The Yale
Shakespeare

✳

The Yale
Shakespeare

Edited by Wilbur L. Cross
and
Tucker Brooke

*Published under the direction of
the Department of English, Yale University*

Barnes
&Noble
Books
NEW YORK

Note: This Barnes & Noble Books edition of the complete *Yale Shakespeare* has been newly typeset from the text of the multi-volume set originally published by Yale University Press.

Introduction © 1993 by Barnes & Noble, Inc.
The Comedy of Errors copyright 1926 by Yale University Press
The Two Gentlemen of Verona copyright 1926 by Yale University Press
The Taming of the Shrew copyright 1921, 1954 by Yale University Press
Love's Labour's Lost copyright 1925 by Yale University Press
A Midsummer Night's Dream copyright 1918 by Yale University Press
The Merchant of Venice copyright 1923, 1959 by Yale University Press
As You Like It copyright 1919, 1954 by Yale University Press
Much Ado About Nothing copyright 1917 by Yale University Press
The Merry Wives of Windsor copyright 1922 by Yale University Press
Twelfth Night copyright 1922, 1954 by Yale University Press
The Tragedy of Troilus and Cressida copyright 1927, 1956 by Yale University Press
All's Well That Ends Well copyright 1926 by Yale University Press
Measure for Measure copyright 1926, 1954 by Yale University Press
The First Part of King Henry the Sixth copyright 1918 by Yale University Press
The Second Part of King Henry the Sixth copyright 1923 by Yale University Press
The Third Part of King Henry the Sixth copyright 1923 by Yale University Press
The Tragedy of Richard the Third copyright 1927 by Yale University Press
The Tragedy of King Richard the Second copyright 1921, 1957 by Yale University Press
The Life and Death of King John copyright 1927 by Yale University Press
The First Part of King Henry the Fourth copyright 1917, 1947 by Yale University Press
The Second Part of King Henry the Fourth copyright 1921 by Yale University Press
The Life of Henry the Fifth copyright 1918, 1955 by Yale University Press
The Life of King Henry the Eighth copyright 1925 by Yale University Press
The Tragedy of Titus Andronicus copyright 1926 by Yale University Press
The Tragedy of Romeo and Juliet copyright 1917, 1954 by Yale University Press
The Tragedy of Julius Caesar copyright 1919, 1959 by Yale University Press
The Tragedy of Hamlet copyright 1917, 1947 by Yale University Press
The Tragedy of Othello copyright 1918, 1947 by Yale University Press
The Tragedy of King Lear copyright 1917, 1947 by Yale University Press
The Tragedy of Macbeth copyright 1918, 1954 by Yale University Press
The Tragedy of Antony and Cleopatra copyright 1921, 1955 by Yale University Press
The Tragedy of Coriolanus copyright 1924 by Yale University Press
The Life of Timon of Athens copyright 1919 by Yale University Press
Pericles, Prince of Tyre copyright 1925 by Yale University Press
The Tragedy of Cymbeline copyright 1924 by Yale University Press
The Winter's Tale copyright 1918 by Yale University Press
The Tempest copyright 1918, 1955 by Yale University Press
Venus and Adonis, Lucrece, and the Minor Poems copyright 1927 by Yale University Press
The Sonnets copyright 1923 by Yale University Press
All rights reserved.

This edition published by Barnes & Noble, Inc.,
by arrangement with Yale University Press.

1993 Barnes & Noble Books

Book design by Charles Ziga, Ziga Design

Project editor: Laura Victoria Levin

ISBN 1-56619-104-1

Printed and bound in the United States of America

M 9 8 7 6 5 4 3 2

❦ CONTENTS ❦

THE TRAGEDIES AND THE POEMS

William Shakespeare's date of birth is not precisely known, but it probably preceded his baptism on April 26, 1564, in Stratford-on-Avon, by only a few days. It is by tradition, then, that Shakespeare's birthday is given as St. George's Day, April 23, which is also the day on which he died in 1616. Although our records of one man's life four centuries ago are limited, we do know something of William Shakespeare's parentage and early family life. William Shakespeare was the third child and first son of John and Mary Shakespeare. Of his four sisters and three brothers, most died in infancy or early childhood, and only one has descendants surviving to this day. He was technically a commoner, yet it is interesting to note his family's ancestral proximity to aristocracy, particularly on his mother's side, and his purchase, later in life, of a heraldic coat of arms for his father.

William Shakespeare's paternal grandfather was probably Richard Shakespeare (d. 1561), a farmer of Snitterfield, four miles northeast of Stratford. Richard Shakespeare's son John was a glover who, early records show, by 1552 had settled in a house on Henley Street in Stratford. It was in the Henley Street house that William Shakespeare was born and spent his early life. At various times, John Shakespeare was active in the town government: In 1561 he was elected one of two chamberlains of the borough; in 1565 he became an alderman; and in 1568 he became high bailiff—in essence, mayor of the town. Sometime in the early 1580s, perhaps around the time of William Shakespeare's marriage in 1582, John Shakespeare was plunged into a period of financial disrepair and social disgrace, recovering both wealth and status in part, it is assumed, through the assistance of his son William. John Shakespeare died in Stratford on September 8, 1601.

Sometime around 1557, John Shakespeare married Mary Arden, the youngest daughter of Robert Arden (d. 1556), a wealthy landowner of Wilmecote, a couple of miles north of Stratford. Robert Arden's father, William Shakespeare's maternal great-grandfather, was Thomas Arden who was living at Wilmecote in 1501 and who probably belonged to the aristocratic family of the Ardens of Park Hall. After seven years and a day of widowhood, Mary Shakespeare died in Stratford September 9, 1608.

In November of 1582, the banns for the marriage of William Shakespeare to Anne Hathaway were issued in the Episcopal Diocese of Worcester. Anne Hathaway was probably the eldest daughter, and one of seven children, of Richard Hathaway. There is no record of her birth, but from evidence offered by her burial tomb, we assume that she was seven or eight years older than her husband, who would have then been eighteen years old. She was most certainly pregnant at time of their marriage, and she is perhaps best remembered for the sole, puzzling reference to her in Shakespeare's will: "Item, I give unto my wife my second best bed with the furniture." Anne Hathaway outlived her husband by some seven years and was buried beside him at Stratford on August 8, 1623. Her epitaph reads: "Here lieth interred the body of Anne, wife of Mr. William Shakespeare, who departed this life the 6th day of August, 1623, being of the age of 67 years."

Beyond these simple details, little is known about Anne Hathaway or, for that matter, of her marriage to William Shakespeare.

The birth of their first child, Susanna, was registered on May 26, 1583, less than six months after the couple was married. Twins Hamnet (sometimes spelled Hamlet) and Judith soon followed, on February 2, 1584. Tragically, Hamnet, William Shakespeare's only son, died having lived little more than eleven years and was buried August 11, 1596. Both of Shakespeare's daughters lived to old age: Susanna until July 11, 1649, and Judith until February 9, 1662. Susanna's daughter, Shakespeare's granddaughter was the only one of Shakespeare's grandchildren to survive to adulthood and marry; however she died without issue on February 17, 1670, the last of William Shakespeare's direct descendants.

As William Shakespeare's theatrical career in London progressed, he purchased land and houses in Stratford and vicinity, most notably, "New Place," for which Shakespeare paid 60 pounds sterling in 1597 and to which Shakespeare retired in 1610. New Place was the second largest house in Stratford and over a century old at the time of purchase. The house was kept in the Shakespeare family until the passing of his granddaughter in 1670, when it was sold to another family and, in 1702, demolished to make way for a new house. In addition to other cottages in Stratford, late in his life (1613) Shakespeare also purchased a house in Blackfriars, London. Records also show that Shakespeare traded in corn and malt, sold a load of stone to the Stratford Corporation for use in repairing a bridge across the Avon, and lent money on at least one occasion to an acquaintance in London. This portrait of Shakespeare as a successful trader in land and goods might seem at odds with the prevailing image of a playwright-poet; however, it must be noted that his wealth was derived not from the sale of his writing *per se*, but rather from the largess of his various patrons and from his position as a primary actor-shareholder in the company which performed his plays.

Perhaps the most tantalizing piece of information about Shakespeare's life appears in the 1596 draft (as well as in a 1599 draft) of a Grant of Arms to Shakespeare's father, which reads, in part:

> *Being therefore solicited and [by] credible report informed that John Shakespeare of Stratford-upon-Avon in the county of Warwick, whose parents and late antecessors were for their valiant and faithful service advanced and rewarded by the most prudent prince King Henry the Seventh of famous memory, sithence which time they have continued in those parts in good reputation and credit.... I have therefore assigned, granted, and by these presents confirmed this shield or coat of arms; viz., Gold on a bend sable a spear of the first, the point steeled, proper; and for his crest or cognizance a falcon, his wings displayed, argent, standing on a wreath of his colors, supporting a spear—gold—steeled as aforesaid, set upon a helmet with mantels and tassels as hath been accustomed and more plainly appeareth depicted on this margent. Signifying hereby that it shall be lawful for the said John Shakespeare, Gent., and for his children, issue, and posterity at all times convenient to make show of and to bear blazoned the same achievement on their shield or coat of arms, escutcheons, crest, cognizance or seals, rings, signets, pennons, guidons, edifices, utensils, liveries, tombs, or monuments, or otherwise ...*

Reasonable conjecture indicates that the coat of arms awarded to

John Shakespeare was, in fact, a reflection of his son's ambition and prosperity, in all likelihood paid for by William Shakespeare himself. Indeed, two other wealthy actors—Augustine Phillips and Thomas Pope, members of Shakespeare's company—also purchased arms to which, it was later charged, they had no hereditary right, as did some twenty-one other contemporaries. By acquiring a coat of arms for his father, William Shakespeare could then claim its insignia and the status conferred therein as part of his own heritage. The arms granted to John Shakespeare are displayed on the monument above William Shakespeare's grave as well as on the tombstone of his daughter Susanna.

William Shakespeare died on April 23, 1616, at New Place in Stratford-on-Avon. The traditional story is that Shakespeare spent his final evening with the playwright Ben Jonson and others celebrating his birthday, perhaps with a bit too much to drink. Inscribed with the date of Shakespeare's death on his tomb in the chancel of the Holy Trinity Church is the following:

Judicio Pylium, genio Socratem, arte Maronem Terra tegit, populus moeret, Olympus habet.

Stay, passenger, why goest thou by so fast?
Read, if thou canst, whom envious death hath placed
Within this monument: Shakespeare, with whom
Quick nature died; whose name doth deck his tomb
Far more than cost; sith all that he hath writ
Leaves living art but page to serve his wit.

His accumulation of wealth is well-evidenced in the bequests of his will. His accrual of honors is equally apparent from the many eulogies published after his death, of which perhaps the most eloquent was proffered by Ben Jonson, who was Shakespeare's friend and perhaps also his fiercest competitor and frequent critic. It reads in part:

To draw no envy, Shakespeare, on thy name,
Am I thus ample to thy book and fame,
While I confess thy writings to be such
As neither man nor muse can praise too much....

I therefore will begin:—Soul of the age!
The applause, delight, the wonder of our stage!
My Shakespeare, rise! I will not lodge thee by
Chaucer or Spenser, or bid Beaumont lie
A little further, to make thee a room.
Thou art a monument without a tomb,
And art alive still, while thy book doth live
And we have wits to read and praise to give....

But stay, I see thee in the hemisphere
Advanc'd and made a constellation there.
Shine forth, thou star of poets, and with rage,
Or influence, chide or cheer the drooping stage,
Which since thy flight fro hence hath mourn'd like night,
And despairs day but for thy volume's light.

Shakespeare in London

It is probable that William Shakespeare began working as an actor in London sometime during the 1580s. However, the first record of Shakespeare as an actor-shareholder in the Lord Chamberlain's company of players does not appear until March 1595, in the accounts of the Treasurer of the Royal Chamber. In this register, William Shakespeare is listed along with William Kempe and Richard Burbage as having performed for Queen Elizabeth I on the previous December 26 and 28 at Greenwich Palace, where one of the plays performed was, quite possibly, *The Comedy Of Errors*. The register reveals that the three were paid the rather handsome sum of ten pounds each per performance.

Will Kempe was famous for his stage appearances in the role of the clown in the plays of Shakespeare and others—he was the original Dogberry in *Much Ado About Nothing*—in addition to being renowned for his morris dancing. Richard Burbage is considered the first great English tragedian, who originated the roles of Hamlet, Lear, Othello, and Richard III, among others. Shakespeare himself is known to have appeared as a principal actor in two plays by Ben Jonson, *Every Man In His Humor* (1598) and *Sejanus* (1603). Indeed, tradition has it that the Lord Chamberlain's Men were determined to reject *Every Man In His Humor*, but Shakespeare ultimately persuaded his partners to put it on.

The Lord Chamberlain's Men presented their first public performances in the Theatre, an outdoor theatre also used on off-days for bull and bear baiting, built just outside the city limits by James Burbage, father of Richard Burbage. When their land-lease expired, the story goes, they dismantled the Theatre and used its timbers to build the Globe on the other side of London. Records dated 1599 show that Richard Burbage and his brother Cuthbert shared one half interest in the Globe; the other half interest was split by William Shakespeare with Will Kempe and three others; that is to say, Shakespeare owned a very profitable one-tenth share in the theatre.

After the death of Queen Elizabeth I in 1603, the players were taken up by King James I, becoming the King's Men. The 1603 commission to the King's Men charges them "freely to use and exercise the art and faculty of playing comedies, tragedies, histories, interludes, morals, pastorals, stage-plays, and such other, like as they have already studied or hereafter shall use or study, as well as for the recreation of our loving subjects as for our solace and pleasure when we shall think good to see them, during our pleasure," and effectively places the players under his protection. Shakespeare's company frequently performed at the courts of Elizabeth I and James I, as well as on its own outdoors, public stages; in 1608 they also took over the Blackfriars Theatre, one of the earliest indoor theatres, for winter performances. The Globe was leveled in a fire in 1613, after a performance of *King Henry VIII*, Shakespeare's last play. The Globe was soon rebuilt, but by then Shakespeare had retired and his death in 1616 along with that of Richard Burbage in 1619 coupled with pressure from Puritan forces, began a lengthy period of instability for the King's Men, finally coming to an end with the closing of the theatres by Parliament in 1642.

By 1592, when the first extant reference to Shakespeare as a dramatist appears, William Shakespeare's presence in London as an actor and dramatist of some visibility seems well-established. Dramatist Robert Greene, in an epilogue to *Groatsworth Of Wit Bought With A Million Of Repentance*, published just after Greene's death in September of that year, refers somewhat obliquely to Shakespeare as "an upstart crow, beautified with our feathers, that with his Tiger's heart wrapt in a player's hide supposes he is as well able to bombast out a blank verse as the best of you; and being an absolute *Johannes fac totum*, is in his own conceit the only Shake-scene in a country." In December of that

same year, an apology of sorts was issued by Henry Chettle, the editor of Greene's diatribe. In his Preface to *Kind-Heart's Dream*, Chettle calls Greene's *Groatsworth of Wit* doubly offensive because the targets cannot avenge themselves on a dead man, and he adds in what appears to be a reference to Shakespeare: "I am as sorry as if the original fault had been my fault, because myself have seen his demeanor no less civil than [t]he excellent in the quality he professes. Besides, divers of worship have reported his uprightness of dealing, which argues his honesty, and his facetious grace in writing that approves his art."

It is very probable that Chettle felt an apology necessary to preserve his own career in the face of Shakespeare's growing popularity. An anonymous poet, who in a verse dated 1594 praises the way in which "Shakespeare paints poor Lucrece' rape," offers a testament to the popularity of Shakespeare's dramatic poem. In the *Palladis Tamia* of Francis Meres (1598), William Shakespeare's name appears near the end of a list of great classical poets that begins with Homer and continues with:

> As the soul of Euphorbus was thought to live in Pythagoras: so the sweet witty soul of Ovid lives in mellifluous and honey-tongued Shakespeare, witness his Venus and Adonis, his Lucrece, his sugared Sonnets among his private friends. . . . As Plautus and Seneca are accounted the best for comedy and tragedy among the Latins: so Shakespeare among the English is the most excellent in both kinds for the stage. . . . As Epius Stolo said that the muses would speak with Plautus' tongue, if they would speak Latin: so I say that the Muses would speak with Shakespeare's fine filed phrase, if they would speak English.

That same year, another poet by the name of Richard Barnfield added his praise of Shakespeare's "honey-flowing vein" in his *Remembrance Of Some English Poets*, declaring: "Well may the body die, but fame dies never." Notes by Gabriel Harvey in 1598 observe: "The younger sort takes much delight in Shakespeare's Venus and Adonis; but his Lucrece and his tragedy of Hamlet, Prince of Denmark, have it in them to please the wiser sort." A 1599 sonnet entitled "Ad Gulielmum Shakespeare," authored by John Weever, begins:

> Honey-tongued Shakespeare, when I saw thine issue,
> I swore Apollo got them and none other;
> Their rosy-tainted features, clothed in tissue,
> Some heavenborn goddess said to be their mother . . .

Moreover, by this time Shakespeare's name had such currency that it was being used to promote publications by other authors, in addition to being mocked, notably by Cambridge undergraduates in their 1600 spoof of college life: "We shall have nothing but pure Shakespeare and shreds of poetry that he hath gathered at the theatres."

As a poet, William Shakespeare's name first appears appended to his 1593 dedication of *Venus And Adonis* to the Earl of Southampton, one of Shakespeare's more generous patrons, and in the subsequent year in the dedication to *Lucrece*, also to the Earl of Southampton, in which Shakespeare declares: "The love I dedicate to your Lordship is without end; whereof this pamphlet without beginning is but a superfluous moiety. The warrant I have of your honorable disposition, not the worth of my untutored lines, makes it assured of acceptance. What I have done is yours, what I have to do is yours, being part in all I have, devoted yours."

As a dramatist, Shakespeare's name first appears on the title page of the second and third editions of *Richard III* (1598) and on the title page of the earliest extant edition of *Love's Labour's Lost* (also dated 1598). In a similar vein, the 1608 edition of *King Lear* is headed by this proclamation: "M. William Shakespeare: His true Chronicle History of the Life and Death of King Lear and his three Daughters. With the unfortunate life of Edgar, son and heir to the Earl of Gloster, and his sullen and assumed humor of Tom of Bedlam: As it was played before the King's Majesty at Whitehall upon St. Stephen's Night in Christmas Holidays, by his Majesty's Servants playing usually at the Globe on the Bankside."

In 1623, seven years after the death of Shakespeare, two shareholders of the King's Men, John Heminge—who probably originated the role of Falstaff—and Henry Condell—who, it is speculated, was the first to play the role of Horatio in *Hamlet*—collected Shakespeare's works into a single volume (called the First Folio), offering it to the public at the price of twenty shillings. Their dedication praises their patrons, the Earl of Pembroke and the Earl of Montgomery, and adds:

> There is a great difference whether any book choose his patrons or find them. This hath done both. For so much were your Lordship's likings of the several parts, when they were acted, as before they were published the volume asked to be yours. We have but collected them, and done an office to the dead, to procure his orphans guardians: without ambition either of self-profit or fame, only to keep the memory of so worthy a friend and fellow alive as was our SHAKESPEARE . . .

In their Epistle to the readers of the first edition of Shakespeare's collected works, Heminge and Condell close with this exhortation:

> Read him, therefore, and again and again; and if then you do not like him, surely you are in some manifest danger not to understand him, and so we leave you to other of his friends whom if you need can be your guides. If you need them not, you can lead yourselves and others, and such readers we wish him.

—Sharon Mazer, Ph. D.

Adapted for this edition from Shakespeare of Stratford, *by Tucker Brooke* (The Yale Shakespeare, *1926*).

The Comedy of Errors

Edited by
ROBERT DUDLEY FRENCH

Dramatis Personae

SOLINUS, *Duke of Ephesus*

AEGEON, *a Merchant of Syracuse*

ANTIPHOLUS OF EPHESUS
ANTIPHOLUS OF SYRACUSE } *Twin Brothers, and Sons to Aegeon and Aemilia, but unknown to each other*

DROMIO OF EPHESUS
DROMIO OF SYRACUSE } *Twin Brothers, and Slaves to the two Antipholuses*

BALTHAZAR, *a Merchant*

ANGELO, *a Goldsmith*

A MERCHANT, *Friend to Antipholus of Syracuse*

A SECOND MERCHANT, *to whom Angelo is a debtor*

DR. PINCH, *a Schoolmaster, and a Conjurer*

AEMILIA, *Wife to Aegeon, an Abbess at Ephesus*

ADRIANA, *Wife to Antipholus of Ephesus*

LUCIANA, *Sister to Adriana*

LUCE, *Servant to Adriana*

A COURTESAN

GAOLER, OFFICERS, AND OTHER ATTENDANTS

SCENE—*Ephesus.*

The Comedy of Errors

INTRODUCTION

SOURCES OF THE PLAY

The plot of *The Comedy of Errors* was derived, directly or indirectly, from the *Menæchmi* of Plautus. Some scholars, mindful of Shakespeare's 'small Latin,' are inclined to believe that his education in the classics had not gone far enough to enable him to read Plautus in the original; and it has been suggested that he may have used an English prose translation, prepared by a certain 'W. W.' This translation, to be sure, was not published until 1595, some years later than the date usually assigned to Shakespeare's play; but the printer, in his note to the reader, hints that the work had existed in manuscript for some time. There is a possibility that Shakespeare had seen it before he wrote his *Errors*. Some verbal resemblances between his play and 'W. W.'s' translation have been pointed out, but they are too slight and too infrequent to be taken as proof that this work was a direct source of *The Comedy of Errors*. It is just as probable that Shakespeare went directly to the Latin text for his material.

The general resemblance between *The Comedy of Errors* and the *Menæchmi* may be indicated by reproducing the argument of the Latin play, which appears in the 1595 translation as follows:

> *Two Twinborne sonnes, a Sicill marchant had,*
> *Menechmus one, and Sosicles the other:*
> *The first his Father lost a little Lad,*
> *The Grandsire namde the latter like his brother.*
> *This (growne a man) long travell tooke to seeke*
> *His Brother, and to Epidamnum came,*
> *Where th' other dwelt inricht, and him so like,*
> *That Citizens there take him for the same:*
> *Father, wife, neighbours, each mistaking either,*
> *Much pleasant Error, ere they meete togither.*

Examination of the two plays shows that the similarity extends to the details of the action. Menæchmus the Citizen, in the Latin play, promises to dine with Erotium, a courtesan; but the dinner goes to Menæchmus the Traveller, who has just landed, accompanied by his slave, Messenio, and is mistaken for his brother by the courtesan and her servants. Erotium gives her guest a cloak to take to the dyers and a chain to be repaired by a goldsmith; and Menæchmus the Citizen is later called to account for these articles, which he has not seen since he stole them from his wife and bestowed them on Erotium. Menæchmus the Traveler, encountering his brother's wife, who mistakes him for her husband, is completely at a loss to understand her reproaches. As a result of their behavior in these bewildering circumstances, both brothers are separately suspected of madness, and Medicus, a physician, essays his powers as a conjurer to reduce the malady. Certainly there are scenes in *The Comedy of Errors* which bear a resemblance to these incidents and situations, and they seem to point toward a familiarity, on Shakespeare's part, with the details of Plautus' play, as well as with its general outline.

Shakespeare's treatment of this source material shows characteristic independence. Of the nine persons of the Plautine comedy, he has retained but six: the Menæchmi (Antipholi), Messenio (Dromio of Syracuse), Mulier (Adriana), Erotium (the Courtesan), and Medicus (Dr. Pinch). Such stock characters as the Cook and the Parasite have been discarded, while Luciana has been substituted for Senex, the doddering father-in-law of Menæchmus the Citizen. Dromio of Ephesus, Solinus, Ægeon, Æmilia, Luce, and the Merchants have been added. Similar incidents and situations are given very different treatment by the two poets. The relations between Adriana and her husband are treated less cynically by Shakespeare than in the Latin play, and the dinner with the courtesan is made to appear the natural result of the injured feelings of a man who finds himself unaccountably locked out of his own house: we certainly hear nothing, in *The Comedy of Errors*, of jewelry or a cloak stolen from Adriana and bestowed upon the courtesan. Antipholus of Syracuse, moreover, is less ready to profit by valuable tokens, forced upon him by people obviously laboring under some strange misapprehension, than his prototype, Menæchmus the Traveller, who not only proposes to make off with the courtesan's cloak and chain, but endeavors to wheedle more booty out of her maid.

Of more importance than these differences in treatment are certain significant additions to the rather simple plot, which appear in *The Comedy of Errors*, broadening the humor and making the comedy a richer play than the *Menæchmi*. In Plautus, only one of the twin heroes is attended by his slave, and there is no suggestion of the delightful absurdity of a second pair of identical twins, attendant upon the first. The presence of the two Dromios has enabled Shakespeare to begin the merry game of confusion earlier in the play and to continue it to the end with unfailing variety in the complications. The substitution of Luciana for Senex not only replaces a stock character with a very real and appealing person, but also provides an opportunity for an added sentimental interest and for some love-making in rhymed verse, which anticipates the poetry of *Romeo and Juliet*. Another important addition is the introduction of Ægeon and Æmilia, which places the boisterous farce in a graceful setting of romantic comedy. This embellishment of the plot has every appearance of being Shakespeare's invention, though possible sources have been pointed out in Ariosto's *Suppositi* and in the old and famous story of Apollonius of Tyre. The scene in which Antipholus of Ephesus knocks vainly at his own door, while his brother is entertained within, does not appear in the *Menæchmi* but resembles a scene in the *Amphitruo*, another comedy by Plautus.

All these important differences between *The Comedy of Errors* and its remote Latin original may, of course, be the fruits of Shakespeare's own labors over his source material; but a plausible case has been made out for the existence of an intermediary step in the evolution of the plot. It has been conjectured that the comedy is the rewriting of an old play, which had become the property of Shakespeare's company. Support has been found for this theory in the use of the doggerel fourteen-syllable line in some of the dialogue, since this form of verse is employed in the

surviving examples of mid-sixteenth century academic comedy. Another bit of evidence, pointing in the same direction, has been found in the corrupt Latin epithets bestowed upon the twin heroes in some of the stage directions of the Folio. It has been suggested that these epithets, which are reproduced in the notes,[1] may have found their way into Shakespeare's play from a garbled transcript of the old comedy which he was rewriting. From the fact that doggerel is used for so much of the dialogue in the first scene of the third act, and from the presence, in that scene alone, of the 'ghost' Balthazar and of Luce, who appears to be the 'kitchen-vestal,' elsewhere named Nell, Mr. J. Dover Wilson argues that we have in a certain part of that scene a portion of the old play, taken over by Shakespeare practically without revision.

This 'lost source' of Shakespeare's play has been identified, by those who argue for its existence, with a performance styled *The Historie of Error*, which was 'shown at Hampton Court on New Yere's daie at night [1576-7], enacted by the children of Powles.' Since the productions given by the boys of St. Paul's were usually derived from classic sources, it seems a plausible conjecture that this lost play was founded upon the *Menæchmi*. The play was given again at Windsor in 1583, if we may believe that the *History of Ferrar* (sic), referred to in the Accounts of the Revels at Court, was the same work.

In the absence of tangible evidence, however, it cannot be definitely stated, either that this lost play was founded upon Plautus, or that it found its way eventually into Shakespeare's hands and formed the basis of his *Comedy of Errors*. Although the theory has gained acceptance, it should be remembered that it rests largely on conjecture and that it begins by assuming the existence of lost evidence which it needs for its support. When all has been said, the fact remains that no principal source for Shakespeare's play, other than the Latin text of the *Menæchmi*, has yet been brought to light.

THE HISTORY OF THE PLAY

In 1594, 'betwixt All-hollontide and Christmas,' the gentlemen of Gray's Inn devised revels to grace the coming holiday season, electing one of their number to preside over their festivities as 'Prince of Purpoole.' An account of their revels, obviously written by some choice spirit who had shared in the proceedings and relished their flavor to the full, found its way into print, nearly a century later, in a tract printed for 'W. Canning, at his Shop in the Temple Cloysters MDCLXXXVIII' under the title *Gesta Grayorum: or the History of the High and Mighty Prince, Henry Prince of Purpoole . . . Who Reigned and Died A.D. 1594.*

This out-of-the-way little volume is valuable for more reasons than one, but its interest for Shakespearians lies in the account which it gives of what happened at Gray's Inn on the night of Holy Innocents (December 28). On that evening, the spirit of revelry seems to have reached its height. An 'ambassador' from the Inner Temple, 'attended by a great number of brave Gentlemen,' put in an appearance about nine of the clock, and it appears that special entertainment of some sort had been devised for their pleasure; but unfortunately 'there arose such a disordered Tumult and Crowd upon the Stage, that there was no opportunity to effect that which was intended.' Indeed, the disorders ran

[1] See notes on I.ii.S.d. and II.i.S.d.

to such length that at last the Lord Ambassador and his train, thinking they were not being 'so kindly entertained as was before expected,' withdrew in some displeasure. 'After their Departure,' the account goes on to record, 'the Throngs and Tumults did somewhat cease, although so much of them continued, as was able to disorder and confound any good Invention whatsoever. In regard whereof, as also for that the Sports intended were especially for the gracing the *Templarians* it was thought good not to offer any thing of Account, saving Dancing and Revelling with Gentlewomen; and after such Sports, a Comedy of Errors (like to *Plautus* his *Menechmus*) was played by the Players. So that Night was begun, and continued to the End, in nothing but Confusion and Errors; whereupon it was ever afterwards called, *The Night of Errors.*'

The players referred to in the account of this night of confusion and errors undoubtedly were the Lord Chamberlain's Men (Shakespeare's company), and the play thrust so inauspiciously upon this tumultuous stage, where the confusion was so great as to 'disorder and confound any good Invention whatsoever,' must have been Shakespeare's *Comedy of Errors*. This is the earliest recorded production of the play, but there is no reason to believe that it was a first performance. Indeed, there is evidence indicating that the comedy had been played before the Queen that very afternoon. Payment to the Lord Chamberlain's Men was made for a performance at the Court, then at Greenwich, on December 28, and it is a reasonable assumption that the company put on the same bill which they were later to present before the lawyers at Gray's Inn. It should be added that the evening performance was probably not a makeshift, as one might infer from the account in the *Gesta Grayorum*. Undoubtedly, the Prince of Purpoole and his councillors had devised some amateur theatricals of their own for the amusement of their guests from the Inner Temple and found themselves obliged to cancel that part of the entertainment when the spirit of revelry passed beyond their control, in the giddy hours of the early evening; but it seems unlikely that they then called in the players to step into the breach. It is more reasonable to assume, with Sir A. Quiller-Couch, that the performance by the professional company had been prearranged, and that 'the players had been preëmpted from Greenwich to present just such an extravaganza upon Plautus as would tickle the scholarly taste and amuse the "studious lawyers" amid their bowers.'

It is generally agreed that the *Comedy of Errors* was not a new play when it was performed at Gray's Inn in 1594. Every test of versification and language places the comedy among Shakespeare's earliest works; and in the list of his plays given by Francis Meres in the *Palladis Tamia* (1598), 'his *Errors*' stands second, between *The Two Gentlemen of Verona* and *Love's Labour's Lost*. A bit of evidence pointing to a date about 1591 has been found in the text of the play. Dromio of Syracuse, finding out countries in the ample person of Nell, the kitchen-wench, discovers France 'in her forehead, armed and reverted, making war against her heir.' This is usually supposed to be a reference to the armed resistance of the Catholic League against Henry of Navarre, named heir to the throne by Henry III in 1589. Such an allusion would have fallen rather flat after the coronation of Navarre in 1593, but would certainly have taken effect in 1591, when English troops were in France, supporting the cause of the Protestant king against his revolted subjects. This historical allusion, together with a reference, a few lines farther on, to 'whole armadoes of carracks' in connection with Spain, has been taken as

evidence to support the date 1591-2, now generally assigned to the play.

The stage history of the comedy, begun amid the tumult of the stormy night at Gray's Inn, has not been conspicuously prosperous. From the Revels Accounts, we learn that '*The Plaie of Errors*, by Shaxberd,' was acted before King James at Whitehall on December 28, 1604. No subsequent performance of the play has been recorded until 1741, when it was revived at Drury Lane. Opening on November 11, the comedy was acted on four successive nights and was put on again on December 10. No bill of the actors in this revival has been preserved, but it is said that Charles Macklin played the part of Dromio of Syracuse.

At Covent Garden, the comedy was revived several times during the eighteenth century. As early as 1734, a comedy in two acts 'taken from Plautus and Shakespeare,' called *See if You Like It, or 'Tis all a Mistake*, was performed there, but we do not know just what relation this play bore to *The Comedy of Errors*. Shakespeare's play was not presented at Covent Garden until April 14, 1762, when it was acted but once. On January 22, 1779, a revised version was performed at the same theatre, probably with the alterations of Thomas Hull, actor, writer, and general utility man of the company. During the next year a farce by W. Woods, called *The Twins, or Which is Which?*, 'altered from Shakespeare's Comedy of Errors,' was produced at the Theatre Royal in Edinburgh; and in April, 1790, a three-act version of Shakespeare's play was performed at Covent Garden. Hull's version came back into its own when it was used as the basis of a production by John Philip Kemble at Covent Garden, on January 9, 1808.

Several actors, well known to the playgoers of the eighteenth century, seem to have increased their reputation by their connection with the play; notably, Quick, as Dromio of Ephesus, and Munden, as Dromio of Syracuse. At a performance given for his benefit, Rees played Dromio of Ephesus opposite Munden, imitating the latter's voice and manner closely. In Kemble's production, Munden held his usual rôle, with Blanchard, who was considerably shorter and could not possibly be mistaken for him, playing Dromio of Ephesus.

The most singular chapter in the history of *The Comedy of Errors* opened on December 11, 1819, when the play was given at Covent Garden as an opera, 'in five acts with Alterations, Additions, and with Songs, Duets, Glees, and Chorusses, Selected entirely from the Plays, Poems and Sonnets of Shakespeare.' This singular production drew together an assortment of Shakespeare's lyrics which included several songs from *As You Like It*, two of the Sonnets, the 'Willow Song' from *Othello*, and 'St. Withold footed thrice the Wold' from *Lear*. In order to introduce all these songs of diverse nature into *The Comedy of Errors*, the reviser found that 'a few additional scenes and passages were absolutely necessary'; and he set himself to his task with as little regard for the expense of scenery as for the text of Shakespeare. The last scene of the third act opened with a magnificent set including mountains 'whose tops are covered with snow,' a river, and a rustic bridge. Horns were heard without, and the purpose of the set was shortly disclosed by the entrance of a hunting party, who sang 'a quartetto and chorus from *Love's Labour's Lost*.' 'This literary murder,' says Genest, 'was committed by Reynolds'; and he goes on to assure the author that 'the only senti-

ments which the real friends of Shakespeare can feel towards him are indignation at his attempt, and contempt for the bungling manner in which he has executed it.' Other friends of Shakespeare than Genest may well feel a little chagrin at the thought that this unpalatable gallimaufry was presented twenty-seven times in its first season and was frequently revived, and that Frederick Reynolds was so encouraged by his success with *The Comedy of Errors* that he continued his assaults upon the plays, presenting operatic versions of *Twelfth Night, The Tempest, Two Gentlemen of Verona*, and *The Merry Wives of Windsor*. It may be said, in extenuation of the sins of the theatre-going public, that Reynolds could avail himself of the services of those 'lovely singing actresses,' Mrs. Stephens and Maria Tree, who acted Adriana and Luciana in his production of the *Errors*.

A revival of the play, not in its strange operatic garb, was given by Samuel Phelps, who played it at Sadler's Wells in November, 1855, and again in January, 1856. This production was followed, in the spring of 1864, on the occasion of the Shakespeare Tercentenary, by an interesting performance given at the Princess' Theatre and through the provinces. The play was acted continuously without the fall of the curtain, and with a strikingly beautiful stage mounting. The two brothers, Charles and Harry Webb, played the two Dromios, giving an extraordinary interpretation, which kept the audience in bewilderment by their similarity in appearance and actions. At a performance by the Webbs in Liverpool in this year, S. B. Bancroft acted Antipholus of Syracuse and John Hare appeared as Dr. Pinch.

In January, 1883, J. S. Clarke, the brother-in-law of Edwin Booth, put on a 'pictorial revival,' for which Lewis Wingfield designed the setting and costumes. On this occasion, Clarke and Harry Paulton, who acted the two Dromios, seem to have secured their comic effect by emphasizing the differences between the twin slaves as much as the similarity. In more recent years, the play has been included in the repertory of the Benson company, for their London season in 1905, with F. R. Benson as Antipholus of Syracuse and the two Dromios by George Weir and Arthur Whitby. The most recent revival, on the London stage, was a performance given as a curtain-raiser to a production of *The Bells* at the Savoy Theatre during the summer of 1924. The comedy was played very rapidly and was well received.

Outside of England, *The Comedy of Errors* has had no very noteworthy history. When performed at the Künstlertheater in Munich, in September, 1910, under the direction of Max Reinhardt of Berlin, the play was referred to as 'a novelty'; though it is to be said that the same authority describes the production as 'the culminating success of an artistic and clever management' (*Athenæum*, October 1, 1910). In America, the play was not acted until 1804, when a production was given at the Park Theatre, New York, on May 25. The most notable revival in this country was that of William H. Crane and Stuart Robson in 1878. Robson and Crane, who acted the two Dromios, were not in the least alike in appearance, but, with the aid of dress and make-up, they achieved a remarkable resemblance. 'Intellectual vacuity was expressed in a blank stare, a rocking gait, fingers sucked or tapped and pressed together, and irresolute swaying, while voices raised in whimpering protest or bleating in appeal called answering laughter from the audience.'

ACT FIRST ❧ SCENE FIRST

[A Hall in the Duke's Palace]
Enter the Duke of Ephesus, with the Merchant [Ægeon] of Syracusa,
Gaoler, and other attendants.

Merch. Proceed, Solinus, to procure my fall,
And by the doom of death end woes and all.
   Duke. Merchant of Syracusa, plead no more.
I am not partial to infringe our laws:
The enmity and discord which of late   5
Sprung from the rancorous outrage of your duke
To merchants, our well-dealing countrymen,
Who, wanting guilders to redeem their lives,
Have seal'd his rigorous statutes with their bloods,
Excludes all pity from our threat'ning looks.   10
For, since the mortal and intestine jars
'Twixt thy seditious countrymen and us,
It hath in solemn synods been decreed,
Both by the Syracusians and ourselves,
To admit no traffic to our adverse towns: 15
Nay, more, if any, born at Ephesus,
Be seen at Syracusian marts and fairs;
Again, if any Syracusian born
Come to the bay of Ephesus: he dies,
His goods confiscate to the duke's dispose;   20
Unless a thousand marks be levied,
To quit the penalty and to ransom him.
Thy substance, valu'd at the highest rate,
Cannot amount unto a hundred marks;
Therefore, by law thou art condemn'd to die.   25
   Merch. Yet this my comfort: when your words are done,
My woes end likewise with the evening sun.
   Duke. Well, Syracusian, say, in brief the cause
Why thou departedst from thy native home,
And for what cause thou cam'st to Ephesus.   30
   Merch. A heavier task could not have been impos'd
Than I to speak my griefs unspeakable:
Yet, that the world may witness that my end
Was wrought by nature, not by vile offence,
I'll utter what my sorrow gives me leave.   35
In Syracusa was I born, and wed
Unto a woman, happy but for me,
And by me too, had not our hap been bad.
With her I liv'd in joy: our wealth increas'd
By prosperous voyages I often made   40
To Epidamnum; till my factor's death,
And the great care of goods at random left,
Drew me from kind embracements of my spouse;
From whom my absence was not six months old,
Before herself,—almost at fainting under   45
The pleasing punishment that women bear,—
Had made provision for her following me,
And soon and safe arrived where I was.
There had she not been long but she became
A joyful mother of two goodly sons;   50
And, which was strange, the one so like the other,

As could not be distinguish'd but by names.
That very hour, and in the self-same inn,
A meaner woman was delivered
Of such a burthen, male twins, both alike.   55
Those,—for their parents were exceeding poor,—
I bought, and brought up to attend my sons.
My wife, not meanly proud of two such boys,
Made daily motions for our home return:
Unwilling I agreed. Alas! too soon   60
We came aboard.
A league from Epidamnum had we sail'd,
Before the always-wind-obeying deep
Gave any tragic instance of our harm:
But longer did we not retain much hope;   65
For what obscured light the heavens did grant
Did but convey unto our fearful minds
A doubtful warrant of immediate death;
Which, though myself would gladly have embrac'd,
Yet the incessant weepings of my wife,   70
Weeping before for what she saw must come,
And piteous plainings of the pretty babes,
That mourn'd for fashion, ignorant what to fear,
Forc'd me to seek delays for them and me.
And this it was, for other means was none: 75
The sailors sought for safety by our boat,
And left the ship, then sinking-ripe, to us:
My wife, more careful for the latter-born,
Had fasten'd him unto a small spare mast,
Such as seafaring men provide for storms;   80
To him one of the other twins was bound,
Whilst I had been like heedful of the other.
The children thus dispos'd, my wife and I,
Fixing our eyes on whom our care was fix'd,
Fasten'd ourselves at either end the mast;   85
And floating straight, obedient to the stream,
Was carried towards Corinth, as we thought.
At length the sun, gazing upon the earth,
Dispers'd those vapours that offended us,
And, by the benefit of his wished light   90
The seas wax'd calm, and we discovered
Two ships from far making amain to us,
Of Corinth that, of Epidaurus this:
But ere they came,—O let me say no more!
Gather the sequel by that went before.   95
   Duke. Nay, forward, old man; do not break off so;
For we may pity, though not pardon thee.
   Merch. O, had the gods done so, I had not now
Worthily term'd them merciless to us!
For, ere the ships could meet by twice five leagues,   100
We were encounter'd by a mighty rock,
Which being violently borne upon,
Our helpful ship was splitted in the midst;
So that, in this unjust divorce of us
Fortune had left to both of us alike   105
What to delight in, what to sorrow for.
Her part, poor soul! seeming as burdened

---

4 **partial:** *enough inclined in your behalf*   8 **guilders:** *money; cf. n.*   11 **intestine;** *cf. n.*
14 **Syracusians:** *i.e. Syracusans*   20 **confiscate:** *confiscated*   **dispose:** *disposal*   21 **marks:**
a mark was worth 13s. 4d., about $3.35   34 **nature:** *natural affection; cf. n.*   41 **Epidam-**
num; *cf. n.*   **factor's:** *agent's*

52 **As:** *that they*   54 **meaner:** *of lower rank*   58 **meanly:** *moderately*   59 **motions:**
proposals   64 **instance:** *indication*   67 **fearful:** *frightened*   68 **doubtful:** *dread-*
ful   72 **plainings:** *wailings*   73 **for fashion:** *from imitation of others*   77 **sinking-**
ripe: *on the point of sinking*   78 **latter-born;** *cf. n.*   92 **amain:** *swiftly*   93 **Epi-**
daurus; *cf. n.*   95 **that:** *what*

With lesser weight, but not with lesser woe,
Was carried with more speed before the wind,
And in our sight they three were taken up   *110*
By fishermen of Corinth, as we thought.
At length, another ship had seiz'd on us;
And, knowing whom it was their hap to save,
Gave healthful welcome to their ship-wrack'd guests;
And would have reft the fishers of their prey,   *115*
Had not their bark been very slow of sail;
And therefore homeward did they bend their course.
Thus have you heard me sever'd from my bliss,
That by misfortunes was my life prolong'd,
To tell sad stories of my own mishaps.   *120*

    Duke. And, for the sake of them thou sorrowest for,
Do me the favour to dilate at full
What hath befall'n of them and thee till now.

    Merch. My youngest boy, and yet my eldest care,
At eighteen years became inquisitive   *125*
After his brother; and importun'd me
That his attendant—so his case was like,
Reft of his brother, but retain'd his name—
Might bear him company in the quest of him;
Whom whilst I labour'd of a love to see,   *130*
I hazarded the loss of whom I lov'd.
Five summers have I spent in farthest Greece,
Roaming clean through the bounds of Asia,
And, coasting homeward, came to Ephesus;
Hopeless to find, yet loath to leave unsought   *135*
Or that or any place that harbours men.
But here must end the story of my life;
And happy were I in my timely death,
Could all my travels warrant me they live.

    Duke. Hapless Ægeon, whom the fates have mark'd   *140*
To bear the extremity of dire mishap!
Now, trust me, were it not against our laws,
Against my crown, my oath, my dignity,
Which princes, would they, may not disannul,
My soul should sue as advocate for thee.   *145*
But though thou art adjudged to the death,
And passed sentence may not be recall'd
But to our honour's great disparagement,
Yet will I favour thee in what I can:
Therefore, merchant, I'll limit thee this day   *150*
To seek thy life by beneficial help.
Try all the friends thou hast in Ephesus;
Beg thou, or borrow, to make up the sum,
And live; if no, then thou art doom'd to die.
Gaoler, take him to thy custody.   *155*

    Gaol. I will my lord.

    Merch. Hopeless and helpless doth Ægeon wend,
But to procrastinate his lifeless end.   *Exeunt.*

❦ SCENE SECOND ❦

[The Mart]

Enter Antipholus Erotes [of Syracuse], a Merchant, and Dromio [of Syracuse].

    Mer. Therefore, give out you are of Epidamnum,
Lest that your goods too soon be confiscate.
This very day, a Syracusian merchant
Is apprehended for arrival here;
And, not being able to buy out his life,   *5*
According to the statute of the town
Dies ere the weary sun set in the west.
There is your money that I had to keep.

    Ant. S. Go bear it to the Centaur, where we host,
And stay there, Dromio, till I come to thee.   *10*
Within this hour it will be dinner-time:
Till that, I'll view the manners of the town,
Peruse the traders, gaze upon the buildings,
And then return and sleep within mine inn,
For with long travel I am stiff and weary.   *15*
Get thee away.

    Dro. S. Many a man would take you at your word,
And go indeed, having so good a mean.   *Exit Dromio.*

    Ant. S. A trusty villain, sir, that very oft,
When I am dull with care and melancholy,   *20*
Lightens my humour with his merry jests.
What, will you walk with me about the town,
And then go to my inn and dine with me?

    Mer. I am invited, sir, to certain merchants,
Of whom I hope to make much benefit;   *25*
I crave your pardon. Soon at five o'clock,
Please you, I'll meet with you upon the mart,
And afterward consort you till bed-time:
My present business calls me from you now.

    Ant. S. Farewell till then: I will go lose myself,   *30*
And wander up and down to view the city.

    Mer. Sir, I commend you to your own content.   *[Exit.]*

    Ant. S. He that commends me to mine own content,
Commends me to the thing I cannot get.
I to the world am like a drop of water   *35*
That in the ocean seeks another drop;
Who, falling there to find his fellow forth,
Unseen, inquisitive, confounds himself:
So I, to find a mother and a brother,
In quest of them, unhappy, lose myself.   *40*

Enter Dromio of Ephesus.

Here comes the almanac of my true date.
What now? How chance thou art return'd so soon?

    Dro. E. Return'd so soon! rather approach'd too late:
The capon burns, the pig falls from the spit,
The clock hath strucken twelve upon the bell;   *45*
My mistress made it one upon my cheek:
She is so hot because the meat is cold;
The meat is cold because you come not home;
You come not home because you have no stomach;

---

114 healthful: *salutary*   **122 dilate:** *narrate*   **133 clean:** *entirely*   **136 Or . . . or:** *either
. . . or*   **138 timely:** *speedy*   **139 warrant me:** *give me assurance that*   **144 disannul:**
annul   **151 life;** *cf. n.*

SCENE TWO, S. d. Antipholus Erotes; *cf. n.*   **9 host:** *lodge*   **13 Peruse:** *observe*   **18
mean:** *means (the money entrusted to him)*   **19 villain:** *fellow*   **26 Soon at:**
about   **28 consort you:** *keep you company*   **37 forth:** *out*   **38 confounds himself:**
i.e. is lost   **41 almanac of my true date;** *cf. n.*   **45 twelve:** *somewhat past the Elizabethan
dinner hour*   **49 stomach:** *appetite*

You have no stomach, having broke your fast;   *50*
But we, that know what 'tis to fast and pray,
Are penitent for your default to-day.

   Ant. S. Stop in your wind, sir: tell me this, I pray:
Where have you left the money that I gave you?

   Dro. E. O, sixpence, that I had o' Wednesday last   *55*
To pay the saddler for my mistress' crupper?
The saddler had it, sir; I kept it not.

   Ant. S. I am not in a sportive humour now.
Tell me, and dally not, where is the money?
We being strangers here, how dar'st thou trust   *60*
So great a charge from thine own custody?

   Dro. E. I pray you, jest, sir, as you sit at dinner.
I from my mistress come to you in post;
If I return, I shall be post indeed,
For she will score your fault upon my pate.   *65*
Methinks your maw, like mine, should be your clock
And strike you home without a messenger.

   Ant. S. Come, Dromio, come, these jests are out of season;
Reserve them till a merrier hour than this.
Where is the gold I gave in charge to thee?   *70*

   Dro. E. To me, sir? why, you gave no gold to me.

   Ant. S. Come on, sir knave, have done your foolishness,
And tell me how thou hast dispos'd thy charge.

   Dro. E. My charge was but to fetch you from the mart
Home to your house, the Phœnix, sir, to dinner: *75*
My mistress and her sister stays for you.

   Ant. S. Now, as I am a Christian, answer me,
In what safe place you have bestow'd my money;
Or I shall break that merry sconce of yours
That stands on tricks when I am undispos'd.   *80*
Where is the thousand marks thou hadst of me?

   Dro. E. I have some marks of yours upon my pate,
Some of my mistress' marks upon my shoulders,
But not a thousand marks between you both.
If I should pay your worship those again,   *85*
Perchance you will not bear them patiently.

   Ant. S. Thy mistress' marks! what mistress, slave, hast thou?

   Dro. E. Your worship's wife, my mistress at the Phœnix;
She that doth fast till you come home to dinner,
And prays that you will hie you home to dinner.   *90*

   Ant. S. What! wilt thou flout me thus unto my face,
Being forbid? There, take you that, sir knave.   *[Strikes him.]*

   Dro. E. What mean you, sir? for God's sake, hold your hands!
Nay, an you will not, sir, I'll take my heels.

                              Exit Dromio Ep.

   Ant. S. Upon my life, by some device or other   *95*
The villain is o'er-raught of all my money.
They say this town is full of cozenage;
As, nimble jugglers that deceive the eye,
Dark-working sorcerers that change the mind,
Soul-killing witches that deform the body,   *100*
Disguised cheaters, prating mountebanks,
And many such-like liberties of sin:
If it prove so, I will be gone the sooner.
I'll to the Centaur, to go seek this slave:
I greatly fear my money is not safe.   *Exit. 105*

ACT SECOND ❧ SCENE FIRST

[The House of Antipholus of Ephesus]
Enter Adriana, wife to Antipholus Sereptus, with Luciana her Sister.

   Adr. Neither my husband nor the slave return'd,
That in such haste I sent to seek his master!
Sure, Luciana, it is two o'clock.

   Luc. Perhaps some merchant hath invited him,
And from the mart he's somewhere gone to dinner.   *5*
Good sister, let us dine and never fret.
A man is master of his liberty:
Time is their master, and, when they see time,
They'll go or come: if so, be patient, sister.

   Adr. Why should their liberty than ours be more?   *10*

   Luc. Because their business still lies out o' door.

   Adr. Look, when I serve him so, he takes it ill.

   Luc. O, know he is the bridle of your will.

   Adr. There's none but asses will be bridled so.

   Luc. Why, headstrong liberty is lash'd with woe.   *15*
There's nothing situate under heaven's eye
But hath his bound, in earth, in sea, in sky:
The beasts, the fishes, and the winged fowls,
Are their males' subjects and at their controls.
Men, more divine, the masters of all these,   *20*
Lords of the wide world, and wild wat'ry seas,
Indu'd with intellectual sense and souls,
Or more pre-eminence than fish and fowls,
Are masters to their females and their lords:
Then, let your will attend on their accords.   *25*

   Adr. This servitude makes you to keep unwed.

   Luc. Not this, but troubles of the marriage-bed.

   Adr. But, were you wedded, you would bear some sway.

   Luc. Ere I learn love, I'll practise to obey.

   Adr. How if your husband start some other where?   *30*

   Luc. Till he come home again, I would forbear.

   Adr. Patience unmov'd! no marvel though she pause;
They can be meek that have no other cause.
A wretched soul, bruis'd with adversity,
We bid be quiet when we hear it cry;   *35*
But were we burden'd with like weight of pain,
As much, or more we should ourselves complain:
So thou, that hast no unkind mate to grieve thee,
With urging helpless patience wouldst relieve me;
But, if thou live to see like right bereft,   *40*
This fool-begg'd patience in thee will be left.

   Luc. Well, I will marry one day, but to try.
Here comes your man; now is your husband nigh.

   Adr. Say, is your tardy master now at hand?   *Enter Dromio E.*

   Dro. E. Nay, he's at two hands with me, and that my   *45*
two ears can witness.

   Adr. Say, didst thou speak with him? Know'st thou his
mind?

   Dro. E. Ay, ay, he told his mind upon mine ear.
Beshrew his hand, I scarce could understand it.   *50*

   Luc. Spake he so doubtfully, thou couldst not feel his
meaning?

   Dro. E. Nay, he struck so plainly, I could too well feel his

---

52 penitent: *i.e. doing penance*   **63** post: *haste; cf. n.*   **73** dispos'd: *disposed of*   **75** Phœnix; *cf. n.*   **78** bestow'd: *deposited*   **79** sconce: *head*   **80** stands on: *insists on*   **94** S. d. Ep.: *i.e. of Ephesus*   **96** o'er-raught: *cheated*   **97** cozenage: *cheating*   **102** liberties of sin: *sinful liberties, license*

II.i.S.d. Antipholus Sereptus; *cf. n.*   **15** lash'd: *scourged; cf. n.*   **17** his: *its*   **30** some other where: *i.e. after some other woman*   **33** other cause: *cause to be otherwise*   **39** helpless: *unavailing*   **41** fool-begg'd: *foolishly demanded*   **50** Beshrew: *ill luck to*

blows; and withal so doubtfully, that I could scarce
understand them.   *55*

    Adr. But say, I prithee, is he coming home?
It seems he hath great care to please his wife.

    Dro. E. Why, mistress, sure my master is horn-mad.

    Adr. Horn-mad, thou villain!

    Dro. E. I mean not cuckold-mad; but, sure, his is   *60*
stark mad.
When I desir'd him to come home to dinner,
He ask'd me for a thousand marks in gold:
' 'Tis dinner time,' quoth I; 'My gold!' quoth he:
'Your meat doth burn,' quoth I; 'My gold!' quoth he: *65*
'Will you come home?' quoth I; 'My gold!' quoth he,
'Where is the thousand marks I gave thee, villain?'
'The pig,' quoth I, 'is burn'd;' 'My gold!' quoth he:
'My mistress, sir,'—quoth I; 'Hang up thy mistress!
I know not thy mistress; out on thy mistress!'   *70*

    Luc. Quoth who?

    Dro. E. Quoth my master:
'I know,' quoth he, 'no house, no wife, no mistress.'
So that my errand, due unto my tongue,
I thank him, I bear home upon my shoulders;   *75*
For, in conclusion, he did beat me there.

    Adr. Go back again, thou slave, and fetch him home.

    Dro. E. Go back again, and be new beaten home?
For God's sake, send some other messenger.

    Adr. Back, slave, or I will break thy pate across.   *80*

    Dro. E. And he will bless that cross with other beating:
Between you, I shall have a holy head.

    Adr. Hence, prating peasant! fetch thy master home.

    Dro. E. Am I so round with you as you with me,
That like a football you do spurn me thus?   *85*
You spurn me hence, and he will spurn me hither:
If I last in this service, you must case me in leather.   *[Exit.]*

    Luc. Fie, how impatience loureth in your face!

    Adr. His company must do his minions grace,
Whilst I at home starve for a merry look.   *90*
Hath homely age the alluring beauty took
From my poor cheek? then, he hath wasted it:
Are my discourses dull? barren my wit?
If voluble and sharp discourse be marr'd,
Unkindness blunts it more than marble hard: *95*
Do their gay vestments his affections bait?
That's not my fault; he's master of my state:
What ruins are in me that can be found
By him not ruin'd? then is he the ground
Of my defeatures. My decayed fair   *100*
A sunny look of his would soon repair;
But, too unruly deer, he breaks the pale
And feeds from home: poor I am but his stale.

    Luc. Self-harming jealousy! fie, beat it hence!

    Adr. Unfeeling fools can with such wrongs dispense.   *105*
I know his eye doth homage otherwhere,
Or else what lets it but he would be here?
Sister, you know he promis'd me a chain:
Would that alone, alone he would detain,
So he would keep fair quarter with his bed!   *110*

I see, the jewel best enamelled
Will lose his beauty; yet the gold bides still
That others touch, and often touching will
Wear gold; and no man that hath a name,
By falsehood and corruption doth it shame.   *115*
Since that my beauty cannot please his eye,
I'll weep what's left away, and weeping die.

    Luc. How many fond fools serve mad jealousy!

                    Exit [with Adriana].

❧ Scene Second ❧

[A public Place]
Enter Antipholus Erotes [of Syracuse].

    Ant. S. The gold I gave to Dromio is laid up
Safe at the Centaur; and the heedful slave
Is wander'd forth, in care to seek me out.
By computation, and mine host's report,
I could not speak with Dromio since at first   *5*
I sent him from the mart. See, here he comes.

Enter Dromio Siracusia.

How now, sir! is your merry humour alter'd?
As you love strokes, so jest with me again.
You know no Centaur? You receiv'd no gold?
Your mistress sent to have me home to dinner?   *10*
My house was at the Phœnix? Wast thou mad,
That thus so madly thou didst answer me?

    Dro. S. What answer, sir? when spake I such a word?

    Ant. S. Even now, even here, not half an hour since.

    Dro. S. I did not see you since you sent me hence,   *15*
Home to the Centaur, with the gold you gave me.

    Ant. S. Villain, thou didst deny the gold's receipt,
And told'st me of a mistress and a dinner;
For which, I hope, thou felt'st I was displeas'd.

    Dro. S. I am glad to see you in this merry vein: *20*
What means this jest? I pray you, master, tell me.

    Ant. S. Yea, dost thou jeer, and flout me in the teeth?
Think'st thou I jest? Hold, take thou that, and that.

                       Beats Dro.

    Dro. S. Hold, sir, for God's sake! now your jest is earnest:
Upon what bargain do you give it me?   *25*

    Ant. S. Because that I familiarly sometimes
Do use you for my fool, and chat with you,
Your sauciness will jest upon my love,
And make a common of my serious hours.
When the sun shines let foolish gnats make sport,   *30*
But creep in crannies when he hides his beams.
If you will jest with me, know my aspect,
And fashion your demeanour to my looks,
Or I will beat this method in your sconce.

    Dro. S. Sconce, call you it? so you would leave battering, *35*
I had rather have it a head: an you use these blows long, I
must get a sconce for my head and insconce it too; or else I
shall seek my wit in my shoulders. But, I pray, sir, why am I
beaten?

    Ant. S. Dost thou not know?   *40*

58 horn-mad; *cf. n.*   **84 round;** *cf. n.*   **87 case:** *encase*   **89 minions:** *darlings*   **99
ground:** *cause*   **100 defeatures:** *disfigurements*   **fair:** *beauty*   **103 stale:** *dupe, laughingstock*   **105 dispense:** *put up*   **107 lets:** *hinders*   **110 keep fair quarter with:** *be true to*

111-115 I see … shame; *cf. n.*   **118 fond:** *doting*   **24 earnest;** *cf. n.*   **29**
Cf. n.   **32 aspect:** *countenance; cf. n.*   **37 sconce:** *helmet; cf. n.*   **38 insconce:** *fortify*

Dro. S. Nothing, sir, but that I am beaten.

Ant. S. Shall I tell you why?

Dro. S. Ay, sir, and wherefore; for they say every why
hath a wherefore.

Ant. S. Why, first,—for flouting me; and then,   45
wherefore,—

For urging it the second time to me.

Dro. S. Was there ever any man thus beaten out of season,
When in the why and the wherefore is neither rime nor
reason?   50
Well, sir, I thank you.

Ant. S. Thank me, sir? for what?

Dro. S. Marry, sir, for this something that you gave me
for nothing.

Ant. S. I'll make you amends next, to give you nothing   55
for something. But say, sir, is it dinner-time?

Dro. S. No, sir: I think the meat wants that I have.

Ant. S. In good time, sir; what's that?

Dro. S. Basting.

Ant. S. Well, sir, then 'twill be dry.   60

Dro. S. If it be, sir, I pray you eat none of it.

Ant. S. Your reason?

Dro. S. Lest it make you choleric, and purchase me
another dry basting.

Ant. S. Well, sir, learn to jest in good time: there's a   65
time for all things.

Dro. S. I durst have denied that, before you were so
choleric.

Ant. S. By what rule, sir?

Dro. S. Marry, sir, by a rule as plain as the plain bald   70
pate of Father Time himself.

Ant. S. Let's hear it.

Dro. S. There's no time for a man to recover his hair
that grows bald by nature.

Ant. S. May he not do it by fine and recovery?   75

Dro. S. Yes, to pay a fine for a periwig and recover the
lost hair of another man.

Ant. S. Why is Time such a niggard of hair, being, as it is,
so plentiful an excrement?

Dro. S. Because it is a blessing that he bestows on beasts: 80
and what he hath scanted men in hair, he hath given them
in wit.

Ant. S. Why, but there's many a man hath more hair
than wit.

Dro. S. Not a man of those but he hath the wit to lose   85
his hair.

Ant. S. Why, thou didst conclude hairy men plain dealers
without wit.

Dro. S. The plainer dealer, the sooner lost: yet he loseth
it in a kind of jollity.   90

Ant. S. For what reason?

Dro. S. For two; and sound ones too.

Ant. S. Nay, not sound, I pray you.

Dro. S. Sure ones then.

Ant. S. Nay, not sure, in a thing falsing.   95

Dro. S. Certain ones, then.

Ant. S. Name them.

Dro. S. The one, to save the money that he spends in
tiring; the other, that at dinner they should not drop in
his porridge.   100

Ant. S. You would all this time have proved there is no
time for all things.

Dro. S. Marry, and did, sir; namely, no time to recover
hair lost by nature.

Ant. S. But your reason was not substantial, why there   105
is no time to recover.

Dro. S. Thus I mend it: Time himself is bald, and
therefore to the world's end will have bald followers.

Ant. S. I knew 'twould be a bald conclusion. But soft!
who wafts us yonder?   110

Enter Adriana and Luciana.

Adr. Ay, ay, Antipholus, look strange, and frown:
Some other mistress hath thy sweet aspects;
I am not Adriana, nor thy wife.
The time was once when thou unurg'd wouldst vow
That never words were music to thine ear,   115
That never object pleasing in thine eye,
That never touch well welcome to thy hand,
That never meat sweet-savour'd in thy taste,
Unless I spake, or look'd, or touch'd, or carv'd to thee.
How comes it now, my husband, O, how comes it,   120
That thou art then estranged from thyself?
Thyself I call it, being strange to me,
That, undividable, incorporate,
Am better than thy dear self's better part.
Ah, do not tear away thyself from me!   125
For know, my love, as easy mayst thou fall
A drop of water in the breaking gulf,
And take unmingled thence that drop again,
Without addition or diminishing,
As take from me thyself and not me too.   130
How dearly would it touch thee to the quick,
Shouldst thou but hear I were licentious,
And that this body, consecrate to thee,
By ruffian lust should be contaminate!
Wouldst thou not spit at me and spurn at me,   135
And hurl the name of husband in my face,
And tear the stain'd skin off my harlot-brow,
And from my false hand cut the wedding-ring
And break it with a deep-divorcing vow?
I know thou canst; and therefore, see thou do it.   140
I am possess'd with an adulterate blot;
My blood is mingled with the crime of lust:
For if we two be one and thou play false,
I do digest the poison of thy flesh,
Being strumpeted by thy contagion.   145
Keep then fair league and truce with thy true bed;
I live distain'd, thou undishonoured.

Ant. S. Plead you to me, fair dame? I know you not:
In Ephesus I am but two hours old,
As strange unto your town as to your talk;   150
Who, every word by all my wit being scann'd,
Wants wit in all one word to understand.

Luc. Fie, brother! how the world is chang'd with you!

---

58 In good time: *forsooth*   **63 choleric:** *irascible; cf. n.*   **64 dry basting:** *severe beat-*
ing   **70 Marry:** *originally an oath by the Virgin Mary*   **75 fine and recovery:** *a legal*
term; cf. n.   **79 excrement:** *outgrowth*   **81 he hath ... hair;** *cf. n.*   **90 jollity;**
cf. n.   **95 falsing:** *deceptive*

99 tiring: *dressing the hair; cf. n.*   **109 bald:** *senseless*   **110 wafts:** *beckons*   **124 better**
part: *soul, spirit*   **126 fall:** *let fall*   **131 dearly:** *grievously*   **145 strumpeted:** *made a*
strumpet   **147 distain'd:** *stained; cf. n.*

When were you wont to use my sister thus?
She sent for you by Dromio home to dinner.   *155*

  Ant. S. By Dromio?

  Dro. S. By me?

  Adr. By thee; and this thou didst return from him,
That he did buffet thee, and in his blows,
Denied my house for his, me for his wife.   *160*

  Ant. S. Did you converse, sir, with this gentlewoman?
What is the course and drift of your compact?

  Dro. S. I, sir? I never saw her till this time.

  Ant. S. Villain, thou liest; for even her very words
Didst thou deliver to me on the mart.   *165*

  Dro. S. I never spake with her in all my life.

  Ant. S. How can she thus, then, call us by our names,
Unless it be by inspiration?

  Adr. How ill agrees it with your gravity
To counterfeit thus grossly with your slave,   *170*
Abetting him to thwart me in my mood!
Be it my wrong you are from me exempt,
But wrong not that wrong with a more contempt.
Come, I will fasten on this sleeve of thine:
Thou art an elm, my husband, I a vine,   *175*
Whose weakness, married to thy stronger state,
Makes me with thy strength to communicate:
If aught possess thee from me, it is dross,
Usurping ivy, brier, or idle moss;
Who, all for want of pruning, with intrusion   *180*
Infect thy sap and live on thy confusion.

  Ant. S. To me she speaks; she moves me for her theme!
What, was I married to her in my dream?
Or sleep I now and think I hear all this?
What error drives our eyes and ears amiss?   *185*
Until I know this sure uncertainty,
I'll entertain the offer'd fallacy.

  Luc. Dromio, go bid the servants spread for dinner.

  Dro. S. O, for my beads! I cross me for a sinner.
This is the fairy land: O spite of spites!   *190*
We talk with goblins, owls, and sprites:
If we obey them not, this will ensue,
They'll suck our breath, or pinch us black and blue.

  Luc. Why prat'st thou to thyself and answer'st not?
Dromio, thou drone, thou snail, thou slug, thou sot!   *195*

  Dro. S. I am transformed, master, am not I?

  Ant. S. I think thou art, in mind, and so am I.

  Dro. S. Nay, master, both in mind and in my shape.

  Ant. S. Thou hast thine own form.

  Dro. S. No, I am an ape.   *200*

  Luc. If thou art chang'd to aught, 'tis to an ass.

  Dro. S. 'Tis true; she rides me, and I long for grass.
'Tis so, I am an ass; else it could never be
But I should know her as well as she knows me.

  Adr. Come, come, no longer will I be a fool,   *205*
To put the finger in the eye and weep,
Whilst man and master laughs my woes to scorn.
Come, sir, to dinner. Dromio, keep the gate.
Husband, I'll dine above with you to-day,

And shrive you of a thousand idle pranks.   *210*
Sirrah, if any ask you for your master,
Say he dines forth, and let no creature enter.
Come, sister. Dromio, play the porter well.

  Ant. S. Am I in earth, in heaven, or in hell?
Sleeping or waking? mad or well-advis'd?   *215*
Known unto these, and to myself disguis'd!
I'll say as they say, and persever so,
And in this mist at all adventures go.

  Dro. S. Master, shall I be porter at the gate?

  Adr. Ay; and let none enter, lest I break your pate.   *220*

  Luc. Come, come, Antipholus, we dine too late.

                   [Exeunt.]

ACT THIRD ❧ SCENE FIRST

[Before the House of Antipholus of Ephesus]
Enter Antipholus of Ephesus, his man Dromio,
Angelo the Goldsmith, and Balthazar the Merchant.

  Ant. E. Good Signior Angelo, you must excuse us all;
My wife is shrewish when I keep not hours;
Say that I linger'd with you at your shop
To see the making of her carkanet,
And that to-morrow you will bring it home.   *5*
But here's a villain, that would face me down
He met me on the mart, and that I beat him,
And charg'd him with a thousand marks in gold,
And that I did deny my wife and house.
Thou drunkard, thou, what didst thou mean by this?   *10*

  Dro. E. Say what you will, sir, but I know what I know;
That you beat me at the mart, I have your hand to show:
If the skin were parchment and the blows you gave were ink,
Your own handwriting would tell you what I think.

  Ant. E. I think thou art an ass.   *15*

  Dro. E.   Marry, so it doth appear
By the wrongs I suffer and the blows I bear.
I should kick, being kick'd; and, being at that pass,
You would keep from my heels and beware of an ass.

  Ant. E. You are sad, Signior Balthazar: pray God, our   *20*
cheer
May answer my good will and your good welcome here.

  Bal. I hold your dainties cheap, sir, and your welcome dear.

  Ant. E. O, Signoir Balthazar, either at flesh or fish,
A table-full of welcome makes scarce one dainty dish.   *25*

  Bal. Good meat, sir, is common; that every churl
affords.

  Ant. E. And welcome more common, for that's nothing
but words.

  Bal. Small cheer and great welcome makes a merry feast.   *30*

  Ant. E. Ay, to a niggardly host and more sparing guest:
But though my cates be mean, take them in good part;
Better cheer may you have, but not with better heart.
But soft! my door is lock'd. Go bid them let us in.

  Dro. E. Maud, Bridget, Marian, Cicely, Gillian, Ginn!   *35*

---

171 mood: *anger*   **172 exempt:** *separated*   **178 possess . . . me:** *dispossess me of thee*   **179 idle:** *barren, unfruitful*   **181 confusion:** *ruin*   **182 moves:** *appeals to* **theme:** *subject*   **186** *Until I unravel this undeniable mystery*   **187 entertain . . . fallacy:** *accept the unreal situation*   **189 beads:** *rosary*   **195 sot:** *fool*   **206 put . . . eye:** *play the child*   **207 laughs:** *cf. n.*

210 shrive you: *call you to confession*   **212 forth:** *away from home*   **215 well-advis'd:** *in my right mind*   **4 carkanet:** *gold collar*   **8 charg'd him with:** *asked him to account for*   **32 cates:** *dainties*   **35 Gillian:** *Juliana* **Ginn:** *Jenny(?)*

Dro. S. [Within.] Mome, malt-horse, capon, coxcomb,
idiot, patch!
Either get thee from the door or sit down at the hatch.
Dost thou conjure for wenches, that thou call'st for such store,
When one is one too many? Go, get thee from the door.   40

Dro. E. What patch is made our porter?—My master
stays in the street.

Dro. S. [Within.] Let him walk from whence he came,
lest he catch cold on's feet.

Ant. E. Who talks within there? ho, open the door!   45

Dro. S. [Within.] Right, sir; I'll tell you when, an you'll
tell me wherefore.

Ant. E. Wherefore? for my dinner: I have not din'd to-day.

Dro. S. Nor to-day here you must not; come again when
you may.   50

Ant. E. What art thou that keep'st me out from the
house I owe?

Dro. S. [Within.] The porter for this time, sir, and my
name is Dromio.

Dro. E. O villain, thou hast stolen both mine office and   55
my name!
The one ne'er got me credit, the other mickle blame.
If thou hadst been Dromio to-day in my place,
Thou wouldst have chang'd thy face for a name, or thy
name for an ass.   60

Luce. [Within.] What a coil is there, Dromio! who are
those at the gate?

Dro. E. Let my master in, Luce.

Luce. [Within.] Faith, no; he comes too late;
And so tell your master.   65

Dro. E.   O Lord! I must laugh.
Have at you with a proverb: Shall I set in my staff?

Luce: [Within.] Have at you with another: that's—
when? can you tell?

Dro. S. [Within.] If thy name be call'd Luce,—   70
Luce, thou hast answer'd him well.

Ant. E. Do you hear, you minion? you'll let us in, I trow?

Luce. [Within.] I thought to have ask'd you.

Dro. S. [Within.]   And you said, no.

Dro. E. So come, help: well struck! there was blow for blow.

Ant. E. Thou baggage, let me in.

Luce. [Within.]   Can you tell for whose sake?

Dro. E. Master, knock the door hard.

Luce. [Within.]   Let him knock till it ache.

Ant. E. You'll cry for this, minion, if I beat the door down.

Luce. [Within.] What needs all that, and a pair of stocks in
the town?

Adr. [Within.] Who is that at the door that keeps all
this noise?

Dro. S. [Within.] By my troth your town is troubled   85
with unruly boys.

Ant. E. Are you there, wife? you might have come before.

Adr. [Within.] Your wife, sir knave! go, get you from the
door.

Dro. E. If you went in pain, master, this 'knave' would   90
go sore.

Ang. Here is neither cheer, sir, nor welcome: we would
fain have either.

Bal. In debating which was best, we shall part with neither.

Dro. E. They stand at the door, master: bid them welcome   95
hither.

Ant. E. There is something in the wind, that we cannot
get in.

Dro. E. You would say so, master, if your garments   100
were thin.
Your cake here is warm within; you stand here in the cold:
It would make a man mad as a buck to be so bought and
sold.

Ant. E. Go fetch me something: I'll break ope the gate.   105

Dro. S. [Within.] Break any breaking here, and I'll break
your knave's pate.

Dro. E. A man may break a word with you, sir, and
words are but wind:
Ay, and break it in your face, so he break it not behind.   110

Dro. S. [Within.] It seems thou wantest breaking: out
upon thee, hind!

Dro. E. Here's too much 'out upon thee!' I pray thee,
let me in.

Dro. S. [Within.] Ay, when fowls have no feathers, and   115
fish have no fin.

Ant. E. Well, I'll break in. Go borrow me a crow.

Dro. E. A crow without feather? Master, mean you so?
For a fish without a fin, there's a fowl without a feather:
If a crow help us in, sirrah, we'll pluck a crow together.   120

Ant. E. Go get thee gone: fetch me an iron crow.

Bal. Have patience, sir; O let it not be so!
Herein you war against your reputation,
And draw within the compass of suspect
The unviolated honour of your wife.   125
Once this,—your long experience of her wisdom,
Her sober virtue, years, and modesty,
Plead on her part some cause to you unknown;
And doubt not, sir, but she will well excuse
Why at this time the doors are made against you.   130
Be rul'd by me: depart in patience,
And let us to the Tiger all to dinner;
And about evening come yourself alone,
To know the reason of this strange restraint.
If by strong hand you offer to break in   135
Now in the stirring passage of the day,
A vulgar comment will be made of it,
And that supposed by the common rout
Against your yet ungalled estimation,
That may with foul intrusion enter in   140
And dwell upon your grave when you are dead;
For slander lives upon succession,
For ever hous'd where it gets possession.

Ant. E. You have prevail'd: I will depart in quiet,
And, in despite of mirth, mean to be merry.   145
I know a wench of excellent discourse,
Pretty and witty, wild and yet too gentle:
There will we dine. This woman that I mean,

36 Mome: *buffoon*   **malt-horse:** *brewer's horse, hence a term of contempt*   **38 hatch:** *half-door, wicket*   **44 on's:** *in his*   **52 owe:** *own*   **57 mickle:** *much*   **58-60** *Cf. n.*   **61 S. d. Within;** *cf. n.*   **coil:** *fuss*   **67 set in my staff:** *'make myself at home' (?)*   **68, 69 when? can you tell;** *cf. n.*   **72 minion:** *hussy*

94 part: *depart*   **103, 104 bought and sold;** *imposed upon*   **112 hind:** *slave*   **117 crow:** *crowbar*   **124 draw … suspect:** *bring into suspicion*   **126 Once this:** *once for all, in short*   **130 made:** *fastened*   **136 stirring passage:** *hour of busy traffic*   **137 vulgar:** *public*   **138 supposed:** *conjectured*   **139 ungalled:** *unblemished*   **142 Cf. n.*   **145 in despite of mirth:** *i.e. though I do not feel like being merry*

My wife—but I protest, without desert—
Hath oftentimes upbraided me withal: 150
To her will we to dinner. *[To Angelo.]* Get you home,
And fetch the chain; by this I know 'tis made:
Bring it, I pray you, to the Porpentine;
For there's the house: that chain will I bestow,
Be it for nothing but to spite my wife,   155
Upon mine hostess there. Good sir, make haste.
Since mine own doors refuse to entertain me,
I'll knock elsewhere, to see if they'll disdain me.
    Ang. I'll meet you at that place some hour hence.
    Ant. E. Do so. This jest shall cost me some expense.   160
                    Exeunt.

❧ SCENE SECOND ❧

[The Same]
Enter Luciana with Antipholus of Syracusia.

    Luc. And may it be that you have quite forgot
A husband's office? Shall, Antipholus,
Even in the spring of love, thy love-springs rot?
Shall love, in building, grow so ruinous?
If you did wed my sister for her wealth,   5
Then, for her wealth's sake use her with more kindness:
Or, if you like elsewhere, do it by stealth;
Muffle your false love with some show of blindness:
Let not my sister read it in your eye;
Be not thy tongue thy own shame's orator;   10
Look sweet, speak fair, become disloyalty;
Apparel vice like virtue's harbinger;
Bear a fair presence, though your heart be tainted;
Teach sin the carriage of a holy saint;
Be secret-false: what need she be acquainted?   15
What simple thief brags of his own attaint?
'Tis double wrong to truant with your bed,
And let her read it in thy looks at board:
Shame hath a bastard fame, well managed;
Ill deeds are doubled with an evil word.   20
Alas, poor women! make us but believe,
Being compact of credit, that you love us;
Though others have the arm, show us the sleeve;
We in your motion turn, and you may move us.
Then, gentle brother, get you in again;   25
Comfort my sister, cheer her, call her wife:
'Tis holy sport to be a little vain,
When the sweet breath of flattery conquers strife.
    Ant. S. Sweet mistress,—what your name is else, I know not,
Nor by what wonder you do hit of mine,—   30
Less in your knowledge and your grace you show not
Than our earth's wonder; more than earth divine.
Teach me, dear creature, how to think and speak:
Lay open to my earthy-gross conceit,
Smother'd in errors, feeble, shallow, weak,   35
The folded meaning of your words' deceit.

Against my soul's pure truth why labour you
To make it wander in an unknown field?
Are you a god? would you create me new?
Transform me, then, and to your power I'll yield.   40
But if that I am I, then well I know
Your weeping sister is no wife of mine,
Nor to her bed no homage do I owe:
Far more, far more, to you do I decline.
O train me not, sweet mermaid, with thy note,   45
To drown me in thy sister flood of tears!
Sing, siren, for thyself, and I will dote:
Spread o'er the silver waves thy golden hairs,
And as a bed I'll take them and there lie;
And in that glorious supposition think   50
He gains by death that hath such means to die:
Let Love, being light, be drowned if she sink!
    Luc. What, are you mad, that you do reason so?
    Ant. S. Not mad, but mated; how, I do not know.
    Luc. It is a fault that springeth from your eye.   55
    Ant. S. For gazing on your beams, fair sun, being by.
    Luc. Gaze where you should, and that will clear your sight.
    Ant. S. As good to wink, sweet love, as look on night.
    Luc. Why call you me love? call my sister so.
    Ant. S. Thy sister's sister.   60
    Luc.   That's my sister.
    Ant. S.   No;
It is thyself, mine own self's better part;
Mine eye's clear eye, my dear heart's dearer heart;
My food, my fortune, and my sweet hope's aim,   65
My sole earth's heaven, and my heaven's claim.
    Luc. All this my sister is, or else should be.
    Ant. S. Call thyself sister, sweet, for I aim thee.
Thee will I love and with thee lead my life:
Thou hast no husband yet nor I no wife.   70
Give me thy hand.
    Luc.   O, soft, sir! hold you still:
I'll fetch my sister, to get her good will   *Exit.*

Enter Dromio Siracusia.

    Ant. S. Why, how now, Dromio! where run'st thou so fast?
    Dro. S. Do you know me, sir? am I Dromio? am I your   75
man? am I myself?
    Ant. S. Thou art Dromio, thou art my man, thou art
thyself.
    Dro. S. I am an ass, I am a woman's man and besides
myself.   80
    Ant. S. What woman's man? and how besides thyself?
    Dro. S. Marry, sir, besides myself, I am due to a woman;
one that claims me, one that haunts me, one that will have me.
    Ant. S. What claim lays she to thee?
    Dro. S. Marry, sir, such claim as you would lay to your   85
horse; and she would have me as a beast: not that, I being a
beast, she would have me; but that she, being a very beastly
creature, lays claim to me.
    Ant. S. What is she?
    Dro. S. A very reverent body; aye, such a one as a man   90
may not speak of, without he say, 'Sir-reverence.' I have but
lean luck in the match, and yet is she a wondrous fat marriage.

---

149 desert: *i.e. my deserving it*   **153 Porpentine:** *porcupine (house-sign)*   **SCENE TWO**
S. d. Luciana; *cf. n.*   **3 love-springs:** *shoots of love*   **4 in building:** *even before completely
built*   **11 become disloyalty;** *cf. n.*   **15 what:** *why*   **16 attaint:** *disgrace*   **22 compact of credit:** *wholly made up of credulity*   **27 vain:** *extravagant in language*   **30 hit
of:** *guess*   **34 conceit:** *understanding*   **36 folded:** *concealed*

44 decline: *incline*   **45 train:** *entice*   **52** *Cf. n.*   **53 reason:** *argue*   **54 mated:**
bewildered; also, furnished with a mate   **56 being by:** *when you are near*   **58 wink:** *close
the eyes*   **66** *Cf. n.*   **68 aim:** *mean*   **91 'Sir-reverence';** *cf. n.* **lean:** *poor*

Ant. S. How dost thou mean a fat marriage?

Dro. S. Marry, sir, she's the kitchen-wench, and all
grease; and I know not what use to put her to, but to   *95*
make a lamp of her and run from her by her own light. I
warrant her rags and the tallow in them will burn a Poland
winter; if she lives till doomsday, she'll burn a week longer
than the whole world.

Ant. S. What complexion is she of?   *100*

Dro. S. Swart, like my shoe, but her face nothing like so
clean kept: for why she sweats; a man may go over shoes in
the grime of it.

Ant. S. That's a fault that water will mend.

Dro. S. No, sir, 'tis in grain; Noah's flood could not do it.

Ant. S. What's her name?

Dro. S. Nell, sir; but her name and three quarters,—that's
an ell and three-quarters,—will not measure her from hip
to hip.

Ant. S. Then she bears some breadth?   *110*

Dro. S. No longer from head to foot than from hip to hip:
she is spherical, like a globe; I could find out countries in her.

Ant. S. In what part of her body stands Ireland?

Dro. S. Marry, sir, in her buttocks: I found it out by the
bogs.   *115*

Ant. S. Where Scotland?

Dro. S. I found it by the barrenness; hard in the palm of
the hand.

Ant. S. Where France?

Dro. S. In her forehead, armed and reverted, making   *120*
war against her heir.

Ant. S. Where England?

Dro. S. I looked for the chalky cliffs, but I could find no
whiteness in them; but I guess it stood in her chin, by the
salt rheum that ran between France and it.   *125*

Ant. S. Where Spain?

Dro. S. Faith, I saw it not; but I felt it hot in her breath.

Ant. S. Where America, the Indies?

Dro. S. O, sir! upon her nose, all o'er embellished with
rubies, carbuncles, sapphires, declining their rich aspect to the
hot breath of Spain, who sent whole armadoes of carracks
to be ballast at her nose.

Ant. S. Where stood Belgia, the Netherlands?

Dro. S. O, sir! I did not look so low. To conclude, this
drudge, or diviner, laid claim to me; call'd me Dromio; swore
I was assured to her; told me what privy marks I had about me,
as the mark of my shoulder, the mole in my neck, the great wart
on my left arm, that I, amazed, ran from her as a witch:
And, I think, if my breast had not been made of faith and
my heart of steel,   *140*
She had transform'd me to a curtal dog and made me turn
i' the wheel.

Ant. S. Go hie thee presently post to the road:
An if the wind blow any way from shore,
I will not harbour in this town to-night: *145*
If any bark put forth, come to the mart,
Where I will walk till thou return to me.

If every one knows us and we know none,
'Tis time, I think, to trudge, pack, and be gone.

Dro. S. As from a bear a man would run for life,   *150*
So fly I from her that would be my wife.   *Exit.*

Ant. S. There's none but witches do inhabit here,
And therefore 'tis high time that I were hence.
She that doth call me husband, even my soul
Doth for a wife abhor; but her fair sister,   *155*
Possess'd with such a gentle sovereign grace,
Of such enchanting presence and discourse,
Hath almost made me traitor to myself:
But, lest myself be guilty to self-wrong,
I'll stop mine ears against the mermaid's song.   *160*

Enter Angelo with the chain.

Ang. Master Antipholus!

Ant. S. Ay, that's my name.

Ang. I know it well, sir: lo, here is the chain.
I thought to have ta'en you at the Porpentine:
The chain unfinish'd made me stay thus long.   *165*

Ant. S. What is your will that I shall do with this?

Ang. What please yourself, sir: I have made it for you.

Ant. S. Made it for me, sir! I bespoke it not.

Ang. Not once, nor twice, but twenty times you have.
Go home with it and please your wife withal;   *170*
And soon at supper-time I'll visit you,
And then receive my money for the chain.

Ant. S. I pray you, sir, receive the money now,
For fear you ne'er see chain nor money more.

Ang. You are a merry man, sir: fare you well.   *Exit.*

Ant. S. What I should think of this, I cannot tell:
But this I think, there's no man is so vain
That would refuse so fair an offer'd chain.
I see, a man here needs not live by shifts,
When in the streets he meets such golden gifts.   *180*
I'll to the mart, and there for Dromio stay:
If any ship put out, then straight away.   *Exit.*

ACT FOURTH ❧ SCENE FIRST

[A Public Place]
Enter a [second] Merchant, Goldsmith [Angelo], and an Officer.

Mer. You know since Pentecost the sum is due,
And since I have not much importun'd you;
Nor now I had not, but that I am bound
To Persia, and want guilders for my voyage:
Therefore make present satisfaction,   *5*
Or I'll attach you by this officer.

Ang. Even just the sum that I do owe to you
Is growing to me by Antipholus;
And in the instant that I met with you
He had of me a chain: at five o'clock   *10*
I shall receive the money for the same.
Pleaseth you walk with me down to his house,
I will discharge my bond, and thank you too.

---

101 **Swart:** *swarthy*   102 **for why:** *because*   105 **in grain:** *fast dyed*   120, 121 **armed
. . . heir;** *cf. n.*   124 **them:** *i.e. her teeth*   131 **armadoes:** *fleets*   **carracks:** *large merchant
ships*   132 **ballast:** *ballasted, loaded*   135 **diviner:** *sorceress*   136 **assured:** *betrothed*   138 **that:** *so that*   141 **curtal:** *having a docked tail*   **turn i' the wheel;**
cf. n.   143 **presently:** *immediately*   **road:** *harbor*

159 **to:** *of*   177 **vain:** *silly*   6 **attach:** *arrest*   8 **growing:** *accruing*

Enter Antipholus Ephes. [and the Ephesian]
Dromio from the Courtesan's.

Off. That labour may you save: see where he comes.   *15*

Ant. E. While I go to the goldsmith's house, go thou
And buy a rope's end: that will I bestow
Among my wife and her confederates,
For locking me out of my doors by day.
But soft! I see the goldsmith. Get thee gone;   *20*
Buy thou a rope, and bring it home to me.

Dro. E. I buy a thousand pound a year! I buy a rope! *Exit Dro.*

Ant. E. A man is well holp up that trusts to you:
I promised your presence and the chain;
But neither chain nor goldsmith came to me.   *25*
Belike you thought our love would last too long,
If it were chain'd together, and therefore came not.

Ang. Saving your merry humour, here's the note
How much your chain weighs to the utmost carat,
The fineness of the gold, and chargeful fashion,   *30*
Which doth amount to three odd ducats more
Than I stand debted to this gentleman:
I pray you see him presently discharg'd,
For his is bound to sea and stays but for it.

Ant. E. I am not furnish'd with the present money;   *35*
Besides, I have some business in the town.
Good signior, take the stranger to my house,
And with you take the chain, and bid my wife
Disburse the sum on the receipt thereof:
Perchance I will be there as soon as you.   *40*

Ang. Then, you will bring the chain to her yourself?

Ant. E. No; bear it with you, lest I come not time enough.

Ang. Well, sir, I will. Have you the chain about you?

Ant. E. An if I have not, sir, I hope you have,
Or else you may return without your money.   *45*

Ang. Nay, come, I pray you, sir, give me the chain:
Both wind and tide stays for this gentleman,
And I, to blame, have held him here too long.

Ant. E. Good Lord! you use this dalliance to excuse
Your breach of promise to the Porpentine.   *50*
I should have chid you for not bringing it,
But, like a shrew, you first begin to brawl.

Mer. The hour steals on; I pray you, sir, dispatch.

Ang. You hear how he importunes me: the chain!

Ant. E. Why, give it to my wife and fetch your money.   *55*

Ang. Come, come, you know I gave it you even now.
Either send the chain or send me by some token.

Ant. E. Fie! now you run this humour out of breath.
Come, where's the chain? I pray you, let me see it.

Mer. My business cannot brook this dalliance.   *60*
Good sir, say whe'r you'll answer me or no:
If not, I'll leave him to the officer.

Ant. E. I answer you! what should I answer you?

Ang. The money that you owe me for the chain.

Ant. E. I owe you none till I receive the chain.   *65*

Ang. You know I gave it you half an hour since.

Ant. E. You gave me none: you wrong me much to say so.

Ang. You wrong me more, sir, in denying it:
Consider how it stands upon my credit.

Mer. Well, officer, arrest him at my suit.   *70*

Off. I do;
And charge you in the duke's name to obey me.

Ang. This touches me in reputation.
Either consent to pay this sum for me,
Or I attach you by this officer.   *75*

Ant. E. Consent to pay thee that I never had!
Arrest me, foolish fellow, if thou dar'st.

Ang. Here is thy fee: arrest him, officer.
I would not spare my brother in this case,
If he should scorn me so apparently.   *80*

Off. I do arrest you, sir: you hear the suit.

Ant. E. I do obey thee till I give thee bail.
But, sirrah, you shall buy this sport as dear
As all the metal in your shop will answer.

Ang. Sir, sir, I shall have law in Ephesus,   *85*
To your notorious shame, I doubt it not.

Enter Dromio Sira. from the Bay.

Dro. S. Master, there is a bark of Epidamnum
That stays but till her owner comes aboard,
And then she bears away. Our fraughtage, sir,
I have convey'd aboard, and I have bought   *90*
The oil, the balsamum, and acqua-vitæ.
The ship is in her trim; the merry wind
Blows fair from land; they stay for nought at all
But for their owner, master, and yourself.

Ant. E. How now! a madman! Why, thou peevish sheep,   *95*
What ship of Epidamnum stays for me?

Dro. S. A ship you sent me to, to hire waftage.

Ant. E. Thou drunken slave, I sent thee for a rope,
And told thee to what purpose, and what end.

Dro. S. You sent me for a rope's end as soon: *100*
You sent me to the bay, sir, for a bark.

Ant. E. I will debate this matter at more leisure,
And teach your ears to list me with more heed.
To Adriana, villain, hie thee straight:
Give her this key, and tell her, in the desk   *105*
That's cover'd o'er with Turkish tapestry,
There is a purse of ducats: let her send it.
Tell her I am arrested in the street,
And that shall bail me. Hie thee, slave, be gone!
On, officer, to prison till it come.   *110*

Exeunt [all except Dromio].

Dro. S. To Adriana! that is where we din'd,
Where Dowsabel did claim me for her husband:
She is too big, I hope, for me to compass.
Thither I must, although against my will,
For servants must their masters' minds fulfil.   *Exit.* *115*

❧ SCENE SECOND ❧

[A Room in the House of Antipholus of Ephesus]
Enter Adriana and Luciana.

Adr. Ah, Luciana, did he tempt thee so?
Mightst thou perceive austerely in his eye

---

17 **bestow:** *employ*   22 **I buy ... year:** *cf. n.*   23 **holp:** *helped*   26 **Belike:** *probably*   30 **chargeful fashion:** *costly workmanship*   32 **debted:** *indebted*   34 **stays:** *waits*   42 **time:** *in time*   57 **send ... token:** *cf. n.*   61 **whe'r:** *whether*   **answer me:** *discharge the debt to me*   69 **stands upon:** *concerns*

80 **apparently:** *openly*   89 **fraughtage:** *freight*   91 **balsamum** *balsam*   **acqua-vitæ:** *brandy*   92 **in her trim:** *rigged, ready to sail*   95 **peevish:** *foolish*   **sheep:** *cf. n.*   97 **waftage:** *passage*   103 **list:** *listen to*   112 **Dowsabel** *cf. n.*   2 **austerely:** *seriously*

That he did plead in earnest? yea or no?
Look'd he or red or pale? or sad or merrily?
What observation mad'st thou in this case   5
Of his heart's meteors tilting in his face?

  Luc. First he denied you had in him no right.

  Adr. He meant he did me none; the more my spite.

  Luc. Then swore he that he was a stranger here.

  Adr. And true he swore, though yet forsworn he were.   10

  Luc. Then pleaded I for you.

  Adr.   And what said he?

  Luc. That love I begg'd for you he begg'd of me.

  Adr. With what persuasion did he tempt thy love?

  Luc. With words that in an honest suit might move.   15
First, he did praise my beauty, then my speech.

  Adr. Didst speak him fair?

  Luc.   Have patience, I beseech.

  Adr. I cannot, nor I will not hold me still:
My tongue, though not my heart, shall have his will.   20
He is deformed, crooked, old and sere,
Ill-fac'd, worse bodied, shapeless everywhere;
Vicious, ungentle, foolish, blunt, unkind,
Stigmatical in making, worse in mind.

  Luc. Who would be jealous, then, of such a one?   25
No evil lost is wail'd when it is gone.

  Adr. Ah, but I think him better than I say,
And yet would herein others' eyes were worse.
Far from her nest the lapwing cries away:
My heart prays for him, though my tongue do curse.   30

               Enter S[yracusan] Dromio.

  Dro. S. Here, go: the desk! the purse! sweet, now, make
haste.

  Luc. How hast thou lost thy breath?

  Dro. S.   By running fast.

  Adr. Where is thy master, Dromio? is he well?   35

  Dro. S. No, he's in Tartar limbo, worse than hell.
A devil in an everlasting garment hath him,
One whose hard heart is button'd up with steel;
A fiend, a fairy, pitiless and rough;
A wolf, nay, worse, a fellow all in buff;   40
A back-friend, a shoulder-clapper, one that countermands
The passages of alleys, creeks and narrow lands;
A hound that runs counter and yet draws dry-foot well;
One that, before the judgment, carries poor souls to hell.

  Adr. Why, man, what is the matter?   45

  Dro. S. I do not know the matter: he is 'rested on the case.

  Adr. What, is he arrested? tell me at whose suit.

  Dro. S. I know not at whose suit he is arrested well;
But he's in a suit of buff which 'rested him, that can I tell.
Will you send him, mistress, redemption, the money in   50
his desk?

  Adr. Go fetch it, sister.—This I wonder at:

                   Exit Luciana.

That he, unknown to me, should be in debt:
Tell me, was he arrested on a band?

  Dro. S. Not on a band, but on a stronger thing: 55
A chain, a chain. Do you not hear it ring?

  Adr. What, the chain?

  Dro. S. No, no, the bell: 'tis time that I were gone:
It was two ere I left him, and now the clock strikes one.

  Adr. The hours come back! that did I never hear.   60

  Dro. S. O yes; if any hour meet a sergeant, a' turns
back for very fear.

  Adr. As if Time were in debt! how fondly dost thou reason!

  Dro. S. Time is a very bankrupt, and owes more than
he's worth to season.   65
Nay, he's a thief too: have you not heard men say,
That Time comes stealing on by night and day?
If Time be in debt and theft, and a sergeant in the way,
Hath he not reason to turn back an hour in a day?

               Enter Luciana.

  Adr. Go, Dromio: there's the money, bear it straight,   70
And bring thy master home immediately.
Come, sister: I am press'd down with conceit,—
Conceit, my comfort and my injury.

          Exit [with Luciana and Dromio].

❧ SCENE THIRD ❧

[A Public Place]
Enter Antipholus Siracusia.

  Ant. S. There's not a man I meet but doth salute me,
As if I were their well acquainted friend;
And every one doth call me by my name.
Some tender money to me; some invite me;
Some other give me thanks for kindnesses;   5
Some offer me commodities to buy:
Even now a tailor call'd me in his shop
And show'd me silks that he had bought for me,
And therewithal, took measure of my body.
Sure, these are but imaginary wiles,   10
And Lapland sorcerers inhabit here.

          Enter Dromio [of] Syr[acuse].

  Dro. S. Master, here's the gold you sent me for.
What, have you got the picture of old Adam new apparelled?

  Ant. S. What gold is this? What Adam dost thou mean?

  Dro. S. Not that Adam that kept the Paradise, but that   15
Adam that keeps the prison: he that goes in the calf's skin
that was killed for the Prodigal: he that came behind you,
sir, like an evil angel, and bid you forsake your liberty.

  Ant. S. I understand thee not.

  Dro. S. No? why, 'tis a plain case: he that went, like a   20
base-viol, in a case of leather; the man, sir, that, when gentlemen are tired, gives them a sob, and 'rests them; he, sir, that
takes pity on decayed men and give them suits of durance; he
that sets up his rest to do more exploits with his mace than
a morris-pike.   25

  Ant. S. What, thou meanest an officer?

---

6 *Cf. n.*   8 **spite:** *vexation*   20 **his:** *its*   21 **sere:** *withered*   22 **shapeless:** *mis-shapen*   24 **Stigmatical:** *branded by deformity*   30 *Cf .n.*   36 **Tartar:** *Tartarean, infernal* **limbo:** *cant term for prison*   37 **everlasting:** *i.e. made of buff, a very durable material*   39 **fairy;** *cf. n.*   41 **A back-friend, a shoulder-clapper;** *cf. n.* **counter-mands:** *prohibits*   42 **creeks:** *narrow winding passages*   43 **counter;** *cf. n.* **draws dry-foot:** *traces the scent of the game*   44 *Cf. n.*   46 **on the case;** *cf. n.*   54 **band:** *bond*

61 **a':** *he (it)*   63 **fondly:** *foolishly*   64, 65 **owes ... season:** *cf. n.*   73 **conceit:** *imaginings*   11 **Lapland sorcerers;** *cf. n.*   13 *Cf. n.*   16, 17 **calf's skin ... Prodigal;** *cf .n.*   22 **sob:** *slight rest given a horse to recover its wind.*   23 **suits of durance:** *durable garments, i.e. prison dress*   24 **sets up his rest:** *stakes his all* **mace:** *club carried by a bailiff or constable*   25 **morris-pike:** *Moorish pike*

Dro. S. Ay, sir, the sergeant of the band; he that brings any man to answer it that breaks his band; one that thinks a man always going to bed, and says, 'God give you good rest!'

Ant. S. Well, sir, there rest in your foolery.   *30*
Is there any ship puts forth to-night? may we be gone?

Dro. S. Why, sir, I brought you word an hour since that the bark Expedition put forth to-night; and then were you hindered by the sergeant to tarry for the hoy Delay. Here are the angels that you sent for to deliver you.   *35*

Ant. S. The fellow is distract, and so am I;
And here we wander in illusions:
Some blessed power deliver us from hence!

           Enter a Courtesan.

Cour. Well met, well met, Master Antipholus.
I see, sir, you have found the goldsmith now: *40*
Is that the chain you promis'd me to-day?

Ant. S. Satan, avoid! I charge thee tempt me not!

Dro. S. Master, is this Mistress Satan?

Ant. S. It is the devil.

Dro. S. Nay, she is worse, she is the devil's dam, and   *45*
here she comes in the habit of a light wench: and thereof comes that the wenches say, 'God damn me;' that's as much as to say, 'God make me a light wench.' It is written, they appear to men like angels of light: light is an effect of fire, and fire will burn; *ergo*, light wenches will burn. Come not near her. *50*

Cour. Your man and you are marvellous merry, sir. Will you go with me? we'll mend our dinner here.

Dro. S. Master, if you do, expect spoon-meat, so bespeak a long spoon.

Ant. S. Why, Dromio?   *55*

Dro. S. Marry, he must have a long spoon that must eat with the devil.

Ant. S. Avoid then, fiend! what tell'st thou me of supping?
Thou art, as you are all, a sorceress:
I conjure thee to leave me and be gone.   *60*

Cour. Give me the ring of mine you had at dinner,
Or, for my diamond, the chain you promis'd,
And I'll be gone, sir, and not trouble you.

Dro. S. Some devils ask but the parings of one's nail,
A rush, a hair, a drop of blood, a pin,   *65*
A nut, a cherry-stone;
But she, more covetous, would have a chain.
Master, be wise: an if you give it her,
The devil will shake her chain and fright us with it.

Cour. I pray you, sir, my ring, or else the chain: *70*
I hope you do not mean to cheat me so.

Ant. S. Avaunt, thou witch! Come, Dromio, let us go.

Dro. S. 'Fly pride,' says the peacock: mistress, that you know.

           Exit [Dromio of Syracuse with his master].

Cour. Now, out of doubt, Antipholus is mad,   *75*
Else would he never so demean himself.
A ring he hath of mine worth forty ducats,
And for the same he promis'd me a chain:
Both one and other he denies me now.
The reason that I gather he is mad,   *80*
Besides this present instance of his rage,

Is a mad tale he told to-day at dinner,
Of his own doors being shut against his entrance.
Belike his wife, acquainted with his fits,
On purpose shut the doors against his way.   *85*
My way is now to hie home to his house,
And tell his wife, that, being lunatic,
He rush'd into my house, and took perforce
My ring away. This course I fittest choose,
For forty ducats is too much to lose.   *[Exit.]*   *90*

❧ Scene Fourth ❧

[A Street]
Enter Antipholus Ephes. with a Gaoler.

Ant. E. Fear me not, man; I will not break away:
I'll give thee, ere I leave thee, so much money,
To warrant thee, as I am 'rested for.
My wife is in a wayward mood to-day,
And will not lightly trust the messenger.   *5*
That I should be attach'd in Ephesus,
I tell you, 'twill sound harshly in her ears.

           Enter Dromio Eph. with a rope's end.

Here comes my man: I think he brings the money.
How now, sir! have you that I sent you for?

Dro. E. Here's that, I warrant you, will pay them all.   *10*

Ant. E. But where's the money?

Dro. E. Why, sir, I gave the money for the rope.

Ant. E. Five hundred ducats, villain, for a rope?

Dro. E. I'll serve you, sir, five hundred at the rate.

Ant. E. To what end did I bid thee hie thee home?   *15*

Dro. E. To a rope's end, sir; and to that end am I return'd.

Ant. E. And to that end, sir, I will welcome you.

           [Beats him.]

Off. Good sir, be patient.

Dro. E. Nay, 'tis for me to be patient; I am in adversity.

Off. Good now, hold thy tongue.   *20*

Dro. E. Nay, rather persuade him to hold his hands.

Ant. E. Thou whoreson, senseless villain!

Dro. E. I would I were senseless, sir, that I might not feel your blows.

Ant. E. Thou art sensible in nothing but blows, and so is   *25*
an ass.

Dro. E. I am an ass indeed; you may prove it by my long ears. I have served him from the hour of my nativity to this instant, and have nothing at his hands for my service but blows. When I am cold, he heats me with beating; when I am   *30*
warm, he cools me with beating: I am waked with it when I sleep, raised with it when I sit, driven out of doors with it when I go from home, welcomed home with it when I return; nay, I bear it on my shoulders, as a begggar wont her brat; and, I think, when he hath lamed shall beg with it from   *35*
door to door.

           Enter Adriana, Luciana, Courtesan, and a
           Schoolmaster, called Pinch

Ant. E. Come, go along; my wife is coming yonder.

---

34 hoy: *a small vessel*   **35 angels:** *gold coins worth about ten shillings apiece*   **36 distract:** *distracted, mad*   **42 avoid:** *avaunt*   **46 light:** *wanton*   **52 mend our dinner:** *i.e. supplement it by further refreshments*   **73 'Fly … peacock.** *cf. n.*   **76 demean:** *conduct*

20 Good now: *pray you*   **25 sensible:** *sensitive*   **34 wont:** *is wont to*

Dro. E. Mistress, *respice finem*, respect your end; or rather,
to prophesy like the parrot, 'Beware the rope's end.'   40
    Ant. E. Wilt thou still talk?   *Beats Dro.*
    Cour. How say you now? is not your husband mad?
    Adr. His incivility confirms no less.
Good Doctor Pinch, you are a conjurer;
Establish him in his true sense again,   45
And I will please you what you will demand.
    Luc. Alas, how fiery and how sharp he looks!
    Cour. Mark how he trembles in his ecstasy!
    Pinch. Give me your hand and let me feel your pulse.
    Ant. E. There is my hand, and let it feel your ear.   50
                            [Strikes him.]
    Pinch. I charge thee, Satan, hous'd within this man,
To yield possession to my holy prayers,
And to thy state of darkness hie thee straight:
I conjure thee by all the saints in heaven.
    Ant. E. Peace, doting wizard, peace! I am not mad.   55
    Adr. O that thou wert not, poor distressed soul!
    Ant. E. You minion, you, are these your customers?
Did this companion with the saffron face
Revel and feast it at my house to-day,
Whilst upon me the guilty doors were shut   60
And I denied to enter in my house?
    Adr. O husband, God doth know you din'd at home;
Where would you had remain'd until this time,
Free from these slanders and this open shame!
    Ant. E. Din'd at home! Thou villain, what say'st thou?   65
    Dro. E. Sir, sooth to say, you did not dine at home.
    Ant. E. Were not my doors lock'd up and I shut out?
    Dro. E. Perdy, your doors were lock'd and you shut out.
    Ant. E. And did not she herself revile me there?
    Dro. E. Sans fable, she herself revil'd you there.   70
    Ant. E. Did not her kitchen-maid rail, taunt, and scorn me?
    Dro. E. Certes, she did; the kitchen-vestal scorn'd you.
    Ant. E. And did not I in rage depart from thence?
    Dro. E. In verity you did: my bones bear witness,
That since have felt the vigour of his rage.   75
    Adr. Is 't good to soothe him in these contraries?
    Pinch. It is no shame: the fellow finds his vein,
And, yielding to him, humours well his frenzy.
    Ant. E. Thou hast suborn'd the goldsmith to arrest me.
    Adr. Alas! I sent you money to redeem you,   80
By Dromio here, who came in haste for it.
    Dro. E. Money by me! heart and good will you might;
But surely, master, not a rag of money.
    Ant. E. Went'st not thou to her for a purse of ducats?
    Adr. He came to me, and I deliver'd it.   85
    Luc. And I am witness with her that she did.
    Dro. E. God and the rope-maker bear me witness
That I was sent for nothing but a rope!
    Pinch. Mistress, both man and master is possess'd:
I know it by their pale and deadly looks.   90
They must be bound and laid in some dark room.
    Ant. E. Say, wherefore didst thou lock me forth to-day?
And why dost thou deny the bag of gold?

    Adr. I did not, gentle husband, lock thee forth.
    Dro. E. And, gentle master, I receiv'd no gold;   95
But I confess, sir, that we were lock'd out.
    Adr. Dissembling villain! thou speak'st false in both.
    Ant. E. Dissembling harlot! thou art false in all,
And art confederate with a damned pack
To make a loathsome abject scorn of me;   100
But with these nails I'll pluck out these false eyes
That would behold in me this shameful sport.

     Enter three or four, and offer to bind him. He strives.

    Adr. O, bind him, bind him! let him not come near me.
    Pinch. More company! the fiend is strong within him.
    Luc. Ay me, poor man, how pale and wan he looks!   105
    Ant. E. What, will you murther me? Thou gaoler, thou,
I am thy prisoner: wilt thou suffer them
To make a rescue?
    Off.   Masters, let him go:
He is my prisoner, and you shall not have him.   110
    Pinch. Go bind this man, for he is frantic too.
         [They bind Dromio of Ephesus.]
    Adr. What wilt thou do, thou peevish officer?
Hast thou delight to see a wretched man
Do outrage and displeasure to himself?
    Off. His is my prisoner; If I let him go,   115
The debt he owes will be requir'd of me.
    Adr. I will discharge thee ere I go from thee:
Bear me forthwith unto his creditor,
And, knowing how the debt grows, I will pay it.
Good Master Doctor, see him safe convey'd   120
Home to my house. O most unhappy day!
    Ant. E. O most unhappy strumpet!
    Dro. E. Master, I am here enter'd in bond for you.
    Ant. E. Out on thee, villain! wherefore dost thou mad me?
    Dro. E. Will you be bound for nothing? be mad, good   125
master: cry, 'the devil!'
    Luc. God help, poor souls, how idly do they talk!
    Adr. Go bear him hence. Sister, go you with me.—

   Exeunt. Mane[n]t Offic[er,] Adri[ana,] Luci[ana,] Courtesan.

Say now, whose suit is he arrested at?
    Off. One Angelo, a goldsmith; do you know him?   130
    Adr. I know the man. What is the sum he owes?
    Off. Two hundred ducats.
    Adr.   Say, how grows it due?
    Off. Due for a chain your husband had of him.
    Adr. He did bespeak a chain for me, but had it not.   135
    Cour. When as your husband all in rage to-day
Came to my house, and took away my ring—
The ring I saw upon his finger now—
Straight after did I meet him with a chain.
    Adr. It may be so, but I did never see it.   140
Come, gaoler, bring me where the goldsmith is:
I long to know the truth hereof at large.

     Enter Antipholus Siracusia with his Rapier drawn,
            and Dromio Sirac.

    Luc. God, for thy mercy! they are loose again.
    Adr. And come with naked swords. Let's call more help   145

---

40 prophesy ... end; *cf. n.*   44 conjurer; *cf. n.*   46 please: *pay*   48 ecstasy:
madness   57 customers: *guests (used contemptuously)*   68 Perdy: *a corruption of 'par
Dieu'*   70 Sans: *without*   72 kitchen-vestal; *cf. n.*   76 soothe; *humor*   83 rag:
bit   90 deadly: *deathly*   91 bound ... dark room: *old-fashioned treatment of madness*

112 peevish: *foolish*   122 unhappy: *mischievous*   136 When as: *when*

To have them bound again   *Run all out.*
Off.   Away! they'll kill us.
                              Exeunt omnes, as fast as may be, frighted.
                                   [Manent Antipholus and Dromio.]
    Ant. S. I see these witches are afraid of swords.
    Dro. S. She that would be your wife now ran from you.
    Ant. S. Come to the Centaur; fetch our stuff from   *150*
thence:
I long that we were safe and sound aboard.
    Dro. S. Faith, stay here this night; they will surely do us
no harm; you saw they speak us fair, give us gold: methinks
they are such a gentle nation, that, but for the mountain   *155*
of mad flesh that claims marriage of me, I could find in
my heart to stay here still, and turn witch.
    Ant. S. I will not stay to-night for all the town;
Therefore away, to get our stuff aboard.   *Exeunt.*

ACT FIFTH ❧ SCENE FIRST

[A Street before an Abbey]
Enter the Merchant and [Angelo,] the Goldsmith.

    Ang. I am sorry, sir, that I have hinder'd you;
But, I protest, he had the chain of me,
Though most dishonestly he doth deny it.
    Mer. How is the man esteem'd here in the city?
    Ang. Of very reverend reputation, sir,   *5*
Of credit infinite, highly belov'd,
Second to none that lives here in the city:
His word might bear my wealth at any time.
    Mer. Speak softly: yonder, as I think, he walks.

Enter Antipholus [of Syracuse] and Dromio [of Syracuse] again.

    Ang. 'Tis so; and that self chain about his neck   *10*
Which he forswore most monstrously to have.
Good sir, draw near to me, I'll speak to him.
Signior Antipholus, I wonder much
That you would put me to this shame and trouble;
And not without some scandal to yourself,   *15*
With circumstance and oaths so to deny
This chain which now you wear so openly:
Beside the charge, the shame, imprisonment,
You have done wrong to this my honest friend,
Who, but for staying on our controversy,   *20*
Had hoisted sail and put to sea to-day.
This chain you had of me; can you deny it?
    Ant. S. I think I had: I never did deny it.
    Mer. Yes, that you did, sir, and forswore it too.
    Ant. S. Who heard me to deny it or forswear it?   *25*
    Mer. These ears of mine, thou know'st, did hear thee.
Fie on thee, wretch! 'tis pity that thou liv'st
To walk where any honest men resort.
    Ant. S. Thou art a villain to impeach me thus:
I'll prove mine honour and mine honesty   *30*
Against thee presently, if thou dar'st stand.
    Mer. I dare, and do defy thee for a villain.

They draw. Enter Adriana, Luciana, Courtesan, and others.

150 stuff: *baggage*   **8** *Cf. n.*   **10 self:** *same*   **16 circumstance:** *particulars*

    Adr. Hold! hurt him not, for God's sake! he is mad.
Some get within him, take his sword away.
Blind Dromio too, and bear them to my house.   *35*
    Dro. S. Run, master, run; for God's sake, take a house!
This is some priory: in, or we are spoil'd!
                         Exeunt [Antipholus of Syracuse and
                              Dromio of Syracuse] to the Priory.

Enter Lady Abbess.

    Abb. Be quiet, people. Wherefore throng you hither?
    Adr. To fetch my poor distracted husband hence.
Let us come in, that we may bind him fast,   *40*
And bear him home for his recovery.
    Ang. I knew he was not in his perfect wits.
    Mer. I am sorry now that I did draw on him.
    Abb. How long hath this possession held the man?
    Adr. This week he hath been heavy, sour, sad,   *45*
And much different from the man he was;
But till this afternoon his passion
Ne'er brake into extremity of rage.
    Abb. Hath he not lost much wealth by wrack of sea?
Buried some dear friend? Hath not else his eye   *50*
Stray'd his affection in unlawful love—
A sin prevailing much in youthful men,
Who give their eyes the liberty of gazing?
Which of these sorrows is he subject to?
    Adr. To none of these, except it be the last;   *55*
Namely, some love that drew him oft from home.
    Abb. You should for that have reprehended him.
    Adr. Why, so I did.
    Abb.   Ay, but not rough enough.
    Adr. As roughly as my modesty would let me.   *60*
    Abb. Haply, in private.
    Adr.   And in assemblies too.
    Abb. Ay, but not enough.
    Adr. It was the copy of our conference:
In bed, he slept not for my urging it;   *65*
At board, he fed not for my urging it;
Alone, it was the subject of my theme;
In company I often glanced it:
Still did I tell him it was vile and bad.
    Abb. And thereof came it that the man was mad: *70*
The venom clamours of a jealous woman
Poisons more deadly than a mad dog's tooth.
It seems, his sleeps were hinder'd by thy railing,
And thereof comes it that his head is light.
Thou say'st his meat was sauc'd with thy upbraidings: *75*
Unquiet meals make ill digestions;
Thereof the raging fire of fever bred:
And what's a fever but a fit of madness?
Thou say'st his sports were hinder'd by thy brawls:
Sweet recreation barr'd, what doth ensue   *80*
But moody and dull melancholy,
Kinsman to grim and comfortless despair,
And at her heels a huge infectious troop
Of pale distemperatures and foes to life?
In food, in sport, and life-preserving rest   *85*
To be disturb'd, would mad or man or beast:

34 within him: *within his guard*   **36 take:** *i.e. take refuge in*   **49 wrack of sea:** *ship-*
wreck   **51 Stray'd:** *led astray*   **64 copy:** *theme*   **68 glanced:** *hinted at*   **84 distem-**
peratures: *disorders*

The consequence is then, thy jealous fits
Hath scar'd thy husband from the use of wits.

   Luc. She never reprehended him but mildly
When he demean'd himself rough, rude, and wildly.   *90*
Why bear you these rebukes and answer not?

   Adr. She did betray me to my own reproof.
Good people, enter, and lay hold on him.

   Abb. No, not a creature enters in my house.

   Adr. Then, let your servants bring my husband forth.   *95*

   Abb. Neither: he took this place for sanctuary,
And it shall privilege him from your hands
Till I have brought him to his wits again,
Or lose my labour in assaying it.

   Adr. I will attend my husband, be his nurse,   *100*
Diet his sickness, for it is my office,
And will have no attorney but myself;
And therefore let me have him home with me.

   Abb. Be patient; for I will not let him stir
Till I have us'd the approved means I have,   *105*
With wholesome syrups, drugs, and holy prayers,
To make of him a formal man again.
It is a branch and parcel of mine oath,
A charitable duty of my order;
Therefore depart and leave him here with me.   *110*

   Adr. I will not hence and leave my husband here;
And ill it doth beseem your holiness
To separate the husband and the wife.

   Abb. Be quiet, and depart: thou shalt not have him.

                             [Exit.]

   Luc. Complain unto the duke of this indignity.   *115*

   Adr. Come, go: I will fall prostrate at his feet,
And never rise until my tears and prayers
Have won his Grace to come in person hither,
And take perforce my husband from the abbess.

   Sec. Mer. By this, I think, the dial points at five: *120*
Anon, I'm sure, the duke himself in person
Comes this way to the melancholy vale,
The place of death and sorry execution,
Behind the ditches of the abbey here.

   Ang. Upon what cause?   *125*

   Sec. Mer. To see a reverend Syracusian merchant,
Who put unluckily into this bay
Against the laws and statutes of this town,
Beheaded publicly for his offence.

   Ang. See where they come: we will behold his death.   *130*

   Luc. Kneel to the duke before he pass the abbey.

   *Enter the Duke of Ephesus, and [Ægeon] the Merchant of
Syracuse, bare head, with the Headsman, and other Officers.*

   Duke. Yet once again proclaim it publicly,
If any friend will pay the sum for him,
He shall not die; so much we tender him.   *135*

   Adr. Justice, most sacred duke, against the abbess!

   Duke. She is a virtuous and a reverend lady:
It cannot be that she hath done thee wrong.

   Adr. May it please your Grace, Antipholus, my husband,
Who I made Lord of me and all I had,   *140*
At your important letters, this ill day

A most outrageous fit of madness took him,
That desperately he hurried through the street,—
With him his bondman, all as mad as he,—
Doing displeasure to the citizens   *145*
By rushing in their houses, bearing thence
Rings, jewels, anything his rage did like.
Once did I get him bound and sent him home,
Whilst to take order for the wrongs I went
That here and there his fury had committed.   *150*
Anon, I wot not by what strong escape,
He broke from those that had the guard of him,
And with his mad attendant and himself,
Each one with ireful passion, with drawn swords
Met us again, and, madly bent on us,   *155*
Chas'd us away, till, raising of more aid,
We came again to bind them. Then they fled
Into this abbey, whither we pursu'd them;
And here the abbess shuts the gates on us,
And will not suffer us to fetch him out,   *160*
Nor send him forth that we may bear him hence.
Therefore, most gracious duke, with thy command
Let him be brought forth, and borne hence for help.

   Duke. Long since thy husband serv'd me in my wars,
And I to thee engag'd a prince's word,   *165*
When thou didst make him master of thy bed,
To do him all the grace and good I could.
Go, some of you, knock at the abbey gate
And bid the lady abbess come to me.
I will determine this before I stir.   *170*

                Enter a Messenger.

   Mess. O mistress, mistress, shift and save yourself!
My master and his man are both broke loose,
Beaten the maids a-row and bound the doctor,
Whose beard they have sing'd off with brands of fire;
And ever as it blaz'd they threw on him   *175*
Great pails of puddled mire to quench the hair.
My master preaches patience to him, and the while
His man with scissors nicks him like a fool;
And sure, unless you send some present help,
Between them they will kill the conjurer.   *180*

   Adr. Peace, fool! thy master and his man are here,
And that is false thou dost report to us.

   Mess. Mistress, upon my life, I tell you true;
I have not breath'd almost, since I did see it.
He cries for you and vows, if he can take you,   *185*
To scorch your face, and to disfigure you.   *Cry within.*
Hark, hark! I hear him, mistress: fly, be gone!

   Duke. Come, stand by me; fear nothing. Guard with
halberds!

   Adr. Ay me, it is my husband! Witness you,   *190*
That he is borne about invisible:
Even now we hous'd him in the abbey here,
And now he's there, past thought of human reason.

   Enter Antipholus [of Ephesus] and Dromio of Ephesus.

   Ant. E. Justice, most gracious duke! O grant me justice,
Even for the service that long since I did thee,   *195*

---

107 formal: *rational*   108 parcel: *part*   123 sorry: *sad*   135 so much ... him: *so
much leniency do we offer him*   140 Who: *whom*   141 important: *importunate, urgent*

149 order for: *measured for settling*   S. d. Messenger: *i.e. one of Adriana's servants*   173
Beaten: *have beaten* a-row: *one after another*   178 nicks ... fool: *cf. n.*
179 present: *immediate* ·   186 scorch: *cf. n.*

When I bestrid thee in the wars and took
Deep scars to save thy life; even for the blood
That then I lost for thee, now grant me justice.
　　Æge. Unless the fear of death doth make me dote,
I see my son Antipholus and Dromio!　　　　　　　　　*200*
　　Ant. E. Justice, sweet prince, against that woman there!
She whom thou gav'st to me to be my wife,
That hath abused and dishonour'd me,
Even in the strength and height of injury!
Beyond imagination is the wrong　　　　　　　　　　　*205*
That she this day hath shameless thrown on me.
　　Duke. Discover how, and thou shalt find me just.
　　Ant. E. This day, great duke, she shut the doors upon me,
While she with harlots feasted in my house.
　　Duke. A grievous fault! Say, woman, didst thou so?　　*210*
　　Adr. No, my good lord: myself, he, and my sister
To-day did dine together. So befall my soul
As this is false he burthens me withal!
　　Luc. Ne'er may I look on day, nor sleep on night,
But she tells to your highness simple truth!　　　　　*215*
　　Ang. O perjur'd woman! They are both forsworn:
In this the madman justly chargeth them.
　　Ant. E. My liege, I am advised what I say:
Neither disturbed with the effect of wine,
Nor heady-rash, provok'd with raging ire,　　　　　　*220*
Albeit my wrongs might make one wiser mad.
This woman lock'd me out this day from dinner:
That goldsmith there, were he not pack'd with her,
Could witness it, for he was with me then;
Who parted with me to go fetch a chain,　　　　　　　*225*
Promising to bring it to the Porpentine,
Where Balthazar and I did dine together.
Our dinner done, and he not coming thither,
I went to seek him: in the street I met him,
And in his company that gentleman.　　　　　　　　*230*
There did this perjur'd goldsmith swear me down
That I this day of him receiv'd the chain,
Which, God he knows, I saw not; for the which
He did arrest me with an officer.
I did obey, and sent my peasant home　　　　　　　*235*
For certain ducats; he with none return'd.
Then fairly I bespoke the officer
To go in person with me to my house.
By the way we met
My wife, her sister, and a rabble more　　　　　　　*240*
Of vile confederates: along with them
They brought one Pinch, a hungry lean-fac'd villain,
A mere anatomy, a mountebank,
A threadbare juggler, and a fortune-teller,
A needy, hollow-ey'd, sharp-looking wretch,　　　　　*245*
A living dead man. This pernicious slave,
Forsooth, took on him as a conjurer,
And, gazing in mine eyes, feeling my pulse,
And with no face, as 'twere, out-facing me,
Cries out, I was possess'd. Then all together　　　　*250*
They fell upon me, bound me, bore me thence,
And in a dark and dankish vault at home
There left me and my man, both bound together;

Till, gnawing with my teeth my bonds in sunder,
I gain'd my freedom, and immediately　　　　　　　*255*
Ran hither to your Grace; whom I beseech
To give me ample satisfaction
For these deep shames and great indignities.
　　Ang. My lord, in truth, thus far I witness with him,
That he din'd not at home, but was lock'd out.　　　*260*
　　Duke. But had he such a chain of thee, or no?
　　Ang. He had, my lord; and when he ran in here,
These people saw the chain about his neck.
　　Sec. Mer. Besides, I will be sworn these ears of mine
Heard you confess you had the chain of him,　　　　*265*
After you first forswore it on the mart;
And thereupon I drew my sword on you;
And then you fled into this abbey here,
From whence, I think, you are come by miracle.
　　Ant. E. I never came within these abbey walls;　　　*270*
Nor ever didst thou draw thy sword on me;
I never saw the chain, so help me heaven!
And this is false you burthen me withal.
　　Duke. Why, what an intricate impeach is this!
I think you all have drunk of Circe's cup.　　　　　*275*
If here you hous'd him, here he would have been;
If he were mad, he would not plead so coldly;
You say he din'd at home; the goldsmith here
Denies that saying. Sirrah, what say you?
　　Dro. E. Sir, he din'd with her there, at the Porpentine.　*280*
　　Cour. He did, and from my finger snatch'd that ring.
　　Ant. E. 'Tis true, my liege; this ring I had of her.
　　Duke. Saw'st thou him enter at the abbey here?
　　Cour. As sure, my liege, as I do see your Grace.
　　Duke. Why, this is strange. Go call the abbess hither.　*285*
I think you are all mated or stark mad.
　　　　　　　　　　　　　　　　　Exit one to the Abbess.
　　Æge. Most mighty duke, vouchsafe me speak a word:
Haply I see a friend will save my life,
And pay the sum that may deliver me.
　　Duke. Speak freely, Syracusian, what thou wilt.　　　*290*
　　Æge. Is not your name, sir, called Antipholus?
And is not that your bondman Dromio?
　　Dro. E. Within this hour I was his bondman, sir;
But he, I thank him, gnaw'd in two my cords:
Now am I Dromio and his man, unbound.　　　　　*295*
　　Æge. I am sure you both of you remember me.
　　Dro. E. Ourselves we do remember, sir, by you;
For lately we were bound, as you are now.
You are not Pinch's patient, are you, sir?
　　Æge. Why look you strange on me? you know me well.　*300*
　　Ant. E. I never saw you in my life till now.
　　Æge. O, grief hath chang'd me since you saw me last,
And careful hours, with Time's deformed hand,
Have written strange defeatures in my face:
But tell me yet, dost thou not know my voice?　　　*305*
　　Ant. E. Neither.
　　Æge. Dromio, nor thou?
　　Dro. E. No, trust me, sir, not I.
　　Æge. I am sure thou dost.
　　Dro. E. Ay, sir; but I am sure I do not; and whatsoever　*310*
a man denies, you are now bound to believe him.

---

196 **bestrid:** *stood over (to defend when fallen)*　209 **harlots:** *lewd fellows*　213 **burthens:**
charges　214 **on night:** *at night*　218 **I . . . say:** *I speak with due deliberation*　223
pack'd: *in league*　235 **peasant:** *servant*　243 **anatomy:** *skeleton*

274 **impeach:** *accusation*　275 **Circe's cup;** *cf. n.*　277 **coldly:** *coolly*　303 **careful:**
full of care　**deformed:** *deforming*

Æge. Not know my voice! O time's extremity,
Hast thou so crack'd and splitted my poor tongue
In seven short years, that here my only son
Knows not my feeble key of untun'd cares?   *315*
Though now this grained face of mine be hid
In sap-consuming winter's drizzled snow,
And all the conduits of my blood froze up,
Yet hath my night of life some memory,
My wasting lamps some fading glimmer left,   *320*
My dull deaf ears a little use to hear:
All these old witnesses—I cannot err—
Tell me thou art my son Antipholus.
    Ant. E. I never saw my father in my life.
    Æge. But seven years since, in Syracusa, boy,   *325*
Thou know'st we parted: but perhaps, my son,
Thou sham'st to acknowledge me in misery.
    Ant. E. The duke and all that know me in the city
Can witness with me that it is not so:
I ne'er saw Syracusa in my life.   *330*
    Duke. I tell thee, Syracusian, twenty years
Have I been patron to Antipholus,
During which time he ne'er saw Syracusa.
I see thy age and dangers make thee dote.

Enter the Abbess, with Antipholus Siracusa and Dromio Sir.

    Abb. Most mighty duke, behold a man much wrong'd   *335*
                             All gather to see them.
    Adr. I see two husbands, or mine eyes deceive me!
    Duke. One of these men is Genius to the other;
And so of these, which is the natural man,
And which the spirit? Who deciphers them?   *340*
    Dro. S. I, sir, am Dromio: command him away.
    Dro. E. I, sir, am Dromio: pray let me stay.
    Ant. S. Ægeon art thou not? or else his ghost?
    Dro. S. O, my old master! who hath bound him here?
    Abb. Whoever bound him, I will loose his bonds,   *345*
And gain a husband by his liberty.
Speak, old Ægeon, if thou be'st the man
That hadst a wife once call'd Æmilia,
That bore thee at a burthen two fair sons.
O, if thou be'st the same Ægeon, speak,   *350*
And speak unto the same Æmilia!
    Æge. If I dream not, thou art Æmilia:
If thou art she, tell me where is that son
That floated with thee on the fatal raft?
    Abb. By men of Epidamnum, he and I   *355*
And the twin Dromio, all were taken up;
But by and by rude fishermen of Corinth
By force took Dromio and my son from them,
And me they left with those of Epidamnum.
What then became of them, I cannot tell;   *360*
I to this fortune that you see me in.
    Duke. Why, here begins his morning story right:
These two Antipholus', these two so like,
And these two Dromios, one in semblance,—
Besides her urging of her wreck at sea,—   *365*
These are the parents to these children,
Which accidentally are met together.

Antipholus, thou cam'st from Corinth first?
    Ant. S. No, sir, not I; I came from Syracuse.
    Duke. Stay, stand apart; I know not which is which.   *370*
    Ant. E. I came from Corinth, my most gracious lord,—
    Dro. E. And I with him.
    Ant. E. Brought to this town by that most famous warrior,
Duke Menaphon, your most renowned uncle.
    Adr. Which of you two did dine with me to-day?   *375*
    Ant. S. I, gentle mistress.
    Adr. And are not you my husband?
    Ant. E. No; I say nay to that.
    Ant. S. And so do I; yet did she call me so;
And this fair gentlewoman, her sister here,   *380*
Did call me brother. *[To Luciana.]* What I told you then,
I hope I shall have leisure to make good,
If this be not a dream I see and hear.
    Ang. That is the chain, sir, which you had of me.
    Ant. S. I think it be, sir; I deny it not.   *385*
    Ant. E. And you, sir, for this chain arrested me.
    Ang. I think I did sir; I deny it not.
    Adr. I sent you money, sir, to be your bail,
By Dromio; but I think he brought it not.
    Dro. E. No, none by me.   *390*
    Ant. S. This purse of ducats I receiv'd from you,
And Dromio, my man, did bring them me.
I see we still did meet each other's man,
And I was ta'en for him, and he for me;
And thereupon these errors are arose.   *395*
    Ant. E. These ducats pawn I for my father here.
    Duke. It shall not need: thy father hath his life.
    Cour. Sir, I must have that diamond from you.
    Ant. E. There, take it; and much thanks for my good
cheer.   *400*
    Abb. Renowned duke, vouchsafe to take the pains
To go with us into the abbey here,
And hear at large discoursed all our fortunes;
And all that are assembled in this place,
That by this sympathized one day's error   *405*
Have suffer'd wrong, go keep us company,
And we shall make full satisfaction.
Thirty-three years have I but gone in travail
Of you, my sons; and, till this present hour
My heavy burthen ne'er delivered.   *410*
The duke, my husband, and my children both,
And you the calendars of their nativity,
Go to a gossip's feast, and go with me:
After so long grief such festivity!
    Duke. With all my heart I'll gossip at this feast.   *415*
        Exeunt omnes. Mane[n]t the two Dromios and two Brothers.
    Dro. S. Master, shall I fetch your stuff from shipboard?
    Ant. E. Dromio, what stuff of mine hast thou embark'd?
    Dro. S. Your goods that lay at host, sir, in the Centaur.
    Ant. S. He speaks to me, I am your master, Dromio:
Come, go with us; we'll look to that anon: *420*
Embrace thy brother there; rejoice with him.
                     Exit [with his Brother].
    Dro. S. There is a fat friend at your master's house,
That kitchen'd me for you to-day at dinner:

---

315 my . . . cares; *cf. n.*   **316** grained: *furrowed*   **338** Genius: *attendant spirit*   **340**
deciphers: *distinguishes*   **362-367** *Cf. n.*   **393** still: *continually*   **405** sympathized: *shared by all*   **408** Thirty-three years;
cf. n.   **412** calendars . . . nativity; *cf. n.*   **413** gossip's: *baptismal sponsor's*   **415** gossip:
make merry   **418** lay at host: *were put up*   **423** kitchen'd: *entertained (in the ktichen)*

She now shall be my sister, not my wife.

   Dro. E. Methinks you are my glass, and not my brother: *425*
I see by you I am a sweet-fac'd youth.
Will you walk in to see their gossiping?

   Dro. S. Not I, sir; you are my elder.

   Dro. E. That's a question: how shall we try it?

   Dro. S. We'll draw cuts for the senior: till then lead
thou first.

   Dro. E. Nay, then, thus:
We came into the world like brother and brother;
And now let's go hand in hand, not one before another.

                         Exeunt.

❧   FINIS   ❧

430 cuts: *lots*

Notes

I.i.8. *guilders.* The word is anachronistically used here, and in IV.i.4, in a general sense for 'money,' without particular reference to the Dutch coin.

I.i.11. *intestine.* This word occurs in *1 Henry IV*, I.i.12, where it means 'internal, civil,' and refers to wars within the state. Though it can hardly have that precise meaning here, it seems to carry a similar implication of a violent disturbance of the peace between people who ought to dwell in amity with one another. By his use of the word 'seditious,' in the next line, Solinus implies that the strife between Syracuse and Ephesus has been in the nature of a civil war.

I.i.34. *nature.* Ægeon wishes it to be remembered, after his death, that it was not the commission of a crime which brought him to his end, but the natural affection which led him to Ephesus, in quest of his son.

I.i.41. *Epidamnum.* 'Epidamium' in the Folio. The correct name of the town is Epidamnum (afterwards called by the Romans 'Dyrrhachium'). It is the modern Durazzo in Albania, on the Adriatic. The fact that the accusative form 'Epidamnum' is used in the translation of the *Menæchmi* published in 1595 has been taken as evidence that Shakespeare saw that translation in manuscript before he wrote *The Comedy of Errors.* Cf. Appendix A.

I.i.78. *latter-born.* From line 124, we learn that it was the younger of the twins who was rescued with his father; and some editors, forgetting that Ægeon is describing the confusion of a shipwreck, have emended the text to correct the apparent inconsistency.

I.i.93. *Epidaurus.* 'Epidarus' in the Folio. A town in Argolis, on the Saronic Gulf. Corinth had a port situated on the same gulf.

I.i.151. *life.* Craig accepts this emendation, proposed by Rowe, for 'helpe' in the Folio; but *health*, which has been adopted by some other editors, seems equally satisfactory.

I.ii.S. d. *Enter Antipholus Erotes.* 'Erotes' is probably a corruption of 'Erraticus,' i.e. the Wanderer. Compare the note on II.i.S. d. below.

I.ii.41. *almanac of my true date.* Because both master and man were born in the same hour, Antipholus can refer to his slave as the almanac by which he can discover the date of his birth.

I.ii.63. *post.* Dromio plays upon two meanings of the word. In the next line, he refers to the post, in a tavern or shop, upon which accounts were 'scored' with chalk or notches.

I.ii.75. *Phœnix.* Probably the sign over the shop of Antipholus of Ephesus, who is a merchant; but private houses, as well as inns and shops, were sometimes distinguished by names that had reference to some distinctive carving or other decoration.

II.i.S. d. *wife to Antipholus Sereptus.* The distinguishing epithet 'Sereptus' is an apparent error for 'Surreptus,' the Lost or Stolen. In the *Menæchmi* of Plautus, one of the twins was stolen from his parents and the other wandered about in search of him. Compare the note on I.ii.S. d. above. The possible relation of these corrupt Latin epithets to a lost source of the play is discussed in Appendix A.

II.i.15. *lash'd.* Perhaps there is a play upon another meaning of the word; viz. 'bound, fastened.'

II.i.57. *horn-mad.* Merely, 'mad as a horned beast,' i.e. a bull or buck; but Adriana is probably right in suspecting a reference to the ancient jest to the effect that the cuckold wore invisible horns.

II.i.82. *round.* Dromio plays upon two meanings of the word: (1) spherical, (2) plain-spoken.

II.i.111-115. *I see, the jewel best enamelled Will lose his beauty; yet the gold bides still That others touch, and often touching will Wear gold; and no man that hath a name, By falsehood and corruption doth it shame.* 'The best enamelled jewel tarnishes; but the gold setting keeps its lustre however it may be worn by the touch; similarly, a man of assured reputation, can commit domestic infidelity without blasting it.' (Herford.) This interpretation of the passage seems quite as satisfactory as those offered by editors who have emended the reading of the Folio more extensively. Theobald's suggestion of *wear*, for the Folio *where*, appears to be the only necessary emendation. At best, the meaning is obscure, and it may be a correct conjecture that some lines have dropped out of the text, which is obviously corrupt.

II.ii.24. *earnest.* Used with quibbling reference to 'earnest money,' i.e. money paid to bind a bargain.

II.ii.29. *And make a common of my serious hours.* 'That is, intrude on them when you please. The allusion is to those tracts of ground destined to common use, which are thence called commons' (Steevens).

II.ii.32. *aspect.* Probably there is an allusion to the astrological use of the word to denote the favorable or unfavorable influences of the planets.

II.ii.37. *sconce.* The dialogue contains a play on three meanings of the word. Antipholus uses it in the slang sense of 'head'; and Dromio, when he speaks of 'battering,' refers to the meaning, 'a small fort,' to which he returns when he uses the word 'insconce' in line 38. In this line it obviously means some form of head-armor.

II.ii.63. *choleric.* Overdone meat was supposed to induce irascibility. Compare *The Taming of the Shrew*, IV.i.167-169:

> 'I tell thee, Kate, 'twas burnt and dried away;
> And I expressly am forbid to touch it,
> For it engenders choler, planteth anger.'

II.ii.75. *fine and recovery.* A legal process by which entailed estates might be transferred from one owner to another.

II.ii.81. *he hath the wit to lose his hair.* In this expression, which seems to have been in the nature of a proverb, Dr. Johnson suspects a reference to the loss of hair through diseases contracted in licentiousness.

II.ii.90. *jollity.* The word hardly seems to fit the context, and some editors read 'policy,' following a conjecture by Staunton.

II.ii.99. *tiring.* The Folio reads 'trying'; corrected by Pope. A tire was a headdress or wig.

II.ii.147. *distain'd.* The word is used elsewhere by Shakespeare with the meaning given in the gloss. The emendation 'unstain'd,' accepted by Craig, appears, at first sight, to fit the context better; but the line as it stands may be taken as a climax to Adriana's outburst against the injustice of the so-called 'double standard,' a matter to which she seems to refer in the obscure passage at II.i.109-113. There seems to be no necessity for following the most recent Cambridge editors in transposing lines 149 and 150.

II.ii.207. *laughs.* The common (Northern English) verbal plural in—s. Compare 'poisons,' V.i.72.

III.i.58-60. *If thou hadst been Dromio to-day in my place, Thou wouldst have chang'd thy face for a name, or thy name for an ass.* If you had been in my place to-day, you would have been glad to wear some other man's face (and so, under his name, pass unrecognized by Antipholus); for otherwise, you would have endured such a beating as to convince you that you were an ass rather than Dromio. Compare lines 15, 16 above.

III.i.61. S. d. *Luce. [Within.]* The stage direction of the Folio, at this point, reads *Enter Luce*; and below, at line 84, *Enter Adriana.* Dyce was probably right in his suggestion that 'both maid and mistress made their appearance on the balcony termed the upper stage, though they undoubtedly were supposed not to see the persons at the door.'

III.i.68, 69. *when? can you tell?* A convenient rejoinder, by which an importunate request or query might be turned aside. Compare *1 Henry IV*, II.i.34.

III.i.142. *For slander lives upon succession.* That is, slander lives on, in possession of a man's reputation, after his death.

III.ii.S. d. *Luciana.* Erroneously called 'Iuliana' in the Folio, which similarly assigns her first speech to 'Iulia.' The others are correctly marked 'Luc.'

III.ii.11. *become disloyalty.* Make even your disloyalty appear becoming by assuming an affectionate attitude toward your wife.

III.ii.52. *Let Love, being light, be drowned if she sink.* Antipholus believes that love is in no danger of being destroyed: it is too buoyant to be drowned. Compare *Venus and Adonis*, 149, 150:

> 'Love is a spirit all compact of fire,
> Not gross to sink, but light, and will aspire.'

III.ii.66. *My sole earth's heaven, and my heaven's claim.* 'All the happiness that I wish on earth, and all that I claim from heaven hereafter' (Malone).

III.ii.91. *'Sir-reverence.'* A contraction of 'save your reverence,' a phrase used by way of apology for a remark that might give offence.

III.ii.120, 121. *armed and reverted, making war against her heir.* There is undoubtedly a quibbling allusion here to the armed resistance of the Holy League to Henry of Navarre, designated heir to the French throne by Henry III in 1589, and finally crowned King of France, as Henry IV, at Chartres, February, 1594. 'Mistress Nell's brazen forehead seemed to push back her rough and rebellious hair, as France resisted the claim of the Protestant heir to the throne' (Clarke). English interest in the civil war in France had been quickened by the fact that, in 1591, Elizabeth sent an expedition under Sir John Norris and the Earl of Essex to aid Henry in the siege of Rouen.

III.ii.141. *turn i' the wheel.* 'There is comprehended, under the Curres of the

coursest kinde, a certaine dog in kitchen-service excellent. For when any meat is to be roasted, they go into a wheel, which they turning round about with the weight of their bodies, so dilligently looke to their businesse, that no drudge nor scullion can do the feate more cunningly. Whom the popular sort hereupon call Turnespets.' (Topsell: *Historie of Foure-Footed Beastes*, 1607.)

IV.i.22. *I buy a thousand pound a year.* The point of Dromio's remark is obscure, but he seems to mean that in buying a rope he is purchasing an annuity likely to yield him an income of a thousand beatings (poundings) a year.

IV.i.57. *send me by some token.* Send me with some sign to attest my right to receive payment for the chain.

IV.i.95. *sheep.* Shakespeare frequently puns upon this word, which was pronounced short, almost like *ship*.

IV.i.112. *Dowsabel.* Her name is Nell (cf. III.ii.107 above); but Dromio ironically applies to her the poetic name, derived from *douce et belle*, frequently used by the Elizabethans to designate a fair lass. Compare Drayton's semi-humorous *Ballad of Dowsabell* (1593).

IV.ii.6. *his heart's meteors tilting in his face.* Warburton finds here an allusion to the aurora borealis, which, as he remarks, sometimes has 'the appearance of lines of armies meeting in the shock.'

IV.ii.30. *Far from her nest the lapwing cries away.* That is, to divert attention from the nest and the young birds. This instinctive habit of the lapwing is frequently referred to in Elizabethan literature.

IV.ii.39. *fairy.* Some editors alter the word, to read *fury,* but emendation is unnecessary. Dromio has in mind the baleful and malevolent disposition sometimes attributed to fairies.

IV.ii.41. *A back-friend, a shoulder-clapper.* The sergeant usually approached from the rear and arrested his man by laying his hand roughly on the shoulder. *Back-friend* has also the meaning of false friend.

IV.ii.43. *runs counter.* A hunting term, meaning to follow the scent in the direction opposite to that which the game has taken. The word *counter* was also used of the two Compters, or debtors' prisons, in London, and officers who made arrests for debt were known as 'sergeants of the counter.'

IV.ii.44. *One that, before the judgment, carries poor souls to hell.* Before the passage of the Debtors' Act of 1869, arrests in civil cases could be made, by what was called 'mesne process,' before final judgment was given. The quibbling reference to the Last Judgment is obvious. 'Hell' was a name given to a prison for confinement of debtors, a sponging house, such as those in Wood Street and the Poultry.

IV.ii.46. *on the case.* 'Dromio S. here appears to quibble on the distinction between "matter" and "case" as a distinction between "contents" and "form." No doubt there is a further reference to the well-known "action on the case," which was a general action for the relief of a civil wrong not especially provided for' (Arden ed.).

IV.ii.64, 65. *owes more than he's worth to season.* Dromio plays upon the familiar expression 'time and season,' where 'season' means 'favorable opportunity.' Time never furnishes us many opportunities as he ought. The thought is the direct opposite of that expressed in *Macbeth*, I.iii.163: 'Time and the hour runs through the roughest day.'

IV.iii.11. *Lapland sorcerers.* Down to the days of Milton, who refers to 'Lapland witches' in *Paradise Lost*, ii. 665, Lapland was frequently mentioned in English literature as the especial home or rendezvous of witches and sorcerers.

IV.iii.13. *What, have you got the picture of old Adam new apparelled?* Dromio is naturally amazed to discover that his master appears to have shaken off the sergeant, whom he calls *the picture of old Adam* because he was 'in buff,' an expression used colloquially of the bare skin. *New apparelled* cannot be so easily explained, but the idea may be, 'Have you got the sergeant a new *suit?*'

IV.iii.16, 17. *calf's skin that was killed for the Prodigal.* St. Luke's Gospel, 15. 23.

IV.iii.73. *'Fly pride,' says the peacock.* An accusation of dishonesty coming from this woman, whom Dromio takes to be dishonest, seems to him as out of place as the warning against pride proverbially attributed to the peacock.

IV.iv.40. *prophesy like the parrot, 'Beware the rope's end.'* Parrots were frequently taught to use such ill-omened phrases as this, in order to raise a laugh against the person for whom the bird appeared to prophesy an evil fate. There is probably a quibble in the expression *Beware the rope's end*, which is a free translation of *respice funem*, frequently used punningly with *respice finem*.

IV.iv.44. *conjurer.* As a schoolmaster, Dr. Pinch was in a position to deal with evil spirits in Latin, the only language which they were popularly supposed to understand. Compare *Hamlet*, I.i.51: 'Thou art a scholar; speak to it, Horatio.'

IV.iv.72. *kitchen-vestal.* 'Her charge being, like that of the vestal virgins, to keep the fire burning' (Johnson).

V.i.8. *His word might bear my wealth at any time.* I should always have been ready to trust him for all I was worth.

V.i.178. *nicks him like a fool.* Court jesters frequently wore their hair trimmed unevenly to give them a ludicrous appearance.

V.i.186. *scorch.* The reading of the Folio. Some editors believe the word is a misprint for *scotch,* to hack or cut.

V.i.275. *Circe's cup.* A draught from Circe's cup transformed men into beasts. The Duke means that some such enchantment appears to have fallen on his subjects, rendering them as irrational as animals.

V.i.315. *my feeble key of untun'd cares.* 'The weak and discordant tone of my voice, that is changed by grief' (Douce).

V.i.362-367. In the Folio, these lines follow line 352. The rearrangement, first suggested by Capell, has been adopted by most modern editors.

V.i.408. *Thirty-three years.* This figure is hardly consistent with two of Ægeon's statements; viz. that his eldest son was eighteen when they separated (I.i.125); and that seven years have since elapsed (V.i.326); but Shakespeare was frequently careless in such matters.

V.i.412. *calendars of their nativity.* I.e. the two Dromios. Compare the note on I.ii.41.

THE TEXT OF THE PRESENT EDITION

The earliest known text of *The Comedy of Errors* is that of the First Folio of 1623.

By permission of the Oxford University Press, the text of the present edition is based upon that of the Oxford Shakespeare, edited by the late W. J. Craig. Departures from Craig's text are indicated below.

1. So far as possible, the stage directions of the Folio have been restored. Necessary additions have been inserted in square brackets.

2. Punctuation and spelling have been normalized to accord with modern English practice; e. g. courtesan, almanac (instead of courtezan, almanack). In the case of the words murther, burden, burthen, etc., the actual form employed by the Folio has been retained.

3. The following alterations in Craig's text have been introduced, readings of the present edition standing before the colon, while those of Craig follow it. Except in the two instances indicated, these changes restore the reading of the Folio.

I.i.15	To admit: T' admit
87	was: were
119	misfortunes: misfortune
127	so: for
II.i.110	yet the: and though
111	and: yet
ii. 121	then: thus
147	distain'd: unstain'd
152	wants: want
191	sprites: elvish sprites
207	laughs: laugh
III.i.143	hous'd: housed
ii. 107	that's: that is
127	saw it: saw
IV.i.17	end: that will I: end, that I will
57	me by: by me
iii. 22	sob: fob
58	then: thee
iv. 101	these false: those false
V.i.72	Poisons: Poison
81	moody: moody moping
88	Hath: Have
140	Who: Whom
186	scorch: scotch
193	there: here
219	disturbed: disturb'd
246	living dead: living-dead
250	all together: altogether (F)
410	burthen ne'er: burdens ne'er (burthen are F)
413	go: joy

The Two Gentlemen of Verona

Edited by
KARL YOUNG

Dramatis Personae

DUKE [OF MILAN], *Father to Silvia*
VALENTINE } *the two Gentlemen*
PROTEUS }
ANTONIO, *Father to Proteus*
THURIO, *a foolish Rival to Valentine*
EGLAMOUR, *Agent for Silvia in her escape*
HOST, *where Julia lodges (in Milan)*
OUTLAWS, *with Valentine*
SPEED, *a clownish Servant to Valentine*
LAUNCE, *the like to Proteus*
PANTHINO, *Servant to Antonio*

JULIA, *Beloved of Proteus*
SILVIA, *Beloved of Valentine*
LUCETTA, *Waiting-Woman to Julia*
SERVANTS, MUSICIANS

SCENE—*Verona; Milan; and a forest on the frontier of Mantua.*

The Two Gentlemen of Verona

INTRODUCTION

SOURCES OF THE PLAY

Although a considerable number of literary origins have been proposed for one part or another of *The Two Gentlemen of Verona*, the source of the main action is represented best, so far as we now know, by the story of Felix and Felismena in *Diana Enamorada*, a pastoral romance of adventurous incidents written in Spanish by Jorge de Montemayor, and first printed in 1542. This story, we may assume, was accessible to Shakespeare in other forms than the Spanish. Bartholomew Yonge's English translation of *Diana* was not published until 1598; but he tells us that it had been in manuscript for sixteen years, and we know that before 1598 two other English translations of parts of Montemayor's work existed in unpublished form. A French translation of relevant parts of *Diana* was printed in 1578 and 1587. It is possible also that the lost play *Felix and Philiomena*, acted at Greenwich in 1584, treated the same fiction.

Directly or indirectly, then, the main plot of Shakespeare's play seems to derive from Montemayor's story; and although we cannot be sure as to contributions from intermediate sources, a comparison of the play and the Spanish romance probably discloses fairly enough at least the general nature of Shakespeare's indebtedness to predecessors, and the direction of his originality. Among the chief matters in which the play resembles the narrative are the following: Proteus' employing Julia's maid as intermediary, and Julia's exhibition of coyness in receiving his letter (I.ii); the breach in the intimacy of the lovers caused by the sending of Proteus to court; the pursuit of Proteus by Julia in disguise; Julia's lodging at an inn and overhearing Proteus' serenade to Silvia (IV.ii); the disguised Julia's taking service with Proteus as his page, and being sent by him to advance his suit to Silvia; the conversation between Julia and Silvia concerning Proteus' former love, and Silvia's rejection of his addresses (IV.iv); and Julia's final reunion with Proteus in the forest. One may add that the Felix (Proteus) of Montemayor has a conventional page who provides at least something of the rôle of Launce.

The more obvious departures of the play from the inherited story are the following: the presence of Valentine, about whom are developed the theme of manly friendship and the incidents of Proteus' treachery; the addition of Thurio, Eglamour, and Speed; the development of the rôle of the Duke as the father of Silvia; and the suppression of Celia's (Silvia's) headlong passion for the supposed boy, Felismena (Julia), and hence the elimination of Celia's voluntary death from hopeless love. These external changes, however, are far less important than the more subtle and profound departures of Shakespeare in characterization and in poetry. The superiority of the dramatist in these respects could be adequately demonstrated only through more ample and detailed comparisons than are possible here. The basis for one significant comparison may, however, be provided. Part of the most appealing conversation between Celia (Silvia) and the disguised Felismena (Julia) in the romance is recounted as follows (Yonge's translation, 1598, p. 64. Cf. Hazlitt's *Shakespeare's Library*, Part I, Vol. I, pp. 298, 299). Felismena is the speaker:

'There is not anie thing (saide Celia) that I would not do for thee, though I were determined not to loue him at all, who for my sake hath forsaken another. For it is no small point of wisedome for me, to learne by other womens harmes to be more wise, and warie in mine owne. Beleeue not good Lady (saide I) that there is any thing in the worlde, that can make Don Felix forget you. And if he hath cast off another for your sake, woonder not thereat, when your beautie and wisedome is so great, and the others so small, that there is no reason to thinke, that he will (though he hath woorthelie forsaken her for your sake) or euer can forget you for any woman else in the worlde. Doest thou then know Felismena (saide Celia) the lady whom thy Master did once loue and serue in his owne countrey? I know her (saide I) although not so well as it was needfull for me, to haue preuented so many mishaps, (and this I spake softly to my selfe). For my fathers house was neere to hers, but seeing your great beautie adorned with such perfections and wisedome, Don Felix can not be blamed, if he hath forgotten his first loue, onely to embrace and honour yours. To this did Celia answer merily, and smiling. Thou hast learned quickly of thy Master to sooth. Not so faire Ladie, saide I, but to serue you woulde I faine learne: for flatterie cannot be, where (in the iudgement of all) there are so manifest signes and proofes of this due commendation. Celia began in good earnest to aske me what manner of woman Felismena was; whom I answered, that touching her beautie, Some thought her to be very faire, but I was neuer of that opinion, bicause she hath many daies since wanted the chiefest thing that is requisite for it. What is that, said Celia? Content of minde, saide I, bicause perfect beautie can neuer be, where the same is not adioyned to it.'

The reader who will turn from this passage to the corresponding lines of the play (IV.iv. 105-175) may judge of Shakespeare's achievement in delicacy and richness of characterization, in pathos, and in poetry.

THE HISTORY OF THE PLAY

We possess no text of *The Two Gentlemen of Verona* earlier than that in the First Folio of 1623, and for determining the precise date of composition we have inadequate evidence. Although the play is mentioned first, so far as we know, by Francis

Meres in his *Palladis Tamia*, of 1598, certain features of style and dramatic technique indicate that it was written considerably earlier. Competent critics have proposed dates ranging between 1590 and 1595, the majority preferring the period 1591-1592. Since the extant text shows both signs of youth and characteristics which may be due to revision, we are not prohibited from surmising that Shakespeare wrote the play as early as 1590-1591, and that he or some one else made changes as late as 1594-1595. All we know for certain is that, as it stands, the play discloses bits of immature workmanship and irregularities which may arise from textual alteration.

In view of the fact that in later comedies Shakespeare improved upon virtually all features of *The Two Gentlemen of Verona*, we need not be surprised at the infrequency of stage-performances of this play. The first production of which we have a record is that by David Garrick at Drury Lane on December 22, 1762. The version presented included 'Alterations and Additions' by Benjamin Victor. Victor's literary audacity may be illustrated by his addition to the last act of two scenes designed for bringing Launce and Speed upon the stage again. The play was performed five times with success; but at the sixth performance occurred a riot motivated, apparently, partly by personal hostility to Garrick and partly by a desire for the restoration of admission at half-price. A more faithful presentation of Shakespeare's text occurred at Covent Garden on April 13, 1784; and in January, 1790, John Philip Kemble gave three performances of the original play at Drury Lane. On April 21, 1808, at Covent Garden, Kemble presented Victor's version, with alterations of his own. Somewhat later, the play was degraded into an opera by Frederic Reynolds, and produced at Covent Garden on November 29, 1821, and on numerous subsequent dates. Shakespeare's own play was revived at Bath on March 23, 1822, and at Drury Lane, by Macready, on December 29, 1841. Charles Kean is said[1] to have produced it both in England and in America during the period 1840-1850, and during the following decade Samuel Phelps gave performances at Sadler's Wells.

During recent years notable productions have been achieved by Osmund Tearle at Stratford-upon-Avon in 1890, by Augustin Daly in New York and London in 1895, and by J. H. Leigh at the Court Theatre, London, in April, 1904. In observance of the Shakespeare Tercentenary, members of the University of Wisconsin gave two performances of the play in May, 1916.

---

1 Cf. Harold Child, in *The Two Gentlemen of Verona*, edited by Sir Arthur Quiller-Couch and John Dover Wilson (Cambridge, 1921), p. 106. I have found no other statement concerning these performances by Charles Kean.

ACT FIRST ❦ SCENE FIRST

[Verona. An open place]
[Enter] Valentine [and] Proteus; and [later,] Speed.

Val. Cease to persuade, my loving Proteus;
Home-keeping youth have ever homely wits.
Were 't not affection chains thy tender days
To the sweet glances of thy honour'd love,
I rather would entreat thy company   *5*
To see the wonders of the world abroad
Than, living dully sluggardiz'd at home,
Wear out thy youth with shapeless idleness.
But since thou lov'st, love still, and thrive therein,
Even as I would when I to love begin.   *10*
  Pro. Wilt thou be gone? Sweet Valentine, adieu!
Think on thy Proteus, when thou haply seest
Some rare noteworthy object in thy travel.
Wish me partaker in thy happiness
When thou dost meet good hap; and in thy danger,   *15*
If ever danger do environ thee,
Commend thy grievance to my holy prayers,
For I will be thy beadsman, Valentine.
  Val. And on a love-book pray for my success?
  Pro. Upon some book I love I'll pray for thee.   *20*
  Val. That's on some shallow story of deep love,
How young Leander cross'd the Hellespont.
  Pro. That's a deep story of a deeper love;
For he was more than over shoes in love.
  Val. 'Tis true; for you are over boots in love,   *25*
And yet you never swum the Hellespont.
  Pro. Over the boots? nay, give me not the boots.
  Val. No, I will not, for it boots thee not.
  Pro.   What?
  Val. To be in love, where scorn is bought with groans;   *30*
Coy looks with heart-sore sighs; one fading moment's mirth
With twenty watchful, weary, tedious nights:
If haply won, perhaps a hapless gain;
If lost, why then a grievous labour won;
However, but a folly bought with wit,   *35*
Or else a wit by folly vanquished.
  Pro. So, by your circumstance, you call me fool.
  Val. So, by your circumstance, I fear you'll prove.
  Pro. 'Tis love you cavil at; I am not Love.
  Val. Love is your master, for he masters you;   *40*
And he that is so yoked by a fool,
Methinks, should not be chronicled for wise.
  Pro. Yet writers say, as in the sweetest bud
The eating canker dwells, so eating love
Inhabits in the finest wits of all.   *45*
  Val. And writers say, as the most forward bud
Is eaten by the canker ere it blow,
Even so by love the young and tender wit
Is turned to folly, blasting in the bud,
Losing his verdure even in the prime,   *50*

And all the fair effects of future hopes.
But wherefore waste I time to counsel thee
That art a votary to fond desire?
Once more adieu! my father at the road
Expects my coming, there to see me shipp'd.   *55*
  Pro. And thither will I bring thee, Valentine.
  Val. Sweet Proteus, no; now let us take our leave.
To Milan let me hear from thee by letters
Of thy success in love, and what news else
Betideth here in absence of thy friend;   *60*
And I likewise will visit thee with mine.
  Pro. All happiness bechance to thee in Milan!
  Val. As much to you at home! and so, farewell.   *Exit.*
  Pro. He after honour hunts, I after love.
He leaves his friends to dignify them more;   *65*
I leave myself, my friends, and all, for love.
Thou, Julia, thou hast metamorphos'd me;
Made me neglect my studies, lose my time,
War with good counsel, set the world at nought;
Made wit with musing weak, heart sick with thought.   *70*

[Enter Speed.]

  Speed. Sir Proteus, save you! Saw you my master?
  Pro. But now he parted hence, to embark for Milan.
  Speed. Twenty to one, then, he is shipp'd already,
And I have play'd the sheep, in losing him.
  Pro. Indeed, a sheep doth very often stray,   *75*
An if the shepherd be a while away.
  Speed. You conclude that my master is a shepherd, then,
and I a sheep?
  Pro. I do.
  Speed. Why then my horns are his horns, whether I   *80*
wake or sleep.
  Pro. A silly answer, and fitting well a sheep.
  Speed. This proves me still a sheep.
  Pro. True, and thy master a shepherd.
  Speed. Nay, that I can deny by a circumstance.   *85*
  Pro. It shall go hard but I'll prove it by another.
  Speed. The shepherd seeks the sheep, and not the sheep
the shepherd; but I seek my master, and my master seeks
not me: therefore I am no sheep.
  Pro. The sheep for fodder follow the shepherd, the shep- *90*
herd for food follows not the sheep; thou for wages fol-
lowest thy master, thy master for wages follows not thee:
therefore thou art a sheep.
  Speed. Such another proof will make me cry 'baa.'
  Pro. But, dost thou hear? gavest thou my letter to Julia? *95*
  Speed. Ay, sir; I, a lost mutton, gave your letter to her, a
laced mutton; and she, a laced mutton, gave me, a lost
mutton, nothing for my labour.
  Pro. Here's too small a pasture for such store of muttons.
  Speed. If the ground be overcharged, you were best stick *100*
her.
  Pro. Nay, in that you are astray; 'twere best pound you.
  Speed. Nay, sir, less than a pound shall serve me for carrying
your letter.

---

8 **shapeless:** *aimless*   9 **still:** *always*   12 **haply:** *by chance*   17 **Commend ... to:** *commit to the attention of*   18 **beadsman:** *one employed to pray for others*   19 **love-book:** *book treating of love (instead of prayer-book)*   22 **Leander;** *cf. n.*   27 **give ... boots** *do not make game of me*   28 **boots:** *profits*   35 **However:** *in any case*   37 **circumstance:** *circumlocution*   38 **circumstance:** *state of affairs*   44 **canker:** *cankerworm*   45 **Inhabits:** *dwells*   47 **blow:** *bloom*   50 **prime:** *spring*

51 **fair ... hopes:** *realization of hopes of future bliss*   53 **fond:** *foolish*   54 **road:** *anchorage*   55 **shipp'd;** *cf. n.*   56 **bring:** *accompany*   59 **success:** *fortune (good or bad)*   70 **thought:** *sorrow*   73, 74 **shipp'd ... sheep;** *cf. n.*   76 **An if:** *if*   80 **horns:** *fancifully attributed to cuckolds*   85 **circumstance:** *detailed proof*   94 **'baa':** *quibble on 'bah'*   97 **laced mutton:** *courtesan; cf. n.*   100 **overcharged:** *overburdened*   100 **stick:** *stab*   102 **pound:** *confine within an enclosure (with quibble)*

Pro. You mistake; I mean the pound,—a pinfold.   *105*

Speed. From a pound to a pin? Fold it over and over,
'Tis threefold too little for carrying a letter to your lover.

Pro. But what said she?

Speed. [*Nodding.*] Ay.

Pro. Nod, ay? why, that's noddy.   *110*

Speed. You mistook, sir. I say she did nod; and you ask
me if she did nod; and I say, 'Ay.'

Pro. And that set together is—noddy.

Speed. Now you have taken the pains to set it together,
take it for your pains.   *115*

Pro. No, no; you shall have it for bearing the letter.

Speed. Well, I perceive I must be fain to bear with you.

Pro. Why, sir, how do you bear with me?

Speed. Marry, sir, the letter very orderly; having nothing
but the word 'noddy' for my pains.   *120*

Pro. Beshrew me, but you have a quick wit.

Speed. And yet it cannot overtake your slow purse.

Pro. Come, come; open the matter in brief. What said she?

Speed. Open your purse, that the money and the matter
may be both at once delivered.   *125*

Pro. Well, sir, here is for your pains [*giving him money*].
What said she?

Speed. Truly, sir, I think you'll hardly win her.

Pro. Why, couldst thou perceive so much from her?

Speed. Sir, I could perceive nothing at all from her; no,   *130*
not so much as a ducat for delivering your letter. And
being so hard to me that brought your mind, I fear she'll
prove as hard to you in telling your mind. Give her no token
but stones, for she's as hard as steel.

Pro. What! said she nothing?   *135*

Speed. No, not so much as 'Take this for thy pains.'
To testify your bounty, I thank you, you have testerned; in
requital whereof, henceforth carry your letters yourself. And
so, sir, I'll commend you to my master.

Pro. Go, go, be gone, to save your ship from wrack;   *140*
Which cannot perish, having thee aboard,
Being destin'd to a drier death on shore.—   [*Exit Speed.*]
I must go send some better messenger.
I fear my Julia would not deign my lines,
Receiving them from such a worthless post.   *Exit.*   *145*

❧ SCENE SECOND ❧

[The Same. The Garden of Julia's House]
Enter Julia and Lucetta.

Jul. But say, Lucetta, now we are alone,
Wouldst thou then counsel me to fall in love?

Luc. Ay, madam, so you stumble not unheedfully.

Jul. Of all the fair resort of gentlemen
That every day with parle encounter me,   *5*
In thy opinion which is worthiest love?

Luc. Please you repeat their names, I'll show my mind
According to my shallow simple skill.

Jul. What think'st thou of the fair Sir Eglamour?

Luc. As of a knight well-spoken, neat and fine;   *10*
But, were I you, he never should be mine.

Jul. What think'st thou of the rich Mercatio?

Luc. Well of his wealth; but of himself, so so.

Jul. What think'st thou of the gentle Proteus?

Luc. Lord, Lord! to see what folly reigns in us!   *15*

Jul. How now! what means this passion at his name?

Luc. Pardon, dear madam; 'tis a passing shame
That I, unworthy body as I am,
Should censure thus on lovely gentlemen.

Jul. Why not on Proteus, as of all the rest?   *20*

Luc. Then thus: of many good I think him best.

Jul. Your reason?

Luc. I have no other but a woman's reason:
I think him so because I think him so.

Jul. And wouldst thou have me cast my love on him?   *25*

Luc. Ay, if you thought your love not cast away.

Jul. Why, he of all the rest hath never mov'd me.

Luc. Yet he of all the rest, I think, best loves ye.

Jul. His little speaking shows his love but small.

Luc. Fire that's closest kept burns most of all.   *30*

Jul. They do not love that do not show their love.

Luc. O! they love least that let men know their love.

Jul. I would I knew his mind.

Luc.   Peruse this paper, madam.
                                [*Gives a letter.*]

Jul. 'To Julia.'—Say from whom?   *35*

Luc.   That the contents will show.

Jul. Say, say, who gave it thee?

Luc. Sir Valentine's page, and sent, I think, from Proteus.
He would have given it you, but I, being in the way,
Did in your name receive it. Pardon the fault, I pray.   *40*

Jul. Now, by my modesty, a goodly broker!
Dare you presume to harbour wanton lines?
To whisper and conspire against my youth?
Now, trust me, 'tis an office of great worth,
And you an officer fit for the place.   *45*
There, take the paper; see it be return'd;
Or else return no more into my sight.

Luc. To plead for love deserves more fee than hate.

Jul. Will ye be gone?

Luc.   That you may ruminate.   *Exit.*   *50*

Jul. And yet I would I had o'erlook'd the letter.
It were a shame to call her back again
And pray her to a fault for which I chid her.
What 'fool is she, that knows I am a maid,
And would not force the letter to my view!   *55*
Since maids, in modesty, say 'No' to that
Which they would have the profferer construe 'Ay.'
Fie, fie! how wayward is this foolish love
That, like a testy babe, will scratch the nurse
And presently all humbled kiss the rod!   *60*
How churlishly I chid Lucetta hence,
When willingly I would have had her here!
How angerly I taught my brow to frown,
When inward joy enforc'd my heart to smile!

105 **pinfold:** *enclosure for stray animals*   110 **noddy:** *simpleton*   117 **fain:** *pleased*   119 **Marry:** *by the Virgin Mary; cf. n.*   121 **Beshrew:** *curse (used playfully)*   123 **open:** *disclose*   129 **perceive:** *receive*   131 **ducat:** *a gold or silver coin*   133 **in telling:** *when you tell her*   134 **stones:** *jewels (possibly)*   137 **testerned:** *'tipped' with a tester, or sixpence*   142 **destin'd . . . shore,** *cf. n.*   144 **deign:** *accept graciously*   145 **post:** *messenger (with quibble)*   4 **resort:** *gathering*   5 **parle:** *conversation*

9 **Sir Eglamour;** *cf. n.*   17 **passing:** *surpassing*   19 **censure:** *pass judgment*   27 **mov'd:** *made a proposal to*   41 **broker:** *go-between*   51 **o'erlook'd:** *looked over, read*   54 **'fool:** *a fool*   59 **testy:** *fretful*   60 **presently:** *immediately*   63 **angerly:** *angrily*

My penance is, to call Lucetta back   65
And ask remission for my folly past.
What ho! Lucetta!

[Enter Lucetta.]

Luc.   What would your ladyship?
Jul. Is it near dinner-time?
Luc.   I would it were,   70
That you might kill your stomach on your meat,
And not upon your maid.
Jul. What is 't that you took up so gingerly?
Luc. Nothing.
Jul. Why didst thou stoop, then?   75
Luc.   To take a paper up
That I let fall.
Jul.   And is that paper nothing?
Luc. Nothing concerning me.
Jul. Then let it lie for those that it concerns.   80
Luc. Madam, it will not lie where it concerns,
Unless it have a false interpreter.
Jul. Some love of yours hath writ to you in rime.
Luc. That I might sing it, madam, to a tune.
Give me a note; your ladyship can set.   85
Jul. As little by such toys as may be possible;
Best sing it to the tune of 'Light o' Love.'
Luc. It is too heavy for so light a tune.
Jul. Heavy! belike it hath some burden, then?
Luc. Ay; and melodious were it, would you sing it.   90
Jul. And why not you?
Luc.   I cannot reach so high.
Jul. Let's see your song. *[Taking the letter.]* How now,
minion!
Luc. Keep tune there still, so you will sing it out.   95
And yet, methinks, I do not like this tune.
Jul. You do not?
Luc.   No, madam; it is too sharp.
Jul. You, minion, are too saucy.
Luc. Nay, now you are too flat,   100
And mar the concord with too harsh a descant.
There wanteth but a mean to fill your song.
Jul. The mean is drown'd with your unruly bass.
Luc. Indeed, I bid the base for Proteus.
Jul. This babble shall not henceforth trouble me.   105
Here is a coil with protestation!—   *[Tears the letter.]*
Go, get you gone, and let the papers lie:
You would be fingering them, to anger me.
Luc. She makes it strange; but she would be best pleas'd
To be so anger'd with another letter.   *[Exit.]*   110
Jul. Nay, would I were so anger'd with the same!
O hateful hands, to tear such loving words!
Injurious wasps, to feed on such sweet honey,
And kill the bees that yield it with your stings!
I'll kiss each several paper for amends.   115
Look, here is writ 'kind Julia.' Unkind Julia!
As in revenge of thy ingratitude,

I throw thy name against the bruising stones,
Trampling contemptuously on thy disdain.
And here is writ 'love-wounded Proteus.'   120
Poor wounded name! my bosom as a bed
Shall lodge thee till thy wound be throughly heal'd;
And thus I search it with a sovereign kiss.
But twice or thrice was 'Proteus' written down.
Be calm, good wind, blow not a word away   125
Till I have found each letter in the letter,
Except mine own name; that some whirlwind bear
Unto a ragged, fearful hanging rock,
And throw it thence into the raging sea!
Lo! here in one line is his name twice writ,   130
'Poor forlorn Proteus, passionate Proteus,
To the sweet Julia.' That I'll tear away;
And yet I will not, sith so prettily
He couples it to his complaining names.
Thus will I fold them one upon another.   135
Now kiss, embrace, contend, do what you will.

[Enter Lucetta.]

Luc. Madam,
Dinner is ready, and your father stays.
Jul. Well, let us go.
Luc. What! shall these papers lie like telltales here?   140
Jul. If you respect them, best to take them up.
Luc. Nay, I was taken up for laying them down;
Yet here they shall not lie, for catching cold.
Jul. I see you have a month's mind to them.
Luc. Ay, madam, you may say what sights you see;   145
I see things too, although you judge I wink.
Jul. Come, come; will 't please you go?   *Exeunt.*

❧ SCENE THIRD ❧

[The Same. A Room in Antonio's House]
Enter Antonio and Panthino; [and later,] Proteus.

Ant. Tell me, Panthino, what sad talk was that
Wherewith my brother held you in the cloister?
Pant. 'Twas of his nephew Proteus, your son.
Ant. Why, what of him?
Pant.   He wonder'd that your lordship   5
Would suffer him to spend his youth at home,
While other men, of slender reputation,
Put forth their sons to seek preferment out:
Some to the wars, to try their fortune there;
Some to discover islands far away;   10
Some to the studious universities.
For any or for all these exercises
He said that Proteus your son was meet,
And did request me to importune you
To let him spend his time no more at home,   15
Which would be great impeachment to his age,
In having known no travel in his youth.
Ant. Nor need'st thou much importune me to that

71 kill: *i.e. subdue, satisfy* **stomach;** *cf. n.* **71, 72 meat . . . maid;** *cf. n.* **80 concerns:** *is of importance* **85 set;** *cf. n.* **87 'Light o' Love':** *name of a tune then familiar* **88 heavy:** *serious* **89 burden;** *cf. n.* **100 flat;** *cf. n.* **101, 102 descant . . . mean;** *cf. n.* **104 bid the base;** *cf. n.* **106 coil with protestation:** *turmoil over solemn declaration* **109 makes it strange:** *pretends aloofness* **111 would . . . same;** *cf. n.* **113 wasps:** *i.e. her fingers* **117 As:** *thus*

122 throughly: *thoroughly* **123 search:** *probe, cleanse* **138 stays:** *waits* **141 respect:** *prize* **142 taken up:** *rebuked* **143 for:** *for fear of* **144 month's mind:** *strong inclination* **146 wink:** *close the eyes* **1 sad:** *serious* **14 importune:** *urge* **16 impeachment:** *reproach*

Whereon this month I have been hammering.
I have consider'd well his loss of time,   *20*
And how he cannot be a perfect man,
Not being tried and tutor'd in the world.
Experience is by industry achiev'd,
And perfected by the swift course of time.
Then tell me, whither were I best to send him?   *25*
    Pant. I think your lordship is not ignorant
How his companion, youthful Valentine,
Attends the emperor in his royal court.
    Ant. I know it well.
    Pant. 'Twere good, I think, your lordship sent him thither.
There shall he practise tilts and tournaments,
Hear sweet discourse, converse with noblemen,
And be in eye of every exercise
Worthy his youth and nobleness of birth.
    Ant. I like thy counsel; well hast thou advis'd;   *35*
And that thou mayst perceive how well I like it,
The execution of it shall make known.
Even with the speediest expedition
I will dispatch him to the emperor's court.
    Pant. To-morrow, may it please you, Don Alphonso   *40*
With other gentlemen of good esteem
Are journeying to salute the emperor,
And to commend their service to his will.
    Ant. Good company; with them shall Proteus go,
And—in good time! Now will we break with him.   *45*

[Enter Proteus.]

    Pro. Sweet love! sweet lines! sweet life!
Here is her hand, the agent of her heart;
Here is her oath for love, her honour's pawn.
O that our fathers would applaud our loves,
To seal our happiness with their consents!   *50*
O heavenly Julia!
    Ant. How now! what letter are you reading there?
    Pro. May 't please your lordship, 'tis a word or two
Of commendations sent from Valentine,
Deliver'd by a friend that came from him.   *55*
    Ant. Lend me the letter; let me see what news.
    Pro. There is no news, my lord; but that he writes
How happily he lives, how well belov'd
And daily graced by the emperor;
Wishing me with him, partner of his fortune.   *60*
    Ant. And how stand you affected to his wish?
    Pro. As one relying on your lordship's will
And not depending on his friendly wish.
    Ant. My will is something sorted with his wish.
Muse not that I thus suddenly proceed;   *65*
For what I will, I will, and there an end.
I am resolv'd that thou shalt spend some time
With Valentinus in the emperor's court.
What maintenance he from his friends receives,
Like exhibition thou shalt have from me.   *70*
To-morrow be in readiness to go.
Excuse it not, for I am peremptory.

    Pro. My lord, I cannot be so soon provided.
Please you, deliberate a day or two.
    Ant. Look, what thou want'st shall be sent after thee.   *75*
No more of stay; to-morrow thou must go.
Come on, Panthino; you shall be employ'd
To hasten on his expedition.   *[Exeunt Antonio and Panthino.]*
    Pro. Thus have I shunn'd the fire for fear of burning,
And drench'd me in the sea, where I am drown'd.   *80*
I fear'd to show my father Julia's letter,
Lest he should take exceptions to my love;
And with the vantage of mine own excuse
Hath he expected most against my love.
O! how this spring of love resembleth   *85*
    The uncertain glory of an April day,
Which now shows all the beauty of the sun,
    And by and by a cloud takes all away!

[Enter Panthino.]

    Pant. Sir Proteus, your father calls for you.
He is in haste; therefore, I pray you, go.   *90*
    Pro. Why, this it is: my heart accords thereto,
And yet a thousand times it answers, 'no.'   *Exeunt.*

ACT SECOND ❧ SCENE FIRST

[Milan. A Room in the Duke's Palace]
Enter Valentine [and] Speed; [and later,] Silvia.

    Speed. Sir, your glove. *[Offering a glove.]*
    Val.   Not mine; my gloves are on.
    Speed. Why, then this may be yours, for this is but one.
    Val. Ha! let me see: ay, give it me, it's mine;
Sweet ornament that decks a thing divine!   *5*
Ah Silvia! Silvia!
    Speed. *[Calling.]* Madam Silvia! Madam Silvia!
    Val. How now, sirrah?
    Speed. She is not within hearing, sir.
    Val. Why, sir, who bade you call her?   *10*
    Speed. Your worship, sir; or else I mistook.
    Val. Well, you'll still be too forward.
    Speed. And yet I was last chidden for being too slow.
    Val. Go to, sir. Tell me, do you know Madam Silvia?
    Speed. She that your worship loves?   *15*
    Val. Why, how know you that I am in love?
    Speed. Marry, by these special marks: first, you have learned,
like Sir Proteus, to wreathe your arms, like a malcontent; to
relish a love-song, like a robin-redbreast; to walk alone, like
one that had the pestilence; to sigh, like a schoolboy that   *20*
had lost his A B C; to weep, like a young wench that had buried her grandam; to fast, like one that takes diet; to watch, like
one that fears robbing; to speak puling, like a beggar at
Hallowmas. You were wont, when you laughed, to crow like
cock; when you walked, to walk like one of the lions; when   *25*
you fasted, it was presently after dinner; when you looked

---

19 hammering: *planning*   **28 emperor;** *cf. n.*   **33 be in eye of:** *have opportunity of seeing*   **43 commend:** *commit*   **45 in good time;** *cf. n.*   **break with:** *disclose our purpose to*   **48 pawn:** *pledge*   **54 commendations:** *greetings*   **59 graced:** *honored*   **64 something sorted:** *rather in agreement*   **65 Muse:** *grumble*   **70 exhibition:** *allowance of money*   **72 Excuse:** *beg off from*   **peremptory:** *determined*

73 provided: *equipped*   **82 take exceptions:** *make objections*   **84 excepted . . . against:** *objected to*   **2, 3 on . . . one;** *cf. n.*   **8 sirrah:** *form of address to inferiors*   **14 Go to:** *an expression of disapprobation*   **18 wreathe:** *fold*   **19 relish:** *sing*   **21 A B C:** *primer*   **22 watch:** *lie awake, or sit up at night*   **23 puling:** *whiningly*   **24 Hallowmas;** *cf. n.*   **25 one . . . lions;** *cf. n.*

sadly, it was for want of money; and now you are metamorphosed with a mistress, that, when I look on you, I can hardly
think you my master.

Val. Are all these things perceived in me?   30

Speed. They are all perceived without ye.

Val. Without me? they cannot.

Speed. Without you? nay, that's certain; for, without you
were so simple, none else would; but you are so without these
follies, that these follies are within you and shine through   35
you like the water in an urinal, that not an eye that sees
you but is a physician to comment on your malady.

Val. But tell me, dost thou know my lady Silvia?

Speed. She that you gaze on so as she sits at supper?

Val. Hast thou observed that? even she, I mean.   40

Speed. Why, sir, I know her not.

Val. Does thou know her by my gazing on her, and yet
knowest her not?

Speed. Is she not hard-favoured, sir?

Val. Not so fair, boy, as well-favoured.   45

Speed. Sir, I know that well enough.

Val. What dost thou know?

Speed. That she is not so fair, as, of you, well-favoured.

Val. I mean that her beauty is exquisite, but her favour
infinite.   50

Speed. That's because the one is painted and the other
out of all count.

Val. How painted? and how out of count?

Speed. Marry, sir, so painted to make her fair, that no
man counts of her beauty.   55

Val. How esteemest thou me? I account of her beauty.

Speed. You never saw her since she was deformed.

Val. How long hath she been deformed?

Speed. Ever since you loved her.

Val. I have loved her ever since I saw her, and still I   60
see her beautiful.

Speed. If you love her, you cannot see her.

Val. Why?

Speed. Because Love is blind. O! that you had mine eyes;
or your own eyes had the lights they were wont to have   65
when you chid at Sir Proteus for going ungartered!

Val. What should I see then?

Speed. Your own present folly and her passing deformity;
for he, being in love, could not see to garter his hose; and
you, being in love, cannot see to put on your hose.   70

Val. Belike, boy, then, you are in love; for last morning
you could not see to wipe my shoes.

Speed. True, sir; I was in love with my bed. I thank you,
you swinged me for my love, which makes me the bolder
to chide you for yours.   75

Val. In conclusion, I stand affected to her.

Speed. I would you were set, so your affection would cease.

Val. Last night she enjoined me to write some lines to one
she loves.

Speed. And have you?   80

Val. I have.

Speed. Are they not lamely writ?

Val. No, boy, but as well as I can do them.
Peace! here she comes.

[Enter Silvia.]

Speed. [Aside.] O excellent motion! O exceeding puppet!   85
Now will he interpret to her.

Val. Madam and mistress, a thousand good morrows.

Speed. [Aside.] O! 'give ye good even: here's a million of
manners.

Sil. Sir Valentine and servant, to you two thousand.   90

Speed. [Aside.] He should give her interest, and she gives it him.

Val. As you enjoin'd me, I have writ your letter
Unto the secret nameless friend of yours;
Which I was much unwilling to proceed in
But for my duty to your ladyship.   *[Gives a letter.]*

Sil. I thank you, gentle servant. 'Tis very clerkly done.   95

Val. Now trust me, madam, it came hardly off;
For, being ignorant to whom it goes
I writ at random, very doubtfully.

Sil. Perchance you think too much of so much pains?   100

Val. No, madam; so it stead you, I will write,
Please you command, a thousand times as much.
And yet—

Sil. A pretty period! Well, I guess the sequel;
And yet I will not name it; and yet I care not;   105
And yet take this again; and yet I thank you,
Meaning henceforth to trouble you no more.

Speed. [Aside.] And yet you will; and yet another 'yet.'

Val. What means your ladyship? do you not like it?

Sil. Yes, yes: the lines are very quaintly writ;   110
But since unwillingly, take them again.
Nay, take them.   *[Gives back the letter.]*

Val.   Madam, they are for you.

Sil. Ay, ay; you writ them, sir, at my request,
But I will none of them; they are for you.   115
I would have had them writ more movingly.

Val. Please you, I'll write your ladyship another.

Sil. And when it's writ, for my sake read it over;
And if it please you, so; if not, why, so.

Val. If it please me, madam, what then?   120

Sil. Why, if it please you, take it for your labour;
And so, good morrow, servant.   *Exit Silvia.*

Speed. O jest unseen, inscrutable, invisible,
As a nose on a man's face, or a weathercock on a steeple!
My master sues to her, and she hath taught her suitor,   125
He being her pupil, to become her tutor.
O excellent device! was there ever heard a better,
That my master, being scribe, to himself should write the letter?

Val. How now, sir! what are you reasoning with yourself?

Speed. Nay, I was riming; 'tis you that have the reason.   130

Val. To do what?

Speed. To be a spokesman from Madam Silvia.

Val. To whom?

Speed. To yourself. Why, she wooes you by a figure.

Val. What figure?   135

Speed. By a letter, I should say.

Val. Why, she hath not writ to me?

---

28 that: *so that*   **34 would:** *i.e. would perceive them*   **36 urinal:** *transparent receptacle for testing urine*   **44 hard-favoured:** *ugly*   **45 well-favoured:** *charming*   **49 favour:** *charm*   **55 counts of:** *takes account of*   **66 going ungartered:** *a convention of love-sickness*   **74 swinged:** *beat*   **77 set:** *seated*

85, 86 motion ... puppet ... interpret; *cf. n.*   **88 'give:** *God give*   **90 servant;** *cf. n.*   **96 clerkly:** *in a scholarly manner*   **101 stead:** *benefit*   **104 period:** *full pause*   **106 again:** *back*   **110 quaintly:** *skilfully*   **129 reasoning:** *talking of*   **134 by a figure:** *indirectly*

Speed. What need she, when she hath made you write to
yourself? Why, do you not perceive the jest?

 Val. No, believe me.   *140*

 Speed. No believing you, indeed, sir. But did you perceive
her earnest?

 Val. She gave me none, except an angry word.

 Speed. Why, she hath given you a letter.

 Val. That's the letter I writ to her friend.   *145*

 Val. And that letter hath she delivered, and there an end.

 Val. I would it were no worse.

 Speed. I'll warrant you, 'tis as well:

'For often have you writ to her, and she, in modesty,
Or else for want of idle time, could not again reply; *150*
Or fearing else some messenger that might her mind discover,
Herself hath taught her love himself to write unto her
  lover.'

All this I speak in print, for in print I found it.
Why muse you, sir? 'Tis dinner-time.   *155*

 Val. I have dined.

 Speed. Ay, but hearken, sir. Though the chameleon Love
can feed on the air, I am one that am nourished by my victuals, and would fain have meat. O! be not like your mistress;
be moved, be moved.   *Exeunt.*

✣ SCENE SECOND ✣

[Verona. A Room in Julia's House]
Enter Proteus [and] Julia; [and later,] Panthino.

 Pro. Have patience, gentle Julia.

 Jul. I must, where is no remedy.

 Pro. When possibly I can, I will return.

 Jul. If you turn not, you will return the sooner.
Keep this remembrance for thy Julia's sake.   *5*
            [Gives him a ring.]

 Pro. Why, then, we'll make exchange. Here, take you this.
            [Gives her another.]

 Jul. And seal the bargain with a holy kiss.

 Pro. Here is my hand for my true constancy;
And when that hour o'erslips me in the day   *10*
Wherein I sigh not, Julia, for thy sake,
The next ensuing hour some foul mischance
Torment me for my love's forgetfulness!
My father stays my coming; answer not.
The tide is now,—nay, not thy tide of tears;   *15*
That tide will stay me longer than I should.
Julia, farewell.   *[Exit Julia.]*
    What! gone without a word?
Ay, so true love should do; it cannot speak;
For truth hath better deeds than words to grace it. *20*

[Enter Panthino.]

 Pant. Sir Proteus, you are stay'd for.

 Pro.   Go; I come, I come.
Alas! this parting strikes poor lovers dumb.
              Exeunt.

✣ SCENE THIRD ✣

[The Same. A Street]
Enter Launce, [leading a dog; and later enter] Panthino.

 Launce. Nay, 'twill be this hour ere I have done weeping; all
the kind of the Launces have this very fault. I have received
my proportion, like the prodigious son, and am going with Sir
Proteus to the imperial's court. I think Crab my dog be the
sourest-natured dog that lives. My mother weeping, my *5*
father wailing, my sister crying, our maid howling, our cat
wringing her hands, and all our house in a great perplexity,
yet did not this cruel-hearted cur shed one tear. He is a stone,
a very pebble stone, and has no more pity in him than a dog.
A Jew would have wept to have seen our parting; why, my *10*
grandam, having no eyes, look you, wept herself blind at my
parting. Nay, I'll show you the manner of it. This shoe is my
father; no, this left shoe is my father; no, no, this left shoe is
my mother; nay, that cannot be so neither; yes, it is so; it is
so; it hath the worser sole. This shoe, with the hole in it, is *15*
my mother, and this my father. A vengeance on 't! there 'tis.
Now, sir, this staff is my sister; for, look you, she is as white
as a lily and as small as a wand. This hat is Nan, our maid. I
am the dog; no, the dog is himself, and I am the dog,—O!
the dog is me, and I am myself; ay, so, so. Now come I to *20*
my father: 'Father, your blessing.' Now should not the shoe
speak a word for weeping. Now should I kiss my father; well,
he weeps on. Now come I to my mother. O, that she could
speak now like a wood woman! Well, I kiss her; why, there
'tis; here's my mother's breath up and down. Now come I *25*
to my sister; mark the moan she makes. Now the dog all this
while sheds not a tear nor speaks a word; but see how I lay
the dust with my tears.

[Enter Panthino.]

 Pant. Launce, away, away, aboard! Thy master is shipped,
and thou art to post after with oars. What's the matter? *30*
why weepest thou, man? Away, ass! you'll lose the tide if you
tarry any longer.

 Launce. It is no matter if the tied were lost; for it is the
unkindest tied that ever any man tied.

 Pant. What's the unkindest tide?   *35*

 Launce. Why, he that's tied here, Crab, my dog.

 Pant. Tut, man, I mean thou'lt lose the flood; and, in losing the flood, lose thy voyage, and, in losing thy voyage, lose
thy master; and, in losing thy master, lose thy service; and,
in losing thy service,—Why dost thou stop my mouth? *40*

 Launce. For fear thou shouldst lose thy tongue.

 Pant. Where should I lose my tongue?

 Launce. In thy tale.

 Pant. In thy tail!

 Launce. Lose the tide, and the voyage, and the master, *45*
and the service, and the tied! Why, man, if the river were dry,
I am able to fill it with my tears; if the wind were down,
I could drive the boat with my sighs.

 Pant. Come, come away, man; I was sent to call thee.

 Launce. Sir, call me what thou darest.   *50*

 Pant. Wilt thou go?

 Launce. Well, I will go.   *Exeunt.*

142, 143 earnest … none; *cf. n.* **150 again reply:** *reply* **154 speak in print:** *speak
precisely; cf. n.* **156 dined:** *i.e. feasted on the sight of Silvia* **4 turn:** *change, prove
unfaithful* **15 tide;** *cf. n. on I.i.54*

2 kind: *family, kindred* **3 proportion, prodigious:** *malapropisms for 'portion' and 'prodigal'* **4 imperial's:** *emperor's* **24 wood:** *mad, distracted; cf. n.* **25 up and down:**
exactly **31 tide;** *cf. n. on I.i.48*

❧ SCENE FOURTH ❧

[Milan. A Room in the Duke's Palace]
Enter Valentine, Silvia, Thurio, [and] Speed;
[and later,] Duke [and] Proteus.

Sil. Servant!
Val. Mistress?
Speed. Master, Sir Thurio frowns on you.
Val. Ay, boy, it's for love.
Speed. Not of you.   5
Val. Of my mistress, then.
Speed. 'Twere good you knock'd him.   *[Exit.]*
Sil. Servant, you are sad.
Val. Indeed, madam, I seem so.
Thu. Seem you that you are not?   10
Val. Haply I do.
Thu. So do counterfeits.
Val. So do you.
Thu. What seem I that I am not?
Val. Wise.   15
Thu. What instance of the contrary?
Val. Your folly.
Thu. And how quote you my folly?
Val. I quote it in your jerkin.
Thu. My jerkin is a doublet.   20
Val. Well, then, I'll double your folly.
Thu. How?
Sil. What, angry, Sir Thurio! do you change colour?
Val. Give him leave, madam; he is a kind of chameleon.
Thu. That hath more mind to feed on your blood than   25
live in your air.
Val. You have said, sir.
Thu. Ay, sir, and done too, for this time.
Val. I know it well, sir: you always end ere you begin.
Sil. A fine volley of words, gentlemen, and quickly shot   30
off.
Val. 'Tis indeed, madam; we thank the giver.
Sil. Who is that, servant?
Val. Yourself, sweet lady; for you gave the fire. Sir Thurio
borrows his wit from your ladyship's looks, and spends what 35
he borrows kindly in your company.
Thu. Sir, if you spend word for word with me, I shall make
your wit bankrupt.
Val. I know it well, sir; you have an ex-chequer of words,
and, I think, no other treasure to give your followers; for it 40
appears by their bare liveries that they live by your bare words.
Sil. No more, gentlemen, no more. Here comes my father.

[Enter Duke.]

Duke. Now, daughter Silvia, you are hard beset.
Sir Valentine, your father's in good health:
What say you to a letter from your friends   45
Of much good news?
Val.   My Lord, I will be thankful
To any happy messenger from thence.
Duke. Know ye Don Antonio, your countryman?
Val. Ay, my good lord; I know the gentleman   50
To be of worth and worthy estimation,
And not without desert so well reputed.
Duke. Hath he not a son?
Val. Ay, my good lord; a son that well deserves
The honour and regard of such a father.   55
Duke. You know him well?
Val. I know him as myself; for from our infancy
We have convers'd and spent our hours together;
And though myself have been an idle truant,
Omitting the sweet benefit of time   60
To clothe mine age with angel-like perfection,
Yet hath Sir Proteus,—for that's his name,—
Made use and fair advantage of his days;
His years but young, but his experience old;
His head unmellow'd, but his judgment ripe;   65
And, in a word,—for far behind his worth
Come all the praises that I now bestow,—
He is complete in feature and in mind
With all good grace to grace a gentleman.
Duke. Beshrew me, sir, but if he make this good,   70
He is as worthy for an empress' love
As meet to be an emperor's counsellor.
Well, sir, this gentleman is come to me
With commendation from great potentates;
And here he means to spend his time awhile.   75
I think, 'tis no unwelcome news to you.
Val. Should I have wish'd a thing, it had been he.
Duke. Welcome him then according to his worth.
Silvia, I speak to you; and you, Sir Thurio;
For Valentine, I need not cite him to it.   80
I;ll send him hither to you presently.   *[Exit.]*
Val. This is the gentleman I told your ladyship
Had come along with me, but that his mistress
Did hold his eyes lock'd in her crystal looks.
Sil. Belike that now she hath enfranchis'd them   85
Upon some other pawn for fealty.
Val. Nay, sure, I think she holds them prisoners still.
Sil. Nay, then he should be blind; and, being blind,
How could he see his way to seek out you?
Val. Why, lady, Love hath twenty pair of eyes.   90
Thu. They say that Love hath not an eye at all.
Val. To see such lovers, Thurio, as yourself.
Upon a homely object Love can wink.
Sil. Have done, have done. Here comes the gentleman.
                                     [Exit Thurio.]   95

[Enter Proteus.]

Val. Welcome, dear Proteus! Mistress, I beseech you,
Confirm his welcome with some special favour.
Sil. His worth is warrant for his welcome hither,
If this be he you oft have wish'd to hear from.
Val. Mistress, it is. Sweet lady, entertain him   100
To be my fellow-servant to your ladyship.
Sil. Too low a mistress for so high a servant.
Pro. Not so, sweet lady; but too mean a servant
To have a look of such a worthy mistress.
Val. Leave off discourse of disability.   105
Sweet lady, entertain him for your servant.

18 quote: *observe; cf. n.*   20 jerkin, doublet; *cf. n.*   26 live ... air; *cf. n.*   48
happy messenger: *bearer of good news*   58 convers'd: *been companions*   60 Omitting: *disregarding*   65 unmellow'd: *untinged
with grey*   68 feature: *outward form*   80 cite: *urge*   84 lock'd ... looks;
cf. n.   85 Belike: *'tis likely* enfranchis'd: *released from confinement*   100 entertain:
take into service

Pro. My duty will I boast of, nothing else.

Sil. And duty never yet did want his meed.
Servant, you are welcome to a worthless mistress.

Pro. I'll die on him that says so but yourself.   *110*

Sil. That you are welcome?

Pro.   That you are worthless.

[Enter Thurio.]

Thu. Madam, my lord your father would speak with you.

Sil. I wait upon his pleasure. Come, Sir Thurio,
Go with me. Once more, new servant, welcome.   *115*
I'll leave you to confer of home-affairs;
When you have done, we look to hear from you.

Pro. We'll both attend upon your ladyship.

                                    [Exeunt Silvia and Thurio.]

Val. Now, tell me, how do all from whence you came?

Pro. Your friends are well and have them much   *120*
commended.

Val. And how do yours?

Pro.   I left them all in health.

Val. How does your lady, and how thrives your love?

Pro. My tales of love were wont to weary you;   *125*
I know you joy not in a love-discourse.

Val. Ay, Proteus, but that life is alter'd now.
I have done penance for contemning love;
Whose high imperious thoughts have punish'd me
With bitter fists, with penitential groans,   *130*
With nightly tears and daily heart-sore sighs;
For, in revenge of my contempt of love,
Love hath chas'd sleep from my enthralled eyes,
And made them watchers of mine own heart's sorrow.
O, gentle Proteus! Love's a mighty lord,   *135*
And hath so humbled me as I confess
There is no woe to his correction,
Nor to his service no such joy on earth.
Now no discourse, except it be of love;
Now can I break my fast, dine, sup, and sleep,   *140*
Upon the very naked name of love.

Pro. Enough; I read your fortune in your eye.
Was this the idol that you worship so?

Val. Even she; and is she not a heavenly saint?

Pro. No; but she is an earthly paragon.   *145*

Val. Call her divine.

Pro.   I will not flatter her.

Val. O! flatter me, for love delights in praises.

Pro. When I was sick, you gave me bitter pills,
And I must minister the like to you.   *150*

Val. Then speak the truth by her; if not divine,
Yet let her be a principality,
Sovereign to all the creatures on the earth

Pro. Except my mistress.

Val.   Sweet, except not any,   *155*
Except thou wilt except against my love.

Pro. Have I not reason to prefer mine own?

Val. And I will help thee to prefer her too.
She shall be dignified with this high honour,—
To bear my lady's train, lest the base earth   *160*
Should from her vesture chance to steal a kiss,

And, of so great a favour growing proud,
Disdain to root the summer-swelling flower,
And make rough winter everlastingly.

Pro. Why, Valentine, what braggardism is this?   *165*

Val. Pardon me, Proteus; all I can is nothing
To her whose worth makes other worthies nothing.
She is alone.

Pro.   Then, let her alone.

Val. Not for the world. Why, man, she is mine own,   *170*
And I as rich in having such a jewel
As twenty seas, if all their sand were pearl,
The water nectar, and the rocks pure gold.
Forgive me that I do not dream on thee,
Because thou see'st me dote upon my love.   *175*
My foolish rival, that her father likes
Only for his possessions are so huge,
Is gone with her along, and I must after,
For love, thou know'st, is full of jealousy.

Pro. But she loves you?   *180*

Val. Ay, and we are betroth'd; nay, more, our marriage-
hour,
With all the cunning manner of our flight,
Determin'd of: how I must climb her window,
The ladder made of cords, and all the means   *185*
Plotted and 'greed on for my happiness.
Good Proteus, go with me to my chamber,
In these affairs to aid me with thy counsel.

Pro. Go on before; I shall inquire you forth.
I must unto the road, to disembark   *190*
Some necessaries that I needs must use,
And then I'll presently attend you.

Val. Will you make haste?

Pro. I will.   *Exit [Valentine].*
Even as one heat another heat expels,   *195*
Or as one nail by strength drives out another,
So the remembrance of my former love
Is by a newer object quite forgotten.
Is it mine [eye], or Valentinus' praise,
Her true perfection, or my false transgression,   *200*
That makes me reasonless to reason thus?
She's fair; and so is Julia that I love,—
That I did love, for now my love is thaw'd,
Which, like a waxen image 'gainst a fire,
Bears no impression of the thing it was.   *205*
Methinks my zeal to Valentine is cold,
And that I love him not as I was wont.
O! but I love his lady too-too much;
And that's the reason I love him so little.
How shall I dote on her with more advice,   *210*
That thus without advice begin to love her?
'Tis but her picture I have yet beheld,
And that hath dazzled my reason's light;
But when I look on her perfections,
There is no reason but I shall be blind.   *215*
If I can check my erring love, I will;
If not, to compass her I'll use my skill.   *[Exit.]*

---

108 meed: *reward*   **110 die on:** *die in fight with*   **120, 121 them much commended:**
sent kind remembrances   **137 to:** *comparable to*   **152 principality;** *cf. n.*   **156 except
against:** *object to*   **158 prefer:** *advance in station*

168 alone: *peerless*   **177 for:** *because*   **189 forth:** *out*   **190 road:** *anchorage; cf. n. on
I.i.55*   **195 Even ... expels;** *cf. n.*   **210 advice:** *deliberation*   **212 picture:** *i.e. outer
form*   **215 no reason but:** *no doubt that*   **217 compass:** *obtain*

❧ Scene Fifth ❧

[The Same. A Street]
Enter Speed and Launce [severally].

Speed. Launce! by mine honesty, welcome to Milan!

Launce. Forswear not thyself, sweet youth, for I am not welcome. I reckon this always that a man is never undone till he be hanged; nor never welcome to a place till some certain shot be paid and the hostess say, 'Welcome!'   5

Speed. Come on, you madcap, I'll to the alehouse with you presently; where, for one shot of five pence, thou shalt have five thousand welcomes. But, sirrah, how did thy master part with Madam Julia?

Launce. Marry, after they closed in earnest, they parted   10
very fairly in jest.

Speed. But shall she marry him?

Launce. No.

Speed. How then? Shall he marry her?

Launce. No, neither.   15

Speed. What, are they broken?

Launce. No, they are both as whole as a fish.

Speed. Why then, how stands the matter with them?

Launce. Marry, thus: when it stands well with him, it stands well with her.   20

Speed. What an ass art thou! I understand thee not.

Launce. What a block art thou, that thou canst not! My staff understands me.

Speed. What thou sayest?

Launce. Ay, and what I do too. Look thee,   25
I'll but lean, and my staff understands me.

Speed. It stands under thee, indeed.

Launce. Why, stand-under and under-stand is all one.

Speed. But tell me true, will 't be a match?

Launce. Ask my dog. If he say ay, it will; if he say no,   30
it will; if he shakes his tail and say nothing, it will.

Speed. The conclusion is, then, that it will.

Launce. Thou shalt never get such a secret from me but by a parable.

Speed. 'Tis well that I get it so. But, Launce, how sayest   35
thou, that my master is become a notable lover?

Launce. I never knew him otherwise.

Speed. Than how?

Launce. A notable lubber, as thou reportest him to be.

Speed. Why, thou whoreson ass, thou mistakest me.   40

Launce. Why, fool, I meant not thee; I meant thy master.

Speed. I tell thee, my master is become a hot lover.

Launce. Why, I tell thee, I care not though he burn himself in love. If thou wilt, go with me to the alehouse; if not, thou art an Hebrew, a Jew, and not worth the name of a   45
Christian.

Speed. Why?

Launce. Because thou hast not so much charity in thee as to go to the ale with a Christian. Wilt thou go?

Speed. At thy service.   50

                                                  Exeunt.

❧ Scene Sixth ❧

[The Same. A Room in the Duke's Palace]
Enter Proteus solus.

Pro. To leave my Julia, shall I be forsworn;
To love fair Silvia, shall I be forsworn;
To wrong my friend, I shall be much forsworn;
And even that power which gave me first my oath
Provokes me to this threefold perjury.   5
Love bade me swear, and Love bids me forswear.
O sweet-suggesting Love! if thou hast sinn'd,
Teach me, thy tempted subject, to excuse it.
At first I did adore a twinkling star,
But now I worship a celestial sun.   10
Unheedful vows may heedfully be broken;
And he wants wit that wants resolved will
To learn his wit to exchange the bad for better.
Fie, fie, unreverend tongue! to call her bad,
Whose sovereignty so oft thou hast preferr'd   15
With twenty thousand soul-confirming oaths.
I cannot leave to love, and yet I do;
But there I leave to love where I should love.
Julia I lose and Valentine I lose.
If I keep them, I needs must lose myself;   20
If I lose them, thus find I by their loss,
For Valentine, myself; for Julia, Silvia.
I to myself am dearer than a friend,
For love is still most precious in itself;
And Silvia—witness heaven that made her fair!—   25
Shows Julia but a swarthy Ethiope.
I will forget that Julia is alive,
Remembering that my love to her is dead;
And Valentine I'll hold an enemy,
Aiming at Silvia as a sweeter friend.   30
I cannot now prove constant to myself
Without some treachery us'd to Valentine.
This night he meaneth with a corded ladder
To climb celestial Silvia's chamber-window,
Myself in counsel, his competitor.   35
Now presently, I'll give her father notice
Of their disguising and pretended flight;
Who, all enrag'd, will banish Valentine;
For Thurio, he intends, shall wed his daughter;
But, Valentine being gone, I'll quickly cross   40
By some sly trick blunt Thurio's dull proceeding.
Love, lend me wings to make my purpose swift,
As thou hast lent me wit to plot this drift!   *Exit.*

❧ Scene Seventh ❧

[Verona. A Room in Julia's House]
Enter Julia and Lucetta.

Jul. Counsel, Lucetta; gentle girl, assist me;
And e'en in kind love I do conjure thee,
Who art the table wherein all my thoughts

---

4 **shot:** *tavern-reckoning*   10 **closed:** *came to terms, or (possibly) embraced*   35, 36 **how sayest thou:** *what have you to say to this*   44-46 **go ... Christian;** *cf. n.*

7 **sweet-suggesting:** *sweetly seductive*   13 **learn:** *teach*   17 **leave:** *cease*   35 **competitor:** *associate, confidant*   37 **pretended:** *intended*   41 **blunt:** *stupid*   43 **drift:** *scheme*   3 **table:** *tablet for memoranda*

Are visibly character'd and engrav'd,
To lesson me and tell me some good mean　　　　　5
How, with my honour, I may undertake
A journey to my loving Proteus.
 Luc. Alas! the way is wearisome and long.
 Jul. A true-devoted pilgrim is not weary
To measure kingdoms with his feeble steps;　　　10
Much less shall she that hath Love's wings to fly,
And when the flight is made to one so dear,
Of such divine perfection, as Sir Proteus.
 Luc. Better forbear till Proteus make return.
 Jul. O! know'st thou not his looks are my soul's food?　15
Pity the dearth that I have pined in,
By longing for that food so long a time.
Didst thou but know the inly touch of love,
Thou wouldst as soon go kindle fire with snow
As seek to quench the fire of love with words.　　20
 Luc. I do not seek to quench your love's hot fire,
But qualify the fire's extreme rage,
Lest it should burn above the bounds of reason.
 Jul. The more thou damm'st it up, the more it burns.
The current that with gentle murmur glides,　　　25
Thou know'st, being stopp'd, impatiently doth rage;
But when his fair course is not hindered,
He makes sweet music with th' enamell'd stones,
Giving a gentle kiss to every sedge
He overtaketh in his pilgrimage;　　　　　　　30
And so by many winding nooks he strays
With willing sport, to the wild ocean.
Then let me go and hinder not my course.
I'll be as patient as a gentle stream
And make a pastime of each weary step,　　　　35
Till the last step have brought me to my love;
And there I'll rest, as after much turmoil
A blessed soul doth in Elysium.
 Luc. But in what habit will you go along?
 Jul. Not like a woman; for I would prevent　　　40
The loose encounters of lascivious men.
Gentle Lucetta, fit me with such weeds
As may beseem some well-reputed page.
 Luc. Why, then, your ladyship must cut your hair.
 Jul. No, girl; I'll knit it up in silken strings　　　45
With twenty odd-conceited true-love knots.
To be fantastic may become a youth
Of greater time than I shall show to be.
 Luc. What fashion, madam, shall I make your breeches?
 Jul. That fits as well as 'Tell me, good my lord,　　50
What compass will you wear your farthingale?'
Why, even what fashion thou best lik'st, Lucetta.
 Luc. You must needs have them with a cod-piece, madam.
 Jul. Out, out, Lucetta! that will be ill-favour'd.
 Luc. A round hose, madam, now's not worth a pin,　　55
Unless you have a cod-piece to stick pins on.
 Jul. Lucetta, as thou lov'st me, let me have
What thou think'st meet and is most mannerly,
But tell me, wench, how will the world repute me
For undertaking so unstaid a journey?　　　　60

I fear me, it will make me scandaliz'd.
 Luc. If you think so, then stay at home and go not.
 Jul. Nay, that I will not.
 Luc. Then never dream on infamy, but go.
If Proteus like your journey when you come,　　　65
No matter who's displeas'd when you are gone.
I fear me, he will scarce be pleas'd withal.
 Jul. That is the least, Lucetta, of my fear.
A thousand oaths, an ocean of his tears,
And instances of infinite of love　　　　　　70
Warrant me welcome to my Proteus.
 Luc. All these are servants to deceitful men.
 Jul. Base men, that use them to so base effect;
But truer stars did govern Proteus' birth;
His words are bonds, his oaths are oracles,　　　75
His love sincere, his thoughts immaculate,
His tears pure messengers sent from his heart,
His heart as far from fraud as heaven from earth.
 Luc. Pray heaven he prove so when you come to him!
 Jul. Now, as thou lov'st me, do him not that wrong　80
To bear a hard opinion of his truth.
Only deserve my love by loving him,
And presently go with me to my chamber,
To take a note of what I stand in need of
To furnish me upon my longing journey.　　　　85
All that is mine I leave at thy dispose,
My goods, my lands, my reputation;
Only, in lieu thereof, dispatch me hence.
Come, answer not, but to it presently!
I am impatient of my tarriance.　　　*Exeunt.*　90

ACT THIRD ❧ SCENE FIRST

[Milan. An anteroom in the Duke's Palace]
Enter Duke, Thurio, [and] Proteus; [and later,] Valentine, Launce,
[and] Speed.

 Duke. Sir Thurio, give us leave, I pray, awhile;
We have some secrets to confer about.　　　*[Exit Thurio.]*
Now tell me Proteus, what's your will with me?
 Pro. My gracious lord, that which I would discover
The law of friendship bids me to conceal;　　　5
But when I call to mind your gracious favours
Done to me, undeserving as I am,
My duty pricks me on to utter that
Which else no worldly good should draw from me.
Know, worthy prince, Sir Valentine, my friend,　　10
This night intends to steal away your daughter.
Myself am one made privy to the plot.
I know you have determin'd to bestow her
On Thurio, whom your gentle daughter hates;
And should she thus be stol'n away from you,　　15
It would be much vexation to your age.
Thus, for my duty's sake, I rather chose
To cross my friend in his intended drift,
Than, by concealing it, heap on your head

4 **character'd**: *inscribed*　18 **inly**: *inward*　41 **encounters**: *accostings*　47 **fantastic**: *fanciful, capricious*　48 **time**: *years*　51 **farthingale**: *hooped petticoat*　53 **cod-piece**; *cf. n.*　54 **ill-favour'd**: *ill-looking*　55 **round hose**; *cf. n.*　60 **unstaid**: *unbecoming*

61 **scandaliz'd**: *disgraced, subject to scandal*　67 **withal**: *with it*　70 **infinite**: *infinity*　85 **longing**: *prompted by longing*　86 **dispose**: *disposal*　90 **tarriance**: *delay*　1 **give ... leave**: *polite form of dismissal*　4 **discover**: *disclose*　18 **drift**: *scheme*

A pack of sorrows which would press you down, 20
Being unprevented, to your timeless grave.

  Duke. Proteus, I thank thee for thine honest care,
Which to requite, command me while I live.
This love of theirs myself have often seen,
Haply when they have judg'd me fast asleep, 25
And oftentimes have purpos'd to forbid
Sir Valentine her company and my court;
But fearing lest my jealous aim might err
And so unworthily disgrace the man,—
A rashness that I ever yet have shunn'd,— 30
I gave him gentle looks, thereby to find
That which thyself hast now disclos'd to me.
And, that thou mayst perceive my fear of this,
Knowing that tender youth is soon suggested,
I nightly lodge her in an upper tower, 35
The key whereof myself have ever kept;
And thence she cannot be convey'd away.

  Pro. Know, noble lord, they have devis'd a mean
How he her chamber-window will ascend
And with a corded ladder fetch her down; 40
For which the youthful lover now is gone
And this way comes he with it presently;
Where, if it please you, you may intercept him.
But, good my lord, do it so cunningly
That my discovery be not aimed at; 45
For love of you, not hate unto my friend,
Hath made me publisher of this pretence.

  Duke. Upon mine honour, he shall never know
That I had any light from thee of this.

  Pro. Adieu, my lord; Sir Valentine is coming.   *[Exit.]* 50

[Enter Valentine.]

  Duke. Sir Valentine, whither away so fast?

  Val. Please it your Grace, there is a messenger
That stays to bear my letters to my friends,
And I am going to deliver them.

  Duke. Be they of much import? 55

  Val. The tenour of them doth but signify
My health and happy being at your court.

  Duke. Nay then, no matter; stay with me awhile;
I am to break with thee of some affairs
That touch me near, wherein thou must be secret. 60
'Tis not unknown to thee that I have sought
To match my friend Sir Thurio to my daughter.

  Val. I know it well, my lord; and sure, the match
Were rich and honourable; besides, the gentleman
Is full of virtue, bounty, worth, and qualities 65
Beseeming such a wife as your fair daughter.
Cannot your Grace win her to fancy him?

  Duke. No, trust me; she is peevish, sullen, froward,
Proud, disobedient, stubborn, lacking duty;
Neither regarding that she is my child, 70
Nor fearing me as if I were her father;
And, may I say to thee, this pride of hers,
Upon advice, hath drawn my love from her;
And, where I thought the remnant of mine age

Should have been cherish'd by her childlike duty, 75
I now am full resolv'd to take a wife
And turn her out to who will take her in.
Then let her beauty be her wedding-dower;
For me and my possessions she esteems not.

  Val. What would your Grace have me to do in this? 80

  Duke. There is a lady of Verona here,
Whom I affect; but she is nice and coy
And nought esteems my aged eloquence.
Now therefore, would I have thee to my tutor,—
For long agone I have forgot to court; 85
Besides, the fashion of the time is chang'd,—
How and which way I may bestow myself
To be regarded in her sun-bright eye.

  Val. Win her with gifts, if she respect not words.
Dumb jewels often in their silent kind 90
More than quick words do move a woman's mind.

  Duke. But she did scorn a present that I sent her.

  Val. A woman sometime scorns what best contents her.
Send her another; never give her o'er,
For scorn at first makes after-love the more. 95
If she do frown, 'tis not in hate of you,
But rather to beget more love in you;
If she do chide, 'tis not to have you gone;
For why the fools are mad if left alone.
Take no repulse, whatever she doth say; 100
For 'get you gone,' she doth not mean 'away!'
Flatter and praise, commend, extol their graces;
Though ne'er so black, say they have angels' faces.
That man that hath a tongue, I say, is no man,
If with his tongue he cannot win a woman. 105

  Duke. But she I mean is promis'd by her friends
Unto a youthful gentleman of worth,
And kept severely from resort of men,
That no man hath access by day to her.

  Val. Why then, I would resort to her by night. 110

  Duke. Ay, but the doors be lock'd and keys kept safe,
That no man hath recourse to her by night.

  Val. What lets but one may enter at her window?

  Duke. Her chamber is aloft, far from the ground,
And built so shelving that one cannot climb it 115
Without apparent hazard of his life.

  Val. Why then, a ladder quaintly made of cords,
To cast up, with a pair of anchoring hooks,
Would serve to scale another Hero's tower,
So bold Leander would adventure it. 120

  Duke. Now, as thou art a gentleman of blood,
Advise me where I may have such a ladder.

  Val. When would you use it? Pray, sir, tell me that.

  Duke. This very night; for Love is like a child,
That longs for everything that he can come by. 125

  Val. By seven o'clock I'll get you such a ladder.

  Duke. But hark thee; I will go to her alone.
How shall I best convey the ladder thither?

  Val. It will be light, my lord, that you may bear it
Under a cloak that is of any length. 130

---

82 **nice:** *fastidious*   85 **forgot:** *forgotten how*   87 **bestow:** *conduct*   89 **respect:** *heed*   90 **kind:** *nature*   99 **For why:** *because*   101 *When she says 'away!' she does not mean 'get you gone!'*   103 **black:** *dark-complexioned*   109, 112 **That:** *so that*   113 **lets:** *hinders*   116 **apparent:** *obvious*   117 **quaintly:** *skilfully*   119, 120 **Hero's . . . Leander;** *cf. n. on I.i.22*   120 **So:** *provided that*   121 **blood:** *good parentage*   130 **of any length:** *tolerably long*

21 **timeless:** *untimely*   28 **aim:** *conjecture*   34 **suggested:** *led astray*   45 **discovery:** *disclosure* **aimed at:** *guessed*   47 **pretence:** *intention*   59 **break with thee of:** *disclose to thee*   67 **fancy:** *love*   73 **advice:** *deliberation*   74 **where:** *whereas*

Duke. A cloak as long as thine will serve the turn?

Val. Ay, my good lord.

Duke.   Then let me see thy cloak;

I'll get me one of such another length.

Val. Why, any cloak will serve the turn, my lord.   *135*

Duke. How shall I fashion me to wear a cloak?

I pray thee, let me feel thy cloak upon me.

                   [Pulls open Valentine's cloak.]

What letter is this same? What's here?—To *Silvia!*

And here an engine fit for my proceeding!

I'll be so bold to break the seal for once.   *[Reads.]*   *140*

'My thoughts do harbour with my Silvia nightly;

   And slaves they are to me that send them flying.

O! could their master come and go as lightly,

   Himself would lodge where senseless they are lying!

My herald thoughts in thy pure bosom rest them;   *145*

   While I, their king, that thither them importune,

Do curse the grace that with such grace hath bless'd them,

   Because myself do want my servants' fortune.

I curse myself, for they are sent by me,

That they should harbour where their lord would be.'   *150*

What's here?

         'Silvia, this night I will enfranchise thee.'

'Tis so; and here's the ladder for the purpose.

Why, Phaethon,—for thou art Merops' son,—

Wilt thou aspire to guide the heavenly car   *155*

And with thy daring folly burn the world?

Wilt thou reach stars, because they shine on thee?

Go, base intruder! overweening slave!

Bestow thy fawning smiles on equal mates,

And think my patience, more than thy desert,   *160*

Is privilege for thy departure hence.

Thank me for this more than for all the favours

Which all too much I have bestow'd on thee.

But if thou linger in my territories

Longer than swiftest expedition   *165*

Will give thee time to leave our royal court,

By heaven! my wrath shall far exceed the love

I ever bore my daughter or thyself.

Be gone! I will not hear thy vain excuse;

But, as thou lov'st thy life, make speed from hence.   *[Exit.]*

Val. And why not death rather than living torment?

To die is to be banish'd from myself;

And Silvia is myself. Banish'd from her

Is self from self,—a deadly banishment!

What light is light, if Silvia be not seen?   *175*

What joy is joy, if Silvia be not by?

Unless it be to think that she is by

And feed upon the shadow of perfection.

Except I be by Silvia in the night,

There is no music in the nightingale;   *180*

Unless I look on Silvia in the day,

There is no day for me to look upon.

She is my essence; and I leave to be,

If I be not by her fair influence

Foster'd, illumin'd, cherish'd, kept alive.   *185*

I fly not death, to fly his deadly doom.

Tarry I here, I but attend on death;

But, fly I hence, I fly away from life.

        [Enter Proteus and Launce.]

Pro. Run, boy; run, run, and seek him out.

Launce. Soho! soho!   *190*

Pro. What seest thou?

Launce. Him we go to find. There's not a hair on's head

but 'tis a Valentine.

Pro. Valentine?

Val. No.   *195*

Pro. Who then? His spirit?

Val. Neither.

Pro. What then?

Val. Nothing.

Launce. Can nothing speak? Master, shall I strike?   *200*

Pro. Who would'st thou strike?

Launce. Nothing.

Pro. Villain, forbear.

Launce. Why, sir, I'll strike nothing. I pray you,—

Pro. Sirrah, I say, forbear.—Friend Valentine, a word.   *205*

Val. My ears are stopp'd and cannot hear good news,

So much of bad already hath possess'd them.

Pro. Then in dumb silence will I bury mine,

For they are harsh, untuneable and bad.

Val. Is Silvia dead?   *210*

Pro. No, Valentine.

Val. No Valentine, indeed, for sacred Silvia!

Hath she forsworn me?

Pro. No, Valentine.

Val. No Valentine, if Silvia have forsworn me!   *215*

What is your news?

Launce. Sir, there is a proclamation that you are vanished.

Pro. That thou art banished, O, that's the news,

From hence, from Silvia, and from me thy friend.

Val. O, I have fed upon this woe already,   *220*

And now excess of it will make me surfeit.

Doth Silvia know that I am banished?

Pro. Ay, ay; and she hath offer'd to the doom—

Which, unrevers'd, stands in effectual force—

A sea of melting pearl, which some call tears.   *225*

Those at her father's churlish feet she tender'd;

With them, upon her knees, her humble self;

Wringing her hands, whose whiteness so became them

As if but now they waxed pale for woe.

But neither bended knees, pure hands held up,   *230*

Sad sighs, deep groans, nor silver-shedding tears,

Could penetrate her uncompassionate sire;

But Valentine, if he be ta'en, must die.

Besides, her intercession chaf'd him so,

When she for thy repeal was suppliant,   *235*

That to close prison he commanded her,

With many bitter threats of biding there.

Val. No more; unless the next word that thou speak'st

Have some malignant power upon my life.

If so, I pray thee, breathe it in mine ear,   *240*

As ending anthem of my endless dolour.

Pro. Cease to lament for that thou canst not help,
And study help for that which thou lament'st.
Time is the nurse and breeder of all good.
Here if thou stay, thou canst not see thy love;   *245*
Besides, thy staying will abridge thy life.
Hope is a lover's staff; walk hence with that
And manage it against despairing thoughts.
Thy letters may be here, though thou art hence;
Which, being writ to me, shall be deliver'd   *250*
Even in the milk-white bosom of thy love.
The time now serves not to expostulate.
Come, I'll convey thee through the city-gate,
And, ere I part with thee, confer at large
Of all that may concern thy love-affairs.   *255*
As thou lov'st Silvia, though not for thyself,
Regard thy danger, and along with me!

Val. I pray thee, Launce, and if thou seest my boy,
Bid him make haste and meet me at the North-gate.

Pro. Go, sirrah, find him out. Come, Valentine.   *260*

Val. O my dear Silvia! hapless Valentine!

[Exeunt Valentine and Proteus.]

Launce. I am but a fool, look you; and yet I have the wit
to think my master is a kind of a knave; but that's all one, if
he be but one knave. He lives not now that knows me to be
in love; yet I am in love; but a team of horse shall not pluck
that from me, nor who 'tis I love; and yet 'tis a woman; but
what woman, I will not tell myself; and yet 'tis a milkmaid;
yet 'tis not a maid, for she hath had gossips; yet 'tis a maid,
for she is her master's maid, and serves for wages. She hath
more qualities than a water-spaniel,—which is much in a   *270*
bare Christian. *[Pulling out a paper.]* Here is the catalog of her
condition. 'Imprimis: She can fetch and carry.' Why, a horse
can do no more; nay, a horse cannot fetch, but only carry;
therefore, is she better than a jade. 'Item: She can milk'; look
you, a sweet virtue in a maid with clean hands.   *275*

[Enter Speed.]

Speed. How now, Signior Launce! what news with your
mastership?

Launce. With my master's ship? why, it is at sea.

Speed. Well, your old vice still: mistake the word. What
news, then, in your paper?   *280*

Launce. The blackest news that ever thou heardest.

Speed. Why, man, how black?

Launce. Why, as black as ink.

Speed. Let me read them.

Launce. Fie on thee, jolthead! thou canst not read.   *285*

Speed. Thou liest; I can.

Launce. I will try thee. Tell me this: who begot thee?

Speed. Marry, the son of my grandfather.

Launce. O, illiterate loiterer! it was the son of thy grandmother. This proves that thou canst not read.   *290*

Speed. Come, fool, come; try me in thy paper.

Launce. There; and Saint Nicholas be thy speed!

Speed. *[Reads.]* 'Imprimis: She can milk.'

Launce. Ay, that she can.

Speed. 'Item: She brews good ale.'   *295*

Launce. And thereof comes the proverb, 'Blessing of your
heart, you brew good ale.'

Speed. 'Item: She can sew.'

Launce. That's as much as to say, 'Can she so?'

Speed. 'Item: She can knit.'   *300*

Launce. What need a man care for a stock with a wench,
when she can knit him a stock?

Speed. 'Item: She can wash and scour.'

Launce. A special virtue; for then she need not be washed
and scoured.   *305*

Speed. 'Item: She can spin.'

Launce. Then may I set the world on wheels, when she
can spin for her living.

Speed. 'Item: She hath many nameless virtues.'

Launce. That's as much as to say, bastard virtues; that,   *310*
indeed, know not their fathers, and therefore have no names.

Speed. Here follow her vices.

Launce. Close at the heels of her virtues.

Speed. 'Item: She is not be to [kissed] fasting, in respect
of her breath.'   *315*

Launce. Well, that fault may be mended with a breakfast.
Read on.

Speed. 'Item: She hath a sweet mouth.'

Launce. That makes amends for her sour breath.

Speed. 'Item: She doth talk in her sleep.'   *320*

Launce. It's no matter for that, so she sleep not in her talk.

Speed. 'Item: She is slow in words.'

Launce. O villain, that set this down among her vices! To
be slow in words is a woman's only virtue. I pray thee, out
with 't, and place it for her chief virtue.   *325*

Speed. 'Item: She is proud.'

Launce. Out with that too; it was Eve's legacy, and cannot
be ta'en from her.

Speed. 'Item: She hath no teeth.'

Launce. I care not for that neither, because I love crusts. *330*

Speed. 'Item: She is curst.'

Launce. Well, the best is, she hath no teeth to bite.

Speed. 'Item: She will often praise her liquor.'

Launce. If her liquor be good, she shall; if she will not,
I will; for good things should be praised.   *335*

Speed. 'Item: She is too liberal.'

Launce. Of her tongue she cannot, for that's writ down she
is slow of; of her purse she shall not, for that I'll keep shut.
Now, of another thing she may, and that cannot I help. Well,
proceed.   *340*

Speed. 'Item: She hath more hair than wit, and more faults
than hairs, and more wealth than faults.'

Launce. Stop there; I'll have her. She was mine, and not
mine, twice or thrice in that last article. Rehearse that once
more.   *345*

Speed. 'Item: She hath more hair than wit,'

Launce. More hair than wit it may be; I'll prove it. The
cover of the salt hides the salt, and therefore it is more than
the salt; the hair that covers the wit is more than the wit, for
the greater hides the less. What's next?   *350*

Speed. 'And more faults than hairs,'—

248 manage: *wield*   252 expostulate: *discuss*   256 though: *even though*   263, 264
that's ... knave; *cf. n.*   265 horse: *horses*   268 gossips: *sponsors for a child of
hers*   270 water-spaniel; *cf. n.* bare: *mere*   272 condition: *characteristics* Imprimis:
in the first place   274 jade; *cf. n.*   285 jolthead: *blockhead*   289 loiterer:
idler   292 Saint Nicholas: *patron saint of scholars*

301 stock: *dowry*   302 stock: *stocking*   307 set ... wheels: *live at ease*   309 nameless: *inexpressible*   318 sweet mouth: *sweet tooth*   327 Eve's legacy; *cf. n.*   331 curst:
shrewish   333 praise: *appraise*   336 liberal: *bold, wanton*   341 more ... wit: *a proverbial expression*

Launce. That's monstrous! O, that that were out!

Speed. 'And more wealth than faults.'

Launce. Why, that word makes the faults gracious. Well, I'll have her; and if it be a match, as nothing is impossible,— *355*

Speed. What then?

Launce. Why, then will I tell thee,—that thy master stays for thee at the North-gate.

Speed. For me?

Launce. For thee! ay; who are thou? He hath stayed for *360* a better man than thee.

Speed. And must I go to him?

Launce. Thou must run to him, for thou hast stayed so long that going will scarce serve the turn.

Speed. Why didst not tell me sooner? Pox of your love- *365* letters!   *[Exit.]*

Launce. Now will he be swing'd for reading my letter. An unmannerly slave, that will thrust himself into secrets. I'll after, to rejoice in the boy's correction.   *[Exit.]*

❧ Scene Second ❧

[The Same. A Room in the Duke's Palace]
Enter Duke [and] Thurio; [and later,] Proteus.

Duke. Sir Thurio, fear not but that she will love you,
Now Valentine is banish'd from her sight.

Thu. Since his exile she hath despis'd me most,
Forsworn my company and rail'd at me,
That I am desperate of obtaining her.   *5*

Duke. This weak impress of love is as a figure
Trenched in ice, which with an hour's heat
Dissolves to water and doth lose his form.
A little time will melt her frozen thoughts,
And worthless Valentine shall be forgot.   *10*

[Enter Proteus.]

How now, Sir Proteus! Is your countryman
According to our proclamation gone?

Pro. Gone, my good lord.

Duke. My daughter takes his going grievously.

Pro. A little time, my lord, will kill that grief.   *15*

Duke. So I believe; but Thurio thinks not so.
Proteus, the good conceit I hold of thee,—
For thou hast shown some sign of good desert,—
Makes me the better to confer with thee.

Pro. Longer than I prove loyal to your Grace   *20*
Let me not live to look upon your Grace.

Duke. Thou know'st how willingly I would effect
The match between Sir Thurio and my daughter.

Pro. I do, my lord.

Duke. And also, I think, thou are not ignorant   *25*
How she opposes her against my will.

Pro. She did, my lord, when Valentine was here.

Duke. Ay, and perversely she persevers so.
What might we do to make the girl forget
The love of Valentine, and love Sir Thurio?   *30*

Pro. The best way is to slander Valentine
With falsehood, cowardice, and poor descent,

Three things that women highly hold in hate.

Duke. Ay, but she'll think that it is spoke in hate.

Pro. Ay, if his enemy deliver it;   *35*
Therefore it must with circumstance be spoken
By one whom she esteemeth as his friend.

Duke. Then you must undertake to slander him.

Pro. And that, my lord, I shall be loath to do:
'Tis an ill office for a gentleman,   *40*
Especially against his very friend.

Duke. Where your good word cannot advantage him,
Your slander never can endamage him;
Therefore the office is indifferent,
Being entreated to it by your friend.   *45*

Pro. You have prevail'd, my lord. If I can do it,
By aught that I can speak in his dispraise,
She shall not long continue love to him.
But say this weed her love from Valentine,
It follows not that she will love Sir Thurio.   *50*

Thu. Therefore, as you unwind her love from him,
Lest it should ravel and be good to none,
You must provide to bottom it on me;
Which must be done by praising me as much
As you in worth disprise Sir Valentine.   *55*

Duke. And, Proteus, we dare trust you in this kind,
Because we know, on Valentine's report,
You are already Love's firm votary
And cannot soon revolt and change your mind.
Upon this warrant shall you have access   *60*
Where you with Silvia may confer at large;
For she is lumpish, heavy, melancholy,
And, for your friend's sake, will be glad of you;
Where you may temper her, by your persuasion
To hate young Valentine and love my friend.   *65*

Pro. As much as I can do I will effect.
But you, Sir Thurio, are not sharp enough;
You must lay lime to tangle her desires
By wailful sonnets, whose composed rimes
Should be full-fraught with serviceable vows.   *70*

Duke. Ay,
Much is the force of heaven-bred poesy.

Pro. Say that upon the altar of her beauty
You sacrifice your tears, your sighs, your heart.
Write till your ink be dry, and with your tears   *75*
Moist it again, and frame some feeling line
That may discover such integrity;
For Orpheus' lute was strung with poets' sinews,
Whose golden touch could soften steel and stones,
Make tigers tame and huge leviathans   *80*
Forsake unsounded deeps to dance on sands.
After your dire-lamenting elegies,
Visit by night your lady's chamber-window
With some sweet consort; to their instruments
Tune a deploring dump; the night's dead silence   *85*
Will well become such sweet-complaining grievance.
This, or else nothing, will inherit her.

Duke. This discipline shows thou hast been in love.

---

354 gracious: *acceptable*   **369 correction:** *punishment*   **5 desperate:** *without hope*   **7 Trenched:** *cut*   **14 grievously:** *sorrowfully*   **17 conceit:** *opinion*

36 circumstance: *much detail*   **41 very:** *true*   **44 indifferent:** *neither good nor bad*   **45 your friend:** *i.e. the Duke*   **52 ravel:** *become entangled*   **53 bottom it;** *cf. n.*   **62 lumpish:** *spiritless*   **64 temper:** *mould*   **68 lime:** *bird lime* **tangle:** *ensnare*   **70 serviceable:** *devoted*   **77 discover such integrity:** *disclose such true devotion*   **78 sinews:** *nerves*   **84 consort:** *company of musicians*   **85 dump:** *mournful melody*   **86 grievance:** *grieving*   **87 inherit:** *obtain*   **88 discipline:** *instruction*

Thu. And thy advice this night I'll put in practice.
Therefore, sweet Proteus, my direction-giver,   90
Let us into the city presently
To sort some gentlemen well skill'd in music.
I have a sonnet that will serve the turn
To give the onset to thy good advice.
     Duke. About it, gentlemen!   95
     Pro. We'll wait upon your grace till after supper,
And afterward determine our proceedings.
     Duke. Even now about it! I will pardon you.   *Exeunt.*

ACT FOURTH ❧ Scene First

[A forest between Milan and Verona]
Enter Valentine, Speed, and [at another door] certain Outlaws.

1. Out. Fellows, stand fast; I see a passenger.
2. Out. If there be ten, shrink not, but down with 'em.
3. Out. Stand, sir, and throw us that you have about ye.
If not, we'll make you sit and rifle you.
     Speed. Sir, we are undone; these are the villains   5
That all the travellers do fear so much.
     Val. My friends,—
     1. Out. That's not so, sir; we are your enemies.
     2. Out. Peace! we'll hear him.
     3. Out. Ay, by my beard, will we, for he is a proper   10
man.
     Val. Then know, that I have little wealth to lose.
A man I am cross'd with adversity;
My riches are these poor habiliments,
Of which if you should here disfurnish me,   15
You take the sum and substance that I have.
     2. Out. Whither travel you?
     Val. To Verona.
     1. Out. Whence came you?
     Val. From Milan.   20
     3. Out. Have you long sojourn'd there?
     Val. Some sixteen months; and longer might have stay'd,
If crooked fortune had not thwarted me.
     2. Out. What! were you banish'd thence?
     Val. I was.   25
     2. Out. For what offence?
     Val. For that which now torments me to rehearse.
I kill'd a man, whose death I much repent;
But yet I slew him manfully, in fight,
Without false vantage or base treachery.   30
     1. Out. Why, ne'er repent it, if it were done so.
But were you banish'd for so small a fault?
     Val. I was, and held me glad of such a doom.
     2. Out. Have you the tongues?
     Val. My youthful travel therein made me happy,   35
Or else I often had been miserable.
     3. Out. By the bare scalp of Robin Hood's fat friar,
This fellow were a king for our wild faction!
     1. Out. We'll have him. Sirs, a word.

     Speed. Master, be one of them;   40
It is an honourable kind of thievery.
     Val. Peace, villain!
     2. Out. Tell us this: have you anything to take to?
     Val. Nothing but my fortune.
     3. Out. Know then, that some of us are gentlemen,   45
Such as the fury of ungovern'd youth
Thrust from the company of awful men.
Myself was from Verona banished
For practising to steal away a lady,
An heir, and near allied unto the duke.   50
     2. Out. And I from Mantua, for a gentleman
Who, in my mood, I stabb'd unto the heart.
     1. Out. And I for such like petty crimes as these.
But to the purpose; for we cite our faults,
That they may hold excus'd our lawless lives;   55
And, partly, seeing you are beautified
With goodly shape, and by your own report
A linguist, and a man of such perfection
As we do in our quality much want—
     2. Out. Indeed, because you are a banish'd man,   60
Therefore, above the rest, we parley to you.
Are you content to be our general?
To make a virtue of necessity
And live, as we do, in this wilderness?
     3. Out. What say'st thou? Wilt thou be of our consort?   65
Say ay, and be the captain of us all.
We'll do thee homage and be rul'd by thee,
Love thee as our commander and our king.
     1. Out. But if thou scorn our courtesy, thou diest.
     2. Out. Thou shalt not live to brag what we have offer'd.   70
     Val. I take your offer and will live with you,
Provided that you do no outrages
On silly women, or poor passengers.
     3. Out. No; we detest such vile, base practices.
Come, go with us; we'll bring thee to our crews,   75
And show thee all the treasure we have got,
Which, with ourselves, all rest at thy dispose.   *Exeunt.*

❧ Scene Second ❧

[Milan. The Court of the Duke's Palace]
Enter Proteus; [and later,] Thurio, Julia, Host, Musician[s], [and]
Silvia.

     Pro. Already have I been false to Valentine,
And now I must be as unjust to Thurio.
Under the colour of commending him,
I have access my own love to prefer.
But Silvia is too fair, too true, too holy,   5
To be corrupted with my worthless gifts.
When I protest true loyalty to her,
She twits me with my falsehood to my friend;
When to her beauty I commend my vows,
She bids me think how I have been forsworn   10
In breaking faith with Julia whom I lov'd:

92 sort: *select*   94 give . . . to: *make a beginning of following*   98 pardon: *excuse*
1 passenger: *passer-by, traveler*   10 proper: *handsome*   33 glad . . . doom: *i.e. glad to
get off so cheaply*   34 tongues: *foreign languages*   37 friar: *Friar Tuck*

43 anything to take to: *any means of subsistence*   47 awful: *commanding respect*   49
practising: *plotting*   52 mood: *anger*   59 quality: *occupation*   61 the rest: *any other
reason*   65 consort: *fellowship*   73 silly: *helpless*   3 colour: *pretence*   9 commend:
deliver*

And notwithstanding all her sudden quips,
The least whereof would quell a lover's hope,
Yet, spaniel-like, the more she spurns my love,
The more it grows, and fawneth on her still.   *15*
But here comes Thurio. Now must we to her window,
And give some evening music to her ear.

[Enter Thurio, and Musicians.]

Thu. How now, Sir Proteus! are you crept before us?
Pro. Ay, gentle Thurio; for you know that love
Will creep in service where it cannot go.   *20*
Thu. Ay; but I hope, sir, that you love not here.
Pro. Sir, but I do; or else I would be hence.
Thu. Who? Silvia?
Pro. Ay, Silvia, for your sake.
Thu. I thank you for your own. Now, gentlemen,   *25*
Let's tune, and to it lustily a while.

[Enter Host and Julia behind. Julia in boy's clothes.]

Host. Now, my young guest, methinks you're allycholly. I
pray you, why is it?
Jul. Marry, mine host, because I cannot be merry.
Host. Come, we'll have you merry. I'll bring you where   *30*
you shall hear music, and see the gentleman that you asked
for.
Jul. But shall I hear him speak?
Host. Ay, that you shall.
Jul. That will be music.   *[Music plays.]*   *35*
Host. Hark! hark!
Jul. Is he among these?
Host. Ay; but peace! let's hear 'em.

Song.

'Who is Silvia? what is she?   *40*
    That all our swains commend her?*
Holy, fair, and wise is she;
    The heaven such grace did lend her,
That she might admired be.

'Is she kind as she is fair?   *45*
    For beauty lives with kindness:*
Love doth to her eyes repair,
    To help him of his blindness;
And, being help'd, inhabits there.

'Then to Silvia let us sing,   *50*
    That Silvia is excelling;*
She excels each mortal thing
    Upon the dull earth dwelling.
To her let us garlands bring.'

Host. How now! are you sadder than you were before?   *55*
How do you, man? The music likes you not.
Jul. You mistake; the musician likes me not.
Host. Why, my pretty youth?
Jul. He plays false, father.
Host. How? Out of tune on the strings?   *60*
Jul. Not so; but yet so false that he grieves my very
heartstrings.
Host. You have a quick ear.

Jul. Ay; I would I were deaf; it makes me have a slow
heart.   *65*
Host. I perceive you delight not in music.
Jul. Not a whit,—when it jars so.
Host. Hark! what fine change is in the music!
Jul. Ay, that change is the spite.
Host. You would have them always play but one thing?   *70*
Jul. I would always have one play but one thing.
But, host, doth this Sir Proteus that we talk on
Often resort unto this gentlewoman?
Host. I will tell you what Launce, his man, told me: he
lov'd her out of all nick.   *75*
Jul. Where is Launce?
Host. Gone to seek his dog; which to-morrow, by his
master's command, he must carry for a present to his lady.
Jul. Peace! stand aside; the company parts.
Pro. Sir Thurio, fear not you. I will so plead   *80*
That you shall say my cunning drift excels.
Thu. Where meet me?
Pro. At Saint Gregory's well.
Thu. Farewell.   *[Exeunt Thurio and Musicians.]*

[Enter Silvia above, at her window.]

Pro. Madam, good even to your ladyship.   *85*
Sil. I thank you for your music, gentlemen.
Who is that that spake?
Pro. One, lady, if you knew his pure heart's truth,
You would quickly learn to know him by his voice.
Sil. Sir Proteus, as I take it.   *90*
Pro. Sir Proteus, gentle lady, and your servant.
Sil. What is your will?
Pro.   That I may compass yours.
Sil. You have your wish; my will is even this:
That presently you hie you home to bed.   *95*
Thou subtle, perjur'd, false, disloyal man!
Think'st thou I am so shallow, so conceitless,
To be seduced by thy flattery,
That hast deceiv'd so many with thy vows?
Return, return, and make thy love amends.   *100*
For me, by this pale queen of night I swear,
I am so far from granting thy request
That I despise thee for thy wrongful suit,
And by and by intend to chide myself
Even for this time I spend in talking to thee.   *105*
Pro. I grant, sweet love, that I did love a lady;
But she is dead.
Jul. [Aside.] 'Twere false, if I should speak it;
For I am sure she is not buried.
Sil. Say that she be; yet Valentine thy friend   *110*
Survives, to whom, thyself art witness,
I am betroth'd; and art thou not asham'd
To wrong him with thy importunacy?
Pro. I likewise hear that Valentine is dead.
Sil. And so suppose am I; for in his grave,   *115*
Assure thyself my love is buried.
Pro. Sweet lady, let me rake it from the earth.
Sil. Go to thy lady's grave and call hers thence;
Or, at the least, in hers sepulchre thine.

---

12 quips: *sharp utterances*   **20 go:** *walk*   **27 allycholly:** *i.e. melancholy*   **49 inhabits:**
dwells   **56 likes:** *pleases*

64 slow: *heavy*   **68 change:** *modulation*   **75 out ... nick:** *beyond all reckoning*   *81*
drift: *scheme*   **96 subtle:** *crafty*   **97 conceitless:** *witless*

Jul. [Aside.] He heard not that.   *120*

Pro. Madam, if your heart be so obdurate.
Vouchsafe me yet your picture for my love,
The picture that is hanging in your chamber.
To that I'll speak, to that I'll sigh and weep;
For since the substance of your perfect self   *125*
Is else devoted, I am but a shadow,
And to your shadow will I make true love.

Jul. [Aside.] If 'twere a substance, you would, sure,
deceive it,
And make it but a shadow, as I am.   *130*

Sil. I am very loath to be your idol, sir;
But, since your falsehood shall become you well
To worship shadows and adore false shapes,
Send to me in the morning and I'll send it.
And so, good rest.   *135*

Pro.   As wretches have o'er night
That wait for execution in the morn.

     [Exeunt Proteus and Silvia, severally.]

Jul. Host, will you go?

Host. By my halidom, I was fast asleep.

Jul. Pray you, where lies Sir Proteus?   *140*

Host. Marry, at my house. Trust me, I think 'tis almost day.

Jul. Not so; but it hath been the longest night
That e'er I watch'd, and the most heaviest.   *[Exeunt.]*

❧ SCENE THIRD ❧

[The Same]
Enter Eglamour, [and later,] Silvia.

Egl. This is the hour that Madam Silvia
Entreated me to call, and know her mind:
There's some great matter she'd employ me in.
Madam, Madam!

     [Enter Silvia above, at her window.]

Sil.   Who calls?   *5*

Egl.   Your servant, and your friend;
One that attends your ladyship's command.

Sil. Sir Eglamour, a thousand times good morrow.

Egl. As many, worthy lady, to yourself.
According to your ladyship's impose,   *10*
I am thus early come to know what service
It is your pleasure to command me in.

Sil. O Eglamour, thou art a gentleman—
Think not I flatter, for I swear I do not—
Valiant, wise, remorseful, well-accomplish'd.   *15*
Thou art not ignorant what dear good will
I bear unto the banish'd Valentine,
Nor how my father would enforce me marry
Vain Thurio, whom my very soul abhors.
Thyself hast lov'd; and I have heard thee say   *20*
No grief did ever come so near thy heart
As when thy lady and thy true love died,
Upon whose grave thou vow'dst pure chastity.
Sir Eglamour, I would to Valentine,

To Mantua, where I hear he makes abode;   *25*
And, for the ways are dangerous to pass,
I do desire thy worthy company,
Upon whose faith and honour I repose.
Urge not my father's anger, Eglamour,
But think upon my grief, a lady's grief,   *30*
And on the justice of my flying hence,
To keep me from a most unholy match,
Which heaven and fortune still rewards with plagues.
I do desire thee, even from a heart
As full of sorrows as the sea of sands,   *35*
To bear me company and go with me.
If not, to hide what I have said to thee,
That I may venture to depart alone.

Egl. Madam, I pity much your grievances;
Which since I know they virtuously are plac'd,   *40*
I give consent to go along with you,
Recking as little what betideth me
As much I wish all good befortune you.
When will you go?

Sil.   This evening coming.   *45*

Egl. Where shall I meet you?

Sil.   At Friar Patrick's cell,
Where I intend holy confession.

Egl. I will not fail your ladyship.
Good morrow, gentle lady.   *50*

Sil. Good morrow, kind Sir Eglamour.

     Exeunt [severally].

❧ SCENE FOURTH ❧

[The Same]
Enter Launce [with his dog; and later enter]
Proteus, Julia, [and] Silvia.

Launce. When a man's servant shall play the cur with him,
look you, it goes hard; one that I brought up of a puppy; one
that I saved from drowning, when three or four of his blind
brothers and sisters went to it. I have taught him, even as one
would say precisely, 'Thus I would teach a dog.' I was sent   *5*
to deliver him as a present to Mistress Silvia from my master,
and I came no sooner into the dining-chamber but he steps
me to her trencher and steals her capon's leg. O! 'tis a foul
thing when a cur cannot keep himself in all companies. I
would have, as one should say, one that takes upon him to   *10*
be a dog indeed, to be, as it were, a dog at all things. If I had
not had more wit than he, to take a fault upon me that he
did, I think verily he had been hanged for 't; sure as I live, he
had suffered for 't. You shall judge. He thrusts me himself into
the company of three or four gentleman-like dogs under the   *15*
duke's table. He had not been there—bless the mark—a piss-
ing-while, but all the chamber smelt him. 'Out with the dog!'
says one; 'What cur is that?' says another; 'Whip him out!' says
the third; 'Hang him up!' says the duke. I, having been acquainted with the smell before, knew it was Crab, and goes   *20*
me to the fellow that whips the dogs. 'Friend,' quoth I, 'you
mean to whip the dog?' 'Ay, marry, do I,' quoth he. 'You do

---

126 else: *elsewhere*   **shadow:** *lifeless person*   **127 shadow:** *portrait*   **139 halidom:** *any-thing regarded as sacred*   **140 lies:** *lodges, sleeps*   **143 watch'd:** *remained awake through*   **10 impose:** *command*   **15 remorseful:** *full of pity*   **16 dear:** *affectionate*

26 for: *because*   **39 grievances:** *distresses*   **43 befortune:** *befall*   **2 of:** *from*   **4 to it:** *to their deaths*   **7 me;** *cf. n.*   **8 trencher:** *wooden plate*   **9 keep:** *restrain*   **11 a dog at:** *adept at*   **16 bless the mark;** *cf. n.*

him the more wrong,' quoth I; ' 'twas I did the thing you wot
of.' He makes me no more ado, but whips me out of the
chamber. How many masters would do this for his servant? 25
Nay, I'll be sworn, I have sat in the stocks for puddings he
hath stolen, otherwise he had been executed; I have stood on
the pillory for geese he hath killed, otherwise he had suffered
for 't. Thou thinkest not of this now. Nay, I remember the
trick you served me when I took my leave of Madam Silvia. 30
Did not I bid thee still mark me and do as I do? When didst
thou see me heave up my leg and make water against a gentlewoman's farthingale! Didst thou ever see me do such a trick?

[Enter Proteus, and Julia in boy's clothes.]

Pro. Sebastian is thy name? I like thee well,
And will employ thee in some service presently. 35
    Jul. In what you please; I will do what I can.
    Pro. I hope thou wilt. *[To Launce.]* How now, you
whoreson peasant!
Where have you been these two days loitering?
    Launce. Marry, sir, I carried Mistress Silvia the dog you 40
bade me.
    Pro. And what says she to my little jewel?
    Launce. Marry, she says, your dog was a cur, and tells you,
currish thanks is good enough for such a present.
    Pro. But she received my dog? 45
    Launce. No, indeed, did she not; here have I brought him
back again.
    Pro. What! didst thou offer her this from me?
    Launce. Ay, sir; the other squirrel was stolen from me
by the hangman boys in the marketplace; and then I offered 50
her mine own, who is a dog as big as ten of yours, and there-
fore the gift the greater.
    Pro. Go, get thee hence, and find my dog again,
Or ne'er return again into my sight.
Away, I say! Stay'st thou to vex me here?   *[Exit Launce.]*
A slave that still an end turns me to shame.
Sebastian, I have entertained thee,
Partly that I have need of such a youth,
That can with some discretion do my business,
For 't is no trusting to yond foolish lout; 60
But chiefly for thy face and thy behaviour,
Which, if my augury deceive me not,
Witness good bringing up, fortune, and truth.
Therefore, know thou, for this I entertain thee.
Go presently, and take this ring with thee; 65
Deliver it to Madam Silvia.
She lov'd me well deliver'd it to me.
    Jul. It seems you lov'd not her, to leave her token.
She's dead, belike?
    Pro.   Not so; I think she lives. 70
    Jul. Alas!
    Pro. Why dost thou cry 'alas'?
    Jul.   I cannot choose
But pity her.
    Pro. Wherefore should'st thou pity her? 75
    Jul. Because methinks that she lov'd you as well
As you do love your lady Silvia.

She dreams on him that has forgot her love;
You dote on her that cares not for your love.
'Tis pity love should be so contrary; 80
And thinking on it makes me cry, 'alas'!
    Pro. Well, give her that ring and therewithal
This letter. That's her chamber. Tell my lady
I claim the promise for her heavenly picture.
Your message done, hie home unto my chamber, 85
Where thou shalt find me sad and solitary.   *[Exit.]*
    Jul. How many women would do such a message?
Alas, poor Proteus! thou hast entertain'd
A fox to be the shepherd of thy lambs.
Alas, poor fool! why do I pity him 90
That with his very heart despiseth me?
Because he loves her, he despiseth me;
Because I love him, I must pity him.
This ring I gave him when he parted from me,
To bind him to remember my good will; 95
And now am I—unhappy messenger—
To plead for that which I would not obtain,
To carry that which I would have refus'd,
To praise his faith which I would have disprais'd.
I am my master's true-confirmed love, 100
But cannot be true servant to my master,
Unless I prove false traitor to myself.
Yet will I woo for him; but yet so coldly
As heaven it knows, I would not have him speed.

[Enter Silvia, attended.]

Gentlewoman, good day! I pray you, be my mean 105
To bring me where to speak with Madam Silvia.
    Sil. What would you with her, if that I be she?
    Jul. If you be she, I do entreat your patience
To hear me speak the message I am sent on.
    Sil. From whom? 110
    Jul. From my master, Sir Proteus, madam.
    Sil. O! he sends you for a picture?
    Jul. Ay, madam.
    Sil. Ursula, bring my picture there.

[A picture brought.]

Go, give your master this. Tell him from me, 115
One Julia, that his changing thoughts forget,
Would better fit his chamber than this shadow.
    Jul. Madam, please you peruse this letter.—
Pardon me, madam, I have unadvis'd
Deliver'd you a paper that I should not. 120
This is the letter to your ladyship.
    Sil. I pray thee, let me look on that again.
    Jul. It may not be; good madam, pardon me.
    Sil. There, hold.
I will not look upon your master's lines. 125
I know they are stuff'd with protestations
And full of new-found oaths, which he will break
As easily as I do tear his paper.
    Jul. Madam, he sends your ladyship this ring.
    Sil. The more shame for him that he sends it me; 130
For I have heard him say a thousand times,
His Julia gave it him at his departure.
Though his false finger have profan'd the ring,

---

23 wot: *know*   **26 puddings:** *animals' intestines* (sometimes stuffed)   **38 whoreson:**
used in coarse playfulness   **49 squirrel;** *cf. n.*   **50 hangman:** *fit for the hangman*   **56
still an end:** *continually*   **64 entertain:** *take into service*   **67 deliver'd:** *who delivered*   **68 leave:** *part with*

90 poor fool: *referring to herself*   **104 speed:** *be successful*   **119 unadvis'd:** *inadvertently*

Mine shall not do his Julia so much wrong.

Jul. She thanks you.   *135*

Sil. What say'st thou?

Jul. I thank you, madam, that you tender her.
Poor gentlewoman! my master wrongs her much.

Sil. Dost thou know her?

Jul. Almost as well as I do know myself: *140*
To think upon her woes, I do protest
That I have wept a hundred several times.

Sil. Belike she thinks that Proteus hath forsook her.

Jul. I think she doth, and that's her cause of sorrow.

Sil. Is she not passing fair?   *145*

Jul. She hath been fairer, madam, than she is.
When she did think my master lov'd her well,
She, in my judgment, was as fair as you;
But since she did neglect her looking-glass
And threw her sun-expelling mask away,   *150*
The air hath starv'd the roses in her cheeks
And pinch'd the lily-tincture of her face,
That now she is become as black as I.

Sil. How tall was she?

Jul. About my stature; for, at Pentecost,   *155*
When all our pageants of delight were play'd,
Our youth got me to play the woman's part,
And I was trimm'd in Madam Julia's gown,
Which served me as fit, by all men's judgments,
As if the garment had been made for me.   *160*
Therefore I know she is about my height.
And at that time I made her weep agood,
For I did play a lamentable part.
Madam, 'twas Ariadne passioning
For Theseus' perjury and unjust flight;   *165*
Which I so lively acted with my tears
That my poor mistress, moved therewithal,
Wept bitterly, and would I might be dead
If I in thought felt not her very sorrow!

Sil. She is beholding to thee, gentle youth.—   *170*
Alas, poor lady, desolate and left!
I weep myself to think upon thy words.
Here, youth, there is my purse. I give thee this
For thy sweet mistress' sake, because thou lov'st her.
Farewell.   *175*

Jul. And she shall thank you for 't, if e'er you know her.—
            [Exit Silvia, with Attendants.]

A virtuous gentlewoman, mild and beautiful.
I hope my master's suit will be but cold,
Since she respects my mistress' love so much.   *180*
Alas, how love can trifle with itself!
Here is her picture; let me see; I think,
If I had such a tire, this face of mine
Were full as lovely as is this of hers;
And yet the painter flatter'd her a little,   *185*
Unless I flatter with myself too much.
Her hair is auburn, mine is perfect yellow:
If that be all the differences in his love,
I'll get me such a colour'd periwig.
Her eyes are grey as glass, and so are mine.   *190*

Ay, but her forehead's low, and mine's as high.
What should it be that he respects in her
But I can make respective in myself,
If this fond Love were not a blinded god?
Come, shadow, come, and take this shadow up,   *195*
For 'tis thy rival. O thou senseless form!
Thou shalt be worshipp'd, kiss'd, lov'd, and ador'd,
And, were there sense in his idolatry,
My substance should be statue in thy stead.
I'll use thee kindly for thy mistress' sake,   *200*
That us'd me so; or else, by Jove I vow,
I should have scratch'd out your unseeing eyes,
To make my master out of love with thee.   *[Exit.]*

ACT FIFTH ❦ SCENE FIRST

[Milan. An Abbey]
Enter Eglamour, [and later,] Silvia.

Egl. The sun begins to gild the western sky,
And now it is about the very hour
That Silvia at Friar Patrick's cell should meet me.
She will not fail; for lovers break not hours,
Unless it be to come before their time,   *5*
So much they spur their expedition.
See, where she comes.

[Enter Silvia.]

            Lady, a happy evening!

Sil. Amen, amen! go on, good Eglamour,
Out at the postern by the abbey-wall.   *10*
I fear I am attended by some spies.

Egl. Fear not; the forest is not three leagues off;
If we recover that, we're sure enough.   *Exeunt.*

❦ SCENE SECOND ❦

[The Same. A Room in the Duke's Palace]
Enter Thurio, Proteus, Julia; [and later,] Duke.

Thu. Sir Proteus, what says Silvia to my suit?

Pro. O, sir, I find her milder than she was;
And yet she takes exceptions at your person.

Thu. What! that my leg is too long?

Pro. No, that it is too little.   *5*

Thu. I'll wear a boot to make it somewhat rounder.

[Jul. Aside.] But love will not be spurr'd to what it loathes.

Thu. What says she to my face?

Pro. She says it is a fair one.

Thu. Nay then, the wanton lies; my face is black.   *10*

Pro. But pearls are fair, and the old saying is,
'Black men are pearls in beauteous ladies' eyes.'

[Jul. Aside.] 'Tis true, such pearls as put out ladies' eyes;
For I had rather wink than look on them.

Thu. How likes she my discourse?   *15*

---

137 tender: *regard tenderly*   **155 Pentecost:** *Whitsuntide*   **156 pageants of delight:** *delightful theatrical representations*   **158 trimm'd:** *dressed*   **162 agood:** *in earnest*   **164 passioning:** *sorrowing*   **170 beholding:** *indebted*   **179 cold:** *ineffectual*   **180 my mistress':** *repeating the fiction of l. 167*   **183 tire:** *headdress*

193 respective: *worthy of respect*   **195 shadow ... shadow;** *cf. n. on IV.ii.128*   **take ... up:** *pun on sense of 'oppose'*   **10 postern:** *small back or side door*   **13 recover:** *reach*   **sure:** *safe*   **3 takes exceptions at:** *objects to*   **9 fair;** *cf. n.*   **11 pearls:** *cataracts*

Pro. Ill, when you talk of war.

Thu. But well, when I discourse of love and peace?

Jul. [Aside.] But better, indeed, when you hold your peace.

Thu. What says she to my valour?

Pro. O, sir, she makes no doubt of that.   20

Jul. [Aside.] She needs not, when she knows it cowardice.

Thu. What says she to my birth?

Pro. That you are well deriv'd.

Jul. [Aside.] True; from a gentleman to a fool.

Thu. Considers she my possessions?   25

Pro. O, ay; and pities them.

Thu. Wherefore?

Jul. [Aside.] That such an ass should owe them.

Pro. That they are out by lease.

Jul. Here comes the duke.   30

[Enter Duke.]

Duke. How now, Sir Proteus! how now, Thurio!
Which of you saw Sir Eglamour of late?

Thu. Not I.

Pro.   Nor I.

Duke.   Saw you my daughter?   35

Pro.   Neither.

Duke. Why then,
She's fled unto that peasant Valentine,
And Eglamour is in her company.
'Tis true; for Friar Laurence met them both,   40
As he in penance wander'd through the forest.
Him he knew well, and guess'd that it was she,
But, being mask'd, he was not sure of it.
Besides, she did intend confession
At Patrick's cell this even, and there she was not.   45
These likelihoods confirm her flight from hence.
Therefore, I pray you, stand not to discourse,
But mount you presently and meet with me
Upon the rising of the mountain-foot,
That leads towards Mantua, whither they are fled.   50
Dispatch, sweet gentlemen, and follow me.   *[Exit.]*

Thu. Why, this it is to be a peevish girl,
That flies her fortune when it follows her.
I'll after, more to be reveng'd on Eglamour
Than for the love of reckless Silvia.   *[Exit.]*   55

Pro. And I will follow, more for Silvia's love
Than hate of Eglamour that goes with her.   *[Exit.]*

Jul. And I will follow, more to cross that love
Than hate for Silvia that is gone for love.   *[Exit.]*

❧ Scene Third ❧

[Frontiers of Mantua. The Forest]
[Enter] Silvia [and] Outlaws.

1. Out. Come, come,
Be patient; we must bring you to our captain.

Sil. A thousand more mischances than this one
Have learn'd me how to brook this patiently.

2. Out. Come, bring her away.   5

1. Out. Where is the gentleman that was with her?

3. Out. Being nimble-footed, he hath outrun us;
But Moyses and Valerius follow him.
Go thou with her to the west end of the wood;
There is our captain. We'll follow him that's fled.   10
The thicket is beset; he cannot 'scape.
     [Exeunt all except the First Outlaw and Silvia.]

1. Out. Come, I must bring you to our captain's cave.
Fear not; he bears an honourable mind,
And will not use a woman lawlessly.   15

Sil. O Valentine! this I endure for thee.   *Exeunt.*

❧ Scene Fourth ❧

[Another Part of the Forest]
Enter Valentine; [and later,] Proteus, Silvia,
Julia, Duke, Thurio, [and] Outlaws.

Val. How use doth breed a habit in a man!
This shadowy desert, unfrequented woods,
I better brook than flourishing peopled towns.
Here can I sit alone, unseen of any,
And to the nightingale's complaining notes   5
Tune my distresses and record my woes.
O thou that dost inhabit in my breast,
Leave not the mansion so long tenantless,
Lest, growing ruinous, the building fall
And leave no memory of what it was!   10
Repair me with thy presence, Silvia!
Thou gentle nymph, cherish thy forlorn swain!

[Noise within.]

What halloing and what stir is this to-day?
These are my mates, that make their wills their law,
Have some unhappy passenger in chase.   15
They love me well; yet I have much to do
To keep them from uncivil outrages.
Withdraw thee, Valentine: who's this comes here?

[Steps aside.]

[Enter Proteus, Silvia, and Julia.]

Pro. Madam, this service I have done for you—
Though you respect not aught your servant doth—   20
To hazard life and rescue you from him
That would have forc'd your honour and your love.
Vouchsafe me, for my meed, but one fair look;
A smaller boon than this I cannot beg,
And less than this, I am sure, you cannot give.   25

Val. [Aside.] How like a dream is this I see and hear!
Love, lend me patience to forbear awhile.

Sil. O, miserable, unhappy that I am!

Pro. Unhappy were you, madam, ere I came;
But by my coming I have made you happy.   30

Sil. By thy approach thou mak'st me most unhappy.

Jul. [Aside.] And me, when he approacheth to your presence.

Sil. Had I been seized by a hungry lion,
I would have been a breakfast to the beast,

---

23 deriv'd: *descended; hence the quibble following*   **25, 26 possessions . . . pities;**
cf. n.   **28 owe:** *own*   **29 out by lease:** *let out to others*   **38 peasant:** *base person*
son   **49 mountain-foot:** *foothill*   **52 peevish:** *perverse*   **4 learn'd:** *thought*   **brook:**
endure

2 desert: *any uninhabited region*   **6 record:** *sing*   **7 inhabit:** *lodge*   **12 swain:**
lover   **15 Have:** *who have*   **20 respect:** *heed*   **31 approach:** *amatory advance*
(probably)

Rather than have false Proteus rescue me.   35
O! heaven be judge how I love Valentine,
Whose life's as tender to me as my soul;
And full as much—for more there cannot be—
I do detest false perjur'd Proteus.
Therefore be gone, solicit me no more.   40
   Pro. What dangerous action, stood it next to death,
Would I not undergo for one calm look!
O, 'tis the curse in love, and still approv'd,
When women cannot love where they're belov'd!
   Sil. When Proteus cannot love where he's belov'd.   45
Read over Julia's heart, thy first best love,
For whose dear sake thou didst then rend thy faith
Into a thousand oaths; and all those oaths
Descended into perjury to love me.
Thou hast no faith left now, unless thou'dst two,   50
And that's far worse than none. Better have none
Than plural faith, which is too much by one.
Thou counterfeit to thy true friend!
   Pro.   In love
Who respects friend?   55
   Sil.   All men but Proteus.
   Pro. Nay, if the gentle spirit of moving words
Can no way change you to a milder form,
I'll woo you like a soldier, at arms' end,
And love you 'gainst the nature of love,—force ye.   60
   Sil. O heaven!
   Pro.   I'll force thee yield to my desire.
   Val. [Coming forward.] Ruffian, let go that rude uncivil
touch;
Thou friend of an ill fashion!   65
   Pro.   Valentine!
   Val. Thou common friend, that's without faith or love—
For such is a friend now! Treacherous man,
Thou hast beguil'd my hopes! Naught but mine eye
Could have persuaded me. Now I dare not say   70
I have one friend alive; thou wouldst disprove me.
Who should be trusted now, when one's right hand
Is perjur'd to the bosom? Proteus,
I am sorry I must never trust thee more,
But count the world a stranger for thy sake.   75
The private wound is deep'st. O time most curst!
'Mongst all foes that a friend should be the worst!
   Pro. My shame and guilt confounds me.
Forgive me, Valentine. If hearty sorrow
Be a sufficient ransom for offence,   80
I tender 't here; I do as truly suffer
As e'er I did commit.
   Val.   Then I am paid;
And once again I do receive thee honest.
Who by repentance is not satisfied   85
Is nor of heaven nor earth; for these are pleas'd.
By penitence the Eternal's wrath's appeas'd;
And, that my love may appear plain and free,
All that was mine in Silvia I give thee.
   Jul. O me unhappy!   *[Swoons.]* 90
   Pro. Look to the boy.
   Val. Why, boy! why, wag! how now! what's the matter?

Look up; speak.
   Jul. O good sir, my master charg'd me
To deliver a ring to Madam Silvia,   95
Which out of my neglect was never done.
   Pro. Where is that ring, boy?
   Jul.   Here 'tis; this is it. *[Gives a ring.]*
   Pro. How! let me see.
Why this is the ring I gave to Julia.   100
   Jul. O, cry you mercy, sir; I have mistook;
This is the ring you sent to Silvia.
                                  [Shows another ring.]
   Pro. But how cam'st thou by this ring?
At my depart I gave this unto Julia.
   Jul. And Julia herself did give it me;   105
And Julia herself hath brought it hither.
   Pro. How! Julia!
   Jul. Behold her that gave aim to all thy oaths,
And entertain'd them deeply in her heart.
How oft hast thou with perjury cleft the root!   110
O Proteus! let this habit make thee blush.
Be thou asham'd that I have took upon me
Such an immodest raiment, if shame live
In a disguise of love.
It is the lesser blot, modesty finds,   115
Women to change their shapes than men their minds.
   Pro. Than men their minds! 'tis true. O heaven! were man
But constant, he were perfect. That one error
Fills him with faults; makes him run through all the sins:
Inconstancy falls off ere it begins.   120
What is in Silvia's face, but I may spy
More fresh in Julia's with a constant eye?
   Val. Come, come, a hand from either.
Let me be blest to make this happy close;
'Twere pity two such friends should be long foes.   125
   Pro. Bear witness, heaven, I have my wish for ever.
   Jul. And I mine.

[Enter Outlaws with Duke and Thurio.]

   Out. A prize! a prize! a prize!
   Val. Forbear, forbear, I say; it is my lord the duke.
Your Grace is welcome to a man disgrac'd,   130
Banished Valentine.
   Duke.   Sir Valentine!
   Thu. Yonder is Silvia; and Silvia's mine.
   Val. Thurio, give back, or else embrace thy death;
Come not within the measure of my wrath;   135
Do not name Silvia thine; if once again,
Verona shall not hold thee. Here she stands;
Take but possession of her with a touch,—
I dare thee but to breathe upon my love.
   Thu. Sir Valentine, I care not for her, I.   140
I hold him but a fool that will endanger
His body for a girl that loves him not.
I claim her not, and therefore she is thine.
   Duke. The more degenerate and base art thou,
To make sure means for her as thou hast done,   145
And leave her on such slight conditions.

---

37 **tender:** *precious*   42 **calm:** *i.e. gentle*   43 **still approv'd:** *continually confirmed by*
experience   55 **respects:** *takes into account*   59 **arms' end:** *sword's point*   67 **common:**
base   82 **commit:** *transgress*   84 **receive:** *acknowledge*

101 **cry you mercy:** *I beg your pardon*   108 **gave aim to:** *was the object of*   110 **root:**
bottom of the heart   111 **habit:** *garb*   113, 114 **if . . . love;** *cf. n.*   120 **Inconstancy**
. . . begins; *cf. n.*   124 **close:** *union*   134 **give back:** *fall back*   135 **measure:**
reach   145 **means:** *efforts*   146 **on . . . conditions:** *so easily*

Now, by the honour of my ancestry,
I do applaud thy spirit, Valentine,
And think thee worthy of an empress' love.
Know then, I here forget all former griefs, *150*
Cancel all grudge, repeal thee home again,
Plead a new state in thy unrivall'd merit,
To which I thus subscribe: Sir Valentine,
Thou art a gentleman and well deriv'd;
Take thou thy Silvia, for thou hast deserv'd her. *155*
 Val. I thank your Grace; the gift hath made me happy.
I now beseech you, for your daughter's sake,
To grant one boon that I shall ask of you.
 Duke. I grant it, for thine own, whate'er it be.
 Val. These banish'd men, that I have kept withal *160*
Are men endu'd with worthy qualities:
Forgive them what they have committed here,
And let them be recall'd from their exile.
They are reformed, civil, full of good,
And fit for great employment, worthy lord. *165*

 Duke. Thou hast prevail'd; I pardon them, and thee;
Dispose of them as thou know'st their deserts.
Come, let us go; we will include all jars
With triumphs, mirth, and rare solemnity.
 Val. And as we walk along, I dare be bold *170*
With our discourse to make your Grace to smile.
What think you of this page, my lord?
 Duke. I think the boy hath grace in him; he blushes.
 Val. I warrant you, my lord, more grace than boy.
 Duke. What mean you by that saying? *175*
 Val. Please you, I'll tell you as we pass along,
That you will wonder what hath fortuned.
Come, Proteus; 'tis your penance but to hear
The story of your loves discovered;
That done, our day of marriage shall be yours; *180*
One feast, one house, one mutual happiness. *Exeunt.*

❦ FINIS ❦

---

151 repeal: *recall from exile* **152 Plead … merit;** *cf. n.* **160 kept withal:** *lived with*

168 include: *conclude* **jars:** *discords* **169 triumphs:** *public festivities* **solemnity:** *festivity* **177 fortuned:** *happened*

Notes

Dramatis Personæ. In the First Folio the *Dramatis Personæ* ('The names of all the Actors') appear at the end of the play.

I.i.22. *Leander.* A youth who nightly swam across the Hellespont to visit his beloved Hero. One night he was drowned in his attempt; whereupon Hero also leaped to her death in the Hellespont. Cf. III.i.119, 120.

I.i.55. *shipp'd.* Although it may be shown that in Shakespeare's time there was probably some sort of water-route between Verona and Milan, we may assume that the dramatist is merely casual here, having vaguely in mind a departure by sea from London rather than pretending to accuracy in Italian geography and topography.

I.i.73, 74. *shipp'd . . . sheep.* It appears that in pronunciation these two words were sufficiently similar to allow a pun. Cf. note on I.i.54.

I.i.97. *laced mutton.* Apparently a play upon the words 'lost' and 'laced' in this speech is intended. Presumably the similarity between the two words in pronunciation was greater than now.

I.i.118. *Marry.* A mild interjection, originally the name of the Virgin Mary used as an oath or invocation.

I.i.141. *destin'd to a drier death on shore.* A reference to the proverbial notion, 'He that is born to be hanged shall never be drowned.'

I.ii.9. *Sir Eglamour.* This personage is not to be confused with Silvia's friend, who appears later.

I.ii.71. *stomach.* A play upon the two meanings, 'anger' and 'appetite.'

I.ii.71, 72. *meat . . . maid.* Probably a quibble, 'meat' being pronounced like 'mate.'

I.ii.85. *set.* 'Set to music.' The next line quibblingly implies the meaning, 'set store by.'

I.ii.89. *burden.* Refrain, or, more exactly, a musical figure repeated, throughout the song, in the bass (French *bourdon*) or underpart.

I.ii.100. *flat.* A quibble on the word in its musical meaning and in the sense of 'downright.'

I.ii.101, 102. *And mar the concord with too harsh a descant. There wanteth but a mean to fill your song.* 'Descant' means the air sung extempore upon a given bass. The 'mean' is the intermediate part (alto or tenor) between the treble and bass. Here the word 'mean' seems to refer also to the correct pitch of any musical note, precisely between 'sharp' and 'flat' of lines 88 and 90.

I.ii.104. *bid the base.* A phrase from the game of prisoner's base. Possibly Lucetta 'bids the base' by challenging Julia to pursue her, thus setting free Proteus, the prisoner at the base.

I.ii.111. *would I were so anger'd with the same.* 'Would that the same letter still existed, and inspired no more anger than I now feel.'

I.iii.28. *emperor.* We need not infer that Shakespeare had in mind the occasional sojourns of Charles V (Emperor, 1519-1556) at Milan. 'Emperor' here probably refers only to the Duke of Milan.

I.iii.45. *in good time.* The phrase is equivalent to '*à propos,*' and is often used when a character arrives opportunely.

II.i.2, 3. *on . . . one.* In the sixteenth century these two words were often spelled alike, and in pronunciation were sufficiently similar to allow a pun.

II.i.24. *Hallowmas.* All Saints' Day, November 1. On this day beggars often received special alms, including 'soul-cake.'

II.i.25. *one of the lions.* Possibly a reference to lions in the Tower of London, or to lions on a royal standard displayed in the theater, or to lions in general.

II.i.85, 86. *motion . . . puppet . . . interpret.* In a puppet-play, or 'motion,' the manipulator of the puppets supplied a discourse designed to 'interpret' the action.

II.i.90. *servant.* A man who pays authorized attentions to a lady, without her pledging herself by accepting them.

II.i.142, 143. *earnest . . . none.* A pun upon 'earnest' as an adjective, and as a noun meaning 'money paid as an installment to secure a bargain.'

II.i.154. *speak in print.* The source of the four lines that Speed found 'in print' is not known. They are evidently composed in 'King Cambyses' vein.'

II.iii.24. *wood.* Possibly there is a pun upon the noun, as indicating a shoe made of wood.

II.iv.18. *quote.* A quibble is probably intended upon 'quote' in the next line, pronounced to sound like 'coat.'

II.iv.20. *jerkin, doublet.* The doublet was a loose upper garment; the jerkin, a long jacket worn over the doublet, or in place of it.

II.iv.26. *live in your air.* The chameleon was supposed to live on air. See II.i.181.

II.iv.84. *lock'd in her crystal looks.* This expression probably arises from a belief that a spirit might be enclosed in a crystal sphere and made to obey commands.

II.iv.152. *principality.* A member of the seventh order of celestial beings. The hierarchy of these beings may be arranged as follows: (1) Seraphim, (2) Cherubim, (3) Thrones, (4) Dominions, (5) Virtues, (6) Powers, (7) Principalities, (8) Archangels, and (9) Angels.

II.iv.195. *Even as one heat another heat expels.* Apparently a reference to an old practice of exposing a burned part of the body to a fire, in the belief that external heat expelled the heat from the burn. Cf. *Romeo and Juliet*, I.ii.46: 'Tut! man, one fire burns out another's burning.'

II.v.44-46. *go to the ale with a Christian.* A reference to 'Church-ale,' a village festival at which ale was sold to raise funds for a church.

II.vii.53. *cod-piece.* A part of a man's breeches made indelicately conspicuous in Shakespeare's time.

II.vii.55. *round hose.* An article of clothing which covered both legs and loins, and which puffed out at the hips.

III.i.147. *Do curse the grace that with such grace hath bless'd them. grace . . . grace:* 'graciousness . . . favour.' The first 'grace' may mean either 'gracious person' or 'one of the Graces.'

III.i.154. *Phaethon . . . Merops' son.* Phaethon's father was Phoebus, and his mother was Clymene, wife of Merops. Phaethon rashly persuaded his father to allow him to drive the chariot of the sun for one day. Failing to control the horses, he came too near the earth, a result referred to in lines 155 and 156. In the classical reference the Duke presumably means merely to taunt Valentine with rashness. It has been suggested, however, that the name Merops provides a pun on the 'ropes' of the ladder.

III.i.184. *influence.* Probably refers to the 'influence' of a star, in the astrological sense of blessing or protection.

III.i.186. *I fly not death, to fly his deadly doom.* 'I do not escape death by flying from the Duke's sentence of death.'

III.i.190. *Soho.* A hunting cry used when a hare is seen. Hence the pun upon 'hair' in Launce's next speech.

III.i.193, 194. *Valentine. Valentine?* The pun is upon 'valentine' as a token of true-love and 'Valentine' as a proper name. The same pun occurs in lines 212, 215.

III.i.263, 264. *that's all one, if he be but one knave.* 'That's no matter, if he be but slightly a knave.' 'But one knave' implies degrees in knave:y, 'two knaves' being a term for excessive knavery.

III.i.270. *water-spaniel.* This animal was thought to be especially given to fawning.

III.i.274. *jade.* Probably a pun upon the meanings 'an ill-conditioned horse' and 'a woman of low morals.'

III.i.345. *Eve's legacy.* Apparently Launce takes 'proud' of the preceding speech as meaning 'hot-blooded' or 'lascivious.' Possibly there is also an allusion to pride as the original deadly sin.

III.ii.53. *bottom it.* 'Wind it as a skein or ball of thread on a core, or bottom, of thread or harder material.'

IV.iv.7. *me.* This equivalent of the Latin 'ethical dative' is used merely to show a certain interest felt by the person indicated. The same use is seen in lines 14 and 20.

IV.iv.16. *bless the mark.* In its origin probably a formula to avert an evil omen; and hence used also as an apology when something improper or obnoxious is being said.

IV.iv.49. *squirrel.* Possibly an expression commonly applied to a small dog; or possibly a contemptuous epithet suggested by the fact that sometimes squirrels were actually carried about by ladies.

V.ii.9. *fair.* The meaning may be 'pale,' with a suggestion of effeminacy; or 'fair-faced,' in the sense of 'deceptive.'

V.ii.25, 26. *possessions . . . pities.* Probably a quibble upon 'possessions' in the sense of 'property' and 'possessions by spirits.' Hence there is probably a double meaning in 'pities': 'despises' (the property) and 'pities' (the possessions by spirits).

V.iv.113, 114. *if shame live In a disguise of love.* 'If there be any shame in a disguise assumed because of love'; or, possibly, referring to Proteus' duplicity, 'if there be any shame in one who falsely pretends to love.'

V.iv.120. *Inconstancy falls off ere it begins.* Probably this means, 'An inconstant man begins to be faithless even before he has declared his love.'

V.iv.152. *Plead a new state in thy unrivall'd merit.* The meaning of this line is uncertain. The following possibilities are offered: (1) 'Plead (in excuse for my change) that your exhibition of such merit creates a new situation'; (2) 'Plead for a new standing for myself in thy unrivall'd merit'; (3) 'Argue for (or utter) a new estimate of thy unrivall'd merit.'

The Text of the Present Edition

The earliest known text of *The Two Gentlemen of Verona* is that of the First Folio of 1623.

By permission of the Oxford University Press, the text of the present edition is that of the Oxford Shakespeare edited by W. J. Craig. Departures from Craig's text, and from that of the First Folio, are indicated below.

1. Minor changes in spelling and pronunciation have not been listed.

2. Craig's text and the present one follow the division into acts and scenes indicated in the First Folio; but the Latin designations in the Folio (e.g. *Actus primus, Scena prima*) are replaced by English equivalents.

In the First Folio the *Dramatis Personæ* ('The names of all the Actors') appear at the end of the play.

3. The stage-directions and list of *dramatis personæ* of the First Folio have been restored as far as possible, all additions being enclosed within square brackets. Aside from editorial additions within brackets, the stage-directions of the present edition differ from those of the First Folio only in the following instances, the readings of the Folio appearing after the colons:

   I.iii.92 S.d. *Exeunt.: Exeunt. Finis.*
   II.iv.217 S.d. *[Exit.]: Exeunt.*
   III.i.369 S.d. *[Exit.]: Exeunt.*
   IV.iv.203 S.d. *[Exit.]: Exeunt.*
   V.ii.7 S.d. *[Jul. Aside.]: Pro.*
   13 S.d. *[Jul. Aside.]: Thu.*
   59 S.d. *[Exit.]: Exeunt.*

4. In the text of the speeches the present edition departs from the text of Craig, and restores the readings of the First Folio, in the following instances, Craig's readings appearing after the colons:

   I.i.108 *Speed. [Nodding.] Ay.: [Speed nods.] Did she nod? Speed. Ay.*

   ii. 54 'fool: fool
   II.iii.15 in it: in
   iv. 90 pair: pairs
   199 [eye]: eye
   v. 44 alehouse: alehouse so
   45 an: a
   III.i.315 [kissed]: kissed
   IV.iv.5 I would: would I
   82 Well,: Well, well,

5. In the present edition, and in that of Craig, the text of the speeches departs from the text of the First Folio in the following instances, the readings of the Folio appearing after the colons:

   I. i.66 leave: love
   74 a sheep: Sheepe
   136 testerned: cestern'd
   ii. 103 your: you
   iii. 88 father calls: Fathers call's
   II.iii.33 tied: tide
   34 tied that ever any man tied.: Tide, that euer any man tide.
   36 tied: tide
   46 tied: tide
   iv. 57 know: knew
   104 mistress: a Mistresse
   167 makes: make
   199 Is it: It is
   199 Valentinus': *Valentines*
   v. 2 Milan: *Padua*
   36 that my: that that my
   III.i.81 of Verona: in *Verona*
   150 would be: should be
   IV.i.36 miserable: often miserable
   50 An heir, and near: And heire and Neece,
   ii. 114 his: her
   iii. 19 abhors: abhor'd
   iv. 50 hangman: Hangmans
   64 thou: thee
   68 to leave: not leaue
   V.ii.32 Sir Eglamour: *Eglamoure*
   iv. 72 trusted now,: trusted

The Taming of the Shrew

Edited by
THOMAS G. BERGIN

✺

Dramatis Personae

A LORD
CHRISTOPHER SLY, *a Tinker*
HOSTESS, PAGE, PLAYERS, } *persons in Act I,*
HUNTSMEN, AND SERVANTS } *Scene 1*
BAPTISTA, *a rich Gentleman of Padua*
VINCENTIO, *an old Gentleman of Pisa*
LUCENTIO, *Son to Vincentio; in love with Bianca*
PETRUCHIO, *a Gentleman of Verona; Suitor*
  to Katherina
GREMIO }
HORTENSIO } *Suitors to Bianca*
TRANIO }
BIONDELLO } *Servants to Lucentio*

GRUMIO }
CURTIS }
NATHANIEL }
PHILIP } *Servants to Petruchio*
JOSEPH }
NICHOLAS }
PETER }
PEDANT, *set up to impersonate Vincentio*
KATHERINA, THE SHREW } *Daughters to Baptista*
BIANCA }
WIDOW
TAILOR, HABERDASHER, AND SERVANTS

SCENE—*Padua, and Petruchio's house in*
  the country.

The Taming of the Shrew

Introduction

Text and Date

The text of this edition follows that of the First Folio (1623), the earliest printed version of the play. The First Quarto edition (1631) is based on the First Folio as are the versions of all subsequent Folio editions (of which there are three).

We have had before us the facsimile edition of the First Folio (Oxford, 1902) and have made our basic principle fidelity to the text. We have, however, indicated some act and scene divisions missing in the Folio and supplied a few stage directions which have become conventional. We have also modernized the spelling, except in cases where the spelling reveals the pronunciation of the time, and we have repunctuated in line with modern practice. Apart from such changes all departures from the Folio reading, for the most part of very minor nature, are indicated in the glosses or notes.

Sources of the Play

In discussing the sources of *The Taming of the Shrew* one must bear in mind that as the play stands it contains three plot ingredients: the beggar transported to a higher realm, the wife tamed, and a pair of lovers united by the machinations of quick-witted servants. All of these elements are of considerable antiquity. The beggar motif goes back as far at least as the *Arabian Nights*. The theme of shrew-taming, in the words of Sir Arthur Quiller-Couch, is 'as old as the hills,' though we may note that it is also the subject of several folk ballads closer to Shakespeare's own time, for example, *A Merry Jest of a Shrewd and Curst Wife Lapped in Morel's Skin for her Good Behavior* (mid-16th century). The devices of the subplot go back through Ariosto to Roman comedy.

The remote sources are clear enough in the main. When we touch on the question of Shakespeare's immediate source we enter more dangerous ground—not by any means unsurveyed but rather too carefully and contradictorily charted. For we must begin with an examination of the relationship of our play to the earlier work *The Taming of a Shrew* (referred to for brevity as *A Shrew*), a problem that has teased Shakespearean editors and critics over the years and which still awaits a solution satisfactory to all. While the first printed edition of *The Shrew* appears in the First Folio (1623), *A Shrew* was published in 1594, and Henslowe's Diary notes, for June of that same year, a performance of a play of that name by the Lord Chamberlain's servants (i.e., Shakespeare's company) at Newington Butts. *A Shrew* is made of coarser stuff than *The Shrew*; it is by comparison of unpolished texture, and the characterization is cruder; indeed it is by nature a farce. At the same time it is in certain respects a more finished product than *The Shrew*: Sly is not ignored after the introductory scenes but consistent use is made of him for comment and at the end he goes off content with the moral of wife-beating, and—another example of tidiness—Katherina is provided with a second sister who pairs off with Hortensio.

The similarities, however, are much more noteworthy than the differences. Both plays begin with the prank played on Sly; the main plot follows an identical development with many scenes the same in action and often in wording; the subplot, borrowed from Gascoigne's *The Supposes* (1556), a translation of Ludovico Ariosto's *I Suppositi* (1509), is likewise similar, though here some minor differences may be noted. The role of Tranio, the elderly suitor (Gremio), the Pedant's relationship to the disguised servant, the device used to persuade the Pedant to undertake the imposture, the confronting of the true and false fathers, the names Petruchio and Licio (though assigned to minor characters in Gascoigne's play)—all these are elements found in both *The Supposes* and the subplot of *The Shrew* though not in *A Shrew*. It seems clear that Shakespeare was not content, as far as the secondary plot was concerned, to take the material from *A Shrew* but went back to Gascoigne whose play thus becomes doubly, at first and second hand as it were, the source of the subplot of *The Shrew*.

Yet this is merely to lay the groundwork for the main problem of the relationship between *A Shrew* and *The Shrew*. Given the priority of printing dates and Henslowe's reference, the normal assumption would be that *A Shrew* is the older play and Shakespeare, in accordance with the habits of the times and indeed his own practice, used it as a basis for his own creation. This is in fact a perfectly tenable theory. But there are others. One, advanced relatively recently by P. Alexander (in the *Time Literary Supplement*, Sept. 16, 1926), holds that the printed version of *A Shrew* is a memorial reconstruction (i.e. a version taken down from the memorization of actors) of the play that we know as *The Shrew*, explaining the differences above noted as adaptations deemed necessary for the presentation before provincial audiences. According to this theory Henslowe actually saw *The Shrew*. This theory has convinced one of the editors of the New Cambridge edition of the play, Dover Wilson, though not his colleague, Quiller-Couch.

Yet a third hypothesis, advanced by Ten Brink (in the *Shakespeare-Jahrbuch*, *12* [1877], 94), suggests that both plays go back to the common source of an original Shrew play, *eine Jugendarbeit Shakespeares* in Ten Brink's opinion. The most recent advocate of the Ten Brink theory is Hardin Craig who, without attributing the source to Shakespeare's own hand, postulates 'a lost original shrew play.' Craig argues that such a hypothesis not only would explain the discrepancies in the plays but also 'has the advantage of showing that everybody is right and everybody is wrong. That is, *A Shrew* might readily be mistaken for the source of *The Shrew*, because *A Shrew* is a version of that source. It might readily be regarded as a "bad" quarto of *The Shrew* because it is a "bad" quarto of the source of *The Shrew*.'[1]

---

1 '*The Shrew* and *A Shrew*; Possible Settlement of an Old Debate,' in *Elizabethan Studies and Other Essays in Honor of George F. Reynolds*, Boulder, 1945, p. 154.

Those who argue for the memorial reconstruction theory are at least spared the burden of finding a suitable author for the early play, save of course insofar as they may regard both works as collaborative enterprises. Critics who cannot accept *A Shrew* as Shakespeare's work have so far failed to reach unanimous accord on any one author; it has been assigned, in the words of Bond 'in turn to every near and important predecessor of Shakespeare save Lyly and Nash'; many modern critics have seen in it the hand of some imitator of Marlowe, and Quiller-Couch indeed finds 'nothing incredible' in the supposition that Marlowe may have written it himself 'with or without collaborators.' Pope, without waiting for the theory of memorial reconstruction, claimed *A Shrew* for Shakespeare himself, a claim recently restated by Courthope in his *History of English Poetry*.

As for the authorship of *The Shrew*, although various editors have sensed the presence of another hand than Shakespeare's, especially in the subplot, opinion has been by no means unanimous on this point and most recently editions, though hesitantly, and with various shades of reservation, attribute the work to Shakespeare. Bond, for example, after enumerating the scenes that have by common consent been assigned to Shakespeare adds for the rest, 'while admitting the presence of other work, I do Not feel that we have ground enough for denying Shakespeare's revision, however hasty, of the whole.' Quiller-Couch, too, seems reluctant to accept a collaborator; for his colleague, Dover Wilson, Shakespeare either 'created or recreated the play,' and Craig in his recent edition of Shakespeare's plays (New York, 1952) also thinks of it as 'probably' Shakespeare's play.

There can be no general agreement on the date of the play, in view of the various theories of its relationship to *A Shrew*. Some rather complicated reasoning by Bond leads him to date the play as of 1594–95, Craig opts for 1593, and Dover Wilson would place it 'before the summer of 1592 or at any rate before 2 May 1594.'[2]

2 For further discussion of the genesis of *The Shrew*, in addition to the authorities cited, see: R. A. Houk, 'Evolution of *The Taming of the Shrew*,' PMLA, December 1942, pp. 1009–38; and 'Strata in the *Taming of the Shrew*,' *Studies in Philology*, 1942, 291–302; H. Dugdale Sykes, *The Authorship of 'The Taming of a Shrew*,' Shakespeare Association, 1919; E. P. Kuhl, 'The Authorship of *The Taming of the Shrew*,' PMLA, 40, 551–618; G. I. Duthie, '*The Taming of a Shrew* and *The Taming of the Shrew*' (*Review of English Studies*, 19 (1948), 337–56).

ACT FIRST ❧ SCENE FIRST

Enter Beggar [Christopher Sly] and Hostess.

Sly. I'll pheeze you, in faith.

Hostess. A pair of stocks, you rogue!

Sly. Y'are a baggage: the Slys are no rogues; look
in the chronicles; we came in with Richard Con-
queror. Therefore, *paucas pallabris*; let the world   5
slide. Sessa!

Hostess. You will not pay for the glasses you have
burst?

Sly. No, not a denier. Go, by St. Jeronimy, go to
thy cold bed and warm thee.   10

Hostess. I know my remedy: I must go fetch the
third-borough.   *[Exit.]*

Sly. Third or fourth or fifth borough, I'll answer
him by law. I'll not budge an inch, boy: let him come
and kindly.   *Falls asleep.* 15

Wind horns. Enter a Lord from hunting, with his train.

Lord. Huntsman, I charge thee, tender well my hounds:
Broach Merriman, the poor cur is emboss'd,
And couple Clowder with the deep-mouth'd brach.
Saw'st thou not, boy, how Silver made it good
At the hedge-corner in the coldest fault?   20
I would not lose the dog for twenty pound.

1. Huntsman. Why Bellman is as good as he, my lord;
He cried upon it at the merest loss
And twice today pick'd out the dullest scent.
Trust me, I take him for the better dog.   25

Lord. Thou art a fool: if Echo were as fleet,
I would esteem him worth a dozen such.
But sup them well and look unto them all.
Tomorrow I intend to hunt again.

1. Huntsman. I will, my lord.   30

Lord. What's here? one dead or drunk? See, doth he
breathe?

2. Huntsman. He breathes, my lord. Were he not warm'd
with ale
This were a bed but cold to sleep so soundly.   35

Lord. O monstrous beast! how like a swine he lies!
Grim death, how foul and loathsome is thine image!
Sirs, I will practice on this drunken man.
What think you, if he were convey'd to bed,
Wrapp'd in sweet clothes, rings put upon his fingers,   40
A most delicious banquet by his bed,
And brave attendants near him when he wakes,
Would not the beggar then forget himself?

1. Huntsman. Believe me, lord, I think he cannot choose.

2. Huntsman. It would seem strange unto him when he   45
wak'd.

Lord. Even as a flatt'ring dream or worthless fancy.
Then take him up and manage well the jest.
Carry him gently to my fairest chamber
And hang it round with all my wanton pictures,   50
Balm his foul head in warm distilled waters
And burn sweet wood to make the lodging sweet.
Procure me music ready when he wakes
To make a dulcet and a heavenly sound;
And if he chance to speak be ready straight,   55
And with a low submissive reverence
Say, 'What is it your honor will command?'
Let one attend him with a silver basin
Full of rose water and bestrew'd with flowers;
Another bear the ewer, the third a diaper,   60
And say, "Will't please your lordship cool your hands?'
Some one be ready with a costly suit
And ask him what apparel he will wear,
Another tell him of his hounds and horse
And that his lady mourns at his disease.   65
Persuade him that he hath been lunatic;
And when he says he is, say that he dreams,
For he is nothing but a mighty lord.
This do, and do it kindly, gentle sirs.
It will be pastime passing excellent,   70
If it be husbanded with modesty.

1. Huntsman. My lord, I warrant you we will play our part,
As he shall think, by our true diligence,
He is no less than what we say he is.

Lord. Take him up gently, and to bed with him,   75
And each one to his office when he wakes.

                                  [Sly is borne out.] Sound trumpets.
Sirrah, go see what trumpet 'tis that sounds: *[Exit Servingman.]*
Belike some noble gentleman that means,
Traveling some journey, to repose him here.   80

Enter Servingman.

How now! who is it?

Servingman.   An't please your honor, players
That offer service to your lordship.

Enter Players.

Lord. Bid them come near.

                          Now, fellows, you are welcome.   85

Players. We thank your honor.

Lord. Do you intend to stay with me tonight?

A Player. So please your lordship to accept our duty.

Lord. With all my heart. This fellow I remember
Since once he play'd a farmer's eldest son: 90
'Twas where you woo'd the gentlewoman so well.
I have forgot your name; but sure that part
Was aptly fitted and naturally perform'd.

A Player. I think 'twas Soto that your honor means.

Lord. 'Tis very true: thou didst it excellent.   95
Well, you are come to me in happy time,
The rather for I have some sport in hand

ACT 1, SCENE 1 SD ENTER . . . HOSTESS (SD is used throughout to indicate stage directions.)
F *Enter Begger and Hostess, Christopher Sly.* **1 Sly:** *F Begger throughout Cf. n.* **pheeze
you:** *do for you* **2 stocks:** *The hostess threatens Sly with being put in the stocks* **4
Richard:** *Sly's error for 'William'* **5 paucas pallabris:** *few words (corrupt Spanish).* **6
Sessa:** *be quiet (French cessez)* **9 denier:** *small copper coin, 'tenth of an English pennie'* **St.
Jeronimy;** *Cf. n.* **12 third-borough:** *constable; F Head-borough* **16 tender well:** *take
good care of* **17 Broach:** *F Brach Cf. n.* **emboss'd:** *foaming at the mouth from hard
running* **18 couple:** *Cf. n. brach bitch* **20 in the coldest fault** *where the scent was
nearly lost* **23 cried upon it:** *gave tongue* **merest loss:** *when it was quite lost* **36
practice:** *play a trick* **42 brave:** *finely dressed*

47 even: *read 'e'en'* **51 Balm:** *perfume* **55 straight:** *at once* **60 diaper:**
towel **67 when he says he is:** *i.e. when Sly says he is now mad* **69 kindly:** *naturally* **70 passing:** *surpassingly* **71 husbanded:** *managed* **modesty:** *moderation* **72
warrant:** *read 'warn't'* **73 As:** *so that* **79 Belike:** *probably* **82 An't:** *if it SD* Enter
Players: *Cf. n.* **84 come near:** *enter* **88 A Player:** *F Player* **duty:** *expression of
respect* **93 naturally:** *read 'nat'rally'* **94 A Player:** *F Sincklo Cf. n.* **Soto:**
Cf. n. **97 The rather for:** *the more so because*

Wherein your cunning can assist me much.
There is a lord will hear you play tonight;
But I am doubtful of your modesties, Lest, over-eyeing   *100*
of his odd behavior—
For yet his honor never heard a play—
You break into some merry passion
And so offend him; for I tell you, sirs,
If you should smile he grows impatient.   *105*

    A Player. Fear not, my lord, we can contain ourselves
Were he the veriest antic in the world.

    Lord. Go, sirrah, take them to the buttery
And give them friendly welcome every one.
Let them want nothing that my house affords.   *110*
                       Exit one with the Players.
Sirrah, go you to Barthol'mew my page
And see him dress'd in all suits like a lady:
That done, conduct him to the drunkard's chamber
And call him 'madam'; do him obeisance.
Tell him from me—as he will win my love—   *115*
He bear himself with honorable action
Such as he hath observ'd in noble ladies
Unto their lords, by them accomplished:
Such duty to the drunkard let him do
With soft low tongue and lowly courtesy,   *120*
And say, 'What is't your honor will command
Wherein your lady and your humble wife
May show her duty and make known her love?'
And then, with kind embracements, tempting kisses,
And with declining head into his bosom,   *125*
Bid him shed tears, as being overjoy'd
To see her noble lord restor'd to health
Who for this seven years hath esteemed him
No better than a poor and loathsome beggar.
And if the boy have not a woman's gift   *130*
To rain a shower of commanded tears
An onion will do well for such a shift,
Which in a napkin being close convey'd
Shall in despite enforce a watery eye.
See this dispatch'd with all the haste thou canst: *135*
Anon I'll give thee more instructions.   *Exit a Servingman.*
I know the boy will well usurp the grace,
Voice, gait, and action of a gentlewoman.
I long to hear him call the drunkard husband,
And how my men will stay themselves from laughter   *140*
When they do homage to this simple peasant.
I'll in to counsel them: haply my presence
May well abate the over merry spleen
Which otherwise would grow into extremes.   *[Exeunt.]*

❧ Scene Second ❧

*Enter aloft the drunkard [Sly], with attendants, some with apparel,
[others with] basin and ewer, and other appurtenances, and Lord.*

    Sly. For God's sake! a pot of small ale.

    1. Servingman. Will't please your lordship drink a cup of
sack?

    2. Servingman. Will't please your honor taste of these
conserves?   *5*

    3. Servingman. What raiment will your honor wear today?

    Sly. I am Christophero Sly; call not me honor nor
lordship. I ne'er drank sack in my life; and if you
give me any conserves, give me conserves of beef.
Ne'er ask me what raiment I'll wear for I have no   *10*
more doublets than backs, no more stockings than
legs nor no more shoes than feet: nay, sometime more
feet than shoes or such shoes as my toes look through
the overleather.

    Lord. Heaven cease this idle humor in your honor!   *15*
O that a mighty man of such descent,
Of such possessions and so high esteem
Should be infused with so foul a spirit!

    Sly. What! would you make me mad? Am not I
Christopher Sly, old Sly's son, of Burton-heath; by   *20*
birth a pedlar, by education a cardmaker, by trans-
mutation a bearherd, and now by present profession
a tinker? Ask Marian Hacket, the fat ale-wife of
Wincot, if she know me not: if she say I am not
fourteen pence on the score for sheer ale score me   *25*
up for the lyingest knave in Christendom. What! I
am not bestraught: here's—

    3. Servingman. O! this it is that makes your lady mourn.

    2. Servingman. O! this is it that makes your servants droop.

    Lord. Hence comes it that your kindred shuns your   *30*
house.
As beaten hence by your strange lunacy.
O noble lord, bethink thee of thy birth,
Call home thy ancient thoughts from banishment
And banish hence these abject lowly dreams.   *35*
Look how thy servants do attend on thee,
Each in his office ready at thy beck.
Wilt thou have music? hark! Apollo plays,   *Music.*
And twenty caged nightingales do sing.
Or wilt thou sleep? we'll have thee to a couch   *40*
Softer and sweeter than the lustful bed
On purpose trimm'd up for Semiramis.
Say thou wilt walk, we will bestrow the ground;
Or wilt thou ride? thy horses shall be trapp'd,
Their harness studded all with gold and pearl.   *45*
Dost thou love hawking? thou hast hawks will soar
Above the morning lark; or wilt thou hunt?

---

98 cunning: *skill*   **100 modesties:** *discretion* **over-eyeing:** *observing*   **103 merry passion:** *fits of laughter*   **107 antic:** *eccentric*   **108 buttery:** *room where drink is kept*   **110
want:** *lack*   **111 page;** *Cf. n.*   **112 in all suits:** *in every respect*   **118 them:** *pleonastic,
referring to ladies* **accomplished:** *performed*   **119 duty:** *service*   **128 him:** *himself*   **132 shift:** *purpose*   **133 napkin:** *handkerchief* **close:** *secretly*   **134 watery:** *read
'wat'ry'*   **136 anon:** *presently*   **137 usurp:** *imitate*   **140 stay:** *keep*   **143 spleen:**
mood (the spleen was thought to be the seat of passions)

SD aloft: *i.e. on the balcony at the back of the stage.* **ewer:** *wide-mouthed pitcher*   **3
sack:** *Spanish and Canary wine*   **9 conserves of beef:** *salt beef*   **15 idle humor:** *absurd
fancy*   **20 Sly's:** *F. Sies* **Burton-heath:** *perhaps Barton-on-the-Heath, a Warwickshire village*   **21 cardmaker:** *cards are instruments for combing wool*   **22 bearherd:** *one who leads
about a tame bear*   **24 Wincot:** *a place, once a hamlet, near Stratford*   **25 sheer ale:** *i.e.
ale only*   **27 bestraught:** *Sly means 'distraught'*   **28 3. Servingman:** *F 3 Man*   **34
ancient thoughts:** *former reason*   **38 Apollo:** *god of music*   **42 Semiramis:** *legendary
lustful queen of Assyria*   **44 trapp'd:** *adorned*   **46 will soar:** *which will soar*

Thy hounds shall make the welkin answer them
And fetch shrill echoes from the hollow earth.

   1. Servingman. Say thou wilt course, thy greyhounds   *50*
are as swift
As breathed stags, ay, fleeter than the roe.

   2. Servingman. Dost thou love pictures? we will fetch
thee straight
Adonis painted by a running brook   *55*
And Cytherea all in sedges hid,
Which seem to move and wanton with her breath
Even as the waving sedges play with wind.

   Lord. We'll show thee Io as she was a maid
And how she was beguiled and surpris'd   *60*
As lively painted as the deed was done.

   3. Servingman. Or Daphne roaming through a thorny wood,
Scratching her legs that one shall swear she bleeds;
And at that sight shall sad Apollo weep,
So workmanly the blood and tears are drawn.   *65*

   Lord. Thou art a lord and nothing but a lord;
Thou hast a lady far more beautiful
Than any woman in this waning age.

   1. Servingman. And till the tears that she hath shed for thee
Like envious floods o'errun her lovely face   *70*
She was the fairest creature in the world,
And yet she is inferior to none.

   Sly. Am I a lord? and have I such a lady?
Or do I dream? or have I dream'd till now?
I do not sleep; I see, I hear, I speak;   *75*
I smell sweet savors and I feel soft things:
Upon my life, I am a lord indeed
And not a tinker nor Christopher Sly.
Well, bring our lady hither to our sight
And once again, a pot o' th' smallest ale.   *80*

   2. Servingman. Will't please your mightiness to wash
your hands?
O, how we joy to see your wit restor'd!
O, that once more you knew but what you are!
These fifteen years you have bin in a dream.   *85*
Or when you wak'd so wak'd as if you slept.

   Sly. These fifteen years! by my fay, a goodly nap.
But did I never speak of all that time?

   1. Servingman. O yes, my lord, but very idle words;
For though you lay here in this goodly chamber,   *90*
Yet would you say ye were beaten out of door
And rail upon the hostess of the house
And say you would present her at the leet
Because she brought stone jugs and no seal'd quarts.
Sometimes you would call out for Cicely Hacket.   *95*

   Sly. Ay, the woman's maid of the house.

   3. Servingman. Why, sir, you know no house nor no
such maid
Nor no such men as you have reckon'd up,
As Stephen Sly, and old John Naps of Greece,   *100*
And Peter Turf, and Henry Pimpernell,

And twenty more such names and men as these
Which never were nor no man ever saw.

   Sly. Now, Lord be thanked for my good amends!

   All. Amen.   *105*

     Enter [the Page, as a] Lady, with Attendants.

   Sly. I thank thee; thou shalt not lose by it.

   Page. How fares my noble lord?

   Sly. Marry, I fare well for here is cheer enough.
Where is my wife?

   Page. Here, noble lord: what is thy will with her?   *110*

   Sly. Are you my wife and will not call me husband?
My men should call me lord: I am your goodman.

   Page. My husband and my lord, my lord and husband;
I am your wife in all obedience.

   Sly. I know it well. What must I call her?   *115*

   Lord. Madam.

   Sly. Al'ce madam or Joan madam?

   Lord. Madam and nothing else: so lords call ladies.

   Sly. Madam wife, they say that I have dream'd
And slept above some fifteen year or more.   *120*

   Page. Ay, and the time seems thirty unto me,
Being all this time abandon'd from your bed.

   Sly. 'Tis much. Servants, leave me and her alone.
Madam, undress you and come now to bed.

   Page. Thrice noble lord, let me entreat of you   *125*
To pardon me yet for a night or two,
Or, if not so, until the sun be set:
For your physicians have expressly charg'd,
In peril to incur your former malady,
That I should yet absent me from your bed.   *130*
I hope this reason stands for my excuse.

   Sly. Ay, it stands so, that I may hardly tarry so
long; but I would be loath to fall into my dreams
again: I will therefore tarry in despite of the flesh
and the blood.   *135*

     Enter a Messenger.

   Messenger. Your honor's players, hearing your
amendment,
Are come to play a pleasant comedy;
For so your doctors hold it very meet,
Seeing too much sadness hath congeal'd your blood,   *140*
And melancholy is the nurse of frenzy:
Therefore they thought it good you hear a play
And frame your mind to mirth and merriment,
Which bars a thousand harms and lengthens life.

   Sly. Marry, I will let them play. It is not a comonty,   *145*
a Christmas gambold, or a tumbling-trick?

   Page. No, my good lord, it is more pleasing stuff.

   Sly. What! household stuff?

   Page. It is a kind of history.

   Sly. Well, we'll see't. Come, madam wife, sit by my side   *150*
And let the world slip: we shall nere be younger.   *Flourish.*

---

48 **welkin:** *sky*   50 **course:** *hunt hares with greyhounds*   52 **breathed:** *in full breath* **roe:** *a type of small deer*   55 **Adonis:** *Cf. n.*   56 **Cytherea:** *Venus*   57 **wanton:** *sway lasciviously*   58 **even:** *read 'e'en'*   59 **Io:** *Greek maiden loved by Zeus*   62 **Daphne:** *Cf. n.*   65 **workmanly:** *skillfully*   68 **waning:** *degenerate*   80 **smallest:** *weakest*   83 **wit:** *reason*   87 **by my:** *read 'bim'* **fay:** *faith*   88 **of:** *in*   93 **leet:** *manorial court where, among others, those accused of using false measures were tried*   94 **seal'd:** *stamped with official seal indicating capacity*   95 **Cicely:** *read 'Cic'ly'*   100, 101 **As Stephen Sly ... Henry Pimpernell;** *Cf. n.*

104 **amends:** *recovery* SD **Page, as a Lady:** *F Lady throughout*   122 **abandon'd:** *banished*   129 **to incur:** *of incurring*   131 **reason:** *pronounced 'raisin,' allowing play on 'raising'*   145 **comonty:** *Sly's version of 'comedy'*   146 **gambold:** *gambol, 'stunt'*   151 **nere:** *never* SD **Flourish:** *meaning 'sound the trumpets'*

❧ SCENE THIRD ❧

Enter Lucentio and his man Tranio.

Lucentio. Tranio, since for the great desire I had
To see fair Padua, nursery of arts,
I am arriv'd for fruitful Lumbardy,
The pleasant garden of great Italy,
And by my father's love and leave am arm'd *5*
With his good will and thy good company,
My trusty servant well approv'd in all,
Here let us breathe and haply institute
A course of learning and ingenious studies.
Pisa, renowned for grave citizens, *10*
Gave me my being and my father first,
A merchant of great traffic through the world,
Vincentio come of the Bentivolii.
Vincentio's son, brought up in Florence,
It shall become to serve all hopes conceiv'd, *15*
To deck his fortune with his virtuous deeds:
And therefore, Tranio, for the time I study,
Virtue and that part of philosophy
Will I apply that treats of happiness
By virtue specially to be achiev'd. *20*
Tell me thy mind, for I have Pisa left
And am to Padua come, as he that leaves
A shallow plash to plunge him in the deep
And with satiety seeks to quench his thirst.
  Tranio. Me pardonato, gentle master mine: *25*
I am in all affected as yourself,
Glad that you thus continue your resolve
To suck the sweets of sweet philosophy.
Only, good master, while we do admire
This virtue and this moral discipline, *30*
Let's be no stoics nor no stocks, I pray;
Or so devote to Aristotle's checks
As Ovid be an outcast quite abjur'd.
Balk logic with acquaintance that you have
And practice rhetoric in your common talk. *35*
Music and poesy use to quicken you;
The mathematics and the metaphysics,
Fall to them as you find your stomach serves you.
No profit grows where is no pleasure tane;
In brief, sir, study what you most affect. *40*
  Lucentio. Gramercies, Tranio, well dost thou advise.
If, Biondello, thou wert come ashore,
We could at once put us in readiness
And take a lodging fit to entertain
Such friends as time in Padua shall beget. *45*
But stay awhile: what company is this?
  Tranio. Master, some show to welcome us to town.

*Enter Baptista with his two daughters, Katherina and Bianca,
Gremio, a Pantaloon, [and] Hortensio, suitor to Bianca. Lucentio
[and] Tranio stand by.*

Baptista. Gentlemen, importune me no farther, *50*
For how I firmly am resolv'd you know;
That is, not to bestow my youngest daughter
Before I have a husband for the elder.
If either of you both love Katherina,
Because I know you well and love you well, *55*
Leave shall you have to court her at your pleasure.
  Gremio. To cart her rather; she's too rough for me.
There, there, Hortensio, will you any wife?
  Katherina. I pray you, sir, is it your will
To make a stale of me amongst these mates? *60*
  Hortensio. Mates, maid! how mean you that? no mates
for you
Unless you were of gentler, milder mold.
  Katherina. I' faith, sir, you shall never need to fear:
Iwis it is not halfway to her heart; *65*
But if it were, doubt not her care should be
To comb your noddle with a three-legg'd stool
And paint your face and use you like a fool.
  Hortensio. From all such divels, good Lord deliver us!
  Gremio. And me too, good Lord! *70*
  Tranio. Husht, master! here is some good pastime toward.
That wench is stark mad or wonderful froward.
  Lucentio. But in the other's silence do I see
Maid's mild behavior and sobriety.
Peace, Tranio! *75*
  Tranio. Well said, master; mum! and gaze your fill.
  Baptista. Gentlemen, that I may soon make good
What I have said—Bianca, get you in:
And let it not displease thee, good Bianca,
For I will love thee nere the less, my girl. *80*
  Katherina. A pretty pet! it is best
Put finger in the eye, an she knew why.
  Bianca. Sister, content you in my discontent.
Sir, to your pleasure humbly I subscribe:
My books and instruments shall be my company, *85*
  On them to look and practice by myself.
  Lucentio. Hark, Tranio! thou mayst hear Minerva speak.
  Hortensio. Signior Baptista, will you be so strange?
Sorry am I that our good will effects
Bianca's grief. *90*
  Gremio. Why will you mew her up,
Signior Baptista, for this fiend of hell
And make her bear the penance of her tongue?
  Baptista. Gentlemen, content ye; I am resolv'd.
Go in, Bianca. *[Exit Bianca.]* *95*
And for I know she taketh most delight
In music, instruments, and poetry,
Schoolmasters will I keep within my house,
Fit to instruct her youth. If you, Hortensio,
Or Signior Gremio, you, know any such, *100*
Prefer them hither; for to cunning men
I will be very kind, and liberal
To mine own children in good bringing up;
And so, farewell. Katherina, you may stay
For I have more to commune with Bianca. *Exit. 105*

2, 3 Padua: . . . Lumbardy; *Cf. n.* **3 for:** *in* **7 approv'd:** *tried* **8 institute:**
begin **9 ingenious:** *intellectual* **15 serve:** *fulfill* **19 apply:** *study* **23 plash:**
pool **25 Me pardonato:** *begging your pardon* (bad Italian) **26 affected:** *disposed* **31**
stocks: *wooden creatures, like posts—with play on 'stoics'* **32 devote:** *devoted* **checks:**
restraints **33 As:** *so that* **Ovid:** *the poet of love* **34 Balk logic:** *bandy arguments, use*
dialectic **36 poesy:** *monosyllabic here* **quicken:** *stimulate* **37 metaphysics;**
Cf. n. **38 stomach:** *inclination* **39 tane:** *taken* **40 affect:** *care for* **41 Gramerc-**
ies: *many thanks* **SD Pantaloon;** *Cf. n.* **Katherina:** *F Katerina, and so pronounced* **suitor:**
F sister **by:** *aside*

57 cart; *Cf. n.* **60 stale:** *laughingstock* **mates:** (low) *fellows, with pun on 'stalemate,' chess*
term **61 mates:** *husbands* **65 Iwis:** *indeed* **68 paint your face:** *i.e. with*
scratches **71 toward:** *at hand* **72 froward:** *bold* **76 master:** *F. Mr.* **81, 82 it**
is best . . . knew why: *let her cry—if she only knew what cause she has* **87 Minerva:**
goddess of wisdom **88 strange:** *unkind* (to Bianca) **91 mew:** *shut, a term from fal-*
conry **96 for:** *since* **101 prefer:** *recommend* **cunning:** *well-trained, able*

Katherina. Why, and I trust I may go too; may I not?
What! shall I be appointed hours, as though, belike,
I knew not what to take and what to leave? Ha!   *Exit.*

Gremio. You may go to the divel's dam: your gifts
are so good, here's none will hold you. Their love is   110
not so great, Hortensio, but we may blow our nails
together and fast it fairly out; our cake's dough on
both sides. Farewell: yet, for the love I bear my
sweet Bianca, if I can by any means light on a fit
man to teach her that wherein she delights, I will wish   115
him to her father.

Hortensio. So will I, Signor Gremio: but a word, I
pray. Though the nature of our quarrel yet never
brooked parle, know now, upon advice, it toucheth us
both—that we may yet again have access to our fair   120
mistress and be happy rivals in Bianca's love—to
labor and effect one thing specially.

Gremio. What's that, I pray?

Hortensio. Marry, sir, to get a husband for her sister.

Gremio. A husband! a divel.   125

Hortensio. I say, a husband.

Gremio. I say, a divel. Thinkst thou, Hortensio,
though her father be very rich, any man is so very
a fool to be married to hell?

Hortensio. Tush, Gremio! though it pass your   130
patience and mine to endure her loud alarums, why,
man, there be good fellows in the world, an a man
could light on them, would take her with all faults,
and money enough.

Gremio. I cannot tell; but I had as lief take her   135
dowry with this condition, to be whipped at the high-
cross every morning.

Hortensio. Faith, as you say, there's small choice in
rotten apples. But come; since this bar in law makes
us friends, it shall be so far forth friendly main-   140
tained, till by helping Baptista's eldest daughter to
a husband, we set his youngest free for a husband,
and then have to't afresh. Sweet Bianca! Happy man
be his dole! He that runs fastest gets the ring. How
say you, Signior Gremio?   145

Gremio. I am agreed: and would I had given him
the best horse in Padua to begin his wooing, that
would thoroughly woo her, wed her, and bed her, and
rid the house of her. Come on.

>   *Exeunt ambo. Mane[n]t Tranio and Lucentio.*

Tranio. I pray, sir, tell me, is it possible   150
That love should of a sudden take such hold?

Lucentio. O Tranio! till I found it to be true
I never thought it possible or likely.
But see, while idly I stood looking on,
I found the effect of love in idleness   155
And now in plainness do confess to thee,
That art to me as secret and as dear

As Anna to the Queen of Carthage was,
Tranio, I burn, I pine, I perish, Tranio,
If I achieve not this young modest girl.   160
Counsel me, Tranio, for I know thou canst.
Assist me, Tranio, for I know thou wilt.

Tranio. Master, it is no time to chide you now;
Affection is not rated from the heart:
If love have touch'd you, nought remains but so,   165
Redime te captam, quam queas minimo.

Lucentio. Gramercies, lad; go forward. This contents;
The rest will comfort, for thy counsel's sound.

Tranio. Master, you look'd so longly on the maid,
Perhaps you mark'd not what's the pith of all.   170

Lucentio. O yes, I saw sweet beauty in her face,
Such as the daughter of Agenor had,
That made great Jove to humble him to her hand
When with his knees he kiss'd the Cretan strond.

Tranio. Saw you no more? mark'd you not how her   175
sister
Began to scold and raise up such a storm
That mortal ears might hardly endure the din?

Lucentio. Tranio, I saw her coral lips to move
And with her breath she did perfume the air.   180
Sacred and sweet was all I saw in her.

Tranio. Nay, then, 'tis time to stir him from his trance.
I pray, awake, sir: if you love the maid
Bend thoughts and wits to achieve her. Thus it stands:
Her elder sister is so curst and shrewd   185
That till the father rid his hands of her,
Master, your love must live a maid at home;
And therefore has he closely mew'd her up,
Because she will not be annoy'd with suitors.

Lucentio. Ah, Tranio, what a cruel father's he!   190
But art thou not advis'd he took some care
To get her cunning schoolmasters to instruct her?

Tranio. Ay, marry, am I, sir; and now 'tis plotted.

Lucentio. I have it, Tranio.

Tranio.   Master, for my hand,   195
Both our inventions meet and jump in one.

Lucentio. Tell me thine first.

Tranio.   You will be schoolmaster
And undertake the teaching of the maid;
That's your device.   200

Lucentio.   It is; may it be done?

Tranio. Not possible, for who shall bear your part
And be in Padua here Vincentio's son?
Keep house and ply his book, welcome his friends,
Visit his countrymen and banquet them?   205

Lucentio. *Basta,* content thee; for I have it full.
We have not yet been seen in any house
Nor can we be distinguish'd by our faces
For man or master: then, it follows thus:
Thou shalt be master, Tranio, in my stead,   210
Keep house, and port, and servants, as I should.
I will some other be; some Florentine,

109 to the divel's dam: *to the devil* gifts: *endowments* 110, 111 Their love is not so great: *The love of women is not so important; Cf. n.* 111, 112 blow our nails together: *be patient* fairly: *well* 113, 114 our cake's ... sides: *our goose is cooked* 115 wish: *recommend* 119 brooked parle: *permitted negotiation* advice: *reflection* 129 to be: *as to be* 132 be: *are (old plural)* 136 high-cross: *cross in the central square or market of a town* 143 have to't afresh: *resume our rivalry* 143, 144 Happy man be his dole: *may his lot be that of a happy man* SD ambo: *both (Gremio and Hortensio)* Mane[n]t: *remain* 155 the effect: *read 'th'effect'* love in idleness; *Cf. n.*

158 Anna; *Cf. n.* 164 rated: *driven out by scolding* 165 Redime ... minimo; *Cf. n.* 167 Gramercies: *many thanks* 169 longly: *longingly or persistently* 170 pith: *essential point* 172 daughter of Agenor; *Cf. n.* 174 strond: *strand* 184 to achieve: *read 't'achieve' (cf. 1. 227)* 185 curst: *bad tempered* shrewd: *shrewdish* 189 Because she will not: *so that she may not* 191 advis'd: *aware* 195 for: *I'll bet* 196 jump: *join* 201 may: *can* 206 Basta: *enough (Italian)* full: *all planned* 210 port: *style of living*

Some Neapolitan, or meaner man of Pisa.
'Tis hatch'd and shall be so: Tranio, at once
Uncase thee, take my color'd hat and cloak.   215
When Biondello comes he waits on thee;
But I will charm him first to keep his tongue.
     Tranio. So had you need.
In brief, sir, sith it your pleasure is
And I am tied to be obedient—   220
For so your father charg'd me at our parting;
'Be serviceable to my son,' quoth he,
Although I think 'twas in another sense—
I am content to be Lucentio
Because so well I love Lucentio.   225
     Lucentio. Tranio, be so, because Lucentio loves,
And let me be a slave, t'achieve that maid
Whose sudden sight hath thrall'd my wounded eye.
Here comes the rogue.

Enter Biondello.

               Sirrah, where have you bin?
     Biondello. Where have I been! Nay, how now! where are
you?
Master, has my fellow Tranio stolne your clothes,
Or you stolne his? or both? pray, what's the news?
     Lucentio. Sirrah, come hither: 'tis no time to jest,   235
And therefore frame your manners to the time.
Your fellow Tranio, here, to save my life,
Puts my apparel and my count'nance on
And I for my escape have put on his;
For in a quarrel since I came ashore   240
I kill'd a man and fear I was descried.
Wait you on him, I charge you, as becomes,
While I make way from hence to save my life.
You understand me?
     Biondello.   I, sir! nere a whit.   245
     Lucentio. And not a jot of Tranio in your mouth.
Tranio is chang'd into Lucentio.
     Biondello. The better for him: would I were so too!
     Tranio. So could I, faith, boy, to have the next wish after,
That Lucentio indeed had Baptista's youngest daughter.   250
But, sirrah, not for my sake, but your master's, I advise
You use your manners discreetly in all kind of companies:
When I am alone, why, then I am Tranio;
But in all places else your master, Lucentio.
     Lucentio. Tranio, let's go.   255
One thing more rests, that thyself execute,
To make one among these wooers: if thou ask me why,
Sufficeth my reasons are both good and weighty.   *Exeunt.*

The Presenters above speak.

     1. Servingman. My lord, you nod; you do not mind
the play.   260
     Sly. Yes, by Saint Anne, I do. A good matter,
surely; comes there any more of it?
     Page. My lord, 'tis but begun.

     Sly. 'Tis a very excellent piece of work, madam
lady: would 'twere done!   *They sit and mark.*

❧ SCENE FOURTH ❧

Enter Petruchio, and his man Grumio.

     Petruchio. Verona, for awhile I take my leave
To see my friends in Padua; but, of all
My best beloved and approved friend,
Hortensio; and I trow this is his house.
Here, sirrah Grumio; knock, I say.   5
     Grumio. Knock, sir? whom should I knock? is there
any man has rebused your worship?
     Petruchio. Villain, I say, knock me here soundly.
     Grumio. Knock you here, sir? why, sir, what am I,
sir, that I should knock you here, sir?   10
     Petruchio. Villain, I say, knock me at this gate
And rap me well or I'll knock your knave's pate.
     Grumio. My master is grown quarrelsome. I should knock
you first
And then I know after who comes by the worst.   15
     Petruchio. Will it not be?
Faith, sirrah, and you'll not knock, I'll ring it;
I'll try how you can *sol, fa,* and sing it.
               He wrings him by the ears.
     Grumio. Help, masters, help! my master is mad.
     Petruchio. Now, knock when I bid you, sirrah villain!   20

Enter Hortensio.

     Hortensio. How now, what's the matter? My old
friend Grumio! and my good friend Petruchio! How
do you all at Verona?
     Petruchio. Signior Hortensio, come you to part the fray?
Con tutto il cuore ben trovato, may I say.   25
     *Hortensio. Alla nostra casa ben venuto, molto
honorato signior mio Petruchio.*
Rise, Grumio, rise: we will compound this quarrel.
     Grumio. Nay, 'tis no matter, sir, what he 'leges in
Latin. If this be not a lawful cause for me to leave   30
his service, look you, sir, he bid me knock him and
rap him soundly, sir: well, was it fit for a servant to
use his master so; being, perhaps, for aught I see,
two-and-thirty, a peep out?
Whom would to God, I had well knock'd at first,   35
Then had not Grumio come by the worst.
     Petruchio. A senseless villain! Good Hortensio,
I bade the rascal knock upon your gate
And could not get him for my heart to do it.
     Grumio. Knock at the gate? O heavens! Spake you not   40
these words plain, 'Sirrah, knock me here, rap

213 **meaner:** *of lower class*   215 **Uncase thee:** *take off your coat*   **color'd:** *Tranio, as becomes a servant, is wearing a sober costume; Lucentio is more gaily clad*   217 **charm:** *compel by enchantment*   219 **sith:** *since*   228 **thrall'd:** *enthralled*   230 **Sirrah:** *usual form of addressing servants*   233 **stolne:** *stolen*   238 **count'nance:** *outward appearance*   249–254 **So could I . . . your master, Lucentio:** *F sets as prose*   256 **rests:** *remains*   **execute:** *carry out*   SD **Presenters:** *actors*   **speak:** *F speakes*   259 **mind:** *pay attention to*

SD **mark:** *watch*   4 **trow:** *believe*   7 **rebused:** *Grumio's version of 'abused'*   8 **me:** *i.e. 'for me' (the ethical dative); Grumio willfully misunderstands me here as 'my ear'*   **soundly:** *vigorously*   12 **pate:** *head*   17 **and:** *if*   **ring:** *with play on 'wring'; see following SD*   18 **sol, fa:** *notes on the scale, said to the accompaniment of the stage business*   19 **masters:** *F mistris*   25 **Con . . . trovato:** *with all my heart well met* (literally, 'found'); F Con tutti le core bene trobatto   26, 27 **Alla . . . Petruchio:** *Welcome to our house, my most honored Signor Petruchio*   **ben:** *F bene*   **molto:** *F multo*   **honorato:** *F honorata*   28 **compound:** *settle*   29 **'leges:** *alleges*   30 **Latin:** *so the foregoing 'foreign talk' seems to Grumio*   34 **two-and-thirty, a peep out:** *expression derived from an old card game, meaning 'intoxicated'*   **peep:** *pip, one of the suit markings on a playing card*   35, 6 **Whom would . . . the worst:** *F sets as prose*

me here, knock me well, and knock me soundly?' And
come you now with 'knocking at the gate'?

    Petruchio. Sirrah, be gone, or talk not, I advise you.

    Hortensio. Petruchio, patience; I am Grumio's pledge.   *45*
Why, this a heavy chance 'twixt him and you,
Your ancient, trusty, pleasant servant Grumio.
And tell me now, sweet friend, what happy gale
Blows you to Padua here from old Verona?

    Petruchio. Such wind as scatters young men through   *50*
    the world
To seek their fortunes farther than at home,
Where small experience grows. But in a few,
Signior Hortensio, thus it stands with me:
Antonio, my father, is deceas'd   *55*
And I have thrust myself into this maze,
Happily to wive and thrive as best I may.
Crowns in my purse I have and goods at home
And so am come abroad to see the world.

    Hortensio. Petruchio, shall I then come roundly to thee   *60*
And wish thee to a shrewd ill-favor'd wife?
Thou'dst thank me but a little for my counsel
And yet I'll promise thee she shall be rich,
And very rich: but thou'rt too much my friend
And I'll not wish thee to her.   *65*

    Petruchio. Signior Hortensio, 'twixt such friends as we
Few words suffice; and therefore, if thou know
One rich enough to be Petruchio's wife,
As wealth is burthen of my wooing dance,
Be she as foul as was Florentius' love,   *70*
As old as Sibyl, and as curst and shrowd
As Socrates' Zentippe, or a worse,
She moves me not, or not removes, at least,
Affection's edge in me, were she as rough
As are the swelling Adriatic seas.   *75*
I come to wive it wealthily in Padua;
If wealthily, then happily in Padua.

    Grumio. Nay, look you, sir, he tells you flatly what
his mind is; why, give him gold enough and marry
him to a puppet or an aglet-baby or an old trot with   *80*
ne'er a tooth in her head, though she have as many
diseases as two-and-fifty horses: why, nothing comes
amiss so money comes withal.

    Hortensio. Petruchio, since we are stepp'd thus far in,
I will continue that I broach'd in jest.   *85*
I can, Petruchio, help thee to a wife
With wealth enough and young and beauteous,
Brought up as best becomes a gentlewoman.
Her only fault—and that is faults enough—
Is that she is intolerable curst   *90*
And shrowd and froward, so beyond all measure,
That were my state far worser than it is
I would not wed her for a mine of gold.

    Petruchio. Hortensio, peace! thou know'st not gold's
    effect.   *95*
Tell me her father's name, and 'tis enough;

For I will board her though she chide as loud
As thunder when the clouds in autumn crack.

    Hortensio. Her father is Baptista Minola,
An affable and courteous gentleman;   *100*
Her name is Katherina Minola,
Renown'd in Padua for her scolding tongue.

    Petruchio. I know her father though I know not her,
And he knew my deceased father well.
I will not sleep, Hortensio, till I see her;   *105*
And therefore let me be thus bold with you,
To give you over at this first encounter
Unless you will accompany me thither.

    Grumio. I pray you, sir, let him go while the humor
lasts. A my word, and she knew him as well as I do   *110*
she would think scolding would do little good upon
him. She may perhaps call him half a score knaves
or so; why, that's nothing: and he begin once, he'll
rail in his rope-tricks. I'll tell you what, sir, an she stand
him but a little, he will throw a figure in her   *115*
face and so disfigure her with it that she shall have
no more eyes to see withal than a cat. You know him
not, sir.

    Hortensio. Tarry, Petruchio, I must go with thee
For in Baptista's keep my treasure is.   *120*
He hath the jewel of my life in hold,
His youngest daughter, beautiful Bianca,
And her witholds from me and other more,
Suitors to her and rivals in my love,
Supposing it a thing impossible,   *125*
For those defects I have before rehears'd,
That ever Katherina will be woo'd.
Therefore this order hath Baptista tane,
That none shall have access unto Bianca
Till Katherine the curst have got a husband.   *130*

    Grumio. Katherine the curst!
A title for a maid of all titles the worst.

    Hortensio. Now shall my friend Petruchio do me grace
And offer me, disguis'd in sober robes,
To old Baptista as a schoolmaster   *135*
Well seen in music, to instruct Bianca,
That so I may, by this device, at least
Have leave and leisure to make love to her
And unsuspected court her by herself.

Enter Gremio, and Lucentio disguised.

    Grumio. Here's no knavery! See, to beguile the old   *140*
folks, how the young folks lay their heads together!
Master, master, look about you: who goes there, ha?

    Hortensio. Peace, Grumio! it is the rival of my love.
Petruchio, stand by awhile.

    Grumio. A proper stripling, and an amorous!   *145*

    Gremio. O! very well; I have perus'd the note.
Hark you, sir; I'll have them very fairly bound:
All books of love, see that at any hand,
And see you read no other lectures to her.

---

46 this: *this is* **heavy:** *sad*   **53 in a few:** *i.e. words*   **58 crowns:** *coins*   **60 come
roundly:** *speak plainly*   **69 burthen:** *the accompaniment*   **70 foul:** *ugly* **Florentius'**
Cf. n.   **71 Sibyl:** *legendary female prophet Cf. n.*   **shrowd:** *shrewd*   **72 Zentippe:** *Xan-
thippe, Socrates' shrewish wife*   **74 as:** *F is as*   **80 aglet-baby:** *small figure carved on the
tag of a point of lace* (French *aiguillette*) **trot:** *hag*   **85 that:** *what*   **90 intolerable:**
intolerably   **91 froward:** *contrary*   **92 state:** *financial condition*

97 board: *appproach, woo* **chide:** *scold*   **107 give you over:** *leave you*   **110 A:**
on   **114 rope-tricks:** *tricks worthy of the rope* (i.e. *hanging*) *with play on 'rhetorics'; cf.
figure, 1. 115*   **114 stand:** *withstand*   **117 cat:** *perhaps because a cat has eyes half closed
in daytime, with incidental play on 'cat' and 'Kate'*   **123 me and other more:** *F me.
Other more*   **128 order . . . tane:** *measures . . . taken*   **133 grace:** *a favor*   **136 seen:**
instructed   **145 proper stripling:** *fine young man* (ironical)   **146 note:** *memorandum*   **148 at any hand:** *in any case*

You understand me. Over and beside   *150*
Signior Baptista's liberality,
I'll mend it with a largess. Take your paper too
And let me have them very well perfum'd,
For she is sweeter than perfume itself
To whom they go to. What will you read to her?   *155*
    Lucentio. What ere I read to her, I'll plead for you,
As for my patron, stand you so assur'd,
As firmly as yourself were still in place;
Yea, and perhaps with more successful words
Than you unless you were a scholar, sir.   *160*
    Gremio. O! this learning, what a thing it is.
    Grumio. O! this woodcock, what an ass it is.
    Petruchio. Peace, sirrah!
    Hortensio. Grumio, mum! God save you, Signior Gremio!
    Gremio. And you are well met, Signior Hortensio.   *165*
Trow you whither I am going? To Baptista Minola.
I promis'd to inquire carefully
About a schoolmaster for the fair Bianca,
And, by good fortune, I have lighted well
On this young man; for learning and behavior   *170*
Fit for her turn; well read in poetry
And other books, good ones, I warrant ye.
    Hortensio. 'Tis well: and I have met a gentleman
Hath promis'd me to help me to another,
A fine musician to instruct our mistress: *175*
So shall I no whit be behind in duty
To fair Bianca, so belov'd of me.
    Gremio. Belov'd of me, and that my deeds shall prove.
    Grumio. And that his bags shall prove.
    Hortensio. Gremio, 'tis now no time to vent our love.   *180*
Listen to me, and if you speak me fair
I'll tell you news indifferent good for either.
Here is a gentleman whom by chance I met,
Upon agreement from us to his liking,
Will undertake to woo curst Katherine;   *185*
Yea, and to marry her if her dowry please.
    Gremio. So said, so done, is well.
Hortensio, have you told him all her faults?
    Petruchio. I know she is an irksome, brawling scold:
If that be all, masters, I hear no harm.   *190*
    Gremio. No, sayst me so, friend? What countryman?
    Petruchio. Born in Verona, old Antonio's son:
My father dead, my fortune lives for me;
And I do hope good days and long to see.
    Gremio. O, sir, such a life, with such a wife, were   *195*
strange!
But if you have a stomach, to't a God's name:
You shall have me assisting you in all.
But will you woo this wildcat?
    Petruchio.   Will I live?   *200*
    Grumio. [*Aside.*] Will he woo her? ay, or I'll hang her.
    Petruchio. Why came I hither but to that intent?
Think you a little din can daunt mine ears?
Have I not in my time heard lions roar?
Have I not heard the sea, puff'd up with winds,   *205*

Rage like an angry boar chafed with sweat?
Have I not heard great ordnance in the field
And heaven's artillery thunder in the skies?
Have I not in a pitched battle heard
Loud larums, neighing steeds, and trumpets' clang?   *210*
And do you tell me of a woman's tongue,
That gives not half so great a blow to hear
As will a chestnut in a farmer's fire?
Tush, tush! fear boys with bugs.
    Grumio. [*Aside.*]   For he fears none.   *215*
    Gremio. Hortensio, hark:
This gentleman is happily arriv'd,
My mind presumes, for his own good and ours.
    Hortensio. I promis'd we would be contributors,
And bear his charge of wooing, whatsoere.   *220*
    Gremio. And so we will, provided that he win her.
    Grumio. [*Aside.*] I would I were as sure of a good dinner.

                Enter Tranio brave, and Biondello.

    Tranio. Gentlemen, God save you! If I may be bold,
Tell me, I beseech you, which is the readiest way
To the house of Signior Baptista Minola?   *225*
    Biondello. He that has the two fair daughters: is't he
you mean?
    Tranio. Even he, Biondello!
    Gremio. Hark you, sir; you mean not her to—
    Tranio. Perhaps, him and her, sir: what have you to do?   *230*
    Petruchio. Not her that chides, sir, at any hand, I pray.
    Tranio. I love no chiders, sir. Biondello, let's away.
    Lucentio. Well begun, Tranio.
    Hortensio.   Sir, a word ere you go:
Are you a suitor to the maid you talk of, yea or no?   *235*
    Tranio. And if I be, sir, is it any offence?
    Gremio. No, if without more words, you will get you hence.
    Tranio. Why, sir, I pray, are not the streets as free
For me as for you?
    Gremio.   But so is not she.   *240*
    Tranio. For what reason, I beseech you?
    Gremio. For this reason, if you'll know,
That she's the choice love of Signior Gremio.
    Hortensio. That she's the chosen of Signior Hortensio.
    Tranio. Softly, my masters! if you be gentlemen   *245*
Do me this right; hear me with patience.
Baptista is a noble gentleman
To whom my father is not all unknown,
And were his daughter fairer than she is
She may more suitors have, and me for one.   *250*
Fair Leda's daughter had a thousand wooers;
Then well one more may fair Bianca have,
And so she shall; Lucentio shall make one
Though Paris came in hope to speed alone.
    Gremio. What! this gentleman will out-talk us all.   *255*
    Lucentio. Sir, give him head. I know he'll prove a jade.
    Petruchio. Hortensio, to what end are all these words?
    Hortensio. Sir, let me be so bold as ask you,

152 paper: *i.e. note; cf. 1.146*   **153 them:** *i.e. the books; cf. l. 147*   **158 as yourself:** *as if you yourself* **in place:** *present*   **162 woodcock:** *bird easily caught, hence symbol of stupidity*   **166 trow:** *know*   **174 help me:** *F help one*   **179 bags:** *moneybags*   **180 vent:** *express*   **182 indifferent:** *equally*   **183 gentleman:** *disyllabic here, 'gemman'*   **184 upon agreement:** *on terms*   **192 Antonio's:** *F. Butonio's*   **197 a:** *in*

206 chafed: *heated, irritated*   **207 ordnance:** *cannon*   **208 heaven's:** *monosyllable* **artillery:** *trisyllable*   **210 larums:** *alarms*   **214 fear:** *frighten* **bugs:** *bogeymen*   **218 ours:** *F yours*   **220 charge:** *expense* **SD brave:** *finely dressed*   **251 Leda's daughter:** *Helen of Troy*   **252 one more:** *i.e. than she now has*   **254 Paris:** *Trojan prince who won Helen from her husband, King Menelaus* **came:** *were to come* **speed:** *succeed*   **256 jade:** *worthless nag*

Did you yet ever see Baptista's daughter?
    Tranio. No, sir; but hear I do that he hath two,   260
The one as famous for a scolding tongue
As is the other for beauteous modesty.
    Petruchio. Sir, sir, the first's for me; let her go by.
    Gremio. Yea, leave that labor to great Hercules
And let it be more than Alcides' twelve.   265
    Petruchio. Sir, understand you this of me in sooth:
The youngest daughter, whom you hearken for,
Her father keeps from all access of suitors
And will not promise her to any man
Until the elder sister first be wed;   270
The younger then is free, and not before.
    Tranio. If it be so, sir, that you are the man
Must stead us all, and me amongst the rest;
And if you break the ice and do this feat,
Achieve the elder, set the younger free   275
For our access, whose hap shall be to have her
Will not so graceless be to be ingrate.
    Hortensio. Sir, you say well, and well you do conceive;
And since you do profess to be a suitor
You must, as we do, gratify this gentleman   280
To whom we all rest generally beholding.
    Tranio. Sir, I shall not be slack: in sign whereof,
Please ye we may contrive this afternoon
And quaff carouses to our mistress' health
And do as adversaries do in law,   285
Strive mightily but eat and drink as friends.
    Grumio.   ⎱
    Biondello. ⎰ O excellent motion! Fellows, let's be gone.
    Hortensio. The motion's good indeed, and be it so:—
Petruchio, I shall be your *ben venuto*.   *Exeunt.* 290

ACT SECOND ❧ SCENE FIRST

Enter Katherina and Bianca [with her hands tied].

    Bianca. Good sister, wrong me not nor wrong yourself
To make a bondmaid and a slave of me;
That I disdain: but for these other gawds,
Unbind my hands, I'll pull them off myself,
Yea, all my raiment, to my petticoat;   5
Or what you will command me will I do,
So well I know my duty to my elders.
    Katherina. Of all thy suitors, here I charge thee, tell
Whom thou lov'st best: see thou dissemble not.
    Bianca. Believe me, sister, of all the men alive   10
I never yet beheld that special face
Which I could fancy more than any other.
    Katherina. Minion, thou liest. Is't not Hortensio?
    Bianca. If you affect him, sister, here I swear
I'll plead for you myself but you shall have him.   15
    Katherina. O! then, belike, you fancy riches more:

You will have Gremio to keep you fair.
    Bianca. Is it for him you do envy me so?
Nay, then you jest and now I well perceive
You have but jested with me all this while.   20
I prithee, sister Kate, untie my hands.
    Katherina. If that be jest then all the rest was so.
                                            Strikes her.

Enter Baptista.

    Baptista. Why, how now, dame! whence grows this
insolence?
Bianca, stand aside. Poor girl! she weeps.   25
Go ply thy needle; meddle not with her.
For shame, thou hilding of a divelish spirit,
Why dost thou wrong her that did nere wrong thee?
When did she cross thee with a bitter word?
    Katherina. Her silence flouts me and I'll be reveng'd.   30
                                      Flies after Bianca.
    Baptista. What! in my sight? Bianca, get thee in.
                                       Exit [Bianca].
    Katherina. What! will you not suffer me? Nay, now I see
She is your treasure, she must have a husband;
I must dance barefoot on her wedding day,
And, for your love to her, lead apes in hell.   35
Talk not to me: I will go sit and weep
Till I can find occasion of revenge.   *[Exit.]*
    Baptista. Was ever gentleman thus griev'd as I?
But who comes here?

Enter Gremio, [with] Lucentio in the habit of a mean man;
Petruchio, with [Hortensio as a Musician; and] Tranio, with his
boy [Biondello] bearing a lute and books.

    Gremio. Good morrow, neighbor Baptista.   40
    Baptista. Good morrow, neighbor Gremio. God save
you, gentlemen!
    Petruchio. And you, good sir. Pray, have you not a daughter
Call'd Katherina, fair and virtuous?
    Baptista. I have a daughter, sir, call'd Katherina.   45
    Gremio. You are too blunt: go to it orderly.
    Petruchio. You wrong me, Signior Gremio: give me leave.
I am a gentleman of Verona, sir,
That, hearing of her beauty and her wit,
Her affability and bashful modesty,   50
Her wondrous qualities and mild behavior,
Am bold to show myself a forward guest
Within your house, to make mine eye the witness
Of that report which I so oft have heard.
And, for an entrance to my entertainment,   55
I do present you with a man of mine,   *[Presenting Hortensio.]*
Cunning in music and the mathematics,
To instruct her fully in those sciences,
Whereof I know she is not ignorant.
Accept of him, or else you do me wrong: 60
His name is Licio, born in Mantua.
    Baptista. Y'are welcome, sir; and he, for your good sake.
But for my daughter Katherina, this I know,

265 Alcide's: *Hercules Cf. n.*   **267 hearken:** *lie in wait, long*   **273 stead:** *help*   **274 feat:** *F seeke*   **276 whose hap shall be:** *whoever has the good luck*   **277 to:** *as to*   **ingrate:** *ungrateful*   **280 gratify:** *reward*   **281 generally:** *read 'gen'rally'*   **283 contrive:** *while away*   **284 carouses:** *full glasses of liquor*   **290 I . . . venuto:** *I shall sponsor you, see to your reception*   **3 gawds:** *adornments; F goods*   **13 Minion:** *minx*

17 fair: *richly dressed*   **18 envy:** (stressed — ⏑) *dislike*   **27 hilding:** *wretch*   **34 dance barefoot on her wedding day;** *Cf. n.*   **35 lead apes in hell:** *proverbial destiny of old maids Cf. Much Ado About Nothing II.1.39.*   **58 To instruct:** *read 't'instruct'*

She is not for your turn, the more my grief.

   Petruchio. I see you do not mean to part with her   65
Or else you like not of my company.

   Baptista. Mistake me not; I speak but as I find.
Whence are you, sir? what may I call your name?

   Petruchio. Petruchio is my name, Antonio's son,
A man well known throughout all Italy.   70

   Baptista. I know him well: you are welcome for his sake.

   Gremio. Saving your tale, Petruchio, I pray,
Let us, that are poor petitioners, speak too.
Bacare! you are marvelous forward.

   Petruchio. O, pardon me, Signior Gremio, I would   75
fain be doing.

   Gremio. I doubt it not, sir; but you will curse your wooing.
Neighbor, this is a gift very grateful, I am sure of
it. To express the like kindness myself, that have
been more kindly beholding to you than any, freely   80
give unto you this young scholar, *[Presenting Lucentio.]* that
hath been long studying at Rheims; as cunning in Greek,
Latin, and other languages, as the other in music and mathematics. His name is Cambio; pray accept his service.

   Baptista. A thousand thanks, Signior Gremio; Welcome,   85
good Cambio.—*[To Tranio.]* But, gentle sir, methinks you
walk like a stranger: may I be so bold to know the cause of
your coming?

   Tranio. Pardon me, sir, the boldness is mine own,
That, being a stranger in this city here,   90
Do make myself a suitor to your daughter,
Unto Bianca, fair and virtuous.
Nor is your firm resolve unknown to me
In the preferment of the eldest sister.
This liberty is all that I request,   95
That, upon knowledge of my parentage,
I may have welcome 'mongst the rest that woo
And free access and favor as the rest.
And, toward the education of your daughters
I here bestow a simple instrument,   100
And this small packet of Greek and Latin books:
If you accept them, then their worth is great.

   Baptista. Lucentio is your name, of whence, I pray?

   Tranio. Of Pisa, sir; son to Vincentio.

   Baptista. A mighty man of Pisa; by report   105
I know him well. You are very welcome, sir.
[To Hortensio.] Take you that lute, *[To Lucentio.]* and you
the set of books;
You shall go see your pupils presently.
Holla, within!   110

             Enter a Servant.

     Sirrah, lead these gentlemen
To my daughters and tell them both
These are their tutors: bid them use them well.
             [Exit Servant, with Lucentio and
             Hortensio, Biondello following.]
We will go walk a little in the orchard
And then to dinner. You are passing welcome   115

And so I pray you all to think yourselves.

   Petruchio. Signior Baptista, my business asketh haste
And every day I cannot come to woo.
You knew my father well, and in him me,
Left solely heir to all his lands and goods,   120
Which I have better'd rather than decreas'd:
Then tell me, if I get your daughter's love
What dowry shall I have with her to wife?

   Baptista. After my death the one half of my lands,
And in possession twenty thousand crowns.   125

   Petruchio. And, for that dowry, I'll assure her of
Her widowhood, be it that she survive me,
In all my lands and leases whatsoever.
Let specialties be therefore drawn between us
That convenants may be kept on either hand.   130

   Baptista. Ay, when the special thing is well obtain'd,
That is, her love; for that is all in all.

   Petruchio. Why, that is nothing; for I tell you, father,
I am as peremptory as she proud-minded;
And where two raging fires meet together   135
They do consume the thing that feeds their fury:
Though little fire grows great with little wind,
Yet extreme gusts will blow out fire and all;
So I to her, and so she yields to me;
For I am rough and woo not like a babe.   140

   Baptista. Well mayst thou woo and happy be thy speed!
But be thou arm'd for some unhappy words.

   Petruchio. Ay, to the proof; as mountains are for winds,
That shake not, though they blow perpetually.

        Enter Hortensio, with his head broke.

   Baptista. How now, my friend! why dost thou look so pale?

   Hortensio. For fear, I promise you, if I look pale.

   Baptista. What, will my daughter prove a good musician?

   Hortensio. I think she'll sooner prove a soldier.
Iron may hold with her but never lutes.

   Baptista. Why, then thou canst not break her to the lute?   150

   Hortensio. Why, no; for she hath broke the lute to me.
I did but tell her she mistook her frets
And bow'd her hand to teach her fingering;
When, with a most impatient divelish spirit,
'Frets, call you these?' quoth she; 'I'll fume with them';   155
And, with that word, she stroke me on the head,
And through the instrument my pate made way.
And there I stood amazed for a while
As on a pillory, looking through the lute,
While she did call me rascal, fiddler,   160
And twangling Jack, with twenty such vilde terms
As had she studied to misuse me so.

   Petruchio. Now, by the world, it is a lusty wench!
I love her ten times more than ere I did:
O! how I long to have some chat with her!   165

   Baptista. *[To Hortensio.]* Well, go with me, and be not so
discomfited.
Proceed in practice with my younger daughter;

---

127 widowhood: *widow's share of estate*   **129 specialties:** *specific contracts*   **134 peremptory:** *stressed* – — ҆– —   **138 extreme:** *stressed* ҆– —   **141 speed:** *fortune*   **143 to
the proof:** *as if in proved (i.e. tested)* **armor**   **144 shake:** *F shakes*   **148 soldier:** *three
syllables here*   **149 hold:** *with resist*   **152 frets:** *ridges on the neck of the lute where the
strings are pressed*   **153 bow'd:** *bent*   **155 Frets . . . fume with them:** *plays on 'fret' and
'fume'*   **156 stroke:** *struck*   **161 twangling:** *twanging* **vilde:** *vile*   **162 As had: . . .
i.e. as if she had made special preparation to abuse me   **163 lusty:** *lively*

---

64 turn: *purpose*   **66 like not of:** *do not care for*   **72-74 saving . . . forward:** *F sets as prose*
72 Saving: *with all due respect*   **74 Bacare:** *back (burlesque Latin)*   **marvelous:** *marvelously*   **77, 78 your wooing. Neighbor:** *F your wooing neighbors*   **78-88 Neighbor . . . your
coming:** *F sets as verse*   **81 you:** *F omits*   **114 orchard:** *garden*   **115 passing:** *exceedingly*

She's apt to learn and thankful for good turns.
Signior Petruchio, will you go with us   170
Or shall I send my daughter Kate to you?

Exit [Baptista, with Gremio, Tranio,
and Hortensio]. Manet Petruchio.

Petruchio. I pray you do; I will attend her here
And woo her with some spirit when she comes.
Say that she rail; why then I'll tell her plain
She sings as sweetly as a nightingale: 175
Say that she frown; I'll say she looks as clear
As morning roses newly wash'd with dew:
Say she be mute and will not speak a word;
Then I'll commend her volubility,
And say she uttereth piercing eloquence.   180
If she do bid me pack I'll give her thanks
As though she bid me stay by her a week;
If she deny to wed I'll crave the day
When I shall ask the banes, and when be married.
But here she comes; and now, Petruchio, speak.   185

Enter Katherina.

Good morrow, Kate; for that's your name, I hear.
Katherina. Well have you heard, but something hard of
hearing:
They call me Katerina that do talk of me.
Petruchio. You lie, in faith; for you are call'd plain Kate,   190
And bonny Kate, and sometimes Kate the curst;
But, Kate, the prettiest Kate in Christendom;
Kate or Kate-Hall, my super-dainty Kate,
For dainties are all Kates: and therefore, Kate,
Take this of me, Kate of my consolation;   195
Hearing thy mildness prais'd in every town,
Thy virtues spoke of, and thy beauty sounded—
Yet not so deeply as to thee belongs—
Myself am mov'd to woo thee for my wife.
Katherina. Mov'd! in good time: let him that mov'd you   200
hether.
Remove you hence. I knew you at the first,
You were a movable.
Petruchio.   Why, what's a movable?
Katherina. A joint stool.   205
Petruchio.   Thou hast hit it: come sit on me.
Katherina. Asses are made to bear and so are you.
Petruchio. Women are made to bear and so are you.
Katherina. No such jade as you, if me you mean.
Petruchio. Alas! good Kate, I will not burthen thee;   210
For, knowing thee to be but young and light—
Katherina. Too light for such a swain as you to catch
And yet as heavy as my weight should be.
Petruchio. Should be! should—buzz!
Katherina.   Well tane, and like a   215
buzzard.
Petruchio. O slow-wing'd turtle! shall a buzzard take thee?

Katherina. Ay, for a turtle, as he takes a buzzard.
Petruchio. Come, come, you wasp; i' faith you are too
angry.   220
Katherina. If I be waspish best beware my sting.
Petruchio. My remedy is then to pluck it out.
Katherina. Ay, if the fool could find it where it lies.
Petruchio. Who knows not where a wasp does wear his
sting?   225
In his tail.
Katherina. In his tongue.
Petruchio.   Whose tongue?
Katherina. Yours, if you talk of tales; and so farewell.
Petruchio. What! with my tongue in your tail? nay,   230
come, again.
Good Kate, I am a gentleman.
Katherina.   That I'll try.

She strikes him.

Petruchio. I swear I'll cuff you if you strike again.
Katherina. So may you lose your arms: 235
If you strike me you are no gentleman,
And if no gentleman, why then no arms.
Petruchio. A herald, Kate? O! put me in thy books.
Katherina. What is your crest? a coxcomb?
Petruchio. A combless cock, so Kate will be my hen.   240
Katherina. No cock of mine; you crow too like a craven.
Petruchio. Nay, come, Kate, come; you must not look so
sour.
Katherina. It is my fashion when I see a crab.
Petruchio. Why, here's no crab, and therefore look not   245
sour.
Katherina. There is, there is.
Petruchio. Then show it me.
Katherina.   Had I a glass I would.
Petruchio. What, you mean my face?   250
Katherina.   Well aim'd of such a
young one.
Petruchio. Now, by Saint George, I am too young for you.
Katherina. Yet you are wither'd.
Petruchio.   'Tis with cares.   255
Katherina.   I care not.
Petruchio. Nay, hear you, Kate: in sooth you scape
not so.
Katherina. I chafe you if I tarry: let me go.
Petruchio. No, not a whit: I find you passing gentle.   260
'Twas told me you were rough and coy and sullen,
And now I find report a very liar;
For thou art pleasant, gamesome, passing courteous,
But slow in speech, yet sweet as springtime flowers.
Thou canst not frown, thou canst not look a sconce,   265
Nor bite the lip as angry wenches will,
Nor hast thou pleasure to be cross in talk;
But thou with mildness entertain'st thy wooers,
With gentle conference, soft and affable.
Why does the world report that Kate doth limp?   270
O sland'rous world! Kate, like the hazel-twig
Is straight and slender, and as brown in hue

---

169 apt: *ready*   **180 uttereth:** *read 'utt'reth'*   **181 pack:** *be off*   **183 deny:** *re-*
fuse   **184 banes:** *banns*   **187-197 hard ... sounded;** *Cf. n.*   **193 Kate-Hall;**
Cf. n.   **200 in good time:** *indeed*   **203 movable:** *pun on 'piece of furniture'*   **205**
joint stool: *stool made by a joiner*   **207, 208 bear:** *i.e. 1) a man, 2) children*   **209 jade:**
worthless nag, worthless person   **212 swain:** *young rustic*   **214 be:** *pun on 'bee'*   **buzz:** *1)*
hum, 2) tush   **buzzard:** *1) kind of hawk, 2) blockhead, 3) large insect*   **217 turtle:** *turtledove*

219 Ay, for a turtle; ... *Cf. n.*   **229 talk of tales:** *talk idly*   **237 arms:** *pun on 'coat*
of arms'   **238 herald:** *and hence authority on heraldry*   **books:** *heraldic registers, with pun*
on 'in your good books'   **239 coxcomb:** *badge of the court food*   **240 combless:** *gentle,*
with crest cut down   **241 craven:** *cowardly (cock-fighting term)*   **244 crab:** *crab*
apple   **251 aim'd of:** *guessed for*   **257 scape:** *escape*   **259 chafe:** *irritate*   **261 coy:**
haughty   **265 a sconce:** *askance*   **269 conference:** *conversation*

As hazelnuts and sweeter than the kernels.
O! let me see thee walk: thou dost not halt.
   Katherina. Go, fool, and whom thou keep'st command.   275
   Petruchio. Did ever Dian so become a grove
As Kate this chamber with her princely gait?
O! be thou Dian and let her be Kate,
And then let Kate be chaste and Dian sportful!
   Katherina. Where did you study all this goodly speech?   280
   Petruchio. It is extempore, from my mother-wit.
   Katherina. A witty mother! witless else her son.
   Petruchio. Am I not wise?
   Katherina.   Yes; keep you warm.
   Petruchio. Marry, so I mean, sweet Katherina, in thy bed;
And therefore, setting all this chat aside,
Thus in plain terms: your father hath consented
That you shall be my wife, your dowry 'greed on;
And will you, nill you, I will marry you.
Now, Kate, I am a husband for your turn;   290
For, by this light, whereby I see thy beauty—
Thy beauty that doth make me like thee well—
Thou must be married to no man but me.

       Enter Baptista, Gremio, [and] Tranio.

For I am he am born to tame you, Kate,
And bring you from a wild Kate to a Kate   295
Conformable as other household Kates.
Here comes your father: never make denial;
I must and will have Katherine to my wife.
   Baptista. Now, Signior Petruchio, how spend you with
my daughter?   300
   Petruchio. How but well, sir? how but well?
It were impossible I should speed amiss.
   Baptista. Why, how now, daughter Katherine! in your
dumps.
   Katherina. Call you me daughter? now, I promise you   305
You have show'd a tender fatherly regard
To wish me wed to one half lunatic,
A madcap ruffian and a swearing Jack
That thinks with oaths to face the matter out.
   Petruchio. Father, 'tis thus: yourself and all the world.   310
That talk'd of her have talk'd amiss of her.
If she be curst it is for policy,
For she's not froward but modest as the dove,
She is not hot but temperate as the morn;
For patience she will prove a second Grissel   315
And Roman Lucrece for her chastity;
And to conclude, we have 'greed so well together
That upon Sunday is the wedding day.
   Katherina. I'll see thee hang'd on Sunday first.
   Gremio. Hark, Petruchio: she says she'll see thee hang'd first.
   Tranio. Is this your speeding? nay, then good night our
part!
   Petruchio. Be patient, gentlemen, I choose her for
myself;

If she and I be pleas'd, what's that to you?   325
'Tis bargain'd 'twixt us twain, being alone,
That she shall still be curst in company.
I tell you, 'tis incredible to believe
How much she loves me. O! the kindest Kate,
She hung about my neck, and kiss on kiss   330
She vied so fast, protesting oath on oath,
That in a twink she won me to her love.
O! you are novices; 'tis a world to see
How tame, when men and women are alone,
A meacock wretch can make the curstest shrew.   335
Give me thy hand, Kate: I will unto Venice
To buy apparel 'gainst the wedding day.
Provide the feast, father, and bid the guests;
I will be sure my Katherine shall be fine.
   Baptista. I know not what to say; but give me your hands.
God send you joy, Petruchio! 'tis a match.
   Gremio. }
   Tranio. } Amen, say we: we will be witnesses.
   Petruchio. Father, and wife, and gentlemen, adieu.
I will to Venice; Sunday comes apace.   345
We will have rings and things and fine array;
And, kiss me, Kate, we will be married a' Sunday.
                 Exeunt Petruchio and Katherine.
   Gremio. Was ever match clapp'd up so suddenly?
   Baptista. Faith, gentlemen, now I play a marchant's part
And venture madly on a desperate mart.   350
   Tranio. 'Twas a commodity lay fretting by you;
'Twill bring you gain or perish on the seas.
   Baptista. The gain I seek is quiet in the match.
   Gremio. No doubt but he hath got a quiet catch.
But now, Baptista, to your younger daughter: 355
Now is the day we long have looked for;
I am your neighbor, and was suitor first.
   Tranio. And I am one that love Bianca more
Than words can witness or your thoughts can guess.
   Gremio. Youngling, thou canst not love so dear as I.   360
   Tranio. Greybeard, thy love doth freeze.
   Gremio.   But thine doth fry.
Skipper, stand back, 'tis age that nourisheth.
   Tranio. But youth in ladies' eyes that flourisheth.
   Baptista. Content you, gentlemen; I will compound   365
this strife:
'Tis deeds must win the prize, and he, of both,
That can assure my daughter greatest dower
Shall have my Bianca's love.
Say, Signior Gremio, what can you assure her?   370
   Gremio. First, as you know, my house within the city
Is richly furnished with plate and gold:
Basins and ewers to lave her dainty hands;
My hangings all of Tyrian tapestry;
In ivory coffers I have stuff'd my crowns;   375
In cypress chests my arras counterpoints,

---

274 halt: *limp*   **275 whom thou keep'st command:** *i.e. tell your servants (not me) what to do*   **276 Dian:** *Diana, chaste goddess of the hunt*   **284 warm:** *with reference to the proverbial expression 'wit enough to keep oneself warm'; as we should say 'enough sense to come in out of the rain'*   **289 nill you:** *will you not*   **295 wild Kate:** *pun on 'cat' as in 1.298*   **303 in your dumps:** *downcast*   **305 promise:** *assure*   **306 You have:** *read 'you've'*   **309 face:** *brazen*   **312 for policy:** *with calculated purpose*   **313 froward:** *perverse*   **314 temperate:** *read 'temp'rate'*   **315, 316 Grissel . . . Lucrece;** *Cf. n.*   **317 we have:** *read 'we've'*   **321 speeding:** *success*

331 vied so fast: *i.e. rivaled me in eagerness to exchange kisses*   **332 twink:** *twinkling*   **333 world:** *worth a world; i.e. wonderful*   **335 meacock:** *meet or cowardly*   **339 fine:** *handsomely dressed*   **340 give me your hands:** *i.e. to join them in betrothal*   **348 clapp'd up:** *arranged*   **349 marchant's:** *merchant's*   **350 mart:** *market*   **351 fretting:** *of cloth ravaged by moths, hence 'wasting away,' with pun on Kate's fretful temper*   **363 Skipper:** *one whose gait reveals lack of maturity and dignity, 'prancer'*   **365 Content you:** *be calm*   **compound:** *settle*   **367 he, of both:** *whichever of the two*   **374 Tyrian:** *purple, dark red*   **376 arras counterpoints:** *tapestry woven in squares of contrasting colors, made in Arras, France*

Costly apparel, tents, and canopies.
Fine linen, Turkey cushions boss'd with pearl,
Valance of Venice gold in needlework,
Pewter and brass, and all things that belong   380
To house or housekeeping. Then, at my farm
I have a hundred milch-kine to the pail,
Six score fat oxen standing in my stalls
And all things answerable to this portion.
Myself am strook in years, I must confess;   385
And if I die tomorrow, this is hers,
If whilst I live she will be only mine.
   Tranio. That 'only' came well in. Sir, list to me:
I am my father's heir and only son,
If I may have your daughter to my wife   390
I'll leave her houses three or four as good,
Within rich Pisa walls, as any one
Old Signior Gremio has in Padua;
Besides two thousand ducats by the year
Of fruitful land, all which shall be her jointer.   395
What, have I pinch'd you, Signior Gremio?
   Gremio. Two thousand ducats by the year of land!
My land amounts not to so much in all:
That she shall have besides an argosy
That now is lying in Marcellus' road.   400
What, have I chok'd you with an argosy?
   Tranio. Gremio, 'tis known my father hath no less
Than three great argosies, besides two galliasses
And twelve tight galleys; these I will assure her
And twice as much, whatere thou offer'st next.   405
   Gremio. Nay, I have off'red all, I have no more;
And she can have no more than all I have.
If you like me, she shall have me and mine.
   Tranio. Why, then the maid is mine from all the world
By your firm promise. Gremio is outvied.   410
   Baptista. I must confess your offer is the best
And, let your father make her the assurance,
She is your own; else, you must pardon me,
If you should die before him, where's her dower?
   Tranio. That's but a cavil: he is old, I young.   415
   Gremio. And may not young men die as well as old?
   Baptista. Well, gentlemen,
I am thus resolv'd. On Sunday next, you know,
My daughter Katherine is to be married:
Now, on the Sunday following, shall Bianca   420
Be bride to you if you make this assurance;
If not, to Signior Gremio:
And so I take my leave and thank you both.   *Exit.*
   Gremio. Adieu, good neighbor. Now I fear thee not:
Sirrah young gamester, your father were a fool   425
To give thee all and in his waning age
Set foot under thy table. Tut! a toy!
An old Italian fox is not so kind, my boy.   *Exit.*
   Tranio. A vengeance on your crafty wither'd hide!

Yet I have fac'd it with a card of ten.   430
'Tis in my head to do my master good:
I see no reason, but suppos'd Lucentio
Must get a father, called 'suppos'd Vincentio';
And that's a wonder: fathers commonly
Do get their children, but in this case of wooing   435
A child shall get a sire if I fail not of my cunning.   *Exit.*

ACT THIRD ❧ SCENE FIRST

Enter Lucentio, Hortensio, and Bianca.

   Lucentio. Fiddler, forbear; you grow too forward, sir.
Have you so soon forgot the entertainment
Her sister Katherine welcom'd you withal?
   Hortensio. But, wrangling pedant, know this lady is
The patroness of heavenly harmony;   5
Then give me leave to have prerogative,
And when in music we have spent an hour
Your lecture shall have leisure for as much.
   Lucentio. Preposterous ass, that never read so far
To know the cause why music was ordain'd!   10
Was it not to refresh the mind of man
After his studies or his usual pain?
Then give me leave to read philosophy,
And while I pause, serve in your harmony.
   Hortensio. Sirrah, I will not bear these braves of thine.   15
   Bianca. Why, gentlemen, you do me double wrong
To strive for that which resteth in my choice.
I am no breeching scholar in the schools;
I'll not be tied to hours nor 'pointed times,
But learn my lessons as I please myself.   20
And, to cut off all strife, here sit we down;
Take you your instrument, play you the whiles;
His lecture will be done ere you have tun'd.
   Hortensio. You'll leave his lecture when I am in tune?
   Lucentio. That will be never; tune your instrument.   25
   Bianca. Where left we last?
   Lucentio. Here, madam:—
'Hic ibat Simois; hic est Sigeria tellus;
   Hic steterat Priami regia celsa senis.
   Bianca. Conster them.   30
   Lucentio. Hic ibat, as I told you before, *Simois,*
I am Lucentio, *hic est,* son unto Vincentio of Pisa,
Sigeria tellus, disguised thus to get your love;
Hic steterat, and that Lucentio that comes a wooing,
Priami, is my man Tranio, *regia,* bearing my port,   35
celsa senis, that we might beguile the old pantaloon.
   Hortensio. Madam, my instrument's in tune.
   Bianca. Let's hear.—O fie! the treble jars.
   Lucentio. Spit in the hole, man, and tune again.

Bianca. Now let me see if I can conster it: *Hic ibat*   40
Simois, I know you not, *hic est Sigeria tellus,* I trust
you not; *Hic steterat Priami,* take heed he hear us
not, *regia,* presume not, *celsa senis,* despair not.

    Hortensio. Madam, 'tis now in tune.

    Lucentio.   All but the bass.   45

    Hortensio. The bass is right; 'tis the base knave that jars.
[*Aside.*] How fiery and forward our pedant is!
Now, for my life, the knave doth court my love;
Pedascule, I'll watch you better yet.

    Bianca. In time I may believe, yet I mistrust.   50

    Lucentio. Mistrust it not; for, sure, Æacides
Was Ajax, call'd so from his grandfather.

    Bianca. I must believe my master; else, I promise you,
I should be arguing still upon that doubt;
But let it rest. Now, Licio, to you.   55
Good master, take it not unkindly, pray,
That I have been thus pleasant with you both.

    Hortensio. You may go walk and give me leave a while;
My lessons make no music in three parts.

    Lucentio. Are you so formal, sir? [*Aside.*] Well, I must wait
And watch withal; for, but I be deceiv'd,
Our fine musician groweth amorous.

    Hortensio. Madam, before you touch the instrument
To learn the order of my fingering,
I must begin with rudiments of art   65
To teach you gamouth in a briefer sort,
More pleasant, pithy, and effectual,
Than hath been taught by any of my trade;
And there it is in writing, fairly drawn.

    Bianca. Why, I am past my gamouth long ago.   70

    Hortensio. Yet read the gamouth of Hortensio.

    Bianca.

    ' *"Gamouth" I am, the ground of all accord,*
      "A re," to plead Hortensio's passion;
    "B mi," Bianca, take him for thy lord,
      "C fa ut," that loves with all affection;   75
    "D sol re," one cliffe, two notes have I;
      "E la mi," show pity or I die.'

Call *you* this gamouth? tut, I like it not.
Old fashions please me best; I am not so nice
To change true rules for odd inventions.   80

            Enter a Messenger.

    Messenger. Mistress, your father prays you leave your books
And help to dress your sister's chamber up;
You know tomorrow is the wedding day.

    Bianca. Farewell, sweet masters both; I must be
gone.   [*Exeunt Bianca and Messenger.*]

    Lucentio. Faith, mistress, then I have no cause to stay.
                                [*Exit.*]

    Hortensio. But I have cause to pry into this pedant.
Methinks he looks as though he were in love.
Yet if thy thoughts, Bianca, be so humble

To cast thy wand'ring eyes on every stale,   90
Seize thee that list; if once I find thee ranging,
Hortensio will be quit with thee by changing.   *Exit.*

❧ Scene Second ❧

Enter Baptista, Gremio, Tranio, Katherina, Bianca [Lucentio,] and
others, attendants.

    Baptista. [To Tranio.] Signior Lucentio, this is the
'pointed day
That Katherine and Petruchio should be married,
And yet we hear not of our son-in-law.
What will be said? what mockery will it be   5
To want the bridegroom when the priest attends
To speak the ceremonial rites of marriage!
What says Lucentio to this shame of ours?

    Katherina. No shame but mine; I must, forsooth, be forc'd
To give my hand oppos'd against my heart   10
Unto a mad-brain rudesby, full of spleen,
Who woo'd in haste and means to wed at leisure.
I told you, I, he was a frantic fool,
Hiding his bitter jests in blunt behavior;
And to be noted for a merry man,   15
He'll woo a thousand, point the day of marriage,
Make friends, invite, and proclaim the banes;
Yet never means to wed where he hath woo'd.
Now must the world point at poor Katherine
And say, 'Lo! there is mad Petruchio's wife,   20
If it would please him come and marry her.'

    Tranio. Patience, good Katherine, and Baptista too.
Upon my life, Petruchio means but well,
Whatever fortune stays him from his word.
Though he be blunt, I know him passing wise;   25
Though he be merry, yet withal he's honest.

    Katherina. Would Katherine had never seen him though!
            Exit weeping [followed by Bianca and others].

    Baptista. Go, girl: I cannot blame thee now to weep,
For such an injury would vex a very saint,
Much more a shrew of thy impatient humor.   30

               Enter Biondello.

    Biondello. Master, master! news! and such old news
as you never heard of!

    Baptista. Is it new and old too? how may that be?

    Biondello. Why, is it not news to hear of Petruchio's
coming?   35

    Baptista. Is he come?

    Biondello. Why, no, sir.

    Baptista. What then?

    Biondello. He is coming.

    Baptista. When will he be here?

    Biondello. When he stands where I am and sees you there. 40

    Tranio. But, say, what to thine old news?

    Biondello. Why, Petruchio is coming, in a new hat
and an old jerkin; a pair of old breeches thrice turn'd;

47–49 *Cf. n.*   49 **Pedascule:** *pedant (synthetic Latin)*   51, 52 *Cf. n.*   53–57
Cf. n.   61 **but:** *unless*   66 **gamouth:** *gamut, i.e. the diatonic scale; Cf. n.*   72 **ground:**
beginning, basis   74 **B mi:** *F Beeme*   76 **cliffe:** *clef (key in music)*   79 **nice:** *capricious*   80 **to:** *as to*   **change:** *F charge*   **odd:** *F old*   81 **Messenger:** *F Nicke Cf. n.*

90 **stale:** *lure, decoy*   91 **Seize thee that list:** *let them take thee that will*   **ranging:** *roving*   92 **be quit:** *get even*   **by changing:** *by loving another*   5 **mockery:** *read 'mock'ry'*   11 **rudesby:** *bumpkin*   **spleen:** *impulsive temper*   15 **noted for:** *known as*   16 **point:** *appoint*   17 **banes:** *banns*   31 **old:** *rare; F omits Cf. n.*

a pair of boots that have been candle-cases, one 45
buckled, another lac'd; an old rusty sword tane
out of the town-armory, with a broken hilt, and
chapeless; with two broken points: his horse hipp'd
with an old mothy saddle and stirrups of no kindred;
besides, possessed with the glanders and like to mose 50
in the chine; troubled with the lampass, infected with
the fashions, full of windgalls, sped with spavins,
rayed with the yellows, past cure of the fives, stark
spoil'd with the staggers, begnawn with the bots,
swayed in the back, and shoulder-shotten; near- 55
legg'd before, and with a half-chekt bit, and a head-
stall of sheep's leather, which, being restrain'd to
keep him from stumbling, hath been often burst and
now repaired with knots; one girth six times piec'd,
and a woman's crupper of velure, which hath two 60
letters for her name fairly set down in studs, and
here and there piec'd with packthread.

    Baptista. Who comes with him?

    Biondello. O, sir! his lackey, for all the world caparison'd
like the horse; with a linen stock on one 65
leg and a kersey boot-hose on the other, gart'red
with a red and blue list; an old hat, and the 'humor
of forty fancies' prick'd in't for a feather: a monster,
a very monster in apparel, and not like a Christain
footboy or a gentleman's lackey. 70

    Tranio. 'Tis some odd humor pricks him to this fashion,
Yet oftentimes he goes but mean-apparell'd.

    Baptista. I am glad he's come, howsoere he comes.

    Biondello. Why, sir, he comes not.

    Baptista. Didst thou not say he comes? 75

    Biondello. Who? that Petruchio came?

    Baptista. Ay, that Petruchio came.

    Biondello. No, sir; I say his horse comes, with him
on his back.

    Baptista. Why, that's all one. 80

    Biondello.

    Nay, by Saint Jamy,
    I hold you a penny,
    A horse and a man
    Is more than one 85
    And yet not many.

          Enter Petruchio and Grumio.

    Petruchio. Come, where be these gallants? who is at home?

    Baptista. You are welcome, sir.

    Petruchio.   And yet I come not well.

    Baptista. And yet you halt not. 90

    Tranio.   Not so well apparell'd
As I wish you were.

    Petruchio. Were it better, I should rush in thus.
But where is Kate? where is my lovely bride?
How does my father? Gentles, methinks you frown. 95
And wherefore gaze this goodly company
As if they saw some wondrous monument,
Some comet, or unusual prodigy?

    Baptista. Why, sir, you know this is your wedding day.
First were we sad, fearing you would not come; 100
Now sadder that you come so unprovided.
Fie! doff this habit, shame to your estate,
An eyesore to our solemn festival.

    Tranio. And tell us what occasion of import
Hath all so long detain'd you from your wife 105
And sent you hither so unlike yourself?

    Petruchio. Tedious it were to tell and harsh to hear.
Sufficeth, I am come to keep my word
Though in some part enforced to digress;
Which, at more leisure, I will so excuse 110
As you shall well be satisfied with all.
But where is Kate? I stay too long from her;
The morning wears, 'tis time we were at church.

    Tranio. See not your bride in these unreverent robes.
Go to my chamber; put on clothes of mine. 115

    Petruchio. Not I, believe me; thus I'll visit her.

    Baptista. But thus, I trust, you will not marry her.

    Petruchio. Good sooth, even thus; therefore ha' done with
words:
To me she's married, not unto my clothes. 120
Could I repair what she will wear in me
As I can change these poor acouterments,
'Twere well for Kate and better for myself.
But what a fool am I to chat with you
When I should bid good morrow to my bride 125
And seal the title with a lovely kiss!

                   Exit [with Grumio].

    Tranio. He hath some meaning in his mad attire.
We will persuade him, be it possible,
To put on better ere he go to church.

    Baptista. I'll after him and see the event of this. 130

          Exit [with Gremio and Attendants].

    Tranio. But to her love concerneth us to add
Her father's liking; which to bring to pass,
As I before imparted to your worship,
I am to get a man—whatere he be
It skills not much, we'll fit him to our turn— 135
And he shall be Vincentio of Pisa,
And make assurance here in Padua,
Of greater sums than I have promised.
So shall you quietly enjoy your hope,
And marry sweet Bianca with consent. 140

    Lucentio. Were it not that my fellow schoolmaster

---

45 **candle-cases:** *i.e. worn out and used as receptacles for candle ends*   48 **chapeless:** *the chape is the metal tip at the end of the sheath* **points:** *garters* **hipp'd:** *lamed in the hip*   49 **of no kindred:** *not matching*   50 **glanders:** *swellings under the jaw*   50, 51 **mose in the chine:** *a dark discharge from the nostrils (a horse disease)*   51 **lampass:** *infected mouth (in horses)*   52 **fashions:** *farcins, i.e. small tumors on horse's body* **windgalls:** *swelling on fetlock joints* **spavins:** *a disease of the hock*   53 **rayed:** *befouled* **yellows:** *kind of jaundice* **fives:** *(a) vives, i.e. swellings at base of the ear*   53, 54 **stark spoil'd with the staggers:** *a prey to a kind of horse palsy*   54 **begnawn with the bots:** *gnawed by small intestinal worms*   55 **swayed:** *with rolling gate, due to back strain; F Waid* **shoulder-shotten:** *with dislocated shoulder*   55, 56 **near-legg'd before:** *with forefeet that knock together*   56 **half-chekt:** *'half-checked' or 'half-cheeked,' loose*   56, 57 **head-stall:** *part of the bridle surrounding the head* **sheep's leather:** *inferior leather, not pigskin as would become a person of consequence* **restrain'd:** *drawn tight*   59 **piec'd:** *patched*   60 **crupper:** *strap fastened to back of saddle and passing around the horse's tail* **velure:** *velvet*   64 **caparison'd:** *decked out*   65 **stock:** *stocking*   66 **kersey boot-hose:** *coarse woolen stocking worn under the riding boot*   67 **list:** *strip of cloth*   67, 68 **'humor of forty fancies':** *parcel of ribons tied together (instead of the conventional feather) Cf. n.*   70 **footboy:** *attendant in livery*   71 **pricks:** *drives*   83 **hold:** *bet*   87 **gallants:** *fine fellows*

91, 92 **Not ... were:** *set as one line in F*   95 **Gentles:** *gentlemen*   102 **habit:** *costume* **estate:** *social position*   109 **enforced to digress:** *compelled to deviate from my promise* (II.1.338–341)   118 **Good sooth:** *indeed* **even:** *read 'e'en'*   121 **wear:** *wear out*   126 **lovely:** *loving*   130 **event:** *outcome; read 'th'event'*   131 **But to her love:** *F. But, sir, Love*   135 **skills:** *matters*

Doth watch Bianca's steps so narrowly
'Twere good, methinks, to steal our marriage;
Which once perform'd, let all the world say no,
I'll keep mine own despite of all the world.   145
   Tranio. That by degrees we mean to look into
And watch our vantage in this business
We'll overreach the greybeard, Gremio,
The narrow-prying father, Minola,
The quaint musician, amorous Licio;   150
All for my master's sake, Lucentio.

              Enter Gremio.

Signior Gremio, came you from the church?
   Gremio. As willingly as ere I came from school.
   Tranio. And is the bride and bridegroom coming home?
   Gremio. A bridegroom say you? 'Tis a groom indeed,   155
A grumbling groom, and that the girl shall find.
   Tranio. Curster than she? why, 'tis impossible.
   Gremio. Why, he's a devil, a devil, a very fiend.
   Tranio. Why, she's a devil, a devil, the devil's dam.
   Gremio. Tut! she's a lamb, a dove, a fool to him.   160
I'll tell you, Sir Lucentio: when the priest
Should ask, if Katherine should be his wife,
'Ay, by goggs woones!' quoth he; and swore so loud
That, all amaz'd, the priest let fall the book
And, as he stoop'd again to take it up   165
This mad-brain'd bridegroom took him such a cuff
That down fell priest and book and book and priest.
'Now, take them up,' quoth he, 'if any list.'
   Tranio. What said the wench when he rose again?
   Gremio. Trembled and shook; for why, he stamp'd   170
and swore,
As if the vicar meant to cozen him.
But after many ceremonies done
He calls for wine: 'A health!' quoth he, as if
He had been aboard, carousing to his mates   175
After a storm; quaff'd off the muscadel
And threw the sops all in the sexton's face,
Having no other reason
But that his beard grew thin and hungerly,
And seem'd to ask him sops as he was drinking.   180
This done, he took the bride about the neck
And kiss'd her lips with such a clamorous smack
That at the parting all the church did echo,
And I, seeing this, came thence for very shame;
And after me, I know, the rout is coming.   185
Such a mad marriage never was before.
Hark, hark! I hear the minstrels play.

              Music plays.

   Enter Petruchio, Katherina, Bianca, Baptista, Hortensio
      [with Grumio and train].

   Petruchio. Gentlemen and friends, I thank you for your
pains.   190

I know you think to dine with me today
And have prepar'd great store of wedding cheer,
But so it is, my haste doth call me hence
And therefore here I mean to take my leave.
   Baptista. Is't possible you will away tonight?   195
   Petruchio. I must away today, before night come.
Make it no wonder; if you knew my business,
You would entreat me rather go than stay.
And, honest company, I thank you all,
That have beheld me give away myself   200
To this most patient, sweet, and virtuous wife.
Dine with my father, drink a health to me,
For I must hence; and farewell to you all.
   Tranio. Let us entreat you stay till after dinner.
   Petruchio. It may not be.   205
   Gremio.   Let me entreat you.
   Petruchio. It cannot be.
   Katherina.   Let me entreat you.
   Petruchio. I am content.
   Katherina.   Are you content to stay?   210
   Petruchio. I am content you shall entreat me stay,
But yet not stay, entreat me how you can.
   Katherina. Now if you love me, stay.
   Petruchio.   Grumio, my horse!
   Grumio. Ay, sir, they be ready; the oats have eaten the   215
horses.
   Katherina. Nay then,
Do what thou canst, I will not go today;
No, nor tomorrow, not till I please myself.
The door is open, sir, there lies your way;   220
You may be jogging whiles your boots are green;
For me, I'll not be gone till I please myself.
'Tis like you'll prove a jolly surly groom,
That take it on you at the first so roundly.
   Petruchio. O Kate! content thee; prethee, be not angry.   225
   Katherina. I will be angry; what hast thou to do?
Father, be quiet; he shall stay my leisure.
   Gremio. Ay, marry, sir, now it begins to work.
   Katherina. Gentlemen, forward to the bridal dinner:
I see a woman may be made a fool   230
If she had not a spirit to resist.
   Petruchio. They shall go forward, Kate, at thy command.
Obey the bride, you that attend on her;
Go to the feast, revel and domineer,
Carouse full measure to her maidenhead,   235
Be mad and merry, or go hang yourselves;
But for my bonny Kate, she must with me.
Nay, look not big, nor stamp, nor stare, nor fret;
I will be master of what is mine own.
She is my goods, my chattels; she is my house,   240
My household stuff, my field, my barn,
My horse, my ox, my ass, my anything;
And here she stands, touch her whoever dare;
I'll bring mine action on the proudest he
That stops my way in Padua. Grumio,   245
Draw forth thy weapon, we are beset with thieves;

---

143 **steal our marriage:** *elope* 147 **vantage:** *advantage* **business:** *three syllables here* 150 **quaint:** *artful* **amorous:** *read 'am'rous'* 155 **groom:** *i.e., rough as a serv-ingman* 159 **dam:** *the very mother of the devil; cf. I.3.109* 163 **goggs woones:** *corrup-tion of 'God's wounds,' a common oath* 166 **took:** *dealt* 168 **list:** *choose to* 170–187 *F sets these lines as prose* 172 **cozen:** *cheat (with invalid ceremony)* 175 **He had:** *read 'he'd'* **aboard:** *aboard ship* 176 **muscadel:** *sweet wine, commonly drunk at wed-dings* 177 **sops:** *dregs* 174 **hungerly:** *sparsely* 180 **sops:** *pieces of cake dipped in wine* 182 **clamorous:** *read 'clam'rous'* 185 **rout:** *mob*

197 **Make it no wonder:** *do not be surprised* 214 **horse:** *horses* 221 **green:** *fresh; proverbial for getting an early start* 223 **jolly:** *overbearing* 224 **roundly:** *unceremoni-ously* 225 **prethee:** *prithee, I pray thee;* 234 **domineer:** *carouse* 238 **big:** *pompous (addressed to the crowd, not Katherina)* 242 **anything:** *with allusion to the langauge of the Tenth Commandment* 244 **bring mine action:** *bring a law suit*

Rescue thy mistress, if thou be a man.
Fear not, sweet wench; they shall not touch thee, Kate:
I'll buckler thee against a million.

              Exeunt Petruchio, Katherina [and Grumio].
   Baptista. Nay, let them go, a couple of quiet ones.   250
   Gremio. Went they not quickly I should die with laughing.
   Tranio. Of all mad matches never was the like.
   Lucentio. Mistress, what's your opinion of your sister?
   Bianca. That being mad herself, she's madly mated.
   Gremio. I warrant him, Petruchio is Kated.   255
   Baptista. Neighbors and friends, though bride and
bridegroom wants
For to supply the places at the table,
You know there wants no junkets at the feast.
Lucentio, you shall supply the bridegroom's place,   260
And let Bianca take her sister's room.
   Tranio. Shall sweet Bianca practice how to bride it?
   Baptista. She shall, Lucentio. Come, gentlemen, let's go.

                                Exeunt.

❧ SCENE THIRD ❧

Enter Grumio.

   Grumio. Fie, fie, on all tired jades, on all mad
masters, and all foul ways! Was ever man so beaten?
was ever man so ray'd? was ever man so weary? I
am sent before to make a fire, and they are coming
after to warm them. Now were not I a little pot and   5
soon hot, my very lips might freeze to my teeth, my
tongue to the roof of my mouth, my heart in my
belly, ere I should come by a fire to thaw me; but I,
with blowing the fire, shall warm myself; for, considering the weather, a taller man than I will take   10
cold. Holla, ho! Curtis.

Enter Curtis.

   Curtis. Who is that calls so coldly?
   Grumio. A piece of ice; if thou doubt it, thou mayst
slide from my shoulder to my heel with no greater
a run but my head and my neck. A fire, good Curtis.   15
   Curtis. Is my master and his wife coming, Grumio?
   Grumio. O! ay, Curtis, ay; and therefore, fire, fire;
cast on no water.
   Curtis. Is she so hot a shrew as she's reported?
   Grumio. She was, good Curtis, before this frost but   20
thou knowest winter tames man, woman, and beast;
for it hath tam'd my old master, and my new mistress, and myself, fellow Curtis.
   Curtis. Away, you three-inch fool! I am no beast.
   Grumio. Am I but three inches? why, thy horn is a   25
foot; and so long am I at the least. But wilt thou
make a fire or shall I complain on thee to our mistress, whose hand—she being now at hand—thou
shalt soon feel, to thy cold comfort, for being slow

in thy hot office?   30
   Curtis. I prethee, good Grumio, tell me, how goes
the world?
   Grumio. A cold world, Curtis, in every office but
thine; and therefore, fire. Do thy duty, and have thy
duty, for my master and mistress are almost frozen   35
to death.
   Curtis. There's fire ready; and therefore, good
Grumio, the news?
   Grumio. Why, 'Jack, boy! ho, boy!' and as much
news as wilt thou.   40
   Curtis. Come, you are so full of cony-catching.
   Grumio. Why therefore fire, for I have caught
extreme cold. Where's the cook? Is supper ready, the
house trimm'd, rushes strew'd, cobwebs swept; the
servingmen in their new fustian, their white stock-   45
ings, and every officer his wedding-garment on?
Be the jacks fair within, the jills fair without, the
carpets laid and everything in order?
   Curtis. All ready; and therefore, I pray thee, news?
   Grumio. First, know, my horse is tired; my master   50
and mistress falne out.
   Curtis. How?
   Grumio. Out of their saddles into the dirt—and
thereby hangs a tale.
   Curtis. Let's ha't, good Grumio   55
   Grumio. Lend thine ear.
   Curtis. Here.
   Grumio. There.   *[Strikes him.]*
   Curtis. This 'tis to feel a tale, not to hear a tale.
   Grumio. And therefore 'tis called a sensible tale,   60
and this cuff was but to knock at your ear and be-
seech listening. Now I begin: *Imprimis*, we came down
a foul hill, my master riding behind my mistress—
   Curtis. Both of one horse?
   Grumio. What's that to thee?   65
   Curtis. Why, a horse.
   Grumio. Tell thou the tale; but hadst thou not
cross'd me thou shouldst have heard how her horse
fell and she under her horse; thou shouldst have
heard in how miry a place, how she was bemoil'd: 70
how he left her with the horse upon her; how he
beat me because her horse stumbled; how she waded
through the dirt to pluck him off me: how he swore;
how she pray'd, that never pray'd before; how I
cried; how the horses ran away; how her bridle was   75
burst; how I lost my crupper; with many things of
worthy memory, which now shall die in oblivion, and
thou return unexperienc'd to thy grave.
   Curtis. By this reck'ning he is more shrew than she.
   Grumio. Ay; and that, thou and the proudest of   80
you all shall find when he comes home. But what talk
I of this? Call forth Nathaniel, Joseph, Nicholas,
Philip, Walter, Sugarsop, and the rest; let their

---

249 buckler: *shield*   **257 wants:** *are lacking*   **259 junkets:** *sweetmeats*   **SCENE 3**
Cf. n.   **3 ray'd:** *dirtied*   **5 little pot:** *proverbial reference to small stature and quick*
temper   **10 taller:** *with play on the meaning 'finer'*   **15 run:** *take-off*   **24 I am no**
beast: *Curtis resents being called a fellow of Grumio who has just designated himself 'a*
beast'   **25 horn:** *i.e. as proverbially worn by a cuckold*

30 office: *duty, task*   **35 duty:** *due, reward (proverbial)*   **39 'Jack, boy! ho, boy!':** *from*
a song (catch) relating the 'news' that the cat is in the well   **41 cony-catching:** *evasive tricks,*
with play on the catch of l. 39   **44 trimm'd:** *made trim, orderly*   **rushes strew'd:** *i.e. on*
the floor   **45 fustian:** *coarse cotton cloth*   **their:** *F the*   **46 officer:** *servant*   **47 jacks:**
1) servingmen, 2) half-pint drinking vessels   **jills:** *1) maidservants, 2) smaller drinking vessels*
(gills)   **47, 48 carpets:** *table-covers*   **51 falne:** *fallen*   **60 sensible:** *1) making sense,*
2) capable of being felt   **62 Imprimis:** *first of all (Latin)*   **64 of:** *on*   **70 bemoil'd:**
covered with mud

heads be slickly comb'd, their blue coats brush'd and
their garters of an indifferent knit; let them curtsy   85
with their left legs and not presume to touch a hair
of my master's horsetail till they kiss their hands.
Are they all ready?

    Curtis. They are.

    Grumio. Call them forth.   90

    Curtis. Do you hear? ho! you must meet my master
to countenance my mistress.

    Grumio. Why, she hath a face of her own.

    Curtis. Who knows not that?

    Grumio. Thou, it seems, that calls for company to   95
countenance her.

    Curtis. I call them forth to credit her.

    Grumio. Why, she comes to borrow nothing of
them.

        Enter four or five Servingmen.

    Nathaniel. Welcome home, Grumio!   100

    Philip. How now, Grumio?

    Joseph. What, Grumio!

    Nicholas. Fellow Grumio!

    Nathaniel. How now, old lad!

    Grumio. Welcome, you; how now, you; what, you;   105
fellow, you; and thus much for greeting. Now, my
spruce companions, is all ready and all things neat?

    Nathaniel. All things is ready. How near is our
master?

    Grumio. E'en at hand, alighted by this; and there-   110
fore be not—Cock's passion, silence! I hear my
master.

        Enter Petruchio and Kate.

    Petruchio. Where be these knaves? What! no man at door
To hold my stirrup nor to take my horse?
Where is Nathaniel, Gregory, Philip?—   115

    All Servingmen. Here, here, sir; here, sir.

    Petruchio. Here, sir! here, sir! here, sir! here, sir!
You loggerheaded and unpolish'd grooms!
What, no attendance? no regard? no duty?
Where is the foolish knave I sent before?   120

    Grumio. Here, sir; as foolish as I was before.

    Petruchio. You peasant swain! you whoreson malt-
horse drudge!
Did I not bid thee meet me in the park
And bring along these rascal knaves with thee.   125

    Grumio. Nathaniel's coat, sir, was not fully made
And Gabrel's pumps were all unpink'd i' th' heel;
There was no link to color Peter's hat
And Walter's dagger was not come from sheathing;
There were none fine but Adam, Rafe, and Gregory;   130
The rest were ragged, old, and beggarly.
Yet, as they are, here are they come to meet you.

    Petruchio. Go, rascals, go, and fetch my supper in.

                             Exeunt Servants.
'Where is the life that late I led?'
Where are those—? Sit down, Kate, and welcome.   135
    Food, food, food, food!

        Enter Servants with supper.

Why, when, I say?—Nay, good sweet Kate, be merry.—
Off with my boots, you rogues! you villains! When?
'It was the friar of orders grey,
As he forth walked on his way':   140
Out, you rogue! you pluck my foot awry;
Take that, and mend the plucking of the other.

                            [Strikes him.]

Be merry, Kate. Some water, here; what, ho!

        Enter one with water.

Where's my spaniel Troilus? Sirrah, get you hence
And bid my cousin Ferdinand come hither: *[Exit Servant.]*
One, Kate, that you must kiss and be acquainted with.
Where are my slippers? Shall I have some water?
Come, Kate, and wash, and welcome heartily.—
You whoreson villain! will you let it fall?   *[Strikes him.]*

    Katherina. Patience, I pray you; 'twas a fault unwilling.   150

    Petruchio. A whoreson, beetle-headed, flap-ear'd knave!
Come, Kate, sit down; I know you have a stomach.
Will you give thanks, sweet Kate, or else shall I?—
What's this? mutton?

    1. Servingman.   Ay.   155

    Petruchio.   Who brought it?

    Peter.   I.

    Petruchio. 'Tis burnt; and so is all the meat.
What dogs are these! Where is the rascal cook?
How durst you, villains, bring it from the dresser,   160
And serve it thus to me that love it not?

        [Throws the meat about the stage.]
There, take it to you, trenchers, cups, and all.
You heedless joltheads and unmanner'd slaves!
What, do you grumble? I'll be with you straight.

    Katherina. I pray you, husband, be not so disquiet: 165
The meat was well if you were so contented.

    Petruchio. I tell thee, Kate, 'twas burnt and dried away
And I expressly am forbid to touch it,
For it engenders choler, planteth anger,
And better 'twere that both of us did fast,   170
Since, of ourselves, ourselves are choleric,
Than feed it with such overroasted flesh.
Be patient; tomorrow't shall be mended,
And for this night we'll fast for company.
Come, I will bring thee to thy bridal chamber.   *Exeunt.*

        Enter Servants severally.

    Nathaniel. Peter, didst ever see the like?

    Peter. He kills her in her own humor.

        Enter Curtis, a Servant.

---

84 slickly: *smoothly*   **85 indifferent knit:** *moderately handsome Cf. n.*   **92 countenance:** *do honor to*   **96 countenance:** *give a face to*   **97 credit:** *Curtis means 'pay respect to,' Grumio plays with the other meaning 'extend credit'*   **111 Cock's:** *corruption of 'God's'*   **118 loggerheaded:** *blockheaded*   **122 peasant swain:** *country lout* **whoreson:** *contemptible* **malt-horse drudge:** *i.e. slow and clumsy as the horse used to grind malt in a brewery*   **127 unpink'd:** *with ornamental embroidery frayed or missing*   **128 link:** *pitchtorch, used to give old hats a new blacking*   **129 sheathing:** *having sheath made or repaired*   **130 fine:** *well turned out*

134 'Where . . . led': *line of an old song; cf. 2 Henry IV, V.3.131*   **136 Food . . . food:** *F Soud . . . soud Cf. n.*   **138 When:** *exclamation of impatience; cf. Richard II, I.1.163*   **139, 140 'It . . . way':** *fragment of an old song*   **152 stomach:** *1) appetite, 2) temper*   **160 dresser:** *sideboard*   **162 trenchers:** *wooden plates*   **164 with you:** *even with you* **straight:** *immediately*   **169 choler:** *the humor that makes one short-tempered, choleric*   **171 for:** *in*   **177 kills . . . humor:** *subdues her by employing her own kind of bad temper* **SD Enter Curtis:** *F I.173*

Grumio. Where is he?

Curtis. In her chamber, making a sermon of continency
to her: *180*
And rails and swears and rates, that she, poor soul,
Knows not which way to stand, to look, to speak,
And sits as one new-risen from a dream.
Away, away! for he is coming hither.   *[Exeunt.]*

Enter Petruchio.

Petruchio. Thus have I politicly begun my reign   *185*
And 'tis my hope to end successfully.
My falcon now is sharp and passing empty
And till she stoop she must not be full gorg'd,
For then she never looks upon her lure.
Another way I have to man my haggard,   *190*
To make her come and know her keeper's call;
That is, to watch her as we watch these kites
That bate and beat and will not be obedient.
She eat no meat today, nor none shall eat;
Last night she slept not, nor tonight she shall not: *195*
As with the meat, some undeserved fault
I'll find about the making of the bed
And here I'll fling the pillow, there the bolster,
This way the coverlet, another way the sheets.
Ay, and amid this hurly I intend   *200*
That all is done in reverend care of her,
And in conclusion she shall watch all night;
And if she chance to nod I'll rail and brawl
And with the clamor keep her still awake.
This is a way to kill a wife with kindness,   *205*
And thus I'll curb her mad and headstrong humor.
He that knows better how to tame a shrew,
Now let him speak: 'tis charity to shrew.   *Exit.*

❧ Scene Fourth ❧

Enter Tranio and Hortensio

Tranio. Is't possible, friend Licio, that Mistress Bianca
Doth fancy any other but Lucentio?
I tell you, sir, she bears me fair in hand.

Hortensio. Sir, to satisfy you in what I have said,
Stand by and mark the manner of his teaching.   *5*
                                        [They stand aside.]

Enter Bianca [and Lucentio].

Lucentio. Now mistress, profit you in what you read?
Bianca. What, master, read you? first resolve me that.
Lucentio. I read that I profess, the Art of Love.
Bianca. And may you prove, sir, master of your art!
Lucentio. While you, sweet dear, prove mistress of my   *10*
heart.

Hortensio. Quick proceeders, marry! Now, tell me, I pray,
You that durst swear that your mistress Bianca
Lov'd none in the world so well as Lucentio.
Tranio. O despiteful love! unconstant womankind!   *15*
I tell thee, Licio, this is wonderful.
Hortensio. Mistake no more: I am not Licio,
Nor a musician, as I seem to be;
But one that scorns to live in this disguise,
For such a one as leaves a gentleman   *20*
And makes a god of such a cullion.
Know, sir, that I am call'd Hortensio.
Tranio. Signior Hortensio, I have often heard
Of your entire affection to Bianca,
And since mine eyes are witness of her lightness   *25*
I will with you, if you be so contented,
Forswear Bianca and her love forever.
Hortensio. See, how they kiss and court! Signior Lucentio,
Here is my hand and here I firmly vow
Never to woo her more, but do forswear her,   *30*
As one unworthy all the former favors
That I have fondly flatter'd her withal.
Tranio. And here I take the like unfeigned oath,
Never to marry with her though she would entreat.
Fie on her! see how beastly she doth court him.   *35*
Hortensio. Would all the world but he had quite
forsworn!
For me, that I may surely keep mine oath,
I will be married to a wealthy widow
Ere three days pass, which hath as long lov'd me   *40*
As I have lov'd this proud disdainful haggard.
And so farewell, Signior Lucentio.
Kindness in women, not their beauteous looks,
Shall win my love; and so I take my leave
In resolution as I swore before.   *[Exit]*
Tranio. Mistress Bianca, bless you with such grace
As longeth to a lover's blessed case!
Nay, I have tane your napping, gentle love,
And have forsworn you with Hortensio.
Bianca. Tranio, you jest. But have you both forsworn me? *50*
Tranio. Mistress, we have.
Lucentio.   Then we are rid of Licio.
Tranio. I' faith, he'll have a lusty widow now,
That shall be woo'd and wedded in a day.
Bianca. God give him joy!   *55*
Tranio. Ay, and he'll tame her.
Bianca.   He says so, Tranio.
Tranio. Faith, he is gone unto the taming-school.
Bianca. The taming-school! what, is there such a place?
Tranio. Ay, mistress, and Petruchio is the master,   *60*
That teacheth tricks eleven and twenty long
To tame a shrew and charm her chattering tongue.

Enter Biondello.

Biondello. O master, master! I have watch'd so long
That I'm dog-weary, but at last I spied
An ancient angel coming down the hill   *65*

179–183 F sets these lines as prose   **181 rates:** *berates* **that:** *so that*   **187 sharp ... empty:** *fasting and hence keen for prey*   **188 stoop:** *1) swoop (falconry), 2) bow to author-ity* **full gorg'd:** *well fed*   **189 then:** *i.e. when well fed* **lure:** *decoy used to recall a falcon* Cf. n.   **190 man:** *tame* **haggard:** *wild female hawk*   **192 watch:** *to keep from sleep* **kites:** *scavenging birds*   **193 bate and beat:** *flap and flutter, words similarly pro-nounced*   **194 eat:** *ate*   **195 Last night ... shall not:** Cf. n.   **200 hurly:** *commo-tion* **intend:** *pretend*   **202 watch:** *stay awake*   **205 kill a wife with kindness:* Cf. n.   **207, 208 shrew ... shrew:** *both pronounced with -ow*   **3 bears me fair in hand:** *leads me on*   **4, 5** F assigns these lines to Lucentio   **6** F assigns this line to Horten-sio   **7 resolve:** *answer*   **8** F assigns this line to Hortensio   **8–11** Cf. n.

12 marry: *a mild oath, originally to Mary the Virgin* ＊   **14 none:** *F me*   **19 scorns:** *F scorne*   **21 cullion:** *(three syllables here) low creature*   **32 her:** *F them*   **47 longeth:* belongeth*   **48 tane:** *taken*   **56 and:** *if*   **61 tricks eleven and twenty long:* Cf. n.   **65 ancient angel:** *fellow of the old stamp (angel, here 'coin')*

Will serve the turn.
 Tranio.   What is he, Biondello?
 Biondello. Master, a marcantant or a pedant—
I know not what; but formal is apparel,
In gait and countenance surely like a father.   *70*
 Lucentio. And what of him, Tranio?
 Tranio. If he be credulous and trust my tale
I'll make him glad to seem Vincentio,
And give assurance to Baptista Minola
As if he were the right Vincentio.   *75*
Take in your love and then let me alone.

     [*Exeunt Lucentio and Bianca.*]

    Enter a Pedant.

 Pedant. God save you, sir!
 Tranio.   And you, sir! you are welcome.
Travel you far on, or are you at the farthest?
 Pedant. Sir, at the farthest for a week or two, *80*
But then up farther and as far as Rome;
And so to Tripoli if God lend me life.
 Tranio. What countryman, I pray?
 Pedant.   Of Mantua.
 Tranio. Of Mantua, sir! marry, God forbid! *85*
And come to Padua, careless of your life?
 Pedant. My life, sir! how, I pray? for that goes hard.
 Tranio. 'Tis death for anyone in Mantua
To come to Padua. Know you not the cause?
Your ships are stay'd at Venice and the duke— *90*
For private quarrel 'twixt your duke and him—
Hath publish'd and proclaim'd it openly.
'Tis marvel, but that you are but newly come,
You might have heard it else proclaim'd about.
 Pedant. Alas, sir! it is worse for me than so, *95*
For I have bills for money by exchange
From Florence and must here deliver them.
 Tranio. Well, sir, to do you courtesy,
This will I do and this I will advise you:
First, tell me, have you ever been at Pisa? *100*
 Pedant. Ay, sir, in Pisa have I often bin;
Pisa, renowned for grave citizens.
 Tranio. Among them, know you one Vincentio?
 Pedant. I know him not but I have heard of him;
A merchant of incomparable wealth. *105*
 Tranio. He is my father, sir; and, sooth to say,
In count'nance somewhat doth resemble you.
 Biondello. [Aside.] As much as an apple doth an
oyster, and all one.
 Tranio. To save your life in this extremity *110*
This favor will I do for his sake,
And think it not the worst of all your fortunes
That you are like to Sir Vincentio.
His name and credit shall you undertake
And in my house you shall be friendly lodg'd. *115*
Look that you take upon you as you should!
You understand me, sir; so shall you stay
Till you have done your business in the city.
If this be court'sy, sir, accept of it.

 Pedant. O sir, I do; and will repute you ever *120*
The patron of my life and liberty.
 Tranio. Then go with me to make the matter good.
This, by the way, I let you understand:
My father is here look'd for every day
To pass assurance of a dower in marriage *125*
'Twixt me and one Baptista's daughter here.
In all these circumstances I'll instruct you.
Go with me to clothe you as becomes you. *Exeunt.*

ACT FOURTH ❧ Scene First

    Enter Katherina and Grumio.

 Grumio. No, no, forsooth; I dare not for my life.
 Katherina. The more my wrong, the more his spite appears.
What, did he marry me to famish me?
Beggars, that come unto my father's door,
Upon entreaty have a present alms; *5*
If not, elsewhere they meet with charity.
But I, who never knew how to entreat
Nor never needed that I should entreat,
Am starv'd for meat, giddy for lack of sleep,
With oaths kept waking and with brawling fed. *10*
And that which spites me more than all these wants,
He does it under name of perfect love,
As who should say, if I should sleep or eat
'Twere deadly sickness or else present death.
I prithee go and get me some repast; *15*
I care not what, so it be wholesome food.
 Grumio. What say you to a neat's foot?
 Katherina. 'Tis passing good: I prithee let me have it.
 Grumio. I fear it is too choleric a meat.
How say you to a fat tripe finely broil'd? *20*
 Katherina. I like it well: good Grumio, fetch it me.
 Grumio. I cannot tell; I fear 'tis choleric.
What say you to a piece of beef and mustard?
 Katherina. A dish that I do love to feed upon.
 Grumio. Ay, but the mustard is too hot a little. *25*
 Katherina. Why then, the beef, and let the mustard rest.
 Grumio. Nay then, I will not; you shall have the mustard
Or else you get no beef of Grumio.
 Katherina. Then both or one, or anything thou wilt.
 Grumio. Why then, the mustard without the beef. *30*
 Katherina. Go, get thee gone, thou false deluding
slave,   *Beats him.*
That feed'st me with the very name of meat.
Sorrow on thee and all the pack of you
That triumph thus upon my misery! *35*
Go, get thee gone, I say.

    Enter Petruchio, and Hortensio with meat.

 Petruchio. How fares my Kate? What, sweeting, all amort?
 Hortensio. Mistress, what cheer?
 Katherina.   Faith, as cold as can be.

---

66 Will serve: *who will serve* **67 What:** *who* **68 marcantant:** *Biondello's pronunciation of Italian mercantante (merchant)* **70 countenance:** *read 'count'nance'* **76 Take in:** *F Par. Take me* **87 goes hard:** *is serious* **90 stay'd:** *detained* **109 all one:** *no matter* **114 undertake:** *assume* **116 take upon you:** *comport yourself*

125 pass: *convey* (legal term) **127 circumstances:** *details* **2 more:** *greater* **5 present:** *immediate* **13 As who should say:** *as if to say* **17 neat:** *ox or calf* **19 choleric:** *productive of temper; cf. III.3.169* **37 all amort:** *out of spirits*

Petruchio. Pluck up thy spirits; look cheerfully upon me.   *40*
Here, love; thou seest how diligent I am
To dress thy meat myself and bring it thee.
I am sure, sweet Kate, this kindness merits thanks.
What! not a word? Nay then, thou lov'st it not
And all my pains is sorted to no proof.   *45*
Here, take away this dish.
     Katherina.   I pray you, let it stand.
     Petruchio. The poorest service is repaid with thanks
And so shall mine, before you touch the meat.
     Katherina. I thank you, sir.   *50*
     Hortensio. Signior Petruchio, fie! you are to blame.
Come, Mistress Kate, I'll bear you company.
     Petruchio. Eat it up all, Hortensio, if thou lov'st me.
Much good do it unto thy gentle heart!
Kate, eat apace. And now, my honey love,   *55*
Will we return unto thy father's house
And revel it as bravely as the best,
With silken coats and caps and golden rings,
With ruffs and cuffs and fardingales and things;
With scarfs and fans and double change of brav'ry,   *60*
With amber bracelets, beads, and all this knav'ry.
What! hast thou din'd? The tailor stays thy leisure
To deck thy body with his ruffling treasure.

               Enter Tailor.

Come, tailor, let us see these ornaments;
Lay forth the gown.—   *65*

             Enter Haberdasher.

                     What news with you, sir?
     Haberdasher. Here is the cap your worship did bespeak.
     Petruchio. Why, this was molded on a porringer;
A velvet dish: fie, fie! 'tis lewd and filthy:
Why, 'tis a cockle or a walnut shell,   *70*
A knack, a toy, a trick, a baby's cap—
Away with it! come, let me have a bigger.
     Katherina. I'll have no bigger, this doth fit the time
And gentlewomen wear such caps as these.
     Petruchio. When you are gentle you shall have one too—   *75*
And not till then.
     Hortensio. [*Aside.*] That will not be in haste.
     Katherina. Why, sir, I trust I may have leave to speak,
And speak I will; I am no child, no babe.
Your betters have endur'd me say my mind   *80*
And if you cannot, best you stop your ears.
My tongue will tell the anger of my heart
Or else my heart, concealing it, will break,
And rather than it shall I will be free
Even to the uttermost, as I please, in words.   *85*
     Petruchio. Why, thou sayst true; it is a paltry cap,
A custard-coffin, a bauble, a silken pie.
I love thee well in that thou lik'st it not.
     Katherina. Love me or love me not, I like the cap

And it I will have or I will have none.   *Exit Haberdasher.*   *90*
     Petruchio. Thy gown? why, ay: come, tailor, let us see't.
O mercy, God! what masquing stuff is here?
What's this? a sleeve? 'tis like a demi-cannon.
What! up and down, carv'd like an apple tart?
Here's snip and nip and cut and slish and slash,   *95*
Like to a censer in a barber's shop.
Why, what, a devil's name, tailor, call'st thou this?
     Hortensio. [*Aside.*] I see, she's like to have neither cap
nor gown.
     Tailor. You bid me make it orderly and well,   *100*
According to the fashion and the time.
     Petruchio. Marry, and did; but if you be rememb'red,
I did not bid you mar it to the time.
Go, hop me over every kennel home,
For you shall hop without my custom, sir.   *105*
I'll none of it: hence! make your best of it.
     Katherina. I never saw a better-fashion'd gown,
More quaint, more pleasing, nor more commendable.
Belike you mean to make a puppet of me.
     Petruchio. Why, true; he means to make a puppet of   *110*
thee.
     Tailor. She says your worship means to make a puppet
of her.
     Petruchio. O monstrous arrogance!
Thou liest, thou thread, thou thimble,   *115*
Thou yard, three-quarters, half yard, quarter, nail!
Thou flea, thou nit, thou winter-cricket thou!
Brav'd in mine own house with a skein of thread!
Away! thou rag, thou quantity, thou remnant,
Or I shall so bemete thee with thy yard   *120*
As thou shalt think on prating whilst thou liv'st!
I tell thee, I, that thou hast marr'd her gown.
     Tailor. Your worship is deceiv'd; the gown is made
Just as my master had direction.
Grumio gave order how it should be done.   *125*
     Grumio. I gave him no order; I gave him the stuff.
     Tailor. But how did you desire it should be made?
     Grumio. Marry, sir, with needle and thread.
     Tailor. But did you not request to have it cut?
     Grumio. Thou hast fac'd many things.   *130*
     Tailor. I have.
     Grumio. Face not me; thou hast brav'd many men; brave
not me; I will neither be fac'd nor brav'd. I say unto thee, I
bid thy master cut out the gown but I did not bid him cut
it to pieces; *ergo*, thou liest.   *135*
     Tailor. Why, here is the note of the fashion to
testify.
     Petruchio. Read it.
     Grumio. The note lies in's throat if he say I said so.
     Tailor. 'Imprimis, a loose-bodied gown.'   *140*
     Grumio. Master, if ever I said loose-bodied gown,
sew me in the skirts of it and beat me to death with
a bottom of brown thread. I said, a gown.

92 masquing: *fit only for masquerade*   **93 demi-cannon:** *kind of large cannon*   **96
censer:** *brazier with perforated cover, used by barbers to burn perfumes and thus sweeten air of
the shop*   **98 to have:** *read 't'have'*   **102 did:** *I did*   **be remembʹred:** *remember*   **104
kennel:** *gutter*   **108 quaint:** *pretty*   **116 nail:** *measure of two and a quarter inches*   **117
nit:** *egg of a louse*   **118 Brav'd:** *defied*   **with:** *by*   **119 quantity:** *small fragment*   **120
bemete:** *measure*   **121 think on prating:** *remember your idle talk*   **130 fac'd:**
trimmed   **132 face:** *affront*   **brav'd:** *dressed in finery*   **brave:** *defy*   **135 ergo:** *therefore*
(Latin)   **143 bottom:** *ball*

45 sorted to no proof: *attended by no corresponding result; fruitless*   **57 bravely:** *finely
dressed*   **59 fardingales:** *hoopskirts*   **60 brav'ry:** *finery*   **61 knav'ry:** *coquettish adornment*   **62 stays:** *awaits*   **63 ruffling:** *ornamented with ruffles*   **SD Haberdasher:** *F
Fel.*   **67 bespeak:** *order*   **69 lewd:** *vile*   **70 cockle:** *sea shell*   **71 knack:** *knick-
knack*   **trick:** *trifle*   **73 fit the time:** *suit the present fashion*   **87 custard-coffin:** *raised
crust of pastry*   **pie:** *shaped like a meat pie, i.e. circular and five or six inches high*

Petruchio. Proceed.

Tailor. 'With a small compass'd cape.'   *145*

Grumio. I confess the cape.

Tailor. 'With a trunk sleeve.'

Grumio. I confess two sleeves.

Tailor. 'The sleeves curiously cut.'

Petruchio. Ay, there's the villainy.   *150*

Grumio. Error i' th' bill, sir; error i' th' bill. I
commanded the sleeves should be cut out and sewed
up again and that I'll prove upon thee, though thy
little finger be armed in a thimble.

Tailor. This is true that I say; and I had thee in   *155*
place where, thou shouldst know it.

Grumio. I am for thee straight. Take thou the bill,
give me thy mete-yard, and spare not me.

Hortensio. God-a-mercy, Grumio! then he shall have
no odds.   *160*

Petruchio. Well, sir, in brief, the gown is not for me.

Grumio. You are i' th' right, sir; 'tis for my mistress.

Petruchio. Go, take it up unto thy master's use.

Grumio. Villain, not for thy life! take up my mistress' gown for thy master's use!   *165*

Petruchio. Why sir, what's your conceit in that?

Grumio. O, sir, the conceit is deeper than you think for.
Take up my mistress' gown to his master's use!
O, fie, fie, fie!

Petruchio. [*Aside.*] Hortensio, say thou wilt see the tailor *170*
paid.
Go take it hence; be gone and say no more.

Hortensio. Tailor, I'll pay thee for thy gown tomorrow;
Take no unkindness of his hasty words.
Away! I say; commend me to thy master.   *Exit Tailor.* *175*

Petruchio. Well, come, my Kate; we will unto your father's,
Even in these honest mean habiliments.
Our purses shall be proud, our garments poor,
For 'tis the mind that makes the body rich;
And as the sun breaks through the darkest clouds   *180*
So honor peereth in the meanest habit.
What, is the jay more precious than the lark
Because his feathers are more beautiful?
Or is the adder better than the eel
Because his painted skin contents the eye?   *185*
O no, good Kate; neither art thou the worse
For this poor furniture and mean array.
If thou account'st it shame, lay it on me.
And therefore frolic; we will hence forthwith
To feast and sport us at thy father's house.   *190*
Go call my men, and let us straight to him;
And bring our horses unto Long-lane end;
There will we mount, and thither walk on foot.
Let's see; I think 'tis now some seven o'clock
And well we may come there by dinnertime.   *195*

Katherina. I dare assure you, sir, 'tis almost two
And 'twill be suppertime ere you come there.

Petruchio. It shall be seven ere I go to horse.
Look, what I speak or do or think to do,

You are still crossing it. Sirs, let' alone: *200*
I will not go today; and ere I do,
It shall be what o'clock I say it is.

Hortensio. Why, so this gallant will command the sun.

                                                    Exeunt.

❧ Scene Second ❧

Enter Tranio, and the Pedant dressed like Vincentio.

Tranio. Sir, this is the house: please it you that I call?

Pedant. Ay, what else? and, but I be deceived,
Signior Baptista may remember me,
Near twenty years ago, in Genoa,
Where we were lodgers at the Pegasus.   *5*

Tranio. 'Tis well; and hold your own in any case
With such austerity as longeth to a father.

Pedant. I warrant you. But sir, here comes your boy;
'Twere good he were school'd.

Enter Biondello.

Tranio. Fear you not him. Sirrah Biondello,   *10*
Now do your duty throughly, I advise you:
Imagine 'twere the right Vincentio.

Biondello. Tut! fear not me.

Tranio. But hast thou done thy errand to Baptista?

Biondello. I told him that your father was at Venice,   *15*
And that you look'd for him this day in Padua.

Tranio. Th' art a tall fellow: hold thee that to drink.
Here comes Baptista. Set your countenance, sir.

Enter Baptista and Lucentio.

Signior Baptista, you are happily met.
[*To the Pedant.*] Sir, this is the gentleman I told you of. *20*
I pray you, stand good father to me now,
Give me Bianca for my patrimony.

Pedant. Soft, son!
Sir, by your leave: having come to Padua
To gather in some debts, my son Lucentio   *25*
Made me acquainted with a weighty cause
Of love between your daughter and himself.
And—for the good report I hear of you,
And for the love he beareth to your daughter,
And she to him—to stay him not too long,   *30*
I am content, in a good father's care,
To have him match'd; and if you please to like
No worse than I, upon some agreement
Me shall you find ready and willing
With one consent to have her so bestow'd;   *35*
For curious I cannot be with you,
Signior Baptista, of whom I hear so well.

Baptista. Sir, pardon me in what I have to say:
Your plainness and your shortness please me well.
Right true it is, your son Lucentio here   *40*
Doth love my daughter and she loveth him—
Or both dissemble deeply their affections—

---

145 **compass'd:** *i.e. with the edge forming a circle*   147 **trunk sleeve:** *very full sleeve; Cf.
l. 93 above*   149 **curiously:** *carefully*   155 **and:** *and if*   155, 156 **in place where:** *in
a suitable place*   157 **bill:** *with pun on usual meaning and the sense of 'halberd'*   158
mete-yard: *yardstick*   163 **unto thy master's use:** *i.e. for whatever purpose he can find
for it*   166 **conceit:** *meaning*   181 **peereth:** *appears* **habit:** *dress*   187 **furniture:**
adornment, costume   188 **account'st:** *F accountedst*

1 **Sir:** *F Sirs* **this is:** *read 'this'*   5 *F assigns this line to Tranio* **Pegasus:** *common name
for an inn*   7 **longeth:** *belongs*   11 **throughly:** *thoroughly*   17 **tall:** *clever* **hold:** *take
(Tranio tips him)*   18 **countenance:** *read 'count'nance'* **SD** *F adds Pedant booted and
bare-headed Cf. n.*   20 **this is:** *read 'this'*   23, 4 **Soft . . . Padua:** *F sets as one line*   36
curious: *cautious*

And therefore, if you say no more than this,
That like a father you will deal with him
And pass my daughter a sufficient dower, 45
The match is made; and all is done;
Your son shall have my daughter with consent.

   Tranio. I thank you, sir. Where then, do you know best
We be affied and such assurance tane
As shall with either part's agreement stand? 50

   Baptista. Not in my house, Lucentio; for, you know,
Pitchers have ears, and I have many servants.
Besides, old Gremio is heark'ning still,
And happily we might be interrupted.

   Tranio. Then at my lodging and it like you: 55
There doth my father lie, and there this night
We'll pass the business privately and well.
Send for your daughter by your servant here;
My boy shall fetch the scrivener presently.
The worst is this, that, at so slender warning, 60
You are like to have a thin and slender pittance.

   Baptista. It likes me well. Cambio, hie you home
And bid Bianca make her ready straight;
And, if you will, tell what hath happened:
Lucentio's father is arriv'd in Padua, 65
And how she's like to be Lucentio's wife.

   Lucentio. I pray the gods she may with all my heart!

                                   Exit Lucentio.

   Tranio. Dally not with the gods, but get thee gone.
Signior Baptista, shall I lead the way? 70
Welcome! one mess is like to be your cheer.
Come, sir; we will better it in Pisa.

   Baptista. I follow you.   *Exeunt.*

    Enter Lucentio and Biondello.

   Biondello. Cambio!

   Lucentio. What sayst thou, Biondello? 75

   Biondello. You saw my master wink and laugh upon
you?

   Lucentio. Biondello, what of that?

   Biondello. Faith, nothing; but has left me here behind to expound the meaning or moral of his signs 80
and tokens.

   Lucentio. I pray thee, moralize them.

   Biondello. Then thus. Baptista is safe, talking with
the deceiving father of a deceitful son.

   Lucentio. And what of him? 85

   Biondello. His daughter is to be brought by you to
the supper.

   Lucentio. And then?

   Biondello. The old priest at Saint Luke's church is
at your command at all hours. 90

   Lucentio. And what of all this?

   Biondello. I cannot tell, except they are busied
about a counterfeit assurance: take you assurance
of her, *cum previlegio ad impremendum solem.* To th'
church! take the priest, clark, and some sufficient 95

49 **affied:** *formally betrothed*   53 **heark'ning still:** *always listening*   54 **happily:** *per-haps*   55 **and it like:** *if it please*   56 **lie:** *lodge*   57 **pass:** *transact*   59 **scrivener:** *notary; read 'scriv'ner'*   61 **pittance:** *meal*   62 **likes:** *pleases*   66 **like:** *likely*   67 *F assigns this line to Biondello Cf. n.*   68 *F adds SD Enter Peter Cf. n.*   71 **mess:** *dish* **cheer:** *entertainment*   79 **has:** *he has*   82 **moralize:** *explain*   92 **except:** *F ex-pect*   93 **assurance:** *betrothal*   94 **cum . . . solem:** *Cf. n.*

honest witnesses.
If this be not that you look for, I have no more to say,
But bid Bianca farewell forever and a day.

   Lucentio. Hear'st thou, Biondello?

   Biondello. I cannot tarry: I knew a wench married 100
in an afternoon as she went to the garden for parsley
to stuff a rabbit; and so may you, sir; and so, adieu,
sir. My master hath appointed me to go to Saint
Luke's, to bid the priest be ready to come against
you come with your appendix.   *Exit.*

   Lucentio. I may, and will, if she be so contented.
She will be pleas'd; then wherefore should I doubt?
Hap what hap may, I'll roundly go about her;
It shall go hard if Cambio go without her.   *Exit.*

❧ Scene Third ❧

   Enter Petruchio, Katherina, Hortensio [with Servants.]

   Petruchio. Come on, a God's name; once more toward
our father's.
Good Lord, how bright and goodly shines the moon!

   Katherina. The moon! the sun: it is not moonlight now.

   Petruchio. I say it is the moon that shines so bright. 5

   Katherina. I know it is the sun that shines so bright.

   Petruchio. Now, by my mother's son, and that's myself,
It shall be moon or star or what I list,
Or ere I journey to your father's house.
Go on and fetch our horses back again. 10
Evermore cross'd and cross'd; nothing but cross'd!

   Hortensio. Say as he says or we shall never go.

   Katherina. Forward, I pray, since we have come so far,
And be it moon or sun or what you please.
And if you please to call it a rush-candle, 15
Henceforth I vow it shall be so for me.

   Petruchio. I say it is the moon.

   Katherina.   I know it is the moon.

   Petruchio. Nay, then you lie; it is the blessed sun.

   Katherina. Then God be bless'd, it is the blessed sun! 20
But sun it is not when you say it is not,
And the moon changes even as your mind.
What you will have it nam'd, even that it is;
And so it shall be so for Katherine.

   Hortensio. Petruchio, go thy ways; the field is won. 25

   Petruchio. Well, forward, forward! thus the bowl should run
And not unluckily against the bias.
But soft! company is coming here.

    Enter Vincentio.

[*To Vincentio.*] Good morrow, gentle mistress: where away?
Tell me, sweet Kate, and tell me truly too, 30
Hast thou beheld a fresher gentlewoman?
Such war of white and red within her cheeks!
What stars do spangle heaven with such beauty
As those two eyes become that heavenly face?
Fair lovely maid, once more good day to thee. 35
Sweet Kate, embrace her for her beauty's sake.

104 **against:** *by the time that*   105 **appendix:** *addition or adjunct, here 'wife'*   1 **a:** *in*   9 **Or ere:** *before*   15 **rush-candle:** *rush, dipped in grease to serve as candle*   19 **is:** *F in*   26 **bowl:** *wooden ball used in game of bowls*   27 **bias:** *Cf. n.*

Hortensio. A will make the man mad, to make a woman
of him.

Katherina. Young budding virgin, fair and fresh and sweet,
Whether away, or where is thy abode?   40
Happy the parents of so fair a child;
Happier the man, whom favorable stars
Allot thee for his lovely bedfellow!

Petruchio. Why, how now, Kate! I hope thou art not mad;
This is a man, old, wrinkled, faded, wither'd,   45
And not a maiden, as thou sayst he is.

Katherina. Pardon, old father, my mistaking eyes
That have been so bedazzled with the sun
That everything I look on seemeth green.
Now I perceive thou art a reverent father;   50
Pardon, I pray thee, for my mad mistaking.

Petruchio. Do, good old grandsire; and withal make
known.
Which way thou travellest: if along with us,
We shall be joyful of thy company.   55

Vincentio. Fair sir, and you my merry mistress,
That with your strange encounter much amaz'd me,
My name is called Vincentio; my dwelling, Pisa;
And bound I am to Padua, there to visit
A son of mine, which long I have not seen.   60

Petruchio. What is his name?

Vincentio.   Lucentio, gentle sir.

Petruchio. Happily met; the happier for thy son.
And now by law, as well as reverent age,
I may entitle thee my loving father: 65
The sister to my wife, this gentlewoman,
Thy son by this hath married. Wonder not
Nor be not griev'd: she is of good esteem,
Her dowry wealthy, and of worthy birth;
Beside, so qualified as may beseem   70
The spouse of any noble gentleman.
Let me embrace with old Vincentio
And wander we to see thy honest son,
Who will of thy arrival be full joyous.

Vincentio. But is this true? or is it else your pleasure,   75
Like pleasant travelers, to break a jest
Upon the company you overtake?

Hortensio. I do assure thee, father, so it is.

Petruchio. Come, go along, and see the truth hereof;
For our first merriment hath made thee jealous.   80
                                        Exeunt [all but Hortensio].

Hortensio. Well, Petruchio, this has put me in heart.
Have to my widow! and if she be froward,
Then hast thou taught Hortensio to be untoward.   *Exit.*

❧ SCENE FOURTH ❧

Enter Biondello, Lucentio, and Bianca;
Gremio is out before.

Biondello. Softly and swiftly, sir, for the priest is ready.

Lucentio. I fly, Biondello, but they may chance to
need thee at home; therefore leave us.   *Exit [with Bianca].*

Biondello. Nay, faith, I'll see the church a your
back; and then come back to my master's as soon as   5
I can.   *[Exit.]*

Gremio. I marvel Cambio comes not all this while.

Enter Petruchio, Kate, Vincentio, [and] Grumio with Attendants.

Petruchio. Sir, here's the door, this is Lucentio's house:
My father's bears more toward the market place;
Thither must I and here I leave you, sir.   10

Vincentio. You shall not choose but drink before you go.
I think I shall command your welcome here
And, by all likelihood, some cheer is toward.   *Knock.*

Gremio. They're busy within; you were best knock louder.

Pedant looks out of the window.

Pedant. What's he that knocks as he would beat   15
down the gate?

Vincentio. Is Signior Lucentio within, sir?

Pedant. He's within, sir, but not to be spoken
withal.

Vincentio. What if a man bring him a hundred   20
pound or two, to make merry withal?

Pedant. Keep your hundred pounds to yourself; he
shall need none so long as I live.

Petruchio. Nay, I told you your son was well beloved in Padua. Do you hear, sir? To leave frivolous   25
circumstances, I pray you tell Signior Lucentio that
his father is come from Pisa and is here at the door
to speak with him.

Pedant. Thou liest; his father is come from Padua
and here looking out at the window.   30

Vincentio. Art thou his father?

Pedant. Ay sir, so his mother says, if I may believe
her.

Petruchio. [To Vincentio.] Why how now, gentleman! why this is flat knavery, to take upon you   35
another man's name.

Pedant. Lay hands on the villain; I believe, a means
to cozen somebody in this city under my countenance.

Enter Biondello.

Biondello. I have seen them in the church together;
God send 'em good shipping! But who is here? mine   40
old master, Vincentio! now we are undone and
brought to nothing.

Vincentio. Come hither, crack-hemp.

Biondello. I hope I may choose, sir.

Vincentio. Come hither, you rogue. What, have you   45
forgot me?

37 A: *he*   **40 Whether:** *whither*   **where:** *F whether*   **43 Allot:** *F A lots*   **49 green:**
metaphorically, 'young'   **50 reverent:** *read 'rev'rent'*   **56 mistress:** *read 'misteress'*   **57**
encounter: *greeting*   **68 esteem:** *reputation*   **70 so qualified:** *having such quali-*
ties   **76 pleasant:** *i.e. fond of pleasantries*   **80 jealous:** *suspicious*   **82 froward:** *pre-*
serves   **83 untoward:** *hard to manage*

SCENE 4 *Cf. n.*   **SD out before:** *on the forestage, where he is unaware of the others*   **4, 5**
a your back: *on your back; I'll see you into the church*   **5 master's:** *F mistris*   **9 bears:**
stands   **15 What's he:** *who is he*   **19 withal:** *with*   **25, 26 frivolous circumstances:**
unimportant details   **35 flat:** *downright*   **37 a:** *he*   **40 good shipping:** *i.e. 'fair sail-*
ing'   **43 crack-hemp:** *gallows bird*   **44 I . . . sir:** *Allow me, sir! Cf. n.*

Biondello. Forgot you! no sir. I could not forget you, for I never saw you before in all my life.

Vincentio. What, you notorious villain! didst thou never see thy master's father, Vincentio?   50

Biondello. What, my old, worshipful old master? yes, marry, sir: see where he looks out of the window.

Vincentio. Is't so, indeed?   *He beats Biondello.*

Biondello. Help, help, help! here's a madman will murder me.   *[Exit.]*   55

Pedant. Help, son! help, Signior Baptista!   *[Exit from above.]*

Petruchio. Prithee, Kate, let's stand aside and see the end of this controversy.   *[They retire.]*

Enter Pedant [below] with Servants, Baptista, [and] Tranio.

Tranio. Sir, what are you that offer to beat my servant?   60

Vincentio. What am I, sir! nay, what are you, sir? O immortal gods! O fine villain! A silken doublet! a velvet hose! a scarlet cloak! and a copatain hat! O, I am undone! I am undone! while I play the good husband at home, my son and my servant spend all   65 at the university.

Tranio. How now! what's the matter?

Baptista. What, is the man lunatic?

Tranio. Sir, you seem a sober ancient gentleman by your habit, but your words show you a madman.   70 Why sir, what cerns it you if I wear pearl and gold? I thank my good father, I am able to maintain it.

Vincentio. Thy father! O villain! he is a sailmaker in Bergamo.

Baptista. You mistake, sir, you mistake, sir. Pray,   75 what do you think is his name?

Vincentio. His name! as if I knew not his name! I have brought him up ever since he was three years old, and his name is Tranio.

Pedant. Away, away, mad ass! his name is Lucentio   80 and he is mine only son, and heir to the lands of me, Signior Vincentio.

Vincentio. Lucentio! O he hath murd'red his master. Lay hold on him, I charge you in the duke's name. O my son, my son! tell me, thou villain, where is my   85 son Lucentio?

Tranio. Call forth an officer.

[Enter one with an Officer.]

Carry this mad knave to the jail. Father Baptista, I charge you see that he be forthcoming.

Vincentio. Carry me to the jail!   90

Gremio. Stay, officer: he shall not go to prison.

Baptista. Talk not, Signior Gremio. I say he shall go to prison.

Gremio. Take heed, Signior Baptista, lest you be cony-catched in this business. I dare swear this is the   95 right Vincentio.

Pedant. Swear, if thou dar'st.

Gremio. Nay, I dare not swear it.

Tranio. Then thou wert best say that I am not Lucentio.   100

Gremio. Yes, I know thee to be Signior Lucentio.

Baptista. Away with the dotard; to the jail with him!

Vincentio. Thus strangers may be hal'd and abused; O monstrous villain!

Enter Biondello, Lucentio, and Bianca.

Biondello. O we are spoil'd; and yonder he is: deny   105 him, forswear him, or else we are all undone.

Exeunt Biondello, Tranio, and Pedant as fast as may be.

Lucentio. Pardon, sweet father.   *Kneel.*

Vincentio.   Lives my sweet son?

Bianca. Pardon, dear father.

Baptista.   How hast thou offended?   110 Where is Lucentio?

Lucentio.   Here's Lucentio, Right son to the right Vincentio, That have by marriage made thy daughter mine While counterfeit supposes blear'd thine eyne.   115

Gremio. Here's packing, with a witness, to deceive us all!

Vincentio. Where is that damned villain Tranio That fac'd and brav'd me in this matter so?

Baptista. Why, tell me, is not this my Cambio?   120

Bianca. Cambio is chang'd into Lucentio.

Lucentio. Love wrought these miracles. Bianca's love Made me exchange my state with Tranio While he did bear my countenance in the town, And happily I have arriv'd at the last   125 Unto the wished haven of my bliss. What Tranio did, myself enforc'd him to; Then pardon him, sweet father, for my sake.

Vincentio. I'll slit the villain's nose, that would have sent me to the jail.   130

Baptista. But do you hear, sir? Have you married my daughter without asking my good will?

Vincentio. Fear not, Baptista; we will content you, go to: but I will in, to be reveng'd for this villainy.   *Exit.*

Baptista. And I, to sound the depth of this knavery.   *Exit.*

Lucentio. Look not pale, Bianca; thy father will not frown.   *Exeunt [Lucentio and Bianca.]*

Gremio. My cake is dough, but I'll in among the rest Out of hope of all but my share of the feast.   *[Exit.]*

Katherina. Husband, let's follow, to see the end of   140 this ado.

Petruchio. First kiss me, Kate, and we will.

Katherina. What! in the midst of the street?

Petruchio. What! art thou asham'd of me?

Katherina. No sir, God forbid; but asham'd to kiss.   145

Petruchio. Why, then let's home again. Come sirrah, let's away.

Katherina. Nay, I will give thee a kiss; now pray thee, love, stay.

Petruchio. Is not this well?: Come, my sweet Kate;   150 Better once than never, for never too late.   *Exeunt.*

---

50 master's: *F Mistris*   **57 Prithee:** *F Preethe*   **63 copatain hat:** *high sugar-loaf hat*   **65 husband:** *frugal manager*   **70 habit:** *outward semblance*   **71 cerns:** *concerns*   **95 cony-catched:** *duped*   SD **Exeunt:** *F Exit*

115 supposes: *substitutions, probably with allusion to Gascoigne's play; see Sources of the Play* **eyne:** *eyes*   **116 packing:** *plotting* **with a witness:** *with a vengeance*   **124 countenance:** *read 'count'nance'*   **134 go to:** *expressions of remonstrance (or, sometimes, impatience)*   **138 My cake is dough:** *proverbial for failure of an enterprise; cf. 1.3.108–109*   **141 ado:** *commotion*   **151 Better . . . late:** *i.e. 'better late than never'*

ACT FIFTH ❧ SCENE FIRST

Enter Baptista, Vincentio, Gremio, the Pedant, Lucentio, and
Bianca, Tranio, Biondello, Grumio, [Petruchio, Katherina, Hortensio,]
and Widow; the Servingmen with Tranio bringing in a banquet.

Lucentio. At last, though long, our jarring notes agree;
And time it is, when raging war is done,
To smile at scapes and perils overblown.
My fair Bianca, bid my father welcome
While I with self-same kindness welcome thine.   5
Brother Petruchio, sister Katherina,
And thou, Hortensio, with thy loving widow,
Feast with the best and welcome to my house;
My banket is to close our stomachs up
After our great good cheer. Pray you, sit down;   10
For now we sit to chat as well as eat.

Petruchio. Nothing but sit and sit, and eat and eat!

Baptista. Padua affords this kindness, son Petruchio.

Petruchio. Padua affords nothing but what is kind.

Hortensio. For both our sakes I would that word were   15
true.

Petruchio. Now, for my life, Hortensio fears his widow.

Widow. Then never trust me, if I be afeard.

Petruchio. You are very sensible and yet you miss my sense:
I mean, Hortensio is afeard of you.   20

Widow. He that is giddy thinks the world turns round.

Petruchio. Roundly replied.

Katherina.   Mistress, how mean you that?

Widow. Thus I conceive by him.

Petruchio. Conceives by me! How likes Hortensio that?   25

Hortensio. My widow says, thus she conceives her tale.

Petruchio. Very well mended. Kiss him for that, good widow.

Katherina. 'He that is giddy thinks the world turns round':
I pray you, tell me what you meant by that.

Widow. Your husband, being troubled with a shrew,   30
Measures my husband's sorrow by his woe,
And now you know my meaning.

Katherina. A very mean meaning.

Widow.   Right, I mean you.

Katherina. And I am mean indeed, respecting you.   35

Petruchio. To her, Kate!

Hortensio. To her, widow!

Petruchio. A hundred marks, my Kate does put her down.

Hortensio. That's my office.

Petruchio. Spoke like an officer; ha' to thee, lad.   40

Drinks to Hortensio.

Baptista. How likes Gremio these quick-witted folks?

Gremio. Believe me, sir, they butt together well.

Bianca. Head and butt! an hasty-witted body
Would say your head and butt were head and horn.

Vincentio. Ay, mistress bride, hath that awaken'd you?   45

Bianca. Ay, but not frighted me; therefore I'll sleep again.

Petruchio. Nay, that you shall not, since you have begun,
Have at you for a bitter jest or two.

Bianca. Am I your bird? I mean to shift my bush;
And then pursue me as you draw your bow.   50
You are welcome all.

Exit Bianca [with Katherina and Widow].

Petruchio. She hath prevented me. Here, Signior Tranio;
This bird you aim'd at, though you hit her not:
Therefore a health to all that shot and miss'd.

Tranio. O sir! Lucentio slipp'd me, like his greyhound,   55
Which runs himself and catches for his master.

Petruchio. A good swift simile but something currish.

Tranio. 'Tis well, sir, that you hunted for yourself;
'Tis thought your deer does hold you at a bay.

Baptista. O ho, Petruchio! Tranio hits you now.   60

Lucentio. I thank thee for that gird, good Tranio.

Hortensio. Confess, confess, hath he not hit you here?

Petruchio. A has a little gall'd me, I confess;
And, as the jest did glance away from me,
'Tis ten to one it maim'd you two outright.   65

Baptista. Now, in good sadness, son Petruchio,
I think thou hast the veriest shrew of all.

Petruchio. Well, I say no: and therefore, for assurance,
Let's each one send unto his wife,
And he whose wife is most obedient   70
To come at first when he doth send for her
Shall win the wager which we will propose.

Hortensio. Content. What's the wager?

Lucentio.   Twenty crowns.

Petruchio. Twenty crowns!   75
I'll venture so much of my hawk or hound,
But twenty times so much upon my wife.

Lucentio. A hundred then.

Hortensio.   Content.

Petruchio.   A match! 'tis done.   80

Hortensio. Who shall begin?

Lucentio.   That will I.
Go Biondello, bid your mistress come to me.

Biondello. I go.   *Exit.*

Baptista. Son, I'll be your half, Bianca comes.   85

Lucentio. I'll have no halves; I'll bear it all myself.

Enter Biondello.

How now! what news?

Biondello.   Sir, my mistress sends you word
That she is busy and she cannot come.

Petruchio. How! she is busy and she cannot come!   90
Is that an answer?

Gremio.   Ay, and a kind one too;
Pray God, sir, your wife send you not a worse.

Petruchio. I hope, better.

Hortensio. Sirrah Biondello, go and entreat my wife   95
To come to me forthwith.   *Exit Biondello.*

Petruchio.   O ho! entreat her!
Nay, then she must needs come.

Hortensio.   I am afraid, sir,
Do what you can, yours will not be entreated.   100

Enter Biondello.

SD banket: *dessert; spelled banket 1.9*   **1 long:** *after a long time*   **2 done:** *F come*   **9**
stomachs: *with second sense of 'quarrel'*   **17 fears:** *used by Petruchio in current sense; the widow*
takes it in the sense of 'frighten'   **18 afeard:** *suspicious*   **22 Roundly:** *frankly*   **24 Thus**
I conceive by him: *that is my impression of his state. Petruchio plays on the other meaning in his*
reply   **40 ha' to:** *here's to*   **48 Have at you:** *here goes*   **bitter:** *sharp; F better*

49 bird: *in the sense of a target*   **52 prevented:** *anticipated*   **55 slipp'd:** *unleashed*   **59**
deer: *with a pun on 'dear'*   **at a bay:** *at bay*   **61 gird:** *taunt*   **63 A:** *he*   **gall'd:**
scratched   **66 good sadness:** *all seriousness*   **68 for assurance:** *to make sure*   **for:** *F*
sir   **76 of:** *on*   **80 A match:** *i.e. it's a bet*   **85 be your half:** *take half of your bet*

Now where's my wife?

Biondello. She says you have some goodly jest in hand.
She will not come; she bids you come to her.

Petruchio. Worse and worse; she will not come! O vilde,
Intolerable, not to be endur'd!   *105*
Sirrah Grumio, go to your mistress; say
I command her come to me.   *Exit [Grumio].*

Hortensio.   I know her answer.

Petruchio. What?

Hortensio. She will not.   *110*

Petruchio. The fouler fortune mine, and there an end.

Enter Katherina.

Baptista. Now, by my hollidam, here comes Katherina!

Katherina. What is your will, sir, that you send for me?

Petruchio. Where is your sister, and Hortensio's wife?

Katherina. They sit conferring by the parlor fire.   *115*

Petruchio. Go fetch them hither; if they deny to come,
Swinge me them soundly forth unto their husbands.
Away, I say, and bring them hither straight.   *[Exit Katherina.]*

Lucentio. Here is a wonder, if you talk of a wonder.

Hortensio. And so it is. I wonder what it bodes.   *120*

Petruchio. Marry, peace it bodes, and love, and quiet life,
An awful rule and right supremacy;
And, to be short, what not that's sweet and happy.

Baptista. Now fair befall thee, good Petruchio!
The wager thou hast won and I will add   *125*
Unto their losses twenty thousand crowns,
Another dowry to another daughter,
For she is chang'd, as she had never been.

Petruchio. Nay, I will win my wager better yet
And show more sign of her obedience,   *130*
Her new-built virtue and obedience.

Enter Kate, Bianca, and Widow.

See where she comes and brings your froward wives
As prisoners to her womanly persuasion.
Katerine, that cap of yours becomes you not:
Off with that bauble, throw it under foot.   *135*

Widow. Lord! let me never have a cause to sigh
Till I be brought to such a silly pass!

Bianca. Fie! what a foolish duty call you this?

Lucentio. I would your duty were as foolish too;
The wisdom of your duty, fair Bianca,   *140*
Hath cost me five hundred crowns since suppertime.

Bianca. The more fool you are for laying on my duty.

Petruchio. Katherine, I charge thee, tell these headstrong
women
What duty they do owe their lords and husbands.   *145*

Widow. Come, come, you're mocking; we will have no
telling.

Petruchio. Come on, I say; and first begin with her.

Widow. She shall not.

Petruchio. I say she shall: and first begin with her.

Katherina. Fie, fie! unknit that threat'ning unkind brow   *150*
And dart not scornful glances from those eyes
To wound thy lord, thy king, thy governor.

It blots thy beauty as frosts do bite the meads,
Confounds thy fame as whirlwinds shake fair buds,   *155*
And in no sense is meet or amiable.
A woman mov'd is like a fountain troubled,
Muddy, ill-seeming, thick, bereft of beauty;
And while it is so, none so dry or thirsty
Will deign to sip or touch one drop of it.   *160*
Thy husband is thy lord, thy life, thy keeper,
Thy head, thy sovereign; one that cares for thee,
And for thy maintenance commits his body
To painful labor both by sea and land,
To watch the night in storms, the day in cold,   *165*
Whilst thou li'st warm at home, secure and safe;
And craves no other tribute at thy hands
But love, fair looks, and true obedience;
Too little payment for so great a debt.
Such duty as the subject owes the prince,   *170*
Even such a woman oweth to her husband;
And when she is froward, peevish, sullen, sour,
And not obedient to his honest will,
What is she but a foul contending rebel
And graceless traitor to her loving lord?—   *175*
I am asham'd that women are so simple
To offer war where they should kneel for peace,
Or seek for rule, supremacy, and sway,
When they are bound to serve, love, and obey.
Why are our bodies soft and weak and smooth,   *180*
Unapt to toil and trouble in the world,
But that our soft conditions and our hearts
Should well agree with our external parts?
Come, come, you forward and unable worms!
My mind hath been as big as one of yours,   *185*
My heart as great, my reason haply more,
To bandy word for word and frown for frown;
But now I see our lances are but straws,
Our strength as weak, our weakness past compare,
That seeming to be most which we indeed least are.   *190*
Then vail your stomachs, for it is no boot,
And place your hands below your husband's foot:
In token of which duty, if he please,
My hand is ready; may it do him ease.

Petruchio. Why, there's a wench! Come on and kiss me,   *195*
Kate.

Lucentio. Well, go thy ways, old lad, for thou shalt ha't.

Vincentio. 'Tis a good hearing when children are toward.

Lucentio. But a harsh hearing when women are froward.

Petruchio. Come, Kate, we'll to bed.   *200*
We three are married, but you two are sped.
'Twas I won the wager, *[to Lucentio.]* though you hit the white;
And, being a winner, God give you good night!

Exit Petruchio [with Katherina].

Hortensio. Now, go thy ways; thou hast tam'd a curst shrow.

Lucentio. 'Tis a wonder, by your leave, she will be tam'd so.

[Exeunt.]

❧ FINIS ❧

---

104 **vilde:** *vile*   112 **hollidam:** *halidom (salvation)*   116 **deny:** *refuse*   117 **Swinge:** *whip*   121 **awful rule:** *order commanding respect*   124 **fair befall thee:** *good luck to you*   133 **prisoners:** *read 'pris'ners'*   141 **five hundred:** *Lucentio is exaggerating—or has made some side-bets*   142 **laying:** *betting*   143–145 **Katherine . . . husbands:** *F sets as prose*

155 **fame:** *reputation*   157 **mov'd:** *angry*   181 **Unapt:** *unsuited*   182 **conditions:** *characteristics*   191 **Then . . . boot:** *so bring down your pride, for it is of no use*   198 **toward:** *obedient*   201 **sped:** *done for*   202 **white:** *center of the target, with play on the name Bianca, meaning 'white'*

I.i. Editors, following Pope, have disregarded the Folio and have labeled the first two scenes of the play 'The Induction.' Our text follows the Folio here as well as in the beginnings of Acts IV and V which were altered by Pope and Warburton.

I.i.1. *Sly.* A Stephen Sly lived in Stratford in Shakespeare's lifetime, and although the name Slie does appear in *A Shrew*, it is likely that Shakespeare is making use of his native country and its inhabitants. A family by the name of Hacket did live in Wincot, so the reference to Marian Hacket, the fat ale-wife of Wincot (I.2 23–24) enforces this view. There is added interest in the fact that a Will Sly was a member of Shakespeare's company.

I.i.9. *St. Jeronimy.* Many editors amend to read 'Go by, Jeronimy,' a phrase from Kyd's *Spanish Tragedy* (III.12.31) and said to be current in Shakespeare's day as an expression of impatience or dismissal. The rest of the line may echo Hieronimo's speech in the same play (II.5.1.): 'What outcries pluck me from my naked bed?'

I.i.17, 18. *Broach. Brach* of 1. 17 seems clearly an error in the Folio (perhaps the printer's eyes strayed to the end of the following line) not only because Merriman is a name commonly given a dog and not a bitch but more cogently because the construction requires a verb. Various emendations have been suggested: *tash* meaning 'to put on a separate leash,' in contrast to the treatment accorded Clowder who is to be 'coupled' (i.e. put on double leash) with another dog: *bath* (or *bathe*) not inappropriate for an 'embossed' dog, and *broach* meaning to 'bleed,' Dover Wilson's and Kittredge's choice. The possible spelling of this verb, *broch*, would be close to the Folio and would indicate another likely treatment of the distressed animal. It seems on the whole the happiest choice. For a discussion of this passage see the article on hunting by J. W. Fortescue in *Shakespeare's England, 2,* 348–50.

I.i.82. *Players.* Bands of strolling players traveled the English countryside presenting their plays wherever they could find an audience, in a market square, a town hall, or in the hall of a nobleman's residence. Particularly in the years 1596–97 when the plague closed the London theatres, Shakespeare's company traveled in the provinces. Hamlet's welcome to the player's (*Hamlet* II.2) indicates the popularity of such groups.

I.i.SD. *Enter Players.* The stage direction indicates a constant feature of Elizabethan dramatic practice: the necessity for a time interval between an actor's entrance through a door in the back of the stage and his appearance as a speaking character on the forestage. He had to cover a distance of some thirty feet and usually the stage directions indicate entries several lines before the characters speak in order to allow for this. Practically all editors have altered the position of stage directions to suit the proscenium-arch stage, and the Shakespearean playing has thus been lost.

I.i.94. *A Player.* The Folio's *Sincklo* indicates that this part was played by one Sincklow of the King's company whose name also appears in the Quarto (1600) of *2 Henry IV*, the First Folio version of *3 Henry VI*, and elsewhere, although he does not seem to have been sufficiently important to merit inclusion among the 'Principall Actors' listed at the beginning of the Folio.

I.i.94. *Soto.* Soto is one of the minor roles in Fletcher's *Woman Pleased* (1620). The reference here is either a later insertion or Fletcher's play goes back to some earlier production of the Shakespearean company.

I.i.111. *page.* It was the custom of acting companies to employ boys to play the female roles. It was not until the Restoration that the parts were played by women. For an interesting account of a boy actor see Bryher's novel, *The Player's Boy* (New York, 1953).

I.ii.55. *Adonis.* The story of Adonis, the young hunter beloved of Venus and slain by a wild boar, is retold in Shakespeare's own *Venus and Adonis.*

I.ii.62. *Daphne.* Daphne, a Greek girl loved by Apollo, escaped his pursuit by being turned into the laurel. Lines 62–65 off this scene suggest Golding's translation of Ovid's *Metamorphoses*, which Shakespeare had read.

I.ii.100, 101. *As Stephen Sly . . . Henry Pimpernell.* Possibly the proper names in these lines are names of real people. There was a Stephen Sly of Stratford, and *Greece* may be a corruption of Greet, a Gloucestershire village, home of 'old John Naps.' See Sydney Lee, *Life of Shakespeare*, p. 167.

I.iii.2–3. *Padua . . . Lumbardy.* Padua is a town in northeastern Italy, famous for its University. Lumbardy (Lombardy) is here rather loosely used as a general term for northern Italy. It includes the region modern Italians know as Venetia, where Padua is located.

I.iii.37. *Metaphysics.* Tranio is here talking about the subjects studied in universities of the time.

I.iii.SD. *Pantaloon.* This is the name of one of the *maschere* or stock characters in the old Italian *commedia dell' arte.* Traditionally the name was used for the role of an old man, often the butt of other characters. Presumably Gremio is here garbed in the costume of such a character, with slippers, spectacles, and baggy pantaloons. Shakespeare (*As You Like It*, II.7) so describes the sixth of man's seven ages:

> The sixth age shifts
> Into the lean and slipper'd pantaloon
> With spectacles on nose and pouch on side,
> His youthful hose, well saved, a world too wide
> For his shrunk shank; and his big manly voice
> Turning again to childish trebles, pipes
> And whistles in his sound.

I.iii.57. *cart.* Disorderly women were sometimes punished by being driven around the town in an open cart, exposed to the jeers of the populace.

I.iii.110, 111. *Their love is not so great.* Some editors believe that *their* refers to the love between Katherina and her father (which is not so great as to prevent him from appreciating Bianca); others interpret it as referring to the love between Bianca and Baptista. Dover Wilson, following the Quarto and earlier editors, prints *There, love . . . .* Later Folios read *our* for *their.*

I.iii.155. *love in idleness.* This is the popular name of the pansy, here probably used literally; cf. *A Midsummer Night's Dream* II, 1.172 ff.

I.iii.158. *Anna.* She was the sister and confidante of Dido, queen of Carthage; cf. *Aeneid*, Bk IV.

I.iii.165. *Redime . . . minimo.* The Latin means 'Ransom your captive self as cheaply as you can.' The phrase quoted (incorrectly) from Terence (*Eunuchus* I.1.29) appears in Lyly's Latin grammar where Shakespeare apparently found it.

I.iii.172. *daughter of Agenor.* Zeus, in the form of a bull, carried off Europa, daughter of Agenor, to Crete; cf. Ovid. *Metamorphoses*, II, 858 ff.

I.iv.70. *Florentius.* Florentius is the knight who in Gower's version (in the *Confessio Amantis*) of the old fairy tale promised to marry an old hag in return for the solution of a riddle that would save his life. Much against his will he kept his promise, and his bride turned into a beautiful maiden. Chaucer also tells this story in 'The Wife of Bath's Tale.'

I.iv.71. *Sybil.* The Cumean Sybil was granted extreme longevity by Apollo who bestowed on her as many years as the grains of sand which she could hold in her hand.

I.iv.265. *Alcides.* The Pythian oracle at Delphi ordered Hercules to serve Eurystheus, king of Tiryus, for the space of twelve years. During this time he performed twelve feats of extraordinary bravery and strength which are commonly referred to as 'the twelve labors of Hercules.'

II.i.34. *dance barefoot on her wedding day.* It was popularly believed that an unmarried elder sister could gain a husband by dancing barefoot at the wedding of her younger sister; thus the phrase is proverbial description of an old maid.

II.i.189–199. Several puns occur in these lines: *hard—heard* (pronounced 'hard'), *bonny—bony* (the F spelling), *Kates—cates* (sweetmeats), and *sounded* 'proclaimed,' with a quibble in the following line on the meaning 'plumbed.'

II.i.195. *Kate-Hall.* Kate-Hall may refer to St. Catherine's Hall at Cambridge or to 'a dining house at Katherine Hall' (New Cambridge ed.) where Queen Elizabeth stopped during a royal progress in 1591.

II.i.220. *Ay, for a turtle . . . .* Bond reads *she* for *he*, suggesting that the initial letter may have been lost in the final *s* of *as.* He interprets Katherina's speech thus: 'A fool may well think her meek and manageable, as she thinks him' or else, 'as she takes a buzzard for a buzzard,' i.e. a fool for a fool. But it is perhaps better to take *buzzard* in the third sense given above, 'a large insect,' usually a large moth or cockchafer (OED).

II.i.317, 318. *Grissel . . . Lucrece.* Griselda, wife of the Marquis of Saluzzo, in Boccaccio's tale (*Decameron* X, 10) blindly obeyed her husband, and hence became the paragon of wifely docility. Lucrece, a Roman matron who, violated by Sextus, son of King Tarquin of Rome, killed herself, became the symbol of chastity and wifely honor. Cf. Shakespeare's *The Rape of Lucrece.*

III.i.4. *know this lady's.* Hammer first suggested this emendation which clarifies the meaning and gives the line its proper number of syllables.

III.i.28, 29. *Hic ibat . . . celsa senis.* 'Here flowed Simois; here is the Trojan land; here stood old Priam's lofty palace.' Ovid, *Heroides* I. 33–4.

III.i.37–39. This is the F arrangement. Some editors, however, reproduce these lines as verse, thus:

Hortensio. Madam, my instrument's in tune.
Bianca.   Let's hear.
O fie! the treble jars.
Lucentio.   Spit in the hole, man,
And tune again.

III.i.47–49. F assigns these lines to Lucentio.

III.i.51–52. F assigns these lines to Bianca.

III.i.53–57. F assigns these lines to Hortensio.

III.i.66. *gamouth. Gamouth* is the Elizabethan spelling of *gamut*, the name for the diatonic scale. This derives from the Greek *gamma* which was the name of the first note in the scale. The suffix *-ut* denotes the first note of a hexachord and the resultant word acquires the meaning of all the notes in the scale.

III.i.81. *Messenger.* The Folio *Nicke* may quite possibly refer to Nicholas Tooley, listed among the 'Principall actors of all these plays' in the First Folio. This hardly seems a part for a 'principal actor' but we may assume he played other parts as well.

III.ii.31. *old.* The reference to *old* in the following line suggests that its omission in this one is an error. Many editors (following Capell) amend to read: 'news, old news, and such news.' We are inclined to agree with Dover Wilson that the insertion of the word after *such* seems 'the simplest and most natural' reading.

III.ii.67–68. *humor of forty fancies.* Doubtless Dover Wilson is right in his assertion that 'no one knows what this phrase means.' Our note follows Halliwell; other guesses include 'some ballad or drollery' (Warburton), 'a collection of short poems such as were called fancies' (Steevens), 'a fantastic ornament comprising the humor of forty different fancies' (Malone).

III. iii. Pope, disregarding the act division indicated in the Folio text, chose to begin the fourth act at this point. All subsequent editors have followed this arbitrary emendation. The present text follows the Folio.

III.iii.85. *indifferent knit.* The ambiguous word is *indifferent*, variously explained as 'not different' (Johnson), 'particolor' (Malone) and with adverbial meaning (Bond) as we have taken it.

III.iii.136. *Food . . . food.* The Folio *soud* has baffled the commentators. Some have taken it as an indication of a sound expressing fatigue, some see in it an echo of the refrain of an old song. 'Soudledum, soudledum' (Halliwell) and Hammer took it as representing the humming of Petruchio. Dover Wilson's emendation *Food*, which we have followed, certainly seems appropriate to the circumstances and the stage business, and is understandable as a printer's confusion of long *s* and *f.*

III.iii.189. *lure.* A lure was a small wicker container covered with feathers used first in training a hawk. Meat was placed inside and the falconer swung the lure in a circle over his head to create a whistling sound. The hawk pouncing on the lure received her food. After the hawk was trained, the mere swinging up of the lure would recall her.

III.iii.195. *Last night . . . shall. not* Either this is a guess on Petruchio's part or Shakespeare has forgotten that the pair has been married only today.

III.iii.205. *kill a wife with kindness.* Of this line Bond wisely remarks: 'This being a common phrase for mistaken indulgence, we need not suppose an allusion to Heywood's *A Woman Killed with Kindness*, 1607, nor adjust the date of our play thereto.'

III.iv.8–11. *Art of Love.* An allusion to Ovid's *Ars amatoria*. These lines contain a series of common puns, namely *art—heart—hart* (pronounced alike), *dear—deer*, and *proceeders*, with a play on its usual meaning and the sense of candidates for degree, with reference to the master of art of l. 9.

III.iv.61. *tricks eleven and twenty long.* This is an allusion to the card game referred to in I.4.33, and means 'tricks suitable to the needs of the case.'

IV.ii.SD. *Enter Baptista and Lucentio.* Since the Pedant is already on the stage, the stage direction in the Folio is either an afterthought or an instruction to the Pedant to remove his hat at the entrance of Baptista and Lucentio. Such directions for stage business are rather rare in the Folio.

IV.ii.67. *I pray . . . my heart.* The Folio's assignment of l. 67 to Biondello has caused some editors to change the *Cambio* of l. 62 to *Biondello*. Yet here Perry's reasoning (Yale Shakespeare, 1928) is quite convincing: Lucentio is Baptista's servant and so would naturally be ordered about by him; furthermore it is essential to the plot to have Bianca fetched by Lucentio. We may assume that Lucentio moves off to another part of the stage, where he awaits Biondello. The Folio provides only one *Exit* but the stage direction of l. 72 seems to indicate that the pair has joined up, either on stage as indicated or just off stage. I would take it that Tranio's speech in l. 68, though picking up Lucentio's phrase, is addressed to Biondello in dismissal. The Folio SD of l. 68 has baffled editors; Bond suggests Peter may be the name of an actor, playing the part of a servant come to tell Tranio that dinner awaits.

IV.ii.94. *cum . . . solem.* This is an ancient copyright formula meaning 'with privilege of exclusive printing' (*cum privilegio ad imprimendum solum*); it is here used metaphorically by Biondello, whose Latin is not perfect. Cf. the same metaphorical use of *appendix* in l. 105.

IV.iii.27. *bias.* In lawn bowling the balls employed are weighted on one side so that they will roll in an arc thus enabling a bowler to go around a ball of an opponent which lies between him and the jack or small white ball which is the target. If the ball is properly bowled it will run *with* and not *against* the bias.

IV. iv. Again our text follows the Folio. Warburton began Act V at this point, and all subsequent editors have followed him rather than the Folio.

IV.iv.44. *I . . . sir.* This expression was used to a disagreeable person who barred one's path in the street, according to the New Cambridge editors; cf. *The Merchant of Venice*, 1.2.41.

Love's Labour's Lost

Edited by **WILBUR CROSS**
and
TUCKER BROOKE

❧

Dramatis Personae

FERDINAND, *King of Navarre*

BEROWNE
LONGAVILLE } *three Lords attending upon*
DUMAINE } *the King in his retirement*

BOYET } *Lords attending upon*
MARCADE } *the Princess of France*

DON ADRIANO DE ARMADO, *a fantastical*
   Spaniard
NATHANIEL, *a Curate*
DULL, *a Constable*
HOLOFERNES, *a Schoolmaster*

COSTARD, *a Clown*
MOTH, *Page to Don Adriano de Armado*
A FORESTER
PRINCESS OF FRANCE

ROSALINE
MARIA } *Ladies attending on the Princess*
KATHARINE

JAQUENETTA, *a country Wench*
OFFICERS AND OTHER ATTENDANTS UPON THE
   KING AND PRINCESS

SCENE—*Navarre.*

Love's Labour's Lost

INTRODUCTION

SOURCES OF THE PLAY

The central idea of *Love's Labour's Lost*—that a scholarly prince binds himself and his chosen associates to a quasi-monastic scheme of life, which is immediately shattered by the intrusion of amorous sentiment[1]—would seem much too obvious to be the original invention of Shakespeare; yet no earlier work, either of fiction or of history, has been discovered which can reasonably be regarded as a source of the play, and modern scholarship can only repeat, as regards the main plot, the confession of the first great detector of Shakespearean sources, Langbaine (1691): 'Loves Labour Lost (*sic*), a Comedy: the Story of which I can give no Account of.' Even more, then, than *A Midsummer Night's Dream* and *The Tempest*, *Love's Labour's Lost* stands out as an example of Shakespeare's rare practice of inventing rather than adapting a dramatic plot.

Like the main plot, the constituent elements which make up the play owe little, apparently, to Shakespeare's reading. They seem rather to be drawn from two non-literary sources upon which the play depends in nearly equal degree. The less conspicuous half of it—involving the characters of Costard, Jaquenetta, Dull, Holofernes, and Nathaniel, and the show of the Nine Worthies—is a heightened study of English country types, evidently founded upon personal observation. The other half, dealing with the French lords and ladies, seems based—in so far as it has a basis outside the poet's imagination—upon the political talk of London in the period about 1589.[2] In 1880 (Sir) Sidney Lee pointed out three features of this part of the play which bear an analogy to contemporary history:

(1) The King of Navarre, Berowne, Longaville, and Dumaine have names which are identical or practically so with those of four conspicuous leaders in the French civil war of 1589–1593: Henri IV (Henry of Navarre); his two generals, Marshal Biron and the Duke of Longueville; and his great opponent, the Duke du Maine, or de Mayenne, brother to the Duke of Guise.[3]

(2) In 1586 Catherine de Medici, Queen-Mother of France, conducted a diplomatic conference with Henry of Navarre at St.-Bris, at which the Queen attempted to influence the course of negotiations by means of a band of gay and charming ladies in waiting.[4]

(3) In 1582–1583 an official deputation of Muscovites was at Queen Elizabeth's court to treat concerning the marriage of the Czar Ivan to a kinswoman of the English Queen. They made themselves ridiculous and became the butt of a practical joke. (See V. ii. 121 and note.)

The pertinence of these parallels is hardly questionable, but the flippancy and vagueness with which Shakespeare utilizes the historical incidents certainly suggest that his knowledge comes from current talk rather than from definite printed accounts. The dramatist, of course, was not purporting to write contemporary history, as Marlowe was when he produced his *Massacre at Paris*. Doubtless Shakespeare first devised his fiction of Navarre and France at a period when it was possible to weave into it recent names and incidents still too vague in their connotation for English auditors to jar against the playful spirit of the comedy.[5] He seems to have conceived of his Navarre, Berowne, Longaville, and Dumaine as living in some pleasant remote time, and it is entirely possible that the real nucleus of the Navarre-France portion of the story is to be found in some such passage as that of Monstrelet's history,[6] cited by Hunter in 1845, the relevancy of which Lee and nearly all subsequent critics have denied. Monstrelet writes as follows: 'At this same season [*ca.* 1403], Charles king of Navarre came to Paris to wait on the king. He negotiated so successfully with the king and his privy council, that he obtained a gift of the castle of Nemours, with some of its dependent castlewicks, which territory was made a duchy. He instantly did homage for it, and at the same time surrendered to the king the castle of Cherbourg, the county of Évreux, and all other lordships he possessed within the kingdom of France, renouncing all claim or profit in them to the king and his successors, on consideration that with this duchy of Nemours the king of France engaged to pay him two hundred thousand gold crowns of the coin of the king our lord.' In this rather complicated transaction Shakespeare may have found the suggestion for the still more complex business of the play, in which likewise a deceased King Charles (cf. II. i. 167) of Navarre and a total sum of two hundred thousand crowns (cf. II. i. 132-136) are involved.[7]

The French and English halves of the play are joined together by the characters of Armado and his page Moth, who are neither French nor convincingly English. In these two figures literary precedent is more evident than elsewhere, and it is clearly John Lyly whom Shakespeare is following. Compare the talk of Armado and Moth in II. i with the following scene between a braggart and his page in Lyly's *Endimion*.[8]

---

1 This idea is evidently a kind of reverse of that in Tennyson's poem, *The Princess*.

2 Several recent writers see English topical references in the Princess of France's visit to Navarre. Thus Mr. Arthur Acheson (*Shakespeare's Lost Years in London*, 1920, p. 119, 165 ff.) conjectures that *Love's Labour's Lost* 'was written late in 1591, or early in 1592, as a reflection of the Queen's progress [August, 1591] to Cowdray House, the home of the Earl of Southampton's maternal grandfather, Viscount Montague, and that the shooting of deer by the Princess and her ladies fancifully records phases of the entertainments arranged for the Queen during her visit.' Cf. note on IV. i. 114.

3 Dumaine is prominent in Marlowe's *Massacre at Paris* as an enemy of Navarre. It is very likely, as Hart and Charlton diffidently suggest, that Shakespeare confused him with Marshal d'Aumont, who, though originally anti-Huguenot, was one of the first to recognize Navarre after Henri III's death (1589) and shared with him in the victory at Ivry (1590). Longueville gained a great victory for the Huguenots at Senlis in 1589. Lee's further assumption that Moth is named after La Motte, a French ambassador at Elizabeth's court in earlier days, lacks probability.

4 Lefranc would substitute for the meeting at St.-Bris an earlier meeting of Catherine and Navarre at Nérac in 1580.

5 See Shakespeare's Original Text and His Revision.

6 Monstrelet, who died in 1453, continued the Chronicles of Froissart from the year 1400. The passage quoted comes near the commencement of his work (bk. i, ch. 17). A number of French editions were available in Shakespeare's time, but there appears to have been no translation into English before that of Thomas Johnes in 1809.

7 Professor Lefranc (*Sous le Masque de 'William Shakespeare'*) makes an important addition by showing that discussions concerning Navarre's holdings in the province of Aquitaine were rife between him and the King of France about 1580.

8 Act V, sc. ii. The date of *Endimion* is probably 1586.

'*Sir Tophas.* Epi, loue hath iustled my libertie from the wall, and taken the vpper hand of my reason.

Epiton. Let mee then trippe vp the heeles of your affection, and thrust your goodwill into the gutter.

Sir To. No, Epi, Loue is a Lorde of misrule, and keepeth Christmas in my corps.

Epi. No doubt there is good cheere: what dishes of delight doth his Lordshippe feast you withal?

Sir To. First, with a great platter of plum-porridge of pleasure, wherein is stued the mutton of mistrust.

Epi. Excellent loue lappe.

Sir To. Then commeth a Pye of patience, a Henne of honnie, a Goose of gall, a Capon of care, and many other Viandes, some sweete and some sowre; which proueth loue to bee, as it was saide of in olde yeeres, *Dulce venenum.*

Epi. A braue banquet.

Sir To. But, Epi, I praye thee feele on my chinne, some thing prycketh mee. What dost thou feele or see?

Epi. There are three or foure little haires.

Sir To. I pray thee call it my bearde. Howe shall I bee troubled when this younge springe shall growe to a great wood!

Epi. O, sir, your chinne is but a quyller yet, you will be most maiesticall when it is full fledge. But I maruell that you loue *Dipsas,* that old Crone,' etc.

The chief literary influence in *Love's Labour's Lost* is certainly Lyly's, poor though the latter's work seems by contrast. Shakespeare at once differentiates himself from the artificial prose comedy of Lyly by his vindication of common sense against affectation and by his deep interest in sonorous verse effects. It is not unlikely that the play is also related superficially to Marlowe's *Massacre at Paris* (written toward the end of 1589), in which the historical Navarre and Dumaine are both introduced, and which opens with Navarre's marriage to the Princess of France.[9]

SHAKESPEARE'S ORIGINAL TEXT AND HIS REVISION

The date of composition of Shakespeare's original (lost) version of *Love's Labour's Lost* and its relation to the text of 1598, corrected and augmented for performance at court, have been the subject of long discussion, to which daring contributions have been made within the last half-dozen years. The conjectured dates of original composition range, according to Dr. Furness' table, from 1588 or earlier till after 1596. Metrical evidence, persisting even in the augmented text, supports the assumption of Furnivall, Dowden, and Sir Sidney Lee that *Love's Labour's Lost* is the earliest of all Shakespeare's plays. Hart (Arden ed., x–xvii) finds other internal evidence pointing 'to 1590 for the date of the earliest form of the play.' Such till recently has been the generally accepted opinion.

In the *Modern Language Review* (July, October, 1918) Mr. H. B. Charlton published a monograph on 'The Date of *Love's Labour's Lost,*' in which he argues for the latter part of 1592 as the time of first composition and assumes only a slight revision immediately previous to the performance of 1597–8. Subsequent writers have apparently inclined to accept Mr. Charlton's rather iconoclastic

conclusions. Professor J. Q. Adams[10] agrees that '1592 is the earliest date that can possibly be assigned to the play,' and conjectures that it was composed during the inhibition of acting from June till December of that year. The recent Cambridge editors (1923) go farther and, joining Mr. Charlton's deductions to some fancied evidences in the play of hostility to Sir Walter Raleigh and his associates, arrive at 1593 for the year of writing: 'We give it as our belief, and no more, that *Love's Labour's Lost* was written in 1593 for a private performance in the house of some grandee who had opposed Raleigh and Raleigh's "men"—possibly the Earl of Southampton's.'

I venture to suggest briefly some reasons for thinking that the probability of an early version of *Love's Labour's Lost*, written not later than 1590 and standing very near the beginning of Shakespeare's dramatic work, remains unimpaired.[11] Mr. Charlton agrees that Shakespeare's use of topical names (Navarre, Berowne, Longaville, Dumaine) is a concession to English interest, in contemporary events in France. This interest, he maintains, really began with the sending of an expeditionary force to the aid of Henry of Navarre in July, 1591, while 'the summer and autumn of 1592 marked the highest level of English public interest in the French wars.[12] It seems clear, on the other hand, that if Shakespeare gave his sentimental students these topical names out of consideration for public interest in their namesakes, he could only have done so before the public, or he himself, had yet acquired any clear notion of the character and achievements of the latter. To call the King of Navarre Ferdinand rather than Henry and ignore his pretensions to the French crown, to say nothing (virtually) of the military fame of the four gentlemen and associate Dumaine in friendship with the rest, or alternatively, to confuse Dumaine with d'Aumont,[13] would have affronted common intelligence if attempted very long after the death of Henri III (August 2, 1589) had brought them all upon the centre of the political stage. I take it that the period between Henri III's assassination and the battle of Ivry (March 14, 1590) was the latest at which an English dramatist could have thought of thus irrelevantly employing the names of the leading French generals for the heroes of a comedy of love and the simple life.

Mr. Charlton's assumption that the revision of the play was slight is contradicted by the large amount of discrepancy between mature and immature work, and also by the curious and cumbrous structure of the existing text, in which the first three acts together are only half the length of the last two and not as long as the colossal second scene of Act V.

The first three acts doubtless represent the scale upon which the comedy was originally written. The earliest critic who attempted to distinguish closely between the two texts (of *ca.* 1590 and *ca.* 1597) appears to have been Spedding, whose apportionment, made in 1839, is quoted by Dr. Furnivall.[14] In a paper on 'The Original Version of *Love's Labour's Lost*' (1918) Professor

---

9 Dr. Johnson made the plausible conjecture that Shakespeare's character of Holofernes owes something to the pedantic schoolmaster, Rombus, in Sir Philip Sidney's pastoral play, *The Lady of May*, acted before Queen Elizabeth in 1578.

10 *Life of Shakespeare*, 1923, p. 142 f. Compare Professor O. F. Emerson in an article on 'Shakespeare's Sonneteering,' *Studies in Philology*, April, 1923, p. 122.

11 I do not deal with the special allusions which Mr. Charlton finds in individual passages of the play to books and events of the period 1590–1592. In most cases the dates implied do not seem to me decisive, and Mr. Charlton's unsupported hypothesis that practically everything in the play was in it from the beginning removes the matter from the field of argument.

12 Dr. Furnivall refers to Stow's statement that in September, 1589, 'the citizens of London furnished a thousand men to be sent over into France, to the aiding of Henry, late King of Navarre, then challenging the crown of France.' Mr. Charlton rather perversely, as it seems to me, refuses to believe that there can have been sufficient public interest at this date.

13 See Sources of the Play, p. 91, note 3.

14 Facsimile of 1598 Quarto, pp. viii, ix; Leopold Shakespere, p. xxiii.

H. D. Gray has attempted with interesting results to discover the scope of the original play, basing his arguments upon evidences of organic unity and 'youthful love of symmetry,' as well as upon style. In the recent Cambridge edition Mr. Dover Wilson has made a similar attempt,[15] independently and by means of totally different criteria—chiefly the bibliographical phenomena of the Quarto and Folio texts. The various results are of course contradictory in many details, but the investigators all agree in assigning a large preponderance of the first three acts to the original version and the larger part of the last two to the revision.

THE HISTORY OF THE PLAY

The known history of *Love's Labour's Lost* begins with the evidence found on the title-page of the earliest edition[16] the Quarto of 1598. This reads: 'A Pleasant Conceited Comedie Called, Loues labors lost. As it vvas presented before her Highnes this last Christmas. Newly corrected and augmented By W. Shakespeare.' Her Highness was Queen Elizabeth and the Christmas performance alluded to probably took place during the season of December, 1597–January, 1598.[17] The statement that the play had been newly corrected and augmented is substantiated beyond all question by the text itself, particularly in the fourth and fifth acts.[18]

Love's Labour's Lost is the earliest of Shakespeare's plays concerning which we have notice of a special performance at court and probably also the earliest to name Shakespeare as author on the printed title-page. It is mentioned in Meres' *Palladis Tamia* (1598), third in the list of six comedies ascribed to the poet, and again in the same year in Robert Tofte's *Alba*, where the allusion is casual and more complimentary to the actors than to the dramatist:

'*Loues Labor Lost, I once did see a Play*
Ycleped so, so called to my paine,
Which I to heare to my small Ioy did stay,
Giuing attendance on my froward Dame,
    My misgiuing minde presaging to me Ill,
    Yet was I drawne to see it gainst my Will.

'*This Play no Play, but Plague was vnto me,*
For there I lost the Loue I liked most:
And what to others seemde a Iest to be,
I that in earnest found vnto my cost:
    To euery one (saue me) twas Comicall,
    Whilst Tragick like to me it did befall.

'*Each Actor plaid in cunning wise his part,*
But chiefly Those entrapt in Cupids snare:
Yet all was fained, twas not from the hart,

They seemde to grieue, but yet they felt no care:
    Twas I that Griefe (indeed) did beare in brest,
    The others did but make a show in Iest.'

The sonnets of Berowne (IV. ii. 104–117) and Longaville (IV. iii. 55–68) and Dumaine's 'ode' (IV. iii. 99–118) were reprinted by William Jaggard in 1599 in the pirated volume called *The Passionate Pilgrim*, and Dumaine's poem was also included in the anthology, *England's Helicon*, in 1600. Later William Drummond of Hawthornden lists the comedy as one of the 'Bookes red be me, *anno* 1606,' when Drummond was staying in London. Property rights in the published play are affirmed when, on January 22, 1606/7, Burby, the publisher of the 1598 Quarto (who seems not to have entered it himself), transferred *Love's Labour's Lost*, along with *Romeo and Juliet* and *The Taming of a Shrew* to Nicholas Linge. Less than a year later Linge surrendered all three plays (November 19, 1607) to John Smethwick, who was later one of the partners in the Folio Shakespeare.

Though probably never notably popular, *Love's Labour's Lost* showed unusual staying powers during the Shakespearean era. First produced at the opening of the poet's career, it was rewritten, as we have seen, in 1597–8 for the particular amusement of Queen Elizabeth. A little over a year after her death it was again selected for court performance in order to divert her successor, Anne of Denmark (Queen of James I), as is witnessed by the following very interesting letter from Sir Walter Cope to Viscount Cranborne (i.e. Sir Robert Cecil, later Lord Salisbury):

'Sir,—I haue sent and bene all thys morning huntyng for players Juglers & Such kinde of Creaturs, but fynde them harde to fynde; wherefore leauing notes for them to seek me, Burbage ys come, and sayes there is no new playe that the quene hath not seene, but they haue reuyued an olde one, cawled *Loves Labore Lost*, which for wytt & mirthe he sayes will please her exceedingly. And thys ys appointed to be played to morrowe night at my Lord of Sowthamptons, unless yow send a wrytt to remove the *corpus cum causa* to your howse in Strande. Burbage ys my messenger ready attending your pleasure.' This is dated '1604,' and the performance referred to is fixed by Mr. Chambers as between January 8 and January 15, 1604/5.[19] The audit office accounts for 1604–5 record the acting 'By his Majesty's players' of 'A play of Loues Labours Lost' between New Year's Day and Twelfth Day (January 6).

A certain degree of continued popularity is indicated by the publication of another Quarto edition of *Love's Labour's Lost* in 1631, during the period, that is, between the appearance of the first and second Folio editions of Shakespeare, when relatively few of his plays were being called for in separate form. The statement on the title-page of this Quarto, 'As it was acted by his Majesty's Servants at the Blackfriars and the Globe,' if correct, proves that revivals must have occurred after 1608–9, when Shakespeare's company first began to use the Blackfriars' Theatre.

Later the play fell into total obscurity for over a century. No performances or adaptations are known during the period of the Restoration or the first half of the eighteenth century. Dryden in 1672[20] groups *Love's Labour's Lost* with *The Winter's Tale* and *Measure for Measure* as examples of the worst of Shakespeare's plays, 'which were either grounded on impossibilities, or at least so meanly written, that the comedy neither caused your mirth,

---

15 The results are summarized on p. 116, of the Cambridge edition.

16 Mr. Pollard has argued that this Quarto was probably preceded by a piratical earlier edition of which no trace remains. The evidence is purely bibliographical and circumstantial, but carries weight.

17 The Elizabethan year began with March 25. Hence if the Quarto was printed between January 1 and March 24, 'this last Christmas' would be Christmas, 1598, by our reckoning. Halliwell-Phillipps (Furness, p. 336) suggested a connection of the performance of the play with a recorded payment in December, 1597, 'for altering and making readie of soundrie chambers at Whitehall against Christmas, and for the plaies, and for making readie in the hall for her Maiestie.' Shakespeare's company acted at court on December 26 of both years, 1597 and 1598, and also on the following January 1 (1598 and 1599).

18 See notes on IV. iii. 313–317 and V. ii. 861–867.

19 *Elizabethan Stage*, iv. 139 f.

20 *The Conquest of Granada*, Pt. II. Defence of the Epilogue.

nor the serious part your concernment.' Jeremy Collier (1699) says briefly of it that 'the poet plays the fool egregiously, for the whole play is a very silly one'; and Gildon (1710) brands it as 'one of the worst of Shakespear's Plays, nay, I think I may say, the very worst.'

When *As You Like It* was revived in 1740, the cuckoo song from the close of *Love's Labour's Lost* was interpolated into the acting version of the other play, where it long continued to be used.[21] This would seem to be the only part of *Love's Labour's Lost* that ever appeared on the eighteenth-century stage. The first known adaptation of our play was printed in 1762 with the title: 'The Students. A Comedy Altered from Shakespeare's Love's Labours Lost, and Adapted to the Stage.' Though equipped with elaborate prologue and epilogue in heroic couplets, there is no evidence that this work ever reached the stage for which it had been 'adapted.' Only about 800 lines of the original play are retained;[22] the characters of Holofernes and Nathaniel are omitted entirely, and the mask of Muscovites and show of Nine Worthies are replaced by a 'comic dance' in dumb-show. The alterations of Shakespeare's main plot are rather remarkable. Berowne puts on a coat intended for Costard, and having thus easily rendered himself irrecognizable, carries messages between the lords and ladies. In this way he secures information enough about the real sentiments of them all to dominate the situation and force an immediate happy ending instead of the year's postponement proposed by the Princess. His closing words express the author's high sense of his improvement upon the original:

> '*Our wooing now doth end like an old play;*
> *Jack hath his Jill; these ladies' courtesie*
> *Hath nobly made our sport a Comedy.*'

Another apparently unacted revision of *Love's Labour's Lost*, likewise anonymous, is preserved in a single copy at the British Museum. It dates from about the year 1800. This version also eliminates Holofernes and Nathaniel and concludes with the la-

dies' consent to immediate matrimony, brought about in a manner quite different from that employed in *The Students.* The characters of Costard and Jaquenetta (Jaquelina) are much romanticized, and they too are made happy at the end. Armado is presented as a demi-villain, and eavesdropping is employed even more copiously than in the original play.

On September 30, 1839, the first recorded performance of *Love's Labour's Lost* since Shakespearean times was given at Covent Garden. Madame Vestris played Rosaline; Harley, Armado; and Anderson, Berowne. The piece was performed nine times and three slightly differing versions of the acting text were published. In 1857 Samuel Phelps presented the play at the Sadler's Wells Theatre, Phelps himself taking the part of Armado. In 1885 and again in 1907 it was produced at the Memorial Theatre, Stratford-on-Avon, as the Shakespeare Birthday play (April 23), Mr. F. R. Benson playing Berowne on the latter occasion. The English Drama Society gave it in Bloomsbury Hall, April 24, 1906. Other productions are recorded by the companies of Charles Fry, Ben Greet, and Florence Glossop-Harris. An acting version, 'adapted by Elsie Fogerty for Girls' Schools,' was published in 1912. Recently, under the management of Miss Lillian Baylis, *Love's Labour's Lost* has appeared frequently in the repertory of the Royal Victoria Hall ('Old Vic.') in London; e.g. in the spring of 1918 and during the season that began September 22, 1923. The most recent production was that given by the Oxford University Dramatic Society in Wadham College garden, June 21, 1924. The enthusiastic tone of the critics of these late performances[23] shows that the play is now gaining in the esteem of audiences as during the past generation it has gained in the favor of critics and general readers.

The most important American productions of *Love's Labour's Lost* were those arranged by Augustin Daly in New York, in 1874, and again in 1891. The German Shakespeare scholar, Rudolph Genée, brought out in 1887 a considerably altered version in three acts for the German stage. In recent times this has usually been supplanted by translations which adhere more closely to the original.

---

21 Cf. Furness, p. 316, note on line 976. Both the cuckoo song and the other song of winter were printed in 1671 in an anthology called *The New Academy of Compliments.*

22 As counted by F. Schult, *Bühnenbearbeitungen von Shakespeares "Love's Labour's Lost,"* 1910.

23 See reviews, for example, in the *Manchester Guardian*, September 28, 1923, and June 27, 1924.

ACT FIRST ❧ SCENE FIRST

[The King of Navarre's Park]
Enter Ferdinand King of Navarre, Berowne, Longaville, and
Dumaine.

King. Let fame, that all hunt after in their lives,
Live register'd upon our brazen tombs,
And then grace us in the disgrace of death;
When, spite of cormorant devouring Time,
Th' endeavour of this present breath may buy   5
That honour which shall bate his scythe's keen edge,
And make us heirs of all eternity.
Therefore, brave conquerors,—for so you are,
That war against your own affections
And the huge army of the world's desires,—   10
Our late edict shall strongly stand in force:
Navarre shall be the wonder of the world;
Our court shall be a little academe,
Still and contemplative in living art.
You three, Berowne, Dumaine, and Longaville,   15
Have sworn for three years' term to live with me,
My fellow-scholars, and to keep those statutes
That are recorded in this schedule here:
Your oaths are pass'd; and now subscribe your names,
That his own hand may strike his honour down   20
That violates the smallest branch herein.
If you are arm'd to do, as sworn to do,
Subscribe to your deep oaths, and keep it too.
    Long. I am resolv'd; 'tis but a three years' fast:
The mind shall banquet, though the body pine: 25
Fat paunches have lean pates, and dainty bits
Make rich the ribs, but bankrupt quite the wits.
    Dum. My loving lord, Dumaine is mortified:
The grosser manner of these world's delights
He throws upon the gross world's baser slaves: 30
To love, to wealth, to pomp, I pine and die;
With all these living in philosophy.
    Ber. I can but say their protestation over;
So much, dear liege, I have already sworn,
That is, to live and study here three years.   35
But there are other strict observances;
As, not to see a woman in that term,
Which I hope well is not enrolled there:
And one day in a week to touch no food,
And but one meal on every day beside;   40
The which I hope is not enrolled there:
And then, to sleep but three hours in the night,
And not be seen to wink of all the day,—
When I was wont to think no harm all night
And make a dark night too of half the day,—   45
Which I hope well is not enrolled there.
O! these are barren tasks, too hard to keep,
Not to see ladies, study, fast, not sleep.
    King. Your oath is pass'd to pass away from these.
    Ber. Let me say no, my liege, an if you please.   50

I only swore to study with your Grace,
And stay here in your court for three years' space.
    Long. You swore to that, Berowne, and to the rest.
    Ber. By yea and nay, sir, then I swore in jest.
What is the end of the study? let me know.   55
    King. Why, that to know which else we should not know.
    Ber. Things hid and barr'd, you mean, from common sense?
    King. Ay, that is study's godlike recompense.
    Ber. Come on then; I will swear to study so,
To know the thing I am forbid to know;   60
As thus: to study where I well may dine,
When I to feast expressly am forbid;
Or study where to meet some mistress fine,
When mistresses from common sense are hid;
Or, having sworn too hard-a-keeping oath,   65
Study to break it, and not break my troth.
If study's gain be thus, and this be so,
Study knows that which yet it doth not know.
Swear me to this, and I will ne'er say no.
    King. These be the stops that hinder study quite,   70
And train our intellects to vain delight.
    Ber. Why, all delights are vain; but that most vain
Which, with pain purchas'd, doth inherit pain:
As, painfully to pore upon a book,
To seek the light of truth; while truth the while   75
Doth falsely blind the eyesight of his look:
Light seeking light doth light of light beguile:
So, ere you find where light in darkness lies,
Your light grows dark by losing of your eyes.
Study me how to please the eye indeed,   80
By fixing it upon a fairer eye,
Who dazzling so, that eye shall be his heed,
And give him light that it was blinded by.
Study is like the heaven's glorious sun,
That will not be deep-search'd with saucy looks: 85
Small have continual plodders ever won,
Save base authority from others' books.
These earthly godfathers of heaven's lights,
That give a name to every fixed star,
Have no more profit of their shining nights   90
Than those that walk and wot not what they are.
Too much to know is to know nought but fame;
And every godfather can give a name.
    King. How well he's read, to reason against reading!
    Dum. Proceeded well, to stop all good proceeding!   95
    Long. He weeds the corn, and still lets grow the weeding.
    Ber. The spring is near, when green geese are abreeding.
    Dum. How follows that?
    Ber.   Fit in his place and time.
    Dum. In reason nothing.   100
    Ber.   Something, then, in rime.
    King. Berowne is like an envious sneaping frost
That bites the first-born infants of the spring.
    Ber. Well, say I am: why should proud summer boast
Before the birds have any cause to sing?   105
Why should I joy in any abortive birth?

LOVE'S LABOUR'S LOST; *cf. n.*   4 cormorant: *ravenous*   6 bate: *blunt*   12 Navarre;
cf. n.   13 academe: *academy*   14 living art: *the art of living; cf. n.*   19 subscribe:
sign   22 arm'd: *ready*   26 pates: *heads*   27 wits: *faculties of the mind*   28 mortified: *dead so far as pleasures and passions are concerned*   32 all these: *i.e. love, wealth,
pomp*   38 there: *i.e. in the schedule*   43 wink of: *close the eyes during*   47 barren:
fruitless, futile   50 an if: *if*

54 By yea and nay: *i.e. by the most positive oath of affirmation and denial*   57 common
sense: *ordinary sight or perception*   62 feast: *cf. n.*   67, 68 Cf. n.   73 Cf. n.   76
his: *its*   77 beguile: *deprive*   79 light: *i.e. sight*   80–83 Study me ... blinded
by; *cf. n.*   85 saucy: *bold*   86 Small: *little*   88–93 Cf. n.   91 wot: *know*   95
Proceeded; *cf. n.*   97 green geese: *grass-fed goslings, i.e. simpletons*   101 Cf. n.   102
sneaping: *nipping*   103 infants: *buds or flowers*

At Christmas I no more desire a rose
Than wish a snow in May's new-fangled shows;
But like of each thing that in season grows.
So you, to study now it is too late,   *110*
Climb o'er the house to unlock the little gate.
    King. Well, sit you out: go home, Berowne: adieu!
    Ber. No, my good lord; I have sworn to stay with you:
And though I have for barbarism spoke more
Than for that angel knowledge you can say,   *115*
Yet confident I'll keep what I have sworn,
And bide the penance of each three years' day.
Give me the paper; let me read the same;
And to the strictest decrees I'll write my name.
    King. How well this yielding rescues thee from shame!   *120*
    Ber. 'Item. That no woman shall come with-in a mile of my
court.' Hath this been proclaimed?
    Long. Four days ago.
    Ber. Let's see the penalty. 'On pain of losing her tongue.'
Who devised this penalty?   *125*
    Long. Marry, that did I.
    Ber.   Sweet lord, and why?
    Long. To fright them hence with that dread penalty.
    [Ber.]. A dangerous law against gentility!
    'Item. If any man be seen to talk with a woman within   *130*
the term of three years, he shall endure such public shame
as the rest of the court can possibly devise.'
This article, my liege, yourself must break;
For well you know here comes in embassy
The French king's daughter with yourself to speak—   *135*
A maid of grace and complete majesty—
About surrender up of Aquitaine
To her decrepit, sick, and bed-rid father.
Therefore this article is made in vain,
Or vainly comes th' admired princess hither.   *140*
    King. What say you, lords? why, this was quite forgot.
    Ber. So study evermore is overshot:
While it doth study to have what it would,
It doth forget to do the thing it should;
And when it hath the thing it hunteth most,   *145*
'Tis won as towns with fire; so won, so lost.
    King. We must of force dispense with this decree;
She must lie here on mere necessity.
    Ber. Necessity will make us all forsworn
Three thousand times within this three years' space: *150*
For every man with his affects is born,
Not by might master'd, but by special grace.
If I break faith, this word shall speak for me:
I am forsworn 'on mere necessity.'
So to the laws at large I write my name: *[Signs.] 155*
And he that breaks them in the least degree
Stands in attainder of eternal shame.
Suggestions are to others as to me;
But I believe, although I seem so loath,
I am the last that will last keep his oath.   *160*
But is there no quick recreation granted?
    King. Ay, that there is. Our court, you know, is haunted

With a refined traveller of Spain,
A man in all the world's new fashion planted,
That hath a mint of phrases in his brain;   *165*
One who the music of his own vain tongue
Doth ravish like enchanting harmony;
A man of complements, whom right and wrong
Have chose as umpire of their mutiny.
This child of fancy, that Armado hight,   *170*
For interim to our studies shall relate
In high-born words the worth of many a knight
From tawny Spain lost in the world's debate.
How you delight, my lords, I know not, I;
But, I protest, I love to hear him lie,   *175*
And I will use him for my minstrelsy.
    Ber. Armado is a most illustrious wight,
A man of fire-new words, fashion's own knight.
    Long. Costard the swain and he shall be our sport;
And, so to study, three years is but short.   *180*

     Enter a Constable [Dull] with Costard with a Letter.

    Const. Which is the duke's own person?
    Ber. This, fellow. What wouldst?
    Const. I myself reprehend his own person, for I am his
Grace's tharborough: but I would see his own person in flesh
and blood.   *185*
    Ber. This is he.
    Const. Signior Arm—Arm—commends you. There's villainy
abroad: this letter will tell you more.
    Cost. Sir, the contempts thereof are as touching me.
    King. A letter from the magnificent Armado.   *190*
    Ber. How low soever the matter, I hope in God for high
words.
    Long. A high hope for a low heaven: God grant us patience!
    Ber. To hear, or forbear laughing?
    Long. To hear meekly, sir, and to laugh moderately,   *195*
or to forbear both.
    Ber. Well, sir, be it as the style shall give us
cause to climb in the merriness.
    Cost. The matter is to me, sir, as concerning Jaquenetta.
The manner of it is, I was taken with the manner.   *200*
    Ber. In what manner?
    Cost. In manner and form following, sir; all those three: I
was seen with her in the manor-house, sitting with her upon
the form, and taken following her into the park; which, put
together, is, in manner and form following. Now, sir,   *205*
for the manner,—it is the manner of a man to speak to a
woman, for the form,—in some form.
    Ber. For the following, sir?
    Cost. As it shall follow in my correction; and
God defend the right!   *210*
    King. Will you hear this letter with attention?
    Ber. As we would hear an oracle.
    Cost. Such is the simplicity of man to hearken after the
flesh.
    King. [Reads.] 'Great deputy, the welkin's vice-gerent,   *215*

and sole dominator of Navarre, my soul's earth's God, and
body's fostering patron,—'

Cost. Not a word of Costard yet.

King. [*Reads.*] 'So it is,—'

Cost. It may be so; but if he say it is so, he is, in telling 220
true, but so.—

King. Peace!

Cost. Be to me and every man that dares not fight.

King. No words!

Cost. Of other men's secrets, I beseech you.   225

King. [*Reads.*]. 'So it is, besieged with sable-coloured melancholy, I did commend the black-oppressing humour to the
most wholesome physic of thy health-giving air; and, as I am a
gentleman, betook myself to walk. The time when? About the
sixth hour; when beasts most graze, birds best peck, and men
sit down to that nourishment which is called supper: so much
for the time when. Now for the ground which; which, I mean,
I walked upon: it is ycleped thy park. Then for the place
where; where, I mean, I did encounter that most obscene and
preposterous event, that draweth from my snow-white pen 235
the ebon-coloured ink, which here thou viewest, beholdest,
surveyest, or seest. But to the place where, it standeth north-
north-east and by east from the west corner of thy curious-
knotted garden. There did I see that low-spirited swain, that
base minnow of thy mirth,—'   240

Cost. Me?

King. [*Reads.*] 'that unlettered small-knowing soul,—'

Cost. Me?

King. [*Reads.*] 'that shallow vessel,—'

Cost. Still me?   245

King. [*Reads.*] 'which, as I remember, hight Costard,—'

Cost. O me!

King. [*Reads.*] 'sorted and consorted, contrary to thy established proclaimed edict and continent canon, with—with,—O!
with—but with this I passion to say wherewith,—'   250

Cost. With a wench.

King. [*Reads.*] 'with a child of our grandmother Eve, a
female; or, for thy more sweet understanding, a woman. Him
I,—as my ever-esteemed duty pricks me on,—have sent to
thee, to receive the meed of punishment, by thy sweet   255
Grace's officer, Anthony Dull; a man of good repute,
carriage, bearing, and estimation.'

Dull. Me, an 't shall please you; I am Anthony Dull.

King. [*Reads.*] 'For Jaquenetta,—so is the weaker vessel called
which I apprehended with the aforesaid swain,—I keep her 260
as a vessel of thy law's fury; and shall, at the least of thy sweet
notice, bring her to trial. Thine, in all compliments of devoted
and heart-burning heat of duty,   *Don Adriano de Armado.*'

Ber. This is not so well as I looked for, but the best that
ever I heard.   265

King. Ay, the best for the worst. But, sirrah, what say you
to this?

Cost. Sir, I confess the wench.

King. Did you hear the proclamation?

Cost. I do confess much of the hearing it, but little of 270
the marking of it.

King. It was proclaimed a year's imprisonment to be taken
with a wench.

Cost. I was taken with none, sir: I was taken with a damsel.

King. Well, it was proclaimed 'damsel.'   275

Cost. This was no damsel neither, sir: she was a virgin.

King. It is so varied too; for it was proclaimed 'virgin.'

Cost. If it were, I deny her virginity: I was taken with a
maid.

King. This maid will not serve your turn, sir.   280

Cost. This maid will serve my turn, sir.

King. Sir, I will pronounce your sentence: you shall fast a
week with bran and water.

Cost. I had rather pray a month with mutton and porridge.

King. And Don Armado shall be your keeper.   285
My Lord Berowne, see him deliver'd o'er:
And go we, lords, to put in practice that
Which each to other hath so strongly sworn.

            [*Exeunt King, Longaville, and Dumaine.*]

Ber. I'll lay my head to any good man's hat,
These oaths and laws will prove an idle scorn.   290
Sirrah, come on.

Cost. I suffer for the truth, sir: for true it is I was taken
with Jaquenetta, and Jaquenetta is a true girl; and therefore welcome the sour cup of prosperity! Affliction may one day smile
again; and till then, sit thee down, sorrow!   *Exeunt.* 295

❧ SCENE SECOND ❧

[The Same]
Enter Armado and Moth his Page.

Arm. Boy, what sign is it when a man of great spirit grows
melancholy?

Boy. A great sign, sir, that he will look sad.

Arm. Why, sadness is one and the self-same thing, dear imp.

Boy. No, no; O Lord, sir, no.   5

Arm. How canst thou part sadness and melancholy, my
tender juvenal?

Boy. By a familiar demonstration of the working, my tough
senior.

Arm. Why tough senior? why tough senior?   10

Boy. Why tender juvenal? why tender juvenal?

Arm. I spoke it, tender juvenal, as a congruent epitheton appertaining to thy young days, which we may nominate tender.

Boy. And I, tough senior, as an appertinent title to your old
time, which we may name tough.   15

Arm. Pretty, and apt.

Boy. How mean you, sir? I pretty, and my saying apt? or I
apt, and my saying pretty?

Arm. Thou pretty, because little.

Boy. Little pretty, because little. Wherefore apt?   20

Arm. And therefore apt, because quick.

Boy. Speak you this in my praise, master?

Arm. In thy condign praise.

Boy. I will praise an eel with the same praise.

Arm. What! that an eel is ingenious?   25

Boy. That an eel is quick.

Arm. I do say thou art quick in answers: thou heat'st my
blood.

---

233 ycleped: *called*   **238 curious-knotted:** *fancifully laid out in intricate beds*   **248
sorted:** *associated*   **249 continent:** *i.e. containing a summary of offenses*   **250 passion:**
grieve   **271 marking of:** *paying attention to*

275 damsel: *a young unmarried woman of good birth*   **284 mutton:** *slang for 'loose
woman'*   **289 lay:** *wager*   **4 imp:** *child*   **12 congruent epitheton:** *suitable epithet*   **13 nominate:** *call*   **14 appertinent:** *appropriate*

Boy. I am answered, sir.

Arm. I love not to be crossed.   30

Boy. [*Aside.*] He speaks the mere contrary; crosses love not him.

Arm. I have promised to study three years with the duke.

Boy. You may do it in an hour, sir.

Arm. Impossible.   35

Boy. How many is one thrice told?

Arm. I am ill at reckoning; it fitteth the spirit of a tapster.

Boy. You are a gentleman and a gamester, sir.

Arm. I confess both: they are both the varnish of a complete man.   40

Boy. Then, I am sure you know how much the gross sum of deuce-ace amounts to.

Arm. It doth amount to one more than two.

Boy. Which the base vulgar do call three.

Arm. True.   45

Boy. Why, sir, is this such a piece of study? Now, here is three studied, ere ye'll thrice wink; and how easy it is to put 'years' to the word 'three,' and study three years in two words, the dancing horse will tell you.

Arm. A most fine figure!   50

Boy. To prove you a cipher.

Arm. I will hereupon confess I am in love; and as it is base for a soldier to love, so am I in love with a base wench. If drawing my sword against the humour of affection would deliver me from the reprobate thought of it, I would take Desire prisoner, and ransom him to any French courtier for a new devised curtsy. I think scorn to sigh: methinks I should outswear Cupid. Comfort me, boy: what great men have been in love?

Boy. Hercules, master.

Arm. Most sweet Hercules! More authority, dear boy,   60 name more; and, sweet my child, let them be men of good repute and carriage.

Boy. Samson, master: he was a man of good carriage, great carriage, for he carried the towngates on his back like a porter; and he was in love.   65

Arm. O well-knit Samson! strong-jointed Samson! I do excel thee in my rapier as much as thou didst me in carrying gates. I am in love too. Who was Samson's love, my dear Moth?

Boy. A woman, master.

Arm. Of what complexion?   70

Boy. Of all the four, or the three, or the two, or one of the four.

Arm. Tell me precisely of what complexion.

Boy. Of the sea-water green, sir.

Arm. Is that one of the four complexions?   75

Boy. As I have read, sir; and the best of them too.

Arm. Green indeed is the colour of lovers; but to have a love of that colour, methinks Samson had small reason for it. He surely affected her for her wit.

Boy. It was so, sir, for she had a green wit.   80

Arm. My love is most immaculate white and red.

Boy. Most maculate thoughts, master, are masked under such colours.

Arm. Define, define, well-educated infant.

Boy. My father's wit, and my mother's tongue, assist me!   85

Arm. Sweet invocation of a child; most pretty and pathetical!

Boy. If she be made of white and red,
   Her faults will ne'er be known,
For blushing cheeks by faults are bred,   90
   And fears by pale white shown:
Then if she fear, or be to blame,
   By this you shall not know,
For still her cheeks possess the same
   Which native she doth owe.   95
A dangerous rime, master, against the reason of white and red.

Arm. Is there not a ballet, boy, of the King and the Beggar?

Boy. The world was very guilty of such a ballet some three ages since; but I think now 'tis not to be found; or, if it were, it would neither serve for the writing nor the tune.   100

Arm. I will have that subject newly writ o'er, that I may example my digression by some mighty precedent. Boy, I do love that country girl that I took in the park with the rational hind Costard: she deserves well.

Boy. [*Aside.*] To be whipped; and yet a better love than   105 my master.

Arm. Sing, boy: my spirit grows heavy in love.

Boy. And that's great marvel, loving a light wench.

Arm. I say, sing.

Boy. Forbear till this company be past.   110

*Enter Clown [Costard], Constable [Dull], and Wench
[Jaquenetta].*

Const. Sir, the duke's pleasure is, that you keep Costard safe: and you must suffer him to take no delight nor no penance, but a' must fast three days a week. For this damsel, I must keep her at the park; she is allowed for the day-woman.   115 Fare you well.

Arm. I do betray myself with blushing. Maid!

Maid. [*Jaq.*] Man?

Arm. I will visit thee at the lodge.

Maid. That's hereby.   120

Arm. I know where it is situate.

Maid. Lord, how wise you are!

Arm. I will tell thee wonders.

Maid. With that face?

Arm. I love thee.   125

Maid. So I heard you say.

Arm. And so farewell.

Maid. Fair weather after you!

Const. Come, Jaquenetta, away!

                Exeunt [Dull and Jaquenetta].

Arm. Villain, thou shalt fast for thy offences ere thou be   130 pardoned.

Clow. Well, sir, I hope, when I do it, I shall do it on a full stomach.

Arm. Thou shalt be heavily punished.

Clow. I am more bound to you than your fellows, for   135 they are but lightly rewarded.

Arm. Take away this villain: shut him up.

Boy. Come, you transgressing slave: away!

Clow. Let me not be pent up, sir: I will fast, being loose.

31 crosses: *coins (which had crosses on them)*   **49 dancing horse;** *cf. n.*   **50 figure:** *illustration*   **54 humour of affection:** *caprice of being in love*   **57 think:** *think it*   **70 complexion:** *disposition; cf. n.*   **79 affected:** *liked* **wit:** *understanding*   **80 green wit;** *cf. n.*

87 pathetical: *touching*   **95 native:** *naturally* **owe:** *own, possess*   **97** *Cf. n.* **ballet:** *ballad*   **99 ages:** *generations*   **102 digression:** *deviation from my nature, i.e. debasement*   **103 rational:** *reasoning, i.e. not stupid*   **105 love:** *lover*   **114 a':** *he*   **115 allowed:** *approved of* **day-woman:** *dairy-woman*

Boy. No, sir; that were fast and loose: thou shalt to prison.

Clow. Well, if ever I do see the merry days of desolation
that I have seen, some shall see—

Boy. What shall some see?

Clow. Nay, nothing, Master Moth, but what they look
upon. It is not for prisoners to be too silent in their words; *145*
and therefore I will say nothing: I thank God I have as little
patience as another man, and therefore I can be quiet.

         Exit [Costard; also Moth].

Arm. I do affect the very ground, which is base, where
her shoe, which is baser, guided by her foot, which is basest,
doth tread. I shall be forsworn,—which is a great argument *150*
of falsehood,—if I love. And how can that be true love
which is falsely attempted? Love is a familiar; Love is a devil:
there is no evil angel but Love. Yet was Samson so tempted,
and he had an excellent strength; yet was Solomon so seduced,
and he had a very good wit. Cupid's butt-shaft is too hard *155*
for Hercules' club, and therefore too much odds for a
Spaniard's rapier. The first and second cause will not serve
my turn; the passado he respects not, the duello he regards
not: his disgrace is to be called boy, but his glory is to subdue
men. Adieu, valour! rust, rapier! be still, drum! for your *160*
manager is in love; yea, he loveth. Assist me some extemporal
god of rime, for I am sure I shall turn sonnet. Devise, wit;
write, pen; for I am for whole volumes in folio.   *Exit.*

ACT SECOND ❦ SCENE FIRST

[The King of Navarre's Park. A Pavilion and Tents at a distance]
Enter the Princess of France, with three attending Ladies [Rosaline,
Maria, Katharine,] and three Lords [Boyet and attending Lords].

Boyet. Now, madam, summon up your dearest spirits:
Consider whom the king your father sends,
To whom he sends, and what's his embassy:
Yourself, held precious in the world's esteem,
To parley with the sole inheritor   *5*
Of all perfections that a man may owe,
Matchless Navarre; the plea of no less weight
Than Aquitaine, a dowry for a queen.
Be now as prodigal of all dear grace
As Nature was in making graces dear,   *10*
When she did starve the general world beside,
And prodigally gave them all to you.

Prin. Good Lord Boyet, my beauty, though but mean,
Needs not the painted flourish of your praise:
Beauty is bought by judgment of the eye,   *15*
Not utter'd by base sale of chapmen's tongues.
I am less proud to hear you tell my worth
Than you much willing to be counted wise
In spending your wit in the praise of mine.
But now to task the tasker: good Boyet,   *20*
You are not ignorant, all-telling fame
Doth noise abroad, Navarre hath made a vow,

Till painful study shall outwear three years,
No woman may approach his silent court:
Therefore to's seemeth it a needful course,   *25*
Before we enter his forbidden gates,
To know his pleasure; and in that behalf,
Bold of your worthiness, we single you
As our best-moving fair solicitor.
Tell him, the daughter of the King of France,   *30*
On serious business, craving quick dispatch,
Importunes personal conference with his Grace.
Haste, signify so much; while we attend,
Like humble-visag'd suitors, his high will.

 Boyet. Proud of employment, willingly I go. *Exit Boyet.* *35*

 Prin. All pride is willing pride, and yours is so.
Who are the votaries, my loving lords,
That are vow-fellows with this virtuous duke?

 [A] Lord. Longaville is one.

 Prin.   Know you the man? *40*

 1. Lad. [Maria]. I know him, madam: at a marriage feast,
Between Lord Perigort and the beauteous heir
Of Jacques Falconbridge solemnized,
In Normandy saw I this Longaville.
A man of sovereign parts he is esteem'd;   *45*
Well fitted in the arts, glorious in arms:
Nothing becomes him ill that he would well.
The only soil of his fair virtue's gloss,—
If virtue's gloss will stain with any soil,—
Is a sharp wit match'd with too blunt a will; *50*
Whose edge hath power to cut, whose will still wills
It should none spare that come within his power.

 Prin. Some merry mocking lord, belike; is 't so?

 1. Lad. They say so most that most his humours know.

 Prin. Such short-liv'd wits do wither as they grow. *55*
Who are the rest?

 2. Lad. [Kath.] The young Dumaine, a well-accomplish'd
youth,
Of all that virtue love for virtue lov'd:
Most power to do most harm, least knowing ill, *60*
For he hath wit to make an ill shape good,
And shape to win grace though he had no wit.
I saw him at the Duke Alençon's once;
And much too little of that good I saw
Is my report to his great worthiness.   *65*

 3. Lad. [Ros.] Another of these students at that time
Was there with him, if I have heard a truth.
Berowne they call him; but a merrier man,
Within the limit of becoming mirth,
I never spent an hour's talk withal.   *70*
His eye begets occasion for his wit;
For every object that the one doth catch
The other turns to a mirth-moving jest,
Which his fair tongue, conceit's expositor,
Delivers in such apt and gracious words,   *75*
That aged ears play truant at his tales,
And younger hearings are quite ravished;
So sweet and voluble is his discourse.

---

140 fast and loose: *cheating game of a sharper* **141 desolation;** *cf. n.* **148 affect:**
love **150 argument:** *proof* **152 familiar:** *familiar spirit, i.e. demon* **155 butt-shaft:**
arrow, without barb, for shooting at butts (targets) **157 cause:** *cause of quarrel* **158
passado:** *pass, or thrust, in fencing* **duello:** *duel* **161 manager:** *wielder of weapons* **162
turn sonnet:** *grow into a sonnet(?), turn sonneteer(?)* **1 dearest:** *best* **7 Navarre:** *King
of Navarre* **plea:** *suit* **16 utter'd:** *sold* **chapmen's:** *shopmen's*

25 to's: *to us* **28 Bold:** *confident* **29 best-moving fair:** *persuasive and just* **33
attend:** *await* **38 duke:** *i.e. king (cf. I. i. 181, I. ii. 135)* **42 Lord Perigort;**
cf. n. **47 would:** *i.e. would do* **50 blunt:** *harsh* **51 still:** *ever* **59 Of:** *by* **61
shape:** *form, or figure* **65 report:** *testimony; cf. n.* **70 withal:** *with* **74 conceit's
expositor:** *expounder of fancy* **76 Cf. n.**

Prin. God bless my ladies! are they all in love,
That every one her own hath garnished   *80*
With such bedecking ornaments of praise?
    [A] Lord. Here comes Boyet.

                              Enter Boyet.

    Prin.   Now, what admittance, lord?
    Boyet. Navarre had notice of your fair approach;
And he and his competitors in oath   *85*
Were all address'd to meet you, gentle lady,
Before I came. Marry, thus much I have learnt;
He rather means to lodge you in the field,
Like one that comes here to besiege his court,
Than seek a dispensation for his oath,   *90*
To let you enter his unpeopled house.

    Enter Navarre, Longaville, Dumaine, and Berowne.

Here comes Navarre.
    King. Fair princess, welcome to the court of Navarre.
    Prin. 'Fair' I give you back again; and 'welcome' I have
not yet: the roof of this court is too high to be yours, and   *95*
welcome to the wide fields too base to be mine.
    King. You shall be welcome, madam, to my court.
    Prin. I will be welcome, then: conduct me thither.
    King. Hear me, dear lady; I have sworn an oath.
    Prin. Our Lady help my lord! he'll be forsworn.   *100*
    King. Not for the world, fair madam, by my will.
    Prin. Why, will shall break it; will, and nothing else.
    King. Your ladyship is ignorant what it is.
    Prin. Were my lord so, his ignorance were wise,
Where now his knowledge must prove ignorance.   *105*
I hear your grace hath sworn out house-keeping:
'Tis deadly sin to keep that oath, my lord,
And sin to break it.
But pardon me, I am too sudden-bold:
To teach a teacher ill beseemeth me.   *110*
Vouchsafe to read the purpose of my coming,
And suddenly resolve me in my suit.   *[Gives a paper.]*
    King. Madam, I will, if suddenly I may.
    Prin. You will the sooner that I were away,
For you'll prove perjur'd if you make me stay.   *115*
    Ber. Did not I dance with you in Brabant once?
    Ros. Did not I dance with you in Brabant once?
    Ber. I know you did.
    Ros.   How needless was it then
To ask the question!   *120*
    Ber.   You must not be so quick.
    Ros. 'Tis 'long of you that spur me with such questions.
    Ber. Your wit's too hot, it speeds too fast, 'twill tire.
    Ros. Not till it leave the rider in the mire.
    Ber. What time o' day?   *125*
    Ros. The hour that fools should ask.
    Ber. How fair befall your mask!
    Ros. Fair fall the face it covers!
    Ber. And send you many lovers!
    Ros. Amen, so you be none.   *130*
    Ber. Nay, then will I be gone.
    King. Madam, your father here doth intimate

The payment of a hundred thousand crowns;
Being but the one half of an entire sum
Disbursed by my father in his wars.   *135*
But say that he, or we,—as neither have,—
Receiv'd that sum, yet there remains unpaid
A hundred thousand more; in surety of the which,
One part of Aquitaine is bound to us,
Although not valu'd to the money's worth.   *140*
If then the king your father will restore
But that one half which is unsatisfied,
We will give up our right in Aquitaine,
And hold fair friendship with his majesty.
But that, it seems, he little purposeth,   *145*
For here he doth demand to have repaid
A hundred thousand crowns; and not demands,
On payment of a hundred thousand crowns,
To have his title live in Aquitaine;
Which we much rather had depart withal,   *150*
And have the money by our father lent,
Than Aquitaine, so gelded as it is.
Dear princess, were not his requests so far
From reason's yielding, your fair self should make
A yielding 'gainst some reason in my breast,   *155*
And go well satisfied to France again.
    Prin. You do the king my father too much wrong,
And wrong the reputation of your name,
In so unseeming to confess receipt
Of that which hath so faithfully been paid.   *160*
    King. I do protest I never heard of it;
And if you prove it, I'll repay it back
Or yield up Aquitaine.
    Prin.   We arrest your word.
Boyet, you can produce acquittances   *165*
For such a sum from special officers
Of Charles his father.
    King.   Satisfy me so.
    Boyet. So please your Grace, the packet is not come
Where that and other specialties are bound: *170*
To-morrow you shall have a sight of them.
    King. It shall suffice me: at which interview
All liberal reason I will yield unto.
Meantime, receive such welcome at my hand
As honour, without breach of honour, may   *175*
Make tender of to thy true worthiness.
You may not come, fair princess, in my gates;
But here without you shall be so receiv'd,
As you shall deem yourself lodg'd in my heart,
Though so denied fair harbour in my house.   *180*
Your own good thoughts excuse me, and farewell:
To-morrow shall we visit you again.
    Prin. Sweet health and fair desires consort your Grace!
    King. Thy own wish wish I thee in every place!   *Exit [King].*
    Ber. Lady, I will commend you to mine own heart.   *185*
    Ros. Pray you, do my commendations; I would be glad
to see it.
    Ber. I would you heard it groan.
    Ros. Is the fool sick?

---

85 **competitors:** *associates*   86 **address'd:** *ready*   95 **roof of this court:** *i.e. the heaven*   105 **Where:** *whereas*   106 **sworn out house-keeping:** *forsworn hospitality*   112 **suddenly:** *quickly*   122 **'long:** *along, because*   127 **fair befall:** *mercy on*

134 *Cf. n.*   150 **depart withal:** *part with*   152 **gelded:** *maimed*   155 **A . . . reason:** *a rather unreasonable yielding*   159 **unseeming:** *seeming not*   164 **arrest:** *take up, challenge*   170 **specialties:** *corroborative documents*   179 **As:** *that*   183 **consort:** *accompany*

Ber. Sick at the heart.   *190*

Ros. Alack! let it blood.

Ber. Would that do it good?

Ros. My physic says, 'ay.'

Ber. Will you prick't with your eye?

Ros. No point, with my knife.   *195*

Ber. Now, God save thy life!

Ros. And yours from long living!

Ber. I cannot stay thanksgiving.   *Exit [i.e. Retires].*

Dum. [Advancing.] Sir, I pray you a word: what lady is that
same?   *200*

Boyet. The heir of Alençon, Katharine her name.

Dum. A gallant lady. Monsieur, fare you well.   *Exit.*

Long. I beseech you a word: what is she in the white.

Boyet. A woman sometimes, an you saw her in the light?

Long. Perchance light in the light. I desire her name.   *205*

Boyet. She hath but one for herself; to desire that were a
shame.

Long. Pray you, sir, whose daughter?

Boyet. Her mother's, I have heard.

Long. God's blessing on your beard!   *210*

Boyet. Good sir, be not offended.
She is an heir of Falconbridge.

Long. Nay, my choler is ended.
She is a most sweet lady.

Boyet. Not unlike, sir; that may be.   *Exit Longaville.*

Enter Berowne [i.e. he advances].

Ber. What's her name, in the cap?

Boyet. Rosaline, by good hap.

Ber. Is she wedded or no?

Boyet. To her will, sir, or so.

Ber. You are welcome, sir. Adieu.   *220*

Boyet. Farewell to me, sir, and welcome to you.

Exit Berowne.

Mar. That last is Berowne, the merry madcap lord:
Not a word with him but a jest.

Boyet.   And every jest but a word.

Prin. It was well done of you to take him at his word. *225*

Boyet. I was as willing to grapple, as he was to board.

Kath. Two hot sheeps, marry!

Boyet.   And wherefore not ships?
No sheep, sweet lamb, unless we feed on your lips.

Kath. You sheep, and I pasture: shall that finish the jest? *230*

Boyet. So you grant pasture for me. *[Offering to kiss her.]*

Kath.   Not so, gentle beast.
My lips are no common, though several they be.

Boyet. Belonging to whom?

Kath.   To my fortunes and me.

Prin. Good wits will be jangling; but, gentles, agree.
This civil war of wits were much better us'd
On Navarre and his book-men, for here 'tis abus'd.

Boyet. If my observation,—which very seldom lies,
By the heart's still rhetoric disclosed with eyes,—   *240*
Deceive me not now, Navarre is infected.

Prin. With what?

Boyet. With that which we lovers entitle affected.

Prin. Your reason.

Boyet. Why, all his behaviours did make their retire   *245*
To the court of his eye, peeping thorough desire.
His heart, like an agate, with your print impress'd,
Proud with his form, in his eye pride express'd.
His tongue, all impatient to speak and not see,
Did stumble with haste in his eyesight to be;   *250*
All senses to that sense did make their repair,
To feel only looking on fairest of fair:
Methought all his senses were lock'd in his eye,
As jewels in crystal for some prince to buy;
Who, tend'ring their own worth from where they were glass'd,
Did point you to buy them, along as you pass'd.
His face's own margent did quote such amazes,
That all eyes saw his eyes enchanted with gazes.
I'll give you Aquitaine, and all that is his,
An you give him for my sake but one loving kiss.   *260*

Prin. Come to our pavilion: Boyet is dispos'd.

Boyet. But to speak that in words which his eye hath disclos'd.
I only have made a mouth of his eye,
By adding a tongue which I know will not lie.

Ros. Thou art an old love-monger, and speak'st skilfully. *265*

Mar. He is Cupid's grandfather, and learns news of him.

Kath. Then was Venus like her mother, for her father is but
grim.

Boyet. Do you hear, my mad wenches?

Ros.   No.   *270*

Boyet.   What, then, do you see?

Ros. Ay, our way to be gone.

Boyet.   You are too hard for me.
Exeunt Omnes.

ACT THIRD ❧ SCENE FIRST

[The King of Navarre's Park]
Enter Braggart [Armado] and his Boy [Moth].

Arm. Warble, child; make passionate my sense of hearing.

Moth. [Singing.] Concolinel,—

Arm. Sweet air! Go, tenderness of years; take this key, give
enlargement to the swain, bring him festinately hither; I must
employ him in a letter to my love.   *5*

Moth. Master, will you win your love with a French brawl?

Arm. How meanest thou? brawling in French?

Moth. No, my complete master; but to jig off a tune at the
tongue's end, canary to it with your feet, humour it with turning up your eyelids, sigh a note and sing a note, sometime   *10*
through the throat, [as] if you swallowed love by singing love,
sometime through [the] nose, as if you snuffed up love by
smelling love; with your hat penthouse-like o'er the shop of
your eyes; with your arms crossed on your thin belly-doublet

---

243 affected: *loving, sentimental*   **246 court:** *governing center*   **248 with his:** *with
its*   **249 to speak and not see:** *not to be able to see rather than to speak*   **252 To feel
only looking:** *that they might feel only in looking*   **256 point:** *invite*   **257 margent:**
margin; cf. n. **quote:** *note*   **261 dispos'd:** *inclined to be merry*   **262 But:** *i.e. disposed
only*   **2 Concolinel:** *cf. n.*   **4 festinately:** *quickly*   **6 brawl:** *dance; cf. n.* **9
canary:** *dance; cf. n.*   **13 penthouse-like:** *porch-like*

---

191 let it blood; *cf. n.*   **195 No point;** *cf. n.*   **201 Katharine;** *cf. n.*   **204 an:**
if   **205 light in the light:** *of light conduct if known*   **210 Cf. n.**   **215 unlike:** *unlikely*   **221 Cf. n.**   **227 Kath.;** *cf. n.*   **233 common, though several;** *cf. n.*   **238
abus'd:** *misused*   **240 rhetoric:** *language*

like a rabbit on a spit; or your hands in your pocket like a   *15*
man after the old painting; and keep not too long in one
tune, but a snip and away. These are complements, these are
humours, these betray nice wenches, that would be betrayed
without these; and make them men of note,—do you note?
men,—that most are affected to these.   *20*

Arm. How hast thou purchased this experience?

Moth. By my penny of observation.

Arm. But O—but O,—

Moth. 'The hobby-horse is forgot.'

Arm. Callest thou my love 'hobby-horse'?   *25*

Moth. No, master; the hobby-horse is but a colt, and your
love perhaps a hackney. But have you forgot your love?

Arm. Almost I had.

Moth. Negligent student! learn her by heart.

Arm. By heart, and in heart, boy.   *30*

Moth. And out of heart, master: all those three I will prove.

Arm. What wilt thou prove?

Moth. A man, if I live; and this, by, in, and without, upon
the instant: by heart you love her, because your heart cannot
come by her; in heart you love her, because your heart is in   *35*
love with her; and out of heart you love her, being out of
heart that you cannot enjoy her.

Arm. I am all these three.

Moth. And three times as much more, and yet nothing at all.

Arm. Fetch hither the swain: he must carry me a letter.   *40*

Moth. A message well sympathized: a horse to be ambassador for an ass.

Arm. Ha, ha! what sayest thou?

Moth. Marry, sir, you must send the ass upon the horse, for
he is very slow-gaited. But I go.   *45*

Arm. The way is but short: away!

Moth. As swift as lead, sir.

Arm. The meaning, pretty ingenious?
Is not lead a metal heavy, dull, and slow?

Moth. Minime, honest master; or rather, master, no.   *50*

Arm. I say, lead is slow.

Moth.   You are too swift, sir, to say so.
Is that lead slow which is fir'd from a gun?

Arm. Sweet smoke of rhetoric!
He reputes me a cannon; and the bullet, that's he: *55*
I shoot thee at the swain.

Moth.   Thump, then, and I flee.

                                         [Exit.]

Arm. A most acute juvenal; volable and free of grace!
By thy favour, sweet welkin, I must sigh in thy face:
Most rude melancholy, valour gives thee place.   *60*
My herald is return'd.

         Enter Page [Moth] and Clown [Costard].

Moth. A wonder, master! here's a costard broken in a shin.

Arm. Some enigma, some riddle: come, thy *l'envoy*, begin.

Cost. No egma, no riddle, no *l'envoy*, no salve in the mail,
sir. O! sir, plantain, a plain plantain: no *l'envoy*, no *l'envoy*,   *65*
no salve, sir, but a plantain.

Arm. By virtue, thou enforcest laughter; thy silly thought,
my spleen; the heaving of my lungs provokes me to ridiculous
smiling: O! pardon me, my stars. Doth the inconsiderate take
salve for *l'envoy*, and the word *l'envoy* for a salve?   *70*

Moth. Do the wise think them other? is not *l'envoy* a salve?

Arm. No, page: it is an epilogue or discourse, to make plain
Some obscure precedence that hath tofore been sain.
I will example it:
The fox, the ape, and the humble-bee   *75*
Were still at odds, being but three.
There's the moral. Now the *l'envoy*.

Moth. I will add the *l'envoy*. Say the moral again.

Arm. The fox, the ape, and the humble-bee
Were still at odds, being but three.   *80*

Moth. Until the goose came out of door,
And stay'd the odds by adding four.
Now will I begin your moral, and do you follow with my
l'envoy.
The fox, the ape, and the humble-bee   *85*
Were still at odds, being but three.

Arm. Until the goose came out of door,
Staying the odds by adding four.

Moth. A good *l'envoy*, ending in the goose.
Would you desire more?   *90*

Cost. The boy hath sold him a bargain, a goose, that's flat.
Sir, your pennyworth is good, an your goose be fat.
To sell a bargain well is as cunning as fast and loose.
Let me see: a fat *l'envoy*, ay, that's a fat goose.

Arm. Come hither, come hither. How did this argument   *95*
begin?

Moth. By saying that a costard was broken in a shin.
Then call'd you for the *l'envoy*.

Cost. True, and I for a plantain: thus came your argument
in;   *100*
Then the boy's fat *l'envoy*, the goose that you bought;
And he ended the market.

Arm. But tell me: how was there a costard broken in a shin?

Moth. I will tell you sensibly.

Cost. Thou hast no feeling of it, Moth: I will speak   *105*
that *l'envoy*.
I, Costard, running out, that was safely within,
Fell over the threshold and broke my shin.

Arm. We will talk no more of this matter.

Cost. Till there be more matter in the shin.   *110*

Arm. Sirrah Costard, I will enfranchise thee.

Cost. O! marry me to one Frances: I smell some *l'envoy*,
some goose, in this.

Arm. By my sweet soul, I mean setting thee at liberty,
enfreedoming thy person: thou wert immured, restrained,   *115*
captivated, bound.

Cost. True, true, and now you will be my purgation
and let me loose.

Arm. I give thee thy liberty, set thee from durance;
and in lieu thereof, impose on thee nothing but this: *120*
—*[Giving a letter.]* Bear this significant to the country
maid Jaquenetta. *[Giving money.]* There is remuneration; for
the best ward of mine honour is rewarding my dependents.
Moth, follow.   *[Exit.]*

Moth. Like the sequel, I. Signior Costard, adieu.   *Exit.*

---

17 complements: *accomplishments*   **18 nice:** *coy*   **22 penny:** *i.e., purchasing me-*
dium   **24** *Cf. n.*   **27 hackney:** *i.e. loose woman*   **41 well sympathized:** *i.e. the mes-*
sage is well suited to the bearer   **50 Minime:** *by no means*   **57 Thump:** *bang!*   **58**
volable: *quick of wit*   **59 welkin:** *sky*   **62 costard:** *head*   **64 mail:** *bag; cf. n.*

68 spleen: *mirth*   **71 l'envoy a salve;** *cf. n.*   **73 sain:** *said*   **82 adding:** *i.e. mak-*
ing   **91 hath . . . bargain;** *cf. n.*   **102 market;** *c.f. n.*   **104 sensibly:** *feelingly*   **121**
significant: *token, i.e. letter*   **123 ward:** *guard*

Cost. My sweet ounce of man's flesh! my incony Jew!—
Now will I look to his remuneration. Remuneration! O that's
the Latin word for three farthings: three farthings, remuneration. 'What's the price of this inkle?' 'One penny.' 'No, I'll
give you a remuneration': why, it carries it. Remuneration! *130*
why, it is a fairer name than French crown. I will never
buy and sell out of this word.

Enter Berowne.

Ber. O my good knave Costard, exceedingly well met!
Cost. Pray you, sir, how much carnation ribbon may a
man buy for a remuneration? *135*
Ber. What is a remuneration?
Cost. Marry, sir, halfpenny farthing.
Ber. Oh! Why then, three-farthing-worth of silk.
Cost. I thank your worship. God be wi' you!
Ber. O stay, slave; I must employ thee. *140*
As thou wilt win my favour, good my knave,
Do one thing for me that I shall entreat.
Cost. When would you have it done, sir?
Ber. O, this afternoon.
Cost. Well, I will do it, sir. Fare you well. *145*
Ber. O, thou knowest not what it is.
Cost. I shall know, sir, when I have done it.
Ber. Why, villain, thou must know first.
Cost. I will come to your worship to-morrow morning.
Ber. It must be done this afternoon. Hark, slave, it is *150*
but this:
The princess comes to hunt here in the park,
And in her train there is a gentle lady:
When tongues speak sweetly, then they name her name,
And Rosaline they call her: ask for her *155*
And to her white hand see thou do commend
This seal'd-up counsel. *[Gives him a shilling.]* There's thy
guerdon: go.
Cost. Gardon, O sweet gardon! better than remuneration;
a 'leven-pence farthing better. Most sweet gardon! I will *160*
do it, sir, in print. Gardon! remuneration!
Ber. O! And I,—
Forsooth, in love! I, that have been love's whip;
A very beadle to a humorous sigh;
A critic, nay, a night-watch constable, *165*
A domineering pedant o'er the boy,
Than whom no mortal so magnificent!
This wimpled, whining, purblind, wayward boy,
This senior-junior, giant-dwarf, Dan Cupid;
Regent of love-rimes, lord of folded arms, *170*
The anointed sovereign of sighs and groans,
Liege of all loiterers and malcontents,
Dread prince of plackets, king of codpieces,
Sole imperator and great general
Of trotting 'paritors: O my little heart! *175*
And I to be a corporal of his field,
And wear his colours like a tumbler's hoop!
What! I love! I sue! I seek a wife!

A woman that is like a German clock,
Still a-repairing, ever out of frame, *180*
And never going aright, being a watch,
But being watch'd that it may still go right!
Nay, to be perjur'd, which is worst of all;
And, among three, to love the worst of all;
A whitely wanton with a velvet brow, *185*
With two pitch balls stuck in her face for eyes.
Ay, and, by heaven, one that will do the deed,
Though Argus were her eunuch and her guard.
And I to sigh for her! to watch for her!
To pray for her! Go to: it is a plague *190*
That Cupid will impose for my neglect
Of his almighty dreadful little might.
Well, I will love, write, sigh, pray, sue, groan:
Some men must love my lady, and some Joan. *[Exit.]*

ACT FOURTH ❧ SCENE FIRST

[The King of Navarre's Park]
*Enter the Princess, a Forester, her Ladies, and
her Lords.*

Prin. Was that the king, that spurr'd his horse so hard
Against the steep uprising of the hill?
Boyet. I know not; but I think it was not he.
Prin. Whoe'er a' was, a' show'd a mounting mind.
Well, lords, to-day we shall have our dispatch; *5*
On Saturday we will return to France.
Then, forester, my friend, where is the bush
That we must stand and play the murtherer in?
For. Hereby, upon the edge of yonder coppice;
A stand where you may make the fairest shoot. *10*
Prin. I thank my beauty, I am fair that shoot,
And thereupon thou speak'st the fairest shoot.
For. Pardon me, madam, for I meant not so.
Prin. What, what? first praise me, and again say no?
O short-liv'd pride! Not fair? alack for woe! *15*
For. Yes, madam, fair.
Prin.   Nay, never paint me now:
Where fair is not, praise cannot mend the brow.
Here, good my glass.—*[Gives money.]* Take this for telling true:
Fair payment for foul words is more than due. *20*
For. Nothing but fair is that which you inherit.
Prin. See, see! my beauty will be sav'd by merit.
O heresy in fair, fit for these days!
A giving hand, though foul, shall have fair praise.
But come, the bow: now mercy goes to kill, *25*
And shooting well is then accounted ill.
Thus will I save my credit in the shoot:
Not wounding, pity would not let me do 't;
If wounding, then it was to show my skill,
That more for praise than purpose meant to kill. *30*
And out of question so it is sometimes,
Glory grows guilty of detested crimes,

---

126 incony: *fine*   **129 inkle:** *tape*   **130 it carries it:** *it carries off the palm*   **131
name:** *word*   **139 wi':** *with*   **157 counsel:** *private communication*   **158 guerdon:** *reward*   **161 in print:** *precisely*   **164 beadle ... sigh;** *cf. n.*   **167 magnificent:** *pompous, overbearing*   **168 wimpled:** *veiled* **purblind:** *totally blind*   **169** *Cf. n.*   **173
plackets:** *petticoats, or slits in petticoats or skirts* **codpieces:** *baggy appendages to the front of
breeches*   **175 'paritors:** *apparitors, officials of the ecclesiastical court*   **177 like ... hoop:**
like the flaunting ribbons attached to a tumbler's hoop

180 frame: *order*   **185 whitely:** *pale-skinned*   **188 Argus:** *a monster having a hundred
eyes*   **194 Joan:** *stock name for a peasant wench; cf. IV.iii. 183 and V.ii. 967*   **9 coppice:**
thicket   **10 stand:** *hunter's station*   **18 fair:** *beauty*   **19 my glass:** *mirror, i.e. the
Forester*   **21 inherit:** *possess*   **22 merit:** *good deeds*   **23 heresy;** *cf. n.*   **24 giving:**
generous   **31 out of question:** *undoubtedly*

When, for fame's sake, for praise, an outward part,
We bend to that the working of the heart;
As I for praise alone now seek to spill   35
The poor deer's blood, that my heart means no ill.

Boyet. Do not curst wives hold that self-sovereignty
Only for praise' sake, when they strive to be
Lords o'er their lords?

Prin. Only for praise; and praise we may afford   40
To any lady that subdues a lord.

Enter Clown [Costard].

Boyet. Here comes a member of the commonwealth.

Cost. God dig-you-den all! Pray you, which is the head lady?

Prin. Thou shalt know her, fellow, by the rest that have no
heads.   45

Cost. Which is the greatest lady, the highest?

Prin. The thickest, and the tallest.

Cost. The thickest, and the tallest: it is so; truth
is truth.
An your waist, mistress, were as slender as my wit,   50
One o' these maids' girdles for your waist should be fit.
Are not you the chief woman? you are the thickest here.

Prin. What's your will, sir? what's your will?

Cost. I have a letter from Monsieur Berowne to one Lady
Rosaline.   55

Prin. O thy letter, thy letter! He's a good friend of mine.
Stand aside, good bearer. Boyet, you can carve;
Break up this capon.

Boyet.   I am bound to serve.—
This letter is mistook; it importeth none here: 60
It is writ to Jaquenetta.

Prin.   We will read it, I swear.
Break the neck of the wax, and every one give ear.

Boyet. [Reads.] 'By heaven, that thou art fair, is most infalli-
ble; true, that thou art beauteous; truth itself, that thou art   65
lovely. More fairer than fair, beautiful than beauteous, truer
than truth itself, have commiseration on thy heroical vassal.
The magnanimous and most illustrate king Cophetua set eye
upon the pernicious and indubitate beggar Zenelophon, and he
it was that might rightly say *veni, vidi, vici;* which to anato-   70
mize in the vulgar—O base and obscure vulgar!—*videlicet,* he
came, saw, and overcame: he came, one; saw, two; overcame,
three. Who came? the king: Why did he come? to see: Why
did he see? to overcome: To whom came he? to the beggar:
What saw he? the beggar. Who overcame he? the beggar.   75
The conclusion is victory: on whose side? the king's; the cap-
tive is enriched: on whose side? the beggar's. The catastrophe is
a nuptial: on whose side? the king's, no, on both in one, or
one in both. I am the king, for so stands the comparison; thou
the beggar, for so witnesseth thy lowliness. Shall I command   80
thy love? I may: Shall I enforce thy love? I could: Shall I en-
treat thy love? I will. What shalt thou exchange for rags? robes;
for tittles? titles; for thyself? me. Thus, expecting thy reply, I
profane my lips on thy foot, my eyes on thy picture, and my
heart on thy every part.   85
Thine, in the dearest design of Industry,

Don Adriano de Armado.
Thus dost thou hear the Nemean lion roar
'Gainst thee, thou lamb, that standest as his prey:
Submissive fall his princely feet before,   90
And he from forage will incline to play.
But if thou strive, poor soul, what art thou then?
Food for his rage, repasture for his den.'

Prin. What plume of feathers is he that indited this letter?
What vane? what weathercock? did you ever hear better?   95

Boyet. I am much deceiv'd but I remember the style.

Prin. Else your memory is bad, going o'er it erewhile.

Boyet. This Armado is a Spaniard, that keeps here in court;
A phantasime, a Monarcho, and one that makes sport
To the prince and his book-mates.   100

Prin.   Thou fellow, a word.
Who gave thee this letter?

Cost.   I told you; my lord.

Prin. To whom shouldst thou give it?

Cost.   From my lord to my lady.

Prin. From which lord, to which lady?

Cost. From my lord Berowne, a good master of mine,
To a lady of France, that he call'd Rosaline.

Prin. Thou hast mistaken his letter. Come, lords, away.
Here, sweet, put up this: 'twill be thine another day.   110

Exeunt [Princess and Train].

Boyet. Who is the suitor? who is the suitor?

Ros.   Shall I teach you to know?

Boyet. Ay, my continent of beauty.

Ros.   Why, she that bears the bow.
Finely put off!   115

Boyet. My lady goes to kill horns; but, if thou marry,
Hang me by the neck if horns that year miscarry.
Finely put on!

Ros. Well then, I am the shooter.

Boyet.   And who is your deer?

Ros. If we choose by the horns, yourself: come not near.
Finely put on, indeed!

Mar. You still wrangle with her, Boyet, and she strikes at
the brow.

Boyet. But she herself is hit lower. Have I hit her now?   125

Ros. Shall I come upon thee with an old saying, that was a
man when King Pepin of France was a little boy, as touching
the hit it?

Boyet. So I may answer thee with one as old, that was a
woman when Queen Guinever of Britain, was a little   130
wench, as touching the hit it.

Ros.   'Thou canst not hit it, hit it, hit it,
Thou canst not hit it, my good man.

Boyet.   'An I cannot, cannot, cannot,
An I cannot, another can.'

Exit [Rosaline].

Cost. By my troth, most pleasant: how both did fit it!

Mar. A mark marvellous well shot, for they both did hit it.

Boyet. A mark! O mark but that mark; a mark, says my   135
lady!

---

33 outward part: *extraneous quality*   **37 curst:** *shrewish*   **42 commonwealth:** *i.e. common people*   **43 dig-you-den:** *give you good evening*   **48 The thickest, etc.:** *cf. n.*   **58
capon:** *love-letter; cf. n.*   **60 importeth:** *concerns*   **68 illustrate:** *illustrious*   **69 indubitate:** *indubitable*   **Zenelophon:** *Penelophon (in the old ballad)*   **70 anatomize:** *analyze, explain*   **83 expecting:** *awaiting*   **86 Industry:** *gallantry*

88 Nemean lion; *cf. n.*   **91 from forage:** *abandoning rapacity*   **93 repasture:** *repast*   **94 plume of feathers:** *featherhead*   **96 but:** *unless*   **97 erewhile:** *just
now*   **98 keeps:** *lives*   **99 phantasime:** *fantastic fellow*   **Monarcho;** *cf. n.*   **110
sweet:** *i.e. Rosaline*   **be thine:** *be of use to thee*   **113 continent:** *container, repository*   **114
bears the bow;** *cf. n.*   **115 put off:** *turned aside*   **116 horns;** *cf. n.*   **123 still:**
ever   **127 King Pepin;** *cf. n.*   **133 fit it:** *make their points*

Let the mark have a prick in 't, to mete at, if it may be.

Mar. Wide o' the bow hand! i' faith your hand is out.

Cost. Indeed a' must shoot nearer, or he'll ne'er hit the
clout.   *140*

Boyet. An if my hand be out, then belike your hand is in.

Cost. Then will she get the upshoot by cleaving the pin.

Mar. Come, come, you talk greasily; your lips grow foul.

Cost. She's too hard for you at pricks; sir: challenge her to
bowl.   *145*

Boyet. I fear too much rubbing. Good night, my good
owl.   [*Exeunt Boyet and Maria.*]

Cost. By my soul, a swain! a most simple clown!
Lord, lord, how the ladies and I have put him down!
O' my troth, most sweet jests! most incony vulgar wit!   *150*
When it comes so smoothly off, so obscenely, as it were, so fit.
Armado, o' the one side, O! a most dainty man.
To see him walk before a lady, and to bear her fan!
To see him kiss his hand! and how most sweetly a' will swear!
And his page o' t'other side, that handful of wit!   *155*
Ah! heavens, it is a most pathetical nit.   *Shout within.*
Sola, sola!   [*Exit running.*]

❧ Scene Second ❧

[The Same]
Enter Dull, Holofernes the Pedant, and Nathaniel.

Nath. Very reverend sport, truly: and done in the testimony
of a good conscience.

Hol. The deer was, as you know, *sanguis*, in blood; ripe as
the pomewater, who now hangeth like a jewel in the ear of
cælo, the sky, the welkin, the heaven; and anon falleth like   *5*
a crab on the face of *terra*, the soil, the land, the earth.

Nath. Truly, Master Holofernes, the epithets are sweetly
varied, like a scholar at the least: but, sir, I assure ye, it was
a buck of the first head.

Hol. Sir Nathaniel, *haud credo;*.   *10*

Dull. 'Twas not a *haud credo*; 'twas a pricket.

Hol. Most barbarous intimation! yet a kind of insinuation,
as it were, *in via*, in way, of explication; *facere*, as it were, replication, or, rather, *ostentare*, to show, as it were, his inclination,—after his undressed, unpolished, uneducated, unpruned,
untrained, or, rather, unlettered, or, ratherest, unconfirmed
fashion,—to insert again my *haud credo* for a deer.

Dull. I said the deer was not a *haud credo*; 'twas a pricket.

Hol. Twice sod simplicity, *bis coctus!*
O thou monster Ignorance, how deformed dost thou look!   *20*

Nath. Sir, he hath not fed of the dainties that are bred
in a book.
He hath not eat paper, as it were; he hath not drunk ink: his
intellect is not replenished; he is only an animal, only sensible
in the duller parts: *25*
And such barren plants are set before us, that we thankful
should be,

Which we [of] taste and feeling are, for those parts that do
fructify in us more than he;
For as it would ill become me to be vain, indiscreet, or a fool:
So were there a patch set on learning, to see him in a school:
But, *omne bene*, say I; being of an old Father's mind,
Many can brook the weather that love not the wind.

Dull. You two are book-men: can you tell me by your wit,
What was a month old at Cain's birth, that's not five weeks   *35*
old as yet?

Hol. Dictynna, goodman Dull: Dictynna, goodman Dull.

Dull. What is Dictynna?

Nath. A title to Phoebe, to Luna, to the moon.

Hol. The moon was a month old when Adam was no more;
And raught not to five weeks when he came to five-score.
The allusion holds in the exchange.

Dull. 'Tis true indeed: the collusion holds in the exchange.

Hol. God comfort thy capacity! I say, the allusion holds in
the exchange.   *45*

Dull. And I say the pollution holds in the exchange, for the
moon is never but a month old; and I say beside that 'twas a
pricket that the princess killed.

Hol. Sir Nathaniel, will you hear an extemporal epitaph
on the death of the deer? and, to humour the ignorant,   *50*
[I have] call'd the deer the princess killed, a pricket.

Nath. *Perge*, good Master Holofernes, *perge;* so it shall please
you to abrogate scurrility.

Hol. I will something affect the letter; for it argues facility.
'The preyful princess pierc'd and prick'd a pretty pleasing   *55*
pricket;
Some say a sore; but not a sore, till now made sore with
shooting.
The dogs did yell; put L to sore, then sorel jumps from
thicket;   *60*
Or pricket, sore, or else sorel; the people fall a hooting.
If sore be sore, then L to sore makes fifty sores one sorel!
Of one sore, I a hundred make, by adding but one more L.'

Nath. A rare talent!

Dull. [*Aside.*] If a talent be a claw, look how he claws   *65*
him with a talent.

Hol. This is a gift that I have, simple, simple; a foolish
extravagant spirit, full of forms, figures, shapes, objects, ideas,
apprehensions, motions, revolutions. These are begot in the ventricle of memory, nourished in the womb of *pia mater*,   *70*
and delivered upon the mellowing of occasion. But the gift is
good in those in whom it is acute, and I am thankful for it.

Nath. Sir, I praise the Lord for you, and so may my parishioners; for their sons are well tutored by you, and their daughters profit very greatly under you: you are a good member   *75*
of the commonwealth.

Hol. *Mehercle!* if their sons be ingenuous, they shall want
no instruction; if their daughters be capable, I will put it to
them. But, *vir sapit qui pauca loquitur*. A soul feminine
saluteth us.   *80*

Enter Jaquenetta and the Clown [Costard].

---

137 **prick:** *point in the center of the target* **mete:** *measure, aim* 138 **Wide . . . hand:** *too far to the left* 140 **clout:** *white mark of cloth in the center of the target* 142 **upshoot:** *upshot, leading shot in a competition* **pin:** *wooden pin holding up the clout* 143 **greasily:** *grossly* 145 **bowl:** *bowling* 156 **pathetical nit:** *pleasing little fellow* 4 **pomewater:** *a kind of apple* 9 **first head:** *fifth year* 10 **haud credo:** *I do not think so* 11 **pricket:** *buck of the second year* 13 **facere . . . replication:** *to make reply* 16 **unconfirmed:** *ignorant* 19 **sod:** *sodden* **bis coctus:** *twice cooked, insipid*

28 **Which we:** *we who* 29 **than he:** *i.e. than in him* 31 **patch:** *clown, fool; cf. n.* 32 **omne bene:** *all's well* 33 *Cf. n.* 37 **Dictynna:** *a name given to Diana; cf. n.* 41 **raught:** *reached* 42 **allusion:** *jest, riddle; cf. n.* 49 **extemporal:** *extemporary* 52 **Perge:** *proceed* 54 **affect the letter:** *make use of alliteration* 57 **sore:** *a deer of the fourth year* 59 **sorel:** *a deer of the third year* 65 **talent:** *talon* 65 **claws:** *scratches pleasingly, flatters* 70 **ventricle:** *a division of the brain here called pia mater* 77 **Mehercle:** *a small oath* 79 **vir sapit, etc.;** *cf. n.*

Jaq. God give you good morrow, Master parson.

Hol. Master parson, *quasi* pers-on? And if one should be pierced, which is the one?

Cost. Marry, Master schoolmaster, he that is likest to a   *85* hogshead.

Hol. Of piercing a hogshead! a good lustre of conceit in a turf of earth; fire enough for a flint, pearl enough for a swine: 'tis pretty; it is well.

Jaq. Good Master parson [*giving a letter to Nathaniel*],   *90* be so good as read me this letter: it was given me by Costard, and sent me from Don Armado: I beseech you, read it.

Hol. Fauste, precor gelida quando pecus omne sub umbra Ruminat, and so forth. Ah! good old Mantuan. I may speak of thee as the traveller doth of Venice: *95*

> —*Venetia, Venetia,*
>
>   *Chi non te vede, non te pretia.*

Old Mantuan! old Mantuan! Who understandeth thee not, loves thee not. *Ut, re, sol, la, mi, fa.* Under pardon, sir, what are the contents? or, rather, as Horace says in his—   *100* What, my soul, verses?

Nath. Ay, sir, and very learned.

Hol. Let me hear a staff, a stanze, a verse: *lege, domine.*

Nath. 'If love make me forsworn, how shall I swear to love? Ah! never faith could hold, if not to beauty vow'd;   *105* Though to myself forsworn, to thee I'll faithful prove; Those thoughts to me were oaks, to thee like osiers bow'd. Study his bias leaves and makes his book thine eyes, Where all those pleasures live that art would comprehend: If knowledge be the mark, to know thee shall suffice.   *110* Well learned is that tongue that well can thee commend; All ignorant that soul that sees thee without wonder; Which is to me some praise, that I thy parts admire. Thy eye Jove's lightning bears, thy voice his dreadful thunder, Which, not to anger bent, is music and sweet fire.   *115* Celestial as thou art, O pardon love this wrong, That sings heaven's praise with such an earthly tongue!'

Hol. You find not the apostrophas, and so miss the accent: let me supervise the canzonet. Here are only numbers ratified; but, for the elegancy, facility, and golden cadence of poesy, *120 caret.* Ovidius Naso was the man: and why, indeed, Naso, but for smelling out the odoriferous flowers of fancy, the jerks of invention? *Imitari* is nothing; so doth the hound his master, the ape his keeper, the tired horse his rider. But, damosella virgin, was this directed to you?   *125*

Jaq. Ay, sir; from one Monsieur Berowne, one of the strange queen's lords.

Hol. I will overglance the superscript. '*To the snow-white hand of the most beauteous Lady Rosaline.*' I will look again on the intellect of the letter, for the nomination of the party *130* writing to the person written unto: '*Your ladyship's, in all desired employment, Berowne.*'—Sir Nathaniel, this Berowne is one of the votaries with the king; and here he hath framed a letter to a sequent of the stranger queen's, which, accidentally, or by the way of progression, hath miscarried. Trip and go, *135* my sweet; deliver this paper into the royal hand of the king;

it may concern much. Stay not thy compliment; I forgive the duty: adieu.

Jaq. Good Costard, go with me. Sir, God save your life!

Cost. Have with thee, my girl.   *Exit [with Jaquenetta]. 140*

Nath. Sir, you have done this in the fear of God, very religiously; and, as a certain Father saith—

Hol. Sir, tell not me of the Father; I do fear colourable colours. But to return to the verses: did they please you, Sir Nathaniel?   *145*

Nath. Marvellous well for the pen.

Hol. I do dine to-day at the father's of a certain pupil of mine; where, if before repast it shall please you to gratify the table with a grace, I will, on my privilege I have with the parents of the foresaid child or pupil, undertake your *ben venuto*; where I will prove those verses to be very unlearned, neither savouring of poetry, wit, nor invention. I beseech your society.

Nath. And thank you too; for society—saith the text—is the happiness of life.

Hol. And, certes, the text most infallibly concludes it.   *155* —[*To Dull.*] Sir, I do invite you too: you shall not say me nay: *pauca verba.* Away! the gentles are at their game, and we will to our recreation.   *Exeunt.*

❧ Scene Third ❧

[The Same]
Enter Berowne, with a paper in his hand, alone.

Ber. The king he is hunting the deer; I am coursing myself: they have pitched a toil; I am toiling in a pitch,—pitch that defiles: defile! a foul word! Well, sit thee down, sorrow! for so they say the fool said, and so say I, and I the fool: well proved, wit! By the Lord, this love is as mad as Ajax: it kills   *5* sheep: it kills me, I a sheep: well proved again o' my side! I will not love; if I do, hang me; i' faith, I will not. O but her eye!—by this light, but for her eye, I would not love her; yes, for her two eyes. Well, I do nothing in the world but lie, and lie in my throat. By heaven, I do love, and it hath taught me to rime, and to be melancholy; and here is part of my rime, and here my melancholy. Well, she hath one o' my sonnets already: the clown bore it, the fool sent it, and the lady hath it: sweet clown, sweeter fool, sweetest lady! By the world, I would not care a pin if the other three were in. Here comes one with a paper: God give him grace to groan!

> *He stands aside [or climbs into a tree].*

> *The King entreth.*

King. Ay me!

Ber. [*Aside.*] Shot, by heaven! Proceed, sweet Cupid: thou hast thumped him with thy bird-bolt under the left pap. In faith, secrets!   *20*

King. 'So sweet a kiss the golden sun gives not To those fresh morning drops upon the rose, As thy eye-beams, when their fresh rays have smote The night of dew that on my cheeks down flows. Nor shines the silver moon one half so bright   *25* Through the transparent bosom of the deep,

As doth thy face through tears of mine give light:
Thou shin'st in every tear that I do weep;
No drop but as a coach doth carry thee:
So ridest thou triumphing in my woe.   30
Do but behold the tears that swell in me,
And they thy glory through my grief will show:
But do not love thyself; then thou wilt keep
My tears for glasses, and still make me weep.
O queen of queens! how far dost thou excel,   35
No thought can think, nor tongue of mortal tell.'
How shall she know my griefs? I'll drop the paper.—
Sweet leaves, shade folly! Who is he comes here?

Enter Longaville. The King steps aside.

What, Longaville! and reading! listen, ear.
   Ber. Now, in thy likeness, one more fool appear!   40
   Long. Ay me! I am forsworn.
   Ber. Why, he comes in like a perjure, wearing papers.
   King. In love, I hope: sweet fellowship in shame!
   Ber. One drunkard loves another of the name.
   Long. Am I the first that have been perjur'd so?   45
   Ber. I could put thee in comfort: not by two that I know:
Thou mak'st the triumviry, the corner-cap of society,
The shape of love's Tyburn, that hangs up simplicity.
   Long. I fear these stubborn lines lack power to move.
O sweet Maria, empress of my love!   50
These numbers will I tear, and write in prose.
   Ber. O! rimes are guards on wanton Cupid's hose:
Disfigure not his slop.
   Long.   This same shall go.   *He reads the Sonnet.*
'Did not the heavenly rhetoric of thine eye,   55
'Gainst whom the world cannot hold argument,
Persuade my heart to this false perjury?
Vows for thee broke deserve not punishment.
A woman I forswore; but I will prove,
Thou being a goddess, I forswore not thee: 60
My vow was earthly, thou a heavenly love;
Thy grace, being gain'd, cures all disgrace in me.
Vows are but breath, and breath a vapour is:
Then thou, fair sun, which on my earth dost shine,
Exhal'st this vapour-vow; in thee it is: 65
If broken, then, it is no fault of mine:
If by me broke, what fool is not so wise
To lose an oath to win a paradise!'
   Ber. This is the liver-vein, which makes flesh a deity,
A green goose a goddess; pure, pure idolatry.   70
God amend us, God amend! we are much out o' the way.
   Long. By whom shall I send this?—Company! stay.
                           [Steps aside.]

Enter Dumaine.

   Ber. All hid, all hid; an old infant play.
Like a demi-god here sit I in the sky,
And wretched fools' secrets heedfully o'er-eye.   75
More sacks to the mill! O heavens! I have my wish.

Dumaine transform'd: four woodcocks in a dish!
   Dum. O most divine Kate!
   Ber. O most profane coxcomb!
   Dum. By heaven, the wonder of a mortal eye!   80
   Ber. By earth, she is not, corporal; there you lie.
   Dum. Her amber hairs for foul have amber quoted.
   Ber. An amber-colour'd raven was well noted.
   Dum. As upright as the cedar.
   Ber.   Stoop, I say;   85
Her shoulder is with child.
   Dum.   As fair as day.
   Ber. Ay, as some days; but then no sun must shine.
   Dum. O that I had my wish!
   Long.   And I had mine!   90
   King. And [I] mine too, good Lord!
   Ber. Amen, so I had mine. Is not that a good word?
   Dum. I would forget her; but a fever she
Reigns in my blood, and will remember'd be.
   Ber. A fever in your blood! why, then incision   95
Would let her out in saucers: sweet misprision!
   Dum. Once more I'll read the ode that I have writ.
   Ber. Once more I'll mark how love can vary wit.
                  Dumaine reads his Sonnet.

   Dum. 'On a day, alack the day!*
Love, whose month is ever May,   100
Spied a blossom passing fair
Playing in the wanton air:
Through the velvet leaves the wind,
All unseen, can passage find;
That the lover, sick to death,   105
Wish'd himself the heaven's breath.
Air, quoth he, thy cheeks may blow;
Air, would I might triumph so!
But alack! my hand is sworn
Ne'er to pluck thee from thy thorn: 110
Vow, alack! for youth unmeet,
Youth so apt to pluck a sweet.
Do not call it sin in me,
That I am forsworn for thee;
Thou for whom e'en Jove would swear   115
Juno but an Ethiop were;
And deny himself for Jove,
Turning mortal for thy love.'

This will I send, and something else more plain,
That shall express my true love's fasting pain.   120
O would the King, Berowne, and Longaville
Were lovers too! Ill, to example ill,
Would from my forehead wipe a perjur'd note;
For none offend where all alike do dote.
   Long. [Advancing.] Dumaine, thy love is far from charity,   125
That in love's grief desir'st society:
You may look pale, but I should blush, I know,
To be o'erheard and taken napping so.
   King. [Advancing.] Come, sir, you blush: as his your
case is such;   130
You chide at him, offending twice as much:

---

42 **perjure:** *perjurer* **papers:** *papers on the breast describing a perjurer's offenses* 47 **trium-**
viry: *triumvirate* **corner-cap:** *biretta, three-cornered cap, of a Catholic priest* 48 **Tyburn:**
triangular gallows at Tyburn, London 52 **guards:** *trimmings* 53 **slop:** *loose trou-*
sers 69 **liver-vein:** *i.e. style of a man in love (the liver being the supposed seat of the*
affections) 73 **All hid:** *i.e. as in the game of hide and seek*

77 **woodcocks:** *proverbially silly birds* 82 **quoted:** *set down, regarded* 85 **Stoop:**
cf. n. 95 **incision:** *blood-letting* 96 **saucers:** *receptacles for the blood* **misprision:** *mis-*
take 116 **Ethiop:** *i.e. black as a negro* 120 **fasting:** *hungry, longing* 122 **example:**
furnish a precedent for

You do not love Maria; Longaville
Did never sonnet for her sake compile,
Nor never lay his wreathed arms athwart
His loving bosom to keep down his heart.   135
I have been closely shrouded in this bush,
And mark'd you both, and for you both did blush.
I heard your guilty rimes, observ'd your fashion,
Saw sighs reek from you, noted well your passion:
Ay me! says one; O Jove! the other cries;   140
One, her hairs were gold, crystal the other's eyes:
[To Longaville.] You would for paradise break faith and troth;
[To Dumaine.] And Jove, for your love, would infringe an oath.
What will Berowne say, when that he shall hear
Faith infringed, which such zeal did swear?   145
How will he scorn! how will he spend his wit!
How will he triumph, leap and laugh at it!
For all the wealth that ever I did see,
I would not have him know so much by me.
    Ber. Now step I forth to whip hypocrisy.   150
                              [Descends from the tree.]
Ah! good my liege, I pray thee, pardon me:
Good heart! what grace hast thou, thus to reprove
These worms for loving, that art most in love?
Your eyes do make no coaches; in your tears   155
There is no certain princess that appears:
You'll not be perjur'd, 'tis a hateful thing:
Tush! none but minstrels like of sonneting.
But are you not asham'd! nay, are you not,
All three of you, to be thus much o'ershot?   160
You found his mote; the king your mote did see;
But I a beam do find in each of three.
O what a scene of foolery have I seen,
Of sighs, of groans, of sorrow, and of teen!
O me! with what strict patience have I sat,   165
To see a king transformed to a gnat;
To see great Hercules whipping a gig,
And profound Solomon to tune a jig,
And Nestor play at push-pin with the boys,
And critic Timon laugh at idle toys!   170
Where lies thy grief? O! tell me, good Dumaine.
And, gentle Longaville, where lies thy pain?
And where my liege's? all about the breast:
A caudle, ho!
    King.   Too bitter is thy jest.   175
Are we betray'd thus to thy over-view?
    Ber. Not you by me, but I betray'd to you:
I, that am honest; I, that hold it sin
To break the vow I engaged in;
I am betray'd, by keeping company   180
With men like [men,] men of inconstancy.
When shall you see me write a thing in rime?
Or groan for Joan? or spend a minute's time
In pruning me? When shall you hear that I
Will praise a hand, a foot, a face, an eye,   185
A gait, a state, a brow, a breast, a waist,
A leg, a limb?—

    King.   Soft! Whither away so fast?
A true man or a thief that gallops so?
    Ber. I post from love; good lover, let me go.   190

        Enter Jaquenetta and Clown [Costard].

    Jaq. God bless the king!
    King.   What present hast thou there?
    Cost. Some certain treason.
    King.   What makes treason here?
    Cost. Nay, it makes nothing, sir.   195
    King.   If it mar nothing neither,
The treason and you go in peace away together.
    Jaq. I beseech your Grace, let this letter be read:
Our parson misdoubts it; 'twas treason, he said.
    King. Berowne, read it over.   200
        He [i.e. Berowne] reads the letter [in dumbshow].
Where hadst thou it?
    Jaw. Of Costard.
    King. Where hadst thou it?
    Cost. Of Dun Adramadio, Dun Adramadio.   205
                              [Berowne tears the letter.]
    King. How now! what is in you? why dost thou tear it?
    Ber. A toy, my liege, a toy: your Grace needs not fear it.
    Long. It did move him to passion, and therefore let's hear it.
    Dum. [Picking up the pieces.] It is Berowne's writing, and
here is his name.   210
    Ber. [To Costard.] Ah, you whoreson loggerhead, you
were born to do me shame.
Guilty, my lord, guilty; I confess, I confess.
    King. What?
    Ber. That you three fools lack'd me fool to make up   215
the mess;
He, he, and you, and you my liege, and I,
Are pick-purses in love, and we deserve to die.
O dismiss this audience, and I shall tell you more.
    Dum. Now the number is even.   220
    Ber.   True, true; we are four.
Will these turtles be gone?
    King.   Hence, sirs; away!
    Cost. Walk aside the true folk, and let the traitors stay.
                          [Exeunt Costard and Jaquenetta.]
    Ber. Sweet lords, sweet lovers, O! let us embrace.   225
As true we are as flesh and blood can be:
The sea will ebb and flow, heaven show his face;
Young blood doth not obey an old decree.
We cannot cross the cause why we were born;
Therefore, of all hands must we be forsworn.   230
    King. What! did these rent lines show some love of thine?
    Ber. 'Did they,' quoth you? Who sees the heavenly Rosaline,
That, like a rude and savage man of Inde,
At the first opening of the gorgeous east,
Bows not his vassal head, and, strooken blind,   235
Kisses the base ground with obedient breast?
What peremptory eagle-sighted eye
Dares look upon the heaven of her brow,
That is not blinded by her majesty?

---

149 by: *about*   158 like of: *like*   160 o'ershot: *wide of the mark*   161 You: *i.e. Longaville* his: *i.e. Dumaine's*   164 teen: *grief, pain*   166 gnat: *a singing insect*   167 gig: *top*   168 tune: *play, or hum*   169 push-pin: *a child's game with pins*   170 critic: *cynic* toys: *trifles*   174 caudle: *a warm gruel, containing wine and spice, for the sick*   181 Cf. n.   184 pruning: *adorning*   186 state: *attitude, pose*

192 present: *paper to be presented*   194 makes: *does*   199 misdoubts: *suspects*   216 mess: *four persons at one table*   222 turtles: *turtle-doves, lovers*   223 sirs: *cf. n.*   229 cross ... born: *i.e. hold out against love*   230 of all hands: *on all hands, in any case*   234 the first ... east: *i.e. the rising of the sun*   235 strooken: *struck*   237 peremptory: *determined, bold*

King. What zeal, what fury, hath inspir'd thee now?   *240*
My love, her mistress, is a gracious moon;
She, an attending star, scarce seen a light.
    Ber. My eyes are then no eyes, nor I Berowne.
O, but for my love, day would turn to night!
Of all complexions the cull'd sovereignty   *245*
Do meet, as at a fair, in her fair cheek;
Where several worthies make one dignity,
Where nothing wants that want itself doth seek.
Lend me the flourish of all gentle tongues,—
Fie, painted rhetoric! O she needs it not: *250*
To things of sale a seller's praise belongs;
She passes praise; then praise too short doth blot.
A wither'd hermit, five-score winters worn,
Might shake off fifty, looking in her eye:
Beauty doth varnish age, as if new-born,   *255*
And gives the crutch the cradle's infancy.
O 'tis the sun that maketh all things shine!
    King. By heaven, thy love is black as ebony.
    Ber. Is ebony like her? O wood divine!
A wife of such wood were felicity.   *260*
O who can give an oath? where is a book?
That I may swear beauty doth beauty lack,
If that she learn not of her eye to look:
No face is fair that is not full so black.
    King. O paradox! Black is the badge of hell,   *265*
The hue of dungeons and the school of night;
And beauty's crest becomes the heavens well.
    Ber. Devils soonest tempt, resembling spirits of
light.
O, if in black my lady's brows be deck'd,   *270*
It mourns that painting [and] usurping hair
Should ravish doters with a false aspect;
And therefore is she born to make black fair.
Her favour turns the fashion of the days,
For native blood is counted painting now;   *275*
And therefore red, that would avoid dispraise,
Paints itself black, to imitate her brow.
    Dum. To look like her are chimney-sweepers black.
    Long. And since her time are colliers counted bright.
    King. And Ethiops of their sweet complexion crack.   *280*
    Dum. Dark needs no candles now, for dark is light.
    Ber. Your mistresses dare never come in rain,
For fear their colours should be wash'd away.
    King. 'Twere good yours did; for, sir, to tell you plain,
I'll find a fairer face not wash'd to-day.   *285*
    Ber. I'll prove her fair, or talk till doomsday here.
    King. No devil will fright thee then so much as she.
    Dum. I never knew man hold vile stuff so dear.
    Long. Look, here's thy love: *[Showing his shoe.]* my foot
and her face see.   *290*
    Ber. O, if the streets were paved with thine eyes,
Her feet were much too dainty for such tread.
    Dum. O vile! then, as she goes, what upward lies
The street should see as she walk'd overhead.
    King. But what of this? Are we not all in love?   *295*
    Ber. Nothing so sure; and thereby all forsworn.

    King. Then leave this chat; and good Berowne, now prove
Our loving lawful, and our faith not torn.
    Dum. Ay, marry, there; some flattery for this evil.
    Long. O some authority how to proceed;   *300*
Some tricks, some quillets, how to cheat the devil.
    Dum. Some salve for perjury.
    Ber.   O, 'tis more than need.
Have at you, then, affection's men-at-arms!
Consider what you first did swear unto: *305*
To fast, to study, and to see no woman;
Flat treason 'gainst the kingly state of youth.
Say, can you fast? your stomachs are too young,
And abstinence engenders maladies.
And where that you have vow'd to study, lords,   *310*
In that each of you hath forsworn his book,
Can you still dream and pore and thereon look?
For when would you, my lord, or you, or you,
Have found the ground of study's excellence
Without the beauty of a woman's face?   *315*
From women's eyes this doctrine I derive:
They are the ground, the books, the academes,
From whence doth spring the true Promethean fire.
Why, universal plodding poisons up
The nimble spirits in the arteries,   *320*
As motion and long-during action tires
The sinewy vigour of the traveller.
Now, for not looking on a woman's face,
You have in that forsworn the use of eyes,
And study too, the causer of your vow;   *325*
For where is any author in the world
Teaches such beauty as a woman's eye?
Learning is but an adjunct to ourself,
And where we are our learning likewise is:
Then when ourselves we see in ladies' eyes,   *330*
Do we not likewise see our learning there?
O we have made a vow to study, lords,
And in that vow we have forsworn our books:
For when would you, my liege, or you, or you,
In leaden contemplation have found out   *335*
Such fiery numbers as the prompting eyes
Of beauty's tutors have enrich'd you with?
Other slow arts entirely keep the brain,
And therefore, finding barren practisers,
Scarce show a harvest of their heavy toil;   *340*
But love, first learned in a lady's eyes,
Lives not alone immured in the brain,
But, with the motion of all elements,
Courses as swift as thought in every power,
And gives to every power a double power,   *345*
Above their functions and their offices.
It adds a precious seeing to the eye:
A lover's eyes will gaze an eagle blind;
A lover's ear will hear the lowest sound,
When the suspicious head of theft is stopp'd: *350*
Love's feeling is more soft and sensible
Than are the tender horns of cockled snails:

247 *I.e. several beauties make one surpassing beauty*   **249 flourish:** *enchancement*   **250 painted:** *showy, artificial*   **266 school of night:** *cf. n.*   **266** *Cf. n.*   **268 resembling:** *taking the form of; cf. n.*   **271 usurping:** *false*   **274 favour:** *face*   **279 counted:** *accounted*   **280 crack:** *boast*   **287 then:** *i.e. at doomsday*

301 quillets: *quibbles*   **304 affection's:** *love's*   **311 In that:** *in as much as*   **book:** *true book, i.e woman's face or eyes; cf. line 333*   **313–318** *Cf. n.*   **318 Promethean:** *divine*   **319 poisons up;** *cf. n.*   **320 arteries;** *cf. n.*   **335 leaden:** *heavy, dull*   **336 numbers:** *verses, poems*   **338 keep:** *remain in*   **350** *Cf. n.*   **352 cockled:** *inclosed in a shell*

Love's tongue proves dainty Bacchus gross in taste.
For valour, is not Love a Hercules,
Still climbing trees in the Hesperides?   355
Subtle as Sphinx; as sweet and musical
As bright Apollo's lute, strung with his hair;
And when Love speaks, the voice of all the gods
Make heaven drowsy with the harmony.
Never durst poet touch a pen to write   360
Until his ink were temper'd with Love's sighs;
O! then his lines would ravish savage ears,
And plant in tyrants mild humility.
From women's eyes this doctrine I derive:
They sparkle still the right Promethean fire;   365
They are the books, the arts, the academes,
That show, contain, and nourish all the world;
Else none at all in aught proves excellent.
Then fools you were these women to forswear,
Or, keeping what is sworn, you will prove fools.   370
For wisdom's sake, a word that all men love,
Or for love's sake, a word that loves all men,
Or for men's sake, the authors of these women;
Or women's sake, by whom we men are men,
Let us once lose our oaths to find ourselves,   375
Or else we lose ourselves to keep our oaths.
It is religion to be thus forsworn;
For charity itself fulfils the law;
And who can sever love from charity?
     King. Saint Cupid, then! and, soldiers, to the field!   380
     Ber. Advance your standards, and upon them, lords!
Pell-mell, down with them! but be first advis'd,
In conflict that you get the sun of them.
     Long. Now to plain-dealing; lay these glozes by:
Shall we resolve to woo these girls of France?   385
     King. And win them too: therefore let us devise
Some entertainment for them in their tents.
     Ber. First, from the park let us conduct them thither;
Then homeward every man attach the hand
Of his fair mistress: in the afternoon   390
We will with some strange pastime solace them,
Such as the shortness of the time can shape;
For revels, dances, masks, and merry hours
Forerun fair Love, strewing her way with flowers.
     King. Away, away! no time shall be omitted,   395
That will betime, and may by us be fitted.
     Ber. Allons! allons! Sow'd cockle reap'd no corn;
And justice always whirls in equal measure:
Light wenches may prove plagues to men forsworn;
If so, our copper buys no better treasure.   *Exeunt.*

ACT FIFTH ❧ SCENE FIRST

[The King of Navarre's Park]
Enter the Pedant [Holofernes], the Curate [Nathaniel], and Dull.

     Hol. Satis quod sufficit.
     Nath. I praise God for you, sir: your reasons at dinner have

been sharp and sententious; pleasant without scurrility, witty
without affection, audacious without impudency, learned without opinion, and strange without heresy. I did converse this   5
quondam day with a companion of the king's, who is intituled,
nominated, or called, Don Adriano de Armado.
     Hol. Novi hominem tanquam te: his humour is lofty, his dis-
course peremptory, his tongue filed, his eye ambitious, his gait
majestical, and his general behaviour vain, ridiculous, and   10
thrasonical. He is too picked, too spruce, too affected,
too odd, as it were, too peregrinate, as I may call it.
     Nath. A most singular and choice epithet.

                              Draw out his table-book.
     Hol. He draweth out the thread of his verbosity finer
than the staple of his argument. I abhor such fanatical   15
phantasimes, such insociable and point-devise companions;
such rackers of orthography, as to speak 'dout,' fine, when he
should say 'doubt'; 'det,' when he should pronounce 'debt,'
—d, e, b, t, not d, e, t: he clepeth a calf, cauf; half, hauf;
neighbour *vocatur* nebour, neigh abbreviated ne. This is   20
abhominable, which he would call abominable,—it insinuateth
me of insanie: *ne intelligis, domine?* To make frantic, lunatic.
     Nath. Laus Deo bene intelligo.
     Hol. Bon, bon, fort bon! Priscian a little scratched; 'twill
serve.   25

     Enter Braggart [Armado], Boy [Moth, and Costard].

     Nath. Videsne quis venit?
     Hol. Video, et gaudeo.
     Arm. [To Moth.] Chirrah!
     Hol. Quare chirrah, not sirrah?
     Arm. Men of peace, well encountered.   30
     Hol. Most military sir, salutation.
     Moth. [Aside to Costard.] They have been at a great feast of
languages, and stolen the scraps.
     Cost. O! they have lived long on the alms-basket of words.
I marvel thy master hath not eaten thee for a word; for   35
thou art not so long by the head as *honorificabilitudinitatibus:*
thou art easier swallowed than a flap-dragon.
     Moth. Peace! the peal begins.
     Arm. [To Holofernes.] Monsieur, are you not lettered?
     Moth. Yes, yes; he teaches boys the horn-book. What is   40
a, b, spelt backward, with the horn on his head?
     Hol. Ba, *pueritia,* with a horn added.
     Moth. Ba! most silly sheep with a horn. You hear his
learning.
     Hol. Quis, quis, thou consonant?   45
     Moth. The third of the five vowels, if you repeat them;
or the fifth, if I.
     Hol. I will repeat them,—a, e, i,—
     Moth. The sheep; the other two concludes it,—o, u.
     Arm. Now, by the salt wave of the Mediterraneum, a   50
sweet touch, a quick venew of wit! snip, snap, quick and
home! it rejoiceth my intellect: true wit!

355 **Hesperides:** *i.e. the garden of the Hesperides*   358 **voice:** *i.e. responsive voice*   372 **loves:** *cherishes, benefits*   378 *Cf. n.*   383 **sun:** *advantage of position*   384 **glozes:** *sophistries*   396 **betime:** *betide, chance*   397 **Sow'd cockle:** *cf. n.*   400 **copper:** *base coin*   1 **Satis quod sufficit:** *Enough is as good as a feast*   2 **reasons:** *arguments, discourse*

4 **affection:** *affectation*   5 **opinion:** *self conceit* **strange:** *novel, original*   8 **Novi ... te:** *I know the man as well as I know you*   9 **filed:** *polished*   11 **tharsonical:** *boastful* **picked:** *fastidious*   12 **peregrinate:** *traveled, foreign*   15 **staple:** *fiber*   16 **point-devise:** *precise*   17 **fine:** *mincingly; cf. n.*   19 **clepeth:** *calls*   20 **vocatur:** *is called, pronounced*   22 **insanie:** *insanity* **ne ... domine:** *do you understand, sir?*   23 **Laus ... intelligo:** *God be praised, I understand well*   24 **Priscian;** *cf. n.*   26 **Videsne ... venit:** *Do you see who comes?*   27 **Video, et gaudeo:** *I see and am pleased*   29 **Quare:** *why*   36 **honorific-etc.;** *cf. n.*   37 **flap-dragon:** *a raisin set on fire in brandy*   40 **horn-book:** *primer; cf. n.*   42 **pueritia:** *childishness, child*   49 **o, u:** *i.e. oh, you*   51 **venew:** *venue, sally*

Moth. Offered by a child to an old man; which is wit-old.

Hol. What is the figure? what is the figure?

Moth. Horns.   55

Hol. Thou disputest like an infant; go, whip thy gig.

Moth. Lend me your horn to make one, and I will whip about your infamy *circum circa*. A gig of a cuckold's horn.

Cost. An I had but one penny in the world, thou shouldst have it to buy gingerbread. Hold, there is the very remuner-   60 ation I had of thy master, thou halfpenny purse of wit, thou pigeon-egg of discretion. O, an the heavens were so pleased that thou wert but my bastard, what a joyful father wouldst thou make me! Go to; thou hast it *ad dunghill*, at the fingers' ends, as they say.   65

Hol. O! I smell false Latin! dunghill for *unguem*.

Arm. Arts-man, *præambula*: we will be singled from the barbarous. Do you not educate youth at the charge-house on the top of the mountain?

Hol. Or *mons*, the hill.   70

Arm. At your sweet pleasure, for the mountain.

Hol. I do, sans question.

Arm. Sir, it is the king's most sweet pleasure and affection to congratulate the princess at her pavilion in the posteriors of this day, which the rude multitude call the afternoon.   75

Hol. The posterior of the day, most generous sir, is liable, congruent, and measurable for the afternoon: the word is well culled, chose, sweet and apt, I do assure you, sir; I do assure.

Arm. Sir, the king is a noble gentleman, and my familiar, I do assure ye, very good friend. For what is inward between us, let it pass: I do beseech thee, remember thy courtesy; I beseech thee, apparel thy head: and among other importunate and most serious designs, and of great import indeed, too, but let that pass: for I must tell thee, it will please his Grace, by the   85 world, sometime to lean upon my poor shoulder, and with his royal finger, thus dally with my excrement, with my mustachio: but, sweet heart, let that pass. By the world, I recount no fable: some certain special honours it pleaseth his greatness to impart to Armado, a soldier, a man of travel, that hath seen   90 the world: but let that pass. The very all of all is, but, sweet heart, I do implore secrecy, that the king would have me pres- ent the princess, sweet chuck, with some delightful ostentation, or show, or pageant, or antick, or fire-work. Now, understand- ing that the curate and your sweet self are good at such erup- tions and sudden breaking out of mirth, as it were, I have acquainted you withal, to the end to crave your assistance.

Hol. Sir, you shall present before her the Nine Worthies. Sir Nathaniel, as concerning some entertainment of time, some show in the posterior of this day, to be rendered by our as-   100 sistants, the king's command, and this most gallant, illustrate, and learned gentleman, before the princess; I say, none so fit as to present the Nine Worthies.

Nath. Where will you find men worthy enough to present them?   105

Hol. Joshua, yourself; myself, or this gallant gentleman, Judas Maccabæus; this swain, because of his great limb, or joint, shall pass Pompey the Great; the page, Hercules,—

Arm. Pardon, sir; error: he is not quantity enough for that Worthy's thumb: he is not so big as the end of his club.   110

Hol. Shall I have audience? he shall present Hercules in minority: his enter and exit shall be strangling a snake; and I will have an apology for that purpose.

Moth. An excellent device! so, if any of the audience hiss, you may cry, 'Well, done, Hercules! now thou crushest the   115 snake!' that is the way to make an offence gracious, though few have the grace to do it.

Arm. For the rest of the Worthies?—

Hol. I will play three myself.

Moth. Thrice-worthy gentleman!   120

Arm. Shall I tell you a thing?

Hol. We attend.

Arm. We will have, if this fadge not, an antick. I beseech you, follow.

Hol. Via, goodman Dull! thou hast spoken no word all   125 this while.

Dull. Nor understood none neither, sir.

Hol. Allons! we will employ thee.

Dull. I'll make one in a dance, or so; or I will play on the tabor to the Worthies, and let them dance the hay.   130

Hol. Most dull, honest Dull, to our sport, away!   *Exeunt.*

❧ SCENE SECOND ❧

[The same. Before the Princess's Pavilion]
Enter the Ladies [i.e. Princess, Katharine, Rosaline, and Maria].

Prin. Sweet hearts, we shall be rich ere we depart,
If fairings come thus plentifully in.
A lady wall'd about with diamonds!
Look you what I have from the loving king.

Ros. Madam, came nothing else along with that?   5

Prin. Nothing but this! yes, as much love in rime
As would be cramm'd up in a sheet of paper,
Writ o' both sides the leaf, margent and all,
That he was fain to seal on Cupid's name.

Ros. That was the way to make his godhead wax;   10
For he hath been five thousand year a boy.

Kath. Ay, and a shrewd unhappy gallows too.

Ros. You'll ne'er be friends with him: a' kill'd your sister.

Kath. He made her melancholy, sad, and heavy;
And so she died: had she been light, like you,   15
Of such a merry, nimble, stirring spirit,
She might ha' been a grandam ere she died;
And so may you, for a light heart lives long.

Ros. What's your dark meaning, mouse, of this light word?

Kath. A light condition in a beauty dark.   20

Ros. We need more light to find your meaning out.

Kath. You'll mar the light by taking it in snuff;
Therefore, I'll darkly end the argument.

Ros. Look, what you do, you do it still i' the dark.

Kath. So do not you, for you are a light wench.   25

Ros. Indeed I weigh not you, and therefore light.

Kath. You weigh me not. O! that's you care not for me.

---

53 wit-old: *i.e. wittol, cuckold*   **58 circum circa:** *round and round; cf. n.*   **64 ad dung- hill;** *cf. n.*   **67 Arts-man:** *professor of the liberal arts*   **præmbula:** *come forward*   **68 charge-house:** *schoolhouse; cf. n.*   **76 generous:** *well-born*   **liable:** *suitable*   **81 inward:** *private*   **82 remember . . . courtesy:** *put on your hat*   **87 excrement:** *excrescence, hair on lip*   **93 chuck:** *a pet name*   **103 Nine Worthies;** *cf. n.*   **108 pass:** *pass for (?), surpass (?)*

111, 112 Hercules in miniority; *cf. n.*   **123 fadge:** *succeed*   **antick:** *grotesque entertain- ment*   **125 Via:** *On your way!*   **130 tabor:** *a small drum*   **hay:** *country dance*   **2 fairings:** *presents, originally such as were bought at a fair*   **9 That:** *so that (there being no blank space left)*   **10 wax:** *grow (with quibble on sealing wax)*   **12 shrewd . . . gallows:** *cunning, roguish knave*   **13 Cf. n.**   **20 condition:** *temperament*   **22 in snuff:** *in anger, ill (with pun on the snuff of a candle)*   **26 weigh;** *cf. n.*

Ros. Great reason; for, 'past cure is still past care.'
Prin. Well bandied both; a set of wit well play'd.
But Rosaline, you have a favour too: *30*
Who sent it? and what is it?
 Ros.   I would you knew:
An if my face were but as fair as yours,
My favour were as great; be witness this.
Nay, I have verses too, I thank Berowne: *35*
The numbers true; and, were the numb'ring too,
I were the fairest goddess on the ground:
I am compar'd to twenty thousand fairs.
Oh, he hath drawn my picture in his letter!
 Prin. Anything like?   *40*
 Ros. Much in the letters, nothing in the praise.
 Prin. Beauteous as ink; a good conclusion.
 Kath. Fair as a text B in a copy-book.
 Ros. 'Ware pencils, ho! let me not die your debtor,
My red dominical, my golden letter: *45*
O, that your face were not so full of O's!
 Prin. A pox of that jest! and I beshrew all shrows!
But, Katharine, what was sent to you from fair
Dumaine?
 Kath. Madam, this glove.   *50*
 Prin.   Did he not send you twain?
 Kath. Yes, madam; and moreover,
Some thousand verses of a faithful lover:
A huge translation of hypocrisy,
Vilely compil'd, profound simplicity.   *55*
 Mar. This, and these pearls to me sent Longaville:
The letter is too long by half a mile.
 Prin. I think no less. Dost thou not wish in heart
The chain were longer and the letter short?
 Mar. Ay, or I would these hands might never part. *60*
 Prin. We are wise girls to mock our lovers so.
 Ros. They are worse fools to purchase mocking so.
That same Berowne I'll torture ere I go.
O that I knew he were but in by the week!
How I would make him fawn, and beg, and seek, *65*
And wait the season, and observe the times,
And spend his prodigal wits in bootless rimes,
And shape his service wholly to my hests,
And make him proud to make me proud that jests!
So perttaunt-like would I o'ersway his state *70*
That he should be my fool, and I his fate.
 Prin. None are so surely caught, when they are
catch'd,
As wit turn'd fool: folly, in wisdom hatch'd,
Hath wisdom's warrant and the help of school *75*
And wit's own grace to grace a learned fool.
 Ros. The blood of youth burns not with such excess
As gravity's revolt to wantonness.
 Mar. Folly in fools bears not so strong a note
As foolery in the wise, when wit doth dote; *80*
Since all the power thereof it doth apply
To prove, by wit, worth in simplicity.

Enter Boyet.

Prin. Here come Boyet, and mirth is in his face.
Boyet. O, I am stabb'd with laughter! Where's her Grace?
Prin. Thy news, Boyet?   *85*
Boyet.   Prepare, madam, prepare!—
Arm, wenches, arm! encounters mounted are
Against your peace: Love doth approach disguis'd,
Armed in arguments; you'll be surpris'd:
Muster your wits; stand in your own defence; *90*
Or hide your heads like cowards, and fly hence.
 Prin. Saint Denis to Saint Cupid! What are they
That charge their breath against us? say, scout, say.
 Boyet. Under the cool shade of a sycamore
I thought to close mine eyes some half an hour, *95*
When, lo! to interrupt my purpos'd rest,
Toward that shade I might behold addrest
The king and his companions: warily
I stole into a neighbour thicket by,
And overheard what you shall overhear;   *100*
That, by and by, disguis'd they will be here.
Their herald is a pretty knavish page,
That well by heart hath conn'd his embassage:
Action and accent did they teach him there;
'Thus must thou speak, and thus thy body bear.' *105*
And ever and anon they made a doubt
Presence majestical would put him out;
'For,' quoth the king, 'an angel shalt thou see;
Yet fear not thou, but speak audaciously.'
The boy replied, 'An angel is not evil;   *110*
I should have fear'd her had she been a devil.'
With that all laugh'd and clapp'd him on the
shoulder,
Making the bold wag by their praises bolder.
One rubb'd his elbow thus, and fleer'd, and swore *115*
A better speech was never spoke before;
Another, with his finger and his thumb,
Cry'd 'Via! we will do 't, come what will come';
The third he caper'd and cried, 'All goes well';
The fourth turn'd on the toe, and down he fell. *120*
With that, they all did tumble on the ground,
With such a zealous laughter, so profound,
That in this spleen ridiculous appears,
To check their folly, passion's solemn tears.
 Prin. But what, but what? come they to visit us? *125*
 Boyet. They do, they do; and are apparell'd thus,
Like Muscovites or Russians, as I guess.
Their purpose is to parle, to court and dance;
And every one his love-feat will advance
Unto his several mistress, which they'll know *130*
By favours several which they did bestow.
 Prin. And will they so? the gallants shall be task'd:
For, ladies, we will every one be mask'd,
And not a man of them shall have the grace,
Despite of suit, to see a lady's face.   *135*
Hold, Rosaline, this favour thou shalt wear,
And then the king will court thee for his dear:
Hold, take thou this, my sweet, and give me thine,
So shall Berowne take me for Rosaline,

---

30 favour: *gift; also face* **36 numbers:** *rhythm* **numb'ring:** *estimate* **41 letters;**
cf. n. **43 text B;** *cf. n.* **44 'Ware pencils;** *cf. n.* **45 red dominical;** *cf. n.* **46
O's:** *marks left by the smallpox* **47 shrows:** *shrews* **54 translation of hypocrisy;**
cf. n. **64 in … week;** *cf. n.* **68 hests:** *behests; cf. n.* **70 perttaunt-like;** *cf. n.*

87 encounters: *assailants* **92 Saint Denis:** *patron saint of France* **97 addrest:** *coming
straight* **101 by and by:** *soon* **106 made a doubt:** *expressed fear* **109 audaciously:**
boldly **115 fleer'd:** *grinned* **123 spleen ridiculous:** *ridiculous merriment* **124 solemn:** *sober* **127 Like Muscovites;** *cf. n.* **132 task'd:** *given a task or problem*

And change you favours too; so shall your loves   140
Woo contrary, deceiv'd by these removes.
   Ros. Come on, then; wear the favours most in sight.
   Kath. But in this changing what is your intent?
   Prin. The effect of my intent is, to cross theirs:
They do it but in mockery merriment;   145
And mock for mock is only my intent.
Their several counsels they unbosom shall
To loves mistook and so be mock'd withal
Upon the next occasion that we meet,
With visages display'd, to talk and greet.   150
   Ros. But shall we dance, if they desire us to 't?
   Prin. No, to the death, we will not move a foot:
Nor to their penn'd speech render we no grace;
But while 'tis spoke each turn away her face.
   Boyet. Why, that contempt will kill the speaker's heart,   155
And quite divorce his memory from his part.
   Prin. Therefore I do it; and I make no doubt,
The rest will ne'er come in, if he be out.
There's no such sport as sport by sport o'erthrown,
To make theirs ours and ours none but our own: 160
So shall we stay, mocking intended game,
And they, well mock'd, depart away with shame.
                                Sound Trumpets.
   Boyet. The trumpet sounds: be mask'd; the maskers come.
                            [The Ladies mask.]

   Enter Blackamoors with music; the Boy [Moth] with
    a speech, and the rest of the Lords disguised.

   Moth. 'All hail, the richest beauties on the earth!'
   Boyet. Beauties no richer than rich taffeta.
   Moth. 'A holy parcel of the fairest dames,
               The Ladies turn their backs to him.
That ever turn'd their—backs—to mortal views!'
   Ber. 'Their eyes,' villain, 'their eyes.'
   Moth. 'That ever turn'd their eyes to mortal views! Out—' 170
   Boyet. True; 'out,' indeed.
   Moth. 'Out of your favours, heavenly spirits, vouchsafe
Not to behold'—
   Ber. 'Once to behold,' rogue.
   Moth. 'Once to behold with your sun-beamed eyes,   175
—with your sun-beamed eyes'—
   Boyet. They will not answer to that epithet;
You were best call it 'daughter-beamed eyes.'
   Moth. They do not mark me, and that brings me out.
   Ber. Is this your perfectness? be gone, you rogue!   180
                              [Exit Moth.]
   Ros. What would these strangers? know their minds,
Boyet:
If they do speak our language, 'tis our will
That some plain man recount their purposes: 185
Know what they would.
   Boyet. What would you with the princess?
   Ber. Nothing but peace and gentle visitation.
   Ros. What would they, say they?
   Boyet. Nothing but peace and gentle visitation.   190
   Ros. Why, that they have; and bid them so be gone.
   Boyet. She says, you have it, and you may be gone.

   King. Say to her, we have measur'd many miles,
To tread a measure with her on this grass.   195
   Boyet. They say that they have measur'd many a mile,
To tread a measure with you on this grass.
   Ros. It is not so. Ask them how many inches
Is in one mile: if they have measur'd many,
The measure then of one is easily told.   200
   Boyet. If to come hither you have measur'd miles,
And many miles, the princess bids you tell
How many inches do fill up one mile.
   Ber. Tell her we measure them by weary steps.
   Boyet. She hears herself.   205
   Ros.   How many weary steps,
Of many weary miles you have o'ergone,
Are number'd in the travel of one mile?
   Ber. We number nothing that we spend for you:
Our duty is so rich, so infinite,   210
That we may do it still without accompt.
Vouchsafe to show the sunshine of your face,
That we, like savages may worship it.
   Ros. My face is but a moon, and clouded too.
   King. Blessed are clouds, to do as such clouds do!   215
Vouchsafe, bright moon, and these thy stars, to shine,
These clouds remov'd, upon our wat'ry eyne.
   Ros. O vain petitioner! beg a greater matter;
Thou now requests but moonshine in the water.
   King. Then, in our measure vouchsafe but one change.   220
Thou bid'st me beg; this begging is not strange.
   Ros. Play, music, then! Nay, you must do it soon.
                                [Music plays.]
Not yet! no dance! thus change I like the moon.
   King. Will you not dance? How come you thus estrang'd?
   Ros. You took the moon at full, but now she's chang'd.   225
   King. Yet still she is the moon, and I the man.
The music plays; vouchsafe some motion to it.
   Ros. Our ears vouchsafe it.
   King.   But your legs should do it.
   Ros. Since you are strangers, and come here by chance,   230
We'll not be nice: take hands: we will not dance.
   King. Why take we hands then?
   Ros.   Only to part friends.
Curtsy, sweet hearts; and so the measure ends.
   King. More measure of this measure: be not nice.   235
   Ros. We can afford no more at such a price.
   King. Prize you yourselves. What buys your company?
   Ros. Your absence only.
   King.   That can never be.
   Ros. Then cannot we be bought: and so, adieu;   240
Twice to your visor, and half once to you!
   King. If you deny to dance, let's hold more chat.
   Ros. In private, then.
   King.   I am best pleas'd with that.
                        [They converse apart.]
   Ber. White-handed mistress, one sweet word with thee.   245
   Prin. Honey, and milk, and sugar; there are three.
   Ber. Nay then, two treys, an if you grow so nice,

---

141 **removes:** *exchanges*   160 **theirs:** *their sport*   161 **intended game:** *the jest they intend*   166 **taffeta:** *i.e. the taffeta, or silk, masks*

195 **measure:** *stately dance*   211 **accompt:** *reckoning*   217 **eyne:** *eyes*   219 **requests:** *requestest*   220 **change:** *round or 'figure' in dancing*   226 **man:** *i.e. man in
the moon*   237 **Prize:** *set a price on*   241 **Twice:** *i.e. twice adieu*   247 **treys:** *threes*

Metheglin, wort, and malmsey: well run, dice!
There's half a dozen sweets.
   Prin.   Seventh sweet, adieu: 250
Since you can cog, I'll play no more with you.
   Ber. One word in secret.
   Prin.   Let it not be sweet.
   Ber. Thou griev'st my gall.
   Prin.   Gall! bitter.   255
   Ber.   Therefore meet.
                     [They converse apart.]
   Dum. Will you vouchsafe with me to change a word?
   Mar. Name it.
   Dum.   Fair lady,—
   Mar.   Say you so? Fair lord!   260
Take that for your 'fair lady.'
   Dum.   Please it you,
As much in private, and I'll bid adieu.
                     [They converse apart.]
   Kath. What! was your vizard made without a tongue? 265
   Long. I know the reason, lady, why you ask.
   Kath. O for your reason; quickly, sir; I long.
   Long. You have a double tongue within your mask,
And would afford my speechless vizard half.
   Kath. 'Veal,' quoth the Dutchman. Is not 'veal' a calf? 270
   Long. A calf, fair lady!
   Kath.   No, a fair lord calf.
   Long. Let's part the word.
   Kath.   No, I'll not be your half:
Take all, and wean it: it may prove an ox.   275
   Long. Look, how you butt yourself in these sharp mocks.
Will you give horns, chaste lady? do not so.
   Kath. Then die a calf, before your horns do grow.
   Long. One word in private with you, ere I die.
   Kath. Bleat softly then; the butcher hears you cry. 280
                     [They converse apart.]
   Boyet. The tongues of mocking wenches are as keen
As is the razor's edge invisible,
Cutting a smaller hair than may be seen,
Above the sense of sense; so sensible
Seemeth their conference; their conceits have wings 285
Fleeter than arrows, bullets, wind, thought, swifter things.
   Ros. Not one word more, my maids: break off, break off.
   Ber. By heaven, all dry-beaten with pure scoff!
   King. Farewell, mad wenches: you have simple wits.
                    Exeunt [King and Lords].
   Prin. Twenty adieus, my frozen Muscovits.   290
Are these the breed of wits so wonder'd at?
   Boyet. Tapers they are, with your sweet breaths puff'd
out.
   Ros. Well-liking wits they have; gross, gross; fat, fat.
   Prin. O poverty in wit, kingly-poor flout!   295
Will they not, think you, hang themselves to-night?
Or ever, but in vizards, show their faces?
This pert Berowne was out of countenance quite.
   Ros. They were all in lamentable cases.
The king was weeping-ripe for a good word.   300

   Prin. Berowne did swear himself out of all suit.
   Mar. Dumaine was at my service, and his sword:
'No point,' quoth I: my servant straight was mute.
   Kath. Lord Longaville said, I came o'er his heart;
And trow you what he call'd me?   305
   Prin.   Qualm, perhaps.
   Kath. Yes, in good faith.
   Prin.   Go, sickness as thou art!
   Ros. Well, better wits have worn plain statute-caps.
But will you hear? the king is my love sworn.   310
   Prin. And quick Berowne hath plighted faith to me.
   Kath. And Longaville was for my service born.
   Mar. Dumaine is mine, as sure as bark on tree.
   Boyet. Madam, and pretty mistresses, give ear:
Immediately they will again be here   315
In their own shapes; for it can never be
They will digest this harsh indignity.
   Prin. Will they return?
   Boyet.   They will, they will, God knows;
And leap for joy, though they are lame with blows: 320
Therefore change favours; and, when they repair,
Blow like sweet roses in this summer air.
   Prin. How blow? how blow? speak to be understood.
   Boyet. Fair ladies, mask'd, are roses in their bud:
Dismask'd, their damask sweet commixture shown, 325
Are angels vailing clouds, or roses blown.
   Prin. Avaunt, perplexity! What shall we do,
If they return in their own shapes to woo?
   Ros. Good madam, if by me you'll be advis'd,
Let's mock them still, as well known as disguis'd. 330
Let us complain to them what fools were here,
Disguis'd like Muscovites, in shapeless gear;
And wonder what they were, and to what end
Their shallow shows and prologue vilely penn'd,
And their rough carriage so ridiculous,   335
Should be presented at our tent to us.
   Boyet. Ladies, withdraw: the gallants are at hand.
   Prin. Whip to your tents, as roes runs o'er land.
           Exeunt [Princess, Ros., Kath., and Maria].

      Enter the King and the rest [of the Lords].

   King. Fair sir, God save you! Where is the princess?
   Boyet. Gone to her tent. Please it your majesty, 340
Command me any service to her thither?
   King. That she vouchsafe me audience for one word.
   Boyet. I will; and so will she, I know, my lord.   *Exit.*
   Ber. This fellow pecks up wit, as pigeons pease,
And utters it again when God doth please: 345
He is wit's pedlar, and retails his wares
At wakes and wassails, meetings, markets, fairs;
And we that sell by gross, the Lord doth know,
Have not the grace to grace it with such show.
This gallant pins the wenches on his sleeve; 350
Had he been Adam, he had tempted Eve:
He can carve too, and lisp: why, this is he
That kiss'd his hand away in courtesy.
This is the ape of form, monsieur the nice,

---

248 Metheglin: *mead containing honey* **wort:** *sweet unfermented beer* **malmsey:** *a sweet wine* **251 cog:** *cheat* **256 meet:** *fitting* **265 tongue;** *cf. n.* **270 Veal:** *i.e. well; cf. n.* **273 part:** *divide; cf. n.* **284 sense of sense:** *i.e. perception* **sensible:** *sensitive* **285 conference:** *conversation* **conceits:** *fancies* **288 dry-beaten:** *cudgelled* **294 Well-liking:** *plump* **295 kingly-poor flout:** *a fling poor for a king* **300 weeping-ripe for:** *ready to weep for want of*

303 No point; *cf. II. i. 195* **306 Qualm:** *calm; cf. n.* **309 statute-caps:** *woollen caps; cf. n.* **317 digest:** *put up with, 'swallow'* **325 commixture:** *complexion* **326 vailing:** *letting fall* **blown:** *full blown* **338 runs:** *run* **347 wakes:** *night festivals* **wassails:** *drinking bouts* **352 can carve:** *knows the art of amorous glance and gesture*

That, when he plays at tables, chides the dice   *355*
In honourable terms: nay, he can sing
A mean most meanly, and in ushering
Mend him who can: the ladies call him sweet;
The stairs, as he treads on them, kiss his feet.
This is the flower that smiles on every one,   *360*
To show his teeth as white as whales-bone;
And consciences, that will not die in debt,
Pay him the due of honey-tongu'd Boyet.
    King. A blister on his sweet tongue, with my heart,
That put Armado's page out of his part!   *365*

    Enter the Ladies [with Boyet].

    Ber. See where it comes! Behaviour, what wert thou,
Till this man show'd thee? and what art thou now?
    King. All hail, sweet madam, and fair time of the day!
    Prin. 'Fair,' in 'all hail,' is foul, as I conceive.
    King. Construe my speeches better, if you may.   *370*
    Prin. Then wish me better: I will give you leave.
    King. We came to visit you, and purpose now
To lead you to our court: vouchsafe it then.
    Prin. This field shall hold me, and so hold your vow:
Nor God, nor I, delights in perjur'd men.   *375*
    King. Rebuke me not for that which you provoke:
The virtue of your eye must break my oath.
    Prin. You nickname virtue; vice you should have spoke;
For virtue's office never breaks men's troth.
Now, by my maiden honour, yet as pure   *380*
As the unsullied lily, I protest,
A world of torments though I should endure,
I would not yield to be your house's guest;
So much I hate a breaking cause to be
Of heavenly oaths, vow'd with integrity.   *385*
    King. O, you have liv'd in desolation here,
Unseen, unvisited, much to our shame.
    Prin. Not so, my lord; it is not so, I swear;
We have had pastimes here and pleasant game.
A mess of Russians left us but of late.   *390*
    King. How, madam! Russians?
    Prin.   Ay, in truth, my lord;
Trim gallants, full of courtship and of state.
    Ros. Madam, speak true. It is not so, my lord:
My lady, to the manner of the days,   *395*
In courtesy gives undeserving praise.
We four, indeed, confronted were with four
In Russian habit: here they stay'd an hour,
And talk'd apace; and in that hour, my lord,
They did not bless us with one happy word.   *400*
I dare not call them fools; but this I think,
When they are thirsty, fools would fain have drink.
    Ber. This jest is dry to me. Gentle sweet,
Your wit makes wise things foolish: when we greet,
With eyes best seeing, heaven's fiery eye,   *405*
By light we lose light: your capacity
Is of that nature that to your huge store
Wise things seem foolish and rich things but poor.
    Ros. This proves you wise and rich, for in my eye—
    Ber. I am a fool, and full of poverty.   *410*

    Ros. But that you take what doth to you belong,
It were a fault to snatch words from my tongue.
    Ber. O, I am yours, and all that I possess.
    Ros. All the fool mine?
    Ber.   I cannot give you less.   *415*
    Ros. Which of the vizards was it that you wore?
    Ber. Where? when? what vizard? why demand you this?
    Ros. There, then, that vizard; that superfluous case
That hid the worse, and show'd the better face.
    King. We were descried: they'll mock us now down-right. *420*
    Dum. Let us confess, and turn it to a jest.
    Prin. Amaz'd, my lord? Why looks your highness sad?
    Ros. Help! hold his brows! he'll sound. Why look you pale?
Sea-sick, I think, coming from Muscovy.
    Ber. Thus pour the stars down plagues for perjury.   *425*
Can any face of brass hold longer out?—
Here stand I, lady; dart thy skill at me;
Bruise me with scorn, confound me with a flout;
Thrust thy sharp wit quite through my ignorance;
Cut me to pieces with thy keen conceit;   *430*
And I will wish thee never more to dance,
Nor never more in Russian habit wait.
O, never will I trust to speeches penn'd,
Nor to the motion of a schoolboy's tongue,
Nor never come in vizard to my friend,   *435*
Nor woo in rime, like a blind harper's song.
Taffeta phrases, silken terms precise,
Three-pil'd hyperboles, spruce affectation,
Figures pedantical; these summer flies
Have blown me full of maggot ostentation: *440*
I do forswear them; and I here protest,
By this white glove,—how white the hand, God knows,—
Henceforth my wooing mind shall be express'd
In russet yeas and honest kersey noes:
And, to begin, wench,—so God help me, la!—   *445*
My love to thee is sound, sans crack or flaw.
    Ros. Sans 'sans,' I pray you.
    Ber.   Yet I have a trick
Of the old rage: bear with me, I am sick;
I'll leave it by degrees. Soft! let us see: *450*
Write, 'Lord have mercy on us' on those three;
They are infected, in their hearts it lies;
They have the plague, and caught it of your eyes:
These lords are visited; you are not free,
For the Lord's tokens on you do I see.   *455*
    Prin. No, they are free that gave these tokens to us.
    Ber. Our states are forfeit: seek not to undo us.
    Ros. It is not so. For how can this be true,
That you stand forfeit, being those that sue?
    Ber. Peace! for I will not have to do with you.   *460*
    Ros. Nor shall not, if I do as I intend.
    Ber. Speak for yourselves: my wit is at an end.
    King. Teach us, sweet madam, for our rude transgression
Some fair excuse.
    Prin.   The fairest is confession.   *465*
Were you not here, but even now, disguis'd?

---

355 tables: *backgammon*   **357 mean:** *tenor*   **361 whales-bone:** *whale's bone, walrus tusk*   **367 man;** *cf. n.*   **378 nickname:** *misname*   **390 mess;** *cf. IV. iii. 216*   **395 to the manner:** *after the fashion*   **403 dry:** *without savor* (with pun on 'thirsty')

423 sound: *swoon*   **431 wish:** *invite*   **435 friend:** *mistress*   **436 blind harper;** *cf. n.*   **438 Three-pil'd:** *having three piles, superfine*   **444 russet:** *homespun, homely* **kersey:** *coarse woollen, plain*   **451 'Lord have mercy';** *cf. n.*   **454 visited:** *plague-smitten*   **455 Lord's tokens:** *cf. n.*   **457 states:** *estates*   **459 sue:** *equivocally for prosecute and entreat*

King. Madam, I was.

Prin.   And were you well advis'd?

King. I was, fair madam.

Prin.   When you then were here, 470
What did you whisper in your lady's ear?

King. That more than all the world I did respect her.

Prin. When she shall challenge this, you will reject her.

King. Upon mine honour, no.

Prin.   Peace! peace! forbear; 475
Your oath once broke, you force not to forswear.

King. Despise me, when I break this oath of mine.

Prin. I will; and therefore keep it. Rosaline,
What did the Russian whisper in your ear?

Ros. Madam, he swore that he did hold me dear 480
As precious eyesight, and did value me
Above this world; adding thereto, moreover,
That he would wed me, or else die my lover.

Prin. God give thee joy of him! the noble lord
Most honourably doth uphold his word. 485

King. What mean you, madam? by my life, my troth,
I never swore this lady such an oath.

Ros. By heaven you did; and to confirm it plain,
You gave me this: but take it, sir, again.

King. My faith and this the princess I did give: 490
I knew her by this jewel on her sleeve.

Prin. Pardon me, sir, this jewel did she wear;
And Lord Berowne, I thank him, is my dear.
What, will you have me, or your pearl again?

Ber. Neither of either; I remit both twain. 495
I see the trick on 't: here was a consent,
Knowing aforehand of our merriment,
To dash it like a Christmas comedy.
Some carry-tale, some please-man, some slight zany,
Some mumble-news, some trencher-knight, some Dick, 500
That smiles his cheek in years, and knows the trick
To make my lady laugh when she's dispos'd,
Told our intents before; which once disclos'd,
The ladies did change favours, and then we,
Following the signs, woo'd but the sign of she. 505
Now, to our perjury to add more terror,
We are again forsworn, in will and error.
Much upon this it is: *[To Boyet.]* and might not you
Forestall our sport, to make us thus untrue?
Do not you know my lady's foot by the squire, 510
And laugh upon the apple of her eye?
And stand between her back, sir, and the fire,
Holding a trencher, jesting merrily?
You put our page out: go, you are allow'd;
Die when you will, a smock shall be your shroud. 515
You leer upon me, do you? there's an eye
Wounds like a leaden sword.

Boyet.   Full merrily
Hath this brave manage, this career, been run.

Ber. Lo! he is tilting straight. Peace! I have done. 520

Enter Clown [i.e. Costard].

Welcome, pure wit! thou partest a fair fray.

Cost. O Lord, sir, they would know
Whether the three Worthies shall come in or no.

Ber. What, are there but three?

Cost.   No, sir; but it is vara fine, 525
For every one pursents three.

Ber.   And three times thrice is nine.

Cost. Not so, sir; under correction, sir, I hope, it is not so.
You cannot beg us, sir, I can assure you, sir; we know what
we know: 530
I hope, sir, three times thrice, sir,—

Ber.   Is not nine?

Cost. Under correction, sir, we know where-until it doth
amount.

Ber. By Jove, I always took three threes for nine. 535

Cost. O Lord, sir! it were pity you should get your
living by reckoning, sir.

Ber. How much is it?

Cost. O Lord, sir! the parties themselves, the actors,
sir, will show whereuntil it doth amount: for mine own 540
part, I am, as they say, but to parfect one man in one poor
man, Pompion the Great, sir.

Ber. Art thou one of the Worthies?

Cost. It pleased them to think me worthy of Pompey the
Great: for mine own part, I know not the degree of the 545
Worthy, but I am to stand for him.

Ber. Go, bid them prepare.

Cost. We will turn it finely off, sir; we will take some care.

Exit.

King. Berowne, they will shame us; let them not approach.

Ber. We are shame-proof, my lord; and 'tis some policy. 550
To have one show worse than the king's and his company.

King. I say they shall not come.

Prin. Nay, my good lord, let me o'errule you now.
That sport best pleases that doth least know how;
Where zeal strives to content, and the contents 555
Dies in the zeal of that which it presents;
Their form confounded makes most form in mirth,
When great things labouring perish in their birth.

Ber. A right description of our sport, my lord.

Enter Braggart [i.e. Armado].

Arm. Anointed, I implore so much expense of thy 560
royal sweet breath as will utter a brace of words.

[Armado converses with the King, and delivers a paper to him]

Prin. Doth this man serve God?

Ber. Why ask you?

Prin. A' speaks not like a man of God his making.

Arm. That is all one, my fair, sweet, honey monarch; for, I
protest, the schoolmaster is exceeding fantastical; too-too vain;
too-too vain: but we will put it, as they say, to *fortuna de la
guerra.* I wish you the peace of mind, most royal couplement!

Exit.

King. Here is like to be a good presence of Worthies. He
presents Hector of Troy; the swain, Pompey the Great; 570
the parish curate, Alexander; Armado's page, Hercules;
the pedant, Judas Maccabæus:
And if these four Worthies in their first show thrive,

---

468 well advis'd: *in right mind*   **476 force not:** *i.e. find it easy*   **496 consent:** *conspiracy*   **498 Christmas comedy:** *absurd burlesque*   **499 please-man:** *flatterer* **zany:** *clown*   **500 trencher-knight:** *serving-man, parasite*   **501 years:** *i.e. wrinkles, such as belong to years*   **509 upon this:** *in this fashion*   **510 squire:** *square, rule*   **511 apple:** *pupil*   **514 allow'd:** *priviledged to jest*   **519 manage:** *horsemanship* **career:** *swift encounter of knights*

529 beg us: *prove us fools; cf. n.*   **542 Pompion:** *pumpkin*   **555, 556 Cf. n.**   **559 our sport:** *i.e. the diguise as Muscovites*   **564 God his:** *God's*   **567, 568 fortuna … guerra:** *the fortune of war*   **568 couplement:** *couple, pair*

These four will change habits and present the other five.
 Ber. There is five in the first show.   *575*
 King. You are deceived, 'tis not so.
 Ber. The pedant, the braggart, the hedge-priest, the fool,
and the boy:—
Abate throw at novum, and the whole world again
Cannot pick out five such, take each one in his vein. *580*
 King. The ship is under sail, and here she comes amain.

   Enter [Costard armed, for] Pompey.

 Cost. 'I Pompey am,—'
 Boyet.   You lie, you are not he.
 Cost. 'I Pompey am,—'
 Boyet.   With libbard's head on knee. *585*
 Ber. Well said, old mocker: I must needs be friends
with thee.
 Cost. 'I Pompey am, Pompey surnam'd the Big,—'
 Dum. 'The Great.'
 Cost. It is 'Great,' sir; 'Pompey surnam'd the Great; *590*
That oft in field, with targe and shield, did make my foe to
sweat:
And travelling along this coast, I here am come by chance,
And lay my arms before the legs of this sweet lass of
 France.'   *595*
If your ladyship would say, 'Thanks, Pompey,' I had done.
 Prin. Great thanks, great Pompey.
 Cost. 'Tis not so much worth; but I hope
I was perfect. I made a little fault in 'Great.'
 Ber. My hat to a halfpenny, Pompey proves the best *600*
Worthy.

   Enter Curate [Nathaniel] for Alexander.

 Nath. 'When in the world I liv'd, I was the world's commander;
By east, west, north, and south, I spread my conquering
might:
My scutcheon plain declares that I am Alisander,—' *605*
 Boyet. Your nose says, no, you are not; for it stands too right.
 Ber. Your nose smells 'no,' in this, most tender-smelling knight.
 Prin. The conqueror is dismay'd. Proceed, good Alexander.
 Nath. 'When in the world I liv'd, I was the world's
commander;—'   *610*
 Boyet. Most true; 'tis right: you were so, Alisander.
 Ber. Pompey the Great,—
 Cost. Your servant, and Costard.
 Ber. Take away the conqueror, take away Alisander.
 Cost. [*To Nathaniel.*] O! sir, you have over-thrown Alisander
the conqueror! You will be scraped out of the painted cloth for
this: your lion, that holds his poll-axe sitting on a close-stool,
will be given to Ajax: he will be the ninth Worthy. A conqueror, and afeard to speak! run away for shame, Alisander!
[*Nathaniel retires.*] There, an 't shall please you: a foolish mild
man; an honest man, look you, and soon dashed! He is a
marvellous good neighbour, faith, and a very good bowler; but,
for Alisander,—alas, you see how 'tis,—a little o'erparted. But
there are Worthies a-coming will speak their mind in some
other sort.   *625*
 Prin. Stand aside, good Pompey.

   Enter Pedant [Holofernes] for Judas, and the Boy [Moth] for
        Hercules.

 Hol. 'Great Hercules is presented by this imp,
Whose club kill'd Cerberus, that three-headed *canus*;
And, when he was a babe, a child, a shrimp, *630*
Thus did he strangle serpents in his *manus*.
Quoniam he seemeth in minority,
Ergo I come with this apology.''
Keep some state in thy exit, and vanish.—   *Exit Boy.*
'Judas I am.—'   *635*
 Dum. A Judas!
 Hol. Not Iscariot, sir.
'Judas I am, yeleped Maccabæus.'
 Dum. Judas Maccabæus clipt is plain Judas.
 Ber. A kissing traitor. How art thou prov'd Judas? *640*
 Hol. 'Judas I am.—'
 Dum. The more shame for you, Judas.
 Hol. What mean you, sir?
 Boyet. To make Judas hang himself.
 Hol. Begin, sir; you are my elder.   *645*
 Ber. Well follow'd: Judas was hanged on an elder.
 Hol. I will not be put out of countenance.
 Ber. Because thou hast no face.
 Hol. What is this?
 Boyet. A cittern-head.   *650*
 Dum. The head of a bodkin.
 Ber. A death's face in a ring.
 Long. The face of an old Roman coin, scarce seen.
 Boyet. The pommel of Cæsar's falchion.
 Dum. The carved-bone face on a flask.   *655*
 Ber. Saint George's half-cheek in a brooch.
 Dum. Ay, and in a brooch of lead.
 Ber. Ay, and worn in the cap of a toothdrawer.
And now forward; for we have put thee in countenance.
 Hol. You have put me out of countenance. *660*
 Ber. False: we have given thee faces.
 Hol. But you have outfaced them all.
 Ber. An thou wert a lion, we would do so.
 Boyet. Therefore, as he is an ass, let him go.
And so adieu, sweet Jude! nay, why dost thou stay? *665*
 Dum. For the later end of his name.
 Ber. For the ass to the Jude? give it him:—Jud-as, away!
 Hol. This is not generous, not gentle, not humble.
 Boyet. A light for Monsieur Judas! it grows dark, he may
stumble.   [*Hol. retires.*] *670*
 Prin. Alas! poor Maccabæus, how hath he been baited.

   Enter Braggart [i.e. Armado, for Hector].

 Ber. Hide thy head, Achilles: here comes Hector in arms.
 Dum. Though my mocks come home by me,
I will now be merry.
 King. Hector was but a Troyan in respect of this. *675*
 Boyet. But is this Hector?
 King. I think Hector was not so clean-timbered.
 Long. His calf is too big for Hector's.
 Dum. More calf, certain.

---

577 hedge-priest: *poor, illiterate priest* **579 Abate . . . novum:** *except for a rare throw of the dice; cf. n.* **585 libbard's:** *leopard's; cf. n.* **611 right:** *straight; cf. n.* **616 painted cloth;** *cf. n.* **617 lion . . . poll-axe;** *cf. n.* **623 o'erparted:** *i.e. given a part too difficult for him*

629 canus: *canis, dog* **631 manus:** *hands* **632 Quoniam:** *since* **633 Ergo:** *therefore* **640 A kissing traitor;** *cf. n.* **645 elder;** *cf. n.* **650 cittern:** *cithern, guitar* **651 bodkin:** *small dagger* **652 death's face:** *death's head* **655 flask:** *powder flask* **658 toothdrawer;** *cf. n.* **673 by:** *about, near* **675 Troyan:** *Trojan, contemptible fellow* **677 clean-timbered:** *well-built*

Boyet. No; he is best indued in the small.   *680*

Ber. This cannot be Hector.

Dum. He's a god or a painter; for he makes faces.

Arm. 'The armipotent Mars, of lances the almighty,
Gave Hector a gift,—'

Dum. A gilt nutmeg.   *685*

Ber. A lemon.

Long. Stuck with cloves.

Dum. No, cloven.

Arm. Peace!

'The armipotent Mars, of lances the almighty,   *690*
Gave Hector a gift, the heir of Ilion;
A man so breath'd, that certain he would fight ye
From morn till night, out of his pavilion.
I am that flower,—'

Dum.   That mint.   *695*

Long.   That columbine.

Arm. Sweet Lord Longaville, rein thy tongue.

Long. I must rather give it the rein, for it runs against Hector.

Dum. Ay, and Hector's a greyhound.

Arm. The sweet war-man is dead and rotten; sweet   *700*
chucks, beat not the bones of the buried; when he breathed, he
was a man. But I will forward with my device. *[To the Princess.]*
Sweet royalty, bestow on me the sense of hearing.

                                 Berowne steps forth.

Prin. Speak, brave Hector; we are much delighted.

Arm. I do adore thy sweet Grace's slipper.   *705*

Boyet. *[Aside to Dumaine.]* Loves her by the foot.

Dum. *[Aside to Boyet.]* He may not by the yard.

Arm. 'This Hector far surmounted Hannibal,—'

            [Berowne returns with Costard.]

Cost. The party is gone; fellow Hector, she is gone;
she is two months on her way.   *710*

Arm. What meanest thou?

Cost. Faith, unless you play the honest Troyan, the poor
wench is cast away: she's quick; the child brags in her belly
already: 'tis yours.

Arm. Dost thou infamonize me among potentates?   *715*
Thou shalt die.

Cost. Then shall Hector be whipped for Jaquenetta that is
quick by him, and hanged for Pompey that is dead by him.

Dum. Most rare Pompey!

Boyet. Renowned Pompey!   *720*

Ber. Greater than great, great, great, great
Pompey! Pompey the Huge!

Dum. Hector trembles.

Ber. Pompey is moved. More Ates, more Ates! stir them on!
stir them on!   *725*

Dum. Hector will challenge him.

Ber. Ay, if a' have no more man's blood in 's belly than
will sup a flea.

Arm. By the north pole, I do challenge thee.

Cost. I will not fight with a pole, like a northern man: *730*
I'll slash; I'll do it by the sword. I bepray you, let me
borrow my arms again.

Dum. Room for the incensed Worthies!

Cost. I'll do it in my shirt.

Dum. Most resolute Pompey!   *735*

Moth. Master, let me take you a button-hole lower.
Do you not see, Pompey is uncasing for the combat? What
mean you? you will lose your reputation.

Arm. Gentlemen and soldiers, pardon me; I will not
combat in my shirt.   *740*

Dum. You may not deny it; Pompey hath made the
challenge.

Arm. Sweet bloods, I both may and will.

Ber. What reason have you for 't?

Arm. The naked truth of it is, I have no shirt. I go   *745*
woolward for penance.

Boyet. True, and it was enjoined him in Rome for want of
linen; since when, I'll be sworn, he wore none but a dish-clout
of Jaquenetta's, and that a' wears next his heart for a favour.

            Enter a Messenger, Monsieur Marcade.

Mar. God save you, madam!

Prin. Welcome, Marcade;   *755*
But that thou interrupt'st our merriment.

Mar. I am sorry, madam; for the news I bring
Is heavy in my tongue. The king your father—

Prin. Dead, for my life!

Mar. Even so: my tale is told.   *760*

Ber. Worthies, away! The scene begins to cloud.

Arm. For mine own part, I breathe free breath.
I have seen the day of wrong through the little hole of discretion, and I will right myself like a soldier.   *Exeunt Worthies.*

King. How fares your majesty?   *765*

Prin. Boyet, prepare: I will away to-night.

King. Madam, not so: I do beseech you, stay.

Prin. Prepare, I say. I thank you, gracious lords,
For all your fair endeavours; and entreat,
Out of a new-sad soul, that you vouchsafe   *770*
In your rich wisdom to excuse or hide
The liberal opposition of our spirits,
If over-boldly we have borne ourselves
In the converse of breath; your gentleness
Was guilty of it. Farewell, worthy lord!   *775*
A heavy heart bears not a humble tongue,
Excuse me so, coming too short of thanks
For my great suit so easily obtain'd.

King. The extreme parts of time extremely forms
All causes to the purpose of his speed,   *780*
And often, at his very loose, decides
That which long process could not arbitrate:
And though the mourning brow of progeny
Forbid the smiling courtesy of love
The holy suit which fain it would convince;   *785*
Yet, since love's argument was first on foot,
Let not the cloud of sorrow justle it
From what it purpos'd; since, to wail friends lost
Is not by much so wholesome-profitable
As to rejoice at friends but newly found.   *790*

Prin. I understand you not: my griefs are double.

Ber. Honest plain words best pierce the ear of grief;

---

680 **small:** *small of the leg*   692 **breath'd:** *endowed with breath, vigorous*   709 **party:**
i.e. Jaquenetta   715 **infamonize:** *infamize*   724 **Ates:** *mischief; cf. n.*   730 **northern**
man: *countryman from the north, boor*

736 **take ... lower:** *(1) help you to strip, (2) humiliate you*   746 **woolward:** *i.e. with*
wool, instead of linen, next to the skin   763, 764 **hole of discretion;** *cf. n.*   772 **liberal:**
over-free   774 **converse of breath:** *conversation*   776 **humble:** *suited to the offering of*
thanks and apologies   779, 780 *Cf. n.*   781 **loose:** *loosing, parting*   785 **convince:**
give proof of   791 **double:** *excessive (?)*

And by these badges understand the king.
For your fair sakes have we neglected time,
Play'd foul play with our oaths. Your beauty, ladies,   *795*
Hath much deform'd us, fashioning our humours
Even to the opposed end of our intents;
And what in us hath seem'd ridiculous,—
As love is full of unbefitting strains;
All wanton as a child, skipping and vain;   *800*
Form'd by the eye, and, therefore, like the eye,
Full of straying shapes, of habits and of forms,
Varying in subjects, as the eye doth roll
To every varied object in his glance:—
Which parti-coated presence of loose love   *805*
Put on by us, if, in your heavenly eyes,
Have misbecom'd our oaths and gravities,
Those heavenly eyes, that look into these faults,
Suggested us to make. Therefore, ladies,
Our love being yours, the error that love makes   *810*
Is likewise yours: we to ourselves prove false,
By being once false for ever to be true
To those that make us both,—fair ladies, you:
And even that falsehood, in itself a sin,
Thus purifies itself and turns to grace.   *815*
   Prin. We have receiv'd your letters full of love;
Your favours, the embassadors of love;
And, in our maiden council, rated them
At courtship, pleasant jest, and courtesy,
As bombast and as lining to the time.   *820*
But more devout than this in our respects
Have we not been; and therefore met your loves
In their own fashion, like a merriment.
   Dum. Our letters, madam, show'd much more than jest.
   Long. So did our looks.   *825*
   Ros.   We did not quote them so.
   King. Now, at the latest minute of the hour,
Grant us your loves.
   Prin.   A time, methinks, too short
To make a world-without-end bargain in.   *830*
No, no, my lord, your Grace is perjur'd much,
Full of dear guiltiness; and therefore this:
If for my love,—as there is no such cause,—
You will do aught, this shall you do for me:
Your oath I will not trust; but go with speed   *835*
To some forlorn and naked hermitage,
Remote from all the pleasures of the world;
There stay, until the twelve celestial signs
Have brought about the annual reckoning.
If this austere insociable life   *840*
Change not your offer made in heat of blood;
If frosts and fasts, hard lodging and thin weeds,
Nip not the gaudy blossoms of your love,
But that it bear this trial and last love;
Then, at the expiration of the year,   *845*
Come challenge me, challenge me by these deserts,
And, by this virgin palm now kissing thine,
I will be thine; and, till that instant, shut
My woful self up in a mourning house,

Raining the tears of lamentation   *850*
For the remembrance of my father's death.
If this thou do deny, let our hands part;
Neither intitled in the other's heart.
   King. If this, or more than this, I would deny,
To flatter up these powers of mine with rest,   *855*
The sudden hand of death close up mine eye!
Hence ever then my heart is in thy breast.
   Ber. And what to me, my love? and what to me?
   Ros. You must be purged too, your sins are rack'd:
You are attaint with faults and perjury;   *860*
Therefore, if you my favour mean to get,
A twelvemonth shall you spend, and never rest,
But seek the weary beds of people sick.
   Dum. But what to me, my love? but what to me?
   Kath. A wife! A beard, fair health, and honesty;   *865*
With three-fold love I wish you all these three.
   Dum. O! shall I say, I thank you, gentle wife?
   Kath. Not so, my lord. A twelvemonth and a day
I'll mark no words that smooth-fac'd wooers say:
Come when the king doth to my lady come;   *870*
Then, if I have much love, I'll give you some.
   Dum. I'll serve thee true and faithfully till then.
   Kath. Yet swear not, lest ye be forsworn again.
   Long. What says Maria?
   Mar.   At the twelvemonth's end   *875*
I'll change my black gown for a faithful friend.
   Long. I'll stay with patience; but the time is long.
   Mar. The liker you; few taller are so young.
   Ber. Studies my lady? mistress, look on me.
Behold the window of my heart, mine eye,   *880*
What humble suit attends thy answer there;
Impose some service on me for thy love.
   Ros. Oft have I heard of you, my Lord Berowne,
Before I saw you; and the world's large tongue
Proclaims you for a man replete with mocks,   *885*
Full of comparisons and wounding flouts,
Which you on all estates will execute
That lie within the mercy of your wit:
To weed this wormwood from your fruitful brain,
And therewithal to win me, if you please,—   *890*
Without the which I am not to be won,—
You shall this twelvemonth term, from day to day,
Visit the speechless sick, and still converse
With groaning wretches; and your task shall be
With all the fierce endeavour of your wit   *895*
To enforce the pained impotent to smile.
   Ber. To move wild laughter in the throat of
death?
It cannot be; it is impossible:
Mirth cannot move a soul in agony.   *900*
   Ros. Why, that's the way to choke a gibing spirit,
Whose influence is begot of that loose grace
Which shallow laughing hearers give to fools.
A jest's prosperity lies in the ear
Of him that hears it, never in the tongue   *905*
Of him that makes it: then, if sickly ears,
Deaf'd with the clamours of their own dear groans,

---

793 **badges;** *cf. n.*   797 *In a way quite opposite to our intentions*   799 **strains:** *impulses*   805
parti-coated: *motley-coated*   809 **Suggested:** *tempted*   820 **bombast:** *padding*   821 **de-**
vout: *serious*   **respects:** *reflections*   826 **quote;** *cf. IV. iii. 82*   832 **dear:** *amiable*   839
Completed the twelve months of the year   842 **weeds:** *clothing*   844 **last:** *remain*

853 **intitled:** *having any right*   857 *Cf. n*   858–865 *Cf. n.*   859 **rack'd:** *i.e. unnaturally*
extended   877 **stay:** *wait*   878 **liker;** *cf. n.*   884 **large:** *lavish*   886 **comparisons:**
personalities   887 **estates:** *ranks*   900 **agony:** *i.e. of death*   907 **dear:** *intense*

Will hear your idle scorns, continue then,
And I will have you and that fault withal;
But if they will not, throw away that spirit,   910
And I shall find you empty of that fault,
Right joyful of your reformation.
    Ber. A twelvemonth! well, befall what will befall,
I'll jest a twelvemonth in an hospital.
    Prin. [*To the King.*] Ay, sweet my lord; and so I take   915
my leave.
    King. No, madam; we will bring you on your way.
    Ber. Our wooing doth not end like an old play;
Jack hath not Jill; these ladies' courtesy
Might well have made our sport a comedy.   920
    King. Come, sir, it wants a twelvemonth and a day,
And then 'twill end.
    Ber.   That's too long for a play.

         Enter Braggart [Armado].

    Arm. Sweet majesty, vouchsafe me,—
    Prin. Was not that Hector?   925
    Dum. The worthy knight of Troy.
    Arm. I will kiss thy royal finger, and take leave. I am a
votary; I have vowed to Jaquenetta to hold the plough for her
sweet love three year. But, most esteemed greatness, will you
hear the dialogue that the two learned men have compiled   930
in praise of the owl and the cuckoo? it should have followed
in the end of our show.
    King. Call them forth quickly; we will do so.
    Arm. Holla! approach.

         Enter all.

This side is *Hiems*, Winter; this *Ver*, the Spring;   935
the one maintained by the owl, th' other by the
cuckoo. *Ver*, begin.

         The Song.

         [*Spring.*]

  '*When daisies pied and violets blue*   940
    And lady-smocks all silver-white
And cuckoo-buds of yellow hue
    Do paint the meadows with delight,

The cuckoo then, on every tree,
Mocks married men; for thus sings he,   945
         Cuckoo;
Cuckoo, cuckoo: O, word of fear,
Unpleasing to a married ear!

'When shepherds pipe on oaten straws,
    And merry larks are ploughmen's clocks,   950
When turtles tread, and rooks, and daws,
    And maidens bleach their summer smocks.
The cuckoo then, on every tree,
Mocks married men; for thus sings he,
         Cuckoo;   955
Cuckoo, cuckoo: O, word of fear,
Unpleasing to a married ear!'

         Winter.

'When icicles hang by the wall,
    And Dick the shepherd blows his nail,   960
And Tom bears logs into the hall,
    And milk comes frozen home in pail,
When blood is nipp'd, and ways be foul,
Then nightly sings the staring owl,
         Tu-who;   965
Tu-whit, tu-who—a merry note,
While greasy Joan doth keel the pot.

'When all aloud the wind doth blow,
    And coughing drowns the parson's saw,
And birds sit brooding in the snow,   970
    And Marian's nose looks red and raw,
When roasted crabs hiss in the bowl,
Then nightly sings the staring owl,
         Tu-who;
Tu-whit, tu-who—a merry note,   975
While greasy Joan doth keel the pot.'

    Arm. The words of Mercury are harsh after the songs
of Apollo. You, that way: we, this way.   *Exeunt Omnes.*

           ❧ FINIS ❧

---

909 withal: *also*   **917 bring:** *attend*   **937** *Cf. n.*   **941 lady-smocks:** *cardamine pratensis, May-flower*   **942 cuckoo-buds:** *buttercups or cowslips*   **951 turtles:** *turtle-doves*   **967 keel:** *cool by stirring*   **969 saw:** *maxim or wise talk*   **972 crabs:** *wild, sour apples*   **bowl:** *i.e. wassail-bowl*

Dramatis Personæ. A list of characters for this play was first supplied by Rowe in 1709. Berowne (spelled 'Biron' in the second and later Folios and in most modern editions) is accented on the second syllable, and rimes with 'moon' (cf. IV.iii.241). Longaville rimes with 'ill' (IV.iii.122) but sometimes also with 'compile' (IV.iii.133) and with 'mile' (V.ii.57). Boyet rimes with 'debt' (V.ii.362); Rosaline with 'mine' (IV.i.56) and 'thine' (V.ii.138). Moth was probably pronounced as if spelled 'Mote' (cf. IV.iii.161, where the common noun, mote, is spelled 'Moth' in the early editions). Armado is often spelled 'Armatho,' which probably indicates the pronunciation (Spanish d = th).

Unusual irregularities are found in the quarto and folio editions of *Love's Labour's Lost* in the naming of the characters. The confusion is particularly striking in IV.ii, where the names of Holofernes and Nathaniel are transposed through most of the scene. Throughout the play the Princess is often called 'Queen'; and the names of Armado, Holofernes, Nathaniel, Costard, and Dull are erratically supplanted in stage directions and speech headings by the titles, Braggart, Pedant, Curate, Clown, and Constable, while Moth is often referred to as Page or Boy. Some recent editors have attempted to discriminate on the evidence of these phenomena between the original and the revised portions of the play. Thus Mr. Dover Wilson argues that passages using the designations 'Braggart,' 'Pedant,' etc., belong to the revision of 1597, whereas passages that give the proper names 'Armado,' Holofernes,' etc., are part of the original play. But this leads to risky conclusions.

Love's Labour's Lost. The spelling of the title is that of the third Folio. The earlier Folios have Loues Labour's Lost. The first Quarto has on the title-page Loues labors lost, but as running-title *Loues Labor's lost.* 'Labour's' was evidently intended as a contraction of 'Labour is.' Meres, however, referred to the play as *Loue labors lost,* clearly regarding 'labors' as the nominative plural. Likewise the play is known in France as *Les Peines de l'Amour Perdues* and in Germany as *Verlorene Liebesmüh.*

I.i.12. *Navarre shall be the wonder of the world.* The opening speech of the King shows the influence of Marlowe's versification in its special sonorousness, alliteration, and exhilaration. Compare with the present line Marlowe's *Dido,* l. 730: 'Lest I be made a wonder to the world.'

I.i.14. *Still and contemplative in living art.* Quietly contemplating the art of perfect living. The line alludes to the common mediæval distinction between the contemplative and the active life. Mr. J. S. Reid (Iowa *Philological Quarterly,* July, 1922) suggests that 'living art' refers particularly to the Stoic term, *ars vivendi,* ethical (as distinguished from physical and logical) philosophy.

I.i.62. *feast.* Theobald's emendation for the 'fast' of the early editions.

I.i.67, 68. *If study's gain be thus, and this be so, Study knows that which yet it doth not know.* If the benefit of study consists only in the development of casuistry, then there is no such thing as knowledge: instead of discovering the true, study merely merges the true and the false.

I.i.73. *Which, with pain purchas'd, doth inherit pain.* In which the final result of painful striving is only further pain.

I.i.80–83. *Study me how to please the eye indeed, By fixing it upon a fairer eye, Who dazzling so, that eye shall be his heed. And give him light that it was blinded by.* 'Me.' (l. 80) is the 'ethical dative'; 'Who' (l. 82) refers to the eye mentioned in l. 80 or to its owner; and 'it' (l. 83) is the object of 'by.' The passage may be paraphrased: Rather study how really to please your eye by fixing it upon that of a sweetheart, whereupon your own eye will be dimmed; but the 'fairer eye' will be your sole attention and give light to you whom it has blinded.

I.i.88–93. *These earthly godfathers of heaven's lights, That give a name to every fixed star, Have no more profit of their shining nights Than those that walk and wot not what they are. Too much to know is to know nought but fame; And every godfather can give a name.* The learned astronomers who give names to the stars have no more real control of them than have the ignorant. Encyclopedic knowledge is but parrot-like, no more essential than the bestowal of a name at the baptism of an infant.

I.i.95. *Proceeded.* Almost certainly used in the technical sense of taking an academic degree. Berowne employs his own intellectual subtlety to discourage others from similarly training themselves.

I.i.101. *In reason nothing. Ber. Something, then, in rime.* Shakespeare is very fond of playing on the alliterative phrase, rime and reason. Compare I.ii.96.

I.i.108. *May's new-fangled shows.* Since the rest of the passage is in alternate rime, it is assumed that the poet intended this line to end with a word riming

with 'birth' (l. 104). Many editors have therefore substituted 'earth' (Theobald) or 'mirth' (Walker) for 'shows'; but neither seems natural, and it is quite likely that Shakespeare himself made the slip through inadvertence.

I.i.111. *Climb o'er the house to unlock the little gate.* Take an absurdly impractical course. The line is printed as in the Quarto. The Folio has the inferior version: 'That were to clymbe ore the house to vnlocke the gate.'

I.i.116. *Yet confident I'll keep what I have sworn.* The second Folio reads 'swore,' which most modern editors introduce for the sake of rime.

I.ii.49. *the dancing horse.* A famous performing horse named Morocco, first definitely mentioned in 1591 but apparently known as early as 1589. He was particularly accomplished in arithmetic.

I.ii.70. *Of what complexion?* The four 'complexions' of the body were variously ascribed to the four elements (earth, air, water, fire) and to the four 'humours' (phlegm, choler, blood, melancholy).

I.ii.80. *she had a green wit.* Perhaps Moth implies a pun on the green withes with which Samson was bound (Judges 16. 7): 'And Samson said unto her, If they bind me with seven green withs that were never dried, then shall I be weak, and be as another man.'

I.ii.97. *a ballet . . . of the King and the Beggar.* The ballad of King Cophetua and the Beggar-maid is a favorite subject of allusion in Shakespeare and his contemporaries. Compare Armado's later mention of it in his letter (IV.i.68 ff.). The extant version, printed in Percy's *Reliques,* appears to be post-Elizabethan.

I.ii.141. *the merry days of desolation.* Perhaps Costard means 'dissipation.'

II.i.42. *Lord Perigort.* Of course, an invented name, Périgord, near Bordeaux, was an important district during the Hundred Years' War between France and England. Shakespeare would have found it mentioned repeatedly in Holinshed in connection with the French campaigns of Henry VI's reign. Falconbridge, in the next line, appears to have been a name the poet liked. It is not French, but is applied to important characters both in *King John* and in *3 Henry VI.* See note on the latter play, I.i.243, in this edition.

II.i.64, 65. *And much too little of that good I saw Is my report to his great worthiness.* My testimony to his worthiness is summed up in saying that I had much too little opportunity to observe it.

II.i.76. *That aged ears play truant at his tales.* The aged are tempted away from business to listen to his tales.

II.i.134. *Being but the one half of an entire sum.* That is, the sum which Navarre's father had lent to France amounted to two hundred thousand crowns. See Sources of the Play, p. 91.

II.i.191. *let it blood.* Alluding to the nearly inevitable practice of blood-letting in sickness.

II.i.195. *No point.* A pun on the English word, 'point' (i.e. my eye is not sharp enough), and the French negative, *ne . . . point.* Maria makes the same poor joke in V.ii.303.

II.i.201. *The heir of Alençon, Katharine her name.* Both the Quarto and Folio texts here print 'Rosalin' instead of Katharine, and in line 217 'Katherin(e)' instead of Rosaline. This is one of the chief points used by Mr. Dover Wilson in an ingenious elaboration of a theory proposed by Mr. Charlton in 1917 (*The Library,* vol. viii, pp. 355–370); namely, that Shakespeare, in the first version of the play, intended the ladies to be masked and Boyet to mix their names when the lovers inquire of him, and that in the revised version he intended to omit this motive of confused identity because of its employment later in V.ii. Mr. Wilson thinks that an unintentional blending of the two versions can be seen in the text of the present scene. There are very strong reasons against these assumptions. The only basis for the idea that the three ladies (unlike the Princess) wear masks in this scene is Berowne's exclamation, 'Now fair befall your mask!' (l. 127), and the reply of Rosaline ('Katharine' in the Quarto). This is far from conclusive. On the other hand, the evident purpose of the scene is to allow each of the lords an opportunity of falling in love with a lady with whom, by hypothesis, he has previously had only the slightest acquaintance, but with whose peculiarities of face and coloring they are all shown to be perfectly familiar when they next appear (see Berowne's soliloquy, III.i.161 ff., and the whole of IV.iii). It is impossible to believe that any author, skilled or unskilled, could have had the idea of frustrating so essential a piece of dramatic business by having the ladies unrecognizably masked and making them converse at cross purposes with the wrong gallants.

II.i.210. *God's blessing on your beard.* Longaville means to imply that Boyet's flippant answers are inconsistent with his venerable beard. In pronunciation

'beard' and 'heard' rimed better than at present, the latter word still retaining the long vowel of its infinitive.

II.i.221. *Farewell to me, sir, and welcome to you.* Say 'farewell' to me, and I will say you are welcome (to depart).

II.i.227. *Kath. Two hot sheeps, marry.* The Quarto assigns this speech to 'Lady Ka.' and the Folio to 'La. Ma.' Nearly all editors follow the latter, which, however, is probably a compositor's error occasioned by the fact that Maria is the speaker just above (l. 222). The three following lady's speeches (ll. 230, 232, 235), assigned in both the early editions simply to 'La.' or 'Lad.,' evidently belong to the same lady who speaks in l. 227. The Quarto's introduction of Katharine into the conversation is a dramatic gain.

II.i.233. *My lips are no common, though several they be.* A quasi-legal pun. Several land, as opposed to common, was that in separate or private ownership. Katharine also calls her lips several as being more than one, or as being parted.

II.i.257. *margent.* Alluding to the habit of printing explanatory notes on the margin (rather than the foot) of the page.

III.i.2. *Concolinel.* Not satisfactorily explained. It has been interpreted as a corruption of the Irish words 'Can cailin gheal' (pronounced con colleen yal), i.e. 'sing, maiden fair.' Marshall suggests that it is French, 'Quand Colinelle,' which is at least as likely.

III.i.6. *brawl.* French *branle.* Defined as the oldest of figure dances.

III.i.9. *canary.* The canary was a very lively dance, allowing the improvisation of new steps.

III.i.24. *The hobby-horse is forgot.* The 'hobby-horse,' a dancer made up to look like a horse, was a favorite figure in morris dances, and a special subject of Puritan invective. The line, 'O, the hobby-horse is forgot,' which Shakespeare uses again in *Hamlet,* III.ii.129, 130, has been supposed to come from a ballad.

III.i.64. *no salve in the mail, sir.* That is, no quacksalver's remedy. Costard apprehends that Armado is calling for exotic (and hence suspect) remedies for the broken shin.

III.i.71. *is not l'envoy a salve?* A pun on the Latin *salve,* used in salutations. The *envoi,* or concluding section, of a mediæval *ballade* ordinarily contained an address to the person to whom the poem was written.

III.i.91. *The boy hath sold him a bargain.* This is usually explained as 'has got the better of him, made a fool of him,'—a sense which the idiom, to sell one a bargain, undoubtedly had. But I think the context shows that Costard, in the innocence of his rustic heart, really conjectures that *l'envoy* means goose, and that the goose mentioned in the incomprehensible as speeches he has just listened to a veritable bird, over the price of which Armado and Moth have been haggling.

III.i.102. *And he ended the market.* There was a proverb: 'Three women and a goose make a market.'

III.i.164. *A very beadle to a humorous sigh.* The beadle was an inferior kind of constable who whipped small offenders. See *2 Henry VI* II.i.148. 'Humorous' is here used in the sense of sentimental.

III.i.169. *This senior-junior, giant-dwarf, Dan Cupid.* The early editions, both quarto and folio, read 'This signior Iunios giant-dwarf, dan Cupid.' It may be better, instead of Hanmer's emendation as given in the text, to print with Hart: 'This signior junior,' i.e. Mr. Youngster.

IV.i.23. *O heresy in fair, fit for these days!* The recent Cambridge editors, following a suggestion of Hart, see in this line and in lines 30–33 below 'a direct allusion to the conversion of Henry IV' to Romanism, July, 1593. The detached lines mentioned fit the historical situation well enough, but the Princess' speech as a whole does not. In his early plays Shakespeare is very fond of introducing passages of reflective moralizing such as this, generally without any suggestion of topical interest.

IV.i.48. *The thickest, and the tallest.* As Marshall remarks, Costard's otherwise dull and uncivil joke gains point if one remembers that the ladies' parts were performed by boys. The wit apparently lies in the fact that the Princess was represented by the oldest and stoutest of this group, whose figure was outgrowing its suitability to feminine rôles.

IV.i.58. *Break up this capon.* To break up a fowl was to carve it. Capon is used figuratively, like the French *poulet,* for a love-letter.

IV.i.88. *the Nemean lion.* The lion slain by Hercules in performances of his first labor. Here and in *Hamlet.* I.iv.91 Shakespeare erroneously accents the first syllable. Hart notes that Golding's Ovid gave him a precedent for the pronunciation.

IV.i.99. *Monarcho.* 'The monarch'; a crazy Italian who lived about the English court. He was subject to delusions of grandeur, and though he died about 1580, was still a familiar subject of allusion twenty years later.

IV.i.113. *she that bears the bow.* Rosaline is punning on 'shooter' and 'suitor,' which were pronounced alike, and often quibblingly confused. In Boyet's speech, line 111, the early editions all print 'shooter' for 'suitor.' In Shakespeare's time, it should be remembered, firearms had not replaced the bow in the fashionable sport of deer-slaying. Several writers see a special application in the deer-shooting allusions of this and the next scene to Queen Elizabeth's well-known fondness for the cross-bow. Cf. Sources of the Play.

IV.i.116. *if horns that year miscarry.* If the crop of horns is not good. Boyet succumbs to the inevitable jest about cuckolds' horns, produced by unfaithful wives.

IV.i.127. *King Pepin of France.* Charlemagne's father, a very ancient monarch.

IV.ii.32. *So were there a patch set of learning, to see him in a school.* The word 'patch' is used ambiguously. If Dull were seen in a school, (1) a patch (fool) would be put to study, and (2) a patch (disfigurement, disgrace) would be put on learning.

IV.ii.33. *Many can brook the weather that love not the wind.* Apparently a proverbial saying, similar to "There is no accounting for tastes," or 'It takes many sorts of men to make a world.' To brook the weather means to put up with foul weather.

IV.ii.37. *Dictynna.* This rare epithet of Diana is found in Golding's Ovid and in Tottel's Miscellany. It made trouble for the early compositors, who spell it 'Dictisima' and 'Dictima.'

IV.ii.42. *The allusion holds in the exchange.* That is, the point of the jest is still seen when Holofernes recasts (in ll. 40, 41) the form in which Dull has given it (l. 35).

IV.ii.79. *vir sapit qui pauca loquitur.* That man is wise who speaks little. The sentence is borrowed directly from Lyly's Latin grammar.

IV.ii.93, 94. *Fauste, precor gelida quando pecus omne sub umbra Ruminat . . . good old Mantuan.* Holofernes quotes the opening words of the first eclogue of Mantuanus (Baptista Spagnoli of Mantua, d. 1516), whose Latin poems were an elementary textbook in the schools of the day. The early editions read 'Facile' instead of 'Fauste,' which the recent Cambridge editors think an intentional misquotation. It is more probably a compositor's misreading of Shakespeare's manuscript.

IV.ii.96, 97. *Venetia, Venetia, Chi non te vede, non te pretia.* Archaic Italian: 'Venice, Venice, he who has not seen thee cannot value thee.' The words are gibberish as they appear in the early editions. Theobald first explained them.

IV.ii.99. *Ut, re, sol, la, mi, fa.* Notes of the old musical scale in incorrect order. They should run: 'ut (later replaced by "do"), re, mi, fa, sol, la.'

IV.ii.100. *As Horace says in his—.* What saying of Horace Holofernes has in mind the commentators have failed to discover.

IV.ii.118. *You find not the apostrophas.* You pronounce syllables which should be omitted. Or perhaps, as Gollancz suggests, Holofernes means the reverse (diereses): You omit syllables which should be pronounced.

IV.ii.119. *numbers ratified.* Metre sanctioned by convention.

IV.ii.127. *from one Monsieur Berowne, one of the strange queen's lords.* A very confusing and probably corrupt passage. What Jaquenetta here says is directly opposed to her assertion (ll. 91, 92) that the letter was sent to her from Don Armado; and the designation of Berowne as 'one of the strange queen's lords' is equally absurd. The recent Cambridge editors add another to a great list of implausible explanations by theorizing that 'Berowne' is a compositor's error for 'Boyet' (written 'Bo' or 'Boy'), and that Jaquenetta understands Holofernes to mean by 'directed' imparted. They assume, therefore, that Boyet juggled the two letters.

IV.ii.135. *Trip and go.* A common phrase, borrowed from the words of a popular morris dance song.

IV.ii.153, 154. *society—saith the text—is the happiness of life.* Nathaniel's source for the remark has not been found. Perhaps he is inventing the 'text' like the 'certain Father' of line 142. There is a much quoted Latin hexameter line, repeated by Marlowe in *Doctor Faustus,* which may have been in Shakespeare's mind: 'Solamen miseris socios habuisse doloris,' it is a comfort to the wretched to have companions in their pain.

IV.iii.5. *as mad as Ajax: it kills sheep.* Alluding to the story that Ajax, disappointed of the award of Achilles' armor, went mad and attacked a flock of sheep, which he took for a hostile army.

IV.iii.85. *Stoop, I say.* 'Stoop' is generally explained as equivalent to stooping, crooked; but there seems no justification for such a use. It is probably the verbal imperative, addressed *sotto voce* to Dumaine: Come off your stilts, abandon your exalted nonsense.

IV.iii.181. *With men like men, men of inconstancy.* There is little to choose between many of the emendations of this line, which is clearly imperfect both in metre and in sense as printed in the early editions: 'With men like men of

inconstancie.' The reading here accepted, which appears to be original with Craig, makes the line mean 'with ordinary, inconstant men.'

IV.iii.222. *sirs.* Costard and Jaquenetta are addressed.

IV.iii.266. *the school of night.* Perhaps 'that which teaches night to be what it is: dark and sinister.' Most editors have preferred to adopt an emendation that originated with Theobald and Warburton: the *scowl* of night. The recent Cambridge editors lend their support to a fantastic notion of Mr. Acheson to the effect that 'the school of night' is a topical allusion to a society composed of Sir Walter Raleigh, the poet Chapman, Marlowe, etc., whom it is supposed Shakespeare was ridiculing in this play.

IV.iii.266. *And beauty's crest becomes the heavens well.* An obscure line. The most obvious meaning is rather flat: 'And beauty's distinguishing mark (or perfection) well becomes the regions of light.'

IV.iii.268. *Devils soonest tempt, resembling spirits of light.* Perhaps an allusion to 2 Corinthians 11. 14: 'And no marvel, for Satan himself is transformed into an angel of light.' The idea recurs in *Hamlet* II.ii.586–588, and in *Measure for Measure* II.iv.16, 17.

IV.iii.313–338. The wording and argument of these lines are repeated in more extended form later in the speech. Compare especially lines 334–337 and 364–368. It is generally recognized that an earlier and a later, expanded and improved, version of the same speech have been accidentally amalgamated in the text which reached the printers. Mr. Dover Wilson argues that the opening lines of Berowne (303–309) were intended to begin both versions, and that they were followed in the earlier version by ll. 310–331 and in the later by ll. 332–379. See note on V.ii.861–867.

IV.iii.319. *poisons up.* Completely poisons. Theobald's emendation, 'prisons up,' is plausible and has been adopted by many editors.

IV.iii.320. *The nimble spirits in the arteries.* The arteries were supposed to contain, not blood simply, but 'vital spirits.'

IV.iii.350. *When the suspicious head of theft is stopp'd.* The 'suspicious head of theft' may be interpreted either actively, i.e. the acutely watchful ears of a thief; or passively, i.e. the ears of one suspicious of being robbed. I think the former the more likely.

IV.iii.378. *For charity itself fulfils the law.* Cf. Romans 13. 8: 'for he that loveth another hath fulfilled the law.'

IV.iii.397. *Sow'd cockle reap'd no corn.* An elliptical and proverbial expression: if we plant weeds, we shall not reap corn; unless we make the proper preparations, we shall not gain the desired results.

V.i.17. *to speak 'dout,' fine, when he should say, 'doubt.'* Holofernes belongs to the pedantic group which sought during the Renaissance to bring the spelling and pronunciation of English words as close as possible to the real or fancied Latin original. Thus the earlier *doute* was written and sounded *doubt* on the authority of Latin *dubitum*, and the earlier *dette* made into *debt* on the analogy of Latin *debitum*. The new, unhistorical spellings managed to establish themselves, but not the pronunciations upon which Holofernes and his class insisted.

V.i.24. *Priscian a little scratched.* That is, your Latin is passable, but hackneyed. Priscian wrote, during the fifth century, A.D., works which were long the standard textbooks on Latin grammar. Previous editors have assumed that 'scratched Priscian' must be equivalent to 'breaking Priscian's head,' i.e. speaking ungrammatical Latin. Hence Theobald misingeniously invented an error by changing Sir Nathaniel's correct sentence to 'Laus deo, *bone* intelligo,' and altered Holofernes' French (misprinted 'Bome boon for boon' in the original editions) into '*Bone?*—bone for *bene*.' But the schoolmaster's meaning is that the sentence is Priscian (correct Latin), but scratched by overuse. He would never admit that a positive error in grammar 'will serve.'

V.i.36. *honorificabilitudinitatibus.* Dative (or ablative) plural of a genuine mediæval Latin word used by Dante and other writers. It was famous as the longest of all words. It means something like 'the state of being capable of honors.'

V.i.40. *horn-book.* A rudimentary implement of education. It consisted in a paper containing the letters of the alphabet, Lord's Prayer, etc., fastened to a piece of board and protected by a covering of transparent horn.

V.i.58. *circum circa.* This is Theobald's rather over-ingenious emendation of '*vnum cita*' in the early editions. Hart proposes '*unciatim,*' inch by inch, and the late Cambridge editors *nimis cito*, all too quickly. Furness thinks *unum cita* a meaningless bit of schoolboy slang.

V.i.64. *ad dunghill.* This, as Holofernes suspects, is a perversion of *ad unguem*, probably current in the grammar-schools.

V.i.68, 69. *the charge-house on the top of the mountain.* Charge-house, defined as boarding-school in the Oxford Dictionary, is not otherwise exemplified. The mention of the top of the mountain has been suspected of containing some topical reference. Critics who wish to identify Holofernes with John Florio take

mountain as suggesting Montaigne, whose essays Florio translated. The date of Florio's Montaigne, 1603, seems sufficient to discredit this theory.

V.i.103. *the Nine Worthies.* They were variously listed, the most common enumeration being:—Three pagans (Hector, Alexander, and Cæsar); three Jews (Joshua, David, and Judas Maccabæus); and three Christians (King Arthur, Charlemagne, and Godfrey of Bouillon). Hercules and Pompey seem to have been first included by Shakespeare.

V.i.111, 112. *Hercules in minority.* The myth related that the infant Hercules' first exploit was to strangle two serpents which Juno had sent to destroy him. Hart quotes a line from Golding's Ovid (*Metamorphoses* ix. 79, 80), which may have stuck in the poet's memory: 'It is my Cradle game To vanquish Snakes.'

V.ii.13. *You'll ne'er be friends with him: a' kill'd your sister.* M. Abel Lefranc (*Sous le Masque de 'William Shakespeare,'* 1919, ii. p. 73–80) identifies this sister of Katharine with Hélène de Tournon, an attendant of Marguerite de Valois, Queen of Navarre, who actually died of love in 1577. But the incident is so similar to Viola's famous story of her sister in *Twelfth Night* that it seems more likely to have come from something in the personal experience of the poet than from anything in the source material of *Love's Labour's Lost.*

V.ii.26. *I weigh not you.* A pun, as the next line shows, on two idioms: (1) 'I do not equal you in weight,' and (2) 'I don't care about you.'

V.ii.41. *Much in the letters, nothing in the praise.* Furness explains 'The resemblance was great in the dark colour of the letters, but not at all in the substance of the praise.'

V.ii.43. *Fair as a text B in a copy-book.* A large ornamental capital in the old 'Gothic' hand: a 'black-letter.'

V.ii.44. *'Ware pencils, ho!* If we come to painting each other's portraits, take care.

V.ii.45. *red dominical.* The red letter in old almanacs to mark the Sundays of the year. The mediæval name for Sunday was 'dies dominica.'

V.ii.54. *A huge translation of hypocrisy.* Katharine affects to think Dumaine's verses imitated from foreign rimers.

V.ii.64. *in by the week.* Permanently caught.

V.ii.68. *hests.* The only argument for this word (which editors unanimously admit to be decisive) is the requirement of a rime for 'jests' in the next line. The First Quarto and First Folio read 'deuice,' for which the Second Folio substituted 'behests.' So in line 78 wantonness is a Second Folio emendation of 'wantons be.'

V.ii.70. *So perttaunt-like would I o'ersway his state.* Not very satisfactorily explained. The numerous conjectural emendations—pedant-like, portent-like, pendant-like, planet-like, etc.—are unconvincing. Marshall argues that perttaunt-like may be the term *'pur tant'* (for so much) used in the card game of Post and Pair, quoting a line from John Davies' *Wittes Pilgrimage* (1610?): 'Then to Pur Tant hee's in subjection.' (Cf. Works of John Davies of Hereford, ed. Grosart, vol.ii.p. 38.)

V.ii.127. *Like Muscovites or Russians.* Russian costumes were not uncommon in English courtly masquerades. Sir Sidney Lee suggests a particular allusion to a visit of Russian nobles to Elizabeth's court in 1583.

V.ii.265. *What! was your wizard made without a tongue?* Mr. W. J. Lawrence explains (*Times Lit. Suppl.*, June 7, 1923) that Elizabethan masks were kept in place by a tongue held between the wearer's teeth.

V.ii.270. *'Veal,' quoth the Dutchman.* 'Veal' may be the Dutchman's pronunciation of 'well,' or the German *viel* (much), or a pun on 'veil' in the sense of mask. The editors' efforts to evolve wit and sense out of this dialogue are all far-fetched. Katharine is evidently punning on Longaville's name in the words 'long' (l. 267) and 'veal.'

V.ii.273. *Let's part the word.* The recent Cambridge editors explain: 'half the word "calf" is a "ca" which are the first two letters of Catharine, and "half" means "wife." '

V.ii.306. *Qualm, perhaps.* Pronounced 'calm'; hence the pun. The same jest occurs in *2 Henry IV* II.iv.30, 31.

V.ii.309. *statute-caps.* An act of Parliament in 1571 required all ordinary citizens to wear woollen caps on Sundays and holidays. Hart quotes a still more apposite regulation for the apparel of London apprentices (in 1582), forbidding them at any time to wear within the city any head covering except a woollen cap. The object was to encourage the wool trade. It is worth noting that Shakespeare's uncle incurred a fine in 1583 for refusing to wear a cloth cap on Sundays and holidays.

V.ii.367. *Till this man show'd thee.* Theobald first read 'man' for the 'madman' of the early editions, which spoils the scansion of the line and certainly does not improve the sense. A plausible explanation of the intrusion of the superfluous 'mad—' is that the compositor's eye caught the first syllable of 'madman' in the next line.

V.ii.436. *like a blind harper's song.* Harping was proverbially the resource of the blind.

V.ii.451. *'Lord have mercy on us.'* The words put up on plague-stricken houses.

V.ii.455. *the Lord's tokens.* Spots on the body, marking the plague. Berowne jestingly so calls the lords' tokens, i.e. the gifts of his three associates to the ladies who are wearing them. There is perhaps in these plague mentions a suggestion of the great London plague of 1592–1593, but Mr. Charlton argues that such jesting would not be natural while the actual plague was raging.

V.ii.529. *You cannot beg us.* This slangy way of saying, 'We are no idiots,' seems to have arisen from the practice of suing for the guardianship of wealthy incompetents.

V.ii.555, 556. *Where zeal strives to content, and the contents Dies in the zeal of that which it presents.* Where the unintelligent zeal of the actors strives to content the audience, and the gist (contents) of the entertainment is destroyed by this very zeal in performance.

V.ii.579. *Abate throw at novum.* Alluding to a game called novem quinque, in which the two principal throws were nine and five. The Cambridge editors explain the words as 'referring to the presentation of nine worthies by five players.'

V.ii.585. *With libbard's head on knee.* Theobald explained this by quoting Cotgrave's definition of the French word *masquine:* 'The representation of a lion's head, etc., upon the elbow or knee of some old-fashioned garments.'

V.ii.606. *it stands too right.* The point seems to be that Alexander's head sat crookedly on his shoulders. Shakespeare can have got this fact from North's Plutarch. Boyet may, however, simply mean that Nathaniel's nose is not aquiline enough for that of a worthy.

V.ii.616. *You will be scraped out of the painted cloth for this.* That is, you will lose your place as one of the worthies. Painted cloths were a more humble substitute for tapestry in wall-coverings, and the nine worthies were a common subject of their decoration.

V.ii.617. *your lion, that holds his poll-axe sitting on a close-stool.* Theobald illustrated this Rabelaisian witticism very neatly by quoting the description of Alexander's arms in Gerard Leigh's *Accidence of Armory,* 1591: 'a lion or [of gold color] seiante [sitting] in a chair, holding a battle-axe argent.'

V.ii.640. *A kissing traitor.* Alluding to the kiss of Judas Iscariot. Berowne gets the hint for this gibe from Dumaine's *clipt* in the line above. Dumaine uses the word in the sense of abbreviated, and Berowne seizes upon another sense, from 'clip,' to embrace.

V.ii.646. *Judas was hanged on an elder.* An old belief. Sir John Mandeville reported that the tree was still standing.

V.ii.658. *worn in the cap of a toothdrawer.* The brooch in the toothdrawer's cap appears to have been a distinguishing mark of his costume. Halliwell quoted a passage from the works of John Taylor, the Water-Poet (1630):—'In Queen Elizabeth's days there was a fellow that wore a brooch in his hat like a toothdrawer.' One of the costume sketches made by Inigo Jones for a mask at James I's court represents a toothdrawer wearing a very high hat with a brooch in the left side. (See publications of the (Old) Shakespeare Society, vol. 39, 1848.)

V.ii.724. *More Ates.* Ate was goddess of discord. She is introduced at the opening of Peele's *Arraignment of Paris* and again in the fourth book of the *Fairy Queen.*

V.ii.763. *I have seen the day of wrong through the little hole of discretion.* 'To see day at a little hole' was a proverbial saying.

V.ii.779, 780. *The extreme parts of time extremely forms All causes to the purpose of his speed.* The closing moments of a period force concentration upon the matter in hand, or subordinate everything else to the necessity of making the most of time. 'Forms' is the old northern English plural, frequent in Shakespeare. Cf. 'runs' in line 338.

V.ii.793. *And by these badges understand the king.* Badges are distinguishing marks. Berowne goes on to explain what they are; namely, the various evidences of the deep sincerity of the wooers' love.

V.ii.857. *Hence ever then.* The Folio reading. The Quarto has 'Hence herrite then,' which Professor Pollard ingeniously explains as 'Hence hermit then.'

V.ii.858–864. These six lines evidently come from the earlier version of the play. The expanded version is found in ll. 879–912. See note on IV.iii.313–317. Mr. Dover Wilson suggests that ll. 913, 914 originally followed 864, and that the whole passage 865–912 was interpolated in the revision, Dumaine being then given in l. 863 the line of Berowne (858) which the poet intended to delete along with Rosaline's original answer (859–864).

V.ii.878. *The liker you; few taller are so young.* Time in being long is the more like Longaville, who is 'long' both by name and by being tall for his age.

V.ii.935. *This side is Hiems, Winter; this Ver, the Spring.* The poetical argument between winter and spring was a famous subject of the mediæval *debate.* One version, entitled *Conflictus Hiemis et Veris,* is ascribed to the celebrated Alcuin (A.D. 735–804).

A Midsummer Night's Dream

Edited by
WILLARD HIGLEY DURHAM

Dramatis Personae

THESEUS, *Duke of Athens*

EGEUS, *Father to Hermia*

LYSANDER ⎫
DEMETRIUS ⎬ *in love with Hermia*

PHILOSTRATE, *Master of the Revels to Theseus*

QUINCE, *a Carpenter*

SNUG, *a Joiner*

BOTTOM, *a Weaver*

FLUTE, *a Bellows-Mender*

SNOUT, *a Tinker*

STARVELING, *a Tailor*

HIPPOLYTA, *Queen of the Amazons, betrothed to Theseus*

HERMIA, *Daughter to Egeus, in love with Lysander*

HELENA, *in love with Demetrius*

OBERON, *King of the Fairies*

TITANIA, *Queen of the Fairies*

PUCK, *or Robin Goodfellow*

PEASE-BLOSSOM

COBWEB

MOTH

MUSTARD-SEED ⎬ *Fairies*

OTHER FAIRIES ATTENDING THEIR KING AND QUEEN

ATTENDANTS ON THESEUS AND HIPPOLYTA

SCENE—*Athens, and a Wood near it.*

A Midsummer Night's Dream

INTRODUCTION

SOURCES OF THE PLAY

For *A Midsummer Night's Dream,* as for one other early play, *Love's Labour's Lost,* and another very late one, *The Tempest,* Shakespeare seems to have devised a plot with relative independence. At any rate, nothing has been found which may properly be called the 'source' of *A Midsummer Night's Dream.* The most that can be said is that there are resemblances of detail between this play and some earlier narratives.

None of these, however, are of any great importance. It is possible, for example, that in writing about Theseus and Hippolyta, Shakespeare had in mind Chaucer's *Knight's Tale;* for there too this 'Duke of Athens' and his bride 'do observance to a morn of May,' and there the name of Philostrate appears. Shakespeare knew also North's translation of Plutarch's *Lives,* which contains a 'Life of Theseus,' and he very probably borrowed some details from this. He could have read the story of Pyramus and Thisbe in several versions, such as that in Chaucer's *Legend of Good Women,* in Ovid's *Metamorphoses,* or in Golding's translation of Ovid (1565). It is barely possible that he derived the suggestion for Oberon's magic 'love-juice' from the Spanish *Diana Enamorada* by Jorge de Montemayor; but if he read an English translation, it must have been in manuscript, for none was published until 1598. He could have found accounts of Robin Goodfellow in several books, and he seems to have met the name Titania in Ovid, where it is applied to Diana; yet his conception of the fairies and of Bottom and the other 'hempen homespuns' is not derived from books, but from the traditions of the countryside, from his own observation of simple men, and from his own imagination.

THE HISTORY OF THE PLAY

A Midsummer Night's Dream was first printed, in quarto, in 1600. A second quarto bears the same date on the title-page, but this was actually printed about 1619. The existence of the play some years before 1600 is proved by the fact that it is mentioned by Francis Meres in his *Palladis Tamia,* which was published in 1598. Those who seek to determine the date of composition more definitely than this are obliged to base their opinions upon internal evidence. Some critics see in Titania's speech about the confusion of the seasons (II. i. 90–116) a reference to the unusually cold, wet summer of 1594. Others, believing that the play was written to honor some great wedding, have attempted, without conspicuous success, to determine whose that wedding was.

The result of these and other conjectures and of inferences drawn from the manner in which Shakespeare here handled his verse is that there is general agreement that the play was written not earlier than 1593 and not later than 1595.

In its original and complete form the play has been, until relatively recent years, among the less popular of Shakespeare's works, although in 1631 the Bishop of Lincoln got into trouble with the Puritans by allowing it to be performed—in whole or in part—at his house on a Sunday. An abridgment of the play with the title *The Merry Conceited Humours of Bottom the Weaver* was apparently acted in private during the period when the theaters were closed (1642–1660). Whether the performance which Pepys saw in 1662 and thought 'the most insipid ridiculous play that ever I saw in my life' was a representation of the play as Shakespeare wrote it is not certain, but in 1692 at any rate the original was displaced by an operatic version with music by Purcell, and from then until well on in the nineteenth century the records show only such perversions and adaptations as that produced by David Garrick in 1755, in which some very stupid songs replaced much of Shakespeare's text and in which the parts of Lysander and Hermia were given to Italian singers.

The credit for the restoration to the stage of something like the original play must be given to Tieck, a German translator of Shakespeare, who produced it at Berlin in 1827 with the incidental music by Mendelssohn which has since become famous. Some of the best performances of recent years have been given in Germany, notably the production by Max Reinhardt, which combined remarkable excellences with lapses of taste characteristically German.

In England and America productions reasonably faithful to the original text have been both frequent and popular since the performance by Mme. Vestris in 1840 at Covent Garden in London. The spectacular possibilities of the play and the popularity of Mendelssohn's music have so appealed to managers that the text has often been swamped in scenery and sound, but there must have been good acting in Augustin Daly's production (1888), when Theseus was played by Joseph Holland, Demetrius by John Drew, Lysander by Otis Skinner, and Helena by Ada Rehan. In 1903 the New Amsterdam Theater in New York was opened with a performance of the play characterized rather by lavish expenditure of money than by intelligence of acting or direction; at another revival in 1906, Miss Annie Russell attempted to play the part of Puck; and in 1915 Granville Barker offered to New York his London production, one which certainly displayed intelligence although its gilded fairies and its substitution of supposedly suggestive 'decorations' in place of realistic scenery aroused much hostile criticism.

ACT FIRST ❧ SCENE FIRST

[Athens. The Palace of Theseus]
Enter Theseus, Hippolyta, with [Philostrate and] others.

The. Now, fair Hippolyta, our nuptial hour
Draws on apace: four happy days bring in
Another moon; but O! methinks how slow
This old moon wanes; she lingers my desires,
Like to a step-dame, or a dowager   *5*
Long withering out a young man's revenue.
   Hip. Four days will quickly steep themselves in night;
Four nights will quickly dream away the time; ·
And then the moon, like to a silver bow
New-bent in heaven, shall behold the night   *10*
Of our solemnities.
   The.   Go, Philostrate,
Stir up the Athenian youth to merriments;
Awake the pert and nimble spirit of mirth;
Turn melancholy forth to funerals;   *15*
The pale companion is not for our pomp.   *[Exit Philostrate.]*
Hippolyta, I woo'd thee with my sword,
And won thy love doing thee injuries;
But I will wed thee in another key,
With pomp, with triumph, and with revelling.   *20*

Enter Egeus and his daughter Hermia, Lysander, and Demetrius.

   Ege. Happy be Theseus, our renowned duke!
   The. Thanks, good Egeus: what's the news with thee?
   Ege. Full of vexation come I, with complaint
Against my child, my daughter Hermia.
Stand forth, Demetrius. My noble lord,   *25*
This man hath my consent to marry her.
Stand forth, Lysander: and, my gracious duke,
This man hath bewitch'd the bosom of my child:
Thou, thou, Lysander, thou hast given her rimes,
And interchang'd love-tokens with my child;   *30*
Thou hast by moonlight at her window sung,
With feigning voice, verses of feigning love;
And stol'n the impression of her fantasy
With bracelets of thy hair, rings, gawds, conceits,
Knacks, trifles, nosegays, sweetmeats, messengers   *35*
Of strong prevailment in unharden'd youth;
With cunning hast thou filch'd my daughter's heart;
Turn'd her obedience, which is due to me,
To stubborn harshness. And, my gracious duke,
Be it so she will not here before your Grace   *40*
Consent to marry with Demetrius,
I beg the ancient privilege of Athens,
As she is mine, I may dispose of her;
Which shall be either to this gentleman,
Or to her death, according to our law   *45*
Immediately provided in that case.
   The. What say you, Hermia? be advis'd, fair maid.
To you your father should be as a god;
One that compos'd your beauties, yea, and one
To whom you are but as a form in wax   *50*
By him imprinted, and within his power

To leave the figure or disfigure it.
Demetrius is a worthy gentleman.
   Her. So is Lysander.
   The.   In himself he is;   *55*
But, in this kind, wanting your father's voice,
The other must be held the worthier.
   Her. I would my father look'd but with my eyes.
   The. Rather your eyes must with his judgment look.
   Her. I do entreat your Grace to pardon me.   *60*
I know not by what power I am made bold,
Nor how it may concern my modesty
In such a presence here to plead my thoughts;
But I beseech your Grace that I may know
The worst that may befall me in this case,   *65*
If I refuse to wed Demetrius.
   The. Either to die the death, or to abjure
For ever the society of men.
Therefore, fair Hermia, question your desires;
Know of your youth, examine well your blood,   *70*
Whether, if you yield not to your father's choice,
You can endure the livery of a nun,
For aye to be in shady cloister mew'd,
To live a barren sister all your life,
Chanting faint hymns to the cold fruitless moon.   *75*
Thrice blessed they that master so their blood,
To undergo such maiden pilgrimage;
But earthlier happy is the rose distill'd,
Than that which withering on the virgin thorn
Grows, lives, and dies, in single blessedness.   *80*
   Her. So will I grow, so live, so die, my lord,
Ere I will yield my virgin patent up
Unto his lordship, whose unwished yoke
My soul consents not to give sovereignty.
   The. Take time to pause; and, by the next new moon,— *85*
The sealing-day betwixt my love and me
For everlasting bond of fellowship,—
Upon that day either prepare to die
For disobedience to your father's will,
Or else to wed Demetrius, as he would;   *90*
Or on Diana's altar to protest
For aye austerity and single life.
   Dem. Relent, sweet Hermia; and Lysander, yield
Thy crazed title to my certain right.
   Lys. You have her father's love, Demetrius;   *95*
Let me have Hermia's: do you marry him.
   Ege. Scornful Lysander! true, he hath my love,
And what is mine my love shall render him;
And she is mine, and all my right of her
I do estate unto Demetrius.   *100*
   Lys. I am, my lord, as well deriv'd as he,
As well possess'd; my love is more than his;
My fortunes every way as fairly rank'd,
If not with vantage, as Demetrius';
And, which is more than all these boasts can be,   *105*
I am belov'd of beauteous Hermia.
Why should not I then prosecute my right?
Demetrius, I'll avouch it to his head,

---

4 lingers: *delays fulfillment of*   **5, 6** *Cf. n.*   **14 pert:** *lively*   **16 pomp:** *ceremonial procession*   **20 triumph:** *festive entertainment*   **32 feigning;** *cf. n.*   **33 fantasy:** *imagination; cf. n.*   **34 gawds:** *gewgaws* **conceits:** *fancy articles*   **35 Knacks:** *knickknacks*   **46 Immediately:** *expressly*

52 disfigure: *destroy*   **56 kind:** *respect, i.e., as husband*   **62 concern:** *befit*   **73 mew'd:** *shut up*   **77 pilgrimage:** *the journey of life*   **78 distill'd:** *reduced to essence*   **82 virgin patent:** *privilege of virginity*   **91 protest:** *vow*   **94 crazed:** *unsound*   **100 estate unto:** *bestow upon*   **102 possess'd:** *endowed*

Made love to Nedar's daughter, Helena,
And won her soul; and she, sweet lady, dotes,   *110*
Devoutly dotes, dotes in idolatry,
Upon this spotted and inconstant man.

    The. I must confess that I have heard so much,
And with Demetrius thought to have spoke thereof;
But, being over-full of self-affairs,   *115*
My mind did lose it. But, Demetrius, come;
And come, Egeus; you shall go with me,
I have some private schooling for you both.
For you, fair Hermia, look you arm yourself
To fit your fancies to your father's will,   *120*
Or else the law of Athens yields you up,
Which by no means we may extenuate,
To death, or to a vow of single life.
Come, my Hippolyta: what cheer, my love?
Demetrius and Egeus, go along: *125*
I must employ you in some business
Against our nuptial, and confer with you
Of something nearly that concerns yourselves.

    Ege. With duty and desire we follow you.

        Exeunt. Manet Lysander and Hermia.

    Lys. How now, my love! Why is your cheek so pale?   *130*
How chance the roses there do fade so fast?

    Her. Belike for want of rain, which I could well
Beteem them from the tempest of mine eyes.

    Lys. Ay me! for aught that ever I could read,
Could ever hear by tale or history,   *135*
The course of true love never did run smooth;
But, either it was different in blood,—

    Her. O cross! too high to be enthrall'd to low.

    Lys. Or else misgraffed in respect of years,—

    Her. O spite! too old to be engag'd to young.   *140*

    Lys. Or else it stood upon the choice of friends,—

    Her. O hell! to choose love by another's eye.

    Lys. Or, if there were a sympathy in choice,
War, death, or sickness did lay siege to it,
Making it momentany as a sound,   *145*
Swift as a shadow, short as any dream,
Brief as the lightning in the collied night,
That, in a spleen, unfolds both heaven and earth,
And ere a man hath power to say, 'Behold!'
The jaws of darkness do devour it up: *150*
So quick bright things come to confusion.

    Her. If then true lovers have been ever cross'd,
It stands as an edict in destiny:
Then let us teach our trial patience,
Because it is a customary cross,   *155*
As due to love as thoughts and dreams and sighs,
Wishes and tears, poor fancy's followers.

    Lys. A good persuasion: therefore, hear me, Hermia.
I have a widow aunt, a dowager
Of great revenue, and she hath no child: *160*
From Athens is her house remote seven leagues;
And she respects me as her only son.

There, gentle Hermia, may I marry thee,
And to that place the sharp Athenian law
Cannot pursue us. If thou lov'st me then,   *165*
Steal forth thy father's house to-morrow night,
And in the wood, a league without the town,
Where I did meet thee once with Helena,
To do observance to a morn of May,
There will I stay for thee.   *170*

    Her.   My good Lysander!
I swear to thee by Cupid's strongest bow,
By his best arrow with the golden head,
By the simplicity of Venus' doves,
By that which knitteth souls and prospers loves,   *175*
And by that fire which burn'd the Carthage queen,
When the false Troyan under sail was seen,
By all the vows that ever men have broke,—
In number more than ever women spoke,—
In that same place thou hast appointed me,   *180*
To-morrow truly will I meet with thee.

    Lys. Keep promise, love. Look, here comes Helena.

        Enter Helena.

    Her. God speed fair Helena! Whither away?

    Hel. Call you me fair? that fair again unsay.
Demetrius loves your fair: O happy fair!   *185*
Your eyes are lode-stars! and your tongue's sweet air
More tuneable than lark to shepherd's ear,
When wheat is green, when hawthorn buds appear.
Sickness is catching: O! were favour so,
Yours would I catch, fair Hermia, ere I go;   *190*
My ear should catch your voice, my eye your eye,
My tongue should catch your tongue's sweet melody.
Were the world mine, Demetrius being bated,
The rest I'll give to be to you translated.
O! teach me how you look, and with what art   *195*
You sway the motion of Demetrius' heart.

    Her. I frown upon him, yet he loves me still.

    Hel. O! that your frowns would teach my smiles such skill.

    Her. I give him curses, yet he gives me love.

    Hel. O! that my prayers could such affection move.   *200*

    Her. The more I hate, the more he follows me.

    Hel. The more I love, the more he hateth me.

    Her. His folly, Helena, is no fault of mine.

    Hel. None, but your beauty: would that fault were mine!

    Her. Take comfort: he no more shall see my face;   *205*
Lysander and myself will fly this place.
Before the time I did Lysander see,
Seem'd Athens as a paradise to me:
O! then, what graces in my love do dwell,
That he hath turn'd a heaven unto a hell.   *210*

    Lys. Helen, to you our minds we will unfold.
To-morrow night, when Phœbe doth behold
Her silver visage in the wat'ry glass,
Decking with liquid pearl the bladed grass,—
A time that lovers' flights doth still conceal,—   *215*
Through Athens' gates have we devis'd to steal.

    Her. And in the wood, where often you and I

115 self-affairs: *my own concerns*   **127 Against:** *in preparation for*   **128 nearly that:** *that closely*   **S. d. Manet** (i.e., manet) *remain*   **133 Beteem:** *grant*   **139 misgraffed:** *badly matched*   **145 momentany:** *momentary*   **147 collied:** *blackened*   **148 spleen:** *sudden fit of passion*   **151 confusion:** *ruin*   **152 ever:** *always*   **157 fancy's:** *love's*   **162 respects:** *looks upon*

176 Carthage queen: *Dido*   **177 Troyan:** *Æneas*   **183 fair:** *beauty*   **186 lode-stars:** *guiding-stars*   **187 tuneable:** *tuneful*   **189 favour:** *charm*   **193 bated:** *excepted*   **194 translated:** *transformed*   **209, 210** *Cf. n.*   **212 Phœbe:** *the moon*   **215 still:** *always*

Upon faint primrose-beds were wont to lie,
Emptying our bosoms of their counsel sweet,
There my Lysander and myself shall meet;　　　*220*
And thence from Athens turn away our eyes,
To seek new friends and stranger companies.
Farewell, sweet playfellow: pray thou for us;
And good luck grant thee thy Demetrius!
Keep word, Lysander: we must starve our sight　　　*225*
From lovers' food till morrow deep midnight.

　　　　　　　　　　　　　　　　Exit Hermia.

　Lys. I will, my Hermia.—Helena, adieu:
As you on him, Demetrius dote on you!　　　*Exit Lysander.*
　Hel. How happy some o'er other some can be!
Through Athens I am thought as fair as she;　　　*230*
But what of that? Demetrius thinks not so;
He will not know what all but he do know;
And as he errs, doting on Hermia's eyes,
So I, admiring of his qualities.
Things base and vile, holding no quantity,　　　*235*
Love can transpose to form and dignity.
Love looks not with the eyes, but with the mind,
And therefore is wing'd Cupid painted blind.
Nor hath Love's mind of any judgment taste;
Wings and no eyes figure unheedy haste:　　　*240*
And therefore is Love said to be a child,
Because in choice he is so oft beguil'd.
As waggish boys in game themselves forswear,
So the boy Love is perjur'd everywhere;
For ere Demetrius look'd on Hermia's eyne,　　　*245*
He hail'd down oaths that he was only mine;
And when this hail some heat from Hermia felt,
So he dissolv'd, and showers of oaths did melt.
I will go tell him of fair Hermia's flight:
Then to the wood will he to-morrow night　　　*250*
Pursue her; and for this intelligence
If I have thanks, it is a dear expense:
But herein mean I do enrich my pain,
To have his sight thither and back again.　　　*Exit.*

❧ Scene Second ❧

[A Room in Quince's House]
Enter Quince the Carpenter, Snug the Joiner, Bottom the Weaver,
Flute the Bellows-mender, Snout the Tinker, and Starveling the
Tailor.

　Quin. Is all our company here?
　Bot. You were best to call them generally, man by man,
according to the scrip.
　Quin. Here is the scroll of every man's name, which is
thought fit, through all Athens, to play in our interlude　　　*5*
before the duke and the duchess on his wedding-day at night.
　Bot. First, good Peter Quince, say what the play treats on;
then read the names of the actors, and so grow to a point.
　Quin. Marry, our play is, The most lamentable comedy, and
most cruel death of Pyramus and Thisby.　　　*10*

　Bot. A very good piece of work, I assure you, and a merry.
Now, good Peter Quince, call forth your actors by the scroll.
Masters, spread yourselves.
　Quin. Answer as I call you. Nick Bottom, the weaver.
　Bot. Ready. Name what part I am for, and proceed.　　　*15*
　Quin. You, Nick Bottom, are set down for Pyramus.
　Bot. What is Pyramus? a lover, or a tyrant?
　Quin. A lover, that kills himself most gallantly for love.
　Bot. That will ask some tears in the true performing of it:
if I do it, let the audience look to their eyes; I will move　　　*20*
storms, I will condole in some measure. To the rest: yet my
chief humour is for a tyrant. I could play Ercles rarely, or a
part to tear a cat in, to make all split.

　　　'The raging rocks
　　　And shivering shocks　　　*25*
　　　Shall break the locks
　　　　Of prison gates:
　　　And Phibbus' car
　　　Shall shine from far
　　　And make and mar　　　*30*
　　　　The foolish Fates.'

This was lofty! Now name the rest of the players. This is
Ercles' vein, a tyrant's vein; a lover is more condoling.
　Quin. Francis Flute, the bellows-mender.
　Flu. Here, Peter Quince.　　　*35*
　Quin. You must take Thisby on you.
　Flu. What is Thisby? a wandering knight?
　Quin. It is the lady that Pyramus must love.
　Flu. Nay, faith, let not me play a woman; I have a
beard coming.　　　*40*
　Quin. That's all one: you shall play it in a mask,
and you may speak as small as you will.
　Bot. An I may hide my face, let me play Thisby too.
I'll speak in a monstrous little voice, 'Thisne, Thisne!' 'Ah,
Pyramus, my lover dear; thy Thisby dear, and lady dear!'　　　*45*
　Quin. No, no; you must play Pyramus; and Flute, you
Thisby.
　Bot. Well, proceed.
　Quin. Robin Starveling, the tailor.
　Star. Here, Peter Quince.　　　*50*
　Quin. Robin Starveling, you must play Thisby's mother.
Tom Snout, the tinker.
　Snout. Here, Peter Quince.
　Quin. You, Pyramus's father; myself, Thisby's father; Snug,
the joiner, you the lion's part: and, I hope, here is a play　　　*55*
fitted.
　Snug. Have you the lion's part written? pray you, if it be,
give it me, for I am slow of study.
　Quin. You may do it extempore, for it is nothing but
roaring.　　　*60*
　Bot. Let me play the lion too. I will roar, that I will do
any man's heart good to hear me; I will roar, that I will
make the duke say, 'Let him roar again, let him roar again.'
　Quin. An you should do it too terribly, you would fright
the duchess and the ladies, that they would shriek; and that　　　*65*
were enough to hang us all.
　All. That would hang us, every mother's son.

218 faint: *pale (?), faintly perfumed (?)*　**219 counsel:** *inmost thought*　**235, 236**
Cf. n.　**243 game:** *jest*　**245 eyne:** *eyes*　**251 intelligence:** *information*　**252 dear**
expense: *cf. n.*　**2 generally;** *cf. n.*　**3 scrip:** *written paper*　**9 Marry:** *an oath from*
the name of the Virgin Mary

22 Ercles: *Hercules*　**23 tear a cat:** *rant*　**28 Phibbus':** *Phœbus', the sun-god's*　**43**
An: *if*　**44 Thisne;** *cf. n.*

Bot. I grant you, friends, if that you should fright the ladies
out of their wits, they would have no more discretion but to
hang us; but I will aggravate my voice so that I will roar   70
you as gently as any sucking dove; I will roar you an
'twere any nightingale.

Quin. You can play no part but Pyramus; for Pyramus
is a sweet-faced man; a proper man, as one shall see in a
summer's day; a most lovely, gentleman-like man; therefore,   75
you must needs play Pyramus.

Bot. Well, I will undertake it. What beard were I best to
play it in?

Quin. Why, what you will.

Bot. I will discharge it in either your straw-colour beard,   80
your orange-tawny beard, your purple-in-grain beard, or
your French-crown colour beard, your perfect yellow.

Quin. Some of your French crowns have no hair at all, and
then you will play bare-faced. But masters, here are your parts;
and I am to entreat you, request you, and desire you, to   85
con them by to-morrow night, and meet me in the palace
wood, a mile without the town, by moonlight: there will we
rehearse; for if we meet in the city, we shall be dogged with
company, and our devices known. In the meantime I will
draw a bill of properties, such as our play wants. I pray   90
you, fail me not.

Bot. We will meet; and there we may rehearse more
obscenely and courageously. Take pains, be perfect; adieu.

Quin. At the duke's oak we meet.

Bot. Enough; hold, or cut bow-strings.   *Exeunt.*

ACT SECOND ❧ SCENE FIRST

[A Wood near Athens]
Enter a Fairy at one door, and Robin Goodfellow at another.

Puck. How now, spirit! whither wander you?
Fai. Over hill, over dale,
    Thorough bush, thorough brier,
Over park, over pale,
    Thorough flood, thorough fire,   5
I do wander everywhere,
Swifter than the moon's sphere;
And I serve the fairy queen,
To dew her orbs upon the green:
The cowslips tall her pensioners be;   10
In their gold coats spots you see;
Those be rubies, fairy favours,
In their freckles live their savours:
I must go seek some dew-drops here,
And hang a pearl in every cowslip's ear.   15
Farewell, thou lob of spirits: I'll be gone;
Our queen and all her elves come here anon.
Puck. The king doth keep his revels here to-night.
Take heed the queen come not within his sight;

For Oberon is passing fell and wrath,   20
Because that she as her attendant hath
A lovely boy, stol'n from an Indian king;
She never had so sweet a changeling;
And jealous Oberon would have the child
Knight of his train, to trace the forests wild;   25
But she, perforce, withholds the loved boy,
Crowns him with flowers, and makes him all her joy.
And now they never meet in grove, or green,
By fountain clear, or spangled starlight sheen,
But they do square; that all their elves, for fear,   30
Creep into acorn-cups and hide them there.
Fai. Either I mistake your shape and making quite,
Or else you are that shrewd and knavish sprite
Call'd Robin Goodfellow: are you not be
That frights the maidens of the villagery;   35
Skim milk, and sometimes labour in the quern,
And bootless make the breathless housewife churn;
And sometime make the drink to bear no barm;
Mislead night wanderers, laughing at their harm?
Those that Hobgoblin call you and sweet Puck,   40
You do their work, and they shall have good luck:
Are you not he?
Puck.   Fairy, thou speak'st aright;
I am that merry wanderer of the night.
I jest to Oberon, and make him smile   45
When I a fat and bean-fed horse beguile,
Neighing in likeness of a filly foal:
And sometime lurk I in a gossip's bowl,
In very likeness of a roasted crab;
And, when she drinks, against her lips I bob   50
And on her wither'd dewlap pour the ale.
The wisest aunt, telling the saddest tale,
Sometime for three-foot stool mistaketh me;
Then slip I from her bum, down topples she,
And 'tailor' cries, and falls into a cough;   55
And then the whole quire hold their hips and laugh;
And waxen in their mirth, and neeze, and swear
A merrier hour was never wasted there.
But, room, fairy! here comes Oberon.
Fai. And here my mistress. Would that he were gone!   60

Enter the King of Fairies [Oberon] at one door with his train;
and the Queen [Titania] at another with hers.

Obe. Ill met by moonlight, proud Titania.
Tita. What! jealous Oberon. Fairies, skip hence:
I have forsworn his bed and company.
Obe. Tarry, rash wanton! am not I thy lord?   65
Tita. Then, I must be thy lady; but I know
When thou hast stol'n away from fairy land
And in the shape of Corin sat all day,
Playing on pipes of corn, and versing love
To amorous Phillida. Why art thou here,   70
Come from the furthest steep of India?

---

71 an 'twere: *as if it were*   74 proper: *fine, handsome*   80 discharge: *perform*   81
purple-in-grain: *fast-dyed Purple*   82 French-crown colour: *color of a gold coin*   86
con: *learn by heart*   90 bill: *list*   95 Cf. n.   SCENE ONE S. d at one door;
cf. n. Robin Goodfellow; *cf. n.*   3 Thorough: *through*   4 pale: *fence*   7 moon's
sphere; *cf. n.*   9 orbs; *cf. n.*   10 pensioners; *cf. n.*   12 favours: *love-tokens*   16
lob: *bumpkin*   17 anon: *presently*

20 passing fell: *exceedingly angry* wrath: *wroth*   23 changeling; *cf. n*   25 trace: *traverse*   29 sheen: *bright*   30 square: *quarrel* that: *so that*   32 making: *form*   33
shrewd: *malicious, mischievous*   36 quern: *hand-mill for grinding grain*   37 bootless:
fruitlessly   38 barm: *froth*   48 gossip's bowl; *cf. n.*   49 crab: *crab-apple*   52 saddest: *soberest*   55 tailor; *cf. n.*   56 quire: *company*   57 waxen: *increase* neeze:
sneeze   68 Corin; *cf. n.*   69 versing love: *making love-verses*   71 steep: *mountain
range*

But that, forsooth, the bouncing Amazon,
Your buskin'd mistress and your warrior love,
To Theseus must be wedded, and you come
To give their bed joy and prosperity.   *75*

    Obe. How canst thou thus for shame, Titania,
Glance at my credit with Hippolyta,
Knowing I know thy love to Theseus?
Didst thou not lead him through the glimmering night
From Perigenia, whom he ravished?   *80*
And make him with fair Ægle break his faith,
With Ariadne, and Antiopa?

    Tita. These are the forgeries of jealousy:
And never, since the middle summer's spring,
Met we on hill, in dale, forest, or mead,   *85*
By paved fountain, or by rushy brook,
Or in the beached margent of the sea,
To dance our ringlets to the whistling wind,
But with thy brawls thou hast disturb'd our sport.
Therefore the winds, piping to us in vain,   *90*
As in revenge, have suck'd up from the sea
Contagious fogs; which, falling in the land,
Hath every pelting river made so proud
That they have overborne their continents:
The ox hath therefore stretch'd his yoke in vain,   *95*
The ploughman lost his sweat, and the green corn
Hath rotted ere his youth attain'd a beard:
The fold stands empty in the drowned field,
And crows are fatted with the murrion flock;
The nine men's morris is fill'd up with mud,   *100*
And the quaint mazes in the wanton green
For lack of tread are undistinguishable:
The human mortals want their winter here:
No night is now with hymn or carol blest:
Therefore the moon, the governess of floods,   *105*
Pale in her anger, washes all the air,
That rheumatic diseases do abound:
And thorough this distemperature we see
The seasons alter: hoary-headed frosts
Fall in the fresh lap of the crimson rose,   *110*
And on old Hiems' thin and icy crown
An odorous chaplet of sweet summer buds
Is, as in mockery, set. The spring, the summer,
The childing autumn, angry winter, change
Their wonted liveries, and the mazed world,   *115*
By their increase, now knows not which is which.
And this same progeny of evil comes
From our debate, from our dissension:
We are their parents and original.

    Obe. Do you amend it then; it lies in you.   *120*
Why should Titania cross her Oberon?
I do but beg a little changeling boy,
To be my henchman.

    Tita.   Set your heart at rest;

The fairy land buys not the child of me.   *125*
His mother was a votaress of my order:
And, in the spiced Indian air, by night,
Full often hath she gossip'd by my side,
And sat with me on Neptune's yellow sands,
Marking the embarked traders on the flood;   *130*
When we have laugh'd to see the sails conceive
And grow big-bellied with the wanton wind;
Which she, with pretty and with swimming gait
Following,—her womb then rich with my young squire,—
Would imitate, and sail upon the land,   *135*
To fetch me trifles, and return again,
As from a voyage, rich with merchandise.
But she, being mortal, of that boy did die;
And for her sake I do rear up her boy,
And for her sake I will not part with him.   *140*

    Obe. How long within this wood intend you stay?

    Tita. Perchance, till after Theseus' wedding-day.
If you will patiently dance in our round,
And see our moonlight revels, go with us;
If not, shun me, and I will spare your haunts.   *145*

    Obe. Give me that boy, and I will go with thee.

    Tita. Not for thy fairy kingdom. Fairies, away!
We shall chide downright, if I longer stay.

              Exeunt [Titania and her train].

    Obe. Well, go thy way: thou shalt not from this grove
Till I torment thee for this injury.   *150*
My gentle Puck, come hither. Thou remember'st
Since once I sat upon a promontory,
And heard a mermaid on a dolphin's back
Uttering such dulcet and harmonious breath,
That the rude sea grew civil at her song,   *155*
And certain stars shot madly from their spheres
To hear the sea-maid's music.

    Puck.   I remember.

    Obe. That very time I saw, but thou couldst not,
Flying between the cold moon and the earth,   *160*
Cupid all arm'd: a certain aim he took
At a fair vestal throned by the west,
And loos'd his love-shaft smartly from his bow,
As it should pierce a hundred thousand hearts;
But I might see young Cupid's fiery shaft   *165*
Quench'd in the chaste beams of the wat'ry moon,
And the imperial votaress passed on,
In maiden meditation, fancy-free.
Yet mark'd I where the bolt of Cupid fell:
It fell upon a little western flower,   *170*
Before milk-white, now purple with love's wound,
And maidens call it Love-in-idleness.
Fetch me that flower; the herb I show'd thee once:
The juice of it on sleeping eyelids laid
Will make or man or woman madly dote   *175*
Upon the next live creature that it sees.
Fetch me this herb; and be thou here again
Ere the leviathan can swim a league.

    Puck. I'll put a girdle round about the earth
In forty minutes.   *Exit.* *180*

    Obe.   Having once this juice,

---

73 buskin'd: *wearing a buskin, a high-heeled hunter's boot*   **77 Glance:** *hint maliciously*   **80 Perigenia;** *cf. n.*   **81, 82 Ægle ... Antiopa;** *cf. n.*   **83 forgeries:** *idle inventions*   **84 spring:** *beginning*   **86 paved fountain:** *spring with pebble-covered bottom*   **87 margent:** *margin*   **88 ringlets:** *circular dances*   **92 Contagious:** *noxious*   **93 pelting:** *petty*   **94 continents:** *boundaries*   **99 murrion:** *diseased*   **100 nine men's morris;** *cf. n.*   **101 wanton:** *luxuriant*   **103–105** *Cf. n.*   **107 rheumatic diseased:** *colds, etc.*   **108 distemperature:** *disorder of the winds and moon (?), ill humor (?)*   **111 Hiems':** *winter's*   **114 chiding:** *fruitful*   **115 mazed:** *bewildered*   **116 increase:** *produce*   **123 henchman:** *page of honor*

126 votaress: *woman under vows*   **148 chide:** *quarrel*   **150 injury:** *affront*   **151–173** *Cf. n.*   **152 Since:** *when*   **172 Love-in-idleness:** *the pansy*   **175 or ... or:** *either ... or*   **178 leviathan:** *whale*

I'll watch Titania when she is asleep,
And drop the liquor of it in her eyes:
The next thing then she waking looks upon,
Be it on lion, bear, or wolf, or bull,   *185*
On meddling monkey, or on busy ape,
She shall pursue it with the soul of love:
And ere I take this charm off from her sight,
As I can take it with another herb,
I'll make her render up her page to me.   *190*
But who comes here? I am invisible,
And I will overhear their conference.

                 Enter Demetrius, Helena following him.

    Dem. I love thee not, therefore pursue me not.
Where is Lysander and fair Hermia?
The one I'll slay, the other slayeth me.   *195*
Thou told'st me they were stol'n into this wood;
And here am I, and wood within this wood,
Because I cannot meet my Hermia.
Hence! get thee gone, and follow me no more.
    Hel. You draw me, you hard-hearted adamant: *200*
But yet you draw not iron, not my heart
Is true as steel: leave you your power to draw,
And I shall have no power to follow you.
    Dem. Do I entice you? Do I speak you fair?
Or, rather, do I not in plainest truth   *205*
Tell you I do not nor I cannot love you?
    Hel. And even for that do I love you the more.
I am your spaniel; and, Demetrius,
The more you beat me, I will fawn on you:
Use me but as your spaniel, spurn me, strike me,   *210*
Neglect me, lose me; only give me leave,
Unworthy as I am, to follow you.
What worser place can I beg in your love,
And yet a place of high respect with me,
Than to be used as you use your dog?   *215*
    Dem. Tempt not too much the hatred of my spirit,
For I am sick when I do look on you.
    Hel. And I am sick when I look not on you.
    Dem. You do impeach your modesty too much,
To leave the city, and commit yourself   *220*
Into the hands of one that loves you not;
To trust the opportunity of night
And the ill counsel of a desert place
With the rich worth of your virginity.
    Hel. Your virtue is my privilege: for that   *225*
It is not night when I do see your face,
Therefore I think I am not in the night;
Nor doth this wood lack worlds of company,
For you in my respect are all the world:
Then how can it be said I am alone,   *230*
When all the world is here to look on me?
    Dem. I'll run from thee and hide me in the brakes,
And leave thee to the mercy of wild beasts.
    Hel. The wildest hath not such a heart as you.
Run when you will, the story shall be chang'd;   *235*
Apollo flies, and Daphne holds the chase;

The dove pursues the griffin; the mild hind
Makes speed to catch the tiger: bootless speed,
When cowardice pursues and valour flies.
    Dem. I will not stay thy questions: let me go;   *240*
Or, if thou follow me, do not believe
But I shall do thee mischief in the wood.
    Hel. Ay, in the temple, in the town, the field,
You do me mischief. Fie, Demetrius!
Your wrongs do set a scandal on my sex.   *245*
We cannot fight for love, as men may do;
We should be woo'd and were not made to woo.
                                                      [*Exit Demetrius.*]
I'll follow thee and make a heaven of hell,
To die upon the hand I love so well.   *Exit.*
    Obe. Fare thee well, nymph: ere he do leave this grove,   *250*
Thou shalt fly him, and he shall seek thy love.

                         Enter Puck.

Hast thou the flower there? Welcome, wanderer.
    Puck. Ay, there it is.
    Obe.   I pray thee, give it me.
I know a bank where the wild thyme blows,   *255*
Where oxlips and the nodding violet grows
Quite over-canopied with luscious woodbine,
With sweet musk-roses, and with eglantine:
There sleeps Titania some time of the night,
Lull'd in these flowers with dances and delight;   *260*
And there the snake throws her enamell'd skin,
Weed wide enough to wrap a fairy in:
And with the juice of this I'll streak her eyes,
And make her full of hateful fantasies.
Take thou some of it, and seek through this grove: *265*
A sweet Athenian lady is in love
With a disdainful youth: anoint his eyes;
But do it when the next thing he espies
May be the lady. Thou shalt know the man
By the Athenian garments he hath on.   *270*
Effect it with some care, that he may prove
More fond of her than she upon her love.
And look thou meet me ere the first cock crow.
    Puck. Fear not, my lord, your servant shall do so.   *Exeunt.*

                    ❧ SCENE SECOND ❧

                  [Another Part of the Wood]
              Enter Queen of Fairies, with her train.

    Tita. Come, now a roundel and a fairy song;
Then, for the third part of a minute, hence;
Some to kill cankers in the musk-rose buds,
Some war with rere-mice for their leathern wings,
To make my small elves coats, and some keep back   *5*
The clamorous owl, that nightly hoots, and wonders
At our quaint spirits. Sing me now asleep;
Then to your offices, and let me rest.

---

197 wood … wood: *mad … wood*   **200 adamant:** *hard stone with magnetic power*   **219 impeach:** *call in question*   **225 for that:** *because*   **229 respect:** *regard*   **232 brakes:** *thickets*   **236 Cf. n.*

237 griffin: *fabulous monster, half lion, half eagle*   **240 stay … questions:** *listen to thy talk*   **255 blows:** *blooms*   **258 eglantine:** *sweetbriar*   **262 Weed:** *garment*   **263 streak:** *stroke*   **1 roundel:** *dance in a circle*   **4 rere-mice:** *bats*   **7 quaint:** *pretty, dainty*   **8 offices:** *duties*

Fairies sing.

             I.   *10*

'You spotted snakes with double tongue,
   Thorny hedge-hogs, be not seen;
Newts, and blind-worms, do no wrong;
   Come not near our fairy queen.'

'Philomel, with melody,   *15*
   Sing in our sweet lullaby;
Lulla, lulla, lullaby; lulla, lulla, lullaby:
Never harm,
Nor spell, nor charm,
Come our lovely lady nigh;   *20*
So, good night, with lullaby.'

            II.

'Weaving spiders come not here;
   Hence, you long-legg'd spinners, hence!
Beetles black, approach not near;   *25*
   Worm nor snail, do no offence.

      Philomel, with melody, &c.'

Fai. Hence, away! now all is well.
   One aloof stand sentinel.   *She sleeps. [Exeunt Fairies.]*

Enter Oberon [and squeezes the flower on Titania's eyelids].

Obe. What thou seest when thou dost wake,   *30*
Do it for thy true-love take;
Love and languish for his sake:
Be it ounce, or cat, or bear,
Pard, or boar with bristled hair,
In thy eye that shall appear   *35*
When thou wak'st, it is thy dear.
Wake when some vile thing is near.   *[Exit.]*

Enter Lysander and Hermia.

Lys. Fair love, you faint with wandering in the wood;
And to speak troth, I have forgot our way:
We'll rest us, Hermia, if you think it good,   *40*
And tarry for the comfort of the day.
   Her. Be it so, Lysander: find you out a bed,
For I upon this bank will rest my head.
   Lys. One turf shall serve as pillow for us both;
One heart, one bed, two bosoms, and one troth.   *45*
   Her. Nay, good Lysander; for my sake, my dear,
Lie further off yet, do not lie so near.
   Lys. O! take the sense, sweet, of my innocence,
Love takes the meaning in love's conference.
I mean that my heart unto yours is knit,   *50*
So that but one heart we can make of it;
Two bosoms interchained with an oath;
So then two bosoms and a single troth.
Then by your side no bed-room me deny,
For, lying so, Hermia, I do not lie.   *55*
   Her. Lysander riddles very prettily:
Now much beshrew my manners and my pride,

If Hermia meant to say Lysander lied.
But, gentle friend, for love and courtesy
Lie further off; in human modesty,   *60*
Such separation as may well be said
Becomes a virtuous bachelor and a maid,
So far be distant; and, good night, sweet friend.
Thy love ne'er alter till thy sweet life end!
   Lys. Amen, amen, to that fair prayer, say I;   *65*
And then end life when I end loyalty!

                 [Retires a little distance.]

Here is my bed: sleep give thee all his rest!
   Her. With half that wish the wisher's eyes be press'd!

                     They sleep.

Enter Puck.

Puck. Through the forest have I gone,
   But Athenian found I none,   *70*
   On whose eyes I might approve
This flower's force in stirring love.
Night and silence! who is here?
Weeds of Athens he doth wear:
This is he, my master said,   *75*
Despised the Athenian maid:
And here the maiden, sleeping sound,
On the dank and dirty ground.
Pretty soul! she durst not lie
Near this lack-love, this kill-courtesy.   *80*
Churl, upon thy eyes I throw
All the power this charm doth owe.
When thou wak'st, let love forbid
Sleep his seat on thy eyelid:
So awake when I am gone;   *85*
For I must now to Oberon.   *Exit.*

Enter Demetrius and Helena, running.

Hel. Stay, though thou kill me, sweet Demetrius.
   Dem. I charge thee, hence, and do not haunt me thus.
   Hel. O! wilt thou darkling leave me? do not so.
   Dem. Stay, on thy peril: I alone will go.   *90*

                 Exit Demetrius.

   Hel. O! I am out of breath in this fond chase.
The more my prayer, the lesser is my grace.
Happy is Hermia, wheresoe'er she lies;
For she hath blessed and attractive eyes.
How came her eyes so bright? Not with salt tears: *95*
If so, my eyes are oftener wash'd than hers.
No, no, I am as ugly as a bear;
For beasts that meet me run away for fear;
Therefore no marvel though Demetrius
Do, as a monster, fly my presence thus.   *100*
What wicked and dissembling glass of mine
Made me compare with Hermia's sphery eyne?
But who is here? Lysander! on the ground!
Dead? or asleep? I see no blood, no wound.
Lysander, if you live, good sir, awake.   *105*
   Lys. [*Awaking.*] And run through fire I will for thy sweet
sake.

---

15 **Philomel:** *the nightingale*   33 **ounce:** *lynx*   **cat:** *wildcat*   34 **Pard:** *leopard*   39
troth: *truth*   57 **beshrew:** *'mischief on'*

71 **approve:** *test*   82 **owe:** *possess*   89 **darkling:** *in the dark*   91 **fond:** *foolish; also,*
loving   92 **grace:** *good fortune*   102 **sphery:** *starry*

Transparent Helena! Nature shows art,
That through thy bosom makes me see thy heart.
Where is Demetrius? O! how fit a word   *110*
Is that vile name to perish on my sword.

    Hel. Do not say so, Lysander; say not so.
What though he love your Hermia? Lord! what though?
Yet Hermia still loves you: then be content.

    Lys. Content with Hermia! No: I do repent   *115*
The tedious minutes I with her have spent.
Not Hermia, but Helena I love:
Who will not change a raven for a dove?
The will of man is by his reason sway'd,
And reason says you are the worthier maid.   *120*
Things growing are not ripe until their season;
So I, being young, till now ripe not to reason;
And touching now the point of human skill,
Reason becomes the marshal to my will,
And leads me to your eyes; where I o'erlook   *125*
Love's stories written in love's richest book.

    Hel. Wherefore was I to this keen mockery born?
When at your hands did I deserve this scorn?
Is 't not enough, is 't not enough, young man,
That I did never, no, nor never can,   *130*
Deserve a sweet look from Demetrius' eye,
But you must flout my insufficiency?
Good troth, you do me wrong, good sooth, you do,
In such disdainful manner me to woo.
But fare you well: perforce I must confess   *135*
I thought you lord of more true gentleness.
O! that a lady of one man refus'd,
Should of another therefore be abus'd.   *Exit.*

    Lys. She sees not Hermia. Hermia, sleep thou there;
And never mayst thou come Lysander near.   *140*
For, as a surfeit of the sweetest things
The deepest loathing to the stomach brings;
Or, as the heresies that men do leave
Are hated most of those they did deceive:
So thou, my surfeit and my heresy,   *145*
Of all he hated, but the most of me!
And, all my powers, address your love and might
To honour Helen, and to be her knight.   *Exit.*

    Her. [*Awaking.*] Help me, Lysander, help me! do thy best   *150*
To pluck this crawling serpent from my breast.
Ay me, for pity! what a dream was here!
Lysander, look how I do quake with fear:
Methought a serpent eat my heart away,
And you sat smiling at his cruel prey.   *155*
Lysander! what! remov'd?—Lysander! lord!
What! out of hearing? gone? no sound, no word?
Alack! where are you? speak, an if you hear;
Speak, of all loves! I swound almost with fear.
No! then I well perceive you are not nigh: *160*
Either death or you I'll find immediately.   *Exit.*

ACT THIRD ❧ SCENE FIRST

[The Wood. Titania lying asleep]
Enter the Clowns [Quince, Snug, Bottom,
Flute, Snout, and Starveling].

    Bot. Are we all met?

    Quin. Pat, pat; and here's a marvellous convenient place for our rehearsal. This green plot shall be our stage, this haw-thornbrake our tiring-house; and we will do it in action as we will do it before the duke.   *5*

    Bot. Peter Quince,—

    Quin. What sayst thou, bully Bottom?

    Bot. There are things in this comedy of Pyramus and Thisby that will never please. First, Pyramus must draw a sword to kill himself, which the ladies cannot abide.   *10*
How answer you that?

    Snout. By 'r lakin, a parlous fear.

    Star. I believe we must leave the killing out, when all is done.

    Bot. Not a whit: I have a device to make all well. Write   *15* me a prologue; and let the prologue seem to say, we will do no harm with our swords, and that Pyramus is not killed in-deed; and, for the more better assurance, tell them that I, Pyramus, am not Pyramus, but Bottom the weaver: this will put them out of fear.   *20*

    Quin. Well, we will have such a prologue, and it shall be written in eight and six.

    Bot. No, make it two more: let it be written in eight and eight.

    Snout. Will not the ladies be afeard of the lion?   *25*

    Star. I fear it, I promise you.

    Bot. Masters, you ought to consider with yourselves: to bring in,—God shield us!—a lion among ladies, is a most dreadful thing; for there is not a more fearful wild-fowl than your lion living, and we ought to look to it.   *30*

    Snout. Therefore, another prologue must tell he is not a lion.

    Bot. Nay, you must name his name, and half his face must be seen through the lion's neck; and he himself must speak through, saying thus, or to the same defect, 'Ladies,' or 'Fair   *35* ladies,' 'I would wish you,' or, 'I would request you,' or, 'I would entreat you, not to fear, not to tremble: my life for yours. If you think I come hither as a lion, it were pity of my life: no, I am no such thing: I am a man as other men are'; and there indeed let him name his name, and tell them   *40* plainly he is Snug the joiner.

    Quin. Well, it shall be so. But there is two hard things, that is, to bring the moonlight into a chamber; for you know, Pyra-mus and Thisby meet by moonlight.

    Snug. Doth the moon shine that night we play our play?   *45*

    Bot. A calendar, a calendar! look in the almanac; find out moonshine, find out moonshine.

    Quin. Yes, it doth shine that night.

    Bot. Why, then may you leave a casement of the great chamber-window, where we play, open; and the moon may   *50* shine in at the casement.

---

123 point: *summit*   **155 prey:** *preying*   **159 of:** *for the sake of*   **swound:** *swoon*

SCENE ONE S. d.   **Clowns:** *men of the lower class; also, comedians*   **4 tiring-house:** *dress-ing-room*   **7 bully:** *a friendly term equivalent to 'good old'*   **12 By 'r lakin** *By Our Lady*   **parlous:** *perilous*   **22 eight and six:** *alternate verses of eight and six syllables*

Quin. Ay; or else one must come in with a bush of thorns
and a lantern, and say he comes to disfigure, or to present, the
person of Moonshine. Then, there is another thing: we must
have a wall in the great chamber; for Pyramus and Thisby,   55
says the story, did talk through the chink of a wall.

Snug. You can never bring in a wall. What say you,
Bottom?

Bot. Some man or other must present Wall; and let him
have some plaster, or some loam, or some rough-cast about   60
him, to signify wall; and let him hold his fingers thus, and
through that cranny shall Pyramus and Thisby whisper.

Quin. If that may be, then all is well. Come, sit down,
every mother's son, and rehearse your parts. Pyramus, you
begin: when you have spoken your speech, enter into that   65
brake; and so every one according to his cue.

Enter Robin [behind].

Puck. What hempen home-spuns have we swaggering here,
So near the cradle of the fairy queen?
What! a play toward; I'll be an auditor;
An actor too perhaps, if I see cause.   70

Quin. Speak, Pyramus.—Thisby, stand forth.

Bot. Thisby, the flowers of odious savours sweet,—

Quin. Odorous, odorous.

Bot. —odours savours sweet:
So hath thy breath, my dearest Thisby dear.   75
But hark, a voice! stay thou but here awhile,
And by and by I will to thee appear.—   *Exit.*

Puck. —A stranger Pyramus than e'er play'd here!   *[Exit.]*

Flu. Must I speak now?

Quin. Ay, marry, must you; for you must understand, he 80
goes but to see a noise that he heard, and is to come again.

Flu. Most radiant Pyramus, most lily-white of hue,
Of colour like the red rose on triumphant brier,
Most brisky juvenal, and eke most lovely Jew,
As true as truest horse that yet would never tire,   85
I'll meet thee, Pyramus, at Ninny's tomb.

Quin. 'Ninus' tomb,' man. Why, you must not speak that
yet; that you answer to Pyramus: you speak all your part at
once, cues and all. Pyramus, enter: your cue is past; it is
'never tire.'   90

Flu. O!—As true as truest horse, that yet would never tire.

[Enter Puck, and Bottom with an ass's head.]

Bot. If I were fair, Thisby, I were only thine.

Quin. O monstrous! O strange! we are haunted.
Pray, masters! fly, masters!—Help!

The Clowns all exeunt.

Puck. I'll follow you, I'll lead you about a round,   95
Through bog, through bush, through brake, through brier:
Sometime a horse I'll be, sometime a hound,
A hog, a headless bear, sometime a fire;
And neigh, and bark, and grunt, and roar, and burn,
Like horse, hound, hog, bear, fire, at every turn.   *Exit.* 100

Bot. Why do they run away? this is a knavery of them
to make me afeard.

Enter Snout.

Snout. O Bottom, thou art changed! what do I see on thee?

Bot. What do you see? you see an ass-head of your own,
do you?   *[Exit Snout.]* 105

Enter Peter Quince.

Quin. Bless thee, Bottom! bless thee! thou are translated.
Exit.

Bot. I see their knavery: this is to make an ass of me; to
fright me, if they could. But I will not stir from this place,
do what they can: I will walk up and down here, and I   110
will sing, that they shall hear I am not afraid.

    'The ousel-cock, so black of hue,
        With orange-tawny bill,
    The throstle with his note so true,
        The wren with little quill.'   115

Tita. [*Awakening.*] What angel wakes me from my flowery bed?

Bot.   'The finch, the sparrow, and the lark,
            The plain-song cuckoo gray,
        Whose note full many a man doth mark,
            And dares not answer, nay;'   120

for indeed, who would set this wit to so foolish a bird? who
would give a bird the lie, though he cry 'cuckoo' never so?

Tita. I pray thee, gentle mortal, sing again:
Mine ear is much enamour'd of thy note;
So is mine eye enthralled to thy shape;   125
And thy fair virtue's force, perforce, doth move me,
On the first view, to say, to swear, I love thee.

Bot. Methinks, mistress, you should have little reason for
that: and yet, to say the truth, reason and love keep little
company together now-a-days. The more the pity, that   130
some honest neighbours will not make them friends. Nay,
I can gleek upon occasion.

Tita. Thou art as wise as thou art beautiful.

Bot. Not so, neither; but if I had wit enough to get out
of this wood, I have enough to serve mine own turn.   135

Tita. Out of this wood do not desire to go:
Thou shalt remain here, whether thou wilt or no.
I am a spirit of no common rate;
The summer still doth tend upon my state;
And I do love thee: therefore, go with me;   140
I'll give thee fairies to attend on thee,
And they shall fetch thee jewels from the deep,
And sing, while thou on pressed flowers dost sleep:
And I will purge thy mortal grossness so
That thou shalt like an airy spirit go.   145
Pease-blossom! Cobweb! Moth! and Mustard-seed!

Enter four Fairies.

Peas. Ready.

Cob.   And I.

Moth.   And I.

Mus.   And I.   150

All Four.   Where shall we go?

Tita. Be kind and courteous to this gentleman;
Hop in his walks, and gambol in his eyes;

52 bush of thorns; *cf. n.*   67 hempen home-spuns: *rude fellows*   69 toward: *in
preparation*   84 juvenal: *an affected word for 'youth'* eke: *also*   100 fire: *will o' the
wisp*

104, 105 you … own; *cf. n.*   112 ousel-cock: *male blackbird*   115 quill: *note*   118
plain-song; *cf. n.*   132 gleek: *jest*   146 Moth; *cf. n.*

Feed him with apricocks and dewberries,
With purple grapes, green figs, and mulberries.   *155*
The honey-bags steal from the humble-bees,
And for night-tapers crop their waxen thighs,
And light them at the fiery glow-worm's eyes,
To have my love to bed, and to arise;
And pluck the wings from painted butterflies   *160*
To fan the moonbeams from his sleeping eyes:
Nod to him, elves, and do him courtesies.

    Peas. Hail, mortal!
    Cob. Hail!
    Moth. Hail!   *165*
    Mus. Hail!
    Bot. I cry your worships mercy, heartily: I beseech your
worship's name.
    Cob. Cobweb.
    Bot. I shall desire you of more acquaintance, good   *170*
Master Cobweb: if I cut my finger, I shall make bold with
you. Your name, honest gentleman?
    Peas. Pease-blossom.
    Bot. I pray you, commend me to Mistress Squash, your
mother, and to Master Peascod, your father. Good Master   *175*
Pease-blossom, I shall desire you of more acquaintance too.
Your name, I beseech you, sir?
    Mus. Mustard-seed.
    Bot. Good Master Mustard-seed, I know your patience
well: that same cowardly, giant-like ox-beef hath devoured   *180*
many a gentleman of your house. I promise you, your kindred
hath made my eyes water ere now. I desire you of more
acquaintance, good Master Mustard-seed.
    Tita. Come, wait upon him; lead him to my bower.
The moon, methinks, looks with a watery eye;   *185*
And when she weeps, weeps every little flower,
Lamenting some enforced chastity.
Tie up my love's tongue, bring him silently.   *Exeunt.*

❦ SCENE SECOND ❦

[Another Part of the Wood]
Enter King of Fairies, solus.

    Obe. I wonder if Titania be awak'd;
Then, what it was that next came in her eye,
Which she must dote on in extremity.

Enter Puck.

Here comes my messenger.
                 How now, mad spirit!   *5*
What night-rule now about this haunted grove?
    Puck. My mistress with a monster is in love.
Near to her close and consecrated bower,
While she was in her dull and sleeping hour,
A crew of patches, rude mechanicals,   *10*
That work for bread upon Athenian stalls,
Were met together to rehearse a play

Intended for great Theseus' nuptial day.
The shallowest thick-skin of that barren sort,
Who Pyramus presented in their sport,   *15*
Forsook his scene, and enter'd in a brake:
When I did him at this advantage take,
An ass's nowl I fixed on his head:
Anon his Thisbe must be answered,
And forth my mimick comes. When they him spy,   *20*
As wild geese that the creeping fowler eye,
Or russet-pated choughs, many in sort,
Rising and cawing at the gun's report,
Sever themselves, and madly sweep the sky;
So, at his sight, away his fellows fly,   *25*
And, at our stamp, here o'er and o'er one falls;
He murder cries, and help from Athens calls.
Their sense thus weak, lost with their fears thus strong,
Made senseless things begin to do them wrong;
For briers and thorns at their apparel snatch;   *30*
Some sleeves, some hats, from yielders all things catch.
I led them on in this distracted fear,
And left sweet Pyramus translated there;
When in that moment, so it came to pass,
Titania wak'd and straightway lov'd an ass.   *35*
    Obe. This falls out better than I could devise.
But hast thou yet latch'd the Athenian's eyes
With the love-juice, as I did bid thee do?
    Puck. I took him sleeping,—that is finish'd too,—
And the Athenian woman by his side;   *40*
That, when he wak'd, of force she must be ey'd.

Enter Demetrius and Hermia.

    Obe. Stand close: this is the same Athenian.
    Puck. This is the woman; but not this the man.
    Dem. O! why rebuke you him that loves you so?
Lay breath so bitter on your bitter foe.   *45*
    Her. Now I but chide; but I should use thee worse,
For thou, I fear, hast given me cause to curse.
If thou hast slain Lysander in his sleep,
Being o'er shoes in blood, plunge in the deep,
And kill me too.   *50*
The sun was not so true unto the day
As he to me. Would he have stol'n away
From sleeping Hermia? I'll believe as soon
This whole earth may be bor'd, and that the moon
May through the centre creep, and so displease   *55*
Her brother's noontide with the Antipodes.
It cannot be but thou hast murder'd him;
So should a murderer look, so dead, so grim.
    Dem. So should the murder'd look, and so should I,
Pierc'd through the heart with your stern cruelty;   *60*
Yet you, the murderer, look as bright, as clear,
As yonder Venus in her glimmering sphere.
    Her. What's this to my Lysander? where is he?
Ah! good Demetrius, wilt thou give him me?
    Dem. I had rather give his carcass to my hounds.   *65*
    Her. Out, dog! out, cur! thou driv'st me past the bounds
Of maiden's patience. Hast thou slain him then?

---

167 **cry . . . mercy:** *beg . . . pardon*   174 **Squash:** *unripe peapod*   175 **Peascod:** *peapod*   187 **enforced:** *violated*   6 **night-rule:** *diversion of the nigh:* **haunted:** *much frequented*   8 **close:** *secret*   10 **patches:** *clowns, fools* **mechanicals:** *workingmen*

14 **barren sort:** *dull company*   18 **nowl:** *noddle, pate*   22 **russet-pated:** *grey-head-
ed* **choughs:** *jackdaws*   26 **our stamp;** *cf. n.*   37 **latch'd:** *moistened (?).*   41 **force:**
necessity   56 **with:** *among*

Henceforth he never number'd among men!
O! once tell true, tell true, e'en for my sake;
Durst thou have look'd upon him being awake,　　　　70
And hast thou kill'd him sleeping? O brave touch!
Could not a worm, an adder, do so much?
An adder did it; for with doubler tongue
Than thine, thou serpent, never adder stung.
　　Dem. You spend your passion on a mispris'd mood:　　75
I am not guilty of Lysander's blood,
Nor is he dead, for aught that I can tell.
　　Her. I pray thee, tell me then that he is well.
　　Dem. An if I could, what should I get therefore?
　　Her. A privilege never to see me more.　　　　80
And from thy hated presence part I so;
See me no more, whether he be dead or no.　　　　*Exit.*
　　Dem. There is no following her in this fierce vein:
Here therefore for awhile I will remain.
So sorrow's heaviness doth heavier grow　　　　85
For debt that bankrupt sleep doth sorrow owe;
Which now in some slight measure it will pay,
If for this tender here I make some stay.　　　　*Lie down.*
　　Obe. What hast thou done? thou hast mistaken quite,
And laid the love-juice on some true-love's sight:　　90
Of thy misprision must perforce ensue
Some true-love turn'd, and not a false turn'd true.
　　Puck. Then fate o'er-rules, that, one man holding troth,
A million fail, confounding oath on oath.
　　Obe. About the wood go swifter than the wind,　　95
And Helena of Athens look thou find:
All fancy-sick she is, and pale of cheer
With sighs of love, that costs the fresh blood dear.
By some illusion see thou bring her here:
I'll charm his eyes against she do appear.　　　　100
　　Puck. I go, I go; look how I go;
Swifter than arrow from the Tartar's bow.　　　　*Exit.*
　　Obe. Flower of this purple dye,
　　　　Hit with Cupid's archery,
　　　　Sink in apple of his eye.　　　　105
　　　　When his love he doth espy,
　　　　Let her shine as gloriously
　　　　As the Venus of the sky.
　　　　When thou wak'st, if she be by,
　　　　Beg of her for remedy.　　　　110

　　　　　　Enter Puck.

　　Puck. Captain of our fairy band,
　　　　Helena is here at hand,
　　　　And the youth, mistook by me,
　　　　Pleading for a lover's fee.
　　　　Shall we their fond pageant see?　　　　115
　　　　Lord, what fools these mortals be!
　　Obe. Stand aside: the noise they make
　　　　Will cause Demetrius to awake.
　　Puck. Then will two at once woo one;
　　　　That must needs be sport alone;　　　　120
　　　　And those things do best please me
　　　　That befall preposterously.

　　　　　Enter Lysander and Helena.

　　Lys. Why should you think that I should woo in scorn?
Scorn and derision never come in tears:
Look, when I vow, I weep; and vows so born,　　　　125
In their nativity all truth appears.
How can these things in me seem scorn to you,
Bearing the badge of faith to prove them true?
　　Hel. You do advance your cunning more and more.
When truth kills truth, O devilish-holy fray!　　　　130
These vows are Hermia's: will you give her o'er?
Weigh oath with oath, and you will nothing weigh:
Your vows, to her and me, put in two scales,
Will even weigh, and both as light as tales.
　　Lys. I had no judgment when to her I swore.　　　135
　　Hel. Nor none, in my mind, now you give her o'er.
　　Lys. Demetrius loves her, and he loves not you.
　　Dem. [*Awaking.*] O Helen! goddess, nymph, perfect,
divine!
To what, my love, shall I compare thine eyne?　　　140
Crystal is muddy. O! how ripe in show
Thy lips, those kissing cherries, tempting grow;
This pure congealed white, high Taurus' snow,
Fann'd with the eastern wind, turns to a crow
When thou hold'st up thy hand. O! let me kiss　　　145
This princess of pure white, this seal of bliss.
　　Hel. O spite! O hell! I see you all are bent
To set against me for your merriment:
If you were civil and knew courtesy,
You would not do me thus much injury.　　　　150
Can you not hate me, as I know you do,
But you must join in souls to mock me too?
If you were men, as men you are in show,
You would not use a gentle lady so;
To vow, and swear, and superpraise my parts,　　　155
When I am sure you hate me with your hearts.
You both are rivals, and love Hermia,
And now both rivals, to mock Helena:
A trim exploit, a manly enterprise,
To conjure tears up in a poor maid's eyes　　　　160
With your derision! none of noble sort
Would so offend a virgin, and extort
A poor soul's patience, all to make you sport.
　　Lys. You are unkind, Demetrius; be not so;
For you love Hermia; this you know I know:　　　165
And here, with all good will, with all my heart,
In Hermia's love I yield you up my part:
And yours of Helena to me bequeath,
Whom I do love, and will do to my death.
　　Hel. Never did mockers waste more idle breath.　　170
　　Dem. Lysander, keep thy Hermia; I will none:
If e'er I lov'd her, all that love is gone.
My heart to her but as guest-wise sojourn'd,
And now to Helen it is home return'd,
There to remain.　　　　175
　　Lys.　　　　　Helen, it is not so.
　　Dem. Disparage not the faith thou dost not know,
Lest to thy peril thou aby it dear.
Look! where thy love comes: yonder is thy dear.

---

71 touch: *exploit*　　**72 worm:** *snake*　　**75 on a mispris'd mood:** *in a mistaken anger*
(?)　　**88 tender:** *offer*　　**91 misprision:** *mistake*　　**97 cheer:** *face*　　**98 costs ... dear;*
cf. n.　　**100 against:** *in expectation of the time when*　　**120 alone:** *having no equal*

126 *By their birth appear wholly true*　　**130** *Cf. n.*　　**143 Taurus':** *lofty mountain range in*
Asiatic Turkey　　**159 trim:** *fine*　　**162 extort:** *wrest away*　　**178 aby:** *pay a penalty for*

Enter Hermia.

Her. Dark night, that from the eye his function takes,   *180*
The ear more quick of apprehension makes;
Wherein it doth impair the seeing sense,
It pays the hearing double recompense.
Thou art not by mine eye, Lysander, found;
Mine ear, I thank it, brought me to thy sound.   *185*
But why unkindly didst thou leave me so?
    Lys. Why should he stay, whom love doth press to go?
    Her. What love could press Lysander from my side?
    Lys. Lysander's love, that would not let him bide,
Fair Helena, who more engilds the night   *190*
Than all yon fiery oes and eyes of light.
Why seek'st thou me? could not this make thee know,
The hate I bare thee made me leave thee so?
    Her. You speak not as you think: it cannot be.
    Hel. Lo! she is one of this confederacy.   *195*
Now I perceive they have conjoin'd all three
To fashion this false sport in spite of me.
Injurious Hermia! most ungrateful maid!
Have you conspir'd, have you with these contriv'd
To bait me with this foul derision?   *200*
Is all the counsel that we two have shar'd,
The sisters' vows, the hours that we have spent,
When we have chid the hasty-footed time
For parting us, O! is all forgot?
All school-days' friendship, childhood innocence?   *205*
We, Hermia, like two artificial gods,
Have with our needles created both one flower,
Both on one sampler, sitting on one cushion,
Both warbling of one song, both in one key,
As if our hands, our sides, voices, and minds,   *210*
Had been incorporate. So we grew together,
Like to a double cherry, seeming parted,
But yet an union in partition;
Two lovely berries moulded on one stem;
So, with two seeming bodies, but one heart;   *215*
Two of the first, like coats in heraldry,
Due but to one, and crowned with one crest.
And will you rent our ancient love asunder,
To join with men in scorning your poor friend?
It is not friendly, 'tis not maidenly: *220*
Our sex, as well as I, may chide you for it,
Though I alone do feel the injury.
    Her. I am amazed at your passionate words.
I scorn you not: it seems that you scorn me.
    Hel. Have you not set Lysander, as in scorn,   *225*
To follow me and praise my eyes and face,
And made your other love, Demetrius,—
Who even but now did spurn me with his foot,—
To call me goddess, nymph, divine and rare,
Precious, celestial? Wherefore speaks he this   *230*
To her he hates? and wherefore doth Lysander
Deny your love, so rich within his soul,
And tender me, forsooth, affection,
But by your setting on, by your consent?
What though I be not so in grace as you,   *235*

So hung upon with love, so fortunate,
But miserable most, to love unlov'd?
This you should pity rather than despise.
    Her. I understand not what you mean by this.
    Hel. Ay, do, persever, counterfeit sad looks,   *240*
Make mouths upon me when I turn my back;
Wink each at other; hold the sweet jest up:
This sport, well carried, shall be chronicled.
If you have any pity, grace, or manners,
You would not make me such an argument.   *245*
But, fare ye well: 'tis partly mine own fault,
Which death or absence soon shall remedy.
    Lys. Stay, gentle Helena! hear my excuse:
My love, my life, my soul, fair Helena!
    Hel. O excellent!   *250*
    Her.   Sweet, do not scorn her so.
    Dem. If she cannot entreat, I can compel.
    Lys. Thou canst compel no more than she entreat:
Thy threats have no more strength than her weak prayers.
Helen, I love thee; by my life, I do: *255*
I swear by that which I will lose for thee,
To prove him false that says I love thee not.
    Dem. I say I love thee more than he can do.
    Lys. If thou say so, withdraw, and prove it too.
    Dem. Quick, come!   *260*
    IIer.   Lysander, whereto tends all this?
    Lys. Away, you Ethiop!
    Dem.   No, no, he'll . . .
Seem to break loose; take on, as you would follow,
But yet come not: you are a tame man, go!   *265*
    Lys. [*To Hermia.*] Hang off, thou cat, thou burr! vile thing,
let loose,
Or I will shake thee from me like a serpent.
    Her. Why are you grown so rude? what change is this?
Sweet love,—   *270*
    Lys.   Thy love! out, tawny Tartar, out!
Out, loathed medicine! hated potion, hence!
    Her. Do you not jest?
    Hel.   Yes, sooth; and so do you.
    Lys. Demetrius, I will keep my word with thee.   *275*
    Dem. I would I had your bond, for I perceive
A weak bond holds you: I'll not trust your word.
    Lys. What! should I hurt her, strike her, kill her dead?
Although I hate her, I'll not harm her so.
    Her. What! can you do me greater harm than hate?   *280*
Hate me! wherefore? O me! what news, my love?
Am not I Hermia? Are not you Lysander?
I am as fair now as I was erewhile.
Since night you lov'd me; yet, since night you left me:
Why, then you left me,—O, the gods forbid!—   *285*
In earnest, shall I say?
    Lys.   Ay, by my life;
And never did desire to see thee more.
Therefore be out of hope, of question, doubt;
Be certain, nothing truer: 'tis no jest,   *290*
That I do hate thee and love Helena.
    Her. O me! you juggler! you canker-blossom!
You thief of love! what! have you come by night

---

191 oes: *small circular spangles; also, o's*   **197 spite:** *contempt*   **198 Injurious:** *in-sulting*   **206 artificial:** *skilled in constructive art*   **214 lovely:** *loving*   **216, 217** *Cf. n.*   **218 rent:** *rend*

240 sad: *serious*   **242 hold . . . up:** *carry . . . on*   **245 argument:** *subject* (of merriment)   **263** *Cf. n.*   **292 canker-blossom:** *worm that destroys the blossom*

And stol'n my love's heart from him?

 Hel.   Fine, i' faith!   *295*
Have you no modesty, no maiden shame,
No touch of bashfulness? What! will you tear
Impatient answers from my gentle tongue?
Fie, fie! you counterfeit, you puppet you!

 Her. Puppet! why, so: ay, that way goes the game. *300*
Now I perceive that she hath made compare
Between our statures: she hath urg'd her height;
And with her personage, her tall personage,
Her height, forsooth, she hath prevail'd with him.
And are you grown so high in his esteem,   *305*
Because I am so dwarfish and so low?
How low am I, thou painted maypole? speak;
How low am I? I am not yet so low
But that my nails can reach unto thine eyes.

 Hel. I pray you, though you mock me, gentlemen, *310*
Let her not hurt me: I was never curst;
I have no gift at all in shrewishness;
I am a right maid for my cowardice:
Let her not strike me. You perhaps may think,
Because she is something lower than myself, *315*
That I can match her.

 Her.   Lower! hark, again.

 Hel. Good Hermia, do not be so bitter with me.
I evermore did love you, Hermia,
Did ever keep your counsels, never wrong'd you; *320*
Save that, in love unto Demetrius,
I told him of your stealth unto this wood.
He follow'd you; for love I follow'd him;
But he hath chid me hence, and threaten'd me
To strike me, spurn me, nay, to kill me too: *325*
And now, so you will let me quiet go,
To Athens will I bear my folly back,
And follow you no further: let me go:
You see how simple and how fond I am.

 Her. Why, get you gone. Who is 't that hinders you? *330*

 Hel. A foolish heart, that I leave here behind.

 Her. What! with Lysander?

 Hel.   With Demetrius.

 Lys. Be not afraid: she shall not harm thee, Helena.

 Dem. No, sir; she shall not, though you take her part. *335*

 Hel. O! when she's angry, she is keen and shrewd.
She was a vixen when she went to school:
And though she be but little, she is fierce.

 Her. 'Little' again! nothing but 'low' and 'little'!
Why will you suffer her to flout me thus? *340*
Let me come to her.

 Lys.   Get you gone, you dwarf;
You minimus, of hindering knot-grass made;
You bead, you acorn!

 Dem.   You are too officious *345*
In her behalf that scorns your services.
Let her alone; speak not to Helena;
Take not her part, for, if thou dost intend
Never so little show of love to her,
Thou shalt aby it.   *350*

 Lys.   Now she holds me not;

Now follow, if thou dar'st, to try whose right,
Or thine or mine, is most in Helena.

 Dem. Follow! nay, I'll go with thee, check by jole.

        Exeunt Lysander and Demetrius.

 Her. You, mistress, all this coil is long of you: *355*
Nay, go not back.

 Hel.   I will not trust you, I,
Nor longer stay in your curst company.
Your hands than mine are quicker for a fray,
My legs are longer though, to run away. *[Exit.]*

 Her. I am amaz'd, and know not what to say. *[Exit.]*

 Obe. This is thy negligence: still thou mistak'st,
Or else commit'st thy knaveries wilfully.

 Puck. Believe me, king of shadows, I mistook.
Did not you tell me I should know the man *365*
By the Athenian garments he had on?
And so far blameless proves my enterprise,
That I have 'nointed an Athenian's eyes;
And so far am I glad it so did sort,
As this their jangling I esteem a sport. *370*

 Obe. Thou see'st these lovers seek a place to fight:
Hie therefore, Robin, overcast the night;
The starry welkin cover thou anon
With drooping fog as black as Acheron;
And lead these testy rivals so astray, *375*
As one come not within another's way.
Like to Lysander sometime frame thy tongue,
Then stir Demetrius up with bitter wrong;
And sometime rail thou like Demetrius;
And from each other look thou lead them thus, *380*
Till o'er their brows death-counterfeiting sleep
With leaden legs and batty wings doth creep:
Then crush this herb into Lysander's eye;
Whose liquor hath this virtuous property,
To take from thence all error with his might, *385*
And make his eyeballs roll with wonted sight.
When they next wake, all this derision
Shall seem a dream and fruitless vision;
And back to Athens shall the lovers wend,
With league whose date till death shall never end. *390*
Whiles I in this affair do thee employ,
I'll to my queen and beg her Indian boy;
And then I will her charmed eye release
From monster's view, and all things shall be peace.

 Puck. My fairy lord, this must be done with haste, *395*
For night's swift dragons cut the clouds full fast,
And yonder shines Aurora's harbinger;
At whose approach, ghosts, wandering here and there,
Troop home to churchyards: damned spirits all,
That in cross-ways and floods have burial, *400*
Already to their wormy beds are gone;
For fear lest day should look their shames upon,
They wilfully themselves exile from light,
And must for aye consort with black-brow'd night.

 Obe. But we are spirits of another sort. *405*
I with the morning's love have oft made sport;
And, like a forester, the groves may tread,
Even till the eastern gate, all fiery-red,

---

303 **personage:** *figure* 311 **curst:** *savage* 313 **right:** *real* 315 **something:** *somewhat* 343 **minimus:** *diminutive creature* **hindering knot-grass;** *cf. n.* 348 **intend:** *pretend*

354 **jole:** *jaw* 355 **coil:** *turmoil* **long of:** *because of* 369 **sort:** *turn out* 374 **Acheron:** *one of the rivers of Hades* 378 **wrong:** *insult* 384 **virtuous:** *powerful* 385 **with his might:** *by its efficacy* 406 **the morning's love;** *cf. n.*

Opening on Neptune, with fair blessed beams
Turns into yellow gold his salt green streams.   *410*
But, notwithstanding, haste; make no delay:
We may effect this business yet ere day.   *[Exit Oberon.]*

    Puck. Up and down, up and down;
       I will lead them up and down:
       I am fear'd in field and town;   *415*
       Goblin, lead them up and down.
Here comes one.

          Enter Lysander.

    Lys. Where art thou, proud Demetrius? speak thou now.
    Puck. Here, villain! drawn and ready. Where art thou?
    Lys. I will be with thee straight.   *420*
    Puck.   Follow me, then,
To plainer ground.   *[Exit Lysander as following the voice.]*

          Enter Demetrius.

    Dem.   Lysander! speak again.
Thou runaway, thou coward, art thou fled?
Speak! In some bush? Where dost thou hide thy head?   *425*
    Puck. Thou coward! art thou bragging to the stars,
Telling the bushes that thou look'st for wars,
And wilt not come? Come, recreant; come, thou child;
I'll whip thee with a rod: he is defil'd
That draws a sword on thee.   *430*
    Dem.   Yea, art thou there?
    Puck. Follow my voice: we'll try no manhood here.

                        Exeunt.

          [Enter Lysander.]

    Lys. He goes before me and still dares me on:
When I come where he calls, then he is gone.
The villain is much lighter-heel'd than I: *435*
I follow'd fast, but faster he did fly;
That fallen am I in dark uneven way,
And here will rest me.   *Lie down.*
          Come, thou gentle day!
For if but once thou show me thy grey light,   *440*
I'll find Demetrius and revenge this spite.   *[Sleeps.]*

       Enter Robin and Demetrius.

    Puck. Ho! ho! ho! Coward, why com'st thou not?
    Dem. Abide me, if thou dar'st; for well I wot
Thou runn'st before me, shifting every place,
And dar'st not stand, nor look me in the face.   *445*
Where art thou now?
    Puck.   Come hither: I am here.
    Dem. Nay then, thou mock'st me. Thou shalt buy this dear,
If ever I thy face by daylight see:
Now, go thy way. Faintness constraineth me   *450*
To measure out my length on this cold bed:
By day's approach look to be visited.

              [Lies down and sleeps.]

          Enter Helena.

    Hel. O weary night! O long and tedious night,
Abate thy hours! shine, comforts, from the east!
That I may back to Athens by daylight,   *455*
From these that my poor company detest:

And sleep, that sometimes shuts up sorrow's eye,
Steal me awhile from mine own company.   *Sleep.*
    Puck. Yet but three? Come one more;
       Two of both kinds make up four.   *460*
       Here she comes, curst and sad:
       Cupid is a knavish lad,
       Thus to make poor females mad.

          Enter Hermia.

    Her. Never so weary, never so in woe,
Bedabbled with the dew and torn with briers,   *465*
I can no further crawl, no further go;
My legs can keep no pace with my desires.
Here will I rest me till the break of day.
Heavens shield Lysander, if they mean a fray!

            [Lies down and sleeps.]

    Puck.   On the ground   *470*
          Sleep sound:
          I'll apply
          To your eye,
    Gentle lover, remedy.

          [Squeezing the juice on Lysander's eyes.]
          When thou wak'st,   *475*
          Thou tak'st
          True delight
          In the sight
    Of thy former lady's eye:
And the country proverb known,   *480*
That every man should take his own,
In your waking shall be shown:
       Jack shall have Jill;
       Nought shall go ill;
The man shall have his mare again,   *485*
And all shall be well.   *[Exit Puck.]*
           They sleep all the Act.

ACT FOURTH ❧ SCENE FIRST

[The Same]
*Enter Queen of Fairies and Clown and Fairies, and the King behind
them [unseen].*

    Tita. Come, sit thee down upon this flowery bed,
While I thy amiable cheeks do coy,
And stick musk-roses in thy sleek smooth head,
And kiss thy fair large ears, my gentle joy.
    Bot. Where's Pease-blossom?   *5*
    Peas. Ready.
    Bot. Scratch my head, Pease-blossom. Where's Mounsieur
Cobweb?
    Cob. Ready.
    Bot. Mounsieur Cobweb, good mounsieur, get your   *10*
weapons in your hand, and kill me a red-hipped humble-bee
on the top of a thistle; and, good mounsieur, bring me the
honey-bag. Do not fret yourself too much in the action,
mounsieur; and, good mounsieur, have a care the honey-bag
break not; I would be loath to have you overflown with a   *15*
honey-bag, signior. Where's Mounsieur Mustard-seed?

---

419 drawn: *with drawn sword*   **454 Abate:** *shorten*

S. d. Act: *intermission*   **2 amiable:** *lovely*   **coy:** *caress*

Must. Ready.

Bot. Give me your neaf, Mounsieur Mustard-seed. Pray you, leave your courtesy, good mounsieur.

Must. What's your will?   20

Bot. Nothing, good mounsieur, but to help Cavalery Cobweb to scratch. I must to the barber's, mounsieur, for methinks I am marvelous hairy about the face; and I am such a tender ass, if my hair do but tickle me, I must scratch.   25

Tita. What, wilt thou hear some music, my sweet love?

Bot. I have a reasonable good ear in music: let us have the tongs and the bones.

Tita. Or say, sweet love, what thou desir'st to eat.

Bot. Truly, a peck of provender: I could munch your   30 good dry oats. Methinks I have a great desire to a bottle of hay: good hay, sweet hay, hath no fellow.

Tita. I have a venturous fairy that shall seek The squirrel's hoard, and fetch thee thence new nuts.

Bot. I had rather have a handful or two of dried pease.   35 But, I pray you, let none of your people stir me. I have an exposition of sleep come upon me.

Tita. Sleep thou, and I will wind thee in my arms. Fairies, be gone, and be all ways away.   *[Exeunt Fairies.]* So doth the woodbine the sweet honeysuckle Gently entwist; the female ivy so Enrings the barky fingers of the elm. O! how I love thee; how I dote on thee!   *[They sleep.]*

Enter Robin Goodfellow.

Obe. [Advancing.] Welcome, good Robin. See'st thou this sweet sight?   45 Her dotage now I do begin to pity: For, meeting her of late behind the wood, Seeking sweet favours for this hateful fool, I did upbraid her and fall out with her; For she his hairy temples then had rounded   50 With coronet of fresh and fragrant flowers; And that same dew, which sometime on the buds Was wont to swell like round and orient pearls, Stood now within the pretty flowerets' eyes Like tears that did their own disgrace bewail.   55 When I had at my pleasure taunted her, And she in mild terms begg'd my patience, I then did ask of her her changeling child; Which straight she gave me, and her fairy sent To bear him to my bower in fairy land.   60 And now I have the boy, I will undo This hateful imperfection of her eyes: And, gentle Puck, take this transformed scalp From off the head of this Athenian swain, That, he awaking when the other do,   65 May all to Athens back again repair, And think no more of this night's accidents But as the fierce vexation of a dream. But first I will release the fairy queen.
        [Touching her eyes with an herb.]

Be as thou wast wont to be;   70 See as thou wast wont to see: Dian's bud o'er Cupid's flower Hath such force and blessed power.

Now, my Titania; wake you, my sweet queen.

Tita. My Oberon! what visions have I seen!   75 Methought I was enamour'd of an ass.

Obe. There lies your love.

Tita.   How came these things to pass? O! how mine eyes do loathe his visage now.

Obe. Silence a while. Robin, take off this head.   80 Titania, music call; and strike more dead Than common sleep of all these five the sense.

Tita. Music, ho! music! such as charmeth sleep.

        Music, still.

Puck. When thou wak'st, with thine own fool's eyes peep.

Obe. Sound, music! Come, my queen, take hands with me, And rock the ground whereon these sleepers be. Now thou and I are new in amity, And will to-morrow midnight solemnly Dance in Duke Theseus' house triumphantly, And bless it to all fair prosperity.   90 There shall the pairs of faithful lovers be Wedded, with Theseus, all in jollity.

Puck. Fairy king, attend, and mark: I do hear the morning lark.

Obe. Then, my queen, in silence sad,   95 Trip we after the night's shade; We the globe can compass soon, Swifter than the wandering moon.

Tita. Come, my lord; and in our flight Tell me how it came this night   100 That I sleeping here was found With these mortals on the ground.
        Sleepers lie still. Exeunt [Fairies]. Wind Horns.

Enter Theseus, Hippolyta, Egeus, and all his train.

The. Go, one of you, find out the forester; For now our observation is perform'd; And since we have the vaward of the day,   105 My love shall hear the music of my hounds. Uncouple in the western valley; let them go: Dispatch, I say, and find the forester. We will, fair queen, up to the mountain's top, And mark the musical confusion   110 Of hounds and echo in conjunction.

Hip. I was with Hercules and Cadmus once, When in a word of Crete they bay'd the bear With hounds of Sparta: never did I hear Such gallant chiding; for, besides the groves,   115 The skies, the fountains, every region near Seem'd all one mutual cry. I never heard So musical a discord, such sweet thunder.

The. My hounds are bred out of the Spartan kind, So flew'd, so sanded; and their heads are hung   120 With ears that sweep away the morning dew;

---

18 neaf: *fist*   **19 leave your courtesy:** *omit formality*   **21 Cavalery:** *i.e., cavalier*   **28 the tongs and the bones:** *rude musical instruments*   **31 bottle:** *bundle*   **48 favours:** *flowers as gifts*   **53 orient:** *lustrous*   **65 other:** *others*   **66 repair:** *return*   **68 fierce:** *extravagant*

S. d. *cf. n.*   **89 triumphantly:** *festively*   **S. d. Wind:** *blow*   **104 observation:** *observance of the rites of May Day*   **105 vaward:** *early part*   **107 Uncouple:** *unleash them*   **108 Dispatch:** *make haste*   **113 bay'd:** *brought to bay*   **115 chiding:** *noise* (of hounds)   **120 flew'd:** *having large chaps*   **sanded:** *of a sandy color*

Crook-knee'd, and dew-lapp'd like Thessalian bulls;
Slow in pursuit, but match'd in mouth like bells,
Each under each. A cry more tuneable
Was never holla'd to, nor cheer'd with horn,   *125*
In Crete, in Sparta, nor in Thessaly:
Judge, when you hear. But, soft! what nymphs are these?
    Ege. My lord, this is my daughter here asleep;
And this, Lysander; this Demetrius is;
This Helena, old Nedar's Helena: *130*
I wonder of their being here together.
    The. No doubt they rose up early to observe
The rite of May, and, hearing our intent,
Came here in grace of our solemnity.
But speak, Egeus, is not this the day   *135*
That Hermia should give answer of her choice?
    Ege. It is, my lord.
    The. Go, bid the huntsmen wake them with their horns.

               Horns and they wake. Shout within.
                      They all start up.

Good morrow, friends. Saint Valentine is past:
Begin these wood-birds but to couple now?   *140*
    Lys. Pardon, my lord.
    The.   I pray you all, stand up.
I know you two are rival enemies:
How comes this gentle concord in the world,
That hatred is so far from jealousy,   *145*
To sleep by hate, and fear no enmity?
    Lys. My lord, I shall reply amazedly,
Half asleep, half waking: but as yet, I swear,
I cannot truly say how I came here;
But, as I think,—for truly would I speak,   *150*
And now I do bethink me, so it is,—
I came with Hermia hither: our intent
Was to be gone from Athens, where we might,
Without the peril of the Athenian law—
    Ege. Enough, enough, my lord; you have enough: *155*
I beg the law, the law, upon his head.
They would have stol'n away; they would, Demetrius,
Thereby to have defeated you and me;
You of your wife, and me of my consent,
Of my consent that she should be your wife.   *160*
    Dem. My lord, fair Helen told me of their stealth,
Of this their purpose hither, to this wood;
And I in fury hither follow'd them,
Fair Helena in fancy following me.
But, my good lord, I wot not by what power,—   *165*
But by some power it is,—my love to Hermia,
Melted as the snow, seems to me now
As the remembrance of an idle gawd
Which in my childhood I did dote upon;
And all the faith, the virtue of my heart,   *170*
The object and the pleasure of mine eye,
Is only Helena. To her, my lord,
Was I betroth'd ere I saw Hermia:
But, like a sickness, did I loathe this food;
But, as in health, come to my natural taste,   *175*
Now do I wish it, love it, long for it,
And will for evermore be true to it.

    The. Fair lovers, you are fortunately met:
Of this discourse we more will hear anon.
Egeus, I will overbear your will,   *180*
For in the temple, by and by, with us,
These couples shall eternally be knit:
And, for the morning now is something worn,
Our purpos'd hunting shall be set aside.
Away with us, to Athens: three and three,   *185*
We'll hold a feast in great solemnity.
Come, Hippolyta.   *Exit Duke [with Hippolyta] and Lords.*
    Dem. These things seem small and undistinguishable,
Like far-off mountains turned into clouds.
    Her. Methinks I see these things with parted eye,   *190*
When everything seems double.
    Hel.   So methinks:
And I have found Demetrius, like a jewel,
Mine own, and not mine own.
    Dem.   Are you sure   *195*
That we are awake? It seems to me
That yet we sleep, we dream. Do you not think
The duke was here, and bid us follow him?
    Her. Yea: and my father.
    Hel.   And Hippolyta.   *200*
    Lys. And he did bid us follow to the temple.
    Dem. Why then, we are awake. Let's follow him;
And by the way let us recount our dreams.   *Exeunt Lovers.*

               Bottom wakes.

    Bot. When my cue comes, call me, and I will answer:
my next is, 'Most fair Pyramus.' Heigh-ho! Peter Quince!   *205*
Flute, the bellows-mender! Snout, the tinker! Starveling!
God's my life! stolen hence, and left me asleep! I have had
a most rare vision. I have had a dream, past the wit of man
to say what dream it was: man is but an ass, if he go about
to expound this dream. Methought I was—there is no man *210*
can tell what. Methought I was,—and methought I had,
—but man is but a patched fool, if he will offer to say what
methought I had. The eye of man hath not heard, the ear of
man hath not seen, man's hand is not able to taste, his tongue
to conceive, nor his heart to report, what my dream was.   *215*
I will get Peter Quince to write a ballad of this dream: it
shall be called Bottom's Dream, because it hath no bottom;
and I will sing it in the latter end of a play, before the
duke: peradventure, to make it the more gracious, I shall
sing it at her death.   *Exit.*

❧ Scene Second ❧

[A Room in Quince's House]
Enter Quince, Flute, Snout, and Starveling.

    Quin. Have you sent to Bottom's house? is he come home
yet?
    Star. He cannot be heard of. Out of doubt he is
transported.
    Flu. If he come not, then the play is marred: it goes not   *5*
forward, doth it?

---

123 mouth: *voice*   **bells:** *i.e., a chime of bells*   **127 soft:** *stop*   **134 in grace of:** *i.e., to grace*   **139 Saint Valentine;** *cf. n.*   **145 jealousy:** *suspicion*   **154 Without:** *beyond*

190 parted eye: *i.e., the two eyes not in focus*   **193, 194** *Cf. n.*   **212 patched:** *motley*   **220 gracious:** *acceptable*   **at her death;** *cf. n.*   **4 transported:** *transformed* (?)

Quin. It is not possible: you have not a man in all Athens able to discharge Pyramus but he.

Flu. No; he hath simply the best wit of any handicraft man in Athens.   *10*

Quin. Yea, and the best person too; and he is a very paramour for a sweet voice.

Flu. You must say, 'paragon': a paramour is, God bless us! a thing of naught.

Enter Snug the Joiner.

Snug. Masters, the duke is coming from the temple, and   *15* there is two or three lords and ladies more married: if our sport had gone forward, we had all been made men.

Flu. O sweet bully Bottom! Thus hath he lost sixpence a day during his life; he could not have 'scaped sixpence a day: an the duke had not given him sixpence a day for playing   *20* Pyramus, I'll be hanged; he would have deserved it: sixpence a day in Pyramus, or nothing.

Enter Bottom.

Bot. Where are these lads? where are these hearts?

Quin. Bottom! O most courageous day! O most happy hour!

Bot. Masters, I am to discourse wonders: but ask me not   *25* what; for if I tell you, I am no true Athenian. I will tell you everything, right as it fell out.

Quin. Let us hear, sweet Bottom.

Bot. Not a word of me. All that I will tell you is, that the duke hath dined. Get your apparel together, good strings to   *30* your beards, new ribbons to your pumps; meet presently at the palace; every man look o'er his part; for the short and the long is, our play is preferred. In any case, let Thisby have clean linen; and let not him that plays the lion pare his nails, for they shall hang out for the lion's claws. And, most dear   *35* actors, eat no onions nor garlic, for we are to utter sweet breath, and I do not doubt but to hear them say, it is a sweet comedy. No more words: away! go; away!   *Exeunt.*

ACT FIFTH   SCENE FIRST

[The Palace of Theseus]
Enter Theseus, Hippolyta, [Philostrate,] and Lords.

Hip. 'Tis strange, my Theseus, that these lovers speak of.

The. More strange than true. I never may believe
These antic fables, nor these fairy toys.
Lovers and madmen have such seething brains,
Such shaping fantasies, that apprehend   *5*
More than cool reason ever comprehends.
The lunatic, the lover, and the poet,
Are of imagination all compact:
One sees more devils than vast hell can hold,
That is the madman; the lover, all as frantic,   *10*
Sees Helen's beauty in a brow of Egypt:
The poet's eye, in a fine frenzy rolling,

Doth glance from heaven to earth, from earth to heaven;
And, as imagination bodies forth
The forms of things unknown, the poet's pen   *15*
Turns them to shapes, and gives to airy nothing
A local habitation and a name.
Such tricks hath strong imagination,
That, if it would but apprehend some joy,
It comprehends some bringer of that joy;   *20*
Or in the night, imagining some fear,
How easy is a bush suppos'd a bear!

Hip. But all the story of the night told over,
And all their minds transfigur'd so together,
More witnesseth than fancy's images,   *25*
And grows to something of great constancy,
But, howsoever, strange and admirable.

Enter lovers, Lysander, Demetrius, Hermia, and Helena.

The. Here come the lovers, full of joy and mirth.
Joy, gentle friends! joy, and fresh days of love
Accompany your hearts!   *30*

Lys.   More than to us
Wait in your royal walks, your board, your bed!

The. Come now; what masques, what dances shall we have,
To wear away this long age of three hours
Between our after-supper and bed-time?   *35*
Where is our usual manager of mirth?
What revels are in hand? Is there no play,
To ease the anguish of a torturing hour?
Call Philostrate.

Philost.   Here, mighty Theseus.   *40*

The. Say, what abridgment have you for this evening?
What masque? what music? How shall we beguile
The lazy time, if not with some delight?

Philost. There is a brief how many sports are ripe;
Make choice of which your highness will see first.   *45*
                        [Gives a paper.]

The. 'The battle with the Centaurs, to be sung
By an Athenian eunuch to the harp.'
We'll none of that: that have I told my love,
In glory of my kinsman Hercules.
'The riot of the tipsy Bacchanals,   *50*
Tearing the Thracian singer in their rage.'
That is an old device; and it was play'd
When I from Thebes came last a conqueror.
'The thrice three Muses mourning for the death
Of Learning, late deceas'd in beggary.'   *55*
That is some satire keen and critical,
Not sorting with a nuptial ceremony.
'A tedious brief scene of young Pyramus
And his love Thisbe; very tragical mirth.'
Merry and tragical! tedious and brief!   *60*
That is, hot ice and wondrous strange snow.
How shall we find the concord of this discord?

Philost. A play there is, my lord, some ten words long,
Which is as brief as I have known a play;

---

14 a thing of naught: *something wicked*   **23 hearts:** *good fellows*   **33 preferred:** *accepted* (?), *offered for acceptance* (by the duke) (?)   **3 antic:** *fantastic*   **toys:** *trifling tales*   **5 apprehend:** *perceive*   **8 compact:** *composed*   **11 Helen:** *Helen of Troy*   **brow of Egypt:** *gypsy's face*

19, 20 *Cf. n.*   **25 More witnesseth:** *is evidence of more*   **26 constancy:** *consistency*   **27 admirable:** *to be wondered at*   **35 after-supper:** *dessert*   **41 abridgment:** *pastime*   **51 Thracian singer:** *Orpheus*   **52 device:** *something devised for dramatic representation*   **56 critical:** *censorious*   **57 sorting with:** *befitting*

But by ten words, my lord, it is too long,   *65*
Which makes it tedious; for in all the play
There is not one word apt, one player fitted.
And tragical, my noble lord, it is;
For Pyramus therein doth kill himself.
Which when I saw rehears'd, I must confess,   *70*
Made mine eyes water; but more merry tears
The passion of loud laughter never shed.

    The. What are they that do play it?

    Philost. Hard-handed men, that work in Athens here,
Which never labour'd in their minds till now,   *75*
And now have toil'd their unbreath'd memories
With this same play, against your nuptial.

    The. And we will hear it.

    Philost.   No, my noble lord;
It is not for you: I have heard it over,   *80*
And it is nothing, nothing in the world;
Unless you can find sport in their intents,
Extremely stretch'd and conn'd with cruel pain,
To do you service.

    The.   I will hear that play;   *85*
For never anything can be amiss,
When simpleness and duty tender it.
Go, bring them in: and take your places, ladies.

                        [Exit Philostrate.]

    Hip. I love not to see wretchedness o'er-charg'd,
And duty in his service perishing.   *90*

    The. Why, gentle sweet, you shall see no such thing.

    Hip. He says they can do nothing in this kind.

    The. The kinder we, to give them thanks for nothing.
Our sport shall be to take what they mistake:
And what poor duty cannot do, noble respect   *95*
Takes it in might, not merit.
Where I have come, great clerks have purposed
To greet me with premeditated welcomes;
Where I have seen them shiver and look pale,
Make periods in the midst of sentences,   *100*
Throttle their practis'd accent in their fears,
And, in conclusion, dumbly have broke off,
Not paying me a welcome. Trust me, sweet,
Out of this silence yet I pick'd a welcome;
And in the modesty of fearful duty   *105*
I read as much as from the rattling tongue
Of saucy and audacious eloquence.
Love, therefore, and tongue-tied simplicity
In least speak most, to my capacity.

              [Enter Philostrate.]

    Philost. So please your Grace, the Prologue is address'd.   *110*

    The. Let him approach.   *Flour[ish of] Trum[pets].*

        Enter the Prologue (Quince).

    Prol. If we offend, it is with our good will.
That you should think, we come not to offend,
But with good will. To show our simple skill,
That is the true beginning of our end.   *115*
Consider then we come but in despite.
We do not come as minding to content you,

Our true intent is. All for your delight,
We are not here. That you should here repent you,
The actors are at hand; and, by their show,   *120*
You shall know all that you are like to know.

    The. This fellow doth not stand upon points.

    Lys. He hath rid his prologue like a rough colt; he knows
not the stop. A good moral, my lord: it is not enough to
speak, but to speak true.   *125*

    Hip. Indeed he hath played on his prologue like a child
on a recorder; a sound, but not in government.

    The. His speech was like a tangled chain; nothing impaired,
but all disordered. Who is next?

Enter Pyramus and Thisbe, Wall, Moonshine, and Lion, Tawyer
with a trumpet before them.

    Prol. Gentles, perchance you wonder at this show;
But wonder on, till truth make all things plain.
This man is Pyramus, if you would know;
This beauteous lady Thisby is, certain.
This man, with lime and rough-cast, doth present   *135*
Wall, that vile Wall which did these lovers sunder;
And through Wall's chink, poor souls, they are content
To whisper, at the which let no man wonder.
This man, with lantern, dog, and bush of thorn,
Presenteth Moonshine; for, if you will know,   *140*
By moonshine did these lovers think no scorn
To meet a Ninus' tomb, there, there to woo.
This grisly beast, which Lion hight by name,
The trusty Thisby, coming first by night,
Did scare away, or rather did affright;   *145*
And, as she fled, her mantle she did fall,
Which Lion vile with bloody mouth did stain.
Anon comes Pyramus, sweet youth and tall,
And finds his trusty Thisby's mantle slain:
Whereat, with blade, with bloody blameful blade,   *150*
He bravely broach'd his boiling bloody breast;
And Thisby, tarrying in mulberry shade,
His dagger drew, and died. For all the rest,
Let Lion, Moonshine, Wall, and lovers twain,
At large discourse, while here they do remain.   *155*

                  Exeunt all but Wall.

    The. I wonder, if the lion be to speak.

    Dem. No wonder, my lord: one lion may, when many
asses do.

    Wall. In this same interlude it doth befall
That I, one Snout by name, present a wall;   *160*
And such a wall, as I would have you think,
That had in it a crannied hole or chink,
Through which the lovers, Pyramus and Thisby,
Did whisper often very secretly.
This loam, this rough-cast, and this stone doth show   *165*
That I am that same wall; the truth is so;
And this the cranny is, right and sinister,
Through which the fearful lovers are to whisper.

    The. Would you desire lime and hair to speak better?

    Dem. It is the wittiest partition that ever I heard   *170*
discourse, my lord.

---

76 unbreath'd: *unpractised*   **82, 83 intents . . . conn'd;** *cf. n.*   **89 o'ercharg'd:** *overbur-*
dened   **96** *I.e., takes the will for the deed*   **97 clerks:** *scholars*   **109 capacity:** *under-*
standing   **110 address'd:** *ready*   **S. d. Flourish:** *blast*

122 stand upon points: *pun on senses 'mind punctuation' and 'be over-careful'*   **124 stop:**
both 'period' and 'method of stopping a horse'   **127 recorder:** *wind instrument of flute*
type   **S. d. Tawyer;** *cf. n.*   **143 hight:** *is called*   **146 fall:** *let fall*   **148 tall:**
goodly   **167 sinister:** *left*

The. Pyramus draws near the wall: silence!

Enter Pyramus.

Pyr. O grim-look'd night! O night with hue so black!
O night which ever art when day is not!
O night! O night alack, alack, alack!   *175*
I fear my Thisby's promise is forgot.
And thou, O wall! O sweet, O lovely wall!
That stand'st between her father's ground and mine;
Thou wall, O wall! O sweet, and lovely wall!
Show me thy chink to blink through with mine eyne.   *180*
                          [*Wall holds up his fingers.*]
Thanks, courteous wall: Jove shield thee well for this!
But what see I? No Thisby do I see.
O wicked wall! through whom I see no bliss;
Curs'd be thy stones for thus deceiving me!
    The. The wall, methinks, being sensible, should curse *185*
again.
    Pyr. No, in truth, sir, he should not. 'Deceiving me,' is This-
by's cue: she is to enter now, and I am to spy her through the
wall. You shall see, it will fall pat as I told you. Yonder she
comes.   *190*

Enter Thisbe.

This. O wall! full often hast thou heard my moans,
For parting my fair Pyramus and me:
My cherry lips have often kiss'd thy stones,
Thy stones with lime and hair knit up in thee.
    Pyr. I see a voice: now will I to the chink,   *195*
To spy an I can hear my Thisby's face.
Thisby!
    This. My love! thou art my love, I think.
    Pyr. Think what thou wilt, I am thy lover's grace;
And, like Limander, am I trusty still.   *200*
    This. And I like Helen, till the Fates me kill.
    Pyr. Not Shafalus to Procrus was so true.
    This. As Shafalus to Procrus, I to you.
    Pyr. O! kiss me through the hole of this vile wall.
    This. I kiss the wall's hole, not your lips at all.   *205*
    Pyr. Wilt thou at Ninny's tomb meet me straightway?
    This. 'Tide life, 'tide death, I come without delay.
    Wall. Thus have I, Wall, my part discharged so;
And, being done, thus Wall away doth go.   *Exeunt Clowns.*
    The. Now is the mural down between the two neighbours.
    Dem. No remedy, my lord, when walls are so wilful to
hear without warning.
    Hip. This is the silliest stuff that ever I heard.
    The. The best in this kind are but shadows, and the worst
are no worse, if imagination amend them.   *215*
    Hip. It must be your imagination then, and not theirs.
    The. If we imagine no worse of them than they of them-
selves, they may pass for excellent men. Here come two noble
beasts in, a man and a lion.

Enter Lion and Moonshine.

Lion. You, ladies, you, whose gentle hearts do fear   *220*
The smallest monstrous mouse that creeps on floor,
May now perchance both quake and tremble here,

When lion rough in wildest range doth roar.
Then know that I, one Snug the joiner, am
A lion-fell, nor else no lion's dam:
For, if I should as lion come in strife   *225*
Into this place, 'twere pity on my life.
    The. A very gentle beast, and of a good conscience.
    Dem. The very best at a beast, my lord, that e'er I saw.
    Lys. This lion is a very fox for his valour.
    The. True; and a goose for his discretion.   *230*
    Dem. Not so, my lord; for his valour cannot carry his
discretion, and the fox carries the goose.
    The. His discretion, I am sure, cannot carry his valour,
for the goose carries not the fox. It is well: leave it to his
discretion, and let us listen to the moon.   *235*
    Moon. This lanthorn doth the horned moon present;—
    Dem. He should have worn the horns on his head.
    The. He is no crescent, and his horns are invisible within
the circumference.
    Moon. This lanthorn doth the horned moon present;   *240*
Myself the man i' the moon do seem to be.
    The. This is the greatest error of all the rest.
The man should be put into the lantern: how is it else the
man i' the moon?
    Dem. He dares not come there for the candle, for, you *245*
see, it is already in snuff.
    Hip. I am aweary of this moon: would he would change!
    The. It appears, by his small light of discretion, that he is in
the wane; but yet, in courtesy, in all reason, we must stay
the time.   *250*
    Lys. Proceed, Moon.
    Moon. All that I have to say, is, to tell you that the lant-
horn is the moon; I, the man in the moon; this thorn-bush,
my thorn-bush; and this dog, my dog.
    Dem. Why, all these should be in the lantern; for all   *255*
these are in the moon. But, silence! here comes Thisbe.

Enter Thisbe.

This. This is old Ninny's tomb. Where is my love?
    Lion. Oh—.   *The Lion roars; Thisbe runs off.*
    Dem. Well roared, Lion.
    The. Well run, Thisbe.   *260*
    Hip. Well shone, Moon. Truly, the moon shines with a
good grace.   [*The Lion tears Thisbe's mantle, and exit.*]
    The. Well moused, Lion.
    Dem. And then came Pyramus.
    Lys. And so the lion vanished.   *265*

Enter Pyramus.

Pyr. Sweet moon, I thank thee for thy sunny beams;
I thank thee, moon, for shining now so bright,
For, by thy gracious, golden, glittering beams,
I trust to taste of truest Thisby's sight.
    But stay, O spite!   *270*
    But mark, poor knight,
What dreadful dole is here!
    Eyes, do you see?
    How can it be?
O dainty duck! O dear!   *275*

---

185 sensible: *capable of perception*   **189 fall:** *happen*   **199 lover's grace:** *i.e.,*
lover   **200 Limander;** *cf. n.*   **207 'Tide:** *come*   **210 mural:** *wall; cf. n.*

225 lion-fell: *lion's skin*   **238 horns:** *cf. n.*   **246 for:** *because of*   **247 in snuff:** *with*
a pun on the sense 'in hasty anger'   **250 stay:** *await*   **264 moused:** *torn (as a cat tears*
a mouse)

Thy mantle good,
    What! stain'd with blood!
Approach, ye Furies fell!
    O Fates, come, come,   280
    Cut thread and thrum;
Quail, crush, conclude, and quell!

The. This passion, and the death of a dear friend, would
go near to make a man look sad.

Hip. Beshrew my heart, but I pity the man.   285

Pyr. O! wherefore, Nature, didst thou lions frame?
Since lion vile hath here deflower'd my dear?
Which is—no, no—which was the fairest dame
That liv'd, that lov'd, that lik'd, that look'd with cheer.
    Come tears, confound;   290
    Out, sword, and wound
The pap of Pyramus:
    Ay, that left pap,
    Where heart doth hop:
Thus die I, thus, thus, thus   *[Stabs himself.]*   295
    Now am I dead,
    Now am I fled;
My soul is in the sky:
    Tongue, lose thy light!
    Moon, take thy flight!   *[Exit Moonshine.]*   300
Now die, die, die, die, die.

Dem. No die, but an ace, for him; for he is but one.

Lys. Less than an ace, man, for he is dead; he is nothing.

The. With the help of a surgeon, he might yet recover,
and prove an ass.   305

Hip. How chance Moonshine is gone before Thisbe
comes back and finds her lover?

The. She will find him by starlight. Here she comes; and
her passion ends the play.

Enter Thisbe.

Hip. Methinks she should not use a long one for such   310
a Pyramus: I hope she will be brief.

Dem. A mote will turn the balance, which Pyramus, which
Thisbe, is the better: he for a man, God warrant us; she for
a woman, God bless us.

Lys. She hath spied him already with those sweet eyes.   315

Dem. And thus she moans, *videlicet:*—

This.
    Asleep, my love?
    What, dead, my dove?
O Pyramus, arise!   320
    Speak, speak! Quite dumb?
    Dead, Dead! A tomb
Must cover thy sweet eyes.
    These lily lips,
    This cherry nose,   325
These yellow cowslip cheeks,
    Are gone, are gone:
    Lovers, make moan!
His eyes were green as leeks.
    O, Sisters Three,   330
    Come, come to me,

With hands as pale as milk;
    Lay them in gore,
    Since you have shore
With shears his thread of silk.   335
    Tongue, not a word:
    Come, trusty sword:
Come, blade, my breast imbrue: *[Stabs herself.]*
    And farewell, friends;
    Thus Thisby ends: 340
Adieu, adieu, adieu.

The. Moonshine and Lion are left to bury the dead.

Dem. Ay, and Wall too.

Bot. No, I assure you; the wall is down that parted their
fathers. Will it please you to see the epilogue, or to hear   345
a Bergomask dance between two of our company?

The. No epilogue, I pray you; for your play needs no excuse. Never excuse; for when the players are all dead, there
need none to be blamed. Marry, if he that writ it had played
Pyramus, and hanged himself in Thisbe's garter, it would   350
have been a fine tragedy: and so it is, truly, and very notably
discharged. But come, your Bergomask: let your epilogue alone.
                                                 [Here a dance of clowns.]
The iron tongue of midnight hath told twelve;
Lovers, to bed; 'tis almost fairy time.
I fear we shall out-sleep the coming morn,   355
As much as we this night have overwatch'd.
This palpable-gross play hath well beguil'd
The heavy gait of night. Sweet friends, to bed.
A fortnight hold we this solemnity,
In nightly revels, and new jollity.   *[Exeunt.]*   360

Enter Puck.

Puck. Now the hungry lion roars,
And the wolf behowls the moon;
Whilst the heavy ploughman snores,
All with weary task fordone.
Now the wasted brands do glow,   365
Whilst the screech-owl, screeching loud,
Puts the wretch that lies in woe
In remembrance of a shroud.
Now it is the time of night
That the graves, all gaping wide,   370
Every one lets forth his sprite,
In the church-way paths to glide:
And we fairies, that do run
By the triple Hecate's team,
From the presence of the sun,   375
Following darkness like a dream,
Now are frolic; not a mouse
Shall disturb this hallow'd house:
I am sent with broom before,
To sweep the dust behind the door.   380

Enter King and Queen of Fairies, with their train.

Obe. Through the house give glimmering light
By the dead and drowsy fire;
Every elf and fairy sprite
Hop as light as bird from brier;

281 **thread and thrum:** *the warp and its fastening, i.e., everything*   282 **Quail:** *overpower*   **quell:** *kill*   283 **passion:** *violent expression of sorrow*   302 **No … ace;**
cf. n.   312 **which … which:** *whether … or*   313 **warrant:** *defend*   330 **Sisters
Three:** *the three Fates*

338 **imbrue:** *stain with blood*   346 **Bergomask dance:** *a rustic dance originating in
Italy*   356 **overwatch'd:** *overwaked*   357 **palpable-gross:** *stupid*   364 **fordone:** *exhausted*   374 *Cf. n.*   377 **frolic:** *merry*

And this ditty after me   *385*
Sing and dance it trippingly.
   Tita. First, rehearse your song by rote,
To each word a warbling note:
Hand in hand, with fairy grace,
Will we sing, and bless this place.   *[Sing and dance.]*   *390*
   Obe. Now, until the break of day,
Through this house each fairy stray.
To the best bride-bed will we,
Which by us shall blessed be;
And the issue there create   *395*
Ever shall be fortunate.
So shall all the couples three
Ever true in loving be;
And the blots of Nature's hand
Shall not in their issue stand: *400*
Never mole, hare-lip, nor scar,
Nor mark prodigious, such as are
Despised in nativity,
Shall upon their children be.
With this field-dew consecrate,   *405*
Every fairy take his gait,
And each several chamber bless,
Through this palace, with sweet peace;
Ever shall in safety rest,

And the owner of it blest.   *410*
   Trip away;
   Make no stay;
Meet me all by break of day.

                 [Exeunt King, Queen, and train.]
   Puck. If we shadows have offended,
Think but this, and all is mended,   *415*
That you have but slumber'd here
While these visions did appear.
And this weak and idle theme,
No more yielding but a dream,
Gentles, do not reprehend: *420*
If you pardon, we will mend.
And, as I'm an honest Puck,
If we have unearned luck
Now to 'scape the serpent's tongue,
We will make amends ere long;   *425*
Else the Puck a liar call:
So, good night unto you all.
Give me your hands, if we be friends,
And Robin shall restore amends.   *[Exit.]*

❧   Finis   ❧

---

395 create: *created*   **405 field-dew consecrate:** *i.e., fairy holy water*   **409 Ever shall:**
i.e., ever shall it; cf. n.

428 hands: *applause*

NOTES

I.i.5, 6. The passage of time seems as slow to Theseus as to a young man under the guardianship of a stepmother or to one who is kept from the enjoyment of his estate by his father's widow who lingers on in possession of a life-interest therein.

I.i.32. *feigning . . . feigning.* The two words 'fain' and 'feign' were often spelled alike in the sixteenth century. Hence 'feigning' may have here its modern sense or it may mean 'love-sick,' 'yearning.' A third possibility, which I am inclined to accept, is that by 'feigning voice' Egeus means 'a repressed voice,' i.e., that Lysander sang softly so as to avoid unwelcome attention.

I.i.33. *stol'n . . . fantasy.* 'Secretly and without permission stamped your image upon her imagination.'

I.i.209, 210. 'How powerful must be the graces of my beloved one, seeing that they have made Athens a place of torture for me; i.e., since so long as she remained in it she could not marry Lysander.' (Deighton.)

I.i.235, 236. 'Love, forgetting proportionate values, can so transform things base and vile that they take on form and dignity.'

I.i.252. *dear expense.* Helena seems to mean that she will pay dearly for Demetrius' thanks—if indeed she receives them—because she will be assisting him to pursue her rival.

I.ii.2. *generally.* Bottom obviously means just the opposite of this, i.e., separately. His intended meaning is usually fairly clear, but it would be a foolhardy editor who should attempt to translate 'Bottomese' too precisely. Cf. 'obscenely' in line 92 of this scene.

I.ii.44. *Thisne.* This word may mean 'in this way' (in which case it should be written without a capital), or it may represent Bottom's first attempt to say Thisbe in a 'monstrous little voice.'

I.ii.95. *hold, or cut bow-strings.* 'This phrase is of the proverbial kind, and was born in the days of archery: when a party was made at butts [archery], assurance of meeting was given in the words of that phrase; the sense of the person using them being that he would "hold" or keep promise, or they might "cut his bowstrings," demolish him for an archer.' (Capell.) This explanation is not certain, but the phrase undoubtedly means, 'Be there without fail.'

II.i.S. d. *at one door.* This refers to one of the side doors on the Elizabethan stage, and not, of course, to the imagined locality.

Robin Goodfellow. This is the proper name of the character referred to indiscriminately in the old copies as Robin or Puck. The latter was often used in the sixteenth century as a generic name for a kind of sprite or goblin. Nash, in his *Terrors of the Night* (1594), says that such mischievous beings 'did most of their merry prankes in the Night. Then ground they malt, and had hempen shirts for their labours, daunst in greene meadowes, pincht maids in their sleep that swept not their houses cleane, and led poor Trauellers out of their way notoriously.'

II.i.7. *moon's sphere.* According to the Ptolemaic system of astronomy accepted in Shakespeare's day, the sun, moon, and stars revolved about the earth fixed in transparent spheres.

II.i.9. *orbs.* The circles of dark green grass often seen in old pastures, once supposed to be produced by the care of fairies in watering such spots.

II.i.10 *pensioners.* Queen Elizabeth had a bodyguard of tall and handsome gentlemen, many of them noble, who were called her pensioners.

II.i.23. *changeling.* Fairies were supposed sometimes to steal a mortal child and to leave a substitute, usually of inferior intelligence, in its place. This substituted being was called a changeling; but here the word is used in reference to the stolen child.

II.i.48. *gossip's bowl.* A drink, often called Lamb's-wool, made of ale, nutmeg, sugar, and roasted crab-apples. Originally served to the sponsors (gossips) at christenings, it was often used on other social occasions.

II.i.55. *tailor.* This exclamation has called forth much learned discussion, the most amusing result of which has been Furness's suggestion that there is here a pun upon a word the reverse of 'header.'

II.i.68. *Corin.* Corin and Phillida (Phyllis) were conventional names for a shepherd and shepherdess.

II.i.80. *Perigenia.* 'This Sinnis had a goodly fair daughter called Perigouna, which fled away when she saw her father slain. . . . But Theseus finding her, called her, and sware by his faith he would use her gently, and do her no hurt, nor displeasure at all.' (North's *Plutarch*, ed. Skeat, p. 279.)

II.i.81, 82. *Ægle . . . Antiopa.* 'For some say that Ariadne hung herself for sorrow, when she saw that Theseus had cast her off. Other . . . think that Theseus left her, because he was in love with another, as by these verses should appear: Ægles, the nymph, was loved of Theseus, Who was the daughter of Panopeus. . . .

Philochorus, and some other hold opinion, that [Theseus] went thither with Hercules against the Amazons: and that to honour his valiantness, Hercules gave him Antiopa the Amazon. . . . Bion . . . saith, that he brought her away by deceit and stealth . . . and that Theseus enticed her to come into his ship . . . and so soon as she was aboard, he hoised his sail, and so carried her away.' (North's *Plutarch*, ed. Skeat, pp. 284–286.)

II.i.100. *nine men's morris.* A game played upon a sort of chessboard dug in the turf.

II.i.103–105. No interpretation of this puzzling passage is entirely satisfactory. E. K. Chambers paraphrases it thus: 'The summer is so bad that men wish it were winter. Not only have we offended the winds, but we have neglected the hymns and carols due from us to the moon. Therefore she too is wrathful, and does her part to spoil the weather.' Furness, on the other hand, explains it as follows: 'Here in Warwickshire, says Titania, in effect (for of course she and Oberon are in the Forest of Arden, with never a thought of Athens; who ever heard of the nine mens morris on the slopes of Pentelicus?), "here the poor human mortals have no summer with its sports, and now they have had no winter with its hymns and carols." ' If the latter be the meaning, 'therefore' is to be understood as 'because of our quarrel.'

II.i.151–173. There is general agreement that this passage contains some allegory; but as to the extent and interpretation of this there is great diversity of opinion. It is fairly certain that the 'fair vestal throned by the west' is Queen Elizabeth. The imagery of the whole passage was very likely suggested by the allegorical figures which appeared in the pageants and 'triumphs' of the day, and it is not impossible that there is specific reference to the 'Princely Pleasures' with which the Earl of Leicester entertained Queen Elizabeth at Kenilworth in 1575.

II.i.236. The story here 'changed,' i.e., reversed, is that of Apollo's pursuit of the nymph Daphne, who was transformed into a laurel tree and thus escaped.

III.i.52. *bush of thorns.* English peasants saw 'the man in the moon' as bearing a bundle of sticks on his back.

III.i.104, 105. *you see an ass-head of your own.* A popular retort which is flung out by Bottom with no consciousness of its special appropriateness.

III.i.118. *plain-song.* Just what characterization of the cuckoo's song is intended is not clear. Perhaps the comparison is between the simple musical interval of the cuckoo's song and that which often occurs at the end of a phrase in the chanting of the psalms. The bird's cry of 'Cuckoo' gives rise in the following lines to one of the common Elizabethan jokes about cuckolds.

III.i.146. *Moth.* The meaning of this name appears when it is given its Elizabethan pronunciation, 'mote,' i.e., a minute particle, as of dust in a sunbeam.

III.ii.26. *our stamp.* Those who are puzzled by the unexpected 'our' instead of 'my,' or who fail to see the alarming effect of the stamping of so diminutive a being, may escape the difficulty by adopting the emendation (first suggested by Allen) *at one stamp*, i.e., 'in one rush.' But cf. IV.i.84, 85.

III.ii.98. *costs the fresh blood dear.* An allusion to the once popular belief that sighing lowers vitality.

III.ii.130. 'If Lysander's present protestations are true, they destroy the truth of his former vows to Hermia, and the contest between these two truths, which in themselves are holy, must in the issue be devilish and end in the destruction of both.' (W. A. Wright.)

III.ii.216, 217. There is some doubt as to the extent to which Shakespeare here pushes his allusion to heraldry, but the following note is satisfactory enough: 'Helen exemplifies her position by a simile,—"we had *two of the first*, i.e., *bodies*, like the double coats [of arms] in heraldry that belong to man and wife *as one person*, but which, like our *single heart*, have but *one crest*." ' (Douce.)

III.ii.263. The punctuation adopted in the text is the result of an attempt to make sense out of the reading of the First Quarto: *No, no; heele Seeme.* As the speech stands Demetrius must be supposed to address Hermia, and then, breaking off, to taunt Lysander. There is almost certainly some corruption of the text, and it might be better to read with the First Folio: *No, no, Sir, seeme to breake loose.* Then the No, no, Sir! would have the force of the modern colloquialism, 'No you don't'!

III.ii.343. *hindering knot-grass.* The knot-grass, a low, tough weed, hinders growth in gardens, and was popularly supposed to be a means of stunting a child's growth.

III.ii.406. *the morning's love.* It is not certain whether this phrase refers to Cephalus, according to classical mythology a mighty hunter and the lover of Aurora, the dawn, or whether it is a figurative description of Aurora herself, or whether it means simply the sun. It is clear, however, that Oberon is contrasting

his freedom to sport by day with the fate of those spirits which are exiled from the sunshine.

IV.i.S.D. *Music, still.* This stage direction of the Folio is puzzling. Since Oberon later directs the music to sound, this may be a direction to the musicians to be ready, but not to play. Another possibility is that the meaning is simply 'soft music.'

IV.i.139. *Saint Valentine.* An allusion to the old belief that the birds began to mate on St. Valentine's day. Cf. Chaucer, *The Parlement of Foules:*

'For this was on seynt Valentynys day,
  Whan every bryd comyth there to chese his make . . .'

IV.i.193, 194. 'Helena, I think, means to say that having found Demetrius unexpectedly, she considered her property in him as insecure as that which a person has in a jewel that he has found by accident; which he knows not whether he shall retain, and which, therefore, may properly enough be called his own and not his own.' (Malone.)

IV.i.220. *at her death.* Does Bottom here mean Thisbe's death? But he is speaking, not of *the* play, but of *a* play. And why 'more gracious' after Thisbe's death? Theobald was very likely right in reading 'after death.' Were Bottom to rise, after dying a heroic death, and sing his 'ballad,' that would be gracious indeed.

V.i.19, 20. 'The mere idea of a joy is enough incentive to a strong imagination to conjure up and believe in the actual presence of a something which causes that joy.' (Chambers.)

V.i.82, 83. *intents . . . conn'd.* 'Intents' is here used in a double sense. Philostrate speaks of the clowns' endeavors to please as carried to the limit of their ability and of their having learned the play, the result of their endeavor, with painful toil.

V.i.S. d. *Tawyer.* This reference in the stage direction of the First Folio to one of the actors in the company to which Shakespeare belonged is an interesting evidence that the Folio was printed from a stage-copy.

V.i.200. *Limander.* Limander and Helen are blunders for Leander and Hero, just as Shafalus and Procrus are the closest the clowns can come to Cephalus and Procris. The two pairs of lovers thus referred to were typical instances of devotion.

V.i.210. *Now is the mural down.* In place of this the First Quarto, which is the most reliable authority for the text of this play, has, *Now is the moon used.* That this latter version is almost certainly corrupt is shown, however, not only by the difficulty of finding in it a satisfactory meaning, but also by the fact that the First Folio substitutes, *Now is the morall downe.* Although the reading of the Folio can be interpreted as a pun on the senses 'moral obstacle' and 'wall all' (i.e., mure all), it still seems unlikely to be what Shakespeare wrote. In despair most editors have taken refuge in the emendation of Pope here adopted, despite the fact that it is open to serious objection both on literary grounds and because the noun 'mural' does not elsewhere appear as part of Shakespeare's vocabulary. The true reading seems irretrievably lost.

V.i.238. *horns.* Moon's lantern had sides of horn instead of glass, so that there is a double significance in his reference to the horned, i.e., crescent, moon. Thereupon Demetrius makes the inevitable Elizabethan joke about the horns which were supposed to grow upon the head of the married man whose wife was unfaithful to him.

V.i.302. *No . . . ace.* Demetrius attempts to make a pun on a second sense of 'die,' i.e., one of a pair of dice. Some editors have attempted to help out

Demetrius' wit by taking the word as related to 'duo,' i.e., two. The Elizabethan pronunciation of 'ace' gives Theseus a chance for another pun.

V.i.374. Hecate is called triple because she was as Luna a heavenly goddess, as Diana an earthly one, and as Hecate one of the lower world. When, as the moon-goddess, she disappears at the coming of the sun, the fairies accompany her car.

V.i.409, 410. It is not improbable that these lines were printed in the wrong order and should be transposed.

The Text of the Present Edition

The text of the present volume is, by permission of the Oxford University Press, that of the *Oxford Shakespeare,* edited by the late W. J. Craig, except for the following deviations:

1. The stage directions are those of the First Folio or the First Quarto, any alterations or additions being enclosed in square brackets. The indication of a second scene in the fifth act has been omitted and the lines renumbered accordingly.

2. A few minor changes in punctuation and in spelling (such as almanac for almanack, gawd for gaud, laugh for loff, and antic for antique) have been made. The spelling lanthorn has been retained only in the speeches of Moon, where it adds clearness to a jest.

3. The following alterations, all revisions to the readings of the First Quarto (save where otherwise indicated), have been made in the text, the reading of the Quarto and the present text preceding the colon, and that of Craig following it:

I.i.71	Whether: Wh'r
194	I'll: I'd
ii. 71	an (Q. and): as
II.i.7	moon's: moone's
71	steep (F1): steppe
80	Perigenia: Perigouna
93	Hath: Have
255	where: whereon
ii. 2	third part: third (misprint ?)
III.i.72	of: have
137	whether: whe'r
ii. 49	the: knee
82	whether: whe'r
98	costs: cost
146	This: That (misprint ?)
173	to: with
193	bare: bear
202	sisters' vows (Q. sisters vowes): sister-vows
204	is all: is it all
207	needles: neelds
272	potion: poison
IV.i.19	courtesy (F1): curtsy
80	Silence a while: Silence, awhile
167	as: as doth
174	a: in
V.i.269	beams: streams

The Merchant of Venice

Edited by
WILLIAM LYON PHELPS

Dramatis Personae

THE DUKE OF VENICE
MOROCHUS, *a Prince, and a Suitor to Portia*
THE PRINCE OF ARRAGON, *Suitor also to Portia*
BASSANIO, *an Italian Lord, Suitor likewise to Portia*
ANTONIO, *A Merchant of Venice*
SALARINO ⎫
SALANIO ⎪ *Gentlemen of Venice, and*
GRATIANO ⎬ *Companions with Bassanio*
LORENZO ⎭
SHYLOCK, *the rich Jew, and Father to Jessica*
TUBAL, *a Jew, Shylock's Friend*

PORTIA, *the rich Italian Lady*
NERISSA, *her waiting-Gentlewoman*
JESSICA, *Daughter to Shylock*

GOBBO, *an old man, Father to Lancelot*
LANCELOT GOBBO, *the Clown*
STEPHANO, *a Messenger*
LEONARDO, *Servant to Bassanio*
BALTHAZAR, *Servant to Portia*

GAOLER AND ATTENDANTS, MAGNIFICOES
OF VENICE, OFFICERS OF THE COURT OF
JUSTICE, SERVANTS TO PORTIA

SCENE—*Alternately at Venice and at Portia's
house, Belmont, on the mainland.*

The Merchant of Venice

INTRODUCTION

It is usually said that there are two separate stories in this play: the Pound of Flesh story, and the story of the Three Caskets. But Professor R. G. Moulton in his admirable book, *Shakespeare as a Dramatic Artist,* emphasizes the fact that there are four strands in the plot, the Pound of Flesh, the Three Caskets, the Elopement of Jessica and Lorenzo and the Episode of the Rings. He points out cleverly and perhaps fancifully the exact moment when Shakespeare brings all four elements together.

There was an old ballad of Gernutus, printed in Percy's *Reliques* (1765), which gives the pound of flesh incident in detail. The difficulty is that no one can prove whether this ballad preceded Shakespeare's *Merchant,* and may thus be considered a source, or followed hard upon the appearance of the play, and is thus merely a tribute to its popularity. The chief source is probably an Italian work, *Il Pecorone,* written in 1378 by Giovanni Fiorentino, and published in 1565. No English translation of this is extant; but as Elizabethan England was familiar with a very large number of vernacular translations from the Italian, it is probable that Shakespeare had access to one in this instance. *Il Pecorone* is a collection of tales, and one of them has the story of a rich woman at Belmont, who is eventually married to a young gentleman, whose friend, in order to lend him money, had come within the danger of an avaricious Jew, who demanded as surety a pound of flesh. The situation is saved by the lady in the court room, who obtains her marriage ring with subsequent pleasantries. The Jew story, however, was a common one in all European literatures.

The Caskets story appears in the *Gesta Romanorum,* a collection of tales dating in England from the thirteenth century. Its editor, Herrtage, describes it as a 'collection of fictitious narratives in Latin, compiled from Oriental apologues, monkish legends, classical stories, tales of chroniclers, popular traditions, and other sources, which it would be now difficult and perhaps impossible to discover.' An English translation was well known in Shakespeare's day, and this book may have been the source of the Caskets plot in *The Merchant of Venice.*

Shakespeare may have invented the Lorenzo-Jessica love story; some think he obtained it from a tale by Massuccio di Salerno, *cir.* 1470, but I doubt it.

In addition to these probable and possible sources, Gosson, in his *Schoole of Abuse* (1579), mentions a play acted at the Bull Inn, called *The Jew.* From his brief description of it, many editors have been convinced that this drama is the prototype of Shakespeare's play, and the real source; but as no copy of it has yet been found, all statements concerning it are largely conjecture.

Shakespeare was undoubtedly influenced by Marlowe's tragedy of blood, *The Jew of Malta,* which was written sometime between 1589 and 1593, and was immensely popular, as it deserved to be. This Jew was a monster rather than a human being; but he was certainly the most famous Jew on the Elizabethan stage until the first matinée of *The Merchant of Venice.* His daughter similarly loves a Christian youth, throws down moneybags from a balcony at night, and ultimately flees from home; and her father's combination of parental and financial emotion infallibly suggests Shylock's ejaculations.

Dr. Johnson, as quoted by Furness, made an epitome of *Il Pecorone,* from which the following extracts are here given (Giannetto=Bassanio; Ansaldo=Antonio):

'Poor Giannetto's head was day and night full of the thoughts of his bad success. When Ansaldo inquired what was the matter, he confessed he could never be contented till he should be in a condition to regain all that he had lost. When Ansaldo found him resolved, he began to sell everything he had to furnish this other fine ship with merchandise; but as he wanted still ten thousand ducats, he applied himself to a Jew at Mestri, and borrowed them on condition that if they were not paid on the feast of St. John in the next month of June, the Jew might take a pound of flesh from any part of his body he pleased. . . .

'Giannetto governed excellently, and caused justice to be administered impartially. . . . But one day, as he stood at the window of the palace with his bride, he saw a number of people pass along the piazza, with lighted torches in their hands. What is the meaning of this? said he. The lady answered, They are artificers going to make their offerings at the Church of St. John, this day being his festival. Giannetto instantly recollected Ansaldo, gave a great sigh, and turned pale. . . . The lady told him to mount on horseback, and go by land the nearest way, to take some attendants, and an hundred thousand ducats; and not to stop until he arrived at Venice. . . .

'. . . The lady now arrives in Venice, in her lawyer's dress. . . . Giannetto proposed to the Jew to apply to this lawyer. With all my heart, says the Jew; but let who will come, I will stick to my bond. They came to this judge and saluted him. Giannetto did not remember him; for he had disguised his face with the juice of certain herbs. Giannetto and the Jew each told the merits of the cause to the judge; who, when he had taken the bond and read it, said to the Jew, I must have you take the hundred thousand ducats, and release this honest man, who will always have a grateful sense of the favour done to him. The Jew replied, I will do no such thing. The judge answered, it will be better for you. The Jew was positive to yield nothing. Upon this they go to the tribunal appointed for such judgments; and our judge says to the Jew, Do you cut a pound of this man's flesh where you choose. The Jew ordered him to be stripped naked; and takes in his hand a razor, which had been made on purpose. Giannetto seeing this, turning to the judge, This, says he, is not the favour I asked of you. Be quiet, says he, the pound of flesh is not yet cut off. As soon as the Jew was going to begin, Take care what you do, says the judge, if you take more or less than a pound, I will order your head to be struck off; and beside, if you shed one drop of blood you shall be put to death.' [Then follows the discomfiture of the Jew, who finding that he cannot get even the principal of the loan, tears up the bond in a rage, receiving no further punishment. The judge declines to accept any money from

Giannetto, but succeeds in inducing him to give her the ring, whereupon follow the now familiar complications. Giannetto wept when his lady pretended that he had been unfaithful; reconciliation followed, and they lived happily forever after.]

For the original of the Caskets story, the following extracts are given from the *Gesta Romanorum,* as printed in Furness.

'Then was the emperour right glad of her safety and comming, and had great compassion on her, saying: Ah faire lady, for the love of my sonne thou hast suffered much woe, neverthelesse if thou be worthie to be his wife, soone shall I prove.

'And when he had thus said, he commanded to bring forth three vessels, the first was made of pure gold, beset with precious stones without, and within full of dead mens bones, and thereupon was ingraven this posey: Whoso chooseth me shall finde that he deserveth.

'The second vessel was made of fine silver, filled with earth and wormes, and the superscription was thus: Whoso chooseth me shall finde that his nature desireth.

'The third vessel was made of lead, full within of precious stones, and the superscription, Whoso chooseth me shall finde that God hath disposed to him.'

But whatever incidents Shakespeare may or may not have drawn from sources, the oftener one compares his play with these stories, the greater seems his genius. His characters are complex human beings; and the speech of Portia on mercy is only one of the evidences of the richness of the mind and character whence it came.

Shylock is a man as well as a Jew; and while Shakespeare took the national attitude toward Jews, and wished his readers and the spectators to rejoice in Shylock's discomfiture, he allowed Shylock to state his own case fairly, and in his comparison of himself with Christians, to reveal his human feelings. It is absurd to suppose that Shakespeare intended Shylock to be a hero, or to carry the sympathy of the audience; on the other hand, Shakespeare was not writing anti-Semitic propaganda, but a play for the theatre, in which the interest is immensely heightened by making every character a recognizable human being.

The History of the Play

It is generally believed that *The Merchant of Venice* was written between 1594 and 1598; but all we know is that it was written before 1598. In that year Francis Meres published his *Palladis Tamia,* where, in a comparison of English poets with the classics, he mentions Shakespeare as a leading contemporary dramatist, and in the list of his productions gives *Merchant of Venice.*

Henslowe's Diary, under date of 25 August, 1594, shows that a new play which he describes as 'the Venesyon comodey,' was performed. No one can prove that this is a reference to the *Merchant of Venice.* Inasmuch as most editors and critics delight in conjecture, it is surprising that no one has tried to prove that this is a play wherein Shakespeare dramatizes his adventures with the 'Venison' of Sir Thomas Lucy, of Charlecote Park.

A quarto edition was printed in 1600, and upon this the Folio text of 1623 was based. In 1619 a spurious edition, bearing the false date 1600, was foisted upon the world. Till 1906 it was generally regarded as the earliest edition and allowed vastly more authority than it in fact deserves.

No one knows when the play was first performed. A version by George Granville, Viscount Lansdowne, was played at London in 1701, and 'held the stage for exactly forty years.' It is printed in Furness as a literary curiosity.

Of the famous actors who have interpreted Shylock, Richard Burbage, the Elizabethan star, may have been the first. In 1741, Charles Macklin, an Irishman, restored the Shakespearean version to the stage, for which he should receive everlasting credit. When he was nearly a hundred years old, he made his last appearance in the rôle of Shylock. The next great actor to take the part was Edmund Kean, in 1814, whose original interpretation made a powerful impression.

In the latter part of the nineteenth century, the greatest impersonation was that by Edwin Booth, who displayed all the resources of his genius. In many ways, it was his finest rôle. Henry Irving attracted wide attention by making Shylock a sympathetic character, but he was neither Elizabethan nor particularly impressive. Richard Mansfield, with his uncanny intelligence, gave a memorable presentation, in which the fiendish character of Shylock was predominant, and yet his humanity not lost. Contemporary with him was the great German actor, Ernst von Possart, who made *Der Kaufmann von Venedig* a favorite play with Continental audiences. He was one of the best of all Shylocks. At the present writing (1922) the only important English-speaking actors of the Jew are Edward Sothern, who, with Julia Marlowe as Portia, gives an admirable production; Walter Hampden; and David Warfield.

ACT FIRST ❧ SCENE FIRST

[Venice. A Street]
Enter Antonio, Salarino, and Salanio.

Ant. In sooth, I know not why I am so sad:
It wearies me; you say it wearies you;
But how I caught it, found it, or came by it,
What stuff 'tis made of, whereof it is born,
I am to learn;   *5*
And such a want-wit sadness makes of me,
That I have much ado to know myself.
   Salar. Your mind is tossing on the ocean;
There, where your argosies with portly sail,—
Like signiors and rich burghers on the flood,   *10*
Or, as it were, the pageants of the sea,—
Do overpeer the petty traffickers,
That curtsy to them, do them reverence,
As they fly by them with their woven wings.
   Salan. Believe me, sir, had I such venture forth,   *15*
The better part of my affections would
Be with my hopes abroad. I should be still
Plucking the grass to know where sits the wind;
Peering in maps for ports, and piers, and roads;
And every object that might make me fear   *20*
Misfortune to my ventures out of doubt
Would make me sad.
   Salar.   My wind, cooling my broth,
Would blow me to an ague, when I thought
What harm a wind too great might do at sea.   *25*
I should not see the sandy hour-glass run
But I should think of shallows and of flats,
And see my wealthy Andrew dock'd in sand
Vailing her high-top lower than her ribs
To kiss her burial. Should I go to church   *30*
And see the holy edifice of stone,
And not bethink me straight of dangerous rocks,
Which touching but my gentle vessel's side
Would scatter all her spices on the stream,
Enrobe the roaring waters with my silks;   *35*
And, in a word, but even now worth this,
And now worth nothing? Shall I have the thought
To think on this, and shall I lack the thought
That such a thing bechanc'd would make me sad?
But tell not me: I know Antonio   *40*
Is sad to think upon his merchandise.
   Ant. Believe me, no: I thank my fortune for it,
My ventures are not in one bottom trusted,
Nor to one place; nor is my whole estate
Upon the fortune of this present year: *45*
Therefore, my merchandise makes me not sad.
   Salar. Why, then you are in love.
   Ant.   Fie, fie!
   Salar. Not in love neither? Then let's say you are sad,
Because you are not merry: and 'twere as easy   *50*
For you to laugh and leap, and say you are merry,

Because you are not sad. Now, by two-headed Janus,
Nature hath fram'd strange fellows in her time:
Some that will evermore peep through their eyes
And laugh like parrots at a bag-piper,   *55*
And other of such vinegar aspect
That they'll not show their teeth in way of smile,
Though Nestor swear the jest be laughable.

Enter Bassanio, Lorenzo, and Gratiano.

   Salan. Here comes Bassanio, your most noble kinsman,
Gratiano, and Lorenzo. Fare ye well: *60*
We leave you now with better company.
   Salar. I would have stay'd till I had made you merry,
If worthier friends had not prevented me.
   Ant. Your worth is very dear in my regard.
I take it, your own business calls on you,   *65*
And you embrace the occasion to depart.
   Salar. Good morrow, my good lords.
   Bass. Good signiors both, when shall we laugh? say when?
You grow exceeding strange: must it be so?
   Salar. We'll make our leisures to attend on yours.   *70*

[Exeunt Salarino and Salanio.]

   Lor. My Lord Bassanio, since you have found Antonio,
We too will leave you; but, at dinner-time,
I pray you, have in mind where we must meet.
   Bass. I will not fail you.
   Gra. You look not well, Signior Antonio;   *75*
You have too much respect upon the world:
They lose it that do buy it with much care:
Believe me, you are marvellously chang'd.
   Ant. I hold the world but as the world, Gratiano;
A stage where every man must play a part,   *80*
And mine a sad one.
   Gra.   Let me play the fool:
With mirth and laughter let old wrinkles come,
And let my liver rather heat with wine
Than my heart cool with mortifying groans.   *85*
Why should a man, whose blood is warm within,
Sit like his grandsire cut in alabaster?
Sleep when he wakes, and creep into the jaundice
By being peevish? I tell thee what, Antonio—
I love thee, and it is my love that speaks—   *90*
There are a sort of men whose visages
Do cream and mantle like a standing pond,
And do a wilful stillness entertain,
With purpose to be dress'd in an opinion
Of wisdom, gravity, profound conceit;   *95*
As who should say, 'I am Sir Oracle,
And when I ope my lips let no dog bark!'
O, my Antonio, I do know of these,
That therefore only are reputed wise
For saying nothing; when, I am very sure,   *100*
If they should speak, would almost damn those ears
Which, hearing them, would call their brothers fools.

---

1 sooth: *truth*   **9 argosies:** *large merchant ships*   **11 pageants:** *festival cars or floats*   **12 overpeer:** *tower over*   **13 curtsy:** *bow with the swell*   **16 affections:** *emotions*   **17 still:** *always*   **21 out of doubt:** *undoubtedly*   **28 wealthy:** *richly laden*   **29 Vailing:** *letting down*   **high-top:** *topmost*   **36, 37 but even ... nothing:** *think how in a moment I may be deprived of all this wealth*   **37 thought:** *anxiety*   **39 bechanc'd:** *if it happened*

52 Janus: *images of the god Janus had two faces, one laughing, one sad*   **56 other:** *others*   **58 Nestor:** *the oldest and gravest of the Greek heroes at Troy*   **63 prevented:** *anticipated*   **64** *I regard your worthiness very highly*   **76 respect ... world:** *concern about business*   **81 sad:** *serious*   **85 mortifying:** *self-denying*   **92 cream and mantle:** *grow a scum*   **standing:** *stagnant*   **94 opinion:** *reputation*   **95 conceit:** *thought*   **101 damn those ears;** *cf. n.*

I'll tell thee more of this another time:
But fish not, with this melancholy bait,
For this fool-gudgeon, this opinion.   *105*
Come, good Lorenzo. Fare ye well awhile:
I'll end my exhortation after dinner.
   Lor. Well, we will leave you then till dinner-time.
I must be one of these same dumb-wise men,
For Gratiano never lets me speak.   *110*
   Gra. Well, keep me company but two years moe,
Thou shalt not know the sound of thine own tongue.
   Ant. Farewell: I'll grow a talker for this gear.
   Gra. Thanks, i' faith; for silence is only commendable
In a neat's tongue dried and a maid not vendible.   *115*

Exit [Gratiano with Lorenzo].

   Ant. Is that anything now?
   Bass. Gratiano speaks an infinite deal of nothing, more than
any man in all Venice. His reasons are as two grains of wheat
hid in two bushels of chaff: you shall seek all day ere you find
them, and, when you have them, they are not worth the   *120*
search.
   Ant. Well, tell me now, what lady is the same
To whom you swore a secret pilgrimage,
That you to-day promis'd to tell me of?
   Bass. 'Tis not unknown to you, Antonio,   *125*
How much I have disabled mine estate,
By something showing a more swelling port
Than my faint means would grant continuance:
Nor do I now make moan to be abridg'd
From such a noble rate; but my chief care   *130*
Is, to come fairly off from the great debts
Wherein my time, something too prodigal,
Hath left me gag'd. To you, Antonio,
I owe the most, in money and in love;
And from your love I have a warranty   *135*
To unburthen all my plots and purposes
How to get clear of all the debts I owe.
   Ant. I pray you, good Bassanio, let me know it;
And if it stand, as you yourself still do,
Within the eye of honour, be assur'd,   *140*
My purse, my person, my extremest means,
Lie all unlock'd to your occasions.
   Bass. In my school-days, when I had lost one shaft,
I shot his fellow of the self-same flight
The self-same way with more advised watch,   *145*
To find the other forth, and by adventuring both,
I oft found both. I urge this childhood proof,
Because what follows is pure innocence.
I owe you much, and, like a wilful youth,
That which I owe is lost; but if you please   *150*
To shoot another arrow that self way
Which you did shoot the first, I do not doubt,
As I will watch the aim, or to find both,
Or bring your latter hazard back again,
And thankfully rest debtor for the first.   *155*

   Ant. You know me well, and herein spend but time
To wind about my love with circumstance;
And out of doubt you do me now more wrong
In making question of my uttermost
Than if you had made waste of all I have: *160*
Then do but say to me what I should do
That in your knowledge may by me be done,
And I am prest unto it: therefore speak.
   Bass. In Belmont is a lady richly left,
And she is fair, and, fairer than that word,   *165*
Of wondrous virtues: sometimes from her eyes
I did receive fair speechless messages:
Her name is Portia; nothing undervalu'd
To Cato's daughter, Brutus' Portia:
Nor is the wide world ignorant of her worth,   *170*
For the four winds blow in from every coast
Renowned suitors; and her sunny locks
Hang on her temples like a golden fleece;
Which makes her seat of Belmont Colchos' strond,
And many Jasons come in quest of her.   *175*
O my Antonio! had I but the means
To hold a rival place with one of them,
I have a mind presages me such thrift,
That I should questionless be fortunate.
   Ant. Thou knowest that all my fortunes are at sea;   *180*
Neither have I money, nor commodity
To raise a present sum: therefore go forth;
Try what my credit can in Venice do:
That shall be rack'd, even to the uttermost,
To furnish thee to Belmont, to fair Portia.   *185*
Go, presently inquire, and so will I,
Where money is, and I no question make
To have it of my trust or for my sake.   *Exeunt.*

❧ SCENE SECOND ❧

[Belmont. A Room in Portia's House]
Portia with her waiting woman Nerissa.

   Por. By my troth, Nerissa, my little body is aweary of this
great world.
   Ner. You would be, sweet madam, if your miseries were in
the same abundance as your good fortunes are: and yet, for
aught I see, they are as sick that surfeit with too much as   *5*
they that starve with nothing. It is no mean happiness therefore to be seated in the mean: superfluity comes sooner by
white hairs, but competency lives longer.
   Por. Good sentences and well pronounced.
   Ner. They would be better if well followed.   *10*
   Por. If to do were as easy as to know what were good to
do, chapels had been churches, and poor men's cottages
princes' palaces. It is a good divine that follows his own
instructions: I can easier teach twenty what were good to
be done, than be one of the twenty to follow mine own   *15*

---

105 fool-gudgeon: *an easily caught fish*   **111 moe:** *more*   **113 gear:** *indefinite word for business of any kind*   **115 In a neat's, etc.;** *cf. n.*   **118 reasons:** *sensible ideas*   **124 That;** *cf. n.*   **127** *By living in a somewhat more lavish way*   **129 abridg'd:** *obliged to desist*   **130 rate:** *standard of life*   **132 time:** *time of life, youth*   **133 gag'd:** *entangled*   **140 eye:** *view, scope*   **144 flight:** *power of flight, range*   **146 forth:** *out*   **148 innocence;** *cf. n.*   **151 self:** *same*   **153 or:** *either*

156 spend but: *only waste*   **159 question:** *doubt*   **163 prest:** *ready*   **164 richly left:** *a wealthy heiress*   **165, 166 fair . . . virtues:** *beautiful and accomplished*   **166 sometimes:** *formerly*   **168 nothing undervalu'd:** *in no way inferior*   **169 Portia;** *cf. n.*   **174 Colchos';** *cf. n.*   **177 hold . . . with:** *make a show equal to*   **178 thrift:** *thriving*   **184 rack'd:** *strained*   **186 presently:** *instantly*   **187 of my trust, etc.:** *either on my credit or from some friend*   **7 seated . . . mean:** *moderately endowed*   **comes . . . by:** *brings on*   **9 sentences:** *sentiments*

teaching. The brain may devise laws for the blood, but a hot temper leaps o'er a cold decree: such a hare is madness the youth, to skip o'er the meshes of good counsel the cripple. But this reasoning is not in the fashion to choose me a husband. O me, the word 'choose!' I may neither choose whom I would _20_ nor refuse whom I dislike; so is the will of a living daughter curbed by the will of a dead father. Is it not hard, Nerissa, that I cannot choose one nor refuse none?

Ner. Your father was ever virtuous, and holy men at their death have good inspirations; therefore, the lottery that he _25_ hath devised in these three chests of gold, silver, and lead, whereof who chooses his meaning chooses you, will, no doubt, never be chosen by any rightly but one who you shall rightly love. But what warmth is there in your affection towards any of these princely suitors that are already come? _30_

Por. I pray thee, over-name them, and as thou namest them, I will describe them; and, according to my description, level at my affection.

Ner. First, there is the Neapolitan prince.

Por. Ay, that's a colt indeed, for he doth nothing but _35_ talk of his horse; and he makes it a great appropriation to his own good parts that he can shoe him himself. I am much afeard my lady his mother played false with a smith.

Ner. Then is there the County Palatine.

Por. He doth nothing but frown, as who should say, _40_ 'An you will not have me, choose.' He hears merry tales, and smiles not: I fear he will prove the weeping philosopher when he grows old, being so full of unmannerly sadness in his youth. I had rather be married to a death's-head with a bone in his mouth than to either of these. God defend me from _45_ these two!

Ner. How say you by the French lord, Monsieur Le Bon?

Por. God made him, and therefore let him pass for a man. In truth, I know it is a sin to be a mocker; but, he! why, he hath a horse better than the Neapolitan's, a better bad habit _50_ of frowning than the Count Palatine; he is every man in no man; if a throstle sing, he falls straight a-capering; he will fence with his own shadow: if I should marry him, I should marry twenty husbands. If he would despise me, I would forgive him, for if he love me to madness, I shall never requite him. _55_

Ner. What say you, then, to Falconbridge, the young baron of England?

Por. You know I say nothing to him, for he understands not me, nor I him: he hath neither Latin, French, nor Italian; and you will come into the court and swear that I have a _60_ poor pennyworth in the English. He is a proper man's picture, but, alas! who can converse with a dumb-show? How oddly he is suited! I think he bought his doublet in Italy, his round hose in France, his bonnet in Germany, and his behaviour everywhere.

Ner. What think you of the Scottish lord, his neighbour? _65_

Por. That he hath a neighbourly charity in him, for he borrowed a box of the ear of the Englishman, and swore he would pay him again when he was able: I think the Frenchman became his surety and sealed under for another.

Ner. How like you the young German, the Duke of _70_ Saxony's nephew?

Por. Very vilely in the morning, when he is sober, and most vilely in the afternoon, when he is drunk: when he is best, he is a little worse than a man, and when he is worst, he is little better than a beast. An the worst fall that ever fell, I _75_ hope I shall make shift to go without him.

Ner. If he should offer to choose, and choose the right casket, you should refuse to perform your father's will, if you should refuse to accept him.

Por. Therefore, for fear of the worst, I pray thee, set a deep glass of Rhenish wine on the contrary casket, for, if the devil be within and that temptation without, I know he will choose it. I will do anything, Nerissa, ere I will be married to a sponge.

Ner. You need not fear, lady, the having any of these lords: they have acquainted me with their determinations; which is, _85_ indeed, to return to their home and to trouble you with no more suit, unless you may be won by some other sort than your father's imposition depending on the caskets.

Por. If I live to be as old as Sibylla, I will die as chaste as Diana, unless I be obtained by the manner of my father's _90_ will. I am glad this parcel of wooers are so reasonable, for there is not one among them but I dote on his very absence, and I pray God grant them a fair departure.

Ner. Do you not remember, lady, in your father's time, a Venetian, a scholar and a soldier, that came hither in the _95_ company of the Marquis of Montferrat?

Por. Yes, yes: it was Bassanio; as I think, he was so called.

Ner. True, madam: he, of all the men that ever my foolish eyes looked upon, was the best deserving a fair lady. _100_

Por. I remember him well, and I remember him worthy of thy praise.

Enter a Servingman.

How now! what news?

Serv. The four strangers seek for you, madam, to take their leave; and there is a forerunner come from a fifth, _105_ the Prince of Morocco, who brings word the prince his master will be here to-night.

Por. If I could bid the fifth welcome with so good heart as I can bid the other four farewell, I should be glad of his approach: if he have the condition of a saint and the _110_ complexion of a devil, I had rather he should shrive me than wive me. Come, Nerissa. Sirrah, go before.
Whiles we shut the gate upon one wooer, another knocks at the door.   *Exeunt.*

❧ SCENE THIRD ❧

[Venice. A public Place]
Enter Bassanio with Shylock the Jew.

Shy. Three thousand ducats; well?
Bass. Ay, sir, for three months.
Shy. For three months; well?
Bass. For the which, as I told you, Antonio shall be bound.
Shy. Antonio shall become bound; well?   _5_
Bass. May you stead me? Will you pleasure me? Shall I know your answer?

---

27 **his meaning:** *the chest he meant*   32 **level:** *aim*   35 **colt:** *'brainless youth'*   36 **appropriation:** *peculiar merit*   39 **County Palatine:** *a count possessing royal privileges*   41 **An:** *if* **choose;** *cf. n.*   42 **weeping philosopher:** *Heraclitus*   47 **by:** *concerning*   52 **throstle:** *thrush*   59 **Latin;** *cf. n.*   61 **proper:** *handsome*   63 **suited:** *dressed* **doublet:** *tight-fitting coat* **round hose:** *a variety of knee-breeches*   68 **Frenchman;** *cf. n.*   69 **sealed under:** *pledged himself*

87 **sort:** *lot*   88 **imposition:** *injunction*   89 **Sibylla;** *cf. n.*   109 **four;** *cf. n.*   110 **condition:** *disposition*   6 **stead:** *assist*

Shy. Three thousand ducats, for three months, and Antonio
bound.

Bass. Your answer to that.   10

Shy. Antonio is a good man.

Bass. Have you heard any imputation to the contrary?

Shy. Ho, no, no, no, no: my meaning in saying he is a
good man is to have you understand me that he is sufficient.
Yet his means are in supposition: he hath an argosy bound   15
to Tripolis, another to the Indies; I understand moreover upon
the Rialto, he hath a third at Mexico, a fourth for England,
and other ventures he hath, squandered abroad. But ships are
but boards, sailors but men: there be land-rats and water-rats,
land-thieves, and water-thieves,—I mean pirates,—and then   20
there is the peril of waters, winds, and rocks. The man is,
notwithstanding, sufficient. Three thousand ducats; I think,
I may take his bond.

Bass. Be assured you may.

Shy. I will be assured I may; and, that I may be assured,   25
I will bethink me. May I speak with Antonio?

Bass. If it please you to dine with us.

Shy. Yes, to smell pork; to eat of the habitation which your
prophet the Nazarite conjured the devil into. I will buy with
you, sell with you, talk with you, walk with you, and so   30
following; but I will not eat with you, drink with you, nor
pray with you. What news on the Rialto? Who is he comes
here?

Enter Antonio.

Bass. This is Signior Antonio.

Shy. [*Aside.*] How like a fawning publican he looks!   35
I hate him for he is a Christian;
But more for that in low simplicity
He lends out money gratis, and brings down
The rate of usance here with us in Venice.
If I can catch him once upon the hip,   40
I will feed fat the ancient grudge I bear him.
He hates our sacred nation, and he rails,
Even there where merchants most do congregate,
On me, my bargains, and my well-won thrift,
Which he calls interest. Cursed be my tribe,   45
If I forgive him!

Bass.   Shylock, do you hear?

Shy. I am debating of my present store,
And, by the near guess of my memory,
I cannot instantly raise up the gross   50
Of full three thousand ducats. What of that?
Tubal, a wealthy Hebrew of my tribe,
Will furnish me. But soft! how many months
Do you desire? [*To Antonio.*] Rest you fair, good signior;
Your worship was the last man in our mouths.   55

Ant. Shylock, albeit I neither lend nor borrow
By taking nor by giving of excess,
Yet, to supply the ripe wants of my friend,
I'll break a custom. [*To Bassanio.*] Is he yet possess'd
How much ye would?   60

Shy.   Ay, ay, three thousand ducats.

Ant. And for three months.

Shy. I had forgot; three months; you told me so.
Well then, your bond; and let me see. But hear you;
Methought you said you neither lend nor borrow   65
Upon advantage.

Ant.   I do never use it.

Shy. When Jacob graz'd his uncle Laban's sheep,—
This Jacob from our holy Abram was,
As his wise mother wrought in his behalf,   70
The third possessor: ay, he was the third,—

Ant. And what of him? did he take interest?

Shy. No; not take interest; not, as you would say,
Directly interest: mark what Jacob did.
When Laban and himself were compromis'd.   75
That all the eanlings which were streak'd and pied
Should fall as Jacob's hire, the ewes, being rank,
In end of autumn turned to the rams;
And, when the work of generation was
Between these woolly breeders in the act,   80
The skilful shepherd peel'd me certain wands,
And, in the doing of the deed of kind,
He stuck them up before the fulsome ewes,
Who, then conceiving, did in eaning time
Fall parti-colour'd lambs, and those were Jacob's.   85
This was a way to thrive, and he was blest:
And thrift is blessing, if men steal it not.

Ant. This was a venture, sir, that Jacob serv'd for;
A thing not in his power to bring to pass,
But sway'd and fashion'd by the hand of heaven.   90
Was this inserted to make interest good?
Or is your gold and silver ewes and rams?

Shy. I cannot tell; I make it breed as fast:
But note me, signior.

Ant.   Mark you this, Bassanio,   95
The devil can cite Scripture for his purpose.
An evil soul, producing holy witness,
Is like a villain with a smiling cheek,
A goodly apple rotten at the heart.
O, what a goodly outside falsehood hath!   100

Shy. Three thousand ducats; 'tis a good round sum.
Three months from twelve, then let me see the rate.

Ant. Well, Shylock, shall we be beholding to you?

Shy. Signior Antonio, many a time and oft
In the Rialto you have rated me   105
About my moneys and my usances:
Still have I borne it with a patient shrug,
For sufferance is the badge of all our tribe.
You call me misbeliever, cut-throat dog,
And spit upon my Jewish gaberdine,   110
And all for use of that which is mine own.
Well then, it now appears you need my help:
Go to then; you come to me, and you say,
'Shylock, we would have moneys:' you say so;
You, that did void your rheum upon my beard,   115
And foot me as you spurn a stranger cur
Over your threshold: moneys is your suit.
What should I say to you? Should I not say,

---

15 supposition: *not in cash or in the bank*   **17 Rialto:** *the Exchange*   **for:** *bound for*   **18
squandered:** *scattered*   **29 Nazarite;** *cf. n.*   **35 fawning publican:** *see Luke 18. 10-
14.*   **37 low simplicity:** *meek folly*   **39 usance:** *interest*   **40 upon the hip:** *a wrestling
grip*   **50 gross:** *total sum*   **57 excess:** *interest*   **58 ripe:** *immediate*   **59 possess'd:**
informed

68 Jacob: *see Gen. 30. 37.*   **75 compromis'd:** *agreed*   **76 eanlings:** *new lambs*   **81
peel'd me;** *cf. n.*   **82 kind:** *nature*   **83 fulsome:** *lustful*   **85 Fall:** *give birth to*   **103
beholding:** *indebted*   **110 gaberdine:** *cloak or long coat*   **115 void your rheum:** *clear
your throat*

'Hath a dog money? Is it possible
A cur can lend three thousand ducats?' or   *120*
Shall I bend low, and in a bondman's key,
With bated breath, and whispering humbleness,
Say this:—
'Fair sir, you spet on me on Wednesday last;
You spurn'd me such a day; another time   *125*
You call'd me dog; and for these courtesies
I'll lend you thus much moneys?'
     Ant. I am as like to call thee so again,
To spet on thee again, to spurn thee too.
If thou wilt lend this money, lend it not   *130*
As to thy friends,—for when did friendship take
A breed for barren metal of his friend?—
But lend it rather to thine enemy;
Who if he break, thou mayst with better face
Exact the penalty.   *135*
     Shy.   Why, look you, how you storm!
I would be friends with you, and have your love,
Forget the shames that you have stain'd me with,
Supply your present wants, and take no doit
Of usance for my moneys, and you'll not hear me: *140*
This is kind I offer.
     Bass. This were kindness.
     Shy.   This kindness will I show.
Go with me to a notary, seal me there
Your single bond; and, in a merry sport,   *145*
If you repay me not on such a day,
In such a place, such sum or sums as are
Express'd in the condition, let the forfeit
Be nominated for an equal pound
Of your fair flesh, to be cut off and taken   *150*
In what part of your body pleaseth me.
     Ant. Content, i' faith: I'll seal to such a bond,
And say there is much kindness in the Jew.
     Bass. You shall not seal to such a bond for me:
I'll rather dwell in my necessity.   *155*
     Ant. Why, fear not, man; I will not forfeit it:
Within these two months, that's a month before
This bond expires, I do expect return
Of thrice three times the value of this bond.
     Shy. O father Abram! what these Christians are,   *160*
Whose own hard dealings teaches them suspect
The thoughts of others. Pray you, tell me this;
If he should break his day, what should I gain
By the exaction of the forfeiture?
A pound of man's flesh, taken from a man,   *165*
Is not so estimable, profitable neither,
As flesh of muttons, beefs, or goats. I say,
To buy his favour, I extend this friendship:
If he will take it, so; if not, adieu;
And, for my love, I pray you wrong me not.   *170*
     Ant. Yes, Shylock, I will seal unto this bond.
     Shy. Then meet me forthwith at the notary's;
Give him direction for this merry bond,
And I will go and purse the ducats straight,
See to my house, left in the fearful guard   *175*
Of an unthrifty knave, and presently

---

124 **spet:** *spat*   139 **doit:** *Dutch coin of small value*   143 *Bass.; cf. n.*   145 **Your single:** *merely your*   149 **equal:** *exact*   175 **fearful:** *fearfully insecure*

I will be with you.   *Exit.*
     Ant.   Hie thee, gentle Jew.
This Hebrew will turn Christian: he grows kind.
     Bass. I like not fair terms and a villain's mind.   *180*
     Ant. Come on: in this there can be no dismay;
My ships come home a month before the day.   *Exeunt.*

ACT SECOND ❧ SCENE FIRST

[Belmont. A Room in Portia's House]
Enter Morochus, a tawny Moor, all in white, and three or four
followers accordingly, with Portia, Nerissa and their train. Flo[urish
of] Cornets.

     Mor. Mislike me not for my complexion,
The shadow'd livery of the burnish'd sun,
To whom I am a neighbour and near bred.
Bring me the fairest creature northward born,
Where Phœbus' fire scarce thaws the icicles,   *5*
And let us make incision for your love,
To prove whose blood is reddest, his or mine.
I tell thee, lady, this aspect of mine
Hath fear'd the valiant: by my love, I swear
The best regarded virgins of our clime   *10*
Have lov'd it too: I would not change this hue,
Except to steal your thoughts, my gentle queen.
     Por. In terms of choice I am not solely led
By nice direction of a maiden's eyes;
Besides, the lottery of my destiny   *15*
Bars me the right of voluntary choosing:
But if my father had not scanted me
And hedg'd me by his wit, to yield myself
His wife who wins me by that means I told you,
Yourself, renowned prince, then stood as fair   *20*
As any comer I have look'd on yet
For my affection.
     Mor.   Even for that I thank you:
Therefore, I pray you, lead me to the caskets
To try my fortune. By this scimitar,—   *25*
That slew the Sophy, and a Persian prince
That won three fields of Sultan Solyman,—
I would outstare the sternest eyes that look,
Outbrave the heart most daring on the earth,
Pluck the young sucking cubs from the she-bear,   *30*
Yea, mock the lion when he roars for prey,
To win thee, lady. But, alas the while!
If Hercules and Lichas play at dice
Which is the better man, the greater throw
May turn by fortune from the weaker hand: *35*
So is Alcides beaten by his page;
And so may I, blind fortune leading me,
Miss that which one unworthier may attain,
And die with grieving.
     Por.   You must take your chance;   *40*

Scene One S. d. **accordingly:** *in similar dress*   2 **shadow'd:** *dark*   7 **reddest;** *cf. n.*   9 **fear'd:** *frightened*   11, 12 **I would not,** etc.; *cf. n.*   14 **nice:** *captious*   17 **scanted:** *restricted*   18 **wit:** *intelligence*   26 **Sophy:** *Shah of Persia*   27 **Solyman:** *He fought the Persians in 1535*   33 **Lichas:** *the servant of Hercules*   36 **Alcides:** *Alcæus was the father of Hercules' stepfather*

And either not attempt to choose at all,
Or swear before you choose, if you choose wrong,
Never to speak to lady afterward
In way of marriage: therefore be advis'd.

   Mor. Nor will not: come, bring me unto my chance.   45

   Por. First, forward to the temple: after dinner
Your hazard shall be made.

   Mor.   Good fortune then!
To make me blest or cursed'st among men!   *Cornets. Exeunt.*

❧   Scene Second   ❧

[Venice. A Street]
Enter the Clown alone.

   Laun. Certainly my conscience will serve me to run from
this Jew my master. The fiend is at mine elbow, and tempts
me, saying to me, 'Gobbo, Launcelot Gobbo, good Launcelot,'
or 'good Gobbo,' or 'good Launcelot Gobbo, use your legs,
take the start, run away.' My conscience says, 'No; take   5
heed, honest Launcelot; take heed, honest Gobbo;' or, as aforesaid, 'honest Launcelot Gobbo; do not run; scorn running with
thy heels.' Well, the most courageous fiend bids me pack: *'Via!'*
says the fiend; 'away!' says the fiend; 'for the heavens, rouse up
a brave mind,' says the fiend, 'and run.' Well, my conscience,
hanging about the neck of my heart, says very wisely to me,
'My honest friend Launcelot, being an honest man's son,'—or
rather an honest woman's son;—for, indeed, my father did
something smack, something grow to, he had a kind of
taste;—well, my conscience says, 'Launcelot, budge not.'   15
'Budge,' says the fiend. 'Budge not,' says my conscience. 'Conscience,' say I, 'you counsel well;' 'fiend,' say I, 'you counsel
well:' to be ruled by my conscience, I should stay with the Jew
my master, who, God bless the mark! is a kind of devil; and,
to run away from the Jew, I should be ruled by the fiend,   20
who saving your reverence, is the devil himself. Certainly, the
Jew is the very devil incarnation; and, in my conscience, my
conscience is but a kind of hard conscience, to offer to counsel me to stay with the Jew. The fiend gives the more friendly
counsel: I will run, fiend; my heels are at your commandment; I
will run.

Enter Old Gobbo, with a basket.

   Gob. Master young man, you; I pray you, which is the way
to Master Jew's?

   Laun. *[Aside.]* O heavens! this is my true-begotten father,
who, being more than sand-blind, high-gravel blind, knows   30
me not: I will try confusions with him.

   Gob. Master young gentleman, I pray you, which is the way
to Master Jew's?

   Laun. Turn up on your right hand at the next turning, but,
at the next turning of all, on your left; marry, at the very   35
next turning, turn of no hand, but turn down indirectly to
the Jew's house.

   Gob. By God's sonties, 'twill be a hard way to hit. Can you

tell me whether one Launcelot, that dwells with him, dwell
with him or no?   40

   Laun. Talk you of young Master Launcelot? *[Aside.]*
Mark me now; now will I raise the waters. Talk you of young
Master Launcelot?

   Gob. No master, sir, but a poor man's son: his father,
though I say it, is an honest, exceeding poor man, and,   45
God be thanked, well to live.

   Laun. Well, let his father be what a' will, we talk of young
Master Launcelot.

   Gob. Your worship's friend, and Launcelot, sir.

   Laun. But I pray you, *ergo,* old man, *ergo,* I beseech you,   50
talk you of young Master Launcelot?

   Gob. Of Launcelot, an 't please your mastership.

   Laun. *Ergo,* Master Launcelot. Talk not of Master
Launcelot, father; for the young gentleman,—according to
Fates and Destinies and such odd sayings, the Sisters Three   55
and such branches of learning,—is, indeed, deceased; or, as
you would say in plain terms, gone to heaven.

   Gob. Marry, God forbid! the boy was the very staff of my
age, my very prop.

   Laun. *[Aside.]* Do I look like a cudgel or a hovel-post, a   60
staff or a prop? Do you know me, father?

   Gob. Alack the day! I know you not, young gentleman: but
I pray you, tell me, is my boy,—God rest his soul!—alive or
dead?

   Laun. Do you not know me, father?   65

   Gob. Alack, sir, I am sand-blind; I know you not.

   Laun. Nay, indeed, if you had your eyes, you might fail of
the knowing me: it is a wise father that knows his own child.
Well, old man, I will tell you news of your son. Give me your
blessing; truth will come to light; murder cannot be hid   70
long; a man's son may, but, in the end, truth will out.

   Gob. Pray you, sir, stand up. I am sure you are not
Launcelot, my boy.

   Laun. Pray you, let's have no more fooling about it, but
give me your blessing: I am Launcelot, your boy that was,   75
your son that is, your child that shall be.

   Gob. I cannot think you are my son.

   Laun. I know not what I shall think of that; but I am
Launcelot, the Jew's man, and I am sure Margery your wife
is my mother.   80

   Gob. Her name is Margery, indeed: I'll be sworn, if thou
be Launcelot, thou art mine own flesh and blood. Lord worshipped might he be! what a beard hast thou got! thou hast
got more hair on thy chin than Dobbin my phill-horse has on
his tail.   85

   Laun. It should seem then that Dobbin's tail grows
backward: I am sure he had more hair on his tail than I have
on my face, when I last saw him.

   Gob. Lord! how art thou changed. How dost thou and thy
master agree? I have brought him a present. How 'gree you   90
now?

   Laun. Well, well: but, for mine own part, as I have set up
my rest to run away, so I will not rest till I have run some
ground. My master's a very Jew: give him a present! give him
a halter: I am famished in his service: you may tell every finger

---

44 **advis'd:** *cautious*   7, 8 **with thy heels:** *indignantly*   8 **'Via!':** *Italian, meaning "get-ap"*   9 **for . . . heavens:** *for heaven's sake!*   14 **smack, etc.;** *cf. n.*   15 **budge:** *flinch, give ground*   19 **God bless the mark;** *cf. n.*   21 **saving your reverence:** *(no offence intended!)*   22 **incarnation;** *cf. n.*   30 **sand-blind:** *half-blind; cf. n.*   38 **sonties;** *cf. n.*

46 **well to live:** *well to do*   51, 52 *Cf. n.*   60 **hovel-post:** *a supporting stick*   82, 83 **Lord . . . be:** *Praise the Lord!*   83 **what a beard;** *cf. n.*   84 **phill-horse:** *shaft-horse*   92, 93 **set up my rest:** *staked all, resolved absolutely* (card-game term)   95 **tell:** *count; cf. n.*

I have with my ribs. Father, I am glad you are come: give
me your present to one Master Bassanio, who, indeed, gives
rare new liveries. If I serve not him, I will run as far as God
has any ground. O rare fortune! here comes the man: to him,
father; for I am a Jew, if I serve the Jew any longer.   *100*

Enter Bassanio, with a follower [Leonardo] or two.

Bass. You may do so; but let it be so hasted that supper
be ready at the farthest by five of the clock. See these letters
delivered; put the liveries to making; and desire Gratiano to
come anon to my lodging.   *[Exit a Servant.]*

    Laun. To him, father.   *105*

    Gob. God bless your worship!

    Bass. Gramercy! wouldst thou aught with me?

    Gob. Here's my son, sir, a poor boy,—

    Laun. Not a poor boy, sir, but the rich Jew's man; that
would, sir,—as my father shall specify,—   *110*

    Gob. He hath a great infection, sir, as one would say,
to serve—

    Laun. Indeed, the short and the long is, I serve the Jew,
and have a desire, as my father shall specify,—

    Gob. His master and he, saving your worship's reverence, *115*
are scarce cater-cousins,—

    Laun. To be brief, the very truth is that the Jew having
done me wrong, doth cause me,—as my father, being, I hope,
an old man, shall frutify unto you,—

    Gob. I have here a dish of doves that I would bestow *120*
upon your worship, and my suit is,—

    Laun. In very brief, the suit is impertinent to myself, as
your worship shall know by this honest old man; and, though
I say it, though old man, yet poor man, my father.

    Bass. One speak for both. What would you?   *125*

    Laun. Serve you, sir.

    Gob. That is the very defect of the matter, sir.

    Bass. I know thee well; thou hast obtain'd thy suit:
Shylock thy master spoke with me this day,
And hath preferr'd thee, if it be preferment   *130*
To leave a rich Jew's service, to become
The follower of so poor a gentleman.

    Laun. The old proverb is very well parted between my
master Shylock and you, sir: you have the grace of God,
sir, and he hath enough.   *135*

    Bass. Thou speak'st it well. Go, father, with thy son.
Take leave of thy old master, and inquire
My lodging out. *[To his followers.]* Give him a livery
More guarded than his fellows': see it done.

    Laun. Father, in. I cannot get a service, no; I have ne'er *140*
a tongue in my head. Well, *[Looking on his palm]* if any man
in Italy have a fairer table which doth offer to swear upon a
book, I shall have good fortune. Go to; here's a simple line of
life: here's a small trifle of wives: alas! fifteen wives is nothing:
a 'leven widows and nine maids is a simple coming-in for *145*
one man; and then to 'scape drowning thrice, and to be in
peril of my life with the edge of a feather-bed; here are simple
'scapes. Well, if Fortune be a woman, she's a good wench for
this gear. Father, come; I'll take my leave of the Jew in the

twinkling of an eye.   *Exit Clown [with Old Gobbo].*   *150*

    Bass. I pray thee, good Leonardo, think on this:
These things being bought, and orderly bestow'd,
Return in haste, for I do feast to-night
My best-esteem'd acquaintance: hie thee, go.

    Leon. My best endeavours shall be done herein.   *155*

Enter Gratiano.

    Gra. Where is your master?

    Leon.   Yonder, sir, he walks.

                                              [Exit.]

    Gra. Signior Bassanio!—

    Bass. Gratiano!

    Gra. I have a suit to you.   *160*

    Bass.   You have obtain'd it.

    Gra. You must not deny me: I must go with you to
Belmont.

    Bass. Why, then you must. But hear thee, Gratiano;
Thou art too wild, too rude and bold of voice;   *165*
Parts that become thee happily enough,
And in such eyes as ours appear not faults;
But where thou art not known, why, there they show
Something too liberal. Pray thee, take pain
To allay with some cold drops of modesty   *170*
Thy skipping spirit, lest, through thy wild behaviour,
I be misconstru'd in the place I go to,
And lose my hopes.

    Gra.   Signior Bassanio, hear me:
If I do not put on a sober habit,   *175*
Talk with respect, and swear but now and then,
Wear prayer-books in my pocket, look demurely,
Nay more, while grace is saying, hood mine eyes
Thus with my hat, and sigh, and say 'amen;'
Use all the observance of civility,   *180*
Like one well studied in a sad ostent
To please his grandam, never trust me more.

    Bass. Well, we shall see your bearing.

    Gra. Nay, but I bar to-night; you shall not gauge me
By what we do to-night.   *185*

    Bass.   No, that were pity:
I would entreat you rather to put on
Your boldest suit of mirth, for we have friends
That purpose merriment. But fare you well:
I have some business.   *190*

    Gra. And I must to Lorenzo and the rest;
But we will visit you at supper-time.   *Exeunt.*

❧ Scene Third ❧

[The Same. A Room in Shylock's House]
Enter Jessica and the Clown.

    Jes. I am sorry thou wilt leave my father so:
Our house is hell, and thou, a merry devil,
Didst rob it of some taste of tediousness.
But fare thee well; there is a ducat for thee:

98, 99 **God has any ground:** *He had little in Venice*   107 **Gramercy:** *grand merci, many
thanks*   116 **cater-cousins:** *speaking acquaintances*   119 **frutify:** *i.e., notify (?)*   122
impertinent: *i.e., pertinent, relating*   130 **preferr'd:** *recommended* **preferment:** *advancement*   133 **The old proverb;** *cf. n.*   139 **guarded:** *adorned with facings*   142 **table;**
cf. n.   145 **simple coming-in:** *small inheritance*

154 **hie thee:** *hurry up*   169 **liberal:** *unrestrained*   175 **habit:** *behavior*   178 **hood:**
hats were worn at meals, but removed during grace   181 **studied:** *rehearsed* **sad ostent:**
serious appearance   3 **taste:** *small bit*

And, Launcelot, soon at supper shalt thou see   *5*
Lorenzo, who is thy new master's guest:
Give him this letter; do it secretly;
And so farewell: I would not have my father
See me in talk with thee.

    Laun. Adieu! tears exhibit my tongue. Most beautiful   *10*
pagan, most sweet Jew! If a Christian did not play the knave
and get thee, I am much deceived. But, adieu! these foolish
drops do somewhat drown my manly spirit: adieu!   *Exit.*

    Jes. Farewell, good Launcelot.
Alack, what heinous sin is it in me   *15*
To be asham'd to be my father's child!
But though I am a daughter to his blood,
I am not to his manners. O Lorenzo!
If thou keep promise, I shall end this strife,
Become a Christian, and thy loving wife.   *Exit. 20*

❧ SCENE FOURTH ❧

[The Same. A Street]
Enter Gratiano, Lorenzo, Salarino, and Salanio.

    Lor. Nay, we will slink away in supper-time,
Disguise us at my lodging, and return
All in an hour.

    Gra. We have not made good preparation.
    Salar. We have not spoke us yet of torch-bearers.   *5*
    Salan. 'Tis vile, unless it may be quaintly order'd,
And better, in my mind, not undertook.

    Lor. 'Tis now but four o'clock: we have two hours
To furnish us.

Enter Launcelot, with a letter.

        Friend Launcelot, what's the news?   *10*
    Laun. An it shall please you to break up this, it shall
seem to signify.

    Lor. I know the hand: in faith, 'tis a fair hand;
And whiter than the paper it writ on
Is the fair hand that writ.   *15*

    Gra.   Love news, in faith.
    Laun. By your leave, sir.
    Lor. Whither goest thou?
    Laun. Marry, sir, to bid my old master, the Jew, to sup
tonight with my new master, the Christian.   *20*
    Lor. Hold here, take this: tell gentle Jessica
I will not fail her; speak it privately.
Go, gentlemen,   *[Exit Clown.]*
Will you prepare you for this masque to-night?
I am provided of a torch-bearer.   *25*
    Salar. Ay, marry, I'll be gone about it straight.
    Salan. And so will I.
    Lor.   Meet me and Gratiano
At Gratiano's lodging some hour hence.
    Salar. 'Tis good we do so.   *Exit [with Salanio]. 30*
    Gra. Was not that letter from fair Jessica?
    Lor. I must needs tell thee all. She hath directed
How I shall take her from her father's house;
What gold and jewels she is furnish'd with;

What page's suit she hath in readiness.   *35*
If e'er the Jew her father come to heaven,
It will be for his gentle daughter's sake;
And never dare misfortune cross her foot,
Unless she do it under this excuse,
That she is issue to a faithless Jew.   *40*
Come, go with me: peruse this as thou goest.
Fair Jessica shall be my torch-bearer.   *Exit [with Gratiano].*

❧ SCENE FIFTH ❧

[The Same. Before Shylock's House]
Enter Jew and his man that was the Clown.

    Shy. Well, thou shalt see, thy eyes shall be thy judge,
The difference of old Shylock and Bassanio:—
What, Jessica!—thou shalt not gormandize,
As thou hast done with me;—What, Jessica!—
And sleep and snore, and rend apparel out—   *5*
Why, Jessica, I say!
    Laun.   Why, Jessica!
    Shy. Who bids thee call? I do not bid thee call.
    Laun. Your worship was wont to tell me that
I could do nothing without bidding.   *10*

Enter Jessica.

    Jes. Call you? What is your will?
    Shy. I am bid forth to supper, Jessica:
There are my keys. But wherefore should I go?
I am not bid for love; they flatter me:
But yet I'll go in hate, to feed upon   *15*
The prodigal Christian. Jessica, my girl,
Look to my house. I am right loath to go:
There is some ill a-brewing towards my rest
For I did dream of money-bags to-night.
    Laun. I beseech you, sir, go: my young master doth   *20*
expect your reproach.
    Shy. So do I his.
    Laun. And they have conspired together: I will not say you
shall see a masque; but if you do, then it was not for nothing
that my nose fell a-bleeding on Black-Monday last, at six   *25*
o'clock i' the morning, falling out that year on Ash-Wednesday
was four year in the afternoon.
    Shy. What! are there masques? Hear you me, Jessica:
Lock up my doors; and when you hear the drum,
And the vile squealing of the wry-neck'd fife,   *30*
Clamber not you up to the casements then,
Nor thrust your head into the public street
To gaze on Christian fools with varnish'd faces,
But stop my house's ears, I mean my casements;
Let not the sound of shallow foppery enter   *35*
My sober house. By Jacob's staff I swear
I have no mind of feasting forth to-night;
But I will go. Go you before me, sirrah;
Say I will come.

10 exhibit, etc.: *express what my tongue would say*   **5 spoke us of:** *ordered*   **6 quaintly:**
ingeniously   **11 break up:** *break the seals of*

40 faithless: *without Christian faith*   **5 rend:** *wear*   **19 to-night:** *last night*   **25 nose,**
etc.: *a sign of bad luck, universally believed*   **Black-Monday:** *Easter Monday*   **26,27 falling**
out, etc.: *mere nonsense*   **30 wry-neck'd:** *played with the head twisted*   **33 with var-**
nish'd faces: *wearing painted masks (or perhaps painted with cosmetics)*   **35 foppery:**
folly   **36 Jacob's staff:** *cf. Gen. 32. 10; Heb. 11. 21*   **37 forth:** *out*

Laun. I will go before, sir. Mistress, look out at window,   *40*
for all this;
There will come a Christian by,
Will be worth a Jewess' eye.   *[Exit Launcelot.]*

Shy. What says that fool of Hagar's offspring, ha?
Jes. His words were, 'Farewell, mistress;' nothing else.   *45*
Shy. The patch is kind enough, but a huge feeder;
Snail-slow in profit, and he sleeps by day
More than the wild cat: drones hive not with me;
Therefore I part with him, and part with him
To one that I would have him help to waste   *50*
His borrow'd purse. Well, Jessica, go in:
Perhaps I will return immediately:
Do as I bid you; shut doors after you:
'Fast bind, fast find,'
A proverb never stale in thrifty mind.   *Exit. 55*

Jes. Farewell; and if my fortune be not crost,
I have a father, you a daughter, lost.   *Exit.*

❧ Scene Sixth ❧

[The Same]
Enter the Maskers, Gratiano and Salarino.

Gra. This is the penthouse under which Lorenzo
Desir'd us to make stand.
Salar.   His hour is almost past.
Gra. And it is marvel he out-dwells his hour,
For lovers ever run before the clock.   *5*
Salar. O! ten times faster Venus' pigeons fly
To seal love's bonds new-made, than they are wont
To keep obliged faith unforfeited!
Gra. That ever holds: who riseth from a feast
With that keen appetite that he sits down?   *10*
Where is the horse that doth untread again
His tedious measures with the unbated fire
That he did pace them first? All things that are,
Are with more spirit chased than enjoy'd.
How like a younker or a prodigal   *15*
The scarfed bark puts from her native bay,
Hugg'd and embraced by the strumpet wind!
How like the prodigal doth she return,
With over-weather'd ribs and ragged sails,
Lean, rent, and beggar'd by the strumpet wind!   *20*
Salar. Here comes Lorenzo: more of this hereafter.

Enter Lorenzo.

Lor. Sweet friends, your patience for my long abode;
Not I, but my affairs, have made you wait:
When you shall please to play the thieves for wives,
I'll watch as long for you then. Approach;   *25*
Here dwells my father Jew. Ho! who's within?

[Enter] Jessica above [in boy's clothes].

Jes. Who are you? Tell me, for more certainty,
Albeit I'll swear that I do know your tongue.

Lor. Lorenzo, and thy love.
Jes. Lorenzo, certain; and my love indeed,   *30*
For whom love I so much? And now who knows
But you, Lorenzo, whether I am yours?
Lor. Heaven and thy thoughts are witness that thou art.
Jes. Here, catch this casket; it is worth the pains.
I am glad 'tis night, you do not look on me,   *35*
For I am much asham'd of my exchange;
But love is blind, and lovers cannot see
The pretty follies that themselves commit;
For if they could, Cupid himself would blush
To see me thus transformed to a boy.   *40*
Lor. Descend, for you must be my torch-bearer.
Jes. What! must I hold a candle to my shames?
They in themselves, good sooth, are too-too light.
Why, 'tis an office of discovery, love,
And I should be obscur'd.   *45*
Lor.   So are you, sweet,
Even in the lovely garnish of a boy.
But come at once;
For the close night doth play the runaway,
And we are stay'd for at Bassanio's feast.   *50*
Jes. I will make fast the doors, and gild myself
With some more ducats, and be with you straight.

[Exit above.]

Gra. Now, by my hood, a Gentile and no Jew.
Lor. Beshrew me, but I love her heartily;
For she is wise, if I can judge of her,   *55*
And fair she is, if that mine eyes be true,
And true she is, as she hath prov'd herself;
And therefore, like herself, wise, fair, and true,
Shall she be placed in my constant soul.

Enter Jessica.

What art thou come? On, gentlemen; away!   *60*
Our masquing mates by this time for us stay.
                    Exit [with Jessica and Salarino].

Enter Antonio.

Ant. Who's there?
Gra. Signior Antonio!
Ant. Fie, fie, Gratiano! where are all the rest?
'Tis nine o'clock; our friends all stay for you.   *65*
No masque to-night: the wind is come about;
Bassanio presently will go aboard:
I have sent twenty out to seek for you.
Gra. I am glad on 't: I desire no more delight
Than to be under sail and gone to-night.   *Exeunt. 70*

❧ Scene Seventh ❧

[Belmont. A Room in Portia's House]
Enter Portia, with Morocco, and both their Trains.

Por. Go, draw aside the curtains, and discover
The several caskets to this noble prince.
Now make your choice.

43 **Jewess' eye**; *cf. n.*   44 **Hagar's**; *cf. Gen. 16.*   46 **patch**: *the dress of fools, hence term of contempt; cf. cross-patch*   47 **profit**: *acquired proficiency, training*   1 **penthouse**: *an attached shed, lean-to*   6 **Venus' pigeons**: *doves drew her chariot*   8 **obliged**: *contracted*   11 **untread**: *retrace*   15 **younker**: *eager youth*   16 **scarfed**; *cf. n.*   22 **abode**: *delay*

32 **yours**: *i.e., whether you love me*   36 **exchange**: *transformation*   44 **discovery**: *revealing*   47 **garnish**: *dress*   49 **close**: *secret*   54 **Beshrew**: *curse, a mild oath*   1 **discover**: *reveal*

Mor. The first, of gold, which this inscription bears:
Who chooseth me shall gain what many men desire.　　　5
The second, silver, which this promise carries:
Who chooseth me shall get as much as he deserves.
This third, dull lead, with warning all as blunt:
Who chooseth me must give and hazard all he hath.
How shall I know if I do choose the right?　　　10
　　Por. The one of them contains my picture, prince:
If you choose that, then I am yours withal.
　　Mor. Some god direct my judgment! Let me see:
I will survey the inscriptions back again:
What says this leaden casket?　　　15
Who chooseth me must give and hazard all he hath.
Must give: For what? for lead? hazard for lead?
This casket threatens. Men that hazard all
Do it in hope of fair advantages:
A golden mind stoops not to shows of dross;　　　20
I'll then nor give nor hazard aught for lead.
What says the silver with her virgin hue?
Who chooseth me shall get as much as he deserves.
As much as he deserves! Pause there, Morocco,
And weigh thy value with an even hand.　　　25
If thou be'st rated by thy estimation,
Thou dost deserve enough; and yet enough
May not extend so far as to the lady:
And yet to be afeard of my deserving
Were but a weak disabling of myself.　　　30
As much as I deserve! Why, that's the lady:
I do in birth deserve her, and in fortunes,
In graces, and in qualities of breeding;
But more than these, in love I do deserve.
What if I stray'd no further, but chose here?　　　35
Let's see once more this saying grav'd in gold:
Who chooseth me shall gain what many men desire.
Why, that's the lady: all the world desires her;
From the four corners of the earth they come,
To kiss this shrine, this mortal-breathing saint:　　　40
The Hyrcanian deserts and the vasty wilds
Of wide Arabia are as throughfares now
For princes to come view fair Portia:
The watery kingdom, whose ambitious head
Spits in the face of heaven, is no bar　　　45
To stop the foreign spirits, but they come,
As o'er a brook, to see fair Portia.
One of these three contains her heavenly picture.
Is 't like that lead contains her? 'Twere damnation
To think so base a thought: it were too gross　　　50
To rib her cerecloth in the obscure grave.
Or shall I think in silver she's immur'd,
Being ten times undervalu'd to tried gold?
O sinful thought! Never so rich a gem
Was set in worse than gold. They have in England　　　55
A coin that bears the figure of an angel
Stamped in gold, but that's insculp'd upon;
But here an angel in a golden bed
Lies all within. Deliver me the key:

Here do I choose, and thrive I as I may!　　　60
　　Por. There, take it, prince; and if my form lie there
Then I am yours.　　　　*[He unlocks the golden casket.]*
　　Mor.　　　　　O hell! what have we here?
A carrion Death, within whose empty eye
There is a written scroll. I'll read the writing.　　　65

　　'*All that glisters is not gold;*
　　Often have you heard that told:
　　Many a man his life hath sold
　　But my outside to behold:
　　Gilded tombs do worms infold.　　　70
　　Had you been as wise as bold,
　　Young in limbs, in judgment old,
　　Your answer had not been inscroll'd:
　　Fare you well; your suit is cold.'

Cold, indeed; and labour lost:　　　75
Then, farewell, heat, and welcome, frost!
Portia, adieu. I have too griev'd a heart
To take a tedious leave: thus losers part.　　*Exit [with his Train].*
　　Por. A gentle riddance. Draw the curtains: go.
Let all of his complexion choose me so.　　　80
　　　　　　　　　Flo[urish of] Cornets. Exeunt.

❧ SCENE EIGHTH ❧

[Venice. A Street]
Enter Salarino and Salanio.

　　Salar. Why, man, I saw Bassanio under sail:
With him is Gratiano gone along;
And in their ship I'm sure Lorenzo is not.
　　Salan. The villain Jew with outcries rais'd the duke,
Who went with him to search Bassanio's ship.　　　5
　　Salar. He came too late, the ship was under sail:
But there the duke was given to understand
That in a gondola were seen together
Lorenzo and his amorous Jessica.
Besides, Antonio certified the duke　　　10
They were not with Bassanio in his ship.
　　Salan. I never heard a passion so confus'd,
So strange, outrageous, and so variable,
As the dog Jew did utter in the streets:
'My daughter! O my ducats! O my daughter!　　　15
Fled with a Christian! O my Christian ducats!
Justice! the law! my ducats, and my daughter!
A sealed bag, two sealed bags of ducats,
Of double ducats, stol'n from me by my daughter!
And jewels! two stones, two rich and precious stones,　　　20
Stol'n by my daughter! Justice! find the girl!
She hath the stones upon her, and the ducats.'
　　Salar. Why, all the boys in Venice follow him,
Crying, his stones, his daughter, and his ducats.
　　Salan. Let good Antonio look he keep his day,　　　25
Or he shall pay for this.
　　Salar.　　　　　　Marry, well remember'd.
I reason'd with a Frenchman yesterday,
Who told me,—in the narrow seas that part

---

8 **all as blunt:** *equally blunt*　　12 **withal:** *therewith*　　25 **with an even hand:** *impartially*　　26 **rated . . . estimation:** *valued according to thy worth*　　30 **disabling:** *disparagement*　　33 *In natural and acquired advantages*　　36 **grav'd:** *engraved*　　40 **shrine:** *image*　　41 **Hyrcanian:** *south of the Caspian Sea*　　42 **throughfares:** *thoroughfares*　　51 **rib:** *enclose*　　**cerecloth:** *winding sheet*　　53 **undervalu'd:** *inferior in value*　　56 **angel:** *gold coin worth 10s.*　　57 **insculp'd upon:** *engraved on the outside*

12 **passion:** *sorrow*　　28 **reason'd:** *talked*

The French and English,—there miscarried 30
A vessel of our country richly fraught.
I thought upon Antonio when he told me,
And wish'd in silence that it were not his.

Salan. You were best to tell Antonio what you hear;
Yet do not suddenly, for it may grieve him. 35

Salar. A kinder gentleman treads not the earth.
I saw Bassanio and Antonio part:
Bassanio told him he would make some speed
Of his return: he answer'd 'Do not so;
Slubber not business for my sake, Bassanio, 40
But stay the very riping of the time;
And for the Jew's bond which he hath of me,
Let it not enter in your mind of love:
Be merry, and employ your chiefest thoughts
To courtship and such fair ostents of love 45
As shall conveniently become you there:'
And even there, his eye being big with tears,
Turning his face, he put his hand behind him,
And with affection wondrous sensible
He wrung Bassanio's hand; and so they parted. 50

Salan. I think he only loves the world for him.
I pray thee, let us go and find him out,
And quicken his embraced heaviness
With some delight or other.

Salar. Do we so. *Exeunt.* 55

❧ SCENE NINTH ❧

[Belmont. A Room in Portia's House]
Enter Nerissa, and a Servitor.

Ner. Quick, quick, I pray thee; draw the curtain straight:
The Prince of Arragon hath ta'en his oath,
And comes to his election presently.

Enter Arragon, his train, and Portia. Flor[ish of] Cornets.

Por. Behold, there stand the caskets, noble prince:
If you choose that wherein I am contain'd, 5
Straight shall our nuptial rites be solemniz'd;
But if you fail, without more speech, my lord,
You must be gone from hence immediately.

Ar. I am enjoin'd by oath to observe three things:
First, never to unfold to any one 10
Which casket 'twas I chose; next, if I fail
Of the right casket, never in my life
To woo a maid in way of marriage;
Lastly,
If I do fail in fortune of my choice, 15
Immediately to leave you and be gone.

Por. To these injunctions every one doth swear
That comes to hazard for my worthless self.

Ar. And so have I address'd me. Fortune now
To my heart's hope! Gold, silver, and base lead. 20
Who chooseth me must give and hazard all he hath:
You shall look fairer, ere I give or hazard.

What says the golden chest? ha! let me see:
Who chooseth me shall gain what many men desire.
What many men desire! that 'many' may be meant 25
By the fool multitude, that choose by show,
Not learning more than the fond eye doth teach,
Which pries not to the interior, but, like the martlet,
Builds in the weather on the outward wall,
Even in the force and road of casualty. 30
I will not choose what many men desire,
Because I will not jump with common spirits
And rank me with the barbarous multitude.
Why, then to thee, thou silver treasure-house;
Tell me once more what title thou dost bear: 35
Who chooseth me shall get as much as he deserves.
And well said too; for who shall go about
To cozen fortune and be honourable
Without the stamp of merit? Let none presume
To wear an undeserved dignity. 40
O! that estates, degrees, and offices
Were not deriv'd corruptly, and that clear honour
Were purchas'd by the merit of the wearer.
How many then should cover that stand bare;
How many be commanded that command; 45
How much low peasantry would then be glean'd
From the true seed of honour; and how much honour
Pick'd from the chaff and ruin of the times
To be new varnish'd! Well, but to my choice:
Who chooseth me shall get as much as he deserves. 50
I will assume desert. Give me a key for this,
And instantly unlock my fortunes here.

[He opens the silver casket.]

Por. Too long a pause for that which you find there.

Ar. What's here? the portrait of a blinking idiot,
Presenting me a schedule! I will read it. 55
How much unlike art thou to Portia!
How much unlike my hopes and my deservings!
Who chooseth me shall have as much as he deserves.
Did I deserve no more than a fool's head?
Is that my prize? are my deserts no better? 60

Por. To offend, and judge, are distinct offices,
And of opposed natures.

Ar.   What is here?

'The fire seven times tried this:
Seven times tried that judgment is 65
That did never choose amiss.
Some there be that shadows kiss;
Such have but a shadow's bliss:
There be fools alive, I wis,
Silver'd o'er; and so was this. 70
Take what wife you will to bed,
I will ever be your head:
So be gone, sir: you are sped.'

Still more fool I shall appear

26 By: *for*   **27 fond:** *foolish*   **28 martlet:** *martin (see Macbeth I.vi.5).*   **30 force and road:** *'in vi et via,' i.e., where accident occurs with the greatest violence and frequency*   **32 jump:** *agree*   **33 rank me:** *class myself*   **37 go about:** *undertake*   **38 cozen:** *cheat honourable: worshipful, honored*   **41 estates:** *status, position* **degrees:** *ranks*   **42 deriv'd:** *inherited*   **44 cover:** *wear their hats (in token of social dignity)*   **47 true . . . honour:** *scions of the great*   **48 chaff and ruin:** *riff-raff*   **51 assume:** *claim*   **61 To offend, etc.:** *the criminal need not judge his own case*   **69 I wis:** *corruption of 'gewis,' certainly*

40 Slubber: *spoil by scamping*   **43 mind of love:** *loving mind*   **45 ostents:** *displays*   **46 conveniently:** *properly*   **49 sensible:** *charged with feeling*   **53 embraced heaviness:** *the sorrow that he so clings to*   **3 election:** *choice*   **18 comes to hazard:** *incurs risk*   **19 address'd me:** *prepared myself*

By the time I linger here: *75*
With one fool's head I came to woo,
But I go away with two.
Sweet, adieu. I'll keep my oath,
Patiently to bear my wroth.   *[Exit Arragon with his Train.]*
    Por. Thus hath the candle sing'd the moth.   *80*
O, these deliberate fools! when they do choose,
They have the wisdom by their wit to lose.
    Ner. The ancient saying is no heresy:
'Hanging and wiving goes by destiny.'
    Por. Come, draw the curtain, Nerissa.   *85*

Enter Messenger.

    Mes. Where is my lady?
    Por.   Here; what would my lord?
    Mes. Madam, there is alighted at your gate
A young Venetian, one that comes before
To signify the approaching of his lord;   *90*
From whom he bringeth sensible regreets,
To wit,—besides commends and courteous breath,—
Gifts of rich value. Yet I have not seen
So likely an embassador of love.
A day in April never came so sweet,   *95*
To show how costly summer was at hand,
As this fore-spurrer comes before his lord.
    Por. No more, I pray thee: I am half afeard
Thou wilt say anon he is some kin to thee,
Thou spend'st such high-day wit in praising him.   *100*
Come, come, Nerissa; for I long to see
Quick Cupid's post that comes so mannerly.
    Ner. Bassanio, lord Love, if thy will it be!   *Exeunt.*

ACT THIRD ❧ SCENE FIRST

[Venice. A Street]
Enter Salanio and Salarino.

    Salan. Now, what news on the Rialto?
    Salar. Why, yet it lives there unchecked that Antonio hath a
ship of rich lading wracked on the narrow seas; the Goodwins,
I think they call the place; a very dangerous flat, and fatal,
where the carcasses of many a tall ship lie buried, as they   *5*
say, if my gossip Report be an honest woman of her word.
    Salan. I would she were as lying a gossip in that as ever
knapped ginger, or made her neighbours believe she wept for
the death of a third husband. But it is true,—without any slips
of prolixity or crossing the plain highway of talk,—that the   *10*
good Antonio, the honest Antonio,—O, that I had a title
good enough to keep his name company!—
    Salar. Come, the full stop.
    Salan. Ha! what sayst thou? Why, the end is, he hath lost
a ship.   *15*
    Salar. I would it might prove the end of his losses.
    Salan. Let me say 'amen' betimes, lest the devil cross my
prayer, for here he comes in the likeness of a Jew.

Enter Shylock.

How now, Shylock! what news among the merchants?
    Shy. You knew, none so well, none so well as you, of   *20*
my daughter's flight.
    Salar. That's certain: I, for my part, knew the tailor that
made the wings she flew withal.
    Salan. And Shylock, for his own part, knew the bird was
fledged; and then it is the complexion of them all to leave   *25*
the dam.
    Shy. She is damned for it.
    Salar. That's certain, if the devil may be her judge.
    Shy. My own flesh and blood to rebel!
    Salar. Out upon it, old carrion! rebels it at these years?   *30*
    Shy. I say my daughter is my flesh and blood.
    Salar. There is more difference between thy flesh and hers
than between jet and ivory; more between your bloods than
there is between red wine and Rhenish. But tell us, do you
hear whether Antonio have had any loss at sea or no?   *35*
    Shy. There I have another bad match: a bankrupt, a prodi-
gal, who dare scarce show his head on the Rialto; a beggar,
that was used to come so smug upon the mart; let him look to
his bond: he was wont to call me usurer; let him look to his
bond: he was wont to lend money for a Christian courtesy;   *40*
let him look to his bond.
    Salar. Why, I am sure, if he forfeit thou wilt not take his
flesh: what's that good for?
    Shy. To bait fish withal: if it feed nothing else, it will feed
my revenge. He hath disgraced me, and hindered me half   *45*
a million, laughed at my losses, mocked at my gains, scorned
my nation, thwarted my bargains, cooled my friends, heated
mine enemies; and what's his reason? I am a Jew. Hath not a
Jew eyes? hath not a Jew hands, organs, dimensions, senses, affections, passions? fed with the same food, hurt with the   *50*
same weapons, subject to the same diseases, healed by the same
means, warmed and cooled by the same winter and summer, as
a Christian is? If you prick us, do we not bleed? if you tickle
us, do we not laugh? if you poison us, do we not die? and if
you wrong us, shall we not revenge? If we are like you in   *55*
the rest, we will resemble you in that. If a Jew wrong a Christian, what is his humility? Revenge. If a Christian wrong a
Jew, what should his sufferance be by Christian example? Why,
revenge. The villainy you teach me I will execute, and it shall
go hard but I will better the instruction.   *60*

Enter a man from Antonio.

    Man. Gentlemen, my master Antonio is at his house, and
desires to speak with you both.
    Salar. We have been up and down to seek him.

Enter Tubal.

    Salan. Here comes another of the tribe: a third cannot be
matched, unless the devil himself turn Jew.   *65*

Exeunt Gentlemen [i.e. Salanio, Salarino, and Antonio's man].

    Shy. How now, Tubal! what news from Genoa? Hast thou
found my daughter?
    Tub. I often came where I did hear of her, but cannot find
her.
    Shy. Why there, there, there, there! a diamond gone,   *70*
cost me two thousand ducats in Frankfort! The curse never fell

---

87 my lord; *cf. n.*   **91 sensible:** *substantial, meaning his gifts* **regreets:** *greetings*   **94 likely:**
promising   **100 high-day:** *holiday, meaning ornate, dressed for holiday*   **3 wracked:**
wrecked   **3 narrow seas:** *English Channel*   **8 knapped:** *munched (pronounce the 'k')*

23 withal: *with; cf. n.*   **25 complexion:** *disposition*   **57 humility:** *sufferance*

upon our nation till now; I never felt it till now: two thousand ducats in that; and other precious, precious jewels. I would my daughter were dead at my foot, and the jewels in her ear! would she were hearsed at my foot, and the ducats in her 75 coffin! No news of them? Why, so: and I know not what's spent in the search: Why thou—loss upon loss! the thief gone with so much, and so much to find the thief; and no satisfaction, no revenge: nor no ill luck stirring but what lights on my shoulders; no sighs but of my breathing; no tears but 80 of my shedding.

Tub. Yes, other men have ill luck too. Antonio, as I heard in Genoa,—

Shy. What, what, what? ill luck, ill luck?

Tub. —hath an argosy cast away, coming from Tripolis. 85

Shy. I thank God! I thank God! Is it true? is it true?

Tub. I spoke with some of the sailors that escaped the wrack.

Shy. I thank thee, good Tubal. Good news, good news! ha, ha! Where? in Genoa? 90

Tub. Your daughter spent in Genoa, as I heard, one night, fourscore ducats.

Shy. Thou stick'st a dagger in me: I shall never see my gold again: fourscore ducats at a sitting! fourscore ducats!

Tub. There came divers of Antonio's creditors in my 95 company to Venice, that swear he cannot choose but break.

Shy. I am very glad of it: I'll plague him; I'll torture him: I am glad of it.

Tub. One of them showed me a ring that he had of your daughter for a monkey. 100

Shy. Out upon her! Thou torturest me, Tubal: it was my turquoise; I had it of Leah when I was a bachelor: I would not have given it for a wilderness of monkeys.

Tub. But Antonio is certainly undone.

Shy. Nay, that's true, that's very true. Go, Tubal, fee me 105 an officer; bespeak him a fortnight before. I will have the heart of him, if he forfeit; for, were he out of Venice, I can make what merchandise I will. Go, go, Tubal, and meet me at our synagogue; go, good Tubal; at our synagogue, Tubal.

Exeunt.

❦ Scene Second ❧

[Belmont. A Room in Portia's House]
Enter Bassanio, Portia, Gratiano, [Nerissa,] and all their Train.

Por. I pray you, tarry: pause a day or two
Before you hazard; for, in choosing wrong,
I lose your company: therefore, forbear awhile.
There's something tells me, but it is not love,
I would not lose you; and you know yourself, 5
Hate counsels not in such a quality.
But lest you should not understand me well,—
And yet a maiden hath no tongue but thought,—
I would detain you here some month or two
Before you venture for me. I could teach you 10
How to choose right, but then I am forsworn;
So will I never be: so may you miss me;
But if you do, you'll make me wish a sin,

That I had been forsworn. Beshrew your eyes,
They have o'erlook'd me and divided me: 15
One half of me is yours, the other half yours,
Mine own, I would say; but if mine, then yours,
And so all yours. O! these naughty times
Put bars between the owners and their rights;
And so, though yours, not yours. Prove it so, 20
Let fortune go to hell for it, not I.
I speak too long; but 'tis to peise the time,
To eke it and to draw it out in length,
To stay you from election.
        Bass.   Let me choose; 25
For as I am, I live upon the rack.
    Por. Upon the rack, Bassanio! then confess
What treason there is mingled with your love.
    Bass. None but that ugly treason of mistrust,
Which makes me fear th' enjoying of my love: 30
There may as well be amity and life
'Tween snow and fire, as treason and my love.
    Por. Ay, but I fear you speak upon the rack,
Where men enforced do speak anything.
    Bass. Promise me life, and I'll confess the truth. 35
    Por. Well then, confess, and live.
    Bass.   'Confess' and 'love'
Had been the very sum of my confession:
O happy torment, when my torturer
Doth teach me answers for deliverance! 40
But let me to my fortune and the caskets.
    Por. Away then! I am lock'd in one of them:
If you do love me, you will find me out.
Nerissa and the rest, stand all aloof.
Let music sound while he doth make his choice; 45
Then, if he lose, he makes a swan-like end,
Fading in music: that the comparison
May stand more proper, my eye shall be the stream
And watery death-bed for him. He may win;
And what is music then? then music is 50
Even as the flourish when true subjects bow
To a new-crowned monarch: such it is
As are those dulcet sounds in break of day
That creep into the dreaming bridegroom's ear,
And summon him to marriage. Now he goes, 55
With no less presence, but with much more love,
Than young Alcides, when he did redeem
The virgin tribute paid by howling Troy
To the sea-monster: I stand for sacrifice;
The rest aloof are the Dardanian wives, 60
With bleared visages, come forth to view
The issue of the exploit. Go, Hercules!
Live thou, I live: with much, much more dismay
I view the fight than thou that mak'st the fray.
Here Music. A Song the whilst Bassanio comments on the 65
caskets to himself.

    'Tell me where is fancy bred,
        Or in the heart or in the head?
        How begot, how nourished?

---

77 **Why thou;** *cf. n.*   90 **Where? in Genoa?;** *cf. n.*   105, 106 **fee . . . officer:** *engage a sheriff's officer for me*   108 **merchandise:** *business*   6 *Hate prompts no such advice*

15 **o'erlook'd:** *looked over, i.e., bewitched*   20,21 **Prove it so,** *etc.; cf. n.*   22 **peise:** *weigh down, retard*   23 **eke:** *add to*   29 **mistrust:** *doubt, uncertainty*   30 **fear:** *feel apprehensive about*   31 **amity and life:** *affectionate intercourse*   51 **flourish:** *trumpets at coronations*   56, 57 **With . . . Alcides:** *cf. n.* **presence:** *dignity of person*   60 **Dardanian:** *Trojan*   67 **fancy:** *love*

Reply, reply.   70
It is engender'd in the eyes,
With gazing fed; and fancy dies
In the cradle where it lies.
     Let us all ring fancy's knell:
     I'll begin it,—Ding, dong, bell.   75

All. Ding, dong, bell.
     Bass. So may the outward shows be least themselves:
The world is still deceiv'd with ornament.
In law, what plea so tainted and corrupt
But, being season'd with a gracious voice,   80
Obscures the show of evil? In religion,
What damned error, but some sober brow
Will bless it and approve it with a text,
Hiding the grossness with fair ornament?
There is no vice so simple but assumes   85
Some mark of virtue on his outward parts.
How many cowards, whose hearts are all as false
As stairs of sand, wear yet upon their chins
The beards of Hercules and frowning Mars,
Who, inward search'd, have livers white as milk;   90
And these assume but valour's excrement
To render them redoubted! Look on beauty,
And you shall see 'tis purchas'd by the weight;
Which therein works a miracle in nature,
Making them lightest that wear most of it: 95
So are those crisped snaky golden locks
Which make such wanton gambols with the wind,
Upon supposed fairness, often known
To be the dowry of a second head,
The skull that bred them in the sepulchre.   100
Thus ornament is but the guiled shore
To a most dangerous sea; the beauteous scarf
Veiling an Indian beauty; in a word,
The seeming truth which cunning times put on
To entrap the wisest. Therefore, thou gaudy gold,   105
Hard food for Midas, I will none of thee;
Nor none of thee, thou pale and common drudge
'Tween man and man: but thou, thou meagre lead,
Which rather threat'nest than dost promise aught,
Thy plainness moves me more than eloquence,   110
And here choose I: joy be the consequence!
     Por. [*Aside.*] How all the other passions fleet to air,
As doubtful thoughts, and rash-embrac'd despair,
And shuddering fear, and green-ey'd jealousy.
O love! be moderate; allay thy ecstasy;   115
In measure rain thy joy; scant this excess;
I feel too much thy blessing; make it less,
For fear I surfeit!
     Bass.   What find I here?

                [*Opening the leaden casket.*]
Fair Portia's counterfeit! What demi-god   120
Hath come so near creation? Move these eyes?
Or whether, riding on the balls of mine,
Seem they in motion? Here are sever'd lips,
Parted with sugar breath; so sweet a bar
Should sunder such sweet friends. Here, in her hairs   125

The painter plays the spider, and hath woven
A golden mesh to entrap the hearts of men
Faster than gnats in cobwebs: but her eyes!—
How could he see to do them? having made one,
Methinks it should have power to steal both his   130
And leave itself unfurnish'd: yet look, how far
The substance of my praise doth wrong this shadow
In underprizing it, so far this shadow
Doth limp behind the substance. Here's the scroll,
The continent and summary of my fortune.   135

     'You that choose not by the view,
     Chance as fair and choose as true!
     Since this fortune falls to you,
     Be content and seek no new.
     If you be well pleas'd with this   140
     And hold your fortune for your bliss,
     Turn you where your lady is
     And claim her with a loving kiss.'

A gentle scroll. Fair lady, by your leave;   [*Kissing her.*]
I come by note, to give and to receive.   145
Like one of two contending in a prize,
That thinks he hath done well in people's eyes,
Hearing applause and universal shout,
Giddy in spirit, still gazing in a doubt
Whether those peals of praise be his or no;   150
So, thrice-fair lady, stand I, even so,
As doubtful whether what I see be true,
Until confirm'd, sign'd, ratified by you.
     Por. You see me, Lord Bassanio, where I stand,
Such as I am: though for myself alone   155
I would not be ambitious in my wish,
To wish myself much better; yet for you
I would be trebled twenty times myself;
A thousand times more fair, ten thousand times
More rich;   160
That only to stand high in your account,
I might in virtues, beauties, livings, friends,
Exceed account: but the full sum of me
Is sum of nothing; which, to term in gross,
Is an unlesson'd girl, unschool'd, unpractis'ed;   165
Happy in this, she is not yet so old
But she may learn; happier than this,
She is not bred so dull but she can learn;
Happiest of all is that her gentle spirit
Commits itself to yours to be directed,   170
As from her lord, her governor, her king.
Myself and what is mine to you and yours
Is now converted: but now I was the lord
Of this fair mansion, master of my servants,
Queen o'er myself; and even now, but now,   175
This house, these servants, and this same myself
Are yours, my lord. I give them with this ring;
Which when you part from, lose, or give away,
Let it presage the ruin of your love,
And be my vantage to exclaim on you.   180
     Bass. Madam, you have bereft me of all words,

---

83 approve: *prove, ratify*   **85 simple:** *pure, unmixed*   **86 his:** *its*   **91 excrement:**
excrescence   **95 lightest:** *i.e., most frivolous*   **96 crisped:** *curled*   **98 Upon supposed**
fairness; *cf. n.*   **101 guiled:** *guileful*   **103 Veiling, etc.;** *cf. n.*   **106 Midas:** *all he*
touched, including food, turned to gold   **113 As:** *such as*   **116 rain;** *cf. n.*

131 unfurnish'd: *unaccompanied by its mate*   **135 continent:** *that which contains*   **145**
note: *authorization in writing*   **163 account:** *calculation*   **164 term in gross:** *sum*
up   **166 Happy:** *fortunate*   **180 vantage:** *opportunity, occasion*

Only my blood speaks to you in my veins;
And there is such confusion in my powers,
As, after some oration fairly spoke
By a beloved prince, there doth appear   185
Among the buzzing pleased multitude;
Where every something, being blent together,
Turns to a wild of nothing, save of joy,
Express'd and not express'd. But when this ring
Parts from this finger, then parts life from hence: 190
O! then be bold to say Bassanio's dead.
   Ner. My lord and lady, it is now our time,
That have stood by and seen our wishes prosper,
To cry, good joy. Good joy, my lord and lady!
   Gra. My Lord Bassanio and my gentle lady,   195
I wish you all the joy that you can wish;
For I am sure you can wish none from me:
And when your honours mean to solemnize
The bargain of your faith, I do beseech you,
Even at that time I may be married too.   200
   Bass. With all my heart, so thou canst get a wife.
   Gra. I thank your lordship, you have got me one.
My eyes, my lord, can look as swift as yours:
You saw the mistress, I beheld the maid;
You lov'd, I lov'd; for intermission   205
No more pertains to me, my lord, than you.
Your fortune stood upon the caskets there,
And so did mine too, as the matter falls;
For wooing here until I sweat again,
And swearing till my very roof was dry   210
With oaths of love, at last, if promise last,
I got a promise of this fair one here
To have her love, provided that your fortune
Achiev'd her mistress.
   Por.   Is this true, Nerissa?   215
   Ner. Madam, it is, so you stand pleas'd withal.
   Bass. And do you, Gratiano, mean good faith?
   Gra. Yes, faith, my lord.
   Bass. Our feast shall be much honour'd in your marriage.
   Gra. We'll play with them the first boy for a thousand   220
ducats.
   Ner. What! and stake down?
   Gra. No; we shall ne'er win at that sport, and stake down.
But who comes here? Lorenzo and his infidel?
What! and my old Venetian friend, Salanio?   225

       Enter Lorenzo, Jessica, and Salanio.

   Bass. Lorenzo, and Salanio, welcome hither,
If that the youth of my new interest here
Have power to bid you welcome. By your leave,
I bid my very friends and countrymen,
Sweet Portia, welcome.   230
   Por.   So do I, my lord:
They are entirely welcome.
   Lor. I thank your honour. For my part, my lord,
My purpose was not to have seen you here;
But meeting with Salanio by the way,   235
He did entreat me, past all saying nay,
To come with him along.

   Salan.   I did, my lord,
And I have reason for it. Signior Antonio
Commends him to you.   *[Gives Bassanio a letter.]*   240
   Bass.   Ere I ope his letter,
I pray you, tell me how my good friend doth.
   Salan. Not sick, my lord, unless it be in mind;
Nor well, unless in mind: his letter there
Will show you his estate.   *[Bassanio] Opens the Letter.*   245
   Gra. Nerissa, cheer yon stranger; bid her welcome.
Your hand, Salanio. What's the news from Venice?
How doth that royal merchant, good Antonio?
I know he will be glad of our success;
We are the Jasons, we have won the fleece.   250
   Salan. I would you had won the fleece that he hath lost.
   Por. There are some shrewd contents in yon same paper,
That steals the colour from Bassanio's cheek:
Some dear friend dead, else nothing in the world
Could turn so much the constitution   255
Of any constant man. What, worse and worse!
With leave, Bassanio; I am half yourself,
And I must freely have the half of anything
That this same paper brings you.
   Bass.   O sweet Portia!   260
Here are a few of the unpleasant'st words
That ever blotted paper. Gentle lady,
When I did first impart my love to you,
I freely told you all the wealth I had
Ran in my veins, I was a gentleman: 265
And then I told you true; and yet, dear lady,
Rating myself at nothing, you shall see
How much I was a braggart. When I told you
My state was nothing, I should then have told you
That I was worse than nothing; for, indeed,   270
I have engag'd myself to a dear friend,
Engag'd my friend to his mere enemy,
To feed my means. Here is a letter, lady;
The paper as the body of my friend,
And every word in it a gaping wound,   275
Issuing life-blood. But is it true, Salanio?
Hath all his ventures fail'd? What, not one hit?
From Tripolis, from Mexico, and England,
From Lisbon, Barbary, and India?
And not one vessel 'scape the dreadful touch   280
Of merchant-marring rocks?
   Salan.   Not one, my lord.
Besides, it should appear, that if he had
The present money to discharge the Jew,
He would not take it. Never did I know   285
A creature, that did bear the shape of man,
So keen and greedy to confound a man.
He plies the duke at morning and at night,
And doth impeach the freedom of the state,
If they deny him justice: twenty merchants,   290
The duke himself, and the magnificoes
Of greatest port, have all persuaded with him;
But none can drive him from the envious plea
Of forfeiture, of justice, and his bond.

---

182 Only: *an adjective, my blood only*   **197 from me:** *at my expense*   **205 intermission;** *cf. n.*   **209 until … again:** *with all my power*   **210 roof:** *roof of my mouth*   **225 Salanio;** *cf. n.*   **229 very:** *true*

245 estate: *state, condition*   **252 shrewd:** *evil*   **255 constitution:** *frame of mind, equanimity*   **256 constant:** *steadfast*   **272 mere:** *absolute*   **277 hit:** *successful venture*   **287 confound:** *destroy*   **289 freedom:** *equal rights*   **291 magnificoes:** *magnates*   **292 port:** *station*   **293 envious:** *hateful*

Jes. When I was with him, I have heard him swear   *295*
To Tubal and to Chus, his countrymen,
That he would rather have Antonio's flesh
Than twenty times the value of the sum
That he did owe him; and I know, my lord,
If law, authority, and power deny not,   *300*
It will go hard with poor Antonio.

    Por. Is it your dear friend that is thus in trouble?

    Bass. The dearest friend to me, the kindest man,
The best-condition'd and unwearied spirit
In doing courtesies, and one in whom   *305*
The ancient Roman honour more appears
Than any that draws breath in Italy.

    Por. What sum owes he the Jew?

    Bass. For me, three thousand ducats.

    Por.   What, no more?   *310*
Pay him six thousand, and deface the bond;
Double six thousand, and then treble that,
Before a friend of this description
Shall lose a hair thorough Bassanio's fault.
First go with me to church and call me wife,   *315*
And then away to Venice to your friend;
For never shall you lie by Portia's side
With an unquiet soul. You shall have gold
To pay the petty debt twenty times over:
When it is paid, bring your true friend along.   *320*
My maid Nerissa and myself meantime,
Will live as maids and widows. Come, away!
For you shall hence upon your wedding-day.
Bid your friends welcome, show a merry cheer;
Since you are dear bought, I will love you dear.   *325*
But let me hear the letter of your friend.

    Bass. 'Sweet Bassanio, my ships have all miscarried, my credi-
tors grow cruel, my estate is very low, my bond to the Jew is
forfeit; and since, in paying it, it is impossible I should live, all
debts are cleared between you and I, if I might but see you
at my death. Notwithstanding, use your pleasure: if your love
do not persuade you to come, let not my letter.'

    Por. O love, dispatch all business, and be gone!

    Bass. Since I have your good leave to go away,
I will make haste; but, till I come again,   *335*
No bed shall e'er be guilty of my stay,
Nor rest be interposer 'twixt us twain.   *Exeunt.*

❧ Scene Third ❧

[Venice. A Street]
Enter the Jew, and Salarino, and Antonio, and the Gaoler.

    Shy. Gaoler, look to him: tell not me of mercy;
This is the fool that lent out money gratis:
Gaoler, look to him.

    Ant.   Hear me yet, good Shylock.

    Shy. I'll have my bond; speak not against my bond: *5*
I have sworn an oath that I will have my bond.
Thou call'dst me dog before thou hadst a cause,
But, since I am a dog, beware my fangs:

The duke shall grant me justice. I do wonder,
Thou naughty gaoler, that thou art so fond   *10*
To come abroad with him at his request.

    Ant. I pray thee, hear me speak.

    Shy. I'll have my bond; I will not hear thee speak:
I'll have my bond, and therefore speak no more.
I'll not be made a soft and dull-eyed fool,   *15*
To shake the head, relent, and sigh, and yield
To Christian intercessors. Follow not;
I'll have no speaking; I will have my bond.   *Exit Jew.*

    Salar. It is the most impenetrable cur
That ever kept with men.   *20*

    Ant.   Let him alone:
I'll follow him no more with bootless prayers.
He seeks my life; his reason well I know.
I oft deliver'd from his forfeitures
Many that have at times made moan to me;   *25*
Therefore he hates me.

    Salar.   I am sure the duke
Will never grant this forfeiture to hold.

    Ant. The duke cannot deny the course of law:
For the commodity that strangers have   *30*
With us in Venice, if it be denied,
'Twill much impeach the justice of the state;
Since that the trade and profit of the city
Consisteth of all nations. Therefore, go:
These griefs and losses have so bated me,   *35*
That I shall hardly spare a pound of flesh
To-morrow to my bloody creditor.
Well, gaoler, on. Pray God, Bassanio come
To see me pay his debt, and then I care not!   *Exeunt.*

❧ Scene Fourth ❧

[Belmont. A Room in Portia's House]
Enter Portia, Nerissa, Lorenzo, Jessica, and a man of Portia's
[Balthazar].

    Lor. Madam, although I speak it in your presence,
You have a noble and a true conceit
Of godlike amity; which appears most strongly
In bearing thus the absence of your lord.
But if you knew to whom you show this honour,   *5*
How true a gentleman you send relief,
How dear a lover of my lord your husband,
I know you would be prouder of the work
Than customary bounty can enforce you.

    Por. I never did repent for doing good,   *10*
Nor shall not now: for in companions
That do converse and waste the time together,
Whose souls do bear an equal yoke of love,
There must be needs a like proportion
Of lineaments, of manners, and of spirit;   *15*
Which makes me think that this Antonio,
Being the bosom lover of my lord,
Must needs be like my lord. If it be so,
How little is the cost I have bestow'd

---

304 unwearied: *most unwearied*   **311 deface:** *cancel by writing across*   **314 thorough:**
through   **324 cheer:** *face*   **1 Gaoler:** *jailor*

10 naughty: *good-for-nought*   **20 kept:** *dwelt*   **29 deny:** *refuse*   **30 commodity:** *trad-*
ing facilities   **33 trade and profit:** *profitable trade*   **35 bated:** *thinned*   **2 conceit:**
conception   **9 customary bounty:** *ordinary benevolence*   **enforce:** *cause to be*

In purchasing the semblance of my soul   20
From out the state of hellish cruelty!
This comes too near the praising of myself;
Therefore, no more of it: hear other things.
Lorenzo, I commit into your hands
The husbandry and manage of my house   25
Until my lord's return: for mine own part,
I have toward heaven breath'd a secret vow
To live in prayer and contemplation,
Only attended by Nerissa here,
Until her husband and my lord's return.   30
There is a monastery two miles off,
And there will we abide. I do desire you
Not to deny this imposition,
The which my love and some necessity
Now lays upon you.   35
   Lor.   Madam, with all my heart:
I shall obey you in all fair commands.
   Por. My people do already know my mind,
And will acknowledge you and Jessica
In place of Lord Bassanio and myself.   40
So fare you well till we shall meet again.
   Lor. Fair thoughts and happy hours attend on you!
   Jes. I wish your ladyship all heart's content.
   Por. I thank you for your wish, and am well pleas'd
To wish it back on you: fare you well, Jessica.   45
                   Exeunt [Jessica and Lorenzo].
Now, Balthazar,
As I have ever found thee honest-true,
So let me find thee still. Take this same letter,
And use thou all the endeavour of a man
In speed to Padua: see thou render this   50
Into my cousin's hand, Doctor Bellario;
And, look, what notes and garments he doth give thee,
Bring them, I pray thee, with imagin'd speed
Unto the tranect, to the common ferry
Which trades to Venice. Waste no time in words,   55
But get thee gone: I shall be there before thee.
   Balth. Madam, I go with all convenient speed.   *[Exit.]*
   Por. Come on, Nerissa: I have work in hand
That you yet know not of: we'll see our husbands
Before they think of us.   60
   Ner.   Shall they see us?
   Por. They shall, Nerissa; but in such a habit
That they shall think we are accomplished
With that we lack. I'll hold thee any wager,
When we are both accoutred like young men,   65
I'll prove the prettier fellow of the two,
And wear my dagger with the braver grace,
And speak between the change of man and boy
With a reed voice, and turn two mincing steps
Into a manly stride, and speak of frays   70
Like a fine bragging youth, and tell quaint lies,
How honourable ladies sought my love,
Which I denying, they fell sick and died:
I could not do withal; then I'll repent,
And wish, for all that, that I had not kill'd them: 75

And twenty of these puny lies I'll tell,
That men shall swear I have discontinu'd school
Above a twelvemonth. I have within my mind
A thousand raw tricks of these bragging Jacks,
Which I will practise.   80
   Ner.   Why, shall we turn to men?
   Por. Fie, what a question's that,
If thou wert near a lewd interpreter!
But come: I'll tell thee all my whole device
When I am in my coach, which stays for us   85
At the park gate; and therefore haste away,
For we must measure twenty miles to-day.   *Exeunt.*

❧ SCENE FIFTH ❧

[The Same. A Garden]
Enter Clown and Jessica.

   Laun. Yes, truly; for, look you, the sins of the father are to
be laid upon the children; therefore, I promise you, I fear you.
I was always plain with you, and so now I speak my agitation
of the matter: therefore be of good cheer; for, truly, I think
you are damned. There is but one hope in it that can do   5
you any good, and that is but a kind of bastard hope
neither.
   Jes. And what hope is that, I pray thee?
   Laun. Marry, you may partly hope that your father got
you not, that you are not the Jew's daughter.   10
   Jes. That were a kind of bastard hope, indeed: so the sins
of my mother should be visited upon me.
   Laun. Truly then I fear you are damned both by father and
mother: thus when I shun Scylla, your father, I fall into
Charybdis, your mother: well, you are gone both ways.   15
   Jes. I shall be saved by my husband; he hath made me a
Christian.
   Laun. Truly the more to blame he: we were Christians enow
before; e'en as many as could well live one by another. This
making of Christians will raise the price of hogs: if we grow 20
all to be pork-eaters, we shall not shortly have a rasher on
the coals for money.
   Jes. I'll tell my husband, Launcelot, what you say: here he
comes.

Enter Lorenzo.

   Lor. I shall grow jealous of you shortly, Launcelot, if   25
you thus get my wife into corners.
   Jes. Nay, you need not fear us, Lorenzo: Launcelot and I
are out. He tells me flatly, there is no mercy for me in heaven,
because I am a Jew's daughter: and he says you are no good
member of the commonwealth, for, in converting Jews to 30
Christians, you raise the price of pork.
   Lor. I shall answer that better to the commonwealth than
you can the getting up of the negro's belly: the Moor is with
child by you, Launcelot.
   Laun. It is much that the Moor should be more than   35
reason; but if she be less than an honest woman, she is
indeed more than I took her for.
   Lor. How every fool can play upon the word! I think the

---

20 semblance . . . soul; *cf. n.*   **25 husbandry and manage:** *care and management*   **33
deny this imposition:** *decline this charge*   **51 cousin's:** *any collateral kin*   **53 imagin'd
speed:** *speed of thought*   **54 tranect;** *cf. n.*   **57 convenient:** *becoming*   **63 accomplished:** *equipped*   **74 could not do withal:** *could not help it*

2 fear: *fear for*   **3 agitation:** *i.e., cogitation*   **7 neither:** *too*   **14, 15 Scylla . . . Charybdis:** *dangers confronting Ulysses*   **16 husband;** *cf. n.*

best grace of wit will shortly turn into silence, and discourse
grow commendable in none only but parrots. Go in, sirrah: *40*
bid them prepare for dinner.

  Laun. That is done, sir; they have all stomachs.

  Lor. Goodly Lord, what a wit-snapper are you! then bid
them prepare dinner.

  Laun. That is done too, sir; only, 'cover' is the word. *45*

  Lor. Will you cover, then, sir?

  Laun. Not so, sir, neither; I know my duty.

  Lor. Yet more quarrelling with occasion! Wilt thou show the
whole wealth of thy wit in an instant? I pray thee, understand
a plain man in his plain meaning: go to thy fellows; bid them
cover the table, serve in the meat, and we will come in to
dinner.

  Laun. For the table, sir, it shall be served in; for the meat,
sir, it shall be covered; for your coming in to dinner, sir, why,
let it be as humours and conceits shall govern.   *Exit Clown. 55*

  Lor. O dear discretion, how his words are suited!
The fool hath planted in his memory
An army of good words: and I do know
A many fools, that stand in better place,
Garnish'd like him, that for a tricksy word *60*
Defy the matter. How cheer'st thou, Jessica?
And now, good sweet, say thy opinion;
How dost thou like the Lord Bassanio's wife?

  Jes. Past all expressing. It is very meet,
The Lord Bassanio live an upright life, *65*
For, having such a blessing in his lady,
He finds the joys of heaven here on earth;
And if on earth he do not mean it, then
In reason he should never come to heaven.
Why, if two gods should play some heavenly match, *70*
And on the wager lay two earthly women,
And Portia one, there must be something else
Pawn'd with the other, for the poor rude world
Hath not her fellow.

  Lor.   Even such a husband *75*
Hast thou of me as she is for a wife.

  Jes. Nay, but ask my opinion too of that.

  Lor. I will anon; first, let us go to dinner.

  Jes. Nay, let me praise you while I have a stomach.

  Lor. No, pray thee, let it serve for table-talk; *80*
Then howsoe'er thou speak'st, 'mong other things
I shall digest it.

  Jes.   Well, I'll set you forth.   *Exeunt.*

ACT FOURTH ❧ SCENE FIRST

[Venice. A Court of Justice]
Enter the Duke, the Magnificoes, Antonio, Bassanio, and Gratiano
[with Salarino, Salanio, and Others].

  Duke. What, is Antonio here?

  Ant. Ready, so please your Grace.

  Duke. I am sorry for thee: thou art come to answer
A stony adversary, an inhuman wretch

Uncapable of pity, void and empty *5*
From any dram of mercy.

  Ant.   I have heard
Your Grace hath ta'en great pains to qualify
His rigorous course; but since he stands obdurate,
And that no lawful means can carry me *10*
Out of his envy's reach, I do oppose
My patience to his fury, and am arm'd
To suffer with a quietness of spirit
The very tyranny and rage of his.

  Duke. Go one, and call the Jew into the court. *15*

  Salar. He's ready at the door: he comes, my lord.

Enter Shylock.

  Duke. Make room, and let him stand before our face.
Shylock, the world thinks, and I think so too,
That thou but lead'st this fashion of thy malice
To the last hour of act; and then 'tis thought *20*
Thou'lt show thy mercy and remorse more strange
Than is thy strange apparent cruelty;
And where thou now exact'st the penalty,—
Which is a pound of this poor merchant's flesh,—
Thou wilt not only loose the forfeiture, *25*
But, touch'd with human gentleness and love,
Forgive a moiety of the principal;
Glancing an eye of pity on his losses,
That have of late so huddled on his back,
Enow to press a royal merchant down, *30*
And pluck commiseration of his state
From brassy bosoms and rough hearts of flint,
From stubborn Turks and Tartars, never train'd
To offices of tender courtesy.
We all expect a gentle answer, Jew. *35*

  Shy. I have possess'd your Grace of what I purpose;
And by our holy Sabbath have I sworn
To have the due and forfeit of my bond:
If you deny it, let the danger light
Upon your charter and your city's freedom. *40*
You'll ask me why I rather choose to have
A weight of carrion flesh than to receive
Three thousand ducats: I'll not answer that:
But say it is my humour: is it answer'd?
What if my house be troubled with a rat, *45*
And I be pleas'd to give ten thousand ducats
To have it ban'd? What, are you answer'd yet?
Some men there are love not a gaping pig;
Some, that are mad if they behold a cat;
And others, when the bagpipe sings i' the nose, *50*
Cannot contain their urine: for affection
Masters our passion, sways it to the mood
Of what it likes, or loathes. Now, for your answer:
As there is no firm reason to be render'd,
Why he cannot abide a gaping pig; *55*
Why he, a harmless necessary cat;
Why he, a woollen bagpipe; but of force
Must yield to such inevitable shame

---

45 **cover:** *cf. n.*   48 **quarrelling with occasion:** *splitting hairs at every opportunity*   55
humours: *whims*   56 **suited:** *elaborately dressed*   61 **Defy the matter:** *spoil the thought*
How cheer'st thou: *what cheer?*   68 **mean it;** *cf. n.*   73 **Pawn'd:** *staked*   3 **answer:**
satisfy

6 **dram:** *drop*   8 **qualify:** *moderate*   14 **tyranny and rage:** *violent dominance*   19
fashion: *pretence*   20 **act:** *performance*   21 **remorse:** *pity*   25 **loose:** *release*   27
moiety: *portion (two syllables only).*   29 **huddled:** *crowded*   38 **due and forfeit:** *forfeit
that is due*   39 **danger:** *damage*   47 **ban'd:** *poisoned*   48 **gaping pig:** *pig roasted
with the mouth open*   51 **affection:** *natural bent of mind*   57 **woollen;** *cf. n.*

As to offend, himself being offended;
so can i give no reason, nor i will not,   60
More than a lodg'd hate and a certain loathing
I bear Antonio, that I follow thus
A losing suit against him. Are you answer'd?
    Bass. This is no answer, thou unfeeling man,
To excuse the current of thy cruelty.   65
    Shy. I am not bound to please thee with my answer.
    Bass. Do all men kill the things they do not love?
    Shy. Hates any man the thing he would not kill?
    Bass. Every offence is not a hate at first.
    Shy. What! wouldst thou have a serpent sting thee twice?   70
    Ant. I pray you, think you question with the Jew:
You may as well go stand upon the beach,
And bid the main flood bate his usual height;
You may as well use question with the wolf,
Why he hath made the ewe bleat for the lamb;   75
You may as well forbid the mountain pines
To wag their high tops, and to make no noise
When they are fretted with the gusts of heaven;
You may as well do anything most hard,
As seek to soften that—than which what's harder?—   80
His Jewish heart: therefore, I do beseech you,
Make no more offers, use no further means;
But with all brief and plain conveniency,
Let me have judgment, and the Jew his will.
    Bass. For thy three thousand ducats here is six.   85
    Shy. If every ducat in six thousand ducats
Were in six parts and every part a ducat,
I would not draw them; I would have my bond.
    Duke. How shalt thou hope for mercy, rendering none?
    Shy. What judgment shall I dread, doing no wrong?   90
You have among you many a purchas'd slave,
Which, like your asses and your dogs and mules,
You use in abject and in slavish parts,
Because you bought them: shall I say to you,
Let them be free, marry them to your heirs?   95
Why sweat they under burdens? let their beds
Be made as soft as yours, and let their palates
Be season'd with such viands? You will answer:
'The slaves are ours:' so do I answer you:
The pound of flesh which I demand of him,   100
Is dearly bought; 'tis mine and I will have it.
If you deny me, fie upon your law!
There is no force in the decrees of Venice.
I stand for judgment: answer; shall I have it?
    Duke. Upon my power I may dismiss this court,   105
Unless Bellario, a learned doctor,
Whom I have sent for to determine this,
Come here to-day.
    Salar.   My lord, here stays without
A messenger with letters from the doctor,   110
New come from Padua.
    Duke. Bring us the letters: call the messenger.
    Bass. Good cheer, Antonio! What, man, courage yet!
The Jew shall have my flesh, blood, bones, and all,
Ere thou shalt lose for me one drop of blood.   115

    Ant. I am a tainted wether of the flock,
Meetest for death: the weakest kind of fruit
Drops earliest to the ground; and so let me:
You cannot better be employ'd, Bassanio,
Than to live still, and write mine epitaph.   120

            Enter Nerissa [dressed like a lawyer's clerk].

    Duke. Came you from Padua, from Bellario?
    Ner. From both, my lord. Bellario greets your Grace.
                                    [Presents a letter.]
    Bass. Why dost thou whet thy knife so earnestly?
    Shy. To cut the forfeiture from that bankrupt there.   125
    Gra. Not on thy sole, but on thy soul, harsh Jew,
Thou mak'st thy knife keen; but no metal can,
No, not the hangman's axe, bear half the keenness
Of thy sharp envy. Can no prayers pierce thee?
    Shy. No, none that thou hast wit enough to make.   130
    Gra. O, be thou damn'd, inexecrable dog!
And for thy life let justice be accus'd.
Thou almost mak'st me waver in my faith
To hold opinion with Pythagoras,
That souls of animals infuse themselves   135
Into the trunks of men: thy currish spirit
Govern'd a wolf, who, hang'd for human slaughter,
Even from the gallows did his fell soul fleet,
And whilst thou lay'st in thy unhallow'd dam,
Infus'd itself in thee; for thy desires   140
Are wolfish, bloody, starv'd, and ravenous.
    Shy. Till thou canst rail the seal from off my bond,
Thou but offend'st thy lungs to speak so loud:
Repair thy wit, good youth, or it will fall
To cureless ruin. I stand here for law.   145
    Duke. This letter from Bellario doth commend
A young and learned doctor to our court.
Where is he?
    Ner.   He attendeth here hard by,
To know your answer, whether you'll admit him.   150
    Duke. With all my heart: some three or four of you
Go give him courteous conduct to this place.
Meantime, the court shall hear Bellario's letter.

    [Clerk]. *'Your Grace shall understand that at the receipt of
    your letter I am very sick; but in the instant that your
    messenger came, in loving visitation was with me a young doc-
    tor of Rome; his name is Balthazar. I acquainted him with the
    cause in controversy between the Jew and Antonio the mer-
    chant: we turned o'er many books together: he is furnished
    nwith my opinion; which, bettered with his own learning,—the
    greatness whereof I cannot enough commend,—comes with him,
    at my importunity, to fill up your Grace's request in my stead.
    I beseech you, let his lack of years be no impediment to let him
    lack a reverend estimation, for I never knew so young a
    body with so old a head. I leave him to your gracious accep-
    tance, whose trial shall better publish his commendation.'*

    Duke. You hear the learn'd Bellario, what he writes:
And here, I take it, is the doctor come.

        Enter Portia for Balthazar [dressed like a doctor of laws].

---

63 **losing:** *moneyless, unprofitable*   65 **current:** *steady flow*   69 **offence:** *resent-*
ment   71 **question:** *converse*   73 **bate:** *reduce*   74, 75 *Cf. n.*   77 **and:** *and bid*
them   88 **draw:** *receive*   93 **parts:** *actions*   98 **season'd:** *gratified*   105 **Upon ...**
power: *by authority vested in me*

120 *Cf. n.*   131 **inexecrable:** *who cannot be execrated enough*   132 **justice;** *cf. n.*   145
cureless: *incurable*   152 **conduct:** *escort*   153 **letter;** *cf. n.*   164 **reverend estimation:**
respectful esteem   166 **publish ... commendation:** *make known his merit*

Give me your hand. Came you from old Bellario?
   Por. I did, my lord.   *170*
   Duke.   You are welcome: take your place.
Are you acquainted with the difference
That holds this present question in the court?
   Por. I am informed throughly of the cause.
Which is the merchant here, and which the Jew?   *175*
   Duke. Antonio and old Shylock, both stand forth.
   Por. Is your name Shylock?
   Shy.   Shylock is my name.
   Por. Of a strange nature is the suit you follow;
Yet in such rule that the Venetian law   *180*
Cannot impugn you as you do proceed.
[To Antonio.] You stand within his danger, do you not?
   Ant. Ay, so he says.
   Por.   Do you confess the bond?
   Ant. I do.   *185*
   Por.   Then must the Jew be merciful.
   Shy. On what compulsion must I? tell me that.
   Por. The quality of mercy is not strain'd,
It droppeth as the gentle rain from heaven
Upon the place beneath: it is twice bless'd;   *190*
It blesseth him that gives and him that takes:
'Tis mightiest in the mightiest; it becomes
The throned monarch better than his crown;
His sceptre shows the force of temporal power,
The attribute to awe and majesty,   *195*
Wherein doth sit the dread and fear of kings;
But mercy is above this sceptred sway,
It is enthroned in the hearts of kings,
It is an attribute to God himself,
And earthly power doth then show likest God's   *200*
When mercy seasons justice. Therefore, Jew,
Though justice be thy plea, consider this,
That in the course of justice none of us
Should see salvation: we do pray for mercy,
And that same prayer doth teach us all to render   *205*
The deeds of mercy. I have spoke thus much
To mitigate the justice of thy plea,
Which if thou follow, this strict court of Venice
Must needs give sentence 'gainst the merchant there.
   Shy. My deeds upon my head! I crave the law,   *210*
The penalty and forfeit of my bond.
   Por. Is he not able to discharge the money?
   Bass. Yes, here I tender it for him in the court;
Yea, twice the sum: if that will not suffice,
I will be bound to pay it ten times o'er,   *215*
On forfeit of my hands, my head, my heart.
If this will not suffice, it must appear
That malice bears down truth. And, I beseech you,
Wrest once the law to your authority:
To do a great right, do a little wrong,   *220*
And curb this cruel devil of his will.
   Por. It must not be. There is no power in Venice
Can alter a decree established:
'Twill be recorded for a precedent,
And many an error by the same example   *225*

Will rush into the state. It cannot be.
   Shy. A Daniel come to judgment! yea, a Daniel!
O wise young judge, how I do honour thee!
   Por. I pray you, let me look upon the bond.
   Shy. Here 'tis, most reverend doctor; here it is.   *230*
   Por. Shylock, there's thrice thy money offer'd thee.
   Shy. An oath, an oath, I have an oath in heaven:
Shall I lay perjury upon my soul?
No, not for Venice.
   Por.   Why, this bond is forfeit;   *235*
And lawfully by this the Jew may claim
A pound of flesh, to be by him cut off
Nearest the merchant's heart. Be merciful:
Take thrice thy money; bid me tear the bond.
   Shy. When it is paid according to the tenour.   *240*
It doth appear you are a worthy judge;
You know the law, your exposition
Hath been most sound: I charge you by the law,
Whereof you are a well-deserving pillar,
Proceed to judgment: by my soul I swear   *245*
There is no power in the tongue of man
To alter me. I stay here on my bond.
   Ant. Most heartily I do beseech the court
To give the judgment.
   Por.   Why then, thus it is: *250*
You must prepare your bosom for his knife.
   Shy. O noble judge! O excellent young man!
   Por. For the intent and purpose of the law
Hath full relation to the penalty,
Which here appeareth due upon the bond.   *255*
   Shy. 'Tis very true! O wise and upright judge!
How much more elder art thou than thy looks!
   Por. Therefore lay bare your bosom.
   Shy.   Ay, 'his breast:'
So says the bond:—doth it not, noble judge?—   *260*
'Nearest his heart:' those are the very words.
   Por. It is so. Are there balance here to weigh
The flesh?
   Shy. I have them ready.
   Por. Have by some surgeon, Shylock, on your charge,   *265*
To stop his wounds, lest he do bleed to death.
   Shy. Is it so nominated in the bond?
   Por. It is not so express'd; but what of that?
'Twere good you do so much for charity.
   Shy. I cannot find it: 'tis not in the bond.   *270*
   Por. You, merchant, have you anything to say?
   Ant. But little: I am arm'd and well prepar'd.
Give me your hand, Bassanio: fare you well!
Grieve not that I am fallen to this for you;
For herein Fortune shows herself more kind   *275*
Than is her custom: it is still her use
To let the wretched man outlive his wealth,
To view with hollow eye and wrinkled brow
An age of poverty; from which lingering penance
Of such a misery doth she cut me off.   *280*
Commend me to your honourable wife:
Tell her the process of Antonio's end;
Say how I lov'd you, speak me fair in death;

172 difference: *dispute*   **174 throughly:** *thoroughly*   **180 rule:** *correct mode of procedure*   **181 impugn:** *oppose*   **182 danger:** *power to hurt*   **188 strain'd:** *constrained, forced*   **195 The attribute:** *what belongs*   **awe and majesty:** *awful majesty*   **201 seasons:** *flavors*   **218 truth:** *equity*   **219 Wrest:** *strain* **to:** *to the advantage of*

227 Daniel; *cf. n.*   **247 stay . . . on:** *await the fulfilment of*   **262 balance:** *scales*   **265 on . . . charge:** *at your expense*   **276 use:** *habit*   **282 process:** *story*   **283 speak . . . fair:** *speak well of me*

And, when the tale is told, bid her be judge
Whether Bassanio had not once a love.   285
Repent but you that you shall lose your friend,
And he repents not that he pays your debt;
For if the Jew do cut but deep enough,
I'll pay it instantly with all my heart.
   Bass. Antonio, I am married to a wife   290
Which is as dear to me as life itself;
But life itself, my wife, and all the world,
Are not with me esteem'd above thy life:
I would lose all, ay, sacrifice them all,
Here to this devil, to deliver you.   295
   Por. Your wife would give you little thanks for that,
If she were by to hear you make the offer.
   Gra. I have a wife, whom, I protest, I love:
I would she were in heaven, so she could
Entreat some power to change this currish Jew.   300
   Ner. 'Tis well you offer it behind her back;
The wish would make else an unquiet house.
   Shy. These be the Christian husbands! I have a daughter;
Would any of the stock of Barabbas
Had been her husband rather than a Christian!   305
We trifle time; I pray thee, pursue sentence.
   Por. A pound of that same merchant's flesh is thine:
The court awards it, and the law doth give it.
   Shy. Most rightful judge!
   Por. And you must cut this flesh from off his breast: 310
The law allows it, and the court awards it.
   Shy. Most learned judge! A sentence! come, prepare!
   Por. Tarry a little: there is something else.
This bond doth give thee here no jot of blood;
The words expressly are 'a pound of flesh:'   315
Then take thy bond, take thou thy pound of flesh;
But, in the cutting it, if thou dost shed
One drop of Christian blood, thy lands and goods
Are, by the laws of Venice, confiscate
Unto the state of Venice.   320
   Gra. O upright judge! Mark, Jew: O learned judge!
   Shy. Is that the law?
   Por.   Thyself shalt see the act;
For, as thou urgest justice, be assur'd
Thou shalt have justice, more than thou desir'st.   325
   Gra. O learned judge! Mark, Jew: a learned judge!
   Shy. I take this offer then: pay the bond thrice,
And let the Christian go.
   Bass.   Here is the money.
   Por. Soft!   330
The Jew shall have all justice; soft! no haste:—
He shall have nothing but the penalty.
   Gra. O Jew! an upright judge, a learned judge!
   Por. Therefore prepare thee to cut off the flesh.
Shed thou no blood; nor cut thou less, nor more,   335
But just a pound of flesh: if thou tak'st more,
Or less, than a just pound, be it but so much
As makes it light or heavy in the substance,
Or the division of the twentieth part
Of one poor scruple, nay, if the scale do turn   340
But in the estimation of a hair,

Thou diest and all thy goods are confiscate.
   Gra. A second Daniel, a Daniel, Jew!
Now, infidel, I have thee on the hip.
   Por. Why doth the Jew pause? take thy forfeiture.   345
   Shy. Give me my principal, and let me go.
   Bass. I have it ready for thee; here it is.
   Por. He hath refus'd it in the open court:
He shall have merely justice, and his bond.
   Gra. A Daniel, still say I; a second Daniel!   350
I thank thee, Jew, for teaching me that word.
   Shy. Shall I not have barely my principal?
   Por. Thou shalt have nothing but the forfeiture,
To be so taken at thy peril, Jew.
   Shy. Why, then the devil give him good of it!   355
I'll stay no longer question.
   Por.   Tarry, Jew:
The law hath yet another hold on you.
It is enacted in the laws of Venice,
If it be prov'd against an alien   360
That by direct or indirect attempts
He seek the life of any citizen,
The party 'gainst the which he doth contrive
Shall seize one half his goods; the other half
Comes to the privy coffer of the state;   365
And the offender's life lies in the mercy
Of the duke only, 'gainst all other voice.
In which predicament, I say, thou stand'st;
For it appears by manifest proceeding,
That indirectly and directly too   370
Thou hast contriv'd against the very life
Of the defendant; and thou hast incurr'd
The danger formerly by me rehears'd.
Down therefore and beg mercy of the duke.
   Gra. Beg that thou mayst have leave to hang thyself: 375
And yet, thy wealth being forfeit to the state,
Thou hast not left the value of a cord;
Therefore thou must be hang'd at the state's charge.
   Duke. That thou shalt see the difference of our spirits,
I pardon thee thy life before thou ask it.   380
For half thy wealth, it is Antonio's;
The other half comes to the general state,
Which humbleness may drive unto a fine.
   Por. Ay, for the state; not for Antonio.
   Shy. Nay, take my life and all; pardon not that: 385
You take my house when you do take the prop
That doth sustain my house; you take my life
When you do take the means whereby I live.
   Por. What mercy can you render him, Antonio?
   Gra. A halter gratis; nothing else, for God's sake!   390
   Ant. So please my lord the duke, and all the court,
To quit the fine for one half of his goods,
I am content; so he will let me have
The other half in use, to render it,
Upon his death, unto the gentleman   395
That lately stole his daughter:
Two things provided more, that, for this favour,
He presently become a Christian;
The other, that he do record a gift,

---

285 love: *devoted friend*   **286 Repent:** *repine, grieve*   **291 Which:** *who*   **306 pursue:** *proceed with*   **336 just:** *precise*   **338 substance:** *amount*   **340 scruple:** *one-third of a dram, twenty grains*   **341 estimation:** *calculation*

363 contrive: *plot*   **365 privy coffer:** *treasury*   **367 'gainst . . . voice:** *in spite of what other persons may judge*   **373 formerly:** *above*   **383 drive:** *reduce*

Here in the court, of all he dies possess'd,   *400*
Unto his son Lorenzo, and his daughter.
     Duke. He shall do this, or else I do recant
The pardon that I late pronounced here.
     Por. Art thou contented, Jew? what dost thou say?
     Shy. I am content.   *405*
     Por.   Clerk, draw a deed of gift.
     Shy. I pray you give me leave to go from hence:
I am not well. Send the deed after me,
And I will sign it.
     Duke.   Get thee gone, but do it.   *410*
     Gra. In christening thou shalt have two godfathers;
Had I been judge, thou shouldst have had ten more,
To bring thee to the gallows, not the font.   *Exit [Shylock].*
     Duke. Sir, I entreat you home with me to dinner.
     Por. I humbly do desire your Grace of pardon: *415*
I must away this night toward Padua,
And it is meet I presently set forth.
     Duke. I am sorry that your leisure serves you not.
Antonio, gratify this gentleman,
For, in my mind, you are much bound to him.   *420*
                Exit Duke [with Magnificoes] and his train.
     Bass. Most worthy gentleman, I and my friend
Have by your wisdom been this day acquitted
Of grievous penalties; in lieu whereof,
Three thousand ducats, due unto the Jew,
We freely cope your courteous pains withal.   *425*
     Ant. And stand indebted, over and above,
In love and service to you evermore.
     Por. He is well paid that is well satisfied;
And I, delivering you, am satisfied,
And therein do account myself well paid: *430*
My mind was never yet more mercenary.
I pray you, know me when we meet again:
I wish you well, and so I take my leave.
     Bass. Dear sir, of force I must attempt you further:
Take some remembrance of us, as a tribute,   *435*
Not as a fee. Grant me two things, I pray you,
Not to deny me, and to pardon me.
     Por. You press me far, and therefore I will yield.
[To Antonio.] Give me your gloves, I'll wear them for your
    sake;   *440*
[To Bassanio.] And, for your love, I'll take this ring from you.
Do not draw back your hand; I'll take no more;
And you in love shall not deny me this.
     Bass. This ring, good sir? alas! it is a trifle;
I will not shame myself to give you this.   *445*
     Por. I will have nothing else but only this;
And now methinks I have a mind to it.
     Bass. There's more depends on this than on the value.
The dearest ring in Venice will I give you,
And find it out by proclamation: *450*
Only for this, I pray you, pardon me.
     Por. I see, sir, you are liberal in offers:
You taught me first to beg, and now methinks
You teach me how a beggar should be answer'd.
     Bass. Good sir, this ring was given me by my wife;   *455*
And when she put it on, she made me vow

That I should never sell nor give nor lose it.
     Por. That 'scuse serves many men to save their gifts.
And if your wife be not a mad-woman,
And know how well I have deserv'd the ring,   *460*
She would not hold out enemy for ever,
For giving it to me. Well, peace be with you.
                Exeunt [Portia and Nerissa].
     Ant. My Lord Bassanio, let him have the ring:
Let his deservings and my love withal
Be valu'd 'gainst your wife's commandment.   *465*
     Bass. Go, Gratiano; run and overtake him;
Give him the ring, and bring him, if thou canst,
Unto Antonio's house. Away! make haste.   *Exit Gratiano.*
Come, you and I will thither presently,
And in the morning early will we both   *470*
Fly toward Belmont. Come, Antonio.   *Exeunt.*

❧ SCENE SECOND ❧

[The Same. A Street]
Enter Portia and Nerissa.

     Por. Inquire the Jew's house out, give him this deed,
And let him sign it. We'll away to-night,
And be a day before our husbands home:
This deed will be well welcome to Lorenzo.

Enter Gratiano.

     Gra. Fair sir, you are well o'erta'en.   *5*
My Lord Bassanio upon more advice
Hath sent you here this ring, and doth entreat
Your company at dinner.
     Por.   That cannot be:
His ring I do accept most thankfully;   *10*
And so, I pray you, tell him: furthermore,
I pray you, show my youth old Shylock's house.
     Gra. That will I do.
     Ner.   Sir, I would speak with you.
[Aside to Portia.] I'll see if I can get my husband's ring,   *15*
Which I did make him swear to keep for ever.
     Por. Thou mayst, I warrant. We shall have old swearing
That they did give the rings away to men;
But we'll outface them, and outswear them too.
Away! make haste: thou know'st where I will tarry.   *20*
     Ner. Come, good sir, will you show me to this house?
                Exeunt.

ACT FIFTH ❧ SCENE FIRST

[Belmont. The Avenue to Portia's House]
Enter Lorenzo and Jessica.

     Lor. The moon shines bright: in such a night as this,
When the sweet wind did gently kiss the trees
And they did make no noise, in such a night
Troilus methinks mounted the Troyan walls,
And sigh'd his soul toward the Grecian tents,   *5*
Where Cressid lay that night.

---

400 of all: *of all of which*   **412 ten more:** *i.e., a jury of twelve*   **419 gratify:** *reward*   **425 cope:** *match, requite*   **434 force:** *necessity*   **attempt:** *tempt, urge*   **450 proclamation:** *advertisement* (through the street crier)

6 advice: *consideration*   **12 old:** *much*   **4 Troilus:** *cf. Shakespeare's play on the theme*

Jes.   In such a night
Did Thisbe fearfully o'ertrip the dew,
And saw the lion's shadow ere himself,
And ran dismay'd away.   *10*
     Lor.   In such a night
Stood Dido with a willow in her hand
Upon the wild sea-banks, and waft her love
To come again to Carthage.
     Jes.   In such a night   *15*
Medea gather'd the enchanted herbs
That did renew old Æson.
     Lor.   In such a night
Did Jessica steal from the wealthy Jew,
And with an unthrift love did run from Venice,   *20*
As far as Belmont.
     Jes.   In such a night
Did young Lorenzo swear he lov'd her well,
Stealing her soul with many vows of faith,
And ne'er a true one.   *25*
     Lor.   In such a night
Did pretty Jessica, like a little shrew,
Slander her love, and he forgave it her.
     Jes. I would out-night you, did nobody come;
But, hark! I hear the footing of a man.   *30*

       Enter Messenger [Stephano].

     Lor. Who comes so fast in silence of the night?
     Mes. A friend.
     Lor. A friend! what friend? your name, I pray you, friend.
     Mes. Stephano is my name; and I bring word
My mistress will before the break of day   *35*
Be here at Belmont: she doth stray about
By holy crosses, where she kneels and prays
For happy wedlock hours.
     Lor.   Who comes with her?
     Mes. None, but a holy hermit and her maid.   *40*
I pray you, is my master yet return'd?
     Lor. He is not, nor we have not heard from him.
But go we in, I pray thee, Jessica,
And ceremoniously let us prepare
Some welcome for the mistress of the house.   *45*

       Enter Clown.

     Clo. Sola, sola! wo ha, ho! sola, sola!
     Lor. Who calls?
     Clo. Sola! did you see Master Lorenzo?
Master Lorenzo! sola, sola!
     Lor. Leave hollaing, man; here.   *50*
     Clo. Sola! where? where?
     Lor. Here.
     Clo. Tell him there's a post come from my master, with his
horn full of good news: my master will be here ere
morning.   *[Exit.]* *55*
     Lor. Sweet soul, let's in, and there expect their coming.
And yet no matter; why should we go in?
My friend Stephano, signify, I pray you,

Within the house, your mistress is at hand;
And bring your music forth into the air.   *[Exit Stephano.]* *60*
How sweet the moonlight sleeps upon this bank!
Here will we sit, and let the sounds of music
Creep in our ears; soft stillness and the night
Become the touches of sweet harmony.
Sit, Jessica: look, how the floor of heaven   *65*
Is thick inlaid with patines of bright gold:
There's not the smallest orb which thou behold'st
But in his motion like an angel sings,
Still quiring to the young-eyed cherubins;
Such harmony is in immortal souls;   *70*
But, whilst this muddy vesture of decay
Doth grossly close it in, we cannot hear it.

       [Enter Musicians.]

Come, ho! and wake Diana with a hymn:
With sweetest touches pierce your mistress' ear,   *75*
And draw her home with music.
     Jes. I am never merry when I hear sweet music.

                                Play music.

     Lor. The reason is, your spirits are attentive:
For do but note a wild and wanton herd,
Or race of youthful and unhandled colts,   *80*
Fetching mad bounds, bellowing and neighing loud,
Which is the hot condition of their blood;
If they but hear perchance a trumpet sound,
Or any air of music touch their ears,
You shall perceive them make a mutual stand,   *85*
Their savage eyes turn'd to a modest gaze
By the sweet power of music: therefore the poet
Did feign that Orpheus drew trees, stones, and floods;
Since nought so stockish, hard, and full of rage,
But music for the time doth change his nature.   *90*
The man that hath no music in himself,
Nor is not mov'd with concord of sweet sounds,
Is fit for treasons, stratagems, and spoils;
The motions of his spirit are dull as night,
And his affections dark as Erebus: *95*
Let no such man be trusted. Mark the music.

       Enter Portia and Nerissa [at a distance].

     Por. That light we see is burning in my hall.
How far that little candle throws his beams!
So shines a good deed in a naughty world.
     Ner. When the moon shone, we did not see the candle.   *100*
     Por. So doth the greater glory dim the less:
A substitute shines brightly as a king
Until a king be by, and then his state
Empties itself, as doth an inland brook
Into the main of waters. Music! hark!   *Muise.* *105*
     Ner. It is your music, madam, of the house.
     Por. Nothing is good, I see, without respect:
Methinks it sounds much sweeter than by day.
     Ner. Silence bestows that virtue on it, madam.
     Por. The crow doth sing as sweetly as the lark   *110*
When neither is attended, and I think
The nightingale, if she should sing by day,

---

8 Thisbe: *cf. Midsummer Night's Dream*   **12 willow:** *emblem of slighted love*   **13 waft:** *beckoned*   **17 renew:** *rejuvenate*   **Æson:** *father of Jason*   **37 crosses:** *those along the road-side*   **46 Sola:** *imitating the post horn*   **48, 49** *Cf. n.*   **56 expect:** *await*   **58 sig-nify:** *make it known*

65, 66 the floor of heaven, etc.; *cf. n.*   **66 patines:** *thin plates, used in celebration of the Eucharist*   **69 quiring:** *singing in harmony*   **78 attentive:** *absorbed, concentrated*   **95 Erebus:** *mythological dark place under Earth*   **107 respect:** *regard to circumstances*   **111 attended:** *given attention*

When every goose is cackling, would be thought
No better a musician than the wren.
How many things by season season'd are   *115*
To their right praise and true perfection!
Peace, ho! the moon sleeps with Endymion,
And would not be awak'd!   *Music ceases.*
    Lor.   That is the voice,
Or I am much deceiv'd, of Portia.   *120*
    Por. He knows me, as the blind man knows the
cuckoo,
By the bad voice.
    Lor.   Dear lady, welcome home.
    Por. We have been praying for our husbands' welfare,   *125*
Which speed, we hope, the better for our words.
Are they return'd?
    Lor.   Madam, they are not yet;
But there is come a messenger before,
To signify their coming.   *130*
    Por.   Go in, Nerissa:
Give order to my servants that they take
No note at all of our being absent hence;
Nor you, Lorenzo; Jessica, nor you.   *A tucket sounds.*
    Lor. Your husband is at hand; I hear his trumpet: *135*
We are no tell-tales, madam; fear you not.
    Por. This night methinks is but the daylight sick;
It looks a little paler: 'tis a day,
Such as the day is when the sun is hid.

        Enter Bassanio, Antonio, Gratiano, and their Followers.

    Bass. We should hold day with the Antipodes,   *140*
If you would walk in absence of the sun.
    Por. Let me give light, but let me not be light;
For a light wife doth make a heavy husband,
And never be Bassanio so for me:
But God sort all! You are welcome home, my lord.   *145*
    Bass. I thank you, madam. Give welcome to my friend:
This is the man, this is Antonio,
To whom I am so infinitely bound.
    Por. You should in all sense be much bound to him,
For, as I hear, he was much bound for you.   *150*
    Ant. No more than I am well acquitted of.
    Por. Sir, you are very welcome to our house:
It must appear in other ways than words,
Therefore I scant this breathing courtesy.
    Gra. [To Nerissa.] By yonder moon I swear you do me   *155*
wrong;
In faith, I gave it to the judge's clerk:
Would he were gelt that had it, for my part,
Since you do take it, love, so much at heart.
    Por. A quarrel, ho, already! what's the matter?   *160*
    Gra. About a hoop of gold, a paltry ring
That she did give me, whose poesy was
For all the world like cutlers' poetry
Upon a knife, 'Love me, and leave me not.'
    Ner. What talk you of the posy, or the value?   *165*
You swore to me, when I did give it you,
That you would wear it till your hour of death,

And that it should lie with you in your grave:
Though not for me, yet for your vehement oaths,
You should have been respective and have kept it.   *170*
Gave it a judge's clerk! no, God's my judge,
The clerk will ne'er wear hair on's face that had it.
    Gra. He will, an if he live to be a man.
    Ner. Ay, if a woman live to be a man.
    Gra. Now, by this hand, I gave it to a youth,   *175*
A kind of boy, a little scrubbed boy,
No higher than thyself, the judge's clerk.
A prating boy, that begg'd it as a fee:
I could not for my heart deny it him.
    Por. You were to blame,—I must be plain with you,—   *180*
To part so slightly with your wife's first gift;
A thing stuck on with oaths upon your finger,
And riveted so with faith unto your flesh.
I gave my love a ring and made him swear
Never to part with it; and here he stands.   *185*
I dare be sworn for him he would not leave it
Nor pluck it from his finger for the wealth
That the world masters. Now, in faith, Gratiano,
You give your wife too unkind a cause of grief:
An 'twere to me, I should be mad at it.   *190*
    Bass. [Aside.] Why, I were best to cut my left hand off,
And swear I lost the ring defending it.
    Gra. My Lord Bassanio gave his ring away
Unto the judge that begg'd it, and indeed
Deserv'd it too; and then the boy, his clerk,   *195*
That took some pains in writing, he begg'd mine;
And neither man nor master would take aught
But the two rings.
    Por.   What ring gave you, my lord?
Not that, I hope, which you receiv'd of me.   *200*
    Bass. If I could add a lie unto a fault,
I would deny it; but you see my finger
Hath not the ring upon it; it is gone.
    Por. Even so void is your false heart of truth.
By heaven, I will ne'er come in your bed   *205*
Until I see the ring.
    Ner.   Nor I in yours,
Till I again see mine.
    Bass.   Sweet Portia,
If you did know to whom I gave the ring,   *210*
If you did know for whom I gave the ring,
And would conceive for what I gave the ring,
And how unwillingly I left the ring,
When naught would be accepted but the ring,
You would abate the strength of your displeasure.   *215*
    Por. If you had known the virtue of the ring,
Or half her worthiness that gave the ring,
Or your own honour to contain the ring,
You would not then have parted with the ring.
What man is there so much unreasonable,   *220*
If you had pleas'd to have defended it
With any terms of zeal, wanted the modesty
To urge the thing held as a ceremony?
Nerissa teaches me what to believe:
I'll die for 't but some woman had the ring.   *225*

---

115 **by . . . season'd:** *by proper time matured*   117 **Endymion:** *Selene, the Moon, saw him asleep and loved him*   **S. d. tucket:** *toccata, a flourish on trumpets*   140, 141 *Cf. n.*   145 **sort:** *dispose*   154 **breathing courtesy:** *words of welcome*   162 **poesy:** *posy on inside of ring*   164 **Upon a knife:** *they put mottoes on knives*   165 **What:** *why*

170 **respective:** *considerate, careful*   176 **scrubbed:** *stunted*   186 **leave:** *give up*   188 **masters:** *owns*   190 **be mad:** *run mad*   218 **contain:** *retain*   222 **wanted the:** *who would have so wanted*   223 **To:** *as to*   **ceremony:** *anything held sacred*

Bass. No, by my honour, madam, by my soul,
No woman had it; but a civil doctor,
Which did refuse three thousand ducats of me,
And begg'd the ring, the which I did deny him,
And suffer'd him to go displeas'd away;   *230*
Even he that did uphold the very life
Of my dear friend. What should I say, sweet lady?
I was enforc'd to send it after him;
I was beset with shame and courtesy;
My honour would not let ingratitude   *235*
So much besmear it. Pardon me, good lady,
For, by these blessed candles of the night,
Had you been there, I think you would have begg'd
The ring of me to give the worthy doctor.
    Por. Let not that doctor e'er come near my house.   *240*
Since he hath got the jewel that I lov'd,
And that which you did swear to keep for me,
I will become as liberal as you;
I'll not deny him anything I have;
No, not my body, nor my husband's bed.   *245*
Know him I shall, I am well sure of it:
Lie not a night from home; watch me like Argus:
If you do not, if I be left alone,
Now by mine honour, which is yet mine own,
I'll have that doctor for my bedfellow.   *250*
    Ner. And I his clerk; therefore be well advis'd
How you do leave me to mine own protection.
    Gra. Well, do you so: let not me take him, then;
For if I do, I'll mar the young clerk's pen.
    Ant. I am the unhappy subject of these quarrels.   *255*
    Por. Sir, grieve not you; you are welcome notwithstanding.
    Bass. Portia, forgive me this enforced wrong;
And in the hearing of these many friends,
I swear to thee, even by thine own fair eyes,
Wherein I see myself,—   *260*
    Por.   Mark you but that!
In both my eyes he doubly sees himself;
In each eye, one: swear by your double self,
And there's an oath of credit.
    Bass.   Nay, but hear me: *265*
Pardon this fault, and by my soul I swear
I never more will break an oath with thee.
    Ant. I once did lend my body for his wealth,
Which, but for him that had your husband's ring,
Had quite miscarried: I dare be bound again,   *270*
My soul upon the forfeit, that your lord
Will never more break faith advisedly.
    Por. Then you shall be his surety. Give him this,
And bid him keep it better than the other.
    Ant. Here, Lord Bassanio; swear to keep this ring.   *275*
    Bass. By heaven! it is the same I gave the doctor!
    Por. I had it of him: pardon me, Bassanio,
For, by this ring, the doctor lay with me.
    Ner. And pardon me, my gentle Gratiano;

For that same scrubbed boy, the doctor's clerk,   *280*
In lieu of this last night did lie with me.
    Gra. Why, this is like the mending of highways
In summer, where the ways are fair enough.
What! are we cuckolds ere we have deserv'd it?
    Por. Speak not so grossly. You are all amaz'd: *285*
Here is a letter; read it at your leisure;
It comes from Padua, from Bellario:
There you shall find that Portia was the doctor,
Nerissa, there, her clerk: Lorenzo here
Shall witness I set forth as soon as you   *290*
And even but now return'd; I have not yet
Enter'd my house. Antonio, you are welcome;
And I have better news in store for you
Than you expect: unseal this letter soon;
There you shall find three of your argosies   *295*
Are richly come to harbour suddenly.
You shall not know by what strange accident
I chanced on this letter.
    Ant.   I am dumb.
    Bass. Were you the doctor and I knew you not?   *300*
    Gra. Were you the clerk that is to make me cuckold?
    Ner. Ay; but the clerk that never means to do it,
Unless he live until he be a man.
    Bass. Sweet doctor, you shall be my bedfellow:
When I am absent, then lie with my wife.   *305*
    Ant. Sweet lady, you have given me life and living;
For here I read for certain that my ships
Are safely come to road.
    Por.   How now, Lorenzo!
My clerk hath some good comforts too for you.   *310*
    Ner. Ay, and I'll give them him without a fee.
There do I give to you and Jessica,
From the rich Jew, a special deed of gift,
After his death, of all he dies possess'd of.
    Lor. Fair ladies, you drop manna in the way   *315*
Of starved people.
    Por.   It is almost morning,
And yet I am sure you are not satisfied
Of these events at full. Let us go in;
And charge us there upon inter'gatories,   *320*
And we will answer all things faithfully.
    Gra. Let it be so: the first inter'gatory
That my Nerissa shall be sworn on is,
Whether till the next night she had rather stay,
Or go to bed now, being two hours to day: *325*
But were the day come, I should wish it dark,
That I were couching with the doctor's clerk.
Well, while I live I'll fear no other thing
So sore as keeping safe Nerissa's ring.   *Exeunt.*

❧ FINIS ❧

---

227 **civil doctor:** *doctor of civil law*   234 **shame ... courtesy:** *shame at trespassing against good manners*   236 **besmear:** *soil*   246 **well:** *very*   247 **Argus:** *he had a hundred eyes*   263 **double:** *full of duplicity*   268 **wealth:** *welfare*   272 **advisedly:** *deliberately*

306 **living:** *means of life*   308 **road:** *harbor*   318, 319 **satisfied ... at full:** *fully informed*   320 **charge ... upon inter'gatories:** *question us on oath*   328 **fear:** *concern myself over*

NOTES

Dramatis Personæ. These were first given, under the heading of 'The Actors Names,' in the third Quarto (1637). Words in brackets have been added by later editors.

I.i.101 *damn those ears,* etc. If they did speak, the people hearing them would immediately call them fools, and thus be in danger of damnation. An allusion to Matthew 5. 22: 'whosoever shall say to his brother . . . Thou fool, shall be in danger of hell fire.'

I.i.115. *In a neat's tongue dried,* etc. A neat is a bovine animal. The meaning of the whole passage is that everybody ought to talk except prudes. Possibly it is a fragment of some popular saying or song.

I.i.124. *That.* The word may refer to either the lady or the pilgrimage; it is impossible to say which, but both are probably implied.

I.i.148. *innocence.* Furness is probably right in thinking innocence here to mean foolishness. Compare the words in the preceding line, 'childhood proof.' Bassanio knew that he had no good reason for asking for more money, when he had not paid what he already owed.

I.i.169. *Cato's daughter, Brutus' Portia.* The Portia of Brutus appears in Shakespeare's *Julius Caesar,* a play which seems not to have been written till half a dozen years after *The Merchant of Venice.*

I.i.174. *Colchos' strond.* Colchis was a legendary country in Asia, on the eastern shore (strond) of the Black Sea. Jason went thither in search of the golden fleece, and with the aid of Medea (whom he later deserted) found and brought away the prize.

I.ii.41. *choose.* This much discussed passage seems to me to mean simply, 'if you don't like me, choose somebody else; choose for yourself.'

I.ii.59. *he hath neither Latin, French, nor Italian.* Englishmen being, then as now, notorious for their ignorance of other languages. Many believe that Shakespeare would not have written this passage if he had been himself thus ignorant; but the criticism is playful, as that about the Englishman's clothes a few lines below.

I.ii.68. *the Frenchman became his surety.* A characteristic English gibe at the consistent but half-hearted way in which the French sided with the Scots in their frequent quarrels with the English. In the Folio (1623) the 'Scottish lord' of line 65 is called simply the 'other lord,' to avoid irritating the Scotch King James, who had become King of England in the interval since the play was first produced.

I.ii.89. *Sibylla.* The Cumaean Sibyl. Apollo promised her that her years should equal the number of grains of sand she held in her hand.

I.ii.109. *The four strangers.* Six have been definitely mentioned, but Shakespeare was careless of minor consistencies.

I.iii.29. *the Nazarite.* Commentators have charged Shakespeare with error in applying this word to Christ, since Nazarene is the ordinary term for 'man of Nazareth.' Nazarite is properly the name of an Old Testament Jewish sect who vowed 'to separate themselves unto the Lord' (Numbers 6. 2); but the distinction between Nazarite and Nazarene was not always observed. The allusion in the word 'habitation' is of course to the transfer of the devils from two men into a herd of swine (Matthew 8. 28 ff.).

I.iii.81. *peel'd me.* 'Me' is here the 'ethical dative,' which is frequent in Shakespeare, but nearly impossible to render in modern English. It slightly stresses the speaker's interest in the action of the verb, but does not otherwise affect the meaning of the sentence and would be omitted in a paraphrase.

I.iii.143. *Bass.* The Folios and first two Quartos give this speech to Bassanio, and are followed by most editors. The third Quarto (an authority of little importance) gives it to Antonio, which seems inherently better. Antonio is carrying on the dialogue with Shylock; furthermore, Bassanio would not be quite a gentleman if he showed any eagerness here to have the loan made. Shakespeare seldom makes a mistake in delicacy of feeling.

II.i.7. *whose blood is reddest.* Even then 'red-blooded' was used as it is now.

II.i.11, 12. *I would not change this hue, Except to steal your thoughts.* The only thing that would induce me to change my bronze skin for white would be the chance of winning you if I were fair.

II.ii.14. *my father did something smack, something grow to, he had a kind of taste.* This means that his father had sensual tastes. Editors explain 'grow to' as a household phrase applied to burnt milk. Launcelot, however, is speaking with relish.

II.ii.19. *God bless the mark!* A deprecatory expression, usually 'God save the mark!' It may have had its origin in Ezekiel 9. 6, where the Lord says: 'Slay utterly old and young, both maids, and little children, and women; but come not near any man upon whom is the mark.' Or it may refer to the mark of Cain, Genesis 4. 15: 'And the Lord said unto him, Therefore whosoever slayeth

Cain, vengeance shall be taken on him sevenfold. And the Lord set a mark upon Cain, lest any finding him should kill him.'

II.ii.22. *the very devil incarnation.* The spurious Quarto of 1619 (falsely dated 1600) substitutes 'incarnall' for 'incarnation,' a change very generally adopted by editors who assumed that quarto to be the genuine first edition of the play. Launcelot's 'devil incarnation' blunderingly confuses three different phrases: devil incarnate, devil's incarnation, and devil in carnation (*i.e.,* pink).

II.ii.30. *being more than sand-blind, high-gravel blind.* Launcelot humorously makes sand-blind a kind of positive to the comparative gravel-blind and superlative stone-blind. 'High-gravel blind' is of course his own invention.

II.ii.38. *By God's sonties.* A corrupted oath: God's saints, or sanctities (or possibly from the French *santé*).

II.ii.51, 52. *But I pray you, ergo, old man, ergo, I beseech you, talk you of young Master Launcelot?* Since you address me respectfully as 'your worship,' and Launcelot is my friend and equal, therefore (*ergo*) is it not *Master* Launcelot that you talk of?

II.ii.83. *what a beard hast thou got!* 'Stage tradition, not improbably from the time of Shakespeare himself, makes Launcelot, at this point, kneel with his back to the sand-blind old Father, who, of course, mistakes his long back hair for a beard, of which his face is perfectly innocent.' (Staunton.)

II.ii.95. *you may tell every finger I have with my ribs.* Topsy-turvy nonsense for 'you may count every rib with your finger.'

II.ii.133. *The old proverb is very well parted.* The proverb was: 'God's grace is gear enough.' Parted means distributed, divided.

II.ii.142. *table,* etc. Palmistry. Table was the technical term for the palm of the hand. As Launcelot opens his hand to inspect the palm, the action suggests to him the idea of laying the hand on the book (Bible) to swear an oath. 'A simple (moderate) line of life' (l. 143) is used humorously for the reverse. Compare 'a small trifle of wives,' 'a simple coming-in for one man' (l. 145). The number of wives was supposed to be indicated by the number of lines running from the ball of the thumb towards the line of life.

II.v.43. *worth a Jewess' eye.* Alluding to a common proverb, 'worth a Jew's eye.' The early editions spell the word 'Iewes' and modern editors find it difficult to decide whether Jewess' or Jew's is intended.

II.vi.16. *scarfed.* Most editors think this refers to flag-decorations. I believe it alludes simply to the spread of sails, which are fresh and strong at the beginning of the voyage, and at the return home are 'ragged . . . Lean, rent, and beggar'd.'

II.ix.87. *what would my lord?* It is generally explained that Portia says this playfully to the servant-messenger. Possibly she supposes, however, from the servant's excited manner that Arragon has returned for some reason, and so makes this impatient query.

III.i.23. *the wings she flew withal.* That is, the boy's dress that was the means of her escape.

III.i.77. *Why thou—* Furness and many other editors believe 'thou' to be a misprint for 'then' (which is actually the reading of the second Folio). But surely Shylock is going to call Jessica a bad name, and either checks himself or can't think of one bad enough.

III.i.90. *Where? in Genoa?* The early editions all have 'here in Genoa,' though Shylock is speaking in Venice. Rowe introduced the emendation, which has been accepted in most modern editions. Furness, however, justifies the original reading by the reasoning that in contrast with rumors of far-off losses on the Goodwins, etc., a loss confirmed in Genoa seems very near and definite.

III.ii.20, 21. *Prove it so, Let fortune go to hell for it, not I.* Should it prove, by the lottery of the caskets, that I am not yours, let chance bear the blame (which could not be adequately punished short of hell), not me.

III.ii.56, 57. *With no less presence, but with much more love, Than young Alcides.* Because Alcides (Hercules) rescued Hesione from the sea-monster, not for love but for the horses promised him by her father Laomedon, King of Troy. Portia compares herself to Hesione in the words, 'I stand for sacrifice' (l. 59). The 'Dardanian wives' (l. 60) are the Trojan matrons.

III.ii.98. *Upon supposed fairness.* This may mean 'on the strength of their fictitious beauty,' as some believe; but the beauty of the hair is real, not fictitious. The phrase probably refers rather to the 'supposed fairness' of the head that the locks adorn, which is really not fair at all.

III.ii.103. *Veiling an Indian beauty.* This is regarded as a very difficult passage, but why? Bassanio has been talking about lovely golden false hair adorning an ugly head, hence concealing it too. Thus the 'beauteous scarf Veiling an Indian

beauty' means the fair veil concealing a black, that is loathsome, beauty. The emphasis is on the word 'Indian,' not 'beauty.'

III.ii.116. *In measure rain thy joy.* The verb is certainly rain, not rein, as some critics have taken it. The meaning is: Pour thy joy moderately.

III.ii.205, 206. *You lov'd, I lov'd; for intermission No more pertains to me, my lord, than you.* There has been much dispute over the meaning of these lines, all due to the punctuation of the early editions, which unanimously omit the semicolon after 'I lov'd' and insert a comma (or period) after 'intermission.' If the old punctuation is retained and understood to mark the logical relations of the parts of the sentence, the best explanation of line 200 would be to interpret 'intermission' as meaning comedy, like 'interlude.' You loved in the style of high drama, I match you with love less dignified perhaps, but real: I am to you as farce to drama. This, however, would leave line 201 far from clear; and it is much more likely that the pointing of the old editions is a striking instance of the tendency in Shakespeare's time to punctuate rhetorically instead of logically. The comma after 'intermission' would thus mark the drop of the actor's voice, not the close of a clause in the sentence.

III.ii.225. *Salanio.* The original editions give the name as Salerio here and throughout the rest of the scene, and several of the most important modern editors, on the strength of this, include Salerio, as well as Salanio and Salarino, among the characters in the play. It is highly unlikely that Shakespeare intended to add this third unnecessary character for the purposes of a single scene: Salerio may be either a slip of the author's pen or a blunder of the compositor.

III.iv.20. *the semblance of my soul.* Antonio, whose likeness to Bassanio makes him also like the very soul of Portia.

III.iv.54. *Unto the tranect, to the common ferry.* The meaning of tranect, evidently an uncommon word, is purposely explained in the words that follow. Since no other example of 'tranect' has been found, Rowe, followed by most modern editors, substitutes 'traject,' which is taken to be an anglicized version of 'traghetto,' the contemporary name of the Venetian ferries.

III.v.15. *I shall be saved by my husband.* See 1 Corinthians 7. 14: 'For the unbelieving husband is sanctified by the wife, and the unbelieving wife is sanctified by the husband.'

III.v.44. *'cover' is the word.* Launcelot here means by cover 'bring the meal to the table.' In his next speech (l. 46) he quibbles on another meaning, 'put on one's hat,' which it would be undutiful for him, a servant, to do in the presence of Lorenzo.

III.v.67. *mean it.* Either, 'do not mean to lead an upright life,' or 'do not observe a mean (temperance, moderation).'

IV.i.57. *a woollen bagpipe.* Covered with woollen cloth. Among the many unnecessary emendations for 'woollen' which have been suggested are swollen, wooden, and wauling (cf. caterwauling). The last is the most plausible.

IV.i.74, 75. *You may as well use question with the wolf, Why he hath made the ewe bleat for the lamb.* An accident in the preparation of the First Quarto caused the omission of the first three words in line 74 and the first four in line 75 in certain copies of that edition. The Folio text was set up from one of the defective copies.

IV.i.120. *Than to live still, and write mine epitaph.* Compare Hamlet to Horatio (*Hamlet*, V.ii.370, 371):

'Absent thee from felicity awhile,
And in this harsh world draw thy breath in pain,
To tell my story.'

IV.i.132. *And for thy life let justice be accus'd.* Possibly meaning that justice is wrong for allowing him to live at all; but I think it means that justice should be condemned for allowing him to live in his present purpose, which though horrible is quite legal.

IV.i.153. *Bellario's letter.* Many say that Bellario had told Portia how to

circumvent Shylock; but this is not only an unnecessary supposition, it spoils the scene. If Portia did not use her mother-wit here, why not let Bellario go himself and thus have Portia run no risk? Doubtless she had persuaded him to be 'very sick.' The subsequent citation of the law proving Shylock guilty of intent to murder may very well have come from Bellario.

IV.i.227. *A Daniel come to judgment.* I.e., a just young judge has arisen. The allusion is to the History of Susanna in the Apocrypha: 'the Lord raised up the holy spirit of a young youth, whose name was Daniel,' and who proceeded to give righteous judgment where his elders had blundered.

V.i.48, 49. *Master Lorenzo? Master Lorenzo!* The only two authoritative texts, those of the First Quarto (1600) and First Folio, both print these words, 'M. Lorenzo & M. Lorenzo,' which may be intended for 'Master Lorenzo and Mistress Lorenzo' (*i.e.*, Jessica).

V.i.65, 66. *the floor of heaven Is thick inlaid with patines of bright gold.* Shakespeare may have forgotten that on a bright, moonlight night one cannot see many stars. Furness, however, suggests that the 'patines' are not stars, but bits of illuminated cloud.

V.i.140, 141. *We should hold day with the Antipodes, If you would walk in absence of the sun.* With you to replace the sun in the night we should think that our day, as it is on the other side of the globe; *i.e.*, you would turn night to day and outshine the sun.

THE TEXT OF THE PRESENT EDITION

The text of the present volume is, by permission, based upon that of the Oxford Shakespeare, compared with the First Folio and Quarto texts. The following changes from the Oxford text have been made:

1. The stage directions are those of the First Folio, necessary additional words being inserted in square brackets.

2. The punctuation has been occasionally altered, and the spelling of a few words normalized; *e.g.*, villainy (villany), nobody (no body), everywhere (every where).

3. The following alterations of text have been introduced, usually in deference to the authority of the genuine (Heyes) Quarto of 1600 (Q) and the First Folio (F). Readings of the present edition precede and those of Craig (Oxford) follow the colon:

I.iii.76	eanlings which (QF): eanlings that
110	spit: spet (QF). Cf. II.vii.45
143	*Bass.* (QF): *Ant.*
161	dealings (QF): dealing (later Folios)
II.ii.22	incarnation (QF): incarnal (spurious quarto)
84	phill-horse (QF): thill-horse (Theobald)
102	farthest (QF): very furthest
II.ix.4	stand (QF): stands (misprint?)
III.i.38	was used (QF): used (Rowe)
70	there, there, there, there! (QF): there there, there!
III.ii.253	steals (QF): steal (Pope)
III.iv.54	tranect (QF): traject (Rowe)
IV.i.22	strange apparent (QF): strange-apparent (Walker)
57	woollen (QF): wauling (Capell)
286	but (Q): not (F)
383	unto (QF): into (misprint?)
V.i.200	hope, which (QF): hope, that
253	let not me (QF): let me not
324	Whether (QF): Whe'r

As You Like It

Edited by
S. C. BURCHELL

Dramatis Personae

DUKE SENIOR, *living in exile in the Forest of Arden*

DUKE FREDERICK, *his Brother and Usurper of the Dukedom*

AMIENS } *Lords attending on*
JAQUES } *the banished Duke*

LE BEAU, *a Courtier attending on Duke Frederick*

CHARLES, *Wrestler to Duke Frederick*

OLIVER
JAQUES DE BOYS } *Sons of Sir Rowland de Boys*
ORLANDO

ADAM
DENNIS } *Servants to Oliver*

TOUCHSTONE, *a Clown*

SIR OLIVER MARTEXT, *a Vicar*

CORIN } *Shepherds*
SILVIUS

WILLIAM, *a country Fellow in love with Audrey*

HYMEN

ROSALIND, *Daughter to the banished Duke*

CELIA, *Daughter to Duke Frederick*

PHEBE, *a Shepherdess*

AUDREY, *a country Wench*

LORDS, PAGES, FORESTERS, ATTENDANTS

As You Like It

INTRODUCTION

TEXT AND DATE

As You Like It was not printed until the First Folio of 1623. As this is the only authoritative text, it has been the concern of the present edition to depart from the Folio reading only when absolutely necessary. Essential stage directions not found in the Folio have been placed in square brackets, while words added to the text have been noted at the foot of the page. Obvious errors have been silently corrected and the spelling has been modernized (as has the punctuation) except in the case of a spelling indicative of Elizabethan pronunciation.

However, the question of the date of the play's composition presents significant difficulties. The play was entered on the Stationer's Register as a book to be stayed (that is, not printed, in order to prevent unauthorized use of the text) on August 4 of an unspecified year. But the order of entries in the Register and the inclusion of *Henry V, Much Ado about Nothing,* and Jonson's *Every Man in his Humour* on the same list make it almost certain that it was the year 1600. This information, however, tells us little about the time of actual composition.

John Dover Wilson, in *The New Shakespeare* (Cambridge, 1926), advances the hypothesis that a first version of the play was written in the summer of 1593 and drastically revised to its present form sometime around 1600. His argument is based upon a number of interesting points of internal evidence: the existence of many blank-verse lines in prose passages of the text as we now have it, the presence of obvious inconsistencies (Celia being 'taller' than Rosalind), certain references to the Martin Marprelate controversy, the publication of Lodge's *Rosalynde* in 1590, and most significant of all, the overt references to Christopher Marlowe.

At one point in the play Touchstone mentions a man being struck more dead than 'a great reckoning in a little room.' Dover Wilson feels that this is a direct reference to Marlowe's death in a tavern brawl on May 30, 1593, with the additional echo of a line from the *Jew of Malta* (see note to *As You Like It,* III.3.11, 12). Marlowe is again referred to in III.5.82, where his *Hero and Leander,* published in 1598, is quoted. A topical allusion of this sort would suggest that Shakespeare wrote the play some time after the year 1598. But Touchstone's remark must be taken as particularly inconclusive evidence that the play was first written in 1593. At best it can be interpreted only as an unconscious reference on Shakespeare's part and, if conscious, talk about Marlowe's death must have been common for many years after 1593. Even as late as 1600 a London audience could be assumed to have understood the allusion. However, it is most significant that Francis Meres in his discussion of Shakespeare's plays, published in 1598, makes no mention of *As You Like It.*

Though Dover Wilson's theory is of great interest and ingeniously conceived, internal and external evidence seem to point most clearly to a date of composition sometime between 1598

and 1600. Until further evidence is disclosed it is impossible to be more definite. Certainly the first mention of the play occurs in 1600.

SOURCES OF THE PLAY

For *As You Like It* Shakespeare characteristically derived his basic plot from another author. In this case all essential material comes from Thomas Lodge's novel, *Rosalynde: Euphues Golden Legacie,* published in 1590. In a note to his 'gentlemen readers' Lodge remarks, 'If you like it, so'—and it is generally assumed that this gave rise to Shakespeare's title. Shakespeare has abandoned the mannered euphuistic style of his source but has retained many of the pastoral elements which can be seen in his idyllic Forest of Arden, far away from the artificiality of court life. This popular Elizabethan theme can be found in a multitude of other works, among them Spenser's *Shepheardes Calender* (1579) and Sidney's *Arcadia* (1590).

Lodge's novel (in turn based on a Middle English poem, *The Coke's Tale of Gamelyn)* is a traditional pastoral romance. Shakespeare, while changing some names, has followed the essential pattern of Lodge's narrative. Rosalynde is the daughter of the banished king of France who falls in love with Rosader (Orlando) when she sees him in a wrestling match. She and her cousin Alinda (Celia) are banished by the usurping king and go in the disguises of Ganymede and Aliena to the Forest of the Ardennes. Here they meet Rosader who has fled from the wrath of his wicked brother Saladyne (Oliver). There is a romance between Rosalynde and Rosader, as in Shakespeare's play; and Saladyne, himself exiled by the evil king, reforms and falls in love with Alinda. News is finally brought to the forest that the peers of France have risen against the usurper, who is defeated, and Rosader is made heir to the throne.

It is obvious that *As You Like It* owes much to Lodge's novel, but Shakespeare has made some significant changes and additions. He has focused the action most clearly on the Forest of Arden passages, cutting out a great deal of the introductory matter, particularly the long section on Rosader's quarrel with his wicked brother, which he compressed to one brief interview. He also concentrated upon the romance of Rosalynde and Rosader and, unlike Lodge, gave merely a brief account of Saladyne's love for Alinda. But changes of this sort are obviously necessitated by the transition from a narrative to a dramatic form and reflect little of Shakespeare's originality.

The significant difference between *As You Like It* and *Rosalynde* lies in the approach to the pastoral tradition. The characters that Shakespeare has added—Touchstone, Jaques, and Audrey—create a tone of realism and form an ironic double image commenting upon the stilted world of pastoral romance.

Perhaps more important even than the treatment of these three characters is Shakespeare's treatment of Rosalind: she is no longer the stock figure that Lodge's Rosalynde was, and the whole action of the play is centered sharply on her, thus eliminating the diffusion characteristic of the novel. She has become a witty, paradoxical young lady, a blend of realism and of romance—fit company for Orlando and fit company too for Touchstone and Jaques.

ACT FIRST ❧ SCENE FIRST

Enter Orlando and Adam.

Orl. As I remember, Adam, it was upon this fashion: he bequeathed me by will but poor a thousand crowns and, as thou say'st, charged my brother on his blessing to breed me well; and there begins my sadness. My brother Jaques he keeps at school, and report speaks goldenly of his profit. For my 5 part, he keeps me rustically at home, or—to speak more properly—stays me here at home unkept, for call you that keeping for a gentleman of my birth that differs not from the stalling of an ox? His horses are bred better; for, besides that they are fair with their feeding, they are taught their manage, 10 and to that end riders dearly hir'd. But I, his brother, gain nothing under him but growth, for the which his animals on his dunghills are as much bound to him as I. Besides this nothing that he so plentifully gives me, the something that nature gave me, his countenance seems to take from me. He lets 15 me feed with his hinds, bars me the place of a brother and, as much as in him lies, mines my gentility with my education. This is it, Adam, that grieves me and the spirit of my father, which I think is within me, begins to mutiny against this servitude. I will no longer endure it, though yet I know 20 no wise remedy how to avoid it.

Enter Oliver.

Adam. Yonder comes my master, your brother.

Orl. Go apart, Adam, and thou shalt hear how he will shake me up.

Oli. Now, sir, what make you here? 25

Orl. Nothing. I am not taught to make anything.

Oli. What mar you then, sir?

Orl. Marry, sir, I am helping you to mar that which God made, a poor unworthy brother of yours, with idleness.

Oli. Marry, sir, be better employed, and be naught a while.

Orl. Shall I keep your hogs and eat husks with them? What prodigal portion have I spent that I should come to such penury?

Oli. Know you where you are, sir?

Orl. O, sir, very well. Here in your orchard. 35

Oli. Know you before whom, sir?

Orl. Ay, better than him I am before knows me. I know you are my eldest brother, and in the gentle condition of blood you should so know me. The courtesy of nations allows you my better, in that you are the first born, but the 40 same tradition takes not away my blood, were there twenty brothers betwixt us. I have as much of my father in me as you, albeit I confess your coming before me is nearer to his reverence.

Oli. What, boy! 45

Orl. Come, come, elder brother, you are too young in this.

Oli. Wilt thou lay hands on me, villain?

Orl. I am no villain; I am the youngest son of Sir Rowland de Boys. He was my father, and he is thrice a villain that 50 says such a father begot villains. Wert thou not my brother, I would not take this hand from thy throat till this other had pull'd out thy tongue for saying so. Thou hast rail'd on thyself.

Adam. Sweet masters, be patient. For your father's 55 remembrance, be at accord.

Oli. Let me go, I say!

Orl. I will not till I please; you shall hear me. My father charg'd you in his will to give me good education. You have train'd me like a peasant, obscuring and hiding from me all 60 gentleman-like qualities. The spirit of my father grows strong in me, and I will no longer endure it. Therefore allow me such exercises as may become a gentleman, or give me the poor allottery my father left me by testament. With that I will go buy my fortunes. 65

Oli. And what wilt thou do? Beg when that is spent? Well, sir, get you in. I will not long be troubled with you; you shall have some part of your will. I pray you, leave me.

Orl. I will no further offend you than becomes me for my good. 70

Oli. Get you with him, you old dog.

Adam. Is 'old dog' my reward? Most true, I have lost my teeth in your service. God be with my old master. He would not have spoke such a word.   *Exeunt Orlando, Adam.*

Oli. Is it even so? Begin you to grow upon me? I will 75 physic your rankness, and yet give no thousand crowns neither. Holla, Dennis!

Enter Dennis.

Den. Calls your worship?

Oli. Was not Charles, the Duke's wrastler, here to speak with me? 80

Den. So please you, he is here at the door and importunes access to you.

Oli. Call him in. *[Exit Dennis.]* 'Twill be a good way, and tomorrow the wrastling is.

Enter Charles.

Cha. Good morrow to your worship. 85

Oli. Good Monsieur Charles, what's the new news at the new court?

Cha. There's no news at the court, sir, but the old news: that is, the old Duke is banished by his younger brother, the new Duke, and three or four loving lords have put themselves into voluntary exile with him, whose lands and revenues enrich the new Duke. Therefore he gives them good leave to wander.

Oli. Can you tell if Rosalind, the Duke's daughter, be banished with her father?

Cha. O, no. For the Duke's daughter, her cousin, so 95 loves her, being ever from their cradles bred together, that she would have followed her exile, or have died to stay behind her. She is at the court and no less beloved of her uncle than his own daughter, and never two ladies loved as they do.

Oli. Where will the old Duke live? 100

Cha. They say he is already in the Forest of Arden, and a

---

1 he; *cf. n.*   **3 poor a:** *a miserable* **breed:** *raise*   **5 school:** *college* **goldenly:** *glowingly*   **6 rustically:** *like a peasant*   **7 stays:** *keeps* **unkept:** *uncared for*   **10 manage:** *training paces*   **11 dearly:** *expensively*   **15 countenance:** *behavior*   **16 hinds:** *field servants*   **17 mines:** *undermines*   **25 make you:** *are you doing*   **27 mar;** *cf. n.*   **30 Marry:** *contraction of 'by the Virgin Mary'* **be naught:** *keep quiet*   **32 prodigal portion;** *cf. n.*   **34 where:** *in whose presence (Orlando takes the literal meaning)*   **37 Ay:** *F 1 (F is the First Folio of 1623)*   **38 gentle condition of blood:** *natural kindness of our relationship*   **39 courtesy of nations:** *conventions of civilized society*   **44 reverence;** *cf. n.*   **46 young:** *brash*

48 villain; *cf. n.*   **63 exercises:** *occupations*   **64 allottery:** *share*   **75 grow:** *presume*   **76 physic** *purge* **rankness:** *insolence, foulness*   **79 wrastler;** *cf. n.*   **86 Monsieur;** *cf. n.*   **101 Forest of Arden;** *cf. n.*

many merry men with him. And there they live like the
old Robin Hood of England. They say many young gentlemen
flock to him every day and fleet the time carelessly as they
did in the golden world.   *105*

Oli. What, you wrastle tomorrow before the new Duke?

Cha. Marry, do I, sir. And I came to acquaint you
with a matter: I am given, sir, secretly to understand that your
younger brother Orlando hath a disposition to come in disguis'd against me to try a fall. Tomorrow, sir, I wrastle for   *110*
my credit, and he that escapes me without some broken limb
shall acquit him well. Your brother is but young and tender,
and for your love I would be loath to foil him, as I must for
my own honor if he come in. Therefore, out of my love to
you, I came hither to acquaint you withal, that either you   *115*
might stay him from his intendment or brook such disgrace
well as he shall run into; in that it is a thing of his own
search, and altogether against my will.

Oli. Charles, I thank thee for thy love to me, which thou
shalt find I will most kindly requite. I had myself notice of   *120*
my brother's purpose herein, and have by underhand means
labored to dissuade him from it; but he is resolute. I'll tell
thee, Charles, it is the stubbornest young fellow of France—full
of ambition, an envious emulator of every man's good parts,
a secret and villainous contriver against me, his natural   *125*
brother. Therefore use thy discretion; I had as lief thou didst
break his neck as his finger. And thou wert best look to 't; for
if thou dost him any slight disgrace, or if he do not mightily
grace himself on thee, he will practise against thee by poison,
entrap thee by some treacherous device, and never leave thee
till he hath tane thy life by some indirect means or other. For
I assure thee—and almost with tears I speak it—there is not
one so young and so villainous this day living. I speak but
brotherly of him; but should I anatomize him to thee as he is,
I must blush and weep, and thou must look pale and wonder.

Cha. I am heartily glad I came hither to you. If he come
tomorrow, I'll give him his payment. If ever he go alone
again, I'll never wrastle for prize more. And so God keep your
worship.   *Exit.*

[Oli.] Farewell, good Charles. Now will I stir this game-   *140*
ster. I hope I shall see an end of him, for my soul—yet I
know not why—hates nothing more than he. Yet he's gentle,
never school'd and yet learned, full of noble device, of all sorts
enchantingly beloved, and indeed so much in the heart of the
world and especially of my own people who best know   *145*
him, that I am altogether misprised. But it shall not be so
long; this wrestler shall clear all. Nothing remains but that I
kindle the boy thither, which now I'll go about.   *Exit.*

❧ Scene Second ❧

Enter Rosalind and Celia.

Cel. I pray thee, Rosalind, sweet my coz, be merry.

Ros. Dear Celia, I show more mirth than I am mistress of,

and would you yet I were merrier? Unless you could teach me
to forget a banished father, you must not learn me how to
remember any extraordinary pleasure.   *5*

Cel. Herein I see thou lov'st me not with the full weight
that I love thee. If my uncle, thy banished father, had banished thy uncle, the Duke my father, so thou hadst been still
with me, I could have taught my love to take thy father for
mine; so wouldst thou, if the truth of thy love to me were   *10*
so righteously temper'd as mine is to thee.

Ros. Well, I will forget the condition of my estate to rejoice
in yours.

Cel. You know my father hath no child but I, nor none is
like to have. And truly, when he dies, thou shalt be his   *15*
heir; for what he hath taken away from thy father perforce I
will render thee again in affection. By mine honor, I will. And
when I break that oath, let me turn monster. Therefore, my
sweet Rose, my dear Rose, by merry.

Ros. From henceforth I will, coz, and devise sports. Let   *20*
me see. What think you of falling in love?

Cel. Marry, I prithee do, to make sport withal. But love no
man in good earnest, nor no further in sport neither than with
safety of a pure blush thou mayst in honor come off again.

Ros. What shall be our sport then?   *25*

Cel. Let us sit and mock the good housewife Fortune from
her wheel, that her gifts may henceforth be bestowed equally.

Ros. I would we could do so, for her benefits are mightily
misplaced and the bountiful blind woman doth most mistake
in her gifts to women.   *30*

Cel. 'Tis true. For those that she makes fair she scarce
makes honest, and those that she makes honest she makes very
ill-favoredly.

Ros. Nay, now thou goest from Fortune's office to Nature's.
Fortune reigns in gifts of the world, not in the lineaments   *35*
of Nature.

Enter Clown [Touchstone].

Cel. No? When Nature hath made a fair creature, may she
not by Fortune fall into the fire? Though Nature hath given us
wit to flout at Fortune, hath not Fortune sent in this fool to
cut off the argument?   *40*

Ros. Indeed there is Fortune too hard for Nature, when
Fortune makes Nature's natural the cutter-off of Nature's wit.

Cel. Peradventure this is not Fortune's work neither but
Nature's, who perceiveth our natural wits too dull to reason of
such goddesses and hath sent this natural for our whetstone.   *45*
For always the dullness of the fool is the whetstone of the
wits. How now, wit? Whether wander you?

Touch. Mistress, you must come away to your father.

Cel. Were you made the messenger?

Touch. No, by mine honor, but I was bid to come for you.

Ros. Where learned you that oath, fool?

Touch. Of a certain knight, that swore by his honor they
were good pancakes and swore by his honor the mustard was
naught. Now I'll stand to it, the pancakes were naught and the
mustard was good. And yet was not the knight forsworn.   *55*

---

104 fleet: *pass*   **105 golden world;** *cf. n.*   **113 loath:** *unwilling* **foil:** *throw*   **115 withal:** *with this*   **116 intendment:** *intent*   **116, 117 brook ... well:** *endure*   **121 underhand:** *unobtrusive*   **125, 126 natural brother:** *blood brother* **had as lief:** *had as soon*   **127 wert best:** *had better* **look to 't:** *take care*   **129 grace:** *do credit to* **practise:** *scheme*   **131 tane:** *taken*   **134 anatomize:** *analyze*   **137 go alone:** *walk without aid*   **140 stir:** *incite* **gamester:** *athlete*   **143 device:** *purpose* **sorts:** *types of people*   **144 enchantingly:** *as if by enchantment*   **146 misprised:** *despised*   **147 clear all:** *settle everything*   **147 kindle ... thither:** *incite him to challenge the wrestler*   **1 coz:** *cousin*

3 I: *F omits*   **4 learn me:** *instruct me*   **8 so:** *provided that*   **11 righteously temper'd:** *thoroughly consistent*   **12 estate:** *fortune*   **16 perforce:** *by force*   **20 sports:** *amusements*   **22 prithee:** *pray you; F prethee*   **23, 24 with ... blush:** *with modesty* **come off:** *escape*   **26 housewife Fortune;** *cf. n.*   **32 honest:** *virtuous*   **33 ill-favoredly:** *ugly looking*   **34 office:** *function*   **36 Nature;** *cf. n.*   **42 natural:** *idiot*   **44 reason of:** *discuss*   **45 and:** *F omits* **whetstone;** *cf. n.*   **47 Whether:** *whither*   **54 naught:** *worthless* **stand to it:** *maintain*   **55 was ... forsworn:** *did not swear falsely*

Cel. How prove you that in the great heap of your
knowledge?

Ros. Ay, marry, now unmuzzle your wisdom.

Touch. Stand you both forth now. Stroke your chins and
swear by your beards that I am a knave.   60

Cel. By our beards—if we had them—thou art.

Touch. By my knavery—if I had it—then I were. But if you
swear by that that is not, you are not forsworn. No more was
this knight swearing by his honor, for he never had any; or,
if he had, he had sworn it away before ever he saw those   65
pancakes or that mustard.

Cel. Prithee, who is't that thou mean'st?

Touch. One that old Frederick, your father, loves.

Cel. My father's love is enough to honor him enough.
Speak no more of him. You'll be whipt for taxation one of   70
these days.

Touch. The more pity that fools may not speak wisely what
wise men do foolishly.

Cel. By my troth, thou sayest true; for, since the little wit
that fools have was silenced, the little foolery that wise men   75
have makes a great show. Here comes Monsieur Le Beau.

Enter Le Beau.

Ros. With his mouth full of news.

Cel. Which he will put on us as pigeons feed their young.

Ros. Then shall we be news-cramm'd.

Cel. All the better; we shall be the more marketable.   80
Bon jour, Monsieur Le Beau, what's the news?

Le Beau. Fair Princess, you have lost much good sport.

Cel. Sport? Of what color?

Le Beau. What color, madam? How shall I answer you?

Ros. As wit and fortune will.   85

Touch. Or as the Destinies decree.

Cel. Well said. That was laid on with a trowel.

Touch. Nay, if I keep not my rank.

Ros. Thou losest thy old smell.

Le Beau. You amaze me, ladies. I would have told you   90
of good wrastling, which you have lost the sight of.

Ros. Yet tell us the manner of the wrastling.

Le Beau. I will tell you the beginning, and if it please your
ladyships, you may see the end; for the best is yet to do. And
here where you are they are coming to perform it.   95

Cel. Well, the beginning that is dead and buried.

Le Beau. There comes an old man and his three sons.

Cel. I could match this beginning with an old tale.

Le Beau. Three proper young men of excellent growth
and presence.   100

Ros. With bills on their necks: 'Be it known unto all
men by these presents.'

Le Beau. The eldest of the three wrastled with Charles, the
Duke's wrastler; which Charles in a moment threw him and
broke three of his ribs, that there is little hope of life in him.
So he serv'd the second, and so the third. Yonder they lie,
the poor old man their father making such pitiful dole over
them that all the beholders take his part with weeping.

Ros. Alas!

Touch. But what is the sport, Monsieur, that the ladies   110
have lost?

Le Beau. Why, this that I speak of.

Touch. Thus men may grow wiser every day. It is the first
time that ever I heard breaking of ribs was sport for ladies.

Cel. Or I, I promise thee.   115

Ros. But is there any else longs to see this broken music
in his sides? Is there yet another dotes upon rib-breaking?
Shall we see this wrastling, cousin?

Le Beau. You must if you stay here; for here is the place appointed for the wrastling, and they are ready to perform it.   120

Cel. Yonder sure they are coming. Let us now stay and
see it.

*Flourish. Enter Duke [Frederick], Lords, Orlando, Charles, and
Attendants.*

Duke. Come on. Since the youth will not be entreated,
his own peril on his forwardness.   125

Ros. Is yonder the man?

Le Beau. Even he, madam.

Cel. Alas, he is too young; yet he looks successfully.

Duke. How now, daughter and cousin, are you crept
hither to see the wrastling?   130

Ros. Ay, my liege, so please you give us leave.

Duke. You will take little delight in it, I can tell you. There
is such odds in the man. In pity of the challenger's youth I
would fain dissuade him, but he will not be entreated. Speak
to him, ladies; see if you can move him.   135

Cel. Call him hether, good Monsieur Le Beau.

Duke. Do so. I'll not be by.

Le Beau. Monsieur the Challenger, the princess calls for you.

Orl. I attend them with all respect and duty.

Ros. Young man, have you challeng'd Charles the Wrastler?

Orl. No, fair princess, he is the general challenger. I
come but in as others do, to try with him the strength of
my youth.

Cel. Young gentleman, your spirits are too bold for your
years. You have seen cruel proof of this man's strength. If   145
you saw yourself with your eyes or knew yourself with your
judgment, the fear of your adventure would counsel you
to a more equal enterprise. We pray you for your own sake
to embrace your own safety and give over this attempt.

Ros. Do, young sir. Your reputation shall not therefore   150
be misprised. We will make it our suit to the Duke that
the wrastling might not go forward.

Orl. I beseech you, punish me not with your hard thoughts,
wherein I confess me much guilty to deny so fair and excellent
ladies anything. But let your fair eyes and gentle wishes go   155
with me to my trial; wherein if I be foil'd, there is but one
sham'd that was never gracious; if kill'd, but one dead
that is willing to be so. I shall do my friends no wrong, for I
have none to lament me; the world no injury, for in it I have
nothing. Only in the world I fill up a place, which may   160
be better supplied when I have made it empty.

Ros. The little strength that I have, I would it were
with you.

---

69 Celia; *cf. n.* enough; *cf. n.*   70 taxation: *insolent criticism, slander*   74 troth:
faith   78 put on: *force on*   80 marketable: *plumper and therefore more valuable*   81
Bon jour; *cf. n.*   83 color: *sort*   89 smell; *cf. n.*   90 amaze: *perplex*   94 to do:
to be done   98 old tale; *cf. n.*   99 proper: *admirable*   100 presence: *carriage*   101
bills: *signs*   102 presents; *cf. n.*   104 which; *cf. n.*   105 that: *so that*   107 dole:
lamentation

116 any: *anyone* longs: *who longs* broken music; *cf. n.*   124 entreated: *persuaded*   125 forwardness: *foolhardiness*   128 looks successfully: *seems able to succeed*   133 such . . . man; *cf. n.*   134 fain: *be glad to*   136 hether; *cf. n.*   139
them; *cf. n.*   151 misprised: *despised* suit: *petition*   157 gracious: *in good favor*

Cel. And mine to eke out hers.

Ros. Fare you well. Pray heaven I be deceiv'd in you.   *165*

Cel. Your heart's desires be with you.

Cha. Come, where is this young gallant that is so
desirous to lie with his mother earth?

Orl. Ready, sir; but his will hath in it a more modest
working.   *170*

Duke. You shall try but one fall.

Cha. No, I warrant your grace you shall not entreat
him to a second, that have so mightily persuaded him from a
first.

Orl. You mean to mock me after; you should not have   *175*
mock'd me before. But come your ways.

Ros. Now Hercules be thy speed, young man.

Cel. I would I were invisible, to catch the strong
fellow by the leg.   *[Charles and Orlando] Wrestle.*

Ros. O excellent young man!   *180*

Cel. If I had a thunderbolt in mine eye, I can tell who
should down.   *[Charles is thrown.] Shout.*

Duke. No more, no more.

Orl. Yes, I beseech your grace; I am not yet well breath'd.

Duke. How dost thou, Charles?   *185*

Le Beau. He cannot speak, my lord.

Duke. Bear him away. What is thy name, young man?

Orl. Orlando, my liege, the youngest son of Sir
Rowland de Boys.

Duke. I would thou hadst been son to some man else.   *190*
The world esteem'd thy father honorable,
But I did find him still mine enemy.
Thou should'st have better pleas'd me with this deed,
Hadst thou descended from another house.
But fare thee well; thou art a gallant youth.   *195*
I would thou hadst told me of another father.
                              Exeunt Duke, [Le Beau, and Lords].

Cel. Were I my father, coz, would I do this?

Orl. I am more proud to be Sir Rowland's son,
His youngest son, and would not change that calling
To be adopted heir to Frederick.   *200*

Ros. My father lov'd Sir Rowland as his soul,
And all the world was of my father's mind.
Had I before known this young man his son,
I should have given him tears unto entreaties,
Ere he should thus have ventur'd.   *205*

Cel.   Gentle cousin,
Let us go thank him and encourage him.
My father's rough and envious disposition
Sticks me at heart. Sir, you have well deserv'd.
If you do keep your promises in love   *210*
But justly as you have exceeded all promise,
Your mistress shall be happy.

Ros. *[presenting a locket].* Gentleman,
Wear this for me, one out of suits with fortune
That could give more, but that her hand lacks means.   *215*
Shall we go, coz?

Cel.   Ay; fare you well, fair gentleman.

Orl. Can I not say 'I thank you'? My better parts
Are all thrown down, and that which here stands up
Is but a quintain, a mere lifeless block.   *220*

Ros. He calls us back. My pride fell with my fortunes.
I'll ask him what he would. Did you call, sir?
Sir, you have wrastled well and overthrown
More than your enemies.

Cel.   Will you go, coz?   *225*

Ros. Have with you. Fare you well.   *Exeunt.*

Orl. What passion hangs these weights upon my tongue?
I cannot speak to her, yet she urg'd conference.

                              Enter Le Beau.

O poor Orlando, thou art overthrown;
Or Charles or something weaker masters thee.   *230*

Le Beau. Good sir, I do in friendship counsel you
To leave this place. Albeit you have deserv'd
High commendation, true applause, and love,
Yet such is now the Duke's condition
That he misconsters all that you have done.   *235*
The Duke is humorous. What he is indeed
More suits you to conceive than I to speak of.

Orl. I thank you, sir. And pray you, tell me this:
Which of the two was daughter of the Duke,
That here was at the wrastling?   *240*

Le Beau. Neither his daughter, if we judge by manners.
But yet indeed the taller is his daughter.
The other is daughter to the banish'd Duke
And here detain'd by her usurping uncle
To keep his daughter company, whose loves   *245*
Are dearer than the natural bond of sisters.
But I can tell you that of late this Duke
Hath tane displeasure 'gainst his gentle niece,
Grounded upon no other argument
But that the people praise her for her virtues,   *250*
And pity her for her good father's sake.
And, on my life, his malice 'gainst the lady
Will suddenly break forth. Sir, fare you well.
Hereafter, in a better world than this,
I shall desire more love and knowledge of you.   *255*

Orl. I rest much bounden to you. Fare you well.
                                                        [Exit Le Beau.]

Thus must I from the smoke into the smother,
From tyrant Duke unto a tyrant brother.
But heavenly Rosalind!

❧ SCENE THREE ❧

Enter Celia and Rosalind.

Cel. Why, cousin, why, Rosalind! Cupid have mercy, not a
word?

Ros. Not one to throw at a dog.

Cel. No, thy words are too precious to be cast away upon

---

165 deceiv'd in: *mistaken about (i.e. his strength)*   **169, 170 modest working:** *moderate
intention*   **177 Hercules be thy speed:** *May Hercules give you good fortune*   **184 well
breath'd:** *fully exercised*   **190 some man else:** *some other man*   **192 still:** *always*   **193
thou hadst:** *to be read 'thou'dst'*   **199 calling:** *name*   **204 unto:** *in addition to*   **209
Sticks me at heart:** *stabs me in the heart*   **211 But justly:** *as exactly*   **214 out of suits:**
out of favor; cf. n

218 parts: *qualities*   **220 quintain;** *cf. n.*   **226 Have with you:** *I'm coming with
you*   **227 passion:** *a strong emotion*   **228 urg'd conference:** *invited conversation*   **234
condition:** *mood*   **235 misconsters:** *misconstrues*   **236 humorous:** *temperamental;
cf. n.*   **242 taller;** *cf. n.*   **243 other is:** *to be read 'other's'*   **248 tane:** *taken*   **249
argument:** *cause*   **256 bounden:** *obligated*   **257 from . . . smother:** *'out of the frying
pan into the fire'*   **SD Rosalind;** *cf. n. (SD is used throughout to indicate stage direction.)*

curs; throw some of them at me. Come, lame me with   5
reasons.

Ros. Then there were two cousins laid up, when the one
should be lam'd with reasons and the other mad without any.

Cel. But is all this for your father?

Ros. No, some of it is for my child's father. O, how full   10
of briers is this working-day world.

Cel. They are but burs, cousin, thrown upon thee in holiday
foolery. If we walk not in the trodden paths, our very petticoats will catch them.

Ros. I could shake them off my coat. These burs are in   15
my heart.

Cel. Hem them away.

Ros. I would try, if I could cry 'hem' and have him.

Cel. Come, come, wrastle with thy affections.

Ros. O, they take the part of a better wrastler than myself.   20

Cel. O, a good wish upon you! You will try in time,
in despite of a fall. But, turning these jests out of service, let
us talk in good earnest. Is it possible on such a sudden you
should fall into so strong a liking with old Sir Rowland's
youngest son?   25

Ros. The Duke my father lov'd his father dearly.

Cel. Doth it therefore ensue that you should love his son
dearly? By this kind of chase I should hate him, for my father
hated his father dearly. Yet I hate not Orlando.

Ros. No, faith. Hate him not, for my sake.   30

Cel. Why should I not? Doth he not deserve well?

Enter Duke with Lords.

Ros. Let me love him for that, and you do love him
because I do. Look, here comes the Duke.

Cel. With his eyes full of anger.

Duke. Mistress, dispatch you with your safest haste   35
And get you from our court.

Ros.   Me, uncle?

Duke.   You, cousin.
Within these ten days if that thou beest found
So near our public court as twenty miles,   40
Thou diest for it.

Ros.   I do beseech your Grace,
Let me the knowledge of my fault bear with me.
If with myself I hold intelligence,
Or have acquaintance with mine own desires;   45
If that I do not dream, or be not frantic—
As I do trust I am not—then, dear uncle,
Never so much as in a thought unborn
Did I offend your highness.

Duke.   Thus do all traitors.   50
If their purgation did consist in words,
They are as innocent as grace itself.
Let it suffice thee that I trust thee not.

Ros. Yet your mistrust cannot make me a traitor.
Tell me whereon the likelihood depends.   55

Duke. Thou art thy father's daughter; there's enough.

Ros. So was I when your highness took his dukedom;

So was I when your highness banish'd him.
Treason is not inherited, my lord;
Or if we did derive it from our friends,   60
What's that to me? My father was no traitor.
Then, good my liege, mistake me not so much
To think my poverty is treacherous.

Cel. Dear sovereign, hear me speak.

Duke. Ay, Celia, we stay'd her for your sake,   65
Else had she with her father rang'd along.

Cel. I did not then entreat to have her stay;
It was your pleasure, and your own remorse.
I was too young that time to value her,
But now I know her. If she be a traitor,   70
Why so am I. We still have slept together,
Rose at an instant, learn'd, play'd, eat together,
And wheresoe'er we went, like Juno's swans,
Still we went coupled and inseparable.

Duke. She is too subtile for thee. And her smoothness,   75
Her very silence and her patience,
Speak to the people, and they pity her.
Thou art a fool. She robs thee of thy name,
And thou wilt show more bright and seem more virtuous
When she is gone. Then open not thy lips.   80
Firm and irrevocable is my doom
Which I have pass'd upon her: she is banish'd.

Cel. Pronounce that sentence then on me, my liege.
I cannot live out of her company.

Duke. You are a fool. You, niece, provide yourself.   85
If you outstay the time, upon mine honor
And in the greatness of my word, you die.

                                    Exeunt Duke, etc.

Cel. O my poor Rosalind, whether wilt thou go?
Wilt thou change fathers? I will give thee mine.
I charge thee be not thou more griev'd than I am.   90

Ros. I have more cause.

Cel.   Thou hast not, cousin.
Prithee, be cheerful. Know'st thou not the Duke
Hath banish'd me, his daughter?

Ros.   That he hath not.   95

Cel. No? Hath not? Rosalind lacks then the love
Which teacheth thee that thou and I am one.
Shall we be sund'red? Shall we part, sweet girl?
No! Let my father seek another heir.
Therefore devise with me how we may fly,   100
Whether to go, and what to bear with us.
And do not seek to take your change upon you,
To bear your griefs yourself and leave me out.
For by this heaven, now at our sorrows pale,
Say what thou canst, I'll go along with thee.   105

Ros. Why, whether shall we go?

Cel. To seek my uncle in the Forest of Arden.

Ros. Alas, what danger will it be to us—
Maids as we are—to travel forth so far?
Beauty provoketh thieves sooner than gold.   110

Cel. I'll put myself in poor and mean attire

---

8 reasons; *cf. n.*   **17 Hem:** *clear away with a cough*   **18** 'hem' . . . him; *cf. n.*   **19**
affections: *feelings*   **22 in despite of:** *notwithstanding*   **turning . . . service:** *putting
aside*   **28 chase:** *pursuit of an argument*   **31 deserve well;** *cf. n.*   **35 dispatch you:**
remove yourself   **44 hold intelligence:** *communicate*   **46 If that:** *if*   **51 purgation:**
absolution from guilt   **52 grace:** *virtue*   **55 likelihood:** *possibility*

60 friends: *relatives*   **63 To:** *as to*   **66 rang'd:** *wandered*   **68 remorse:** *compassion*   **71 still:** *always*   **72 Rose:** *risen* **at an instant:** *at the same time* **eat:** *eaten*
(pronounced 'et')   **73 Juno's swans;** *cf. n.*   **75 subtile:** *subtle, acute*   **79 show:** *appear* **virtuous:** *full of good qualities*   **81 doom:** *sentence*   **87 in . . . word:** *by my word
as ruler*   **101 Whether:** *whither*   **102 change;** *cf. n.*   **111 mean:** *lowly*

And with a kind of umber smirch my face;
The like do you. So shall we pass along
And never stir assailants.

   Ros.   Were it not better,   *115*
Because that I am more than common tall,
That I did suit me all points like a man:
A gallant curtelaxe upon my thigh,
A boar spear in my hand, and—in my heart
Lie there what hidden woman's fear there will— *120*
We'll have a swashing and a martial outside,
As many other mannish cowards have
That do outface it with their semblances.

   Cel. What shall I call thee when thou art a man?
   Ros. I'll have no worse a name than Jove's own page, *125*
And therefore look you call me Ganymede.
But what will you be call'd?

   Cel. Something that hath a reference to my state:
No longer Celia but Aliena.

   Ros. But, cousin, what if we assay'd to steal *130*
The clownish Fool out of your father's court?
Would he not be a comfort to our travel?

   Cel. He'll go along o'er the wide world with me.
Leave me alone to woo him. Let's away
And get our jewels and our wealth together, *135*
Devise the fittest time and safest way
To hide us from pursuit that will be made
After my flight. Now go we in content
To liberty, and not to banishment.   *Exeunt.*

ACT SECOND   SCENE FIRST

Enter Duke Senior, Amiens, and two or three Lords like Foresters.

   Duke S. Now, my co-mates and brothers in exile,
Hath not old custom made this life more sweet
Than that of painted pomp? Are not these woods
More free from peril than the envious court?
Here feel we not the penalty of Adam,   *5*
The seasons' difference?—as, the icy fang
And churlish chiding of the winter's wind
Which when it bites and blows upon my body
E'en till I shrink with cold, I smile and say:
'This is no flattery; these are counselors   *10*
That feelingly persuade me what I am.'
Sweet are the uses of adversity,
Which, like the toad, ugly and venomous,
Wears yet a precious jewel in his head.
And this our life, exempt from public haunt, *15*
Finds tongues in trees, books in the running brooks,
Sermons in stones, and good in everything.

   Ami. I would not change it. Happy is your grace
That can translate the stubborness of Fortune
Into so quiet and so sweet a style.   *20*

   Duke S. Come, shall we go and kill us venison?
And yet it irks me the poor dappled fools,
Being native burghers of this desert city,
Should in their own confines with forked heads
Have their round hanches gor'd.   *25*

   1 Lord.   Indeed, my lord,
The melancholy Jaques grieves at that,
And in that kind swears you do more usurp
Than doth your brother that hath banish'd you.
Today my Lord of Amiens and myself   *30*
Did steal behind him as he lay along
Under an oak whose anticke root peeps out
Upon the brook that brawls along this wood.
To the which place a poor sequest'red stag,
That from the hunter's aim had tane a hurt, *35*
Did come to languish. And indeed, my lord,
The wretched animal heav'd forth such groans
That their discharge did stretch his leathern coat
Almost to bursting, and the big round tears
Cours'd one another down his innocent nose *40*
In piteous chase. And thus the hairy fool,
Much marked of the melancholy Jaques,
Stood on th' extremest verge of the swift brook,
Augmenting it with tears.

   Duke S.   But what said Jaques?   *45*
Did he not moralize this spectacle?

   1 Lord. O yes, into a thousand similes.
First, for his weeping into the needless stream:
'Poor deer,' quoth he, 'thou mak'st a testament
As worldlings do, giving thy sum of more   *50*
To that which had too much.' Then, being there alone,
Left and abandoned of his velvet friends:
''Tis right,' quoth he, 'thus misery doth part
The flux of company.' Anon a careless herd,
Full of the pasture, jumps along by him   *55*
And never stays to greet him. 'Ay,' quoth Jaques,
'Sweep on, you fat and greasy citizens;
'Tis just the fashion. Wherefore do you look
Upon that poor and broken bankrupt there?'
Thus most invectively he pierceth through   *60*
The body of the country, city, court,
Yea, and of this our life, swearing that we
Are mere usurpers, tyrants, and what's worse,
To fright the animals and to kill them up
In their assign'd and native dwelling place. *65*

   Duke S. And did you leave him in this contemplation?
   2 Lord. We did, my Lord, weeping and commenting
Upon the sobbing deer.

   Duke S.   Show me the place.
I love to cope him in these sullen fits,   *70*
For then he's full of matter.

   1 Lord. I'll bring you to him straight.   *Exeunt.*

---

112 umber: *brown pigment*   **114 stir:** *incite*   **116 than common:** *than usually*   **117 all points:** *in all respects*   **118 curtelaxe:** *broad sword*   **121 swashing:** *swaggering*   **123 outface it:** *brazen it out*   **semblances:** *appearances*   **126 Ganymede;** *cf. n.*   **129 Aliena:** *the cast off* (Latin)   **130 assay'd:** *attempted*   **134 woo:** *persuade*   **138 in content:** *satisfied*   **1 exile:** *stressed — —́*   **3 painted:** *artificial, cf. n.*   **5 the penalty of Adam;** *cf. n.*   **6 as:** *for example*   **7 churlish:** *rough*   **9 E'en:** *F Even*   **12 uses:** *benefits*   **13 toad;** *cf. n.*   **15 public haunt:** *resorts of men*   **18 Amiens;** *cf. n.*   **20 style:** *i.e. of life*

23 desert: *uninhabited*   **24 confines:** *territory*   **forked heads:** *hunting arrows*   **25 hanches:** *haunches*   **27 Jaques;** *cf. n.*   **28 in that kind:** *in that respect*   **31 along:** *stretched out*   **32 anticke:** *old* (stressed —́ —)   **33 brawls:** *courses*   **34 sequest'red:** *separated from the herd*   **42 of:** *by*   **43 verge:** *bank*   **46 moralize:** *make a sermon on*   **48 needless:** *i.e. not needing any more water*   **50 worldlings:** *people of the world*   **51 there;** *cf. n.*   **52 of:** *by*   **velvet;** *cf. n.*   **53 part:** *part from*   **54 flux:** *stream*   **Anon:** *presently*   **60 invectively:** *with denunciation*   **61 the:** (before *country*) *F omits*   **64 kill . . . up:** *kill off*   **70 cope:** *meet*   **71 matter:** *substance*   **72 straight:** *immediately*

❧ Scene Second ❧

Enter Duke [Frederick], with Lords.

Duke. Can it be possible that no man saw them?
It cannot be; some villains of my court
Are of consent and sufferance in this.
   1 Lord. I cannot hear of any that did see her.
The ladies, her attendants of her chamber,   *5*
Saw her abed, and in the morning early
They found the bed untreasur'd of their mistress.
   2 Lord. My lord, the roynish Clown at whom so oft
Your Grace was wont to laugh is also missing.
Hisperia, the princess' gentlewoman,   *10*
Confesses that she secretly o'erheard
Your daughter and her cousin much commend
The parts and graces of the wrastler
That did but lately foil the sinewy Charles.
And she believes, wherever they are gone,   *15*
That youth is surely in their company.
   Duke. Send to his brother; fetch that gallant hither.
If he be absent, bring his brother to me.
I'll make him find him. Do this suddenly,
And let not search and inquisition quail   *20*
To bring again these foolish runaways.   *Exeunt.*

❧ Scene Third ❧

Enter Orlando and Adam.

Orl. Who's there?
   Adam. What, my young master! O my gentle master,
O my sweet master, O you memory
Of old Sir Rowland. Why, what make you here?
Why are you virtuous? Why do people love you?   *5*
And wherefore are you gentle, strong, and valiant?
Why would you be so fond to overcome
The bonny prizer of the humorous Duke?
Your praise is come too swiftly home before you.
Know you not, master, to some kind of men   *10*
Their graces serve them but as enemies?
No more do yours: your virtues, gentle master,
Are sanctified and holy traitors to you.
O what a world is this, when what is comely
Envenoms him that bears it.   *15*
   Orl. Why, what's the matter?
   Adam.   O unhappy youth,
Come not within these doors. Within this roof
The enemy of all your graces lives.
Your brother—no, no brother, yet the son   *20*
(Yet not the son, I will not call him son)
Of him I was about to call his father—
Hath heard your praises and this night he means
To burn the lodging where you use to lie,
And you within it. If he fail of that,   *25*
He will have other means to cut you off.

I overheard him and his practices.
This is no place: this house is but a butchery.
Abhor it, fear it, do not enter it.
   Orl. Why, whether, Adam, would'st thou have   *30*
me go?
   Adam. No matter whether, so you come not here.
   Orl. What, would'st thou have me go and beg my
food?
Or with a base and boist'rous sword enforce   *35*
A thievish living on the common road?
This I must do, or know not what to do;
Yet this I will not do, do how I can.
I rather will subject me to the malice
Of a diverted blood and bloody brother.   *40*
   Adam. But do not so. I have five hundred crowns,
The thrifty hire I saved under your father,
Which I did store to be my foster nurse
When service should in my old limbs lie lame
And unregarded age in corners thrown.   *45*
Take that; and He that doth the ravens feed,
Yea, providently caters for the sparrow,
Be comfort to my age. Here is the gold;
All this I give you. Let me be your servant.
Though I look old, yet I am strong and lusty;   *50*
For in my youth I never did apply
Hot and rebellious liquors in my blood,
Nor did not with unbashful forehead woo
The means of weakness and debility.
Therefore my age is as a lusty winter,   *55*
Frosty but kindly. Let me go with you;
I'll do the service of a younger man
In all your business and necessities.
   Orl. O good old man, how well in thee appears
The constant service of the antique world,   *60*
When service sweat for duty, not for meed.
Thou art not for the fashion of these times,
Where none will sweat but for promotion,
And having that, do choke their service up
Even with the having; it is not so with thee.   *65*
But, poor old man, thou prun'st a rotten tree
That cannot so much as a blossom yield,
In lieu of all thy pains and husbandry.
But come thy ways; we'll go along together,
And ere we have thy youthful wages spent,   *70*
We'll light upon some settled low content.
   Adam. Master, go on and I will follow thee
To the last gasp with truth and loyalty.
From seventeen years till now almost fourscore
Here lived I; but now live here no more.   *75*
At seventeen years many their fortunes seek,
But at fourscore it is too late a week.
Yet Fortune cannot recompense me better
Than to die well, and not my master's debtor.   *Exeunt.*

---

3 Are ... sufferance: *have agreed and contrived*   **8 roynish:** *mangy*   **13 wrastler:** *here three syllables, 'wrasteler.'*   **19 suddenly:** *immediately*   **20 inquisition:** *investigation* **quail:** *falter*   **SD Enter ... Adam;** *cf. n.*   **3 memory:** *reminder*   **4 make you:** *are you doing*   **5 virtuous:** *full of good qualities*   **7 fond:** *foolish*   **8 bonny prizer:** *sturdy prize fighter*   **15 envenoms:** *poisons*   **19 graces:** *virtues*   **24 use:** *are accustomed*

27 practices: *plots*   **28 place:** *i.e. for Orlando* **butchery:** *slaughterhouse*   **30 whether:** *whither*   **35 boist'rous:** *violent*   **40 diverted blood:** *unnatural relationship*   **42 thrifty hire:** *wages economically saved*   **60 constant:** *faithful* **antique:** *ancient (stressed* `— —`*).*   **62 sweat:** *sweated* **meed:** *reward*   **68 In lieu of:** *in return for*   **69 come thy ways:** *come along*   **71 low:** *lowly* **content:** *peace*   **77 too late a week:** *far too late*

❧ SCENE FOURTH ❧

Enter Rosalind for Ganymede, Celia for Aliena, and Clown, alias
Touchstone.

Ros. O Jupiter, how weary are my spirits!

Touch. I care not for my spirits, if my legs were not
weary.

Ros. I could find in my heart to disgrace my man's
apparel and to cry like a woman. But I must comfort the   *5*
weaker vessel, as doublet and hose ought to show
itself courageous to petticoat. Therefore courage, good
Aliena.

Cel. I pray you, bear with me. I cannot go no further.

Touch. For my part, I had rather bear with you than   *10*
bear you. Yet I should bear no cross if I did bear you, for
I think you have no money in your purse.

Ros. Well, this is the Forest of Arden.

Touch. Ay, now am I in Arden, the more fool I. When I
was at home I was in a better place, but travelers must be   *15*
content.

Enter Corin and Silvius.

Ros. Ay, be so, good Touchstone. Look you, who
comes here—a young man and an old in solemn talk.

Cor. That is the way to make her scorn you still.

Sil. O Corin, that thou knew'st how I do love her.   *20*

Cor. I partly guess, for I have lov'd ere now.

Sil. No, Corin. Being old, thou canst not guess,
Though in thy youth thou wast as true a lover
As ever sigh'd upon a midnight pillow.
But if thy love were ever like to mine—   *25*
As sure I think did never man love so—
How many actions most ridiculous
Hast thou been drawn to by thy fantasy?

Cor. Into a thousand that I have forgotten.

Sil. O thou didst then ne'er love so heartily.   *30*
If thou rememb'rest not the slightest folly
That ever love did make thee run into,
Thou hast not lov'd.
Or if thou hast not sat as I do now,
Wearing thy hearer in thy mistress' praise,   *35*
Thou hast not lov'd.
Or if thou hast not broke from company
Abruptly as my passion now makes me,
Thou hast not lov'd.
O Phebe, Phebe, Phebe!   *Exit.*   *40*

Ros. Alas, poor shepherd! Searching of thy wound,
I have by hard adventure found mine own.

Touch. And I mine. I remember when I was in love, I
broke my sword upon a stone and bid him take that for
coming a-night to Jane Smile. And I remember the kissing   *45*
of her batler and the cow's dugs that her pretty chopt
hands had milk'd. And I remember the wooing of a peascod
instead of her, from whom I took two cods, and giving
them her again, said with weeping tears: 'Wear these for my

sake.' We that are true lovers run into strange capers. But   *50*
as all is mortal in nature, so is all nature in love mortal
in folly.

Ros. Thou speak'st wiser than thou art ware of.

Touch. Nay, I shall ne'er be ware of mine own wit till
I break my shins against it.   *55*

Ros. Jove, Jove, this shepherd's passion
Is much upon my fashion.

Touch. And mine. But it grows something stale
with me.

Cel. I pray you, one of you question yond man,   *60*
If he for gold will give us any food.
I faint almost to death.

Touch.   Holla, you clown!

Ros. Peace, fool! He's not thy kinsman.

Cor.   Who calls?   *65*

Touch. Your betters, sir.

Cor.   Else are they very wretched.

Ros. Peace, I say! Good even to you, friend.

Cor. And to you, gentle sir, and to you all.

Ros. I prithee, shepherd, if that love or gold   *70*
Can in this desert place buy entertainment,
Bring us where we may rest ourselves and feed.
Here's a young maid with travel much oppress'd,
And faints for succor.

Cor.   Fair sir, I pity her,   *75*
And wish for her sake more than for mine own
My fortunes were more able to relieve her.
But I am shepherd to another man,
And do not shear the fleeces that I graze.
My master is of churlish disposition,   *80*
And little recks to find the way to heaven
By doing deeds of hospitality.
Besides, his cote, his flocks, and bounds of feed
Are now on sale; and at our sheepcote now,
By reason of his absence, there is nothing   *85*
That you will feed on. But what is, come see,
And in my voice most welcome shall you be.

Ros. What is he that shall buy his flock and pasture?

Cor. That young swain that you saw here but erewhile,
That little cares for buying anything.   *90*

Ros. I pray thee, if it stand with honesty,
Buy thou the cottage, pasture, and the flock,
And thou shalt have to pay for it of us.

Cel. And we will mend thy wages. I like this place
And willingly could waste my time in it.   *95*

Cor. Assuredly the thing is to be sold.
Go with me. If you like, upon report,
The soil, the profit, and this kind of life,
I will your very faithful feeder be
And buy it with your gold right suddenly.   *Exeunt.*

---

1 weary; *cf. n.*   **6 weaker vessel:** *woman*   **doublet and hose:** *Elizabethan male costume of jacket and tights*   **11 cross;** *cf. n.*   **13 Arden;** *cf. n.*   **28 fantasy:** *love*   **30 ne'er:** *F* never   **35 Wearing:** *wearying*   **41 Searching of:** *probing*   **42 hard adventure:** *misfortune*   **45 a-night:** *at night*   **46 batler:** *a stick for beating clothes*   **chopt:** *chapped*   **47 peascod:** *peapod*

50 capers: *pranks*   **mortal;** *cf. n.*   **53 ware:** *aware*   **58 something:** *somewhat*   **60 yond:** *yonder*   **63 clown:** *peasant*   **64 kinsman;** *cf. n.*   **71 entertainment:** *hospitality*   **74 succor:** *aid*   **80 churlish:** *niggardly*   **81 recks:** *cares*   **83 cote:** *cottage*   **bounds of feed:** *extent of pasturage*   **87 in my voice:** *for my part*   **88 What:** *who*   **89 but erewhile:** *just now*   **91 stand:** *be consistent*   **93 have to pay:** *have money to pay*   **94 mend:** *raise*   **95 waste:** *pass*   **99 feeder:** *servant*

❧ Scene Five ❧

Enter Amiens, Jaques, and others.

Song

Ami.   *Under the greenwood tree*
            Who loves to lie with me,
            And turn his merry note
            Unto the sweet bird's throat,
        Come hither, come hither, come hither!   5
            Here shall he see
            No enemy
            But winter and rough weather.

Jaq. More, more, I prithee, more.
Ami. It will make you melancholy, Monsieur Jaques.   10
Jaq. I thank it. More, I prithee, more. I can suck melancholy
out of a song as a weasel sucks eggs. More, I prithee, more.
Ami. My voice is ragged; I know I cannot please you.
Jaq. I do not desire you to please me; I do desire you to
sing. Come, more: another stanzo. Call you 'em stanzos?   15
Ami. What you will, Monsieur Jaques.
Jaq. Nay, I care not for their names; they owe me nothing.
Will you sing?
Ami. More at your request than to please myself.
Jaq. Well then, if ever I thank any man, I'll thank you.   20
But that they call compliment is like th' encounter of two
dog-apes. And when a man thanks me heartily, methinks
I have given him a penny, and he renders me the beggarly
thanks. Come, sing. And you that will not, hold your tongues.
Ami. Well, I'll end the song. Sirs, cover the while; the Duke
will drink under this tree. He hath been all this day to look you.
Jaq. And I have been all this day to avoid him. He is
too disputable for my company. I think of as many matters as
he, but I give heaven thanks and make no boast of them.
Come, warble, come.   30

Song

                                        All together here.

Who doth ambition shun
And loves to lie i' th' sun,
Seeking the food he eats
And pleas'd with what he gets,
Come hither, come hither, come hither!   35
    Here shall he see
    No enemy
    But winter and rough weather.

Jaq. I'll give you a verse to this note that I made yester-
day in despite of my invention.   40
Ami. And I'll sing it.
Jaq. Thus it goes:

If it do come to pass
That any man turn ass,
Leaving his wealth and ease,   45
A stubborn will to please,
Ducdame, ducdame, ducdame!

Here shall he see
Gross fools as he,
And if he will come to me.   50

Ami. What's that 'ducdame'?
Jaq. 'Tis a Greek invocation to call fools into a circle. I'll go
sleep if I can; if I cannot, I'll rail against all the first born of
Egypt.
Ami. And I'll go seek the Duke. His banket is prepar'd   55
                                            Exeunt.

❧ Scene Sixth ❧

Enter Orlando and Adam.

Adam. Dear master, I can go no further. O, I die for food!
Here lie I down and measure out my grave. Farewell, kind
master.
Orl. Why, how now, Adam? No greater heart in thee? Live
a little, comfort a little, cheer thyself a little. If this   5
uncouth forest yield anything savage, I will either be food for
it or bring it for food to thee. Thy conceit is nearer death
than thy powers. For my sake, be comfortable; hold death
awhile at the arm's end. I will here be with thee presently,
and if I bring thee not something to eat, I will give thee   10
leave to die; but if thou diest before I come, thou art a
mocker of my labor. Well said. Thou look'st cheerly, and I'll
be with thee quickly. Yet thou liest in the bleak air. Come, I
will bear thee to some shelter, and thou shalt not die for lack
of a dinner, if there live anything in this desert. Cheerly, good
Adam.   *Exeunt.*

❧ Scene Seventh ❧

Enter Duke Senior, [Amiens,] and Lord, like Outlaws.

Duke S. I think he be transform'd into a beast,
For I can nowhere find him like a man.
1 Lord. My lord, he is but even now gone hence.
Here was he merry, hearing of a song.
Duke S. If he, compact of jars, grow musical,   5
We shall have shortly discord in the spheres.
Go seek him; tell him I would speak with him.

Enter Jaques.

1 Lord. He saves my labor by his own approach.
Duke S. Why, how now, monsieur! What a life is this
That your poor friends must woo your company.   10
What, you look merrily.
Jaq. A fool, a fool. I met a fool i' th' forest,
A motley fool—a miserable world.
As I do live by food I met a fool,
Who laid him down and bask'd him in the sun,   15
And rail'd on Lady Fortune in good terms,
In good set terms; and yet a motley fool.

---

3 turn: *adapt*   **13 ragged:** *uneven*   **15 stanzo:** *stanza*   **17 names:** *i.e. signatures on a bond of debt*   **21 that:** *what* **compliment:** *courtesy*   **22 dog-apes:** *dog-faced baboons*   **25 cover the while:** *set the table now*   **26 look:** *look for*   **28 disputable:** *prone to argue*   **39 note:** *tune*   **40 in . . . invention:** *without using my imagination*   **47 Ducdame;** *cf. n.*

50 And if: *an if, if only*   **52 circle;** *cf. n.*   **53, 54 first born of Egypt;** *cf. n.*   **55 banket:** *banquet, a light meal of fruit and wine*   **5 comfort a little:** *take comfort*   **6 uncouth:** *unknown*   **7 conceit:** *imagination*   **9 presently:** *immediately*   **12 Well said:** *well done* **cheerly:** *cheerful*   **1 be:** *is (the subjunctive form)*   **5 compact of jars:** *made up of discord*   **6 discord . . . spheres;** *cf. n.*   **11 merrily:** *cheerful*   **13 motley;** *cf. n.*   **17 good set terms:** *precise terms*

'Good morrow, fool,' quoth I. 'No, sir,' quoth he,
'Call me not fool till heaven hath sent me fortune.'
And then he drew a dial from his poke,   20
And looking on it with lackluster eye,
Says, very wisely: 'It is ten o'clock.'
'Thus we may see,' quoth he, 'how the world wags.
'Tis but an hour ago since it was nine,
And after one hour more 'twill be eleven.   25
And so from hour to hour we ripe and ripe,
And then from hour to hour we rot and rot.
And thereby hangs a tale.' When I did hear
The motley fool thus moral on the time,
My lungs began to crow like Chanticleer   30
That fools should be so deep contemplative.
And I did laugh sans intermission,
An hour by his dial. O noble fool,
A worthy fool! Motley's the only wear.
    Duke S. What fool is this?   35
    Jaq. O worthy fool—one that hath been a courtier
And says, if ladies be but young and fair,
They have the gift to know it. And in his brain,
Which is as dry as the remainder biscuit
After a voyage, he hath strange places cramm'd   40
With observation, the which he vents
In mangled forms. O that I were a fool!
I am ambitious for a motley coat.
    Duke S. Thou shalt have one.
    Jaq.   It is my only suit.   45
Provided that you weed your better judgments
Of all opinion that grows rank in them,
That I am wise. I must have liberty
Withal, as large a charter as the wind
To blow on whom I please, for so fools have.   50
And they that are most galled with my folly,
They most must laugh. And why, sir, must they so?
The 'why' is plain as way to parish church:
He that a fool doth very wisely hit
Doth very foolishly, although he smart,   55
Not to seem senseless of the bob. If not,
The wise man's folly is anatomiz'd
E'en by the squand'ring glances of the fool.
Invest me in my motley. Give me leave
To speak my mind, and I will through and through   60
Cleanse the foul body of th' infected world,
If they will patiently receive my medicine.
    Duke S. Fie on thee. I can tell what thou would'st do.
    Jaq. What, for a counter, would I do but good?
    Duke S. Most mischievous foul sin in chiding sin;   65
For thou thyself hath been a libertine
As sensual as the brutish sting itself.
And all th' embossed sores and headed evils
That thou with license of free foot hast caught,
Would'st thou disgorge into the general world.   70
    Jaq. Why, who cries out on pride

That can therein tax any private party?
Doth it not flow as hugely as the sea,
Till that the weary very means do ebb?
What woman in the city do I name,   75
When that I say the city woman bears
The cost of princes on unworthy shoulders?
Who can come in and say that I mean her,
When such a one as thee, such is her neighbor?
Or what is he of basest function   80
That says his bravery is not on my cost,
Thinking that I mean him, but therein suits
His folly to the mettle of my speech?
There then. How then? What then? Let me see wherein
My tongue hath wrong'd him. If it do him right,   85
Then he hath wrong'd himself; if he be free,
Why then my taxing, like a wild goose, flies
Unclaim'd of any man. But who comes here?

    Enter Orlando [with sword drawn].

    Orl. Forbear, and eat no more.
    Jaq.   Why, I have eat none yet.   90
    Orl. Nor shalt not, till necessity be serv'd.
    Jaq. Of what kind should this cock come of?
    Duke S. Art thou thus bolden'd, man, by thy distress,
Or else a rude despiser of good manners,
That in civility thou seem'st so empty?   95
    Orl. You touch'd my vein at first. The thorny point
Of bare distress hath tane from me the show
Of smooth civility; yet am I inland bred
And know some nurture. But forbear, I say.
He dies that touches any of this fruit   100
Till I and my affairs are answered.
    Jaq. And you will not be answer'd with reason,
I must die.
    Duke S. What would you have? Your gentleness shall force
More than your force move us to gentleness.   105
    Orl. I almost die for food, and let me have it.
    Duke S. Sit down and feed, and welcome to our table.
    Orl. Speak you so gently? Pardon me, I pray you.
I thought that all things had been savage here,
And therefore put I on the countenance   110
Of stern commandment. But—whate'er you are
That in this desert inaccessible
Under the shade of melancholy boughs
Lose and neglect the creeping hours of time—
If ever you have look'd on better days,   115
If ever been where bells have knoll'd to church,
If ever sat at any good man's feast,
If ever from your eyelids wip'd a tear
And know what 'tis to pity and be pitied,
Let gentleness my strong enforcement be.   120
In the which hope I blush and hide my sword.
    Duke S. True it is that we have seen better days,
And have with holy bell been knoll'd to church,
And sat at good men's feasts, and wip'd our eyes

---

20 dial: *sundial* **poke:** *pocket* **23 wags:** *moves along* **26 hour;** *cf. n.* **ripe:** *grow ripe, cf. n.* **29 moral:** *moralize* **30 Chanticleer;** *cf. n.* **31 deep:** *deeply* **32 sans:** *without* **39 remainder biscuit:** *stale hardtack* **41 vents:** *utters* **45 suit;** *cf. n.* **47 rank:** *luxuriant* **49 Withal:** *too* **charter:** *license* **51 galled:** *irritated* **55 Doth very foolishly:** *acts very foolishly* **56 Not to:** *F omits* **senseless:** *insensible* **bob:** *taunt* **57 anatomiz'd:** *analyzed* **58 E'en:** *F Even* **squand'ring:** *random* **59 Invest:** *clothe* **64 counter:** *coin of little value, i.e. a wager* **67 sting:** *lust* **68 embossed:** *swollen* **70 general:** *whole (to be read 'gen'ral')*

72 tax: *criticize* **74 weary very means;** *cf. n.* **81 bravery:** *elaborate dress (to be read 'brav'ry')* **on my cost:** *at my expense* **83 mettle:** *substance* **86 free:** *not guilty* **89 Forbear:** *abstain* **93 bolden'd:** *emboldened* **95 civility:** *courtesy* **96 touch'd my vein:** *hit my feelings* **98 inland bred:** *civilized* **99 nurture:** *good breeding* **101 answered:** *provided for* **102 And:** *an (if)* **reason;** *cf. n.* **111 commandment:** *authority* **116 knoll'd:** *tolled* **120 enforcement:** *support*

Of drops that sacred pity hath engend'red.   125
And therefore sit you down in gentleness,
And take upon command what help we have
That to your wanting may be minist'red.
    Orl. Then but forbear your food a little while,
Whiles like a doe I go to find my fawn   130
And give it food. There is an old poor man,
Who after me hath many a weary step
Limp'd in pure love. Till he be first suffic'd,
Oppress'd with two weak evils, age and hunger,
I will not touch a bit.   135
    Duke S.   Go find him out,
And we will nothing waste till you return.
    Orl. I thank ye, and be blest for your good comfort.

                                          Exit.

    Duke S. Thou seest we are not all alone unhappy.
This wide and universal theater   140
Presents more woeful pageants than the scene
Wherein we play in.
    Jaq.   All the world's a stage,
And all the men and women merely players.
They have their exits and their entrances,   145
And one man in his time plays many parts,
His acts being seven ages. At first the infant,
Mewling and puking in the nurse's arms.
Then the whining schoolboy with his satchel
And shining morning face, creeping like snail   150
Unwillingly to school. And then the lover,
Sighing like furnace, with a woeful ballad
Made to his mistress' eyebrow. Then a soldier,
Full of strange oaths and bearded like the pard,
Jealous in honor, sudden and quick in quarrel,   155
Seeking the bubble Reputation
E'en in the cannon's mouth. And then the justice,
In fair round belly with good capon lin'd,
With eyes severe and beard of formal cut,
Full of wise saws and modern instances;   160
And so he plays his part. The sixt age shifts
Into the lean and slipper'd pantaloon,
With spectacles on nose and pouch on side;
His youthful hose well sav'd, a world too wide
For his shrunk shank, and his big manly voice,   165
Turning again toward childish treble, pipes
And whistles in his sound. Last scene of all,
That ends this strange eventful history,
Is second childishness and mere oblivion—
Sans teeth, sans eyes, sans taste, sans everything.   170

        Enter Orlando with Adam.

    Duke S. Welcome. Set down your venerable burthen,
And let him feed.
    Orl. I thank you most for him.
    Adam.   So had you need;
I scarce can speak to thank you for myself.   175
    Duke S. Welcome; fall to. I will not trouble you

As yet to question you about your fortunes.
Give us some music and, good cousin, sing.

                    Song

Ami.   *Blow, blow, thou winter wind*
      Thou art not so unkind   180
        As man's ingratitude.
    Thy tooth is not so keen
    Because thou art not seen,
      Although thy breath be rude.
Heigh ho, sing heigh ho, unto the green holly!   185
Most friendship is feigning, most loving mere folly:
      Then heigh ho, the holly,
      This life is most jolly.

    Freeze, freeze, thou bitter sky,
    That dost not bite so nigh   190
      As benefits forgot.
    Though thou the waters warp,
    Thy sting is not so sharp
      As friend rememb'red not.
Heigh ho, sing, etc.   195

    Duke S. If that you were the good Sir Rowland's son,
As you have whisper'd faithfully you were,
And as mine eye doth his effigies witness
Most truly limn'd and living in your face,
Be truly welcome hither. I am the Duke   200
That lov'd your father. The residue of your fortune,
Go to my cave and tell me. Good old man,
Thou art right welcome, as thy master is.
Support him by the arm. Give me your hand,
And let me all your fortunes understand.   *Exeunt.*

ACT THIRD ❧ SCENE FIRST

Enter Duke [Frederick], Lords, and Oliver.

    Duke. Not see him since? Sir, sir, that cannot be.
But were I not the better part made mercy,
I should not seek an absent argument
Of my revenge, thou present. But look to it:
Find out thy brother, wheresoe'er he is;   5
Seek him with candle; bring him dead or living
Within this twelvemonth, or turn thou no more
To seek a living in our territory.
Thy lands and all things that thou dost call thine,
Worth seizure, do we seize into our hands,   10
Till thou canst quit thee by thy brother's mouth
Of what we think against thee.
    Oli. O that your highness knew my heart in this.
I never lov'd my brother in my life.
    Duke. More villain thou. Well, push him out of doors,   15
And let my officers of such a nature

---

127 **upon command:** *at your pleasure*   **128 wanting:** *need*   **134 weak:** *causing weakness*   **138 comfort:** *help*   **148 Mewling:** *crying, mewing like a cat*   **154 pard:** *leopard*   **155 Jealous in:** *suspiciously careful of*   **157 E'en:** *F* Even   **160 saws:** *maxims* **modern instances:** *everyday illustrations*   **161 sixt:** *sixth*   **162 pantaloon:** *old dotard, cf. n.*   **167 his:** *its*   **169 mere:** *total*   **170 Sans:** *without*   **171 burthen:** *burden*

192 warp: *i.e. by turning into ice*   **198 effigies:** *likeness (stressed — ´ —)*   **199 limn'd:** *portrayed*   **2 made mercy:** *made of mercy*   **3 argument:** *object, i.e. Orlando*   **6 candle;** *cf. n.*   **7 turn:** *return*   **11 quit:** *absolve*   **16 of such a nature:** *whose business it is*

Make an extent upon his house and lands.
Do this expediently, and turn him going.   *Exeunt.*

❧ SCENE SECOND ❧

Enter Orlando.

Orl. Hang there, my verse, in witness of my love.
And thou, thrice crowned Queen of Night, survey
With thy chaste eye, from thy pale sphere above,
Thy huntress' name that my full life doth sway.
O Rosalind, these trees shall be my books   5
And in their barks my thoughts I'll character,
That every eye which in this forest looks
Shall see thy virtue witness'd everywhere.
Run, run, Orlando! Carve on every tree
The fair, the chaste, and unexpressive she.   *Exit.* 10

Enter Corin and Clown [Touchstone].

Cor. And how like you this shepherd's life, Master
Touchstone?

Touch. Truly, shepherd, in respect of itself it is a good
life; but in respect that it is a shepherd's life, it is naught.
In respect that it is solitary, I like it very well; but in   15
respect that it is private, it is a very vild life. Now, in respect
it is in the fields, it pleaseth me well; but in respect it is not
in the court, it is tedious. As it is a spare life, look you, it fits
my humor well; but as there is no more plenty in it, it goes
much against my stomach. Hast any philosophy in thee,   20
shepherd?

Cor. No more but that I know the more one sickens, the
worse at ease he is; and that he that wants money, means, and
content is without three good friends; that the property of rain
is to wet, and fire to burn; that good pasture makes fat   25
sheep; and that a great cause of the night is lack of the sun;
that he that hath learned no wit by nature nor art may
complain of good breeding, or comes of a very dull kindred.

Touch. Such a one is a natural philosopher.
Wast ever in court, shepherd?   30

Cor. No, truly.

Touch. Then thou art damn'd.

Cor. Nay, I hope.

Touch. Truly thou art damn'd like an ill-roasted egg,
all on one side.   35

Cor. For not being at court? Your reason.

Touch. Why, if thou never wast at court, thou never saw'st
good manners. If thou never saw'st good manners, then thy
manners must be wicked; and wickedness is sin, and sin is
damnation. Thou art in a parlous state, shepherd.   40

Cor. Not a whit, Touchstone. Those that are good
manners at the court are as ridiculous in the country as the behavior of the country is most mockable at the court. You told

me you salute not at the court, but you kiss your hands. That
courtesy would be uncleanly if courtiers were shepherds.   45

Touch. Instance briefly. Come, instance.

Cor. Why, we are still handling our ewes, and their fells
you know are greasy.

Touch. Why, do not your courtier's hands sweat? And is
not the grease of a mutton as wholesome as the sweat of a   50
man? Shallow, shallow. A better instance, I say. Come.

Cor. Besides, our hands are hard.

Touch. Your lips will feel them the sooner. Shallow again.
A more sounder instance, come.

Cor. And they are often tarr'd over with the surgery of   55
our sheep. And would you have us kiss tar? The courtier's
hands are perfum'd with civet.

Touch. Most shallow man, thou worm's meat in respect of a
good piece of flesh indeed, learn of the wise and perpend: civet
is of baser birth than tar, the very uncleanly flux of a cat.   60
Mend the instance, shepherd.

Cor. You have too courtly a wit for me. I'll rest.

Touch. Wilt thou rest damn'd? God help thee, shallow man.
God make incision in thee; thou art raw.

Cor. Sir, I am a true laborer. I earn that I eat, get that I   65
wear; owe no man hate, envy no man's happiness; glad of
other men's good, content with my harm; and the greatest of
my pride is to see my ewes graze and my lambs suck.

Touch. That is another simple sin in you—to bring the ewes
and the rams together and to offer to get your living by the   70
copulation of cattle; to be bawd to a bellwether and to
betray a she-lamb of a twelvemonth to a crooked-pated old
cuckoldly ram, out of all reasonable match. If thou beest not
damn'd for this, the divell himself will have no shepherds. I
cannot see else how thou shouldst scape.   75

Cor. Here comes young Master Ganymede, my new
mistress' brother.

Enter Rosalind [reading from a paper].

Ros.   *From the east to western Ind,*
           No jewel is like Rosalind.
           Her worth being mounted on the wind,   80
           Through all the world bears Rosalind.
           All the pictures fairest lin'd
           Are but black to Rosalind.
           Let no face be kept in mind
           But the fair of Rosalind.   85

Touch. I'll rhyme you so eight years together, dinners
and suppers and sleeping hours excepted. It is the right
butter-women's rank to market.

Ros. Out, fool!

Touch. For a taste: 90

           If a hart do lack a hind,
           Let him seek out Rosalind.
           If the cat will after kind,

---

44 but: *unless*   **46 Instance:** *give an example*   **47 still:** *always* **fells:** *fleeces* **55**
tarr'd; *cf. n.*   **57 civet:** *perfume derived from the civet cat*   **58 worm's meat:** *food for*
worms **in respect of:** *in comparison with*   **59 perpend:** *consider*   **60 flux:** *dis-*
charge   **61 Mend:** *improve*   **64 incision:** *an operation (to cure his folly)* **raw:** *inexperi-*
enced, simple (with a pun on 'sore')   **65 that:** *what*   **69 simple:** *foolish*   **70 offer:**
undertake   **71 bellwether:** *the leading sheep in a flock carries a bell*   **73 cuckoldly;**
cf. n. **out . . . match:** *a quite unsuitable match*   **74 divell:** *devil*   **78 Ind;** *cf. n.*   **82**
lin'd: *drawn*   **84 fair:** *i.e. fair face*   **87 right:** *precise*   **88 butter-women's rank;**
cf. n.   **89 Out:** *away with you*   **90 taste:** *sample*   **93 after kind:** *follow nature*

---

17 extent: *seizure*   **18 expediently:** *expeditiously*   **2 Queen of Night:** *the moon;*
cf. n.   **4 huntress' names;** *cf. n.* **full:** *entire* **sway:** *rule*   **6 character:** *inscribe*   **7**
That: *so that*   **10 unexpressive:** *indescribable*   **14 naught:** *worthless*   **16 private:** *lone-*
ly **vild:** *vile*   **18 spare:** *frugal*   **20 philosophy:** *science, general knowledge*   **27 wit:**
knowledge   **28 complain . . . breeding:** *complain of the lack of good breeding*   **38 man-**
ners; *cf. n.*

So be sure will Rosalind.
Winter garments must be lin'd;   95
So must slender Rosalind.
They that reap must sheaf and bind,
Then to cart with Rosalind.
Sweetest nut hath sourest rind:
Such a nut is Rosalind.   100
He that sweetest rose will find,
Must find love's prick and Rosalind.

This is the very false gallop of verses. Why do you infect
yourself with them?

Ros. Peace, you dull fool. I found them on a tree.   105

Touch. Truly the tree yields bad fruit.

Ros. I'll graff it with you, and then I shall graff it with a
medlar. Then it will be the earliest fruit i' th' country: for
you'll be rotten ere you be half ripe, and that's the right
virtue of the medlar.   110

Touch. You have said; but whether wisely or no, let
the forest judge.

Enter Celia with a writing.

Ros. Peace! Here comes my sister reading; stand aside.

Cel.   *Why should this a desert be?*
               For it is unpeopled? No.   115
       Tongues I'll hang on every tree
               That shall civil sayings show:
       Some, how brief the life of man
               Runs his erring pilgrimage,
       That the stretching of a span   120
               Buckles in his sum of age;
       Some, of violated vows
               'Twixt the souls of friend and friend.
       But upon the fairest boughs,
               Or at every sentence end,   125
       Will I 'Rosalinda' write,
               Teaching all that read to know
       The quintessence of every sprite
               Heaven would in little show.
       Therefore heaven nature charg'd   130
               That one body should be fill'd
       With all graces wide enlarg'd.
               Nature presently distill'd
       Helen's cheek but not her heart,
               Cleopatra's majesty,   135
       Atalanta's better part,
               Sad Lucretia's modesty.
       Thus Rosalind of many parts
               By heavenly synod was devis'd,
       Of many faces, eyes, and hearts,   140
               To have the touches dearest priz'd.
       Heaven would that she these gifts should have,
               And I to live and die her slave.

Ros. O most gentle Jupiter, what tedious homily of love
have you wearied your parishioners withal and never cried: 145
'Have patience, good people.'

Cel. How now? Back, friends. Shepherd, go off a little; go
with him, sirrah.

Touch. Come, shepherd. Let us make an honorable retreat,
though not with bag and baggage, yet with scrip and   150
scrippage.   *Exeunt.*

Cel. Didst thou hear these verses?

Ros. O yes, I heard them all, and more too; for some of
them had in them more feet than the verses would bear.

Cel. That's no matter. The feet might bear the verses.   155

Ros. Ay, but the feet were lame and could not bear
themselves without the verse, and therefore stood lamely in
the verse.

Cel. But didst thou hear without wondering how thy
name should be hang'd and carved upon these trees?   160

Ros. I was seven of the nine days out of the wonder
before you came; for look here what I found on a palm tree. I
was never so berhym'd since Pythagoras' time that I was an
Irish rat, which I can hardly remember.

Cel. Trow you who hath done this?   165

Ros. Is it a man?

Cel. And a chain that you once wore—about his neck.
Change you color?

Ros. I prithee, who?

Cel. O Lord, Lord, it is a hard matter for friends to   170
meet. But mountains may be remov'd with earthquakes,
and so encounter.

Ros. Nay, but who is it?

Cel. Is it possible?

Ros. Nay, I prithee now with most petitionary vehe-   175
mence, tell me who it is.

Cel. O wonderful, wonderful, and most wonderful wonderful! And yet again wonderful and after that, out of all hooping.

Ros. Good my complexion! Dost thou think, though I am
caparison'd like a man, I have a doublet and hose in my   180
disposition? One inch of delay more is a South Sea of
discovery. I prithee, tell me who is it quickly and speak apace.
I would thou couldst stammer, that thou mightst pour this conceal'd man out of thy mouth as wine comes out of a narrow-
mouth'd bottle, either too much at once or none at all. I   185
prithee, take the cork out of thy mouth that I may
drink thy tidings.

Cel. So you may put a man in your belly?

Ros. Is he of God's making? What manner of man? Is his
head worth a hat? Or his chin worth a beard?   190

Cel. Nay, he hath but a little beard.

Ros. Why, God will send more, if the man will be thankful.
Let me stay the growth of his beard, if thou delay me not the
knowledge of his chin.

Cel. It is young Orlando, that tripp'd up the wrastler's   195
heels and your heart, both in an instant.

Ros. Nay, but the divell take mocking. Speak sad brow and
true maid.

---

98 to cart; *cf. n.*   **107 graff:** *graft* **you:** *a pun on 'yew'*   **108 medlar;** *cf. n.*   **109
right virtue:** *proper characteristic*   **114 a:** *F omits*   **115 For:** *because*   **117 civil:** *polite*   **119 erring:** *wandering*   **121 Buckles in:** *limits*   **128 quintessence:** *the most
highly refined essence (stressed ∸ — ∸)*   **129 in little:** *in miniature*   **132 wide enlarg'd:**
in fullest manifestation   **134 Helen's:** *Helen of Troy, the immediate cause of the Trojan
War*   **135 Cleopatra's:** *queen of Egypt, mistress of Caesar and Antony*   **136 Atalanta's:**
Grecian huntress famed for fleetness of foot   **137 Lucretia's:** *Roman woman dishonored by
Tarquin*   **139 synod:** *council*

144 Jupiter; *cf. n.*   **150 bag and baggage:** *equipment (a military term)*   **150, 151 scrip
and scrippage:** *a wallet and its contents*   **163 Pythagoras' time;** *cf. n.* **that:** *when*   **164
Irish rat;** *cf. n.*   **165 Trow:** *know*   **175 petitionary vehemence:** *vehement petition*   **178 out of all hooping:** *beyond all shouting*   **179 Good my complexion;**
cf. n.   **180 caparison'd:** *outfitted*   **181, 182 South Sea of discovery;** *cf. n.* **apace:** *with
haste*   **197, 198 Speak . . . maid:** *speak solemnly and truly*

Cel. I'faith, coz, 'tis he.

Ros. Orlando?   *200*

Cel. Orlando.

Ros. Alas the day! What shall I do with my doublet and hose? What did he when thou saw'st him? What said he? How look'd he? Wherein went he? What makes he here? Did he ask for me? Where remains he? How parted he with thee? And *205* when shalt thou see him again? Answer me in one word.

Cel. You must borrow me Gargantua's mouth first; 'tis a word too great for any mouth of this age's size. To say 'ay' and 'no' to these particulars is more than to answer in a catechism.   *210*

Ros. But doth he know that I am in this forest and in man's apparel? Looks he as freshly as he did the day he wrastled?

Cel. It is as easy to count atomies as to resolve the proposi- tions of a lover. But take a taste of my finding him, and   *215* relish it with good observance: I found him under a tree, like a dropp'd acorn.

Ros. It may well be call'd Jove's tree, when it drops forth such fruit.

Cel. Give me audience, good madam.   *220*

Ros. Proceed.

Cel. There lay he stretch'd along like a wounded knight.

Ros. Though it be pity to see such a sight, it well becomes the ground.

Cel. Cry 'holla' to the tongue, I prithee; it curvets un-   *225* seasonably. He was furnish'd like a hunter.

Ros. O ominous: he comes to kill my heart.

Cel. I would sing my song without a burthen; thou bring'st me out of tune.

Ros. Do you not know I am a woman? When I think,   *230* I must speak. Sweet, say on.

Enter Orlando and Jaques.

Cel. You bring me out. Soft, comes he not here?

Ros. 'Tis he. Slink by and note him.

Jaq. I thank you for your company; but, good faith, I had as lief have been myself alone.   *235*

Orl. And so had I; but yet for fashion sake I thank you too for your society.

Jaq. God buy you. Let's meet as little as we can.

Orl. I do desire we may be better strangers.

Jaq. I pray you mar no more trees with writing love   *240* songs in their barks.

Orl. I pray you mar no moe of my verses with reading them ill-favoredly.

Jaq. Rosalind is your love's name?

Orl. Yes, just.   *245*

Jaq. I do not like her name.

Orl. There was no thought of pleasing you when she was christen'd.

Jaq. What stature is she of?

Orl. Just as high as my heart.   *250*

Jaq. You are full of pretty answers. Have you not been acquainted with goldsmiths' wives and conn'd them out of rings?

Orl. Not so. But I answer your right painted cloth, from whence you have studied your questions.   *255*

Jaq. You have a nimble wit; I think 'twas made of Atalan- ta's heels. Will you sit down with me? And we two will rail against our mistress, the World, and all our misery.

Orl. I will chide no breather in the world but myself, against whom I know most faults.   *260*

Jaq. The worst fault you have is to be in love.

Orl. 'Tis a fault I will not change for your best virtue. I am weary of you.

Jaq. By my troth, I was seeking for a fool when I found you.   *265*

Orl. He is drown'd in the brook. Look but in and you shall see him.

Jaq. There I shall see mine own figure.

Orl. Which I take to be either a fool or a cipher.

Jaq. I'll tarry no longer with you. Farewell, good Signior *270* Love.

Orl. I am glad of your departure. Adieu, good Monsieur Melancholy.   *[Exit Jaques.]*

Ros. I will speak to him like a saucy lacky and under that habit play the knave with him. Do you hear, forester?   *275*

Orl. Very well. What would you?

Ros. I pray you, what is't o'clock?

Orl. You should ask me what time o' day. There's no clock in the forest.

Ros. Then there is no true lover in the forest, else sigh- *280* ing every minute and groaning every hour would detect the lazy foot of Time as well as a clock.

Orl. And why not the swift foot of Time? Had not that been as proper?

Ros. By no means, sir. Time travels in divers paces with *285* divers persons. I'll tell you who Time ambles withal, who Time trots withal, who Time gallops withal, and who he stands still withal.

Orl. I prithee, who does he trot withal?

Ros. Marry, he trots hard with a young maid between *290* the contract of her marriage and the day it is solemniz'd. If the interim be but a sennight, Time's pace is so hard that it seems the length of seven year.

Orl. Who ambles Time withal?

Ros. With a priest that lacks Latin and a rich man that *295* hath not the gout; for the one sleeps easily because he cannot study, and the other lives merrily because he feels no pain: the one lacking the burthen of lean and wasteful learning, the other knowing no burthen of heavy tedious penury. These Time ambles withal.   *300*

Orl. Who doth he gallop withal?

Ros. With a thief to the gallows. For though he go as softly as foot can fall, he thinks himself too soon there.

Orl. Who stays it still withal?

Ros. With lawyers in the vacation; for they sleep between *305* term and term, and then they perceive not how Time moves.

---

204 Wherein went he?: *how was he dressed?*   **207 Gargantua's mouth;** *cf. n.*   **212 freshly:** *vigorous*   **214 atomies:** *motes*   **resolve:** *answer*   **propositions:** *questions*   **216 good observance:** *careful attention*   **218 Jove's tree;** *cf. n.*   **219 such:** F omits   **220 audience:** *attention*   **225 'holla':** *stop*   **curvets:** *prances*   **226 furnish'd:** *dressed*   **227 heart:** *with a pun on 'hart'*   **228 burthen:** *refrain*   **228, 229 bring'st me out:** *confuse, bring out of tune*   **233 note:** *observe*   **235 myself alone:** *by myself*   **238 buy:** F contrac- tion of 'be with'   **242 moe:** *more*   **243 ill-favoredly:** *incorrectly*   **245 just:** *exactly*

252 goldsmiths' wives . . . rings; *cf. n.*   **254 right:** *regular*   **painted cloth;** *cf. n.*   **256, 257 Atalanta's heels;** *cf. n.*   **259 breather:** *living person*   **269 cipher:** *zero*   **274, 275 under that habit:** *in that guise*   **281 detect:** *show*   **285 divers:** *different*   **286 withal:** *with*   **292 sennight:** *a week* (seven nights)   **298 wasteful:** *causing bodily waste*   **306 term:** *period of court session*

Orl. Where dwell you, pretty youth?

Ros. With this shepherdess, my sister, here in the skirts of the forest, like fringe upon a petticoat.

Orl. Are you native of this place?   310

Ros. As the cony that you see dwell where she is kindled.

Orl. Your accent is something finer than you could purchase in so removed a dwelling.

Ros. I have been told so of many. But, indeed, an old religious uncle of mine taught me to speak, who was in   315 his youth an inland man—one that knew courtship too well, for there he fell in love. I have heard him read many lectors against it, and I thank God I am not a woman, to be touch'd with so many giddy offences as he hath generally tax'd their whole sex withal.   320

Orl. Can you remember any of the principal evils that he laid to the charge of women?

Ros. There were none principal. They were all like one another as halfpence are, every one fault seeming monstrous till his fellow fault came to match it.   325

Orl. I prithee, recount some of them.

Ros. No, I will not cast away my physic but on those that are sick. There is a man haunts the forest that abuses our young plants with carving 'Rosalind' on their barks, hangs odes upon hawthornes and elegies on brambles—all,   330 forsooth, deifying the name of Rosalind. If I could meet that fancy-monger, I would give him some good counsel, for he seems to have the quotidian of love upon him.

Orl. I am he that is so love-shak'd. I pray you, tell me your remedy.   335

Ros. There is none of my uncle's marks upon you. He taught me how to know a man in love; in which cage of rushes I am sure you are not prisoner.

Orl. What were his marks?

Ros. A lean cheek, which you have not; a blue eye and   340 sunken, which you have not; an unquestionable spirit, which you have not; a beard neglected, which you have not. But I pardon you for that for, simply, your having in beard is a younger brother's revenue. Then your hose should be ungarter'd, your bonnet unbanded, your sleeve unbutton'd,   345 your shoe untied, and every thing about you demonstrating a careless desolation. But you are no such man: you are rather point device in your accoutrements, as loving yourself, than seeming the lover of any other.

Orl. Fair youth, I would I could make thee believe I love.

Ros. Me believe it? You may as soon make her that you love believe it, which I warrant she is apter to do than to confess she does. That is one of the points in the which women still give the lie to their consciences. But, in good sooth, are you he that hangs the verses on the trees,   355 wherein Rosalind is so admired?

Orl. I swear to thee, youth, by the white hand of Rosalind, I am that he, that unfortunate he.

Ros. But are you so much in love as your rhymes speak?

Orl. Neither rhyme nor reason can express how much.   360

Ros. Love is merely a madness and, I tell you, deserves as well a dark house and a whip as madmen do. And the reason why they are not so punish'd and cured is that the lunacy is so ordinary that the whippers are in love too. Yet I profess curing it by counsel.   365

Orl. Did you ever cure any so?

Ros. Yes, one, and in this manner: he was to imagine me his love, his mistress, and I set him every day to woo me. At which time would I—being but a moonish youth—grieve, be effeminate, changeable, longing and liking, proud,   370 fantastical, apish, shallow, inconstant, full of tears, full of smiles; for every passion something, and for no passion truly anything, as boys and women are for the most part cattle of this color. Would now like him, now loathe him; then entertain him, then forswear him; now weep for him,   375 then spit at him; that I drave my suitor from his mad humor of love to a living humor of madness, which was to forswear the full stream of the world and to live in a nook merely monastic. And thus I cur'd him, and this way will I take upon me to wash your liver as clean as a sound   380 sheep's heart, that there shall not be one spot of love in't.

Orl. I would not be cured, youth.

Ros. I would cure you, if you would but call me Rosalind, and come every day to my cote and woo me.

Orl. Now, by the faith of my love, I will. Tell me   385 where it is.

Ros. Go with me to it, and I'll show it you. And by the way you shall tell me where in the forest you live. Will you go?

Orl. With all my heart, good youth.   390

Ros. Nay, you must call me Rosalind. Come, sister. Will you go?   *Exeunt.*

❧ SCENE THIRD ❧

Enter Clown [Touchstone], Audrey, and Jaques.

Touch. Come apace, good Audrey. I will fetch up your goats, Audrey. And how, Audrey, am I the man yet? Doth my simple feature content you?

Aud. Your features! Lord warrant us, what features?

Touch. I am here with thee and thy goats as the most   5 capricious poet, honest Ovid, was among the Goths.

Jaq. [aside]. O knowledge ill-inhabited, worse than Jove in a thatch'd house.

Touch. When a man's verses cannot be understood, nor a man's good wit seconded with the forward child, Under-   10 standing, it strikes a man more dead than a great reckoning in a little room. Truly, I would the gods had made thee poetical.

Aud. I do not know what poetical is. Is it honest in deed and word? Is it a true thing?

Touch. No, truly, for the truest poetry is the most   15

---

feigning, and lovers are given to poetry. And what they swear
in poetry may be said, as lovers, they do feign.

Aud. Do you wish then that the gods had made me poetical?

Touch. I do truly, for thou swear'st to me thou art
honest. Now if thou wert a poet, I might have some hope   20
thou didst feign.

Aud. Would you not have me honest?

Touch. No, truly, unless thou wert hard favor'd. For honesty
coupled to beauty is to have honey a sauce to sugar.

Jaq. [aside]. A material fool.   25

Aud. Well, I am not fair, and therefore I pray the gods
make me honest.

Touch. Truly, and to cast away honesty upon a foul slut
were to put good meat into an unclean dish.

Aud. I am not a slut, though I thank the gods I am foul.   30

Touch. Well, praised be the gods for thy foulness; slut-
tishness may come hereafter. But be it as it may be, I will
marry thee, and to that end I have been with Sir Oliver
Martext, the vicar of the next village, who hath promis'd to
meet me in this place of the forest and to couple us.   35

Jaq. [aside]. I would fain see this meeting.

Aud. Well, the gods give us joy.

Touch. Amen. A man may, if he were of fearful heart,
stagger in this attempt; for here we have no temple but the
wood, no assembly but horn-beasts. But what though?   40
Courage. As horns are odious, they are necessary. It is said
many a man knows no end of his goods. Right. Many a man
has good horns and knows no end of them. Well, that is the
dowry of his wife; 'tis none of his own getting. Horns? Even
so. Poor men alone? No, no. The noblest deer hath them   45
as huge as the rascal. Is the single man therefore blessed? No.
As a wall'd town is more worthier than a village, so is the forehead of a married man more honorable than the bare brow of
a bachelor. And by how much defense is better than no skill,
by so much is a horn more precious than to want.   50

Enter Sir Oliver Martext.

Here comes Sir Oliver. Sir Oliver Martext, you are well
met. Will you dispatch us here under this tree, or shall we go
with you to your chapel?

Sir Oliver. Is there none here to give the woman?

Touch. I will not take her on gift of any man.   55

Sir Oliver. Truly, she must be given or the marriage is not lawful.

Jaq. Proceed, proceed. I'll give her.

Touch. Good even, good Master What-ye-call't. How do
you, sir? You are very well met. Goddild you for your last
company. I am very glad to see you. Even a toy in hand   60
here, sir. Nay, pray be cover'd.

Jaq. Will you be married, motley?

Touch. As the ox hath his bow, sir, the horse his
curb, and the falcon her bells, so man hath his desires;
and as pigeons bill, so wedlock would be nibbling.   65

Jaq. And will you, being a man of your breeding, be
married under a bush like a beggar? Get you to church and
have a good priest that can tell you what marriage is. This fellow

will but join you together as they join wainscote; then one of you
will prove a shrunk panel and, like green timber, warp, warp.   70

Touch. I am not in the mind but I were better to be
married of him than of another, for he is not like to marry
me well. And not being well married, it will be a good
excuse for me hereafter to leave my wife.

Jaq. Go thou with me and let me counsel thee.   75

Touch. Come, sweet Audrey.
We must be married, or we must live in bawdry.
Farewell, good Master Oliver: not

> O sweet Oliver,
> O brave Oliver,   80
> Leave me not behind thee.

but

> Wind away,
> Be gone, I say!
> I will not to wedding with thee.   85

Sir Oliver. 'Tis no matter. Ne'er a fantastical knave of
them all shall flout me out of my calling.   *Exeunt.*

❧ SCENE FOURTH ❧

Enter Rosalind and Celia.

Ros. Never talk to me; I will weep.

Cel. Do, I prithee. But yet have the grace to consider that
tears do not become a man.

Ros. But have I not cause to weep?

Cel. As good cause as one would desire. Therefore weep.   5

Ros. His very hair is of the dissembling color.

Cel. Something browner than Judas'. Marry, his kisses are
Judas' own children.

Ros. I' faith, his hair is of a good color.

Cel. An excellent color. Your chestnut was ever the only   10
color.

Ros. And his kissing is as full of sanctity as the touch of
holy bread.

Cel. He hath bought a pair of cast lips of Diana. A nun of
winter's sisterhood kisses not more religiously; the very ice   15
of chastity is in them.

Ros. But why did he swear he would come this morning,
and comes not?

Cel. Nay, certainly there is no truth in him.

Ros. Do you think so?   20

Cel. Yes. I think he is not a pickpurse nor a horse-stealer,
but for his verity in love, I do think him as concave as a
covered goblet or a worm-eaten nut.

Ros. Not true in love?

Cel. Yes, when he is in. But I think he is not in.   25

Ros. You have heard him swear downright he was.

Cel. 'Was' is not 'is.' Besides, the oath of a lover is no
stronger than the word of a tapster; they are both the
confirmer of false reckonings. He attends here in the forest
on the Duke your father.   30

---

20 honest: *chaste*   **23 hard favor'd:** *ugly*   **25 material:** *full of ideas*   **28 foul:** *ugly*   **33
Sir;** *cf. n.*   **35 couple:** *join, marry*   **38 heart;** *cf. n.*   **40 horn-beasts;** *cf. n.*   **But what
though?:** *but what of that?*   **46 rascal:** *a young or inferior deer*   **50 want:** *lack*   **52
dispatch:** *i.e. marry*   **58 Master What-ye-call't;** *cf. n.*   **59 Goddild:** *God reward you*   **60
toy:** *trifling matter*   **61 be cover'd:** *put on your hat*   **62 motley:** *fool*   **63 bow:** *yoke*

77 bawdry: *sin*   **79 O sweet Oliver;** *cf. n.*   **83 Wind away:** *go away*   **87 flout:**
jeer   **6 dissembling color;** *cf. n.*   **14 cast:** *cast off*   **lips of Diana:** *Diana was the
goddess of chastity*   **15 winter's sisterhood:** *i.e. the bond of chastity*   **22 verity:** *truth*
concave: *hollow, insincere*   **27 a:** *F omits*   **28 tapster:** *tavern waiter*   **29 reckonings:**
accounts, charges

Ros. I met the Duke yesterday and had much question with
him. He ask'd me of what parentage I was; I told him of as
good as he. So he laugh'd and let me go. But what talk we of
fathers when there is such a man as Orlando?

Cel. O, that's a brave man! He writes brave verses,   35
speaks brave words, swears brave oaths, and breaks them
bravely—quite traverse athwart the heart of his lover, as a
puisny tilter that spurs his horse but on one side breaks his
staff like a noble goose. But all's brave that youth mounts
and folly guides. Who comes here?   40

Enter Corin.

Cor. Mistress and master, you have oft inquired
After the shepherd that complain'd of love,
Who you saw sitting by me on the turf
Praising the proud disdainful shepherdess
That was his mistress.   45

Cel.   Well, and what of him?

Cor. If you will see a pageant truly play'd
Between the pale complexion of true love
And the red glow of scorn and proud disdain,
Go hence a little and I shall conduct you,   50
If you will mark it.

Ros.   O, come, let us remove.
The sight of lovers, feedeth those in love.
Bring us to this sight, and you shall say
I'll prove a busy actor in their play.   *Exeunt.*   55

❧ Scene Fifth ❧

Enter Silvius and Phebe.

Sil. Sweet Phebe, do not scorn me. Do not, Phebe.
Say that you love me not, but say not so
In bitterness. The common executioner,
Whose heart th' accustom'd sight of death makes hard,
Falls not the ax upon the humbled neck   5
But first begs pardon. Will you sterner be
Than he that dies and lives by bloody drops?

Enter Rosalind, Celia, and Corin.

Phebe. I would not be thy executioner.
I fly thee, for I would not injure thee.
Thou tell'st me there is murder in mine eye.   10
'Tis pretty, sure, and very probable
That eyes, that are the frail'st and softest things,
Who shut their coward gates on atomies,
Should be called tyrants, butchers, murtherers.
Now I do frown on thee with all my heart,   15
And if mine eyes can wound, now let them kill thee.
Now counterfeit to swound. Why, now fall down!
Or if thou canst not, O for shame, for shame.
Lie not, to say mine eyes are murtherers.
Now show the wound mine eye hath made in thee.   20
Scratch thee but with a pin and there remains
Some scar of it; lean but upon a rush,

The cicatrice and capable impressure
Thy palm some moment keeps. But now mine eyes,
Which I have darted at thee, hurt thee not;   25
Nor I am sure there is no force in eyes
That can do hurt.

Sil.   O dear Phebe,
If ever, as that ever may be near,
You meet in some fresh cheek the power of fancy,   30
Then shall you know the wounds invisible
That Love's keen arrows make.

Phebe   But till that time
Come not thou near me. And when that time comes,
Afflict me with thy mocks; pity me not,   35
As till that time I shall not pity thee.

Ros. And why, I pray you? Who might be your mother
That you insult, exult, and all at once,
Over the wretched? What, though you have no beauty—
As, by my faith, I see no more in you   40
Than without candle may go dark to bed—
Must you be therefore proud and pitiless?
Why, what means this? Why do you look on me?
I see no more in you than in the ordinary
Of Nature's sale-work. 'Od's my little life,   45
I think she means to tangle my eyes too.
No, faith, proud mistress, hope not after it;
'Tis not your inky brows, your black silk hair,
Your bugle eyeballs, nor your cheek of cream
That can entame my spirits to your worship.   50
You foolish shepherd, wherefore do you follow her
Like foggy south, puffing with wind and rain?
You are a thousand times a properer man
Than she a woman. 'Tis such fools as you
That makes the world full of ill-favor'd children.   55
'Tis not her glass but you that flatters her,
And out of you she sees herself more proper
Than any of her lineaments can show her.
But, mistress, know yourself. Down on your knees
And thank heaven, fasting, for a good man's love.   60
For I must tell you friendly in your ear:
Sell when you can; you are not for all markets.
Cry the man mercy, love him, take his offer.
Foul is most foul, being foul to be a scoffer.
So take her to thee, shepherd. Fare you well.   65

Phebe. Sweet youth, I pray you, chide a year together.
I had rather hear you chide than this man woo.

Ros. He's falne in love with your foulness, and she'll fall in
love with my anger. If it be so, as fast as she answers thee
with frowning looks, I'll sauce her with bitter words. Why   70
look you so upon me?

Phebe. For no ill will I bear you.

Ros. I pray you, do not fall in love with me,
For I am falser than vows made in wine.
Besides, I like you not. If you will know my house,   75
'Tis at the tuft of olives here hard by.
Will you go, sister? Shepherd, ply her hard.

31 **question:** *conversation*   35 **brave:** *fine*   37 **traverse athwart;** *cf. n.*   38 **puisny:**
insignificant, incompetent (pronounced 'puny')   48 **pale complexion;** *cf. n.*   51 **mark:**
observe   52 **remove:** *depart*   5 **Falls:** *lets fall*   7 **dies and lives:** *makes his living*   14 **murtherers:** *murderers*   17 **counterfeit:** *pretend* **swound:** *swoon*   22 **but;**
F omits

23 **cicatrice:** *impression* **capable impressure:** *firm imprint*   30 **fancy:** *love*   41 **candle . . .
bed;** *cf. n.*   45 **sale-work:** *product of poor quality* **'Od's:** *God save*   49 **bugle:** *a black glass
bead, here meaning 'black'*   50 **entame:** *subdue* **to your worship:** *to worship you*   52 **south:**
south wind, cf. n.   53 **properer:** *handsomer*   56 **glass:** *mirror*   63 **Cry . . . mercy:** *beg
for mercy*   64 **Foul . . . scoffer;** *cf. n.*   66 **together:** *on end*   67 **I had:** *to be read
'I'd'*   68 **falne:** *fall'n*   70 **sauce:** *rebuke*

Come, sister. Shepherdess, look on him better
And be not proud, though all the world could see
None could be so abus'd in sight as he.   *80*
Come, to our flock.   *Exeunt [Rosalind, Celia, Corin].*
      Phebe. Dead shepherd, now I find thy saw of might:
'Whoever lov'd that lov'd not at first sight?'
      Sil. Sweet Phebe.
      Phebe. Hah! What say'st thou, Silvius?   *85*
      Sil. Sweet Phebe, pity me.
      Phebe. Why, I am sorry for thee, gentle Silvius.
      Sil. Wherever sorrow is, relief would be.
If you do sorrow at my grief in love,
By giving love your sorrow and my grief   *90*
Were both extermin'd.
      Phebe. Thou hast my love. Is not that neighborly?
      Sil. I would have you.
      Phebe.   Why, that were covetousness.
Silvius, the time was that I hated thee,   *95*
And yet it is not that I bear thee love.
But since that thou canst talk of love so well,
Thy company, which erst was irksome to me,
I will endure; and I'll employ thee too.
But do not look for further recompense   *100*
Than thine own gladness that thou art employ'd.
      Sil. So holy and so perfect is my love,
And I in such a poverty of grace,
That I shall think it a most plenteous crop
To glean the broken ears after the man   *105*
That the main harvest reaps. Loose now and then
A scatt'red smile, and that I'll live upon.
      Phebe. Know'st thou the youth that spoke to me erewhile?
      Sil. Not very well. But I have met him oft,
And he hath bought the cottage and the bounds   *110*
That the old Carlot once was master of.
      Phebe. Think not I love him, though I ask for him.
'Tis but a peevish boy, yet he talks well.
But what care I for words? Yet words do well
When he that speaks them pleases those that hear.   *115*
It is a pretty youth—not very pretty.
But sure he's proud, and yet his pride becomes him.
He'll make a proper man: the best thing in him
Is his complexion. And faster than his tongue
Did make offense his eyes did heal it up.   *120*
He is not very tall, yet for his years he's tall.
His leg is but so-so, and yet 'tis well.
There was a pretty redness in his lip,
A little riper and more lusty red
Than that mix'd in his cheek. 'Twas just the difference   *125*
Betwixt the constant red and mingled damask.
There be some women, Silvius, had they mark'd him
In parcels as I did, would have gone near
To fall in love with him. But for my part,
I love him not nor hate him not; and yet   *130*
I have more cause to hate him than to love him,
For what had he to do to chide at me?

He said mine eyes were black and my hair black,
And, now I am rememb'red, scorn'd at me.
I marvel why I answer'd not again.   *135*
But that's all one: omittance is no quittance.
I'll write to him a very tanting letter,
And thou shalt bear it. Wilt thou, Silvius?
      Sil. Phebe, with all my heart.
      Phebe.   I'll write it straight.   *140*
The matter's in my head and in my heart:
I will be bitter with him and passing short.
Go with me, Silvius.   *Exeunt.*

ACT FOURTH ❦ SCENE FIRST

Enter Rosalind, and Celia, and Jaques.

      Jaq. I prithee, pretty youth, let me be better acquainted
with thee.
      Ros. They say you are a melancholy fellow.
      Jaq. I am so. I do love it better than laughing.
      Ros. Those that are in extremity of either are   *5*
abominable fellows, and betray themselves to every modern
censure worse than drunkards.
      Jaq. Why, 'tis good to be sad and say nothing.
      Ros. Why, then 'tis good to be a post.
      Jaq. I have neither the scholar's melancholy, which is   *10*
emulation; nor the musician's, which is fantastical; nor the
courtier's, which is proud; nor the soldier's, which is ambitious;
nor the lawyer's, which is politic; nor the lady's, which is nice;
nor the lover's, which is all these. But it is a melancholy of
mine own, compounded of many simples, extracted from   *15*
many objects, and indeed the sundry contemplation of my
travels, in which my often rumination wraps me in a most
humorous sadness.
      Ros. A traveler! By my faith, you have great reason to
be sad. I fear you have sold your own lands to see other   *20*
men's. Then to have seen much and to have nothing is
to have rich eyes and poor hands.
      Jaq. Yes, I have gain'd my experience.

Enter Orlando.

      Ros. And your experience makes you sad. I had rather
have a fool to make me merry than experience to make   *25*
me sad, and to travel for it too.
      Orl. Good day and happiness, dear Rosalind.
      Jaq. Nay, then, God buy you, and you talk in blank verse.
      Ros. Farewell, Monsieur Traveler. Look you lisp and wear
strange suits, disable all the benefits of your own country,   *30*
be out of love with your nativity, and almost chide God
for making you that countenance you are; or I will scarce
think you have swam in a gundello. *[Exit Jaques.]* Why, how
now, Orlando? Where have you been all this while? You a

---

78 better: *more kindly*   **80 abus'd in sight:** *deceived by eyesight*   **82 Dead shepherd;** *cf. n.*   **91 extermin'd:** *banished*   **92 neighborly;** *cf. n.*   **98 erst:** *at first*   **103 poverty of grace:** *lack of favor*   **107 scatt'red:** *stray*   **108 erewhile:** *a little while ago;* F *erewhile.*   **110 bounds:** *acreage*   **111 Carlot;** *cf. n.*   **126 constant:** *uniform* **mingled damask:** *a mixture of red and white, like the damask rose*   **127 be:** *are*   **128 In parcels:** *bit by bit*   **131 I:** F *omits*

134 I am rememb'red: *I recall*   **136 omittance . . . quittance;** *cf. n.*   **137 tanting:** *taunting*   **142 passing short:** *exceedingly curt*   **1 be:** F *omits*   **8 sad:** *here with two meanings: 'melancholy' and 'heavy'*   **11 emulation:** *envy*   **13 politic:** *crafty* **nice:** *delicate*   **15 simples:** *herbs, ingredients*   **28 buy:** *be with* **and:** *an* (if)   **29 lisp:** *talk in an affected manner*   **30 disable:** *disparage*   **31 nativity:** *birthplace*   **33 swam . . . gundello:** *ridden in a gondola, i.e. been to Venice*

lover? And you serve me such another trick, never come   35
in my sight more.

Orl. My fair Rosalind, I come within an hour of my
promise.

Ros. Break an hour's promise in love? He that will divide
a minute into a thousand parts and break but a part of the   40
thousand part of a minute in the affairs of love, it may be
said of him that Cupid hath clapp'd him o' th' shoulder.
But I'll warrant him heart-whole.

Orl. Pardon me, dear Rosalind.

Ros. Nay. And you be so tardy, come no more in my   45
sight; I had as lief be woo'd of a snail.

Orl. Of a snail?

Ros. Ay, of a snail. For though he comes slowly, he carries
his house on his head—a better jointure, I think, than you
make a woman. Besides, he brings his destiny with him.   50

Orl. What's that?

Ros. Why, horns; which such as you are fain to be
beholding to your wives for. But he comes armed in his
fortune, and prevents the slander of his wife.

Orl. Virtue is no horn-maker, and my Rosalind is virtuous.

Ros. And I am your Rosalind.

Cel. It pleases him to call you so. But he hath a
Rosalind of a better leer than you.

Ros. Come, woo me, woo me; for now I am in a holiday
humor and like enough to consent. What would you say   60
to me now, and I were your very very Rosalind?

Orl. I would kiss before I spoke.

Ros. Nay, you were better speak first; and when you were
gravel'd for lack of matter, you might take occasion to kiss.
Very good orators, when they are out, they will spit; and   65
for lovers lacking—God warn us—matter, the cleanliest
shift is to kiss.

Orl. How if the kiss be denied?

Ros. Then she puts you to entreaty, and there begins
new matter.   70

Orl. Who could be out, being before his beloved mistress?

Ros. Marry, that should you if I were your mistress, or I
should think my honesty ranker than my wit.

Orl. What of my suit?

Ros. Not out of your apparel, and yet out of your suit.   75
Am I not your Rosalind?

Orl. I take some joy to say you are, because I would
be talking of her.

Ros. Well, in her person, I say I will not have you.

Orl. Then, in mine own person, I die.   80

Ros. No, faith, die by attorney. The poor world is almost six
thousand years old, and in all this time there was not any
man died in his own person, *videlicet,* in a love cause. Troilus
had his brains dash'd out with a Grecian club, yet he did what
he could to die before; and he is one of the patterns of   85
love. Leander, he would have liv'd many a fair year though
Hero had turn'd nun, if it had not been for a hot midsummer
night; for, good youth, he went but forth to wash him in the

Hellespont, and being taken with the cramp, was drown'd;
and the foolish chroniclers of that age found it was 'Hero   90
of Cestos.' But these are all lies. Men have died from time
to time and worms have eaten them, but not for love.

Orl. I would not have my right Rosalind of this mind,
for I protest her frown might kill me.

Ros. By this hand, it will not kill a fly. But come. Now   95
I will be your Rosalind in a more coming-on disposition;
and ask me what you will, I will grant it.

Orl. Then love me, Rosalind.

Ros. Yes, faith, will I—Fridays and Saturdays and all.

Orl. And wilt thou have me?   100

Ros. Ay, and twenty such.

Orl. What sayest thou?

Ros. Are you not good?

Orl. I hope so.

Ros. Why then, can one desire too much of a good thing?
Come, sister, you shall be the priest and marry us. Give me
your hand, Orlando. What do you say, sister?

Orl. Pray thee, marry us.

Cel. I cannot say the words.

Ros. You must begin, 'Will you, Orlando . . .'   110

Cel. Go to. Will you, Orlando, have to wife this Rosalind?

Orl. I will.

Ros. Ay, but when?

Orl. Why, now. As fast as she can marry us.

Ros. Then you must say, 'I take thee, Rosalind, for   115
wife.'

Orl. I take thee, Rosalind, for wife.

Ros. I might ask you for your commission, but I do
take thee, Orlando, for my husband. There's a girl goes
before the priest, and certainly a woman's thought runs   120
before her actions.

Orl. So do all thoughts; they are wing'd.

Ros. Now tell me how long you would have her after
you have possess'd her?

Orl. For ever and a day.   125

Ros. Say 'a day' without the 'ever.' No, no, Orlando.
Men are April when they woo, December when they wed;
maids are May when they are maids, but the sky changes
when they are wives. I will be more jealous of thee than a
Barbary cock-pigeon over his hen, more clamorous than a   130
parrot against rain, more new-fangled than an ape, more
giddy in my desires than a monkey. I will weep for nothing,
like Diana in the fountain, and I will do that when you are
dispos'd to be merry. I will laugh like a hyen, and that
when thou art inclin'd to sleep.   135

Orl. But will my Rosalind do so?

Ros. By my life, she will do as I do.

Orl. O, but she is wise.

Ros. Or else she could not have the wit to do this.
The wiser, the waywarder. Make the doors upon a   140
woman's wit, and it will out at the casement; shut that, and
'twill out at the keyhole; stop that, 'twill fly with the smoke
out at the chimney.

Orl. A man that had a wife with such a wit, he might
say, 'Wit, whether wilt?'   145

35 **And:** *an* (if).   42 **clapp'd:** *seized on the shoulder as if to arrest*   45 **And:** *an* (if)   46
of: *by*   49 **jointure:** *marriage portion*   52 **horns;** *cf. n.*   53 **beholding:** *behold-*
en   **armed:** *i.e. with horns*   55 **horn-maker:** *cuckold-maker*   58 **leer:** *appearance*   61
and: *an* (if)   64 **gravel'd:** *nonplussed*   65 **out:** *out of material*   66 **God warn us:**
God warrant (protect) *us*   **cleanliest shift:** *cleverest device*   73 **ranker:** *more flour-*
ishing   74 **suit;** *cf. n.*   81 **by attorney:** *by proxy*   83 **videlicet:** *namely*   **Troilus;**
cf. n.   85 **patterns:** *models*   86 **Leander;** *cf. n.*

90 **found:** *gave the verdict* (in a legal sense)   93 **right:** *true*   118 **commission:** *author-*
ity   119 **goes before:** *anticipates*   130 **Barbary:** *Oriental*   131 **against:** *in expectation*
of   **new-fangled:** *fond of novelty*   132 **giddy:** *capricious*   133 **Diana;** *cf. n.*   134
hyen: *hyena*   140 **Make:** *shut*   145 **'Wit . . . wilt?';** *cf. n.*

Ros. Nay, you might keep that check for it till you met your wive's wit going to your neighbor's bed.

Orl. And what wit could wit have to excuse that?

Ros. Marry, to say she came to seek you there. You shall never take her without her answer unless you take   *150* her without her tongue. O, that woman that cannot make her fault her husband's occasion, let her never nurse her child herself, for she will breed it like a fool.

Orl. For these two hours, Rosalind, I will leave thee.

Ros. Alas, dear love, I cannot lack thee two hours.   *155*

Orl. I must attend the Duke at dinner. By two o'clock I will be with thee again.

Ros. Ay, go your ways, go your ways. I knew what you would prove; my friends told me as much, and I thought no less. That flattering tongue of yours won me. 'Tis   *160* but one cast away, and so come death. Two o'clock is your hour.

Orl. Ay, sweet Rosalind.

Ros. By my troth, and in good earnest, and so God mend me, and by all pretty oaths that are not dangerous, if you   *165* break one jot of your promise or come one minute behind your hour, I will think you the most pathetical break-promise and the most hollow lover and the most unworthy of her you call Rosalind that may be chosen out of the gross band of the unfaithful. Therefore beware my censure and keep your   *170* promise.

Orl. With no less religion than if thou wert indeed my Rosalind. So adieu.

Ros. Well, Time is the old justice that examines all such offenders, and let Time try. Adieu.   *Exit [Orlando]. 175*

Cel. You have simply misus'd our sex in your love prate. We must have your doublet and hose pluck'd over your head and show the world what the bird hath done to her own nest.

Ros. O coz, coz, coz, my pretty little coz, that thou didst know how many fathom deep I am in love! But it   *180* cannot be sounded; my affection hath an unknown bottom, like the Bay of Portugal.

Cel. Or rather bottomless—that as fast as you pour affection in, it runs out.

Ros. No; that same wicked bastard of Venus that was   *185* begot of thought, conceiv'd of spleen, and born of madness, that blind rascally boy that abuses everyone's eyes because his own are out—let him be judge how deep I am in love. I'll tell thee, Aliena, I cannot be out of sight of Orlando. I'll go find a shadow and sigh till he come.   *190*

Cel. And I'll sleep.   *Exeunt.*

❧ SCENE SECOND ❧

Enter Jaques and Lords, Foresters.

Jaq. Which is he that killed the deer?

Lord. Sir, it was I.

Jaq. Let's present him to the Duke like a Roman conqueror, and it would do well to set the deer's horns upon his head for a branch of victory. Have you no song, forester, for this   *5* purpose?

Lord. Yes, sir.

Jaq. Sing it. 'Tis no matter how it be in tune, so it make noise enough.   *Music.*

Song

What shall he have that kill'd the deer?   *10*
His leathern skin and horns to wear.
Then sing him home. The rest shall bear
This burthen:

Take thou no scorn to wear the horn.
It was a crest ere thou wast born.   *15*
Thy father's father wore it,
And thy father bore it.
The horn, the horn, the lusty horn
Is not a thing to laugh to scorn.   *Exeunt.*

❧ SCENE THIRD ❧

Enter Rosalind and Celia.

Ros. How say you now? Is it not past two o'clock? And here much Orlando.

Cel. I warrant you, with pure love and troubled brain

Enter Silvius

he hath tane his bow and arrows and is gone forth to sleep. Look who comes here.   *5*

Sil. My errand is to you, fair youth.
My gentle Phebe did bid me give you this.

[Presenting a letter.]

I know not the contents but, as I guess
By the stern brow and waspish action
Which she did use as she was writing of it,   *10*
It bears an angry tenure. Pardon me,
I am but as a guiltless messenger.

Ros. Patience herself would startle at this letter
And play the swaggerer. Bear this, bear all.
She says I am not fair, that I lack manners;   *15*
She calls me proud, and that she could not love me
Were man as rare as Phoenix. 'Od's my will,
Her love is not the hare that I do hunt.
Why writes she so to me? Well, shepherd, well?
This is a letter of your own device.   *20*

Sil. No, I protest. I know not the contents;
Phebe did write it.

Ros.   Come, come, you are a fool,
And turn'd into the extremity of love.
I saw her hand: she has a leathern hand,   *25*
A freestone colored hand. I verily did think
That her old gloves were on, but 'twas her hands.
She has a housewive's hand; but that's no matter.
I say she never did invent this letter.
This is a man's invention and his hand.   *30*

Sil. Sure it is hers.

Ros. Why, 'tis a boisterous and a cruel style,
A style for challengers. Why, she defies me,

146 check: *rebuke*   **147 wive's:** *wife's, an old genitive*   **152 occasion;** *cf. n.*   **155 lack:** *do without*   **164, 165 mend me:** *change my fortune*   **167 pathetical:** *pitiable*   **169 gross:** *whole*   **170 censure:** *condemnation*   **172 religion:** *fidelity*   **176 simply:** *completely* **misus'd:** *abused*   **178 bird . . . nest;** *cf. n.*   **185 bastard of Venus;** *cf. n.*   **186 thought:** *melancholy* **spleen:** *impulse*

12, 13 The rest . . . burthen; *cf. n.*   **19 laugh to scorn:** *ridicule*   **2 here much Orlando:** *i.e. spoken with irony*   **11 tenure:** *tenor, purport* (to be read 'tenor')   **17 Phoenix;** *cf. n.*   **24 turn'd:** *brought* **the extremity:** *to be read 'th' extremity.'*   **26 freestone colored:** *the color of brown stone*   **32 boisterous:** *to be read 'boist'rous.'*

Like Turk to Christian. Women's gentle brain
Could not drop forth such giant rude invention,   35
Such Ethiop words, blacker in their effect
Than in their countenance. Will you hear the letter?
   Sil. So please you, for I never heard it yet;
Yet heard too much of Phebe's cruelty.
   Ros. She Phebes me! Mark how the tyrant writes.   *Read.*

   Art thou God to shepherd turn'd
   That a maiden's heart hath burn'd?

Can a woman rail thus?
   Sil. Call you this railing?   *Read.*

Ros.   *Why, thy Godhead laid apart,*   45
   Warr'st thou with a woman's heart?

Did you ever hear such railing?

   Whiles the eyes of man did woo me
   That could do no vengeance to me.

Meaning me a beast.   50

   If the scorn of your bright eyne
   Have power to raise such love in mine,
   Alack, in me what strange effect
   Would they work in mild aspect?
   Whiles you chid me, I did love;   55
   How then might your prayers move!
   He that brings this love to thee
   Little knows this love in me.
   And by him seal up thy mind
   Whether that thy youth and kind   60
   Will the faithful offer take
   Of me and all that I can make;
   Or else by him my love deny,
   And then I'll study how to die.

   Sil. Call you this chiding?   65
   Cel. Alas, poor shepherd.
   Ros. Do you pity him? No, he deserves no pity. Wilt thou
love such a woman? What, to make thee an instrument and
play false strains upon thee? Not to be endur'd. Well, go
your way to her—for I see love hath made thee a tame   70
snake—and say this to her: that if she loves me, I charge
her to love thee; if she will not, I will never have her unless
thou entreat for her. If you be a true lover, hence, and not a
word. For here comes more company.   *Exit Silvius.*

Enter Oliver.

   Oli. Good morrow, fair ones. Pray you, if you know,   75
Where in the purlieus of this forest stands
A sheepcote fenc'd about with olive trees?
   Cel. West of this place, down in the neighbor bottom.
The rank of osiers by the murmuring stream,
Left on your right hand, brings you to the place.   80
But at this hour the house doth keep itself;
There's none within.

   Oli. If that an eye may profit by a tongue,
Then should I know you by description:
Such garments and such years. 'The boy is fair,   85
Of female favor, and bestows himself
Like a ripe sister; the woman low
And browner than her brother.' Are not you
The owner of the house I did inquire for?
   Cel. It is no boast, being ask'd, to say we are.   90
   Oli. Orlando doth commend him to you both,
And to that youth he calls his Rosalind
He sends this bloody napkin. Are you he?
   Ros. I am. What must we understand by this?
   Oli. Some of my shame, if you will know of me   95
What man I am, and how and why and where
This handkercher was stain'd.
   Cel.   I pray you tell it.
   Oli. When last the young Orlando parted from you,
He left a promise to return again   100
Within an hour; and pacing through the forest,
Chewing the food of sweet and bitter fancy,
Lo, what befell! He threw his eye aside,
And mark what object did present itself
Under an old oak, whose boughs were moss'd with age   105
And high top bald with dry antiquity:
A wretched ragged man, o'ergrown with hair,
Lay sleeping on his back. About his neck
A green and gilded snake had wreath'd itself,
Who with her head nimble in threats approach'd   110
The opening of his mouth. But suddenly,
Seeing Orlando, it unlink'd itself
And with indented glides did slip away
Into a bush. Under which bush's shade
A lioness, with udders all drawn dry,   115
Lay couching head on ground, with catlike watch
When that the sleeping man should stir; for 'tis
The royal disposition of that beast
To prey on nothing that doth seem as dead.
This seen, Orlando did approach the man   120
And found it was his brother, his elder brother.
   Cel. O, I have heard him speak of that same brother,
And he did render him the most unnatural
That liv'd amongst men.
   Oli.   And well he might so do,   125
For well I know he was unnatural.
   Ros. But to Orlando: did he leave him there,
Food to the suck'd and hungry lioness?
   Oli. Twice did he turn his back and purpos'd so.
But kindness, nobler ever than revenge.   130
And nature stronger that his just occasion
Made him give battle to the lioness,
Who quickly fell before him. In which hurtling
From miserable slumber I awaked.
   Cel. Are you his brother?   135
   Ros.   Was't you he rescu'd?
   Cel. Was't you that did so oft contrive to kill him?
   Oli. 'Twas I, but 'tis not I. I do not shame

---

34 Turk; *cf. n.*   **35 giant rude:** *extremely rude*   **36 Ethiop:** *black*   **37 countenance:**
to be read 'count'nance'   **40 Phebes:** *treats cruelly, acts like Phebe*   **45 Godhead:** *divini-*
ty **laid apart:** *put aside*   **51 eyne:** *archaic plural of 'eye'*   **54 aspect:** *stressed — ´*   **59**
seal up thy mind: *send under seal*   **60 youth and kind:** *youthful nature*   **76 purlieus:**
borders of a forest   **78 bottom:** *valley*   **79 osiers:** *willows*   **81 keep itself:** *take care*
of itself (i.e. is empty)

86 favor: *feature* **bestows:** *carries*   **87 ripe:** *grown up* **low:** *short*   **93 napkin:** *hand-*
kerchief   **97 handkercher:** *handkerchief*   **103 threw . . . aside:** *looked to one side*   **105**
old: *this word causes an irregular line but it appears in all folios*   **112 unlink'd:** *un-*
coiled   **113 indented:** *winding*   **123 render:** *describe*   **131 occasion:** *opportu-*
nity   **133 hurtling:** *tumult*   **137 contrive:** *plot*

To tell you what I was, since my conversion
So sweetly tastes, being the thing I am.   *140*

    Ros. But for the bloody napkin?

    Oli.   By and by.
When from the first to last, betwixt us two
Tears our recountments had most kindly bath'd,
As how I came into that desert place—   *145*
In brief, he led me to the gentle Duke,
Who gave me fresh array and entertainment,
Committing me unto my brother's love;
Who led me instantly unto his cave,
There stripp'd himself, and here upon his arm   *150*
The lioness had torn some flesh away,
Which all this while had bled. And now he fainted
And cried, in fainting, upon Rosalind.
Brief, I recover'd him, bound up his wound,
And after some small space, being strong at heart,   *155*
He sent me hither, stranger as I am,
To tell this story that you might excuse
His broken promise; and to give this napkin,
Dy'd in his blood, unto the shepherd youth
That he in sport doth call his Rosalind.   *[Rosalind faints.]*

    Cel. Why, how now, Ganymede, sweet Ganymede!

    Oli. Many will swoon when they do look on blood.

    Cel. There is more in it. Cousin Ganymede!

    Oli. Look, he recovers.

    Ros. I would I were at home.   *165*

    Cel.   We'll lead you thither.
I pray you, will you take him by the arm?

    Oli. Be of good cheer, youth. You a man? You lack a
man's heart.

    Ros. I do so, I confess it. Ah, sirrah, a body would   *170*
think this was well counterfeited. I pray you tell your brother
how well I counterfeited. Heigh-ho!

    Oli. This was not counterfeit; there is too great testimony
in your complexion that it was a passion of earnest.

    Ros. Counterfeit, I assure you.   *175*

    Oli. Well then, take a good heart and counterfeit to be a man.

    Ros. So I do. But, i' faith, I should have been a woman by right.

    Cel. Come, you look paler and paler. Pray you, draw
homewards. Good sir, go with us.

    Oli. That will I, for we must bear answer back how   *180*
you excuse my brother, Rosalind.

    Ros. I shall devise something, but I pray you commend
my counterfeiting to him. Will you go?   *Exeunt.*

ACT FIVE ❧ SCENE FIRST

Enter Clown [Touchstone] and Audrey.

    Touch. We shall find a time, Audrey. Patience, gentle
Audrey.

    Audrey. Faith, the priest was good enough, for all the old
gentleman's saying.

    Touch. A most wicked Sir Oliver, Audrey, a most vile   *5*

Martext. But, Audrey, there is a youth here in the forest lays
claim to you.

    Audrey. Ay, I know who 'tis. He hath no interest in me in
the world. Here comes the man you mean.

Enter William.

    Touch. It is meat and drink to me to see a clown.   *10*
By my troth, we that have good wits have much to
answer for. We shall be flouting; we cannot hold.

    William. Good ev'n, Audrey.

    Audrey. God ye good ev'n, William.

    William. And good ev'n to you, sir.   *15*

    Touch. Good ev'n, gentle friend. Cover thy head, cover thy
head. Nay, prithee be cover'd. How old are you, friend?

    William Five and twenty, sir.

    Touch. A ripe age. Is thy name William?

    William. William, sir.   *20*

    Touch. A fair name. Wast born i' th' forest here?

    William. Ay, sir, I thank God.

    Touch. 'Thank God': a good answer. Art rich?

    William. Faith, sir, so-so.

    Touch. 'So-so' is good, very good, very excellent   *25*
good. And yet it is not; it is but so-so. Art thou wise?

    William. Ay, sir, I have a pretty wit.

    Touch. Why, thou say'st well. I do now remember a saying:
'The fool doth think he is wise, but the wise man knows himself
to be a fool.' The heathen philosopher, when he had a desire to
eat a grape, would open his lips when he put it into his mouth,
meaning thereby that grapes were made to eat and lips to open.
You do love this maid?

    William. I do, sir.

    Touch. Give me your hand. Art thou learned?   *35*

    William. No, sir.

    Touch. Then learn this of me: to have is to have. For it is a
figure in rhetoric that drink, being pour'd out of a cup into
a glass, by filling the one doth empty the other. For all your
writers do consent that *ipse* is he; now you are not   *40*
ipse, for I am he.

    William. Which he, sir?

    Touch. He, sir, that must marry this woman. Therefore, you
clown, abandon (which is in the vulgar 'leave') the society (which
in the boorish is 'company') of this female (which in the common
is 'woman'); which together is, abandon the society of this female.
Or, clown, thou perishest; or, to thy better understanding, diest;
or, to wit, I kill thee, make thee away, translate thy life into
death, thy liberty into bondage. I will deal in poison with thee,
or in bastinado, or in steel; I will bandy with thee in faction; I
will o'errun thee with policy; I will kill thee a hundred and fifty
ways. Therefore tremble and depart.

    Audrey. Do, good William.

    William. God rest you merry, sir.   *Exit.*

Enter Corin.

    Cor. Our master and mistress seeks you. Come away, away.

    Touch. Trip, Audrey, trip, Audrey. I attend, I attend. *Exeunt.*

---

144 recountments: *stories*   **154 Brief:** *briefly*   **recover'd:** *revived*   **174 passion of ear-nest:** *a genuine swoon*

10 clown: *rustic*   **12 flouting:** *mocking*   **hold:** *refrain*   **14 God ye:** *God give you*   *27*
wit: *intelligence*   **40 ipse:** *he himself (Latin)*   **50 bastinado:** *cudgel*   **bandy:** *contend*   **faction:** *dissension*   **51 o'errun:** *overwhelm*   **policy:** *craft*   **54 God ... merry:** *God keep you in good spirits*

✤ SCENE TWO ✤

Enter Orlando and Oliver.

Orl. Is't possible that on so little acquaintance you should like her? That, but seeing, you should love her? And loving, woo? And wooing, she should grant? And will you persever to enjoy her?

Oli. Neither call the giddiness of it in question, the   *5* poverty of her, the small acquaintance, my sudden wooing, nor sudden consenting. But say with me, 'I love Aliena'; say with her, that she loves me; consent with both, that we may enjoy each other. It shall be to your good: for my father's house and all the revenue that was old Sir Rowland's will I   *10* estate upon you, and here live and die a shepherd.

Enter Rosalind.

Orl. You have my consent. Let your wedding be tomorrow; thither will I invite the Duke and all's contented followers. Go you and prepare Aliena for, look you, here comes my Rosalind.

Ros. God save you, brother.   *15*

Oli. And you, fair sister.   *[Exit.]*

Ros. O my dear Orlando, how it grieves me to see thee wear thy heart in a scarf.

Orl. It is my arm.

Ros. I thought thy heart had been wounded with the   *20* claws of a lion.

Orl. Wounded it is, but with the eyes of a lady.

Ros. Did your brother tell you how I counterfeited to sound when he show'd me your handkercher?

Orl. Ay, and greater wonders than that.   *25*

Ros. O, I know where you are. Nay, 'tis true. There was never anything so sudden but the fight of two rams and Cae-sar's thrasonical brag of 'I came, saw, and overcame.' For your brother and my sister no sooner met, but they look'd; no sooner look'd, but they lov'd; no sooner lov'd, but they   *30* sigh'd; no sooner sigh'd, but they ask'd one another the reason; no sooner knew the reason, but they sought the remedy. And in these degrees have they made a pair of stairs to marriage, which they will climb incontinent, or else be incontinent before marriage. They are in the very wrath of love, and   *35* they will together. Clubs cannot part them.

Orl. They shall be married tomorrow, and I will bid the Duke to the nuptial. But O, how bitter a thing it is to look into happiness through another man's eyes. By so much the more shall I tomorrow be at the height of heart-heaviness,   *40* by how much I shall think my brother happy in having what he wishes for.

Ros. Why then, tomorrow I cannot serve your turn for Rosalind?

Orl. I can live no longer by thinking.   *45*

Ros. I will weary you then no longer with idle talking. Know of me then—for now I speak to some purpose—that I know you are a gentleman of good conceit. I speak not this that you should bear a good opinion of my knowledge, insomuch I say I know you are. Neither do I labor for a   *50* greater esteem than may in some little measure draw a belief

from you, to do yourself good and not to grace me. Believe then, if you please, that I can do strange things. I have, since I was three year old, convers'd with a magician most profound in his art, and yet not damnable. If you do love Rosalind so near the heart as your gesture cries it out, when your brother marries Aliena shall you marry her. I know into what straits of fortune she is driven, and it is not impossible to me—if it appear not inconvenient to you—to set her before your eyes tomorrow human as she is, and without any danger.   *60*

Orl. Speak'st thou in sober meanings?

Ros. By my life, I do—which I tender dearly, though I say I am a magician. Therefore put you in your best array, bid your friends; for if you will be married tomorrow, you shall, and to Rosalind, if you will.   *65*

Enter Silvius and Phebe.

Look, here comes a lover of mine and a lover of hers.

Phebe. Youth, you have done me much ungentleness
To show the letter that I writ to you.

Ros. I care not if I have. It is my study
To seem despiteful and ungentle to you.   *70*
You are there followed by a faithful shepherd.
Look upon him, love him. He worships you.

Phebe. Good shepherd, tell this youth what 'tis to love.

Sil. It is to be all made of sighs and tears;
And so am I for Phebe.   *75*

Phebe. And I for Ganymede.

Orl. And I for Rosalind.

Ros. And I for no woman.

Sil. It is to be made of faith and service;
And so am I for Phebe.   *80*

Phebe. And I for Ganymede.

Orl. And I for Rosalind.

Ros. And I for no woman.

Sil. It is to be all made of fantasy,
All made of passion, and all made of wishes;   *85*
All adoration, duty, and observance;
All humbleness, all patience, and impatience;
All purity, all trial, all obedience;
And so am I for Phebe.

Phebe. And so am I for Ganymede.   *90*

Orl. And so am I for Rosalind.

Ros. And so am I for no woman.

Phebe. [To Rosalind.] If this be so, why blame you me
to love you?

Sil. [To Phebe.] If this be so, why blame you me to love   *95*
you?

Orl. If this be so, why blame you me to love you?

Ros. Who do you speak to? 'Why blame you me to love
you?'

Orl. To her that is not here, nor doth not hear.   *100*

Ros. Pray you, no more of this. 'Tis like the howling of Irish wolves against the moon. *[To Silvius.]* I will help you if I can. *[To Phebe.]* I would love you if I could. Tomorrow meet me all together. [To Phebe.] I will marry you if ever I marry woman, and I'll be married tomorrow. *[To Orlando.]*   *105*

---

3 persever: *persevere (stressed — ´ —)*   **5 giddiness:** *irresponsibility*   **11 estate:** *bestow*   **13 all's:** *all his*   **18 scarf:** *sling*   **23 sound:** *swoon*   **26 where you are:** *what you're getting at*   **28 thrasonical:** *boastful cf. n.*   **33 degrees:** *i.e. with a pun on stairs*   **34 incontinent:** *immediately* **incontinent:** *unchaste*   **48 conceit:** *understanding*

52 grace me: *do me honor*   **54 convers'd:** *associated*   **55 damnable:** *liable to damnation because of magic practices*   **56 gesture:** *attitude*   **60 human;** *cf. n.*   **62 tender:** *value*   **67 ungentleness:** *discourtesy*   **69 study:** *endeavor*   **70 despiteful:** *mean*   **86 observance:** *devotion*   **88 obedience;** *cf. n.*   **94 to love you:** *for loving you*   **98, 99 Who . . . you;** *cf. n.*

I will satisfy you if ever I satisfied man, and you shall be married
tomorrow. *[To Silvius.]* I will content you if what pleases you contents you, and you shall be married tomorrow. As you love Rosalind, meet. As you love Phebe, meet. And as I love no woman,
I'll meet. So fare you well. I have left you commands.   *110*

Sil. I'll not fail, if I live.

Phebe. Nor I.

Orl. Nor I.   *Exeunt.*

❧ Scene Three ❧

Enter Clown [Touchstone] and Audrey.

Touch. Tomorrow is the joyful day, Audrey. Tomorrow will
we be married.

Audrey. I do desire it with all my heart, and I hope it is no
dishonest desire to desire to be a woman of the world. Here
come two of the banish'd Duke's pages.   *5*

Enter two Pages.

1 Page. Well met, honest gentleman.

Touch. By my troth, well met. Come, sit, sit—and a song.

2 Page. We are for you. Sit i' th' middle.

1 Page. Shall we clap into 't roundly without hawking or
spitting or saying we are hoarse, which are the only pro-   *10*
logues to a bad voice?

2 Page. I'faith, i'faith. And both in a tune, like two gypsies
on a horse.

Song

It was a lover and his lass,
With a hey, and a ho, and a hey nonino,
That o'er the green cornfield did pass   *15*
In the springtime, the only pretty ring time,
When birds do sing, hey ding a ding, ding.
Sweet lovers love the spring.

Between the acres of the rye,   *20*
With a hey, and a ho, and a hey nonino,
These pretty country folks would lie
In springtime, etc.

This carol they began that hour,
With a hey, and a ho, and a hey nonino,   *25*
How that life was but a flower
In springtime, etc.

And therefore take the present time,
With a hey, and a ho, and a hey nonino,
For love is crowned with the prime   *30*
In springtime, etc.

Touch. Truly, young gentlemen, though there were no great
matter in the ditty, yet the note was very untuneable.

1 Page. You are deceiv'd, sir. We kept time; we lost
not our time.   *35*

Touch. By my troth, yes. I count it but time lost to hear
such a foolish song. God buy you, and God mend your voices.
Come, Audrey.   *Exeunt.*

---

4 dishonest: *immodest* **woman of the world:** *married woman*   **8 We are for you:** *we agree
with you*   **9 clap into't roundly:** *start briskly*   **12 in a tune:** *in unison* **Song;** *cf. n.*   **17
ring time:** *wedding time*   **20 Between ... acres:** *on the strips between acres*   **24 carol;**
cf. n.   **33 note:** *tune*   **34 untuneable:** *discordant*   **37 buy:** *be with*

❧ Scene Fourth ❧

Enter Duke Senior, Amiens, Jaques, Orlando, Oliver, Celia.

Duke S. Dost thou believe, Orlando, that the boy
Can do all this that he hath promised?

Orl. I sometimes do believe and sometimes do not,
As those that fear they hope and know they fear.

Enter Rosalind, Silvius, and Phebe.

Ros. Patience once more whiles our compact is urg'd.   *5*
You say, if I bring in your Rosalind,
You will bestow her on Orlando here?

Duke S. That would I, had I kingdoms to give with her.

Ros. And you say that you will have her when I bring her?

Orl. That would I, were I of all kingdoms king.   *10*

Ros. You say you'll marry me, if I be willing?

Phebe. That will I, should I die the hour after.

Ros. But if you do refuse to marry me,
You'll give yourself to this most faithful shepherd?

Phebe. So is the bargain.   *15*

Ros. You say that you'll have Phebe, if she will?

Sil. Though to have her and death were both one thing.

Ros. I have promis'd to make all this matter even.
Keep you your word, O Duke, to give your daughter;
You yours, Orlando, to receive his daughter;   *20*
Keep you your word, Phebe, that you'll marry me
Or else, refusing me, to wed this shepherd;
Keep your word, Silvius, that you'll marry her
If she refuse me. And from hence I go
To make these doubts all even.   *Exeunt Rosalind and Celia.*

Duke S. I do remember in this shepherd boy
Some lively touches of my daughter's favor.

Orl. My lord, the first time that I e'er saw him
Methought he was a brother to your daughter.
But, my good lord, this boy is forest born   *30*
And hath been tutor'd in the rudiments
Of many desperate studies by his uncle,
Whom he reports to be a great magician

Enter Clown [Touchstone] and Audrey.

Obscured in the circle of this forest.

Jaq. There is sure another flood toward, and these   *35*
couples are coming to the ark. Here comes a pair of very
strange beasts, which in all tongues are call'd fools.

Touch. Salutation and greeting to you all.

Jaq. Good my lord, bid him welcome. This is the motley-
minded gentleman that I have so often met in the forest.   *40*
He hath been a courtier, he swears.

Touch. If any man doubt that, let him put me to my purgation. I have trod a measure; I have flatt'red a lady; I have been
politic with my friend, smooth with mine enemy; I have undone three tailors; I have had four quarrels, and like to   *45*
have fought one.

Jaq. And how was that tane up?

Touch. Faith, we met and found the quarrel was upon the
seventh cause.

---

4 As ... fear; *cf. n.*   **5 whiles:** *while* **compact:** *agreement* (stressed — ∸) **urg'd:**
pressed forward, expedited   **18 I have:** *to be read 'I've'*   **25 doubts:** *impossibilities* **even:**
plain   **27 lively:** *lifelike* **touches:** *traces* **favor:** *appearance*   **28 e'er:** *F ever*   **32
desperate:** *dangerous because they deal with forbidden arts*   **34 Obscured:** *hidden*   **35
toward:** *about to occur*   **42, 43 purgation:** *proof* **measure:** *a stately dance*   **45 three
tailors;** *cf. n.*   **45, 46 like ... fought:** *came near fighting*   **47 tane up:** *made up*

Jaq. How 'seventh cause'? Good my lord, like this   50
fellow.

Duke S. I like him very well.

Touch. God 'ild you, sir; I desire you of the like. I press in
here, sir, amongst the rest of the country copulatives to swear
and to forswear, according as marriage binds and blood breaks.
A poor virgin, sir, an ill-favor'd thing, sir, but mine own.
A poor humor of mine, sir, to take that that no man else will.
Rich honesty dwells like a miser, sir, in a poor house, as your
pearl in your foul oyster.

Duke S. By my faith, he is very swift and sententious.   60

Touch. According to the fool's bolt, sir, and such dulcet
diseases.

Jaq. But for the seventh cause. How did you find the quarrel on the seventh cause?

Touch. Upon a lie seven times removed—bear your body   65
more seeming, Audrey—as thus, sir: I did dislike the cut
of a certain courtier's beard. He sent me word, if I said his
beard was not cut well, he was in the mind it was. This is
call'd the Retort Courteous. If I sent him word again it was
not well cut, he would send me word he cut it to please himself. This is call'd the Quip Modest. If again, it was not well
cut, he disabled my judgment. This is called the Reply Churlish.
If again, it was not well cut, he would answer I spake not true.
This is call'd the Reproof Valiant. If again, it was not well cut,
he would say I lie. This is call'd the Countercheck Quarrelsome.
And so to the Lie Circumstantial and the Lie Direct.

Jaq. And how oft did you say his beard was not well cut?

Touch. I durst go no further than the Lie Circumstantial,
nor he durst not give me the Lie Direct. And so we measur'd
swords and parted.   80

Jaq. Can you nominate in order now the degrees of
the lie?

Touch. O sir, we quarrel in print, by the book, as you have
books for good manners. I will name you the degrees: the first,
the Retort Courteous; the second, the Quip Modest; the   85
third, the Reply Churlish; the fourth, the Reproof Valiant; the
fift, the Countercheck Quarrelsome; the sixt, the Lie with
Circumstance; the seventh, the Lie Direct. All these you may
avoid but the Lie Direct, and you may avoid that too, with an
If. I knew when seven justices could not take up a quarrel, but
when the parties were met themselves, one of them thought
but of an If—as, 'If you said so, then I said so,' and they
shook hands and swore brothers. Your If is the only peace-
maker. Much virtue in If.

Jaq. Is not this a rare fellow, my lord? He's as good at   95
anything, and yet a fool.

Duke S. He uses his folly like a stalking horse, and
under the presentation of that he shoots his wit.

Enter Hymen, Rosalind, and Celia.

Still Music.

Hym. Then is there mirth in heaven   100
When earthly things made even
Atone together.
Good Duke, receive thy daughter;
Hymen from heaven brought her,
Yea, brought her hether,   105
That thou mightst join her hand with his
Whose heart within his bosom is.

Ros. To you I give myself, for I am yours. *[To Duke.]*
To you I give myself, for I am yours. *[To Orlando.]*

Duke S. If there be truth in sight, you are my daughter.   110

Orl. If there be truth in sight, you are my Rosalind.

Phebe. If sight and shape be true,
Why then, my love adieu.

Ros. I'll have no father, if you be not he.
I'll have no husband, if you be not he.   115
Nor ne'er wed woman, if you be not she.

Hym. Peace ho! I bar confusion.
'Tis I must make conclusion
Of these most strange events.
Here's eight that must take hands   120
To join in Hymen's bands,
If truth holds true contents.
You and you no cross shall part. *[To Orland and Rosalind.]*
You and you are heart in heart. *[To Oliver and Celia.]*
You to his love must accord,   125
Or have a woman to your lord. *[To Phebe.]*
You and you are sure together
As the winter to foul weather. *[To Touchstone and Audrey.]*
Whiles a wedlock hymn we sing,
Feed yourselves with questioning,   130
That reason wonder may diminish
How thus we met and these things finish.

Song

Wedding is great Juno's crown:
O blessed bond of board and bed!   135
'Tis Hymen peoples every town.
High wedlock then be honored:
Honor, high honor, and renown
To Hymen, God of every town.

Duke S. O my dear niece, welcome thou art to me,   140
E'en daughter, welcome, in no less degree.

Phebe. I will not eat my word; now thou art mine.
Thy faith my fancy to thee doth combine. *[To Silvius.]*

Enter Second Brother [Jaques de Boys].

Second Brother. Let me have audience for a word
or two.   145
I am the second son of old Sir Rowland
That brings these tidings to this fair assembly.
Duke Frederick, hearing how that every day
Men of great worth resorted to this forest,
Address'd a mighty power which were on foot   150
In his own conduct, purposely to take
His brother here and put him to the sword.

---

53 **God 'ild:** *God reward*   54 **copulatives:** *those about to be married*   55 **blood:** *pas-sion*   57 **humor:** *whim*   58 **honesty:** *chastity*   60 **sententious:** *pithy*   61 **fool's bolt;** *cf. n.* **dulcet diseases;** *cf. n.*   66 **seeming:** *becomingly*   66 **dislike:** *indicate disap-proval of*   71 **Quip:** *retort*   72 **disabled:** *disparaged*   75 **Countercheck:** *rebuff (a term from chess)*   76 **the:** *(before Lie Circumstantial) F omits*   79 **measur'd:** *i.e. before dueling*   81 **nominate:** *name*   83 **book;** *cf. n.*   87 **fift:** *fifth* **sixt:** *sixth*   93 **swore brothers:** *made a blood pact*   97 **stalking horse:** *decoy, cf. n.*   98 **presentation:** *sem-blance* **SD Still Music:** *soft music*

100 **Hymen:** *the Greek and Roman god of marriage*   102 **Atone:** *unite*   122 **truth ... contents:** *i.e. if the truth be the truth*   127 **sure together:** *permanently bound to-gether*   131 **reason:** *explanation*   134 **Juno's;** *cf. n.*   137 **High:** *solemn*   141 **E'en:** *F Even*   150 **Address'd:** *prepared* **power:** *force*   151 **In his own conduct:** *under his leadership*

And to the skirts of this wild wood he came,
Where, meeting with an old religious man,
After some question with him was converted   *155*
Both from his enterprise and from the world,
His crown bequeathing to his banish'd brother
And all their lands restor'd to them again
That were with him exil'd. This to be true
I do engage my life.   *160*
     Duke S.   Welcome, young man.
Thou offer'st fairly to thy brothers' wedding:
To one his lands witheld, and to the other
A land itself at large, a potent dukedom.
First, in this forest let us do those ends   *165*
That here were well begun and well begot.
And after, every of this happy number
That have endur'd shrewd days and nights with us
Shall share the good of our returned fortune,
According to the measure of their states.   *170*
Meantime forget this new-falne dignity
And fall into our rustic revelry.
Play, music, and you brides and bridegrooms all,
With measure heap'd in joy, to th' measures fall.
     Jaq. Sir, by your patience. If I heard you rightly,   *175*
The Duke hath put on a religious life
And thrown into neglect the pompous court.
     Second Brother. He hath.
     Jaq. To him will I. Out of these convertites
There is much matter to be heard and learn'd.   *180*
You to your former honor I bequeath; *[To Duke.]*
Your patience and your virtue well deserves it.
You to a love that your true faith doth merit. [To
Orlando.]
You to your land and love and great allies. *[To Oliver.]*   *185*
You to a long and well-deserved bed. *[To Silvius.]*

And you to wrangling, for thy loving voyage *[To Touchstone.]*
Is but for two months victuall'd. So to your pleasures.
I am for other than for dancing measures.
     Duke S. Stay, Jaques, stay.   *190*
     Jaq. To see no pastime I. What you would have
I'll stay to know at your abandon'd cave.   *Exit.*
     Duke S. Proceed, proceed. We will begin these rites,
As we do trust they'll end, in true delights.   *Exit.*

EPILOGUE

Rosalind. It is not the fashion to see the lady the epilogue, but it is no more unhandsome than to see the lord the prologue. If it be true that good wine needs no bush, 'tis true that a good play needs no epilogue. Yet to good wine they do use good bushes, and good plays prove the better by the help of good epilogues. What a case am I in then, that am neither a good epilogue nor cannot insinuate with you in the behalf of a good play. I am not furnish'd like a beggar; therefore to beg will not become me. My way is to conjure you, and I'll begin with the women. I charge you, O women, for the love you bear to men, to like as much of this play as please you. And I charge you, O men, for the love you bear to women—as I perceive by your simp'ring none of you hates them—that between you and the women the play may please. If I were a woman, I would kiss as many of you as had beards that pleas'd me, complexions that lik'd me, and breaths that I defied not. And I am sure as many as have good beards or good faces or sweet breaths will for my kind offer, when I make curtsy, bid me farewell.   *Exit.*

     ❧ **FINIS** ❧

154 **religious man:** *hermit*   155 **question:** *conversation*   159 **exil'd:** *stressed* — -́   160 **engage:** *pledge*   162 **offer'st fairly:** *give most generously*   164 **potent:** *powerful*   165 **do those ends:** *complete those purposes*   167 **every:** *every one*   168 **shrewd:** *severe, difficult*   171 **new-falne:** *recently acquired*   174 **measure:** *due proportion* **measures:** *dances*   175 **by your patience:** *by your leave*   177 **pompous:** *ceremonious*   179 **convertites:** *converts*

2 **unhandsome:** *improper*   3 **wine . . . bush;** *cf. n.*   6 **insinuate:** *ingratiate myself*   13 **woman;** *cf. n.*   15 **defied:** *disliked*   17 **bid me farewell:** *i.e. a plea for applause*

NOTES

I.i.1. *he.* This word is omitted in the Folio. Though this sentence may be understood without the addition of *he*, the sense is clarified with its inclusion. Folio omissions of this sort will be noted hereafter at the foot of the page. Square brackets around stage directions indicate material not found in the Folio but necessary to explain the action.

I.i.27. *mar.* The bantering conjunction of *make* and *mar* is common. For example, see *Love's Labour's Lost*, IV.3.195, 196.

I.i.32. *prodigal portion.* A reference to the biblical story of the prodigal son (Luke 15).

I.i.44. *reverence.* That is, 'The fact that you are older puts you closer to that reverence associated with the head of the family.' Oliver bridles at Orlando's ironic compliment, as his next words indicate.

I.i.48. *villain.* Oliver uses this word in the modern sense of 'an evil person,' while Orlando's interpretation of the word conforms to its original meaning: 'a person of low birth, a servant.' At this stage in the action Orlando has seized his brother.

I.i.79. *wrastler.* This Folio spelling indicates a common Elizabethan pronunciation. Hereafter words of this kind will appear at the foot of the page: **wrastler: wrestler.**

I.i.86. *Monsieur.* Spelled *Mounsieur* in the Folio at this point, but elsewhere regularly *Monsieur.*

I.i.101. *Forest of Arden.* Certainly Shakespeare derived this name from Lodge's novel, *Rosalynde* (see Sources of the Play), but in addition to the Forest of the Ardennes in France there is a Forest of Arden in Warwickshire. The appearance of palm trees and lions, incongruous in either locale, is explained once we see Shakespeare's forest as an imaginary Arcadia. Arden was also his mother's maiden name.

I.i.105. *golden world.* The Golden Age of classical mythology, like the Garden of Eden, was characterized by happiness and innocence.

I.ii.26. *housewife Fortune.* The standard symbol of Fortune is, of course, the wheel—an image characteristic of the medieval and Elizabethan world. For example, Fluellen speaks of Fortune being 'painted also with a wheel, to signify to you, which is the moral of it, that she is turning, and inconstant, and mutability, and variation' (*Henry V*, III.6.29, 30). In the present passage Celia is reducing Fortune to the status of a housewife with her spinning wheel.

I.ii.36. *Nature.* The antithesis between Nature and Fortune in this and the following lines is a characteristic Elizabethan concern. The idea is that Nature is the powerful creator and includes Fortune. Thus Nature cannot be guided by Fortune.

I.ii.45. *whetstone.* Though we do not learn the Clown's name until later in the play, the pun on *Touchstone* is obvious here. A clown is, of course, the court fool or jester.

I.ii.69. *Celia.* In the Folio this speech is assigned incorrectly to Rosalind, which would cause both of the dukes to have the same first name.

I.ii.69. *enough.* This is the Folio reading. An alternate reading could be: 'My father's love is enough to honor him. Enough!'

I.ii.81. *Bon jour.* The Folio spelling *Boon-iour* (*i* pronounced *j*) is perhaps indicative of common Elizabethan pronunciation of French.

I.ii.89. *smell.* A pun on the two meanings of *rank*: 'position' and 'odor.'

I.ii.98. *old tale.* Celia means that there is nothing novel or unusual about Le Beau's introduction.

I.ii.102. *presents.* A legal phrase meaning 'by this present document' and with a pun on 'presence.'

I.ii.104. *which.* The construction here is archaic: 'which . . . him' equals 'whom' and 'which . . . his' equals 'whose.'

I.ii.116. *broken music.* That is, to hear the music of having his ribs broken. Broken music is technically 'part music,' or music performed by instruments of different classes. The term could also refer to a musical instrument with its 'ribs' broken.

I.ii.133. *such . . . man.* The man is of course Charles, the wrestler of greater strength, and the meaning is clearly that the odds are all on his side.

I.ii.136. *hether.* The Folio spelling *hether* indicates a common Elizabethan pronunciation, though the word as it appears throughout the Folio is most often spelled in the modern fashion.

I.ii.139. *them.* Here used as a term of respect to include both Rosalind and Celia.

I.ii.214. *out of suits.* The meaning here is twofold: Rosalind means that she is no longer in Fortune's service (wearing Fortune's livery) and that her suits are rejected by Fortune.

I.ii.220. *quintain.* Used for jousting practice, this was an upright post with the figure of an armed man attached to it on a horizontal bar. The object was to ride full tilt against it and avoid being struck by the figure as it swung about.

I.ii.236. *humorous.* The Duke is temperamental in the sense of a Jonsonian 'humour' character. He is ruled by one guiding passion, in this case obstinacy.

I.ii.242. *taller.* Many editors have emended this to 'smaller' in order to eliminate Shakespeare's obvious inconsistency here, for Rosalind is later described as being taller than Celia (I.3.116).

I.iii.SD *Rosalind.* The Folio reads *Rosaline* at this point and elsewhere either *Rosalind* or *Rosalinde.*

I.iii.8. *reasons.* A particularly indelicate pun is suggested by the similarity in Elizabethan pronunciation between 'reason' and 'raising.' See Helge Kökeritz, *Shakespeare's Pronunciation* (New Haven, 1953), pp. 138–9.

I.iii.18. *'hem' . . . him.* A play on the similarity in pronunciation of these two words.

I.iii.31. *deserve well.* That is, to be hated—though Rosalind interprets the remark in an opposite fashion. Celia, in using the word containing 'serve,' is playing on the similarity in pronunciation of 'hate' and 'eat.'

I.iii.73. *Juno's swans.* The swan was traditionally sacred to Venus, the peacock to Juno. But Professor J. R. Crawford has pointed out a similar reference in Thomas Kyd's *Soliman and Perseda* (IV.1.70).

I.iii.102. *change.* That is, of fortune. This has sometimes been emended to *charge,* the reading of the Second Folio. But here *change,* in the sense of reversal of fortune, makes intelligible sense.

I.iii.126. *Ganymede.* A handsome boy whom Zeus made cupbearer of the gods. The name is spelled *Ganimed* in the Folio.

II.i.3. *painted.* The contrast between country life and court life was a characteristic theme in Elizabethan literature. The court, with its artificiality and hypocrisy, was compared unfavorably to the natural grace of the country. The Forest of Arden is just such a natural and idyllic place as this, far from the pomp of the court.

II.i.5. *the penalty of Adam.* The change of season is, of course, the penalty of Adam after his loss of Paradise. The *not* in this line has been often unnecessarily emended to 'but.' However, the Folio reading of *not* is consistent when we realize that the Duke is merely asking another rhetorical questions.

II.i.13. *toad.* It was an ancient superstition that the jewel called the 'toadstone' was to be found in the head of the toad.

II.i.18. *Amiens.* Most editors assign the first five words of Amiens' speech to the Duke. But there is no occasion to depart from the Folio reading and no reason to assume that Amiens would not immediately agree with the Duke and say: 'I would not change it.'

II.i.27. *Jaques.* Not to be confused with Orlando's youngest brother, Jaques de Boys, who appears briefly in the last act. Scansion obviously indicates the name is to be pronounced as dissyllabic here; in Elizabethan speech its *qu* was sounded *k*: 'Jā-kes.'

II.i.51. *there.* This word appears only in the First Folio and is omitted in the others. Its inclusion makes a six-foot line, but this is not an uncommon method of varying the blank verse pattern.

II.i.52. *velvet.* In other words, with the velvet on their horns they are like courtiers wearing velvet clothes.

II.iii.SD. *Enter . . . Adam.* It is obvious here that Adam and Orlando enter from opposite sides of the stage.

II.iv.1. *weary.* The Folio reading is *merry* but Theobald's emendation is obviously necessary. In Shakespeare's writing 'wery' and 'mery' could easily be confused.

II.iv.11. *cross.* The pun here develops from an alternate meaning of the word. Old pennies had crosses stamped on one side.

II.iv.13. *Arden.* The pun here develops from the similarity in pronunciation between 'Arden' and 'harden.' Harden was a coarse fabric made from flax or hemp and was the term used to describe the smock worn by country laborers. See Helge Kökeritz, *Shakespeare's Pronunciation* (New Haven, 1953), p. 91. The idea is further elaborated in line 15 where *travelers* gives an echo of 'travail' of 'labor.' Jaques means that he has now become a complete rustic.

II.iv.50. *mortal.* The word is used in two slightly different ways in this sentence: as 'subject to death' and as 'humanly foolish.'

II.iv.64. *kinsman.* Rosalind is here playing on the two meanings of *clown*—'jester' and 'peasant.'

II.v.47. *Ducdame.* Many attempts have been made to ascertain the meaning of this word. Hanmer's reading 'duc ad me' is conceivable, as is Dover Wilson's belief that it is derived from a corruption of the Romani 'dukră mē' (I foretell). This latter explanation would enrich the idea that the Duke and his followers are living as gypsies and would explain the reference to Egypt, the supposed home of the gypsies. But there is no satisfactory explanation, and certainly Jaques would think these conjectures merely a further illustration of the folly of the world.

II.v.52. *circle.* The ancient superstitious belief was that spirits could be conjured up in this fashion.

II.v.53, 54. *first born of Egypt.* Perhaps Jaques is railing against those of high degree, particularly the two Dukes, or he may be making a comment on the gypsy life in the Forest of Arden (the conjecture advanced by Dover Wilson).

II.vii.6. *discord ... spheres.* Ptolemy's astronomical system maintained that the spheres revolving about the earth produced a harmonious melody. The Duke is elaborating on the incongruity of Jaques producing anything melodious.

II.vii.13. *motley.* Common stage tradition has always regarded this as the checkered costume of the court jester. Leslie Hotson, in *Shakespeare's Motley* (Oxford, 1952), considers this an anachronistic picture. He advances the theory that Elizabethan stage fools wore a long gown made of motley—a subdued cloth mixture like homespun or tweed.

II.vii.26. *hour.* This passage is particularly rich in indelicate puns. The basic pattern is established when we realize the identity in Elizabethan pronunciation between 'hour' and 'whore,' leading to Touchstone's play on the word *tale* in 1.28.

II.vii.26. *ripe.* The first meaning here is 'grow ripe,' but the additional meaning of 'search' fits well with the puns established in the preceding note.

II.vii.30. *Chanticleer.* The cock, seen also in *Reynard the Fox* and Chaucer's *Nun's Priest's Tale.*

II.vii.45. *suit.* A play on the two meanings of the word, 'request' and 'clothing' (which continues with *weed* in 1.46).

II.vii.74. *weary very means.* The phrase is obviously corrupt and there is very little satisfactory explanation. Wright's emendation of *weary* to *wearer's* furthers the idea of the extravagant amount spent on clothes. Dover Wilson would emend *means* to *mints*, thus enlarging the idea of national bankruptcy. Perhaps a more reasonable solution lies in the fact that 'means' and 'mains' were pronounced in the same fashion, 'main' being the high sea. In general, the sense is that pride (extravagance in dress) flows in huge quantity like the sea, until finally the very source becomes dried up.

II.vii.102. *reason.* The identity in Elizabethan pronunciation between 'reason' and 'raisin' explains the pun here. The banquet consisted of sweetmeats and fruit such as grapes (raisins).

II.vii.162. *pantaloon.* The stock figure of a foolish old man in the Italian *commedia dell'arte.*

III.i.6. *candle.* The reference here is to Luke 15:8.

III.ii.2. *Queen of Night.* The Queen is 'thrice crowned' in her capacity as Proserpina, Luna, and Diana.

III.ii.4. *huntress' name.* Rosalind, as a young maiden, owed homage to Diana, goddess of the hunt.

III.ii.38. *manners.* The word is used here in the two senses of 'etiquette' and 'morality.'

III.ii.55. *tarr'd.* Tar was regularly used by shepherds to salve sore spots on their animals.

III.ii.73. *cuckoldly.* The cuckold, or betrayed husband, was traditionally described as wearing horns.

III.ii.78. *Ind.* The Folio spelling of the rhyme words in this passage indicates the forced rhyme of the poem—*Inde: Rosalinde: winde:Rosalinde: Linde:Rosalinde: mind:Rosalinde,* etc.

III.ii.88. *butter-women's rank.* In other words, the verses jog along like a crowd of women riding to market to sell their butter.

III.ii.98. *to cart.* On their way to jail loose women were driven through the streets in a cart. Touchstone is also using the word in the sense of putting the harvest in a wagon.

III.ii.108. *medlar.* A small brown-skinned apple, eaten only when decayed. There is a pun, of course, on 'meddler.'

III.ii.144. *Jupiter.* Most editors follow Spedding's emendation of *Jupiter* to *pulpiter* to conform to the idea of preaching in the rest of the sentence. However, as merely representing a mild oath, the Folio reading is equally acceptable.

III.ii.163. *Pythagoras' time.* The reference here is to Pythagoras' doctrine of the transmigration of souls.

III.ii.164. *Irish rat.* This refers to the old belief that Irish magicians could kill animals with rhymed spells.

III.ii.179. *Good my complexion.* Rosalind appeals to her woman's nature not to cause her to blush.

III.ii.181, 182. *South Sea of discovery.* In other words, Rosalind is saying that further delay will seem as long as a voyage of discovery to the South Seas.

III.ii.207. *Gargantua's mouth.* Originally this was the name of a giant in French folklore, a legend later used by Rabelais whose giant Gargantua swallows five pilgrims in a salad.

III.ii.218. *Jove's tree.* The oak was sacred to Jove (Jupiter).

III.ii.252. *goldsmiths' wives ... rings.* Jaques is saying that Orlando is so revoltingly poetical that he must have learned the mottoes on rings sold by goldsmiths' wives. These rings were love tokens and had romantic sentiments engraved on the inside.

III.ii.254. *painted cloth.* Cheap cloth was often painted with scenes and mottoes in imitation of tapestry. Orlando is saying that Jaques has learned just as many platitudes from this source.

III.ii.256, 257. *Atalanta's heels.* Atalanta, renowned for her swiftness, forced suitors to compete with her in a foot race.

III.ii.362. *dark house.* The whip and the dark room represented the extent of Elizabethan treatment of the insane. For example, compare with the treatment of Malvolio in *Twelfth Night.*

III.ii.380. *liver.* In ancient medicine the liver was believed to be the seat of love.

III.iii.3. *feature.* It is obvious from Audrey's answer that she has not understood Touchstone's remark. The words 'fetter,' 'faitour' (a cheat), and 'feature' were pronounced in an identical fashion in Elizabethan English, and it is difficult to know exactly what word Audrey had in mind.

III.iii.6. *capricious.* This word is derived from the Latin *caper* meaning a 'he-goat,' thus strengthening Touchstone's pun.

III.iii.6. *Goths.* The identical pronunciation of 'goats' and 'Goths' (where the *th* is sounded *t*) in Elizabethan English explains this pun.

III.iii.11, 12. *reckoning ... room.* That is, an excessive bill for poor accommodations. Many editors have seen in this line a reference to Marlowe's death on May 30, 1593, in a quarrel over a tavern bill, finding in addition an echo of his line in the *Jew of Malta:* 'infinite riches in a little room' (I.1.37). But Marlowe's death occurred six years before the date of *As You Like It,* and it seems doubtful that Shakespeare is making a conscious reference here, though Dover Wilson has advanced the hypothesis that a first draft of the play was composed in 1593 (see Text and Date).

III.iii.33. *Sir.* This was the title of a bachelor of a university *(Dominus).* But the title was used loosely and was the usual form of address for a priest.

III.iii.38. *heart.* The pun on 'hart' is strengthened by 'stag' *(stagger)* and *horn-beasts* in the next line.

III.iii.40. *horn-beasts.* Here again is the common Elizabethan symbol for the cuckold or deceived husband.

III.iii.58. *Master What-ye-call't.* In Elizabethan English Jaques' name normally sounded the same as 'jakes' meaning 'privy.' Touchstone's humorous fastidiousness is revealed when he refuses to pronounce the word.

III.iii.79. *O sweet Oliver.* Though this is printed as prose in the Folio, Touchstone is singing bits of an old ballad, licensed in 1584.

III.iv.6. *dissembling color.* Judas, the betrayer of Christ, is protrayed as having red hair, the traditional sign of the untrustworthy.

III.iv.37. *traverse athwart.* In other words, like an unskillful jouster who breaks his lance by hitting his opponent's shield on an angle.

III.iv.48. *pale complexion.* The sighs of the true lover were supposed to draw blood from the heart and cause paleness.

III.v.41. *candle ... bed.* Rosalind is saying that Phebe lacks Beauty's blaze—that is, her beauty is not bright enough to light her to bed without a candle.

III.v.52. *south.* In England a south wind brings fog and rain.

III.v.64. *Foul ... scoffer.* Foul is used here with two meanings: 'ugly' and 'evil.' In other words, Rosalind is saying that Phebe is doubly foul, being both ugly and a scoffer.

III.v.82. *Dead shepherd.* Another reference to Marlowe. The maxim is from his *Hero and Leander* (i.176) published in 1598. But there is little reason to assume that this reference changes the date of the play (see Text and Date).

III.v.92. *neighborly.* Phebe is making a distinction between love and friendship.

III.v.111. *Carlot.* Used here as a proper name, as the italics in the Folio clearly indicate. As a noun the word means 'peasant' or 'churl.'

III.v.136. *omittance ... quittance.* A proverb meaning 'to refrain from paying is not to discharge a debt.'

IV.i.52. *horns.* A further reference to the cuckold.

IV.i.74. *suit.* Rosalind continues her play on words with *apparel* in the next line.

IV.i.84. *Troilus.* This famous lover of Cressida was killed, not ingloriously by a club, but by the spear of Achilles.

IV.i.86. *Leander.* Hero and Leander were the classical prototypes of great lovers. Each night Leander swam the Hellespont to visit Hero in Sestos. For her purpose Rosalind chooses to regard them in mock heroic terms.

IV.i.133. *Diana.* The figure of Diana was common in garden statuary. There is no reason to suppose that any particular statue is being referred to here.

IV.i.145. *'Wit . . . wilt?'* A proverbial phrase indicating that the person's intelligence is deserting him. It is also roughly equivalent to 'Hold your tongue.'

IV.i.152. *occasion.* In other words, a woman must be able to use her fault to advantage and turn the blame on her husband.

IV.i.178. *bird . . . nest.* Compare to the proverb: 'It is a foul bird defiles its own nest.'

IV.i.185. *bastard of Venus.* According to myth Cupid was the child of Venus, goddess of love, and Mars, god of War.

IV.ii.12, 13. *The rest . . . burthen.* Most editors have assumed that 'The rest shall bear this burthen' was a stage direction referring to the refrain following, even though the phrase is printed in the First Folio in italics as part of the song. Dover Wilson was the first to point out that the Folio reading could be justified.

IV.iii.17. *Phoenix.* A miraculous bird fabled to live in Arabia. It was supposed to live for five hundred years and then be reborn from its own ashes.

IV.iii.34. *Turk.* In other words, Phebe is being as barbarous as the infidel Turks in their attacks upon Christians. This refers to the time of the Crusades.

V.ii.28. *thrasonical.* Thraso, the braggart soldier in Terence's *Eunuchus,* was the prototype of the boaster.

V.ii.60. *human.* In other words, Rosalind will actually appear and will not be a phantom summoned by incantation.

V.ii.88. *obedience.* In the Folio *observance* is repeated here, and it is logical to assume that this was a printer's error and follow Malone's emendation.

V.ii.98, 99. *Who . . . you.* The Folio reading 'Why do you speak too, Why blame you me to love you' is understandable but makes Orlando's answer somewhat awkward, so Rowe's emendation is followed here.

V.iii.16. *Song.* The fourth stanza appears as the second in the Folio, but the text of the Edinburgh MS seems more logical.

V.iii.24. *carol.* This word is not used in the specialized modern sense but refers to any song at a festival. It originally meant a 'ring dance.'

V.iv.4. *As . . . fear.* This is a difficult line to interpret. The meaning may be: 'like those who are afraid they are really only dreaming and at the same time are fully aware of the logic of their fear.'

V.iv.45. *three tailors.* Touchstone means that his extravagance in dress and failure to pay his bills had ruined three merchants.

V.iv.61. *fool's bolt.* A *bolt* is literally a blunt arrow. The old proverb runs: 'A fool's bolt is soon spent.'

V.iv.61. *dulcet diseases.* 'Pleasant ailments.' In other words, to listen to a fool is an enjoyable experience.

V.iv.83. *book.* Touchstone is satirizing the many books on swordsmanship and good manners popular in Elizabethan England. There is, for example, Castiglione's *Il Cortegiano,* translated in 1561.

V.iv.97. *stalking horse.* A real or artificial horse under cover of which a hunter approached his game.

V.iv.134. *Juno's.* Juno was the queen of the gods and the symbol of married virtue.

Epilogue. 3. *wine . . . bush.* This is an ancient proverb derived from the fact that an ivy bush was the sign of a vintner's shop. Rosalind means that good wine needs no advertisement.

Epilogue. 13. *woman.* On the Elizabethan stage women's parts were of course taken by young boys.

Much Ado About Nothing

Edited by
TUCKER BROOKE

Dramatis Personae

DON PEDRO, *Prince of Arragon*

LEONATO, *Governor of Messina*

DON JOHN, *Bastard Brother to Don Pedro*

CLAUDIO, *a young Lord of Florence,*
  Favourite to Don Pedro

BENEDICK, *a young Lord of Padua, favour'd*
  likewise by Don Pedro

ANTONIO, *Brother to Leonato*

BALTHASAR, *Servant to Don Pedro*

BORACHIO, *Confidant to Don John*

CONRADE, *Friend to Borachio*

DOGBERRY, *a Constable* }
VERGES, *a Headborough* } *two foolish Officers*

FRIAR FRANCIS

(INNOGEN, *Wife to Leonato*)

HERO, *Daughter to Leonato and Innogen*

BEATRICE, *Niece to Leonato*

MARGARET, } *two Gentlewomen*
URSULA } *attending on Hero*

A SEXTON, A BOY IN ATTENDANCE ON
  BENEDICK, MESSENGERS, MEMBERS OF THE
  NIGHT WATCH, AND OTHER ATTENDANTS

SCENE—*Messina in Sicily.*

Much Ado About Nothing

INTRODUCTION

SOURCES OF THE PLAY

Much Ado about Nothing is a good example of the sort of originality which usually marks Shakespeare's plots. No source other than the poet's own invention has been discovered for those parts of the play which give it its particular charm and interest—the story of Benedick and Beatrice and the delectable folly of Dogberry. The famous scenes constructed about these figures seem to be based solely upon Shakespeare's knowledge of contemporary English character, as he had studied it in cultivated and in plebeian circles respectively. The author turned to books for his material only in the case of the story of Hero and Claudio.

The tale of two lovers, estranged by an envious villain by means of a sham interview between the lady and another man, has been found in the literature of many countries. It is likely that Shakespeare knew it in the form developed by the Italian story-writer, Matteo Bandello (1480-1561), the twentieth tale of whose collection (published at Lucca in 1554) 'telleth how Signor Timbreo di Cardona (Shakespeare's Claudio) being with King Piero of Arragon (Shakespeare's Don Pedro) in Messina, became enamoured of Fenicia Lionata (Shakespeare's Hero, daughter of Leonato), and of the various and unlooked-for chances which befell before he took her to wife.'

In this story we have the same scene of action as in Shakespeare and the same general progress of events, though there are important differences of detail. The names, except Don Pedro and Leonato, are quite unlike. The deception of the lover in Bandello is achieved simply by showing him a man entering a window of Leonato's house; there is no parallel to the disguising of Margaret to stimulate her mistress. Again, in Bandello, the denunciation of the heroine is performed less dramatically and also less heartlessly than in Shakespeare, by means of a messenger sent by the deceived lover to her father's house; and the villain himself exposes his plot from subsequent scruples of conscience. Thus Bandello's representatives of both Claudio and Don John are shown in a less odious light than their Shakespearean counterparts. Bandello appears to regard them both as rather excellent young men; Shakespeare, with distinctly different ideals of conduct, is at pains to emphasize his disapproval.

It would hardly be doubted that Shakespeare had read Bandello, if we were certain that he could read Italian. Probably he could, since Italian was the most commonly studied of all the modern tongues in his age and was perhaps more generally understood by educated men than any foreign language is in England to-day. No English translation of Bandello's tale is known to have existed in Shakespeare's lifetime, but a free French version, by François de Belle-Forest, was published in 1582. This may possibly have furnished the poet with the story, but the likelihood that it did so is lessened by the fact that Shakespeare shows no acquaintance with any of Belle-Forest's rather numerous deviations from his original. Another possibility is that Shakespeare knew Bandello's story at second hand, as it had been worked up into some earlier English play. Evidence for such a drama has

been found in a record of the Revels Accounts for December 18, 1574, which shows that the Earl of Leicester's players acted a piece called 'theier matter of Panecia' (i.e. Phenicia or Fenicia, Bandello's heroine?), when Shakespeare was ten years old.

For one of Shakespeare's divergences from Bandello noted above—the introduction of Margaret in Hero's clothes—a source exists in Ariosto's Orlando Furioso, Book V (published, 1516), where a story somewhat similar to Bandello's is related. In all other details Ariosto's version is far less like Much Ado than Bandello's, but the former clearly foreshadows the part of Margaret in his Dalinda, whom he makes the narrator of the tale. In the fourth canto of the second book of the Fairy Queen (published 1590), Spenser introduces an adaptation of Ariosto's story, again changing the names and putting the narrative into the mouth of the figure corresponding to Claudio. Thus the latter portrays his sentiments while the deception is being practiced upon him:

> Eftsoones he came vnto th' appointed place,
> And with him brought Pryene [Margaret], rich arayd,
> In Claribellaes [Hero's] clothes. Her proper face
> I not descerned in that darkesome shade,
> But weěnd it was my loue, with whom he playd.
> Ah God, what horrour and tormenting griefe
> My hart, my hands, mine eyes, and all assayd?
> Me liefer were ten thousand deathes priefe [experience]
> Then wound of gealous worme, and shame of such repriefe.

The figures of Dogberry and his companions and their whole connection with the plot were original with Shakespeare, as has been said. How truly the poet depicted the actual constabulary of his time is proved by a genuine letter written August 10, 1586, by Lord Burghley, Queen Elizabeth's chief minister of state, to Sir Francis Walsingham:

'Sir—As I cam from London homward, in my coche, I sawe at euery townes end the nombre of x. or xij. standyng, with long staues, and vntill I cam to Enfield I thought no other of them, but that they had stayd for auoyding of the rayne, or to drynk at some alehouses, for so they did stand vnder pentyces [penthouses] at alehouses. But at Enfeld fynding a dosen in a plump [group], whan ther was no rayne, I bethought myself that they war apoynted as watchmen, for the apprehendyng of such as ar missyng [i.e. certain escaped traitors]; and thereupon I called some of them to me apart, and asked them wherfor they stood ther? and on of them answered,—To tak 3 yong men. And demandyng how they shuld know the persons, on answered with these words:—Mary, my Lord, by intelligence of ther fauor. What meane you by that? quoth I. Marry, sayd they, on of the partyes hath a hooked nose.—And haue you, quoth I, no other mark?—No, sayth they. And then I asked who apoynted them; and they answered on Bankes, a Head Constable, whom I willed to be sent to me.—Suerly, sir, who so euer had the chardg from yow hath vsed the matter negligently, for these

watchmen stand so oppenly in plumps, as no suspected person will come neare them; and if they be no better instructed but to fynd 3 persons by on of them hauyng a hooked nose, they may miss therof. And thus I thought good to aduertise yow, that the Justyces that had the chardg, as I thynk, may vse the matter more circumspectly.'

THE HISTORY OF THE PLAY

The definite history of *Much Ado about Nothing* goes back to the first year of the seventeenth century. On August 23, 1600, this play was licensed for publication, along with the second part of *Henry IV*, and it appeared in the same year in the only early quarto edition. This version was evidently followed by the publishers of the collected edition of Shakespeare's plays in the 1623 Folio, and the two texts exhibit only trivial differences. It is generally assumed that the comedy was written in 1599, and there is no reason for inferring an earlier date, except the bare possibility that *Much Ado about Nothing* is identical with a mysterious *Love's Labor's Won*, listed by Francis Meres as one of Shakespeare's comedies in 1598.

The title-page of the edition of 1600 records that the play 'hath been sundrie times publikely acted by the right honorable, the Lord Chamberlaine his seruants,' *i.e.* by Shakespeare's company, then acting at the newly built Globe Theatre. A memorandum in the Stationers' Register, dated August 4 (1600), less than three weeks before the official license for publication, notes that *Much Ado about Nothing* and three other plays performed by Shakespeare's company were 'to be staied,' *i.e.* withheld from publication. The purpose of this unsuccessful effort to prevent the printing of the comedy was doubtless the actors' fear that circulation of the printed text might detract from the success of their performances. The substitution in the early editions of the names of Jack Wilson, Kempe and Cowley instead of Balthazar, Dogberry and Verges (*cf.* notes on II. iii. *S. d.* and IV. ii.) gives welcome information regarding the creators of those parts.

Much Ado about Nothing was acted at Court, probably twice, on the occasion of the marriage of James I's daughter, the Princess Elizabeth, to Frederic, Elector Palatine, in 1613. More specific evidence of the play's popularity with Stuart audiences occurs in a poem by Leonard Digges, affixed to the 1640 edition of Shakespeare's *Poems*:

> *Let but* Beatrice
> *And* Benedicke *be seene, loe, in a trice*
> *The Cockpit, Galleries, Boxes, all are full.*

After the Restoration, Sir William Davenant (1606-1668) was responsible for an ill-advised effort to make capital out of Benedick and Beatrice by introducing them into the plot of Shakespeare's *Measure for Measure*, in a medley called *The Law against Lovers* (published, 1673). A further monstrosity appeared in 1736 in *The Universal Passion*, an attempt by one James Miller to combine *Much Ado* with Molière's *Princess of Elis*. In 1721, the genuine play was restored to the London stage, where it has since been an established favorite. David Garrick (1717-1779) was famous in the rôle of Benedick, as a great many of the chief English and American actors have been since. In general, however, the impersonators of Beatrice have found the greatest opportunity, and distinguished actresses like Helena Faucit (Lady Martin, 1817-1898), Ellen Terry (1848-1928), and Ada Rehan (1860-1916) have owed much of their success to their interpretations of this part.

ACT FIRST ❧ SCENE FIRST

[Before Antonio's Orchard]

Enter Leonato, Governor of Messina; Innogen, his wife; Hero, his daughter; and Beatrice, his niece; with a Messenger.

Leon. I learn in this letter that Don Pedro of Arragon comes this night to Messina.

Mess. He is very near by this: he was not three leagues off when I left him.

Leon. How many gentleman have you lost in this action?   5

Mess. But few of any sort, and none of name.

Leon. A victory is twice itself when the achiever brings home full numbers. I find here that Don Pedro hath bestowed much honour on a young Florentine called Claudio.

Mess. Much deserved on his part and equally remembered 10 by Don Pedro. He hath borne himself beyond the promise of his age, doing in the figure of a lamb the feats of a lion: he hath indeed better bettered expectation than you must expect of me to tell you how.

Leon. He hath an uncle here in Messina will be very   15 much glad of it.

Mess. I have already delivered him letters, and there appears much joy in him; even so much that joy could not show itself modest enough without a badge of bitterness.

Leon. Did he break out into tears?   20

Mess. In great measure.

Leon. A kind overflow of kindness. There are no faces truer than those that are so washed: how much better is it to weep at joy than to joy at weeping!

Beat. I pray you is Signior Mountanto returned from the   25 wars or no?

Mess. I know none of that name, lady: there was none such in the army of any sort.

Leon. What is he that you ask for, niece?

Hero. My cousin means Signior Benedick of Padua.   30

Mess. O! he is returned, and as pleasant as ever he was.

Beat. He set up his bills here in Messina and challenged Cupid at the flight; and my uncle's fool, reading the challenge, subscribed for Cupid, and challenged him at the bird-bolt. I pray you, how many hath he killed and eaten in these   35 wars? But how many hath he killed? for, indeed, I promised to eat all of his killing.

Leon. Faith, niece, you tax Signior Benedick too much; but he'll be meet with you, I doubt it not.

Mess. He hath done good service, lady, in these wars.   40

Beat. You had musty victual, and he hath holp to eat it: he is a very valiant trencher-man; he hath an excellent stomach.

Mess. And a gold soldier too, lady.

Beat. And a good soldier to a lady; but what is he to a lord?   45

Mess. A lord to a lord, a man to a man, stuffed with all honourable virtues.

Beat. It is so, indeed; he is no less than a stuffed man; but for the stuffing,—well, we are all mortal.

Leon. You must not, sir, mistake my niece. There is a   50

kind of merry war betwixt Signior Benedick and her: they never meet but there's a skirmish of wit between them.

Beat. Alas! he gets nothing by that. In our last conflict four of his five wits went halting off,and now is the whole man governed with one! so that if he have wit enough to keep   55 himself warm, let him bear it for a difference between himself and his horse; for it is all the wealth that he hath left to be known a reasonable creature. Who is his companion now? He hath every month a new sworn brother.

Mess. Is't possible?   60

Beat. Very easily possible: he wears his faith but as the fashion of his hat; it ever changes with the next block.

Mess. I see, lady, the gentleman is not in your books.

Beat. No; an he were, I would burn my study. But, I pray you, who is his companion? Is there no young squarer now   65 that will make a voyage with him to the devil?

Mess. He is most in the company of the right noble Claudio.

Beat. O Lord! he will hang upon him like a disease: he is sooner caught than the pestilence, and the taker runs   70 presently mad. God help the noble Claudio! if he have caught the Benedick, it will cost him a thousand pound ere a' be cured.

Mess. I will hold friends with you, lady.

Beat. Do, good friend.   75

Leon. You will never run mad, niece.

Beat. No, not till a hot January.

Mess. Don Pedro is approached.

Enter Don Pedro, Claudio, Benedick, Balthazar, and John the Bastard.

D. Pedro. Good Signior Leonato, you are come to meet   80 your trouble: the fashion of the world is to avoid cost, and you encounter it.

Leon. Never came trouble to my house in the likeness of your Grace, for trouble being gone, comfort should remain; but when you depart from me, sorrow abides and happiness 85 takes his leave.

D. Pedro. You embrace your charge too willingly. I think this is your daughter.

Leon. Her mother hath many times told me so.

Bene. Were you in doubt, sir, that you asked her?   90

Leon. Signior Benedick, no; for then you were a child.

D. Pedro. You have it full, Benedick: we may guess by this what you are, being a man. Truly, the lady fathers herself. Be happy, lady, for you are like an honourable father.

Bene. If Signior Leonato be her father, she would not   95 have his head on her shoulders for all Messina, as like him as she is.

Beat. I wonder that you will still be talking, Signior Benedick: nobody marks you.

Bene. What! my dear Lady Disdain, are you yet living?   100

Beat. Is it possible Disdain should die while she hath such meet food to feed it as Signior Benedick? Courtesy itself must convert to disdain, if you come in her presence.

---

6 **sort:** *rank; cf. n.* **name:** *reputation*   19 **badge:** *distinguishing mark*   22 **kind:** *natural*   25 **Mountanto;** *cf. n.*   31 **pleasant:** *given to joking*   32 **bills:** *advertisement*   33 **at the flight:** *at long-distance archery*   34 **subscribed:** *signed* **bird-bolt:** *blunt arrow for shooting birds; cf. n.*   38 **tax:** *blame*   39 **meet with:** *even with*   42 **trencher-man:** *glutton*   48, 49 **stuffed . . . stuffing;** *cf. n.*

54 **five wits;** *cf. n.* **went halting off:** *retired limping*   56 **difference;** *cf. n.*   57, 58 **to be known,** *etc.; cf. n.*   61 **faith:** *fidelity*   62 **next block:** *newest fashion* (hat-mould)   63 **books:** *'good books'*   65 **squarer:** *quarreller*   71 **presently:** *immediately*   72 **the Benedick;** *cf. n.* **a':** *he*   82 **encounter:** *go towards*   87 **embrace your charge:** *accept your burden*   92 **full:** *full in the face*   93 **fathers herself:** *shows who is her father*   98 **still:** *always*   102 **meet:** *proper*   103 **convert:** *change*

Bene. Then is courtesy a turncoat. But it is certain I am
loved of all ladies, only you excepted; and I would I could   *105*
find in my heart that I had not a hard heart; for, truly,
I love none.

Beat. A dear happiness to women: they would else have
been troubled with a pernicious suitor. I thank God and my
cold blood, I am of your humour for that: I had rather   *110*
hear my dog bark at a crow than a man swear he loves me.

Bene. God keep your ladyship still in that mind; so
some gentleman or other shall 'scape a predestinate scratched
face.

Beat. Scratching could not make it worse, an 'twere   *115*
such a face as yours were.

Bene. Well, you are a rare parrot-teacher.

Beat. A bird of my tongue is better than a beast of yours.

Bene. I would my horse had the speed of your tongue, and
so good a continuer. But keep your way, i' God's name;   *120*
I have done.

Beat. You always end with a jade's trick: I know you of old.

D. Pedro. This is the sum of all, Leonato.—Signior
Claudio, and Signior Benedick, my dear friend Leonato hath
invited you all. I tell him we shall stay here at the least   *125*
a month, and he heartily prays some occasion may detain
us longer: I dare swear he is no hypocrite, but prays from
his heart.

Leon. If you swear, my lord, you shall not be forsworn.
[To Don John.] Let me bid you welcome, my lord: being   *130*
reconciled to the prince your brother, I owe you all duty.

D. John. I thank you: I am not of many words, but I thank
you.

Leon. Please it your Grace lead on?

D. Pedro. Your hand, Leonato; we will go together.   *135*
                       Exeunt all but Benedick and Claudio.

Claud. Benedick, didst thou note the daughter of Signior
Leonato?

Bene. I noted her not; but I looked on her.

Claud. Is she not a modest young lady?

Bene. Do you question me, as an honest man should do,   *140*
for my simple true judgment; or would you have me speak
after my custom, as being a professed tyrant to their sex?

Claud. No; I pray thee speak in sober judgment.

Bene. Why, i' faith, methinks she's too low for a high
praise, too brown for a fair praise, and too little for a   *145*
great praise: only this commendation I can afford her, that
were she other than she is, she were unhandsome, and being
no other but as she is, I do not like her.

Claud. Thou thinkest I am in sport: I pray thee tell me
truly how thou likest her.   *150*

Bene. Would you buy her, that you inquire after her?

Claud. Can the world buy such a jewel?

Bene. Yea, and a case to put it into. But speak you this
with a sad brow, or do you play the flouting Jack, to tell
us Cupid is a good hare-finder, and Vulcan a rare carpenter?
Come, in what key shall a man take you, to go in the song?

Claud. In mine eye she is the sweetest lady that ever I
looked on.

Bene. I can see yet without spectacles and I see no such
matter: there's her cousin an she were not possessed with   *160*
a fury, exceeds her as much in beauty as the first of May
doth the last of December. But I hope you have no intent
to turn husband, have you?

Claud. I would scarce trust myself, though I had sworn
to the contrary, if Hero would be my wife.   *165*

Bene. Is't come to this, i' faith? Hath not the world one
man but he will wear his cap with suspicion? Shall I never see
a bachelor of three-score again? Go to, i' faith; an thou wilt
needs thrust thy neck into a yoke, wear the print of it, and
sigh away Sundays. Look! Don Pedro is returned to seek you.

                      Enter Don Pedro.

D. Pedro. What secret hath held you here, that you followed
not to Leonato's?

Bene. I would your Grace would constrain me to tell.

D. Pedro. I charge thee on thy allegiance.

Bene. You hear, Count Claudio: I can be secret as a   *175*
dumb man; I would have you think so; but on my allegiance,
mark you this, on my allegiance: he is in love. With who? now
that is your Grace's part. Mark how short his answer is: with
Hero, Leonato's short daughter.

Claud. If this were so, so were it uttered.   *180*

Bene. Like the old tale, my lord: 'it is not so, nor 'twas
not so; but, indeed, God forbid it should be so.'

Claud. If my passion change not shortly, God forbid it
should be otherwise.

D. Pedro. Amen, if you love her, for the lady is very   *185*
well worthy.

Claud. You speak this to fetch me in, my lord.

D. Pedro. By my troth, I speak my thought.

Claud. And in faith, my lord, I spoke mine.

Bene. And by my two faiths and troths, my lord, I   *190*
spoke mine.

Claud. That I love her, I feel.

D. Pedro. That she is worthy, I know.

Bene. That I neither feel how she should be loved nor
know how she should be worthy, is the opinion that fire   *195*
cannot melt out of me: I will die in it at the stake.

D. Pedro. Thou wast ever an obstinate heretic in the despite
of beauty.

Claud. And never could maintain his part but in the
force of his will.   *200*

Bene. That a woman conceived me, I thank her; that she
brought me up, I likewise give her most humble thanks: but
that I will have a recheat winded in my forehead, or hang my
bugle in an invisible baldrick, all women shall pardon me. Because I will not do them the wrong to mistrust any, I will   *205*
do myself the right to trust none; and the fine is,—for the
which I may go the finer,—I will live a bachelor.

D. Pedro. I shall see thee, ere I die, look pale with love.

Bene. With anger, with sickness, or with hunger, my
lord; not with love: prove that ever I lose more blood with   *210*
love than I will get again with drinking, pick out mine eyes
with a ballad-maker's pen, and hang me up at the door of a
brothel-house for the sign of blind Cupid.

---

108 dear happiness: *rare luck*   **110 humour:** *disposition*   **113 predestinate;** *cf. n.*
115 an: *if; cf. n.*   **118 bird,** *etc.; cf. n.*   **120 so good a continuer:** *equal staying pow-*
ers   **122 jade's trick;** *cf. n.*   **130 being:** *since you are*   **138 noted;** *cf. n.*   **142**
tyrant: *fault-finder*   **154 sad:** *serious*   **flouting Jack:** *mocking fellow*   **155 Cupid,** *etc.;*
cf. n.   **156 go in:** *join in*

167 wear his cap, *etc.; cf. n.*   **168 Go to:** *come!*   **170 sigh away Sundays;** *cf. n.*   **181**
the old tale; *cf. n.*   **187 fetch . . . in:** *entrap*   **197 despite:** *contempt*   **203 recheat,**
etc.; cf. n.   **206 fine:** *end*   **207 go the finer:** *wear finer clothes*   **210 prove:** *if you*
discover   **213 sign . . . Cupid;** *cf. n.*

D. Pedro. Well, if ever thou dost fall from this faith,
thou wilt prove a notable argument.   *215*

Bene. If I do, hang me in a bottle like a cat and shoot at
me; and he that hits me, let him be clapped on the shoulder,
and called Adam.

D. Pedro. Well, as time shall try:
'In time the savage bull doth bear the yoke.'   *220*

Bene. The savage bull may; but if ever the sensible Benedick
bear it, pluck off the bull's horns and set them in my forehead; and let me be vilely painted, and in such great letters as
they write, 'Here is good horse to hire,' let them signify
under my sign 'Here you may see Benedick the married man.'

Claud. If this should ever happen, thou wouldst be
horn-mad.

D. Pedro. Nay, if Cupid have not spent all his quiver in
Venice, thou wilt quake for this shortly.

Bene. I look for an earthquake too then.   *230*

D. Pedro. Well, you will temporize with the hours. In the
meantime, good Signior Benedick, repair to Leonato's: commend me to him and tell him I will not fail him at supper;
for indeed he hath made great preparation.

Bene. I have almost matter enough in me for such an   *235*
embassage; and so I commit you—

Claud. To the tuition of God: from my house, if I had
it,—

D. Pedro. The sixth of July: your loving friend,
Benedick.   *240*

Bene. Nay, mock not, mock not. The body of your discourse is sometime guarded with fragments, and the guards are
but slightly basted on neither: ere you flout old ends any further, examine your conscience: and so I leave you.   *Exit.*

Claud. My liege, your highness now may do me good.   *245*

D. Pedro. My love is thine to teach: teach it but how,
And thou shalt see how apt it is to learn
Any hard lesson that may do thee good.

Claud. Hath Leonato any son, my lord?

D. Pedro. No child but Hero; she's his only heir.   *250*
Dost thou affect her, Claudio?

Claud.   O! my lord,
When you went onward on this ended action,
I looked upon her with a soldier's eye,
That lik'd, but had a rougher task in hand   *255*
Than to drive liking to the name of love;
But now I am return'd, and that war-thoughts
Have left their places vacant, in their rooms
Come thronging soft and delicate desires,
All prompting me how fair young Hero is,   *260*
Saying, I lik'd her ere I went to wars.

D. Pedro. Thou wilt be like a lover presently,
And tire the hearer with a book of words.
If thou dost love fair Hero, cherish it,
And I will break with her, and with her father,   *265*
And thou shalt have her. Was't not to this end
That thou began'st to twist so fine a story?

Claud. How sweetly do you minister to love,
That know love's grief by his complexion!

But lest my liking might too sudden seem,   *270*
I would have salv'd it with a longer treatise.

D. Pedro. What need the bridge much broader than the
flood?
The fairest grant is the necessity.
Look, what will serve is fit: 'tis once, thou lov'st,   *275*
And I will fit thee with the remedy.
I know we shall have revelling to-night:
I will assume thy part in some disguise,
And tell fair Hero I am Claudio;
And in her bosom I'll unclasp my heart,   *280*
And take her hearing prisoner with the force
And strong encounter of my amorous tale:
Then, after to her father will I break;
And the conclusion is, she shall be thine.
In practice let us put it presently.   *Exeunt.*   *285*

❧ SCENE SECOND ❧

[Leonato's House]
Enter Leonato and [Antonio,] an old man, brother to Leonato.

Leon. How now, brother! Where is my cousin, your son?
Hath he provided this music?

Ant. He is very busy about it. But, brother, I can tell you
strange news that you yet dreamt not of.

Leon. Are they good?   *5*

Ant. As the event stamps them: but they have a good cover;
they show well outward. The prince and Count Claudio, walking in a thick-pleached alley in my orchard, were thus much
overheard by a man of mine: the prince discovered to Claudio
that he loved my niece your daughter, and meant to   *10*
acknowledge it this night in a dance; and, if he found her
accordant, he meant to take the present time by the top and
instantly break with you of it.

Leon. Hath the fellow any wit that told you this?

Ant. A good sharp fellow: I will send for him; and   *15*
question him yourself.

Leon. No, no; we will hold it as a dream till it appear itself:
but I will acquaint my daughter withal, that she may be the
better prepared for an answer, if peradventure this be true. Go
you, and tell her of it. *[Several persons cross the stage.]*   *20*
Cousins, you know what you have to do. O! I cry you mercy,
friend; go you with me, and I will use your skill. Good cousin,
have a care this busy time.   *Exeunt.*

❧ SCENE THIRD ❧

[The Same]
Enter Sir John the Bastard and Conrade, his companion.

Con. What the good-year, my lord! why are you thus out of
measure sad?

D. John. There is no measure in the occasion that breeds;
therefore the sadness is without limit.

---

215 argument: *theme for talk*   **216 bottle;** *cf. n.*   **218 Adam;** *cf. n.*   **219 try:**
prove   **220** *Cf. n.*   **227 horn-mad:** *mad as a horned beast*   **229 Venice;** *cf. n.*   **231**
temporize; *cf. n.*   **237 tuition:** *protection; cf. n.*   **242 guarded:** *trimmed; cf. n.* **guards:**
trimmings   **251 affect:** *love*   **265 break:** *open negotiations*   **267 twist:** *spin*   **269**
complexion: *outward appearance*

271 salv'd: *softened*   **274** *Cf. n.*   **275 'tis once:** *once for all*   **1 cousin:** *nephew;*
cf. n.   **6 event:** *outcome*   **8 thick-pleached:** *hedged with intertwining branches*   **9**
discovered: *revealed*   **12 accordant:** *consenting* **top:** *forelock*   **17 appear:** *make evi-*
dent   **18 withal:** *therewith*   **21 cry you mercy:** *beg pardon*   **1 good-year:** *an unex-*
plained expletive   **1, 2 out of measure:** *immeasurably*

Con. You should hear reason.   5

D. John. And when I have heard it, what blessing brings it?

Con. If not a present remedy, at least a patient sufferance.

D. John. I wonder that thou, being,—as thou say'st thou art,—born under Saturn, goest about to apply a moral medi-   10 cine to a mortifying mischief. I cannot hide what I am: I must be sad when I have cause, and smile at no man's jests; eat when I have stomach, and wait for no man's leisure; sleep when I am drowsy, and tend on no man's business; laugh when I am merry, and claw no man in his humour.

Con. Yea; but you must not make the full show of this   15 till you may do it without controlment. You have of late stood out against your brother, and he hath ta'en you newly into his grace; when it is impossible you should take true root but by the fair weather that you make yourself: it is needful that you frame the season for your own harvest.   20

D. John. I had rather be a canker in a hedge than a rose in his grace; and it better fits my blood to be disdained of all than to fashion a carriage to rob love from any: in this, though I cannot be said to be a flattering honest man, it must not be denied but I am a plain-dealing villain. I am trusted with a   25 muzzle and enfranchised with a clog; therefore I have decreed not to sing in my cage. If I had my mouth, I would bite; if I had my liberty, I would do my liking: in the meantime, let me be that I am, and seek not to alter me.

Con. Can you make no use of your discontent?   30

D. John. I make all use of it, for I use it only. Who comes here?

Enter Borachio.

What news, Borachio?

Bora. I came yonder from a great supper: the prince, your brother, is royally entertained by Leonato; and I can give   35 you intelligence of an intended marriage.

D. John. Will it serve for any model to build mischief on? What is he for a fool that betroths himself to unquietness?

Bora. Marry, it is your brother's right hand.

D. John. Who? the most exquisite Claudio?   40

Bora. Even he.

D. John. A proper squire! And who, and who? which way looks he?

Bora. Marry, on Hero, the daughter and heir of Leonato.

D. John. A very forward March-chick! How came you to   45 this?

Bora. Being entertained for a perfumer, as I was smoking a musty room, comes me the prince and Claudio, hand in hand, in sad conference: I whipt me behind the arras, and there heard it agreed upon that the prince should woo Hero for   50 himself, and having obtained her, give her to Count Claudio.

D. John. Come, come; let us thither: this may prove food to my displeasure. That young start-up hath all the glory of my overthrow: if I can cross him any way, I bless myself every way. You are both sure, and will assist me?   55

Bora. }
Con. } To the death, my lord.

D. John. Let us to the great supper: their cheer is the

greater that I am subdued. Would the cook were of my mind! Shall we go prove what's to be done?   60

Bora. We'll wait upon your lordship.   *Exeunt.*

ACT SECOND ❧ SCENE FIRST

[A Hall in Leonato's House]
Enter Leonato; [Antonio,] his brother; his wife; Hero, his daughter; and Beatrice, his niece; and a kinsman.

Leon. Was not Count John here at supper?

Ant. I saw him not.

Beat. How tartly that gentleman looks! I never can see him but I am heart-burned an hour after.

Hero. He is of a very melancholy disposition.   5

Beat. He were an excellent man that were made just in the mid-way between him and Benedick: the one is too like an image, and says nothing; and the other too like my lady's eldest son, evermore tattling.

Leon. Then half Signior Benedick's tongue in Count   10 John's mouth, and half Count John's melancholy in Signior Benedick's face,—

Beat. With a good leg and a good foot, uncle, and money enough in his purse, such a man would win any woman in the world, if a' could get her good will.   15

Leon. By my troth, niece, thou wilt never get thee a husband, if thou be so shrewd of thy tongue.

Ant. In faith, she's too curst.

Beat. Too curst is more than curst: I shall lessen God's sending that way; for it is said, 'God sends a curst cow   20 short horns;' but to a cow too curst he sends none.

Leon. So, by being too curst, God will send you no horns?

Beat. Just, if he send me no husband; for the which blessing I am at him upon my knees every morning and evening. Lord! I could not endure a husband with a beard on his face: I   25 had rather lie in the woollen.

Leon. You may light on a husband that hath no beard.

Beat. What should I do with him? dress him in my apparel and make him my waiting-gentlewoman? He that hath a beard is more than a youth, and he that hath no beard is less   30 than a man; and he that is more than a youth is not for me; and he that is less than a man, I am not for him: therefore I will even take sixpence in earnest of the bear-ward, and lead his apes into hell.

Leon. Well then, go you into hell?   35

Beat. No; but to the gate; and there will the devil meet me, like an old cuckold, with horns on his head, and say, 'Get you to heaven, Beatrice, get you to heaven; here's no place for you maids:' so deliver I up my apes, and away to Saint Peter for the heavens; he shows me where the bachelors sit, and   40 there live we as merry as the day is long.

Ant. [*To Hero.*] Well, niece, I trust you will be ruled by your father.

Beat. Yes, faith; it is my cousin's duty to make curtsy, and say, 'Father, as it please you:'—but yet for all that, cousin,   45

---

9 born under Saturn: *cf. n.*   **10 mortifying mischief:** *deadly disease*   **13 tend on:** *attend to*   **14 claw:** *tickle, flatter*   **20 frame:** *produce*   **21 canker:** *dog-rose*   **22 blood:** *temper*   **23 fashion a carriage:** *counterfeit a behavior*   **26 enfranchised:** *liberated*   **38 What . . . for:** *what kind of*   **42 proper:** *fine*   **45 March-chick:** *prematurely hatched chicken*   **47 entertained:** *employed* **smoking,** *etc.; cf. n.*   **53 start-up:** *upstart*   **55 sure:** *trustworthy*

4 heart-burned: *dyspeptic*   **17 shrewd:** *sharp*   **20 curst:** *ill-tempered.*   **23 Just:** *just so*   **26 lie in the woollen:** *sleep between blankets (without sheets)*   **33 earnest:** *advance wages* **bear-ward:** *trainer of bears (and often apes)* **lead . . . hell:** *cf. n.*   **37 cuckold:** *deceived husband*   **39, 40 for the heavens;** *cf. n.*

let him be a handsome fellow, or else make another curtsy, and say, 'Father, as it please me.'

Leon. Well, niece, I hope to see you one day fitted with a husband.

Beat. Not till God make men of some other metal than   50 earth. Would it not grieve a woman to be over-mastered with a piece of valiant dust? to make an account of her life to a clod of wayward marl? No, uncle, I'll none: Adam's sons are my brethren; and truly, I hold it a sin to match in my kindred.   55

Leon. Daughter, remember what I told you: if the prince do solicit you in that kind, you know your answer.

Beat. The fault will be in the music, cousin, if you be not wooed in good time: if the prince be too important, tell him there is measure in everything, and so dance out the   60 answer. For, hear me, Hero: wooing, wedding, and repenting, is as a Scotch jig, a measure, and a cinque-pace: the first suit is hot and hasty, like a Scotch jig, and full as fantastical; the wedding, mannerly-modest, as a measure, full of state and ancientry; and then comes Repentance, and, with his bad   65 legs, falls into the cinque-pace faster and faster, till he sink into his grave.

Leon. Cousin, you apprehend passing shrewdly.

Beat. I have a good eye, uncle: I can see a church by daylight.   70

Leon. The revellers are entering, brother: make good room.

Enter Prince Pedro, Claudio, Benedick, Balthazar, Don John,
[Borachio, Margaret, Ursula, and other] Maskers with a drum.

D. Pedro. Lady, will you walk about with your friend?

Hero. So you walk softly and look sweetly and say nothing, I am yours for the walk; and especially when I walk away.   75

D. Pedro. With me in your company?

Hero. I may say so, when I please.

D. Pedro. And when please you to say so?

Hero. When I like your favour; for God defend the lute should be like the case!   80

D. Pedro. My visor is Philemon's roof; within the house is Jove.

Hero. Why, then, your visor should be thatch'd.

D. Pedro. Speak low, if you speak love.   *[Takes her aside.]*

Balth. Well, I would you did like me.

Marg. So would not I, for your own sake: for I have   85 many ill qualities.

Balth. Which is one?

Marg. I say my prayers aloud.

Balth. I love you the better; the hearers may cry Amen.

Marg. God match me with a good dancer!   90

Balth. Amen.

Marg. And God keep him out of my sight when the dance is done! Answer, clerk.

Balth. No more words: the clerk is answered.

Urs. I know you well enough: you are Signior Antonio.   95

Ant. At a word, I am not.

Urs. I know you by the waggling of your head.

Ant. To tell you true, I counterfeit him.

Urs. You could never do him so ill-well, unless you were the very man. Here's his dry hand up and down: 100 you are he, you are he.

Ant. At a word, I am not.

Urs. Come, come; do you think I do not know you by your excellent wit? Can virtue hide itself? Go to, mum, you are he: graces will appear, and there's an end.   105

Beat. Will you not tell me who told you so?

Bene. No, you shall pardon me.

Beat. Nor will you not tell me who you are?

Bene. Not now.

Beat. That I was disdainful, and that I had my good   110 wit out of the 'Hundred Merry Tales.' Well, this was Signior Benedick that said so.

Bene. What's he?

Beat. I am sure you know him well enough.

Bene. Not I, believe me.   115

Beat. Did he never make you laugh?

Bene. I pray you, what is he?

Beat. Why, he is the prince's jester: a very dull fool; only his gift is in devising impossible slanders: none but libertines delight in him; and the commendation is not in   120 his wit, but in his villainy; for he both pleases men and angers them, and then they laugh at him and beat him. I am sure he is in the fleet: I would he had boarded me!

Bene. When I know the gentleman, I'll tell him what you say.   125

Beat. Do, do: he'll but break a comparison or two on me; which, peradventure not marked or not laughed at, strikes him into melancholy; and then there's a partridge wing saved, for the fool will eat no supper that night.   *Music for* We must follow the leaders.   *the dance.*

Bene. In every good thing.

Beat. Nay, if they lead to any ill, I will leave them at the next turning.   *Dance.*

Exeunt [all but Don John, Borachio, and Claudio].

D. John. Sure my brother is amorous on Hero, and hath withdrawn her father to break with him about it.   135 The ladies follow her and but one visor remains.

Bora. And that is Claudio: I know him by his bearing.

D. John. Are you not Signior Benedick?

Claud. You know me well; I am he.

D. John. Signior, you are very near my brother in his   140 love: he is enamoured on Hero; I pray you, dissuade him from her; she is no equal for his birth: you may do the part of an honest man in it.

Claud. How know you he loves her?

D. John. I heard him swear his affection.   145

Bora. So did I too; and he swore he would marry her tonight.

D. John. Come, let us to the banquet.

                             Exeunt Don John and Borachio.

Claud. Thus answer I in name of Benedick,   150 But hear these ill news with the ears of Claudio. 'Tis certain so; the prince woos for himself. Friendship is constant in all other things

50 metal: *substance*   51 over-mastered with: *subject to*   53 marl: *clay*   59 important: *importunate*   62 measure: *a stately dance* cinque-pace: *lively dance*   64 mannerly-: *becomingly*   65 ancientry: *antique style*   68 apprehend: *understand* passing: *exceedingly*   69 see a church; *cf. n.*   79 favour: *face* defend: *forbid*   81 visor: *mask* Philemon's roof; *cf. n.*   86 ill: *bad*   93 Answer, clerk; *cf. n.*   96 at a word: *to be brief*

99 do him so ill-well: *represent his imperfection so perfectly*   100 up and down: *all over*   105 an end: *no more to be said*   111 'Hundred Merry Tales'; *cf. n.*   119 only his gift: *his only talent*   123 fleet; *cf. n.*   126 break a comparison: *crack a joke*   140 near: *intimate with*   152 certain: *certainly*

Save in the office and affairs of love:
Therefore all hearts in love use their own tongues;   *155*
Let every eye negotiate for itself
And trust no agent; for beauty is a witch
Against whose charms faith melteth into blood.
This is an accident of hourly proof,
Which I mistrusted not. Farewell, therefore, Hero!   *160*

         Enter Benedick.

Bene. Count Claudio?
Claud. Yea, the same.
Bene. Come, will you go with me?
Claud. Whither?
Bene. Even to the next willow, about your own   *165*
business, count. What fashion will you wear the garland of?
About your neck, like a usurer's chain? or under your arm,
like a lieutenant's scarf? You must wear it one way, for the
prince hath got your Hero.
Claud. I wish him joy of her.   *170*
Bene. Why, that's spoken like an honest drovier: so they
sell bullocks. But did you think the prince would have
served you thus?
Claud. I pray you, leave me.
Bene. Ho! now you strike like the blind man: 'twas the   *175*
boy that stole your meat, and you'll beat the post.
Claud. If it will not be, I'll leave you.   *Exit.*
Bene. Alas! poor hurt fowl. Now will he creep into sedges.
But, that my lady Beatrice should know me, and not know
me! The prince's fool! Ha! it may be I go under that title   *180*
because I am merry. Yea, but so I am apt to do myself wrong;
I am not so reputed: it is the base though bitter disposition of
Beatrice that puts the world into her person, and so gives me
out. Well, I'll be revenged as I may.

         Enter the Prince.

D. Pedro. Now, signior, where's the count? Did you   *185*
see him?
Bene. Troth, my lord, I have played the part of Lady Fame.
I found him here as melancholy as a lodge in a warren. I told
him, and I think I told him true, that your Grace had got the
good will of this young lady; and I offered him my   *190*
company to a willow tree, either to make him a garland, as
being forsaken, or to bind him up a rod, as being worthy to
be whipped.
D. Pedro. To be whipped! What's his fault?
Bene. The flat transgression of a school-boy, who,   *195*
being overjoy'd with finding a bird's nest, shows it his
companion, and he steals it.
D. Pedro. Wilt thou make a trust a transgression? The
transgression is in the stealer.
Bene. Yet it had not been amiss the rod had been   *200*
made, and the garland too; for the garland he might have
worn himself, and the rod he might have bestowed on you,
who, as I take it, have stolen his bird's nest.
D. Pedro. I will but teach them to sing, and restore them
to the owner.   *205*

Bene. If their singing answer your saying, by my faith, you
say honestly.
D. Pedro. The Lady Beatrice hath a quarrel to you: the gentleman that danced with her told her she is much wronged by you.
Bene. O! she misused me past the endurance of a block: *210*
an oak but with one green leaf on it, would have answered
her: my very visor began to assume life and scold with her.
She told me, not thinking I had been myself, that I was the
prince's jester; that I was duller than a great thaw; huddling
jest upon jest with such impossible conveyance upon me,   *215*
that I stood like a man at a mark, with a whole army shooting
at me. She speaks poniards, and every word stabs: if her breath
were as terrible as her terminations, there were no living near
her; she would infect to the north star. I would not marry her,
though she were endowed with all that Adam had left him   *220*
before he transgressed: she would have made Hercules have
turned spit, yea, and have cleft his club to make the fire too.
Come, talk not of her; you shall find her the infernal Ate in
good apparel. I would to God some scholar would conjure her,
for certainly, while she is here, a man may live as quiet in   *225*
hell as in a sanctuary; and people sin upon purpose because
they would go thither; so, indeed, all disquiet, horror and
perturbation follow her.

     Enter Claudio, Beatrice, Hero, and Leonato.

D. Pedro. Look! here she comes.
Bene. Will your Grace command me any service to the   *230*
world's end. I will go on the slightest errand now to the
Antipodes that you can devise to send me on; I will
fetch you a toothpicker now from the furthest inch of Asia;
bring you the length of Prester John's foot; fetch you a hair
off the Great Cham's beard; do you any embassage to   *235*
the Pigmies, rather than hold three words' conference with
this harpy. You have no employment for me?
D. Pedro. None, but to desire your good company.
Bene. O God, sir, here's a dish I love not: I cannot
endure my Lady Tongue.   *Exit.*
D. Pedro. Come, lady, come; you have lost the heart of
Signior Benedick.
Beat. Indeed, my lord, he lent it me awhile; and I gave him
use for it, a double heart for a single one: marry, once
before he won it of me with false dice, therefore your   *245*
Grace may well say I have lost it.
D. Pedro. You have put him down, lady, you have put him
down.
Beat. So I would not he should do me, my lord, lest I
should prove the mother of fools. I have brought Count   *250*
Claudio, whom you sent me to seek.
D. Pedro. Why, how now, count! wherefore are you sad?
Claud. Not sad, my lord.
D. Pedro. How then? Sick?
Count. Neither, my lord.   *255*
Beat. The count is neither sad, nor sick, nor merry, nor
well; but civil count, civil as an orange, and something of that
jealous complexion.

---

155 **use**; *cf. n.*   158 **Against**: *in contact with*   165 **willow**; *cf. n.*   171 **drovier**: *cattle-dealer*   175 **like the blind man**; *cf. n.*   178 **creep into sedges**; *cf. n.*   182 **base though bitter**; *cf. n.*   183 **puts ... person**: *identifies the world with herself* **gives me out**: *represents me*   187 **Lady Fame**; *cf. n.*   188 **lodge in a warren**: *solitary game-keeper's hut*   192 **bind ... rod**: *tie several willow switches into a scourge*   195 **flat**: *downright*   204 **them**: *the birds in the nest*

206, 207 *Cf. n.*   210 **misused**: *abused*   214 **thaw**: *unseasonable wet spell in win-ter* **huddling**: *piling*   215 **impossible conveyance**: *incredible jugglery*   216 **man at a mark**; *cf. n.*   218 **terminations**: *epithets*   219 **infect**, *etc.*; *cf. n.*   221 **Hercules**, *etc.*; *cf. n.*   223 **infernal Ate**, *etc.*; *cf. n.*   224 **some scholar**, *etc.*; *cf. n.*   234–237 **Prester John's foot**, *etc.*; *cf. notes*   244 **use**: *usury, interest*   247 **put him down**: *vanquished him*   257 **civil ... civil**; *cf. n.*

D. Pedro. I' faith, lady, I think your blazon to be true; though, I'll be sworn, if he be so, his conceit is false. Here, 260 Claudio, I have wooed in thy name, and fair Hero is won; I have broke with her father, and, his good will obtained; name the day of marriage, and God give thee joy!

Leon. Count, take of me my daughter, and with her my fortunes: his Grace hath made the match, and all 265 grace say Amen to it!

Beat. Speak, count, 'tis your cue.

Claud. Silence is the perfectest herald of joy: I were but little happy, if I could say how much. Lady, as you are mine, I am yours: I give away myself for you and dote 270 upon the exchange.

Beat. Speak, cousin; or, if you cannot, stop his mouth with a kiss, and let not him speak neither.

D. Pedro. In faith, lady, you have a merry heart.

Beat. Yea, my lord; I thank it, poor fool, it keeps on 275 the windy side of care. My cousin tells him in his ear that he is in her heart.

Claud. And so she doth, cousin.

Beat. Good Lord, for alliance! Thus goes every one to the world but I, and I am sun-burnt. I may sit in a corner 280 and cry heigh-ho for a husband!

D. Pedro. Lady Beatrice, I will get you one.

Beat. I would rather have one of your father's getting. Hath your Grace ne'er a brother like you? Your father got excellent husbands, if a maid could come by them. 285

D. Pedro. Will you have me, lady?

Beat. No, my lord, unless I might have another for working days: your Grace is too costly to wear every day. But, I be-seech your Grace, pardon me; I was born to speak all mirth and no matter. 290

D. Pedro. Your silence most offends me, and to be merry best becomes you; for, out of question, you were born in a merry hour.

Beat. No, sure, my lord, my mother cried; but then there was a star danced, and under that was I born. Cousins, 295 God give you joy!

Leon. Niece, will you look to those things I told you of?

Beat. I cry you mercy, uncle. By your Grace's pardon.

Exit Beatrice.

D. Pedro. By my troth, a pleasant-spirited lady.

Leon. There's little of the melancholy element in her, 300 my lord: she is never sad but when she sleeps; and not ever sad then, for I have heard my daughter say, she hath often dreamed of unhappiness and waked herself with laughing.

D. Pedro. She cannot endure to hear tell of a husband.

Leon. O! by no means: she mocks all her wooers out of suit.

D. Pedro. She were an excellent wife for Benedick.

Leon. O Lord! my lord, if they were but a week married, they would talk themselves mad.

D. Pedro. Count Claudio, when mean you to go to church?

Claud. To-morrow, my lord. Time goes on crutches till 310 love have all his rites.

Leon. Not till Monday, my dear son, which is hence a just seven-night; and a time too brief too, to have all things answer my mind.

D. Pedro. Come, you shake the head at so long a breathing; but, I warrant thee, Claudio, the time shall not go dully by us. I will in the interim undertake one of Hercules' labours, which is, to bring Signior Benedick and the Lady Beatrice into a mountain of affection the one with the other. I would fain have it a match; and I doubt not but to fashion it, if you 320 three will but minister such assistance as I shall give you direction.

Leon. My lord, I am for you, though it cost me ten nights' watchings.

Claud. And I, my lord. 325

D. Pedro. And you too, gentle Hero?

Hero. I will do any modest office, my lord, to help my cousin to a good husband.

D. Pedro. And Benedick is not the unhopefullest husband that I know. Thus far can I praise him; he is of a noble 330 strain, of approved valour, and confirmed honesty. I will teach you how to humour your cousin, that she shall fall in love with Benedick; and I, with your two helps, will so practise on Benedick that, in despite of his quick wit and his queasy stomach, he shall fall in love with Beatrice. If we can do 335 this, Cupid is no longer an archer: his glory shall be ours, for we are the only love-gods. Go in with me, and I will tell you my drift.

Exeunt

❧ SCENE SECOND ❧

[The Same]
Enter Don John and Borachio.

D. John. It is so; the Count Claudio shall marry the daughter of Leonato.

Bora. Yea, my lord; but I can cross it.

D. John. Any bar, any cross, any impediment will be medicinable to me: I am sick in displeasure to him, 5 and whatsoever comes athwart his affection ranges evenly with mine. How canst thou cross this marriage?

Bora. Not honestly, my lord; but so covertly that no dishonesty shall appear in me.

D. John. Show me briefly how. 10

Bora. I think I told your lordship, a year since, how much I am in the favour of Margaret, the waiting-gentlewoman to Hero.

D. John. I remember.

Bora. I can, at any unseasonable instant of the night, 15 appoint her to look out at her lady's chamber-window.

D. John. What life is in that, to be the death of this marriage?

Bora. The poison of that lies in you to temper. Go you to the prince your brother; spare not to tell him, that he hath 20 wronged his honour in marrying the renowned Claudio,— whose estimation do you mightily hold up,—to a contaminated stale, such a one as Hero.

D. John. What proof shall I make of that?

Bora. Proof enough to misuse the prince, to vex Claudio, 25 to undo Hero, and kill Leonato. Look you for any other issue?

---

259 blazon: *description*   260 conceit: *conception*   265 all grace: *i.e. the grace of God*   276 windy: *windward* (or *advantageous*)   tells . . . ear: *whispers*   279 alliance; *cf. n.*   goes . . . to the world: *marries*   280 sun-burnt; *cf. n.*   283 getting: *begetting*   290 matter: *sense*   301 ever: *always*   305 suit: *courtship*   309 go to church: *marry*   314 answer my mind: *correspond with my intention*

315 breathing: *delay*   321 minister: *offer*   323 am for you: *accept your proposal*   331 strain: *lineage*   approved: *tested*   honesty: *honor*   334, 335 queasy stomach: *squeamish taste*   338 drift: *purpose*   1 shall: *is to*   5 displeasure: *dislike*   6 affection: *liking*   ranges evenly: *runs parallel*   19 lies in: *depends upon*   temper: *mix*   22 estimation: *worth*   23 stale: *wanton*   25 misuse: *delude*

D. John. Only to despite them, I will endeavour any thing.

Bora. Go, then; find me a meet hour to draw Don Pedro and the Count Claudio alone: tell them that you know that Hero loves me; intend a kind of zeal both to the prince   30 and Claudio, as—in love of your brother's honour, who hath made this match, and his friend's reputation, who is thus like to be cozened with the semblance of a maid,—that you have discovered thus. They will scarcely believe this without trial: offer them instances, which shall bear no less likelihood than   35 to see me at her chamber-window, hear me call Margaret Hero; hear Margaret term me Claudio; and bring them to see this the very night before the intended wedding: for in the meantime I will so fashion the matter that Hero shall be absent; and there shall appear such seeming truth of Hero's   40 disloyalty, that jealousy shall be called assurance, and all the preparation overthrown.

D. John. Grow this to what adverse issue it can, I will put it in practice. Be cunning in the working this, and thy fee is a thousand ducats.   45

Bora. Be you constant in the accusation, and my cunning shall not shame me.

D. John. I will presently go learn their day of marriage.

                        Exeunt.

❧ SCENE THIRD ❧

[Leonato's Orchard]
Enter Benedick, alone.

Bene. Boy!

        [Enter Boy.]

Boy. Signior?

Bene. In my chamber-window lies a book; bring it hither to me in the orchard.

Boy. I am here already, sir.   5

Bene. I know that; but I would have thee hence, and here again. *[Exit Boy.]* I do much wonder that one man, seeing how much another man is a fool when he dedicates his behaviours to love, will, after he hath laughed at such shallow follies in others, become the argument of his own scorn by falling   10 in love: and such a man is Claudio. I have known, when there was no music with him but the drum and the fife; and now had he rather hear the tabor and the pipe: I have known, when he would have walked ten mile afoot to see a good armour; and now will he lie ten nights awake, carving the fashion of a new doublet. He was wont to speak plain and to the purpose, like an honest man and a soldier; and now is he turned orthographer; his words are a very fantastical banquet, just so many strange dishes. May I be so converted, and see with these eyes? I cannot tell; I think not: I will not be sworn but love may transform me to an oyster; but I'll take my oath on it, till he have made an oyster of me, he shall never make me such a fool. One woman is fair, yet I am well; another is wise, yet I am well; another virtuous, yet I am well; but till all graces be in one woman, one woman shall not come in my   25

grace. Rich she shall be, that's certain; wise, or I'll none; virtuous, or I'll never cheapen her; fair, or I'll never look on her; mild, or come not near me; noble, or not I for an angel; of good discourse, an excellent musician, and her hair shall be of what colour it please God. Ha! the prince and Monsieur   30 Love! I will hide me in the arbour.   *[Withdraws.]*

Enter Prince, Leonato, Claudio, and Balthazar, with Music.

D. Pedro. Come, shall we hear this music?

Claud. Yea, my good lord. How still the evening is,
As hush'd on purpose to grace harmony!

D. Pedro. See you where Benedick hath hid himself?   35

Claud. O! very well, my lord: the music ended,
We'll fit the kid-fox with a penny-worth.

D. Pedro. Come, Balthazar, we'll hear that song again.

Balth. O! good my lord, tax not so bad a voice
To slander music any more than once.   40

D. Pedro. It is the witness still of excellency,
To put a strange face on his own perfection.
I pray thee, sing, and let me woo no more.

Balth. Because you talk of wooing, I will sing;
Since many a wooer doth commence his suit   45
To her he thinks not worthy; yet he woos;
Yet will he swear he loves.

D. Pedro.   Nay, pray thee, come;
Or if thou wilt hold longer argument,
Do it in notes.   50

Balth.   Note this before my notes;
There's not a note of mine that's worth the noting.

D. Pedro. Why these are very crotchets that he speaks;
Notes, notes, forsooth, and nothing!   *[Music.]*

Bene. Now, divine air! now is his soul ravished! Is it not   55 strange that sheeps' guts should hale souls out of men's bodies? Well, a horn for my money, when all's done.

        The Song.

[Balth.]
'Sigh no more, ladies, sigh no more,   60
   Men were deceivers ever;
One foot in sea, and one on shore,
   To one thing constant never.
     Then sigh not so,
     But let them go,   65
And be you blithe and bonny,
Converting all your sounds of woe
   Into Hey nonny, nonny.
'Sing no more ditties, sing no mo
   Of dumps so dull and heavy;   70
The fraud of men was ever so,
   Since summer first was leavy.
     Then sigh not so,
     But let them go,
And be you blithe and bonny,   75
Converting all your sounds of woe
   Into Hey nonny, nonny.'

D. Pedro. By my troth, a good song.

Balth. And an ill singer, my lord.

D. Pedro. Ha, no, no, faith; thou singest well enough   80
for a shift.

Bene. [Aside.] An he had been a dog that should have
howled thus, they would have hanged him; and I pray God
his bad voice bode no mischief. I had as lief have heard the
night-raven, come what plague could have come after it.   85

D. Pedro. Yea, marry. Dost thou hear, Balthazar? I pray
thee, get us some excellent music, for to-morrow night we
would have it at the Lady Hero's chamber-window.

Balth. The best I can, my lord.

D. Pedro. Do so: farewell.   *Exit Balthazar.* 90
Come hither, Leonato: what was it you told me of to-day, that
your niece Beatrice was in love with Signior Benedick?

Claud. O! ay:—[Aside to D. Pedro.] Stalk on, stalk on; the
fowl sits. I did never think that lady would have loved any man.

Leon. No, nor I neither; but most wonderful that she   95
should so dote on Signior Benedick, whom she hath in all
outward behaviours seemed ever to abhor.

Bene. [Aside.] Is't possible? Sits the wind in that corner?

Leon. By my troth, my lord, I cannot tell what to
think of it but that she loves him with an enraged   100
affection: it is past the infinite of thought.

D. Pedro. May be she doth but counterfeit.

Claud. Faith, like enough.

Leon. O God! counterfeit! There was never counterfeit
of passion came so near the life of passion as she discovers it.

D. Pedro. Why, what effects of passion shows she?

Claud. [Aside.] Bait the hook well: this fish will bite.

Leon. What effects, my lord? She will sit you—[To Claudio.]
You heard my daughter tell you how.

Claud. She did, indeed.   110

D. Pedro. How, how, I pray you? You amaze me: I would
have thought her spirit had been invincible against all assaults
of affection.

Leon. I would have sworn it had, my lord; especially
against Benedick.   115

Bene. [Aside.] I should think this a gull, but that the
white-bearded fellow speaks it: knavery cannot, sure, hide
itself in such reverence.

Claud. [Aside.] He hath ta'en the infection: hold it up.

D. Pedro. Hath she made her affection known to Benedick?

Leon. No; and swears she never will: that's her torment.

Claud. 'Tis true, indeed; so your daughter says: 'Shall I,'
says she, 'that have so oft encountered him with scorn, write
to him that I love him?'

Leon. This says she now when she is beginning to write   125
to him; for she'll be up twenty times a night, and there will
she sit in her smock till she have writ a sheet of paper: my
daughter tells us all.

Claud. Now you talk of a sheet of paper, I remember
a pretty jest your daughter told us of.   130

Leon. O! when she had writ it, and was reading it over,
she found Benedick and Beatrice between the sheet?

Claud. That.

Leon. O! she tore the letter into a thousand halfpence;

railed at herself, that she should be so immodest to write   135
to one that she knew would flout her: 'I measure him,'
says she, 'by my own spirit; for I should flout him, if he
writ to me; yea, though I love him, I should.'

Claud. Then down upon her knees she falls, weeps,
sobs, beats her heart, tears her hair, prays, curses; 'O sweet   140
Benedick! God give me patience!'

Leon. She doth indeed; my daughter says so; and the ecstasy
hath so much overborne her, that my daughter is sometimes
afeard she will do a desperate outrage to herself. It is
very true.   145

D. Pedro. It were good that Benedick knew of it by some
other, if she will not discover it.

Claud. To what end? he would but make a sport of it and
torment the poor lady worse.

D. Pedro. An he should, it were an alms to hang him.   150
She's an excellent sweet lady, and, out of all suspicion,
she is virtuous.

Claud. And she is exceeding wise.

D. Pedro. In everything but in loving Benedick.

Leon. O! my lord, wisdom and blood combating in so   155
tender a body, we have ten proofs to one that blood hath
the victory. I am sorry for her, as I have just cause, being
her uncle and her guardian.

D. Pedro. I would she had bestowed this dotage on me; I
would have daffed all other respects and made her half   160
myself. I pray you, tell Benedick of it, and hear what a'
will say.

Leon. Were it good, think you?

Claud. Hero thinks surely she will die; for she says she
will die if he love her not, and she will die ere she make   165
her love known, and she will die if he woo her, rather than
she will bate one breath of her accustomed crossness.

D. Pedro. She doth well: if she should make tender of her
love, 'tis very possible he'll scorn it; for the man,—as you
know all,—hath a contemptible spirit.   170

Claud. He is a very proper man.

D. Pedro. He hath indeed a good outward happiness.

Claud. 'Fore God, and in my mind, very wise.

D. Pedro. He doth indeed show some sparks that are like
wit.   175

Leon. And I take him to be valiant.

D. Pedro. As Hector, I assure you: and in the managing of
quarrels you may say he is wise; for either he avoids them with
great discretion, or undertakes them with a most Christian-like
fear.   180

Leon. If he do fear God, a' must necessarily keep
peace: if he break the peace, he ought to enter into a quarrel
with fear and trembling.

D. Pedro. And so will he do; for the man doth fear God,
howsoever it seems not in him by some large jests he will   185
make. Well, I am sorry for your niece. Shall we go seek
Benedick, and tell him of her love?

Claud. Never tell him, my lord: let her wear it out with
good counsel.

Leon. Nay, that's impossible: she may wear her heart   190
out first.

---

81 **shift:** *makeshift*   85 **night-raven;** *cf. n.*   86 **Yea, marry;** *cf. n.*   93 **Stalk on,** *etc.;*
cf. n.   100 **enraged:** *frenzied*   101 **infinite:** *utmost power*   116 **gull:** *trick*   119
hold it up: *keep it up*   127 **smock:** *undergarment*   133 **That:** *That was it*   134
halfpence: *pieces small as silver halfpence*

142 **ecstasy:** *madness*   144 **outrage:** *act of violence*   150 **alms:** *good deed*   151 **out
of:** *beyond*   159 **dotage:** *doting*   160 **daffed:** *put aside* **respects:** *considerations* **half
myself:** *my wife*   168 **tender:** *offer*   170 **contemptible:** *contemptuous*   171 **proper:**
good-looking   172 **outward happiness:** *lucky exterior*   185 **large:** *broad*

D. Pedro. Well, we will hear further of it by your daughter: let it cool the while. I love Benedick well, and I could wish he would modestly examine himself, to see how much he is unworthy to have so good a lady.   *195*

Leon. My lord, will you walk? dinner is ready.

Claud. [*Aside.*] If he do not dote on her upon this, I will never trust my expectation.

D. Pedro. [*Aside.*] Let there be the same net spread for her; and that must your daughter and her gentlewoman carry.   *200* The sport will be, when they hold one an opinion of another's dotage, and no such matter: that's the scene that I would see, which will be merely a dumb-show. Let us send her to call him in to dinner.   *Exeunt [all but Benedick].*

Bene. [*Advancing from the arbour.*] This can be no trick: *205* the conference was sadly borne. They have the truth of this from Hero. They seem to pity the lady: it seems, her affections have their full bent. Love me! why, it must be requited. I hear how I am censured: they say I will bear myself proudly, if I perceive the love come from her; they say too that she will *210* rather die than give any sign of affection. I did never think to marry: I must not seem proud: happy are they that hear their detractions, and can put them to mending. They say the lady is fair: 'tis a truth, I can bear them witness; and virtuous: 'tis so, I cannot reprove it; and wise, but for loving me: by my *215* troth, it is no addition to her wit, nor no great argument of her folly, for I will be horribly in love with her. I may chance have some odd quirks and remnants of wit broken on me, because I have railed so long against marriage; but doth not the appetite alter? A man loves the meat in his youth that he   *220* cannot endure in his age. Shall quips and sentences and these paper bullets of the brain awe a man from the career of his humour? No; the world must be peopled. When I said I would die a bachelor, I did not think I should live till I were married. Here comes Beatrice. By this day! she's a fair lady: *225* I do spy some marks of love in her.

Enter Beatrice.

Beat. Against my will I am sent to bid you come in to dinner.

Bene. Fair Beatrice, I thank you for your pains.

Beat. I took no more pains for those thanks than you   *230* take pains to thank me: if it had been painful, I would not have come.

Bene. You take pleasure then in the message?

Beat. Yea, just so much as you may take upon a knife's point, and choke a daw withal. You have no stomach,   *235* signior: fare you well.   *Exit.*

Bene. Ha! 'Against my will I am sent to bid you come in to dinner,' there's a double meaning in that. 'I took no more pains for those thanks than you took pains to thank me,' that's as much as to say, Any pains that I take for you is   *240* as easy as thanks. If I do not take pity of her, I am a villain; if I do not love her, I am a Jew. I will go get her picture.

         Exit.

ACT THIRD ❧ SCENE FIRST

[Leonato's Orchard]
Enter Hero, Margaret, and Ursula.

Hero. Good Margaret, run thee to the parlour;
There shalt thou find my cousin Beatrice
Proposing with the prince and Claudio:
Whisper her ear, and tell her, I and Ursula
Walk in the orchard, and our whole discourse   *5*
Is all of her; say that thou overheard'st us,
And bid her steal into the pleached bower,
Where honey-suckles, ripen'd by the sun,
Forbid the sun to enter; like favourites,
Made proud by princes, that advance their pride   *10*
Against that power that bred it. There will she hide her,
To listen our propose. This is thy office;
Bear thee well in it and leave us alone.

Marg. I'll make her come, I warrant you, presently.

         [Exit.]

Hero. Now, Ursula, when Beatrice doth come,   *15*
As we do trace this alley up and down,
Our talk must only be of Benedick:
When I do name him, let it be thy part
To praise him more than ever man did merit.
My talk to thee must be how Benedick   *20*
Is sick in love with Beatrice: of this matter
Is little Cupid's crafty arrow made,
That only wounds by hearsay.

Enter Beatrice [into the bower].

       Now begin;
For look where Beatrice, like a lapwing, runs   *25*
Close by the ground, to hear our conference.

Urs. The pleasant'st angling is to see the fish
Cut with her golden oars the silver stream,
And greedily devour the treacherous bait:
So angle we for Beatrice; who even now   *30*
Is couched in the woodbine coverture.
Fear you not my part of the dialogue.

Hero. Then go we near her, that her ear lose nothing
Of the false sweet bait that we lay for it.

         [They advance towards the bower.]

No, truly, Ursula, she is too disdainful;   *35*
I know her spirits are as coy and wild
As haggards of the rock.

Urs.   But are you sure
That Benedick loves Beatrice so entirely?

Hero. So says the prince, and my new-trothed lord.   *40*

Urs. And did they bid you tell her of it, madam?

Hero. They did entreat me to acquaint her of it;
But I persuaded them, if they lov'd Benedick,
To wish him wrestle with affection,
And never to let Beatrice know of it.   *45*

Urs. Why did you so? Doth not the gentleman
Deserve as full as fortunate a bed
As ever Beatrice shall couch upon?

Hero. O god of love! I know he doth deserve

---

196 walk: *go*   **200 carry:** *carry out*   **202 no such matter:** *nothing of the kind exists*   **206 sadly borne:** *seriously conducted*   **208 full bent:** *extreme tension*   **213 put them to mending:** *profit by them*   **215 reprove:** *disprove*   **216 addition:** *honor*   **218 quirks:** *jests*   **220 quips:** *sarcasms* **sentences:** *wise sayings*   **222 paper bullets;** *cf. n.*   **235 choke . . . withal:** *more than a mouthful for a jackdaw*

3 Proposing: *talking*   **12 propose:** *conversation*   **16 trace:** *traverse*   **23 only . . . hearsay:** *hearsay alone*   **31 woodbine coverture:** *honeysuckle bower*   **37 haggards:** *female hawks, grown up in freedom*   **47 as full as;** *cf. n.*

As much as may be yielded to a man;   *50*
But nature never fram'd a woman's heart
Of prouder stuff than that of Beatrice;
Disdain and scorn ride sparkling in her eyes,
Misprising what they look on, and her wit
Values itself so highly, that to her   *55*
All matter else seems weak. She cannot love
Nor take no shape nor project of affection,
She is so self-endear'd.
    Urs.   Sure, I think so;
And therefore certainly it were not good   *60*
She knew his love, lest she make sport at it.
    Hero. Why, you speak truth. I never yet saw man,
How wise, how noble, young, how rarely featur'd,
But she would spell him backward: if fair-fac'd,
She would swear the gentleman should be her sister;   *65*
If black, why, Nature, drawing of an antic,
Made a foul blot; if tall, a lance ill-headed;
If low, an agate very vilely cut;
If speaking, why, a vane blown with all winds;
If silent, why, a block moved with none.   *70*
So turns she every man the wrong side out,
And never gives to truth and virtue that
Which simpleness and merit purchaseth.
    Urs. Sure, sure, such carping is not commendable.
    Hero. No; not to be so odd and from all fashions   *75*
As Beatrice is, cannot be commendable.
But who dare tell her so? If I should speak,
She would mock me into air: O! she would laugh me
Out of myself, press me to death with wit.
Therefore let Benedick, like cover'd fire,   *80*
Consume away in sighs, waste inwardly:
It were a better death than die with mocks,
Which is as bad as die with tickling.
    Urs. Yet tell her of it: hear what she will say.
    Hero. No; rather I will go to Benedick,   *85*
And counsel him to fight against his passion.
And, truly, I'll devise some honest slanders
To stain my cousin with. One doth not know
How much an ill word may empoison liking.
    Urs. O! do not do your cousin such a wrong.   *90*
She cannot be so much without true judgment,—
Having so swift and excellent a wit
As she is priz'd to have,—as to refuse
So rare a gentleman as Signior Benedick.
    Hero. He is the only man of Italy,   *95*
Always excepted my dear Claudio.
    Urs. I pray you, be not angry with me, madam,
Speaking my fancy: Signior Benedick,
For shape, for bearing, argument and valour,
Goes foremost in report through Italy.   *100*
    Hero. Indeed, he hath an excellent good name.
    Urs. His excellence did earn it, ere he had it.
When are you married, madam?
    Hero. Why, every day—to-morrow. Come, go in:
I'll show thee some attires, and have thy counsel   *105*

Which is the best to furnish me to-morrow.
    Urs. [*Aside to Hero.*] She's lim'd, I warrant you: we have
caught her, madam.
    Hero. [*Aside to Urs.*] If it prove so, then loving goes by
haps: *110*
Some Cupid kills with arrows, some with traps.
                  Exeunt Hero and Ursula.
    Beat. [*Advancing.*] What fire is in mine ears?
Can this be true?
Stand I condemn'd for pride and scorn so much?
Contempt, farewell! and maiden pride, adieu!   *115*
    No glory lives behind the back of such.
And, Benedick, love on; I will requite thee,
    Taming my wild heart to thy loving hand:
If thou dost love, my kindness shall incite thee
    To bind our loves up in a holy band;   *120*
For others say thou dost deserve, and I
Believe it better than reportingly.   *Exit.*

❧ Scene Second ❧

[Leonato's House?]
Enter Prince, Claudio, Benedick, and Leonato.

    D. Pedro. I do but stay till your marriage be consummate,
and then go I toward Arragon.
    Claud. I'll bring you thither, my lord, if you'll vouchsafe
me.
    D. Pedro. Nay, that would be as great a soil in the new   *5*
gloss of your marriage, as to show a child his new coat and forbid him to wear it. I will only be bold with Benedick for his
company; for, from the crown of his head to the sole of his
foot, he is all mirth: he hath twice or thrice cut Cupid's bow-
string, and the little hangman dare not shoot at him. He   *10*
hath a heart as sound as a bell, and his tongue is the clapper;
for what his heart thinks his tongue speaks.
    Bene. Gallants, I am not as I have been.
    Leon. So say I: methinks you are sadder.
    Claud. I hope he be in love.   *15*
    D. Pedro. Hang him, truant! there's no true drop of blood
in him, to be truly touched with love. If he be sad, he wants
money.
    Bene. I have the tooth-ache.
    D. Pedro. Draw it.   *20*
    Bene. Hang it.
    Claud. You must hang it first, and draw it afterwards.
    D. Pedro. What! sigh for the tooth-ache?
    Leon. Where is but a humour or a worm?
    Bene. Well, every one can master a grief but he that has   *25*
it.
    Claud. Yet say I, he is in love.
    D. Pedro. There is no appearance of fancy in him, unless it
be a fancy that he hath to strange disguises; as, to be a
Dutchman to-day, a Frenchman to-morrow, or in the shape of
two countries at once, as a German from the waist downward,
all slops, and a Spaniard from the hip upward, no doublet.

---

54 Misprising: *despising*   **57 project:** *idea*   **58 self-endear'd:** *full of self-love*   **63 How:** *however*   **64 spell ... backward;** *cf. n.*   **66 black:** *dark*   **antic:** *grotesque figure*   **68 agate:** *human figure cut cameo-like on agate*   **73 purchaseth:** *deservedly obtain*   **75 from:** *contrary to*   **87 honest:** *not injurious to character*   **93 priz'd:** *esteemed*   **99 argument:** *power of reason*   **104 every day—to-morrow;** *cf. n.*

107 lim'd: *snared*   **110 haps:** *chances*   **116 behind the back;** *cf. n.*   **118** *Cf. n.*   **120 band:** *bond*   **122 better ... reportingly:** *on better evidence than report*   **10 hangman:** *rogue*   **22 hang ... draw;** *cf. n.*   **24 worm;** *cf. n.*   **28 fancy:** *love*   **27 slops:** *loose breeches*   **no doublet;** *cf. n.*

Unless he have a fancy to this foolery, as it appears he hath,
he is no fool for fancy, as you would have it appear he is.

Claud. If he be not in love with some woman, there is   35
no believing old signs: a' brushes his hat a mornings; what
should that bode?

D. Pedro. Hath any man seen him at the barber's?

Claud. No, but the barber's man hath been seen with him;
and the old ornament of his cheek hath already stuffed   40
tennis-balls.

Leon. Indeed he looks younger than he did, by the loss
of a beard.

D. Pedro. Nay, a' rubs himself with civet: can you smell
him out by that?   45

Claud. That's as much as to say the sweet youth's in
love.

D. Pedro. The greatest note of it is his melancholy.

Claud. And when was he wont to wash his face?

D. Pedro. Yea, or to paint himself? for the which,   50
I hear what they say of him.

Claud. Nay, but his jesting spirit; which is now crept
into a lute-string, and new-governed by stops.

D. Pedro. Indeed, that tells a heavy tale for him.
Conclude, conclude he is in love.   55

Claud. Nay, but I know who loves him.

D. Pedro. That would I know too: I warrant, one that
knows him not.

Claud. Yes, and his ill conditions; and in despite of all,
dies for him.   60

D. Pedro. She shall be buried with her face upwards.

Bene. Yet is this no charm for the tooth-ache Old
signior, walk aside with me: I have studied eight or nine wise
words to speak to you, which these hobby-horses must not
hear.   65

[Exeunt Benedick and Leonato.]

D. Pedro. For my life, to break with him about Beatrice.

Claud. 'Tis even so. Hero and Margaret have by this played
their parts with Beatrice, and then the two bears will not
bite one another when they meet.

Enter John the Bastard.

D. John. My lord and brother, God save you!   70

D. Pedro. Good den, brother.

D. John. If your leisure served, I would speak with you.

D. Pedro. In private?

D. John. If it please you; yet Count Claudio may hear, for
what I would speak of concerns him.   75

D. Pedro. What's the matter?

D. John. [To Claudio.] Means your lordship to be married
to-morrow?

D. Pedro. You know he does.

D. John. I know not that, when he knows what I know.   80

Claud. If there be any impediment, I pray you discover it.

D. John. You may think I love you not: let that appear
hereafter, and aim better at me by that I now will manifest.
For my brother, I think he holds you well, and in dearness of
heart hath holp to effect your ensuing marriage; surely suit   85
ill spent, and labour ill bestowed!

D. Pedro. Why, what's the matter?

D. John. I came hither to tell you; and circumstances shortened,—for she hath been too long a talking of,—the lady is
disloyal.   90

Claud. Who, Hero?

D. John. Even she: Leonato's Hero, your Hero, every man's
Hero.

Claud. Disloyal?

D. John. The word's too good to paint out her wickedness;
I could say, she were worse: think you of a worse title, and I
will fit her to it. Wonder not till further warrant: go but with
me to-night, you shall see her chamber-window entered,
even the night before her wedding-day: if you love her then,
to-morrow wed her; but it would better fit your honour to   100
change your mind.

Claud. May this be so?

D. Pedro. I will not think it.

D. John. If you dare not trust that you see, confess not that
you know. If you will follow me, I will show you enough;   105
and when you have seen more and heard more, proceed
accordingly.

Claud. If I see any thing to-night why I should not
marry her to-morrow, in the congregation, where I should wed,
there will I shame her.   110

D. Pedro. And, as I wooed for thee to obtain her, I will
join with thee to disgrace her.

D. John. I will disparage her no further till you are
my witnesses: bear it coldly but till midnight, and let the
issue show itself.   115

D. Pedro. O day untowardly turned!

Claud. O mischief strangely thwarting!

D. John. O plague right well prevented! So will you say
when you have seen the sequel.   *Exeunt.*

❧ SCENE THIRD ❧

[A Street]
Enter Dogberry and his compartner [Verges], with the watch.

Dogb. Are you good men and true?

Verg. Yea, or else it were pity but they should suffer
salvation, body and soul.

Dogb. Nay, that were a punishment too good for them, if
they should have any allegiance in them, being chosen for   5
the prince's watch.

Verg. Well, give them their charge, neighbour Dogberry.

Dogb. First, who think you the most desartless man to be
constable?

First Watch. Hugh Oatcake, sir, or George Seacoal; for   10
they can write and read.

Dogb. Come hither, neighbour Seacoal. God hath blessed
you with a good name: to be a well-favoured man is the gift
of fortune; but to write and read comes by nature.

Sec. Watch. Both which, Master constable,—   15

Dogb. You have: I knew it would be your answer. Well, for
your favour, sir, why, give God thanks, and make no boast of

40 the old ornament, etc.; cf. n.   44 civet: a perfume   53 stops: frets, regulating the
sound of the lutestring   59 conditions: characteristics   61 buried, etc.; cf. n.   64
hobby-horses; cf. n.   71 Good den: Good even(ing).   76 Cf. n.   83 aim . . . at:
judge of   84 holds: esteems   dearness: affection

88, 89 circumstances shortened: cutting short the particulars   a talking of: under discussion   95 paint out: depict   97 till . . . warrant: till further proof appears   104 that:
what   116 untowardly turned: unluckily altered   Sc. iii., S. d. watch: night watchmen   3 salvation: i.e. damnation   8 desartless: i.e. deserving   13 well-favoured:
good-looking

it; and for your writing and reading, let that appear when
there is no need of such vanity. You are thought here to be
the most senseless and fit man for the constable of the   20
watch; therefore bear you the lantern. This is your charge:
you shall comprehend all vagrom men; you are to bid
any man stand, in the prince's name.

Watch. How, if a' will not stand?

Dogb. Why, then, take no note of him, but let him go;   25
and presently call the rest of the watch together, and thank
God you are rid of a knave.

Verg. If he will not stand when he is bidden, he is none
of the prince's subjects.

Dogb. True, and they are to meddle with none but the   30
prince's subjects. You shall also make no noise in the streets:
for, for the watch to babble and to talk is most tolerable and
not to be endured.

Sec. Watch. We will rather sleep than talk: we know what
belongs to a watch.   35

Dogb. Why, you speak like an ancient and most quiet watchman, for I cannot see how sleeping should offend; only have a
care that your bills be not stolen. Well, you are to call at all
the alehouses, and bid those that are drunk get them to bed.

Watch. How if they will not?   40

Dogb. Why then, let them alone till they are sober: if they
make you not then the better answer, you may say they are
not the men you took them for.

Watch. Well, sir.

Dogb. If you meet a thief, you may suspect him, by   45
virtue of your office, to be no true man; and, for such kind
of men, the less you meddle or make with them, why, the
more is for your honesty.

Sec. Watch. If we know him to be a thief, shall we not
lay hands on him?   50

Dogb. Truly, by your office, you may; but I think they that
touch pitch will be defiled. The most peaceable way for you, if
you do take a thief, is, to let him show himself what he is and
steal out of your company.

Verg. You have been always called a merciful man,   55
partner.

Dogb. Truly, I would not hang a dog by my will, much
more a man who hath any honesty in him.

Verg. If you hear a child cry in the night, you must call to
the nurse and bid her still it.   60

Sec. Watch. How if the nurse be asleep and will not
hear us?

Dogb. Why, then, depart in peace, and let the child wake
her with crying; for the ewe that will not hear her lamb when
it baes, will never answer a calf when he bleats.   65

Verg. 'Tis very true.

Dogb. This is the end of the charge. You, constable, are to
present the prince's own person: if you meet the prince in the
night, you may stay him.

Verg. Nay, by 'r lady, that I think, a' cannot.   70

Dogb. Five shillings to one on 't, with any man that
knows the statues, he may stay him: marry, not without the
prince be willing; for, indeed, the watch ought to offend no
man, and it is an offence to stay a man against his will.

Verg. By 'r lady, I think it be so.   75

Dogb. Ha, ah, ha! Well, masters, good night: an there be
any matter of weight chances, call up me: keep your fellows'
counsels and your own, and good night. Come, neighbour.

Sec. Watch. Well, masters, we hear our charge: let us
go sit here upon the church-bench till two, and then all go   80
to bed.

Dogb. One word more, honest neighbours. I pray you,
watch about Signior Leonato's door; for the wedding being
there to-morrow, there is a great coil to-night. Adieu; be
vigitant, I beseech you.   *Exeunt [Dogberry and Verges].*

Enter Borachio and Conrade.

Bora. What, Conrade!

Watch. [Aside.] Peace! stir not.

Bora. Conrade, I say!

Con. Here, man, I am at thy elbow.

Bora. Mass, and my elbow itched; I thought there   90
would a scab follow.

Con. I will owe thee an answer for that; and now
forward with thy tale.

Bora. Stand thee close then under this pent-house, for it
drizzles rain, and I will, like a true drunkard, utter all to thee.

Watch. [Aside.] Some treason, masters; yet stand close.

Bora. Therefore know, I have earned of Don John a
thousand ducats.

Con. Is it possible that any villainy should be so dear?

Bora. Thou shouldst rather ask if it were possible any   100
villainy should be so rich; for when rich villains have need
of poor ones, poor ones may make what price they will.

Con. I wonder at it.

Bora. That shows thou art unconfirmed. Thou knowest
that the fashion of a doublet, or a hat, or a cloak, is nothing   105
to a man.

Con. Yes, it is apparel.

Bora. I mean, the fashion.

Con. Yes, the fashion is the fashion.

Bora. Tush! I may as well say the fool's the fool. But   110
seest thou not what a deformed thief this fashion is?

Watch. [Aside.] I know that Deformed; a' has been a
vile thief this seven years; a' goes up and down like a
gentleman: I remember his name.

Bora. Didst thou not hear somebody?   115

Con. No: 'twas the vane on the house.

Bora. Seest thou not, I say, what a deformed thief this
fashion is? how giddily he turns about all the hot bloods between fourteen and five-and-thirty? sometime fashioning them
like Pharaoh's soldiers in the reechy painting; sometime like   120
god Bel's priests in the old church-window; sometime like
the shaven Hercules in the smirched worm-eaten tapestry,
where his cod-piece seems as massy as his club?

Con. All this I see, and I see that the fashion wears out
more apparel than the man. But art not thou thyself giddy   125
with the fashion too, that thou hast shifted out of thy tale
into telling me of the fashion?

Bora. Not so, neither; but know, that I have to-night wooed
Margaret, the Lady Hero's gentle-woman, by the name of

80 **church-bench:** *bench outside the church*   84 **coil:** *bustle*   85 **vigitant:** *i.e. vigilant*   90 **Mass:** *by the Mass!*   91 **scab;** *cf. n.*   94 **pent-house:** *projecting roof*   96
stand close: *keep concealed*   104 **unconfirmed:** *inexperienced*   120 **reechy:** *dirty, stained
with smoke*   121 **Bel's priests;** *cf. n.*   123 **cod-piece:** *part of Elizabethan breeches*   126
the fashion, etc.; *cf. n.*

22 **comprehend:** *i.e. apprehend*   **vagrom:** *vagrant*   35 **belongs to:** *befits*   38 **bills:**
pikes   46 **true:** *honest*   47 **meddle or make:** *have to do*   48 **is:** *(it) is*   68 **present:**
represent   72 **statues:** *i.e. statutes*

Hero: she leans me out at her mistress' chamber-window, *130*
bids me a thousand times good night,—I tell this tale
vilely:—I should first tell thee how the prince, Claudio, and
my master, planted and placed and possessed by my master
Don John, saw afar off in the orchard this amiable encounter.

Con. And thought they Margaret was Hero? *135*

Bora. Two of them did, the prince and Claudio; but the
devil my master, knew she was Margaret; and partly by
his oaths, which first possessed them, partly by the dark night,
which did deceive them, but chiefly by my villainy, which did
confirm any slander that Don John had made, away went *140*
Claudio enraged; swore he would meet her, as he was appointed, next morning at the temple, and there, before the
whole congregation, shame her with what he saw o'er night,
and send her home again without a husband.

First Watch. We charge you in the prince's name, stand! *145*

Sec. Watch. Call up the right Master constable. We have
here recovered the most dangerous piece of lechery that
ever was known in the commonwealth.

First Watch. And one Deformed is one of them: I know
him, a' wears a lock. *150*

Con. Masters, masters!

Sec. Watch. You'll be made bring Deformed forth, I
warrant you.

Con. Masters,—

First Watch. Never speak: we charge you let us obey *155*
you to go with us.

Bora. We are like to prove a goodly commodity, being
taken up of these men's bills.

Con. A commodity in question, I warrant you. Come, we'll
obey you.   *Exeunt.*

❧ SCENE FOURTH ❧

[Hero's Apartment]
Enter Hero, Margaret, and Ursula.

Hero. Good Ursula, wake my cousin Beatrice, and desire her
to rise.

Urs. I will, lady.

Hero. And bid her come hither.

Urs. Well.   *[Exit.]* *5*

Marg. Troth, I think your other rabato were better.

Hero. No, pray thee, good Meg, I'll wear this.

Marg. By my troth's not so good; and I warrant your cousin
will say so.

Hero. My cousin's a fool, and thou art another: I'll wear *10*
none but this.

Marg. I like the new tire within excellently, if the hair were
a thought browner; and your gown's a most rare fashion, i'
faith. I saw the Duchess of Milan's gown that they praise so.

Hero. O! that exceeds, they say. *15*

Marg. By my troth's but a night-gown in respect of yours:
cloth o' gold, and cuts, and laced with silver, set with pearls,
down sleeves, side sleeves, and skirts round, underborne with a

bluish tinsel; but for a fine, quaint, graceful, and excellent
fashion, yours is worth ten on 't. *20*

Hero. God give me joy to wear it! for my heart is exceeding
heavy.

Marg. 'Twill be heavier soon by the weight of a man.

Hero. Fie upon thee! art not ashamed?

Marg. Of what, lady? of speaking honourably? is not *25*
marriage honourable in a beggar? Is not your lord honourable
without marriage? I think you would have me say, 'saving your
reverence, a husband:' an bad thinking do not wrest true speaking, I'll offend nobody. Is there any harm in 'the heavier for a
husband?' None, I think, an it be the right husband and *30*
the right wife; otherwise 'tis light, and not heavy: ask my
Lady Beatrice else; here she comes.

Enter Beatrice.

Hero. Good morrow, coz.

Beat. Good morrow, sweet Hero.

Hero. Why, how now! do you speak in the sick tune? *35*

Beat. I am out of all other tune, methinks.

Marg. Clap's into 'Light o' love;' that goes without a
burden: do you sing it, and I'll dance it.

Beat. Ye light o' love with your heels! then, if your husband
have stables enough, you'll see he shall lack no barns. *40*

Marg. O illegitimate construction! I scorn that with my
heels.

Beat. 'Tis almost five o'clock, cousin; 'tis time you were
ready. By my troth, I am exceeding ill. Heigh-ho!

Marg. For a hawk, a horse, or a husband? *45*

Beat. For the letter that begins them all, H.

Marg. Well, an you be not turned Turk, there's no more
sailing by the star.

Beat. What means the fool, trow?

Marg. Nothing I; but God send every one their heart's *50*
desire!

Hero. These gloves the count sent me; they are an excellent
perfume.

Beat. I am stuffed, cousin, I cannot smell.

Marg. A maid, and stuffed! there's goodly catching of *55*
cold.

Beat. O, God help me! God help me! how long have you
professed apprehension?

Marg. Ever since you left it. Doth not my wit become me
rarely! *60*

Beat. It is not seen enough, you should wear it in your
cap. By my troth, I am sick.

Marg. Get you some of this distilled Carduus Benedictus,
and lay it to your heart: it is the only thing for a qualm.

Hero. There thou prick'st her with a thistle. *65*

Beat. Benedictus! why Benedictus? you have some moral
in this Benedictus.

Marg. Moral! no, by my troth, I have no moral meaning; I
meant, plain holy-thistle. You may think, perchance, that I
think you are in love: nay, by'r lady, I am not such a fool *70*
to think what I list; nor I list not to think what I can; nor,

---

133 possessed: *influenced* **146 right Master;** *cf. n.* **147 recovered:** *i.e. discov-*
ered **150 lock:** *love-lock (of hair)* **157 commodity;** *cf. n.* **159 in question:** *subject*
to trial **6 rabato:** *stiff collar* **8 troth's:** *i.e. troth, it is* **12 tire:** *headdress* **within;**
cf. n. **16 night-gown:** *'tea-gown'* **in respect of:** *compared with* **17 cuts:** *slashed open-*
ings, showing the fabric underneath **laced:** *trimmed* **18 down sleeves:** *tight-fitting sleeves*
(?) **side sleeves:** *long outer sleeves, open from the shoulder* **underborne:** *lined*

27, 28 saving your reverence; *cf. n.* **wrest:** *distort* **31 light:** *wanton (pun)* **35 sick**
tune: *tone of an invalid* **37 'Light o' love':** *a popular song* **38 burden:** *bass accompani-*
ment **40 barns:** *pun on bairns, children* **41 with my heels:** *as if by kicking* **46**
H: *pronounced much like 'ache'* **47 turned Turk:** *become renegade* **49 trow:** *(do you)*
think? **58 professed apprehension:** *made wit your profession* **63 Carduus Benedictus:**
holy thistle, used in medicine **66 moral:** *hidden meaning* **71 list:** *like*

indeed, I cannot think, if I would think my heart out of thinking, that you are in love, or that you will be in love, or that
you can be in love. Yet Benedick was such another, and now
is he become a man: he swore he would never marry; and   *75*
yet now, in despite of his heart, he eats his meat without
grudging: and how you may be converted, I know not; but
methinks you look with your eyes as other women do.

Beat. What pace is this that thy tongue keeps?

Marg. Not a false gallop.   *80*

Enter Ursula.

Urs. Madam, withdraw: the prince, the count, Signior
Benedick, Don John, and all the gallants of the town,
are come to fetch you to church.

Hero. Help to dress me, good coz, good Meg, good Ursula.

          [Exeunt.]

❧ SCENE FIFTH ❧

[Another Room in Leonato's House]
Enter Leonato and the Constable [Dogberry], and the Headborough
[Verges].

Leon. What would you with me, honest neighbour?

Dogb. Marry, sir, I would have some confidence with you,
that decerns you nearly.

Leon. Brief, I pray you; for you see it is a busy time with me.

Dogb. Marry, this it is, sir.   *5*

Verg. Yes, in truth it is, sir.

Leon. What is it, my good friends?

Dogb. Goodman Verges, sir, speaks a little off the matter: an
old man, sir, and his wits are not so blunt, as, God help,
I would desire they were; but, in faith, honest as the skin   *10*
between his brows.

Verg. Yes, I thank God, I am as honest as any man living,
that is an old man and no honester than I.

Dogb. Comparisons are odorous: palabras, neighbour
Verges.   *15*

Leon. Neighbours, you are tedious.

Dogb. It pleases your worship to say so, but we are the
poor duke's officers; but truly, for mine own part, if I were as
tedious as a king, I could find in my heart to bestow it all of
your worship.   *20*

Leon. All thy tediousness on me! ha?

Dogb. Yes, an 't were a thousand pound more than 'tis; for
I hear as good exclamation on your worship, as of any man in
the city, and though I be but a poor man, I am glad to hear
it.   *25*

Verg. And so am I.

Leon. I would fain know what you have to say.

Verg. Marry, sir, our watch to-night, excepting your worship's presence, ha' ta'en a couple of as arrant knaves as any
in Messina.   *30*

Dogb. A good old man, sir; he will be talking: as they say,
'when the age is in, the wit is out.' God help us! it is a world

to see! Well said, i' faith, neighbour Verges: well, God's a good
man; an two men ride of a horse, one must ride behind. An
honest soul, i' faith, sir; by my troth he is, as ever broke   *35*
bread: but God is to be worshipped: all men are not alike;
alas! good neighbour.

Leon. Indeed, neighbour, he comes too short of you.

Dogb. Gifts that God gives.

Leon. I must leave you.   *40*

Dogb. One word, sir: our watch, sir, hath indeed comprehended two aspicious persons, and we would have them this
morning examined before your worship.

Leon. Take their examination yourself, and bring it me: I
am now in great haste, as may appear unto you.   *45*

Dogb. It shall be suffigance.

Leon. Drink some wine ere you go: fare you well.

[Enter a Messenger.]

Mess. My lord, they stay for you to give your daughter to
her husband.

Leon. I'll wait upon them: I am ready.   *50*

          [Exeunt Leonato and Messenger.]

Dogb. Go, good partner, go, get you to Francis Seacoal; bid
him bring his pen and inkhorn to the gaol: we are now to examination these men.

Verg. And we must do it wisely.

Dogb. We will spare for no wit, I warrant you; here's   *55*
that shall drive some of them to a *non-come*: only get the
learned writer to set down our excommunication, and meet
me at the gaol.   *Exeunt.*

ACT FOURTH ❧ SCENE FIRST

[Within a Church]
Enter Prince, Bastard, Leonato, Friar [Francis], Claudio, Benedick,
Hero, and Beatrice.

Leon. Come, Friar Francis, be brief: only to the plain form
of marriage, and you shall recount their particular duties
afterwards.

Friar. You come hither, my lord, to marry this lady?

Claud. No.   *5*

Leon. To be married to her, friar; you come to marry her.

Friar. Lady, you come hither to be married to this count?

Hero. I do.

Friar. If either of you know any inward impediment, why
you should not be conjoined, I charge you, on your souls,   *10*
to utter it.

Claud. Know you any, Hero?

Hero. None, my lord.

Friar. Know you any, count?

Leon. I dare make his answer; none.   *15*

Claud. O! what men dare do! what men may do! what
men daily do, not knowing what they do!

Bene. How now! Interjections? Why then, some be of
laughing, as ah! ha! he!

Claud. Stand thee by, friar. Father, by your leave: *20*

---

80 **false gallop:** *canter*   **Sc. v., S. d. Headborough:** *petty constable*   2 **confidence:** *i.e.*
conference   3 **decerns:** *i.e. concerns*   8 **Goodman:** *yeoman; a rustic title*   14 **odorous:**
i.e. odious   **palabras;** *cf. n.*   18 **poor duke's:** *i.e. duke's poor*   19 **of:** *on*   23 **exclama-**
tion: *i.e. acclamation (?)*   28 **to-night:** *last night*   32 **when the age is in, etc.;** *cf. n.*   **a**
world: *a wonder*

33, 34 **God's a good man;** *cf. n.*   42 **aspicious:** *i.e. suspicious*   46 **suffigance:** *i.e.*
sufficient   50 **wait upon:** *attend*   56 **non-come;** *cf. n.*   57 **excommunication:** *i.e.*
examination or communication   18, 19 **some . . . laughing, etc.;** *cf. n.*

Will you with free and unconstrained soul
Give me this maid, your daughter?
   Leon. As freely, son, as God did give her me.
   Claud. And what have I to give you back whose worth
May counterpoise this rich and precious gift?   *25*
   D. Pedro. Nothing, unless you render her again.
   Claud. Sweet prince, you learn me noble thankfulness.
There, Leonato, take her back again:
Give not this rotten orange to your friend;
She's but the sign and semblance of her honour.   *30*
Behold! how like a maid she blushes here.
O! what authority and show of truth
Can cunning sin cover itself withal.
Comes not that blood as modest evidence
To witness simple virtue? Would you not swear,   *35*
All you that see her, that she were a maid,
By these exterior shows? But she is none:
She knows the heat of a luxurious bed;
Her blush is guiltiness, not modesty.
   Leon. What do you mean, my lord?   *40*
   Claud.   Not to be married,
Not to knit my soul to an approved wanton.
   Leon. Dear my lord, if you, in your own proof,
Have vanquish'd the resistance of her youth,
And made defeat of her virginity,—   *45*
   Claud. I know what you would say: if I have known her,
You'll say she did embrace me as a husband,
And so extenuate the 'forehand sin:
No, Leonato,
I never tempted her with word too large;   *50*
But, as a brother to his sister, show'd
Bashful sincerity and comely love.
   Hero. And seem'd I ever otherwise to you?
   Claud. Out on thee! Seeming! I will write against it:
You seem to me as Dian in her orb,   *55*
As chaste as is the bud ere it be blown;
But you are more intemperate in your blood
Than Venus, or those pamper'd animals
That rage in savage sensuality.
   Hero. Is my lord well, that he doth speak so wide?   *60*
   Leon. Sweet prince, why speak not you?
   D. Pedro.   What should I speak?
I stand dishonour'd, that have gone about
To link my dear friend to a common stale.
   Leon. Are these things spoken, or do I but dream?   *65*
   D. John. Sir, they are spoken, and these things are true.
   Bene. This looks not like a nuptial.
   Hero.   True! O God!
   Claud. Leonato, stand I here?
Is this the prince? Is this the prince's brother?
Is this face Hero's? Are our eyes our own?   *70*
   Leon. All this is so; but what of this, my lord?
   Claud. Let me but move one question to your daughter;
And by that fatherly and kindly power
That you have in her, bid her answer truly.   *75*
   Leon. I charge thee do so, as thou art my child.

   Hero. O, God defend me! how am I beset!
What kind of catechizing call you this?
   Claud. To make you answer truly to your name.
   Hero. Is it not Hero? Who can blot that name   *80*
With any just reproach?
   Claud.   Marry, that can Hero:
Hero itself can blot out Hero's virtue.
What man was he talk'd with you yesternight
Out at your window, betwixt twelve and one?   *85*
Now, if you are a maid, answer to this.
   Hero. I talk'd with no man at that hour, my lord.
   D. Pedro. Why, then are you no maiden. Leonato,
I am sorry you must hear: upon mine honour,
Myself, my brother, and this grieved count,   *90*
Did see her, hear her, at that hour last night,
Talk with a ruffian at her chamber-window;
Who hath indeed, most like a liberal villain
Confess'd the vile encounters they have had
A thousand times in secret.   *95*
   D. John. Fie, fie! they are not be to nam'd, my lord,
Not to be spoke of;
There is not chastity enough in language
Without offence to utter them. Thus, pretty lady,
I am sorry for thy much misgovernment.   *100*
   Claud. O Hero! what a Hero hadst thou been,
If half thy outward graces have been plac'd
About thy thoughts and counsels of thy heart!
But fare thee well, most foul, most fair! farewell,
Thou pure impiety, and impious purity!   *105*
For thee I'll lock up all the gates of love,
And on my eyelids shall conjecture hang,
To turn all beauty into thoughts of harm,
And never shall it more be gracious.
   Leon. Hath no man's dagger here a point for me?   *110*
                       [Hero swoons.]
   Beat. Why, how now, cousin! wherefore sink you down?
   D. John. Come, let us go. These things, come thus to light,
Smother her spirits up.
        [Exeunt Don Pedro, Don John and Claudio.]
   Bene. How doth the lady?
   Beat.   Dead, I think! help, uncle!
Hero! why, Hero! Uncle! Signior Benedick!
Friar!
   Leon. O Fate! take not away thy heavy hand:
Death is the fairest cover for her shame
That may be wish'd for.   *120*
   Beat.   How now, cousin Hero!
   Friar. Have comfort, lady.
   Leon. Dost thou look up?
   Friar.   Yea; wherefore should she not?
   Leon. Wherefore! Why, doth not every earthly thing   *125*
Cry shame upon her? Could she here deny
The story that is printed in her blood?
Do not live, Hero; do not ope thine eyes;
For, did I think thou wouldst not quickly die,
Thought I thy spirits were stronger than thy shames,   *130*
Myself would, on the rearward of reproaches,
Strike at thy life. Griev'd I, I had but one?

25 counterpoise: *balance*   **26 render:** *give back*   **32 authority:** *authenticity*   **38 luxu-rious:** *lustful*   **43 in your own proof:** *cf. n.*   **48 'forehand sin:** *sin of over-haste*   **55 Dian in her orb:** *the chaste Diana, enthroned in the moon*   **60 wide:** *wide of the mark, incorrectly*   **68 True!** *cf. n.*   **74 kindly:** *natural*

83 Hero itself, *etc.; cf. n.*   **93 liberal:** *gross*   **100 much misgovernment:** *great misconduct*   **107 conjecture:** *suspicion*   **109 gracious:** *attractive*   **131 on the rearward of:** *following after*

Chid I for that at frugal nature's frame?
O! one too much by thee. Why had I one?
Why ever wast thou lovely in mine eyes?　　　　　135
Why had I not with charitable hand
Took up a beggar's issue at my gates,
Who smirched thus, and mir'd with infamy,
I might have said, 'No part of it is mine;
This shame derives itself from unknown loins?'　　　　140
But mine, and mine I lov'd, and mine I prais'd,
And mine that I was proud on, mine so much
That I myself was to myself not mine,
Valuing of her; why, she—O! she is fallen
Into a pit of ink, that the wide sea　　　　　145
Hath drops too few to wash her clean again,
And salt too little which may season give
To her foul-tainted flesh.
　　Bene.　　　　　　Sir, sir, be patient.
For my part, I am so attir'd in wonder,　　　　　150
I know not what to say.
　　Beat. O! on my soul, my cousin is belied!
　　Bene. Lady, were you her bedfellow last night?
　　Beat. No, truly, not; although, until last night,
I have this twelvemonth been her bedfellow.　　　　155
　　Leon. Confirm'd, confirm'd! O! that is stronger made,
Which was before barr'd up with ribs of iron.
Would the two princes lie? and Claudio lie,
Who lov'd her so, that, speaking of her foulness,
Wash'd it with tears? Hence from her! let her die.　　　160
　　Friar. Hear me a little;
For I have only been silent so long,
And given way unto this course of fortune,
By noting of the lady: I have mark'd
A thousand blushing apparitions　　　　　165
To start into her face; a thousand innocent shames
In angel whiteness bear away those blushes;
And in her eye there hath appear'd a fire,
To burn the errors that these princes hold
Against her maiden truth. Call me a fool;　　　　170
Trust not my reading nor my observations,
Which with experimental seal doth warrant
The tenour of my book; trust not my age,
My reverence, calling, nor divinity,
If this sweet lady lie not guiltless here　　　　　175
Under some biting error.
　　Leon.　　　　　Friar, it cannot be.
Thou seest that all the grace that she hath left
Is, that she will not add to her damnation
A sin of perjury: she not denies it.　　　　　180
Why seek'st thou then to cover with excuse
That which appears in proper nakedness?
　　Friar. Lady, what man is he you are accus'd of?
　　Hero. They know that do accuse me, I know none;
If I know more of any man alive　　　　　185
Than that which maiden modesty doth warrant,
Let all my sins lack mercy! O, my father!
Prove you that any man with me convers'd
At hours unmeet, or that I yesternight
Maintain'd the change of words with any creature,　　　190

Refuse me, hate me, torture me to death.
　　Friar. There is some strange misprision in the princes.
　　Bene. Two of them have the very bent of honour;
And if their wisdoms be misled in this,
The practice of it lives in John the bastard,　　　　195
Whose spirits toil in frame of villainies.
　　Leon. I know not. If they speak but truth of her,
These hands shall tear her; if they wrong her honour,
The proudest of them shall well hear of it.
Time hath not yet so dried this blood of mine,　　　200
Nor age so eat up my invention,
Nor fortune made such havoc of my means,
Nor my bad life reft me so much of friends,
But they shall find, awak'd in such a kind,
Both strength of limb and policy of mind,　　　　205
Ability in means and choice of friends,
To quit me of them throughly.
　　Friar.　　　　　　Pause awhile,
And let my counsel sway you in this case.
Your daughter here the princes left for dead;　　　210
Let her awhile be secretly kept in,
And publish it that she is dead indeed:
Maintain a mourning ostentation;
And on your family's old monument
Hang mournful epitaphs and do all rites　　　　215
That appertain unto a burial.
　　Leon. What shall become of this? What will this do?
　　Friar. Marry, this well carried shall on her behalf
Change slander to remorse; that is some good:
But not for that dream I on this strange course,　　　220
But on this travail look for greater birth.
She dying, as it must be so maintain'd,
Upon the instant that she was accus'd,
Shall be lamented, pitied and excus'd
Of every hearer; for it so falls out　　　　　225
That what we have we prize not to the worth
Whiles we enjoy it, but being lack'd and lost,
Why, then we rack the value, then we find
The virtue that possession would not show us
Whiles it was ours. So will it fare with Claudio:　　　230
When he shall hear she died upon his words,
The idea of her life shall sweetly creep
Into his study of imagination,
And every lovely organ of her life
Shall come apparell'd in more precious habit,　　　235
More moving-delicate, and full of life
Into the eye and prospect of his soul,
Than when she liv'd indeed: then shall he mourn,—
If ever love had interest in his liver,—
And wish he had not so accused her,　　　　240
No, though he thought his accusation true.
Let this be so, and doubt not but success
Will fashion the event in better shape
Than I can lay it down in likelihood.
But if all aim but this be levell'd false,　　　　245

192 misprision: *misunderstanding*　**193 bent:** *natural inclination*　**195 practice:** *trickery*　**196 frame:** *contrivance*　**201 invention:** *power of mind*　**204 kind:** *manner*　**207 quit … of:** *avenge … on*　**211 secretly kept in:** *kept hidden*　**213 mourning ostentation:** *show of mourning*　**228 rack:** *stretch*　**233 study of imagination:** *imaginative study*　**234 organ:** *faculty*　**235 habit:** *dress*　**236 moving-delicate:** *touchingly delicate*　**237 prospect:** *view*　**239 liver:** *supposed seat of love*　**242 success:** *the result*　**244 lay … likelihood:** *conjecture*　**245** *Cf. n.*

133 frame: *established order*　**143** *Cf. n.*　**144 Valuing:** *when estimating the value*　**145 that:** *so that*　**147 season:** *savor*　**150 attir'd:** *wrapped up*　**172 experimental seal:** *seal of experience*　**173 book;** *cf. n.*　**190 change:** *exchange*

The supposition of the lady's death
Will quench the wonder of her infamy:
And if it sort not well, you may conceal her,—
As best befits her wounded reputation,—
In some reclusive and religious life,   250
Out of all eyes, tongues, minds and injuries.

Bene. Signior Leonato, let the friar advise you:
And though you know my inwardness and love
Is very much unto the prince and Claudio,
Yet, by mine honour, I will deal in this   255
As secretly and justly as your soul
Should with your body.

Leon.   Being that I flow in grief,
The smallest twine may lead me.

Friar. 'Tis well consented: presently away;   260
For to strange sores strangely they strain the cure.
Come, lady, die to live: this wedding day
Perhaps is but prolong'd: have patience and endure.

Exit [with Leonato and Hero.]

Bene. Lady Beatrice, have you wept all this while?

Beat. Yea, and I will weep a while longer.   265

Bene. I will not desire that.

Beat. You have no reason; I do it freely.

Bene. Surely I do believe your fair cousin is wronged.

Beat. Ah! how much might the man deserve of me that
would right her.   270

Bene. Is there any way to show such friendship?

Beat. A very even way, but no such friend.

Bene. May a man do it?

Beat. It is a man's office, but not yours.

Bene. I do love nothing in the world so well as you: is   275
not that strange?

Beat. As strange as the thing I know not.
It were as possible for me to say I loved nothing so well as
you; but believe me not, and yet I lie not; I confess
nothing, nor I deny nothing. I am sorry for my cousin.   280

Bene. By my sword, Beatrice, thou lovest me.

Beat. Do not swear by it, and eat it.

Bene. I will swear by it that you love me; and I will
make him eat it that says I love not you.

Beat. Will you not eat your word?   285

Bene. With no sauce that can be devised to it. I protest
I love thee.

Beat. Why then, God forgive me!

Bene. What offence, sweet Beatrice?

Beat. You have stayed me in a happy hour: 290
I was about to protest I loved you.

Bene. And do it with all thy heart.

Beat. I love you with so much of my heart that none
is left to protest.

Bene. Come, bid me do anything for thee.   295

Beat. Kill Claudio.

Bene. Ha! not for the wide world.

Beat. You kill me to deny it. Farewell.

Bene. Tarry, sweet Beatrice.

Beat. I am gone, though I am here: there is no love   300
in you: nay, I pray you, let me go.

Bene. Beatrice,—

Beat. In faith, I will go.

Bene. We'll be friends first.

Beat. You dare easier be friends with me than fight   305
with mine enemy.

Bene. Is Claudio thine enemy?

Beat. Is he not approved in the height a villain, that hath
slandered, scorned, dishonoured my kinswoman? O! that
I were a man. What! bear her in hand until they come to   310
take hands, and then, with public accusation, uncovered slander,
unmitigated rancour,—O God, that I were a man! I would eat
his heart in the market-place.

Bene. Hear me, Beatrice,—

Beat. Talk with a man out at a window! a proper saying!   315

Bene. Nay, but Beatrice,—

Beat. Sweet Hero! she is wronged, she is slandered, she is undone.

Bene. Beat—

Beat. Princes and counties! Surely, a princely testimony,
a goodly Count Comfect; a sweet gallant, surely! O! that I   320
were a man for his sake, or that I had any friend would be a
man for my sake! But manhood is melted into curtsies, valour
into compliment, and men are only turned into tongue, and
trim ones too: he is now as valiant as Hercules, that only
tells a lie and swears it. I cannot be a man with wishing,   325
therefore I will die a woman with grieving.

Bene. Tarry, good Beatrice. By this hand, I love thee.

Beat. Use it for my love some other way than swearing by it.

Bene. Think you in your soul the Count Claudio hath
wronged Hero?   330

Beat. Yea, as sure as I have a thought or a soul.

Bene. Enough! I am engaged, I will challenge him. I
will kiss your hand, and so leave you. By this hand, Claudio
shall render me a dear account. As you hear of me, so think
of me. Go, comfort your cousin: I must say she is dead;   335
and so, farewell.

[Exeunt.]

✣ Scene Second ✣

[A Prison]

*Enter the Constables [Dogberry and Verges] and the Town Clerk
[Sexton] in gowns, [with the Watch, Conrade and] Borachio.*

Dogb. Is our whole dissembly appeared?

Verg. O! a stool and a cushion for the sexton.

Sexton. Which be the malefactors?

Dogb. Marry, that am I and my partner.

Verg. Nay, that's certain: we have the exhibition to   5
examine.

Sexton. But which are the offenders that are to be examined?
let them come before Master constable.

Dogb. Yea, marry, let them come before me. What is
your name, friend?   10

Bora. Borachio.

Dogb. Pray write down Borachio. Yours, sirrah?

Con. I am a gentleman, sir, and my name is Conrade.

Dogb. Write down Master gentleman Conrade. Masters,
do you serve God?   15

Con. ⎫
Bora. ⎭ Yea, sir, we hope.

---

248 sort: *turn out*   **250 reclusive:** *secluded*   **251 injuries:** *insults*   **253 inwardness:**
intimacy   **258 flow in:** *overflow with*   **261 Cf. n.**   **263 prolong'd:** *postponed*   **272**
even: *smooth, easy*   **300 gone:** *absent in spirit*

308 height: *highest degree*   **310 bear . . . in hand:** *delude*   **311 uncovered:** *open*   **319**
counties: *counts*   **320 Comfect:** *sweetmeat*   **Sc. ii;** *cf. n.*   **1 dissembly:** *i.e. assem-*
bly   **4 Dogb.;** *cf. n.*   **5 exhibition:** *i.e. commission* (?)

Dogb. Write down that they hope they serve God: and write
God first; for God defend but God should go before such villains! Masters, it is proved already that you are little better   20
than false knaves, and it will go near to be thought so
shortly. How answer you for yourselves?

Con. Marry, sir, we say we are none.

Dogb. A marvellous witty fellow, I assure you; but I will
go about with him. Come you hither, sirrah; a word in your   25
ear: sir, I say to you, it is thought you are false knaves.

Bora. Sir, I say to you we are none.

Dogb. Well, stand aside. 'Fore God, they are both in a tale.
Have you writ down, that they are none?

Sexton. Master constable, you go not the way to examine: 30
you must call forth the watch that are their accusers.

Dogb. Yea, marry, that's the eftest way. Let the watch come
forth. Masters, I charge you, in the prince's name, accuse these
men.

First Watch. This man said, sir, that Don John, the   35
prince's brother, was a villain.

Dogb. Write down Prince John a villain. Why, this is flat
perjury, to call a prince's brother villain.

Bora. Master constable,—

Dogb. Pray thee, fellow, peace: I do not like thy look, I   40
promise thee.

Sexton. What heard you him say else?

Sec. Watch. Marry, that he had received a thousand ducats
of Don John for accusing the Lady Hero wrongfully.

Dogb. Flat burglary as ever was committed.   45

Verg. Yea, by the mass, that it is.

Sexton. What else, fellow?

First Watch. And that Count Claudio did mean, upon his
words, to disgrace Hero before the whole assembly, and not
marry her.   50

Dogb. O villain! thou wilt be condemned into everlasting redemption for this.

Sexton. What else?

Sec. Watch. This is all.

Sexton. And this is more, masters, than you can deny.   55
Prince John is this morning secretly stolen away: Hero
was in this manner accused, in this very manner refused, and,
upon the grief of this, suddenly died. Master constable, let
these men be bound, and brought to Leonato's: I will go before and show him their examination.   *[Exit.]* 60

Dogb. Come, let them be opinioned.

Verg. Let them be in the hands—

Con. Off, coxcomb!

Dogb. God's my life! where's the sexton? let him write
down the prince's officer coxcomb. Come, bind them.   65
Thou naughty varlet!

Con. Away! you are an ass; you are an ass.

Dogb. Dost thou not suspect my place? Dost thou not suspect my years? O that he were here to write me down an ass!
but, masters, remember that I am an ass; though it be not written down, yet forget not that I am an ass. No, thou villain,
thou art full of piety, as shall be proved upon thee by good
witness. I am a wise fellow; and, which is more, an officer;
and, which is more, a householder; and, which is more, as

pretty a piece of flesh as any in Messina; and one that knows
the law, go to; and a rich fellow enough, go to; and a
fellow that hath had losses; and one that hath two gowns, and
everything handsome about him. Bring him away. O that I
had been writ down an ass!   *Exeunt.*

ACT FIFTH ❧ SCENE FIRST

[Before Leonato's House.]
Enter Leonato and his brother [Antonio].

Ant. If you go on thus, you will kill yourself;
And 'tis not wisdom thus to second grief
Against yourself.

Leon.   I pray thee, cease thy counsel,
Which falls into mine ears as profitless   5
As water in a sieve: give not me counsel;
Nor let no comforter delight mine ear
But such a one whose wrongs do suit with mine:
Bring me a father that so lov'd his child,
Whose joy of her is overwhelm'd like mine,   10
And bid him speak of patience;
Measure his woe the length and breadth of mine,
And let it answer every strain for strain,
As thus for thus and such a grief for such,
In every lineament, branch, shape, and form: 15
If such a one will smile, and stroke his beard;
Bid sorrow wag, cry 'hem' when he should groan,
Patch grief with proverbs; make misfortune drunk
With candle-wasters; bring him yet to me,
And I of him will gather patience.   20
But there is no such man; for, brother, men
Can counsel and speak comfort to that grief
Which they themselves not feel; but, tasting it,
Their counsel turns to passion, which before
Would give preceptial medicine to rage,   25
Fetter strong madness in a silken thread,
Charm ache with air and agony with words.
No, no; 'tis all men's office to speak patience
To those that wring under the load of sorrow,
But no man's virtue nor sufficiency   30
To be so moral when he shall endure
The like himself. Therefore give me no counsel:
My griefs cry louder than advertisement.

Ant. Therein do men from children nothing differ.

Leon. I pray thee, peace! I will be flesh and blood;   35
For there was never yet philosopher
That could endure the toothache patiently,
However they have writ the style of gods
And made a push at chance and sufferance.

Ant. Yet bend not all the harm upon yourself;   40
Make those that do offend you suffer too.

Leon. There thou speak'st reason: nay, I will do so.
My soul doth tell me Hero is belied;

---

21 **go near to:** *almost*   24 **witty:** *cunning*   25 **go about with:** *circumvent*   28 **in a tale:** *agreed on one story*   32 **eftest:** *quickest (?)*   61 **opinioned:** *i.e. pinioned*   61, 62 *Cf. n.*   66 **naughty:** *good-for-naught*   68 **suspect:** *i.e. respect*   72 **piety:** *i.e. impiety*   74 **householder:** *head of a household*

75 **as pretty . . . flesh:** *as fine a fellow*   2 **second:** *assist*   8 **suit:** *agree*   13 **strain:** *strong feeling*   17 **wag:** *pass on; cf. n.*   19 **candle-wasters:** *sleepless revellers or students*   25 **preceptial:** *made up of precepts*   27 **air:** *mere breath*   29 **wring:** *writhe*   31 **moral:** *full of wisdom*   33 **advertisement:** *advice*   38 **style of:** *language worthy of*   39 **push;** *cf. n.* **sufferance:** *suffering*

And that shall Claudio know; so shall the prince,
And all of them that thus dishonour her.
 Ant. Here come the prince and Claudio hastily.   45

     Enter Prince and Claudio.

 D. Pedro. Good den, good den.
 Claud.   Good day to both of you.
 Leon. Hear you, my lords,—
 D. Pedro.   We have some haste, Leonato.
 Leon. Some haste, my lord! well, fare you well, my lord:
Are you so hasty now?—well, all is one.
 D. Pedro. Nay, do not quarrel with us, good old man.
 Ant. If he could right himself with quarrelling,
Some of us would lie low.   55
 Claud.   Who wrongs him?
 Leon. Marry, thou dost wrong me; thou dissembler, thou.
Nay, never lay thy hand upon thy sword;
I fear thee not.
 Claud.   Marry, beshrew my hand,   60
If it should give your age such case of fear.
In faith, my hand meant nothing to my sword.
 Leon. Tush, tush, man! never fleer and jest at me:
I speak not like a dotard nor a fool,
As, under privilege of age, to brag   65
What I have done being young, or what would do,
Were I not old. Know, Claudio, to thy head,
Thou hast so wrong'd mine innocent child and me
That I am forc'd to lay my reverence by,
And, with grey hairs and bruise of many days, 70
Do challenge thee to trial of a man.
I say thou hast belied mine innocent child:
Thy slander hath gone through and through her heart,
And she lies buried with her ancestors;
O! in a tomb where never scandal slept,   75
Save this of hers, fram'd by thy villainy!
 Claud. My villainy?
 Leon   Thine, Claudio; thine, I say.
 D. Pedro. You say not right, old man.
 Leon   My lord, my lord, 80
I'll prove it on his body, if he dare,
Despite his nice fence and his active practice,
His May of youth and bloom of lustihood.
 Claud. Away! I will not have to do with you.
 Leon. Canst thou so daff me? Thou hast kill'd my child; 85
If thou kill'st me, boy, thou shalt kill a man.
 Ant. He shall kill two of us, and men indeed:
But that's no matter; let him kill one first:
Win me and wear me; let him answer me.
Come, follow me, boy; come, sir boy, come, follow me. 90
Sir boy, I'll whip you from your foining fence;
Nay, as I am a gentleman, I will.
 Leon. Brother,—
 Ant. Content yourself. God knows I lov'd my niece;
And she is dead, slander'd to death by villains, 95
That dare as well answer a man indeed
As I dare take a serpent by the tongue.
Boys, apes, braggarts, Jacks, milksops!
 Leon.   Brother Antony,—

 Ant. Hold you content. What, man! I know them, yea, 100
And what they weigh, even to the utmost scruple,
Scambling, out-facing, fashion-monging boys,
That lie and cog and flout, deprave and slander,
Go anticly, show outward hideousness,
And speak off half a dozen dangerous words, 105
How they might hurt their enemies, if they durst;
And this is all!
 Leon. But, brother Antony,—
 Ant.   Come, 'tis no matter:
Do not you meddle, let me deal in this.   110
 D. Pedro. Gentlemen both, we will not wake your patience.
My heart is sorry for your daughter's death;
But, on my honour, she was charg'd with nothing
But what was true and very full of proof.
 Leon. My lord, my lord—   115
 D. Pedro.   I will not hear you.
 Leon.   No?
Come, brother, away. I will be heard.—
 Ant. And shall, or some of us will smart for it.

      Exeunt Leonato and Antonio.

     Enter Benedick.

 D. Pedro. See, see; here comes the man we went to seek. 120
 Claud. Now, signior, what news?
 Bene. Good day, my lord.
 D. Pedro. Welcome, signior: you are almost come to part almost a fray.
 Claud. We had like to have had our two noses snapped 125
off with two old men without teeth.
 D. Pedro. Leonato and his brother. What thinkest thou? Had we
fought, I doubt we should have been too young for them.
 Bene. In a false quarrel there is no true valour. I came
to seek you both.   130
 Claud. We have been up and down to seek thee; for we are
high-proof melancholy, and would fain have it beaten away.
Wilt thou use thy wit?
 Bene. It is in my scabbard; shall I draw it?
 D. Pedro. Dost thou wear thy wit by thy side? 135
 Claud. Never any did so, though very many have been
beside their wit. I will bid thee draw, as we do the minstrels;
draw, to pleasure us.
 D. Pedro. As I am an honest man, he looks pale. Art thou
sick, or angry?   140
 Claud. What, courage, man! What though care killed a
cat, thou hast mettle enough in thee to kill care.
 Bene. Sir, I shall meet your wit in the career, an you
charge it against me. I pray you choose another subject.
 Claud. Nay then, give him another staff: this last was 145
broke cross.
 D. Pedro. By this light, he changes more and more:
I think he be angry indeed.
 Claud. If he be, he knows how to turn his girdle.
 Bene. Shall I speak a word in your ear?   150
 Claud. God bless me from a challenge!
 Bene. [*Aside to Claudio.*] You are a villain; I jest not: I will

---

52 all is one: *'tis all the same* **60 beshrew:** *curse* **63 fleer:** *sneer* **67 to thy head:**
to thy face **82 fence:** *skill in fencing* **83 lustihood:** *vigor* **89 Win me, etc.;**
cf. n. **91 foining:** *thrusting*

102 Scambling: *contentious* **out-facing:** *swaggering* **103 cog:** *cheat* **deprave:** *vilify* **104 anticly:** *dressed like clowns* **111 wake your patience;** *cf. n.* **133 high-proof:**
in the highest degree **137 beside their wit:** *out of their wits* **draw;** *cf. n.* **143 in the**
career: *at full speed* **144 charge:** *direct* **145 staff:** *lance* **broke cross;** *cf. n.* **149**
turn his girdle; *cf. n.*

make it good how you dare, with what you dare, and when
you dare. Do me right, or I will protest your cowardice. You
have killed a sweet lady, and her death shall fall heavy on   155
you. Let me hear from you.

Claud. Well I will meet you, so I may have good cheer.

D. Pedro. What, a feast, a feast?

Claud. I' faith, I thank him; he hath bid me to a calf's-
head and a capon, the which if I do not carve most   160
curiously, say my knife's naught. Shall I not find a woodcock too?

Bene. Sir, your wit ambles well; it goes easily.

D. Pedro. I'll tell thee how Beatrice praised thy wit the
other day. I said, thou hadst a fine wit. 'True,' says she, 'a fine
little one.' 'No,' said I, 'a great wit.' 'Right,' said she, 'a   165
great gross one.' 'Nay,' said I, 'a good wit.' 'Just,' said she, 'it
hurts nobody.' 'Nay,' said I, 'the gentlemen is wise.' 'Certain,'
said she, 'a wise gentleman.' 'Nay,' said I, 'he hath the tongues.'
'That I believe,' said she, 'for he swore a thing to me on
Monday night, which he forswore on Tuesday morning: 170
there's a double tongue; there's two tongues.' Thus did she, an
hour together, trans-shape thy particular virtues; yet at last she
concluded with a sigh, thou wast the properest man in Italy.

Claud. For the which she wept heartily and said she
cared not.   175

D. Pedro. Yea, that she did; but yet, for all that, an if she
did not hate him deadly, she would love him dearly. The old
man's daughter told us all.

Claud. All, all; and moreover, God saw him when he
was hid in the garden.   180

D. Pedro. But when shall we set the savage bull's horns
on the sensible Benedick's head?

Claud. Yea, and text underneath, 'Here dwells Benedick
the married man!'

Bene. Fare you well, boy: you know my mind. I will   185
leave you now to your gossip-like humour: you break jests as
braggarts do their blades, which, God be thanked, hurt not.
My lord, for your many courtesies I thank you: I must dis-
continue your company. Your brother the bastard is fled
from Messina: you have, among you, killed a sweet and   190
innocent lady. For my Lord Lack-beard there, he and I shall
meet; and till then, peace be with him.   [*Exit.*]

D. Pedro. He is in earnest.

Claud. In most profound earnest; and, I'll warrant you,
for the love of Beatrice.   195

D. Pedro. And hath challenged thee?

Claud. Most sincerely.

D. Pedro. What a pretty thing man is when he goes in his
doublet and hose and leaves off his wit!

Claud. He is then a giant to an ape; but then is an ape   200
a doctor to such a man.

D. Pedro. But, soft you; let me be: pluck up, my heart,
and be sad! Did he not say my brother was fled?

*Enter Constable [Dogberry, Verges, and Watch, with] Conrade
and Borachio.*

Dogb. Come, you, sir: if justice cannot tame you, she
shall ne'er weigh more reasons in her balance. Nay, an you   205
be a cursing hypocrite once, you must be looked to.

D. Pedro. How now! two of my brother's men bound! Borachio, one!

Claud. Hearken after their offence, my lord.

D. Pedro. Officers, what offence have these men done?   210

Dogb. Marry, sir, they have committed false report; moreover, they have spoken untruths; secondarily, they are slanders;
sixth and lastly, they have belied a lady; thirdly, they have
verified unjust things; and to conclude, they are lying knaves.

D. Pedro. First, I ask thee what they have done; thirdly,   215
I ask thee what's their offence; sixth and lastly, why they are
committed; and, to conclude, what you lay to their charge?

Claud. Rightly reasoned, and in his own division; and,
by my troth, there's one meaning well suited.

D. Pedro. Who have you offended, masters, that you are   220
thus bound to your answer? this learned constable is too
cunning to be understood. What's your offence?

Bora. Sweet prince, let me go no further to mine answer:
do you hear me, and let this count kill me. I have deceived
even your very eyes: what your wisdoms could not discover,   225
these shallow fools have brought to light; who, in the night
overheard me confessing to this man how Don John your
brother incensed me to slander the Lady Hero; how you
were brought into the orchard and saw me court Margaret
in Hero's garments; how you disgraced her, when you should
marry her. My villainy they have upon record; which I had
rather seal with my death than repeat over to my shame. The
lady is dead upon mine and my master's false accusation;
and, briefly, I desire nothing but the reward of a villain.

D. Pedro. Runs not this speech like iron through your blood?

Claud. I have drunk poison whiles he utter'd it.

D. Pedro. But did my brother set thee on to this?

Bora. Yea; and paid me richly for the practice of it.

D. Pedro. He is compos'd and fram'd of treachery:
And fled he is upon this villainy.   240

Claud. Sweet Hero! now thy image doth appear
In the rare semblance that I lov'd it first.

Dogb. Come, bring away the plaintiffs: by this time our
sexton hath reformed Signior Leonato of the matter. And
masters, do not forget to specify, when time and place shall   245
serve, that I am an ass.

Verg. Here, here comes Master Signior Leonato, and the sexton too.

Enter Leonato [, Antonio, and the Sexton].

Leon. Which is the villain? Let me see his eyes,
That, when I note another man like him,   250
I may avoid him. Which of these is he?

Bora. If you would know your wronger, look on me.

Leon. Art thou the slave that with thy breath hast kill'd
Mine innocent child?

Bora.   Yea, even I alone.   255

Leon. No, not so, villain; thou beliest thyself:
Here stand a pair of honourable men;
A third is fled, that had a hand in it.
I thank you, princes, for my daughter's death:
Record it with your high and worthy deeds.   260
'Twas bravely done, if you bethink you of it.

154 Do me right: *give me satisfaction*   **protest:** *proclaim*   **161 curiously:** *daintily*   **naught:**
worthless   **woodcock:** *a stupid bird*   **168 a wise gentleman;** *cf. n.*   **172 trans-shape:**
distort   **199 leaves off his wit;** *cf. n.*   **201 doctor:** *learned man; cf. n.*   **202 soft
you:** *gently!*   **pluck up:** *rouse thyself*

209 Hearken after: *inquire into*   **212 slanders:** *i.e. slanderers*   **214 verified:** *i.e. testified*   **219 well suited;** *cf. n.*   **221 to your answer:** *to answer for your conduct*   **228
incensed:** *instigated*   **243 plaintiffs:** *i.e. defendants*   **244 reformed:** *i.e. informed*   **245 specify:** *i.e. testify (?)*

Claud. I know not how to pray your patience;
Yet I must speak. Choose your revenge yourself;
Impose me to what penance your invention
Can lay upon my sin: yet sinn'd I not   265
But in mistaking.

    D. Pedro.   By my soul, nor I:
And yet, to satisfy this good old man,
I would bend under any heavy weight
That he'll enjoin me to.   270

    Leon. I cannot bid you bid my daughter live;
That were impossible: but, I pray you both,
Possess the people in Messina here
How innocent she died; and if your love
Can labour aught in sad invention,   275
Hang her an epitaph upon her tomb,
And sing it to her bones: sing it to-night.
To-morrow morning come you to my house,
And since you could not be my son-in-law,
Be yet my nephew. My brother hath a daughter,   280
Almost the copy of my child that's dead,
And she alone is heir to both of us:
Give her the right you should have given her cousin,
And so dies my revenge.

    Claud.   O noble sir,   285
Your over-kindness doth wring tears from me!
I do embrace your offer; and dispose
For henceforth of poor Claudio.

    Leon. To-morrow then I will expect your coming;
To-night I take my leave. This naughty man   290
Shall face to face be brought to Margaret,
Who, I believe, was pack'd in all this wrong,
Hir'd to it by your brother.

    Bora.   No, by my soul she was not;
Nor knew not what she did when she spoke to me;   295
But always hath been just and virtuous
In anything that I do know by her.

    Dogb. Moreover, sir,—which, indeed, is not under white
and black,—this plaintiff here, the offender, did call me ass:
I beseech you, let it be remembered in his punishment.   300
And also, the watch heard them talk of one Deformed: they
say he wears a key in his ear and a lock hanging by it, and
borrows money in God's name, the which he hath used so
long and never paid, that now men grow hard-hearted, and
will lend nothing for God's sake. Pray you, examine him   305
upon that point.

    Leon. I thank thee for thy care and honest pains.

    Dogb. Your worship speaks like a most thankful and
reverend youth, and I praise God for you.

    Leon. There's for thy pains.   310

    Dogb. God save the foundation!

    Leon. Go, I discharge thee of thy prisoner, and I thank thee.

    Dogb. I leave an arrant knave with your worship; which
I beseech your worship to correct yourself, for the example
of others. God keep your worship! I wish your worship   315
well; God restore you to health! I humbly give you leave to
depart, and if a merry meeting may be wished, God prohibit
it! Come, neighbour.   *Exeunt [Dogberry and Verges].*

    Leon. Until to-morrow morning, lords, farewell.

    Ant. Farewell, my lords: we look for you to-morrow.   320

    D. Pedro. We will not fail.

    Claud.   To-night I'll mourn with Hero.
       [Exeunt Don Pedro and Claudio.]

    Leon [To the Watch.] Bring you these fellows on. We'll
talk with Margaret,   325
How her acquaintance grew with this lewd fellow.   *Exeunt.*

❧ SCENE SECOND ❧

[Leonato's Orchard.]
Enter Benedick and Margaret.

    Bene. Pray thee, sweet Mistress Margaret, deserve well at my
hands by helping me to the speech of Beatrice.

    Marg. Will you then write me a sonnet in praise of my
beauty?

    Bene. In so high a style, Margaret, that no man living   5
shall come over it; for, in most comely truth, thou deservest it.

    Marg. To have no man come over me! why, shall I always
keep below stairs?

    Bene. Thy wit is as quick as the greyhound's mouth; it
catches.   10

    Marg. And yours as blunt as the fencer's foils, which hit,
but hurt not.

    Bene. A most manly wit, Margaret; it will not hurt a
woman: and so, I pray thee, call Beatrice. I give thee the
bucklers.   15

    Marg. Give us the swords, we have bucklers of our own.

    Bene. If you use them, Margaret, you must put in the pikes
with a vice; and they are dangerous weapons for maids.

    Marg. Well, I will call Beatrice to you, who I think hath
legs.   20

    Bene. And therefore will come.   *Exit Margaret.*

    '*The god of love,*
      That sits above,
    And knows me, and knows me,
      How pitiful I deserve,—'   25

I mean, in singing; but in loving, Leander the good swimmer,
Troilus the first employer of pandars, and a whole book full of
these quondam carpet-mongers, whose names yet run smoothly
in the even road of a blank verse, why, they were never so
truly turned over and over as my poor self, in love. Marry,   30
I cannot show it in rime; I have tried: I can find out no rime
to 'lady' but 'baby,' an innocent rime; for 'scorn,' 'horn,' a
hard rime; for 'school,' 'fool,' a babbling rime; very ominous
endings: no, I was not born under a riming planet, nor I
cannot woo in festival terms.   35

Enter Beatrice.

Sweet Beatrice, wouldst thou come when I called thee?

    Beat. Yea, signior; and depart when you bid me.

    Bene. O, stay but till then!

---

264 Impose: *subject*   **273 Possess:** *inform*   **292 pack'd:** *implicated*   **297 by:** *concern-ing*   **298, 299 under black and white:** *in writing*   **311 foundation;** *cf. n.*   **317 prohibit:** *i.e. permit (?)*

5 style; *cf. n.*   **8 keep below stairs:** *remain a servant*   **14, 15 give … bucklers:** *yield*   **18 vice;** *cf. n.*   **26, 27 Leander … Troilus:** *cf. n.*   **28 quondam carpet-mongers:** *carpet-knights of old*   **32 innocent:** *silly*   **34 riming planet;** *cf. n.*   **35 festival terms:** *language not used every day*

Beat. 'Then' is spoken; fare you well now: and yet, ere I go,
let me go with that I came for; which is, with knowing   40
what hath passed between you and Claudio.

Bene. Only foul words; and thereupon I will kiss thee.

Beat. Foul words is but foul wind, and foul wind is but foul
breath, and foul breath is noisome; therefore I will depart
unkissed.   45

Bene. Thou hast frighted the word out of his right sense, so
forcible is thy wit. But I must tell thee plainly, Claudio undergoes my challenge, and either I must shortly hear from him, or
I will subscribe him a coward. And, I pray thee now, tell me,
for which of my bad parts didst thou first fall in love with   50
me?

Beat. For them all together; which maintained so politic a
state of evil that they will not admit any good part to intermingle with them. But for which of my good parts did you first
suffer love for me?   55

Bene. 'Suffer love,' a good epithet! I do suffer love indeed,
for I love thee against my will.

Beat. In spite of your heart, I think. Alas, poor heart! If you
spite it for my sake, I will spite it for yours; for I will never
love that which my friend hates.   60

Bene. Thou and I are too wise to woo peaceably.

Beat. It appears not in this confession: there's not one wise
man among twenty that will praise himself.

Bene. An old, an old instance, Beatrice, that lived in the
time of good neighbours. If a man do not erect in this age   65
his own tomb ere he dies, he shall live no longer in monument than the bell rings and the widow weeps.

Beat. And how long is that, think you?

Bene. Question: why, an hour in clamour and a quarter
rheum: therefore it is most expedient for the wise,—if   70
Don Worm, his conscience, find no impediment to the
contrary,— to be the trumpet of his own virtues, as I am to
myself. So much for praising myself, who, I myself will bear
witness, is praiseworthy. And now tell me, how doth your
cousin?   75

Beat. Very ill.

Bene. And how do you?

Beat. Very ill too.

Bene. Serve God, love me, and mend. There will I leave
you too, for here comes one in haste.   80

Enter Ursula.

Urs. Madam, you must come to your uncle. Yonder's old coil
at home: it is proved, my Lady Hero hath been falsely
accused, the prince and Claudio mightily abused; and Don
John is the author of all, who is fled and gone. Will you
come presently?   85

Beat. Will you go hear this news, signior?

Bene. I will live in thy heart, die in thy lap, and be buried
in thy eyes; and moreover I will go with thee to thy uncle's.

                                        Exeunt.

❧ SCENE THIRD ❧

[Within the Church]
Enter Claudio, Prince, and three or four with tapers.

Claud. Is this the monument of Leonato?
A Lord. It is, my lord.

[Claud., reading the] Epitaph.

'Done to death by slanderous tongues
   Was the Hero that here lies:
Death, in guerdon of her wrongs,   5
   Gives her fame which never dies.
So the life that died with shame
Lives in death with glorious fame.'

Hang thou there upon the tomb,
Praising her when I am dumb.   10
Now, music, sound, and sing your solemn hymn.

Song
'Pardon, goddess of the night,
Those that slew thy virgin knight;
For the which, with songs of woe,
Round about her tomb they go.   15
   Midnight, assist our moan;
   Help us to sigh and groan,
Heavily, heavily:
   Graves, yawn and yield your dead,
   Till death be uttered,   20
    Heavily, heavily.'

Claud. Now, unto thy bones good night!
yearly will I do this rite.

D. Pedro. Good morrow, masters: put your torches out.
The wolves have prey'd; and look, the gentle day,   25
Before the wheels of Phœbus, round about
  Dapples the drowsy east with spots of grey.
Thanks to you all, and leave us: fare you well.

Claud. Good morrow, masters: each his several way.

D. Pedro. Come, let us hence, and put on other weeds;   30
And then to Leonato's we will go.

Claud. And Hymen now with luckier issue speed's,
Than this for whom we render'd up this woe!   *Exeunt.*

❧ SCENE FOURTH ❧

[Leonato's House]
Enter Leonato, Antonio, Benedick, [Beatrice,] Margaret, Ursula,
Friar and Hero.

Friar. Did I not tell you she was innocent?
Leon. So are the prince and Claudio, who accus'd her
Upon the error that you heard debated:
But Margaret was in some fault for this,
Although against her will, as it appears   5
In the true course of all the question.

Ant. Well, I am glad that all things sort so well.

46 his: *its*   **47, 48 undergoes:** *is subject to* (?)   **49 subscribe:** *write down*   **52 politic:**
prudently governed   **64 instance:** *saying* (?)   **65 time of good neighbours;** *cf. n.*   **69**
Question: *that is the question* **clamour:** *i.e. sound of the bell*   **70 rheum:** *tears*   **70,**
71 Don Worm; *cf. n.*   **79 mend:** *recover health*   **81 old coil:** *a great ado*   **83 abused:**
deceived

9, 10 *Cf. n.*   **20 uttered;** *cf. n.*   **25 have prey'd:** *have ceased to prey (night is over)*   **30**
weeds: *garments*   **32 luckier issue:** *better fortune* **speed's:** *grant us help*   **33 this;**
cf. n.   **3 debated:** *discussed*   **6 In the true course, etc.;** *cf. n.*

Bene. And so am I, being else by faith enforc'd
To call young Claudio to a reckoning for it.
   Leon. Well, daughter, and you gentlewomen all,   *10*
Withdraw into a chamber by yourselves,
And when I send for you, come hither, mask'd;
The prince and Claudio promis'd by this hour
To visit me.   *Exeunt ladies.*
        You know your office, brother;   *15*
You must be father to your brother's daughter,
And give her to young Claudio.
   Ant. Which I will do with confirm'd countenance.
   Bene. Friar, I must entreat your pains, I think.
   Friar. To do what, signior?   *20*
   Bene. To bind me, or undo me; one of them.
Signior Leonato, truth it is, good signior,
Your niece regards me with an eye of favour.
   Leon. That eye my daughter lent her: 'tis most true.
   Bene. And I do with an eye of love requite her.   *25*
   Leon. The sight whereof I think, you had from me,
From Claudio, and the prince. But what's your will?
   Bene. Your answer, sir, is enigmatical:
But, for my will, my will is your good will
May stand with ours, this day to be conjoin'd   *30*
In the state of honourable marriage:
In which, good friar, I shall desire your help.
   Leon. My heart is with your liking.
   Friar.   And my help.
Here come the prince and Claudio.   *35*

     Enter Prince and Claudio, with Attendants.

   D. Pedro. Good morrow to this fair assembly.
   Leon. Good morrow, prince; good morrow, Claudio:
We here attend you. Are you yet determin'd
To-day to marry with my brother's daughter?
   Claud. I'll hold my mind, were she an Ethiop.   *40*
   Leon. Call her forth, brother: here's the friar ready.
                      [Exit Antonio.]
   D. Pedro. Good morrow, Benedick. Why, what's the matter,
That you have such a February face,
So full of frost, of storm and cloudiness?
   Claud. I think he thinks upon the savage bull.   *45*
Tush! fear not, man, we'll tip thy horns with gold,
And all Europa shall rejoice at thee,
As once Europa did at lusty Jove,
When he would play the noble beast in love.
   Bene. Bull Jove, sir, had an amiable low: *50*
And some such strange bull leap'd your father's cow,
And got a calf in that same noble feat,
Much like to you, for you have just his bleat.
   Claud. For this I owe you: here come other reckonings.

   Enter Antonio [with] Hero, Beatrice, Margaret, Ursula [masked].

Which is the lady I must seize upon?   *55*
   Ant. This same is she, and I do give you her.
   Claud. Why, then she's mine. Sweet, let me see your face.
   Leon. No, that you shall not, till you take her hand
Before this friar, and swear to marry her.
   Claud. Give me your hand: before this holy friar,   *60*

I am your husband, if you like of me.
   Hero. And when I liv'd, I was your other wife:
                        [Unmasking.]
And when you lov'd, you were my other husband.
   Claud. Another Hero!
   Hero.   Nothing certainer   *65*
One Hero died defil'd, but I do live,
And surely as I live, I am a maid.
   D. Pedro. The former Hero! Hero that is dead!
   Leon. She died, my lord, but whiles her slander liv'd.
   Friar. All this amazement can I qualify: *70*
When after that the holy rites are ended,
I'll tell you largely of fair Hero's death:
Meantime, let wonder seem familiar,
And to the chapel let us presently.
   Bene. Soft and fair, friar. Which is Beatrice?   *75*
   Beat. [Unmasking.] I answer to that name.
What is your will?
   Bene. Do not you love me?
   Beat.   Why, no; no more than reason.
   Bene. Why, then, your uncle and the prince and Claudio *80*
Have been deceived; for they swore you did.
   Beat. Do not you love me?
   Bene.   Troth, no; no more than reason.
   Beat. Why, then, my cousin, Margaret, and Ursula,
Are much deceiv'd; for they did swear you did.   *85*
   Bene. They swore that you were almost sick for me.
   Beat. They swore that you were well-nigh dead for me.
   Bene. 'Tis no such matter. Then, you do not love me?
   Beat. No, truly, but in friendly recompense.
   Leon. Come, cousin, I am sure you love the gentleman. *90*
   Claud. And I'll be sworn upon 't that he loves her;
For here's a paper written in his hand,
A halting sonnet of his own pure brain,
Fashion'd to Beatrice.
   Hero.   And here's another,   *95*
Writ in my cousin's hand, stolen from her pocket,
Containing her affection unto Benedick.
   Bene. A miracle! here's our own hands against our hearts.
Come, I will have thee; but, by this light, I take thee
for pity.   *100*
   Beat. I would not deny you; but, by this good day, I yield
upon great persuasion, and partly to save your life, for I was
told you were in a consumption.
   Bene. Peace! I will stop your mouth.   *[Kisses her.]*
   D. Pedro. How dost thou, 'Benedick, the married man'? *105*
   Bene. I'll tell thee what, prince; a college of witcrackers cannot flout me out of my humour. Dost thou think I care for a
satire or an epigram? No; if a man will be beaten with brains,
a' shall wear nothing handsome about him. In brief, since I do
purpose to marry, I will think nothing to any purpose that *110*
the world can say against it; and therefore never flout at me
for what I have said against it, for man is a giddy thing, and
this is my conclusion. For thy part, Claudio, I did think to
have beaten thee; but, in that thou art like to be my kinsman,
live unbruised, and love my cousin.   *115*
   Claud. I had well hoped thou wouldst have denied Beatrice,
that I might have cudgelled thee out of thy single life, to make

---

8 by faith: *by my pledged word*   **18 confirm'd:** *steady*   **21 undo:** *(1) unbind, (2)
ruin*   **45** *Cf. n.*   **47, 48 Europa:** *cf. n.*   **54 owe you:** *i.e. owe you an answer*

61 like of: *care for*   **70 qualify:** *moderate*   **72 largely:** *fully*   **73 let wonder,** *etc.;
cf. n.*   **83 Troth:** *by my troth*   **93 his own pure:** *purely his own*   **105** *Cf. n.*   **108
beaten with brains,** *etc.; cf. n.*

thee a double-dealer; which, out of question, thou wilt be, if
my cousin do not look exceeding narrowly to thee.

Bene. Come, come, we are friends. Let's have a dance   *120*
ere we are married, that we may lighten our own hearts
and our wives' heels.

Leon. We'll have dancing afterward.

Bene. First, of my word; therefore play, music! Prince, thou
art sad; get thee a wife, get thee a wife: there is no staff   *125*
more reverend than one tipped with horn.

Enter Messenger.

Mes. My lord, your brother John is ta'en in flight,
And brought with armed men back to Messina.

Bene. Think not on him till to-morrow; I'll devise thee
brave punishments for him. Strike up, pipers!   *Dance.*

❧ FINIS ❧

NOTES

I.i.S. d. *[Before Antonio's Orchard]*, etc. The quarto edition of this play (1600) makes no division into either acts or scenes. The folio edition (1623) divides the acts correctly, but does not mark the separate scenes, except in the case of the present one, the first. Neither of the early editions indicates where the action of the various scenes occurs. In the present instance modern editors have usually located the scene 'Before Leonato's House.' Line 83-85 and 232, however, suggest that Leonato and his family have come to meet their distinguished guests near the edge of the town, and lines 7-9 of scene ii point to the neighborhood of Antonio's orchard (*i.e.* garden) as the place of meeting. See L. Mason, *Modern Philology,* xi. 379-89.

I.i.S. d. *Innogen, his wife.* Leonato's wife is mentioned only in this stage direction and in that at the opening of Act II. Modern editors have therefore regularly omitted her name in both places. It is possible that Shakespeare gave her a small part in the first draft of the play, and subsequently cut it out for the sake of compression.

I.i.6 *sort.* The interpretation of this word given in the footnote is preferred by most editors; but it is possible to take the word in the more general sense which it bears at present: 'kind.'

I.i.25 *Mountanto.* A team in fencing, 'upper-cut,' used by Beatrice to characterize Benedick's lively and pugnacious disposition.

I.i.32-34 *challenged Cupid . . . bird-bolt.* The jest is that Benedick vaingloriously challenged Cupid to a contest at shooting hearts, to which Leonato's fool replied by suggesting himself as Benedick's proper competitor and the childish bird-bolt as his proper weapon.

I.i.48, 49 *stuffed . . . stuffing.* Beatrice calls Benedick a 'stuffed' man because of his proneness to over-eat; then, playing with the phrase, suggests that his 'stuffing'—what is in him, what he is made of—is of no very fine quality.

I.i.54 *five wits.* 'Not the five senses, but the five other wits: the memory, fantasy, estimation, imagination, and common wit. Benedick is left the last only.'

I.i.56 *bear it for a difference.* Alluding to a term in heraldry, where a 'difference' was some slight mark added to differentiate coats of arms otherwise indistinguishable.

I.i.57, 58 *to be known,* etc. This infinitive clause is the subject of the sentence. Bare recognition as a rational creature, not a dumb animal, is all the intellectual wealth Benedick has left.

I.i.72 *the Benedick.* Beatrice affects to think the harmful result of Benedick's company a physical disease, like the colic.

I.i.113 *a predestinate scratched face.* The gentleman destined to marry Beatrice is predestined to have his face scratched by her. If she refuses to marry, he will escape that destiny.

I.i.115 *an.* The conjunction 'and,' one old meaning of which was 'if.' Here and regularly elsewhere the old editions spell 'and,' which modern editors alter for the sake of clearness.

I.i.118 *A bird of my tongue,* etc. 'A bird taught to speak like me,' alluding to Benedick's gibe, 'parrot-teacher.' The latter part of the sentence implies that only a beast could be taught to speak like Benedick.

I.i.122 *a jade's trick.* Some such trick of a bad horse as slipping the head out of the collar and escaping. Beatrice gibes at Benedick's sudden breaking off of the dispute.

I.i.138 *noted.* Benedick puns on one of the less obvious meanings of the word. Possibly the sense he has in mind is to provide with notes, set to music: 'I did not set the young lady to music,' *i.e.* did not go into raptures over her.

I.i.155 *Cupid . . . carpenter.* It would be an obvious absurdity to select the blind god, Cupid, to spy out the sitting hare, or to name Vulcan, the god of the flaming forge, as a proper person to work with the carpenter's inflammable materials.

I.i.167 *wear his cap with suspicion.* 'Deceived husbands, according to the ancient jest, wore invisible horns. Every husband, therefore, would suspect his cap of concealing horns.' (MacCracken.)

I.i.170 *sigh away Sundays.* It is hardly clear whether Sundays are particularly named because the days normally most happily spent or because the discontented husband would be most conscious of his yoke in the special domesticity of Sundays.

I.i.181 *Like the old tale,* etc. An old children's tale, somewhat similar to that of Bluebeard, survived till the eighteenth century, in which occurred the words: 'It is not so, nor it was not so, and God forbid it should be so.'

I.i.203 *recheat winded in my forehead . . . invisible baldrick.* Another allusion to the invisible 'horns'; cf. note on l. 167. The recheat was a horn blast blown (*winded*) to recall the hounds from the chase; the baldrick, a strap worn across the shoulder and supporting the horn.

I.i.213 *for the sign of blind Cupid.* Alluding to the pictorial signs hung up before places of business in Shakespeare's time. Benedick, treated as he suggests and hung up at the door, would make a proper illustration for 'The Blind Cupid.'

I.i.216 *hang me in a bottle like a cat,* etc. 'Bottle' means probably the wicker basket used to hold the cat used as the mark in archery contests.

I.i.218 *called Adam.* A special title of honor for the successful archer, doubtless from the fame of the archer-outlaw of the ballads, Adam Bell.

I.i.220 *'In time the savage bull doth bear the yoke.'* A line quoted from memory, and not quite accurately, from Thomas Kyd's famous *Spanish Tragedy* (composed about 1587).

I.i.228, 229 *Cupid . . . Venice.* Venice was famed for frivolity.

I.i.231. *temporize.* The meaning is not certain. 'Come to terms' is one explanation; another, rather more probable, is 'become tempered', *i.e.* grow milder. 'With the hours' means 'in the course of time.'

I.i.236-240 *and so I commit you . . . your loving friend, Benedick.* The words of Benedick suggest to Claudio the conventional mode of concluding formal letters, which he and Don Pedro proceed to parody. The sixth of July, formerly celebrated as Midsummer Day, is mentioned because of its suggestion of 'midsummer madness.'

I.i.242 *guarded with fragments,* etc. Metaphors from tailoring. Benedick means that Don Pedro and Claudio cannot in conscience afford to mock at trite phrases ('flout old ends'), for their own conversation is often made up of just such materials very poorly assimilated.

I.i.274 *The fairest grant is the necessity.* The best gift is the one which just fits the need of the recipient; *i.e.* it is a mistake to be excessive.

I.ii.1 *my cousin, your son.* Antonio's son is not elsewhere mentioned, and V.i.284 suggests that he has no son. The inconsistency may be due to oversight. The 'cousins' and 'cousin' addressed by Leonato in ll. 21 and 22 are probably more distant relatives, dependants of his household.

I.iii.9 *born under Saturn.* According to the old belief, persons born under the domination of the planet Saturn acquired the morose disposition hence called *saturnine.*

I.iii.47 *smoking a musty room.* Elizabethan rooms, strewn with stale rushes, often required perfuming in order to dispel unpleasant odors.

I.iii.48 *comes me.* Shakespeare very frequently employs a dative personal pronoun, as here, in a sense not found in modern usage. It is sometimes called the 'ethical' dative and merely suggests the interest of the person referred to in the act mentioned.

II.i.33, 34 *lead his apes into hell.* An allusion to a very common ancient saying that women who died old maids 'led apes in hell.' The origin of the phrase is uncertain; it may refer to the weakness of elderly spinsters for pet animals. Small apes held the place in their affection in Tudor times which cats hold to-day.

II.i.39, 40 *for the heavens.* The phrase can be interpreted either (1) 'on my way to heaven,' St. Peter being the gate-keeper whom one met before entering; or (2) as a petty oath equivalent to 'by heaven' or perhaps 'for dear life.'

II.i.69 *I can see a church by daylight.* 'I am not wholly blind.' The church would be the most conspicuous object in nearly any old town.

II.i.81 *Philemon's roof.* A reference to the story in Ovid's *Metamorphoses* (bk. viii) of how the peasant couple, Philemon and Baucis, entertained Jupiter under their humble roof. Hence, *thatch'd* in line 82, peasant cottages having thatched roofs.

II.i.93 *Answer, clerk.* Balthazar's *Amen* in the previous speech reminds Margaret of the parish clerk, whose business was to read out the responses at church in a loud voice.

II.i.111 *the 'Hundred Merry Tales.'* A popular collection of coarse anecdotes.

II.i.123 *fleet.* Properly a company of vessels sailing together, Beatrice uses the word of the company of masqueraders present. The nautical suggestion of the word leads her to continue the figure in the word *boarded,* which implies the attack of one vessel on another.

II.i.155 *use.* It is disputed whether this word is a plain indicative or a subjunctive, equivalent to 'let all hearts . . . use.' The latter seems more probable.

II.i.165, 166 *willow . . . garland.* Referring to the garlands of weeping willow worn by forsaken lovers.

II.i.175 *like the blind man,* etc. An allusion to an incident at the close of the first chapter of the Spanish novel, *Lazarillo de Tormes.*

II.i.178 *creep into sedges.* Waterfowl, when wounded, creep for shelter into the sedges along the river bank. So Claudio will go off and pine by himself.

II.i.182 *base though bitter.* The adjectives have been condemned as unintelligible in their context; but Benedick means to condemn the disposition of Beatrice

as 'base,' *i.e.* unworthy, unjust, while admitting that her words have a sting (bitterness) which 'base' criticisms do not usually possess.

II.i.187 *Lady Fame.* The Vergilian deity *Fama*, Rumor, who goes about the world spreading news.

II.i.206, 207 *If their singing,* etc. 'If the birds sings as you say (*i.e.* if Hero consents to do as you intend and marry Claudio) . . . what you say is creditable to you.'

II.i.216 *like a man at a mark.* In archery contests a man stood beside the mark to check off the contestants' arrows as they struck. It was a perilous position when the archers shot badly.

II.i.219 *infect to the north star.* The infection of her breath would reach beyond planetary space.

II.i.221 *made Hercules have turned spit,* etc. Beatrice would have treated Hercules worse than Omphale, who in the legend put him into domestic service. Turning the spit was the meanest office in the Elizabethan kitchen. It was often performed by dogs.

II.i.223 *infernal Ate in good apparel.* Beatrice is like Ate, the goddess of discord, in everything except that she wears the clothes of a fashionable gentlewoman.

II.i.224 *I would . . . some scholar would conjure her.* Scholars were reputed to be able to raise up and banish evil spirits.

II.i.234 *Prester John's foot.* Prester John was a fabled Christian king, supposed to live in some remote part of Asia or Africa.

II.i.235 *the Great Cham's beard.* The Great Cham or Grand Khan was the ruler of the Mongols.

II.i.235 *the Pigmies.* The fabulous race who fought with cranes.

II.i.236 *harpy.* The Harpies were rapacious female monsters who afflicted voyagers.

II.i.257 *civil . . . civil.* A pun on civil and Seville, commonly spelled and pronounced alike. Seville oranges are bitter-sweet, neither one thing nor the other. Hence the application to Claudio. Yellow, the color of oranges, is also the color (complexion) of jealousy (l. 258).

II.i.279 *alliance.* I.e. relationship by marriage. Beatrice teases Claudio for addressing her as 'cousin' as if he were already married to her cousin Hero.

II.i.280 *sun-burnt.* Probably, a mild way of saying 'unattractive'; but some editors explain it as 'exposed to the sun,' unsheltered, *i.e.* a lone woman.

II.ii.37 *term me Claudio.* Editors have found difficulty in understanding why Margaret should address Borachio by any name but his own; but how is Margaret, who is not privy to the design against her mistress, to be prevented from suspecting a plot when she hears herself loudly called 'Hero,' unless Borachio has previously persuaded her to act out a little play in which they are to simulate the happiness of the declared lovers?

II.iii.5 *I am here already, sir.* The boy indulges in hyperbole: 'I will go so fast that you may say I am back again already.' Benedick pretends to take his words literally.

II.iii.13 *the tabor and the pipe.* Drum and fife (l. 12) are of course the instruments of martial music; tabor (a small drum) and pipe are the corresponding instruments which appear in times of peaceful revelry.

II.iii.28 *noble . . . angel.* A pun, frequent in Shakespeare, on the names of two coins of his day. A 'noble' was worth one-third of a sovereign (*i.e.* 6s. 8d.), an 'angel' half a sovereign (10s.).

II.iii.30 *of what colour it pleases God.* That is, her hair must not be dyed.

II.iii.S. d. *Balthazar.* The folio edition here substitutes for 'Balthazar' the name of the actor who took his part: *Iacke Wilson.* Compare the note on IV. ii.

II.iii.37 *kid-fox.* Since 'kid fox' does not appear to have been a current name for a young fox, many of the best editors are disposed to alter the text to 'the hid fox.'

II.iii.41, 42 *It is the witness still of excellency,* etc. 'It is always (*still*) a proof of excellence that, in demeanour, it is unconscious, or unknowing, of its own perfection.' (Furness.)

II.iii.53 *crotchets.* A pun on two meanings of the word: (1) whims, (2) notes of music.

II.iii.54 *notes, notes, forsooth, and nothing!* A pun is evident here, 'nothing' being pronounced by Elizabethans much or precisely like 'noting.' It has been suggested that a similar pun is involved in the title of the play, *Much Ado about Nothing* (or *Noting, i.e.* eavesdropping).

II.iii.85 *night-raven.* The voice of this bird (which has not been certainly identified) was supposed to betoken some 'plague,' especially sickness or death.

II.iii.86 *Yea, marry.* These words have no reference, of course, to the speech of Benedick, who has hidden himself apart from the others (cf. l. 35). Furness explains that while Benedick speaks the Prince has been talking to Claudio about the music for Hero 'to-morrow night' (l. 87) and that he here assents to Claudio's suggestion.

II.iii.93 *Stalk on,* etc. A figure from game-stalking. The 'fowl' is Benedick, whom they hope to catch 'sitting.'

II.iii.222 *paper bullets of the brain.* Quips and sentences, Benedick foresees, will be shot at him like bullets, but being taken from books, they are but paper bullets, which do no real injury. For *career* in the sense of full speed, cf. V.i.144.

III.i.47 *as full as.* Possibly a misprint for *at full as,* 'fully as.'

III.i.64 *spell him backward.* Alluding to the practice of conjurors, who spell prayers and holy names backwards in order to produce incantations. The meaning is: turn his virtues into vices.

III.i.104 *every day—to-morrow.* The meaning seems to be: 'I am married every day—it is constantly in my thoughts; but the actual time is to-morrow.' Perhaps, however, Hero refers to the postponement of the ceremony (cf. II.i.310 ff.) and means: 'Every day it is set for the next.'

III.i.116 *behind the back.* I.e. when their back is turned, when people talk about them.

III.i.118 *Taming my wild heart to thy loving hand.* A figure suggested by the taming of a hawk, which comes to know the hand of the falconer.

III.ii.22 *hang . . . draw.* Alluding to the punishment of traitors, who were hanged, drawn, and quartered.

III.ii.24 *a humour or a worm.* Contemporary dental theory ascribed toothache, among other causes, to the presence of humors, *i.e.* unhealthy secretions, and to actual worms in the teeth.

III.ii.27 *no doublet.* That is, no doublet is to be seen, because, like a Spaniard, the upper part of his body is quite enveloped by his cloak.

III.ii.40, 41 *the old ornament of his cheek hath already stuffed tennis-balls.* He has cut off his beard. The tennis-balls of the day were sometimes stuffed with human hair.

III.ii.61 *buried with her face upwards.* Suicides were sometimes buried with their faces downward. The Prince means that Beatrice will not be responsible for her own death.

III.ii.64 *hobby-horses.* Originally morris-dancers dressed to look like horses; hence any ridiculously frivolous persons.

III.ii.76 This line should perhaps be assigned to Claudio.

III.iii.91 *scab.* Modern usage of 'scab' for a scurvy fellow renders the pun still intelligible.

III.iii.121 *god Bel's priests.* Threescore and ten priests of Bel are mentioned in the Apocryphal book of *Daniel.*

III.iii.126 *the fashion wears out more apparel than the man.* That is, new clothes are required oftener to conform to changes of fashion than for actual use.

III.iii.146 *right Master constable.* An absurd title. The speaker is thinking of such respectful phrases as 'right worshipful.'

III.iii.157, 158 *commodity . . . bills.* 'Bills' is used punningly with reference, first, to the bills (halberds) of the watch; second, to the common commercial phrase, 'to take up a commodity on one's bills,' *i.e.* buy merchandise on credit.

III.iv.12 *within.* Furness prefers to take 'tire within' as meaning the inner trimming of the head dress. *Within* may, however, mean 'in an inner room.'

III. iv.27, 28 *saving your reverence.* A common expression, sometimes abbreviated sir-reverence.' It means that no disrespect to the hearer is intended.

III.v.14 *palabras.* A scrap of Spanish: *pocas palabras,* few words.

III.v.32 *when the age is in,* etc. An original adaptation of an old proverb: 'When ale is in, wit is out.'

III.v.33, 34 *God's a good man.* A proverbial saying.

III.v.56 *non-come.* Dogberry probably means 'non plus,' but confuses that bit of learning with another: 'non compos mentis.'

IV.i.18, 19 *some be of laughing, as ah! ha! he!* Alluding to the way Latin and English grammars of the day listed the interjections according to the emotions they expressed.

IV.i.43 *in your own proof.* 'In making trial of her yourself.' (Wright.)

IV.i.68 *True!* Hero's exclamation refers to Don John's speech, not Benedick's.

IV.i.83 *Hero itself,* etc. 'The very name, by becoming a byword and a reproach, can blot out virtue.' (Furness.)

IV.i.143 *That I myself was to myself not mine.* I.e. Hero was so much a part of me that by comparison I was not myself.

IV.i.173 *The tenour of my book.* 'Book' is used in the general sense of the learning gained from books, the tenor or general nature of which is warranted (*i.e.* confirmed) by the Friar's practical observations of life.

IV.i.245 *But if all aim but this be levell'd false.* 'If every other aim miscarry.'

IV.i.261 *For to strange sores strangely they strain the cure.* 'Strange diseases require desperately strange cures.'

IV. ii. The early editions, both quarto and folio, prefix to the speeches of Dogberry and Verges in this scene the names of the actors who originally took

their parts; *viz.,* Kempe and Cowley respectively. The phrase 'in gowns' in the opening stage direction means that the constables and town clerk (sexton) wore their gowns of office.

IV.ii.4 *Dogb.* In this case the early editions give the speech to 'Andrew,' perhaps a nickname of the clown or Merry-Andrew, Kempe.

IV.ii.61, 62. In the early editions these lines form a single speech, printed thus: 'Let them be in the hands of Coxcombe.' The folio gives the words to the Sexton, the quarto to Cowley (*i.e.* Verges). Malone suggested the accepted reading, which cannot be regarded as certain.

V.i.17 *Bid sorrow wag.* Capell's emendation. The early editions have 'And sorrow, wagge,' which apparently makes no sense.

V.i.39 *made a push.* The most probable meaning is made a 'pish!', *i.e.* mocked.

V.i.89 *Win me and wear me.* A proverbial phrase: 'He may have me if he wins me (by the sword).'

V.i.111 *wake your patience.* 'We will not keep your patience wakeful or excited.' It would be more natural to say 'wake your impatience,' but the Prince is too polite to use the uncomplimentary term.

V.i.137 *draw.* The word is used punningly, with special reference to bidding the minstrels draw their bows across the strings of their instruments.

V.i.145 *broke cross.* Like 'in the career' above (l. 143), this is a figure from the tilting matches of the day. Only a very awkward tilter would aim so badly as to break his staff 'cross,' *i.e.* not by a direct blow, but by allowing it to strike lengthwise across his opponent's body.

V.i.149 *turn his girdle.* A common proverbial saying of rather vague force. Probably it means no more than 'change his mood,' but it has also been explained as 'prepare to fight,' referring to the alleged custom of wrestlers to turn the buckles of their girdles to the back before beginning.

V.i.168 *a wise gentleman.* Evidently the words, as repeated by Beatrice, had some colloquial derogatory force now lost. Perhaps they were a cant name for a fool.

V.i.198, 199 *goes in his doublet and hose and leaves off his wit.* Doublet and hose formed the Elizabethan undress costume, a cloak being worn over them on formal occasions. The Prince suggests ironically that man's wit is a mere outward embellishment which he can leave off as easily as he can his cloak and go about in his natural stupidity.

V.i.200 *He is then a giant to an ape,* etc. In physical proportions man is much greater than an ape (*i.e.* an Elizabethan pet ape, a small monkey), but in mental power the ape is far superior.

V.i.219 *one meaning well suited.* One meaning provided with many different suits of clothes; alluding to the previous speech of Don Pedro, where practically the same idea is expressed in four different ways.

V.i.311 *God save the foundation.* A customary phrase, used by those who received assistance from a charitable foundation, quite out of place here since Leonato is not a 'foundation.'

V.ii.5 *so high a style.* A pun on the two words, 'style' and 'stile,' is intended; 'come over' in the next line implying both 'excel' the style and 'climb over' the stile.

V.ii.18 *with a vice.* A play on 'vice,' the screw by which the sharp pointed 'pike' was fastened in the centre of the buckler, and 'vice,' sin.

V.ii.26, 27 *Leander . . . Troilus.* Allusions probably to Marlowe's *Hero and Leander* and Chaucer's *Troilus and Criseide* respectively.

V.ii.34 *not born under a riming planet.* Alluding to the old-fashioned belief in the influence exerted upon each man's temperament by the particular planet which was most conspicuous when he was born.

V.ii.65 *in the time of good neighbours.* In the time when people's neighbours used to speak well of them—a very long time ago.

V.ii.70, 71 *Don Worm, his conscience.* The old moralists represented conscience as a gnawing worm. The title 'Don' is given it from mock respect.

V.iii.9, 10 *Hang thou there upon the tomb,* etc. Dr. Furness holds that these lines are not Claudio's comment while affixing the epitaph, but part of the epitaph itself; but compare Claudio's similar riming comment below, ll. 22, 23.

V.iii.20 *Till death be uttered.* There has been much unnecessary discussion of the meaning of this passage. It is clear if we understand *uttered* in the common Elizabethan sense of 'sent abroad,' 'put into circulation.' The word is regularly so used with regard to books placed on sale, news made public, etc. The meaning here is, then, that the graves are to yawn and yield their dead until death is scattered abroad among the world of men.

V.iii.33 *Than this,* etc. 'This' probably refers to Hero: 'May Hymen grant us a happier outcome than he granted to her whose marriage was the means of her death.' Hymen is the god of marriage. Dr. Furness explains 'Than this' as a contraction for 'than in this (issue).'

V.iv.6. *In the true course of all the question.* 'Now that the whole question has been truly followed up.'

V.iv.45 *I think he thinks upon the savage bull.* A jesting reminiscence of the conversation between Don Pedro and Benedick, I.i.219-226.

V.iv.47, 48 *Europa . . . Europa.* In the first instance the continent of Europe, in the second the mythological maiden, supposed to have been carried off by Jupiter in the form of a bull, and to have given her name to the land whither she was brought.

V.iv.73 *let wonder seem familiar.* 'Act as if your curiosity had already been satisfied.'

V.iv.105 *'Benedick, the married man.'* See I.i.225.

V.iv.108 *beaten with brains.* Subjected to ridicule. If a man fears ridicule, Benedick says, he will not dare to have anything handsome about him (whether clothes or a wife), which might attract attention to him.

V.iv.118 *a double-dealer.* Used punningly, first of one who gives up his single life for the double life of matrimony, and then with an allusion to double-dealing, inconstancy.

THE TEXT OF THE PRESENT EDITION

The text of the present volume is, by permission of the Oxford University Press, that of the Oxford Shakespeare, edited by the late W. J. Craig, except for the following deviations:

1. The stage directions are based on those in the two original editions of the play, a few obvious errors in the latter being corrected and words there missing added within square brackets.

2. About half a dozen words are differently spelled: *e.g.,* antic (antick), lantern (lanthorn), villainy (villany), haggard (haggerd).

3. Five changes of punctuation or wording have been made, *viz.*:

I.i.123	Leonato.—	*for*	Leonato:
II.iii.86	marry. Dost	*for*	marry; dost
II.iii.108	sit you—	*for*	sit you;
III.i.104	day—	*for*	day,
V.i.102	Scambling	*for*	Scrambling

The Merry Wives of Windsor

Edited by
GEORGE VAN SANTVOORD

Dramatis Personae

SIR JOHN FALSTAFF
FENTON, *a young Gentleman*
SHALLOW, *a Country Justice*
SLENDER, *Cousin to Shallow*
FORD }
PAGE } *two Gentlemen dwelling at Windsor*
WILLIAM PAGE, *a Boy, Son to Page*
SIR HUGH EVANS, *a Welsh Parson*
DOCTOR CAIUS, *a French Physician*
HOST *of the Garter Inn*
BARDOLPH }
PISTOL } *Followers of Falstaff*
NYM }

ROBIN, *Page to Falstaff*
SIMPLE, *Servant to Slender*
RUGBY, *Servant to Doctor Caius*

MISTRESS FORD
MISTRESS PAGE
ANNE PAGE, *her Daughter, in love with Fenton*
MISTRESS QUICKLY, *Servant to Doctor Caius*

SERVANTS TO PAGE, FORD ETC.

SCENE—*Windsor; and the Neighbourhood.*

The Merry Wives of Windsor

INTRODUCTION

SOURCES OF THE PLAY

The Merry Wives of Windsor ranks next after *Love's Labour's Lost, A Midsummer Night's Dream,* and *The Tempest* among Shakespeare's plays, as owing least to any definite sources for its plot. It is a comedy of contemporary manners, and most of its details seem to be original with Shakespeare.

There are two elements in the plot for which parallels can be found in contemporary English and Italian literature. The first of these is the incident of the women who discover that one gallant is courting them simultaneously, and their luring him on successively, only to make a laughingstock of him in the end. A story of this sort which Shakespeare may have seen is found in William Painter's *Palace of Pleasure,* published at London in 1566. The 49th tale in Painter's first volume is a free adaptation of an Italian story told by Straparola and by Ser Giovanni Fiorentino, whose novels were printed in Italy about 1550. In Painter's story, Philenio Sisterno, a scholar of Bologna, meets three ladies at a ball, and professes his devotion to each in turn. The ladies' discovery of his deceit and their determination to make a mockery of him have some slight resemblance to the story of Mrs. Ford and Mrs. Page and their revenge on Falstaff.

'Esmerentiana, the wife of Seignior Lamberto, not for any euill, but in sporting wise said vnto her companions: "Gentle-women, I have gotten this night in dauncing, a curteous louer, a very faire Gentleman, and of so good behauiour as any one in the world": and from point to point, (she) rehearsed vnto them all that he had said. Which Panthemia and Simphorosia vnder-standing, answered, that the like had chaunced vnto them, and they departed not from the feaste before eche of them knewe him that was their louer: whereby they perceiued that his woordes proceded not of faithful Loue, but rather of follie and dissimula-tion, and they separated not from thence vntill all three with one accorde, had conspired every one to give him mocke.' Each of the ladies then sends Philenio an invitation to visit her and each tricks him when he comes to her house. Esmerentiana's husband returns unexpectedly, and she claps Philenio into a hiding-place which she had filled with 'fagots of sharp thorns.' Panthemia leads him into a closet, and a loose board in the floor precipitates him into an outhouse, where he spends a miserable night. Sim-phorosia gives him drugged wine, which he drinks all unsus-pecting. Her servants then strip him and fling him into the street, where he lies unconscious until morning.

Another element in Shakespeare's plot, which may have been suggested by several contemporary stories, is that of the lover who unwittingly confides his plans to the jealous husband of his lady. This theme is found in the *Tale of the two lovers of Pisa* in Tarlton's *Newes out of Purgatorie,* a collection of stories published in 1590. In this tale, Mutio, an old doctor of Pisa, discovers that Lionello is courting Margaret, the beautiful woman he has just married. Lionello informs his friend of his plans for meeting Margaret, so Mutio is able to break in upon them each time. Margaret is quick of wit, and manages to conceal her lover—once

in a 'dry-vat' full of feathers; again 'between two ceilings of a chamber,' and finally in an old chest where valuable papers are stored. This time Mutio is sure Lionello is in the house, so he sets fire to the room, and Margaret saves her lover by bidding the servants carry out the chest.

Similar stories by Straparola and Ser Giovanni Fiorentino have interesting parallels to Mrs. Ford's trick of concealing Falstaff in the buck-basket. In these stories the wife makes use of 'a chest with clothes in front,' or 'a heap of wet clothes from the wash' for hiding her lover. But it is doubtful if English translations of them were available at the time *The Merry Wives* was written. A translation of one of them (printed in 1632) describes the hus-band in words that might apply to Shakespeare's Ford, as 'a person naturally inclin'd to jealousy (a passion extraordinarily reigning in Italy).' Recent scholars have been interested in ele-ments in the play that may be derived from ancient Roman comedy.

Except for such details as may be drawn from these sources, *The Merry Wives of Windsor* is of Shakespeare's own invention. It is the only one of his plays which deals exclusively with English country society.

THE HISTORY OF THE PLAY

The Merry Wives of Windsor was entered on the Stationers' Regis-ter on January 18, 1602. It was published the same year as a small Quarto, which was reprinted in 1619. The text of both is very corrupt. Comparison of them with the text of the Folio, published in 1623, seems to indicate that the publisher of the Quarto secured his version of the play by taking it down as best he could from the mouths of the players, perhaps with some assistance from one of them.

The play was probably written in 1599. In the epilogue to the *Second Part of Henry IV* (produced about 1598), Shakespeare had written: 'If you be not too much cloy'd with fat meat, our humble author will continue the story with Sir John in it . . . where for anything I know Falstaff shall die of a sweat, unless a' be killed already with your hard opinions.' *The Merry Wives* seems to offer the promised continuation of Sir John's adventures.

Two interesting traditions have long been current about the play. The first of these is that it was written at the command of Queen Elizabeth, and in a period of fourteen days. John Dennis, writing in 1702, says of the play: 'I know very well that it hath pleased one of the greatest queens that ever was in the world. . . . This comedy was written at her command, and by her direction, and she was so eager to see it acted that she commanded it to be finished in fourteen days; and was afterwards, as tradition tells us, very well pleased at the representation.' Rowe repeated the story in his *Life of Shakespeare,* adding of Queen Elizabeth: 'She

was so well pleased with that admirable character of Falstaff in the two parts of *Henry the Fourth,* that she commanded him to continue it for one play more, and to show him in love. This is said to be the occasion of his writing *The Merry Wives of Windsor.* How well she was obeyed, the play itself is an admirable proof.'

The other tradition is that in Justice Shallow, Shakespeare is satirizing Sir Thomas Lucy of Charlecote, near Stratford, who had prosecuted him in his youth for poaching. According to a note by Archdeacon Davies, written probably between 1688 and 1707, Shakespeare was 'much given to all unluckinesse in stealing venison and Rabbits particularly from Sr. Lucy, . . . but his reveng is so great that he is his Justice Clodpate, and calls him a great man and that in allusion to his name bore three lowses rampant for his Arms.' Rowe, in 1709, adds to this: 'Amongst other extravagancies, in *The Merry Wives of Windsor* he has made him a deer-stealer, that he might at the same time remember his Warwickshire prosecutor under the name of Justice Shallow; he has given him very near the same coat of arms which Dugdale, in his Antiquities of that county, describes for a family there, and makes the Welsh parson descant very pleasantly upon them.'

Of the earliest performances of the play we know from the title-page of the 1602 Quarto that it was 'divers times acted, both before her Majesty and elsewhere.' Shakespeare's company presented it at Whitehall before King James during the winter of 1604-1605; and another court performance occurred in 1612-1613. The play was presented before Charles I also; for in the records of Sir Henry Herbert is the entry: 'before the king and queene this yeare of our Lord 1638. . . . At the Cocpit the 15th of November. The merry wifes of winser.'

Of the actors in these productions we know nothing definite. John Heminge, a member of Shakespeare's company and one of editors of the 1623 Folio, is said to have been the original Falsaff; and after the Restoration John Lowen (1576-1659) was remembered as having excelled in the part 'before the wars.'

The Merry Wives was one of the first plays revived after the Commonwealth. On December 5, 1660, Pepys records seeing it with 'the humours of the country gentlemen and the French doctor very well done, but the rest but very poorly, and Sir J. Falstaffe as bad as any.' In 1661 he went again to the theatre 'such is the power of the Devil over me . . . and saw the Merry Wives ill done.' And in 1667 yet another production of the play 'did not please me at all in no part.'

When the Drury Lane Theatre opened in 1663 *The Merry Wives* was one of the productions which 'being well performed were very satisfactory to the town'; and forty years later John Dennis still remembered Wintersel's success as Falstaff 'in King Charles the Second's reign.'

In 1702 Dennis produced an adaptation of *The Merry Wives* under the title of *The Comical Gallant, or the Amours of Sir John Falstaff.* Falstaff's beating at the end of the play is shifted to Ford, to punish him for his jealousy, and Sir John is spared the humiliation of appearing in women's clothes, but he has a far more degrading part to play when he is bullied by Mrs. Page, disguised as a roistering captain. Dennis' piece 'was received but coldly,' and the original play was soon afterward successfully revived by Betterton, with Mrs. Bracegirdle, and later Peg Woffington, in the rôle of Mrs. Ford.

During the eighteenth century the part of Falstaff was ably interpreted by Quin, Henderson, and Cooke. Horace Walpole wrote on hearing of Quin's death, 'Pray, who is to give an idea of Falstaff, now Quin is dead?' John Henderson (1747-1785) won great applause in the part. Rogers in his table-talk says 'his Hamlet and his Falstaff were equally good.' Kemble revised the play in 1797, and successfully produced his version a few years later, playing Ford to the Falstaff of George Frederick Cooke. Cooke later visited the United States, where he died in 1811. *The Merry Wives* had already been produced in this country in 1770, at the Southwark Theatre in Philadelphia.

During the nineteenth century the play has been a favorite source for librettos for operas. In 1824 Frederick Reynolds was 'censured as an interpolator, for converting Shakespeare's plays into operas'; but his production of the *Merry Wives* ran for thirty-two performances at Drury Lane, and was a great success. In 1838 Balfe's opera, *Falstaff,* with an Italian libretto by Maggioni, was produced at London. Nine years later a German version, *Die lustigen Weiber von Windsor* with music by Nicolai, was given in Berlin. Nicolai's work was soon afterwards produced in Paris with some amusingly Gallic touches—Fenton is transformed into a young poet; Caius becomes a bullying captain; and Anne Page's character suffers by being made deceitful and dishonest. Perhaps to balance these French features *Rule Britannia* was introduced into a chorus toward the end of the piece. The greatest of the operatic versions of the play is Verdi's *Falstaff* (1893).

During all this time the original comedy has maintained its popularity on the stage. Among innumerable modern productions may be mentioned that at the New Theatre in New York (1910), and those of Sir Herbert Tree, who 'made Falstaff such a merry rogue that you forgot his cowardice and his grossness in laughing at his conceit and his mock bravery.' Tree's productions of the play in England and America were elaborately mounted, and generally accompanied by the music for the lyrics composed by Arthur Sullivan in 1874. The play is a favorite for amateur performances. It was presented by the Yale Dramatic Association in 1909.

ACT FIRST ❧ SCENE FIRST

[Windsor. Before Page's House]
Enter Justice Shallow, Slender, [and] Sir Hugh Evans; [and later]
Master Page, Falstaff, Bardolph, Nym, Pistol, Anne Page, Mistress
Ford, Mistress Page, [and] Simple.

Shal. Sir Hugh, persuade me not; I will make a Star-chamber matter of it; if he were twenty Sir John Falstaffs he shall not abuse Robert Shallow, esquire.

Slen. In the county of Gloucester, justice of peace, and *coram.* 5

Shal. Ay, cousin Slender, and *cust-alorum.*

Slen. Ay, and *rato-lorum* too; and a gentleman born, Master Parson; who writes himself *armigero,* in any bill, warrant, quittance, or obligation,—*armigero.*

Shal. Ay, that I do; and have done any time these three 10 hundred years.

Slen. All his successors gone before him hath done 't; and all his ancestors that come after him may: they may give the dozen white luces in their coat.

Shal. It is an old coat. 15

Eva. The dozen white louses do become an old coat well; it agrees well, *passant;* it is a familiar beast to man, and signifies love.

Shal. The luce is the fresh fish; the salt fish is an old coat.

Slen. I may quarter, coz? 20

Shal. You may, by marrying.

Eva. It is marring indeed, if he quarter it.

Shal. Not a whit.

Eva. Yes, py'r lady; if he has a quarter of your coat, there is but three skirts for yourself, in my simple conjectures: but that is all one. If Sir John Falstaff have committed disparagements unto you, I am of the Church, and will be glad to do my benevolence to make atonements and comprises between you.

Shal. The Council shall hear it; it is a riot.

Eva. It is not meet the Council hear a riot; there is no fear 30 of Got in a riot. The Council, look you, shall desire to hear the fear of Got, and not to hear a riot; take your vizaments in that.

Shal. Ha! o' my life, if I were young again, the sword should end it.

Eva. It is petter that friends is the sword, and end it; and 35 there is also another device in my prain, which, peradventure, prings goot discretions with it. There is Anne Page, which is daughter to Master Thomas Page, which is pretty virginity.

Slen. Mistress Anne Page? She has brown hair, and speaks small like a woman. 40

Eva. It is that fery person for all the 'orld, as just as you will desire; and seven hundred pounds of moneys, and gold and silver, is her grandsire, upon his death's-bed,—Got deliver to a joyful resurrections!—give, when she is able to overtake seventeen years old. It were a goot motion if we leave our 45 pribbles and prabbles, and desire a marriage between Master Abraham and Mistress Anne Page.

Shal. Did her grandsire leave her seven hundred pound?

Eva. Ay, and her father is make her a petter penny.

Shal. I know the young gentlewoman; she has good gifts. 50

Eva. Seven hundred pounds and possibilities is goot gifts.

Shal. Well, let us see honest Master Page. Is Falstaff there?

Eva. Shall I tell you a lie? I do despise a liar as I do despise one that is false; or as I despise one that is not true. The knight, Sir John, is there; and, I beseech you, be ruled by 55 your well-willers. I will peat the door for Master Page. *[Knocks.]* What, hoa! Got pless your house here!

Page. [Within.] Who's there?

Eva. Here is Got's plessing, and your friend, and Justice Shallow; and here young Master Slender, that peradventures 60 shall tell you another tale, if matters grow to your likings.

[Enter Page.]

Page. I am glad to see your worships well. I thank you for my venison, Master Shallow.

Shal. Master Page, I am glad to see you: much good do it your good heart! I wished your venison better; it was ill 65 killed. How doth good Mistress Page?—and I thank you always with my heart, la! with my heart.

Page. Sir, I thank you.

Shal. Sir, I thank you; by yea and no, I do.

Page. I am glad to see you, good Master Slender. 70

Slen. How does your fallow greyhound, sir? I heard say he was outrun on Cotsall.

Page. It could not be judged, sir.

Slen. You'll not confess, you'll not confess.

Shal. That he will not: 'tis your fault, 'tis your fault. 75 'Tis a good dog.

Page. A cur, sir.

Shal. Sir, he's a good dog, and a fair dog; can there be more said? he is good and fair. Is Sir John Falstaff here?

Page. Sir, he is within; and I would I could do a good 80 office between you.

Eva. It is spoke as a Christians ought to speak.

Shal. He hath wronged me, Master Page.

Page. Sir, he doth in some sort confess it.

Shal. If it be confessed, it is not redressed: is not that so, 85 Master Page? He hath wronged me; indeed, he hath;—at a word, he hath,—believe me: Robert Shallow, esquire, saith, he is wronged.

Page. Here comes Sir John.

[Enter Sir John Falstaff, Pistol, Bardolph, and Nym.]

Fal. Now, Master Shallow, you'll complain of me to the 90 king?

Shal. Knight, you have beaten my men, killed my deer, and broke open my lodge.

Fal. But not kissed your keeper's daughter?

Shal. Tut, a pin! this shall be answered. 95

Fal. I will answer it straight: I have done all this. That is now answered.

Shal. The Council shall know this.

Fal. 'Twere better for you if it were known in counsel: you'll be laughed at. 100

SCENE ONE S. d.; *cf. n.*   **Sir:** *old title for a priest,*   **1, 2 Star-chamber matter;** *cf. n.*   **5** **coram;** *cf. n.*   **6, 7 cust-alorum . . . rato-lorum;** *cf. n.*   **8 armigero:** *esquire* **bill:** *bill of exchange* **quittance:** *discharge from debt*   **13 give:** *display*   **14 luces:** *pikes (fish); cf. n.*   **17 passant:** *walking* (heraldry)   **19** *Cf. n.*   **20 quarter;** *cf. n.*   **28 compremises:** *i.e., compromises*   **29 Council:** *i.e., the Privy Council sitting in Star Chamber*   **32 vizaments:** *i.e., avisements, deliberations*   **39 Mistress:** *formal title for women*   **40 small:** *shrilly*   **41 'orld:** *i.e., world*   **46 pribbles and prabbles:** *quibbles and brabbles* (?), *i.e., petty disputings*

50 gifts: *qualities of mind*   **51 possibilities:** *expectations*   **71 fallow:** *fawn-color*   **72 Cotsall;** *cf. n.*   **75 fault:** *misfortune*   **95 pin:** *trifle* **answered:** *atoned for*   **96 straight:** *immediately*   **99 in counsel:** *in secret*

Eva. *Pauca verba*, Sir John; goot worts.

Fal. Good worts! good cabbage. Slender, I broke your head: what matter have you against me?

Slen. Marry, sir, I have matter in my head against you; and against your cony-catching rascals, Bardolph, Nym, and Pistol. [They carried me to the tavern, and made me drunk, and afterwards picked my pocket.]   105

Bard. You Banbury cheese!

Slen. Ay, it is no matter.

Pist. How now, Mephistophilus!   110

Slen. Ay, it is no matter.

Nym. Slice, I say! *pauca, pauca*; slice! that's my humour.

Slen. Where's Simple, my man? can you tell, cousin?

Eva. Peace, I pray you. Now let us understand: there is three umpires in this matter, as I understand; that is—   115
Master Page, *fidelicet*, Master Page; and there is myself, *fidelicet*, myself; and the three party is, lastly and finally, mine host of the Garter.

Page. We three, to hear it and end it between them.

Eva. Fery goot: I will make a prief of it in my note-   120
book; and we will afterwards 'ork upon the cause with as great discreetly as we can.

Fal. Pistol!

Pist. He hears with ears.

Eva. The tevil and his tam! what phrase is this, 'He   125
hears with ear'? Why, it is affectations.

Fal. Pistol, did you pick Master Slender's purse?

Slen. Ay, by these gloves, did he,—or I would I might never come in mine own great chamber again else,—of seven groats in mill-sixpences, and two Edward shovel-boards, that cost   130
me two shilling and two pence a-piece of Yead Miller, by these gloves.

Fal. Is this true, Pistol?

Eva. No; it is false, if it is a pick-purse.

Pist. Ha, thou mountain foreigner!—Sir John and master   135
mine,
I combat challenge of this latten bilbo.
Word of denial in thy labras here!
Word of denial: froth and scum, thou liest.

Slen. By these gloves, then, 'twas he.   140

Nym. Be avised, sir, and pass good humours. I will say, 'marry trap,' with you, if you run the nuthook's humour on me: that is the very note of it.

Slen. By this hat, then, he in the red face had it; for though I cannot remember what I did when you made me drunk,   145
yet I am not altogether an ass.

Fal. What say you, Scarlet and John?

Bard. Why, sir, for my part, I say, the gentleman had drunk himself out of his five sentences.

Eva. It is his 'five senses'; fie, what the ignorance is!   150

Bard. And being fap, sir, was, as they say, cashier'd; and so conclusions pass'd the careires.

Slen. Ay, you spake in Latin then too; but 'tis no matter.

I'll ne'er be drunk whilst I live again, but in honest, civil, godly company, for this trick: if I be drunk, I'll be drunk with those that have the fear of God, and not with drunken knaves.

Eva. So Got udge me, that is a virtuous mind.

Fal. You hear all these matters denied, gentlemen; you hear it.

[Enter Anne Page with wine; Mistress Ford and Mistress Page following.]

Page. Nay, daughter, carry the wine in; we'll drink   160
within.

[Exit Anne Page.]

Slen. O heaven! this is Mistress Anne Page.

Page. How now, Mistress Ford!

Fal. Mistress Ford, by my troth, you are very well met: by your leave, good mistress.   *[Kisses her.]* 165

Page. Wife, bid these gentlemen welcome. Come, we have a hot venison pasty to dinner: come, gentlemen, I hope we shall drink down all unkindness.   *[Exeunt all except Shallow, Slender, and Evans.]*

Slen. I had rather than forty shillings I had my Book of Songs and Sonnets here.   170

[Enter Simple.]

How now, Simple! Where have you been? I must wait on myself, must I? You have not the Book of Riddles about you, have you?

Sim. Book of Riddles! why, did you not lend it to Alice Shortcake upon All-Hallowmas last, a fortnight afore   175
Michaelmas?

Shal. Come, coz; come, coz; we stay for you. A word with you, coz; marry, this, coz: there is, as 'twere a tender, a kind of tender, made afar off by Sir Hugh here: do you understand me?   180

Slen. Ay, sir, you shall find me reasonable: if it be so, I shall do that that is reason.

Shal. Nay, but understand me.

Slen. So I do, sir.

Eva. Give ear to his motions, Master Slender: I will   185
description the matter to you, if you pe capacity of it.

Slen. Nay, I will do as my cousin Shallow says. I pray you pardon me; he's a justice of peace in his country, simple though I stand here.

Eva. But that is not the question; the question is   190
concerning your marriage.

Shal. Ay, there's the point, sir.

Eva. Marry, is it, the very point of it; to Mistress Anne Page.

Slen. Why, if it be so, I will marry her upon any   195
reasonable demands.

Eva. But can you affection the 'oman? Let us command to know that of your mouth or of your lips; for divers philosophers hold that the lips is parcel of the mouth: therefore, precisely, can you carry your good will to the maid?   200

Shal. Cousin Abraham Slender, can you love her?

Slen. I hope, sir, I will do as it shall become one that would do reason.

101 **Pauca verba:** *few words* **worts:** *i.e., words* 102 **worts:** *vegetables* 105 **cony-catch-ing:** *cheating* 106, 107 **They ... pocket:** *cf. n.* 108 **Banbury cheese:** *cf. n.* 110 **Mephistophilus:** *devil; cf. n.* 112 **Slice:** *of cheese* (?); *cf. n.* **humour:** *cf. n.* 116 **fidelicet:** *i.e., videlicet, namely* 118 **Garter:** *an inn at Windsor* 129 **great chamber:** *hall* **groats:** *coins valued at fourpence* 130 **mill-sixpences:** *coins with raised borders* **Ed-ward shovel-boards:** *broad shillings; cf. n.* 131 **Yead:** *abbreviation of Edward* 135 **mountain foreigner:** *Welshman* 137 **latten bilbo:** *brass sword* 138 **labras:** *lips* 141 **avised:** *advised* 142 **marry trap:** *be off with you* (?) 142 **run ... humour:** *cf. n.* 143 **very note:** *exact information* 147 **Scarlet and John:** *cf. n.* 151 **fap:** *drunk* **cashier'd:** *slang for robbed* 152 **careires:** *cf. n.*

157 **udge:** *i.e., judge* 170, 171 **Book of Songs and Sonnets:** *cf. n.* 175 **All-Hallowmas:** *All Saints' Day, November 1* 176 **Michaelmas:** *St. Michael's Day, September 29* 177 **stay:** *wait* 178 **tender:** *offer* 179 **afar off:** *indirectly* 188, 189 **simple though:** *as sure as* 199 **parcel:** *part*

Eva. Nay, Got's lords and his ladies! you must speak possable, if you can carry her your desires towards her.　205

Shal. That you must. Will you, upon good dowry, marry her?

Slen. I will do a greater thing than that, upon your request, cousin, in any reason.

Shal. Nay, conceive me, conceive me, sweet coz: what I　210 do, is to pleasure you, coz. Can you love the maid?

Slen. I will marry her, sir, at your request; but if there be no great love in the beginning, yet heaven may decrease it upon better acquaintance, when we are married and have more occasion to know one another: I hope, upon familiarity　215 will grow more contempt: but if you say, 'Marry her,' I will marry her; that I am freely dissolved, and dissolutely.

Eva. It is a fery discretion answer; save, the faul is in the 'ort 'dissolutely': the 'ort is, according to our meaning, 'resolutely.' His meaning is goot.　220

Shal. Ay, I think my cousin meant well.

Slen. Ay, or else I would I might be hanged, la!

Shal. Here comes fair Mistress Anne.

[Enter Anne Page.]

Would I were young for your sake, Mistress Anne.

Anne. The dinner is on the table; my father desires　225 your worships' company.

Shal. I will wait on him, fair Mistress Anne.

Eva. Od's plessed will! I will not be absence at the grace.

　　　　　　　　　　　[Exeunt Shallow and Evans.]

Anne. Will 't please your worship to come in, sir?

Slen. No, I thank you, forsooth, heartily; I am very well.　230

Anne. The dinner attends you, sir.

Slen. I am not a-hungry, I thank you forsooth. Go, sirrah, for all you are my man, go wait upon my cousin Shallow. *[Exit Simple.]* A justice of peace sometime may be beholding to his friend for a man. I keep but three men and a boy yet, till my mother be dead; but what though? yet I live like a poor gentleman born.

Anne. I may not go in without your worship: they will not sit till you come.　240

Slen. I' faith, I'll eat nothing; I thank you as much as though I did.

Anne. I pray you, sir, walk in.

Slen. I had rather walk here, I thank you. I bruised my shin th' other day with playing at sword and dagger with　245 a master of fence; three veneys for a dish of stewed prunes;— and, by my troth, I cannot abide the smell of hot meat since. Why do your dogs bark so? be there bears i' the town?

Anne. I think there are, sir; I heard them talked of.

Slen. I love the sport well; but I shall as soon quarrel　250 at it as any man in England. You are afraid, if you see the bear loose, are you not?

Anne. Ay, indeed, sir.

Slen. That's meat and drink to me, now: I have seen Sackerson loose twenty times, and have taken him by the　255 chain; but, I warrant you, the women have so cried and shrieked at it, that it passed: but women, indeed, cannot abide 'em; they are very ill-favoured rough things.

[Enter Page.]

Page. Come, gentle Master Slender, come; we stay for you.

Slen. I'll eat nothing, I thank you, sir.　260

Page. By cock and pie, you shall not choose, sir! come, come.

Slen. Nay, pray you, lead the way.

Page. Come on, sir.

Slen. Mistress Anne, yourself shall go first.　265

Anne. Not I, sir; pray you, keep on.

Slen. Truly, I will not go first: truly, la! I will not do you that wrong.

Anne. I pray you, sir.

Slen. I'll rather be unmannerly than trouble-some. You　270 do yourself wrong, indeed, la!　　　　　　　　*Exeunt.*

❧ Scene Second ❧

[The Same]
Enter Evans and Simple.

Eva. Go your ways, and ask of Doctor Caius' house, which is the way: and there dwells one Mistress Quickly, which is in the manner of his nurse, or his try nurse, or his cook, or his laundry, his washer, and his wringer.

Sim. Well, sir.　5

Eva. Nay, it is petter yet. Give her this letter; for it is a 'oman that altogether's acquaintance with Mistress Anne Page: and the letter is, to desire and require her to solicit your master's desires to Mistress Anne Page. I pray you, be gone: I will make an end of my dinner; there's pippins and seese to come.

　　　　　　　　　　　　　　　　　　　Exeunt

❧ Scene Third ❧

[A Room in the Garter Inn]
Enter Falstaff, Host, Bardolph, Nym, Pistol, [and] Page [Robin].

Fal. Mine host of the Garter!

Host. What says my bully-rook? Speak scholarly and wisely.

Fal. Truly, mine host, I must turn away some of my followers.

Host. Discard, bully Hercules; cashier: let them wag; trot,　5 trot.

Fal. I sit at ten pounds a week.

Host. Thou'rt an emperor, Cæsar, Keisar, and Pheezar. I will entertain Bardolph; he shall draw, he shall tap: said I well, bully Hector?　10

Fal. Do so, good mine host.

Host. I have spoke; let him follow. *[To Bardolph.]* Let me see thee froth and lime: I am at a word; follow.　　　*[Exit.]*

Fal. Bardolph, follow him. A tapster is a good trade: an old cloak makes a new jerkin; a withered serving-man, a fresh　15 tapster. Go; adieu.

Bard. It is life that I have desired. I will thrive.

---

205 **possable:** *i.e., positively*　210 **conceive:** *understand*　211 **pleasure:** *please*　218 **faul:** *i.e., fault*　219 **'ort:** *i.e., word*　228 **Od's** *i.e., God's*　231 **attends:** *awaits*　232 **sirrah:** *fellow*　246 **fence:** *fencing*　**veneys:** *fencing-bouts*　250 **the sport:** *i.e., bear-baiting*　255 **Sackerson;** *cf. n.*　257 **passed:** *beat everything*　258 **ill-favoured:** *ugly*

261 **By cock and pye:** *a petty oath*　3 **manner:** *capacity*　10 **seese:** *i.e., cheese*　2 **bully-rook:** *fine fellow (slang)*　5 **wag:** *go their way*　7 **I sit at:** *my expenses are*　8 **Keisar, and Pheezar;** *cf. n.*　9 **entertain:** *employ as servant*　**draw:** *draw liquor*　**tap:** *act as tapster*　13 **froth and lime;** *cf. n.*　**at a word:** *reader*　15 **jerkin:** *jacket*

Pist. O base Hungarian wight! wilt thou the spigot wield?

[Exit Bardolph.]

Nym. He was gotten in drink; is not the humour conceited?

Fal. I am glad I am so acquit of this tinderbox; his thefts   20
were too open; his filching was like an unskilful singer; he
kept not time.

Nym. The good humour is to steal at a minim's rest.

Pist. 'Convey,' the wise it call. 'Steal!' foh! a fico for the
phrase!   25

Fal. Well, sirs, I am almost out at heels.

Pist. Why, then, let kibes ensue.

Fal. There is no remedy; I must cony-catch, I must shift.

Pist. Young ravens must have food.

Fal. Which of you know Ford of this town?   30

Pist. I ken the wight: he is of substance good.

Fal. My honest lads, I will tell you what I am about.

Pist. Two yards, and more.

Fal. No quips now, Pistol! Indeed, I am in the waist two
yards about; but I am now about no waste; I am about   35
thrift. Briefly, I do mean to make love to Ford's wife: I spy
entertainment in her; she discourses, she carves, she gives the
leer of invitation: I can construe the action of her familiar
style; and the hardest voice of her behaviour, to be Englished
rightly, is, 'I am Sir John Falstaff's.'   40

Pist. He hath studied her well, and translated her well,
out of honesty into English.

Nym. The anchor is deep: will that humour pass?

Fal. Now, the report goes she has all the rule of her
husband's purse; he hath a legion of angels.   45

Pist. As many devils entertain, and 'To her, boy,' say I.

Nym. The humour rises; it is good: humour me the angels.

Fal. I have writ me here a letter to her; and here another to
Page's wife, who even now gave me good eyes too, examined
my parts with most judicious œillades: sometimes the beam   50
of her view gilded my foot, sometimes my portly belly.

Pist. Then did the sun on dunghill shine.

Nym. I thank thee for that humour.

Fal. O! she did so course o'er my exteriors with such a
greedy intention, that the appetite of her eye did seem to   55
scorch me up like a burning-glass. Here's another letter to her:
she bears the purse too; she is a region in Guiana, all gold and
bounty. I will be 'cheater to them both, and they shall be ex-
chequers to me: they shall be my East and West Indies, and I
will trade to them both. Go bear thou this letter to Mistress   60
Page; and thou this to Mistress Ford. We will thrive, lads,
we will thrive.

Pist. Shall I Sir Pandarus of Troy become, And by my side
wear steel? then, Lucifer take all!

Nym. I will run no base humour: here, take the humour-   65
letter. I will keep the haviour of reputation.

Fal. [To Robin.] Hold, sirrah, bear you these letters tightly:
Sail like my pinnace to these golden shores
Rogues, hence! avaunt! vanish like hailstones, go;

Trudge, plod away o' the hoof; seek shelter, pack!   70
Falstaff will learn the humour of this age,
French thrift, you rogues: myself and skirted page.

[Exeunt Falstaff and Robin.]

Pist. Let vultures gripe thy guts! for gourd and fullam holds,
And high and low beguile the rich and poor.
Tester I'll have in pouch when thou shalt lack,   75
Base Phrygian Turk!

Nym. I have operations [in my head,] which be humours
of revenge.

Pist. Wilt thou revenge?

Nym. By welkin and her star!   80

Pist. With wit or steel?

Nym. With both the humours, I:
I will discuss the humour of this love to Page.

Pist.   And I to Ford shall eke unfold
How Falstaff, varlet vile,   85
His dove will prove, his gold will hold,
And his soft couch defile.

Nym. My humour shall not cool: I will incense Page to deal
with poison; I will possess him with yellowness, for the
revolt of mine is dangerous: that is my true humour.   90

Pist. Thou art the Mars of malcontents: I second thee;
troop on.   *[Exeunt.]*

❧ SCENE FOURTH ❧

[A Room in Doctor Caius's House]
Enter Mistress Quickly, Simple, [and] John Rugby; [and later]
Doctor Caius, and Fenton.

Quick. What, John Rugby!—
I pray thee, go to the casement, and see if you can see my
master, Master Doctor Caius, coming: if he do, i' faith, and
find anybody in the house, here will be an old abusing of
God's patience and the king's English.   5

Rug. I'll go watch.

Quick. Go: and we'll have a posset for 't soon at night, in
faith, at the latter end of a sea-coal fire. *[Exit Rugby.]* An honest, willing, kind fellow, as ever servant shall come in house
withal; and, I warrant you, no tell-tale, nor no breed-bate: 10
his worst fault is, that he is given to prayer; he is something
peevish that way, but nobody but has his fault; but let that
pass. Peter Simple you say your name is?

Sim. Ay, for fault of a better.

Quick. And Master Slender's your master?   15

Sim. Ay, forsooth.

Quick. Does he not wear a great round beard like a glover's
paring-knife?

Sim. No, forsooth: he hath but a little whey-face, with a
little yellow beard—a Cain-coloured beard.   20

Quick. A softly-sprighted man, is he not?

Sim. Ay, forsooth; but he is as tall a man of his hands as

---

18 wight: *man; cf. n.*   **19 gotten:** *begotten*   **conceited:** *ingenious*   **20 acquit:**
rid   **23 minim's rest:** *time of a half measure* (music)   **24 Convey:** *thieves' slang for*
steal   **fico:** *fig*   **26 out at heels:** *out of money*   **27 kibes:** *chilblains*   **28 shift:**
devise a trick   **31 ken:** *know*   **37 carves:** *shows courtesy*   **38 action:** *gesture*   **42**
honesty: *chastity*   **43 anchor ... deep;** *cf. n.*   **45 angels:** *gold coins valued at about*
half a sovereign   **50 œillades:** *amorous glances*   **57 Guiana;** *cf. n.*   **58 'cheater;**
cf. n.   **63 Sir Pandarus;** *cf. n.*   **66 haviour:** *behavior*   **67 tightly:** *safely*   **69**
avaunt: *be off*

70 pack: *depart*   **72 French thrift;** *cf. n.*   **skirted:** *wearing a coat with skirts*   **73 gourd**
and fullam; *cf. n.*   **74 high and low:** *i.e., high and low numbers on dice*   **75 Tester:**
sixpence   **pouch:** *purse*   **80 welkin:** *sky*   **83 discuss:** *tell*   **88, 89 deal with:** *em-*
ploy   **possess ... yellowness:** *make him jealous*   **89, 90 the revolt of mine:** *i.e., my*
revolt   **4 old:** *great*   **7 posset:** *hot milk curdled with ale*   **soon at night:** *as soon as*
night comes   **8 sea-coal:** *mineral coal* (i.e., not charcoal) *brought by sea*   **10 withal:**
with   **breed-bate:** *mischief-maker*   **12 peevish:** *silly*   **14 fault:** *lack*   **20 Cain-**
coloured; *cf. n.*   **21 softly-sprighted:** *gentle* (?)   **22 tall:** *valiant*

any is between this and his head: he hath fought with a
warrener.

Quick. How say you?—O! I should remember him: does   25
he not hold up his head, as it were, and strut in his gait?

Sim. Yes, indeed, does he.

Quick. Well, heaven send Anne Page no worse fortune! Tell
Master Parson Evans I will do what I can for your master:
Anne is a good girl, and I wish—   30

[Enter Rugby.]

Rug. Out, alas! here comes my master.

Quick. We shall all be shent. Run in here, good young man;
go into this closet. He will not stay long *[Shuts Simple in the
closet.]* What, John Rugby! John, what, John, I say! Go, John,
go inquire for my master; I doubt he be not well, that he   35
comes not home.   *[Exit Rugby.] [Singing.]*
'And down, down, adown-a,' &c.

[Enter Doctor Caius.]

Caius. Vat is you sing? I do not like dese toys. Pray you, go
and vetch me in my closet *une boitine verde*; a box, a green-a
box: do intend vat I speak? a green-a box.   40

Quick. Ay, forsooth; I'll fetch it you. *[Aside.]* I am glad he
went not in himself: if he had found the young man, he
would have been horn-mad.

Caius. Fe, fe, fe, fe! ma foi, il fait fort chaud. Je m'en vais à
la cour,—la grande affaire.   45

Quick. Is it this, sir?

Caius. Oui; mettez le au mon pocket; dé-pêchez, quickly.—
Vere is dat knave Rugby?

Quick. What, John Rugby! John!

[Enter Rugby.]

Rug. Here, sir.   50

Caius. You are John Rugby, and you are Jack Rugby: come,
take-a your rapier, and come after my heel to de court.

Rug. 'Tis ready, sir, here in the porch.

Caius. By my trot, I tarry too long.—Od's me! Qu'ay
j'oublié? dere is some simples in my closet, dat I will not   55
for de varld I shall leave behind.

Quick. *[Aside]* Ay me! he'll find the young man there,
and be mad.

Caius. O diable! diable! vat is in my closet?—Villain! larron!
[Pulling Simple out.] Rugby, my rapier!   60

Quick. Good master, be content.

Caius. Verefore shall I be content-a?

Quick. The young man is an honest man.

Caius. Vat shall de honest man do in my closet? dere is
no honest man dat shall come in my closet.   65

Quick. I beseech you, be not so phlegmatic. Hear the truth
of it: he came of an errand to me from Parson Hugh.

Caius. Vell.

Sim. Ay, forsooth, to desire her to—

Quick. Peace, I pray you.   70

Caius. Peace-a your tongue!—Speak-a your tale.

Sim. To desire this honest gentlewoman, your maid, to
speak a good word to Mistress Anne Page for my master in
the way of marriage.

Quick. This is all, indeed, la! but I'll ne'er put my finger   75
in the fire, and need not.

Caius. Sir Hugh send-a you?—Rugby, *baillez* me some
paper: tarry you little-a while. *[Writes.]*

Quick. *[Aside to Simple.]* I am glad he is so quiet: if he had
been throughly moved, you should have heard him so loud,   80
and so melancholy. But, notwithstanding, man, I'll do your
master what good I can; and the very yea and the no is, the
French doctor, my master,—I may call him my master, look
you, for I keep his house; and I wash, wring, brew, bake,
scour, dress meat and drink, make the beds, and do all   85
myself,—

Sim. *[Aside to Quickly.]* 'Tis a great charge to come under
one body's hand.

Quick. *[Aside to Simple.]* Are you avis'd o' that? you shall
find it a great charge: and to be up early and down late;   90
but notwithstanding,—to tell you in your ear,—I would have
no words of it,—my master himself is in love with Mistress
Anne Page: but notwithstanding that, I know Anne's mind,
that's neither here nor there.

Caius. You jack'nape, give-a dis letter to Sir Hugh; by   95
gar, it is a challenge: I vill cut his troat in de Park; and I vill
teach a scurvy jack-a-nape priest to meddle or make. You may
be gone; it is not good you tarry here: by gar, I vill cut all his
two stones; by gar, he shall not have a stone to trow at his dog.
                    [Exit Simple.]

Quick. Alas! he speaks but for his friend.   100

Caius. It is no matter-a for dat:—do not you tell-a me dat
I shall have Anne Page for myself? By gar, I vill kill de Jack
priest; and I have appointed mine host of de *Jartiere* to
measure our weapon. By gar, I vill myself have Anne Page.

Quick. Sir, the maid loves you, and all shall be well.   105
We must give folks leave to prate: what, the good-jer!

Caius. Rugby, come to the court vit me. By gar, if I have
not Anne Page, I shall turn your head out of my door. Follow
my heels, Rugby.   *[Exeunt Caius and Rugby.]*

Quick. You shall have An fool's-head of your own. No,   110
I know Anne's mind for that: never a woman in Windsor
knows more of Anne's mind than I do; nor can do more
than I do with her, I thank heaven.

Fent. *[Within.]* Who's within there? ho!

Quick. Who's there, I trow? Come near the house,   115
I pray you.

[Enter Fenton.]

Fent. How now, good woman! how dost thou?

Quick. The better, that it pleases your good worship to ask.

Fent. What news? how does pretty Mistress Anne?

Quick. In truth, sir, and she is pretty, and honest, and   120
gentle; and one that is your friend, I can tell you that by
the way; I praise heaven for it.

Fent. Shall I do any good, thinkest thou? Shall I not lose
my suit?

Quick. Troth, sir, all is in his hands above; but notwith-   125
standing, Master Fenton, I'll be sworn on a book, she loves
you. Have not your worship a wart above your eye?

Fent. Yes, marry have I; what of that?

---

24 **warrener:** *gamekeeper*   32 **shent:** *scolded*   35 **doubt:** *fear*   38 **toys:** *foolish
things*   40 **intend:** *hear* (Fr. entendre)   43 **horn-mad:** *stark-mad*   54 **trot:**
troth   55 **simples:** *medicinal herbs*   66 **phlegmatic:** *i.e., choleric* (?)

77 **baillez:** *fetch*   80 **throughly:** *thoroughly*   87 **charge:** *burden*   95 **jack'nape:** *coxcomb*   97 **meddle or make:** *interfere*   102 **Jack:** *term of contempt*   104 **measure our
weapon:** *i.e., as umpire in a duel*   106 **good-jer:** *an expression of disgust*   110 **An fool's-
head;** *cf. n.*   115 **trow:** *wonder*   **Come near:** *enter*   120 **honest:** *chaste*

Quick. Well, thereby hangs a tale. Good faith, it is such another Nan; but, I detest, an honest maid as ever broke   *130* bread: we had an hour's talk of that wart. I shall never laugh but in that maid's company;—but, indeed, she is given too much to allicholy and musing. But for you—well, go to.

Fent. Well, I shall see her to-day. Hold, there's money for thee; let me have thy voice in my behalf: if thou seest her   *135* before me, commend me.

Quick. Will I? i' faith, that we will: and I will tell your worship more of the wart the next time we have confidence; and of other wooers.

Fent. Well, farewell; I am in great haste now.   *140*

Quick. Farewell to your worship. [*Exit Fenton.*] Truly, an honest gentleman: but Anne loves him not; for I know Anne's mind as well as another does. Out upon 't! what have I forgot?

Exit.

ACT SECOND ❧ SCENE FIRST

[Before Page's House]

Enter Mistress Page, [with a letter; and later] Mistress Ford, Master Page, Master Ford, Pistol, Nym, [Mistress] Quickly, Host, [and] Shallow.

Mrs. Page. What! have I 'scaped love-letters in the holiday-time of my beauty, and am I now a subject for them? Let me see.   [*Reads.*]

'Ask me no reason why I love you; for though Love use Reason for his physician, he admits him not for his counsellor.   *5* You are not young, no more am I; got to then, there's sympathy; you are merry, so am I; ha! ha! then, there's more sympathy; you love sack, and so do I; would you desire better sympathy? Let it suffice thee, Mistress Page, at the least, if the love of a soldier can suffice, that I love thee. I will not say,   *10* pity me,—'tis not a soldier-like phrase; but I say, love me. By me,

> *Thine own true knight,*
> *By day or night,*
> *Or any kind of light,*   *15*
> *With all his might*
> *For thee to fight,* JOHN FALSTAFF.'

What a Herod of Jewry is this! O wicked, wicked world! one that is well-nigh worn to pieces with age, to show himself a young gallant! What an unweighed behaviour hath this   *20* Flemish drunkard picked, with the devil's name! out of my conversation, that he dares in this manner assay me? Why, he hath not been thrice in my company! What should I say to him? I was then frugal of my mirth:—heaven forgive me! Why, I'll exhibit a bill in the parliament for the putting down of   *25* men. How shall I be revenged on him? for revenged I will be, as sure as his guts are made of puddings.

[Enter Mistress Ford.]

Mrs. Ford. Mistress Page! trust me, I was going to your house.

Mrs. Page. And, trust me, I was coming to you. You look   *30* very ill.

Mrs. Ford. Nay, I'll ne'er believe that: I have to show to the contrary.

Mrs. Page. Faith, but you do, in my mind.

Mrs. Ford. Well, I do then; yet, I say I could show you   *35* to the contrary. O, Mistress Page! give me some counsel.

Mrs. Page. What's the matter, woman?

Mrs. Ford. O woman, if it were not for one trifling respect, I could come to such honour!

Mrs. Page. Hang the trifle, woman; take the honour.   *40* What is it?—dispense with trifles;—what is it?

Mrs. Ford. If I would but go to hell for an eternal moment or so, I could be knighted.

Mrs. Page. What? thou liest. Sir Alice Ford! These knights will hack; and so thou shouldst not alter the article of thy   *45* gentry.

Mrs. Ford. We burn daylight: here, read, read; perceive how I might be knighted. I shall think the worse of fat men as long as I have an eye to make difference of men's liking: and yet he would not swear; praised women's modesty; and gave   *50* such orderly and well-behaved reproof to all uncomeliness, that I would have sworn his disposition would have gone to the truth of his words; but they do no more adhere and keep place together than the Hundredth Psalm to the tune of 'Green Sleeves.' What tempest, I trow, threw this whale, with so   *55* many tuns of oil in his belly, ashore at Windsor? How shall I be revenged on him? I think, the best way were to entertain him with hope, till the wicked fire of lust have melted him in his own grease. Did you ever hear the like?

Mrs. Page. Letter for letter, but that the name of Page and Ford differs! To thy great comfort in this mystery of ill opinions, here's the twin brother of thy letter: but let thine inherit first; for, I protest, mine never shall. I warrant, he hath a thousand of these letters, writ with blank space for different names, sure more, and these are the second edition. He will print   *65* them, out of doubt; for he cares not what he puts into the press, when he would put us two: I had rather be a giantess, and lie under Mount Pelion. Well, I will find you twenty lascivious turtles ere one chaste man.

Mrs. Ford. Why, this is the very same; the very hand,   *70* the very words. What doth he think of us?

Mrs. Page. Nay, I know not: it makes me almost ready to wrangle with mine own honesty. I'll entertain myself like one that I am not acquainted withal; for, sure, unless he know some strain in me, that I know not myself, he would never   *75* have boarded me in this fury.

Mrs. Ford. Boarding call you it? I'll be sure to keep him above deck.

Mrs. Page. So will I: if he come under my hatches, I'll never to sea again. Let's be revenged on him: let's appoint him a   *80* meeting; give him a show of comfort in his suit, and lead him on with a fine-baited delay, till he hath pawned his horses to mine host of the Garter.

Mrs. Ford. Nay, I will consent to act any villany against him, that may not sully the chariness of our honesty. O,   *85*

---

133 allicholy: *i.e., melancholy* **go to:** *no more of that!*   **6, 7 sympathy:** *agreement*   **8 sack:** *white Spanish wine*   **18 Herod of Jewry;** *cf. n.*   **20 unweighed:** *inconsiderate* **Flemish drunkard;** *cf. n.*   **21 conversation:** *conduct*   **24 exhibit:** *submit for consideration*   **25 putting down:** *destroying*   **27 puddings:** *stuffed intestines, sausages*

45 hack: *grow common* (?); *cf. n.* **article . . . gentry:** *character of your rank*   **47 burn daylight:** *waste time*   **49 make difference:** *discriminate between* **liking:** *looks*   **51 uncomeliness:** *rude behavior*   **52, 53 disposition . . . words;** *cf. n.*   **53 adhere:** *agree*   **54 Green Sleeves;** *cf. n.*   **57 entertain:** *fill his thoughts*   **69 turtles:** *turtle doves, symbolic of faithful love*   **73 entertain:** *treat*   **82 fine-baited:** *subtly alluring*   **85 chariness:** *scrupulous integrity*

that my husband saw this letter! it would give eternal food
to his jealousy.

Mrs. Page. Why, look where he comes; and my good man
too: he's as far from jealousy, as I am from giving him cause;
and that, I hope, is an unmeasurable distance.   90

Mrs. Ford. You are the happier woman.

Mrs. Page. Let's consult together against this greasy knight.
Come hither.   *[They retire.]*

[Enter Ford, with Pistol; and Page, with Nym.]

Ford. Well, I hope it be not so.

Pist. Hope is a curtal dog in some affairs: Sir John   95
affects thy wife.

Ford. Why, sir, my wife is not young.

Pist. He woos both high and low, both rich and poor,
Both young and old, one with another, Ford.
He loves the galimaufry: Ford, perpend.   100

Ford. Love my wife!

Pist. With liver burning hot: prevent, or go thou,
Like Sir Actæon he, with Ringwood at thy heels.—
O! odious is the name!

Ford. What name, sir?   105

Pist. The horn, I say. Farewell:
Take heed; have open eye, for thieves do foot by night:
Take heed, ere summer comes or cuckoo-birds do sing.
Away, sir Corporal Nym!
Believe it, Page; he speaks sense.   *[Exit.]*

Ford. *[Aside.]* I will be patient: I will find out this.

Nym. *[To Page.]* And this is true; I like not the humour of
lying. He hath wronged me in some humours: I should have
borne the humoured letter to her, but I have a sword and
it shall bite upon my necessity. He loves your wife; there's   115
the short and the long. My name is Corporal Nym; I speak,
and I avouch 'tis true: my name is Nym, and Falstaff loves
your wife. Adieu. I love not the humour of bread and cheese;
[and there's the humour of it.] Adieu.   *[Exit.]*

Page. 'The humour of it,' quoth 'a! here's a fellow   120
frights humour out of his wits.

Ford. I will seek out Falstaff.

Page. I never heard such a drawling, affecting rogue.

Ford. If I do find it: well.

Page. I will not believe such a Cataian, though the   125
priest o' the town commended him for a true man.

Ford. 'Twas a good sensible fellow; well.

Page. How now, Meg!

[Mrs. Page and Mrs. Ford come forward.]

Mrs. Page. Whither go you, George?—Hark you.

Mrs. Ford. How now, sweet Frank! why art thou melancholy?

Ford. I melancholy! I am not melancholy. Get you home, go.

Mrs. Ford. Faith, thou hast some crotchets in thy head now.
Will you go, Mistress Page?

Mrs. Page. Have with you. You'll come to dinner, George?
[Aside to Mrs. Ford.] Look, who comes yonder: she shall be our
messenger to this paltry knight.

Mrs. Ford. *[Aside to Mrs. Page.]* Trust me, I thought on her:
she'll fit it.

[Enter Mistress Quickly.]

Mrs. Page. You are come to see my daughter Anne?

Quick. Ay, forsooth; and, I pray, how does good Mistress   140
Anne?

Mrs. Page. Go in with us, and see: we'd have an hour's talk
with you.   *[Exeunt Mrs. Page, Mrs. Ford, and Mrs. Quickly.]*

Page. How now, Master Ford!

Ford. You heard what this knave told me, did you not?   145

Page. Yes; and you heard what the other told me?

Ford. Do you think there is truth in them?

Page. Hang 'em, slaves! I do not think the knight would
offer it: but these that accuse him in his intent towards our
wives, are a yoke of his discarded men; very rogues, now   150
they be out of service.

Ford. Were they his men?

Page. Marry, were they.

Ford. I like it never the better for that. Does he lie at
the Garter?   155

Page. Ay, marry, does he. If he should intend this voyage
towards my wife, I would turn her loose to him; and what
he gets more of her than sharp words, let it lie on my head.

Ford. I do not misdoubt my wife, but I would be loth to
turn them together. A man may be too confident: I would   160
have nothing 'lie on my head': I cannot be thus satisfied.

Page. Look, where my ranting host of the Garter comes.
There is either liquor in his pate or money in his purse
when he looks so merrily.—

[Enter Host.]

How now, mine host!   165

Host. How now, bully-rook! thou'rt a gentleman. Cavaliero-
justice, I say!

[Enter Shallow.]

Shal. I follow, mine host, I follow. Good even and
twenty, good Master Page! Master Page, will you go with us?
we have sport in hand.   170

Host. Tell him, cavaliero-justice; tell him, bully-rook.

Shal. Sir, there is a fray to be fought between Sir Hugh the
Welsh priest and Caius the French doctor.

Ford. Good mine host o' the Garter, a word with you.

[Drawing him aside.]

Host. What sayest thou, my bully-rook?   175

Shal. *[To Page.]* Will you go with us to behold it? My
merry host hath had the measuring of their weapons, and, I
think, hath appointed them contrary places; for, believe me,
I hear the parson is no jester. Hark, I will tell you what our
sport shall be.   *[They converse apart.]*   180

Host. Hast thou no suit against my knight, my guest-
cavalier?

Ford. None, I protest: but I'll give you a pottle of burnt
sack to give me recourse to him and tell him my name is
Brook, only for a jest.   185

Host. My hand, bully: thou shalt have egress and regress;
said I well? and thy name shall be Brook. It is a merry knight.
Will you go, mynheers?

Shal. Have with you, mine host.

95 curtal: *having tail docked* affects: *is fond of*   100 galimaufry: *medley* perpend: *consider*   102 liver: *supposed seat of love*   103 Actæon ... Ringwood; *cf. n.*   107 foot:
walk   108 cuckoo-birds; *cf. n.*   123 affecting: *affected*   125 Cataian: *Chinese; cf. n.*
132 crotchets: *whims*   134 Have with you: *I'll go along with you*

150 yoke: *pair* very: *thorough*   159 misdoubt: *mistrust*   166, 167 Cavaliero-justice;
cf. n.   168, 169 Good even and twenty; *cf. n.*   178 contrary: *different*   183 pottle:
tankard burnt sack: *warm wine*   184 recourse: *access*   188 mynheers: *sirs*

Page. I have heard, the Frenchman hath good skill in   *190*
his rapier.

Shal. Tut, sir! I could have told you more. In these
times you stand on distance, your passes, stoccadoes, and I
know not what: 'tis the heart, Master Page; 'tis here, 'tis here.
I have seen the time with my long sword I would have   *195*
made you four tall fellows skip like rats.

Host. Here, boys, here, here! shall we wag?

Page. Have with you. I had rather hear them scold than
fight.   *[Exeunt Host, Shallow, and Page.]*

Ford. Though Page be a secure fool, and stands so firmly
on his wife's frailty, yet I cannot put off my opinion so easily.
She was in his company at Page's house, and what they made
there, I know not. Well, I will look further into 't; and I have
a disguise to sound Falstaff. If I find her honest, I lose not my
labour; if she be otherwise, 'tis labour well bestowed.   *205*
                               [Exit.]

❧ Scene Second ❧

[A Room in the Garter Inn]
Enter Falstaff *[and]* Pistol; *[and later]* Robin, *[Mistress]* Quickly,
Bardolph, *[and]* Ford.

Fal. I will not lend thee a penny.

Pist. Why, then the world's mine oyster,
Which I with sword will open.
[I will retort the sum in equipage.]

Fal. Not a penny. I have been content, sir, you should lay   *5*
my countenance to pawn: I have grated upon my good friends
for three repreives for you and your coach-fellow Nym; or else
you had looked through the grate, like a geminy of baboons. I
am damned in hell for swearing to gentlemen my friends, you
were good soldiers and tall fellows; and when Mistress   *10*
Bridget lost the handle of her fan, I took 't upon mine
honour thou hadst it not.

Pist. Didst thou not share? hadst thou not fifteen pence?

Fal. Reason, you rogue, reason: thinkest thou, I'll endanger
my soul gratis? At a word, hang no more about me; I am no
gibbet for you: go: a short knife and a throng!—to your manor
of Pickt-hatch! go. You'll not bear a letter for me, you rogue!—
you stand upon your honour!—Why, thou unconfinable baseness, it is as much as I can do to keep the terms of mine
honour precise. I, I, I, myself sometimes, leaving the fear of   *20*
God on the left hand and hiding mine honour in my necessity, am fain to shuffle, to hedge and to lurch; and yet you,
rogue, will ensconce your rags, your cat-a-mountain looks,
your red-lattice phrases, and your bold-beating oaths, under
the shelter of your honour! You will not do it, you!   *25*

Pist. I do relent: what wouldst thou more of man?

[Enter Robin.]

Rob. Sir, here's a woman would speak with you.

Fal. Let her approach.

[Enter Mistress Quickly.]

Quick. Give your worship good morrow.

Fal. Good morrow, good wife.   *30*

Quick. Not so, an 't please your worship.

Fal. Good maid, then.

Quick. I'll be sworn
As my mother was, the first hour I was born.

Fal. I do believe the swearer. What with me?   *35*

Quick. Shall I vouchsafe your worship a word or two?

Fal. Two thousand, fair woman; and I'll vouchsafe thee the
hearing.

Quick. There is one Mistress Ford, sir,—I pray, come a little
nearer this ways:—I myself dwell with Master Doctor Caius.   *40*

Fal. Well, on: Mistress Ford, you say,—

Quick. Your worship says very true:—I pray your worship,
come a little nearer this ways.

Fal. I warrant thee, nobody hears; mine own people,
mine own people.   *45*

Quick. Are they so? God bless them, and make them
his servants!

Fal. Well: Mistress Ford; what of her?

Quick. Why, sir, she's a good creature. Lord, Lord! your
worship's a wanton! Well, heaven forgive you, and all of   *50*
us, I pray!

Fal. Mistress Ford; come, Mistress Ford,—

Quick. Marry, this is the short and the long of it. You have
brought her into such a canaries as 'tis wonderful: the best
courtier of them all, when the court lay at Windsor, could   *55*
never have brought her to such a canary; yet there has been
knights, and lords, and gentlemen, with their coaches, I warrant you, coach after coach, letter after letter, gift after gift;
smelling so sweetly—all musk, and so rushling, I warrant you,
in silk and gold; and in such alligant terms; and in such   *60*
wine and sugar of the best and the fairest, that would have
won any woman's heart; and, I warrant you, they could never
get an eye-wink of her. I had myself twenty angels given me
this morning; but I defy all angels, in any such sort, as they
say, but in the way of honesty: and, I warrant you,   *65*
they could never get her so much as sip on a cup with the
proudest of them all; and yet there has been earls, nay, which
is more, pensioners; but, I warrant you, all is one with her.

Fal. But what says she to me? be brief, my good she-
Mercury.   *70*

Quick. Marry, she hath received your letter; for the which
she thanks you a thousand times; and she gives you to notify
that her husband will be absence from his house between ten
and eleven.

Fal. Ten and eleven?   *75*

Quick. Ay, forsooth; and then you may come and see the
picture, she says, that you wot of: Master Ford, her husband,
will be from home. Alas! the sweet woman leads an ill life with
him; he's a very jealousy man; she leads a very frampold life
with him, good heart.   *80*

Fal. Ten and eleven. Woman, commend me to her; I
will not fail her.

Quick. Why, you say well. But I have another messenger to
your worship: Mistress Page hath her hearty commendations to
you too: and let me tell you in your ear, she's as fartuous a   *85*
civil modest wife, and one, I tell you, that will not miss you

---

193 distance: *interval between fencers*   **passes:** *lunges*   **stoccadoes:** *thrusts*   **196 made you:**
made ('you' is 'ethical')   **200 secure:** *unsuspicious*   **4 retort:** *i.e., repay*   **equipage:** *cf. n.*
6 countenance; *cf. n.*   **7 coach-fellow:** *mate*   **8 geminy:** *pair*   **11 handle;** *cf. n.*
took 't: *swore*   **16 short knife:** *for cutting purses*   **17 Pickt-hatch;** *cf. n.*   **22 shuffle:**
equivocate   **hedge:** *cheat*   **lurch:** *lie in ambush*   **23 cat-a-mountain:** *wildcat*   **24 red-**
lattice phrases: *alehouse talk*   **bold-beating:** *blustering*

54 canaries: *i.e., quandary (?)*   **59 rushling:** *i.e., rustling*   **60 alligant:** *i.e., eloquent*   **68**
pensioners: *gentlemen of the sovereign's bodyguard*   **69, 70 she-Mercury:** *female messen-*
ger   **77 wot:** *know*   **79 frampold:** *quarrelsome*   **85 fartuous:** *i.e., virtuous*

morning nor evening prayer, as any is in Windsor, whoe'er be the other: and she bade me tell your worship that her husband is seldom from home; but, she hopes there will come a time. I never knew a woman so dote upon a man: surely, I think 90 you have charms, la; yes, in truth.

Fal. Not I, I assure thee: setting the attraction of my good parts aside, I have no other charms.

Quick. Blessing on your heart for 't!

Fal. But, I pray thee, tell me this: has Ford's wife and 95 Page's wife acquainted each other how they love me?

Quick. That were a jest indeed! they have not so little grace, I hope: that were a trick, indeed! But Mistress Page would desire you to send her your little page, of all loves: her husband has a marvellous infection to the little page; and, truly, Master Page is an honest man. Never a wife in Windsor leads a better life than she does: do what she will, say what she will, take all, pay all, go to bed when she list, rise when she list, all is as she will: and, truly she deserves it; for if there be a kind woman in Windsor, she is one. You must send her your page; no remedy.

Fal. Why, I will.

Quick. Nay, but do so, then: and, look you, he may come and go between you both; and in any case have a nay-word, that you may know one another's mind, and the boy never need to understand anything; for 'tis not good that children 110 should know any wickedness: old folks, you know, have discretion, as they say, and know the world.

Fal. Fare thee well: commend me to them both. There's my purse; I am yet thy debtor.—Boy, go along with this woman.— *[Exeunt Mistress Quickly and Robin.]* This news distracts me. 115

Pist. This punk is one of Cupid's carriers.
Clap on more sails; pursue; up with your fights;
Give fire! she is my prize, or ocean whelm them all!
                              [Exit.]

Fal. Sayest thou so, old Jack? go thy ways; I'll make more of thy old body than I have done. Will they yet look after 120 thee? Wilt thou, after the expense of so much money, be now a gainer? Good body, I thank thee. Let them say 'tis grossly done; so it be fairly done, no matter.

[Enter Bardolph.]

Bard. Sir John, there's one Master Brook below would fain speak with you, and be acquainted with you: and hath 125 sent your worship a morning's draught of sack.

Fal. Brook is his name?

Bard. Ay, sir.

Fal. Call him in. *[Exit Bardolph.]* Such Brooks are welcome to me, that o'erflow such liquor. Ah, ha! Mistress Ford 130 and Mistress Page, have I encompassed you? go to; *via!*

[Enter Bardolph, with Ford, disguised.]

Ford. Bless you, sir!

Fal. And you, sir; would you speak with me?

Ford. I make bold to press with so little preparation upon you. 135

Fal. You're welcome. What's your will?—Give us leave, drawer.   *[Exit Bardolph.]*

Ford. Sir, I am a gentleman that have spent much: my name is Brook.

Fal. Good Master Brook, I desire more acquaintance of you.

Ford. Good Sir John, I sue for yours: not to charge you; for I must let you understand I think myself in better plight for a lender than you are: the which hath something emboldened me to this unseasoned intrusion; for, they say, if money go before, all ways do lie open.. 145

Fal. Money is a good soldier, sir, and will on.

Ford. Troth, and I have a bag of money here troubles me: if you will help to bear it, Sir John, take all, or half, for easing me of the carriage.

Fal. Sir, I know not how I may deserve to be your 150 porter.

Ford. I will tell you, sir, if you will give me the hearing.

Fal. Speak, good Master Brook; I shall be glad to be your servant.

Ford. Sir, I hear you are a scholar,—I will be brief with you, and you have been a man long known to me, though 155 I had never so good means, as desire, to make myself acquainted with you. I shall discover a thing to you, wherein I must very much lay open mine own imperfection; but, good Sir John, as you have one eye upon my follies, as you hear them unfolded, turn another into the register of your own, 160 that I may pass with a reproof the easier, sith you yourself know how easy it is to be such an offender.

Fal. Very well, sir; proceed.

Ford. There is a gentlewoman in this town, her husband's name is Ford. 165

Fal. Well, sir.

Ford. I have long loved her, and, I protest to you, bestowed much on her; followed her with a doting observance; engrossed opportunities to meet her; fee'd every slight occasion that could but niggardly give me sight of her; not only bought many 170 presents to give her, but have given largely to many to know what she would have given. Briefly, I have pursued her as love hath pursued me; which hath been on the wing of all occasions. But whatsoever I have merited, either in my mind or in my means, meed, I am sure, I have received none; unless 175 experience be a jewel that I have purchased at an infinite rate; and that hath taught me to say this,
'Love like a shadow flies when substance love pursues;
Pursuing that that flies, and flying what pursues.'

Fal. Have you received no promise of satisfaction at her 180 hands?

Ford. Never.

Fal. Have you importuned her to such a purpose?

Ford. Never.

Fal. Of what quality was your love, then? 185

Ford. Like a fair house built upon another man's ground; so that I have lost my edifice by mistaking the place where I erected it.

Fal. To what purpose have you unfolded this to me?

Ford. When I have told you that, I have told you all. Some say, that though she appear honest to me, yet in other places she enlargeth her mirth so far that there is shrewd construction made of her. Now, Sir John, here is the heart of my purpose: you are a gentleman of excellent breeding, admirable discourse,

---

93 parts: *qualities*   **99 of all loves:** *for love's sake*   **100 infection:** *i.e., affection*   **103 list:** *please*   **108 nay-word:** *password*   **116 punk:** *strumpet*   **carriers:** *messengers*   **117 fights;** *cf. n.*   **118 my prize;** *cf. n.*   **123 grossly:** *heavily*   **129 Brooks;** *cf. n.*   **131 encompassed:** *outwitted*   **via:** *go on*   **136 Give us leave:** *withdraw*

141 charge: *cause expense to*   **144 unseasoned:** *ill-timed*   **157 discover:** *disclose*   **160 register:** *record*   **161 sith:** *since*   **168 engrossed:** *bought up wholesale*   **169 fee'd:** *employed*   **178, 179** *Cf. n.*   **192 shrewd:** *evil*

of great admittance, authentic in your place and person, *195*
generally allowed for your many warlike, courtlike, and learned
preparations.

Fal. O, sir!

Ford. Believe it, for you know it. There is money; spend it,
spend it; spend more; spend all I have; only give me so *200*
much of your time in exchange of it, as to lay an amiable
siege to the honesty of this Ford's wife: use your art of
wooing, win her to consent to you; if any man may, you may
as soon as any.

Fal. Would it apply well to the vehemency of your *205*
affection, that I should win what you would enjoy?
Methinks you prescribe to yourself very preposterously.

Ford. O, understand my drift. She dwells so securely on the
excellency of her honour, that the folly of my soul dares not
present itself: she is too bright to be looked against. Now, *210*
could I come to her with any detection in my hand, my
desires had instance and argument to commend themselves: I
could drive her then from the ward of her purity, her reputation, her marriage-vow, and a thousand other her defences,
which now are too-too strongly embattled against me. *215*
What say you to 't, Sir John?

Fal. Master Brook, I will first make bold with your money;
next, give me your hand; and last, as I am a gentleman, you
shall, if you will, enjoy Ford's wife.

Ford. O good sir! *220*

Fal. I say you shall.

Ford. Want no money, Sir John; you shall want none.

Fal. Want no Mistress Ford, Master Brook; you shall want
none. I shall be with her, I may tell you, by her own appointment; even as you came in to me, her assistant or go- *225*
between parted from me: I say I shall be with her between ten
and eleven; for at that time the jealous rascally knave her husband will be forth. Come you to me at night; you shall know
how I speed.

Ford. I am blest in your acquaintance. Do you know *230*
Ford, sir?

Fal. Hang him, poor cuckoldly knave! I know him not. Yet
I wrong him, to call him poor: they say the jealous wittolly
knave hath masses of money; for the which his wife seems to
me well-favoured. I will use her as the key of the cuckoldly *235*
rogue's coffer; and there's my harvest-home.

Ford. I would you knew Ford, sir, that you might avoid
him, if you saw him.

Fal. Hang him, mechanical salt-butter rogue! I will stare
him out of his wits; I will awe him with my cudgel: it *240*
shall hang like a meteor o'er the cuckold's horns. Master
Brook, thou shalt know I will predominate over the peasant, and thou shalt lie with his wife. Come to me soon at
night. Ford's a knave, and I will aggravate his style; thou,
Master Brook, shalt know him for knave and cuckold. Come
to me soon at night. *[Exit.]*

Ford. What a damned Epicurean rascal is this! My heart is
ready to crack with impatience. Who says this is improvident jealousy? my wife hath sent to him, the hour is fixed,
the match is made. Would any man have thought this? *250*
See the hell of having a false woman! My bed shall be abused,
my coffers ransacked, my reputation gnawn at; and I shall
not only receive this villainous wrong, but stand under the
adoption of abominable terms, and by him that does me
this wrong. Terms! names! Amaimon sounds well; Lucifer, *255*
well; Barbason, well; yet they are devils' additions, the
names of fiends: but Cuckold! Wittol!—Cuckold! the devil
himself hath not such a name. Page is an ass, a secure ass:
he will trust his wife; he will not be jealous. I will rather trust
a Fleming with my butter, Parson Hugh the Welshman *260*
with my cheese, an Irishman with my aqua-vitæ bottle, or a
thief to walk my ambling gelding, than my wife with herself: then she plots, then she ruminates, then she devises; and
what they think in their hearts they may effect, they will
break their hearts but they will effect. God be praised for *265*
my jealousy! Eleven o'clock the hour: I will prevent this, detect my wife, be revenged on Falstaff, and laugh at Page.
I will about it; better three hours too soon than a minute too
late. Fie, fie, fie! cuckold! cuckold! cuckold! *Exit.*

❧ SCENE THIRD ❧

[A Field near Windsor]
Enter Caius [and] Rugby; [and later] Page, Shallow, Slender,
[and] Host.

Caius. Jack Rugby!

Rug. Sir?

Caius. Vat is de clock, Jack?

Rug. 'Tis past the hour, sir, that Sir Hugh promised to
meet. *5*

Caius. By gar, he has save his soul, dat he is no come: he
has pray his Pible vell, dat he is no come. By gar, Jack Rugby,
he is dead already, if he be come.

Rug. He is wise, sir; he knew your worship would kill him,
if he came. *10*

Caius. By gar, de herring is no dead so as I vill kill him.
Take your rapier, Jack; I vill tell you how I vill kill him.

Rug. Alas, sir! I cannot fence.

Caius. Villainy, take your rapier.

Rug. Forbear; here's company. *15*

[Enter Host, Shallow, Slender, and Page.]

Host. Bless thee, bully Doctor!

Shal. Save you, Master Doctor Caius!

Page. Now, good Master Doctor!

Slen. Give you good morrow, sir.

Caius. Vat be all you, one, two, tree, four, come for? *20*

Host. To see thee fight, to see thee foin, to see thee traverse;
to see thee here, to see thee there; to see thee pass thy punto,
thy stock, thy reverse, thy distance, thy montant. Is he dead,
my Ethiopian? is he dead, my Francisco? ha, bully! What says
my Æsculapius? my Galen? my heart of elder? ha! is he *25*
dead, bully stale? is he dead?

---

195 **admittance:** *fashion* **authentic:** *powerful* 196 **allowed:** *approved* 197 **prepara-**
tions: *accomplishments* 201 **amiable:** *amorous* 212 **instance:** *evidence* 213 **ward:**
posture of defence (fencing) 228 **forth:** *away from home* 232 **cuckoldly:** *having an*
unfaithful wife 233 **wittolly:** *cuckoldly* 235 **well-favoured:** *good-looking* 239 **me-**
chanical: *vulgar* **salt-butter:** *rank* (?) 242 **predominate:** *have ascendancy* 244 **aggra-**
vate: *add to* **style:** *title* 247 **Epicurean:** *sensual*

253, 254 **stand . . . terms;** *cf. n.* 255, 256 **Amaimon, Barbason:** *devils* **additions:**
titles 257 **Wittol:** *contented cuckold* 21 **foin:** *thrust* (fencing) **traverse:** *march back*
and forth 22, 23 **punto . . . montant:** *fencing terms; cf. n.* 24 **Francisco:** *i.e.,*
Frenchman 25 **Æsculapius:** *Greek god of medicine* **Galen:** *Greek physician of second*
century A. D. **heart of elder:** *coward; cf. n.* 26 **stale;** *cf. n.*

Caius. By gar, he is de coward Jack priest of de vorld; he is not show his face.

Host. Thou art a Castilian King Urinal! Hector of Greece, my boy!   30

Caius. I pray you, bear vitness that me have stay six or seven, two, tree hours for him, and he is no come.

Shal. He is the wiser man, Master Doctor: he is a curer of souls, and you a curer of bodies; if you should fight, you go against the hair of your professions. Is it not true, Master Page?   35

Page. Master Shallow, you have yourself been a great fighter, though now a man of peace.

Shal. Bodykins, Master Page, though I now be old and of the peace, if I see a sword out, my finger itches to make one. Though we are justices and doctors and churchmen, Master   40 Page, we have some salt of our youth in us; we are the sons of women, Master Page.

Page. 'Tis true, Master Shallow.

Shal. It will be found so, Master Page. Master Doctor Caius, I am come to fetch you home. I am sworn of the   45 peace: you have showed yourself a wise physician, and Sir Hugh hath shown himself a wise and patient churchman. You must go with me, Master Doctor.

Host. Pardon, guest-justice.—A word, Monsieur Mockwater.

Caius. Mock-vater! vat is dat?   50

Host. Mock-water, in our English tongue, is valour, bully.

Caius. By gar, den, I have as mush mock-vater as de Englishman.—Scurvy jack-dog priest! by gar, me vill cut his ears.

Host. He will clapper-claw thee tightly, bully.

Caius. Clapper-de-claw! vat is dat?   55

Host. That is, he will make thee amends.

Caius. By gar, me do look, he shall clapper-de-claw me; for, by gar, me vill have it.

Host. And I will provoke him to 't, or let him wag.

Caius. Me tank you for dat.   60

Host. And moreover, bully,—But first, Master guest, and Master Page, and eke Cavaliero Slender, go you through the town to Frogmore.   *[Aside to them.]*

Page. Sir Hugh is there, is he?

Host. He is there: see what humour he is in; and I will   65 bring the doctor about by the fields. Will it do well?

Shal. We will do it.

Page, Shal., and Slen. Adieu, good Master Doctor.
                              [Exeunt Page, Shallow, and Slender.]

Caius. By gar, me vill kill de priest; for he speak for a jack-an-ape to Anne Page.   70

Host. Let him die. Sheathe thy impatience; throw cold water on thy choler: go about the fields with me through Frogmore: I will bring thee where Mistress Anne Page is, at a farmhouse a-feasting; and thou shalt woo her. Cried game; said I well?

Caius. By gar, me tank you for dat: by gar, I love you;   75 and I shall procure-a you de good guest, de earl, de knight, de lords, de gentlemen, my patients.

Host. For the which I will be thy adversary toward Anne Page: said I well?

Caius. By gar, 'tis good; vell said.   80

Host. Let us wag, then.

Caius. Come at my heels, Jack Rugby.   *Exeunt.*

ACT THIRD ❧ SCENE FIRST

[A Field near Frogmore]
Enter Evans [and] Simple; [and later] Page, Shallow, Slender, Host, Caius, [and] Rugby.

Eva. I pray you now, good Master Slender's serving-man, and friend Simple by your name, which way have you looked for Master Caius, that calls himself doctor of physic?

Sim. Marry, sir, the pittie-ward, the parkward, every way; old Windsor way, and every way but the town way.   5

Eva. I most fehemently desire you you will also look that way.

Sim. I will, sir.   *[Exit.]*

Eva. Pless my soul! how full of chollors I am, and trempling of mind! I shall be glad if he have deceived me. How melancholies I am! I will knog his urinals about his knave's costard when I have goot opportunities for the 'ork: pless my soul!

                                                        [Sings.]

'To shallow rivers, to whose falls
Melodious birds sing madrigals;
There will we make our peds of roses,   15
And a thousand fragrant posies.
To shallow—'

Mercy on me! I have a great dispositions to cry.   *[Sings.]*

Melodious birds sing madrigals,—
When as I sat in Pabylon,—   20
And a thousand vagram posies.
To shallow,—'

                              [Enter Simple.]

Sim. Yonder he is coming, this way, Sir Hugh.

Eva. He's welcome.   *[Sings.]*

'To shallow rivers, to whose falls—'   25

Heaven prosper the right!—what weapons is he?

Sim. No weapons, sir. There comes my master, Master Shallow, and another gentleman, from Frogmore, over the stile, this way.

Eva. Pray you, give me my gown; or else keep it in your   30 arms.   *[Reads in a book.]*

                    [Enter Page, Shallow, and Slender.]

Shal. How now, Master Parson! Good morrow, good Sir Hugh. Keep a gamester from the dice, and a good student from his book, and it is wonderful.

Slen. [Aside.] Ah, sweet Anne Page!   35

Page. Save you, good Sir Hugh!

Eva. Pless you from His mercy sake, all of you!

Shal. What, the sword and the word! do you study them both, Master Parson?

Page. And youthful still in your doublet and hose! this   40 raw rheumatic day?

Eva. There is reasons and causes for it.

Page. We are come to you to do a good office, Master Parson.

---

29 **Hector of Greece:** *i.e., valiant warrior*   35 **hair:** *grain*   38 **Bodykins:** *God's body*   39 **make one:** *join in*   41 **salt:** *quality*   49 **Mockwater:** *physician* (slang)   54 **clapper-claw:** *thrash*   63 **Frogmore:** *cf. n.*   74 **Cried game;** *cf. n.*

4 **pittie-ward:** *toward the little park; cf. n.*   9 **chollors:** *choler, ie., anger*   11 **knog:** *knock* **costard:** *apple, used jokingly for head*   12 **'ork:** *i.e., work*   13–20 *Cf. n.*   21 **vagram:** *i.e., fragrant*   40 **doublet and hose;** *cf. n.*

Eva. Fery well: what is it?   45

Page. Yonder is a most reverend gentleman, who, belike
having received wrong by some person, is at most odds with
his own gravity and patience that ever you saw.

Shal. I have lived fourscore years and upward; I never heard
a man of his place, gravity, and learning, so wide of his   50
own respect.

Eva. What is he?

Page. I think you know him; Master Doctor Caius, the
renowned French physician.

Eva. Got's will, and his passion of my heart! I had as   55
lief you would tell me of a mess of porridge.

Page. Why?

Eva. He has no more knowledge in Hibbocrates and Galen,—
and he is a knave besides; a cowardly knave as you would
desires to be acquainted withal.   60

Page. I warrant you, he's the man should fight with him.

Slen. [*Aside.*] O, sweet Anne Page!

Shal. It appears so, by his weapons. Keep them asunder:
here comes Doctor Caius.

[*Enter Host, Caius, and Rugby.*]

Page. Nay, good Master Parson, keep in your weapon.   65

Shal. So do you, good Master Doctor.

Host. Disarm them, and let them question: let them keep
their limbs whole and hack our English.

Caius. I pray you, let-a me speak a word vit your ear:
verefore will you not meet-a me?   70

Eva. [*Aside to Caius.*] Pray you, use your patience: in
good time.

Caius. By gar, you are de coward, de Jack dog, John ape.

Eva. [*Aside to Caius.*] Pray you, let us not be laughing-stogs
to other men's humours; I desire you in friendship, and I   75
will one way or other make you amends. [*Aloud.*] I will knog
your urinals about your knave's cogscomb [for missing your
meetings and appointments.]

Caius. Diable!—Jack Rugby,—mine host de *Jarretierre*,—
have I not stay for him to kill him? have I not, at de   80
place I did appoint?

Eva. As I am a Christians soul, now, look you, this is the
place appointed: I'll be judgment by mine host of the Garter.

Host. Peace, I say, Gallia and Gaul; French and Welsh,
soul-curer and body-curer!   85

Caius. Ay, dat is very good; excellent.

Host. Peace, I say! hear mine host of the Garter. Am I politic? am I subtle? am I a Machiavel? Shall I lose my doctor?
no; he gives me the potions and the motions. Shall I lose my
parson, my priest, my Sir Hugh? no; he gives me the   90
proverbs and the no-verbs. [Give me thy hand, terrestrial;
so;]—give me thy hand celestial; so. Boys of art, I have deceived you both; I have directed you to wrong places: your
hearts are mighty, your skins are whole, and let burnt sack be
the issue. Come, lay their swords to pawn. Follow me, lads   95
of peace; follow, follow, follow.

Shal. Trust me, a mad host!—Follow, gentlemen, follow.

Slen. [*Aside.*] O, sweet Anne Page!

[*Exeunt Shallow, Slender, Page, and Host.*]

Caius. Ha! do I perceive dat? have you make-a de sot of us,
ha, ha?   100

Eva. This is well; he has made us his vlouting-stog. I
desire you that we may be friends and let us knog our
prains together to be revenge on this same scall, scurvy,
cogging companion, the host of the Garter.

Caius. By gar, vit all my heart. He promise to bring   105
me vere is Anne Page: by gar, he deceive me too.

Eva. Well, I will smite his noddles. Pray you, follow.

[*Exeunt.*]

❧ Scene Second ❧

[A Street in Windsor]
[Enter] Mist[ress] Page [and] Robin; [and later] Ford, Page,
Shallow, Slender, Host, Evans, [and] Caius.

Mrs. Page. Nay, keep your way, little gallant: you were wont
to be a follower, but now you are a leader. Whether had you
rather lead mine eyes, or eye your master's heels?

Rob. I had rather, forsooth, go before you like a man than
follow him like a dwarf.   5

Mrs. Page. O! you are a flattering boy: now I see you'll
be a courtier.

[*Enter Ford.*]

Ford. Well met, Mistress Page. Whither go you?

Mrs. Page. Truly, sir, to see your wife: is she at home?

Ford. Ay; and as idle as she may hang together, for want   10
of company. I think if your husbands were dead, you two
would marry.

Mrs. Page. Be sure of that,—two other husbands.

Ford. Where had you this pretty weather-cock?

Mrs. Page. I cannot tell what the dickens his name is my   15
husband had him of. What do you call your knight's name,
sirrah?

Rob. Sir John Falstaff.

Ford. Sir John Falstaff!

Mrs. Page. He, he; I can never hit on's name. There is   20
such a league between my good man and he! Is your wife at
home indeed?

Ford. Indeed she is.

Mrs. Page. By your leave, sir: I am sick till I see her.

[*Exeunt Mistress Page and Robin.*]

Ford. Has Page any brains? hath he any eyes? hath he any   25
thinking? Sure, they sleep; he hath no use of them. Why, this
boy will carry a letter twenty mile, as easy as a cannon will
shoot point-blank twelve score. He pieces out his wife's inclination; he gives her folly motion and advantage: and now she's
going to my wife, and Falstaff's boy with her. A man may   30
hear this shower sing in the wind: and Falstaff's boy with her!
Good plots! they are laid; and our revolted wives share damnation together. Well; I will take him, then torture my wife,
pluck the borrowed veil of modesty from the so seeming Mistress Page, divulge Page himself for a secure and wilful Actæon;
and to these violent proceedings all my neighbours shall cry

47 **odds:** *strife*   50, 51 **so . . . respect:** *so indifferent to his reputation*   58 **Hibbocrates:**
i.e., Hippocrates, Greek physician and writer of fifth century B. C.   67 **question:** *talk*   84
Gallia: *i.e., Wales (Fr. Galles)*   88 **Machiavel:** *intriguer*   92 **art:** *learning*   95 **issue:**
conclusion

99 **sot:** *fool*   101 **vlouting-stog:** *i.e., floutingstock, laughingstock*   103 **scall:** *i.e., scald,*
sccurvy **cogging:** *cheating*   2 **Whether:** *(I wonder) whether*   21 **league:** *friend-*
ship   28 **pieces out:** *ekes out*   29 **motion:** *instigation*   31 **hear . . . wind:** *i.e., the*
matter is perfectly obvious   36 **cry aim:** *express their approval; cf. n.*

aim. *[Clock strikes.]* The clock gives me my cue, and my assurance bids me search; there I shall find Falstaff. I shall be rather praised for this than mocked; for it is as positive as the earth is firm, that Falstaff is there: I will go. *40*

[Enter Page, Shallow, Slender, Host, Sir Hugh Evans, Caius, and Rugby.]

Shal., Page, &c. Well met, Master Ford.

Ford. Trust me, a good knot. I have good cheer at home; and I pray you all go with me.

Shal. I must excuse myself, Master Ford.

Slen. And so must I, sir: we have appointed to dine *45*
with Mistress Anne, and I would not break with her for more money than I'll speak of.

Shal. We have lingered about a match between Anne Page and my cousin Slender, and this day we shall have our answer.

Slen. I hope I have your good will, father Page. *50*

Page. You have, Master Slender; I stand wholly for you: but my wife, Master Doctor, is for you altogether.

Caius. Ay, by gar; and de maid is love-a me: my nursh-a Quickly tell me so mush.

Host. What say you to young Master Fenton? he capers, *55*
he dances, he has eyes of youth, he writes verses, he speaks holiday, he smells April and May: he will carry 't, he will carry 't; 'tis in his buttons; he will carry 't.

Page. Not by my consent, I promise you. The gentleman is of no having: he kept company with the wild prince and *60*
Poins; he is of too high a region; he knows too much. No, he shall not knit a knot in his fortunes with the finger of my substance: if he take her, let him take her simply; the wealth I have waits on my consent, and my consent goes not that way.

Ford. I beseech you heartily, some of you go home with me to dinner: besides your cheer, you shall have sport; I will show you a monster. Master Doctor, you shall go; so shall you, Master Page; and you, Sir Hugh.

Shal. Well, fare you well: we shall have the freer wooing at Master Page's. *[Exeunt Shallow and Slender.]*

Caius. Go home, John Rugby; I come anon. *[Exit Rugby.]*

Host. Farewell, my hearts: I will to my honest knight Falstaff, and drink canary with him. *[Exit]*

Ford. [Aside.] I think I shall drink in pipe-wine first with him; I'll make him dance. Will you go, gentles? *75*

All. Have with you to see this monster. *Exeunt.*

❧ SCENE THIRD ❧

[A Room in Ford's House]

Enter M[istress] Ford [and] M[istress] Page; [and later] Servants, Robin, Falstaff, Ford, Page, Caius, [and] Evans.

Mrs. Ford. What, John! what, Robert!

Mrs. Page. Quickly, quickly:—Is the buck-basket—

Mrs. Ford. I warrant. What, Robin, I say!

[Enter Servants with a basket.]

Mrs. Page. Come, come, come.

Mrs. Ford. Here, set it down. *5*

Mrs. Page. Give your men the charge; we must be brief.

Mrs. Ford. Marry, as I told you before, John, and Robert, be ready here hard by in the brewhouse; and when I suddenly call you, come forth, and without any pause or staggering, take this basket on your shoulders: that done, trudge with it in all haste, and carry it among the whitsters in Datchet-mead, and there empty it in the muddy ditch, close by the Thames side.

Mrs. Page. You will do it?

Mrs. Ford. I have told them over and over; they lack no direction. Be gone, and come when you are called. *15*
         [Exeunt Servants.]

Mrs. Page. Here comes little Robin.

[Enter Robin.]

Mrs. Ford. How now, my eyas-musket! what news with you?

Rob. My master, Sir John, is come in at your back-door, Mistress Ford, and requests your company.

Mrs. Page. You little Jack-a-Lent, have you been true to us?

Rob. Ay, I'll be sworn. My master knows not of your being here, and hath threatened to put me into everlasting liberty if I tell you of it; for he swears he'll turn me away.

Mrs. Page. Thou'rt a good boy; this secrecy of thine shall be a tailor to thee and shall make thee a new doublet and *25*
hose. I'll go hide me.

Mrs. Ford. Do so. Go tell thy master I am alone. *[Exit Robin.]* Mistress Page, remember you your cue.

Mrs. Page. I warrant thee; if I do not act it, hiss me.
         [Exit.]

Mrs. Ford. Go to, then: we'll use this unwholesome *30*
humidity, this gross watery pumpion; we'll teach him to know turtles from jays.

[Enter Falstaff.]

Fal. 'Have I caught my heavenly jewel?' Why, now let me die, for I have lived long enough: this is the period of my ambition: O this blessed hour! *35*

Mrs. Ford. O, sweet Sir John!

Fal. Mistress Ford, I cannot cog, I cannot prate, Mistress Ford. Now shall I sin in my wish: I would thy husband were dead. I'll speak it before the best lord, I would make thee my lady. *40*

Mrs. Ford. I your lady, Sir John! alas, I should be a pitiful lady.

Fal. Let the court of France show me such another. I see how thine eye would emulate the diamond: thou hast the right arched beauty of the brow that becomes the ship-tire, the *45*
tire-valiant, or any tire of Venetian admittance.

Mrs. Ford. A plain kerchief, Sir John: my brows become nothing else; nor that well neither.

Fal. By the Lord, thou art a traitor to say so: thou wouldst make an absolute courtier; and the firm fixture of thy foot *50*
would give an excellent motion to thy gait in a semi-circled farthingale. I see what thou wert, if Fortune thy foe were not, Nature thy friend. Come, thou canst not hide it.

42 knot: *company* **57 holiday:** *in choice language* **57, 58 he will ... buttons:** *he'll win; he has it in him* **60 having:** *property* **60, 61 prince and Poins:** *cf. n.* **region:** *height in the heavens* **63 simply:** *by herself* **73 canary:** *a sweet wine* **74 pipe-wine:** *wine in the cask; cf. n.* **2 buck-basket:** *basket for soiled linen* **6 charge:** *order* **11 whitsters:** *bleachers of linen* **Datchet-mead;** *cf. n.* **17 eyas-musket:** *young sparrow-hawk* **20 Jack-a-Lent:** *puppet used as target in a game* **31 pumpion:** *pumpkin* **33** *Cf. n.* **34 period:** *final point* **37 cog:** *fawn* **45 ship-tire:** *headdress shaped like a ship* **46 tire-valiant:** *fantastic headdress* **50 absolute:** *perfect* **51, 52 semi-circled farthingale:** *petticoat, the hoops of which did not come round in front* **Fortune thy foe;** *cf. n.*

Mrs. Ford. Believe me, there's no such thing in me.

Fal. What made me love thee? let that persuade thee   55
there's something extraordinary in thee. Come, I cannot cog
and say thou art this and that, like a many of these lisping
hawthornbuds, that come like women in men's apparel, and
smell like Bucklersbury in simple-time; I cannot; but I love
thee; none but thee; and thou deservest it.   60

Mrs. Ford. Do not betray me, sir. I fear you love Mistress
Page.

Fal. Thou mightst as well say, I love to walk by the Counter-gate, which is as hateful to me as the reek of a lime-kiln.

Mrs. Ford. Well, heaven knows how I love you; and you   65
shall one day find it.

Fal. Keep in that mind; I'll deserve it.

Mrs. Ford. Nay, I must tell you, so you do, or else I could
not be in that mind.

Rob. [Within.] Mistress Ford! Mistress Ford! here's Mis-   70
tress Page at the door, sweating and blowing and looking
wildly, and would needs speak with you presently.

Fal. She shall not see me: I will ensconce me behind the
arras.

Mrs. Ford. Pray you, do so: she's a very tattling woman.   75

[Falstaff hides himself.]

[Enter Mistress Page and Robin.]

What's the matter? how now!

Mrs. Page. O Mistress Ford! what have you done? You're
shamed, you are overthrown, you're undone for ever!

Mrs. Ford. What's the matter, good Mistress Page?

Mrs. Page. O well-a-day, Mistress Ford! having an honest   80
man to your husband, to give him such cause of suspicion!

Mrs. Ford. What cause of suspicion?

Mrs. Page. What cause of suspicion! Out upon you! how am
I mistook in you!

Mrs. Ford. Why, alas, what's the matter?   85

Mrs. Page. Your husband's coming hither, woman, with all
the officers in Windsor, to search for a gentleman that he says
is here now in the house by your consent, to take an ill advantage of his absence: you are undone.

Mrs. Ford. [Aside.] Speak louder.—'Tis not so, I hope.   90

Mrs. Page. Pray heaven it be not so, that you have such a
man here! but 'tis most certain your husband's coming with
half Windsor at his heels, to search for such a one. I come before to tell you. If you know yourself clear, why, I am glad of
it; but if you have a friend here, convey, convey him out.   95
Be not amazed; call all your senses to you: defend your reputation, or bid farewell to your good life for ever.

Mrs. Ford. What shall I do?—There is a gentleman, my dear
friend; and I fear not mine own shame so much as his peril: I
had rather than a thousand pound he were out of the house.

Mrs. Page. For shame! never stand 'you had rather' and 'you
had rather': your husband's here at hand; bethink you of some
conveyance: in the house you cannot hide him. O, how have
you deceived me! Look, here is a basket: if he be of any reasonable stature, he may creep in here; and throw foul linen   105
upon him, as if it were going to bucking: or—it is whiting-
time—send him by your two men to Datchet-mead.

Mrs. Ford. He's too big to go in there. What shall I do?

Fal. [Coming forward.] Let me see 't, let me see 't, O, let
me see 't! I'll in, I'll in. Follow your friend's counsel. I'll in.   110

Mrs. Page. What, Sir John Falstaff! Are these your letters,
knight?

Fal. I love thee, and none but thee; help me away: let me
creep in here. I'll never—   *[Gets into the basket; they cover
him with foul linen.]*

Mrs. Page. Help to cover your master, boy. Call your   115
men, Mistress Ford. You dissembling knight!

Mrs. Ford. What, John! Robert! John!   *[Exit Robin.]*

[Enter Servants.]

Go take up these clothes here quickly; where's the cowl-staff?
look, how you drumble! carry them to the laundress in
Datchet-mead; quickly, come.   120

[Enter Ford, Page, Caius, and Sir Hugh Evans.]

Ford. Pray you, come near: if I suspect without cause, why
then make sport at me; then let me be your jest; I deserve it.
How now! what goes here? whither bear you this?

Serv. To the laundress, forsooth.

Mrs. Ford. Why, what have you to do whither they bear   125
it? You were best meddle with buck-washing.

Ford. Buck! I would I could wash myself of the buck! Buck,
buck, buck! Ay, buck; I warrant you, buck; and of the season
too; it shall appear. *[Exeunt Servants with the basket.]* Gentlemen, I have dreamed to-night; I'll tell you my dream.   130
Here, here, here be my keys: ascend my chambers; search,
seek, find out: I'll warrant we'll unkennel the fox. Let me
stop this way first. *[Locking the door.]* So, now uncape.

Page. Good Master Ford, be contented: you wrong yourself
too much.   135

Ford. True, Master Page. Up, gentlemen; you shall see
sport anon: follow me, gentlemen.   *[Exit.]*

Eva. This is fery fantastical humours and jealousies.

Caius. By gar, 'tis no de fashion of France; it is not
jealous in France.   140

Page. Nay, follow him, gentlemen; see the issue of his
search.   *[Exeunt Page, Caius, and Evans.]*

Mrs. Page. Is there not a double excellency in this?

Mrs. Ford. I know not which pleases me better; that my
husband is deceived, or Sir John.   145

Mrs. Page. What a taking was he in when your husband
asked who was in the basket!

Mrs. Ford. I am half afraid he will have need of washing;
so throwing him into the water will do him a benefit.

Mrs. Page. Hang him, dishonest rascal! I would all of   150
the same strain were in the same distress.

Mrs. Ford. I think my husband hath some special suspicion
of Falstaff's being here; for I never saw him so gross in his
jealousy till now.

Mrs. Page. I will lay a plot to try that; and we will yet   155
have more tricks with Falstaff: his dissolute disease will scarce
obey this medicine.

Mrs. Ford. Shall we send that foolish carrion Mistress

---

58 **hawthorn-buds:** *dandies*   59 **Bucklersbury;** *cf. n.*   63, 64 **Counter-gate:** *gate of
debtors' prison*   73 **ensconce:** *conceal.*   74 **arras:** *hanging screen of tapestry placed round
the walls of a room*   94 **clear:** *innocent*   101 **stand:** *lose time over*   106 **bucking:**
washing **whiting-time:** *bleaching-time*

118 **cowl-staff:** *pole for carrying a basket between two persons*   119 **drumble:** *dawdle*   126
buck-washing: *washing of clothes*   128 **of the season:** *in season*   130 **to-night:** *last
night*   132 **unkennel:** *drive from cover*   133 **uncape:** *uncouple; cf. n.*   146 **taking:**
fright

Quickly to him, and excuse his throwing into the water; and give him another hope, to betray him to another punishment?

Mrs. Page. We will do it: let him be sent for to-morrow, eight o'clock, to have amends.

[Enter Ford, Page, Caius, and Sir Hugh Evans.]

Ford. I cannot find him: may be the knave bragged of that he could not compass.

Mrs. Page. [Aside to Mrs. Ford.] Heard you that? *165*

Mrs. Ford. [Aside to Mrs. Page.] Ay, ay, peace.—You use me well, Master Ford, do you?

Ford. Ay, I do so.

Mrs. Ford. Heaven make you better than your thoughts!

Ford. Amen! *170*

Mrs. Page. You do yourself mighty wrong, Master Ford.

Ford. Ay, ay; I must bear it.

Eva. If there pe any pody in the house, and in the chambers, and in the coffers, and in the presses, heaven forgive my sins at the day of judgment! *175*

Caius. By gar, nor I too, dere is no bodies.

Page. Fie, fie, Master Ford! are you not ashamed? What spirit, what devil suggests this imagination? I would not ha' your distemper in this kind for the wealth of Windsor Castle.

Ford. 'Tis my fault, Master Page: I suffer for it. *180*

Eva. You suffer for a pad conscience: your wife is as honest a 'omans as I will desires among five thousand, and five hundred too.

Caius. By gar, I see 'tis an honest woman.

Ford. Well; I promised you a dinner. Come, come, *185* walk in the Park: I pray you, pardon me; I will hereafter make known to you why I have done this. Come, wife; come, Mistress Page. I pray you, pardon me; pray heartily, pardon me.

Page. Let's go in, gentlemen; but, trust me, we'll mock him. I do invite you to-morrow morning to my house to breakfast; after, we'll a-birding together: I have a fine hawk for the bush. Shall it be so?

Ford. Anything.

Eva. If there is one, I shall make two in the company.

Caius. If dere be one or two, I shall make-a de turd. *195*

Ford. Pray you go, Master Page.

Eva. I pray you now, remembrance tomorrow on the lousy knave, mine host.

Caius. Dat is good; by gar, vit all my heart.

Eva. A lousy knave! to have his gibes and his mockeries!

Exeunt.

❧ SCENE FOURTH ❧

[A Room in Page's House]

Enter Fenton [and] Anne Page; [and later] Shallow, Slender, [Mistress] Quickly, Page, [and] Mist[ress] Page.

Fent. I see I cannot get thy father's love; Therefore no more turn me to him, sweet Nan.

Anne. Alas! how then?

Fent.   Why, thou must be thyself.
He doth object, I am too great of birth, *5*
And that my state being gall'd with my expense,

I seek to heal it only by his wealth.
Besides these, other bars he lays before me,
My riots past, my wild societies;
And tells me 'tis a thing impossible *10*
I should love thee but as a property.

Anne. May be he tells you true.

Fent. No, heaven so speed me in my time to come!
Albeit I will confess thy father's wealth
Was the first motive that I woo'd thee, Anne: *15*
Yet, wooing thee, I found thee of more value
Than stamps in gold or sums in sealed bags;
And 'tis the very riches of thyself
That now I aim at.

Anne.   Gentle Master Fenton, *20*
Yet seek my father's love; still seek it, sir:
If opportunity and humblest suit
Cannot attain it, why, then,—hark you hither.

[They converse apart.]

[Enter Shallow, Slender, and Mistress Quickly.]

Shal. Break their talk, Mistress Quickly: my kinsman shall speak for himself. *25*

Slen. I'll make a shaft or a bolt on 't. 'Slid, 'tis but venturing.

Shal. Be not dismayed.

Slen. No, she shall not dismay me: I care not for that, but that I am afeard. *30*

Quick. Hark ye; Master Slender would speak a word with you.

Anne. I come to him. *[Aside.]* This is my father's choice. O, what a world of veil ill-favour'd faults Looks handsome in three hundred pounds a year! *35*

Quick. And how does good Master Fenton? Pray you, a word with you.

Shal. She's coming; to her, coz. O boy, thou hadst a father!

Slen. I had a father, Mistress Anne; my uncle can tell you good jests of him. Pray you, uncle, tell Mistress Anne the *40* jest, how my father stole two geese out of a pen, good uncle.

Shal. Mistress Anne, my cousin loves you.

Slen. Ay, that I do; as well as I love any woman in Gloucestershire.

Shal. He will maintain you like a gentlewoman. *45*

Slen. Ay, that I will, come cut and long-tail, under the degree of a squire.

Shal. He will make you a hundred and fifty pounds jointure.

Anne. Good Master Shallow, let him woo for himself. *50*

Shal. Marry, I thank you for it; I thank you for that good comfort. She calls you, coz: I'll leave you.

Anne. Now, Master Slender.

Slen. Now, good Mistress Anne.—

Anne. What is your will? *55*

Slen. My will? od's heartlings! that's a pretty jest, indeed! I ne'er made my will yet, I thank heaven; I am not such a sickly creature, I give heaven praise.

Anne. I mean, Master Slender, what would you with me?

Slen. Truly, for mine own part, I would little or nothing *60* with you. Your father and my uncle have made motions: if it

---

174 presses: *clothespresses* **179 kind:** *way* **191 a-birding:** *hawking; cf. n.* **2 turn:** *refer* **6 state:** *estate* **gall'd with my expense:** *exhausted by my squandering*

17 stamps: *coins* **24 Break:** *interrupt* **26 shaft . . . bolt;** *cf. n.* **'Slid:** *God's eyelid* **46 cut:** *with docked tail* **56 od's heartlings:** *God's little heart*

be any luck, so; if not, happy man be his dole! They can tell
you how things go better than I can: you may ask your father;
here he comes.

[Enter Page and Mistress Page.]

Page. Now, Master Slender: love him, daughter Anne.   65
Why, how now! what does Master Fenton here?
You wrong me, sir, thus still to haunt my house:
I told you, sir, my daughter is dispos'd of.
    Fent. Nay, Master Page, be not impatient.
    Mrs. Page. Good Master Fenton, come not to my child.   70
    Page. She is no match for you.
    Fent. Sir, will you hear me?
    Page.   No, good Master Fenton.
Come, Master Shallow; come, son Slender, in.
Knowing my mind, you wrong me, Master Fenton.   75
                    [Exeunt Page, Shallow, and Slender.]
    Quick. Speak to Mistress Page.
    Fent. Good Mistress Page, for that I love your daughter
In such a righteous fashion as I do,
Perforce, against all checks, rebukes and manners,
I must advance the colours of my love   80
And not retire: let me have your good will.
    Anne. Good mother, do not marry me to yond fool.
    Mrs. Page. I mean it not; I seek you a better husband.
    Quick. That's my master, Master Doctor.
    Anne. Alas! I had rather be set quick i' the earth, And   85
bowl'd to death with turnips.
    Mrs. Page. Come, trouble not yourself. Good Master Fenton,
I will not be your friend nor enemy:
My daughter will I question how she loves you,
And as I find her, so am I affected.   90
Till then, farewell, sir: she must needs go in;
Her father will be angry.
    Fent. Farewell, gentle mistress. Farewell, Nan.
                    [Exeunt Mistress Page and Anne.]
    Quick. This is my doing now: 'Nay,' said I, 'will you cast
away your child on a fool, and a physician? Look on Master   95
Fenton.' This is my doing.
    Fent. I thank thee: and I pray thee, once to-night
Give my sweet Nan this ring. There's for thy pains.
    Quick. Now heaven send thee good fortune!   *[Exit Fenton.]*
A kind heart he hath: a woman would run through fire   100
and water for such a kind heart. But yet I would my master
had Mistress Anne; or I would Master Slender had her; or,
in sooth, I would Master Fenton had her. I will do what I
can for them all three, for so I have promised, and I'll be
as good as my word; but speciously for Master Fenton. Well,
I must of another errand to Sir John Falstaff from my two
mistresses: what a beast am I to slack it!   *[Exit.]*

❧ SCENE FIFTH ❧

[A Room in the Garter Inn]
Enter Falstaff [and] Bardolph;
[and later Mistress] Quickly, [and] Ford.

Fal. Bardolph, I say,—
Bard. Here, sir.
Fal. Go fetch me a quart of sack; put a toast in 't. *[Exit
Bardolph.]* Have I lived to be carried in a basket, and to be
thrown in the Thames like a barrow of butcher's offal? Well,   5
if I be served such another trick, I'll have my brains ta'en out,
and buttered, and give them to a dog for a new year's gift.
The rogues slighted me into the river with as little remorse as
they would have drowned a blind bitch's puppies, fifteen i' the
litter; and you may know by my size that I have a kind of   10
alacrity in sinking: if the bottom were as deep as hell, I should
down. I have been drowned but that the shore was shelvy and
shallow; a death that I abhor, for the water swells a man, and
what a thing should I have been when I had been swelled! I
should have been a mountain of mummy.   15

[Enter Bardolph with sack.]

Bard. Here's Mistress Quickly, sir, to speak with you.
Fal. Come, let me pour in some sack to the Thames water,
for my belly's as cold as if I had swallowed snowballs for pills
to cool the reins. Call her in.
Bard. Come in, woman.   20

[Enter Mistress Quickly.]

Quick. By your leave. I cry you mercy: give your worship
good morrow.
Fal. Take away these chalices. Go brew me a pottle of sack
finely.
Bard. With eggs, sir?   25
Fal. Simple of itself; I'll no pullet-sperm in my brewage.
[Exit Bardolph.]—How now!
Quick. Marry, sir, I come to your worship from Mistress
Ford.
Fal. Mistress Ford! I have had ford enough; I was thrown   30
into the ford; I have my belly full of ford.
Quick. Alas the day! good heart, that was not her fault: she
does so take on with her men; they mistook their erection.
Fal. So did I mine, to build upon a foolish woman's
promise.   35
Quick. Well, she laments, sir, for it, that it would yearn
your heart to see it. Her husband goes this morning a-birding:
she desires you once more to come to her between eight and
nine. I must carry her word quickly: she'll make you amends,
I warrant you.   40
Fal. Well, I will visit her: tell her so; and bid her think
what a man is: let her consider his frailty, and then judge of
my merit.
Quick. I will tell her.
Fal. Do so. Between nine and ten, sayest thou?   45
Quick. Eight and nine, sir.
Fal. Well, be gone: I will not miss her.
Quick. Peace be with you, sir.   *[Exit.]*
Fal. I marvel I hear not of Master Brook; he sent me word
to stay within. I like his money well. O! here he comes.   50

[Enter Ford.]

---

62 **happy man be his dole:** *happiness be his portion (a proverbial phrase)*   79 **checks:** *re-
proofs*   80 **colours:** *standards*   85 **quick:** *alive*   90 **affected:** *inclined*   97 **once:** *sometime*   105 **speciously:** *i.e., especially*

8 **slighted:** *tossed carelessly*   15 **mummy:** *dead flesh*   19 **reins:** *kidneys*   21 **cry you
mercy:** *beg your pardon*   23 **pottle:** *two-quart measure*   33 **erection:** *i.e., direction*   36
yearn: *grieve*

Ford. Bless you, sir!

Fal. Now, Master Brook, you come to know what hath passed between me and Ford's wife?

Ford. That, indeed, Sir John, is my business.

Fal. Master Brook, I will not lie to you: I was at her 55
house the hour she appointed me.

Ford. And sped you, sir?

Fal. Very ill-favouredly, Master Brook.

Ford. How so, sir? did she change her determination?

Fal. No, Master Brook; but the peaking cornuto her 60
husband, Master Brook, dwelling in a continual 'larum of
jealousy, comes me in the instant of our encounter, after we
had embraced, kissed, protested, and, as it were, spoke the
prologue of our comedy; and at his heels a rabble of his
companions, thither provoked and instigated by his distem- 65
per, and, forsooth, to search his house for his wife's love.

Ford. What! while you were there?

Fal. While I was there.

Ford. And did he search for you, and could not find you?

Fal. You shall hear. As good luck would have it, comes in 70
one Mistress Page; gives intelligence of Ford's approach; and in
her invention, and Ford's wife's distraction, they conveyed me
into a buck-basket.

Ford. A buck-basket!

Fal. By the Lord, a buck-basket! rammed me in with foul 75
shirts and smocks, socks, foul stockings, greasy napkins; that,
Master Brook, there was the rankest compound of villainous
smell that ever offended nostril.

Ford. And how long lay you there?

Fal. Nay, you shall hear, Master Brook, what I have 80
suffered to bring this woman to evil for your good. Being thus
crammed in the basket, a couple of Ford's knaves, his hinds,
were called forth by their mistress to carry me in the name of
foul clothes to Datchet-lane: they took me on their shoulders;
met the jealous knave their master in the door, who asked 85
them once or twice what they had in their basket. I quaked for
fear lest the lunatic knave would have searched it; but Fate, or-
daining he should be a cuckold, held his hand. Well; on went
he for a search, and away went I for foul clothes. But mark
the sequel, Master Brook: I suffered the pangs of three several 90
deaths: first, an intolerable fright, to be detected with a jealous
rotten bell-wether; next, to be compassed, like a good bilbo, in
the circumference of a peck, hilt to point, heel to head; and
then, to be stopped in, like a strong distillation, with stinking
clothes that fretted in their own grease: think of that, a man of 95
my kidney, think of that, that am as subject to heat as butter;
a man of continual dissolution and thaw: it was a miracle to
'scape suffocation. And in the height of this bath, when I was
more than half stewed in grease, like a Dutch dish, to be
thrown into the Thames, and cooled, glowing hot, in that 100
surge, like a horse-shoe; think of that, hissing hot, think of
that, Master Brook!

Ford. In good sadness, sir, I am sorry that for my sake you
have suffered all this. My suit then is desperate; you'll undertake her no more? 105

Fal. Master Brook, I will be thrown into Etna, as I have
been into Thames, ere I will leave her thus. Her husband is

this morning gone a-birding: I have received from her another
embassy of meeting; 'twixt eight and nine is the hour, Master
Brook. 110

Ford. 'Tis past eight already, sir.

Fal. Is it? I will then address me to my appointment. Come
to me at your convenient leisure, and you shall know how I
speed, and the conclusion shall be crowned with your enjoying
her: adieu. You shall have her, Master Brook; Master 115
Brook, you shall cuckold Ford.   *[Exit.]*

Ford. Hum! ha! is this a vision? is this a dream? do I sleep?
Master Ford, awake! awake, Master Ford! there's a hole made
in your best coat, Master Ford. This 'tis to be married: this
'tis to have linen and buck-baskets! Well, I will proclaim 120
myself what I am: I will now take the lecher; he is at my
house; he cannot 'scape me; 'tis impossible he should; he cannot creep into a half-penny purse, nor into a pepper-box; but,
lest the devil that guides him should aid him, I will search
impossible places. Though what I am I cannot avoid, yet 125
to be what I would not, shall not make me tame: if I have
horns to make one mad, let the proverb go with me; I'll be
horn-mad.   *[Exit.]*

ACT FOURTH   SCENE FIRST

[A Street]
Enter Mistress Page, [Mistress] Quickly, [and] William; [and later]
Evans.

Mrs. Page. Is he at Master Ford's already, thinkest thou?

Quick. Sure he is by this, or will be presently; but truly, he
is very courageous mad about his throwing into the water.
Mistress Ford desires you to come suddenly.

Mrs. Page. I'll be with her by and by: I'll but bring my 5
young man here to school. Look, where his master comes;
'tis a playing-day, I see.

[Enter Sir Hugh Evans.]

How now, Sir Hugh! no school to-day?

Eva. No; Master Slender is let the boys leave to play.

Quick. Blessing of his heart! 10

Mrs. Page. Sir Hugh, my husband says my son profits
nothing in the world at his book: I pray you, ask him some
questions in his accidence.

Eva. Come hither, William; hold up your head; come.

Mrs. Page. Come on, sirrah; hold up your head; answer 15
your master, be not afraid.

Eva. William, how many numbers is in nouns?

Will. Two.

Quick. Truly, I thought there had been one number more,
because they say, 'Od's nouns.' 20

Eva. Peace your tattlings! What is *fair*, William?

Will. Pulcher.

Quick. Polecats! there are fairer things than polecats, sure.

Eva. You are a very simplicity 'oman: I pray you peace.
What is *lapis*, William? 25

Will. A stone.

Eva. And what is a *stone*, William?

58 **ill-favouredly:** *badly*   60 **peaking:** *sneaking* **cornuto:** *cuckold*   61 **'larum:**
alarm   65 **distemper:** *ill humour*   76 **that:** *so that*   82 **hinds:** *servants*   91 **with:**
by   92 **bilbo;** *cf. n.*   95 **fretted:** *consumed*   103 **sadness:** *seriousness*

109 **embassy:** *message*   112 **address:** *prepare*   4 **suddenly:** *at once*   5 **by and by:**
immediately   20 **Od's nouns:** *God's wounds*

Will. A pebble.

Eva. No, it is *lapis:* I pray you remember in your prain.

Will. Lapis.   30

Eva. That is a good William. What is he, William, that does lend articles?

Will. Articles are borrowed of the pronoun, and be thus declined, *Singulariter, nominativo, hic, hæc, hoc.*

Eva. Nominativo, hig, hag, hog; pray you, mark: *genitivo,*   35
hujus. Well, what is your accusative case?

Will. Accusativo, hinc.

Eva. I pray you, have your remembrance, child; *accusativo, hung, hang, hog.*

Quick. Hang-hog is Latin for bacon, I warrant you.   40

Eva. Leave your prabbles, 'oman. What is the focative case, William?

Will. O *vocativo,* O.

Eva. Remember, William; focative is *caret.*

Quick. And that's a good root.   45

Eva. 'Oman, forbear.

Mrs. Page. Peace!

Eva. What is your genitive case plural, William?

Will. Genitive case?

Eva. Ay.   50

Will. Genitive, horum, harum, horum.

Quick. Vengeance of Jenny's case! fie on her! Never name her, child, if she be a whore.

Eva. For shame, 'oman!

Quick. You do ill to teach the child such words. He   55
teaches him to hick and to hack, which they'll do fast enough of themselves, and to call 'horum'; fie upon you!

Eva. 'Oman, art thou lunatics? hast thou no understandings for thy cases and the numbers of the genders? Thou art as foolish Christian creatures as I would desires.   60

Mrs. Page. Prithee, hold thy peace.

Eva. Show me now, William, some declensions of your pronouns.

Will. Forsooth, I have forgot.

Eva. It is *qui, quæ, quod;* if you forget your *quis,* your   65
quæs, and your *quods,* you must be preeches. Go your ways and play; go.

Mrs. Page. He is a better scholar than I thought he was.

Eva. He is a good sprag memory. Farewell, Mistress Page.

Mrs. Page. Adieu, good Sir Hugh. *[Exit Sir Hugh.]* Get   70
you home, boy. Come, we stay too long.   *Exeunt.*

❧ SCENE SECOND ❧

[A Room in Ford's House]
Enter Falstaff, Mist[ress] Ford; [and later] Mist[ress] Page, Servants, Ford, Page, Caius, Evans, [and] Shallow.

Fal. Mistress Ford, your sorrow hath eaten up my sufferance. I see you are obsequious in your love, and I profess requital to a hair's breadth; not only, Mistress Ford, in the simple office of love, but in all the accoutrement, complement and ceremony of it. But are you sure of your husband now?   5

Mrs. Ford. He's a-birding, sweet Sir John.

---

40 Hang-hog: *cf. n.*   **44 caret:** *is wanting* (Latin)   **56 hick:** *hiccup*   **66 preeches:** *i.e., breeched, flogged*   **69 sprag:** *i.e., sprack, alert*   **1, 2 sufferance:** *sufferings* **obsequious:** *devoted*

Mrs. Page. [Within.] What ho! gossip Ford! what ho!

Mrs. Ford. Step into the chamber, Sir John.   *[Exit Falstaff.]*

[Enter Mistress Page.]

Mrs. Page. How now, sweetheart! who's at home besides yourself?   10

Mrs. Ford. Why, none but mine own people.

Mrs. Page. Indeed!

Mrs. Ford. No, certainly.—*[Aside to her.]* Speak louder.

Mrs. Page. Truly, I am so glad you have nobody here.

Mrs. Ford. Why?   15

Mrs. Page. Why, woman, your husband is in his old lines again: he so takes on yonder with my husband; so rails against all married mankind; so curses all Eve's daughters, of what complexion soever; and so buffets himself on the forehead, crying, 'Peer out, peer out!' that any madness I ever yet beheld   20
seemed but tameness, civility and patience, to this his distemper he is in now. I am glad the fat knight is not here.

Mrs. Ford. Why, does he talk of him?

Mrs. Page. Of none but him; and swears he was carried out, the last time he searched for him, in a basket: protests to   25
my husband he is now here, and hath drawn him and the rest of their company from their sport, to make another experiment of his suspicion. But I am glad the knight is not here; now he shall see his own foolery.

Mrs. Ford. How near is he, Mistress Page?   30

Mrs. Page. Hard by; at street end; he will be here anon.

Mrs. Ford. I am undone! the knight is here.

Mrs. Page. Why then you are utterly shamed, and he's but a dead man. What a woman are you! Away with him, away with him! better shame than murder.   35

Mrs. Ford. Which way should he go? how should I bestow him? Shall I put him into the basket again?

[Enter Falstaff.]

Fal. No, I'll come no more i' the basket. May I not go out ere he come?

Mrs. Page. Alas! three of Master Ford's brothers watch the   40
door with pistols, that none shall issue out; otherwise you might slip away ere he came. But what make you here?

Fal. What shall I do? I'll creep up into the chimney.

Mrs. Ford. There they always use to discharge their birding-pieces.   45

Mrs. Page. Creep into the kiln-hole.

Fal. Where is it?

Mrs. Ford. He will seek there, on my word. Neither press, coffer, chest, trunk, well, vault, but he hath an abstract for the remembrance of such places, and goes to them by his note: 50
there is no hiding you in the house.

Fal. I'll go out, then.

Mrs. Page. If you go out in your own semblance, you die, Sir John. Unless you go out disguised,—

Mrs. Ford. How might we disguise him?   55

Mrs. Page. Alas the day! I know not. There is no woman's gown big enough for him; otherwise, he might put on a hat, a muffler, and a kerchief, and so escape.

Fal. Good hearts, devise something: any extremity rather than a mischief.   60

---

7 gossip: *friend*   **16 lines:** *rage*   **19 complexion:** *sort*   **44 use:** *are accustomed*   **49 abstract:** *catalogue*

Mrs. Ford. My maid's aunt, the fat woman of Brainford, has a gown above.

Mrs. Page. On my word, it will serve him; she's as big as he is: and there's her thrummed hat and her muffler too. Run up, Sir John.   65

Mrs. Ford. Go, go, sweet Sir John: Mistress Page and I will look some linen for your head.

Mrs. Page. Quick, quick! we'll come dress you straight; put on the gown the while.   *[Exit Falstaff.]*

Mrs. Ford. I would my husband would meet him in this 70 shape: he cannot abide the old woman of Brainford; he swears she's a witch; forbade her my house, and hath threatened to beat her.

Mrs. Page. Heaven guide him to thy husband's cudgel, and the devil guide his cudgel afterwards!   75

Mrs. Ford. But is my husband coming?

Mrs. Page. Ay, in good sadness, is he; and talks of the basket too, howsoever he hath had intelligence.

Mrs. Ford. We'll try that; for I'll appoint my men to carry the basket again, to meet him at the door with it, as they 80 did last time.

Mrs. Page. Nay, but he'll be here presently: let's go dress him like the witch of Brainford.

Mrs. Ford. I'll first direct my men what they shall do with the basket. Go up; I'll bring linen for him straight.   *[Exit.]*

Mrs. Page. Hang him, dishonest varlet! we cannot misuse him enough.
We'll leave a proof, by that which we will do,
Wives may be merry, and yet honest too:
We do not act that often jest and laugh;   90
'Tis old but true, 'Still swine eats all the draff.'   *[Exit.]*

[Enter Mistress Ford, and two servants.]

Mrs. Ford. Go, sirs, take the basket again on your shoulders: your master is hard at door; if he bid you set it down, obey him. Quickly; dispatch.   *[Exit.]*

First Serv. Come, come, take it up.   95

Sec. Serv. Pray heaven, it be not full of knight again.

First Serv. I hope not; I had as lief bear so much lead.

[Enter Ford, Page, Shallow, Caius, and Sir Hugh Evans.]

Ford. Ay, but if it prove true, Master Page, have you any way then to unfool me again? Set down the basket, villains. Somebody call my wife. Youth in a basket! O you panderly 100 rascals! there's a knot, a ging, a pack, a conspiracy against me: now shall the devil be shamed. What, wife, I say! Come, come forth! Behold what honest clothes you send forth to bleaching!

Page. Why, this passes! Master Ford, you are not to go loose any longer; you must be pinioned.   105

Eva. Why, this is lunatics! this is mad as a mad dog!

Shal. Indeed, Master Ford, this is not well, indeed.

Ford. So say I too, sir.—

[Enter Mistress Ford.]

Come hither Mistress Ford; the honest woman, the modest wife, the virtuous creature, that hath the jealous fool to her 110 husband! I suspect without cause, mistress, do I?

Mrs. Ford. Heaven be my witness, you do, if you suspect me in any dishonesty.

Ford. Well said, brazen-face! hold it out. Come forth, sirrah!
                    [Pulling clothes out of the basket.]

Page. This passes!   115

Mrs. Ford. Are you not ashamed? let the clothes alone.

Ford. I shall find you anon.

Eva. 'Tis unreasonable. Will you take up your wife's clothes? Come away.

Ford. Empty the basket, I say!   120

Mrs. Ford. Why, man, why?

Ford. Master Page, as I am an honest man, there was one conveyed out of my house yesterday in this basket: why may not he be there again? In my house I am sure he is; my intelligence is true; my jealousy is reasonable. Pluck me out all the linen.   125

Mrs. Ford. If you find a man there he shall die a flea's death.

Page. Here's no man.

Shal. By my fidelity, this is not well, Master Ford, this wrongs you.   130

Eva. Master Ford, you must pray, and not follow the imaginations of your own heart: this is jealousies.

Ford. Well, he's not here I seek for.

Page. No, nor nowhere else but in your brain.

Ford. Help to search my house this one time: if I find 135 not what I seek, show no colour for my extremity; let me for ever be your table-sport; let them say of me, 'As jealous as Ford, that searched a hollow walnut for his wife's leman.' Satisfy me once more; once more search with me.

Mrs. Ford. What ho, Mistress Page! come you and the 140 old woman down; my husband will come into the chamber.

Ford. Old woman! What old woman's that?

Mrs. Ford. Why, it is my maid's aunt of Brainford.

Ford. A witch, a quean, an old cozening quean! Have I not forbid her my house? She comes of errands, does she? We are simple men; we do not know what's brought to pass under the profession of fortune-telling. She works by charms, by spells, by the figure, and such daubery as this is, beyond our element: we know nothing. Come down, you witch, you hag, you; come down, I say!   150

Mrs. Ford. Nay, good, sweet husband! good gentlemen, let him not strike the old woman.

[Enter Falstaff in woman's clothes, and Mistress Page.]

Mrs. Page. Come, Mother Prat; come, give me your hand.

Ford. I'll 'prat' her.—*[Beating him.]* Out of my door, you witch, you rag, you baggage, you polecat, you ronyon! out, 155 out! I'll conjure you, I'll fortune-tell you.   *[Exit Falstaff.]*

Mrs. Page. Are you not ashamed? I think you have killed the poor woman.

Mrs. Ford. Nay, he will do it. 'Tis a goodly credit for you.

Ford. Hang her, witch!   160

Eva. By yea and no, I think the 'oman is a witch indeed: I like not when a 'oman has a great peard; I spy a great peard under his muffler.

Ford. Will you follow, gentlemen? I beseech you, follow: see but the issue of my jealousy. If I cry out thus upon no trail, never trust me when I open again.

---

61 **fat woman of Brainford**; *cf. n.*   64 **thrummed**: *made of coarse yarn*   86 **dishonest**: *unchaste*   91 **draff**: *swill*   94 **dispatch**: *hasten*   101 **ging**: *gang*   **pack**: *confederacy*

136 **show no colour**: *suggest no excuse*   **extremity**: *extravagance*   138 **leman**: *lover*   144 **quean**: *hussy*   **cozening**: *deceiving*   148 **figure**: *effigy; cf. n.*   **daubery**: *false show*   155 **ronyon**: *mangy woman*

Page. Let's obey his humour a little further. Come,
gentlemen.   [*Exeunt Ford, Page, Shallow, Caius, and Evans.*]
   Mrs. Page. Trust me, he beat him most pitifully.
   Mrs. Ford. Nay, by the mass, that he did not; he beat   *170*
him most unpitifully methought.
   Mrs. Page. I'll have the cudgel hallowed and hung o'er the
altar: it hath done meritorious service.
   Mrs. Ford. What think you? May we, with the warrant of
womanhood and the witness of a good conscience, pursue   *175*
him with any further revenge?
   Mrs. Page. The spirit of wantonness is, sure, scared out of
him: if the devil have him not in fee-simple, with fine and
recovery, he will never, I think, in the way of waste, attempt
us again.   *180*
   Mrs. Ford. Shall we tell our husbands how we have served him?
   Mrs. Page. Yes, by all means; if it be but to scrape the
figures out of your husband's brains. If they can find in their
hearts the poor unvirtuous fat knight shall be any further
afflicted, we two will still be the ministers.   *185*
   Mrs. Ford. I'll warrant they'll have him publicly shamed,
and methinks there would be no period to the jest, should
he not be publicly shamed.
   Mrs. Page. Come, to the forge with it then; shape it:
I would not have things cool.   *Exeunt.* *190*

❧ SCENE THIRD ❧

[A Room in the Garter Inn]
Enter Host and Bardolph.

Bard. Sir, the Germans desire to have three of your horses:
the duke himself will be to-morrow at court, and they are
going to meet him.
   Host. What duke should that be comes so secretly? I hear
not of him in the court. Let me speak with the gentlemen;   *5*
they speak English?
   Bard. Ay, sir; I'll call them to you.
   Host. They shall have my horses, but I'll make them pay;
I'll sauce them: they have had my house a week at command;
I have turned away my other guests: they must come off;   *10*
I'll sauce them. Come.   *Exeunt.*

❧ SCENE FOURTH ❧

[A Room in Ford's House]
Enter Page, Ford, Mistress Page, Mistress Ford, and Evans.

Eva. 'Tis one of the pest discretions of a 'oman as ever I
did look upon.
   Page. And did he send you both these letters at an instant?
   Mrs. Page. Within a quarter of an hour.
   Ford. Pardon me, wife. Henceforth do what thou wilt;   *5*
I rather will suspect the sun with cold
Than thee with wantonness: now doth thy honour stand,
In him that was of late an heretic,
As firm as faith.

Page.   'Tis well, 'tis well; no more.   *10*
Be not as extreme in submission
As in offence;
But let our plot go forward: let our wives
Yet once again, to make us public sport,
Appoint a meeting with this old fat fellow,   *15*
Where we may take him and disgrace him for it.
   Ford. There is no better way than that they spoke of.
   Page. How? to send him word they'll meet him in the Park
at midnight? Fie, fie! he'll never come.
   Eva. You say he has been thrown into the rivers, and has   *20*
been grievously peaten as an old 'oman: methinks there should
be terrors in him that he should not come; methinks his flesh
is punished, he shall have no desires.
   Page. So think I too.
   Mrs. Ford. Devise but how you'll use him when he comes,   *25*
And let us two devise to bring him thither.
   Mrs. Page. There is an old tale goes that Herne the hunter,
Sometime a keeper here in Windsor forest,
Doth all the winter-time, at still midnight,
Walk round about an oak, with great ragg'd horns;   *30*
And there he blasts the tree, and takes the cattle,
And makes milch-kine yield blood, and shakes a chain
In a most hideous and dreadful manner:
You have heard of such a spirit, and well you know
The superstitious idle-headed eld   *35*
Receiv'd and did deliver to our age
This tale of Herne the hunter for a truth.
   Page. Why, yet there want not many that do fear
In deep of night to walk by this Herne's oak.
But what of this?   *40*
   Mrs. Ford.   Marry, this is our device;
That Falstaff at that oak shall meet with us,
[*Disguis'd like Herne with huge horns on his head.*]
   Page. Well, let it not be doubted but he'll come,
And in this shape when you have brought him thither,   *45*
What shall be done with him? what is your plot?
   Mrs. Page. That likewise have we thought upon, and thus:
Nan Page my daughter, and my little son,
And three or four more of their growth, we'll dress
Like urchins, ouphs, and fairies, green and white,   *50*
With rounds of waxen tapers on their heads,
And rattles in their hands. Upon a sudden,
As Falstaff, she, and I, are newly met,
Let them from forth a sawpit rush at once
With some diffused song: upon their sight,   *55*
We two in great amazedness will fly:
Then let them all encircle him about,
And, fairy-like, to-pinch the unclean knight;
And ask him why, that hour of fairy revel,
In their so sacred paths he dares to tread   *60*
In shape profane.
   Mrs. Ford.   And till he tell the truth,
Let the supposed fairies pinch him sound
And burn him with their tapers.
   Mrs. Page.   The truth being known,   *65*
We'll all present ourselves, dis-horn the spirit,
And mock him home to Windsor.

---

178 fee-simple: *absolute possession* **fine and recovery;** *cf. n.*   **179 waste:** *spoliation*   **183 figures:** *phantasms*   **185 ministers:** *agents*   **187 period:** *fitting conclusion*   **1 Germans;** *cf. n.*   **10 come off:** *pay down*

31 blasts: *blights*   **takes:** *bewitches*   **35 eld:** *people of olden time*   **50 urchins:** *goblins*   **ouphs:** *elves*   **55 diffused:** *confused*   **58 to-pinch:** *pinch soundly*   **63 sound:** *soundly*

Ford.   The children must
Be practis'd well to this, or they'll ne'er do 't.

Eva. I will teach the children their behaviours; and I will   *70*
be like a jack-an-apes also, to burn the knight with my taber.

Ford. That will be excellent. I'll go buy them vizards.

Mrs. Page. My Nan shall be the queen of all the fairies,
Finely attired in a robe of white.

Page. That silk will I go buy:—*[Aside.]* and in that time   *75*
Shall Master Slender steal my Nan away,
And marry her at Eton. Go, send to Falstaff straight.

Ford. Nay, I'll to him again in name of Brook;
He'll tell me all his purpose. Sure, he'll come.

Mrs. Page. Fear not you that. Go, get us properties,   *80*
And tricking for our fairies.

Eva. Let us about it: it is admirable pleasures and fery
honest knaveries.   *[Exeunt Page, Ford, and Evans.]*

Mrs. Page. Go, Mistress Ford,
Send Quickly to Sir John, to know his mind.   *85*
                        [Exit Mistress Ford.]
I'll to the doctor: he hath my good will,
And none but he, to marry with Nan Page.
That Slender, though well landed, is an idiot;
And him my husband best of all affects:
The doctor is well money'd, and his friends   *90*
Potent at court: he, none but he, shall have her,
Though twenty thousand worthier come to crave her.   *[Exit.]*

❧ SCENE FIFTH ❧

[A Room in the Garter Inn]
Enter Host [and] Simple; [and later] Falstaff, Bardolph, Evans,
Caius, [and Mistress] Quickly.

Host. What wouldst thou have, boor? what, thick-skin?
speak, breathe, discuss; brief, short, quick, snap.

Sim. Marry, sir, I come to speak with Sir John Falstaff from
Master Slender.

Host. There's his chamber, his house, his castle, his standing-   *5*
bed and truckle-bed: 'tis painted about with the story of the
Prodigal, fresh and new. Go knock and call: he'll speak like
an Anthropophaginian unto thee: knock, I say.

Sim. There's an old woman, a fat woman, gone up into his
chamber: I'll be so bold as stay, sir, till she come down; I   *10*
come to speak with her, indeed.

Host. Ha! a fat woman! the knight may be robbed: I'll call.
Bully knight! Bully Sir John! speak from thy lungs military:
art thou there? it is thine host, thine Ephesian, calls.

Fal. [Above.] How now, mine host!   *15*

Host. Here's a Bohemian-Tartar tarries the coming down
of thy fat woman. Let her descend, bully; let her descend;
my chambers are honourable: fie! privacy? fie!

[Enter Falstaff.]

Fal. There was, mine host, an old fat woman even now
with me, but she's gone.   *20*

Sim. Pray you, sir, was 't not the wise woman of Brainford?

Fal. Ay, marry, was it, mussel-shell: what would you with
her?

Sim. My master, sir, Master Slender, sent to her, seeing her
go thorough the streets, to know, sir, whether one Nym, sir,   *25*
that beguiled him of a chain, had the chain or no.

Fal. I spake with the old woman about it.

Sim. And what says she, I pray, sir?

Fal. Marry, she says that the very same man that beguiled
Master Slender of his chain cozened him of it.   *30*

Sim. I would I could have spoken with the woman herself: I
had other things to have spoken with her too, from him.

Fal. What are they? let us know.

Host. Ay, come; quick.

Sim. I may not conceal them, sir.   *35*

Host. Conceal them, or thou diest.

Sim. Why, sir, they were nothing but about Mistress Anne
Page; to know if it were my master's fortune to have her or
no.

Fal. 'Tis, 'tis his fortune.   *40*

Sim. What, sir?

Fal. To have her, or no. Go; say the woman told me so.

Sim. May I be bold to say so, sir?

Fal. Ay, sir: like who more bold?

Sim. I thank your worship: I shall make my master glad   *45*
with these tidings.   *[Exit.]*

Host. Thou art clerkly, thou art clerkly, Sir John. Was there
a wise woman with thee?

Fal. Ay, that there was, mine host; one that hath taught me
more wit than ever I learned before in my life: and I paid   *50*
nothing for it neither, but was paid for my learning.

[Enter Bardolph.]

Bard. Out, alas, sir! cozenage, mere cozenage!

Host. Where be my horses? speak well of them, varletto.

Bard. Run away, with the cozeners; for so soon as I came
beyond Eton, they threw me off, from behind one of them,   *55*
in a slough of mire; and set spurs and away, like three German
devils, three Doctor Faustuses.

Host. They are gone but to meet the duke, villain. Do not
say they be fled: Germans are honest men.

[Enter Sir Hugh Evans.]

Eva. Where is mine host?   *60*

Host. What is the matter, sir?

Eva. Have a care of your entertainments: there is a friend of
mine come to town, tells me, there is three cozen-germans that
has cozened all the hosts of Readins, of Maidenhead, of Colebrook, of horses and money. I tell you for good will, look   *65*
you: you are wise and full of gibes and vlouting-stogs, and 'tis
not convenient you should be cozened. Fare you well.   *[Exit.]*

[Enter Doctor Caius.]

Caius. Vere is mine host de Jarteer?

Host. Here, Master Doctor, in perplexity and doubtful
dilemma.   *70*

Caius. I cannot tell vat is dat; but it is tell-a me dat you

---

72 vizards: *masks*   **77 Eton;** *cf. n.*   **80 properties:** *stage requisites*   **81 tricking:**
adornment   **6 truckle-bed:** *trundle-bed, pushed under standing-bed when not in use*   **8**
Anthropophaginian: *cannibal*   **14 Ephesian:** *boon companion*   **16 Bohemian-Tartar:**
wild fellow

22 mussel-shell; *cf. n.*   **25 thorough:** *through*   **35 conceal:** *i.e., reveal*   **44 like**
... bold: *like the boldest*   **47 clerkly:** *scholarly*   **52 mere:** *pure*   **53 varletto:** *rascal*
servant   **57 Doctor Faustuses;** *cf. n.*   **63 cozen-germans;** *cf. n.*   **64 Readins:** *Read-*
ing   **64, 65 Colebrook:** *Colnbrook, four miles east of Windsor*

make grand preparation for a duke de Jamany: by my trot,
dere is no duke dat de court is know to come. I tell you for
good vill: adieu.   *[Exit.]*

   Host. Hue and cry, villain! go. Assist me, knight; I am   *75*
undone. Fly, run, hue and cry, villain! I am undone!
                         [Exeunt Host and Bardolph.]

   Fal. I would all the world might be cozened, for I have
been cozened and beaten too. If it should come to the ear of
the court how I have been transformed, and how my transformation hath been washed and cudgelled, they would melt   *80*
me out of my fat drop by drop, and liquor fishermen's boots
with me: I warrant they would whip me with their fine wits
till I were as crest-fallen as a dried pear. I never prospered
since I forswore myself at primero. Well, if my mind were but
long enough to say my prayers, I would repent.   *85*

             [Enter Mistress Quickly.]

Now, whence come you?
   Quick. From the two parties, forsooth.
   Fal. The devil take one party and his dam the other! and
so they shall be both bestowed. I have suffered more for
their sakes, more than the villainous inconstancy of man's   *90*
disposition is able to bear.
   Quick. And have not they suffered? Yes, I warrant; speciously one of them: Mistress Ford, good heart, is beaten black
and blue, that you cannot see a white spot about her.
   Fal. What tellest thou me of black and blue? I was beaten
myself into all the colours of the rainbow; and I was like to be
apprehended for the witch of Brainford: but that my admirable
dexterity of wit, my counterfeiting the action of an old
woman, delivered me, the knave constable had set me i' the
stocks, i' the common stocks, for a witch.   *100*
   Quick. Sir, let me speak with you in your chamber; you
shall hear how things go, and, I warrant, to your content.
Here is a letter will say somewhat. Good hearts! what ado here
is to bring you together! Sure, one of you does not serve
heaven well, that you are so crossed.   *105*
   Fal. Come up into my chamber.   *Exeunt.*

❧ SCENE SIXTH ❧

[Another Room in the Garter Inn]
Enter Fenton [and] Host.

   Host. Master Fenton, talk not to me: my mind is heavy; I will
give over all.
   Fent. Yet hear me speak. Assist me in my purpose,
And, as I am a gentleman, I'll give thee
A hundred pound in gold more than your loss.   *5*
   Host. I will hear you, Master Fenton; and I will, at the least,
keep your counsel.
   Fent. From time to time I have acquainted you
With the dear love I bear to fair Anne Page;
Who mutually hath answer'd my affection,   *10*
So far forth as herself might be her chooser,
Even to my wish. I have a letter from her
Of such contents as you will wonder at;

The mirth whereof so larded with my matter,
That neither singly can be manifested,   *15*
Without the show of both; wherein fat Falstaff
Hath a great scene: the image of the jest
I'll show you where at large.   *[Showing the letter.]*
   Hark, good mine host:
To-night at Herne's oak, just 'twixt twelve and one,   *20*
Must my sweet Nan present the Fairy Queen;
The purpose why, is here: in which disguise,
While other jests are something rank on foot,
Her father hath commanded her to slip
Away with Slender, and with him at Eton   *25*
Immediately to marry: she hath consented:
Now, sir,
Her mother, even strong against that match
And firm for Doctor Caius, hath appointed
That he shall likewise shuffle her away,   *30*
While other sports are tasking of their minds;
And at the deanery, where a priest attends,
Straight marry her: to this her mother's plot
She, seemingly obedient, likewise hath
Made promise to the doctor. Now, thus it rests: *35*
Her father means she shall be all in white,
And in that habit, when Slender sees his time
To take her by the hand and bid her go,
She shall go with him: her mother hath intended,
The better to denote her to the doctor,   *40*
For they must all be mask'd and vizarded—
That quaint in green she shall be loose enrob'd,
With ribands pendent, flaring 'bout her head;
And when the doctor spies his vantage ripe,
To pinch her by the hand; and on that token   *45*
The maid hath given consent to go with him.
   Host. Which means she to deceive, father or mother?
   Fent. Both, my good host, to go along with me:
And here it rests, that you'll procure the vicar
To stay for me at church 'twixt twelve and one,   *50*
And, in the lawful name of marrying,
To give our hearts united ceremony.
   Host. Well, husband your device; I'll to the vicar.
Bring you the maid, you shall not lack a priest.
   Fent. So shall I evermore be bound to thee;   *55*
Besides, I'll make a present recompense.   *Exeunt.*

ACT FIFTH ❧ SCENE FIRST

[A room in the Garter Inn]
Enter Falstaff [and Mistress] Quickly; and [later] Ford.

   Fal. Prithee, no more prattling; go: I'll hold. This is the
third time; I hope good luck lies in odd numbers. Away! go.
They say there is divinity in odd numbers, either in nativity,
chance or death. Away!
   Quick. I'll provide you a chain, and I'll do what I can to   *5*
get you a pair of horns.

---

72 Jamany: *i.e., Germany*   **81 liquor:** *grease*   **83 crest-fallen ... pear,** *cf. n.*   **84 primero:** *a card game*   **105 crossed:** *thwarted*   **10 mutually:** *reciprocally*

14 larded: *interspersed*   **17 image:** *idea*   **21 present:** *represent*   **23 something:** *somewhat* **rank:** *abundantly*   **28 even:** *equally*   **31 tasking:** *occupying*   **42 quaint:** *ele-
gantly*   **52 united ceremony:** *union of the marriage rite*   **1 hold:** *keep the
engagement*

Fal. Away, I say; time wears: hold up your head, and mince.

           [Exit Mistress Quickly.]

      [Enter Ford.]

How now, Master Brook! Master Brook, the matter will be
known to-night, or never. Be you in the Park about midnight,
at Herne's oak, and you shall see wonders.   *10*

Ford. Went you not to her yesterday, sir, as you told me
you had appointed?

Fal. I went to her, Master Brook, as you see, like a poor
old man; but I came from her, Master Brook, like a poor old
woman. That same knave Ford, her husband, hath the finest *15*
mad devil of jealousy in him, Master Brook, that ever governed
frenzy. I will tell you: he beat me grievously, in the shape of a
woman; for in the shape of a man, Master Brook, I fear not
Goliath with a weaver's beam, because I know also life is a
shuttle. I am in haste: go along with me; I'll tell you all, *20*
Master Brook. Since I plucked geese, played truant, and
whipped top, I knew not what it was to be beaten till lately.
Follow me: I'll tell you strange things of this knave Ford, on
whom to-night I will be revenged, and I will deliver his wife
into your hand. Follow. Strange things in hand, Master *25*
Brook! Follow.   *Exeunt.*

❧ SCENE SECOND ❧

[Windsor Park]
Enter Page, Shallow, [and] Slender.

Page. Come, come; we'll couch i' the castle-ditch till we see
the light of our fairies. Remember, son Slender, my daughter.

Slen. Ay, forsooth; I have spoke with her and we have a
nayword how to know one another. I come to her in white,
and cry, 'mum'; she cries, 'budget'; and by that we know *5*
one another.

Shal. That's good too: but what needs either your 'mum,' or
her 'budget'? the white will decipher her well enough. It hath
struck ten o'clock.

Page. The night is dark; light and spirits will become it *10*
well. Heaven prosper our sport! No man means evil but the
devil, and we shall know him by his horns. Let's away; follow
me.   *Exeunt.*

❧ SCENE THIRD ❧

[A Street leading to the Park]
Enter Mist[ress] Page, Mist[ress] Ford, [and] Caius.

Mrs. Page. Master Doctor, my daughter is in green: when
you see your time, take her by the hand, away with her to the
deanery, and dispatch it quickly. Go before into the Park: we
two must go together.

Caius. I know vat I have to do. Adieu.   *5*

Mrs. Page. Fare you well, sir. *[Exit Caius.]* My husband will
not rejoice so much at the abuse of Falstaff, as he will chafe at
the doctor's marrying my daughter: but 'tis no matter; better a
little chiding than a great deal of heart-break.

Mrs. Ford. Where is Nan now and her troop of fairies, *10*
and the Welsh devil, Hugh?

Mrs. Page. They are all couched in a pit hard by Herne's
oak, with obscured lights; which, at the very instant of Falstaff's and our meeting, they will at once display to the night.

Mrs. Ford. That cannot choose but amaze him.   *15*

Mrs. Page. If he be not amazed, he will be mocked; if
he be amazed, he will every way be mocked.

Mrs. Ford. We'll betray him finely.

Mrs. Page. Against such lewdsters and their lechery,
Those that betray them do no treachery.   *20*

Mrs. Ford. The hour draws on: to the oak, to the oak!

              Exeunt.

❧ SCENE FOURTH ❧

[Windsor Park]
Enter Evans [disguised] and [others as] Fairies.

Eva. Trib, trib, fairies: come; and remember your parts: Be
pold, I pray you; follow me into the pit, and when I give the
watch-'ords, do as I pid you. Come, come; trib, trib. *Exeunt.*

❧ SCENE FIFTH ❧

[Another Part of the Park]
Enter Falstaff [disguised as Herne; and later] Mistress Page,
Mistress Ford, Evans, Anne Page, [and others, as] Fairies; [also]
Page, Ford, [Mistress] Quickly, Slender, Fenton, Caius, [and]
Pistol.

Fal. The Windsor bell hath struck twelve; the minute draws
on. Now, the hot-blooded gods assist me! Remember, Jove,
thou wast a bull for thy Europa; love set on thy horns. O powerful love! that, in some respects, makes a beast a man; in
some other, a man a beast. You were also, Jupiter, a swan for *5*
the love of Leda; O omnipotent love! how near the god drew
to the complexion of a goose! A fault done first in the form of
a beast; O Jove, a beastly fault! and then another fault in the
semblance of a fowl: think on 't, Jove; a foul fault! When gods
have hot backs, what shall poor men do? For me, I am here *10*
a Windsor stag; and the fattest, I think, i' the forest: send me
a cool rut-time, Jove, or who can blame me to piss my tallow?
Who comes here? my doe?

    [Enter Mistress Ford and Mistress Page.]

Mrs. Ford. Sir John! art thou there, my deer? my male deer?

Fal. My doe with the black scut! Let the sky rain potatoes;
let it thunder to the tune of 'Green Sleeves'; hail kissing-comfits and snow eringoes; let there come a tempest of provocation, I will shelter me here.

Mrs. Ford. Mistress Page is come with me, sweetheart.

Fal. Divide me like a brib'd buck, each a haunch: I will *20*
keep my sides to myself, my shoulders for the fellow of this
walk, and my horns I bequeath your husbands. Am I a

---

7 mince: *walk prudishly* **19, 20 life is a shuttle;** *cf. n.* **1 couch:** *lie* **5 mum . . .**
budget; *cf. n.* **8 decipher:** *indicate*

19 lewdsters: *lechers* **3 Europa;** *cf. n.* **6 Leda;** *cf. n.* **15 scut:** *tail* (of a deer) **po-**
tatoes: *sweet potatoes* (supposed to incite love) **16 kissing-comfits:** *perfumed sweet-*
meats **17 eringoes:** *candied sea-holly* **20 brib'd:** *cut into portions* **21 fellow:**
keeper **22 walk:** *forest*

woodman, ha? Speak I like Herne the hunter? Why, now is
Cupid a child of conscience; he makes restitution. As I am a
true spirit, welcome!　　　　　　　　　　　　*[Noise within.]* 25
　　Mrs. Page. Alas! what noise?
　　Mrs. Ford. Heaven forgive our sins!
　　Fal. What should this be?
　　Mrs. Ford.　⎫
　　Mrs. Page.　⎬ Away, away! *[They run off.]*
　　　　　　　　　　　　　　　　　　　　　　　　　　　30
　　Fal. I think the devil will not have me damned, lest the oil that is
in me should set hell on fire; he would never else cross me thus.

Enter [Sir Hugh Evans, disguised as before; Pistol, as Hobgoblin;
Anne Page, and others, as] Fairies [with tapers.]

　　Anne. Fairies, black, grey, green, and white, 35
You moonshine revellers, and shades of night,
You orphan heirs of fixed destiny,
Attend your office and your quality.
Crier Hobgoblin, make the fairy oyes.
　　Pist. Elves, list your names: silence, you airy toys! 40
Cricket, to Windsor chimneys shalt thou leap:
Where fires thou find'st unrak'd and hearths unswept,
There pinch the maids as blue as bilberry:
Our radiant queen hates sluts and sluttery.
　　Fal. They are fairies; he that speaks to them shall die: 45
I'll wink and couch: no man their works must eye.
　　　　　　　　　　　　　　　　[Lies down upon his face.]
　　Eva. Where's Bede? Go you, and where you find a maid
That, ere she sleep, has thrice her prayers said,
Raise up the organs of her fantasy,
Sleep she as sound as careless infancy; 50
But those as sleep and think not on their sins,
Pinch them, arms, legs, backs, shoulders, sides, and shins.
　　Anne. About, about!
Search Windsor castle, elves, within and out:
Strew good luck, ouphs, on every sacred room, 55
That it may stand till the perpetual doom,
In state as wholesome as in state 'tis fit,
Worthy the owner, and the owner it.
The several chairs of order look you scour
With juice of balm and every precious flower: 60
Each fair instalment, coat, and several crest,
With loyal blazon, ever more be blest!
And nightly, meadow-fairies, look you sing,
Like to the Garter's compass, in a ring:
The expressure that it bears, green let it be, 65
More fertile-fresh than all the field to see;
And, *Honi soit qui mal y pense* write
In emerald tufts, flowers purple, blue, and white,
Like sapphire, pearl, and rich embroidery,
Buckled below fair knighthood's bending knee: 70
Fairies use flowers for their charactery.
Away! disperse! But, till 'tis one o'clock,
Our dance of custom round about the oak
Of Herne the hunter, let us not forget.
　　Eva. Pray you, lock hand in hand; yourselves in order set; 75
And twenty glow-worms shall our lanterns be,

To guide our measure round about the tree.
But, stay; I smell a man of middle-earth.
　　Fal. Heavens defend me from that Welsh fairy, lest he
transform me to a piece of cheese! 80
　　Pist. Vile worm, thou wast o'erlook'd even in thy birth.
　　Anne. With trial-fire touch me his finger-end:
If he be chaste, the flame will back descend
And turn him to no pain; but if he start,
It is the flesh of a corrupted heart. 85
　　Pist. A trial! come.
　　Eva.　　　　　　Come, will this wood take fire?
　　　　　　　　　　　　　[They burn him with their tapers.]
　　Fal. Oh, oh, oh!
　　Anne. Corrupt, corrupt, and tainted in desire!
About him, fairies, sing a scornful rime; 90
And, as you trip, still pinch him to your time.

　　　　　　　　　　The Song.
'Fie on sinful fantasy!
Fie on lust and luxury!
Lust is but a bloody fire, 95
Kindled with unchaste desire,
Fed in heart, whose flames aspire,
As thoughts do blow them higher and higher.
Pinch him, fairies, mutually;
Pinch him for his villainy; 100
Pinch him, and burn him, and turn him about,
Till candles and star-light and moonshine be out.'

[During this song they pinch Falstaff. Doctor Caius comes one
way, and steals away a boy in green; Slender another way, and
takes off a boy in white; and Fenton comes, and steals away
Anne Page. A noise of hunting is heard within. All the fairies
run away. Falstaff rises.]

[Enter Page, Ford, Mistress Page, and Mistress Ford.]

　　Page. Nay, do not fly: I think we have watch'd you now:
Will none but Herne the hunter serve your turn?
　　Mrs. Page. I pray you, come, hold up the jest no higher. 110
Now, good Sir John, how like you Windsor wives?
See you these, husband? do not these fair yokes
Become the forest better than the town?
　　Ford. Now sir, who's a cuckold now? Master Brook,
Falstaff's a knave, a cuckoldly knave; here are his horns, 115
Master Brook: and, Master Brook, he hath enjoyed nothing
of Ford's but his buck-basket, his cudgel, and twenty pounds
of money, which must be paid too, Master Brook; his horses
are arrested for it, Master Brook.
　　Mrs. Ford. Sir John, we have had ill luck; we could 120
never meet. I will never take you for my love again, but I
will always count you my deer.
　　Fal. I do begin to perceive that I am made an ass.
　　Ford. Ay, and an ox too; both the proofs are extant.
　　Fal. And these are not fairies? I was three or four times 125
in the thought they were not fairies; and yet the guiltiness of
my mind, the sudden surprise of my powers, drove the grossness of the foppery into a received belief, in despite of the teeth
of all rime and reason, that they were fairies. See now how wit
may be made a Jack-a-lent, when 'tis upon ill employment! 130

23 woodman: *hunter; cf. n.*　**24 child of conscience;** *cf. n.*　**S.d. Hobgoblin:**
Puck　**37 orphan heirs;** *cf. n.*　**37 office:** *duty*　**quality:** *profession*　**39 oyes:** *hear*
ye! (the court crier's call)　**43 bilberry:** *blueberry*　**46 wink:** *close my eyes*　**49**
Cf. n.　**59 chairs of order;** *cf. n.*　**61 instalment:** *stall*　**62 blazon:** *armorial bear-*
ings　**64 compass:** *circle*　**65 expressure:** *picture*　**71 charactery:** *writing*

78 middle-earth: *world of mortals*　**81 o'erlook'd:** *bewitched*　**94 luxury:** *lascivi-*
ousness　**95 bloody fire:** *fire in the blood*　**99 mutually:** *all at once*　**112 yokes;**
cf. n.　**119 arrested:** *seized by warrant*　**127 powers:** *faculties*　**128 foppery:** *deceit*

Eva. Sir John Falstaff, serve Got, and leave your desires, and fairies will not pinse you.

Ford. Well said, fairy Hugh.

Eva. And leave you your jealousies too, I pray you.

Ford. I will never mistrust my wife again, till thou art   *135* able to woo her in good English.

Fal. Have I laid my brain in the sun and dried it, that it wants matter to prevent so gross o'er-reaching as this? Am I ridden with a Welsh goat too? shall I have a coxcomb of frize? 'Tis time I were choked with a piece of toasted cheese.   *140*

Eva. Seese is not goot to give putter: your pelly is all putter.

Fal. 'Seese' and 'putter'! have I lived to stand at the taunt of one that makes fritters of English? This is enough to be the decay of lust and late-walking through the realm.

Mrs. Page. Why, Sir John, do you think, though we   *145* would have thrust virtue out of our hearts by the head and shoulders, and have given ourselves without scruple to hell, that ever the devil could have made your our delight?

Ford. What, a hodge-pudding? a bag of flax?

Mrs. Page. A puffed man?   *150*

Page. Old, cold, withered, and of intolerable entrails?

Ford. And one that is as slanderous as Satan?

Page. And as poor as Job?

Ford. And as wicked as his wife?

Eva. And given to fornications, and to taverns, and sack   *155* and wine and metheglins, and to drinkings and swearings and starings, pribbles and prabbles?

Fal. Well, I am your theme: you have the start of me; I am dejected; I am not able to answer the Welsh flannel. Ignorance itself is a plummet o'er me: use me as you will.   *160*

Ford. Marry, sir, we'll bring you to Windsor, to one Master Brook, that you have cozened of money, to whom you should have been a pander: over and above that you have suffered, I think, to repay that money will be a biting affliction.

[*Mrs. Ford.* Nay, husband, let that go to make amends;   *165* Forgive that sum, and so we'll all be friends.

Ford. Well, here's my hand: all is forgiven at last.]

Page. Yet be cheerful, knight: thou shalt eat a posset tonight at my house; where I will desire thee to laugh at my wife, that now laughs at thee. Tell her, Master Slender   *170* hath married her daughter.

Mrs. Page. [*Aside.*] Doctors doubt that: if Anne Page be my daughter, she is, by this, Doctor Caius' wife.

[Enter Slender.]

Slen. Whoa, ho! ho! father Page!

Page. Son, how now! how now, son! have you dispatched?

Slen. Dispatched! I'll make the best in Gloucestershire know on 't; would I were hanged, la, else!

Page. Of what, son?

Slen. I came yonder at Eton to marry Mistress Anne Page, and she's a great lubberly boy: if it had not been i' the   *180* church, I would have swinged him, or he should have swinged me. If I did not think it had been Anne Page, would I might never stir! and 'tis a postmaster's boy.

Page. Upon my life, then, you took the wrong.

Slen. What need you tell me that? I think so, when I took a

boy for a girl. If I had been married to him, for all he was in woman's apparel, I would not have had him.

Page. Why, this is your own folly. Did not I tell you how you should know my daughter by her garments?

Slen. I went to her in white, and cried, 'mum,' and she   *195* cried 'budget,' as Anne and I had appointed; and yet it was not Anne, but a postmaster's boy.

[*Eva.* Jeshu! Master Slender, cannot you see put marry poys?

Page. O I am vexed at heart: what shall I do?]

Mrs. Page. Good George, be not angry: I knew of your   *200* purpose; turned my daughter into green; and, indeed, she is now with the doctor at the deanery, and there married.

[Enter Caius.]

Caius. Vere is Mistress Page? By gar, I am cozened: I ha' married *un garçon, a boy; un paysan,* by gar, a boy; it is not Anne Page: by gar, I am cozened.   *205*

Mrs. Page. Why, did you not take her in green?

Caius. Ay, by gar, and 'tis a boy: by gar, I'll raise all Windsor.   *[Exit.]*

Ford. This is strange. Who hath got the right Anne?

Page. My heart misgives me: here comes Master Fenton.   *210*

[Enter Fenton and Anne Page.]

How now, Master Fenton!

Anne. Pardon, good father! good my mother, pardon!

Page. Now, mistress, how chance you went not with Master Slender?

Mrs. Page. Why went you not with Master Doctor, maid?

Fent. You do amaze her: hear the truth of it.
You would have married her most shamefully,
Where there was no proportion held in love.
The truth is, she and I, long since contracted,
Are now so sure that nothing can dissolve us.   *215*
The offence is holy that she hath committed,
And this deceit loses the name of craft,
Of disobedience, or unduteous title,
Since therein she doth evitate and shun
A thousand irreligious cursed hours,   *220*
Which forced marriage would have brought upon her.

Ford. Stand not amaz'd: here is no remedy:
In love the heavens themselves do guide the state:
Money buys lands, and wives are sold by fate.

Fal. I am glad, though you have ta'en a special stand to   *225*
strike at me, that your arrow hath glanced.

Page. Well, what remedy?—Fenton, heaven give thee joy!
What cannot be eschew'd must be embrac'd.

Fal. When night dogs run all sorts of deer are chas'd.

Mrs. Page. Well, I will muse no further. Master Fenton,   *230*
Heaven give you many, many merry days!
Good husband, let us every one go home,
And laugh this sport o'er by a country fire;
Sir John and all.

Ford.   Let it be so. Sir John,   *235*
To Master Brook you yet shall hold your word;
For he to-night shall lie with Mistress Ford.   *Exeunt.*

❧ FINIS ❧

---

139 coxcomb: *fool's cap*   **frize:** *woollen cloth, made in Wales*   **149 hodge-pudding:** *pudding of many ingredients* (?)   **156 metheglins:** *mead, a fermented drink*   **159 dejected:** *humbled*   **flannel:** *cloth, commonly made in Wales*   **159, 160 Ignorance ... me;** *cf. n.*   **181 swinged:** *beaten*   **183 postmaster:** *master of post horses*

214 contracted: *betrothed*   **219 evitate:** *avoid*   **225 stand:** *place from which to shoot*   **230 muse:** *complain*

NOTES

I.i.S.d. At the head of each scene of this play in the Folio of 1623 is prefixed a list of all the characters who appear during the scene. Except for these lists, and the *exeunt* at the close of each scene, the Folio is practically without stage-directions. It has been suggested that whoever prepared the play for the Folio was probably influenced by the 'classical method' of dividing plays into scenes, followed in the volume of Ben Jonson's plays published in 1616. By this method a new scene begins every time there is a change of actors on the stage. Thus the exit or entrance of a character marks the beginning of a new scene, and to each scene is prefixed a list of the actors who are actually on the stage during its course.

I.i.1, 2. *Star-chamber matter.* The Star Chamber was a court deriving its name from the *'chambre des estoiles'* at Westminster, where it sat, beginning with the reign of Edward III. It was proverbially harsh and arbitrary.

I.i.5. *coram.* Slender is confusing the Latin words *quorum* and *coram. Quorum* was the first word of a clause in the commission which named justices, and so came to be a title of certain justices. *Coram* was the first word Shallow would use as justice, in attestation of the legal documents he speaks of in lines 8 and 9: *'Coram me Roberto Shallow, armigero,'* i.e., 'before me Robert Shallow, Esquire.'

I.i.6, 7. *cust-alorum . . . rato-lorum.* Blunders for *Custos Rotulorum,* Keeper of the Rolls, the principal justice of the peace of a county.

I.i.14. *luces.* This is evidently a hit at the Warwickshire gentleman, Sir Thomas Lucy of Charlecote, whose game Shakespeare poached while a youth at Stratford. His arms were 'three luces hauriant argent.' Cf. The History of the Play.

I.i.19. An obscure passage. 'May not the whole point of the matter lie in Shallow's use of the word "salt," the heraldic term used especially for vermin? If so, "salt fish"="leaping louse," with a quibble on "salt" as opposed to "fresh fish." There is a further allusion to the predilection of vermin for "old coats," used quibblingly in the sense of "coats of arms" ' (Gollancz).

I.i.20. *quarter.* In heraldry, to combine the arms of another family with one's own by placing them in one of the four compartments of the shield.

I.i.72. *Cotsall.* The Cotswolds, a hilly region in Gloucestershire, celebrated for the 'Cotswold games,' where coursing and other rural sports flourished.

I.i.106, 107. Here and elsewhere, passages of the text found in the Quarto of 1602, but not in the Folio, are marked by square brackets.

I.i.108. *Banbury cheese.* Proverbially thin, 'nothing but paring.' Bardolph is ridiculing Slender's leanness.

I.i.110. *Mephistophilus.* The evil spirit attendant upon the hero in Marlowe's tragedy, *Doctor Faustus* (1588).

I.i.112. *Slice.* Either Nym is still ridiculing Slender's thinness, or he is using the word in its slang sense, meaning to cut, whether to cut with a sword, or 'cut and run.'

I.i.112. *humour.* According to medieval physiology there were four chief 'humours' (or fluids) in the human body—blood, phlegm, choler and black bile. The relative proportion of these determined whether a person's temperament were sanguine, phlegmatic, choleric or melancholy. In Shakespeare's time 'humour' was the most overworked word in the language, 'racked and tortured with constant abuse,' as Ben Jonson said. It is a favorite with Nym and Pistol.

I.i.130. *Edward shovel-boards.* Shilling pieces coined in the reign of Edward VI (1547-1553), commonly used in a game which consisted in pushing coins toward a mark. They were sufficiently rare to bring a premium in Shakespeare's day.

I.i.142. *run . . . humour.* 'If you say I am a thief (Steevens). Nuthook was the slang for constable.

I.i.147. *Scarlet and John.* Two of Robin Hood's men. Falstaff is ridiculing Bardolph's red face.

I.i.151. *careires.* A term used to designate galloping a horse at full speed, backward and forward. Probably Bardolph's 'conclusions pass'd the careires' meant 'the words ran high, at full gallop.' Commentators have been as much puzzled by it as is Slender.

I.i.170, 171. *Book of Songs and Sonnets.* 'Songes and Sonnets, written by the Right Honourable Lord Henry Howard, late Earle of Surrey, and others,' printed in 1557, and very popular during the reign of Queen Elizabeth.

I.i.255. *Sackerson.* A famous bear exhibited at Paris Garden in Southwark.

I.iii.8. *Keisar, and Pheezar.* Keisar is another form of Cæsar, the general term for emperor. Pheezar is probably from 'pheeze,' to beat.

I.iii.13. *froth and lime.* The host calls for an immediate exhibition of Bardolph's abilities as a tapster. Frothing a pot of beer made it appear fuller than it really was; mixing lime with the sack made it sparkle in the glass.

I.iii.18. Pistol's line is 'a parody on a line taken from one of the old bombast plays' (Steevens).

I.iii.43. *anchor . . . deep.* 'The scheme for debauching Ford's wife is deep.'

I.iii.57. *Guiana.* In 1596 Sir Walter Raleigh returned from an expedition to South America and published a book entitled "The Discoverie of the Large, Rich, and Bewtiful Empyre of Guiana, with a relation of the great and golden Citie of Manoa, which the Spaniards call El Dorado.'

I.iii.58. *'cheator.* An officer appointed to look after the King's escheats (i.e., properties which fell to a lord by forfeit or fine). He would have abundant opportunity of defrauding people of their estates, hence Falstaff's pun.

I.iii.63. *Sir Pandarus.* The go-between in the story of Troilus and Cressida. Pistol makes him a knight.

I.iii.72. *French thrift.* 'An economy then practised in France of making a single page serve in lieu of a train of attendants' (Clarke).

I.iii.73. *gourd and fullam.* Gourds were hollow dice; fullams were dice loaded at one corner.

I.iv.20. *Cain-coloured.* 'In old pictures and tapestries Cain and Judas were always represented as having yellow beards, or what we now call sandy-coloured' (Hudson).

I.iv.110. *An fool's-head.* Mistress Quickly is punning on 'Anne' and 'an' with reference to Caius' speech in line 108.

II.i.18. *Herod of Jewry.* Herod was the arch-villain in the old mystery plays.

II.i.20. *Flemish drunkard.* The Flemish were notorious for their intemperance.

II.i.45. *hack.* This word is a puzzle. 'Grow cheap,' 'kick,' 'deny,' and 'do mischief' are some of the meanings that have been suggested for it. It occurs again in the play, IV.i.56. Whatever the exact meaning, the general sense is clearly that Mrs. Page does not set a high value upon knighthood.

II.i.52, 53. *disposition would have gone to the truth of his words.* That is, his character would have been in accordance with his speech.

II.i.54. *Green Sleeves.* An old ballad-tune, usually sung with vulgar words, popular 'from the time of Elizabeth to the present day.'

II.i.104. *Actæon . . . Ringwood.* Actæon was a hunter in classical mythology, who accidentally saw Diana bathing, and was transformed by her into a stag. He was then slain by his dogs. Like him Ford will have 'horns' (the symbol of a cuckold, or deceived husband) if Falstaff's plans succeed. Ringwood was a typical dog's name.

II.i.109. *cuckoo-birds.* The cuckoo's note was supposed to foretell cuckoldom. Cf. *Love's Labour's Lost*, V.ii.946.

"The cuckoo then on every tree
Mocks married men,' etc.

II.i.126. *Cataian.* Often used as a term of reproach. From Cataia, or Cathay, the old name for China.

II.i.168, 169. *Cavaliero-justice.* The host is bestowing an additional title on Justice Shallow. Cavaliero meant a gentleman trained in arms; hence a gallant.

II.i.170, 171. *Good even and twenty.* 'Good evening and twenty of 'em!'

II.ii.4. *equipage.* Pistol may mean 'I'll pay you in commodities,' i.e., swords, bucklers, etc.; or (as Greg suggests) the sense may be 'I will return the money to you in all fairness' (equity).

II.ii.6. *countenance.* Falstaff means he had gone surety for Pistol's borrowings. He is punning on the two meanings of countenance: (1) face, and (2) patronage.

II.ii.11. *handle.* Fans were often set in handles of gold and silver.

II.ii.17. *Pickt-hatch.* A district of ill-repute in London, the houses having hatches or half-doors guarded with spikes to prevent marauders from 'leaping the hatch.' (Cf. *King Lear*, III. vi.70.)

II.ii.117. *fights.* A kind of screen used during naval engagements to protect the crew of a vessel.

II.ii.118. *my prize.* Perhaps an intimation of the fate of Mistress Quickly. In *Henry V* we find Pistol has married her.

II.ii.129. *Brooks.* Throughout the play as printed in the Folio, Ford's assumed name is Broome. Falstaff's pun here, and the authority of the two Quartos, have led modern editors to follow Pope in reading Brook throughout the play. Wright suggests the name may have been altered at the instance of someone named Brook, who had influence with the actors or their patron.

II.ii.177, 178. Cf. Ben Jonson's

"Follow a shadow, it still flies you;
Seem to fly it, it will pursue:
So court a mistress, she denies you;
Let her alone, she will court you."

II.ii.252, 253. *stand under the adoption of abominable terms.* Have to submit to being called by vile names.

II.iii.22, 23. *punto ... montant.* The punto was a blow with the point of the sword, the stock or stoccado (cf. II.i. 196) a thrust, the reverse a backhand stroke, and the montant an upward blow.

II.iii.25. *heart of elder.* 'In contradistinction to "heart of oak," elder wood having nothing but soft pith at heart' (Clarke). *Stale.* Slang term for physician. The word means urine, and alludes to the practice of examining patients' water in diagnosing cases.

II.iii.63. *Frogmore.* Now best known as the site of the mansion in Little Park, Windsor, built for the late King Edward VII while Prince of Wales.

II.iii.74. *Cried game.* 'The sport is arranged and proclaimed' (Hart). The phrase is from bear-baiting.

III.i.4. *pittie-ward.* Towards the Petty or Little Park, as distinguished from the Windsor Great Park.

III.i.13-20. Stanzas from a popular song by Christopher Marlowe. In line 20 Sir Hugh substitutes for one of Marlowe's lines a line from a metrical version of Psalm 137.

III.i.40. *doublet and hose.* The ordinary men's dress in Elizabethan times was the doublet, a close-fitting garment extending to the hips, and hose. Out of doors, and in cold weather a cloak or *gown* (line 30) was worn outside this. The latter still survives in the academic gown.

III.ii.36. *cry aim.* Archers when about to shoot were encouraged by cries of 'Aim!'

III.ii.60, 61. *prince and Poins.* This is a reference to the adventures of Falstaff in *Henry IV*, where he is the associate of Prince Hal and his companions.

III.ii.74. *pipe-wine.* There is a pun here upon pipe in its double sense of a cask and a musical instrument. It is suggested by Falstaff's mention in line 73, of canary, which was the name of a lively dance, as well as a sort of wine.

III.iii.11. *Datchet-mead.* An open meadow by the river, where clothes were washed out of doors as they are in France to-day. The village of Datchet is two miles east of Windsor, on the left bank of the Thames.

III.iii.33. Falstaff is quoting the opening line of the second song of Sir Philip Sidney's *Astrophel and Stella*, which begins:

'Have I caught my heavenly jewel
Teaching sleepe most faire to be?'

III.iii.52. *Fortune thy foe.* An allusion to a popular old song beginning 'Fortune my foe, why dost thou frown on me?'

III.iii.59. *Bucklersbury.* A street off Cheapside in London, inhabited by herbalists, who sold all sorts of simples or medicinal herbs.

III.iii.133. *uncape.* Ford is here using the language of the hunting-field. 'The collar of the grayhound was sometimes called his cape; a term equally applicable to the couple (or leash) of the running hound' (Madden). Hence to uncape would mean to uncouple, or set free, the hounds.

III.iii.191. *a-birding.* Birding was hawking with a sparrow hawk. Page's hawk is especially trained 'for the bush'; that is he flies at small birds which take refuge in a bush, where they can be shot.

III.iv.26. *a shaft or a bolt.* A shaft was a long slender arrow, a bolt a short thick one. Slender's whole phrase means 'I'll do it one way or another.'

III.v.92. *bilbo.* The swords of Bilbao, in Spain, were noted for the temper and elasticity of their blades. The test of a good sword was that it could be bent into a circle.

IV.i.40. *Hang-hog ... bacon.* Probably suggested by an anecdote of Sir Nicholas Bacon. A prisoner named Hog had been condemned to death and prayed for mercy on the ground of kindred. 'Ay,' replied the judge, 'but you and I cannot be of kindred unless you be hanged, for Hog is not Bacon till it be well hanged.'

IV.ii.61. *fat woman of Brainford.* 'The witch of Brentford,' a well-known personage of Shakespeare's day, kept a tavern at Brentford, a town on the Thames about twelve miles directly east of Windsor. In the 1602 Quarto of *The Merry Wives*, and in Dekker and Webster's *Westward Ho!* she is spoken of as 'Gillian of Brainford.'

IV.ii.148. *figure.* To 'work by the figure' meant to operate on a wax effigy of a person for the purpose of enchantment.

IV.ii.178. *fine and recovery.* The means by which an estate tail was converted into a few simple, so that the owner might dispose of it as he wished.

IV.iii.1. *The Germans.* Perhaps an allusion to the visit to Windsor in 1592 of Count Frederick of Mompelgard, afterwards Duke of Wurtemberg and Teck (cf. IV.v.72). In the text of the 1602 edition of the play there is evidently a reference to his title in the lines:

There is three sorts of cosen garmombles
Is cosen all the Hosts of Maidenhead and Readings.

Post horses were furnished him gratis during his stay, through a pass of Lord Howard.

IV.iv.77. *Eton.* Town in Buckinghamshire across the Thames from Windsor, famous for the school founded there in 1440 by Henry VI.

IV.v.22. *mussel-shell.* 'He calls poor Simple mussel-shell because he stands with his mouth open' (Johnson).

IV.v.57. *Doctor Faustuses.* Faustus was the famous mediæval scholar who obtained magic power for twenty-four years by selling his soul to the devil. He is the hero of Marlowe's tragedy of *Doctor Faustus*.

IV.v.63. *cozen-germans.* A pun on cousin-german, relative, and cozening, or cheating, Germans.

IV.v.83. *crest-fallen as a dried pear.* 'Pears when they are dried become flat, and lose the erect and oblong form that distinguishes them from apples' (Steevens).

V.i.20. *life is a shuttle.* Falstaff is thinking of Job 7. 6: 'My days are swifter than a weaver's shuttle, and are spent without hope.'

V.ii.5. *mum ... budget.* 'To play mum-budget' was 'to be tongue-tyed, to say never a word.'

V.v.3. *Europa.* The sister of Cadmus, who was carried off by Jove in the shape of a bull. Her story is told by Ovid, *Metamorphoses*, ii. 833 ff.

V.v.6. *Leda.* Courted by Jupiter in the shape of a swan. The story is given in the *Odyssey*, Book xi, and in Ovid's *Metamorphoses* vi. 109 ff.

V.v.23. *woodman.* Falstaff is priding himself on his knowledge of the rules for cutting up and apportioning a buck.

V.v.24. *child of conscience.* Cupid is conscientious, and will requite him for his past misfortunes.

V.v.37. *orphan heirs.* Fairies were believed to be of spontaneous birth, and so were 'created orphans by fate.'

V.v.49. 'Exalt her imagination by pleasant dreams.'

V.v.59. *chairs of order.* The stalls in St. George's Chapel at Windsor assigned to the Knights of the Garter, an order of Knighthood, founded about 1347 by Edward III (1327-1377). The emblem of the order is a blue garter with the motto *'Honi soit qui mal y pense.'*

V.v.112. *yokes.* Alluding to the antlers on Falstaff's head, which bore some resemblance to the projections on the top of ox-yokes.

V.v.159, 160. *Ignorance ... me.* 'Ignorance has sounded me,' or 'got to the bottom of me."

The Text of the Present Edition

The text of the present volume is, by permission of the Oxford University Press, that of the Oxford Shakespeare, edited by the late W. J. Craig, except for the following deviations:

1. In accordance with the plan of this series, the stage-directions of the First Folio have been preserved so far as possible. Modern additions to these are enclosed in square brackets, and passages of the text found only in the Quarto are similarly marked.

2. A few unimportant changes have been made in punctuation and the spelling of a few words has been normalized, as anything for any thing, Gloucester, Gloucestershire for Gloster, Glostershire, lantern for lanthorn, mussel-shell for muscle-shell, œillades for œilliades, Poins for Pointz, till for 'till, villainy, villainous for villany, villanous, warlike for war-like.

3. The following changes in punctuation or wording have been made, all of them being reversions to the readings of the Folio. The readings of the present edition precede the colon and Craig's follow in each case:

I.iv.20	Cain-coloured: cane-coloured	
	(Folio Caine-colourd)	
II.i.88	look where: look, where	
II.ii.17	Pickt-hatch: Picht-hatch	
II.iii.74	Cried game;: Cried I aim?	
	(Folio Cried-game,)	
III.i.84	Gaul: Guallia	
	(Folio Gaule)	
III.iii.87	in Windsor: of Windsor	
III.v.57	sped: how sped	
III.v.127	one: me	
IV.i.9	let: get	
IV.i.40	Hang-hog: Hang hog	

IV.i.57	horum;: horum?		IV.v.44	sir: like: Sir Tike;
IV.i.59	of: and		IV.vi.17	scene: scare
IV.ii.16	lines: lunes		V.iii.9	heart-break: heart break
IV.ii.109	Mistress Ford; Mistress Ford,: Mistress Ford;			(Folio hearte-break)
IV.ii.163	his: her		V.v.49	Raise: Rein
IV.v.24	master: Master		V.v.51	as: that

Twelfth Night or What You Will

Edited by
WILLIAM P. HOLDEN

Dramatis Personae

ORSINO, DUKE OF ILLYRIA

SEBASTIAN, *Brother to Viola*

ANTONIO, *Sea Captain, Friend to Sebastian*

A SEA CAPTAIN, *Friend to Viola*

VALENTINE }
CURIO } *Gentlemen attending on the Duke*

SIR TOBY BELCH, *Kinsman of Olivia*

SIR ANDREW AGUECHEEK, *Suitor of Olivia*

MALVOLIO, *Steward to Olivia*

FABIAN, *an Attendant to Olivia*

THE CLOWN FESTE, *Olivia's Fool*

OLIVIA, *a Countess*

VIOLA, *in love with the Duke; Sister to Sebastian*

MARIA, *Olivia's Gentlewoman*

LORDS, A PRIEST, SAILORS, OFFICERS,
    MUSICIANS, AND OTHER ATTENDANTS

SCENE—*Illyria and the coast nearby.*

Twelfth Night

INTRODUCTION

TEXT AND DATE

The earliest text of *Twelfth Night*, that of the First Folio (1623), is excellent: the spelling and punctuation are generally clear, and the lines offer few difficulties of meaning. The compositor has several times encountered words or passages which he did not understand, such as *staniel* (II.5.106) and *pavin* (V.1.199), and he fails to realize that Malvolio is reading from a letter in II.5.127 ff. The text appears to have been set up from a particularly accurate and complete promptbook; this conclusion is supported by the survival of a number of careful instructions: 'Enter Viola and Malvolio at several doors' (II.2.1), and 'Malvolio within' (IV.2), both of which indicate the construction and employment of the stage on which the play would have been produced. In addition the scene divisions, entrances, and exits are unusually complete. The copy is in all ways among the best of Shakespeare's plays.

John Manningham from the Middle Temple recorded in his diary for February 2, 1602, a performance which he had seen:

> At our feast wee had a play called
> "Twelve Night, or What you Will," much
> like the Commedy of Errores, or Menechmi
> in Plautus, but most like and neere to
> that in Italian called Inganni . . .

Within the play itself, the evidence supports Manningham. The song 'O Mistress Mine' (II.3.34 ff.) was printed in 1509 in Morley's *Consort Lessons;* and 'Corydon's Farewell to Phyllis,' from which Sir Toby sings the first line (II.3.91), appeared in Jones' *First Booke of Songes* in 1600. Fabian's 'pension of thousands to be paid from the Sophy' (II.5.160) seems to be a reflection of rumors of the moment concerning the fabulous wealth of the shah of Persia; the stories had started with the published report of Sir Robert Shirley's trip to Persia in 1599. The 'icicle on a Dutchman's beard' (III.2.24) sounds like a reference to the Arctic voyages of Barentz, an account of which was entered in the Stationers' Register in 1598. The 'new map with the augmentation of the Indies' (III.2.69) seems to have been Edward Wright's, done in 1600; Wright used the Mercator projection (Maria's *lines*), then new to England. Finally, Valentino Orsino, duke of Bracciano, visited the English court in January 1600; and the Lord Chamberlain's men (Shakespeare's company) performed before the court on January 6, or Twelfth Night. The presence of Orsino's name in the play suggests that the first performance may have been on Twelfth Night 1600.

However, it appears that the text underwent revisions of an undetermined extent in the years immediately after 1600. In 1606 a statue was passed against the profane use of God's name on the stage; and *Jove* occurs in a number of places where 'God' would be much more natural. Sir Toby's 'Jove bless thee, Master Parson' (IV.2.10) is extremely strained; indeed, it sounds as though the revisions were intended to make the rule on profanity ridiculous. And Malvolio's 'Jove, not I, is the doer of this' (III.4.78) is inappropriate to the steward's character. Again, there

is an indication of revision when the Duke asks Cesario to sing (II.4.2) and is told that Feste the Jester is not there. The song was probably first assigned to Cesario and, in a later performance, to Feste; the revisions of the script did not include the elimination of the old speech in which the Duke asked Cesario to sing.

SOURCES OF THE PLAY

The romantic plot of *Twelfth Night*—the story of the Duke Orsino, Olivia, and Viola—is derived from a large number of sources; it is not possible to name a single direct ancestor. H. H. Furness' variorum edition (1901) and Morton Luce's *Rich's 'Apolonius and Silla'* (1912) contain the most complete accounts of the versions, dramatic and nondramatic, from which Shakespeare might have drawn.

Shakespeare's immediate source for the narrative is unknown, not through lack of an earlier telling but because of the multiplicity of versions, a number of which seem to have furnished him with various details, ranging from bits of narrative to names of characters and, possibly, verbal elements for his lines. The mention, quoted above, in Manningham's diary of 'that in Italian called *Inganni*' is extremely ambiguous: he may have been referring to a single play which he mistakenly regarded as the immediate source of *Twelfth Night;* he may have been referring to a group of plays loosely known as the *Inganni;* or he may simply have been referring to the common dramatic theme of the *inganni,* that is 'deceits' or 'tricks.' Finally, it is possible that he confused the word *inganni* with *ingannati,* 'deceived,' 'tricked.' There are three Italian plays with the name *Gl' Inganni:* the authors and the dates of printing are Nicolo Secchi, 1562; Curzio Gonzaga, 1592; and Domico Cornaccini, 1604. All three have plots which resemble the central plot of *Twelfth Night,* but it is unlikely that they are Shakespeare's sources. It might be noted that Gonzaga's play does have the name Cesare for the lady in disguise. The date of printing of the Carnaccini would perhaps have made it too late.

The probability is much greater that Shakespeare got elements for his story of the Duke Orsino in love with the Countess Olivia, and Viola, the disguised page in love with, and in the service of, the Duke, from the anonymous play, *Gl' Ingannati.* The title is sufficiently close to Manningham's *Inganni. Gl' Ingannati* was first acted in 1531 and was published six years later as part of the volume *Il Sacrificio,* a collection of assorted works dedicated to faithless mistresses and written by members of a Sienese literary coterie, the *Intronati.* One of the deserted lovers is mentioned by name, Agnol Malevoli, which might have suggested either Malvolio or Aguecheek. The action of *Gl' Ingannati* includes a brother and sister who look alike, and a trick of disguise by means of which the sister remains unknown near the man she loves. The ending is comic, with the proper transfer of

affections and the solving of the mystery of the brother and sister. Among the characters there are a pretentious pedant, a dupe, and a nurse, possibly suggestions for Malvolio, Sir Andrew, and Maria. The lady in disguise takes the name of Fabio, certainly close to Shakespeare's Fabian, and in the prologue there is a mention of 'la notte di Beffana' or Twelfth Night. In short, the resemblances between the two plays are too numerous to allow the dismissal of *Gl' Ingannati* as a remote antecedent of *Twelfth Night.*

However, the connection between the two is not compelling simply because there existed in Italian, French, and English a number of versions of the same story; and Shakespeare is known to have been familiar with other writings of the authors of several of the versions. He had read, for example, the prose stories of Geraldo Cinthio, and in his *Hecatommithi* (1565) there is a retelling of the plot *Gl' Ingannati.* Cinthio begins his version with a shipwreck, an event added to the dramatic version, and Shakespeare takes over the shipwreck, probably not directly, in *Twelfth Night.* Story 36 of the second part of Matteo Bandello's *Novelle* (1554) is again the story of the lady in love who disguises herself as a man, and of her brother who looks like her. Bandello has changed the names, but the narrative remains that of *Gl' Ingannati.* In Bandello there may be some verbal anticipations of Shakespeare. For instance, 'L'amoroso verme voracement con grandissimo cordoglio rodeva il cuore' perhaps suggest Viola's 'But let concealment, like a worm i' the bud, Feed on her damask cheek' (II.4.121). However, verbal similarities prove little about Bandello as a source for Shakespeare, since he is known to have been familiar with a French translation of Bandello. In François de Belleforest's *Histoires Tragiques,* vol. 4 (1570), there is another version of Bandello's retelling of *Gl' Ingannati;* and in the same collection there are other narratives which Shakespeare used for his plots. Belleforest keeps the names of the characters from Bandello, but omits and adds details to point up his narrative.

A number of other rewritings of *Gl' Ingannati,* all less notable, survive. Shakespeare may have been acquainted with the French play by Charles Estienne, *Les Abusés* (1543); but it is more probable that Shakespeare saw or knew about the production of a Latin adaptation, *Lælia,* presented at Queens' College, Cambridge, about 1595. Two Spanish plays are similar to *Gl' Ingannati.* They are *Los Engañados* (1567) by Lope de Rueda and the anonymous and undated *La Española de Florencia.*

But the version of *Gl' Ingannati* most easily available to Shakespeare was an English retelling in a collection of prose narratives by Barnabie Riche, *Riche his Farewell to Militarie Profession* (1581). The story, the second in the volume, is titled 'The Historie of Apolonius and Silla.'

In Cyprus the young and noble Silla fell in love with the Duke Apolonius, a guest of her father. Apolonius did not return her love and went to his home, Constantinople. Silla determined to follow him; accompanied by her devoted servant Pedro, who passed as her brother, she boarded a ship. The voyage ended in a shipwreck; all were lost except Silla, but she was thus freed from the unwelcome love-making of the captain. Silla saved her life by clinging to a chest which turned out to be filled with the captain's clothing and money. So she dressed herself as a man, called herself Silvio, the name of her brother with whom she was identical in appearance, and went unknown into the service of the Duke Apolonius in Constantinople. He sent her a number of times as messenger to the widow Julina with whom he was in love. Julina refused the attentions of the Duke, but fell in love with the young man Silvio and confessed her love to him. Meantime, the real Silvio, the brother of Silla in disguise, had arrived in Constantinople in search of his sister. Julina saw him, mistook him for the servant, and was betrothed to him; but he then left still in search of his sister. Julina presently found that she was to have a child by him.

When Apolonius learned that his servant Silvio had seduced Julina he threw Silvio in a dungeon. Later Apolonius attempted to compel Silvio to marry Julina; but Silvio revealed to Julina the disguise and her (Silla's) love for Apolonius. Having heard the story from Julina, Apolonius decided that he was really in love with Silla and they were married. The story of their love got to the brother Silvio, and he returned to Constantinople to see his sister. Apolonius took the real Silvio to Julina and they were married.

In Riche's version, a prose tale centered on narrative, there is very little characterization, and the events move with a looseness which would be impossible for the stage. Shakespeare has added details of character and a tighter plot to produce from the leisurely 'history' a dramatic unit of swiftness and point. In essence, the narrative consists of two combined themes of deception. The first is the story of the siblings who look alike and who cause a series of ironic complications on the stage until the final scene in which they appear together and solve the mystery for the other characters in the play. (The audience is at no point mystified.) This device Latin comedy had taken from Greek, and Shakespeare had used it in *The Comedy of Errors.* The second device, the trick of the lady in disguise as a man and serving her beloved without his knowledge, Shakespeare had used in *Two Gentlemen of Verona.* Within the more complex pattern of the narrative of *Gl' Ingannati* (and Riche's retelling), the two themes of deception are combined; in addition, the beloved of the lady in disguise loves another woman and sends his page, really the lady who loves him, as a messenger to his lady. Thinking the page is a man, the woman falls in love with him. Finally, the complications are resolved and the page, revealed as a woman, wins the love of her master. Both the trick of disguise and the shift in sex were peculiarly plausible to the Shakespearean audience, accustomed to boy-actors in female roles.

No source is known for the comic subplot of Malvolio and his tormentors, Maria, Sir Toby, Sir Andrew, Feste, and Fabian. But the subplot has pleased audiences more than the main plot; and the play has been known commonly by the false title of *Malvolio.* The two plots are connected by more than mere events. Both hinge upon the original theme of *Gl' Ingannati,* 'the deceived.' If the lover, the Duke Orsino, is deceived, so is the lover, Malvolio; and so are, in one way or another, most of the other characters of the play.

ACT FIRST ❧ SCENE FIRST

Enter Orsino, Duke of Illyria, Curio, and other Lords.

Duke. If music be the food of love, play on!
Give me excess of it, that surfeiting,
The appetite may sicken and so die.
That strain agen! It had a dying fall;
O, it came o'er my ear like the sweet sound   5
That breathes upon a bank of violets,
Stealing and giving odor. Enough, no more;
'Tis not so sweet now as it was before.
O spirit of love, how quick and fresh art thou,
That notwithstanding thy capacity,   10
Receiveth as the sea. Nought enters there,
Of what validity and pitch soe'er,
But falls into abatement and low price
Even in a minute. So full of shapes is fancy
That it alone is high fantastical.   15
  Curio. Will you go hunt, my lord?
  Duke.   What, Curio?
  Curio. The hart.
  Duke. Why, so I do, the noblest that I have.
O, when mine eyes did see Olivia first,   20
Methought she purg'd the air of pestilence.
That instant was I turn'd into a hart,
And my desires like fell and cruel hounds
Ere since pursue me. How now, what news from her?

Enter Valentine.

  Valentine. So please my lord, I might not be admitted,   25
But from her handmaid do return this answer:
The element itself, till seven years' heat,
Shall not behold her face at ample view;
But like a cloistress she will veiled walk,
And water once a day her chamber round   30
With eye-offending brine: all this to season
A brother's dead love, which she would keep fresh
And lasting in her sad remembrance.
  Duke. O, she that hath a heart of that fine frame
To pay this debt of love but to a brother,   35
How will she love when the rich golden shaft
Hath kill'd the flock of all affections else
That live in her; when liver, brain, and heart,
These sovereign thrones, are all supplied and fill'd,
Her sweet perfections, with one self king.   40
Away before me to sweet beds of flow'rs;
Love-thoughts lie rich when canopied with bow'rs.   *Exeunt.*

❧ SCENE SECOND ❧

Enter Viola, a Captain, and Sailors.

  Viola. What country, friends, is this?
  Captain. This is Illyria, lady.
  Viola. And what should I do in Illyria?
My brother he is in Elysium.
Perchance he is not drown'd. What think you sailors?   5
  Captain. It is perchance that you yourself were sav'd.
  Viola. O my poor brother, and so perchance may he be!
  Captain. True, madam, and to comfort you with chance,
Assure yourself, after our ship did split,
When you, and those poor number sav'd with you,   10
Hung on our driving boat, I saw your brother,
Most provident in peril, bind himself
(Courage and hope both teaching him the practice)
To a strong mast that liv'd upon the sea:
Where, like Arion on the dolphin's back,   15
I saw him hold acquaintance with the waves
So long as I could see.
  Viola. For saying so, there's gold.
Mine own escape unfoldeth to my hope,
Whereto thy speech serves for authority   20
The like of him. Know'st thou this country?
  Captain. Ay, madam, well, for I was bred and born
Not three hours' travel from this very place.
  Viola. Who governs here?
  Captain. A noble duke in nature as in name.   25
  Viola. What is his name?
  Captain. Orsino.
  Viola. Orsino. I have heard my father name him.
He was a bachelor then.
  Captain. And so is now, or now so very late: 30
For but a month ago I went from hence,
And then 'twas fresh in murmur (as you know
What great ones do, the less will prattle of)
That he did seek the love of fair Olivia.
  Viola. What's she?   35
  Captain. A virtuous maid, the daughter of a count
That died some twelvemonth since; then leaving her
In the protection of his son, her brother,
Who shortly also died; for whose dear love,
They say, she hath abjur'd the sight   40
And company of men.
  Viola.   O that I serv'd that lady,
And might not be deliver'd to the world
Till I had made mine own occasion mellow,
What my estate is.   45
  Captain.   That were hard to compass,
Because she will admit no kind of suit,
No, not the Duke's.
  Viola. There is a fair behavior in thee, Captain,
And though that nature with a beauteous wall   50

1–3 If music . . . so die; *cf. n.*   **4 agen:** *again* **fall:** *cadence, rhythm*   **5 sound:** *both the sound of music and of the wind*   **9–14 O spirit . . . in a minute;** *cf. n.*   **9 quick:** *alive*   **12 pitch:** *high point of a falcon's flight*   **14 Even:** *monosyllabic* **shapes:** *figures, forms* **fancy:** *imagination, the mind of the lover; cf. n.*   **15 high fantastical:** *highly changeable and imaginative*   **18 hart:** *the adult male deer*   **19 the noblest;** *cf. n.*   **21 Methought:** *it seemed to me*   **22 hart:** *possibly a pun on 'heart'; cf. n.*   **23 fell:** *savage, fierce*   **24 Ere:** *e'er, ever*   **25 might not:** *could not*   **27 element:** *sky* **heat** *the course of the sun*   **29 cloistress:** *nun in a convent*   **31 eye-offending brine:** *the salt tears irritate the eye* **to season:** *both 'to spice' and 'to preserve'*   **33 remembrance:** *probably four syllables*   **34 frame:** *construction*   **36 golden shaft:** *Cupid's golden arrow brings love; cf. n.*   **37 else:** *other*   **38 liver, brain, and heart:** *supposed centers of love, thought, and emotion, respectively*   **40 one self king:** *one and the same person, her husband*

3 Illyria: *on the east coast of the Adriatic*   **4 Elysium:** *heaven (Greek mythology) cf. n.*   **8 chance:** *what may have happened*   **11 driving:** *'driving before the wind' or 'drifting'*   **12 provident:** *foreseeing and thrifty*   **14 liv'd:** *survived by floating*   **15 Arion:** *F* **Orion**; *cf. n.*   **19 unfoldeth to my hope:** *reveals itself so as to give me hope (for my brother)*   **21 the like:** *the same escape* **country:** *probably three syllables*   **22 bred:** *conceived*   **32 'twas fresh in murmur:** *there was a current rumor*   **35 What's she:** *'who's she' and 'what sort of person is she'*   **43 deliver'd:** *given over to, disclosed, revealed; cf. n.*   **44 Till . . . mellow:** *till I had arranged my own proper opportunity (to disclose)*   **45 estate:** *position in society* **to compass:** *to achieve*   **49 behavior:** *both 'conduct' and 'appearance'*   **50 though that:** *though*

Doth oft close in pollution, yet of thee
I will believe thou hast a mind that suits
With this thy fair and outward character.
I prethee (and I'll pay thee bounteously)
Conceal me what I am, and be my aid   55
For such disguise as haply shall become
The form of my intent. I'll serve this Duke,
Thou shalt present me as an eunuch to him;
It may be worth thy pains. For I can sing,
And speak to him in many sorts of music   60
That will allow me very worth his service.
What else may hap, to time I will commit;
Only shape thou thy silence to my wit.

    Captain. Be you his eunuch, and your mute I'll be;
When my tongue blabs, then let mine eyes not see.   65

    Viola. I thank thee. Lead me on.   *Exeunt.*

❧ SCENE THIRD ❧

Enter Sir Toby and Maria.

    Toby. What a plague means my niece to take the death of
her brother thus? I am sure care's an enemy to life.

    Maria. By my troth, Sir Toby, you must come in earlier
a nights. Your cousin, my lady, takes great exceptions to your
ill hours.   5

    Toby. Why, let her except before excepted.

    Maria. Ay, but you must confine yourself within the modest
limits of order.

    Toby. Confine? I'll confine myself no finer than I am. These
clothes are good enough to drink in, and so be these boots   10
too. And they be not, let them hang themselves in their own
straps.

    Maria. That quaffing and drinking will undo you. I heard
my lady talk of it yesterday, and of a foolish knight that you
brought in one night here to be her wooer.   15

    Toby. Who? Sir Andrew Aguecheek?

    Maria. Ay, he.

    Toby. He's as tall a man as any's in Illyria.

    Maria. What's that to th' purpose?

    Toby. Why, he has three thousand ducats a year.   20

    Maria. Ay, but he'll have but a year in all these ducats.
He's a very fool and a prodigal.

    Toby. Fie that you'll say so! He plays o' th' viol-de-gamboys
and speaks three or four languages word for word without
book, and hath all the good gifts of nature.   25

    Maria. He hath indeed, almost natural. For besides that he's
a fool, he's a great quarreler; and but that he hath the gift of a

coward to allay the gust he hath in quarreling, 'tis thought
among the prudent he would quickly have the gift of a grave.

    Toby. By this hand, they are scoundrels and substractors   30
that say so of him. Who are they?

    Maria. They that add, moreover, he's drunk nightly in your
company.

    Toby. With drinking healths to my niece. I'll drink to her
as long as there is a passage in my throat and drink in   35
Illyria. He's a coward and a coistrel that will not drink to my
niece till his brains turn o' th' toe like a parish top. What,
wench? *Castiliano vulgo;* for here comes Sir Andrew Agueface.

Enter Sir Andrew.

    Andrew. Sir Toby Belch. How now, Sir Toby Belch?

    Toby. Sweet Sir Andrew.   40

    Andrew. Bless you, fair shrew.

    Maria. And you too, sir.

    Toby. Accost, Sir Andrew, accost.

    Andrew. What's that?

    Toby. My niece's chambermaid.   45

    Andrew. Good Mistress Accost, I desire better acquaintance.

    Maria. My name is Mary, sir.

    Andrew. Good Mistress Mary Accost.

    Toby. You mistake, knight. 'Accost' is front her, board her,
woo her, assail her.   50

    Andrew. By my troth I would not undertake her in this
company. Is that the meaning of 'accost'?

    Maria. Fare you well, gentlemen.

    Toby. And thou let part so, Sir Andrew, would thou mightst
never draw sword agen.   55

    Andrew. And you part so, mistress, I would I might never
draw sword agen. Fair lady, do you think you have fools in
hand?

    Maria. Sir, I have not you by th' hand.

    Andrew. Marry, but you shall have, and here's my hand.   60

    Maria. Now, sir, thought is free. I pray you bring your
hand to th' butt'ry bar and let it drink.

    Andrew. Wherefore, sweetheart? What's your metaphor?

    Maria. It's dry, sir.

    Andrew. Why, I think so. I am not such an ass but I   65
can keep my hand dry. But what's your jest?

    Maria. A dry jest, sir.

    Andrew. Are you full of them?

    Maria. Ay, sir, I have them at my fingers' ends. Marry, now
I let go your hand, I am barren.   *Exit.*   70

    Toby. O knight, thou lack'st a cup of canary. When did I
see thee so put down?

    Andrew. Never in your life, I think, unless you see canary
put me down. Methinks sometimes I have no more wit than a

---

53 character: *personal appearance*   **54 I prethee:** *I prithee, I pray thee*   **57 The form
of my intent:** *my outward purpose*   **61 allow me . . . service:** *make me very worth while
as his servant*   **63 to my wit:** *in accordance with my cleverness; cf. n.*   **64 mute:** *silent
servant (in contrast with Viola as the sexless servant)*   **3 by my troth:** *truly*   **4 a
nights:** *of nights*   **cousin:** *used loosely for 'kinsman,' 'cousin,' 'aunt,' 'nephew,' 'niece'*   **6
except before excepted:** *object uselessly to what I do; cf. n.*   **7 modest:** *decent, restrained*   **order:** *good conduct*   **9 finer:** *'tighter' and 'better,' both of clothing and conduct,
with a quibble on 'confine'*   **10 be:** *a regular plural*   **11 And:** *if; cf. n.*   **13 undo:**
ruin   **18 tall:** *both 'tall' and 'brave' (ironically of Sir Andrew)*   **20 ducats:** *an Italian
coin; cf. n.*   **22 very:** *true, genuine*   **23 viol-de-gamboys:** *'leg-viola,' predecessor of the
violincello (Italian, viola da gamba)*   **24, 25 without book:** *by memory*   **26 almost
natural:** *almost like a fool; cf. n.*

28 gust . . .: *in taste . . . for*   **30 substractors:** *detractors, calumniators*   **32 nightly:**
'nightly' and possibly 'knightly,' 'like a knight'   **36 coistrel:** *a groom, a base fellow*   **37
parish top;** *cf. n.*   **38 wrench:** *young girl; cf. n.*   **Castiliano vulgo;** *cf. n.*   **Agueface:** *pale
and thin-faced. Ague, an acute fever, commonly malaria*   **40 Sweet:** *'dear,' a conventional
form of address*   **41 shrew:** *a scolding man or woman*   **43–48 Accost . . . Accost;**
cf. n.   **46 Andrew:** *F Ma [ria]*   **48 Mistress Mary Accost:** *F mistris Mary, accost*   **49
front her:** *face her*   **board:** *'to greet'; but also 'to go on board,' as of a ship (French, abor-
der)*   **And thou let part so:** *if you let her go thus*   **57 agen:** *again*   **56 And:** *if*   **57, 58
fools in hand:** *fools to do business with*   **60 Marry:** *originally 'the Virgin Mary,' but here
a mild oath, 'indeed,' 'to be sure'*   **62 butt'ry bar;** *cf. n.*   **it:** *your hand, i.e. 'Have a
drink'*   **64 It's dry, sir;** *cf. n.*   **70 barren:** *barren of jokes*   **71 canary:** *a sweet wine
from the Canary Islands*   **72 put down:** *discomforted*   **74 methinks:** *it seems to
me*   **74, 75 no more wit than a Christian:** *no more intelligence than the average man*

Christian or an ordinary man has. But I am a great eater   *75*
of beef and I believe that does harm to my wit.

Toby. No question.

Andrew. And I thought that, I'd forswear it. I'll ride home
tomorrow, Sir Toby.

Toby. Pourquoi, my dear knight?   *80*

Andrew. What is 'pourquoi'? Do, or not do? I would I had
bestowed that time in the tongues that I have in fencing,
dancing, and bear-baiting. O, had I but followed the arts!

Toby. Then hadst thou had an excellent head of hair.

Andrew. Why, would that have mended my hair?   *85*

Toby. Past question, for thou seest it will not curl by nature.

Andrew. But it becomes me well enough, does't not?

Toby. Excellent. It hangs like flax on a distaff; and I hope
to see a huswife take thee between her legs and spin it
off.   *90*

Andrew. Faith, I'll home tomorrow, Sir Toby. Your niece
will not be seen, or if she be, it's four to one she'll none of
me. The Count himself here hard by woos her.

Toby. She'll none o' th' Count. She'll not match above her
degree, neither in estate, years, nor wit; I have heard her   *95*
swear't. Tut, there's life in't, man.

Andrew. I'll stay a month longer. I am a fellow o' th'
strangest mind i' th' world. I delight in masques and revels
sometimes altogether.

Toby. Art thou good at these kick-chawses, knight?   *100*

Andrew. As any man in Illyria, whatsoever he be, under
the degree of my betters, and yet I will not compare with an
old man.

Toby. What is thy excellence in a galliard, knight?

Andrew. Faith, I can cut a caper.   *105*

Toby. And I can cut the mutton to't.

Andrew. And I think I have the back-trick simply as strong
as any man in Illyria.

Toby. Wherefore are these things hid? Wherefore have these
gifts a curtain before 'em? Are they like to take dust, like   *110*
Mistress Mall's picture? Why dost thou not go to church in a
galliard and come home in a coranto? My very walk should be
a jig. I would not so much as make water but in a sink-a-pace.
What dost thou mean? Is it a world to hide virtues in? I did
think by the excellent constitution of thy leg, it was   *115*
form'd under the star of a galliard.

Andrew. Ay, 'tis strong, and it does indifferent well in a
dam'd color'd stock. Shall we sit about some revels?

Toby. What shall we do else? Were we not born under
Taurus?   *120*

Andrew. Taurus? That's sides and heart.

Toby. No, sir; it is legs and thighs. Let me see thee caper.
Ha, higher; ha, ha, excellent!   *Exeunt.*

❧ SCENE FOURTH ❧

Enter Valentine, and Viola in man's attire.

Valentine. If the Duke continue these favors towards you,
Cesario, you are like to be much advanc'd. He hath known
you but three days and already you are no stranger.

Viola. You either fear his humor or my negligence, that
you call in question the continuance of his love. Is he   *5*
inconstant, sir, in his favors?

Valentine. No, believe me.

Enter Duke, Curio, and Attendants.

Viola. I thank you. Here comes the Count.

Duke. Who saw Cesario, ho?

Viola. On your attendance, my lord, here.   *10*

Duke. Stand you awhile aloof. Cesario,
Thou know'st no less but all. I have unclasp'd
To thee the book even of my secret soul.
Therefore, good youth, address thy gait unto her;
Be not denied access, stand at her doors,   *15*
And tell them there thy fixed foot shall grow
Till thou have audience.

Viola.   Sure, my noble lord,
If she be so abandon'd to her sorrow
As it is spoke, she never will admit me.   *20*

Duke. Be clamorous and leap all civil bounds
Rather than make unprofited return.

Viola. Say I do speak with her, my lord, what then?

Duke. O, then unfold the passion of my love;
Surprise her with discourse of my dear faith;   *25*
It shall become thee well to act my woes.
She will attend it better in thy youth
Than in a nuncio's of more grave aspect.

Viola. I think not so, my lord.

Duke.   Dear lad, believe it;   *30*
For they shall yet belie thy happy years
That say thou art a man. Diana's lip
Is not more smooth and rubious; thy small pipe
Is as the maiden's organ, shrill and sound,
And all is semblative a woman's part.   *35*
I know thy constellation is right apt
For this affair. Some four or five attend him,
All if you will; for I myself am best
When least in company. Prosper well in this,
And thou shalt live as freely as thy lord   *40*
To call his fortunes thine.

Viola.   I'll do my best
To woo your lady: *[Aside.]* yet a barful strife!
Whoe'er I woo, myself would be his wife.   *Exeunt.*

75, 76 great … wit; *cf. n.* **wit:** *intellect, mind*   **78 And:** *if*   **80 Pourquoi:** *why*
(French)   **83 bear-baiting;** *cf. n.*   **the arts:** *liberal learning such as languages*   **85
mended:** *improved*   **86 curl by nature:** *F coole my nature; cf. n.*   **87 becoms me:** *F
becoms we*   **88 like flax on a distaff:** *like straight strings of flax on a stick used in spinning*   **89 huswife:** *housewife, pronounced 'huzzif'*   **93 hard by:** *near by*   **95 degree:**
position in society **estate:** *fortune*   **99 altogether:** *in all respects*   **100 kick-chawses:**
trifles (French, quelque chose*)*   **101, 102 under the degree of my betters:** *except of a social
rank higher than mine*   **102, 103 an old man:** *probably 'an experienced person'*   **104
galliard:** *a quick dance in triple time*   **105 caper:** *a frolicsome leap; also a spice used with
mutton*   **107 back-trick:** *a step backward in a dance; cf. n.*   **110 like:** *likely* **take:**
collect   **111 Mistress Mall's picture:** *any woman's portrait; cf. n.*   **112 coranto:** *a swift
running dance (French* courante*)* **should:** *would*   **113 sink-a-pace:** *a rapid dance of five
steps (French* cinque-pas*). cf. n.*   **116 under the star of a galliard:** *i.e. under a dancing
star*   **118 dam'd color'd;** *cf. n.* **stock:** *stocking* **sit:** *set; cf. n.*   **121 Taurus:** *the bull,
one of the signs of the Zodiac; cf. n.*   **That's sides:** *F That sides*

4 his humor or my negligence: *his changeableness or my neglect (as a servant)*   **11 you:**
all except Cesario   **12 no less but all:** *everything*   **13 even:** *monosyllabic*   **14 address
thy gait:** *direct thy steps*   **15 access:** *stressed — ́* **doors;** *cf. n.*   **21 clamorous:**
noisy **civil:** *polite*   **22 unprofited:** *unproductive*   **25 surprise:** *to overcome suddenly
(French* surprendre*)* **dear:** *'extreme,' commonly used as an intensive*   **28 nuncio's:** *messenger's* **aspect:** *stressed — ́*   **33 rubious:** *ruby red* **pipe:** *throat*   **34 sound:**
clear   **35 semblative a woman's part:** *like a woman's actions* **a:** *possibly 'of a'*   **36 thy
constellation:** *thy nature; cf. n.* **apt:** *suited*   **37 him:** *Cesario (on his visit to
Olivia)*   **40 freely:** *without restriction*   **43 a barful strife:** *a conflict full of hin-
drances*   **43, 44 woo … woo …:** *would a verbal quibble; cf. n.*

❧ SCENE FIFTH ❧

Enter Maria and Clown.

Maria. Nay, either tell me where thou hast been, or I will not open my lips so wide as a bristle may enter in way of thy excuse. My lady will hang thee for thy absence.

Clown. Let her hang me. He that is well hang'd in this world needs to fear no colors.   5

Maria. Make that good.

Clown. He shall see none to fear.

Maria. A good lenten answer. I can tell thee where the saying was born, of 'I fear no colors.'

Clown. Where, good Mistress Mary?   10

Maria. In the wars; and that may you be bold to say in your foolery.

Clown. Well, God give them wisdom that have it; and those that are fools, let them use their talents.

Maria. Yet you will be hang'd for being so long absent,   15
or to be turn'd away. Is not that as good as a hanging to you?

Clown. Many a good hanging prevents a bad marriage; and for turning away, let summer bear it out.

Maria. You are resolute then?

Clown. Not so neither; but I am resolv'd on two   20
points.

Maria. That if one break, the other will hold; or if both break, your gaskins fall.

Clown. Apt, in good faith; very apt. Well, go thy way. If Sir Toby would leave drinking, thou wert as witty a   25
piece of Eve's flesh as any in Illyria.

Maria. Peace, you rogue; no more o' that. Here comes my lady. Make your excuse wisely, you were best.   *[Exit.]*

Enter Lady Olivia with Malvolio.

Clown. Wit, and't be thy will, put me into good fooling. Those wits that think they have thee do very oft prove   30
fools; and I that am sure I lack thee may pass for a wise man. For what says Quinapalus? 'Better a witty fool than a foolish wit.' God bless thee, lady.

Olivia. Take the fool away.

Clown. Do you not hear, fellows? Take away the lady.   35

Olivia. Go to, y'are a dry fool. I'll no more of you. Besides, you grow dishonest.

Clown. Two faults, madonna, that drink and good counsel will amend. For give the dry fool drink, then is the fool not dry. Bid the dishonest man mend himself: if he mend, he   40
is no longer dishonest; if he cannot, let the botcher mend him. Anything that's mended is but patch'd; virtue that transgresses is but patch'd with sin, and sin that amends is but patch'd with virtue. If that this simple syllogism will serve, so; if it will not, what remedy? As there is no true cuckold but   45
calamity, so beauty's a flower. The lady bade take away the fool; therefore I say again, take her away.

Olivia. Sir, I bade them take away you.

Clown. Misprison in the highest degree. Lady, *cucullus non facit monachum.* That's as much to say as, I wear not   50
motley in my brain. Good madonna, give me leave to prove you a fool.

Olivia. Can you do it?

Clown. Dexteriously, good madonna.

Olivia. Make your proof.   55

Clown. I must catechize you for it, madonna. Good my mouse of virtue, answer me.

Olivia. Well, sir, for want of other idleness, I'll bide your proof.

Clown. Good madonna, why mourn'st thou?   60

Olivia. Good fool, for my brother's death.

Clown. I think his soul is in hell, madonna.

Olivia. I know his soul is in heaven, fool.

Clown. The more fool, madonna, to mourn for your brother's soul, being in heaven. Take away the fool, gentlemen.   65

Olivia. What think you of this fool, Malvolio? Doth he not mend?

Malvolio. Yes, and shall do till the pangs of death shake him. Infirmity that decays the wise doth ever make the better fool.   70

Clown. God send you, sir, a speedy infirmity for the better increasing your folly. Sir Toby will be sworn that I am no fox, but he will not pass his word for twopence that you are no fool.

Olivia. How say you to that, Malvolio?   75

Malvolio. I marvel your ladyship takes delight in such a barren rascal. I saw him put down the other day with an ordinary fool that has no more brain than a stone. Look you now, he's out of his guard already. Unless you laugh and minister occasion to him, he is gagg'd. I protest I take these wise   80
men that crow so at these set kind of fools no better than the fools' zanies.

Olivia. O, you are sick of self-love, Malvolio, and taste with a distemper'd appetite. To be generous, guiltless, and of free disposition, is to take those things for bird-bolts that you   85
deem cannon bullets. There is no slander in an allow'd fool, though he do nothing but rail; nor no railing in a known discreet man, though he do nothing but reprove.

Clown. Now Mercury endue thee with leasing, for thou speak'st well of fools.   90

Enter Maria.

Maria. Madam, there is at the gate a young gentleman much desires to speak with you.

Olivia. From the Count Orsino, is it?

Maria. I know not, madam. 'Tis a fair young man and well attended.   95

Olivia. Who of my people hold him in delay?

Maria. Sir Toby, madam, your kinsman.

---

5 to fear no colors: *'to fear nothing,' proverbial; cf. n.*   **8 lenten:** *thin, poor*   **13, 14 Well, God … talents:** *Cf. n.*   **18 for:** *as for*   **away:** *Cf. n.*   **let summer bear it out:** *let the warm weather make it (the loss of my job) endurable*   **22 if one [point] break:** *'point' in the argument and 'point' as a string used to hold up breeches*   **23 gaskins:** *loose breeches*   **25, 26 If Sir Toby … Illyria:** *Cf. n.*   **28 you were best:** *it would be best for you*   **29 and't:** *if it*   **32 Quinapalus:** *an invention of the Clown*   **36 Go to:** *go away, cease*   **dry:** *'barren,' 'unfruitful,' rather than 'ironical'*   **37 dishonest:** *unreliable (because he has been absent)*   **38 madonna:** *my lady (Italian mia donna)*   **39 dry:** *'thirsty' and 'barren'*   **41 botcher:** *a mender, especially a tailor or cobbler who does repairs*   **42–45 Anything … virtue:** *cf. n.*   **45, 46 As there … flower:** *cf. n.*

49 Misprison: *mistake*   **cucullus … monachum:** *the cowl doesn't make the monk*   **50 motley:** *clothing of a mixed color, worn by stage fools; cf. n.*   **54 Dexteriously:** *variant of 'dexterously'*   **56, 57 Good my mouse:** *'my good mouse'; 'mouse' was a common term of endearment*   **67 mend:** *get better as to his jokes*   **68 shall do:** *shall become more foolish*   **77 barren:** *empty (of wit)*   **put down … with:** *defeated … by*   **79 out of his guard:** *without an answer of wit*   **79, 80 minister occasion:** *give opportunity or opening*   **81 set kind:** *conventional sort*   **82 zanies:** *cf. n.*   **83 of:** *with*   **84 distemper'd:** *ill, unhealthy*   **85 bird-bolts:** *blunt-headed arrows for shooting birds*   **86 no slander in an allow'd fool:** *cf. n.*   **89 Mercury:** *Mercury was full of guile and tricks*   **endue:** *supply with*   **leasing:** *lying*

Olivia. Fetch him off, I pray you. He speaks nothing but madman. Fie on him *[Exit Maria.]* Go you, Malvolio. If it be a suit from the Count, I am sick or not at home. What you will, to dismiss it. *(Exit Malvolio.)* Now you see, sir, how your fooling grows old and people dislike it. 100

Clown. Thou hast spoke for us, madonna, as if thy eldest son should be a fool; whose scull Jove cram with brains, for here he comes. 105

Enter Sir Toby.

One of thy kin has a most weak *pia mater.*

Olivia. By mine honor, half drunk. What is he at the gate, cousin?

Toby. A gentleman.

Olivia. A gentleman? What gentleman? 110

Toby. 'Tis a gentleman here. A plague o' these pickle-herring! How now, sot?

Clown. Good Sir Toby.

Olivia. Cousin, cousin, how have you come so early by this lethargy? 115

Toby. Lechery, I defy lechery. There's one at the gate.

Olivia. Ay, marry, what is he?

Toby. Let him be the divel and he will, I care not. Give me faith, say I. Well, it's all one. *Exit.*

Olivia. What's a drunken man like, fool? 120

Clown. Like a drown'd man, a fool, and a madman. One draught above heat makes him a fool, the second mads him, and a third drowns him.

Olivia. Go, thou, and seek the crowner, and let him sit o' my coz; for he's in the third degree of drink: he's drown'd. 125 Go look after him.

Clown. He is but mad yet, madonna, and the fool shall look to the madman. *[Exit.]*

Enter Malvolio.

Malvolio. Madam, yond young fellow swears he will speak with you. I told him you were sick; he takes on him to 130 understand so much and therefore comes to speak with you. I told him you were asleep; he seems to have a foreknowledge of that too, and therefore comes to speak with you. What is to be said to him, lady? He's fortified against any denial.

Olivia. Tell him he shall not speak with me. 135

Malvolio. Has been told so; and he says he'll stand at your door like a sheriff's post and be the supporter to a bench, but he'll speak with you.

Olivia. What kind o' man is he?

Malvolio. Why, of mankind. 140

Olivia. What manner of man?

Malvolio. Of very ill manner. He'll speak with you, will you or no.

Olivia. Of what personage and years is he?

Malvolio. Not yet old enough for a man nor young enough

for a boy: as a squash is before 'tis a pescod, or a codling when 'tis almost an apple. 'Tis with him in standing water, between boy and man. He is very well favor'd and he speaks very shrewishly. One would think his mother's milk were scarce out of him. 150

Olivia. Let him approach. Call in my gentlewoman.

Malvolio. Gentlewoman, my lady calls. *Exit.*

Enter Maria.

Olivia. Give me my veil; come, throw it o'er my face. We'll once more hear Orsino's embassy.

Enter Viola.

Viola. The honorable lady of the house, which is she? 155

Olivia. Speak to me; I shall answer for her. Your will?

Viola. Most radiant, exquisite, and unmatchable beauty. I pray you tell me if this be the lady of the house, for I never saw her. I would be loath to cast away my speech, for besides that it is excellently well penn'd, I have taken great pains 160 to con it. Good beauties, let me sustain no scorn. I am very comptible, even to the least sinister usage.

Olivia. Whence came you, sir?

Viola. I can say little more than I have studied, and that question's out of my part. Good gentle one, give me 165 modest assurance if you be the lady of the house, that I may proceed in my speech.

Olivia. Are you a comedian?

Viola. No, my profound heart; and yet (by the very fangs of malice I swear) I am not that I play. Are you the lady 170 of the house?

Olivia. If I do not usurp myself, I am.

Viola. Most certain, if you are she, you do usurp yourself; for what is yours to bestow is not yours to reserve. But this is from my commission. I will on with my speech in your 175 praise and then show you the heart of my message.

Olivia. Come to what is important in't. I forgive you the praise.

Viola. Alas, I took great pains to study it, and 'tis poetical.

Olivia. It is the more like to be feigned; I pray you keep it in. I heard you were saucy at my gates, and allow'd your approach rather to wonder at you than to hear you. If you be not mad, be gone; if you have reason, be brief. 'Tis not that time of moon with me to make one in skipping a dialogue. 185

Maria. Will you hoist sail, sir? Here lies your way.

Viola. No, good swabber; I am to hull here a little longer. Some mollification for your giant, sweet lady. Tell me your mind; I am a messenger.

Olivia. Sure you have some hideous matter to deliver, 190 when the courtesy of it is so fearful. Speak your office.

99 madman: *like a lunatic* **102 old:** *stale* **104 should be:** *were going to be* (in the future) **105 he:** *Sir Toby, drunk* **106 pia mater:** *innermost membrane enveloping the brain* **107 What:** *'what' and 'who'* **111 A plague:** *cf. n.* **112 sot:** *fool, clown* **114 Cousin:** *loosely for 'kinsman' or 'uncle'* **115 lethargy:** *torpor* (of drunkenness) **117 marry:** *to be sure* **118 divel:** *devil* **and:** *if* **119 faith:** *to resist the devil* **it's all one:** *no difference* **121, 122 One draught above heat:** *one drink above the amount to make him normally warm* **124 crowner:** *variant of 'coroner'* **124, 125 sit o' my coz:** *hold an inquest on my cousin or kinsman* (Sir Toby) **130 on him:** *upon himself* **136 Has:** *he has* (from 'h' has') **137 sheriff's post . . . supporter to a bench;** *cf. n.*

146 squash: *unripe pea pod* **pescod:** *peascod, ripe pea pod* **codling:** *unripe apple* **147 standing water:** *the tide at ebb or flood when it flows neither way* **148 well favor'd:** *of good appearance or face* **149 shrewishly:** *irritably* **SD Enter Viola:** *F Enter Violena; cf. n.* (SD is used throughout to indicate stage direction.) **158 if this be;** *cf. n.* **161 con:** *learn, memorize* **sustain:** *endure, receive* (from you) **162 comptible:** *spelling variant of 'countable'* (sensitive) **the least sinister usage:** *the least hostile treatment* **166 modest:** *moderate* **168 comedian:** *actor* **169 my profound heart;** *cf. n.* **169, 170 the very fangs of malice:** *the very worst reports and rumors about me* **173 you do usurp yourself:** *i.e. you should be married* **175 from:** *in addition to, outside* **177 forgive you:** *excuse you* (from delivering) **183 reason:** *sanity* **183–85 'Tis not that time . . . dialogue;** *cf. n.* **186 Here lies your way:** *i.e. go* **187 swabber:** *minor officer in charge of cleaning a ship* **to hull:** *to float without sail* **188 giant:** (guarding) *monster; cf. n.* **191 when the courtesy of it is so fearful:** *when the manner of delivering it is so frightening* **office:** *message, business*

Viola. It alone concerns your ear. I bring no overture of
war, no taxation of homage. I hold the olive in my hand.
My words are as full of peace as matter.

Olivia. Yet you began rudely. What are you? What 195
would you?

Viola. The rudeness that hath appear'd in me have I learn'd
from my entertainment. What I am, and what I would, are as
secret as maidenhead: to your ears, divinity; to any other's,
profanation. 200

Olivia. Give us the place alone; we will hear this divinity.
[Exit Maria.] Now, sir, what is your text?

Viola. Most sweet lady.

Olivia. A comfortable doctrine, and much may be said
of it. Where lies your text? 205

Viola. In Orsino's bosom.

Olivia. In his bosom? In what chapter of his bosom?

Viola. To answer by the method, in the first of his
heart.

Olivia. O, I have read it; it is heresy. Have you no 210
more to say?

Viola. Good madam, let me see your face.

Olivia. Have you any commission from your lord to negotiate with my face? You are now out of your text; but we
will draw the curtain and show you the picture. *[Unveils.]* 215
Look you, sir, such a one I was this present. Is't not well
done?

Viola. Excellently done, if God did all.

Olivia. 'Tis in grain, sir; 'twill endure wind and weather.

Viola. 'Tis beauty truly blent, whose red and white, 220
Nature's own sweet and cunning hand laid on.
Lady, you are the cruel'st she alive
If you will lead these graces to the grave,
And leave the world no copy.

Olivia. O, sir, I will not be so hardhearted. I will give 225
out divers schedules of my beauty. It shall be inventoried and
every particle and utensil label'd to my will: as, item, two lips
indifferent red; item, two grey eyes, with lids to them; item,
one neck, one chin, and so forth. Were you sent hither to
praise me? 230

Viola. I see you what you are; you are too proud;
But if you were the divel, you are fair.
My lord and master loves you. O, such love
Could be but recompens'd though you were crown'd
The nonpareil of beauty. 235

Olivia. How does he love me?

Viola. With adorations, fertill tears,
With groans that thunder love, with sighs of fire.

Olivia. Your lord does know my mind; I cannot love him.
Yet I suppose him virtuous, know him noble, 240
Of great estate, of fresh and stainless youth;
In voices well divulg'd, free, learn'd, and valiant,
And in dimension and the shape of nature
A gracious person. But yet I cannot love him.

He might have took his answer long ago. 245

Viola. If I did love you in my master's flame,
With such a suff'ring, such a deadly life,
In your denial I would find no sense;
I would not understand it.

Olivia. Why, what would you? 250

Viola. Make me a willow cabin at your gate
And call upon my soul within the house;
Write loyal cantons of contemned love
And sing them loud even in the dead of night;
Hallow your name to the reverberate hills 255
And make the babbling gossip of the air
Cry out 'Olivia.' O, you should not rest
Between the elements of air and earth
But you should pity me.

Oliva. You might do much. 260
What is your partentage?

Viola. Above my fortunes, yet my state is well. I am a
gentleman.

Olivia. Get you to your lord.
I cannot love him. Let him send no more 265
Unless, perchance, you come to me again
To tell me how he takes it. Fare you well.
I thank you for your pains. Spend this for me.

Viola. I am no fee'd post, lady; keep your purse;
My master, not myself, lacks recompense. 270
Love make his heart of flint that you shall love;
And let your fervor, like my master's, be
Plac'd in contempt. Farewell, fair cruelty. *Exit.*

Olivia. 'What is your parentage?'
'Above my fortunes, yet my state is well. 275
I am a gentleman.' I'll be sworn thou art.
Thy tongue, thy face, thy limbs, actions, and spirit
Do give thee fivefold blazon. Not too fast; soft, soft;
Unless the master were the man. How now?
Even so quickly may one catch the plague? 280
Methinks I feel this youth's perfections
With an invisible and subtle stealth
To creep in at mine eyes. Well, let it be.
What ho, Malvolio!

Enter Malvolio.

Malvolio. Here, madam, at your service. 285

Olivia. Run after that same peevish messenger
The County's man. He left this ring behind him,
Would I or not. Tell him I'll none of it.
Desire him not to flatter with his lord
Nor hold him up with hopes. I am not for him. 290
If that the youth will come this way tomorrow,
I'll give him reasons for't. Hie thee, Malvolio.

Malvolio. Madam, I will. *Exit.*

Olivia. I do I know not what, and fear to find
Mine eye too great a flatterer for my mind. 295

Fate, show thy force: ourselves we do not owe.
What is decreed must be, and be this so.　　　　　　*[Exit.]*

　　　　　　　　　　　　　　　　　Finis, Actus primus.

ACT SECOND ❧ SCENE FIRST

Enter Antonio and Sebastian.

Antonio. Will you stay no longer? Nor will you not that I
go with you?

Sebastian. By your patience, no. My stars shine darkly over
me; the malignancy of my fate might perhaps distemper yours.
Therefore I shall crave of you your leave that I may bear　　5
my evils alone. It were a bad recompense for your love to
lay any of them on you.

Antonio. Let me yet know of you whither you are bound.

Sebastian. No, sooth, sir. My determinate voyage is mere
extravagancy. But I perceive in you so excellent a touch of　　10
modesty that you will not extort from me what I am willing
to keep in; therefore it charges me in manners the rather to
express myself. You must know of me then, Antonio, my
name is Sebastian, which I call'd Roderigo. My father was that
Sebastian of Messaline whom I know you have heard of.　　15
He left behind him myself and a sister, both born in an hour.
If the heavens had been pleas'd, would we had so ended. But
you, sir, alter'd that, for some hour before you took me from
the breach of the sea was my sister drown'd.

Antonio. Alas the day!　　　　　　　　　　　　　20

Sebastian. A lady, sir, though it was said she much resembled me, was yet of many accounted beautiful. But though I
could not with such estimable wonder overfar believe that, yet
thus far I will boldly publish her: she bore a mind that envy
could not but call fair. She is drown'd already, sir, with　　25
salt water, though I seem to drown her remembrance again
with more.

Antonio. Pardon me, sir, your bad entertainment.

Sebastian. O good Antonio, forgive me your trouble.

Antonio. If you will not murther me for my love, let　　30
me be your servant.

Sebastian. If you will not undo what you have done, that is,
kill him whom you have recover'd, desire it not. Fare ye well
at once. My bosom is full of kindness; and I am yet so near
the manners of my mother that, upon the least　　　　35
occasion more, mine eyes will tell tales of me. I am bound
to the Count Orsino's court. Farewell.　　　　　　*Exit.*

Antonio. The gentleness of all the gods go with thee.
I have many enemies in Orsino's court,
Else would I very shortly see thee there.　　　　　40
But come what may, I do adore thee so
That danger shall seem sport and I will go.　　　　*Exit.*

❧ SCENE SECOND ❧

Enter Viola and Malvolio at several doors.

Malvolio. Were not you ev'n now with the Countess Olivia?

Viola. Even now, sir. On a moderate pace I have since
arriv'd but hither.

Malvolio. She returns this ring to you, sir. You might have saved
me my pains to have taken it away yourself. She adds, moreover,　　5
that you should put your lord into a desperate assurance she will
none of him. And one thing more, that you be never so hardy to
come again in his affairs, unless it be to report your lord's taking of
this. Receive it so.

Viola. She took the ring of me. I'll none of it.　　　　10

Malvolio. Come, sir, you peevishly threw it to her; and her
will is, it should be so return'd. If it be worth stooping for, there
it lies, in your eye; if not, be it his that finds it.　　　　*Exit.*

Viola. I left no ring with her. What means this lady?
Fortune forbid my outside have not charmed her.　　　　15
She made good view of me; indeed, so much
That methought her eyes had lost her tongue,
For she did speak in starts distractedly.
She loves me sure; the cunning of her passion
Invites me in this churlish messenger.　　　　　　20
None of my lord's ring? Why, he sent her none.
I am the man. If it be so, as 'tis,
Poor lady, she were better love a dream.
Disguise, I see thou art a wickedness
Wherein the pregnant enemy does much.　　　　　25
How easy is it for the proper false
In women's waxen hearts to set their forms.
Alas, O, frailty is the cause, not we,
For such as we are made, if such we be.
How will this fadge? My master loves her dearly;　　　　30
And I (poor monster) fond as much on him;
And she (mistaken) seems to dote on me.
What will become of this? As I am man,
My state is desperate for my master's love.
As I am woman (now alas the day!),　　　　　　35
What thriftless sighs shall poor Olivia breathe?
O Time, thou must untangle this, not I;
It is too hard a knot for me t' untie.　　　　　　*[Exit]*

❧ SCENE THIRD ❧

Enter Sir Toby and Sir Andrew.

Toby. Approach, Sir Andrew. Not to be abed after midnight
is to be up betimes, and *diluculo surgere,* thou know'st.

Andrew. Nay, by my troth, I know not; but I know to be
up late is to be up late.

296 owe: *possess, own, control*　**1 Nor . . . not;** *cf. n.*　**3 patience:** *allowance, leave*　**3, 4
My stars . . . distemper yours;** *cf. n.*　**9 sooth:** *truly*　**determinate:** *determined upon*　**10
extravagancy:** *an extravagant fancy*　**touch:** *feeling*　**12 it charges me in manners:** *I am compelled in good manners*　**15 Messaline:** *perhaps Mitylene, but identification is unnecessary*　**16 in
an hour:** *in the same hour*　**19 the breach of the sea:** *the breaking waves, usually on a coast*　**23
with such estimable wonder:** *with so much admiring wonder (for her)*　**24 publish:** *declare, describe publicly*　**28 your bad entertainment:** *the poor hospitality I have given you*　**29 your
trouble:** *for causing you trouble*　**30 murther me for my love:** *i.e. kill me by leaving me*　**for:** *in
reward for*　**33 recover'd:** *saved*　**38 gentleness:** *kindliness*

SD Enter . . . at several doors; *cf. n.*　**2 On a moderate pace:** *at a moderate walking
pace*　**5 to have taken it:** *if you had taken it*　**6, 7 a desperate assurance she will
none of him:** *an extreme assurance leaving no hope that she will have any part of him*　**7,
8 so hardy to come:** *so venturesome as to come*　**15 not:** *emphatic negative attached to*
forbid　**16 made good view of me:** *looked favorably at me*　**17 methought:** *it seemed
to me*　**her eyes had lost her tongue:** *what she saw had caused her to lose her tongue*　**19
cunning:** *craftiness*　**20 in:** *through*　**25 pregnant enemy:** *strong enemy; cf. n.*　**26
the proper false:** *i.e. those who appear to be respectable and genuine but are deceivers*　**27
forms:** *'impressions' as of a seal, and 'appearance'*　**28, 29 Alas . . . such we be;** *cf. n.*　**30
fadge:** *fit, be suitable*　**31 monster:** *because of both sexes*　**fond:** *dote*　**34 desperate:**
pronounced 'desp'rate'　**36 thriftless:** *unprofitable*　**2 betimes:** *early*　**diluculo surgere:**
to get up at dawn; F Deliculo cf. n.　**3 by my troth:** *truly*

Toby. A false conclusion; I hate it as an unfill'd can. To   5
be up after midnight and to go to bed then, is early; so that
to go to bed after midnight is to go to bed betimes. Does not
our lives consist of the four elements?

Andrew. Faith, so they say; but I think it rather consists
of eating and drinking.   10

Toby. Th' art a scholar. Let us therefore eat and drink.
Marian, I say, a stoup of wine.

Enter Clown.

Andrew. Here comes the fool, i' faith.

Clown. How now, my hearts? Did you never see the picture
of We Three?   15

Toby. Welcome, ass. Now let's have a catch.

Andrew. By my troth, the fool has an excellent breast. I had
rather than forty shillings I had such a leg and so sweet a
breath to sing as the fool has. In sooth, thou wast in very gracious fooling last night when thou spok'st of Pigrogromitus,   20
of the Vapians passing the equinoctial of Queubus. 'Twas very
good, i' faith. I sent thee sixpence for thy leman. Hadst it?

Clown. I did impeticos thy gratillity, for Malvolio's nose is
no whipstock. My lady has a white hand, and the Myrmidons
are no bottle-ale houses.   25

Andrew. Excellent. Why, this is the best fooling, when all
is done. Now a song.

Toby. Come on, there is sixpence for you. Let's have a song.

Andrew. There's a testril of me too. If one knight
give a ———   30

Clown. Would you have a love song, or a song of good life?

Toby. A love song, a love song.

Andrew. Ay, ay. I care not for good life.

Clown sings.

O mistress mine, where are you roaming?
O, stay and hear, your true love's coming,   35
That can sing both high and low.
Trip no further, pretty sweeting;
Journeys end in lovers meeting,
Every wise man's son doth know.

Andrew. Excellent good, i' faith.   40

Toby. Good, good.

Clown [sings].

What is love? 'Tis not hereafter;
Present mirth hath present laughter;
What's to come is still unsure.   45
In delay there lies no plenty;
Then come kiss me, sweet and twenty:
Youth's a stuff will not endure.

Andrew. A mellifluous voice, as I am true knight.

Toby. A contagious breath.   50

Andrew. Very sweet and contagious, i' faith.

Toby. To hear by the nose, it is dulcet in contagion. But
shall we make the welkin dance indeed? Shall we rouse the
night owl in a catch that will draw three souls out of one
weaver? Shall we do that?   55

Andrew. And you love me, let's do't. I am dog at a catch.

Clown. By'r Lady, sir, and some dogs will catch well.

Andrew. Most certain. Let our catch be 'Thou knave.'

Clown. 'Hold thy peace, thou knave,' knight? I shall be
constrain'd in't to call thee knave, knight.   60

Andrew. 'Tis not the first time I have constrained one to
call me knave. Begin, fool. It begins, 'Hold thy peace.'

Clown. I shall never begin if I hold my peace.

Andrew. Good, i' faith; come, begin.

Catch sung. Enter Maria.

Maria. What a caterwauling do you keep here? If my   65
lady have not call'd up her steward Malvolio and bid him turn
you out of doors, never trust me.

Toby. My lady's a Catayan, we are politicians, Malvolio's a
Peg-a-Ramsey, and *[Sings.]* 'Three merry men be we.' Am
not I consanguineous? Am I not of her blood? Tilly vally,   70
lady *[Sings.],* 'There dwelt a man in Babylon, lady, lady.'

Clown. Beshrew me, the knight's in admirable fooling.

Andrew. Ay, he does well enough if he be dispos'd, and so
do I too. He does it with a better grace, but I do it more
natural.   75

Toby. [Sings.] 'O the *twelfe* day of December.'

Maria. For the love o' God, peace.

Enter Malvolio.

Malvolio. My masters, are you mad? Or what are you? Have
you no wit, manners, nor honesty, but to gabble like tinkers at this time of night? Do ye make an alehouse of my   80
lady's house, that ye squeak out your coziers' catches without
any mitigation or remorse of voice? Is there no respect of
place, persons, nor time in you?

Toby. We did keep time, sir, in our catches. Sneck up.

Malvolio. Sir Toby, I must be round with you. My lady   85
bade me tell you that though she harbors you as her kinsman,
she's nothing allied to your disorders. If you can separate yourself and your misdemeanors, you are welcome to the house. If
not, and it would please you to take leave of her, she is
very willing to bid you farewell.   90

Toby. [Sings.] 'Farewell, dear heart, since I must needs be
gone.'

Maria. Nay, good Sir Toby.

Clown. [Sings.] 'His eyes do show his days are almost
done.'   95

---

5 **can:** *metal vessel for holding liquor*   7, 8 **Does not ... elements;** *cf. n.*   12 **stoup:** *a
drinking vessel*   14 **hearts:** *a term of endearment*   14, 15 **the picture of We Three;**
cf. n.   16 **a catch:** *a musical round in which one singer 'catches' at the words of another*   17
breast: *lungs, hence voice in singing*   19, 20 **gracious:** *graceful, elegant*   20, 21 **Pigro-
gomitus ... Queubus:** *the names are meaningless*   22 **leman:** *sweetheart*   23–25 **I did
impeticos thy gratillity ... bottle-ale houses;** *cf. n.*   29 **testril:** *diminutive of 'tester,'
'sixpence'* **of:** *from*   30 **give a ———:** *F give a*   31 **good life:** *virtuous living*   34
O mistress mine; *cf. n.*   45 **still:** *always*   47 **sweet and twenty:** *'sweet and twenty times
sweet' or 'sweet and twenty years old'*   50 **A contagious breath:** *'a catchy voice or tune,' also
'a bad breath'*

52 **To hear ... contagion;** *cf. n.*   53 **the welkin:** *the sky*   54 **a catch:** *a round* (of
singing)   54, 55 **draw three souls out of one weaver;** *cf. n.*   56 **And:** *if*   **I am dog
at a catch:** *I am an expert at a round* (of singing)   57 **By'r Lady:** *'by our Lady'* (the
Virgin Mary), *a petty oath*   58 **'Thou knave';** *cf. n.*   65 **caterwauling:** *the cry of the
cat at rutting time*   68 **Catayan:** *person of no account, scoundrel* **politicians:** *Statesmen
concerned with important question* *cf. n.*   69 **a Peg-a-Ramsey:** *probably 'a lewd, coarse
person'; cf. n.* **'Three merry men be we';** *cf. n.*   70 **consanguineous:** *related* **Tilly
vally:** *nonsense*   71 **'There dwelt a man';** *cf. n.*   72 **Beshrew me:** *'curse me,' a mild
oath*   75 **natural:** *'naturally,' but also 'a fool' 'like a fool'*   76 **'O the twelfe day of
December'; cf. n.** **twelfe:** *twelfth*   79 **wit:** *sense* **honesty:** *respectability*   81 **coziers'
catches:** *cobblers' musical rounds*   82 **mitigation or remorse:** *lessening or regret*   82
respect of: *respect for*   84 **Sneck up:** *snick up, go hang*   85 **round:** *plain*   89 **and:**
if   91 **'Farewell, dear heart';** *cf. n.*

Malvolio. Is't even so?

Toby. [*Sings.*] 'But I will never die.'

Clown. Sir Toby, there you lie.

Malvolio. This is much credit to you.

Toby. [*Sings.*] 'Shall I bid him go?'   100

Clown. [*Sings.*] 'What and if you do?'

Toby. [*Sings.*] 'Shall I bid him go, and spare not?'

Clown. [*Sings.*] 'O, no, no, no, no, you dare not.'

Toby. Out o' tune, sir? Ye lie. Art any more than a steward? Dost thou think because thou art virtuous, there shall be   105 no more cakes and ale?

Clown. Yes, by St. Anne, and ginger shall be hot i' th' mouth too.

Toby. Th' art i' th' right. Go, sir, rub your chain with crumbs. A stoup of wine, Maria.   110

Malvolio. Mistress Mary, if you priz'd my lady's favor at anything more than contempt, you would not give means for this uncivil rule. She shall know of it, by this hand.   *Exit.*

Maria. Go shake your ears.

Andrew. 'Twere as good a deed as to drink when a   115 man's ahungry, to challenge him the field and then to break promise with him and make a fool of him.

Toby. Do't, knight. I'll write thee a challenge; or I'll deliver thy indignation to him by word of mouth.

Maria. Sweet Sir Toby, be patient for tonight. Since   120 the youth of the Count's was today with my lady, she is much out of quiet. For Monsieur Malvolio, let me alone with him. If I do not gull him into a nayword and make him a common recreation, do not think I have wit enough to lie straight in my bed. I know I can do it.   125

Toby. Possess us, possess us. Tell us something of him.

Maria. Marry, sir, sometimes he is a kind of Puritan.

Andrew. O, if I thought that, I'd beat him like a dog.

Toby. What, for being a Puritan? Thy exquisite reason, dear knight.   130

Andrew. I have no exquisite reason for't, but I have reason good enough.

Maria. The div'l a Puritan that he is, or anything constantly but a time-pleaser, an affection'd ass, that cons state without book and utters it by great swarths. The best persuaded of   135 himself, so cramm'd (as he thinks) with excellencies that it is his grounds of faith that all that look on him love him; and on that vice in him will my revenge find notable cause to work.

Toby. What wilt thou do?   140

Maria. I will drop in his way some obscure epistles of love wherein by the color of his beard, the shape of his leg, the manner of his gait, the expressure of his eye, forehead, and complexion, he shall find himself most feelingly personated. I can write very like my lady your niece; on a forgotten matter we can hardly make distinction of our hands.

Toby. Excellent. I smell a device.

Andrew. I have't in my nose too.

Toby. He shall think by the letters that thou wilt drop that they come from my niece, and that she's in love with him.   150

Maria. My purpose is indeed a horse of that color.

Andrew. And your horse now would make him an ass.

Maria. Ass, I doubt not.

Andrew. O, 'twill be admirable.

Maria. Sport royal, I warrant you. I know my physic   155 will work with him. I will plant you two and let the fool make a third, where he shall find the letter. Observe his construction of it. For this night, to bed and dream on the event. Farewell.
                                                        Exit.

Toby. Good night, Penthesilea.

Andrew. Before me, she's a good wench.   160

Toby. She's a beagle true bred, and one that adores me. What o' that?

Andrew. I was ador'd once too.

Toby. Let's to bed, knight. Thou hadst need send for more money.   165

Andrew. If I cannot recover your niece, I am a foul way out.

Toby. Send for money, knight. If thou hast her not i' th' end, call me Cut.

Andrew. If I do not, never trust me, take it how you will.

Toby. Come, come; I'll go burn some sack. 'Tis too late to go to bed now. Come, knight; come, knight.   *Exeunt.*

❧ SCENE FOURTH ❧

Enter Duke, Viola, Curio, and others.

Duke. Give me some music. Now good morrow, friends. Now, good Cesario, but that piece of song, That old and anticke song we heard last night. Methought it did relieve my passion much, More than light airs and recollected terms   5 Of these most brisk and giddy-paced times. Come, but one verse.

Curio. He is not here, so please your lordship, that should sing it.

Duke. Who was it?   10

Curio. Feste the jester, my lord, a fool that the Lady Olivia's father took much delight in. He is about the house.

Duke. Seek him out, and play the tune the while.
                                        [*Exit Curio.*] *Music plays.*

Come hither, boy. If ever thou shalt love,   15 In the sweet pangs of it remember me; For such as I am, all true lovers are, Unstaid and skittish in all motions else Save in the constant image of the creature That is belov'd. How dost thou like this tune?   20

---

98 there you lie: *you are a liar*   **101 and if:** *if*   **106 cakes and ale;** *cf. n.*   **107 St. Anne;** *cf. n.*   **ginger;** *cf. n.*   **109, 110 rub your chain with crumbs;** *cf. n.*   **a stoup:** *a cup*   **112 give means:** *i.e. bring the wine*   **113 uncivil rule:** *disorderly revel*   **by this hand:** *a mild exclamation*   **114 Go shake your ears:** *i.e. you are an ass*   **115 as good a deed as to drink;** *cf. n.*   **116 to challenge him the field:** *to challenge him to the field of battle*   **120 Sweet:** *dear*   **123 gull:** *trick*   **a nayword:** *a byword;* F *an ayword*   **124 recreation:** *'pastime' or 'amusement'*   **126 Possess us:** *give us the facts*   **127 Marry:** *indeed*   **a kind of Puritan;** *cf. n.*   **133 div'l:** *devil*   **134 a time-pleaser:** *a sycophant, a toady*   **affection'd:** *affected*   **cons state without book:** *studies and learns a stately manner by heart*   **135 swarths:** *quantities; cf. n.*   **The best persuaded of himself:** *the highest opinion of himself*   **137 grounds of faith:** *firm belief*   **143 expressure:** *expression*   **144 personated:** *represented*   **146 distinction of our hands:** *difference in our handwritings*

153 Ass: *both 'ass' and 'as'*   **155 physic:** *'medicine' in the sense of 'cure' for Malvolio's conceit*   **156, 157 let the fool make a third;** *cf. n.*   **he:** *Malvolio*   **157 construction:** *interpretation*   **158 the event:** *the outcome*   **159 Penthesilea:** *Queen of the Amazons (ironically)*   **160 Before me:** *I swear by myself*   **161 a beagle:** *a small rabbit hound*   **166 recover:** *'win,' 'gain,' possibly with the legal force of 'gain title to'*   **a foul way out:** *miserably out of money*   **169 Cut:** *a horse with a short tail*   **171 burn some sack:** *warm some sherry*   **1 morrow:** *morning*   **3 anticke:** *antique, old-fashioned (stressed* —́ —*)*   **5 recollected:** *studied, learned*   **18 in all motions else:** *in all other emotions or feelings*

Viola. It gives a very echo to the seat
Where love is thron'd.
    Duke.   Thou dost speak masterly.
My life upon't, young though thou art, thine eye
Hath stay'd upon some favor that it loves.   25
Hath it not, boy?
    Viola.   A little, by your favor.
    Duke. What kind of woman is't?
    Viola.   Of your complexion.
    Duke. She is not worth thee then. What years, i' faith?   30
    Viola. About your years, my lord.
    Duke. Too old, by heaven. Let still the woman take
An elder than herself; so wears she to him,
So sways she level in her husband's heart.
For, boy, however we do praise ourselves,   35
Our fancies are more giddy and unfirm,
More longing, wavering, sooner lost and worn,
Than women's are.
    Viola.   I think it well, my Lord.
    Duke. Then let thy love be younger than thyself,   40
Or thy affection cannot hold the bent;
For women are as roses whose fair flow'r,
Being once display'd, doth fall that very hour.
    Viola. And so they are; alas, that they are so.
To die, even when they to perfection grow.   45

               Enter Curio and Clown.

    Duke. O fellow, come, the song we had last night.
Mark it, Cesario; it is old and plain.
The spinsters and the knitters in the sun,
And the free maids that weave their thread with bones,
Do use to chant it. It is silly sooth,   50
And dallies with the innocence of love
Like the old age.
    Clown. Are you ready, sir?
    Duke. I prethee sing.   *Music.*

               The Song   55

Come away, come away, death,
And in sad cypress let me be laid.
Fie, away; fie, away, breath;
I am slain by a fair cruel maid.
My shroud of white, stuck all with yew,   60
O, prepare it.
My part of death, no one so true
Did share it.

Not a flower, not a flower sweet
On my black coffin let there be strown.   65
Not a friend, not a friend greet
My poor corpse, where my bones shall be thrown.
A thousand thousand sighs to save,

Lay me, O, where
Sad true lover never find my grave,   70
To weep there.

    Duke. There's for thy pains.
    Clown. No pains, sir. I take pleasure in singing, sir.
    Duke. I'll pay thy pleasure then.
    Clown. Truly, sir, and pleasure will be paid one time or   75
another.
    Duke. Give me now leave to leave thee.
    Clown. Now the melancholy god protect thee, and the tailor
make thy doublet of changeable taffeta, for thy mind is a very
opal. I would have men of such constancy put to sea, that   80
their business might be everything, and their intent everywhere;
for that's it that always makes a good voyage of nothing.
Farewell.   *Exit.*
    Duke. Let all the rest give place.
               [Exeunt Curio and Attendants.]
                    Once more, Cesario,   85
Get thee to yond same sovereign cruelty.
Tell her my love, more noble than the world,
Prizes not quantity of dirty lands.
The parts that fortune hath bestow'd upon her,
Tell her I hold as giddily as fortune.   90
But 'tis that miracle and queen of gems
That nature pranks her in, attracts my soul.
    Viola. But if she cannot love you, sir.
    Duke. I cannot be so answer'd.
    Viola.   Sooth, but you must.   95
Say that some lady, as perhaps there is,
Hath for your love as great a pang of heart
As you have for Olivia. You cannot love her.
You tell her so. Must she not then be answer'd?
    Duke. There is no woman's sides   100
Can bide the beating of so strong a passion
As love doth give my heart; no woman's heart
So big to hold so much; they lack retention.
Alas, their love may be call'd appetite,
No motion of the liver, but the palate   105
That suffer surfeit, cloyment, and revolt.
But mine is all as hungry as the sea
And can digest as much; make no compare
Between that love a woman can bear me
And that I owe Olivia.   110
    Viola.   Ay, but I know.
    Duke. What dost thou know?
    Viola. Too well what love women to men may owe.
In faith, they are as true of heart as we.
My father had a daughter lov'd a man   115
As it might be perhaps, were I a woman,
I should your lordship.
    Duke.   And what's her history?
    Viola. A blank, my lord. She never told her love,
But let concealment like a worm i' th' bud,   120

21 the seat: *the heart*   **23 masterly:** *in an experienced manner*   **25 favor:** *'face'; in l. 25 Viola puns on 'favor'*   **32 still:** *always*   **33 so wears she to him:** *so she adapts herself to him*   **34 so sways she level:** *so she keeps constant her husband's love*   **36 Our fancies:** *men's loves*   **37 worn:** *worn out; cf. n.*   **41 hold the bent:** *'keep the intensity,' as in a bent bow; or 'hold the direction'*   **45 even:** *monosyllabic*   **48 spinsters:** *spinners*   **49 free:** *happy, carefree*   **weave their thread with bones:** *make bone or thread lace with bone bobbins*   **50 Do use to:** *are accustomed to*   **silly sooth:** *simple truth*   **51 dallies with:** *treats lightly of*   **52 the old age:** *the former times (of virtue)*   **54 I prethee:** *I pray thee*   **56 Come away:** *'come away from there,' i.e. 'come here'*   **57 cypress:** *a coffin of cypress wood, boughs of cypress, or thin black cloth (all associated with mourning)*   **58 Fie, away:** *fie, go away; cf. n.*   **60 yew:** *the yew tree, associated with mourning*   **62, 63 My part . . . share it;** *cf. n.*

75 pleasure will be paid: *indulgence exacts its penalty; cf. n.*   **78 the melancholy: god;** *cf. n.*   **79 doublet:** *a closely fitted jacket*   **taffeta:** *a thin silk cloth*   **80 opal:** *a semiprecious stone of changeable color*   **80–82 I would have . . . voyage of nothing;** *Cf. n.*   **84 give place:** *leave*   **86 sovereign cruelty:** *supremely cruel person (Olivia)*   **88 dirty:** *'made of earth or dirt' and 'filthy'*   **89 parts:** *possessions, attributes*   **fortune:** *luck, chance*   **90 giddily:** *lightly*   **92 pranks her in:** *decks her or dresses her in*   **94 cannot:** *F It cannot; Cf. n.*   **95 Sooth:** *truly*   **100, 101 woman's sides Can bide;** *Cf. n.*   **bide:** *withstand, endure*   **103 they lack retention:** *women lack the capacity of retaining*   **105, 106 No motion . . . and revolt;** *Cf. n.*   **114 owe:** *have toward; so also l. 110*

Feed on her damask cheek. She pin'd in thought;
And with a green and yellow melancholy,
She sat like Patience on a monument,
Smiling at grief. Was not this love indeed?
We men may say more, swear more; but indeed   *125*
Our shows are more than will; for still we prove
Much in our vows, but little in our love.

   Duke. But died thy sister of her love, my boy?
   Viola. I am all the daughters of my father's house,
And all the brothers too; and yet I know not.   *130*
Sir, shall I to this lady?
   Duke.   Ay, that's the theme.
To her in haste. Give her this jewel. Say
My love can give no place, bide no denay.   *Exeunt.*

❧ SCENE FIFTH ❧

Enter Sir Toby, Sir Andrew, and Fabian.

   Toby. Come thy ways, Signior Fabian.
   Fabian. Nay, I'll come. If I lose a scruple of this sport, let
me be boil'd to death with melancholy.
   Toby. Wouldst thou not be glad to have the niggardly
rascally sheep-biter come by some notable shame?   *5*
   Fabian. I would exult, man. You know he brought me out
o' favor with my lady about a bear-baiting here.
   Toby. To anger him we'll have the bear again; and we will
fool him black and blue, shall we not, Sir Andrew?
   Andrew. And we do not, it is pity of our lives.   *10*

Enter Maria.

   Toby. Here comes the little villain. How now, my metal of
India?
   Maria. Get ye all three into the box tree. Malvolio's coming
down this walk. He has been yonder i' the sun practicing behavior to his own shadow this half hour. Observe him, for   *15*
the love of mockery; for I know this letter will make a contemplative idiot of him. Close, in the name of jesting. *[The others
hide.]* Lie thou there, *[Throws down a letter.]* for here comes
the trout that must be caught with tickling.   *Exit.*

Enter Malvolio.

   Malvolio. 'Tis but fortune, all is fortune. Maria once told   *20*
me she did affect me; and I have heard herself come thus near,
that should she fancy, it should be one of my complexion. Besides, she uses me with a more exalted respect than anyone else
that follows her. What should I think on't?
   Toby. Here's an overweening rogue.   *25*
   Fabian. O, peace! Contemplation makes a rare turkey cock
of him. How he jets under his advanc'd plumes!
   Andrew. 'Slight, I could so beat the rogue.

   Toby. Peace, I say.
   Malvolio. To be Count Malvolio.   *30*
   Toby. Ah, rouge!
   Andrew. Pistol him, pistol him.
   Toby. Peace, peace.
   Malvolio. There is example for't. The Lady of the Strachy
married the yeoman of the wardrobe.   *35*
   Andrew. Fie on him, Jezebel.
   Fabian. O, peace! Now he's deeply in. Look how imagina-
tion blows him.
   Malvolio. Having been three months married to her, sitting
in my state.   *40*
   Toby. O, for a stonebow to hit him in the eye!
   Malvolio. Calling my officers about me, in my branch'd
velvet gown; having come from a day bed, where I have left
Olivia sleeping.
   Toby. Fire and brimstone!   *45*
   Fabian. O, peace, peace!
   Malvolio. And then to have the humor of state; and after
a demure travel of regard—telling them I know my place,
as I would they should do theirs—to ask for my kinsman
Toby.   *50*
   Toby. Bolts and shackles!
   Fabian. O, peace, peace, peace, now, now!
   Malvolio. Seven of my people with an obedient start make
out for him. I frown the while, and perchance wind up my
watch, or play with my— some rich jewel. Toby   *55*
approaches; curtsies there to me.
   Toby. Shall this fellow live?
   Fabian. Though our silence be drawn from us with cars, yet
peace.
   Malvolio. I extend my hand to him thus, quenching my   *60*
familiar smile with an austere regard of control.
   Toby. And does not Toby take you a blow o' the lips then?
   Malvolio. Saying, 'Cousin Toby, my fortunes having cast me
on your niece, give me this prerogative of speech.'
   Toby. What, what?   *65*
   Malvolio. 'Your must amend your drunkenness.'
   Toby. Out, scab.
   Fabian. Nay, patience, or we break the sinews of our plot.
   Malvolio. 'Besides, you waste the treasure of your time
with a foolish knight.'   *70*
   Andrew. That's me, I warrant you.
   Malvolio. 'One Sir Andrew.'
   Andrew. I knew 'twas I, for many do call me fool.
   Malvolio. What employment have we here?

                         [Takes up the letter.]

   Fabian. Now is the woodcock near the gin.   *75*
   Toby. O, peace, and the spirit of humors intimate reading
aloud to him.
   Malvolio. By my life, this is my lady's hand. These be

121 **damask:** *of variegated color, here pink and white as of a damask rose*   122–124 **And
with ... smiling at grief;** *Cf. n.*   126 **Our shows ... will;** *Cf. n.* **still**   134 **can give
no place:** *cannot yield* **denay:** *denial*   1 **Come thy ways:** *come along on your way*   2
a scruple: *a bit; Cf. n.*   3 **let me ... melancholy;** *Cf. n.*   5 **sheep-biter:** *a dog that
bites sheep, a sneaking fellow*   6, 7 **You know ... a bear-baiting here;** *Cf. n.*   10 **And:
if**   11, 12 **my metal of India:** *my golden one; Cf. n.*   14, 15 **behavior:** *elegant conduct*   16, 17 **make a contemplative idiot of him:** *fill him with idiotic thoughts*   17
Close: *hide*   19 **trout ... tickling;** *Cf. n.*   21 **she did affect me:** *Olivia was inclined
to love me*   22 **complexion:** *personality, temperament; Cf. n.*   24 **follows her:** *is in her
service*   27 **jets under his advanc'd plumes:** *struts under his stiffened feathers*   28
'Slight: *'by God's light,' a mild oath*

29 **Toby;** *Cf. n.*   32 **Pistol him:** *shoot him*   34 **The Lady of the Strachy;** *Cf. n.*   35
the yeoman of the wardrobe: *the servant in charge of the clothing and linen of a noble
family*   36 **Fie on him, Jezebel;** *Cf. n.*   38 **blows him:** *puffs him up*   40 **state:**
dignity, seat of state   41 **a stonebow:** *a crossbow or catapult for shooting stones*   42
branch'd: *embroidered with figures of branches or flowers*   43 **a day bed:** *a couch*   47
the humor of state: *the manner and disposition of authority*   48 **a demure travel of
regard:** *a grave survey of observation; Cf. n.*   49, 50 **my kinsman Toby:** *Malvolio omits
the title 'Sir'*   53, 54 **make out:** *go out*   55 **my— some rich:** *F my some rich;
Cf. n.*   58 **with cars:** *by force, by terrible violence; Cf. n.*   61 **control:** *authority*   62
take you: *give you*   67 **Out, scab:** *away, scurvy fellow*   74 **employment:** *affair, matter*   75 **woodcock ... gin:** *gin snare, trap*   76, 77 **the spirit ... to him;** *Cf. n.*

her very C's,, her U's, and her T's, and thus makes she her
great P's. It is in contempt of question her hand.   80

  Andrew. Her C's, her U's, and her T's; why that?
  Malvolio. [*Reads.*] 'To the unknown belov'd, this, and my
good wishes.' Her very phrases. By your leave, wax. Soft. And
the impressure her Lucrece, with which she uses to seal. 'Tis
my lady. To whom should this be?   85
  Fabian. This wins him, liver and all.
  Malvolio. [*Reads.*]

> *Jove knows I love,*
> *But who?*
> *Lips, do not move,*
> *No man must know.*   90

'No man must know.' What follows? The numbers alter'd. 'No
man must know.' If this should be thee, Malvolio?
  Toby. Marry, hang thee, brock.
  Malvolio. [*Reads.*]

> *I may command where I adore,*
> *But silence like a Lucrece knife,*   95
> *With bloodless stroke my heart doth gore.*
> *M. O. A. I. doth sway my life.*

  Fabian. A fustian riddle.
  Toby. Excellent wench, say I.
  Malvolio. 'M. O. A. I. doth sway my life.' Nay, but   100
first let me see, let me see, let me see.
  Fabian. What dish o' poison has she dress'd him!
  Toby. And with what wing the staniel checks at it!
  Malvolio. 'I may command where I adore.' Why, she may
command me: I serve her; she is my lady. Why, this is   105
evident to any formal capacity. There is no obstruction in this.
And the end; what should that alphabetical position
portend? If I could make that resemble something in me?
Softly. 'M. O. A. I.'
  Toby. O, ay, make up that. He is now at a cold scent.   110
  Fabian. Sowter will cry upon't for all this, though it
be as rank as a fox.
  Malvolio. M., Malvolio, Why, that begins my name.
  Fabian. Did not I say he would work it out? The cur is
excellent at faults.   115
  Malvolio. M. But then there is no consonancy in the
sequel. That suffers under probation. A should follow, but
O does.
  Fabian. And O shall end, I hope.
  Toby. Ay, or I'll cudgel him and make him cry O.   120
  Malvolio. And then I comes behind.
  Fabian. Ay, and you had any eye behind you, you might
see more detraction at your heels than fortunes before you.
  Malvolio. 'M. O. A. I.' This simulation is not as the former;

and yet to crush this a little, it would bow to me, for every   125
one of these letters are in my name. Soft, here follows prose.
  [*Reads.*] 'If this fall into thy hand, revolve. In my stars I
am above thee, but be not afraid of greatness. Some are born
great, some achieve greatness, and some have greatness thrust
upon 'em. Thy fates open their hands; let thy blood and spirit
embrace them; and to inure thyself to what thou art like to be,
cast thy humble slough and appear fresh. Be opposite with
a kinsman, surly with servants. Let thy tongue tang arguments
of state. Put thyself into the trick of singularity. She thus advises thee that sighs for thee. Remember who commended thy
yellow stockings and wish'd to see thee ever cross-garter'd. I
say remember; go to; thou art made if thou desir'st to be so.
If not, let me see thee a steward still, the fellow of servants,
and not worthy to touch Fortune's fingers. Farewell. She that
would alter services with thee,   140

                                   'The Fortunate-Unhappy.'
Daylight and champian discovers not more. This is open,
I will be proud, I will read politic authors, I will baffle Sir
Toby, I will wash off gross acquaintance, I will be point devise, the very man. I do not now fool myself to let imagination jade me; for every reason excites to this, that my lady
loves me. She did commend my yellow stockings of late;
she did praise my leg being cross-garter'd; and in this she manifests herself to my love, and with a kind of injunction drives
me to these habits of her liking. I thank my stars, I am happy.
I will be strange, stout, in yellow stockings and cross-garter'd,
even with the swiftness of putting on. Jove and my stars be
praised. Here is yet a postscript.
  [*Reads.*] 'Thou canst not choose but know who I am. If
thou entertain'st my love, let it appear in thy smiling. Thy   155
smiles become thee well. Therefore in my presence still smile,
dear my sweet, I prethee.' Jove, I thank thee. I will smile,
I will do everything that thou wilt have me.   *Exit.*

  Fabian. I will not give my part of this sport for a pension
of thousands to be paid from the Sophy.   160
  Toby. I could marry this wench for this device.
  Andrew. So could I too.
  Toby. And ask no other dowry with her but such another
jest.

                            Enter Maria.

  Andrew. Nor I neither.   165
  Fabian. Here comes my noble gull-catcher.
  Toby. Wilt thou set thy foot o' my neck?
  Andrew. Or o' mine either?
  Toby. Shall I play my freedom at tray-trip and become
thy bondslave?   170
  Andrew. I' faith, or I either?

79, 80 her very C's ... P's *in contempt of question: beyond question*   **83 By your
leave, wax;** *Cf. n.* **Soft:** *careful, slow*   **84 uses:** *is accustomed to*   **86 liver:** *the seat of
passion*   **91 The numbers alter'd:** *the meters or accents of verse altered*   **93 brock:** *badger*   **98 fustian:** *ridiculously lofty; Cf. n.*   **99 Excellent wench:** *clever girl* (of
Maria)   **102 What:** *what a* **dress'd:** *prepared*   **103 And with ... at it;** *Cf. n.* **staniel:**
an inferior hawk; F Stallion   **106 formal capacity:** *normal intellect* **obstruction:** *difficulty*   **107 what should:** *what would* **position:** *order*   **109 Softly:** *easily, carefully*   **110 make up that:** *put that together* **a cold scent:** *an old and difficult trail, a false
trail*   **111, 112 Sowter ... fox;** *Cf. n.*   **115 faults:** *gaps or breaks in the scent;
Cf. n.*   **116, 117 But then ... probation;** *Cf. n.*   **119 And O shall end;** *Cf. n.*   **122
and:** *if* **any eye behind you;** *Cf. n.*   **123 more detraction at your heels:** *more loss of
face and humiliation coming directly after you*   **124 simulation:** *puzzle, hidden meaning*

125 and yet ... bow to me; *Cf. n.*   **126 Soft:** *carefully, slowly*   **127 revolve:** *think,
consider* **my stars:** *my fate, my position*   **128 born:** *F become*   **129 achieve:** *F atcheeves
Cf. n.*   **131 inure:** *get used to* **like:** *likely*   **132 cast ... fresh;** *Cf. n.*   **133 tang:**
sound with, echo with;   **134 singularity:** *eccentricity*   **136 cross-garter'd;**
Cf. n.   **137 go to:** *go on*   **140 alter services:** *exchange positions;*   **140–142
thee,/'The Fortunate-Unhappy.'/Daylight:** *F thee, the fortunate unhappy daylight;
Cf. n.*   **142 champian:** *variant of 'champaign,' 'open country'*   **143 politic authors:**
writers on government; F pollticke; Cf. n.   **baffle:** *to subject (especially a knight) to disgrace*   **144 point devise:** *perfectly correct*   **146 jade me:** *befool me*   **148 in this:**
in this letter   **151 strange:** *aloof* **stout:** *brave, proud*   **152 Jove;** *Cf. n.*   **156 still:**
always   **157 dear:** *F deero* **I prethee:** *I pray thee*   **160 the Sophy:** *the shah of Persia;
Cf. n.*   **165 Nor I neither:** *an emphatic negative*   **166 gull-catcher:** *one who catches
gulls; gulls are persons easily tricked; compare 'gullible'*   **167 Wilt ... neck;** *Cf. n.*   **169
play:** *gamble* **tray-trip:** *a game of dice*

Toby. Why, thou hast put him in such a dream that when the image of it leaves him, he must run mad.

Maria. Nay, but say true, does it work upon him?

Toby. Like aqua-vite with a midwife.   *175*

Maria. If you will then see the fruits of the sport, mark his first approach before my lady. He will come to her in yellow stockings, and 'tis a color she abhors; and cross-garter'd, a fashion she detests; and he will smile upon her, which will now be so unsuitable to her disposition, being addicted   *180* to a melancholy as she is, that it cannot but turn him into a notable contempt. If you will see it, follow me.

Toby. To the gates of Tartar, thou most excellent divel of wit.

Andrew. I'll make one too.   *Exeunt.*

Finis, Actus secundus.

ACT THIRD ❧ SCENE FIRST

Enter Viola and Clown.

Viola. Save thee, friend, and thy music. Dost thou live by thy tabor?

Clown. No, sir, I live by the church.

Viola. Art thou a churchman?

Clown. No such matter, sir. I do live by the church; for   *5* I do live at my house, and my house doth stand by the church.

Viola. So thou mayst say the king lies by a beggar, if a beggar dwell near him; or the church stands by thy tabor, if thy tabor stand by the church.   *10*

Clown. You have said, sir. To see this age! A sentence is but a chev'ril glove to a good wit. How quickly the wrong side may be turn'd outward!

Viola. Nay, that's certain. They that dally nicely with words may quickly make them wanton.   *15*

Clown. I would therefore my sister had had no name, sir.

Viola. Why, man?

Clown. Why, sir, her name's a word, and to dally with that word might make my sister wanton. But indeed words are   *20* very rascals since bonds disgrac'd them.

Viola. Thy reason, man?

Clown. Troth, sir, I can yield you none without words, and words are grown so false I am loath to prove reason with them.   *25*

Viola. I warrant thou art a merry fellow and car'st for nothing.

Clown. Not so, sir; I do care for something; but in my conscience, sir, I do not care for you. If that be to care for nothing, sir, I would it would make you invisible.   *30*

Viola. Art not thou the Lady Olivia's fool?

Clown. No, indeed, sir. The Lady Olivia has no folly. She will keep no fool, sir, till she be married; and fools are as like husbands as pilchers are to her-rings, the husbands the bigger. I am indeed not her fool, but her corrupter of words.   *35*

Viola. I saw thee late at the Count Orsino's.

Clown. Foolery, sir, does walk about the orb like the sun: it shines everywhere. I would be sorry, sir, but the fool should be as oft with your master as with my mistress. I think I saw your wisdom there.   *40*

Viola. Nay, and thou pass upon me, I'll no more with thee. Hold, there's expenses for thee.   *[Gives a coin.]*

Clown. Now Jove in his next commodity of hair send thee a beard.

Viola. By my troth, I'll tell thee, I am almost sick for   *45* one, though I would not have it grow on my chin. Is thy lady within?

Clown. Would not a pair of these have bred, sir?

Viola. Yes, being kept together and put to use.

Clown. I would play Lord Pandarus of Phrygia, sir, to   *50* bring a Cressida to this Troilus.

Viola. I understand you, sir. 'Tis well begg'd.

[Gives another coin.]

Clown. The matter, I hope, is not great, sir, begging but a beggar: Cressida was a beggar. My lady is within, sir. I will conster to them whence you come. Who you are and what   *55* you would are out of my welkin. I might say 'element' but the word is overworn.   *Exit.*

Viola. This fellow is wise enough to play the fool,
And to do that well craves a kind of wit.
He must observe their mood on whom he jests,   *60*
The quality of persons, and the time;
Not, like the haggard, check at every feather
That comes before his eye. This is a practice
As full of labor as a wise man's art;
For folly that he wisely shows is fit;   *65*
But wise men, folly-fall'n, quite taint their wit.

Enter Sir Toby and [Sir] Andrew.

Toby. Save you, gentleman.

Viola. And you, sir.

Andrew. Dieu vous garde, monsieur.

Viola. Et vous aussi. Vostre serviteur.   *70*

Andrew. I hope, sir, you are, and I am yours.

Toby. Will you encounter the house? My niece is desirous you should enter, if your trade be to her.

Viola. I am bound to your niece, sir; I mean, she is the list of my voyage.   *75*

Toby. Taste your legs, sir; put them to motion.

Viola. My legs do better understand me, sir, than I understand what you mean by bidding me taste my legs.

---

34 pilchers: *pilchards, small fish related to the herring*   **36 late:** *lately*   **37 the orb:** *the world*   **38 I would;** *Cf. n.*   **40 your wisdom;** *Cf. n.*   **41 and thou pass upon me:** *if you thrust at me (with your jokes)*   **42 expenses:** *reimbursement*   **43 Jove in his next commodity of hair:** *Jove when he next sends a lot or assignment of hair*   **48 these:** *these coins*   **49 put to use:** *loaned at interest*   **50, 51 Pandarus . . . Cressida . . . Troilus;** *Cf. n.*   **54 Cressida was a beggar;** *Cf. n.*   **55 conster:** *construe, explain*   **56 welkin: sky**   **element:** *both 'sky' and 'element' in the modern sense*   **59 craves a kind of wit:** *demands a kind of intelligence*   **62 Not, like:** *F And like the*   **haggard:** *the untrained hawk*   **check at every feather:** *forsake her quarry for other game*   **63 practice:** *skill*   **65 fit:** *suitable*   **66 wise men:** *F wisemens*   **folly-fall'n:** *when they have fallen into folly*   **67 Save you:** *God save you*   **69, 70 Dieu . . . serviteur:** *God protect you, sir . . . And you also. Your servant (French)*   **72 encounter:** *meet, i.e. go into; Cf. n.*   **73 if your trade be to her:** *if your business concern her*   **74 bound:** *to bound for*   **list:** *limit, end*   **76 Taste:** *try*   **77 understand:** *both 'comprehend' and 'stand under'*

---

175 aqua vite: *any distilled liquor* (Latin *aqua vitae*, 'water of life'), *Cf. n.*   **182 a notable contempt:** *a state of being particularly despised* (by Olivia)   **183 Tartar:** *Tartarus the section of hell reserved for the most evil* (Roman mythology)   **divel:** *devil*   **185 I'll make one too:** *I'll go along too*   **1 Save thee:** *God save thee*   **live by:** *make a living by*   **3 tabor:** *drum* (which the stage clown commonly carried)   **8 king:** *F kings*   **lies by:** *dwells by*   **11 A sentence:** *any unit of meaning*   **12 a chev'ril glove:** *a kid glove*   **14 dally nicely:** *play foolishly or fastidiously*   **15 wanton:** *capricious, unmanageable*   **20 wanton:** *lascivious, lewd; Cf. n.*   **21 since bonds disgrac'd them;** *Cf. n.*   **23 Troth:** *truly*   **24 to prove reason:** *to test rightness*   **26, 27 car'st for nothing:** *you never worry*

Toby. I mean, to go, sir, to enter.

Viola. I will answer you with gait and entrance; but we   80
are prevented.

Enter Olivia and Gentlewoman [Maria].

Most excellent accomplish'd lady, the heavens rain odors
on you!

Andrew. [Aside.] That youth's a rare courtier. 'Rain odors.'
Well!   85

Viola. My matter hath no voice, lady, but to your own
most pregnant and vouchsafed ear.

Andrew. [Aside.] 'Odors,' 'pregnant,' and 'vouchsafed.' I'll
get 'em all three already.

Olivia. Let the garden door be shut and leave me to my   90
hearing. *[Exeunt Sir Toby, Sir Andrew, and Maria.]* Give me
your hand, sir.

Viola. My duty, madam, and most humble service.

Olivia. What is your name?

Viola. Cesario is your servant's name, fair princess.   95

Olivia. My servant, sir? 'Twas never merry world
Since lowly feigning was call'd compliment.
Y' are servant to the Count Orsino, youth.

Viola. And he is yours, and his must needs be yours.
Your servant's servant is your servant, madam.   100

Olivia. For him, I think not on him; for his thoughts,
Would they were blanks, rather than fill'd with me.

Viola. Madam, I come to whet your gentle thoughts
On his behalf.

Olivia.   O, by your leave, I pray you.   105
I bade you never speak again of him;
But would you undertake another suit,
I had rather hear you to solicit that
Than music from the spheres.

Viola.   Dear lady.   110

Olivia. Give me leave, beseech you. I did send,
After the last enchantment you did here,
A ring in chase of you. So did I abuse
Myself, my servant, and, I fear me, you.
Under your hard construction must I sit,   115
To force that on you in a shameful cunning
Which you knew none of yours. What might you think?
Have you not set mine honor at the stake
And baited it with all th' unmuzzled thoughts
That tyrannous heart can think? To one of your receiving   120
Enough is shown; a cypress, not a bosom,
Hides my heart. So let me hear you speak.

Viola. I pity you.

Olivia.   That's a degree to love.

Viola. No, not a grize; for 'tis a vulgar proof   125
That very oft we pity enemies.

Olivia. Why then methinks 'tis time to smile agen.

O world, how apt the poor are to be proud!
If one should be a prey, how much the better
To fall before the lion than the wolf!   *Clock strikes.* 130
The clock upbraids me with the waste of time.
Be not afraid, good youth; I will not have you.
And yet when wit and youth is come to harvest,
Your wife is like to reap a proper man.
There lies your way, due west.   135

Viola.   Then westward ho!
Grace and good disposition attend your ladyship.
You'll nothing, madam, to my lord by me?

Olivia. Stay.
I prethee tell me what thou think'st of me.   140

Viola. That you do think you are not what you are.

Olivia. If I think so, I think the same of you.

Viola. Then think you right. I am not what I am.

Olivia. I would you were as I would have you be.

Viola. Would it be better, madam, than I am?   145
I wish it might, for now I am your fool.

Olivia. O, what a deal of scorn looks beautiful
In the contempt and anger of his lip!
A murd'rous guilt shows not itself more soon
Than love that would seem hid: love's night is noon.   150
Cesario, by the roses of the spring,
By maidhood, honor, truth, and everything,
I love thee so, that maugre all thy pride,
Nor wit nor reason can my passion hide.
Do not extort thy reasons from this clause,   155
For that I woo, thou therefore hast no cause.
But rather reason thus with reason fetter:
Love sought is good, but given unsought is better.

Viola. By innocence I swear and by my youth,
I have one heart, one bosom, and one truth,   160
And that no woman has, nor never none
Shall mistress be of it, save I alone.
And so adieu, good madam. Never more
Will I my master's tears to you deplore.

Olivia. Yet come again; for thou perhaps mayst move   165
That heart which now abhors, to like his love.   *Exeunt.*

❧ Scene Second ❧

Enter Sir Toby, Sir Andrew, and Fabian.

Andrew: No, faith, I'll not stay a jot longer.

Toby. Thy reason, dear venom; give thy reason.

Fabian. You must needs yield your reason, Sir Andrew.

Andrew. Marry, I saw your niece do more favors to the
Count's servingman than ever she bestow'd upon me. I   5
saw't i' th' orchard.

Toby. Did she see the while, old boy? Tell me that.

Andrew. As plain as I see you now.

Fabian. This was a great argument of love in her toward
you.   10

80 gait: *walking;* F *gate; Cf. n.*   81 prevented: *anticipated*   82 excellent: *excellently*   86 hath no voice: *can be told no one*   87 pregnant: *receptive* vouchsafed: *graciously given*   89 already: *fully prepared* (for my future use). all ready   96, 97 'Twas never . . . compliment; *Cf. n.*   99 yours: *your servant* (in love) his: *his servant*   102 blanks: *blank thoughts*   103 to whet: *to sharpen* (particularly by rubbing)   108 I had: *pronounced 'I'd'*   109 music from the spheres; *Cf. n.*   111 beseech: *I beseech*   112 enchantment: *magic of making me love you* here: F *heare*   113 abuse: *deceive*   115 construction: *interpretation* (of my character)   116, 117 To force . . . none of yours; *Cf. n.*   118, 119 at the stake . . . unmuzzled thoughts; *Cf. n.* baited it: *harassed it*   120 your receiving: *your receptive capacity; Cf. n.*   121 a cypress: *a transparent black cloth used in sign of mourning*   122 Hides . . . speak; *Cf. n.*   125 a grize: *a grece, a flight of steps, a degree* a vulgar proof: *a common experience*   127 'tis time to smile agen; *Cf. n.*

130 the lion . . . the wolf; *Cf. n.*   134 proper: *worthy, handsome*   135, 136 due west. Then westword ho; *Cf. n.*   137 disposition: *frame of mind*   141, 142 That you do think . . . the same of you; *Cf. n.*   146 I am your fool: *you make a fool of me*   147 what a deal: *what a great deal*   150 love's night is noon: *love makes itself plain*   153 maugre: *despite*   154 Nor . . . nor: *neither . . . nor*   155-158 Do not extort . . . better; *Cf. n.*   161 nor never none: *nor ever one*   166 his: *the Duke's*   2 venom: *venomous person; Cf. n.*   4 Marry: *to be sure*   6 orchard: *probably 'garden' in the modern sense; Cf. n.*   7 see: *watch; Cf. n.*

Andrew. 'Slight. Will you make an ass o' me?

Fabian. I will prove it legitimate, sir, upon the oaths of judgment and reason.

Toby. And they have been grand-jurymen since before Noah was a sailor.   *15*

Fabian. She did show favor to the youth in your sight only to exasperate you, to awake your dormouse valor, to put fire in your heart and brimstone in your liver. You should then have accosted her; and with some excellent jests, fire-new from the mint, you should have bang'd the youth into dumbness.   *20* This was look'd for at your hand, and this was balk'd. The double gilt of this opportunity you let time wash off, and you are now sail'd into the north of my lady's opinion where you will hang like an icicle on a Dutchman's beard, unless you do redeem it by some laudable attempt either of valor or policy. *25*

Andrew. And't be any way, it must be with valor, for policy I hate. I had lief be a Brownist as a politician.

Toby. Why then, build me thy fortunes upon the basis of valor. Challenge me the Count's youth to fight with him; hurt him in eleven places. My niece shall take note of it; and   *30* assure thyself there is no love broker in the world can more prevail in man's commendation with woman than report of valor.

Fabian. There is no way but this, Sir Andrew.

Andrew. Will either of you bear me a challenge to him?   *35*

Toby. Go, write it in a martial hand. Be curst and brief. It is no matter how witty, so it be eloquent and full of intention. Taunt him with the license of ink. If thou thou'st him some thrice, it shall not be amiss; and as many lies as will lie in thy sheet of paper, although the sheet were big   *40* enough for the bed of Ware of England, set 'em down, go about it. Let there be gall enough in thy ink, though thou write with a goose-pen, no matter. About it!

Andrew. Where shall I find you?

Toby. We'll call thee at the cubiculo. Go.   *45*

                                               Exit Sir Andrew.

Fabian. This is a dear manikin to you, Sir Toby.

Toby. I have been dear to him, lad, some two thousand strong or so.

Fabian. We shall have a rare letter from him; but you'll not deliver 't.   *50*

Toby. Never trust me then; and by all means stir on the youth to an answer. I think oxen and wainropes cannot hale them together. For Andrew, if he were open'd and you find so much blood in his liver as will clog the foot of a flea, I'll eat the rest of th' anatomy.   *55*

Fabian. And his opposite, the youth, bears in his visage no great presage of cruelty.

Enter Maria.

Toby. Look where the youngest wren of mine comes.

Maria. If you desire the spleen and will laugh yourselves

into stitches, follow me. Yond gull Malvolio is turned   *60* heathen, a very renegatho; for there is no Christian that means to be saved by believing rightly can ever believe such impossible passages of grossness. He's in yellow stockings.

Toby. And cross-garter'd?

Maria. Most villainously, like a pedant that keeps a   *65* school i' th' church. I have dogg'd him like his murtherer. He does obey every point of the letter that I dropp'd to betray him. He does smile his face into more lines than is in the new map with the augmentation of the Indies. You have not seen such a thing as 'tis. I can hardly forbear hurling things at him. I know my lady will strike him. If she do, he'll smile and tak't for a great favor.

Toby. Come bring us, bring us where he is.   *Exeunt omnes.*

❧ SCENE THREE ❧

Enter Sebastian and Antonio.

Sebastian. I would not by my will have troubled you,
But since you make your pleasure of your pains,
I will no further chide you.

Antonio. I could not stay behind you. My desire
(More sharp than filed steel) did spur me forth;   *5*
And not all love to see you (though so much
As might have drawn one to a longer voyage)
But jealousy what might befall your travel,
Being skilless in these parts; which to a stranger,
Unguided and unfriended, often prove   *10*
Rough and unhospitable. My willing love,
The rather by these arguments of fear,
Set forth in your pursuit.

Sebastian.   My kind Antonio,
I can no other answer make but thanks,   *15*
And thanks; and ever oft good turns
And shuffl'd off with such uncurrent pay.
But were my worth, as is my conscience, firm,
You should find better dealing. What's to do?
Shall we go see the relics of this town?   *20*

Anotonio. Tomorrow, sir. Best first go see your lodging?

Sebastian. I am not weary and 'tis long to night.
I pray you let us satisfy our eyes
With the memorials and the things of fame
That do renown this city.   *25*

Antonio.   Would you'ld pardon me.
I do not without danger walk these streets.
Once in a sea fight 'gainst the Count his galleys
I did some service of such note indeed
That, were I tane here, it would scarce be answer'd.   *30*

Sebastian. Belike you slew great number of his people.

Antonio. Th' offence is not of such a bloody nature,
Albeit the quality of the time and quarrel
Might well have given us bloody argument.

12 **'Slight:** *'God's light,' an oath*   13 **legitimate:** *legitimately, logically*   14 **grand-jurymen:** *competent to judge evidence*   17 **dormouse:** *i.e. sleepy; Cf. n.*   18 **brimstone in your liver:** *make your liver hot*   19 **fire-new:** *brand-new*   21 **balk'd:** *missed*   22 **double gilt;** *Cf. n.*   24 **an icicle on a Dutchman's beard;** *Cf. n.*   26 **And't:** *if it*   27 **Brownist;** *Cf. n.*   28, 29 **build me . . . Challenge me:** *ethical datives*   36 **curst:** *perversely cross*   38 **with the license of ink:** *with all the excessive liberty that written language allows*   38, 39 **If thou thou'st him:** *if you call him 'thou'; Cf. n.*   41 **the bed of Ware;** *Cf. n.*   42 **gall;** *Cf. n.*   43 **goose-pen;** *Cf. n.*   45 **the cubiculo:** *the sleeping chamber* (*Latin* in cubiculo)   46 **dear manikin:** *dear little man; Cf. n.*   47 **dear:** *expensive*   52 **wainropes:** *wagon ropes* **hale:** *haul*   54 **blood in his liver:** *i.e. courage; Cf. n.*   58 **youngest wren of mine;** *Cf. n.*   59 **If you desire the spleen;** *Cf. n.*

60 **gull:** *dupe*   61 **renegatho:** *renegade; Cf. n.*   63 **passages of grossness:** *statements* (in the letter) *of exaggerated misinformation*   65 **pedant:** *schoolteacher*   66 **murtherer:** *variant form of 'murderer'*   69 **new map . . . Indies;** *Cf. n.*   6 **all love:** *extreme desire*   8 **jealousy:** *solicitude*   9 **skilless in:** *without knowledge of*   16 **And thanks . . . turns;** *Cf. n.*   17 **shuffl'd off:** *set aside, discounted* **uncurrent:** *valueless as currency* (i.e. 'thanks')   18 **my worth:** *the money I have* **my conscience:** *my conscience concerning your favors*   20 **relics:** *monuments*   28 **the Count his galleys:** *the Count's galleys*   30 **tane:** *taken* **it would scarce be answer'd:** *it would be difficult to explain away*   31 **Belike:** *perhaps*   33 **Albeit:** *although*

It might have since been answer'd in repaying   *35*
What we took from them, which for traffic's sake
Most of our city did. Only myself stood out;
For which, if I be lapsed in this place,
I shall pay dear.
   Sebastian.   Do not then walk too open.   *40*
   Antonio. It doth not fit me. Hold, sir, here's my purse.
In the south suburbs at the Elephant
Is best to lodge. I will bespeak our diet,
Whiles you beguile the time and feed your knowledge
With viewing of the town. There shall you have me.   *45*
   Sebastian. Why I your purse?
   Antonio. Haply your eye shall light upon some toy
You have desire to purchase; and your store
I think is not for idle markets, sir.
   Sebastian. I'll be your purse-bearer and leave you for   *50*
An hour.
   Antonio. To th' Elephant.
   Sebastian.   I do remember.   *Exeunt.*

❧ SCENE FOURTH ❧

Enter Olivia and Maria.

Olivia. I have sent after him; he says he'll come.
How shall I feast him? What bestow of him?
For youth is bought more oft than begg'd or borrow'd.
I speak too loud. Where's Malvolio? He is sad and civil,
And suits well for a servant with my fortunes.   *5*
Where is Malvolio?
   Maria. He's coming, madam, but in very strange manner.
He is sure possess'd, madam.
   Olivia. Why, what's the matter? Does he rave?
   Maria. No, madam, he does nothing but smile. Your   *10*
ladyship were best to have some guard about you if he come,
for sure the man is tainted in's wits.
   Olivia. Go call him hither.

Enter Malvolio.

                 I am as mad as he,
If sad and merry madness equal be.   *15*
How now, Malvolio?
   Malvolio. Sweet lady, ho, ho!
   Olivia. Smil'st thou?
I sent for thee upon a sad occasion.
   Malvolio. Sad lady, I could be sad. This does make   *20*
some obstruction in the blood, this cross-gartering; but what
of that? If it please the eye of one, it is with me as the
very true sonnet is, 'Please one and please all.'
   Olivia. Why, how doest thou, man? What is the matter
with thee?   *25*
   Malvolio. Not black in my mind, though yellow in my legs.

It did come to his hands, and commands shall be executed.
I think we do know the sweet Roman hand.
   Olivia. Wilt thou go to bed, Malvolio?
   Malvolio. To bed? Ay, sweetheart, and I'll come to thee.   *30*
   Olivia. God comfort thee. Why dost thou smile so and
kiss thy hand so oft?
   Maria. How do you, Malvolio?
   Malvolio. At your request? Yes, nightingales answer daws.
   Maria. Why appear you with this ridiculous boldness   *35*
before my lady?
   Malvolio. 'Be not afraid of greatness.' 'Twas well writ.
   Olivia. What mean'st thou by that, Malvolio?
   Malvolio. 'Some are born great.'
   Olivia. Ha?   *40*
   Malvolio. 'Some achieve greatness.'
   Olivia. What say'st thou?
   Malvolio. 'And some have greatness thrust upon them.'
   Olivia. Heaven restore thee.
   Malvolio. 'Remember who commended thy yellow   *45*
stockings.'
   Olivia. Thy yellow stockings?
   Malvolio. 'And wish'd to see thee cross-garter'd.'
   Olivia. Cross-garter'd?'
   Malvolio. 'Go to, thou art made, if thou desir'st to be so.'   *50*
   Olivia. Am I made?
   Malvolio. 'If not, let me see thee a servant still.'
   Olivia. Why, this is very midsummer madness.

Enter Servant.

   Servant. Madam, the young gentleman of the Count
Orsino's is return'd. I could hardly entreat him back. He   *55*
attends your ladyship's pleasure.
   Olivia. I'll come to him. *[Exit Servant.]* Good Maria, let this
fellow be look'd to. Where's my cousin Toby? Let some of my
people have a special care of him. I would not have him
miscarry for the half of my dowry.   *60*
                    Exit [Olivia with Maria].
   Malvolio. O, ho, do you come near to me now? No worse
man that Sir Toby to look to me. This concurs directly with
the letter. She sends him on purpose that I may appear stubborn to him, for she incites me to that in the letter. 'Cast   *65*
thy humble slough,' says she. 'Be opposite with a kinsman,
surly with servants. Let thy tongue tang with arguments of
state. Put thyself into the trick of singularity.' And consequently sets down the manner how: as, a sad face, a reverend
carriage, a slow tongue, in the habit of some sir of note, and   *70*
so forth. I have lim'd her, but it is Jove's doing and Jove make
me thankful. And when she went away now, 'Let this fellow
be look'd to.' Fellow? Not 'Malvolio,' nor after my degree, but
'fellow.' Why, everything adheres togither, that no dram of a
scruple, no scruple of a scruple, no obstacle, no incredulous   *75*
or unsafe circumstance—what can be said? Nothing that can
be, can come between me and the full prospect of my hopes.
Well, Jove, not I, is the doer of this and he is to be thanked.

36 for traffic's sake: *for trade's sake* **38 lapsed:** *pounced upon as an offender* **42 the Elephant:** *A London inn sign; Cf. n.* **47 some toy:** *some trifle* **48 store:** *store of money* **49 idle markets:** *useless purchasings* **2 of him:** *on him (Cesario)* **4 sad and civil:** *serious and sedate* **8 possess'd:** *possessed by the devil* **12 in's:** *in his* **15 sad:** *serious* **20 sad:** *'unhappy' and 'uncomfortable'* **21 this cross-gartering;** *cf. n.* **23 sonnet:** *any short poem* **'Please one and please all';** *cf. n.* **24 Olivia. Why, how:** *F. Mal. Why how*

28 Roman hand: *the Italian style, like modern handwriting; cf. n.* **34 At your request ... daws;** *cf. n.* **50 Go to:** *go on* **made;** *cf. n.* **53 midsummer madness;** *cf. n.* **59, 60 miscarry:** *come to harm* **64, 65 stubborn:** *hard, stiff, rigid* **67 tang with:** *sound with, echo with;* F *langer with; cf. n.* **68–70 And consequently ... and so forth;** *cf. n.* **69 sad:** *serious* **70 the habit of some sir:** *the clothing of some gentleman* **71 lim'd:** *caught; cf. n.* **72 fellow:** *probably in the sense of 'companion,' not as Olivia uses it in addressing an inferior* **73 degree:** *position* **74 togither:** *together* **dram:** *one-eighth fluid ounce* **scruple:** *both 'doubt' and 'one twenty-fourth of an ounce' (apothecaries' weight)* **75 incredulous:** *incredible*

Enter [Sir] Toby, Fabian, and Maria.

Toby. Which way is he, in the name of sanctity? If all the divels of hell be drawn in little and Legion himself possess'd 80 him, yet I'll speak to him.

Fabian. Here he is, here he is. How is't with you, sir? How is't with you, man?

Malvolio. Go off, I discard you. Let me enjoy my private. Go off. 85

Maria. Lo, how hollow the fiend speaks within him. Did I not tell you? Sir Toby, my lady prays you to have a care of him.

Malvolio. Ah, ha, does she so?

Toby. Go to, go to; peace, peace; we must deal gently 90 with him. Let me alone. How do you, Malvolio? How is't with you? What, man, defy the divel? Consider, he's an enemy to mankind.

Malvolio. Do you know what you say?

Maria. La you, and you speak ill of the divel, how he 95 takes it at heart. Pray God he be not bewitch'd.

Fabian. Carry his water to th' wise woman.

Maria. Marry, and it shall be done tomorrow morning if I live. My lady would not lose him for more than I'll say.

Malvolio. How now, mistress? 100

Maria. O Lord.

Toby. Prethee, hold thy peace. This is not the way. Do you not see you move him? Let me alone with him.

Fabian. No way but gentleness; gently, gently. The fiend is rough and will not be roughly us'd. 105

Toby. Why, how now my bawcock? How dost thou, chuck?

Malvolio. Sir.

Toby. Ay, biddy, come with me. What, man, 'tis not for gravity to play at cherry-pit with Satan. Hang him, foul collier! 110

Maria. Get him to say his prayers; good Sir Toby, get him to pray.

Malvolio. My prayers, minx?

Maria. No, I warrant you, he will not hear of godliness.

Malvolio. Go hang yourselves all. You are idle shallow 115 things. I am not of your element. You shall know more hereafter. *Exit.*

Toby. Is't possible?

Fabian. If this were play'd upon a stage now, I could condemn it as an improbable fiction. 120

Toby. His very genius hath taken the infection of the device, man.

Maria. Nay, pursue him now, lest the device take air and taint.

Fabian. Why, we shall make him mad indeed.

Maria. The house will be the quieter. 125

Toby. Come, we'll have him in a dark room and bound. My niece is already in the belief that he's mad. We may carry it thus for our pleasure and his penance, till our very pastime, tired out of breath, prompt us to have mercy on him; at which time we will bring the device to the bar and crown thee 130 for a finder of madmen. But see, but see.

Enter Sir Andrew.

Fabian. More matter for a May morning.

Andrew. Here's the challenge; read it. I warrant there's vinegar and pepper in't.

Fabian. Is't so saucy? 135

Andrew. Ay, is't? I warrant him. Do but read.

Toby. Give me. *[Reads.]* 'Youth, whatsoever thou art, thou art but a scurvy fellow.'

Fabian. Good and valiant.

Toby. [Reads.] 'Wonder not nor admire not in thy mind 140 why I do call thee so, for I will show thee no reason for't.'

Fabian. A good note that keeps you from the blow of the law.

Toby. [Reads.] 'Thou com'st to the Lady Olivia, and in my sight she uses thee kindly. But thou liest in thy throat; 145 that is not the matter I challenge thee for.'

Fabian. Very brief and to exceeding good sense—less.

Toby. [Reads.] 'I will waylay thee going home; where if it be thy chance to kill me—'

Fabian. Good. 150

Toby. [Reads.] 'Thou kill'st me like a rogue and a villain.'

Fabian. Still you keep o' th' windy side of the law. Good.

Toby. [Reads.] 'Fare thee well, and God have mercy upon one of our souls. He may have mercy upon mine, but my 155 hope is better, and so look to thyself. Thy friend as thou usest him, and they sworn enemy,

　　　　　　　　　　'Andrew Aguecheek.'

If this letter move him not, his legs cannot. I'll give't him.

Maria. You may have very fit occasion for't. He is now 160 in some commerce with my lady and will by and by depart.

Toby. Go, Sir Andrew. Scout me for him at the corner of the orchard like a bumbaily. So soon as ever thou seest him, draw; and as thou draw'st, swear horrible; for it comes to pass oft that a terrible oath with a swaggering accent sharply 165 twang'd off, gives manhood more approbation then ever proof itself would have earn'd him. Away.

Andrew. Nay, let me alone for swearing. *Exit.*

Toby. Now will not I deliver his letter; for the behavior of the young gentleman gives him out to be of good capacity 170 and breeding; his employment between his lord and my niece confirms no less. Therefore this letter, being so excellently ignorant, will breed no terror in the youth. He will find it comes from a clodpoll. But, sir, I will deliver his challenge by word of mouth, set upon Aguecheek a notable report of 175 valor, and drive the gentleman (as I know his youth will aptly receive it) into a most hideous opinion of his rage, skill, fury, and impetuosity. This will so fright them both that they will kill one another by the look, like cockatrices.

Enter Olivia and Viola.

Fabian. Here he comes with your niece. Give them way 180 till he take leave, and presently after him.

80 **drawn in little**: *brought in a small space; cf. n.* **Legion**; *cf. n.* **82, 83 How is't with you, man?**; *cf. n.* **84 private**: *privacy* **90 Go to**: *go on* **95 La**: *Oh!* **and**: *if* **96 bewitch'd**; *cf. n.* **97 Carry . . . woman**; *cf. n.* **102 Prethee**: *I pray thee* **106 bawcock**: *good fellow (French beau coq)* **107 chuck**: *chick* **109 biddy**: *chicken* **110 gravity**: *dignity* **cherry-pit**: *a child's game; cf. n.* **collier**: *coal peddler; cf. n.* **115 idle**: *empty, trifling* **121 genius**: *nature* **123 take air and taint**: *be exposed and thus contaminated* **126 in a dark room and bound**; *cf. n.* **127, 128 carry it**: *carry the trick on* **130 the bar**: *the bar of judgment*

132 matter for a May morning: *material for a May-day comedy* **135 saucy**: *a quibble on 'spicy' and 'impudent' or 'sharp'* **136 Ay, is't?** F1, *ist?* **138 scurvy**: *scabby, dirty* **142, 143 A good note . . . law**; *cf. n.* **153 windy**: *windward, safe* **155, 156 my hope**: *my hope of winning* **160 You may**: F*Yon may* **for't**: F*fot't* **161 by and by**: *immediately, soon* **162 me**: *ethical dative* **163 orchard**: *probably 'garden'* **bumbaily**: *bumbailiff, an agent employed in making arrests* **166 approbation**: *confirmation* **proof**: *testing* **168 let me alone**: *leave that (swearing) to me* **174 a clodpoll**: *a clod-head, a fool* **179 cockatrices**: *basilisks; cf. n.* **180 Give them way**: *give them privacy, let them alone* **181 presently**: *immediately*

Toby. I will meditate the while upon some horrid
message for a challenge. *[Exeunt Sir Toby, Fabian, and Maria.]*

Olivia. I have said too much unto a heart of stone,
And laid mine honor too unchary on't.   185
There's something in me that reproves my fault;
But such a headstrong potent fault it is
That it but mocks reproof.

Viola. With the same havior that your passion bears,
Goes on my master's griefs.   190

Olivia. Here, wear this jewel for me; 'tis my picture.
Refuse it not; it hath no tongue to vex you.
And I beseech you come again tomorrow.
What shall you ask of me that I'll deny,
That honor, sav'd, may upon asking give?   195

Viola. Nothing but this: your true love for my master.

Olivia. How with mine honor may I give him that
Which I have given to you?

Viola.   I will acquit you.

Olivia. Well, come again tomorrow. Fare thee well. A   200
fiend like thee might bear my soul to hell.   *[Exit.]*

Enter [Sir] Toby and Fabian.

Toby. Gentleman, God save thee.

Viola. And you, sir.

Toby. That defense thou hast, betake thee to't. Of what
nature the wrongs are thou hast done him, I know not; but
thy intercepter, full of despite, bloody as the hunter, attends
thee at the orchard end. Dismount thy tuck, be yare in thy
preparation; for thy assailant is quick, skillful, and deadly.

Viola. You mistake, sir. I am sure no man hath any quarrel
to me. My remembrance is very free and clear from any   210
image of offense done to any man.

Toby. You'll find it otherwise, I assure you. Therefore,
it you hold your life at any price, betake you to your guard;
for your opposite hath in him what youth, strength, skill,
and wrath can furnish man withal.   215

Viola. I pray you, sir, what is he?

Toby. He is knight dubb'd with unhatch'd rapier and on
carpet consideration, but he is a divel in private brawl. Souls
and bodies hath he divorc'd three; and his incensement at this
moment is so implacable that satisfaction can be none but   220
by pangs of death and sepulcher. 'Hob, nob' is his word.
'Give't or take't.'

Viola. I will return again into the house and desire some
conduct of the lady. I am no fighter. I have heard of some
kind of men that put quarrels purposely on others to taste   225
their valor. Belike this is a man of that quirk.

Toby. Sir, no. His indignation derives itself out of a very
competent injury; therefore get you on and give him his desire.
Back you shall not to the house, unless you undertake that
with me which with as much safety you might answer him.   230
Therefore on, or strip your sword stark naked; for meddle you
must, that's certain, or forswear to wear iron about you.

Viola. This is as uncivil as strange. I beseech you, do me
this courteous office, as to know of the knight what my offense
to him is. It is something of my negligence, nothing of my   235
purpose.

Toby. I will do so. Signior Fabian, stay you by this gentleman till my return.   *Exit Toby.*

Viola. Pray you, sir, do you know of this matter?

Fabian. I know the knight is incens'd againt you, even   240
to a mortal arbitrement; but nothing of the circumstance more.

Viola. I beseech you, what manner of man is he?

Fabian. Nothing of that wonderful promise, to read him by
his form, as you are like to find him in the proof of his
valor. He is indeed, sir, the most skillful, bloody, and fatal   245
opposite that you could possibly have found in any part of
Illyria. Will you walk towards him? I will make your peace
with him if I can.

Viola. I shall be much bound to you for't. I am one that
had rather go with sir priest than sir knight. I care not   250
who knows so much of my mettle.   *Exeunt.*

Enter [Sir] Toby and [Sir] Andrew.

Toby. Why, man, he's a very divel; I have not seen such a
firago. I had a pass with him, rapier, scabbard, and all, and he
gives me the stuck-in with such a mortal motion that it is
inevitable; and on the answer he pays you as surely as your   255
feet hits the ground they step on. They say he has been fencer
to the Sophy.

Andrew. Pox on't, I'll not meddle with him.

Toby. Ay, but he will not now be pacified. Fabiran can
scarce hold him yonder.   260

Andrew. Plague on't, and I thought he had been valiant and
so cunning in fence, I'd have seen him damn'd ere I'd have
challeng'd him. Let him let the matter slip, and I'll give him
my horse, grey Capilet.

Toby. I'll make the motion. Stand here; make a good   265
show on't. This shall end without the perdition of souls.
[Aside.] Marry, I'll ride your horse as well as I ride you.

Enter Fabian and Viola.

I have his horse to take up the quarrel. I have persuaded him
the youth's a divel.

Fabian. He is as horribly conceited of him, and pants   270
and looks pale as if a bear were at his heels.

Toby. There's no remedy, sir. He will fight with you for's
oath sake. Marry, he hath better bethought him of his quarrel,
and he finds that now scarce to be worth talking of. Therefore
draw for the supportance of his vow. He protests he will   275
not hurt you.

Viola. *[Aside.]* Pray God defend me! A little thing would
make me tell them how much I lack of a man.

Fabian. Give ground if you see him furious.

Toby. Come, Sir Andrew, there's no remedy. The gentleman
will for his honor's sake have one bout with you. He cannot

---

185 **unchary on't:** *carelessly on it* (the heart of stone)   189 **havior:** *behavior*   190 **Goes . . . griefs:** *my master's grieving love for you goes on; cf. n.*   191 **jewel:** *any ornament or trinket; here perhaps 'locket'*   195 **honor, sav'd:** *honor preserved*   204 **betake thee to't:** F *betake the too't*   206 **despite:** *scorn, defiance*   207 **Dismount thy tuck:** *take out thy rapier*   **yare:** *quick*   215 **withal:** *with*   217 **with unhatch'd rapier . . . carpet consideration;** *cf. n.*   221 **Hob, nob:** *have or have not, give or take*   224 **conduct:** *protective escort*   226 **Belike:** *probably, possibly*   **quirk:** *peculiarity*   228 **competent injury:** *sufficiently serious injury;* F *computent*   229, 230 **unless you undertake . . . answer him;** *cf. n.*   231 **meddle:** *engage* (in the fight)   232 **forswear to wear iron:** *repudiate on oath* (your right) *to wear a sword*

234 **to know of the knight:** *to find out from the knight*   241 **mortal arbitrement:** *deadly settlement*   244 **proof:** *testing*   250 **sir priest:** *i.e. 'dominus,' a common title of address for the clergy*   251 **mettle:** *quality of temperament*   253 **firago:** *virago; cf. n.*   **pass:** *bout*   254 **the stuck-in:** *the thrust or lunge*   255 **the answer:** *the return hit*   256 **hits;** *cf. n.*   257 **the Sophy:** *the shah of Persia*   258 **Pox on't:** *the plague on it; cf. n.*   261 **and:** *if*   264 **Capilet;** *cf. n.*   266 **the perdition of souls:** *i.e. killing*   268 **to take up:** *to settle*   270 **He is as horribly conceited of him:** *he is imagining all sorts of dreadful things about him*   272 **for's:** *for his*   275 **supportance:** *keeping*

by the duello avoid it; but he has promised me as he is a gentleman and a soldier, he will not hurt you. Come on, to't.

Andrew. Pray God he keep his oath!   *[Draws.]*

Enter Antonio.

Viola. I do assure you 'tis against my will.   *[Draws.]*
Antonio. Put up your sword. If this young gentleman
Have done offense, I take the fault on me;
If you offend him, I for him defy you.
Toby. You, sir? Why, what are you?
Antonio. [*Draws.*] One, sir, that for his love dares yet   290
do more
Than you have heard him brag to you he will.
Toby. Nay, if you be an undertaker, I am for you.   *[Draws.]*

Enter Officers.

Fabian. O good Sir Toby, hold. Here come the officers.
Toby. [*To Antonio.*] I'll be with you anon.   295
Viola. [*To Sir Andrew.*] Pray, sir, put your sword up,
if you please.
Andrew. Marry, will I, sir; and for that I promis'd you,
I'll be as good as my word. He will bear you easily and
reins well.   300
1 Officer. This is the man; do thy office.
2 Officer. Antonio, I arrest thee at the suit
Of Count Orsino.
Antonio.   You do mistake me, sir.
1 Officer. No, sir, no jot. I know your favor well,   305
Though now you have no sea cap on your head.
Take him away. He knows I know him well.
Antonio. I must obey. [*To Viola.*] This comes with
seeking you.
But there's no remedy; I shall answer it.   310
What will you do, now my necessity
Makes me to ask you for my purse? It grieves me
Much more for what I cannot do for you
Than what befalls myself. You stand amaz'd,
But be of comfort.   315
2 Officer. Come, sir, away.
Antonio. I must entreat of you some of that money.
Viola. What money, sir?
For the fair kindness you have show'd me here,
And part being prompted by your present trouble,   320
Out of my lean and low ability
I'll lend you something. My having is not much;
I'll make division of my present with you.
Hold, there's half my coffer.
Antonio.   Will you deny me now?   325
Is't possible that my deserts to you
Can lack persuasion? Do not tempt my misery,
Lest that it make me so unsound a man
As to upbraid you with those kindnesses
That I have done for you.   330
Viola.   I know of none,
Nor know I you by voice or any feature.

I hate ingratitude more in a man
Than lying, vainness, babbling drunkenness,
Or any taint of vice whose strong corruption   335
Inhabits our frail blood.
Antonio.   O heavens themselves!
2 Officer. Come, sir, I pray you go.
Antonio. Let me speak a little. This youth that you see here
I snatch'd one half out of the jaws of death;   340
Reliev'd him with such sanctity of love;
And to his image which methought did promise
Most venerable worth, did I devotion.
1 Officer. What's that to us? The time goes by. Away.
Antonio. But O, how vild an idol proves this god!   345
Thou hast, Sebastian, done good feature shame.
In nature there's no blemish but the mind.
None can be called deform'd but the unkind.
Virtue is beauty; but the beauteous evil
Are empty trunks, o'erflourish'd by the devil.   350
1 Officer. The man grows mad; away with him. Come,
come, sir.
Antonio. Lead me on.   *Exit [with Officers.]*
Viola. Methinks his words do from such passion fly
That he believes himself; so do not I.   355
Prove true, imagination, O, prove true,
That I, dear brother, be now tane for you!
Toby. Come hither, knight; come hiter, Fabian.
We'll whisper o'er a couplet or two of most sage saws.
Viola. He nam'd Sebastian. I my brother know   360
Yet living in my glass. Even such and so
In favor was my brother, and he went
Still in this fashion, color, ornament,
For him I imitate. O, if it prove,
Tempests are kind, and salt waves fresh in love!   *[Exit.]*
Toby. A very dishonest paltry boy, and more a coward than
a hare. His dishonesty appears in leaving his friend here in
necessity and denying him; and for his cowardship, ask Fabian.
Fabian. A coward, a most devout coward; religious in it.
Andrew. 'Slid, I'll after him again and beat him.   370
Toby. Do; cuff him soundly, but never draw thy sword.
Andrew. And I do not.
Fabian. Come, let's see the event.
Toby. I dare lay any money 'twill be nothing yet.   *Exeunt.*
                                                   [Finis, Actus tertius.]

ACT FOURTH ❧ SCENE FIRST

Enter Sebastian and Clown.

Clown. Will you make me believe that I am not sent for
you?

---

282 **the duello:** *the rules of polite dueling; cf. n.*   293 **an undertaker:** *one who takes up a
challenge*   295 **anon:** *presently*   298 **and for that:** *and for the horse*   299 **reins:** *F
raines*   305 **favor:** *face*   314 **amaz'd:** *'dazed,' stronger than in modern usage*   320
part: *in part*   322 **My having:** *what I have*   323 **my present:** *what I have now*   324
my coffer: *my money*   326 **my deserts to you:** *what you owe me*   327 **persuasion:** *the
power to persuade*

334 **vainness:** *'uselessness' or 'personal conceit'*   342 **image:** *appearance; cf. n.*   343 **venerable:** *worthy of veneration*   345 **vild:** *vile; cf. n.*   348 **unkind:** *'cruel' and 'unnatural'*   349 **beauteous evil:** *evil beautiful in appearance*   350 **empty trunks,
o'erflourish'd:** *empty bodies covered with blossoms or vendure; cf. n.*   354 **fly:** *come violently*   355 **so do not I:** *'I do not believe him,' and 'I do not believe myself' (in the hope
that my brother is alive)*   357 **tane:** *taken*   359 **sage saws:** *wise sayings*   361 **Yet
living in my glass:** *i.e. whenever I look in the mirror*   362 **favor:** *face*   363 **still:**
always   364 **For:** *because*   366 **dishonest:** *dishonorable*   367
hare; *cf. n.*   370 **'Slid:** *'God's lid' (eyelid); a mild oath*   372 **And:** *if*   373 **the event:**
the result, the outcome   374 **yet:** *nevertheless*   **Exeunt:** *F. Exit.*

Sebastian. Go to, go to, thou art a foolish fellow. Let me be clear of thee.

    Clown. Well held out, i' faith. No, I do not know you;   5
nor I am not sent to you by my lady to bid you come speak with her; nor your name is not Master Cesario; nor this is not my nose neither. Nothing that is so is so.

    Sebastian. I prethee vent thy folly somewhere else. Thou know'st not me.   10

    Clown. Vent my folly! He has heard that word of some great man and now applies it to a fool. Vent my folly! I am afraid this great lubber the world will prove a cockney. I prethee now ungird thy strangeness, and tell me what I shall vent to my lady? Shall I vent to her that thou art coming?   15

    Sebastian. I prethee, foolish Greek, depart from me. There's money for thee. If you tarry longer, I shall give worse payment.

    Clown. By my troth, thou hast an open hand. These wise men that give fools money get themselves a good report,   20
after fourteen years' purchase.

Enter [Sir] Andrew, [Sir] Toby, and Fabian.

    Andrew. Now, sir, have I met you again. There's for you.
                                   [Strikes Sebastian.]

    Sebastian. Why, there's for thee, and there, and there. Are all the people mad?   *[Beats Sir Andrew.]*   25

    Toby. Hold, sir, or I'll throw your dagger o'er the house.
                                  [Holds Sebastian.]

    Clown. This will I tell my lady straight. I would not be in some of your coats for twopence.   *[Exit.]*

    Toby. Come on, sir; hold.   30

    Andrew. Nay, let him alone. I'll go another way to work with him. I'll have an action of battery against him if there be any law in Illyria. Though I stroke him first, yet it's no matter for that.

    Sebastian. Let go thy hand.   35

    Toby. Come, sir, I will not let you go. Come, my young soldier, put up your iron. You are well flesh'd. Come on.

    Sebastian. I will be free from thee.   *[Frees himself.]*
What wouldst thou now?
If thou dar'st tempt me further, draw thy sword.   *[Draws.]*   40

    Toby. What, what? Nay then, I must have an ounce or two of this malapert blood from you.   *[Draws.]*

Enter Olivia.

    Olivia. Hold, Toby. On thy life I charge thee, hold.

    Toby. Madam.

    Olivia. Will it be ever thus? Ungracious wretch,   45
Fit for the mountains and the barbarous caves,
Where manners ne'er were preach'd. Out of my sight.
Be not offended, dear Cesario.
Rudesby, be gone.   *[Exeunt Sir Toby, Sir Andrew, and Fabian.]*
I prethee, gentle friend,   50
Let thy fair wisdom, not thy passion, sway
In this uncivil and unjust extent

Against thy peace. Go with me to my house,
And hear thou there how many fruitless pranks
This ruffian hath botch'd up, that thou thereby   55
Mayst smile at this. Thou shalt not choose but go.
Do not deny. Beshrew his soul for me.
He started one poor heart of mine, in thee.

    Sebastian. What relish is in this? How runs the stream?
Or am I mad, or else this is a dream   60
Let fancy still my sense in Lethe steep;
If it be thus to dream, still let me sleep.

    Olivia. Nay, come, I prethee. Would thou'dst be rul'd by me?

    Sebastian. Madam, I will.

    Olivia.   O, say so, and so be.   *Exeunt.*

❧ SCENE SECOND ❧

Enter Maria and Clown.

    Maria. Nay, I prethee put on this gown and this beard. Make him believe thou art Sir Topas the curate. Do it quickly. I'll call Sir Toby the whilst.   *[Exit.]*

    Clown. Well, I'll put it on, and I will dissemble myself in't, and I would I were the first that ever dissembled in such a   5
gown. I am not tall enough to become the function well, nor lean enough to be thought a good student; but to be said an honest man and a good housekeeper goes as fairly as to say a careful man and a great scholar. The competitors enter.

Enter [Sir] Toby [and Maria].

    Toby. Jove bless thee, Master Parson.   10

    Clown. Bonos dies, Sir Toby; for as the old hermit of Prague that never saw pen and ink very wittily said to a niece of King Gorboduc, 'That that is is'; so I being Master Parson, am Master Parson. For what is 'that' but that? And 'is' but is?

    Toby. To him, Sir Topas.   15

    Clown. What ho, I say. Peace in this prison.

    Toby. The knave counterfeits well; a good knave.

Malvolio within.

    Malvolio. Who calls there?

    Clown. Sir Topas the curate, who comes to visit Malvolio the lunatic.   20

    Malvolio. Sir Topas, Sir Topas, good Sir Topas, go to my lady.

    Clown. Out, hyperbolical fiend! How vexest thou this man? Talkest thou nothing but of ladies?

    Toby. Well said, Master Parson.   25

    Malvolio. Sir Topas, never was man thus wronged; good Sir Topas, do not think I am mad. They have laid me here in hideous darkness.

---

57 Beshrew: *curse*   **58 started:** *startled* **heart:** *'heart' or 'hart'; cf. n.*   **59 relish:** *taste*   **60 Or . . . or either . . . or**   **61 Lethe:** *the river of forgetfulness in the underworld* (Greek mythology)   **62 still:** *always*   **2 Sir:** *common title of address for the clergy* **Topas;** *cf. n.*   **3 the whilst:** *meanwhile*   **4 dissemble:** *disguise*   **6 the function:** *the function of a cleric*   **7 student:** *student*   **8 a good housekeeper:** *one who lives well*   **9 the competitors:** *the associates*   **11 Bonos dies:** *good day* (a pretense at ecclesiastical Latin)   **11 the old hermit of Prague:** *probably the clown's invention*   **12, 13 King Gorboduc;** *cf. n.*   **17 knave:** *boy, fellow* **SD Malvolio within;** *cf. n.*   **23 hyperbolical:** *enormous*

---

3 Go to: *go on*   **5 held out:** *kept up, continued*   **9 I prethee:** *I pray thee*   **13 lubber:** *lout* **a cockney:** *an affected, foppish person; cf. n.*   **14 ungird thy strangeness:** *let loose thy strange manner*   **16 Greek:** *'merry companion' or 'unintelligible speaker'*   **21 after fourteen years' purchase:** *at a high price; cf. n.*   **32 action of battery:** *a suit at law for beating* (me)   **33 stroke:** *struck*   **37 You are well flesh'd:** *you have had a good taste; cf. n.*   **42 malapert:** *impudent*   **49 Rudesby:** *unmannerly fellow*   **51 fair:** *just* **sway:** *rule*   **52 uncivil:** *uncivilized* **extent:** *probably 'display,' possibly 'assault'*

Clown. Fie, thou dishonest Satan. I call thee by the most
modest terms, for I am one of those gentle ones that will   30
use the divel himself with courtesy. Say'st thou that house
is dark?

Malvolio. As hell, Sir Topas.

Clown. Why, it hath bay windows transparent as barricadoes, and the clear stores toward the south north are as lus-   35
trous as ebony. And yet complainest thou of obstruction?

Malvolio. I am not mad, Sir Topas; I say to you this house
is dark.

Clown. Madman, thou errest. I say there is no darkness
but ignorance, in which thou art more puzzl'd than the   40
Egyptians in their fog.

Malvolio. I say this house is as dark as ignorance, though
ignorance were as dark as hell; and I say there was never
man thus abus'd. I am no more mad than you are; make the
trial of it in any constant question.   45

Clown. What is the opinion of Pythagoras concerning
wild fowl?

Malvolio. That the soul of our grandam might happily
inhabit a bird.

Clown. What think'st thou of his opinion?   50

Malvolio. I think nobly of the soul and no way approve
his opinion.

Clown. Fare thee well. Remain thou still in darkness. Thou
shalt hold th' opinion of Pythagoras ere I will allow of thy
wits, and fear to kill a woodcock, lest thou dispossess the   55
soul of thy grandam. Fare thee well.

Malvolio. Sir Topas, Sir Topas.

Toby. My most exquisite Sir Topas.

Clown. Nay, I am for all waters.

Maria. Thou mightst have done this without thy beard   60
and gown. He sees thee not.

Toby. To him in thine own voice, and bring me word
how thou find'st him. *[To Maria.]* I would we were well rid of
this knavery. If he may be conveniently deliver'd, I would he
were; for I am now so far in offense with my niece that I cannot pursue with any safety this sport to the upshot. *[To the
Clown.]* Come by and by to my chamber. *Exit [with Maria.]*

Clown. [Sings.]

Hey Robin, jolly Robin
Tell me how thy lady does.

Malvolio. Fool.   70

Clown. 'My lady is unkind, perdie.'

Malvolio. Fool.

Clown. 'Alas, why is she so?'

Malvolio. Fool, I say.

Clown. 'She loves another.' Who calls, ha?   75

Malvolio. Good fool, as ever thou wilt deserve well at
my hand, help me to a candle, and pen, ink, and paper. As I
am a gentleman, I will live to be thankful to thee for't.

Clown. Master Malvolio?

Malvolio. Ay, good fool.   80

Clown. Alas, sir, how fell you besides your five wits?

Malvolio. Fool, there was never man so notoriously abus'd.
I am as well in my wits, fool, as thou art.

Clown. But as well: then you are mad indeed, if you be
no better in your wits than a fool.   85

Malvolio. They have here propertied me; keep me in
darkness, send ministers to me, asses, and do all they can to
face me out of my wits.

Clown. Advise you what you say. The minister is here.
Malvolio, Malvolio, thy wits the heavens restore. Endeavor   90
thyself to sleep, and leave thy vain bibble babble.

Malvolio. Sir Topas.

Clown. Maintain no words with him, good fellow. Who, I,
sir? Not I, sir. God buy you, good Sir Topas. Marry, amen. I
will, sir, I will.   95

Malvolio. Fool, fool, fool, I say.

Clown. Alas, sir, be patient. What say you, sir? I am shent
for speaking to you.

Malvolio. Good fool, help me to some light and some paper.
I tell thee I am as well in my wits as any man in Illyria.   100

Clown. Well-a-day, that you were, sir.

Malvolio. By this hand, I am. Good fool, some ink, paper,
and light; and convey what I will set down to my lady. It shall
advantage thee more than ever the bearing of letter did.

Clown. I will help you to't. But tell me true, are you   105
not mad indeed? Or do you but counterfeit?

Malvolio. Believe me, I am not; I tell thee true.

Clown. Nay, I'll ne'er believe a madman till I see his brains.
I will fetch you light and paper and ink.

Malvolio. Fool, I'll requite it in the highest degree. I   110
prethee be gone.

Clown. [Sings.]

I am gone, sir,
And anon, sir,
I'll be with you again,
    In a trice,   115
    Like to the old Vice,
Your need to sustain.
Who with dagger of lath,
In his rage and his wrath,
    Cries 'Ah, ha,' to the divel.   120
Like a mad lad,
'Pare thy nails, dad.'
Adieu, goodman divel.   *Exit.*

❧ SCENE THIRD ❧

Enter Sebastian.

Sebastian. This is the air; that is the glorious sun;
This pearl she gave me, I do feel't and see't;
And though 'tis wonder that enwraps me thus,
Yet 'tis not madness. Where's Antonio then?

29 **dishonest:** *dishonorable*   30 **modest:** *moderate*   31 **house:** *'house' and 'darkened room'*   34, 35 **barricadoes:** *barricades*   **clear stores:** *clerestories, the upper part of a church or building with a series of windows*   40, 41 **the Egyptians in their fog;** *cf. n.*   45 **constant:** *consistent*   46 **Pythagoras;** *cf. n.*   48 **happily:** *haply, by chance*   59 **for all waters:** *good for any trade, occupation*   64 **deliver'd:** *let out*   66 **this sport to the upshot:** *this sport to the outcome; cf. n.*   **to:** *F omits*   67 **by and by:** *immediately*   68 **Hey Robin;** *cf. n.*   71 **perdie:** *certainly (French par dieu)*

81 **how fell you besides:** *how fell you out of*   **five wits;** *cf. n.*   86 **propertied me:** *made me a property, a mere thing*   87 **face me out of my wits:** *impudently claim that I am mad*   89 **Advise you:** *be careful of*   94 **God buy you:** *good-by; cf. n.*   **Marry;** *cf. n.*   97 **shent:** *reproved*   101 **Well-a-day:** *woe, alas*   104 **advantage:** *be of advantage to*   113 **anon:** *straightway, at once*   112–114 **I am gone, sir . . . again;** *cf. n.*   116–122 **Like to the old Vice . . . 'Pare thy nails, dad';** *cf. n.*   123 **Adieu, goodman divel;** *cf. n.*

I could not find him at the Elephant;   5
Yet there he was, and there I found this credit
That he did range the town to seek me out.
His counsel now might do me golden service;
For though my soul disputes well with my sense
That this may be some error, but no madness,   10
Yet doth this accident and flood of fortune
So far exceed all instance, all discourse,
That I am ready to distrust mine eyes
And wrangle with my reason that persuades me
To any other trust but that I am mad,   15
Or else the lady's mad. Yet if 'twere so,
She could not sway her house, command her followers,
Take and give back affairs and their dispatch
With such a smooth, discreet, and stable bearing
As I perceive she does. There's something in't   20
That is deceivable. But here the lady comes.

Enter Olivia and Priest.

Olivia. Blame not this haste of mine. If you mean well,
Now go with me and with this holy man
Into the chantry by. There before him
And underneath that consecrated roof,   25
Plight me the full assurance of your faith,
That my most jealous and too doubtful soul
May live at peace. He shall conceal it
Whiles you are willing it shall come to note,
What time we will our celebration keep   30
According to my birth. What do you say?
Sebastian. I'll follow this good man and go with you
And having sworn truth, ever will be true.
Olivia. Then lead the way, good father; and heavens so shine
That they may fairly note this act of mine.   *Exeunt.*

Finis, Actus quartus.

ACT FIFTH ❧ SCENE FIRST

Enter Clown and Fabian.

Fabian. Now as thou lov'st me, let me see his letter.
Clown. Good Master Fabian, grant me another request.
Fabian. Anything.
Clown. Do not desire to see this letter.
Fabian. This is to give a dog and in recompense desire   5
my dog again.

Enter Duke, Viola, Curio, and Lords.

Duke. Belong you to the Lady Olivia, friends?
Clown. Ay, sir, we are some of her trappings.
Duke. I know thee well. How doest thou, my good fellow?
Clown. Truly, sir, the better for my foes and the worse   10
for my friends.
Duke. Just the contrary: the better for thy friends.

Clown. No, sir, the worse.
Duke. How can that be?
Clown. Marry, sir, they praise me and make an ass of   15
me; now my foes tell me plainly I am an ass. So that by my
foes, sir, I profit in the knowledge of myself, and by my
friends I am abused. So that conclusions to be as kisses, if
your four negatives make your two affirmatives, why then,
the worse for my friends and the better for my foes.   20
Duke. Why, this is excellent.
Clown. By my troth, sir, no; though it please you to be
one of my friends.
Duke. Thou shalt not be the worse for me. There's gold.
Clown. But that it would be double dealing, sir, I would 25
you could make it another.
Duke. O, you give me ill counsel.
Clown. Put your grace in your pocket, sir, for this once,
and let your flesh and blood obey it.
Duke. Well, I will be so much a sinner to be a double   30
dealer. There's another.
Clown. *Primo, secundo, tertio* is a good play, and the old
saying is 'The third pays for all.' The triplex, sir, is a good
tripping measure; or the bells of St. Bennet, sir, may put
you in mind, one, two, three.   35
Duke. You can fool no more money out of me at this
throw. If you will let your lady know I am here to speak
with her, and bring her along with you, it may awake my
bounty further.
Clown. Marry, sir, lullaby to your bounty till I come agen.
I go, sir; but I would not have you to think that my desire
of having is the sin of covetousness. But as you say, sir, let
your bounty take a nap; I will awake it anon.   *Exit.*

Enter Antonio and Officers.

Viola. Here comes the man, sir, that did rescue me.
Duke. That face of his I do remember well.
Yet when I saw it last, it was besmear'd   45
As black as Vulcan in the smoke of war.
A baubling vessel was he captain of,
For shallow draught and bulk unprizable,
With which such scathful grapple did he make
With the most noble bottom of our fleet   50
That very envy and the tongue of loss
Cried fame and honor on him. What's the matter?
1 Officer. Orsino, this is that Antonio
That took the Phoenix and her fraught from Candy;
And this is he that did the Tiger board   55
When your young nephew Titus lost his leg.
Here in the streets, desperate of shame and state,
In private brabble did we apprehend him.
Viola. He did me kindness, sir, drew on my side;
But in conclusion put strange speech upon me.   60

---

6 **this credit:** *this report believed*   9 **my soul disputes well with my sense:** *my mind
agrees well with my senses*   12 **instance:** *example*   **discourse:** *logic, reason*   14 **wrangle:**
dispute   17 **sway:** *rule*   18 **dispatch:** *management*   21 **deceivable:** *deceptive*   24
the chantry by: *the chapel near by; cf. n.*   26 **Plight me . . . your faith;** *cf. n.*   27
jealous: *jealous*   29 **Whiles:** *until*   **note:** *notice*   30 **What time:** *at which time*   31
my birth: *my station*   5 **This is to give a dog;** *cf. n.*   8 **trappings:** *train, attendants*   9 **doest;** *cf. n.*

18 **abused:** *'deceived' and 'wronged'*   18–20 **So that conclusions . . . for my foes;**
cf. n.   25 **But that:** *but for the fact that*   **double dealing:** *both 'double giving' and 'deceit'*   28 **grace:** *both 'Duke' and 'generosity'*   32 **Primo, secundo, tertio;** *cf. n.*   33
'The third pays for all'; *cf. n.*   **triplex:** *triple time in music*   34 **St. Bennet:** *St. Benedict;
cf. n.*   37 **throw:** *throw of the dice*   46 **Vulcan:** *Roman god of fire and patron of metal
workers*   47 **a baubling vessel:** *a trifling vessel, an unimportant ship*   48 **unprizable:**
incapable of being valued, worthless   49 **scathful:** *harmful*   50 **bottom:** *ship*   51 **very:**
even   **loss:** *those losing the battle*   54 **fraught:** *cargo*   **Candy:** *'Candia' and 'Crete'*   57
desperate of shame and state: *reckless of shame and of his condition*   58 **brabble:**
brawl   59 **drew:** *drew his sword*   60 **put strange speech upon me:** *spoke to me strangely*

I know not what 'twas but distraction.
 Duke. Notable pirate, thou salt-water thief,
What foolish boldness brought thee to their mercies
Whom thou in terms so bloody and so dear   65
Hast made thine enemies?
 Antonio.   Orsino, noble sir,
Be pleas'd that I shake off these names you give me.
Antony never yet was thief or pirate,
Though I confess, on base and ground enough,   70
Orsino's enemy. A witchcraft drew me hither.
That most ingrateful boy there by your side
From the rude sea's enrag'd and foamy mouth
Did I redeem. A wrack past hope he was.
His life I gave him and did thereto add   75
My love without retention or restraint,
All his in dedication. For his sake
Did I expose myself (pure for his love)
Into the danger of this adverse town;
Drew to defend him when he was beset;   80
Where being apprehended, his false cunning
(Not meaning to partake with me in danger)
Taught him to face me out of his acquaintance,
And grew a twenty years removed thing
While one would wink; denied me mine own purse,   85
Which I had recommended to his use
Not half an hour before.
 Viola.   How can this be?
 Duke. When came he to this town?
 Antonio. Today, my lord; and for three months before,   90
No intrim, not a minute's vacancy,
Both day and night did we keep company.

Enter Olivia and Attendants.

 Duke. Here comes the countess; now heaven walks on earth.
But for thee, fellow: fellow, thy words are madness.
Three months this youth hath tended upon me,   95
But more of that anon. Take him aside.
 Olivia. What would my lord, but that he may not have,
Wherein Olivia may seem serviceable?
Cesario, you do not keep promise with me.
 Viola. Madam.   100
 Duke. Gracious Olivia.
 Olivia. What do you say, Cesario? Good my lord.
 Viola. My lord would speak; my duty hushes me.
 Olivia. If it be ought to the old tune, my lord,
It is as fat and fulsome to mine ear   105
As howling after music.
 Duke.   Still so cruel?
 Olivia. Still so constant, lord.
 Duke. What, to perverseness? You uncivil lady,
To whose ingrate and unauspicious altars   110
My soul the faithfull'st off'rings have breath'd out
That e'er devotion tender'd. What shall I do?
 Olivia. Even what it please my lord, that shall become him.

 Duke. Why should I not (had I the heart to do it),
Like to th' Egyptian thief at point of death,   115
Kill what I love? (A savage jealousy
That sometimes savors nobly.) But hear me this:
Since you to nonregardance cast my faith,
And that I partly know the instrument
That screws me from my true place in your favor,   120
Live you the marble-breasted tyrant still.
But this your minion, whom I know you love,
And whom, by heaven I swear, I tender dearly,
Him will I tear out of that cruel eye
Where he sits crowned in his master's spite.   125
Come, boy, with me. My thoughts are ripe in mischief.
I'll sacrifice the lamb that I do love,
To spite a ravin's heart within a dove.   *[Going.]*
 Viola. And I most jocund, apt, and willingly,
To do you rest a thousand deaths would die.   *[Following.]*
 Olivia. Where goes Cesario?
 Viola.   After him I love
More than I love these eyes, more than my life,
More by all mores than ere I shall love wife.
If I do feign, you witnesses above   135
Punish my life for tainting of my love.
 Olivia. Ay me detested! How am I beguil'd!
 Viola. Who does beguile you? Who does do you wrong?
 Olivia. Hast thou forgot thyself? Is it so long?
Call forth the holy father.   *[Exit an Attendant.]*
 Duke.   *[To Viola.]* Come, away.
 Olivia. Whither, my lord? Cesario, husband, stay.
 Duke. Husband?
 Olivia.   Ay, husband. Can he that deny?
 Duke. Her husband, sirrah?   145
 Viola.   No, my lord, not I.
 Olivia. Alas, it is the baseness of thy fear
That makes thee strangle thy propriety.
Fear not, Cesario; take thy fortunes up;
Be that thou know'st thou art, and then thou art   150
As great as that thou fear'st.

Enter Priest.

                    O welcome, father!
Father, I charge thee by thy reverence
Here to unfold—though lately we intended
To keep in darkness what occasion now   155
Reveals before 'tis ripe—what thou dost know
Hath newly pass'd between this youth and me.
 Priest. A contract of eternal bond of love,
Confirm'd by mutual joinder of your hands,
Attested by the holy close of lips,   160
Strength'ned by interchangement of your rings;
And all the ceremony of this compact
Seal'd in my function, by my testimony;
Since when, my watch hath told me, toward my grave
I have travel'd but two hours.   165
 Duke. O thou dissembling cub, what will thou be

---

62 **distraction:** *madness*   63 **thief:** *'robber,' a strong word*   65 **dear:** *costly; cf. n.*   74 **wrack:** *wreck*   78 **pure:** *purely, only*   79 **adverse:** *hostile*   83 **to face me out of his acquaintance:** *shamelessly to pretend not to know me*   84, 85 **And grew . . . would wink;** *cf. n.*   86 **had recommended:** *had given in charge, had urged*   90 **three months;** *cf. n.*   91 **intrim:** *interim*   97 **but that he may not have:** *except what he may not have (my love)*   105 **fat:** *superabundant, unnecessary* **fulsome:** *offensive to the taste*   110 **ingrate:** *ungrateful* **unauspicious:** *unpropitious*   111 **My soul . . . have breath'd;** *cf. n.*   113 **Even** *monosyllabic*

115 **th' Egyptian thief;** *cf. n.*   118 **nonregardance:** *neglect, lack of regard*   122 **minion:** *favorite*   123 **tender:** *hold*   125 **in his master's spite:** *despite his master*   129 **apt:** *properly*   130 **To do you rest:** *to give you peace*   134 **mores:** *customs*   136 **for tainting:** *for corrupting (by feigning)*   142 **husband;** *cf. n.*   145 **sirrah:** *'sir'; the form is familiar or contemptuous*   148 **thy propriety:** *thy identity*   151 **that thou fear'st:** *i.e. the Duke*

When time hath sow'd a grizzle on thy case?
Or will not else thy craft so quickly grow
That thine own trip shall be thine overthrow?
Farewell, and take her; but direct thy feet   170
Where thou and I henceforth may never meet.
    Viola. My lord, I do protest.
    Olivia.   O, do not swear.
Hold little faith, though thou hast too much fear.

Enter Sir Andrew.

    Andrew. For the love of God, a surgeon. Send one   175
presently to Sir Toby.
    Olivia. What's the matter?
    Andrew. H'as broke my head across and has given Sir
Toby a bloody coxcomb too. For the love of God, your help.
I had rather than forty pound I were at home.   180
    Olivia. Who has done this, Sir Andrew?
    Andrew. The Count's gentleman, one Cesario. We took him
for a coward, but he's the very divel incardinate.
    Duke. My gentleman Cesario?
    Andrew. Od's lifelings, here he is. You broke my head for
nothing, and that that I did, I was set on to do't by Sir Toby.
    Viola. Why do you speak to me? I never hurt you.
You drew your sword upon me without cause,
But I bespake you fair and hurt you not.

Enter [Sir] Toby and Clown.

    Andrew. If a bloody coxcomb be a hurt, you have hurt   190
me. I think you set nothing by a bloody coxcomb. Here comes
Sir Toby halting; you shall hear more. But if he had not been
in drink, he would have tickl'd you othergates than he did.
    Duke. How now, gentleman? How is't with you?
    Toby. That's all one. Has hurt me, and there's th' end   195
on't. Sot, didst see Dick Surgeon, sot?
    Clown. O, he's drunk, Sir Toby, an hour agone. His eyes
were set at eight i' th' morning.
    Toby. Then he's a rogue and a passy measures pavin.
I hate a drunken rogue.   200
    Olivia. Away with him! Who hath made this havoc with
them?
    Andrew. I'll help you, Sir Toby, because we'll be
dress'd together.
    Toby. Will you help an ass-head and a coxcomb and a   205
knave, a thin-fac'd knave, a gull?
    Olivia. Get him to bed and let his hurt be look'd to.
            [Exeunt Clown, Fabian, Sir Toby, and Sir Andrew.]

Enter Sebastian.

    Sebastian. I am sorry, madam, I have hurt your
kinsman;
But had it been the brother of my blood,   210
I must have done no less with wit and safety.

You throw a strange regard upon me, and by that
I do perceive it hath offended you.
Pardon me, sweet one, even for the vows
We made each other but so late ago.   215
    Duke. One face, one voice, one habit, and two persons,
A natural perspective, that is and is not.
    Sebastian. Antonio, O my dear Antonio,
How have the hours rack'd and tortur'd me
Since I have lost thee!   220
    Antonio. Sebastian are you?
    Sebastian.   Fear'st thou that, Antonio?
    Antonio. How have you made division of yourself?
An apple cleft in two is not more twin
Than these two creatures. Which is Sebastian?   225
    Olivia. Most wonderful.
    Sebastian. Do I stand there? I never had a brother;
Nor can there be that deity in my nature
Of here and everywhere. I had a sister
Whom the blind waves and surges have devour'd.   230
Of charity, what kin are you to me?
What countryman? What name? What parentage?
    Viola. Of Messaline; Sebastian was my father;
Such a Sebastian was my brother too.
So went he suited to his watery tomb.   235
If spirits can assume both form and suit,
You come to fright us.
    Sebastian.   A spirit I am indeed,
But am in that dimension grossly clad,
Which from the womb I did participate.   240
Were you a woman, as the rest goes even,
I should my tears let fall upon your cheek
And say, 'Thrice welcome, drowned Viola!'
    Viola. My father had a mole upon his brow.
    Sebastian. And so had mine.   245
    Viola. And died that day when Viola from her birth
Had numb'red thirteen years.
    Sebastian. O, that record is lively in my soul!
He finished indeed his mortal act
That day that made my sister thirteen years.   250
    Viola. If nothing lets to make us happy both
But this my masculine usurp'd attire,
Do not embrace me till each circumstance
Of place, time, fortune do cohere and jump
That I am Viola; which to confirm,   255
I'll bring you to a captain in this town,
Where lie my maiden weeds; by whose gentle help
I was preserv'd to serve this noble Count.
All the occurrence of my fortune since
Hath been between this lady and this lord.   260
    Sebastian. [*To Olivia.*] So comes it, lady, you have been
mistook.
But nature to her bias drew in that.
You would have been contracted to a maid,
Nor are you therein, by my life, deceiv'd;   265
You are betroth'd both to a maid and man.

---

167 a grizzle: *gray hair* **case:** *sheath or skin, particularly of a fox* **169 trip:** *trickery;*
cf. n. **174 Hold little faith:** *keep a little faith* **176 presently:** *at once* **178 H'as:** *he*
has **179 coxcomb:** *head* **183 incardinate:** *possibly a quibble on 'incarnate,' 'in the flesh,'*
and 'incardinate,' 'like a cardinal'; cf. n. **185 Od's lifelings:** *'God's little lives'; a mild*
oath **189 bespake you fair:** *spoke to you politely* **192 halting:** *limping* **193 oth-**
ergates: *otherwise* **195 That's all one:** *it makes no difference* **196 sot:** *'fool'; possibly*
'habitual drinker' **197 agone:** *ago* **198 set:** *'fixed' or 'gone down,' i.e. 'closed'* **199**
passy measures pavin: *an eight-bar double-slow dance;* F. *panyn;*
cf. n. **201 havoc;** *cf. n.* **203–4 be dress'd:** *have our wounds dressed* **205 a cox-**
comb: *a simpleton* **206 a gull:** *a dupe* **211 with wit and safety:** *with intelligent regard*
for my safety

212 a strange regard: *an estranged look* **216 habit:** *dress* **217 A natural perspective,**
that is and is not; *cf. n.* **229 Of here and everywhere:** *of omnipresence* **231 Of**
charity: *in kindness* **235 suited:** *dressed* **236 suit:** *dress* **239 dimension:** *form* -
grossly: *materially, in the flesh* **240 participate:** *partake, inherit* **241 as the rest goes**
even; *cf. n.* **248 record:** *memory* (stressed — ´) **251 lets:** *hinders; cf. n.* **254**
jump: *agree completely* **257 weeds:** *clothes* **263 But nature to her bias drew in that;**
cf. n. **266 a maid:** *i.e. a chaste man*

Duke. Be not amaz'd; right noble is his blood.
If this be so, as yet the glass seems true,
I shall have share in this most happy wrack.
[To Viola.] Boy, thou hast said to me a thousand times   *270*
Thou never should'st love woman like to me.
    Viola. And all those sayings will I over swear
And all those swearings keep as true in soul
As doth that orbed continent the fire
That severs day from night.   *275*
    Duke.   Give me thy hand
And let me see thee in thy woman's weeds.
    Viola. The captain that did bring me first on shore
Hath my maid's garments. He upon some action
Is now in durance at Malvolio's suit,   *280*
A gentleman and follower of my lady's.
    Olivia. He shall enlarge him. Fetch Malvolio hither.
And yet alas, now I remember me,
They say, poor gentleman, he's much distract.

         Enter Clown, with a letter, and Fabian.

A most extracting frenzy of mine own   *285*
From my remembrance clearly banish'd his.
How does he, sirrah?
    Clown. Truly, madam, he holds Belzebub at the stave's end
as well as a man in his case may do. Has here writ a letter
to you. I should have given't you today morning. But as a   *290*
madman's epistles are no gospels, so it skills not much when
they are deliver'd.
    Olivia. Open't and read it.
    Clown. Look then to be well edified, when the fool
delivers the madman. *[Reads.]* 'By the Lord, madam.'   *295*
    Olivia. How now, art thou mad?
    Clown. No, madam, I do but read madness. And your lady-
ship will have it as it ought to be, you must allow *vox.*
    Olivia. Prethee read i' thy right wits.
    Clown. So I do, madonna; but to read his right wits is   *300*
to read thus. Therefore, perpend, my princess, and give ear.
    Olivia. *[To Fabian.]* Read it you, sirrah.
    Fabian. *(Reads.)* 'By the Lord, madam, you wrong me, and
the world shall know it. Though you have put me into
darkness and given your drunken cousin rule over me, yet   *305*
have I the benefit of my senses as well as your ladyship. I have
your own letter that induced me to the semblance I put on;
with the which I doubt not but to do myself much right, or
you much shame. Think of me as you please. I leave my duty
a little unthought of, and speak out of my injury.   *310*
                 'The Madly Us'd Malvolio.'
    Olivia. Did he write this?
    Clown. Ay, madam.
    Duke. This savors not much of distraction.
    Olivia. See him deliver'd, Fabrian; bring him hither.   *315*
                       [Exit Fabian.]
My lord, so please you, these things further thought on,

To think me as well a sister as a wife,
One day shall crown th' alliance on't, so please you,
Here at my house and at my proper cost.
    Duke. Madam, I am most apt t'embrace your offer.   *320*
[To Viola.] Your master quits you; and for your service
done him,
So much against the mettle of your sex,
So far beneath your soft and tender breeding,
And since you call'd me master for so long,   *325*
Here is my hand; you shall from this time be
Your master's mistress.
    Olivia.   A sister; you are she.

         Enter [Fabian with] Malvolio.

    Duke. Is this the madman?
    Olivia.   Ay, my lord, this same.   *330*
How now, Malvolio?
    Malvolio.   Madam, you have done me wrong,
Notorious wrong.
    Olivia.   Have I, Malvolio? No.
    Malvolio. Lady, you have. Pray you peruse that letter.   *335*
You must not now deny it is your hand.
Write from it if you can, in hand or phrase,
Or say 'tis not your seal, not your invention.
You can say none of this. Well, grant it then;
And tell me in the modesty of honor,   *340*
Why you have given me such clear lights of favor,
Bade me come smiling and cross-garter'd to you,
To put on yellow stockings and to frown
Upon Sir Toby and the lighter people;
And, acting this in an obedient hope,   *345*
Why have you suffer'd me to be imprison'd,
Kept in a dark house, visited by the priest,
And made the most notorious geck and gull
That e'er invention play'd on? Tell me why?
    Olivia. Alas, Malvolio, this is not my writing,   *350*
Though I confess much like the character;
But out of question, 'tis Maria's hand.
And now I do bethink me, it was she
First told me thou wast mad; then cam'st in smiling,
And in such form which here were presuppos'd   *355*
Upon thee in the letter. Prethee be content.
This practice hath most shrewdly pass'd upon thee;
But when we know the grounds and authors of it,
Thou shalt be both the plaintiff and the judge
Of thine own cause.   *360*
    Fabian.   Good madam, hear me speak,
And let no quarrel nor no brawl to come,
Taint the condition of this present hour,
Which I have wond'red at. In hope it shall not,
Most freely I confess myself and Toby   *365*
Set this device against Malvolio here,
Upon some stubborn and uncourteous parts
We had conceiv'd against him. Maria writ

---

267 **amaz'd:** *dazed*   268 **the glass:** *the perspective glass of 1.217 above*   269 **wrack:**
wreck (the shipwreck)   272 **over swear:** *swear over again*   274 **orbed:** *continent;
cf. n.*   279 **some action:** *some legal charge*   280 **in durance:** *imprisoned*   282 **enlarge
him:** *free him*   284 **distract:** *distracted, insane*   285 **extracting:** *distracting*   286 **his:**
my remembrance of him (Malvolio)   287 **sirrah:** *'sir,' used to an inferior*   288 **he hold
Belzebub at the stave's end:** *he hold the devil off; cf. n.*   291 **it skills not much:** *not
much it makes not much difference*   297 **And:** *if*   298 **vox:** *'voice', i.e. a loud voice or
the voice of a madman.*   300 **madonna:** *my lady*   301 **perpend:** *ponder, consider*   309, 310 **I leave . . . my injury;** *cf. n.*

317 **a sister:** *i.e. a sister-in-law*   319 **proper cost:** *own expense*   320 **apt:** *prone to,
ready*   321 **quits you:** *releases you*   323 **mettle:** *quality of temperament*   337 **from it:**
differently from it   340 **in the modesty of honor:** *with regard for the propriety of (your)
honor*   344 **lighter:** *lesser*   345 **acting:** *refers to Malvolio*   348 **geck:** *fool, dupe* **gull:**
dupe   355, 356 **presuppos'd Upon thee:** *put upon you beforehand*   357 **shrewdly pass'd
upon thee:** *maliciously been put upon you*   362 **nor no:** *'nor,' an emphatic negative*   367
Upon: *on account of* **stubborn:** *haughty* **parts:** *personal attributes, characteristics*

The letter at Sir Toby's great importance,
In recompense whereof he hath married her.   370
How with a sportful malice it was follow'd
May rather pluck on laughter than revenge,
If that the injuries be justly weigh'd
That have on both sides pass'd.
    Olivia. Alas poor fool, how have they baffl'd thee!   375
    Clown. Why, 'some are born great, some achieve greatness,
and some have greatness thrown upon them.' I was one, sir, in
this interlude, one Sir Topas, sir; but that's all one. 'By the
Lord, fool, I am not mad.' But do you remember, 'Madam,
why laugh you at such a barren rascal? And you smile not,   380
he's gagg'd'? And thus the whirligig of time brings in his
revenges.
    Malvolio. I'll be reveng'd on the whole pack of you!
                                                 [Exit.]
    Olivia. He hath been most notoriously abus'd.
    Duke. Pursue him and entreat him to a peace.   385
He hath not told us of the captain yet.
When that is known and golden time convents,
A solemn combination shall be made
Of our dear souls. Meantime, sweet sister,
We will not part from hence. Cesario, come   390
(For so you shall be while you are a man);
But when in other habits you are seen,
Orsino's mistress and his fancy's queen.
                        Exeunt [all but the Clown].

                  Clown sings.

When that I was and a little tiny boy,
   With hey, ho, the wind and the rain,   395
A foolish thing was but a toy,
   For the rain it raineth every day.

But when I came to man's estate,
   With hey, ho, the wind and the rain,
'Gainst knaves and thieves men shut their gate,   400
   For the rain it raineth every day.

But when I came, alas, to wive,
   With hey, ho, the wind and the rain,
By swaggering could I never thrive,
   For the rain it raineth every day.   405

But when I came unto my beds,
   With hey, ho, the wind and the rain,
With tosspots still had drunken heads,
   For the rain it raineth every day.

A great while ago the world begun,   410
   With hey, ho, the wind and the rain:
But that's all one, our play is done,
   And we'll strive to please you every day.

                           [Exit.]

              ❧ FINIS ❧

---

369 importance: *importunity*   **371 it:** *the plot*   **372 pluck on:** *draw on, urge on*   **375 baffl'd thee:** *disgraced you publicly*   **378 interlude:** *an early form of dramatic comedy or entertainment*   **381 And:** *if*   **whirligig:** *circling course*   **386 the captain:** *Antonio, in jail*   **387 convents:** *comes together, suits*   **392 habits:** *clothing*

394–413 When that I was ... to please you every day; *cf. n.*   **394 and a:** *the and is superfluous; cf. n.*   **tiny:** *F.* tine   **398–408 But when I came to man's estate ... With tosspots still had drunken heads;** *cf. n.*   **395, 399, 403 With hey, ho, the wind and the rain;** *F.* with hey ho, etc.   **397, 401, 405 For the rain it raineth every day;** *F.* for the raine, etc.   **411 With hey, ho, the wind and the rain;** *F.* hey hot, etc.   **414 And we'll strive to please you every day;** *cf. n.*

NOTES

[**The Actors'** . . . **nearby**]: A list of characters and the location of the scene do not appear in the First Folio. Rowe (1709) first gave the characters. Both the names *Orsino* and *Valentine* appear to have been suggested by a visit of Don Valentino Orsino, Duke of Bracciano, to the English Court in January 1600. Tradition and, less certainly, the text, make Sir Toby the uncle of Olivia. The name of Feste the clown is the contemporary form of *feast, celebration,* and is thus related to the title of the play.

Twelfth Night or What You Will. The Folio spells the title 'twelfe,' the old form and pronunciation of the ordinal. Twelfth Night is the night of Epiphany, January 6, the twelfth day after Christmas. Traditionally commemorating the Magi and the manifestation of Christ to the Gentiles, the holiday marked the end of the Christmas festivities. The title may mean that the play was written for one particular Twelfth Night celebration, perhaps at court, or that the spirit of the play is consonant with the Christmas holidays. 'What You Will' simply enforces the air of lightness of 'Twelfth Night.'

I.i.1–3. *If music . . . so die.* If music is the food for love, play on to excess so that love's appetite for music, having too much, may sicken and die. It is most improbable that the Duke is wishing that his love for Olivia may also die.

I.i.9–14. *O spirit . . . in a minute.* O spirit of love, how alive and fresh you are in that, despite your power of receiving, you still devour things as does the sea. Nothing goes into love of whatever value and high esteem but that it falls into belittlement and low value at once. The central idea of the passage is the leveling power of love.

I.i.14. *fancy.* In Shakespearean English the term has a number of meanings and is most commonly used in psychology and esthetics. The most probable meaning here is the imagination or the mind of the man in love.

I.i.19. *the noblest.* His nobest *hart* (deer) and 'heart,' Olivia.

I.i.22. *hart.* A second pun on *hart* and 'heart.' The specific reference is to the story of Acteon who saw Diana bathing naked. As punishment, she transformed him into a hart and pursued him to his death with his own hounds. Shakespeare's most probable source is Ovid's *Metamorphoses*, Bk. 3, ll. 143–252 (Loeb ed.).

I.i.36. *golden shaft.* Cupid had two arrows; one was of gold, had a sharp point, and kindled love; the other was of lead, had a blunt point, and brought dislike. See the *Metamorphoses*, Bk. I,ll. 469–71 (Loeb ed.).

I.ii.4. *Elysium.* Viola picks a word that sounds like 'Illyria.'

I.ii.15. *Arion.* Orion of the Folio is either a phonetic spelling or a misreading of Shakespeare, the copyist, or the printer. The lines closely follow Ovid's account in the *Fasti*, 2, 113–16 (Loeb ed.). Arion, a bard on a voyage, jumped overboard to escape the sailors who would have murdered him for his money. A dolphin offered his back, and thereon the poet paid for his passage by playing on his lyre.

I.ii.43. *delivered.* Viola does not wish to be *delivered* or disclosed to the world; she is an unprotected woman in a strange country and she will remain in disguise until an opportune time for revealing her name and proper position in society.

I.ii.63. *to my wit.* The word has a large number of meanings in Shakespearean English. Here 'cleverness,' 'resourcefulness,' and 'intelligence' are the most probable synonyms.

I.iii.6. *except before excepted.* The legalism, *exceptis excipiendis,* 'those things expected which have been excepted,' was a phrase commonly employed in the writing of leases and allowed for conditions which had already been set up prior to the writing of the lease.

I.iii.11. *And.* Alternate form of 'an,' to mean 'if.' 'And' with this meaning is the standard spelling of the First Folio. 'An' is more common before 1600.

I.iii.20. *ducat.* The silver ducat of Italy was worth about 3*s.* 6*d.* in Shakespeare's time.

I.iii.26. *almost natural.* A natural is an idiot. Maria is punning on the word.

I.iii.37. *parish top.* Townships and parishes kept large tops which were made to spin by being whipped with eel skins. The origin of the practice may be in religious ritual; at any rate, there was communal top-spinning. See Alice B. Gomme's *The Traditional Games of England* (2 vols. 1894, 1898), *2,* 301–3. Evidence does not support Steevens' statement that the purpose of the top was 'that the peasants might be kept warm by exercise, and out of mischief, while they could not work.' Nares' *Glossary* (ed. 1859) lists references but without confirmation of Steevens.

I.iii.38. *wench.* The use here is familiar, not derogatory.

I.iii.38. *Castiliano, vulgo.* The exact meaning is unknown. Sir Toby wants Maria to be soberly polite to Sir Andrew. The Castilian people had a special

reputation for politeness. Hanmer emended the phrase to *Castiliano volto,* which he glosses 'her most civil and worthy looks.'

I.iii.43–48. *Accost . . . Accost.* Sir Toby tells Sir Andrew to greet Maria; Sir Andrew does not know the meaning of *accost* and thinks it is Maria's name. Maria is a *chambermaid* (1. 45) only in the sense of 'lady-in-waiting' to Olivia.

I.iii.62. *butt'ry bar.* The buttery bar was the bar, usually in the cellar, where the butts or barrels of liquor were stored. The word is unrelated to 'butter.'

I.iii.64. *It's dry, sir.* Maria begins a series of puns with several meanings for *dry,* namely, 'witty,' 'in need of a drink,' and 'impotent' or 'old.' A moist hand was believed to be a sign of youth and of liberality in money and love. Sir Andrew misses the point, but Maria continues the pun with 'at my fingers' ends' and 'I am barren.'

I.iii.75, 76. *great . . . wit.* The Englishman's diet was traditionally heavy and the quantity of beef in it was supposed to make him dull-witted.

I.iii.83. *bear-baiting.* An amusement in which a bear was tied or chained to a stake and unmuzzled dogs were set on it. The sport was extremely popular among all classes and was commonly carried on in the theaters.

I.iii.86. *curl by nature.* Sir Toby is punning on 'art' as opposed to 'nature' and probably on 'tongs' (curling tongs) and 'tongues' in 1. 82.

I.iii.107. *back-trick.* Minor verbal quibbles of an obscene sort probably occur in *caper, mutton,* and *back-trick.*

I.iii.111. *Mistress Mall's picture.* Attempts to identify Mall as Maria or as Mall Catpurse, the criminal Mary Frith, born probably about 1584, are not convincing.

I.iii.113. *sink-a-pace.* The obvious pun on the word depends on 'make water.'

I.iii.118. *dam'd color'd.* There is no satisfactory explanation of the phrase. Rowe's emendation, *flame-color'd,* is commonly accepted. There is the possibility that *dam'd* may mean 'dark' or 'black.'

I.iii.118. *sit.* The two verbs 'sit' and 'set' were confused in Shakespearean as in modern English. 'Sit' is from Old English *sittan;* 'set' is from Old English *settan.*

I.iii.121. *Taurus.* The twelve signs of the Zodiac, named after astral constellations and related to time, were supposed to govern various parts of the human body. By consulting as astrological almanac the physician might determine the proper treatment for disease in a particular part of the body at a particular time of the year. The bull Taurus, according to some authorities, governed sides and heart; according to others, neck and throat. But Sir Toby's speech should not be taken seriously.

I.iv.15. *doors.* The plural is perhaps derived from the doors, commonly divided, of the Elizabethan house.

I.iv.36. *thy constellation.* According to astrological theory the character of a person was determined at the moment of his birth by the 'constellation' or arrangement of stars at that time.

I.iv.43, 44. *woo . . . woo . . . would.* The quibble depends on the fact that 'would' was sometimes pronounced like 'wooed' in Modern English.

I.v.5. *to fear no colors.* Maria's interpretation of the proverbial phrase suggests that *no colors* may have meant originally 'no flags,' and thus came from army usage. The clown is punning on 'collar,' the hangman's rope.

I.v.13, 14. *Well, God . . . talents.* May God let those who are intelligent use their intelligence, and may fools (both professional fools and foolish people) use their abilities. *Talents* means 'native abilities' and, by a pun on 'talons,' 'claws' or 'guile.' In addition, if Feste is using the northern pronunciation of *fools,* there is a pun on 'fools' and 'fowls' to match 'talents' and 'talons.'

I.v.18 *away.* There is the remote possibility of a quibble on 'a whey,' that is, 'a turning sour' from the *summer.*

I.v.25, 26. *If Sir Toby . . . Illyria.* If Sir Toby would stop drinking, you would make as clever a wife (for him) as any in Illyria.

I.v.42–45. *Anything . . . virtue.* Anything that is cured (and patched) is but patched; virtue that sins is mixed with sin, and evil that reforms is mixed with good. That is, all men are a mixture of good and bad. The clown is parodying formal logic.

I.v.45, 46. *As there . . . flower.* Every man is married to luck; when his luck is bad, he is betrayed, he is a cuckold. And beauty (Olivia's beauty) is transitory. The clown is saying that all men and women must resign themselves to fate.

I.v.50. *motley.* The clown's motley was of pieces of cloth of different colors, or of a cloth woven of threads of mixed colors.

I.v.82. *zanies.* The understudies, imitators and butts of professional fools. The term is also a snynonym for 'clown' or 'fool.'

I.v.86. *no slander in an allow'd fool.* A fool who is allowed or privileged to practice his foolery (part of which is to insult people) cannot be guilty of slander.

I.v.111. *A plague.* Sir Toby traditionally belches before these words.

I.v.137. *sheriff's post . . . supporter to a bench.* Carved and painted posts were put by the doors of town officials. *Supporter* is used in the sense of 'prop' or 'post.'

I.v.SD. *Enter Viola.* The First Folio reading of *Enter Violenta* is a possible reflection of Italian background for the narrative but more probably a misreading by the compositor of 'Viola enter.'

I.v.158. *if this be.* A typical example of the present subjunctive, now more restricted in use.

I.v.169. *my profound heart.* My deeply penetrating lady. 'Heart' is a common form of address to a lady.

I.v.183–185. *'Tis not that time . . . dialogue.* The moon has not now influenced me enough to make me a party to skipping over and confusing a conversation. The moon was believed to produce lunacy, or moon-madness. The common addition of *so* after *in* is unnecessary.

I.v.188. *giant.* The traditional guard of the lady in medieval romances. The word is applied ironically to Maria who is small. Other references to her size are *Penthesilea* (II.3.159); *little villian* (II.5.11); and *youngest wren of mine* (III.2.58).

I.v.219. *in grain.* The grain was red dyestuff consisting of the dried bodies of the insect *coccus cacti.*

I.v.227. *item.* The term, adverbial in origin, meant 'also,' 'likewise'; it was used for introducing a new article, fact, or statement in a formal list.

I.v.276. *thou art.* Olivia in her soliloquy shifts from the formal 'you' to the intimate 'thou' as she thinks of Cesario and her love for him.

I.v.287. *County's.* Words ending in *t* tended to keep the old plural and possessive in *es.* This fact resulted in the back formation, 'county.'

I.v.295. *Mine eye . . . mind.* My eye has taken too favorable an impression (of Cesario) for my intellect to approve.

II.i.1. *Nor . . . not.* The double negative is an emphatic negative in Shakespearean English, as in Old English and in modern dialectal English.

II.i.3, 4. *My stars . . . distemper yours.* The arrangement of the stars at the moment of one's birth was thought to determine one's future destiny. During one's life an examination of those stars would tell whether the time was propitious. Thus Sebastian is saying: 'The astrological interpretation of my stars is bad; my bad fate might perhaps infect your fate.'

II.ii.SD. *Enter . . . at several doors.* The scene is near Olivia's house. The stage direction means that Viola and Malvolio enter each by one of the different doors at the rear of the Shakespearean stage. The usual stage had two doors, right and left, with a third possible entrance through the curtain under the balcony at the center of the back or inner stage.

II.ii.25. *pregnant enemy.* 'Pregnant' to mean 'strong' is common before and during Shakespeare's time. In ll. 26 and 27 there is the possible suggestion of Satan disguised as a serpent to seduce Eve.

II.ii.28, 29. *Alas . . . such we be.* The First Folio is commonly emended as follows: 'Alas, our frailty is the cause, not we, For such as we are made of, such we be.' The alterations are attractive but unnecessary to a satisfactory meaning of the passage: 'Alas, O, frailty is the cause, not woman; on account of the way that we women are made, since we are of that sort.' The two final clauses are close to repetitious, and the repetition of *such* is a rhetorical trick which obscures the syntax.

II.iii.2. *diluculo surgere.* Diluculo surgere saluberrimum est, 'To get up at dawn is most healthful.' The maxim is from the Latin grammar of William Lily and John Colet, first printed in 1549. The book came to be known as the Eton Latin Grammar, and in its numerous editions and revisions has been a standard text for English schoolboys into the 20th century.

II.iii.7, 8. *Does not . . . elements.* It was believed that life depended on the correct mixture of the four elements of the universe, air, fire, earth, and water. Note the plural subject and singular verg.

II.iii.14, 15. *the picture of We Three.* A picture or signboard at an inn with the heads of two fools displayed, and the inscription: 'We three loggerheads be.' The onlooker is the third.

I.iii.23–25. *I did impeticos thy gratillity . . . bottle-ale houses.* The meaning is obscure. By *impeticos,* the Clown means 'put into the pocket of my long gown or petticoat.' Clowns frequently wore long coats. *Gratillity* is simply an improvised diminutive for 'gratuity.' The following is a possible paraphrase of the passage: 'I did pocket your small gratuity, for Malvolio's nose can soon smell out money; my lady-love has elegant tastes, and the Myrmidons (where we drink) are no cheap drinking houses.' That is, the Clown is saying that he can use the money. *Whipstock* is 'whip handle.'

II.iii.34. *O mistress mine.* The Clown's song, either by Shakespeare or by an unknown author, was first printed in Thomas Morley's *Consort Lessons* (1599).

II.iii.52. *To hear . . . contagion.* If we can hear with our noses, the fool's voice and breath are pleasant to listen to but bad to smell.

II.iii.54, 55. *draw three souls out of one weaver.* Weavers were famous for their singing and their love of song.

II.iii.58. *'Thou knave.'* The words of the catch are: 'Hold thy peace, thou knave; and I prithee hold thy peace.' H. H. Furness in *A New Variorum,* p. 118, gives the words and music. The earliest printing which he reports is in *Deutero-melia* (1609).

II.iii.68. *Catayan.* Chinese, a person from Cathay. They were believed to be dishonest and shiftless.

II.iii.69. *a Peg-a-Ramsey.* The reference appears to be to the coarse and immoral heroine of an old ballad 'Bonny Peggy Ramsey,' the words and music of which are reprinted in Thomas D'Urfey's *Wit and Mirth* (6 vols. 1719–20), *5,* 139. For a discussion of the music see William Chappell's *Old English Popular Music* (2 vols. 1893), *1,* 248. The ballad begins:

> Bonny Peggy Ramsey that any Man may se,
> And bonny was her Face, with a fair freckel'd Eye . . .

Sir Toby is thus saying ironically of Malvolio, who is about to enter, that he is handsome, coarse, and immoral.

II.iii.69. *'Three merry men be we'.* The words of the song perhaps appear in George Peele's *The Old Wives' Tale* (1595), Act II:

> Three merry men, and three merry men,
> And three merry men be we;
> I in the wood, and thou on the ground,
> And Jack sleeps in the tree.

Furness in *A New Variorum,* p. 120, prints words and music.

II.iii.71. *'There dwelt a man.'* 'The Constancy of Susanna' is a ballad on the story of Susanna and the Elders:

> There dwelt a man in Babylon,
>   of reputation great by fame;
> He tooke to wife a faire woman,
>   Susanna she was call'd by name;
> A woman faire and vertuous:
>   Lady, lady,
> Why should wee not to her learne thus
>   to live godly?

It is reprinted in the *Roxburghe Ballads,* ed. W. Chappell (9 vols. 1871–99) *1,* 190–3.

II.iii.76. *'O the twelfe day of December.'* The phrase is probably from a lost ballad. It is unlikely that Sir Toby is misquoting either 'Musselburgh Field' (the suggestion of G. L. Kittredge) or 'The Twelve Days of Christmas' (the suggestion of I. B. Cauthen, Jr.) 'Musselburgh Field' begins: 'On the tenth day of December . . .'; it is reprinted in F. J. Child's *The English and Scottish Popular Ballads* (5 vols. 1882–94), *3,* 378–9. 'The Twelve Days of Christmas' begins: 'On the twelfth day of Christmas . . .'; it is reprinted in Cecil J. Sharp's and Charles L. Marson's *Folk Songs from Somerset* (5 vols. 1908–09, *2,* 52–5, 74–5.

II.iii.91. *'Fairwell, dear heart.'* From 'Corydon's Farewell to Phyllis,' a song in Robert Jones' *First Booke of Songes and Ayres* (1600), ed. E. H. Fellowes (1925), pp. 25–5. Sir Toby and the Clown sing snatches from the first two stanzas only:

> Farewell, dear love, since thou wilt needs be gon,
> Mine eyes do show my life is almost done.
> Nay, I will never die, so long as I can spy.
> There be many moe though that she do go.
> There be many moe, I fear not.
> Why, then, let her go, I care not!
>
> Farewell, farewell, since this I find is true,
> I will not spend more time in wooing you.
> But I will seeke elsewhere if I may find her there.
> Shall I bid her go? What and if I do?
> Shall I bid her go, and spare not?
> O no, no, no, no, no, I dare not.

II.iii.106. *cakes and ale.* The traditional refreshment for holidays and saints' days.

II.iii.107. *St. Anne.* The mother of the Virgin Mary. The oath is colorless. Unconvincing efforts have been made to connect the Clown's use of the oath

with St. Anne as the giver of 'wealth and living great' on the basis of an unidentified quotation in Robert Chambers' *Book of Days* (2 vols. 1863–64), *2*, 389.

II.iii.107. *ginger.* Used to spice ale, ginger was believed to reduce drunkenness. Ginger was also esteemed as an aphrodisiac.

II.iii.109, 110. *rub your chain with crumbs.* As steward of the house, Malvolio wears a chain with keys. The chain survives on the wine steward in the modern restaurant. Toby tells Malvolio: 'Polish your chain with bread crumbs,' i.e. 'Get back into your proper place,' 'Mind your own business.'

II.iii.115. *as good a deed as to drink.* A traditional comparison.

II.iii.127. *a kind of Puritan.* Maria means that Malvolio is oversolemn and overpunctilious, two characteristics associated with the modern use of the word 'Puritan.' Sir Andrew misunderstands her and thinks that she has said that Malvolio is of the reforming or dissenting party in the Church, that is, that he is not a good Church of England man. Sir Toby then protests the harshness of Sir Andrew's judgment and Maria (ll. 133ff.) explains that Malvolio is not a Puritan but simply a conceited fool. Malvolio has already (II.3.78–82) done something which no stage Puritan would have done: he has spoken slightingly of tinkers and coziers (cobblers), traditional mainstays of the dissenting sects. In point of fact, Malvolio does not conform to the type of the stage Puritan common in the drama of the period. Malvolio has the sobriety and the conceit of the stage Puritan, but in the further complexities of his character he goes as far beyond the stock figure as Falstaff goes beyond the *miles gloriosus,* the conventional braggart soldier of Roman comedy.

II.iii.135. *swarths.* A 'swarth' or 'swath' is the space covered by the sweep of the mower's scythe in cutting one side of a field.

II.iii.156, 157. *let the fool make a third.* In the plot Fabian and not Feste makes the third. The change may be an oversight on Shakespeare's part, or an indication of revision.

II.iv.37. *worn.* Hanmer's emendation, *won,* is commonly accepted.

II.iv.58. *Fie, away.* Rowe's emendation, *Fly away,* is commonly accepted.

II.iv.62, 63. *My part . . . share it.* My portion of death, no lover so true did share (with me).

II.iv.75. *pleasure will be paid.* The line is proverbial. See *The Oxford Dictionary of English Proverbs* (1948), p. 507.

II.iv.78. *the melancholy god.* Possibly Saturn, but more probably the Clown is only saying that the Duke enjoys his melancholy.

II.iv.80–82. *I would have . . . voyage of nothing.* I would have men of such fickleness make a voyage, that they might have business everywhere and intend to go everywhere; for that's what always brings back a good cargo of nothing. I.e. if you aim at everything, you achieve nothing.

II.iv.94. *I cannot.* The next line, 'Sooth, but you must [be so answer'd],' justifies the emendation.

II.iv.100, 101. *woman's sides Can bide.* Note the omission of the relative, common in early Modern English.

II.iv.105, 106. *No motion . . . and revolt.* No genuine movement of the liver, the seat of true love, but a mere physical sensation in the palate which is subject to excess, satiety, and disgust. The singular subject with a plural verb is not uncommon in Shakespearean English.

II.iv.122–124. *And with . . . smiling at grief.* Green and yellow are colors commonly associated with sadness and decay. The sense of the passage is that Viola's sister sat calmly, like a statue of Patience, and smiled in the midst of her grief. It is possible that the figure of Patience was suggested by Chaucer's *Parliament of Fowls,* ll. 242–3:

> *Dame Pacience syttynge there I fond,*
> *With face pale, upon an hil of sond . . .*

Both Viola's sister and Chaucer's Patience are pale and are seated. In addition, Griselda of Chaucer's 'Clerk's Tale' is a monumental figure of patience in the face of suffering similar to that of Viola's sister.

II.iv.126. *Our shows . . . will.* Our display of love is more than our actual will to love.

II.v.2. *a scruple.* Literally, one twenty-fourth of an ounce, apothecaries' weight.

II.v.3. *let me . . . melancholy.* The sense of the passage hinges on a pun. 'Boil' and 'bile' were pronounced alike, and black bile produced melancholy. The point may be that poisoners were boiled to death, but that melancholy was a cold and not a hot humor.

II.v.6, 7. *You know . . . a bear-baiting here.* Malvolio's dislike of bear-baiting connects him with the satirical portrayals of Puritans. But the trait does not make him a dissenter; it only emphasizes his puritanical or 'precise' mien.

II.v.11, 12. *my metal of India.* The East Indies were the fabled source for gold in the period. The First Folio reads *Mettle,* a common variant of 'metal.' There is probably a pun on 'metal' and 'mettle.'

II.v.19. *trout . . . tickling.* It was believed that trout could be caught by tickling them about the gills.

II.v.22. *complexion.* The mixture of the four humors, blood, bile, black bile, and phlegm, in the body. The predominance of one humor produced a personality of that humor. Thus the Duke Orsino might be said to be melancholic because of a predominance of black bile.

II.v.29. *Toby.* This line and Sir Toby's 'Peace, peace' (l. 33) are commonly assigned to Fabian.

II.v.34. *The Lady of the Strachy.* Her identity is unknown, and no satisfactory emendation of *Strachy* has been suggested. The meaning of the passage is obvious: Malvolio has in mind some story of a lady of high position who married one of the servants. The following are the more important of the emendations which have been proposed: *Trachy* or Thrace (Warburton); *starchy* or linen (Stevens); *Tragedy* (Bulloch); *county* (Kinnear); *Malfi,* or the Duchess of Malfi (Dunlap and Luce). However, Charles J. Sisson has discovered evidence suggesting that the reference is satirical and to the King's Revels company, and that it was interpolated after 1616.

II.v.36. *Fie on him, Jezebel.* 'Fie' is an exclamation of disgust. Sir Andrew says: 'Fie on Malvolio, who is a Jezebel.' Jezebel was the haughty wife of Ahab. See 1 Kings 16 and 19 and 2 Kings 9.

II.v.48. *a demure travel of regard.* Here and elsewhere Malvolio's English is pedantically heavy.

II.v.55. *my—some rich jewel.* The dash is a necessary addition to the unpunctuated phrase in the First Folio. Malvolio is about to say 'my chain.'

II.v.58. *with cars.* The reference appears to be to a method of torture or execution in which the victim was bound to cars or carts which then went in opposite directions. Compare '. . . but a team of horse shall not pluck that from me,' in *Two Gentlemen of Verona,* III.1.264, or the phrase, current to the present, 'Wild horses cannot get that out of me.'

II.v.75. *woodcock . . . gin.* The woodcock was proverbially a stupid bird which walked easily into the gin or snare. *Gin* is a shortened form of 'engine.'

II.v.76, 77. *the spirit . . . to him.* May the spirit of whims suggest to him that he read it aloud. *Humors* here does not seem to have the usual medical meaning, nor does it mean 'wit' or 'merriment.'

II.v.79, 80. *her very C's . . . P's.* Malvolio happens to spell out two Elizabethan obscenities. There are no C's or P's in the address of the letter as he reads it.

II.v.83. *By your leave, wax.* The letter would be folded upon itself and sealed, and would have no envelope. Malvolio apologetically asks the seal for permission to break it. The request is conventional.

II.v.84. *Lucrece.* The beautiful and chaste wife of Tarquinius Collatinus was raped by Sextus, son of Tarquin, king of Rome. Lucrece told her father and her husband of what had happened and then committed suicide. The story is the subject of Shakespeare's poem, *The Rape of Lucrece* (1594).

II.v.91. *The numbers alter'd.* Numbers may be a contraction of 'number is.'

II.v.93. *brock.* The more common phrase is 'stinking brock.' There is also a tradition that the badger is conceited and noisy.

II.v.98. *fustian.* Originally a coarse cloth made of cotton and flax.

II.v.106. *And with . . . at it.* The falcon—here a *staniel* or inferior kind of hawk—*checks* when it leaves the pursuit of the game it has been sent after and follows other prey. Sir Toby is saying: 'How quickly the fool leaves the truth and goes off on a false trail.'

II.v.111, 112. *Sowter . . . fox.* The dog will bark on the trail, however, though the deception is as plain as the smell of a fox. 'Souter' or 'sowter' means 'maker or mender of shoes' and is used of any bungler, botcher, or ignorant workman. *Sowter* is here the name of the bungling dog.

II.v.115. *faults.* Fabian is punning. He means not only 'breaks in the scent' but also that Malvolio is excellent at getting himself into *faults* or difficulties.

II.v.116, 117. *But then . . . probation.* But there is no consistency in what follows. It becomes strained under testing.

II.v.119. *And O shall end.* And the trick will end with Malvolio's exclaiming 'O' in disgust. Obscure verbal quibbles of an indecent sort occur from l.116 through 120.

II.v.122. *any eye behind you.* It is unlikely that there is here any reference, as some editors have supposed, to Chaucer's figure of Prudence with three eyes (*Troilus and Cressida,* bk. V. ll. 744–5):

> *Prudence, allas, oon of thyne eyen thre*
> *Me lakked alwey, ere that I come here!*

II.v.125. *and yet . . . bow to me.* And yet, if I were to force the meaning of this 'M. O. A. I' a little, it would indicate me.

II.v.128, 129. *born . . . achieve.* The emendations make the passage consistent with III.4.39 and 43, and with V.1.376.

II.v.132. *cast . . . fresh.* Cast off your humble manner as a snake casts off his old skin, and appear new.

II.v.133. *tang . . . state.* Sound out with theories of statecraft. *Tang* also means 'to taste,' 'to smack.'

II.v.136. *cross-garter'd.* The garters held up the stockings or attached the breeches to the stockings. Cross-gartering was an eccentric fashion in which the garters were crossed both above and below the knee.

II.v.140. *alter services.* In addition to the 'services' of the steward, it may be that Maria has cleverly suggested the 'services' of the courtly lover to his lady.

II.v.140–142. *Fortunate-Unhappy.* Compare 'Fortunatus Infelix,' a common posy or short motto used as an inscription for a ring, picture, poem, or emblem.

II.v.143. *politic authors.* The *pollticke* of the Folio possibly indicates the pronunciation.

II.v.152. *Jove.* The use of the word here and elsewhere suggests alteration in the text after 1606 and that, consequently, the text of the First Folio is later than 1606. A statute of 1606 forbade the profane use of God's name on the stage. The Clown Feste speaks of Jove in I.5.104 and III.1.43, but the reference is appropriate to his intelligence and character. Malvolio's use of *Jove* and its use in several other places in the play (II.5.157; III.4.71,78; and particularly IV.2.10) sound strange or unnatural. It is probable that the original text read *God.*

II.v.160. *the Sophy.* The brothers Sir Robert and Sir Anthony Shirley had gone in 1599 on an expedition to Persia. Sir Anthony had left Persia after five months; Sir Robert had stayed. An account of the trip appeared in *Sir A. Shierlies Journey Overland to Venice* (1600). The 'pension of thousands to be paid from the Sophy' may refer to reports of fabulous wealth to be had from the shah.

II.v.167. *Wilt . . . neck.* Sir Toby offers to submit utterly to Maria's wit in the fashion of victims of military conquest.

II.v.175. *Like aqua-vite with a midwife.* There is no certain explanation of the phrase. Either midwives used distilled liquor to induce labor, or midwives by tradition drank excessively.

III.i.20. *wanton.* There is the remote possibility of a quibble on 'want one,' i.e. 'want a name.'

III.i.21. *since bonds disgrac'd them.* I.e. since a man's word is no longer as good as his bond, mankind has been disgraced or put to shame by the formal and necessary pledges (bonds) imposed by law.

III.i.38. *I would.* Shakespearean English, like modern American English, is not strict in the use of 'would' and 'should.'

III.i.40. *your wisdom.* An ironic variation on the conventional title of address, 'Your worship.'

III.i.50, 51. *Pandarus . . . Cressida . . . Troilus.* Troilus, a son of Priam, a king of Troy, loved Cressida of Troy. Cressida's uncle, Pandarus, acted as a go-between and Cressida returned Troilus' love. In an exchange of prisoners between the Greeks and the Trojans, Cressida was sent to the Greek camp to join her father Calchas who had fled to the Greeks. In the Greek camp Diomede courted Cressida and supplanted Troilus in her affections. Troilus and Diomede fought inconclusively, and finally Troilus was killed in battle by Achilles. Shakespeare's *Troilus and Cressida* was produced about 1602; he was familiar with a number of versions of the story, most notably Chaucer's.

III.i.54. *Cressida was a beggar.* Robert Henryson (d. 1506) continued the story of Cressida in *The Testament of Cressid.* Diomede deserted Cressida who became a harlot in the Greek camp. The gods afflicted her with leprosy and she had to beg by the roadside. The victorious Troilus rode by, but he did not recognize her. She learned who he was and, after having sent him a ring he had given her, died.

III.i.72. *encounter.* Here and with *taste* (l. 76) Sir Toby is playing pedantically with his words.

III.i.80. *gait.* The *gate* of the Folio suggests that a pun was possibly intended.

III.i.96, 97. *'Twas never . . . compliment.* The world has never been a happy one since the pretense of humility (with the word *servant*) came to be a convention of polite behavior. The phrase 'merry world' has the force of 'good old days.'

III.i.109. *music from the spheres.* It was believed that the universe consisted of a series of spheres, one inside the other, and all centered on the earth. The spheres revolved, carrying within them the various heavenly bodies, and giving off a divine harmony inaudible to man.

III.i.116, 117. *To force . . . none of yours.* That I forced on you by a shameful trick a ring which you knew was not yours at all.

III.i.118, 119. *at the stake . . . unmuzzled thoughts.* The figure is another reference to the popular sport of bear-baiting. The verb 'to bait' means 'to cause to bite.'

III.i.120. The line is irregular: it consists of an alexandrine (twelve syllables

of six iambics) with an extra unaccented syllable at the end. J. Dover Wilson in his edition (1930) rearranges the lines:

> To one of your receiving enough is shown,
> A cypress, not a bosom, hides my heart:
> So let me bear you speak.
> Viola.   I pity you.
> Olivia. That's a degree to love.
> Viola.   No, not a grise;
> For 'tis a vulgar proof,
> That very oft we pity enemies.

III.i.122. *Hides . . . speak.* The first syllable is accented and is followed by four iambics, a total of nine syllables. This type of headless line is common in the earlier drama and there is no compelling reason for regularizing it by emending *Hides* to 'Hideth.'

III.i.127. *'tis time to smile agen.* I.e. it is time for me to smile once more and to forget you, if you are my enemy or if you can only pity me.

III.i.130. *the lion . . . the wolf.* The lion is the noble Duke Orsino; the wolf is the cruel Cesario.

III.i.135, 136. *due west. Then westward ho.* Olivia's implication in the phrase 'due west' is that she is dismissing Cesario forever from her favor; she sends Cesario toward the setting sun. Cesario (Viola) answers with a more cheerful phrase, 'Westward ho!' The Thames boatman cried 'Westward ho!' and 'Eastword ho!' to prospective passengers to indicate the direction of the next trip on the river.

III.i.141, 142. *That you do think . . . the same of you.* Viola says that Olivia thinks she is in love with a man, and that she is not. Olivia, not understanding the statement, and thinking that Viola has meant either that Olivia is not really in love, or that she is mad, answers that she (Olivia) believes the same thing of Viola ('you do think you are not what you are'), that is, that Viola really does love Olivia, or that Viola is mad to reject Olivia's love.

III.i.155–158. *Do not extort . . . better.* Do not extract by force your arguments from the fact that, because I woo you, you have no reason to accept. But rather make your logic firm with this reasonable proposition: love which is sought is good, but love which is given unsought is better.

III.ii.2. *venom.* Here and elsewhere Sir Toby plays with words by using them out of their ordinary context.

III.ii.6. *orchard.* From Old English *ortyeard.* The first element *ort-* is probably from the Latin *[h]ortus,* 'garden'; *-yeard* is the modern 'yard.'

III.ii.7. *see.* The Folio is commonly emended to *see thee.*

III.ii.17. *dormouse.* The dormouse was traditionally a sleepy animal.

III.ii.22. *double gilt.* The *double gilt* or gilding (a double dipping or plating of an object by a goldsmith) was the opportunity, doubly golden, to prove superiority both as a lover and as a fighter.

III.ii.24. *an icicle on a Dutchman's beard.* The phrase may be connected with the voyages, famous around 1600, of the Dutchman Barentz to the Arctic regions in 1596. An account by Gerritt de Veer had appeared in Amsterdam in 1598 and was entered in English in the Stationers' Register in 1598 (ed. E. Arber, *3,* 118): '. . . A true description of Three voyages by sea . . . and of the feirce Beares and other Sea monsters, and marveylous could, and howe in the last voyage, the shippe is besett in Iyce . . . by Jerrett De Veer . . .'

III.ii.27. *Brownist.* A member of the religious sect founded by Robert Browne (1550?–1633?). Browne opposed both the Episcopal and the Presbyterian forms of church government and advocated the Independent or Congregationalist form. He preached separation around 1578–80, but he later submitted to the Church of England and for forty years was a rector in Northamptonshire.

III.ii.38, 39. *If thou thou'st him.* 'Thou' corresponded to the French *tu* and German *du,* proper for addressing children, close relatives, friends, and inferiors, but an insult when used with strangers.

III.ii.41. *the bed of Ware.* The great bed of Ware is a 16th-century carved oak bed, ten feet nine inches square. It was one of the sights of Shakespeare's time and is referred to in a number of contemporary plays. The bed is now in the Victoria and Albert Museum, London.

III.ii.42. *gall.* An excrescence produced on the oak by the action of insects. Oak galls were used in the manufacture of ink. The pun is on *gall* 'bitterness.'

III.ii.43. *goose-pen.* The implication is that Sir Andrew's style will be silly.

III.ii.46. *dear manikin.* In the phrase there is the suggestion of 'puppet' or artist's lay figure to be twisted and manipulated at will.

III.ii.54. *blood in his liver.* It was believed that the liver was the seat of courage; blood in the liver produced courage. Compare 'lily-livered,' meaning 'cowardly.'

III.ii.58. *youngest wren of mine.* Sir Toby means that Maria is young and small in stature; the wren is a particularly small bird. 'My youngest little bird' is

an adequate rendering of the phrase. The common emendation of *mine* of the Folio to *nine* involves the explanation that wrens lay from nine to ten eggs and that the last of the brood is supposed to be the smallest.

III.ii.59. *If you desire the spleen.* The spleen was believed to be the source of, among other things, laughter.

III.ii.61. *renegatho.* The spelling possibly represents an attempt to produce in the pronunciation the Spanish voiced spirant *d.*

III.ii.69. *new map . . . Indies.* The *new map* of the East Indies and North America was done in 1600 by Edward Wright with the assistance of Richard Hakluyt, author of the various *Voyages,* and John Davis, navigator. It is described and reproduced in *Shakespeare's England* (Oxford Press ed., 2 vols. 1916), *1,* 173–4. The *lines* which Maria speaks of are those of Mercator's projection, a system new to English maps of the period.

III.iii.16. *And thanks . . . turns.* The short line is commonly emended for scansion. The compositor or the copyist may have dropped part of the speech.

III.iii.42. *the Elephant.* A. C. Southern in the *Times Literary Supplement,* June 12, 1953, has shown that in 1598 'there was an inn known as The Elephant on the Bankside' and that an inn with that name probably was there at least until 1605. The common London inn sign, The Elephant and Castle, survives notably in the underground station south of Waterloo.

III.iv.21. *this cross-gartering.* Malvolio now has his garters crossed both above and below the knee.

III.iv.23. *'Please one and please all.'* The phrase is common. However, Malvolio may be quoting specifically from a ballad entered in the Stationers' Register in 1592 (ed. E. Arger, *2,* 602): '. . . the Crowe shee sittes upon the wall: please One and please all.' The ballad was signed 'R.T.,' possibly for Richard Tarlton, actor and clown. It is reprinted in *A Collection of Seventy-nine Black-letter Ballads,* ed. Joseph Lilly (1867), pp. 255–9. The first stanza follows:

> *Please one and please all,*
> *Be they great be they small,*
> *Be they little be they lowe,*
> *So pypeth the Crowe,*
> > *sitting upon a wall:*
> > *please one and please all,*
> > *please one and please all.*

III.iv.28. *Roman hand.* There were two styles of handwriting in use around 1600. The old secretary hand, almost illegible to modern readers, was common. The Italian style (*Roman hand*), fairly close to modern script, was being used increasingly and was particularly popular with women.

III.iv.34. *At your request . . . daws.* The speech is ironic. Malvolio says: 'Should I answer the request of my inferior, Maria? Of course. Nightingales answer the calls of jackdaws or crows.'

III.iv.50. *made.* Here and in the following lines there is possibly a verbal quibble on 'made' and 'maid,' (servant). In addition, *madness* (l. 53) may have been pronounced almost like 'maidness.'

III.iv.53. *midsummer madness.* It was believed that midsummer produced insanity. Compare 'dog-days.' June 23, Midsummer Eve, was a time of magic.

III.iv.67. *tang with.* The *langer* of the First Folio is not recorded as a verb in the NED; and *tang* is in the letter which Malvolio is quoting from II.5.133.

III.iv.68–70. *And consequently . . . and so forth.* Malvolio stops quoting from the letter and seemingly explores its implications as to his future conduct for winning Olivia. There is the slight possibility that the sentence is a later interpolation.

III.iv.71. *lim'd.* Birds were caught by spreading birdlime, a sticky substance, on twigs or on trees.

III.iv.80. *drawn in little.* It is unlikely that the figure has the force of 'portrayed in miniature.' Devils were notorious for their ability to contract into a small space. The phrase would thus mean 'contracted.'

III.iv.80. *Legion.* Mark 5:8–9: 'For he [Jesus] said unto him, Come out of the man, thou unclean spirit. And he asked him, What is thy name? And he answered, saying, My name is Legion: for we are many.'

III.iv.82, 83. *How is't with you, man?.* Wright assigned the line to Sir Toby.

III.iv.96. *bewitch'd.* Possession by a witch's spell and possession by the devil are two different things; in popular usage the two are interchangeable. Maria combines the two.

III.iv.97. *Carry . . . woman.* 'Take his urine to the wise woman for diagnosis.' A 'wise woman' pretended to cure disease, bewitchment, and possession by devils. In addition, she usually told fortunes.

III.iv.110. *cherry-pit.* A child's game in which the players throw cherry stones

into a small hole. Sir Toby means that it is below Malvolio's dignity to be intimate with Satan.

III.iv.110. *collier.* The devil is associated with coal because of his blackness and possibly because of the traditional flames of hell.

III.iv.126. *in a dark room and bound.* The standard treatment for insanity. Whipping was also believed to be beneficial. Insanity was commonly regarded as amusing.

III.iv.142, 143. *A good note . . . law.* A clever remark (since *scurvy* is vague) which keeps you from being legally liable.

III.iv.179. *cockatrices.* Fabulous reptiles hatched by serpents from cocks' eggs. Both the breath and glance of a cockatrice were fatal.

III.iv.190. *Goes . . . griefs.* Note the disagreement of subject and verb in the inverted sentence.

III.iv.217. *with unhatch'd rapier . . . carpet consideration.* With an unhacked rapier and for affairs of peace rather than of war. That is, when Sir Andrew was dubbed a knight his sword had never been used in battle, and he got his honor perhaps through influence, favor, or service at court (*carpet consideration*) rather than for fighting. The term 'carpet knight' is common in this derogatory sense. *Unhatch'd* is 'unhacked,' 'undented.'

III.iv.229, 230. *unless you undertake . . . answer him.* Unless you undertake a duel with me, which with as much safety you might undertake with him in answering his challenge.

III.iv.253. *firago.* The substitution of initial *f* for *v* indicates a hypercorrect pronunciation, particularly common among speakers of southern English, some of whom tended to use, incorrectly, initial *v* in place of *f.*

III.iv.256. *hits.* Feet is perhaps regarded collectively; but 16th- and 17th-century grammar is frequently loose.

III.iv.258. *Pox on't.* The curse is a common one and refers to the great pox, or syphilis, rather than to the smallpox.

III.iv.264. *Capilet.* Diminutive form of *caple* or *capul* and derived probably from Latin, *cabullus,* 'horse.' The word is common to Middle English and Icelandic.

III.iv.282. *the duello.* A standard work on the subject was *Vincento Saviolo His Practice* (1595).

III.iv.342. *image.* Image here means 'ideal representation' or 'ideal appearance' to be worshiped within the friendship code of courtly love.

III.iv.345. *vild.* There is commonly an excrescent *d* in words ending in *l* and *n.* Compare French *son,* English 'sound'; or the substandard 'drownded.'

III.iv.350. *empty trunks, o'erflourish'd.* The sense of the passage is that the devil deceitfully 'overflourishes' or decorates the empty bodies to give them a beautiful appearance. It is unlikely that *trunks* refers to ornamented chests for clothing. *Trunks* as 'bodies' continues the figure of the mind and the body from the lines immediately preceding.

III.iv.367. *hare.* The hare was traditionally a cowardly animal.

IV.i.13. *a cockney.* The terms seems to come from Middle English *cocken-ey,* 'cock's egg,' or a small and malformed egg. The various attached meanings are 'milksop,' 'a townsman,' and 'a Londoner.'

IV.i.21. *after fourteen years' purchase.* A normal purchase price for land was the amount of rent which would be collected from it in twelve years. Thus, *fourteen years' purchase* would be a high price.

IV.i.37. *You are well flesh'd.* 'To flesh' is to give a taste of the game killed to a hawk or hound in order to incite it further to the chase.

IV.i.58. *started . . . heart.* 'To start' is the hunting term for forcing an animal to leave its lair.

IV.ii.2. *Topas.* The topaz stone was believed to cure insanity; Shakespeare may have had in mind Chaucer's comic knight of 'The Tale of Sir Thopas.'

IV.ii.12,13. *King Gorboduc.* A legendary king of Britain, Gorboduc's story is told by Geoffrey of Monmouth. The king is a leading figure in an early blank-verse tragedy by Thomas Sackville and Thomas Norton, *Gorboduc,* or *Ferrex and Porrex* (1562). The 'niece of King Gorboduc' is an invention of the clown.

IV.ii.SD. *Malvolio within.* The stage direction indicates that Malvolio is either inside the inner stage, a small enclosed area at the center and rear of the Elizabethan stage, or at the wicket of one of the doors at either side of the inner stage. The latter is improbable since he is the focal point of the scene. In a court performance he would probably be in a small house or 'mansion' made of canvas on a frame and set out on the stage.

IV.ii.40, 41. *the Egyptians in their fog.* Exodus 10:22 'And Moses stretched forth his hand toward heaven; and there was a thick darkness in all the land of Egypt three days.'

IV.ii.46. *Pythagoras.* The Greek philosopher of the 6th century B.C. was believed to have been the originator of the doctrine of the transmigration of

souls. The doctrine was common knowledge, but Shakespeare might have had it from Ovid, specifically from the *Metamorphoses*.

IV.ii.66. *this sport to the upshot.* The *upshot* is the final shot in a match at archery. *To*, Rowe's emendation, was either dropped from the copy or merged with the preceding *t* of *sport*.

IV.ii.68. *Hey Robin.* The song has been attributed doubtfully to Sir Thomas Wyatt. It is reprinted in Percy's *Reliques* (ed. 1847), *1*, 196–9. The song begins:

> *A Robyn,*
> *Jolly Robyn,*
> *Tell me how they leman [lady-love] doeth,*
> *And thou shalt knowe of myn.*
>
> *'My Lady is unkynd, perde,'*
> *Alack! why is she so?*
> *'She loveth an other better than me;*
> *And yet she will say no.'*

IV.ii.81. *five wits.* The *wits* or powers of the mind were numbered five, by analogy with the five senses, and were common wit, imagination, fantasy, estimation, and memory.

IV.ii.94. *God buy you.* The modern 'goodbye' is from 'God be with you.' Some variants are the following: 'God bu'y you,' 'God buy ye,' 'God buy to ye,' and 'God bu'y.'

IV.ii.94. *Marry.* It is unlikely that the exclamation retains any of its original meaning of 'the Virgin Mary,' even it its use here with *amen*.

IV.ii.112–114. *I am gone, sir . . . again.* The lines are possibly a fragment from a lost song. E. W. Naylor in *Shakespeare and Music* (1896), p. 190, assigns music to them.

IV.ii.116–122. *Like to the old Vice . . . 'Pare thy nails, dad'.* The Vice was the comic character in the morality plays and stood either for a particular vice or for sin in general. He would sometimes *sustain* the *need* of the hero by helping him in his contest with the devil. The Vice traditionally carried a *dagger of lath* with which he would offer to pare Satan's nails. Shakespeare's fools are in a number of respects the decendants of the Vice.

IV.ii.123. *Adieu, goodman divel.* An insulting and even dangerous way to take leave of the devil, since *goodman* was the form of address for a person below the rank of gentleman.

IV.iii.24. *the chantry by.* A chantry is properly a chapel devoted to the celebration of masses for the dead and supported by an endowment for that purpose. The term is used here in the more general sense of 'small church.'

IV.iii.26. *Plight me . . . your faith.* 'Pledge me full promise of your fidelity [in the betrothal ceremony at church].' The actual marriage ceremony was frequently preceded by a separate betrothal ceremony which was regarded very seriously both by the betrothed and by the church. The marriage ceremony of the Anglican Church consists of a betrothal followed by a marriage.

V.i.5. *This is to give a dog.* The following entry, for March 26, 1603, is in John Manningham's Diary, ed. John Bruce (Camden Society, 1868), pp. 148–9: 'Mr. Francis Curle told me howe one Dr. Bullein, the Queenes kinsman, had a dog which he doted one, soe much that the Queene understanding of it requested he would graunt hir one desyre, and he should have what soever he would aske. Shee demaunded his dogge; he gave it, and "Nowe, Madame," quoth he, "you promised to give me my desyre." "I will," quothe she. "Then I pray you give me my dog againe." '

V.i.9. *doest.* The form is correct, but unusual in the First Folio which generally prints *dost*.

V.i.18–20. *So that conclusions . . . for my foes.* The best of many explications of the passage is by J. Dover Wilson and Hardin Craig. The mock logic hinges on the fact that a kiss is made of four lips which are *negatives*. The lips are joined by two mouths which are the *two affirmatives*. The clown says that if conclusions are like this, then the conclusion that he is not an ass has only half the value of the conclusion that he is one. In addition to the obvious juggling of the words *negatives* and *affirmatives* in the parody of logic, there is a play on *ass* in the sense of 'professional clown' and *ass* in the ordinary sense of 'fool.'

V.i.32. *Primo, secundo, tertio.* The term appears to come either from a game of dice (see l. 37) or from an undefined child's game, the philosophers' table.

V.i.33. *The third pays for all.* Proverbial. See *The Oxford Dictionary of English Proverbs* (1948), p. 651. The meaning is probably: 'The third time wins all.' Compare 'The third time never fails,' 'The third time is a charm,' and 'The third time's lucky.'

V.i.34. *St. Bennet.* Any church dedicated to St. Benedict (480–543). There was a St. Bennet Hithe, Paul's Wharf, near the Globe theater. The church was burned in the fire of London in 1666.

V.i.65. *dear.* In Shakespearean English the word is frequently no more than an intensifying adjective with the meaning of 'extreme,' 'serious,' or 'grievous.'

V.i.84, 85. *And grew . . . would wink.* And became as strange as someone who had not seen me for twenty years in the time it would take one to wink.

V.i.90. *three months.* The fact that this is impossible by any time scheme that can be devised for the play is unimportant.

V.i.111. *My soul . . . have breath'd.* Irregular grammar is common in Shakespearean English when the object precedes the verb.

V.i.115. *th' Egyptian thief.* In the story of 'Theagenes and Cariclia' from the *Ethiopica* of the Greek Hellodorus, possibly of the 3d century A.D. There was an English version by Thomas Underdowne, *An Æthiopian Historie*, published in 1569 (ed. C. Whibley, *The Tudor Translations*, 1895). Thyamis, an Egyptian robber-chief in danger of capture, intends to kill his beautiful prisoner, Cariclia, with whom he is in love. In the darkness of the cave he slays another woman by mistake. 'And if the barbarous people be once in despaire of their owne safetie, they have a custome to kill all those by whome they set much, and whose companie they desire after death, or els would keepe them from the violence and wrong of their enemies.' (Whibley, p. 38.)

V.i.142. *husband.* The word is used here and below in the sense that the betrothal ceremony in the chantry was the legal equivalent of marriage. There were two sorts of betrothal ceremonies, *sponsalia per verba de futuro*, and *sponsalia per verba de praesenti*. Under the betrothal de praesenti, the more binding of the two, the couple pledged themselves as man and wife from the moment of the betrothal—the agreement is of the present. That a betrothal de praesenti has taken place is indicated by the use of the word *husband*. The couple are husband and wife although they will not actually be married in the chruch until the marriage ceremony takes place at a later date. Edward R. Hardy, Jr., has observed to the editor that the priest in his speech, ll. 158–163, seems to echo the proclamation of the marriage from the Book of Common Prayer with the phrases 'joinder of your hands' and 'interchangement of your rings.' Finally, Sebastian says *betroth'd* in l. 266; and Olivia in ll. 317–18 clearly speaks of the double marriage ceremony to be performed at her house in the future. For an account of the two kinds of betrothals and the canon law on each, see George E. Howard's *A History of Matrimonial Institutions* (3 vols. Chicago and London, 1904), *1*, 313–20, 337–63.

V.i.169. *trip.* The sense is 'you will trip yourself up.' The term is perhaps from wrestling.

V.i.183. *incardinate.* It seems unlikely that the word is a pointless verbal blunder from Sir Andrew. If there is a quibble on *incardinate*, 'to institute to a cardinalship' and 'devil incarnate,' the line is an example of the anti-Roman Catholic jest, common in the English drama of the period.

V.i.199. *passy measures pavin.* The *panyn* of the Folio appears to be a misprint for *pavin*. The clown has just said that the surgeon is drunk and has been since 'eight i' th' morning.' Sir Toby's phrase 'a passy measures pavin' is a reference to dancing, perhaps suggested by the word *eight* from the clown. 'Passy measures' is Sir Toby's variant on 'passemeasure' from the Italian *passemezzo*, a slow dance. The tune consists of 'strains' which contain an even number of bars, most commonly eight. The same structure holds for the 'pavin' or, as it is more commonly spelled, 'pavan.' The pavan is a slow dance of Italian or Spanish origin. The name is perhaps from the Spanish *pavo*, 'peacock.' Thus, when the clown tells Sir Toby that the surgeon was drunk at 'eight i' th' morning,' Sir Toby answers: 'Then he's a rogue, and he's an eight-bar double-slow dance.' I.e. he's a laggard and should hurry up.

V.i.201. *havoc.* Originally the signal to an army for the seizure of spoil and for pillage.

V.i.217. *A natural perspective, that is and is not.* A *perspective* or 'prospective' was a glass made so as to produce an optical illusion or distortion from nature. By 'a natural perspective' the Duke means that here nature has produced the illusion and not art. The phrase 'that is and is not' means that although the two people are real, they are not really one and the same person as the various characters in the play have supposed.

V.i.241. *as the rest goes even.* As the other facts (which you have just told me) make you my sister. Compare the phrase 'comes out even,' i.e. is consistent, logical, right.

V.i.251. *lets.* 'Let,' 'to allow,' is from Old English *lætan;* 'let,' 'to hinder,' is from Old English *lettan.* The second survives in the phrase 'without let or hindrance.'

V.i.263. *But nature to her bias drew in that.* But nature drew into natural course or line of inclination (*bias*), and corrected, that mistake which you made of falling in love with a woman. The figure, a common one in Shakespeare, is from bowling; the balls were loaded so that they rolled in a curved line or 'bias.'

V.i.274. *orbed continent.* Probably 'the sun.' 'As the sun keeps the fire that

severs day from night.' But 'orbed continent' may also mean the curved path or sphere which, under the Ptolomaic system, is the course of the sun around the earth, the center of the universe. The meaning would then be: 'As the sphere of the sun keeps in place the fire of the sun that severs day from night.'

V.i.288. *he holds Belzebub at the stave's end.* Belzebub or Beelzebub is loosely a synonym for Satan. The figure is from the game of dueling with staves or heavy sticks.

V.i.309, 310. *I leave . . . my injury.* I leave my duty of respect to you somewhat out of mind and instead speak from the consciousness of my injury.

V.i.394–413. *When that I was . . . To please you every day.* Critical opinion of the Clown's song has varied from Warburton's 'This wretched stuff . . .' to Knight's 'We hold this song to be the most philosophical Clown's song upon record . . . It is the history of a life . . .' For a survey of the pronouncements, see Furness, *A New Variorum*, pp. 313–14. No earlier version of the song is known.

V.i.394. *and a.* Furness states that the redundant *and* is common in ballads; J. Dover Wilson, that it is an insertion by the playhouse musician; Kittredge, that *and* carried a note of music.

V.i.392–402. *But when I came to man's estate . . . With tosspots still had drunken heads.* It is impossible, as well as unnecessary, to extract precise meaning from these lines. However, it can be argued that the following is the general meaning. The second stanza, beginning 'But when I came to man's estate,' says that his foolishness, which was of no account while he was 'a little tiny boy,' caused men to shut their gates against him, because they shut their gates against fools and knaves. The third stanza, beginning 'But when I came, alas, to wive,' says that after he got married he did not prosper because he was still a swaggerer. The fourth stanza, beginning 'But when I came unto my beds,' might mean: 'When I went to bed, like other tosspots, I kept having drunken heads.' But this interpretation necessitates the insertion of 'I' before 'had drunken heads,' and a strain on the use of the plural 'heads.' It is necessary to accept the song for what it is; like much popular poetry, it lacks precise meaning, but it is roughly intelligible and a perfectly appropriate ending for the comedy.

V.i.414. *And we'll strive to please you every day.* A conventional promise from the acting company to the audience, which might consist largely of regular patrons.

The Tragedy of Troilus and Cressida

Edited by
JACKSON J. CAMPBELL

Dramatis Personae

PRIAM, *King of Troy*

HECTOR
TROILUS
PARIS } *his Sons*
DEIPHOBUS
HELENUS

AENEAS } *Trojan Commanders*
ANTENOR

CALCHAS, *a Trojan Priest, taking part
  with the Greeks*

PANDARUS, *Uncle to Cressida*

AGAMEMNON, *the Grecian General*

MENELAUS, *his Brother*

ACHILLES
AJAX
ULYSSES } *Grecian Commanders*
NESTOR
DIOMEDES
PATROCLUS

THERSITES, *a deformed and scurrilous Grecian*

ALEXANDER, *Servant to Cressida*

SERVANT TO TROILUS, SERVANT TO PARIS,
  SERVANT TO DIOMEDES

HELEN, *Wife to Menelaus*

ANDROMACHE, *Wife to Hector*

CASSANDRA, *Daughter to Priam; a Prophetess*

CRESSIDA, *Daughter to Calchas*

TROJAN AND GREEK SOLDIERS,
  AND ATTENDANTS

The Tragedy of
Troilus and Cressida

INTRODUCTION

TEXT AND DATE

There are two good texts of *Troilus and Cressida*, a Quarto and the Folio, either of which could justifiably be used as the basis for a modern edition. Unusual circumstances attended the publication of each text, but, after certain shufflings on the part of the printers, in each case a text was issued which has a certain degree of authority.

The history of the Quarto starts with an entry in the Stationers' Register for February 7, 1603: 'Master Roberts, Entered for his copie in full Court holden this day to print when he hath gotten sufficient aucthority for yt, The booke of Troilus and Cresseda, as yt is acted by my lord Chamberlens Men.' This license probably refers to Shakespeare's play, but it was evidently not acted upon, for no *Troilus and Cressida* came out at this time. Six years later, however, another entry was made in the Stationers' Register licensing the publishers Bonian and Walley to print a play called *The History of Troylus and Cressida*, which had been acted by Shakespeare's company. Soon after this entry of January 1609, possibly in the spring, the Quarto appeared.

There are two variant states of this 1609 Quarto. The first has a title page which reads: 'THE / Historie of Troylus / and Cresseida./ As it was acted by the Kings Maiesties / servants at the Globe. / Written by William Shakespeare. / [Design] / LONDON / Imprinted by G. Eld for R. Bonian and H. Walley, and / are to be sold at the spred Eagle in Paules / Church-yeard, over against the / great North doore. / 1609.' While the printing of this issue was going forward, for some unknown reason the printer stopped printing, canceled the title page, reset the type of the upper half of it, and added a prefatory epistle before the text.[1] Some of the extant copies of Q have the earlier title page, and some the later,[2] but it is clear that for the body of the text all the copies are from one single edition and were printed from the same forms. The new title page and the Epistle raise several problems which have never been completely solved, in that they imply that the play had not been acted, despite the statements of the first title page and the Stationers' Register that it had. This claim that the play had never been 'clapper-claw'd with the palms of the vulgar' may or may not be true, since the Epistle is patently an advertising blurb designed to increase sales among the would-be wits. In any case, it can safely be said that the play was not particularly popular; no performance of it is recorded elsewhere, and it was not printed again until the publication of the Folio in 1623.

In the First Folio *Troilus and Cressida* was originally scheduled to follow *Romeo and Juliet* in the section of the book containing the tragedies. Three pages of type had already been set up when the printer stopped work, probably because of difficulties with the copyright, and the play was eventually printed between the histories and the tragedies, after *Henry VIII* and before *Coriolanus*. In this new position there was added a prologue which does not appear in Q.

Several theories have been put forward to explain these curious changes in F, as there have been to explain the changes in Q, but in both cases the explanations offered often do not get far out of the realm of theory and into the area of fact. A recent series of articles,[3] however, has established with clear proof the relationship between the text of the Folio and the text of the Quarto. The first three pages in F were set up in type directly from a copy of Q. After the resumption of printing, with *Troilus* in its new location, the 'copy' used was a copy of Q which had been collated with an independently authoritative manuscript, whether a promptbook or foul papers. A good many changes were made in the Q text during the collation, including some which correct printer's errors and some which introduce completely new readings. F prefaces the play with a prologue which does not exist in Q, and in addition augments the text with some forty-odd new lines scattered throughout the play, most of which are unmistakably genuine. Even the prologue, poor as it is as poetry, cannot be proved to be by another hand. Thus, in a sense, F is a derivative text, but at the same time it is often more authoritative than the text it was derived from. For this reason, the present edition follows the Folio text as closely as possible. If Q had been used, it would have been necessary to make a conflate text by adding lines from F; and certainly if F's changes have any authority at all, either from the author or the playhouse, it cannot be said that Q is the sole substantive text. When it has been advisable to use the Q reading for individual words, F's reading is given in the glosses: for example, I.l.21 leavening F *leau'ing*. When neither the F nor Q reading is satisfactory, the text has been emended. This has occurred only when it was absolutely necessary, and the emendations are printed in square brackets and explained in the notes. Any added stage directions which do not appear in F are also printed in square brackets. Punctuation has been kept as close as practicable to that of F and Q, but in many cases it has been changed to conform with modern practice. In accordance with the general policy of this series, spellings which indicate Renaissance pronunciation have been retained, although the Folio's inconsistencies in spelling of words like *nere, ne're, ene, e'ne*, when they indicate nothing about pronunciation, have been reduced to consistency.

---

1 This Epistle is printed on page 325 of this edition.

2 By some sort of slip on the part of the binder, the Yale Elizabethan Club copy contains both title pages and the Epistle.

3 Peter Alexander, "*Troilus and Cressida*, 1609," *The Library*, 4th ser., *9* (1928), 265-86; Philip Williams, "Shakespeare's *Troilus and Cressida*: The Relationship of the Quarto and the Folio," *Studies in Bibliography*, *3* (University of Virginia, 1950), 131-43; Alice Walker, "The Textual Problem of *Troilus and Cressida*," *Modern Language Review*, *45* (1950), 459-64; W. W. Greg, "The Printing of Shakespeare's *Troilus and Cressida* in the First Folio," *Papers of the Bibliographical Society of America*, *45* (1951), 273-82; Alice Walker, *Textual Problems of the First Folio* (Cambridge, England, 1953).

Dating the composition of the play with any exactitude is virtually impossible. If we take the 1603 entry in the Stationers' Register to refer to Shakespeare's play, as most scholars are willing to do, we at least have a *terminus ad quem* for its composition. It is not included in Francis Meres' list of Shakespeare's plays in *Palladis Tamia* in 1598,[4] so we can take that date as the earlier limit. To narrow the date down further, a great many ingenious arguments have been offered of varying credibility, most of them depending on alleged topical allusions in the play. This play has long been associated with the so-called War of the Theaters, and although many scholars do not accept the identification of certain characters in this play with certain of Shakespeare's contemporaries, there remains the suspicion that this play has some connection with Ben Johnson's *Poetaster*, which was produced in 1601. The amount of connection is in dispute, and many of the topical allusions are doubtful. Even though such vagueness is unsatisfactory, it is probably unwise to date the play more precisely than 'shortly before 1603.'

SOURCES OF THE PLAY

Troilus and Cressida is one of the most difficult of Shakespeare's plays to deal with in regard to its sources. We know in general where he could have gotten his Troy material, but we lack conclusive proofs to demonstrate the immediate origin of the play.

This play is, of course, a composite work, combining two threads of action, the Troilus-Cressida love story and the military plot involving the larger struggle between the Greeks and the Trojans. The Troilus portion is easier to deal with, since its main source lies in Chaucer's great poem, *Troilus and Criseyde*. The story had had a complicated earlier history, and in spite of claims that it was originally a classical story, it was really the invention of medieval writers. Although several of the personages in the story appear in Homer's *Iliad*, they are there little more than names, and the love narrative did not appear in any recognizable form until it was written in the *Roman de Troie* by Benoit de Sainte-Maure, a French poet of the 12th century. It was copied with few changes into the *Historia Trojana*, a 13th-century Latin prose work by Guido delle Colonne. The story was extracted from the mass of Trojan history in which it was embedded by Boccaccio, whose *Filostrato* expands the story and treats it as a center of focus for an artistic unity. Chaucer, in writing his version, followed Boccaccio's poem, but expanded it and developed the characterizations until it became what is probably the only unquestioned masterpiece dealing with this story.

A comparison of Shakespeare's play with Chaucer's poem reveals many points in which Shakespeare was following the plot outline of Chaucer, but it at the same time makes us conscious of a wide difference in tone and attitude toward the various characters. Shakespeare has sometimes been accused of debasing Chaucer's characters, as he has been accused of debasing the Homeric characters in the military plot. The characters had been considerably degraded, however, before they came to Shakespeare. The edition of Chaucer's works printed by Thynne in 1532 included a poem by the 15th-century Scots poet, Robert Henryson, entitled *The Testament of Cressid*. This poem continues the

Cressida story and reduces her to a beggar and a leper before her death. Throughout the 16th century Henryson's poem was thought to be part of Chaucer's work, in spite of the fact that it is written in the lowland dialect of Scotland, and the just punishment of the heroine evidently appealed to many readers. There are a very great number of treatments of the story during the 16th century, ranging from a Latin play by Nicholas Grimald, through lyrics, songs, and broadside ballads, to mere chance references in similes and metaphors. By Shakespeare's time the story had become common property of the people, known undoubtedly to many who had never read Chaucer or Henryson. Pandarus was taken as the type for the pimp or go-between, and such was his fame that before the middle of the century *pander* had become a common noun. Cressida was so well established in the popular mind as a loose, unfaithful woman that the phrase 'a woman of Cressid's kind,' meaning a whore, had become a cliché.[5] Thus Shakespeare's characterizations of these people represent not so much his reinterpretation of the story as his acceptance of the tradition as it came down to him.

The same thing is true of his treatment of the personages in the military plot. Throughout the Middle Ages and on into the Renaissance, the Troy story was almost always told with sympathy for the Trojans, and several Western nations fancifully traced their origins to some colonizing Trojan hero who wandered as a displaced person after the war. Homer in the original was little known in England until the 16th century, and the derogatory medieval conception of Greek characters like Achilles, Ajax, and Agamemnon continued even after some Englishmen had begun reading Homer. The two earlier authorities whom Shakespeare seems to have used were Lydgate's *Troy Book* and Caxton's *Recuyell of the Historyes of Troye*. Lydgate's poem is a compendium of virtually all the stories connected with Troy, drawn principally from Guido delle Colonne's *Historia Trojana*. Caxton's *Recuyell* is a translation of *Le Recueil de Troyennes Ystoires* by a French prose writer, Raoul le Fevre. Details of plot incident from Shakespeare's play have been traced to each of these sources,[6] but it must be admitted that few really convincing verbal parallels have been cited. Any material Shakespeare got from them had been pretty thoroughly assimilated by the time it reissued from his pen, for his dependence on them is not nearly so obvious as was his use of his sources for the English history plays or the Gloucester plot of *Lear*.

Shakespeare probably made use also of George Chapman's famous translation of Homer, although at the time this play appears to have been written only eight books of the translation had been printed. Books I, II, VII through XI, and XVIII, which were issued in 1598, do include a brief characterization of Thersites, who is completely missing in Caxton and Lydgate.[7] Again in this case, however, it must be stated that no truly inescapable cases of verbal parallelism have been discovered, and we can by no means ignore the possibility that Shakespeare might have read his Homer, or parts of it, in a Latin translation or even in the Greek.

---

4 Leslie Hotson's contention in his *Shakespeare's Sonnets Dated* (London, 1949) that this play is the puzzling *Loves Labours Wonne* of Meres' list is not at all convincing.

5 The change in conception of the Troilus story during the 16th century is treated in full by Hyder Rollins, 'The Troilus-Cressida Story from Chaucer to Shakespeare,' *PMLA, 32* (1917), 383-429. Some few facts are added to this body of information by W. B. D. Henderson, 'Shakespeare's *Troilus and Cressida* Yet Deeper in its Tradition,' *The Parrott Presentation Volume* (Princeton, 1935), pp. 127-56.

6 One or two minor items have been traced to Robert Greene's *Euphues His Censure to Philautus*, published in 1587.

7 Recently Robert Presson has argued that Shakespeare followed Chapman in many basic details, and followed Lydgate very little.

As always in considering Shakespeare's sources, we have the picture of his using diverse materials, in this case Chaucer, Lydgate, Caxton, Homer, and probably a certain amount of popular, bookless tradition; but his combination of those materials into a unified, two-plot play, written at least in part in language which compares favorably with his greatest, is a unique achievement. There have been serious critical doubts about his complete success in the over-all structure and tone of the play, but few critics have denied that it contains many magnificently conceived scenes and speeches.

Before leaving the subject, some mention should be made of the theory that there was an earlier Troilus play which Shakespeare used as his source. As is the case with *Hamlet*, there is not now in existence any play which Shakespeare might have revised to become the play we have, but many scholars have long suspected that there was once such a play. We have record of several 16th-century plays on the Troy theme, two of which are mentioned in Henslowe's diary at the end of the century. *Troy* was performed in 1596, and a play was being written by Dekker and Chettle on the subject in 1599. Since these have not survived,[8] we can never be sure just how much influence they had on Shakespeare's play. He probably drew little from them directly, since they belonged to a rival company, but considering the obvious popularity of this material there is the bare possibility that still other Troy plays were available to him. A play by Thomas Heywood called *The Iron Age* treats most of the events covered by Shakespeare and shows some striking similarities to *Troilus;* but it was very probably written after Shakespeare's play, unless, as has been conjectured, the *Troy* mentioned by Henslowe is an earlier version of *Iron Age.*[9] Many readers have criticized the treatment Shakespeare gives to the conclusion of his play, and some have surmised that in his revision of some earlier play, he lost interest for some reason toward the end and gave the battle scenes in the last act very few of his master touches. Although this may be true, it is a mistake to argue that the scenes are not Shakespeare's simply because no great poetry appears. A large-scale battle scene such as that which runs from V.4 to V.9 was a rapid paced spectacle of movement and action, and the sketchy verbal scenario supplied for it is quite adequate to allow stirring production effects. The theory of Shakespeare's revision of any earlier play, which in turn, presumably, drew from Chaucer, Lydgate, and Caxton, must remain merely a plausible possibility until such a play is discovered.

A NEVER WRITER, TO AN EVER READER. NEWS.

Eternal reader, you have here a new play, never stal'd with the Stage, never clapped-claw'd with the palms of the vulgar, and yet passing full of the palm comical, for it is a birth of your brain that never undertook anything comical vainly. And were but the vain names of comedies changed for the titles of commodities, or of plays for pleas, you should see all those grand censors, that now style them such vanities, flock to them for the main grace of their gravities, especially this author's comedies, that are so fram'd to the life that they serve for the most common commentaries of all the actions of our lives, showing such a dexterity and power of wit that the most displeased with plays are pleas'd with his comedies. And all such dull and heavy-witted worldlings as were never capable of the wit of a comedy, coming by report of them to his representations, have found that wit there that they never found in themselves and have parted better witted than they came, feeling an edge of wit set upon them more than ever they dreamed they had brain to grind it on. So much and such savored salt of wit is in his comedies that they seem, for their height of pleasure, to be born in that sea that brought forth Venus. Amongst all there is none more witty than this; and had I time I would comment upon it, though I know it needs not, for so much as will make you think your testern well bestowed, but for so much worth even poor I know to be stuff'd in it. It deserves such a labour as well as the best comedy in Terence or Plautus. And believe this, that when he is gone and his comedies out of sale, you will scramble for them and set up a new English Inquisition. Take this for a warning, and at the peril of your pleasure's loss and judgment's, refuse not nor like this the less for not being sullied with the smoky breath of the multitude, but thank fortune for the scape it hath made amongst you, since by the grand possessors' wills I believe you should have pray'd for them rather than been pray'd. And so I leave all such to be pray'd for, for the state of their wits' healths, that will not praise it. Vale.[10]

8 A 'plot' or sketch of entrances and exits for some Troilus play has survived. It is generally thought that it belongs to the lost play of Dekker and Chettle.

9 This play and the other Elizabethan works dealing with the Troy story are studied by J. S. P. Tatlock, 'The Siege of Troy in Elizabethan Literature, Especially in Shakespeare and Heywood,' *PMLA, 30* (1915), 673-770.

10 This epistle appeared in the second issue of the Quarto of *Troilus and Cressida.*

THE PROLOGUE

In Troy there lies the scene. From isles of Greece
The princes orgillous, their high blood chaf'd,
Have to the port of Athens sent their ships
Fraught with the ministers and instruments
Of cruel war. Sixty-and-nine that wore   5
Their crownets regal, from th' Athenian bay
Put forth toward Phrygia and their vow is made
To ransack Troy, within whose strong immures
The ravish'd Helen, Menelaus' queen,
With wanton Paris sleeps, and that's the quarrel.   10
To Tenedos they come,
And the deep-drawing [barks] do there disgorge
Their warlike fraughtage. Now on Dardan plains
The fresh and yet unbruised Greeks do pitch
Their brave pavilions. Priam's six-gated city,   15
Dardan and Timbria, Helias, Chetas, Troien,
And Antenonidus, with massy staples
And corresponsive and fulfilling bolts
[Sperr] up the sons of Troy.
Now expectations, tickling skittish spirits,   20
On one and other side, Troyan and Greek,
Sets all on hazard. And hither am I come,
A prologue arm'd, but not in confidence
Of author's pen, or actor's voice, but suited
In like conditions as our argument,   25
To tell you, fair beholders, that our play
Leaps ore the vaunt and firstlings of those broils,
Beginning in the middle, starting thence away
To what may be digested in a play.
Like, or find fault; do as your pleasures are: 30
Now good or bad, 'tis but the chance of war.

ACT FIRST ❧ SCENE FIRST

Enter Pandarus and Troilus.

Troilus. Call here my varlet; I'll unarm again.
Why should I war without the walls of Troy
That find such cruel battle here within?
Each Troyan that is master of his heart,
Let him to field; Troilus, alas, hath none.   5
  Pandarus. Will this gear nere be mended?
  Troilus. The Greeks are strong, and skillful to their strength,
Fierce to their skill, and to their fierceness valiant;
But I am weaker than a woman's tear,
Tamer than sleep, fonder than ignorance,   10
Less valiant than the virgin in the night,
And skilless as unpractic'd infancy.
  Pandarus. Well, I have told you enough of this.
For my part, I'll not meddle nor make no farther.

He that will have a cake out of the wheat must needs tarry   15
the grinding.
  Troilus. Have I not tarried?
  Pandarus. Ay, the grinding; but you must tarry the bolting.
  Troilus. Have I not tarried?
  Pandarus. Ay, the bolting; but you must tarry the   20
[leavening].
  Troilus. Still have I tarried.
  Pandarus. Ay, to the leavening; but here's yet in the word
hereafter: the kneading, the making of the cake, the heating of
the oven, and the baking. Nay, you must stay the cooling,   25
too, or you may chance to burn your lips.
  Troilus. Patience herself, what goddess ere she be,
Doth lesser blench at sufferance than I do.
At Priam's royal table do I sit,
And when fair Cressid comes into my thoughts—   30
So, traitor, then she comes, when she is thence.
  Pandarus. Well, she look'd yesternight fairer than ever I
saw her look, or any woman else.
  Troilus. I was about to tell thee: when my heart,
As wedged with a sigh, would rive in twain   35
Lest Hector or my father should perceive me,
I have (as when the sun doth light ascorn)
Buried this sign in wrinkle of a smile;
But sorrow, that is couch'd in seeming gladness,
Is like that mirth fate turns to sudden sadness.   40
  Pandarus. And her hair were not somewhat darker than Helen's
—well, go to—there were no more comparison between the women.
But for my part, she is my kinswoman; I would not, as they term it,
praise her, but I would somebody had heard her talk yesterday as I
did. I will not dispraise your sister Cassandra's wit, but—   45
  Troilus. O Pandarus! I tell thee Pandarus—
When I do tell thee, 'There my hopes lie drown'd,'
Reply not in how many fadoms deep
They lie indrench'd. I tell thee, 'I am mad
In Cressid's love.' Thou answer'st, 'She is fair,'   50
Pour'st in the open ulcer of my heart
Her eyes, her hair, her cheek, her gait, her voice;
Handlest in thy discourse, O, that her hand,
In whose comparison all whites are ink,
Writing their own reproach, to whose soft seizure   55
The cygnet's down is harsh, and spirit of sense
Hard as the palm of ploughman. This thou tell'st me,
As true thou tell'st me, when I say I love her.
But saying thus, instead of oil and balm
Thou lay'st in every gash that love hath given me   60
The knife that made it.
  Pandarus. I speak no more than truth.
  Troilus. Thou dost not speak so much.
  Pandarus. Faith, I'll not meddle in't. Let her be as she is.
If she be fair, 'tis the better for her; and she be not, she   65
has the mends in her own hands.
  Troilus. Good Pandarus! How now, Pandarus?
  Pandarus. I have had my labor for my travel, ill thought on
of her and ill thought on of you; gone between and between,
but small thanks for my labor.   70

---

2 orgillous: *orgulous, proud*   **8 immures:** *walls*   **12 barks:** *F barke* (F refers throughout
to the First Folio of 1623.)   **13 Dardan:** *the plains around Troy*   **15 brave:** *splendid*   **17 Antenonidus;** *Cf. n.*   **18 fulfilling:** *which fill their sockets completely*   **19
Sperr up:** *pen up, enclose; F Stirre; Cf. n.*   **22 hazard:** *chance*   **23-5 prologue arm'd
... argument;** *Cf. n.*   **25 argument:** *plot, story*   **27 ore:** *o'er, over* **vaunt:** *van, beginning*   **1 varlet:** *servant*   **6 gear:** *matter, affair* **nere:** *ne'er, never*   **7 to:** *in addition
to*   **10 fonder:** *more foolish*

20 bolting: *sifting*   **21 leavening:** *F leau'ing*   **23, 24 here's ... hereafter;** *Cf. n.*   **28
blench:** *flinch*   **31 So ... thence;** *Cf. n.*   **37 ascorn:** *in mockery.*   **41 And:** *and if*
Cf. n.   **42 go to:** *never mind* **were:** *would be*   **44 her:** *F it*   **48 fadoms:** *fathoms*   **55 seizure:** *grasp*   **56 spirit of sense;** *Cf. n.*   **66 mends:** *remedy*   **68 travel:**
travail, pains   **69 thought on of:** *thought of by*

Troilus. What, art thou angry, Pandarus? What, with me?

Pandarus. Because she's kin to me, therefore she's not so fair as Helen. And she were not kin to me, she would be as fair on Friday as Helen is on Sunday. But what care I? I care not and she were a black-a-moor; 'tis all one to me.   75

Troilus. Say I she is not fair?

Pandarus. I do not care whether you do or no. She's a fool to stay behind her father. Let her to the Greeks, and so I'll tell her the next time I see her. For my part, I'll meddle nor make no more i' th' matter.   80

Troilus. Pandarus?

Pandarus. Not I.

Troilus. Sweet Pandarus.

Pandarus. Pray you, speak no more to me. I will leave all as I found it, and there an end.   *Exit Pandarus.*   85

Sound alarum.

Troilus. Peace, you ungracious clamors! Peace, rude sounds!
Fools on both sides! Helen must needs be fair,
When with your blood you daily paint her thus.
I cannot fight upon this argument;
It is too starv'd a subject for my sword.   90
But Pandarus—O gods! how do you plague me!
I cannot come to Cressid but by Pandar,
And he's as tetchy to be woo'd to woo
As she is stubborn-chaste against all suit.
Tell me, Apollo, for thy Daphne's love,   95
What Cressid is, what Pandar, and what we.
Her bed is India; there she lies, a pearl;
Between our Ilium and where she resides
Let it be call'd the wild and wand'ring flood,
Ourself the merchant, and this sailing Pandar   100
Our doubtful hope, our convoy and our bark.

Alarum. Enter Aeneas.

Aeneas. How now, Prince Troilus? Wherefore not afield?

Troilus. Because not there. This woman's answer sorts,
For womanish it is to be from thence.
What news, Aeneas, from the field today?   105

Aeneas. That Paris is returned home, and hurt.

Troilus. By whom, Aeneas?

Aeneas.   Troilus, by menelaus.

Troilus. Let Paris bleed! 'Tis but a scar to scorn.
Paris is gor'd with Menelaus' horn.   *Alarum.*   110

Aeneas. Hark, what good sport is out of town today!

Troilus. Better at home, if 'would I might' were 'may.'
But to the sport abroad, are you bound thither?

Aeneas. In all swift haste.

Troilus.   Come, go we then togither.   115
Exeunt.

❧ SCENE SECOND ❧

Enter Cressida and her Man.

Cressida. Who were those went by?

Man.   Queen Hecuba and Helen.

Cressida. And whether go they?

Man.   Up to the eastern tower,
Whose height commands as subject all the vale,   5
To see the battle. Hector, whose patience
Is as a virtue fix'd, today was mov'd.
He chides Andromache and strooke his armorer,
And, like as there were husbandry in war,
Before the sun rose he was harness'd light   10
And to the field goes he, where every flower
Did as a prophet weep what it foresaw
In Hector's wrath.

Cressida.   What was his cause of anger?

Man. The noise goes; this: there is among the Greeks   15
A lord of Troyan blood, nephew to Hector;
They call him Ajax.

Cressida.   Good, and what of him?

Man. They say he is a very man *per se*
And stands alone.   20

Cressida. So do all men, unless they are drunk, sick, or have no legs.

Man. This man, lady, hath robb'd many beasts of their particular additions. He is as valiant as the lion, churlish as the bear, slow as the elephant; a man into whom nature hath so 25 crowded humors that his valor is crush'd into folly, his folly sauced with discretion. There is no man hath a virtue that he hath not a glimpse of, nor any man an attaint but he carries some stain of it. He is melancholy without cause and merry against the hair. He hath the joints of everything, but every- 30 thing so out of joint that he is a gouty Briareus, many hands and no use; or pur-blinded Argus, all eyes and no sight.

Cressida. But how should this man, that makes me smile, make Hector angry?

Man. They say he yesterday cop'd Hector in the battle   35 and stroke him down, the disdain and shame whereof hath ever since kept Hector fasting and waking.

Enter Pandarus.

Cressida. Who comes here?

Man. Madam, your uncle Pandarus.

Cressida. Hector's a gallant man.   40

Man. As may be in the world, lady.

Pandarus. What's that? What's that?

Cressida. Good morrow, uncle Pandarus.

Pandarus. Good morrow, cousin Cressid. What do you talk of? Good morrow, Alexander. How do you, cousin?   45
When were you at Ilium?

Cressida. This morning, uncle.

Pandarus. What were you talking of when I came?
Was Hector arm'd and gone ere you came to Ilium?
Helen was not up, was she?   50

---

1 **those went:** *those who went*   3 **whether:** *whiter*   8 **stroke:** *struck*   9 **like as:** *as if*   **husbandry:** *thrift, good management*   10 **harness'd:** *girded with armor* **noise:** *rumor*   16 **nephew;** *Cf. n.*   19 **per se:** *par excellence, superlative, unique*   24 **additions:** *qualities, characteristics*   26 **humors;** *Cf. n.*   26, 27 **valor . . . discretion;** *Cf. n.*   28 **attaint:** *stain on honor*   30 **against the hair:** *against the grain, out of due season*   31 **Briareus:** *a monster in Greek mythology who had a hundred hands and fifty heads*   32 **Argus:** *a giant in Greek mythology who had a hundred eyes*   33 **should:** *could*   35 **cop'd:** *fought*   36 **stroke:** *struck*   45 **cousin;** *Cf. n.*

Cressida. Hector was gone but Helen was not up.
Pandarus. E'en so. Hector was stirring early.
Cressida. That were we talking of, and of his anger.
Pandarus. Was he angry?
Cressida. So he says here.   55
Pandarus. True, he was so. I know the cause too. He'll lay about him today, I can tell them that. And there's Troilus will not come far behind him; let them take heed of Troilus. I can tell them that too.
Cressida. What, is he angry too?   60
Pandarus. Who, Troilus? Troilus is the better man of the two.
Cressida. O Jupiter! There's no comparison.
Pandarus. What, not between Troilus and Hector? Do you know a man if you see him?   65
Cressida. Ay, if I ever saw him before and knew him.
Pandarus. Well, I say Troilus is Troilus.
Cressida. Then you say as I say, for I am sure he is not Hector.
Pandarus. No, [nor] Hector is not Troilus in some degrees.
Cressida. 'Tis just to each of them. He is himself.
Pandarus. Himself? Alas, poor Troilus, I would he were.
Cressida. So he is.
Pandarus. Condition I had gone barefoot to India.
Cressida. He is not Hector.   75
Pandarus. Himself? No, he's not himself; would a were himself. Well, the gods are above; time must friend or end. Well, Troilus, well. I would my heart were in her body! No, Hector is not a better man than Troilus.
Cressida. Excuse me.   80
Pandarus. He is elder.
Cressida. Pardon me, pardon me.
Pandarus. Th' other's not come to't. You shall tell me another tale when th' other's come to't. Hector shall not have his will this year.   85
Cressida. He shall not need it, if he have his own.
Pandarus. Nor his qualities.
Cressida. No matter.
Pandarus. Nor his beauty.
Cressida. 'Twould not become him; his own's better.   90
Pandarus. You have no judgment, niece. Helen herself swore th' other day that Troilus for a brown favor, for so 'tis, I must confess—not brown neither—
Cressida. No, but brown.
Pandarus. Faith, to say truth, brown and not brown.   95
Cressida. To say the truth, true and not true.
Pandarus. She prais'd his complexion above Paris.
Cressida. Why, Paris hath color enough.
Pandarus. So he has.
Cressida. Then Troilus should have too much, if she   100
prais'd him above; his complexion is higher than his. He having color enough, and the other higher, is too flaming a praise for a good complexion. I had as lieve Helen's golden tongue had commended Troilus for a copper nose.
Pandarus. I swear to you I think Helen loves him   105
better than Paris.
Cressida. Then she's a merry Greek indeed!

Pandarus. Nay, I am sure she does. She came to him th' other day into the compass'd window—and you know he has not past three or four hairs on his chin—   110
Cressida. Indeed, a tapster's arithmetic may soon bring his particulars therein to a total.
Pandarus. Why, he is very young, and yet will he within three pound lift as much as his brother Hector.
Cressida. Is he so young a man, and so old a lifter?   115
Pandarus. But to prove to you that Helen loves him: she came and puts me her white hand to his cloven chin—
Cressida. Juno have mercy! How came it cloven?
Pandarus. Why, you know 'tis dimpled. I think his smiling becomes him better than any man in all Phrygia.   120
Cressida. O, he smiles valiantly.
Pandarus. Does he not?
Cressida. O yes, and 'twere a cloud in autumn.
Pandarus. Why, go to then. But to prove to you that Helen loves Troilus—   125
Cressida. Troilus will stand to the proof, if you'll prove it so.
Pandarus. Troilus? Why, he esteems her no more than I esteem an addle egg.
Cressida. If you love an addle egg as well as you love an idle head, you would eat chickens i' th' shell.   130
Pandarus. I cannot choose but laugh to think how she tickled his chin. Indeed she has a marvel's white hand, I must needs confess.
Cressida. Without the rack.
Pandarus. And she takes upon her to spy a white hair   135
on his chin.
Cressida. Alas, poor chin! Many a wart is richer.
Pandarus. But there was such laughing. Queen Hecuba laugh'd that her eyes ran ore.
Cressida. With millstones.   140
Pandarus. And Cassandra laugh'd.
Cressida. But there was more temperate fire under the pot of her eyes. Did her eyes run ore too?
Pandarus. And Hector laugh'd.
Cressida. At what was all this laughing?   145
Pandarus. Marry, at the white hair that Helen spied on Troilus' chin.
Cressida. And't had been a green hair, I should have laugh'd too.
Pandarus. They laugh'd not so much at the hair, as at   150
his pretty answer.
Cressida. What was his answer?
Pandarus. Quoth she, 'Here's but two and fifty hairs on your chin, and one of them is white.'
Cressida. This is her question.   155
Pandarus. That's true; make no question of that. 'Two and fifty hairs,' quoth he, 'and one white. That white hair is my father, and all the rest are his sons.' 'Jupiter!' quoth she, 'which of these hairs is Paris, my husband?' 'The forked one,' quoth he. 'Pluck't out and give it him.' But there was such *160*
laughing, and Helen so blush'd, and Paris so chaf'd, and all the rest so laugh'd, that it pass'd!

---

70 nor: *F not*   **74 Condition:** *on condition that; Cf. n.*   **76 a:** *he; Cf. n.*   **77 time . . . end;** *Cf. n.*   **78 heart:** *feelings*   **85 will;** *Cf. n.*   **92 brown favor:** *dark complexion*   **100 should:** *would*   **101 higher:** *more vivid, colorful*   **103 lieve:** *lief*   **107 merry Greek:** *a gay, lively person* (slang)

109 compass'd window: *bay window*   **111 tapster's arithmetic:** *Cf. n.*   **115 lifter:** *with a pun on 'shoplifter'*   **117 puts me:** *puts* (me, so-called ethical dative, superfluous in modern usage)   **129 addle egg:** *rotten egg*   **132 marvel's:** *marvelous*   **134 Without the rack:** *without being tortured*   **140 With millstones:** *a proverbial expression, indicating no tears at all*   **146 Marry:** *a mild oath, having reference to the Virgin Mary*   **148 And't:** *if it; I.1.41.; Cf. n.*   **151 pretty:** *clever, apt*   **159 forked:** *'horned,' perhaps with the usual reference to cuckold's horns*   **162 pass'd:** *exceeded all bounds*

Cressida. So let it now, for it has been a great while going by.

Pandarus. Well, cousin, I told you a thing yesterday.   *165*
Think on't.

Cressida. So I do.

Pandarus. I'll be sworn 'tis true. He will weep you an 'twere a man born in April.   *Sound a retreat.*

Cressida. And I'll spring up in his tears an 'twere a   *170*
nettle against May.

Pandarus. Hark! They are coming from the field. Shall we stand up here and see them as they pass toward Ilium? Good niece, do, sweet niece Cressida.

Cressida. At your pleasure.   *175*

Pandarus. Here, here, here's an excellent place. Here we may see most bravely. I'll tell you them all by their names as they pass by, but mark Troilus above the rest.

Enter Aeneas [and passes over the stage].

Cressida. Speak not so loud.

Pandarus. That's Aeneas. Is not that a brave man? He's   *180*
one of the flowers of Troy, I can [tell] you. But mark Troilus; you shall see anon.

Cressida. Who's that?

Enter Antenor [and passes over the stage].

Pandarus. That's Antenor. He has a shrowd wit, I can tell you, and he's a man good enough. He's one o' th' sound-   *185*
est judgment in Troy whosoever, and a proper man of person. When comes Troilus? I'll show you Troilus anon. If he see me, you shall see him nod at me.

Cressida. Will he give you the nod?

Pandarus. You shall see.   *190*

Cressida. If he do, the rich shall have more.

Enter Hector [and passes over the stage].

Pandarus. That's Hector, that, that, look you, that! There's a fellow! Go thy way, Hector. There's a brave man, niece. O brave Hector! Look how he looks. There's a countenance! Is't not a brave man?   *195*

Cressida. O brave man!

Pandarus. Is a not? It does a man's heart good. Look you what hacks are on his helmet; look you yonder. Do you see? Look you there. There's no jesting; [there's] laying on, tak't off who will, as they say. There be hacks!   *200*

Cressida. Be those with swords?

Enter Paris [and passes over the stage].

Pandarus. Swords, anything, he cares not. And the divel come to him, it's all one. By God's lid, it does one's heart good. Yonder comes Paris, yonder comes Paris! Look ye yon- der, niece. Is't not a gallant man too, is't not? Why, this is   *205*
brave now. Who said he came hurt home today? He's not hurt. Why, this will do Helen's heart good now, ha? Would I could see Troilus now. You shall [see] Troilus anon.

Cressida. Who's that?

Enter Hellenus [and passes over the stage.]

Pandarus. That's Hellenus. I marvel where Troilus is. That's Hellenus. I think he went not forth today. That's Hellenus.

Cressida. Can Hellenus fight, uncle?

Pandarus. Hellenus? No. Yes, he'll fight indifferent well. I marvel where Troilus is. Hark, do you not hear the people cry 'Troilus'? Hellenus is a priest.   *215*

Cressida. What sneaking fellow comes yonder?

Enter Troilus [and passes over the stage].

Pandarus. Where? Yonder? That's Deiphobus. 'Tis Troilus! There's a man, niece! Hem? Brave Troilus, the prince of chivalry!

Cressida. Peace, for shame, peace!

Pandarus. Mark him, [note] him. O brave Troilus! Look   *220*
well upon him, niece. Look you how his sword is bloodied, and his helm more hack'd than Hector's. And how he looks, and how he goes. O admirable youth! He nere saw three-and-twenty. Go thy way, Troilus, go thy way. Had I a sister were a Grace or a daughter a goddess, he should take his choice.   *225*
O admirable man! Paris? Paris is dirt to him, and I warrant, Helen, to change, would give money to boot.

Enter common soldiers [and pass over the stage].

Cressida. Here come more.

Pandarus. Asses, fools, dolts! Chaff and bran, chaff and bran. Porredge after meat. I could live and die i' th' eyes of Troilus. Nere look, nere look; the eagles are gone! Crows and daws, crows and daws. I had rather be such a man as Troilus than Agamemnon and all Greece.

Cressida. There is among the Greeks Achilles, a better man than Troilus.   *235*

Pandarus. Achilles? A drayman, a porter, a very camel.

Cressida. Well, well.

Pandarus. Well, well? Why, have you any discretion? Have you any eyes? Do you know what a man is? Is not birth, beauty, good shape, discourse, manhood, learning, gentleness, virtue, youth,   *240*
liberality, and so forth, the spice and salt that seasons a man?

Cressida. Ay, a minc'd man. And then to be bak'd with no date in the pie, for then the man's date's out.

Pandarus. You are such another woman, one knows not at what ward you lie.   *245*

Cressida. Upon my back, to defend my belly; upon my wit, to defend my wiles; upon my secrecy, to defend mine honesty; my mask, to defend my beauty; and you to defend all these; and at all these wards I lie, at a thousand watches.

Pandarus. Say one of your watches.   *250*

Cressida. Nay, I'll watch you for that; and that's one of the chiefest of them too. If I cannot ward what I would not have hit, I can watch you for telling how I took the blow, unless it swell past hiding, and then it's past watching.

Enter Boy.

Pandarus. You are such another!   *255*

Boy. Sir, my lord would instantly speak with you.

Pandarus. Where?

Boy. At your own house.

---

171 against: *in expectation of*   **177 bravely:** *excellently*   **181 tell:** *F omits*   **184 shrowd:** *shrewd*   **186 whosoever:** *no matter who*   **proper man of person:** *man of attractive appearance*   **189 nod;** *Cf. n.*   **193 brave;** *Cf. n.*   **197 Is a not?:** *Is he not?*   **199 there's laying on:** *real fighting; F laying on*   **tak't off:** *depreciate it*   **200 be:** *are*   **202 divel:** *'devil,' so spelled consistently throughout this play*   **203 God's lid:** *'by God's eyelid,' a mild oath*   **208 shall see:** *F shall*

210 marvel: *wonder*   **213 indifferent:** *middlingly*   **220 note:** *F not*   **223 nere:** *never*   **230 Porredge:** *porridge*   **i' th' eyes of Troilus:** *in Troilus' company*   **243 date's out;** *Cf. n.*   **244 such another woman:** *such a perverse woman*   **245 ward:** *a defensive posture in fencing*   **248 mask;** *Cf. n.*   **249 lie:** *F has a superfluous at after lie*   **251 watch;** *Cf. n.*   **254 swell past hiding:** *a reference to pregnancy*

Pandarus. Good, boy, tell him I come. I doubt he be hurt.
Fare ye well, good niece.   *[Exit Boy.]*   260
    Cressida. Adieu, uncle.
    Pandarus. I'll be with you, niece, by and by.
    Cressida. To bring, uncle.
    Pandarus. Ay, a token from Troilus.
    Cressida. By the same token, you are a bawd.   *Exit Pandarus.*
Words, vows, gifts, tears, and love's full sacrifice
He offers in another's enterprise.
But more in Troilus thousandfold I see
Than in the glass of Pandar's praise may be;
Yet hold I off. Women are angels wooing;   270
Things won are done; joy's soul lies in the doing.
That she belov'd knows nought that knows not this:
Men prize the thing ungain'd more than it is.
That she was never yet that ever knew
Love got so sweet as when desire did sue.   275
Therefore this maxim out of love I teach:
'Achievement is command; ungain'd beseech.'
[Then] though my heart's contents firm love doth bear,
Nothing of that shall from mine eyes appear.   *Exit.*

❧ SCENE THIRD ❧

Sennet. Enter Agamemnon, Nestor, Ulysses, Diomedes, Menelaus,
with others.

    Agamemnon. Princess,
What grief hath set the jaundice on your cheeks?
The ample proposition that hope makes
In all designs begun on earth below
Fails in the promised largeness. Checks and disasters   5
Grow in the veins of actions highest rear'd;
As knots, by the conflux of meeting sap,
Infect the sound pine and diverts his grain,
Tortive and errant, from his course of growth.
Nor, princes, is it matter new to us   10
That we come short of our suppose so far
That after seven years' siege yet Troy walls stand.
Sith every action that hath gone before
Whereof we have record, trial did draw
Bias and thwart, not answering the aim,   15
And that unbodied figure of the thought
That gave't surmised shape. Why then, you princes,
Do you with cheeks abash'd behold our works
And think them shame, which are indeed nought else
But the protractive trials of great love   20
To find persistive constancy in men?
The fineness of which metal is not found
In Fortune's love; for then the bold and coward,
The wise and fool, the artist and unread,
The hard and soft, seem all affin'd and kin.   25

But in the wind and tempest of her frown
Distinction with a loud and powerful fan,
Puffing at all, winnows the light away,
And what hath mass or matter by itself
Lies rich in virtue and unmingled.   30
    Nestor. With due observance of thy godly seat,
Great Agamemnon, Nestor shall apply
Thy latest words. In the reproof of chance
Lies the true proof of men. The sea being smooth,
How many shallow bauble boats dare sail   35
Upon her patient breast, making their way
With those of nobler bulk!
But let the ruffian Boreas once enrage
The gentle Thetis, and anon behold
The strong-ribb'd bark through liquid mountains cut,   40
Bounding between the two moist elements
Like Perseus' horse. Where's then the saucy boat
Whose weak untimber'd sides but even now
Corrival'd greatness? Either to harbor fled
Or made a toast for Neptune. Even so,   45
Doth valor's show and valor's worth divide
In storms of Fortune. For in her ray and brightness
The herd hath more annoyance why the brize
Than by the tiger; but when the splitting wind
Makes flexible the knees of knotted oaks,   50
And flies fled under shade, why then the thing of courage,
As rous'd with rage, with rage doth sympathize,
And with an accent tun'd in selfsame key
Retorts to chiding Fortune.
    Ulysses.   Agamemnon,   55
Thou great commander, nerve, and bone of Greece,
Heart of our numbers, soul and only spirit
In whom the tempers and the minds of all
Should be shut up, hear what Ulysses speaks.
Besides th' applause and approbation   60
The which, *[To Agamemnon.]* most mighty for thy place and
sway,
And thou *[To Nestor.]* most reverend for thy stretch'd-out life,
I give to both your speeches; which were such
As Agamemnon and the hand of Greece   65
Should hold up high in brass; and such again
As venerable Nestor, hatch'd in silver,
Should with a bond of air, strong as the axletree
In which the heavens ride, knit all Greeks' ears
To his experienc'd tongue; yet let it please both,   70
Tho great, and wise, to hear Ulysses speak.
    Agamemnon. Speak, Prince of Ithaca, and be't of less expect
That matter needless, of importless burthen,
Divide thy lips than we are confident,
When rank Thersites opes [masty] jaws,   75
We shall hear music, wit, and oracle.
    Ulysses. Troy, yet upon his basis, had been down,

---

259 doubt: *respect, fear*   **263 To bring;** *Cf. n.*   **269 glass:** *mirror*   **270 wooing:**
when being wooed   **272 she:** *woman*   **275 Love got:** *love already achieved*   **277**
Achievement . . . beseech; *Cf. n.*   **beseech:** *entreaty*   **278 Then:** *F That*   **3 proposi-**
tion: *offer*   **7 conflux:** *stressed* — —   **8 diverts;** *Cf. n.*   **9 Tortive:** *distorted,*
twisted   **11 suppose:** *expectation*   **13 Sith:** *since*   **14 trial:** *the testing by experience,*
the actual events   **15 Bias:** *lopsided, not quite perfect; Cf. n.*   **20 protractive:** *protracted,*
drawn out   **21 persistive:** *persistent*   **23 Fortune's;** *Cf. n.*   **24 artist:** *scholar*   **25**
affin'd: *related*

30 unmingled: *pure, not mixed* (read here as four syllables)   **32 apply:** *moralize*   **33**
reproof: *resistance, refusing to accept*   **35 bauble:** *weak, toylike*   **38 Boreas:** *the north*
wind   **39 Thetis:** *originally a sea goddess, here used to mean the sea in general*   **42**
Perseus' horse: *Pegasus*   **46 valor's . . . worth:** *apparent bravery and actual bravery*   **48**
brize: *gadfly*   **51 flies fled:** *flies have fled* **shade:** *shelter*   **54 Retorts;** *Cf. n.*   **56**
nerve: *sinew*   **60 th' applause;** *F the applause: Q is better metrically since* approbation *has*
five syllables here   **61 To Agamemnon;** *Cf. n.*   **66 in brass:** *engraved on a brass tab-*
let   **67 hatch'd:** *etched; Cf. n.*   **68 air:** *breath*   **69 knit:** *tie, join*   **72 expect:**
expectation, build-up   **73 importless:** *meaningless* **burthen:** *substance, purport*   **75**
rank: *vile, offensive* **opes:** *opens* **masty:** *massive, powerful; F Masticke; Cf. n.*   **77 his:**
its **basis:** *base, foundation* **had been:** *would have been*

And the great Hector's sword had lack'd a master
But for these instances.
The specialty of rule hath been neglected,   80
And look how many Grecian tents do stand
Hollow upon this plain, so many hollow factions.
When that the general is not like the hive,
To whom the foragers shall all repair,
What honey is expected? Degree being vizarded,   85
Th' unworthiest shews as fairly in the mask.
The heavens themselves, the planets, and this center
Observe degree, priority, and place,
Insisture, course, proportion, season, form.
Office, and custom, in all line of order;   90
And therefore is the glorious planet Sol
In noble eminence enthron'd and spher'd
Amidst the other, whose med'cinable eye
Corrects the ill aspects of planets evil,
And posts, like the commandment of a king,   95
Sans check, to good and bad. But when the planets
In evil mixture to disorder wander,
What plagues and what portents, what mutiny,
What raging of the sea, shaking of earth,
Commotion in the winds! Frights, changes, horrors   100
Divert and crack, rend and deracinate
The unity and married calm of states
Quite from their fixure. O, when degree is shak'd,
Which is the ladder to all high designs,
The enterprise is sick. How could communities,   105
Degrees in schools, and brotherhoods in cities,
Peaceful commerce from dividable shores,
The primogenitive and due of birth,
Prerogative of age, crowns, scepters, laurels,
But by degree, stand in authentic place?   110
Take but degree away, untune that string,
And hark, what discord follows! Each thing meets
In mere oppugnancy. The bounded waters
Should lift their bosoms higher than the shores
And make a sop of all this solid globe.   115
Strength should be lord of imbecility,
And the rude son should strike his father dead.
Force should be right; or rather, right and wrong,
Between whose endless jar justice resides,
Should lose her names, and so should justice too.   120
Then everything includes itself in power,
Power into will, will into appetite,
And appetite, an universal wolf,
So doubly seconded with will and power,
Must make perforce an universal prey   125
And last eat up himself. Great Agamemnon,
This chaos, when degree is suffocate,
Follows the choking;
And this neglection of degrees is it
That by a pace goes backward in a purpose   130

It hath to climb. The general's disdain'd
By him one step below, he by the next,
That next by him beneath; so every step,
Exampled by the first pace that is sick
Of his superior, grows to an envious fever   135
Of pale and bloodless emulation.
And 'tis this fever that keeps Troy on foot,
Not her own sinews. To end a tale of length,
Troy in our weakness lives, not in her strength.
    Nestor. Most wisely hath Ulysses here discover'd   140
The fever whereof all our power is sick.
    Agamemnon. The nature of the sickness found, Ulysses,
What is the remedy?
    Ulysses. The great Achilles, whom opinion crowns,
The sinew and the forehand of our host,   145
Having his ear full of his airy fame,
Grows dainty of his worth, and in his tent
Lies mocking our designs. With him Patroclus
Upon a lazy bed the livelong day
Breaks scurril jests,   150
And with ridiculous and awkward action
(Which, slanderer, he imitation calls)
He pageants us. Sometime, great Agamemnon,
Thy topless deputation he puts on,
And like a strutting player whose conceit   155
Lies in his hamstring and doth think it rich
To hear the wooden dialogue and sound
'Twixt his stretch'd footing and the scaffolage—
Such to-be-pitied and orewrested seeming
He acts thy greatness in. And when he speaks,   160
'Tis like a chime a-mending, with terms unsquar'd,
Which, from the tongue of roaring Typhon dropp'd,
Would [seem] hyperboles. At this fusty stuff
The large Achilles, on his press'd bed lolling,
From his deep chest laughs out a loud applause,   165
Cries 'Excellent! 'Tis Agamemnon just!
Now play me Nestor; hum, and stroke thy beard
As he, being dress'd to some oration.'
That's done, as near as the extremest ends
Of parallels, as like as Vulcan and his wife;   170
Yet god Achilles still cries 'Excellent!
'Tis Nestor right. Now play him me, Patroclus,
Arming to answer in a night alarm.'
And then, forsooth, the faint defects of age
Must be the scene of mirth: to cough and spit,   175
And with a palsy fumbling on his gorget,
Shake in and out the rivet. And at this sport
Sir Valor dies; cries 'O, enough, Patroclus!
Or give me ribs of steel; I shall split all
In pleasure of my spleen.' And in this fashion   180
All our abilities, gifts, natures, shapes,

---

79 instances: *specific causes*   **80 specialty of rule:** *prerogatives of ruling or command-ing*   **85 Degree:** *subordination in rank*   **vizarded:** *masked*   **86 shews:** *shows*   **87 center:** *the earth; Cf. n.*   **89 Insisture:** *regularity, constancy*   **91 Sol;** *Cf. n.*   **93 the other:** *the other planets*   **med'cinable:** *curative, having the effect of medicine*   **94 aspects;** *Cf. n.*   **95 posts:** *speeds.*   **96 Sans:** *check without hindrance or hesitation*   **101 deracinate:** *uproot*   **103 fixure:** *fixed stability*   **104 designs:** *plans, purposes*   **107 dividable:** *separate*   **108 primogenitive:** *primogeniture*   **110 authentic:** *true, legal*   **113 oppugnancy:** *opposition*   **114 Should:** *would*   **115 sop:** *a thing soaked or soggy*   **116 should:** *would*   **imbecility:** *physical weakness*   **120 her:** *their; Cf. n.*   **121 includes itself in:** *is embraced in*   **127 suffocate:** *suffocated*   **130, 131 purpose … climb;** *Cf. n.*

134 sick: *envious*   **136 emulation:** *envy, imitation (five syllables here)*   **140 discover'd:** *pointed out, revealed*   **144 opinion:** *fame, public approval*   **145 forehand:** *mainstay*   **147 dainty:** *fastidious, conceited*   **150 scurril:** *scurrilous*   **153 pageants:** *acts out, mimics*   **154 topless deputation:** *supreme dignity deputed to the commander*   **155 conceit:** *faculty of mind*   **156 hamstring:** *tendons behind the knee, governing leg movement*   **158 stretch'd footing:** *exaggerated paces*   **scaffolage:** *wooden stage*   **159 orewrested:** *too tight, strained; Cf. n.*   **161 a-mending:** *being mended*   **162 Typhon:** *mythical Greek giant associated with hurricanes*   **163 seem;** *F seemes*   **167 hum:** *hem and haw*   **168 being dress'd to:** *preparing for*   **oration:** *four syllables*   **170 Vulcan and his wife;** *Cf. n.*   **172 me:** *an ethical dative, without special meaning*   **173 answer:** *i.e. answer a summons to battle*   **176 gorget:** *a piece of armor for the throat*   **180 spleen:** *merriment*

Severals and generals of grace exact,
Achievements, plots, orders, preventions,
Excitements to the field, or speech for truce,
Success or loss, what is or is not, serves   185
As stuff for these two to make paradoxes.

   Nestor. And in the imitation of these twain,
Who, as Ulysses says, opinion crowns
With an imperial voice, many are infect.
Ajax is grown self-will'd and bears his head   190
In such a rein, in full as proud a place
As broad Achilles, and keeps his tent like him,
Make factious feasts, rails on our state of war,
Bold as an oracle, and sets Thersites—
A slave whose gall coins slanders like a mint—   195
To match us in comparisons with dirt,
To weaken and discredit our exposure,
How rank soever rounded in with danger.

   Ulysses. They tax our policy and call it cowardice,
Count wisdom as no member of the war,   200
Forestall prescience, and esteem no act
But that of hand. The still and mental parts
That do contrive how many hands shall strike
When fitness call them on, and know by measure
Of their observant toil the enemies' weight—   205
Why, this hath not a finger's dignity.
They call this bedwork, mapp'ry, closet war;
So that the ram that batters down the wall,
For the great swing and rudeness of his poise,
They place before his hand that made the engine,   210
Or those that with the fineness of their souls
By reason guide his execution.

   Nestor. Let this be granted, and Achilles' horse
Makes many Thetis' sons.   *Tucket.*

   Agamemnon. What trumpet? Look, Menelaus.   215
   Menelaus. From Troy.

            Enter Aeneas.

   Agamemnon. What would you 'fore our tent?
   Aeneas. Is this great Agamemnon's tent, I pray you?
   Agamemnon. Even this.
   Aeneas. May one that is a herald, and a prince,   220
Do a fair message to his kingly ears?
   Agamemnon. With surety stronger than Achilles' arm
'Fore all the Greekish heads, which with one voice
Call Agamemnon head and general.
   Aeneas. Fair leave and large security. How may   225
A stranger to those most imperial looks
Know them from eyes of other mortals?
   Agamemnon.   How?
   Aeneas. Ay.
I ask that I might waken reverence,   230
And on the cheek be ready with a blush
Modest as morning when she coldly eyes
The youthful Phoebus.
Which is that god in office, guiding men?

Which is the high and mighty Agamemnon?   235
   Agamemnon. This Troyan scorns us, or the men of Troy
Are ceremonious courtiers.
   Aeneas. Courtiers as free, as debonair, unarm'd,
As bending angels; that's their fame in peace.
But when they would seem soldiers, they have galls,   240
Good arms, strong joints, true swords; and, Jove's accord,
Nothing so full of heart. But peace, Aeneas!
Peace, Troyan. Lay thy finger on thy lips.
The worthiness of praise distains his worth
If that [the] prais'd himself brings the praise forth.   245
But what the repining enemy commends,
That breath fame blows; that praise sole pure transcends.
   Agamemnon. Sir, you of Troy, call you yourself Aeneas?
   Aeneas. Ay, Greek, that is my name.
   Agamemnon. What's your affair, I pray you?   250
   Aeneas. Sir, pardon; 'tis for Agamemnon's ears.
   Agamemnon. He hears nought privately that comes from Troy.
   Aeneas. Nor I from Troy come not to whisper him.
I bring a trumpet to awake his ear,
To set his sense on the attentive bent   255
And then to speak.
   Agamemnon.   Speak frankly as the wind.
It is not Agamemnon's sleeping hour.
That thou shalt know, Troyan, he is awake,
He tells thee so himself.   260
   Aeneas.   Trumpet, blow loud.
Send thy brass voice through all these lazy tents,
And every Greek of mettle, let him know
What Troy means fairly shall be spoke aloud.
                The trumpets sound.
We have, great Agamemnon, here in Troy,   265
A prince call'd Hector—Priam is his father—
Who in this dull and long-continu'd truce
Is rusty grown. He bade me take a trumpet
And to this purpose speak: Kings, princes, lords,
If there be one amongst the fair'st of Greece   270
That holds his honor higher than his ease,
That seeks his praise more than he fears his peril,
That knows his valor and knows not his fear,
That loves his mistress more than in confession,
With truant vows to her own lips he loves,   275
And dare avow her beauty and her worth
In other arms than hers—to him this challenge.
Hector, in view of Troyans and of Greeks,
Shall make it good, or do his best to do it.
He hath a lady wiser, fairer, truer   280
Than ever Greek did compass in his arms,
And will tomorrow with his trumpet call,
Midway between your tents and walls of Troy,
To rouse a Grecian that is true in love.
If any come, Hector shall honor him;   285
If none, he'll say in Troy when he retires,
The Grecian dames are sunburnt and not worth
The splinter of a lance. Even so much.
   Agamemnon. This shall be told our lovers, Lord Aeneas.
If none of them have soul in such a kind,   290
We left them all at home. But we are soldiers,

And may that soldier a mere recreant prove,
That means not, hath not, or is not in love.
If then one is, or hath, or means to be,
That one meets Hector; if none else, I'll be he.   295
   Nestor. Tell him of Nestor, one that was a man
When Hector's grandsire suck'd. He is old now,
But if there be not in our Grecian mold
One noble man that hath one spark of fire
To answer for his love, tell him from me,   300
I'll hide my silver beard in a gold beaver
And in my vantbrace put this wither'd brawn,
And meeting him, will tell him that my lady
Was fairer than his grandam, and as chaste
As may be in the world. His youth in flood,   305
I'll [prove] this truth with my three drops of blood.
   Aeneas. Now heavens forbid such scarcity of youth.
   Ulysses. Amen.
   Agamemnon. Fair Lord Aeneas, let me touch your hand;
To our pavilion shall I lead you first.   310
Achilles shall have word of this intent,
So shall each lord of Greece from tent to tent.
Yourself shall feast with us before you go
And find the welcome of a noble foe.
            Exeunt. [Manent] Ulysses and Nestor.
   Ulysses. Nestor.   315
   Nestor. What says Ulysses?
   Ulysses. I have a young conception in my brain;
Be you my time to bring it to some shape.
   Nestor. What is't?
   Ulysses. This 'tis: 320
Blunt wedges rive hard knots. The seeded pride
That hath to this maturity blown up
In rank Achilles must or now be cropp'd
Or, shedding, breed a nursery of like evil
To overbulk us all.   325
   Nestor.   Well, and how?
   Ulysses. This challenge that the gallant Hector sends,
However it is spread in general name,
Relates in purpose only to Achilles.
   Nestor. The purpose is perspicuous even as substance,   330
Whose grossness little characters sum up;
And, in the publication, make no strain
But that Achilles, were his brain as barren
As banks of Lybia (though Apollo knows
'Tis dry enough), will with great speed of judgment,   335
Ay, with celerity, find Hector's purpose
Pointing on him.
   Ulysses.   And wake him to the answer, think you?
   Nestor. Yes, 'tis most meet. Who may you else oppose
That can from Hector bring his honor off,   340
If not Achilles? Though't be a sportful combat,
Yet in this trial much opinion dwells;
For here the Troyans taste our dear'st repute
With their fin'st palate; and trust to me, Ulysses,

Our imputation shall be oddly pois'd   345
In this wild action. For the success,
Although particular, shall give a scantling
Of good or bad unto the general,
And in such indexes, although small pricks
To their subsequent volumes, there is seen   350
The baby figure of the giant mass
Of things to come at large. It is suppos'd
He that meets Hector issues from our choice;
And choice, being mutual act of all our souls,
Makes merit her election and doth boil,   355
As 'twere, from forth us all, a man distill'd
Out of our virtues; who miscarrying,
What heart from hence receives the conqu'ring part
To steel a strong opinion to themselves!
Which entertain'd, limbs are in his instruments,   360
In no less working, than are swords and bows
Directive by the limbs.
   Ulysses.   Give pardon to my speech:
Therefore 'tis meet Achilles meet not Hector.
Let us, like merchants, show our foulest wares   365
And think perchance they'll sell; if not,
The lustre of the better yet to show
Shall show the better. Do not consent
That ever Hector and Achilles meet;
For both our honor and our shame in this   370
Are dogg'd with two strange followers.
   Nestor. I see them not with my old eyes. What are they?
   Ulysses. What glory our Achilles shares from Hector,
Were he not proud, we all should wear with him.
But he already is too insolent,   375
And we were better parch in Afric sun
Than in the pride and salt scorn of his eyes
Should he 'scape Hector fair. If he were foil'd,
Why then we did our main opinion crush
In taint of our best man. No, make a lott'ry,   380
And by device let blockish Ajax draw
The sort to fight with Hector. Among ourselves
Give him allowance as the worthier man,
For that will physic the great Myrmidon
Who broils in loud applause, and make him fall   385
His crest that prouder than blue iris bends.
If the dull brainless Ajax come safe off,
We'll dress him up in voices; if he fail,
Yet go we under our opinion still,
That we have better men. But hit or miss,   390
Our project's life this shape of sense assumes,
Ajax employ'd plucks down Achilles' plumes.
   Nestor. Now, Ulysses, I begin to relish thy advice,
And I will give a taste of it forthwith
To Agamemnon. Go we to him straight.   395
Two curs shall tame each other. Pride alone
Must tarre the mastiffs on, as 'twere their bone.

---

301 **beaver:** *helmet with face guard*   302 **vantbrace:** *armor for the arms*   305 **His youth in flood:** *though he be in his prime*   306 **prove:** *F* pawn   SD **Manent** *F* Manet: *Q omits*   317 **young conception:** *germ of an idea*   321 **rive:** *split, sever*   **seeded:** *mature, gone to seed*   323 **or:** *either*   324 **nursery:** *read 'nurs'ry'*   330 **perspicuous:** *clear, evident*   **even:** *read 'e'en'*   **substance:** *material riches*   331 **characters:** *figures*   332 **publication:** *the proclamation of Hector's challenge*   **make no strain:** *never fear, have no difficulty in believing*   334 **Lybia:** *North African desert country*   339 **meet:** *fitting*   340 **bring ... off:** *come out with honor unscathed*   342 **opinion:** *reputation*

345 **imputation:** *good name*   **oddly pois'd:** *in delicate balance*   346-348 **For ... general;** *Cf. n.*   346 **success:** *outcome*   347 **scantling:** *portion, amount*   349-352 **And in ... large;** *Cf. n.*   350 **subsequent:** *stressed —́ —*   355 **Makes ... election:** *elects the one with greatest merit*   358 **conqu'ring part:** *the winning side, i.e. the Trojan*   359 **steel:** *bolster up*   360-362 **Which ... the limbs;** *Cf. n.*   362 **Directive:** *subject to direction, directable*   367 **to show:** *to be shown*   377 **salt:** *bitter*   379 **main opinion:** *chief reason for our glorious reputation*   380 **taint:** *the staining of honor*   381 **device:** *stratagem*   **blockish:** *stupid*   382 **sort:** *lot*   383 **allowance:** *acknowledgment*   384 **physic:** *cure*   **great Myrmidon:** *Achilles*   385 **broils in:** *seethes in, revels in*   **fall:** *lower, let fall*   388 **voices:** *loud praises*   397 **tarre:** *urge, incite*

ACT SECOND ❧ SCENE FIRST

Enter Ajax and Thersites.

Ajax. Thersites?

Thersites. Agamemnon—how if he had biles, full, all over, generally?

Ajax. Thersites?

Thersites. And those biles did run? Say so. Did not the *5*
general run? Were not that a botchy core?

Ajax. Dog!

Thersites. Then there would come some matter from him.
I see none now.

Ajax. Thou bitch-wolf's son, canst [thou] not hear? Feel, *10*
then!   *Strikes him.*

Thersites. The plague of Greece upon thee, thou mongrel,
beef-witted lord!

Ajax. Speak then, you whinid'st leaven, speak! I will beat
thee into handsomeness. *15*

Thersites. I shall sooner rail thee into wit and holiness;
but I think thy horse will sooner con an oration than you
learn a prayer without book. Thou canst strike, canst thou?
A red murrain [o'] thy jade's tricks.

Ajax. Toadstool, learn me the proclamation. *20*

Thersites. Dost thou think I have no sense, thou strik'st
me thus?

Ajax. The proclamation!

Thersites. Thou art proclaim'd a fool, I think.

Ajax. Do not, porpentine, do not! My fingers itch. *25*

Thersites. I would thou didst itch from head to foot,
and I had the scratching of thee. I would make thee the
loathsom'st scab in Greece.

Ajax. I say, the proclamation!

Thersites. Thou grumblest and railest every hour on Achilles,
and thou art as full of envy at his greatness as Cerberus is at
Proserpina's beauty; ay, that thou bark'st at him.

Ajax. Mistress Thersites!

Thersites. Thou shouldst strike him.

Ajax. Cobloaf! *35*

Thersites. He would pun thee into shivers with his fist,
as a sailor breaks a bisquit.

Ajax. You whoreson cur!

Thersites. Do, do!

Ajax. Thou stool for a witch! *40*

Thersites. Ay, do, do, thou sodden-witted lord! Thou hast no
more brain than I have in mine elbows. An asinico may tutor
thee. Thou scurvy valiant ass, thou art but to thrash Troyans,
and thou art bought and sold among those of any wit like a
barbarian slave. If thou use to beat me, I will begin at thy *45*
heel and tell what thou art by inches, thou thing of no
bowels, thou!

Ajax. You dog!

Thersites. You scurvy lord!

Ajax. You cur! *50*

Thersites. Mars his idiot! Do, rudeness; do, camel, do do!

Enter Achilles and Patroclus.

Achilles. Why, how now, Ajax? Wherefore do you this?
How now, Thersites? What's the matter, man?

Thersites. You see him there, do you?

Achilles. Ay. What's the matter? *55*

Thersites. Nay, look upon him.

Achilles. So I do. What's the matter?

Thersites. Nay, but regard him well.

Achilles. Well? Why, I do so.

Thersites. But yet you look not well upon him; for *60*
whomsoever you take him to be, he is Ajax.

Achilles. I know that, fool.

Thersites. Ay, but that fool knows not himself.

Ajax. Therefore I beat thee.

Thersites. Lo, lo, lo, lo, what modicums of wit he utters. *65*
His evasions have ears thus long. I have bobb'd his brain more
than he has beat my bones. I will buy nine sparrows for a
penny, and his piamater is not worth the ninth part of a sparrow. This lord, Achilles, Ajax—who wears his wit in his belly,
and his guts in his head—I'll tell you what I say of him. *70*

Achilles. What?

Thersites. I say this Ajax—

Achilles. Nay, good Ajax.

Thersites. Has not so much wit—

Achilles. Nay, I must hold you. *75*

Thersites. As will stop the eye of Helen's needle, for
whom he comes to fight.

Achilles. Peace, fool.

Thersites. I would have peace and quietness, but the fool
will not—he, there! That he! Look you there! *80*

Ajax. O thou damn'd cur, I shall—

Achilles. Will you set your wit to a fool's?

Thersites. No, I warrant you, for a fool's will shame it.

Patroclus. Good words, Thersites.

Achilles. What's the quarrel? *85*

Ajax. I bade [the] vile owl go learn me the tenor of the
proclamation, and he rails upon me.

Thersites. I serve thee not.

Ajax. Well, go to, go to.

Thersites. I serve here voluntary. *90*

Achilles. Your last service was sufferance, 'twas not voluntary;
no man is beaten voluntary. Ajax was here the voluntary, and
you as under an impress.

Thersites. Ene so, a great deal of your wit, too, lies in your
sinews, or else there be liars. Hector shall have a great catch *95*
if he knock out either of your brains. He were as good crack
a fusty nut with no kernel.

Achilles. What, with me too, Thersites?

Thersites. There's Ulysses and old Nestor, whose wit was
moldy ere their grandsires had nails on their toes, yoke *100*
you like draft oxen and make you plough up the war.

Achilles. What? What?

Thersites. Yes, good sooth. To Achilles! to Ajax! to—

Ajax. I shall cut out your tongue.

Thersites. 'Tis no matter; I shall speak as much as thou *105*
afterwards.

Patroclus. No more words, Thersites.

---

2 biles: *boils* **6 botchy:** *ulcerous* **8 matter:** *pun on 'sense' and 'pus'* **10 canst thou:** *F
canst y* **14 whinid'st** *finewed'st, most mouldy; Cf. n.* **15 handsomeness:** *politeness* **17
con:** *learn* **18 without book:** *by heart* **19 murrain:** *plague* **o':** *F o'th* **jade's tricks:**
tricks of a mean horse **20 learn me:** *inform me of* **21 sense:** *sensibility, feeling* **25 porpentine:** *porcupine* **31, 32 Cerberus . . . Proserpina's;** *Cf. n.* **35 Cobloaf:** *small, rounded
loaf* **36 pun:** *pound* **42 asinico:** *young ass* **44 bought and sold:** *manipulated and
deceived as of no account* **51 Mars his idiot:** *Mars' idiot; Cf. n.*

66 evasions . . . long: *they are asslike, stupid* **bobb'd:** *beaten, pummeled* **68 piamater:**
brain **82 set:** *oppose* **86 vile:** *F thee vile* **93 impress:** *forced service* **94 Ene:**
even **95 be:** *are* **96 He were as good:** *he might as well* **97 fusty:** *stale* **103
good sooth:** *in truth, surely* **To Achilles! to Ajax!;** *Cf. n.*

Thersites. I will hold my peace when Achilles' brooch bids
me, shall I?

Achilles. There's for you, Patroclus.   110

Thersites. I will see you hang'd like clotpolls ere I come any
more to your tents. I will keep where there is wit stirring and
leave the faction of fools.   *Exit.*

Patroclus. A good riddance.

Achilles. Marry, this, sir, is proclaim'd through all our host:
That Hector, by the fifth hour of the sun,
Will with a trumpet 'twixt our tents and Troy
Tomorrow morning call some knight to arms
That hath a stomach, and such a one that dare
Maintain—I know not what. 'Tis trash. Farewell.   120

Ajax. Farewell? Who shall answer him?

Achilles. I know not. 'Tis put to lottery; otherwise he knew
his man.

Ajax. O, meaning you? I will go learn more of it.   *[Exeunt.]*

❧ SCENE SECOND ❧

Enter Priam, Hector, Troilus, Paris, and Helenus.

Priam. After so many hours, lives, speeches spent,
Thus once again says Nestor from the Greeks:
'Deliver Helen, and all damage else
(As honor, loss of time, travail, expense,
Wounds, friends, and what else dear that is consum'd   5
In hot digestion of this cormorant war)
Shall be stroke off.' Hector, what say you to't?

Hector. Though no man lesser fears the Greeks than I,
As far as touches my particular,
Yet dread Priam,   10
There is no lady of more softer bowels,
More spongy to suck in the sense of fear,
More ready to cry out, 'Who knows what follows?'
Than Hector is. The wound of peace is surety,
Surety secure. But modest doubt is call'd   15
The beacon of the wise, the tent that searches
To th' bottom of the worst. Let Helen go.
Since the first sword was drawn about this question,
Every tithe soul 'mongst many thousand dismes
Hath been as dear as Helen. I mean, of ours.   20
If we have lost so many tenths of ours
To guard a thing not ours, nor worth to us,
Had it our name, the value of one ten,
What merit's in that reason which denies
The yielding of her up.   25

Troilus.   Fie, fie, my brother!
Weigh you the worth and honor of a king
So great as our dread father in a scale
Of common ounces? Will you with counters sum
The past proportion of his infinite,   30
And buckle in a waist most fathomless
With spans and inches so diminutive

As fears and reason? Fie, for godly shame!

Helenus. No marvel, though you bite so sharp at reasons,
You are so empty of them. Should not our father   35
Bear the great sway of his affairs with reasons,
Because your speech hath none that tells him so.

Troilus. You are for dreams and slumbers, brother priest;
You fur your gloves with reason. Here are your reasons:
You know an enemy intends you harm;   40
You know a sword employ'd is perilous
And reason flies the object of all harm.
Who marvels, then, when Helenus beholds
A Grecian and his sword, if he do set
The very wings of reason to his heels,   45
And fly like chidden Mercury from Jove
Or like a star disorb'd? Nay, if we talk of reason,
Let's shut our gates and sleep. Manhood and honor
Should have hard hearts, would they but fat their thoughts
With this cramm'd reason. Reason and respect   50
Make livers pale and lustihood deject.

Hector. Brother, she is not worth what she doth cost
The holding.

Troilus.   What's aught, but as 'tis valu'd?

Hector. But value dwells not in particular will.   55
It holds his estimate and dignity
As well wherein 'tis precious of itself
As in the prizer. 'Tis [mad] idolatry
To make the service greater than the god,
And the will dotes that is inclinable   60
To what infectiously itself affects,
Without some image of th' affected merit.

Troilus. I take today a wife, and my election
Is led on in the conduct of my will;
My will enkindled by mine eyes and ears,   65
Two traded pilots 'twixt the dangerous shores
Of will and judgment. How may I avoid,
Although my will distaste what it elected,
The wife I chose? There can be no evasion
To blench from this, and to stand firm by honor.   70
We turn not back the silks upon the merchant
When we have spoil'd them; nor the remainder viands
We do not throw in unrespective [sieve]
Because we now are full. It was thought meet
Paris should do some vengeance on the Greeks.   75
Your breath of full consent bellied his sails.
The seas and winds, old wranglers, took a truce
And did him service. He touch'd the ports, desir'd,
And for an old aunt whom the Greeks held captive,
He brought a Grecian queen whose youth and freshness   80
Wrinkles Apollo's and makes stale the morning.
Why keep we her? The Grecians keep our aunt.
Is she worth keeping? Why, she is a pearl
Whose price hath launch'd above a thousand ships,
And turn'd crown'd kings to merchants.   85
If you'll avouch 'twas wisdom Paris went,

---

108 brooch; *Cf. n.*   **111 clotpolls:** *blockheads*   **119 stomach:** *appetite for fighting*   **122
knew:** *would know* **SD Exeunt** *F Exit;* *Q omits*   **6 cormorant:** *a predatory bird*   **9
touches my particular:** *concerns me in particular*   **11 softer bowels:** *sensitivity, compas-*
sion   **14 surety:** *overconfident security*   **16 tent:** *swab for probing wounds*   **19 tithe:**
tenth; Cf. n. **dismes:** *(pronounced 'dimes') tens (of men lost)*   **23 Had it our name:**
even if she were one of us   **29 counters:** *beads on an abacus*   **30 past:** *exceeding* **infinite:**
infinite greatness   **31 fathomless:** *measureless*

34 reasons: *homophonous pun on 'reasons' and 'raisins'*   **39 fur . . . reason:** *use reason for
everything*   **46 And fly . . . Jove;** *Cf. n.*   **47 disorb'd:** *displaced from its orbit*   **49
fat:** *make fat, feed*   **50 respect:** *circumspection*   **51 livers:** *the reputed source of courage
and 'gall'* **deject:** *dejected*   **55 particular will:** *the volition of an individual*   **56 his:**
its **dignity:** *worthiness*   **58 prizer:** *person who prizes* **mad;** *F made*   **60-62 And the
. . . merit;** *Cf. n.*   **60 dotes:** *is foolish*   **66 traded:** *experienced*   **67 avoid:** *cast
off*   **68 distaste:** *not like*   **70 blench:** *flinch*   **73 sieve:** *F same*   **78 touch'd:**
reached   **79 old aunt:** *cf. I.2.16 Cf. n.*   **81 Wrinkles:** *makes appear wrinkled and ugly*

As you must needs, for you all cried, 'Go, go';
If you'll confess he brought home noble prize,
As you must needs, for you all clapp'd your hands
And cried, 'Inestimable'; why do you now   90
The issue of your proper wisdoms rate
And do a deed that fortune never did,
Beggar the estimation which you priz'd
Richer than sea and land? O theft most base
That we have stolne what we do fear to keep!   95
But thieves unworthy of a thing so stolne,
That in their country did them that disgrace,
We fear to warrant in our native place.

Enter Cassandra with her hair about her ears.

Cassandra. Cry, Troyans, cry!
Priam.   What noise? What shriek is this?
Troilus. 'Tis our mad sister. I do know her voice.
Cassandra. Cry, Troyans!
Hector. It is Cassandra.
Cassandra. Cry, Troyans, cry! Lend me ten thousand eyes
And I will fill them with prophetic tears.   105
   Hector. Peace, sister, peace.
   Cassandra. Virgins and boys, mid-age and wrinkled old,
Soft infancy, that nothing can but cry,
Add to my clamor! Let us pay betimes
A moity of that mass of moan to come.   110
Cry, Troyans, cry! Practice your eyes with tears.
Troy must not be, nor goodly Ilion stand.
Our firebrand brother Paris burns us all.
Cry, Troyans, cry; a Helen and a woe.
Cry, cry, Troy burns, or else let Helen go.   *Exit.*   115
   Hector. Now, youthful Troilus, do not these high strains
Of divination in our sister work
Some touches of remorse? Or is your blood
So madly hot that no discourse of reason
Nor fear of bad success in a bad cause   120
Can qualify the same?
   Troilus.   Why, brother Hector,
We may not think the justness of each act
Such and no other than event doth form it,
Nor once deject the courage of our minds   125
Because Cassandra's mad. Her brainsick raptures
Cannot distaste the goodness of a quarrel
Which hath our several honors all engag'd
To make it gracious. For my private part,
I am no more touch'd than all Priam's sons,   130
And Jove forbid there should be done amongst us
Such things as might offend the weakest spleen
To fight for and maintain.
   Paris. Else might the world convince of levity
As well my undertakings as your counsels;   135
But I attest the gods, your full consent
Gave wings to my propension and cut off
All fears attending on so dire a project.
For what, alas, can these my single arms?

What propugnation is in one man's valor   140
To stand the push and enmity of those
This quarrel would excite? Yet I protest,
Were I alone to pass the difficulties,
And had as ample power as I have will,
Paris should nere retract what he hath done   145
Nor faint in the pursuit.
   Priam.   Paris, you speak
Like one besotted on your sweet delights.
You have the honey still, but these the gall;
So to be valiant is no praise at all.   150
   Paris. Sir, I propose not merely to myself
The pleasure such a beauty brings with it;
But I would have the soil of her fair rape
Wip'd off in honorable keeping her.
What treason were it to the ransack'd queen,   155
Disgrace to your great worths, and shame to me,
Now to deliver her possession up
On terms of base compulsion! Can it be
That so degenerate a strain as this
Should once set footing in your generous bosoms?   160
There's not the meanest spirit on our party
Without a heart to dare, or sword to draw,
When Helen is defended; nor none so noble
Whose life were ill bestow'd or death unfam'd
Where Helen is the subject. Then, I say,   165
Well may we fight for her whom we know well
The world's large spaces cannot parallel.
   Hector. Paris and Troilus, you have both said well;
And on the cause and question now in hand
Have gloz'd, but superficially; not much   170
Unlike young men, whom Aristotle thought
Unfit to hear moral philosophy.
The reasons you allege do more conduce
To the hot passion of distemp'red blood
Than to make up a free determination   175
'Twixt right and wrong; for pleasure and revenge
Have ears more deaf than adders to the voice
Of any true decision. Nature craves
All dues be rend'red to their owners. Now
What nearer debt in all humanity   180
Than wife is to the husband? If this law
Of nature be corrupted through affection,
And that great minds, of partial indulgence
To their benumbed wills, resist the same,
There is a law in each well ord'red nation   185
To curb those raging appetites that are
Most disobedient and refractory.
If Helen then be wife to Sparta's king,
As it is known she is, these moral laws
Of nature and of nation speak aloud   190
To have her back return'd. Thus to persist
In doing wrong extenuates not wrong,
But makes it much more heavy. Hector's opinion
Is this in way of truth. Yet neretheless,
My spritely brethren, I propend to you   195

---

91 issue: *result* **rate:** *berate, chide* **93 Beggar:** *make poor, belittle* **95 That:** *in that.* **stolne:** *stol'n* **98 warrant:** *make good, defend* **110 moity:** *moiety, part* **119 discourse of reason:** *process of reasoning* **120 success:** *result, final issue* **126 raptures:** *ecstatic visions* **127 distaste:** *destroy the savor of* **129 gracious:** *righteous* **132 spleen:** *heart, courage* **134 convince:** *convict* **136 attest:** *call to witness* **137 propension:** *inclination, desire* **139 can:** *can do* **single:** *unaided*

140 propugnation: *defense* **143 pass:** *experience, bear the brunt of* **145 nere:** *never* **retract:** *draw back from* **153 soil:** *stain* **rape:** *abduction* **155 ransack'd:** *abducted* **160 generous:** *high-born* **161 on our party:** *on our side* **170 gloz'd:** *commented* **171 Aristotle:** *Cf. n.* **177 adders:** *Cf. n.* **182 affection:** *appetite, inclination* **183 partial:** *excessive (three syllables here)* **194 neretheless:** *nevertheless* **195 propend:** *bow to, give in to*

In resolution to keep Helen still;
For 'tis a cause that hath no mean dependence
Upon our joint and several dignities.

  Troilus. Why, there you touch'd the life of our design.
Were it not glory that we more affected   200
Than the performance of our heaving spleens,
I would not wish a drop of Troyan blood
Spent more in her defense. But worthy Hector,
She is a theme of honor and renown,
A spur to valiant and magnanimous deeds,   205
Whose present courage may beat down our foes,
And fame in time to come canonize us.
For I presume brave Hector would not lose
So rich advantage of a promis'd glory
As smiles upon the forehead of this action   210
For the wide world's revenue.

  Hector.   I am yours,
You valiant offspring of great Priamus.
I have a roisting challenge sent amongst
The dull and factious nobles of the Greeks   215
Will strike amazement to their drowsy spirits.
I was advertis'd their great general slept,
Whilst emulation in the army crept.
This I presume will wake him.   *Exeunt.*

❧ Scene Third ❧

Enter Thersites solus.

  Thersites. How now, Thersites? What, lost in the labyrinth
of thy fury? Shall the elephant Ajax carry it thus? He beats me,
and I rail at him. O worthy satisfaction! Would it were otherwise; that I could beat him whilst he rail'd at me. 'Sfoot, I'll
learn to conjure and raise divels, but I'll see some issue of my
spiteful execrations. Then there's Achilles, a rare enginer! If
Troy be not taken till these two undermine it, the walls will
stand till they fall of themselves. O thou great thunder-darter
of Olympus, forget that thou art Jove, the king of gods; and
Mercury, loose all the serpentine craft of thy caduceus, if thou
take not that little little less than little wit from them that they
have, which short-arm'd ignorance itself knows is so abundant
scarce it will not in circumvention deliver a fly from a spider
without drawing the massy irons and cutting the web. After
this, the vengeance on the whole camp! Or rather the bone   15
ache, for that, methinks, is the curse dependent on those that
war for a placket. I have said my prayers and divel, Envy, say
'Amen.' What ho? My Lord Achilles?

Enter Patroclus.

  Patroclus. Who's there? Thersites? Good Thersites, come in
and rail.   20

  Thersites. If I could have rememb'red a gilt counterfeit, thou
wouldst not have slipp'd out of my contemplation. But it is no
matter. Thyself upon thyself! The common curse of mankind,
folly and ignorance, be thine in great revenue! Heaven bless
thee from a tutor, and discipline come not near thee. Let thy
blood be thy direction till thy death, then if she that lays thee
out says thou art a fair corse, I'll be sworn and sworn upon't
she never shrouded any but lazars. Amen. Where's Achilles?

  Patroclus. What, art thou devout? Wast thou in a prayer?

  Thersites. Ay. The heavens hear me!   30

Enter Achilles.

  Achilles. Who's there?

  Patroclus. Thersites, my lord.

  Achilles. Where, where? Art thou come? Why, my cheese,
my digestion, why hast thou not serv'd thyself into my table
so many meals? Come, what's Agamemnon?   35

  Thersites. Thy commander, Achilles. Then tell me, Patroclus,
what's Achilles?

  Patroclus. Thy lord, Thersites. Then tell me, I pray thee,
what's thyself?

  Thersites. Thy knower, Patroclus. Then tell me, Patroclus, 40
what art thou?

  Patroclus. Thou mayst tell that know'st.

  Achilles. O, tell, tell!

  Thersites. I'll decline the whole question. Agamemnon
commands Achilles, Achilles is my lord, I am Patroclus'   45
knower, and Patroclus is a fool.

  Patroclus. You rascal!

  Thersites. Peace, fool, I have not done.

  Achilles. He is a privileg'd man. Proceed, Thersites.

  Thersites. Agamemnon is a fool, Achilles is a fool,   50
Thersites is a fool, and, as aforesaid, Patroclus is a fool.

  Achilles. Derive this. Come.

  Thersites. Agamemnon is a fool to offer to command Achilles; Achilles is a fool to be commanded of Agamemnon; Thersites is a fool to serve such a fool; and Patroclus is a fool   55
positive.

  Patroclus. Why am I a fool?

Enter Agamemnon, Ulysses, Nestor, Diomedes, Ajax, and Calchas.

  Thersites. Make that demand to the Creator; it suffices me
thou art. Look you, who comes here?

  Achilles. Patroclus, I'll speak with nobody. Come in   60
with me, Thersites.   *Exit.*

  Thersites. Here is such patchery, such juggling and such
knavery! All the argument is a cuckold and a whore—a good
quarrel to draw emulations, factions, and bleed to death upon.
Now the dry suppeago on the subject, and war and lechery   65
confound all!   *[Exit.]*

  Agamemnon. Where is Achilles?

  Patroclus. Within his tent but ill dispos'd, my lord.

  Agamemnon. Let it be known to him that we are here.
He [shent] our messengers and we lay by   70
Our appertainments, visiting of him.
Let him be told [so, lest] perchance he think
We dare not move the question of our place
Or know not what we are.

---

201 **heaving spleens:** *unruly feelings of resentment*   207 **canonize:** *stressed* — ´—
211 **revenue:** *stressed* — ´—   214 **roisting:** *roistering, bullying*   216 **Will:** *which will*
amazement: *wonder, bewilderment*   217 **advertis'd:** *informed* stressed — ´— —   218
emulation: *ambitious rivalry*   2 **carry it:** *behave himself*   4 **'Sfoot:** *'God's foot,' a mild
oath*   5 **but:** *unless*   6 **enginer:** *a contriver of military engines*   10 **caduceus:** *Mercury's
wand*   12 **short-arm'd:** *incapable of reaching far*   14 **massy irons:** *great swords*   15, 16
bone ache: *syphilis*   17 **placket:** *petticoat, woman*   21, 22 **gilt counterfeit ... slipp'd;**
Cf. n.

24 **bless:** *preserve*   26 **blood:** *passion*   27 **corse:** *corpse*   28 **lazars:** *lepers*   33
cheese; *Cf. n.*   44 **decline:** *run through (as in grammatical declining)*   52 **Derive:**
explain, show reasons   54 **of:** *by*   58 **demand:** *question*   62 **patchery:** *roguery*   65
suppeago: *serpigo (a skin disease)* SD **Exit:** *not in F or Q*   70 **shent:** *reviled, scolded;* F
sent; Q sate; *Cf. n.*   71 **appertainments:** *rights, prerogatives*   72 **so, lest:** *F of, so*   73
move: *assert* **place:** *position of authority*

Patroclus.   I shall so say to him.   *[Exit.]*   *75*

Ulysses. We saw him at the opening of his tent. He is not sick.

Ajax. Yes, lion-sick, sick of proud heart. You may call it melancholy if [you] will favor the man; but, by my head, it is pride. But why? Why? Let him show us the cause?   *80* A word, my lord.

Nestor. What moves Ajax thus to bay at him?

Ulysses. Achilles hath inveigled his fool from him.

Nestor. Who, Thersites?

Ulysses. He.   *85*

Nestor. Then will Ajax lack matter, if he have lost his argument.

Ulysses. No. You see he is his argument that has his argument, Achilles.

Nestor. All the better; their fraction is more our wish   *90* than their faction. But it was a strong counsel that a fool could disunite.

Ulysses. The amity that wisdom knits not, folly may easily untie.

Enter Patroclus.

Here comes Patroclus.   *95*

Nestor. No Achilles with him?

Ulysses. The elephant hath joints, but none for courtesy. His legs are legs for necessity, not for [flexure].

Patroclus. Achilles bids me say he is much sorry If anything more than your sport and pleasure   *100* Did move your greatness and this noble state To call upon him. He hopes it is no other But for your health and your digestion sake, And after-dinner's breath.

Agamemnon.   Hear you, Patroclus.   *105* We are too well acquainted with these answers. But his evasion, wing'd thus swift with scorn, Cannot outfly our apprehensions. Much attribute he hath, and much the reason Why we ascribe it to him; yet all his virtues,   *110* Not virtuously if his own part beheld, Do in our eyes begin to lose their gloss; [Yea, like] fair fruit in an unwholesome dish, Are like to rot untasted. Go and tell him We came to speak with him; and you shall not sin   *115* If you do say we think him overproud And underhonest, in self-assumption greater Than in the note of judgment. And worthier than himself Here tends the savage strangeness he puts on, Disguise the holy strength of their command,   *120* And underwrite in an observing kind His humorous predominance, yea, watch His pettish lines, his ebbs, his flows, as if The passage and whole carriage of this action Rode on his tide. Go tell him this, and add   *125*

That if he overhold his price so much, We'll none of him. But let him, like an engine Not portable, lie under this report: Bring action hither; this cannot go to war. A stirring dwarf we do allowance give   *130* Before a sleeping giant. Tell him so.

Patroclus. I shall, and bring his answer presently.   *[Exit.]*

Agamemnon. In second voice we'll not be satisfied; We come to speak with him. Ulysses, enter you.   *Exit Ulysses.*

Ajax. What is he more than another?   *135*

Agamemnon. No more than what he thinks he is.

Ajax. Is he so much? Do you not think he thinks himself a better man than I am?

Agamemnon. No question.

Ajax. Will you subscribe his thought and say he is?   *140*

Agamemnon. No, noble Ajax. You are as strong, as valiant, as wise, no less noble, much more gentle, and altogether more tractable.

Ajax. Why should a man be proud? How doth pride grow? I know not what it is.   *145*

Agamemnon. Your mind is the clearer, Ajax, and your virtues the fairer. He that is proud eats up himself. Pride is his own glass, his own trumpet, his own chronicle; and whatever praises itself but in the deed, devours the deed in the praise.

Enter Ulysses.

Ajax. I do hate a proud man as I hate the engend'ring   *150* of toads.

Nestor. Yet he loves himself. Is't not strange?

Ulysses. Achilles will not to the field tomorrow.

Agamemnon. What's his excuse?

Ulysses.   He doth relie on none,   *155* But carries on the stream of his dispose Without observance or respect of any, In will peculiar and in self-admission.

Agamemnon. Why, will he not upon our fair request. Untent his person and share the air with us?   *160*

Ulysses. Things small as nothing, for request's sake only, He makes important. Possess'd he is with greatness, And speaks not to himself, but with a pride That quarrels at self-breath. Imagin'd [worth] Holds in his blood such swolne and hot discourse   *165* That 'twixt his mental and his active parts Kingdom'd Achilles in commotion rages And batters gainst itself. What should I say? He is so plaguy proud that the death tokens of it Cry, 'No recovery.'   *170*

Agamemnon.   Let Ajax to go him. Dear lord, go you and greet him in his tent. 'Tis said he holds you well and will be led At your request a little from himself.

Ulysses. O Agamemnon, let it not be so!   *175* We'll consecrate the steps that Ajax makes When they go from Achilles. Shall the proud lord That bastes his arrogance with his own seam

---

Exit: *not in F or Q*   **79 you:** *F omits*   **86–89 matter... Achilles;** *Cf. n.*   **90 fraction:** *division, separation*   **91 faction:** *uniting together as friends* **counsel;** *Cf. n.*   **93 knits not;** *Cf. n.*   **98 flexure:** *bending; F* flight; *Cf. n.*   **103 digestion:** *digestion's*   **104 breath:** *exercise*   **108 apprehensions:** *here five syllables*   **109 attribute:** *reputation, praise*   **111 Not ... beheld:** *not looked at or considered on his part in the proper way*   **113 Yea, like:** *F* Yea, and like   **118 note of judgment:** *mark of good judgment*   **118–122 And worthier ... predominance;** *Cf. n.*   **119 tends:** *awaits* **savage strangeness:** *rude aloofness*   **121 underwrite:** *submit to*   **122 humorous:** *capricious*   **123 lines:** *lunes, fits of temper*

126 overhold: *overestimate*   **130 allowance:** *praise, approbation*   **132 presently:** *at once* SD **Exit:** *not in F or Q*   **133 second voice:** *his words repeated by another person, words at second hand*   **147 his:** *its*   **148 glass:** *mirror* **chronicle:** *history*   **156 dispose:** *predisposition*   **158 peculiar:** *unique, a law unto himself* **self-admission:** *self-approbation*   **161 for request's sake:** *merely because they are requested*   **164 self-breath:** *his own words* **worth:** *F* wroth   **165 swolne:** *swollen* **discourse:** *quarrel, controversy*   **167 Kingdom'd;** *Cf. n.*   **178 seam:** *grease, drippings*

And never suffers matter of the world
Enter his thoughts—save such as do revolve   *180*
And ruminate himself—shall he be worshipp'd
Of what we hold an idol more than he?
No, this thrice worthy and right valiant lord
Must not so stale his palm, nobly acquir'd,
Nor by my will assubjugate his merit,   *185*
As amply titled as Achilles is,
By going to Achilles.
That were to enlard his fat-already pride
And add more coals to Cancer, when he burns
With entertaining great Hyperion.   *190*
This lord go to him? Jupiter forbid,
And say in thunder, 'Achilles go to him!'
   Nestor. [Aside.] O, this is well! He rubs the vein of him.
   Diomedes. [Aside.] And how his silence drinks up this
applause!   *195*
   Ajax. If I go to him, with my armed fist I'll pash him
ore the face.
   Agamemnon.   O no, you shall not go.
   Ajax. And a be proud with me, I'll feeze his pride.
Let me go to him.   *200*
   Ulysses. Not for the worth that hangs upon our quarrel.
   Ajax. A paltry insolent fellow.
   Nestor. [Aside.] How he describes himself!
   Ajax. Can he not be sociable?
   Ulysses. [Aside.] The raven chides blackness.   *205*
   Ajax. I'll let his humor's blood.
   Agamemnon. [Aside.] He will be the physician that should
be the patient.
   Ajax. And all men were o' my mind—
   Ulysses. [Aside.] Wit would be out of fashion.   *210*
   Ajax. A should not bear it so; a should eat swords first.
Shall pride carry it?
   Nestor. [Aside.] And 'twould, you'ld carry half.
   Ulysses. [Aside.] A would have ten shares.
   Ajax. I will knead him. I'll make him supple.   *215*
   Nestor. [Aside.] He's not yet through warm. Force him
with praises. Pour in, pour in; his ambition is dry.
   Ulysses. [To Agamemnon.] My lord, you feed too much
on this dislike.
   Nestor. Our noble general, do not do so.   *220*
   Diomedes. You must prepare to fight without Achilles.
   Ulysses. Why, 'tis this naming of him doth him harm.
Here is a man—but 'tis before his face;
I will be silent.
   Nestor.   Wherefore should you so?   *225*
He is not emulous, as Achilles is.
   Ulysses. Know the whole world, he is as valiant.
   Ajax. A whoreson dog, that shall palter thus with us.
Would he were a Troyan!
   Nestor. What a vice were it in Ajax now—   *230*
   Ulysses. If he were proud.
   Diomedes. Or covetous of praise.
   Ulysses. Ay, or surly borne.

   Diomedes. Or strange, or self-affected.
   Ulysses. Thank the heavens, lord, thou art of sweet   *235*
composure.
Praise him that got thee, she that gave thee suck;
[Fam'd] be thy tutor, and thy parts of nature
Thrice fam'd beyond, beyond all erudition.
But he that disciplin'd thy arms to fight,   *240*
Let Mars divide eternity in twain
And give him half; and for thy vigor,
Bull-bearing Milo his addition yield
To sinewy Ajax. I will not praise thy wisdom,
Which, like a bourn, a pale, a shore, confines   *245*
Thy spacious and dilated parts. Here's Nestor
Instructed by the antiquary times;
He must, he is, he cannot but be wise.
But pardon, father Nestor, were your days
As green as Ajax' and your brains so temper'd,   *250*
You should not have the eminence of him
But be as Ajax.
   Ajax.   Shall I call you father?
   Ulysses. Ay, my good son.
   Diomedes.   Be rul'd by him, Lord Ajax.   *255*
   Ulysses. There is no tarrying here; the hart Achilles
Keeps thicket. Please it our general,
To call together all his state of war.
Fresh kings are come to Troy; tomorrow
We must with all our main of power stand fast.   *260*
And here's a lord—come knights from East to West
And cull their flower, Ajax shall cope the best.
   Agamemnon. Go we to counsel. Let Achilles sleep.
Light boats may sail swift, though greater bulks draw deep.
                                        Exeunt.

ACT THIRD ❧ SCENE FIRST

Music sounds within. Enter Pandarus and a Servant.

   Pandarus. Friend, you! Pray you, a word. Do not you
follow the young Lord Paris?
   Servant. Ay, sir, when he goes before me.
   Pandarus. You depend upon him, I mean.
   Servant. Sir, I do depend upon the Lord.   *5*
   Pandarus. You depend upon a noble gentleman; I must
needs praise him.
   Servant. The Lord be praised.
   Pandarus. You know me, do you not?
   Servant. Faith, sir, superficially.   *10*
   Pandarus. Friend, know me better; I am the Lord Pandarus.
   Servant. I hope I shall know your honor better.
   Pandarus. I do desire it.
   Servant. You are in the state of grace?
   Pandarus. Grace? Not so, friend. Honor and lordship   *15*
are my title. What music is this?
   Servant. I do but partly know, sir; it is music in parts.
   Pandarus. Know you the musicians?
   Servant. Wholly, sir.

---

182 Of what we hold: *by him whom we regard*   **184 stale:** *cheapen* **palm:** *honors*   **185 assubjugate:** *debase* **187 to enlard:** *to fatten; read 't'enlard'* **189 coals to Cancer;** *Cf. n.*   **196 pash:** *bash, strike* **199 a:** *he; so also in l.211* **feeze:** *settle, chastise* **206 let his humor's blood:** *relieve him of humorous blood by bleeding; Cf. n.* **211 eat swords;** *Cf. n.* **214 shares:** *i.e. as of stock; Cf. n.* **216 He's … warm;** *Cf. n.* **through:** *thoroughly* **Force:** *farce, stuff* **218 My lord;** *Cf. n.* **226 emulous:** *envious* **228 palter:** *shuffle, dodge* **233 surly borne:** *of surly bearing*

234 strange: *aloof* **self-affected:** *egotistical* **237 got:** *begot* **238 Fam'd:** *F Fame* **243 Milo;** *Cf. n.* **addition:** *particular quality (i.e. of strength)* **245 bourn:** *boundary* **pale:** *fence* **246 dilated parts:** *expansive qualities of excellence* **247 antiquary:** *ancient* **250 green:** *young, few* **251 should … eminence of:** *would not be superior to* **260 main:** *strength* **262 cope:** *meet* **2 follow:** *i.e. as a servant, follower* **12 honor;** *Cf. n.* **17 in parts:** *in harmony*

Pandarus. Who play they to?   20

Servant. To the hearers, sir.

Pandarus. At whose pleasure, friend?

Servant. At mine, sir, and theirs that love music.

Pandarus. Command, I mean, friend.

Servant. Who shall I command, sir?   25

Pandarus. Friend, we understand not one another. I am too courtly and thou art too cunning. At whose request do these men play?

Servant. That's to't indeed, sir. Marry, sir, at the request of Paris my lord, who's there in person; with him the mortal   30 Venus, the heartblood of beauty, love's invisible soul.

Pandarus. Who? My cousin Cressida?

Servant. No, sir; Helen. Could you not find out that by her attributes?

Pandarus. It should seem, fellow, that thou hast not seen   35 the Lady Cressida. I come to speak with Paris from the Prince Troilus. I will make a complimental assault upon him, for my business seethes.

Servant. Sodden business! There's a stewed phrase indeed!

Enter Paris and Helena.

Pandarus. Fair be to you, my lord, and to all this fair   40 company. Fair desires in all fair measure fairly guide them, especially to you, fair queen! Fair thoughts be your fair pillow.

Helen. Dear lord, you are full of fair words.

Pandarus. You speak your fair pleasure, sweet queen. Fair prince, here is good broken music.   45

Paris. You have broke it, cousin, and by my life you shall make it whole again. You shall piece it out with a piece of your performance. Nell, he is full of harmony.

Pandarus. Truly, lady, no.

Helen. O, sir—   50

Pandarus. Rude, in sooth; in good sooth, very rude.

Paris. Well said, my lord, well. You say so in fits.

Pandarus. I have business to my lord, dear queen. My lord, will you vouchsafe me a word?

Helen. Nay, this shall not hedge us out. We'll hear you   55 sing, certainly.

Pandarus. Well, sweet queen, you are pleasant with me. But, marry, thus, my lord: my dear lord and most esteemed friend, your brother Troilus—

Helen. My Lord Pandarus, honey sweet lord—   60

Pandarus. Go to, sweet queen, go to.—Commends himself most affectionately to you—

Helen. You shall not bob us out of our melody; if you do, our melancholy upon your head.

Pandarus. Sweet queen, sweet queen! That's a sweet   65 queen, i' faith—

Helen. And to make a sweet lady sad is a sour offense.

Pandarus. Nay, that shall not serve your turn; that shall it not, in truth, la! Nay, I care not for such words; no, no.— And, my lord, he desires you that if the king call for him   70 at supper, you will make his excuse.

Helen. My Lord Pandarus!

Pandarus. What says my sweet queen, my very, very sweet queen?

Paris. What exploit's in hand? Where sups he tonight?   75

Helen. Nay, but my lord—

Pandarus. What says my sweet queen? My cousin will fall out with you.

Helen. You must not know where he sups.

Paris. With my disposer, Cressida.   80

Pandarus. No, no; no such matter. You are wide. Come, your disposer is sick.

Paris. Well, I'll make excuse.

Pandarus. Ay, good my lord. Why should you say Cressida? No, your poor disposer's sick.   85

Paris. I spy!

Pandarus. You spy? What do you spy? Come, give me an instrument now, sweet queen.

Helen. Why, this is kindly done.

Pandarus. My niece is horrible in love with a thing you   90 have, sweet queen.

Helen. She shall have it, my lord, if it be not my Lord Paris.

Pandarus. He? No, she'll none of him; they two are twain.

Helen. Falling in after falling out may make them three.   95

Pandarus. Come, come, I'll hear no more of this. I'll sing you a song now.

Helen. Ay, ay, prithee now. By my troth, sweet lord, thou hast a fine forehead.

Pandarus. Ay, you may, you may.   100

Helen. Let the song be love; this love will undo us all. O, Cupid, Cupid, Cupid!

Pandarus. Love? Ay, that it shall, i' faith.

Paris. Ay, good now; love, love, nothing but love.

Pandarus. In good troth, it begins so.   105

> *Love, love, nothing but love, still more!*
>   *For O, love's bow*
>   *Shoots buck and doe.*
>   *The shaft confounds*
>   *Not that it wounds*   110
>   *But tickles still the sore.*
>   *These lovers cry;*
>   *O ho, they die!*
> *Yet that which seems the wound to kill,*
>   *Doth turn 'O ho!' to 'Ha, ha, he!'*   115
>   *So dying love lives still.*
>   *O ho! awhile, but ha, ha, ha!*
> *O ho! groans out for ha, ha, ha!—Hey ho!*

Helen. In love, i' faith, to the very tip of the nose!

Paris. He eats nothing but doves, love, and that breeds   120 hot blood, and hot blood begets hot thoughts, and hot thoughts beget hot deeds, and hot deeds is love.

Pandarus. Is this the generation of love? Hot blood, hot thoughts, and hot deeds? Why, they are vipers! Is love a generation of vipers? Sweet lord, who's afield today?   125

Paris. Hector, Deiphobus, Helenus, Antenor, and all the gallantry of Troy. I would fain have arm'd today but my Nell would not have it so. How chance my brother Troilus went not?

Helen. He hangs the lip at something. You know all, Lord Pandarus?   130

31 **love's invisible soul;** *Cf. n.*   37 **complimental assault;** *Cf. n.*   39 **Sodden;** *Cf. n.* SD **Helena;** *Cf. n.*   40 **Fair;** *Cf. n.*   45 **broken music:** *music in parts, harmony*   51 **sooth:** *truth*   52 **fits;** *Cf. n.*   55 **hedge us out:** *put us off*   63 **bob:** *cheat*

79 **Helen;** *Cf. n.*   80 **disposer:** *mistress, lady*   81 **wide:** *wide of the truth, have missed the mark*   94 **twain:** *separated by disagreements, at variance*   103 **Love;** *Cf. n.*   109 **confounds:** *destroys*   110 **that:** *that which*   114 **wound to kill:** *killing wound*   120 **doves;** *Cf. n.*   124 **vipers;** *Cf. n.*

Pandarus. Not I, honey sweet queen. I long to hear how
they sped today. You'll remember your brother's excuse?

    Paris. To a hair.

    Pandarus. Farewell, sweet queen.

    Helen. Commend me to your niece.   *135*

    Pandarus. I will, sweet queen.   *[Exit.]*

                          Sound a retreat.

    Paris. They're come from field. Let us to Priam's hall
To greet the warriors. Sweet Helen, I must woo you
To help unarm our Hector. His stubborn buckles,
With these your white enchanting fingers touch'd,   *140*
Shall more obey than to the edge of steel
Or force of Greekish sinews. You shall do more
Than all the island kings—disarm great Hector.

    Helen. 'Twill make us proud to be his servant, Paris.
Yea, what he shall receive of us in duty   *145*
Gives us more palm in beauty than we have,
Yea, overshines ourself.

    Paris. Sweet, above thought I love thee!   *Exeunt.*

❧ SCENE SECOND ❧

Enter Pandarus and Troilus' Man.

    Pandarus. How now? Where's thy master? At my cousin
Cressida's?

    Man. No, sir; he stays for you to conduct him thither.

Enter Troilus.

    Pandarus. O, here he comes. How now, how now?

    Troilus. Sirrah, walk off.   *5*

    Pandarus. Have you seen my cousin?

    Troilus. No, Pandarus. I stalk about her door
Like a strange soul upon the Stygian banks
Staying for waftage. O, be thou my Charon
And give me swift transportation to those fields   *10*
Where I may wallow in the lily beds
Propos'd for the deserver. O gentle Pandarus,
From Cupid's shoulder pluck his painted wings
And fly with me to Cressid.

    Pandarus. Walk here i' th' orchard. I'll bring her straight.   *15*

                          Exit Pandarus.

    Troilus. I am giddy; expectation whirls me round.
Th' imaginary relish is so sweet
That it enchants my sense. What will it be
When that the wat'ry palates taste indeed
Love's thrice repured nectar? Death, I fear me,   *20*
Sounding destruction, or some joy too fine,
Too subtle, potent, and too sharp in sweetness
For the capacity of my ruder powers.
I fear it much, and I do fear besides
That I shall lose distinction in my joys,   *25*
As doth a battle when they charge on heaps
The enemy flying.

Enter Pandarus.

    Pandarus. She's making her ready; she'll come straight. You
must be witty now. She does so blush, and fetches her wind
so short, as if she were fray'd with a sprite. I'll fetch her.   *30*
It is the prettiest villain; she fetches her breath so short
as a new-tane sparrow.   *Exit Pandarus.*

    Troilus. Even such a passion doth embrace my bosom.
My heart beats thicker than a feverous pulse,
And all my powers do their bestowing lose,   *35*
Like vassalage at unawares encount'ring
The eye of majesty.

Enter Pandarus and Cressida.

    Pandarus. Come, come, what need you blush? Shame's a
baby. Here she is now; swear the oaths now to her that you
have sworn to me. What, are you gone again? You must be   *40*
watch'd ere you be made tame, must you? Come your ways,
come your ways. And you draw backward, we'll put you i' th'
fills. Why do you not speak to her? Come, draw this curtain
and let's see your picture. Alas, the day! How loath you are to
offend daylight! And 'twere dark you'd close sooner. So, so,   *45*
rub on, and kiss the mistress. How now? A kiss in fee-farm?
Build there, carpenter; the air is sweet. Nay, you shall fight
your hearts out ere I part you. The falcon as the tercel, for all
the ducks i' th' river. Go to, go to!

    Troilus. You have bereft me of all words, lady.   *50*

    Pandarus. Words pay no debts. Give her deeds. But she'll be-
reave you o' th' deeds too, if she call your activity in question.
What, billing again? Here's 'In witness whereof the parties interchangeably—' Come in, come in! I'll go get a fire.   *[Exit.]*

    Cressida. Will you walk in, my lord?   *55*

    Troilus. O Cressida, how often have I wish'd me thus!

    Cressida. Wish'd, my lord? The gods grant—O my lord!

    Troilus. What should they grant? What makes this pretty
abruption? What too curious dreg espies my sweet lady in
the fountain of our love?   *60*

    Cressida. More dregs than water, if my tears have eyes.

    Troilus. Fears make divels of cherubins; they never see truly.

    Cressida. Blind fear that seeing reason leads finds [safer] foot-
ing than blind reason stumbling without fear. To fear the
worst oft cures the worse.   *65*

    Troilus. O, let my lady apprehend no fear. In all Cupid's
pageant there is presented no monster.

    Cressida. [Nor] nothing monstrous neither?

    Troilus. Nothing but our undertakings, when we vow to
weep seas, live in fire, eat rocks, tame tigers; thinking it harder
for our mistress to devise imposition enough than for us to undergo any difficulty imposed. This is the monstruosity in love,
lady; that the will is infinite and the execution confin'd; that
the desire is boundless and the act a slave to limit.

    Cressida. They say all lovers swear more performance than   *75*
they are able, and yet reserve an ability that they never perform, vowing more than the perfection of ten, and discharging
less than the tenth part of one. They that have the voice of
lions and the acts of hares, are they not monsters?

Exit: *not in F or Q*   143 island: *i.e. the Greek islands*   146 palm: *renown*   148
Sweet . . . thee; *Cf. n.*   3 stays: *waits*   5 Sirrah: *a term of address used to inferiors*   8,
9 Stygian . . . Charon; *Cf. n.* waftage: *passage*   12 Propos'd: *promised*   15 straight:
immediately   20 repured: *refined; F reputed*   21 Sounding: *swooning*   26 battle:
army on heaps: *in great numbers*

29 fetches her wind: *breathes*   30 fray'd: *frightened* It: *she* (baby talk)   32 new-tane:
newly taken or captured   33 Even: *read 'e'en'*   34 thicker: *faster*   35 bestowing: *use,
employment*   41 watch'd: *kept from sleeping; Cf. n.*   43 fills: *shafts, as of a horse-drawn
wagon* curtain: *veil*   45 close: *come together*   46 rub on: *press on* (a term from bowling) in fee-farm: *indefinitely; Cf. n.*   48 falcon . . . tercel; *Cf. n.*   53, 54 'In . . .
interchangeably': *a legal phrase used in mutual contracts* SD Exit: *not in F or Q*   59
abruption: *breaking off* curious: *minute*   63 safer: *F safe*   67 pageant: *masque, pantomime*   68 Nor: *F Not*   72 monstruosity: *monstrosity*   73 will: *desire, appetite*

Troilus. Are there such? Such are not we! Praise us as we   *80*
are tasted; allow us as we prove. Our head shall go bare till
merit crown it. No perfection in reversion shall have a praise
in present. We will not name desert before his birth, and being
born, his addition shall be humble. Few words to fair faith.
Troilus shall be such to Cressid. As what envy can say worst   *85*
shall be a mock for his truth; and what truth can speak truest,
not truer than Troilus.

Cressida. Will you walk in, my lord?

Enter Pandarus.

Pandarus. What, blushing still? Have you not done talking
yet?   *90*

Cressida. Well, uncle, what folly I commit I dedicate to you.

Pandarus. I thank you for that. If my lord get a boy of you,
you'll give him me. Be true to my lord. If he flinch, chide me
for it.

Troilus. You know now your hostages—your uncle's   *95*
word and my firm faith.

Pandarus. Nay, I'll give my word for her too. Our kindred
though they be long ere they are woo'd, they are constant
being won. They are burrs, I can tell you; they'll stick
where they are thrown.   *100*

Cressida. Boldness comes to me now and brings me heart.
Prince Troilus, I have lov'd you night and day
For many weary months.

Troilus. Why was my Cressid then so hard to win?

Cressida. Hard to seem won. But I was won, my lord,   *105*
With the first glance that ever—pardon me!
If I confess much you will play the tyrant.
I love you now, but not till now so much
But I might master it. In faith, I lie.
My thoughts were like unbridled children [grown]   *110*
Too headstrong for their mother. See, we fools!
Why have I blabb'd? Who shall be true to us
When we are so unsecret to ourselves?
But though I lov'd you well, I woo'd you not;
And yet, good faith, I wish'd myself a man,   *115*
Or that we women had men's privilege
Of speaking first. Sweet, bid me hold my tongue,
For in this rapture I shall surely speak
The thing I shall repent. See, see, your silence,
Coming in dumbness, from my weakness draws   *120*
My soul of counsel from me. Stop my mouth.

Troilus. And shall, albeit sweet music issues thence.

Pandarus. Pretty, i' faith.

Cressida. My lord, I do beseech you, pardon me;
'Twas not my purpose thus to beg a kiss.   *125*
I am asham'd. O heavens, what have I done!
For this time will I take my leave, my lord.

Troilus. Your leave, sweet Cressid?

Pandarus. Leave! And you take leave till tomorrow
morning—   *130*

Cressida. Pray you, content you.

Troilus. What offends you, lady?

Cressida. Sir, mine own company.

Troilus. You cannot shun yourself.

Cressida.   Let me go and try.   *135*

I have a kind of self resides with you;
But an unkind self, that itself will leave
To be another's fool. Where is my wit?
I would be gone. I speak I know not what.

Troilus. Well know they what they speak that [speak]   *140*
so wisely.

Cressida. Perchance, my lord, I shew more craft than love,
And fell so roundly to a large confession
To angle for your thoughts. But you are wise,
Or else you love not; for to be wise and love   *145*
Exceeds man's might. That dwells with gods above.

Troilus. Oh, that I thought it could be in a woman
(As if it can, I will presume in you)
To feed for aye her lamp and flames of love;
To keep her constancy in plight and youth,   *150*
Outliving beauties outward, with a mind
That doth renew swifter than blood decays;
Or that persuasion could but thus convince me
That my integrity and truth to you
Might be affronted with the match and weight   *155*
Of such a winnowed [purity] in love.
How were I then uplifted! But, alas,
I am as true as truth's simplicity,
And simpler than the infancy of truth.

Cressida. In that I'll war with you.   *160*

Troilus.   O virtuous fight,
When right with right wars who shall be most right.
True swains in love shall in the world to come
Approve their truths by Troilus. When their rhymes,
Full of protest, of oath, and big compare,   *165*
Wants similies, truth tir'd with iteration—
As true as steel, as plantage to the moon,
As sun to day, as turtle to her mate,
As iron to adamant, as earth to th' center—
Yet after all comparisons of truth,   *170*
As truth's authentic author to be cited,
'As true as Troilus' shall crown up the verse,
And sanctify the numbers.

Cressida.   Prophet may you be!
If I be false, or swerve a hair from truth,   *175*
When time is old and hath forgot itself,
When water drops have worn the stones of Troy
And blind oblivion swallow'd cities up,
And mighty states characterless are grated
To dusty nothing; yet let memory   *180*
From false to false among false maids in love
Upbraid my falsehood. When they've said 'As false
As air, as water, as wind, as sandy earth,
As fox to lamb, as wolf to heifer's calf,
Pard to the hind, or stepdame to her son,'   *185*
Yea, let them say, to stick the heart of falsehood,
'As false as Cressida.'

Pandarus. Go to, a bargain made! Seal it, seal it. I'll be the
witness. Here I hold your hand, here my cousin's. If ever you
prove false one to another, since I have taken such pains to

---

81 tasted: *tested* **allow:** *estimate* **82 in reversion:** *in the future* **83 his:** *its* **85, 86**
envy . . . his truth; *Cf. n.* **92 get:** *beget* **110 grown:** F *grow* **120 Coming:** *forward, apt; Cf. n.* **121 soul of counsel:** *innermost thoughts*

140 speak so: F *speaks so* **143 roundly:** *frankly, straight-forwardly* **150 in plight and**
youth: *in health and youth, ever young* **151 beauties outward:** *external beauties* **155**
affronted: *met with, matched with* **156 purity:** F *puriritie* **164 Approve:** *attest,*
confirm **165 protest:** *stressed — ‐́ compare:** *comparisons* **166 Wants:**
want **167 plantage:** *plants, vegetation; Cf. n.* **168 turtle:** *turtle dove* **169 ada-**
mant: *loadstone* **179 characterless:** *stressed — ‐́ — —* **185 Pard:** *leopard* **186**
stick: *stab*

bring you together, let all pitiful goers-between be call'd to
the world's end after my name. Call them all Pandars. Let all
constant men be Troiluses, all false women Cressids, and all
brokers-between Pandars! Say 'Amen.'

Troilus. Amen.   *195*

Cressida. Amen.

Pandarus. Amen. Whereupon I will shew you a chamber,
which bed, because it shall not speak of your pretty encounters,
press it to death. Away! And Cupid grant all tongue-tied maidens
here Bed, chamber, and Pandar to provide this gear.   *200*

                                  Exeunt.

❧ SCENE THIRD ❧

*Enter Ulysses, Diomedes, Nestor, Agamemnon, Menelaus, and
Calchas. Flourish.*

Calchas. Now, princes, for the service I have done you,
Th' advantage of the time prompts me aloud
To call for recompense. Appear it to your mind
That through the sight I bear in things to love,
I have abandon'd Troy, left my possession,   *5*
Incurr'd a traitor's name, expos'd myself
From certain and possess'd conveniences
To doubtful fortunes, sequest'ring from me all
That time, acquaintance, custom, and condition
Made tame and most familiar to my nature;   *10*
And here, to do you service, am become
As new into the world, strange, unacquainted.
I do beseech you, as in way of taste,
To give me now a little benefit
Out of those many regist'red in promise   *15*
Which, you say, live to come in my behalf.

     Agamemnon. What wouldst thou of us, Troyan?
Make demand.

     Calchas. You have a Troyan prisoner call'd Antenor,
Yesterday took. Troy holds him very dear.   *20*
Oft have you (often have you thanks therefore)
Desir'd my Cressid in right great exchange,
Whom Troy hath still denied. But this Antenor
I know is such a wrest in their affairs
That their negotiations all must slack,   *25*
Wanting his manage; and they will almost
Give us a prince of blood, a son of Priam,
In change of him. Let him be sent, great princes,
And he shall buy my daughter, and her presence
Shall quite strike off all service I have done   *30*
In most accepted pain.

     Agamemnon.   Let Diomedes bear him
And bring us Cressid hither. Calchas shall have
What he requests of us. Good Diomed,
Furnish you fairly for this interchange.   *35*
Withal bring word if Hector will tomorrow
Be answer'd in his challenge. Ajax is ready.

     Diomedes. This shall I undertake, and 'tis a burthen
Which I am proud to bear.   *Exit.*

Enter Achilles and Patroclus in their tent.

     Ulysses. Achilles stand i' th' entrance of his tent.   *40*
Please it our general to pass strangely by him
As if he were forgot; and princes all,
Lay negligent and loose regard upon him.
I will come last. 'Tis like he'll question me
Why such unplausive eyes are bent, why turn'd on him.   *45*
If so, I have derision medicinable
To use between your strangeness and his pride,
Which his own will shall have desire to drink.
It may do good. Pride hath no other glass
To show itself but pride; for supple knees   *50*
Feed arrogance and are the proud man's fees.

     Agamemnon. We'll execute your purpose and put on
A form of strangeness as we pass along.
So do each lord, and either greet him not
Or else disdainfully, which shall shake him more   *55*
Than if not look'd on. I will lead the way.

     Achilles. What, comes the general to speak with me?
You know my mind. I'll fight no more 'gainst Troy.

     Agamemnon. What says Achilles? Would he ought with us?

     Nestor. Would you, my lord, ought with the general?   *60*

     Achilles. No.

     Nestor. Nothing, my lord.

     Agamemnon. The better.   *[Exeunt Agamemnon and Nestor.]*

     Achilles. Good day, good day.

     Menelaus. How do you? How do you?   *[Exit.]*   *65*

     Achilles. What, does the cuckold scorn me?

     Ajax. How now, Patroclus?

     Achilles. Good morrow, Ajax.

     Ajax. Ha.

     Achilles. Good morrow.   *70*

     Ajax. Ay, and good next day too.   *[Exit.]*

     Achilles. What mean these fellows? Know they not Achilles?

     Patroclus. They pass by strangely. They were us'd to bend
To send their smiles before them to Achilles,
To come as humbly as they us'd to creep   *75*
To holy altars.

     Achilles.   What, am I poor of late?
'Tis certain, greatness, once falne out with fortune,
Must fall out with men too. What the declin'd is
He shall as soon read in the eyes of others   *80*
As feel in his own fall; for men, like butterflies,
Shew not their mealy wings but to the summer;
And not a man for being simply man
Hath any honor, but honor'd for those honors
That are without him, as place, riches, and favor,   *85*
Prizes of accident as oft as merit;
Which when they fall, as being slippery standers,
The love that lean'd on them as slippery too,
Doth one pluck down another, and together
Die in the fall. But 'tis not so with me;   *90*
Fortune and I are friends. I do enjoy
At ample point all that I did possess,
Save these men's looks, who do, methinks, find out

SD **Exeunt;** *Cf. n.* SD **Flourish:** *fanfare*   **4 sight … love;** *Cf. n.*   **5 possession:** *property*   **8 sequest'ring:** *setting aside*   **10 tame:** *usual, familiar*   **13 taste:** *sample*   **16 live to come:** *exist to be used in the future*   **24 wrest:** *vital instrument; cf. I.3.159; Cf. n.*   **26 Wanting his manage:** *lacking his management*   **31 pain:** *hardships; Cf. n.*   **32 bear:** *take*   **35 Furnish you:** *equip yourself*

41 strangely: *aloofly*   **43 loose:** *disrespectful, negligent*   **44 like:** *likely*   **45 unplausive:** *not applauding, disapproving*   **46 medicinable:** *pronounced 'med'cinable'*   **49 glass:** *mirror*   **Exit:** *F Exeunt; this blanket SD is the F substitute for the several exits supplied by modern editors at ll. 63 and 65*   **78 falne:** *fall'n*   **85 without him:** *outside of him*   **92 At ample point:** *fully*

Something not worth in me such rich beholding
As they have often given. Here is Ulysses.   95
I'll interrupt his reading. How now, Ulysses?
   Ulysses. Now, great Thetis' son.
   Achilles.   What are you reading?
   Ulysses. A strange fellow here
Writes me that man, how dearly ever parted,   100
How much in having, or without or in,
Cannot make boast to have that which he hath,
Nor feels not what he owes, but by reflection;
As when his virtues shining upon others
Heat them, and they retort that heat again   105
To the first giver.
   Achilles.   This is not strange, Ulysses.
The beauty that is borne here in the face
The bearer knows not, but commends itself
[To others' eyes; not doth the eye itself,   110
That most pure spirit of sense, behold itself,]
Not going from itself; but eye to eye oppos'd
Salutes each other with each other's form.
For speculation turns not to itself
Till it hath travel'd and is married there   115
Where it may see itself. This is not strange at all.
   Ulysses. I do not strain at the position—
It is familiar—but at the author's drift;
Who in his circumstance expressly proves
That no [man] is the lord of anything.   120
Though in and of him there is much consisting,
Till he communicate his parts to others,
Nor doth he of himself know them for aught
Till he behold them formed in th' applause
Where [th' are] extended; who, like an arch, reverb'rate   125
The voice again, or like a gate of steel,
Fronting the sun, receives and renders back
His figure and his heat. I was much rapt in this,
And apprehended here immediately
The unknown Ajax.   130
Heavens, what a man is there! A very horse,
That has he knows not what. Nature, what things there are
Most abject in regard and dear in use!
What things again most dear in the esteem
And poor in worth! Now shall we see tomorrow   135
An act that very chance doth throw upon him—
Ajax renown'd. O heavens, what some men do,
While some men leave to do!
How some men creep in skittish Fortune's hall
Whiles others play the idiots in her eyes!   140
How one man eats into another's pride,
While pride is feasting in his wantonness!
To see these Grecian lords! Why, even already
They clap the lubber Ajax on the shoulder
As if his foot were on brave Hector's breast   145
And great Troy shrinking.
   Achilles.   I do believe it,

For they pass'd by me as misers do by beggars,
Neither gave to me good word nor look.
What, are my deeds forgot?   150
   Ulysses. Time hath, my lord, a wallet at his back
Wherein he puts alms for Oblivion,
A great-siz'd monster of ingratitudes.
Those scraps are good deeds past,
Which are devour'd as fast as they are made,   155
Forgot as soon as done. Perseverance, dear my lord,
Keeps honor bright. To have done is to hang
Quite out of fashion like a rusty mail,
In monumental mock'ry. Take the instant way,
For honor travels in a strait so narrow   160
Where one but goes abreast. Keep then the path;
For emulation hath a thousand sons
That one by one pursue. If you give way
Or hedge aside from the direct forthright,
Like to an ent'red tide, they all rush by   165
And leave you hindmost;
Or like a gallant horse falne in the first rank
Lie there for pavement to the abject [rear],
Orerun and trampled on. Then what they do in present,
Though less than yours in past, must oertop yours.   170
For Time is like a fashionable host
That slightly shakes his parting guest by th' hand,
And with his arms outstretch'd, as he would fly,
Grasps in the comer. The welcome ever smiles,
And [farewell] goes out sighing. O, let not virtue seek   175
Remuneration for the thing it was;
For beauty, wit,
High birth, vigor of bone, desert in service,
Love, friendship, charity, are subjects all
To envious and calumniating time.   180
One touch of nature makes the whole world kin:
That all with one consent praise new-born gauds
Though they are made and molded of things past,
And [give] to dust that is a little gilt
More laud than gilt oredusted.   185
The present eye praises the present object.
Then marvel not, thou great and complete man,
That all the Greeks begin to worship Ajax,
Since things in motion [sooner] catch the eye
Than what not stirs. The cry went out on thee,   190
And still it might, and yet it may again,
If thou wouldst not entomb thyself alive
And case thy reputation in thy tent,
Whose glorious deeds, but in these fields of late,
Made emulous missions 'mongst the gods themselves   195
And drave great Mars to faction.
   Achilles.   Of this my privacy
I have strong reasons.
   Ulysses.   But 'gainst your privacy
The reasons are more potent and heroical.   200
'Tis known, Achilles, that you are in love
With one of Priam's daughters.
   Achilles. Ha? Known?

---

100 **how ... parted:** *howsoever well supplied with parts, or talents*   101 **or ... or:** *either ... or*   103 **owes:** *owns*   105 **retort:** *return*   110, 111 **To ... itself:** *not in F*   114 **speculation:** *seeing, sight*   115 **married:** *joined*   117 **strain:** *F* straine it   118 **drift:** *general direction of the author's argument*   119 **circumstance:** *detailed proof*   120 **man:** *F* may   121 **consisting:** *residing, inhering*   125 **th' are:** *F* they are   **extended:** *magnified, spread*   **arch:** *vaulted roof*   132 **Nature:** *a mild oath or expletive*   133 **abject:** *poor, mean*   **dear in use:** *precious in the using*   139, 140 **How ... eyes;** *Cf. n.*   142 **feasting;** *Cf. n.*   144 **lubber:** *lout, blockhead*

151 **wallet:** *large bag*   152 **alms:** *gifts* (i.e. the scraps of l. 154)   **Oblivion:** *secondary accent on last syllable*   158 **mail:** *coat of mail*   159 **instant:** *present*   161 **one but goes:** *walks*   162 **emulation:** *rivalry*   164 **forthright:** *straightaway*   168 **rear:** *rear ranks; Cf. n.*   175 **farewell:** *F* farewels   181 **touch:** *quality, trait*   184 **give;** *Cf. n.*   187 **complete:** *whole, perfect (stressed ⌣ —)*   189 **sooner;** *F* begin to; *Cf. n.*   190 **out on:** *Q* once on   195 **emulous:** *envious*   196 **drave:** *drove*

Ulysses. Is that a wonder?
The providence that's in a watchful state　　　　　　　*205*
Knows almost every grain of Pluto's gold,
Finds bottom in th' uncomprehensive deeps,
Keeps place with thought, and almost like the gods
[Does] thoughts unveil in their dumb cradles.
There is a mystery, with whom relation　　　　　　　*210*
Durst never meddle, in the soul of state,
Which hath an operation more divine
Than breath or pen can give expressure to.
All the commerce that you have had with Troy
As perfectly is ours as yours, my lord.　　　　　　　*215*
And better would it fit Achilles much
To throw down Hector than Polixena.
But it must grieve young Pyrrhus now at home,
When fame shall in [our islands] sound her trump
And all the Greekish girls shall tripping sing,　　　*220*
'Great Hector's sister did Achilles win,
But our great Ajax bravely beat down him.'
Farewell, my lord. I as your lover speak;
The fool slides ore the ice that you should break.　　*[Exit.]*

　　Patroclus. To this effect, Achilles, have I mov'd you.　*225*
A woman impudent and mannish grown
Is not more loath'd than an effeminate man
In time of action. I stand condemn'd for this;
They think my little stomach to the war
And your great love to me restrains you thus.　　　*230*
Sweet, rouse yourself; and the weak wanton Cupid
Shall from your neck unloose his amorous fold,
And like a dew drop from the lion's mane
Be shook to airy air.
　　Achilles.　　　　　Shall Ajax fight with Hector?　*235*
　　Patroclus. Ay, and perhaps receive much honor by him.
　　Achilles. I see my reputation is at stake;
My fame is shrowdly gor'd.
　　Patroclus.　　　　　O then, beware.
Those wounds heal ill that men do give themselves.　*240*
Omission to do what is necessary
Seals a commission to a blank of danger,
And danger like an ague subtly taints
Even then when we sit idly in the sun.
　　Achilles. Go call Thersites hither, sweet Patroclus.　*245*
I'll send the fool to Ajax and desire him
T' invite the Troyan lords after the combat
To see us here unarm'd. I have a woman's longing,
An appetite that I am sick withal,
To see great Hector in his weeds of peace,　　　　*250*

　　　　　　　　Enter Thersites.

To talk with him and to behold his visage,
Even to my full of view. A labor sav'd.
　　Thersites. A wonder.
　　Achilles. What?
　　Thersites. Ajax goes up and down the field asking for　*255*
himself.

　　Achilles. How so?
　　Thersites. He must fight singly tomorrow with Hector, and
is so prophetically proud of an heroical cudgeling that he raves
in saying nothing.　　　　　　　　　　　　　　*260*
　　Achilles. How can that be?
　　Thersites. Why, he stalks up and down like a peacock—a
stride and a stand; ruminates like an hostess that hath no arithmetic but her brain to set down her reckoning; bites his lip
with a politic regard, as who should say, 'There were wit　*265*
in this head and 'twould out'; and so there is, but it lies as
coldly in him as fire in a flint, which will not show without
knocking. The man's undone forever; for if Hector break not
his neck i' th' combat, he'll break't himself in vainglory. He
knows not me. I said, 'Good morrow, Ajax'; and he replies,　*270*
'Thanks, Agamemnon.' What think you of this man that takes
me for the general? He's grown a very land-fish, languageless, a
monster. A plague of opinion! A man may wear it on both
sides, like a leather jerkin.
　　Achilles. Thou must be my ambassador to him, Thersites.　*275*
　　Thersites. Who, I? Why, he'll answer nobody. He professes
not answering. Speaking is for beggars; he wears his tongue
in's arms. I will put on his presence; let Patroclus make his
demands to me; you shall see the pageant of Ajax.
　　Achilles. To him, Patroclus. Tell him I humbly desire the val-
iant Ajax to invite the most valorous Hector to come unarm'd
to my tent, and to procure safe-conduct for his person of the
magnanimous and most illustrious, six-or-seven-times-honor'd
captain, general of the Grecian army, Agamemnon, et cetera.
Do this.　　　　　　　　　　　　　　　　　　*285*
　　Patroclus. Jove bless great Ajax!
　　Thersites. Hum.
　　Patroclus. I come from the worthy Achilles.
　　Thersites. Ha?
　　Patroclus. Who most humbly desires you to invite　　*290*
Hector to his tent.
　　Thersites. Hum.
　　Patroclus. And to procure safe-conduct from Agamemnon.
　　Thersites. Agamemnon?
　　Patroclus. Ay, my lord.　　　　　　　　　　　*295*
　　Thersites. Ha!
　　Patroclus. What say you to't?
　　Thersites. God buy you, with all my heart.
　　Patroclus. Your answer, sir.
　　Thersites. If tomorrow be a fair day, by eleven o'clock it　*300*
will go one way or other. Howsoever, he shall pay for me ere
he has me.
　　Patroclus. Your answer, sir.
　　Thersites. Fare you well, with all my heart.
　　Achilles. Why, but he is not in this tune, is he?　　*305*
　　Thersites. No, but he's out o' tune thus. What music
will be in him when Hector has knock'd out his brains,
I know not, but I am sure, none, unless the fiddler Apollo
get his sinews to make catlings on.
　　Achilles. Come, thou shalt bear a letter to him straight.　*310*
　　Thersites. Let me carry another to his horse, for that's the
more capable creature.
　　Achilles. My mind is troubled like a fountain stirr'd,

---

206 Knows ... gold; *Cf. n.*　**207 uncomprehensive:** *incomprehensible*　**208 Keeps place with:** *consorts with*　**209 Does:** Q *Do;* F *Doe*　**210 relation:** *act of relating, telling*　**211 state:** *the State*　**213 expressure:** *expression*　**214 commerce:** *stressed — –*　**217 Polixena;** *Cf. n.*　**218 Pyrrhus:** *Neoptolemus, son of Achilles*　**219 our islands:** F *her island*　**trump:** *trumpet*　**224 fool ... break;** *Cf. n.*　**229 stomach:** *liking*　**232 fold:** *embrace*　**238 shrowdly gor'd:** *sharply (shrewdly) wounded*　**242 commission ... blank;** *Cf. n.*　**244, 252 Even:** *read 'e'en'*　**250 weeds:** *clothes*

264 reckoning: *bill, computation*　**265 political regard:** *serious look*　**were:** *is*　**266 and:** *if*　**'twould:** *it would come;* F *twoo'd*　**272 land-fish:** *a fish living on land, an unnatural creature*　**273 of:** *on*　**opinion:** *reputation, fame*　**278 put on:** *act out*　**298 buy:** *be with*　**309 catlings:** *catgut strings for musical instruments*　**312 capable:** *intelligent*

And I myself see not the bottom of it.

Thersites. Would the fountain of your mind were clear   *315*
again, that I might water an ass at it. I had rather be a tick in
a sheep than such a valiant ignorance.   [*Exeunt.*]

ACT FOURTH ❧ Scene First

Enter at one door Aeneas with a torch; at another Paris, Deiphobus,
Antenor, Diomed the Grecian, with torches.

Paris. See, ho! Who is that there?
Deiphobus.   It is the Lord Aeneas.
Aeneas. Is the prince there in person?
Had I so good occasion to lie long
As you, Prince Paris, nothing but heavenly business   *5*
Should rob my bedmate of my company.
  Diomedes. That's my mind too. Good morrow, Lord Aeneas.
  Paris. A valiant Greek, Aeneas; take his hand.
Witness the process of your speech, [wherein]
You told how Diomed in a whole week by days   *10*
Did haunt you in the field.
  Aeneas.   Health to you, valiant sir,
During all question of the gentle truce;
But when I meet you arm'd, as black defiance
As heart can think or courage execute!   *15*
  Diomedes. The one and other Diomed embraces.
Our bloods are now in calm, and so long, health.
But when contention and occasion meets,
By Jove, I'll play the hunter for thy life
With all my force, pursuit, and policy.   *20*
  Aeneas. And thou shalt hunt a lion that will fly
With his face backward. In humane gentleness,
Welcome to Troy; now, by Anchises' life,
Welcome indeed. By Venus' hand I swear,
No man alive can love in such a sort   *25*
The thing he means to kill more excellently.
  Diomedes. We sympathize. Jove let Aeneas live,
If to my sword his fate be not the glory,
A thousand complete courses of the sun,
But in mine emulous honor let him die,   *30*
With every joint a wound, and that tomorrow.
  Aeneas. We know each other well.
  Diomedes. We do, and long to know each other worse.
  Paris. This is the most despiteful'st gentle greeting,
The noblest hateful love that ere I heard of.   *35*
What business, lord, so early?
  Aeneas. I was sent for to the king, but why, I know not.
  Paris. His purpose meets you. It was to bring this Greek
To Calchas' house, and there to render him,
For the enfree'd Antenor, the fair Cressid.   *40*
Let's have your company; or if you please
Haste there before us. I constantly do think,
Or rather call my thought a certain knowledge,
My brother Troilus lodges there tonight.

Rouse him and give him note of our approach,   *45*
With the whole quality whereof. I fear
We shall be much unwelcome.
  Aeneas.   That I assure you.
Troilus had rather Troy were borne to Greece
Then Cressid borne from Troy.
  Paris.   There is no help.   *50*
The bitter disposition of the time
Will have it so. On, lord, we'll follow you.
  Aeneas. Good morrow, all.   *Exit Aeneas.*
  Paris. And tell me, noble Diomed; faith, tell me true,   *55*
Even in the soul of sound good fellowship,
Who in your thoughts merits fair Helen most,
Myself or Menelaus?
  Diomedes.   Both alike.
He merits well to have her that doth seek her,   *60*
Not making any scruple of her soilure,
With such a hell of pain and world of charge.
And you as well to keep her that defend her,
Not palating the taste of her dishonor,
With such a costly loss of wealth and friends.   *65*
He, like a puling cuckold, would drink up
The lees and dregs of a flat tamed piece.
You, like a lecher, out of whorish loins
Are pleas'd to breed out your inheritors.
Both merits pois'd, each weighs nor less nor more,   *70*
But he as he; which heavier for a whore?
  Paris. You are too bitter to your countrywoman.
  Diomedes. She's bitter to her country. Hear me, Paris.
For every false drop in her bawdy veins
A Grecian's life hath sunk; for every scruple   *75*
Of her contaminated carrion weight
A Troyan hath been slain. Since she could speak,
She hath not given so many good words breath
As for her Greeks and Troyans suff'red death.
  Paris. Fair Diomed, you do as chapmen do,   *80*
Dispraise the thing that you desire to buy;
But we in silence hold this virtue well;
We'll not commend what we intend to sell.
Here lies our way.   *Exeunt.*

❧ Scene Second ❧

Enter Troilus and Cressida.

Troilus. Dear, trouble not yourself. The morn is cold.
Cressida. Then, sweet my lord, I'll call mine uncle down.
He shall unbolt the gates.
  Troilus.   Trouble him not.
To bed, to bed. Sleep kill those pretty eyes,   *5*
And give as soft attachment to thy senses
As infants empty of all thought.
  Cressida.   Good morrow, then.
  Troilus. I prithee now, to bed.
  Cressida.   Are you aweary of me?   *10*

---

9 process: *course, gist* **wherein:** *F within*   **10 by days:** *day by day*   **13 question:**
discussion   **23 Anchises':** *Anchises was Aeneas' father*   **24 Venus':** *Venus was Aeneas'*
mother   **27 sympathize:** *agree, are of the same mind*   **29 complete:** *stressed ˉ —*   **30**
emulous: *envious*   **38 His purpose meets you:** *his reason is right here before you*   **42**
constantly: *confidently*

46 quality: *substance, occasion of the visit*   **61 soilure:** *soiled state, dishonor*   **62 charge:**
trouble expense   **67 tamed:** *opened, with seal broken* (with senses pointing both ways in the
pun on *piece*)   **piece:** *cask of wine; also a slang term for a woman*   **70 pois'd:** *weighed* **nor**
less: *F no lesse*   **71 which . . . whore?;** *Cf. n.*   **75 scruple:** *a very small unit of weight*   **80**
chapmen: *petty merchants*   **83 We'll . . . sell;** *Cf. n.*   **5 kill:** *overpower, subdue*

Troilus. O Cressida! But that the busy day,
Wak'd by the lark, hath rous'd the ribald crows,
And dreaming night will hide our eyes no longer,
I would not from thee.
    Cressida.   Night hath been too brief.   *15*
    Troilus. Beshrew the witch! With venomous wights she stays
As [tediously] as hell, but flies the grasps of love
With wings more momentary swift than thought.
You will catch cold, and curse me.
    Cressida. Prithee, tarry. You men will never tarry.   *20*
O foolish Cressid, I might have still held off,
And then you would have tarried. Hark, there's one up?
    Pandarus. *Within.* What's all the doors open here?
    Troilus. It is your uncle.   *Enter Pandarus.*
    Cressida. A pestilence on him. Now will he be mocking.   *25*
I shall have such a life!
    Pandarus. How now, how now? How go maidenheads? Hear
you, maid, where's my cousin Cressid?
    Cressida. Go hang yourself, you naughty mocking uncle!
You bring me to do—and then you flout me too.   *30*
    Pandarus. To do what? To do what? Let her say what!
What have I brought you to do?
    Cressida. Come, come, beshrew your heart. You'll nere be
good, nor suffer others.
    Pandarus. Ha, ha! Alas, poor wretch. A poor chipochia,   *35*
hast not slept tonight? Would he not, a naughty man,
let it sleep? A bugbear take him!   *One knocks.*
    Cressida. Did not I tell you? Would he were knock'd i' th'
head!
Who's that at door? Good uncle, go and see.   *40*
My lord, come you again into my chamber.
You smile and mock me, as if I meant naughtily.
    Troilus. Ha, ha.
    Cressida. Come, you are deceiv'd; I think of no such thing.
How earnestly they knock! Pray you, come in.   *Knock.*
I would not for half Troy have you seen here.   *Exeunt.*
    Pandarus. Who's there? What's the matter? Will you beat
down the door? How now, what's the matter?

[Enter Aeneas.]

    Aeneas. Good morrow, lord, good morrow.
    Pandarus. Who's there? My Lord Aeneas? By my troth, I   *50*
knew you not. What news with you so early?
    Aeneas. Is not Prince Troilus here?
    Pandarus. Here? What should he do here?
    Aeneas. Come, he is here, my lord; do not deny him.
It doth import him much to speak with me.   *55*
    Pandarus. Is he here, say you? 'Tis more than I know, I'll
be sworn. For my own part, I came in late. What should he
do here?
    Aeneas. Who! Nay then. Come, come, you'll do him wrong
ere y' are ware. You'll be so true to him to be false to him.   *60*
Do not you know of him, but yet go fetch him hither; go.
                                  [Exit Pandarus.]

Enter Troilus.

    Troilus. How now! What's the matter?
    Aeneas. My lord, I scarce have leisure to salute you,

My matter is so rash. There is at hand
Paris, your brother, and Deiphobus,   *65*
The Grecian Diomed, and our Antenor
Deliver'd to us; and for him forthwith,
Ere the first sacrifice, within this hour,
We must give up to Diomedes' hand
The Lady Cressida.   *70*
    Troilus.   Is it concluded so?
    Aeneas. By Priam and the general state of Troy.
They are at hand and ready to effect it.
    Troilus. How my achievements mock me!
I will go meet them. And my Lord Aeneas,   *75*
We met by chance; you did not find me here.
    Aeneas. Good, good, my lord. The secrets of nature
Have not more gift in taciturnity.   *Exeunt.*

Enter Pandarus and Cressid.

    Pandarus. Is't possible? No sooner got but lost! The divel
take Antenor! The young prince will go mad. A plague   *80*
upon Antenor! I would they had broke's neck!
    Cressida. How now? What's the matter? Who was here?
    Pandarus. Ah, ha!
    Cressida. Why sigh you so profoundly? Where's my lord?
Gone?   *85*
Tell me, sweet uncle, what's the matter?
    Pandarus. Would I were as deep under the earth as I am
above!
    Cressida. O, the gods! What's the matter?
    Pandarus. Prithee, get thee in. Would thou hadst nere   *90*
been born; I knew thou wouldst be his death.
O poor gentleman! A plague upon Antenor!
    Cressida. Good uncle, I beseech you, on my knees I beseech
you, what's the matter?
    Pandarus. Thou must be gone, wench, thou must be   *95*
gone. Thou art chang'd for Antenor. Thou must to thy father,
and be gone from Troilus. 'Twill be his death; 'twill be his
bane. He cannot bear it.
    Cressida. O, you immortal gods! I will not go.
    Pandarus. Thou must.   *100*
    Cressida. I will not, uncle! I have forgot my father;
I know no touch of consanguinity;
No kin, no love, no blood, no soul, so near me
As the sweet Troilus. O, you gods divine!
Make Cressid's name the very crown of falsehood
If ever she leave Troilus! Time, force, and death   *105*
Do to this body what extremity you can.
But the strong base and building of my love
Is as the very center of the earth,
Drawing all things to it. I will go in and weep.
    Pandarus. Do, do.   *110*
    Cressida. Tear my bright hair, and scratch my praised cheeks.
Crack my clear voice with sobs, and break my heart
With sounding Troilus, I will not go from Troy.   *Exeunt.*

---

11 **But that:** *except that*   16 **venomous wights:** *evil creatures*   17 **tediously:** *F* hidi-
ously   35 **chipochia;** *Cf. n.*   55 **doth import him much:** *is very important to him*

64 **rash:** *urgent*   69 **Diomedes':** *F* Diomed   77 **secrets:** *possibly three syllables
here*   96 **chang'd:** *exchanged*   98 **bane:** *destruction, death*

❧ SCENE THIRD ❧

Enter Paris, Troilus, Aeneas, Deiphobus, Antenor, and Diomedes.

Paris. It is great morning, and the hour prefix'd
Of her delivery to this valiant Greek
Comes fast upon. Good my brother Troilus,
Tell you the lady what she is to do,
And haste her to the purpose.   5
Troilus.   Walk into her house.
I'll bring her to the Grecian presently;
And to his hand when I deliver her,
Think it an altar and thy brother Troilus
A priest, there off'ring to it his [own] heart.   10
Paris. I know what 'tis to love,
And would, as I shall pity, I could help.
Please you walk in, my lords.   *Exeunt.*

❧ SCENE FOURTH ❧

Enter Pandarus and Cressid.

Pandarus. Be moderate, be moderate.
Cressida. Why tell you me of moderation?
The grief is fine, full perfect that I taste,
And [violenteth] in a sense as strong
As that which causeth it. How can I moderate it?   5
If I could temporize with my affection
Or brew it to a weak and colder palate,
The like allayment could I give my grief.
My love admits no qualifying [dross];

Enter Troilus.

No more my grief, in such a precious loss.   10
Pandarus. Here, here, here he comes, a sweet duck.
Cressida. O Troilus! Troilus!
Pandarus. What a pair of spectacles is here! Let me embrace
too. 'O heart,' as the goodly saying is,

    O heart, heavy heart   15
    Why sighest thou without breaking?

Where he answers again,

    Because thou canst not ease thy smart
    By friendship nor by speaking.

There was never a truer rhyme. Let us cast away nothing,   20
for we may live to have need of such a verse. We see it,
we see it. How now, lambs?
Troilus. Cressid, I love thee in so strange a purity
That the bless'd gods, as angry with my fancy,
More bright in zeal than the devotion which   25
Cold lips blow to their deities, take thee from me.
Cressida. Have the gods envy?
Pandarus. Ay, ay, ay, ay. 'Tis too plain a case.
Cressida. And is it true that I must go from Troy?
Troilus. A hateful truth!   30
Cressida.   What, and from Troilus too?
Troilus. From Troy, and Troilus.

Cressida.   Is't possible?
Troilus. And suddenly, where injury of chance
Puts back leave-taking, justles roughly by   35
All time of pause, rudely beguiles our lips
Of all rejoindure, forcibly prevents
Our lock'd embrasures, strangles our dear vows,
Even in the birth of our own laboring breath.
We two, that with so many thousand sighs   40
Did buy each other, must poorly sell ourselves
With the rude brevity and discharge of [one].
Injurious time now with a robber's haste
Crams his rich thiev'ry up, he knows not how.
As many farewells as be stars in heaven,   45
With distinct breath, and consign'd kisses to them,
He fumbles up into a loose adieu,
And scants us with a single famish'd kiss,
Distasting with the salt of broken tears.
Aeneas. Within. My lord, is the lady ready?   50
Troilus. Hark, you are call'd. Some say the genius so
Cries 'Come!' to him that instantly must die.
Bid them have patience; she shall come anon.
Pandarus. Where are my tears? Rain, to lay this wind,
Or my heart will be blown up by the root.   *[Exit.]*   55
Cressida. I must then to the Grecians?
Troilus.   No remedy.
Cressida. A woeful Cressid 'mongst the merry Greeks.
When shall we see again?
Troilus.   Hear me, my love;   60
Be thou but true of heart—
Cressida. I, true! How now? What wicked deem is this?
Troilus. Nay, we must use expostulation kindly,
For it is parting from us.
I speak not 'Be thou true' as fearing thee,   65
For I will throw my glove to death himself
That there's no maculation in thy heart;
But 'Be thou true' say I to fashion in
My sequent protestation. Be thou true,
And I will see thee.   70
Cressida.   O, you shall be expos'd,
My lord, to dangers as infinite as imminent.
But I'll be true.
Troilus.   And I'll grow friend with danger.
Wear this sleeve.   75
Cressida.   And you this glove.
When shall I see you?
Troilus. I will corrupt the Grecian sentinels,
To give thee nightly visitation.
But yet be true.   80
Cressida.   O heavens! 'Be true' again?
Troilus. Hear why I speak it, love.
The Grecian youths are full of quality;
Their loving well compos'd with gift of nature,
[Flowing] and swelling ore with arts and exercise.   85
How novelties may move, and parts with person,
Alas, a kind of godly jealousy,
Which I beseech you call a virtuous sin,

---

34 injury of chance: *fortuitous ill treatment*   **37 rejoindure:** *reunion; Cf. n.*   **38 embrasures:** *embraces*   **42 one:** *F* our   **44 thiev'ry:** *F* theiverie   **46 distinct ... consign'd:** *both stressed* — —   **49 Distasting:** *destroying the taste* tears; *Cf. n.*   **51 genius;** *Cf. n.*   **54 wind:** *i.e. of sighs*   **59 When ... again;** *Cf. n.*   **62 deem:** *surmise, supposition*   **67 maculation:** *stain*   **83 quality:** *natural gifts*   **85 Flowing:** *F* flawing; *Cf. n.*   **86 parts with person:** *accomplishments with personal charm*

1 great morning: *full daylight*   **2 delivery:** *read 'deliv'ry'*   **10 his own heart:** *F* his heart   **4 violenteth:** *rages violently; F* no lesse   **9 dross:** *impurity; F* cross   **24 fancy:** *love*

Makes me afraid.

   Cressida.   O heavens! You love me not!   *90*

   Troilus. Die I a villain then!

In this I do not call your faith in question

So mainly as my merit. I cannot sing,

Nor heel the high lavolt, nor sweeten talk,

Nor play at subtle games—fair virtues all,   *95*

To which the Grecians are most prompt and pregnant.

But I can tell that in each grace of these

There lurks a still and dumb-discoursive divel

That tempts most cunningly. But be not tempted!

   Cressida. Do you think I will?   *100*

   Troilus.   No,

But something may be done that we will not,

And sometimes we are divels to ourselves,

When we will tempt the frailty of our powers,

Presuming on their changeful potency.   *105*

   Aeneas. Within. Nay, good my lord?

   Troilus.   Come, kiss and let us part.

   Paris. Within. Brother Troilus?

   Troilus.   Good brother, come you hither

And bring Aeneas and the Grecian with you.   *110*

   Cressida. My lord, will you be true?

   Troilus. Who, I? Alas, it is my vice, my fault.

Whiles others fish with craft for great opinion,

I with great truth catch mere simplicity;

Whilst some with cunning gild their copper crowns,   *115*

With truth and plainness I do wear mine bare.

     Enter [Paris, Aeneas, Deiphobus, Antenor, and Diomed.]

Fear not my truth. The moral of my wit

Is plain and true; there's all the reach of it.

Welcome, Sir Diomed; here is the lady,

Which for Antenor we deliver you.   *120*

At the port, lord, I'll give her to thy hand,

And by the way possess thee what she is.

Entreat her fair; and by my soul, fair Greek,

If ere thou stand at mercy of my sword,

Name Cressid and thy life shall be as safe   *125*

As Priam is in Ilion.

   Diomedes.   Fair Lady Cressid,

So please you, save the thanks this prince expects.

The lustre in your eye, heaven in your cheek,

Pleads your fair [usage], and to Diomed   *130*

You shall be mistress and command him wholly.

   Troilus. Grecian, thou dost not use me courteously,

To shame the zeal of my petition to thee

In praising her. I tell thee, lord of Greece,

She is as far high soaring ore thy praises   *135*

As thou unworthy to be call'd her servant.

I charge thee use her well, even for my charge,

For by the dreadful Pluto, if thou dost not,

Though the great bulk Achilles be thy guard,

I'll cut thy throat.   *140*

   Diomedes.   O, be not mov'd, Prince Troilus.

Let me be privileg'd by my place and message

To be a speaker free. When I am hence,

I'll answer to my lust. And know, my lord,

I'll nothing do on charge. To her own worth   *145*

She shall be priz'd; but that you say, 'Be't so,'

I'll speak it in my spirit and honor, 'No.'

   Troilus. Come, to the port. I'll tell thee, Diomed,

This brave shall oft make thee to hide thy head.

Lady, give me your hand; and as we walk   *150*

To our own selves bend we our needful talk.   *Sound trumpet.*

   Paris. Hark, Hector's trumpet!

   Aeneas.   How have we spent this morning!

The prince must think me tardy and remiss

That swore to ride before him in the field.   *155*

   Paris. 'Tis Troilus' fault. Come, come, to field with him.

     Exeunt [Troilus, Cressida, Diomed, and Paris].

   Deiphobus. Let us make ready straight.

   Aeneas. Yea, with a bridegroom's fresh alacrity

Let us address to tend on Hector's heels.

The glory of our Troy doth this day lie   *160*

On his fair worth and single chivalry.   *[Exeunt.]*

❧ Scene Fifth ❧

Enter Ajax, armed, Achilles, Patroclus, Agamemnon, Menelaus,
Ulysses, Nestor, Calchas, etc.

   Agamemnon. Here art thou in appointment fresh and fair,

Anticipating time. With starting courage,

Give with thy trumpet a loud note to Troy,

Thou dreadful Ajax, that the appalled air

May pierce the head of the great combatant   *5*

And hale him hither.

   Ajax.   Thou trumpet, there's my purse;

Now crack thy lungs, and split thy brazen pipe!

Blow, villain, till thy sphered bias cheek

Outswell the colic of puff'd Aquilon.   *10*

Come, stretch thy chest and let thy eyes spout blood;

Thou blowest for Hector.

   Ulysses. No trumpet answers.

   Achilles.   'Tis but early days.

   Agamemnon. Is not [yond] Diomed with Calchas' daughter?

   [Enter Diomed and Cressida.]

   Ulysses. 'Tis he. I ken the manner of his gait;

He rises on the toe. That spirit of his

In aspiration lifts him from the earth.

   Agamemnon. Is this the Lady Cressid?

   Diomedes.   Even she.   *20*

   Agamemnon. Most dearly welcome to the Greeks, sweet lady.

   Nestor. Our general doth salute you with a kiss.

   Ulysses. Yet is the kindness but particular;

'Twere better she were kiss'd in general.

   Nestor. And very courtly counsel. I'll begin.   *25*

So much for Nestor.

   Achilles. I'll take that winter from your lips, fair lady.

Achilles bids you welcome.

Menelaus. I had good argument for kissing once.

Patroclus. But that's no argument for kissing now.   30

For thus popp'd Paris in his hardiment

And parted thus you and your argument.

Ulysses. O deadly gall, and theme of all our scorns,

For which we lose our heads, to gild his horns.

Patroclus. The first was Menelaus' kiss, this mine;   35

Patroclus kisses you.

Menelaus.   O, this is trim!

Patroclus. Paris and I kiss evermore for him.

Menelaus. I'll have my kiss, sir. Lady, by your leave.

Cressida. In kissing do you render or receive?   40

Patroclus. Both take and give.

Cressida.   I'll make my match to live,

The kiss you take is better than you give.

Therefore no kiss.

Menelaus. I'll give you boot. I'll give you three for one.   45

Cressida. You are an odd man. Give even or give none.

Menelaus. An odd man, lady? Every man is odd.

Cressida. No. Paris is not; for you know 'tis true

That you are odd, and he is even with you.

Menelaus. You fillip me o' th' head.   50

Cressida.   No, I'll be sworn.

Ulysses. It were no match, your nail against his horn.

May I, sweet lady, beg a kiss of you?

Cressida. You may.

Ulysses.   I do desire it.   55

Cressida.   Why beg then?

Ulysses. Why then, for Venus' sake, give me a kiss

When Helen is a maid again, and his.

Cressida. I am your debtor. Claim it when 'tis due.

Ulysses. Never's my day, and then a kiss of you.   60

Diomedes. Lady, a word. I'll bring you to your father.

          [Exeunt Diomed and Cressida.]

Nestor. A woman of quick sense.

Ulysses.   Fie, fie upon her!

There's a language in her eye, her cheek, her lip;

Nay, her foot speaks. Her wanton spirits look out   65

At every joint and motive of her body.

O, these encounterers so glib of tongue,

That give a coasting welcome [ere] it comes,

And wide unclasp the tables of their thoughts

To every tickling reader! Set them down   70

For sluttish spoils of opportunity,

And daughters of the game.

Enter all of Troy: Hector, Paris, Aeneas, Helenus, and attendants.
          Flourish.

All. The Troyans' trumpet.

Agamemnon.   Yonder comes the troop.

Aeneas. Hail, all you state of Greece. What shall be done   75

To him that victory commands? Or do you purpose

A victor shall be known? Will you the knights

Shall to the edge of all extremity

Pursue each other, or shall be divided

By any voice or order of the field?   80

Hector bade ask.

Agamemnon.   Which way would Hector have it?

Aeneas. He cares not. He'll obey conditions.

Agamemnon. 'Tis done like Hector; but securely done,

A little proudly, and great deal disprizing   85

The knight oppos'd.

Aeneas.   If not Achilles, sir,

What is your name?

Achilles.   If not Achilles, nothing.

Aeneas. Therefore, Achilles. But what ere, know this: 90

In the extremity of great and little,

Valor and pride excel themselves in Hector;

The one almost as infinite as all,

The other blank as nothing. Weigh him well,

And that which looks like pride is courtesy.   95

This Ajax is half made of Hector's blood,

In love whereof, half Hector stays at home;

Half heart, half hand, half Hector comes to seek

This blended knight, half Troyan and half Greek.

Achilles. A maiden battle then? O, I perceive you.   100

          [Enter Diomedes.]

Agamemnon. Here is Sir Diomed. Go, gentle knight;

Stand by our Ajax. As you and Lord Aeneas

Consent upon the order of their fight,

So be it, either to the uttermost

Or else a [breath]. The combatants being kin   105

Half stints their strife before their strokes begin.

Ulysses. They are oppos'd already.

Agamemnon. What Troyan is that same that looks so heavy?

Ulysses. The youngest son of Priam, a true knight,

Not yet mature yet matchless, firm of word,   110

Speaking in deeds and deedless in his tongue;

Not soon provok'd, nor being provok'd, soon calm'd.

His heart and hand both open and both free;

For what he has, he gives; what thinks, he shews;

Yet gives he not till judgment guide his bounty,   115

Nor dignifies an impair thought with breath;

Manly as Hector, but more dangerous,

For Hector in his blaze of wrath subscribes

To tender objects, but he, in heat of action,

Is more vindicative than jealous love.   120

They call him Troilus, and on him erect

A second hope as fairly built as Hector.

Thus says Aeneas, one that knows the youth,

Even to his inches, and with private soul

Did in great Ilion thus translate him to me.   *Alarum.*   125

Agamemnon. They are in action.

Nestor. Now, Ajax, hold thine own.

Troilus. Hector, thou sleep'st. Awake thee!

Agamemnon. His blows are well dispos'd there,

Ajax.   *Trumpets cease.*   130

Diomedes. You must no more.

Aeneas. Princes, enough, so please you.

Ajax. I am not warm yet. Let us fight again.

---

31 **hardiment:** *audacity*   32 **And ... argument:** *Cf. n.*   34 **horns:** *i.e. cuckold's horns*   42 **make ... live:** *bet my life*   45 **boot:** *to boot, extra advantages*   50 **fillip:** *hit (a reference to his cuckold's horns)*   58 **his:** *i.e. Menelaus'*   62 **sense:** *pun on two meanings: 'intelligence' and 'sensuality'*   66 **motive:** *unit, part that produces motion*   67 **encounterers:** *flirts, 'forward' women*   68 **a coasting:** *Cf. n.*   **ere:** *F ete*   69 **tables:** *tablets*   70 **tickling:** *avid, curious*   72 **game:** *Cf. n.*   77 **Will you:** *do you wish*

83 **conditions:** *four syllables here*   85 **disprizing:** *depreciating; Q misprising*   96 **Ajax ... blood:** *Cf. n.*   100 **maiden battle:** *a draw, an issueless combat*   105 **breath:** *breathing space; F breach*   109 **knight:** *Cf. n.*   113 **free:** *generous, noble*   116 **impair:** *unsuitable, unconsidered (stressed* ⌣ — *)*   120 **vindicative:** *vindictive*   124 **to his inches:** *his exact height, i.e. very intimately*   **with private soul:** *in confidence*   125 **translate:** *reveal, interpret*

Diomedes. As Hector pleases.

Hector.   Why then will I no more.   *135*
Thou art, great lord, my father's sister's son,
A cousin german to great Priam's seed.
The obligation of our blood forbids
A gory emulation 'twixt us twain.
Were thy commixion Greek and Troyan so   *140*
That thou couldst say, 'This hand is Grecian all
And this is Troyan, the sinews of this leg
All Greek, and this all Troy; my mother's blood
Runs on the dexter cheek, and this sinister
Bounds in my father's,' by Jove multipotent,   *145*
Thou shouldst not bear from me a Greekish member
Wherein my sword had not impressure made
Of our rank feud. But the just gods gainsay
That any drop thou borrow'dst from thy mother,
My sacred aunt, should by my mortal sword   *150*
Be drained. Let me embrace thee, Ajax.
By him that thunders, thou hast lusty arms!
Hector would have them fall upon him thus.
Cousin, all honor to thee.

Ajax.   I thank thee, Hector.   *155*
Thou art too gentle and too free a man.
I came to kill thee, cousin, and bear hence
A great addition earned in thy death.

Hector. Not Neoptolymus so mirable,
On whose bright crest fame with her loud'st oyes   *160*
Cries, 'This is he,' [could] promise to himself
A thought of added honor torn from Hector.

Aeneas. There is expectance here from both the sides
What further you will do.

Hector.   We'll answer it;   *165*
The issue is embracement. Ajax, farewell.

Ajax. If I might in entreaties find success,
As seld I have the chance, I would desire
My famous cousin to our Grecian tents.

Diomedes. 'Tis Agamemnon's wish, and great Achilles   *170*
Doth long to see unarm'd the valiant Hector.

Hector. Aeneas, call my brother Troilus to me,
And signify this loving interview
To the expecters of our Troyan part.
Desire them home. Give me thy hand, my cousin;   *175*
I will go eat with thee and see your knights.

Enter Agamemnon and the rest.

Ajax. Great Agamemnon comes to meet us here.

Hector. The worthiest of them tell me name by name;
But for Achilles, mine own searching eyes
Shall find him by his large and portly size.   *180*

Agamemnon. Worthy of arms, as welcome as to one
That would be rid of such an enemy.
But that's no welcome. Understand more clear;
What's past and what's to come is strew'd with husks
And formless ruin of oblivion;   *185*
But in this extant moment, faith and troth,

Strain'd purely, from all hollow bias drawing,
Bids thee with most divine integrity
From heart of very heart, great Hector, welcome.

Hector. I thank thee, most imperious Agamemnon.   *190*

Agamemnon. My well-fam'd lord of Troy, no less to you.

Menelaus. Let me confirm my princely brother's greeting.
You brace of warlike brothers, welcome hither.

Hector. Who must we answer?

Aeneas.   The noble Menelaus.   *195*

Hector. O, you, my lord! By Mars his gauntlet, thanks.
Mock not that I affect th' untraded oath;
Your quondam wife swears still by Venus' glove.
She's well, but bade me not commend her to you.

Menelaus. Name her not now, sir; she's a deadly theme.   *200*

Hector. O pardon! I offend.

Nestor. I have, thou gallant Troyan, seen thee oft,
Laboring for destiny, make cruel way
Through ranks of Greekish youth, and I have seen thee
As hot as Perseus, spur thy Phrygian steed,   *205*
And seen thee scorning forfeits and subduements
When thou hast hung thy advanced sword i' th' air,
Not letting it decline on the declin'd;
That I have said unto my standers-by,
'Lo, Jupiter is yonder, dealing life.'   *210*
And I have seen thee pause and take thy breath
When that a ring of Greeks have hemm'd thee in,
Like an Olympian wrestling. This have I seen,
But this thy countenance, still lock'd in steel,
I never saw till now. I knew thy grandsire   *215*
And once fought with him. He was a soldier good,
But by great Mars, the captain of us all,
Never like thee. Let an old man embrace thee,
And, worthy warrior, welcome to our tents.

Aeneas. 'Tis the old Nestor.   *220*

Hector. Let me embrace thee, good old chronicle,
That hast so long walk'd hand in hand with time.
Most reverend Nestor, I am glad to clasp thee.

Nestor. I would my arms could match thee in contention
As they contend with thee in courtesy.   *225*

Hector. I would they could.

Nestor. Ha? By this white beard, I'd fight with thee
tomorrow.
Well, welcome, welcome. I have seen the time.

Ulysses. I wonder now how yonder city stands,   *230*
When we have here her base and pillar by us.

Hector. I know your favor, Lord Ulysses, well.
Ah sir, there's many a Greek and Troyan dead
Since first I saw yourself and Diomed
In Ilion on your Greekish embassy.   *235*

Ulysses. Sir, I foretold you then what would ensue.
My prophecy is but half his journey yet,
For yonder walls that pertly front your town,
Yond towers, whose wanton tops do buss the clouds,
Must kiss their own feet.   *240*

Hector.   I must not believe you.
There they stand yet. And modestly I think,

---

139 emulation: *rivalry*   **140 commixion:** *mixture*   **144 dexter:** *right.* **sinister:** *left*
(stressed — ´ —)   **145 multipotent:** *very powerful*   **148 gainsay:** *forbid*   **156 free:**
generous, noble   **159 Neoptolymus;** *Cf. n.* **mirable:** *admirable, marvelous*   **160 oyes;**
Cf. n.   **161 could:** *F could'st*   **163 expectance:** *expectation, wondering*   **166 issue:**
result   **168 seld:** *seldom* **desire:** *invite*   **174 expecters . . . part:** *Trojans who are waiting*   **175 Desire them:** *request them to go* **SD Enter . . . rest;** *Cf. n.*   **180 portly:**
majestic, imposing   **185 oblivion:** *four distinct syllables here*

187 from . . . drawing: *withdrawing from bias; cf. I.3.15; Cf. n.*   **191 My . . . you:** *you
probably addressed to Troilus*   **196 Mars his gauntlet:** *Mars' gauntlet*   **197 untraded:**
unusual, not customary   **198 quondam:** *former*   **205 Perseus;** *cf. I.3.42 gloss*   **206
subduements:** *situations in which opponent is subdued*   **214 still:** *continually*   **215 grandsire;** *Cf. n.*   **221 chronicle:** *history book (here used figuratively)*   **232 favor:** *face, aspect*   **238 pertly:** *boldly*   **239 buss:** *kiss*   **242 modestly:** *without exaggeration*

The fall of every Phrygian stone will cost
A drop of Grecian blood. The end crowns all,
And that old common arbitrator, Time,   245
Will one day end it.
   Ulysses.   So to him we leave it.
Most gentle and most valiant Hector, welcome.
After the general, I beseech you next
To feast with me and see me at my tent.   250
   Achilles. I shall forestall thee, Lord Ulysses, thou.
Now Hector I have fed mine eyes on thee;
I have with exact view perus'd thee, Hector,
And quoted joint by joint.
   Hector.   Is this Achilles?   255
   Achilles. I am Achilles.
   Hector. Stand fair, I prithee; let me look on thee.
   Achilles. Behold thy fill.
   Hector.   Nay, I have done already.
   Achilles. Thou art too brief. I will the second time,   260
As I would buy thee, view thee limb by limb.
   Hector. O, like a book of sport thou'lt read me ore;
But there's more in me than thou understandst.
Why dost thou so oppress me with thine eye?
   Achilles. Tell me, you heavens, in which part of his body   265
Shall I destroy him? Whether there, or there, or there,
That I may give the local wound a name,
And make distinct the very breach whereout
Hector's great spirit flew. Answer me, heavens.
   Hector. It would discredit the bless'd gods, proud man,   270
To answer such a question. Stand again.
Think'st thou to catch my life so pleasantly
As to prenominate in nice conjecture
Where thou wilt hit me dead?
   Achilles.   I tell thee, yea.   275
   Hector. Wert thou the oracle to tell me so,
I'd not believe thee. Henceforth guard thee well,
For I'll not kill thee there, nor there, nor there,
But by the forge that stithied Mars his helm,
I'll kill thee everywhere, yea, ore and ore!   280
You wisest Grecians, pardon me this brag.
His insolence draws folly from my lips.
But I'll endeavor deeds to match these words,
Or may I never—
   Ajax.   Do not chafe thee, cousin.   285
And you, Achilles, let these threats alone,
Till accident or purpose bring you to't.
You may [have] every day enough of Hector
If you have stomach. The general state, I fear,
Can scarce entreat you to be odd with him.   290
   Hector. I pray you, let us see you in the field.
We have had pelting wars since you refus'd
The Grecians' cause.
   Achilles.   Dost thou entreat me, Hector?
Tomorrow do I meet thee fell as death;   295
Tonight, all friends.
   Hector.   Thy hand upon that match!
   Agamemnon. First, all you peers of Greece, go to my tent;
There in the full convive you. Afterwards,

As Hector's leisure and your bounties shall   300
Concur together, severally entreat him.
Beat loud the taborins, let the trumpets blow,
That this great soldier may his welcome know.
                Exeunt [all but Troilus and Ulysses].
   Troilus. My Lord Ulysses, tell me, I beseech you,
In what place of the field doth Calchas keep?   305
   Ulysses. At Menelaus' tent, most princely Troilus.
There Diomed doth feast with him tonight,
Who neither looks on heaven nor on earth,
But gives all gaze and bent of amorous view
On the fair Cressid.   310
   Troilus. Shall I, sweet lord, be bound to thee so much,
After we part from Agamemnon's tent,
To bring me thither?
   Ulysses.   You shall command me, sir.
As gentle tell me, of what honor was   315
This Cressida in Troy? Had she no lover there
That wails her absence?
   Troilus. O sir, to such as boasting shew their scars
A mock is due. Will you walk on, my lord?
She was belov'd, she lov'd; she is, and doth;   320
But still sweet love is food for Fortune's tooth.   *Exeunt.*

ACT FIFTH ❧ SCENE FIRST

Enter Achilles and Patroclus.

   Achilles. I'll heat his blood with Greekish wine tonight,
Which with my scimitar I'll cool tomorrow.
Patroclus, let us feast him to the height.
   Patroclus. Here comes Thersites.

Enter Thersites.

   Achilles.   How now, thou core of envy?   5
Thou crusty batch of nature, what's the news?
   Thersites. Why, thou picture of what thou seem'st, and idol
of idiot-worshipers, here's a letter for thee.
   Achilles. From whence, fragment?
   Thersites. Why, thou full dish of fool, from Troy.   10
   Patroclus. Who keeps the tent now?
   Thersites. The surgeon's box, or the patient's wound.
   Patroclus. Well said, adversity, and what need these tricks?
   Thersites. Prithee be silent, boy. I profit not by thy talk.
Thou art thought to be Achilles' male varlot.   15
   Patroclus. Male varlot, you rogue? What's that?
   Thersites. Why, his masculine whore. Now the rotten
diseases of the South, guts-griping ruptures, catarrhs, loads of
gravel i' th' back, lethargies, cold palsies, and the like take
and take again such prepostrous discoveries!   20
   Patroclus. Why, thou damnable box of envy, thou, what
meanst thou to curse thus?
   Thersites. Do I curse thee?
   Patroclus. Why no, you ruinous butt! You whoreson
indistinguishable cur!   25

---

253 **exact:** *here stressed* — —   254 **quoted:** *scrutinized*   273 **prenominate:** *specify or name beforehand* **nice:** *precise*   279 **stithied:** *forged*   285 **chafe thee:** *arouse yourself*   288 **may have:** *F* may   290 **odd:** *at odds*   292 **pelting:** *petty, insignificant*   295 **fell:** *fierce, cruel*   299 **convive you:** *be convivial, feast*

301 **severally entreat him:** *individually invite (treat) him*   302 **taborins:** *drums*   320 **doth;** *Cf. n.*   12 **surgeon's box;** *Cf. n.*   15 **varlot;** *Cf. n.*   18, 19 **loads . . . back:** *kidney stones* **lethargies:** *apoplexies* **palsies;** *Cf. n.*   20 **discoveries:** *revelations*   24 **butt:** *cask of wine, hogshead*

Thersites. No? Why art thou then exasperate, thou idle, immaterial skein of sleyd silk? Thou green sarcenet flap for a sore eye, thou tassel of a prodigal's purse, thou! Ah, how the poor world is pest'red with such water-flies, diminutives of nature!

Patroclus. Out, gall!   *30*

Thersites. Finch egg!

Achilles. My sweet Patroclus, I am thwarted quite
From my great purpose in tomorrow's battle.
Here is a letter from Queen Hecuba,
A token from her daughter, my fair love,   *35*
Both taxing me and gaging me to keep
An oath that I have sworn. I will not break it.
Fall Greeks, fail fame, honor or go or stay,
My major vow lies here; this I'll obey.
Come, come Thersites, help to trim my tent;   *40*
This night in banqueting must all be spent.
Away, Patroclus.   *[Exeunt Achilles and Patroclus.]*

Thersites. With too much blood and too little brain, these two may run mad; but if with too much brain and too little blood they do, I'll be a curer of madmen. Here's Agamemnon, an honest fellow enough, and one that loves quails, but he has not so much brain as ear wax; and the goodly transformation of Jupiter there, his brother, the bull, the primitive statue and oblique memorial of cuckolds, a thrifty shoeing horn in a chain, hanging at his brother's leg—to what form but that *50* he is, should wit larded with malice and malice forced with wit turn him to? To an ass were nothing; he is both ass and ox. To an ox were nothing; he is both ox and ass. To be a dog, a mule, a cat, a fitchew, a toad, a lizard, an owl, a puttock, or a herring without a roe, I would not care; but to be Menelaus, *55* I would conspire against destiny. Ask me not what I would be, if I were not Thersites. For I care not to be the louse of a lazar, so I were not Menelaus. Hoy-day, spirits and fires!

Enter Hector, Ajax, Agamemnon, Ulysses, Nestor, Diomed, with lights.

Agamemnon. We go wrong, we go wrong.

Ajax.   No, yonder 'tis.   *60*
There where we see the light.

Hector.   I trouble you.

Ajax. No, not a whit.

Enter Achilles.

Ulysses.   Here comes himself to guide you.

Achilles. Welcome, brave Hector. Welcome, princes all.   *65*

Agamemnon. So now, fair prince of Troy, I bid good night.
Ajax commands the guard to tend on you.

Hector. Thanks and good night to the Greeks' general.

Menelaus. Good night, my lord.

Hector. Good night, sweet Lord Menelaus.   *70*

Thersites. Sweet draught! 'Sweet,' quoth a? Sweet sink, sweet sewer!

Achilles. Good night and welcome, both at once, to those
That go or tarry.

Agamemnon.   Good night.   *75*

     [Exeunt Agamemnon and Menelaus.]

Achilles. Old Nestor tarries, and you too Diomed;
Keep Hector company an hour or two.

Diomedes. I cannot, lord. I have important business,
The tide whereof is now. Good night, great Hector.

Hector. Give me your hand.   *80*

Ulysses.   Follow his torch. He goes
To Calchas' tent. I'll keep you company.

Troilus. Sweet sir, you honor me.

Hector.   And so good night.

     [Exeunt Diomed, Troilus, and Ulysses.]

Achilles. Come, come, enter my tent.   *85*

     Exeunt [Achilles, Hector, Ajax, and Nestor].

Thersites. That same Diomed's a false-hearted rogue, a most unjust knave. I will no more trust him when he leers than I will a serpent when he hisses. He will spend his mouth and promise, like Brabbler the hound, but when he performs, astronomers foretell it, that it is prodigious—there will come *90* some change. The sun borrows of the moon when Diomed keeps his word. I will rather leave to see Hector than not to dog him. They say he keeps a Troyan drab, and uses the traitor Calchas his tent. I'll after. Nothing but lechery! All incontinent varlots!   *[Exit.]*

❧ SCENE SECOND ❧

Enter Diomed.

Diomedes. What, are you up here, ho? Speak.

Calchas. [Within.] Who calls?

Diomedes. Diomed. Calchas, I think, where's your daughter?

Calchas. [Within.] She comes to you.

Enter Troilus and Ulysses.

Ulysses. Stand where the torch may not discover us.   *5*

Enter Cressid.

Troilus. Cressid comes forth to him.

Diomedes. How now, my charge?

Cressida. Now, my sweet guardian, hark; a word with you.

Troilus. Yea, so familiar?

Ulysses. She will sing any man at first sight.   *10*

Thersites. And any man may [sing] her, if he can take her [cliff]; she's noted.

Diomedes. Will you remember?

Cressida. Remember? Yes.

Diomedes. Nay, but do then; and let your mind be   *15*
coupled with your words.

Troilus. What should she remember?

Ulysses. List!

Cressida. Sweet honey Greek, tempt me no more to folly.

Thersites. Roguery!   *20*

Diomedes. Nay, then—

Cressida. I'll tell you what.

Diomedes. Foh, foh! Come, tell a pin! You are a forsworn—

Cressida. In faith, I cannot. What would you have me do?

Thersites. A juggling trick, to be secretly open.   *25*

26, 27 **immaterial:** *insignificant, flimsy* **sleyd:** *raw, untwisted* **sarcenet:** *fine silk*   36 **gaging:** *binding, engaging*   38 **or . . . or:** *either . . . or.* **SD Exeunt . . . Patroclus:** *F has merely Exit.* **Q has no SD**   46 **quails:** *women, prostitutes*   47-49 **transformation . . . cuckolds;** *Cf. n.* **shoeing horn:** *shoe horn, tool; Cf. n.*   50 **that:** *that which*   51 **forced:** *stuffed, farced*   54 **fitchew:** *polecat* **puttock:** *small hawk*   71 **draught:** *privy* **sink:** *cesspool.* **SD** *F has no SD here.*

79 **tide:** *time* **SD Exeunt . . . Ulysses** *Cf. n.*   89 **Brabbler;** *Cf. n.*   92 **leave to see:** *leave off seeing*   94 **Calchas his:** *Calchas'; see II.1.54 Cf. n.* **after:** *follow after* **SD Exit:** *F Exeunt*   5 **discover:** *reveal*   11 **sing:** *F find*   12 **cliff:** *clef, key; F life*   14 **Cressida.:** *Mistakenly labeled Cal. in both F and Q*   23 **tell a pin:** *tell, nothing!*

Diomedes. What did you swear you would bestow on me?

Cressida. I prithee, do not hold me to mine oath.
Bid me do anything but that, sweet Greek.

Diomedes. Good night.

Troilus. Hold, patience.   30

Ulysses. How now, Troyan?

Cressida. Diomed.

Diomedes. No, no. Good night. I'll be your fool no more.

Troilus. Thy better must.

Cressida.   Hark, one word in your ear,   35

Troilus. O plague and madness!

Ulysses. You are moved, prince. Let us depart, I pray you,
Lest your displeasure should enlarge itself
To wrathful terms. This place is dangerous;
The time right deadly. I beseech you go.   40

Troilus. Behold, I pray you.

Ulysses.   Nay, good my lord, go off.
You flow to great distraction. Come, my lord.

Troilus. I pray thee, stay.

Ulysses.   You have not patience; come.   45

Troilus. I pray you, stay. By hell and hell torments,
I will not speak a word.

Diomedes.   And so good night.

Cressida. Nay, but you part in anger.

Troilus.   Doth that grieve thee?   50
O wither'd truth!

Ulysses.   Why, how now, lord?

Troilus.   By Jove,
I will be patient.

Cressida.   Guardian? Why, Greek!   55

Diomedes. Foh, foh! Adieu. You palter.

Cressida. In faith, I do not. Come hither once again.

Ulysses. You shake, my lord, at something. Will you go?
You will break out.

Troilus.   She strokes his cheek!   60

Ulysses.   Come, come.

Troilus. Nay, stay. By Jove, I will not speak a word!
There is between my will and all offenses
A guard of patience. Stay a little while.

Thersites. How the divel Luxury with his fat rump and   65
potato finger tickles these together. Fry, lechery, fry!

Diomedes. But will you, then?

Cressida. In faith, I will. Lo, never trust me else.

Diomedes. Give me some token for the surety of it.

Cressida. I'll fetch you one.   *Exit.*   70

Ulysses. You have sworn patience.

Troilus.   Fear me not, sweet lord.
I will not be myself, nor have cognition
Of what I feel. I am all patience.

Enter Cressid.

Thersites. Now, the pledge! Now, now, now!   75

Cressida. Here, Diomed; keep this sleeve.

Troilus. O beauty! Where is thy faith?

Ulysses. My lord.

Troilus. I will be patient; outwardly I will.

Cressida. You look upon that sleeve? Behold it well.   80
He lov'd me, O false wench! Give't me again.

Diomedes. Whose was't?

Cressida. It is no matter now I have't again.
I will not meet with you tomorrow night.
I prithee, Diomed, visit me no more.   85

Thersites. Now she sharpens. Well said, whetstone.

Diomedes. I shall have it.

Cressida.   What, this?

Diomedes.   Ay, that.

Cressida. O all you gods! O pretty, pretty pledge!   90
Thy master now lies thinking in his bed
Of thee and me, and sighs, and takes my glove,
And gives memorial dainty kisses to it,
As I kiss thee. Nay, do not snatch it from me.
He that takes that [doth take] my heart withal.   95

Diomedes. I had your heart before; this follows it.

Troilus. I did swear patience.

Cressida. You shall not have it, Diomed; faith, you shall not.
I'll give you something else.

Diomedes. I will have this. Whose was it?   100

Cressida.   It is no matter.

Diomedes. Come, tell me whose it was!

Cressida. 'Twas one that lov'd me better than you will.
But now you have it, take it.

Diomedes.   Whose was it?   105

Cressida. By all Diana's waiting women yond,
And by herself, I will not tell you whose.

Diomedes. Tomorrow will I wear it on my helm,
And grieve his spirit that dares not challenge it.

Troilus. Wert thou the divel and wor'st it on thy horn,   110
It should be challeng'd.

Cressida.   Well, well, 'tis done. 'Tis past;
And yet it is not. I will not keep my word.

Diomedes. Why then, farewell.
Thou never shalt mock Diomed again.   115

Cressida. You shall not go. One cannot speak a word
But it straight starts you.

Diomedes.   I do not like this fooling.

Thersites. Nor I, by Pluto! But that that likes not me,
pleases me best.   120

Diomedes. What, shall I come? The hour?

Cressida.   Ay, come. O Jove!
Do come. I shall be plagu'd.

Diomedes.   Farewell till then.   *Exit.*

Cressida. Good night. I prithee, come.   125
Troilus, farewell. One eye yet looks on thee,
But with my heart the other eye doth see.
Ah, poor our sex! This fault in us I find:
The error of our eye directs our mind.
What error leads must err. O then, conclude   130
Minds sway'd by eyes are full of turpitude.   *Exit.*

Thersites. A proof of strength she could not publish more;
Unless she say, 'My mind is now turn'd whore.'

Ulysses. All's done, my lord.

Troilus.   It is.   135

Ulysses.   Why stay we then?

Troilus. To make a recordation to my soul
Of every syllable that here was spoke.

---

28 do anything: *F* do not anything   **43 flow:** *go toward*   **56 palter:** *equivocate, deal crookedly*   **65 Luxury:** *lechery*   **66 potato;** *Cf. n.*   **72 Fear me not:** *you can depend on me*

94 Nay . . . me; *Cf. n.*   **95 doth take:** *F rakes; F2 takes*   **106 Diana's waiting women:** *the moon's attendants, the stars*   **119 likes not me:** *does not please me; Cf. n.*   **123 plagu'd:** *harassed (perhaps in the sense of punishment)*   **137 make a recordation:** *to make a record on, engrave on*

But if I tell how these two did coact,
Shall I not lie in publishing a truth?   *140*
Sith yet there is a credence in my heart,
An esperance so obstinately strong
That doth invert that test of eyes and ears,
As if those organs had deceptious functions,
Created only to calumniate.   *145*
Was Cressid here?
     Ulysses.   I cannot conjure, Troyan.
     Troilus. She was not, sure.
     Ulysses.   Most sure she was.
     Troilus. Why, my negation hath no taste of madness.   *150*
     Ulysses. Nor mine, my lord. Cressid was here but now.
     Troilus. Let it not be believ'd for womanhood!
Think we had mothers. Do not give advantage
To stubborn critics, apt without a theme
For depravation to square the general sex   *155*
By Cressid's rule. Rather think this not Cressid.
     Ulysses. What hath she done, prince, that can soil our
mothers?
     Troilus. Nothing at all, unless that this were she.
     Thersites. Will he swagger himself out on's own eyes?   *160*
     Troilus. This she? No, this is Diomed's Cressida.
If beauty have a soul, this is not she;
If souls guide vows, if vows are sanctimony,
If sanctimony be the gods' delight,
If there be rule in unity itself,   *165*
This is not she. O madness of discourse!
That cause sets up with and against thyself
[Bifold] authority, where reason can revolt
Without perdition, and loss assume all reason
Without revolt. This is and is not Cressid.   *170*
Within my soul there doth conduce a fight
Of this strange nature, that a thing inseparate
Divides more wider than the sky and earth,
And yet the spacious breadth of this division
Admits no orifexfor a point as subtle   *175*
As Ariachne's broken woof to enter.
Instance, O instance, strong as Pluto's gates!
Cressid is mine, tied with the bonds of heaven.
Instance, O instance, strong as heaven itself!
The bonds of heaven are slipp'd, dissolv'd, and loos'd,   *180*
And with another knot, five finger tied,
The fractions of her faith, orts of her love,
The fragments, scraps, the bits, and greasy relics
Of her ore-eaten faith are bound to Diomed.
     Ulysses. May worthy Troilus be half attached   *185*
With that which here his passion doth express?
     Troilus. Ay, Greek, and that shall be divulged well
In characters as red as Mars his heart,
Inflam'd with Venus. Never did young man fancy
With so eternal and so fix'd a soul.   *190*

Hark, Greek. As much [as] I do Cressid love,
So much by weight hate I her Diomed.
That sleeve is mine that he'll bear in his helm.
Were it a casque compos'd by Vulcan's skill,
My sword should bite it. Not the dreadful spout   *195*
Which shipmen do the hurricano call,
Constring'd in mass by the almighty [sun],
Shall dizzy with more clamour Neptune's ear
In his descent than shall my prompted sword,
Falling on Diomed.   *200*
     Thersites. He'll tickle it for his concupy.
     Troilus. O Cressid! O false Cressid! False, false, false!
Let all untruths stand by thy stained name
And they'll seem glorious.
     Ulysses.   O, contain yourself.   *205*
Your passion draws ears hither.

     Enter Aeneas.

     Aeneas. I have been seeking you this hour, my lord.
Hector by this is arming him in Troy.
Ajax, your guard, stays to conduct you home.
     Troilus. Have with you, prince. My courteous lord, adieu.   *210*
Farewell, revolted fair. And Diomed,
Stand fast and wear a castle on thy head.
     Ulysses. I'll bring you to the gates.
     Troilus.   Accept distracted thanks.
     Exeunt Troilus, Aeneas, and Ulysses.
     Thersites. Would I could meet that rogue, Diomed. I would
croak like a raven; I would bode, I would bode. Patroclus will
give me anything for the intelligence of this whore. The parrot
will not do more for an almond than he for a commodious
drab. Lechery, lechery, still wars and lechery! Nothing else
holds fashion. A burning divel take them!   *[Exit.]*   *220*

❧ SCENE THIRD ❧

Enter Hector and Andromache.

     Andromache. When was my lord so much urgently temper'd
To stop his ears against admonishment?
Unarm, unarm, and do not fight today.
     Hector. You train me to offend you. Get you gone.
By the everlasting gods, I'll go!   *5*
     Andromache. My dreams will sure prove ominous to the day.
     Hector. No more, I say.

     Enter Cassandra.

     Cassandra.   Where is my brother Hector?
     Andromache. Here, sister, arm'd and bloody in intent.
Consort with me in loud and dear petition,   *10*
Pursue me him on knees; for I have dreamt
Of bloody turbulence, and this whole night
Hath nothing been but shapes and forms of slaughter.
     Cassandra. O, 'tis true!
     Hector.   Ho! Bid my trumpet sound.   *15*
     Cassandra. No notes of sally, for the heavens, sweet brother.

139 coact: *act together*   **141 Sith:** *since*   **142 esperance:** *hope*   **143 that test;** *Cf. n.*
144 deceptious: *deceptive*   **154 critics:** *cynical cavillers*   **155 depravation:** *defamation,*
disparagement **square:** *measure* **general sex:** *female sex in general*   **156 rule:** *ruler, yard-*
stick   **160 on's:** *on his, of his*   **163 sanctimony:** *a holy thing*   **166 discourse:** *reason-*
ing   **167, 168 That cause ... Without revolt;** *Cf. n.* **cause:** *reasoning* **Bifold:** *F By*
foule   **171 doth conduce:** *goes on*   **172 inseparate:** *single, whole, unified*   **175 orifex:**
orifice, opening   **176 Ariachne's broken woof:** *a spider web; Cf. n.*   **177 Instance:**
example, evidence, proof   **181 five finger tied:** *tied by mere human hands*   **182 orts:**
leavings, scraps   **184 ore-eaten:** *eaten over, picked over already*   **185 May:** *can* **attached:**
seriously involved in   **188 characters:** *letters*   **189 fancy:** *love*

191 As much as: *from F2; Q and F* as much **Cressid:** *F Cressida*   **195 spout:** *water-*
spout   **197 Constring'd:** *brought together* **sun:** *F Fenne*   **199 descent:** *depths*
prompted: *ready*   **201 concupy:** *concubine*   **209 stays:** *waits*   **217, 218 parrot ...**
almond; *Cf. n.* **commodious:** *accommodating*   **219 still:** *always* **SD Exit:** *Not in*
F   **1 temper'd:** *disposed*   **4 train:** *invite, lure*   **10 dear:** *honorable*

Hector. Be gone, I say! The gods have heard me swear.

Cassandra. The gods are deaf to hot and peevish vows;
They are polluted off'rings, more abhorr'd
Than spotted livers in the sacrifice.   20

Andromache. O, be persuaded. Do not count it holy
To hurt by being just. It is as lawful,
For we would give much, to use violent thefts
And rob in behalf of charity.

Cassandra. It is the purpose that makes strong the vow,   25
But vows to every purpose must not hold.
Unarm, sweet Hector.

Hector.   Hold you still, I say!
Mine honor keeps the weather of my fate.
Life every man holds dear, but the dear man   30
Holds honor far more precious-dear than life.

Enter Troilus.

How now, young man? Meanst thou to fight today?

Andromache. Cassandra, call my father to persuade.

Exit Cassandra.

Hector. No, faith, young Troilus. Doff thy harness, youth.
I am today i' th' vein of chivalry.   35
Let grow thy sinews till their knots be strong,
And tempt not yet the brushes of the war.
Unarm thee, go. And doubt thou not, brave boy,
I'll stand today for thee and me and Troy.

Troilus. Brother, you have a vice of mercy in you   40
Which better fits a lion than a man.

Hector. What vice is that? Good Troilus, chide me for it.

Troilus. When many times the captive Grecian falls,
Even in the fan and wind of your fair sword,
You bid them rise and live.   45

Hector.   O, 'tis fair play.

Troilus. Fool's play, by heaven, Hector!

Hector.   How now, how now?

Troilus. For th' love of all the gods,
Let's leave the hermit Pity with our mothers;   50
And when we have our armors buckled on,
The venom'd vengeance ride upon our swords,
Spur them to ruthful work, rein them from ruth.

Hector. Fie, savage, fie!

Troilus.   Hector, then 'tis wars.   55

Hector. Troilus, I would not have you fight today.

Troilus. Who should withhold me?
Not fate, obedience, nor the hand of Mars
Beck'ning with fiery truncheon my retire;
Nor Priamus and Hecuba on knees,   60
Their eyes oregalled with recourse of tears,
Nor you my brother with your true sword drawn
Oppos'd to hinder me, should stop my way
But by my ruin.

Enter Priam and Cassandra.

Cassandra. Lay hold upon him, Priam; hold him fast.   65
He is thy crutch. Now if thou lose thy stay,
Thou on him leaning and all Troy on thee,
Fall all together.

Priam.   Come, Hector come. Go back.
Thy wife hath dreamt, thy mother hath had visions,   70
Cassandra doth foresee, and I myself
Am like a prophet suddenly enrapt
To tell thee that this day is ominous.
Therefore, come back.

Hector.   Aeneas is afield,   75
And I do stand engag'd to many Greeks,
Even in the faith of valor, to appear
This morning to them.

Priam.   Ay, but thou shalt not go.

Hector. I must not break my faith.   80
You know me dutiful; therefore dear sir,
Let me not shame respect, but give me leave
To take that course by your consent and voice
Which you do here forbid me, royal Priam.

Cassandra. O Priam, yield not to him.   85

Andromache.   Do not, dear father.

Hector. Andromache, I am offended with you.
Upon the love you bear me, get you in.   *Exit Andromache.*

Troilus. This foolish, dreaming, superstitious girl
Makes all these bodements.   90

Cassandra.   O farewell, dear Hector.
Look how thou diest! Look how thy eye turns pale!
Look how thy wounds [do] bleed at many vents!
Hark how Troy roars, how Hecuba cries out,
How poor Andromache shrills her dolor forth!   95
Behold distraction, frenzy, and amazement,
Like witless antics one another meet,
And all cry, 'Hector! Hector's dead! O Hector!'

Troilus. Away, away.

Cassandra. Farewell. Yes, soft! Hector, I take my leave.   100
Thou dost thyself and all our Troy deceive.   *Exit.*

Hector. You are amaz'd, my liege, at her exclaim.
Go in and cheer the town; we'll forth and fight,
Do deeds of praise and tell you them at night.

Priam. Farewell. The gods with safety stand about thee.   105
                    [Exeunt Priam and Hector severally.] Alarum.

Troilus. They are at it, hark! Proud Diomed, believe
I come to lose my arm or win my sleeve.

Enter Pandar.

Pandarus. Do you hear, my lord? Do you hear?

Troilus. What now?

Pandarus. Here's a letter come from yond poor girl.   110

Troilus. Let me read.

Pandarus. A whoreson tisick, a whoreson rascally tisick so
troubles me, and the foolish fortune of this girl, and what one
thing, what another, that I shall leave you one o' th's days.
And I have a rheum in mine eyes too, and such an ache   115
in my bones, that unless a man were curst, I cannot tell
what to think on't. What says she there?

Troilus. Words, words, mere words, no matter from the
heart;
Th' effect doth operate another way.   *[He tears the letter.]*
Go, wind, to wind! There turn and change together.
My love with words and errors still she feeds,
But edifies another with her deeds.

18 **peevish:** *silly, foolish*   23 **For ... much:** *because we would like to give much; Cf. n.*
29 **keeps the weather of:** *has superiority over, has the wind of*   30 **dear man:** *honorable or noble man; Cf. n.*   34 **harness:** *armor*   37 **brushes:** *attacks, clashes*   41 **lion;**
Cf. n.   44 **fan:** *air current*   53 **ruthful:** *pitiful, i.e. violent and tragic*   59 **truncheon:**
staff or baton, sometimes used as signal to stop fighting

77 **faith of valor:** *promises involving a soldier's honor*   82 **shame respect:** *disgrace the respect
I owe you*   90 **bodements:** *forebodings*   93 **do:** *F doth*   97 **antics:** *madmen*   102
exclaim: *exclamations*   112 **tisick:** *lung congestion, cough*   120 **effect:** *real meaning*

Pandarus. Why, but hear you?

Troilus. Hence, brother lacky! Ignomy and shame   *125*
Pursue thy life and live aye with thy name!   *Exeunt.*

✄ SCENE FOURTH ✄

Alarum. Enter Thersites in excursion.

Thersites. Now they are clapper-clawing one another, I'll go
look on. That dissembling abominable varlet, Diomed, has got
that same scurvy, doting, foolish young knave's sleeve of Troy
there in his helm. I would fain see them meet, that that same
young Troyan ass that loves the whore there might send that   *5*
Greekish whoremasterly villain with the sleeve back to the dissembling, luxurious drab of a sleeveless errant. O' th' tother
side, the policy of those crafty swearing rascals—that [stale]
old-mouse-eaten dry cheese, Nestor, and that same dog-fox
Ulysses—is not prov'd worth a blackberry. They set me up,   *10*
in policy, that mongrel cur Ajax against that dog of as bad a
kind, Achilles. And now is the cur Ajax prouder than the cur
Achilles and will not arm today. Whereupon, the Grecians
began to proclaim barbarism, and policy grows into an ill
opinion.   *15*

Enter Diomed and Troilus.

Soft! Here comes sleeve and th' other.

Troilus. Fly not; for shouldst thou take the River Styx
I would swim after.

Diomedes.   Thou dost miscall retire.
I do not fly, but advantageous care   *20*
Withdrew me from the odds of multitude.
Have at thee!

Thersites. Hold thy whore, Grecian! Now, for thy whore,
Troyan! Now the sleeve, now the sleeve!

     [Exeunt Diomed and Troilus.]

Enter Hector.

Hector. What are thou, Greek? Art thou for Hector's match
Art thou of blood and honor?

Thersites. No, no! I am a rascal, a scurvy railing knave, a
very filthy rogue.

Hector. I do believe thee. Live.   *[Exit.]*

Thersites. God a mercy that thou wilt believe me; but a   *30*
plague break thy neck for frighting me. What's become of the
wenching rogues? I think they have swallowed one another. I
would laugh at that miracle; yet in a sort, lechery eats itself.
I'll seek them.   *Exit.*

✄ SCENE FIFTH ✄

Enter Diomed and Servants.

Diomedes. Go, go, my servant, take thou Troilus' horse.
Present the fair steed to my Lady Cressid.
Fellow, commend my service to her beauty;
Tell her I have chastis'd the amorous Troyan

And am her knight by proof.   *5*
Servant.   I go, my lord.   *[Exit.]*

Enter Agamemnon.

Agamemnon. Renew, renew! The fierce Polidamus
Hath beat down Menon; bastard Margarelon
Hath Doreus prisoner
And stands colossus-wise waving his beam   *10*
Upon the pashed corses of the kings
Epistropus and Cedus. Polixenes is slain;
Amphimacus and Thous deadly hurt;
Patroclus tane or slain, and Palamedes
Sore hurt and bruis'd. The dreadful Sagittary   *15*
Appalls our numbers. Haste we, Diomed,
To reinforcement, or we perish all.

Enter Nestor.

Nestor. Go bear Patroclus' body to Achilles,
And bid the snail-pac'd Ajax arm for shame.
There is a thousand Hectors in the field.   *20*
Now here he fights on Galathe, his horse,
And there lacks works; anon he's there afoot,
And there they fly or die, like scaled sculls
Before the belching whale; then is he yonder,
And there the straying Greeks, ripe for his edge,   *25*
Fall down before him like the mower's swath.
Here, there, and everywhere he leaves and takes,
Dexterity so obeying appetite
That what he will he does, and does so much
That proof is call'd impossibility.   *30*

Enter Ulysses.

Ulysses. O courage, courage, princes! Great Achilles
Is arming, weeping, cursing, vowing vengeance.
Patroclus' wounds have rous'd his drowsy blood,
Together with his mangled Myrmidons
That noseless, handless, hack'd, and chipp'd come to him,   *35*
Crying on Hector. Ajax hath lost a friend
And foams at mouth, and he is arm'd and at it,
Roaring for Troilus, who hath done today
Mad and fantastic execution,
Engaging and redeeming of himself   *40*
With such a careless force and forceless care
As if that luck, in very spite of cunning,
Bade him win all.

Enter Ajax.

Ajax. Troilus! Thou coward, Troilus!   *Exit.*
Diomedes.   Ay, there, there!   *45*
Nestor. So, so, we draw together.   *Exit.*

Enter Achilles.

Achilles.   Where is this Hector?
Come, come, though boy-queller, shew thy face!
Know what it is to meet Achilles angry.
Hector, where's Hector? I will none but Hector.   *[Exeunt.*

124-126 Why ... name; *Cf. n.*   125 Ignomy: *ignominy*   SD in excursion: *running onstage*   7 luxurious: *lecherous*   of a sleeveless errant: *on a useless errand*   8 stale: *F stole*   10 set me up: *set up*   11 in policy: *craftily*   14 proclaim barbarism: *follow anarchic barbarity rather than ordered policy*   20 advantageous care: *care for my own advantage*   25 Hector's match; *Cf. n.*

7-14 Polidamus ... Palamedes; *Cf. n.*   10 beam: *lance*   11 pashed: *smashed, mangled*   corses: *corpses*   14 tane: *taken*   15 Sagittary; *Cf. n.*   23 scaled sculls: *schools of fish*   26 swath: *grain cut by scythe*   30 proof: *accomplished fact*   36 Crying on: *exclaiming about*   39 execution: *five syllables here*   48 queller: *killer*   SD Exeunt; *Cf. n.*

❧ Scene Sixth ❧

Enter Ajax.

Ajax. Troilus, thou coward Troilus, shew thy head!

Enter Diomed.

Diomedes. Troilus, I say! Where's Troilus?
Ajax.   What wouldst thou?
Diomedes. I would correct him.
Ajax. Were I the general, thou shouldst have my office   5
Ere that correction. Troilus, I say! What, Troilus!

Enter Troilus.

Troilus. O traitor Diomed!
Turn thy false face, thou traitor,
And pay thy life thou ow'st me for my horse!
Diomedes. Ha, art thou there?   10
Ajax. I'll fight with him alone. Stand, Diomed.
Diomedes. He is my prize. I will not look upon.
Troilus. Come, both you cogging Greeks. Have at you both!
                    Exeunt Troilus [, Ajax, and Diomed].

Enter Hector.

Hector. Yea, Troilus? O well fought, my youngest brother!

Enter Achilles.

Achilles. Now do I see thee. Have at thee Hector!   15
Hector. Pause, if thou wilt.
Achilles. I do disdain thy courtesy, proud Troyan.
Be happy that my arms are out of use;
My rest and negligence befriends thee now,
But thou anon shalt hear of me again;   20
Till when, go seek thy fortune.   *Exit.*
Hector.   Fare thee well.
I would have been much more a fresher man
Had I expected thee. How now, my brother?

Enter Troilus.

Troilus. Ajax hath tane Aeneas! Shall it be?   25
No, by the flame of yonder glorious heaven,
He shall not carry him. I'll be tane too,
Or bring him off. Fate hear me what I say;
I reck not though thou end my life today.   *Exit.*

Enter One in armor.

Hector. Stand, stand, thou Greek! Thou art a goodly mark.   30
No? Wilt thou not? I like thy armor well;
I'll frush it and unlock the rivets all,
But I'll be master of it. Wilt thou not, beast, abide?
Why then, fly on. I'll hunt thee for thy hide.   *[Exeunt.]*

❧ Scene Seventh ❧

Enter Achilles with Myrmidons.

Achilles. Come here about me, you my Myrmidons.
Mark what I say: Attend me where I wheel,

Strike not a stroke, but keep yourselves in breath;
And when I have the bloody Hector found,
Empale him with your weapons round about.   5
In fellest manner execute your arms.
Follow me, sirs, and my proceeding eye.
It is decreed Hector the great must die.   *Exit [with followers].*

Enter Thersites, Menelaus, and Paris.

Thersites. The cuckold and the cuckold maker are at it. Now
bull! Now dog! Low, Paris, low! Now my double hen'd sparrow! Low, Paris, low! The bull has the game. 'Ware horns, ho!
                    Exit Paris and Menelaus.

Enter Bastard.

Bastard. Turn, slave, and fight!
Thersites. What art thou?
Bastard. A bastard son of Priam's.
Thersites. I am a bastard too. I love bastards. I am a bastard   15
begot, bastard instructed, bastard in mind, bastard in valor, in
everything illegitimate. One bear will not bite another, and
wherefore should one bastard? Take heed; the quarrel's most
ominous to us; if the son of a whore fight for a whore, he
tempts judgment. Farewell, bastard.   20
Bastard. The divel take thee, coward.   *Exeunt.*

❧ Scene Eighth ❧

Enter Hector.

Hector. Most putrified core, so fair without,
Thy goodly armor thus hath cost thy life.
Now is my day's work done. I'll take good breath.
Rest, sword; thou hast thy fill of blood and death.

Enter Achilles and his Myrmidons.

Achilles. Look, Hector, how the sun begins to set;   5
How ugly night comes breathing at his heels,
Even with the vail and darking of the sun.
To close the day up, Hector's life is done.
Hector. I am unarm'd. Forgo this vantage, Greek.
Achilles. Strike, fellows, strike! This is the man I seek.   10
So Ilion, fall thou; now Troy sink down!
Here lies thy heart, thy sinews, and thy bone.
On Myrmidons! Cry you all amain:
'Achilles hath the mighty Hector slain.'   *Retreat.*
Hark, a retreat upon our Grecian part.   15
Greek. The Troyan trumpets sound the like, my lord.
Achilles. The dragon wing of night orespreads the earth
And, sticklerlike, the armies separates.
My half-supp'd sword that frankly would have fed,
Pleas'd with this dainty bait, thus goes to bed.   20
Come, tie his body to my horse's tail;
Along the field I will the Troyan trail.   *Exeunt.*

---

6 **Ere that correction;** *Cf. n.*   12 **look upon:** *to be a spectator*   13 **cogging:** *de-*
frauding **SD Exeunt … Diomed:** *F has merely* Exit Troilus   19 **rest and negligence:**
i.e. his long inactivity has made him rusty   27 **carry:** *prevail, have victory over*   32 **frush:**
smash **SD Exeunt:** *F* Exit   2 **wheel:** *turn, go*

5 **Empale:** *'surround,' as with a fence*   6 **execute:** *employ, make use of*   **arms:** *F* arme   10
Low: *sound of a bull (a horned beast)*   **double hen'd sparrow;** *Cf. n.*   1 **putrified:** *four*
syllables here   3 **breath:** *breathing space, rest*   7 **vail:** *setting*   16 **Greek:** *one of the*
Myrmidons **sound:** *F* sounds   18 **stickler-:** *an arbiter at a duel*   19 **frankly:** *abun-*
dantly, freely

❧ SCENE NINTH ❧

Sound retreat. Shout.
Enter Agamemnon, Ajax, Menelaus, Nestor, Diomed, and the rest,
marching.

Agamemnon. Hark, hark! What shout is that?
Nestor.   Peace, drums.
Soldier [Within.] Achilles! Achilles! Hector's slain! Achilles!
Diomedes. The bruit is, Hector's slain and by Achilles.
  Ajax. If it be so, yet bragless let it be.   5
Great Hector was a man as good as he.
  Agamemnon. March patiently along. Let one be sent
To pray Achilles see us at our tent.
If in his death the gods have us befriended,
Great Troy is ours, and our sharp wars are ended.   *Exeunt.*

❧ SCENE TENTH ❧

Enter Aeneas, Paris, Antenor, and Deiphobus.

Aeneas. Stand, ho! Yet are we masters of the field.
Never go home. Here starve we out the night.

Enter Troilus.

Troilus. Hector is slain.
All.   Hector? The gods forbid!
  Troilus. He's dead; and at the murtherer's horse's tail,   5
In beastly sort dragg'd through the shameful field.
Frown on, you heavens; effect your rage with speed!
Sit, gods, upon your thrones, and smile at Troy!
I say, at once let your brief plagues be mercy,
And linger not our sure destructions on.   10
  Aeneas. My lord, you do discomfort all the host.
  Troilus. You understand me not that tell me so.
I do not speak of flight, of fear, of death,
But dare all imminence that gods and men
Address their dangers in. Hector is gone.   15
Who shall tell Priam so? Or Hecuba?
Let him that will a screechowl aye be call'd
Go in to Troy, and say there, 'Hector's dead.'
There is a word will Priam turn to stone,
Make wells and Niobes of the maids and wives,   20
Cool statues of the youth, and in a word,

Scare Troy out of itself. But march away;
Hector is dead. There is no more to say.
Stay yet. You vile abominable tents,
Thus proudly pight upon our Phrygian plains,   25
Let Titan rise as early as he dare,
I'll through and through you! And thou great-siz'd coward,
No space of earth shall sunder our two hates.
I'll haunt thee like a wicked conscience still,
That moldeth goblins swift as frenzy's thoughts.   30
Strike a free march to Troy. With comfort go.
Hope of revenge shall hide our inward woe.

Enter Pandarus.

  Pandarus. But hear you? Hear you?
  Troilus. Hence, broker-lacky! Ignomy and shame
Pursue thy life and live aye with thy name.   35
                    Exeunt [all but Pandarus].
  Pandarus. A goodly med'cine for mine aching bones. O
world, world, world! Thus is the poor agent despis'd. O
traitors and bawds! How earnestly you are set awork, and
how ill requited! Why should our endeavor be so desir'd,
and the performance so loath'd? What verse for it? What   40
instance for it? Let me see.

Full merrily the humble bee doth sing
Till he hath lost his honey and his sting;
And being once subdu'd in armed tail,
Sweet honey and sweet notes together fail.   45

Good traders in the flesh, set this in your painted cloths.
As many as be here of Pandar's hall,
Your eyes half out, weep out at Pandar's fall;
Or if you cannot weep, yet give some groans,
Though not for me, yet for your aching bones.   50
Brethren and sisters of the hold-door trade,
Some two months hence my will shall here be made.
It should be now, but that my fear is this:
Some galled goose of Winchester would hiss.
Till then, I'll sweat and seek about for eases,   55
And at that time bequeath you my diseases.   *[Exit.]*

❧ FINIS ❧

---

3 **Within:** *Q only*   4 **bruit:** *clamor, rumor*   8 **smile;** *Cf. n.*   14 **imminence:** *impending evil*   15 **Address:** *prepare*

25 **pight:** *pitched*   26 **Titan:** *the sun*   **SD all but Pandarus:** *Q only*   46 **painted cloths:** *wall hangings; Cf. n.*   51 **hold-door:** *pimp, pander* (those who hold the door to ensure privacy)   54 **galled goose of Winchester;** *Cf. n.*   55 **sweat;** *Cf. n.*   **SD Exit:** *F Exeunt*

Prologue.17. *Antenonidus.* The spelling of this name differs from the form we find in earlier writers who name the gates; but since there is no real agreement even among these earlier authorities, the F reading has been allowed to stand.

Prologue.19. *Sperr up.* This is an emendation introduced in Theobald's edition for the unsatisfactory reading in F.

Prologue.23–5. *prologue arm'd . . . argument.* The prologue comes not to boast of the excellence of the author or the actors, and he is dressed in armor simply because it is appropriate to the warlike argument of the play. Some scholars have interpreted this passage as a reference to Jonson's satirical play, *The Poetaster,* and have further interpreted the whole play of *Troilus and Cressida* as Shakespeare's rejoinder to Jonson.

I.i.23, 24. *here's . . . hereafter.* There's yet more hereafter in the word *tarry,* i.e. *the kneading,* etc.

I.i.31. *So . . . thence.* Troilus calls himself a traitor for admitting that Cressida is ever out of his thoughts. Then he goes on to say that whenever she goes from them, she immediately comes back.

I.i.41. *And.* And in this meaning appears frequently throughout any Renaissance play, and in modern editions it is usually spelled *an.* In this play and in F it is almost always spelled *and.*

I.i.56. *spirit of sense.* This phrase has been much discussed, and there is no explanation which is generally agreed upon. Perhaps Shakespeare means the essential, invisible spirit of sensation. In a series of soft things being compared with the softness of Cressida's hand, this intangible, immaterial item is certainly not out of place.

I.i.73, 74. *fair . . . Sunday.* Cressida would be as beautiful in her poorest clothes as Helen in her finest.

I.i.78. *father.* Cressida's father was Calchas, a priest, who had deserted the Trojan cause to go over to the Greeks. Shakespeare, in treating Calchas later on in Act III, makes no reference to the legend that he had been told to do so by Apollo.

I.i.98. *Ilium.* In this play, as in the medieval authorities for the Troilus story, Ilium always means specifically the palace of Priam rather than the entire city of Troy.

I.i.110. *horn.* The horn joke was omnipresent in the Elizabethan period. A man whose wife was unfaithful to him was pictured as having invisible cuckold's horns on his head. The joke appears throughout this play, almost as often as Menelaus is mentioned.

I.i.113. *togither.* This spelling of 'together' is not infrequent in Shakespeare's plays; for the rhyme *thither : togither* see Helge Kökeritz, *Shakespeare's Pronunciation* (New Haven, Yale University Press, 1953), p. 187.

I.ii.16. *nephew.* Actually Ajax was Hector's cousin. Much earlier Priam's sister, Hesione, had been carried off to Greece and there, according to one legend, was married to Telamon and bore Ajax. Thus Ajax was Priam's nephew and Hector's cousin. This relationship is mentioned again in II.2 and IV.5.

I.ii.26. *humors.* In Renaissance medicine the four humors (blood, yellow bile, black bile, and phlegm) were fluids secreted by various organs of the body. These fluids were thought to determine not only physical health but temperament, personality, and behavior. When the secretions were functioning properly and the right proportions of each were maintained, health resulted; but if one humor became excessive, certain aberrations were likely to appear. The word also had an extended, less technical usage, meaning 'caprice' or 'mood.'

I.ii.26, 27. *valor . . . discretion.* His valor is crushed into or mixed thoroughly with folly, and his folly is further mixed or sauced with discretion.

I.ii.45. *cousin.* This word was very loosely applied in Elizabethan English to virtually any collateral relationship. Actually, Cressida was Pandarus' niece.

I.ii.74. *Condition.* By the impossible nature of the condition, we gather that Pandarus is contradicting Cressida.

I.ii.76. *a.* This unaccented form of 'he' was probably a neutral [ə] sound, though the spelling is uniformly *a* in the Renaissance texts. It will be hereafter printed without gloss or comment.

I.ii.77. *time . . . end.* This was a proverbial phrase, meaning something like 'Time will tell.'

I.ii.85. *will.* Some modern editors emend this word to *wit.* Both F and Q have *will,* however, and if we take it to refer to Troilus' will power or strength of will no emendation is necessary.

I.ii.111. *tapster's arithmetic.* The tapsters or drawers of beer in the alehouses were proverbially poor at adding.

I.ii.189. *nod.* The related word, 'noddy,' a simpleton, forms the punning

basis for Cressida's next speech. 'He who is already rich in foolishness (a noddy) shall receive more if Troilus give him a nod.'

I.ii.193. *brave.* Here and elsewhere in the play this word probably has double or triple connotations, since the meaning could be 'courageous,' or simply 'splendid,' 'fine,' or sometimes 'showy,' 'gaudy.'

I.ii.243. *date's out.* The pun here depends on the meaning of *date* with reference to time: 'the man's time is up' or 'he's out of date.'

I.ii.248. *mask.* Renaissance women often wore masks to protect their complexions from the elements.

I.ii.251. *watch.* Puns on the various meanings of *watch* and *ward* run throughout this passage. Cressida means here that she will prevent his telling by keeping watch on him.

I.ii.263. *To bring.* This is a rare Elizabethan slang idiom, possibly meaning 'with a vengeance.'

I.ii.277. *Achievement . . . beseech.* This cryptic epigram is evidently not proverbial but rather original with Cressida. It probably means that men use entreaty when the lady is ungained, but change to peremptory language when the object is achieved.

I.iii.8. *diverts.* Both F and Q read thus, although modern usage demands *divert.* Such plurals formed with *-s* by analogy with the singular were common in Shakespeare's day and constituted an acceptable variant to the form without *-s.*

I.iii.15. *Bias.* The bowling balls of the time were not true spheres but had a bias or added weight on one side. Often in Shakespeare this word is extended metaphorically to other matters, as it is here.

I.iii.23. *Fortune's.* The concept of the goddess Fortune was a favorite idea which the Elizabethans inherited from the Middle Ages. She might befriend a person without reason and bring him success, or just as capriciously plunge him into misery.

I.iii.54. *Retorts.* F reads *Retyres.* Various emendations have been suggested for this meaningless reading. The word *Retorts* was first proposed by Dyce (ed. 1857) and has been accepted by most modern editors, although there is no way of knowing exactly what Shakespeare wrote.

I.iii.61. *To Agamemnon.* There is no indication of the person addressed in the early texts, but this and the following line make sense only if addressed to Agamemnon and Nestor respectively.

I.iii.67. *hatch'd.* The phrase *hatch'd in silver* probably refers to Nestor's white hair.

I.iii.75. *masty.* The rare word *Masticke* in the Folio (this passage does not occur in Q) has occasioned many ingenious explanations. Professor Kökeritz suggests very plausibly that the printer misread *mastie* (mastif) as *mastic,* which he set up in type with a conventional *ck* and a mute *e.*

I.iii.87. *center.* Shakespeare is here using the Ptolemaic concept of the cosmos.

I.iii.91. *Sol.* The sun was considered a planet in Ptolemaic astronomy.

I.iii.94. *aspects.* According to the lore of astrology, certain relative positions or aspects of planets are supposed to have harmful effects on earthly activities.

I.iii.120. *her.* This *her* may be a mere mistake in F for *their,* which is the Q reading. It is perfectly possible, however, that this is the old form for the third person genitive plural (Chaucer's *here*), common in southern texts up to the beginning of the 16th century, although archaic by Shakespeare's time.

I.iii.130, 131. *purpose . . . climb.* The purpose of those who neglect degree is to climb the social ladder to the next step above. This process goes downward, or *backward,* pace by pace through the ranks as specified in the succeeding lines.

I.iii.159. *orewrested.* Shakespeare is drawing a metaphor from stringed musical instruments. The wrest is the pin used for tightening the string.

I.iii.170. *Vulcan and his wife.* The god Vulcan was always pictured as particularly ugly, while Venus was, of course, extremely beautiful.

I.iii.214. *Thetis' sons.* Achilles was Thetis' son. Nestor means that if it be granted that physical force is superior to mental powers, then anyone mounted on Achilles' horse would be as great as Achilles.

I.iii.241, 242. *Jove's . . . heart.* When Jove approves, nothing is so full of courage (as a Trojan).

I.iii.346–348. *For . . . general.* The outcome of the combat, although it actually applies to only two particular persons, shall decide the amount of praise or shame attributed to the Greeks and Trojans in general.

I.iii.349–352. *And in . . . large.* The figure here refers to the table of contents of a book. From the brief indication of the 'index' one sees in reduced form the contents of the whole volume.

I.iii.360–362. *Which . . . . the limbs.* Deighton (ed. 1906) paraphrases this

passage thus: 'And if this belief (i.e. of the Trojans, that they will be victorious) is entertained it will energise the limbs of those who hold it, just as those limbs energise the swords and bows they wield.'

II.i.14. *whinid'st.* Since this word appears nowhere else, it has produced many ingenious emendations. Many editors have avoided it by substituting the Q reading, *unsalted,* but this is also unsatisfactory because salt is not normally required for leavening. The most plausible suggestion has been that of Upton (*Critical Observations,* 1746), who noted that *whinid'st* could be a dialectal pronunciation of 'vinewedest' or 'vinidest' (finewedest), meaning 'most mouldy.' This view is supported by Kökeritz, *Shakespeare's Pronunciation,* p. 323.

II.i.31, 32. *Cerberus . . . Proserpina's.* Cerberus was the three-headed dog who guarded the Greek Hades. Proserpina was the beautiful wife of Pluto, the god of the underworld.

II.i.51. *Mars his idiot.* This construction, called the *his*-genitive, was originally due to a grammatical misconception. The genitive ending *-es* in a word like 'Marses' was sometimes thought to be a separate element, i.e. 'Mars is,' and this 'is' was thought to be equivalent to *his.* It was used very commonly throughout the Renaissance and even later. It appears frequently later on in this play.

II.i.103. *To Achilles! to Ajax!* This is uttered as if a call urging on a team of oxen.

II.i.108. *brooch.* Many modern editors emend this word to *brach.* Since it appears as *brooch,* however, in Q, and all the Folios, it is likely that the word is correct as it stands. It would not be surprising if Thersites were making a highly obscene accusation, for *brooch* or 'broach' in the 16th century meant, among other things, a 'pointed rod, spit or pricker.' (cf. OED).

II.ii.19. *tithe.* This word also meant anything paid by way of offering or sacrifice. The ambiguity adds meaning to this passage.

II.ii.46. *And fly . . . Jove.* F has this line misplaced two lines further along. The Q placement is obviously preferable.

II.ii.60–62. *And the . . . merit.* This passage might be paraphrased: 'That will is foolish which inclines to something which it unwholesomely likes without taking into account some idea of the absolute merit of the thing liked.'

II.ii.171. *Aristotle.* In the *Nicomachean Ethics,* Aristotle indicated that political philosophy was unsuitable for young men. The term *moral* in the 16th century embraced the realm of political ethics as well as other things.

II.ii.177. *adders.* It was a popular belief in Shakespeare's time that adders were deaf, or could stop up their ears at will.

II.iii.21, 22. *gilt counterfeit . . . slipp'd.* Thersites is punning on the meaning of 'slip' as a counterfeit coin.

II.iii.33. *cheese.* The practice of eating cheese after a meal was supposed to aid digestion. Also a noble lord often called in his fool to entertain him after a meal. Achilles thus combines the two in a facetious metaphor.

II.iii.70. *shent.* Neither the Q nor F reading makes sense in this passage, and most modern editors accept the emendation *shent* of Theobald.

II.iii.86–89. *matter . . . Achilles.* Nestor and Ulysses are playing with the word *argument.* Nestor says that Ajax will lack subject matter for this railing if he has lost Thersites. Ulysses replies that he has a new *argument* for railing, namely Achilles, who took away Thersites.

II.iii.91. *counsel.* Q has *composure,* which makes sense in this passage, but not very different sense from the F reading.

II.iii.93. *knits not.* The punctuation here is from the Q. F has *knits, not folly* etc., which contains the obverse of the same idea.

II.iii.98. *flexure.* Although the F reading makes sense of a sort, the Q word is preferable, since this whole passage controverts an old notion, still current in Shakespeare's day, that elephants have no joints. It adds an idea from a proverb that elephants, like great men, are too proud to bow, or 'make a leg.'

II.iii.118–122. *And worthier . . . predominance.* A worthier man than he here attends his rule aloofness, foregoes the deference due to the holy strength of his position (commander-in-chief), and submits in a passive way to his capricious superiority.

II.iii.167. *Kingdom'd.* Achilles is metaphorically considered a kingdom containing warring factions.

II.iii.189. *coals to Cancer.* Cancer is the sign of the zodiac which the sun enters at the summer solstice. Thus this line means 'and add more heat to summer.'

II.iii.206. *let his humor's blood.* In the word *humor's* the apostrophe undoubtedly means that it is a contracted form of *humorous,* which is the reading of Q. *Humorous* means here both 'full of humors' and 'capricious.'

II.iii.211. *eat swords.* This may be a printer's error for *eat's words,* i.e. *eat his words.* However, there are other scornful references in Shakespeare to eating swords (*Much Ado about Nothing,* IV.1.281, 282; *Anthony and Cleopatra,* III.13.234).

II.iii.214. *shares.* This line is sometimes taken as a topical allusion to the financial arrangements of Shakespeare's company. When the Globe theater was built in 1599, its ownership was divided into ten shares. Thus Ulysses would seem to mean that Ajax would have all (pride), not just half.

II.iii.216. *He's . . . warm.* Both F and Q give this sentence to Ajax' preceding speech. It makes more sense, however, as part of Nestor's speech, and most modern editors print it so. None of the asides in this scene are so marked in F, but it is clear there are several speeches Ajax is not meant to hear.

II.iii.218. *My lord.* Although the F does not indicate it with a scene direction, Ulysses quite obviously shifts his address to Agamemnon at this point.

II.iii.243. *Milo.* Milo was a semilegendary athlete of Greece who bore a four-year-old bull forty yards, killed it with one blow, and ate it.

III.i.12. *honor.* The servant is punning on the word *honor,* as he does in the next speech on the word *grace.* Pandarus does not catch the joke.

III.i.31. *love's invisible soul.* Helen, as a very symbol of love and beauty, a mortal Venus, is here hyperbolically considered the very essence or spirit of love.

III.i.37. *complimental assault.* Pandarus in this speech and in his next is using rather affectedly courtly language. *Complimental* refers to paying his compliments or respects in a formal way.

III.i.39. *Sodden.* This is the old past participle of 'seethe.' The servant twists Pandarus' word by applying another meaning common at the time. Hot steaming baths were used as a remedy for veneral disease, and a person in them was in a sense *sodden.* This naturally suggests the 'stews' or brothels of his next pun.

III.i.SD. *Helena.* This older form of the name Helen is used nowhere else in the play.

III.i.40. *Fair.* Throughout this speech Pandarus is employing a rather exaggerated rhetorical trick with his frequent repetition of the word fair as an adjective, adverb, and noun, sometimes meaning 'good,' 'fine,' sometimes 'beautiful.'

III.i.52. *fits.* Paris' remark is not entirely clear; perhaps he means Pandarus deprecates his singing only now and then, by *fits.* A pun is possible, for *fits* also meant the stanzas or sections of a song.

III.i.79. *Helen.* Helen's speech here is sometimes made part of Pandarus' preceding speech, and it perhaps fits better there; but since neither F nor Q give any authority for such a shift, and since it is understandable, with a slightly different sense, in Helen's mouth, the F reading has been retained.

III.i.103. *Love.* The tenor of this song is highly bawdy, since the pun on *die,* 'experience orgasm' and 'expire,' runs throughout. *Hey ho,* at the end, may be not part of the song but a sigh of Pandarus after finishing.

III.i.120. *doves.* Doves were, of course, sacred to Venus, and Paris indicates that eating them has an aphrodisiac effect.

III.i.124. *vipers.* Pandarus is jokingly bringing the idea around to the familiar phrase 'generation of vipers' from the Bible (Matt. 3:7), where, of course, it is used in a completely different context.

III.i.148. *Sweet . . . thee.* This sentence is part of Helen's preceding speech in F, but is given to the uxorious Paris in Q.

III.ii.8, 9. *Stygian . . . Charon.* Charon was the boatman who ferried souls across the river Styx to the Greek underworld. The field of lilies in the next line are the Elysian fields.

III.ii.41. *watch'd.* Hawks were often tamed by wearing them down through lack of sleep.

III.ii.46. *in fee-farm.* A *fee-farm* was a grant of land in fee for an indefinite period of time.

III.ii.48. *falcon . . . tercel.* The *falcon* is the female bird and the *tercel* the male. Pandarus is also using a phrase from betting jargon, saying that he would back Cressida against Troilus for any amount.

III.ii.85, 86. *envy . . . his truth.* The worst thing malice can say of him will be to mock him for his fidelity and truth.

III.ii.120. *Coming.* Many editors emend this word to *Cunning,* but this F and Q reading *Coming* makes excellent sense.

III.ii.167. *plantage.* In some quarters the belief persists to the present that the growth of vegetation is influenced by the moon.

III.ii.SD. *Exeunt.* Troilus and Cressida start off stage after l. 200, and Pandarus stays behind a moment to deliver his leering couplet to the audience.

III.iii.4. *sight . . . love.* This passage has been often discussed and emended, and certainly *things to come* would be a more intelligible reading. Both F and Q have *things to love,* however. Possibly Shakespeare meant 'through the insight I have into things which should be loved,' namely life, security, and the winning side. The soothsayer Calchas had previously been informed by the Delphic oracle that Troy would lose the war.

III.iii.31. *pain.* The phrase *most accepted* may refer to Calchas' acceptance of the hardships, or it may imply that the Greeks have readily accepted his painful services.

III.iii.139, 140. *How ... eyes.* How some men sneak unnoticed into capricious Fortune's hall, while others, from her point of view, play the fool.

III.iii.142. *feasting.* Many editors prefer the Q reading, *fasting*, here, but the F makes perfectly good sense and is more directly applicable to Achilles.

III.iii.168. *rear.* This word is an emendation suggested by Hanmer (ed. 1745). The F has *abject, neere.* Lines 167, 168 are missing in Q.

III.iii.184 *give.* F and Q have *go.* Theobald first used this emendation in his edition of 1733, and it has been accepted by most subsequent editors.

III.iii.189. *sooner.* The words *begin to* in F were probably drawn down mistakenly from the line above by a copyist or a typesetter.

III.iii.206. *Knows ... gold.* 'Knows minutely of the most unsearchable things.' Shakespeare, along with many others in his time, seems to amalgamate the persons of Pluto, god of the lower world, and Plutus, the god of riches.

III.iii.217. *Polixena.* Daughter of Priam and Hecuba, with whom Achilles had fallen in love. Though not in Homer, this twist in the Troy story was added in later Greek times, and the medieval writers on Troy emphasized it as one of the motives for Achilles' withdrawal from the battle.

III.iii.224. *fool ... break.* This line has been variously interpreted. Possibly it means that Achilles should break the thin ice Ajax is sliding over, and thus keep him in his place. Some scholars have taken this as a reference to an actual event which Shakespeare knew about, and have used it as an argument for dating the play.

III.iii.242. *commission ... blank.* 'Puts you at the complete mercy of danger.' The metaphor here is drawn from the practice of issuing blank commissions to the collectors of imposts, to be filled in at their discretion.

IV.i.71. *which ... whore?* This line has been much discussed. The Q reads *the heavier for a whore,* and neither F nor Q has a question mark. Using the common concept of a whore as a 'light' woman, however, the F reading becomes quite intelligible as a question, and the line supports the idea of equal balance which Diomedes has stated in the previous line.

IV.i.83. *We'll ... sell.* This line has caused trouble, mainly because Paris obviously has no intention of selling Helen, except at the very dear price of defeat. It is clear, however, that he is reversing the practice of the chapmen and of Diomedes in favor of silence concerning his commodity.

IV.ii.35. *chipochia.* This word is probably best explained as an anglicized form of the Italian *cappocchia,* 'simpleton.' Pandarus is here speaking mock baby talk, however, and this may be a mere invented nonce word of endearment.

IV.iv.37. *rejoindure.* This is merely an elaborated spelling of *rejoinder* from *re-* and *joinder* (union) as in *Twelfth Night,* V.1.159.

IV.iv.49. *tears.* After this word in F, but not in Q, there occurs the SD *Enter Aeneas.* This is probably a mistake, for further along at l. 106 Aeneas still speaks *Within.*

IV.iv.51. *genius.* In Roman mythology each person was thought to have an attendant spirit or genius which presided over his destiny during life.

IV.iv.59. *When ... again.* Through a typesetter's error this line is given to Troilus in F. Q has it as part of Cressida's speech.

IV.iv.85. *Flowing.* This emendation was suggested by Stanton. There is some reason to suspect that there was post-Shakespearean tampering with the text in this passage, either in the theater or the printing shop, for the Q leaves out this word and the entire preceding line. The Q line *And swelling ... exercise* is a normal pentameter line, and the addition of this word in the F turns it into a hexameter. The F reading has been retained, however, since not only this word but the whole of l. 84 is involved, and it would be hard to prove that that line is not Shakespeare's.

IV.iv.SD. *Paris, Aeneas ...* The F SD reads *Enter the Greeks,* but of course Diomedes is the only Greek who takes part in the ensuing scene.

IV.iv.133. *zeal ... thee.* This is the Q reading, except that the word *seal* of both Q and F was emended to *zeal* by Warburton (ed. 1747). The somewhat garbled F reading for this passage runs: *To shame the seale of my petition towards/ I praising her.*

IV.iv.157. *Let ... straight.* This line is marked *Dio.* in F, and it does not occur in Q. Since it is entirely inappropriate for Diomedes, most editors assume that the *Dio.* was a mistake for *Dei.* and assign the speech to Deiphobus.

IV.v.SD. *Calchas.* Calchas' name stands thus in the SD of both F and Q, although he does not speak in this scene, and from Diomedes' speech at l. 61 it would seem that he is not present.

IV.v.32. *And ... argument.* This line was evidently dropped inadvertently by the compositor of F, for the line is needed to explain the action at this point. At the word *thus* Patroclus evidently steps between Menelaus and Cressida and kisses her in his stead.

IV.v.68. *a coasting.* So spelled in both F and Q. It may be that this should

be read *accosting,* but it may also be from the verb 'to coast,' to move alongside, as of a ship. In either case the whole sentence is clearer if *welcome* be taken as the direct object and *a coasting* as the indirect object of *give.*

IV.v.72. *game.* After this word F, but not Q, has *Exeunt,* but judging from the ensuing scene no one leaves the stage.

IV.v.96. *Ajax ... blood.* Ajax, as son of Hesione, Hector's aunt, was closely related to Hector by blood. Cf. I.2.16.N.

IV.v.109. *knight.* After this word in F, but not in Q, there follow the words, *they call him Troilus.* They evidently are out of place, for they anticipate and duplicate part of l. 121. The later position is preferable, since the identification appears as the culmination of the description.

IV.v.159. *Neoptolymus.* It is not clear just whom Hector is talking about. Neoptolemus (or Pyrrhus, mentioned above at III.3.218) was Achilles' son, and according to some versions of the Troy legend was eventually responsible for the conclusion of the war, but at this time he had no reputation which could be termed *mirable.* Samuel Johnson suggested that Shakespeare might have taken Neoptolemus to be the family name, and therefore he is here speaking of Achilles.

IV.v.160. *Oyes.* Both F and Q read (*O yes*), but this was a frequent spelling for the cry 'Oyez,' 'here ye,' an expression still used in the law courts.

IV.v.SD. *Enter ... rest.* This stage direction occurs in F but not in Q. It is puzzling since they have probably not left the stage. Perhaps they watched the fight from a distance (possibly from the inner stage) and at this point come forward to the group around the fighters.

IV.v.215. *grandsire.* Laomedon, father of Priam, years before had been active in some of the incidents leading up to the Trojan War. Nestor's great age at present led the medieval authorities to assume that he also had been an actor in the events of two generations before, although the Greek stories record no fight between Laomedon and Nestor. At I.3.297 Shakespeare has Nestor refer to Laomedon in a slightly different way.

IV.v.320. *doth.* The F spells this word *dooth,* and it is possible that it did make a perfect rhyme with *tooth,* whatever their common vowel sound.

V.i.12. *surgeon's box.* Thersites punningly takes *tent* to mean 'a probe for a wound.'

V.i.15. *varlot.* This is the reading of both F and Q and thus it has been retained. There is a temptation to emend the word to *harlot,* as many editors have done, particularly because of Thersites' explanation in l. 17. Perhaps an amalgamation of the word *harlot* and *varlet* was intentional with Thersites. However, *varlots* appears in Q at V.1.95, where no such ambiguity is intended.

V.i.19. *palsies.* After this word the Q adds: *raw eyes, dirt-rotten livers, wheezing lungs, bladders full of impostume* (pus), *sciaticas, lime-kilns* (burnings) *i' th' palm, incurable bone-ache, and the riveled fee-simple of the tetter* (absolute ownership of the skin disease). The words *and the like* in F are thought to be a substitution at some later time when the long quarto list of diseases was shortened.

V.i.47–49. *transformation ... cuckolds.* In the Europa story Jupiter transformed himself into a bull. Thus the bull, a horned creature, may be considered, as Thersites puts it, to be *the primitive statue and oblique memorial of cuckolds,* such as Menelaus.

V.i.49. *shoeing horn.* There is probably here another reference to cuckoldry, plus the idea of Menelaus' ineffectual dependence on Agamemnon (hanging on a chain at his leg).

V.i.SD. *Exeunt ... Ulysses* A simple *Exeunt* after l. 85 in Q and F was probably meant as a blanket affair to get the two parties off the stage severally.

V.i.89. *Brabbler.* A hound which bayed a great deal but hunted poorly was often called a *brabbler* or a 'babbler.'

V.ii.66. *potato.* Potatoes were commonly thought to be aphrodisiac.

V.ii.94. *Nay ... me.* This sentence is given to Diomedes in both Q and F. The apparent action of the scene, however, makes it likely that it is part of Cressida's speech.

V.ii.119. *likes not me.* Q has *likes not you,* which also makes sense. Whereas the Q reading indicates spite toward Diomedes, the paradox of the line as it stands in F underlines the general perverseness of Thersites and the malignant and cynical pleasure he takes in unpleasant and sometimes disgusting things.

V.ii.143. *that test.* Q has *th' attest,* which is perhaps the better reading, but F makes good enough sense to stand.

V.ii.167, 168. *That cause ... Without revolt.* These knotty lines are clearer if we realize that Troilus has by this time reasoned himself into a palpable contradiction and is acutely conscious of the fact. He is saying that it is madly irrational for reason to point two ways; that would be the same as saying that reason can revolt or stop operating without being lost (perdition), or that lost reason or unreason can pass an unrevolted reason. He is virtually charging himself with sophistry in his argument that this is not Cressida.

V.ii.176. *Ariachne's broken woof.* The name Ariachne seems to be an amalgam-

ation of Arachne and Ariadne, but in this context Shakespeare is clearly referring to the Arachne story. In a weaving contest with Athene, Arachne produced a magnificent piece of cloth, which Athene destroyed. Arachne thereupon hung herself, but Athene saved her by changing the rope into a spider web and Arachne into a spider.

V.ii.217, 218. *parrot . . . almond.* Elizabethan parrots asked for almonds rather than crackers.

V.iii.23. *For . . . much.* This line appears in F as: *For we would count give much to as violent thefts.* Tyrwhitt first suggested deleting *count* and changing *as* to *use.* This is no more than a guess, but since it is impossible to as certain exactly what Shakespeare wrote at this point, many later editors have accepted the emendation.

V.iii.30. *dear man.* Many editors have replaced this *dear* with some other word, such as *brave, clear, true.* This, however, spoils Shakespeare's intentional word play on the two meanings of *dear.*

V.iii.41. *lion.* Lions were thought to be merciful to those that humbled themselves.

V.iii.124, 126. *Why . . . name.* These two speeches are duplicated at the end of the play (V.10.33–35). In the Q they appear only at the end of the play. This duplication in F probably means that some sort of revision had taken place; perhaps they were written originally for this position, then shifted to the end.

V.iv.25. *Hector's match.* Custom allowed a high-born person to fight only with his peers.

V.v.7–14. *Polidamus . . . Palamedes.* All the names in this speech are names of warriors whom Shakespeare chose at random from the earlier accounts of the Troy story in order to give an impression of feverish battle at this point. Patroclus is the only one who is a character of any importance in this play.

Margarelon was a bastard son of Priam, and it may be he whom Thersites talks to at V.7.13 ff.

V.v.15. *Sagittary.* A supernatural creature reputed to have fought for the Trojans. It was part horse, part man, and an uncommonly accurate archer.

V.v.SD. *Exeunt.* The stage direction is *Exit* in F and Q, but no previous exits have been indicated for Agamemnon or Ulysses. It is very probable that each of them left the stage after his speech, in spite of the fact that there is no indication of it in the text.

V.vi.6. *Ere that correction.* Ajax disputes Diomedes' right to fight Troilus since he wants to do so himself. He says if he were general he would rather give up his command than let Diomedes have the privilege of 'correcting' Troilus.

V.vii.10. *double hen'd sparrow.* This, the reading of F, may be wrong, but it has been allowed to stand since all the many suggested emendations are uncertain. The Q has *double hen'd Spartan,* and a most plausible suggestion has recently been made that Shakespeare originally wrote *double horn'd Spartan.*

V.x.8. *smile.* Several editors have considered this a contradiction of the idea in the preceding line and have emended to *smite.* This phrase is *smile at,* not *smile on,* however, and this imputation of callous derision to the gods is in keeping with Troilus' general bitterness and cynicism at the end of the play.

V.x.46. *painted cloths.* Elizabethan rooms often had mottoes and quotations worked into the tapestries or painted hangings. Pandarus is suggesting that his obscene little poem be set on the cloths of a brothel.

V.x.54. *galled goose of Winchester.* The licensed brothels were under the jurisdiction of the Archbishop of Winchester; thus a *galled goose* was probably a prostitute with venereal disease.

V.x.55. *sweat.* Induced sweating was used as a cure for venereal disease.

All's Well That Ends Well

Edited by
ARTHUR E. CASE

Dramatis Personae

KING OF FRANCE

DUKE OF FLORENCE

BERTRAM, *Count of Rousillon*

LAFEU, *an old Lord*

PAROLLES, *a parasitical Follower of Bertram*

SEVERAL YOUNG FRENCH LORDS, THAT SERVE
   WITH BERTRAM IN THE FLORENTINE WARS

RINALDO, *a Steward* } *Servants to the Countess*

LAVACHE, *a Clown* } *of Rousillon*

COUNTESS OF ROUSILLON, *Mother to Bertram*

HELENA, *Daughter to* Gerard de Narbon,
   a famous physician, some time since dead

AN OLD WIDOW OF FLORENCE

VIOLENTA } *Neighbors and friends to the Widow*

MARIANA }

LORDS ATTENDING ON THE KING, OFFICERS,
   SOLDIERS, ETC.

SCENE—*Partly in France and partly in Tuscany.*

All's Well That Ends Well

INTRODUCTION

SOURCES OF THE PLAY

The source of the main plot of *All's Well that Ends Well* is the ninth novel of the third day of Boccaccio's *Decameron,* as translated by William Painter in *The Palace of Pleasure* (1566). Painter's synopsis of the story is as follows:

'Giletta a phisician's doughter of Narbon, healed the Frenche Kyng of a fistula, for reward whereof she demaunded Beltramo Counte of Rossiglione to husbande. The Counte beyng maried againste his will, for despite fled to Florence and loved an other. Giletta his wife, by pollicie founde meanes to lye with her husbande, in place of his lover, and was begotten with child of two soonnes: which knowen to her husbande, he received her againe, and afterwardes he lived in great honor and felicitie.'

The most significant features of Boccaccio's story which Shakespeare altered are these: Giletta is rich; she is not the foster-sister of Bertram, though brought up with him; and the King of France is not present to act as *deus ex machina* in the final reconciliation. Boccaccio's tale is related chiefly for the sake of the plot, and so far as the character-portraits of Helena, Bertram and the King are concerned Shakespeare's debt to his original is negligible. There are no counterparts in the novel for the Countess, Lafeu, Lavache or any of the persons of the sub-plot which recounts the adventures and downfall of Parolles. For this subplot and for the character of Parolles no sources have been found, although various books have been suggested from which Shakespeare might have drawn a few minor incidents or expressions.

THE HISTORY OF THE PLAY

The early history of *All's Well that Ends Well* has long been the subject of controversy. In 1598 Francis Meres, in his *Palladis Tamia,* referred to Shakespeare as the author of a play called *Love's Labour's Won.* It has been almost universally assumed that this play has not been lost, but that it was re-named before publication. Five or six of Shakespeare's comedies have been identified with *Love's Labour's Won* by various editors, but the theory of Dr. Farmer, put forth in 1767, that the play is the one known to us as *All's Well that Ends Well,* has been concurred in by the majority of critics. The internal evidence, on which alone this theory rests, is fairly convincing. The older title certainly fits the plot of the play admirably. Moreover, two speeches in the fifth act seem to refer directly to that title, and in the second of these speeches there is also an unmistakable allusion to the present name of the play:

Will you be mine, now you are doubly won?

V.iii.350

All is well ended if this suit be won....

Epilogue

If Dr. Farmer's conjecture is correct, *All's Well* must have been written by 1598, but many critics place its composition much earlier than this, and a few place it as late as 1606. The evidence (which is

again entirely internal) is extremely confusing. The frequent rhymed passages and the letters in verse are characteristic of Shakespeare's earlier work: on the other hand, there are many speeches (e.g. that of the King, I. ii. 30-54) in the involved elliptical style of the author's later period. Perhaps the most satisfactory, and certainly the most commonly received, solution of the problem is to assume that *All's Well* as we have it is the revised form of an early play. This view is strengthened by the existence of some awkward breaks in the text (notably that at I. i.153) which may be due to the imperfect joining of the older and the newer versions.

All's Well that Ends Well was first printed in the Folio of 1623, and it did not achieve a separate publication until 1734.[1] There is no record of its having been performed in Shakespeare's lifetime or, indeed, for more than a century after his death. The play was included in a seventeenth century 'Catalogue of part of His Ma[tes] Servants Players as they were formerly acted at the Blackfryers & now allowed of to his Ma[tes] Servants at y[e] New Theatre,'[2] but there is nothing to show that Killigrew ever took advantage of this license. At length, on February 24, 1740–1, the following advertisement appeared in *The London Daily Post, and General Advertiser:* 'For the Benefit of Mrs. Giffard. At the Late Theatre in *Goodman's-Fields,* Saturday, March 7, will be performed A Concert . . . N.B. Between the Two Parts of the Concert, will be reviv'd a Play, call'd All's Well That Ends Well. Written by Shakespear, and never performed since his Time. . . . the part of Helena by Mrs. Giffard, with an Epilogue adapted to that Character. . . .'

This performance seems to have been sufficiently successful to incite emulation. The play was put on ten times at Drury Lane during the season of 1741-2 with T. Cibber as Parolles and Mrs. Woffington as Helena. Covent Garden followed suit in 1746, when a performance for Cibber's benefit was arranged for April 1, but as Cibber returned to Drury Lane before that date Woodward took over his part with great success. In the next seventeen years the play was revived several times, chiefly at the instance of Woodward, who was, according to Davies, fond of the rôle of Parolles. Between 1763 and 1900 *All's Well* was acted only about once a decade. Among those who produced it in the nineteenth century were Samuel Phelps and Charles Fry. Most of the nineteenth century revivals made use of a bowdlerized version of the play arranged by Kemble.

The most recent English productions of *All's Well* were those of the Old Vic in London and of the Memorial Theater in Stratford-on-Avon, both in 1922. The same year saw a German production at the Schauspielhaus in Graz. Dr. E. Mühlbach lists, in the *Shakespeare-Jahrbuch* for 1921, eight German performances in the years 1911-1920. There seems to be no record of any American performance.

---

1 The 'edition' of 1714 noted by Lowndes is merely a copy of the play removed from the eight-volume edition of Rowe.

2 This catalogue is reproduced on pp. 316-317 of *A History of Restoration Drama* by Allardyce Nicoll, who gives its date as c. Jan 12, 1668-9.

ACT FIRST ❧ SCENE FIRST

[Rousillon. A Room in the Countess's Palace]
Enter young Bertram, Count of Rousillon, his Mother [the Countess],
and Helena, [and] Lord Lafeu, all in black.

Count. In delivering my son from me, I bury a second
husband.

Ber. And I, in going, madam, weep o'er my father's death
anew; but I must attend his majesty's command, to whom I
am now in ward, evermore in subjection. 5

Laf. You shall find of the king a husband, madam; you,
sir, a father. He that so generally is at all times good must of
necessity hold his virtue to you, whose worthiness would stir
it up where it wanted rather than lack it where there is such
abundance. 10

Count. What hope is there of his majesty's amendment?

Laf. He hath abandoned his physicians, madam, under
whose practices he hath persecuted time with hope, and finds
no other advantage in the process but only the losing of hope
by time. 15

Count. This young gentlewoman had a father,—O, that
'had!' how sad a passage 'tis!—whose skill was almost as great
as his honesty; had it stretched so far, would have made nature
immortal, and death should have play for lack of work.
Would, for the king's sake, he were living! I think it would 20
be the death of the king's disease.

Laf. How called you the man you speak of, madam?

Count. He was famous, sir, in his profession, and it was his
great right to be so: Gerard de Narbon.

Laf. He was excellent indeed, madam: the king very 25
lately spoke of him admiringly and mourningly. He was
skilful enough to have lived still, if knowledge could be set
up against mortality.

Ber. What is it, my good lord, the king languishes of?

Laf. A fistula, my lord. 30

Ber. I heard not of it before.

Laf. I would it were not notorious. Was this gentlewoman
the daughter of Gerard de Narbon?

Count. His sole child, my lord; and bequeathed to my overlooking. I have those hopes of her good that her education 35
promises: her dispositions she inherits, which makes fair gifts
fairer; for where an unclean mind carries virtuous qualities,
there commendations go with pity; they are virtues and traitors
too: in her they are the better for their simpleness; she derives
her honesty and achieves her goodness. 40

Laf. Your commendations, madam, get from her tears.

Count. 'Tis the best brine a maiden can season her praise in.
The remembrance of her father never approaches her heart but
the tyranny of her sorrows takes all livelihood from her cheek.
No more of this, Helena; go to, no more, lest it be rather 45
thought you affect a sorrow, than to have—

Hel. I do affect a sorrow indeed, but I have it too.

Laf. Moderate lamentation is the right of the dead, excessive
grief the enemy to the living.

Count. If the living be enemy to the grief, the excess 50
makes it soon mortal.

Ber. Madam, I desire your holy wishes.

Laf. How understand we that?

Count. Be thou blest, Bertram; and succeed thy father
In manners, as in shape! thy blood and virtue 55
Contend for empire in thee, and thy goodness
Share with thy birthright! Love all, trust a few,
Do wrong to none: be able for thine enemy
Rather in power than use, and keep thy friend
Under thy own life's key: be check'd for silence, 60
But never tax'd for speech. What heaven more will
That thee may furnish, and my prayers pluck down,
Fall on thy head! *[To Lafeu.]* Farewell, my lord;
'Tis an unseason'd courtier; good my lord,
Advise him. 65

Laf. He cannot want the best
That shall attend his love.

Count. Heaven bless him! Farewell, Bertram. *[Exit.]*

Ber. [*To Helena*] The best wishes that can be forged in your
thoughts be servants to you! Be comfortable to my mother, 70
your mistress, and make much of her.

Laf. Farewell, pretty lady: you must hold the credit of your
father. *[Exeunt Bertram and Lafeu.]*

Hel. O, were that all! I think not on my father,
And these great tears grace his remembrance more 75
Than those I shed for him. What was he like?
I have forgot him: my imagination
Carries no favour in 't but Bertram's.
I am undone: there is no living, none,
If Bertram be away. 'Twere all one 80
That I should love a bright particular star
And think to wed it, he is so above me:
In his bright radiance and collateral light
Must I be comforted, not in his sphere.
Th' ambition in my love thus plagues itself: 85
The hind that would be mated by the lion
Must die for love. 'Twas pretty, though a plague,
To see him every hour; to sit and draw
His arched brows, his hawking eye, his curls,
In our heart's table; heart too capable 90
Of every line and trick of his sweet favour:
But now he's gone, and my idolatrous fancy
Must sanctify his relics. Who comes here?

Enter Parolles.

One that goes with him: I love him for his sake;
And yet I know him a notorious liar, 95
Think him a great way fool, solely a coward;
Yet these fix'd evils sit so fit in him,
That they take place, when virtue's steely bones
Looks bleak i' th' cold wind: withal, full oft we see

---

4 **attend:** *pay heed to* 4, 5 **to . . . ward:** *under whose guardianship I now am* 7 **generally:** *universally* 8 **hold:** *continue to display* 11 **amendment:** *improvement in health* 13 **persecuted . . . hope:** *spent much time in hoping* 17 **passage:** *expression* 23, 24 **his great right:** *clearly his due* 27, 28 **set up against:** *opposed to* 30 **fistula:** *a sinuous ulcer* 34, 35 **overlooking:** *supervision* 36 **dispositions:** *natural inclinations* 37 **virtuous qualities:** *admirable intellectual qualities* 38 **go with pity:** *are given with regret* 39 **simpleness:** *lack of complexity* 44 **livelihood:** *liveliness* 47 *Cf. n.*

50, 51 *Cf. n.* 53 *Cf. n.* 55 **thy:** *may thy* 57 **Share . . . birthright:** *equal your inherited nobility* 58, 59 **be . . . use:** *be able to conquer your enemy, but spare him* 59, 60 **keep . . . key:** *protect your friend with your life* **check'd:** *reproached* 61 **tax'd:** *rebuked* **will:** *may desire* 62 **That . . . furnish:** *that may adorn your character* 66, 67 **He . . . love:** *cf. n.* 69, 70 *Cf. n.* **Be comfortable to:** *console* 72 **hold the credit:** *uphold the good name* 75, 76: **And . . . him:** *cf. n.* 78 **favour:** *face* 80, 81 **'Twere . . . should:** *I might as well* **particular:** *individual* 83, 84 *Cf. n.* 89 **hawking:** *hawklike* 90 **table:** *tablet* **capable:** *ready to receive the impress* 91 **trick:** *peculiarity* 93 **sanctify his relics:** *worship his memory* 96 **a great way:** *largely* **solely:** *altogether* 97 **sit . . . him:** *become him so well* 98 **take place:** *find acceptance* **steely:** *unbending* 99 **Looks:** *Cf. n.* **withal:** *therewith*

Cold wisdom waiting on superfluous folly.   100

Par. Save you, fair queen!

Hel. And you, monarch!

Par. No.

Hel. And no.

Par. Are you meditating on virginity?   105

Hel. Ay. You have some stain of soldier in you; let me ask you a question. Man is enemy to virginity; how may we barricado it against him?

Par. Keep him out.

Hel. But he assails; and our virginity, though valiant in   110 the defence, yet is weak. Unfold to us some warlike resistance.

Par. There is none: man, setting down before you, will undermine you and blow you up.

Hel. Bless our poor virginity from underminers and blowers up! Is there no military policy, how virgins might blow up   115 men?

Par. Virginity being blown down, man will quicklier be blown up: marry, in blowing him down again, with the breach yourselves made, you lose your city. It is not politic in the commonwealth of nature to preserve virginity. Loss of   120 virginity is rational increase, and there was never virgin got till virginity was first lost. That you were made of is metal to make virgins. Virginity, by being once lost, may be ten times found: by being ever kept, it is ever lost. 'Tis too cold a companion: away with 't!   125

Hel. I will stand for 't a little, though therefore I die a virgin.

Par. There's little can be said in 't; 'tis against the rule of nature. To speak on the part of virginity is to accuse your mothers, which is most infallible disobedience. He that   130 hangs himself is a virgin: virginity murders itself, and should be buried in highways, out of all sanctified limit, as a desperate offendress against nature. Virginity breeds mites, much like a cheese, consumes itself to the very paring, and so dies with feeding his own stomach. Besides, virginity is   135 peevish, proud, idle, made of self-love, which is the most inhibited sin in the canon. Keep it not; you cannot choose but lose by 't! Out with 't! within the year it will make itself two, which is a goodly increase, and the principal itself not much the worse. Away with 't!   140

Hel. How might one do, sir, to lose it to her own liking?

Par. Let me see: marry, ill, to like him that ne'er it likes. 'Tis a commodity will lose the gloss with lying; the longer kept, the less worth: off with 't, while 'tis vendible; answer the time of request. Virginity, like an old courtier, wears her   145 cap out of fashion; richly suited, but unsuitable: just like the brooch and the toothpick, which wear not now. Your date is better in your pie and your porridge than in your cheek: and your virginity, your old virginity, is like one of our French withered pears; it looks ill, it eats drily; marry, 'tis a   150 withered pear; it was formerly better; marry, yet 'tis a withered pear. Will you anything with it?

Hel. Not my virginity yet.

There shall your master have a thousand loves,

A mother, and a mistress, and a friend,   155

A phœnix, captain, and an enemy,

A guide, a goddess, and a sovereign,

A counsellor, a traitress, and a dear,

His humble ambition, proud humility,

His jarring concord, and his discord dulcet,   160

His faith, his sweet disaster; with a world

Of pretty, fond, adoptious christendoms,

That blinking Cupid gossips. Now shall he—

I know not what he shall. God send him well!

The court's a learning-place, and he is one—   165

Par. What one, i' faith?

Hel. That I wish well. 'Tis pity—

Par. What's pity?

Hel. That wishing well had not a body in 't,

Which might be felt; that we, the poorer born,   170

Whose baser stars do shut us up in wishes,

Might with effects of them follow our friends,

And show what we alone must think, which never

Returns us thanks.

Enter [a] Page.

Page. Monsieur Parolles, my lord calls for you.   *[Exit]*   175

Par. Little Helen, farewell: if I can remember thee, I will think of thee at court.

Hel. Monsieur Parolles, you were born under a charitable star.

Par. Under Mars, I.   180

Hel. I especially think, under Mars.

Par. Why under Mars?

Hel. The wars hath so kept you under that you must needs be born under Mars.

Par. When he was predominant.   185

Hel. When he was retrograde, I think rather.

Par. Why think you so?

Hel. You go so much backward when you fight.

Par. That's for advantage.

Hel. So is running away, when fear proposes the safety: 190 but the composition that your valour and fear makes in you is a virtue of a good wing, and I like the wear well.

Par. I am so full of businesses I cannot answer thee acutely. I will return perfect courtier; in the which, my instruction shall serve to naturalize thee, so thou wilt be capable of a   195 courtier's counsel, and understand what advice shall thrust upon thee; else thou diest in thine unthankfulness, and thine ignorance makes thee away: farewell. When thou hast leisure, say thy prayers; when thou hast none, remember thy friends. Get thee a good husband, and use him as he uses thee: so, farewell.   200

[Exit.]

Hel. Our remedies oft in ourselves do lie,

Which we ascribe to heaven: the fated sky

Gives us free scope; only doth backward pull

Our slow designs when we ourselves are dull.

100 superfluous: *luxurious*   103, 104 *Cf. n.*   106 stain: *trace*   112 setting down: *setting down his batteries*   118 marry: *by the Virgin Mary*   121 rational: *reasonable*   122 metal: *material*   126 stand: *fight*   128 in 't: *for it*   130 infallible: *unquestionable*   132 sanctified limit; *cf. n.*   135 his; *cf. n.*   136 inhibited: *forbidden*   137, 138 Out with 't: *put it to use*   142 that . . . likes: *whom it does not please*   143 lying: *lying unused*   144, 145 answer . . . request: *meet the demand*   146 suited: *dressed*   147 wear not: *are not in fashion*   date: *used punningly*   153 Not: *not with*

154–165 *Cf. n.*   160 dulcet: *sweet*   162 adoptious christendoms: *nicknames*   163 blinking: *blind*   gossips: *is sponsor for*   171 *Whose less exalted destinies confine us to wishing merely*   172 effects: *execution*   173 alone must: *can only*   185, 186 *Cf. n.*   189 for advantage: *for strategic purposes*   191 composition: *compromise*   192 virtue . . . wing; *cf. n.*   wear: *fashion*   194 in the which: *in which (court etiquette)*.   195 naturalize: *familiarize*   capable of: *able to comprehend*   198 makes thee away: *will destroy you*   198, 199 When . . . friends; *cf. n.*   202 fated sky: *destiny*

What power is it which mounts my love so high,   *205*
That makes me see, and cannot feed mine eye?
The mightiest space in fortune nature brings
To join like likes, and kiss like native things.
Impossible be strange attempts to those
That weigh their pains in sense, and do suppose   *210*
What hath been cannot be: who ever strove
To show her merit, that did miss her love?
The king's disease—my project may deceive me,
But my intents are fix'd and will not leave me.

❧ SCENE SECOND ❧

[Paris. A Room in the King's Palace.]
Flourish [of] Cornets. Enter the King of France, with letters, and
divers Attendants.

King. The Florentines and Senoys are by th' ears;
Have fought with equal fortune, and continue
A braving war.

     1. Lord.   So 'tis reported, sir.

     King. Nay, 'tis most credible: we here receive it   *5*
A certainty, vouch'd from our cousin Austria,
With caution that the Florentine will move us
For speedy aid; wherein our dearest friend
Prejudicates the business, and would seem
To have us make denial.   *10*

     1. Lord.   His love and wisdom,
Approv'd so to your majesty, may plead
For amplest credence.

     King.   He hath arm'd our answer,
And Florence is denied before he comes:
Yet, for our gentlemen that mean to see   *15*
The Tuscan service, freely have they leave
To stand on either part.

     2. Lord.   It well may serve
A nursery to our gentry, who are sick   *20*
For breathing and exploit.

     King.   What's he comes here?

Enter Bertram, Lafeu and Parolles.

     1. Lord. It is the Count Rousillon, my good lord, Young
Bertram.

     King.   Youth, thou bear'st thy father's face.   *25*
Frank nature, rather curious than in haste,
Hath well compos'd thee. Thy father's moral parts
Mayst thou inherit too! Welcome to Paris.

     Ber. My thanks and duty are your majesty's.

     King. I would I had that corporal soundness now,   *30*
As when thy father and myself in friendship
First tried our soldiership! He did look far
Into the service of the time, and was

Discipled of the bravest: he lasted long;
But on us both did haggish age steal on,   *35*
And wore us out of act. It much repairs me
To talk of your good father. In his youth
He had the wit which I can well observe
To-day in our young lords; but they may jest
Till their own scorn return to them unnoted   *40*
Ere they can hide their levity in honour.
So like a courtier, contempt nor bitterness
Were in his pride or sharpness; if they were,
His equal had awak'd them; and his honour,
Clock to itself, knew the true minute when   *45*
Exception bid him speak, and at this time
His tongue obey'd his hand: who were below him
He us'd as creatures of another place,
And bow'd his eminent top to their low ranks,
Making them proud of his humility   *50*
In their poor praise he humbled. Such a man
Might be a copy to these younger times,
Which, follow'd well, would demonstrate them now
But goers backward.

     Ber.   His good remembrance, sir,   *55*
Lies richer in your thoughts than on his tomb;
So in approof lives not his epitaph
As in your royal speech.

     King. Would I were with him! He would always say,—
Methinks I hear him now: his plausive words   *60*
He scatter'd not in ears, but grafted them,
To grow there and to bear,—'Let me not live,'—
This his good melancholy oft began,
On the catastrophe and heel of pastime,
When it was out,—'Let me not live,' quoth he,   *65*
'After my flame lacks oil, to be the snuff
Of younger spirits, whose apprehensive senses
All but new things disdain; whose judgments are
Mere fathers of their garments; whose constancies
Expire before their fashions.' This he wish'd: *70*
I, after him, do after him wish too,
Since I nor wax nor honey can bring home,
I quickly were dissolved from my hive,
To give some labourers room.

     2. Lord.   You're loved, sir;   *75*
They that least lend it you shall lack you first.

     King. I fill a place, I know 't. How long is 't, count,
Since the physician at your father's died?
He was much fam'd.

     Ber.   Some six months since, my lord.   *80*

     King. If he were living, I would try him yet:
Lend me an arm: the rest have worn me out
With several applications: nature and sickness
Debate it at their leisure. Welcome, count;
My son's no dearer.   *85*

---

205 **mounts . . . high:** *fixes my love on so high an object*   207, 208 *Cf. n.*   209 **strange attempts:** *unusual undertakings*   210 **weigh . . . sense:** *estimate their labor by reason*   212 **miss:** *fail to attain*   213 **deceive:** *disappoint*   1 **Senoys:** *Siennese, dwellers in Sienna*   **by th' ears:** *in combat*   3 **braving:** *defiant*   1. Lord; *cf. n.*   5, 6 **receive . . . certainty:** *are made certain of it*   6 **cousin Austria:** *fellow ruler of Austria*   7 **move:** *petition*   9 **Prejudicates the business:** *gives his opinion of the matter in advance*   9, 10 **would . . . us:** *seems to wish us to*   12 **Approv'd so:** *so often proved*   14 **arm'd:** *strengthened*   15 **Florence:** *the Duke of Florence*   18 **stand . . . part:** *fight on either side*   19 **serve:** *serve as*   21 **breathing:** *exercise*   26 **Frank:** *liberal*   **curious:** *painstaking*   32, 33 **did . . . service:** *saw much of the wars*

34 **Discipled of:** *taught by*   36 **wore . . . act:** *wore out our ability*   **repairs:** *refreshes*   39–41 **but . . . honour;** *cf. n.*   42–44 **So . . . them;** *cf. n.*   45 **Clock to itself:** *its own counselor*   **true:** *proper*   46 **Exception:** *disapproval*   **bid:** *bade*   47 **obey'd his hand:** *obeyed its (the clock's) hand, spoke fittingly*   **who:** *those who*   50, 51 **Making . . . humbled;** *cf. n.*   57, 58 *Cf. n.*   60 **plausive:** *winning*   62 **bear:** *bear fruit*   64 **On . . . heel:** *at the conclusion of*   65 **out:** *finished*   66 **snuff:** *object of distaste*   67 **apprehensive:** *fastidious*   69 **Mere . . . garments:** *capable merely of devising new fashions*   73 **dissolved:** *removed*   76 **least lend it you:** *give you least* (love)   83 **several applications:** *various remedies*   84 **Debate it:** *contend*

Ber.   Thank your majesty.
         Exit [King, attended by all the others]. Flourish.

❧ SCENE THIRD ❧

[Rousillon. A Room in the Countess's Palace]
Enter Countess, Steward, and Clown.

Count. I will now hear: what say you of this gentlewoman?

Stew. Madam, the care I have had to even your content, I wish might be found in the calendar of my past endeavours; for then we wound our modesty and make foul the clearness of our deservings, when of ourselves we publish them.   *5*

Count. What does this knave here? Get you gone, sirrah: the complaints I have heard of you I do not all believe: 'tis my slowness that I do not; for I know you lack not folly to commit them, and have ability enough to make such knaveries yours.   *10*

Clo. 'Tis not unknown to you, madam, I am a poor fellow.

Count. Well, sir.

Clo. No, madam, 'tis not so well that I am poor, though many of the rich are damned. But, if I may have your ladyship's good will to go to the world, Isbel the woman and   *15* I will do as we may.

Count. Wilt thou needs be a beggar?

Clo. I do beg your good will in this case.

Count. In what case?

Clo. In Isbel's case and mine own. Service is no   *20* heritage; and I think I shall never have the blessing of God till I have issue o' my body, for they say barnes are blessings.

Count. Tell me thy reason why thou wilt marry.

Clo. My poor body, madam, requires it: I am driven on by the flesh; and he must needs go that the devil drives.   *25*

Count. Is this all your worship's reason?

Clo. Faith, madam, I have other holy reasons, such as they are.

Count. May the world know them?

Clo. I have been, madam, a wicked creature, as you and   *30* all flesh and blood are; and, indeed, I do marry that I may repent.

Count. Thy marriage, sooner than thy wickedness.

Clo. I am out o' friends, madam; and I hope to have friends for my wife's sake.   *35*

Count. Such friends are thine enemies, knave.

Clo. Y'are shallow, madam, in great friends; for the knaves come to do that for me which I am aweary of. He that ears my land spares my team, and gives me leave to in the crop: if I be his cuckold, he's my drudge. He that comforts my wife *40* is the cherisher of my flesh and blood; he that cherishes my flesh and blood loves my flesh and blood; he that loves my flesh and blood is my friend: *ergo,* he that kisses my wife is my friend. If men could be contented to be what they are, there were no fear in marriage; for young Charbon the puritan,   *45* and old Poysam the papist, howsome'er their hearts are severed in religion, their heads are both one; they may joul horns together like any deer i' the herd.

Count. Wilt thou ever be a foul-mouthed and calumnious knave?   *50*

Clo. A prophet I, madam; and I speak the truth the next way:

'For I the ballad will repeat,
Which men full true shall find:
Your marriage comes by destiny,   *55*
Your cuckoo sings by kind.'

Count. Get you gone, sir: I'll talk with you more anon.

Stew. May it please you, madam, that he bid Helen come to you: of her I am to speak.

Count. Sirrah, tell my gentlewoman I would speak with   *60* her; Helen, I mean.

Clo. 'Was this fair face the cause, quoth she,*
   Why the Grecians sacked Troy?
Fond done, done fond,
   Was this King Priam's joy?   *65*
With that she sighed as she stood,
With that she sighed as she stood,
   And gave this sentence then;
Among nine bad if one be good,
Among nine bad if one be good,   *70*
   There's yet one good in ten.'

Count. What! one good in ten? you corrupt the song, sirrah.

Clo. One good woman in ten, madam; which is a purifying o' the song. Would God would serve the world so all the year! we'd find no fault with the tithe-woman if I were the   *75* parson. One in ten, quoth a'! An we might have a good woman born but o'er every blazing star, or at an earthquake, 'twould mend the lottery well: a man may draw his heart out ere a' pluck one.

Count. You'll be gone, sir knave, and do as I command you!

Clo. That man should be at woman's command, and yet no hurt done! Though honesty be no puritan, yet it will do no hurt; it will wear the surplice of humility over the black gown of a big heart. I am going, forsooth: the business is for Helen to come hither.   *Exit.*   *85*

Count. Well, now.

Stew. I know, madam, you love your gentlewoman entirely.

Count. Faith, I do: her father bequeathed her to me; and she herself, without other advantage, may lawfully make title to as much love as she finds: there is more owing her than is   *90* paid, and more shall be paid her than she'll demand.

Stew. Madam, I was very late more near her than I think she wished me: alone she was, and did communicate to herself her own words to her own ears; she thought, I dare vow for her, they touched not any stranger sense. Her matter was,   *95* she loved your son: Fortune, she said, was no goddess, that had put such difference betwixt their two estates; Love no god, that would not extend his might, only where qualities were level; [Dian no] queen of virgins, that would suffer her poor knight surprised, without rescue in the first assault or ransom after- *100* ward. This she delivered in the most bitter touch of sorrow that e'er I heard virgin exclaim in; which I held my duty

---

2 **even your content:** *act in accord with your desires*   3 **calendar:** *catalogue*   15 **go ... world:** *marry*   16 **do ... may:** *do our best*   22 **barnes:** *children*   27 **holy:** *religious*   37 **shallow ... friends:** *ignorant of the ways of friendship*   38 **ears:** *plows*   39 **in the crop:** *gather the harvest*   45, 46 **young ... papist;** *cf. n.*   47, 48 **joul ... together;** *cf. n.*

52 **next:** *nearest*   56 **cuckoo;** *cf. n.*   **by kind:** *by nature*   64 **Fond:** *foolishly*   77 **o'er:** *during the appearance of*   **blazing star:** *comet*   82–84 **Though ... heart;** *cf. n.*   84 **big:** *proud*   **business:** *thing to be done*   89 **make title:** *prove her right*   92 **late:** *recently*   95 **touched ... sense:** *were not overheard*   **Her matter was:** *the substance of her speech*   99 **knight:** *votaress*   100 **surprised:** *to be surprised*   101 **delivered:** *spoke*

speedily to acquaint you withal, sithence in the loss that may
happen it concerns you something to know it.

    Count. You have discharged this honestly: keep it to   *105*
yourself. Many likelihoods informed me of this before, which
hung so tottering in the balance that I could neither believe
nor misdoubt. Pray you, leave me: stall this is in your
bosom;and I thank you for your honest care. I will speak
with you further anon.   *Exit Steward.*   *110*

             Enter Helen.

Even so it was with me when I was young:
If ever we are nature's, these are ours; this thorn
Doth to our rose of youth rightly belong;
Our blood to us, this to our blood is born:
It is the show and seal of nature's truth,   *115*
Where love's strong passion is impress'd in youth:
By our remembrances of days foregone,
Such were our faults, or then we thought them none.
Her eye is sick on 't: I observe her now.

    Hel. What is your pleasure, madam?   *120*

    Count.   You know, Helen,
I am a mother to you.

    Hel. Mine honourable mistress.

    Count.   Nay, a mother:
Why not a mother? When I said, 'a mother,'   *125*
Methought you saw a serpent: what's in 'mother'
That you start at it? I say, I am your mother;
And put you in the catalogue of those
That were enwombed mine: 'tis often seen
Adoption strives with nature, and choice breeds   *130*
A native slip to us from foreign seeds;
You ne'er oppress'd me with a mother's groan,
Yet I express to you a mother's care.
God's mercy, maiden! does it curd thy blood
To say I am thy mother? What's the matter,   *135*
That this distemper'd messenger of wet,
The many-colour'd Iris, rounds thine eye?
Why? that you are my daughter?

    Hel.   That I am not.

    Count. I say, I am your mother.   *140*

    Hel.   Pardon, madam;
The Count Rousillon cannot be my brother:
I am from humble, he from honour'd name;
No note upon my parents, his all noble:
My master, my dear lord he is; and I   *145*
His servant live, and will his vassal die.
He must not be my brother.

    Count.   Nor I your mother?

    Hel. You are my mother, madam: would you were,—
So that my lord your son were not my brother,—   *150*
Indeed my mother! or were you both our mothers,
I care no more for than I do for heaven,
So I were not his sister. Can't no other,
But, I your daughter, he must be my brother?

    Count. Yes, Helen, you might be my daughter-in-law: *155*
God shield you mean it not! daughter and mother

So strive upon your pulse. What, pale again?
My fear hath catch'd your fondness: now I see
The mystery of your loveliness, and find
Your salt tears' head: now to all sense 'tis gross: *160*
You love my son: invention is asham'd,
Against the proclamation of thy passion,
To say thou dost not: therefore tell me true;
But tell me then, 'tis so: for, look, thy cheeks
Confess it, th' one to th' other; and thine eyes   *165*
See it so grossly shown in thy behaviours
That in their kind they speak it: only sin
And hellish obstinacy tie thy tongue,
That truth should be suspected. Speak, is't so?
If it be so, you have wound a goodly clew;   *170*
If it be not, forswear 't: howe'er, I charge thee,
As heaven shall work in me for thine avail,
To tell me truly.

    Hel.   Good madam, pardon me!

    Count. Do you love my son?   *175*

    Hel.   Your pardon, noble mistress!

    Count. Love you my son?

    Hel.   Do not you love him, madam?

    Count. Go not about; my love hath in 't a bond
Whereof the world takes note: come, come, disclose   *180*
The state of your affection, for your passions
Have to the full appeach'd.

    Hel.   Then, I confess,
Here on my knee, before high heaven and you
That before you, and next unto high heaven,   *185*
I love your son.
My friends were poor, but honest; so's my love:
Be not offended, for it hurts not him
That he is lov'd of me: I follow him not
By any token of presumptuous suit;   *190*
Nor would I have him till I do deserve him;
Yet never know how that desert should be.
I know I love in vain, strive against hope;
Yet, in this captious and intenible sieve
I still pour in the waters of my love,   *195*
And lack not to lose still. Thus, Indian-like,
Religious in mine error, I adore
The sun, that looks upon his worshipper,
But knows of him no more. My dearest madam,
Let not your hate encounter with my love   *200*
For loving where you do: but, if yourself,
Whose aged honour cites a virtuous youth,
Did ever in so true a flame of liking
Wish chastely and love dearly, that your Dian
Was both herself and Love, O! then, give pity   *205*
To her, whose state is such that cannot choose
But lend and give where she is sure to lose,
That seeks not to find that her search implies,
But, riddle-like, lives sweetly where she dies.

---

157 strive . . . pulse: *affect your pulse in turn*   **158 catch'd:** *discovered*   **160 head:** *source* **gross:** *palpable*   **161 invention:** *dissimulation*   **162 Against:** *in the face of*   **166 grossly:** *openly*   **167 in their kind:** *after their own manner*   **169 That . . . suspected:** *in order to cast doubt upon the truth*   **170 wound . . . clew:** *made a fine snarl*   **171 howe'er:** *in any event*   **172** *If you wish Heaven to move me to help you*   **179 Go not about:** *do not quibble*   **182 appeach'd:** *accused you*   **194 captious:** *deceptive* **intenible:** *incapable of retaining*   **196 lack . . . still:** *have an inexhaustible supply to pour forth*   **200 encounter with:** *oppose*   **202 cites:** *is proof of*   **206 that:** *that which*   **209 riddle-like:** *paradoxically*

103 sithence: *since* **loss:** *misfortune*   **108 misdoubt:** *disbelieve* **stall this:** *keep this (knowledge)*   **112 these:** *these (feelings)*   **114 blood:** *disposition*   **115 show:** *evidence*   **119 on 't:** *because of it*   **131 native slip:** *grafted branch*   **136, 137** *Cf. n.*   **144 note:** *mark of distinction*   **153 Can't no other:** *can it not be otherwise*

Count. Had you not lately an intent—speak truly—   *210*
To go to Paris?
    Hel.   Madam, I had.
    Count.   Wherefore? tell true.
    Hel. I will tell truth; by grace itself I swear.
You know my father left me some prescriptions   *215*
Of rare and prov'd effects, such as his reading
And manifest experience had collected
For general sovereignty; and that he will'd me
In heedfull'st reservation to bestow them,
As notes whose faculties inclusive were   *220*
More than they were in note. Amongst the rest,
There is a remedy, approv'd, set down
To cure the desperate languishings whereof
The king is render'd lost.
    Count.   This was your motive   *225*
For Paris, was it? speak.
    Hel. My lord your son made me to think of this;
Else Paris and the medicine and the king
Had from the conversation of my thoughts
Haply been absent then.   *230*
    Count.   But think you, Helen,
If you should tender your supposed aid,
He would receive it? He and his physicians
Are of a mind; he, that they cannot help him,
They, that they cannot help. How shall they credit   *235*
A poor unlearned virgin, when the schools,
Embowell'd of their doctrine, have left off
The danger to itself?
    Hel.   There's something in 't,
More than my father's skill, which was the great'st   *240*
Of his profession, that his good receipt
Shall for my legacy be sanctified
By the luckiest stars in heaven: and, would your honour
But give me leave to try success, I'd venture
The well-lost life of mine on his Grace's cure,   *245*
By such a day, an hour.
    Count.   Dost thou believe 't?
    Hel. Ay, madam, knowingly.
    Count. Why, Helen, thou shalt have my leave and love,
Means, and attendants, and my loving greetings   *250*
To those of mine in court. I'll stay at home
And pray God's blessing into thy attempt.
Be gone to-morrow; and be sure of this,
What I can help thee to thou shalt not miss.

ACT SECOND ❧ SCENE FIRST

[Paris. A Room in the King's Palace]
Enter the King, [attended,] with divers young Lords taking leave
for the Florentine war; Count Rousillon and Parolles. Flourish [of]
cornets.

    King. Farewell, young lords: these warlike principles
Do not throw from you: and you, my lords, farewell:

Share the advice betwixt you; if both gain all,
The gift doth stretch itself as 'tis receiv'd,
And is enough for both.   *5*
    1. Lord.   'Tis our hope, sir,
After well enter'd soldiers, to return
And find your Grace in health.
    King. No, no, it cannot be; and yet my heart
Will not confess he owes the malady   *10*
That doth my life besiege. Farewell, young lords;
Whether I live or die, be you the sons
Of worthy Frenchmen: let higher Italy—
Those bated that inherit but the fall
Of the last monarchy—see that you come   *15*
Not to woo honour, but to wed it; when
The bravest questant shrinks, find what you seek
That fame may cry you loud: I say, farewell.
    2. Lord. Health, at your bidding, serve your majesty!
    King. Those girls of Italy, take heed of them: *20*
They say our French lack language to deny
If they demand: beware of being captives,
Before you serve.
    Both Lords.   Our hearts receive your warnings.
    King. Farewell. *[To another Lord]* Come hither to me.   *25*
                        [They converse.]
    1. Lord. [To Bertram.] O my sweet lord, that you will stay
behind us!
    Par. 'Tis not his fault, the spark.
    2. Lord.   O, 'tis brave wars!   *30*
    Par. Most admirable: I have seen those wars.
    Ber. I am commanded here, and kept a coil with 'Too
young,' and 'the next year,' and ''tis too early.'
    Par. An thy mind stand to 't, boy, steal away bravely.
    Ber. I shall stay here the forehorse to a smock,   *35*
Creaking my shoes on the plain masonry,
Till honour be bought up and no sword worn
But one to dance with! By heaven! I'll steal away.
    1. Lord. There's honour in the theft.
    Par.   Commit it, count.   *40*
    2. Lord. I am your accessary; and so farewell.
    Ber. I grow to you, and our parting is a tortured body.
    1. Lord. Farewell, captain.
    2. Lord. Sweet Monsieur Parolles!
    Par. Noble heroes, my sword and yours are kin. Good   *45*
sparks and lustrous, a word, good metals: you shall find in the
regiment of the Spinii one Captain Spurio, with his cicatrice,
an emblem of war, here on his sinister cheek: it was this
very sword entrenched it: say to him, I live, and observe his
reports for me.   *50*
    2. Lord. We shall, noble captain.
    Par. Mars dote on you for his novices!   *[Exeunt Lords.]*
What will ye do?
    Ber. Stay the king.
    Par. Use a more spacious ceremony to the noble lords;   *55*
you have restrained yourself within the list of too cold an
adieu: be more expressive to them; for they wear themselves in

---

218 **general sovereignty:** *universal efficacy*   219 **reservation:** *safe-keeping*   220 **notes:** *prescriptions* **faculties:** *powers* **inclusive:** *all-embracing*   221 **in note:** *stated in writing*   224 **render'd lost:** *reported to be sick unto death*   229 **conversation:** *intercourse*   230 **Haply:** *perhaps*   237 **Embowell'd ... doctrine:** *exhausted of their learning* **left off:** *abandoned*   251 **those of mine:** *my kinsmen*   252 **into:** *upon*

7 **After ... soldiers:** *after we are well embarked on our military careers*   10 **owes:** *owns*   13–15 **let ... monarchy;** *cf. n.*   17 **questant:** *seeker*   18 **cry you loud:** *proclaim you loudly*   32 **kept a coil:** *pestered*   35 **forehorse ... smock:** *usher to a lady*   37 **bought up:** *entirely appropriated by others*   38 **But ... with;** *cf. n.*   41 **accessary:** *accessory*   42 **our ... body;** *cf. n.*   52 **novices:** *devotees*   53 **ye:** *i.e. Bertram*   54 **Stay the king:** *await the king's pleasure*   55 **spacious ceremony:** *elaborate courtesy*   56 **list:** *boundary*   57, 58 **wear ... in time:** *are an ornament to the time*

the cap of the time, there do muster true gait, eat, speak, and
move under the influence of the most received star; and
though the devil lead the measure, such are to be followed. *60*
After them, and take a more dilated farewell.

Ber. And I will do so.

Par. Worthy fellows; and like to prove most sinewy
swordmen.   *Exeunt [Bertram and Parolles].*

Enter Lafeu.

Laf. *[Kneeling.]* Pardon, my lord, for me and for my tidings.

King. I'll see thee to stand up.

Laf. Then here's a man stands that has brought his pardon.
I would you had kneel'd, my lord, to ask me mercy,
And that at my bidding you could so stand up.

King. I would I had, so I had broke thy pate, *70*
And ask'd thee mercy for 't.

Laf. Good faith, across: but, my good lord, 'tis thus;
Will you be cur'd of your infirmity?

King. No.

Laf. O! will you eat no grapes, my royal fox? *75*
Yes, but you will my noble grapes an if
My royal fox could reach them. I have seen a medicine
That's able to breathe life into a stone,
Quicken a rock, and make you dance canary
With spritely fire and motion; whose simple touch *80*
Is powerful to araise King Pepin, nay,
To give great Charlemain a pen in's hand
And write to her a love-line.

King.   What 'her' is this?

Laf. Why, Doctor She. My lord, there's one arriv'd, *85*
If you will see her: now, by my faith and honour,
If seriously I may convey my thoughts
In this my light deliverance, I have spoke
With one, that in her sex, her years, profession,
Wisdom, and constancy, hath amaz'd me more *90*
Than I dare blame my weakness. Will you see her
(For that is her demand) and know her business?
That done, laugh well at me.

King.   Now, good Lafeu,
Bring in the admiration, that we with thee *95*
May spend our wonder too, or take off thine
By wondering how thou took'st it.

Laf.   Nay, I'll fit you,
And not be all day neither.   *[He retires to the door.]*

King. Thus he his special nothing ever prologues. *100*

Laf. *[to Helena, without.]* Nay, come your ways.

Enter Helen.

King.   This haste hath wings indeed.

Laf. Nay, come your ways;
This is his majesty, say your mind to him:
A traitor you do look like, but such traitors *105*
His majesty seldom fears: I am Cressid's uncle,
That dare leave two together. Fare you well.   *Exit*

King. Now, fair one, does your business follow us?

Hel. Ay, my good lord.

Gerard de Narbon was my father; *110*
In what he did profess well found.

King.   I knew him.

Hel. The rather will I spare my praises towards him;
Knowing him is enough. On's bed of death
Many receipts he gave me; chiefly one, *115*
Which, as the dearest issue of his practice,
And of his old experience the only darling,
He bade me store up as a triple eye,
Safer than mine own two, more dear. I have so;
And, hearing your high majesty is touch'd *120*
With that malignant cause wherein the honour
Of my dear father's gift stands chief in power,
I come to tender it and my appliance,
With all bound humbleness.

King.   We thank you, maiden, *125*
But may not be so credulous of cure,
When our most learned doctors leave us, and
The congregated college have concluded
That labouring art can never ransom nature
From her inaidible estate; I say we must not *130*
So stain our judgment or corrupt our hope,
To prostitute our past-cure malady
To empirics, or to dissever so
Our great self and our credit, to esteem
A senseless help when help past sense we deem. *135*

Hel. My duty then, shall pay me for my pains:
I will no more enforce mine office on you;
Humbly entreating from your royal thoughts
A modest one to bear me back again.

King. I cannot give thee less, to be call'd grateful. *140*
Thou thought'st to help me, and such thanks I give
As one near death to those that wish him live;
But what at full I know, thou know'st no part,
I knowing all my peril, thou no art.

Hel. What I can do can do no hurt to try, *145*
Since you set up your rest 'gainst remedy.
He that of greatest works is finisher
Oft does them by the weakest minister:
So holy writ in babes hath judgment shown,
When judges have been babes; great floods have flown *150*
From simple sources, and great seas have dried
When miracles have by the greatest been denied.
Oft expectation fails, and most oft there
Where most it promises; and oft it hits
Where hope is coldest and despair most sits. *155*

King. I must not hear thee: fare thee well, kind maid.
Thy pains, not us'd, must by thyself be paid:
Proffers not took reap thanks for their reward.

Hel. Inspired merit so by breath is barr'd.
It is not so with Him that all things knows, *160*
As 'tis with us that square our guess by shows;
But most it is presumption in us when
The help of heaven we count the act of men.
Dear sir, to my endeavours give consent;

Of heaven, not me, make an experiment.   165
I am not an imposture that proclaim
Myself against the level of mine aim;
But know I think, and think I know most sure
My art is not past power nor you past cure.

King. Art thou so confident? Within what space   170
Hop'st thou my cure?

Hel.   The greatest grace lending grace,
Ere twice the horses of the sun shall bring
Their fiery torcher his diurnal ring,
Ere twice in murk and occidental damp   175
Moist Hesperus hath quench'd her sleepy lamp,
Or four and twenty times the pilot's glass
Hath told the thievish minutes how they pass,
What is infirm from your sound parts shall fly,
Health shall live free and sickness freely die.   180

King. Upon thy certainty and confidence
What dar'st thou venture?

Hel.   Tax of impudence,
A strumpet's boldness, a divulged shame,
Traduc'd by odious ballads: my maiden's name   185
Sear'd otherwise; nay worse—if worse—extended
With vilest torture let my life be ended.

King. Methinks in thee some blessed spirit doth speak
His powerful sound within an organ weak;
And what impossibility would slay   190
In common sense, sense saves another way.
Thy life is dear; for all that life can rate
Worth name of life, in thee hath estimate;
Youth, beauty, wisdom, courage, all
That happiness and prime can happy call: 195
Thou this to hazard needs must intimate
Skill infinite or monstrous desperate.
Sweet practiser, thy physic I will try,
That ministers thine own death if I die.

Hel. If I break time, or flinch in property   200
Of what I spoke, unpitied let me die,
And well deserv'd. Not helping, death's my fee;
But, if I help, what do you promise me?

King. Make thy demand.

Hel.   But will you make it even?   205

King. Ay, by my sceptre, and my hopes of heaven.

Hel. Then shalt thou give me with thy kingly hand
What husband in thy power I will command:
Exempted be from me the arrogance
To choose from forth the royal blood of France,   210
My low and humble name to propagate
With any branch or image of thy state;
But such a one, thy vassal, whom I know
Is free for me to ask, thee to bestow.

King. Here is my hand; the premises observ'd,   215
Thy will by my performance shall be serv'd:
So make the choice of thy own time, for I,
Thy resolv'd patient, on thee still rely.
More should I question thee, and more I must,

(Though more to know could not be more to trust)   220
From whence thou cam'st, how tended on; but rest
Unquestion'd welcome and undoubted blest.
Give me some help here, ho! If thou proceed
As high as word, my deed shall match thy deed.

*Flourish. Exit [with Attendants;
Helena follows.]*

❧ SCENE SECOND ❧

*[Rousillon. A Room in the Countess's Palace]
Enter Countess and Clown.*

Count. Come on, sir; I shall now put you to the height of
your breeding.

Clo. I will show myself highly fed and lowly taught. I know
my business is but to the court.

Count. To the court! why what place make you special,   5
when you put off that with such contempt? 'But to the court!'

Clo. Truly, madam, if God have lent a man any manners,
he may easily put it off at court. He that cannot make a leg,
put off's cap, kiss his hand, and say nothing, has neither leg,
hands, lip, nor cap; and indeed such a fellow, to say   10
precisely, were not for the court: but for me, I have an
answer will serve all men.

Count. Marry, that's a bountiful answer that fits all
questions.

Clo. It is like a barber's chair that fits all buttocks; the   15
pin-buttock, the quatch-buttock, the brawn-buttock, or any
buttock.

Count. Will your answer serve fit to all questions?

Clo. As fit as ten groats is for the hand of an attorney, as
your French crown for your taffeta punk, as Tib's rush for   20
Tom's forefinger, as a pancake for Shrove-Tuesday, a morris
for Mayday, as the nail to his hole, the cuckold to his horn, as
a scolding quean to a wrangling knave, as the nun's lip to the
friar's mouth, nay, as the pudding to his skin.

Count. Have you, I say, an answer of such fitness for all   25
questions?

Clo. From below your duke to beneath your constable, it
will fit any question.

Count. It must be an answer of most monstrous size that
must fit all demands.   30

Clo. But a trifle neither, in good faith, if the learned should
speak truth of it. Here it is, and all that belongs to 't; ask me
if I am a courtier; it shall do you no harm to learn.

Count. To be young again, if we could! I will be a fool in
question, hoping to be the wiser by your answer. I pray   35
you, sir, are you a courtier?

Clo. O Lord, sir! there's a simple putting off. More, more, a
hundred of them.

Count. Sir, I am a poor friend of yours, that loves you.

Clo. O Lord, sir! Thick, thick, spare not me.   40

167 **against ... aim:** *equal to my task*   174 **diurnal ring:** *daily round*   176 **her;**
cf. n.   177 **glass:** *hour-glass*   178 **told:** *counted*   183 **Tax:** *accusation*   186 **nay ...**
worse; *cf. n.*   192 **rate:** *consider*   193 **in ... estimate:** *has great value for you*   195
prime: *youth*   196 **Thou ... hazard:** *your risking this* **intimate:** *indicate*   198 **prac-**
tiser: *practitioner*   200 *If I delay beyond the appointed time, or come short in perfor-*
mance   205 **make it even:** *fulfill it*   209 **Exempted be:** *far be*

221 **tended on:** *attended*   223, 224 **If ... word:** *if you perform your promises*   1 **put**
... height: *make thorough trial*   5 **make you special:** *do you consider extraordinary*   8
put it off: *make his way* **leg:** *bow*   16 **pin-buttock:** *thin buttock* **quatch-buttock:** *flat*
buttock **brawn-buttock:** *brawny buttock*   20 **crown:** *a coin* **taffeta punk:** *prostitute*
dressed in taffeta   20, 21 **Tib's ... forefinger;** *cf. n.* **morris:** *morris-dance*   23 **quean:**
woman

Count. I think, sir, you can eat none of this homely meat.

Clo. O Lord, sir! Nay, put me to 't, I warrant you.

Count. You were lately whipped, sir, as I think.

Clo. O Lord, sir! Spare not me.

Count. Do you cry, 'O Lord, sir!' at your whipping,   45
and 'Spare not me'? Indeed your 'O Lord, sir!' is very sequent
to your whipping: you would answer very well to a whipping,
if you were but bound to 't.

Clo. I ne'er had worse luck in my life in my 'O Lord, sir!'
I see things may serve long, but not serve ever.   50

Count. I play the noble housewife with the time,
To entertain 't so merrily with a fool.

Clo. O Lord, sir! why, there 't serves well again.

Count. An end, sir: to your business. Give Helen this,
And urge her to a present answer back: 55
Commend me to my kinsmen and my son.
This is not much.

Clo. Not much commendation to them?

Count. Not much employment for you: you understand me.

Clo. Most fruitfully: I am there before my legs.   60

Count. Haste you again.   *Exeunt [severally].*

❧ SCENE THIRD ❧

[Paris. A Room in the King's Palace]
Enter Count, Lafeu, and Parolles.

Laf. They say miracles are past; and we have our philosophical persons, to make modern and familiar, things supernatural
and causeless. Hence is it that we make trifles of terrors, ensconcing ourselves into seeming knowledge, when we should
submit ourselves to an unknown fear.   5

Par. Why, 'tis the rarest argument of wonder that hath
shot out in our latter times.

Ber. And so 'tis.

Laf. To be relinquished of the artists,—

Par. So I say—both of Galen and Paracelsus.   10

Laf. Of all the learned and authentic fellows,—

Par. Right; so I say.

Laf. That gave him out incurable,—

Par. Why, there 'tis; so say I too.

Laf. Not to be helped,—   15

Par. Right; as 'twere, a man assured of a—

Laf. Uncertain life, and sure death.

Par. Just, you say well: so would I have said.

Laf. I may truly say it is a novelty to the world.

Par. It is, indeed: if you will have it in showing, you   20
shall read it in What-do-you-call there.

Laf. A showing of a heavenly effect in an earthly actor.

Par. That's it I would have said; the very same.

Laf. Why, your dolphin is not lustier: 'fore me, I speak
in respect—   25

Par. Nay, 'tis strange, 'tis very strange, that is the brief

and the tedious of it; and he's of a most facinerious spirit that
will not acknowledge it to be the—

Laf. Very hand of heaven—

Par. Ay, so I say.   30

Laf. In a most weak—

Par. And debile minister, great power, great transcendence:
which should, indeed, give us a further use to be made
than alone the recovery of the king, as to be—

Laf. Generally thankful.   35

Enter King, Helen, and Attendants.

Par. I would have said it; you say well. Here comes the
king.

Laf. Lustig, as the Dutchman says: I'll like a maid the
better, whilst I have a tooth in my head. Why, he's able to
lead her a coranto.   40

Par. Mort du vinaigre! Is not this Helen?

Laf. 'Fore God, I think so.

King. Go, call before me all the lords in court.

[Exit an Attendant.]

Sit, my preserver, by thy patient's side: 45
And with this healthful hand, whose banish'd sense
Thou hast repeal'd, a second time receive
The confirmation of my promised gift,
Which but attends thy naming.

Enter three or four Lords.

Fair maid, send forth thine eye: this youthful parcel   50
Of noble bachelors stand at my bestowing,
O'er whom both sovereign power and father's voice
I have to use; thy frank election make;
Thou hast power to choose, and they none to forsake.

Hel. To each of you one fair and virtuous mistress   55
Fall, when Love please; marry, to each but one.

Laf. I'd give bay Curtal, and his furniture,
My mouth no more were broken than these boys'
And writ as little beard.

King.   Peruse them well: 60
Not one of those but had a noble father.

She addresses her to a Lord.

Hel. Gentlemen,
Heaven hath through me restor'd the king to health.

All. We understand it, and thank heaven for you.

Hel. I am a simple maid, and therein wealthiest   65
That I protest I simply am a maid.
Please it your majesty, I have done already:
The blushes in my cheeks thus whisper me,
'We blush, that thou shouldst choose; but, be refus'd,
Let the white death sit on thy cheek for ever;   70
We'll ne'er come there again.'

King.   Make choice, and see;
Who shuns thy love, shuns all his love in me.

Hel. Now, Dian, from thy altar do I fly,
And to imperial Love, that god most high,   75
Do my sighs stream. Sir, will you hear my suit?

1. Lord. And grant it.

41 homely meat: *humble food*   46 very sequent to: *a natural outcome of*   48 bound
to 't: *obliged to*   51 I am indeed provident of my time   52 entertain 't: *occupy it*   60
fruitfully: *fully*   2 modern: *trivial*   3, 4 ensconcing ... into: *sheltering ourselves
within*   9 relinquished ... artists: *given up by all the scholars*   11 authentic: *authoritative* fellows: *members (of the college of physicians)*   13 gave him out: *pronounced
him*   18 Just: *precisely*   20 in showing: *in black and white*

27 facinerious; *cf. n.*   38 Lustig: *brisk*   40 coranto: *a lively dance*   41 Mort du
vinaigre; *cf. n.*   46 sense: *faculties*   47 repeal'd: *called back*   49 attends:
awaits   50 parcel: *group*   54 forsake: *deny*   56 to ... one; *cf. n.*   57 bay ...
furniture: *my bay horse and his harness*   58 broken: *lacking teeth*   59 writ: *laid claim
to*   70 white death: *deathly pallor*

Hel.   Thanks, sir; all the rest is mute.
Laf. I had rather be in this choice than throw ames-ace
for my life.   *80*
    Hel. The honour, sir, that flames in your fair eyes,
Before I speak, too threateningly replies:
Love make your fortunes twenty times above
Her that so wishes, and her humble love!
    2. Lord. No better, if you please.   *85*
    Hel.   My wish receive,
Which great Love grant! and so I take my leave.
    Laf. Do all they deny her? An they were sons of mine,
I'd have them whipp'd or I would send them to the Turk
to make eunuchs of.   *90*
    Hel. [*To third Lord.*] Be not afraid that I your hand
should take;
I'll never do you wrong, for your own sake:
Blessing upon your vows; and in your bed
Find fairer fortune, if you ever wed!   *95*
    Laf. These boys are boys of ice, they'll none have her: sure,
they are bastards to the English; the French ne'er got 'em.
    Hel. You are too young, too happy, and too good,
To make yourself a son out of my blood.
    4. Lord. Fair one, I think not so.   *100*
    Laf. There's one grape yet. I am sure thy father drunk
wine. But if thou be'st not an ass, I am a youth of fourteen:
I have known thee already.
    Hel. [*To Bertram.*] I dare not say I take you; but I give
Me and my service, ever whilst I live,   *105*
Into your guiding power. This is the man.
    King. Why then, young Bertram, take her; she's thy wife.
    Ber. My wife, my liege! I shall beseech your highness
In such a business give me leave to use
The help of mine own eyes.   *110*
    King.   Know'st thou not, Bertram,
What she has done for me?
    Ber.   Yes, my good lord;
But never hope to know why I should marry her.
    King. Thou know'st she has rais'd me from my sickly bed.
    Ber. But follows it, my lord, to bring me down
Must answer for your raising? I know her well:
She had her breeding at my father's charge.
A poor physician's daughter my wife! Disdain
Rather corrupt me ever!   *120*
    King. 'Tis only title thou disdain'st in her, the which
I can build up. Strange is it that our bloods,
Of colour, weight, and heat, pour'd all together,
Would quite confound distinction, yet stands off
In differences so mighty. If she be   *125*
All that is virtuous, save what thou dislik'st,
A poor physician's daughter, thou dislik'st
Of virtue for the name; but do not so:
From lowest place when virtuous things proceed,
The place is dignified by the doer's deed: *130*
Where great additions swell's, and virtue none,
It is a dropsied honour. Good alone

Is good, without a name: vileness is so:
The property by what it is should go,
Not by the title. She is young, wise, fair;   *135*
In these to nature she's immediate heir,
And these breed honour: that is honour's scorn
Which challenges itself as honour's born,
And is not like the sire: honours thrive
When rather from our acts we them derive   *140*
Than our foregoers. The mere word's a slave,
Debosh'd on every tomb, on every grave,
A lying trophy, and as oft is dumb
Where dust and damn'd oblivion is the tomb
Of honour'd bones indeed. What should be said?   *145*
If thou canst like this creature as a maid,
I can create the rest: virtue and she
Is her own dower; honour and wealth from me.
    Ber. I cannot love her, nor will strive to do 't.
    King. Thou wrong'st thyself if thou shouldst strive   *150*
to choose.
    Hel. That you are well restor'd, my lord, I'm glad:
Let the rest go.
    King. My honour's at the stake, which to defeat
I must produce my power. Here, take her hand,   *155*
Proud scornful boy, unworthy this good gift,
That dost in vile misprision shackle up
My love and her desert; that canst not dream
We, poising us in her defective scale,
Shall weigh thee to the beam; that wilt not know,   *160*
It is in us to plant thine honour where
We please to have it grow. Check thy contempt:
Obey our will, which travails in thy good:
Believe not thy disdain, but presently
Do thine own fortunes that obedient right   *165*
Which both thy duty owes and our power claims;
Or I will throw thee from my care for ever
Into the staggers and the careless lapse
Of youth and ignorance, both my revenge and hate
Loosing upon thee, in the name of justice,   *170*
Without all terms of pity. Speak; thine answer.
    Ber. Pardon, my gracious lord; for I submit
My fancy to your eyes. When I consider
What great creation and what dole of honour
Flies where you bid it, I find that she, which late   *175*
Was in my nobler thoughts most base, is now
The praised of the king; who, so ennobled,
Is, as 'twere, born so.
    King.   Take her by the hand,
And tell her she is thine: to whom I promise   *180*
A counterpoise, if not to thy estate
A balance more replete.
    Ber.   I take her hand.
    King. Good fortune and the favour of the king
Smile upon this contract, whose ceremony   *185*
Shall seem expedient on the now-born brief,

---

133 vileness is so: *vileness is vileness, although it be not called so*   **134 property:**
quality   **136** *She is indebted to nature for these gifts*   **138 challenges:** *proclaims*   **141
foregoers:** *ancestors*   **142 Debosh'd:** *perverted*   **154 which to defeat:** *to prevent the loss of
which*   **157 misprision;** *cf. n.*   **159 poising us:** *adding our weight*   **defective:** *light*   **161
in us:** *in our power*   **163 travails in:** *works toward*   **165** *Serve your own interests by obedience*   **168 staggers:** *bewilderment*   **careless lapse:** *unheeded fall*   **176 nobler:** *too
noble*   **182 more replete:** *more than equal*   **186** *Shall seem to follow immediately upon
this new-made contract*

---

78 all . . . mute: *you assent with your lips only*   **79, 80** *Cf. n.*   **119, 120 Disdain . . .
ever:** *rather let your displeasure cast me down forever*   **121 title:** *want of title*   **123 Of:**
in respect of   **124 confound distinction:** *defy differentiation*   **stands off:** *diverge*   **127,
128 thou . . . name:** *you despise virtue because it lacks a high-sounding title*   **131** *When great
titles exalt us, yet we have no virtue*   **132 dropsied:** *swollen by disease*

And be perform'd to-night: the solemn feast
Shall more attend upon the coming space,
Expecting absent friends. As thou lov'st her,
Thy love's to me religious; else, does err.   *190*

*Exeunt [King, Bertram, Helena, Lords, and Attendants.] Parolles
and Lafeu stay behind, commenting of this wedding.*

Laf. Do you hear, monsieur? a word with you.
Par. Your pleasure, sir?
Laf. Your lord and master did well to make his
recantation.   *195*
Par. Recantation! My lord! my master!
Laf. Ay; is it not a language I speak?
Par. A most harsh one, and not to be understood
without bloody succeeding. My master!
Laf. Are you companion to the Count Rousillon?   *200*
Par. To any count; to all counts; to what is man.
Laf. To what is count's man: count's master is of another
style.
Par. You are too old, sir; let it satisfy you, you are too old.
Laf. I must tell thee, sirrah, I write man; to which title   *205*
age cannot bring thee.
Par. What I dare too well do, I dare not do.
Laf. I did think thee, for two ordinaries, to be a pretty
wise fellow: thou didst make tolerable vent of thy travel; it
might pass; yet the scarfs and the bannerets about thee did   *210*
manifoldly dissuade me from believing thee a vessel of too
great a burthen. I have now found thee; when I lose thee
again, I care not; yet art thou good for nothing but taking up,
and that thou'rt scarce worth.
Par. Hadst thou not the privilege of antiquity upon thee,—
Laf. Do not plunge thyself too far in anger, lest thou hasten
thy trial; which if—Lord have mercy on thee for a hen! So,
my good window of lattice, fare thee well: thy casement I need
not open, for I look through thee. Give me thy hand.
Par. My lord, you give me most egregious indignity.   *220*
Laf. Ay, with all my heart; and thou art worthy of it.
Par. I have not, my lord, deserved it.
Laf. Yes, good faith, every dram of it; and I will not
bate thee a scruple.
Par. Well, I shall be wiser—   *225*
Laf. Ev'n as soon as thou canst, for thou hast to pull at a
smack o' the contrary. If ever thou be'st bound in thy scarf
and beaten, thou shalt find what it is to be proud of thy
bondage. I have a desire to hold my acquaintance with thee,
or rather my knowledge, that I may say in the default,   *230*
he is a man I know.
Par. My lord, you do me most insupportable vexation.
Laf. I would it were hell-pains for thy sake, and my
poor doing eternal: for doing I am past; as I will by thee,
in what motion age will give me leave.   *Exit*   *235*
Par. Well, thou hast a son shall take this disgrace off me;
scurvy, old, filthy, scurvy lord! Well, I must be patient; there
is no fettering of authority. I'll beat him, by my life, if I

can meet him with any convenience, an he were double and
double a lord. I'll have no more pity of his age than I   *240*
would have of—I'll beat him, an if I could but meet him again!

[Re-]enter Lafeu.

Laf. Sirrah, your lord and master's married; there's news
for you: you have a new mistress.
Par. I most unfeignedly beseech your lordship to make
some reservation of your wrongs: he is my good lord: *245*
whom I serve above is my master.
Laf. Who? God?
Par. Ay, sir.
Laf. The devil it is that's thy master. Why dost thou garter
up thy arms o' this fashion? dost make hose of thy sleeves?   *250*
do other servants so? Thou wert best set thy lower part where
thy nose stands. By mine honour, if I were but two hours
younger, I'd beat thee: methinks thou art a general offence,
and every man should beat thee: I think thou wast created
for men to breathe themselves upon thee.   *255*
Par. This is hard and undeserved measure, my lord.
Laf. Go to, sir; you were beaten in Italy for picking a kernel
out of a pomegranate; you are a vagabond and no true
traveller: you are more saucy with lords and honourable personages than the commission of your birth and virtue gives   *260*
you heraldry. You are not worth another word, else I'd call
you knave. I leave you.   *Exit.*

Enter Count Rousillon.

Par. Good, very good; it is so then: good, very good,
let it be concealed awhile.
Ber. Undone, and forfeited to cares for ever!   *265*
Par. What's the matter, sweet heart?
Ber. Although before the solemn priest I have sworn,
I will not bed her.
Par. What, what, sweet heart?
Ber. O my Parolles, they have married me!   *270*
I'll to the Tuscan wars, and never bed her.
Par. France is a dog-hole, and it no more merits
The tread of a man's foot. To the wars!
Ber. There's letters from my mother: what the import is.
I know not yet.   *275*
Par. Ay, that would be known. To the wars, my boy!
to the wars!
He wears his honour in a box, unseen,
That hugs his kicky-wicky here at home,
Spending his manly marrow in her arms,   *280*
Which should sustain the bound and high curvet
Of Mars's fiery steed. To other regions
France is a stable; we that dwell in 't jades;
Therefore, to the war!
Ber. It shall be so: I'll send her to my house,   *285*
Acquaint my mother with my hate to her,
And wherefore I am fled; write to the king
That which I durst not speak: his present gift
Shall furnish me to those Italian fields,
Where noble fellows strike. Wars is no strife   *290*
To the dark house and the detested wife.

189 **Expecting:** *tarrying for*   199 **succeeding:** *consequence*   205 **write:** *call myself*   208 **ordinaries:** *meals*   209 **vent:** *display*   212 **found thee:** *found you
out*   213 **taking up:** *contradicting* (used punningly)   217 **hen:** *coward*   225
Cf. n.   226, 227 **pull . . . contrary:** *draw at a taste of the opposite quality* (folly)   230
in the default: *when it is necessary*   234 **as . . . thee;** *cf. n.*   234, 235 **in . . . leave:** *as
fast as my age permits*

255 **breathe:** *exercise*   260 **commission:** *warrant*   261 **heraldry:** *rank*   265 **forfeited:** *given up*   281 **curvet:** *leap*   283 **jades:** *draft horses*   289 **furnish me to:** *equip
me for*   291 **To:** *compared to*

Par. Will this capriccio hold in thee? art sure?

Ber. Go with me to my chamber and advise me.
I'll send her straight away: to-morrow
I'll to the wars, she to her single sorrow. *295*

Par. Why, these balls bound; there's noise in it.
'Tis hard:
A young man married is a man that's marr'd:
Therefore away, and leave her bravely; go:
The king has done you wrong: but, hush! 'tis so. *300*

        Exit [with Bertram].

❧ SCENE FOURTH ❧

[Same. Another Room in the Palace]
Enter Helena and Clown.

Hel. My mother greets me kindly: is she well?

Clo. She is not well; but yet she has her health; she's very
merry, but yet she is not well: but thanks be given, she's very
well, and wants nothing i' the world; but yet she is not well.

Hel. If she be very well, what does she ail that she's not *5*
very well?

Clo. Truly, she's very well indeed, but for two things.

Hel. What two things?

Clo. One, that she's not in heaven, whither God send her
quickly! the other, that she's in earth, from whence God *10*
send her quickly!

Enter Parolles.

Par. Bless you, my fortunate lady!

Hel. I hope, sir, I have your good will to have mine own
good fortune.

Par. You had my prayers to lead them on; and to keep *15*
them on, have them still. O! my knave, how does my old
lady?

Clo. So that you had her wrinkles, and I her money, I
would she did as you say.

Par. Why, I say nothing. *20*

Clo. Marry, you are the wiser man; for many a man's
tongue shakes out his master's undoing. To say nothing, to do
nothing, to know nothing, and to have nothing, is to be a
great part of your title; which is within a very little of nothing.

Par. Away! [Before God,] th'art a knave. *25*

Clo. You should have said, sir, before a knave thou'rt a
knave; that is, before me thou'rt a knave: this had been truth,
sir.

Par. Go to, thou art a witty fool; I have found thee.

Clo. Did you find me in yourself, sir? or were you taught *30*
to find me? The search, sir, was profitable; and much fool
may you find in you, even to the world's pleasure and the
increase of laughter.

Par. A good knave, i'faith, and well fed.
Madam, my lord will go away to-night; *35*
A very serious business calls on him.
The great prerogative and rite of love,
Which, as your due, time claims, he does acknowledge,
But puts it off to a compell'd restraint;

Whose want, and whose delay, is strew'd with sweets, *40*
Which they distil now in the curbed time,
To make the coming hour o'erflow with joy,
And pleasure drown the brim.

Hel.   What's his will else?

Par. That you will take your instant leave o' the king, *45*
And make this haste as your own good proceeding,
Strengthen'd with what apology you think
May make it probable need.

Hel.   What more commands he?

Par. That, having this obtain'd, you presently *50*
Attend his further pleasure.

Hel. In everything I wait upon his will.

Par. I shall report it so.   *Exit Parolles.*

Hel. [To Clown.]   I pray you come, sirrah.

        Exit [followed by Clown].

❧ SCENE FIFTH ❧

[Another Room in the Same]
Enter Lafeu and Bertram.

Laf. But I hope your lordship thinks not him a soldier.

Ber. Yes, my lord, and of very valiant approof.

Laf. You have it from his own deliverance.

Ber. And by other warranted testimony.

Laf. Then my dial goes not true: I took this lark for a *5*
bunting.

Ber. I do assure you, my lord, he is very great in knowledge, and accordingly valiant.

Laf. I have then sinned against his experience and transgressed against his valour; and my state that way is *10*
dangerous, since I cannot yet find in my heart to repent. Here
he comes; I pray you, make us friends; I will pursue the amity.

Enter Parolles.

Par. [To Bertram.] These things shall be done, sir.

Laf. Pray you, sir, who's his tailor?

Par. Sir? *15*

Laf. O! I know him well, I, sir. He, sir, 's a good workman,
a very good tailor.

Ber. [Aside to Parolles.] Is she gone to the king?

Par. She is.

Ber. Will she away to-night? *20*

Par. As you'll have her.

Ber. I have writ my letters, casketed my treasure,
Given orders for our horses, and to-night,
When I should take possession of the bride,
End ere I do begin. *25*

Laf. A good traveller is something at the latter end of a
dinner; but one that lies three thirds, and uses a known truth
to pass a thousand nothings with, should be once heard and
thrice beaten. God save you, captain.

Ber. Is there any unkindness between my lord and you, *30*
monsieur?

292 **capriccio:** *whim* **hold:** *persist* 296 **these ... it;** *cf. n.* 5 **what:** *in what
way* 24 **title:** *value* 30 **in yourself:** *by yourself (used punningly)* 39 **Postpones it
because of an unavoidable necessity**

41 **curbed time:** *time of restraint* 46 **And make this haste appear to arise from your own
desires** 48 **make ... need:** *make the necessity plausible* 50 **this:** *i.e. permission to depart*
presently: *at once* 2 **very ... approof:** *proved valor* 5 **my ... true:** *I am mistaken* 8 **accordingly:** *to a corresponding degree* 12 **pursue:** *further*

Par. I know not how I have deserved to run into my lord's
displeasure.

Laf. You have made shift to run into 't, boots and spurs
and all, like him that leaped into the custard; and out of   *35*
it you'll run again, rather than suffer question for your
residence.

Ber. It may be you have mistaken him, my lord.

Laf. And shall do so ever, though I took him at's prayers.
Fare you well, my lord; and believe this of me, there can be   *40*
no kernel in this light nut; the soul of this man is his
clothes. Trust him not in matter of heavy consequence; I have
kept of them tame, and know their natures. Farewell, monsieur: I have spoken better of you than you have or will to deserve at my hand; but we must do good against evil. *[Exit.]*   *45*

Par. An idle lord, I swear.

Ber. I think [not] so.

Par. Why do you not know him?

Ber. Yes, I do know him well; and common speech
Gives him a worthy pass. Here comes my clog.   *50*

Enter Helena [followed by Clown].

Hel. I have, sir, as I was commanded from you,
Spoke with the king, and have procur'd his leave
For present parting; only, he desires
Some private speech with you.

Ber.   I shall obey his will.   *55*
You must not marvel, Helen, at my course,
Which holds not colour with the time, nor does
The ministration and required office
On my particular: prepar'd I was not
For such a business; therefore am I found   *60*
So much unsettled. This drives me to entreat you
That presently you take your way for home;
And rather muse than ask why I entreat you;
For my respects are better than they seem,
And my appointments have in them a need   *65*
Greater than shows itself at the first view
To you than know them not. This to my mother.

[Giving a letter.]

'Twill be two days ere I shall see you, so
I leave you to your wisdom.

Hel.   Sir, I can nothing say,   *70*
But that I am your most obedient servant.

Ber. Come, come, no more of that.

Hel.   And ever shall
With true observance seek to eke out that
Wherein toward me my homely stars have fail'd   *75*
To equal my great fortune.

Ber.   Let that go:
My haste is very great. Farewell: hie home.

Hel. Pray sir, your pardon.

Ber.   Well, what would you say?   *80*

Hel. I am not worthy of the wealth I owe,
Nor dare I say 'tis mine, and yet it is;
But, like a timorous thief, most fain would steal
What law does vouch mine own.

Ber.   What would you have?   *85*

Hel. Something, and scarce so much: nothing, indeed.
I would not tell you what I would, my lord:—
Faith, yes;
Strangers and foes do sunder, and not kiss.

Ber. I pray you, stay not, but in haste to horse.   *90*

Hel. I shall not break your bidding, good my lord.
[To Clown.] Where are my other men? *[To Parolles.]*
Monsieur, farewell.   *Exit.*

Ber. Go thou toward home; where I will never come
Whilst I can shake my sword or hear the drum.
Away! and for our flight.   *95*

Par.   Bravely, *coragio!*   *[Exeunt.]*

ACT THIRD ❧ SCENE FIRST.

[Florence. A Room in the Duke's Palace]
Flourish. Enter the Duke of Florence [and] the two Frenchmen [the
Lords], with a troop of soldiers.

Duke. So that from point to point now have you heard
The fundamental reasons of this war,
Whose great decision hath much blood let forth,
And more thirsts after.

1. Lord.   Holy seems the quarrel   *5*
Upon your Grace's part; black and fearful
On the opposer.

Duke. Therefore we marvel much our cousin France
Would in so just a business shut his bosom
Against our borrowing prayers.   *10*

1. Lord.   Good my lord,
The reasons of our state I cannot yield,
But like a common and an outward man,
That the great figure of a council frames
By self-unable motion: therefore dare not   *15*
Say what I think of it, since I have found
Myself in my incertain grounds to fail
As often as I guess'd.

Duke.   Be it his pleasure.

2. Lord. But I am sure the younger of our nature,   *20*
That surfeit on their ease, will day by day
Come here for physic.

Duke.   Welcome shall they be,
And all the honours that can fly from us
Shall on them settle. You know your places well;   *25*
When better fall, for your avails they fell.
To-morrow to the field.   *Flourish. [Exeunt.]*

---

32 run into: *incur*   **35 like … custard;** *cf. n.*   **34, 35 suffer … residence:** *bear being
questioned for your presence there*   **39 do so:** *i.e. take him amiss* (pun on 'mistake')   **43
of them:** *some of* (such creatures)   **50 pass:** *reputation*   **53 present parting:** *immediate
departure*   **57 holds … with:** *does not seem suitable to*   **59 particular:** *part*   **63
muse:** *wonder*   **64 respects:** *motives*   **65 appointments:** *commands*   **need:** *necessity*

91 break: *disobey*   **96 coragio:** *courage*   **3 decision:** *act of deciding*   **12 yield:**
tell   **13 But like:** *except as*   **outward:** *having no access to councils of state*   **14, 15 That
… motion;** *cf. n.*   **19 Be … pleasure:** *let us suppose it his will*   **26 better fall:** *better
places fall vacant*   **for your avails:** *to your advantage*

❧ Scene Second ❧

[Rousillon. A Room in the Countess's Palace]
Enter Countess and Clown.

Count. It hath happened all as I would have had it, save
that he comes not along with her.

Clo. By my troth, I take my young lord to be a very
melancholy man.

Count. By what observance, I pray you?   5

Clo. Why, he will look upon his boot and sing; mend the
ruff and sing; ask questions and sing; pick his teeth and sing.
I know a man that had this trick of melancholy hold a goodly
manor for a song.

Count. [*Opening a letter.*] Let me see what he writes,   10
and when he means to come.

Clo. I have no mind to Isbel since I was at court. Our old
lings and our Isbels o' the country are nothing like your old
ling and your Isbels o' the court: the brains of my Cupid's
knocked out, and I begin to love, as an old man loves   15
money, with no stomach.

Count. What have we here?

Clo. E'en that you have there.   *Exit.*

[Countess reads] a Letter. 'I have sent you a daughter-in-law:
she hath recovered the king, and undone me. I have wedded   20
her, not bedded her; and sworn to make the "not" eternal.
You shall hear I am run away: know it before the report come.
If there be breadth enough in the world, I will hold a long
distance. My duty to you.

> Your unfortunate son,   25
> Bertram.'

This is not well, rash and unbridled boy,
To fly the favours of so good a king!
To pluck his indignation on thy head
By the misprising of a maid too virtuous   30
For the contempt of empire!

[Re-]enter clown.

Clo. O madam! yonder is heavy news within between
two soldiers and my young lady.

Count. What is the matter?

Clo. Nay, there is some comfort in the news, some   35
comfort; your son will not be killed so soon as I thought
he would.

Count. Why should he be killed?

Clo. So say I, madam, if he run away, as I hear he does: the
danger is in standing to 't; that's the loss of men, though it   40
be the getting of children. Here they come will tell you more;
for my part, I only hear your son was run away.   *[Exit.]*

Enter Helen and two Gentlemen [the French Lords].

1. Gen. Save you, good madam.

Hel. Madam, my lord is gone, for ever gone.

2. Gen. Do not say so.   45

Count. Think upon patience. Pray you, gentlemen,
I have felt so many quirks of joy and grief,
That the first face of neither, on the start,

Can woman me unto 't. Where is my son, I pray you?

2. Gen. Madam, he's gone to serve the Duke of Florence: 50
We met him thitherward; for thence we came,
And, after some dispatch in hand at court,
Thither we bend again.

Hel. Look on his letter, madam; here's my passport.
'When thou canst get the ring upon my finger, which never 55
shall come off, and show me a child begotten of thy body
that I am father to, then call me husband: but in such a
"then" I write a "never."'
This is a dreadful sentence.

Count. Brought you this letter, gentlemen?   60

1. Gen.   Ay, madam;
And for the contents' sake are sorry for our pains.

Count. I prithee, lady, have a better cheer;
If thou engrossest all the griefs are thine,
Thou robb'st me of a moiety: he was my son,   65
But I do wash his name out of my blood,
And thou art all my child. Towards Florence is he?

2. Gen. Ay, madam.

Count.   And to be a soldier?

2. Gen. Such is his noble purpose; and, believe 't,   70
The duke will lay upon him all the honour
That good convenience claims.

Count.   Return you thither?

1. Gen. Ay, madam, with the swiftest wing of speed.

Hel. 'Till I have no wife, I have nothing in France.'   75
'Tis bitter.

Count. Find you that there?

Hel.   Ay, madam.

1. Gen. 'Tis but the boldness of his hand, haply, which
his heart was not consenting to.   80

Count. Nothing in France until he have no wife!
There's nothing here that is too good for him
But only she; and she deserves a lord
That twenty such rude boys might tend upon,
And call her hourly mistress. Who was with him?   85

1. Gen. A servant only, and a gentleman
Which I have some time known.

Count.   Parolles, was it not?

1. Gen. Ay, my good lady, he.

Count. A very tainted fellow, and full of wickedness.   90
My son corrupts a well-derived nature
With his inducement.

1. Gen.   Indeed, good lady,
The fellow has a deal of that too much,
Which holds him much to have.   95

Count. Y'are welcome, gentlemen.
I will entreat you, when you see my son,
To tell him that his sword can never win
The honour that he loses: more I'll entreat you
Written to bear along.   100

2. Gen.   We serve you, madam,
In that and all your worthiest affairs.

Count. Not so, but as we change our courtesies.

---

5 **observance:** *observation*   8, 9 **hold ... for:** *value ... at*   13 **lings:** *a kind of fish*   20 **recovered:** *healed*   23 **hold:** *keep*   29 **pluck:** *bring down*   30 **misprising:** *despising*   31 *For even an emperor to look down upon*   48 **on the start:** *on sudden appearance*

49 **woman me unto 't:** *make me show a woman's emotions*   51 **thitherward:** *on his way thither*   52 **dispatch:** *business*   63 **cheer:** *countenance*   64 *If you take exclusive possession of all the sorrows that are yours*   65 **moiety:** *half*   72 **good convenience claims:** *propriety permits*   91 **well-derived nature:** *excellent natural disposition*   92 **With his inducement:** *through his influence*   94, 95 *Cf. n.*   102 **worthiest:** *most worthy*   103 *You are my servants only in the language of compliment*

Will you draw near?   *Exit [with the two Gentlemen].*
Hel. 'Till I have no wife, I have nothing in France.'   *105*
Nothing in France until he has no wife!
Thou shalt have none, Rousillon, none in France;
Then hast thou all again. Poor lord! is 't I
That chase thee from thy country, and expose
Those tender limbs of thine to the event   *110*
Of the none-sparing war? and is it I
That drive thee from the sportive court, where thou
Wast shot at with fair eyes, to be the mark
Of smoky muskets? O you leaden messengers,
That ride upon the violent speed of fire,   *115*
Fly with false aim; move the still-pairing air,
That sings with piercing; do not touch my lord!
Whoever shoots at him, I set him there;
Whoever charges on his forward breast,
I am the caitiff that do hold him to 't;   *120*
And, though I kill him not, I am the cause
His death was so effected: better 'twere
I met the ravin lion when he roar'd
With sharp constraint of hunger; better 'twere
That all the miseries which nature owes   *125*
Were mine at once. No, come thou home, Rousillon,
Whence honour but of danger wins a scar,
As oft it loses all: I will be gone;
My being here it is that holds thee hence:
Shall I stay here to do 't? no, no, although   *130*
The air of paradise did fan the house,
And angels offic'd all: I will be gone,
That pitiful rumour may report my flight,
To consolate thine ear. Come, night; end, day!
For with the dark, poor thief, I'll steal away.   *Exit.*   *135*

⁂ SCENE THIRD ⁂

[Florence. Before the Duke's Palace]

Flourish. Enter the Duke of Florence, Rousillon, drum and
trumpets, Soldiers, Parolles.
Duke. The general of our horse thou art; and we,
Great in our hope, lay our best love and credence
Upon thy promising fortune.
Ber.   Sir, it is   *5*
A charge too heavy for my strength, but yet
We'll strive to bear it for your worthy sake
To th' extreme edge of hazard.
Duke.   Then go thou forth,   *10*
And fortune play upon thy prosperous helm
As thy auspicious mistress!
Ber.   This very day,
Great Mars, I put myself into thy file:
Make me but like my thoughts, and I shall prove   *15*
A lover of thy drum, hater of love.   *Exeunt omnes.*

⁂ SCENE FOURTH ⁂

[Rousillon. A Room in the Countess's Palace]
Enter Countess and Steward.

Count. Alas! and would you take the letter of her?
Might you not know she would do as she has done,
By sending me a letter? Read it again.

[Steward reads a] Letter. 'I am Saint Jacques' pilgrim,
thither gone: *5*
Ambitious love hath so in me offended
That bare-foot plod I the cold ground upon
With sainted vow my faults to have amended.
Write, write, that from the bloody course of war,
My dearest master, your dear son, may hie: *10*
Bless him at home in peace, whilst I from far
His name with zealous fervour sanctify:
His taken labours bid him me forgive;
I, his despiteful Juno, sent him forth
From courtly friends, with camping foes to live,   *15*
Where death and danger dogs the heels of worth:
He is too good and fair for Death and me;
Whom I myself embrace, to set him free.'
Count. Ah, what sharp stings are in her mildest words!
Rinaldo, you did never lack advice so much,   *20*
As letting her pass so: had I spoke with her,
I could have well diverted her intents,
Which thus she hath prevented.
Stew.   Pardon me, madam:
If I had given you this at over-night,
She might have been o'erta'en; and yet she writes,   *25*
Pursuit would be but vain.
Count.   What angel shall
Bless this unworthy husband? he cannot thrive,
Unless her prayers, whom heaven delights to hear,   *30*
And loves to grant, reprieve him from the wrath
Of greatest justice. Write, write, Rinaldo,
To this unworthy husband of his wife.
Let every word weigh heavy of her worth
That he does weigh too light: my greatest grief,   *35*
Though little he do feel it, set down sharply.
Dispatch the most convenient messenger:
When haply he shall hear that she is gone,
He will return; and hope I may that she,
Hearing so much, will speed her foot again,   *40*
Led hither by pure love. Which of them both
Is dearest to me I have no skill in sense
To make distinction. Provide this messenger.
My heart is heavy and mine age is weak;
Grief would have tears, and sorrow bids me speak.   *Exeunt.*

❦ Scene Fifth ❦

[Without the Walls of Florence]
A tucket afar off. Enter old Widow of Florence, her daughter
[Diana], Violenta and Mariana, with other citizens.

Wid. Nay, come; for if they do approach the city, we shall
lose all the sight.

Dia. They say the French count has done most honourable
service.

Wid. It is reported that he has taken their greatest com- 5
mander, and that with his own hand he slew the duke's
brother. We have lost our labour; they are gone a contrary
way: hark! you may know by their trumpets.

Mar. Come; let's return again, and suffice ourselves with
the report of it. Well, Diana, take heed of this French 10
earl: the honour of a maid is her name, and no legacy is
so rich as honesty.

Wid. I have told my neighbor how you have been solicited
by a gentleman his companion.

Mar. I know that knave, hang him! one Parolles: a filthy 15
officer he is in those suggestions for the young earl. Beware of
them, Diana; their promises, enticements, oaths, tokens, and all
these engines of lust, are not the things they go under: many a
maid hath been seduced by them; and the misery is, example,
that so terrible shows in the wrack of maidenhood, cannot 20
for all that dissuade succession, but that they are limed with
the twigs that threatens them. I hope I need not to advise you
further; but I hope your own grace will keep you where you
are, though there were no further danger known but the
modesty which is so lost. 25

Dia. You shall not need to fear me.

Wid. I hope so.

Enter Helen [in the dress of a Pilgrim].

Look, here comes a pilgrim:
I know she will lie at my house; thither they send one another.
I'll question her. 30
God save you, pilgrim! whither are [you] bound?

Hel. To Saint Jaques le Grand.
Where do the palmers lodge, I do beseech you?

Wid. At the Saint Francis, here beside the port.

Hel. Is this the way? 35

Wid.   Ay, marry, is 't.   *A march afar.*
                                    Hark you!
They come this way. If you will tarry, holy pilgrim,
But till the troops come by,
I will conduct you where you shall be lodg'd: 40
The rather, for I think I know your hostess
As ample as myself.

Hel.   Is it yourself?

Wid. If you shall please so, pilgrim.

Hel. I thank you, and will stay upon your leisure. 45

Wid. You came, I think, from France?

Hel.   I did so.

Wid. Here you shall see a countryman of yours
That has done worthy service.

Hel.   His name, I pray you. 50

Dia. The Count Rousillon: know you such a one?

Hel. But by the ear, that hears most nobly of him;
His face I know not.

Dia.   Whatsome'er he is,
He's bravely taken here. He stole from France, 55
As 'tis reported: for the king had married him
Against his liking. Think you it is so?

Hel. Ay, surely, mere the truth: I know his lady.

Dia. There is a gentleman that serves the count
Reports but coarsely of her. 60

Hel.   What's his name?

Dia. Monsieur Parolles.

Hel.   O, I believe with him.
In argument of praise, or to the worth
Of the great count himself, she is too mean 65
To have her name repeated: all her deserving
Is a reserved honesty, and that
I have not heard examin'd.

Dia.   Alas, poor lady!
'Tis a hard bondage to become the wife 70
Of a detesting lord.

Wid. I write, good creature, wheresoe'er she is,
Her heart weighs sadly. This young maid might do her
A shrewd turn if she pleas'd.

Hel.   How do you mean? 75
May be the amorous count solicits her
In the unlawful purpose.

Wid.   He does, indeed;
And brokes with all that can in such a suit
Corrupt the tender honour of a maid: 80
But she is arm'd for him and keeps her guard
In honestest defence.

Drum and colours. Enter Count Rousillon, Parolles, and the
whole army.

Mar.   The gods forbid else! 85

Wid. So, now they come.
That is Antonio, the duke's eldest son;
That, Escalus.

Hel.   Which is the Frenchman?

Dia.   He; 90
That with the plume: 'tis a most gallant fellow;
I would he lov'd his wife: if he were honester,
He were much goodlier. Is 't not a handsome gentleman?

Hel. I like him well.

Dia. 'Tis pity he is not honest. Yond's that same knave 95
That leads him to these places: were I his lady,
I would poison that vile rascal.

Hel.   Which is he?

Dia. That jackanapes with scarfs. Why is he melancholy?

Hel. Perchance he's hurt i' the battle. 100

Par. Lose our drum! well.

Mar. He's shrewdly vexed at something.
Look, he has spied us.

Wid. Marry, hang you!

Scene Five S.d. tucket: *trumpet call* Violenta; *cf. n.*   16 suggestions for: *allurements*
in behalf of   18 go under: *pretend to be*   20 shows: *appears*   21 dissuade succession:
prevent recurrence limed: *ensnared*   26 fear me: *have fears for me*   34 port: *gate*   42
ample: *well*   45 stay upon: *await*

52 by the ear: *by hearsay*   54 Whatsome'er: *whatever*   58 mere the truth: *the simple
truth*   64 In . . . praise: *as a subject of formal laudation* to the worth: *compared with
the worth*   65 mean: *humble*   67 honesty: *chastity*   68 examin'd: *questioned*   72
write: *warrant*   74 shrewd: *evil*   79 brokes with: *traffics in*   85 forbid else: *forbid
it should be otherwise*   95 Yond's: *yonder's*   102 shrewdly: *keenly*

Mar. And your courtesy, for a ring-carrier!   *105*

        Exit [Bertram, with Parolles and the army].

Wid. The troop is past. Come, pilgrim, I will bring you
Where you shall host: of enjoin'd penitents
There's four or five, to great Saint Jaques bound,
Already at my house.

Hel.   I humbly thank you.   *110*
Please it this matron and this gentle maid
To eat with us to-night, the charge and thanking
Shall be for me; and, to requite you further,
I will bestow some precepts of this virgin
Worthy the note.   *115*

Both.   We'll take your offer kindly.   *Exeunt.*

❧ SCENE SIXTH ❧

[Camp before Florence]
Enter Count Rousillon and the Frenchmen [the Lords], as at first.

1. Lord. Nay, good my lord, put him to 't: let him have
his way.

2. Lord. If your lordship find him not a hilding hold me
no more in your respect.

1. Lord. On my life, my lord, a bubble.   *5*

Ber. Do you think I am so far deceived in him?

1. Lord. Believe it, my lord, in mine own direct knowledge,
without any malice, but to speak of him as my kinsman, he's a
most notable coward, an infinite and endless liar, an hourly
promise-breaker, the owner of no one good quality worthy   *10*
your lordship's entertainment.

2. Lord. It were fit you knew him, lest, reposing too far in
his virtue, which he hath not, he might at some great and
trusty business in a main danger fail you.

Ber. I would I knew in what particular action to try him.   *15*

2. Lord. None better than to let him fetch off his drum,
which you hear him so confidently undertake to do.

1. Lord. I, with a troop of Florentines, will suddenly surprise him: such I will have whom I am sure he knows not
from the enemy. We will bind and hoodwink him so, that   *20*
he shall suppose no other but that he is carried into the leaguer
of the adversaries, when we bring him to our own tents. Be
but your lordship present at his examination: if he do not, for
the promise of his life and in the highest compulsion of base
fear, offer to betray you and deliver all the intelligence in   *25*
his power against you, and that with the divine forfeit of his
soul upon oath, never trust my judgment in anything.

2. Lord. O, for the love of laughter, let him fetch his drum!
he says he has a stratagem for 't. When your lordship sees the
bottom of his success in 't, and to what metal this counter-   *30*
feit lump of ours will be melted, if you give him not John
Drum's entertainment, your inclining cannot be removed. Here
he comes.

Enter Parolles.

1. Lord. O, for the love of laughter, hinder not the honour
of his design! let him fetch off his drum in any hand.   *35*

Ber. How now, monsieur! this drum sticks sorely in your
disposition.

2. Lord. A pox on 't! let it go: 'tis but a drum.

Par. 'But a drum!' Is 't 'but a drum'? A drum so lost! There
was excellent command, to charge in with our horse upon   *40*
our own wings, and to rend our own soldiers!

2. Lord. That was not to be blamed in the command of the
service: it was a disaster of war that Cæsar himself could not
have prevented if he had been there to command.

Ber. Well, we cannot greatly condemn our success: some   *45*
dishonour we had in the loss of that drum; but it is not to
be recovered.

Par. It might have been recovered.

Ber. It might; but it is not now.

Par. It is to be recovered. But that the merit of service is   *50*
seldom attributed to the true and exact performer, I would
have that drum or another, or *hic jacet*.

Ber. Why, if you have a stomach, to 't, monsieur; if you
think your mystery in stratagem can bring this instrument
of honour again into his native quarter, be magnanimous in   *55*
the enterprise and go on; I will grace the attempt for a worthy
exploit: if you speed well in it, the duke shall both speak
of it and extend to you what further becomes his greatness, even
to the utmost syllable of your worthiness.

Par. By the hand of a soldier, I will undertake it.   *60*

Ber. But you must not now slumber in it.

Par. I'll about it this evening: and I will presently pen down
my dilemmas, encourage myself in my certainty, put myself
into my mortal preparation, and by midnight look to hear
further from me.   *65*

Ber. May I be bold to acquaint his Grace you are gone
about it?

Par. I know not what the success will be, my lord, but the
attempt I vow.

Ber. I know th' art valiant, and, to the possibility of thy   *70*
soldiership, will subscribe for thee. Farewell.

Par. I love not many words.   *Exit.*

1. Lord. No more than a fish loves water. Is not this a
strange fellow, my lord, that so confidently seems to undertake
this business, which he knows is not to be done; damns   *75*
himself to do, and dares better be damned than to do 't?

2. Lord. You do not know him, my lord, as we do: certain
it is, that he will steal himself into a man's favour, and for a
week escape a great deal of discoveries; but when you find him
out you have him ever after.   *80*

Ber. Why, do you think he will make no deed at all of this
that so seriously he does address himself unto?

1. Lord. None in the world; but return with an invention
and clap upon you two or three probable lies. But we have
almost imbost him, you shall see his fall to-night; for,   *85*
indeed, he is not for your lordship's respect.

2. Lord. We'll make you some sport with the fox ere we

---

105 **ring-carrier:** *go-between* 107 **host:** *lodge* **enjoin'd penitents:** *pilgrims performing imposed penances* 114 **bestow ... of:** *give some advice to* 115 **Worthy the note:** *worth noting* 1 **to 't:** *to the test* 3 **hilding:** *coward* 5 **bubble:** *sham* 11 **entertainment:** *maintaining* 14 **main:** *very great* 16 **fetch off:** *rescue* 20 **hoodwink:** *blind- fold* 21 **no other but:** *nothing else than* **leaguer:** *camp* 24 **in:** *under* **highest:** *strong- est* 30 **bottom:** *extent* 31, 32 **John Drum's entertainment;** *cf. n.* **inclining:** *partiality*

35 **in any hand:** *at all events* 42, 43 **command of the service:** *commanders of the army* 52 **hic jacet;** *cf. n.* 53 **stomach:** *inclination* **to 't:** *attempt it* 54 **mystery: skill** 56 **grace:** *honor* 57 **speed:** *succeed* 59 **utmost syllable:** *last jot* 62 **about: go about** 62, 63 **pen ... dilemmas:** *write out the difficulties to be overcome* **encourage ... certainty:** *make sure of my success* 63, 64 **put ... preparation:** *prepare for the possibility of death* 70 **possibility:** *extent* 75 **damns:** *condemns* 78 **steal:** *insinuate* 82 **address ... unto:** *undertake* 84 **clap:** *foist* 85 **imbost:** *surrounded* 86 **for:** *worthy of*

case him. He was first smoked by the old Lord Lafeu: when
his disguise and he is parted, tell me what a sprat you shall
find him; which you shall see this very night.   *90*

1. Lord. I must go look my twigs: he shall be caught.

Ber. Your brother he shall go alone with me.

1. Lord. As 't please your lordship: I'll leave you.   *[Exit.]*

Ber. Now will I lead you to the house, and show you
The lass I spoke of.   *95*

2. Lord.   But you say she's honest.

Ber. That's all the fault. I spoke with her but once,
And found her wondrous cold; but I sent to her,
By this same coxcomb that we have i' the wind,
Tokens and letters which she did re-send;   *100*
And this is all I have done. She's a fair creature;
Will you go see her?

2. Lord.   With all my heart, my lord.

                                                                    Exeunt.

❧ Scene Seventh ❧

[Florence. A Room in the Widow's House]
Enter Helen and Widow.

Hel. If you misdoubt me that I am not she,
I know not how I shall assure you further,
But I shall lose the grounds I work upon.

Wid. Though my estate be fall'n, I was well born,
Nothing acquainted with these businesses;   *5*
And would not put my reputation now
In any staining act.

Hel.   Nor would I wish you.
First, give me trust, the count he is my husband,
And what to your sworn counsel I have spoken   *10*
Is so from word to word; and then you cannot,
By the good aid that I of you shall borrow,
Err in bestowing it.

Wid.   I should believe you:
For you have show'd me that which well approves   *15*
Y'are great in fortune.

Hel.   Take this purse of gold,
And let me buy your friendly help thus far,
Which I will over-pay and pay again
When I have found it. The count he woos your daughter,   *20*
Lays down his wanton siege before her beauty,
Resolv'd to carry her: let her in fine consent,
As we'll direct her how 'tis best to bear it.
Now, his important blood will nought deny
That she'll demand: a ring the county wears,   *25*
That downward hath succeeded in his house
From son to son, some four or five descents
Since the first father wore it: this ring he holds
In most rich choice; yet, in his idle fire,
To buy his will, it would not seem too dear,   *30*
Howe'er repented after.

Wid.   Now I see
The bottom of your purpose.

Hel. You see it lawful then. It is no more,
But that your daughter, ere she seems as won,   *35*
Desires this ring, appoints him an encounter,
In fine, delivers me to fill the time,
Herself most chastely absent. After,
To marry her, I'll add three thousand crowns
To what is past already.   *40*

Wid.   I have yielded.
Instruct my daughter how she shall persever,
That time and place with this deceit so lawful
May prove coherent. Every night he comes
With musics of all sorts and songs compos'd   *45*
To her unworthiness: it nothing steads us
To chide him from our eaves, for he persists
As if his life lay on 't.

Hel.   Why then to-night
Let us assay our plot; which, if it speed,   *50*
Is wicked meaning in a lawful deed,
And lawful meaning in a lawful act,
Where both not sin, and yet a sinful fact.
But let's about it.   *[Exeunt.]*

Act Fourth ❧ Scene First

[Without the Florentine Camp]
Enter one of the Frenchmen [First Lord] with five or six other
Soldiers in ambush.

1. Lord. He can come no other way but by this hedge-
corner. When you sally upon him, speak what terrible language
you will: though you understand it not yourselves, no matter;
for we must not seem to understand him, unless some one
among us, whom we must produce for an interpreter.   *5*

1. Sold. Good captain, let me be the interpreter.

1. Lord. Art not acquainted with him? knows he not thy
voice?

1. Sold. No, sir, I warrant you.

1. Lord. But what linsey-woolsey hast thou to speak to   *10*
us again?

1. Sold. E'en such as you speak to me.

1. Lord. He must think us some band of strangers i' th' adversary's entertainment. Now, he hath a smack of all neighbour-
ing languages; therefore we must every one be a man of his   *15*
own fancy, not to know what we speak one to another;
so we seem to know, is to know straight our purpose: chough's
language, gabble enough, and good enough. As for you,
interpreter, you must seem very politic. But couch, ho!
here he comes, to beguile two hours in a sleep, and then to   *20*
return and swear the lies he forges.

Enter Parolles.

Par. Ten o'clock: within these three hours 'twill be time
enough to go home. What shall I say I have done? It must be

---

88 case: *flay* **smoked:** *found out*   **89 sprat:** *a worthless fish*   **91 look my twigs:** *see to
my snares*   **97 all the fault:** *the only drawback*   **99 have ... wind:** *are in pursuit
of*   **3** Cf. n.   **5 Nothing acquainted:** *entirely unfamiliar*   **6, 7 put ... act:** *do
anything tending to injure my reputation*   **10 to ... counsel:** *to you in sworn secrecy*   **11
from word to word:** *every word*   **15 approves:** *proves*   **22 carry:** *conquer* **in fine:**
in short   **24 bear it:** *conduct the affair*   **24 important:** *importunate*   **25 county:**
count   **29 rich choice:** *high estimation* **idle fire:** *foolish passion*

42 persever: *proceed*   **44 prove coherent:** *agree*   **46 steads:** *avails*   **50 assay:**
try   **10 linsey-woolsey:** *nondescript (language)*   **13 strangers:** *foreigners*   **17 straight:**
immediately **chough's:** *crow's*   **19 couch:** *hide*

a very plausive invention that carries it. They begin to smoke
me, and disgraces have of late knocked too often at my   25
door. I find my tongue is too foolhardy; but my heart hath the
fear of Mars before it and of his creatures, not daring the
reports of my tongue.

1. Lord. [*Aside.*] This is the first truth that e'er thine own
tongue was guilty of.   30

Par. What the devil should move me to undertake the recovery of this drum, being not ignorant of the impossibility, and
knowing I had no such purpose? I must give myself some
hurts and say I got them in exploit. Yet slight ones will not
carry it: they will say, 'Came you off with so little?' and   35
great ones I dare not give. Wherefore, what's the instance? Tongue,
I must put you into a butter-woman's mouth, and buy myself
another of Bajazet's mule, if you prattle me into these perils.

1. Lord. Is it possible he should know what he is, and be
that he is?   40

Par. I would the cutting of my garments would serve the
turn, or the breaking of my Spanish sword.

1. Lord. We cannot afford you so.

Par. Or the baring of my beard, and to say it was in
stratagem.   45

1. Lord. 'Twould not do.

Par. Or to drown my clothes, and say I was stripped.

1. Lord. Hardly serve.

Par. Though I swore I leapt from the window of the
citadel—   50

1. Lord. How deep?

Par. Thirty fathom.

1. Lord. Three great oaths would scarce make that be
believed.

Par. I would I had any drum of the enemy's: 55
I would swear I recovered it.

1. Lord. You shall hear one anon.

Par. A drum now of the enemy's!

Alarum within.

1. Lord. Throca movousus, cargo, cargo, cargo.   60
All. Cargo, cargo, cargo, villianda par corbo, cargo.

[*They seize and blindfold him.*]

Par. O! ransom, ransom! Do not hide mine eyes.

Inter. Boskos thromuldo boskos.

Par. I know you are the Muskos' regiment;
And I shall lose my life for want of language.   65
If there be here German, or Dane, low Dutch,
Italian, or French, let him speak to me:
I'll discover that which shall undo
The Florentine.

Inter.   Boskos vauvado: 70
I understand thee, and can speak thy tongue:
Kerelybonto, sir,
Betake thee to thy faith, for seventeen poniards
Are at thy bosom.

Par.   O!   75

Inter.   O! pray, pray, pray.
Manka revania dulche.

1. Lord.   Oscorbidulchos volivorco.

Inter. The general is content to spare thee yet,

And, hoodwink'd as thou art, will lead thee on   80
To gather from thee: haply thou may'st inform
Something to save thy life.

Par.   O! let me live,
And all the secrets of our camp I'll show,
Their force, their purposes; nay, I'll speak that   85
Which you will wonder at.

Inter.   But wilt thou faithfully?

Par. If I do not, damn me.

Inter.   *Acordo linta.*
Come on; thou art granted space.   90

Exit [with Parolles guarded].
A short alarum within.

1. Lord. Go, tell the Count Rousillon and my brother
We have caught the woodcock, and will keep him muffled
Till we do hear from them.

Sold.   Captain, I will.

1. Lord. A' will betray us all unto ourselves: 95
Inform on that.

Sold.   So I will, sir.   [*Exit.*]

1. Lord. Till then, I'll keep him dark and safely lock'd. *Exit.*

❧ Scene Second ❧

[Florence. A Room in the Widow's House]
Enter Bertram and the maid called Diana.

Ber. They told me that your name was Fontibell.
Dia. No, my good lord, Diana.
Ber.   Titled goddess;
And worth it, with addition! But, fair soul,
In your fine frame hath love no quality?   5
If the quick fire of youth light not your mind,
You are no maiden, but a monument:
When you are dead, you should be such a one
As you are now, for you are cold and stern;
And now you should be as your mother was   10
When your sweet self was got.

Dia. She then was honest.

Ber.   So should you be.

Dia   No:
My mother did but duty; such, my lord,   15
As you owe to your wife.

Ber.   No more o' that!
I prithee do not strive against my vows.
I was compell'd to her; but I love thee
By love's own sweet constraint, and will for ever   20
Do thee all rights of service.

Dia   Ay, so you serve us
Till we serve you; but when you have our roses,
You barely leave our thorns to prick ourselves
And mock us with our bareness.   25

Ber.   How have I sworn!

Dia. 'Tis not the many oaths that makes the truth,
But the plain single vow that is vow'd true.
What is not holy, that we swear not by,
But take the high'st to witness: then, pray you, tell me,   30

24 **plausive:** *plausible* **carries it:** *succeeds*   36 **instance:** *proof*   38 **Bajazet's mule;**
cf. n.   43 **afford you so:** *let you off so cheaply*   44 **baring:** *shaving* **Alarum:** *trumpet*
blast 73 **faith:** *religion*

81 **gather:** *obtain information*   90 **space:** *a reprieve*   92 **woodcock:** *fool* **muffled:**
blindfolded   96 **Inform on:** *relate*   4 **addition:** *a higher title of honor*   5 **quality:**
standing   13 **should:** *would*   24 **barely:** *merely*

If I should swear by Jove's great attributes
I lov'd you dearly, would you believe my oaths,
When I did love you ill? This has no holding,
To swear by him whom I protest to love,
That I will work against him: therefore your oaths　　35
Are words and poor conditions, but unseal'd,
At least in my opinion.
　　　Ber.　　　　　　　　Change it, change it.
Be not so holy-cruel: love is holy;
And my integrity ne'er knew the crafts　　　　40
That you do charge men with. Stand no more off,
But give thyself unto my sick desires,
Who then recovers: say thou art mine, and ever
My love as it begins shall so persever.
　　　Dia. I see that men make rope's in such a scarre　　45
That we'll forsake ourselves. Give me that ring.
　　　Ber. I'll lend it thee, my dear; but have no power
To give it from me.
　　　Dia.　　　　　　　Will you not, my lord?
　　　Ber. It is an honour longing to our house,　　　50
Bequeathed down from many ancestors,
Which were the greatest obloquy i' the world
In me to lose.
　　　Dia.　　　　Mine honour's such a ring:
My chastity's the jewel of our house,　　　　55
Bequeathed down from many ancestors,
Which were the greatest obloquy i' the world
In me to lose. Thus your own proper wisdom
Brings in the champion honour on my part
Against your vain assault.　　　　　　　60
　　　Ber.　　　　　　　Here, take my ring:
My house, mine honour, yea, my life, be thine,
And I'll be bid by thee.
　　　Dia. When midnight comes, knock at my chamberwindow:
I'll order take my mother shall not hear.　　　65
Now will I charge you in the band of truth,
When you have conquer'd my yet maiden bed,
Remain there but an hour, nor speak to me.
My reasons are most strong, and you shall know them
When back again this ring shall be deliver'd:　　70
And on your finger in the night I'll put
Another ring that, what in time proceeds,
May token to the future our past deeds.
Adieu, till then; then, fail not. You have won
A wife of me, though there my hope be done.　　75
　　　Ber. A heaven on earth I have won by wooing thee. 　*[Exit.]*
　　　Dia. For which live long to thank both heaven and me!
You may so in the end.
My mother told me just how he would woo
As if she sat in's heart; she says all men　　　80
Have the like oaths: he had sworn to marry me
When his wife's dead; therefore I'll lie with him
When I am buried. Since Frenchmen are so braid,
Marry that will, I live and die a maid:
Only in this disguise I think 't no sin　　　85
To cozen him that would unjustly win.　　　*Exit.*

---

31 **Jove's;** *cf. n.*　　33 **holding:** *consistency*　　36 **conditions:** *covenants*　**unseal'd;**
cf. n.　　40 **crafts:** *deceits*　　43 **Who then recovers:** *which then recover*　45 *Cf. n.*　　50
longing: *belonging*　　58 **proper:** *own (used intensively)*　　59 **on my part:** *in my be-*
half　　66 **band:** *bond*　　72 **what . . . proceeds:** *whatever happens in the future*　　73
token: *be witness of*　　83 **braid:** *deceitful*　　86 **cozen:** *deceive*

❧ SCENE THIRD ❦

[The Florentine Camp]

Enter the two French Captains [the Lords] and some two or three
Soldiers.

　1. Lord. You have not given him his mother's letter?

　2. Lord. I have delivered it an hour since: there is something
in 't that stings his nature, for on the reading it he changed
almost into another man.

　1. Lord. He has much worthy blame laid upon him for　　5
shaking off so good a wife and so sweet a lady.

　2. Lord. Especially he hath incurred the everlasting displeasure of the king, who had even tuned his bounty to sing happiness to him. I will tell you a thing, but you shall let it dwell
darkly with you.　　　　　　　　　　　　　　10

　1. Lord. When you have spoken it, 'tis dead, and I am
the grave of it.

　2. Lord. He hath perverted a young gentlewoman here in
Florence, of a most chaste renown; and this night he fleshes
his will in the spoil of her honour: he hath given her his　　15
monumental ring, and thinks himself made in the unchaste
composition.

　1. Lord. Now, God delay our rebellion! as we are ourselves,
what things are we!

　2. Lord. Merely our own traitors: and as in the common　20
course of all treasons, we still see them reveal themselves, till
they attain to their abhorred ends, so he that in this action
contrives against his own nobility, in his proper stream o'erflows himself.

　1. Lord. Is it not meant damnable in us, to be trumpeters 25
of our unlawful intents? We shall not then have his company
to-night?

　2. Lord. Not till after midnight, for he is dieted to his hour.

　1. Lord. That approaches apace: I would gladly have him see
his company anatomized, that he might take a measure of　　30
his own judgments, wherein so curiously he had set this
counterfeit.

　2. Lord. We will not meddle with him till he come, for
his presence must be the whip of the other.

　1. Lord. In the meantime what hear you of these wars?　　35

　2. Lord. I hear there is an overture of peace.

　1. Lord. Nay, I assure you, a peace concluded.

　2. Lord. What will Count Rousillon do then? will he travel
higher, or return again into France?

　1. Lord. I perceive by this demand, you are not altogether 40
of his council.

　2. Lord. Let it be forbid, sir; so should I be a great deal
of his act.

　1. Lord. Sir, his wife some two months since fled from his
house: her pretence is a pilgrimage to Saint Jaques le Grand; 45
which holy undertaking with most austere sanctimony she
accomplished; and, there residing, the tenderness of her
nature became as a prey to her grief; in fine, made a groan
of her last breath, and now she sings in heaven.

　2. Lord. How is this justified?　　　　　　　　50

---

5 **worthy:** *deserved*　　9, 10 **dwell . . . with:** *be kept secret by*　　14 **fleshes:** *gratifies*　15
spoil: *spoliation*　　16 **monumental:** *commemorative*　　17 **composition:** *compact*　18
God . . . rebellion: *God make us slow to rebel*　　20 **our own traitors:** *traitors to our-*
selves　　22 **ends:** *destruction*　　23, 24 **o'erflows:** *drowns*　　25, 26 **Is . . . intents;**
cf. n.　　28 **dieted to:** *fully occupied until*　　30 **company:** *companion*　　31 **curiously:**
carefully　　39 **higher:** *further into Italy*　　42, 43 **of his act:** *a partner in his actions*　45
pretence: *purpose*　　50 **justified:** *confirmed as true*

1. Lord. The stronger part of it by her own letters, which makes her story true, even to the point of her death: her death itself, which could not be her office to say is come, was faithfully confirmed by the rector of the place.

2. Lord. Hath the count all this intelligence?   55

1. Lord. Ay, and the particular confirmations, point from point, to the full arming of the verity.

2. Lord. I am heartily sorry that he'll be glad of this.

1. Lord. How mightily sometimes we make us comforts of our losses!   60

2. Lord. And how mightily some other times we drown our gain in tears! The great dignity that his valour hath here acquired for him shall at home be encountered with a shame as ample.

1. Lord. The web of our life is of a mingled yarn, good   65
and ill together: our virtues would be proud if our faults whipped them not; and our crimes would despair if they were not cherished by our virtues.

Enter a Messenger.

How now! where's your master?

Mess. He met the duke in the street, sir, of whom he   70
hath taken a solemn leave: his lordship will next morning for France. The duke hath offered him letters of commendations to the king.

2. Lord. They shall be no more than needful there, if they were more than they can commend.   75

Enter Count Rousillon.

1. Lord. They cannot be too sweet for the king's tartness. Here's his lordship now. How now, my lord! is 't not after midnight?

Ber. I have to-night dispatched sixteen businesses, a month's length apiece, by an abstract of success: I have congied with   80
the duke, done my adieu with his nearest, buried a wife, mourned for her, writ to my lady mother I am returning, entertained my convoy, and between these main parcels of dispatch effected many nicer needs: the last was the greatest, but that I have not ended yet.   85

2. Lord. If the business be of any difficulty, and this morning your departure hence, it requires haste of your lordship.

Ber. I mean, the business is not ended, as fearing to hear of it hereafter. But shall we have this dialogue between the fool and the soldier? Come, bring forth this counterfeit module: 90
has deceived me, like a double-meaning prophesier.

2. Lord. Bring him forth.   *[Exeunt Soldiers.]*
Has sat i' the stocks all night, poor gallant knave.

Ber. No matter; his heels have deserved it, in usurping his spurs so long. How does he carry himself?   95

1. Lord. I have told your lordship already, the stocks carry him. But to answer you as you would be understood, he weeps like a wench that had shed her milk: he hath confessed himself to Morgan—whom he supposes to be a friar—from the time of his remembrance to this very instant disaster of his   100
setting i' the stocks: and what think you he hath confessed?

Ber. Nothing of me, has a'?

2. Lord. His confession is taken, and it shall be read to his face: if your lordship be in 't, as I believe you are, you must have the patience to hear it.   105

Enter Parolles with his Interpreter [and other Soldiers].

Ber. A plague upon him! muffled! he can say nothing of me: hush! hush!

1. Lord. Hoodman come! *Portotartarossa.*

Inter. He calls for the tortures: what will you say without 'em?   110

Par. I will confess what I know without constraint: if ye pinch me like a pasty, I can say no more.

Inter. Bosko chimurcho.

1. Lord. Boblibindo chicurmurco.

Inter. You are a merciful general. Our general bids you   115
answer to what I shall ask you out of a note.

Par. And truly, as I hope to live.

Inter. 'First, demand of him how many horse the duke is strong.' What say you to that?

Par. Five or six thousand; but very weak and unserviceable: the troops are all scattered, and the commanders very poor rogues, upon my reputation and credit, and as I hope to live.

Inter. Shall I set down your answer so?

Par. Do: I'll take the sacrament on 't, how and which way you will.   125

Ber. All's one to him. What a past-saving slave is this!

1. Lord. Y' are deceived, my lord: this is Monsieur Parolles, the gallant militarist—that was his own phrase—that had the whole theoric of war in the knot of his scarf, and the practice in the chape of his dagger.   130

2. Lord. I will never trust a man again for keeping his sword clean; nor believe he can have everything in him by wearing his apparel neatly.

Inter. Well, that's set down.

Par. Five or six thousand horse, I said—I will say true—   135
or thereabouts, set down, for I'll speak truth.

1. Lord. He's very near the truth in this.

Ber. But I con him no thanks for 't, in the nature he delivers it.

Par. Poor rogues, I pray you, say.   140

Inter. Well, that's set down.

Par. I humbly thank you, sir. A truth's a truth; the rogues are marvellous poor.

Inter. 'Demand of him, of what strength they are a-foot.' What say you to that?   145

Par. By my troth, sir, if I were to live this present hour, I will tell true. Let me see: Spurio, a hundred and fifty; Sebastian, so many; Corambus, so many; Jacques, so many; Guiltian, Cosmo, Lodowick, and Gratii, two hundred fifty each; mine own company, Chitopher, Vaumond, Bentii, two hundred fifty each: so that the muster-file, rotten and sound, upon my life, amounts not to fifteen thousand poll; half of the which dare not shake the snow from off their cassocks, lest they shake themselves to pieces.

Ber. What shall be done to him?   155

1. Lord. Nothing, but let him have thanks. Demand of him my condition, and what credit I have with the duke.

Inter. Well, that's set down. 'You shall demand of him,

51 **stronger:** *greater*   54 **rector:** *governor*   57 **arming:** *corroboration*   74 **shall:** *would*   80 **abstract of success:** *successful summary proceeding*   **congied with:** *taken leave of*   81 **done ... nearest:** *said farewell to his suite*   82, 83 **entertained:** *engaged*   **main ... dispatch:** *chief pieces of business*   90 **module:** *model*   94 **usurping:** *unworthily wearing*   100 **instant:** *present*

129 **theoric:** *theory*   130 **chape:** *the metal part of the sheath*   138 **con ... thanks:** *am not grateful to him*   **in the nature:** *in view of the way in which*   146 **live ... hour:** *live but an hour*   153 **cassocks:** *military cloaks*   157 **condition:** *character*

whether one Captain Dumaine be i' the camp, a Frenchman;
what his reputation is with the duke; what his valour, 　*160*
honesty, and expertness in wars; or whether he thinks it were
not possible, with well-weighing sums of gold, to corrupt him
to a revolt.' What say you to this? what do you know of it?

Par. I beseech you, let me answer to the particular of the
inter'gatories: demand them singly. 　*165*

Inter. Do you know this Captain Dumaine?

Par. I know him: a' was a botcher's 'prentice in Paris, from
whence he was whipped for getting the shrieve's fool with
child; a dumb innocent, that could not say him nay.

　　　　　　　　　[Dumaine lifts up his hand in anger.]

Ber. Nay, by your leave, hold your hands; though I 　*170*
know his brains are forfeit to the next tile that falls.

Inter. Well, is this captain in the Duke of Florence's camp?

Par. Upon my knowledge he is, and lousy.

1. Lord. Nay, look not so upon me; we shall hear of your
lordship anon. 　*175*

Inter. What is his reputation with the duke?

Par. The duke knows him for no other but a poor officer of
mine, and writ to me this other day to turn him out o' the
band: I think I have his letter in my pocket.

Inter. Marry, we'll search. 　*180*

Par. In good sadness, I do not know: either it is there, or it
is upon a file with the duke's other letters in my tent.

Inter. Here 'tis; here's a paper; shall I read it to you?

Par. I do not know if it be it or no.

Ber. Our interpreter does it well. 　*185*

1. Lord. Excellently.

Inter. 'Dian, the count's a fool, and full of gold—'

Par. That is not the duke's letter, sir; that is an advertisement to a proper maid in Florence, one Diana, to take heed of
the allurement of one Count Rousillon, a foolish idle boy, 　*190*
but for all that very ruttish. I pray you, sir, put it up again.

Inter. Nay, I'll read it first, by your favour.

Par. My meaning in 't, I protest, was very honest in the behalf of the maid; for I knew the young count to be a dangerous and lascivious boy, who is a whale to virginity, and 　*195*
devours up all the fry it finds.

Ber. Damnable both-sides rogue!

Inter. 'When he swears oaths, bid him drop gold, and take it;
After he scores, he never pays the score:
Half won is match well made; match, and well make it; 　*200*
He ne'er pays after-debts; take it before,
And say a soldier, Dian, told thee this:
Men are to mell with, boys are not to kiss;
For count of this, the count's a fool, I know it,
Who pays before, but not when he does owe it. 　*205*
Thine, as he vow'd to thee in thine ear,
　　　　　　　　　　　　　Parolles.'

Ber. He shall be whipped through the army with this rime
in's forehead.

1. Lord. This is your devoted friend, sir, the manifold 　*210*
linguist and the armipotent soldier.

Ber. I could endure anything before but a cat, and now he's
a cat to me.

Inter. I perceive, sir, by our general's looks, we shall be fain
to hang you. 　*215*

Par. My life, sir, in any case! not that I am afraid to die,
but that, my offences being many, I would repent out the remainder of nature. Let me live, sir, in a dungeon, i' the stocks,
or anywhere, so I may live.

Inter. We'll see what may be done, so you confess freely: 　*220*
therefore, once more to this Captain Dumaine. You have
answered to his reputation with the duke and to his valour:
what is his honesty?

Par. He will steal, sir, an egg out of a cloister; for rapes and
ravishments he parallels Nessus; he professes not keeping of 　*225*
oaths; in breaking 'em he is stronger than Hercules; he will lie,
sir, with such volubility, that you would think truth were a
fool; drunkenness is his best virtue, for he will be swine-drunk,
and in his sleep he does little harm, save to his bed-clothes
about him; but they know his conditions, and lay him in 　*230*
straw. I have but little more to say, sir, of his honesty: he
has everything that an honest man should not have; what an
honest man should have, he has nothing.

1. Lord. I begin to love him for this.

Ber. For this description of thine honesty? A pox upon 　*235*
him for me! he's more and more a cat.

Inter. What say you to his expertness in war?

Par. Faith, sir, has led to the drum before the English tragedians—to belie him I will not—and more of his soldiership
I know not; except, in that country, he had the honour to 　*240*
be the officer at a place there called Mile-end, to instruct for
the doubling of files. I would do the man what honour I can,
but of this I am not certain.

1. Lord. He hath out-villained villainy so far, that the rarity
redeems him. 　*245*

Ber. A pox on him! he's a cat still.

Inter. His qualities being at this poor price, I need not to
ask you if gold will corrupt him to revolt.

Par. Sir, for a cardecu he will sell the fee-simple of his
salvation, the inheritance of it; and cut th' entail from all 　*250*
remainders, and a perpetual succession for it perpetually.

Inter. What's his brother, the other Captain Dumaine?

2. Lord. Why does he ask him of me?

Inter. What's he?

Par. E'en a crow o' the same nest; not altogether so great 　*255*
as the first in goodness, but greater a great deal in evil. He
excels his brother for a coward, yet his brother is reputed one
of the best that is. In a retreat he outruns any lackey; marry,
in coming on he has the cramp.

Inter. If your life be saved, will you undertake to betray 　*260*
the Florentine?

Par. Ay, and the captain of his horse, Count Rousillon.

Inter. I'll whisper with the general, and know his pleasure.

Par. [*Aside.*] I'll no more drumming; a plague of all drums!
Only to seem to deserve well, and to beguile the supposi- 　*265*
tion of that lascivious young boy the count, have I run into
this danger. Yet who would have suspected an ambush where
I was taken?

Inter. There is no remedy, sir, but you must die. The general says, you, that have so traitorously discovered the secrets of

---

164 particular: *detail*　**167 botcher's:** *mending tailor's*　**168 shrieve's fool:** *feeble-minded girl under the sheriff's guardianship*　**181 good sadness:** *all seriousness*　**188, 189 advertisement:** *admonition*　**191 ruttish:** *lascivious*　**196 fry:** *young fish*　**199 scores:** *incurs a debt*　**200** *Cf. n.*　**203 mell:** *deal*　**209 in's:** *on his*　**211 armipotent:** *powerful in arms*

217, 218 *I desire to spend the rest of my life in repentance*　**225 Nessus;** *cf. n.*　**238 led:** *carried*　**247 at ... price:** *of such low value*　**249 cardecu:** *quart d' écu, a small French coin*　**249–251 sell ... perpetually;** *cf. n.*　**259 coming on:** *advancing*　**265, 266 supposition:** *imagination*

your army, and made such pestiferous reports of men very
nobly held, can serve the world for no honest use: therefore
you must die. Come, headsman, off with his head.

   Par. O Lord, sir, let me live, or let me see my death!

   Inter. That shall you, and take your leave of all your friends.

                              [Unmuffling him.]

So, look about you: know you any here?

   Ber. Good morrow, noble captain.

   2. Lord. God bless you, Captain Parolles.

   1. Lord. God save you, noble captain.   *280*

   2. Lord. Captain, what greeting will you to my Lord Lafeu?
I am for France.

   1. Lord. Good captain, will you give me a copy of the
sonnet you writ to Diana in behalf of the Count Rousillon?
an I were not a very coward I'd compel it of you; but   *285*
fare you well.   *Exeunt [all except Parolles and Interpreter].*

   Inter. You are undone, captain, all but your scarf; that has a
knot on 't yet.

   Par. Who cannot be crushed with a plot?

   Inter. If you could find out a country where but women *290*
were that had received so much shame, you might begin an
impudent nation. Fare ye well, sir; I am for France too:
we shall speak of you there.   *Exit.*

   Par. Yet am I thankful: if my heart were great
'Twould burst at this. Captain I'll be no more;   *295*
But I will eat and drink, and sleep as soft
As captain shall: simply the thing I am
Shall make me live. Who knows himself a braggart,
Let him fear this; for it will come to pass
That every braggart shall be found an ass.   *300*
Rust, sword! cool, blushes! and Parolles, live
Safest in shame! being fool'd, by foolery thrive!
There's place and means for every man alive.
I'll after them   *Exit.*

❧ SCENE FOURTH ❧

[Florence. A Room in the Widow's House]
Enter Helen, Widow, and Diana.

   Hel. That you may well perceive I have not wrong'd you,
One of the greatest in the Christian world
Shall be my surety; 'fore whose throne 'tis needful,
Ere I can perfect mine intents, to kneel.
Time was I did him a desired office,   *5*
Dear almost as his life; which gratitude
Through flinty Tartar's bosom would peep forth,
And answer, thanks. I duly am inform'd
His Grace is at Marseilles; to which place
We have convenient convoy. You must know,   *10*
I am supposed dead: the army breaking,
My husband hies him home; where, heaven aiding,
And by the leave of my good lord the king,
We'll be before our welcome.

   Wid.   Gentle madam,   *15*
You never had a servant to whose trust

Your business was more welcome.

   Hel.   Nor you, mistress,
Ever a friend whose thoughts more truly labour
To recompense your love. Doubt not but heaven   *20*
Hath brought me up to be your daughter's dower,
As it hath fated her to be my motive
And helper to a husband. But, O strange men!
That can such sweet use make of what they hate,
When saucy trusting of the cozen'd thoughts   *25*
Defiles the pitchy night: so lust doth play
With what it loathes for that which is away
But more of this hereafter. You, Diana,
Under my poor instructions yet must suffer
Something in my behalf.   *30*

   Dia.   Let death and honesty
Go with your impositions, I am yours,
Upon your will to suffer.

   Hel.   Yet, I pray you:
But with the word the time will bring on summer, *35*
When briers shall have leaves as well as thorns,
And be as sweet as sharp. We must away;
Our wagon is prepar'd, and time revives us:
All's well that ends well: still the fine's the crown;
Whate'er the course, the end is the renown.   *Exeunt.* *40*

❧ SCENE FIFTH ❧

[Rousillon. A Room in the Countess's Palace]
Enter Clown, old Lady [the Countess], and Lafeu.

   Laf. No, no, no; your son was misled with a snipt-taffeta
fellow there, whose villainous saffron would have made all the
unbaked and doughy youth of a nation in his colour: your
daughter-in-law had been alive at this hour, and your son here
at home, more advanced by the king than by that red-tailed *5*
humble-bee I speak of.

   Count. I would I had not known him; it was the death of
the most virtuous gentlewoman that ever nature had praise for
creating. If she had partaken of my flesh, and cost me the
dearest groans of a mother, I could not have owed her a *10*
more rooted love.

   Laf. 'Twas a good lady, 'twas a good lady: we may pick a
thousand sallets ere we light on such another herb.

   Clo. Indeed, sir, she was the sweet-marjoram of the sallet,
or, rather the herb of grace.   *15*

   Laf. They are not herbs, you knave; they are nose-herbs.

   Clo. I am no great Nebuchadnezzar, sir; I have not much
skill in grass.

   Laf. Whether dost thou profess thyself, a knave, or a fool?

   Clo. A fool, sir, at a woman's service, and a knave at a *20*
man's.

   Laf. Your distinction?

   Clo. I would cozen the man of his wife, and do his service.

   Laf. So you were a knave at his service, indeed.

   Clo. And I would give his wife my bauble, sir, to do her *25*
service.

---

22 motive: *promoter*   **25 saucy:** *wanton*   **31, 32 Let ... impositions;** *cf. n.*   **33**
Upon: *in accordance with*   **34 Yet:** *for a while*   **35 with the word:** *almost as I*
speak   **39 fine's:** *end is*   **1 snipt-taffeta:** *dressed in slashed taffeta garments*   **2 saffron:**
yellow dye (used in pastry)   **10 dearest:** *most grievous*   **13 sallets:** *salads*   **15 herb of**
grace: *rue*   **16 herbs:** *edible herbs*   **nose-herbs:** *scented flowers*

282 I am for: *I am about to set out for*   **285 very:** *complete*   **4 perfect mine intents:**
carry out my purposes   **9 Marseilles;** *cf. n.*   **11 breaking:** *disbanding*   **14 be ...**
welcome: *arrive before we are expected*

Laf. I will subscribe for thee, thou art both knave and fool.

Clo. At your service.

Laf. No, no, no.

Clo. Why, sir, if I cannot serve you, I can serve as great   *30*
a prince as you are.

Laf. Who's that? a Frenchman?

Clo. Faith, sir, a' has an English name; but his fisnomy is
more hotter in France than there.

Laf. What prince is that?   *35*

Clo. The black prince, sir; *alias,* the prince of darkness;
alias, the devil.

Laf. Hold thee, there's my purse. I give thee not this to
suggest thee from thy master thou talkest of: serve him still.

Clo. I am a woodland fellow, sir, that always loved a   *40*
great fire; and the master I speak of ever keeps a good fire.
But, sure, he is the prince of the world; let his nobility remain
in's court. I am for the house with the narrow gate, which I
take to be too little for pomp to enter: some that humble
themselves may; but the many will be too chill and tender,   *45*
and they'll be for the flowery way that leads to the broad
gate and the great fire.

Laf. Go thy ways, I begin to be aweary of thee; and I tell
thee so before, because I would not fall out with thee. Go thy
ways: let my horses be well looked to, without any tricks.   *50*

Clo. If I put any tricks upon 'em, sir, they shall be jade's
tricks, which are their own right by the law of nature.

                                              Exit.

Laf. A shrewd knave and an unhappy.

Count. So a' is. My lord that's gone made himself much
sport out of him: by his authority he remains here, which   *55*
he thinks is a patent for his sauciness; and, indeed, he has
no pace, but runs where he will.

Laf. I like him well; 'tis not amiss. And I was about to tell
you, since I heard of the good lady's death, and that my lord
your son was upon his return home, I moved the king my   *60*
master to speak in the behalf of my daughter; which, in the minority of them both, his majesty, out of a self-gracious remembrance, did first propose. His highness hath promised me to do it;
and to stop by the displeasure he hath conceived against your
son, there is no fitter matter. How does your ladyship like it?   *65*

Count. With very much content, my lord, and I wish it
happily effected.

Laf. His highness comes post from Marseilles, of as able body
as when he numbered thirty: a' will be here to-morrow, or I am
deceived by him that in such intelligence hath seldom failed.   *70*

Count. It rejoices me that I hope I shall see him ere I die. I
have letters that my son will be here to-night: I shall beseech
your lordship to remain with me till they meet together.

Laf. Madam, I was thinking with what manners I might
safely be admitted.   *75*

Count. You need but plead your honourable privilege.

Laf. Lady, of that I have made a bold charter; but I thank
my God it holds yet.

[Re-]enter Clown.

Clo. O madam! yonder's my lord your son with a patch of

velvet on's face: whether there be a scar under it or no, the velvet knows; but 'tis a goodly patch of velvet. His left cheek is a
cheek of two pile and a half, but his right cheek is worn bare.

Laf. A scar nobly got, or a noble scar, is a good livery of
honour; so belike is that.

Clo. But it is your carbonadoed face.   *85*

Laf. Let us go see your son, I pray you: I long to talk
with the young noble soldier.

Clo. Faith, there's a dozen of 'em, with delicate fine hats
and most courteous feathers, which bow the head and nod at
every man.   *Exeunt.*   *90*

ACT FIFTH ❧ SCENE FIRST

[Marseilles. A Street]
Enter Helen, Widow, and Diana, with two Attendants.

Hel. But this exceeding posting, day and night,
Must wear your spirits low; we cannot help it:
But since you have made the days and nights as one,
To wear your gentle limbs in my affairs,
Be bold you do so grow in my requital   *5*
As nothing can unroot you. In happy time!

Enter a gentle Astringer.

This man may help me to his majesty's ear,
If he would spend his power. God save you, sir.

Gent. And you.

Hel. Sir, I have seen you in the court of France.   *10*

Gent. I have been sometimes there.

Hel. I do presume, sir, that you are not fallen
From the report that goes upon your goodness;
And therefore, goaded with most sharp occasions,
Which lay nice manners by, I put you to   *15*
The use of your own virtues, for the which
I shall continue thankful.

Gent.   What's your will?

Hel. That it will please you
To give this poor petition to the king,   *20*
And aid me with that store of power you have
To come into his presence.

Gent. The king's not here.

Hel.   Not here, sir!

Gent.   Not, indeed: *25*
He hence remov'd last night, and with more haste
Than is his use.

Wid.   Lord, how we lose our pains!

Hel. All's well that ends well yet,
Though time seem so adverse and means unfit.   *30*
I do beseech you, whither is he gone?

Gent. Marry, as I take it, to Rousillon,
Whither I am going.

Hel.   I do beseech you, sir,
Since you are like to see the king before me,   *35*

33 **fisnomy:** *physiognomy*   **39 suggest:** *entice*   **51, 52 jade's tricks;** *cf. n.*   **53 shrewd:**
sharp of speech   **unhappy:** *mischievous*   **56 patent:** *license*   **57 pace:** *training*   **62
out … remembrance:** *graciously and of his own motion*   **69 numbered thirty:** *was thirty
years old*   **74, 75 with … admitted:** *how I might becomingly gain admittance*   **77 made
… charter:** *made daring use*

82 two … half; *cf. n.*   **83 livery:** *badge*   **85 carbonadoed:** *scored across, slashed*   **1
posting:** *hastening*   **5 bold:** *sure*   **grow … requital:** *strengthen my intention to reward
you*   **6 In … time:** *this happens favorably*   **S. d. gentle Astringer:** *gentleman-fal-
coner*   **8 spend:** *use*   **13 goes upon:** *is current concerning*   **14 sharp occasions:** *keen
necessities*   **15 lay … by:** *put aside finical manners*   **put you to:** *urge upon you*   **27
use:** *custom*

Commend the paper to his gracious hand;
Which I presume shall render you no blame
But rather make you thank your pains for it.
I will come after you with what good speed
Our means will make us means.   40

Gent.   This I'll do for you.

Hel. And you shall find yourself to be well thank'd,
Whate'er falls more. We must to horse again:
Go, go, provide.   *[Exeunt.]*

❧ SCENE SECOND ❧

[Rousillon. The inner Court of the Countess's Palace]
Enter Clown and Parolles.

Par. Good Monsieur Lavache, give my Lord Lafeu this
letter. I have ere now, sir, been better known to you, when I
have held familiarity with fresher clothes; but I am now, sir,
muddied in Fortune's mood, and smell somewhat strong of
her strong displeasure.   5

Clo. Truly, Fortune's displeasure is but sluttish if it smell
so strongly as thou speakest of: I will henceforth eat no fish
of Fortune's buttering. Prithee, allow the wind.

Par. Nay, you need not to stop your nose, sir: I spake
but by a metaphor.   10

Clo. Indeed, sir, if your metaphor stink, I will stop my nose;
or against any man's metaphor. Prithee, get thee further.

Par. Pray you, sir, deliver me this paper.

Clo. Foh! prithee, stand away: a paper from Fortune's close-
stool to give to a nobleman! Look, here he comes himself.   15

Enter Lafeu.

Here is a purr of Fortune's, sir, or of Fortune's cat—but not a
musk-cat—that has fallen into the unclean fishpond of her displeasure, and, as he says, is muddied withal. Pray you, sir, use
the carp as you may, for he looks like a poor, decayed, ingenious, foolish, rascally knave. I do pity his distress in my   20
similes of comfort, and leave him to your lordship.   *[Exit.]*

Par. My lord, I am a man whom Fortune hath cruelly
scratched.

Laf. And what would you have me do? 'tis too late to pare
her nails now. Wherein have you played the knave with   25
Fortune that she should scratch you, who of herself is a good
lady, and would not have knaves thrive long under [her]?
There's a cardecu for you. Let the justices make you and
Fortune friends; I am for other business.

Par. I beseech your honour to hear me one single word.   30

Laf. You beg a single penny more: come, you shall ha 't;
save your word.

Par. My name, my good lord, is Parolles.

Laf. You beg more than [one] word then. Cox my passion!
give me your hand. How does your drum?   35

Par. O, my good lord! you were the first that found me.

Laf. Was I, in sooth? and I was the first that lost thee.

Par. It lies in you, my lord, to bring me in some grace, for
you did bring me out.

Laf. Out upon thee, knave! dost thou put upon me at   40
once both the office of God and the devil? one brings thee in
grace and the other brings thee out. *[Trumpets sound.]* The
king's coming; I know by his trumpets. Sirrah, inquire further
after me; I had talk of you last night: though you are a fool
and a knave, you shall eat: go to, follow.   45

Par. I praise God for you.

                                              [Exeunt.]

❧ SCENE THIRD ❧

[The Same. A Room in the Countess's Palace]
Flourish. Enter King, old Lady [the Countess], Lafeu, the two French
Lords, with Attendants.

King. We lost a jewel of her, and our esteem
Was made much poorer by it: but your son,
As mad in folly, lack'd the sense to know
Her estimation home.

Count.   'Tis past, my liege;   5
And I beseech your majesty to make it
Natural rebellion, done i' the blaze of youth,
When oil and fire, too strong for reason's force,
O'erbears it and burns on.

King.   My honour'd lady,   10
I have forgiven and forgotten all,
Though my revenges were high bent upon him,
And watch'd the time to shoot.

Laf.   This I must say—
But first I beg my pardon—the young lord   15
Did to his majesty, his mother, and his lady,
Offence of mighty note, but to himself
The greatest wrong of all: he lost a wife
Whose beauty did astonish the survey
Of richest eyes, whose words all ears took captive,   20
Whose dear perfection hearts that scorn'd to serve
Humbly call'd mistress.

King.   Praising what is lost
Makes the remembrance dear. Well, call him hither;
We are reconcil'd, and the first view shall kill   25
All repetition. Let him not ask our pardon:
The nature of his great offence is dead,
And deeper than oblivion we do bury
Th' incensing relics of it. Let him approach,
A stranger, no offender; and inform him   30
So 'tis our will he should.

Gent.   I shall, my liege.   *[Exit.]*

King. What says he to your daughter? have you spoke?

Laf. All that he is hath reference to your highness.

King. Then shall we have a match. I have letters sent me,   35
That sets him high in fame.

Enter Count Bertram.

Laf.   He looks well on 't.

---

43 **Whate'er falls more:** *whatever else occurs*   3 **held familiarity:** *been acquainted*   4
mood: *anger*   8 **allow the wind:** *let me get to windward of you*   28, 29 **Let . . . friends;**
cf. n.   34 **Cox my passion:** *God's passion*   38 **in some grace:** *into some favor*

1 **our esteem:** *the value of our kingdom*   3 **As:** *as if*   4 **estimation:** *worth*   **home:**
thoroughly   6 **make:** *consider*   12 **high bent upon:** *strongly directed against*   20 **rich-**
est: *most experienced*   26 **repetition:** *reference to what is past*   34 **hath reference to:** *is*
dependent upon   37 **He . . . on 't:** *his appearance bears it out*

King. I am not a day of season,
For thou mayst see a sunshine and a hail
In me at once; but to the brightest beams   40
Distracted clouds give way: so stand thou forth;
The time is fair again.
    Ber.   My high-repented blames,
Dear sovereign, pardon to me.
    King.   All is whole;   45
Not one word more of the consumed time.
Let's take the instant by the forward top,
For we are old, and on our quick'st decrees
Th' inaudible and noiseless foot of time
Steals ere we can effect them. You remember   50
The daughter of this lord?
    Ber. Admiringly, my liege:
At first I stuck my choice upon her, ere my heart
Durst make too bold a herald of my tongue,
Where the impression of mine eye enfixing,   55
Contempt his scornful perspective did lend me,
Which warp'd the line of every other favour;
Scorn'd a fair colour, or express'd it stolen;
Extended or contracted all proportions
To a most hideous object. Thence it came   60
That she, whom all men prais'd, and whom myself,
Since I have lost, have lov'd, was in mine eye
The dust that did offend it.
    King.   Well excus'd:
That thou didst love her, strikes some scores away   65
From the great compt. But love that comes too late,
Like a remorseful pardon slowly carried,
To the great sender turns a sour offence,
Crying, 'That's good that's gone.' Our rash faults
Make trivial price of serious things we have,   70
Not knowing them until we know their grave:
Oft our displeasures, to ourselves unjust,
Destroy our friends and after weep their dust:
Our own love waking cries to see what's done,
While shameful hate sleeps out the afternoon.   75
Be this sweet Helen's knell, and now forget her.
Send forth your amorous token for fair Maudlin:
The main consents are had; and here we'll stay
To see our widower's second marriage-day,
Which better than the first, O dear heaven, bless!   80
Or, ere they meet, in me, O nature, cesse!
    Laf. Come on, my son, in whom my house's name
Must be digested, give a favour from you
To sparkle in the spirits of my daughter,
That she may quickly come.   *[Bertram gives a ring.]*   85
                By my old beard,
And every hair that's on 't, Helen, that's dead,
Was a sweet creature; such a ring as this,
The last that e'er I took her leave at court,
I saw upon her finger.   90
    Ber.   Hers it was not.
    King. Now, pray you, let me see it; for mine eye,
While I was speaking, oft was fasten'd to 't.—

This ring was mine; and, when I gave it Helen,
I bade her, if her fortunes ever stood   95
Necessitied to help, that by this token
I would relieve her. Had you that craft to reave her
Of what should stead her most?
    Ber.   My gracious sovereign,
Howe'er it pleases you to take it so,   100
The ring was never hers.
    Count.   Son, on my life,
I have seen her wear it; and she reckon'd it
At her life's rate.
    Laf.   I am sure I saw her wear it.   105
    Ber. You are deceiv'd, my lord, she never saw it:
In Florence was it from a casement thrown me,
Wrapp'd in a paper, which contain'd the name
Of her that threw it. Noble she was, and thought
I stood ingag'd: but when I had subscrib'd   110
To mine own fortune, and inform'd her fully
I could not answer in that course of honour
As she had made the overture, she ceas'd
In heavy satisfaction, and would never
Receive the ring again.   115
    King.   Plutus himself,
That knows the tinct and multiplying medicine,
Hath not in nature's mystery more science
Than I have in this ring: 'twas mine, 'twas Helen's,
Whoever gave it you. Then, if you know   120
That you are well acquainted with yourself,
Confess 'twas hers, and by what rough enforcement
You got it from her. She call'd the saints to surety,
That she would never put it from her finger,
Unless she gave it to yourself in bed,   125
Where you have never come, or sent it us
Upon her great disaster.
    Ber.   She never saw it.
    King. Thou speak'st it falsely, as I love mine honour,
And mak'st conjectural fears to come into me   130
Which I would fain shut out. If it should prove
That thou art so inhuman—'twill not prove so—
And yet I know not: thou didst hate her deadly,
And she is dead; which nothing, but to close
Her eyes myself, could win me to believe,   135
More than to see this ring. Take him away.
                       [Guards seize Bertram.]
My fore-past proofs, howe'er the matter fall,
Shall tax my fears of little vanity,
Having vainly fear'd too little. Away with him!
We'll sift this matter further.   140
    Ber.   If you shall prove
This ring was ever hers, you shall as easy
Prove that I husbanded her bed in Florence,
Where yet she never was.   *[Exit guarded.]*
    King. I am wrapp'd in dismal thinkings.   145

    Enter a Gentleman [the Astringer].

---

38 of season: *seasonable*   **43 high-repented blames:** *deeply repented faults*   **46 consumed:** *past*   **47 instant:** *present moment*   **forward top:** *forelock*   **56 perspective:** *instrument for producing optical illusions*   **58 express'd:** *declared*   **66 compt:** *account*   **75 Cf. n.**   **81 cesse:** *cease*   **83 digested:** *amalgamated*   **89 The last:** *the last time*

96 Necessitied to help: *in need of help*   **110 ingag'd:** *unengaged*   **110, 111 subscrib'd . . . fortune:** *admitted the state of my fortunes*   **112, 113 I . . . overture:** *I could not pursue the honorable course she suggested*   **114 heavy satisfaction:** *sorrowful acquiescence*   **117 tinct:** *tincture*   **multiplying medicine:** *chemical which multiplies gold*   **118 science:** *knowledge*   **120, 121 if . . . yourself:** *if you know what is best for yourself*   **127 Upon:** *at the time of*   **137, 138 My . . . little;** *cf. n.*

Gent.   Gracious sovereign,
Whether I have been to blame or no, I know not:
Here's a petition from a Florentine,
Who hath for four or five removes come short
To tender it herself. I undertook it,   *150*
Vanquish'd thereto by the fair grace and speech
Of the poor suppliant, who by this I know
Is here attending: her business looks in her
With an importing visage, and she told me,
In a sweet verbal brief, it did concern   *155*
Your highness with herself.

    [King reads] a Letter. 'Upon his many protestations to marry
me when his wife was dead, I blush to say it, he won me.
Now is the Count Rousillon a widower: his vows are forfeited
to me, and my honour's paid to him. He told from Florence,
taking no leave, and I follow him to his country for justice.
Grant it me, O king! in you it best lies; otherwise a seducer
flourishes, and a poor maid is undone.

                                        Diana Capilet.'

    Laf. I will buy me a son-in-law in a fair, and toll for   *165*
this: I'll none of him.

    King. The heavens have thought well on thee, Lafeu,
To bring forth this discovery. Seek these suitors. Go speedily
and bring again the count.   *[Exeunt some Attendants.]*

                        Enter Bertram [guarded].

I am afeard the life of Helen, lady,   *170*
Was foully snatch'd.

    Count.   Now, justice on the doers!

    King. I wonder, sir, sith wives are monsters to you,
And that you fly them as you swear them lordship,
Yet you desire to marry.   *175*

            Enter Widow, Diana, and Parolles [with Attendants].

                        What woman's that?

    Dia. I am, my lord, a wretched Florentine,
Derived from the ancient Capilet:
My suit, as I do understand, you know,
And therefore know how far I may be pitied.   *180*

    Wid. I am her mother, sir, whose age and honour
Both suffer under this complaint we bring,
And both shall cease, without your remedy.

    King. Come hither, count; do you know these women?

    Ber. My lord, I neither can nor will deny   *185*
But that I know them: do they charge me further?

    Dia. Why do you look so strange upon your wife?

    Ber. She's none of mine, my lord.

    Dia.   If you shall marry,
You give away this hand, and that is mine;   *190*
You give away heaven's vows, and those are mine;
You give away myself, which is known mine;
For I by vow am so embodied yours
That she which marries you must marry me:
Either both or none.   *195*

    Laf. [To Bertram.] Your reputation comes too short for
my daughter: you are no husband for her.

    Ber. My lord, this is a fond and desperate creature,
Whom sometime I have laugh'd with: let your highness
Lay a more noble thought upon mine honour   *200*
Than for to think that I would sink it here.

    King. Sir, for my thoughts, you have them ill to friend,
Till your deeds gain them: fairer prove your honour,
Than in my thought it lies.

    Dia.   Good my lord,   *205*
Ask him upon his oath, if he does think
He had not my virginity.

    King. What sayst thou to her?

    Ber.   She's impudent, my lord;
And was a common gamester to the camp.   *210*

    Dia. He does me wrong, my lord; if I were so,
He might have bought me at a common price:
Do not believe him. O! behold this ring,
Whose high respect and rich validity
Did lack a parallel; yet for all that   *215*
He gave it to a commoner o' the camp,
If I be one.

    Count.   He blushes, and 'tis hit:
Of six preceding ancestors, that gem
Conferr'd by testament to the sequent issue,   *220*
Hath it been ow'd and worn. This is his wife:
That ring's a thousand proofs.

    King.   Methought you said
You saw one here in court could witness it.

    Dia. I did, my lord, but loath am to produce   *225*
So bad an instrument: his name's Parolles.

                                [Exit Parolles covertly.]

    Laf. I saw the man to-day, if man he be.

    King. Find him, and bring him hither.   *[Exit an Attendant.]*

    Ber.   What of him?   *230*
He's quoted for a most perfidious slave,
With all the spots of the world tax'd and debosh'd,
Whose nature sickens but to speak a truth.
Am I or that or this for what he'll utter,
That will speak anything?   *235*

    King.   She hath that ring of yours.

    Ber. I think she has: certain it is I lik'd her,
And boarded her i' the wanton way of youth.
She knew her distance and did angle for me,
Madding my eagerness with her restraint,   *240*
As all impediments in fancy's course
Are motives of more fancy; and, in fine,
Her infinite cunning, with her modern grace,
Subdued me to her rate: she got the ring,
And I had that which any inferior might   *245*
At market-price have bought.

    Dia.   I must be patient;
You, that have turn'd off a first so noble wife,
May justly diet me. I pray you yet—
Since you lack virtue I will lose a husband—   *250*
Send for your ring; I will return it home,
And give me mine again.

149 removes: *days' journeys*   **149, 150 come . . . tender:** *fallen short of tendering*   **153, 154 looks . . . visage:** *seems, from her appearance, to be important*   **156 with:** *as well as*   **162 in . . . lies:** *it is most in your power*   **165 toll for:** *take out a license to sell*   **173 sith:** *since*   **178 Derived:** *descended*   **183 cease:** *die*

202 you . . . friend: *they are unfriendly to you*   **210 gamester:** *harlot*   **214 respect:** *esteem*   **validity:** *value*   **218 'tis hit:** *it is discovered*   **226 instrument:** *agent*   **231 quoted:** *cited*   **234** *Am I to be judged according to what he will say?*   **240 Madding:** *maddening*   **243 modern:** *commonplace*   **244 Subdued . . . rate:** *forced me to agree to her price*   **249 diet me:** *deprive me of my due*

Ber.   I have it not.

King. What ring was yours, I pray you?

Dia.   Sir, much like   255
The same upon your finger.

King. Know you this ring? This ring was his of late.

Dia. And this was it I gave him, being a-bed.

King. The story then goes false you threw it him
Out of a casement.   260

Dia.   I have spoke the truth.

[Re-]enter Parolles [with Attendant.]

Ber. My lord, I do confess the ring was hers.

King. You boggle shrewdly, every feather starts you.
Is this the man you speak of?

Dia.   Ay, my lord.   265

King. Tell me, sirrah, but tell me true, I charge you,
Not fearing the displeasure of your master—
Which on your just proceeding I'll keep off—
By him and by this woman here what know you?

Par. So please your majesty, my master hath been an   270
honourable gentleman. Tricks he hath had in him, which
gentlemen have.

King. Come, come to the purpose: did he love this woman?

Par. Faith, sir, he did love her; but how?

King. How, I pray you?   275

Par. He did love her, sir, as a gentleman loves a woman.

King. How is that?

Par. He loved her, sir, and loved her not.

King. As thou art a knave, and no knave,—what an
equivocal companion is this!   280

Par. I am a poor man, and at your majesty's command.

Laf. He's a good drum, my lord, but a naughty orator.

Dia. Do you know he promised me marriage?

Par. Faith, I know more than I'll speak.

King. But wilt thou not speak all thou knowest?   285

Par. Yes, so please your majesty. I did go between them, as
I said; but more than that, he loved her, for, indeed, he was
mad for her, and talked of Satan, and of limbo, and of Furies,
and I know not what: yet I was in that credit with them at
that time, that I knew of their going to bed, and of other   290
motions, as promising her marriage, and things which would
derive me ill will to speak of: therefore I will not speak what
I know.

King. Thou hast spoken all already, unless thou canst say
they are married: but thou art too fine in thy evidence;   295
therefore stand aside. This ring, you say, was yours?

Dia. Ay, my good lord.

King. Where did you buy it? or who gave it you?

Dia. It was not given me, nor I did not buy it.

King. Who lent it you?   300

Dia.   It was not lent me neither.

King. Where did you find it, then?

Dia.   I found it not.

King. If it were yours by none of all these ways, How
could you give it him?   305

Dia.   I never gave it him.

Laf. This woman's an easy glove, my lord: she goes off and
on at pleasure.

King. This ring was mine: I gave it his first wife.

Dia. It might be yours or hers, for aught I know.   310

King. Take her away; I do not like her now.
To prison with her; and away with him.
Unless thou tell'st me where thou hadst this ring
Thou diest within this hour.

Dia.   I'll never tell you.   315

King. Take her away.

Dia.   I'll put in bail, my liege.

King. I think thee now some common customer.

Dia. By Jove, if ever I knew man, 'twas you.

King. Wherefore hast thou accus'd him all this while?   320

Dia. Because he's guilty, and he is not guilty.
He knows I am no maid, and he'll swear to 't;
I'll swear I am a maid, and he knows not.
Great king, I am no strumpet, by my life;
I am either maid, or else this old man's wife.   325

[Pointing to Lafeu.]

King. She does abuse our ears: to prison with her!

Dia. Good mother, fetch my bail.   *[Exit Widow.]*
Stay, royal sir;
The jeweller that owes the ring is sent for,
And he shall surety me. But for this lord,   330
Who hath abus'd me, as he knows himself,
Though yet he never harm'd me, here I quit him:
He knows himself my bed he hath defil'd,
And at that time he got his wife with child:
Dead though she be, she feels her young one kick: 335
So there's my riddle: one that's dead is quick;
And now behold the meaning.

Enter Helen and Widow.

King.   Is there no exorcist
Beguiles the truer office of mine eyes?
Is 't real that I see?   340

Hel.   No, my good lord;
'Tis but the shadow of a wife you see;
The name and not the thing.

Ber.   Both, both. O pardon!

Hel. O my good lord! when I was like this maid,   345
I found you wondrous kind. There is your ring;
And, look you, here's your letter; this it says:
'When from my finger you can get this ring,
And are by me with child, &c.' This is done:
Will you be mine, now you are doubly won?   350

Ber. If she, my liege, can make me know this clearly,
I'll love her dearly, ever, ever dearly.

Hel. If it appear not plain, and prove untrue,
Deadly divorce step between me and you!
O! my dear mother, do I see you living?   355

Laf. Mine eyes smell onions; I shall weep anon.
[To Parolles.] Good Tom Drum, lend me a handkercher:
so, I thank thee. Wait on me home, I'll make sport with thee:
let thy curtsies alone, they are scurvy ones.

King. Let us from point to point this story know,   360

---

263 boggle shrewdly: *change about vilely*   **starts:** *startles*   **268 on ... proceeding:** *if you act honorably*   **269 By:** *concerning*   **282 drum:** *drummer*   **naughty:** *worthless*   **291 motions:** *acts*   **295 fine:** *finical*

318 customer: *harlot*   **332 quit:** *acquit*   **336 quick:** *alive, with child (used punningly)*   **338 exorcist:** *raiser of dead spirits*

To make the even truth in pleasure flow.
[To Diana.] If thou be'st yet a fresh uncropped flower,
Choose thou thy husband, and I'll pay thy dower;
For I can guess that by thy honest aid
Thou kept'st a wife herself, thyself a maid.   365
Of that, and all the progress, more and less,
Resolvedly more leisure shall express:
All yet seems well; and if it end so meet,
The bitter past, more welcome is the sweet.   *Flourish.*

❧ EPILOGUE ❧

Spoken by the King.

The king's a beggar, now the play is done:
All is well ended if this suit be won
That you express content; which we will pay,
With strife to please you, day exceeding day:
Ours be your patience then, and yours our parts;   5
Your gentle hands lend us, and take our hearts.

Exeunt omnes.

❧ FINIS ❧

361 **even:** *straightforward*   366 **progress:** *course of the affair*   367 **Resolvedly:** *until all is explained*   368 **meet:** *fittingly*

6 **hands:** *applause*

NOTES

I.i.47. *I do affect a sorrow indeed, but I have it too.* Helena means that she affects a grief for her father, but feels a real grief at the departure of Bertram. Her other cryptic utterances in this scene hint at her love for Bertram, which she conceals behind a veil of obscure and ambiguous speech.

I.i.50, 51. *If the living be enemy to the grief, the excess makes it soon mortal.* 'If Bertram returned your love, your joy would overbalance your grief.'

I.i.53. *How understand me that?* Lafeu's question refers to the Countess' remark: he has just perceived that it contained some hidden meaning. Perhaps, as Coleridge suggests, Lafeu and Bertram speak at once.

I.i.66, 67. *He cannot want the best That shall attend his love.* The sense is obscure. Perhaps it is that Bertram can never lack the best service of those who, like Lafeu, follow him because they love him.

I.i.69, 70. *The best wishes that can be forged in your thoughts be servants to you!* 'May your dearest wishes be fulfilled.'

I.i.75, 76. *And these great tears grace his remembrance more Than those I shed for him.* The tears she now sheds for Bertram are, to those who mistake their cause, a greater tribute to her father than those she shed at his death.

I.i.83, 84. *In his bright radiance and collateral light Must I be comforted, not in his sphere.* An allusion to the Ptolemaic system of astronomy, according to which there were eight concentric spheres surrounding the earth. Each star or planet was limited to one of these spheres, but its light penetrated the others.

I.i.99. *Looks.* The third person plural present indicative of Shakespearean verbs not infrequently end in s: cf. II. iii. 124, III. iv. 16, III. v. 22.

I.i.103, 104. *No. And no.* Parolles disclaims any right to the title of monarch, and Helena in turn repudiates the name of queen.

I.i.132. *should be buried in highways, out of all sanctified limit.* It was forbidden to bury suicides in consecrated ground: they were frequently interred at a crossroads.

I.i.135. *his.* The regular possessive case of 'it' in Shakespeare. 'Its' occurs but seldom.

I.i.154–165. Helena catalogues the endearing nicknames by which Bertram will address his (supposititious) sweethearts at the French court. Under the stress of dissembling her emotion she speaks somewhat incoherently.

I.i.185, 186. *predominant, retrograde.* Astrological terms. A planet is generally benign in its influence when it is predominant, and malignant when it is retrograde.

I.i.192. *a virtue of a good wing.* A reference to the popular sport of falconry. The insinuation is that Parolles is apt in flight, which would be a virtue in a hawk, but which is a reproach to a soldier.

I.i.198, 199. *When thou hast leisure, say thy prayers; when thou hast none, remember thy friends.* Parolles is already affecting the cynical philosophy which he believes suitable to a courtier. The advice may be paraphrased, 'Say your prayers when you can find nothing better to do, and remember your friends only when you are too busy to serve them.'

I.i.207, 208. *The mightiest space in fortune nature brings To join like likes, and kiss like native things.* 'Across the gulf of the greatest disparity in fortune, nature brings kindred spirits to join each other, and to kiss like people born to each other's society.'

I.ii. 1. Lord. The 1. Lord and 2. Lord of this scene are, in the Folio, called '1 Lo. G.' and '2 Lo. E.' The initials, as Capell suggested, are probably those of the actors who played these parts. These initials are used in all the other scenes (II. i, III. i, ii, vi, IV. i, iii) in which the two French lords appear, although the title preceding the initial is sometimes 'Lord,' sometimes 'French' and sometimes 'Cap[tain].' At the beginning of IV. i the 1. Lord is described by the Folio as '1 Lord E.,' and the error in the initial persists throughout the scene. It is clear from the dialogue in III. vi and IV. iii that it is '1 Lord G.' who undertakes and carries out the capture of Parolles.

I.ii.39–41. *but they may jest Till their own scorn return to them unnoted Ere they can hide their levity in honour.* 'Your father had the same airy flights of satirical wit with the young lords of the present time, but they do not what he did, hide their unnoted levity in honour, cover petty faults with great merit.' (Johnson.)

I.ii.42–44. *So like a courtier, contempt nor bitterness Were in his pride or sharpness; if they were, His equal had awak'd them.* 'As was fitting in a courtier, he exhibited neither contempt in his pride, nor bitterness in his sharp strokes of wit, except when he was provoked by an equal.'

I.ii.50, 51. *Making them proud of his humility In their poor praise he humbled.* 'Making them proud by his humble acceptance of their praises, which he rendered inadequate by the nobility of his actions.'

I.ii.57, 58. *So in approof lives not his epitaph As in your royal speech.* 'His virtues are testified to nowhere so eloquently as in your royal speech.'

I.iii.45, 46. *young Charbon the puritan, and old Poysam the papist.* The two names are probably corruptions of 'Chairbonne' and 'Poisson,' referring to the lenten diets of the two sects.

I.iii.47, 48. *joul horns together.* The standing Elizabethan jest alluding to the horns that were supposed to grow upon the forehead of a wronged husband.

I.iii.56. *cuckoo.* Another stock pleasantry on the same subject, playing on the words 'cuckoo' and 'cuckold.' Cf. *Love's Labour's Lost,* V. ii. 940–948.

I.iii.82–84. The puritan clergy thought the surplice savoured too much of Roman Catholicism: they preferred to wear a simple black gown. However, as the laws of the church required the use of the surplice, they wore it, but *over* the gown.

I.iii.136, 137. *That this distemper'd messenger of wet, The many-colour'd Iris, rounds thine eye.* Henley explains that this as a reference to 'that suffusion of colours which glimmers around the sight when the eyelashes are wet with tears.'

II.i.13–15. *let higher Italy—Those bated that inherit but the fall Of the last monarchy—.* A much-disputed passage. The meaning may be, 'Let the Italian nobles, except those whose rank is the gift of the last revolution (and whose opinions on matters of honour are therefore of no account).'

II.i.38. *But one to dance with!* Ceremonial swords were a part of court dress.

II.i.42. *our parting is a tortured body.* 'Parting us is as painful as dismembering a body.'

II.i.90, 91. *more Than I dare blame my weakness.* 'To such a degree that I cannot attribute it entirely to credulity on my part.'

II.i.121, 122. *wherein the honour Of my dear father's gift stands chief in power.* 'In the cure of which my father's gift is reputed most powerful.'

II.i.176. *her.* This is the reading of the Folio, and there is nothing to show that Shakespeare is not responsible for this mistake in the sex of Hesperus.

II.i.186. *nay worse—if worse—extended.* This is the most satisfactory emendation of the obviously corrupt reading of the Folio: 'ne worse of worst extended.'

II.ii.20, 21. *as Tib's rush for Tom's forefinger.* Rush rings were frequently exchanged by country lovers who decided to dispense with the marriage ceremony.

II.iii.27. *facinerious.* Parolles' error for 'facinorous' (='infamous').

II.iii.41. *Mort du vinaigre.* Literally, 'By the death of the vinegar,' i.e. 'By the Crucifixion.'

II.iii.56. *to each but one.* This may mean either 'but one wife to each of you' or 'to each of you, with one exception (i.e. Bertram).'

II.iii.79, 80. *I had rather be in this choice than throw ames-ace for my life.* 'Ames-ace'=two aces, the lowest throw at dice. Lafeu ironically contrasts such ill luck with the good luck of being in this choice.

II.iii.157. *misprision.* A play on two meanings of the word: 'wrongful imprisonment' and 'lack of appreciation.'

II.iii.225. *Well, I shall be wiser—.* Presumably Parolles intends to conclude with some such words as 'than to attack an old man,' but Lafeu purposely misunderstands him.

II.iii.234. *as I will by thee.* Lafeu plays on the word 'past': the meaning is 'I will pass by thee.'

II.iii.297. *these balls bound; there's noise in it.* 'The noise which these balls make when they bounce shows that they are good': i. e. 'Your words show that you have proper spirit.'

II.v.35. *like him that leaped into the custard.* It was a favorite amusement at city entertainments for a jester to leap into a large custard.

III.i.14, 15. *That the great figure of a council frames By self-unable motion.* 'Who forms his ideas of a great council by the sole aid of his own insufficient mental powers.'

III.ii.94, 95. *The fellow has a deal of that too much, Which holds him much to have.* 'The fellow has too much of that quality (persuasiveness) which stands him in such good stead.'

III.iv.4. *Saint Jacques' pilgrim.* The shrine has not been identified.

III.iv.14. *his despiteful Juno.* A reference to the labors of Hercules, imposed upon him by Juno.

III.v.S. d. *Violenta.* No speech is assigned to Violenta by the Folio. It is possible that she was a speaking character in an earlier version of the play, and that her lines were cancelled in a subsequent revision, while the presence of her name in this stage-direction was overlooked.

III.vi.31. *John Drum's entertainment.* Giving a man a beating, or throwing him out of doors, was sometimes called John (or Tom) Drum's entertainment.

III.vi.52. *hic jacet.* 'Here lies—': the common beginning of epitaphs. Parolles means that he would get the drum or die in the attempt.

III.vii.3. *But I shall lose the grounds I work upon.* 'Unless I give up the only advantage I possess.' The only further proof of her identity which Helena can offer is the evidence of Bertram, and to disclose herself to him would be to defeat her purpose.

IV.i.38. *Bajazet's mule.* Probably Parolles' error for 'Balaam's ass.' He wishes to exchange a prattling tongue for one which speaks but seldom, and then only by inspiration.

IV.ii.31. *Jove's.* Quite possibly Shakespeare wrote 'God's,' which was altered to the present word in deference to the laws against blasphemy on the stage. The general meaning of the passage would then be, 'Who would believe me, if I swore by God that I would break His laws?'

IV.ii.36. *unseal'd.* A bond without a seal is invalid.

IV.ii.45. *I see that men make rope's in such a scarre.* This line is hopelessly corrupt.

IV.iii.25, 26. *Is it not meant damnable in us, to be trumpeters of our unlawful intents?* 'Do we not court damnation in parading our unlawful intentions?' Most editors emend 'most' for 'meant.'

IV.iii.200. *Half won is match well made; match, and well make it.* 'A bargain in which you receive half your price in advance is a good one; adopt this course.'

IV.iii.225. *Nessus.* The centaur who attempted to carry off Deïaneira.

IV.iii.249–251. The legal phrases in this speech are all taken from the form for the absolute conveyance of real property.

IV.iv.9. *Marseilles.* This should be pronounced as a tri-syllabic word. The spellings of the Folio are *Marcellae* and *Marcellus*.

IV.iv.31, 32. *Let death and honesty Go with your impositions.* 'Even unto death, if your commands are honest.'

IV.v.51, 52. *jade's tricks.* Used punningly: a jade is a horse, a jade's trick is a sharp practice.

IV.v.82. *two pile and a half.* The quality of velvet is determined by the height of the pile or nap, under the terms 'double-pile,' 'triple-pile,' etc.

V.ii.28, 29. *Let the justices make you and Fortune friends.* 'Let the justices of the peace award you a maintenance out of the funds for the poor.'

V.iii.75. *While shameful hate sleeps out the afternoon.* 'While shameful hate, having done its worst, is indifferent to the distress it has caused.'

V.iii.137, 138. *My fore-past proofs, howe'er the matter fall, Shall tax my fears of little vanity, Having vainly fear'd too little.* 'No matter what my conclusions may be, I shall not be ashamed of having feared too much, since it is clear from what I have heard that until now I have been too unsuspecting.'

THE TEXT OF THE PRESENT EDITION

The text of the present edition is based, by permission of the Oxford University Press, upon that of the Oxford Shakespeare, edited by the late W. J. Craig, which has been collated with the Folio of 1623. The following deviations have been made from Craig's text:

1. The stage-directions are those of the Folio: additional directions, where necessary, have been printed within square brackets.

2. A number of minor changes in punctuation, not affecting the meaning of the passages involved, have been made without comment. The spelling of a few words has been normalized: e. g. warlike has been substituted for war-like, theoric for theorick, villainy for villany and wagon for waggon.

3. The forms 'y'are' and 'th'art,' where they occur in the Folio, have been restored in place of the 'you're' and 'thou'rt' of Craig's text. The Folio has also been followed in the use of such elisions as 'th' inaudible.'

4. The following changes of text have been made, in almost every instance in accord with the Folio. The readings of the present edition precede the colon: those of Craig follow it:

I.i.46 to have—: have it.
   50 *Count.*: *Hel.*
   80 'Twere: It were
   99 Looks bleak i' th': Look bleak in the
  112 setting: sitting
  143 commodity will: commodity that will
  183 hath: have
ii.63 This: Thus
  75 You're loved: You are lov'd
iii.77 o'er: for
  159 loveliness: loneliness
  246 an: and

II.i.3 gain all,: gain, all (F)
25, 26 Farewell. *[To another Lord.]* Come hither to me. *[They converse.]*: Farewell. Come hither to me. *[Exit attended.]*
  54 Stay the king.: Stay: the king. *Re-enter King; Parolles and Bertram retire.*
  66 see: fee
  70 I would I had, so: I would I had: so
  97 wondering: wond'ring
  99 *[He retires to the door.]*: *[Exit.]*
  101 *Laf. [to Helena without.]* Nay, come your ways. *Enter Helen.*: *Re-enter Lafeu with Helena. Laf.* Nay, come your ways.
  155 sits (shifts F): fits
  166 imposture (impostrue F): imposter
  172 greatest: great'st
  176 her: his
  194 courage, all: courage, virtue, all
ii.58 them?: them. (F)
  59 me.: me?
iii.10 *Par.* So I say—both of Galen and Paracelsus.: *Par.* So I say. *Laf.* Both of Galen and Paracelsus. *Par.* So I say.
  21 in What-do-you-call there. (in what do you call there F): in—what do you call there—.
  27 he's: he is
  27 facinerious: facinorous
31–35 *Laf.* In a most weak— *Par.* And debile . . . as to be— *Laf.* Generally thankful.: *Laf.* In a most weak and debile . . . as to be generally thankful.
  52 sovereign: sov'reign
  124 stands: stand
  158 that: thou
  212 burthen: burden
  225 wiser—: wiser.
  226 Ev'n: E'en
  260 commission: heraldry
  261 heraldry: commission
  266 What's: What is
  282 regions: regions!
  290 Wars: War
iv.14 fortune: fortunes
  25 Away! [Before God,] th'art a knave.: Away! Thou'rt a knave.
53–55 *Par.* I shall report it so. *Exit Parolles. Hel. [to Clown.]* I pray you come, sirrah. *Exit [followed by Clown.]*: *Par.* I shall report it so. *Hel.* I pray you. Come, sirrah. *[Exeunt.]*
v.16 well, I, sir. He, sir's,: well, Ay sir; he, sir, is
92, 93 *[To Clown.]* Where are my other men? *[To Parolles.]* Monsieur, farewell. *Exit.*: *Ber. [To Parolles.]* Where are my other men, monsieur? *[To Helena.]* Farewell. *[Exit Helena.]*
III.ii.8 hold: sold
  13 lings: ling
  11 none-sparing: non-sparing
  116 still-pairing (still-peering F): still-piecing
iii.11 prosperous: prosp'rous
iv.16 dogs: dog
v.22 threatens: threaten
  54 Whatsome'er: Whatsoe'er
  72 I write,: Ay, right;
vi.31 ours: ore
  53 stomach, to 't: stomach to 't
  55 his: its
  85 imbost: embossed
vii.8, 20 count he: county
  38 After,: After this,
IV.i.12 E'en: Even
  38 mule: mute
  49 leapt: leaped
  57 You shall. Thou shalt
  61 *Cargo, cargo, cargo,*: *Cargo, cargo,*
ii.30 high'st: Highest
  31 Jove's: God's
  43 recovers: recover
  45 scarre: scarr
  72 that, what in time proceeds,: that what in time proceeds
iii.25 meant: most

52   makes: make
80   congied: conge'd
90   module: has: model; he has
159   Dumaine: Dumain (and so throughout)
236   he's: he is
238   has: he has
247, 248   not to ask: not ask
v.13   sallets: salads
14   sallet: salad
16   herbs: salad-herbs
33   fisnomy: phisnomy
54, 69   a': he
V.i.30   seem: seems

iii.36   sets: set
55   enfixing: infixing
69   rash: rasher
80   Which: *Count.* Which
110   ingag'd: engag'd
S.d.   *[Exeunt some Attendants.]: Exeunt the gentle Astringer, and*
       some Attendants.
S.d.   *Enter Widow, Diana and Parolles [with Attendants].: Re-enter*
       the gentle Astringer, with Widow and Diana.
184   count: county
218   hit: it
S.d.   *[Exit Parolles covertly.]:* [omits]
282   He's: He is

Measure for Measure

Edited by
DAVIS HARDING

Dramatis Personae

VINCENTIO, *the Duke*
ANGELO, *the Deputy*
ESCALUS, *an ancient Lord*
CLAUDIO, *a young Gentleman*
LUCIO, *a Fantastic*
Two other like Gentleman
[VARRIUS, *a Gentleman attending on the Duke*]
Provost
THOMAS }
PETER } *two friars*
[A JUSTICE]
ELBOW, *a simple Constable*
FROTH, *a foolish Gentleman*
CLOWN, [*Pompey, Tapster to Mistress Overdone*]

ABHORSON, *an Executioner*

BARNARDINE, *a dissolute Prisoner*
ISABELLA, *Sister to Claudio*
MARIANA, *betrothed to Angelo*
JULIET, *beloved of Claudio*
FRANCISCA, *a Nun*
MISTRESS OVERDONE, *a Bawd*

LORDS, OFFICERS, CITIZENS, BOY, AND
  ATTENDANTS

SCENE—*Vienna.*

Measure for Measure

INTRODUCTION

TEXT AND DATE

It is now generally accepted that there was a performance of *Measure for Measure* at Court on St. Stephen's Day, Dec. 26, 1604. Probably the play as we know it was finished earlier in the same year. Two apparent references to King James (I.1.72-77; II.4.26-30) and a possible reference to the plague year of 1603 (I.2.77) suggest that at least portions of the play were written after March 14, 1603, when James ascended the English throne. But the alleged references are by no means certain, and recently J. Dover Wilson has complicated the problem of a date for *Measure for Measure* by arguing that the play shows evidence of one or more revisions over a period of years. On the whole, however, the style would seem to support the belief that Shakespeare gave the play its final shaping in 1604.

There is no evidence that *Measure for Measure* was published during Shakespeare's lifetime. Consequently, the Folio of 1623 provides the only authoritative text. Unfortunately, the condition of this text entirely justifies Wilson's conclusion that the copy from which it was printed was not an autograph or playhouse manuscript but the work of a rather careless transcriber, who may even have assembled the play from the 'parts' of individual actors. Many entrances and exits are omitted from the Folio text and the stage directions are very thin—facts which give some plausibility to the 'assemblage' theory.

The present edition is based, therefore, upon the text of the First Folio. Emendations have been sparingly introduced. A few obvious printer's errors and mislineations are silently corrected. Otherwise, all departures from the Folio text are duly recorded. Significant emendations are discussed in the notes.

SOURCES OF THE PLAY

Measure for Measure remains one of Shakespeare's most puzzling plays. Revaluations of the play in the last twenty years have greatly enriched our understanding of its thought and poetry, but each new interpretation seems to have raised almost as many questions as it has answered. It is therefore especially gratifying to know the direct source of *Measure for Measure*. Such a source will always furnish interesting materials for a study of Shakespeare's methods and may often suggest fruitful approaches to the problem of interpretation.

The direct source of *Measure for Measure* is George Whetstone's *The right excellent and famous Historye of Promos and Cassandra: Divided into Commical Discourses*, in two parts, published in 1578. The play was apparently never acted. Four years later, Whetstone published a prose version in a collection of short stories called *An Heptameron of Civill Discourses*. Whetstone himself had derived his plot from one of the tales in the *Hecatommithi* of Giraldi Cinthio, published in Sicily in 1565. At some time before 1573, the latter had also dramatized the tale in a play entitled *Epitia*. It is possible that Shakespeare knew the Cinthio versions, and it is all but certain that he knew the *Heptameron*, narrated by 'Madame Isabella,' which may have suggested the name of his heroine. But the only essential debt is to the play of *Promos and Cassandra*.

Whetstone makes the city Julio, in Hungary, the setting for his drama. It begins with the reading of letters from Corvinus, King of Hungary, designating one Promos as the new deputy-governor of Julio and giving him full powers 'to weede from good the yll.' In his speech of acceptance, Promos stresses the need for judicial integrity and impartiality. 'Each shall be doomde,' he says, 'even as his merite is,' but he pointedly asserts the desirability of tempering justice with mercy. Then, as in *Measure for Measure*, the reader is transported into the heart of the city for a glance at the prevailing lawlessness. Sexual corruption is especially evident. We are introduced to Lamia, a notorious strumpet and her 'man,' Rosko, the prototypes of Mistress Overdone and Pompey. From Rosko we learn that Promos has already acted; he has revived an old law making fornication a capital offense and a young man named Andrugio has been arrested and sentenced to death. Lamia is distressed by this piece of news, envisaging a hopeless life of chastity and poverty, but Rosko heartens her with the information that Phallax, the deputy's 'secondary,' is notoriously susceptible to 'lace mutton.' In the meantime, Andrugio appeals to his sister, Cassandra, to intercede on his behalf before the governor. She quickly consents. In the first of two interviews with Promos, she pleads with him to 'over-rule the force of lawe with mercie' and urges as extenuating factors her brother's 'yong yeares,' his overmastering passion, and his intention to marry his mistress, Polina. Promos tells her to return on the morrow. Cassandra, it immediately develops, has moved him more by her person than by her eloquence. In a brief soliloquy following her departure, he laments the 'sodaine change' her beauty and 'modest wordes' have wrought in him. Promos now reveals his passion for Cassandra to Phallax, and is advised by the latter to offer Cassandra a choice of alternatives: either she must yield up her body to the governor or her brother must die. Confronted with this choice on the occasion of their second meeting, Cassandra indignantly tells Promos 'my selfe wyll dye ere I my honor stayne.' The governor's promise of a subsequent marriage is spurned, and Cassandra hurries off to inform her brother of the new development. Unlike Claudio in *Measure for Measure*, Andrugio shows no trace of horror at the vile offer of the governor. Arguing that 'in forst faultes is no intent of yll,' he begs Cassandra to do as Promos wishes.

Up to this point in the action, the events of *Promos and Cassandra* are closely paralleled by those in *Measure for Measure*. But now Shakespeare and Whetstone part company. Cassandra at length yields to her brother's entreaties and makes the sacrifice which she has been led to believe will save his life. But she is mistaken. Promos fulfills neither of his two promises; he makes it clear that he has no intention of marrying her and, instead of releasing her brother, gives order that he be executed forthwith

and his head presented to Cassandra on a platter. A friendly jailer, however, frees Andrugio, who betakes himself to the woods. For the head of Andrugio, he substitutes 'A dead man's head that suffered th' other day,' and it is this head with he displays to Cassandra. Distraught with grief, Cassandra now resolves to go to King Corvinus with the whole story. This resolution is made at the end of Act IV, Scene 4, of the First Part. Not until the last scene of the Second Part is final justice meted out.

Between these limits, the action moves sluggishly. The alliance between corruption in government, represented by Phallax, and corruption in civil life, represented by Lamia and Rosko, has produced a flourishing immorality. As Shakespeare was later to do, Whetstone intersperses his main action with subplot scenes designed to illustrate this immorality. Corvinus arrives in the city at the end of Act I (of the Second Part) and, shortly afterwards, issues a proclamation announcing his intention to sit in judgment upon grievances. First, Phallax is exposed; Corvinus orders his goods confiscated and strips him of his office. Then Cassandra comes forward and lodges her accusation against the governor. For having unjustly done Andrugio to death, Promos receives the sentence of execution; but he must first marry Cassandra 'to repayre hir honour.' Cassandra now undergoes an astonishing change of heart.

Nature wyld mee my brother love; now dutie commaunds mee
To preferre before kyn or friend, my husband's safetie.

Meanwhile Andrugio has heard of the death sentence passed upon Promos, and magnanimously resolves to give himself up in order that he may not see Cassandra 'plunged in distres.' Promos is already on his way to execution when Andrugio, in a timely arrival, reveals his true identity to the king. Impressed by this unselfish action, Corvinus sets Andrugio free after extracting a promise that he will marry Polina. A repentant Promos fares even better. At Cassandra's request, the king not only restores him to his freedom but—surprisingly—to his office as well. And on this pleasant note the play ends.

The plot of Promos and Cassandra has much to recommend it, and no reader will fail to notice the extent to which Shakespeare is indebted to it. But it has one grave flaw. The marriage of Cassandra to her seducer and the would-be murderer of her brother is as distasteful as it is psychologically unsound. Whet-

stone's attempt to motivate it by representing Cassandra as falling in love with Promos succeeds only in drawing attention to its initial absurdity. It was clearly his recognition of this flaw which led Shakespeare to make his most striking alteration in the plot of the original story. By introducing the Mariana story and the device of the bed-trick, he contrives to save the virtue of his heroine Isabella and, at the same time, does no disservice to Mariana, whose love for Angelo, it is made clear, had triumphantly survived the passage of time and his original dislike for her. Shakespeare's only other major alteration is the increased scope he gives to the activities of the Duke. In the old play, 'Corvinus, King of Hungary' is simply the agent by means of which the action is finally resolved—a *deus ex machina*. In *Measure for Measure*, the powerful figure of the Duke in the background in touch at all times with the developing situation and always controlling it, transfers our main attention from the plot to the issues which have set it in motion.

The theme of Whetstone's play is weakly defined and executed. Indeed, if the reader is not alert, he tends to lose sight of the theme altogether until suddenly confronted with it in the parting advice which King Corvinus gives Promos.

Henceforth, forethinke of thy forepassed faultes,
And measure grace with Justice evermore.
Unto the poore have evermore an eye,
And let not might out countenaunce their right.
Thy officers trust not in every tale,
In cheife, when they are meanes in strifes and sutes:
Though thou be just, yet coyne maye them corrupt;
And if by them thou dost injustice showe,
Tys thou shalt beare the burden of their faultes.

As these lines suggest, for Whetstone the idea that the good governor should temper strict justice with mercy is ancillary to the more general propositions that 'might' should not be confused with 'right' and that the ruler is ultimately responsible for the actions of his subordinates. It was the mercy theme, however, which commended itself to Shakespeare's poetic imagination, and around which he carefully constructed his play. To this theme Shakespeare attached a dignity and importance for which there is no precedent in Whetstone. It may be added that *Measure for Measure* is the only play of Shakespeare with a thematic title.

ACT FIRST ❧ SCENE FIRST

Enter Duke, Escalus, Lords [and Attendants].

Duke. Escalus.

Escalus. My lord.

Duke. Of government the properties to unfold,
Would seem in me t' affect speech and discourse,
Since I am put to know that your own science   5
Exceeds, in that, the lists of all advice
My strength can give you. Then no more remains,
But that, to your sufficiency, as your worth is able,
And let them work. The nature of our people,
Our city's institutions, and the terms   10
For common justice, y' are as pregnant in
As art and practice hath enriched any
That we remember. There is our commission,
From which we would not have you warp. Call hither,
I say, bid come before us Angelo.   *[Exit an Attendant.]* 15
What figure of us think you he will bear?
For you must know, we have with special soul
Elected him our absence to supply,
Lent him our terror, dress'd him with our love,
And given his deputation all the organs   20
Of our own power. What think you of it?

Escalus. If any in Vienna be of worth
To undergo such ample grace and honor,
It is Lord Angelo.

Enter Angelo.

Duke.   Look where he comes.   25

Angelo. Always obedient to your Grace's will,
I come to know your pleasure.

Duke.   Angelo,
There is a kind of character in thy life,
That to th' observer doth thy history   30
Fully unfold. Thyself and thy belongings
Are not thine own so proper, as to waste
Thyself upon thy virtues, they on thee.
Heaven doth with us as we with torches do,
Not light them for themselves; for if our virtues   35
Did not go forth of us, 'twere all alike
As if we had them not. Spirits are not finely touch'd
But to fine issues, nor Nature never lends
The smallest scruple of her excellence,
But, like a thrifty goddess, she determines   40
Herself the glory of a creditor,
Both thanks and use. But I do bend my speech
To one that can my part in him advertise.
Hold therefore, Angelo:
In our remove be thou at full ourself.   45
Mortality and mercy in Vienna

Live in thy tongue and heart. Old Escalus,
Though first in question, is thy secondary.
Take thy commission.

Angelo.   Now, good my lord,   50
Let there be some more test made of my mettle,
Before so noble and so great a figure
Be stamp'd upon it.

Duke.   No more evasion.
We have with a leaven'd and prepared choice   55
Proceeded to you; therefore take your honors.
Our haste from hence is of so quick condition
That it prefers itself, and leaves unquestion'd
Matters of needful value. We shall write to you,
As time and our concernings shall importune,   60
How it goes with us, and do look to know
What doth befall you here. So fare you well:
To th' hopeful execution do I leave you
Of your commissions.

Angelo.   Yet give leave, my lord,   65
That we may bring you something on the way.

Duke. My haste may not admit it;
Nor need you, on mine honor, have to do
With any scruple. Your scope is as mine own,
So to enforce or qualify the laws.   70
As to your soul seems good. Give me your hand.
I'll privily away. I love the people,
But do not like to stage me to their eyes.
Though it do well, I do not relish well
Their loud applause and Aves vehement,   75
Nor do I think the man of safe discretion
That does affect it. Once more, fare you well.

Angelo. The heavens give safety to your purposes!

Escalus. Lead forth and bring you back in happiness!

Duke. I thank you. Fare you well.   *Exit.* 80

Escalus. I shall desire you, sir, to give me leave
To have free speech with you; and it concerns me
To look into the bottom of my place.
A power I have, but of what strength and nature
I am not yet instructed.   85

Angelo. 'Tis so with me. Let us withdraw together,
And we may soon our satisfaction have
Touching that point.

Escalus.   I'll wait upon your Honor.

Exeunt.

❧ SCENE SECOND ❧

Enter Lucio and two other Gentlemen.

Lucio. If the Duke, with the other dukes, come not to composition with the king of Hungary, why then all the dukes fall upon the king.

1. Gentleman. Heaven grant us its peace, but not the king of Hungary's!   5

2. Gentleman. Amen.

ACT FIRST *Cf. n.*   3 **to unfold:** *read* 't'unfold'   4 **t' affect:** *to love*   5 **put:** *made*
6 **lists:** *limits*   8, 9 **But . . . work;** *Cf. n.*   11 **pregnant:** *expert*   14 **warp:**
deviate   16 **figure:** *representation*   17 **soul:** *affection*   19 **terror:** *i.e. authority to
punish*   20 **deputation:** *vice-regency*   29 **character:** *hidden meaning* (literally, cipher
for secret correspondence)   31 **belongings:** *qualities*   32 **proper:** *exclusively*   32, 33
as to . . . thee; *Cf. n.*   34, 35 **Heaven . . . themselves;** *Cf. n.*   37 **Spirits:** *one syllable
here, either* 'spir'ts' *or* 'sprites' **finely touch'd:** *nobly endowed*   38 **issues:** *purposes*   38–42 **Nature . . . use;** *Cf. n.*   39 **scruple:** *third part of a dram*   40 **determines:** *decrees for*   42 **use:** *interest*   43 **one . . . advertise** (stressed — ᷉ —) *Cf. n.*
44 **Hold;** *Cf. n.*   45 **remove:** *absence*   46 **mortality:** *death*

48 **question:** *appointment* **secondary:** *subordinate*   51 **mettle:** *essential worth; a quibble
on* 'metal'   55 **We have:** *read* 'we've' **leaven'd:** *well-considered*   57–59 **Our . . . value;**
Cf. n.   60 **concernings:** *business*   66 **bring you something:** *escort you a short distance*   69 **scope:** *liberty to act*   73 **stage:** *me exhibit myself*   74 **do well:** *be fit*   75
Aves: *acclamations*   83 **bottom of my place:** *full extent of my authority*   2 **composition:**
agreement

Lucio. Thou conclud'st like the sanctimonious pirate, that went to sea with the Ten Commandments, but scraped one out of the table.

2. Gentleman. 'Thou shalt not steal'?   10

Lucio. Ay, that he razed.

1. Gentleman. Why, 'twas a commandment to command the captain and all the rest from their functions: they put forth to steal. There's not a soldier of us all that, in the thanksgiving before meat, do relish the petition well that prays for peace.   15

2. Gentleman. I never heard any soldier dislike it.

Lucio. I believe thee, for I think thou never wast where grace was said.

2. Gentleman. No? A dozen times at least.

1. Gentleman. What? In meter?   20

Lucio. In any proportion or in any language.

1. Gentleman. I think, or in any religion.

Lucio. Ay, why not? Grace is grace, despite of all controversy: as, for example, thou thyself art a wicked villain, despite of all grace.   25

2. Gentleman. Well, there went but a pair of shears between us.

Lucio. I grant: as there may between the lists and the velvet. Thou art the list.

1. Gentleman. And thou the velvet. Thou art good velvet; 30 thou'rt a three-pil'd piece, I warrant thee. I had as lief be a list of an English kersey as be pil'd, as thou art pil'd, for a French velvet. Do I speak feelingly now?

Lucio. I think thou dost; and indeed with most painful feeling of thy speech. I will, out of thine own confession, learn to begin thy health; but, whilst I live, forget to drink after thee.

1. Gentleman. I think I have done myself wrong, have I not?

2. Gentleman. Yes, that thou hast, whether thou art tainted or free.   40

Enter Bawd [Mistress Overdone].

Lucio. Behold, behold, where Madam Mitigation comes!

1. Gentleman. I have purchas'd as many diseases under her roof as come to—

2. Gentleman. To what, I pray?

Lucio. Judge.   45

2. Gentleman. To three thousand dolors a year.

1. Gentleman. Ay, and more.

Lucio. A French crown more.

1. Gentleman. Thou art always figuring diseases in me; but thou art full of error. I am sound.   50

Lucio. Nay, not—as one would say—healthy, but so sound as things that are hollow. Thy bones are hollow; impiety has made a feast of thee.

1. Gentleman. [To Mistress Overdone.] How now! Which of your hips has the most profound sciatica?   55

Mistress Overdone. Well, well; there's one yonder arrested and carried to prison was worth five thousand of you all.

2. Gentleman. Who's that, I pray thee?

Mistress Overdone. Marry, sir, that's Claudio, Signior Claudio.   60

1. Gentleman. Claudio to prison? 'Tis not so.

Mistress Overdone. Nay, but I know 'tis so. I saw him arrested, saw him carried away, and, which is more, within these three days his head to be chopp'd off.

Lucio. But, after all this fooling, I would not have it so.   65 Art thou sure of this?

Mistress Overdone. I am too sure of it; and it is for getting Madam Julietta with child.

Lucio. Believe me, this may be. He promis'd to meet me two hours since, and he was ever precise in promise-keeping. 70

2. Gentleman. Besides, you know, it draws something near to the speech we had to such a purpose.

1. Gentleman. But most of all agreeing with the proclamation.

Lucio. Away! Let's go learn the truth of it.   75

　　　　　　　Exit [Lucio with the Gentlemen].

Mistress Overdone. Thus, what with the war, what with the sweat, what with the gallows and what with poverty, I am custom-shrunk.

Enter Clown [Pompey].

How now? What's the news with you?

Pompey. Yonder man is carried to prison.   80

Mistress Overdone. Well, what has he done?

Pompey. A woman.

Mistress Overdone. But what's his offense?

Pompey. Groping for trouts in a peculiar river.

Mistress Overdone. What? Is there a maid with child by him?

Pompey. No, but there's a woman with maid by him. You have not heard of the proclamation, have you?

Mistress Overdone. What proclamation, man?

Pompey. All houses in the suburbs of Vienna must be pluck'd down.   90

Mistress Overdone. And what shall become of those in the city?

Pompey. They shall stand for seed: they had gone down too, but that a wise burgher put in for them.

Mistress Overdone. But shall all our houses of resort in   95 the suburbs be pull'd down?

Pompey. To the ground, mistress.

Mistress Overdone. Why, here's a change indeed in the commonwealth! What shall become of me?

Pompey. Come, fear not you! Good counselors lack no   100 clients. Though you change your place, you need not change your trade. I'll be your tapster still. Courage! There will be pity taken on you; you that have worn your eyes almost out in the service, you will be considered.

Mistress Overdone. What's to do here, Thomas Tapster?   105 Let's withdraw.

Pompey. Here comes Signior Claudio, led by the provost to prison; and there's Madam Juliet.   *Exeunt.*

Enter Provost, Claudio, Juliet, Officers, Lucio, and two Gentlemen.

Claudio. Fellow, why dost thou show me thus to th' world? Bear me to prison, where I am committed.   110

---

15 petition . . . peace; *Cf. n.*   **21 proportion;** *Cf. n.*   **26, 27 there . . . us:** *we were cut from the same cloth*   **28 lists:** *the outer edging made of plain material, pileless*   **31 three-pil'd;** *Cf. n.*   **32 kersey:** *stout coarse cloth*   **33 velvet:** *courtesan* **feelingly:** *to the purpose*   **34–36 and . . . thee;** *Cf. n.*   **37 done myself wrong:** *given myself away*   **42, 43 I . . . to;** *Cf. n.*   **46 dolors:** *pun on 'dollars'*   **48 French crown:** *a gold coin, a bald head*   **55 sciatica:** *regarded as a symptom of venereal disease*

77 sweat: *the plague*   **78 custom-shrunk:** *reduced to fewer customers*   **82 woman;** *Cf. n.*   **84 Groping . . . river;** *Cf. n.*   **86 maid;** *Cf. n.*   **89 suburbs;** *cf. n.*   **93 had gone:** *would have gone*   **94 put in:** *interceded*   **105 Thomas Tapster;** *Cf. n.*   **107 provost:** *jailor*   **SD Enter Provost . . . Gentlemen;** *Cf. n.* (SD is used throughout to indicate stage direction.)

Provost. I do it not in evil disposition,
But from Lord Angelo by special charge.
  Claudio. Thus can the demigod Authority
Make us pay down for our offense by weight
The words of heaven; on whom it will, it will;   *115*
On whom it will not, so: yet still 'tis just.
  Lucio. Why how now Claudio? Whence comes this restraint?
  Claudio. From too much liberty, my Lucio, liberty.
As surfeit is the father of much fast,
So every scope by the immoderate use   *120*
Turns to restraint. Our natures do pursue,
Like rats that ravin down their proper bane,
A thirsty evil, and when we drink we die.
  Lucio. If I could speak so wisely under an arrest, I would
send for certain of my creditors. And yet, to say the truth,   *125*
I had as lief have the foppery of freedom as the mortality
of imprisonment. What's thy offense, Claudio?
  Claudio. What but to speak of would offend again.
  Lucio. What, is't murder?
  Claudio. No.   *130*
  Lucio. Lechery?
  Claudio. Call it so.
  Provost. Away, sir! You must go.
  Claudio. One word, good friend. Lucio, a word with you.
  Lucio. A hundred, if they'll do you any good.   *135*
Is lechery so look'd after?
  Claudio. Thus stands it with me: upon a true contract
I got possession of Julietta's bed.
You know the lady; she is fast my wife,
Save that we do the denunciation lack   *140*
Of outward order. This we came not to,
Only for propagation of a dower
Remaining in the coffer of her friends,
From whom we thought it meet to hide our love
Till time had made them for us. But it chances   *145*
The stealth of our most mutual entertainment
With character too gross is writ on Juliet.
  Lucio. With child, perhaps?
  Claudio.   Unhappily, even so.
And the new deputy now for the Duke—   *150*
Whether it be the fault and glimpse of newness,
Or whether that the body public be
A horse whereon the governor doth ride,
Who, newly in the seat, that it may know
He can command, lets it straight feel the spur;   *155*
Whether the tyranny be in his place,
Or in his eminence that fills it up,
I stagger in—but this new governor
Awakes me all the enrolled penalties
Which have, like unscour'd armor, hung by th' wall   *160*
So long that nineteen zodiacs have gone round,
And none of them been worn; and for a name
Now puts the drowsy and neglected act
Freshly on me: 'tis surely for a name.

  Lucio. I warrant it is. And thy head stands so tickle on   *165*
thy shoulders that a milkmaid, if she be in love, may sigh
it off. Send after the Duke and appeal to him.
  Claudio. I have done so, but he's not to be found.
I prithee, Lucio, do me this kind service.
This day my sister should the cloister enter,   *170*
And there receive her approbation.
Acquaint her with the danger of my state,
Implore her, in my voice, that she make friends
To the strict deputy. Bid herself assay him—
I have great hope in that; for in her youth   *175*
There is a prone and speechless dialect,
Such as move men; beside, she hath prosperous art
When she will play with reason and discourse,
And well she can persuade.
  Lucio. I pray she may: as well for the encouragement of   *180*
the like, which else would stand under grievous imposition,
as for the enjoying of thy life, who I would be sorry should
be thus foolishly lost at a game of tick-tack. I'll to her.
  Claudio. I thank you, good friend Lucio.
  Lucio. Within two hours.   *185*
  Claudio.   Come, officer, away!   *Exeunt.*

❧ SCENE THIRD ❧

Enter Duke and Friar Thomas.

  Duke. No, holy Father, throw away that thought:
Believe not that the dribbling dart of love
Can pierce a complete bosom. Why I desire thee
To give me secret harbor hath a purpose
More grave and wrinkled than the aims and ends   *5*
Of burning youth.
  Friar.   May your Grace speak of it?
  Duke. My holy sir, none better knows than you
How I have ever lov'd the life remov'd
And held in idle price to haunt assemblies   *10*
Where youth and cost, witless bravery keeps.
I have deliver'd to Lord Angelo—
A man of stricture and firm abstinence—
My absolute power and place here in Vienna,
And he supposes me travel'd to Poland;   *15*
For so I have strew'd it in the common ear,
And so it is receiv'd. Now, pious sir,
You will demand of me why I do this?
  Friar. Gladly, my lord.
  Duke. We have strict statutes and most biting laws—   *20*
The needful bits and curbs to headstrong steeds—
Which for this fourteen years we have let slip;
Even like an oregrown lion in a cave,
That goes not out to prey. Now, as fond fathers,
Having bound up the threat'ning twigs of birch,   *25*
Only to stick it in their children's sight

115 **words of heaven;** *Cf. n.*   122 **ravin:** *swallow greedily* **proper bane:** *poison peculiar to them* 126 **foppery:** *folly* **mortality:** *state of being subject to decay or death* *Cf. n.* 137 **contract** *(stressed — ´)* 159 **she . . . wife;** *Cf. n.* 140 **denunciation:** *proclamation of banns by the church* 142 **propagation:** *increase* 143 **friends:** *kinsfolk* 151 **fault . . . newness;** *Cf. n.* 156 **place:** *office* 158 **stagger in:** *am in doubt about* 159 **the enrolled:** *read 'th' enrolled'* 160 **unscour'd:** *rusty* 161 **zodiacs . . . round:** *years have passed* 162 **for a name:** *to acquire a reputation*

165 **tickle:** *unstable* 171 **receive her approbation:** *(five syllables here)* *enter upon her novitiate* 173 **voice:** *name* 174 **assay:** *attempt, accost* 176 **prone:** *enticing* **prone and speechless dialect;** *Cf. n.* 177 **she hath prosperous:** *read 'she'th prosp'rous'* 183 **tick-tack:** *a kind of backgammon in which pegs were fitted into holes* 2 **dribbling:** *feeble* 3 **complete:** *(stressed — ´ —)* *perfect* 10 **in idle price:** *as valueless* 11 **cost:** *extravagance* **bravery:** *ostentation* 13 **stricture:** *strictness* 16 **I have:** *read 'I've'* 18 **demand:** *ask* 21 **steeds:** *Cf. n.* 22 **slip;** *Cf. n.* 23 **Even:** *read 'E'en'* **oregrown:** *grown fat or old* 24 **fond:** *foolish*

For terror, not to use, in time the rod
Becomes more mock'd than fear'd; so our decrees,
Dead to infliction, to themselves are dead,
And Liberty plucks Justice by the nose;   30
The baby beats the nurse, and quite athwart
Goes all decorum.
    Friar.   It rested in your Grace
To unloose this tied-up justice when you pleas'd;
And it in you more dreadful would have seem'd   35
Than in Lord Angelo.
    Duke.   I do fear, too dreadful:
Sith 'twas my fault to give the people scope,
'Twould be my tyranny to strike and gall them
For what I bid them do: for we bid this be done,   40
When evil deeds have their permissive pass
And not the punishment. Therefore, indeed, my Father,
I have on Angelo impos'd the office,
Who may, in th' ambush of my name, strike home,
And yet my nature never in the sight   45
To do it slander. And to behold his sway,
I will, as 'twere a brother of your order,
Visit both prince and people. Therefore, I prithee,
Supply me with the habit, and instruct me
How I may formally in person bear   50
Like a true friar. Moe reasons for this action
At our more leisure shall I render you;
Only this one: Lord Angelo is precise,
Stands at a guard with envy; scarce confesses
That his blood flows, or that his appetite   55
Is more to bread than stone. Hence shall we see,
If power change purpose, what our seemers be.
                              Exit [with Friar].

❧ SCENE FOURTH ❧

Enter Isabel and Francisca, a Nun.

Isabella. And have you nuns no farther privileges?
Nun. Are not these large enough?
Isabella. Yes, truly. I speak not as desiring more,
But rather wishing a more strict restraint
Upon the sisterhood, the votarists of Saint Clare.   5

Lucio within.

Lucio. Ho! Peace be in this place!
Isabella.   Who's that which calls?
Nun. It is a man's voice. Gentle Isabella,
Turn you the key, and know his business of him.
You may, I may not. You are yet unsworn.   10
When you have vow'd, you must not speak with men
But in the presence of the prioress;
Then, if you speak, you must not show your face,
Or, if you show your face, you must not speak.
He calls again. I pray you, answer him.   *[Exit.]*   15
    Isabella. Peace and prosperity! Who is't that calls?

[Enter Lucio.]

    Lucio. Hail, virgin, if you be, as those cheek-roses
Proclaim you are no less! Can you so stead me
As bring me to the sight of Isabella,
A novice of this place, and the fair sister   20
To her unhappy brother, Claudio?
    Isabella. Why 'her unhappy brother'? let me ask,
The rather for I now must make you know
I am that Isabella, and his sister.
    Lucio. Gentle and fair, your brother kindly greets you.   25
Not to be weary with you, he's in prison.
    Isabella. Woe me! for what?
    Lucio. For that which, if myself might be his judge,
He should receive his punishment in thanks.
He hath got his friend with child.   30
    Isabella. Sir, make me not your story.
    Lucio.   'Tis true.
I would not, though 'tis my familiar sin
With maids to seem the lapwing and to jest,
Tongue far from heart, play with all virgins so.   35
I hold you as a thing enskied and sainted,
By your renouncement an immortal spirit,
And to be talk'd with in sincerity,
As with a saint.
    Isabella. You do blaspheme the good in mocking me.   40
    Lucio. Do not believe it. Fewness and truth, 'tis thus:
Your brother and his lover have embrac'd.
As those that feed grow full, as blossoming time
That from the seedness the bare fallow brings
To teeming foison, even so her plenteous womb   45
Expresseth his full tilth and husbandry.
    Isabella. Someone with child by him? My cousin Juliet?
    Lucio. Is she your cousin?
    Isabella. Adoptedly, as schoolmaids change their names
By vain though apt affection.   50
    Lucio.   She it is.
    Isabella. O, let him marry her!
    Lucio.   This is the point.
The Duke is very strangely gone from hence;
Bore many gentlemen—myself being one—   55
In hand and hope of action; but we do learn
By those that know the very nerves of state,
His givings-out were of an infinite distance
From his true-meant design. Upon his place,
And with full line of his authority,   60
Governs Lord Angelo, a man whose blood
Is very snow-broth; one who never feels
The wanton stings and motions of the sense
But doth rebate and blunt his natural edge
With profits of the mind, study and fast.   65
He—to give fear to use and liberty,
Which have for long run by the hideous law,
As mice by lions—hath pick'd out an act,
Under whose heavy sense your brother's life

---

28 Becomes: *F omits*   29 infliction: *execution*   30 Liberty: *license*   34 To unloose: *read 't' unloose*   38 Sith: *since*   39 gall: *hurt*   40–42 for . . . punishment; *Cf. n.*   45, 46 And . . . slander; *Cf. n.*   50 bear: *conduct myself*   51 Moe: *more*   52 more: *greater*   53 precise: *puritanical*   54 Stands . . . envy: *guards against malice*   56 to: *inclined to*

18 stead: *help*   26 weary: *tedious*   30 friend: *sweetheart, mistress*   31 make . . . story: *tell me no tales*   34 lapwing: *Cf. n.*   36 enskied: *heavenly*   41 Fewness and truth: *briefly and truly*   44 seedness: *seeding*   45 foison *rich harvest.* even; *read 'e'en'*   46 tilth: *tillage*   52 marry; *Cf. n.*   55, 56 Bore . . . in hand: *kept them in expectation*   57 nerves: *sinews*   58 givings-out: *announced plans;* F *giving-out*   60 line: *scope*   62 snow-broth: *melting snow*   63 motions: *impulses* sense: *sexual desire*   64 rebate: *dull*   66 use and liberty: *licentious custom*

Falls into forfeit; he arrests him on it,   *70*
And follows close the rigor of the statute,
To make him an example. All hope is gone,
Unless you have the grace by your fair prayer
To soften Angelo. And that's my pith of business
'Twixt you and your poor brother.   *75*
    Isabella. Doth he so seek his life?
    Lucio.   Has censur'd him
Already and, as I hear, the provost hath
A warrant for his execution.
    Isabella. Alas! What poor ability's in me   *80*
To do him good?
    Lucio.   Assay the power you have.
    Isabella. My power? Alas! I doubt—
    Lucio.   Our doubts are traitors,
And make us lose the good we oft might win,   *85*
By fearing to attempt. Go to Lord Angelo,
And let him learn to know, when maidens sue,
Men give like gods; but when they weep and kneel,
All their petitions are as freely theirs
As they themselves would owe them.   *90*
    Isabella. I'll see what I can do.
    Lucio.   But speedily.
    Isabella. I will about it straight,
No longer staying but to give the Mother
Notice of my affair. I humbly thank you.   *95*
Commend me to my brother. Soon at night
I'll send him certain word of my success.
    Lucio. I take my leave of you.
    Isabella.   Good sir, adieu. *Exeunt.*

ACT SECOND ❧ SCENE FIRST

Enter Angelo, Escalus, and Servants, Justice.

    Angelo. We must not make a scarecrow of the law,
Setting it up to fear the birds of prey,
And let it keep one shape, till custom make it
Their perch and not their terror.
    Escalus. ·   Ay, but yet   *5*
Let us be keen and rather cut a little,
Than fall and bruise to death. Alas! This gentleman,
Whom I would save, had a most noble father.
Let but your Honor know—
Whom I believe to be most strait in virtue—   *10*
That, in the working of your own affections,
Had time coher'd with place or place with wishing,
Or that the resolute acting of your blood
Could have attain'd th' effect of your own purpose,
Whether you had not sometime in your life   *15*
Err'd in this point which now you censure him,
And pull'd the law upon you.
    Angelo. 'Tis one thing to be tempted, Escalus,
Another thing to fall. I not deny,
The jury, passing on the prisoner's life,   *20*

May in the sworn twelve have a thief or two
Guiltier than him they try; what's open made to justice,
That justice seizes: what knows the laws
That thieves do pass on thieves? 'Tis very pregnant
The jewel that we find, we stoop and tak't   *25*
Because we see it; but what we do not see
We tread upon, and never think of it.
You may not so extenuate his offense
For I have had such faults; but rather tell me,
When I, that censure him, do so offend,   *30*
Let mine own judgment pattern out my death,
And nothing come in partial. Sir, he must die.

Enter Provost.

    Escalus. Be it as your wisdom will.
    Angelo.   Where is the provost?
    Provost. Here, if it like your Honor.   *35*
    Angelo.   See that Claudio
Be executed by nine tomorrow morning:
Bring him his confessor, let him be prepar'd;
For that's the utmost of his pilgrimage.   *[Exit Provost.]*
    Escalus. Well, heaven forgive him, and forgive us all!   *40*
Some rise by sin, and some by virtue fall:
Some run from brakes of vice, and answer none,
And some condemned for a fault alone.

Enter Elbow, Froth, Clown [Pompey], Officers.

    Elbow. Come, bring them away. If these be good people
in a commonweal that do nothing but use their abuses   *45*
in common houses, I know no law. Bring them away.
    Angelo. How now, sir! What's your name? And what's the
matter?
    Elbow. If it please your Honor, I am the poor Duke's consta-
ble, and my name is Elbow. I do lean upon justice, sir, and do
bring in here before your good Honor two notorious benefactors.
    Angelo. Benefactors! Well, what benefactors are they? Are
they not malefactors?
    Elbow. If it please your Honor, I know not well what they
are; but precise villains they are, that I am sure of, and void of
all profanation in the world that good Christians ought to have.
    Escalus. This comes off well: here's a wise officer.
    Angelo. Go to: what quality are they of? Elbow is your
name? Why dost thou not speak, Elbow?
    Pompey. He cannot, sir. He's out at elbow.   *60*
    Angelo. What are you, sir?
    Elbow. He, sir! A tapster, sir; parcel-bawd; one that serves a
bad woman, whose house, sir, was, as they say, pluck'd down
in the suburbs; and now she professes a hot-house, which I
think is a very ill house too.   *65*
    Escalus. How know you that?
    Elbow. My wife, sir, whom I detest before heaven and your
Honor—
    Escalus. How! Thy wife?
    Elbow. Ay, sir; whom I thank heaven is an honest woman—
    Escalus. Dost thou detest her therefore?

76–82 Doth . . . have; *Cf. n.*   **77 censur'd:** *sentenced*   **79 execution:** *five syllables
here*   **85 make:** *F makes*   **89 as freely theirs:** *as freely granted them*   **90 owe:** *possess*   **94 Mother:** *the abbess or prioress*   **96 Soon at night:** *early tonight*   **97 success:**
the consequence, good or bad   **2 fear:** *frighten*   **7 fall:** *let fall, as an executioner's ax*   **9
know:** *consider*   **12 coher'd:** *agreed*   **13 your:** *F our*

23, 24 what . . . thieves; *Cf. n.*   **24 pregnant:** *evident*   **29 For:** *because*   **32 come
in partial:** *intervene*   **38 confessor:** *stressed ́– — ́–*   **39 utmost of his pilgrimage:**
limit of his earthly life   **42 brakes of vice;** *Cf. n.*   **brakes;** *thickets* **vice;** *F ice*   **46
common houses:** *brothels*   **55 precise:** *precious, arrant*   **56 profanation:** *for 'profession'*   **58 quality:** *occupation*   **62 parcel-bawd:** *part bawd, part tapster*   **64 hot-
house:** *properly a bathhouse, but commonly a brothel*   **67 detest:** *for 'protest' or 'attest'*

Elbow. I say, sir, I will detest myself also, as well as she, that this house, if it be not a bawd's house, it is pity of her life, for it is a naughty house.

Escalus. How dost thou know that, Constable?   75

Elbow. Marry, sir, by my wife; who, if she had bin a woman cardinally given, might have bin accus'd in fornication, adultery, and all uncleanliness there.

Escalus. By the woman's means?

Elbow. Ay, sir, by Mistress Overdone's means; but as she   80
spit in his face, so she defied him.

Pompey. Sir, if it please your Honor, this is not so.

Elbow. Prove it before these varlets here, thou honorable man, prove it.

Escalus. Do you hear how he misplaces?   85

Pompey. Sir, she came in, great with child, and longing— saving your Honor's reverence—for stew'd prunes. Sir, we had but two in the house, which at that very distant time stood, as it were, in a fruit dish, a dish of some threepence; your Honors have seen such dishes; they are not China dishes,   90
but very good dishes—

Escalus. Go to, go to: no matter for the dish, sir.

Pompey. No, indeed, sir, not of a pin; you are therein in the right: but to the point. As I say, this Mistress Elbow, being, as I say, with child, and being great-bellied, and longing, as I   95
said, for prunes, and having but two in the dish, as I said, Master Froth here, this very man, having eaten the rest, as I said, and, as I say, paying for them very honestly; for, as you know, Master Froth, I could not give you threepence again.

Froth. No, indeed.   100

Pompey. Very well: you being then, if you be rememb'red, cracking the stones of the foresaid prunes—

Froth. Ay, so I did, indeed.

Pompey. Why, very well: I telling you then, if you be remem- b'red, that such a one and such a one were past cure of the   105
thing you wot of, unless they kept very good diet, as I told you—

Froth. All this is true.

Pompey. Why, very well then—

Escalus. Come, you are a tedious fool: to the purpose. What was done to Elbow's wife, that he hath cause to   110
complain of? Come me to what was done to her.

Pompey. Sir, your Honor cannot come to that yet.

Escalus. No, sir, nor I mean it not.

Pompey. Sir, but you shall come to it, by your Honor's leave. And I beseech you look into Master Froth here, sir: 115
a man of fourscore pound a year, whose father died at Hallowmas. Was't not at Hallowmas, Master Froth?

Froth. Allhallond-Eve.

Pompey. Why very well: I hope here be truths. He, sir, sit- ting, as I say, in a lower chair, sir—'twas in the Bunch of   120
Grapes, where indeed you have a delight to sit, have you not?

Froth. I have so, because it is an open room and good for winter.

Pompey. Why, very well then: I hope here be truths.

Angelo. This will last out a night in Russia,   125
When nights are longest there. I'll take my leave,
And leave you to the hearing of the cause,
Hoping you'll find good cause to whip them all.

Escalus. I think no less. Good morrow to your Lordship.

> *Exit [Angelo].*

Now, sir, come on: what was done to Elbow's wife, once more?

Pompey. Once, sir? There was nothing done to her once.

Elbow. I beseech you, sir, ask him what this man did to my wife.

Pompey. I beseech your Honor, ask me.

Escalus. Well, sir, what did this gentleman to her?   135

Pompey. I beseech you, sir, look in this gentleman's face. Good Master Froth, look upon his Honor; 'tis for a good purpose. Doth your Honor mark his face?

Escalus. Ay, sir, very well.

Pompey. Nay, I beseech you, mark it well.   140

Escalus. Well, I do so.

Pompey. Doth your Honor see any harm in his face?

Escalus. Why, no.

Pompey. I'll be suppos'd upon a book, his face is the worst thing about him. Good, then: if his face be the worst thing   145
about him, how could Master Froth do the constable's wife any harm? I would know that of your Honor.

Escalus. He's in the right. Constable, what say you to it?

Elbow. First, and it like you, the house is a respected house; next, this is a respected fellow; and his mistress is a   150
respected woman.

Pompey. By this hand, sir, his wife is a more respected person than any of us all.

Elbow. Varlet, thou liest: thou liest, wicked varlet. The time is yet to come that she was ever respected with man,   155
woman, or child.

Pompey. Sir, she was respected with him before he married with her.

Escalus. Which is the wiser here? Justice or Iniquity? Is this true?

Elbow. O thou caitiff! O thou varlet! O thou wicked   160
Hannibal! I respected with her before I was married to her? If ever I was respected with her, or she with me, let not your Worship think me the poor Duke's officer. Prove this, thou wicked Hannibal, or I'll have my action of battery on thee.

Escalus. If he took you a box o' th' ear, you might have   165
your action of slander, too.

Elbow. Marry, I thank your good Worship for it. What is't your Worship's pleasure I shall do with this wicked caitiff?

Escalus. Truly, officer, because he hath some offenses in him that thou wouldst discover if thou couldst, let him continue   170
in his courses till thou know'st what they are.

Elbow. Marry, I thank your Worship for it. Thou seest, thou wicked varlet, now, what's come upon thee: thou art to continue now, thou varlet, thou art to continue.

Escalus. Where were you born, friend?   175

Froth. Here in Vienna, sir.

Escalus. Are you of fourscore pounds a year?

Froth. Yes, an't please you, sir.

Escalus. So. *[To Pompey.]* What trade are you of, sir?

Pompey. A tapster, a poor widow's tapster.   180

Escalus. Your mistress' name?

Pompey. Mistress Overdone.

Escalus. Hath she had any more than one husband?

Pompey. Nine, sir; Overdone by the last.

Escalus. Nine! Come hither to me, Master Froth. Master   185
Froth, I would not have you acquainted with tapsters; they

---

77 **cardinally:** *for 'carnally' and usually so pronounced*   85 **misplaces:** *i.e. words*   87
stew'd prunes; *Cf. n.*   88 **distant:** *for 'instant'*   111 **Come me:** *come* (me so-called ethical dative)   118 **Allhallond-Eve:** *Hallowe'en*   120 **lower:** *easy or reclining*   120,
121 **Bunch of Grapes;** *Cf. n.*   122 **open:** *public*

144 **suppos'd:** *for 'deposed'* (under oath)   149, 150 **respected:** *for 'suspected'*   159 **Justice or Iniquity?;** *Cf. n.*   161 **Hannibal:** *for 'cannibal'*   165 **took:** *struck*

will draw you, Master Froth, and you will hang them. Get
you gone, and let me hear no more of you.

Froth. I thank your Worship. For mine own part, I never
come into any room in a taphouse, but I am drawn in. *190*

Escalus. Well, no more of it, Master Froth. Farewell.

[*Exit Froth.*]

Come you hither to me, Master tapster. What's your name,
Master tapster?

Pompey. Pompey.

Escalus. What else? *195*

Pompey. Bum, sir.

Escalus. Troth, and your bum is the greatest thing about
you so that, in the beastliest sense, you are Pompey the Great.
Pompey, you are partly a bawd, Pompey, howsoever you color
it in being a tapster, are you not? Come, tell me true: *200*
it shall be the better for you.

Pompey. Truly, sir, I am a poor fellow that would live.

Escalus. How would you live, Pompey? By being a bawd?
What do you think of the trade, Pompey? Is it a lawful trade?

Pompey. If the law would allow it, sir. *205*

Escalus. But the law will not allow it, Pompey; nor it
shall not be allowed in Vienna.

Pompey. Does your Worship mean to geld and splay all
the youth of the city?

Escalus. No, Pompey. *210*

Pompey. Truly, sir, in my poor opinion, they will to't then.
If your Worship will take order for the drabs and the knaves,
you need not to fear the bawds.

Escalus. There is pretty orders beginning, I can tell you:
it is but heading and hanging. *215*

Pompey. If you head and hang all that offend that way but
for ten year together, you'll be glad to give out a commission
for more heads. If this law hold in Vienna ten year, I'll rent
the fairest house in it after threepence a bay. If you live to see
this come to pass, say Pompey told you so. *220*

Escalus. Thank you, good Pompey; and, in requital of your
prophecy, hark you: I advise you, let me not find you before
me again upon any complaint whatsoever; no, not for dwelling
where you do. If I do, Pompey, I shall beat you to your tent,
and prove a shrewd Caesar to you. In plain dealing, Pompey, I
shall have you whipt. So, for this time, Pompey, fare you well.

Pompey. I thank your Worship for your good counsel.
[*Aside.*] But I shall follow it as the flesh and fortune shall bet-
ter determine. Whip me! No, no, let carman whip his jade.
The valiant heart's not whipt out of his trade. *Exit.* *230*

Escalus. Come hither to me, Master Elbow; come hither, Master
Constable. How long have you been in this place of constable?

Elbow. Seven year and a half, sir.

Escalus. I thought, by the readiness in the office, you had
continued in it some time. You say, seven years together? *235*

Elbow. And a half, sir.

Escalus. Alas, it hath been great pains to you! They do you
wrong to put you so oft upon't. Are there not men in your
ward sufficient to serve it?

Elbow. Faith, sir, few of any wit in such matters. As *240*
they are chosen, they are glad to choose me for them. I do
it for some piece of money, and go through with all.

Escalus. Look you bring me in the names of some six or
seven, the most sufficient of your parish.

Elbow. To your Worship's house, sir? *245*

Escalus. To my house. Fare you well. [*Exit Elbow.*]
What's o'clock, think you?

Justice. Eleven, sir.

Escalus. I pray you home to dinner with me.

Justice. I humbly thank you. *250*

Escalus. It grieves me for the death of Claudio. But there's
no remedy.

Justice. Lord Angelo is severe.

Escalus.   It is but needful.
Mercy is not itself, that oft looks so; *255*
Pardon is still the nurse of second woe.
But yet poor Claudio! There is no remedy.
Come, sir.   *Exeunt.*

❧ Scene Second ❧

Enter Provost, [and a] Servant.

Servant. He's hearing of a cause. He will come straight.
I'll tell him of you.

Provost.   Pray you, do. [*Exit Servant.*] I'll know
His pleasure; maybe he will relent. Alas!
He hath but as offended in a dream. *5*
All sects, all ages smack of this vice—and he
To die for't!

Enter Angelo.

Angelo. Now, what's the matter, Provost?

Provost. Is it your will Claudio shall die tomorrow?

Angelo. Did I not tell thee, yea? Hadst thou not order? *10*
Why dost thou ask again?

Provost.   Lest I might be too rash.
Under your good correction, I have seen,
When, after execution, Judgment hath
Repented o'er his doom. *15*

Angelo.   Go to: let that be mine.
Do you your office, or give up your place,
And you shall well be spar'd.

Provost.   I crave your Honor's pardon.
What shall be done, sir, with the groaning Juliet? *20*
She's very near her hour.

Angelo.   Dispose of her
To some more fitter place; and that with speed.

[Enter Servant.]

Servant. Here is the sister of the man condemn'd
Desires access to you. *25*

Angelo.   Hath he a sister?

Provost. Ay, my good lord, a very virtuous maid,
And to be shortly of a sisterhood,
If not already.

Angelo.   Well, let her be admitted. [*Exit Servant.*] *30*
See you the fornicatress be remov'd.
Let her have needful, but not lavish, means;
There shall be order for't.

---

187 draw: *you, Cf. n.*   197 bum; *Cf. n.*   208 geld: *castrate* splay: *spay*   212 take order: *take measures* drabs: *whores*   215 heading: *beheading*   219 after: *at the rate of* bay; *Cf. n.* 224, 225 I shall . . . you; *Cf. n.*   229 carman: *teamster* jade: *poor-spirited horse*   238 put . . . upon't: *impose the office . . . upon you, Cf. n.*   239 sufficient: *able*

256 still: *always*   6 sects: *classes of people*   13 Under . . . correction: *begging your pardon*

Enter Lucio and Isabella.

Provost.   'Save your Honor!

Angelo. Stay a little while. *[To Isabella.]* Y' are   35
welcome: what's your will?

Isabella. I am a woeful suitor to your Honor,
Please but your Honor hear me.

Angelo.   Well: what's your suit?

Isabella. There is a vice that most I do abhor,   40
And most desire should meet the blow of justice,
For which I would not plead, but that I must;
For which I must not plead, but that I am
At war 'twixt will and will not.

Angelo.   Well: the matter?   45

Isabella. I have a brother is condemn'd to die.
I do beseech you, let it be his fault,
And not my brother.

Provost. [Aside.] Heaven give thee moving graces!

Angelo. Condemn the fault, and not the actor of it?   50
Why, every fault's condemn'd ere it be done.
Mine were the very cipher of a function,
To fine the faults whose fine stands in record,
And let go by the actor.

Isabella.   O just, but severe law!   55
I had a brother then. Heaven keep your Honor!

Lucio. [Aside to Isabella.] Give't not o'er so: to him again,
entreat him,
Kneel down before him, hang upon his gown;
You are too cold. If you should need a pin,   60
You could not with more tame a tongue desire it.
To him, I say!

Isabella. Must he needs die?

Angelo.   Maiden, no remedy.

Isabella. Yes: I do think that you might pardon him,   65
And neither heaven nor man grieve at the mercy.

Angelo. I will not do't.

Isabella.   But can you, if you would?

Angelo. Look, what I will not, that I cannot do.

Isabella. But might you do't, and do the world no wrong,   70
If so your heart were touch'd with that remorse
As mine is to him!

Angelo. He's sentenc'd: 'tis too late.

Lucio. [Aside to Isabella.]   You are too cold.

Isabella. Too late? Why, no: I that do speak a word,   75
May call it back again. Well, believe this,
No ceremony that to great ones 'longs,
Not the king's crown, nor the deputed sword,
The marchal's truncheon, nor the judge's robe,
Become them with one half so good a grace   80
As mercy does.
If he had been as you, and you as he,
You would have slipp'd like him; but he, like you,
Would not have been so stern.

Angelo.   Pray you, be gone.   85

Isabella. I would to heaven I had your potency,
And you were Isabel! Should it then be thus?
No: I would tell what 'twere to be a judge,

And what a prisoner.

Lucio. [Aside to Isabella.] Ay, touch him; there's the vein.   90

Angelo. Your brother is a forfeit of the law,
And you but waste your words.

Isabella.   Alas, alas.
Why, all the souls that were were forfeit once,
And He that might the vantage best have took,   95
Found out the remedy. How would you be,
If He, which is the top of judgment, should
But judge you as you are? O think on that!
And mercy then will breathe within your lips,
Like man new made.   100

Angelo.   Be you content, fair maid.
It is the law, not I, condemn your brother.
Were he my kinsman, brother or my son,
It should be thus with him: he must die tomorrow.

Isabella. Tomorrow? O, that's sudden,   105
Spare him, spare him!
He's not prepar'd for death. Even for our kitchens
We kill the fowl of season. Shall we serve heaven
With less respect than we do minister
To our gross selves? Good, good my lord, bethink you: 110
Who is it that hath died for this offence?
There's many have committed it.

Lucio.   *[Aside to Isabella.]* Ay, well said.

Angelo. The law hath not been dead, though it hath slept.
Those many had not dar'd to do that evil,   115
If the first that did th' edict infringe
Had answer'd for his deed. Now 'tis awake,
Takes note of what is done, and like a prophet
Looks in a glass that shows what future evils,
Either new, or by remissness new-conceiv'd,   120
And so in progress to be hatch'd and born,
Are now to have no successive degrees,
But, ere they live, to end.

Isabella.   Yet show some pity.

Angelo. I show it most of all when I show justice,   125
For then I pity those I do not know,
Which a dismiss'd offense would after gall,
And do him right that, answering one foul wrong,
Lives not to act another. Be satisfied.
Your brother dies tomorrow. Be content.   130

Isabella. So you must be the first that gives this sentence,
And he, that suffers. O, it is excellent
To have a giant's strength, but it is tyrannous
To use it like a giant!

Lucio. [Aside to Isabella.] That's well said.   135

Isabella. Could great men thunder
As Jove himself does, Jove would nere be quiet,
For every pelting, petty officer
Would use his heaven for thunder,
Nothing but thunder! Merciful heaven!   140
Thou rather with thy sharp and sulphurous bolt
Splits the unwedgeable and gnarled oak
Than the soft myrtle; but man, proud man,
Dress'd in a little brief authority,

47, 48 let ... brother: *let the fault die and not my brother*   **52 cipher:** *zero, a mere nothing;*   **53, 54 To fine ... actor:** *Cf. n.*   **53 record:** *stressed* — ́—   **61 tame:** *spiritless*   **71 remorse:** *pity*   **76 back:** *not in F*   **77 ceremony:** *symbol of greatness* **'longs:** *belongs*   **79 truncheon:** *staff of office*   **86 potency:** *power*

95 vantage: *advantage (to punish mankind)*   **97 top of judgment:** *supreme judge*   **100 new made:** *regenerate, hence in his original innocence*   **107 Even:** *read 'E'en'*   **108 of season:** *when it is in season*   **116 edict** *stressed* — ́—   **119 glass:** *crystal glass, of the kind used in divination*   **120 new:** *F now*   **122 successive** *stressed* ́— —́ —   **degrees:** *descendants*   **123 ere:** *F here*   **137 nere:** *never*   **138 pelting:** *paltry*   **142 Splits:** *splitst* **unwedgeable:** *not to be split even with wedges*

Most ignorant of what he's most assur'd—   *145*
His glassy essence—like an angry ape,
Plays such fantastic tricks before high heaven
As makes the angels weep; who, with our spleens,
Would all themselves laugh mortal.
 Lucio. [*Aside to Isabella.*] O, to him, to him, wench!   *150*
He will relent.
He's coming. I perceive't.
 Provost. [*Aside.*] Pray heaven she win him!
 Isabella. We cannot weigh our brother with ourself:
Great men may jest with saints: 'tis wit in them,   *155*
But in the less foul profanation.
 Lucio. [*Aside to Isabella.*] Thou'rt i' th' right, girl: more o'
that.
 Isabella. That in the captain's but a choleric word,
Which in the soldier is flat blasphemy.   *160*
 Lucio. [*Aside to Isabella.*] Art avis'd o' that? More on't.
 Angelo. Why do you put these sayings upon me?
 Isabella. Because Authority, though it err like others,
Hath yet a kind of medicine in itself,
That skins the vice o' th' top. Go to your bosom: *165*
Knock there, and ask your heart what it doth know
That's like my brother's fault. If it confess
A natural guiltiness such as is his,
Let it not sound a thought upon your tongue
Against my brother's life.   *170*
 Angelo. [*Aside.*] She speaks, and 'tis
Such sense that my sense breeds with it. [*Aloud.*]
Fare you well.
 Isabella. Gentle my lord, turn back.
 Angelo. I will bethink me. Come again tomorrow.   *175*
 Isabella. Hark how I'll bribe you. Good my lord, turn back.
 Angelo. How! Bribe me?
 Isabella. Ay, with such gifts that heaven shall share with
you.
 Lucio. [*Aside to Isabella.*] You had marr'd all else.   *180*
 Isabella. Not with fond sickles of the tested gold,
Or stones whose rates are either rich or poor
As fancy values them; but with true prayers
That shall be up at heaven and enter there
Ere sunrise: prayers from preserved souls,   *185*
From fasting maids whose minds are dedicate
To nothing temporal.
 Angelo. Well: come to me tomorrow.
 Lucio. [*Aside to Isabella.*] Go to: 'tis well. Away!
 Isabella. Heaven keep your Honor safe!   *190*
 Angelo. [*Aside.*] Amen.
For I am that way going to temptation,
Where prayers cross.
 Isabella. At what hour tomorrow
Shall I attend your lordship?   *195*
 Angelo. At any time 'fore noon.
 Isabella. 'Save your Honor!
     [*Exeunt Isabella, Lucio, and Provost.*]
 Angelo. From thee: even from thy virtue.
What's this? What's this? Is this her fault or mine?

The tempter, or the tempted, who sins most?   *200*
Ha!
Not she; nor doth she tempt. But it is I
That, lying by the violet in the sun,
Do as the carrion does, not as the flower,
Corrupt with virtuous season. Can it be   *205*
That modesty may more betray our sense
Than woman's lightness? Having waste ground enough,
Shall we desire to raze the sanctuary,
And pitch our evils there? O, fie, fie, fie!
What dost thou? Or what art thou, Angelo?   *210*
Dost thou desire her foully for those things
That make her good? O, let her brother live!
Thieves for their robbery have authority
When judges steal themselves. What! do I love her,
That I desire to hear her speak again,   *215*
And feast upon her eyes? What is't I dream on?
O cunning enemy that, to catch a saint,
With saints dost bait thy hook! Most dangerous
Is that temptation that doth goad us on
To sin in loving virtue. Never could the strumpet,   *220*
With all her double vigor, art and nature,
Once stir my temper; but this virtuous maid
Subdues me quite. Ever till now,
When men were fond, I smil'd and wonder'd how.   *Exit.*

❧ Scene Third ❧

Enter Duke [disguised as a friar] and Provost.

 Duke. Hail to you, Provost! So I think you are.
 Provost. I am the provost. What's your will, good Friar?
 Duke. Bound by my charity and my bless'd order,
I come to visit the afflicted spirits
Here in the prison. Do me the common right   *5*
To let me see them and to make me know
The nature of their crimes, that I may minister
To them accordingly.
 Provost. I would do more than that, if more were needful.

Enter Julietta.

Look, here comes one: a gentlewoman of mine,   *10*
Who, falling in the flames of her own youth,
Hath blister'd her report. She is with child,
And he that got it, sentenc'd: a young man
More fit to do another such offense,
Than die for this.   *15*
 Duke. When must he die?
 Provost. As I do think, tomorrow.
[*To Julietta.*] I have provided for you. Stay a while,
And you shall be conducted.
 Duke. Repent you, fair one, of the sin you carry?   *20*
 Julietta. I do, and bear the shame most patiently.
 Duke. I'll teach you how you shall arraign your conscience,
And try your penitence, if it be sound,
Or hollowly put on.
 Julietta. I'll gladly learn.   *25*

---

146 **glassy essence:** *fragile being* 148 **spleens:** *the spleen was the organ once regarded as the seat of the emotions* 149 **laugh mortal:** *laugh themselves to death* 152 **coming:** *on the verge of relenting* 154 **weigh ... ourself:** *judge others by ourselves* 156 **less:** *lesser men* 161 **avis'd:** *informed* 165 **skins:** *covers the sore without healing it* 168 **natural:** *read 'nat'ral'* 171, 172 **She ... it;** *Cf. n.* 181 **sickles:** *shekels* 182 **rates:** *F rate* 193 **prayers cross:** *Cf. n.* 197 **'Save:** *God save*

205 **Corrupt ... season;** *Cf. n.* 206 **sense:** *sensuality* 207 **lightness:** *wantonness* 209 **evils:** *Cf. n.* 224 **fond:** *doting* 1 **So:** *such* 11 **flames:** *F flawes* 12 **blister'd her report:** *besmirched her reputation* 24 **hollowly:** *insincerely*

Duke. Love you the man that wrong'd you?

Julietta. Yes, as I love the woman that wrong'd him.

Duke. So then it seems your most offenseful act
Was mutually committed?

Julietta.   Mutually.   30

Duke. Then was your sin of heavier kind than his.

Julietta. I do confess it, and repent it, Father.

Duke. 'Tis meet so, daughter: but lest you do repent,
As that the sin hath brought you to this shame,
Which sorrow is always toward ourselves, not heaven,   35
Showing we would not spare heaven as we love it,
But as we stand in fear—

Julietta. I do repent me, as it is an evil,
And take the shame with joy.

Duke.   There rest.   40
Your partner, as I hear, must die tomorrow,
And I am going with instruction to him.
Grace go with you, *Benedicite.*   *Exit.*

Julietta. Must die tomorrow! O injurious love,
That respites me a life, whose very comfort   45
Is still a dying horror!

Provost.   'Tis pity of him.   *Exeunt.*

❦ SCENE FOURTH ❦

Enter Angelo.

Angelo. When I would pray and think, I think and pray
To several subjects. Heaven hath my empty words,
Whilst my invention, hearing not my tongue,
Anchors on Isabel: heaven in my mouth,
As if I did but only chew his name,   5
And in my heart the strong and swelling evil
Of my conception. The state, whereon I studied,
Is like a good thing, being often read,
Grown sear'd and tedious; yea, my gravity,
Wherein, let no man hear me, I take pride,   10
Could I, with boot, change for an idle plume,
Which the air beats for vain. O place! O form!
How often dost thou with thy case, thy habit,
Wrench awe from fools, and tie the wiser souls
To thy false seeming! Blood, thou art blood: 15
Let's write 'good Angel' on the devil's horn,
Is't not the devil's crest? How now! who's there?

Enter Servant.

Servant. One Isabel, a sister, desires access to you.

Angelo. Teach her the way. *[Exit Servant.]* O heavens!
Why does my blood thus muster to my heart,   20
Making both it unable for itself,
And dispossessing all my other parts
Of necessary fitness?
So play the foolish throngs with one that swounds:
Come all to help him, and so stop the air   25
By which he should revive; and even so

The general, subject to a well-wish'd king,
Quit their own part, and in obsequious fondness
Crowd to his presence, where their untaught love
Must needs appear offense.   30

Enter Isabella.

            How now, fair maid!

Isabella. I am come to know your pleasure.

Angelo. That you might know it, would much better please me
Than to demand what 'tis. Your brother cannot live.

Isabella. Even so. Heaven keep your Honor!   35

Angelo. Yet may he live a while; and, it may be,
As long as you or I. Yet he must die.

Isabella. Under your sentence?

Angelo. Yea.

Isabella. When, I beseech you? that in his reprieve,   40
Longer or shorter, he may be so fitted
That his soul sicken not.

Angelo. Ha! fie, these filthy vices! It were as good
To pardon him that hath from nature stolne
A man already made, as to remit   45
Their saucy sweetness that do coin heaven's image
In stamps that are forbid: 'tis all as easy
Falsely to take away a life true made,
As to put metal in restrained meanes
To make a false one.   50

Isabella. 'Tis set down so in heaven, but not in earth.

Angelo. Say you so? Then I shall pose you quickly.
Which had you rather, that the most just law
Now took your brother's life; or, to redeem him,
Give up your body to such sweet uncleanness   55
As she that he hath stain'd?

Isabella.   Sir, believe this,
I had rather give my body than my soul.

Angelo. I talk not of your soul. Our compell'd sins
Stand more for number than for accompt.   60

Isabella.   How say you?

Angelo. Nay, I'll not warrant that; for I can speak
Against the thing I say. Answer to this:
I, now the voice of the recorded law,
Pronounce a sentence on your brother's life.   65
Might there not be a charity in sin
To save this brother's life?

Isabella.   Please you to do't,
I'll take it as a peril to my soul.
It is no sin at all, but charity.   70

Angelo. Pleas'd you to do't, at peril of your soul,
Were equal poise of sin and charity.

Isabella. That I do beg his life, if it be sin,
Heaven let me bear it! You granting of my suit,
If that be sin, I'll make it my morn prayer   75
To have it added to the faults of mine
And nothing of your answer.

Angelo.   Nay, but hear me.
Your sense pursues not mine: either you are ignorant,

---

33 meet: *proper*   **35 sorrow is:** *read 'sorrow's'*   **36 spare heaven as:** *refrain from offending heaven because*   **44–46 O . . . horror;** *Cf. n.*   **2 several:** *different*   **3 invention:** *imagination*   **7 conception:** *thought*   **9 sear'd:** *dry; F feard*   **11 boot:** *advantage*   **plume:** *a feather or panache, emblematic of frivolity*   **12 vain:** *quibble on 'vane'*   **13 case:** *external show*   **habit:** *dress*   **16, 17 Let's write . . . crest;** *Cf. n.*   **21 unable:** *weak*   **24 swounds:** *swoons*

27 general: *common people*   **28 obsequious:** *dutiful*   **32 know;** *Cf. n.*   **41 fitted:** *prepared for death*   **44 stolne:** *stolen*   **45 remit:** *pardon*   **46 saucy:** *lascivious*   **47 stamps** *dies for making coins*   **all:** *quite*   **47–50 'tis . . . one;** *Cf. n.*   **48 Falsely:** *illegally*   **49 restrained:** *forbidden*   **meanes:** *mints*   **51 'Tis . . . earth;** *Cf. n.*   **52 pose you:** *put a hard question to you*   **58 I had:** *read 'I'd'*   **59 compell'd:** *stressed —́ —*   **60 for accompt:** *(pronounced 'account'); Cf. n.*   **62 that:** *i.e. Angelo's argument in ll. 59, 60*   **77 nothing of your answer:** *nothing for which you can be held accountable*

Or seem so craftily; and that's not good.   80
   Isabella. Let me be ignorant, and in nothing good,
But graciously to know I am no better.
   Angelo. Thus wisdom wishes to appear most bright
When it doth tax itself, as these black masks
Proclaim an enshield beauty ten times louder   85
Than beauty could, display'd. But mark me.
To be received plain, I'll speak more gross:
Your brother is to die.
   Isabella. So.
   Angelo. And his offense is so, as it appears,   90
Accountant to the law upon that pain.
   Isabella. True.
   Angelo. Admit no other way to save his life—
As I subscribe not that, nor any other,
But in the loss of question—that you, his sister,   95
Finding yourself desir'd of such a person,
Whose credit with the judge, or own great place,
Could fetch your brother from the manacles
Of the all-building law; and that there were
No earthly mean to save him, but that either   100
You must lay down the treasures of your body
To this suppos'd, or else to let him suffer,
What would you do?
   Isabella. As much for my poor brother as myself:
That is, were I under the terms of death,   105
Th' impression of keen whips I'ld wear as rubies,
And strip myself to death, as to a bed
That longing have been sick for, ere I'ld yield
My body up to shame.
   Angelo.   Then must your brother die.   110
   Isabella. And 'twere the cheaper way:
Better it were a brother died at once,
Than that a sister, by redeeming him,
Should die for ever.
   Angelo. Were not you then as cruel as the sentence   115
That you have slander'd so?
   Isabella. Ignomy in ransom and free pardon
Are of two houses: lawful mercy
Is nothing kin to foul redemption.
   Angelo. You seem'd of late to make the law a tyrant,   120
And rather prov'd the sliding of your brother
A merriment than a vice.
   Isabella. O, pardon me, my lord! It oft falls out,
To have what we would have, we speak not what we mean.
I something do excuse the thing I hate,   125
For his advantage that I dearly love.
   Angelo. We are all frail.
   Isabella.   Else let my brother die,
If not a fedary, but only he
Owe and succeed they weakness.   130
   Angelo. Nay, women are frail too.
   Isabella. Ay, as the glasses where they view themselves,
Which are as easy broke as they make forms.
Women! Help heaven! Men their creation mar

In profiting by them. Nay, call us ten times frail,   135
For we are soft as our complexions are,
And credulous to false prints.
   Angelo.   I think it well:
And from this testimony of your own sex—
Since I suppose we are made to be no stronger   140
Than faults may shake our frames—let me be bold.
I do arrest your words. Be that you are,
That is, a woman; if you be more, you're none.
If you be one, as you are well express'd
By all external warrants, show it now,   145
By putting on the destin'd livery.
   Isabella. I have no tongue but one. Gentle my lord,
Let me entreat you speak the former language.
   Angelo. Plainly conceive, I love you.
   Isabella. My brother did love Juliet.   150
And you tell me that he shall die for't.
   Angelo. He shall not, Isabel, if you give me love.
   Isabella. I know your virtue hath a licence in't,
Which seems a little fouler than it is,
To pluck on others.   155
   Angelo.   Believe me, on mine honor,
My words express my purpose.
   Isabella. Ha! little honor to be much believ'd
And most pernicious purpose! Seeming, seeming!
I will proclaim thee, Angelo; look for't!   160
Sign me a present pardon for my brother,
Or with an outstretch'd throat I'll tell the world aloud
What man thou art.
   Angelo.   Who will believe thee, Isabel?
My unsoil'd name, th' austereness of my life,   165
My vouch against you, and my place i' th' state,
Will so your accusation overweigh,
That you shall stifle in your own report
And smell of calumny. I have begun,
And now I give my sensual race the rein.   170
Fit thy consent to my sharp appetite;
Lay by all nicety and prolixious blushes,
That banish what they sue for: redeem thy brother
By yielding up thy body to my will,
Or else he must not only die the death,   175
But thy unkindness shall his death draw out
To ling'ring sufferance. Answer me tomorrow,
Or, by the affection that now guides me most,
I'll prove a tyrant to him. As for you,
Say what you can, my false oreweighs your true.   *Exit.* 180
   Isabella. To whom should I complain? Did I tell this,
Who would believe me? O perilous mouths!
That bear in them one and the selfsame tongue,
Either of condemnation or approof,
Bidding the law make curtsy to their will,   185
Hooking both right and wrong to th' appetite,
To follow as it draws. I'll to my brother.
Though he hath falne by prompture of the blood,
Yet hath he in him such a mind of honor,
That, had he twenty heads to tender down   190

---

80 **craftily:** *F* crafty   81 **me:** *F omits*   84 **tax:** *reprove*   85 **enshield:** *concealed; Cf. n.*   87 **gross:** *plainly*   91 **pain:** *punishment*   94 **subscribe:** *admit*   95 **in . . . question:** *in idle conversation* (?)   97 **place:** *official position*   99 **all-building:** *upon which all is founded*   100 **mean:** *means*   108 **have:** *I have*   117 **Ignomy:** *ignominy*   121 **sliding:** *backsliding*   129, 130 **If . . . weakness;** *Cf. n.*   129 **fedary:** *associate*   130 **Owe:** *possess* **succeed:** *inherit*   133 **forms:** *images, reflections*   134–135 **Men . . . them;** *Cf. n.*

137 **credulous:** *susceptible* **prints:** *impressions*   142 **I . . . words:** *I take them as security*   146 **destin'd livery:** *i.e. the frailty of your sex*   147 **tongue:** *language*   148 **former language:** *i.e. the unambiguous language employed earlier*   153–155 **I . . . others;** *Cf. n.*   166 **vouch:** *testimony*   170 **race:** *nature, with a quibble*   172 **nicety:** *coyness, reserve* **prolixious:** *superfluous*   177 **sufferance:** *pain*   178 **affection:** *lust*   184 **approof:** *approbation*   188 **falne:** *fallen* **prompture:** *instigation*

On twenty bloody blocks, he'd yield them up,
Before his sister should her body stoop
To such abhorr'd pollution.
Then, Isabel, live chaste, and, brother, die:
More than our brother is our chastity.   *195*
I'll tell him yet of Angelo's request,
And fit his mind to death, for his soul's rest.   *Exit.*

ACT THIRD ❧ SCENE FIRST

Enter Duke [as a friar], Claudio, and Provost.

Duke. So then you hope of pardon from Lord Angelo?
Claudio. The miserable have no other medicine
But only hope:
I have hope to live, and am prepar'd to die.
Duke. Be absolute for death. Either death or life   *5*
Shall thereby be the sweeter. Reason thus with life:
If I do lose thee, I do lose a thing
That none but fools would keep. A breath thou art,
Servile to all the skyey influences,
That dost this habitation, where thou keep'st,   *10*
Hourly afflict. Merely, thou art Death's fool,
For him thou labor'st by thy flight to shun,
And yet run'st toward him still. Thou art not noble,
For all th' accommodations that thou bear'st
Are nurs'd by baseness. Thou'rt by no means valiant,   *15*
For thou dost fear the soft and tender fork
Of a poor worm. Thy best of rest is sleep,
And that thou oft provok'st; yet grossly fear'st
Thy death, which is no more. Thou art not thyself,
For thou exists on many a thousand grains   *20*
That issue out of dust. Happy thou art not;
For what thou hast not, still thou striv'st to get,
And what thou hast, forget'st. Thou art not certain,
For thy complexion shifts to strange effects,
After the moon. If thou art rich, thou'rt poor;   *25*
For, like an ass whose back with ingots bows,
Thou bear'st thy heavy riches but a journey,
And Death unloads thee. Friend hast thou none,
For thine own bowels, which do call thee sire,
The mere effusion of thy proper loins,   *30*
Do curse the gout, serpigo, and the rheum,
For ending thee no sooner. Thou hast nor youth nor age,
But, as it were, an after-dinner's sleep,
Dreaming on both; for all thy blessed youth
Becomes as aged, and doth beg the alms   *35*
Of palsied Eld: and when thou art old and rich,
Thou hast neither heat, affection, limb, nor beauty,
To make thy riches pleasant. What's yet in this
That bears the name of life? Yet in this life
Lie hid moe thousand deaths; yet death we fear,   *40*
That makes these odds all even.

Claudio.   I humbly thank you.
To sue to live, I find I seek to die,
And, seeking death, find life: let it come on.

Enter Isabella.

Isabella. What, ho! Peace here. Grace and good company! *45*
Provost. Who's there? Come in, the wish deserves a welcome.
Duke. Dear sir, ere long I'll visit you again.
Claudio. Most holy sir, I thank you.
Isabella. My business is a word or two with Claudio.
Provost. And very welcome. Look, Signior; here's your sister.
Duke. Provost, a word with you.
Provost. As many as you please.
Duke. Bring me to hear them speak, where I may be
conceal'd.   *[Duke and Provost withdraw.]*
Claudio. Now, sister, what's the comfort?   *55*
Isabella. Why,
As all comforts are: most good, most good indeed.
Lord Angelo, having affairs to heaven,
Intends you for his swift ambassador,
Where you shall be an everlasting leiger.   *60*
Therefore, your best appointment make with speed;
Tomorrow you set on.
Claudio.   Is there no remedy?
Isabella. None but such remedy as, to save a head,
To cleave a heart in twain.   *65*
Claudio.   But is there any?
Isabella. Yes, brother, you may live.
There is a divelish mercy in the judge,
If you'll implore it, that will free your life,
But fetter you till death.   *70*
Claudio.   Perpetual durance?
Isabella. Ay, just—perpetual durance, a restraint,
Though all the world's vastidity you had,
To a determin'd scope.
Claudio.   But in what nature?   *75*
Isabella. In such a one as, you consenting to't,
Would bark your honor from that trunk you bear,
And leave you naked.
Claudio.   Let me know the point.
Isabella. O, I do fear thee, Claudio, and I quake,   *80*
Let thou a feverous life shouldst entertain,
And six or seven winters more respect
Than a perpetual honor. Dar'st thou die?
The sense of death is most in apprehension,
And the poor beetle that we tread upon   *85*
In corporal sufferance finds a pang as great
As when a giant dies.
Claudio.   Why give you me this shame?
Think you I can a resolution fetch
From flow'ry tenderness? If I must die,   *90*
I will encounter darkness as a bride,
And hug it in mine arms.
Isabella. There spake my brother: there my father's grave
Did utter forth a voice. Yes, thou must die:

---

5 absolute: *wholly determined*   9 skyey influences; *Cf. n.*   14–15 For . . . baseness;
Cf. n.   16–17 For . . . worm; *Cf. n.*   23 certain: *constant*   24–5 For . . . moon;
Cf. n.   29 bowels: *offspring*   30 effusion: *pouring-out*   31 serpigo: *spreading skin disease F Sapego* rheum: *excessive moisture in the body, causing catarrh*   32–4 Thou . . .
both; *Cf. n.*   34–6 for . . . Eld; *Cf. n.*   36 thou art: *read 'thou'rt'*   37 limb:
vigor   40 moe *i.e. more than those mentioned*

SD Enter Isabella; *Cf. n.*   53 me to hear them: *F them to hear me*   SD Duke and
Provost withdraw; *Cf. n.*   60 leiger: *resident ambassador*   61 appointment: *preparation*   68 divelish: *F devilish*   71 durance *imprisonment*   72 just: *exactly*   73, 74
Though . . . scope; *Cf. n.*   73 Though: *F through* vastidity: *immensity*   77 bark:
strip   81 feverous: *read 'fev'rous'* entertain: *maintain*   86 corporal sufferance: *read
'corp'ral suff'rance'* finds: *experiences*   89 a resolution fetch: *derive courage*

Thou art too noble to conserve a life   *95*
In base appliances. This outward-sainted deputy,
Whose settled visage and deliberate word
Nips youth i' th' head, and follies doth enew
As falcon doth the fowl, is yet a divel.
His filth within being cast, he would appear   *100*
A pond as deep as hell.
   Claudio.   The prenzie Angelo!
   Isabella. O, 'tis the cuning livery of hell,
The damned'st body to invest and cover
In prenzie guards! Dost thou think, Claudio?   *105*
If I would yield him my virginity,
Thou mightst be freed.
   Claudio.   O heavens! it cannot be.
   Isabella. Yes, he would give't thee, from this rank offense,
So to offend him still. This night's the time   *110*
That I should do what I abhor to name,
Or else thou diest tomorrow.
   Claudio.   Thou shalt not do't.
   Isabella. O! were it but my life,
I'd throw it down for your deliverance   *115*
As frankly as a pin.
   Claudio.   Thanks, dear Isabel.
   Isabella. Be ready, Claudio, for your death tomorrow.
   Claudio. Yes. Has he affections in him,
That thus can make him bite the law by th' nose,   *120*
When he would force it: Sure it is no sin;
Or of the deadly seven it is the least.
   Isabella. Which is the least?
   Claudio. If it were damnable, he being so wise,
Why would he for the momentary trick   *125*
Be perdurably fin'd? O Isabel!
   Isabella. What says my brother?
   Claudio.   Death is a fearful thing.
   Isabella. And shamed life a hateful.
   Claudio. Ay, but to die, and go we know not where,   *130*
To lie in cold obstruction and to rot,
This sensible warm motion to become
A kneaded clod; and the delighted spirit
To bathe in fiery floods, or to reside
In thrilling region of thick-ribbed ice,   *135*
To be imprison'd in the viewless winds,
And blown with restless violence round about
The pendent world; or to be worse than worst
Of those that lawless and incertain thought
Imagine howling: 'tis too horrible!   *140*
The weariest and most loathed worldly life
That age, ache, penury and imprisonment
Can lay on nature is a paradise
To what we fear of death.
   Isabella. Alas! alas!   *145*
   Claudio.   Sweet sister, let me live.
What sin you do to save a brother's life,
Nature dispenses with the deed so far

That it becomes a virtue.
   Isabella.   O you beast!   *150*
O faithless coward! O dishonest wretch!
Wilt thou be made a man out of my vice?
Is't not a kind of incest, to take life
From thine own sister's shame? What should I think?
Heaven shield my mother play'd my father fair,   *155*
For such a warped slip of wilderness
Nere issu'd from his blood. Take my defiance,
Die, perish! Might but my bending down
Reprieve thee from thy fate, it should proceed.
I'll pray a thousand prayers for thy death,   *160*
No word to save thee.
   Claudio. Nay, hear me, Isabel.
   Isabella.   O, fie, fie, fie!
Thy sin's not accidental, but a trade.
Mercy to thee would prove itself a bawd,   *165*
'Tis best that thou diest quickly.   *[Going.]*
   Claudio.   O hear me, Isabella.
                          [Duke comes forward.]
   Duke. Vouchsafe a word, young sister, but one word.
   Isabella. What is your will?
   Duke. Might you dispense with your leisure, I would by   *170*
and by have some speech with you: the satisfaction I would
require is likewise your own benefit.
   Isabella. I have no superfluous leisure: my stay must be
stolen out of other affairs; but I will attend you a while.
   Duke. *[Aside to Claudio.]* Son, I have overheard what   *175*
pass'd between you and your sister. Angelo had never the purpose
to corrupt her; only he hath made an assay of her virtue to
practice his judgment with the disposition of natures. She, having
the truth of honor in her, hath made him that gracious denial
which he is most glad to receive. I am confessor to Angelo,   *180*
and I know this to be true; therefore prepare yourself to death.
Do not satisfy your resolution with hopes that are fallible: to-
morrow you must die. Go to your knees and make ready.
   Claudio. Let me ask my sister pardon. I am so out of love
with life that I will sue to be rid of it.   *185*
   Duke. Hold you there: farewell.   *[Exit Claudio.]*

                [Enter Provost.]

Provost, a word with you.
   Provost. What's your will, Father?
   Duke. That now you are come, you will be gone. Leave me
a while with the maid. My mind promises with my habit   *190*
no loss shall touch her by my company.
   Provost. In good time.   *Exit.*
   Duke. The hand that hath made you fair hath made you
good. The goodness that is cheap in beauty makes beauty brief
in goodness; but grace, being the soul of your complexion,   *195*
shall keep the body of it ever fair. The assault that Angelo
hath made to you, fortune hath convey'd to my understanding;
and, but that frailty hath examples for his falling, I should
wonder at Angelo. How will you do to content this substitute,
and to save your brother?   *200*

---

96 in base appliances: *by base means*   **97 settled:** *composed*   **98 enew:** *drive into the water* (term from falconry) *F emmew*   **100 cast:** *emptied, as a pond of mud and refuse*   **102 prenzie:** *puritanical* (?); *Cf. n.*   **105 guards:** *trimmings*   **110 still:** *always*   **119 affections:** *passions*   **120 bite by th' nose:** *treat with contempt*   **121 force:** *enforce*   **126 perdurably fin'd:** *eternally punished*   **131 obstruction:** *stagnation* (of the blood)   **133 kneaded;** *i.e. like dough* **delighted:** *accustomed to delight*   **135 thrilling:** *piercing* (with cold) **region:** *tract; Cf. n.*   **136 viewless:** *invisible*   **148 dispenses with:** *pardons*

155 shield: *forbid*   **156 slip of wilderness:** *worthless slip or scion*   **159 proceed:** *take place*   **170, 171 by and by:** *immediately*   **177, 178 practice his judgment:** *experiment*   **178 disposition of natures:** *evaluation of character*   **182 satisfy your resolution:** *fortify your courage*   **186 Hold you there:** *persist in that course*   **191 loss:** *harm*   **192 In good time:** *well and good*   **194 cheap:** *lightly esteemed*   **196 assault:** *love-proposal*   **199 substitute:** *i.e. Angelo*

Isabella. I am now going to resolve him. I had rather my brother die by the law than my son should be unlawfully born. But O, how much is the good Duke deceived in Angelo! If ever he return and I can speak to him, I will open my lips in vain, or discover his government.　　　　　　　　　　*205*

Duke. That shall not be much amiss: yet, as the matter now stands, he will avoid your accusation; he made trial of you only. Therefore, fasten your ear on my advisings: to the love I have in doing good a remedy presents itself. I do make myself believe that you may most uprighteously do a poor wronged lady a merited benefit, redeem your brother from the angry law, do no stain to your own gracious person, and much please the absent Duke, if peradventure he shall ever return to have hearing of this business.

Isabella. Let me hear you speak farther. I have spirit to　*215* do anything that appears not foul in the truth of my spirit.

Duke. Virtue is bold, and goodness never fearful. Have you not heard speak of Mariana, the sister of Frederick, the great soldier who miscarried at sea?

Isabella. I have heard of the lady, and good words went　*220* with her name.

Duke. She should this Angelo have married, was affianced to her by oath, and the nuptial appointed: between which time of the contract and limit of the solemnity, her brother Frederick was wrack'd at sea, having in that perished vessel the dowry　*225* of his sister. But mark how heavily this befell to the poor gentlewoman: there she lost a noble and renowned brother, in his love toward her ever most kind and natural; with him the portion and sinew of her fortune, her marriage dowry; with both, her combinate husband, this well-seeming Angelo.　*230*

Isabella. Can this be so? Did Angelo so leave her?

Duke. Left her in her tears, and dried not one of them with his comfort; swallowed his vows whole, pretending in her discoveries of dishonor: in few, bestowed her on her own lamentation, which she yet wears for his sake; and he, a marble to　*235* her tears, is washed with them, but relents not.

Isabella. What a merit were it in death to take this poor maid from the world! What corruption in this life, that it will let this man live! But how out of this can she avail?

Duke. It is a rupture that you may easily heal; and　*240* the cure of it not only saves your brother, but keeps you from dishonor in doing it.

Isabella. Show me how, good Father.

Duke. This forenamed maid hath yet in her the continuance of her first affection: his unjust unkindness, that in all reason should have quenched her love, hath, like an impediment in the current, made it more violent and unruly. Go you to Angelo: answer his requiring with a plausible obedience, agree with his demands to the point. Only refer yourself to this advantage: first, that your stay with him may not be long, that　*250* the time may have all shadow and silence in it, and the place answer to convenience. This being granted in course—and now follows all—we shall advise this wronged maid to stead up your appointment, go in your place. If the encounter acknowledge itself hereafter, it may compel him to her recompense;　*255*

and here, by this is your brother saved, your honor untainted, the poor Mariana advantaged, and the corrupt deputy scaled. The maid will I frame and make fit for his attempt. If you think well to carry this, as you may, the doubleness of the benefit defends the deceit from reproof. What think you of it?　*260*

Isabella. The image of it gives me content already, and I trust it will grow to a most prosperous perfection.

Duke. It lies much in your holding up. Haste you speedily to Angelo. If for this night he entreat you to his bed, give him promise of satisfaction. I will presently to St. Luke's; there,　*265* at the moated grange, resides this dejected Mariana. At that place call upon me, and dispatch with Angelo, that it may be quickly.

Isabella. I thank you for this comfort. Fare you well, good Father.　　　　　　　　　　　　　　　　　*Exit. 270*

　　　Enter Elbow, Clown [Pompey, and] Officers.

Elbow. Nay, if there be no remedy for it but that you will needs buy and sell men and women like beasts, we shall have all the world drink brown and white bastard.

Duke. O heavens! What stuff is here?

Pompey. 'Twas never merry world, since, of two usuries,　*275* the merriest was put down, and the worser allow'd by order of law a furr'd gown to keep him warm; and furr'd with fox and lamb skins too, to signify that craft, being richer than innocency, stands for the facing.

Elbow. Come your way, sir. Bless you, good Father Friar.　*280*

Duke. And you, good brother father. What offense hath this man made you, sir?

Elbow. Marry, sir, he hath offended the law; and, sir, we take him to be a thief too, sir, for we have found upon him, sir, a strange picklock, which we have sent to the deputy.　*285*

Duke. Fie, sirrah! A bawd, a wicked bawd!
The evil that thou causest to be done,
That is thy means to live. Do thou but think
What 'tis to cram a maw or clothe a back
From such a filthy vice. Say to thyself,　　　　　*290*
From their abominable and beastly touches
I drink, I eat, array myself, and live.
Canst thou believe thy living is a life,
So stinkingly depending? Go mend, go mend.

Pompey. Indeed, it does stink in some sort, sir; but yet,　*295* sir, I would prove—

Duke. Nay, if the divel have given thee proofs for sin,
Thou wilt prove his. Take him to prison, officer.
Correction and instruction must both work
Ere this rude beast will profit.　　　　　　　　*300*

Elbow. He must before the deputy, sir; he has given him warning. The deputy cannot abide a whoremaster: if he be a whoremonger, and comes before him, he were as good go a mile on his errand.

Duke. That we were all, as some would seem to be,　*305* Free from our faults, as faults from seeming, free!

　　　　　　　Enter Lucio.

201 resolve: *free from uncertainty*　　**205 discover:** *reveal*　**government:** *conduct*　**207 avoid:** *make void, refute*　　**222 was affianced:** *i.e. Angelo*　**223 by:** *F omits.*　**223, 224 between . . . solemnity;** *Cf. n.*　　**230 combinate:** *betrothed*　　**234 in few:** *in a few words*　**bestowed her on:** *i.e. abandoned her to*　　**235 marble:** *i.e. hardhearted*　　**239 avail:** *benefit*　　**248 plausible:** *fair-seeming*　　**249 refer yourself to:** *have recourse to*　　**251 shadow:** *darkness*　　**252 in course:** *as a matter of course*　　**253 stead up:** *assume*

257 scaled: *weighed, as by scales*　　**258 frame:** *instruct*　　**261 image:** *mental picture*　　**266 grange:** *a secluded country house*　**dejected:** *rejected, dispirited*　　**267 dispatch:** *come to an agreement*　　**SD Exit;** *Cf. n.*　　**273 bastard:** *a sweet Spanish wine*　　**275 two usuries;** *Cf. n.*　　**279 facing:** *trimming*　　**281 brother father;** *Cf. n.*　　**285 picklock:** *skeleton key*　　**292 array:** *F away*　　**294 stinkingly depending:** *depending upon such a stinking means of support*　　**303, 304 go . . . errand:** *i.e. give himself up for lost*　　**306 Free:** *F omits*

Elbow. His neck will come to your waist—a cord, sir.

Pompey. I spy comfort: I cry bail. Here's a gentleman and
a friend of mine.

Lucio. How now, noble Pompey! What, at the wheels   310
of Caesar? Art thou led in triumph? What, is there none of
Pygmalion's images, newly made woman, to be had now, for
putting the hand in the pocket and extracting it clutched?
What reply? ha? What say'st thou to this tune, matter and
method? Is't not drowned i' th' last rain, ha? What say'st   315
thou, Trot? Is the world as it was, man? Which is the way?
Is it sad, and few words, or how? The trick of it?

Duke. Still thus, and thus, still worse!

Lucio. How doth my dear morsel, thy mistress?
Procures she still, ha?   320

Pompey. Troth, sir, she hath eaten up all her beef, and she
is herself in the tub.

Lucio. Why, 'tis good. It is the right of it; it must be so.
Ever your fresh whore and your powder'd bawd: an unshunned
consequence, it must be so. Art going to prison, Pompey?   325

Pompey. Yes, faith, sir.

Lucio. Why, 'tis not amiss, Pompey. Farewell. Go, say I sent
thee thither. For debt, Pompey? or how?

Elbow. For being a bawd, for being a bawd.

Lucio. Well, then, imprison him. If imprisonment be   330
the due of a bawd, why, 'tis his right. Bawd is he, doubtless,
and of antiquity too: bawd-born. Farewell, good Pompey.
Commend me to the prison, Pompey. You will turn good
husband now, Pompey, you will keep the house.

Pompey. I hope, sir, your good Worship will be my bail.   335

Lucio. No, indeed will I not, Pompey; it is not the wear.
I will pray, Pompey, to increase your bondage: if you take it
not patiently, why, your mettle is the more. Adieu, trusty
Pompey. 'Bless you, Friar.

Duke. And you.   340

Lucio. Does Bridget paint still, Pompey, ha?

Elbow. Come your ways, sir. Come.

Pompey. You will not bail me then, sir?

Lucio. Then, Pompey, nor now. What news abroad, Friar?
What news?   345

Elbow. Come your ways, sir. Come.

Lucio. Go to kennel, Pompey. Go.

           [Exeunt Elbow, Pompey, and Officers.]
What news, Friar, of the Duke?

Duke. I know none. Can you tell me of any?

Lucio. Some say he is with the emperor of Russia; other   350
some, he is in Rome. But where is he, think you?

Duke. I know not where; but wheresoever, I wish him well.

Lucio. It was a mad fantastical trick of him to steal from the
state, and usurp the beggary he was never born to. Lord Angelo dukes it well in his absence; he puts trangression to't.   355

Duke. He does well in't.

Lucio. A little more lenity to lechery would do no harm in
him. Something too crabbed that way, Friar.

Duke. It is too general a vice, and severity must cure it.

Lucio. Yes, in good sooth, the vice is of a great kindred;   360
it is well allied. But it is impossible to extirp it quite, Friar,

till eating and drinking be put down. They say this Angelo was
not made by man and woman after this downright way of creation. Is it true, think you?

Duke. How should he be made, then?   365

Lucio. Some report a sea-maid spawn'd him; some that he
was begot between two stock-fishes. But it is certain that when
he makes water his urine is congeal'd ice, that I know to be
true. And he is a motion generative, that's infallible.

Duke. You are pleasant, sir, and speak apace.   370

Lucio. Why, what a ruthless thing is this in him, for the rebellion of a cod-piece to take away the life of a man! Would
the Duke that is absent have done this? Ere he would have
hang'd a man for the getting a hundred bastards, he would
have paid for the nursing a thousand. He had some feeling   375
of the sport; he knew the service, and that instructed him to
mercy.

Duke. I never heard the absent Duke much detected for
women; he was not inclin'd that way.

Lucio. O, sir, you are deceiv'd.   380

Duke. 'Tis not possible.

Lucio. Who? Not the Duke? Yes, your beggar of fifty. And
his use was to put a ducat in her clack-dish. The Duke had
crotchets in him. He would be drunk, too; that let me inform
you.   385

Duke. You do him wrong, surely.

Lucio. Sir, I was an inward of his. A shy fellow was the
Duke; and I believe I know the cause of his withdrawing.

Duke. What, I prethee, might be the cause?

Lucio. No, pardon. 'Tis a secret must be lock'd within   390
the teeth and the lips. But this I can let you understand, the
greater file of the subject held the Duke to be wise.

Duke. Wise! Why, no question but he was.

Lucio. A very superficial, ignorant, unweighing fellow.

Duke. Either this is envy in you, folly, or mistaking.   395
The very stream of his life and the business he hath helm'd
must, upon a warranted need, give him a better proclamation.
Let him be but testimonied in his own bringings-forth, and
he shall appear to the envious a scholar, a statesman, and a
soldier. Therefore, you speak unskillfully; or, if your knowl-   400
edge be more, it is much darkened in your malice.

Lucio. Sir, I know him, and I love him.

Duke. Love talks with better knowledge, and knowledge
with dearer love.

Lucio. Come, sir, I know what I know.   405

Duke. I can hardly believe that, since you know not what
you speak. But, if ever the Duke return—as our prayers are he
may—let me desire you to make your answer before him. If it
be honest you have spoke, you have courage to maintain it. I
am bound to call upon you; and, I pray you, your name?   410

Lucio. Sir, my name is Lucio, well known to the Duke.

Duke. He shall know you better, sir, if I may live to report
you.

Lucio. I fear you not.

363 after: *according to*   **367 stock-fishes:** *dried codfish*   **369 motion generative;** *Cf. n.*
372 cod-piece; *Cf. n.*   **374 getting:** *begetting*   **378 detected:** *accused*   **382 beggar
of fifty:** *beggarwoman fifty years*   **383 clack-dish:** *wooden dish with a lid, clacked to
attract attention*   **384 crotchets:** *odd fancies*   **387 inward:** *intimate* **shy:** *reserved,
fearful*   **390 must:** *which must*   **392 greater file:** *majority*   **394 unweighing:**
thoughtless   **396 helm'd:** *steered*   **397 upon ... need:** *were warrant needed* **give
him a better proclamation:** *proclaim him to be a better man*   **398 testimonied:** *attested*
bringings-forth: *achievements*   **400 unskillfully:** *without discernment*   **404 dearer:**
F deare

307 His ... waist; *Cf. n.*   **311 Caesar:** *the conqueror of Pompey*   **312 Pygmalion's
images;** *Cf. n.*   **313 it:** *F omits* **clutched:** *i.e. full of money*   **314 tune:** *temper,
humor*   **316 Trot:** *contemptuous term for an old woman*   **317 sad:** *serious* **trick:** *fashion* **321, 322 she ... tub;** *Cf. n.*   **324 unshunned:** *inevitable*   **333 husband:** *in its
etymological sense, housekeeper*   **336 wear:** *fashion*   **338 mettle:** *spirit with a quibble*   **354 usurp:** *wrongfully assume*   **361 extirp:** *extirpate*

Duke. O! You hope the Duke will return no more, or   415
you imagine me too unhurtful an opposite. But indeed I can
do you little harm; you'll forswear this again!

Lucio. I'll be hang'd first. Thou art deceiv'd in me, Friar.
But no more of this. Canst thou tell if Claudio die tomorrow
or no?   420

Duke. Why should he die, sir?

Lucio. Why? For filling a bottle with a tun-dish. I would
the Duke we talk of were return'd again: this ungenitur'd
agent will unpeople the province with continency. Sparrows
must not build in his house-eaves because they are lecherous.   425
The Duke yet would have dark deeds darkly answered; he
would never bring them to light. Would he were return'd!
Marry, this Claudio is condemned for untrussing. Farewell, good
Friar; I prethee, pray for me. The Duke, I say to thee again,
would eat mutton on Fridays. He's not past it yet, and   430
I say to thee, he would mouth with a beggar, though she smelt
brown bread and garlic. Say that I said so. Farewell.   *Exit.*

Duke. No might nor greatness in mortality
Can censure 'scape. Back-wounding calumny
The whitest virtue strikes. What king so strong   435
Can tie the gall up in the slanderous tongue?
But who comes here?

*Enter Escalus, Provost, and [Officers with] Bawd
[Mistress Overdone].*

Escalus. Go, away with her to prison!

Mistress Overdone. Good my lord, be good to me. Your
Honor is accounted a merciful man, good my lord.   440

Escalus. Double and treble admonition, and still forfeit in
the same kind! This would make mercy swear, and play the
tyrant.

Provost. A bawd of eleven years' continuance, may it please
your Honor.   445

Mistress Overdone. My lord, this is one Lucio's information
against me. Mistress Kate Keepdown was with child by him in
the Duke's time; he promis'd her marriage. His child is a year
and a quarter old, come Philip and Jacob. I have kept it
myself, and see how he goes about to abuse me!   450

Escalus. That fellow is a fellow of much license. Let him
be call'd before us. Away with her to prison! Go to: no more
words. *[Exeunt Officers with Mistress Overdone.]* Provost, my
brother Angelo will not be alter'd; Claudio must die tomorrow.
Let him be furnish'd with divines, and have all charitable   455
preparation. If my brother wrought by my pity, it should not
be so with him.

Provost. So please you, this friar hath been with him, and
advis'd him for th' entertainment of death.

Escalus. Good even, good Father.   460

Duke. Bliss and goodness on you!

Escalus. Of whence are you?

Duke. Not of this country, though my chance is now
To use it for my time. I am a brother
Of gracious order, late come from the See,   465
In special business from his Holiness.

Escalus. What news abroad i' th' world?

Duke. None, but that there is so great a fever on goodness, that
the dissolution of it must cure it. Novelty is only in request, and
it is as dangerous to be aged in any kind of course, as it is   470
virtuous to be constant in any undertaking. There is scarce truth
enough alive to make societies secure, but security enough to
make fellowships accurs'd. Much upon this riddle runs the wisdom of the world. This news is old enough, yet it is every day's
news. I pray you, sir, of what disposition was the Duke?   475

Escalus. One that, above all other strifes, contended
especially to know himself.

Duke. What pleasure was he given to?

Escalus. Rather rejoicing to see another merry, than merry at
anything which professed to make him rejoice: a gentleman   480
of all temperance. But leave we him to his events, with a
prayer they may prove prosperous; and let me desire to know
how you find Claudio prepar'd. I am made to understand that
you have lent him visitation.

Duke. He professes to have received no sinister measure   485
from his judge, but most willingly humbles himself to the
determination of justice; yet had he framed to himself, by the
instruction of his frailty, many deceiving promises of life,
which I, by my good leisure, have discredited to him, and
now is he resolv'd to die.   490

Escalus. You have paid the heavens your function, and the
prisoner the very debt of your calling. I have labor'd for the
poor gentleman to the extremest shore of my modesty; but my
brother-justice have I found so severe, that he hath forc'd me
to tell him he is indeed Justice.   495

Duke. If his own life answer the straitness of his proceeding,
it shall become him well; wherein if he chance to fail, he hath
sentenc'd himself.

Escalus. I am going to visit the prisoner. Fare you well.

Duke. Peace be with you!   *[Exeunt Escalus and Provost.]*   500
He, who the sword of heaven will bear
Should be as holy as severe;
Pattern in himself to know,
Grace to stand, and virtue go;
More nor less to others paying   505
Than by self-offenses weighing.
Shame to him whose cruel striking
Kills for faults of his own liking!
Twice treble shame on Angelo,
To weed my vice and let his grow!   510
O, what may man within him hide,
Though angel on the outward side!
How may likeness made in crimes,
Making practice on the times,
To draw with idle spider's strings   515
Most ponderous and substantial things?
Craft against vice I must apply:
With Angelo tonight shall lie
His old betrothed, but despised:
So disguise shall, by th' disguised,   520
Pay with falsehood, false exacting,
And perform an old contracting.   *Exit.*

---

416 **opposite:** *adversary*   422 **tun-dish:** *funnel*   423 **ungenitur'd:** *impotent*   428
untrussing: *undoing the trousers*   430 **mutton;** *Cf. n.*   430, 431 **He's ... thee;**
Cf. n.   **not:** *F now*   433 **mortality:** *human life*   441 **forfeit:** *liable to penalty*   449
Philip and Jacob; *Cf. n.*   456 **wrought:** *by my pity acted as mercifully as I would*   459
entertainment: *expectation*   464 **time:** *present time*   465 **See:** *i.e. of Rome*

469 **dissolution:** *death* **only:** *especially*   472 **security:** *Cf. n.*   476 **strifes:** *endeavors*   481 **to his events:** *to the outcome of his affairs*   484 **visitation:** *priestly visit*   485
sinister: *unjust*   487 **determination:** *sentence* **framed:** *fabricated* **instruction:** *prompting*   491 **paid ... function:** *done your duty toward God*   493 **shore:** *limit* **modesty:**
sense of propriety   501–522 **He ... contracting;** *Cf. n.*   504 **and virtue go:** *if virtue
fail*   513–516 **How ... things;** *Cf. n.*

ACT FOURTH ❧ SCENE FIRST

Enter Mariana, and Boy singing.

'Take, O take those lips away,
That so sweetly were forsworn;
And those eyes, the break of day,
Lights that do mislead the morn:
But my kisses bring again, bring again,   5
Seals of love, but seal'd in vain, seal'd in vain.'

Enter Duke [disguised as before].

Mariana. Break off thy song, and haste thee quick away.
Here comes a man of comfort, whose advice
Hath often still'd my brawling discontent.   *[Exit Boy.]*
I cry you mercy, sir, and well could wish   10
You had not found me here so musical.
Let me excuse me, and believe me so,
My mirth it much displeas'd, but pleas'd my woe.
    Duke. 'Tis good; though music oft hath such a charm
To make bad good, and good provoke to harm.   15
I pray you tell me, hath anybody inquir'd for me here today?
Much upon this time have I promis'd here to meet.
    Mariana. You have not been inquir'd after. I have sat here
all day.

Enter Isabella.

    Duke. I do constantly believe you. The time is come even   20
now. I shall crave your forbearance a little; may be I will call
upon you anon, for some advantage to yourself.
    Mariana. I am always bound to you.   *Exit.*
    Duke. Very well met, and well come.
What is the news from this good deputy?   25
    Isabella. He hath a garden circummur'd with brick,
Whose western side is with a vineyard back'd;
And to that vineyard is a planched gate,
That makes his opening with this bigger key.
This other doth command a little door   30
Which from the vineyard to the garden leads.
There have I made my promise,
Upon the heavy middle of the night,
To call upon him.
    Duke. But shall you on your knowledge find this way?   35
    Isabella. I have tane a due and wary note upon't.
With whispering and most guilty diligence,
In action all of precept, he did show me
The way twice ore.
    Duke.   Are there no other tokens   40
Between you 'greed concerning her observance?
    Isabella. No, none, but only a repair i' th' dark,
And that I have possess'd him my most stay
Can be but brief; for I have made him know
I have a servant comes with me along,   45
That stays upon me, whose persuasion is
I come about my brother.
    Duke.   'Tis well borne up.

I have not yet made known to Mariana
A word of this. What ho, within! Come forth!   50

Enter Mariana.

I pray you, be acquainted with this maid.
She comes to do you good.
    Isabella.   I do desire the like.
    Duke. Do you persuade yourself that I respect you?
    Mariana. Good Friar, I know you do, and have found it.   55
    Duke. Take then this your companion by the hand,
Who hath a story ready for your ear.
I shall attend your leisure, but make haste;
The vaporous night approaches.
    Mariana. Will't please you walk aside?   60

            Exeunt [Mariana and Isabella].

    Duke. O place and greatness! Millions of false eyes
Are stuck upon thee. Volumes of report
Run with these false and most contrarious quests
Upon thy doings; thousand escapes of wit
Make thee the father of their idle dream,   65
And rack thee in their fancies!

Enter Mariana and Isabella.

                            Welcome, how agreed?
    Isabella. She'll take the enterprise upon her, Father,
If you advise it.
    Duke.   It is not my consent,   70
But my entreaty too.
    Isabella.   Little have you to say
When you depart from him but, soft and low,
'Remember now my brother.'
    Mariana.   Fear me not.   75
    Duke. Nor, gentle daughter, fear you not at all.
He is your husband on a pre-contract.
To bring you thus together, 'tis no sin,
Sith that the justice of your title to him
Doth flourish the deceit. Come, let us go: 80
Our corn's to reap, for yet our tilth's to sow.   *Exeunt.*

❧ SCENE SECOND ❧

Enter Provost and Clown [Pompey].

    Provost. Come hither, sirrah. Can you cut off a man's head?
    Pompey. If the man be a bachelor, sir, I can; but if he be a
married man, he's his wife's head, and I can never cut off a
woman's head.
    Provost. Come, sir, leave me your snatches, and yield me   5
a direct answer. Tomorrow morning are to die Claudio and
Barnardine. Here is in our prison a common executioner, who
in his office lacks a helper. If you will take it on you to assist
him, it shall redeem you from your gyves; if not, you shall
have your full time of imprisonment, and your deliverance   10
with an unpitied whipping, for you have been a notorious
bawd.
    Pompey. Sir, I have been an unlawful bawd time out of

1–6 'Take ... vain'; *Cf. n.*   10 cry you mercy: *beg your pardon*   13 My mirth ...
woe; *Cf. n.*   17 meet: *be present*   20 constantly: *firmly*   26 circummur'd: *walled
around*   28 planched: *boarded*   33 heavy: *drowsy*   38 action all of precept: *with
instructive gestures*   39 ore: *o'er, over*   41 observance: *i.e. of the instructions Isabella has
received*   42 repair: *rendezvous*   43 possess'd: *informed*   48 borne up: *contrived*

62 stuck: *fixed* report: *rumor*   63 quests: *inquiries (cries of hounds upon the
scent)*   64 escapes: *sallies*   66 rack: *distort*   80 flourish: *gloss over*   81 tilth:
plowed land; Cf. n   5 snatches: *quibbles*   7 common: *public*   9 gyves: *chains.*   11
unpitied: *pitiless*

mind, but yet I will be content to be a lawful hangman. I would be glad to receive some instruction from my fellow   *15*
partner.
Provost. What ho, Abhorson! Where's Abhorson, there?

Enter Abhorson.

Abhorson. Do you call, sir?
Provost. Sirrah, here's a fellow will help you tomorrow in your execution. If you think it meet, compound with him   *20*
by the year, and let him abide here with you; if not, use him for the present and dismiss him. He cannot plead his estima-
tion with you; he hath been a bawd.
Abhorson. A bawd, sir? Fie upon him! He will discredit our mystery.   *25*
Provost. Go to, sir: you weigh equally. A feather will turn the scale.   *Exit.*
Pompey. Pray, sir, by your good favor—for surely, sir, a good favor you have, but that you have a hanging look—do
you call, sir, your occupation a mystery?   *30*
Abhorson. Ay, sir, a mystery.
Pompey. Painting, sir, I have heard say, is a mystery; and your whores, sir, being members of my occupation, using paint-
ing, do prove my occupation a mystery. But what mystery there should be in hanging, if I should be hang'd, I cannot   *35*
imagine.
Abhorson. Sir, it is a mystery.
Pompey. Proof?
Abhorson. Every true man's apparel fits your thief. If it be too little for your thief, your true man thinks   *40*
it big enough. If it be too big for your thief, your thief thinks it little enough; so every true man's apparel fits your thief.

Enter Provost.

Provost. Are you agreed?
Pompey. Sir, I will serve him, for I do find that your hangman is a more penitent trade than your bawd; he doth   *45*
oftener ask forgiveness.
Pompey. You, sirrah, provide your block and your ax tomor-row four o'clock.
Abhorson. Come on, bawd. I will instruct thee in my trade. Follow.   *50*
Pompey. I do desire to learn, sir; and, I hope, if you have occasion to use me for your own turn, you shall find me yare.
For, truly, sir, for your kindness I owe you a good turn.
Provost. Call hether Barnardine and Claudio.
                          Exeunt [Pompey and Abhorson].
Th' one has my pity, not a jot the other,   *55*
Being a murtherer, though he were my brother.

Enter Claudio.

Look, here's the warrant, Claudio, for thy death.
'Tis now dead midnight, and by eight tomorrow
Thou must be made immortal. Where's Barnardine?
Claudio. As fast lock'd up in sleep as guiltless labor   *60*
When it lies starkly in the traveler's bones.
He will not wake.
Provost.   Who can do good on him?

Well, go, prepare yourself. *[Knocking within.]* But hark, what
noise?   *65*
Heaven give your spirits comfort. *[Exit Claudio.]* By and By.
I hope it is some pardon or reprieve
For the most gentle Claudio.

Enter Duke [disguised as before].

                  Welcome, Father.
Duke. The best and wholesom'st spirits of the night   *70*
Envelop you, good Provost. Who call'd here of late?
Provost. None since the curfew rung.
Duke. Not Isabel?
Provost.   No.
Duke. They will, then, ere't be long.   *75*
Provost. What comfort is for Claudio?
Duke. There's some in hope.
Provost.   It is a bitter deputy.
Duke. Not so, not so: his life is parallel'd
Even with the stroke and line of his great justice.   *80*
He doth with holy abstinence subdue
That in himself which he spurs on his power
To qualify in others. Were he meal'd with that
Which he corrects, then were he tyrannous,
But this being so, he's just. *[Knocking within.]* Now are   *85*
they come.   *[Exit Provost.]*
This is a gentle provost. Sildom when
The steeled gaoler is the friend of men. *[Knocking.]*
How now! What noise? That spirit's possess'd with haste
That wounds th' unsisting postern with these strokes.   *90*

[Enter Provost.]

Provost. There he must stay until the officer
Arise to let him in; he is call'd up.
Duke. Have you no countermand for Claudio yet,
But he must die tomorrow?
Provost.   None, sir, none.   *95*
Duke. As near the dawning, Provost, as it is,
You shall hear more ere morning.
Provost.   Happily
You something know: yet I believe there comes
No countermand. No such example have we.   *100*
Besides, upon the very siege of justice,
Lord Angelo hath to the public ear
Profess'd the contrary.

Enter a Messenger.

Duke. This is his Lord's man.
Provost. And here comes Claudio's pardon.   *105*
Messenger. My Lord hath sent you this note, and by me this
further charge: that you swerve not from the smallest article of
it, neither in time, matter, or other circumstance. Good mor-
row; for, as I take it, it is almost day.
Provost. I shall obey him.   *[Exit Messenger.]*   *110*
Duke. [Aside.] This is his pardon, purchas'd by such sin
For which the pardoner himself is in:
Hence hath offense his quick celerity,
When it is borne in high authority.

---

20 meet: *fitting* **compound:** *come to terms*   **22 estimation:** *good reputation*   **25 mys-tery:** *craft, trade*   **28 favor:** *countenance*   **39–42 Every . . . thief;** *Cf. n.*   **40 true:** *honest*   **45, 46 he . . . forgiveness:** *Cf. n.*   **52 yare:** *nimble* F y'are   **54 hether:** *hither*   **61 starkly:** *stiffly*

66 By and by: *right away* (in answer to the knocking)   **80 Even:** *read 'E'en'* **stroke and line;** *Cf. n.*   **83 qualify:** *temper* **meal'd:** *stained*   **87 Sildom when:** *it is seldom that*   **88 steeled:** *hardened*   **90 unsisting:** *unresisting*   **98 Happily:** *per-chance*   **101 siege:** *seat*

When Vice makes Mercy, Mercy's so extended,   115
That for the fault's love is th' offender friended.
Now, sir, what news?

Provost. I told you. Lord Angelo, belike thinking me remiss
in mine office, awakens me with this unwonted putting on—
methinks strangely, for he hath not us'd it before.   120

Duke. Pray you, let's hear.

[Provost reads] The Letter.

*Whatsoever you may hear to the contrary, let Claudio be exe-
cuted by four of the clock; and, in the afternoon, Barnardine.
For my better satisfaction, let me have Claudio's head sent
me by five. Let this be duly performed, with a thought that   125
more depends on it than we must yet deliver. Thus fail not
to do your office, as you will answer it at your peril.*
What say you to this, sir?

Duke. What is that Barnardine who is to be executed in
th' afternoon?   130

Provost. A Bohemian born, but here nurs'd up and bred;
one that is a prisoner nine years old.

Duke. How came it that the absent Duke had not either
deliver'd him to his liberty or executed him? I have heard
it was ever his manner to do so.   135

Provost. His friends still wrought reprieves for him; and,
indeed, his fact, till now in the government of Lord Angelo,
came not to an undoubtful proof.

Duke. It is now apparent?

Provost. Most manifest, and not denied by himself.   140

Duke. Hath he borne himself penitently in prison? How
seems he to be touch'd?

Provost. A man that apprehends death no more dreadfully
but as a drunken sleep: careless, reckless, and fearless of
what's past, present, or to come; insensible of mortality,   145
and desperately mortal.

Duke. He wants advice.

Provost. He will hear none. He hath evermore had the liberty of the prison: give him leave to escape hence, he would
not. Drunk many times a day, if not many days entirely   150
drunk. We have very oft awak'd him, as if to carry him to
execution, and show'd him a seeming warrant for it; it hath
not moved him at all.

Duke. More of him anon. There is written in your brow,
Provost, honesty and constancy. If I read it not truly, my   155
ancient skill beguiles me; but in the boldness of my cunning I
will lay myself in hazard. Claudio, whom here you have warrant to execute, is no greater forfeit to the law than Angelo
who hath sentenc'd him. To make you understand this in a
manifested effect, I crave but four days' respite, for the which
you are to do me both a present and a dangerous courtesy.

Provost. Pray, sir, in what?

Duke. In the delaying death.

Provost. Alack! how may I do it, having the hour limited,
and an express command, under penalty, to deliver his head   165
in the view of Angelo? I may make my case as Claudio's,
to cross this in the smallest.

Duke. By the vow of mine order I warrant you, if my
instructions may be your guide. Let this Barnardine be this
morning executed, and his head borne to Angelo.   170

Provost. Angelo hath seen them both, and will discover the
favor.

Duke. O! death's a great disguiser, and you may add to it.
Shave the head, and dye the beard; and say it was the desire of
the penitent to be so bar'd before his death. You know the   175
course is common. If anything fall to you upon this, more
than thanks and good fortune, by the Saint whom I profess,
I will plead against it with my life.

Provost. Pardon me, good Father; it is against my oath.

Duke. Were you sworn to the Duke or to the deputy?   180

Provost. To him, and to his substitutes.

Duke. You will think you have made no offense, if the
Duke avouch the justice of your dealing?

Provost. But what likelihood is in that?

Duke. Not a resemblance, but a certainty. Yet since I see   185
you fearful, that neither my coat, integrity, nor persuasion can
with ease attempt you, I will go further than I meant, to pluck
all fears out of you. Look you, sir; here is the hand and seal of
the Duke: you know the character, I doubt not, and the signet
is not strange to you.   190

Provost. I know them both.

Duke. The contents of this is the return of the Duke. You
shall anon over-read it at your pleasure, where you shall find
within these two days, he will be here. This is a thing that Angelo knows not, for he this very day receives letters of strange   195
tenor, perchance of the Duke's death, perchance entering into
some monastery, but by chance nothing of what is writ. Look,
th' unfolding star calls up the shepherd. Put not yourself into
amazement how these things should be; all difficulties are but
easy when they are known. Call your executioner, and off   200
with Barnardine's head. I will give him a present shrift and advise him for a better place. Yet you are amaz'd, but this shall
absolutely resolve you. Come away; it is almost clear dawn.

Exit [with Provost].

❧ SCENE THIRD ❧

Enter Clown [Pompey].

Pompey. I am as well acquainted here as I was in our house
of profession: one would think it were Mistress Overdone's
own house, for here be many of her old customers. First,
here's young Master Rash; he's in for a commodity of brown
paper and old ginger, nine-score and seventeen pounds, of   5
which he made five marks, ready money. Marry, then ginger
was not much in request, for the old women were all dead.
Then is there here one Master Caper, at the suit of Master
Threepile the mercer, for some four suits of peach-color'd
satin, which now peaches him a beggar. Then have we here   10
young Dizzy, and young Master Deepvow, and Master Cop-
perspur, and Master Starve-lackey, the rapier and dagger man,
and young Drop-heir that kill'd lusty Pudding, and Master

119 **putting on:** *incitement*   132 **prisoner . . . old:** *prisoner for nine years*   136 **still:** *constantly*   137 **fact:** *crime*   138 **undoubtful:** *certain*   143 **dreadfully:** *with dread*   145
mortality: *death*   146 **mortal:** *lacking in any hope of immortality*   147 **advice:** *spiritual
counsel*   157 **lay . . . hazard:** *jeopardize myself* (a dicing metaphor)   159, 160 **in . . . effect:**
by presenting concrete evidence   164 **limited:** *designated*   167 **cross:** *thwart*

168 **warrant you:** *guarantee your security*   172 **favor:** *difference in feature*   174 **dye:** *F
tie; Cf. n.*   175 **bar'd:** *shaved*   185 **resemblance:** *probability*   189 **character:** *handwriting*   198 **unfolding star:** *morning star, when the flocks leave the fold*   199 **amazement:** *perplexity*   201 **shrift:** *confession and absolution*   203 **resolve:** *assure*   2
profession: *business*   4–7 **commodity . . . dead;** *Cf. n.*   10 **peaches:** *impeaches*

Forthright the tilter, and brave Master Shoe-tie, the great
traveler, and wild Half-can that stabb'd Pots, and, I think,   *15*
forty more; all great doers in our trade, and are now 'for the
Lord's sake.'

Enter Abhorson.

Abhorson. Sirrah, bring Barnardine hither.

Pompey. Master Barnardine! You must rise and be hang'd,
Master Barnardine.   *20*

Abhorson. What ho! Barnardine!

Barnardine. [*Within.*] A pox o' your throats!
Who makes that noise there? What are you?

Pompey. Your friends, sir, the hangman. You must be so
good, sir, to rise and be put to death.   *25*

Barnardine. [*Within.*] Away! you rogue, away! I am sleepy.

Abhorson. Tell him he must awake, and that quickly too.

Pompey. Pray, Master Barnardine, awake till you are executed, and sleep afterwards.

Abhorson. Go in to him, and fetch him out.   *30*

Pompey. He is coming, sir, he is coming. I hear his straw
rustle.

Enter Barnardine.

Abhorson. Is the ax upon the block, sirrah?

Pompey. Very ready, sir.

Barnardine. How now, Abhorson! What's the news with   *35*
you?

Abhorson. Truly, sir, I would desire you to clap into your
prayers: for, look you, the warrant's come.

Barnardine. You rogue, I have been drinking all night;
I am not fitted for't.   *40*

Pompey. O, the better, sir: for he that drinks all night,
and is hang'd betimes in the morning, may sleep the sounder
all the next day.

Enter Duke [disguised as before].

Abhorson. Look you, sir; here comes your ghostly father.
Do we jest now, think you?   *45*

Duke. Sir, induced by my charity, and hearing how hastily
you are to depart, I am come to advise you, comfort you, and
pray with you.

Barnardine. Friar, not I: I have been drinking hard all night,
and I will have more time to prepare me, or they shall beat   *50*
out my brains with billets. I will not consent to die this day,
that's certain.

Duke. O, sir, you must; and therefore, I beseech you look
forward on the journey you shall go.

Barnardine. I swear I will not die today for any man's   *55*
persuasion.

Duke. But hear you—

Barnardine. Not a word: if you have anything to say to me,
come to my ward; for thence will not I today.   *Exit.*

Enter Provost.

Duke. Unfit to live or die. O gravel heart!   *60*
After him, fellows: bring him to the block.

[Exeunt Abhorson and Pompey.]

Provost. Now, sir, how do you find the prisoner?

Duke. A creature unprepar'd, unmeet for death,
And to transport him in the mind he is
Were damnable.   *65*

Provost.   Here in the prison, Father,
There died this morning of a cruel fever
One Ragozine, a most notorious pirate,
A man of Claudio's years—his beard and head
Just of his color. What if we do omit   *70*
This reprobate till he were well inclin'd,
And satisfy the deputy with the visage
Of Ragozine, more like to Claudio?

Duke. O, 'tis an accident that heaven provides!
Dispatch it presently. The hour draws on   *75*
Prefix'd by Angelo. See this be done,
And sent according to command, whiles I
Persuade this rude wretch willingly to die.

Provost. This shall be done, good Father, presently.
But Barnardine must die this afternoon.   *80*
And how shall we continue Claudio,
To save me from the danger that might come
If he were known alive?

Duke.   Let this be done.
Put them in secret holds, both Barnardine and Claudio.   *85*
Ere twice the sun hath made his journal greeting
To th' under generation, you shall find
Your safety manifested.

Provost. I am your free dependant.

Duke. Quick, dispatch, and send the head to Angelo.   *90*
                              Exit [Provost].

Now will I write letters to Angelo—
The Provost, he shall bear them—whose contents
Shall witness to him I am near at home,
And that, by great injunctions, I am bound
To enter publicly. Him I'll desire   *95*
To meet me at the consecrated fount
A league below the city; and from thence,
By cold gradation and well-balanc'd form,
We shall proceed with Angelo.

Enter Provost.

Provost. Here is the head. I'll carry it myself.   *100*

Duke. Convenient is it. Make a swift return,
For I would commune with you of such things
That want no ear but yours.

Provost.   I'll make all speed.   *Exit.*

Isabella. [*Within.*] Peace, ho, be here!   *105*

Duke. The tongue of Isabel. She's come to know
If yet her brother's pardon be come hither.
But I will keep her ignorant of her good,
To make her heavenly comforts of despair,
When it is least expected.   *110*

Enter Isabella.

Isabella.   Ho, by your leave!

Duke. Good morning to you, fair and gracious daughter.

14 tilter: *fencer* **Shoe-tie;** *Cf. n.* **16, 17 'for . . . sake':** *cry of prisoners asking alms from jail windows* **23 What:** *who* **37 clap into:** *go at once into* **40 I . . . for't;** *Cf. n.* **44 ghostly:** *spiritual* **51 billets:** *blocks of wood* **58 ward:** *cell* **60 gravel:** *stony*

64 transport: *i.e. to the next world* **70 omit:** *pass by* **75 presently:** *immediately* **81 continue:** *keep* **86 journal:** *daily* **87 th' under:** *the Antipodes;* F *yond.* **89 free dependant:** *willing servant* **98 cold gradation:** *deliberate degrees* **102 commune:** *stressed — —*

Isabella. The better, given me by so holy a man.
Hath yet the deputy sent my brother's pardon?
    Duke. He hath releas'd him, Isabel, from the world.   *115*
His head is off and sent to Angelo.
    Isabella. Nay, but it is not so.
    Duke. It is no other. Show your wisdom, daughter,
In your close patience.
    Isabella. O! I will to him and pluck out his eyes!   *120*
    Duke. You shall not be admitted to his sight.
    Isabella. Unhappy Claudio! Wretched Isabel!
Injurious world! Most damned Angelo!
    Duke. This nor hurts him nor profits you a jot.
Forbear it therefore; give your cause to heaven.   *125*
Mark what I say, which you shall find
By every syllable a faithful verity.
The Duke comes home tomorrow—nay, dry your eyes—
One of our covent, and his confessor,
Gives me this instance. Already he hath carried   *130*
Notice to Escalus and Angelo,
Who do prepare to meet him at the gates,
There to give up their power. If you can, pace your wisdom
In that good path that I would wish it go,
And you shall have your bosom on this wretch,   *135*
Grace of the Duke, revenges to your heart,
And general honor.
    Isabella.   I am directed by you.
    Duke. This letter then to Friar Peter give—
'Tis that he sent me of the Duke's return.   *140*
Say, by this token, I desire his company
At Mariana's house tonight. Her cause and yours,
I'll perfect him withal, and he shall bring you
Before the Duke; and to the head of Angelo
Accuse him home and home. For my poor self,   *145*
I am combined by a sacred vow
And shall be absent. Wend you with this letter.
Command these fretting waters from your eyes
With a light heart. Trust not my holy order,
If I pervert your course. Who's here?   *150*

Enter Lucio.

    Lucio. Good even. Friar, where's the provost?
    Duke. Not within, sir.
    Lucio. O pretty Isabella, I am pale at mine heart to see
thine eyes so red: thou must be patient. I am fain to dine
and sup with water and bran. I dare not for my head fill   *155*
my belly; one fruitful meal would set me to't. But they say
the Duke will be here tomorrow. By my troth, Isabel, I lov'd
thy brother. If the old fantastical Duke of dark corners
had been at home, he had lived.   *[Exit Isabella.]*
    Duke. Sir, the Duke is marvelous little beholding to   *160*
your reports; but the best is, he lives not in them.
    Lucio. Friar, thou knowest not the Duke so well as I do.
He's a better woodman than thou tak'st him for.
    Duke. Well, you'll answer this one day. Fare ye well.
    Lucio. Nay, tarry, I'll go along with thee. I can tell thee   *165*
pretty tales of the Duke.

    Duke. You have told me too many of him already, sir, if
they be true; if not true, none were enough.
    Lucio. I was once before him for getting a wench with
child.   *170*
    Duke. Did you such a thing?
    Lucio. Yes, marry, did I; but I was fain to forswear it.
They would else have married me to the rotten medlar.
    Duke. Sir, your company is fairer than honest. Rest you
well.   *175*
    Lucio. By my troth, I'll go with thee to the lane's end.
If bawdy talk offend you, we'll have very little of it. Nay,
Friar, I am a kind of burr: I shall stick.   *Exeunt.*

❧ SCENE FOURTH ❧

Enter Angelo and Escalus.

    Escalus. Every letter he hath writ hath disvouch'd other.
    Angelo. In most uneven and distracted manner. His actions
show much like to madness. Pray heaven his wisdom be not
tainted. And why meet him at the gates, and redeliver our
authorities there?   *5*
    Escalus. I guess not.
    Angelo. And why should we proclaim it in an hour before
his ent'ring, that if any crave redress of injustice, they should
exhibit their petitions in the street?
    Escalus. He shows his reason for that: to have a dispatch   *10*
of complaints, and to deliver us from devices hereafter, which
shall then have no power to stand against us.
    Angelo. Well, I beseech you let it be proclaim'd. Betimes i'
th' morn I'll call you at your house. Give notice to such men
of sort and suit as are to meet him.   *15*
    Escalus. I shall, sir: fare you well.
    Angelo. Good night.   *Exit [Escalus].*
This deed unshapes me quite, makes me unpregnant
And dull to all proceedings. A deflower'd maid,
And by an eminent body that enforc'd   *20*
The law against it! But that her tender shame
Will not proclaim against her maiden loss,
How might she tongue me! Yet reason dares her no:
For my authority bears off a credent bulk,
That no particular scandal once can touch   *25*
But it confounds the breather. He should have liv'd,
Save that his riotous youth, with dangerous sense,
Might in the times to come have tane revenge,
By so receiving a dishonor'd life
With ransom of such shame. Would yet he had liv'd!   *30*
Alack, when once our grace we have forgot,
Nothing goes right: we would, and we would not.   *Exit.*

119 close: *secret i.e. by concealing your suffering*   **120 I will:** *read 'I'll'*   **129 covent:** *convent*
confessor: *stressed* ´— —´   **130 instance:** *piece of news*   **133 pace:** *direct*   **135 bosom:**
heart's desire   **143 perfect:** *make him fully acquainted with*   **145 home and home:** *sharply,*
decisively   **146 combined:** *bound*   **147 Wend you:** *go your way*   **154 fain:** *com-*
pelled   **158 fantastical:** *capricious* **of dark corners:** *i.e. he transacts his affairs in dark cor-*
ners   **161 in them:** *according to them*   **163 woodman:** *hunter, i.e. of women*

173 medlar: *a fruit rotten before it is ripe*   **174 fairer:** *more amiable*   **1 disvouch'd:**
contradicted   **11 devices:** *cunning plots*   **13–17 Well . . . night;** *Cf. n.*   **13 Betimes:**
early   **15 sort and suit:** *rank and standing*   **18 unshapes:** *confounds* **unpregnant:**
unapt   **22 her maiden loss:** *loss of her virginity*   **23 tongue:** *accuse* **dares her no:**
intimidates her into saying nothing   **24 credent bulk:** *weight of credibility*   **25 particular:**
personal   **28 tane:** *ta'en, taken*   **30 he had:** *read 'he'd'*

❧ SCENE FIFTH ❧

Enter Duke [in his own habit] and Friar Peter.

Duke. These letters at fit time deliver me.
The provost knows our purpose and our plot.
The matter being afoot, keep your instruction,
And hold you ever to our special drift,
Though sometimes you do blench from this to that,   5
As cause doth minister. Go call at Flavius' house,
And tell him where I stay; give the like notice
To Valencius, Rowland, and to Crassus,
And bid them bring the trumpets to the gate.
But send me Flavius first.   10
   Friar Peter.   It shall be speeded well.   *[Exit.]*

Enter Varrius.

Duke. I thank thee, Varrius; thou hast made good haste.
Come, we will walk. There's other of our friends
Will greet us here anon, my gentle Varrius. *Exeunt.*

❧ SCENE SIXTH ❧

Enter Isabella and Mariana.

Isabella. To speak so indirectly I am loath.
I would say the truth; but to accuse him so,
That is your part. Yet I'm advis'd to do it,
He says, to veil full purpose.
   Mariana.   Be rul'd by him.   5
   Isabella. Besides, he tells me that if peradventure
He speak against me on the adverse side,
I should not think it strange, for 'tis a physic
That's bitter to sweet end.
   Mariana. I would Friar Peter—   10

Enter [Friar] Peter.

   Isabella.   O, peace! The friar is come.
Friar Peter. Come, I have found you out a stand most fit,
Where you may have such vantage on the Duke
He shall not pass you. Twice have the trumpets sounded.
The generous and gravest citizens   15
Have hent the gates, and very near upon
The Duke is ent'ring; therefore hence, away.   *Exeunt.*

ACT FIFTH ❧ SCENE FIRST

*Enter Duke, Varrius, Lords, Angelo, Escalus, Lucio,
[Provost, Officers, and] Citizens at several doors.*

Duke. My very worthy cousin, fairly met.
Our old and faithful friend, we are glad to see you.
   Angelo.⎫
          ⎬Happy return be to your royal Grace!
   Escalus.⎭
                                5

Duke. Many and hearty thankings to you both.
We have made inquiry of you; and we hear
Such goodness of your justice, that our soul
Cannot but yield you forth to public thanks,
Forerunning more requital.   10
   Angelo.   You make my bonds still greater.
   Duke. O, your desert speaks loud, and I should wrong it,
To lock it in the wards of covert bosom,
When it deserves with characters of brass,
A forted residence 'gainst the tooth of time   15
And razure of oblivion. Give me your hand,
And let the subject see, to make them know
That outward courtesies would fain proclaim
Favors that keep within. Come, Escalus,
You must walk by us on our other hand;   20
And good supporters are you.

Enter [Friar] Peter and Isabella.

Friar Peter. Now is your time. Speak loud and kneel before
him.
   Isabella. Justice, O royal Duke! Vail your regard
Upon a wrong'd—I would fain have said, a maid!   25
O worthy Prince, dishonor not your eye
By throwing it on any other object
Till you have heard me in my true complaint
And given me justice, justice, justice, justice!
   Duke. Relate your wrongs. In what? By whom? Be brief.   30
Here is Lord Angelo shall give you justice.
Reveal yourself to him.
   Isabella.   O worthy Duke!
You bid me seek redemption of the divel.
Hear me yourself; for that which I must speak   35
Must either punish me, not being believ'd,
Or wring redress from you. Hear me, O hear me, here!
   Angelo. My Lord, her wits, I fear me, are not firm.
She hath bin a suitor to me for her brother,
Cut off by course of justice—   40
   Isabella.   By course of justice!
   Angelo. And she will speak most bitterly and strange.
   Isabella. Most strange, but yet most truly, will I speak.
That Angelo's forsworn, is it not strange?
That Angelo's a murtherer, is't not strange?   45
That Angelo is an adulterous thief,
A hypocrite, a virgin-violator,
Is it not strange, and strange?
   Duke.   Nay, it is ten times strange.
   Isabella. It is not truer he is Angelo   50
Than this is all as true as it is strange.
Nay, it is ten times true; for truth is truth
To th' end of reck'ning.
   Duke.   Away with her! Poor soul,
She speaks this in th' infirmity of sense.   55
   Isabella. O Prince, I conjure thee, as thou believ'st
There is another comfort than this world,
That thou neglect me not with that opinion
That I am touch'd with madness. Make not impossible
That which but seems unlike. 'Tis not impossible   60

---

1 me: *ethical dative*   **4 drift:** *purpose*   **5 blench:** *turn aside*   **9 trumpets:** *trumpeters*   **2 I would:** *read 'I'd'*   **4 veil full purpose:** *conceal our full plan*   **12 stand:** *station*   **13 vantage:** *advantage of position*   **15 generous:** *of noble birth*   **16 hent:** *reached*   **1 cousin:** *title of respect*   **2 we are:** *read 'we're'*

7 We have *read: 'we've'*   **13 wards:** *prison cells*   **covert bosom:** *i.e. keep it secret in my heart*   **14 characters:** *letters*   **15 forted:** *fortified*   **16 razure:** *effacement*   **24 Vail your regard:** *look down*   **39 She hath:** *read 'she'th'*   **55 in ... sense:** *out of a sick mind*   **60 unlike:** *improbable*

But one, the wicked'st caitiff on the ground,
May seem as shy, as grave, as just, as absolute
As Angelo; even so may Angelo,
In all his dressings, caracts, titles, forms,
Be an arch-villain. Believe it, royal Prince.   65
If he be less, he's nothing; but he's more,
Had I more name for badness.
    Duke.   By mine honesty,
If she be mad—as I believe no other—
Her madness hath the oddest frame of sense,   70
Such a dependency of thing on thing,
As ere I heard in madness.
    Isabella.   O gracious Duke,
Harp not on that; nor do not banish reason
For inequality, but let your reason serve   75
To make the truth appear where it seems hid,
And hide the false seems true.
    Duke.   Many that are not mad
Have sure more lack of reason. What would you say?
    Isabella. I am the sister of one Claudio,   80
Condemn'd upon the act of fornication
To lose his head, condemn'd by Angelo.
I, in probation of a sisterhood,
Was sent to by my brother, one Lucio
As then the messenger—   85
    Lucio.   That's I, and't like your Grace.
I came to her from Claudio, and desir'd her
To try her gracious fortune with Lord Angelo
For her poor brother's pardon.
    Isabella.   That's he indeed.   90
    Duke. You were not bid to speak.
    Lucio.   No, my good lord,
Nor wish'd to hold my peace.
    Duke.   I wish you now, then.
Pray you, take note of it, and when you have   95
A business for yourself, pray heaven you then
Be perfect.
    Lucio. I warrant your Honor.
    Duke. The warrant's for yourself: take heed to't.
    Isabella. This gentleman told somewhat of my tale—   100
    Lucio. Right.
    Duke. It may be right, but you are i' the wrong
To speak before your time. Proceed.
    Isabella.   I went
To this pernicious caitiff deputy—   105
    Duke. That's somewhat madly spoken.
    Isabella.   Pardon it,
The phrase is to the matter.
    Duke. Mended again. The matter: proceed.
    Isabella. In brief, to set the needless process by,   110
How I persuaded, how I pray'd, and kneel'd
How he refell'd me, and how I replied—
For this was of much length—the vild conclusion
I now begin with grief and shame to utter.
He would not, but by gift of my chaste body   115
To his concupiscible intemperate lust,
Release my brother; and, after much debatement,

My sisterly remorse confutes mine honor,
And I did yield to him. But the next morn betimes,
His purpose surfeiting, he sends a warrant   120
For my poor brother's head.
    Duke.   This is most likely!
    Isabella. O, that it were as like as it is true!
    Duke. By heaven, fond wretch! Thou know'st not what thou
speak'st,   125
Or else thou art suborn'd against his honor
In hateful practice. First, his integrity
Stands without blemish; next, it imports no reason
That with such vehemency he should pursue
Faults proper to himself. If he had so offended,   130
He would have weigh'd thy brother by himself,
And not have cut him off. Someone hath set you on.
Confess the truth, and say by whose advice
Thou cam'st here to complain.
    Isabella.   And is this all?   135
Then, O you blessed ministers above,
Keep me in patience; and with ripen'd time
Unfold the evil which is here wrapt up
In countenance! Heaven shield your Grace from woe,
As I, thus wrong'd, hence unbelieved go!   140
    Duke. I know you'd fain be gone. An officer!
To prison with her! Shall we thus permit
A blasting and a scandalous breath to fall
On him so near us? This needs must be a practice.
Who knew of your intent and coming hither?   145
    Isabella. One that I would were here, Friar Lodowick.
    Duke. A ghostly father, belike. Who knows that
Lodowick?
    Lucio. My lord, I know him; 'tis a meddling friar.
I do not like the man. Had he been lay, my lord,   150
For certain words he spake against your Grace
In your retirement, I had swing'd him soundly.
    Duke. Words against me! This' a good friar, belike!
And to set on this wretched woman here
Against our substitute! Let this friar be found.   155
    Lucio. But yesternight, my lord, she and that friar,
I saw them at the prison: a saucy friar,
A very scurvy fellow.
    Friar Peter. Blessed be your royal Grace!
I have stood by, my lord, and I have heard   160
Your royal ear abus'd. First, hath this woman
Most wrongfully accus'd your substitute,
Who is as free from touch or soil with her,
As she from one ungot.
    Duke.   We did believe no less.   165
Know you that Friar Lodowick that she speaks of?
    Friar Peter. I know him for a man divine and holy—
Not scurvy, nor a temporary meddler,
As he's reported by this gentleman;
And, on my trust, a man that never yet   170
Did, as he vouches, misreport your Grace.
    Lucio. My lord, most villainously—believe it.
    Friar Peter. Well: he in time may come to clear himself,
But at this instant he is sick, my lord,

---

62 absolute: *perfect*   64 dressings: *outward shows*   caracts: *distinctive marks*   72 ere: *e'er, ever*
75 inequality: *injustice*   77 hide: *eclipse*   seems: *which seems*   83 probation: *novitiate*
86 and't like: *if it please*   93 wish'd: *bidden, with a quibble*   108 to: *applicable to*   110
set . . . by: *pass over*   112 refell'd: *refuted*   113 vild: *vile*   116 concupiscible: *lewd*

118 remorse: *pity*   124 fond: *foolish*   126 suborn'd: *bribed to bear false witness*   127
practice: *stratagem*   130 proper: *belonging*   139 countenance: *authority*   144 practice: *plot*   150 lay: *a layman*   152 swing'd: *beaten*   153 This': *this is*   163 soil: *defilement*   164 ungot: *unborn*   168 temporary: *in worldly affairs*

Of a strange fever. Upon his mere request,   *175*
Being come to knowledge that there was complaint
Intended 'gainst Lord Angelo, came I hether,
To speak, as from his mouth, what he doth know
Is true and false; and what he with his oath
And all probation will make up full clear,   *180*
Whensoever he's convented. First, for this woman,
To justify this worthy nobleman,
So vulgarly and personally accus'd,
Her shall you hear disproved to her eyes,
Till she herself confess it.   *185*
 Duke.   Good Friar, let's hear it.

     [Isabella withdraws, guarded.] Enter Mariana.

Do you not smile at this, Lord Angelo?
O heaven, the vanity of wretched fools!
Give us some seats. Come, cousin Angelo,
In this I'll be impartial. Be you judge   *190*
Of your own cause. Is this the witness, Friar?
First, let her show her face, and after speak.
 Mariana. Pardon, my lord. I will not show my face
Until my husband bid me.
 Duke. What, are you married?   *195*
 Mariana. No, my lord.
 Duke. Are you a maid?
 Mariana. No, my lord.
 Duke. A widow, then?
 Mariana. Neither, my lord.   *200*
 Duke. Why, you are nothing, then—neither maid, widow,
nor wife?
 Lucio. My lord, she may be a punk; for many of them are
neither maid, widow, nor wife.
 Duke. Silence that fellow. I would he had some cause   *205*
To prattle for himself.
 Lucio. Well, my lord.
 Mariana. My lord, I do confess I nere was married,
And I confess besides I am no maid:
I have known my husband, yet my husband   *210*
Knows not that ever he knew me.
 Lucio. He was drunk, then, my lord; it can be no better.
 Duke. For the benefit of silence, would thou wert so too!
 Lucio. Well, my lord.
 Duke. This is no witness for Lord Angelo.   *215*
 Mariana. Now I come to't, my lord:
She that accuses him of fornication,
In selfsame manner doth accuse my husband;
And charges him, my lord, with such a time,
When, I'll depose, I had him in mine arms,   *220*
With all th' effect of love.
 Angelo. Charges she moe than me?
 Mariana.   Not that I know.
 Duke. No? You say your husband?
 Mariana. Why, just, my lord, and that is Angelo,   *225*
Who thinks he knows that he nere knew my body,
But knows he thinks that he knows Isabel's.
 Angelo. This is a strange abuse. Let's see thy face.
 Mariana. My husband bids me. Now I will unmask.

           [Unveiling.]

This is that face, thou cruel Angelo,
Which once thou swor'st was worth the looking on.
This is the hand which, with a vow'd contract,
Was fast belock'd in thine. This is the body
That took away the match from Isabel,   *235*
And did supply thee at thy garden-house
In her imagin'd person.
 Duke.   Know you this woman?
 Lucio. Carnally, she says.
 Duke.   Sirrah, no more!   *240*
 Lucio. Enough, my lord.
 Angelo. My lord, I must confess I know this woman,
And five years since there was some speech of marriage
Betwixt myself and her, which was broke off,
Partly for that her promised proportions   *245*
Came short of composition, but in chief
For that her reputation was disvalued
In levity: since which time of five years
I never spake with her, saw her, nor heard from her,
Upon my faith and honor.   *250*
 Mariana.   Noble Prince,
As there comes light from heaven and words from breath,
As there is sense in truth and truth in virtue,
I am affianc'd this man's wife as strongly
As words could make up vows; and, my good lord,   *255*
But Tuesday night last gone in's garden-house
He knew me as a wife. As this is true,
Let me in safety raise me from my knees
Or else forever be confixed here
A marble monument.   *260*
 Angelo.   I did but smile till now:
Now, good my lord, give me the scope of justice—
My patience here is touch'd. I do perceive
These poor informal women are no more
But instruments of some more mightier member   *265*
That sets them on. Let me have way, my lord,
To find this practice out.
 Duke.   Ay, with my heart;
And punish them to your height of pleasure.
Thou foolish Friar, and thou pernicious woman,   *270*
Compact with her that's gone, think'st thou thy oaths,
Though they would swear down each particular saint,
Were testimonies against his worth and credit
That's seal'd in approbation? You, Lord Escalus,
Sit with my cousin. Lend him your kind pains   *275*
To find out this abuse, whence 'tis deriv'd.
There is another friar that set them on.
Let him be sent for.
 Friar Peter. Would he were here, my lord; for he indeed
Hath set the women on to this complaint.   *280*
Your provost knows the place where he abides
And he may fetch him.
 Duke.   Go do it instantly.   *[Exit Provost.]*
And you, my noble and well-warranted cousin,
Whom it concerns to hear this matter forth,   *285*
Do with your injuries as seems you best,

175 **Upon . . . request:** *solely because he requested it* 177 **hether:** *hither* 180 **probation:** *proof* 181 **Whensoever:** *read 'whensoe'er'* **convented:** *summoned* 183 **vulgarly:** *publicly* SD **Isabella withdraws;** *Cf. n.* 190 **be impartial:** *take no part* 192 **her:** *F your* 203 **punk:** *prostitute* 208 **nere:** *ne'er, never* 228 **abuse:** *deception*

233 **contract:** *stressed* — ´ 235 **match:** *appointment* 236 **supply:** *gratify* 245 **promised:** *F promis'd* **proportions:** *dowry* 246 **composition:** *agreement* 248 **levity:** *loose conduct* 259 **confixed:** *firmly fixed* 262 **scope:** *free play* 264 **informal:** *foolish* 271 **Compact:** *leagued* 272 **particular:** *read 'partic'lar'* 273 **against:** *read 'gainst'*

In any chastisement. I for a while
Will leave you, but stir not you till you have
Well determin'd upon these slanderers.

    Escalus. My lord, we'll do it throughly.   *Exit [Duke].* 290
Signior Lucio, did not you say you knew that Friar Lodowick
   to be a dishonest person?

    Lucio. Cucullus non facit monachum: honest in nothing, but
in his clothes; and one that hath spoke most villainous
speeches of the Duke.   295

    Escalus. We shall entreat you to abide here till he come and
enforce them against him. We shall find this friar a notable
fellow.

    Lucio. As any in Vienna, on my word.

    Escalus. Call that same Isabel here once again. I would   300
speak with her. *[Exit an Attendant.]* Pray you, my lord, give
me leave to question; you shall see how I'll handle her.

    Lucio. Not better than he, by her own report.

    Escalus. Say you?

    Lucio. Marry, sir, I think, if you handled her privately, she
would sooner confess: perchance, publicly, she'll be asham'd.

Enter Duke [in his friar's habit], Provost, Isabella [and Officers].

    Escalus. I will go darkly to work with her.

    Lucio. That's the way: for women are light at midnight.

    Escalus. Come on, mistress. Here's a gentlewoman denies
all that you have said.   310

    Lucio. My lord, here comes the rascal I spoke of—here
with the provost.

    Escalus. In very good time. Speak not you to him, till we
call upon you.

    Lucio. Mum.   315

    Escalus. Come, sir. Did you set these women on to
slander Lord Angelo? They have confess'd you did.

    Duke. 'Tis false.

    Escalus. How! know you where you are?

    Duke. Respect to your great place! And let the divel   320
Be sometime honor'd for his burning throne.
Where is the Duke? 'Tis he should hear me speak.

    Escalus. The Duke's in us, and we will hear you speak.
Look you speak justly.

    Duke. Boldly at least. But O, poor souls,   325
Come you to seek the lamb here of the fox?
Good night to your redress! Is the Duke gone?
Then is your cause gone, too. The Duke's unjust,
Thus to retort your manifest appeal
And put your trial in the villain's mouth   330
Which here you come to accuse.

    Lucio. This is the rascal! This is he I spoke of.

    Escalus. Why, thou unreverend and unhallow'd Friar!
Is't not enough thou hast suborn'd these women
To accuse this worthy man but, in foul mouth,   335
And in the witness of his proper ear,
To call him villain?
And then to glance from him to th' Duke himself,
To tax him with injustice? Take him hence.
To th' rack with him! We'll touse him joint by joint,   340
But we will know his purpose. What! 'Unjust'!

    Duke. Be not so hot. The Duke
Dare no more stretch this finger of mine than he
Dare rack his own: his subject am I not,
Nor here provincial. My business in this state   345
Made me a looker-on here in Vienna,
Where I have seen corruption boil and bubble
Till it orerun the stew. Laws for all faults,
But faults so countenanc'd, that the strong statutes
Stand like the forefeits in a barber shop,   350
As much in mock as mark.

    Escalus. Slander to th' state! Away with him to prison!

    Angelo. What can you vouch against him, Signior Lucio?
Is this the man that you did tell us of?

    Lucio. 'Tis he, my lord. Come hither, goodman bald-   355
pate. Do you know me?

    Duke. I remember you, sir, by the sound of your voice. I
met you at the prison in the absence of the Duke.

    Lucio. O, did you so? And do you remember what you
said of the Duke?   360

    Duke. Most notedly, sir.

    Lucio. Do you so, sir? And was the Duke a fleshmonger, a
fool, and a coward, as you then reported him to be?

    Duke. You must, sir, change persons with me, ere you
make that my report. You, indeed, spoke so of him; and   365
much more, much worse.

    Lucio. O thou damnable fellow! Did not I pluck thee
by the nose for thy speeches?

    Duke. I protest I love the Duke as I love myself.

    Angelo. Hark how the villain would close now, after   370
his treasonable abuses!

    Escalus. Such a fellow is not to be talk'd withal.
Away with him to prison! Where is the provost?
Away with him to prison! Lay bolts enough upon him, let
him speak no more. Away with those giglets too, and   375
with the other confederate companion!

        [The Provost lays hands on the Duke.]

    Duke. Stay, sir: stay a while.

    Angelo. What! Resists he? Help him. Lucio.

    Lucio. Come, sir; come, sir; come, sir. Foh, sir! Why,   380
you bald-pated, lying rascal, you must be hooded, must you?
Show your knave's visage, with a pox to you! Show your
sheep-biting face, and be hang'd an hour! Will't not off?

        [Pulls off the friar's hood, and discovers the Duke.]

    Duke. Thou art the first knave that ere mad'st a Duke.   385
First, Provost, let me bail these gentle three.
[To Lucio.] Sneak not away, sir, for the friar and you
Must have a word anon. Lay hold on him.

    Lucio. This may prove worse than hanging.

    Duke. *[To Escalus.]* What you have spoke I pardon.   390
Sit you down,
We'll borrow place of him. *[To Angelo.]* Sir, by your leave.
Hast thou or word, or wit, or impudence
That yet can do thee office? If thou hast,
Rely upon it till my tale be heard,   395
And hold no longer out.

    Angelo.   O my dread lord!
I should be guiltier than my guiltiness

---

290 **throughly:** *thoroughly*   293 **Cucullus … monachum:** *the hood does not make the monk*   297 **notable:** *worth watching*   307 **darkly:** *obscurely*   308 **light:** *wanton, a quibble*   321 **burning throne;** *Cf. n.*   329 **retort:** *throw back*   336 **in … ear:** *in his own hearing*   340 **touse:** *tear*   **him:** *F you*

345 **provincial:** *within his jurisdiction*   348 **stew:** *cauldron, brothel*   350, 351 **forfeits … mark;** *Cf. n.*   361 **notedly:** *particularly*   370 **close:** *come to terms*   372 **withal:** *with*   375 **giglets:** *lewd women*   382, 383 **sheep-biting:** *skulking*   393 **or … or:** *either … or*   396 **hold … out:** *maintain no longer silence*

To think I can be undiscernible,
When I perceive your Grace, like power divine,   *400*
Hath look'd upon my passes. Then, good Prince,
No longer session hold upon my shame,
But let my trial be mine own confession.
Immediate sentence, then, and sequent death
Is all the grace I beg.   *405*
  Duke.   Come hither, Mariana.
Say, wast thou ere contracted to this woman?
  Angelo. I was, my lord.
  Duke. Go take her hence, and marry her instantly.
Do you the office, Friar—which consummate,   *410*
Return him here again. Go with him, Provost.
    Exit [*Angelo, with Mariana, Friar Peter, and Provost*].
  Escalus. My lord, I am more amaz'd at his dishonor
Than at the strangeness of it.
  Duke.   Come hither, Isabel.   *415*
Your friar is now your prince. As I was then
Advertising and holy to your business,
Not changing heart with habit, I am still
Attorney'd at your service.
  Isabella.   O, give me pardon,   *420*
That I, your vassal, have employ'd and pain'd
Your unknown sovereignty.
  Duke.   You are pardon'd, Isabel.
And now, dear maid, be you as free to us.
Your brother's death, I know, sits at your heart,   *425*
And you may marvel why I obscur'd myself,
Laboring to save his life, and would not rather
Make rash remonstrance of my hidden power
Than let him so be lost. O most kind maid,
It was the swift celerity of his death   *430*
That brain'd my purpose: but peace be with him.
That life is better life, past fearing death,
Than that which lives to fear. Make it your comfort,
So happy is your brother.

    Enter Angelo, Mariana, [*Friar*] Peter, Provost.

  Isabella.   I do, my lord.   *435*
  Duke. For this new-married man approaching here,
Whose salt imagination yet hath wrong'd
Your well-defended honor, you must pardon
For Mariana's sake. But as he adjudg'd your brother—
Being criminal, in double violation   *440*
Of sacred chastity, and of promise-breach,
Thereon dependent, for your brother's life—
The very mercy of the law cries out
Most audible, even from his proper tongue,
'An Angelo for Claudio, death for death!'   *445*
Haste still pays haste, and leisure answers leisure,
Like doth quit like, and Measure still for Measure.
Then, Angelo, thy fault's thus manifested,
Which though thou wouldst deny, denies thee vantage.
We do condemn thee to the very block   *450*
Where Claudio stoop'd to death, and with like haste.

Away with him!
  Mariana. O, my most gracious lord!
I hope you will not mock me with a husband.
  Duke. It is your husband mock'd you with a husband.   *455*
Consenting to the safeguard of your honor,
I thought your marriage fit. Else imputation,
For that he knew you, might reproach your life
And choke your good to come. For his possessions,
Although by confutation they are ours,   *460*
We do instate and widow you with all,
To buy you a better husband.
  Mariana.   O my dear lord!
I crave no other, nor no better man.
  Duke. Never crave him; we are definitive.   *465*
  Mariana. Gentle my liege—
  Duke.   You do but lose your labor.
Away with him to death! [*To Lucio.*] Now, sir, to you.
  Mariana. O my good lord! Sweet Isabel, take my part:
Lend me your knees, and, all my life to come,   *470*
I'll lend you all my life to do you service.
  Duke. Against all sense you do importune her:
Should she kneel down in mercy of this fact,
Her brother's ghost his paved bed would break,
And take her hence in horror.   *475*
  Mariana.   Isabel,
Sweet Isabel, do yet but kneel by me:
Hold up your hands, say nothing, I'll speak all.
They say best men are moulded out of faults,
And, for the most, become much more the better   *480*
For being a little bad: so may my husband.
O, Isabel! will you not lend a knee?
  Duke. He dies for Claudio's death.
  Isabella. [*Kneeling.*]   Most bounteous sir,
Look, if it please you, on this man condemn'd,   *485*
As if my brother liv'd. I partly think
A due sincerity governed his deeds,
Till he did look on me. Since it is so,
Let him not die. My brother had but justice,
In that he did the thing for which he died: *490*
For Angelo,
His act did not oretake his bad intent,
And must be buried but as an intent
That perish'd by the way. Thoughts are no subjects,
Intents but merely thoughts.   *495*
  Mariana.   Merely, my lord.
  Duke. Your suit's unprofitable: stand up, I say.
I have bethought me of another fault.
Provost, how came it Claudio was beheaded
At an unusual hour?   *500*
  Provost. It was commanded so.
  Duke. Had you a special warrant for the deed?
  Provost. No, my good lord; it was by private message.
  Duke. For which I do discharge you of your office.
Give up your keys.   *505*
  Provost.   Pardon me, noble lord:
I thought it was a fault, but knew it not,

399 be undiscernible: *remain unrevealed* **401 passes:** *devices* **402 session hold:** *sit in judgment* **410 consummate:** *performed* **417 Advertising:** *stressed* — ´ — ´ *and* **holy:** *ministering and devoted* **419 Attorney'd:** *i.e. as an advocate or special pleader* **424 free:** *generous* **426 marvel:** *probably to be read 'mar'l'* **428 rash remonstrance:** *hasty manifestation* **430 celerity:** *read 'celer'ty'* **431 brain'd:** *shattered* **434 So:** *thus* **437 salt:** *lascivious* **440 criminal:** *guilty* **447 Measure ... Measure:** *Cf. n.* **449 vantage:** *the advantage of any such denial*

457 imputation: *censure* **460 confutation:** *the fact of Angelo's proven guilt; Cf. n.* **461 instate and widow:** *give you as a widow's legacy* **465 definitive:** *firmly resolved* **473 fact:** *evil deed* **474 paved bed:** *i.e. vaulted with stone; Cf. n.* **480 for the most:** *in most cases* **487 sincerity:** *read 'sincer'ty'* **494 Thoughts are no subjects:** *thoughts are not punishable by the state*

Yet did repent me, after more advice;
For testimony whereof, one in the prison,
That should by private order else have died   510
I have reserv'd alive.
   Duke.   What's he?
   Provost.   His name is Barnardine.
   Duke. I would thou hadst done so by Claudio.
Go, fetch him hither: let me look upon him.   *[Exit Provost.]*
   Escalus. I am sorry, one so learned and so wise
As you, Lord Angelo, have still appear'd,
Should slip so grossly, both in the heat of blood,
And lack of temper'd judgment afterward.
   Angelo. I am sorry that such sorrow I procure;   520
And so deep sticks it in my penitent heart
That I crave death more willingly than mercy.
'Tis my deserving, and I do entreat it.

   Enter Barnardine and Provost, Claudio [muffled], Julietta.

   Duke. Which is that Barnardine?
   Provost.   This, my lord.   525
   Duke. There was a friar told me of this man.
Sirrah, thou art said to have a stubborn soul,
That apprehends no further than this world,
And squar'st thy life according. Thou'rt condemn'd:
But, for those earthly faults, I quit them all,   530
And pray thee take this mercy to provide
For better times to come. Friar, advise him:
I leave him to your hand. What muffled fellow's that?
   Provost. This is another prisoner that I sav'd,
Who should have died when Claudio lost his head—   535
As like almost to Claudio as himself.   *[Unmuffles Claudio.]*
   Duke. [To Isabella.] If he be like your brother, for his sake
Is he pardon'd, and, for your lovely sake—
Give me your hand and say you will be mine—
He is my brother too. But fitter time for that.   540
By this Lord Angelo perceives he's safe—
Methinks I see a quick'ning in his eye.
Well, Angelo, your evil quits you well.
Look that you love your wife; her worth, worth yours.
I find an apt remission in myself,   545
And yet here's one in place I cannot pardon.
[To Lucio.] You, sirrah, that knew me for a fool, a coward,

One all of luxury, an ass, a madman:
Wherein have I so deserv'd of you,
That you extol me thus?   550
   Lucio. 'Faith, my lord, I spoke it but according to the trick.
If you will hang me for it, you may; but I had rather it would
please you, I might be whipped.
   Duke. Whipp'd first, sir, and hang'd after.
Proclaim it, Provost, round about the city,   555
If any woman wrong'd by this lewd fellow—
As I have heard him swear himself there's one
Whom he begot with child—let her appear,
And he shall marry her. The nuptial finish'd,
Let him be whipp'd and hang'd.   560
   Lucio. I beseech your Highness, do not marry me to a
whore. Your Highness said even now, I made you a Duke.
Good my lord, do not recompense me in making me a
cuckold.
   Duke. Upon mine honor, thou shalt marry her.   565
Thy slanders I forgive; and therewithal
Remit thy other forfeits. Take him to prison,
And see our pleasure herein executed.
   Lucio. Marrying a punk, my lord, is pressing to death, whip-
ping, and hanging.   570
   Duke. Slandering a prince deserves it.
                       [Exeunt officers with Lucio.]
She, Claudio, that you wrong'd, look you restore.
Joy to you, Mariana! Love her, Angelo.
I have confess'd her and I know her virtue.   575
Thanks, good friend Escalus, for thy much goodness:
There's more behind that is more gratulate.
Thanks, Provost, for thy care and secrecy;
We shall employ thee in a worthier place.
Forgive him, Angelo, that brought you home   580
The head of Ragozine for Claudio's:
Th' offense pardons itself. Dear Isabel,
I have a motion much imports your good,
Whereto if you'll a willing ear incline,
What's mine is yours, and what is yours is mine.   585
So, bring us to our palace, where we'll show
What's yet behind, that's meet you all should know.

                             [Exeunt.]

❧ FINIS ❧

---

508 **advice:** *consideration*   517 **still:** *always*   527 **thou art:** *read 'thou'rt'*   529
squar'st: *shapes*   530 **quit:** *remit*   532 **advise:** *give spiritual counsel*   543 **quits:** *re-*
quites   545 **apt remission:** *ready forgiveness*   546 **in place:** *present*

548 **luxury:** *lechery*   551 **according to the trick:** *as a joke*   567 **Remit . . . forfeits:**
cancel your other punishments   569 **pressing to death:** *i.e. by the placing of heavy weights*
on the chest   577 **behind:** *to come* **gratulate:** *pleasing*   583 **motion:** *proposal*

NOTES

[The Actors' Names] Based upon the list of characters appended to the Folio text of the play. Bracketed names appear in the text but not on the list. The list supplies the Duke's name, Vincentio, which does not appear in the text.

I. The Folio divides this play into acts and scenes throughout. These divisions are 'theatrical'—that is, they are adapted to the special conditions of the Elizabethan stage. Modern editors generally do not begin a new scene at I.2.108, and generally divide Act III into two scenes.

I.i.8, 9. *But . . . work.* Possibly two half-lines have been omitted here, but the text is not unintelligible as it stands. The Duke has just praised Escalus for a knowledge of government exceeding his own. Nothing remains, then, except that Escalus apply his best abilities to his *sufficiency*—that is, his fitness for government—and let them work together.

I.i.32, 33. *as to . . . thee.* 'As to justify you in wasting your energy upon the mere cultivation of your virtues or in limiting the effect of your virtues to your own character' (Durham).

I.i.34, 35. *Heaven . . . themselves.* Cf. Matthew 5:15, 'Neither do men light a candle, and put it under a bushel, but on a candlestick; and it giveth light unto all that are in the house.'

I.i.38–42. *Nature . . . use.* 'She requires and allots to herself the same advantages that creditors usually enjoy—thanks for the endowments she has bestowed, and extraordinary exertions in those whom she has thus favored, by way of interest (use)' (Malone).

I.i.43. *one . . . advertise.* One who can, in his own right, make known his abilities as my deputy.

I.i.44. *Hold.* Possibly reflecting stage business. The Duke extends the commission to Angelo, whose initial reluctance to accept it is emphasized by Shakespeare. Some editors, however, believe that the Duke is here exhorting Angelo to hold fast to those virtues he has just described him as possessing. There is little to choose between the two interpretations. It is quite likely that the text has been cut.

I.i.53–5. *Our . . . value.* The need for our hasty departure is so compelling that we must give it preference over important matters which would otherwise require our attention.

I.ii.15. *petition . . . peace.* The authorized form of grace under Queen Elizabeth ended with the words, 'God save our Queen and Realm, and send us peace in Christ.'

I.ii.21. *proportion.* There are many contemporary references to the tediously long graces fashionable at the time. Lucio is quibbling on one of the meanings of the word 'meter.'

I.ii.31. *three-pil'd.* Three-piled—that is, deep-napped—velvet was velvet of the very finest quality. The First Gentleman quibbles on this meaning of the term and *pil'd* meaning 'peeled' or 'bald,' with reference to one of the supposed effects of the French Disease, syphilis.

I.ii.34–36. *and . . . thee.* Lucio mockingly interprets the First Gentleman's *feelingly* (l. 33) as 'painfully,' and so as a confession of a mouth-sore stemming from venereal infection. He therefore says that, although he will start a round of healths in his name, he will avoid drinking after him: that is, out of the same cup.

I.ii.42,43. *I . . . to.* In the Folio, this speech as well as the preceding one is given to Lucio. Pope was the first of a succession of editors to give the speech to the First Gentleman, from whom it seems slightly more appropriate in view of the subsequent dialogue. In this case, the First Gentleman's remark (ll. 49, 50) must be interpreted as whimsy. Lucio capitalizes on another verbal indiscretion.

I.ii.82. *woman.* The verb 'to do' (see the preceding line) was frequently used in this bawdy sense by Elizabethans. Cf. the name Mistress Overdone.

I.ii.84. *Groping . . . river.* Peculiar means 'privately-owned' and fishing in private waters constituted poaching. One way of catching trout was to tickle them out of their hiding-places. *Peculiar* had also acquired a colloquial meaning of 'mistress.'

I.ii.86. *maid.* 'Maids' are the young of skate and other fish and, as Wilson points out, Pompey had just mentioned 'groping for trouts.' The explanation, if correct, adds little point and much coarseness to the quibble.

I.ii.89. *suburbs.* That is, outside the walls of the city, the customary location for Renaissance brothels. The *suburbs* of London were notorious for them.

I.ii.105. *Thomas Tapster.* Mistress Overdone addresses Pompey by the name commonly given, in Shakespeare's day, to any tapster.

I.ii.SD. *Enter Provost . . . Gentlemen.* The Folio begins a new scene at this point, perhaps an evidence of revision for, if ll.79–108 were not present in an

earlier text of the play, the Folio division could be defended. The transition from ll. 1–79 to 109 ff. would then have been sharp enough to warrant a new scene.

I.ii.115. *words of heaven.* The *words of heaven*, according to Henley, are those found in Romans 9:15, 'For he [God] saith to Moses, I will have mercy on whom I will have mercy, and I will have compassion on whom I will have compassion.' In addition, the passage reflects the conventional Renaissance belief that the ruling prince was a viceroy of God. The meaning, then, would seem to be: the demigod—in this case, Angelo—can make us pay exactly *(by weight)* for our offenses, and his judgments, by virtue of his deputed authority, are as uncontrollable as those of Heaven itself.

I.ii.126. *mortality.* The Folio reading. Most editors emend to *morality*. But the word *morality* does not appear elsewhere in Shakespeare whereas *mortality* appears often. The word is ultimately derived from Latin *mortalitas* which Cooper (*Thesaurus*, 1578) defines: 'Mortality, frailety, estate subject to decay.'

I.ii.159. *she . . . wife.* In Shakespeare's day, there were two types of betrothal contract: a contract in words of the future tense *(sponsalia per verba de futuro)* and a contract in words of the present tense *(sponsalia per verbe de praesenti).* The former was roughly equivalent to the modern 'engagement' and could be broken off at will. The latter constituted valid and binding matrimony in the eyes of the law. Consummation of the marriage, however, was not to take place before the union had received the benediction of the church, or its licensed representative. 'The husband and wife who have intercourse with each other before the church has blessed their marriage, sin and should be put to penance; they will be compelled by spiritual censures to celebrate their marriage before the face of the church; but they were married already when they exchanged a consent *per verba de praesenti . . .*' (Pollock and Maitland, *The History of English Law,* 1911, 2,372–3). Claudio's contract was clearly *de praesenti.* Technically, therefore, Claudio was guilty of fornication, but it must be added that Shakespeare's contemporaries would have regarded his sin as highly venial. Despite the teaching of the church, cohabitation on the basis of unblessed *de praesenti* contracts was widely practiced.

I.ii.151. *fault . . . newness.* The meaning of this highly compressed phrase cannot be communicated in a few words. 'Whether it be the fault of newness, a fault arising from the mind being dazzled by a new authority, of which the new governor had yet had only a glimpse . . .' (Malone).

I.ii.176. *prone and speechless dialect.* The phrase is usually interpreted as an instance of hendiadys—silently earnest or eager. It is difficult, however, to find a precise meaning for *prone*, perhaps because Shakespeare deliberately makes it ambiguous: *prone,* suggesting the posture of supplication, a familiar meaning of Latin *pronus,* but with overtones of an indelicate sexual connotation it seems to have had for Elizabethans. The play is full of such double-entendres.

I.iii.21. *steeds.* The Folio has *weedes,* which badly confuses the metaphor, although the reading can be defended. Most editors have adopted the emendation in the text, first suggested by Theobald. Cf. the preceding scene, ll. 162–5.

I.iii.22. *slip.* The Folio reading, which most editors emend to *sleep.* But the Elizabethan pronunciation of the two words was virtually identical and, in fact, *sleep* was sometimes spelled *slip.* See Helge Kökeritz, *Shakespeare's Pronunciation* (1953), pp. 146, 191. Both meanings are in this passage metaphorically appropriate—perhaps reflecting Shakespeare's intention.

I.iii.40–42. *for . . . punishment.* For we virtually bid people abuse their liberties when evil deeds are permitted to pass without punishment.

I.iii.45, 46. *And . . . slander.* The Folio reads *fight* for *sight* and *do in slander* for *do it slander.* The emended reading was first proposed by Hanmer. The meaning seems to be that, while Angelo is accomplishing the necessary reforms in the name of the Duke, the latter's nature will remain so completely out of sight that no slander can possibly attach itself to his name.

I.iv.34. *lapwing.* A bird notorious for its trickery in leading hunters away from its young. Lucio makes a distinction between what he says and what he really feels,—'tongue far from heart.'

I.iv.52. *marry.* Sexual intercourse on the basis of an unblessed *de praesenti* contract could be partly expiated by a subsequent celebration of the marriage 'in the face of the church.'

I.iv.76-82. *Doth . . . have.* These lines have been rearranged by modern editors. In the Folio, the lines end with *so, already, warrant, poor, good.* The words *for his* (l. 79) are contracted into *For's* in the Folio.

II.i.23, 24. *what . . . thieves.* Angelo has just said that justice can penalize only those offenses which are known to it. But there is no way for justice (the laws) to know when thieves pass judgment on thieves.

II.i.42. *brakes of vice.* The Folio reading *brakes of ice* has never been convincingly defended. The emendation adopted in the text was first proposed by Rowe. However enigmatic the phrasing may be, the general meaning is clear from the context: 'Some escape from a thicket-like tangle of vices without punishment; others are condemned for a single fault.'

II.i.87. *stew'd prunes.* There seems to have been a theory that this fruit was effective both in the prevention and cure of venereal disease, hence its popularity in brothels. Perhaps word-play is involved, too. 'Stews' was a common Elizabethan term for 'brothel.'

II.i.120, 121. *Bunch of Grapes.* It was the custom in Elizabethan times to give such names to the different rooms of an inn.

II.i.159. *Justice or Iniquity?* That is, Elbow or Pompey. There is a glancing allusion here to the old morality plays, in some of which the Vice is actually named Iniquity.

II.i.187. *draw you.* A quibble on the name Froth as well as on 'hang, draw, and quarter.' They will *draw you*—that is, empty you, deprive you of all your money and possessions.

II.i.197. *bum.* The buttocks, but also the fantastically stuffed trunk hose which emphasized the buttocks and which were very much in vogue at the time.

II.i.219. *bay.* A unit of measurement in contemporary architecture. 'Applied to a house,' the NED says, 'it appears to be the space lying under one gable, or included between two party walls.' The bays of the Globe Theater were twelve and a half feet square. See John C. Adams, *The Globe Playhouse*, pp. 20-1.

II.i.224, 225. *I shall . . . you.* The reference is to the decisive defeat of Pompey by Caesar at the battle of Pharsalus in 48 B.C.

II.i.238. *put . . . upon't.* It was the practice for the ward or parish to choose its own constable; the latter, if he wished, might then pay someone else to act as his deputy.

II.ii.53, 54. *To fine . . . actor. To fine* means 'to punish.' Angelo asserts that justice would be nothing if, instead of punishing the criminals, its sole function was to condemn their crimes—crimes already condemned in the statute books.

II.ii.171, 172. *She . . . it.* Here the two meanings of *sense*, upon which Shakespeare plays over and over again, are found in close juxtaposition. The lines recall I.2.175–179.

II.ii.193. *prayers cross.* As Isabella has just used the term *Honor*, it is a title of respect. Taking the word in its normal sense, Angelo pretends to see in Isabella's remark a prayer at cross purposes with the wish which has formed in his own heart. There is probably also an oblique reference to the Lord's Prayer—'Lead us not into temptation, but deliver us from evil.'

II.ii.205. *Corrupt . . . season.* I am corrupted by those very qualities which make her virtuous, just as it is the same sun which makes carrion putrid and the violet lovely and fragrant.

II.ii.209. *evils.* It has been said that privies were once known as *evils* but the NED does not record this meaning. To support the general conception, there is a scriptural parallel in 2 Kings 10:27.

II.iii.44–46. *O . . . horror.* Some editors would read *law* for *love*. But the meaning seems clear enough. Their illicit love has injured both Claudio and Julietta in that it has brought Claudio a sentence of death and respited Julietta a comfortless life, almost worse than death itself. In Shakespeare's source-play, Whetstone's *Promos and Cassandra*, Polina, the counterpart of Julietta, in a long soliloquy, blames love for her misfortunes and those of her condemned lover (Part I, Act V, Scene 3).

II.iv.16, 17. *Let's write . . . crest.* For *Is't not* (Warburton, Hanmer) the Folio reads *'Tis not*. The horn is the devil's crest. In *As You Like It* (IV.2.14–15), Jacques sings of a horn which is also a crest. Playing on his own name (*good Angel*), Angelo here seems to be drawing a parallel between himself and the devil, the master-hypocrite, perhaps in his self-revulsion identifying himself with the devil, as Iago with other feelings does in *Othello*.

II.iv.32. *know.* In his mind, Angelo translates Isabella's innocent 'I have come to know your pleasure' into the language of sexual gratification. To *know* a woman was to have sexual relations with her.

II.iv.47–50. *'tis . . . one.* That is, it is no worse wrongfully to take away the life of a man who has been legitimately born than it is to beget an illegitimate child. The coining metaphor is further developed. For 'meanes' as a variant spelling of 'mints,' see Kökeritz, *Shakespeare's Pronunciation*, p. 215.

II.iv.51. *'Tis . . . earth.* 'What you have stated is undoubtedly the divine law: murder and fornication are both forbid by the canons of scripture; but on earth the latter offence is considered as less heinous than the former' (Malone).

II.iv.60. *for accompt.* That is, we are not called to such strict account for the sins which are forced upon us as for those we commit voluntarily. Only the number of *compell'd sins*, therefore, has real significance.

II.iv.85. *enshield.* Dover Wilson would read *enshelled*, calling attention to Ben Jonson's *Masque of Blackness* (produced Jan. 5, 1605), in which the female masquers, one of whom was Queen Anne, made their appearance in a large concave shell resembling mother-of-pearl.

II.iv.129, 130. *If . . . weakness.* Angelo has just admitted that all men are frail, and *thy weakness* is the weakness of the male sex: 'If no one else has shared my brother's weakness, if he alone has inherited the male frailty to which you refer, then let him die.'

II.iv.134, 135. *Men . . . them.* The primary meaning, as Wilson saw, is suggested by the preceding metaphor. Women are as fragile as mirrors and, like mirrors, they too *make forms*—that is, men. Hence, when men take advantage of woman's frailty, they are marring the sex which brought them into being.

II.iv.153–155. *I . . . others.* 'Your virtue assumes an air of licentiousness, which is not natural to you, on purpose to try me' (Steevens). This speech explains why Isabella at first receives Angelo's blunt declaration of love (1. 149) so calmly.

III.i.9. *skyey influences.* The received opinion in Shakespeare's day was that the stars and planets influenced not only weather conditions but the affairs and lives of men. A man's fate was in his 'stars.' Cf. the note to III.1.24–5.

III.i.14–15. *For . . . baseness.* 'For all the conveniences and comforts you possess are provided by the base offices and occupations of others.' But the phrase 'Are nurs'd by baseness' may mean 'Are cherished out of low and selfish motives.'

III.i.16–17. *For . . . worm.* Editors generally take *worm* in its common Elizabethan sense of 'snake.' But by the *poor worm*, Shakespeare may mean the grave or coffin worm to which, by analogy with 'snake,' he ascribes a forked tongue in a delicate mockery of man's pretensions to valor.

III.i.24–5. *For . . . moon.* 'Your temperament is influenced in many strange directions by the operation of the moon.' The moon, a symbol of mutability, was believed to affect human character and conduct.

III.i.32–4. *Thou . . . both.* 'When we are young, we busy ourselves in forming schemes for succeeding time, and miss the gratifications that are before us; when we are old, we amuse the languor of age with the recollection of youthful pleasures or performances: so that our life, of which no part is filled with the business of the present time, resembles our dreams after dinner, when the events of the morning are mingled with the designs of the evening' (Johnson).

III.i.34–6. *for . . . Eld.* A passage which has never been satisfactorily explained, possibly because it may be corrupt. Perhaps 'in your youth you are forced into a dependence on old age, and are like palsied eld in begging alms.' The central idea is that, in our youth, when we are in a position to enjoy life, we lack the means to do so. by the time we are old and rich, we have lost the power of enjoyment.

III.i.SD. *Enter Isabella.* Folio stage entrances tend to reflect playhouse conditions. It takes a few moments for the actor, entering from back or side, to reach the center of the stage. Modern editors often find it convenient to drop Folio entrances a few lines.

III.i.SD. Modern editors indicate that the Duke and Provost leave the stage at this point but the Folio gives no 'Exeunt.' Nor does the Folio provide a re-entry for the Duke at 1.168. Probably the Duke and Provost simply withdraw to one side of the stage or, if the action of the scene was initiated on the inner stage, to the outer stage.

III.i.73, 74. *Though . . . scope.* Though you were free to range over the wide world, you would still be mentally confined to the idea of your own ignominy.

III.i.102. *prenzie.* The only two occurrences of this word in the language, according to the NED, appear here within the space of a few lines. Cf. *prenzie guards* in 1. 105. There has been no satisfactory elucidation of the word's meaning. The context seems to require a meaning akin to 'puritanical' or 'prim.' Hotson, however, believes that *prenzie* is Shakespeare's translation of the now obsolete Italian word for 'prince' (*prenze*) and that *prenzie guards* means therefore 'prince-robes,' clothes with rich trimming. The explanation is not very convincing.

III.i.135. *region.* The conception of Hell as alternating between severe cold and intense heat was medieval in origin. Both Dante (*Inferno*, canto VI) and Milton (*Paradise Lost*, II, 587–603) draw upon the conception.

III.i.223, 224. *between . . . solemnity.* The contract of Angelo, like that of Claudio, was of the *de praesenti* type, constituting legal matrimony. Also, like that of Claudio, it had not been solemnized 'in the face of the church.'

III.i.SD. *Exit.* Modern editors, with the exception of Wilson, begin a new scene at this point, although one is not designated in the Folio and, in fact, is scarcely necessary. Isabella makes her exit, but the Duke remains on stage and is present when Elbow and his officers enter with their prisoner, Pompey.

III.i.275. *two usuries.* Procuring and moneylending. Contemporary references show that moneylenders were accustomed to wear gowns furred in this manner. Here the fox skin connotes craft and the lamb skin, innocence.

III.i.281. *brother father.* The Duke good-humoredly mocks Elbow's awkward form of address. Elbow was probably represented on the stage as old and doddering.

III.i.307. *His . . . waist.* Elbow makes capital of the fact that the hempen rope which Franciscan friars wore as a girdle was also the kind of rope generally used in hangings.

III.i.312. *Pygmalion's images.* According to legend, Pygmalion made a statue of a woman so beautiful that he fell in love with it. When he embraced it, the statue came to life. Lucio mocks the tendency of bawds to exaggerate the beauty and chastity of the prostitutes they represent. 'Have you no women to sell who are as beautiful and unstained as Pygmalion's statue when it first came to life?'

III.i.321, 322. *she . . . tub.* Pompey quibbles on two kinds of tubs: one for corning beef, the other, into which salt was put, for sweating individuals suffering from venereal disease. Hence, *powder'd* (1. 324) means 'salted.'

III.i.369. *motion generative.* A puppet was known as a *motion.* Lucio seems to imply that, although Angelo has the organs of generation, he makes no more use of them than if he were a puppet.

III.i.372. *cod-piece.* A baggy and often indelicately conspicuous appendage to the front of the breeches.

III.i.430. *mutton.* The primary reference is to fasting on Fridays during Lent, but Lucio glances at another meaning of *mutton* common at the time, 'prostitute.'

III.i.430, 431. *He's . . . thee.* Hanmer's emendation. The Folio reads 'He's now past it, yet (and I say to thee),' which can be defended. But the context suggests that the emended reading is preferable. Lucio, furthermore, is not one to qualify his remarks. For Shakespeare to have him do so here would be out of character.

III.i.449. *Philip and Jacob.* The feast of St. Philip and St. James was celebrated on May 1. Jacobus is the Latin equivalent of James.

III.i.472. *security.* The Duke alludes to the practice of one friend standing security for another, which often led to broken friendships when bonds were forfeited.

III.i.501–522. *He . . . contracting.* Many critics believe these octo-syllabic couplets were not written by Shakespeare. There is some clumsiness in the phrasing and in general no clear purpose would seem to be served by a chorus at this point. Wilson, while believing that the verse itself is un-Shakespearean, calls attention to the similarity between this chorus and the Gower choruses in *Pericles.* The problem appears insoluble.

III.i.513–516. *How . . . things.* A most difficult passage and perhaps corrupt. Editors attempt to construe it with the preceding verses, but it might be better to view the lines as interrogatory and transitional. This interpretation is supported by the Folio punctuation of the passage, restored in the present edition. The Duke asks himself how, by adopting spider-like methods of deceit, roughly similar to those of Angelo ('Craft against vice' and 'Pay with falsehood, false exacting'), he can take advantage of the current situation to encompass (*To draw* meaning 'draw together') the *substantial* ends he had earlier outlined to Isabella (see III.1.254–257). Angelo has made the relationship between Claudio and Julietta a criminal one and it is by a 'likeness made in crimes'—that is, by the device of the bed-trick—that the Duke hopes to ensnare Angelo.

IV.i.1–6. *Take . . . vain.* This song appears also in Fletcher's *Bloody Brother* (V.2) with, however, the addition of a second stanza. There is no way of knowing whether Shakespeare or Fletcher was its author. The most likely explanation is that Shakespeare wrote the song as we have it in this play and that then Fletcher added the new (and more erotic) stanza to make the song conform to his special purposes in *The Bloody Brother.* On this point, see William R. Bowden, *The English Dramatic Lyric,* 16034–42, p. 28.

IV.i.13. *My mirth . . . woe* That is, the music did not make me mirthful but served only to assuage my sorrow.

IV.i.81 *tilth* Folio *tithe's,* for which no editor has been able to find a satisfactory meaning. The emendation, first proposed by Warburton, restores both sense and point to the proverb-like saying.

IV.ii.39–42. *Every . . . thief.* The Folio ends Abhorson's speech with *thief* (1. 39) and gives the rest of it to Pompey. The alteration, first made by Capell, has been adopted by almost all subsequent editors. The argument of the hangman is based upon the fact that it was customary for Elizabethan hangmen to inherit the clothing worn by their victims at the time of execution. His reasoning, as Heath pointed out, runs exactly parallel to that of Pompey. 'As the latter puts

in his claim to the whores, as members of his occupation, and, in virtue of their painting, would enroll his own fraternity in the mystery of painters; so the former equally lays claims to the thieves, as members of his profession, and in their right, endeavors to rank his brethren, the hangmen, under the mystery of fitters of apparel, or tailors.'

IV.i.45, 46. *he . . . forgiveness.* Another custom of hangmen was to ask forgiveness from those they were about to execute.

IV.i.80. *stroke and line.* Angelo's manner of life is consistent with his ideals of rendering justice; he practices what he preaches. There may be a quibble on *stroke* (blow of the executioner's ax) and *line* (the hangman's cord).

IV.ii.174. *dye.* The Folio reading *tie* can be defended, but see Act IV, Scene 3, ll. 69, 70. Harrison suggests that to tie a beard was to trim it short. The emendation adopted in the text was first proposed by Simpson.

IV.iii.4–7. *commodity . . . dead.* By Act of Parliament in 1571, not more than 10 per cent interest could be charged on loans. Moneylenders, however, could, and frequently did, evade the statute by the legal device known as 'commodities.' Before making a loan of cash, the moneylender would require the borrower to purchase a 'commodity' of goods, usually of little or no value. Thus, in the case of Master Rash, the 'commodity' was 'brown paper and old ginger.' For this he paid £197 and received a loan of five marks (£3.6s.8d.). But, unfortunately, there turned out to be no market for the ginger, since all the old women, who were notoriously fond of it, had died. Pompey, as usual, is indulging his penchant for lighthearted exaggeration.

IV.iii.14. *Shoe-tie.* The significance of this name is explained by a passage in Nashe's *Unfortunate Traveller* (McKerrow, 2, 300-1), quoted by Hart and Wilson. 'From Spaine what bringeth our Traveller? . . . I have not yet tucht all, for he hath in either shoo as much taffatie for his tyings as wold serve for an ancient; which serveth him (if you wil have the mysterie of it) of the owne accord for a shoo-rag.'

IV.iii.40. *I . . . for't.* To take the life of a man when he had not confessed, and been absolved from, his sins was to place his eternal life in jeopardy. So Hamlet will not kill King Claudius while he is praying but prefers to wait until he is 'drunk asleep or in his rage' or in the performance of some act 'That hath no relish of salvation in't.'

IV.iv.13–17. *Well . . . night* Set as prose in the Folio, possibly a printer's mistake. The passage is easily translated into blank verse and in many editions it is so rearranged. In this case, the end words successive lines would be *proclaim'd, house, suit, well.*

V.i.SD. *Isabella withdraws.* The Folio has no stage direction to indicate that Isabella leaves the stage at this time. Yet the Duke, at 1. 271, refers to her as *gone* and, at 1. 300, Escalus orders that Isabella be called *here once again.* She is given a re-entry at 1. 307. Capell was the first to establish her exit after 1. 186 and modern editors have followed his precedent. Despite the remarks of Friar Peter, 1. 184, that the Duke will hear Isabella 'disproved to her eyes,' the latter seems not to have heard the testimony of Mariana. See ll. 309, 310. The problem appears insoluble on the basis of available evidence. Wilson suggests that there may have been some tampering with the text at this point.

V.i.321. *burning throne.* The Duke implies that the devil has ascended the seat of justice in the person of Angelo—'another version,' comments Hart, 'of the good angel on the devil's crest.'

V.i.350, 351. *forfeits . . . mark.* The *forfeits,* as Hart shows, 'were teeth extracted by barbers who doubled as dentists. To advertise their dual function, barbers were wont to hang teeth on a string and exhibit them in their shops. Thus, the extracted teeth stand in the same relation to the 'strong statutes' as the 'threat'ning twigs of birch' in I.3.25.

V.i.447. *Measure . . . Measure.* Cf. Matthew 7:2. 'For with what judgment ye judge, ye shall be judged: and with what measure ye mete, it shall be measured to you again.' And see the next three verses in Matthew.

V.i.460. *confutation.* So Folio. Most editors emend to 'confiscation.' In the longhand of the time, the letters 'c' and 't' looked very much alike and it is easy to see how the compositor could have made a mistake, reading 'confutation' for 'confiscation.' The Folio reading, however, can be defended.

V.i.474. *paved bed.* Common graves were not *paved.* Hart believes there may be a reference to the 'custom' of burying executed criminals under the stone flooring of the jail. But it seems more likely that the Duke is alluding to the family crypt or vault.

The First Part of King Henry the Sixth

Edited by
TUCKER BROOKE

Dramatis Personae

KING HENRY THE SIXTH
DUKE OF BEDFORD, *Uncle to the King, Regent of France*
DUKE OF GLOUCESTER, *Uncle to the King, and Protector*
DUKE OF EXETER   } *Great-Uncles*
BISHOP OF WINCHESTER } *to the King*
RICHARD PLANTAGENET, *Son of Richard, late*
   Earl of Cambridge; afterwards Duke of York
DUKE OF SOMERSET
EARL OF WARWICK
EARL OF SALISBURY
EARL OF SUFFOLK
LORD TALBOT, *afterwards Earl of Shrewsbury*
JOHN TALBOT, *his Son*
EDMUND MORTIMER, *Earl of March*
SIR JOHN FASTOLFE
SIR WILLIAM GLANSDALE
SIR THOMAS GARGRAVE
SIR WILLIAM LUCY
VERNON, *of the White-Rose, or York, Faction*
BASSET, *of the Red-Rose, or Lancaster, Faction*
WOODVILE, *Lieutenant of the Tower*
MAYOR OF LONDON

A LAWER OF THE TEMPLE
LORDS, WARDERS OF THE TOWER, MORTIMER'S KEEPERS,
   HERALDS, OFFICERS, SOLDIERS, MESSENGERS,
   AND ATTENDANTS

CHARLES, *Dauphin of France (legitimately, King Charles VII)*
REIGNIER, *Duke of Anjou, and titular King of Naples*
DUKE OF BURGUNDY
DUKE OF ALENÇON
BASTARD OF ORLEANS
GOVERNOR OF PARIS
GENERAL OF THE FRENCH FORCES IN BORDEAUX
MASTER-GUNNER OF ORLEANS, AND HIS SON
AN OLD SHEPHERD, *Father to Joan la Pucelle*
MARGARET, *Daughter to Reignier*
COUNTESS OF AUVERGNE
JOAN LA PUCELLE, *commonly called Joan of Arc*
FRENCH HERALD, SERGEANT, AND SENTINELS; PORTER
   TO THE COUNTESS OF AUVERGNE; FIENDS APPEARING
   TO LA PUCELLE

SCENE—*London and Westminster; various parts of France.*

The First Part of King Henry the Sixth

INTRODUCTION

SOURCES OF THE PLAY

The historical material in *1 Henry VI* is arranged with a total disregard to chronology, as the notes on various passages indicate. The earliest event portrayed is the funeral of Henry V on November 7, 1422; the latest the recovery of Talbot's body after his death on July 17, 1453. In some parts, the play is certainly based upon Shakespeare's favorite authority, the second edition of Raphael Holinshed's Chronicle of England (1587). Close following of this book is evident when the introduction of Joan of Arc (I.ii.46-151) is compared with Holinshed's words: 'In time of this siege at Orleance . . . vnto Charles the Dolphin, at Chinon, as he was in verie great care and studie how to wrestle against the English nation . . . was caried a yoong wench of an eighteene yeeres old, called Ione Are, by name of hir father (a sorie sheepheard) Iames of Are, and Isabell hir mother; brought vp poorelie in their trade of keeping cattell . . . Of fauour was she counted likesome, of person stronglie made and manlie, of courage great, hardie, and stout withall: an vnderstander of counsels though she were not at them; great semblance of chastitie both of bodie and behauiour. . . . A person (as their bookes make hir) raised vp by power diuine, onelie for succour to the French estate then deepelie in distresse. . . . From saint Katharins church of Fierbois in Touraine (where she neuer had beene and knew not) in a secret place there among old iron, appointed she hir sword to be sought out and brought hir, that with fiue floure delices was grauen on both sides, wherewith she fought and did manie slaughters by hir owne hands. . . . Vnto the Dolphin into his gallerie when first she was brought, and he shadowing himselfe behind, setting other gaie lords before him to trie hir cunning, from all the companie, with a salutation . . . she pickt him out alone; who thereupon had hir to the end of the gallerie, where she held him an houre in secret and priuate talke, that of his priuie chamber was thought verie long, and therefore would haue broken it off; but he made them a sign to let hir saie on. In which (among other), as likelie it was, she set out vnto him the singular feats (forsooth) giuen her to vnderstand by reuelation diuine, that in vertue of that sword shee should atchiue; which were, how with honor and victorie shee would raise the siege at Orleance, set him in state of the crowne of France, and driue the English out of the countrie, thereby he to inioie the kingdome alone. Heerevpon he hartened at full, appointed hir a sufficient armie with absolute power to lead them, and they obedientlie to doo as she bad them.'

The first edition of Holinshed (1577) and the other earlier English chroniclers are here briefer and quite different, containing no suggestion of the words out of which lines 60-68, 98-101, 118 ff. of the play are developed.[1] Holinshed, however, is by no means the basis of the entire play. Several scenes—those of Talbot and the Countess of Auvergne, the rose-plucking in the Temple Garden, Plantagenet's interview with Mortimer, and Suffolk's capture of Margaret—have no discovered source. The first of these was probably borrowed from the legend of some popular warrior or outlaw,[2] the others are fanciful embellishments of history.

In some cases, again, the drama deserts Holinshed in order to make use of the older and generally more detailed chronicle of Edward Halle (*The Union of Lancaster and York,* 1548). This seems to be true of the dialogue between Talbot and his son in IV. v and vi. Holinshed contents himself with a bare summary of the battle at Castillon: 'though he [Talbot] first with manfull courage, and sore fighting wan the entrie of their [the French] campe; yet at length they compassed him about, and shooting him through the thigh with an handgun, slue his horsse, and finally killed him lieng on the ground, whome they durst neuer looke in the face, while he stood on his feet.[3] It was said, that after he perceiued there was no remedie, but present losse of the battell, he counselled his sonne, the lord Lisle, to saue himselfe by flight, sith the same could not redound to anie great reproch in him, this being the first iournie [day of battle] in which he had beene present. Manie words he vsed to persuade him to haue saued his life; but nature so wrought in the son, that neither desire of life, nor feare of death, could either cause him to shrinke, or conueie himselfe out of the danger, and so there manfullie ended his life with his said father.'

Halle, on the other hand, paints the whole scene far more graphically, and suggests some of the actual words which the dramatist puts into Talbot's mouth: 'When the Englishmen were come to the place where the Frenchmen were encamped, in the which (as Eneas Siluius testifieth) were iii. C. peces of brasse, beside diuers other small peces, and subtill Engynes to the Englishmen vnknowen, and nothing suspected, they lyghted al on fote, the erle of Shrewesbury only except, which because of his age, rode on a litle hakeney, and fought fiercely with the Frenchmen, & gat thentre of their campe, and by fyne force entered into the same. This conflicte continued in doubtfull iudgement of victory ii. longe houres: durynge which fight the lordes of Montamban and Humadayre, with a great companye of Frenchmen entered the battayle, and began a new felde, & sodaynly the Gonners perceiuynge the Englishmen to approche nere, discharged their ordinaunce, and slew iii. C. persons, nere to the erle, who perceiuynge the imminent ieopardy, and subtile labirynth, in the which he and hys people were enclosed and illaqueate, despicynge his awne sauegarde, and desirynge the life of his entierly and welbeloued

---

1 Holinshed is certainly the source also of IV.i.18 ff.

2 The resemblance to Robin Hood stories, suggested by several critics, is of the vaguest.
3 These words, repeated from Halle, are echoed in I.i.138-140 of the play.

sonne the lord Lisle, willed, aduertised, and counsailled hym to departe out of the felde, and to saue hym selfe. But when the sonne had aunswered that it was neither honest nor natural for him, to leue his father in the extreme ieopardye of his life, and that he woulde taste of that draught, which his father and Parent should assay and begyn: The noble erle & comfortable capitayn sayd to him: Oh sonne sonne, I thy father, which onely hath bene the terror and scourge of the French people so many yeres, which hath subuerted so many townes, and profligate and discomfited so many of them in open battayle, and marcial conflict, neither can here dye, for the honor of my countery, without great laude and perpetuall fame, nor flye or departe without perpetuall shame and continualle infamy. But because this is thy first iourney and enterprise, neither thy flyeng shall redounde to thy shame, nor thy death to thy glory: for as hardy a man wisely flieth, as a temerarious person folishely abidethe, therefore ye fleyng of me shalbe ye dishonor, not only of me & my progenie, but also a discomfiture of all my company: thy departure shall saue thy lyfe, and make the able another tyme, if I be slayn to reuenge my death and to do honor to thy Prince and profyt to his Realme. But nature so wrought in the sonne, that neither desire of lyfe, nor thought of securitie, could withdraw or pluck him from his natural father: Who consideryng the constancy of his chyld, and the great daunger that they stode in, comforted his souldiours, cheared his Capitayns, and valeauntly set on his enemies, and slew of them more in number than he had in his company. But his enemies hauyng a greater company of men, & more abundaunce of ordinaunce then before had bene sene in a battayle, fyrst shot him through the thyghe with a handgonne, and slew his horse, & cowardly killed him, lyenge on the ground, whome they neuer durste loke in the face, whyle he stode on his fete, and with him, there dyed manfully hys sonne the lord Lisle. . . .'

Verbal echoes of the passage above are probably to be found in lines 18, 40, 45, 46 of IV.v and in line 30 of the next scene.[4]

THE HISTORY OF THE PLAY

The drama now known as *1 Henry VI* is first heard of as 'Harry the Sixth' on March 3, 1592. Upon that afternoon it was acted at the Rose Theatre by Lord Strange's Men (Shakespeare's company), who had begun their temporary occupancy of the Rose about a fortnight before (February 19). Philip Henslowe's diary notes that the play was new on March 3, and that the first performance brought the manager the unusually large sum of £3 16s. 8d. It was then repeated with gradually diminishing frequency and returns: the diary records fourteen (possibly fifteen) productions up to June 19, 1592. *Harry the Sixth* appears to have been, as Fleay calls it, the most popular play of its season.

4 It is fair to observe that the verbal indebtedness to Halle is not as close as the indebtedness to Holinshed in the extract given on p. 437, and is very likely a debt at second hand. That is, Halle's dialogue between father and son may have been utilized by the original author of the play, and Shakespeare, rewriting the scene without direct reference to Halle, may have removed much of Halle's wording, though leaving enough to show that Shakespeare's authority, Holinshed, did not furnish all the material. Moreover, it is impossible to say whether the original dramatist used Halle's Chronicle itself or resorted to the later work of Grafton (1569), for Grafton incorporates the entire passage verbatim. The only change he makes is to remove three words of Halle, which he evidently regarded as archaic. Instead of 'illaqueate' he reads 'wrapped'; instead of 'profligate and discomfited,' 'discomfited' alone; and instead of 'temerarious,' 'rashe.'

Clear evidence of its effect upon the audiences at this time is given in Thomas Nashe's *Pierce Penniless*, written in the summer of 1592 and licensed for the press on August 8. Nashe uses the play to illustrate his argument that the drama may exert a valuable moral influence. 'How would it haue ioyed braue *Talbot* (the terror of the French),' he writes, 'to thinke that after he had lyne two hundred yeares in his Tombe, he should triumphe againe on the Stage, and haue his bones newe embalmed with the teares of ten thousand spectators at least (at seuerall times), who, in the Tragedian that represents his person, imagine they behold him fresh bleeding.' (McKerrow's ed. I.212.)

There is no reason for doubting that the play referred to in both the documents of 1592 just cited is *1 Henry VI*. There seems nothing, however, to justify the usual assumption that this play had already received Shakespeare's additions, and was therefore in 1592 a revised version of a still earlier drama. Henslowe directly and Nashe by implication testify that their play was new. The same conclusion is warranted by the evident sensation it created in 1592 and particularly by the absence of the smallest hint of its existence previously. The only fair inference, then, from the facts known is that the play of *Harry the Sixth*, dealing largely with Talbot's wars in France, was composed about the beginning of the year 1592, and that this was later remodelled by Shakespeare into *1 Henry VI*.

It is not easy to say when the remodelling and the consequent revival of the play on the stage occurred. In the absence of positive records, critics have naturally inclined to the assumption that a work clearly not equal to Shakespeare's ordinary performances must have been produced very early in his career. Against this are to be weighed the following considerations: (1) The success of Henslowe's play was proved but not completely exploited in 1592. According to the usual methods of the time a revised version would not be called for till after the lapse of several years. Marlowe's *Doctor Faustus*, originally produced about 1589, still held the stage in no seriously altered form from September, 1594, till October, 1597. The first extensive adaptation recorded was paid for, November 22, 1602. *The Jew of Malta*, acted without change from February, 1592, till June, 1596, was revived in 1601. The old *Hamlet*, performed between 1589 and 1594, was rewritten by Shakespeare about 1601.

(2) *1 Henry VI*, as we have it, is arranged to serve as a prologue to *2* and *3 Henry VI*. Shakespeare clearly revised our play with these dramas in his mind, and probably not till after he had completed his revision of them.

(3) The earlier (pre-Shakespearean) versions of *2* and *3 Henry VI* were printed in 1594 and 1595 respectively, these texts presumably becoming accessible to the publishers after the revised dramas supplanted them for stage purposes. The fact that no such text of the early *1 Henry VI* was printed would suggest that that play was reserved either till it was too late to warrant publishers to trade upon its former popularity or till Shakespeare's company began to take more stringent measures to prevent the publication of any play-texts.

(4) A mutual connection exists between *1 Henry VI* and *Henry V* (cf. note on IV.ii.10, 11). Several passages in our play seem reminiscent of the other (written in 1599). It is a plausible hypothesis at least that *1 Henry VI* was revised in order on the one hand to profit by the popular interest in *Henry V* and on the other to link that play with *2 Henry VI*,

thus completing the chain of history dramas from *Richard II* to *Richard III*.[5]

(5) The most positive evidence of the date of the Shakespearean additions to *1 Henry VI* is that discussed in the note on IV.vii.63-71. Unless some earlier printed source than is now known can be found for Talbot's epitaph, it will be hard to establish a date prior to 1599 for the revised play.

The idea that Shakespeare could not about 1600 have done work as apparently immature as that which he contributed to *1 Henry VI*, or have sanctioned the performance at that time of so poor a play, is not in consonance with facts. Shakespeare's company undoubtedly produced worse plays during this period when the public taste seemed to warrant them (e.g., *A Yorkshire Tragedy* in 1605), and the Shakespearean parts of *1 Henry VI* are assuredly not as unworthy of the author of *Henry V* as is *The Merry Wives of Windsor* (ca. 1600) unworthy of the author of *Twelfth Night* and *Much Ado About Nothing*.

On November 8, 1623, the publishers of the Shakespeare Folio, Blount and Jaggard, entered our play for publication under the rather surprising title of 'The thirde parte of Henry ye Sixt.' The work now known as *1 Henry VI* is certainly meant, for *2* and *3 Henry VI* (in their early forms) had both been previously licensed,[6] and the Blount-Jaggard license specifically refers only to such of Shakespeare's plays 'as are not formerly entred to other men.' It is probable that in thus listing as the third part the drama which by historical sequence became in the Folio the first part, the publishers meant more than simply that this was the last part remaining unlicensed. It seems fair to assume that they so thought of it because they remembered it as the latest of Shakespeare's *Henry VI* plays to be produced on the stage.

Since Shakespeare's death, *1 Henry VI* has had only the scantiest stage history. Most subsequent adaptations of the Henry VI cycle ignore the first part. However, J. H. Merivale's compilation, *Richard, Duke of York*, acted by Edmund Kean, December 22, 1817, and published the same year, opens with three scenes closely following II.iv, II.v, III.i, and IV.i of our play.

An abridgment of the three *Henry VI* plays ('*Henry VI. A Tragedy in Five Acts. Condensed from Shakespeare, and arranged for the Stage*') was prepared by the eminent actor-manager, Charles Kemble (1775-1854), and first printed from the only known copy in volume ii of the *Henry Irving Shakespeare*. This work begins like Merivale's with the Temple Garden scene, and like it ignores the scenes in France. *1 Henry VI* furnished Kemble

with the material for Act I (approximately) of his adaptation, which seems never to have been acted.

On March 13, 1738, 'by desire of several Ladies of Quality' the play of 'Henry 6th, part 1st,' was performed for the benefit of the actor Dennis Delane (died, 1750), who acted Talbot to the Suffolk of Walker and the Joan of Arc of Mrs. Hallam. The notice 'not acted fifty years,' affixed to the announcement of this performance, appears to be a most conservative under-statement. Another most remarkable production was that given by the F. R. Benson company at the Stratford Memorial Festival in May, 1906. Mr. Benson here 'made a triumphant Talbot, and the audience seemed never weary of recalling him.' (*Athenæum*, May 12, 1906.)

The Authorship of the Play

I. Shakespeare's Concern in It

With regard to the connection of Shakespeare with *1 Henry VI* four different opinions have been put forward:

(1) Shakespeare had no part in the play. This was apparently the view of Richard Farmer, who says (*Essay on the Learning of Shakespeare*, 1767): '*Henry the sixth* hath ever been doubted; and [Nashe's allusion in *Pierce Penniless*] may give us reason to believe it was previous to our Author. . . . I have no doubt but *Henry the sixth* had the same Author with *Edward the third*.' Malone[7] and Drake[8] took the negative position strongly, and Collier flirted with it,[9] while more recently Dowden (*Shakspere: His Mind and Art*, 173; *Shakspere Primer*, etc.) and Furnivall (Introduction to *Leopold Shakspere*) have virtually denied any real trace of Shakespeare in the work.

(2) Shakespeare wrote the entire play. Samuel Johnson favored this hypothesis, arguing that 'from mere inferiority nothing can be inferred; in the productions of wit there will be inequality.' He was supported by his colleague Steevens, who remarks: 'This historical play might have been one of our author's earliest dramatick efforts; and almost every young poet begins his career by imitation. Shakspeare therefore, till he felt his own strength, perhaps servilely conformed to the style and manner of his predecessors.'[10] Charles Knight in the *Pictorial Shakspeare* (1867) asserted with much greater positiveness that all the three parts of *Henry VI* 'are, in the strictest sense of the word, Shakspeare's own plays,' and was followed by the American critics, Verplanck (1847) and Hudson.[11] Such has been the view almost unanimously of the Germans: Schlegel, Bodenstedt, Delius, Ulrici, Sarrazin, Brandl,

---

5 It is often argued that the priority of *1 Henry VI* to *Henry V* is proved by the closing lines of the epilogue to the latter play:

> 'Henry the Sixth, in infant bands crown'd King
> Of France and England, did this king succeed;
> Whose state so many had the managing,
> That they lost France and made his England bleed:
> Which oft our stage hath shown; and, for their sake,
> In your fair minds let this acceptance take.'

Dogmatism on the point is not justifiable, but the performance of *Harry the Sixth* in 1592 (and afterward) by Shakespeare's company explains the allusion quite as well as the assumption that the revised *1 Henry VI* had already been acted. I find it easier to read in the lines of the epilogue a modestly veiled hint that if *Henry V* proved a success, Shakespeare was thinking of following it up by a revised version of *Harry the Sixth*, than to believe that he really meant to imply that the *Henry VI* plays as now known were such excellent works as to make amends for any defects in *Henry V*. The epilogue to *2 Henry IV* promised the audience *Henry V*, 'if you be not too much cloyed.' The epilogue to *Henry V* reminds them how they have in the past applauded *Henry VI*. Is it not the intention to suggest: 'Perhaps you may have those plays again' (with *Harry the Sixth* worked over so as to fill its place in the series)?

6 When Millington assigned the early versions of *2* and *3 Henry VI* to Pavier, April 19, 1602, he called them 'the first and second parte of Henry the VI.'

7 Boswell-Malone Shakespeare, 1823, v. 246: 'I am therefore decisively of opinion that this play was not written by Shakspeare'; ibid., xviii.557: Part I is "the entire or nearly the entire production of some ancient dramatist.'

8 *Shakspeare and his Times*, 1817, ii.293: 'The hand of Shakspeare is nowhere visible throughout the entire of this "Drum-and-Trumpet-Thing," as Mr. Morgan [Maurice Morgann] has justly termed it.'

9 *Annals of the Stage*, 1831, iii.145: 'It is plausibly conjectured that Shakespeare never touched the *First Part of Henry VI* as it stands in his works.'

10 Capell also should apparently be included among the believers in Shakespeare's exclusive authorship. In his introduction he anticipates and very quaintly develops the idea of Steevens's second sentence: 'We are quite in the dark as to when the first part was written; but should be apt to conjecture, that it was some considerable time after the other two; and perhaps when those two were retouched. . . . And those two parts, even with all their re-touchings, being still much inferior to the other plays of that class, he may reasonably [*sic*] be supposed to have underwrit himself on purpose in the first, that he might the better match with those it belong'd to.'

11 'I can but give it as my firm and settled judgment that the main body of the play is certainly Shakespeare's; nor do I perceive any clear and decisive reason for calling in another hand to account for any part of it.'

Creizenach (Gervinus is the honorable exception). The only recent British scholar to espouse this cause is, I believe, Courthope,[12] who in a remarkable Appendix 'On the Authenticity of Some of the Early Plays Assigned to Shakespeare and their Relationship to the Development of his Dramatic Genius' (*History of English Poetry*, vol. iv, 1903) goes even farther than Knight.

(3) Shakespeare collaborated with other dramatists to produce the play. Grant White (*Essay on the Authorship of King Henry the Sixth*, 1859) supposes that 'It is not improbable that Marlowe, Greene, Peele, and Shakespeare were all engaged upon it,' and suggests 'that within two or three years of Shakespeare's arrival in London, that is, about 1587 or 1588, he was engaged to assist Marlowe, Greene, and perhaps Peele, in dramatizing the events of King Henry the Sixth's reign.' Ingram (*Marlowe and his Associates*, 1904) writes that *1 Henry VI* 'furnishes but slight evidence of containing much of the handiwork of the two men, Marlowe and Shakespeare, who are now believed [*sic*] to have jointly remodelled it'; and Hart (*Arden Shakespeare*, 1909) reasons: 'We are at liberty to place Part I, in so far as it is Shakespeare's, as his earliest work with a date of about 1589-90.... I see no reason, therefore, to look for an imaginary earlier completed play.... We can imagine very easily that Shakespeare was invited to lend a hand to Greene and Peele.'

(4) Shakespeare, working by himself, revised an earlier play of different authorship. Theobald seems first to have formulated this theory: 'Though there are several master-strokes in these three plays [of *Henry VI*], which incontestably betray the workmanship of Shakspeare; yet I am almost doubtful whether they were entirely of his writing. And unless they were wrote by him very early, I should rather imagine them to have been brought to him as a director of the stage; and so have received some finishing beauties at his hand.'[13] Such is the opinion of Coleridge, Gervinus, Staunton, Halliwell-Phillipps, and Dyce, the last of whom definitely repudiates the Grant White theory: 'not written by Shakespeare in conjunction with any other author or authors, but ... a comparatively old drama, which he slightly altered and improved.' Fleay gives precise, but highly dubious, details (*Life and Work of Shakspere*, 1886): 'About 1588-9 Marlowe plotted, and, in conjunction with Kyd (or Greene), Peele, and Lodge, wrote *1 Henry VI* for the Queen's men.... In 1591-2 the Queen's men were in distress and sold, among other plays, *1 Henry VI* to Lord Strange's men, who produced it in 1592 with Shakspere's Talbot additions as a new play.' Rives (1874) argues that Shakespeare revised and expanded an old play dealing exclusively with the wars in France, and Henneman (1901) comes to much the same conclusion. Gray (1917) allows Shakespeare's revisionary labor a somewhat less wide, but still very extensive scope. Herford (Eversley Shakespeare), Rolfe, and Sir Sidney Lee limit the signs of his hand to a couple of scenes; while Ward, Gollancz and Schelling stress their belief that Shakespeare was not properly a reviser, but a 'contributor' of 'additions' to the original work.

This last theory, with its differing implications, has vastly the largest number of upholders at the present time, and is indeed the only one that can be brought into reasonable harmony with the evidence. In regard to the particular scenes to be ascribed to Shakespeare there has been no radical variation among good critics. Nearly all credit Shakespeare with II.iv (the Temple Garden dispute); a large majority also with II.v (the death of Mortimer), which naturally links itself with the foregoing, and with the whole or most of IV.ii-vii (Talbot's death). With less assurance V.iii. 45-202 (Suffolk's wooing of Margaret) is added. In all these there are strong indications of Shakespeare. Note the plays on words: 'I love no colours, and without all colour' (II.iv.34); 'And in that ease, I'll tell thee my disease' (II.v.44); 'And they shall find dear deer of us' (IV.ii.54), together with the technical deer-hunting allusions in the last passage and the hawk, dog, horse references in II.iv.11-14.

Compare also the bold use of transferred adjectives, quite Shakespearean and quite unlike the general style of the play as a whole: 'In dumb significants' (II.iv.26), 'this pale and maiden blossom' (II.iv.47), 'this pale and angry rose' (II.iv.109), 'my blood-drinking hate' (II.iv.110), 'death and deadly night' (II.iv.129), 'feet whose strengthless stay is numb' (II.v.13), 'sweet enlargement' (II.v.30), 'the dusky torch of Mortimer' (II.v.122), 'your stately and air-braving towers' (IV.ii.13), 'the process of his sandy hour' (IV.ii.36), 'sleeping neglection' (IV.iii.49), 'That ever living man of memory' (IV.iii.51), 'bring thy father to his drooping chair' (IV.v.5), 'bold-fac'd victory' (IV.vi.12).

Especially Shakespearean are the fanciful metaphors and similes which abound in these scenes: 'Were growing time once ripen'd to my will' (II.iv.101); 'I'll note you in my book of memory' (II.iv.103); 'these gray locks, the pursuivants of Death' (II.v.5); 'These eyes, like lamps whose wasting oil is spent' (II.v.8); 'pithless arms, like to a wither'd vine That droops his sapless branches to the ground' (II.v.11, 12); 'Just death, kind umpire of men's miseries' (II.v.29); 'But now thy uncle is removing hence, As princes do their courts, when they are cloy'd With long continuance in a settled place' (II.v.104-106); 'To wall thee from the liberty of flight' (IV.ii.24); 'girdled with a waist of iron' (IV.iii.20); 'ring'd about with bold adversity' (IV.iv.14); 'Now thou art seal'd the son of chivalry' (IV.vi.29); 'To save a paltry life and slay bright fame' (IV.vi.45); 'Triumphant death, smear'd with captivity' (IV.vii.3); 'inhearsed in the arms Of the most bloody nurser of his harms' (IV.vii.46); 'Twinkling another counterfeited beam' (V.iii.63).

Consideration of the passages just cited, which are fairly representative, though of course not complete, will, I think, suggest a gradual decrease through the scenes concerned in the recognizable Shakespearean quality. The Temple Garden and Mortimer scenes are rather more positively like Shakespeare than the blank verse Talbot passages, and decidedly more so than the rimed Talbot passages (IV.iii.28-46, IV.v.16-vii.50) or the Suffolk-Margaret scene. This is reasonable, since the first two scenes bear most appearance of being spontaneous with the reviser of the play, and since Shakespeare's language is regularly bolder in blank verse than in rime.

It would be hazardous to attempt to infer from the style alone the date at which Shakespeare wrote his scenes.[14] The diction does not seem to me that of the poet's earliest period; and Furnivall has observed that the proportion of extra-syllabled lines in the

---

12 Note, however, the historian Gairdner's passing remark (*Studies in English History*, 1881, 65): 'I dismiss altogether the hypothesis which some have advanced, that the First Part of *Henry VI* was not really Shakespeare's. So far as internal evidence goes, if in ability it be not equal to Shakespeare's best, it is too great for any other writer.'

13 This is the sense also of Maurice Morgann's wild obiter dictum on the play, referred to in the quotation from Drake above. He alludes to Sir John Fastolfe, 'a name for ever dishonoured by a frequent exposure in that Drum-and-trumpet Thing called *The first part of Henry VI.*, written doubtless, or rather exhibited, long before *Shakespeare* was born, tho' afterwards repaired, I think, and furbished up by him with here and there a little sentiment and diction.' (*Essay on the Dramatic Character of Sir John Falstaff*, 1777.)

14 See The History of the Play, p. 438.

Temple Garden scene (about 26 per cent) 'forbids us supposing it is very early work.' It would also be ill-advised to set precise limits for Shakespeare's part in the play. His hand is most evident in the scenes just discussed, but Talbot's death must, I think, have been a conspicuous feature of the original pre-Shakespearean play, and it is unlikely that the reviser here removed all traces of his predecessor. On the other hand, it is entirely reasonable to suspect Shakespearean penciling in scenes where the handling is too light or too perfunctory to leave any definite impression of genius. In particular, Mr. Gray finds evidence of the greater writer in the opening of III.i and in the Vernon-Basset quarrel (III.iv.28ff. and IV.i.78ff.). I am impressed by Henneman's suggestion that IV.i as a whole is the reviser's replica of III.iv (cf. note on IV.i): there seems to be nothing in the later scene which Shakespeare might not have written, and a positive clue may perhaps be found in the fact that Talbot's account of the Battle of Patay is here certainly taken from Holinshed rather than Halle.[15] Another hint of the same kind appears in I.ii in the adoption from Holinshed's second edition of the favorable view of Joan of Arc (which Holinshed explains that he derives from French sources), whereas the remainder of the play gives an inharmonious conception drawn from the earlier English chronicles.[16]

The reviser's hand, presumably Shakespeare's, is evident in the way the close of *1 Henry VI* is shaped to fit it as an introduction to Part II of the trilogy. Henneman states the relationship of the three parts with accuracy, if with undue caution: 'So specifically does I prepare for II and III in certain particulars that it is conceivable that I was written after II and that III had already been planned.' If he means in the case of Part I, not the original composition, but the reviser's adaptation, it is certain, I think, that I follows II. Note that the thirty-ninth line of the play, where Winchester says to Gloucester, 'Thy wife is proud; she holdeth thee in awe,' can only be rationally explained as a preparation for Part II. The gibe means nothing as regards Part I. Again, the conclusion of Part I can only have been worked into an open advertisement for Part II,

> *'Margaret shall now be queen, and rule the king;*
> *But I will rule both her, the king, and realm,'*

after Parts II and III had passed into the possession of Shakespeare's company, and been adapted for representation by them. The 1592 *Harry the Sixth* cannot well be imagined to have ended so, for Pembroke's company appear at this time to have owned the early versions of Parts II and III.[17] It is not reasonable that Strange's company should have employed a conclusion quite out of keeping with their main theme of Talbot's glory and explicable only as preparing the audience for the play of a rival company.

That the original ending of the play was greatly changed by

the reviser appears from textual evidence, which Fleay with characteristic subtlety noted, and, I think, characteristically misinterpreted. The marking of acts and scenes in the only early edition—that of the Folio—is entirely regular as far as the close of Act III (save that the individual scenes of Acts I and II are not divided off); and it is extraordinarily chaotic in Acts IV and V. Practically the whole close of the play (from IV.i through V.iv) is given as Act IV, Act V consisting only of the short last scene (V.v), and being marked at all probably merely in order to secure the conventional total of five acts. The six scenes dealing with Talbot's death (IV.ii-vii) are undivided and carelessly tacked on to IV.i, with which they have only a remote organic connection. From this Fleay argues that the Talbot scenes are a patch of new material, not corresponding to anything in the old play: 'It is plain that they were written subsequently to the rest of the play and inserted at a revival. They had to be inserted in such a manner as not to break the connection between this play and *2 Henry VI;* and were put in the most convenient place, regardless of historic sequence.' I think the reverse is true: that it was the necessity of creating a spurious connection with *2 Henry VI* which produced the disorder. Originally the Talbot scenes probably came nearer the end of the play and stood in closer relationship to their natural complement, the retributive overthrow of Joan (V.ii, iii.1-44, iv.1-93) and the final submission of the Dauphin (V.iv.116-175). On this unhistorical, but very dramatic note of national vindication the old play may be supposed to have concluded. To change this note to that of pessimism and foreboding with which Part II opens was the reviser's problem.[18] It required a complete *volte-face,* which has been executed with dexterity but probably at a cost to the effectiveness of this play (considered individually and not as the introduction to a great tetralogy) for which Shakespeare's improvement of the poetry in the Talbot scenes does not compensate. The patchwork is most painfully evident where the otherwise admirable Suffolk-Margaret-Reignier scene (V.iii.45-202) is pasted in between two sections of the Joan story. The last scene in the play, constituting the entire Actus Quintus of the Folio, clearly belongs altogether to the later recension. The writing of so purely utilitarian a scene was small game for Shakespeare, but the execution is by no means un-Shakespearean.[19]

Henneman's summary of Shakespeare's probable purpose in *1 Henry VI* is, I think, fair and conservative: 'To work up or rewrite the Talbot portions of the Chronicles, probably, though not necessarily, already crystallized into an old play on the triumph of "brave Talbot" over the French, which possessed the hated Joan of Arc scenes and all; to intensify the figure and character of Talbot; to work over or add scenes like those touching Talbot's death; to connect him with the deplorable struggles of the nobles; to invent, by a happy poetical thought, the origin of the factions of the Red and White Roses in the Temple Garden; to sound at once the note of weakness in the king continued in the succeeding Parts, and thus convert the old Talbot material effectually into a Henry VI drama; and to close with the wooing of Margaret as specific introduction to Part II,—something like this seems the task that the dramatist set himself to perform.'

---

15 Holinshed reports that Talbot had 'not past six thousand men' (cf. IV.i.20 and also I.i.112), while Halle gives him five thousand.

16 Two small points, which I have not seen mentioned, may have some bearing on the date of Shakespeare's revision: (1) The Mortimer scene, especially lines 67-81, sounds rather like a reminiscence of *1 Henry IV.* (2) Margaret's vain efforts to make Suffolk attend to her questions and the retribution she takes (V.iii.72-109) repeat Falstaff's tactics with the Chief Justice (*2 Henry IV,* II.i.143-165). It is possible, but hardly so likely, that the sequence was the other way.

17 Pembroke's Men are supposed to have sold these plays and others at the time of their distress in September, 1593—a year and a half after Strange's (Shakespeare's) Men produced *Harry the Sixth.* Cf. Greg, *Henslowe's Diary,* ii.85; Murray, *English Dram. Companies,* i.65. (I do not agree with Murray's suggestion of a possible connection between Shakespeare and the Pembroke company.)

18 The clearest indication of an effort to prepare the audience for this new gloom in the close appears in the croaking speeches of Exeter, affixed to III.i and IV.i.

19 Gervinus pointed out (*Shakespeare,* 2d ed., 1850, i.202) that if the Suffolk-Margaret scene and the last scene were omitted, and the play left to close with 'Winchester's peace' (V.iv), it would have a conclusion much better suited to the chief content.

II. THE AUTHOR OF THE ORIGINAL PLAY

1. Marlowe?

Henslowe's play of *Harry the Sixth,* if it followed somewhat the lines just suggested, undoubtedly deserved the popularity it attained. It was probably more effective on the stage than the expanded work which supplanted it, and in 1591-92 can have been written only by a real poet and a skilled dramatist. There were not many such at this period. Marlowe was one, but I concur warmly in Mr. Gray's opinion that 'Marlowe himself cannot be read into this drama.' Marlowe's influence, however, is unquestionably apparent in the older parts of the play. Note, for example, the following echoes.[20]

I.i.2:
  'Comets, importing change of times and states'
Marlowe's Lucan 527:
  'And comets that presage the fall of kingdoms.'

I.i.3:
  'Brandish your crystal tresses in the sky.'
Tamburlaine 1922:
  'Shaking her silver tresses in the air.'

I.i.22:
  'Like captives bound to a triumphant car.'
Edward II 174:
  'With captive kings at his triumphant car.'

I.i.36:
  'Whom like a school-boy you may over-awe.'
Edward II 1336 f.:
  'As though your highness were a school-boy still,
  And must be awed and governed like a child.'

I.i.46:
  'Instead of gold we'll offer up our arms.'
Jew of Malta 758 f.:
              'Instead of gold,
  We'll send thee bullets wrapped in smoke and fire.'

I.i.149:
  'I'll hale the Dauphin headlong from his throne.'
Tamburlaine 4021:
  'Haling him headlong to the lowest hell.'

I.vi.11, 12:
  'Why ring not out the bells throughout the town?
  Dauphin, command the citizens make bonfires.'
Tamburlaine 1335 f.:
  'Ringing with joy their superstitious bells,
  And making bonfires for my overthrow.'

III.ii.43:
  'That hardly we escap'd the pride of France.'
Tamburlaine 140:
  'Lest you subdue the pride of Christendom.'
Tamburlaine 3568:
  'To overdare the pride of Græcia.'
Dido 482:
  'That after burnt the pride of Asia.'

III.ii.140:
  'But kings and mightiest potentates must die.'
Tamburlaine 4641:
  'For Tamburlaine, the scourge of God, must die.'

III.iii.13:
  'And we will make thee famous through the world.'
Tamburlaine 2173:
  'And makes my deeds infamous through the world.'

III.iii.24:
  'But be extirped from our provinces.'
Faustus 122:
  'And reign sole king of all our provinces.'

IV.vii.32:
  'Now my old arms are young John Talbot's grave.'
Jew of Malta 1192:
  'These arms of mine shall be thy sepulchre.'

V.iv.34:
  'Take her away; for she hath liv'd too long.'
Edward II 2651:
  'Nay, to my death, for too long have I lived.'

V.iv.87, 88:
  'May never glorious sun reflex his beams
  Upon the country where you make adobe.'
Tamburlaine 969 f.:
  'For neither rain can fall upon the earth,
  Nor sun reflex his virtuous beams thereon.'

Marlowe's general influence is also traceable, as in I.vi, where the barbaric magnificence of the Dauphin's promises to Joan plagiarizes those of Tamburlaine to Zenocrate (*Tamb.* 278 ff.), and his promise that Joan's coffin shall be carried before the kings and queens of France recalls the second part of Marlowe's play (II.iii, III.ii). The concluding couplet of this same scene echoes the close of *1 Tamburlaine,* Act III; and the burial of Zenocrate is again clearly parodied in the burial of Salisbury (II.ii).[21]

All this means mimicry, conscious or unconscious. Frequently the imitation degenerates into travesty, as in the weak mouthing of Bedford (I.i.148-156) and the atrocious rot of the whole scene in which Salisbury is stricken (I.iv). Imagine Marlowe making his chief hero say at the height of passion:

> *What chance is this, that suddenly hath cross'd us?*
> *Speak, Salisbury; at least, if thou canst speak,' etc.*

It is easier to conceive the mighty line to have attained the unsurpassable flatness of the messenger's words in II.iii.30, 31:

> *Stay, my Lord Talbot; for my Lady craves*
> *To know the cause of your abrupt departure.'*

The real proof that Marlowe did not write *Harry the Sixth* is the absence of any passion except in scenes which bear marks of revisions. The lines are usually musical and sometimes charming, and the stage action is interesting, but they are not irradiated by the electric intensity that scintillates in Marlowe. Till Shakespeare vivifies him in the fourth act, Talbot himself is but a skeleton in armor.

2. Greene?

Greene has been very often suggested as the author of this play, most recently by Gray, though with reservations, and most positively by Hart. I see nothing that renders such an attribution reasonable: Hart's verbal parallels seem quite without demonstrative value. Greene's essays in the chronicle history drama are notably characteristic, and evidence a method entirely unlike that of this play. He nowhere exhibits any tendency toward patriotic themes or any interest in the facts of

---

20 The line numbers for Marlowe's works are those of the Oxford edition.

21 Several of these similarities have been noted by Anders, *Shakespeare's Books,* p. 121. Sarrazin had previously mentioned the resemblance of Joan's appeal to Burgundy (III.iii) and Tamburlaine's appeal to Theridamas (305 ff.).

history. Rather in his quasi-historic plays, *Friar Bacon and Friar Bungay* and *James IV* (and in *George-a-Greene* if it be his), he yields to an apparently irresistible devotion for pastoral woodland settings, romantic love stories, quaint supernaturalism, and clownish roguery. Unless one can fancy Joan's brief address to her fiends (V.iii.1-24) to be akin in atmosphere or purpose to the magic humbuggery of Bacon and the fairy machinery of Oberon, *1 Henry VI* is wholly unlike Greene in all these points. It is unlike him both in the inflexibility with which it harps on the historical note, and in its absence of humor, sentiment, or pathos. Greene, of course, may have written the play, but it is less like his avowed work than that of any contemporary dramatist.

3. Peele?

It is not by a process of elimination merely that I arrive at George Peele as the most likely author of the old *Harry the Sixth* play. Indications of several kinds point in Peele's direction. He was at the time the work was produced distinctly the most conspicuous exponent of jingoistic national pride—a trait of which Marlowe shows absolutely nothing and Greene hardly more. Peele had composed the patriotic masques to celebrate the Lord Mayoralty of Sir Wolstan Dixie in 1585 and of Sir William Web in 1591. His *Polyhymnia* (1590) lauded in martial strains 'the honourable Triumph at Tilt' when Sir Henry Lea formally resigned his post of Queen's Champion, and he again touched the same theme in *Anglorum Feriae* (1595), written in honor of the thirty-seventh anniversary of Elizabeth's accession. In 1589 he had twice come forth as the spokesman of the nation: in his *Eclogue Gratulatory* to the Earl of Essex 'for his welcome into England from Portugal,' and in his fine *Farewell*, 'Entituled to the famous and fortunate Generals of our English forces: Sir John Norris and Sir Francis Drake.' Later, again, in 1593, he linked the knighthood of his age with that of the past in *The Honour of the Garter*.[22] His plays of the same period, *Edward I* and *The Battle of Alcazar,* are equally filled with the praise of English daring. No known author of 1591 has anything like the same claim on merely extrinsic evidence to be regarded as the author of a play in celebration of the martial exploits of the brave Lord Talbot.[23]

General similarities between Peele's *Edward I* and *1 Henry VI* have been often noted, particularly the unhappy resemblance in the defamation of the Spanish Eleanor and the French Joan of Arc. One of the most insular of Britons, Peele was incapable of glorifying his countrymen without slandering the races they opposed. The undramatic line put into Joan's mouth (III.iii.86),

'Done like a Frenchman: turn, and turn again!'

is fairly characteristic of his bigotry.

The verse of the older portions of the play—saccharine rather than strong, and the loose but animated structure are

what one finds in Peele's recognized dramas. The imitation of Marlowe is equally a feature of those which were produced after *Tamburlaine*.[24]

The Countess of Auvergne episode, with its grace and lack of human warmth, seems to me like Peele's work. In its relation to the military plot, and particularly in the military tableau with which it closes, it is very suggestive of the more elaborated Countess of Salisbury episode in the anonymous *Edward III*. I give my adhesion to the conjecture of Farmer, already quoted, that *'Henry the sixth* [in its earliest form] had the same Author with *Edward the third,'* and believe that author to have been Peele.[25]

---

22 This poem should be compared with Talbot's speech, 'When first this order was ordained,' etc. (IV.i.33ff.).

23 Peele's favorite epigram, which he affixes at least three times to his poems, might well serve as motto for *1 Henry VI:*

> *Gallia victa dedit flores, invicta leones*
>   *Anglia, jus belli in flore, leone suum;*
> *O sic, O semper ferat Anglia laeta (or 'Elizabetha') triumphos,*
>   *Inclyta Gallorum flore, leone suo.'*

24 *Edward I* 954:
> 'It is but temporal that you can inflict.'

Edward II 1550:
> ''Tis but temporal that thou canst inflict.'

Edward I 1165 f.:
> 'This comfort, madam, that your grace doth give
> Blinds me in double duty whilst I live.'

Edward II 1684 f.:
> 'These comforts that you give our woeful queen
> Bind us in kindness all at your command.'

Edward I 2800:
> 'Hence, feigned weeds, unfeigned is my grief.'

Edward II 1964:
> 'Hence, feigned weeds, unfeigned are my woes.'

David & Bethsabe 12-14:
> 'The host of heaven . . . cast
> Their crystal armor at his conquering feet.'

Tamburlaine 1932:
> 'There angels in their crystal armors fight.'

David & Bethsabe 181:
> 'And makes their weapons wound the senseless winds.'

Tamburlaine 1256:
> 'And make our strokes to wound the senseless air'
> ('lure' in first edition).

Battle of Alcazar 190:
> 'The bells of Pluto ring revenge amain.'

Edward II 1956:
> 'Let Pluto's bells ring out my fatal knell.'

Battle of Alcazar 250:
> 'Tamburlaine, triumph not, for thou must die.'

Tamburlaine 4641:
> 'For Tamburlaine, the Scourge of God, must die.'

(The line numbers for Peele's plays are those of the Malone Society editions.)

25 Cf. *The Shakespeare Apocrypha,* p. xxiii.

ACT FIRST ❦ SCENE FIRST

[Westminster Abbey]
Dead March.
Enter the Funeral of King Henry the Fifth, attended on by the Duke
of Bedford, Regent of France; the Duke of Gloucester, Protector;
the Duke of Exeter; Warwick; the Bishop of Winchester; and the
Duke of Somerset [with Heralds, &c.].

Bed. Hung be the heavens with black, yield day to night!
Comets, importing change of times and states,
Brandish your crystal tresses in the sky,
And with them scourge the bad revolting stars,
That have consented unto Henry's death!   *5*
King Henry the Fifth, too famous to live long!
England ne'er lost a king of so much worth.
　Glo. England ne'er had a king until his time.
Virtue he had, deserving to command:
His brandish'd sword did blind men with his beams;   *10*
His arms spread wider than a dragon's wings;
His sparkling eyes, replete with wrathful fire,
More dazzled and drove back his enemies
Than mid-day sun fierce bent against their faces.
What should I say? his deeds exceed all speech: *15*
He ne'er lift up his hand but conquered.
　Exe. We mourn in black: why mourn we not in blood?
Henry is dead and never shall revive.
Upon a wooden coffin we attend,
And death's dishonourable victory   *20*
We with our stately presence glorify,
Like captives bound to a triumphant car.
What! shall we curse the planets of mishap
That plotted thus our glory's overthrow?
Or shall we think the subtle-witted French   *25*
Conjurers and sorcerers, that, afraid of him,
By magic verses have contriv'd his end?
　Win. He was a king bless'd of the King of kings.
Unto the French the dreadful judgment-day
So dreadful will not be as was his sight.   *30*
The battles of the Lord of hosts he fought:
The church's prayers made him so prosperous.
　Glo. The church! where is it? Had not churchmen pray'd,
His thread of life had not so soon decay'd:
None do you like but an effeminate prince,   *35*
Whom like a school-boy you may over-awe.
　Win. Gloucester, whate'er we like thou art protector,
And lookest to command the prince and realm.
Thy wife is proud; she holdeth thee in awe,
More than God or religious churchmen may.   *40*
　Glo. Name not religion, for thou lov'st the flesh,
And ne'er throughout the year to church thou go'st,
Except it be to pray against thy foes.
　Bed. Cease, cease these jars and rest your minds in peace!
Let's to the altar: heralds, wait on us: *45*
Instead of gold we'll offer up our arms,
Since arms avail not, now that Henry's dead.
Posterity, await for wretched years,
When at their mothers' moist eyes babes shall suck,
Our isle be made a marish of salt tears,   *50*

And none but women left to wail the dead.
Henry the Fifth! thy ghost I invoke:
Prosper this realm, keep it from civil broils!
Combat with adverse planets in the heavens!
A far more glorious star thy soul will make,   *55*
Than Julius Cæsar, or bright—

Enter a Messenger.

　Mess. My honourable lords, health to you all!
Sad tidings bring I to you out of France,
Of loss, of slaughter, and discomfiture:
Guyenne, Champagne, Rheims, Orleans,   *60*
Paris, Gisors, Poitiers, are all quite lost.
　Bed. What sayst thou, man, before dead Henry's corse?
Speak softly; or the loss of those great towns
Will make him burst his lead and rise from death.
　Glo. Is Paris lost? is Roan yielded up?   *65*
If Henry were recall'd to life again
These news would cause him once more yield the ghost.
　Exe. How were they lost? what treachery was us'd?
　Mess. No treachery; but want of men and money.
Among the soldiers this is muttered,   *70*
That here you maintain several factions;
And, whilst a field should be dispatch'd and fought,
You are disputing of your generals.
One would have lingering wars with little cost;
Another would fly swift, but wanteth wings;   *75*
A third thinks, without expense at all,
By guileful fair words peace may be obtain'd.
Awake, awake, English nobility!
Let not sloth dim your honours new-begot:
Cropp'd are the flower-de-luces in your arms;   *80*
Of England's coat one half is cut away.
　Exe. Were our tears wanting to this funeral
These tidings would call forth their flowing tides.
　Bed. Me they concern; Regent I am of France.
Give me my steeled coat: I'll fight for France.   *85*
Away with these disgraceful wailing robes!
Wounds will I lend the French instead of eyes,
To weep their intermissive miseries.

Enter to them another Messenger.

　Sec. Mess. Lords, view these letters, full of bad mischance.
France is revolted from the English quite,   *90*
Except some petty towns of no import:
The Dauphin Charles is crowned king in Rheims;
The Bastard of Orleans with him is join'd;
Reignier, Duke of Anjou, doth take his part;
The Duke of Alençon flieth to his side.   *Exit.*   *95*
　Exe. The Dauphin crowned king! all fly to him!
O! whither shall we fly from this reproach?
　Glo. We will not fly, but to our enemies' throats.
Bedford, if thou be slack, I'll fight it out.
　Bed. Gloucester, why doubt'st thou of my forwardness?   *100*
An army have I muster'd in my thoughts,
Wherewith already France is overrun.

The First Part, etc.; *cf. n.*　**1 Hung … black;** *cf. n.*　**10 his:** *its*　**16 lift:** *lifted*　**50 marish:** *marsh; cf. n.*

60, 61 *Cf. n.*　**64 lead:** *leaden wrappings*　**65 Roan:** *Rouen*　**71 several:** *separate*　**72 field … dispatch'd:** *battle … arranged*　**80** *The fleurs de lys are plucked from your coat of arms*　**88 intermissive:** *temporarily interrupted (but now to be renewed)*　**92** *Cf. n.*

Enter another Messenger.

Third Mess. My gracious lords, to add to your laments,
Wherewith you now bedew King Henry's hearse,
I must inform you of a dismal fight   105
Betwixt the stout Lord Talbot and the French.
    Win. What! wherein Talbot overcame? is 't so?
    Third Mess. O, no! wherein Lord Talbot was o'er-thrown:
The circumstance I'll tell you more at large.
The tenth of August last this dreadful lord,   110
Retiring from the siege of Orleans,
Having full scarce six thousand in his troop,
By three-and-twenty thousand of the French
Was round encompassed and set upon.
No leisure had he to enrank his men;   115
He wanted pikes to set before his archers;
Instead whereof sharp stakes pluck'd out of hedges
They pitched in the ground confusedly,
To keep the horsemen off from breaking in.
More than three hours the fight continued;   120
Where valiant Talbot above human thought
Enacted wonders with his sword and lance.
Hundreds he sent to hell, and none durst stand him;
Here, there, and everywhere, enrag'd he flew:
The French exclaim'd the devil was in arms;   125
All the whole army stood agaz'd on him.
His soldiers, spying his undaunted spirit,
A Talbot! A Talbot! cried out amain,
And rush'd into the bowels of the battle.
Here had the conquest fully been seal'd up,   130
If Sir John Fastolfe had not play'd the coward.
He, being in the vaward,—plac'd behind,
With purpose to relieve and follow them,—
Cowardly fled, not having struck one stroke.
Hence grew the general wrack and massacre;   135
Enclosed were they with their enemies.
A base Walloon, to win the Dauphin's grace,
Thrust Talbot with a spear into the back;
Whom all France, with their chief assembled strength,
Durst not presume to look once in the face.   140
    Bed. Is Talbot slain? then I will slay myself,
For living idly here in pomp and ease
Whilst such a worthy leader, wanting aid,
Unto his dastard foemen is betray'd.
    Third Mess. O no! he lives; but is took prisoner,   145
And Lord Scales with him, and Lord Hungerford:
Most of the rest slaughter'd or took likewise.
    Bed. His ransom there is none but I shall pay:
I'll hale the Dauphin headlong from his throne;
His crown shall be the ransom of my friend;   150
Four of their lords I'll change for one of ours.
Farewell, my masters; to my task will I;
Bonfires in France forthwith I am to make,
To keep our great Saint George's feast withal:
Ten thousand soldiers with me I will take,   155
Whose bloody deeds shall make all Europe quake.
    Third Mess. So you had need; for Orleans is besieg'd;
The English army is grown weak and faint;

The Earl of Salisbury craveth supply,
And hardly keeps his men from mutiny,   160
Since they, so few, watch such a multitude.
    Exe. Remember, lords, your oaths to Henry sworn,
Either to quell the Dauphin utterly,
Or bring him in obedience to your yoke.
    Bed. I do remember it; and here take my leave,   165
To go about my preparation.   *Exit Bedford.*
    Glo. I'll to the Tower with all the haste I can,
To view the artillery and munition;
And then I will proclaim young Henry king.   *Exit Gloucester.*
    Exe. To Eltham will I, where the young king is,   170
Being ordain'd his special governor;
And for his safety there I'll best devise.   *Exit.*
    Win. Each hath his place and function to attend:
I am left out; for me nothing remains.
But long I will not be Jack-out-of-office.   175
The king from Eltham I intend to steal,
And sit at chiefest stern of public weal.   *Exit.*

❧ Scene Second ❧

[France. Before Orleans]
Sound a Flourish.
*Enter Charles, Alençon, and Reignier, marching with Drum and
Soldiers.*

    Char. Mars his true moving, even as in the heavens
So in the earth, to this day is not known.
Late did he shine upon the English side;
Now we are victors; upon us he smiles.
What towns of any moment but we have?   5
At pleasure here we lie near Orleans;
Otherwhiles the famish'd English, like pale ghosts,
Faintly besiege us one hour in a month.
    Alen. They want their porridge and their fat bull-beeves:
Either they must be dieted like mules   10
And have their provender tied to their mouths,
Or piteous they will look, like drowned mice.
    Reig. Let's raise the siege: why live we idly here?
Talbot is taken, whom we wont to fear:
Remaineth none but mad-brain'd Salisbury,   15
And he may well in fretting spend his gall;
Nor men nor money hath he to make war.
    Char. Sound, sound alarum! we will rush on them.
Now for the honour of the forlorn French!
Him I forgive my death that killeth me   20
When he sees me go back one foot or fly.   *Exeunt.*

*Here Alarum; they are beaten back by the English, with great loss.
Enter Charles, Alençon, and Reignier.*

    Char. Who ever saw the like? what men have I!
Dogs! cowards! dastards! I would ne'er have fled
But that they left me 'midst my enemies.
    Reig. Salisbury is a desperate homicide;   25
He fighteth as one weary of his life:

110, 111 *Cf. n.*   110 **dreadful:** *redoubtable*   112 **full scarce:** *scarce full, not quite*   116 **wanted pikes;** *cf. n.*   124 **flew;** *cf. n.*   126 **agaz'd on:** *astounded at*   131 **Sir John Fastolfe;** *cf. n.*   132 **vaward,—plac'd behind;** *cf. n.*   136 **with:** *by*   148 *Cf. n.*   154 **Saint George's feast;** *cf. n.*   **withal:** *therewith*

162 **your oaths;** *cf. n.*   163 **quell:** *destroy*   170 **Eltham;** *cf. n.*   177 **at chiefest stern:** *in supreme control*   **Scene Two** S. d. **Flourish:** *trumpet blast*   1 **Mars his true moving:** *Mars' exact movement; cf. n.*   7 **Otherwhiles:** *at times*   14 **wont:** *were wont*   17 **Nor: neither*   18 **alarum:** *call to arms*

The other lords, like lions wanting food,
Do rush upon us as their hungry prey.
   Alen. Froissart, a countryman of ours, records,
England all Olivers and Rowlands bred   *30*
During the time Edward the Third did reign.
More truly now may this be verified;
For none but Samsons and Goliases
It sendeth forth to skirmish. One to ten!
Lean raw-bon'd rascals! who would e'er suppose   *35*
They had such courage and audacity?
   Char. Let's leave this town; for they are hare-brain'd slaves,
And hunger will enforce them to be more eager:
Of old I know them; rather with their teeth
The walls they'll tear down than forsake the siege.   *40*
   Reig. I think, by some odd gimmors or device,
Their arms are set like clocks, still to strike on;
Else ne'er could they hold out so as they do.
By my consent, we'll e'en let them alone.
   Alen. Be it so.   *45*

Enter the Bastard of Orleans.

   Bast. Where's the prince Dauphin? I have news for him.
   Char. Bastard of Orleans, thrice welcome to us.
   Bast. Methinks your looks are sad, your cheer appall'd:
Hath the late overthrow wrought this offence?
Be not dismay'd, for succour is at hand: *50*
A holy maid hither with me I bring,
Which by a vision sent to her from heaven
Ordained is to raise this tedious siege,
And drive the English forth the bounds of France.
The spirit of deep prophecy she hath,   *55*
Exceeding the nine sibyls of old Rome;
What's past and what's to come she can descry.
Speak, shall I call her in? Believe my words,
For they are certain and unfallible.
   Char. Go, call her in. *[Exit Bastard.]* But first, to try   *60*
her skill,
Reignier, stand thou as Dauphin in my place:
Question her proudly; let thy looks be stern:
By this means shall we sound what skill she hath.

Enter Joan Pucelle [with Bastard].

   Reig. Fair maid, is 't thou wilt do these wondrous feats?   *65*
   Joan. Reignier, is 't thou that thinkest to beguile me?
Where is the Dauphin? Come, come from behind;
I know thee well, though never seen before.
Be not amaz'd, there's nothing hid from me:
In private will I talk with thee apart.   *70*
Stand back, you lords, and give us leave a while.
   Reig. She takes upon her bravely at first dash.
   Joan. Dauphin, I am by birth a shepherd's daughter,
My wit untrain'd in any kind of art.
Heaven and our Lady gracious hath it pleas'd   *75*
To shine on my contemptible estate:
Lo! whilst I waited on my tender lambs,
And to sun's parching heat display'd my cheeks.
God's mother deigned to appear to me,

And in a vision full of majesty   *80*
Will'd me to leave my base vocation
And free my country from calamity:
Her aid she promis'd and assur'd success;
In complete glory she reveal'd herself;
And, whereas I was black and swart before,   *85*
With those clear rays which she infus'd on me,
That beauty am I bless'd with which you see.
Ask me what question thou canst possible
And I will answer unpremeditated:
My courage try by combat, if thou dar'st,   *90*
And thou shalt find that I exceed my sex.
Resolve on this, thou shalt be fortunate
If thou receive me for thy warlike mate.
   Char. Thou hast astonish'd me with thy high terms.
Only this proof I'll of thy valour make,   *95*
In single combat thou shalt buckle with me,
And if thou vanquishest, thy words are true;
Otherwise I renounce all confidence.
   Joan. I am prepar'd: here is my keen-cdg'd sword,
Deck'd with five flower-de-luces on each side;   *100*
The which at Touraine, in Saint Katharine's churchyard,
Out of a great deal of old iron I chose forth.
   Char. Then come, o' God's name; I fear no woman.
   Joan. And, while I live, I'll ne'er fly from a man.

Here they fight, and Joan la Pucelle overcomes.

   Char. Stay, stay thy hands! thou art an Amazon,   *105*
And fightest with the sword of Deborah.
   Joan. Christ's mother helps me, else I were too weak.
   Char. Whoe'er helps thee, 'tis thou that must help me:
Impatiently I burn with thy desire;
My heart and hands thou hast at once subdu'd.   *110*
Excellent Pucelle, if thy name be so,
Let me thy servant and not sovereign be;
'Tis the French Dauphin sueth to thee thus.
   Joan. I must not yield to any rites of love,
For my profession's sacred from above: *115*
When I have chased all thy foes from hence,
Then will I think upon a recompense.
   Char. Meantime look gracious on thy prostrate thrall.
   Reig. My lord, methinks, is very long in talk.
   Alen. Doubtless he shrives this woman to her smock;   *120*
Else ne'er could he so long protract his speech.
   Reig. Shall we disturb him, since he keeps no mean?
   Alen. He may mean more than we poor men do know:
These women are shrewd tempters with their tongues.
   Reig. My lord, where are you? what devise you on?   *125*
Shall we give over Orleans, or no?
   Joan. Why, no, I say, distrustful recreants!
Fight till the last gasp; I will be your guard.
   Char. What she says, I'll confirm: we'll fight it out.
   Joan. Assign'd am I to be the English scourge.   *130*
This night the siege assuredly I'll raise:
Expect Saint Martin's summer, halcyon days,
Since I have entered into these wars.
Glory is like a circle in the water,
Which never ceaseth to enlarge itself,   *135*

---

28 hungry: *stimulating hunger*   **30 Olivers and Rowlands:** *knights like the best who followed Charlemagne*   **33 Goliases:** *Goliaths (Golias is the Latin form)*   **41 gimmors:** *mechanical joints*   **42 still:** *continually*   **48 cheer appall'd:** *mood dejected*   **56 nine sibyls;** *cf. n.*

94 high terms: *lofty language*   **96 buckle:** *contend*   **100 Deck'd:** *adorned*   **106 sword of Deborah;** *cf. n.*   **111 Pucelle;** *cf. n.*   **122 mean:** *moderation*   **132 Saint Martin's summer;** *cf. n.*

Till by broad spreading it disperse to nought.
With Henry's death the English circle ends;
Dispersed are the glories it included.
Now am I like that proud insulting ship
Which Cæsar and his fortune bare at once.   *140*
   Char. Was Mahomet inspired with a dove?
Thou with an eagle art inspired then.
Helen, the mother of great Constantine,
Nor yet Saint Philip's daughters were like thee.
Bright star of Venus, fall'n down on the earth,   *145*
How may I reverently worship thee enough?
   Alen. Leave off delays and let us raise the siege.
   Reig. Woman, do what thou canst to save our honours;
Drive them from Orleans and be immortaliz'd.
   Char. Presently we'll try. Come, let's away about it: *150*
No prophet will I trust if she prove false.   *Exeunt.*

❧ SCENE THIRD ❧

[London. Before the Tower]
Enter Gloucester, with his Serving-men [in blue coats].

   Glo. I am come to survey the Tower this day;
Since Henry's death, I fear, there is conveyance.
Where be these warders that they wait not here?
Open the gates! 'Tis Gloucester that calls.   *[Servants knock.]*
   First Ward. [*Within.*] Who's there that knocks so   *5*
imperiously?
   First Serv. It is the noble Duke of Gloucester.
   Sec. Ward. [*Within.*] Whoe'er he be, you may not be let in.
   First Serv. Villains, answer you so the Lord Protector?
   First Ward. [*Within.*] The Lord protect him! so we   *10*
answer him:
We do not otherwise than we are will'd.
   Glo. Who willed you? or whose will stands but mine?
There's none protector of the realm but I.
Break up the gates, I'll be your warrantize: *15*
Shall I be flouted thus by dunghill grooms?

Gloucester's men rush at the Tower gates and Woodvile the
Lieutenant speaks within.

   Wood. What noise is this? what traitors have we here?
   Glo. Lieutenant, is it you whose voice I hear?
Open the gates! here's Gloucester that would enter.
   Wood. [*Within.*] Have patience, noble Duke; I may not   *20*
open,
The Cardinal of Winchester forbids:
From him I have express commandment
That thou nor none of thine shall be let in.
   Glo. Faint-hearted Woodvile, prizest him 'fore me?   *25*
Arrogant Winchester, that haughty prelate,
Whom Henry, our late sovereign, ne'er could brook?
Thou art no friend to God or to the king:
Open the gates, or I'll shut thee out shortly.
   First Serv. Open the gates unto the Lord Protector;   *30*
Or we'll burst them open, if that you come not quickly.

Enter to the Protector at the Tower gates Winchester and his men
in tawny coats.

   Win. How now, ambitious Humphrey! what means this?
   Glo. Peel'd priest, dost thou command me to be shut out?
   Win. I do, thou most usurping proditor,
And not protector, of the king or realm.   *35*
   Glo. Stand back, thou manifest conspirator,
Thou that contriv'dst to murder our dead lord;
Thou that giv'st whores indulgences to sin:
I'll canvass thee in thy broad cardinal's hat,
If thou proceed in this thy insolence.   *40*
   Win. Nay, stand thou back; I will not budge a foot:
This be Damascus, be thou cursed Cain,
To slay thy brother Abel, if thou wilt.
   Glo. I will not slay thee, but I'll drive thee back:
Thy scarlet robes as a child's bearing-cloth   *45*
I'll use to carry thee out of this place.
   Win. Do what thou dar'st; I'll beard thee to thy face.
   Glo. What! am I dar'd and bearded to my face?—
Draw, men, for all this privileged place;
Blue coats to tawny coats. Priest, beware your beard;   *50*
I mean to tug it and to cuff you soundly.
Under my feet I stamp thy cardinal's hat:
In spite of pope or dignities of church,
Here by the cheeks I'll drag thee up and down.
   Win. Gloucester, thou'lt answer this before the pope.   *55*
   Glo. Winchester goose! I cry a rope! a rope!
Now beat them hence; why do you let them stay?
Thee I'll chase hence, thou wolf in sheep's array.
Out, tawny coats! out, scarlet hypocrite!

Here Gloucester's men beat out the Cardinal's men, and enter in
the hurly-burly the Mayor of London and his Officers.

   May. Fie, lords! that you, being supreme magistrates,   *60*
Thus contumeliously should break the peace!
   Glo. Peace, mayor! thou know'st little of my wrongs:
Here's Beaufort, that regards nor God nor King,
Hath here distrain'd the Tower to his use.
   Win. Here's Gloucester, a foe to citizens;   *65*
One that still motions war and never peace,
O'ercharging your free purses with large fines,
That seeks to overthrow religion
Because he is protector of the realm,
And would have armour here out of the Tower,   *70*
To crown himself king and suppress the prince.
   Glo. I will not answer thee with words, but blows.
                        Here they skirmish again.
   May. Nought rests for me, in this tumultuous strife
But to make open proclamation.
Come, officer: as loud as e'er thou canst;   *75*
Cry.
   Off. 'All manner of men, assembled here in arms this day,
against God's peace and the king's, we charge and command
you, in his highness' name, to repair to your several dwelling-
places; and not to wear, handle, or use, any sword, weapon,   *80*
or dagger, henceforward, upon pain of death.'

139, 140 *Cf. n.*   **141** *Cf. n.*   **143** *Cf. n.*   **144** *Cf. n.*   **2 conveyance:** *underhand*
dealing   **15 Break up:** *open forcibly* **warrantize:** *surety*   **23 Cardinal;** *cf. n.*   **25**
Woodvile; *cf. n.*

33 Peel'd: *tonsured*   **34 proditor:** *betrayer*   **37 contriv'dst:** *plottedst; cf. n.*   **38**
Cf. n.   **39 canvass:** *toss, as in a canvas sheet*   **42 Damascus;** *cf. n.*   **45 bearing-**
cloth: *christening robe*   **56 Winchester goose:** *cant name of a foul disease*   **64 distrain'd:**
confiscated   **66 motions:** *advocates*

Glo. Cardinal, I'll be no breaker of the law;
But we shall meet and break our minds at large.
 Win. Gloucester, we will meet; to thy cost, be sure:
Thy heart-blood I will have for this day's work.   *85*
 May. I'll call for clubs if you will not away.
This cardinal's more haughty than the devil.
 Glo. Mayor, farewell: thou dost but what thou mayst.
 Win. Abominable Gloucester! guard thy head;
For I intend to have it ere long.   *90*
     Exeunt [severally, Gloucester and Winchester,
           with their Serving-men].
 May. See the coast clear'd, and then we will depart.
Good God! these nobles should such stomachs bear;
I myself fight not once in forty year.   *Exeunt.*

❧ SCENE FOURTH ❧

[France. Before Orleans]
Enter the Master-Gunner of Orleans and his Boy.

M. Gun. Sirrah, thou know'st how Orleans is besieg'd,
And how the English have the suburbs won.
 Son. Father, I know; and oft have shot at them,
Howe'er unfortunate I miss'd my aim.
 M. Gun. But now thou shalt not. Be thou rul'd by me: *5*
Chief master-gunner am I of this town;
Something I must do to procure me grace.
The prince's espials have informed me
How the English, in the suburbs close entrench'd,
Wont through a secret gate of iron bars   *10*
In yonder tower to overpeer the city,
And thence discover how with most advantage
They may vex us with shot or with assault.
To intercept this inconvenience,
A piece of ordnance 'gainst it I have plac'd;   *15*
And fully even these three days have I watch'd
If I could see them. Now, boy, do thou watch,
For I can stay no longer.
If thou spy'st any, run and bring me word;
And thou shalt find me at the Governor's. *Exit.* *20*
 Son. Father, I warrant you; take you no care;
I'll never trouble you if I may spy them.   *Exit.*

Enter Salisbury and Talbot on the turrets, with [Sir William
Glansdale, Sir Thomas Gargrave, and] Others.

 Sal. Talbot, my life, my joy! again return'd!
How wert thou handled being prisoner?
Or by what means got'st thou to be releas'd,   *25*
Discourse, I prithee, on this turret's top.
 Tal. The Duke of Bedford had a prisoner
Call'd the brave Lord Ponton de Santrailles;
For him I was exchang'd and ransomed.
But with a baser man at arms by far   *30*
Once in contempt they would have barter'd me:
Which I disdaining scorn'd, and craved death
Rather than I would be so vile-esteem'd.
In fine, redeem'd I was as I desir'd.
But, O! the treacherous Fastolfe wounds my heart: *35*

Whom with my bare fists I would execute
If I now had him brought into my power.
 Sal. Yet tell'st thou not how thou wert entertain'd.
 Tal. With scoffs and scorns and contumelious taunts.
In open market-place produc'd they me,   *40*
To be a public spectacle to all:
Here, said they, is the terror of the French,
The scarecrow that affrights our children so.
Then broke I from the officers that led me,
And with my nails digg'd stones out of the ground *45*
To hurl at the beholders of my shame.
My grisly countenance made others fly.
None durst come near for fear of sudden death.
In iron walls they deem'd me not secure;
So great fear of my name 'mongst them was spread *50*
That they suppos'd I could rend bars of steel
And spurn in pieces posts of adamant:
Wherefore a guard of chosen shot I had,
That walk'd about me every minute-while;
And if I did but stir out of my bed   *55*
Ready they were to shoot me to the heart.

Enter the Boy with a linstock.

 Sal. I grieve to hear what torments you endur'd;
But we will be reveng'd sufficiently.
Now it is supper-time in Orleans:
Here, through this grate, I count each one,   *60*
And view the Frenchmen how they fortify:
Let us look in; the sight will much delight thee.
Sir Thomas Gargrave, and Sir William Glansdale,
Let me have your express opinions
Where is best place to make our battery next.   *65*
 Gar. I think at the north gate; for there stand lords.
 Glan. And I, here, at the bulwark of the bridge.
 Tal. For aught I see, this city must be famish'd,
Or with light skirmishes enfeebled.

Here they shoot and Salisbury falls down [together with Gargrave].

 Sal. O Lord! have mercy on us, wretched sinners. *70*
 Gar. O Lord! have mercy on me, woeful man.
 Tal. What chance is this that suddenly hatch cross'd us?
Speak, Salisbury; at least, if thou canst speak:
How far'st thou, mirror of all martial men?
One of thy eyes and thy cheek's side struck off! *75*
Accursed tower! accursed fatal hand
That hath contriv'd this woeful tragedy!
In thirteen battles Salisbury o'ercame;
Henry the Fifth he first train'd to the wars;
Whilst any trump did sound or drum struck up,   *80*
His sword did ne'er leave striking in the field.
Yet liv'st thou, Salisbury? though thy speech doth fail,
One eye thou hast to look to heaven for grace:
The sun with one eye vieweth all the world.
Heaven, be thou gracious to none alive,   *85*
If Salisbury wants mercy at thy hands!
Bear hence his body; I will help to bury it.
Sir Thomas Gargrave, hast thou any life?
Speak unto Talbot; nay, look up to him.

---

83 break: *express (with a pun)* **86 clubs:** *the rallying cry to summon apprentices and other*
citizens **8 espials:** *spies* **11 overpeer:** *look down upon* **23-56** *Cf. n.*

38 entertain'd: *treated* **53 chosen shot:** *sharpshooters* **S. d. linstock:** *stick holding gun-*
ner's match **64 express:** *precise* **68 must be:** *will have to be* **81 leave:** *cease from*

Salisbury, cheer thy spirit with this comfort;   *90*
Thou shalt not die, whiles—
He beckons with his hand and smiles on me,
As who should say, 'When I am dead and gone,
Remember to avenge me on the French.'
Plantagenet, I will; and like thee,   *95*
Play on the lute, beholding the towns burn:
Wretched shall France be only in my name.
          Here an Alarum, and it thunders and lightens.
What stir is this? What tumult's in the heavens?
Whence cometh this alarum and the noise?

         Enter a Messenger.

   Mess. My lord, my lord! the French have gather'd head: *100*
The Dauphin, with one Joan la Pucelle join'd,
A holy prophetess new risen up,
Is come with a great power to raise the siege.
         Here Salisbury lifteth himself up and groans.
   Tal. Hear, hear how dying Salisbury doth groan!
It irks his heart he cannot be reveng'd.   *105*
Frenchmen, I'll be a Salisbury to you:
Pucelle or puzzel, dolphin or dogfish,
Your hearts I'll stamp out with my horse's heels
And make a quagmire of your mingled brains.
Convey me Salisbury into his tent,   *110*
And then we'll try what these dastard Frenchmen dare.
         Alarum. Exeunt [bearing out the bodies].

❧ SCENE FIFTH ❧

[The Same. Before one of the Gates]
Here an Alarum again, and Talbot pursueth the Dauphin and
driveth him. Then enter Joan la Pucelle, driving Englishmen before
her. Then enter Talbot.

   Tal. Where is my strength, my valour, and my force?
Our English troops retire, I cannot stay them;
A woman clad in armour chaseth them.

         Enter Pucelle.

Here, here she comes. I'll have a bout with thee:
Devil, or devil's dam, I'll conjure thee: *5*
Blood will I draw on thee, thou art a witch,
And straightway give thy soul to him thou serv'st.
   Joan. Come, come, 'tis only I that must disgrace thee.
               Here they fight.
   Tal. Heavens, can you suffer hell so to prevail?
My breast I'll burst with straining of my courage,   *10*
And from my shoulders crack my arms asunder,
But I will chastise this high-minded strumpet.
               They fight again.
   Joan. Talbot, farewell; thy hour is not yet come:
I must go victual Orleans forthwith.
     A short Alarum; then [let Pucelle] enter the town with Soldiers.
O'ertake me if thou canst; I scorn thy strength.   *15*
Go, go, cheer up thy hungry-starved men;

Help Salisbury to make his testament:
This day is ours, as many more shall be.   *Exit*
     Tal. My thoughts are whirled like a potter's wheel;
I know not where I am, nor what I do: *20*
A witch, by fear, not force, like Hannibal,
Drives back our troops and conquers as she lists:
So bees with smoke, and doves with noisome stench,
Are from their hives and houses driven away.
They call'd us for our fierceness English dogs;   *25*
Now, like to whelps, we crying run away.   *A short Alarum.*
Hark, countrymen! either renew the fight,
Or tear the lions out of England's coat;
Renounce your soil, give sheep in lions' stead:
Sheep run not half so treacherous from the wolf,   *30*
Or horse or oxen from the leopard,
As you fly from your oft-subdued slaves.
         Alarum. Here another skirmish.
It will not be: retire into your trenches:
You all consented unto Salisbury's death,
For none would strike a stroke in his revenge.   *35*
Pucelle is entered into Orleans
In spite of us or aught that we could do.
O! would I were to die with Salisbury.
The shame hereof will make me hide my head.
         Exit Talbot. Alarum, Retreat, Flourish.

❧ SCENE SIXTH ❧

[The Same]
Enter, on the walls, Pucelle, Dauphin, Reignier, Alençon, and
Soldiers.

   Joan. Advance our waving colours on the walls;
Rescu'd is Orleans from the English:
Thus Joan la Pucelle hath perform'd her word.
   Char. Divinest creature, Astræa's daughter,
How shall I honour thee for this success?   *5*
Thy promises are like Adonis' gardens,
That one day bloom'd and fruitful were the next.
France, triumph in thy glorious prophetess!
Recover'd is the town of Orleans:
More blessed hap did ne'er befall our state.   *10*
   Reig. Why ring not out the bells throughout the town?
Dauphin, command the citizens make bonfires
And feast and banquet in the open streets,
To celebrate the joy that God hath given us.
   Alen. All France will be replete with mirth and joy,   *15*
When they shall hear how we have play'd the men.
   Char. 'Tis Joan, not we, by whom the day is won;
For which I will divide my crown with her;
And all the priests and friars in my realm
Shall in procession sing her endless praise.   *20*
A statelier pyramis to her I'll rear
Than Rhodope's of Memphis ever was:
In memory of her when she is dead,
Her ashes, in an urn more precious

---

95 Plantagenet; *cf. n.*   **like thee;** *cf. n.*   **97 only in:** *at the mere sound of*   **100 head:**
armed forces   **107 puzzel:** *lewd woman*   **dolphin or dogfish;** *cf. n.*   **6** *Cf. n.*   **12**
high-minded: *presumptuous*   **S. d.** *Cf. n.*

21 like Hannibal; *cf. n.*   **28** *Cf. n.*   **29 give:** *display* (as a heraldic emblem)   **S. d.**
Retreat: *signal to recall troops*   **1 Advance:** *raise*   **4 Astræa's daughter;** *cf. n.*   **6**
Adonis' gardens; *cf. n.*   **21 pyramis:** *pyramid*   **22 Rhodope's of Memphis;** *cf. n.*
25 coffer of Darius; *cf. n.*

Than the rich-jewell'd coffer of Darius,   *25*
Transported shall be at high festivals
Before the kings and queens of France.
No longer on Saint Denis will we cry,
But Joan la Pucelle shall be France's saint.
Come in, and let us banquet royally,   *30*
After this golden day of victory.   *Flourish. Exeunt.*

ACT SECOND ❧ SCENE FIRST

[Before Orleans]
Enter a [French] Sergeant of a Band, with two Sentinels.

Serg. Sirs, take your places and be vigilant.
If any noise or soldier you perceive
Near to the walls, by some apparent sign
Let us have knowledge at the court of guard.
Sent. Sergeant, you shall.   *[Exit Sergeant.]*   *5*
             Thus are poor servitors—
When others sleep upon their quiet beds—
Constrain'd to watch in darkness, rain, and cold.

Enter Talbot, Bedford, and Burgundy, with [soldiers bearing]
scaling-ladders; their drums beating a dead march.

Tal. Lord regent, and redoubted Burgundy,
By whose approach the regions of Artois,   *10*
Walloon, and Picardy, are friends to us,
This happy night the Frenchmen are secure,
Having all day carous'd and banqueted:
Embrace we then this opportunity,
As fitting best to quittance their deceit   *15*
Contriv'd by art and baleful sorcery.
Bed. Coward of France! how much he wrongs his fame,
Despairing of his own arm's fortitude,
To join with witches and the help of hell!
Bur. Traitors have never other company.   *20*
But what's that Pucelle whom they term so pure?
Tal. A maid, they say.
Bed.   A maid, and be so martial!
Bur. Pray God she prove not masculine ere long;
If underneath the standard of the French   *25*
She carry armour, as she hath begun.
Tal. Well, let them practise and converse with spirits;
God is our fortress, in whose conquering name
Let us resolve to scale their flinty bulwarks.
Bed. Ascend, brave Talbot; we will follow thee.   *30*
Tal. Not all together: better far, I guess,
That we do make our entrance several ways,
That if it chance the one of us do fail,
The other yet may rise against their force.
Bed. Agreed. I'll to yond corner.   *35*
Bur.   And I to this.
Tal. And here will Talbot mount, or make his grave.
Now, Salisbury, for thee, and for the right
Of English Henry, shall this night appear
How much in duty I am bound to both.   *40*

Sent. Arm, arm! the enemy doth make assault!

[The English] cry, 'St. George' 'A Talbot' The French leap o'er
the walls in their shirts. Enter, several ways, Bastard [of Orleans],
Alençon, Reignier, half ready, and half unready.

Alen. How now, my lords! what! all unready so?
Bast. Unready! ay, and glad we 'scap'd so well.
Reig. 'Twas time, I trow, to wake and leave our beds,
Hearing alarums at our chamber-doors.   *45*
Alen. Of all exploits since first I follow'd arms,
Ne'er heard I of a warlike enterprise
More venturous or desperate than this.
Bast. I think this Talbot be a fiend of hell.
Reig. If not of hell, the heavens, sure, favour him.   *50*
Alen. Here cometh Charles: I marvel how he sped.
Bast. Tut! holy Joan was his defensive guard.

Enter Charles and Joan.

Char. Is this thy cunning, thou deceitful dame?
Didst thou at first, to flatter us withal,
Make us partakers of a little gain,   *55*
That now our loss might be ten times so much?
Joan. Wherefore is Charles impatient with his friend?
At all times will you have my power alike?
Sleeping or waking must I still prevail,
Or will you blame and lay the fault on me?   *60*
Improvident soldiers! had your watch been good,
This sudden mischief never could have fall'n.
Char. Duke of Alençon, this was your default,
That, being captain of the watch to-night,
Did look no better to that weighty charge.   *65*
Alen. Had all your quarters been so safely kept
As that whereof I had the government,
We had not been thus shamefully surpris'd.
Bast. Mine was secure.
Reig.   And so was mine, my lord.   *70*
Char. And for myself, most part of all this night,
Within her quarter and mine own precinct
I was employ'd in passing to and fro,
About relieving of the sentinels:
Then how or which way should they first break in?   *75*
Joan. Question, my lords, no further of the case,
How or which way: 'tis sure they found some place
But weakly guarded, where the breach was made.
And now there rests no other shift but this;
To gather our soldiers, scatter'd and dispers'd,   *80*
And lay new platforms to endamage them.

Alarum. Enter a Soldier, crying, 'A Talbot! a Talbot!' They fly,
leaving their clothes behind.

Sold. I'll be so bold to take what they have left.
The cry of Talbot serves me for a sword;
For I have loaden me with many spoils,
Using no other weapon but his name.   *Exit.*   *85*

Act Second S. d. Band: *body of troops*   **4 court of guard:** *guardhouse*   **S. d. dead
march;** *cf. n.*   **9 Burgundy;** *cf. n.*   **12 secure:** *unsuspecting*   **15 quittance:** *requite*   **27 practise:** *conspire*   **34 other:** *others*

S. d.; Cf. n.   **43 unready:** *undressed*   **72 her:** *Joan's*   **81 platforms:** *plots*

❧ SCENE SECOND ❧

[Within the Town]
Enter Talbot, Bedford, Burgundy [a Captain, and Others].

Bed. The day begins to break, and night is fled,
Whose pitchy mantle over-veil'd the earth.
Here sound retreat, and cease our hot pursuit.   *Retreat.*
   Tal. Bring forth the body of old Salisbury,
And here advance it in the market-place,   5
The middle centre of this cursed town.
Now have I paid my vow unto his soul;
For every drop of blood was drawn from him
There hath at least five Frenchmen died to-night.
And that hereafter ages may behold   10
What ruin happen'd in revenge of him,
Within their chiefest temple I'll erect
A tomb wherein his corse shall be interr'd:
Upon the which, that every one may read,
Shall be engrav'd the sack of Orleans,   15
The treacherous manner of his mournful death,
And what a terror he had been to France.
But, lords, in all our bloody massacre,
I muse we met not with the Dauphin's grace,
His new-come champion, virtuous Joan of Arc,   20
Nor any of his false confederates.
   Bed. 'Tis thought, Lord Talbot, when the fight began,
Rous'd on the sudden from their drowsy beds,
They did amongst the troops of armed men
Leap o'er the walls for refuge in the field.   25
   Bur. Myself—as far as I could well discern
For smoke and dusky vapours of the night—
Am sure I scar'd the Dauphin and his trull,
When arm in arm they both came swiftly running,
Like to a pair of loving turtle-doves   30
That could not live asunder day or night.
After that things are set in order here,
We'll follow them with all the power we have.

Enter a Messenger.

   Mess. All hail, my lords! Which of this princely train
Call ye the warlike Talbot, for his acts   35
So much applauded through the realm of France?
   Tal. Here is the Talbot: who would speak with him?
   Mess. The virtuous lady, Countess of Auvergne,
With modesty admiring thy renown,
By me entreats, great lord, thou wouldst vouchsafe   40
To visit her poor castle where she lies,
That she may boast she hath beheld the man
Whose glory fills the world with loud report.
   Bur. Is it even so? Nay, then, I see our wars
Will turn into a peaceful comic sport,   45
When ladies crave to be encounter'd with.
You may not, my lord, despise her gentle suit.
   Tal. Ne'er trust me then; for when a world of men
Could not prevail with all their oratory,
Yet hath a woman's kindness over-rul'd: 50
And therefore tell her I return great thanks,
And in submission will attend on her.
Will not your honours bear me company?

   Bed. No, truly; 'tis more than manners will;
And I have heard it said, unbidden guests   55
Are often welcomest when they are gone.
   Tal. Well then, alone,—since there's no remedy,—
I mean to prove this lady's courtesy.
Come hither, captain.   *Whispers.*
           You perceive my mind.   60
   Capt. I do, my lord, and mean accordingly.   *Exeunt.*

❧ SCENE THIRD ❧

[Auvergne. Court of the Castle]
Enter Countess [and her Porter].

   Count. Porter, remember what I gave in charge;
And when you have done so, bring the keys to me.
   Port. Madam, I will.   *Exit.*
   Count. The plot is laid: if all things fall out right,
I shall as famous be by this exploit   5
As Scythian Tomyris by Cyrus' death.
Great is the rumour of this dreadful knight,
And his achievements of no less account:
Fain would mine eyes be witness with mine ears,
To give their censure of these rare reports.   10

Enter a Messenger and Talbot.

   Mess. Madam,
According as your ladyship desir'd,
By message crav'd, so is Lord Talbot come.
   Count. And he is welcome. What! is this the man?
   Mess. Madam, it is.   15
   Count.   Is this the scourge of France?
Is this the Talbot, so much fear'd abroad,
That with his name the mothers still their babes?
I see report is fabulous and false:
I thought I should have seen some Hercules,   20
A second Hector, for his grim aspect,
And large proportion of his strong-knit limbs.
Alas! this is a child, a silly dwarf:
It cannot be this weak and writhled shrimp
Should strike such terror to his enemies.   25
   Tal. Madam, I have been bold to trouble you;
But since your ladyship is not at leisure,
I'll sort some other time to visit you.
   Count. What means he now? Go ask him whither he goes.
   Mess. Stay, my Lord Talbot; for my lady craves   30
To know the cause of your abrupt departure.
   Tal. Marry, for that she's in a wrong belief,
I go to certify her Talbot's here.

Enter Porter, with keys.

   Count. If thou be he, then art thou prisoner.
   Tal. Prisoner! to whom?   35
   Count.   To me, bloodthirsty lord;
And for that cause I train'd thee to my house.
Long time thy shadow hath been thrall to me,
For in my gallery thy picture hangs:
But now the substance shall endure the like,   40

---

8 was: *which was*   **19 muse:** *wonder*   **41 lies:** *dwells*

6 Scythian Tomyris; *cf. n.*   **10 censure:** *opinion*   **23** *Cf. n.*   **24 writhled:** *wrinkled*   **28 sort:** *choose*   **33 certify:** *inform*   **37 train'd:** *lured*

And I will chain these legs and arms of thine,
That hast by tyranny, these many years,
Wasted our country, slain our citizens,
And sent our sons and husbands captive.

Tal. Ha, ha, ha!   45

Count. Laughest thou, wretch? thy mirth shall turn to moan.

Tal. I laugh to see your ladyship so fond
To think that you have aught but Talbot's shadow,
Whereon to practise your severity.

Count. Why, art not thou the man?   50

Tal.   I am, indeed.

Count. Then have I substance too.

Tal. No, no, I am but shadow of myself:
You are deceiv'd, my substance is not here;
For what you see is but the smallest part   55
And least proportion of humanity.
I tell you, madam, were the whole frame here,
It is of such a spacious lofty pitch,
Your roof were not sufficient to contain it.

Count. This is a riddling merchant for the nonce;   60
He will be here, and yet he is not here:
How can these contrarieties agree?

Tal. That will I show you presently.

*Winds his horn. Drums strike up; a peal of ordnance. Enter
Soldiers.*

How say you, madam? are you now persuaded
That Talbot is but shadow of himself?   65
These are his substance, sinews, arms, and strength,
With which he yoketh your rebellious necks,
Razeth your cities, and subverts your towns,
And in a moment makes them desolate.

Count. Victorious Talbot! pardon my abuse: 70
I find thou art no less than fame hath bruited,
And more than may be gather'd by thy shape.
Let my presumption not provoke thy wrath;
For I am sorry that with reverence
I did not entertain thee as thou art.   75

Tal. Be not dismay'd, fair lady; nor misconster
The mind of Talbot as you did mistake
The outward composition of his body.
What you have done hath not offended me;
Nor other satisfaction do I crave,   80
But only, with your patience, that we may
Taste of your wine and see what cates you have;
For soldiers' stomachs always serve them well.

Count. With all my heart, and think me honoured
To feast so great a warrior in my house.   *Exeunt.*

❧ SCENE FOURTH ❧

[London. The Temple Garden]
*Enter Richard Plantagenet, Warwick, Somerset, Pole [Earl of
Suffolk], and others [Vernon and a Lawyer].*

Plan. Great lords, and gentlemen, what means this silence?
Dare no man answer in a case of truth?

Suf. Within the Temple hall we were too loud;
The garden here is more convenient.

Plan. Then say at once if I maintain'd the truth,   5
Or else was wrangling Somerset in th' error?

Suf. Faith, I have been a truant in the law,
And never yet could frame my will to it;
And therefore frame the law unto my will.

Som. Judge you, my Lord of Warwick, then, between us.   10

War. Between two hawks, which flies the higher pitch;
Between two dogs, which hath the deeper mouth;
Between two blades, which bears the better temper;
Between two horses, which doth bear him best;
Between two girls, which hath the merriest eye;   15
I have perhaps some shallow spirit of judgment;
But in these nice sharp quillets of the law,
Good faith, I am no wiser than a daw.

Plan. Tut, tut! here is a mannerly forbearance:
The truth appears so naked on my side,   20
That any purblind eye may find it out.

Som. And on my side it is so well apparell'd,
So clear, so shining, and so evident,
That it will glimmer through a blind man's eye.

Plan. Since you are tongue-tied, and so loath to speak,   25
In dumb significants proclaim your thoughts:
Let him that is a true-born gentleman,
And stands upon the honour of his birth,
If he suppose that I have pleaded truth,
From off this brier pluck a white rose with me.   30

Som. Let him that is no coward nor no flatterer,
But dare maintain the party of the truth,
Pluck a red rose from off this thorn with me.

War. I love no colours, and, without all colour
Of base insinuating flattery   35
I pluck this white rose with Plantagenet.

Suf. I pluck this red rose with young Somerset:
And say withal I think he held the right.

Ver. Stay, lords and gentlemen, and pluck no more,
Till you conclude that he, upon whose side   40
The fewest roses are cropp'd from the tree,
Shall yield the other in the right opinion.

Som. Good Master Vernon, it is well objected:
If I have fewest I subscribe in silence.

Plan. And I.   45

Ver. Then for the truth and plainness of the case,
I pluck this pale and maiden blossom here,
Giving my verdict on the white rose side.

Som. Prick not your finger as you pluck it off,
Lest bleeding you do paint the white rose red,   50
And fall on my side so, against your will.

Ver. If I, my lord, for my opinion bleed,
Opinion shall be surgeon to my hurt,
And keep me on the side where still I am.

Som. Well, well, come on: who else?   55

Lawyer. [To Somerset.] Unless my study and my books
be false,
The argument you held was wrong in you,
In sign whereof I pluck a white rose too.

Plan. Now, Somerset, where is your argument?   60

---

44 captivate: *into captivity*   **47 fond:** *foolish*   **58 pitch:** *height*   **60 riddling mer-**
chant: *riddle-monger*   **63 presently:** *immediately*   **76 misconster:** *misconstrue*   **82**
cates: *delicacies*

6 *Cf. n.*   **7** *Cf. n.*   **17 quillets:** *subtleties*   **26 significants:** *signs*   **32 party:**
side   **34 colours:** *pun on meaning 'pretences'*   **36 Plantagenet;** *cf. n. on I.iv.95*   **43**
objected: *proposed*   **44 subscribe:** *submit*

Som. Here, in my scabbard; meditating that
Shall dye your white rose in a bloody red.
  Plan. Meantime, your cheeks do counterfeit our roses;
For pale they look with fear, as witnessing
The truth on our side.   *65*
  Som.   No, Plantagenet,
'Tis not for fear but anger that thy cheeks
Blush for pure shame to counterfeit our roses,
And yet thy tongue will not confess thy error.
  Plan. Hath not thy rose a canker, Somerset?   *70*
  Som. Hath not thy rose a thorn, Plantagenet?
  Plan. Ay, sharp and piercing, to maintain his truth;
Whiles thy consuming canker eats his falsehood.
  Som. Well, I'll find friends to wear my bleeding roses,
That shall maintain what I have said is true,   *75*
Where false Plantagenet dare not be seen.
  Plan. Now, by this maiden blossom in my hand,
I scorn thee and thy faction, peevish boy.
  Suf. Turn not thy scorns this way, Plantagenet.
  Plan. Proud Pole, I will, and scorn both him and thee. *80*
  Suf. I'll turn my part thereof into thy throat.
  Som. Away, away! good William de la Pole:
We grace the yeoman by conversing with him.
  War. Now, by God's will, thou wrong'st him, Somerset:
His grandfather was Lionel, Duke of Clarence,   *85*
Third son to the third Edward, King of England.
Spring crestless yeomen from so deep a root?
  Plan. He bears him on the place's privilege,
Or durst not, for his craven heart, say thus.
  Som. By Him that made me, I'll maintain my words *90*
On any plot of ground in Christendom.
Was not thy father, Richard Earl of Cambridge,
For treason executed in our late king's days?
And, by his treason stand'st not thou attainted,
Corrupted, and exempt from ancient gentry?   *95*
His trespass yet lives guilty in thy blood;
And, till thou be restor'd, thou art a yeoman.
  Plan. My father was attached, not attainted;
Condemn'd to die for treason, but no traitor;
And that I'll prove on better men than Somerset, *100*
Were growing time once ripen'd to my will.
For your partaker Pole and you yourself,
I'll note you in my book of memory,
To scourge you for this apprehension:
Look to it well and say you are well warn'd.   *105*
  Som. Ah, thou shalt find us ready for thee still,
And know us by these colours for thy foes;
For these my friends in spite of thee shall wear.
  Plan. And, by my soul, this pale and angry rose,
As cognizance of my blood-drinking hate,   *110*
Will I for ever and my faction wear,
Until it wither with me to my grave
Or flourish to the height of my degree.
  Suf. Go forward, and be chok'd with thy ambition:
And so farewell until I meet thee next.   *Exit.* *115*
  Som. Have with thee, Pole. Farewell, ambitious Richard.
                Exit.

  Plan. How I am brav'd and must perforce endure it!
  War. This blot that they object against your house
Shall be wip'd out in the next parliament,
Call'd for the truce of Winchester and Gloucester; *120*
And if thou be not then created York,
I will not live to be accounted Warwick.
Meantime in signal of my love to thee,
Against proud Somerset and William Pole,
Will I upon thy party wear this rose.   *125*
And here I prophesy: this brawl to-day,
Grown to this faction in the Temple garden,
Shall send between the red rose and the white
A thousand souls to death and deadly night.
  Plan. Good Master Vernon, I am bound to you, *130*
That you on my behalf would pluck a flower.
  Ver. In your behalf still would I wear the same.
  Lawyer. And so will I.
  Plan. Thanks, gentle sir.
Come, let us four to dinner: I dare say   *135*
This quarrel will drink blood another day.   *Exeunt.*

❧ SCENE FIFTH ❧

[London. A Room in the Tower]
Enter Mortimer, brought in a chair, and Jailors.

  Mor. Kind keepers of my weak decaying age,
Let dying Mortimer here rest himself.
Even like a man new haled from the rack,
So fare my limbs with long imprisonment;
And these gray locks, the pursuivants of death,   *5*
Nestor-like aged, in an age of care,
Argue the end of Edmund Mortimer.
These eyes, like lamps whose wasting oil is spent,
Wax dim, as drawing to their exigent;
Weak shoulders, overborne with burdening grief,   *10*
And pithless arms, like to a wither'd vine
That droops his sapless branches to the ground:
Yet are these feet whose strengthless stay is numb,
Unable to support this lump of clay,
Swift-winged with desire to get a grave,   *15*
As witting I no other comfort have.
But tell me, keeper, will my nephew come?
  First Keep. Richard Plantagenet, my lord, will come:
We sent unto the Temple, unto his chamber,
And answer was return'd that he will come.   *20*
  Mor. Enough: my soul shall then be satisfied.
Poor gentleman! his wrong doth equal mine.
Since Henry Monmouth first began to reign,
Before whose glory I was great in arms,
This loathsome sequestration have I had;   *25*
And even since then hath Richard been obscur'd,
Depriv'd of honour and inheritance.
But now the arbitrator of despairs,
Just death, kind umpire of men's miseries,
With sweet enlargement doth dismiss me hence: *30*
I would his troubles likewise were expir'd,
That so he might recover what was lost.

---

70 **canker:** *canker-worm*   83 **the yeoman;** *cf. n.*   88 **bears him on:** *takes advantage of*   95 **exempt:** *cut off*   98 **attached, not attainted;** *cf. n.*   102 **partaker:** *supporter*   104 **apprehension:** *conception, opinion*   113 **degree:** *rank*   116 **Have with thee:** *let us go*

5 **pursuivants:** *messengers*   6 *Cf. n.*   7 **Edmund Mortimer;** *cf. n.*   9 **exigent:** *end*   25 **sequestration:** *seclusion, imprisonment*

Enter Richard.

First Keep. My lord, your loving nephew now is come.

Mor. Richard Plantagenet, my friend, is he come?

Plan. Ay, noble uncle, thus ignobly us'd,   35
Your nephew, late despised Richard, comes.

Mor. Direct mine arms I may embrace his neck,
And in his bosom spend my latter gasp:
O! tell me when my lips do touch his cheeks,
That I may kindly give one fainting kiss.   40
And now declare, sweet stem from York's great stock,
Why didst thou say of late thou wert despis'd?

Plan. First, lean thine aged back against mine arm;
And in that ease, I'll tell thee my disease.
This day, in argument upon a case,   45
Some words there grew 'twixt Somerset and me;
Among which terms he us'd a lavish tongue
And did upbraid me with my father's death:
Which obloquy set bars before my tongue,
Else with the like I had requited him.   50
Therefore, good uncle, for my father's sake,
In honour of a true Plantagenet,
And for alliance sake, declare the cause
My father, Earl of Cambridge, lost his head.

Mor. That cause, fair nephew, that imprison'd me,   55
And hath detain'd me all my flow'ring youth
Within a loathsome dungeon, there to pine,
Was cursed instrument of his decease.

Plan. Discover more at large what cause that was,
For I am ignorant and cannot guess.   60

Mor. I will, if that my fading breath permit,
And death approach not ere my tale be done.
Henry the Fourth, grandfather to this king,
Depos'd his nephew Richard, Edward's son,
The first-begotten, and the lawful heir   65
Of Edward king, the third of that descent:
During whose reign the Percies of the North,
Finding his usurpation most unjust,
Endeavour'd my advancement to the throne.
The reason mov'd these warlike lords to this   70
Was, for that—young Richard thus remov'd,
Leaving no heir begotten of his body—
I was the next by birth and parentage;
For by my mother I derived am
From Lionel Duke of Clarence, the third son   75
To King Edward the Third; whereas he
From John of Gaunt doth bring his pedigree,
Being but fourth of that heroic line.
But mark: as, in this haughty great attempt
They laboured to plant the rightful heir,   80
I lost my liberty, and they their lives.
Long after this, when Henry the Fifth,
Succeeding his father Bolingbroke, did reign,
Thy father, Earl of Cambridge, then deriv'd
From famous Edmund Langley, Duke of York,   85
Marrying my sister that thy mother was,
Again in pity of my hard distress
Levied an army, weening to redeem

And have install'd me in the diadem;
But, as the rest, so fell that noble earl,   90
And was beheaded. Thus the Mortimers,
In whom the title rested, were suppress'd.

Plan. Of which, my lord, your honour is the last.

Mor. True; and thou seest that I no issue have,
And that my fainting words do warrant death: 95
Thou art my heir; the rest I wish thee gather:
But yet be wary in thy studious care.

Plan. Thy grave admonishments prevail with me.
But yet methinks my father's execution
Was nothing less than bloody tyranny.   100

Mor. With silence, nephew, be thou politic:
Strong-fixed is the house of Lancaster,
And like a mountain, not to be remov'd.
But now thy uncle is removing hence,
As princes do their courts, when they are cloy'd   105
With long continuance in a settled place.

Plan. O uncle! would some part of my young years
Might but redeem the passage of your age.

Mor. Thou dost then wrong me,—as the slaughterer doth,
Which giveth many wounds when one will kill.—   110
Mourn not, except thou sorrow for my good;
Only give order for my funeral:
And so farewell; and fair be all thy hopes,
And prosperous be thy life in peace and war!   *Dies.*

Plan. And peace, no war, befall thy parting soul!   115
In prison hast thou spent a pilgrimage,
And like a hermit overpass'd thy days.
Well, I will lock his counsel in my breast;
And what I do imagine let that rest.
Keepers, convey him hence; and I myself   120
Will see his burial better than his life.

        Exeunt [Jailors, bearing out the body of Mortimer].
Here dies the dusky torch of Mortimer,
Chok'd with ambition of the meaner sort:
And, for those wrongs, those bitter injuries,
Which Somerset hath offer'd to my house,   125
I doubt not but with honour to redress;
And therefore haste I to the parliament,
Either to be restored to my blood,
Or make my ill the advantage of my good.   *Exit.*

ACT THIRD ❧ SCENE FIRST

[London. The Parliament House]
Flourish. Enter King, Exeter, Gloucester, Winchester, Warwick, Som-
erset, Suffolk, Richard Plantagenet. Gloucester offers to put up a bill;
Winchester snatches it, tears it.

Win. Com'st thou with deep premeditated lines,
With written pamphlets studiously devis'd,
Humphrey of Gloucester? If thou canst accuse,
Or aught intend'st to lay unto my charge,

---

38 **latter:** *final*   44 **disease:** *grievance*   53 **alliance sake:** *sake of relationship*   59
Discover: *make known*   64 **nephew:** *blood relative, here first cousin*   67 **whose:** *Henry*
IV's   74 **mother:** *i.e., paternal grandmother*

95 **warrant:** *certify*   96 **the rest . . . gather:** *cf. n.*   128 **blood:** *hereditary rights*   129
Cf. n.   **Act Third, Scene One;** *cf. n.*

Do it without invention, suddenly;   5
As I, with sudden and extemporal speech
Purpose to answer what thou canst object.
   Glo. Presumptuous priest! this place commands my patience
Or thou shouldst find thou hast dishonour'd me.
Think not, although in writing I preferr'd   10
The manner of thy vile outrageous crimes,
That therefore I have forg'd, or am not able
Verbatim to rehearse the method of my pen:
No, prelate; such is thy audacious wickedness,
Thy lewd, pestiferous, and dissentious pranks,   15
As very infants prattle of thy pride.
Thou art a most pernicious usurer,
Froward by nature, enemy to peace;
Lascivious, wanton, more than well beseems
A man of thy profession and degree;   20
And for thy treachery, what's more manifest,
In that thou laid'st a trap to take my life
As well at London Bridge as at the Tower?
Beside, I fear me, if thy thoughts were sifted,
The king, thy sovereign, is not quite exempt   25
From envious malice of thy swelling heart.
   Win. Gloucester, I do defy thee. Lords, vouchsafe
To give me hearing what I shall reply.
If I were covetous, ambitious, or perverse,
As he will have me, how am I so poor?   30
Or how haps it I seek not to advance
Or raise myself, but keep my wonted calling?
And for dissension, who preferreth peace
More than I do, except I be provok'd?
No, my good lords, it is not that offends;   35
It is not that that hath incens'd the duke:
It is, because no one should sway but he;
No one but he should be about the king;
And that engenders thunder in his breast,
And makes him roar these accusations forth.   40
But he shall know I am as good—
   Glo.   As good!
Thou bastard of my grandfather!
   Win. Ay, lordly sir; for what are you, I pray,
But one imperious in another's throne?   45
   Glo. Am I not protector, saucy priest?
   Win. And am not I a prelate of the church?
   Glo. Yes, as an outlaw in a castle keeps,
And useth it to patronage his theft.
   Win. Unreverent Gloucester!   50
   Glo.   Thou art reverent,
Touching thy spiritual function, not thy life.
   Win. Rome shall remedy this.
   War.   Roam thither then.
   Som. My lord, it were your duty to forbear.   55
   War. Ay, see the bishop be not overborne.
   Som. Methinks my lord should be religious,
And know the office that belongs to such.
   War. Methinks his lordship should be humbler;
It fitteth not a prelate so to plead.   60
   Som. Yes, when his holy state is touch'd so near.

   War. State holy, or unhallow'd, what of that?
Is not his Grace protector to the king?
   Plan. [Aside.] Plantagenet, I see, must hold his tongue,
Lest it be said, 'Speak, sirrah, when you should;   65
Must your bold verdict enter talk with lords?'
Else would I have a fling at Winchester.
   King. Uncles of Gloucester and of Winchester,
The special watchmen of our English weal,
I would prevail, if prayers might prevail,   70
To join your hearts in love and amity.
O! what a scandal is it to our crown,
That two such noble peers as ye should jar.
Believe me, lords, my tender years can tell
Civil dissension is a viperous worm,   75
That gnaws the bowels of the commonwealth.
      A noise within; 'Down with the tawny-coats!'
   King. What tumult's this?
   War.   An uproar, I dare warrant,
Begun through malice of the bishop's men.   80
      A noise again; 'Stones! Stones!'

Enter Mayor [of London].

   May. O, my good lords, and virtuous Henry,
Pity the city of London, pity us!
The bishop and the Duke of Gloucester's men,
Forbidden late to carry any weapon,   85
Have fill'd their pockets full of pebble stones,
And banding themselves in contrary parts
Do pelt so fast at one another's pate,
That many have their giddy brains knock'd out:
Our windows are broke down in every street,   90
And we for fear compell'd to shut our shops.

*Enter, in skirmish, [the Serving-men of Gloucester and Winchester]
with bloody pates.*

   King. We charge you, on allegiance to ourself,
To hold your slaught'ring hands, and keep the peace,—
Pray, uncle Gloucester, mitigate this strife.
   First Serv. Nay, if we be forbidden stones, we'll fall to it   95
with our teeth.
   Sec. Serv. Do what ye dare, we are as resolute.
      Skirmish again.
   Glo. You of my houschold, leave this peevish broil,
And set this unaccustom'd fight aside.
   Third Serv. My lord, we know your Grace to be a man   100
Just and upright, and, for your royal birth,
Inferior to none but to his majesty;
And ere that we will suffer such a prince,
So kind a father of the commonweal,
To be disgraced by an inkhorn mate,   105
We and our wives and children all will fight,
And have our bodies slaught'red by thy foes.
   First Serv. Ay, and the very parings of our nails
Shall pitch a field when we are dead.   *Begin again.*
   Glo.   Stay, stay, I say!   110
And, if you love me, as you say you do,
Let me persuade you to forbear a while.
   King. O! how this discord doth afflict my soul!

---

5 invention: *preconceived design*   9 find: *i.e., to thy sorrow*   13 method . . . pen: *summary of what I have written*   22, 23 *Cf. n.*   45 imperious: *playing the emperor*   49 patronage: *maintain, dignify*   51 reverent: *reverend*   53, 54 *Cf. n.*

66 enter talk; *cf. n.*   84–91 *Cf. n.*   105 inkhorn mate: *low pedant*   109 pitch a field: *do battle*

Can you, my Lord of Winchester, behold
My sighs and tears and will not once relent?   *115*
Who should be pitiful if you be not?
Or who should study to prefer a peace
If holy churchmen take delight in broils?
   War. Yield, my Lord Protector; yield, Winchester;
Except you mean with obstinate repulse   *120*
To slay your sovereign and destroy the realm.
You see what mischief and what murder too
Hath been enacted through your enmity:
Then be at peace, except ye thirst for blood.
   Win. He shall submit or I will never yield.   *125*
   Glo. Compassion on the king commands me stoop;
Or I would see his heart out ere the priest
Should ever get that privilege of me.
   War. Behold, my Lord of Winchester, the duke
Hath banish'd moody discontented fury,   *130*
As by his smoothed brows it doth appear:
Why look you still so stern and tragical?
   Glo. Here, Winchester, I offer thee my hand.
   King. Fie, uncle Beaufort! I have heard you preach,
That malice was a great and grievous sin;   *135*
And will not you maintain the thing you teach,
But prove a chief offender in the same?
   War. Sweet king! the bishop hath a kindly gird.
For shame, my Lord of Winchester, relent!
What! shall a child instruct you what to do?   *140*
   Win. Well, Duke of Gloucester, I will yield to thee;
Love for thy love and hand for hand I give.
   Glo. [*Aside.*] Ay; but I fear me, with a hollow heart.
See here, my friends and loving countrymen,
This token serveth for a flag of truce,   *145*
Betwixt ourselves and all our followers.
So help me God, as I dissemble not!
   Win. [*Aside.*] So help me God, as I intend it not!
   King. O loving uncle, kind Duke of Gloucester,
How joyful am I made by this contract!   *150*
Away, my masters! trouble us no more;
But join in friendship, as your lords have done.
   First Serv. Content: I'll to the surgeon's.
   Sec. Serv.   And so will I.
   Third Serv. And I will see what physic the tavern   *155*
affords.   *Exeunt* [*Mayor, Serving-men, &c.*].
   War. Accept this scroll, most gracious sovereign,
Which in the right of Richard Plantagenet
We do exhibit to your majesty.
   Glo. Well urg'd, my Lord of Warwick: for, sweet prince, *160*
An if your Grace mark every circumstance,
You have great reason to do Richard right;
Especially for those occasions
At Eltham-place I told your majesty.
   King. And those occasions, uncle, were of force: *165*
Therefore, my loving lords, our pleasure is
That Richard be restored to his blood.
   War. Let Richard be restored to his blood;
So shall his father's wrongs be recompens'd.
   Win. As will the rest, so willeth Winchester.   *170*
   King. If Richard will be true, not that alone,
But all the whole inheritance I give

That doth belong unto the house of York,
From whence you spring by lineal descent.
   Plan. Thy humble servant vows obedience,   *175*
And humble service till the point of death.
   King. Stoop then and set your knee against my foot;
And, in reguerdon of that duty done,
I girt thee with the valiant sword of York:
Rise, Richard, like a true Plantagenet,   *180*
And rise created princely Duke of York.
   Plan. And so thrive Richard as thy foes may fall!
And as my duty springs, so perish they
That grudge one thought against your majesty!
   All. Welcome, high prince, the mighty Duke of York! *185*
   Som. [*Aside.*] Perish, base prince, ignoble Duke of York!
   Glo. Now will it best avail your majesty
To cross the seas and to be crown'd in France.
The presence of a king engenders love
Amongst his subjects and his loyal friends,   *190*
As it disanimates his enemies.
   King. When Gloucester says the word, King Henry goes;
For friendly counsel cuts off many foes.
   Glo. Your ships already are in readiness.

                 Sennet. Flourish. Exeunt.

           Manet Exeter.

   Exe. Ay, we may march in England or in France,   *195*
Not seeing what is likely to ensue.
This late dissension grown betwixt the peers
Burns under feigned ashes of forg'd love,
And will at last break out into a flame:
As fester'd members rot but by degree,   *200*
Till bones and flesh and sinews fall away,
So will this base and envious discord breed.
And now I fear that fatal prophecy
Which in the time of Henry, nam'd the Fifth,
Was in the mouth of every sucking babe: *205*
That Henry born at Monmouth should win all,
And Henry born at Windsor lose all:
Which is so plain that Exeter doth wish
His days may finish ere that hapless time.   *Exit.*

❧ SCENE SECOND ❧

[France. Before Rouen]
Enter Pucelle, disguised, with four Soldiers [dressed like countrymen,]
with sacks upon their backs.

   Joan. These are the city gates, the gates of Roan,
Through which our policy must make a breach:
Take heed, be wary how you place your words;
Talk like the vulgar sort of market-men
That come to gather money for their corn.   *5*
If we have entrance,—as I hope we shall,—
And that we find the slothful watch but weak,
I'll by a sign give notice to our friends,
That Charles the Dauphin may encounter them.

---

128 **privilege:** *advantage*   138 **gird:** *rebuke*   151 **my masters:** *good fellows* (a term of condescension)   161 **An if:** *if*   165 **occasions:** *reasons*

172–174 *Cf. n.*   178 **reguerdon:** *reward*   179 **girt:** *gird*   184 **grudge . . . thought:** *bear . . . grudging thought*   187, 188 *Cf. n.*   191 **disanimates:** *discourages*   S. d. Sennet; *cf. n.*   203 **that fatal prophecy;** *cf. n.*   **Scene Two** S. d.; *cf. n.*   2 **policy:** *trickery*   7 **that:** *i.e., if*

First Sold. Our sacks shall be a mean to sack the city,   *10*
And we be lords and rulers over Roan;
Therefore we'll knock.   *Knock.*
   Watch. [*Within.*] *Qui est là?*
   Joan. *Paysans, pauvres gens de France:*
Poor market-folks that come to sell their corn.   *15*
   Watch. [*Opening the gates.*] Enter, go in; the market-bell is
rung.
   Joan. Now, Roan, I'll shake thy bulwarks to the ground.
               Exeunt [*Pucelle, &c., into the city*].

Enter Charles, Bastard, Alençon [*and Forces*].

   Char. Saint Denis bless this happy stratagem!   *20*
And once again we'll sleep secure in Roan.
   Bast. Here enter'd Pucelle and her practisants;
Now she is there how will she specify
Where is the best and safest passage in?
   Alen. By thrusting out a torch from yonder tower;   *25*
Which, once discern'd, shows that her meaning is,
No way to that, for weakness, which she enter'd.

Enter Pucelle on the top, thrusting out a torch burning.

   Joan. Behold! this is the happy wedding torch
That joineth Roan unto her countrymen,
But burning fatal to the Talbonites!   [*Exit.*]   *30*
   Bast. See, noble Charles, the beacon of our friend,
The burning torch in yonder turret stands.
   Char. Now shine it like a comet of revenge,
A prophet to the fall of all our foes!
   Alen. Defer no time, delays have dangerous ends;   *35*
Enter, and cry 'The Dauphin!' presently,
And then do execution on the watch.
             Alarum. [*They enter the town.*]

An Alarum. [*Enter*] *Talbot in an Excursion.*

   Tal. France, thou shalt rue this treason with thy tears,
If Talbot but survive thy treachery.   *40*
Pucelle, that witch, that damned sorceress,
Hath wrought this hellish mischief unawares,
That hardly we escap'd the pride of France.   *Exit.*

An Alarum: Excursions. [*Enter from the town*] *Bedford, brought
in sick in a chair. Enter Talbot and Burgundy, without: within,
Pucelle, Charles, Bastard, and Alençon on the Walls.*

   Joan. Good morrow, gallants! Want ye corn for bread?
I think the Duke of Burgundy will fast   *45*
Before he'll buy again at such a rate.
'Twas full of darnel; do you like the taste?
   Bur. Scoff on, vile fiend and shameless courtezan!
I trust ere long to choke thee with thine own,
And make thee curse the harvest of that corn.   *50*
   Char. Your Grace may starve perhaps, before that time.
   Bed. O! let no words, but deeds, revenge this treason!
   Joan. What will you do, good grey-beard? break a lance,
And run a tilt at death within a chair?
   Tal. Foul fiend of France, and hag of all despite,   *55*

Encompass'd with thy lustful paramours!
Becomes it thee to taunt his valiant age
And twit with cowardice a man half dead?
Damsel, I'll have a bout with you again,
Or else let Talbot perish with this shame.   *60*
   Joan. Are you so hot, sir? Yet, Pucelle, hold thy peace;
If Talbot do but thunder, rain will follow.
         They [*i.e., Talbot, &c.,*] *whisper together in counsel.*
God speed the parliament! who shall be the speaker?
   Tal. Dare ye come forth and meet us in the field?
   Joan. Belike your lordship takes us then for fools,   *65*
To try if that our own be ours or no.
   Tal. I speak not to that railing Hecate,
But unto thee, Alençon, and the rest;
Will ye, like soldiers, come and fight it out?
   Alen. Signior, no.   *70*
   Tal. Signior, hang! base muleters of France!
Like peasant foot-boys do they keep the walls,
And dare not take up arms like gentlemen.
   Joan. Away, captains! let's get us from the walls;
For Talbot means no goodness, by his looks.   *75*
God be wi' you, my lord! we came but to tell you
That we are here.
         Exeunt [*Pucelle, &c.,*] *from the Walls.*
   Tal. And there will we be too, ere it be long,
Or else reproach be Talbot's greatest fame!
Vow, Burgundy, by honour of thy house,—   *80*
Prick'd on by public wrongs sustain'd in France,—
Either to get the town again, or die;
And I, as sure as English Henry lives,
And as his father here was conqueror,
As sure as in this late-betrayed town   *85*
Great Cœur-de-lion's heart was buried,
So sure I swear to get the town or die.
   Bur. My vows are equal partners with thy vows
   Tal. But, ere we go, regard this dying prince,
The valiant Duke of Bedford. Come, my lord,   *90*
We will bestow you in some better place,
Fitter for sickness and for crazy age.
   Bed. Lord Talbot, do not so dishonour me:
Here will I sit before the walls of Roan,
And will be partner of your weal or woe.   *95*
   Bur. Courageous Bedford, let us now persuade you.
   Bed. Not to be gone from hence; for once I read,
That stout Pendragon in his litter, sick,
Came to the field and vanquished his foes:
Methinks I should revive the soldiers' hearts,   *100*
Because I ever found them as myself.
   Tal. Undaunted spirit in a dying breast!
Then be it so: heavens keep old Bedford safe!
And now no more ado, brave Burgundy,
But gather we our forces out of hand,   *105*
And set upon our boasting enemy.   *Exit* [*with Burgundy*]

An Alarum. Excursions. Enter Sir John Fastolfe and a Captain.

   Cap. Whither away, Sir John Fastolfe, in such haste?
   Fast. Whither away! to save myself by flight:
We are like to have the overthrow again.

---

16 market-bell: *bell signaling the opening of market*   **22 practisants:** *conspirators*   **24
Where;** *cf. n.*   **27 to:** *is comparable to*   **30 Talbonites;** *cf. n.*   **S. d. Excursion:** *sally
against the enemy*   **43 the pride of France;** *cf. n.*   **S. d. Alençon;** *cf. n.*   **47 darnel:** *a
weed injurious to wheat ('corn')*   **49 thine own:** *thy own bread*   **53 good grey-beard;**
cf. n.   **55 of all despite:** *most despicable*

67 Hecate: *goddess of witchcraft, witch*   **71 muleters:** *muleteers*   **84** *Cf. n.*   **85, 86**
Cf. n.   **92 crazy:** *broker*   **98, 99** *Cf. n.*   **105 out of hand:** *immediately*

Cap. What! will you fly, and leave Lord Talbot?   110
Fast.   Ay,
All the Talbots in the world, to save my life.   *Exit.*
Cap. Cowardly knight! ill fortune follow thee!   *Exit.*

    Retreat. Excursions. Pucelle, Alençon, and Charles fly.

Bed. Now, quiet soul, depart when Heaven please,
For I have seen our enemies' overthrow.   115
What is the trust or strength of foolish man?
They, that of late were daring with their scoffs,
Are glad and fain by flight to save themselves.

    Bedford dies, and is carried in by two in his chair.

    An Alarum. Enter Talbot, Burgundy, and the rest.

Tal. Lost, and recover'd in a day again!
This is a double honour, Burgundy: 120
Yet heavens have glory for this victory!
Bur. Warlike and martial Talbot, Burgundy
Enshrines thee in his heart, and there erects
Thy noble deeds as valour's monument.
Tal. Thanks, gentle duke. But where is Pucelle now?   125
I think her old familiar is asleep.
Now where's the Bastard's braves, and Charles his gleeks?
What! all amort? Roan hangs her head for grief,
That such a valiant company are fled.
Now will we take some order in the town,   130
Placing therein some expert officers,
And then depart to Paris to the king;
For there young Henry with his nobles lie.
Bur. What wills Lord Talbot pleaseth Burgundy.
Tal. But yet, before we go, let's not forget   135
The noble Duke of Bedford late deceas'd,
But see his exequies fulfill'd in Roan:
A braver soldier never couched lance,
A gentler heart did never sway in court;
But kings and mightiest potentates must die,   140
For that's the end of human misery.   *Exeunt.*

❧ Scene Third ❧

    [Between Rouen and Paris]
    Enter Charles, Bastard, Alençon, Pucelle [and Forces].

Joan. Dismay not, princes, at this accident,
Nor grieve that Roan is so recovered:
Care is no cure, but rather corrosive,
For things that are not to be remedied.
Let frantic Talbot triumph for a while,   5
And like a peacock sweep along his tail;
We'll pull his plumes and take away his train,
If Dauphin and the rest will be but rul'd.
Char. We have been guided by thee hitherto,
And of thy cunning had no diffidence: 10
One sudden foil shall never breed distrust.
Bast. Search out thy wit for secret policies,
And we will make thee famous through the world.

Alen. We'll set thy statue in some holy place
And have thee reverenc'd like a blessed saint: 15
Employ thee, then, sweet virgin, for our good.
Joan. Then thus it must be; this doth Joan devise:
By fair persuasions, mix'd with sugar'd words,
We will entice the Duke of Burgundy
To leave the Talbot and to follow us.   20
Char. Ay, marry, sweeting, if we could do that,
France were no place for Henry's warriors;
Nor should that nation boast it so with us,
But be extirped from our provinces.
Alen. For ever should they be 'expuls'd from France,   25
And not have title of an earldom here.
Joan. Your honours shall perceive how I will work
To bring this matter to the wished end.
                         Drum sounds afar off.
Hark! by the sound of drum you may perceive
Their powers are marching unto Paris-ward.   30

    Here sound an English march. [Enter, and pass over, Talbot and
                      his Forces.]

There goes the Talbot, with his colours spread,
And all the troops of English after him.

    French march. [Enter the Duke of Burgundy and his Forces.]

Now in the rearward comes the duke and his:
Fortune in favour makes him lag behind.   35
Summon a parley; we will talk with him.
                         Trumpets sound a parley.
Char. A parley with the Duke of Burgundy!
Bur. Who craves a parley with the Burgundy?
Joan. The princely Charles of France, thy countryman.
Bur. What sayst thou, Charles? for I am marching hence.   40
Char. Speak, Pucelle, and enchant him with thy words.
Joan. Brave Burgundy, undoubted hope of France!
Stay, let thy humble handmaid speak to thee.
Bur. Speak on; but be not over-tedious.
Joan. Look on thy country, look on fertile France,   45
And see the cities and the towns defac'd
By wasting ruin of the cruel foe.
As looks the mother on her lowly babe
When death doth close his tender dying eyes,
See, see the pining malady of France;   50
Behold the wounds, the most unnatural wounds,
Which thou thyself hast giv'n her woeful breast.
O! turn thy edged sword another way;
Strike those that hurt, and hurt not those that help.
One drop of blood drawn from thy country's bosom   55
Should grieve thee more than streams of foreign gore:
Return thee therefore, with a flood of tears,
And wash away thy country's stained spots.
Bur. Either she hath bewitch'd me with her words,
Or nature makes me suddenly relent.   60
Joan. Besides, all French and France exclaims on thee,
Doubting thy birth and lawful progeny.
Who join'st thou with but with a lordly nation
That will not trust thee but for profit's sake?
When Talbot hath set footing once in France,   65

126 **familiar:** *attendant demon*   127 **braves:** *bravado* **gleeks:** *gibes*   128 **all amort:** *'à la mort,' sick to death, prostrated*   130 **some order:** *certain measures*   137 **exequies:** *obsequies*   1 **Dismay:** *lose courage*   3 **corrosive:** *caustic, painful*   10 **diffidence:** *distrust*

16 **Employ thee:** *exert thyself*   19, 20 *Cf. n.*   24 **extirped:** *rooted out*   48 **lowly:** *lying low (?)*   62 **progeny:** *descent*

And fashion'd thee that instrument of ill,
Who then but English Henry will be lord,
And thou be thrust out like a fugitive?
Call we to mind, and mark but this for proof,
Was not the Duke of Orleans thy foe,   *70*
And was he not in England prisoner?
But when they heard he was thine enemy,
They set him free, without his ransom paid,
In spite of Burgundy and all his friends.
See then, thou fight'st against thy countrymen!   *75*
And join'st with them will be thy slaughtermen.
Come, come, return; return, thou wandering lord;
Charles and the rest will take thee in their arms.
    Bur. I am vanquished; these haughty words of hers
Have batter'd me like roaring cannon-shot,   *80*
And made me almost yield upon my knees.
Forgive me, country, and sweet countrymen!
And, lords, accept this hearty kind embrace:
My forces and my power of men are yours.
So, farewell, Talbot; I'll no longer trust thee.   *85*
    Joan. Done like a Frenchman: turn, and turn again!
    Char. Welcome, brave duke! thy friendship makes us fresh.
    Bast. And doth beget new courage in our breasts.
    Alen. Pucelle hath bravely play'd her part in this,
And doth deserve a coronet of gold.   *90*
    Char. Now let us on, my lords, and join our powers:
And seek how we may prejudice the foe.   *Exeunt.*

❧ SCENE FOURTH ❧

[Paris. A Room in the Palace]
Enter the King, Gloucester, Winchester, York, Suffolk, Somerset,
Warwick, Exeter [Vernon, Basset, and Others]. To them, with his
Soldiers, Talbot.

    Tal. My gracious prince, and honourable peers,
Hearing of your arrival in this realm,
I have a while giv'n truce unto my wars,
To do my duty to my sovereign:
In sign whereof, this arm,—that hath reclaim'd   *5*
To your obedience fifty fortresses,
Twelve cities, and seven walled towns of strength,
Beside five hundred prisoners of esteem,—
Lets fall his sword before your highness' feet,
And with submissive loyalty of heart,   *10*
Ascribes the glory of his conquest got,
First to my God, and next unto your Grace.
    King. Is this the Lord Talbot, uncle Gloucester,
That hath so long been resident in France?
    Glo. Yes, if it please your majesty, my liege.   *15*
    King. Welcome, brave captain and victorious lord!
When I was young,—as yet I am not old,—
I do remember how my father said,
A stouter champion never handled sword.
Long since we were resolved of your truth,   *20*
Your faithful service and your toil in war;
Yet never have you tasted our reward,
Or been reguerdon'd with so much as thanks,

Because till now we never saw your face:
Therefore, stand up; and for these good deserts,   *25*
We here create you Earl of Shrewsbury;
And in our coronation take your place.
                  Sennet. Flourish. Exeunt.

Mane[n]t Vernon and Basset.

    Ver. Now, sir, to you, that were so hot at sea,
Disgracing of these colours that I wear
In honour of my noble Lord of York,   *30*
Dar'st thou maintain the former words thou spak'st?
    Bas. Yes, sir: as well as you dare patronage
The envious barking of your saucy tongue
Against my lord the Duke of Somerset.
    Ver. Sirrah, thy lord I honour as he is.   *35*
    Bas. Why, what is he? as good a man as York.
    Ver. Hark ye; not so: in witness, take ye that.   *Strikes him.*
    Bas. Villain, thou know'st the law of arms is such
That, whoso draws a sword, 'tis present death,
Or else this blow should broach thy dearest blood.   *40*
But I'll unto his majesty, and crave
I may have liberty to venge this wrong;
When thou shalt see I'll meet thee to thy cost.
    Ver. Well, miscreant, I'll be there as soon as you;
And, after, meet you sooner than you would.   *Exeunt.*   *45*

ACT FOURTH ❧ SCENE FIRST

[Paris. A Room of State]
Enter King, Gloucester, Winchester, York, Suffolk, Somerset,
Warwick, Talbot, Exeter, and Governor.

    Glo. Lord bishop, set the crown upon his head.
    Win. God save King Henry, of that name the sixth.
    Glo. Now, Governor of Paris, take your oath,—
                  [Governor kneels.]
That you elect no other king but him,
Esteem none friends but such as are his friends,   *5*
And none your foes but such as shall pretend
Malicious practices against his state:
This shall ye do, so help you righteous God!
        [The Governor takes the oath and exit.]

Enter Fastolfe.

    Fast. My gracious sovereign, as I rode from Calais,
To haste unto your coronation,   *10*
A letter was deliver'd to my hands,
Writ to your Grace from the Duke of Burgundy.
    Tal. Shame to the Duke of Burgundy and thee!
I vow'd, base knight, when I did meet thee next,
To tear the garter from thy craven's leg;   *[Plucking it off.]*   *15*
Which I have done, because unworthily
Thou wast installed in that high degree.
Pardon me, princely Henry, and the rest:
This dastard, at the battle of Patay,
When but in all I was six thousand strong,   *20*
And that the French were almost ten to one,

---

66 that instrument of: *instrument of that* (?)   **70–74** *Cf. n.*   **86** *Cf. n.*   **92 preju-**
dice: *injure*   **18** *Cf. n.*   **20 resolved:** *convinced*

26 *Cf. n.*   **38, 39** *Cf. n.*   **Act Fourth, Scene One;** *Cf. n.*   **4 elect:** *accept*   6
pretend: *purpose*   **15 the garter:** *Order of the Garter*   **19 Patay;** *cf. n.*

Before we met or that a stroke was given,
Like to a trusty squire did run away:
In which assault we lost twelve hundred men;
Myself, and divers gentlemen beside,   25
Were there surpris'd and taken prisoners.
Then judge, great lords, if I have done amiss;
Or whether that such cowards ought to wear
This ornament of knighthood, yea, or no?
    Glo. To say the truth, this fact was infamous   30
And ill beseeming any common man,
Much more a knight, a captain and a leader.
    Tal. When first this order was ordain'd, my lords,
Knights of the garter were of noble birth,
Valiant and virtuous, full of haughty courage,   35
Such as were grown to credit by the wars;
Not fearing death, nor shrinking for distress,
But always resolute in most extremes.
He then that is not furnish'd in this sort
Doth but usurp the sacred name of knight,   40
Profaning this most honourable order;
And should—if I were worthy to be judge—
Be quite degraded, like a hedge-born swain
That doth presume to boast of gentle blood.
    King. Stain to thy countrymen! thou hear'st thy doom.   45
Be packing therefore, thou that wast a knight;
Henceforth we banish thee on pain of death.   *[Exit Fastolfe.]*
And now, my Lord Protector, view the letter
Sent from our uncle Duke of Burgundy.
    Glo. *[Viewing superscription.]* What means his Grace,   50
that he hath chang'd his style?
No more, but plain and bluntly, 'To the King!'
Hath he forgot he is his sovereign?
Or doth this churlish superscription
Pretend some alteration in good will?   55
What's here? 'I have, upon especial cause,
Mov'd with compassion of my country's wrack,
Together with the pitiful complaints
Of such as your oppression feeds upon,
Forsaken your pernicious faction,   60
And join'd with Charles, the rightful King of France.'
O, monstrous treachery! Can this be so,
That in alliance, amity, and oaths,
There should be found such false dissembling guile?
    King. What! doth my uncle Burgundy revolt?   65
    Glo. He doth, my lord, and is become your foe.
    King. Is that the worst this letter doth contain?
    Glo. It is the worst, and all, my lord, he writes.
    King. Why then, Lord Talbot there shall talk with him,
And give him chastisement for this abuse.   70
How say you, my lord? are you not content?
    Tal. Content, my liege! Yes: but that I am prevented,
I should have begg'd I might have been employ'd.
    King. Then gather strength, and march unto him straight:
Let him perceive how ill we brook his treason,   75
And what offence it is to flout his friends.
    Tal. I go, my lord; in heart desiring still
You may behold confusion of your foes.   *[Exit.]*

Enter Vernon and Basset.

    Ver. Grant me the combat, gracious sovereign!
    Bas. And me, my lord; grant me the combat too!   80
    York. This is my servant: hear him, noble prince!
    Som. And this is mine: sweet Henry, favour him!
    King. Be patient, lords; and give them leave to speak.
Say, gentlemen, what makes you thus exclaim?
And wherefore crave you combat? or with whom?   85
    Ver. With him, my lord; for he hath done me wrong.
    Bas. And I with him; for he hath done me wrong.
    King. What is that wrong whereof you both complain?
First let me know, and then I'll answer you.
    Bas. Crossing the sea from England into France,   90
This fellow here, with envious carping tongue,
Upbraided me about the rose I wear;
Saying, the sanguine colour of the leaves
Did represent my master's blushing cheeks,
When stubbornly he did repugn the truth   95
About a certain question in the law
Argu'd betwixt the Duke of York and him;
With other vile and ignominious terms:
In confutation of which rude reproach,
And in defence of my lord's worthiness,   100
I crave the benefit of law of arms.
    Ver. And that is my petition, noble lord:
For though he seem with forged quaint conceit,
To set a gloss upon his bold intent,
Yet know, my lord, I was provok'd by him;   105
And he first took exceptions at this badge,
Pronouncing that the paleness of this flower
Bewray'd the faintness of my master's heart.
    York. Will not this malice, Somerset, be left?
    Som. Your private grudge, my Lord of York, will out,   110
Though ne'er so cunningly you smother it.
    King. Good Lord! what madness rules in brainsick men,
When, for so slight and frivolous a cause,
Such factious emulations shall arise!
Good cousins both, of York and Somerset,   115
Quiet yourselves, I pray, and be at peace.
    York. Let this dissension first be tried by fight,
And then your highness shall command a peace.
    Som. The quarrel toucheth none but us alone;
Betwixt ourselves let us decide it, then.   120
    York. There is my pledge; accept it, Somerset.
    Ver. Nay, let it rest where it began at first.
    Bas. Confirm it so, mine honourable lord.
    Glo. Confirm it so! Confounded be your strife!
And perish ye, with your audacious prate!   125
Presumptuous vassals! are you not asham'd,
With this immodest clamorous outrage
To trouble and disturb the king and us?—
And you, my lords, methinks you do not well
To bear with their perverse objections;   130
Much less to take occasion from their mouths
To raise a mutiny betwixt yourselves:
Let me persuade you take a better course.
    Exe. It grieves his highness: good my lords, be friends.
    King. Come hither, you that would be combatants.   135

---

30 fact: *misdeed*   **37 distress:** *physical suffering*   **38 most extremes:** *greatest extremities*   **39 furnish'd in this sort:** *so endowed*   **51 style:** *mode of address*   **55 Pretend:
portend*   **72 prevented:** *anticipated*

79 the combat: *license to fight*   **95 repugn:** *repudiate*   **103 quaint:** *ingenious*   **125
prate:** *prating*   **127 immodest:** *immoderate, presumptuous*   **130 objections:** *accusations*

Henceforth I charge you, as you love our favour,
Quite to forget this quarrel and the cause.
And you, my lords, remember where we are;
In France, amongst a fickle wavering nation.
If they perceive dissension in our looks,   *140*
And that within ourselves we disagree,
How will their grudging stomachs be provok'd
To wilful disobedience, and rebel!
Beside, what infamy will there arise,
When foreign princes shall be certified   *145*
That for a toy, a thing of no regard,
King Henry's peers and chief nobility
Destroy'd themselves, and lost the realm of France!
O! think upon the conquest of my father,
My tender years, and let us not forgo   *150*
That for a trifle that was bought with blood!
Let me be umpire in this doubtful strife.
I see no reason, if I wear this rose,   *[Putting on a red rose.]*
That any one should therefore be suspicious
I more incline to Somerset than York: *155*
Both are my kinsmen, and I love them both.
As well they may upbraid me with my crown,
Because, forsooth, the King of Scots is crown'd.
But your discretions better can persuade
Than I am able to instruct or teach: *160*
And therefore, as we hither came in peace,
So let us still continue peace and love.
Cousin of York, we institute your Grace
To be our regent in these parts of France:
And, good my Lord of Somerset, unite   *165*
Your troops of horsemen with his bands of foot;
And like true subjects, sons of your progenitors,
Go cheerfully together and digest
Your angry choler on your enemies.
Ourself, my Lord Protector, and the rest,   *170*
After some respite will return to Calais;
From thence to England; where I hope ere long
To be presented by your victories,
With Charles, Alençon, and that traitorous rout.
          Exeunt. Mane[n]t York, Warwick, Exeter, Vernon.

War. My Lord of York, I promise you, the king   *175*
Prettily, methought, did play the orator.
York. And so he did; but yet I like it not,
In that he wears the badge of Somerset.
War. Tush! that was but his fancy, blame him not;
I dare presume, sweet prince, he thought no harm.   *180*
York. An if I wist he did,—But let it rest;
Other affairs must now be managed.
          Exeunt. Flourish. Manet Exeter.

Exe. Well didst thou, Richard, to suppress thy voice;
For had the passions of thy heart burst out,
I fear we should have seen deciphered there   *185*
More rancorous spite, more furious raging broils,
Than yet can be imagin'd or suppos'd.
But howsoe'er, no simple man that sees
This jarring discord of nobility,
This shouldering of each other in the court,   *190*
This factious bandying of their favourites,

But that it doth presage some ill event.
'Tis much when sceptres are in children's hands;
But more, when envy breeds unkind division:
There comes the ruin, there begins confusion.   *Exit.*   *195*

❧ SCENE SECOND ❧

[Before Bordeaux]
Enter Talbot, with Trump and Drum, before Bordeaux.

Tal. Go to the gates of Bordeaux, trumpeter;
Summon their general unto the wall.

          [Trumpet] sounds. Enter General aloft [with followers].

English John Talbot, captains, calls you forth,
Servant in arms to Harry King of England;
And thus he would: Open your city gates,   *5*
Be humble to us, call my sovereign yours,
And do him homage as obedient subjects,
And I'll withdraw me and my bloody power;
But, if you frown upon this proffer'd peace,
You tempt the fury of my three attendants,   *10*
Lean famine, quartering steel, and climbing fire;
Who in a moment even with the earth
Shall lay your stately and air-braving towers,
If you forsake the offer of their love.
Gen. Thou ominous and fearful owl of death,   *15*
Our nation's terror and their bloody scourge!
The period of thy tyranny approacheth.
On us thou canst not enter but by death;
For, I protest, we are well fortified,
And strong enough to issue out and fight: *20*
If thou retire, the Dauphin, well appointed,
Stands with the snares of war to tangle thee:
On either hand thee there are squadrons pitch'd,
To wall thee from the liberty of flight;
And no way canst thou turn thee for redress   *25*
But death doth front thee with apparent spoil,
And pale destruction meets thee in the face.
Ten thousand French have ta'en the sacrament,
To rive their dangerous artillery
Upon no Christian soul but English Talbot.   *30*
Lo! there thou stand'st, a breathing valiant man,
Of an invincible unconquer'd spirit:
This is the latest glory of thy praise,
That I, thy enemy, 'due thee withal;
For ere the glass, that now begins to run,   *35*
Finish the process of his sandy hour,
These eyes, that see thee now well coloured,
Shall see thee wither'd, bloody, pale, and dead.   *Drum afar off.*
Hark! hark! the Dauphin's drum, a warning bell,
Sings heavy music to thy timorous soul;   *40*
And mine shall ring thy dire departure out.   *Exit.*
Tal. He fables not; I hear the enemy:
Out, some light horsemen, and peruse their wings.
O! negligent and heedless discipline;

141 within: *among*   142 grudging stomachs: *rebellious tempers*   146 toy: *whim, tri-*
fle   168 digest: *vent, disperse*   S. d. Flourish; *cf. n.*   191 bandying: *contending*

192 But: *but sees, i.e., without seeing*   194 unkind: *unnatural*   Scene Two; *cf. n.*   5
would: *would have you understand*   10, 11 *Cf. n.*   17 period: *full stop, end*   23 either
hand: *both sides of*   25 redress: *aid*   26 apparent spoil: *obvious ruin*   29 rive: *cause
to burst, discharge*   43 peruse their wings: *reconnoitre their flanks*   44 discipline: *tactics*

How are we park'd and bounded in a pale,   45
A little herd of England's timorous deer,
Maz'd with a yelping kennel of French curs!
If we be English deer, be, then, in blood;
Not rascal-like, to fall down with a pinch,
But rather, moody-mad and desperate stags,   50
Turn on the bloody hounds with heads of steel,
And make the cowards stand aloof at bay:
Sell every man his life as dear as mine,
And they shall find dear deer of us, my friends.
God and Saint George, Talbot and England's right,   55
Prosper our colours in this dangerous fight!   *[Exeunt.]*

❧ SCENE THIRD ❧

[Plains in Gascony]
Enter a Messenger that meets York. Enter York with Trumpet and
many Soldiers.

York. Are not the speedy scouts return'd again,
That dogg'd the mighty army of the Dauphin?
   Mess. They are return'd, my lord; and give it out,
That he is march'd to Bordeaux with his power,
To fight with Talbot. As he march'd along,   5
By your espials were discovered
Two mightier troops than that the Dauphin led,
Which join'd with him and made their march for Bordeaux.
   York. A plague upon that villain Somerset,
That thus delays my promised supply   10
Of horsemen that were levied for this siege!
Renowned Talbot doth expect my aid,
And I am louted by a traitor villain,
And cannot help the noble chevalier.
God comfort him in this necessity!   15
If he miscarry, farewell wars in France.

Enter another Messenger [Sir William Lucy].

   Sec. Mess. Thou princely leader of our English strength,
Never so needful on the earth of France,
Spur to the rescue of the noble Talbot,
Who now is girdled with a waist of iron   20
And hemm'd about with grim destruction.
To Bordeaux, warlike duke! To Bordeaux, York!
Else, farewell Talbot, France, and England's honour.
   York. O God! that Somerset, who in proud heart
Doth stop my cornets, were in Talbot's place!   25
So should we save a valiant gentleman
By forfeiting a traitor and a coward.
Mad ire and wrathful fury makes me weep
That thus we die, while remiss traitors sleep.
   Sec. Mess. O! send some succour to the distress'd lord.   30
   York. He dies, we lose; I break my warlike word;
We mourn, France smiles; we lose, they daily get;
All long of this vile traitor Somerset.
   Sec. Mess. Then God take mercy on brave Talbot's soul;
And on his son young John, whom two hours since   35

I met in travel toward his warlike father.
This seven years did not Talbot see his son;
And now they meet where both their lives are done.
   York. Alas! what joy shall noble Talbot have,
To bid his young son welcome to his grave?   40
Away! vexation almost stops my breath
That sunder'd friends greet in the hour of death.
Lucy, farewell: no more my fortune can,
But curse the cause I cannot aid the man.
Maine, Blois, Poitiers, and Tours, are won away,   45
Long all of Somerset and his delay.   *Exit [with his Soldiers].*
   Sec. Mess. Thus, while the vulture of sedition
Feeds in the bosom of such great commanders,
Sleeping neglection doth betray to loss
The conquest of our scarce cold conqueror,   50
That ever living man of memory,
Henry the Fifth. Whiles they each other cross,
Lives, honours, lands, and all hurry to loss.

❧ SCENE FOURTH ❧

[The Same]
Enter Somerset, with his Army [and a Captain of Talbot's].

   Som. It is too late; I cannot send them now:
This expedition was by York and Talbot
Too rashly plotted: all our general force
Might with a sally of the very town
Be buckled with: the over-daring Talbot   5
Hath sullied all his gloss of former honour
By this unheedful, desperate, wild adventure:
York set him on to fight and die in shame,
That, Talbot dead, great York might bear the name.
   Cap. Here is Sir William Lucy, who with me   10
Set from our o'ermatch'd forces forth for aid.
   Som. How now, Sir William! whither were you sent?
   Lucy. Whither, my lord? from bought and sold Lord Talbot;
Who, ring'd about with bold adversity,
Cries out for noble York and Somerset,   15
To beat assailing death from his weak legions:
And whiles the honourable captain there
Drops bloody sweat from his war-wearied limbs,
And, in advantage lingering, looks for rescue,
You, his false hopes, the trust of England's honour,   20
Keep off aloof with worthless emulation.
Let not your private discord keep away
The levied succours that should lend him aid,
While he, renowned noble gentleman,
Yields up his life unto a world of odds: 25
Orleans the Bastard, Charles, Burgundy,
Alençon, Reignier, compass him about,
And Talbot perisheth by your default.
   Som. York set him on; York should have sent him aid.
   Lucy. And York as fast upon your Grace exclaims;   30
Swearing that you withhold his levied host
Collected for this expedition.

---

45 park'd: *enclosed* **pale:** *fence*   **47 Maz'd:** *bewildered*   **48 in blood:** *vigorous*   **49 rascal-like:** *like a lean and jaded deer*   **13 louted:** *mocked*   **25 cornets:** *troops of horse*   **33 long of:** *on account of*

47 vulture of sedition; *cf. n.*   **49 Sleeping neglection:** *slothful neglect*   **50 scarce cold conqueror;** *cf. n.*   **Scene Four;** *cf. n.*   **4 the very town:** *the mere garrison* (unsupported by the relieving armies)   **13 Whither, my lord;** *cf. n.*   **19 in advantage lingering:** *making the most of every desperate chance* (?)   **21 worthless:** *unworthy*

Som. York lies; he might have sent and had the horse:
I owe him little duty, and less love;
And take foul scorn to fawn on him by sending.   *35*
    Lucy. The fraud of England, not the force of France,
Hath now entrapp'd the noble-minded Talbot.
Never to England shall he bear his life,
But dies, betray'd to fortune by your strife.
    Som. Come, go; I will dispatch the horsemen straight: *40*
Within six hours they will be at his aid.
    Lucy. Too late comes rescue: he is ta'en or slain,
For fly he could not if he would have fled;
And fly would Talbot never, though he might.
    Som. If he be dead, brave Talbot, then adieu!   *45*
    Lucy. His fame lives in the world, his shame in you. *Exeunt.*

❧ SCENE FIFTH ❧

[Castillon, near Bordeaux]
Enter Talbot and his Son.

    Tal. O young John Talbot! I did send for thee
To tutor thee in stratagems of war,
That Talbot's name might be in thee reviv'd
When sapless age, and weak unable limbs
Should bring thy father to his drooping chair.   *5*
But,—O malignant and ill-boding stars!
Now thou art come unto a feast of death,
A terrible and unavoided danger:
Therefore, dear boy, mount on my swiftest horse,
And I'll direct thee how thou shalt escape   *10*
By sudden flight: come, dally not, be gone.
    John. Is my name Talbot? and am I your son?
And shall I fly? O! if you love my mother,
Dishonour not her honourable name,
To make a bastard and a slave of me: *15*
The world will say he is not Talbot's blood
That basely fled when noble Talbot stood.
    Tal. Fly, to revenge my death, if I be slain.
    John. He that flies so will ne'er return again.
    Tal. If we both stay, we both are sure to die.   *20*
    John. Then let me stay; and, father, do you fly:
Your loss is great, so your regard should be;
My worth unknown, no loss is known in me.
Upon my death the French can little boast;
In yours they will, in you all hopes are lost.   *25*
Flight cannot stain the honour you have won;
But mine it will that no exploit have done:
You fled for vantage everyone will swear;
But if I bow, they'll say it was for fear.
There is no hope that ever I will stay   *30*
If the first hour I shrink and run away.
Here, on my knee, I beg mortality,
Rather than life preserv'd with infamy.
    Tal. Shall all thy mother's hopes lie in one tomb?
    John. Ay, rather than I'll shame my mother's womb.   *35*
    Tal. Upon my blessing I command thee go.
    John. To fight I will, but not to fly the foe.
    Tal. Part of thy father may be sav'd in thee.
    John. No part of him but will be shame in me.

8 unavoided: *unavoidable*   **22 regard:** *care* (of yourself)

    Tal. Thou never hadst renown, nor canst not lose it.   *40*
    John. Yes, your renowned name: shall flight abuse it?
    Tal. Thy father's charge shall clear thee from that stain.
    John. You cannot witness for me, being slain.
If death be so apparent, then both fly.
    Tal. And leave my followers here to fight and die?   *45*
My age was never tainted with such shame.
    John. And shall my youth be guilty of such blame?
No more can I be sever'd from your side
Than can yourself yourself in twain divide.
Stay, go, do what you will, the like do I;   *50*
For live I will not if my father die.
    Tal. Then here I take my leave of thee, fair son,
Born to eclipse thy life this afternoon.
Come, side by side together live and die,
And soul with soul from France to heaven fly.   *Exeunt.*   *55*

❧ SCENE SIXTH ❧

[The Same]
Alarum: Excursions, wherein Talbot's Son is hemmed about, and
Talbot rescues him.

    Tal. Saint George and victory! fight, soldiers, fight!
The regent hath with Talbot broke his word,
And left us to the rage of France his sword.
Where is John Talbot? Pause, and take thy breath:
I gave thee life and rescu'd thee from death.   *5*
    John. O! twice my father, twice am I thy son:
The life thou gav'st me first was lost and done,
Till with thy warlike sword, despite of fate,
To my determin'd time thou gav'st new date.
    Tal. When from the Dauphin's crest thy sword struck fire,   *10*
It warm'd thy father's heart with proud desire
Of bold-fac'd victory. Then leaden age,
Quicken'd with youthful spleen and warlike rage,
Beat down Alençon, Orleans, Burgundy,
And from the pride of Gallia rescu'd thee.   *15*
The ireful bastard Orleans,—that drew blood
From thee, my boy, and had the maidenhood
Of thy first fight,—I soon encountered
And, interchanging blows, I quickly shed
Some of his bastard blood; and, in disgrace,   *20*
Bespoke him thus, 'Contaminated, base,
And misbegotten blood I spill of thine,
Mean and right poor, for that pure blood of mine
Which thou didst force from Talbot, my brave boy.'
Here, purposing the Bastard to destroy,   *25*
Came in strong rescue. Speak, thy father's care,
Art thou not weary, John? How dost thou fare?
Wilt thou yet leave the battle, boy, and fly,
Now thou art seal'd the son of chivalry?
Fly, to revenge my death when I am dead;   *30*
The help of one stands me in little stead.
O! too much folly is it, well I wot,
To hazard all our lives in one small boat.
If I to-day die not with Frenchmen's rage,
To-morrow I shall die with mickle age: *35*
By me they nothing gain an if I stay;

3 France his: *France's*   **9 determin'd:** *ended*   **25 purposing:** *as I purposed*

'Tis but the short'ning of my life one day.
In thee thy mother dies, our household's name,
My death's revenge, thy youth, and England's fame.
All these and more we hazard by thy stay;   40
All these are sav'd if thou wilt fly away.

John. The sword of Orleans hath not made me smart;
These words of yours draw life-blood from my heart.
On that advantage, bought with such a shame,
To save a paltry life and slay bright fame,   45
Before young Talbot from old Talbot fly,
The coward horse that bears me fall and die!
And like me to the peasant boys of France,
To be shame's scorn and subject of mischance!
Surely, by all the glory you have won,   50
An if I fly, I am not Talbot's son:
Then talk no more of flight, it is no boot;
If son to Talbot, die at Talbot's foot.

Tal. Then follow thou thy desperate sire of Crete,
Thou Icarus. Thy life to me is sweet: 55
If thou wilt fight, fight by thy father's side,
And, commendable prov'd, let's die in pride.

Exeunt.

❧ Scene Seventh ❧

[The Same]

Alarum: Excursions. Enter Old Talbot, led [by a Servant].

Tal. Where is my other life?—mine own is gone;—
O! where's young Talbot? where is valiant John?
Triumphant death, smear'd with captivity,
Young Talbot's valour makes me smile at thee.
When he perceiv'd me shrink and on my knee,   5
His bloody sword he brandish'd over me,
And like a hungry lion did commence
Rough deeds of rage and stern impatience;
But when my angry guardant stood alone,
Tendering my ruin and assail'd of none,   10
Dizzy-ey'd fury and great rage of heart
Suddenly made him from my side to start
Into the clust'ring battle of the French;
And in that sea of blood my boy did drench
His overmounting spirit; and there died   15
My Icarus, my blossom, in his pride.

Enter [Soldiers] with John Talbot, borne.

Serv. O, my dear lord! lo, where your son is borne!
Tal. Thou antic, death, which laugh'st us here to scorn,
Anon, from thy insulting tyranny,
Coupled in bonds of perpetuity,   20
Two Talbots, winged through the lither sky,
In thy despite shall 'scape mortality.
O! thou, whose wounds become hard-favour'd death,
Speak to thy father ere thou yield thy breath;
Brave death by speaking whether he will or no;   25
Imagine him a Frenchman and thy foe.

Poor boy! he smiles, methinks, as who should say,
Had death been French, then death had died to-day.
Come, come, and lay him in his father's arms:
My spirit can no longer bear these harms.   30
Soldiers, adieu! I have what I would have,
Now my old arms are young John Talbot's grave.   *Dies.*

Enter Charles, Alençon, Burgundy, Bastard and Pucelle.

Char. Had York and Somerset brought rescue in,
We should have found a bloody day of this.
Bast. How the young whelp of Talbot's, raging-wood,   35
Did flesh his puny sword in Frenchmen's blood!
Joan. Once I encounter'd him, and thus I said:
'Thou maiden youth, be vanquish'd by a maid':
But with a proud majestical high scorn,
He answer'd thus: 'Young Talbot was not born   40
To be the pillage of a giglot wench.'
So, rushing in the bowels of the French,
He left me proudly, as unworthy fight.
Bur. Doubtless he would have made a noble knight;
See, where he lies inhearsed in the arms   45
Of the most bloody nurser of his harms.
Bast. Hew them to pieces, hack their bones asunder,
Whose life was England's glory, Gallia's wonder.
Char. O, no! forbear; for that which we have fled
During the life, let us not wrong it dead.   50

Enter Lucy [with a French Herald].

Lucy. Herald, conduct me to the Dauphin's tent,
To know who hath obtain'd the glory of the day.
Char. On what submissive message art thou sent?
Lucy. Submission, Dauphin! 'tis a mere French word;
We English warriors wot not what it means.   55
I come to know what prisoners thou hast ta'en,
And to survey the bodies of the dead.
Char. For prisoners ask'st thou? hell our prison is.
But tell me whom thou seek'st.
Lucy. Where is the great Alcides of the field,   60
Valiant Lord Talbot, Earl of Shrewsbury?
Created, for his rare success in arms,
Great Earl of Washford, Waterford, and Valence;
Lord Talbot of Goodrig and Urchinfield,
Lord Strange of Blackmere, Lord Verdon of Alton,   65
Lord Cromwell of Wingfield, Lord Furnivall of Sheffield,
The thrice-victorious Lord of Falconbridge;
Knight of the noble order of Saint George,
Worthy Saint Michael and the Golden Fleece;
Great mareschal to Henry the Sixth   70
Of all his wars within the realm of France?
Joan. Here is a silly stately style indeed!
The Turk, that two-and-fifty kingdoms hath,
Writes not so tedious a style as this.
Him that thou magnifiest with all these titles,   75
Stinking and fly-blown lies here at our feet.
Lucy. Is Talbot slain, the Frenchmen's only scourge,
Your kingdom's terror and black Nemesis?
O! were mine eye-balls into bullets turn'd,
That I in rage might shoot them at your faces!   80

44 On that advantage: *cf. n.*   **48 like:** *liken*   **54 sire of Crete:** *i.e., Dædalus*   **3 smear'd with captivity:** *thyself besmirched with defeat*   **9 guardant:** *guardian*   **10 Tendering:** *solicitous over*   **13 battle:** *main body*   **18 antic:** *buffoon*   **21 lither:** *yielding*   **23 become hard-favour'd:** *beautify ugly*   **25 Brave:** *defy*

35 raging-wood: *mad with rage*   **41 giglot:** *wanton*   **44 Doubtless:** *undoubtedly*   **63–71 Cf. n.*   **72 style:** *title***

O! that I could but call these dead to life!
It were enough to fright the realm of France.
Were but his picture left among you here,
It would amaze the proudest of you all.
Give me their bodies, that I may bear them hence,　　　85
And give them burial as beseems their worth.
　　Joan. I think this upstart is old Talbot's ghost,
He speaks with such a proud commanding spirit.
For God's sake, let him have 'em; to keep them here
They would but stink and putrefy the air.　　　90
　　Char. Go, take their bodies hence.
　　Lucy.　　　　　　　　　　I'll bear them hence:
But from their ashes shall be rear'd
A phœnix that shall make all France afeard.
　　Char. So we be rid of them, do with 'em what thou wilt.　　　95
And now to Paris, in this conquering vein:
All will be ours now bloody Talbot's slain.　　　*Exeunt.*

ACT FIFTH ❦ SCENE FIRST

[London. A Room in the Palace]
Sennet. Enter King, Gloucester, and Exeter.

　　King. Have you perus'd the letters from the pope,
The emperor, and the Earl of Armagnac?
　　Glo. I have, my lord; and their intent is this:
They humbly sue unto your excellence
To have a godly peace concluded of　　　5
Between the realms of England and of France.
　　King. How doth your Grace affect their motion?
　　Glo. Well, my good lord; and as the only means
To stop effusion of our Christian blood,
And stablish quietness on every side.　　　10
　　King. Ay, marry, uncle; for I always thought
It was both impious and unnatural
That such immanity and bloody strife
Should reign among professors of one faith.
　　Glo. Beside, my lord, the sooner to effect　　　15
And surer bind this knot of amity,
The Earl of Armagnac, near knit to Charles,
A man of great authority in France,
Proffers his only daughter to your Grace
In marriage, with a large and sumptuous dowry.　　　20
　　King. Marriage, uncle! alas! my years are young,
And fitter is my study and my books
Than wanton dalliance with a paramour.
Yet call the ambassadors; and, as you please,
So let them have their answers every one:　　　25
I shall be well content with any choice
Tends to God's glory and my country's weal.

Enter Winchester [dressed as Cardinal], and three Ambassadors
[one a Papal Legate].

　　Exe. [Aside.] What! is my Lord of Winchester install'd,
And call'd unto a cardinal's degree?
Then, I perceive that will be verified　　　30

Henry the Fifth did sometime prophesy,—
'If once he come to be a cardinal,
He'll make his cap co-equal with the crown.'
　　King. My lords ambassadors, your several suits
Have been consider'd and debated on.　　　35
Your purpose is both good and reasonable;
And therefore are we certainly resolv'd
To draw conditions of a friendly peace;
Which by my Lord of Winchester we mean
Shall be transported presently to France.　　　40
　　Glo. And for the proffer of my lord your master,
I have inform'd his highness so at large,
As,—liking of the lady's virtuous gifts,
Her beauty, and the value of her dower,—
He doth intend she shall be England's queen.　　　45
　　King. In argument and proof of which contract,
Bear her this jewel, pledge of my affection.
And so, my lord protector, see them guarded
And safely brought to Dover; where inshipp'd
Commit them to the fortune of the sea.　　　50
　　　　　　Exeunt [all but Winchester and the Legate].
　　Win. Stay, my lord legate: you shall first receive
The sum of money which I promised
Should be deliver'd to his holiness
For clothing me in these grave ornaments.
　　Leg. I will attend upon your lordship's leisure.　　　55
　　Win. [Aside.] Now Winchester will not submit, I trow,
Or be inferior to the proudest peer.
Humphrey of Gloucester, thou shalt well perceive
That neither in birth or for authority
The bishop will be overborne by thee:　　　60
I'll either make thee stoop and bend thy knee,
Or sack this country with a mutiny.　　　*Exeunt.*

❦ SCENE SECOND ❦

[France. Plains in Anjou?]
Enter Charles, Burgundy, Alençon, Bastard, Reignier, and Joan.

　　Char. These news, my lord, may cheer our drooping
spirits;
'Tis said the stout Parisians do revolt,
And turn again unto the warlike French.
　　Alen. Then, march to Paris, royal Charles of France,　　　5
And keep not back your powers in dalliance.
　　Joan. Peace be amongst them if they turn to us;
Else, ruin combat with their palaces!

Enter Scout.

　　Scout. Success unto our valiant general,
And happiness to his accomplices!　　　10
　　Char. What tidings send our scouts? I prithee speak.
　　Scout. The English army, that divided was
Into two parties, is now conjoin'd in one,
And means to give you battle presently.
　　Char. Somewhat too sudden, sirs, the warning is:　　　15
But we will presently provide for them.
　　Bur. I trust the ghost of Talbot is not there:
Now he is gone, my lord, you need not fear.

84 amaze: *astound*　　**89, 95 'em;** *cf. n.*　　**1, 2** *Cf. n.*　　**7 affect:** *incline toward*　　**13**
immanity: *ferocity*

31 sometime: *formerly*　　**43 As:** *that*　　**10 accomplices:** *comrades*

Joan. Of all base passions, fear is most accurs'd.
Command the conquest, Charles, it shall be thine;   20
Let Henry fret and all the world repine.
    Char. Then on, my lords; and France be fortunate!
          Exeunt. Alarum. Excursions.

❧ SCENE THIRD ❧

[The Same]
Enter Joan la Pucelle.

  Joan. The regent conquers and the Frenchmen fly.
Now help, ye charming spells and periapts;
And ye choice spirits that admonish me
And give me signs of future accidents: *Thunder.*
You speedy helpers, that are substitutes   5
Under the lordly monarch of the north,
Appear, and aid me in this enterprise!

Enter Fiends.

This speedy and quick appearance argues proof
Of your accustom'd diligence to me.
Now, ye familiar spirits, that are cull'd   10
Out of the powerful regions under earth,
Help me this once, that France may get the field.
          They walk, and speak not.
O! hold me not with silence over-long.
Where I was wont to feed you with my blood,
I'll lop a member off and give it you,   15
In earnest of a further benefit,
So you do condescend to help me now.
          They hang their heads.
No hope to have redress? My body shall
Pay recompense, if you will grant my suit.
          They shake their heads.
Cannot my body nor blood-sacrifice   20
Entreat you to your wonted furtherance?
Then take my soul; my body, soul, and all,
Before that England give the French the foil.
          They depart.
See! they forsake me. Now the time is come,
That France must vail her lofty-plumed crest,   25
And let her head fall into England's lap.
My ancient incantations are too weak,
And hell too strong for me to buckle with:
Now, France, thy glory droopeth to the dust.   *Exit.*

Excursions. Burgundy and York fight hand to hand. French fly
[leaving Joan in York's power].

  York. Damsel of France, I think I have you fast: 30
Unchain your spirits now with spelling charms,
And try if they can gain your liberty.
A goodly prize, fit for the devil's grace!
See how the ugly witch doth bend her brows,
As if with Circe she would change my shape.   35
  Joan. Chang'd to a worser shape thou canst not be.

  York. O! Charles the Dauphin is a proper man;
No shape but his can please your dainty eye.
  Joan. A plaguing mischief light on Charles and thee!
And may ye both be suddenly surpris'd   40
By bloody hands, in sleeping on your beds!
  York. Fell banning hag, enchantress, hold thy tongue!
  Joan. I prithee, give me leave to curse a while.
  York. Curse, miscreant, when thou comest to the stake.
          Exeunt.

Alarum. Enter Suffolk, with Margaret in his hand.

  Suf. Be what thou wilt, thou art my prisoner.   *Gazes on her.*
O fairest beauty! do not fear nor fly,
For I will touch thee but with reverent hands.
I kiss these fingers for eternal peace,
And lay them gently on thy tender side.
What art thou? say, that I may honour thee.   50
  Mar. Margaret my name, and daughter to a king,
The King of Naples, whosoe'er thou art.
  Suf. An earl I am, and Suffolk am I call'd.
Be not offended, nature's miracle,
Thou art allotted to be ta'en by me: 55
So doth the swan her downy cygnets save,
Keeping them prisoners underneath her wings.
Yet if this servile usage once offend,
Go and be free again, as Suffolk's friend.   *She is going.*
O stay! I have no power to let her pass;   60
My hand would free her, but my heart says no.
As plays the sun upon the glassy streams,
Twinkling another counterfeited beam,
So seems this gorgeous beauty to mine eyes.
Fain would I woo her, yet I dare not speak: 65
I'll call for pen and ink and write my mind.
Fie, De la Pole! disable not thyself;
Hast not a tongue? is she not here?
Wilt thou be daunted at a woman's sight?
Ay; beauty's princely majesty is such   70
Confounds the tongue and makes the senses rough.
  Mar. Say, Earl of Suffolk,—if thy name be so,—
What ransom must I pay before I pass?
For I perceive, I am thy prisoner.
  Suf. [Aside.] How canst thou tell she will deny thy suit,   75
Before thou make a trial of her love?
  Mar. Why speak'st thou not? what ransom must I pay?
  Suf. [Aside.] She's beautiful and therefore to be woo'd,
She is a woman, therefore to be won.
  Mar. Wilt thou accept of ransom, yea or no?   80
  Suf. [Aside.] Fond man! remember that thou hast a wife;
Then how can Margaret be thy paramour?
  Mar. I were best to leave him, for he will not hear.
  Suf. [Aside.] There all is marr'd; there lies a cooling card.
  Mar. He talks at random; sure, the man is mad.   85
  Suf. [Aside.] And yet a dispensation may be had.
  Mar. And yet I would that you would answer me.
  Suf. [Aside.] I'll win this Lady Margaret. For whom?
Why, for my king: tush! that's a wooden thing.
  Mar. [Overhearing him.] He talks of wood: it is some   90
carpenter.

---

1 **The regent conquers;** *cf. n.*   2 **periapts:** *amulets*   4 **accidents:** *events*   5 **substi-**
tutes: *agents*   6 **monarch of the north;** *cf. n.*   25 **vail:** *lower*   **S. d. Burgundy**
and York fight; *cf. n.*   31 **spelling:** *working spells*   35 **with Circe:** *Circe-like*

37 **proper:** *handsome*   42 **Fell:** *fierce*   48 **for:** *in token of*   55 **allotted:** *appointed* (by fate)
63 *Cf. n.*   67 **disable:** *disparage*   68 *Cf. n.*   71 **Confounds:** *that it confounds*   **S. d. Aside;**
cf. n.   78, 79 *Cf. n.*   84 **cooling card:** *card* (played by an adversary) *which dashes one's hope*

Suf. [*Aside.*] Yet so my fancy may be satisfied,
And peace established between these realms.
But there remains a scruple in that too;
For though her father be the King of Naples,   95
Duke of Anjou and Maine, yet is he poor,
And our nobility will scorn the match.
    Mar. Hear ye, captain? Are you not at leisure?
    Suf. [*Aside.*] It shall be so, disdain they ne'er so much:
Henry is youthful and will quickly yield.   100
Madam, I have a secret to reveal.
    Mar. [*Aside.*] What though I be enthrall'd? he seems a
    knight,
And will not any way dishonour me.
    Suf. Lady, vouchsafe to listen what I say.   105
    Mar. [*Aside.*] Perhaps I shall be rescu'd by the French;
And then I need not crave his courtesy.
    Suf. Sweet madam, give me hearing in a cause—
    Mar. Tush, women have been captivate ere now.
    Suf. Lady, wherefore talk you so?   110
    Mar. I cry you mercy, 'tis but *quid for quo.*
    Suf. Say, gentle princess, would you not suppose
Your bondage happy to be made a queen?
    Mar. To be a queen in bondage is more vile
Than is a slave in base servility;   115
For princes should be free.
    Suf.   And so shall you,
If happy England's royal king be free.
    Mar. Why, what concerns his freedom unto me?
    Suf. I'll undertake to make thee Henry's queen,   120
To put a golden sceptre in thy hand
And set a precious crown upon thy head,
If thou wilt condescend to be my—
    Mar.   What?
    Suf.   His love.   125
    Mar. I am unworthy to be Henry's wife.
    Suf. No, gentle madam; I unworthy am
To woo so fair a dame to be his wife
And have no portion in the choice myself.
How say you, madam, are you so content?   130
    Mar. An if my father please, I am content.
    Suf. Then call our captains and our colours forth!
And, madam, at your father's castle walls
We'll crave a parley, to confer with him.

       Sound. Enter Reignier on the Walls.

    Suf. See, Reignier, see thy daughter prisoner!   135
    Reig. To whom?
    Suf.   To me.
    Reig.   Suffolk, what remedy?
I am a soldier, and unapt to weep,
Or to exclaim on Fortune's fickleness.   140
    Suf. Yes, there is remedy enough, my lord:
Consent, and for thy honour give consent,
Thy daughter shall be wedded to my king,
Whom I with pain have woo'd and won thereto;
And this her easy-held imprisonment   145
Hath gain'd thy daughter princely liberty.
    Reig. Speaks Suffolk as he thinks?
    Suf.   Fair Margaret knows

That Suffolk doth not flatter, face, or feign.
    Reig. Upon thy princely warrant, I descend   150
To give thee answer of thy just demand.   [*Exit from the walls.*]
    Suf. And here I will expect thy coming.

       Trumpets sound. Enter Reignier [below].

    Reig. Welcome, brave earl, into our territories:
Command in Anjou what your honour pleases.
    Suf. Thanks, Reignier, happy for so sweet a child,   155
Fit to be made companion with a king.
What answer makes your Grace unto my suit?
    Reig. Since thou dost deign to woo her little worth
To be the princely bride of such a lord,
Upon condition I may quietly   160
Enjoy mine own, the country Maine and Anjou,
Free from oppression or the stroke of war,
My daughter shall be Henry's if he please.
    Suf. That is her ransom; I deliver her;
And those two counties I will undertake   165
Your Grace shall well and quietly enjoy.
    Reig. And I again, in Henry's royal name,
As deputy unto that gracious king,
Give thee her hand for sign of plighted faith.
    Suf. Reignier of France, I give thee kingly thanks,   170
Because this is in traffic of a king.
[*Aside.*] And yet, methinks, I could be well content
To be mine own attorney in this case.
I'll over, then, to England with this news,
And make this marriage to be solemniz'd.   175
So farewell, Reignier: set this diamond safe,
In golden palaces, as it becomes.
    Reig. I do embrace thee, as I would embrace
The Christian prince, King Henry, were he here.
    Mar. Farewell, my lord. Good wishes, praise, and prayers.
Shall Suffolk ever have of Margaret.   *She is going.*
    Suf. Farewell, sweet madam! but hark you, Margaret;
No princely commendations to my king?
    Mar. Such commendations as become a maid,
A virgin, and his servant, say to him.   185
    Suf. Words sweetly plac'd and modestly directed.
But madam, I must trouble you again,
No loving token to his majesty?
    Mar. Yes, my good lord; a pure unspotted heart,
Never yet taint with love, I send the king.   190
    Suf. And this withal.   *Kiss her.*
    Mar. That for thyself: I will not so presume,
To send such peevish tokens to a king.

       [*Exeunt Reignier and Margaret.*]

    Suf. O! wert thou for myself! But Suffolk, stay;
Thou mayst not wander in that labyrinth;   195
There Minotaurs and ugly treasons lurk.
Solicit Henry with her wondrous praise:
Bethink thee on her virtues that surmount
And natural graces that extinguish art;
Repeat their semblance often on the seas,   200
That, when thou com'st to kneel at Henry's feet,
Thou mayst bereave him of his wits with wonder.   *Exit.*

---

92 fancy: *love*   **113 to be:** *if you were in consequence*   **139 unapt:** *disinclined*

149 face: *wear a false face*   **171 traffic:** *business*   **190 taint:** *infected*   **193 peevish:** *silly*

❧ SCENE FOURTH ❧

[Rouen]

Enter York, Warwick, Shepherd, [with] Pucelle [guarded].

York. Bring forth that sorceress, condemn'd to burn.

Shep. Ah, Joan! this kills thy father's heart outright
Have I sought every country far and near,
And, now it is my chance to find thee out,
Must I behold thy timeless cruel death?   *5*
Ah, Joan! sweet daughter Joan, I'll die with thee.

Joan. Decrepit miser! base ignoble wretch!
I am descended of a gentler blood:
Thou art no father nor no friend of mine.

Shep. Out, out! My lords, an please you, 'tis not so;   *10*
I did beget her all the parish knows:
Her mother liveth yet, can testify
She was the first fruit of my bachelorship.

War. Graceless! wilt thou deny thy parentage?

York. This argues what her kind of life hath been: *15*
Wicked and vile; and so her death concludes.

Shep. Fie, Joan, that thou wilt be so obstacle!
God knows, thou art a collop of my flesh;
And for thy sake have I shed many a tear:
Deny me not, I prithee, gentle Joan.   *20*

Joan. Peasant, avaunt! You have suborn'd this man,
Of purpose to obscure my noble birth.

Shep. 'Tis true, I gave a noble to the priest,
The morn that I was wedded to her mother.
Kneel down and take my blessing, good my girl.   *25*
Wilt thou not stoop? Now cursed be the time
Of thy nativity! I would the milk
Thy mother gave thee, when thou suck'dst her breast,
Had been a little ratsbane for thy sake!
Or else, when thou didst keep my lambs a-field,   *30*
I wish some ravenous wolf had eaten thee!
Dost thou deny thy father, cursed drab?
O! burn her, burn her! hanging is too good.   *Exit.*

York. Take her away; for she hath liv'd too long,
To fill the world with vicious qualities.   *35*

Joan. First, let me tell you whom you have condemn'd:
Not me begotten of a shepherd swain,
But issu'd from the progeny of kings;
Virtuous and holy; chosen from above,
By inspiration of celestial grace,   *40*
To work exceeding miracles on earth.
I never had to do with wicked spirits:
But you,—that are polluted with your lusts,
Stain'd with the guiltless blood of innocents,
Corrupt and tainted with a thousand vices,—   *45*
Because you want the grace that others have,
You judge it straight a thing impossible.
To compass wonders but by help of devils.
No, misconceived! Joan of Arc hath been
A virgin from her tender infancy,   *50*
Chaste and immaculate in very thought;
Whose maiden blood, thus rigorously effus'd.
Will cry for vengeance at the gates of heaven.

York. Ay, ay: away with her to execution!

War. And hark ye, sirs; because she is a maid,   *55*
Spare for no fagots, let there be enow:
Place barrels of pitch upon the fatal stake,
That so her torture may be shortened.

Joan. Will nothing turn your unrelenting hearts?
Then, Joan, discover thine infirmity,   *60*
That warranteth by law to be thy privilege.
I am with child, ye bloody homicides:
Murder not then the fruit within my womb,
Although ye hale me to a violent death.

York. Now, heaven forfend! the holy maid with child!   *65*

War. The greatest miracle that e'er ye wrought!
Is all your strict preciseness come to this?

York. She and the Dauphin have been juggling:
I did imagine what would be her refuge.

War. Well, go to; we will have no bastards live;   *70*
Especially since Charles must father it.

Joan. You are deceiv'd; my child is none of his:
It was Alençon that enjoy'd my love.

York. Alençon! that notorious Machiavel!
It dies an if it had a thousand lives.   *75*

Joan. O! give me leave, I have deluded you:
'Twas neither Charles, nor yet the duke I nam'd,
But Reignier, King of Naples, that prevail'd.

War. A married man: that's most intolerable.

York. Why, here's a girl! I think she knows not well,   *80*
There were so many, whom she may accuse.

War. It's sign she hath been liberal and free.

York. And yet, forsooth, she is a virgin pure.
Strumpet, thy words condemn thy brat and thee:
Use no entreaty, for it is in vain.   *85*

Joan. Then lead me hence; with whom I leave my curse:
May never glorious sun reflex his beams
Upon the country where you make abode;
But darkness and the gloomy shade of death
Environ you, till mischief and despair   *90*
Drive you to break your necks or hang yourselves!

Exit [guarded].

York. Break thou in pieces and consume to ashes,
Thou foul accursed minister of hell!

Enter Cardinal.

Car. Lord regent, I do greet your excellence
With letters of commission from the king.   *95*
For know, my lords, the states of Christendom,
Mov'd with remorse of these outrageous broils,
Have earnestly implor'd a general peace
Betwixt our nation and the aspiring French;
And here at hand the Dauphin, and his train,   *100*
Approacheth to confer about some matter.

York. Is all our travail turn'd to this effect?
After the slaughter of so many peers,
So many captains, gentlemen, and soldiers,
That in this quarrel have been overthrown,   *105*
And sold their bodies for their country's benefit,
Shall we at last conclude effeminate peace?
Have we not lost most part of all the towns,
By treason, falsehood, and by treachery,
Our great progenitors had conquered?   *110*

Scene Four S. d. Rouen; *cf. n.*   5 timeless: *untimely*   7 miser: *wretch*   17 obstacle:
i.e., obstinate   18 collop: *slice*   23 noble: *coin* (worth 6 s. 8 d.)   49 misconceived:
deluded ones

61 warranteth: *offers security*   74 that notorious Machiavel; *cf. n.*   87 reflex: *cast*

O! Warwick, Warwick! I foresee with grief
The utter loss of all the realm of France.
 War. Be patient, York: if we conclude a peace,
It shall be with such strict and severe covenants
As little shall the Frenchmen gain thereby.   *115*

  Enter Charles, Alençon, Bastard, Reignier [and Others].

 Char. Since, lords of England, it is thus agreed,
That peaceful truce shall be proclaim'd in France,
We come to be informed by yourselves
What the conditions of that league must be.
 York. Speak, Winchester; for boiling choler chokes *120*
The hollow passage of my poison'd voice,
By sight of these our baleful enemies.
 Car. Charles, and the rest, it is enacted thus:
That, in regard King Henry gives consent,
Of mere compassion and of lenity,   *125*
To ease your country of distressful war,
And suffer you to breathe in fruitful peace,
You shall become true liegemen to his crown:
And, Charles, upon condition thou wilt swear
To pay him tribute, and submit thyself,   *130*
Thou shalt be plac'd as viceroy under him,
And still enjoy thy regal dignity.
 Alen. Must he be, then, as shadow of himself?
Adorn his temples with a coronet,
And yet, in substance and authority,   *135*
Retain but privilege of a private man?
This proffer is absurd and reasonless.
 Char. 'Tis known already that I am possess'd
With more than half the Gallian territories,
And therein reverenc'd for their lawful king: *140*
Shall I, for lucre of the rest unvanquish'd,
Detract so much from that prerogative
As to be call'd but viceroy of the whole?
No, lord ambassador; I'll rather keep
That which I have than, coveting for more, *145*
Be cast from possibility of all.
 York. Insulting Charles! hast thou by secret means
Us'd intercession to obtain a league,
And now the matter grows to compromise,
Stand'st thou aloof upon comparison? *150*
Either accept the title thou usurp'st,
Of benefit proceeding from our king
And not of any challenge of desert,
Or we will plague thee with incessant wars.
 Reig. My lord, you do not well in obstinacy *155*
To cavil in the course of this contract:
If once it be neglected, ten to one,
We shall not find like opportunity.
 Alen. [Aside to Charles.] To say the truth, it is your policy
To save your subjects from such massacre *160*
And ruthless slaughters as are daily seen
By our proceeding in hostility;
And therefore take this compact of a truce,
Although you break it when your pleasure serves.
 War. How sayst thou, Charles? shall our condition stand? *165*
 Char. It shall;

Only reserv'd, you claim no interest
In any of our towns of garrison.
 York. Then swear allegiance to his majesty;
As thou art knight, never to disobey   *170*
Nor be rebellious to the crown of England,
Thou, nor thy nobles, to the crown of England.
   [Charles, &c., give tokens of fealty.]
So, now dismiss your army when ye please;
Hang up your ensigns, let your drums be still,
For here we entertain a solemn peace. *Exeunt.* *175*

❧ Scene Fifth ❧

[London. A Room in the Palace]
Enter Suffolk in conference with the King, Gloucester, and Exeter.

 King. Your wondrous rare description, noble earl,
Of beauteous Margaret hath astonish'd me:
Her virtues, graced with external gifts
Do breed love's settled passions in my heart:
And like as rigour of tempestuous gusts *5*
Provokes the mightiest hulk against the tide,
So am I driven by breath of her renown
Either to suffer shipwrack, or arrive
Where I may have fruition of her love.
 Suf. Tush! my good lord, this superficial tale *10*
Is but a preface of her worthy praise:
The chief perfections of that lovely dame—
Had I sufficient skill to utter them—
Would make a volume of enticing lines,
Able to ravish any dull conceit: *15*
And, which is more, she is not so divine,
So full replete with choice of all delights,
But with as humble lowliness of mind
She is content to be at your command:
Command, I mean, of virtuous chaste intents, *20*
To love and honour Henry as her lord.
 King. And otherwise will Henry ne'er presume.
Therefore, my Lord Protector, give consent
That Margaret may be England's royal queen.
 Glo. So should I give consent to flatter sin. *25*
You know, my lord, your highness is betroth'd
Unto another lady of esteem;
How shall we then dispense with that contract,
And not deface your honour with reproach?
 Suf. As doth a ruler with unlawful oaths; *30*
Or one that, at a triumph having vow'd
To try his strength, forsaketh yet the lists
By reason of his adversary's odds.
A poor earl's daughter is unequal odds,
And therefore may be broke without offence. *35*
 Glo. Why, what, I pray, is Margaret more than that?
Her father is no better than an earl,
Although in glorious titles he excel.
 Suf. Yes, my lord, her father is a king,
The King of Naples and Jerusalem; *40*
And of such great authority in France
As his alliance will confirm our peace,

---

121 poison'd; *cf. n.* **141** lucre: *desire of gain* **149** grows to: *approaches* **150** comparison: *quibbling rhetoric* **152 Of benefit:** *by way of bounty*

15 conceit: *imagination* **31** triumph: *tournament*

And keep the Frenchmen in allegiance.

  Glo. And so the Earl of Armagnac may do,
Because he is near kinsman unto Charles.   *45*

  Exe. Beside, his wealth doth warrant a liberal dower,
Where Reignier sooner will receive than give.

  Suf. A dower, my lords! disgrace not so your king,
That he should be so abject, base, and poor,
To choose for wealth and not for perfect love.   *50*
Henry is able to enrich his queen,
And not to seek a queen to make him rich:
So worthless peasants bargain for their wives,
As market-men for oxen, sheep, or horse.
Marriage is a matter of more worth   *55*
Than to be dealt in by attorneyship:
Not whom we will, but whom his Grace affects,
Must be companion of his nuptial bed;
And therefore, lords, since he affects her most
It most of all these reasons bindeth us,   *60*
In our opinions she should be preferr'd.
For what is wedlock forced, but a hell,
An age of discord and continual strife?
Whereas the contrary bringeth bliss,
And is a pattern of celestial peace.   *65*
Whom should we match with Henry, being a king,
But Margaret, that is daughter to a king?
Her peerless feature, joined with her birth,
Approves her fit for none but for a king:
Her valiant courage and undaunted spirit—   *70*
More than in women commonly is seen—
Will answer our hope in issue of a king;
For Henry, son unto a conqueror,
Is likely to beget more conquerors,
If with a lady of so high resolve   *75*
As is fair Margaret he be link'd in love.
Then yield, my lords; and here conclude with me
That Margaret shall be queen, and none but she.

  King. Whether it be through force of your report,
My noble lord of Suffolk, or for that   *80*
My tender youth was never yet attaint
With any passion of inflaming love,
I cannot tell; but this I am assur'd,
I feel such sharp dissension in my breast,
Such fierce alarums both of hope and fear,   *85*
As I am sick with working of my thoughts.
Take, therefore, shipping; post, my lord, to France;
Agree to any covenants, and procure
That Lady Margaret do vouchsafe to come
To cross the seas to England and be crown'd   *90*
King Henry's faithful and anointed queen:
For your expenses and sufficient charge,
Among the people gather up a tenth.
Be gone, I say; for till you do return
I rest perplexed with a thousand cares.   *95*
And you, good uncle, banish all offence:
If you do censure me by what you were,
Not what you are, I know it will excuse
This sudden execution of my will.
And so, conduct me, where from company   *100*
I may revolve and ruminate my grief.   *Exit.*

  Glo. Ay, grief, I fear me, both at first and last.
                Exit Gloucester [with Exeter].

  Suf. Thus Suffolk hath prevail'd; and thus he goes,
As did the youthful Paris once to Greece;
With hope to find the like event in love,   *105*
But prosper better than the Trojan did.
Margaret shall now be queen, and rule the king;
But I will rule both her, the king, and realm.   *Exit.*

❧ FINIS ❧

---

56 by attorneyship: *by the shrewd calculation of third parties*   **68 feature:** *form of body*

92 charge: *money to spend*   **93 gather up a tenth;** *cf. n.*   **100 from company:** *unaccom-panied*   **105 event:** *outcome*

The First Part of Henry the Sixth. The numeral is invariably spelled 'Sixt' in the old editions, the new form of the word being very rare in Shakespeare's time. So 'fift' for 'fifth,' as for instance in the opening stage direction and in line 6 below.

I.i.1. *Hung be the heavens with black.* This meteorological reference receives added point from the Elizabethan practice of draping the stage in black when a tragedy was to be acted. Cf., for example, lines 74, 75 of the Induction to *A Warning for Fair Women* (perhaps by Thomas Heywood), printed in 1599:

> *'The stage is hung with black, and I perceive*
> *The auditors prepar'd for Tragedy.'*

The play cited was acted by Shakespeare's company.

I.i.50. *marish.* Pope's emendation for the *Nourish* (i.e., nurse?) of the Folios, which many modern editors retain.

I.i.60, 61. These lines illustrate the freedom with which the play everywhere alters historic fact. Two of the places named, Orleans and Poitiers, were not in English possession. The others were not lost till periods varying from seven to nearly thirty years after the date represented in the scene. Possibly we should understand that the first Messenger is reporting exaggerated rumors. His statement in regard to Orleans is contradicted by what the third Messenger says in line 157 (cf. also line 111).

I.i.92. Another anachronism. The crowning of Charles VII at Rheims, the culmination of Joan of Arc's triumphs, actually occurred seven years later (July 12, 1429). Charles had, however, been crowned at Poitiers in 1422. The Bastard of Orleans, mentioned in the next line, was Jean, Count Dunois (1402-1468), illegitimate son of the Duke of Orleans and first cousin of Charles VII. He was one of the finest soldiers of his age, and is introduced in a conspicuous rôle in Schiller's play, *Die Jungfrau von Orleans,* as well as in Voltaire's earlier mock-heroic, *La Pucelle d'Orléans.*

I.i.110, 111. *The tenth of August last . . . the siege of Orleans.* These lines and those which follow describe the Battle of Patay (June 18, 1429), of which another account is introduced in IV.i.19-26. The general issue of the battle is correctly given and it is rightly said to have followed the British retirement from the siege of Orleans (May 8, 1429); but the allusion to Patay in the present lines is out of place, since the raising of the siege of Orleans is portrayed in a later part of the play (I.v and vi).

I.i.116. *wanted pikes to set before his archers.* The military tactics of the day directed that the archers, often stationed on the flanks of the army, should be protected from charges of cavalry by rows of pikes fixed in the ground, points outward. Holinshed's statement is that the English set their pikes (stakes) before the archers in the usual way, but had no time afterwards to arrange their line of battle.

I.i.124. *flew.* The Folios have the easy misprint 'slew' (with long s), which a very few editors are quixotic enough to champion.

I.i.131. *Sir John Fastolfe.* This episode of Fastolfe's cowardice is four times employed in the play. Cf. I.iv.35-37; III.ii.107-113; IV.i.9-47. Modern historians represent Fastolfe as a general of distinction and of unblemished valor, but the chroniclers of Shakespeare's day accepted the libel incorporated in the play. The chief interest of the figure here is his connection with the great Falstaff of the Henry IV plays. It is to be noted that the early editions of the present play invariably call Fastolfe Sir John Falstaffe, a fact which suggests that, in the minds of the editors of the First Folio, at least, the two were identified. J. B. Henneman (*Publ. Mod. Lang. Assoc.,* xv, 1900) gives a number of reasons for assuming that when Shakespeare chose the name Falstaff for the fat knight of *Henry IV* and *The Merry Wives of Windsor* (originally called Sir John Oldcastle), he was actuated by reminiscence of Fastolfe in the present play. L. W. V. Harcourt identifies Falstaff with another Sir John Fastolf.

I.i.132. *in the vaward,—plac'd behind.* Almost a contradiction in terms, which editors have sought to harmonize by emendation ('rearward' for *vaward*) or by casuistry. The most reasonable interpretation is perhaps that of H. C. Hart: 'Fastolfe was in support (placed behind) of the vanguard, which was probably led by Talbot himself.'

I.i.148. *His ransom there is none but I shall pay.* An ambiguous line which may be paraphrased in two ways: (1) 'I will pay any ransom that may be named'; (2) 'I alone will pay his ransom,' i.e., leave it to me.

I.i.154. *Saint George's feast.* Properly, April 23 (the day of Shakespeare's death and traditionally his birthday). Bonfires in honor of St. George, however, would be appropriate on any day of English victory.

I.i.162. *your oaths to Henry sworn.* Holinshed relates how Henry V on his deathbed admonished the Dukes of Bedford and Gloucester and the Earls of Salisbury and Warwick never to make a treaty with the Dauphin by which any part of France might be relinquished, and how he commanded Bedford as Regent of France 'with fire and sword to persecute the Dolphin, till he had either brought him to reason and obeisance, or else to driue and expell him out of the realme of France.' He adds: 'The noble men present promised to obserue his precepts, and to performe his desires.'

I.i.170. *Eltham.* A village nine miles southeast of London, on the road to Dartford and Canterbury. The Palace, of which picturesque remains still exist, was a favorite residence of the English sovereigns from the thirteenth to the middle of the sixteenth century. In line 176, *steal* is a modern emendation (by Mason) for 'send' of the Folios. Though not inevitable, the change is supported by the rime, frequent at the close of scenes, and it has been adopted in most recent texts. On the other hand, support for the Folio reading may perhaps be found in the words of Holinshed, who refers to Winchester's alleged purpose 'to set hand on the kings person, and to haue remooued him from Eltham, the place that he was in, to Windsor.'

I.ii.1. *Mars his true moving.* The planet Mars has a very eccentric orbit, and his apparently irregular course puzzled astronomers till explained by Kepler in 1609. Editors have noted a strikingly similar allusion in Thomas Nashe's preface to *Have with you to Saffron Walden* (1596): 'you are as ignorant . . . as the Astronomers are in the true mouings of *Mars,* which to this day they could neuer attaine too.' (McKerrow's Nashe, iii.20.)

I.ii.56. *the nine sibyls of old Rome.* The Cumæan Sibyl offered King Tarquin nine books. The poet has transferred the number to the sibyls themselves, of whom various numbers (but not nine) are reckoned.

I.ii.106. *the sword of Deborah.* Cf. Judges, chapters 4 and 5.

I.ii.111. *Excellent Pucelle, if thy name be so.* Holinshed's Chronicle introduces Joan of Arc as 'Ione Are' or more fully, 'Ione de Are, Pusell de dieu.' The Folio text of the play usually refers to her simply as *Pucelle* (spelled 'Puzel' or 'Pucell'). The stage direction after line 64 of this scene calls her 'Ioane Puzel,' that after line 104 'Ioane de Puzel' (so also in I.vi.3 and V.iii.S. d.). In II.i and V.iv she appears as 'Ioane,' but is only twice called Joan of Arc ('Acre' or 'Aire' in the Folio; cf. II.ii.20 and V.i.49). Mr. Fleay attempted to find in these differences of name a clue to the play's authorship.

I.ii.132. *Saint Martin's summer.* Summer in the midst of autumn. The reference is to the unseasonably warm weather often occurring about St. Martin's Day (November 11).

I.ii.139, 140. The allusion is to a common but probably unhistoric story recorded in Plutarch's Life of Cæsar. During the war with Pompey, when the latter's navy commanded the sea, Cæsar embarked on a small pinnace incognito 'as if he had bene some poore man of meane condition,' with the idea of crossing to his army at Brundisium. A storm arose and the commander of the vessel ordered his men to put back. 'Cæsar, hearing that, straight discouered himselfe vnto the Maister of the pynnasse, who at the first was amazed when he saw him: but Cæsar then taking him by the hand sayd vnto him, Good fellow, be of good cheare, and forwards hardily, feare not, for thou hast Cæsar & his fortune with thee.' (North's translation, 1579.) Peele mentions the episode in a similar manner in his *Farewell* to Norris and Drake (1589):

> *'and let me say*
> *To you, my mates, as Cæsar said to his,*
> *Striving with Neptune's hills; you bear, quoth he,*
> *Cæsar, and Cæsar's fortune in your ships.'*

I.ii.141. *Was Mahomet inspired with a dove?* This alludes to a trick ascribed to Mahomet by several Elizabethan writers. Thomas Nashe has two references to it, and Nashe's most recent editor quotes the following from an earlier work, *Strange Things out of Seb. Munster* (1574): 'For he [Mahomet] accustomed and taught a Doue to be fedde and fetch meate [i.e., food] at his eares, the which Doue his moste subtile and craftye maister called the holy Ghoste. He preached openly, and made his bragges like a most lying villen that this Doue did shew vnto him the most secrete counsel of God, as often as the simple fowle did flye vnto his eares for nourishment.' (McKerrow's Nashe, iv.200.)

I.ii.143. *Helen, the mother of great Constantine.* The reputed discoverer of the True Cross. Two frescoes representing this legend adorned the Guild Chapel at Stratford in Shakespeare's time. See reproductions in Ward, *Shakespeare's Town and Times,* p. 33.

I.ii.144. *Saint Philip's daughters.* Referred to in Acts 21. 9 as 'virgins, which did prophesy.'

I.iii.23. *The Cardinal of Winchester.* Editors have pointed out that the mention of Winchester's cardinalate in this scene is inconsistent with the fact that he is represented as only just made cardinal in V.i.30 ff. and is called bishop in III.i.56 and IV.i.1. Winchester became cardinal in 1427, but the chroniclers report that there had been much previous talk of his probable elevation.

I.iii.25. *Woodvile.* Holinshed records that when Gloucester wished to enter the Tower, 'Richard Wooduile esquier (hauing at that time the charge of the keeping of the Tower) refused his desire; and kept the same Tower against him vndulie and against reason, by the commandement of my said lord of Winchester.' Woodvile became a person of great consequence upon the marriage, nearly forty years later, of his daughter to Edward IV, and in 1466 was created Earl Rivers.

I.iii.37. *Thou that contriv'dst to murder our dead lord.* The fourth of five charges brought against Winchester by Gloucester (in 1426) relates to the former's alleged complicity in an attempt to murder the Prince of Wales, later Henry V. The same scandal has been more obscurely insinuated by Gloucester in I.i.33, 34.

I.iii.38. The disorderly houses on the Southwark bank of the Thames were under the control of the Bishop of Winchester and paid him a revenue. The proximity of these houses to the Rose Theatre, where this play appears to have been first acted (and to the later Globe), doubtless gave point to the allusion.

I.iii.42. *This be Damascus, be thou cursed Cain.* Several popular mediæval works (Mandeville's *Travels,* Higden's *Polychronicon*) gave currency to the belief that Abel was slain on the site of Damascus.

I.iv.23-56. This passage involves several anachronisms. Salisbury's mortal wound was received at Orleans in October, 1428. Talbot was captured at Patay in June, 1429, and was not released by exchange with Santrailles till 1433.

I.iv.95. *Plantagenet.* Montacute, not Plantagenet, was Salisbury's name. Furthermore, the appellation Plantagenet was not adopted by the English royal family till after Salisbury's death. It first appears in public records in 1460, being revived by one of the characters in this play, Richard Duke of York, as a means of expressing superiority of descent over the Lancastrian line (cf. D. N. B. s. v. Plantagenet).

I.iv.95. *like thee.* The reading of the First Folio, meaning 'I will be as unconcernedly remorseless as you have been.' The next line carries with it a subordinate reminiscence of the well-known story of Nero, which led the later Folios to alter *like thee* to 'Nero-like will.' Malone then blended the two readings into the vapid 'like thee, Nero,' a perversion which nearly all modern editors have unfortunately accepted.

I.iv.107. *dolphin or dogfish.* Dogfish, a small shark, was commonly used as an opprobrious epithet. Dolphin is the invariable form of the French title Dauphin in the early editions of the play. Modern editors substitute the present spelling in all cases except this, where the pun requires retention of the older form. It should be remarked that the Dauphin of the play was from the legitimist French point of view King of France (Charles VII) through the entire course of the action, since the death of his father, Charles VI, occurred only two months after that of Henry V. The English, however, ignored Charles VII's pretensions to the throne and continued to employ his old title.

I.v.6. *Blood will I draw on thee, thou art a witch.* Johnson asserted the existence of a superstition that 'he that could draw the witch's blood was free from her power'; but no confirmation of this has apparently been found in Elizabethan literature.

I.v.S. d. Joan here goes from the lower to the upper stage of the Elizabethan theatre, lines 15-18 being spoken from the upper or balcony stage.

I.v.21. *like Hannibal.* The allusion is perhaps to the stratagem recorded by Livy (bk. xxii. c. 16, 17); Hannibal extricated his forces from an unfavorable position by driving against Fabius's army during the night two thousand oxen with blazing fagots tied to their horns.

I.v.28. *tear the lions out of England's coat.* The armorial dress of the kings of England was embroidered with three lions (or leopards).

I.vi.4. *Astræa's daughter.* That is, daughter of Justice, in allusion to the myth that Astræa forsook the world when it became corrupt, and carried her divine scales to the constellation of Libra. Spenser develops the legend elaborately at the opening of the fifth book of the *Fairy Queen;* and Peele's *Descensus Astrææ* turns it into a pageant in honor of the installation of a new lord mayor of London in 1591.

I.vi.6. *Adonis' gardens.* What these were in classic literature has been acrimoniously disputed, but a beautiful and extended description, which perhaps inspired the present line, is given by Spenser, *Fairy Queen,* bk. iii. canto vi.

I.vi.22. *Rhodope's of Memphis.* One of the most beautiful pyramids was said to have been built by Rhodope, a Greek courtesan who married the king of Memphis. The reading in the text is a conjecture of Capell for 'Rhodophes or Memphis' of the Folios.

I.vi.25. *the rich-jewell'd coffer of Darius.* Alexander the Great is said to have kept Homer's poems under his pillow at night and during the day to have carried them 'in the rich iewel cofer of Darius, lately before vanquished by him in battaile.' (Puttenham, *Art of English Poesie,* 1589.)

II.i.S. d. *dead march.* The dead march is in honor of Salisbury, whose body is carried with the army. Cf. line 4 of the next scene. (Hart.)

II.i.9. *redoubted Burgundy.* Philip the Good, Duke of Burgundy, had been alienated from the Dauphin by the treacherous murder of his father in 1419. He was the ally of the English from the time of the treaty of Troyes (1420) till 1435. He was the second cousin of Charles VII and father of the famous Charles the Bold.

II.i.S. d. *The French leap o'er the walls in their shirts.* This entire episode, which the dramatist has transferred to Orleans, is based upon an incident that really occurred in May, 1428 (a year before the relief of Orleans), at Le Mans in the adjacent province of Maine. Holinshed, following earlier chroniclers, records that the Frenchmen, surprised by an early morning counter-attack, 'got vp in their shirts, and lept ouer the walles.'

II.iii.6. *As Scythian Tomyris by Cyrus' death.* The story of Herodotus is that Tomyris, Queen of the Massagetæ, led her troops to battle after her husband's death, slew Cyrus the Great (B. C. 529), and in scorn of his bloodthirstiness dropped his severed head into a wine skin filled with blood. Compare the countess's address to Talbot in line 36.

II.iii.23. *this is a child, a silly dwarf.* The countess exaggerates greatly. Talbot was eighty years of age when he fell in battle, and the examination of his bones, when they were exhumed in 1874, showed that he could not have been undersized. 'The bones generally were remarkably well developed, and had evidently belonged to a muscular man.'

II.iv.6. *Or else was wrangling Somerset in th' error?* Capell changed *error* to 'right' and Rolfe, retaining the old text, wished to interpret *else* as 'in other words.' Neither, probably, is justified. Richard's apparent alternatives amount to the same thing. From craft or from impetuosity he leaves the hearers to whom he appeals but one answer. It is 'heads, I win; tails, Somerset loses.'

II.iv.7. *Faith, I have been a truant in the law.* Shakespeare brilliantly imagines the quarrel of the roses to have started among a group of young aristocrats, studying law in the Temple.

II.iv.83. *the yeoman.* Somerset's slur is explained in his next speech. The execution of Plantagenet's father for treason (as recorded in the play of *Henry V*) deprived his heir of all titles of nobility. Lionel of Clarence, third son of Edward III, was not the grandfather, as Warwick states in line 85, but the great-great-grandfather of Plantagenet. See the genealogical table on next page.

II.iv.98. *attached, not attainted.* Literally, arrested, but not formally condemned, as by bill of attainder, to the legal consequences of treason. It is evident that the speaker is splitting hairs, but it does appear that Richard was permitted to succeed to his inheritances without the formal restoration to his blood which the play represents (III.i.167 ff.). See D. N. B.

II.v.6. *Nestor-like aged, in an age of care.* That is, trebly aged by care. 'The care that has afflicted my life has made me as old as Nestor' (who lived through three mortal lifetimes).

II.v.7. *Edmund Mortimer.* The poet adopts without essential alteration the statement of the chroniclers. Holinshed says: 'Edmund Mortimer, the last earle of March of that name (which long time had beene restreined from his libertie . . .) deceassed without issue; whose inheritance descended to the lord Richard Plantagenet.' Modern commentators point out that the chronicles, and with them Shakespeare, are wrong, since this Mortimer died in freedom in 1424. Apparently, they confused Edmund Mortimer, Earl of March, with his cousin, Sir John Mortimer, who after long captivity was executed in the same year (1424). It is evident, moreover, from the use of the word 'mother' rather than 'grandmother' in line 74, that Shakespeare further confuses Edmund Mortimer, Earl of March, with an older Edmund Mortimer, his uncle, just as he does in the first part of *Henry IV.* (See note on I.iii.147, 148 of that play in the present edition.)

II.v.96. *the rest I wish thee gather.* Probably *gather* is used in the well-authenticated Shakespearean sense of 'infer,' and Mortimer desires cautiously to remind his nephew of the full significance of his heirship; namely, the claim to the crown that it carries with it.

THE FOLLOWING TABLE ILLUSTRATES THE RELATIONSHIPS OF THE VARIOUS MEMBERS OF THE ENGLISH ROYAL FAMILY:

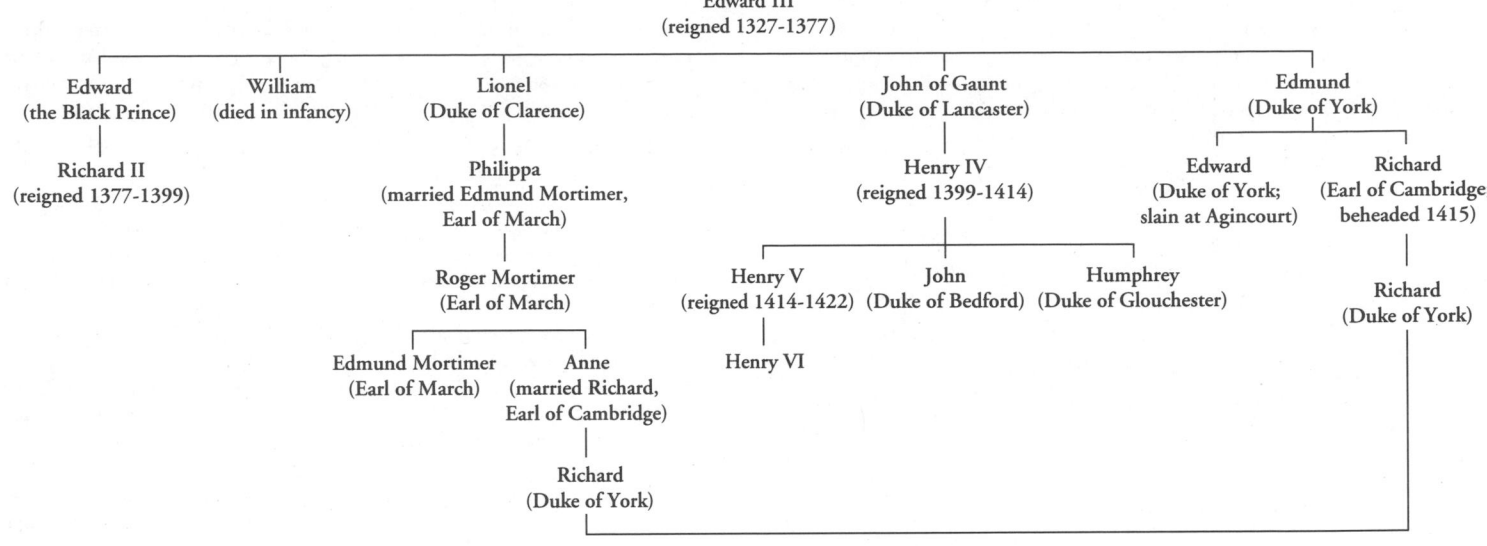

Somerset (John, 1st Duke of Somerset, 1403-1444) was the grandson of John of Gaunt, his father and the
Bishop of Winchester (cf. III. i. 43) being both illegitimate sons of that prince.

II.v.129. 'Or make my injuries an instrument for attaining my ambition.'
The Folios read 'will' instead of *ill,* the latter being one of Theobald's convincing
emendations.

III.i. The historical place of this scene was Leicester, where Parliament met in
1426 (three years before the relief of Orleans depicted in Act I). Line 83 shows,
however, that the dramatist thought of the events as occurring in London. King
Henry, who plays a precocious part in the scene, was actually in his fifth year.

III.i.22, 23. Gloucester's third charge against Winchester, as reported by the
chroniclers, was that he had put men at arms and archers in ambush at the
Southwark end of London Bridge, with intent to slay the Protector if he attempted to pass that way to the young king at Eltham. The reference to the trap
laid at the Tower alludes of course to the incident dramatized in I.iii.

III.i.53, 54. *Rome . . . Roam.* The words were not identical in sound. Elsewhere in Shakespeare *Rome* rimes with 'doom,' 'groom,' 'room,'—words which
have not essentially changed their pronunciation, while *roam* has presumably the
vowel sound in modern 'broad.' Probably the pun in the present line was consciously inexact. Otherwise one might argue that Shakespeare was not its author.

III.i.66. *enter talk.* On the precedent of the participle *entertalking* in Golding's
translation of Ovid (1565-67), Hart changed this phrase to a single word: *en-
tertalk.* The New English Dictionary does not recognize the word.

III.i.84-91. This reference to the use of pebble stones, when weapons were
forbidden the adherents of the contending noblemen, appears to show that the
author of the scene had recourse to the ancient chronicler Fabyan. The episode
is not mentioned by Holinshed.

III.i.172-174. Richard Plantagenet inherited the earldom of Cambridge from his
father and the dukedom of York from his father's elder brother, who had died (at
Agincourt; cf. *Henry V,* IV.vi.) without issue. To these great estates were added by
inheritance from his mother's side the titles of the Mortimers, Earls of March.

III.i.187, 188. King Henry's voyage to France occurred at the close of 1431,
five years after the Parliament of Leicester which furnished the material for the
opening portion of this scene.

III.i.S. d. *Sennet.* A sennet was a trumpet signal to mark the approach or
departure of a procession.

III.i.203. *that fatal prophecy.* The prophecy was very well known in Shakespeare's time—more so, doubtless, than in Henry V's. Holinshed thus reports it:
'The king, being certified [of the birth of his son at Windsor] gaue God thanks
. . . But, when he heard reported the place of his natiuitie, were it that he [had
been] warned by some prophesie, or had some foreknowledge, or else iudged
himselfe of his sonnes fortune, he said vnto the lord Fitz Hugh, his trustie
chamberleine, these words: "My lord, I Henrie, borne at Monmouth, shall small
time reigne, & much get; and Henrie, borne at Windsore, shall long reigne, and
all loose: but as God will, so be it." '

III.ii.S. d. The story of the capture of Rouen is apocryphal. This city

remained in the hands of the English till 1449, eighteen years after Joan of Arc
had been burned there. The particular stratagem here related may have been
suggested by two different anecdotes found in the chroniclers, one referring to
the capture of the castle of Cornill (Corville?) by the English, the other to the
capture of Le Mans by the French.

III.ii.24. *Where.* This is Rowe's emendation, adopted regularly by subsequent
editors. The Folios read *Here,* which may well be defended: Joan's signal is not
to distinguish the safest passageway, but to indicate the practicability of that by
which she entered.

III.ii.30. *Talbonites.* A derivative formed from a Latinized version of Talbot's
name: Talbo, Talbonis (though Talbottus is the form used by Camden). Modern
editors seem all to accept Theobald's cacophonous emendation, 'Talbotites,' N. E. D.
recognizes neither word.

III.ii.43. *the pride of France.* Compare *the pride of Gallia* (IV.vi.15). These
sonorous phrases mean hardly more than 'the French.' They are echoes of Marlowe, who had rung the changes upon 'the pride of Asia,' 'the pride of Græcia.'

III.ii.S. d. *Alençon.* The Folios make Reignier enter here, not Alençon, and
for the speaker's name in lines 25 and 35 above they have 'Reig.,' not 'Alen.'
This, probably, is only a careless slip. It is not at all likely that Alençon and
Reignier were both on the walls (upper stage) in addition to Charles, Joan, and
the Bastard; and the three cases just noted are the only mentions of Reignier in
this scene or the next.

III.ii.53. *good grey-beard.* John, Duke of Bedford, third son of Henry IV,
was only about forty-five years of age when he died in 1435. Here his death is
antedated, being thrown back into the lifetime of Joan, whom he actually survived
by four years, and his age is greatly exaggerated. Bedford is called by Hume 'the
most accomplished prince of his age, a skilful politician, as well as a good general.'
Shakespeare, in the second part of *Henry IV,* paints an unfavorable portrait of
him in his youth, as Prince John of Lancaster.

III.ii.84. *And as his father here was conqueror.* Henry V captured Rouen in 1518,
after a long siege. Shakespeare's play of *Henry V* does not allude to this conquest.

III.ii.85, 86. Holinshed tells how Richard I 'willed his heart to be conueied
vnto Rouen, and there buried; in testimonie of the loue which he had euer borne
vnto that citie for the stedfast faith and tried loialtie at all times found in the
citizens there.'

III.ii.98, 99. This story is told of Uther Pendragon (King Arthur's father)
by Geoffrey of Monmouth, followed by Malory (I.iv) and by Harding. Holinshed's later compilation refers the exploit to Pendragon's brother. Marlowe's
Tamburlaine similarly puts his foes to flight when afflicted with mortal sickness.

III.iii.19, 20. Burgundy's actual abandonment of the English for the French
occurred several years after Joan's death. Knight, however, called attention to a letter
(which the authors of the play can hardly have known), written by Joan to Burgundy
on the very day of Charles VII's coronation at Rheims (July 17, 1429). In this she
makes use of much the same arguments as in the scene before us.

III.iii.70-74. The facts, as accurately stated by the chroniclers, are here greatly distorted. The Duke of Orleans, captured at Agincourt in 1415, was kept prisoner in England till 1440. His release thus took place five years after Burgundy's defection, and is stated to have been largely by reason of Burgundy's efforts.

III.iii.86. *Done like a Frenchman,* etc. The apparent inconsistency of this line in Joan's mouth has been much discussed. It is not in character, but is a clear appeal from the original author of the play to the prejudice of his audience. Hart thinks that Joan, as an inhabitant of Lorraine, 'would not hesitate to speak thus of the French people.' But if Lorraine was not strictly French, neither was Burgundy. Warburton suggested that the line was 'an offering of the poet to his royal mistress's resentment for Henry the Fourth's last great turn in religion, in the year 1593,' i.e., his renunciation of Protestantism.

III.iv.18. *I do remember how my father said.* Malone acutely cited this line in defence of his contention that this play is not by Shakespeare or by the author of the early versions of *2* and *3 Henry VI*. The author of the present play, he argued, did not know that Henry VI was a nine-months' infant when his father died. Shakespeare did know this (cf. Epilogue to *Henry V*), and so did the author of the *True Tragedy* (*3 Henry VI*), neither of whom could therefore have written Part I. On the other hand, it might be explained that we have here one of Shakespeare's purposeful tamperings with dramatic time. There is an advantage in making the King appear older than he really was without reminding the reader that the whole long time from infancy to maturity has elapsed since the play began (with the funeral of Henry V).

III.iv.26. *We here create you Earl of Shrewsbury.* Talbot was thus ennobled in 1442, eleven years after the coronation of Henry, to which the king invites him in the next line.

III.iv.38, 39. 'By the ancient common law ... striking in the king's court of justice, or drawing a sword therein, was a capital felony.' (Blackstone.)

IV.i. Henneman notes the 'curious relation' which this scene bears to the previous one (III.iv). 'Both have the King in Paris; both have identically the same actors; both have the same two situations, viz., Talbot's interview with the King, and the quarrel of Vernon and Basset, the followers respectively of York and Somerset. But the second scene is developed far beyond the former, and the spirit of the two is equally different. One is condensed and compressed; the other elaborated and heightened by fresh details.' Annotators have observed that when Henry VI was crowned at Paris (1431), Talbot was still a prisoner to the French, Exeter was dead, and Gloucester in England serving as the King's lieutenant.

IV.i.19. *Patay.* The Folios erroneously print 'Poictiers,' doubtless from confusion in the compositor's mind with the Black Prince's great victory at Poitiers seventy-three years before (1356). For the battle of Patay, cf. note on I.i.110, 111.

IV.i.S. d. *Flourish.* Modern editors place this 'Flourish' in the stage direction following line 174, after the exit of the king. It probably belongs there.

IV.ii. A lapse of twenty-two years, from Henry's coronation (1431) to Talbot's last campaign (1453), is covered rather skilfully by the concluding portion of the previous scene.

IV.ii.10, 11. *my three attendants, Lean famine, quartering steel, and climbing fire.* These words furnish a significant parallel to those in the Prologue preceding Act I of *Henry V,* lines 6-8:

> 'and at his heels,
> *Leash'd in like hounds, should famine, sword, and fire*
> *Crouch for employment.'*

The figures are not identical, but each bears the Shakespearean stamp, and both (more particularly that in the present play) are reminiscent of a speech which the chroniclers report Henry V to have made to the besieged citizens of Rouen.

IV.iii.47. *vulture of sedition.* A figurative allusion to the vulture which fed in the bosom of the bound Prometheus.

IV.iii.50. *scarce cold conqueror.* Henry V had been dead thirty-one years when Talbot fell, but the hyperbole is dramatically effective and tends in a very Shakespearean way to give cohesion and the sense of rapid movement.

IV.iv. Modern editors designate this scene as occurring on 'Other Plains in Gascony,' but it is evident that there is no change of place, since Lucy continues upon the stage. (The later Folios inserted an 'Exit' after the last line of scene iii, but there is none in the original text.)

IV.iv.13. *Whither, my lord?* Lucy impatiently echoes the question, which he scorns to answer. His concern is with the person from whom, not the one to whom, he is sent.

IV.vi.44. *On that advantage.* Perhaps this can be construed in the sense of 'for the sake of that advantage,' i.e., personal safety. In that case the phrase must be understood as modifying *fly* in line 46. This, however, is strained, and it may be better to interpret 'Fie on that advantage' and supply an exclamation point for the comma at the end of line 45.

IV.vii.63-71. *Great Earl of Washford,* etc. Great interest attaches to this list of Talbot's titles. No source for it has been discovered earlier than an epitaph of Talbot printed in 1599 (in Richard Crompton's *Mansion of Magnanimitie*), which runs thus: 'here lieth the right noble knight, Iohn Talbott, Earle of Shrewsbury, Washford, Waterford, and Valence, Lord Talbot of Goodrige, and Vrchengfield, Lord Strange of the blacke Meere, Lord Verdon of Alton, Lord Crumwell of Wingfield, Lord Louetoft of Worsop, Lord Furniuall of Sheffield, Lord Faulconbrige, knight of the most noble order of S. George, S. Michaell, and the Golden fleece, Great Marshall to king Henry the sixt of his realme of France ...' It will be seen that this agrees almost verbatim with the text of the play, the only alterations in the latter being the omission of one title and the addition of a few words for metrical purposes. The prose of the epitaph is therefore treated in the very manner in which in the Roman plays Shakespeare treated much of the prose of North's Plutarch, and the whole passage has a strong Shakespearean flavor. Are we, then, to infer that Shakespeare made his alteration of the play not earlier than 1599, at about the time when he was writing *Henry V?* See Introduction on The History of the Play.

IV.vii.89, 94. *'em.* The First Folio has 'him' in both cases, owing probably to misreading of 'hem' (i.e., *'em*) in the manuscript.

V.i.1, 2. Two events, separated by a considerable time, are here combined: the intervention of the Emperor Sigismund and the Pope in 1435 to secure peace in France, and the proposal to marry Henry to the daughter of the Count of Armagnac in 1442. Both these incidents long antedated Talbot's death.

V.iii.1. *The regent conquers.* Historically, Bedford was regent of France when Joan was captured in 1430, but York is of course intended both here and in IV.vi.2 (cf. IV.i.163, 164).

V.iii.6. *monarch of the north.* Evil spirits were identified with various quarters of the compass, particularly the east and the north.

V.iii.S. d. *Burgundy and York fight.* So the Folio editions. Modern editors make the fight take place between Joan and York, but without justification. Joan's power has now disappeared and her part is passive. Probably the *Exit* after line 29, though in the old texts, should be omitted, leaving Joan a spectator of the fight which follows.

V.iii.63. *Twinkling another counterfeited beam.* That is, each twinkling beam, reflected by the water, seems doubled.

V.iii.68. *is she not here?* This is the reading of the First Folio. The second, third, and fourth, apparently troubled by the fact that the line has but four feet, added 'thy prisoner' after *here,* and they have been followed by most modern editors, though the words supplied are quite otiose.

V.iii.75. *[Aside].* This stage direction, here and in the following lines, is added by modern editors. It will be observed that the speeches so marked are only partially inaudible.

V.iii.78, 79. A quasi-proverbial saying, found in *Titus Andronicus* (II.i.86, 87) and elsewhere.

V.iv.S. d. *Rouen.* Modern editors place this scene at the 'Camp of the Duke of York, in Anjou,' to connect it with the previous scene which they put 'Before Angiers.' Really there are here two scenes, which, save for the authority of convention, ought to be separated. The first, dealing with the death of Joan in 1431, must be localized at Rouen. The second, beginning at line 94, dramatizes the peace negotiations which took place at Arras in 1435. With the meeting between Joan and her father should be contrasted the different treatment of the same theme in Act IV, scene xi, of Schiller's play. (Schiller, for dramatic effect, places the father's denunciation at Rheims immediately after the coronation of Charles VII.)

V.iv.74. *Alençon! that notorious Machiavel.* The reference to Machiavelli (1469-1527) is an anachronism in York's mouth, but no modern figure was more familiarly talked of by the Elizabethans. By them he was regarded as the symbol of heartless ambition. It is very likely that in coupling Alençon with Machiavel the author intended a by-reference to the notorious Duke of Alençon who came a wooing to Queen Elizabeth in 1579 and aroused the violent antipathy of her subjects.

V.iv.121. *poison'd.* This can perhaps be interpreted to mean that the throat poisoned by choler chokes the voice. Many editors, however, and with good reason, accept Theobald's emendation, 'prison'd.'

V.v.93. *Among the people gather up a tenth.* Levy a special tax of ten per cent on incomes. Suffolk's levy, however, is stated to have been a fifteenth, not a tenth, and in the first scene of the second part of the play we have the correct figure:

> 'That Suffolk should demand a whole fifteenth
> *For costs and charges in transporting her!'*
>   (*2 Henry VI,* I.i.132, 133.)

The Second Part of King Henry the Sixth

Edited by
Tucker Brooke

Dramatis Personae

KING HENRY THE SIXTH
DUKE OF GLOUCESTER, *Uncle to the King*
CARDINAL BEAUFORT, *Great-Uncle to the King*
DUKE OF YORK
EDWARD } *Sons of York*
RICHARD }
DUKE OF SOMERSET
DUKE OF BUCKINGHAM
MARQUESS OF SUFFOLK
EARL OF SALISBURY
EARL OF WARWICK, *Son of Salisbury*
LORD CLIFFORD
YOUNG CLIFFORD, *his Son*
LORD SCALES, *Governor of the Tower*
LORD SAY
SIR JOHN STANLEY
SIR HUMPHREY STAFFORD
WILLIAM STAFFORD, *his Brother*
VAUX, *a Gentleman of the Court*
MATTHEW GOFFE, *a Captain under Lord Scales*
ALEXANDER IDEN, *a Gentleman of Kent*
TWO GENTLEMEN, *Prisoners with Suffolk*
A LIEUTENANT OF A WARSHIP, MASTER,
    AND MASTER'S MATE
WALTER WHITMORE, *an Officer under the Lieutenant*

JACK CADE, *a Rebel Leader*
JOHN HUME }
JOHN SOUTHWELL } *Priests*
ROGER BOLINGBROKE, *a Scholar and Conjurer*
MAYOR OF SAINT ALBANS
CLERK OF CHATHAM
SIMPOX, AN IMPOSTOR
GEORGE BEVIS, JOHN HOLLAND, DICK THE BUTCHER, SMITH
    THE WEAVER, MICHAEL, AND OTHER FOLLOWERS OF CADE
THOMAS HORNER, *an Armourer*
PETER THUMP, *his Apprentice*
TWO MURDERERS
A SPIRIT RAISED BY BOLINGBROKE

MARGARET OF ANJOU, *Queen to King Henry*
ELEANOR, *Duchess of Gloucester*
MARGERY JORDAN, *a Witch*
SIMPCOX'S WIFE

LORDS, LADIES, AND ATTENDANTS; HERALD, PETITIONERS,
    ALDERMEN, A BEADLE, SHERIFF, AND OFFICERS; CITIZENS,
    APPRENTICES, FALCONERS, SOLDIERS, MESSENGERS, ETC.

SCENE—*London and its environs, Saint Albans, Bury St.
    Edmunds, Kenilworth Castle, and several parts of Kent.*

The Second Part of King Henry the Sixth

INTRODUCTION

SOURCES OF THE PLAY

The only real source of the Second Part of *King Henry VI* is the earlier play, *The First Part of the Contention betwixt the two famous Houses of York and Lancaster,* of which imperfect and slightly varying printed editions appeared in 1594, 1600, and 1619. The reviser, Shakespeare, worked with a manuscript text probably superior in a number of passages to that produced by the printers of 1594.

The First Part of the Contention is itself based upon the story of the chroniclers Halle and Holinshed, whose narratives are here so nearly identical that it is hardly important to determine which was employed by the original dramatist.[1] For the episode of Gloucester and the impostor Simpcox a dialogue of Sir Thomas More (1530) may have been used; the story was repeated by the chronicler Grafton (1568) and the martyrologist Foxe (1576), but is not found in Halle or Holinshed.

In revising the play Shakespeare's method was exceedingly painstaking. The 1594 version of the *Contention* contains only about 1250 metrical lines,[2] which in *2 Henry VI* are supplemented by some 2000 lines of new or largely revised material. But there seems to be no evidence that the reviser made use of new source matter. He merely elaborated out of his own fancy scenes and speeches with which the basic play presented him. He added no new character or important dramatic incident, and can hardly be shown to have made any first-hand study of the historical sources.

Thus the consideration of Shakespeare's additions does not really involve a study of the sources of the play (apart from the *Contention*); it involves almost solely the question of the spirit in which Shakespeare improvised new speeches to fit the scenario furnished by the old play.

The simpler and generally clearer tone of the *Contention* is well illustrated in the scenes depicting Suffolk's death and that of Cade. The 147 lines of *2 Henry VI* IV.i are expanded from the following 78 lines of the *Contention*.

'Alarmes within, and the chambers be discharged, like as it were a fight at sea. And then enter the Captaine of the ship and the Maister, and the Maisters Mate, & the Duke of Suffolke disguised, and others with him, and Water Whickmore.

Cap. Bring forward these prisoners that scorn'd to yeeld,
Vnlade their goods with speed and sincke their ship,
Here Maister, this prisoner I giue to you.
This other, the Maisters Mate shall haue,
And Water Whickmore thou shalt haue this man,
And let them paie their ransomes ere they passe.

Suffolke. Water!   He starteth.

Water. How now, what doest feare me?

---

1 Cf. W. G. Boswell-Stone, *Shakespeare's Holinshed*, pp. xi, xii, where passages apparently derived from Holinshed rather than Halle are cited. Compare, on the other hand, the note on II.iii.14 in this edition, which points to Halle rather than Holinshed as authority.

2 Eked out by about 700 lines of prose or corrupted verse.

Thou shalt haue better cause anon.

Suf. It is thy name affrights me, not thy selfe.
I do remember well, a cunning Wyssard told me,
That by Water I should die:
Yet let not that make thee bloudie minded.
Thy name being rightly sounded,
Is Gualter, not Water.

VVater. Gualter or Water, als one to me,
I am the man must bring thee to thy death.

Suf. I am a Gentleman looke on my Ring,
Ransome me at what thou wilt, it shalbe paid.

VVater. I lost mine eye in boording of the ship,
And therefore ere I marchantlike sell blood for gold,
Then cast me headlong downe into the sea.

2. Priso. But what shall our ransomes be?

Mai. A hundreth pounds a piece, either paie that or die.

2. Priso. Then saue our liues, it shall be paid.

VVater. Come sirrha, thy life shall be the ransome I will haue.

Suff. Staie villaine, thy prisoner is a Prince,
The Duke of Suffolke, William de la Poull.

Cap. The Duke of Suffolke folded vp in rags.

Suf. I sir, but these rags are no part of the Duke,
Ioue sometime went disguisde, and why not I?

Cap. I but Ioue was neuer slaine as thou shalt be.

Suf. Base Iadie groome, King Henries blood
The honourable blood of Lancaster,
Cannot be shead by such a lowly swaine,
I am sent Ambassador for the Queene to France,
I charge thee waffe me crosse the channell safe.

Cap. Ile waffe thee to thy death, go Water take him hence,
And on our long boates side, chop off his head.

Suf. Thou darste not for thine owne.

Cap. Yes Poull.

Suffolke. Poull.

Cap. I Poull, puddle, kennell, sinke and durt,
Ile stop that yawning mouth of thine,
Those lips of thine that so oft haue kist the
Queene, shall sweepe the ground, and thou that
Smildste at good Duke Humphreys death,
Shalt liue no longer to infect the earth.

Suffolke. This villain being but Captain of a Pinnais,
Threatens more plagues then mightie Abradas,
The great Masadonian Pyrate,
Thy words addes fury and not remorse in me.

Cap. I but my deeds shall staie thy fury soone.

Suffolke. Hast not thou waited at my Trencher,
When we haue feasted with Queene Margret?
Hast not thou kist thy hand and held my stirrope?
And barehead plodded by my footecloth Mule,

And thought thee happie when I smilde on thee?
This hand hath writ in thy defence,
Then shall I charme thee, hold thy lauish toong.

   Cap. Away with him, Water, I say, and off with his hed.

   1. Priso. Good my Lord, intreat him mildly for your life.

   Suffolke. First let this necke stoupe to the axes edge,
Before this knee do bow to any,
Saue to the God of heauen and to my King:
Suffolkes imperiall toong cannot pleade
To such a Iadie groome.

   Water. Come, come, why do we let him speake,
I long to haue his head for raunsome of mine eye.

   Suffolk. A Swordar and bandeto slaue,
Murthered sweete Tully.
Brutus bastard-hand stabde Iulius Cæsar,
And Suffolke dies by Pyrates on the seas.

                           Exet Suffolke, and *VVater.*

   Cap. Off with his head, and send it to the Queene,
And ransomelesse this prisoner shall go free,
To see it safe deliuered vnto her.
Come lets goe.   *Exet omnes.*'

The scene of Jack Cade's death, corresponding to *2 Henry VI* IV.x, is in the *Contention* less than half as long. It is almost altogether in prose, and quite lacks the conceits and efforts at 'fine writing' which the reviser affects.

'Enter *Iacke Cade* at one doore, and at the other, maister *Alexander Eyden* and his men, and *Iack Cade* lies downe picking of hearbes and eating them.

   Eyden. Good Lord how pleasant is this country life,
This litle land my father left me here,
With my contented minde serues me as well,
As all the pleasures in the Court can yeeld,
Nor would I change this pleasure for the Court.

   Cade. Sounes, heres the Lord of the soyle, Stand villaine, thou wilt betraie mee to the King, and get a thousand crownes for my head, but ere thou goest, ile make thee eate yron like an Astridge, and swallow my sword like a great pinne.

   Eyden. Why sawcy companion, why should I betray thee? Ist not inough that thou hast broke my hedges, And enterd into my ground without the leaue of me the owner, But thou wilt braue me too.

   Cade. Braue thee and beard thee too, by the best blood of the Realme, looke on me well, I haue eate no meate this fiue dayes, yet and I do not leaue thee and thy fiue men as dead as a doore nayle, I pray God I may neuer eate grasse more.

   Eyden. Nay, it neuer shall be saide whilst the world doth stand, that Alexander Eyden an Esquire of Kent, tooke oddes to combat with a famisht man, looke on me, my limmes are equall vnto thine, and euery way as big, then hand to hand, ile combat thee. Sirrha fetch me weapons, and stand you all aside.

   Cade. Now sword, if thou doest not hew this burly-bond churle into chines of beefe, I beseech God thou maist fal into some smiths hand, and be turnd to hobnailes.

   Eyden. Come on thy way.

                   (They fight, and *Cade* fals downe.

   Cade. Oh villaine, thou hast slaine the floure of Kent for chiualrie, but it is famine & not thee that has done it, for come ten thousand diuels, and giue me but the ten meales that I wanted this fiue daies, and ile fight with you all, and so a poxe rot thee, for Iacke Cade must die.   (He dies.

   Eyden. Iack Cade, & was it that monstrous Rebell which I

haue slaine. Oh sword ile honour thee for this, and in my chamber shalt thou hang as a monument to after age, for this great seruice thou hast done to me. Ile drag him hence, and with my sword cut off his head and beare it to the King.   (*Exet.*'

The History of the Play

On March 12, 1593/4, a London publisher, Thomas Millington, registered his copyright in 'a booke intituled, the firste parte of the Contention of the twoo famous houses of York and Lancaster with the death of the good Duke Humfrey, and the banishment and Deathe of the Duke of Suffolk, and the tragicall ende of the proud Cardinall of Winchester, with the notable rebellion of Jack Cade and the Duke of Yorkes ffirste clayme vnto the Crowne.' During the same year the play was published by Millington with a similarly descriptive title-page. In this 1594 edition and in a reprint of it which appeared in 1600 no mention is made of the author's name or of the company which produced the play.

In 1619 the *First Part of the Contention* was again printed, now in combination with the early version of *3 Henry VI (The True Tragedy)*, under the title of 'The Whole Contention betweene the two Famous Houses, Lancaster and Yorke. . . . Diuided into two Parts: And newly corrected and enlarged. Written by *William Shakespeare*, Gent.' The corrections and enlargements here announced are relatively inessential, and the earlier part of the *Whole Contention* amounts to no more than a new edition of the Quarto of 1594, though the publisher's intention was evidently to imply that it contained the large additions by Shakespeare which actually first appeared in the text of *2 Henry VI* in the Shakespeare Folio of 1623.

The close plot relationship between the *First Part of the Contention* and the *True Tragedy* makes it fairly evident that the former play was produced, as we know the latter to have been, by the Earl of Pembroke's Company before that company disbanded in 1593. This troupe had recently acted Marlowe's *Edward II*, and, if the inferences of recent scholars are correct, was at the moment employing Shakespeare's services both as actor and as playwright. Professor J. Q. Adams suggests that Shakespeare's initial revision of the *First Part of the Contention* and of the *True Tragedy* was made (in 1592) in order to enable the Pembroke Company to present them in competition with the original version of *1 Henry VI* (by Peele?), which was at this time proving a great success at the rival theatre of Lord Strange's Men.[3]

We have little knowledge of the stage history of *2 Henry VI* between the time it was amplified out of the earlier *First Part of the Contention* and the Restoration era. The Epilogue to Shakespeare's *Henry V* (1599) indicates that the Henry VI plays had been popular:

> '*Henry the Sixth, in infant bands crown'd King*
> *Of France and England, did this king succeed;*
> *Whose state so many had the managing,*
> *That they lost France and made his England bleed:*
> *Which oft our stage hath shown; and, for their sake,*
> *In your fair minds let this acceptance take.*'

---

3 Cf. J. Q. Adams, *A Life of William Shakespeare*, 1923, pp. 136, 137, and the edition of *1 Henry VI* in the present series, pp. 438, 439, 443.

Ben Jonson's Prologue to *Every Man in his Humour* singles out the York and Lancaster plays (i.e. *2* and *3 Henry VI* and *Richard III*) among 'the ill customs of the age,' which purchase the delight of audiences by unjustifiable dramatic methods. He rebukes the authors who

> *'with three rusty swords,*
> *And help of some few foot and half-foot words,*
> *Fight over York and Lancaster's long jars,*
> *And in the tiring-house bring wounds to scars.'*

Jonson's contemporary and rival, the artist-architect Inigo Jones (1573-1652) has left a vigorous sketch of Jack Cade in costume, which may point to some otherwise unrecorded revival or adaptation of *2 Henry VI* in the reign of James I or Charles I.[4]

A revision of *2 Henry VI* by the Restoration dramatist, John Crowne, was produced at the Duke of York's Theatre about 1681, and published in the same year with the title: *Henry the Sixth; or, The Murder of the Duke of Glocester.* This work begins with the quarrel of Gloucester and Cardinal Beaufort over King Henry's marriage, and, after presenting the death of both Humphrey and Beaufort, closes with the announcement of Suffolk's death and the success of Cade's revolt. The cast of characters is reduced to eleven, all save the Sheriff of London persons of the highest rank. Duke Humphrey was acted by Betterton and the Duchess Eleanor by Mrs. Betterton. Though in general Crowne follows the course of events in Shakespeare's play, as far as the middle of the fourth act, he retains little of Shakespeare's wording[5] and quite alters the spirit of the piece, which he seeks to bring into line with the anti-papal feeling of the closing years of Charles II by representing his odious Cardinal as an example of the vices of the roman clergy.[6]

A sequel[7] to the foregoing play was written by Crowne under the title of *The Miseries of Civil-War.* This is in the main an alteration of *3 Henry VI,* but the first act, as well as the opening pages of the second, deal with matter included in the Second Part, i.e. the progress and final suppression of Jack Cade's rebellion and the first battle of St. Albans.

On February 15, 1723, was acted at Drury Lane Ambrose Philips' play: *Humfrey Duke of Gloucester* (printed the same year). This is a tragedy in the French style, consisting of many brief conversational scenes, which change whenever a character enters or leaves the stage. Only nine dramatis personæ appear, besides an Officer of Justice and two Ruffians. The whole action 'passes within the King's Palace in Westminster,' and within twenty-four hours. Humphrey, York, Salisbury, and Warwick are represented as high-minded gentlemen without much discrimination of character, and the Duchess Eleanor is absurdly idealized, while Beaufort is made a conventional villain. The indebtedness to Shakespeare is much smaller than even in Crowne's pieces, and is not unfairly indicated in Philips' Epistle to the Reader: 'They

who have read Shakespear's Second Part of Henry VI. may, probably, recollect most of the Passages I have borrowed from Him, either Word for Word, or with some small Alteration. Nevertheless, that I may not be thought unwilling to Acknowledge my Obligation to so great a Poet, I desire my Readers will place to his Account One or Two Hints, and One intire Line in the 24th Page, where Eleanor's Penance is related: Four Lines in the 38th Page, where Beaufort speaks of Gloucester's Popularity: Three Parts in Four of the Description of the Duke's dead Body, in Page 71: And about Seventeen Lines in the last Scene; some of which are so very beautifull, that it may be questioned whether there be any Passages in Shakespear that deserve greater Commendation.'

None of the revisions just mentioned enjoyed a real popularity. The most notable revival of *2 Henry VI* in modern times was that produced by the great actor, Edmund Kean, at Drury Lane. According to Genest the first performance took place on December 22, 1817. The play was called *Richard, Duke of York; or, The Contention of York and Lancaster,* and was adapted from the Second Part of *Henry VI,* with smaller borrowings from the First and Third Parts, by J. H. Merivale, in such a way as to give prominence to the rôle of York, which was acted by Kean himself. Queen Margaret was played by Mrs. Glover and Jack Cade by the notable comedian Munden.[8]

In 1863 an adaptation of *2 Henry VI* under the title of *The Wars of the Roses* was played some thirty or forty times at the Surrey Theatre under the direction of the reviser, Mr. Anderson, who, with remarkable versatility, doubled the rôles of York and Cade.[9] In 1864 *2 Henry VI,* translated with considerable modifications into German, was produced at Weimar by Dingelstedt as one of the series of Shakespearean history plays (omitting *1 Henry VI*), which were performed in celebration of the poet's tercentenary.[10] A more recent revival was that of the F. R. Benson Company at the Shakespeare Memorial Festival, Stratford-on-Avon, 1906, when the entire group of history plays, from *Richard II* to *Richard III,* was presented on successive days, the production of *2 Henry VI* occurring on May 3.[11]

THE AUTHORSHIP OF THE PLAY

In the vexed problem of the authorship of the Second Part of *Henry VI* two separate questions are involved:

(a) Who wrote the subsidiary play of *The First Part of the Contention,* preserved for us in the edition of 1594 and the reissues of 1600 and 1619?

(b) By whom were the large and often redundant additions made which distinguish the 1623 text of *2 Henry VI* from the *First Part of the Contention?*

These questions can be only briefly treated here.[12] *The First Part of the Contention* is either a particularly rough and unfinished

---

4 This drawing is reproduced in the Shakespeare Society volume, *Sketches from Inigo Jones, etc.,* 1848.

5 Crowne's Epistle to Sir Charles Sedley says: 'I call'd it in the Prologue Shakespeare's Play, though he has no Title to the 40th part of it. The Text I took out of his Second Part of Henry the Sixth, but as most Texts are serv'd, I left it as soon as I could.' A recent investigator (Gustav Krecke, *Die englischen Bühnenbearbeitungen von Shakespeare's 'King Henry the Sixth,'* Rostock, 1911) estimates that of 2864 lines in Crowne's play 215 are taken direct from Shakespeare.

6 Langbaine, a contemporary, writing in 1691, says: 'This Play was oppos'd by the Popish Faction, who by their Power at Court got it supprest: however it was well receiv'd by the Rest of the Audience.'

7 This, however, was printed in 1680, a year before the earliest edition of *The Murder of the Duke of Glocester,* and it may have been composed earlier.

8 Cf. Charles Lamb: On the Acting of Munden, *Essays of Elia.*

9 This version was never printed and is now lost. Mr. Anderson informed Mr. F. A. Marshall (*Henry Irving Shakespeare,* Introduction to *2 Henry VI*): 'Unfortunately the manuscript with all books and papers were destroyed when the theatre was burnt down in the year 1864.' Another manuscript condensation of the Three Parts of *Henry VI,* prepared by the actor, Charles Kemble, is printed by Mr. Marshall, *ibid.,* vol. ii, pp. 203-246.

10 For a detailed account of these jubilee performances see L. Eckardt: *Shakespeare's englische Historien auf der Weimarer Bühne,* Shakespeare Jahrbuch i. 362-391.

11 An account will be found in the London *Athenæum,* May 12, 1906.

12 They are discussed more fully in a monograph on *The Authorship of the Second and Third Parts of King Henry VI,* Conn. Academy of Arts and Sciences, 1912.

work, or it has been very unfaithfully represented in the published versions. It contains a little less than two thousand lines, of which only about 1250 may be scanned as pentameter verse. In such a case arguments based upon elaborate stylistic analysis are more than usually dangerous. That Marlowe, however, was largely responsible for the play seems now to be the general belief. Evidence of many kinds points to his authorship: (1) the powerful, if rude, singleness and consistency of plot conception; (2) the predominance of Marlovian types of character, boisterous and self-assertive, like York, Suffolk, Queen Margaret, the Duchess Eleanor, Cardinal Beaufort, Warwick, and Cade; (3) a remarkably numerous and striking series of verbal parallels with passages in Marlowe's accepted writings; (4) metrical evidence, which shows the author of the uncorrupted verse portions of the play to have had many of Marlowe's most characteristic peculiarities of poetic style.

The theory that the *Contention* contains, besides Marlowe's work, scenes by other writers, such as Greene, Peele, or Shakespeare himself, has given rise to much discussion. Particularly in regard to the partly humorous scenes in the fourth act, in which Cade and his followers figure, there has been manifested an unwillingness to credit Marlowe's authorship and a desire to recognize that of Shakespeare.[13] I see little prospect of reaching conclusive results on these points. The theory that the *Contention* was written by Marlowe at all, or by any other reputable writer of blank verse, is allowable only on the assumption that there has been much contamination of the extant texts; and the inequality of style is more safely attributed to theatrical manipulation or careless transcribing and printing than to a fundamental division of authorship. The Cade scenes, as they appear in the *Contention,* are not unworthy of the young Shakespeare, but they bear no indelible stamp of his hand, and the wisest attitude toward them is perhaps that agnostically expressed by Mr. F. A. Marshall (*Henry Irving Shakespeare*): 'If Shakespeare's claim to have been part author of *The Contention* and *The True Tragedy* rests chiefly on the humours of Jack Cade and his company of rebels, we may feel ourselves at perfect liberty to believe that he had no share in them whatever.'

(b) That other writers than Shakespeare assisted in the revision of *The First Part of the Contention* and *The True Tragedy* into the Second and Third Parts of *Henry VI* has been often suggested, most recently by Dr. Else von Schaubert, who argues in a very elaborate dissertation[14] that Michael Drayton was author of con-

siderable portions of both the Second and Third Parts. For this view, as well as for that which would make Marlowe himself Shakespeare's assistant in the revision, I see no sufficient evidence.

Whether Shakespeare's revision, as printed in the Folio of 1623, represents the work as completed by him in 1592, or whether it is the result of a series of recastings, is hard to say. It is natural to assume that the text may have been subjected to some alteration as often as the plays were revived on Shakespeare's stage, but there seems no ground for supposing that any very essential changes were made after Shakespeare had attained full maturity as a writer. Stylistically the Shakespearean portions of *1 Henry VI* testify to a later date of composition than the Shakespearean portions of the Second and Third Parts.

The study of the rewritten or additional matter in *2 Henry VI* and *3 Henry VI,* which in the former play exceeds and in the latter amounts to about three-fourths of the total length of the basic play, offers one of the best opportunities to gauge the trend of Shakespeare's poetical abilities near the beginning of his career. As compared with the original author (Marlowe) it is evident that the reviser, Shakespeare, had broader sympathies. He is interested in a greater variety of types of human beings, and exerts himself to do justice to such good but weak personalities as King Henry and Gloucester, who in the original versions had been left shadowy and negative. These characters are greatly improved and much more fully developed in the revised plays. On the other hand, the reviser has evidently less maturity and finality in his view of life than the original author: he sentimentalizes and frequently blurs the outlines of the earlier plays, particularly in his handling of the harsh and limited, but clean-cut evil figures depicted in the *Contention* and *True Tragedy:* York, Suffolk, Margaret, Beaufort, etc. Rhetorical declamation and prettinesses of figurative illustration tempt him to undramatic and frequently inconsistent additions, of which the effect is to lower the dramatic pitch of the scene.[15] This tendency shows itself uncurbed in *2 Henry VI:* in the Third Part the poet gets it under better control.[16]

In metrical matters also the habit of the young Shakespeare displays itself. He has revised the scansion of the verses with almost meticulous conscientiousness and in doing so exhibits mannerisms distinctly different from those of his original. He inclines much more to the use of the feminine-ending or elevensyllable line than the author of the basic plays, and tends to avoid the weak-ending (final pyrrhic) line and the alexandrine.[17]

---

13 Cf. J. Q. Adams, *A Life of William Shakespeare,* p. 137: 'The plays (i.e. *The First Part of the Contention* and *True Tragedy*) show unmistakable signs of Shakespeare's workmanship.' *Ibid.,* p. 136, note 3: 'There is no ground for the supposition that Greene had a share in these plays. . . . On the other hand, it seems quite possible that George Peele was associated with Marlowe in their composition.'

14 *Draytons Anteil an 'Heinrich VI,' 2. u. 3. Teil, Neue Anglistische Arbeiten,* 1920. (The author accepts the old theory that the *Contention* and *True Tragedy* are not earlier plays, but pirated versions of the Shakespearean plays.)

15 A number of passages in which the Shakespearean version deviates significantly from the source play are referred to in the notes to this edition. See those on I. i. 142 f., 233 f.; I. iii. 17-19, 168 f.; II. ii. 39-42; II. iii. 7 f.; III. i. 9-12, 332 f., 357-360; III. ii. 27, 348 f.; IV. i. 1-7; V. ii. 59 f.

16 For detailed discussion see *Authorship of 2 and 3 Henry VI* (Conn. Academy), pp. 194-211: 'Shakespeare's Revision of Marlowe's Work.'

17 *Ibid.,* pp. 177-183: 'Metrical Evidence.'

ACT FIRST ❧ SCENE FIRST

[London. A Room of State in the Palace]
Flourish of Trumpets: then hautboys. Enter King, Duke Humphrey,
Salisbury, Warwick, and Beaufort, on the one side. The Queen,
Suffolk, York, Somerset, and Buckingham on the other.

Suf. As by your high imperial majesty
I had in charge at my depart for France,
As procurator to your excellence,
To marry Princess Margaret for your Grace;
So, in the famous ancient city, Tours,   5
In presence of the Kings of France and Sicil,
The Dukes of Orleans, Calaber, Britaine, and Alençon,
Seven earls, twelve barons, and twenty reverend bishops,
I have perform'd my task, and was espous'd:
And humbly now upon my bended knee,   10
In sight of England and her lordly peers,
Deliver up my title in the queen
To your most gracious hands, that are the substance
Of that great shadow I did represent;
The happiest gift that ever marquess gave,   15
The fairest queen that ever king receiv'd.

King. Suffolk, arise. Welcome, Queen Margaret:
I can express no kinder sign of love
Than this kind kiss. O Lord, that lends me life,
Lend me a heart replete with thankfulness!   20
For thou hast given me in this beauteous face
A world of earthly blessings to my soul,
If sympathy of love unite our thoughts.

Queen. Great King of England and my gracious lord,
The mutual conference that my mind hath had   25
By day, by night, waking, and in my dreams,
In courtly company, or at my beads,
With you, mine alderliefest sovereign,
Makes me the bolder to salute my king
With ruder terms, such as my wit affords,   30
And over-joy of heart doth minister.

King. Her sight did ravish, but her grace in speech,
Her words yclad with wisdom's majesty,
Makes me from wondering fall to weeping joys;
Such is the fulness of my heart's content.   35
Lords, with one cheerful voice welcome my love.

All kneel [and say]. Long live Queen Margaret, England's
happiness!

Queen. We thank you all.   *Flourish.*

Suf. My Lord Protector, so it please your Grace,   40
Here are the articles of contracted peace
Between our sovereign and the French King Charles,
For eighteen months concluded by consent.

Glo. Reads. 'Imprimis, It is agreed between the French king,
Charles, and William De la Pole, Marquess of Suffolk, ambassa-
dor for Henry King of England, that the said Henry shall
espouse the Lady Margaret, daughter unto Reignier King of
Naples, Sicilia, and Jerusalem, and crown her Queen of
England ere the thirtieth of May next ensuing.

'item, That the duchy of Anjou and the county of Maine   50
shall be released and delivered to the king her father—'
[Lets the paper fall.]

King. Uncle, how now!
Glo.   Pardon me, gracious lord;
Some sudden qualm hath struck me at the heart   55
And dimm'd mine eyes, that I can read no further.

King. Uncle of Winchester, I pray, read on.

Win. 'Item, It is further agreed between them, that the duchies of Anjou and Maine shall be released and delivered over to
the king her father; and she sent over of the King of England's
own proper cost and charges, without having any dowry.'

King. They please us well. Lord Marquess, kneel down:
We here create thee the first Duke of Suffolk,
And girt thee with the sword. Cousin of York,
We here discharge your Grace from being regent   65
I' the parts of France, till term of eighteen months
Be full expir'd. Thanks, uncle Winchester,
Gloucester, York, Buckingham, Somerset,
Salisbury, and Warwick;
We thank you all for this great favour done,   70
In entertainment to my princely queen.
Come, let us in, and with all speed provide
To see her coronation be perform'd.

Exit King, [with] Queen, and Suffolk. Mane[n]t the rest.

Glo. Brave peers of England, pillars of the state,
To you Duke Humphrey must unload his grief,   75
Your grief, the common grief of all the land.
What! did my brother Henry spend his youth,
His valour, coin, and people, in the wars?
Did he so often lodge in open field,
In winter's cold, and summer's parching heat,   80
To conquer France, his true inheritance?
And did my brother Bedford toil his wits,
To keep by policy what Henry got?
Have you yourselves, Somerset, Buckingham,
Brave York, Salisbury, and victorious Warwick,   85
Receiv'd deep scars in France and Normandy?
Or hath mine uncle Beaufort and myself,
With all the learned council of the realm,
Studied so long, sat in the council-house
Early and late, debating to and fro   90
How France and Frenchmen might be kept in awe?
And hath his highness in his infancy
Been crown'd in Paris, in despite of foes?
And shall these labours and these honours die?
Shall Henry's conquest, Bedford's vigilance,   95
Your deeds of war and all our counsel die?
O peers of England! shameful is this league,
Fatal this marriage, cancelling your fame,
Blotting your names from books of memory,
Razing the characters of your renown,   100
Defacing monuments of conquer'd France,
Undoing all, as all had never been.

Car. Nephew, what means this passionate discourse,
This peroration with such circumstance?

---

1 **The Second . . . Henry the Sixth;** *cf. n.*   2 **had in charge:** *was commissioned*   **depart:**
departure   3 **procurator:** *proxy*   6 **Sicil:** *René, Margaret's father, titular king of Sicily*
18 **kinder:** *more natural*   25 **mutual:** *intimate*   27 **beads:** *prayers*   28 **alderliefest:**
dearest of all   30 **ruder:** *too rude*   31 **over-joy:** *excessive joy*   33 **yclad:** *garbed*   44
Imprimis: *in the first place*

50 **Item:** *likewise*   57 **Uncle of Winchester:** *Beaufort was the king's half-great-*
uncle   58–61 *Cf. n.*   61 **proper:** *personal*   65 *Cf. n.*   64 **girt:** *gird*   66, 67 **till**
. . . expir'd; *cf. n.*   71 **entertainment:** *service*   **S. d. Manent:** *remain on the*
stage   77 **my brother Henry:** *Henry V*   83 **policy:** *administration*   99 **books of**
memory: *chronicles of honor*   100 **Razing the characters:** *erasing the record*   101 **Defac-**
ing: *effacing*   104 *This so detailed harangue*

For France, 'tis ours; and we will keep it still.   *105*
   Glo. Ay, uncle; we will keep it, if we can;
But now it is impossible we should.
Suffolk, the new-made duke that rules the roast,
Hath given the duchies of Anjou and Maine
Unto the poor King Reignier, whose large style   *110*
Agrees not with the leanness of his purse.
   Sal. Now, by the death of him who died for all,
These counties were the keys of Normandy.
But wherefore weeps Warwick, my valiant son?
   War. For grief that they are past recovery: *115*
For, were there hope to conquer them again,
My sword should shed hot blood, mine eyes no tears.
Anjou and Maine! myself did win them both;
Those provinces these arms of mine did conquer:
And are the cities, that I got with wounds,   *120*
Deliver'd up again with peaceful words?
Mort Dieu!
   York. For Suffolk's duke, may he be suffocate,
That dims the honour of this warlike isle!
France should have torn and rent my very heart   *125*
Before I would have yielded to this league.
I never read but England's kings have had
Large sums of gold and dowries with their wives;
And our King Henry gives away his own,
To match with her that brings no vantages.   *130*
   Glo. A proper jest, and never heard before,
That Suffolk should demand a whole fifteenth
For costs and charges in transporting her!
She should have stay'd in France, and starv'd in France,
Before—   *135*
   Car. My Lord of Gloucester, now ye grow too hot:
It was the pleasure of my lord the king.
   Glo. My Lord of Winchester, I know your mind:
'Tis not my speeches that you do mislike,
But 'tis my presence that doth trouble ye.   *140*
Rancour will out: proud prelate, in thy face
I see thy fury. If I longer stay,
We shall begin our ancient bickerings.
Lordings, farewell; and say, when I am gone,
I prophesied France will be lost ere long.   *Exit Humphrey.*
   Car. So, there goes our protector in a rage.
'Tis known to you he is mine enemy,
Nay, more, an enemy unto you all,
And no great friend, I fear me, to the king.
Consider lords, he is the next of blood,   *150*
And heir apparent to the English crown:
Had Henry got an empire by his marriage,
And all the wealthy kingdoms of the west,
There's reason he should be displeas'd at it.
Look to it, lords; let not his smoothing words   *155*
Bewitch your hearts; be wise and circumspect.
What though the common people favour him,
Calling him, 'Humphrey, the good Duke of Gloucester.'
Clapping their hands, and crying with loud voice,
'Jesu maintain your royal excellence!'   *160*
With 'God preserve the good Duke Humphrey!'

I fear me, lords, for all this flattering gloss,
He will be found a dangerous protector.
   Buck. Why should he then protect our sovereign,
He being of age to govern of himself?   *165*
Cousin of Somerset, join you with me,
And all together, with the Duke of Suffolk,
We'll quickly hoise Duke Humphrey from his seat.
   Car. This weighty business will not brook delay;
I'll to the Duke of Suffolk presently.   *Exit Cardinal.*   *170*
   Som. Cousin of Buckingham, though Humphrey's pride
And greatness of his place be grief to us,
Yet let us watch the haughty cardinal:
His insolence is more intolerable
Than all the princes in the land beside: *175*
If Gloucester be displac'd, he'll be protector.
   Buck. Or thou, or I, Somerset, will be protector,
Despite Duke Humphrey or the cardinal.
              Exit Buckingham, and Somerset.
   Sal. Pride went before, ambition follows him.
While these do labour for their own preferment,   *180*
Behoves it us to labour for the realm.
I never saw but Humphrey, Duke of Gloucester,
Did bear him like a noble gentleman.
Oft have I seen the haughty cardinal
More like a soldier than a man o' the church,   *185*
As stout and proud as he were lord of all,
Swear like a ruffian and demean himself
Unlike the ruler of a commonweal.
Warwick, my son, the comfort of my age,
Thy deeds, thy plainness, and thy housekeeping   *190*
Hath won the greatest favour of the commons,
Excepting none but good Duke Humphrey:
And, brother York, thy acts in Ireland,
In bringing them to civil discipline,
Thy late exploits done in the heart of France,   *195*
When thou wert regent for our sovereign,
Have made thee fear'd and honour'd of the people.
Join we together for the public good,
In what we can to bridle and suppress
The pride of Suffolk and the cardinal,   *200*
With Somerset's and Buckingham's ambition;
And, as we may, cherish Duke Humphrey's deeds,
While they do tend the profit of the land.
   War. So God help Warwick, as he loves the land,
And common profit of his country!   *205*
   York. And so says York, *[Aside.]* for he hath greatest cause.
   Sal. Then let's make haste away, and look unto the main.
   War. Unto the main! O father, Maine is lost!
That Maine which by main force Warwick did win,
And would have kept so long as breath did last.   *210*
Main chance, father, you meant; but I meant Maine,
Which I will win from France, or else be slain.
          Exit Warwick, and Salisbury. Manet York.
   York. Anjou and Maine are given to the French;
Paris is lost; the state of Normandy
Stands on a tickle point now they are gone.   *215*

---

108 **rules the roast:** *domineers*   110 **large style:** *inflated titles*   118 *Cf. n.*   123 **For:**
as for; cf. n.   130 **no vantages:** *nothing but herself*   132 **fifteenth;** *cf. n.*   143 **our . . .**
bickerings; *cf. n.*   151 **heir apparent;** *cf. n.*   153 *Cf. n.*   155 **smoothing:** *ingratiating*

162 **flattering gloss:** *specious flattery*   165 **of age;** *cf. n.*   168 **hoise:** *hoist*   175 **all:**
that of all   177 **Or:** *either*   179 **Pride . . . ambition;** *cf. n.*   186 **as:** *as if*
187 **demean:** *behave*   190 **housekeeping:** *hospitality*   191 **Hath;** *cf. n.*   193 **brother**
York; *cf. n.*   194 **civil:** *orderly*   202 **cherish:** *foster, support*   207 **main:** *the most*
important thing at stake (from game of hazard)   215 **tickle:** *slippery*

Suffolk concluded on the articles,
The peers agreed, and Henry was well pleas'd
To change two dukedoms for a duke's fair daughter.
I cannot blame them all: what is 't to them?
'Tis thine they give away, and not their own.　220
Pirates may make cheap pennyworths of their pillage,
And purchase friends, and give to courtezans,
Still revelling like lords till all be gone;
While as the silly owner of the goods
Weeps over them, and wrings his hapless hands,　225
And shakes his head, and trembling stands aloof,
While all is shar'd and all is borne away,
Ready to starve and dare not touch his own:
So York must sit and fret and bite his tongue
While his own lands are bargain'd for and sold.　230
Methinks the realms of England, France, and Ireland
Bear that proportion to my flesh and blood
As did the fatal brand Althæa burnt
Unto the prince's heart of Calydon.
Anjou and Maine both given unto the French!　235
Cold news for me, for I had hope of France,
Even as I have of fertile England's soil.
A day will come when York shall claim his own;
And therefore I will take the Nevils' parts
And make a show of love to proud Duke Humphrey,　240
And, when I spy advantage, claim the crown,
For that's the golden mark I seek to hit.
Nor shall proud Lancaster usurp my right.
Nor hold the sceptre in his childish fist,
Nor wear the diadem upon his head,　245
Whose churchlike humours fit not for a crown.
Then, York, be still awhile, till time do serve:
Watch thou and wake when others be asleep,
To pry into the secrets of the state;
Till Henry, surfeiting in joys of love,　250
With his new bride and England's dear-bought queen,
And Humphrey with the peers be fall'n at jars:
Then will I raise aloft the milk-white rose,
With whose sweet smell the air shall be perfum'd,
And in my standard bear the arms of York,　255
To grapple with the house of Lancaster;
And, force perforce, I'll make him yield the crown,
Whose bookish rule hath pull'd fair England down. *Exit York.*

❧ Scene Second ❧

[The Same. A Room in the Duke of Gloucester's House]
Enter Duke Humphrey and his wife Eleanor.

Elea. Why droops my lord, like over-ripen'd corn
Hanging the head at Ceres' plenteous load?
Why doth the great Duke Humphrey knit his brows,
As frowning at the favours of the world?
Why are thine eyes fix'd to the sullen earth,　5
Gazing on that which seems to dim thy sight?
What seest thou there? King Henry's diadem,
Enchas'd with all the honours of the world?
If so, gaze on, and grovel on thy face,
Until thy head be circled with the same.　10
Put forth thy hand, reach at the glorious gold:
What! is 't too short? I'll lengthen it with mine;
And having both together heav'd it up,
We'll both together lift our heads to heaven,
And never more abase our sight so low　15
As to vouchsafe one glance unto the ground.
　Hum. O Nell, sweet Nell, if thou dost love thy lord,
Banish the canker of ambitious thoughts:
And may that thought, when I imagine ill
Against my king and nephew, virtuous Henry,　20
Be my last breathing in this mortal world!
My troublous dream this night doth make me sad.
　Elea. What dream'd my lord? tell me, and I'll requite it
With sweet rehearsal of my morning's dream.
　Hum. Methought this staff, mine office-badge in court,　25
Was broke in twain; by whom I have forgot,
But, as I think, it was by the cardinal;
And on the pieces of the broken wand
Were plac'd the heads of Edmund Duke of Somerset,
And William De la Pole, first Duke of Suffolk.　30
This was my dream: what it doth bode, God knows.
　Elea. Tut! this was nothing but an argument
That he that breaks a stick of Gloucester's grove
Shall lose his head for his presumption.
But list to me, my Humphrey, my sweet duke:　35
Methought I sat in seat of majesty
In the cathedral church of Westminster,
And in that chair where kings and queens are crown'd;
Where Henry and Dame Margaret kneel'd to me,
And on my head did set the diadem.　40
　Hum. Nay, Eleanor, then must I chide outright:
Presumptuous dame! ill-nurtur'd Eleanor!
Art thou not second woman in the realm,
And the protector's wife, belov'd of him?
Hast thou not worldly pleasure at command,　45
Above the reach or compass of thy thought?
And wilt thou still be hammering treachery,
To tumble down thy husband and thyself
From top of honour to disgrace's feet?
Away from me, and let me hear no more.　50
　Elea. What, what, my lord! are you so choleric
With Eleanor, for telling but her dream?
Next time I'll keep my dreams unto myself,
And not be check'd.
　Hum. Nay, be not angry; I am pleas'd again.　55

Enter Messenger.

　Mess. My Lord Protector, 'tis his highness' pleasure
You do prepare to ride unto Saint Albans,
Whereas the king and queen do mean to hawk.
　Hum. I go. Come, Nell, thou wilt ride with us?
　　　　　　　　　　Exit Humphrey [with Messenger].
　Elea. Yes, my good lord, I'll follow presently.　60

---

216 **concluded:** *decided*　221 **pennyworths:** *bargains*　224 **While as:** *while*　**silly:** *helpless*　232 **proportion:** *relation*　233, 234 *Cf. n.*　234 **prince's heart:** *heart of the prince*　239 **take the Nevils' parts;** *cf. n.*　246 **churchlike humours:** *pietistic temperament*　252 **at jars:** *into squabbles*　257 **force perforce:** *by violent compulsion*　1 **corn:** *wheat (or other cereal grain)*

8 **Enchas'd:** *adorned*　9 **grovel … face;** *cf. n.*　18 **canker:** *eating sore, ulcer*　25 **office-badge:** *mark of authority* (as Protector)　32 **argument:** *testimony, proof*　38 **that chair;** *cf. n.*　42 **ill-nurtur'd:** *ill-bred, rude*　47 **hammering:** *meditating*　49 *From highest honor to lowest disgrace*　54 **check'd:** *rebuked*

Follow I must; I cannot go before,
While Gloucester bears this base and humble mind.
Were I a man, a duke, and next of blood,
I would remove these tedious stumbling-blocks
And smooth my way upon their headless necks;   65
And, being a woman, I will not be slack
To play my part in Fortune's pageant.
Where are you there? Sir John! nay, fear not, man,
We are alone; here's none but thee and I.

Enter Hume.

Hume. Jesus preserve your royal majesty!   70
Elea. What sayst thou? majesty! I am but Grace.
Hume. But, by the grace of God, and Hume's advice,
Your Grace's title shall be multiplied.
Elea. What sayst thou, man? hast thou as yet conferr'd
With Margery Jordan, the cunning witch,   75
With Roger Bolingbroke, the conjurer?
And will they undertake to do me good?
Hume. This they have promised, to show your highness
A spirit rais'd from depth of under ground,
That shall make answer to such questions   80
As by your Grace shall be propounded him.
Elea. It is enough: I'll think upon the questions.
When from Saint Albans we do make return
We'll see these things effected to the full.
Here, Hume, take this reward; make merry, man,   85
With thy confederates in this weighty cause.   *Exit Eleanor.*
Hume. Hume must make merry with the duchess' gold!
Marry, and shall. But how now, Sir John Hume!
Seal up your lips, and give no words but mum:
The business asketh silent secrecy.   90
Dame Eleanor gives gold to bring the witch:
Gold cannot come amiss, were she a devil.
Yet have I gold flies from another coast:
I dare not say from the rich cardinal
And from the great and new-made Duke of Suffolk;   95
Yet I do find it so: for, to be plain,
They, knowing Dame Eleanor's aspiring humour,
Have hired me to undermine the duchess
And buzz these conjurations in her brain.
They say, 'A crafty knave does need no broker;'   100
Yet am I Suffolk and the cardinal's broker.
Hume, if you take not heed, you shall go near
To call them both a pair of crafty knaves.
Well, so it stands; and thus, I fear, at last
Hume's knavery will be the duchess' wrack,   105
And her attainture will be Humphrey's fall.
Sort how it will I shall have gold for all.   *Exit.*

61 go before: *i.e. occupy the highest place*   68 Sir John; *cf. n.*   71 but Grace;
cf. n.   88 Marry . . . shall: *indeed he shall*   93 flies: *which flies* coast: *quarter*   100
broker: *agent, go-between*   106 attainture: *conviction*

❧ SCENE THIRD ❧

[The Same. A Room in the Palace]
Enter three or four Petitioners, the Armourer's man [Peter]
being one.

1. Pet. My masters, let's stand close: my Lord Protector will
come this way by and by, and then we may deliver our supplications in the quill.
2. Pet. Marry, the Lord protect him, for he's a good man!
Jesu bless him!   5

Enter Suffolk and Queen.

1. Pet. Here a' comes, methinks, and the queen with him.
I'll be the first, sure.
2. Pet. Come back, fool! this is the Duke of Suffolk and
not my Lord Protector.
Suf. How now, fellow! wouldst anything with me?   10
1. Pet. I pray, my lord, pardon me: I took ye for my
Lord Protector.
Queen. [*Glancing at the Superscriptions.*] 'To my Lord
Protector!' Are your supplications to his lordship? Let me see
them: what is thine?   15
1. Pet. Mine is, an 't please your Grace, against John
Goodman, my Lord Cardinal's man, for keeping my house,
and lands, my wife and all, from me.
Suf. Thy wife too! that is some wrong indeed. What's yours?
What's here? 'Against the Duke of Suffolk, for enclosing   20
the commons of Melford!' How now, sir knave!
2. Pet. Alas! sir, I am but a poor petitioner of our whole
township.
Peter. [*Presenting his petition.*] Against my master, Thomas
Horner, for saying that the Duke of York was rightful heir   25
to the crown.
Queen. What sayst thou? Did the Duke of York say he
was rightful heir to the crown?
Peter. That my master was? No, forsooth: my master said
that he was; and that the king was an usurper.   30
Suf. Who is there?

Enter Servant.

Take this fellow in, and send for his master with a pursuivant
presently. We'll hear more of your matter before the king.
                                      Exit [Servant with Peter].
Queen. And as for you, that love to be protected
Under the wings of our protector's grace,   35
Begin your suits anew and sue to him.   *Tears the supplication.*
Away, base cullions! Suffolk, let them go.
All. Come, let's be gone.   *Exeunt [Petitioners].*
Queen. My Lord of Suffolk, say, is this the guise,
Is this the fashion in the court of England?   40
Is this the government of Britain's isle,
And this the royalty of Albion's king?
What! shall King Henry be a pupil still
Under the surly Gloucester's governance?
Am I a queen in title and in style,   45
And must be made a subject to a duke?
I tell thee, Pole, when in the city Tours
Thou ran'st a-tilt in honour of my love,

And stol'st away the ladies' hearts of France,
I thought King Henry had resembled thee   50
In courage, courtship, and proportion:
But all his mind is bent to holiness,
To number Ave-Maries on his beads;
His champions are the prophets and apostles;
His weapons holy saws of sacred writ;   55
His study is his tilt-yard, and his loves
Are brazen images of canoniz'd saints.
I would the college of the cardinals
Would choose him pope, and carry him to Rome,
And set the triple crown upon his head: 60
That were a state fit for his holiness.
        Suf. Madam, be patient: as I was cause
Your highness came to England, so will I
In England work your Grace's full content.
        Queen. Beside the haught protector, have we Beaufort   65
The imperious churchman, Somerset, Buckingham,
And grumbling York; and not the least of these
But can do more in England than the king.
        Suf. And he of these that can do most of all
Cannot do more in England than the Nevils: 70
Salisbury and Warwick are no simple peers.
        Queen. Not all these lords do vex me half so much
As that proud dame, the Lord Protector's wife:
She sweeps it through the court with troops of ladies,
More like an empress than Duke Humphrey's wife.   75
Strangers in court do take her for the queen:
She bears a duke's revenues on her back,
And in her heart she scorns our poverty.
Shall I not live to be aveng'd on her?
Contemptuous base-born callet as she is,   80
She vaunted 'mongst her minions t'other day
The very train of her worst wearing gown
Was better worth than all my father's lands,
Till Suffolk gave two dukedoms for his daughter.
        Suf. Madam, myself have lim'd a bush for her,   85
And plac'd a quire of such enticing birds
That she will light to listen to the lays,
And never mount to trouble you again.
So, let her rest: and, madam, list to me;
For I am bold to counsel you in this.   90
Although we fancy not the cardinal,
Yet must we join with him and with the lords
Till we have brought Duke Humphrey in disgrace.
As for the Duke of York, this late complaint
Will make but little for his benefit: 95
So, one by one, we'll weed them all at last,
And you yourself shall steer the happy helm.

                    Sound a Sennet.

Enter the King, Duke Humphrey, Cardinal, Buckingham, York,
[Somerset,] Salisbury, Warwick, and the Duchess.

        King. For my part, noble lords, I care not which;
Or Somerset or York, all's one to me.

        York. If York have ill demean'd himself in France,   100
Then let him be denay'd the regentship.
        Som. If Somerset be unworthy of the place,
Let York be regent; I will yield to him.
        War. Whether your Grace be worthy, yea or no,
Dispute not that: York is the worthier.   105
        Car. Ambitious Warwick, let thy betters speak.
        War. The cardinal's not my better in the field.
        Buck. All in this presence are thy betters, Warwick.
        War. Warwick may live to be the best of all.
        Sal. Peace, son! and show some reason, Buckingham,   110
Why Somerset should be preferr'd in this.
        Queen. Because the king, forsooth, will have it so.
        Hum. Madam, the king is old enough himself
To give his censure: these are no women's matters.
        Queen. If he be old enough, what needs your Grace   115
To be protector of his excellence?
        Hum. Madam, I am protector of the realm;
And at his pleasure will resign my place.
        Suf. Resign it then and leave thine insolence.
Since thou wert king,—as who is king but thou?—   120
The commonwealth hath daily run to wrack;
The Dauphin hath prevail'd beyond the seas;
And all the peers and nobles of the realm
Have been as bondmen to thy sovereignty.
        Car. The commons hast thou rack'd; the clergy's bags   125
Are lank and lean with thy extortions.
        Som. Thy sumptuous buildings and thy wife's attire
Have cost a mass of public treasury.
        Buck. Thy cruelty in execution
Upon offenders hath exceeded law,   130
And left thee to the mercy of the law.
        Queen. Thy sale of offices and towns in France,
If they were known, as the suspect is great,
Would make thee quickly hop without thy head.
                              Exit Humphrey. [The Queen drops her fan.]
Give me my fan: what, minion! can ye not?   135
                    She gives the Duchess a box on the ear.
I cry you mercy, madam, was it you?
        Duch. Was 't I? yea, I it was, proud Frenchwoman:
Could I come near your beauty with my nails,
I'd set my ten commandments in your face.
        King. Sweet aunt, be quiet; 'twas against her will.   140
        Duch. Against her will! Good king, look to 't in time;
She'll hamper thee and dandle thee like a baby:
Though in this place most master wear no breeches,
She shall not strike Dame Eleanor unreveng'd.   *Exit Eleanor.*
        Buck. Lord Cardinal, I will follow Eleanor,   145
And listen after Humphrey, how he proceeds:
She's tickled now; her fume needs no spurs,
She'll gallop far enough to her destruction.   *Exit Buckingham.*

                    Enter Humphrey.

        Hum. Now, lords, my choler being over-blown
With walking once about the quadrangle,   150
I come to talk of commonwealth affairs.
As for your spiteful false objections,

51 courtship: *courtliness* **proportion:** *figure*   **57 canoniz'd;** *cf. n.*   **65 haught:** *proud*   **70 the Nevils;** *cf. n.*   **80 callet:** *lewd woman*   **82 worst wearing:** *most un-fashionable*   **83 better worth:** *worth more*   **85 lim'd a bush:** *set a snare*   **86 quire:** *choir, chorus*   **birds:** *decoy birds*   **91 fancy:** *love*   **S. d. Sennet:** *trumpet call for march of processions*   **99** *Cf. n.*

101 denay'd: *refused*   **116 protector;** *cf. n.*   **122 The Dauphin;** *cf. n.*   **127 sumptuous buildings;** *cf. n.*   **128 treasury:** *treasure*   **133 suspect:** *suspicion*   **136 cry you mercy:** *beg your pardon*   **139 my ten commandments:** *marks of my ten fingers; cf. n.*   **143 most master:** *the most masterful spirit*   **146 listen after:** *seek news of*   **147 fume:** *passion*

Prove them, and I lie open to the law:
But God in mercy so deal with my soul
As I in duty love my king and country!   *155*
But to the matter that we have in hand.
I say, my sovereign, York is meetest man
To be your regent in the realm of France.

   Suf. Before we make election, give me leave
To show some reason, of no little force,   *160*
That York is most unmeet of any man.

   York. I'll tell thee, Suffolk, why I am unmeet:
First, for I cannot flatter thee in pride;
Next, if I be appointed for the place,
My Lord of Somerset will keep me here,   *165*
Without discharge, money, or furniture,
Till France be won into the Dauphin's hands.
Last time I danc'd attendance on his will
Till Paris was besieg'd, famish'd, and lost.

   War. That can I witness; and a fouler fact   *170*
Did never traitor in the land commit.

   Suf. Peace, headstrong Warwick!

   War. Image of pride, why should I hold my peace?

Enter Armourer [Horner] and his Man [Peter].

   Suf. Because here is a man accus'd of treason:
Pray God the Duke of York excuse himself!   *175*

   York. Doth any one accuse York for a traitor?

   King. What mean'st thou, Suffolk? tell me, what are these?

   Suf. Please it your majesty, this is the man
That doth accuse his master of high treason.
His words were these: that Richard, Duke of York,   *180*
Was rightful heir unto the English crown,
And that your majesty was an usurper.

   King. Say, man, were these thy words?

   Arm. An 't shall please your majesty, I never said nor
thought any such matter: God is my witness, I am falsely   *185*
accused by the villain.

   Pet. By these ten bones, my lords, he did speak them to me
in the garret one night, as we were scouring my Lord of York's
armour.

   York. Base dunghill villain, and mechanical,   *190*
I'll have thy head for this thy traitor's speech.
I do beseech your royal majesty
Let him have all the rigour of the law.

   Arm. Alas! my lord, hang me if ever I spake the words. My
accuser is my prentice; and when I did correct him for his   *195*
fault the other day, he did vow upon his knees he would be
even with me: I have good witness of this: therefore I beseech
your majesty, do not cast away an honest man for a villain's
accusation.

   King. Uncle, what shall we say to this in law?   *200*

   Hum. This doom, my lord, if I may judge.
Let Somerset be regent o'er the French,
Because in York this breeds suspicion;
And let these have a day appointed them
For single combat in convenient place,   *205*
For he hath witness of his servant's malice.
This is the law, and this Duke Humphrey's doom.

   [*King.* Then be it so. My Lord of Somerset,

We make your Grace lord regent o'er the French.]

   Som. I humbly thank your royal majesty.   *210*

   Arm. And I accept the combat willingly.

   Pet. Alas! my lord, I cannot fight: for God's sake, pity my
case! the spite of man prevaileth against me. O Lord, have
mercy upon me! I shall never be able to fight a blow. O Lord,
my heart!   *215*

   Hum. Sirrah, or you must fight, or else be hang'd.

   King. Away with them to prison; and the day of combat
shall be the last of the next month. Come, Somerset, we'll see
thee sent away.   *Flourish. Exeunt.*

❧ SCENE FOURTH ❧

[The Same. The Duke of Gloucester's Garden]
*Enter the Witch [Margery Jordan], the two Priests [Hume and
Southwell], and Bolingbroke.*

   Hume. Come, my masters; the duchess, I tell you, expects
performance of your promises.

   Boling. Master Hume, we are therefore provided. Will her
ladyship behold and hear our exorcisms?

   Hume. Ay; what else? fear you not her courage.   *5*

   Boling. I have heard her reported to be a woman of an
invincible spirit: but it shall be convenient, Master Hume,
that you be by her aloft while we be busy below; and so, I
pray you, go in God's name, and leave us.   *Exit Hume.*
Mother Jordan, be you prostrate, and grovel on the earth;   *10*
John Southwell, read you; and let us to our work.

Enter Eleanor aloft.

   Elea. Well said, my masters, and welcome all.
To this gear the sooner the better.

   Boling. Patience, good lady; wizards know their times:
Deep night, dark night, the silent of the night,   *15*
The time of night when Troy was set on fire;
The time when screech-owls cry, and ban-dogs howl,
And spirits walk, and ghosts break up their graves,
That time best fits the work we have in hand.
Madam, sit you, and fear not: whom we raise   *20*
We will make fast within a hallow'd verge.

*Here do the ceremonies belonging, and make the circle; Boling-
broke or Southwell reads, Conjuro te, &c. It thunders and lightens
terribly; then the Spirit riseth.*

   Spir. Adsum.

   Witch. Asmath!
By the eternal God, whose name and power
Thou tremblest at, answer that I shall ask;   *25*
For till thou speak, thou shalt not pass from hence.

   Spir. Ask what thou wilt. That I had said and done!

   Boling. First, of the king: what shall of him become?

   Spir. The Duke yet lives that Henry shall depose;
But him outlive, and die a violent death.   *30*

[As the Spirit speaks, Southwell writes the answers.]

163 for: *because* **166 discharge:** *formal license to proceed to France* **furniture:** *equipment* **168 Last time;** *cf. n.* **170 fact:** *misdeed* **187 bones:** *fingers* **190 mechanical:** *plebeian* **201 doom:** *judgment* **203 in:** *in regard to*

208, 209 *Cf. n.* **8 aloft:** *i.e. on the balcony of the stage* **12 Well said:** *well done* **13
gear:** *business* **15 silent:** *silent part* **17 ban-dogs:** *chained watch-dogs* **18 break up:**
tear open **21 hallow'd verge:** *magic circle* **S. d. belonging:** *appropriate* **25 that:**
what **27 That:** *would that* **done:** *had it over*

Boling. What fates await the Duke of Suffolk?
Spir. By water shall he die and take his end.
Boling. What shall befall the Duke of Somerset?
Spir. Let him shun castles:
Safer shall he be upon the sandy plains   35
Than where castles mounted stand.
Have done, for more I hardly can endure.
    Boling. Descend to darkness and the burning lake!
False fiend, avoid!   *Thunder and lightning. Exit Spirit.*

Enter the Duke of York and the Duke of Buckingham with their
Guard, and break in.

    York. Lay hands upon these traitors and their trash.   40
Beldam, I think we watch'd you at an inch.
What, madam! are you there? the king and commonweal
Are deeply indebted for this piece of pains:
My Lord Protector will, I doubt it not,
See you well guerdon'd for these good deserts.   45
    Elea. Not half so bad as thine to England's king,
Injurious duke, that threatest where's no cause.
    Buck. True, madam, none at all. What call you this?
                [Showing her the papers.]
Away with them! let them be clapp'd up close
And kept asunder. You, madam, shall with us: 50
Stafford, take her to thee.—
We'll see your trinkets here all forthcoming.
All, away!   *Exit [Guard, with Duchess, etc.].*
    York. Lord Buckingham, methinks you watch'd her well:
A pretty plot, well chosen to build upon!   55
Now, pray, my lord, let's see the devil's writ.
What have we here?   *Reads.*
'The duke yet lives that Henry shall depose;
But him outlive, and die a violent death.'
Why, this is just,   60
'*Aio te, Æacida, Romanos vincere posse.*'
Well, to the rest:
'Tell me what fate awaits the Duke of Suffolk?
By water shall he die and take his end.
What shall betide the Duke of Somerset?   65
Let him shun castles:
Safer shall he be upon the sandy plains
Than where castles mounted stand.'
Come, come, my lords; these oracles
Are hardly attain'd, and hardly understood.   70
The king is now in progress towards Saint Albans;
With him, the husband of this lovely lady:
Thither goes these news as fast as horse can carry them,
A sorry breakfast for my Lord Protector.
    Buck. Your Grace shall give me leave, my Lord of York,   75
To be the post, in hope of his reward.
    York. At your pleasure, my good lord.
Who's within there, ho!

Enter a Servingman.

Invite my Lords of Salisbury and Warwick
To sup with me to-morrow night. Away!   *Exeunt.*   80

ACT SECOND ❧ SCENE FIRST

[St. Albans]
Enter the King, Queen, Protector, Cardinal, and Suffolk, with
Falconers halloing.

    Queen. Believe me, lords, for flying at the brook,
I saw not better sport these seven years' day:
Yet, by your leave, the wind was very high,
And, ten to one, old Joan had not gone out.
    King. But what a point, my lord, your falcon made,   5
And what a pitch she flew above the rest!
To see how God in all his creatures works!
Yea, man and birds are fain of climbing high.
    Suf. No marvel, an it like your majesty,
My Lord Protector's hawks do tower so well;   10
They know their master loves to be aloft,
And bears his thoughts above his falcon's pitch.
    Glo. My lord, 'tis but a base ignoble mind
That mounts no higher than a bird can soar.
    Car. I thought as much; he would be above the   15
clouds.
    Glo. Ay, my Lord Cardinal; how think you by that?
Were it not good your Grace could fly to heaven?
    King. The treasury of everlasting joy.
    Car. Thy heaven is on earth; thine eyes and thoughts   20
Beat on a crown, the treasure of thy heart;
Pernicious protector, dangerous peer,
That smooth'st it so with king and commonweal!
    Glo. What! cardinal, is your priesthood grown peremptory?
Tantæne animis cœlestibus iræ?   25
Churchmen so hot? good uncle, hide such malice;
With such holiness can you do it?
    Suf. No malice, sir; no more than well becomes
So good a quarrel and so bad a peer.
    Glo. As who, my lord?   30
    Suf.   Why, as you, my lord,
An 't like your lordly lord-protectorship.
    Glo. Why, Suffolk, England knows thine insolence.
    Queen. And thy ambition, Gloucester.
    King.   I prithee, peace,   35
Good queen, and whet not on these furious peers;
For blessed are the peacemakers on earth.
    Car. Let me be blessed for the peace I make
Against this proud protector with my sword!
    Glo. [Aside to the Cardinal.] Faith, holy uncle, would   40
'twere come to that!
    Car. [Aside to Gloucester.] Marry, when thou dar'st.
    Glo. [Aside to the Cardinal.] Make up no factious numbers
for the matter;
In thine own person answer thy abuse.   45
    Car. [Aside to Gloucester.] Ay, where thou dar'st not peep:
and if thou dar'st,
This evening on the east side of the grove.
    King. How now, my lords!
    Car.   Believe me, cousin Gloucester,   50
Had not your man put up the fowl so suddenly,

---

41 **Beldam:** *hag* **watch'd:** *caught in the act* **at an inch:** *precisely* 47 **Injurious:** *insulting* 49
clapp'd up close: *closely imprisoned* 55 *Cf. n.* 61 *Cf. n.* 70 **hardly:** *with difficulty* 73 **goes;**
cf. n.

1 **flying ... brook:** *hawking for waterfowl* 2 **day:** *space of time* 4 *Cf. n.* 5 **point:**
position from which to attack the prey 6 **pitch:** *height* 10 **tower:** *soar* 21 **Beat on:**
keep aiming at 23 **smooth'st it:** *insinuatest* 25 *Cf. n.* 27 *Cf. n.* 43 *Do not*
refer the quarrel to your followers

We had had more sport. *[Aside to Gloucester.]* Come with
thy two-hand sword.

   Glo. True, uncle.

   Car. Are ye advis'd? *[Aside to Gloucester.]* The east side   *55*
of the grove.

   Glo. [Aside to the Cardinal.] Cardinal, I am with you.

   King. Why, how now, uncle Gloucester!

   Glo. Talking of hawking; nothing else, my lord.—
[Aside to the Cardinal.] Now, by God's mother, priest, I'll   *60*
shave your crown
For this, or all my fence shall fail.

   Car. [Aside to Gloucester.] Medice, teipsum;
Protector, see to 't well, protect yourself.

   King. The winds grow high; so do your stomachs, lords.   *65*
How irksome is this music to my heart!
When such strings jar, what hope of harmony?
I pray, my lords, let me compound this strife.

             Enter one crying, 'A Miracle.'

   Glo. What means this noise?
Fellow, what miracle dost thou proclaim?   *70*

   One. A miracle! a miracle!

   Suf. Come to the king, and tell him what miracle.

   One. Forsooth, a blind man at Saint Alban's shrine,
Within this half hour hath receiv'd his sight;
A man that ne'er saw in his life before.   *75*

   King. Now, God be prais'd, that to believing souls
Gives light in darkness, comfort in despair!

Enter the Mayor of Saint Albans, and his Brethren, bearing the
man [Simpcox] between two in a chair [followed by Simpcox's
wife and others].

   Car. Here comes the townsmen on procession,
To present your highness with the man.

   King. Great is his comfort in this earthly vale,   *80*
Although by his sight his sin be multiplied.

   Glo. Stand by, my masters; bring him near the king:
His highness' pleasure is to talk with him.

   King. Good fellow, tell us here the circumstance,
That we for thee may glorify the Lord.   *85*
What! hast thou been long blind, and now restor'd?

   Simp. Born blind, an 't please your Grace.

   Wife. Ay, indeed, was he.

   Suf. What woman is this?

   Wife. His wife, an 't like your worship.   *90*

   Glo. Hadst thou been his mother, thou couldst have
better told.

   King. Where wert thou born?

   Simp. At Berwick in the north, an 't like your Grace.

   King. Poor soul! God's goodness hath been great to thee: *95*
Let never day nor night unhallow'd pass,
But still remember what the Lord hath done.

   Queen. Tell me, good fellow, cam'st thou here by chance,
Or of devotion, to this holy shrine?

   Simp. God knows, of pure devotion; being call'd   *100*
A hundred times and oft'ner in my sleep,

By good Saint Alban; who said, 'Simon, come;
Come, offer at my shrine, and I will help thee.'

   Wife. Most true, forsooth; and many time and oft
Myself have heard a voice to call him so.   *105*

   Car. What! art thou lame?

   Simp.   Ay, God Almighty help me!

   Suf. How cam'st thou so?

   Simp.   A fall off of a tree.

   Wife. A plum-tree, master.   *110*

   Glo.   How long hast thou been blind?

   Simp. O! born so, master.

   Glo.   What! and wouldst climb a tree?

   Simp. But that in all my life, when I was a youth.

   Wife. Too true; and bought his climbing very dear.   *115*

   Glo. Mass, thou lov'dst plums well, that wouldst venture so.

   Simp. Alas! master, my wife desir'd some damsons,
And made me climb with danger of my life.

   Glo. A subtle knave! but yet it shall not serve.
Let me see thine eyes: wink now: now open them: *120*
In my opinion yet thou seest not well.

   Simp. Yes, master, clear as day; I thank God and Saint
Albans.

   Glo. Sayst thou me so? What colour is this cloak of?

   Simp. Red, master; red as blood.   *125*

   Glo. Why, that's well said. What colour is my gown of?

   Simp. Black, forsooth; coal-black, as jet.

   King. Why then, thou know'st what colour jet is of?

   Suf. And yet, I think, jet did he never see.

   Glo. But cloaks and gowns before this day a many.   *130*

   Wife. Never, before this day, in all his life.

   Glo. Tell me, sirrah, what's my name?

   Simp. Alas! master, I know not.

   Glo. What's his name?

   Simp. I know not.   *135*

   Glo. Nor his?

   Simp. No, indeed, master.

   Glo. What's thine own name?

   Simp. Saunder Simpcox, an if it please you, master.

   Glo. Then, Saunder, sit there, the lying'st knave in Christendom. If thou hadst been born blind, thou mightst as well
have known all our names as thus to name the several colours
we do wear. Sight may distinguish of colours, but suddenly to
nominate them all, it is impossible. My lords, Saint Alban here
hath done a miracle; and would ye not think that cunning   *145*
to be great, that could restore this cripple to his legs again?

   Simp. O, master, that you could!

   Glo. My masters of St. Albans, have you not beadles in
your town, and things called whips?

   May. Yes, my lord, if it please your Grace.   *150*

   Glo. Then send for one presently.

   May. Sirrah, go fetch the beadle hither straight.

                              Exit [an Attendant].

   Glo. Now fetch me a stool hither by and by. *[A stool*
brought out.] Now, sirrah, if you mean to save yourself
from whipping, leap me over this stool and run away.   *155*

   Simp. Alas! master, I am not able to stand alone:
You go about to torture me in vain.

54-57 *Cf. n.*   **55 advis'd:** *clearly informed*   **62 fence:** *skill in fencing*   **63 Medice,**
teipsum: *Doctor, cure thyself*   **65 stomachs:** *angers*   **67 jar:** *sound a discord*   **68**
compound: *settle, compose*   **73 Saint Alban's shrine;** *cf. n.*   **82 Although the recovery**
of his eyesight expose him to additional temptations   **84 circumstance:** *details*

102 Simon; *cf. n.*   **114 But that:** *only that one tree*   **119 serve:** *serve his purpose, suc-*
ceed   **120 wink:** *close both eyes*   **122 Saint Albans:** *i.e. the saint's shrine*   **130 many:**
multitude   **144 nominate:** *call by name*   **153 by and by:** *at once*   **155 leap me:** *leap*

Enter a Beadle with whips.

Glo. Well, sir, we must have you find your legs. Sirrah
beadle, whip him till he leap over that same stool.

Bead. I will, my lord. Come on, sirrah; off with your   *160*
doublet quickly.

Simp. Alas! master, what shall I do? I am not able to stand.

*After the Beadle hath hit him once, he leaps over the stool, and
runs away: and they follow and cry, 'A miracle!'*

King. O God! seest thou this, and bear'st so long?
Queen. It made me laugh to see the villain run.
Glo. Follow the knave; and take this drab away.   *165*
Wife. Alas! sir, we did it for pure need.
Glo. Let them be whipp'd through every market town
Till they come to Berwick, from whence they came.
          Exit [Mayor, with Beadle, Wife, &c].
Car. Duke Humphrey has done a miracle to-day.
Suf. True; made the lame to leap and fly away.   *170*
Glo. But you have done more miracles than I;
You made in a day, my lord, whole towns to fly.

Enter Buckingham.

King. What tidings with our cousin Buckingham?
Buck. Such as my heart doth tremble to unfold.
A sort of naughty persons, lewdly bent,   *175*
Under the countenance and confederacy
Of Lady Eleanor, the protector's wife,
The ringleader and head of all this rout,
Have practis'd dangerously against your state,
Dealing with witches and with conjurers: *180*
Whom we have apprehended in the fact,
Raising up wicked spirits from under ground,
Demanding of King Henry's life and death,
And other of your highness' privy council,
As more at large your Grace shall understand.   *185*
Car. And so, my Lord Protector, by this means
Your lady is forthcoming yet at London.
This news, I think, hath turn'd your weapon's edge;
'Tis like, my lord, you will not keep your hour.
Glo. Ambitious churchman, leave to afflict my heart: *190*
Sorrow and grief have vanquish'd all my powers;
And, vanquish'd as I am, I yield to thee,
Or to the meanest groom.
King. O God! what mischiefs work the wicked ones,
Heaping confusion on their own heads thereby.   *195*
Queen. Gloucester, see here the tainture of thy nest;
And look thyself be faultless, thou wert best.
Glo. Madam, for myself, to heaven I do appeal,
How I have lov'd my king and commonweal;
And, for my wife, I know not how it stands.   *200*
Sorry I am to hear what I have heard:
Noble she is, but if she have forgot
Honour and virtue, and convers'd with such
As, like to pitch, defile nobility,
I banish her my bed and company,   *205*
And give her, as a prey, to law and shame,

That hath dishonour'd Gloucester's honest name.
King. Well, for this night we will repose us here:
To-morrow toward London back again,
To look into this business thoroughly,   *210*
And call these foul offenders to their answers;
And poise the cause in justice' equal scales,
Whose beam stands sure, whose rightful cause prevails.
          Flourish. Exeunt.

❧ SCENE SECOND ❧

*[London. The Duke of York's Garden]
Enter York, Salisbury, and Warwick.*

York. Now, my good Lords of Salisbury and Warwick,
Our simple supper ended, give me leave,
In this close walk to satisfy myself,
In craving your opinion of my title,
Which is infallible to England's crown.   *5*
Sal. My lord, I long to hear it at full.
War. Sweet York, begin; and if thy claim be good,
The Nevils are thy subjects to command.
York. Then thus:
Edward the Third, my lords, had seven sons: *10*
The first, Edward the Black Prince, Prince of Wales;
The second, William of Hatfield; and the third,
Lionel, Duke of Clarence; next to whom
Was John of Gaunt, the Duke of Lancaster;
The fifth was Edmund Langley, Duke of York;   *15*
The sixth was Thomas of Woodstock, Duke of Gloucester;
William of Windsor was the seventh and last.
Edward the Black Prince died before his father,
And left behind him Richard, his only son,
Who after Edward the Third's death, reign'd as king;   *20*
Till Henry Bolingbroke, Duke of Lancaster,
The eldest son and heir of John of Gaunt,
Crown'd by the name of Henry the Fourth,
Seiz'd on the realm, depos'd the rightful king,
Sent his poor queen to France, from whence she came,   *25*
And him to Pomfret; where as all you know,
Harmless Richard was murther'd traitorously.
War. Father, the duke hath told the truth;
Thus got the house of Lancaster the crown.
York. Which now they hold by force and not by right;   *30*
For Richard, the first son's heir, being dead,
The issue of the next son should have reign'd.
Sal. But William of Hatfield died without an heir.
York. The third son, Duke of Clarence, from whose line
I claim the crown, had issue, Philippe a daughter,   *35*
Who married Edmund Mortimer, Earl of March:
Edmund had issue Roger, Earl of March:
Roger had issue Edmund, Anne, and Eleanor.
Sal. This Edmund, in the reign of Bolingbroke,
As I have read, laid claim unto the crown;   *40*
And but for Owen Glendower, had been king,
Who kept him in captivity till he died.
But, to the rest.
York.   His eldest sister, Anne,

175 sort: *set* naughty: *good-for-naught* lewdly bent: *with evil intent* 178 rout: *company* 179 practis'd: *plotted* 181 in the fact: *red-handed* 183 Demanding of: *inquiring about* 187 forthcoming: *under arrest* 190 leave: *cease* 196 tainture: *fouling* 197 thou wert best: *you had better* 203 convers'd: *had dealings*

212 poise: *weigh* 213 beam: *transverse balancing rod of scales* 3 close: *private* 39–42 This Edmund … died; *cf. n.*

My mother, being heir unto the crown,   45
Married Richard, Earl of Cambridge, who was son
To Edmund Langley, Edward the Third's fifth son.
By her I claim the kingdom: she was heir
To Roger, Earl of March; who was the son
Of Edmund Mortimer, who married Philippe,   50
Sole daughter unto Lionel, Duke of Clarence:
So, if the issue of the eldest son
Succeed before the younger, I am king.
    War. What plain proceeding is more plain than this?
Henry doth claim the crown from John of Gaunt,   55
The fourth son; York claims it from the third.
Till Lionel's issue fails, his should not reign:
It fails not yet, but flourishes in thee,
And in thy sons, fair slips of such a stock.
Then, father Salisbury, kneel we together,   60
And in this private plot be we the first
That shall salute our rightful sovereign
With honour of his birthright to the crown.
    Both. Long live our sovereign Richard, England's king!
    York. We thank you, lords! But I am not your king   65
Till I be crown'd, and that my sword be stain'd
With heart-blood of the house of Lancaster;
And that's not suddenly to be perform'd,
But with advice and silent secrecy.
Do you as I do in these dangerous days,   70
Wink at the Duke of Suffolk's insolence,
At Beaufort's pride, at Somerset's ambition,
At Buckingham and all the crew of them,
Till they have snar'd the shepherd of the flock,
That virtuous prince, the good Duke Humphrey: 75
'Tis that they seek; and they, in seeking that
Shall find their deaths, if York can prophesy.
    Sal. My lord, break we off; we know your mind at full.
    War. My heart assures me that the Earl of Warwick
Shall one day make the Duke of York a king.   80
    York. And, Nevil, this I do assure myself,
Richard shall live to make the Earl of Warwick
The greatest man in England but the king.   *Exeunt.*

❧ SCENE THIRD ❧

[The Same. A Hall of Justice]
Sound Trumpets. Enter the King and State [including Queen,
Gloucester, York, Suffolk, and Salisbury], with Guard, to banish the
Duchess. [Margery Jordan, Hume, Southwell, and Bolingbroke are
also brought in.]

    King. Stand forth, Dame Eleanor Cobham, Gloucester's
wife.
In sight of God and us your guilt is great:
Receive the sentence of the law for sins
Such as by God's book are adjudg'd to death.   5
You four, from hence to prison back again;
From thence, unto the place of execution:
The witch in Smithfield shall be burnt to ashes,
And you three shall be strangled on the gallows.
You, madam, for you are more nobly born,   10
Despoiled of your honour in your life,

Shall, after three days' open penance done,
Live in your country here in banishment,
With Sir John Stanley, in the Isle of Man.
    Elea. Welcome is banishment; welcome were my death.   15
    Glo. Eleanor, the law, thou seest, hath judged thee:
I cannot justify whom the law condemns.
        [Exeunt the Duchess, and the other Prisoners, guarded.]
Mine eyes are full of tears, my heart of grief.
Ah, Humphrey! this dishonour in thine age
Will bring thy head with sorrow to the ground.   20
I beseech your majesty, give me leave to go;
Sorrow would solace and mine age would ease.
    King. Stay, Humphrey, Duke of Gloucester: ere thou go,
Give up thy staff: Henry will to himself
Protector be; and God shall be my hope,   25
My stay, my guide, and lantern to my feet.
And go in peace, Humphrey; no less belov'd
Than when thou wert protector to thy king.
    Queen. I see no reason why a king of years
Should be to be protected like a child.   30
God and King Henry govern England's realm!
Give up your staff, sir, and the king his realm.
    Glo. My staff! here, noble Henry, is my staff:
As willingly do I the same resign
As e'er thy father Henry made it mine;   35
And even as willingly at thy feet I leave it
As others would ambitiously receive it.
Farewell, good king! when I am dead and gone,
May honourable peace attend thy throne.   *Exit Gloucester.*
    Queen. Why, now is Henry king, and Margaret queen;   40
And Humphrey, Duke of Gloucester, scarce himself,
That bears so shrewd a maim: two pulls at once;
His lady banish'd, and a limb lopp'd off,
This staff of honour raught: there let it stand,
Where it best fits to be, in Henry's hand.   45
    Suf. Thus droops this lofty pine and hangs his sprays;
Thus Eleanor's pride dies in her youngest days.
    York. Lords, let him go. Please it your majesty
This is the day appointed for the combat;
And ready are the appellant and defendant,   50
The armourer and his man, to enter the lists,
So please your highness to behold the fight.
    Queen. Ay, good my lord; for purposely therefore
Left I the court, to see this quarrel tried.
    King. O' God's name, see the lists and all things fit: 55
Here let them end it; and God defend the right!
    York. I never saw a fellow worse bested,
Or more afraid to fight, than is the appellant,
The servant of this armourer, my lords.

Enter at one door the Armourer [Horner] and his Neighbours,
drinking to him so much that he is drunk; and he enters with a
drum before him, and his staff with a sand-bag fastened to it:
and at the other door his Man [Peter], with a drum and sand-
bag, and Prentices drinking to him.

    1. Neigh. Here, neighbour Horner, I drink to you in a cup
of sack: and fear not, neighbour, you shall do well enough.

63 With . . . birthright: *acclaiming his hereditary right*   4 *Cf. n.*   7, 8 *Cf. n.*

14 *Cf. n.*   22 would: *needs to have*   26 staff: *badge of office*   30 be to be: *need to*
be   42 so . . . maim: *so sore a mutilation*   pulls: *pluckings of feathers* (?)   44 raught:
seized   47 youngest: *latest, most recent* (?); *cf. n.*   50 appellant: *challenger*   55 O':
in   57 bested: *prepared*   61 sack: *dry Spanish wine*

2. Neigh. And here, neighbour, here's a cup of charneco.

3. Neigh. And here's a pot of good double beer, neighbour:
drink, and fear not your man.

Arm. Let it come, i' faith, and I'll pledge you all; and a   65
fig for Peter!

1. Pren. Here, Peter, I drink to thee; and be not afraid.

2. Pren. Be merry, Peter, and fear not thy master: fight for
credit of the prentices.

Peter. I thank you all: drink, and pray for me, I pray you;
for, I think, I have taken my last draught in this world. Here,
Robin, an if I die, I give thee my apron: and, Will, thou shalt
have my hammer: and here, Tom, take all the money that I
have. O Lord bless me! I pray God, for I am never able to
deal with my master, he hath learnt so much fence already.   75

Sal. Come, leave your drinking and fall to blows. Sirrah,
what's thy name?

Peter. Peter, forsooth.

Sal. Peter! what more?

Peter. Thump.   80

Sal. Thump! then see thou thump thy master well.

Arm. Masters, I am come hither, as it were, upon my man's
instigation, to prove him a knave, and myself an honest man:
and touching the Duke of York, I will take my death I never
meant him any ill, nor the king, nor the queen; and there-   85
fore, Peter, have at thee with a downright blow!

York. Dispatch: this knave's tongue begins to double.
Sound, trumpets, alarum to the combatants.

      They fight, and Peter strikes him down.

Arm. Hold, Peter, hold! I confess, I confess treason.   *[Dies.]*

York. Take away his weapon. Fellow, thank God, and   90
the good wine in thy master's way.

Peter. O God! have I overcome mine enemies in this
presence? O Peter! thou hast prevailed in right!

King. Go, take hence that traitor from our sight;
For by his death we do perceive his guilt: 95
And God in justice hath reveal'd to us
The truth and innocence of this poor fellow,
Which he had thought to have murther'd wrongfully.
Come, fellow, follow us for thy reward.

       Sound a flourish. Exeunt.

❧ Scene Fourth ❧

[The Same. A Street]

Enter Duke Humphrey and his Men, in mourning cloaks.

Glo. Thus sometimes hath the brightest day a cloud;
And after summer evermore succeeds
Barren winter, with his wrathful nipping cold:
So cares and joys abound, as seasons fleet.
Sirs, what's o'clock?   5

Serv.   Ten, my lord.

Glo. Ten is the hour that was appointed me
To watch the coming of my punish'd duchess:
Uneath may she endure the flinty streets,
To tread them with her tender-feeling feet.   10

Sweet Nell, ill can thy noble mind abrook
The abject people, gazing on thy face
With envious looks still laughing at thy shame,
That erst did follow thy proud chariot wheels
When thou didst ride in triumph through the streets.   15
But, soft! I think she comes; and I'll prepare
My tear-stain'd eyes to see her miseries.

*Enter the Duchess in a white sheet, and a taper burning in her
  hand, with the Sheriff, [Sir John Stanley,] and Officers.*

Serv. So please your Grace, we'll take her from the sheriff.

Glo. No, stir not for your lives; let her pass by.

Elea. Come you, my lord, to see my open shame?   20
Now thou dost penance too. Look! how they gaze.
See! how the giddy multitude do point,
And nod their heads, and throw their eyes on thee.
Ah, Gloucester, hide thee from their hateful looks,
And, in thy closet pent up, rue my shame,   25
And ban thine enemies, both mine and thine!

Glo. Be patient, gentle Nell; forget this grief.

Elea. Ay, Gloucester, teach me to forget myself;
For whilst I think I am thy wedded wife,
And thou a prince, protector of this land,   30
Methinks I should not thus be led along,
Mail'd up in shame, with papers on my back,
And follow'd with a rabble that rejoice
To see my tears and hear my deep-fet groans.
The ruthless flint doth cut my tender feet,   35
And when I start, the envious people laugh,
And bid me be advised how I tread.
Ah, Humphrey! can I bear this shameful yoke?
Trowest thou that e'er I'll look upon the world,
Or count them happy that enjoys the sun?   40
No; dark shall be my light, and night my day;
To think upon my pomp shall be my hell.
Sometime I'll say, I am Duke Humphrey's wife;
And he a prince and ruler of the land:
Yet so he rul'd and such a prince he was   45
As he stood by whilst I, his forlorn duchess,
Was made a wonder and a pointing-stock
To every idle rascal follower.
But be thou mild and blush not at my shame;
Nor stir at nothing till the axe of death   50
Hang over thee, as, sure, it shortly will;
For Suffolk, he that can do all in all
With her that hateth thee, and hates us all,
And York, and impious Beaufort, that false priest,
Have all lim'd bushes to betray thy wings;   55
And, fly thou how thou canst, they'll tangle thee:
But fear not thou, until thy foot be snar'd,
Nor never seek prevention of thy foes.

Glo. Ah, Nell! forbear: thou aimest all awry;
I must offend before I be attainted;
And had I twenty times so many foes,   60
And each of them had twenty times their power,
All these could not procure me any scath,

---

62 **charneco:** *sweet Portuguese wine* 84 **take my death:** *pledge my life* 87 **double:**
talk thickly 89 **I confess treason;** *cf. n.* 98 **Which:** *whom* 4 **fleet:** *pass* 9
Uneath: *hardly*

11 **abrook:** *endure* 12 **abject:** *vile* 25 **closet:** *private apartment* 26 **ban:**
curse 32 **Mail'd:** *wrapped* 33 **with:** *by* 34 **deep-fet:** *deep-drawn* 36 **start:**
wince 37 **advised:** *cautious* 40 **that enjoys:** *who enjoy* 47 **pointing-stock:** *butt of
ridicule* 48 **rascal follower:** *worthless hireling* 54 *Cf. I. iii. 84* 57 **prevention:**
forestalling 59 **attainted:** *convicted* 62 **scath:** *injury*

So long as I am loyal, true, and crimeless.
Wouldst have me rescue thee from this reproach?   *65*
Why, yet thy scandal were not wip'd away,
But I in danger for the breach of law.
Thy greatest help is quiet, gentle Nell:
I pray thee, sort thy heart to patience;
These few days' wonder will be quickly worn.   *70*

Enter a Herald.

 Her. I summon your Grace to his majesty's parliament,
holden at Bury the first of this next month.
 Glo. And my consent ne'er ask'd herein before!
This is close dealing. Well, I will be there.   *[Exit Herald.]*
My Nell, I take my leave: and, master sheriff,   *75*
Let not her penance exceed the king's commission.
 Sher. An 't please your Grace, here my commission stays;
And Sir John Stanley is appointed now
To take her with him to the Isle of Man.
 Glo. Must you, Sir John, protect my lady here?   *80*
 Stan. So am I given in charge, may 't please your Grace.
 Glo. Entreat her not the worse in that I pray
You use her well. The world may laugh again;
And I may live to do you kindness if
You do it her: and so, Sir John, farewell.   *85*
 Elea. What! gone, my lord, and bid me not farewell!
 Glo. Witness my tears, I cannot stay to speak.
        Exit Gloucester [with his Men].
 Elea. Art thou gone too? All comfort go with thee!
For none abides with me: my joy is death;
Death, at whose name I oft have been afear'd,   *90*
Because I wish'd this world's eternity.
Stanley, I prithee, go, and take me hence;
I care not whither, for I beg no favour,
Only convey me where thou art commanded.
 Stan. Why, madam, that is to the Isle of Man;   *95*
There to be us'd according to your state.
 Elea. That's bad enough, for I am but reproach:
And shall I then be us'd reproachfully?
 Stan. Like to a duchess, and Duke Humphrey's lady:
According to that state you shall be us'd.   *100*
 Elea. Sheriff, farewell, and better than I fare,
Although thou hast been conduct of my shame.
 Sher. It is my office; and, madam, pardon me.
 Elea. Ay, ay, farewell; thy office is discharg'd.
Come, Stanley, shall we go?   *105*
 Stan. Madam, your penance done, throw off this sheet,
And go we to attire you for our journey.
 Elea. My shame will not be shifted with my sheet:
No; it will hang upon my richest robes,
And show itself, attire me how I can.   *110*
Go, lead the way; I long to see my prison.   *Exeunt.*

ACT THIRD ❧ SCENE FIRST

[The Abbey at Bury St. Edmunds]
Sound a sennet. Enter King, Queen, Cardinal, Suffolk, York, Buckingham, Salisbury, and Warwick, to the Parliament.

 King. I muse my Lord of Gloucester is not come:
'Tis not his wont to be the hindmost man,
Whate'er occasion keeps him from us now.
 Queen. Can you not see? or will ye not observe
The strangeness of his alter'd countenance?   *5*
With what a majesty he bears himself,
How insolent of late he is become,
How proud, how peremptory, and unlike himself?
We know the time since he was mild and affable,
And if we did but glance a far-off look,   *10*
Immediately he was upon his knee,
That all the court admir'd him for submission:
But meet him now, and, be it in the morn,
When everyone will give the time of day,
He knits his brow and shows an angry eye,   *15*
And passeth by with stiff unbowed knee,
Disdaining duty that to us belongs.
Small curs are not regarded when they grin,
But great men tremble when the lion roars;
And Humphrey is no little man in England.   *20*
First note that he is near you in descent,
And should you fall, he is the next will mount.
Me seemeth then it is no policy,
Respecting what a rancorous mind he bears,
And his advantage following your decease,   *25*
That he should come about your royal person
Or be admitted to your highness' council.
By flattery hath he won the commons' hearts,
And when he please to make commotion,
'Tis to be fear'd they all will follow him.   *30*
Now 'tis the spring, and weeds are shallow-rooted;
Suffer them now and they'll o'ergrow the garden,
And choke the herbs for want of husbandry.
The reverent care I bear unto my lord
Made me collect these dangers in the duke.   *35*
If it be fond, call it a woman's fear;
Which fear if better reasons can supplant,
I will subscribe and say I wrong'd the duke.
My Lord of Suffolk, Buckingham, and York,
Reprove my allegation if you can   *40*
Or else conclude my words effectual.
 Suf. Well hath your highness seen into this duke;
And had I first been put to speak my mind,
I think I should have told your Grace's tale.
The duchess, by his subornation,   *45*
Upon my life, began her devilish practices:
Or if he were not privy to those faults,
Yet, by reputing of his high descent,
As, next the king he was successive heir,
And such high vaunts of his nobility,   *50*

---

69 sort: *adapt* **70 worn:** *worn away, expired* **72 Bury:** *Bury St. Edmunds in Suffolk*
the first . . . month; *cf. n.* **74 close:** *secretive, sly* **76 commission:** *warrant* **77**
stays: *stops* **91 this . . . eternity:** *perpetuation of worldly enjoyment* **97 but reproach:**
all disgrace **101 better . . . fare:** *may you fare better than I do* **102 conduct:** *the*
conductor

1 muse: *wonder* **2** *Cf. n.* **9–12** *Cf. n.* **9 since:** *when* **14 give . . . day:** *say*
'good morning' **18 grin:** *show their teeth* **23 policy:** *prudent course* **24 Respecting:**
considering **25** *And considering the profit he would derive from your death* **33 hus-**
bandry: *cultivation of the soil* **35 collect:** *infer* **36 fond:** *foolish* **38 subscribe:**
submit **40 Reprove:** *disprove* **41 effectual:** *conclusive* **45 subornation:** *instiga-*
tion **48 reputing:** *boasting*

Did instigate the bedlam brain-sick duchess,
By wicked means to frame our sovereign's fall.
Smooth runs the water where the brook is deep,
And in his simple show he harbours treason.
The fox barks not when he would steal the lamb: 55
No, no, my sovereign; Gloucester is a man
Unsounded yet, and full of deep deceit.
     Car. Did he not, contrary to form of law,
Devise strange deaths for small offences done?
     York. And did he not, in his protectorship,   60
Levy great sums of money through the realm
For soldiers' pay in France, and never sent it?
By means whereof the towns each day revolted.
     Buck. Tut! these are petty faults to faults unknown,
Which time will bring to light in smooth Duke Humphrey.   65
     King. My lords, at once: the care you have of us,
To mow down thorns that would annoy our foot,
Is worthy praise; but shall I speak my conscience,
Our kinsman Gloucester is as innocent
From meaning treason to our royal person,   70
As is the sucking lamb or harmless dove.
The duke is virtuous, mild, and too well given
To dream on evil, or to work my downfall.
     Queen. Ah! what's more dangerous than this fond affiance!
Seems he a dove? his feathers are but borrow'd,   75
For he's disposed as the hateful raven:
Is he a lamb? his skin is surely lent him,
For he's inclin'd as is the ravenous wolf.
Who cannot steal a shape that means deceit?
Take heed, my lord; the welfare of us all   80
Hangs on the cutting short that fraudful man.

Enter Somerset.

     Som. All health unto my gracious sovereign!
     King. Welcome, Lord Somerset. What news from France?
     Som. That all your interest in those territories
Is utterly bereft you: all is lost.   85
     King. Cold news, Lord Somerset: but God's will be done!
     York. [*Aside.*] Cold news for me; for I had hope of France,
As firmly as I hope for fertile England.
Thus are my blossoms blasted in the bud,
And caterpillars eat my leaves away;   90
But I will remedy this gear ere long,
Or sell my title for a glorious grave.

Enter Gloucester.

     Glo. All happiness unto my lord the king!
Pardon, my liege, that I have stay'd so long.
     Suf. Nay, Gloucester, know that thou art come too soon,   95
Unless thou wert more loyal than thou art:
I do arrest thee of high treason here.
     Glo. Well, Suffolk, thou shalt not see me blush,
Nor change my countenance for this arrest:
A heart unspotted is not easily daunted.   100
The purest spring is not so free from mud

As I am clear from treason to my sovereign.
Who can accuse me? wherein am I guilty?
     York. 'Tis thought, my lord, that you took bribes of France,
And, being protector, stay'd the soldiers' pay;   105
By means whereof his highness hath lost France.
     Glo. Is it but thought so? What are they that think it?
I never robb'd the soldiers of their pay,
Nor ever had one penny bribe from France.
So help me God, as I have watch'd the night,   110
Ay, night by night, in studying good for England.
That doit that e'er I wrested from the king,
Or any groat I hoarded to my use,
Be brought against me at my trial-day!
No; many a pound of mine own proper store,   115
Because I would not tax the needy commons,
Have I dis-pursed to the garrisons,
And never ask'd for restitution.
     Car. It serves you well, my lord, to say so much.
     Glo. I say no more than truth, so help me God!   120
     York. In your protectorship you did devise
Strange tortures for offenders, never heard of,
That England was defam'd by tyranny.
     Glo. Why, 'tis well known that, whiles I was protector,
Pity was all the fault that was in me;   125
For I should melt at an offender's tears,
And lowly words were ransom for their fault.
Unless it were a bloody murtherer,
Or foul felonious thief that fleec'd poor passengers,
I never gave them condign punishment: 130
Murther, indeed, that bloody sin, I tortur'd
Above the felon or what trespass else.
     Suf. My lord, these faults are easy, quickly answer'd:
But mightier crimes are laid unto your charge,
Whereof you cannot easily purge yourself.   135
I do arrest you in his highness' name,
And here commit you to my Lord Cardinal
To keep until your further time of trial.
     King. My Lord of Gloucester, 'tis my special hope
That you will clear yourself from all suspect: 140
My conscience tells me you are innocent.
     Glo. Ah! gracious lord, these days are dangerous.
Virtue is chok'd with foul ambition,
And charity chas'd hence by rancour's hand;
Foul subornation is predominant,   145
And equity exil'd your highness' land.
I know their complot is to have my life;
And if my death might make this island happy,
And prove the period of their tyranny,
I would expend it with all willingness;   150
But mine is made the prologue to their play;
For thousands more, that yet suspect no peril,
Will not conclude their plotted tragedy.
Beaufort's red sparkling eyes blab his heart's malice,
And Suffolk's cloudy brow his stormy hate;   155
Sharp Buckingham unburthens with his tongue

52 frame: *bring to pass*   **59 Devise strange deaths;** *cf. n.*   **64 to:** *in comparison with*   **66 at once:** *addressing you all together* (?), *without more ado* (?)   **68 shall . . . conscience:** *if I am to say what I really think*   **72 too well given:** *of too good character*   **74 fond affiance:** *foolish trust*   **77 lent him:** *i.e. not his own, false*   **79** *What intending deceiver cannot assume a false appearance?*   **83–86** *Cf. n.*   **87 Cold news for me;** *cf. n.*   **97** *Cf. n.*

110 watch'd: *kept vigil through*   **112 doit:** *Dutch coin, worth half a farthing*   **113 groat:** *four-penny coin*   **117 dis-pursed:** *paid out*   **126 should:** *was wont to, would*   **129 passengers:** *wayfarers*   **130 condign:** *adequate*   **132** *Beyond any other kind of felony or misdemeanor*   **138 further:** *future*   **145 subornation:** *instigation to perjury or crime* (cf. l. 45)   **149 period:** *end*   **150 it:** *i.e. my life*   **153 conclude:** *by their deaths bring to conclusion*

The envious load that lies upon his heart;
And dogged York, that reaches at the moon,
Whose overweening arm I have pluck'd back,
By false accuse doth level at my life: 160
And you, my sovereign lady, with the rest,
Causeless have laid disgraces on my head,
And with your best endeavour have stirr'd up
My liefest liege to be mine enemy.
Ay, all of you have laid your heads together; 165
Myself had notice of your conventicles;
And all to make away my guiltless life.
I shall not want false witness to condemn me,
Nor store of treasons to augment my guilt;
The ancient proverb will be well effected: 170
'A staff is quickly found to beat a dog.'
  Car. My liege, his railing is intolerable.
If those that care to keep your royal person
From treason's secret knife and traitor's rage
Be thus upbraided, chid, and rated at, 175
And the offender granted scope of speech,
'Twill make them cool in zeal unto your Grace.
  Suf. Hath he not twit our sovereign lady here
With ignominious words, though clerkly couch'd,
As if she had suborned some to swear 180
False allegations to o'erthrow his state?
  Queen. But I can give the loser leave to chide.
  Glo. Far truer spoke than meant: I lose, indeed;
Beshrew the winners, for they play'd me false!
And well such losers may have leave to speak. 185
  Buck. He'll wrest the sense and hold us here all day.
Lord Cardinal, he is your prisoner.
  Car. Sirs, take away the duke, and guard him sure.
  Glo. Ah! thus King Henry throws away his crutch
Before his legs be firm to bear his body: 190
Thus is the shepherd beaten from thy side,
And wolves are gnarling who shall gnaw thee first.
Ah! that my fear were false, ah! that it were;
For good King Henry, thy decay I fear.

                    Exit Gloucester [guarded].
  King. My lords, what to your wisdoms seemeth best 195
Do or undo, as if ourself were here.
  Queen. What! will your highness leave the parliament?
  King. Ay, Margaret; my heart is drown'd with grief,
Whose flood begins to flow within mine eyes,
My body round engirt with misery, 200
For what's more miserable than discontent?
Ah! uncle Humphrey, in thy face I see
The map of honour, truth, and loyalty;
And yet, good Humphrey, is the hour to come
That e'er I prov'd thee false, or fear'd thy faith. 205
What low'ring star now envies thy estate,
That these great lords, and Margaret our queen,
Do seek subversion of thy harmless life?
Thou never didst them wrong, nor no man wrong;
And as the butcher takes away the calf, 210
And binds the wretch, and beats it when it strays,

Bearing it to the bloody slaughter-house,
Even so, remorseless, have they borne him hence;
And as the dam runs lowing up and down,
Looking the way her harmless young one went, 215
And can do nought but wail her darling's loss;
Even so myself bewails good Gloucester's case,
With sad unhelpful tears, and with dimm'd eyes
Look after him, and cannot do him good;
So mighty are his vowed enemies. 220
His fortunes I will weep; and, 'twixt each groan,
Say 'Who's a traitor, Gloucester he is none.' *Exit.*
  Queen. Free lords, cold snow melts with the sun's hot
beams.
Henry my lord is cold in great affairs, 225
Too full of foolish pity; and Gloucester's show
Beguiles him as the mournful crocodile
With sorrow snares relenting passengers;
Or as the snake, roll'd in a flowering bank,
With shining checker'd slough, doth sting a child 230
That for the beauty thinks it excellent.
Believe me, lords, were none more wise than I,—
And yet herein I judge mine own wit good,—
This Gloucester should be quickly rid the world,
To rid us from the fear we have of him. 235
  Car. That he should die is worthy policy;
And yet we want a colour for his death.
'Tis meet he be condemn'd by course of law.
  Suf. But in my mind that were no policy:
The king will labour still to save his life; 240
The commons haply rise to save his life;
And yet we have but trivial argument,
More than mistrust, that shows him worthy death.
  York. So that, by this, you would not have him die.
  Suf. Ah, York, no man alive so fain as I. 245
  York. 'Tis York that hath more reason for his death.
But, my Lord Cardinal, and you, my Lord of Suffolk,
Say as you think, and speak it from your souls,
Were 't not all one an empty eagle were set
To guard the chicken from a hungry kite, 250
As place Duke Humphrey for the king's protector?
  Queen. So the poor chicken should be sure of death.
  Suf. Madam, 'tis true: and were 't not madness, then,
To make the fox surveyor of the fold?
Who, being accus'd a crafty murtherer, 255
His guilt should be but idly posted over
Because his purpose is not executed.
No; let him die, in that he is a fox,
By nature prov'd an anemy to the flock,
Before his chaps be stain'd with crimson blood, 260
As Humphrey, prov'd by reasons, to my liege.
And do not stand on quillets how to slay him:
Be it by gins, by snares, by subtilty,
Sleeping or waking, 'tis no matter how,
So he be dead; for that is good deceit 265
Which mates him first that first intends deceit.
  Queen. Thrice noble Suffolk, 'tis resolutely spoke.

---

159 overweening: *presumptuous; cf. n.* **160 accuse:** *accusation* **level:** *aim* **164 liefest liege:** *dearest sovereign* **166 conventicles:** *secret meetings* **170 effected:** *put into effect* **173 care:** *endure care, trouble themselves* **178 twit:** *twitted* **179 clerkly couch'd:** *phrased with learned circumlocution* **184 Beshrew:** *curse, fie on!* **192 gnarling:** *snarling (to determine)* **203 map:** *epitome, abstract*

222 Who's: *whoever is* **223 Free:** *noble* **230 slough:** *skin* **237 colour:** *pretext* **242 argument:** *evidence* **243 mistrust:** *suspicion* **245 fain:** *gladly* **249 empty:** *i.e. starving* **256 idly:** *foolishly* **posted over:** *passed over hastily, ignored* **261 prov'd:** *i.e. proved an enemy* **262 stand on quillets:** *waste time with subtle distinctions* **263 gins:** *traps* **266 mates:** *confounds, overwhelms*

Suf. Not resolute, except so much were done,
For things are often spoke and seldom meant;
But, that my heart accordeth with my tongue,   270
Seeing the deed is meritorious,
And to preserve my sovereign from his foe,
Say but the word and I will be his priest.
    Car. But I would have him dead, my Lord of Suffolk.
Ere you can take due orders for a priest: 275
Say you consent and censure well the deed,
And I'll provide his executioner;
I tender so the safety of my liege.
    Suf. Here is my hand, the deed is worthy doing.
    Queen. And so say I.   280
    York. And I: and now we three have spoke it,
It skills not greatly who impugns our doom.

Enter a Post.

    Post. Great lords, from Ireland am I come amain,
To signify that rebels there are up,
And put the Englishmen unto the sword.   285
Send succours, lords, and stop the rage betime,
Before the wound do grow uncurable;
For, being green, there is great hope of help.
    Car. A breach that craves a quick expedient stop!
What counsel give you in this weighty cause?   290
    York. That Somerset be sent as regent thither.
'Tis meet that lucky ruler be employ'd;
Witness the fortune he hath had in France.
    Som. If York, with all his far-fet policy,
Had been the regent there instead of me,   295
He never would have stay'd in France so long.
    York. No, not to lose it all, as thou hast done:
I rather would have lost my life betimes
Than bring a burden of dishonour home,
By staying there so long till all were lost.   300
Show me one scar character'd on thy skin:
Men's flesh preserv'd so whole do seldom win.
    Queen. Nay then, this spark will prove a raging fire,
If wind and fuel be brought to feed it with.
No more, good York; sweet Somerset, be still: 305
Thy fortune, York, hadst thou been regent there,
Might happily have prov'd far worse than his.
    York. What! worse than nought? nay, then a shame take all.
    Som. And in the number thee, that wishest shame.
    Car. My Lord of York, try what your fortune is.   310
Th' uncivil kerns of Ireland are in arms
And temper clay with blood of Englishmen:
To Ireland will you lead a band of men,
Collected choicely, from each county some,
And try your hap against the Irishmen?   315
    York. I will, my lord, so please his majesty.
    Suf. Why, our authority is his consent,
And what we do establish he confirms:
Then, noble York, take thou this task in hand.
    York. I am content: provide me soldiers, lords,   320

Whiles I take order for mine own affairs.
    Suf. A charge, Lord York, that I will see perform'd.
But now return we to the false Duke Humphrey.
    Car. No more of him; for I will deal with him
That henceforth he shall trouble us no more.   325
And so break off; the day is almost spent.
Lord Suffolk, you and I must talk of that event.
    York. My Lord of Suffolk, within fourteen days
At Bristow I expect my soldiers;
For there I'll ship them all for Ireland.   330
    Suf. I'll see it truly done, my Lord of York.

Exeunt. Manet York.

    York. Now, York, or never, steel thy fearful thoughts,
And change misdoubt to resolution:
Be that thou hop'st to be, or what thou art
Resign to death; it is not worth th' enjoying.   335
Let pale-fac'd fear keep with the mean-born man,
And find no harbour in a royal heart.
Faster than spring-time showers comes thought on thought,
And not a thought but thinks on dignity.
My brain, more busy than the labouring spider,   340
Weaves tedious snares to trap mine enemies.
Well, nobles, well; 'tis politicly done,
To send me packing with an host of men:
I fear me you but warm the starved snake,
Who, cherish'd in your breasts, will sting your hearts.   345
'Twas men I lack'd, and you will give them me:
I take it kindly; yet be well assur'd
You put sharp weapons in a madman's hands.
Whiles I in Ireland nourish a mighty band,
I will stir up in England some black storm   350
Shall blow ten thousand souls to heaven or hell;
And this fell tempest shall not cease to rage
Until the golden circuit on my head,
Like to the glorious sun's transparent beams,
Do calm the fury of this mad-bred flaw.   355
And, for a minister of my intent,
I have seduc'd a headstrong Kentishman,
John Cade of Ashford,
To make commotion, as full well he can,
Under the title of John Mortimer.   360
In Ireland have I seen this stubborn Cade
Oppose himself against a troop of kerns,
And fought so long, till that his thighs with darts
Were almost like a sharp-quill'd porpentine:
And, in the end being rescu'd, I have seen   365
Him caper upright like a wild Morisco,
Shaking the bloody darts as he his bells.
Full often, like a shag-hair'd crafty kern,
Hath he conversed with the enemy,
And undiscover'd come to me again,   370
And given me notice of their villainies.
This devil here shall be my substitute;
For that John Mortimer, which now is dead,
In face, in gait, in speech, he doth resemble.
By this I shall perceive the commons' mind,   375

---

270 that: *to prove that*   **273 be his priest:** *i.e. perform his last offices, arrange his death*   **276 censure well:** *approve*   **278 tender:** *value*   **282 skills:** *matters*   **283 amain:** *with speed*   **286 betime:** *betimes, early*   **289 expedient:** *expeditious*   **294 far-fet:** *far-fetched, cunning*   **301 character'd:** *written*   **307 happily:** *haply, perhaps*   **309 in the number:** *among the rest; cf. n.*   **311 uncivil:** *disorderly*   **kerns:** *light-armed irregulars*   **312 temper clay:** *moisten the ground*   **319** *Cf. n.*

329 Bristow: *Bristol*   **332, 333** *Cf. n.*   **343 send me packing:** *pack me off*   **344 starved:** *frozen*   **351 Shall:** *which shall*   **353 circuit:** *circlet, crown*   **355 mad-bred:** *due to mad policies of Henry and his counselors*   **flaw:** *squall of wind*   **356 minister:** *agent*   **357–360** *Cf. n.*   **363 fought:** *i.e. have seen him fight*   **364 porpentine:** *porcupine*   **366 caper upright:** *lead up and down*   **Morisco:** *morris-dancer*   **368 shag-hair'd:** *shaggy*

How they affect the house and claim of York.
Say he be taken, rack'd, and tortured,
I know no pain they can inflict upon him
Will make him say I mov'd him to those arms.
Say that he thrive,—as 'tis great like he will,—   *380*
Why, then from Ireland come I with my strength,
And reap the harvest which that rascal sow'd;
For, Humphrey being dead, as he shall be,
And Henry put apart, the next for me.   *Exit.*

❧ SCENE SECOND ❧

[Bury St. Edmunds. A Room in the Palace]
Enter two or three [murderers] running over the stage, from the
murther of Duke Humphrey.

1. Mur. Run to my Lord of Suffolk; let him know
We have dispatch'd the duke, as he commanded.
2 Mur. O! that it were to do. What have we done?
Didst ever hear a man so penitent?

Enter Suffolk.

1. Mur. Here comes my lord.   *5*
Suf. Now, sirs, have you dispatch'd this thing?
1. Mur. Ay, my good lord, he's dead.
Suf. Why, that's well said. Go, get you to my house;
I will reward you for this venturous deed.
The king and all the peers are here at hand.   *10*
Have you laid fair the bed? is all things well,
According as I gave directions?
1 Mur. 'Tis, my good lord.
Suf. Away! be gone.   *Exeunt [Murderers].*

Sound trumpets. Enter the King, the Queen, Cardinal, Somerset,
with Attendants.

King. Go, call our uncle to our presence straight;
Say, we intend to try his Grace to-day,
If he be guilty, as 'tis published.
Suf. I'll call him presently, my noble lord.   *Exit.*
King. Lords, take your places; and, I pray you all,   *20*
Proceed no straiter 'gainst our uncle Gloucester
Than from true evidence, of good esteem,
He be approv'd in practice culpable.
Queen. God forbid any malice should prevail
That faultless may condemn a nobleman!   *25*
Pray God, he may acquit him of suspicion!
King. I thank thee, Meg; these words content me much.

Enter Suffolk.

How now! why look'st thou pale? why tremblest thou?
Where is our uncle? what's the matter, Suffolk?
Suf. Dead in his bed, my lord; Gloucester is dead.   *30*
Queen. Marry, God forfend!
Car. God's secret judgment: I did dream to-night
The duke was dumb, and could not speak a word.

King swoons.

Queen. How fares my lord? Help, lords! the king is dead.
Som. Rear up his body; wring him by the nose.   *35*
Queen. Run, go, help, help! O Henry, ope thine eyes!
Suf. He doth revive again. Madam, be patient.
King. O heavenly God!
Queen.   How fares my gracious lord?
Suf. Comfort, my sovereign! gracious Henry, comfort!   *40*
King. What! doth my Lord of Suffolk comfort me?
Came he right now to sing a raven's note,
Whose dismal tune bereft my vital powers,
And thinks he that the chirping of a wren,
By crying comfort from a hollow breast,   *45*
Can chase away the first-conceived sound?
Hide not thy poison with such sugar'd words:
Lay not thy hands on me; forbear, I say:
Their touch affrights me as a serpent's sting.
Thou baleful messenger, out of my sight!   *50*
Upon thy eyeballs murderous tyranny
Sits in grim majesty to fright the world.
Look not upon me, for thine eyes are wounding:
Yet do not go away; come, basilisk,
And kill the innocent gazer with thy sight;   *55*
For in the shade of death I shall find joy,
In life but double death, now Gloucester's dead.
Queen. Why do you rate my Lord of Suffolk thus?
Although the duke was enemy to him,
Yet he, most Christian-like, laments his death: *60*
And for myself, foe as he was to me,
Might liquid tears or heart-offending groans
Or blood-consuming sighs recall his life,
I would be blind with weeping, sick with groans,
Look pale as primrose with blood-drinking sighs,   *65*
And all to have the noble duke alive.
What know I how the world may deem of me?
For it is known we were but hollow friends:
It may be judg'd I made the duke away:
So shall my name with slander's tongue be wounded,   *70*
And princes' courts be fill'd with my reproach.
This get I by his death. Ay me, unhappy!
To be a queen, and crown'd with infamy!
King. Ah! woe is me for Gloucester, wretched man.
Queen. Be woe for me, more wretched than he is.   *75*
What! dost thou turn away and hide thy face?
I am no loathsome leper; look on me.
What! art thou, like the adder, waxen deaf?
Be poisonous too and kill thy forlorn queen.
Is all thy comfort shut in Gloucester's tomb?   *80*
Why, then, Dame Margaret was ne'er thy joy.
Erect his statua and worship it,
And make my image but an alehouse sign.
Was I for this nigh wrack'd upon the sea,
And twice by awkward wind from England's bank   *85*
Drove back again unto my native clime?
What boded this, but well forewarning wind
Did seem to say, 'Seek not a scorpion's nest,
Nor set no footing on this unkind shore?'

---

380 *great like: very likely*   **3** *to do: i.e. still undone*   **14** *S. d.; cf. n.*   **18** *If: to determine whether* **published:** *publicly asserted*   **19** *presently: at once*   **21** *straiter: more rigorously*   **22** *of good esteem: worthy of credence*   **23** *approv'd: proved*   **27** *Meg; cf. n.*   **31** *forfend: forbid*   **32** *to-night: last night*

35 *Rear up: support*   **42** *right now: this very moment*   **51** *murderous tyranny: the tyranny of murder*   **54** *basilisk: fabulous reptile whose sight caused death*   **58** *rate: upbraid*   **63** *blood-consuming; cf. n.*   **68** *hollow friends: euphemism for enemies*   **75** *woe: sorry*   **78** *like the adder; cf. n.* **waxen:** *grown*   **85** *awkward: unfavorable*

What did I then, but curs'd the gentle gusts   90
And he that loos'd them forth their brazen caves;
And bid them blow towards England's blessed shore,
Or turn our stern upon a dreadful rock?
Yet Æolus would not be a murtherer,
But left that hateful office unto thee: 95
The pretty vaulting sea refus'd to drown me,
Knowing that thou wouldst have me drown'd on shore
With tears as salt as sea through thy unkindness:
The splitting rocks cower'd in the sinking sands,
And would not dash me with their ragged sides,   100
Because thy flinty heart, more hard than they,
Might in thy palace perish Margaret.
As far as I could ken thy chalky cliffs,
When from thy shore the tempest beat us back,
I stood upon the hatches in the storm,   105
And when the dusky sky began to rob
My earnest-gaping sight of thy land's view,
I took a costly jewel from my neck,
A heart it was, bound in with diamonds,
And threw it towards thy land: the sea receiv'd it,   110
And so I wish'd thy body might my heart:
And even with this I lost fair England's view,
And bid mine eyes be packing with my heart,
And call'd them blind and dusky spectacles
For losing ken of Albion's wished coast.   115
How often have I tempted Suffolk's tongue—
The agent of thy foul inconstancy—
To sit and witch me, as Ascanius did,
When he to madding Dido would unfold
His father's acts, commenc'd in burning Troy!   120
Am I not witch'd like her? or thou not false like him?
Ay me! I can no more. Die, Margaret!
For Henry weeps that thou dost live so long.

Noise within. Enter Warwick and many Commons.

War. It is reported, mighty sovereign,
That good Duke Humphrey traitorously is murder'd   125
By Suffolk and the Cardinal Beaufort's means.
The commons, like an angry hive of bees
That want their leader, scatter up and down,
And care not who they sting in his revenge.
Myself have calm'd their spleenful mutiny,   130
Until they hear the order of his death.
King. That he is dead, good Warwick, 'tis too true;
But how he died God knows, not Henry.
Enter his chamber, view his breathless corpse,
And comment then upon his sudden death.   135
War. That shall I do, my liege. Stay, Salisbury,
With the rude multitude till I return.   *[Exit.]*
King. O! thou that judgest all things, stay my thoughts,
My thoughts that labour to persuade my soul
Some violent hands were laid on Humphrey's life.   140
If my suspect be false, forgive me, God,
For judgment only doth belong to thee.
Fain would I go to chafe his paly lips

With twenty thousand kisses, and to drain
Upon his face an ocean of salt tears,   145
To tell my love unto his deaf dumb trunk,
And with my fingers feel his hand unfeeling:
But all in vain are these mean obsequies,

                              Bed put forth [by Warwick].
And to survey his dead and earthy image
What were it but to make my sorrow greater?   150
War. Come hither, gracious sovereign, view this body.
King. That is to see how deep my grave is made;
For with his soul fled all my worldly solace,
For seeing him I see my life in death.
War. As surely as my soul intends to live   155
With that dread King that took our state upon him
To free us from his Father's wrathful curse,
I do believe that violent hands were laid
Upon the life of this thrice-famed duke.
Suf. A dreadful oath, sworn with a solemn tongue!   160
What instance gives Lord Warwick for his vow?
War. See how the blood is settled in his face.
Oft have I seen a timely-parted ghost,
Of ashy semblance, meagre, pale, and bloodless,
Being all descended to the labouring heart;   165
Who, in the conflict that it holds with death,
Attracts the same for aidance 'gainst the enemy;
Which with the heart there cools, and ne'er returneth
To blush and beautify the cheek again.
But see, his face is black and full of blood,   170
His eyeballs further out than when he liv'd,
Staring full ghastly like a strangled man;
His hair uprear'd, his nostrils stretch'd with struggling:
His hands abroad display'd, as one that grasp'd
And tugg'd for life, and was by strength subdu'd.   175
Look, on the sheets his hair, you see, is sticking;
His well-proportion'd beard made rough and rugged,
Like to the summer's corn by tempest lodg'd.
It cannot be but he was murder'd here;
The least of all these signs were probable.   180
Suf. Why, Warwick, who should do the duke to death?
Myself and Beaufort had him in protection,
And we, I hope, sir, are no murtherers.
War. But both of you were vow'd Duke Humphrey's foes,
And you, forsooth, had the good duke to keep: 185
'Tis like you would not feast him like a friend,
And 'tis well seen he found an enemy.
Queen. Then you, belike, suspect these noblemen
As guilty of Duke Humphrey's timeless death.
War. Who finds the heifer dead, and bleeding fresh,   190
And sees fast by a butcher with an axe,
But will suspect 'twas he that made the slaughter?
Who finds the partridge in the puttock's nest,
But may imagine how the bird was dead,
Although the kite soar with unbloodied beak?   195
Even so suspicious is this tragedy.
Queen. Are you the butcher, Suffolk? where's your knife?
Is Beaufort term'd a kite? where are his talons?
Suf. I wear no knife to slaughter sleeping men;

91 he: *i.e. Æolus* forth: *out of*   92 bid: *I bade*   101 Because: *in order that*   102 perish: *destroy*   103 ken: *discern*   113 be packing with: *accompany in flight*   114 spectacles: *visual organs*   118–120 *Cf. n.*   118 witch: *bewitch*   119 madding: *growing mad*   131 order: *manner*   135 comment upon: *interpret*   136 Salisbury; *cf. n.*   143 chafe: *warm* paly: *pale*

148 obsequies: *acts of duty*   163 timely-parted ghost: *body of one whose soul has departed naturally*   165 Being: *i.e. the blood*   174 abroad display'd: *extended*   178 lodg'd: *beaten down*   180 probable: *sufficient as proof*   193 puttock's: *kite's, hawk's*

But here's a vengeful sword, rusted with ease,   200
That shall be scoured in his rancorous heart
That slanders me with murther's crimson badge.
Say, if thou dar'st, proud Lord of Warwickshire,
That I am faulty in Duke Humphrey's death.

    War. What dares not Warwick, if false Suffolk dare him?

    Queen. He dares not calm his contumelious spirit,
Nor cease to be an arrogant controller,
Though Suffolk dare him twenty thousand times.

    War. Madam, be still, with reverence may I say;
For every word you speak in his behalf   210
Is slander to your royal dignity.

    Suf. Blunt-witted lord, ignoble in demeanour!
If ever lady wrong'd her lord so much,
Thy mother took into her blameful bed
Some stern untutor'd churl, and noble stock   215
Was graft with crab-tree slip; whose fruit thou art,
And never of the Nevils' noble race.

    War. But that the guilt of murther bucklers thee,
And I should rob the deathsman of his fee,
Quitting thee thereby of ten thousand shames,   220
And that my sovereign's presence makes me mild,
I would, false murd'rous coward, on thy knee
Make thee beg pardon for thy passed speech,
And say it was thy mother that thou meant'st;
That thou thyself wast born in bastardy: 225
And after all this fearful homage done,
Give thee thy hire, and send thy soul to hell,
Pernicious blood-sucker of sleeping men.

    Suf. Thou shalt be waking while I shed thy blood,
If from this presence thou dar'st go with me.   230

    War. Away even now, or I will drag thee hence:
Unworthy though thou art, I'll cope with thee,
And do some service to Duke Humphrey's ghost.

                   Exeunt [Suffolk and Warwick].

    King. What stronger breastplate than a heart untainted!
Thrice is he arm'd that hath his quarrel just,   235
And he but naked, though lock'd up in steel,
Whose conscience with injustice is corrupted.   *A noise within.*

    Queen. What noise is this?

Enter Suffolk and Warwick, with their weapons drawn.

    King. Why, how now, lords! your wrathful weapons drawn
Here in our presence! dare you be so bold?   240
Why, what tumultuous clamour have we here?

    Suf. The trait'rous Warwick, with the men of Bury,
Set all upon me, mighty sovereign.

Enter Salisbury.

    Sal. [Speaking to those within.] Sirs, stand apart; the king
shall know your mind.   245
Dread lord, the commons send you word by me,
Unless false Suffolk straight be done to death,
Or banished fair England's territories,
They will by violence tear him from your palace
And torture him with grievous lingering death.   250
They say, by him the good Duke Humphrey died;
They say, in him they fear your highness' death;

And mere instinct of love and loyalty,
Free from a stubborn opposite intent,
As being thought to contradict your liking,   255
Makes them thus forward in his banishment.
They say, in care of your most royal person,
That if your highness should intend to sleep,
And charge that no man should disturb your rest
In pain of your dislike or pain of death,   260
Yet, notwithstanding such a strait edict,
Were there a serpent seen, with forked tongue,
That slily glided towards your majesty,
It were but necessary you were wak'd,
Lest, being suffer'd in that harmful slumber,   265
The mortal worm might make the sleep eternal:
And therefore do they cry, though you forbid,
That they will guard you, whe'r you will or no,
From such fell serpents as false Suffolk is,
With whose envenomed and fatal sting,   270
Your loving uncle, twenty times his worth,
They say, is shamefully bereft of life.

    Commons within. An answer from the king, my Lord of
Salisbury!

    Suf. 'Tis like the commons, rude unpolish'd hinds,   275
Could send such message to their sovereign;
But you, my lord, were glad to be employ'd,
To show how quaint an orator you are:
But all the honour Salisbury hath won
Is that he was the lord ambassador,   280
Sent from a sort of tinkers to the king.

    Within. An answer from the king, or we will all break in!

    King. Go, Salisbury, and tell them all from me,
I thank them for their tender loving care;
And had I not been cited so by them,   285
Yet did I purpose as they do entreat;
For, sure, my thoughts do hourly prophesy
Mischance unto my state by Suffolk's means:
And therefore, by His majesty I swear,
Whose far-unworthy deputy I am,   290
He shall not breathe infection in this air
But three days longer, on the pain of death.   *[Exit Salisbury.]*

    Queen. O Henry! let me plead for gentle Suffolk.

    King. Ungentle queen, to call him gentle Suffolk!
No more, I say; if thou dost plead for him   295
Thou wilt but add increase unto my wrath.
Had I but said, I would have kept my word,
But when I swear, it is irrevocable.
[To Suffolk.] If after three days' space thou here be'st found
On any ground that I am ruler of,   300
The world shall not be ransom for thy life.
Come, Warwick, come, good Warwick, go with me;
I have great matters to impart to thee.

                   Exit [with Warwick, etc.].

    Queen. Mischance and sorrow go along with you!
Heart's discontent and sour affliction   305
Be playfellows to keep you company!
There's two of you; the devil make a third,
And threefold vengeance tend upon your steps!

    Suf. Cease, gentle queen, these execrations,

---

207 controller: *meddling detractor*   **219 deathsman:** *executioner*   **220 Quitting:** *relieving*   **226 fearful homage:** *cowardly submission*

253 mere instinct: *sincere impulse*   **254 opposite intent:** *purpose of opposition*   **268 whe'r:** *whether*   **271 his worth:** *as worthy as he*   **277 quaint:** *clever*   **285 cited:** *urged*   **291 breathe … in:** *infect with his breath*   **297 said:** *affirmed without oath*

And let thy Suffolk take his heavy leave.   310
    Queen. Fie, coward woman and soft-hearted wretch!
Hast thou not spirit to curse thine enemy?
    Suf. A plague upon them! Wherefore should I curse them?
Would curses kill, as doth the mandrake's groan,
I would invent as bitter-searching terms,   315
As curst, as harsh and horrible to hear,
Deliver'd strongly through my fixed teeth,
With full as many signs of deadly hate,
As lean-fac'd Envy in her loathsome cave.
My tongue should stumble in mine earnest words;   320
Mine eyes should sparkle like the beaten flint;
Mine hair be fix'd an end, as one distract;
Ay, every joint should seem to curse and ban:
And even now my burthen'd heart would break,
Should I not curse them. Poison be their drink!   325
Gall, worse than gall, the daintiest that they taste!
Their sweetest shade a grove of cypress trees!
Their chiefest prospect murd'ring basilisks!
Their softest touch as smart as lizard's stings!
Their music frightful as the serpent's hiss,   330
And boding screech-owls make the consort full!
All the foul terrors in dark-seated hell—
    Queen. Enough, sweet Suffolk; thou torment'st thyself;
And these dread curses, like the sun 'gainst glass,
Or like an overcharged gun, recoil,   335
And turn the force of them upon thyself.
    Suf. You bade me ban, and will you bid me leave?
Now, by the ground that I am banish'd from,
Well could I curse away a winter's night,
Though standing naked on a mountain top,   340
Where biting cold would never let grass grow,
And think it but a minute spent in sport.
    Queen. O! let me entreat thee, cease! Give me thy hand,
That I may dew it with my mournful tears;
Nor let the rain of heaven wet this place,   345
To wash away my woeful monuments.
O! could this kiss be printed in thy hand,   *[Kisses his hand.]*
That thou might'st think upon these by the seal,
Through whom a thousand sighs are breath'd for thee.
So, get thee gone, that I may know my grief;   350
'Tis but surmis'd whiles thou art standing by,
As one that surfeits thinking on a want.
I will repeal thee, or, be well assur'd,
Adventure to be banished myself;
And banished I am, if but from thee.   355
Go; speak not to me; even now be gone.
O! go not yet. Even thus two friends condemn'd
Embrace and kiss, and take ten thousand leaves,
Loather a hundred times to part than die.
Yet now farewell; and farewell life with thee!   360
    Suf. Thus is poor Suffolk ten times banished,
Once by the king, and three times thrice by thee.
'Tis not the land I care for, wert thou thence;
A wilderness is populous enough,
So Suffolk had thy heavenly company: 365

For where thou art, there is the world itself,
With every several pleasure in the world,
And where thou art not, desolation.
I can no more: live thou to joy thy life;
Myself to joy in nought but that thou liv'st.   370

        Enter Vaux.

    Queen. Whither goes Vaux so fast? what news, I prithee?
    Vaux. To signify unto his majesty
That Cardinal Beaufort is at point of death;
For suddenly a grievous sickness took him,
That makes him gasp and stare, and catch the air,   375
Blaspheming God, and cursing men on earth.
Sometime he talks as if Duke Humphrey's ghost
Were by his side; sometime he calls the king,
And whispers to his pillow, as to him,
The secrets of his overcharged soul: 380
And I am sent to tell his majesty
That even now he cries aloud for him.
    Queen. Go tell this heavy message to the king.   *Exit [Vaux].*
Ay me! what is this world! what news are these!
But wherefore grieve I at an hour's poor loss,   385
Omitting Suffolk's exile, my soul's treasure?
Why only, Suffolk, mourn I not for thee,
And with the southern clouds contend in tears,
Theirs for the earth's increase, mine for my sorrows?
Now get thee hence: the king, thou know'st, is coming;   390
If thou be found by me thou art but dead.
    Suf. If I depart from thee I cannot live;
And in thy sight to die, what were it else
But like a pleasant slumber in thy lap?
Here could I breathe my soul into the air,   395
As mild and gentle as the cradle-babe,
Dying with mother's dug between its lips;
Where, from thy sight, I should be raging mad,
And cry out for thee to close up mine eyes,
To have thee with thy lips to stop my mouth: 400
So shouldst thou either turn my flying soul,
Or I should breathe it so into thy body,
And then it liv'd in sweet Elysium.
To die by thee were but to die in jest;
From thee to die were torture more than death.   405
O! let me stay, befall what may befall!
    Queen. Away! though parting be a fretful corrosive,
It is applied to a deathful wound.
To France, sweet Suffolk: let me hear from thee;
For wheresoe'er thou art in this world's globe,   410
I'll have an Iris that shall find thee out.
    Suf. I go.
    Queen.   And take my heart with thee.
    Suf. A jewel, lock'd into the woefull'st cask
That ever did contain a thing of worth.   415
Even as a splitted bark, so sunder we:
This way fall I to death.
    Queen.   This way for me.
        Exeunt [at different doors].

---

314 mandrake's groan; *cf. n.*   **316 curst:** *bitter*   **322 an:** *on* **as . . . distract:** *like a madman's*   **327 cypress trees:** *trees symbolical of mourning*   **329 smart:** *painful*   **331 consort:** *band of musicians*   **337 leave:** *cease*   **346 woeful monuments:** *marks of woe (tear stains)*   **348 seal:** *impression of her lips; cf. n.*   **352** *As when a glutton thinks of famine*   **353 repeal thee:** *secure your recall*   **354 Adventure:** *risk*

374 *Cf. n.*   **385 hour's poor loss:** *petty transitory grief*   **386 Omitting:** *ignoring*   **388 southern:** *i.e. fog-laden*   **391 by:** *with*   **397 its;** *cf. n.*   **407 corrosive:** *painful remedy*   **411 Iris:** *Juno's messenger*   **414 into:** *within* **cask:** *casket*

❧ SCENE THIRD ❧

[London. Cardinal Beaufort's Bedchamber]
Enter the King, Salisbury, and Warwick to the Cardinal in bed.

King. How fares my lord? speak, Beaufort, to thy sovereign.
Car. If thou be'st death, I'll give thee England's treasure,
Enough to purchase such another island,
So thou wilt let me live, and feel no pain.
    King. Ah! what a sign it is of evil life   5
Where death's approach is seen so terrible.
    War. Beaufort, it is thy sovereign speaks to thee.
    Car. Bring me unto my trial when you will.
Died he not in his bed? where should he die?
Can I make men live whe'r they will or no?   10
O! torture me no more, I will confess.
Alive again? then show me where he is:
I'll give a thousand pound to look upon him.
He hath no eyes, the dust hath blinded them.
Comb down his hair; look! look! it stands upright,   15
Like lime-twigs set to catch my winged soul.
Give me some drink; and bid the apothecary
Bring the strong poison that I bought of him.
    King. O thou eternal Mover of the heavens!
Look with a gentle eye upon this wretch;   20
O! beat away the busy meddling fiend
That lays strong siege unto this wretch's soul,
And from his bosom purge this black despair.
    War. See how the pangs of death do make him grin!
    Sal. Disturb him not! let him pass peaceably.   25
    King. Peace to his soul, if God's good pleasure be!
Lord Cardinal, if thou think'st on heaven's bliss,
Hold up thy hand, make signal of thy hope.
He dies, and makes no sign. O God, forgive him!
    War. So bad a death argues a monstrous life.   30
    King. Forbear to judge, for we are sinners all.
Close up his eyes, and draw the curtain close;
And let us all to meditation.   *Exeunt.*

ACT FOURTH ❧ SCENE FIRST

[Kent. The Seashore near Dover]
Alarum. Fight at Sea. Ordnance goes off. Enter Lieutenant,
Suffolk, and others [including Master, Master's Mate, Walter
Whitmore, and various prisoners].

Lieu. The gaudy, blabbing, and remorseful day
Is crept into the bosom of the sea,
And now loud-howling wolves arouse the jades
That drag the tragic melancholy night;
Who with their drowsy, slow, and flagging wings   5
Clip dead men's graves, and from their misty jaws
Breathe foul contagious darkness in the air.
Therefore bring forth the soldiers of our prize,
For, whilst our pinnace anchors in the Downs,
Here shall they make their ransom on the sand,   10
Or with their blood stain this discolour'd shore.
Master, this prisoner freely give I thee:

1–7 *Cf. n.*   6 **Clip**: *embrace*   9 **pinnace**: *one-masted vessel* **Downs**; *cf. n.*   11 **discolour'd**; *cf. n.*

And thou that art his mate make boot of this;
The other *[Pointing to Suffolk]*, Walter Whitmore, is thy share.
    1. Gent. What is my ransom, master? let me know.   15
    Mast. A thousand crowns, or else lay down your head.
    Mate. And so much shall you give, or off goes yours.
    Lieu. What! think you much to pay two thousand crowns,
And bear the name and port of gentlemen?
Cut both the villains' throats! for die you shall: 20
The lives of those which we have lost in fight
Be counterpois'd with such a petty sum!
    1. Gent. I'll give it, sir; and therefore spare my life.
    2. Gent. And so will I, and write home for it straight.
    Whit. I lost mine eye in laying the prize aboard,   25
[To Suffolk.] And therefore to revenge it shalt thou die;
And so should these if I might have my will.
    Lieu. Be not so rash: take ransom; let him live.
    Suf. Look on my George; I am a gentleman:
Rate me at what thou wilt, thou shalt be paid.   30
    Whit. And so am I; my name is Walter Whitmore.
How now! why start'st thou? what! doth death affright?
    Suf. Thy name affrights me, in whose sound is death.
A cunning man did calculate my birth,
And told me that by *Water* I should die: 35
Yet let not this make thee be bloody-minded;
Thy name is Gaultier, being rightly sounded.
    Whit. Gaultier, or Walter, which it is I care not.
Never yet did base dishonour blur our name
But with our sword we wip'd away the blot: 40
Therefore, when merchant-like I sell revenge,
Broke be my sword, my arms torn and defac'd,
And I proclaim'd a coward through the world!
    Suf. Stay, Whitmore; for thy prisoner is a prince,
The Duke of Suffolk, William de la Pole.   45
    Whit. The Duke of Suffolk muffled up in rags!
    Suf. Ay, but these rags are no part of the duke:
Jove sometime went disguis'd, and why not I?
    Lieu. But Jove was never slain, as thou shalt be.
    Suf. Obscure and lowly swain, King Henry's blood,   50
The honourable blood of Lancaster,
Must not be shed by such a jaded groom.
Hast thou not kiss'd thy hand and held my stirrup?
Bare-headed plodded by my foot-cloth mule,
And thought thee happy when I shook my head?   55
How often hast thou waited at my cup,
Fed from my trencher, kneel'd down at the board,
When I have feasted with Queen Margaret?
Remember it and let it make thee crest-fall'n;
Ay, and allay this thy abortive pride.   60
How in our voiding lobby hast thou stood
And duly waited for my coming forth?
This hand of mine hath writ in thy behalf,
And therefore shall it charm thy riotous tongue.
    Whit. Speak, captain, shall I stab the forlorn swain?   65
    Lieu. First let my words stab him, as he hath me.
    Suf. Base slave, thy words are blunt, and so art thou.
    Lieu. Convey him hence, and on our longboat's side

13 **make . . . this**: *take your profit from the ransom of this one*   19 **port**: *demeanor*   22
counterpois'd: *balanced, reckoned equal*   25 **laying aboard**: *grappling with*   29 **George**:
cf. n.   30 **Rate me**: *set my ransom*   35 **Water**; *cf. n.*   48–50 *Cf. n.*   50 **King
Henry's blood**; *cf. n.*   52 **jaded**: *contemptible*   54 **foot-cloth mule**; *cf. n.*   61 **voiding lobby**: *antechamber*

Strike off his head.

Suf.   Thou dar'st not for thy own.   70

Lieu. Yes, Pole.

Suf.   Pole!

Lieu.   Pool! Sir Pool! lord!

Ay, kennel, puddle, sink; whose filth and dirt

Troubles the silver spring where England drinks.   75

Now will I dam up this thy yawning mouth

For swallowing the treasure of the realm:

Thy lips, that kiss'd the queen, shall sweep the ground;

And thou, that smil'dst at good Duke Humphrey's death,

Against the senseless winds shalt grin in vain,   80

Who in contempt shall hiss at thee again:

And wedded be thou to the hags of hell,

For daring to affy a mighty lord

Unto the daughter of a worthless king,

Having neither subject, wealth, nor diadem.   85

By devilish policy art thou grown great,

And, like ambitious Sylla, overgorg'd

With gobbets of thy mother's bleeding heart.

By thee Anjou and Maine were sold to France,

The false revolting Normans thorough thee   90

Disdain to call us lord, and Picardy

Hath slain their governors, surpris'd our forts,

And sent the ragged soldiers wounded home.

The princely Warwick, and the Nevils all,

Whose dreadful swords were never drawn in vain,   95

As hating thee, are rising up in arms:

And now the house of York, thrust from the crown

By shameful murther of a guiltless king,

And lofty proud encroaching tyranny,

Burns with revenging fire; whose hopeful colours   100

Advance our half-fac'd sun, striving to shine,

Under the which is writ *Invitis nubibus*.

The commons here in Kent are up in arms;

And to conclude, reproach and beggary

Is crept into the palace of our king,   105

And all by thee. Away! convey him hence.

Suf. O! that I were a god, to shoot forth thunder

Upon these paltry, servile, abject drudges.

Small things make base men proud: this villain here,

Being captain of a pinnace, threatens more   110

Than Bargulus, the strong Illyrian pirate.

Drones suck not eagles' blood, but rob beehives.

It is impossible that I should die

By such a lowly vassal as thyself.

Thy words move rage, and not remorse in me: 115

I go of message from the queen to France;

I charge thee, waft me safely cross the Channel.

Lieu. Walter!

Whit. Come, Suffolk, I must waft thee to thy death.

Suf. Pene gelidus timor occupat artus: it is thee I fear.   120

Whit. Thou shalt have cause to fear before I leave thee.

What! are ye daunted now? now will ye stoop?

1. Gent. My gracious lord, entreat him, speak him fair.

Suf. Suffolk's imperial tongue is stern and rough,

Us'd to command, untaught to plead for favour.   125

Far be it we should honour such as these

With humble suit: no, rather let my head

Stoop to the block than these knees bow to any,

Save to the God of heaven and to my king;

And sooner dance upon a bloody pole   130

Than stand uncover'd to the vulgar groom.

True nobility is exempt from fear:

More can I bear than you dare execute.

Lieu. Hale him away, and let him talk no more.

Suf. Come, soldiers, show what cruelty ye can,   135

That this my death may never be forgot.

Great men oft die by vile besonians.

A Roman sworder and banditto slave

Murder'd sweet Tully; Brutus' bastard hand

Stabb'd Julius Cæsar; savage islanders   140

Pompey the Great; and Suffolk dies by pirates.

Exit Walter with Suffolk.

Lieu. And as for these whose ransom we have set,

It is our pleasure one of them depart:

Therefore come you with us and let him go.

Exit Lieutenant, and the rest. Manet the first Gent.

Enter Walter with the body [of Suffolk].

Whit. There let his head and lifeless body lie,   145

Until the queen his mistress bury it.   *Exit Walter.*

1. Gent. O barbarous and bloody spectacle!

His body will I bear unto the king:

If he revenge it not, yet will his friends;

So will the queen, that living held him dear.   150

[Exit with the body.]

❧ SCENE SECOND ❧

[Blackheath]

Enter Bevis and John Holland.

Bevis. Come, and get thee a sword, though made of a lath: they have been up these two days.

Holl. They have the more need to sleep now then.

Bevis. I tell thee, Jack Cade the clothier means to dress the commonwealth, and turn it, and set a new nap upon it.   5

Holl. So he had need, for 'tis threadbare. Well, I say it was never merry world in England since gentlemen came up.

Bevis. O miserable age! Virtue is not regarded in handicraftsmen.

Holl. The nobility think scorn to go in leather aprons.   10

Bevis. Nay, more; the king's council are no good workmen.

Holl. True; and yet it is said, 'Labour in thy vocation': which is as much to say as, let the magistrates be labouring men; and therefore should we be magistrates.

Bevis. Thou hast hit it; for there's no better sign of a   15 brave mind than a hard hand.

Holl. I see them! I see them! There's Best's son, the tanner of Wingham,—

---

74 **kennel:** *gutter* **sink:** *cesspool*   77 **For:** *for fear of, to prevent*   83 **affy:** *betroth*   87 **ambitious Sylla;** *cf. n.*   88 **gobbets:** *lumps of flesh*   90 **thorough:** *through*   98 **guiltless king:** *i.e. Richard II*   101 **Advance:** *display* **half-fac'd:** *with disk half obscured; cf. n.*   102 **Invitis nubibus:** *in spite of clouds*   111 **Bargulus;** *cf. n.*   116 **of message:** *as messenger*   117 **waft:** *convey by water*   120 **Pene . . . artus;** *cf. n.*

130 **dance . . . pole;** *Cf. n.*   137 **besonians:** *beggars*   138 **sworder:** *gladiator*   140 **savage islanders;** *Cf. n.*   2 **up:** *in arms*   4 **clothier:** *cloth-worker*   7 **came up:** *came into fashion*

Bevis. He shall have the skins of our enemies to make
dog's-leather of.   20

Holl. And Dick the butcher,—

Bevis. Then is sin struck down like an ox, and iniquity's
throat cut like a calf.

Holl. And Smith the weaver,—

Bevis. Argo, their thread of life is spun.   25

Holl. Come, come, let's fall in with them.

> *Drum. Enter Cade, Dick Butcher, Smith the Weaver, and a*
> *Sawyer, with infinite numbers.*

Cade. We John Cade, so termed of our supposed father,—

Butch. [Aside.] Or rather, of stealing a cade of herrings.

Cade. For our enemies shall fall before us, inspired with the
spirit of putting down kings and princes,—Command silence.

Butch. Silence!

Cade. My father was a Mortimer,—

Butch. [Aside.] He was an honest man, and a good
bricklayer.   35

Cade. My mother a Plantagenet,—

Butch. [Aside.] I knew her well; she was a midwife.

Cade. My wife descended of the Lacies,—

Butch. [Aside.] She was, indeed, a pedlar's daughter, and
sold many laces.   40

Weav. [Aside.] But now of late, not able to travel with
her furred pack, she washes bucks here at home.

Cade. Therefore am I of an honourable house.

Butch. [Aside.] Ay, by my faith, the field is honourable;
and there was he born, under a hedge; for his father had   45
never a house but the cage.

Cade. Valiant I am.

Weav. [Aside.] A' must needs, for beggary is valiant.

Cade. I am able to endure much.

Butch. [Aside.] No question of that, for I have seen him   50
whipped three market-days together.

Cade. I fear neither sword nor fire.

Weav. [Aside.] He need not fear the sword, for his coat
is of proof.

Butch. [Aside.] But methinks he should stand in fear of   55
fire, being burnt i' the hand for stealing of sheep.

Cade. Be brave, then; for your captain is brave, and vows
reformation. There shall be in England seven halfpenny loaves
sold for a penny; the three-hooped pot shall have ten hoops;
and I will make it felony to drink small beer. All the realm   60
shall be in common, and in Cheapside shall my palfrey go
to grass. And when I am king,—as king I will be,—

All. God save your majesty!

Cade. I thank you, good people:—there shall be no money;
all shall eat and drink on my score; and I will apparel them   65
all in one livery, that they may agree like brothers, and
worship me their lord.

Butch. The first thing we do, let's kill all the lawyers.

Cade. Nay, that I mean to do. Is not this a lamentable
thing, that of the skin of an innocent lamb should be made   70

parchment? that parchment, being scribbled o'er, should undo
a man? Some say the bee stings; but I say, 'tis the bee's wax,
for I did but seal once to a thing, and I was never mine own
man since. How now! who's there?

> *Enter a Clerk.*

Weav. The clerk of Chatham: he can write and read and   75
cast accompt.

Cade. O monstrous!

Weav. We took him setting of boys' copies.

Cade. Here's a villain!

Weav. Has a book in his pocket with red letters in 't.   80

Cade. Nay, then he is a conjurer.

Butch. Nay, he can make obligations, and write court-hand.

Cade. I am sorry for 't: the man is a proper man, of mine
honour; unless I find him guilty, he shall not die. Come
hither, sirrah, I must examine thee. What is thy name?   85

Clerk. Emmanuel.

Butch. They use to write it on the top of letters. 'Twill
go hard with you.

Cade. Let me alone. Dost thou use to write thy name, or
hast thou a mark to thyself, like a honest plain-dealing man?   90

Clerk. Sir, I thank God, I have been so well brought up,
that I can write my name.

All. He hath confessed: away with him! he's a villain and
a traitor.

Cade. Away with him, I say: hang him with his pen and   95
ink-horn about his neck.   *Exit one with the Clerk.*

> *Enter Michael.*

Mich. Where's our general?

Cade. Here I am, thou particular fellow.

Mich. Fly, fly, fly! Sir Humphrey Stafford and his brother
are hard by, with the king's forces.   100

Cade. Stand, villain, stand, or I'll fell thee down. He shall
be encountered with a man as good as himself: he is but a
knight, is a'?

Mich. No.

Cade. To equal him, I will make myself a knight presently.
[Kneels.] Rise up Sir John Mortimer. *[Rises.]* Now have at him.

> *Enter Sir Humphrey Stafford and his Brother, with drum and*
> *Soldiers.*

Staf. Rebellious hinds, the filth and scum of Kent,
Mark'd for the gallows, lay your weapons down;
Home to your cottages, forsake this groom: 110
The king is merciful, if you revolt.

Bro. But angry, wrathful, and inclin'd to blood,
If you go forward: therefore yield, or die.

Cade. As for these silken-coated slaves, I pass not:
It is to you, good people, that I speak,   115
O'er whom, in time to come I hope to reign;
For I am rightful heir unto the crown.

Staf. Villain! thy father was a plasterer;
And thou thyself a shearman, art thou not?

Cade. And Adam was a gardener.   120

Bro. And what of that?

---

24 Argo: *ergo, therefore*   **27 cade:** *barrel (containing 600 herrings)*   **29 For:** *because*   **fall:** *pun on Latin 'cado' meaning fall*   **38 Lacies:** *family name of the Earls of Lincoln*   **42 furred pack:** *waterproof pack, made of skin with the hair outward*   **washes bucks:** *takes in washing*   **46 cage:** *lock-up*   **48 A' must needs:** *he must be*   **53, 54 of proof:** *tried by long service*   **58 reformation:** *alteration of government*   **59 three-hooped pot:** *wooden quart-pot*   **65 on my score:** *at my expense*   **68 kill … lawyers;** *cf. n.*

76 cast accompt: *calculate*   **78 copies:** *models of handwriting*   **82 obligations:** *contracts*   **court-hand:** *type of handwriting used in legal documents*   **83 proper:** *good-looking*   **87 They … letters;** *cf. n.*   **98 particular:** *as opposed to 'general'*   **104 No:** *i.e. he is no more*   **111 revolt:** *i.e. forsake Cade*   **119 shearman:** *one who shears cloth*

Cade. Marry, this: Edmund Mortimer, Earl of March,
Married the Duke of Clarence' daughter, did he not?

Staf. Ay, sir.

Cade. By her he had two children at one birth.   *125*

Bro. That's false.

Cade. Ay, there's the question; but I say, 'tis true:
The elder of them, being put to nurse,
Was by a beggar-woman stol'n away;
And, ignorant of his birth and parentage,   *130*
Became a bricklayer when he came to age:
His son am I; deny it if you can.

Butch. Nay, 'tis too true; therefore he shall be king.

Weav. Sir, he made a chimney in my father's house, and the
bricks are alive at this day to testify it; therefore deny it not.

Staf. And will you credit this base drudge's words,
That speaks he knows not what?

All. Ay, marry, will we; therefore get ye gone.

Bro. Jack Cade, the Duke of York hath taught you this.

Cade. [Aside.] He lies, for I invented it myself. Go to,   *140*
sirrah; tell the king from me, that, for his father's sake, Henry
the Fifth, in whose time boys went to span-counter for French
crowns, I am content he shall reign; but I'll be protector over
him.

Butch. And furthermore, we'll have the Lord Say's head   *145*
for selling the dukedom of Maine.

Cade. And good reason; for thereby is England mained, and
fain to go with a staff, but that my puissance holds it up.
Fellow kings, I tell you that that Lord Say hath gelded the
commonwealth, and made it an eunuch; and more than   *150*
that, he can speak French; and therefore he is a traitor.

Staf. O gross and miserable ignorance!

Cade. Nay, answer, if you can: the Frenchmen are our
enemies; go to then, I ask but this: can he that speaks with
the tongue of an enemy be a good counsellor, or no?   *155*

All. No, no; and therefore we'll have his head.

Bro. Well, seeing gentle words will not prevail,
Assail them with the army of the king.

Staf. Herald, away; and throughout every town
Proclaim them traitors that are up with Cade;   *160*
That those which fly before the battle ends
May, even in their wives' and children's sight,
Be hang'd up for example at their doors:
And you, that be the king's friends, follow me.

                  Exit [with Brother and Soldiers].

Cade. And you, that love the commons, follow me.   *165*
Now show yourselves men; 'tis for liberty.
We will not leave one lord, one gentleman:
Spare none but such as go in clouted shoon,
For they are thrifty honest men, and such
As would, but that they dare not, take our parts.   *170*

Butch. They are all in order, and march toward us.

Cade. But then are we in order when we are most out of
order. Come, march! forward!   *[Exeunt.]*

❦ SCENE THIRD ❦

[Another Part of Blackheath]

*Alarums to the fight, wherein both the Staffords are slain. Enter
Cade and the rest.*

Cade. Where's Dick, the butcher of Ashford?

Butch. Here, sir.

Cade. They fell before thee like sheep and oxen, and thou
behavedst thyself as if thou hadst been in thine own slaughter-
house: therefore thus will I reward thee; the Lent shall be as   *5*
long again as it is, and thou shalt have a licence to kill for a
hundred lacking one.

Butch. I desire no more.

Cade. And, to speak truth, thou deserv'st no less. This
monument of the victory will I bear; [Puts on Sir Humphrey
Stafford's armour.] and the bodies shall be dragged at my horse'
heels, till I do come to London, where we will have the
Mayor's sword borne before us.

Butch. If we mean to thrive and do good, break open the
gaols and let out the prisoners.   *15*

Cade. Fear not that, I warrant thee. Come; let's march
towards London.   *Exeunt.*

❦ SCENE FOURTH ❦

[London. A Room in the Palace]

*Enter the King with a supplication, and the Queen with Suffolk's
head; the Duke of Buckingham, and the Lord Say.*

Queen. Oft have I heard that grief softens the mind,
And makes it fearful and degenerate;
Think therefore on revenge, and cease to weep.
But who can cease to weep and look on this?
Here may his head lie on my throbbing breast;   *5*
But where's the body that I should embrace?

Buck. What answer makes your Grace to the rebels'
supplication?

King. I'll send some holy bishop to entreat;
For God forbid so many simple souls   *10*
Should perish by the sword! And I myself,
Rather than bloody war shall cut them short,
Will parley with Jack Cade their general.
But stay, I'll read it over once again.

Queen. Ah, barbarous villains! hath this lovely face   *15*
Rul'd like a wandering planet over me,
And could it not enforce them to relent,
That were unworthy to behold the same?

King. Lord Say, Jack Cade hath sworn to have thy head.

Say. Ay, but I hope your highness shall have his.   *20*

King. How now, madam!
Still lamenting and mourning for Suffolk's death?
I fear me, love, if that I had been dead,
Thou wouldest not have mourn'd so much for me.

Queen. No, my love; I should not mourn, but die for thee.

Enter a Messenger.

King. How now! what news? why com'st thou in such haste?

Mess. The rebels are in Southwark; fly, my lord!

---

142 span-counter: *children's game played with coins or counters*   **147** mained:
maimed   **168** clouted shoon: *patched (?), hobnailed (?) shoes*

6 licence to kill; *cf. n.*   **16** Fear: *doubt*   **16** like ... planet: *alluding to planetary
influence*

Jack Cade proclaims himself Lord Mortimer,
Descended from the Duke of Clarence' house,
And calls your Grace usurper openly,   30
And vows to crown himself in Westminster.
His army is a ragged multitude
Of hinds and peasants, rude and merciless:
Sir Humphrey Stafford and his brother's death
Hath given them heart and courage to proceed.   35
All scholars, lawyers, courtiers, gentlemen,
They call false caterpillars, and intend their death.
    King. O graceless men! they know not what they do.
    Buck. My gracious lord, retire to Killingworth,
Until a power be rais'd to put them down.   40
    Queen. Ah! were the Duke of Suffolk now alive,
These Kentish rebels would be soon appeas'd.
    King. Lord Say, the traitors hate thee,
Therefore away with us to Killingworth.
    Say. So might your Grace's person be in danger.   45
The sight of me is odious in their eyes;
And therefore in this city will I stay,
And live alone as secret as I may.

            Enter another Messenger.

    Mess. Jack Cade hath gotten London bridge;
The citizens fly and forsake their houses;   50
The rascal people, thirsting after prey,
Join with the traitor; and they jointly swear
To spoil the city and your royal court.
    Buck. Then linger not, my lord; away! take horse.
    King. Come, Margaret; God, our hope, will succour us.   55
    Queen. My hope is gone, now Suffolk is deceas'd.
    King. [To Lord Say.] Farewell, my lord: trust not the
Kentish rebels.
    Buck. Trust nobody, for fear you be betray'd.
    Say. The trust I have is in mine innocence,   60
And therefore am I bold and resolute.   *Exeunt.*

❧ SCENE FIFTH ❧

[The Same. The Tower]
Enter Lord Scales upon the Tower walking. Then enter two or three
Citizens below.

    Scales. How now! is Jack Cade slain?
    1. Cit. No, my lord, nor likely to be slain; for they have
won the bridge, killing all those that withstand them. The
Lord Mayor craves aid of your honour from the Tower, to
defend the city from the rebels.   5
    Scales. Such aid as I can spare you shall command;
But I am troubled here with them myself;
The rebels have assay'd to win the Tower.
But get you to Smithfield and gather head,
And thither I will send you Matthew Goffe: 10
Fight for your king, your country, and your lives;
And so, farewell, for I must hence again.   *Exeunt.*

❧ SCENE SIXTH ❧

[London. Cannon Street]
Enter Jack Cade and the rest, and strikes his staff on London-stone.

    Cade. Now is Mortimer lord of this city. And here, sitting
upon London-stone, I charge and command that, of the city's
cost, the pissing-conduit run nothing but claret wine this first
year of our reign. And now, henceforward, it shall be treason
for any that calls me other than Lord Mortimer.   5

            Enter a Soldier, running.

    Sold. Jack Cade! Jack Cade!
    Cade. Knock him down there.   *They kill him.*
    Smith. If this fellow be wise, he'll never call ye Jack Cade
more: I think he hath a very fair warning.
    Dick. My lord, there's an army gathered together in   10
Smithfield.
    Cade. Come then, let's go fight with them.
But first, go and set London-bridge on fire, and, if you can,
burn down the Tower too. Come, let's away.   *Exeunt omnes.*

❧ SCENE SEVENTH ❧

[The Same. Smithfield]
Alarums. Matthew Goffe is slain, and all the rest [of the King's
forces]. Then enter Jack Cade, with his Company.

    Cade. So, sirs:—Now go some and pull down the Savoy;
others to the inns of court: down with them all.
    Dick. I have a suit unto your lordship.
    Cade. Be it a lordship, thou shalt have it for that word.
    Dick. Only that the laws of England may come out of your
mouth.
    Holl. [Aside.] Mass, 'twill be sore law then; for he was thrust
in the mouth with a spear, and 'tis not whole yet.
    Smith. [Aside.] Nay, John, it will be stinking law; for his
breath stinks with eating toasted cheese.   10
    Cade. I have thought upon it; it shall be so. Away! burn all
the records of the realm: my mouth shall be the parliament of
England.
    Holl. [Aside.] Then we are like to have biting statutes, unless
his teeth be pulled out.   15
    Cade. And henceforward all things shall be in common.

            Enter a Messenger.

    Mess. My lord, a prize, a prize! here's the Lord Say, which
sold the towns in France; he that made us pay one-and-twenty
fifteens, and one shilling to the pound, the last subsidy.

       Enter George [Bevis] with the Lord Say.

    Cade. Well, he shall be beheaded for it ten times. Ah!   20
thou say, thou serge, nay, thou buckram lord; now art thou within
point-blank of our jurisdiction regal. What canst thou answer
to my majesty for giving up of Normandy unto Monsieur Basimecu, the Dauphin of France? Be it known unto thee by these
presence, even the presence of Lord Mortimer, that I am the   25

---

33 **hinds:** *farm laborers*   39 **Killingworth:** *Kenilworth Castle in Warwickshire*   42 **appeas'd:** *pacified, reduced to quiet*   51 **rascal people:** *rabble*   9 **gather head:** *collect your
forces*

2 **London-stone:** *a Roman milestone in Cannon Street*   3, 4 **pissing-conduit:** *a small water
fountain*   1 **Savoy:** *the London residence of the Duke of Lancaster*   2 **inns of court:** *the
abode of lawyers*   17, 18 **which . . . France;** *cf. n.*   **one-and-twenty fifteens;** *cf. n.*   21
say . . . serge . . . buckram: *various kinds of cloth*   23 **Basimecu:** *obscene term of derision*   24, 25 **these presence:** *humorous error for 'these presents'*

besom that must sweep the court clean of such filth as thou art. Thou hast most traitorously corrupted the youth of the realm in erecting a grammar-school; and whereas, before, our forefathers had no other books but the score and the tally, thou hast caused printing to be used; and, contrary to the king his crown and dignity, thou hast built a paper-mill. It will be proved to thy face that thou hast men about thee that usually talk of a noun and a verb, and such abominable words as no Christian ear can endure to hear. Thou hast appointed justices of peace, to call poor men before them about matters they   35 were not able to answer. Moreover, thou hast put them in prison; and because they could not read, thou hast hanged them; when indeed only for that cause they have been most worthy to live. Thou dost ride in a foot-cloth, dost thou not?

Say. What of that?   40

Cade. Marry, thou ought'st not to let thy horse wear a cloak, when honester men than thou go in their hose and doublets.

Dick. And work in their shirt too; as myself, for example, that am a butcher.   45

Say. You men of Kent,—

Dick. What say you of Kent?

Say. Nothing but this: 'tis *bona terra, mala gens.*

Cade. Away with him! away with him! he speaks Latin.

Say. Hear me but speak, and bear me where you will.   50
Kent, in the Commentaries Cæsar writ,
Is term'd the civil'st place of all this isle:
Sweet is the country, because full of riches;
The people liberal, valiant, active, wealthy;
Which makes me hope you are not void of pity.   55
I sold not Maine, I lost not Normandy;
Yet, to recover them, would lose my life.
Justice with favour have I always done;
Prayers and tears have mov'd me, gifts could never.
When have I aught exacted at your hands,   60
But to maintain the king, the realm, and you?
Large gifts have I bestow'd on learned clerks,
Because my book preferr'd me to the king,
And seeing ignorance is the curse of God,
Knowledge the wing wherewith we fly to heaven,   65
Unless you be possess'd with devilish spirits,
You cannot but forbear to murther me.
This tongue hath parley'd unto foreign kings
For your behoof,—

Cade. Tut! when struck'st thou one blow in the field?   70

Say. Great men have reaching hands: oft have I struck
Those that I never saw, and struck them dead.

Geo. O monstrous coward! what, to come behind folks!

Say. These cheeks are pale for watching for your good.

Cade. Give him a box o' the ear, and that will make 'em   75
red again.

Say. Long sitting, to determine poor men's causes,
Hath made me full of sickness and diseases.

Cade. Ye shall have a hempen caudle then, and the help
of hatchet.   80

Dick. Why dost thou quiver, man?

Say. The palsy, and not fear, provokes me.

Cade. Nay, he nods at us; as who should say, I'll be even with you: I'll see if his head will stand steadier on a pole, or no. Take him away and behead him.   85

Say. Tell me wherein have I offended most?
Have I affected wealth, or honour? speak.
Are my chests fill'd up with extorted gold?
Is my apparel sumptuous to behold?
Whom have I injur'd, that ye seek my death?   90
These hands are free from guiltless bloodshedding,
This breast from harbouring foul deceitful thoughts.
O! let me live.

Cade. [*Aside.*] I feel remorse in myself with his words; but I'll bridle it: he shall die, an it be but for pleading so well for   95
his life. Away with him! he has a familiar under his tongue; he speaks not o' God's name. Go, take him away, I say, and strike off his head presently; and then break into his son-in-law's house, Sir James Cromer, and strike off his head, and bring them both upon two poles hither.   100

All. It shall be done.

Say. Ah, countrymen! if when you make your prayers,
God should be so obdurate as yourselves,
How would it fare with your departed souls?
And therefore yet relent, and save my life.   105

Cade. Away with him! and do as I command ye. [*Exeunt some, with Lord Say.*] The proudest peer in the realm shall not wear a head on his shoulders, unless he pay me tribute; there shall not a maid be married, but she shall pay to me her maidenhead, ere they have it; men shall hold of me *in capite;*   110
and we charge and command that their wives be as free as heart can wish or tongue can tell.

Dick. My lord, when shall we go to Cheapside and take up commodities upon our bills?

Cade. Marry, presently.   115

All. O! brave!

Enter one with the heads [of Lord Say and Sir James Cromer].

Cade. But is not this braver? Let them kiss one another, for they loved well when they were alive. Now part them again, lest they consult about the giving up of some more towns in France. Soldiers, defer the spoil of the city until night: for   120
with these borne before us, instead of maces, will we ride through the streets; and at every corner have them kiss. Away!

Exit [with his followers].

❧ SCENE EIGHTH ❧

[The Same. Southwark]
Alarum and Retreat. Enter again Cade, and all his rabblement.

Cade. Up Fish Street! down St. Magnus' corner! kill and knock down! throw them into Thames!   *Sound a parley.*
What noise is this I hear? Dare any be so bold to sound retreat or parley, when I command them kill?

Enter Buckingham, and Old Clifford [with Forces].

Buck. Ay, here they be that dare and will disturb thee.   5

---

26 besom: *broom*   **29 the score and the tally;** *cf. n.*   **30 printing;** *cf. n.*   **king his:** *king's*   **32 usually:** *habitually*   **37 because ... read:** *lacking 'benefit of clergy'*   **42, 43 hose and doublets;** *cf. n.*   **51, 52** *Cf. n.*   **63 book:** *i.e. learning*   **71 reaching:** *far-reaching*   **79 hempen caudle:** *hangman's noose*   **help of hatchet:** *i.e. cure by decapitation*

87 affected: *set my heart on*   **91 guiltless bloodshedding:** *shedding of guiltless blood*   **96 familiar:** *attendant demon*   **97 o':** *in*   **110 in capite:** *by direct grant* (with a pun).   **114 bills:** *halberds* (with pun on bills of credit)   **1 Fish Street;** *cf. n.*

Know, Cade, we come ambassadors from the king
Unto the commons whom thou hast misled;
And here pronounce free pardon to them all
That will forsake thee and go home in peace.

   Clif. What say ye, countrymen? will ye relent,   *10*
And yield to mercy, whilst 'tis offer'd you,
Or let a rebel lead you to your deaths?
Who loves the king, and will embrace his pardon,
Fling up his cap, and say 'God save his majesty!'
Who hateth him, and honours not his father,   *15*
Henry the Fifth, that made all France to quake,
Shake he his weapon at us, and pass by.

   All. God save the king! God save the king!

   Cade. What! Buckingham and Clifford, are ye so brave? And
you, base peasants, do ye believe him? will you needs be   *20*
hanged with your pardons about your necks? Hath my sword
therefore broke through London Gates, that you should leave
me at the White Hart in Southwark? I thought ye would never
have given out these arms till you had recovered your ancient
freedom; but you are all recreants and dastards, and delight   *25*
to live in slavery to the nobility. Let them break your backs
with burthens, take your houses over your heads, ravish your
wives and daughters before your faces: for me, I will make
shift for one, and so, God's curse light upon you all!

   All. We'll follow Cade, we'll follow Cade!   *30*

   Clif. Is Cade the son of Henry the Fifth,
That thus you do exclaim you'll go with him?
Will he conduct you through the heart of France,
And make the meanest of you earls and dukes?
Alas! he hath no home, no place to fly to;   *35*
Nor knows he how to live but by the spoil,
Unless by robbing of your friends and us.
Were 't not a shame that, whilst you live at jar,
The fearful French, whom you late vanquished,
Should make a start o'er seas and vanquish you?   *40*
Methinks already in this civil broil
I see them lording it in London streets,
Crying *Villiago!* unto all they meet.
Better ten thousand base-born Cades miscarry,
Than you should stoop unto a Frenchman's mercy.   *45*
To France, to France! and get what you have lost;
Spare England, for it is your native coast.
Henry hath money, you are strong and manly;
God on our side, doubt not of victory.

   All. A Clifford! a Clifford! we'll follow the king and Clifford.   *50*

   Cade. [*Aside.*] Was ever feather so lightly blown to and fro
as this multitude? The name of Henry the Fifth hales them to
an hundred mischiefs, and makes them leave me desolate. I see
them lay their heads together to surprise me. My sword make
way for me, for here is no staying. In despite of the devils   *55*
and hell, have through the very middest of you! and heavens
and honour be witness, that no want of resolution in me, but
only my followers' base an ignominious treasons, makes me
betake me to my heels.   *Exit.*

   Buck. What, is he fled? go some, and follow him;   *60*
And he that brings his head unto the king
Shall have a thousand crowns for his reward.
                           Exeunt some of them.

Follow me, soldiers: we'll devise a mean
To reconcile you all unto the king.   *Exeunt omnes.*

❦ Scene Ninth ❦

[Kenilworth Castle]
Sound Trumpets. Enter King, Queen, and Somerset on the Terrace.

   King. Was ever king that joy'd an earthly throne,
And could command no more content than I?
No sooner was I crept out of my cradle
But I was made a king at nine months old:
Was never subject long'd to be a king   *5*
As I do long and wish to be a subject.

Enter Buckingham and Clifford.

   Buck. Health, and glad tidings, to your majesty!
   King. Why, Buckingham, is the traitor Cade surpris'd?
Or is he but retir'd to make him strong?

Enter multitudes with halters about their necks.

   Clif. He's fled, my lord, and all his powers do yield;   *10*
And humbly thus, with halters on their necks,
Expect your highness' doom, of life, or death.

   King. Then, heaven, set ope thy everlasting gates,
To entertain my vows of thanks and praise!
Soldiers, this day have you redeem'd your lives,   *15*
And show'd how well you love your prince and country:
Continue still in this so good a mind,
And Henry, though he be infortunate,
Assure yourselves, will never be unkind:
And so, with thanks and pardon to you all,   *20*
I do dismiss you to your several countries.

   All. God save the king! God save the king!

Enter a Messenger.

   Mess. Please it your Grace to be advertised,
The Duke of York is newly come from Ireland;
And with a puissant and a mighty power   *25*
Of gallowglasses, and stout kerns,
Is marching hitherward in proud array;
And still proclaimeth, as he comes along,
His arms are only to remove from thee
The Duke of Somerset, whom he terms a traitor.   *30*

   King. Thus stands my state, 'twixt Cade and York distress'd;
Like to a ship, that, having scap'd a tempest,
Is straightway calm'd, and boarded with a pirate.
But now is Cade driven back, his men dispers'd;
And now is York in arms to second him.   *35*
I pray thee, Buckingham, go and meet him,
And ask him what's the reason of these arms.
Tell him I'll send Duke Edmund to the Tower;
And, Somerset, we will commit thee thither,
Until his army be dismiss'd from him.   *40*

   Som. My lord,
I'll yield myself to prison willingly,
Or unto death, to do my country good.

---

23 the White Hart; *cf. n.*   24 given out: *yielded up*   38 at jar: *in discord*   38–40
Cf. n.   43 Villiago: *villain*

8 surpris'd: *taken prisoner*   14 entertain: *receive*   21 countries: *districts*   23 advertised: *informed*   26 gallowglasses: *heavy-armed Irish soldiers*   33 with: *by*

King. In any case, be not too rough in terms;
For he is fierce and cannot brook hard language.   45

Buck. I will, my lord; and doubt not so to deal
As all things shall redound unto your good.

King. Come, wife, let's in, and learn to govern better;
For yet may England curse my wretched reign.

Flourish. Exeunt.

❧ SCENE TENTH ❧

[Kent. Iden's Garden]
Enter Cade

Cade. Fie on ambitions! fie on myself, that have a sword,
and yet am ready to famish! These five days have I hid me in
these woods and durst not peep out, for all the country is laid
for me; but now I am so hungry, that if I might have a lease
of my life for a thousand years I could stay no longer. Where-   5
fore, on a brick wall have I climbed into this garden, to see
if I can eat grass, or pick a sallet another while, which is not
amiss to cool a man's stomach this hot weather. And I think
this word 'sallet' was born to do me good: for many a time,
but for a sallet, my brain-pan had been cleft with a brown   10
bill; and many a time, when I have been dry, and bravely
marching, it hath served me instead of a quart-pot to drink
in; and now the word 'sallet' must serve me to feed on.

Enter Iden.

Iden. Lord! who would live turmoiled in the court,
And may enjoy such quiet walks as these?   15
This small inheritance my father left me
Contenteth me, and worth a monarchy.
I seek not to wax great by others' waning,
Or gather wealth I care not with what envy:
Sufficeth that I have maintains my state,   20
And sends the poor well pleased from my gate.

Cade. [*Aside.*] Here's the lord of the soil come to seize
me for a stray, for entering his fee-simple without leave. Ah,
villain! thou wilt betray me, and get a thousand crowns of
the king by carrying my head to him; but I'll make thee   25
eat iron like an ostrich, and swallow my sword like a great
pin, ere thou and I part.

Iden. Why, rude companion, whatsoe'er thou be,
I know thee not; why then should I betray thee?
Is 't not enough to break into my garden,   30
And like a thief to come to rob my grounds,
Climbing my walls in spite of me the owner,
But thou wilt brave me with these saucy terms?

Cade. Brave thee! ay, by the best blood that ever was
broached, and beard thee too. Look on me well: I have eat   35
no meat these five days; yet, come thou and thy five men,
and if I do not leave you all as dead as a door-nail, I pray
God I may never eat grass more.

Iden. Nay, it shall ne'er be said, while England stands,
That Alexander Iden, an esquire of Kent,   40
Took odds to combat a poor famish'd man.
Oppose thy steadfast-gazing eyes to mine,

See if thou canst out-face me with thy looks:
Set limb to limb, and thou art far the lesser;
Thy hand is but a finger to my fist;   45
Thy leg a stick compared with this truncheon;
My foot shall fight with all the strength thou hast;
And if mine arm be heaved in the air
Thy grave is digg'd already in the earth.
As for words, whose greatness answers words,   50
Let this my sword report what speech forbears.

Cade. By my valour, the most complete champion that ever
I heard! Steel, if thou turn the edge, or cut not out the burly-
boned clown in chines of beef ere thou sleep in thy sheath, I
beseech Jove on my knees, thou mayst be turned to hobnails.   55

Here they fight. [Cade falls.]

O, I am slain! Famine and no other hath slain me: let ten
thousand devils come against me, and give me but the ten
meals I have lost, and I'ld defy them all. Wither, garden;
and be henceforth a burying-place to all that do dwell in
this house, because the unconquered soul of Cade is fled.   60

Iden. Is 't Cade that I have slain, that monstrous traitor?
Sword, I will hallow thee for this thy deed,
And hang thee o'er my tomb when I am dead:
Ne'er shall this blood be wiped from thy point,
But thou shalt wear it as a herald's coat,   65
To emblaze the honour that thy master got.

Cade. Iden, farewell; and be proud of thy victory. Tell Kent
from me, she hath lost her best man, and exhort all the world
to be cowards; for I, that never feared any, am vanquished by
famine, not by valour.   *Dies.*   70

Iden. How much thou wrong'st me, heaven be my judge.
Die, damned wretch, the curse of her that bare thee!
And as I thrust thy body in with my sword,
So wish I I might thrust thy soul to hell.
Hence will I drag thee headlong by the heels   75
Unto a dunghill which shall be thy grave,
And there cut off thy most ungracious head;
Which I will bear in triumph to the king,
Leaving thy trunk for crows to feed upon.

Exit [dragging out the body].

ACT FIFTH ❧ SCENE FIRST

[Kent. Fields between Dartford and Blackheath]
Enter York and his army of Irish, with drum and colours.

York. From Ireland thus comes York to claim his right,
And pluck the crown from feeble Henry's head:
Ring, bells, aloud; burn, bonfires, clear and bright,
To entertain great England's lawful king.
Ah *sancta majestas,* who would not buy thee dear?   5
Let them obey that know not how to rule;
This hand was made to handle nought but gold:
I cannot give due action to my words,
Except a sword or sceptre balance it.
A sceptre shall it have, have I a soul,   10

---

3 laid: *beset*   9 sallet: *salad of green herbs*   10 sallet: *light headpiece or helmet*   21
and: *and so is*   20 Sufficeth that: *it is enough that what*   26 eat ... ostrich;
cf. n.

46 truncheon: *a thick staff* (Iden's leg)   51 *Cf. n.*   73 thrust in: *pierce*   5
Cf. n.   8 action: *effect*   9 balance it: *add weight to my hand*   10 have I: *as sure as
I have*

On which I'll toss the flower-de-luce of France.

Enter Buckingham.

Whom have we here? Buckingham, to disturb me?
The king hath sent him, sure: I must dissemble.
    Buck. York, if thou meanest well, I greet thee well.
    York. Humphrey of Buckingham, I accept thy greeting.   *15*
Art thou a messenger, or come of pleasure?
    Buck. A messenger from Henry, our dread liege,
To know the reason of these arms in peace;
Or why thou,—being a subject as I am,—
Against thy oath and true allegiance sworn,   *20*
Should raise so great a power without his leave,
Or dare to bring thy force so near the court.
    York. [*Aside.*] Scarce can I speak, my choler is so great:
O! I could hew up rocks and fight with flint,
I am so angry at these abject terms;   *25*
And now, like Ajax Telamonius,
On sheep or oxen could I spend my fury.
I am far better born than is the king,
More like a king, more kingly in my thoughts;
But I must make fair weather yet awhile,   *30*
Till Henry be more weak, and I more strong.
[*Aloud.*] Buckingham, I prithee, pardon me
That I have given no answer all this while;
My mind was troubled with deep melancholy.
The cause why I have brought this army hither   *35*
Is to remove proud Somerset from the king,
Seditious to his Grace and to the state.
    Buck. That is too much presumption on thy part:
But if thy arms be to no other end,
The king hath yielded unto thy demand: *40*
The Duke of Somerset is in the Tower.
    York. Upon thine honour, is he a prisoner?
    Buck. Upon mine honour, he is a prisoner.
    York. Then, Buckingham, I do dismiss my powers.
Soldiers, I thank you all; disperse yourselves;   *45*
Meet me to-morrow in Saint George's Field,
You shall have pay, and everything you wish,
And let my sovereign, virtuous Henry,
Command my eldest son, nay, all my sons,
As pledges of my fealty and love;   *50*
I'll send them all as willing as I live:
Lands, goods, horse, armour, anything I have
Is his to use, so Somerset may die.
    Buck. York, I commend this kind submission:
We twain will go into his highness' tent.   *55*

Enter King and Attendants.

    King. Buckingham, doth York intend no harm to us,
That thus he marcheth with thee arm in arm?
    York. In all submission and humility
York doth present himself unto your highness.
    King. Then what intend these forces thou dost bring?   *60*
    York. To heave the traitor Somerset from hence,
And fight against that monstrous rebel, Cade,
Who since I heard to be discomfited.

Enter Iden, with Cade's head.

    Iden. If one so rude and of so mean condition
May pass into the presence of a king,   *65*
Lo! I present your Grace a traitor's head,
The head of Cade, whom I in combat slew.
    King. The head of Cade! Great God, how just art thou!
O! let me view his visage, being dead,
That living wrought me such exceeding trouble.   *70*
Tell me, my friend, art thou the man that slew him?
    Iden. I was, an 't like your majesty.
    King. How art thou call'd, and what is thy degree?
    Iden. Alexander Iden, that's my name;
A poor esquire of Kent, that loves his king.   *75*
    Buck. So please it you, my lord, 'twere not amiss
He were created knight for his good service.
    King. Iden, kneel down. [*He kneels.*] Rise up knight.
We give thee for reward a thousand marks,
And will that thou henceforth attend on us.   *80*
    Iden. May Iden live to merit such a bounty,
And never live but true unto his liege!

Enter Queen and Somerset.

    King. See! Buckingham! Somerset comes with the queen:
Go, bid her hide him quickly from the duke.
    Queen. For thousand Yorks he shall not hide his head,   *85*
But boldly stand and front him to his face.
    York. How now! is Somerset at liberty?
Then, York, unloose thy long-imprison'd thoughts
And let thy tongue be equal with thy heart.
Shall I endure the sight of Somerset?   *90*
False king! why hast thou broken faith with me,
Knowing how hardly I can brook abuse?
King did I call thee? no, thou art not king;
Not fit to govern and rule multitudes,
Which dar'st not, no, nor canst not rule a traitor.   *95*
That head of thine doth not become a crown;
Thy hand is made to grasp a palmer's staff,
And not to grace an awful princely sceptre.
That gold must round engirt these brows of mine,
Whose smile and frown, like to Achilles' spear,   *100*
Is able with the change to kill and cure.
Here is a hand to hold a sceptre up,
And with the same to act controlling laws.
Give place: by heaven, thou shalt rule no more
O'er him whom heaven created for thy ruler.   *105*
    Som. O monstrous traitor! I arrest thee, York,
Of capital treason 'gainst the king and crown.
Obey, audacious traitor; kneel for grace.
    York. Wouldst have me kneel? first let me ask of these
If they can brook I bow a knee to man.   *110*
Sirrah, call in my sons to be my bail: [*Exit an Attendant.*]
I know ere they will have me go to ward,
They'll pawn their swords of my enfranchisement.
    Queen. Call hither Clifford; bid him come amain,
To say if that the bastard boys of York   *115*
Shall be the surety for their traitor father.   [*Exit Buckingham.*]
    York. O blood-bespotted Neapolitan,
Outcast of Naples, England's bloody scourge!
The sons of York, thy betters in their birth,

---

11 **toss:** *bear aloft* **flower-de-luce:** *fleur de lys*   15 **Humphrey of Buckingham;** *cf. n.*   26
Ajax Telamonius; *cf. n.*   46 **Saint George's Field;** *cf. n.*   49 **Command:** *demand as hostage*

80 **will:** *command*   100 **Achilles' spear;** *cf. n.*   103 **act:** *put into effect*   109 **these:**
his followers   112 **ward:** *custody*   113 **of:** *in behalf of* **enfranchisement:** *freedom*   114
amain: *with speed*   117 **Neapolitan;** *cf. n.*

Shall be their father's bail; and bane to those   *120*
That for my surety will refuse the boys!

Enter Edward and Richard.

See where they come: I'll warrant they'll make it good.

Enter Clifford [and his son].

Queen. And here comes Clifford, to deny their bail.
Clif. [Kneeling.] Health and all happiness to my lord the king!
York. I thank thee, Clifford: say, what news with thee?   *125*
Nay, do not fright us with an angry look:
We are thy sovereign, Clifford, kneel again;
For thy mistaking so we pardon thee.
Clif. This is my king, York, I do not mistake;
But thou mistak'st me much to think I do.   *130*
To Bedlam with him! is the man grown mad?
King. Ay, Clifford; a bedlam and ambitious humour
Makes him oppose himself against his king.
Clif. He is a traitor; let him to the Tower,
And chop away that factious pate of his.   *135*
Queen. He is arrested, but will not obey:
His sons, he says, shall give their words for him.
York. Will you not, sons?
Edw. Ay, noble father, if our words will serve.
Rich. And if words will not, then our weapons shall.   *140*
Clif. Why, what a brood of traitors have we here!
York. Look in a glass, and call thy image so:
I am thy king, and thou a false-heart traitor.
Call hither to the stake my two brave bears,
That with the very shaking of their chains   *145*
They may astonish these fell-lurking curs:
Bid Salisbury and Warwick come to me.

Enter the Earls of Warwick and Salisbury.

Clif. Are these thy bears? we'll bait thy bears to death,
And manacle the bearard in their chains,
If thou dar'st bring them to the baiting-place.   *150*
Rich. Oft have I seen a hot o'erweening cur
Run back and bite, because he was withheld;
Who, being suffer'd, with the bear's fell paw,
Hath clapp'd his tail between his legs, and cried:
And such a piece of service will you do,   *155*
If you oppose yourselves to match Lord Warwick.
Clif. Hence, heap of wrath, foul indigested lump,
As crooked in thy manners as thy shape!
York. Nay, we shall heat you thoroughly anon.
Clif. Take heed, lest by your heat you burn yourselves.   *160*
King. Why, Warwick, hath thy knee forgot to bow?
Old Salisbury, shame to thy silver hair,
Thou mad misleader of thy brain-sick son!
What! wilt thou on thy death-bed play the ruffian,
And seek for sorrow with thy spectacles?   *165*
O! where is faith? O, where is loyalty?
If it be banish'd from the frosty head,
Where shall it find a harbour in the earth?
Wilt thou go dig a grave to find out war,

And shame thine honourable age with blood?   *170*
Why art thou old, and want'st experience?
Or wherefore dost abuse it, if thou hast it?
For shame! in duty bend thy knee to me,
That bows unto the grave with mickle age.
Sal. My lord, I have consider'd with myself   *175*
The title of this most renowned duke;
And in my conscience do repute his Grace
The rightful heir to England's royal seat.
King. Hast thou not sworn allegiance unto me?
Sal. I have.   *180*
King. Canst thou dispense with heaven for such an oath?
Sal. It is great sin to swear unto a sin,
But greater sin to keep a sinful oath.
Who can be bound by any solemn vow
To do a murderous deed, to rob a man,   *185*
To force a spotless virgin's chastity,
To reave the orphan of his patrimony,
To wring the widow from her custom'd right,
And have no other reason for this wrong
But that he was bound by a solemn oath?   *190*
Queen. A subtle traitor needs no sophister.
King. Call Buckingham, and bid him arm himself.
York. Call Buckingham, and all the friends thou hast,
I am resolv'd for death or dignity.
Clif. The first I warrant thee, if dreams prove true.   *195*
War. You were best to go to bed and dream again,
To keep thee from the tempest of the field.
Clif. I am resolv'd to bear a greater storm
Than any thou canst conjure up to-day;
And that I'll write upon thy burgonet,   *200*
Might I but know thee by thy household badge.
War. Now, by my father's badge, old Nevil's crest,
The rampant bear chain'd to the ragged staff,
This day I'll wear aloft my burgonet,—
As on a mountain-top the cedar shows,   *205*
That keeps his leaves in spite of any storm,—
Even to affright thee with the view thereof.
Clif. And from thy burgonet I'll rend thy bear,
And tread it underfoot with all contempt,
Despite the bearard that protects the bear.   *210*
Y. Clif. And so to arms, victorious father,
To quell the rebels and their complices.
Rich. Fie! charity! for shame! speak not in spite,
For you shall sup with Jesu Christ to-night.
Y. Clif. Foul stigmatic, that's more than thou canst tell.   *215*
Rich. If not in heaven, you'll surely sup in hell.   *Exeunt.*

❧ SCENE SECOND ❧

[Saint Albans]
[Alarums: Excursions.] Enter Warwick.

War. Clifford of Cumberland, 'tis Warwick calls:
And if thou dost not hide thee from the bear,

---

140 Cf. n.   **144 two brave bears**; cf. n.   **146 fell-lurking**: *watching to do mischief*   **149 bearard**: *bear-ward, keeper of bears*   **150 baiting-place**: *bear-pit*   **153 suffer'd**: *allowed to have his way*   **with**: *at a blow of*   **156 oppose yourselves**: *venture*   **157 indigested**: *unformed, shapeless*   **165 with ... spectacles**: *with careful scrutiny*   **169 Will you ensure your own death by promoting war?**

174 That: *i.e. thy knee*   **mickle**: *much*   **181 dispense with**: *get exemption from*   **182 swear**: *pledge oneself*   **187 reave**: *bereave*   **188 custom'd**: *sanctioned by custom*   **191 sophister**: *teacher of equivocation*   **194 resolv'd for**: *determined to win*   **196 You ... best**: *it would be best for you*   **200 burgonet**: *helmet*   **201 household badge**: *distinguishing emblem of a family*   **202, 203** Cf. n.   **204 aloft**: *on top of*   **212 complices**: *accomplices*   **215 stigmatic**: *one branded with deformity*   **2 And if**: *An if, if*

Now, when the angry trumpet sounds alarum,
And dead men's cries do fill the empty air,
Clifford, I say, come forth, and fight with me!   5
Proud northern lord, Clifford of Cumberland,
Warwick is hoarse with calling thee to arms.

Enter York.

How now, my noble lord! what! all afoot?
    York. The deadly-handed Clifford slew my steed;
But match to match I have encounter'd him,   10
And made a prey for carrion kites and crows
Even of the bonny beast he lov'd so well.

Enter Clifford.

    War. Of one or both of us the time is come.
    York. Hold, Warwick! seek thee out some other chase,
For I myself must hunt this deer to death.   15
    War. Then, nobly, York; 'tis for a crown thou fight'st.
As I intend, Clifford, to thrive to-day,
It grieves my soul to leave thee unassail'd.   *Exit War.*
    Clif. What seest thou in me, York? why dost thou pause?
    York. With thy brave bearing should I be in love,   20
But that thou art so fast mine enemy.
    Clif. Nor should thy prowess want praise and esteem,
But that 'tis shown ignobly and in treason.
    York. So let it help me now against thy sword
As I in justice and true right express it.   25
    Clif. My soul and body on the action both!
    York. A dreadful lay! address thee instantly.
    Clif. La fin couronne les œuvres.
                [They fight, and Clifford falls and dies.]
    York. Thus war hath given thee peace, for thou art still.
Peace with his soul, heaven, if it be thy will!   *Exit.*   30

Enter Young Clifford.

    Y. Clif. Shame and confusion! all is on the rout:
Fear frames disorder, and disorder wounds
Where it should guard. O war! thou son of hell,
Whom angry heavens do make their minister,
Throw in the frozen bosoms of our part   35
Hot coals of vengeance! Let no soldier fly:
He that is truly dedicate to war
Hath no self-love; nor he that loves himself
Hath not essentially, but by circumstance,
The name of valour.   *[Seeing his father's body.]*   40
            O, let the vile world end,
And the premised flames of the last day
Knit heaven and earth together;
Now let the general trumpet blow his blast,
Particularities and petty sounds   45
To cease!—Wast thou ordain'd, dear father,
To lose thy youth in peace, and to achieve
The silver livery of advised age,
And in thy reverence and thy chair-days thus
To die in ruffian battle? Even at this sight   50

My heart is turn'd to stone: and while 'tis mine
It shall be stony. York not our old men spares;
No more will I their babes: tears virginal
Shall be to me even as the dew to fire;
And beauty, that the tyrant oft reclaims,   55
Shall to my flaming wrath be oil and flax.
Henceforth I will not have to do with pity:
Meet I an infant of the house of York,
Into as many gobbets will I cut it
As wild Medea young Absyrtus did: 60
In cruelty will I seek out my fame.
Come, thou new ruin of old Clifford's house:
                        [Taking up the body.]
As did Æneas old Anchises bear,
So bear I thee upon my manly shoulders;
But then Æneas bare a living load,   65
Nothing so heavy as these woes of mine.   *[Exit.]*

Enter Richard and Somerset to fight. [Somerset is killed.]

    Rich. So, lie thou there;
For underneath an alehouse' paltry sign,
The Castle in Saint Albans, Somerset
Hath made the wizard famous in his death.   70
Sword, hold thy temper; heart, be wrathful still:
Priests pray for enemies, but princes kill.   *[Exit.]*

Fight. Excursions. Enter King, Queen, and others.

    Queen. Away, my lord! you are slow: for shame, away!
    King. Can we outrun the heavens? good Margaret, stay.
    Queen. What are you made of? you'll nor fight nor fly: 75
Now is it manhood, wisdom, and defence
To give the enemy way, and to secure us
By what we can, which can no more but fly.

                        Alarum afar off.

If you be ta'en, we then should see the bottom
Of all our fortunes: but if we haply scape,   80
As well we may, if not through your neglect,
We shall to London get, where you are lov'd,
And where this breach now in our fortunes made
May readily be stopp'd.

Enter [Young] Clifford.

    Clif. But that my heart's on future mischief set,   85
I would speak blasphemy ere bid you fly;
But fly you must: uncurable discomfit
Reigns in the hearts of all our present parts.
Away, for your relief! and we will live
To see their day and them our fortune give.   90
Away, my lord, away!   *Exeunt.*

---

21 **fast:** *inalterably*   26 **action:** *result of combat*   27 **lay:** *stake* **address thee:** *prepare*   28 **La fin ... œuvres:** *'finis coronat opus,' the result proves the justice of the cause*   35 **part:** *party, side*   39 **not ... circumstance:** *not really but through accident*   41 **premised:** *went before their time (?), foreordained (?)*   45 **Particularities:** *individual affairs*   46 **cease:** *put an end to*   48 **advised:** *experienced, cautious*   49 **reverence:** *state of dignity* **chair-days:** *time of repose*

54 **as ... fire:** *i.e. shall make the flame hotter*   55 **that ... reclaims:** *which often subdues ferocity*   60 **Medea ... Absyrtus:** *cf. n.*   66 **Nothing:** *in no respect*   70 **the wizard:** *i.e. the Spirit (cf. I. iv. 38-40)*   75 **nor ... nor:** *neither ... nor*   77 **secure us:** *make ourselves safe*   78 **which can:** *we who can do*   79, 80 *Cf. n.*   81 **if ... neglect:** *if we do not fail through your negligence*   87 **discomfit:** *discouragement*   88 **all ... parts:** *all of our party here*   90 **their day:** *a day of victory like theirs* **them ... give:** *impose on them a misfortune like this of ours*

❧ Scene Third ❧

[Field near Saint Albans]

*Alarum. Retreat. Enter York, Richard, Warwick, and Soldiers, with
drum and colours.*

York. Of Salisbury, who can report of him,
That winter lion, who in rage forgets
Aged contusions and all brush of time,
And, like a gallant in the brow of youth,
Repairs him with occasion? this happy day   5
Is not itself, nor have we won one foot,
If Salisbury be lost.
    Rich.   My noble father,
Three times to-day I holp him to his horse,
Three times bestrid him; thrice I led him off,   10
Persuaded him from any further act:
But still, where danger was, still there I met him;
And like rich hangings in a homely house,
So was his will in his old feeble body.
But, noble as he is, look where he comes.   15

Enter Salisbury.

Sal. Now, by my sword, well hast thou fought to-day;
By the mass, so did we all. I thank you, Richard:
God knows how long it is I have to live;
And it hath pleas'd him that three times to-day
You have defended me from imminent death.   20
Well, lords, we have not got that which we have:
'Tis not enough our foes are this time fled,
Being opposites of such repairing nature.
    York. I know our safety is to follow them;
For, as I hear, the king is fled to London,   25
To call a present court of parliament:
Let us pursue him ere the writs go forth:—
What says Lord Warwick? shall we after them?
    War. After them! nay, before them, if we can.
Now, by my hand, lords, 'twas a glorious day: 30
Saint Albans battle, won by famous York,
Shall be eterniz'd in all age to come.
Sound, drums and trumpets, and to London all:
And more such days as these to us befall!   *Exeunt.*

❧ Finis ❧

---

2 winter: *aged*   **3 brush:** *wear and tear*   **4 brow:** *forefront*   **5 Repairs . . . occasion:**
grows more vigorous as he is called upon to exert himself   **10 bestrid:** *stood over, to defend
him when prostrate*   **12 still:** *always*   **21 got:** *secured firmly*   **23 opposites:** *adversaries* **of . . . nature:** *so endowed with means
of recovery*   **27 writs;** *cf. n.*

NOTES

The Second Part of Henry the Sixth. The last word is written 'Sixt' in the early editions, that being the regular Elizabethan form of the numeral.

I.i.58-61. *It is further agreed between them, etc.* Editors have not failed to observe that the wording of the document here differs from what Gloucester has just read, ll. 50 ff. Such inconsistency is very common in Shakespeare. Compare I. iv, lines 35 ff. and 63 ff. It is not necessary to explain that Gloucester's eyes were dim, or that his agitation prevented him from getting more than the general import of the passage. The author was writing for auditors, who would not compare the two texts.

I.i.63. *We here create thee the first Duke of Suffolk.* The Earl of Suffolk was created Marquis, September 14, 1444, and was made Duke, June 2, 1448, three years after the coronation of Queen Margaret (May, 1445). The earlier dignity is the one which chronologically belongs in this scene; but the author is doubtless thinking of Holinshed's account of the later one: 'the marquesse of Suffolke, by great fauour of the king, & more desire of the queene, was erected to the title and dignitie of duke of Suffolke, which he a short time inioied.'

I.i.66, 67. *till term of eighteen months Be full expir'd.* York is discharged for the term of the truce with the French king. Cf. line 43 above.

I.i.118. *Anjou and Maine! myself did win them both.* An entirely unhistoric statement (found in the *Contention* version also). The earliest military service that Warwick saw was at the first battle of St. Albans, with which this play concludes (May 22, 1455). The present Earl of Warwick, the King-maker, is probably here confused with his father-in-law, from whom he derived his title. The earlier Earl, who died in 1439, appears in *The First Part of Henry VI* as a general on service in France. This is perhaps an indication that the authors of the *Contention* and of the *First Part* were not the same. (Actually the King-maker did not become Earl of Warwick till 1449. In the historical year of this scene, 1445, the earldom was held by the young son of the Earl who fought in France.)

I.i.123. *For Suffolk's duke, may he be suffocate.* Poor puns are frequent in this play.

I.i.132, 133. *That Suffolk should demand a whole fifteenth For costs and charges in transporting her.* A tax of one-fifteenth on personal property. The lines are suggested by Holinshed: 'for the fetching of hir, the marquesse of Suffolke demanded a whole fifteenth in open parliament.' In the concluding scene of the *First Part* (V.v.92 f.), King Henry authorizes Suffolk to levy a greater tax:

'For your expenses and sufficient charge,
Among the people gather up a tenth.'

I.i.142, 143. *If I longer stay, We shall begin our ancient bickerings.* Allusion to the quarrels of Gloucester and the Cardinal in the *First Part*. This is one of the passages added by the reviser.

I.i.151. *heir apparent to the English crown.* A misuse of the term, according to modern practice, for Gloucester was heir presumptive, not heir apparent; i.e. his right to succeed was contingent upon the chance that Henry would leave no lineal heir.

I.i.153. *all the wealthy kingdoms of the west.* Perhaps an anachronistic allusion to the golden realms of Spanish America.

I.i.164, 165. *Why should he then protect our sovereign, He being of age to govern of himself?* King Henry was twenty-five years old at the time of Gloucester's death in 1447. Gloucester, however, had ceased to be Protector in name, or even in fact, long before. His formal Protectorship was annulled in 1429, when the king was crowned (at the age of seven). Thereafter Gloucester held no higher title than that of 'First Councillor.'

I.i.179. *Pride went before, ambition follows him.* 'Pride' stands for the Cardinal, 'ambition' for Buckingham and Somerset.

I.i.190, 191. *Thy deeds, thy plainness, and thy housekeeping Hath won the greatest favour of the commons.* Many modern editors alter 'hath' to 'have,' but Elizabethan English often prefers a logical to a grammatical agreement between subject and verb. 'Hath' may be explained as agreeing with the nearest of the three subjects, or with the aggregate idea of Warwick's character implied by all three. Frequently the lack of agreement is only apparent, not real (cf. note on I.iv.73).

I.i.193. *brother York, thy acts in Ireland.* Salisbury and York were brothers-in-law (see note on line 239 below). York's 'acts in Ireland' were not performed till later than the historical date of this scene (1445). His highly successful administration of Ireland occurred in 1448-1450. Compare the note on III.i.319.

I.i.233, 234. *As did the fatal brand Althæa burnt Unto the prince's heart of Calydon.* The heart of the prince of Calydon (Meleager) succumbed to death

when his mother in anger burned the piece of firewood ('brand'), which the Fates had prophesied would measure his length of life. This passage, like many others of a flowery and rhetorical nature, is not found in the original (*Contention*) version, and was presumably added by Shakespeare. It has been noted that the myth is here correctly reproduced from Ovid, whereas in *2 Henry IV* (II.ii.76-79) the poet seems to retain only a confused recollection of it.

I.i.239. *And therefore I will take the Nevils' parts.* York's wife was Cecily, youngest sister of Richard Nevil, Earl of Salisbury, and aunt of Warwick. Actually it was the Nevils who took York's part. (Compare note on I.iii.69-71.)

I.ii.9. *grovel on thy face.* Solicit supernatural aid. Compare I.iv.13, 14.

I.ii.38. *in that chair where kings and queens are crown'd.* The 'chair of Scone' at Westminster. The stone of destiny which formed its seat was brought by Edward I from Scotland in 1296.

I.ii.68. *Sir John.* Not a title of knighthood, but a common form of address for priests. In such cases it signifies no more than 'Dominie.'

I.ii.71. *I am but Grace.* 'Your Grace' being the proper salutation for a Duchess. In Shakespeare, however, it is frequently used in addressing kings and queens, as in the next scene of this play, line 66.

I.iii.16–18. *Mine is, an 't please your Grace, against John Goodman, my Lord Cardinal's man, for keeping my house, and lands, my wife and all, from me.* Suf. *Thy wife too! that is some wrong indeed.* This passage, which is considerably developed from its source in the *Contention*, shows in its revised form a strong similarity to the opening scene of the play of *Sir Thomas More*, in which Shakespeare is thought to have had a part. Some of the Jack Cade scenes of the present play likewise betray a close affinity to *Sir Thomas More*.

I.iii.20, 21. *Against the Duke of Suffolk, for enclosing the commons of Melford.* Long Melford is a town in the county of Suffolk. The form of oppression represented by the appropriation and fencing in by wealthy citizens of common land was frequent in the sixteenth century. Some of the latest records of Shakespeare's life deal with his attitude toward the project of enclosing the common at Welcombe near Stratford. His kinsman, Thomas Greene, wrote as follows, November 17, 1614: 'My cosen Shakspear comyng yesterdy to town, I went to see him how he did. He told me that they assured him they ment to inclose no further than to Gospell Bush, and so upp straight (leavyng out part of the Dyngles to the ffield) to the gate in Clopton hedg, and take in Salisburyes peece; and that they mean in Aprill to survey the land, and then to gyve satisfaccion, and not before; and he and Mr. Hall [Shakespeare's son-in-law] say they think there will be nothyng done at all.' On September 1, 1615, Greene wrote in his Diary: 'Mr. Shakspeare told Mr. J. Greene that I was not able to beare the enclosing of Welcombe.'

I.iii.57. *canoniz'd.* The accent is on the second syllable, as regularly in Shakespeare.

I.iii.69-71. *And he of these that can do most of all Cannot do more in England than the Nevils: Salisbury and Warwick are no simple peers.* These lines are not found in the *Contention* version, and may be fairly credited to Shakespeare's Warwickshire memories of the Nevils. This noble family—'of all the great houses of mediaeval England ... incontestibly the toughest and the most prolific' (Oman)—originated in the north, about Raby Castle near Durham. The first earldom they acquired was that of Westmoreland, bestowed by Richard II upon Sir Ralph Nevil in 1397. The latter is the Earl of Westmoreland who appears in Shakespeare's plays of *Henry IV* and *Henry V*. He married, as his second wife, a daughter of John of Gaunt, sister of the Cardinal Beaufort of the present play. Salisbury was their son and Warwick their grandson.

I.iii.99. *Or Somerset or York, all's one to me.* Holinshed records that at the expiration of York's term as Regent of France (in 1446), 'he returned home, and was ioifullie receiued of the king with thanks for his good seruice, as he had full well deserued in time of that his gouernement: and, further, that now, when a new regent was to be chosen and sent ouer, to abide vpon safegard of the countries beyond the seas as yet subiect to the English dominion, the said duke of Yorke was eftsoones (as a man most meet to supplie that roome) appointed to go ouer againe, as regent of France, with all his former allowances.

'But the duke of Summerset, still maligning the duke of Yorkes aduancement, as he had sought to hinder his dispatch at the first when he was sent ouer to be regent, (as before yee haue heard,) he likewise now wrought so, that the king reuoked his grant made to the duke of Yorke for enioieng of that office the terme of other fiue yeeres, and, with helpe of William marquesse of Suffolke, obtained that grant for himselfe.' In connection with the latter part of this extract, see lines 162 ff.

I.iii.115, 116. *If he be old enough, what needs your Grace To be protector of*

his excellence? As before noted, this title had long since lapsed. Observe Gloucester's reply and see note on I.i.164, 165.

I.iii.122. *The Dauphin hath prevail'd beyond the seas.* Since the sovereignty of the French king, Charles VII, was not acknowledged by the English, they continued to designate him by the title ('Dolphin' in Elizabethan spelling) he had borne during his father's lifetime. The particular victories for the Dauphin here referred to are probably those obtained in 1443-1444 over John, the first Duke of Somerset, brother of the Duke who appears in this scene. By the influence of his uncle, Cardinal Beaufort, the first duke was appointed, on March 30, 1443, 'Captain-General of all France and Guienne.' After a campaign of utter disaster, he returned to England and died in May, 1444. His failure was in a way a vindication, not a disgrace, for Gloucester.

I.iii.127. *Thy sumptuous buildings.* The Duke occupied Greenwich Palace, which was greatly enlarged and improved by his Renaissance taste. In Shakespeare's time it was a favorite residence of Queen Elizabeth and King James.

I.iii.138, 139. *Could I come near your beauty with my nails, I'd set my ten commandments in your face.* This undignified scene is historically impossible. The Queen and Duchess never met, for the humiliation and banishment of the latter, depicted in Act II, scene iv, occurred in 1441, four years before Margaret came to England.

I.iii.168, 169. *Last time I danc'd attendance on his will Till Paris was besieg'd, famish'd, and lost.* The loss of Paris occurred in 1437, seven years before the present Duke of Somerset came to his title. York, however, is probably alluding to a scene in the *First Part* (IV.iii.10, 11), where he complains of 'that villain Somerset,

> *That thus delays my promised supply*
> *Of horsemen that were levied for this siege.'*

This is in connection with the siege of Bordeaux and last campaign of Talbot, 1453 (historically long after the date of the present scene). These lines have again been added by the reviser. Compare note on I.i.142, 143.

I.iii.208, 209. These lines are not in the Folio. They have been introduced from the *Contention* version because Somerset's reply (line 210) seems to presuppose them.

I.iv.55. *A pretty plot, well chosen to build upon!* There is a quibble on 'plot': a plot of ground and a stratagem.

I.iv.60, 61. *Why, this is just, 'Aio te, Æacida, Romanos vincere posse.'* The cryptic answer about the Duke of York and Henry, just quoted, is as ambiguous as the famous response given by the oracle to Pyrrhus, King of Epirus, which may be interpreted either, 'I say that you, descendant of Æacus, can conquer the Romans,' or 'I say that the Romans can conquer you.'

I.iv.73. *Thither goes these news as fast as horse can carry them.* An example of Shakespeare's frequent use of an apparently singular verb with a plural subject. Compare note on I.i.190, 191. The irregularity is usually to be explained by the fact that, while Shakespeare ordinarily used the midland verbal inflections which correspond with those of modern English, he was also familiar with the northern inflection, in which the present plural ends in 's,' and with the southern, in which it ends in 'eth.' Modern editors generally normalize the dialectal forms, except where rhyme or metre requires their retention. Other instances in which the Folio reading deviates from modern usage are the following: 'humours fits not' (I.i.246), 'My troublous dreams this night doth make me sad' (I.ii.22), 'What plain proceedings is more plain' (II.i.54), 'count them happy that enjoys the sun' (II.iv.40), 'these dread curses . . . recoil, And turns the force of them upon thyself' (III.ii.334), 'the traitors hateth thee' (IV.iv.43), 'Let them obey that knows not how to rule' (V.i.6), 'what intends these forces' (V.i.60), 'thou mistakes me much' (V.i.130).

II.i.4. *old Joan had not gone out.* Old Joan (a hawk) would not have flown against such a wind.

II.i.25. *Tantæne animis cælestibus iræ?* A quotation from the first book of the Æneid (line 11): 'Are such furies possible to heavenly minds?'

II.i.27. *With such holiness can you do it?* 'Holy as you seem to be, can you hide your malice?' Or perhaps, 'can you be so hot?'

II.i.55-56. The Folio gives these three speeches as one, spoken by Gloucester. Theobald made the change.

II.i.73. *Saint Alban's shrine.* The town and abbey of St. Albans, twenty-two miles north of London, are named after the first Christian martyr in Britain, Saint Alban, who was put to death there, A. D. 304. The sham miracle is narrated by Sir Thomas More on the authority of his father. It was copied from More into Grafton's Chronicle, but not into those of Halle and Holinshed.

II.i.102. *who said, 'Simon, come.'* Theobald has been generally followed in emending Simon to Simpcox, but the latter is merely a derivative of Simon, through Sim-cock (Simon boy). It is more in keeping with the saint's dignity to employ the Biblical name in its purity.

II.ii.39-42. *This Edmund, in the reign of Bolingbroke, As I have read, laid claim unto the crown; And but for Owen Glendower, had been king, Who kept him in captivity till he died.* Here, as in *1 Henry IV*, I.iii.147, 148, and in *1 Henry VI*, II.v., the name Edmund Mortimer causes confusion. The Edmund Mortimer (5th Earl of March), who figured in the reign of Bolingbroke as heir to the throne, was (as York says in lines 43, 44) York's mother's brother. He did not die either in captivity to Glendower, as here stated, or in the Tower of London, as *1 Henry VI* represents. The Edmund Mortimer captured by Glendower was uncle of the other Edmund, being younger brother to Roger, fourth Earl of March. The erroneous statement that Glendower 'kept him in captivity till he died,' which contradicts Shakespeare's treatment of the situation in *1 Henry IV*, seems due to a further confusion of Sir Edmund Mortimer with another prisoner of Glendower, Lord Grey of Ruthin, whom the chroniclers report to have been kept a captive till his death. The *Contention* version of this scene gives a quite different and even more garbled account of these facts.

II.iii.5. *Such as by God's book are adjudg'd to death.* Cf. Exodus 22.18: 'Thou shalt not suffer a witch to live'; and Leviticus 20.6: 'And the soul that turneth after such as have familiar spirits, and after wizards . . . I will even set my face against that soul, and will cut him off from among his people.'

II.iii.8, 9. *The witch in Smithfield shall be burnt to ashes, And you three shall be strangled on the gallows.* Holinshed's account is as follows: 'Margerie Iordeine was burnt in Smithfield, and Roger Bolinbrooke was drawne to Tiburne, and hanged and quartered; taking vpon his death that there was neuer anie such thing by them imagined. John Hun had his pardon, and Southwell died in the Tower the night before his execution.' These lines dealing with the punishment of the Duchess's accomplices are not found in the *Contention* version. Holinshed's statement that Hun, or Hume, 'had his pardon' may have prompted the suggestion in I.ii.88 ff. that he betrayed the Duchess's plot.

II.iii.14. *With Sir John Stanley, in the Isle of Man.* The dramatist appears here to be following Halle's (or Grafton's) Chronicle. Holinshed gives the name correctly as Sir Thomas Stanley. The error is found in the *Contention* version (e.g., in lines corresponding to II.iv.78, 80, 85), and is not an evidence that Shakespeare himself forsook his favorite Holinshed for Halle. (The present line is not in the *Contention*.)

II.iii.47. *Thus Eleanor's pride dies in her youngest days.* Some editors take 'her' as referring to 'pride,' but the Duchess's pride is nowhere represented as a newly acquired characteristic. Probably 'youngest' should be understood, like the Latin *novissimi*, as latest, most recent, in which case the meaning is that Eleanor's pride, so long maintained, dies at last.

II.iii.89. *I confess, I confess treason.* Holinshed makes it clear that the armorer 'was slaine without guilt,'—as a result of intoxication and not of his unrighteous cause. Peter, on the other hand, was a false servant who 'liued not long vnpunished; for being conuict of felonie in court of assise, he was iudged to be hanged, and so was, at Tiburne.' But it was the design of the author of the *Contention*, whom the reviser here follows closely, to emphasize from the start the treasonable purposes of York.

II.iv.71, 72. *I summon your Grace to his majesty's parliament, holden at Bury the first of this next month.* The three days' penance imposed on the Duchess were November 13, 15, 17, 1441. The Parliament at Bury St. Edmunds opened on February 10, 1447. Gloucester arrived on the 18th and died on the 23d.

III.i.1, 2. *I muse my Lord of Gloucester is not come: 'Tis not his wont to be the hindmost man.* The parliament had been in session for a week when Gloucester arrived. See previous note.

III.i.9-12. *We know the time since he was mild and affable, And if we did but glance a far-off look, Immediately he was upon his knee, That all the court admir'd him for submission.* This seems not to have been true of Gloucester, who was of an obstinate disposition. The lines are in the rhetorical style that the reviser of this play particularly affects. They are evolved from a slight hint in the *Contention*:

> 'The time hath bene, but now that time is past,
> That none so humble as Duke Humphrey was.'

III.i.58, 59. *Did he not, contrary to form of law, Devise strange deaths for small offences done?* 'He was accused, it is said, of malpractices during his Protectorate, especially of having caused men adjudged to die to be put to other execution than the law of the land allowed.' (Vickers, *Humphrey Duke of Gloucester*, p. 290.) The charge is found in the chroniclers, and has been suggested earlier in the play (I.iii.129 f.).

III.i.83-85. *Welcome, Lord Somerset. What news from France? Som. That all your interest in those territories Is utterly bereft you: all is lost.* This reports correctly Somerset's disastrous management of affairs in France from the time of his violation of the truce in March, 1449, till his return to England in October, 1450. The events alluded to are about three years later than Gloucester's death, and

about three years earlier than the death of Talbot (July, 1453), which is depicted in the *First Part*.

III.i.87, 88. *Cold news for me; for I had hope of France, As firmly as I hope for fertile England.* These lines are repeated from I.i.236, 237. Holinshed reports that Somerset's ignominious conduct in France 'kindled so great a rancor in the duke's [York's] heart and stomach, that he neuer left persecuting the duke of Summerset, vntill he had brought him to his fatall end and confusion.' In fact, York seems, however, not to have been the persecutor.

III.i.97. *I do arrest thee of high treason here.* The circumstances of Gloucester's arrival in Bury and his arrest are given by Vickers, *op. cit.*, p. 292 f.: 'It was eleven o'clock in the morning when Gloucester rode into the city by the south gate, and passing through the "horsemarket," turned to his left into the Northgate Ward. Here he passed through a mean street, and as he rode along, he asked a passerby, by what name the alley was known. "Forsoothe, my Lord, hit is called the Dede [dead] Lane," came the answer. Then the inborn superstition of "the Good Duke" asserted itself; so with an old prophecy he had read ringing in his ears, and a word of pious resignation on his lips, he rode on to the "North Spytyll" outside the Northgate, otherwise called "Seynt Salvatoures," where he was to lodge. Having eaten his dinner, a deputation came to wait upon him, consisting of the Duke of Buckingham, the Marquis of Dorset, the Earl of Salisbury, Lord Sudley, and Viscount Beaumont. The last in his capacity of High Constable placed the Duke under arrest by the King's command.'

III.i.158-160. *And dogged York, that reaches at the moon, Whose overweening arm I have pluck'd back, By false accuse doth level at my life.* 'On the other hand, the Duke of York had come to the front as the opponent of the Beauforts and as a follower of Duke Humphrey, though he never came anywhere near to supplanting the latter as leader of the opposition to the existing state of government.' (Vickers, *op. cit.*, p. 307) 'To the majority of the English people York passed not as a disturber of the peace, but as a wronged and injured man, goaded into resistance by the machinations of the Court party. In one aspect he was regarded as a great lord of the royal blood excluded from his rightful place at the Council board, and even kept out of the country, by his enemies who had the King's ear. In another he was regarded as the leader and mouthpiece of the Opposition of the day, of the old and popular war-party which inherited the traditions of Henry the Fifth and Humphrey of Gloucester.' (Oman, *Warwick*, p. 42.) Holinshed and other chroniclers had pointed out that the removal of Gloucester left King Henry exposed to attack by the House of York; but it was the author of the *Contention* (closely followed in the lines above) who dramatized the Duke of York as a treacherous self-seeker, held in check by the good Duke Humphrey. The conception, while unfair to York, gave force and unity to the play.

III.i.309. *And in the number thee, that wishest shame.* An allusion to the motto: '*Honi soit qui mal y pense.*'

III.i.319. *Then, noble York, take thou this task in hand.* These lines introduce York's Lieutenancy in Ireland (1448-1450), which in the first scene of the play is alluded to as already past. See note on I.i.193.

III.i.331, 332. *Now, York, or never, steel thy fearful thoughts, And change misdoubt to resolution.* In the original (*Contention*) version these lines have a very different spirit:

'*Now, York, bethink thyself and rouse thee vp,*
Take time whilst it is offered thee so fair.'

The speech as a whole, which has been expanded from twenty-four to fifty-three lines, is a very good example of the change Shakespeare's revision has wrought in York's character. The fearless, positive, and unscrupulous figure of the *Contention* is in the present play half concealed by an addition of sentimental, imaginative, and irresolute fancy.

III.i.357-360. *I have seduc'd a headstrong Kentishman, John Cade of Ashford, To make commotion, as full well he can, Under the title of John Mortimer.* 'A certeine yoong man, of a goodlie stature and right pregnant of wit, was intised to take vpon him the name of Iohn Mortimer, coosine to the duke of Yorke; (although his name was Iohn Cade, or, of some, Iohn Mend-all, an Irishman, as *Polychronicon* saith).' (Holinshed.) The chroniclers do not assert that York was privy to Cade's rebellion. Lines 360-370, reciting Cade's performances in Ireland under the eye of York, are all new with the reviser of the play. They were probably inspired by Holinshed's remark that some authorities called Cade an Irishman.

III.ii.S. d. In the Folio text Suffolk enters with the King, Queen, and the rest, having gone out previously with the Murderers. Thus a new scene should properly begin at this point; and this would be logical since Gloucester's death took place at a lodging at some distance from the king's court. Editors have, however, preferred to retain the Quarto (*Contention*) arrangement, by which the Murderers go out alone. 'Then enter the King and Queene' and all the rest except Suffolk, who is at once directly addressed by the King: 'My Lord of Suffolk, go call our uncle Gloster.'

III.ii.27. *Meg.* In the Folio the word is 'Nell.' So in lines 81, 102, and 122 'Elinor' (or 'Elianor') appears instead of the 'Margaret' which modern editors have substituted. None of the lines in question occur in the *Contention* version. They are to be ascribed to a slip of the reviser's pen, induced, of course, by his familiarity with 'Nell' and 'Eleanor' as applied to the Duchess of Gloucester in earlier scenes. The mistake is of a sort more easily committed by a reviser, applying patches throughout the play, than by an author who thought in terms of the scene as a whole.

III.ii.62, 63. *heart-offending groans Or blood-consuming sighs.* Shakespeare is fond of the old idea that every sigh costs the heart a drop of blood. The notion is here given in double form and then repeated in line 65: 'blood-drinking sighs.' In the *Third Part*, IV.iv.22, we have 'blood-sucking sighs.' Compare *A Midsummer-Night's Dream*, III.ii.98: 'with sighs of love, that costs the fresh blood dear.'

III.ii.78. *What! art thou, like the adder, waxen deaf?* A common allusion which goes back to Psalm 58. 4, 5: 'they are like the deaf adder that stoppeth her ear; Which will not hearken to the voice of charmers, charming never so wisely.' Cf. Shakespeare's 112th Sonnet, lines 10, 11: 'my adder's sense To critic and to flatterrer stopped are.'

III.ii.118-120. *as Ascanius did, When he to madding Dido would unfold His father's acts, commenc'd in burning Troy!* The allusion is new with the reviser, and like many of Shakespeare's classical references is not minutely accurate. It was Æneas himself who told Dido of his acts, and Ascanius, his son, was impersonated on that occasion by Cupid.

III.ii.136, 137. *Stay, Salisbury, With the rude multitude till I return.* Warwick speaks through the door to his father, who does not enter the stage.

III.ii.314. *Would curses kill, as doth the mandrake's groan.* The mandrake, or mandragora, was a poisonous plant with narcotic properties. Its forked root was supposed to resemble the human figure, and to utter a cry when pulled from the ground which would kill or drive mad those who heard it. For the latter penalty, cf. *Romeo and Juliet*, IV.iii.48 f.

'*And shrieks like mandrakes' torn out of the earth,*
That living mortals, hearing them, run mad.'

III.ii.348, 349. *That thou might'st think upon these by the seal, Through whom a thousand sighs are breath'd for thee.* As often in cases of difficult syntax, Samuel Johnson's paraphrase has been found the most accurate: 'That by the impression of my kiss forever remaining on thy hand thou mightest think on those lips through which a thousand sighs will be breathed for thee.' 'These' in line 348 is the antecedent of 'whom' and refers to Margaret's lips. The elaborate and 'precious' style which the reviser affects is well illustrated when lines 347-349 are contrasted with the plain language of the *Contention* version:

'*Oh let this kisse be printed in thy hand,*
That when thou seest it, thou maist thinke on me.'

III.ii.373. *Cardinal Beaufort is at point of death.* Beaufort's death occurred on April 11, 1447, six weeks after that of Gloucester, and three years before the banishment of Suffolk (March 17, 1450). The unfavorable character of Beaufort which the dramatists derived from the Tudor chroniclers is not historically justified. The aged cardinal's death seems in particular to have been peaceful and dignified. See L. B. Radford's judicial and sympathetic biography (*Henry Beaufort, Bishop, Chancellor, Cardinal*, 1908).

III.ii.397. *its lips.* One of the very rare instances of the possessive *its* in Shakespeare. The corresponding line of the *Contention* has 'his lips'; the Folio 'it's lips.'

IV.i.1-7. *The gaudy, blabbing, and remorseful day Is crept into the bosom of the sea, And now loud-howling wolves arouse the jades, etc.* 'These obviously additional lines, inartistically joined to the scene by the word "Therefore" [line 8] bear impress of Shakespeare's earliest Marlovian style, or rather Peeleian, but vastly more powerful and more musical.' (Hart.) The *Contention* version opens very simply with the equivalent of line 8: 'Bring forward these prisoners that scorn'd to yeeld.'

IV.i.9. *whilst our pinnace anchors in the Downs.* The Downs are a roadstead off the east coast of Kent, protected by Goodwin Sands (which are mentioned in *The Merchant of Venice*, III.i.3). This reference to the Downs is not in the *Contention* version. From *King Lear* it would seem that Shakespeare must have had some personal knowledge of the coast of Kent.

IV.i.11. *Or with their blood stain this discolour'd shore.* 'Discolour'd' is used 'proleptically': stain this shore, which will then be discolored by their blood.

IV.i.29. *Look on my George; I am a gentleman.* An image of Saint George in gold was worn by Knights of the Garter.

IV.i.35. *And told me that by Water I should die.* Compare I.iv.32. The "l" in Walter was silent, as in the abbreviated form 'Wat.'

IV.i.48-50. The Folio text of these lines is evidently corrupt, and has been corrected by comparison with the *Contention*. The Folio omits line 48 and gives line 50 as part of the Lieutenant's speech, making Suffolk's answer begin with line 51. (For 'lowly' the Folio reads 'lowsie.')

IV.i.50. *King Henry's blood.* Suffolk had only a vague claim to kinship with the king. Our chief interest in his family connection rests in the circumstance that his wife, Alice Chaucer, appears to have been a granddaughter of the poet.

IV.i.54. *my foot-cloth mule.* A mule caparisoned with an elaborate cloth of state, reaching to the ground. Mules were highly regarded as mounts.

IV.i.87. *ambitious Sylla.* Lucius Cornelius Sulla, or Sylla (ca. 138-78 B. C.), enemy of Marius and author of the first great proscription or legalized massacre in Roman history. He figures in Lodge's play, *The Wounds of Civil War* (printed, 1594).

IV.i.101. *Advance our half-fac'd sun, striving to shine.* 'Edward III bare for his device the rays of the sun dispersing themselves out of a cloud.' (Camden.) The defeat of Warwick at Barnet was due to confusion of the badge of his supporter Oxford with the 'sun with rays' borne by Edward IV. 'Oxford's men, whose banners and armour bore the Radiant Star of the De Veres, were mistaken by their comrades for a flanking column of Yorkists. In the mist their badge had been taken for the Sun with Rays, which was King Edward's cognisance.' (Oman, *Warwick*, p. 232.)

IV.i.111. *Bargulus, the strong Illyrian pirate.* In the *Contention* the passage reads: 'mightie Abradas, The great Masadonian Pyrate,' a borrowing apparently from Greene, who wrote in his *Penelope's Web:* 'Abradas the great Macedonian Pirat thought euery one had a letter of mart that bare sayles in the Ocean.' In his *Menaphon* Greene repeated the sentence verbatim. Nothing further has been discovered concerning Abradas. Bargulus is substituted in the Folio version of the play from Cicero's *De Officiis*, bk. ii, ch. 11: 'Bargulus [properly Bardylis] Illyricus latro . . . magnas opes habuit.' Nicholas Grimald's translation of the *De Officiis* (1556) renders the phrase, 'Bargulus, that Illyrian robber.'

IV.i.120. *Pene gelidus timor occupat artus.* 'Cold fear almost seizes my joints.' The Folio gives the first word as 'Pine,' which most editors omit as meaningless. Theobald interpreted it as 'pœnæ,' (fear) of punishment, and Malone as 'pene,' almost.

IV.i.127-130. *let my head . . . sooner dance upon a bloody pole.* 'There is, indeed, one detail in the drama of the period which may be regarded as symbolical of the whole dramatic tendency of the time, namely, the swinging about of a human head, cut from its body, on the stage. This cut-off head was a stage-property that had survived from the time of the mystery-plays, when it was meant to represent the head of the unfortunate John the Baptist at the gruesome crowning point of the dance of Salome. It survived in several specimens, a favourite stage-property, in the popular theatre, certain, as we may presume, at every appearance of drawing the ironical applause of experienced theatre-goers, and probably known to the actors, whose sense of the comic was at all times keen, by some droll nickname now forgotten. In the three parts of the old drama of *Henry VI* this head appears at different times. Queen Margaret (*2 Henry VI*, IV.iv.) presses it to her bosom as the head of her dead lover, Suffolk. A few scenes later it appears in duplicate and with a different signification, again further on (V.i.) as the head of the rebel Cade.' (Schücking, *Character Problems in Shakespeare's Plays*, 1922, p. 19 f.)

IV.i.140. *savage islanders.* Pompey was slain in Egypt, 48 B. C., not by savage islanders, but by Egyptians and renegade soldiers of his own. The error is not found in the *Contention*. It is a coincidence that in Chapman's *Tragedy of Cæsar and Pompey* (printed 1631) Pompey is murdered on the island of Lesbos.

IV.ii.68. *The first thing we do, let's kill all the lawyers.* The proposal to kill lawyers seems to have been a feature, not of Cade's rebellion, but of the earlier one led by Wat Tyler in 1381.

IV.ii.87. *They use to write it on the top of letters.* Emmanuel ('God with us') was placed as a pious sentiment at the head of letters and other documents.

IV.iii.5-7. *the Lent shall be as long again as it is; and thou shalt have a licence to kill for a hundred lacking one.* The eating of flesh during Lent was forbidden in Elizabeth's reign, and killing of beasts at that time was permitted only by special license to provide for invalids (supposedly) unable to dispense with flesh. A license to kill for ninety-nine a week during a doubled Lent would thus constitute a valuable monopoly. 'For' in line 6 may mean 'at the rate of,' allowing Dick to slaughter ninety-nine beasts a week.

IV.vii.17, 18. *the Lord Say, which sold the towns in France.* Lord Say had been associated with Suffolk in the cession of Anjou and Maine.

IV.vii.18. *he that made us pay one-and-twenty fifteens.* Twenty-one fifteens is a humorous exaggeration. A frequent mode of raising revenue to cover unusual expenditures of the government was to impose a tax of one-fifteenth (sometimes one-tenth) on personal property. Compare note on I.i.132. One of Cade's actual demands was 'that neither fifteens should hereafter be demanded, nor once anie impositions or taxes be spoken of.'

IV.vii.34. *the score and the tally.* Tallies were the two halves of a stick, split and divided between creditor and debtor. Scores were the notches on the tallies which served to certify the transactions.

IV.vii.35. *thou hast caused printing to be used.* An anachronism, since the first book printed in England was not produced till 1477. (Cade's rebellion was in 1450, the outbreak following Suffolk's death by two months.)

IV.vii.42, 43. *when honester men than thou go in their hose and doublets.* Hose and doublet were the indispensable articles of dress, covering the lower and upper parts of the body respectively. The cloak was worn over hose and doublet by the well-to-do. For the horse's 'cloak' or foot-cloth cf. note on IV.i.54.

IV.vii.51, 52. *Kent, in the Commentaries Cæsar writ, Is term'd the civil'st place of all this isle.* The wording, which is almost the same in the *Contention*, is probably borrowed from Golding's translation of Cæsar's Commentaries (1565): 'Of all the inhabitants of this isle the civilest are the Kentishfolke.' Marlowe, a Kentishman, may have introduced the quotation. The less complimentary appraisal in line 48, ' 'tis *bona terra, mala gens*' (good land, bad people), is supplied by the reviser, who adds the words, *mala gens*.

IV.viii.1. *Up Fish Street! down St. Magnus' corner!* Places on the northern, or London, side of London Bridge. St. Magnus' Church was at the foot of the bridge, and Fish Street ran up from the bridge towards Eastcheap (where Shakespeare's Boar's Head Tavern was situated). This scene evidently takes place on the Southwark side of the river.

IV.viii.23. *at the White Hart in Southwark.* Next to the Tabard Inn, which stood near, the White Hart was the best inn in Southwark. Holinshed records that Cade lodged at the White Hart.

IV.viii.38-40. *Were 't not a shame that, whilst you live at jar, The fearful French, whom you late vanquished, Should make a start o'er seas and vanquish you?* Probably an anachronistic allusion to French raids upon the English coast in 1457 (seven years after Cade's rebellion), when Sandwich was captured and sacked and Fowey in Cornwall burned.

IV.x.25, 26. *I'll make thee eat iron like an ostrich.* That ostriches could eat nails and other iron was one of the 'vulgar errors' common in Shakespeare's time.

IV.x.51. *As for words, whose greatness answers words.* So much for words, whose pomposity corresponds to the pompousness of yours. The line is unsatisfactory and probably corrupt.

V.i.5. *Ah sancta majestas, who would not buy thee dear?* A six-foot line, frequently employed by Marlowe for emphasis. It is found in the *Contention* version.

V.i.15. *Humphrey of Buckingham.* Buckingham was brother-in-law of Salisbury and uncle of Warwick. Though a supporter of King Henry, he was friendly with the Yorkists, and was employed on the morning of the first battle of St. Albans (May 22, 1455) as an intermediary between the two forces. York's armed return from Ireland and protest against Somerset occurred in 1452. The incidents of over three years of difficult negotiation are condensed in the present scene.

V.i.26, 27. *And now, like Ajax Telamonius, On sheep or oxen could I spend my fury.* An allusion (not in the *Contention*) to the madness of Ajax, when he slew a flock of sheep in his rage that the arms of Achilles had been adjudged to Ulysses rather than himself. Shakespeare refers to the myth again in *Love's Labour's Lost*, IV.iii.5, 6: 'By the Lord, this love is as mad as Ajax: it kills sheep.'

V.i.46. *Saint George's Field.* A large open drill ground between Southwark and Lambeth, south of the Thames.

V.i.100, 101. *Whose smile and frown, like to Achilles' spear, Is able with the change to kill and cure.* Telephus, who had been wounded by Achilles' spear, could not be cured till the rust of the same weapon was applied to his wound. This classical figure also is missing in the *Contention* version.

V.i.117. *O blood-bespotted Neapolitan.* Alluding to Margaret's father's title of King of the two Sicilies (Sicily and Naples). There may be an implied reference to the famous Sicilian Vespers massacre of 1282.

V.i.140. *And if words will not, then our weapons shall.* The speaker, Richard, was two and a half years old when the first battle of St. Albans was fought.

V.i.144. *Call hither to the stake my two brave bears.* A metaphor from the popular sport of bear-baiting, at which bears were fastened to stakes and attacked by dogs. Warwick and Salisbury are termed bears because of the badge of the 'bear and ragged staff.' Cf. next note.

V.i.202, 203. *Now, by my father's badge, old Nevil's crest, The rampant bear chain'd to the ragged staff.* The heraldry here is erroneous. Warwick's famous badge of the bear and ragged staff was not derived from his father, but inherited, like his earldom, from the Beauchamp family to which his wife belonged. The Nevil crest was a bull.

V.ii.59, 60. *Into as many gobbets will I cut it As wild Medea young Absyrtus did.* Not found in the *Contention*. The story is told in Ovid's *Tristia*. Medea, pursued by her father as she accompanied Jason from Colchos with the golden

fleece, delayed the pursuers by slaying her brother Absyrtus and throwing his dismembered limbs into the sea.

V.ii.79, 80. *If you be ta'en, we then should see the bottom Of all our fortunes.* The king was wounded with an arrow in the battle and fell into the hands of the Yorkists, from whom he suffered no further injury.

V.iii.27. *Let us pursue him ere the writs go forth.* Lords were summoned to parliament by special writ issued in the name of the king. The parliament referred to was not summoned till several years after the battle.

THE TEXT OF THE PRESENT EDITION

The text of the present volume is, by permission of the Oxford University Press, that of the Oxford Shakespeare, edited by the late W. J. Craig. Craig's text has been carefully collated with the Shakespeare Folio of 1623, and the following deviations have been introduced:

1. The stage directions of the Folio have been restored. Necessary words and directions, omitted by the Folio, are added within square brackets.

2. Punctuation and spelling have been normalized to accord with modern English practice; e.g., yclad, warlike, housekeeping, Saint Albans, villainies (instead of y-clad, war-like, house-keeping, Saint Alban's, villanies). The words murder, murther, murderer, murtherer, burden, burthen, etc., have not been normalized, the actual form employed by the Folio being in each case retained.

3. The following changes of text have been introduced, usually in accordance with Folio authority. The readings of the present edition precede the colon, while Craig's readings follow it.

I.i.136   ye F: you
191   Hath F: Have
iii.40   fashion in (Fashions in F): fashion of
48   a-tilt F: a tilt
147   needs F: can need
182   an F: a
iv.6   of an F: of
31   fates await F: fate awaits
47   threatest where's F: threat'st where is
73   goes F: go

II.i.15   he would F: he'd
47   and if F: an if
55   ye F: you
102   Simon (Symon F): Simpcox
122   Saint Albans (Saint Albones F): Saint Alban
182   under ground F: under-ground
iii.31   realm F: helm
iv.39   Trowest F: Trow'st
40   enjoys F: enjoy
III.i.10   And F: An
98   Suffolk F: Suffolk's duke
117   dis-pursed F: disbursed
329   Bristow F: Bristol
343   an host F: a host
ii.149   earthy F: earthly
290   far-unworthy F: far unworthy
322   Mine hair be fix'd an end F: My hair be fix'd on end
331   consort F: concert
396   cradle-babe F: cradle babe
407   corrosive F: corsive
IV.i.22   Be F: Cannot be
48   sometime: sometimes
80   shalt: shall F
120   Pene (Pine F) gelidus . . . it is F: Gelidus . . . 'tis
ii.90   a honest F: an honest
150   an eunuch F: a eunuch
vi.8   ye F: you
vii.39   in F: on
viii.53   an hundred F: a hundred
x.1   ambitions F: ambition
50   for words F: for more words
58   I'ld (I'de F): I'll
V.i.21   Should F: Shouldst
113   of F: for
149, 210   bearard (Berard, Bearard F): bear-ward
ii.3   alarum F: alarm

The Third Part of King Henry the Sixth

Edited by

TUCKER BROOKE

Dramatis Personae

KING HENRY THE SIXTH
EDWARD, PRINCE OF WALES, *his Son*
LOUIS THE ELEVENTH, *King of France*
DUKE OF SOMERSET ⎫
DUKE OF EXETER ⎪
EARL OF NORTHUMBERLAND ⎪
EARL OF OXFORD ⎬ *Lancastrians*
EARL OF WESTMORELAND ⎪
HENRY, EARL OF RICHMOND, *a Boy* ⎪
LORD CLIFFORD ⎭
RICHARD PLANTAGENET, *Duke of York*
EDWARD, EARL OF MARCH,
   later King Edward IV ⎫
EDMUND, EARL OF RUTLAND ⎬ *his Sons*
GEORGE, LATER DUKE OF CLARENCE ⎪
RICHARD, LATER DUKE OF GLOUCESTER ⎭
DUKE OF NORFOLK ⎫
MARQUESS OF MONTAGUE ⎪
EARL OF WARWICK ⎪
EARL OF PEMBROKE ⎬ *Yorkists*
LORD HASTINGS ⎪
LORD STAFFORD ⎭
SIR JOHN MORTIMER ⎫
SIR HUGH MORTIMER ⎬ *Uncles to the Duke of York*

LORD RIVERS, *Brother to Lady Grey*
SIR JOHN MONTGOMERY ⎫
SIR WILLIAM STANLEY ⎬ *Followers of King Edward IV*
SIR JOHN SOMERVILLE, *a Follower of Warwick*
A NOBLEMAN, *bearing a message*
ROBERT ASPALL, *Tutor to Rutland*
LIEUTENANT OF THE TOWER
MAYOR OF YORK
TWO GAMEKEEPERS
A HUNTSMAN
A SON THAT HAS KILLED HIS FATHER
A FATHER THAT HAS KILLED HIS SON

MARGARET OF ANJOU, *Queen to King Henry*
LADY GREY, *later Queen to King Edward*
LADY BONA, *Sister to the French Queen*
A NURSE, *with the infant son of King Edward*

SOLDIERS, ATTENDANTS, MESSENGERS, WATCHMEN, ETC.

SCENE—*London and Westminster, Paris, York, Coventry,
and Chipping Norton; Sandal Castle in Yorkshire;
Battlefields of Wakefield, Towton, Barnet, and
Tewkesbury; Open Country in England.*

The Third Part of King Henry the Sixth

INTRODUCTION

SOURCES OF THE PLAY

The Third Part of *Henry VI*, like the Second Part, is based upon an earlier play, which the reviser expands largely and in an independent spirit, but without the introduction of new plot material, and apparently without further study of the historical sources (chiefly Halle or Holinshed). The sole direct source, then, of *3 Henry VI* appears to have been this basic play, *The True Tragedy of Richard Duke of York,* of which printed editions survive from the years 1595, 1600, and 1619. There is reason for inferring that the manuscript version which Shakespeare employed when he produced *3 Henry VI* gave a somewhat fuller, and perhaps otherwise more faithful, version of the original play than that found in any of the three printed editions.

The revision by which *The True Tragedy* was transformed into *3 Henry VI* was very thorough, but decidedly less thorough than that which *The First Part of the Contention* underwent in passing into *2 Henry VI*. Whereas the latter play contains about 2150 lines of new or recast matter, *3 Henry VI* contains only about 1550; and the reviser's work in *3 Henry VI* consists much more in brief casual additions or in alterations which affect the metre rather than the meaning, rather than in such long rhetorical insertions as particularly characterize *2 Henry VI*. It would appear that when Shakespeare came to rewrite the later of the two plays, he had somewhat abated the revisionary ardor that led to the elaborate poetic improvisations (often of dubious dramatic worth) with which he so generously interspersed the text of *2 Henry VI*.

The best example of the lingering in *3 Henry VI* of the zest for rhetorical embellishment is found in the first thirty-eight lines of V. iv (Margaret's speech), which correspond to the following eleven lines in *The True Tragedy*:

'Welcome to England, my louing friends of Frāce.
And welcome Summerset, and Oxford too.
Once more haue we spread our sailes abroad,
And though our tackling be almost consumde,
And Warwike as our maine mast ouerthrowne,
Yet warlike Lords raise you that sturdie post,
That beares the sailes to bring vs vnto rest,
And Ned and I as willing Pilots should
For once with carefull mindes guide on the sterne,
To beare vs through that dangerous gulfe
That heretofore hath swallowed vp our friends.'

Usually the reviser has shown more moderation. Gloucester's famous soliloquy at the close of III. ii (lines 143–213) has indeed been more than doubled, but it does not dilute or misinterpret the sentiment of the following *True Tragedy* lines out of which it has grown:

'Manet Gloster and speakes.

Glo. I, Edward will vse women honourablie,
Would he were wasted marrow, bones and all,
That from his loines no issue might succeed
To hinder me from the golden time I looke for,
For I am not yet lookt on in the world.
First is there Edward, Clarence, and Henry
And his sonne, and all they (sic) lookt for issue
Of their loines ere I can plant my selfe,
A cold premeditation for my purpose,
What other pleasure is there in the world beside?
I will go clad my bodie in gaie ornaments,
And lull my selfe within a ladies lap,
And witch sweet Ladies with my words and lookes.
Oh monstrous man, to harbour such a thought!
Why loue did scorne me in my mothers wombe.
And for I should not deale in hir affaires,
Shee did corrupt fraile nature in the flesh,
And plaste an enuious mountaine on my backe,
Where sits deformity to mocke my bodie,
To drie mine arme vp like a withered shrimpe.
To make my legges of an vnequall size,
And am I then a man to be belou'd?
Easier for me to compasse twentie crownes.
Tut I can smile, and murder when I smile,
I crie content, to that that greeues me most.
I can adde colours to the Camelion,
And for a need change shapes with Protheus,
And set the aspiring Catilin to schoole.
Can I doe this, and cannot get the crowne?
Tush were it ten times higher, Ile put it downe.'

The finest individual scene in either version of the play, that of the Duke of York's death (I, iv), has been treated by the reviser with marked respect. Here 165 lines in the *True Tragedy* version are altered into 180 lines of *3 Henry VI* with only a conservative minimum of amplification or incidental correction.

THE HISTORY OF THE PLAY

The earliest allusion to any part of *3 Henry VI* is found in Robert Greene's *Groatsworth of Wit* (1592), where one line[1] is parodied in a connection which shows that Shakespeare had already been employed in revising the drama. The Shakespearean text was not printed till the appearance of the Shakespeare Folio

---

1 I. iv. 137. Cf. note on this line, p. 119.

in 1623, but the earlier play, out of which *3 Henry VI* was produced, was published in 1595 with the title: "The true Tragedie of Richard Duke of Yorke, and the death of good King Henrie the Sixt, with the whole contention betweene the two Houses Lancaster and Yorke, as it was sundrie times acted by the Right Honourable the Earle of Pembrooke his seruants.' This was reprinted in 1600 and again, with some minor corrections, in 1619. On the last occasion the *True Tragedy* was published in combination with the early version of *2 Henry VI* (*The First Part of the Contention*) under the blanket title of "The Whole Contention betweene the two Famous Houses, Lancaster and Yorke. With the Tragicall ends of the good Duke Humfrey, Richard Duke of Yorke, and King Henrie the sixt.'

There is little evidence concerning the history of the play in the time of Shakespare and his contemporaries. The title-page of the first edition of the *True Tragedy*, quoted above, shows that it was acted by the Earl of Pembroke's Company of actors, who disbanded in 1593. The Epilogue to Shakespeare's *Henry V* (1599) implies that the Henry VI plays in general had often been shown in Shakespeare's theatre and had been well received. Ben Jonson's Prologue to the revised version of *Every Man in his Humour* (1616) refers to the plays dealing with 'York and Lancaster's long jars' as one of the popular but faulty types of drama of the day.

After the Restoration John Crowne rewrote *3 Henry VI* under the title of *The Miseries of Civil-War*. Crowne's version was published in 1680, 'As it is Acted at the Duke's Theatre By His Royal Highnesses Servants.' The opening scenes, dealing with Cade's rebellion and the first battle of St. Albans, are drawn from *2 Henry VI*.[2] Crowne romanticizes the story in the spirit of his age, making Warwick the unsuccessful lover of Lady Grey and adding further amatory interest by an episodic love affair between King Edward and Lady Eleanor Butler, who in the last act dons male disguisings and meets her death at Edward's hands on the battle field. Only 75 lines out of 2793 in this long piece are drawn directly from Shakespeare.[3]

That critical interest in Shakespeare's plays of Henry VI was not altogether lacking in Crowne's day appears from a note on the three plays in Gerard Langbaine's account of Shakespeare (*Account of the English Dramatic Poets*, 1691): 'These three Plays contain the whole length of this King's Reign, *viz.* Thirty eight Years, six Weeks, and four Days. Altho' this be contrary to the strict Rules of *Dramatick Poetry;* yet it must be owned, even by Mr. *Dryden* himself, That this Picture in *Miniature,* has many Features, which excell even several of his more exact Strokes of Symmetry and Proportion.' It is probable that the Henry VI plays of Shakespeare were read more generally at this time, and with less sense of their inferiority, than in later periods.

In the next generation Theophilus Cibber produced a strange medley of Crowne's *Miseries of Civil-War* and Shakespeare's *Henry VI* under the title: 'An Historical Tragedy of the Civil Wars in the Reign of King Henry VI (Being a Sequel to the Tragedy of Humfrey Duke of Gloucester.[4] And an Introduction to the Tragical History of King Richard III). Alter'd from Shakespeare, in the Year 1720'.[5] In this work the luxuriances of Crowne

are pruned away and a large amount of the Shakespearean text replaced.[6]

In 1795 Richard Valpy, a well-known schoolmaster of Reading on the Thames, brought out a work entitled: 'The Roses; or King Henry the Sixth; An Historical Tragedy Represented at Reading School, Oct. 15th, 16th, and 17th, 1795. Compiled principally from Shakespeare.' This play opens with the announcement of York's death to his sons, Edward and Richard (*3 Henry VI* II. i). It is essentially an acting version, for young performers, of the last four acts of *3 Henry VI*, with occasional borrowings from the two earlier Parts and even, in one instance, from *Richard II*. The printed text was popular enough to reach a second edition in 1810.

A composite drama, called *Richard Duke of York,* was made by J. H. Merivale out of the three parts of *Henry VI,* and acted at Drury Lane Theatre, December 22, 1817, the chief part, that of York, being taken by Edmund Kean. The greater portion of Merivale's abridgment is drawn from *2 Henry VI,* but his fifth act corresponds with the first act of Shakespeare's Third Part.

The actor, Charles Kemble (1775-1854), condensed the three parts of *Henry VI* into a single play, but does not appear to have produced his version on the stage.[7] In 1863 Shepherd and Anderson successfully acted at the Surrey Theatre an adaptation of Shakespeare's *Henry VI,* entitled *The Wars of the Roses,* the manuscript version of which was destroyed by fire in the following year. In 1864 *3 Henry VI* (altered and translated into German) was performed at Weimar as part of a series of Shakespearean history plays produced by Dingelstedt in honor of the poet's tercentenary.[8] A subsequent English revival was that of the F. R. Benson Company at the Shakespeare Memorial Festival, Stratford-on-Avon, May 4, 1906. Mr. Benson himself took the part of Richard of Gloucester.[9]

The Authorship of the Play

The authorship problems in the case of *3 Henry VI*—that is, the questions, who wrote the *True Tragedy* version, and who the altered and additional matter found in the Folio text of *3 Henry VI?,*—are so intimately associated with the similar problems presented by *2 Henry VI* and its source, that the two Parts cannot well be discussed separately. Reference must therefore be made to the edition of *2 Henry VI* in this series, where an attempt is made to state general conclusions regarding the authorship of both Parts.

In summary it may be said that *The True Tragedy* seems to be fundamentally a work of Marlowe, though certainly preserved in a corrupted form, while the revision represented by the 1623 text of *3 Henry VI* is mainly, if not wholly, the work of Shakespeare in the early years of his dramatic novitiate.

The True Tragedy, in comparison with *The First Part of the Contention,* shows less variety of tone and less inequality of style: it is a better unified and more moving drama and contains fewer

2 For further details of this play and of Crowne's other piece, *Henry the Sixth, or the Murder of the Duke of Glocester,* see *2 Henry VI* in this edition.

3 The figures are those given by G. Krecke in his useful dissertation: *Die englischen Bühnenbearbeitungen von Shakespeares 'King Henry the Sixth,'* Rostock, 1911.

4 I.e. Ambrose Philips' tragedy, based on *2 Henry VI,* acted February 15, 1723.

5 The 'Second Edition' is dated 1724; the first appeared apparently in 1723, and the play was performed at Drury Lane on July 5, 1723.

6 According to Krecke (*op cit.*) Cibber's version consists of 985 lines from Shakespeare, 507 from Crowne, and 746 of Cibber's own.

7 The text of this abridgment was first printed, from Kemble's manuscript, in volume ii of the *Henry Irving Shakespeare.*

8 For an account see L. Eckardt: *Shakespeare's englische Historien auf der Weimarer Bühne,* Shakespeare Jahrbuch i. 362–391.

9 The entire group of history plays from *Richard II* to *Richard III* was produced in sequence on this occasion. See the London *Athenæum,* May 12, 1906.

scenes which suggest a doubt concerning the possibility of Marlowe's authorship. Shakespeare's revision of this work in *3 Henry VI* is, as has been already said,[10] less elaborate and more understanding than his revision of the *Contention*. He retains better the spirit of the original and in his alterations, extensive though they indeed are, shows himself more the practical dramatist and less the practicing versifier. An advance in purposeful and economical method appears, for example, in the reviser's rearrangement of the sequence of scenes iv–vii of Act IV,[11] and in his occasional transposition of lines in the original play to other positions where they are more effective. Line 53 of II. i, 'But Hercules himself must yield to odds,' and the opening lines of V. iii,

> '*Thus far our fortune keeps an upward course,*
> *And we are grac'd with wreaths of victory.*'

are found in *The True Tragedy,* but at quite different points from those at which Shakespeare has chosen to employ them. Various details of the relation of the revised to the unrevised play are discussed in the notes; e.g., those on I. i. 14; I, ii. 28–31; II. i. 68 f., 114; II. ii. 89–92; II. iii. 15; II. v. 54; II. vi. 8, 42–44; III. iii. 16–18; IV. ii. 20 f.; IV. iii. S.d.; IV. vii. 50; V. i. S.d.; V. iv. 1–38.

---

10 Cf. Sources of the Play.
11 Cf. notes on IV. iv and IV. vii, p. 555.

ACT FIRST ❧ SCENE FIRST

[London. The Parliament-House]
Alarum. Enter Plantagenet, Edward, Richard, Norfolk, Montague,
Warwick, and Soldiers.

War. I wonder how the king escap'd our hands.
York. While we pursu'd the horsemen of the north,
He slily stole away and left his men:
Whereat the great Lord of Northumberland,
Whose warlike ears could never brook retreat,   5
Cheer'd up the drooping army; and himself,
Lord Clifford, and Lord Stafford, all abreast,
Charg'd our main battle's front, and breaking in
Were by the swords of common soldiers slain.
　Edw. Lord Stafford's father, Duke of Buckingham,   10
Is either slain or wounded dangerous;
I cleft his beaver with a downright blow:
That this is true, father, behold his blood.
　　　　　　　[Showing his bloody sword.]
　Mont. And, brother, here's the Earl of Wilshire's blood,
Whom I encounter'd as the battles join'd.   15
　Rich. Speak thou for me, and tell them what I did.
　　　　[Throwing down the Duke of Somerset's head.]
　York. Richard hath best deserv'd of all my sons.
But is your Grace dead, my Lord of Somerset?
　Norf. Such hope have all the line of John of Gaunt!
　Rich. Thus do I hope to shake King Henry's head.   20
　War. And so do I. Victorious Prince of York,
Before I see thee seated in that throne
Which now the house of Lancaster usurps,
I vow by heaven these eyes shall never close.
This is the palace of the fearful king,   25
And this the regal seat: possess it, York;
For this is thine, and not King Henry's heirs'.
　York. Assist me, then, sweet Warwick, and I will;
For hither we have broken in by force.
　Norf. We'll all assist you; he that flies shall die.   30
　York. Thanks, gentle Norfolk. Stay by me, my lords;
And, soldiers, stay and lodge by me this night.
　　　　　　　　　　　　　　They go up.
　War. And when the king comes, offer him no violence,
Unless he seek to thrust you out perforce. *[The Soldiers retire.]*
　York. The queen this day here holds her parliament,   35
But little thinks we shall be of her council:
By words or blows here let us win our right.
　Rich. Arm'd as we are, let's stay within this house.
　War. The bloody parliament shall this be call'd,
Unless Plantagenet, Duke of York, be king,   40
And bashful Henry depos'd, whose cowardice
Hath made us by-words to our enemies.
　York. Then leave me not, my lords; be resolute;
I mean to take possession of my right.
　War. Neither the king, nor he that loves him best,   45
The proudest he that holds up Lancaster,
Dares stir a wing if Warwick shake his bells.

I'll plant Plantagenet, root him up who dares.
Resolve thee, Richard; claim the English crown.
　　　[Warwick leads York to the throne, who seats himself.]

Flourish. Enter King Henry, Clifford, Northumberland,
Westmoreland, Exeter, and the rest.

　Henry. My lords, look where the sturdy rebel sits,   50
Even in the chair of state! belike he means—
Back'd by the power of Warwick, that false peer—
To aspire unto the crown and reign as king.
Earl of Northumberland, he slew thy father,
And thine, Lord Clifford; and you both have vow'd revenge   55
On him, his sons, his favourites, and his friends.
　North. If I be not, heavens be reveng'd on me!
　Clif. The hope thereof makes Clifford mourn in steel.
　West. What! shall we suffer this? let's pluck him down:
My heart for anger burns; I cannot brook it.   60
　Henry. Be patient, gentle Earl of Westmoreland.
　Clif. Patience is for poltroons, such as he:
He durst not sit there had your father liv'd.
My gracious lord, here in the parliament
Let us assail the family of York.   65
　North. Well hast thou spoken, cousin: be it so.
　Henry. Ah! know you not the city favours them,
And they have troops of soldiers at their beck?
　Exe. But when the duke is slain, they'll quickly fly.
　Henry. Far be the thought of this from Henry's heart,   70
To make a shambles of the parliament-house!
Cousin of Exeter, frowns, words, and threats
Shall be the war that Henry means to use.
Thou factious Duke of York, descend my throne,
And kneel for grace and mercy at my feet;   75
I am thy sovereign
　York.　　　　　I am thine.
　Exe. For shame! come down: he made thee Duke of York.
　York. It was my inheritance, as the earldom was.
　Exe. Thy father was a traitor to the crown.   80
　War. Exeter, thou art a traitor to the crown
In following this usurping Henry.
　Clif. Whom should he follow but his natural king?
　War. True, Clifford; that is Richard, Duke of York.
　Henry. And shall I stand, and thou sit in my throne?   85
　York. It must and shall be so: content thyself.
　War. Be Duke of Lancaster: let him be king.
　West. He is both king and Duke of Lancaster;
And that the Lord of Westmoreland shall maintain.
　War. And Warwick shall disprove it. You forget   90
That we are those which chas'd you from the field
And slew your fathers, and with colours spread
March'd through the city to the palace gates.
　North. Yes, Warwick, I remember it to my grief;
And, by his soul, thou and thy house shall rue it.   95
　West. Plantagenet, of thee, and these thy sons,
Thy kinsmen and thy friends, I'll have more lives
Than drops of blood were in my father's veins.
　Clif. Urge it no more; lest that instead of words
I send thee, Warwick, such a messenger   100
As shall revenge his death before I stir.

S. d. Plantagenet; *cf. n.*　**1** *Cf. n.*　**5** retreat: *trumpet call commanding retirement*　**7**
Lord Clifford: *cf. n.*　**12** beaver: *face-guard of helmet*　**14** brother: *cf. n.*　**17**
Cf. n.　**19** *May all the descendants of John of Gaunt expect the same*　**S. d.** *They go*
up; cf. n.　**35** *Cf. n.*　**46** he: *man*　holds up: *supports the cause of*　**47** shake his
bells: *cf. n.*

49 Resolve thee: *be resolute*　**57** be not: *be not revenged*　**67** the city favours them:
cf. n.　**79** earldom: *of March*　**80** *Cf. n.*　**89** Lord of Westmoreland: *cf. n.*

War. Poor Clifford! how I scorn his worthless threats.

York. Will you we show our title to the crown?

If not, our swords shall plead it in the field.

Henry. What title hast thou, traitor, to the crown?   *105*

Thy father was, as thou art, Duke of York;

Thy grandfather, Roger Mortimer, Earl of March;

I am the son of Henry the Fifth,

Who made the Dauphin and the French to stoop,

And seiz'd upon their towns and provinces.   *110*

War. Talk not of France, sith thou hast lost it all.

Henry. The Lord Protector lost it, and not I:

When I was crown'd I was but nine months old.

Rich. You are old enough now, and yet, methinks, you lose.

Father, tear the crown from the usurper's head.   *115*

Edw. Sweet father, do so; set it on your head.

Mont. [*To York.*] Good brother, as thou lov'st and honour'st arms,

Let's fight it out and not stand cavilling thus.

Rich. Sound drums and trumpets, and the king will fly.   *120*

York. Sons, peace!

Henry. Peace thou! and give King Henry leave to speak.

War. Plantagenet shall speak first: hear him, lords;

And be you silent and attentive too,

For he that interrupts him shall not live.   *125*

Henry. Think'st thou that I will leave my kingly throne,

Wherein my grandsire and my father sat?

No: first shall war unpeople this my realm;

Ay, and their colours, often borne in France,

And now in England to our heart's great sorrow,   *130*

Shall be my winding-sheet. Why faint you, lords?

My title's good, and better far than his.

War. Prove it, Henry, and thou shalt be king.

Henry. Henry the Fourth by conquest got the crown.

York. 'Twas by rebellion against his king.   *135*

Henry. [*Aside.*] I know not what to say: my title's weak.

[*Aloud.*] Tell me, may not a king adopt an heir?

York. What then?

Henry. An if he may, then am I lawful king;

For Richard, in the view of many lords,   *140*

Resign'd the crown to Henry the Fourth,

Whose heir my father was, and I am his.

York. He rose against him, being his sovereign,

And made him to resign his crown perforce.

War. Suppose, my lords, he did it unconstrain'd,   *145*

Think you 'twere prejudicial to his crown?

Exe. No; for he could not so resign his crown

But that the next heir should succeed and reign.

Henry. Art thou against us, Duke of Exeter?

Exe. His is the right, and therefore pardon me.   *150*

York. Why whisper you, my lords, and answer not?

Exe. My conscience tells me he is lawful king.

Henry [*Aside.*] All will revolt from me, and turn to him.

North. Plantagenet, for all the claim thou lay'st,

Think not that Henry shall be so depos'd.   *155*

War. Depos'd he shall be in despite of all.

North. Thou art deceiv'd: 'tis not thy southern power,

Of Essex, Norfolk, Suffolk, nor of Kent,

Which makes thee thus presumptuous and proud,

Can set the duke up in despite of me.   *160*

Clif. King Henry, be thy title right or wrong,

Lord Clifford vows to fight in thy defence:

May that ground gape and swallow me alive,

Where I shall kneel to him that slew my father!

Henry. O Clifford, how thy words revive my heart!   *165*

York. Henry of Lancaster, resign thy crown.

What mutter you, or what conspire you, lords?

War. Do right unto this princely Duke of York,

Or I will fill the house with armed men,

And o'er the chair of state, where now he sits,   *170*

Write up his title with usurping blood.

      He stamps with his foot, and the Soldiers show themselves.

Henry. My Lord of Warwick, hear me but one word:—

Let me for this my life-time reign as king.

York. Confirm the crown to me and to mine heirs,

And thou shalt reign in quiet while thou liv'st.   *175*

Henry. I am content: Richard Plantagenet,

Enjoy the kingdom after my decease.

Clif. What wrong is this unto the prince your son!

War. What good is this to England and himself!

West. Base, fearful, and despairing Henry!   *180*

Clif. How hast thou injur'd both thyself and us!

West. I cannot stay to hear these articles.

North. Nor I.

Clif. Come, cousin, let us tell the queen these news.

West. Farewell, faint-hearted and degenerate king,   *185*

In whose cold blood no spark of honour bides.

North. Be thou a prey unto the house of York,

And die in bands for this unmanly deed!

Clif. In dreadful war mayst thou be overcome,

Or live in peace abandon'd and despis'd!   *190*

      [*Exeunt Northumberland, Clifford, and Westmoreland.*]

War. Turn this way, Henry, and regard them not.

Exe. They seek revenge and therefore will not yield.

Henry. Ah! Exeter.

War.   Why should you sigh, my lord?

Henry. Not for myself, Lord Warwick, but my son,   *195*

Whom I unnaturally shall disinherit.

But be it as it may; I here entail

The crown to thee and to thine heirs for ever;

Conditionally, that here thou take an oath

To cease this civil war, and, whilst I live,   *200*

To honour me as thy king and sovereign;

And neither by treason nor hostility

To seek to put me down and reign thyself.

York. This oath I willingly take and will perform.

      [*Coming from the throne.*]

War. Long live King Henry! Plantagenet, embrace him.   *205*

Henry. And long live thou and these thy forward sons!

York. Now York and Lancaster are reconcil'd.

Exe. Accurs'd be he that seeks to make them foes!

      Sennet. Here they come down.

York. Farewell, my gracious lord; I'll to my castle.

War. And I'll keep London with my soldiers.   *210*

Norf. And I to Norfolk with my followers.

Mont. And I unto the sea from whence I came.

---

106 *Cf. n.*   **107 Thy grandfather:** *on the mother's side*   **111 sith:** *since*   **114 old enough now:** *i.e. thirty-nine years old*   **146 crown:** *legal claim to the crown*   **157 deceiv'd:** *mistaken*   **thy southern power;** *cf. n.*

160 Can: *that can*   **188 bands:** *bonds*   **S.d. Sennet:** *bugle notes to signal the moving of a procession*   **209 castle:** *Sandal Castle, near Wakefield* (Yorkshire)   **212 unto the sea;** *cf. n.*

[Exeunt York and his sons, Warwick, Norfolk, Montague,
Soldiers, and Attendants.]
Henry. And I, with grief and sorrow, to the court.

Enter the Queen [and the Prince of Wales].

Exe. Here comes the queen, whose looks bewray her anger:
I'll steal away.   *[Going.]*   215
 Henry. Exeter, so will I.   *[Going.]*
 Queen. Nay, go not from me; I will follow thee.
 Henry. Be patient, gentle queen, and I will stay.
 Queen. Who can be patient in such extremes?
Ah! wretched man; would I had died a maid,   220
And never seen thee, never borne thee son,
Seeing thou hast prov'd so unnatural a father.
Hath he deserv'd to lose his birthright thus?
Hadst thou but lov'd him half so well as I,
Or felt that pain which I did for him once,   225
Or nourish'd him as I did with my blood,
Thou wouldst have left thy dearest heart-blood there,
Rather than have made that savage duke thine heir,
And disinherited thine only son.
 Prince. Father, you cannot disinherit me: 230
If you be king, why should not I succeed?
 Henry. Pardon me, Margaret; pardon me, sweet son;
The Earl of Warwick and the duke enforc'd me.
 Queen. Enforc'd thee! art thou king, and wilt be forc'd?
I shame to hear thee speak. Ah! timorous wretch;   235
Thou hast undone thyself, thy son, and me;
And given unto the house of York such head
As thou shalt reign but by their sufferance.
To entail him and his heirs unto the crown,
What is it but to make thy sepulchre,   240
And creep into it far before thy time?
Warwick is chancellor and the Lord of Calais;
Stern Faulconbridge commands the narrow seas;
The duke is made protector of the realm;
And yet shalt thou be safe? such safety finds   245
The trembling lamb environed with wolves.
Had I been there, which am a silly woman,
The soldiers should have toss'd me on their pikes
Before I would have granted to that act;
But thou preferr'st thy life before thine honour: 250
And seeing thou dost, I here divorce myself,
Both from thy table, Henry, and thy bed,
Until that act of parliament be repeal'd
Whereby my son is disinherited.
The northern lords that have forsworn thy colours   255
Will follow mine, if once they see them spread;
And spread they shall be, to thy foul disgrace,
And utter ruin of the house of York.
Thus do I leave thee. Come, son, let's away;
Our army is ready; come, we'll after them.   260
 Henry. Stay, gentle Margaret, and hear me speak.
 Queen. Thou hast spoke too much already: get thee gone.
 Henry. Gentle son Edward, thou wilt stay with me?
 Queen. Ay, to be murther'd by his enemies.
 Prince. When I return with victory from the field   265
I'll see your Grace: till then, I'll follow her.

 Queen. Come, son, away; we may not linger thus.
       [Exeunt Queen and the Prince.]
 Henry. Poor queen! how love to me and to her son
Hath made her break out into terms of rage.
Reveng'd may she be on that hateful duke,   270
Whose haughty spirit, winged with desire,
Will cost my crown, and like an empty eagle
Tire on the flesh of me and of my son!
The loss of those three lords torments my heart:
I'll write unto them, and entreat them fair.   275
Come, cousin; you shall be the messenger.
 Exe. And I, I hope, shall reconcile them all.

         Exit [with Henry].

❧ Scene Second ❧

[A Room in Sandal Castle, near Wakefield, in Yorkshire
Flourish. Enter Richard, Edward, and Montague.]

 Rich. Brother, though I be youngest, give me leave.
 Edw. No, I can better play the orator.
 Mont. But I have reasons strong and forcible.

Enter the Duke of York.

 York. Why, how now, sons and brother! at a strife?
What is your quarrel? how began it first?   5
 Edw. No quarrel, but a slight contention.
 York. About what?
 Rich. About that which concerns your Grace and us:
The crown of England, father, which is yours.
 York. Mine, boy? not till King Henry be dead.   10
 Rich. Your right depends not on his life or death.
 Edw. Now you are heir, therefore enjoy it now:
By giving the house of Lancaster leave to breathe,
It will outrun you, father, in the end.
 York. I took an oath that he should quietly reign.   15
 Edw. But for a kingdom any oath may be broken:
I would break a thousand oaths to reign one year.
 Rich. No; God forbid your Grace should be forsworn.
 York. I shall be, if I claim by open war.
 Rich. I'll prove the contrary, if you'll hear me speak. 20
 York. Thou canst not, son; it is impossible.
 Rich. An oath is of no moment, being not took
Before a true and lawful magistrate
That hath authority over him that swears:
Henry had none, but did usurp the place;   25
Then, seeing 'twas he that made you to depose,
Your oath, my lord, is vain and frivolous.
Therefore, to arms! And, father, do but think
How sweet a thing it is to wear a crown,
Within whose circuit is Elysium,   30
And all that poets feign of bliss and joy.
Why do we linger thus? I cannot rest
Until the white rose that I wear be dy'd
Even in the lukewarm blood of Henry's heart.
 York. Richard, enough, I will be king, or die.   35

---

214 bewray: *disclose*   230 *Cf. n.*   237 head: *headway*   243 *Cf. n.*   narrow seas:
English Channel   247 which: *who*   silly: *feeble*   249 granted: *submitted*

272 cost: *assail*   empty: *famished*   273 Tire: *gorge*   275 entreat ... fair: *propitiate
them*   1 give me leave: *let me speak*   22 moment: *weight*   26 made ... depose:
administered the oath   28–31 *Cf. n.*

Brother, thou shalt to London presently,
And whet on Warwick to this enterprise.
Thou, Richard, shalt to the Duke of Norfolk,
And tell him privily of our intent.
You, Edward, shall unto my Lord Cobham,   40
With whom the Kentishmen will willingly rise:
In them I trust; for they are soldiers,
Witty, courteous, liberal, full of spirit.
While you are thus employ'd, what resteth more,
But that I seek occasion how to rise,   45
And yet the king not privy to my drift,
Nor any of the house of Lancaster?

Enter Gabriel [a Messenger].

But, stay: what news? why com'st thou in such post?
   Mess. The queen with all the northern earls and lords
Intend here to besiege you in your castle.   50
She is hard by with twenty thousand men,
And therefore fortify your hold, my lord.
   York. Ay, with my sword. What! think'st thou that we fear
them?
Edward and Richard, you shall stay with me;   55
My brother Montague shall post to London:
Let noble Warwick, Cobham and the rest,
Whom we have left protectors of the king,
With powerful policy strengthen themselves,
And trust not simple Henry nor his oaths.   60
   Mont. Brother, I go; I'll win them, fear it not:
And thus most humbly I do take my leave.   *Exit Montague.*

Enter Mortimer, and his Brother.

   York. Sir John, and Sir Hugh Mortimer, mine uncles!
You are come to Sandal in a happy hour;
The army of the queen mean to besiege us.   65
   Sir John. She shall not need, we'll meet her in the field.
   York. What! with five thousand men?
   Rich. Ay, with five hundred, father, for a need:
A woman's general; what should we fear?   *A march afar off.*
   Edw. I hear their drums; let's set our men in order,   70
And issue forth and bid them battle straight.
   York. Five men to twenty! though the odds be great,
I doubt not, uncle, of our victory.
Many a battle have I won in France,
When as the enemy hath been ten to one: 75
Why should I not now have the like success?

                                   Alarum. Exeunt.

❧ SCENE THIRD ❧

[Field of Battle between Sandal Castle and Wakefield]
Enter Rutland, and his Tutor.

   Rut. Ah, whither shall I fly to 'scape their hands?
Ah! tutor, look, where bloody Clifford comes!

Enter Clifford [and Soldiers].

   Clif. Chaplain, away! thy priesthood saves thy life.
As for the brat of this accursed duke,
Whose father slew my father, he shall die.   5
   Tut. And I, my lord, will bear him company.
   Clif. Soldiers, away with him.
   Tut. Ah! Clifford, murther not this innocent child,
Lest thou be hated both of God and man!
                     Exit [forced off by soldiers].
   Clif. How now! is he dead already? Or is it fear   10
That makes him close his eyes? I'll open them.
   Rut. So looks the pent-up lion o'er the wretch
That trembles under his devouring paws;
And so he walks, insulting o'er his prey,
And so he comes to rend his limbs asunder.   15
Ah! gentle Clifford, kill me with thy sword,
And not with such a cruel threatening look.
Sweet Clifford! hear me speak before I die:
I am too mean a subject for thy wrath;
Be thou reveng'd on men, and let me live.   20
   Clif. In vain thou speak'st, poor boy; my father's blood
Hath stopp'd the passage where thy words should enter.
   Rut. Then let my father's blood open it again:
He is a man, and, Clifford, cope with him.
   Clif. Had I thy brethren here, their lives and thine   25
Were not revenge sufficient for me;
No, if I digg'd up thy forefathers' graves,
And hung their rotten coffins up in chains,
It could not slake mine ire, nor ease my heart.
The sight of any of the house of York   30
Is as a fury to torment my soul;
And till I root out their accursed line,
And leave not one alive, I live in hell.
Therefore—   *[Lifting his hand.]*
   Rut. O! let me pray before I take my death.   35
To thee I pray; sweet Clifford, pity me!
   Clif. Such pity as my rapier's point affords.
   Rut. I never did thee harm: why wilt thou slay me?
   Clif. Thy father hath.
   Rut.   But 'twas ere I was born.   40
Thou hast one son; for his sake pity me,
Lest in revenge thereof, sith God is just,
He be as miserably slain as I.
Ah! let me live in prison all my days;
And when I give occasion of offence,   45
Then let me die, for now thou hast no cause.
   Clif. No cause!
Thy father slew my father; therefore, die.   *[Stabs him.]*
   Rut. Dii faciant laudis summa sit ista tuæ!   *[Dies.]*
   Clif. Plantagenet! I come, Plantagenet!
And this thy son's blood cleaving to my blade
Shall rust upon my weapon, till thy blood,
Congeal'd with this, do make me wipe off both.   *Exit.*

---

36 presently: *at once*   **42, 43** *Cf. n.*   **43 Witty:** *wise* **liberal:** *gentlemanly*   **44 resteth:** *remains to be done*   **46 privy ... drift:** *aware of my intention* **S. d. Gabriel;** *cf. n.*   **48 post:** *haste*   **52 hold:** *castle*   **59 powerful policy:** *cunningly-gained power*   **76 the like:** *equal*

12 pent-up: *caged, rendered fierce*   **14 insulting:** *exulting in triumph*   **40 ere I was born;** *cf. n.*   **49** *'The gods grant that this be the height of thy glory'*

❧ SCENE FOURTH ❧

[Another Part of the Plains]
Alarum. Enter Richard, Duke of York.

York. The army of the queen hath got the field:
My uncles both are slain in rescuing me;
And all my followers to the eager foe
Turn back and fly, like ships before the wind,
Or lambs pursu'd by hunger-starved wolves. 5
My sons, God knows what hath bechanced them:
But this I know, they have demean'd themselves
Like men born to renown by life or death.
Three times did Richard make a lane to me,
And thrice cried, 'Courage, father! fight it out!' 10
And full as oft came Edward to my side,
With purple falchion, painted to the hilt
In blood of those that had encounter'd him:
And when the hardiest warriors did retire,
Richard cried, 'Charge! and give no foot of ground!' 15
And cried, 'A crown, or else a glorious tomb!
A sceptre, or an earthly sepulchre!'
With this, we charg'd again; but, out, alas!
We bodg'd again: as I have seen a swan
With bootless labour swim against the tide, 20
And spend her strength with over-matching waves.

A short alarum within.

Ah, hark! the fatal followers do pursue;
And I am faint and cannot fly their fury;
And were I strong I would not shun their fury:
The sands are number'd that makes up my life; 25
Here must I stay, and here my life must end.

Enter the Queen, Clifford, Northumberland, the young Prince,
and Soldiers.

Come, bloody Clifford, rough Northumberland,
I dare your quenchless fury to more rage:
I am your butt, and I abide your shot.
North. Yield to our mercy, proud Plantagenet. 30
Clif. Ay, to such mercy as his ruthless arm
With downright payment show'd unto my father.
Now Phaethon hath tumbled from his car,
And made an evening at the noontide prick.
York. My ashes, as the phœnix, may bring forth 35
A bird that will revenge upon you all;
And in that hope I throw mine eyes to heaven,
Scorning whate'er you can afflict me with.
Why come you not? what! multitudes, and fear?
Clif. So cowards fight when they can fly no further; 40
So doves do peck the falcon's piercing talons;
So desperate thieves, all hopeless of their lives,
Breathe out invectives 'gainst the officers.
York. O Clifford! but bethink thee once again,
And in thy thought o'er-run my former time; 45
And, if thou canst for blushing, view this face,
And bite thy tongue, that slanders him with cowardice
Whose frown hath made thee faint and fly ere this.
Clif. I will not bandy with thee word for word,

But buckle with thee blows, twice two for one. 50
Queen. Hold, valiant Clifford! for a thousand causes
I would prolong awhile the traitor's life.
Wrath makes him deaf: speak thou, Northumberland.
North. Hold, Clifford! do not honour him so much
To prick thy finger, though to wound his heart. 55
What valour were it, when a cur doth grin,
For one to thrust his hand between his teeth,
When he might spurn him with his foot away?
It is war's prize to take all vantages,
And ten to one is no impeach of valour. 60

[They lay hands on York, who struggles.]

Clif. Ay, ay; so strives the woodcock with the gin.
North. So doth the cony struggle in the net.
York. So triumph thieves upon their conquer'd booty;
So true men yield, with robbers so o'er-matched.
North. What would your Grace have done unto him now? 65
Queen. Brave warriors, Clifford and Northumberland,
Come, make him stand upon this molehill here,
That raught at mountains with outstretched arms,
Yet parted but the shadow with his hand.
What! was it you that would be England's king? 70
Was 't you that revell'd in our parliament,
And made a preachment of your high descent?
Where are your mess of sons to back you now?
The wanton Edward, and the lusty George?
And where's that valiant crook-back prodigy, 75
Dicky your boy, that with his grumbling voice
Was wont to cheer his dad in mutinies?
Or, with the rest, where is your darling Rutland?
Look, York: I stain'd this napkin with the blood
That valiant Clifford with his rapier's point 80
Made issue from the bosom of the boy;
And if thine eyes can water for his death,
I give thee this to dry thy cheeks withal.
Alas, poor York! but that I hate thee deadly,
I should lament thy miserable state. 85
I prithee grieve, to make me merry, York.
What! hath thy fiercy heart so parch'd thine entrails
That not a tear can fall for Rutland's death?
Why art thou patient, man? thou shouldst be mad;
And I, to make thee mad, do mock thee thus. 90
Stamp, rave, and fret, that I may sing and dance.
Thou wouldst be fee'd, I see, to make me sport:
York cannot speak unless he wear a crown.
A crown for York! and, lords, bow low to him:
Hold you his hands whilst I do set it on. 95

[Putting a paper crown on his head.]

Ah, marry, sir, now looks he like a king!
Ay, this is he that took King Henry's chair;
And this is he was his adopted heir.
But how is it that great Plantagenet
Is crown'd so soon, and broke his solemn oath? 100
As I bethink me, you should not be king
Till our King Henry had shook hands with death.
And will you pale your head in Henry's glory,
And rob his temples of the diadem,

---

4 Turn back: *present their backs* **7 demean'd:** *behaved* **12 purple:** *blood-color* **falchion:** *curved sword, sabre* **19 bodg'd:** *gave way* **21 with:** *against* **25 makes;* *cf. n.* **29 butt:** *mark at archery* **33 Phaethon;** *cf. n.* **34 noontide prick:** *midday mark on the sundial* **45 o'er-run:** *review*

50 buckle ... blows: *strive with blows* **56 grin:** *show his teeth* **59 prize:** *privilege* **60 impeach:** *derogation* **61 woodcock:** *a proverbially silly bird* **gin:** *snare* **62 cony:** *rabbit* **67 Cf. n.** **68 raught:** *reached* **73 mess:** *squad of four* **77 cheer:** *incite* **83 withal:** *with* **92 fee'd:** *paid* **102 shook hands:** *met* **103 pale:** *encircle*

Now in his life, against your holy oath?   *105*
O! 'tis a fault too-too unpardonable.
Off with the crown; and, with the crown, his head;
And, whilst we breathe, take time to do him dead.
    Clif. That is my office, for my father's sake.
    Queen. Nay, stay; let's hear the orisons he makes.   *110*
    York. She-wolf of France, but worse than wolves of France,
Whose tongue more poisons than the adder's tooth!
How ill-beseeming is it in thy sex
To triumph, like an Amazonian trull,
Upon their woes whom fortune captivates!   *115*
But that thy face is, vizard-like, unchanging,
Made impudent with use of evil deeds,
I would assay, proud queen, to make thee blush:
To tell thee whence thou cam'st, of whom deriv'd,
Were shame enough to shame thee, wert thou not shameless.
Thy father bears the type of King of Naples,
Of both the Sicils and Jerusalem;
Yet not so wealthy as an English yeoman.
Hath that poor monarch taught thee to insult?
It needs not, nor it boots thee not, proud queen,   *125*
Unless the adage must be verified,
That beggars mounted run their horse to death.
'Tis beauty that doth oft make women proud;
But, God he knows, thy share thereof is small:
'Tis virtue that doth make them most admir'd;   *130*
The contrary doth make thee wonder'd at:
'Tis government that makes them seem divine;
The want thereof makes thee abominable.
Thou art as opposite to every good
As the Antipodes are unto us,   *135*
Or as the south to the septentrion
O tiger's heart wrapp'd in a woman's hide!
How couldst thou drain the life-blood of the child,
To bid the father wipe his eyes withal,
And yet be seen to bear a woman's face?   *140*
Women are soft, mild, pitiful, and flexible;
Thou stern, obdurate, flinty, rough, remorseless.
Bidd'st thou me rage? why, now thou hast thy wish:
Wouldst have me weep? why, now thou hast thy will;
For raging wind blows up incessant showers,   *145*
And when the rage allays, the rain begins.
These tears are my sweet Rutland's obsequies,
And every drop cries vengeance for his death,
'Gainst thee, fell Clifford, and thee, false French-woman.
    North. Beshrew me, but his passions moves me so   *150*
That hardly can I check my eyes from tears.
    York. That face of his the hungry cannibals
Would not have touch'd, would not have stain'd with blood;
But you are more inhuman, more inexorable,—
O! ten times more, than tigers of Hyrcania.   *155*
See, ruthless queen, a hapless father's tears:
This cloth thou dipp'dst in blood of my sweet boy,
And I with tears do wash the blood away.
Keep thou the napkin, and go boast of this;
And if thou tell'st the heavy story right,   *160*

Upon my soul, the hearers will shed tears;
Yea, even my foes will shed fast-falling tears,
And say, 'Alas! it was a piteous deed!'
There, take the crown, and with the crown my curse,
And in thy need such comfort come to thee   *165*
As now I reap at thy too cruel hand!
Hard-hearted Clifford, take me from the world;
My soul to heaven, my blood upon your heads!
    North. Had he been slaughter-man to all my kin,
I should not for my life but weep with him,   *170*
To see how inly sorrow gripes his soul.
    Queen. What! weeping-ripe, my Lord Northumberland?
Think but upon the wrong he did us all,
And that will quickly dry thy melting tears.
    Clif. Here's for my oath; here's for my father's death.   *175*
                     [Stabbing him.]
    Queen. And here's to right our gentle-hearted king.
                     [Stabbing him.]
    York. Open thy gate of mercy, gracious God!
My soul flies through these wounds to seek out thee.   *[Dies.]*
    Queen. Off with his head, and set it on York gates;
So York may overlook the town of York.   *Flourish. Exeunt.*

ACT SECOND & SCENE FIRST

[Chipping Norton in Oxfordshire]
A March. Enter Edward, Richard, and their power.

    Edw. I wonder how our princely father 'scap'd,
Or whether he be 'scap'd away or no
From Clifford's and Northumberland's pursuit.
Had he been ta'en, we should have heard the news;
Had he been slain, we should have heard the news;   *5*
Or had he 'scap'd, methinks we should have heard
The happy tidings of his good escape.
How fares my brother? why is he so sad?
    Rich. I cannot joy until I be resolv'd
Where our right valiant father is become.   *10*
I saw him in the battle range about,
And watch'd him how he singled Clifford forth.
Methought he bore him in the thickest troop
As doth a lion in a herd of neat;
Or as a bear, encompass'd round with dogs,   *15*
Who having pinch'd a few and made them cry,
The rest stand all aloof and bark at him.
So far'd our father with his enemies;
So fled his enemies my warlike father:
Methinks 'tis prize enough to be his son.   *20*
See how the morning opes her golden gates,
And takes her farewell of the glorious sun;
How well resembles it the prime of youth,
Trimm'd like a younker prancing to his love.
    Edw. Dazzle mine eyes, or do I see three suns?   *25*
    Rich. Three glorious suns, each one a perfect sun;
Not separated with the racking clouds,

---

106 too-too: *altogether too*   **108 breathe:** *repose* **do ... dead:** *kill him*   **110 orisons:** *prayers*   **114 trull:** *virago*   **115 captivates:** *makes captive*   **116 vizard-like:** *like a mask*   **117 use:** *habit*   **118 assay:** *attempt*   **121 type:** *title*   **125 boots:** *profits*   **132 government:** *conduct*   **136 septentrion:** *north*   **137** *Cf. n.*   **146 allays:** *abates*   **149 fell:** *vindictive*   **150 Beshrew:** *plague on* **passions:** *wild griefs*   **155 Hyrcania;** *cf. n.*   **159 napkin:** *handkerchief*   **160 heavy:** *grievous*

164 *Cf. n.*   **171 inly:** *inward*   **172 weeping-ripe:** *ready for tears*   **9 resolv'd:** *informed*   **10 Where ... is become:** *what has become of*   **13 bore him:** *behaved himself*   **14 neat:** *cattle*   **20 prize;** *cf. n.*   **22** *Takes leaves of the sun as it sets out on its daily course*   **23 prime:** *springtime*   **24 younker:** *stripling*   **25** *Cf. n.*   **27 racking:** *driving in soft masses*

But sever'd in a pale clear-shining sky.
See, see! they join, embrace and seem to kiss.
As if they vow'd some league inviolable: 30
Now are they but one lamp, one light, one sun.
In this the heaven figures some event.
    Edw. 'Tis wondrous strange, the like yet never heard of.
I think it cites us, brother, to the field;
That we, the sons of brave Plantagenet,   35
Each one already blazing by our meeds,
Should notwithstanding join our lights together,
And over-shine the earth, as this the world.
Whate'er it bodes, henceforward will I bear
Upon my target three fair-shining suns.   40
    Rich. Nay, bear three daughters: by your leave I speak it,
You love the breeder better than the male.

          Enter one blowing.

But what art thou, whose heavy looks foretell
Some dreadful story hanging on thy tongue?
    Mess. Ah! one that was a woeful looker-on,   45
When as the noble Duke of York was slain,
Your princely father, and my loving lord.
    Edw. O! speak no more, for I have heard too much.
    Rich. Say how he died, for I will hear it all.
    Mess. Environed he was with many foes,   50
And stood against them, as the hope of Troy
Against the Greeks that would have enter'd Troy.
But Hercules himself must yield to odds;
And many strokes, though with a little axe,
Hews down and fells the hardest-timber'd oak.   55
By many hands your father was subdu'd;
But only slaughter'd by the ireful arm
Of unrelenting Clifford and the queen,
Who crown'd the gracious duke in high despite;
Laugh'd in his face; and when with grief he wept,   60
The ruthless queen gave him to dry his cheeks
A napkin steeped in the harmless blood
Of sweet young Rutland, by rough Clifford slain:
And after many scorns, many foul taunts,
They took his head, and on the gates of York   65
They set the same; and there it doth remain,
The saddest spectacle that e'er I view'd.
    Edw. Sweet Duke of York! our prop to lean upon,
Now thou art gone, we have no staff, no stay!
O Clifford! boist'rous Clifford! thou hast slain   70
The flower of Europe for his chivalry;
And treacherously hast thou vanquish'd him,
For hand to hand he would have vanquish'd thee.
Now my soul's palace is become a prison:
Ah! would she break from hence, that this my body   75
Might in the ground be closed up in rest,
For never henceforth shall I joy again,
Never, O! never, shall I see more joy.
    Rich. I cannot weep, for all my body's moisture
Scarce serves to quench my furnace-burning heart: 80
Nor can my tongue unload my heart's great burthen;
For self-same wind that I should speak withal

Is kindling coals that fires all my breast,
And burns me up with flames, that tears would quench.
To weep is to make less the depth of grief: 85
Tears then, for babes; blows and revenge for me!
Richard, I bear thy name; I'll venge thy death,
Or die renowned by attempting it.
    Edw. His name that valiant duke hath left with thee;
His dukedom and his chair with me is left.   90
    Rich. Nay, if thou be that princely eagle's bird,
Show thy descent by gazing 'gainst the sun:
For chair and dukedom, throne and kingdom say;
Either that is thine, or else thou wert not his.

    March. Enter Warwick, Marquess Montague, and their Army.

    War. How now, fair lords! What fare? what news   95
abroad?
    Rich. Great Lord of Warwick, if we should recount
Our baleful news, and at each word's deliverance
Stab poniards in our flesh till all were told,
The words would add more anguish than the wounds.   100
O valiant lord! the Duke of York is slain.
    Edw. O Warwick! Warwick! that Plantagenet
Which held thee dearly as his soul's redemption,
Is by the stern Lord Clifford done to death.
    War. Ten days ago I drown'd these news in tears,   105
And now, to add more measure to your woes,
I come to tell you things sith then befallen.
After the bloody fray at Wakefield fought,
Where your brave father breath'd his latest gasp,
Tidings, as swiftly as the posts could run,   110
Were brought me of your loss and his depart.
I, then in London, keeper of the king,
Muster'd my soldiers, gather'd flocks of friends,
[And very well appointed, as I thought,]
March'd towards Saint Albans to intercept the queen,   115
Bearing the king in my behalf along;
For by my scouts I was advertised
That she was coming with a full intent
To dash our late decree in parliament,
Touching King Henry's oath and your succession.   120
Short tale to make, we at Saint Albans met,
Our battles join'd, and both sides fiercely fought:
But whether 'twas the coldness of the king,
Who look'd full gently on his warlike queen,
That robb'd my soldiers of their heated spleen;   125
Or whether 'twas report of her success;
Or more than common fear of Clifford's rigour,
Who thunders to his captives blood and death,
I cannot judge: but, to conclude with truth,
Their weapons like to lightning came and went;   130
Our soldiers', like the night-owl's lazy flight,
Or like a lazy thresher with a flail,
Fell gently down, as if they struck their friends.
I cheer'd them up with justice of our cause,
With promise of high pay, and great rewards: 135
But all in vain; they had no heart to fight,
And we in them no hope to win the day;
So that we fled: the king unto the queen;

32 figures: *foreshadows* **event:** *future happening* **34 cites:** *calls* **36 meeds:*
merits **38 this:** *this light, the sun* **41 by your leave:** *without meaning offense* **51**
the hope of Troy: *Hector* **68, 69** *Cf. n.* **71** *Him who in knightly prowess was the*
pride of Europe **80 furnace-burning:** *burning like a furnace*

90 chair: *seat of authority* **91 bird:** *fledgling* **91, 92** *Cf. n.* **95 What fare:** *how*
do you fare? **111 depart:** *decease* **114 appointed:** *equipped; cf. n.* **117 advertised:*
informed **119 dash:** *frustrate* **125 heated spleen:** *hot valor***

Lord George your brother, Norfolk, and myself,
In haste, post-haste, are come to join with you;   140
For in the marches here we heard you were,
Making another head to fight again.

    Edw. Where is the Duke of Norfolk, gentle Warwick?
And when came George from Burgundy to England?

    War. Some six miles off the duke is with the soldiers;   145
And for your brother, he was lately sent
From your kind aunt, Duchess of Burgundy,
With aid of soldiers to this needful war.

    Rich. 'Twas odds, belike, when valiant Warwick fled:
Oft have I heard his praises in pursuit,   150
But ne'er till now his scandal of retire.

    War. Nor now my scandal, Richard, dost thou hear;
For thou shalt know, this strong right hand of mine
Can pluck the diadem from faint Henry's head,
And wring the awful sceptre from his fist,   155
Were he as famous, and as bold in war
As he is fam'd for mildness, peace, and prayer.

    Rich. I know it well, Lord Warwick; blame me not:
'Tis love I bear thy glories makes me speak.
But in this troublous time what's to be done?   160
Shall we go throw away our coats of steel,
And wrap our bodies in black mourning gowns,
Numb'ring our Ave-Maries with our beads?
Or shall we on the helmets of our foes
Tell our devotion with revengeful arms?   165
If for the last, say 'Ay,' and to it, lords.

    War. Why, therefore Warwick came to seek you out;
And therefore comes my brother Montague.
Attend me, lords. The proud insulting queen,
With Clifford and the haught Northumberland,   170
And of their feather many moe proud birds,
Have wrought the easy-melting king like wax.
He swore consent to your succession,
His oath enrolled in the parliament;
And now to London all the crew are gone,   175
To frustrate both his oath and what beside
May make against the house of Lancaster.
Their power, I think, is thirty thousand strong:
Now, if the help of Norfolk and myself,
With all the friends that thou, brave Earl of March,   180
Amongst the loving Welshmen canst procure,
Will but amount to five and twenty thousand,
Why, *Via!* to London will we march,
And once again bestride our foaming steeds,
And once again cry, 'Charge upon our foes!'   185
But never once again turn back and fly.

    Rich. Ay, now methinks I hear great Warwick speak:
Ne'er may he live to see a sunshine day,
That cries 'Retire,' if Warwick bid him stay.

    Edw. Lord Warwick, on thy shoulder will I lean;   190
And when thou fail'st—as God forbid the hour!—
Must Edward fall, which peril heaven forfend!

    War. No longer Earl of March, but Duke of York:
The next degree is England's royal throne;
For King of England shalt thou be proclaim'd   195
In every borough as we pass along;
And he that throws not up his cap for joy
Shall for the fault make forfeit of his head.
King Edward, valiant Richard, Montague,
Stay we no longer dreaming of renown,   200
But sound the trumpets, and about our task.

    Rich. Then, Clifford, were thy heart as hard as steel,—
As thou hast shown it flinty by thy deeds,—
I come to pierce it, or to give thee mine.

    Edw. Then strike up, drums! God, and Saint George for us!

Enter a Messenger.

    War. How now! what news?
    Mess. The Duke of Norfolk sends you word by me,
The queen is coming with a puissant host;
And craves your company for speedy counsel.
    War. Why then it sorts; brave warriors, let's away.   210
                                Exeunt omnes.

❧ Scene Second ❧

[Before York]

*Flourish. Enter the King, the Queen, Clifford, Northumberland, and
young Prince, with drum and trumpets.*

    Queen. Welcome, my lord, to this brave town of York.
Yonder's the head of that arch-enemy,
That sought to be encompass'd with your crown:
Doth not the object cheer your heart, my lord?

    King. Ay, as the rocks cheer them that fear their wrack: 5
To see this sight, it irks my very soul.
Withhold revenge, dear God! 'tis not my fault,
Nor wittingly have I infring'd my vow.

    Clif. My gracious liege, this too much lenity
And harmful pity must be laid aside.   10
To whom do lions cast their gentle looks?
Not to the beast that would usurp their den.
Whose hand is that the forest bear doth lick?
Not his that spoils her young before her face.
Who 'scapes the lurking serpent's mortal sting?   15
Not he that sets his foot upon her back.
The smallest worm will turn being trodden on,
And doves will peck in safeguard of their brood.
Ambitious York did level at thy crown,
Thou smiling while he knit his angry brows: 20
He, but a duke, would have his son a king,
And raise his issue like a loving sire;
Thou, being a king, bless'd with a goodly son,
Didst yield consent to disinherit him,
Which argu'd thee a most unloving father.   25
Unreasonable creatures feed their young;
And though man's face be fearful to their eyes,
Yet, in protection of their tender ones,
Who hath not seen them, even with those wings
Which sometime they have us'd with fearful flight,   30
Make war with him that climb'd unto their nest,
Offering their own lives in their young's defence?

For shame, my liege! make them your precedent.
Were it not pity that this goodly boy
Should lose his birthright by his father's fault,   35
And long hereafter say unto his child,
'What my great grandfather and grandsire got,
My careless father fondly gave away?'
Ah! what a shame were this. Look on the boy;
And let his manly face, which promiseth   40
Successful fortune, steel thy melting heart
To hold thine own and leave thine own with him.
    King. Full well hath Clifford play'd the orator,
Inferring arguments of mighty force.
But, Clifford, tell me, didst thou never hear   45
That things ill got had ever bad success?
And happy always was it for that son
Whose father for his hoarding went to hell?
I'll leave my son my virtuous deeds behind;
And would my father had left me no more!   50
For all the rest is held at such a rate
As brings a thousand-fold more care to keep
Than in possession any jot of pleasure.
Ah! cousin York, would thy best friends did know
How it doth grieve me that thy head is here!   55
    Queen. My lord, cheer up your spirits: our foes are nigh,
And this soft courage makes your followers faint.
You promis'd knighthood to our forward son:
Unsheathe your sword, and dub him presently.
Edward, kneel down.   60
    King. Edward Plantagenet, arise a knight;
And learn this lesson, draw thy sword in right.
    Prince. My gracious father, by your kingly leave,
I'll draw it as apparent to the crown,
And in that quarrel use it to the death.   65
    Clif. Why, that is spoken like a toward prince.

Enter a Messenger.

    Mess. Royal commanders, be in readiness:
For with a band of thirty thousand men
Comes Warwick, backing of the Duke of York;
And in the towns, as they do march along,   70
Proclaims him king, and many fly to him:
Darraign your battle, for they are at hand.
    Clif. I would your highness would depart the field:
The queen hath best success when you are absent.
    Queen. Ay, good my lord, and leave us to our fortune.   75
    King. Why, that's my fortune too; therefore I'll stay.
    North. Be it with resolution then to fight.
    Prince. My royal father, cheer these noble lords,
And hearten those that fight in your defence:
Unsheathe your sword, good father: cry, 'Saint George!'   80

*March. Enter Edward, Warwick, Richard, Clarence, Norfolk,
Montague, and Soldiers.*

    Edw. Now, perjur'd Henry, wilt thou kneel for grace,
And set thy diadem upon my head;
Or bide the mortal fortune of the field?

    Queen. Go, rate thy minions, proud insulting boy!
Becomes it thee to be thus bold in terms   85
Before thy sovereign and thy lawful king?
    Edw. I am his king, and he should bow his knee;
I was adopted heir by his consent:
Since when, his oath is broke; for, as I hear,
You, that are king, though he do wear the crown,   90
Have caus'd him, by new act of parliament,
To blot out me, and put his own son in.
    Clif. And reason too:
Who should succeed the father but the son?
    Rich. Are you there, butcher? O! I cannot speak.   95
    Clif. Ay, crook-back; here I stand to answer thee,
Or any he the proudest of thy sort.
    Rich. 'Twas you that kill'd young Rutland, was it not?
    Clif. Ay, and old York, and yet not satisfied.
    Rich. For God's sake, lords, give signal to the fight.   100
    War. What sayst thou, Henry, wilt thou yield the crown?
    Queen. Why, how now, long tongu'd Warwick! dare you speak?
When you and I met at Saint Albans last,
Your legs did better service than your hands.
    War. Then 'twas my turn to fly, and now 'tis thine.   105
    Clif. You said so much before, and yet you fled.
    War. 'Twas not your valour, Clifford, drove me thence.
    North. No, nor your manhood that durst make you stay.
    Rich. Northumberland, I hold thee reverently.
Break off the parley; for scarce I can refrain   110
The execution of my big-swoln heart
Upon that Clifford, that cruel child-killer.
    Clif. I slew thy father: call'st thou him a child?
    Rich. Ay, like a dastard and a treacherous coward,
As thou didst kill our tender brother Rutland;   115
But ere sunset I'll make thee curse the deed.
    King. Have done with words, my lords, and hear me speak.
    Queen. Defy them, then, or else hold close thy lips.
    King. I prithee, give no limits to my tongue:
I am a king, and privileg'd to speak.   120
    Clif. My liege, the wound that bred this meeting here
Cannot be cur'd by words; therefore be still.
    Rich. Then, executioner, unsheathe thy sword.
By him that made us all, I am resolv'd
That Clifford's manhood lies upon his tongue.   125
    Edw. Say, Henry, shall I have my right or no?
A thousand men have broke their fasts to-day,
That ne'er shall dine unless thou yield the crown.
    War. If thou deny, their blood upon thy head;
For York in justice puts his armour on.   130
    Prince. If that be right which Warwick says is right,
There is no wrong, but everything is right.
    Rich. Whoever got thee, there thy mother stands;
For well I wot thou hast thy mother's tongue.
    Queen. But thou art neither like thy sire nor dam,   135
But like a foul misshapen stigmatic,
Mark'd by the destinies to be avoided,
As venom toads, or lizards' dreadful stings.

---

33 **precedent:** *example*   38 **fondly:** *foolishly*   44 **Inferring:** *alleging*   47 **happy ... it:**
did things always turn out well   58 **forward:** *ardent*   64 **apparent:** *heir-apparent*   66
toward: *hopeful*   72 **Darraign:** *draw up* **battle:** *line of battle*   73 **depart:** *leave*   76
Cf. n.

84 **rate:** *scold* **minions:** *saucy favorites*   85 **thus ... terms:** *on so insolent a footing*   89–92 *Cf. n.*   93 **reason:** *it was reasonable*   97 **any ... proudest:** *the proudest
one whatever* **sort:** *party*   109 **reverently:** *in respect*   119 **limits:** *limitation*   124
resolv'd: *convinced*   129 **deny:** *refuse*   130 **in ... on:** *fights in a just cause*   133 **got:**
begot   136 **stigmatic:** *one branded by deformity*   138 **venom:** *poisonous*

Rich. Iron of Naples hid with English gilt,—
Whose father bears the title of a king,   *140*
As if a channel should be call'd the sea,—
Sham'st thou not, knowing whence thou art extraught,
To let thy tongue detect thy base-born heart?
   Edw. A wisp of straw were worth a thousand crowns,
To make this shameless callet know herself.   *145*
Helen of Greece was fairer far than thou,
Although thy husband may be Menelaus;
And ne'er was Agamemnon's brother wrong'd
By that false woman as this king by thee.
His father revell'd in the heart of France,   *150*
And tam'd the king, and made the dauphin stoop;
And had he match'd according to his state,
He might have kept that glory to this day;
But when he took a beggar to his bed,
And grac'd thy poor sire with his bridal day,   *155*
Even then that sunshine brew'd a shower for him,
That wash'd his father's fortunes forth of France,
And heap'd sedition on his crown at home.
For what hath broach'd this tumult but thy pride?
Hadst thou been meek our title still had slept,   *160*
And we, in pity of the gentle king,
Had slipp'd our claim until another age.
   Clar. But when we saw our sunshine made thy spring,
And that thy summer bred us no increase,
We set the axe to thy usurping root;   *165*
And though the edge hath something hit ourselves,
Yet know thou, since we have begun to strike,
We'll never leave, till we have hewn thee down,
Or bath'd thy growing with our heated bloods.
   Edw. And in this resolution I defy thee;   *170*
Not willing any longer conference,
Since thou deny'st the gentle king to speak.
Sound trumpets!—let our bloody colours wave!
And either victory, or else a grave.
   Queen. Stay, Edward.   *175*
   Edw. No, wrangling woman, we'll no longer stay: These words
will cost ten thousand lives this day.   *Exeunt omnes.*

❧ SCENE THIRD ❧

[A Field of Battle between Towton and Saxton, in Yorkshire]
Alarum. Excursions. Enter Warwick.

   War. Forspent with toil, as runners with a race,
I lay me down a little while to breathe;
For strokes receiv'd, and many blows repaid,
Have robb'd my strong-knit sinews of their strength,
And spite of spite needs must I rest a while.   *5*

Enter Edward, running.

   Edw. Smile, gentle heaven! or strike, ungentle death!
For this world frowns, and Edward's sun is clouded.

   War. How now, my lord! what hap? what hope of good?

Enter Clarence.

   Clar. Our hap is loss, our hope but sad despair,
Our ranks are broke, and ruin follows us.   *10*
What counsel give you? whither shall we fly?
   Edw. Bootless is flight, they follow us with wings;
And weak we are and cannot shun pursuit.

Enter Richard.

   Rich. Ah! Warwick, why hast thou withdrawn thyself?
Thy brother's blood the thirsty earth hath drunk,   *15*
Broach'd with the steely point of Clifford's lance;
And in the very pangs of death he cried,
Like to a dismal clangor heard from far,
'Warwick, revenge! brother, revenge my death!'
So, underneath the belly of their steeds,   *20*
That stain'd their fetlocks in his smoking blood,
The noble gentleman gave up the ghost.
   War. Then let the earth be drunken with our blood:
I'll kill my horse because I will not fly.
Why stand we like soft-hearted women here,   *25*
Wailing our losses, whiles the foe doth rage;
And look upon, as if the tragedy
Were play'd in jest by counterfeiting actors?
Here on my knee I vow to God above,
I'll never pause again, never stand still,   *30*
Till either death hath clos'd these eyes of mine,
Or fortune given me measure of revenge.
   Edw. O Warwick! I do bend my knee with thine;
And in this vow do chain my soul to thine.
And, ere my knee rise from the earth's cold face,   *35*
I throw my hands, mine eyes, my heart to thee,
Thou setter up and plucker down of kings,
Beseeching thee, if with thy will it stands
That to my foes this body must be prey,
Yet that thy brazen gates of heaven may ope,   *40*
And give sweet passage to my sinful soul!
Now, lords, take leave until we meet again,
Where'er it be, in heaven or in earth.
   Rich. Brother, give me thy hand; and, gentle Warwick,
Let me embrace thee in my weary arms: *45*
I, that did never weep, now melt with woe
That winter should cut off our spring-time so.
   War. Away, away! Once more, sweet lords, farewell.
   Clar. Yet let us all together to our troops,
And give them leave to fly that will not stay,   *50*
And call them pillars that will stand to us;
And if we thrive, promise them such rewards
As victors wear at the Olympian games.
This may plant courage in their quailing breasts;
For yet is hope of life and victory.   *55*
Forslow no longer; make we hence amain.   *Exeunt.*

---

139 *You whose cheap Neapolitan origin is gilded by your English rank*   141 **channel:** *gutter*   142 **extraught:** *extracted*   144 **wisp of straw;** *cf. n.*   145 **callet:** *lewd woman*   147 **Menelaus:** *the typical injured husband*   155 *Cf. n.*   162 **slipp'd:** *let pass, forgone*   164 **increase:** *harvest*   166 **something:** *somewhat*   169 **bath'd thy growing:** *watered thy roots*   172 **deny'st:** *forbiddest*   1 **Forspent:** *utterly exhausted; cf. n.*

9 **hap:** *fortune*   12 **Bootless:** *fruitless*   15 **Thy brother's blood;** *cf. n.*   16 **Broach'd:** *set flowing*   27 **upon:** *on*   32 **measure:** *due proportion*   38 **stands:** *accords*   56 **Forslow:** *delay*

❧ Scene Fourth ❧

[Another Part of the Field]
Excursions. Enter Richard and Clifford.

Rich. Now, Clifford, I have singled thee alone.
Suppose this arm is for the Duke of York,
And this for Rutland; both bound to revenge,
Wert thou environ'd with a brazen wall.

    Clif. Now, Richard, I am with thee here alone.   5
This is the hand that stabb'd thy father York,
And this the hand that slew thy brother Rutland;
And here's the heart that triumphs in their death
And cheers these hands that slew thy sire and brother,
To execute the like upon thyself;   10
And so, have at thee!

                They fight. Warwick comes. Clifford flies.

    Rich. Nay, Warwick, single out some other chase;
For I myself will hunt this wolf to death.   *Exeunt.*

❧ Scene Fifth ❧

[Another Park of the Field]
Alarum. Enter King Henry alone.

Hen. This battle fares like to the morning's war,
When dying clouds contend with growing light,
What time the shepherd, blowing of his nails,
Can neither call it perfect day nor night.
Now sways it this way, like a mighty sea   5
Forc'd by the tide to combat with the wind;
Now sways it that way, like the self-same sea
Forc'd to retire by fury of the wind:
Sometime the flood prevails, and then the wind;
Now one the better, then another best;   10
Both tugging to be victors, breast to breast,
Yet neither conqueror nor conquered:
So is the equal poise of this fell war.
Here on this molehill will I sit me down.
To whom God will, there be the victory!   15
For Margaret my queen, and Clifford too,
Have chid me from the battle; swearing both
They prosper best of all when I am thence.
Would I were dead! if God's good will were so;
For what is in this world but grief and woe?   20
O God! methinks it were a happy life,
To be no better than a homely swain;
To sit upon a hill, as I do now,
To carve out dials quaintly, point by point,
Thereby to see the minutes how they run,   25
How many make the hour full complete;
How many hours bring about the day;
How many days will finish up the year;
How many years a mortal man may live.
When this is known, then to divide the times: 30
So many hours must I tend my flock;
So many hours must I take my rest;
So many hours must I contemplate;
So many hours must I sport myself;
So many days my ewes have been with young;   35
So many weeks ere the poor fools will ean;
So many years ere I shall shear the fleece:
So minutes, hours, days, months, and years,
Pass'd over to the end they were created,
Would bring white hairs unto a quiet grave.   40
Ah! what a life were this! how sweet! how lovely!
Gives not the hawthorn bush a sweeter shade
To shepherds, looking on their silly sheep,
Than doth a rich embroider'd canopy
To kings that fear their subjects' treachery?   45
Oh, yes! it doth; a thousand-fold it doth.
And to conclude, the shepherd's homely curds,
His cold thin drink out of his leather bottle,
His wonted sleep under a fresh tree's shade,
All which secure and sweetly he enjoys,   50
Is far beyond a prince's delicates,
His viands sparkling in a golden cup,
His body couched in a curious bed,
When care, mistrust, and treason wait on him.

Alarum. Enter a Son that hath killed his Father at one door: and
a Father that hath killed his Son at another door.

    Son. Ill blows the wind that profits nobody.   55
This man whom hand to hand I slew in fight
May be possessed with some store of crowns;
And I, that haply take them from him now,
May yet ere night yield both my life and them
To some man else, as this dead man doth me.   60
Who's this? O God! it is my father's face,
Whom in this conflict I unwares have kill'd.
O heavy times, begetting such events!
From London by the king was I press'd forth;
My father, being the Earl of Warwick's man,   65
Came on the part of York, press'd by his master;
And I, who at his hands receiv'd my life,
Have by my hands of life bereaved him.
Pardon me, God, I knew not what I did!
And pardon, father, for I knew not thee!   70
My tears shall wipe away these bloody marks;
And no more words till they have flow'd their fill.

    King. O piteous spectacle! O bloody times!
Whiles lions war and battle for their dens,
Poor harmless lambs abide their enmity.   75
Weep, wretched man, I'll aid thee tear for tear;
And let our hearts and eyes, like civil war,
Be blind with tears, and break o'ercharg'd with grief.

Enter Father, bearing of his Son.

    Fath. Thou that so stoutly hast resisted me,
Give me thy gold, if thou hast any gold,   80
For I have bought it with an hundred blows.
But let me see: is this our foeman's face?
Ah! no, no, no, it is mine only son.
Ah, boy, if any life be left in thee,
Throw up thine eye: see, see! what showers arise,   85

---

34 **sport:** *amuse*   36 **ean:** *give birth*   43 **silly:** *harmless*   50 **secure:** *securely*   51
delicates: *dainties*   53 **curious:** *gorgeous*   54 *Cf. n.*   57 **with:** *of store: quan-*
tity   58 **haply:** *by chance*   62 **unwares:** *unknowingly*   64 **press'd forth:** *led out by*
impressment **S. d.;** *cf. n.*

---

1 **singled:** *selected one victim from the herd* (hunting term).   9 **cheers:** *encourages*   3
blowing of: *warming by breathing on*   24 **dials:** *sundials*   **quaintly:** *ingeniously*

Blown with the windy tempest of my heart,
Upon thy wounds, that kills mine eye and heart.
O! pity, God, this miserable age.
What stratagems, how fell, how butcherly,
Erroneous, mutinous, and unnatural,　　　　　　　　　　　90
This deadly quarrel daily doth beget!
O boy! thy father gave thee life too soon,
And hath bereft thee of thy life too late.

　　King. Woe above woe! grief more than common grief!
O! that my death would stay these ruthful deeds.　　95
O! pity, pity; gentle heaven, pity.
The red rose and the white are on his face,
The fatal colours of our striving houses:
The one his purple blood right well resembles;
The other his pale cheeks, methinks, presenteth:　　100
Wither one rose, and let the other flourish!
If you contend, a thousand lives must wither.

　　Son. How will my mother for a father's death
Take on with me and ne'er be satisfied!

　　Fath. How will my wife for slaughter of my son　105
Shed seas of tears and ne'er be satisfied!

　　King. How will the country for these woeful chances
Misthink the king and not be satisfied!

　　Son. Was ever son so ru'd a father's death?

　　Fath. Was ever father so bemoan'd his son?　　110

　　King. Was ever king so griev'd for subjects' woe?
Much is your sorrow; mine, ten times so much.

　　Son. I'll bear thee hence, where I may weep my fill.
　　　　　　　　　　　　　　　　　　[Exit with the body.]

　　Fath. These arms of mine shall be thy winding-sheet;
My heart, sweet boy, shall be thy sepulchre,　　　115
For from my heart thine image ne'er shall go:
My sighing breast shall be thy funeral bell;
And so obsequious will thy father be,
E'en for the loss of thee, having no more,
As Priam was for all his valiant sons.　　　　　　120
I'll bear thee hence; and let them fight that will,
For I have murther'd where I should not kill.
　　　　　　　　　　　　　　　　Exit [with the body].

　　Hen. Sad-hearted men, much overgone with care,
Here sits a king more woeful than you are.

Alarums. Excursions. Enter the Queen, the Prince, and Exeter.

　　Prince. Fly, father, fly! for all your friends are fled,　125
And Warwick rages like a chafed bull.
Away! for death doth hold us in pursuit.

　　Queen. Mount you, my lord; towards Berwick post amain.
Edward and Richard, like a brace of greyhounds
Having the fearful flying hare in sight,　　　　　130
With fiery eyes sparkling for very wrath,
And bloody steel grasp'd in their ireful hands,
Are at our backs; and therefore hence amain.

　　Exe. Away! for vengeance comes along with them.
Nay, stay not to expostulate; make speed,　　　135
Or else come after: I'll away before.

　　Hen. Nay, take me with thee, good sweet Exeter:
Not that I fear to stay, but love to go
Whither the queen intends. Forward! away!　　　*Exeunt.*

❧ SCENE SIXTH ❧

[The Same]
A loud alarum. Enter Clifford, wounded.

　　Clif. Here burns my candle out; ay, here it dies,
Which, whiles it lasted, gave King Henry light.
O Lancaster! I fear thy overthrow
More than my body's parting with my soul.
My love and fear glu'd many friends to thee;　　5
And, now I fall, thy tough commixtures melts,
Impairing Henry, strength'ning misproud York:
[The common people swarm like summer flies;]
And whither fly the gnats but to the sun?
And who shines now but Henry's enemies?　　　10
O Phœbus! hadst thou never given consent
That Phaethon should check thy fiery steeds,
Thy burning car never had scorch'd the earth;
And, Henry, hadst thou sway'd as kings should do,
Or as thy father and his father did,　　　　　15
Giving no ground unto the house of York,
They never then had sprung like summer flies;
I and ten thousand in this luckless realm
Had left no mourning widows for our death,
And thou this day hadst kept thy chair in peace.　20
For what doth cherish weeds but gentle air?
And what makes robbers bold but too much lenity?
Bootless are plaints, and cureless are my wounds;
No way to fly, nor strength to hold out flight:
The foe is merciless, and will not pity,　　　25
For at their hands I have deserv'd no pity.
The air hath got into my deadly wounds,
And much effuse of blood doth make me faint.
Come, York and Richard, Warwick and the rest;
I stabb'd your fathers' bosoms, split my breast.　*[He faints.]*

*Alarum and Retreat. Enter Edward, Warwick, Richard, and
Soldiers, Montague and Clarence.*

　　Edw. Now breathe we, lords: good fortune bids us pause,
And smooth the frowns of war with peaceful looks.
Some troops pursue the bloody-minded queen,
That led calm Henry, though he were a king,
As doth a sail, fill'd with a fretting gust,　　35
Command an argosy to stem the waves.
But think you, lords, that Clifford fled with them?

　　War. No, 'tis impossible he should escape;
For, though before his face I speak the words,
Your brother Richard mark'd him for the grave;　40
And wheresoe'er he is, he's surely dead.
　　　　　　　　　　　　　　Clifford groans [and dies].

　　Edw. Whose soul is that which takes her heavy leave:

　　Rich. A deadly groan, like life and death's departing.

　　Edw. See who it is: and now the battle's ended,
If friend or foe let him be gently us'd.　　　45

　　Rich. Revoke that doom of mercy, for 'tis Clifford;
Who not contented that he lopp'd the branch
In hewing Rutland when his leaves put forth,
But set his murth'ring knife unto the root

87 Upon: *at sight of*　90 Erroneous: *criminal*　93 late: *recently*　95 ruthful: *pitiable*　100
presenteth: *symbolize*　104 Take on: *rave*　108 Misthink: *think ill of*　118 obsequious: *dutiful
in mourning*　123 overgone: *oppressed*　126 chafed: *angered*　131 very: *veritable*

S. d.; *cf. n.*　5 My . . . fear: *love and fear of me*　6 commixtures: *compounds, substances
held together by glue*　7 Impairing: *weakening*　8 Cf. n.　12 check: *curb, manage*　17 sprung: *propagated*　28 effuse: *shedding.*　36 argosy: *large merchant vessel*　42–44 Cf. n.　46 doom: *judgment*　48 when . . . forth: *in youth*

From whence that tender spray did sweetly spring,   *50*
I mean our princely father, Duke of York.

    War. From off the gates of York fetch down the head,
Your father's head, which Clifford placed there;
Instead whereof let this supply the room:
Measure for measure must be answered.   *55*

    Edw. Bring forth that fatal screech-owl to our house,
That nothing sung but death to us and ours:
Now death shall stop his dismal threatening sound,
And his ill-boding tongue no more shall speak.

    War. I think his understanding is bereft.   *60*
Speak, Clifford; dost thou know who speaks to thee?
Dark cloudy death o'ershades his beams of life,
And he nor sees, nor hears us what we say.

    Rich. O! would he did; and so perhaps he doth;
'Tis but his policy to counterfeit,   *65*
Because he would avoid such bitter taunts
Which in the time of death he gave our father.

    Clar. If so thou think'st, vex him with eager words.

    Rich. Clifford! ask mercy and obtain no grace.

    Edw. Clifford, repent in bootless penitence.   *70*

    War. Clifford! devise excuses for thy faults.

    Clar. While we devise fell tortures for thy faults.

    Rich. Thou didst love York, and I am son to York.

    Edw. Thou pitiedst Rutland, I will pity thee.

    Clar. Where's Captain Margaret, to fence you now?   *75*

    War. They mock thee, Clifford: swear as thou wast wont.

    Rich. What! not an oath? nay, then the world goes hard
When Clifford cannot spare his friends an oath.
I know by that he's dead; and, by my soul,
If this right hand would buy two hours' life,   *80*
That I in all despite might rail at him,
This hand should chop it off, and with the issuing blood
Stifle the villain whose unstaunched thirst
York and young Rutland could not satisfy.

    War. Ay, but he's dead: off with the traitor's head,   *85*
And rear it in the place your father's stands.
And now to London with triumphant march,
There to be crowned England's royal king:
From whence shall Warwick cut the sea to France,
And ask the Lady Bona for thy queen.   *90*
So shalt thou sinew both these lands together;
And, having France thy friend, thou shalt not dread
The scatter'd foe that hopes to rise again;
For though they cannot greatly sting to hurt,
Yet look to have them buzz to offend thine ears.   *95*
First will I see the coronation;
And then to Brittany I'll cross the sea,
To effect this marriage, so it please my lord.

    Edw. Even as thou wilt, sweet Warwick, let it be;
For in thy shoulder do I build my seat,   *100*
And never will I undertake the thing
Wherein thy counsel and consent is wanting.
Richard, I will create thee Duke of Gloucester;
And George, of Clarence; Warwick, as ourself,
Shall do and undo as him pleaseth best.   *105*

    Rich. Let me be Duke of Clarence, George of Gloucester,

For Gloucester's dukedom is too ominous.

    War. Tut! that's a foolish observation:
Richard, be Duke of Gloucester. Now to London.
To see these honours in possession.   *Exeunt.*   *110*

ACT THIRD ❦ SCENE FIRST

[A Chase in the North of England]
Enter Sinklo and Humphrey [two gamekeepers], with cross-bows in
their hands.

    Sink. Under this thick-grown brake we'll shroud ourselves;
For through this laund anon the deer will come;
And in this covert will we make our stand,
Culling the principal of all the deer.

    Hum. I'll stay above the hill, so both may shoot.   *5*

    Sink. That cannot be; the noise of thy cross-bow
Will scare the herd, and so my shoot is lost.
Here stand we both, and aim we at the best:
And, for the time shall not seem tedious,
I'll tell thee what befell me on a day   *10*
In this self place where now we mean to stand.

    Hum. Here comes a man; let's stay till he be past.

Enter the King, with a prayer-book.

    Hen. From Scotland am I stol'n, even of pure love,
To greet mine own land with my wishful sight.
No, Harry, Harry, 'tis no land of thine;   *15*
Thy place is fill'd, thy sceptre wrung from thee,
Thy balm wash'd off wherewith thou was anointed:
No bending knee will call thee Cæsar now,
No humble suitors press to speak for right,
No, not a man comes for redress of thee;   *20*
For how can I help them, and not myself?

    Sink. Ay, here's a deer whose skin's a keeper's fee:
This is the quondam king; let's seize upon him.

    Hen. Let me embrace thee, sour adversity,
For wise men say it is the wisest course.   *25*

    Hum. Why linger we? let us lay hands upon him.

    Sink. Forbear awhile; we'll hear a little more.

    Hen. My queen and son are gone to France for aid;
And, as I hear, the great commanding Warwick
Is thither gone, to crave the French king's sister   *30*
To wife for Edward. If this news be true,
Poor queen and son, your labour is but lost;
For Warwick is a subtle orator,
And Lewis a prince soon won with moving words.
By this account then Margaret may win him,   *35*
For she's a woman to be pitied much:
Her sighs will make a battery in his breast;
Her tears will pierce into a marble heart;
The tiger will be mild whiles she doth mourn;
And Nero will be tainted with remorse,   *40*
To hear and see her plaints, her brinish tears.
Ay, but she's come to beg; Warwick, to give:

---

49 But set; *cf. n.*   **54 supply the room:** *take its place*   **55** *Treatment given must corre-*
spond to treatment received   **60 understanding:** *consciousness*   **67 Which:** *as*   **68**
eager: *biting*   **75 fence:** *shield*   **77 goes hard:** *has come to a hard pass*   **81 despite:**
obloquy   **83 unstaunched:** *insatiable*   **90 Lady Bona;** *cf. n.*   **91 sinew:** *join*

107 *Cf. n.*   **SCENE ONE** S. d. *Sinklo and Humphrey; cf. n.*   **2 laund:** *glade*   **4**
Culling: *selecting*   **9 for:** *in order that*   **11 self:** *very*   **12 stay:** *postpone action*   **14**
wishful: *longing*   **17 balm:** *consecrated oil*   **was:** *wast*   **19 speak for right:** *crave jus-*
tice   **20 of:** *from*   **22 fee:** *perquisite*   **23 quondam:** *one-time, former*   **24**
Cf. n.   **37 battery:** *bruise*   **40 tainted:** *touched*

She on his left side, craving aid for Henry;
He on his right, asking a wife for Edward.
She weeps, and says her Henry is depos'd;   45
He smiles, and says his Edward is install'd;
That she, poor wretch, for grief can speak no more:
Whiles Warwick tells his title, smooths the wrong,
Inferreth arguments of mighty strength,
And in conclusion wins the king from her,   50
With promise of his sister, and what else,
To strengthen and support King Edward's place.
O Margaret! thus 'twill be; and thou, poor soul,
Art then forsaken, as thou went'st forlorn.

   Hum. Say, what art thou, that talk'st of kings and queens?   55
   King. More than I seem, and less than I was born to:
A man at least, for less I should not be;
And men may talk of kings, and why not I?
   Hum. Ay, but thou talk'st as if thou wert a king.
   King. Why, so I am, in mind; and that's enough.   60
   Hum. But, if thou be a king, where is thy crown?
   King. My crown is in my heart, not on my head;
Not deck'd with diamonds and Indian stones,
Nor to be seen: my crown is call'd content;
A crown it is that seldom kings enjoy.   65
   Hum. Well, if you be a king crown'd with content,
Your crown content and you must be contented
To go along with us; for, as we think,
You are the king King Edward hath depos'd;
And we his subjects, sworn in all allegiance,   70
Will apprehend you as his enemy.
   King. But did you never swear, and break an oath?
   Hum. No, never such an oath; nor will not now.
   King. Where did you dwell when I was King of England?
   Hum. Here in this country, where we now remain.   75
   King. I was anointed king at nine months old;
My father and my grandfather were kings,
And you were sworn true subjects unto me:
And tell me, then, have you not broke your oaths?
   Sink. No;   80
For we were subjects but while you were king.
   King. Why, am I dead? do I not breathe a man?
Ah! simple men, you know not what you swear.
Look, as I blow this feather from my face,
And as the air blows it to me again,   85
Obeying with my wind when I do blow,
And yielding to another when it blows,
Commanded always by the greater gust;
Such is the lightness of you common men.
But do not break your oaths; for of that sin   90
My mild entreaty shall not make you guilty.
Go where you will, the king shall be commanded;
And be you kings: command, and I'll obey.
   Sink. We are true subjects to the king, King Edward.
   King. So would you be again to Henry,   95
If he were seated as King Edward is.
   Sink. We charge you, in God's name and the king's,
To go with us unto the officers.
   King. In God's name, lead; your king's name be obey'd:
And what God will, that let your king perform;   100
And what he will, I humbly yield unto.   *Exeunt.*

47 **That:** *so that*   48 **smooths:** *glosses over*   50 **in conclusion:** *finally*   51 **what else:** *anything else he desires*   57 **should not:** *could hardly*   71 **apprehend:** *arrest*

❧ Scene Second ❧

[London. A Room in the Palace]
Enter King Edward, Gloucester, Clarence, Lady Grey.

   K. Edw. Brother of Gloucester, at Saint Albans field
This lady's husband, Sir John Grey, was slain,
His lands then seiz'd on by the conqueror:
Her suit is now, to repossess those lands;
Which we in justice cannot well deny,   5
Because in quarrel of the house of York
The worthy gentleman did lose his life.
   Rich. Your highness shall do well to grant her suit;
It were dishonour to deny it her.
   K. Edw. It were no less: but yet I'll make a pause.   10
   Rich. [Aside to Clarence.] Yea; is it so?
I see the lady hath a thing to grant,
Before the king will grant her humble suit.
   Clar. [Aside to Richard.] He knows the game: how true
he keeps the wind!   15
   Rich. [Aside to Clarence.] Silence!
   K. Edw. Widow, we will consider of your suit,
And come some other time to know our mind.
   Widow. Right gracious lord, I cannot brook delay:
May it please your highness to resolve me now,   20
And what your pleasure is shall satisfy me.
   Rich. [Aside to Clarence.] Ay, widow? then I'll warrant
you all your lands,
An if what pleases him shall pleasure you:
Fight closer, or, good faith, you'll catch a blow.   25
   Clar. [Aside to Richard.] I fear her not, unless she chance
to fall.
   Glo. [Aside to Clarence.] God forbid that! for he'll
take vantages.
   K. Edw. How many children hast thou, widow? tell me.   30
   Clar. [Aside to Richard.] I think he means to beg a
child of her.
   Glo. [Aside to Clarence.] Nay, then, whip me; he'll rather
give her two.
   Widow. Three, my most gracious lord.   35
   Glo. [Aside to Clarence.] You shall have four, if you'll be
rul'd by him.
   K. Edw. 'Twere pity they should lose their father's lands.
   Widow. Be pitiful, dread lord, and grant it then.
   K. Edw. Lords, give us leave: I'll try this widow's wit.   40
   Rich. [Aside to Clarence.] Ay, good leave have you; for
you will have leave,
Till youth take leave and leave you to the crutch.
                               [Retiring with Clarence.]
   K. Edw. Now, tell me, madam, do you love your children?
   Widow. Ay, full as dearly as I love myself.   45
   K. Edw. And would you not do much to do them good?
   Widow. To do them good I would sustain some harm.
   K. Edw. Then get your husband's lands, to do them good.
   Widow. Therefore I came unto your majesty.
   K. Edw. I'll tell you how these lands are to be got.   50
   Widow. So shall you bind me to your highness' service.
   K. Edw. What service wilt thou do me, if I give them?
   Widow. What you command, that rests in me to do.

6, 7 **Cf.** *n.*   10 **pause:** *delay*   14 **wind:** *advantageous position*   17 **of:** *concerning*   18 **And:** *and therefore*   20 **resolve:** *free from anxiety*   26 **fear:** *fear for*

K. Edw. But you will take exceptions to my boon.

Widow. No, gracious lord, except I cannot do it.   55

K. Edw. Ay, but thou canst do what I mean to ask.

Widow. Why, then I will do what your Grace commands.

Rich. [Aside to Clarence.] He plies her hard; and much rain wears the marble.

Clar. [Aside to Richard.] As red as fire! nay, then her   60 wax must melt.

Widow. Why stops my lord? shall I not hear my task?

K. Edw. An easy task: 'tis but to love a king.

Widow. That's soon perform'd, because I am a subject.

K. Edw. Why then, thy husband's lands I freely give thee.   65

Widow. I take my leave with many thousand thanks.

Rich. [Aside to Clarence.] The match is made; she seals it with a curtsy.

K. Edw. But stay thee; 'tis the fruits of love I mean.

Widow. The fruits of love I mean, my loving liege.   70

K. Edw. Ay, but, I fear me, in another sense. What love think'st thou I sue so much to get?

Widow. My love till death, my humble thanks, my prayers: That love which virtue begs and virtue grants.

K. Edw. No, by my troth, I did not mean such love.   75

Widow. Why, then you mean not as I thought you did.

K. Edw. But now you partly may perceive my mind.

Widow. My mind will never grant what I perceive Your highness aims at, if I aim aright.

K. Edw. To tell thee plain, I aim to lie with thee.   80

Widow. To tell you plain, I had rather lie in prison.

K. Edw. Why, then thou shalt not have thy husband's lands.

Widow. Why, then mine honesty shall be my dower; For by that loss I will not purchase them.

K. Edw. Therein thou wrong'st thy children mightily.   85

Widow. Herein your highness wrongs both them and me. But, mighty lord, this merry inclination Accords not with the sadness of my suit: Please you dismiss me, either with 'ay,' or 'no.'

K. Edw. Ay, if thou wilt say 'ay' to my request;   90 No, if thou dost say 'no' to my demand.

Widow. Then, no, my lord. My suit is at an end.

Rich. [Aside to Clarence.] The widow likes him not, she knits her brows.

Clar. [Aside to Richard.] He is the bluntest wooer in   95 Christendom.

K. Edw. [Aside.] Her looks do argue her replete with modesty; Her words do show her wit incomparable; All her perfections challenge sovereignty: One way or other, she is for a king;   100 And she shall be my love, or else my queen. Say that King Edward take thee for his queen?

Widow. 'Tis better said than done, my gracious lord: I am a subject fit to jest withal, But far unfit to be a sovereign.   105

K. Edw. Sweet widow, by my state I swear to thee, I speak no more than what my soul intends; And that is, to enjoy thee for my love.

Widow. And that is more than I will yield unto. I know I am too mean to be your queen,   110 And yet too good to be your concubine.

K. Edw. You cavil, widow: I did mean, my queen.

Widow. 'Twill grieve your Grace my sons should call you father.

K. Edw. No more than when my daughters call thee mother. Thou art a widow, and thou hast some children; And, by God's mother, I, being but a bachelor, Have other some: why, 'tis a happy thing To be the father unto many sons. Answer no more, for thou shalt be my queen.   120

Rich. [Aside to Clarence.] The ghostly father now hath done his shrift.

Clar. [Aside to Richard.] When he was made a shriver, 'twas for shift.

K. Edw. Brothers, you muse what chat we two have had.   125

Rich. The widow likes it not, for she looks very sad.

K. Edw. You'd think it strange if I should marry her.

Clar. To whom, my lord?

K. Edw. Why, Clarence, to myself.

Rich. That would be ten days' wonder at the least.   130

Clar. That's a day longer than a wonder lasts.

Rich. By so much is the wonder in extremes.

K. Edw. Well, jest on, brothers: I can tell you both Her suit is granted for her husband's lands.

Enter a Nobleman.

Nob. My gracious lord, Henry your foe is taken,   135 And brought as prisoner to your palace gate.

K. Edw. See that he be convey'd unto the Tower: And go we, brothers, to the man that took him, To question of his apprehension. Widow, go you along. Lords, use her honourably.   140

Exeunt. Manet Richard.

Rich. Ay, Edward will use women honourably. Would he were wasted, marrow, bones, and all, That from his loins no hopeful branch may spring, To cross me from the golden time I look for! And yet, between my soul's desire and me—   145 The lustful Edward's title buried,— Is Clarence, Henry, and his son young Edward, And all the unlook'd for issue of their bodies, To take their rooms, ere I can place myself: A cold premeditation for my purpose!   150 Why then, I do but dream on sovereignty; Like one that stands upon a promontory, And spies a far-off shore where he would tread, Wishing his foot were equal with his eye; And chides the sea that sunders him from thence,   155 Saying, he'll lade it dry to have his way: So do I wish the crown, being so far off, And so I chide the means that keeps me from it, And so I say I'll cut the causes off, Flatt'ring me with impossibilities.   160 My eye's too quick, my heart o'erweens too much, Unless my hand and strength could equal them. Well, say there is no kingdom then for Richard; What other pleasure can the world afford? I'll make my heaven in a lady's lap,   165

---

118 other some: *some others*   **122 for shift:** *to serve a crafty purpose*   **125 muse:** *wonder*   **131** *Cf. n.*   **149 rooms:** *places*   **150 cold premeditation:** *unfavorable augury*   **156 lade:** *empty*   **158 means:** *intervening obstacles*   **160 me:** *myself*   **161 o'erweens too much:** *is too presumptuous*

54 boon: *petition*   **79 aims at:** *intends*   **aim:** *guess*   **83 honesty:** *virtue*   **88 sadness:** *seriousness*   **97 argue:** *prove*

And deck my body in gay ornaments,
And witch sweet ladies with my words and looks.
O miserable thought! and more unlikely
Than to accomplish twenty golden crowns.
Why, love forswore me in my mother's womb: *170*
And, for I should not deal in her soft laws,
She did corrupt frail nature with some bribe,
To shrink mine arm up like a wither'd shrub;
To make an envious mountain on my back,
Where sits deformity to mock my body;   *175*
To shape my legs of an unequal size;
To disproportion me in every part,
Like to a chaos, or an unlick'd bear-whelp
That carries no impression like the dam.
And am I then a man to be belov'd?   *180*
O monstrous fault! to harbour such a thought.
Then, since this earth affords no joy to me
But to command, to check, to o'erbear such
As are of better person than myself,
I'll make my heaven to dream upon the crown;   *185*
And, whiles I live, to account this world but hell,
Until my misshap'd trunk that bears this head
Be round impaled with a glorious crown.
And yet I know not how to get the crown,
For many lives stand between me and home: *190*
And I, like one lost in a thorny wood,
That rents the thorns and is rent with the thorns,
Seeking a way and straying from the way;
Not knowing how to find the open air,
But toiling desperately to find it out,   *195*
Torment myself to catch the English crown:
And from that torment I will free myself,
Or hew my way out with a bloody axe.
Why, I can smile, and murther whiles I smile,
And cry, 'Content,' to that which grieves my heart,   *200*
And wet my cheeks with artificial tears,
And frame my face to all occasions.
I'll drown more sailors than the mermaid shall;
I'll slay more gazers than the basilisk;
I'll play the orator as well as Nestor,   *205*
Deceive more slily than Ulysses could,
And, like a Sinon, take another Troy.
I can add colours to the chameleon,
Change shapes with Proteus for advantages,
And set the murtherous Machiavel to school.   *210*
Can I do this, and cannot get a crown?
Tut! were it farther off, I'll pluck it down.   *Exit.*

❧ SCENE THIRD ❧

[Paris. A Room in the Palace]

*Flourish. Enter Lewis the French King, his sister Bona; his Admiral
called Bourbon; Prince Edward, Queen Margaret, and the Earl of
Oxford. Lewis sits, and riseth up again.*

Lew. Fair Queen of England, worthy Margaret,
Sit down with us: it ill befits thy state
And birth, that thou shouldst stand while Lewis doth sit.
    Mar. No, mighty King of France: now Margaret
Must strike her sail, and learn a while to serve   *5*
Where kings command. I was, I must confess,
Great Albion's queen in former golden days;
But now mischance hath trod my title down,
And with dishonour laid me on the ground,
Where I must take like seat unto my fortune,   *10*
And to my humble seat conform myself.
    Lew. Why, say, fair queen, whence springs this deep despair?
    Mar. From such a cause as fills mine eyes with tears
And stops my tongue, while heart is drown'd in cares.
    Lew. Whate'er it be, be thou still like thyself,   *15*
And sit thee by our side. *Seats her by him.* Yield not thy neck
To fortune's yoke, but let thy dauntless mind
Still ride in triumph over all mischance.
Be plain, Queen Margaret, and tell thy grief;
It shall be eas'd, if France can yield relief.   *20*
    Mar. Those gracious words revive my drooping thoughts,
And give my tongue-tied sorrows leave to speak.
Now, therefore, be it known to noble Lewis,
That Henry, sole possessor of my love,
Is of a king become a banish'd man,   *25*
And forc'd to live in Scotland a forlorn;
While proud ambitious Edward, Duke of York,
Usurps the regal title and the seat
Of England's true-anointed lawful king.
This is the cause that I, poor Margaret,   *30*
With this my son, Prince Edward, Henry's heir,
Am come to crave thy just and lawful aid;
And if thou fail us, all our hope is done.
Scotland hath will to help, but cannot help;
Our people and our peers are both misled,   *35*
Our treasure seiz'd, our soldiers put to flight,
And, as thou seest, ourselves in heavy plight.
    Lew. Renowned queen, with patience calm the storm,
While we bethink a means to break it off.
    Mar. The more we stay, the stronger grows our foe.   *40*
    Lew. The more I stay, the more I'll succour thee.
    Mar. O! but impatience waiteth on true sorrow:
And see where comes the breeder of my sorrow.

Enter Warwick.

Lew. What's he approacheth boldly to our presence?
    Mar. Our Earl of Warwick, Edward's greatest friend.   *45*
    Lew. Welcome, brave Warwick! What brings thee to France?
                                He descends. She ariseth.
    Mar. Ay, now begins a second storm to rise;
For this is he that moves both wind and tide.
    War. From worthy Edward, King of Albion,

---

167 **witch:** *bewitch, charm*   179 **carries ... dam:** *has nothing of its mother's shape;
cf. n.*   183 **check:** *control*   188 **impaled:** *encircled*   190 **home:** *the goal*   192 **rents:**
tears, rends   204 **basilisk:** *fabulous reptile whose sight was death*   208 **add ... to:** *assume
more colors than*   209 **for advantages:** *as my purpose requires*   210 *Give Machiavelli
himself lessons in murder; cf. n.*

2 **state:** *dignity*   16 **sit thee:** *seat thyself*   16–18 *Cf. n.*   25 **of:** *from being*   26
forlorn: *outcast*   39 **break it off:** *cut it short*   42 **waiteth on:** *attends*   44 **he:** *he
who*

My lord and sovereign, and thy vowed friend,   *50*
I come, in kindness and unfeigned love,
First, to do greetings to thy royal person;
And then to crave a league of amity;
And lastly to confirm that amity
With nuptial knot, if thou vouchsafe to grant   *55*
That virtuous Lady Bona, thy fair sister,
To England's king in lawful marriage.
 Mar. If that go forward, Henry's hope is done.
 War. And, gracious madam,   *Speaking to Bona.*
  in our king's behalf,   *60*
I am commanded, with your leave and favour,
Humbly to kiss your hand, and with my tongue
To tell the passion of my sovereign's heart;
Where fame, late entering at his heedful ears,
Hath plac'd thy beauty's image and thy virtue.   *65*
 Mar. King Lewis and Lady Bona, hear me speak,
Before you answer Warwick. His demand
Springs not from Edward's well-meant honest love,
But from deceit bred by necessity;
For how can tyrants safely govern home,   *70*
Unless abroad they purchase great alliance?
To prove him tyrant this reason may suffice,
That Henry liveth still; but were he dead,
Yet here Prince Edward stands, King Henry's son.
Look, therefore, Lewis, that by this league and marriage   *75*
Thou draw not on thy danger and dishonour;
For though usurpers sway the rule awhile,
Yet heavens are just, and time suppresseth wrongs.
 War. Injurious Margaret!
 Prince.   And why not queen?   *80*
 War. Because thy father Henry did usurp,
And thou no more art prince than she is queen.
 Oxf. Then Warwick disannuls great John of Gaunt,
Which did subdue the greatest part of Spain;
And, after John of Gaunt, Henry the Fourth,   *85*
Whose wisdom was a mirror to the wisest;
And, after that wise prince, Henry the Fifth,
Who by his prowess conquered all France:
From these our Henry lineally descends.
 War. Oxford, how haps it, in this smooth discourse,   *90*
You told not how Henry the Sixth hath lost
All that which Henry the Fifth had gotten?
Methinks these peers of France should smile at that.
But for the rest, you tell a pedigree
Of threescore and two years; a silly time   *95*
To make prescription for a kingdom's worth.
 Oxf. Why, Warwick, canst thou speak against thy liege,
Whom thou obeyedst thirty and six years,
And not bewray thy treason with a blush?
 War. Can Oxford, that did ever fence the right,   *100*
Now buckler falsehood with a pedigree?
For shame! leave Henry, and call Edward king.
 Oxf. Call him my king, by whose injurious doom
My elder brother, the Lord Aubrey Vere,
Was done to death? and more than so, my father,   *105*
Even in the downfall of his mellow'd years,
When nature brought him to the door of death?

No, Warwick, no; while life upholds this arm,
This arm upholds the house of Lancaster.
 War. And I the house of York.   *110*
 Lew. Queen Margaret, Prince Edward, and Oxford,
Vouchsafe at our request to stand aside,
While I use further conference with Warwick.

    They stand aloof.

 Mar. Heaven grant that Warwick's words bewitch him
not!   *115*
 Lew. Now, Warwick, tell me, even upon thy conscience,
Is Edward your true king? for I were loath
To link with him that were not lawful chosen.
 War. Thereon I pawn my credit and mine honour.
 Lew. But is he gracious in the people's eye?   *120*
 War. The more that Henry was unfortunate.
 Lew. Then further, all dissembling set aside,
Tell me for truth the measure of his love
Unto our sister Bona.
 War.   Such it seems   *125*
As may beseem a monarch like himself.
Myself have often heard him say and swear
That this his love was an eternal plant,
Whereof the root was fix'd in virtue's ground,
The leaves and fruit maintain'd with beauty's sun,   *130*
Exempt from envy, but not from disdain,
Unless the Lady Bona quit his pain.
 Lew. Now, sister, let us hear your firm resolve.
 Bona. Your grant, or your denial, shall be mine:
Yet I confess that often ere this day,   *Speaks to War.*   *135*
When I have heard your king's desert recounted,
Mine ear hath tempted judgment to desire.
 Lew. Then, Warwick, thus: our sister shall be Edward's;
And now forthwith shall articles be drawn
Touching the jointure that your king must make,   *140*
Which with her dowry shall be counterpois'd.
Draw near, Queen Margaret, and be a witness
That Bona shall be wife to the English king.
 Prince. To Edward, but not to the English king.
 Mar. Deceitful Warwick! it was thy device   *145*
By this alliance to make void my suit:
Before thy coming Lewis was Henry's friend.
 Lew. And still is friend to him and Margaret:
But if your title to the crown be weak,
As may appear by Edward's good success,   *150*
Then 'tis but reason that I be releas'd
From giving aid which late I promised.
Yet shall you have all kindness at my hand
That your estate requires and mine can yield.
 War. Henry now lives in Scotland at his ease,   *155*
Where having nothing, nothing can he lose.
And as for you yourself, our quondam queen,
You have a father able to maintain you,
And better 'twere you troubled him than France.
 Mar. Peace! impudent and shameless Warwick, peace;   *160*
Proud setter up and puller down of kings;
I will not hence, till, with my talk and tears,
Both full of truth, I make King Lewis behold

---

64 **fame:** *report* 79 **Injurious:** *insulting* 83, 84 *Cf. n.* 84 **disannuls:** *makes nothing of* 96 **prescription:** *right based on immemorial custom* 97, 98 *Cf. n.* 101 **buckler:** *shield, defend* 103 **injurious:** *unjust; cf. n.* 105 **more than so:** *yet more*

118 **lawful:** *lawfully* 121 **unfortunate:** *a breeder of misfortune* 131 *Cf. n.* 132 **quit his pain:** *requite his longing* 134 **grant:** *assent* 136 **desert:** *merit* 140 **jointure:** *property settled on wife at marriage* 141 **counterpois'd:** *equalled* 161 *Cf. n.*

Thy sly conveyance and thy lord's false love;
For both of you are birds of self-same feather. *165*

Post blowing a horn within.

Lew. Warwick, this is some post to us or thee.

Enter the Post.

Post. My lord ambassador, these letters are for you,
           Speaks to Warwick.
Sent from your brother, Marquess Montague:
These from our king unto your majesty. *To Lewis.*
And, madam, these for you; from whom I know not. *To Margaret.*

They all read their letters.

Oxf. I like it well that our fair queen and mistress
Smiles at her news, while Warwick frowns at his.

Prince. Nay, mark how Lewis stamps as he were nettled:
I hope all's for the best.

Lew. Warwick, what are thy news? and yours, fair queen? *175*

Mar. Mine, such as fill my heart with unhop'd joys.

War. Mine, full of sorrow and heart's discontent.

Lew. What! has your king married the Lady Grey?
And now, to soothe your forgery and his,
Sends me a paper to persuade me patience? *180*
Is this the alliance that he seeks with France?
Dare he presume to scorn us in this manner?

Mar. I told your majesty as much before:
This proveth Edward's love and Warwick's honesty.

War. King Lewis, I here protest, in sight of heaven, *185*
And by the hope I have of heavenly bliss,
That I am clear from this misdeed of Edward's;
No more my king, for he dishonours me,—
But most himself, if he could see his shame.
Did I forget that by the house of York *190*
My father came untimely to his death?
Did I let pass th' abuse done to my niece?
Did I impale him with the regal crown?
Did I put Henry from his native right?
And am I guerdon'd at the last with shame? *195*
Shame on himself! for my desert is honour:
And, to repair my honour, lost for him,
I here renounce him and return to Henry.
My noble queen, let former grudges pass,
And henceforth I am thy true servitor. *200*
I will revenge his wrong to Lady Bona,
And replant Henry in his former state.

Mar. Warwick, these words have turn'd my hate to love;
And I forgive and quite forget old faults,
And joy that thou becom'st King Henry's friend. *205*

War. So much his friend, ay, his unfeigned friend,
That, if King Lewis vouchsafe to furnish us
With some few bands of chosen soldiers,
I'll undertake to land them on our coast,
And force the tyrant from his seat by war. *210*
'Tis not his new-made bride shall succour him:
And as for Clarence, as my letters tell me,
He's very likely now to fall from him,
For matching more for wanton lust than honour,
Or than for strength and safety of our country. *215*

Bona. Dear brother, how shall Bona be reveng'd,
But by thy help to this distressed queen?

Mar. Renowned prince, how shall poor Henry live,
Unless thou rescue him from foul despair?

Bona. My quarrel and this English queen's are one. *220*

War. And mine, fair Lady Bona, joins with yours.

Lew. And mine with hers, and thine and Margaret's.
Therefore, at last, I firmly am resolv'd
You shall have aid.

Mar. Let me give humble thanks for all at once. *225*

Lew. Then, England's messenger, return in post,
And tell false Edward, thy supposed king,
That Lewis of France is sending over masquers,
To revel it with him and his new bride.
Thou seest what's past; go fear thy king withal. *230*

Bona. Tell him, in hope he'll prove a widower shortly,
I wear the willow garland for his sake.

Mar. Tell him, my mourning weeds are laid aside,
And I am ready to put armour on.

War. Tell him from me, that he hath done me wrong, *235*
And therefore I'll uncrown him ere 't be long.
There's thy reward: be gone. *Exit Post.*

Lew.   But, Warwick,
Thou and Oxford, with five thousand men,
Shall cross the seas, and bid false Edward battle; *240*
And, as occasion serves, this noble queen
And prince shall follow with a fresh supply.
Yet ere thou go, but answer me one doubt:
What pledge have we of thy firm loyalty?

War. This shall assure my constant loyalty: *245*
That if our queen and this young prince agree,
I'll join mine eldest daughter and my joy
To him forthwith in holy wedlock bands.

Mar. Yes, I agree, and thank you for your motion.
Son Edward, she is fair and virtuous, *250*
Therefore delay not, give thy hand to Warwick;
And, with thy hand, thy faith irrevocable,
That only Warwick's daughter shall be thine.

Prince. Yes, I accept her, for she well deserves it;
And here, to pledge my vow, I give my hand. *255*
     He gives his hand to Warwick.

Lew. Why stay we now? These soldiers shall be levied,
And thou, Lord Bourbon, our high admiral,
Shall waft them over with our royal fleet.
I long till Edward fall by war's mischance,
For mocking marriage with a dame of France. *260*
     Exeunt. Manet Warwick.

War. I came from Edward as ambassador,
But I return his sworn and mortal foe:
Matter of marriage was the charge he gave me,
But dreadful war shall answer his demand.
Had he none else to make a stale but me? *265*
Then none but I shall turn his jest to sorrow.
I was the chief that rais'd him to the crown,
And I'll be chief to bring him down again:
Not that I pity Henry's misery,
But seek revenge on Edward's mockery. *Exit.* *270*

---

164 conveyance: *deceit* **166 post:** *messenger bearing letters* **173 as:** *as if* **179 soothe your forgery:** *palliate your deceit* **190, 191** *Cf. n.* **192** *Cf. n.* **194 native:** *innate* **195 guerdon'd:** *rewarded*

227 supposed: *pretended* **230 what's past:** *what has happened* **fear:** *frighten* **withal:** *therewith* **232 willow garland:** *emblem of unhappy love* **240 bid:** *offer* **247 eldest daughter;** *cf. n.* **249 motion:** *offer* **258 waft:** *convey by water* **259 long till:** *am impatient that* **265 stale:** *dupe* **267 chief:** *principal means*

ACT FOURTH ❧ SCENE FIRST

[London. A Room in the Palace]
Enter Richard, Clarence, Somerset, and Montague.

Rich. Now tell me, brother Clarence, what think you
Of this new marriage with the Lady Grey?
Hath not our brother made a worthy choice?
   Clar. Alas! you know, 'tis far from hence to France;
How could he stay till Warwick made return?   *5*
   Som. My lords, forbear this talk; here comes the king.

Flourish. Enter King Edward, Lady Grey, Pembroke, Stafford,
   Hastings. Four stand on one side, and four on the other.

   Rich. And his well-chosen bride.
   Clar. I mind to tell him plainly what I think.
   K. Edw. Now, brother of Clarence, how like you our
choice,   *10*
That you stand pensive, as half malcontent?
   Clar. As well as Lewis of France, or the Earl of Warwick,
Which are so weak of courage and in judgment
That they'll take no offence at our abuse.
   K. Edw. Suppose they take offence without a cause,   *15*
They are but Lewis and Warwick: I am Edward,
Your king and Warwick's, and must have my will.
   Rich. And shall have your will, because our king:
Yet hasty marriage seldom proveth well.
   K. Edw. Yea, brother Richard, are you offended too?   *20*
   Rich. Not I:
No, God forbid, that I should wish them sever'd
Whom God hath join'd together: ay, and 'twere pity
To sunder them that yoke so well together.
   K. Edw. Setting your scorns and your mislike aside,   *25*
Tell me some reason why the Lady Grey
Should not become my wife and England's queen:
And you too, Somerset and Montague,
Speak freely what you think.
   Clar. Then this is mine opinion: that King Lewis   *30*
Becomes your enemy for mocking him
About the marriage of the Lady Bona.
   Rich. And Warwick, doing what you gave in charge,
Is now dishonoured by this new marriage.
   K. Edw. What if both Lewis and Warwick be appeas'd   *35*
By such invention as I can devise?
   Mont. Yet to have join'd with France in such alliance
Would more have strengthen'd this our commonwealth
'Gainst foreign storms, than any home-bred marriage.
   Hast. Why, knows not Montague, that of itself   *40*
England is safe, if true within itself?
   Mont. Yes; but the safer when 'tis back'd with France.
   Hast. 'Tis better using France than trusting France:
Let us be back'd with God and with the seas
Which he hath given for fence impregnable;   *45*
And with their helps only defend ourselves:
In them and in ourselves our safety lies.
   Clar. For this one speech Lord Hastings well deserves
To have the heir of the Lord Hungerford.
   K. Edw. Ay, what of that? it was my will and grant;   *50*

And for this once my will shall stand for law.
   Rich. And yet methinks your Grace hath not done well,
To give the heir and daughter of Lord Scales
Unto the brother of your loving bride:
She better would have fitted me or Clarence: *55*
But in your bride you bury brotherhood.
   Clar. Or else you would not have bestow'd the heir
Of the Lord Bonville on your new wife's son,
And leave your brothers to go speed elsewhere.
   K. Edw. Alas, poor Clarence, is it for a wife   *60*
That thou art malcontent? I will provide thee.
   Clar. In choosing for yourself you show'd your judgment,
Which being shallow, you shall give me leave
To play the broker on mine own behalf;
And to that end I shortly mind to leave you.   *65*
   K. Edw. Leave me, or tarry, Edward will be king,
And not be tied unto his brother's will.
   L. Grey. My lords, before it pleas'd his majesty
To raise my state to title of a queen,
Do me but right, and you must all confess   *70*
That I was not ignoble of descent;
And meaner than myself have had like fortune.
But as this title honours me and mine,
So your dislikes, to whom I would be pleasing,
Do cloud my joys with danger and with sorrow.   *75*
   K. Edw. My love, forbear to fawn upon their frowns:
What danger or what sorrow can befall thee,
So long as Edward is thy constant friend
And their true sovereign, whom they must obey?
Nay, whom they shall obey, and love thee too,   *80*
Unless they seek for hatred at my hands;
Which if they do, yet will I keep thee safe,
And they shall feel the vengeance of my wrath.
   Rich. [*Aside.*] I hear, yet say not much, but think the more.

Enter a Post.

   K. Edw. Now, messenger, what letters or what news   *85*
From France?
   Post. My sovereign liege, no letters; and few words,
But such as I, without your special pardon,
Dare not relate.
   K. Edw. Go to, we pardon thee: therefore, in brief,   *90*
Tell me their words as near as thou canst guess them.
What answer makes King Lewis unto our letters?
   Post. At my depart these were his very words:
'Go tell false Edward, thy supposed king,
That Lewis of France is sending over masquers,   *95*
To revel it with him and his new bride.'
   K. Edw. Is Lewis so brave? belike he thinks me Henry.
But what said Lady Bona to my marriage?
   Post. These were her words, utter'd with mild disdain:
'Tell him, in hope he'll prove a widower shortly,   *100*
I'll wear the willow garland for his sake.'
   K. Edw. I blame not her, she could say little less;
She had the wrong. But what said Henry's queen?
For I have heard that she was there in place.
   Post. 'Tell him,' quoth she, 'my mourning weeds are done,   *105*

S. d.; *cf. n.*   **8 mind:** *intend*   **11 malcontent:** *dissatisfied*   **14 abuse:** *insult*   **19**
proveth: *turns out*   **25 mislike:** *displeasure*   **36 invention:** *plan*   **41** *Cf. n.*   **43**
using: *making a tool of*   **48, 49** *Cf. n.*

64 *To be my own agent*   **71 not . . . descent;** *cf. n.*   **72 meaner:** *lowlier persons*   **74**
your dislikes: *the displeasure of you*   **76 fawn upon:** *seek to propitiate*   **90 Go to:**
come!   **91 guess:** *approximate*   **97 brave:** *full of bravado*   **104 in place:** *present*   **105 done:** *done with, laid aside*

And I am ready to put armour on.'
   K. Edw. Belike she minds to play the Amazon.
But what said Warwick to these injuries?
   Post. He, more incens'd against your majesty
Than all the rest, discharg'd me with these words: 110
'Tell him from me that he hath done me wrong,
And therefore I'll uncrown him ere 't be long.'
   K. Edw. Ha! durst the traitor breathe out so proud words?
Well, I will arm me, being thus forewarn'd:
They shall have wars, and pay for their presumption. 115
But say, is Warwick friends with Margaret?
   Post. Ay, gracious sovereign; they are so link'd in friendship,
That young Prince Edward marries Warwick's daughter.
   Clar. Belike the elder; Clarence will have the younger.
Now, brother king, farewell, and sit you fast, 120
For I will hence to Warwick's other daughter;
That, though I want a kingdom, yet in marriage
I may not prove inferior to yourself.
You that love me and Warwick, follow me.
                Exit Clarence, and Somerset follows.
   Rich. [*Aside.*] Not I. 125
My thoughts aim at a further matter; I
Stay not for love of Edward, but the crown.
   K. Edw. Clarence and Somerset both gone to Warwick!
Yet am I arm'd against the worst can happen,
And haste is needful in this desperate case. 130
Pembroke and Stafford, you in our behalf
Go levy men, and make prepare for war:
They are already, or quickly will be landed:
Myself in person will straight follow you.
                Exeunt Pembroke and Stafford.
But ere I go, Hastings and Montague, 135
Resolve my doubt   You twain, of all the rest,
Are near to Warwick by blood, and by alliance:
Tell me if you love Warwick more than me?
If it be so, then both depart to him;
I rather wish you foes than hollow friends: 140
But if you mind to hold your true obedience,
Give me assurance with some friendly vow
That I may never have you in suspect.
   Mont. So God help Montague as he proves true!
   Hast. And Hastings as he favours Edward's cause! 145
   K. Edw. Now, brother Richard, will you stand by us?
   Rich. Ay, in despite of all that shall withstand you.
   K. Edw. Why, so! then am I sure of victory.
Now therefore let us hence; and lose no hour
Till we meet Warwick with his foreign power.   *Exeunt.* 150

❧ SCENE SECOND ❧

[A Plain in Warwickshire]
Enter Warwick and Oxford in England, with French Soldiers.

   War. Trust me, my lord, all hitherto goes well;
The common people by numbers swarm to us.

          Enter Clarence and Somerset.

But see where Somerset and Clarence comes!

Speak suddenly, my lords, are we all friends?
   Clar. Fear not that, my lord. 5
   War. Then, gentle Clarence, welcome unto Warwick;
And welcome, Somerset: I hold it cowardice,
To rest mistrustful where a noble heart
Hath pawn'd an open hand in sign of love;
Else might I think that Clarence, Edward's brother, 10
Were but a feigned friend to our proceedings:
But welcome, sweet Clarence; my daughter shall be thine.
And now what rests, but in night's coverture,
Thy brother being carelessly encamp'd,
His soldiers lurking in the towns about, 15
And but attended by a simple guard,
We may surprise and take him at our pleasure?
Our scouts have found the adventure very easy:
That as Ulysses, and stout Diomede,
With sleight and manhood stole to Rhesus' tents, 20
And brought from thence the Thracian fatal steeds;
So we, well cover'd with the night's black mantle,
At unawares may beat down Edward's guard,
And seize himself; I say not, slaughter him,
For I intend but only to surprise him. 25
You, that will follow me to this attempt,
Applaud the name of Henry with your leader.
                They all cry 'Henry!'
Why, then, let's on our way in silent sort.
For Warwick and his friends, God and Saint George!   *Exeunt.*

❧ SCENE THIRD ❧

[Edward's Camp near Warwick]
Enter three Watchmen to guard the King's tent.

   1. Watch. Come on, my masters, each man take his stand;
The king, by this, is set him down to sleep.
   2. Watch. What, will he not to bed?
   1. Watch. Why, no: for he hath made a solemn vow
Never to lie and take his natural rest 5
Till Warwick or himself be quite suppress'd.
   2. Watch. To-morrow then belike shall be the day,
If Warwick be so near as men report.
   3. Watch. But say, I pray, what nobleman is that
That with the king here resteth in his tent? 10
   1. Watch. 'Tis the Lord Hastings, the king's chiefest friend.
   3. Watch. O! is it so? But why commands the king
That his chief followers lodge in towns about him,
While he himself keeps in the cold field?
   2. Watch. 'Tis the more honour, because the more dangerous.
   3. Watch. Ay, but give me worship and quietness;
I like it better than a dangerous honour.
mIf Warwick knew in what estate he stands,
'Tis to be doubted he would waken him.
   1. Watch. Unless our halberds did shut up his passage. 20
   2. Watch. Ay; wherefore else guard we his royal tent,
But to defend his person from night foes?

---

119 *Cf. n.*   120 **sit you fast:** *seat yourself firmly*   132 **prepare:** *preparation*   143
suspect: *suspicion*

4 **suddenly:** *quickly*   5 **Fear:** *doubt*   13 **rests:** *remains to be done* **in . . . coverture:**
under cover of night   20 **sleight:** *craft*   21 **Thracian . . . steeds;** *cf. n.*   25 **surprise:**
capture unawares   28 **sort:** *manner*   16 **worship and quietness:** *honorable quiet*   18
in . . . stands: *Edward's situation*   19 **doubted:** *feared*

Enter Warwick, Clarence, Oxford, Somerset, and French Soldiers,
silent all.

War. This is his tent; and see where stand his guard.
Courage, my masters! honour now or never!
But follow me, and Edward shall be ours.   25
　1. Watch. Who goes there?
　2. Watch. Stay, or thou diest.

Warwick and the rest cry all, 'Warwick! Warwick!' and set upon the
Guard, who fly, crying, 'Arm! Arm!' Warwick and the rest follow-
ing them.

The drum playing and trumpet sounding, enter Warwick, Somerset,
and the rest, bringing the King out in his gown, sitting in a chair.
Richard and Hastings fly over the stage.
　Som.　　　　　　　　　What are they that fly there?
　War. Richard and Hastings: let them go; here is the duke.
　K. Edw. The duke! Why, Warwick, when we parted,   30
Thou call'dst me king!
　War.　　　　　Ay, but the case is alter'd:
When you disgrac'd me in my embassade,
Then I degraded you from being king,
And come now to create you Duke of York.   35
Alas! how should you govern any kingdom,
That know not how to use ambassadors,
Nor how to be contented with one wife,
Nor how to use your brothers brotherly,
Nor how to study for the people's welfare,   40
Nor how to shroud yourself from enemies?
　K. Edw. Yea, brother of Clarence, art thou here too?
Nay, then, I see that Edward needs must down.
Yet, Warwick, in despite of all mischance,
Of thee thyself, and all thy complices,   45
Edward will always bear himself as king:
Though Fortune's malice overthrow my state,
My mind exceeds the compass of her wheel.
　War. Then, for his mind, be Edward England's king:
　　　　　　　　　　　　Takes off his crown.
But Henry now shall wear the English crown,   50
And be true king indeed, thou but the shadow.
My Lord of Somerset, at my request,
See that forthwith Duke Edward be convey'd
Unto my brother, Archbishop of York.
When I have fought with Pembroke and his fellows,   55
I'll follow you, and tell what answer
Lewis and the Lady Bona send to him:
Now for a while farewell, good Duke of York.
　　　　　　　　　　　They lead him out forcibly.
　K. Edw. What fates impose, that men must needs abide;
It boots not to resist both wind and tide.   60
　　　　　　Exeunt [Edward and Somerset, with Guard].
　Oxf. What now remains, my lords, for us to do,
But march to London with our soldiers?
　War. Ay, that's the first thing that we have to do;
To free King Henry from imprisonment,
And see him seated in the regal throne.   *Exeunt.*

❧ Scene Fourth ❧

[London. A Room in the Palace]
Enter Rivers and Lady Grey [Queen Elizabeth].

　Riv. Madam, what makes you in this sudden change?
　L. Grey. Why, brother Rivers, are you yet to learn,
What late misfortune is befall'n King Edward?
　Riv. What! loss of some pitch'd battle against Warwick?
　L. Grey. No, but the loss of his own royal person.   5
　Riv. Then is my sovereign slain?
　L. Grey. Ay, almost slain, for he is taken prisoner;
Either betray'd by falsehood of his guard
Or by his foe surpris'd at unawares:
And, as I further have to understand,   10
Is new committed to the Bishop of York,
Fell Warwick's brother, and by that our foe.
　Riv. These news, I must confess, are full of grief;
Yet, gracious madam, bear it as you may:
Warwick may lose, that now hath won the day.   15
　L. Grey. Till then fair hope must hinder life's decay.
And I the rather wean me from despair
For love of Edward's offspring in my womb:
This is it that makes me bridle passion,
And bear with mildness my misfortune's cross;   20
Ay, ay, for this I draw in many a tear,
And stop the rising of blood-sucking sighs,
Lest with my sighs or tears I blast or drown
King Edward's fruit, true heir to th' English crown.
　Riv. But, madam, where is Warwick then become?   25
　L. Grey. I am inform'd that he comes towards London,
To set the crown once more on Henry's head:
Guess thou the rest; King Edward's friends must down.
But, to prevent the tyrant's violence,—
For trust not him that hath once broken faith,—   30
I'll hence forthwith unto the sanctuary,
To save at least the heir of Edward's right:
There shall I rest secure from force and fraud.
Come, therefore; let us fly while we may fly:
If Warwick take us, we are sure to die.   *Exeunt.*   35

❧ Scene Fifth ❧

[A Park near Middleham Castle in Yorkshire]
Enter Richard, Lord Hastings, and Sir William Stanley.

　Rich. Now, my Lord Hastings and Sir William Stanley,
Leave off to wonder why I drew you hither,
Into this chiefest thicket of the park.
Thus stands the case. You know, our king, my brother,
Is prisoner to the bishop here, at whose hands   5
He hath good usage and great liberty,
And often but attended with weak guard,
Comes hunting this way to disport himself.
I have advertis'd him by secret means,
That if about this hour he make this way,   10
Under the colour of his usual game,
He shall here find his friends, with horse and men
To set him free from his captivity.

S. d. French Soldiers; *cf. n.*   **32** the case is alter'd: *conditions have changed*   **41** shroud:
shelter   **45** complices: *accomplices*   **49** for his mind: *in imagination*   **54** *Cf. n.*   **55**
Pembroke; *cf. n.*

Scene Fourth; *cf. n.*   **2** brother Rivers; *cf. n.*   **22** blood-sucking sighs; *cf. n.*   **31,**
32 *Cf. n.*   Scene Fifth; *cf. n.*

Enter King Edward, and a Huntsman with him.

Hunt. This way, my lord, for this way lies the game.

K. Edw. Nay, this way, man: see where the huntsmen stand.   15
Now, brother of Gloucester, Lord Hastings, and the rest,
Stand you thus close, to steal the bishop's deer?

Rich. Brother, the time and case requireth haste.
Your horse stands ready at the park corner.

K. Edw. But whither shall we then?   20

Hast. To Lynn, my lord; and, shipp'd, from thence to
Flanders.

Rich. Well guess'd, believe me; for that was my meaning.

K. Edw. Stanley, I will requite thy forwardness.

Rich. But wherefore stay we? 'tis no time to talk.   25

K. Edw. Huntsman, what sayst thou? wilt thou go along?

Hunt. Better do so than tarry and be hang'd.

Rich. Come then, away; let's ha' no more ado.

K. Edw. Bishop, farewell: shield thee from Warwick's frown,
And pray that I may repossess the crown.   *Exeunt.*   30

❧ SCENE SIXTH ❧

[A Room in the Tower]

*Flourish. Enter King Henry the Sixth, Clarence, Warwick,
Somerset, young Henry [Earl of Richmond], Oxford, Montague,
and Lieutenant [of the tower].*

K. Hen. Master lieutenant, now that God and friends
Have shaken Edward from the regal seat,
And turn'd my captive state to liberty,
My fear to hope, my sorrows unto joys,
At our enlargement what are thy due fees?   5

Lieu. Subjects may challenge nothing of their sovereigns;
But if a humble prayer may prevail,
I then crave pardon of your majesty.

K. Hen. For what, lieutenant? for well using me?
Nay, be thou sure, I'll well requite thy kindness;   10
For that it made my imprisonment a pleasure;
Ay, such a pleasure as encaged birds
Conceive, when, after many moody thoughts
At last by notes of household harmony
They quite forget their loss of liberty.   15
But, Warwick, after God, thou set'st me free,
And chiefly therefore I thank God and thee;
He was the author, thou the instrument.
Therefore, that I may conquer Fortune's spite
By living low, where Fortune cannot hurt me,   20
And that the people of this blessed land
May not be punish'd with my thwarting stars,
Warwick, although my head still wear the crown,
I here resign my government to thee,
For thou art fortunate in all thy deeds.   25

War. Your Grace hath still been fam'd for virtuous;
And now may seem as wise as virtuous,
By spying and avoiding Fortune's malice;
For few men rightly temper with the stars:
Yet in this one thing let me blame your Grace,   30
For choosing me when Clarence is in place.

Clar. No, Warwick, thou art worthy of the sway,
To whom the heavens, in thy nativity
Adjudg'd an olive branch and laurel crown,
As likely to be blest in peace and war;   35
And therefore I yield thee my free consent.

War. And I choose Clarence only for protector.

K. Hen. Warwick and Clarence, give me both your hands:
Now join your hands, and with your hands your hearts,
That no dissension hinder government: 40
I make you both protectors of this land,
While I myself will lead a private life,
And in devotion spend my latter days,
To sin's rebuke and my Creator's praise.

War. What answers Clarence to his sovereign's will?   45

Clar. That he consents, if Warwick yield consent;
For on thy fortune I repose myself.

War. Why then, though loath, yet must I be content:
We'll yoke together, like a double shadow
To Henry's body, and supply his place;   50
I mean, in bearing weight of government,
While he enjoys the honour and his ease.
And, Clarence, now then it is more than needful
Forthwith that Edward be pronounc'd a traitor,
And all his lands and goods be confiscate.   55

Clar. What else? and that succession be determin'd.

War. Ay, therein Clarence shall not want his part.

K. Hen. But, with the first of all your chief affairs,
Let me entreat, for I command no more,
That Margaret your queen, and my son Edward,   60
Be sent for, to return from France with speed:
For, till I see them here, by doubtful fear
My joy of liberty is half eclips'd.

Clar. It shall be done, my sovereign, with all speed.

K. Hen. My Lord of Somerset, what youth is that,   65
Of whom you seem to have so tender care?

Som. My liege, it is young Henry, Earl of Richmond.

K. Hen. Come hither, England's hope.

Lays his hand on his head.

If secret powers
Suggest but truth to my divining thoughts,   70
This pretty lad will prove our country's bliss.
His looks are full of peaceful majesty,
His head by nature fram'd to wear a crown,
His hand to wield a sceptre, and himself
Likely in time to bless a regal throne.   75
Make much of him, my lords; for this is he
Must help you more than you are hurt by me.

Enter a Post.

War. What news, my friend?

Post. That Edward is escaped from your brother,
And fled, as he hears since, to Burgundy.   80

War. Unsavoury news! but how made he escape?

Post. He was convey'd by Richard, Duke of Gloucester,
And the Lord Hastings, who attended him
In secret ambush on the forest side,
And from the bishop's huntsmen rescu'd him: 85
For hunting was his daily exercise.

War. My brother was too careless of his charge.

---

17 close: *in concealment*   **5 enlargement:** *liberation*   **14 notes ... harmony:** *filling the house with song*   **22 with ... stars:** *by my bad luck*   **29 temper:** *work in harmony*   **67 Henry, Earl of Richmond;** *cf. n.*   **82 convey'd:** *stolen away*   **83 attended:** *awaited*

But let us hence, my sovereign, to provide
A salve for any sore that may betide.

Exeunt. Mane[n]t Somerset, Richmond, and Oxford.

Som. My lord, I like not of this flight of Edward's;   90
For doubtless Burgundy will yield him help,
And we shall have more wars before 't be long.
As Henry's late presaging prophecy
Did glad my heart with hope of this young Richmond,
So doth my heart misgive me, in these conflicts   95
What may befall him to his harm and ours:
Therefore, Lord Oxford, to prevent the worst,
Forthwith we'll send him hence to Brittany,
Till storms be past of civil enmity.

Oxf. Ay, for if Edward repossess the crown,   100
'Tis like that Richmond with the rest shall down.

Som. It shall be so; he shall to Brittany.
Come, therefore, let's about it speedily.   *Exeunt.*

❧ SCENE SEVENTH ❧

[Before York]
Flourish. Enter Edward, Richard, Hastings, and Soldiers.

K. Edw. Now, brother Richard, Lord Hastings, and the rest,
Yet thus far Fortune maketh us amends,
And says that once more I shall interchange
My waned state for Henry's regal crown.
Well have we pass'd, and now repass'd the seas,   5
And brought desired help from Burgundy:
What then remains, we being thus arriv'd
From Ravenspurgh haven before the gates of York,
But that we enter, as into our dukedom?

Rich. The gates made fast! Brother, I like not this;   10
For many men that stumble at the threshold
Are well foretold that danger lurks within.

K. Edw. Tush, man! abodements must not now affright us.
By fair or foul means we must enter in,
For hither will our friends repair to us.   15

Hast. My liege, I'll knock once more to summon them.

Enter, on the Walls, the Mayor of York and his Brethren.

May. My lords, we were forewarned of your coming,
And shut the gates for safety of ourselves;
For now we owe allegiance unto Henry.

K. Edw. But, Master Mayor, if Henry be your king,   20
Yet Edward, at the least, is Duke of York.

May. True, my good lord, I know you for no less.

K. Edw. Why, and I challenge nothing but my dukedom,
As being well content with that alone.

Rich. [Aside.] But when the fox hath once got in his nose,   25
He'll soon find means to make the body follow.

Hast. Why, Master Mayor, why stand you in a doubt?
Open the gates; we are King Henry's friends.

May. Ay, say you so? the gates shall then be open'd.

He descends.

Rich. A wise stout captain, and soon persuaded.   30

Hast. The good old man would fain that all were well,

So 'twere not long of him; but being enter'd,
I doubt not, I, but we shall soon persuade
Both him and all his brothers unto reason.

Enter the Mayor and two Aldermen.

K. Edw. So, Master Mayor: these gates must not be shut   35
But in the night, or in the time of war.
What! fear not, man, but yield me up the keys;   *Takes his keys.*
For Edward will defend the town and thee,
And all those friends that deign to follow me.

March. Enter Montgomery with drum and Soldiers.

Rich. Brother, this is Sir John Montgomery,   40
Our trusty friend, unless I be deceiv'd.

K. Edw. Welcome, Sir John! but why come you in arms?

Mont. To help King Edward in his time of storm,
As every loyal subject ought to do.

K. Edw. Thanks, good Montgomery; but we now forget   45
Our title to the crown, and only claim
Our dukedom till God please to send the rest.

Mont. Then fare you well, for I will hence again:
I came to serve a king and not a duke.
Drummer, strike up, and let us march away.   50

The drum begins to march.

K. Edw. Nay, stay, Sir John, awhile; and we'll debate
By what safe means the crown may be recover'd.

Mont. What talk you of debating? in few words,
If you'll not here proclaim yourself our king,
I'll leave you to your fortune, and be gone   55
To keep them back that come to succour you.
Why shall we fight, if you pretend no title?

Rich. Why, brother, wherefore stand you on nice points?

K. Edw. When we grow stronger then we'll make our claim;
Till then, 'tis wisdom to conceal our meaning.   60

Hast. Away with scrupulous wit! now arms must rule.

Rich. And fearless minds climb soonest unto crowns.
Brother, we will proclaim you out of hand;
The bruit thereof will bring you many friends.

K. Edw. Then be it as you will; for 'tis my right,   65
And Henry but usurps the diadem.

Mont. Ay, now my sovereign speaketh like himself;
And now will I be Edward's champion.

Hast. Sound, trumpet! Edward shall be here proclaim'd;
Come, fellow soldier, make thou proclamation.   70

Flourish. Sound.

Sold. Edward the Fourth, by the grace of God, King of
England and France, and Lord of Ireland, &c.

Mont. And whosoe'er gainsays King Edward's right,
By this I challenge him to single fight.

Throws down his gauntlet.

All. Long live Edward the Fourth!   75

K. Edw. Thanks, brave Montgomery;—and thanks unto
you all:
If Fortune serve me, I'll requite this kindness.
Now, for this night, let's harbour here in York;
And when the morning sun shall raise his car   80

---

89 **betide:** *chance, happen*   90 **like not of:** *am troubled by*   **SCENE SEVEN;** *cf. n.*   8
Ravenspurgh; *cf. n.*   12 **foretold:** *forewarned*   13 **abodements:** *omens*   23 **challenge:**
claim

32 **long of:** *on account of*   40 **Sir John Montgomery;** *cf. n.*   50 **Drummer;** *cf. n.*
S. d. **march:** *sound signal for marching*   58 **stand ... points:** *boggle over technicalities*   61 **scrupulous wit:** *cautious calculation*   63 **out of hand:** *at once*   64 **bruit:**
rumor   80 **car:** *chariot of Phœbus*

Above the border of this horizon,
We'll forward towards Warwick, and his mates;
For well I wot that Henry is no soldier.
Ah, froward Clarence, how evil it beseems thee
To flatter Henry, and forsake thy brother!   85
Yet, as we may, we'll meet both thee and Warwick.
Come on, brave soldiers: doubt not of the day;
And, that once gotten, doubt not of large pay.   *Exeunt.*

❧ Scene Eighth ❧

[London. A Room in the Bishop of London's Palace]
Flourish. Enter the King [Henry], Warwick, Montague, Clarence,
Oxford, and Exeter.

War. What counsel, lords? Edward from Belgia,
With hasty Germans and blunt Hollanders,
Hath pass'd in safety through the narrow seas,
And with his troops doth march amain to London;
And many giddy people flock to him.   5
   King. Let's levy men, and beat him back again.
   Clar. A little fire is quickly trodden out,
Which, being suffer'd, rivers cannot quench.
   War. In Warwickshire I have true-hearted friends,
Not mutinous in peace, yet bold in war;   10
Those will I muster up: and thou, son Clarence,
Shalt stir up in Suffolk, Norfolk, and in Kent,
The knights and gentlemen to come with thee:
Thou, brother Montague, in Buckingham,
Northampton, and in Leicestershire, shalt find   15
Men well inclin'd to hear what thou command'st:
And thou, brave Oxford, wondrous well belov'd,
In Oxfordshire shalt muster up thy friends.
My sovereign, with the loving citizens,
Like to his island girt in with the ocean,   20
Or modest Dian circled with her nymphs,
Shall rest in London till we come to him.
Fair lords, take leave, and stand not to reply.
Farewell, my sovereign.
   K. Hen. Farewell, my Hector, and my Troy's true hope.   25
   Clar. In sign of truth, I kiss your highness' hand.
   K. Hen. Well-minded Clarence, be thou fortunate!
   Mont. Comfort, my lord; and so, I take my leave.
   Oxf. [Kissing Henry's hand.] And thus I seal my truth, and
bid adieu.   30
   K. Hen. Sweet Oxford, and my loving Montague,
And all at once, once more a happy farewell.
   War. Farewell, sweet lords: let's meet at Coventry.
          Exeunt [all but King Henry and Exeter].
   K. Hen. Here at the palace will I rest awhile.
Cousin of Exeter, what thinks your lordship?   35
Methinks the power that Edward hath in field
Should not be able to encounter mine.
   Exe. The doubt is that he will seduce the rest.
   K. Hen. That's not my fear; my meed hath got me fame:
I have not stopp'd mine ears to their demands,   40

Nor posted off their suits with slow delays;
My pity hath been balm to heal their wounds,
My mildness hath allay'd their swelling griefs,
My mercy dried their water-flowing tears;
I have not been desirous of their wealth;   45
Nor much oppress'd them with great subsidies,
Nor forward of revenge, though they much err'd.
Then why should they love Edward more than me?
No, Exeter, these graces challenge grace:
And when the lion fawns upon the lamb,   50
The lamb will never cease to follow him.
       Shout within, 'A Lancaster! A Lancaster!'
   Exe. Hark, hark, my lord! what shouts are these?

Enter Edward, [Richard,] and his Soldiers.

   K. Edw. Seize on the shamefac'd Henry! bear him hence:
And once again proclaim us King of England.
You are the fount that makes small brooks to flow: 55
Now stops thy spring, my sea shall suck them dry,
And swell so much the higher by their ebb.
Hence with him to the Tower! let him not speak.
       Exit [Attendant] with King Henry.
And, lords, towards Coventry bend we our course,
Where peremptory Warwick now remains: 60
The sun shines hot, and if we use delay,
Cold biting winter mars our hop'd-for hay.
   Rich. Away betimes, before his forces join,
And take the great-grown traitor unawares:
Brave warriors, march amain towards Coventry.   *Exeunt.*   65

Act Fifth ❧ Scene First

[Coventry]
Enter Warwick, the Mayor of Coventry, two Messengers, and others,
upon the Walls.

   War. Where is the post that came from valiant Oxford?
How far hence is thy lord, mine honest fellow?
   1. Mess. By this at Dunsmore, marching hitherward.
   War. How far off is our brother Montague?
Where is the post that came from Montague?   5
   2. Mess. By this at Daintry, with a puissant troop.

Enter [Sir John] Somerville.

   War. Say, Somerville, what says my loving son?
And, by thy guess, how nigh is Clarence now?
   Som. At Southam I did leave him with his forces,
And do expect him here some two hours hence.   10
                    [Drum heard.]
   War. Then Clarence is at hand. I hear his drum.
   Som. It is not his, my lord; here Southam lies:
The drum your honour hears marcheth from Warwick.
   War. Who should that be? belike, unlook'd for friends.
   Som. They are at hand, and you shall quickly know.   15

---

84 evil: *ill*   **85 flatter:** *serve obsequiously*   **SCENE EIGHT S. d. Exeter;** *cf. n.*   **8 suffer'd:** *ignored*   **23 stand:** *delay*   **32 at once:** *together*   **38 doubt:** *fear*   **39 meed:** *merit*

41 posted off: *carelessly postponed*   **46 subsidies:** *taxes*   **47 forward of:** *(been) eager for*   **S. d. A Lancaster;** *cf. n.*   **53 shamefac'd:** *shamefast, bashful*   **56 Now . . . spring:** *now that your spring is stopped*   **61, 62** *Cf. n.*   **3 Dunsmore:** *Dunsmore Heath, eight miles east of Coventry*   **6 Daintry:** *Daventry, 20 miles southeast*   **9 Southam:** *15 miles south*   **13 Warwick:** *12 miles southwest*

March. Flourish. Enter Edward, Richard, and Soldiers.

K. Edw. Go, trumpet, to the walls, and sound a parle.
Rich. See how the surly Warwick mans the wall.
War. O, unbid spite! is sportful Edward come?
Where slept our scouts, or how are they seduc'd,
That we could hear no news of his repair?   20
   K. Edw. Now, Warwick, wilt thou ope the city gates,
Speak gentle words, and humbly bend thy knee?—
Call Edward king, and at his hands beg mercy?
And he shall pardon thee these outrages.
   War. Nay, rather, wilt thou draw thy forces hence,—   25
Confess who set thee up and pluck'd thee down?—
Call Warwick patron, and be penitent;
And thou shalt still remain the Duke of York.
   Rich. I thought, at least he would have said the king;
Or did he make the jest against his will?   30
   War. Is not a dukedom, sir, a goodly gift?
   Rich. Ay, by my faith, for a poor earl to give:
I'll do thee service for so good a gift.
   War. 'Twas I that gave the kingdom to thy brother.
   K. Edw. Why then 'tis mine, if but by Warwick's gift.   35
   War. Thou art no Atlas for so great a weight:
And, weakling, Warwick takes his gift again;
And Henry is my king, Warwick his subject.
   K. Edw. But Warwick's king is Edward's prisoner;
And, gallant Warwick, do but answer this,   40
What is the body, when the head is off?
   Rich. Alas! that Warwick had no more forecast,
But, whiles he thought to steal the single ten,
The king was slily finger'd from the deck.
You left poor Henry at the bishop's palace,   45
And, ten to one, you'll meet him in the Tower.
   K. Edw. 'Tis even so: yet you are Warwick still.
   Rich. Come, Warwick, take the time; kneel down, kneel
down:
Nay, when! strike now, or else the iron cools.   50
   War. I had rather chop this hand off at a blow,
And with the other fling it at thy face,
Than bear so low a sail to strike to thee.
   K. Edw. Sail how thou canst, have wind and tide thy friend;
This hand, fast wound about thy coal-black hair,   55
Shall, whiles thy head is warm and new cut off,
Write in the dust this sentence with thy blood:
'Wind-changing Warwick now can change no more.'

Enter Oxford, with drum and colours.

   War. O cheerful colours! see where Oxford comes!
   Oxf. Oxford, Oxford, for Lancaster!   60
                              [He and his Forces enter the city.]
   Rich. The gates are open, let us enter too.
   K. Edw. So other foes may set upon our backs.
Stand we in good array; for they no doubt
Will issue out again and bid us battle:
If not, the city being but of small defence,   65
We'll quickly rouse the traitors in the same.
   War. O! welcome, Oxford! for we want thy help.

Enter Montague, with drum and colours.

   Mont. Montague, Montague, for Lancaster!
                              [He and his Forces enter the city.]
   Rich. Thou and thy brother both shall buy this treason
Even with the dearest blood your bodies bear.   70
   K. Edw. The harder match'd, the greater victory:
My mind presageth happy gain, and conquest.

Enter Somerset, with drum and colours.

   Som. Somerset, Somerset, for Lancaster!
                              [He and his Forces enter the city.]
   Rich. Two of thy name, both Dukes of Somerset,
Have sold their lives unto the house of York;   75
And thou shalt be the third, if this sword hold.

Enter Clarence, with drum and colours.

   War. And lo! where George of Clarence sweeps along,
Of force enough to bid his brother battle;
With whom an upright zeal to right prevails
More than the nature of a brother's love.   80
Come, Clarence, come; thou wilt, if Warwick call.
   Clar. Father of Warwick, know you what this means?
                              [Taking the red rose out of his helmet.]
Look here, I throw my infamy at thee:
I will not ruinate my father's house,
Who gave his blood to lime the stones together,   85
And set up Lancaster. Why, trow'st thou, Warwick,
That Clarence is so harsh, so blunt, unnatural,
To bend the fatal instruments of war
Against his brother and his lawful king?
Perhaps thou wilt object my holy oath: 90
To keep that oath were more impiety
Than Jephthah's, when he sacrific'd his daughter.
I am so sorry for my trespass made
That, to deserve well at my brother's hands,
I here proclaim myself thy mortal foe;   95
With resolution, wheresoe'er I meet thee—
As I will meet thee if thou stir abroad—
To plague thee for thy foul misleading me.
And so, proud-hearted Warwick, I defy thee,
And to my brother turn my blushing cheeks.   100
Pardon me, Edward, I will make amends;
And, Richard, do not frown upon my faults,
For I will henceforth be no more unconstant.
   K. Edw. Now welcome more, and ten times more belov'd,
Than if thou never hadst deserv'd our hate.   105
   Rich. Welcome, good Clarence; this is brotherlike.
   War. O passing traitor, perjur'd, and unjust!
   K. Edw. What, Warwick, wilt thou leave the town, and
fight?
Or shall we beat the stones about thine ears?   110
   War. Alas! I am not coop'd here for defence:
I will away towards Barnet presently,
And bid thee battle, Edward, if thou dar'st.
   K. Edw. Yes, Warwick, Edward dares, and leads the way.
Lords, to the field; Saint George and victory!   *Exeunt.*   115
              March. Warwick and his company follows.

---

16 parle: *parley*   18 unbid: *unwelcome*   20 repair: *approach*   36 Atlas: *capable sup-porter*   42 forecast: *forethought*   43 single: *simple, unimportant*   44 deck: *pack of cards*   45 bishop's palace: *cf. n.*   48 time: *favorable moment*   50 Nay, when: *come! come!*   58 Wind-changing: *fickle as the wind*   64 bid: *offer*   65 of small defence: *ill-fortified*

74 Two of thy name: *cf. n.*   79 to: *for* S. d.: *cf. n.*   85 lime: *cement*   90 object: *urge*   93 my trespass made: *the fault I have already committed*   107 passing: *surpassing*   111 Alas: *forsooth*

❧ SCENE SECOND ❧

[A Field of Battle near Barnet]

*Alarum and Excursions. Enter Edward, bringing forth Warwick,
wounded.*

K. Edw. So, lie thou there: die thou, and die our fear;
For Warwick was a bug that fear'd us all.
Now Montague, sit fast; I seek for thee,
That Warwick's bones may keep thine company.   *Exit.*

     War. Ah! who is nigh? come to me, friend or foe,   5
And tell me who is victor, York or Warwick?
Why ask I that? my mangled body shows,
My blood, my want of strength, my sick heart shows,
That I must yield my body to the earth,
And, by my fall, the conquest to my foe.   10
Thus yields the cedar to the axe's edge,
Whose arms gave shelter to the princely eagle,
Under whose shade the ramping lion slept,
Whose top branch overpeer'd Jove's spreading tree,
And kept low shrubs from winter's powerful wind.   15
These eyes, that now are dimm'd with death's black veil,
Have been as piercing as the mid-day sun,
To search the secret treasons of the world:
The wrinkles in my brows, now fill'd with blood,
Were liken'd oft to kingly sepulchres;   20
For who liv'd king, but I could dig his grave?
And who durst smile when Warwick bent his brow?
Lo! now my glory smear'd in dust and blood;
My parks, my walks, my manors that I had,
Even now forsake me; and of all my lands   25
Is nothing left me but my body's length.
Why, what is pomp, rule, reign, but earth and dust?
And, live we how we can, yet die we must.

     Enter Oxford and Somerset.

     Som. Ah! Warwick, Warwick, wert thou as we are,
We might recover all our loss again.   30
The queen from France hath brought a puissant power;
Even now we heard the news. Ah, couldst thou fly!

     War. Why, then, I would not fly. Ah! Montague,
If thou be there, sweet brother, take my hand,
And with thy lips keep in my soul awhile.   35
Thou lov'st me not; for, brother, if thou didst,
Thy tears would wash this cold congealed blood
That glues my lips and will not let me speak.
Come quickly, Montague, or I am dead.

     Som. Ah! Warwick, Montague hath breath'd his last;   40
And to the latest gasp, cried out for Warwick,
And said, 'Commend me to my valiant brother.'
And more he would have said; and more he spoke,
Which sounded like a clamour in a vault,
That mought not be distinguish'd: but at last   45
I well might hear, deliver'd with a groan,
'O! farewell, Warwick!'

     War. Sweet rest his soul! Fly, lords, and save yourselves;
For Warwick bids you all farewell, to meet in heaven.   *[Dies.]*

     Oxf. Away, away, to meet the queen's great power.   50
     Here they bear away his body. Exeunt.

❧ SCENE THIRD ❧

[Another Part of the Field]

*Flourish. Enter King Edward, in triumph: with Richard, Clarence,
and the rest.*

     K. Edw. Thus far our fortune keeps an upward course,
And we are grac'd with wreaths of victory.
But in the midst of this bright-shining day,
I spy a black, suspicious, threat'ning cloud,
That will encounter with our glorious sun,   5
Ere he attain his easeful western bed:
I mean, my lords, those powers that the queen
Hath rais'd in Gallia have arriv'd our coast,
And, as we hear, march on to fight with us.

     Clar. A little gale will soon disperse that cloud,   10
And blow it to the source from whence it came:
Thy very beams will dry those vapours up,
For every cloud engenders not a storm.

     Rich. The queen is valu'd thirty thousand strong,
And Somerset, with Oxford, fled to her: 15
If she have time to breathe, be well assur'd
Her faction will be full as strong as ours.

     K. Edw. We are advertis'd by our loving friends
That they do hold their course toward Tewkesbury.
We, having now the best at Barnet field,   20
Will thither straight, for willingness rids way;
And, as we march, our strength will be augmented
In every county as we go along.
Strike up the drum! cry 'Courage!' and away.   *Exeunt.*

❧ SCENE FOURTH ❧

[Plains near Tewkesbury]

*Flourish. March. Enter the Queen, young Edward, Somerset,
Oxford, and Soldiers.*

     Queen. Great lords, wise men ne'er sit and wail their loss,
But cheerly seek how to redress their harms.
What though the mast be now blown overboard,
The cable broke, the holding anchor lost,
And half our sailors swallow'd in the flood?   5
Yet lives our pilot still: is 't meet that he
Should leave the helm and like a fearful lad
With tearful eyes add water to the sea,
And give more strength to that which hath too much;
Whiles in his moan the ship splits on the rock,   10
Which industry and courage might have sav'd?
Ah, what a shame! ah, what a fault were this!
Say, Warwick was our anchor; what of that?
And Montague our top-mast; what of him?
Our slaughter'd friends the tackles; what of these?   15
Why, is not Oxford here another anchor?
And Somerset another goodly mast?
The friends of France our shrouds and tacklings?
And, though unskilful, why not Ned and I
For once allow'd the skilful pilot's charge?   20
We will not from the helm, to sit and weep,
But keep our course, though the rough wind say no,

---

2 **bug:** *imaginary terror*   13 **ramping:** *rampant, fierce*   14 **overpeer'd … tree:** *towered
above the oak*   23 **smear'd:** *is soiled*   31 *Cf. n.* **S. d.;** *cf. n.*

8 **arriv'd:** *landed at*   21 **rids way:** *does away with distance*   1–38 *Cf. n.*   2 **cheerly:**
blithely   15 **tackles:** *ropes*

From shelves and rocks that threaten us with wrack.
As good to chide the waves as speak them fair.
And what is Edward but a ruthless sea?   25
What Clarence but a quicksand of deceit?
And Richard but a ragged fatal rock?
All those the enemies to our poor bark.
Say you can swim; alas! 'tis but a while:
Tread on the sand; why, there you quickly sink: 30
Bestride the rock; the tide will wash you off,
Or else you famish; that's a threefold death.
This speak I, lords, to let you understand,
If case some one of you would fly from us,
That there's no hop'd-for mercy with the brothers   35
More than with ruthless waves, with sands and rocks.
Why, courage, then! what cannot be avoided
'Twere childish weakness to lament or fear.
    Prince. Methinks a woman of this valiant spirit
Should, if a coward heard her speak these words,   40
Infuse his breast with magnanimity,
And make him, naked, foil a man at arms.
I speak not this, as doubting any here;
For did I but suspect a fearful man,
He should have leave to go away betimes,   45
Lest in our need he might infect another,
And make him of like spirit to himself.
If any such be here, as God forbid!
Let him depart before we need his help.
    Oxf. Women and children of so high a courage,   50
And warriors faint! why, 'twere perpetual shame.
O brave young prince! thy famous grandfather
Doth live again in thee: long mayst thou live
To bear his image and renew his glories!
    Som. And he, that will not fight for such a hope,   55
Go home to bed, and, like the owl by day,
If he arise, be mock'd and wonder'd at.
    Queen. Thanks, gentle Somerset: sweet Oxford, thanks.
    Prince. And take his thanks that yet hath nothing else.

Enter a Messenger.

    Mess. Prepare you, lords, for Edward is at hand,   60
Ready to fight; therefore be resolute.
    Oxf. I thought no less: it is his policy
To haste thus fast, to find us unprovided.
    Som. But he's deceiv'd; we are in readiness.
    Queen. This cheers my heart to see your forwardness. 65
    Oxf. Here pitch our battle; hence we will not budge.

*Flourish, and march. Enter Edward, Richard, Clarence, and
Soldiers.*

    K. Edw. Brave followers, yonder stands the thorny wood,
Which, by the heavens' assistance and your strength,
Must by the roots be hewn up yet ere night.
I need not add more fuel to your fire,   70
For well I wot ye blaze to burn them out:
Give signal to the fight, and to it, lords.
    Queen. Lords, knights, and gentlemen, what I should say
My tears gainsay; for every word I speak,
Ye see, I drink the water of my eye.   75

Therefore, no more but this: Henry, your sovereign,
Is prisoner to the foe; his state usurp'd,
His realm a slaughter house, his subjects slain,
His statutes cancell'd, and his treasure spent;
And yonder is the wolf that makes this spoil.   80
You fight in justice: then, in God's name, lords,
Be valiant, and give signal to the fight.   *Exeunt.*
                              Alarum. Retreat. Excursions.

❧ SCENE FIFTH ❧

[Another Part of the Same]
*Flourish. Enter Edward, Richard, Clarence [with] Queen, Oxford,
Somerset [as prisoners].*

    K. Edw. Now, here a period of tumultuous broils.
Away with Oxford to Hames Castle straight:
For Somerset, off with his guilty head.
Go, bear them hence; I will not hear them speak.
    Oxf. For my part, I'll not trouble thee with words. 5
    Som. Nor I, but stoop with patience to my fortune.
                              Exeunt [guarded].
    Queen. So part we sadly in this troublous world,
To meet with joy in sweet Jerusalem.
    K. Edw. Is proclamation made, that who finds Edward
Shall have a high reward, and he his life?   10
    Rich. It is: and lo, where youthful Edward comes.

Enter the Prince [led in by Soldiers].

    K. Edw. Bring forth the gallant: let us hear him speak.
What! can so young a thorn begin to prick?
Edward, what satisfaction canst thou make,
For bearing arms, for stirring up my subjects,   15
And all the trouble thou hast turn'd me to?
    Prince. Speak like a subject, proud ambitious York!
Suppose that I am now my father's mouth:
Resign thy chair, and where I stand kneel thou,
Whilst I propose the self-same words to thee,   20
Which, traitor, thou wouldst have me answer to.
    Queen. Ah, that thy father had been so resolv'd!
    Rich. That you might still have worn the petticoat,
And ne'er have stol'n the breech from Lancaster.
    Prince. Let Æsop fable in a winter's night;   25
His currish riddles sorts not with this place.
    Rich. By heaven, brat, I'll plague ye for that word.
    Queen. Ay, thou wast born to be a plague to men.
    Rich. For God's sake, take away this captive scold.
    Prince. Nay, take away this scolding crookback rather. 30
    K. Edw. Peace, wilful boy, or I will charm your tongue.
    Clar. Untutor'd lad, thou art too malapert.
    Prince. I know my duty; you are all undutiful:
Lascivious Edward, and thou perjur'd George,
And thou misshapen Dick, I tell ye all,   35
I am your better, traitors as ye are;
And thou usurp'st my father's right and mine.
    K. Edw. Take that, the likeness of this railer here.
                              Stabs him.

23 shelves: *sandbanks*   27 ragged: *jagged*   34 If case: *if it should happen*   41 magnanimity: *courage*   63 unprovided: *unprepared*   74 gainsay: *forbid*

S. d. Excursions: *sallies across the stage*   1 period: *full stop*   2 Hames Castle;
cf. n.   18 mouth: *representative*   24 breech: *breeches*   25 Æsop; *cf. n.*   26 sorts:
agree   31 charm: *silence*   32 malapert: *impudent*

Rich. Sprawl'st thou? take that, to end thy agony.

            Rich. stabs him.

Clar. And there's for twitting me with perjury. 40

            Clar. stabs him.

Queen. O, kill me too!

Rich. Marry, and shall.   *Offers to kill her.*

K. Edw. Hold, Richard, hold! for we have done too much.

Rich. Why should she live, to fill the world with words?

K. Edw. What! doth she swoon? use means for her recovery.

Rich. Clarence, excuse me to the king, my brother;

I'll hence to London on a serious matter:

mEre ye come there, be sure to hear some news.

 Clar. What? what?

 Rich. Tower! the Tower!   *Exit.* 50

 Queen. O Ned, sweet Ned! speak to thy mother, boy!

Canst thou not speak? O traitors! murtherers!

They that stabb'd Cæsar shed no blood at all,

Did not offend, nor were not worthy blame,

If this foul deed were by, to equal it: 55

He was a man; this, in respect, a child;

And men ne'er spend their fury on a child.

What's worse than murtherer, that I may name it?

No, no, my heart will burst, an if I speak:

And I will speak, that so my heart may burst. 60

Butchers and villains! bloody cannibals!

How sweet a plant have you untimely cropp'd!

You have no children, butchers! if you had,

The thought of them would have stirr'd up remorse:

But if you ever chance to have a child,   65

Look in his youth to have him so cut off

As, deathsmen, you have rid this sweet young prince!

 K. Edw. Away with her! go, bear her hence perforce.

 Queen. Nay, never bear me hence, dispatch me here:

Here sheathe thy sword, I'll pardon thee my death. 70

What! wilt thou not? then, Clarence, do it thou.

 Clar. By heaven, I will not do thee so much ease.

 Queen. Good Clarence, do; sweet Clarence, do thou do it.

 Clar. Didst thou not hear me swear I would not do it?

 Queen. Ay, but thou usest to forswear thyself: 75

'Twas sin before, but now 'tis charity.

What! wilt thou not? Where is that devil's butcher,

Richard, hard-favour'd Richard? Richard, where art thou?

Thou art not here: murther is thy alms-deed;

Petitioners for blood thou ne'er put'st back. 80

 K. Edw. Away, I say! I charge ye, bear her hence.

 Queen. So come to you and yours, as to this prince!

       Exit Queen [led out forcibly].

 K. Edw. Where's Richard gone?

 Clar. To London, all in post; and, as I guess,

To make a bloody supper in the Tower.   85

 K. Edw. He's sudden if a thing comes in his head.

Now march we hence: discharge the common sort

With pay and thanks, and let's away to London

And see our gentle queen how well she fares;

By this, I hope, she hath a son for me.   90

        Exit [with Clarence].

❧ SCENE SIXTH ❧

[London. The Tower]

Enter Henry the Sixth and Richard [meeting], with the Lieutenant
on the Walls.

 Rich. Good day, my lord. What! at your book so hard?

 Hen. Ay, my good lord:—my lord, I should say rather;

'Tis sin to flatter, 'good' was little better:

'Good Gloucester' and 'good devil' were alike,

And both preposterous; therefore, not 'good lord.' 5

 Rich. Sirrah, leave us to ourselves: we must confer.

        [Exit Lieutenant.]

 Hen. So flies the reckless shepherd from the wolf;

So first the harmless sheep doth yield his fleece,

And next his throat unto the butcher's knife.

What scene of death hath Roscius now to act? 10

 Rich. Suspicion always haunts the guilty mind;

The thief doth fear each bush an officer.

 Hen. The bird that hath been limed in a bush,

With trembling wings misdoubteth every bush;

And I, the hapless male to one sweet bird, 15

Have now the fatal object in my eye

Where my poor young was lim'd, was caught, and kill'd.

 Rich. Why, what a peevish fool was that of Crete,

That taught his son the office of a fowl!

And yet, for all his wings, the fool was drown'd. 20

 Hen. I, Dædalus; my poor boy, Icarus;

Thy father, Minos, that denied our course;

The sun, that sear'd the wings of my sweet boy,

Thy brother Edward, and thyself the sea,

Whose envious gulf did swallow up his life. 25

Ah! kill me with thy weapon, not with words.

My breast can better brook thy dagger's point

Than can my ears that tragic history.

But wherefore dost thou come? is 't for my life?

 Rich. Think'st thou I am an executioner? 30

 Hen. A persecutor, I am sure, thou art:

If murth'ring innocents be executing,

Why, then thou art an executioner.

 Rich. Thy son I kill'd for his presumption.

 Hen. Hadst thou been kill'd, when first thou didst presume,

Thou hadst not liv'd to kill a son of mine.

And thus I prophesy: that many a thousand,

Which now mistrust no parcel of my fear,

And many an old man's sigh, and many a widow's,

And many an orphan's water-standing eye, 40

Men for their sons', wives for their husbands',

And orphans for their parents' timeless death,

Shall rue the hour that ever thou wast born.

The owl shriek'd at thy birth, an evil sign;

The night-crow cried, aboding luckless time; 45

Dogs howl'd, and hideous tempest shook down trees!

The raven rook'd her on the chimney's top,

And chattering pies in dismal discords sung.

Thy mother felt more than a mother's pain,

And yet brought forth less than a mother's hope; 50

To wit an indigested and deformed lump,

---

39 **Sprawl'st:** *twitchest in death-agony* 42 **Marry . . . shall:** *I will, forsooth* 48 **be sure:** *expect* 55 **equal:** *compare with* 56 **in respect:** *compared with him* 62 **cropp'd:** *broken off* 63 **You have no children;** *cf. n.* 64 **remorse:** *pity* 67 **deathsmen:** *executioners* **rid:** *made away* 75 **usest:** *hast the habit* 79 **alms-deed:** *charity* 82 **come to:** *befall* 87 **common sort:** *plain soldiery*

10 **Roscius;** *cf. n.* 13 **limed:** *caught with bird-lime* 15 **male:** *male parent* 18 **that of Crete;** *cf. n.* 38 **mistrust no parcel:** *have no inkling* 40 **water-standing:** *flooded with tears* 42 **timeless:** *untimely* 45 **aboding:** *foreboding* 47 **rook'd her:** *squatted* 48 **pies:** *magpies*

Not like the fruit of such a goodly tree.
Teeth hadst thou in thy head when thou wast born,
To signify thou cam'st to bite the world:
And, if the rest be true which I have heard, 55
Thou cam'st—
 Rich. I'll hear no more: die, prophet, in thy speech:
             Stabs him.
For this, amongst the rest, was I ordain'd.
 Hen. Ay, and for much more slaughter after this.
O, God forgive my sins, and pardon thee! 60
 Rich. What! will the aspiring blood of Lancaster
Sink in the ground? I thought it would have mounted.
See how my sword weeps for the poor king's death!
O, may such purple tears be always shed
From those that wish the downfall of our house. 65
If any spark of life be yet remaining,
Down, down to hell; and say I sent thee thither,
           Stabs him again.
I, that have neither pity, love, nor fear.
Indeed, 'tis true, that Henry told me of;
For I have often heard my mother say 70
I came into the world with my legs forward.
Had I not reason, think ye, to make haste,
And seek their ruin that usurp'd our right?
The midwife wonder'd, and the women cried
'O! Jesus bless us, he is born with teeth.' 75
And so I was; which plainly signified
That I should snarl and bite and play the dog.
Then, since the heavens have shap'd my body so,
Let hell make crook'd my mind to answer it.
I have no brother, I am like no brother; 80
And this word 'love,' which greybeards call divine,
Be resident in men like one another
And not in me: I am myself alone.
Clarence, beware; thou keep'st me from the light:
But I will sort a pitchy day for thee; 85
For I will buzz abroad such prophecies
That Edward shall be fearful of his life;
And then, to purge his fear, I'll be thy death.
King Henry and the prince his son are gone:
Clarence, thy turn is next, and then the rest, 90
Counting myself but bad till I be best.
I'll throw thy body in another room,
And triumph, Henry, in thy day of doom.
         Exit [with the body].

For hardy and undoubted champions;
Two Cliffords, as the father and the son;
And two Northumberlands: two braver men
Ne'er spurr'd their coursers at the trumpet's sound;
With them, the two brave bears, Warwick and Montague, 10
That in their chains fetter'd the kingly lion,
And made the forest tremble when they roar'd.
Thus have we swept suspicion from our seat,
And made our footstool of security.
Come hither, Bess, and let me kiss my boy. 15
Young Ned, for thee thine uncles and myself
Have in our armours watch'd the winter's night;
Went all afoot in summer's scalding heat,
That thou might'st repossess the crown in peace;
And of our labours thou shalt reap the gain. 20
 Rich. [*Aside.*] I'll blast his harvest, if your head were laid;
For yet I am not look'd on in the world.
This shoulder was ordain'd so thick to heave;
And heave it shall some weight, or break my back:
Work thou the way, and that shall execute. 25
 King. Clarence and Gloucester, love my lovely queen;
And kiss your princely nephew, brothers both.
 Clar. The duty that I owe unto your majesty
I seal upon the lips of this sweet babe.
 King. Thanks, noble Clarence; worthy brother, thanks. 30
 Rich. And that I love the tree from whence thou sprang'st,
Witness the loving kiss I give the fruit.
[*Aside.*] To say the truth, so Judas kiss'd his master,
And cried 'all hail!' when as he meant all harm.
 King. Now am I seated as my soul delights, 35
Having my country's peace and brothers' loves.
 Clar. What will your Grace have done with Margaret?
Reignier, her father, to the King of France
Hath pawn'd the Sicils and Jerusalem,
And hither have they sent it for her ransom. 40
 King. Away with her, and waft her hence to France.
And now what rests but that we spend the time
With stately triumphs, mirthful comic shows,
Such as befits the pleasure of the court?
Sound drums and trumpets! farewell sour annoy! 45
For here, I hope, begins our lasting joy. *Exeunt omnes.*

⁜ FINIS ⁜

⁜ SCENE SEVENTH ⁜

[The Same. A Room in the Palace]
Flourish. Enter King, Queen [Elizabeth], Clarence, Richard,
Hastings, Nurse [with Infant], and Attendants.

 King. Once more we sit in England's royal throne,
Repurchas'd with the blood of enemies.
What valiant foemen, like to autumn's corn,
Have we mow'd down, in tops of all their pride!
Three Dukes of Somerset, threefold renown'd 5

64 purple tears: *drops of blood* 85 sort: *find out* pitchy: *pitch-black* 86 buzz: *whisper* 88 purge: *remove* 91 bad: *lowly* 4 in tops: *at the height*

6 undoubted: *fearless* 7 as: *to wit* 13 suspicion: *anxiety* 17 watch'd: *kept vigil
through* 21 laid: *laid to rest, dead* 25 thou: *his brain* that: *his arm or shoulder* 40
it: *the sum raised* 43 triumphs: *public rejoicings*

NOTES

The Third Part of Henry the Sixth. Here and elsewhere the old editions read 'Sixt' for sixth. So 'fift' for modern 'fifth.'

I.i.S.d. *Enter Plantagenet.* This is the name under which York is known in *1 Henry VI.* See that play, III.i. 172–174, and the note in this edition. It is perhaps remarkable that the *Second Part* never uses the name.

I.i.1. *I wonder how the king escap'd our hands.* This first line, which is identical in the *True Tragedy* version, contains a violation of historic fact. The king did not escape, or attempt to escape, the Yorkists. He was found by them after the battle with a slight arrow-wound in the neck, and was treated with great outward respect.

I.i.7–9. *Lord Clifford, and Lord Stafford, all abreast, Charg'd our main battle's front, and breaking in Were by the swords of common soldiers slain.* This account of Clifford's death is inconsistent with that given in *2 Henry Vi,* V.ii., where Clifford is slain by York. Compare also line 164 of the present scene and line 48 of I.iii. The inconsistency is in all these cases carried over from the earlier plays of the *Contention* and *True Tragedy.*

I.i.14. *brother.* The Marquis of Montague, Warwick's brother, who fell at Barnet (cf. V.ii.), was not created Lord Montague till after the battle of Towton (1461), which is dramatized in Act II of the present play. He was not York's brother, but his nephew. Has the historical Montague been merged with Faulconbridge, his uncle, who was Salisbury's brother and York's brother-in-law, and who does not appear in *3 Henry VI?* In the *True Tragedy* version Montague likewise addresses York as 'brother' at this point; but in the next scene (lines 4 and 36), where York calls him 'brother,' the *True Tragedy* has 'cosen Montague.' See notes on lines 212 and 243.

I.i.17. *Richard hath best deserv'd of all my sons.* The precocity of Richard of Gloucester is probably the most striking of all the deviations from history in this play and its predecessor, the *Second Part.* Born at Fotheringay Castle, October 2, 1452, Richard was incapable of taking part in the first battle of St. Albans, May 22, 1455. He was less than nineteen at the time of the battle of Tewkesbury (May 4, 1471), with which this play concludes.

I.i.S.d. *They go up.* The chair of state, in which York seats himself, is apparently on the upper stage.

I.i.35. *The queen this day here holds her parliament.* The author represents these events as following immediately upon the first battle of St. Albans (May 22, 1455), but the Parliament which declared York heir to the throne did not in fact meet till October, 1460.

I.i.47. *Dares stir a wing if Warwick shake his bells.* An allusion to falconry. Bells were attached to the legs of falcons. The best illustration I know is a passage in Nicholas Grimald's Latin play, *Christus Redivivus* (1543), II.iii.:

> 'Attamen a dominis cum dimittitur,
> Sinistra hic ales & in sublime uolitat: eam
> Adoritur atque insequitur strenuissime,
> Ac motis pendenteis tibijs campanulæ
> Tubæ sonitum supplent, crescat ut audacitas.'

'Yet, when the hawk is sent forth by its masters, it flies aloft on the left, and attacks the heron most vigorously; and, as its legs move, the hanging bells give forth the sound of a trumpet, so that the bird's daring increases.' (Translated by L. R. Merrill.)

I.i.67. *Ah! know you not the city favours them.* London seems to have sympathized with the Yorkists during the entire struggle, though the citizens took no great part in the fighting. Holinshed says, in regard to the Queen's hostility to the Duke of York: 'She could attempt nothing against him neere to London, because the duke was in more estimation there than either the king hir husband, or hir selfe.' At the close of *2 Henry VI* (V.ii.82) Margaret professes to believe the reverse: 'We shall to London get, where you are lov'd.'

I.i.80. *Thy father was a traitor to the crown.* The Earl of Cambridge was beheaded at Southampton in 1415 for plotting against the life of Henry V. See *King Henry V,* II.ii.

I.i.89. *And that the Lord of Westmoreland shall maintain.* Ralph, second Earl of Westmoreland, representative of the older branch of the Nevil family, which sided with the Lancastrians. His wife was a daughter of Hotspur, and he a half-first-cousin of Warwick.

I.i.106. *Thy father was, as thou art, Duke of York.* Not strictly true, for York inherited the dukedom from his uncle, the elder brother of the Earl of Cambridge. See note on line 80 above.

I.i.157, 158. *'tis not thy southern power, Of Essex, Norfolk, Suffolk, nor of Kent.* Northumberland speaks as a Percy of the north. Warwick was strong in the

counties mentioned, but his power was great also in the north, the Nevil domains being largely in Yorkshire and Durham.

I.i.212. *And I unto the sea from whence I came.* The *True Tragedy* also assigns this speech to Montague, who, however, in the next scene is found at York's castle. The words do not fit the historical Montague. See note on line 243.

I.i.230. *Father, you cannot disinherit me.* The prince was born October 13, 1454, and was therefore only six years old at the time of this scene.

I.i.243. *Stern Faulconbridge commands the narrow seas.* This line is echoed in Marlowe's *Edward II,* line 970: 'The hautie Dane commands the narrow seas.' Faulconbridge is mentioned only here in the play. He is Warwick's uncle, William Nevil, Baron Fauconberg, who commanded at Calais as Warwick's deputy in 1459–1460, led the Yorkist left wing at Towton, and was later made Earl of Kent. The special reference in the present line is to his control of Calais and the Straits of Dover during the year previous to the Parliament of 1460. There is no reason for the assumption of commentators that Fauconberg's son Thomas (also known as Faulconbridge) is referred to. The latter figures at a later period (ca. 1470) and receives much attention in the first part of Heywood's play, *King Edward IV.* I conjecture that Faulconbridge's part in the drama has been amalgamated with that of his nephew Montague, and that the figure referred to in this line is the same as the speaker of lines 14 and 212 above.

I.ii.28–31. *And, father, do but think How sweet a thing it is to wear a crown, Within whose circuit is Elysium, And all that poets feign of bliss and joy.* These beautiful lines, which are not found in the *True Tragedy* version, reproduce very exactly the sentiment and melody of Marlowe's *Tamburlaine.* Compare lines 763–765 of that play:

> 'I thinke the pleasure they enjoy in heauen
> Can not compare with kingly joyes in earth,
> To weare a Crowne enchac'd with pearle and golde.'

And also lines 863, 879 f.,

> 'The . . . sweetnes of a crowne . . .
> That perfect blisse and sole felicitie,
> The sweet fruition of an earthly crowne.'

If the absence of such notable lines from all editions previous to the Shakespeare Folio indicates that they are additions by Shakespeare, they show how capable he was of reproducing the veritable tone of Marlowe.

I.ii.42, 43. *In them I trust; for they are soldiers, Witty, courteous, liberal, full of spirit.* These lines also, which so praise the men of Marlowe's native Kent, first appear in the Folio. For Shakespeare's apparent interest in Kent compare notes on IV.i.9 and IV.vii.51, 52 of the *Second Part.*

I.ii.S.d. *Enter Gabriel.* The name of the actor who represented the messenger has here been preserved. The same thing happens in the stage direction at the opening of Act III. This is good evidence that the Folio text was based on the players' copy used by the prompter. Gabriel is probably Gabriel Spencer, the actor, who was slain by Ben Jonson in a duel, September 22, 1598.

I.iii.40. *But 'twas ere I was born.* The author has altered the relative ages of the Duke of York's sons. Edmund, Earl of Rutland, was next to Edward the heir. He was twelve years old at the time of his death and seven when the elder Clifford was killed at St. Albans. Richard of Gloucester, on the other hand, who is represented in the play as a mature warrior, was not born till 1452, and was but eight years old at the battle of Wakefield. Compare note on I.i.17.

I.iv.25. *The sands are number'd that makes up my life.* Modern editors usually print 'make,' but the other is a genuine plural form, characteristic of the northern English dialect. It is frequently employed by Shakespeare and other standard Elizabethan writers. For other examples in this play compare line 150 of the present scene and also II.i.55, II.i.83, II.v.87, II.vi.6, III.ii.160, IV.ii.3, V.v.26, V.vii.44.

I.iv.33. *Phaethon.* The son of Apollo, who (according to Ovid) attempted to guide the chariot of the sun and was dashed to pieces. Compare II.vi.11–13.

I.iv.67. *Come, make him stand upon this molehill here.* 'Some write that the duke was taken aliue, and in derision caused to stand vpon a molehill.' (Holinshed.)

I.iv.137. *O tiger's heart wrapp'd in a woman's hide!* This line, which occurs in the same form in the *True Tragedy,* has been made famous by Robert Greene's parody in his attack on Shakespeare (*Groatsworth of Wit,* 1592): 'for there is an upstart Crow, beautified with our feathers, that with his *Tygers heart wrapt in a Players hide,* supposes he is as well able to bumbast out a blanke verse as the best of you: and being an absolute *Johannes fac totum,* is in his owne conceit the onely Shake-scene in a countrie.'

I.iv.155. *tigers of Hyrcania.* Proverbially fierce from the time that Vergil made Dido (*Ænid* iv.367) refer to 'Hyrcanæ . . . tigres.' Hyrcania was a province in ancient Persia on the Caspian Sea.

I.iv.164. *There, take the crown, and with the crown my curse.* This gesture, rather absurd in the case of York's paper crown, is suggestive of the abdication of Marlowe's *Edward II* (line 2043): 'Here, take my crowne, the life of Edward too.'

II.i.20. *Methinks 'tis prize enough to be his son.* The *True Tragedy* prints 'pride' instead of 'prize,' and the former may be the proper word.

II.i.25. *Dazzle mine eyes, or do I see three suns?* The apparition here described is related by the chroniclers as occurring just before Edward's victory at Mortimer's Cross (February 2, 1461): 'At which time the sunne (as some write) appeared to the earle of March like three sunnes, and suddenlie ioined altogither in one. Upon which sight he tooke such courage, that he, fiercelie setting on his enimies, put them to flight.' (Holinshed.) The engagement at Mortimer's Cross has been omitted by the dramatist. The present scene should be imagined as occurring at Chipping Norton where Edward and Warwick met after the latter's defeat at the second battle of St. Albans, February 17, 1461, though the allusion in line 140 to 'the marches here' shows that the dramatist thought of Edward as still in the neighborhood of Mortimer's Cross on the Welsh border.

II.i.68, 69. *Sweet Duke of York! our prop to lean upon, Now thou art gone, we have no staff, no stay!* Compare Marlowe's *Massacre at Paris*, lines 1122, 1123:

> 'Sweet Duke of Guise, our prop to leane vpon,
> Now thou art dead, heere is no stay for vs.'

The version of line 69 in the *True Tragedy* is still closer: 'Now thou art gone there is no hope for vs.'

II.i.91, 92. *Nay, if thou be that princely eagle's bird, Show thy descent by gazing 'gainst the sun.* Alluding to the common idea, derived from Pliny, that eagles could gaze at the sun without blinking.

II.i.114. *And very well appointed, as I thought.* This line is omitted in the Folio, probably by inadvertence. Otherwise the speech of Warwick is identical in the Folio and *True Tragedy* versions, save for a few trifling verbal alterations of the reviser.

II.i.147. *your kind aunt, Duchess of Burgundy.* 'Isabel, daughter of John I, King of Portugal, by Philippa of Lancaster, eldest daughter of John of Gaunt: she was therefore third cousin to Edward instead of aunt.' (Rolfe.) Holinshed records that after the death of the Duke of York and his second son Rutland, 'The duches of Yorke, seeing hir husband and sonne slaine, and not knowing what should succeed of hir eldest sonnes chance, sent hir two yonger sonnes, George and Richard, ouer the sea, to the citie of Utrecht in Almaine, where they were of Philip duke of Burgognie well receiued; and so remained there, till their brother Edward had got the crowne and gouernement of the realme.'

II.ii.76. *Why, that's my fortune too; therefore I'll stay.* The king was not at the battle of Towton, but attending the Palm Sunday service at York, ten miles away.

II.ii.89–92. *Since when, his oath is broke; for, as I hear, You, that are king, though he do wear the crown, Have caus'd him, by new act of parliament, To blot out me, and put his own son in.* These lines throw light upon the reviser's method. In the *True Tragedy* they are assigned to Clarence, and line 92 reads: 'To blot our brother out, and put his owne son in.' In the Folio 'our brother' is replaced by 'me,' for no obvious reason except to reduce the length of the line; but by inadvertence the abbreviated speaker's name, '*Cla.*,' is left standing before line 89, and it remained for modern editors to rectify the inconsistency.

II.ii.144, 145. *A wisp of straw were worth a thousand crowns, To make this shameless callet know herself.* A wisp of straw was the mark of shame attached to a scold or other female offender.

II.ii.155. *And grac'd thy poor sire with his bridal day.* Made a present to your father of the expenses of the wedding. There is a gibe at the condition in the marriage contract (*2 Henry VI*, I.i.60, 61) that Margaret be 'sent over of the King of England's own proper cost and charges, without having any dowry.'

II.iii.1, 2. *Forspent with toil, as runners with a race, I lay me down a little while to breathe.* The battle of Towton lasted ten hours, on Palm Sunday, 1461; thirty thousand men were slain, and it was in all respects the most terrible conflict of the Wars of the Roses. The present picture of the discouragement of the Yorkist leaders, exaggerated for dramatic purposes, is suggested by a local advantage which the Lancastrians under Clifford had gained two days before (March 26) at Ferrybridge.

II.iii.15. *Thy brother's blood the thirsty earth hath drunk.* The 'Bastard of Salisbury,' half-brother of Warwick, was slain at Ferrybridge. It is remarkable that in the *True Trgedy* Richard announces to Warwick the death, not of his brother, but of his father Salisbury. The reviser doubtless made the correction for the sake of accuracy, since Holinshed records the historic fact that Salisbury had already been captured at Wakefield and beheaded.

II.v.54. The latter part of this soliloquy, from line 20, corresponds to nothing in the *True Tragedy* and is a good example of the sentimental note found in many of Shakespeare's additions to the original play. There is an evident analogy to the much more mature soliloquy of Richard II on thought (*Richard II*, V.v.1–66) and Henry IV on sleep (*2 Henry IV*, III.i.4ff.). It is equally evident, I think, that lines 20–54 are influenced by the style of Greene's pastoral verse.

II.v.S.d. *Enter Father, bearing of his son.* The Father, whose entrance has been prepared for in the stage direction following line 54, now comes forward.

II.vi.S.d. *Enter Clifford, wounded.* The *True Tragedy* reads 'Enter Clifford wounded, with an arrow in his necke.' Clifford was actually slain, in a small engagement on the day before the battle of Towton, by an arrow in the neck.

II.vi.8. *The common people swarm like summer flies.* This line is not in the Folio, and has been introduced from the *True Tragedy* version (cf. II.i.113). On the other hand, line 17, which also mentions summer flies, is found only in the Folio. Both were probably not intended to remain. With these exceptions, Clifford's speech is virtually the same in the two versions and may pass as a fair sample of the *True Tragedy* style.

II.vi.42–44. The speeches are divided as in the *True Tragedy*. The Folio gives lines 42, 43, and the first four words of 44 to Richard, Edward's speech beginning 'And now.'

II.vi.49. *But set.* An example of confused syntax; 'but' is redundant. Lines 47–51 are a bad example of sentimental amplification of two simple verses in the *True Tragedy*:

> 'Who kild our tender brother Rutland,
> And stabd our princelie father Duke of Yorke.'

II.vi.90. *the Lady Bona.* Daughter to the Duke of Savoy and sister to the French queen. She lived at the court of her brother-in-law, Louis XI. Warwick did advocate this marriage for King Edward, and was displeased when he married Lady Grey; but the negotiations concerning the Lady Bona in 1464 cannot be regarded as the immediate cause of the open rupture between Warwick and Edward five years later.

II.vi.107. *Gloucester's dukedom is too ominous.* The chroniclers comment upon the fact that three Dukes of Gloucester before Richard had come to miserable ends. One was Duke Humphrey, who figures in the first and second parts of *Henry VI*, and another Duke Thomas 'of Woodstock,' whose murder is frequently alluded to in *Richard II*.

III.i.S.d. *Enter Sinklo and Humphrey.* The *True Tragedy* reads 'Enter two keepers with bow and arrowes.' Compare notes on I.ii.S.d., where similarly the Folio substitutes the name of the actor. Sinklo is John Sinkler, an unimportant member of Shakespeare's company. His name occurs in connection with small rôles in the Induction to *The Taming of the Shrew* and in *2 Henry IV*, V.iv. (Quarto version). Humphrey seems to be Humphrey Jeffes, a minor actor associated at different times with various companies.

III.i.24. *Let me embrace thee, sour adversity.* The Folio reads 'Let me embrace the sower Aduersaries.'

III.ii.6, 7. *Because in quarrel of the house of York The worthy gentleman did lose his life.* This statement, which the reviser has taken over from the *True Tragedy*, is incorrect. Sir John Grey was slain at the second battle of St. Albans, fighting on the side of Queen Margaret. In *Richard III*, I.iii.130–133, Shakespeare gives the facts accurately, making Richard say to the Queen:

> 'In all which time you and your husband Grey
> Were factious for the house of Lancaster.
> . . . Was not your husband
> In Margaret's battle at St. Albans slain?'

(In line 2 of the present passage the name of the lady's husband is given as Sir *Richard* Grey in both the *True Tragedy* and the Folio; 'Sir John Grey' is the correction of modern editors.)

III.ii.133. *That's a day longer than a wonder lasts.* A 'nine days' wonder' being the proverbial superlative.

III.ii.180, 181. *an unlick'd bear-whelp That carries no impression like the dam.* Fabulous natural history, reported by both Ovid and Pliny. The young bear was supposed to be born a formless mass of flesh which the mother reduced to symmetry by licking with her tongue.

III.ii.212. *And set the murtherous Machiavel to school.* Machiavelli was born in 1469, five years later than the historical date of this scene; but the anachronism is justified by the fact that Gloucester's character owes much to the current Elizabethan distortion of Machiavelli's doctrine of the Prince.

III.iii.16–18. *Yield not thy neck To fortune's yoke, but let thy dauntless mind Still ride in triumph over all mischance.* Lines strikingly suggestive of Marlowe. Since they do not appear in the *True Tragedy*, they are doubtless to be ascribed

to that poet's influence upon the reviser, not actually to his pen. Compare note on I.ii.28–31.

III.iii.83, 84. *Then Warwick disannuls great John of Gaunt, Which did subdue the greatest part of Spain.* John of Gaunt was engaged in an indecisive campaign in Spain in 1386–1387, and in 1367 had served with his brother, the Black Prince, in a more successful expedition. The theme of his rather apocryphal triumphs was apparently popular in England during the Armada era. Kyd's *Spanish Tragedy* (ca. 1587, I.v.48ff.) refers to 'a valiant Englishman,

> *Braue John of Gaunt, the Duke of Lancaster.*
>
> . . . . .
>
> *He with a puissant armie came to Spaine,*
> *And tooke our King of Castile prisoner.'*

A book (not now extant) was licensed for publication, May 14, 1594, under the title of 'the famous historye of John of Gaunte, sonne to Kinge Edward the Third, with his conquest of Spaine and marriage of his Twoo daughters to the Kinges of Castile and Portugale, &c.'

III.iii.97, 98. *Why, Warwick, canst thou speak against thy liege, Whom thou obeyedst thirty and six years.* The *True Tragedy* reads 'thirtie and eight yeeres.' Warwick was born in 1428 and at the time of the negotiation for the French marriage of Edward (1464) was thirty-six years old. But the dramatists were thinking of the general period during which King Henry's sovereignty had been acknowledged by the Yorkist party: i.e. from his accession in 1422 till the final breach in 1459 or 1460.

III.iii.103–105. *Call him my king, by whose injurious doom My elder brother, the Lord Aubrey Vere, Was done to death? and more than so, my father.* Holinshed reports, under date of February, 1462, that 'the earle of Oxford, far striken in age, and his sonne and heire the lord Awbreie Veer, either through malice of their enimies, or for that they had offended the king, were both, with diuerse of their councellours, attainted, and put to execution; which caused Iohn earle of Oxford euer after to rebell.' Actually, however, the present earl did not declare himself for the house of Lancaster till much later (1470).

III.iii.131. *Exempt from envy, but not from disdain.* This complex sentence (lines 123–128) is taken practically without change from the *True Tragedy*. The idea is that Edward's love is so genuine, so solidly rooted in appreciation of Bona's virtue and beauty, that it need apprehend no misconstruction (*envy*), though its very sincerity lays the king particularly open to pain if Bona should reject his suit.

III.iii.161. *Proud setter up and puller down of kings.* Virtually the same words which Margaret here applies to Warwick have been addressed by King Edward to the deity in II.iii.37: 'Thou setter up and plucker down of kings.'

III.iii.190, 191. *Did I forget that by the house of York My father came untimely to his death?* The lines are taken directly from the *True Tragedy*, but contain no truth. Salisbury, Warwick's father, was captured by the Lancastrians at the battle of Wakefield and by them beheaded. Compare note on II.iii.15.

III.iii.192. *Did I let pass th' abuse done to my niece?* The chronicles report vaguely that Warwick had received some such injury from Edward. (Bulwer-Lytton's novel, *The Last of the Barons*, ascribes the hostility of Warwick and Edward to abuse done Warwick's daughter.)

III.iii.247, 248. *I'll join mine eldest daughter and my joy To him forthwith in holy wedlock bands.* It was Warwick's younger daughter, Anne, who married Prince Edward, the elder having been already married to Clarence. In *Richard III,* I.i.156, the error is corrected. Speaking of Prince Edward's widow, Richard says: 'For then I'll marry Warwick's youngest daughter.'

IV.i.S.d. *Four stand on one side, and four on the other.* The king stands in the middle and the two factions group themselves at opposite sides of the stage.

IV.i.41. *England is safe, if true within itself.* A common sentiment which forms the subject of the concluding lines of Shakespeare's *King John*.

IV.i.48, 49. *For this one speech Lord Hastings well deserves To have the heir of the Lord Hungerford.* This passage and lines 52–56 below are based on Halle's report of a complaint against the king which Clarence made to Warwick: 'This you knowe well enough, that the heire of the Lord Scales he hath maried to his wifes brother, the heire also of the lorde Bonuile and Haryngton he hath geuen to his wifes sonne, and theire of the lorde Hungerford he hath graunted to the lorde Hastynges: thre mariages more meter for hys twoo brethren and kynne then for suche newe foundlynges as he hath bestowed theim on.'

IV.i.71. *That I was not ignoble of descent.* Her mother, born Jacquetta of Luxemburg, was a great lady of Burgundy, who was married in 1433 to the Duke of Bedford, brother of Henry V. Upon Bedford's death she married Sir Richard Woodville, whose daughter the present queen was.

IV.i.119. *Belike the elder; Clarence will have the younger.* Compare note on III. iii. 247, 248. Clarence had married Warwick's elder daughter, Isabel, June

11, 1469, more than a year before the marriage of his younger daughter to Prince Edward.

IV.ii.20, 21. *With sleight and manhood stole to Rhesus' tents, And brought from thence the Thracian fatal steeds.* It had been prophesied that Troy could not be taken if the horses of Rhesus, King of Thrace, drank of the Xanthus River and grazed on the Trojan plain. The tenth book of the *Iliad* tells how Ulysses and Diomede, exponents of craft (*sleight*) and valor (*manhood*) respectively, averted the peril by slaying Rhesus on the night of his arrival and carrying off the horses. The story is referred to by both Ovid and Vergil. This allusion is an addition by the reviser of the play: lines 19–25 appear first in the Folio, whereas the rest of Warwick's speech is virtually unchanged from the *True Tragedy*.

IV.iii.S.d. *French Soldiers.* This stage direction and all the business of the watchmen (lines 1–22, 26, 27) are added by the reviser. Two separate overthrows of King Edward by Warwick have been merged by the dramatists. The capture of the king here depicted took place in July, 1469, before Warwick's reconciliation with King Henry and without the aid of French soldiers. In March, 1470, Edward suddenly regained his power, and Warwick was obliged to flee to France. Here he united with the Lancastrians, and in September (1470) he landed at Dartmouth, accompanied by French troops. Edward then found himself deserted by his followers and fled to Holland.

IV.iii.54. *Unto my brother, Archbishop of York.* George Nevil. It was in fact he who commanded the body of horse that captured Edward, July 28, 1469.

IV.iii.55. *When I have fought with Pembroke and his fellows.* This fight took place a couple of days before Edward's capture. The Earl of Pembroke was defeated near Banbury, July 26, 1469, and beheaded at Northampton the next day.

IV.iv. In the *True Tragedy* this scene follows the present scene five. The reviser's transposition is a dramatic improvement.

IV.iv.2. *brother Rivers.* The queen's oldet brother, Anthony Woodville, Lord Rivers. It was he who married the heiress of Lord Scales. Cf. IV.i.52–54.

IV.iv.22. *blood-sucking sighs.* Alluding to an old belief that sighing exhausted the blood. See note on *2 Henry VI,* III.ii.62, 63.

IV.iv.31, 32. *I'll hence forthwith unto the sanctuary, To save at least the heir of Edward's right.* After Edward's flight from England to Holland, 'his wife queene Elizabeth tooke sanctuarie at Westminster, and there, in great penurie, forsaken of all hir friends, was deliuered of a faire son called Edward.' (Holinshed.) The date of the prince's birth was November, 1470.

IV.v. Two distinct events are combined in this account of Edward's escape from Warwick, as in scene three two separate overthrows of Edward by Warwick have been merged (cf. note on IV.iii.S.d.). Edward's release from surveillance at Middleham Castle occurred, with Warwick's consent, in September, 1469; his precipitate flight to Holland took place just a year later, when Warwick returned to England, September, 1470, at the head of the Lancastrian forces. The strategem by which Edward is rescued in this scene is apocryphal, but is found in the chroniclers.

IV.vi.67. *it is young Henry, Earl of Richmond.* The future King Henry VII. He was the grandson of Katharine of France, widow of Henry V, by her second husband, Owen Tudor. The story of Henry VI's prophecy concerning the boy (who was thirteen years old at the time of this scene) is found in Holinshed. It is an evident fabrication, devised in compliment to the Tudor dynasty.

IV.vii. In the *True Tragedy* this scene and scene six are transposed. Compare note on scene four above. The arrangement of material before the reviser's changes was, then: scene iii., scene v., scene iv., scene vii., scene vi., scene viii.

IV.vii.8. *Ravenspurgh haven.* On the coast of Yorkshire, at the mouth of the Humber River. The site is now submerged. Henry IV (Bolingbroke) landed here in 1399. The landing of Edward IV occurred on March 14, 1471.

IV.vii.40. *Sir John Montgomery.* The name is Sir Thomas Montgomery in Holinshed, who reports that it was at Nottingham, not York, that Montgomery joined the King and persuaded him to make open claim to the crown.

IV.vii.50. *Drummer.* Some copies of the Folio have 'Drumme,' and the *True Tragedy* 'Drum.'

IV.viii.S.d. *Exeter.* The Folio substitutes Somerset's name for Exeter's, but the latter's presence is evidenced by lines 34 ('Cousin of Exeter') and 49 ('No, Exeter'), as well as by the abbreviated name '*Exet.*' before lines 38 and 53. It is likely that the rôles of Somerset and Exeter were played by the same actor.

IV.viii.S.d. *Shout within, 'A Lancaster! A Lancaster!'* Edward's troops have apparently been instructed to pass themselves off as adherents of Henry.

IV.viii.61, 62. *The sun shines hot, and if we use delay, Cold biting winter mars our hop'd-for hay.* I.e. let us make hay while the sun shines.

V.i.45. *You left poor Henry at the bishop's palace.* Compare IV.viii.34, where Henry says: 'Here at the palace will I rest awhile.' Halle records that when Edward entered London, King Henry's friends fled, 'leuinge kyng Henry alone, as an

hoste that shoulde be sacrificed, in the Bishops palace of London adioyninge to Poules churche.'

V.i.74, 75. *Two of thy name, both Dukes of Somerset, Have sold their lives unto the house of York.* Edmund, the second Duke of Somerset, was killed at the first battle of St. Albans (cf.I.i.16). His son Henry, the third duke, was beheaded after the battle of Hexham, May 15, 1464. (This last battle is not mentioned in the play.) The person addressed in the present lines is Edmund, the fourth duke, younger brother of Duke Henry, who was captured and beheaded after Tewkesbury (cf.V.iv.).

V.i.S.d. *Taking the red rose out of his helmet.* The revised play has no stage direction at this point, but the *True Tragedy* inserts the following: 'Sound a Parlie, and Richard and Clarence whispers togither, and then Clarence takes his red Rose out of his hat, and throwes it at Warwike.' The word 'hat' illustrates the fact that the actors were dressed in Elizabethan costume, not in mediæval armor as in modern performances.

V.ii.31. *The queen from France hath brought a puissant power.* Queen Margaret's forces landed at Weymouth on the very day on which the battle of Barnet was fought, Easter Day (April 14), 1471. Somerset made his escape from Barnet and soon joined her. (Cf. note on V.i.74, 75.)

V.ii.S.d. *Here they bear away his body.* The removal of the bodies of those supposedly slain was an important detail on stages which lacked front curtains.

V.iv.1–38. A particularly noteworthy example of the reviser's work. In the *True Tragedy* Margaret's speech consists of but eleven lines, and is less resolute as well as much less ornate. The reviser has deviated from the chroniclers, who report that, on hearing the news of Barnet, Margaret 'like a woman al dismaied for feare, fell to the ground, her harte was perced with sorowe, her speache was in maner passed, all her spirites were tormented with Malencoly.' She was unwilling to risk an immediate battle, but was overruled by Somerset.

V.v.2. *Away with Oxford to Hames Castle straight.* Oxford, who escaped from Barnet, was not at Tewkesbury and was only captured several years later (February, 1474) at St. Michael's Mount in Cornwall. He was then sent to the castle of Hanmes near Calais, where he remained in captivity for ten years.

V.v.25. *Let Æsop fable in a winter's night.* Æsop was reported to have been a slave, dwarfish and deformed in appearance. The prince gibes at the traditional deformity of Richard.

V.v.63. *You have no children, butchers.* On the contrary Edward had several daughters and a newly-born son (cf. n. on IV.iv.31, 32), and Clarence a son.

V.vi.10. *What scene of death hath Roscius now to act?* Roscius was a famous Roman actor (died 62 B.C.) much praised by Cicero. His distinction lay in comic not tragic rôles, but his name was used proverbially by Elizabethan writers of any excellent actor.

V.vi.18, 19. *Why, what a peevish fool was that of Crete, That taught his son the office of a fowl!* I.e. Dædalus, a fabulous contriver of marvelous mechanical inventions. Wishing to escape from Crete against the will of King Minos, he made artificial wings for himself and his son Icarus, fastening them on with wax. Dædalus made the flight in safety, but Icarus flew too near the sun, which melted the wax and caused him to fall into the Ægean.

THE TEXT OF THE PRESENT EDITION

The text of the present volume is, by permission of the Oxford University Press, that of the Oxford Shakespeare, edited by the late W. J. Craig. Craig's

text has been carefully collated with the Shakespeare Folio of 1623, and the following deviations have been introduced:

1. The stage directions of the Folio have been restored. Necessary words and directions, omitted by the Folio, are added within square brackets.

2. Punctuation and spelling have been normalized to accord with modern English practice; e.g., warlike, afoot, sunset, Saint Albans, Tewkesbury, Phaethon (instead of war-like, a-foot, sun-set, Saint Alban's, Tewksbury, Phæthon). The words murder, murther, murder'd, murther'd, burden, burthen, etc., have not been normalized, the actual form employed by the Folio being in each case retained.

3. The following changes of text have been introduced, usually in accordance with Folio authority. The readings of the present edition precede the colon, while Craig's readings follow it.

I.i.11	dangerous F: dangerously
79	It was F: 'Twas
84	that is (that's F): and that's
ii.38	to F: unto
iv.25	makes F: make
116	vizard-like F: visor-like
150	passions F: passion
II.i.55	Hews . . . fells F: Hew . . . fell
83	fires F: fire
84	burns F: burn
171	moe F: more
183	march F: march amain
v.81	an hundred F: a hundred
87	kills F: kill
110	his F: a
S.d.	Alarums F: Alarum
vi.2	whiles F: while
6	melts F: melt
100	in F: on
III.i.17	thou was F: thou wast
ii.33	Nay, then, whip me F: Nay, whip me, then
160	keeps F: keep
214	farther F: further
IV.i.9	brother of Clarence F: brother Clarence
18	shall F: you shall
ii.3	comes F: come
iii.29	here is F: here's
30	parted F: parted last
v.21	shipp'd (shipt F): ship
V.iv.34	If case F: In case
75	my eye F: mine eyes
v.26	sorts F: sort
27	ye F: you
50	Tower F: The Tower
78	Richard, hard-favour'd Richard F: Hard-favour'd Richard
vi.51	indigested and F: indigest
vii.25	that shall (that shalt F): thou shalt
44	befits F: befit

The Tragedy of Richard the Third

WITH THE LANDING OF EARL RICHMOND AND THE BATTLE AT BOSWORTH FIELD

Edited by
JACK R. CRAWFORD

Dramatis Personae

KING EDWARD THE FOURTH
EDWARD, *Prince of Wales;*
afterwards King Edward the Fifth } *Sons to the King*
RICHARD, *Duke of York*
GEORGE, *Duke of Clarence*
RICHARD, *Duke of Gloucester,* } *Brothers to the King*
afterwards King Richard the Third
EDWARD, *a young Son of Clarence*
HENRY, *Earl of Richmond;*
   afterwards King Henry the Seventh
CARDINAL BOURCHIER, *Archbishop of Canterbury*
THOMAS ROTHERHAM, *Archbishop of York*
JOHN MORTON, *Bishop of Ely*
DUKE OF BUCKINGHAM
DUKE OF NORFOLK
EARL OF SURREY, *his Son*
EARL RIVERS, *Brother to King Edward's Queen*
MARQUESS OF DORSET, AND LORD GREY, *her Sons*
EARL OF OXFORD
LORD HASTINGS
EARL OF DERBY, *called also* LORD STANLEY
LORD LOVEL
SIR THOMAS VAUGHAN
SIR RICHARD RATCLIFF
SIR WILLIAM CATESBY
SIR JAMES TYRRELL

SIR JAMES BLUNT
SIR WALTER HERBERT
SIR ROBERT BRAKENBURY, *Lieutenant of the Tower*
SIR WILLIAM BRANDON
SIR CHRISTOPHER URSWICK, *a Priest*
ANOTHER PRIEST
LORD MAYOR OF LONDON
SHERIFF OF WILTSHIRE
TRESSEL AND BERKELEY, *Gentlemen attending on*
   the Lady Anne

ELIZABETH, *Queen of King Edward the Fourth*
MARGARET, *Widow of King Henry the Sixth*
DUCHESS OF YORK, *Mother to King Edward the Fourth,*
   Clarence, and Richard, Duke of Gloucester
LADY ANNE, *Widow of Edward, Prince of Wales, Son to*
   King Henry the Sixth; afterwards married to Richard,
   Duke of Gloucester
LADY MARGARET PLANTAGENET, *a young Daughter*
   of Clarence

LORDS, AND OTHER ATTENDANTS; TWO GENTLEMEN,
   A KEEPER, A PURSUIVANT, SCRIVENER, CITIZENS,
   MURDERERS, MESSENGERS, GHOSTS OF THOSE
   MURDERED BY RICHARD THE THIRD, SOLDIERS, ETC.

SCENE—*England.*

The Tragedy of Richard the Third

INTRODUCTION

SOURCES OF THE PLAY

The second edition of Holinshed's *Chronicles* (1st ed., 1577; 2d ed., 1587) is the chief historical source of *Richard III*. Often the account in Holinshed is a paraphrase of Halle, *The Vnion of the two noble and illustre fameles of Lancastre and Yorke* (1550),[1] which in turn is based upon Sir Thomas More's *History of King Richard the thirde*, published 1513. The authorship of More's history has been attributed to Cardinal Morton, who died in 1500. For matter not in More, Halle was indebted to Polydore Vergil's *Historia Angliæ*, Basel, 1555. Textual references to Holinshed, Halle, and More in this edition are derived from *Shakspere's Holinshed*, edited by W. G. Boswell-Stone, London, 1896. Boswell-Stone's references to More's history are from the text of More's *Workes*, edition of 1557, the paging from J. R. Lumby's edition, 1883.

Matter relating to *Richard III* in the second edition of Holinshed, that is not to be found in the first, is as follows: *Holinshed*, iii. 702 (the fire-new stamp of Dorset's title, I. iii. 263, 264); *Holinshed*, iii. 754 (Richard's friends resorting to him through fear, but wishing and working his destruction, V. ii. 20, 21); *Holinshed*, iii. 757 (Richmond's oration to his army, V. iii. 256); *Holinshed*, iii. 756 (Richard's oration to his army, V. iii. 236); *Holinshed*, iii. 756 (Richmond kept in Brittany by Richard's mother's means, V. iii. 346).

Two plays on Richard's life preceded the first publication of Shakespeare's in 1597. These were Dr. Thomas Legge's *Richardus Tertius*, a tragedy in Latin performed at St. John's College, Cambridge, in 1579, and *The True Tragedie of Richard III, with the conjunction and joining of the two noble houses, Lancaster and Yorke; as it was playd by the Queenes Maiesties Players. 1594.*

Shakespeare owes little or nothing to Dr. Legge's play.[2] There has been considerable difference of opinion concerning the relation of Shakespeare's play to the *True Tragedie*. In general, it is safe to say that there are certain resemblances, such as Richard's cry for "A horse, a horse, a fresh horse," but that Shakespeare's indebtedness hardly extends beyond a few hints. Artistically and dramatically the two plays are from pole to pole apart.[3]

To sum up, Shakespeare's conception of Richard's character consistently follows More; for his incidents, the dramatist used the second edition of Holinshed, inspired perhaps in his choice of subject by the success of the *True Tragedie*. The passages from Holinshed quoted in the notes will illustrate Shakespeare's use of his principal source.

THE HISTORY OF THE PLAY

The date of composition of the play, from internal critical evidence, is about the year 1593. The first Quarto appeared in 1597, and editions were frequent thereafter.

The popularity of *Richard III* on the Elizabethan stage appears to have been great, judging from the number of contemporary references and the frequent parodies of the line "A horse! a horse! My kingdom for a horse!"[4] Richard Burbage (c. 1567-1619) probably was the creator of the rôle; in any event there are important contemporary references to his interpretation of Richard. In the *Return from Parnassus* (1601), Pt. 2, IV. iii. Burbage is portrayed as examining a Cambridge student in the art of acting, making him declaim the opening soliloquy of *Richard III*. Manningham's *Diary* for March 13, 1602, refers to an anecdote "vpon a tyme when Burbidge played Richard III." Bishop Corbet's *Iter Boreale* (written before 1635) particularly notes the fame of Burbage's Richard:

> *"For when he would have sayd 'King Richard dyed,'*
> *And call'd—'A horse! a horse!'—he Burbidge cry'de."*

In 1619 a *Funeral Elegy* on Burbage came out, a poem extant in more than one version, containing a reference to his Richard.

> *"And Crookback, as befits, shall cease to live."*

Other contemporary references may be found in J. Munro, *The Shakespeare Allusion Book*, 1909. On the other hand, we possess today no account of an Elizabethan performance of this tragedy, and but one dated reference to a performance before the closing of the theatres in 1642. In Sir Henry Herbert's *Office Book* for the year 1633 there is a note to the effect that *Richard III* was played at St. James' on November 17, before Charles I and Henrietta Maria. In a prologue prefixed to the 1641 edition of Chapman's *Bussy D'Ambois*, one of the actors is recommended because "as Richard he was liked."

When the theatres were reopened after the Restoration, although many of Shakespeare's plays (freely revised or adapted, it is true) were played, there is no record of *Richard III*. The character of Richard, however, continued to appear in plays by other dramatists, notably in John Crowne's *Henry the Sixth, The Second Part, or The Misery of Civil War* (1681), and John Caryl's *The English Princess, or The Death of Richard the Third* (1667). Thomas Betterton (c. 1635-1710), the famous actor of this period, played the Richard of *The English Princess*. Samuel Pepys saw this play on March 7, 1667; "a most sad, melancholy play, and pretty good; but nothing eminent in it, as some tragedys are." In Crowne's drama Betterton played the Earl of Warwick.

On July 9, 1700, Colley Cibber's famous revision of *Richard III* was produced at Drury Lane, a version of the tragedy destined

---

1 Page references in the notes are to the edition of 1809.

2 For a full discussion of this point, see G. B. Churchill, *Richard III up to Shakespeare*, pp. 265-395.

3 Cf. Churchill, *op. cit.*, p. 398. The text of the *True Tragedie* will be found in Furness' *Variorum*, pp. 505-548.

4 Peele, *The Battle of Alcazar* (1594); Marston, *Scourge of Villainie* (1598); Heywood, *Edward the Fourth* (pub. 1600); Chapman, *Eastward Hoe* (1605); Marston, *Parasitaster, or the Fawne* (1606), *What You Will* (1607); Heywood, *Iron Age* (1611); Brathwaite, *Strappado for the Divell* (1615); Fletcher and Massinger, *Little French Lawyer* (c. 1620).

to hold the stage until today.[5] Cibber (1671-1757) himself played Richard in his own version at various revivals up until 1733, and once thereafter (1739). There is not space here to include an analysis of Cibber's version; the text of it may be found in Oxberry's collected *British Drama*. In Furness' *Variorum* edition of *Richard III*, page 604, will be found a table of the number of lines retained by Cibber, his borrowings from other Shakespearean plays, and his own additions, all of which totalled some thousand odd lines.[6]

The following revivals of *Richard III*, previous to Garrick's London début are recorded by Genest: Dec. 6, 1715, Drury Lane; March 11, 1721, Lincoln's Inn Fields, with Ryan as Richard. The latter continued to play the part until 1740, challenging rivalry with Cibber of the Drury Lane company in the rôle. In 1732 Ryan and the Lincoln's Inn company moved to Covent Garden. Drury Lane revived the play in 1734 and 1739 with Quin as Richard.

On October 19, 1741, at Goodman's Fields, David Garrick (1717-1779) appeared for the first time on the London stage, choosing for his début the character of Richard the Third. Possibly no first night in the history of the English stage has created a greater sensation than this of Garrick's. It was a triumph, establishing him at once as the foremost actor of the day, a position he retained throughout his life. The secret of Garrick's success, apart from the genius with which he was endowed, was the naturalness of his acting. The playing of tragic rôles had become conventionalized into declamation, rant, artificial gestures and poses. For these defects Garrick substituted an "easy and familiar, yet forcible style in speaking and acting."[7] Garrick played Richard seventeen times that season, and fourteen times the next season at Drury Lane. He continued to play the part at intervals throughout his whole career, his last appearance as Richard being on June 5, 1776, the occasion of his retirement from the stage. During this year Mrs. Siddons, the great tragic actress, played Lady Anne twice to Garrick's Richard.

Throughout the whole of this time the tragedy (in Cibber's version) remained a public and professional favorite. Many other well-known actors, besides Garrick, appeared as Richard, among them Quin (famous also as a Falstaff), Ryan, Spranger Barry, Mossop, and Thomas Sheridan. In 1746 Garrick challenged Quin to an alternating duel in the character, Quin appearing one night as a representative of the old flamboyant school of tragedy, and Garrick the next to uphold the naturalistic school. The public verdict was overwhelmingly for Garrick. Charles Macklin (1699-1797), an actor of considerable fame and actual merit before the vogue of Garrick, played Richard four times at the age of eighty-five.

In 1789 John Philip Kemble (1757-1823) first appeared in the character of Richard. Kemble was not a believer in naturalistic acting and returned to the school of "high-erected deportment, expressive action, solemn cadence, (and) stately pauses." Kemble's dignity, however, was free from the faults of the ranting pre-Garrick period. "The declamation of Mr. Kemble seemed to be fetched from the schools of philosophy—it was always pure and correct."[8] Kemble played Richard at Drury Lane at intervals until 1802, and at Covent Garden until he left the stage in 1817.

Mrs. Siddons usually played Queen Elizabeth to her brother's Richard, and another brother, Charles, played Richmond at the revival of 1811. The next year Charles played Richard.

George Frederick Cooke (1756-1812) after playing Richard several times in the provinces, appeared, October 31, 1800, at Covent Garden in the character. When Kemble played in the company with Cooke, the rôle of Richmond was assigned to Kemble. Cooke was the first actor of prominence to play Richard in America. He chose for his début on the American stage the tragedy of *Richard III*, opening in New York on Nov. 21, 1810. He was greatly admired in America, although Lamb has described his Richard as a "butcher-like representation."

In 1805 the "infant Roscius," William Betty, then fourteen years of age and described by his contemporaries as "the tenth wonder of the world," played Richard. Lord Byron had an unfavorable opinion of Master Betty, which he expressed in *English Bards and Scotch Reviewers*.

To Kemble we owe the inauguration of elaborate scenery and the first attempts at accuracy in historical costume in *Richard III*, but the version of Cibber continued to be the text, although Kemble shortened somewhat the Cibber play.

Edmund Kean (1787-1833) attained the greatest fame of any actor of the nineteenth century in Richard. He played it for the first time in London at Drury Lane in 1814, his conception of the character modelled upon the interpretation of George Frederick Cooke, but in reality Kean was so unlike Cooke physically, being small and energetic, that there was little resemblance between the two interpretations. Lord Byron was one of Kean's enthusiastic admirers, as was the poet Keats. It was of Kean's Richard that Coleridge said it was like "reading Shakespeare by flashes of lightning." Kean was a continuer of the Garrick, instead of the Kemble, tradition, to which he added his own peculiar fire and vivacity. As J. P. Kemble pointed out, if one liked the style of Kean, one would not like the style of Kemble. There is, however, no question of the greater popularity of the style of Kean.[9] The contemporary newspapers are extravagant in their praises: "one of the finest pieces of acting we have ever beheld, or perhaps that the stage has ever known"; and "as the curtain fell the audience rose as one man, cheered lustily, applauded wildly, declaring by word and action this new actor was great indeed." Kean twice played Richard in America in 1820 and 1825. Much of the "traditional" stage-business followed today was originated by Kean.

Kean had but one rival in the part for several years, Junius Brutus Booth (1796-1852) at Covent Garden. He first appeared as Richard Feb. 12, 1817, and although he had his followers, his fame has been eclipsed by the popular glory of his great rival.

The next important Richard was William Charles Macready (1793-1873) who produced the tragedy in London at Covent Garden in 1819, to great applause, thus challenging the supremacy of Kean. Drury Lane responded to the challenge and the two Richards appeared nightly at the rival houses. Genest says of Macready, referring to the revival May 23, 1823: "He was very inferior to Kean, till the ghosts appeared . . . he was then superior." Leigh Hunt said: "Mr. Kean's Richard is the more sombre and perhaps deeper part of him; Mr. Macready's the livelier and more animal part—a very considerable one nevertheless."

On March 12, 1821, Macready attempted the practical resto-

---

5 Robert Mantell, the contemporary actor, has recently used the Cibber version.

6 For the classic condemnation of Cibber's version, see Hazlitt, *The Characters of Shakespear's Plays*, essay on *Richard III*.

7 Davies: *Memoirs of the Life of David Garrick.* 1780.

8 James Boaden: *Memoirs of the Life of John Philip Kemble.* 1825. See also Leigh Hunt: *Critical Essays on the Performers of the London Theatres*, 1807, for an analysis of Kemble's acting.

9 The best description of the acting of Kean is to be found in W. Hazlitt: *The Characters of Shakespear's Plays*, essay on *Richard III*.

ration of Shakespeare's text, leaving in, however, some of Cibber's lines that had become identified in the popular mind with *Richard III*.[10] But this partial restoration did not find favor and was abandoned after the second performance of it. In his later revivals in 1831, 1836-7, Macready returned to the Cibber text.

On February 20, 1845, Samuel Phelps (1804-1878) produced *Richard III* at Sadler's Wells, where it ran for about four weeks. Great attention was paid by Phelps to scenery and historical detail. The text used was Shakespeare's with, however, certain cuts. Once more, nevertheless, upon the revival of the tragedy in the season of 1862-3, Phelps returned to the Cibber version.

Perhaps the most elaborate production of *Richard III* yet given was that by Charles Kean (1811-1868) at the Princess Theatre on February 20, 1850. The playbill lists one hundred and twenty-one performers and a formidable array of "authorities" on historical details. All this parade of scholarship did not prevent Charles Kean from using the Cibber version, for which decision he argues at length upon the playbill. Barry Sullivan (1821-1891), in a modified Cibber version, was perhaps the most conspicuous of the lesser actors of the period from Charles Kean to Sir Henry Irving.

Henry Irving (1838-1905) restored Shakespeare's text at the Lyceum on January 29, 1877, with later revivals December 19, 1896, and February 27, 1897. Irving made only the cuts necessary to render the tragedy one of a length suitable for the modern stage, ending with Richard's fall and his second utterance of "a horse a horse, my kingdom for a horse!" Tennyson particularly admired Irving's "Plantagenet look." His interpretation was primarily intellectual.

But two English successors of Irving remain to mention, Sir Herbert Tree (1853-1917) and Sir Francis Robert Benson (1858-1939). Tree's production was noted for its gorgeous pageantry and the emphasis upon the melodramatic note in Richard; Benson's for its general adequacy. Both followed the text of Shakespeare. Finally a word must be said, before turning to the history of the play in America, of the Shakespearean productions at the Old Vic, where an excellent stock company had performed all of Shakespeare's plays.

The first recorded performance of a Shakespearean play in America is that of *Richard III,* Cibber version, March 5, 1750, at the theatre in Nassau Street, New York. The Richard was an American, Thomas Kean. The play was repeated the next season. Robert Upton is the second interpreter of Richard in America, January 23, 1752. There is a record of *Richard III* played by an American company in Annapolis in 1752.

In the same year an English company was brought over by Lewis Hallam, with the financial assistance of his brother William. After playing in the Southern Colonies, this English company played *Richard III* on November 12, 1753, at New York. The Richard was a Mr. Rigby, about whose interpretation theatrical history is silent. Another performance of the tragedy was given by Hallam's company on February 7, 1759.

At Philadelphia *Richard III* was performed at the Southwark Theatre in 1766, and on December 14, 1767, one week after the opening of the new John Street theatre at New York the tragedy was performed. Richard trod the boards several times

more before the Congress, on October 24, 1778, recommended the suspension of all amusements. The majority of these performances were given by Lewis Hallam.

Major Williams, of the British army of occupation, played Richard at New York in 1779. The tragedy continued, after the Revolution, to be one of the most popular of Shakespeare's plays, the most noteworthy of these earlier players being John Hodgkinson, at New York (1793-4) and James Fennel, at Philadelphia's Chestnut Theatre (April 21, 1795). A company at Boston and strolling companies elsewhere in New England likewise included *Richard III* in the repertory. Thomas A. Cooper (1776-1849) completes the list of players of this rôle at the close of the eighteenth century.

The arrival of George Frederick Cooke at New York in 1810 began a new era on the American stage. His Richard was closely imitated by the American actor, John Duff (1787-1831). Between the two visits of Edmund Kean to America (1820 and 1825), came Junius Brutus Booth, who made his first appearance in the part of Richard at the New Park Theatre on October 5, 1821. Junius Booth continued to play Richard for the thirty subsequent years of his career.

Edwin Forrest (1806-1872), the first American born actor of importance, appeared as Richard at the Bowery Theatre, New York, on January 23, 1827. Forrest played Richard as a noble prince, maintaining that a man of Richard's intellectual power would have the skill to conceal his deformity. He published a slightly altered form of Cibber's text.

Before and after the visit of Charles Kean in 1836 and again in 1840, the tragedy underwent some strange vicissitudes upon our stage. Several "child-actors" appeared as Richard, among whom were boys and girls of eleven and less. Ellen Bateman, for example, played Richard at the age of four. More than one woman likewise essayed the character. Charlotte Crampton gave a performance of the tragedy, in which, during the last act, she exhibited a troup of trained horses, thus repeating what had already been done at the London Astley's where *Richard III* was once turned into a spectacular circus. Other actors were fond of using the character of Richard for displaying their powers of mimicry of legitimate players.

It was Edwin Booth (1833-1893) who brought back to our stage the dignity appropriate to this tragedy. As early as 1852 he had made his début as a player in the character of Richard at San Francisco, and appeared for the first time at New York on May 4, 1857. Booth used the Cibber version until 1878, when the distinguished dramatic critic, William Winter, prepared for Booth a version based upon a rearrangement and cutting of Shakespeare's text.

There is not space to consider all the Richards seen in America. A mere enumeration of such names as the Wallacks, John Edward McCullough, Laurence Barrett, Robert Bruce Mantell, and Richard Mansfield will give some hint of the extensive history of this play upon our stage. But in conclusion a word must be said for the production by Arthur Hopkins of John Barrymore as Richard at New York on March 6, 1920. This was perhaps the best opportunity that generation had had to judge of the acting merits of this tragedy.[11]

---

10 *Reminiscences*, 162. Ed. by Sir Frederick Pollock. 1875.

11 For a full account of this play, see *The Stage History of Shakespeare's King Richard the Third*, by Alice I. Perry Wood, Columbia University Press, New York, 1909. The present editor has drawn some of his information from this complete study.

ACT FIRST ❧ SCENE FIRST

[London. A Street]
Enter Richard Duke of Gloucester, solus.

Rich. Now is the winter of our discontent
Made glorious summer by this sun of York;
And all the clouds that lour'd upon our house
In the deep bosom of the ocean buried.
Now are our brows bound with victorious wreaths;   5
Our bruised arms hung up for monuments;
Our stern alarums changed to merry meetings;
Our dreadful marches to delightful measures.
Grim-visag'd war hath smooth'd his wrinkled front;
And now,—instead of mounting barbed steeds,   10
To fright the souls of fearful adversaries,—
He capers nimbly in a lady's chamber
To the lascivious pleasing of a lute.
But I, that am not shap'd for sportive tricks,
Nor made to court an amorous looking-glass;   15
I, that am rudely stamp'd, and want love's majesty
To strut before a wanton ambling nymph;
I, that am curtail'd of this fair proportion,
Cheated of feature by dissembling nature,
Deform'd, unfinish'd, sent before my time   20
Into this breathing world, scarce half made up,
And that so lamely and unfashionable
That dogs bark at me, as I halt by them;
Why, I, in this weak piping time of peace,
Have no delight to pass away the time,   25
Unless to see my shadow in the sun
And descant on mine own deformity:
And therefore, since I cannot prove a lover,
To entertain these fair well-spoken days,
I am determined to prove a villain,   30
And hate the idle pleasures of these days.
Plots have I laid, inductions dangerous,
By drunken prophecies, libels, and dreams,
To set my brother Clarence and the king
In deadly hate the one against the other: 35
And if King Edward be as true and just
As I am subtle, false, and treacherous,
This day should Clarence closely be mew'd up,
About a prophecy, which says that G
Of Edward's heirs the murtherer shall be.   40
Dive, thoughts, down to my soul: here Clarence comes.

Enter Clarence and Brakenbury, guarded.

Brother, good day: what means this armed guard
That waits upon your Grace?
     Clar.   His majesty,
Tendering my person's safety, hath appointed   45

This conduct to convey me to the Tower.
     Rich. Upon what cause?
     Clar.   Because my name is George.
     Rich. Alack! my lord, that fault is none of yours;
He should, for that, commit your godfathers.   50
O! belike his majesty hath some intent
That you should be new-christen'd in the Tower.
But what's the matter, Clarence? may I know?
     Clar. Yea, Richard, when I know; but I protest
As yet I do not: but, as I can learn,   55
He hearkens after prophecies and dreams;
And from the cross-row plucks the letter G,
And says a wizard told him that by G
His issue disinherited should be;
And, for my name of George begins with G,   60
It follows in his thoughts that I am he.
These, as I learn, and such like toys as these,
Have mov'd his highness to commit me now.
     Rich. Why, this it is, when men are rul'd by women:
'Tis not the king that sends you to the Tower;   65
My Lady Grey, his wife, Clarence, 'tis she
That tempers him to this extremity.
Was it not she and that good man of worship,
Anthony Woodville, her brother there,
That made him send Lord Hastings to the Tower,   70
From whence this present day he is deliver'd?
We are not safe, Clarence; we are not safe.
     Clar. By heaven, I think there is no man secure
But the queen's kindred and night-walking heralds
That trudge betwixt the king and Mistress Shore.   75
Heard you not what a humble suppliant
Lord Hastings was for her delivery?
     Rich. Humbly complaining to her deity
Got my lord chamberlain his liberty.
I'll tell you what; I think it is our way,   80
If we will keep in favour with the king,
To be her men and wear her livery:
The jealous o'erworn widow and herself,
Since that our brother dubb'd them gentlewomen,
Are mighty gossips in our monarchy.   85
     Brak. I beseech your Graces both to pardon me;
His majesty hath straitly given in charge
That no man shall have private conference,
Of what degree soever, with your brother,
     Rich. Even so; an 't please your worship, Brakenbury,   90
You may partake of anything we say:
We speak no treason, man: we say the king
Is wise and virtuous, and his noble queen
Well struck in years, fair, and not jealous;
We say that Shore's wife hath a pretty foot,   95
A cherry lip, a bonny eye, a passing pleasing tongue;
And that the queen's kindred are made gentlefolks.
How say you, sir? can you deny all this?
     Brak. With this, my lord, myself have nought to do.

1, 2 winter ... York; *cf. n.*   6 monuments: *memorial trophies*   7 alarums: *calls to arms*   8 measures: *solemn dances*   9 front: *forehead*   10 barbed: *i.e. having the breasts and flanks armed, properly 'barded'*   11 fearful: *timorous*   12 He capers; *cf. n.*   13 lute: *a stringed instrument*   14 sportive: *amorous*   15 amorous; *cf. n.*   17 ambling: *walking affectedly*   18 fair proportion: *goodly form*   19 feature; *cf. n.* dissembling; *cf. n.*   21 breathing: *living*   22 unfashionable: *unfashionably*   23 halt: *limp*   24 weak piping time; *cf. n.*   27 descant: *comment*   29 fair ... days; *cf. n.*   30 villain; *cf. n.*   31 idle: *trifling*   32 inductions: *initial steps in an undertaking*   33 drunken prophecies; *cf. n.*   36 true and just; *cf. n.*   38 mew'd: *cooped*   39 About: *because of; cf. n.*   44 His majesty; *cf. n.*   45 Tendering: *having regard for*

46 conduct: *escort*   51 belike: *perhaps*   56 hearkens: *inquires*   57 cross-row: *i.e. the alphabet; cf. n.*   60 for: *because*   62 toys: *whims, idle fancies*   64 this: *thus*   67 tempers; *cf. n.*   69 Anthony Woodville; *cf. n.*   74 night-walking heralds; *cf. n.*   75 Mistress Shore; *cf. n.*   77 her delivery: *her deliverance of him; cf. n.*   80 way: *course*   83 o'erworn: *faded; cf. n.*   84 dubb'd: *i.e. invested them with the position of*   85 gossips: *meddlesome cronies*   87 straitly: *strictly*   89 degree: *rank*   90 an 't; *cf. n.*   94 Well struck: *advanced; cf. n. on 83 above*   96 bonny: *pleasant, comedy* passing: *exceedingly*

Rich. Naught to do with Mistress Shore! I tell thee, fellow,   *100*
He that doth naught with her, excepting one,
Were best to do it secretly, alone.
    Brak. What one, my lord?
    Rich. Her husband, knave. Wouldst thou betray me?
    Brak. I do beseech your Grace to pardon me; and withal   *105*
Forbear your conference with the noble duke.
    Clar. We know thy charge, Brakenbury, and will obey.
    Rich. We are the queen's abjects, and must obey.
Brother, farewell; I will unto the king;
And whatsoe'er you will employ me in,   *110*
Were it to call King Edward's widow sister,
I will perform it to enfranchise you.
Meantime, this deep disgrace in brotherhood
Touches me deeper than you can imagine.
    Clar. I know it pleaseth neither of us well.   *115*
    Rich. Well, your imprisonment shall not be long;
I will deliver you, or else lie for you:
Meantime, have patience.
    Clar.   I must perforce: farewell.

       Exit Clarence [with Brakenbury, and Guard].

    Rich. Go, tread the path that thou shalt ne'er return.   *120*
Simple, plain Clarence! I do love thee so
That I will shortly send thy soul to heaven,
If heaven will take the present at our hands.
But who comes here? the new-deliver'd Hastings!

       Enter Lord Hastings.

    Hast. Good time of day unto my gracious lord!   *125*
    Rich. As much unto my good lord chamberlain!
Well are you welcome to this open air.
How hath your lordship brook'd imprisonment?
    Hast. With patience, noble lord, as prisoners must:
But I shall live, my lord, to give them thanks   *130*
That were the cause of my imprisonment.
    Rich. No doubt, no doubt; and so shall Clarence too;
For they that were your enemies are his,
And have prevail'd as much on him as you.
    Hast. More pity that the eagles should be mew'd,   *135*
While kites and buzzards play at liberty.
    Rich. What news abroad?
    Hast. No news so bad abroad as this at home:
The king is sickly, weak, and melancholy,
And his physicians fear him mightily.   *140*
    Rich. Now by Saint John, that news is bad indeed.
O! he hath kept an evil diet long,
And over-much consum'd his royal person:
'Tis very grievous to be thought upon.
Where is he, in his bed?   *145*
    Hast.   He is.
    Rich. Go you before, and I will follow you.   *Exit Hastings.*
He cannot live, I hope; and must not die
Till George be pack'd with post-horse up to heaven.
I'll in, to urge his hatred more to Clarence,   *150*
With lies well steel'd with weighty arguments;

And, if I fail not in my deep intent,
Clarence hath not another day to live:
Which done, God take King Edward to his mercy,
And leave the world for me to bustle in!   *155*
For then I'll marry Warwick's youngest daughter.
What though I kill'd her husband and her father?
The readiest way to make the wench amends
Is to become her husband and her father:
The which will I; not all so much for love   *160*
As for another secret close intent,
By marrying her, which I must reach unto.
But yet I run before my horse to market:
Clarence still breathes; Edward still lives and reigns:
When they are gone, then must I count my gains.   *Exit.*   *165*

❧ SCENE SECOND ❧

[London. Another Street]
Enter the corse of Henry the Sixth with Halberds to guard it, Lady
Anne being the Mourner.

    Anne. Set down, set down your honourable load,
If honour may be shrouded in a hearse,
Whilst I a while obsequiously lament
Th' untimely fall of virtuous Lancaster.
Poor key-cold figure of a holy king!   *5*
Pale ashes of the house of Lancaster!
Thou bloodless remnant of that royal blood!
Be it lawful that I invocate thy ghost,
To hear the lamentations of poor Anne,
Wife to thy Edward, to thy slaughter'd son,   *10*
Stabb'd by the self-same hand that made these wounds!
Lo, in these windows that let forth thy life,
I pour the helpless balm of my poor eyes.
O, cursed be the hand that made these holes!
Cursed the heart that had the heart to do it!   *15*
Cursed the blood that let this blood from hence!
More direful hap betide that hated wretch,
That makes us wretched by the death of thee,
Than I can wish to wolves, to spiders, toads,
Or any creeping venom'd thing that lives!   *20*
If ever he have child, abortive be it,
Prodigious, and untimely brought to light,
Whose ugly and unnatural aspect
May fright the hopeful mother at the view;
And that be heir to his unhappiness!   *25*
If ever he have wife, let her be made
More miserable by the death of him
Than I am made by my young lord and thee!
Come, now towards Chertsey with your holy load,
Taken from Paul's to be interred there;   *30*
And still, as you are weary of this weight,
Rest you, whiles I lament King Henry's corse.
    [The Bearers take up the corpse and advance.]

    Enter Richard Duke of Gloucester.

---

101 naught: *wickedness*   **104 betray:** *i.e. trap me into speaking treason*   **108 abjects:** *i.e. the most servile of her subjects; cf. n.*   **111 widow;** *cf. n.*   **112 enfranchise:** *set free*   **117 lie for you:** *be imprisoned in your stead; cf. n.*   **136 play;** *cf. n.*   **140 fear him:** *fear for him*   **141 Saint John;** *cf. n.*   **142 diet:** *mode of life*   **149 post-horse:** *i.e. the speediest possible means*

156 Warwick's ... daughter: *i.e. Lady Anne, the widow of Edward Prince of Wales*   **1 Anne;** *cf. n.*   **3 obsequiously:** *mournfully, as befits a funeral*   **5 key-cold:** *cold in death*   **8 invocate:** *invoke*   **12 windows:** *i.e. wounds*   **13 helpless:** *useless*   **17 hap:** *fortune*   **19 wolves;** *cf. n.*   **22 Prodigious:** *abnormal, monstrous*   **25 unhappiness:** *disposition to mischief*   **29 Chertsey;** *cf. n.*

Rich. Stay, you that bear the corse, and set it down.

Anne. What black magician conjures up this fiend,
To stop devoted charitable deeds?   35

Rich. Villains! set down the corse; or, by Saint Paul,
I'll make a corse of him that disobeys.

[First] Gent. My lord, stand back, and let the coffin pass.

Rich. Unmanner'd dog! stand'st thou when I command?
Advance thy halberd higher than my breast,   40
Or, by Saint Paul, I'll strike thee to my foot,
And spurn upon thee, beggar, for thy boldness.

[The Bearers set down the coffin.]

Anne. What! do you tremble? are you all afraid?
Alas! I blame you not; for you are mortal,
And mortal eyes cannot endure the devil.   45
Avaunt, thou dreadful minister of hell!
Thou hadst but power over his mortal body,
His soul thou canst not have: therefore, be gone.

Rich. Sweet saint, for charity, be not so curst.

Anne. Foul devil, for God's sake hence, and trouble us not;   50
For thou hast made the happy earth thy hell,
Fill'd it with cursing cries and deep exclaims.
If thou delight to view thy heinous deeds,
Behold this pattern of thy butcheries.
O, gentlemen, see! see! dead Henry's wounds   55
Open their congeal'd mouths and bleed afresh.
Blush, blush, thou lump of foul deformity,
For 'tis thy presence that exhales this blood
From cold and empty veins, where no blood dwells.
Thy deed, inhuman and unnatural,   60
Provokes this deluge most unnatural.
O God! which this blood mad'st, revenge his death;
O earth! which this blood drink'st, revenge his death;
Either heaven with lightning strike the murtherer dead,
Or earth, gape open wide, and eat him quick,   65
As thou dost swallow up this good king's blood,
Which his hell-govern'd arm hath butchered!

Rich. Lady, you know no rules of charity,
Which renders good for bad, blessings for curses.

Anne. Villain, thou know'st nor law of God nor man: 70
No beast so fierce but knows some touch of pity.

Rich. But I know none, and therefore am no beast.

Anne. O, wonderful, when devils tell the truth!

Rich. More wonderful when angels are so angry.
Vouchsafe, divine perfection of a woman,   75
Of these supposed crimes, to give me leave,
By circumstance, but to acquit myself.

Anne. Vouchsafe, diffus'd infection of man,
Of these known evils, but to give me leave,
By circumstance, to curse thy cursed self.   80

Rich. Fairer than tongue can name thee, let me have
Some patient leisure to excuse myself.

Anne. Fouler than heart can think thee, thou canst make
No excuse current, but to hang thyself.

Rich. By such despair I should accuse myself.   85

Anne. And by despairing shalt thou stand excus'd

For doing worthy vengeance on thyself,
That didst unworthy slaughter upon others.

Rich. Say that I slew them not.

Anne.   Then say they were not slain: 90
But dead they are, and, devilish slave, by thee.

Rich. I did not kill your husband.

Anne.   Why, then he is alive.

Rich. Nay, he is dead; and slain by Edward's hand.

Anne. In thy foul throat thou liest: Queen Margaret saw   95
Thy murd'rous falchion smoking in his blood;
The which thou once didst bend against her breast,
But that thy brothers beat aside the point.

Rich. I was provoked by her sland'rous tongue,
That laid their guilt upon my guiltless shoulders.   100

Anne. Thou wast provoked by thy bloody mind,
That never dreamt on aught but butcheries.
Didst thou not kill this king?

Rich. I grant ye.

Anne. Dost grant me, hedge-hog? Then, God grant me too   105
Thou mayst be damned for that wicked deed!
O! he was gentle, mild, and virtuous!

Rich. The better for the King of heaven that hath him.

Anne. He is in heaven, where thou shalt never come.

Rich. Let him thank me, that holp to send him thither;   110
For he was fitter for that place than earth.

Anne. And thou unfit for any place but hell.

Rich. Yes, one place else, if you will hear me name it.

Anne. Some dungeon.

Rich.   Your bed-chamber.   115

Anne. Ill rest betide the chamber where thou liest!

Rich. So will it, madam, till I lie with you.

Anne. I hope so.

Rich.   I know so. But gentle Lady Anne,
To leave this keen encounter of our wits,   120
And fall something into a slower method,
Is not the causer of the timeless deaths
Of these Plantagenets, Henry and Edward,
As blameful as the executioner?

Anne. Thou wast the cause, and most accurs'd effect.   125

Rich. Your beauty was the cause of that effect;
Your beauty, that did haunt me in my sleep
To undertake the death of all the world,
So I might live one hour in your sweet bosom.

Anne. If I thought that, I tell thee, homicide,   130
These nails should rent that beauty from my cheeks.

Rich. These eyes could not endure that beauty's wrack;
You should not blemish it if I stood by:
As all the world is cheered by the sun,
So I by that; it is my day, my life.   135

Anne. Black night o'ershade thy day, and death thy life!

Rich. Curse not thyself, fair creature; thou art both.

Anne. I would I were, to be reveng'd on thee.

Rich. It is a quarrel most unnatural,
To be reveng'd on him that loveth thee.   140

Anne. It is a quarrel just and reasonable,
To be reveng'd on him that kill'd my husband.

Rich. He that bereft thee, lady, of thy husband,

---

34 black magician: *i.e. one in league with the devil*   **35 devoted:** *devout*   **40 halberd:** *a spear with a cutting blade*   **49 curst:** *malignant, shrewish*   **52 exclaims:** *exclamations*   **54 pattern:** *example*   **56 Open … afresh:** *cf. n.*   **58 exhales:** *draws forth*   **65 quick:** *alive*   **70 nor … nor:** *neither … nor*   **71 touch:** *sensation, feeling*   **76 crimes:** *cf. n.*   **77 circumstance:** *circumstantial evidence* **but:** *only*   **78 diffus'd:** *disorderly (?); cf. n.*   **79 Of:** *cf. n.*   **82 patient:** *tranquil*   **84 current:** *sterling, genuine*

94 Edward's hand; *cf. n.*   **96 falchion:** *curved sword*   **97 bend:** *direct, aim*   **105 hedge-hog:** *cf. n.*   **110 holp:** *helped*   **116 betide:** *befall*   **121 slower:** *more deliberate*   **122 timeless:** *untimely*   **125 effect:** *agent. In the next line 'effect' has its usual meaning*   **131 rent:** *rend*   **132 wrack:** *destruction, ruin*

Did it to help thee to a better husband.

   Anne. His better doth not breathe upon the earth.   *145*

   Rich. He lives that loves thee better than he could.

   Anne. Name him.

   Rich.   Plantagenet.

   Anne.   Why, that was he.

   Rich. The self-same name, but one of better nature.   *150*

   Anne. Where is he?

   Rich.   Here. [*She*] *spits at him.*

              Why dost thou spit at me?

   Anne. Would it were mortal poison, for thy sake!

   Rich. Never came poison from so sweet a place.   *155*

   Anne. Never hung poison on a fouler toad.

Out of my sight! thou dost infect mine eyes.

   Rich. Thine eyes, sweet lady, have infected mine.

   Anne. Would they were basilisks, to strike thee dead!

   Rich. I would they were, that I might die at once;   *160*

For now they kill me with a living death.

Those eyes of thine from mine have drawn salt tears,

Sham'd their aspects with store of childish drops;

These eyes, which never shed remorseful tear;

No, when my father York and Edward wept   *165*

To hear the piteous moan that Rutland made

When black-fac'd Clifford shook his sword at him;

Nor when thy warlike father like a child

Told the sad story of my father's death,

And twenty times made pause to sob and weep,   *170*

That all the standers-by had wet their cheeks,

Like trees bedash'd with rain: in that sad time,

My manly eyes did scorn an humble tear;

And what these sorrows could not thence exhale,

Thy beauty hath, and made them blind with weeping.   *175*

I never su'd to friend, nor enemy;

My tongue could never learn sweet smoothing words;

But, now thy beauty is propos'd my fee,

My proud heart sues, and prompts my tongue to speak.

                    She looks scornfully at him.

Teach not thy lip such scorn, for it was made   *180*

For kissing, lady, not for such contempt.

If thy revengeful heart cannot forgive,

Lo! here I lend thee this sharp-pointed sword;

Which if thou please to hide in this true breast,

And let the soul forth that adoreth thee,   *185*

I lay it naked to the deadly stroke,

And humbly beg the death upon my knee.

         He lays his breast open: she offers at [*it*]

                     with his sword.

Nay, do not pause; for I did kill King Henry;

But 'twas thy beauty that provoked me.

Nay, now dispatch; 'twas I that stabb'd young Edward;   *190*

              [*She again offers at his breast.*]

But 'twas thy heavenly face that set me on.

                       She falls the sword.

Take up the sword again, or take up me.

   Anne. Arise, dissembler: though I wish thy death,

I will not be thy executioner.

   Rich. Then bid me kill myself, and I will do it.   *195*

   Anne. I have already.

   Rich.   That was in thy rage:

Speak it again, and, even with the word,

This hand, which for thy love did kill thy love,

Shall, for thy love, kill a far truer love: *200*

To both their deaths shalt thou be accessary.

   Anne. I would I knew thy heart.

   Rich. 'Tis figur'd in my tongue.

   Anne. I fear me both are false.

   Rich. Then never man was true.   *205*

   Anne. Well, well, put up your sword.

   Rich. Say, then, my peace is made.

   Anne. That shalt thou know hereafter.

   Rich. But shall I live in hope?

   Anne. All men, I hope, live so.   *210*

   [*Rich.*] Vouchsafe to wear this ring.

   [*Anne.* To take is not to give.]

   Rich. Look, how my ring encompasseth thy finger,

Even so thy breast encloseth my poor heart:

Wear both of them, for both of them are thine.   *215*

And if thy poor devoted servant may

But beg one favour at thy gracious hand,

Thou dost confirm his happiness for ever.

   Anne. What is it?

   Rich. That it may please you leave these sad designs   *220*

To him that hath most cause to be a mourner,

And presently repair to Crosby House;

Where, after I have solemnly interr'd

At Chertsey monastery this noble king,

And wet his grave with my repentant tears,   *225*

I will with all expedient duty see you:

For divers unknown reasons, I beseech you,

Grant me this boon.

   Anne. With all my heart; and much it joys me too

To see you are become so penitent.   *230*

Tressel and Berkeley, go along with me.

   Rich. Bid me farewell.

   Anne.   'Tis more than you deserve;

But since you teach me how to flatter you,

Imagine I have said farewell already.   *235*

         Exit two [*Tressel and Berkeley*] *with Anne.*

   [*Rich.* Sirs, take up the corse.]

   Gent. Towards Chertsey, noble lord?

   Rich. No, to White-Friars; there attend my coming.

                         Exit Corse.

Was ever woman in this humour woo'd?

Was ever woman in this humour won?   *240*

I'll have her; but I will not keep her long.

What! I, that kill'd her husband, and his father,

To take her in her heart's extremest hate;

With curses in her mouth, tears in her eyes,

The bleeding witness of my hatred by;   *245*

Having God, her conscience, and these bars against me,

And I no friends to back my suit withal

But the plain devil and dissembling looks,

And yet to win her, all the world to nothing!

Ha!   *250*

Hath she forgot already that brave prince,

Edward, her lord, whom I, some three months since,

---

156 poison . . . **toad**; *cf. n.*   **159 basilisks**; *cf. n.*   **163 aspects**: *appearance*   **166 Rutland**; *cf. n.*   **171 That**: *so that*   **176 smoothing**: *flattering*   S. d. **falls**: *lets fall*

203 figur'd: *portrayed*   **222 presently**: *immediately*   **Crosby House**; *cf. n.*   **226 expedient**: *expeditious*   **238 White-Friars**; *cf. n.*   **239, 240** *Cf. n.*   **252 three months**; *cf. n.*

Stabb'd in my angry mood at Tewkesbury?
A sweeter and a lovelier gentleman,
Fram'd in the prodigality of nature,   255
Young, valiant, wise, and, no doubt, right royal,
The spacious world cannot again afford:
And will she yet abase her eyes on me,
That cropp'd the golden prime of this sweet prince,
And made her widow to a woeful bed?   260
On me, whose all not equals Edward's moiety?
On me, that halts and am misshapen thus?
My dukedom to a beggarly denier
I do mistake my person all this while:
Upon my life, she finds, although I cannot,   265
Myself to be a marvellous proper man.
I'll be at charges for a looking-glass,
And entertain a score or two of tailors,
To study fashions to adorn my body:
Since I am crept in favour with myself,   270
I will maintain it with some little cost.
But first I'll turn yon fellow in his grave,
And then return lamenting to my love.
Shine out, fair sun, till I have bought a glass,
That I may see my shadow as I pass.   *Exit.*

❧ Scene Third ❧

[London. A Room in the Palace.]
Enter the Queen Mother [Elizabeth], Lord Rivers, and Lord Grey.

Riv. Have patience, madam: there's no doubt his majesty
Will soon recover his accustom'd health.
Grey. In that you brook it ill, it makes him worse:
Therefore, for God's sake, entertain good comfort,
And cheer his Grace with quick and merry words.   5
Q. Eliz. If he were dead, what would betide on me?
Grey. No other harm but loss of such a lord.
Q. Eliz. The loss of such a lord includes all harms.
Grey. The heavens have bless'd you with a goodly son,
To be your comforter when he is gone.   10
Q. Eliz. Ah! he is young; and his minority
Is put unto the trust of Richard Gloucester,
A man that loves not me, nor none of you.
Riv. Is it concluded he shall be protector?
Q. Eliz. It is determin'd, not concluded yet: 15
But so it must be if the king miscarry.

Enter Buckingham and Derby.

Grey. Here come the Lords of Buckingham and Derby.
Buck. Good time of day unto your royal Grace!
Der. God make your majesty joyful as you have been!
Q. Eliz. The Countess Richmond, good my Lord of Derby,   20
To your good prayer will scarcely say amen.
Yet, Derby, notwithstanding she's your wife,
And loves not me, be you, good lord, assur'd
I hate not you for her proud arrogance.

Der. I do beseech you, either not believe   25
The envious slanders of her false accusers;
Or, if she be accus'd on true report,
Bear with her weakness, which, I think, proceeds
From wayward sickness, and no grounded malice.
Q. Eliz. Saw you the king to-day, my Lord of Derby?   30
Der. But now the Duke of Buckingham and I,
Are come from visiting his majesty.
Q. Eliz. What likelihood of his amendment, lords?
Buck. Madam, good hope; his Grace speaks cheerfully.
Q. Eliz. God grant him health! did you confer with him?   35
Buck. Ay, madam: he desires to make atonement
Between the Duke of Gloucester and your brothers,
And between them and my lord chamberlain;
And sent to warn them to his royal presence.
Q. Eliz. Would all were well! But that will never be.   40
I fear our happiness is at the height.

Enter Richard [with Hastings, and Dorset].

Rich. They do me wrong, and I will not endure it:
Who is it that complains unto the king,
That I, forsooth, am stern and love them not?
By holy Paul, they love his Grace but lightly   45
That fill his ears with such dissentious rumours.
Because I cannot flatter and look fair,
Smile in men's faces, smooth, deceive, and cog,
Duck with French nods and apish courtesy,
I must be held a rancorous enemy.   50
Cannot a plain man live and think no harm,
But thus his simple truth must be abus'd
With silken, sly, insinuating Jacks?
Grey. To whom in all this presence speaks your Grace?
Rich. To thee, that hast nor honesty nor grace.   55
When have I injur'd thee? when done thee wrong?
Or thee? or thee? or any of your faction?
A plague upon you all! His royal grace,—
Whom God preserve better than you would wish!—
Cannot be quiet scarce a breathing-while,   60
But you must trouble him with lewd complaints.
Q. Eliz. Brother of Gloucester, you mistake the matter.
The king, on his own royal disposition,
And not provok'd by any suitor else,
Aiming, belike, at your interior hatred,   65
That in your outward action shows itself
Against my children, brothers, and myself,
Makes him to send, that he may learn
The ground [of your ill-will, and so remove it].
Rich. I cannot tell; the world is grown so bad   70
That wrens make prey where eagles dare not perch:
Since every Jack became a gentleman
There's many a gentle person made a Jack.
Q. Eliz. Come, come, we know your meaning, brother
Gloucester;   75
You envy my advancement and my friends'.
God grant we never may have need of you!
Rich. Meantime, God grants that I have need of you:
Our brother is imprison'd by your means,

---

255 **prodigality of nature:** *nature's most prodigal mood*   263 **denier:** *a small copper coin*   266 **proper:** *handsome*   267 **be . . . for:** *buy*   268 **entertain:** *take into service*   272 **in:** *into*   5 **quick:** *lively*   6 **betide on:** *become of*   12 *Cf. n.*   15 *Cf. n.*   16 **miscarry:** *perish*   16 S. d. *Cf. n.*   20 **Countess Richmond;** *cf. n.*

36 **atonement:** *a reconciliation*   39 **warn:** *summon*   48 **cog:** *cheat*   49 **Duck:** *bow*   **apish:** *imitative, false*   53 **Jacks:** *low-bred fellows*   57 **faction:** *party*   60 **breathing-while:** *short time*   61 **lewd:** *worthless, vile*   63 **disposition:** *inclination*   71 **make prey:** *prey*   77 **have need of you:** *am in trouble because of you*

Myself disgrac'd, and the nobility   *80*
Held in contempt; while great promotions
Are daily given to ennoble those
That scarce, some two days since, were worth a noble.
   Q. Eliz. By him that rais'd me to this careful height
From that contented hap which I enjoy'd,   *85*
I never did incense his majesty
Against the Duke of Clarence, but have been
An earnest advocate to plead for him.
My lord, you do me shameful injury,
Falsely to draw me in these vile suspects.   *90*
   Rich. You may deny that you were not the mean
Of my Lord Hastings' late imprisonment.
   Riv. She may, my lord; for—
   Rich. She may, Lord Rivers! why, who knows not so?
She may do more, sir, than denying that: *95*
She may help you to many fair preferments,
And then deny her aiding hand therein,
And lay those honours on your high desert.
What may she not? She may,—ay, marry, may she,—
   Riv. What, marry, may she?   *100*
   Rich. What, marry, may she! marry with a king,
A bachelor and a handsome stripling too.
I wis your grandam had a worser match.
   Q. Eliz. My Lord of Gloucester, I have too long borne
Your blunt upbraidings and your bitter scoffs;   *105*
By heaven, I will acquaint his majesty
Of those gross taunts that oft I have endur'd.
I had rather be a country servant-maid
Than a great queen, with this condition,
To be so baited, scorn'd, and stormed at: *110*
Small joy have I in being England's queen.

         Enter old Queen Margaret.

   Q. Mar. *[Aside.]* And lessen'd be that small, God, I beseech
him!
Thy honour, state, and seat is due to me.
   Rich. What! threat you me with telling of the king?   *115*
[Tell him, and spare not: look, what I have said]
I will avouch 't in presence of the king:
I dare adventure to be sent to the Tower.
'Tis time to speak; my pains are quite forgot.
   Q. Mar. *[Aside.]* Out, devil! I do remember them too well: *120*
Thou kill'dst my husband Henry in the Tower,
And Edward, my poor son, at Tewkesbury.
   Rich. Ere you were queen, ay, or your husband king,
I was a pack-horse in his great affairs,
A weeder-out of his proud adversaries,   *125*
A liberal rewarder of his friends;
To royalize his blood I spent mine own.
   Q. Mar. *[Aside.]* Ay, and much better blood than his, or
thine.
   Rich. In all which time you and your husband Grey   *130*
Were factious for the house of Lancaster;
And, Rivers, so were you. Was not your husband
In Margaret's battle at Saint Alban's slain?

Let me put in your minds, if you forget,
What you have been ere this, and what you are;   *135*
Withal, what I have been, and what I am.
   Q. Mar. *[Aside.]* A murtherous villain, and so still thou art.
   Rich. Poor Clarence did forsake his father, Warwick,
Ay, and forswore himself,—which Jesu pardon!—
   Q. Mar. *[Aside.]* Which God revenge!   *140*
   Rich. To fight on Edward's party for the crown;
And for his meed, poor lord, he is mew'd up.
I would to God my heart were flint, like Edward's;
Or Edward's soft and pitiful, like mine:
I am too childish-foolish for this world.   *145*
   Q. Mar. *[Aside.]* Hie thee to hell for shame, and leave this
world,
Thou cacodemon! there thy kingdom is.
   Riv. My Lord of Gloucester, in those busy days
Which here you urge to prove us enemies,   *150*
We follow'd then our lord, our sovereign king;
So should we you, if you should be our king.
   Rich. If I should be! I had rather be a pedlar.
Far be it from my heart, the thought thereof!
   Q. Eliz. As little joy, my lord, as you suppose   *155*
You should enjoy, were you this country's king,
As little joy you may suppose in me
That I enjoy, being the queen thereof.
   Q. Mar. *[Aside.]* A little joy enjoys the queen thereof;
For I am she, and altogether joyless.   *160*
I can no longer hold me patient.   *[Advancing.]*
Hear me, you wrangling pirates, that fall out
In sharing that which you have pill'd from me!
Which of you trembles not that looks on me?
If not that, I being queen, you bow like subjects,   *165*
Yet that, by you depos'd, you quake like rebels?
Ah! gentle villain, do not turn away.
   Rich. Foul wrinkled witch, what mak'st thou in my sight?
   Q. Mar. But repetition of what thou hast marr'd;
That will I make before I let thee go.   *170*
   Rich. Wert thou not banished on pain of death?
   Q. Mar. I was; but I do find more pain in banishment
Than death can yield me here by my abode.
A husband and a son thou ow'st to me;
And thou, a kingdom; all of you, allegiance: *175*
This sorrow that I have by right is yours,
And all the pleasures you usurp are mine.
   Rich. The curse my noble father laid on thee,
When thou didst crown his warlike brows with paper,
And with thy scorns drew'st rivers from his eyes;   *180*
And then, to dry them, gav'st the duke a clout
Steep'd in the faultless blood of pretty Rutland.
His curses, then from bitterness of soul
Denounc'd against thee, are all fall'n upon thee;
And God, not we, hath plagu'd thy bloody deed.   *185*
   Q. Eliz. So just is God, to right the innocent.
   Hast. O! 'twas the foulest deed to slay that babe,
And the most merciless, that e'er was heard of.
   Riv. Tyrants themselves wept when it was reported.
   Dors. No man but prophesied revenge for it.   *190*

---

83 noble: *a coin, with quibble on the usual meaning*   **84 careful:** *full of cares*   **90**
suspects: *suspicions*   **91 mean:** *agent*   **96 preferments:** *promotions*   **110 baited:** *ha-*
rassed   **116–118** *Cf. n.*   **117 avouch:** *maintain*   **118 adventure:** *venture*   **119**
pains: *labors*   **123 Ere . . . king;** *cf. n.*   **127 royalize:** *make royal*   **131 factious . . .**
Lancaster; *cf. n.*   **133 Margaret's battle;** *cf. n.*

139 forswore himself: *repudiated his oath*   **142 meed:** *reward*   **148 cacodemon:** *evil*
spirit   **157 in me:** *as regards me*   **163 sharing:** *dividing*   **pill'd:** *plundered*   **164–166**
Cf. n.   **167 gentle:** *precious* (ironic)   **168 mak'st:** *dost*   **171 banished;** *cf. n.*   **178**
The curse; *cf. n.*   **181 clout:** *cloth*

Buck. Northumberland, then present, wept to see it.

Q. Mar. What! were you snarling all before I came,
Ready to catch each other by the throat,
And turn you all your hatred now on me?
Did York's dread curse prevail so much with heaven   195
That Henry's death, my lovely Edward's death,
Their kingdom's loss, my woeful banishment,
Should all but answer for that peevish brat?
Can curses pierce the clouds and enter heaven?
Why then, give way, dull clouds, to my quick curses!   200
Though not by war, by surfeit die your king,
As ours by murther, to make him a king!
Edward, thy son, that now is Prince of Wales,
For Edward, our son, that was Prince of Wales,
Die in his youth by like untimely violence!   205
Thyself a queen, for me that was a queen,
Outlive thy glory, like my wretched self!
Long mayst thou live to wail thy children's death,
And see another, as I see thee now,
Deck'd in thy rights, as thou art stall'd in mine!   210
Long die thy happy days before thy death;
And, after many lengthen'd hours of grief,
Die neither mother, wife, nor England's queen!
Rivers, and Dorset, you were standers by,—
And so wast thou, Lord Hastings,—when my son   215
Was stabb'd with bloody daggers: God, I pray him,
That none of you may live your natural age,
But, by some unlook'd accident cut off,—

Rich. Have done thy charm, thou hateful wither'd hag!

Q. Mar. And leave out thee? stay, dog, for thou shalt   220
hear me.
If heaven have any grievous plague in store,
Exceeding those that I can wish upon thee,
O! let them keep it till thy sins be ripe,
And then hurl down their indignation   225
On thee, the troubler of the poor world's peace.
The worm of conscience still begnaw thy soul!
Thy friends suspect for traitors while thou liv'st
And take deep traitors for thy dearest friends!
No sleep close up that deadly eye of thine,   230
Unless it be while some tormenting dream
Affrights thee with a hell of ugly devils!
Thou elvish-mark'd, abortive, rooting hog!
Thou that wast seal'd in thy nativity
The slave of nature and the son of hell!   235
Thou slander of thy heavy mother's womb!
Thou loathed issue of thy father's loins!
Thou rag of honour! thou detested—

Rich. Margaret!

Q. Mar.   Richard!   240

Rich.   Ha!

Q. Mar.   I call thee not.

Rich. I cry thee mercy then, for I did think
That thou hadst call'd me all these bitter names.

Q. Mar. Why, so I did; but look'd for no reply.   245
O, let me make the period to my curse!

Rich. 'Tis done by me, and ends in 'Margaret.'

Q. Eliz. Thus have you breath'd your curse against yourself.

Q. Mar. Poor painted queen, vain flourish of my fortune!
Why strew'st thou sugar on that bottled spider,   250
Whose deadly web ensnareth thee about?
Fool, fool! thou whet'st a knife to kill thyself.
The day will come that thou shalt wish for me
To help thee curse this poisonous bunch-back'd toad.

Hast. False-boding woman, end thy frantic curse.   255
Lest to thy harm thou move our patience.

Q. Mar. Foul shame upon you! you have all mov'd mine.

Riv. Were you well serv'd, you would be taught your duty.

Q. Mar. To serve me well, you all should do me duty,
Teach me to be your queen, and you my subjects: 260
O, serve me well, and teach yourselves that duty!

Dor. Dispute not with her, she is lunatic.

Q. Mar. Peace, Master Marquess! you are malapert:
Your fire-new stamp of honour is scarce current.
O that your young nobility could judge   265
What 'twere to lose it, and be miserable!
They that stand high have many blasts to shake them,
And if they fall, they dash themselves to pieces.

Rich. Good counsel, marry: learn it, learn it, marquess.

Dor. It touches you, my lord, as much as me.   270

Rich. Ay, and much more; but I was born so high:
Our aery buildeth in the cedar's top,
And dallies with the wind, and scorns the sun.

Q. Mar. And turns the sun to shade; alas! alas!
Witness my son, now in the shade of death;   275
Whose bright out-shining beams thy cloudy wrath
Hath in eternal darkness folded up.
Your aery buildeth in our aery's nest:
O God! that seest it, do not suffer it;
As it was won with blood, lost be it so!   280

Buck. Peace, peace! for shame, if not for charity.

Q. Mar. Urge neither charity nor shame to me:
Uncharitably with me have you dealt,
And shamefully my hopes by you are butcher'd.
My charity is outrage, life my shame;   285
And in that shame still live my sorrow's rage!

Buck. Have done, have done.

Q. Mar. O princely Buckingham! I'll kiss thy hand,
In sign of league and amity with thee:
Now fair befall thee and thy noble house!   290
Thy garments are not spotted with our blood,
Nor thou within the compass of my curse.

Buck. Nor no one here; for curses never pass
The lips of those that breathe them in the air.

Q. Mar. I will not think but they ascend the sky,   295
And there awake God's gentle-sleeping peace.
O Buckingham! take heed of yonder dog:
Look, when he fawns, he bites; and when he bites,
His venom tooth will rankle to the death.
Have not to do with him, beware of him;   300
Sin, death, and hell have set their marks on him,
And all their ministers attend on him.

Rich. What doth she say, my Lord of Buckingham?

---

191 Northumberland; *cf. n.*   **198 peevish:** *silly*   **201 surfeit:** *excess of luxurious liv-*
ing   **210 Deck'd:** *dressed*   **stall'd:** *installed*   **227 begnaw:** *gnaw*   **233 elvish-mark'd;**
cf. n.   **rooting hog;** *cf. n.*   **234 seal'd:** *stamped*   **235 slave of nature;** *i.e. because*
branded by nature with a deformity   **246 period:** *conclusion*

249 painted: *feigned, counterfeit*   **vain flourish:** *empty embellishment*   **250 bottled:** *i.e.*
resembling a bottle, swollen   **263 malapert:** *impudent*   **264 fire-new … current;*
cf. n.   **272 aery:** *brood*   **273 dallies:** *trifles*   **285 My … shame;** *cf. n.*   **292
compass:** *range*   **293, 294 curses … air;** *cf. n.*   **295 but:** *otherwise than that*   **299
rankle:** *cause a festering wound*

Buck. Nothing that I respect, my gracious lord.

Q. Mar. What! dost thou scorn me for my gentle counsel, *305*
And soothe the devil that I warn thee from?
O! but remember this another day,
When he shall split thy very heart with sorrow,
And say poor Margaret was a prophetess.
Live each of you the subject to his hate, *310*
And he to yours, and all of you to God's! *Exit.*

Buck. My hair doth stand an end to hear her curses.

Riv. And so doth mine. I muse why she's at liberty.

Rich. I cannot blame her: by God's holy mother,
She hath had too much wrong, and I repent *315*
My part thereof that I have done to her.

Q. Eliz. I never did her any, to my knowledge.

Rich. Yet you have all the vantage of her wrong.
I was too hot to do somebody good,
That is too cold in thinking of it now. *320*
Marry, as for Clarence, he is well repaid;
He is frank'd up to fatting for his pains:
God pardon them that are the cause thereof!

Riv. A virtuous and a Christian-like conclusion,
To pray for them that have done scath to us. *325*

Rich. So do I ever, being well-advis'd;
　　　　　　　　　　　　　　Speaks to himself.
For had I curs'd now, I had curs'd myself.

Enter Catesby.

Cates. Madam, his majesty doth call for you;
And for your Grace; and yours, my gracious lord.

Q. Eliz. Catesby, I come. Lords, will you go with me? *330*

Riv. We wait upon your Grace.
　　　　　　　　　　　Exeunt all but Richard.

Rich. I do the wrong, and first begin to brawl.
The secret mischiefs that I set abroach
I lay unto the grievous charge of others.
Clarence, whom I, indeed, have cast in darkness, *335*
I do beweep to many simple gulls;
Namely, to Derby, Hastings, Buckingham;
And tell them 'tis the queen and her allies
That stir the king against the duke my brother.
Now they believe it; and withal whet me *340*
To be reveng'd on Rivers, Dorset, Grey;
But then I sigh, and, with a piece of scripture,
Tell them that God bids us do good for evil:
And thus I clothe my naked villainy
With odd old ends stol'n forth of holy writ, *345*
And seem a saint when most I play the devil.

Enter two Murtherers.

But soft! here come my executioners.
How now, my hardy, stout, resolved mates!
Are you now going to dispatch this thing?

Mur. We are, my lord; and come to have the warrant, *350*
That we may be admitted where he is.

Rich. Well thought upon; I have it here about me:
　　　　　　　　　　　　　　[Gives the warrant.]
When you have done, repair to Crosby-place.

But, sirs, be sudden in the execution,
Withal obdurate; do not hear him plead; *355*
For Clarence is well-spoken, and perhaps
May move your hearts to pity, if you mark him.

Mur. Tut, tut, my lord, we will not stand to prate.
Talkers are no good doers: be assur'd
We go to use our hands and not our tongues. *360*

Rich. Your eyes drop millstones, when fools' eyes fall tears:
I like you, lads; about your business straight.
Go, go, dispatch.

Mur. 　　　　We will, my noble lord. *[Exeunt.]*

❧ Scene Fourth ❧

[The Same. The Tower]
Enter Clarence and Keeper.

Keep. Why looks your Grace so heavily to-day?

Clar. O, I have pass'd a miserable night,
So full of fearful dreams, of ugly sights,
That, as I am a Christian faithful man,
I would not spend another such a night, *5*
Though 'twere to buy a world of happy days,
So full of dismal terror was the time.

Keep. What was your dream, my lord? I pray you, tell me.

Clar. Methoughts that I had broken from the Tower,
And was embark'd to cross to Burgundy; *10*
And in my company my brother Gloucester,
Who from my cabin tempted me to walk
Upon the hatches: there we look'd toward England,
And cited up a thousand heavy times,
During the wars of York and Lancaster, *15*
That had befall'n us. As we pac'd along
Upon the giddy footing of the hatches,
Methought that Gloucester stumbled; and, in falling,
Struck me, that thought to stay him, overboard,
Into the tumbling billows of the main. *20*
O Lord, methought what pain it was to drown:
What dreadful noise of water in mine ears!
What sights of ugly death within mine eyes!
Methoughts I saw a thousand fearful wracks;
A thousand men that fishes gnaw'd upon; *25*
Wedges of gold, great anchors, heaps of pearl,
Inestimable stones, unvalu'd jewels,
All scatter'd in the bottom of the sea.
Some lay in dead men's skulls; and in those holes
Where eyes did once inhabit, there were crept, *30*
As 'twere in scorn of eyes, reflecting gems,
That woo'd the slimy bottom of the deep,
And mock'd the dead bones that lay scatter'd by.

Keep. Had you such leisure in the time of death
To gaze upon these secrets of the deep? *35*

Clar. Methought I had; and often did I strive
To yield the ghost; but still the envious flood
Stopt in my soul, and would not let it forth
To find the empty, vast, and wandering air;

306 soothe: *flatter*　**312 an:** *on*　**313 muse:** *wonder*　**322 frank'd up:** *i.e. shut up in a sty*　**325 scath:** *harm*　**329 Cf. n.**　**332 brawl:** *quarrel*　**333 set abroach:** *set on foot*　**336 beweep:** *weep over* **gulls:** *dupes*　**337 Namely:** *that is to say*　**340 whet:** *incite*　**341 Dorset;** *cf. n.*　**345 odd old ends:** *odds and ends*　**347 soft:** *stay, stop*

354 sudden: *quick*　**361 millstones;** *cf. n.*　**S. D.:** *Cf. n.*　**1 heavily:** *sorrowfully*　**9 Methoughts:** *it seemed to me*　**10 Burgundy;** *cf. n.*　**13 hatches:** *movable planks forming a kind of deck*　**14 cited up:** *called to mind*　**20 main:** *sea*　**24 wracks:** *wrecks*　**26 Wedges:** *masses*　**27 unvalu'd:** *priceless*　**31 reflecting:** *shining*　**37 yield the ghost: i.e. die* **envious:** *malicious*　**38 Stopt in:** *kept in*

But smother'd it within my panting bulk, 40
Who almost burst to belch it in the sea.
    Keep. Awak'd you not in this sore agony?
    Clar. No, no, my dream was lengthen'd after life;
O! then began the tempest to my soul.
I pass'd methought, the melancholy flood, 45
With that sour ferryman which poets write of,
Unto the kingdom of perpetual night.
The first that there did greet my stranger soul
Was my great father-in-law, renowned Warwick;
Who spake aloud, 'What scourge for perjury 50
Can this dark monarchy afford false Clarence?'
And so he vanish'd: then came wand'ring by
A shadow like an angel, with bright hair
Dabbled in blood; and he shriek'd out aloud,
'Clarence is come,—false, fleeting, perjur'd Clarence, 55
That stabb'd me in the field by Tewkesbury;—
Seize on him, Furies; take him unto torment!'
With that, methought, a legion of foul fiends
Environ'd me, and howled in mine ears
Such hideous cries, that with the very noise 60
I trembling wak'd, and for a season after
Could not believe but that I was in hell,
Such terrible impression made my dream.
    Keep. No marvel, lord, though it affrighted you;
I am afraid, methinks, to hear you tell it. 65
    Clar. Ah Keeper, Keeper! I have done these things,
That now give evidence against my soul,
For Edward's sake; and see how he requites me.
O God! if my deep prayers cannot appease thee,
But thou wilt be aveng'd on my misdeeds, 70
Yet execute thy wrath on me alone:
O, spare my guiltless wife and my poor children!
Keeper, I prithee sit by me a while;
My soul is heavy, and I fain would sleep.
    Keep. I will, my lord. God give your Grace good rest! 75
                          [Clarence sleeps.]

        Enter Brakenbury, the Lieutenant.

    Brak. Sorrow breaks seasons and reposing hours,
Makes the night morning, and the noon-tide night.
Princes have but their titles for their glories,
An outward honour for an inward toil;
And, for unfelt imaginations, 80
They often feel a world of restless cares:
So that, between their titles and low name,
There's nothing differs but the outward fame.

        Enter [the] two Murtherers.

    1. Mur. Ho! who's here?
    Brak. What wouldst thou, fellow? and how cam'st thou 85
hither?
    2. Mur. I would speak with Clarence, and
I came hither on my legs.
    Brak. What! so brief?
    1. Mur. 'Tis better, sir, than to be tedious.— 90

Let him see our commission, and talk no more.
                      [Brakenbury] Reads.
    Brak. I am, in this, commanded to deliver
The noble Duke of Clarence to your hands:
I will not reason what is meant hereby,
Because I will be guiltless from the meaning. 95
There lies the duke asleep, and there the keys.
I'll to the king, and signify to him
That thus I have resign'd to you my charge.
    1. Mur. You may, sir; 'tis a point of wisdom: fare you well.
                      Exit [Brakenbury].
    2. Mur. What! shall we stab him as he sleeps? 100
    1. Mur. No; he'll say 'twas done cowardly, when he wakes.
    2. Mur. Why, he shall never wake until the great judgment day.
    1. Mur. Why, then he'll say we stabbed him sleeping.
    2. Mur. The urging of that word 'judgment' hath bred a
kind of remorse in me. 105
    1. Mur. What! art thou afraid?
    2. Mur. Not to kill him, having a warrant, but to be
damn'd for killing him, from the which no warrant can defend
me.
    1. Mur. I thought thou hadst been resolute. 110
    2. Mur. So I am, to let him live.
    1. Mur. I'll back to the Duke of Gloucester, and tell him
so.
    2. Mur. Nay, I prithee, stay a little: I hope this passionate
humour of mine will change; it was wont to hold me but 115
while one tells twenty.
    1. Mur. How dost thou feel thyself now?
    2. Mur. Some certain dregs of conscience are yet within me.
    1. Mur. Remember our reward when the deed's done.
    2. Mur. Come, he dies: I had forgot the reward. 120
    1. Mur. Where's thy conscience now?
    2. Mur. O, in the Duke of Gloucester's purse.
    1. Mur. When he opens his purse to give us our reward,
thy conscience flies out.
    2. Mur. 'Tis no matter; let it go: there's few or none will 125
entertain it.
    1. Mur. What if it come to thee again?
    2. Mur. I'll not meddle with it; it makes a man a coward; a
man cannot steal, but it accuseth him; a man cannot swear, but
it checks him; a man cannot lie with his neighbour's wife, 130
but it detects him: 'tis a blushing shamefac'd spirit, that mutinies
in a man's bosom; it fills a man full of obstacles; it made me
once restore a purse of gold that, by chance, I found; it beggars
any man that keeps it; it is turned out of towns and cities for a
dangerous thing; and every man that means to live well 135
endeavours to trust to himself and live without it.
    1. Mur. 'Tis even now at my elbow, persuading me not to
kill the duke.
    2. Mur. Take the devil in thy mind, and believe him not:
he would insinuate with thee but to make thee sigh. 140
    1. Mur. I am strong-framed; he cannot prevail with me.
    2. Mur. Spoke like a tall man that respects thy reputation.
Come, shall we fall to work?
    1. Mur. Take him on the costard with the hilts of thy
sword, and then throw him into the malmsey-butt in the 145
next room.

---

40 **bulk:** *body*   45 **melancholy flood;** *cf. n.*   46 **ferryman:** *Charon*   49 **father-in-law;** *cf. n.*   50 **scourge for perjury;** *cf. n.*   53 **A shadow;** *cf. n.*   55 **fleeting:** *vacillating*   56 **stabb'd ... Tewkesbury;** *cf. n.*   64 **No ... though:** *it is not strange that*   74 **fain:** *gladly*   80 **unfelt imaginations:** *i.e. what they imagine they might do but are unable to realize*

105 **remorse:** *scruple*   115 **humour:** *mood*   116 **tells:** *counts*   131 **shamefac'd:** *bashful*   139 **him:** *refers to conscience* **insinuate:** *ingratiate*   142 **tall:** *doughty, valiant*   144 **costard:** *head; cf. n.* **hilts:** *hilt*   145 **malmsey:** *a kind of wine*

2. Mur. O, excellent device! and make a sop of him.

1. Mur. Soft! he wakes.

2. Mur. Strike!

1. Mur. No, we'll reason with him. 150

Clar. Where art thou, keeper? give me a cup of wine.

2. Mur. You shall have wine enough, my lord, anon.

Clar. In God's name, what art thou?

1. Mur. A man, as you are.

Clar. But not, as I am royal. 155

1. Mur. Nor you, as we are, loyal.

Clar. Thy voice is thunder, but thy looks are humble.

1. Mur. My voice is now the king's, my looks mine own.

Clar. How darkly, and how deadly dost thou speak!
Your eyes do menace me: why look you pale? 160
Who sent you hither? Wherefore do you come?

2. Mur. To, to, to—

Clar. To murther me?

Both [Mur.] Ay, ay.

Clar. You scarcely have the hearts to tell me so, 165
And therefore cannot have the hearts to do it.
Wherein, my friends, have I offended you?

1. Mur. Offended us you have not, but the king.

Clar. I shall be reconcil'd to him again.

2. Mur. Never, my lord; therefore prepare to die. 170

Clar. Are you drawn forth among a world of men
To slay the innocent? What is my offence?
Where is the evidence that doth accuse me?
What lawful quest have given their verdict up
Unto the frowning judge? or who pronounc'd 175
The bitter sentence of poor Clarence' death?
Before I be convict by course of law,
To threaten me with death is most unlawful.
I charge you, as you hope for any goodness
[By Christ's dear blood shed for our grievous sins,] 180
That you depart and lay no hands on me:
The deed you undertake is damnable.

1. Mur. What we will do, we do upon command.

2. Mur. And he that hath commanded is our king.

Clar. Erroneous vassals! the great King of kings 185
Hath in the table of his law commanded
That thou shalt do no murther: will you, then,
Spurn at his edict and fulfil a man's?
Take heed; for he holds vengeance in his hand,
To hurl upon their heads that break his law. 190

2. Mur. And that same vengeance doth he hurl on thee,
For false forswearing and for murther too:
Thou didst receive the sacrament to fight
In quarrel of the house of Lancaster.

1. Mur. And, like a traitor to the name of God, 195
Didst break that vow, and, with thy treacherous blade
Unripp'dst the bowels of thy sovereign's son.

2. Mur. Whom thou wast sworn to cherish and defend.

1. Mur. How canst thou urge God's dreadful law to us,
When thou hast broke it in such dear degree? 200

Clar. Alas! for whose sake did I that ill deed?
For Edward, for my brother, for his sake:
He sends you not to murther me for this;
For in that sin he is as deep as I.

If God will be avenged for the deed, 205
O! know you yet, he doth it publicly:
Take not the quarrel from his powerful arm;
He needs no indirect or lawless course
To cut off those that have offended him.

1. Mur. Who made thee then a bloody minister, 210
When gallant-springing, brave Plantagenet,
That princely novice, was struck dead by thee?

Clar. My brother's love, the devil, and my rage.

1. Mur. Thy brother's love, our duty, and thy faults,
Provoke us hither now to slaughter thee. 215

Clar. If you do love my brother, hate not me;
I am his brother, and I love him well.
If you are hir'd for meed, go back again,
And I will send you to my brother Gloucester,
Who shall reward you better for my life 220
Than Edward will for tidings of my death.

2. Mur. You are deceiv'd, your brother Gloucester hates
you.

Clar. O, no! he loves me, and he holds me dear:
Go you to him from me. 225

1. Mur.   Ay, so we will.

Clar. Tell him, when that our princely father York
Bless'd his three sons with his victorious arm,
[And charg'd us from his soul to love each other,]
He little thought of this divided friendship: 230
Bid Gloucester think on this, and he will weep.

1. Mur. Ay, millstones; as he lesson'd us to weep.

Clar. O! do not slander him, for he is kind.

1. Mur. Right;
As snow in harvest. Come, you deceive yourself. 235
'Tis he that sends us to destroy you here.

Clar. It cannot be; for he bewept my fortune,
And hugg'd me in his arms, and swore, with sobs,
That he would labour my delivery.

1. Mur. Why, so he doth, when he delivers you 240
From this earth's thraldom to the joys of heaven.

2. Mur. Make peace with God, for you must die, my lord.

Clar. Have you that holy feeling in your souls,
To counsel me to make my peace with God,
And are you yet to your own souls so blind, 245
That you will war with God by murd'ring me?
O, sirs, consider! they that set you on
To do this deed, will hate you for the deed.

2. Mur. What shall we do?

Clar.   Relent and save your souls. 250

1. Mur. Relent? 'Tis cowardly and womanish.

Clar. Not to relent, is beastly, savage, devilish.
Which of you, if you were a prince's son,
Being pent from liberty, as I am now,
If two such murtherers as yourselves came to you, 255
Would not entreat for life?
My friend, I spy some pity in thy looks;
O! if thine eye be not a flatterer,
Come thou on my side, and entreat for me,
As you would beg, were you in my distress. 260
A begging prince what beggar pities not?

---

147 **sop;** *cf. n.*   159 **darkly:** *frowningly*   174 **quest:** *inquest, jury*   177 **convict:** *con-*
victed   180 *Cf. n.*   185 **Erroneous:** *misguided*   188 **Spurn at:** *oppose contemptu-*
ously   200 **dear:** *grievous, dire*

211 **gallant-springing;** *cf. n.*   212 **novice:** *youth*   213 **My brother's love:** *my love of*
my brother   215 **Provoke:** *urge*   232 **lesson'd:** *taught*   235 **snow in harvest;**
cf. n.   239 **labour:** *busy himself to procure*   241 **thraldom:** *slavery*   254 **pent from:**
shut up from

2. *Mur.* Look behind you, my lord.
1. *Mur.* Take that! and that!   *Stabs him.*
          If all this will not do,
I'll drown you in the malmsey-butt within.   *265*
                              Exit [with the body].
2. *Mur.* A bloody deed, and desperately dispatch'd!
How fain, like Pilate, would I wash my hands
Of this most grievous murther.
1. *Mur.* How now! what mean'st thou, that thou help'st
me not?   *270*
By heaven, the duke shall know how slack you have been.
2. *Mur.* I would he knew that I had sav'd his brother!
Take thou the fee, and tell him what I say;
For I repent me that the duke is slain.
1. *Mur.* So do not I: go, coward as thou art.   *275*
Well, I'll go hide the body in some hole,
Till that the duke give order for his burial:
And when I have my meed, I will away;
For this will out, and then I must not stay.   *Exit.*

ACT SECOND ✖ SCENE FIRST

[London. A room in the Palace]
Flourish. Enter the King [Edward IV] sick, the Queen [Elizabeth],
Lord Marquess Dorset, Rivers, Hastings, Catesby, Buckingham,
[Grey,] Woodville [and Others].

K. Edw. Why, so: now have I done a good day's work.
You peers, continue this united league:
I every day expect an embassage
From my Redeemer to redeem me hence;
And more at peace my soul shall part to heaven,   *5*
Since I have made my friends at peace on earth.
Rivers and Hastings, take each other's hand;
Dissemble not your hatred, swear your love.
Riv. By heaven, my soul is purg'd from grudging hate;
And with my hand I seal my true heart's love.   *10*
Hast. So thrive I, as I truly swear the like!
K. Edw. Take heed, you dally not before your king;
Lest he that is the supreme King of kings
Confound your hidden falsehood, and award
Either of you to be the other's end.   *15*
Hast. So prosper I, as I swear perfect love!
Riv. And I, as I love Hastings with my heart!
K. Edw. Madam, your self is not exempt from this;
Nor you, son Dorset; Buckingham, nor you:
You have been factious one against the other.   *20*
Wife, love Lord Hastings, let him kiss your hand;
And what you do, do it unfeignedly.
Q. Eliz. There, Hastings; I will never more remember
Our former hatred, so thrive I and mine!
K. Edw. Dorset, embrace him; Hastings, love lord marquess.   *25*
Dor. This interchange of love, I here protest,
Upon my part shall be inviolable.

Hast. And so swear I.   *[They embrace.]*
K. Edw. Now, princely Buckingham, seal thou this league
With thy embracements to my wife's allies,   *30*
And make me happy in your unity.
Buck. *[To the Queen.]* Whenever Buckingham doth turn
his hate
Upon your Grace, but with all duteous love
Doth cherish you and yours, God punish me   *35*
With hate in those where I expect most love!
When I have most need to employ a friend,
And most assured that he is a friend,
Deep, hollow, treacherous, and full of guile,
Be he unto me! This do I beg of heaven,   *40*
When I am cold in love to you or yours.   *[They] embrace.*
K. Edw. A pleasing cordial, princely Buckingham,
Is this thy vow unto my sickly heart.
There wanteth now our brother Gloucester here
To make the blessed period of this peace.   *45*
Buck. And, in good time, here comes Sir Richard Ratcliff
and the duke.

Enter Ratcliff and Gloucester.

Rich. Good morrow to my sovereign king and queen;
And princely peers, a happy time of day!
K. Edw. Happy, indeed, as we have spent the day.   *50*
Gloucester, we have done deeds of charity;
Made peace of enmity, fair love of hate,
Between these swelling wrong-incensed peers.
Rich. A blessed labour, my most sovereign lord.
Among this princely heap, if any here,   *55*
By false intelligence, or wrong surmise,
Hold me a foe;
If I unwillingly, or in my rage,
Have aught committed that is hardly borne
To any in this presence, I desire   *60*
To reconcile me to his friendly peace:
'Tis death to me to be at enmity;
I hate it, and desire all good men's love.
First, madam, I entreat true peace of you,
Which I will purchase with my duteous service;   *65*
Of you, my noble cousin Buckingham,
If ever any grudge were lodg'd between us;
Of you, and you, Lord Rivers, and of Dorset,
That all without desert have frown'd on me;
Of you, Lord Woodville, and Lord Scales, of you,   *70*
Dukes, earls, lords, gentlemen; indeed, of all.
I do not know that Englishman alive
With whom my soul is any jot at odds
More than the infant that is born to-night:
I thank my God for my humility.   *75*
Q. Eliz. A holy day shall this be kept hereafter:
I would to God all strifes were well compounded.
My sovereign lord, I do beseech your highness
To take our brother Clarence to your grace.
Rich. Why, madam, have I offer'd love for this,   *80*
To be so flouted in this royal presence?

---

265 malmsey-butt; *cf. n.*   **267 Pilate;** *cf. n.*   **2 united league;** *cf. n.*   **7 Rivers and Hastings;** *cf. n.*   **8 Dissemble:** *disguise*   **11 So . . . like;** *cf. n.*   **12 dally:** *play a part*   **15 Either . . . end;** *cf. n.*   **20 factious:** *quarrelsome*

37 most: *am most*   **44 wanteth:** *is needed*   **46 in good time:** *at a fortunate moment*   **52 of:** *instead of*   **53 swelling:** *inflated with anger*   **55 heap:** *assembly*   **58 unwillingly:** *unintentionally* **rage:** *unthinking passion*   **59 hardly borne:** *taken amiss*   **61 me:** *myself*   **68 Of . . . Dorset;** *cf. n.*   **69 without desert:** *i.e. without desert on my part*   **70 Lord . . . Scales;** *cf. n.*   **71-74** *Cf. n.*   **77 compounded:** *settled*

Who knows not that the gentle duke is dead?   *They all start.*
You do him injury to scorn his corse.

    K. Edw. Who knows not he is dead! who knows he is?

    Q. Eliz. All-seeing heaven, what a world is this!   85

    Buck. Look I so pale, Lord Dorset, as the rest?

    Dor. Ay, my good lord; and no man in the presence
But his red colour hath forsook his cheeks.

    K. Edw. Is Clarence dead? the order was revers'd.

    Rich. But he, poor man, by your first order died,   90
And that a winged Mercury did bear;
Some tardy cripple bare the countermand,
That came too lag to see him buried.
God grant that some, less noble and less loyal,
Nearer in bloody thoughts, and not in blood,   95
Deserve not worse than wretched Clarence did,
And yet go current from suspicion.

Enter Earl of Derby.

    Der. A boon, my sovereign, for my service done!

    K. Edw. I prithee, peace: my soul is full of sorrow.

    Der. I will not rise, unless your highness hear me.   100

    K. Edw. Then say at once, what is it thou request'st.

    Der. The forfeit, sovereign, of my servant's life;
Who slew to-day a riotous gentleman
Lately attendant on the Duke of Norfolk.

    K. Edw. Have I a tongue to doom my brother's death,   105
And shall that tongue give pardon to a slave?
My brother kill'd no man, his fault was thought;
And yet his punishment was bitter death.
Who su'd to me for him? who, in my wrath,
Kneel'd at my feet, and bid me be advis'd?   110
Who spoke of brotherhood? who spoke of love?
Who told me how the poor soul did forsake
The mighty Warwick, and did fight for me?
Who told me, in the field at Tewkesbury,
When Oxford had me down, he rescu'd me,   115
And said, 'Dear brother, live, and be a king'?
Who told me, when we both lay in the field,
Frozen almost to death, how he did lap me
Even in his garments; and did give himself,
All thin and naked, to the numb cold night?   120
All this from my remembrance brutish wrath
Sinfully pluck'd, and not a man of you
Had so much grace to put it in my mind.
But when your carters or your waiting-vassals
Have done a drunken slaughter, and defac'd   125
The precious image of our dear Redeemer,
You straight are on your knees for pardon, pardon;
And I, unjustly too, must grant it you;
But for my brother not a man would speak,
Nor I, ungracious, speak unto myself   130
For him, poor soul. The proudest of you all
Have been beholding to him in his life,
Yet none of you would once beg for his life.
O God! I fear, thy justice will take hold
On me and you and mine and yours for this.   135
Come, Hastings, help me to my closet. Ah, poor Clarence!

*Exeunt some with King and Queen [Hastings, Rivers,
Dorset, and Grey].*

    Rich. This is the fruits of rashness. Mark'd you not
How that the guilty kindred of the queen
Look'd pale when they did hear of Clarence' death?   140
O! they did urge it still unto the king:
God will revenge it. Come, lords; will you go
To comfort Edward with our company?

    Buck. We wait upon your Grace.   *Exeunt.*

❧ SCENE SECOND ❧

[The Same. A Room in the Palace]
*Enter the old Duchess of York, with the two children of Clarence
[Edward and a daughter].*

    Edw. Good grandam, tell us, is our father dead?

    Duch. No, boy.

    Daugh. Why do you weep so oft, and beat your breast,
And cry—'O Clarence, my unhappy son'?

    Edw. Why do you look on us, and shake your head,   5
And call us orphans, wretches, castaways,
If that our noble father were alive?

    Duch. My pretty cousins, you mistake me both;
I do lament the sickness of the king,
As loath to lose him, not your father's death;   10
It were lost sorrow to wail one that's lost.

    Edw. Then you conclude, my grandam, he is dead.
The king, mine uncle, is to blame for it:
God will revenge it; whom I will importune
With earnest prayers all to that effect.   15

    Daugh. And so will I.

    Duch. Peace, children, peace! the king doth love you well.
Incapable and shallow innocents,
You cannot guess who caus'd your father's death.

    Edw. Grandam, we can; for my good uncle Gloucester   20
Told me, the king, provok'd to 't by the queen,
Devis'd impeachments to imprison him:
And when my uncle told me so, he wept,
And pitied me, and kindly kiss'd my cheek;
Bade me rely on him, as on my father,   25
And he would love me dearly as a child.

    Duch. Ah! that deceit should steal such gentle shape,
And with a virtuous visor hide deep vice.
He is my son, ay, and therein my shame,
Yet from my dugs he drew not this deceit.   30

    Edw. Think you my uncle did dissemble, grandam?

    Duch. Ay, boy.

    Edw. I cannot think it. Hark! what noise is this?

*Enter the Queen [Elizabeth] with her hair about her ears; Rivers
and Dorset after her.*

    Q. Eliz. Ah! who shall hinder me to wail and weep,
To chide my fortune, and torment myself?   35
I'll join with black despair against my soul,
And to myself become an enemy.

    Duch. What means this scene of rude impatience?

---

87 presence: *king's company*   92 bare: *bore*   93 lag: *late*   95 blood: *relationship*   97 go ... suspicion; *cf. n.*   106 pardon ... slave; *cf. n.*   110 be advis'd:
deliberate   115 Oxford; *cf. n.*   118 lap: *enwrap*   132 beholding: *under obligation*

6 castaways; *cf. n.*   8 cousins: *relatives, here grandchildren*   18 Incapable: *without
power of understanding*   22 impeachments: *accusations*   24 Cf. n.   27 shape: *outward appearance*   28 visor: *mask*

Q. Eliz. To make an act of tragic violence:
Edward, my lord, thy son, our king, is dead!   40
Why grow the branches when the root is gone?
Why wither not the leaves that want their sap?
If you will live, lament: if die, be brief,
That our swift-winged souls may catch the king's;
Or, like obedient subjects, follow him   45
To his new kingdom of ne'er-changing night.
     Duch. Ah! so much interest have I in thy sorrow
As I had title in thy noble husband.
I have bewept a worthy husband's death,
And liv'd with looking on his images;   50
But now two mirrors of his princely semblance
Are crack'd in pieces by malignant death,
And I for comfort have but one false glass,
That grieves me when I see my shame in him.
Thou art a widow; yet thou art a mother,   55
And hast the comfort of thy children left [thee]:
But death hath snatch'd my husband from mine arms,
And pluck'd two crutches from my feeble hands,
Clarence and Edward. O! what cause have I—
Thine being but a moiety of my moan—   60
To overgo thy woes, and drown thy cries!
     Edw. Ah, aunt, you wept not for our father's death;
How can we aid you with our kindred tears?
     Daugh. Our fatherless distress was left unmoan'd;
Your widow-dolour likewise be unwept.   65
     Q. Eliz. Give me no help in lamentation;
I am not barren to bring forth complaints:
All springs reduce their currents to mine eyes,
That I, being govern'd by the watery moon,
May send forth plenteous tears to drown the world!   70
Ah, for my husband! for my dear Lord Edward!
     Chil. Ah, for our father! for our dear Lord Clarence!
     Duch. Alas, for both! both mine, Edward and Clarence!
     Q. Eliz. What stay had I but Edward? and he's gone.
     Chil. What stay had we but Clarence? and he's gone.   75
     Duch. What stays had I but they? and they are gone.
     Q. Eliz. Was never widow had so dear a loss.
     Chil. Were never orphans had so dear a loss.
     Duch. Was never mother had so dear a loss.
Alas! I am the mother of these griefs: 80
Their woes are parcell'd, mine is general.
She for an Edward weeps, and so do I;
I do for a Clarence weep, so doth not she:
These babes for Clarence weep, [and so do I;
I for an Edward weep,] so do not they: 85
Alas! you three, on me, threefold distress'd,
Pour all your tears; I am your sorrow's nurse,
And I will pamper it with lamentation.
     Dor. Comfort, dear mother: God is much displeas'd
That you take with unthankfulness his doing.   90
In common worldly things 'tis call'd ungrateful,
With dull unwillingness to repay a debt
Which with a bounteous hand was kindly lent;
Much more to be thus opposite with heaven,

For it requires the royal debt it lent you.   95
     Riv. Madam, bethink you, like a careful mother,
Of the young prince your son: send straight for him;
Let him be crown'd; in him your comfort lives.
Drown desperate sorrow in dead Edward's grave,
And plant your joys in living Edward's throne.   100

     Enter Richard [Duke of Gloucester], Buckingham, Derby,
          Hastings, and Ratcliff.

     Rich. Sister, have comfort: all of us have cause
To wail the dimming of our shining star;
But none can help our harms by wailing them.
Madam, my mother, I do cry you mercy;
I did not see your Grace. Humbly on my knee   105
I crave your blessing.
     Duch. God bless thee! and put meekness in thy breast,
Love, charity, obedience, and true duty.
     Rich. Amen; *[Aside.]* and make me die a good old
man!   110
That is the butt-end of a mother's blessing;
I marvel that her Grace did leave it out.
     Buck. You cloudy princes and heart-sorrowing peers,
That bear this heavy mutual load of moan,
Now cheer each other in each other's love: 115
Though we have spent our harvest of this king,
We are to reap the harvest of his son.
The broken rancour of your high-swoll'n hates,
But lately splinter'd, knit, and join'd together,
Must gently be preserv'd, cherish'd, and kept: 120
Me seemth good, that, with some little train,
Forthwith from Ludlow the young prince be fet
Hither to London, to be crown'd our king.
     Riv. Why with some little train, my Lord of Buckingham?
     Buck. Marry, my lord, lest by a multitude   125
The new-heal'd wound of malice should break out;
Which would be so much the more dangerous,
By how much the estate is green and yet ungovern'd;
Where every horse bears his commanding rein,
And may direct his course as please himself,   130
As well the fear of harm, as harm apparent,
In my opinion, ought to be prevented.
     Rich. I hope the king made peace with all of us,
And the compact is firm and true in me.
     Riv. And so in me; and so, I think, in all: 135
Yet, since it is but green, it should be put
To no apparent likelihood of breach,
Which haply by much company might be urg'd:
Therefore I say with noble Buckingham,
That it is meet so few should fetch the prince.   140
     Hast. And so say I.
     Rich. Then be it so: and go we to determine
Who they shall be that straight shall post to Ludlow.
Madam, and you my sister, will you go
To give your censures in this business?   145
          Exeunt. Mane[n]t Buckingham and Richard.
     Buck. My lord, whoever journeys to the prince,
For God's sake, let not us two stay at home:

---

40 Edward; *cf. n.*   **50** images: *i.e. children*   **53** false glass: *i.e. Richard*   **60** moiety:
fractional part, half   **61** overgo: *exceed*   **63** kindred tears: *i.e. tears of kinsmen*   **65**
widow-dolour: *widow's grief*   **67** to: *in capacity to*   **68** reduce: *bring back*   **70**
Cf. n.   **74** stay: *support*   **80** mother ... griefs; *cf. n.*   **81** parcell'd: *i.e. distributed*
among them severally general: *i.e. embraces the griefs of all*   **94** opposite: *in opposition*

103 help: *remedy*   **113** cloudy: *grief-clouded*   **118** broken rancour; *cf. n.* high-swoll'n:
excessively bitter   **119** splinter'd: *bound up with splints*   **121** little train: *few attendants;*
cf. n.   **122** Ludlow; *cf. n.*   **128** estate: *state* green: *new*   **130** please: *may*
please   **138** urg'd: *brought on*   **145** censures: *opinions*

For by the way I'll sort occasion,
As index to the story we late talk'd of,
To part the queen's proud kindred from the prince.   *150*
   Rich. My other self, my counsel's consistory,
My oracle, my prophet! My dear cousin,
I, as a child, will go by thy direction.
Towards Ludlow, then, for we'll not stay behind.   *Exeunt.*

❧ SCENE THIRD ❧

[The Same. A Street]
Enter one Citizen at one door and another at the other.

   1. Cit. Good morrow, neighbour: whither away so fast?
   2. Cit. I promise you, I scarcely know myself:
Hear you the news abroad?
   1. Cit.   Ay; that the king is dead.
   2. Cit. Ill news, by'r lady; seldom comes the better: *5*
I fear, I fear, 'twill prove a giddy world.

Enter another Citizen.

   3. Cit. Neighbours, God speed!
   1. Cit.   Give you good morrow, sir.
   3. Cit. Doth the news hold of good King Edward's death?
   2. Cit. Ay, sir, it is too true; God help the while!   *10*
   3. Cit. Then, masters, look to see a troublous world.
   1. Cit. No, no; by God's good grace, his son shall reign.
   3. Cit. Woe to that land that's govern'd by a child!
   2. Cit. In him there is a hope of government,
Which in his nonage council under him,   *15*
And in his full and ripen'd years himself,
No doubt, shall then and till then govern well.
   1. Cit. So stood the state when Henry the Sixth
Was crown'd at Paris but at nine months old.
   3. Cit. Stood the state so? no, no, good friends, God wot;
For then this land was famously enrich'd
With politic grave counsel; then the king
Had virtuous uncles to protect his Grace.
   1. Cit. Why, so hath this, both by his father and mother.
   3. Cit. Better it were they all came by his father,   *25*
Or by his father there were none at all;
For emulation, who shall now be nearest,
Will touch us all too near, if God prevent not.
O! full of danger is the Duke of Gloucester,
And the queen's sons and brothers haught and proud!   *30*
And were they to be rul'd, and not to rule,
This sickly land might solace as before.
   1. Cit. Come, come, we fear the worst; all will be well.
   3. Cit. When clouds are seen, wise men put on their cloaks;
When great leaves fall, then winter is at hand;   *35*
When the sun sets, who doth not look for night?
Untimely storms make men expect a dearth.
All may be well; but, if God sort it so,
'Tis more than we deserve, or I expect.
   2. Cit. Truly, the hearts of men are full of fear: *40*

You cannot reason almost with a man
That looks not heavily and full of dread.
   3. Cit. Before the days of change, still is it so:
By a divine instinct men's minds mistrust
Pursuing danger; as, by proof, we see   *45*
The waters swell before a boisterous storm.
But leave it all to God. Whither away?
   2. Cit. Marry, we were sent for to the justices.
   3. Cit. And so was I: I'll bear you company.   *Exeunt.*

❧ SCENE FOURTH ❧

[The Same. A Room in the Palace]
Enter [the] Archbishop [of York, the] young [Duke of] York, the
Queen [Elizabeth,] and the Duchess [of York].

   Arch. Last night, I hear, they lay at Stony-Stratford;
And at Northampton they do rest to-night:
To-morrow, or next day, they will be here.
   Duch. I long with all my heart to see the prince.
I hope he is much grown since last I saw him.   *5*
   Q. Eliz. But I hear, no; they say my son of York
Has almost overta'en him in his growth.
   York. Ay, mother, but I would not have it so.
   Duch. Why, my good cousin, it is good to grow.
   York. Grandam, one night, as we did sit at supper,   *10*
My uncle Rivers talk'd how I did grow
More than my brother: 'Ay,' quoth my uncle Gloucester,
'Small herbs have grace, great weeds do grow apace:'
And since, methinks, I would not grow so fast,
Because sweet flowers are slow and weeds make haste.   *15*
   Duch. Good faith, good faith, the saying did not hold
In him that did object the same to thee:
He was the wretched'st thing when he was young,
So long a-growing, and so leisurely,
That, if his rule were true, he should be gracious.   *20*
   Arch. And so, no doubt, he is, my gracious madam.
   Duch. I hope he is; but yet let mothers doubt.
   York. Now, by my troth, if I had been remember'd,
I could have given my uncle's grace a flout,
To touch his growth nearer than he touch'd mine.   *25*
   Duch. How, my young York? I prithee, let me hear it.
   York. Marry, they say my uncle grew so fast,
That he could gnaw a crust at two hours old:
'Twas full two years ere I could get a tooth.
Grandam, this would have been a biting jest.   *30*
   Duch. I prithee, pretty York, who told thee this?
   York. Grandam, his nurse.
   Duch. His nurse! why, she was dead ere thou wast born.
   York. If 'twere not she, I cannot tell who told me.
   Q. Eliz. A parlous boy: go to, you are too shrewd.   *35*
   Duch. Good madam, be not angry with the child.
   Q. Eliz. Pitchers have ears.

Enter a Messenger.

   Arch. Here comes a messenger. What news?

---

148 sort: *contrive*   **149 index:** *introduction, prelude*   **150 queen's proud kindred;**
cf. n.   **151 consistory:** *council-chamber* (figuratively)   **5 by'r:** *by our* (corruption of oath)
seldom . . . better; *cf. n.*   **6 giddy:** *confused*   **9 hold:** *hold good*   **11 troublous:** *trou-*
bled   **13 Woe . . . child;** *cf. n.*   **15 nonage:** *minority*   **19 nine months;** *cf. n.*   **27**
emulation: *jealous rivalry*   **30 haught:** *haughty*   **32 solace:** *be happy*   **38 sort:** *allot*

41 almost: *hardly*   **42 That . . . heavily:** *who does not look as if aware of the serious*
day   **45 by:** *for*   **1 Stony-Stratford;** *cf. n.*   **18 wretched'st:** *puniest*   **23 been re-**
member'd: *recollected*   **28** *Cf. n.*   **35 parlous:** *clever, keen*   **37 Pitchers;** *cf. n.*
S. d. *Cf. n.*

Mess. Such news, my lord, as grieves me to report.
Q. Eliz. How doth the prince?   40
Mess.   Well, madam, and in health.
Duch. What is thy news?
Mess. Lord Rivers and Lord Grey are sent to Pomfret.
With them Sir Thomas Vaughan, prisoners.
Duch. Who hath committed them?   45
Mess.   The mighty dukes,
Gloucester and Buckingham.
Arch.   For what offence?
Mess. The sum of all I can I have disclos'd:
Why, or for what, the nobles were committed   50
Is all unknown to me, my gracious lord.
Q. Eliz. Ay me! I see the ruin of my house!
The tiger now hath seiz'd the gentle hind;
Insulting tyranny begins to jut
Upon the innocent and aweless throne: 55
Welcome destruction, blood, and massacre!
I see, as in a map, the end of all.
Duch. Accursed and unquiet wrangling days,
How many of you have mine eyes beheld!
My husband lost his life to get the crown,   60
And often up and down my sons were toss'd
For me to joy and weep their gain and loss.
And being seated, and domestic broils
Clean over-blown, themselves, the conquerors,
Make war upon themselves; brother to brother,   65
Blood to blood, self against self: O preposterous
And frantic outrage, end thy damned spleen;
Or let me die, to look on earth no more!
Q. Eliz. Come, come, my boy; we will to sanctuary.
Madam, farewell.   70
Duch.   Stay, I will go with you.
Q. Eliz. You have no cause.
Arch. [To the Queen.] My gracious lady, go;
And thither bear your treasure and your goods.
For my part, I'll resign unto your Grace   75
The seal I keep: and so betide to me
As well I tender you and all of yours!
Go; I'll conduct you to the sanctuary.   *Exeunt.*

ACT THIRD ❧ SCENE FIRST

[The Same. A Street]
The Trumpets sound. Enter young Prince [of Wales], the Dukes of
Gloucester and Buckingham, Lord Cardinal [Bourchier, Catesby],
with Others.

Buck. Welcome, sweet prince, to London, to your chamber.
Rich. Welcome, dear cousin, my thoughts' sovereign;
The weary way hath made you melancholy.
Prince. No, uncle; but our crosses on the way
Have made it tedious, wearisome, and heavy: 5
I want more uncles here to welcome me.
Rich. Sweet prince, the untainted virtue of your years

Hath not yet div'd into the world's deceit:
No more can you distinguish of a man
Than of his outward show; which, God he knows,   10
Seldom or never jumpeth with the heart.
Those uncles which you want were dangerous;
Your Grace attended to their sugar'd words,
But look'd not on the poison of their hearts:
God keep you from them, and from such false friends!   15
Prince. God keep me from false friends! but they were none.
Rich. My lord, the Mayor of London comes to greet you.

Enter [the] Lord Mayor [and his Train].

L. May. God bless your Grace with health and happy days!
Prince. I thank you, good my lord; and thank you all.
I thought my mother and my brother York   20
Would long ere this have met us on the way:
Fie! what a slug is Hastings, that he comes not
To tell us whether they will come or no.

Enter Lord Hastings.

Buck. And in good time here comes the sweating lord.
Prince. Welcome, my lord. What, will our mother come?   25
Hast. On what occasion, God he knows, not I,
The queen your mother, and your brother York,
Have taken sanctuary: the tender prince
Would fain have come with me to meet your Grace,
But by his mother was perforce withheld.   30
Buck. Fie! what an indirect and peevish course
Is this of hers! Lord Cardinal, will your Grace
Persuade the queen to send the Duke of York
Unto his princely brother presently?
If she deny, Lord Hastings, go with him,   35
And from her jealous arms pluck him perforce.
Card. My Lord of Buckingham, if my weak oratory
Can from his mother win the Duke of York,
Anon expect him here; but if she be obdurate
To mild entreaties, God [in heaven] forbid   40
We should infringe the holy privilege
Of blessed sanctuary! not for all this land
Would I be guilty of so great a sin.
Buck. You are too senseless-obstinate, my lord,
Too ceremonious and traditional: 45
Weigh it but with the grossness of this age,
You break not sanctuary in seizing him.
The benefit thereof is always granted
To those whose dealings have deserv'd the place
And those who have the wit to claim the place: 50
This prince hath neither claim'd it, nor deserv'd it;
And therefore, in mine opinion, cannot have it:
Then, taking him from thence that is not there,
You break no privilege nor charter there.
Oft have I heard of sanctuary men,   55
But sanctuary children ne'er till now.
Card. My lord, you shall o'er-rule my mind for once.
Come on, Lord Hastings, will you go with me?
Hast. I go, my lord.

---

53 **hind:** *doe*   54 **jut:** *encroach*   55 **aweless:** *i.e. because occupied by a young prince*   57 **map;** *cf. n.*   69 **sanctuary;** *cf. n.*   **S. d. Cardinal;** *cf. n.*   1 **chamber:** *royal residence*   4 **crosses:** *vexations*

11 **jumpeth:** *agrees*   16 *Cf. n.*   **S. d.;** *Cf. n.*   22 **slug:** *sluggard*   30 **perforce:** *by force*   36 **pluck him;** *cf. n.*   39 **Anon:** *soon*   40, 41 **God ... infringe;** *cf. n.*   44 **senseless-obstinate:** *obstinate without reason*   45 **Too ... traditional:** *too given to standing on ceremony and precedent*   46 **grossness:** *lack of nicety; cf. n.*   53 **taking ... there:** *i.e. because, actually, he is not in sanctuary*   56 **children;** *cf. n.*

Prince. Good lords, make all the speedy haste you may.   60
                 Exeunt Cardinal and Hastings.
Say, uncle Gloucester, if our brother come,
Where shall we sojourn till our coronation?
   Rich. Where it think'st best unto your royal self.
If I may counsel you, some day or two
Your highness shall repose you at the Tower: 65
Then where you please, and shall be thought most fit
For your best health and recreation.
   Prince. I do not like the Tower, of any place:
Did Julius Caesar build that place, my lord?
   Buck. He did, my gracious lord, begin that place,   70
Which, since, succeeding ages have re-edified.
   Prince. Is it upon record, or else reported
Successively from age to age, he built it?
   Buck. Upon record, my gracious lord.
   Prince. But say, my lord, it were not register'd,   75
Methinks the truth should live from age to age,
As 'twere retail'd to all posterity,
Even to the general [all-]ending day.
   Rich. [*Aside.*] So wise so young, they say, do never live long.
   Prince. What say you, uncle?   80
   Rich. I say, without characters, fame lives long.
[*Aside.*] Thus, like the formal Vice, Iniquity,
I moralize two meanings in one word.
   Prince. That Julius Cæsar was a famous man;
With what his valour did enrich his wit,   85
His wit set down to make his valour live:
Death makes no conquest of his conqueror,
For now he lives in fame, though not in life.
I'll tell you what, my cousin Buckingham,—
   Buck. What, my gracious lord?   90
   Prince. An if I live until I be a man,
I'll win our ancient right in France again,
Or die a soldier, as I liv'd a king.
   Rich. [*Aside.*] Short summers lightly have a forward spring.

       Enter young York, Hastings, and Cardinal.

   Buck. Now, in good time, here comes the Duke of York.   95
   Prince. Richard of York! how fares our noble brother?
   York. Well, my dear lord; so must I call you now.
   Prince. Ay, brother, to our grief, as it is yours:
Too late he died that might have kept that title,
Which by his death hath lost much majesty.   100
   Rich. How fares our cousin, noble Lord of York?
   York. I thank you, gentle uncle. O, my lord,
You said that idle weeds are fast in growth:
The prince my brother hath outgrown me far.
   Rich. He hath, my lord.   105
   York.   And therefore is he idle?
   Rich. O, my fair cousin, I must not say so.
   York. Then he is more beholding to you than I.
   Rich. He may command me as my sovereign;
But you have power in me as in a kinsman.   110
   York. I pray you, uncle, give me this dagger.
   Rich. My dagger, little cousin? with all my heart.

Prince. A beggar, brother?
   York. Of my kind uncle, that I know will give;
And, being but a toy, which is no grief to give.   115
   Rich. A greater gift than that I'll give my cousin.
   York. A greater gift! O, that's the sword to it.
   Rich. Ay, gentle cousin, were it light enough.
   York. O, then, I see, you'll part but with light gifts;
In weightier things you'll say a beggar nay.   120
   Rich. It is too weighty for your Grace to wear.
   York. I weigh it lightly, were it heavier.
   Rich. What! would you have my weapon, little lord?
   York. I would, that I might thank you, as you call me.
   Rich. How?   125
   York. Little.
   Prince. My Lord of York will still be cross in talk.
Uncle, your Grace knows how to bear with him.
   York. You mean, to bear me, not to bear with me:
Uncle, my brother mocks both you and me.   130
Because that I am little, like an ape,
He thinks that you should bear me on your shoulders.
   Buck. With what a sharp provided wit he reasons!
To mitigate the scorn he gives his uncle,
He prettily and aptly taunts himself: 135
So cunning and so young is wonderful.
   Rich. My lord, will 't please you pass along?
Myself and my good cousin Buckingham
Will to your mother, to entreat of her
To meet you at the Tower and welcome you.   140
   York. What! will you go unto the Tower, my lord?
   Prince. My Lord Protector will have it so.
   York. I shall not sleep in quiet at the Tower.
   Rich. Why, what should you fear?
   York. Marry, my uncle Clarence' angry ghost: 145
My grandam told me he was murther'd there.
   Prince. I fear no uncles dead.
   Rich. Nor none that live, I hope.
   Prince. And if they live, I hope, I need not fear.
But come, my lord; and, with a heavy heart,   150
Thinking on them, go I unto the Tower.
     A Sennet. Exeunt Prince, York, Hastings, and Dorset.
         Mane[n]t Richard, Buckingham, and Catesby.
   Buck. Think you, my lord, this little prating York
Was not incensed by his subtle mother
To taunt and scorn you thus opprobriously?
   Rich. No doubt, no doubt: O! 'tis a perilous boy;   155
Bold, quick, ingenious, forward, capable:
He's all the mother's, from the top to toe.
   Buck. Well, let them rest. Come hither, Catesby; thou art sworn
As deeply to effect what we intend   160
As closely to conceal what we impart.
Thou know'st our reasons urg'd upon the way:
What think'st thou? is it not an easy matter
To make William Lord Hastings of our mind,
For the instalment of this noble duke   165
In the seat royal of this famous isle?
   Cate. He for his father's sake so loves the prince

64 some: *a*   65 the Tower; *cf. n.*   68 of any place: *most of all places*   69 Julius Cæsar; *cf. n.*   77 retail'd: *handed down*   78 [all-]ending day: *i.e. doomsday*   79 So . . . long; *cf. n.*   81 characters: *written documents*   82 Vice, Iniquity; *cf. n.*   83 moralize: *interpret*   85 With what: *that with which*   94 lightly: *commonly*   97 dear; *cf. n.*   99 late: *lately*

115 toy: *trifle*   127 cross: *given to opposition*   132 shoulders; *cf. n.*   133 provided: *ready*   134 scorn: *taunt*   142 *Cf. n.*   151 on: *of* S. d. Sennet; *cf. n.*   153 incensed: *instigated*   155 perilous: *i.e. parlous*   156 forward: *precocious*   capable: *intelligent*   166 seat royal: *royal throne*

That he will not be won to aught against him.

 Buck. What think'st thou, then, of Stanley? will not he?

 Cate. He will do all in all as Hastings doth.   *170*

 Buck. Well then, no more but this: go, gentle Catesby,

And, as it were far off, sound thou Lord Hastings,

How he doth stand affected to our purpose;

And summon him to-morrow to the Tower,

To sit about the coronation.   *175*

If thou dost find him tractable to us,

Encourage him, and tell him all our reasons:

If he be leaden, icy-cold, unwilling,

Be thou so too, and so break off the talk,

And give us notice of his inclination;   *180*

For we to-morrow hold divided councils,

Wherein thyself shalt highly be employ'd.

 Rich. Commend me to Lord William: tell him, Catesby,

His ancient knot of dangerous adversaries

To-morrow are let blood at Pomfret Castle;   *185*

And bid my lord, for joy of this good news,

Give Mistress Shore one gentle kiss the more.

 Buck. Good Catesby, go, effect this business soundly.

 Cate. My good lords both, with all the heed I can.

 Rich. Shall we hear from you, Catesby, ere we sleep?   *190*

 Cate. You shall, my lord.

 Rich. At Crosby House, there shall you find us both.

            Exit Catesby.

 Buck. Now, my lord, what shall we do if we perceive.

Lord Hastings will not yield to our complots?

 Rich. Chop off his head; something we will determine: *195*

And, look, when I am king, claim thou of me

The earldom of Hereford, and all the moveables

Whereof the king my brother was possess'd.

 Buck. I'll claim that promise at your Grace's hand.

 Rich. And look to have it yielded with all kindness.   *200*

Come, let us sup betimes, that afterwards

We may digest our complots in some form.   *Exeunt.*

❧ Scene Second ❧

[The Same. Before Lord Hastings' House]
Enter a Messenger to the door of Hastings.

 Mess. [Knocking.] My lord! my lord!

 Hast. [Within.] Who knocks?

 Mess. One from the Lord Stanley.

 Hast. [Within.] What is 't o'clock?

 Mess. Upon the stroke of four.   *5*

Enter Lord Hastings.

 Hast. Cannot my Lord Stanley sleep these tedious nights?

 Mess. So it appears by that I have to say.

First, he commends him to your noble self.

 Hast. What then?

 Mess. Then certifies your lordship, that this night   *10*

He dreamt the boar had rased off his helm:

Besides, he says there are two councils kept;

And that may be determin'd at the one

Which may make you and him to rue at th' other.

Therefore he sends to know your lordship's pleasure,   *15*

If you will presently take horse with him,

And with all speed post with him toward the north,

To shun the danger that his soul divines.

 Hast. Go, fellow, go, return unto thy lord;

Bid him not fear the separated council: *20*

His honour and myself are at the one,

And at the other is my good friend Catesby;

Where nothing can proceed that toucheth us

Whereof I shall not have intelligence.

Tell him his fears are shallow, without instance: *25*

And for his dreams, I wonder he's so simple

To trust the mockery of unquiet slumbers.

To fly the boar before the boar pursues,

Were to incense the boar to follow us

And make pursuit where he did mean no chase.   *30*

Go, bid thy master rise and come to me;

And we will both together to the Tower,

Where, he shall see, the boar will use us kindly.

 Mess. I'll go, my lord, and tell him what you say.   *Exit.*

Enter Catesby.

 Cate. Many good morrows to my noble lord!   *35*

 Hast. Good morrow, Catesby; you are early stirring.

What news, what news, in this our tottering state?

 Cate. It is a reeling world, indeed, my lord;

And I believe will never stand upright

Till Richard wear the garland of the realm.   *40*

 Hast. How! wear the garland! dost thou mean the crown?

 Cate. Ay, my good lord.

 Hast. I'll have this crown of mine cut from my shoulders

Before I'll see the crown so foul misplac'd.

But canst thou guess that he doth aim at it?   *45*

 Cate. Ay, on my life; and hopes to find you forward

Upon his party for the gain thereof:

And thereupon he sends you this good news,

That this same very day your enemies,

The kindred of the queen, must die at Pomfret.   *50*

 Hast. Indeed, I am no mourner for that news,

Because they have been still my adversaries;

But that I'll give my voice on Richard's side,

To bar my master's heirs in true descent,

God knows I will not do it, to the death.   *55*

 Cate. God keep your lordship in that gracious mind!

 Hast. But I shall laugh at this a twelve-month hence,

That they which brought me in my master's hate,

I live to look upon their tragedy.

Well, Catesby, ere a fortnight make me older,   *60*

I'll send some packing that yet think not on 't.

 Cate. 'Tis a vile thing to die, my gracious lord,

When men are unprepar'd and look not for it.

 Hast. O monstrous, monstrous! and so falls it out

With Rivers, Vaughan, Grey; and so 'twill do   *65*

With some men else, that think themselves as safe

As thou and I; who, as thou know'st, are dear

To princely Richard and to Buckingham.

---

172 **far off:** *indirectly; cf. n.* 175 **sit:** *confer* 184 **knot:** *group* 187 **Mistress Shore;**
cf. n. 194 **complots:** *plots, conspiracies* 197, 198 *Cf. n.* 197 **moveables:** *personal
property* 5 **stroke of four;** *cf. n.* 10 **certifies:** *informs* 11 **boar:** *i.e. Richard* **rased:**
torn

20 **separated council;** *cf. n.* 25 **instance:** *cause, motive* 26 **his dreams;** *cf. n.* 27
To: *as to* 43 **crown:** *head* 52 **still:** *always* 55 **to the death:** *i.e. even if my refusal
cost me my life*

Cate. The princes both make high account of you;
[*Aside.*] For they account his head upon the bridge.   70
    Hast. I know they do, and I have well deserv'd it.

Enter Lord Stanley.

Come on, come on; where is your boar-spear, man?
Fear you the boar, and go so unprovided?
    Stan. My lord, good morrow; good morrow, Catesby:
You may jest on, but by the holy rood,   75
I do not like these several councils, I.
    Hast. My lord, I hold my life as dear as yours;
And never, in my days, I do protest,
Was it so precious to me as 'tis now.
Think you, but that I know our state secure,   80
I would be so triumphant as I am?
    Stan. The lords at Pomfret, when they rode from London,
Were jocund and suppos'd their states were sure,
And they indeed had no cause to mistrust;
But yet you see how soon the day o'ercast.   85
This sudden stab of rancour I misdoubt;
Pray God, I say, I prove a needless coward!
What, shall we toward the Tower? the day is spent.
    Hast. Come, come, have with you. Wot you what,
my lord?   90
To-day the lords you talk of are beheaded.
    Stan. They, for their truth, might better wear their heads,
Than some that have accus'd them wear their hats.
But come, my lord, let's away.

Enter a Pursuivant.

    Hast. Go on before; I'll talk with this good fellow.   95
                    Exeunt Lord Stanley and Catesby.
How now, sirrah! how goes the world with thee?
    Purs. The better that your lordship please to ask.
    Hast. I tell thee, man, 'tis better with me now
Than when thou met'st me last where now we meet:
Then was I going prisoner to the Tower,   100
By the suggestion of the queen's allies;
But now, I tell thee,—keep it to thyself,—
This day those enemies are put to death,
And I in better state than e'er I was.
    Purse. God hold it to your honour's good content!   105
    Hast. Gramercy, fellow: there, drink that for me.
                      Throws him his purse.
                      Exit Pursuivant.
    Purs. I thank your honour.

Enter a Priest.

    Pr. Well met, my lord; I am glad to see your honour.
    Hast. I thank thee, good Sir John, with all my heart.
I am in your debt for your last exercise;   110
Come the next Sabbath, and I will content you.
    Pr. I'll wait upon your lordship.

Enter Buckingham.

    Buck. What, talking with a priest, lord chamberlain?
Your friends at Pomfret, they do need the priest:
Your honour hath no shriving work in hand.   115
    Hast. Good faith, and when I met this holy man,
The men you talk of came into my mind.
What, go you toward the Tower?
    Buck. I do, my lord; but long I cannot stay there:
I shall return before your lordship thence.   120
    Hast. Nay, like enough, for I stay dinner there.
    Buck. [*Aside.*] And supper too, although thou know'st
it not.
Come, will you go?
    Hast.   I'll wait upon your lordship.   *Exeunt.*

❧ SCENE THIRD ❧

[Pomfret. Before the Castle]
Enter Sir Richard Ratcliff, with Halberds, carrying the nobles
[Rivers, Grey, and Vaughan] to death at Pomfret.

    Riv. Sir Richard Ratcliff, let me tell thee this:
To-day shalt thou behold a subject die
For truth, for duty, and for loyalty.
    Grey. God bless the prince from all the pack of you!
A knot you are of damned blood-suckers.   5
    Vaugh. You live that shall cry woe for this hereafter!
    Rat. Dispatch; the limit of your lives is out.
    Riv. O Pomfret, Pomfret! O thou bloody prison!
Fatal and ominous to noble peers!
Within the guilty closure of thy walls   10
Richard the Second here was hack'd to death;
And, for more slander to thy dismal seat,
We give to thee our guiltless blood to drink.
    Grey. Now Margaret's curse is fall'n upon our heads,
When she exclaim'd on Hastings, you, and I,   15
For standing by when Richard stabb'd her son.
    Riv. Then curs'd she Richard, then curs'd she Buckingham.
Then curs'd she Hastings: O! remember, God,
To hear her prayer for them, as now for us;
And for my sister and her princely sons,   20
Be satisfied, dear God, with our true blood,
Which, as thou know'st, unjustly must be split.
    Rat. Make haste; the hour of death is expiate.
    Riv. Come, Grey, come, Vaughan; let us here embrace.
Farewell until we meet again in heaven.   *Exeunt.*

❧ SCENE FOURTH ❧

[London. The Tower]
Enter Buckingham, Derby, Hastings, Bishop of Ely, Norfolk, Ratcliff,
Lovel, with others, at a Table.

    Hast. Now noble peers, the cause why we are met
Is to determine of the coronation:
In God's name, speak, when is the royal day?
    Buck. Is all things ready for the royal time?
    Der. It is; and wants but nomination.   5

70 head … bridge; *cf. n.*   75 rood: *cross*   83 jocund: *carefree, merry* sure: *se-cure*   85 o'ercast: *became overcast*   86 misdoubt: *suspect*   87 needless: *without cause or reason*   88 spent; *cf. n.*   89 have with you: *I will go with you* Wot: *know* S. d. Pursuivant: *junior officer attending on a herald*   99 now we meet; *cf. n.* 101 suggestion: *urging (in a bad sense)*   106 Gramercy: *thanks* 109 Sir John; *cf. n.*   110 exercise: *act of worship, discourse*

113 talking; *cf. n.*   115 shriving; *cf. n.*   S.D. *Cf. n.*   7 out: *at an end*   10 closure: *enclosure*   11 *Cf. n.*   14 Margaret's curse; *cf. n.*   23 expiate: *fully come*   S.D. Derby: *i.e. Stanley*   5 nomination: *appointing*

Ely. To-morrow then I judge a happy day.
Buck. Who knows the Lord Protector's mind herein?
Who is most inward with the noble duke?
Ely. Your Grace, we think, should soonest know his mind.
Buck. We know each other's faces; for our hearts,   10
He knows no more of mine than I of yours;
Nor I of his, my lord, than you of mine.
Lord Hastings, you and he are near in love.
Hast. I thank his Grace, I know he loves me well;
But, for his purpose in the coronation,   15
I have not sounded him, nor he deliver'd
His gracious pleasure any way therein:
But you, my honourable lords, may name the time;
And in the duke's behalf I'll give my voice,
Which, I presume, he'll take in gentle part.   20

Enter Richard.

Ely. In happy time, here comes the duke himself.
Rich. My noble lords and cousins all, good morrow.
I have been long a sleeper; but, I trust,
My absence doth neglect no great design,
Which by my presence might have been concluded.   25
Buck. Had you not come upon your cue, my lord,
William Lord Hastings had pronounc'd your part,
I mean, your voice, for crowning of the king.
Rich. Than my Lord Hastings no man might be bolder:
His lordship knows me well, and loves me well.   30
My Lord of Ely, when I was last in Holborn,
I saw good strawberries in your garden there;
I do beseech you send for some of them.
Ely. Marry, and will, my lord, with all my heart.
                                        Exit Bishop.
Rich. Cousin of Buckingham, a word with you.   35
                                [Takes him aside.]
Catesby hath sounded Hastings in our business,
And finds the testy gentleman so hot,
That he will lose his head ere give consent
His master's child, as worshipfully he terms it,
Shall lose the royalty of England's throne.   40
Buck. Withdraw yourself a while; I'll go with you.
                        Exeunt [Richard and Buckingham].
Der. We have not yet set down this day of triumph.
To-morrow, in my judgment, is too sudden;
For I myself am not so well provided
As else I would be, were the day prolong'd.   45

[Re-]enter the Bishop of Ely.

Ely. Where is my lord, the Duke of Gloucester?
I have sent for these strawberries.
Hast. His Grace looks cheerfully and smooth this morning:
There's some conceit or other likes him well,
When that he bids good morrow with such spirit.   50
I think there's never a man in Christendom
Can lesser hide his love or hate than he;
For by his face straight shall you know his heart.
Der. What of his heart perceive you in his face

By any livelihood he show'd to-day?   55
Hast. Marry, that with no man here he is offended;
For, were he, he had shown it in his looks.
[*Der.* I pray God he be not, I say.]

[Re-]enter Richard and Buckingham.

Rich. I pray you all, tell me what they deserve
That do conspire my death with devilish plots   60
Of damned witchcraft, and that have prevail'd
Upon my body with their hellish charms?
Hast. The tender love I bear your Grace, my lord,
Makes me most forward in this princely presence
To doom th' offenders, whosoe'er they be: 65
I say, my lord, they have deserved death.
Rich. Then be your eyes the witness of their evil.
Look how I am bewitch'd; behold mine arm
Is like a blasted sapling, wither'd up:
And this is Edward's wife, that monstrous witch,   70
Consorted with that harlot strumpet Shore,
That by their witchcraft thus have marked me.
Hast. If they have done this deed, my noble lord,—
Rich. If! thou protector of this damned strumpet,
Talk'st thou to me of ifs? Thou art a traitor: 75
Off with his head! now, by Saint Paul, I swear,
I will not dine until I see the same.
Lovel and Ratcliff, look that it be done:
The rest, that love me, rise, and follow me.
            Exeunt. Mane[n]t Lovel and Ratcliff,
                            with the Lord Hastings.
Hast. Woe, woe, for England! not a whit for me;   80
For I, too fond, might have prevented this.
Stanley did dream the boar did rase our helms;
And I did scorn it, and disdain to fly.
Three times to-day my foot-cloth horse did stumble,
And started when he look'd upon the Tower,   85
As loath to bear me to the slaughter-house.
O! now I need the priest that spake to me:
I now repent I told the pursuivant,
As too triumphing, how mine enemies
To-day at Pomfret bloodily were butcher'd   90
And I myself secure in grace and favour.
O Margaret, Margaret! now thy heavy curse
Is lighted on poor Hastings' wretched head.
Rat. Come, come, dispatch; the duke would be at dinner:
Make a short shrift, he longs to see your head.   95
Hast. O momentary grace of mortal men,
Which we more hunt for than the grace of God!
Who builds his hope in air of your good looks,
Lives like a drunken sailor on a mast;
Ready with every nod to tumble down   100
Into the fatal bowels of the deep.
Lov. Come, come, dispatch; 'tis bootless to exclaim.
Hast. O bloody Richard! miserable England!
I prophesy the fearful'st time to thee
That ever wretched age hath look'd upon.   105
Come, lead me to the block; bear him my head:
They smile at me who shortly shall be dead.   *Exeunt.*

---

6 happy: *suitable*   **8 inward:** *familiar, intimate*   **9 should soonest:** *is most likely*
to   **21 In happy time:** *opportunely*   **26 upon:** *at* cue; *cf. n.*   **28 voice:** *vote*   **32
good strawberries;** *cf. n.*   **37 testy:** *quick-tempered*   **45 prolong'd:** *postponed*   **49
conceit:** *idea, thought* **likes:** *that pleases*

55 livelihood: *animated appearance*   **S.d.** *Cf. n.*   **61 prevail'd:** *effected harm*   **69
blasted sapling;** *cf. n.*   **71 Consorted:** *associated*   **74 If;** *cf. n.*   **81 fond:** *fool-*
ish   **84 foot-cloth;** *cf. n.*   **95 shrift:** *confession*   **98 air . . . looks;** *cf. n.*   **99
drunken . . . mast;** *cf. n.*   **102 bootless:** *useless*

❧ SCENE FIFTH ❧

[London. The Tower Walls]
Enter Richard and Buckingham, in rotten armour, marvellous
ill-favored.

Rich. Come, cousin, canst thou quake, and change thy
colour,
Murther thy breath in middle of a word,
And then again begin, and stop again,
As if thou wert distraught and mad with terror?   5
Buck. Tut! I can counterfeit the deep tragedian,
Speak and look back, and pry on every side,
Tremble and start at wagging of a straw,
Intending deep suspicion: ghastly looks
Are at my service, like enforced smiles;   10
And both are ready in their offices,
At any time, to grace my stratagems.
But what! is Catesby gone?
Rich. He is; and, see, he brings the mayor along.

Enter the [Lord] Mayor and Catesby.

Buck. Lord Mayor,—   15
Rich. Look to the drawbridge there!
Buck.   Hark! a drum.
Rich. Catesby, o'erlook the walls.
Buck. Lord Mayor, the reason we have sent,—
Rich. Look back, defend thee; here are enemies.   20
Buck. God and our innocency defend and guard us!

Enter Lovel and Ratcliff, with Hastings' head.

Rich. Be patient, they are friends, Ratcliff and Lovel.
Lov. Here is the head of that ignoble traitor,
The dangerous and unsuspected Hastings.
Rich. So dear I lov'd the man that I must weep.   25
I took him for the plainest harmless creature
That breath'd upon the earth a Christian;
Made him my book, wherein my soul recorded
The history of all her secret thoughts:
So smooth he daub'd his vice with show of virtue,   30
That, his apparent open guilt omitted,
I mean his conversation with Shore's wife,
He liv'd from all attainder of suspects.
Buck. Well, well, he was the covert'st shelter'd traitor
That ever liv'd.   35
Would you imagine, or almost believe,—
Were 't not that by great preservation
We live to tell it,—that the subtle traitor
This day had plotted, in the council-house,
To murther me and my good Lord of Gloucester?   40
May. Had he done so?
Rich. What! think you we are Turks or infidels?
Or that we would, against the form of law,
Proceed thus rashly in the villain's death,
But that the extreme peril of the case,   45
The peace of England and our person's safety,
Enforc'd us to this execution?

May. Now, fair befall you! he deserv'd his death;
And your good Graces both have well proceeded.
To warn false traitors from the like attempts.   50
Buck. I never look'd for better at his hands,
After he once fell in with Mistress Shore.
Yet had we not determin'd he should die,
Until your lordship came to see his end;
Which now the loving haste of these our friends,   55
Something against our meanings, have prevented:
Because, my lord, I would have had you heard
The traitor speak, and timorously confess
The manner and the purpose of his treasons;
That you might well have signified the same   60
Unto the citizens, who haply may
Misconster us in him, and wail his death.
May. But, my good lord, your Grace's words shall serve,
As well as I had seen and heard him speak:
And do not doubt, right noble princes both,   65
But I'll acquaint our duteous citizens
With all your just proceedings in this case.
Rich. And to that end we wish'd your lordship here,
T' avoid the censures of the carping world.
Buck. Which since you come too late of our intent,   70
Yet witness what you hear we did intend:
And so, my good Lord Mayor, we bid farewell.

Exit [Lord] Mayor.

Rich. Go, after, after, cousin Buckingham.
The mayor towards Guildhall hies him in all post:
There, at your meetest vantage of the time,   75
Infer the bastardy of Edward's children:
Tell them how Edward put to death a citizen,
Only for saying he would make his son
Heir to the crown; meaning indeed his house,
Which by the sign thereof was termed so.   80
Moreover, urge his hateful luxury
And bestial appetite in change of lust;
Which stretch'd unto their servants, daughters, wives,
Even where his raging eye or savage heart
Without control lusted to make a prey.   85
Nay, for a need, thus far come near my person:
Tell them, when that my mother went with child
Of that insatiate Edward, noble York,
My princely father, then had wars in France;
And, by true computation of the time,   90
Found that the issue was not his begot;
Which well appeared in his lineaments,
Being nothing like the noble duke my father.
Yet touch this sparingly, as 'twere far off,
Because, my lord, you know my mother lives.   95
Buck. Doubt not, my lord, I'll play the orator
As if the golden fee for which I plead
Were for myself: and so, my lord, adieu.
Rich. If you thrive well, bring them to Baynard's Castle;
Where you shall find me well accompanied   100
With reverend fathers and well-learned bishops.

S. d. rotten: *rusty*   **5 distraught:** *mentally damaged*   **9 Intending:** *pretending*   **30 daub'd:** *glossed*   **32 conversation:** *criminal conversation*   **33 from:** *free from*   **attainder of suspects:** *stain of suspicions*   **34 covert'st:** *most secret*   **36 almost:** *even*   **42 Turks;** *cf. n.*

48 fair befall: *good fortune attend*   **51, 52** *Cf. n.*   **57 heard:** *to have heard*   **62 Misconster:** *misconstrue*   **66 duteous:** *dutiful*   **69 carping:** *fault-finding*   **70 of our intent;** *cf. n.*   **74 post:** *haste*   **75 meetest vantage:** *most favorable opportunity*   **77 a citizen;** *cf. n.*   **80 sign;** *cf. n.*   **81 luxury:** *lechery*   **86 for a need:** *if necessary*   **thus ... near;** *cf. n.*   **92 Which:** *a fact which*   **well appeared:** *was clearly apparent*   **99 Baynard's Castle;** *cf. n.*

Buck. I go; and towards three or four o'clock
Look for the news that the Guildhall affords.

                     Exit Buckingham.

Rich. Go, Lovel, with all speed to Doctor Shaw;
[*To Catesby.*] Go thou to Friar Penker; bid them both   *105*
Meet me within this hour at Baynard's Castle.

              Exit [Catesby, with Lovel].

Now will I go to take some privy order,
To draw the brats of Clarence out of sight;
And to give order that no manner person
Have any time recourse unto the princes.   *110*

          Exeunt [Richard and Ratcliff].

❧ SCENE SIXTH ❧

[The Same. A Street]
Enter a Scrivener.

  Scriv. Here is the indictment of the good Lord Hastings;
Which in a set hand fairly is engross'd,
That it may be to-day read o'er in Paul's:
And mark how well the sequel hangs together.
Eleven hours I have spent to write it over,   *5*
For yesternight by Catesby was it sent me.
The precedent was full as long a-doing;
And yet within these five hours Hastings liv'd,
Untainted, unexamin'd, free, at liberty.
Here's a good world the while! Who is so gross   *10*
That cannot see this palpable device?
Yet who so bold but says he sees it not?
Bad is the world; and all will come to naught,
When such ill dealing must be seen in thought.

                      Exit.

❧ SCENE SEVENTH ❧

[The Same. The Court of Baynard's Castle]
Enter Richard and Buckingham at several doors.

  Rich. How now, how now! what say the citizens?
  Buck. Now, by the holy mother of our Lord,
The citizens are mum, say not a word.
  Rich. Touch'd you the bastardy of Edward's children?
  Buck. I did; with his contract with Lady Lucy,   *5*
And his contract by deputy in France;
Th' unsatiate greediness of his desire,
And his enforcement of the city wives;
His tyranny for trifles; his own bastardy,
As being got, your father then in France,   *10*
And his resemblance being not like the duke:
Withal I did infer your lineaments,
Being the right idea of your father,
Both in your form and nobleness of mind;

Laid open all your victories in Scotland,   *15*
Your discipline in war, wisdom in peace,
Your bounty, virtue, fair humility;
Indeed, left nothing fitting for your purpose
Untouch'd or slightly handled in discourse;
And when my oratory drew toward end,   *20*
I bid them that did love their country's good
Cry 'God save Richard, England's royal king!'
  Rich. And did they so?
  Buck. No, so God help me, they spake not a word;
But, like dumb statues or breathing stones,   *25*
Star'd each on other, and look'd deadly pale.
Which when I saw, I reprehended them;
And ask'd the mayor what meant this wilful silence:
His answer was, the people were not us'd
To be spoke to but by the recorder.   *30*
Then he was urg'd to tell my tale again:
'Thus saith the duke, thus hath the duke inferr'd;'
But nothing spoke in warrant from himself.
When he had done, some followers of mine own,
At lower end of the hall, hurl'd up their caps,   *35*
And some ten voices cried, 'God save King Richard!'
And thus I took the vantage of those few,
'Thanks, gentle citizens and friends,' quoth I;
'This general applause and cheerful shout
Argues your wisdom and your love to Richard:'   *40*
And even here brake off, and came away.
  Rich. What tongueless blocks were they! would they not speak?
Will not the mayor, then, and his brethren come?
  Buck. The mayor is here at hand. Intend some fear;   *45*
Be not you spoke with but by mighty suit:
And look you get a prayer-book in your hand,
And stand between two churchmen, good my lord:
For on that ground I'll make a holy descant:
And be not easily won to our requests;   *50*
Play the maid's part, still answer nay, and take it.
  Rich. I go; and if you plead as well for them
As I can say nay to thee for myself,
No doubt we bring it to a happy issue.
  Buck. Go, go, up to the leads! the Lord Mayor knocks.   *55*

                    [Exit Richard.]

Enter the [Lord] Mayor, [Aldermen,] and Citizens.

Welcome, my lord: I dance attendance here;
I think the duke will not be spoke withal.

Enter [from the Castle,] Catesby.

Now, Catesby! what says your lord to my request?
  Cate. He doth entreat your Grace, my noble lord,
To visit him to-morrow or next day.   *60*
He is within, with two right reverend fathers,
Divinely bent to meditation;
And in no worldly suits would he be mov'd,
To draw him from his holy exercise.
  Buck. Return, good Catesby, to the gracious duke: *65*
Tell him, myself, the mayor and aldermen,

---

104 Doctor Shaw; *cf. n.*   105 Friar Penker; *cf. n.*   107 privy order: *private measures*   109 manner: *manner of*   110 recourse: *access*   S. d. Scrivener: *professional scribe*   2 engross'd: *written out in a legal hand*   7 precedent: *original rough copy*   9 Untainted: *without suspicion of guilt*   10 gross: *stupid*   14 seen in thought: *i.e. observed but not referred to*   5 Lady Lucy; *cf. n.*   6 contract by deputy; *cf. n.*   11 resemblance: *appearance*   13 right idea: *exact image*

15 victories; *cf. n.*   25 statues: *a trisyllable here; cf. n.*   30 recorder: *a city official*   37 vantage: *advantage*   38 quoth: *said*   40 Argues: *shows*   46-249 *Cf. n.*   46 by mighty suit: *after urgent entreaty*   51 maid's part; *cf. n.*   56 dance attendance: *attend assiduously*

In deep designs, in matter of great moment,
No less importing than our general good,
Are come to have some conference with his Grace.
 Cate. I'll signify so much unto him straight. *Exit.* *70*
 Buck. Ah, ha, my lord, this prince is not an Edward!
He is not lolling on a lewd love-bed,
But on his knees at meditation;
Not dallying with a brace of courtesans,
But meditating with two deep divines; *75*
Not sleeping, to engross his idle body,
But praying, to enrich his watchful soul.
Happy were England, would this virtuous prince
Take on his Grace the sovereignty thereof:
But sure, I fear, we shall not win him to it. *80*
 May. Marry, God defend his Grace should say nay!
 Buck. I fear he will. Here Catesby comes again.

   [Re-]enter Catesby.

Now, Catesby, what says his Grace?
 Cate. He wonders to what end you have assembled
Such troops of citizens to come to him, *85*
His Grace not being warn'd thereof before:
He fears, my lord, you mean no good to him.
 Buck. Sorry I am my noble cousin should
Suspect me that I mean no good to him.
By heaven, we come to him in perfect love; *90*
And so once more return, and tell his Grace. *Exit [Catesby].*
When holy and devout religious men
Are at their beads, 'tis much to draw them thence;
So sweet is zealous contemplation.

  Enter Richard, aloft, between two Bishops. [Catesby returns.]

 L. May. See, where his Grace stands 'tween two clergymen!
 Buck. Two props of virtue for a Christian prince,
To stay him from the fall of vanity;
And, see, a book of prayer in his hand:
True ornaments to know a holy man.
Famous Plantagenet, most gracious prince, *100*
Lend favourable ear to our requests,
And pardon us the interruption
Of thy devotion and right Christian zeal.
 Rich. My lord, there needs no such apology;
I do beseech your Grace to pardon me, *105*
Who, earnest in the service of my God,
Deferr'd the visitation of my friends.
But, leaving this, what is your Grace's pleasure?
 Buck. Even that, I hope, which pleaseth God above,
And all good men of this ungovern'd isle. *110*
 Rich. I do suspect I have done some offence
That seems disgracious in the city's eye;
And that you come to reprehend my ignorance.
 Buck. You have, my lord: would it might please your
Grace, *115*
On our entreaties to amend your fault!
 Rich. Else wherefore breathe I in a Christian land?
 Buck. Know then, it is your fault that you resign
The supreme seat, the throne majestical,
The sceptred office of your ancestors, *120*

Your state of fortune and your due of birth,
The lineal glory of your royal house,
To the corruption of a blemish'd stock;
Whiles, in the mildness of your sleepy thoughts,—
Which here we waken to our country's good,— *125*
The noble isle doth want his proper limbs;
His face defac'd with scars of infamy,
His royal stock graft with ignoble plants,
And almost shoulder'd in the swallowing gulf
Of dark forgetfulness and deep oblivion. *130*
Which to recure we heartily solicit
Your gracious self to take on you the charge
And kingly government of this your land:
Not as protector, steward, substitute,
Or lowly factor for another's gain; *135*
But as successively from blood to blood,
Your right of birth, your empery, your own.
For this, consorted with the citizens,
Your very worshipful and loving friends,
And by their vehement instigation, *140*
In this just cause come I to move your Grace.
 Rich. I cannot tell, if to depart in silence,
Or bitterly to speak in your reproof,
Best fitteth my degree or your condition:
If not to answer, you might haply think *145*
Tongue-tied ambition, not replying, yielded
To bear the golden yoke of sovereignty,
Which fondly you would here impose on me;
If to reprove you for this suit of yours,
So season'd with your faithful love to me, *150*
Then, on the other side, I check'd my friends.
Therefore, to speak, and to avoid the first,
And then, in speaking, not to incur the last,
Definitively thus I answer you.
Your love deserves my thanks; but my desert *155*
Unmeritable shuns your high request.
First, if all obstacles were cut away,
And that my path were even to the crown,
As the ripe revenue and due of birth,
Yet so much is my poverty of spirit, *160*
So mighty and so many my defects,
That I would rather hide me from my greatness,
Being a bark to brook no mighty sea,
Than in my greatness covet to be hid,
And in the vapour of my glory smother'd. *165*
But, God be thank'd, there is no need of me;
And much I need to help you, were there need;
The royal tree hath left us royal fruit,
Which, mellow'd by the stealing hours of time,
Will well become the seat of majesty, *170*
And make, no doubt, us happy by his reign.
On him I lay that you would lay on me,
The right and fortune of his happy stars;
Which God defend that I should wring from him!
 Buck. My lord, this argues conscience in your Grace; *175*

---

70 straight: *at once* **76 engross:** *fatten* **80 win:** *persuade* **93 beads:** *prayers* **99
ornaments:** *the word refers to the bishops as well as to the prayer book* **112 disgracious:**
ungracious

126 want: *lack* **his:** *its* **128 graft:** *engrafted* **130 deep:** *profound* **131 recure:** *restore* (to normal) **132 charge:** *responsibility* **135 factor:** *hireling* **136 successively:**
by right of succession **137 empery:** *empire* **142-174** *Cf. n.* **144 condition:**
rank **145 haply:** *perhaps* **150 season'd with:** *rendered palatable by* **151 check'd:**
should rebuke **156 Unmeritable:** *undeserving* **159 ripe revenue:** *ready inheritance* **167 And ... need;** *cf. n.* **173 happy stars;** *cf. n.*

But the respects thereof are nice and trivial,
All circumstances well considered.
You say that Edward is your brother's son:
So say we too, but not by Edward's wife;
For first was he contract to Lady Lucy,—   *180*
Your mother lives a witness to his vow,—
And afterward by substitute betroth'd
To Bona, sister to the King of France.
These both put off, a poor petitioner,
A care-craz'd mother to a many sons,   *185*
A beauty-waning and distressed widow,
Even in the afternoon of her best days,
Made prize and purchase of his wanton eye,
Seduc'd the pitch and height of his degree
To base declension and loath'd bigamy: *190*
By her, in his unlawful bed, he got
This Edward, whom our manners call the prince.
More bitterly could I expostulate,
Save that, for reverence to some alive,
I give a sparing limit to my tongue.   *195*
Then, good my lord, take to your royal self
This proffer'd benefit of dignity;
If not to bless us and the land withal,
Yet to draw forth your noble ancestry
From the corruption of abusing times,   *200*
Unto a lineal true-derived course.
   L. May. Do, good my lord; your citizens entreat
you.
   Buck. Refuse not, mighty lord, this proffer'd love.
   Cate. O, make them joyful! grant their lawful suit!   *205*
   Rich. Alas! why would you heap this care on me?
I am unfit for state and majesty:
I do beseech you, take it not amiss,
I cannot nor I will not yield to you.
   Buck. If you refuse it, as, in love and zeal,   *210*
Loath to depose the child, your brother's son;
As well we know your tenderness of heart
And gentle, kind, effeminate remorse,
Which we have noted in you to your kindred,
And egally, indeed, to all estates,   *215*
Yet know whe'r you accept our suit or no,
Your brother's son shall never reign our king;
But we will plant some other in the throne,
To the disgrace and downfall of your house:
And in this resolution here we leave you.   *220*
Come, citizens, we will entreat no more.
            Exeunt [Buckingham and Citizens].
   Cate. Call him again, sweet prince; accept their suit:
If you deny them, all the land will rue it.
   Rich. Will you enforce me to a world of cares?
Call them again: I am not made of stones,   *225*
But penetrable to your kind entreaties,
Albeit against my conscience and my soul.
          [Re-]enter Buckingham and the rest.

Cousin of Buckingham, and sage, grave men,
Since you will buckle fortune on my back,
To bear her burthen, whe'r I will or no,   *230*
I must have patience to endure the load:
But if black scandal or foul-fac'd reproach
Attend the sequel of your imposition,
Your mere enforcement shall acquittance me
From all the impure blots and stains thereof;   *235*
For God doth know, and you may partly see,
How far I am from the desire of this.
   L. May. God bless your Grace! we see it, and will say it.
   Rich. In saying so, you shall but say the truth.
   Buck. Then I salute you with this royal title: *240*
Long live King Richard, England's worthy king!
   All. Amen.
   Buck. To-morrow may it please you to be crown'd?
   Rich. Even when you please, for you will have it so.
   Buck. To-morrow then we will attend your Grace: *245*
And so most joyfully we take our leave.
   Rich. [To the Bishops.] Come, let us to our holy work again.
Farewell, my cousin;—farewell, gentle friends.   *Exeunt.*

ACT FOURTH ❧ SCENE FIRST

[London. Before the Tower]
Enter the Queen [Elizabeth], Anne, Duchess of Gloucester, [leading
Lady Margaret Plantagenet], The Duchess of York, and Marquess
Dorset.

   Duch. York. Who meets us here? my niece Plantagenet,
Led in the hand of her kind aunt of Gloucester?
Now, for my life, she's wand'ring to the Tower,
On pure heart's love, to greet the tender prince.
Daughter, well met.   *5*
   Anne.   God give your Graces both
A happy and a joyful time of day!
   Q. Eliz. As much to you, good sister! whither away?
   Anne. No farther than the Tower; and, as I guess,
Upon the like devotion as yourselves,   *10*
To gratulate the gentle princes there.
   Q. Eliz. Kind sister, thanks: we'll enter all together:—

       Enter the Lieutenant [Brakenbury].

And, in good time, here the lieutenant comes.
Master lieutenant, pray you, by your leave,
How doth the prince, and my young son of York?   *15*
   Brak. Right well, dear madam. By your patience,
I may not suffer you to visit them:
The king hath strictly charg'd the contrary.
   Q. Eliz. The king! who's that?
   Brak.   I mean the Lord Protector.   *20*
   Q. Eliz. The Lord protect him from that kingly title!
Hath he set bounds between their love and me?
I am their mother; who shall bar me from them?
   Duch. York. I am their father's mother; I will see them.
   Anne. Their aunt I am in law, in love their mother: *25*

---

176 respects ... nice: *considerations on which your arguments are founded are overscrupulous*   **180 contract:** *contracted; cf. n. line 5*   **181 a witness;** *cf. n.*   **185 care-craz'd:** *shattered by care*   **188 purchase:** *booty*   **189 pitch;** *cf. n.*   **190 declension:** *gradual falling away from a high standard* **bigamy;** *cf. n.*   **193 expostulate:** *expound*   **200 abusing times:** *i.e. the period following Edward's marriage to Elizabeth*   **213 effeminate remorse:** *woman-like pity*   **215 egally:** *equally* **estates:** *classes of persons*   **220 in this resolution:** *with this resolve*

233 imposition: *action in imposing this burden*   **234 acquittance:** *acquit*   **1 niece:** *grandchild*   **4 On:** *out of*   **10 like devotion;** *cf. n.*   **11 gratulate:** *greet*

Then bring me to their sights; I'll bear thy blame,
And take thy office from thee, on my peril.
   Brak. No, madam, no, I may not leave it so:
I am bound by oath, and therefore pardon me.

                             Exit Lieutenant.

           Enter Stanley.

   Stan. Let me but meet you, ladies, on hour hence,   30
And I'll salute your Grace of York as mother,
And reverend looker-on of two fair queens.
[To the Duchess of Gloucester.] Come, madam, you must
straight to Westminster,
There to be crowned Richard's royal queen.   35
   Q. Eliz. Ah! cut my lace asunder,
That my pent heart may have some scope to beat,
Or else I swoon with this dead-killing news.
   Anne. Despiteful tidings! O! unpleasing news!
   Dor. Be of good cheer: mother, how fares your Grace?   40
   Q. Eliz. O, Dorset! speak not to me, get thee gone!
Death and destruction dog thee at thy heels;
Thy mother's name is ominous to children.
If thou wilt outstrip death, go cross the seas,
And live with Richmond, from the reach of hell: 45
Go, hie thee, hie thee, from this slaughter-house,
Lest thou increase the number of the dead,
And make me die the thrall of Margaret's curse,
Nor mother, wife, nor England's counted queen.
   Stan. Full of wise care is this your counsel, madam.   50
[To Dorset.] Take all the swift advantage of the hours;
You shall have letters from me to my son
In your behalf, to meet you on the way:
Be not ta'en tardy by unwise delay.
   Duch. York. O ill-dispersing wind of misery!   55
O my accursed womb, the bed of death!
A cockatrice hast thou hatch'd to the world,
Whose unavoided eye is murtherous!
   Stan. Come, madam, come; I in all haste was sent.
   Anne. And I with all unwillingness will go.   60
O would to God that the inclusive verge
Of golden metal that must round my brow
Were red-hot steel to scar me to the brains!
Anointed let me be with deadly venom,
And die, ere men can say, 'God save the queen!'   65
   Q. Eliz. Go, go, poor soul, I envy not thy glory;
To feed my humour, wish thyself no harm.
   Anne. No! why? When he, that is my husband now
Came to me, as I follow'd Henry's corse;
When scarce the blood was well wash'd from his hands,   70
Which issu'd from my other angel husband,
And that dead saint which then I weeping follow'd;
O! when, I say, I look'd on Richard's face,
This was my wish, 'Be thou,' quoth I, 'accurs'd,
For making me, so young, so old a widow!   75
And, when thou wedd'st, let sorrow haunt thy bed;
And be thy wife—if any be so mad—
More miserable by the life of thee

Than thou hast made me by my dear lord's death!'
Lo! ere I can repeat this curse again,   80
Within so small a time, my woman's heart
Grossly grew captive to his honey words,
And prov'd the subject of mine own soul's curse:
Which hitherto hath held mine eyes from rest;
For never yet one hour in his bed   85
Did I enjoy the golden dew of sleep,
But with his timorous dreams was still awak'd.
Besides, he hates me for my father Warwick,
And will, no doubt, shortly be rid of me.
   Q. Eliz. Poor heart, adieu! I pity thy complaining.   90
   Anne. No more than with my soul I mourn for yours.
   Dor. Farewell! thou woeful welcomer of glory!
   Anne. Adieu, poor soul, that tak'st thy leave of it!
   Duch. York. *[To Dorset.]* Go thou to Richmond, and
good fortune guide thee!   95
[To Anne.] Go thou to Richard, and good angels tend thee!
[To Q. Elizabeth.] Go thou to sanctuary, and good thoughts
possess thee!
I to my grave, where peace and rest lie with me!
Eighty odd years of sorrow have I seen,   100
And each hour's joy wrack'd with a week of teen.
   Q. Eliz. Stay, yet look back with me unto the Tower.
Pity, you ancient stones, those tender babes
Whom envy hath immur'd within your walls,
Rough cradle for such little pretty ones!   105
Rude ragged nurse, old sullen playfellow
For tender princes, use my babies well.
So foolish sorrow bids your stones farewell.   *Exeunt.*

❧ SCENE SECOND ❧

[The Same. A Room of State in the Palace]
Sound a Sennet. Enter Richard in pomp, Buckingham, Catesby,
Ratcliff, Lovel [and a Page].

   K. Rich. Stand all apart! Cousin of Buckingham!
   Buck. My gracious sovereign!
   K. Rich. Give me thy hand. *Sound. [He ascends the throne.]*
Thus high, by thy advice,
And thy assistance, is King Richard seated: 5
But shall we wear these glories for a day?
Or shall they last, and we rejoice in them?
   Buck. Still live they, and for ever let them last!
   K. Rich. Ah! Buckingham, now do I play the touch,
To try if thou be current gold indeed: 10
Young Edward lives: think now what I would speak.
   Buck. Say on, my loving lord.
   K. Rich. Why, Buckingham, I say, I would be king.
   Buck. Why, so you are, my thrice-renowned lord.
   K. Rich. Ha! am I king? 'Tis so: but Edward lives.   15
   Buck. True, noble prince.
   K. Rich.   O bitter consequence,
That Edward still should live! 'True, noble prince!'
Cousin, thou wast not wont to be so dull:
Shall I be plain? I wish the bastards dead;   20

---

28 it: *i.e. my office*   **35 crowned;** *cf. n.*   **38 dead-killing:** *death-dealing*   **39 Despiteful:** *cruel*   **45 Richmond;** *cf. n.* **from:** *beyond*   **48 thrall:** *slave, victim*   **49 counted:** *accounted*   **57 cockatrice;** *cf. n.*   **61 verge:** *circle*   **75 old:** *i.e. old in sorrow*   **77** *Cf. I. ii. 26–28*

88 Warwick; *cf. n.*   **100 Eighty odd;** *cf. n.*   **101 wrack'd with:** *destroyed by* **teen:** *woe*   **104 envy:** *spite*   **106 ragged:** *rough* **sullen:** *dismal*   **9 play the touch:** *play the part of a touchstone; cf. n.*   **17 consequence:** *sequel*

And I would have it suddenly perform'd.
What sayst thou now? speak suddenly, be brief.
   Buck. Your Grace may do your pleasure.
   K. Rich. Tut, tut! thou art all ice, thy kindness freezes:
Say, have I thy consent that they shall die?   *25*
   Buck. Give me some little breath, some pause, dear lord,
Before I positively speak in this:
I will resolve you herein presently.   *Exit Buck.*
   Cate. [*Aside to another.*] The king is angry: see, he gnaws
his lip.   *30*
   K. Rich. [*Descends from his throne.*] I will converse with iron-
witted fools
And unrespective boys: none are for me
That look into me with considerate eyes.
High-reaching Buckingham grows circumspect.   *35*
Boy!
   Page. My lord!
   K. Rich. Know'st thou not any whom corrupting gold
Will tempt unto a close exploit of death?
   Page. I know a discontented gentleman,   *40*
Whose humble means match not his haughty spirit:
Gold were as good as twenty orators,
And will, no doubt, tempt him to anything.
   K. Rich. What is his name?
   Page.   His name, my lord, is Tyrrell. *45*
   K. Rich. I partly know the man: go, call him hither, boy.
     Exit [Page].

The deep-revolving, witty Buckingham
No more shall be the neighbour to my counsels.
Hath he so long held out with me, untir'd,
And stops he now for breath? well, be it so.   *50*

Enter Stanley.

How now, Lord Stanley! what's the news?
   Stan. Know, my loving lord,
The Marquess Dorset, as I hear, is fled
To Richmond, in the parts where he abides.
   K. Rich. Come hither, Catesby: rumour it abroad *55*
That Anne, my wife, is very grievous sick;
I will take order for her keeping close.
Inquire me out some mean poor gentleman,
Whom I will marry straight to Clarence' daughter:
The boy is foolish, and I fear not him.   *60*
Look, how thou dream'st! I say again, give out
That Anne, my queen, is sick, and like to die.
About it; for it stands me much upon
To stop all hopes whose growth may damage me.
     [*Exit Catesby.*]
I must be married to my brother's daughter, *65*
Or else my kingdom stands on brittle glass.
Murther her brothers, and then marry her!
Uncertain way of gain! But I am in
So far in blood, that sin will pluck on sin:
Tear-falling pity dwells not in this eye.   *70*

[Re-]enter [Page with] Tyrrell.

Is thy name Tyrrell?

   Tyr. James Tyrrell, and your most obedient subject.
   K. Rich. Art thou, indeed?
   Tyr.   Prove me, my gracious lord.
   K. Rich. Dar'st thou resolve to kill a friend of mine? *75*
   Tyr. Please you; but I had rather kill two enemies.
   K. Rich. Why, then thou hast it: two deep enemies,
Foes to my rest, and my sweet sleep's disturbers,
Are they that I would have thee deal upon.
Tyrrell, I mean those bastards in the Tower.   *80*
   Tyr. Let me have open means to come to them,
And soon I'll rid you from the fear of them.
   K. Rich. Thou sing'st sweet music. Hark, come hither,
Tyrrell:
Go, by this token: rise, and lend thine ear.   *Whispers.* *85*
There is no more but so: say it is done,
And I will love thee, and prefer thee for it.
   Tyr. I will dispatch it straight.   *Exit.*

[Re-]enter Buckingham.

   Buck. My lord, I have consider'd in my mind
The late request that you did sound me in.   *90*
   K. Rich. Well, let that rest. Dorset is fled to Richmond.
   Buck. I hear the news, my lord.
   K. Rich. Stanley, he is your wife's son: well, look to it.
   Buck. My lord, I claim the gift, my due by promise,
For which your honour and your faith is pawn'd: *95*
Th' earldom of Hereford and the moveables
Which you have promised I shall possess.
   K. Rich. Stanley, look to your wife: if she convey
Letters to Richmond, you shall answer it.
   Buck. What says your highness to my just request? *100*
   K. Rich. I do remember me, Henry the Sixth
Did prophesy that Richmond should be king,
When Richmond was a little peevish boy.
A king! perhaps—
   [*Buck.* My lord!   *105*
   K. Rich. How chance the prophet could not at that time
Have told me, I being by, that I should kill him?
   Buck. My lord, your promise for the earldom,—
   K. Rich. Richmond! When last I was at Exeter,
The mayor in courtesy show'd me the castle,   *110*
And call'd it Rougemont: at which name I started,
Because a bard of Ireland told me once
I should not live long after I saw Richmond.
   Buck. My lord!
   K. Rich. Ay, what's o'clock?   *115*
   Buck. I am thus bold to put your Grace in mind
Of what you promis'd me.
   K. Rich. Well, but what is 't o'clock?
   Buck.   Upon the stroke of ten.
   K. Rich. Well, let it strike.   *120*
   Buck.   Why let it strike?
   K. Rich. Because that, like a Jack, thou keep'st the stroke
Betwixt thy begging and my meditation.
I am not in the giving vein to-day.]
   Buck. May it please you to resolve me in my suit? *125*

74 Prove: *test*   **79 deal upon:** *set to work on*   **86 There . . . so:** *i.e. nothing more than to carry out the whispered instructions*   **87 prefer:** *advance*   **95 pawn'd:** *pledged*   **98 wife;** *cf. n.*   **99 answer:** *answer for*   **101 remember me:** *recollect*   **102 prophesy;** *cf. n.*   **105-124** *Cf. n.*   **106 How chance:** *how chance is that*   **111 Rougemont;** *cf. n.*   **122 Jack;** *cf. n.*   **125 resolve:** *confirm; cf. n.*

28 resolve you: *give you a definite answer*   **33 unrespective:** *heedless*   **35 High-reaching:** *ambitious*   **39 close:** *secret* **exploit:** *deed*   **45** *Cf. n.*   **47 deep-revolving:** *profoundly considering* **witty:** *cunning*   **56 grievous sick;** *cf. n.*   **63 stands . . . upon:** *concerns me greatly*   **65 brother's daughter;** *cf. n.*   **70 Tear-falling:** *causing tears to fall*

K. Rich. Thou troublest me: I am not in the vein.
                                        Exit [King Richard and Train].
    Buck. And is it thus? repays he my deep service
With such contempt? made I him king for this?
O, let me think on Hastings, and be gone
To Brecknock, while my fearful head is on.   *Exit. 130*

❧ SCENE THIRD ❦

[The Same.]
Enter Tyrrell.

Tyr. The tyrannous and bloody act is done;
The most arch deed of piteous massacre
That ever yet this land was guilty of.
Dighton and Forrest, whom I did suborn
To do this piece of ruthful butchery,   *5*
Albeit they were flesh'd villains, bloody dogs,
Melted with tenderness and mild compassion,
Wept like to children in their death's sad story.
'Oh! thus,' quoth Dighton, 'lay the gentle babies:'
'Thus, thus,' quoth Forrest, 'girdling one another   *10*
Within their alabaster innocent arms:
Their lips were four red roses on a stalk,
And in their summer beauty kiss'd each other.
A book of prayers on their pillow lay;
Which one,' quoth Forrest, 'almost chang'd my mind;   *15*
But, O, the devil'—there the villain stopp'd;
When Dighton thus told on: 'We smothered
The most replenished sweet work of nature,
That from the prime creation e'er she fram'd.'
Hence both are gone with conscience and remorse;   *20*
They could not speak; and so I left them both,
To bear this tidings to the bloody king:
And here he comes.

Enter Richard.

            All health, my sovereign lord!
    K. Rich. Kind Tyrrell, am I happy in thy news?   *25*
    Tyr. If to have done the thing you gave in charge
Beget your happiness, be happy, then,
For it is done.
    K. Rich.   But didst thou see them dead?
    Tyr. I did, my lord.   *30*
    K. Rich.   And buried, gentle Tyrrell?
    Tyr. The chaplain of the Tower hath buried them;
But where, to say the truth, I do not know.
    K. Rich. Come to me, Tyrrell, soon, and after supper,
When thou shalt tell the process of their death.   *35*
Meantime, but think how I may do thee good,
And be inheritor of thy desire.
Farewell till then.
    Tyr.   I humbly take my leave.   *[Exit.]*
    K. Rich. The son of Clarence have I pent up close; *40*

His daughter meanly have I match'd in marriage;
The sons of Edward sleep in Abraham's bosom;
And Anne, my wife, hath bid this world good night.
Now, for I know the Britaine Richmond aims
At young Elizabeth, my brother's daughter,   *45*
And, by that knot, looks proudly on the crown,
To her go I, a jolly thriving wooer.

Enter Ratcliff.

    Rat. My lord!
    K. Rich. Good or bad news, that thou com'st in so bluntly?
    Rat. Bad news, my lord: Morton is fled to Richmond;   *50*
And Buckingham, back'd with the hardy Welshmen,
Is in the field, and still his power increaseth.
    K. Rich. Ely with Richmond troubles me more near
Than Buckingham and his rash-levied strength.
Come; I have learn'd that fearful commenting   *55*
Is leaden servitor to dull delay.
Delay leads impotent and snail-pac'd beggary:
Then fiery expedition be my wing,
Jove's Mercury, and herald for a king!
Go, muster men: my counsel is my shield;   *60*
We must be brief when traitors brave the field.   *Exeunt.*

❧ SCENE FOURTH ❦

[The Same. Before the Palace]
Enter old Queen Margaret.

    Q. Mar. So, now prosperity begins to mellow
And drop into the rotten mouth of death.
Here in these confines slily have I lurk'd
To watch the waning of mine enemies.
A dire induction am I witness to,   *5*
And will to France, hoping the consequence
Will prove as bitter, black, and tragical.
Withdraw thee, wretched Margaret: who comes here?

Enter Duchess [of York] and Queen [Elizabeth].

    Q. Eliz. Ah! my poor princes! ah, my tender babes,
My unblown flowers, new-appearing sweets,   *10*
If yet your gentle souls fly in the air
And be not fix'd in doom perpetual,
Hover about me with your airy wings,
And hear your mother's lamentation.
    Q. Mar. Hover about her; say, that right for right   *15*
Hath dimm'd your infant morn to aged night.
    Duch. So many miseries have craz'd my voice,
That my woe-wearied tongue is still and mute.
Edward Plantagenet, why art thou dead?
    Q. Mar. Plantagenet doth quit Plantagenet;   *20*
Edward for Edward pays a dying debt.

130 Brecknock; *cf. n.*   2 arch: *principal*   4 suborn: *procure by bribery*   5 ruthful: *pitiable*   6 flesh'd: *hardened; cf. n.*   8 in: *in relating*   9 Dighton; *cf. n.*   10 Forrest; *cf. n.*   11 alabaster: *marble-white*   18 replenished: *complete, perfect*   19 prime: *first in time* fram'd: *formed*   20 gone: *completely overcome*   35 process: *narrative*   37 inheritor: *possessor*   40 pent up; *cf. n.*

41 daughter; *cf. n.*   42 Abraham's bosom; *cf. n.*   44 Britaine: *Breton; cf. n.*   46 knot: *i.e. marriage alliance*   S. d. Ratcliff; *cf. n.*   50 Morton: *John Morton, Bishop of Ely; cf. n.*   52 power: *body of troops; cf. n.*   53 near: *closely*   54 rash-levied: *hastily raised*   55 fearful commenting: *timorous discussion*   56 leaden: *figuratively for 'slow'*   58 expedition: *haste*   59 Jove's Mercury; *cf. n.*   61 brave: *boastfully dispute*   3 confines: *regions, territories*   6 to France; *cf. n.*   10 unblown: *unblossomed, budding*   15 right for right; *cf. n.*   17 craz'd: *cracked*   20 quit: *requite*

Q. Eliz. Wilt thou, O God! fly from such gentle lambs,
And throw them in the entrails of the wolf?
When didst thou sleep when such a deed was done?

   Q. Mar. When holy Harry died, and my sweet son.   *25*

   Duch. Dead life, blind sight, poor mortal living ghost,
Woe's scene, world's shame, grave's due by life usurp'd,
Brief abstract and record of tedious days,
Rest thy unrest on England's lawful earth,   *[Sitting down.]*
Unlawfully made drunk with innocent blood!   *30*

   Q. Eliz. Ah! that thou wouldst as soon afford a grave
As thou canst yield a melancholy seat;
Then would I hide my bones, not rest them here.
Ah! who hath any cause to mourn but we?
                    [Sitting down by her.]

   Q. Mar. If ancient sorrow be most reverend,   *35*
Give mine the benefit of signiory,
And let my griefs frown on the upper hand,
If sorrow can admit society.   *[Sitting down with them.]*
[Tell o'er your woes again by viewing mine:]
I had an Edward, till a Richard kill'd him;   *40*
I had a husband, till a Richard kill'd him:
Thou hadst an Edward, till a Richard kill'd him;
Thou hadst a Richard, till a Richard kill'd him.

   Duch. I had a Richard too, and thou didst kill him;
I had a Rutland too, thou holp'st to kill him.   *45*

   Q. Mar. Thou hadst a Clarence too, and Richard
kill'd him.
From forth the kennel of thy womb hath crept
A hell-hound that doth hunt us all to death:
That dog, that had his teeth before his eyes,   *50*
To worry lambs, and lap their gentle blood,
That foul defacer of God's handiwork,
That reigns in galled eyes of weeping souls,
That excellent grand-tyrant of the earth,
Thy womb let loose, to chase us to our graves.   *55*
O upright, just, and true-disposing God!
How do I thank thee that this carnal cur
Preys on the issue of his mother's body,
And makes her pew-fellow with others' moan.

   Duch. O, Harry's wife, triumph not in my woes!   *60*
God witness with me, I have wept for thine.

   Q. Mar. Bear with me; I am hungry for revenge,
And now I cloy me with beholding it.
Thy Edward he is dead, that kill'd my Edward;
The other Edward dead, to quit my Edward;   *65*
Young York he is but boot, because both they
Match'd not the high perfection of my loss:
Thy Clarence he is dead that stabb'd my Edward;
And the beholders of this frantic play,
Th' adulterate Hastings, Rivers, Vaughan, Grey,   *70*
Untimely smother'd in their dusky graves.
Richard yet lives, hell's black intelligencer,
Only reserv'd their factor, to buy souls
And send them thither; but at hand, at hand,
Ensues his piteous and unpitied end: *75*

Earth gapes, hell burns, fiends roar, saints pray,
To have him suddenly convey'd from hence.
Cancel his bond of life, dear God! I pray,
That I may live and say, The dog is dead.

   Q. Eliz. O! thou didst prophesy the time would   *80*
come
That I should wish for thee to help me curse
That bottled spider, that foul bunchback'd toad.

   Q. Mar. I call'd thee then vain flourish of my fortune;
I call'd thee then poor shadow, painted queen;   *85*
The presentation of but what I was;
The flattering index of a direful pageant;
One heav'd a-high to be hurl'd down below;
A mother only mock'd with two fair babes;
A dream of what thou wast, a garish flag   *90*
To be the aim of every dangerous shot;
A sign of dignity, a breath, a bubble,
A queen in jest, only to fill the scene.
Where is thy husband now? where be thy brothers?
Where be thy two sons? wherein dost thou joy?   *95*
Who sues and kneels and says, 'God save the queen'?
Where be the bending peers that flatter'd thee?
Where be the thronging troops that follow'd thee?
Decline all this, and see what now thou art:
For happy wife, a most distressed widow;   *100*
For joyful mother, one that wails the name;
For one being sued to, one that humbly sues;
For queen, a very caitiff crown'd with care;
For she that scorn'd at me, now scorn'd of me;
For she being fear'd of all, now fearing one;   *105*
For she commanding all, obey'd of none.
Thus hath the course of justice whirl'd about,
And left thee but a very prey to time;
Having no more but thought of what thou wast,
To torture thee the more, being what thou art.   *110*
Thou didst usurp my place, and dost thou not
Usurp the just proportion of my sorrow?
Now thy proud neck bears half my burthen'd yoke,
From which even here I slip my wearied head,
And leave the burthen of it all on thee.   *115*
Farewell, York's wife, and queen of sad mischance:
These English woes shall make me smile in France.

   Q. Eliz. O thou, were skill'd in curses, stay awhile,
And teach me how to curse mine enemies.

   Q. Mar. Forebear to sleep the night, and fast the day;   *120*
Compare dead happiness with living woe;
Think that thy babes were sweeter than they were,
And he that slew them fouler than he is:
Bettering thy loss makes the bad causer worse:
Revolving this will teach thee how to curse.   *125*

   Q. Eliz. My words are dull; O! quicken them with thine!

   Q. Mar. Thy woes will make them sharp, and pierce like
mine.   *Exit Margaret.*

   Duch. Why should calamity be full of words?

   Q. Eliz. Windy attorneys to their client's woes,   *130*
Airy succeeders of intestate joys,
Poor breathing orators of miseries!

---

28 abstract: *epitome; cf. n.*   **31 thou:** *i.e. the earth*   **36 signiory:** *precedence*   **37 on . . . hand:** *in the first place*   **53, 54** *Cf. n.*   **53 galled:** *sore from weeping; cf. n.*   **54 excellent:** *superlative*   **57 carnal:** *bloody*   **59 pew-fellow:** *associate*   **65 The:** *misprint for 'thy' (?)*   **66 boot:** *something given in addition to make up a deficiency of value*   **70 adulterate:** *adulterous*   **72 intelligencer:** *secret agent, spy*   **73 their:** *refers to hell*

86 presentation: *semblance*   **87 index . . . pageant;** *cf. n.*   **90-92** *Cf. n.*   **90 garish:** *gaudy*   **99 Decline:** *go through formally*   **103 caitiff:** *wretch (literally, captive)*   **107** *Cf. n.*   **120 the:** *during the*   **124 Bettering:** *magnifying*   **125 Revolving:** *thinking over*   **126 quicken:** *enliven*   **131 intestate:** *literally, not having made a will; cf. n.*

Let them have scope: though what they will impart
Help nothing else, yet do they ease the heart.

    Duch. If so, then be not tongue-tied: go with me,   *135*
And in the breath of bitter words let's smother
My damned son, that thy two sweet sons smother'd.

                                     [A trumpet heard.]
The trumpet sounds: be copious in exclaims.

    Enter King Richard and his Train [marching].

    K. Rich. Who intercepts me in my expedition?
    Duch. O! she that might have intercepted thee,   *140*
By strangling thee in her accursed womb,
From all the slaughters, wretch, that thou hast done!
    Q. Eliz. Hid'st thou that forehead with a golden crown,
Where should be branded, if that right were right,
The slaughter of the prince that ow'd that crown,   *145*
And the dire death of my poor sons and brothers?
Tell me, thou villain slave, where are my children?
    Duch. Thou toad, thou toad, where is thy brother Clarence
And little Ned Plantagenet, his son?
    Q. Eliz. Where is the gentle Rivers, Vaughan, Grey?   *150*
    Duch. Where is kind Hastings?
    K. Rich. A flourish, trumpets! strike alarum, drums!
Let not the heavens hear these tell-tale women
Rail on the Lord's anointed. Strike, I say!

                                     Flourish, Alarums.

Either be patient, and entreat me fair,   *155*
Or with the clamorous report of war
Thus will I drown your exclamations.
    Duch. Art thou my son?
    K. Rich. Ay; I thank God, my father, and yourself.
    Duch. Then patiently hear my impatience.   *160*
    K. Rich. Madam, I have a touch of your condition,
That cannot brook the accent of reproof.
    Duch. O, let me speak!
    K. Rich.   Do, then; but I'll not hear.
    Duch. I will be mild and gentle in my words.   *165*
    K. Rich. And brief, good mother; for I am in haste.
    Duch. Art thou so hasty? I have stay'd for thee,
God knows, in torment and in agony.
    K. Rich. And came I not at last to comfort you?
    Duch. No, by the holy rood, thou know'st it well,   *170*
Thou cam'st on earth to make the earth my hell.
A grievous burthen was thy birth to me;
Tetchy and wayward was thy infancy;
Thy school-days frightful, desperate, wild and furious;
Thy prime of manhood daring, bold, and venturous;   *175*
Thy age confirm'd, proud, subtle, sly, and bloody,
More mild, but yet more harmful, kind in hatred.
What comfortable hour canst thou name
That ever grac'd me with thy company?
    K. Rich. Faith, none, but Humphrey Hour, that   *180*
call'd your Grace
To breakfast once forth of my company.
If I be so disgracious in your eye,
Let me march on, and not offend you, madam.
Strike up the drum!   *185*

    Duch.   I prithee, hear me speak.
    K. Rich. You speak too bitterly.
    Duch.   Hear me a word;
For I shall never speak to thee again.
    K. Rich. So!   *190*
    Duch. Either thou wilt die by God's just ordinance,
Ere from this war thou turn a conqueror;
Or I with grief and extreme age shall perish,
And never more behold thy face again.
Therefore take with thee my most grievous curse,   *195*
Which, in the day of battle, tire thee more
Than all the complete armour that thou wear'st!
My prayers on the adverse party fight;
And there the little souls of Edward's children
Whisper the spirits of thine enemies   *200*
And promise them success and victory.
Bloody thou art, bloody will be thy end;
Shame serves thy life and doth thy death attend.   *Exit.*
    Q. Eliz. Though far more cause, yet much less spirit to
curse   *205*
Abides in me: I say amen to her.   *[Going.]*
    K. Rich. Stay, madam; I must talk a word with you.
    Q. Eliz. I have no more sons of the royal blood
For thee to slaughter: for my daughters, Richard,
They shall be praying nuns, not weeping queens;   *210*
And therefore level not to hit their lives.
    K. Rich. You have a daughter call'd Elizabeth,
Virtuous and fair, royal and gracious.
    Q. Eliz. And must she die for this? O! let her live,
And I'll corrupt her manners, stain her beauty;   *215*
Slander myself as false to Edward's bed;
Throw over her the veil of infamy:
So she may live unscarr'd of bleeding slaughter,
I will confess she was not Edward's daughter.
    K. Rich. Wrong not her birth; she is a royal princess.   *220*
    Q. Eliz. To save her life, I'll say she is not so.
    K. Rich. Her life is safest only in her birth.
    Q. Eliz. And only in that safety died her brothers.
    K. Rich. Lo! at their birth good stars were opposite.
    Q. Eliz. No, to their lives ill friends were contrary.   *225*
    K. Rich. All unavoided is the doom of destiny.
    Q. Eliz. True, when avoided grace makes destiny.
My babes were destin'd to a fairer death,
If grace had bless'd thee with a fairer life.
    K. Rich. You speak as if that I had slain my cousins.   *230*
    Q. Eliz. Cousins, indeed; and by their uncle cozen'd
Of comfort, kingdom, kindred, freedom, life.
Whose hand soever lanch'd their tender hearts,
Thy head, all indirectly, gave direction:
No doubt the murderous knife was dull and blunt   *235*
Till it was whetted on thy stone-hard heart,
To revel in the entrails of my lambs.
But that still use of grief makes wild grief tame,
My tongue should to thy ears not name my boys
Till that my nails were anchor'd in thine eyes;   *240*
And I, in such a desperate bay of death,
Like a poor bark, of sails and tackling reft,
Rush all to pieces on thy rocky bosom.

---

134 Help . . . else: *is of no avail otherwise*   **145 ow'd:** *owned*   **151** *Cf. n.*   **155 entreat
me fair:** *use me well*   **161 condition:** *temperament*   **167 stay'd:** *waited*   **173 Tetchy:**
fretful, peevish   **175 prime of:** *early*   **177 kind in hatred:** *i.e. hating while pretending
kindness*   **180 Humphrey Hour:** *Cf. n.*   **183 disgracious:** *out of favor*

203 serves: *i.e. is servant to*   **211 level:** *aim*   **212 Elizabeth;** *cf. n.*   **218 So:** *provided*   **224 opposite;** *cf. n.*   **231 cozen'd:** *cheated*   **233 lanch'd:** *pierced*   **234**
Cf. n.   **242 reft:** *bereft*

K. Rich. Madam, so thrive I in my enterprise
And dangerous success of bloody wars,   *245*
As I intend more good to you and yours
Than ever you or yours by me were harm'd.

Q. Eliz. What good is cover'd with the face of heaven,
To be discover'd, that can do me good?

K. Rich. Th' advancement of your children, gentle lady.   *250*

Q. Eliz. Up to some scaffold, there to lose their heads?

K. Rich. Unto the dignity and height of fortune,
The high imperial type of this earth's glory.

Q. Eliz. Flatter my sorrow with report of it:
Tell me what state, what dignity, what honour,   *255*
Canst thou demise to any child of mine?

K. Rich. Even all I have; ay, and myself and all,
Will I withal endow a child of thine;
So in the Lethe of thy angry soul
Thou drown the sad remembrance of those wrongs   *260*
Which thou supposest I have done to thee.

Q. Eliz. Be brief, lest that the process of thy kindness
Last longer telling than thy kindness' date.

K. Rich. Then know, that from my soul I love thy daughter.

Q. Eliz. My daughter's mother thinks it with her soul.   *265*

K. Rich. What do you think?

Q. Eliz. That thou dost love my daughter from thy soul:
So from thy soul's love didst thou love her brothers;
And from my heart's love I do thank thee for it.

K. Rich. Be not so hasty to confound my meaning: *270*
I mean, that with my soul I love thy daughter,
And do intend to make her Queen of England.

Q. Eliz. Well then, who dost thou mean shall be her king?

K. Rich. Even he that makes her queen: who else
should be?   *275*

Q. Eliz. What! thou?

K. Rich. Even so: how think you of it?

Q. Eliz. How canst thou woo her?

K. Rich.   That I would learn of you,
As one being best acquainted with her humour.   *280*

Q. Eliz. And wilt thou learn of me?

K. Rich.   Madam, with all my heart.

Q. Eliz. Send to her, by the man that slew her brothers,
A pair of bleeding hearts; thereon engrave
Edward and York; then haply will she weep: *285*
Therefore present to her, as sometime Margaret
Did to thy father, steep'd in Rutland's blood,
A handkerchief, which, say to her, did drain
The purple sap from her sweet brother's body,
And bid her wipe her weeping eyes withal.   *290*
If this inducement move her not to love,
Send her a letter of thy noble deeds:
Tell her thou mad'st away her uncle Clarence,
Her uncle Rivers; ay, and for her sake,
Mad'st quick conveyance with her good aunt Anne.   *295*

K. Rich. You mock me, madam; this is not the way
To win your daughter.

Q. Eliz.   There is no other way,
Unless thou couldst put on some other shape,
And not be Richard that hath done all this.   *300*

K. Rich. Say, that I did all this for love of her?

Q. Eliz. Nay, then, indeed, she cannot choose but hate thee,
Having bought love with such a bloody spoil.

K. Rich. Look, what is done cannot be now amended:
Men shall deal unadvisedly sometimes,   *305*
Which after-hours gives leisure to repent.
If I did take the kingdom from your sons,
To make amends I'll give it to your daughter.
If I have kill'd the issue of your womb,
To quicken your increase, I will beget   *310*
Mine issue of your blood upon your daughter:
A grandam's name is little less in love
Than is the doting title of a mother;
They are as children but one step below,
Even of your mettle, of your very blood;   *315*
Of all one pain, save for a night of groans
Endur'd of her for whom you bid like sorrow.
Your children were vexation to your youth,
But mine shall be a comfort to your age.
The loss you have is but a son being king,   *320*
And by that loss your daughter is made queen.
I cannot make you what amends I would,
Therefore accept such kindness as I can.
Dorset, your son, that with a fearful soul
Leads discontented steps in foreign soil,   *325*
This fair alliance quickly shall call home
To high promotions and great dignity:
The king that calls your beauteous daughter wife
Familiarly shall call thy Dorset brother;
Again shall you be mother to a king,   *330*
And all the ruins of distressful times
Repair'd with double riches of content.
What! we have many goodly days to see:
That liquid drops of tears that you have shed
Shall come again, transform'd to orient pearl,   *335*
Advantaging their love with interest
Of ten times double gain of happiness.
Go then, my mother; to thy daughter go:
Make bold her bashful years with your experience;
Prepare her ears to hear a wooer's tale;   *340*
Put in her tender heart th' aspiring flame
Of golden sovereignty; acquaint the princess
With the sweet silent hours of marriage joys:
And when this arm of mine hath chastised
The petty rebel, dull-brain'd Buckingham,   *345*
Bound with triumphant garlands will I come,
And lead thy daughter to a conqueror's bed;
To whom I will retail my conquest won,
And she shall be sole victress, Cæsar's Cæsar.

Q. Eliz. What were I best to say? her father's brother   *350*
Would be her lord? Or shall I say, her uncle?
Or, he that slew her brothers and her uncles?
Under what title shall I woo for thee,
That God, the law, my honour, and her love
Can make seem pleasing to her tender years?   *355*

K. Rich. Infer fair England's peace by this alliance.

Q. Eliz. Which she shall purchase with still lasting war.

K. Rich. Tell her, the king, that may command, entreats.

Q. Eliz. That at her hands which the king's King forbids.

244–247 *Cf. n.*   **245 success:** *result*   **253 type:** *emblem* (crown)   **256 demise:** *convey*   **259 Lethe;** *cf. n.*   **267 from:** *apart from*   **287** *Cf. n.*   **295 conveyance:** *i.e. dishonest dealing;* *cf. n.*   **301** *Cf. n.*

303 spoil: *waste, havoc*   **316 Of . . . pain:** *of equal interest and responsibility*   **317 bid:** *offered*   **324 Dorset;** *cf. n.*   **336 love;** *cf. n.*   **345** *Cf. n.*   **359 king's . . . forbids;** *cf. n.*

K. Rich. Say, she shall be a high and mighty queen.   *360*
Q. Eliz. To vail the title, as her mother doth.
K. Rich. Say, I will love her everlastingly.
Q. Eliz. But how long shall that title 'ever' last?
K. Rich. Sweetly in force unto her fair life's end.
Q. Eliz. But how long fairly shall her sweet life last?   *365*
K. Rich. As long as heaven and nature lengthens it.
Q. Eliz. As long as hell and Richard likes of it.
K. Rich. Say, I, her sovereign, am her subject low.
Q. Eliz. But she, your subject, loathes such sovereignty.
K. Rich. Be eloquent in my behalf to her.   *370*
Q. Eliz. An honest tale speeds best being plainly told.
K. Rich. Then plainly to her tell my loving tale.
Q. Eliz. Plain and not honest is too harsh a style.
K. Rich. Your reasons are too shallow and too quick.
Q. Eliz. O, no! my reasons are too deep and dead;   *375*
Too deep and dead, poor infants, in their graves.
K. Rich. Harp not on that string, madam; that is past.
Q. Eliz. Harp on it still shall I till heartstrings break.
K. Rich. Now, by my George, my garter, and my crown,—
Q. Eliz. Profan'd, dishonour'd, and the third usurp'd.   *380*
K. Rich. I swear,—
Q. Eliz.   By nothing; for this is no oath.
Thy George, profan'd, hath lost his lordly honour;
Thy garter, blemish'd, pawn'd his knightly virtue;
Thy crown, usurp'd, disgrac'd his kingly glory.   *385*
If something thou wouldst swear to be believ'd,
Swear, then, by something that thou hast not wrong'd.
K. Rich. Then, by myself,—
Q. Eliz.   Thyself is self-misus'd.
K. Rich. Now, by the world,—   *390*
Q. Eliz.   'Tis full of thy foul wrongs.
K. Rich. My father's death,—
Q. Eliz.   Thy life hath it dishonour'd.
K. Rich. Why, then, by God,—
Q. Eliz.   God's wrong is most of all.   *395*
If thou didst fear to break an oath with him,
The unity the king my husband made
Thou hadst not broken, nor my brothers died:
If thou hadst fear'd to break an oath by him,
Th' imperial metal, circling now thy head,   *400*
Had grac'd the tender temples of my child,
And both the princes had been breathing here,
Which now, two tender bed-fellows for dust,
Thy broken faith hath made the prey for worms.
What canst thou swear by now?   *405*
K. Rich.   The time to come.
Q. Eliz. That thou hast wronged in the time o'er past;
For I myself have many tears to wash
Hereafter time for time past wrong'd by thee.
The children live, whose fathers thou hast slaughter'd,   *410*
Ungovern'd youth, to wail it with their age:
The parents live, whose children thou hast butcher'd,
Old barren plants, to wail it with their age.
Swear not by time to come; for that thou hast
Misus'd ere us'd, by times ill-us'd o'erpast.   *415*
K. Rich. As I intend to prosper, and repent,
So thrive I in my dangerous affairs

Of hostile arms! myself myself confound!
Heaven and fortune bar me happy hours!
Day, yield me not thy light; nor, night, thy rest!   *420*
Be opposite all planets of good luck
To my proceeding, if, with dear heart's love,
Immaculate devotion, holy thoughts,
I tender not thy beauteous princely daughter!
In her consists my happiness and thine: *425*
Without her, follows to myself, and thee,
Herself, the land, and many a Christian soul,
Death, desolation, ruin, and decay:
It cannot be avoided but by this;
It will not be avoided but by this.   *430*
Therefore, dear mother,—I must call you so,—
Be the attorney of my love to her:
Plead what I will be, not what I have been;
Not my deserts, but what I will deserve:
Urge the necessity and state of times,   *435*
And be not peevish found in great designs.
     Q. Eliz. Shall I be tempted of the devil thus?
     K. Rich. Ay, if the devil tempt you to do good.
     Q. Eliz. Shall I forget myself to be myself?
     K. Rich. Ay, if your self's remembrance wrong yourself. *440*
     Q. Eliz. Yet thou didst kill my children.
     K. Rich. But in your daughter's womb I bury them:
Where, in that nest of spicery, they will breed
Selves of themselves, to your recomforture.
     Q. Eliz. Shall I go win my daughter to thy will?   *445*
     K. Rich. And be a happy mother by the deed.
     Q. Eliz. I go. Write to me very shortly,
And you shall understand from me her mind.
     K. Rich. Bear her my true love's kiss; and so farewell.
                         Exit Q[ueen Elizabeth].
Relenting fool, and shallow changing woman!   *450*

          Enter Ratcliff [followed by Catesby].

How now! what news?
     Rat. Most mighty sovereign, on the western coast
Rideth a puissant navy; to our shores
Throng many doubtful hollow-hearted friends,
Unarm'd, and unresolv'd to beat them back.   *455*
'Tis thought that Richmond is their admiral;
And there they hull, expecting but the aid
Of Buckingham to welcome them ashore.
     K. Rich. Some light-foot friend post to the Duke of
Norfolk: *460*
Ratcliff, thyself, or Catesby; where is he?
     Cate. Here, my good lord.
     K. Rich.   Catesby, fly to the duke.
     Cate. I will, my lord, with all convenient haste.
     K. Rich. Ratcliff, come hither. Post to Salisbury: *465*
When thou com'st thither,—*[To Catesby.]* Dull, unmindful
villain,
Why stay'st thou here, and go'st not to the duke?
     Cate. First, mighty liege, tell me your highness' pleasure,
What from your Grace I shall deliver to him.   *470*
     K. Rich. O, true, good Catesby! bid him levy straight
The greatest strength and power that he can make,

361 **vail:** *lower*   374 **quick:** *hasty*   377, 378 *Cf. n.*   379 **George;** *cf. n.*   387
Cf. n.   394 **God;** *cf. n.*   398 **brothers;** *cf. n.*   409 **Hereafter time:** *the fu-*
ture   415 *Cf. n.*

419 *Cf. n.*   424 **tender:** *hold in high estimation*   436 **found;** *cf. n.*   443
Cf. n.   444 **recomforture:** *renewed comfort*   457 **hull:** *drift; cf. n.*   459 **light-foot:**
nimble **Norfolk;** *cf. n.*   465 **Ratcliff;** *cf. n.* **Salisbury;** *cf. n.*

And meet me suddenly at Salisbury.
　Cate. I go.　　　　　　　　　　　　　　　　　　　*Exit.*
　Rat. What, may it please you, shall I do at Salisbury?　*475*
　K. Rich. Why, what wouldst thou do there before I go?
　Rat. Your highness told me I should post before.
　K. Rich. My mind is chang'd.

Enter Lord Stanley.

　　　　　　　　　　　Stanley, what news with you?
　Stan. None good, my liege, to please you with the hearing;
Nor none so bad but well may be reported.
　K. Rich. Hoyday, a riddle! neither good nor bad!
What need'st thou run so many miles about,
When thou mayst tell thy tale the nearest way?
Once more, what news?　　　　　　　　　　　　　　　*485*
　Stan.　　　　　　Richmond is on the seas.
　K. Rich. There let him sink, and be the seas on him!
White-liver'd runagate! what doth he there?
　Stan. I know not, mighty sovereign, but by guess.
　K. Rich. Well, as you guess?　　　　　　　　　　　*490*
　Stan. Stirr'd up by Dorset, Buckingham, and Morton,
He makes for England, here to claim the crown.
　K. Rich. Is the chair empty? is the sword unsway'd?
Is the king dead? the empire unpossess'd?
What heir of York is there alive but we?　　　　　　*495*
And who is England's king but great York's heir?
Then, tell me, what make he upon the seas?
　Stan. Unless for that, my liege, I cannot guess.
　K. Rich. Unless for that he comes to be your liege,
You cannot guess wherefore the Welshman comes.　　*500*
Thou wilt revolt and fly to him I fear.
　Stan. No, my good lord; therefore mistrust me not.
　K. Rich. Where is thy power, then, to beat him back?
Where be thy tenants and thy followers?
Are they not now upon the western shore,　　　　　*505*
Safe-conducting the rebels from their ships?
　Stan. No, my good lord, my friends are in the north.
　K. Rich. Cold friends to me: what do they in the north,
When they should serve their sovereign in the west?
　Stan. They have not been commanded, mighty king:　*510*
Pleaseth your majesty to give me leave,
I'll muster up my friends, and meet your Grace,
Where and what time your majesty shall please.
　K. Rich. Ay, [ay,] thou wouldst be gone to join with
Richmond:　　　　　　　　　　　　　　　　　　　*515*
But I'll not trust thee.
　Stan.　　　　　　Most mighty sovereign,
You have no cause to hold my friendship doubtful.
I never was, nor never will be false.
　K. Rich. Go, then, and muster men: but leave behind　*520*
Your son, George Stanley: look your heart be firm,
Or else his head's assurance is but frail.
　Stan. So deal with him as I prove true to you.

　　　　　　　　　　　　　　　　　Exit Stanley.

Enter a Messenger.

　Mess. My gracious sovereign, now in Devonshire,
As I by friends am well advertised,　　　　　　　　*525*

Sir Edward Courtney, and the haughty prelate,
Bishop of Exeter, his elder brother,
With many moe confederates are in arms.

Enter another Messenger.

　[Sec.] Mess. In Kent, my liege, the Guildfords are in arms;
And every hour more competitors　　　　　　　　　*530*
Flock to the rebels, and their power grows strong.

Enters another Messenger.

　[Third] Mess. My lord, the army of great Buckingham—
　K. Rich. Out on ye, owls! nothing but songs of death?
　　　　　　　　　　　　　　　　　He striketh him.
There, take thou that, till thou bring better news.
　[Third] Mess. The news I have to tell your majesty　*535*
Is, that by sudden floods and fall of waters,
Buckingham's army is dispers'd and scatter'd;
And he himself wander'd away alone,
No man knows whither.
　K. Rich.　　　　　　I cry thee mercy:　　　　*540*
There is my purse, to cure that blow of thine.
Hath any well-advised friend proclaim'd
Reward to him that brings the traitor in?
　[Third] Mess. Such proclamation hath been made, my lord.

Enter another Messenger.

　[Fourth] Mess. Sir Thomas Lovel, and Lord Marquess　*545*
Dorset,
'Tis said, my liege, in Yorkshire are in arms:
But this good comfort bring I to your highness,
The Britaine navy is dispers'd by tempest.
Richmond, in Dorsetshire, sent out a boat　　　　　*550*
Unto the shore to ask those on the banks
If they were his assistants, yea or no;
Who answer'd him, they came from Buckingham
Upon his party: he, mistrusting them,
Hois'd sail, and made his course again for Britaine.　*555*
　K. Rich. March on, march on, since we are up in arms;
If not to fight with foreign enemies,
Yet to beat down these rebels here at home.

Enter Catesby.

　Cate. My liege, the Duke of Buckingham is taken,
That is the best news: that the Earl of Richmond　*560*
Is with a mighty power landed at Milford
Is colder news, but yet they must be told.
　K. Rich. Away towards Salisbury! while we reason here,
A royal battle might be won and lost.
Some one take order Buckingham he brought　　　　*565*
To Salisbury; the rest march on with me.

　　　　　　　　　　　　　　　Flourish. Exeunt.

---

473 suddenly: *immediately*　482 Hoyday: *exclamation of surprise*　488 White-liver'd
runagate: *cowardly roamer*　499 liege: *sovereign*　500 Welshman; *cf. n.*　502 mistrust; *cf. n.*　522 assurance: *safety*

526 Sir Edward Courtney; *cf. n.*　527 Bishop of Exeter; *cf. n.*　528 moe:
more.　529 the Guildfords; *cf. n.*　530 competitors: *associates*　533 owls . . . death;
cf. n.　538 *Cf. n.*　549 tempest; *cf. n.*　555 Hois'd: *hoisted*　559 *Cf. n.*　561
landed; *cf. n.*

❧ SCENE FIFTH ❧

[The Same. A Room in Lord Derby's House]
Enter Derby and Sir Christopher [Urswick].

Der. Sir Christopher, tell Richmond this from me:
That in the sty of the most deadly boar
My son, George Stanley, is frank'd up in hold:
If I revolt, off goes young George's head;
The fear off that holds off my present aid.   5
So, get thee gone: commend me to thy lord.
Withal, say that the queen hath heartily consented
He should espouse Elizabeth, her daughter.
But, tell me, where is princely Richmond now?
　　Chris. At Pembroke, or at Ha'rford-west, in Wales.   10
　　Der. What men of name resort to him?
　　Chris. Sir Walter Herbert, a renowned soldier,
Sir Gilbert Talbot, Sir William Stanley,
Oxford, redoubted Pembroke, Sir James Blunt,
And Rice ap Thomas, with a valiant crew;   15
And many other of great name and worth:
And towards London do they bend their power,
If by the way they be not fought withal.
　　Der. Well, hie thee to thy lord; I kiss his hand:
My letter will resolve him of my mind.   20
Farewell.   *Exeunt.*

ACT FIFTH ❧ SCENE FIRST

[Salisbury. An open Place]
Enter Buckingham with [the Sheriff and] Halberds, led to execution.

Buck. Will not King Richard let me speak with him?
Sher. No, my good lord; therefore be patient.
Buck. Hastings, and Edward's children, Grey and Rivers,
Holy King Henry, and thy fair son Edward,
Vaughan, and all that have miscarried   5
By underhand, corrupted, foul injustice,
If that your moody discontented souls
Do through the clouds behold this present hour,
Even for revenge mock my destruction!
This is All-Souls' day, fellow, is it not?   10
　　Sher. It is.
　　Buck. Why, then All-Souls' day is my body's doomsday.
This is the day which, in King Edward's time,
I wish'd might fall on me, when I was found
False to his children and his wife's allies;   15
This is the day wherein I wish'd to fall
By the false faith of him whom most I trusted;
This, this All-Souls' day to my fearful soul
Is the determin'd respite of my wrongs.
That high All-Seer which I dallied with   20
Hath turn'd my feigned prayer on my head,
And given in earnest what I begg'd in jest.
Thus doth he force the swords of wicked men
To turn their own points in their masters' bosoms.
Thus Margaret's curse falls heavy on my neck: 25

'When he,' quoth she, 'shall split thy heart with sorrow,
Remember Margaret was a prophetess.'
Come, lead me, officers, to the block of shame:
Wrong hath but wrong, and blame the due of blame.
　　　　　　　Exeunt Buckingham with Officers.

❧ SECOND SECOND ❧

[A Plain near Tamworth]
Enter Richmond, Oxford, [Sir James] Blunt, [Sir Walter] Herbert,
and Others, with drum and colours.

Richm. Fellows in arms, and my lost loving friends,
Bruis'd underneath the yoke of tyranny,
Thus far into the bowels of the land
Have we march'd on without impediment:
And here receive we from our father Stanley   5
Lines of fair comfort and encouragement.
The wretched, bloody, and usurping boar,
That spoil'd your summer fields and fruitful vines,
Swills your warm blood like wash, and makes his trough
In your embowell'd bosoms, this foul swine   10
Is now even in the centry of this isle,
Near to the town of Leicester, as we learn:
From Tamworth thither is but one day's march.
In God's name, cheerly on, courageous friends,
To reap the harvest of perpetual peace   15
By this one bloody trial of sharp war.
　　Oxf. Every man's conscience is a thousand men,
To fight against this guilty homicide.
　　Herb. I doubt not but his friends will turn to us.
　　Blunt. He hath no friends but what are friends for fear,   20
Which in his dearest need will fly from him.
　　Richm. All for our vantage: then, in God's name, march:
True hope is swift, and flies with swallow's wings;
Kings it makes gods, and meaner creatures kings.
　　　　　　　　　Exeunt Omnes.

❧ SCENE THIRD ❧

[Bosworth Field]
Enter King Richard in arms with [the Duke of] Norfolk, Ratcliff,
and the Earl of Surrey.

K. Rich. Here pitch our tent, even here in Bosworth field.
My Lord of Surrey, why look you so sad?
　　Sur. My heart is ten times lighter than my looks.
　　K. Rich. My Lord of Norfolk,—
　　Nor. 　　　　　　　Here, most gracious liege.   5
　　K. Rich. Norfolk, we must have knocks; ha! must we not?
　　Nor. We must both give and take, my loving lord.
　　K. Rich. Up with my tent! here will I lie to-night;
　　　　　　[Soldiers begin to set up the King's tent.]
But where to-morrow? Well, all's one for that.
Who hath descried the number of the traitors?   10
　　Nor. Six or seven thousand is their utmost power.

---

3 **frank'd up;** *cf. n.*　**in hold:** *in custody as a hostage*　4 **If I revolt;** *cf. n.*　10 **Ha'rford-west:** *Haverfordwest*　12-15 *Cf. n.*　15 **crew:** *band*　10 **All-Souls' day:** *November first;*
cf. n.　13 *Cf. n.*　19 **determin'd … wrongs;** *cf. n.*　24 **bosoms;** *cf. n.*　25 *Cf. n.*

3 **bowels:** *center*　6 **Lines:** *letters*　8 **spoil'd:** *despoiled; cf. n.*　10 **embowell'd:** *disem-*
boweled　11 **centry:** *exact center*　20 **friends for fear;** *cf. n.*　S. d. **Earl of Surrey;**
cf. n.　10 **descried:** *caught sight of*

K. Rich. Why, our battalia trebles that account;
Besides, the king's name is a tower of strength,
Which they upon the adverse faction want.
Up with the tent! Come, noble gentlemen,   15
Let us survey the vantage of the ground;
Call for some men of sound direction:
Let's lack no discipline, make no delay;
For lords, to-morrow is a busy day.   *Exeunt.*

Enter [on the other side of the field,] Richmond, Sir William
          Brandon, Oxford, and Dorset.

Richm. The weary sun hath made a golden set,   20
And, by the bright tract of his fiery car,
Gives token of a goodly day to-morrow.
Sir William Brandon, you shall bear my standard.
Give me some ink and paper in my tent:
I'll draw the form and model of our battle,   25
Limit each leader to his several charge,
And part in just proportion our small power.
My Lord of Oxford, you, Sir William Brandon,
And you, Sir Walter Herbert, stay with me.
The Earl of Pembroke keeps his regiment: 30
Good Captain Blunt, bear my good-night to him,
And by the second hour in the morning
Desire the earl to see me in my tent.
Yet one thing more, good captain, do for me;
Where is Lord Stanley quarter'd, do you know?   35
     Blunt. Unless I have mista'en his colours much,—
Which, well I am assur'd, I have not done,—
His regiment lies half a mile at least
South from the mighty power of the king.
     Richm. If without peril it be possible,   40
Sweet Blunt, make some good means to speak with
him,
And give him from me this most needful note.
     Blunt. Upon my life, my lord, I'll undertake it;
And so, God give you quiet rest to-night!   45
     Richm. Good-night, good Captain Blunt. Come,
gentlemen,
Let us consult upon to-morrow's business.
In to my tent! the dew is raw and cold.
                    They withdraw into the tent.

Enter Richard, Ratcliff, Norfolk, and Catesby.

     K. Rich. What is't o'clock?   50
     Cate.   It's supper-time, my lord;
It's nine o'clock.
     K. Rich.   I will not sup to-night.
Give me some ink and paper.
What, is my beaver easier than it was,   55
And all my armour laid into my tent?
     Cate. It is, my liege; and all things are in readiness.
     K. Rich. Good Norfolk, hie thee to thy charge;
Use careful watch; choose trusty sentinels.
     Nor. I go, my lord.   60
     K. Rich. Stir with the lark to-morrow, gentle Norfolk.

     Nor. I warrant you, my lord.   *Exit.*
     K. Rich. Ratcliff!
     Rat. My lord?
     K. Rich.   Send out a pursuivant at arms   65
To Stanley's regiment; bid him bring his power
Before sun-rising, lest his son George fall
Into the blind cave of eternal night.
Fill me a bowl of wine. Give me a watch.
Saddle white Surrey for the field to-morrow.   70
Look that my staves be sound, and not too heavy.
Ratcliff!
     Rat. My lord?
     K. Rich. Saw'st the melancholy Lord Northumberland?
     Rat. Thomas the Earl of Surrey, and himself,   75
Much about cock-shut time, from troop to troop
Went through the army, cheering up the soldiers.
     K. Rich. So, I am satisfied. Give me a bowl of wine:
I have not that alacrity of spirit,
Nor cheer of mind, that I was wont to have.   80
Set it down. Is ink and paper ready?
     Rat. It is, my lord.
     K. Rich. Bid my guard watch; leave me.
Ratcliff, about the mid of night come to my tent
And help to arm me. Leave me, I say.   85
          [King Richard retires into his tent.]
               Exit Ratcliff [with Catesby].

[Richmond's tent opens, and discovers him and his Officers, &c.]
     Enter Derby to Richmond in his tent.

     Der. Fortune and victory sit on thy helm!
     Richm. All comfort that the dark night can afford
Be to thy person, noble father-in-law!
Tell me, how fares our noble mother?
     Der. I, by attorney, bless thee from thy mother, 90
Who prays continually for Richmond's good:
So much for that. The silent hours steal on,
And flaky darkness breaks within the east.
In brief, for so the season bids us be,
Prepare thy battle early in the morning,   95
And put thy fortune to th' arbitrement
Of bloody strokes and mortal-staring war.
I, as I may,—that which I would I cannot,—
With best advantage will deceive the time,
And aid thee in this doubtful shock of arms: 100
But on thy side I may not be too forward,
Lest, being seen, thy brother, tender George,
Be executed in his father's sight.
Farewell: the leisure and the fearful time
Cuts off the ceremonious vows of love   105
And ample interchange of sweet discourse,
Which so long sunder'd friends should dwell upon:
God give us leisure for these rites of love!
Once more, adieu: be valiant, and speed well!
     Richm. Good lords, conduct him to his regiment. 110
I'll strive, with troubled noise, to take a nap,
Lest leaden slumber peise me down to-morrow,

---

12 **battalia:** *battle array; cf. n.*   13 **tower;** *cf. n.*   17 **direction:** *capacity of directing*
S. d. **Dorset;** *cf. n.*   20 **set:** *setting*   21 **tract:** *trace, sunset glow*   26 **Limit:** *as-*
sign **several charge:** *individual command*   30 **keeps:** *stays with*   41 **make . . . means:**
contrive some opportunity   43 **needful:** *important*   55 **beaver:** *face-guard of the helmet*

68 **blind:** *dark*   69 **watch:** *sentinel (?); cf. n.*   71 **staves:** *lance-shafts*   74 **Saw'st:**
sawest thou   76 **cock-shut time:** *evening twilight*   90 **attorney:** *proxy*   93 **flaky:**
i.e. broken into flakes of cloud   96 **arbitrement:** *decision*   97 **mortal-staring:** *fatal-*
visaged   99 **the time:** *i.e. those who are about me*   102 **tender George;** *cf. n.*   104
leisure: *duration of opportunity*   111 **troubled:** *troublesome*   112 **peise:** *weigh*

When I should mount with wings of victory.
Once more, good-night, kind lords and gentlemen.

Exeunt. Manet Richmond.

O thou, whose captain I account myself,   *115*
Look on my forces with a gracious eye!
Put in their hands thy bruising irons of wrath,
That they may crush down with a heavy fall
Th' usurping helmets of our adversaries!
Make us thy ministers of chastisement,   *120*
That we may praise thee in thy victory!
To thee I do commend my watchful soul,
Ere I let fall the windows of mine eyes:
Sleeping and waking, O defend me still!   *Sleeps.*

Enter the Ghost of Prince Edward, Son to Henry the Sixth
[between the two tents].

Ghost. To Richard. Let me sit heavy on thy soul to-morrow! *125*
Think how thou stab'dst me in my prime of youth
At Tewkesbury: despair, therefore, and die!
Ghost to Richmond. Be cheerful, Richmond; for the wronged
souls
Of butcher'd princes fight in thy behalf: *130*
King Henry's issue, Richmond, comforts thee.

Enter the Ghost of Henry the Sixth.

Ghost. [To King Richard.] When I was mortal, my anointed
body
By thee was punched full of [deadly] holes:
Think on the Tower and me; despair and die!   *135*
Henry the Sixth bids thee despair and die.
To Richmond. Virtuous and holy, be thou conqueror!
Harry, that prophesied thou shouldst be king,
Doth comfort thee in sleep: live and flourish!

Enter the Ghost of Clarence.

Ghost. [To King Richard.] Let me sit heavy in thy soul   *140*
to-morrow!
I, that was wash'd to death with fulsome wine,
Poor Clarence, by thy guile betray'd to death!
To-morrow in the battle think on me,
And fall thy edgeless sword: despair, and die!   *145*
To Richmond. Thou offspring of the house of Lancaster,
The wronged heirs of York do pray for thee:
Good angels guard thy battle! live, and flourish!

Enter the Ghosts of Rivers, Grey, and Vaughan.

[Ghost of] Rivers. [To King Richard.] Let me sit heavy
in thy soul to-morrow,   *150*
Rivers, that died at Pomfret! despair, and die!
[Ghost of] Grey. [To King Richard.] Think upon Grey, and
let thy soul despair.
[Ghost of] Vaughan. [To King Richard.] Think upon
Vaughan, and with guilty fear   *155*
Let fall thy lance: despair, and die!—
All to Richmond. Awake! and think our wrongs in Richard's
bosom
Will conquer him! Awake, and win the day!

Enter the Ghost of Lord Hastings.

Ghost. [To King Richard.] Bloody and guilty, guiltily awake; *160*
And in a bloody battle end thy days!
Think on Lord Hastings: despair, and die!—
To Richmond. Quiet, untroubled soul, awake, awake!
Arm, fight, and conquer, for fair England's sake!

Enter the Ghosts of the two young Princes.

Ghosts. [To King Richard.] Dream on thy cousins   *165*
smother'd in the Tower:
Let us be laid within thy bosom, Richard,
And weigh thee down to ruin, shame, and death!
Thy nephews' souls bid thee despair, and die!
To Richmond. Sleep, Richmond, sleep in peace, and wake *170*
in joy;
Good angels guard thee from the boar's annoy!
Live, and beget a happy race of kings!
Edward's unhappy sons do bid thee flourish.

Enter the Ghost of Anne, his wife.

Ghost. To Richard. Richard, thy wife, that wretched   *175*
Anne, thy wife,
That never slept a quiet hour with thee,
Now fills thy sleep with perturbations:
To-morrow in the battle think on me,
And fail thy edgeless sword: despair, and die!   *180*
To Richmond. Thou quiet soul, sleep thou a quiet sleep;
Dreams of success and happy victory!
Thy adversary's wife doth pray for thee.

Enter the Ghost of Buckingham.

Ghost. To Richard. The first was I that help'd thee
to the crown;   *185*
The last was I felt thy tyranny.
O! in the battle think on Buckingham,
And die in terror of thy guiltiness!
Dream on, dream on, of bloody deeds and death:
Fainting, despair; despairing, yield thy breath!   *190*
To Richmond. I died for hope ere I could lend thee aid:
But cheer thy heart, and be thou not dismay'd:
God and good angels fight on Richmond's side;
And Richard fall in height of all his pride!

[The Ghosts vanish. King] Richard
starts out of his dream.

K. Rich. Give me another horse! bind up my wounds!   *195*
Have mercy, Jesu! Soft! I did but dream.
O coward conscience, how dost thou afflict me!
The lights burn blue. It was now dead midnight.
Cold fearful drops stand on my trembling flesh.
What? do I fear myself? there's none else by: *200*
Richard loves Richard; that is, I am I.
Is there a murtherer here? No. Yes, I am:
Then fly: what! from myself? Great reason: why?
Lest I revenge. What? myself upon myself?
Alack! I love myself. Wherefore? for any good   *205*
That I myself have done unto myself?
O no: alas! I rather hate myself
For hateful deeds committed by myself.

---

117 bruising ... wrath; *cf. n.*   **123 windows:** *shutters*   **125** *Cf. n.*   **142 fulsome:**
nauseating   **156 lance;** *cf. n.*

167 laid; *cf. n.*   **172 annoy:** *annoyance*   **191 for hope;** *cf. n.*   **197 coward con-**
science; *cf. n.*   **198 lights ... blue;** *cf. n.*   **now;** *cf. n.*   **200** *Cf. n.*

I am a villain. Yet I lie; I am not.
Fool, of thyself speak well: fool, do not flatter.   210
My conscience hath a thousand several tongues,
And every tongue brings in a several tale,
And every tale condemns me for a villain.
Perjury, [perjury,] in the high'st degree:
Murther, stern murther, in the dir'st degree;   215
All several sins, all us'd in each degree,
Throng all to the bar, crying all, 'Guilty! guilty!'
I shall despair. There is no creature loves me;
And if I die, no soul shall pity me:
Nay, wherefore should they, since that I myself   220
Find in myself no pity to myself?
Methought the souls of all that I had murther'd
Came to my tent; and every one did threat
To-morrow's vengeance on the head of Richard.

Enter Ratcliff.

Rat. My lord!   225
K. Rich. ['Zounds!] Who's there?
Rat. Ratcliff, my lord; 'tis I. The early village cock
Hath twice done salutation to the morn;
Your friends are up, and buckle on their armour.
[*K. Rich.* O Ratcliff! I have dream'd a fearful dream.   230
What thinkest thou, will our friends prove all true?
Rat. No doubt, my lord.]
K. Rich.   O Ratcliff! I fear, I fear,—
Rat. Nay, good my lord, be not afraid of shadows.
K. Rich. By the apostle Paul, shadows to-night   235
Have struck more terror to the soul of Richard
Than can the substance of ten thousand soldiers,
Armed in proof, and led by shallow Richmond.
'Tis not yet near day. Come, go with me;
Under our tents I'll play the eaves-dropper,   240
To hear if any mean to shrink from me.

Exeunt Richard and Ratcliff.

*Enter the Lords [Oxford and Others] to Richmond sitting
in his tent.*

Lords. Good morrow, Richmond!
Richm. Cry mercy, lords, and watchful gentlemen,
That you have ta'en a tardy sluggard here.
Lords. How have you slept, my lord?   245
Richm. The sweetest sleep, and fairest-boding dreams
That ever enter'd in a drowsy head,
Have I since your departure had, my lords.
Methought their souls, whose bodies Richard murther'd,
Came to my tent and cried on victory: 250
I promise you, my heart is very jocund
In the remembrance of so fair a dream.
How far into the morning is it, lords?
Lords. Upon the stroke of four.
Richm. Why, then 'tis time to arm and give direction.   255

His oration to his Soldiers.

More than I have said, loving countrymen,
The leisure and enforcement of the time

Forbids to dwell upon: yet remember this,
God and our good cause fight upon our side;
The prayers of holy saints and wronged souls,   260
Like high-rear'd bulwarks, stand before our faces;
Richard except, those whom we fight against
Had rather have us win than him they follow.
For what is he they follow? truly, gentlemen,
A bloody tyrant and a homicide;   265
One rais'd in blood, and one in blood establish'd;
One that made means to come by what he hath,
And slaughter'd those that were the means to help him;
A base foul stone, made precious by the foil
Of England's chair, where he is falsely set;   270
One that hath ever been God's enemy.
Then, if you fight against God's enemy,
God will in justice ward you as his soldiers;
If you do swear to put a tyrant down,
You sleep in peace, the tyrant being slain;   275
If you do fight against your country's foes,
Your country's fat shall pay your pains the hire;
If you do fight in safeguard of your wives,
Your wives shall welcome home the conquerors;
If you do free your children from the sword,   280
Your children's children quits it in your age.
Then, in the name of God and all these rights,
Advance your standards, draw your willing swords.
For me, the ransom of my bold attempt
Shall be this cold corpse on the earth's cold face;   285
But if I thrive, the gain of my attempt
The least of you shall share his part thereof.
Sound drums and trumpets, boldly and cheerfully;
God and Saint George! Richmond and victory!   *Exeunt.*

*Enter King Richard, Ratcliff, and Catesby [Attendants,
and Forces].*

K. Rich. What said Northumberland as touching Richmond?
Rat. That he was never trained up in arms.
K. Rich. He said the truth: and what said Surrey then?
Rat. He smil'd, and said, 'The better for our purpose.'
K. Rich. He was in the right; and so, indeed, it is.

Clock strikes.

Tell the clock there. Give me a calendar.   295
Who saw the sun to-day?
Rat.   Not I, my lord.
K. Rich. Then he disdains to shine; for by the book
He should have brav'd the east an hour ago:
A black day will it be to somebody.   300
Ratcliff!
Rat. My lord?
K. Rich.   The sun will not be seen to-day;
The sky doth frown and lower upon our army.
I would these dewy tears were from the ground.   305
Not shine to-day! Why, what is that to me
More than to Richmond? for the self-same heaven
That frowns on me looks sadly upon him.

Enter Norfolk.

Nor. Arm, arm, my lord! the foe vaunts in the field.   309

---

217 **bar:** *i.e. of justice*   219 **shall;** *cf. n.*   226 **'Zounds:** *an oath, God's wounds*   230-
232 *Cf. n.*   238 **proof:** *impenetrable armor*   240 **eaves-dropper;** *cf. n.*   243 **Cry
mercy:** *I beg your pardon*   250 **cried on:** *proclaimed; cf. n.*   256 *Cf. n.*   257 **enforcement:** *constraint, limitation*

262 **except:** *wish the exception of*   273 **ward:** *guard*   274 **swear;** *cf. n.*   277 **fat:**
prosperity   283 **Advance:** *raise*   284 **ransom:** *forfeit*   295 **Tell:** *count the strokes
of*   298 **book:** *i.e. the calendar*   299 **brav'd:** *made splendid*   309 **vaunts:** *boasts*

K. Rich. Come, bustle, bustle; caparison my horse.   *310*
Call up Lord Stanley, bid him bring his power:
I will lead forth my soldiers to the plain,
And thus my battle shall be ordered:
My forward shall be drawn [out all] in length,
Consisting equally of horse and foot;   *315*
Our archers shall be placed in the midst:
John Duke of Norfolk, Thomas Earl of Surrey,
Shall have the leading of the foot and horse.
They thus directed, we will follow
In the main battle, whose puissance on either side   *320*
Shall be well winged with our chiefest horse.
This, and Saint George to boot! What think'st thou,
Norfolk?
     Nor. A good direction, warlike sovereign.
This found I on my tent this morning.   *325*
'Jockey of Norfolk, be not so bold,
For Dickon thy master is bought and sold.'
     K. Rich. A thing devised by the enemy!
Go, gentlemen, every man to his charge:
Let not our babbling dreams affright our souls;   *330*
For conscience is a word that cowards use,
Devis'd at first to keep the strong in awe:
Our strong arms be our conscience, swords our law.
March on, join bravely, let us to 't pell-mell;
If not to heaven, then hand in hand to hell.   *335*

[His oration to his Army.]

What shall I say more than I have inferr'd?
Remember whom you are to cope withal:
A sort of vagabonds, rascals, and run-aways,
A scum of Britaines and base lackey peasants,
Whom their o'ercloyed country vomits forth   *340*
To desperate adventures and assur'd destruction.
You sleeping safe, they bring you to unrest;
You having lands, and bless'd with beauteous wives,
They would restrain the one, distain the other.
And who doth lead them but a paltry fellow,   *345*
Long kept in Britaine at our mother's cost?
A milksop, one that never in his life
Felt so much cold as over shoes in snow?
Let's whip these stragglers o'er the seas again;
Lash hence these overweening rags of France,   *350*
These famish'd beggars, weary of their lives;
Who, but for dreaming on this fond exploit,
For want of means, poor rats, had hang'd themselves:
If we be conquer'd, let men conquer us,
And not these bastard Britaines; whom our fathers   *355*
Have in their own land beaten, bobb'd, and thump'd,
And, on record, left them the heirs of shame.
Shall these enjoy our lands? lie with our wives?
Ravish our daughters?   *Drum after off.*
     Hark! I hear their drum.   *360*
Fight, gentlemen of England! fight, bold yeomen!
Draw, archers, draw your arrows to the head!
Spur your proud horses hard, and ride in blood;

Amaze the welkin with your broken staves!

Enter a Messenger.

What says Lord Stanley? will he bring his power?   *365*
     Mess. My lord, he doth deny to come.
     K. Rich. Off with his son George's head!
     Nor. My lord, the enemy is pass'd the marsh:
After the battle let George Stanley die.
     K. Rich. A thousand hearts are great within my bosom: *370*
Advance our standards! set upon our foes!
Our ancient word of courage, fair Saint George,
Inspire us with the spleen of fiery dragons!
Upon them! Victory sits upon our helms.   *[Exeunt.]*

❧ Scene Fourth ❧

[Another Part of the Field]
Alarum: Excursions. Enter [Norfolk and Forces; to him] Catesby.

     Cate. Rescue, my Lord of Norfolk! rescue, rescue!
The king enacts more wonders than a man,
Daring an opposite to every danger:
His horse is slain, and all on foot he fights,
Seeking for Richmond in the throat of death.   *5*
Rescue, fair lord, or else the day is lost!

Alarums. Enter Richard.

     K. Rich. A horse! a horse! my kingdom for a horse!
     Cate. Withdraw, my lord; I'll help you to a horse.
     K. Rich. Slave! I have set my life upon a cast,
And I will stand the hazard of the die.   *10*
I think there be six Richmonds in the field;
Five have I slain to-day, instead of him.—
A horse! a horse! my kingdom for a horse!   *[Exeunt.]*

*Alarum. Enter Richard and Richmond. They fight; Richard is
slain. Retreat and flourish. Enter Richmond, Derby bearing the
crown, with divers other Lords.*

     Richm. God and your arms be prais'd, victorious friends:
The day is ours, the bloody dog is dead.   *15*
     Der. Courageous Richmond, well hast thou acquit thee!
Lo! here, this long-usurped royalty
From the dead temples of this bloody wretch
Have I pluck'd off, to grace thy brows withal:
Wear it, [enjoy it,] and make much of it.   *20*
     Richm. Great God of heaven, say amen to all!
But, tell me, is young George Stanley living?
     Der. He is, my lord, and safe in Leicester town;
Whither, if you please, we may withdraw us.
     Richm. What men of name are slain on either side?   *25*
     Der. John Duke of Norfolk, Walter Lord Ferrers,
Sir Robert Brakenbury, and Sir William Brandon.
     Richm. Inter their bodies as become their births:
Proclaim a pardon to the soldiers fled
That in submission will return to us;   *30*
And then, as we have ta'en the sacrament,

---

310 **caparison:** *put trappings on*   321 **winged:** *flanked*   324 **direction:** *order of battle*   326 **Jockey;** *cf. n.*   327 **Dickon:** *a cognomen of the Devil, with a quibble on the nickname 'Dick' for Richard*   **bought and sold:** *i.e. betrayed for a bribe*   336 *Cf. n.*   337 **cope withal:** *have to do with*   338 **sort:** *set*   344 **distain:** *defile*   346 **Britaine:** *Brittany*   350 **overweening:** *presumptuous*   356 **bobb'd:** *banged*

366 **deny:** *refuse*   367 *Cf. n.*   368 **marsh;** *cf. n.*   373 **spleen:** *wrath*   3 **opposite:** *adversary*   7 *Cf. n.*   9 **cast:** *i.e. of the dice, a gambler's chance*   10 **hazard:** *chance*   11 **six Richmonds;** *cf. n.*   16 **acquit:** *acquitted*   17 **royalty;** *cf. n.*   27 **Brandon;** *cf. n.*

We will unite the white rose and the red:
Smile, heaven, upon this fair conjunction,
That long have frown'd upon their enmity!
What traitor hears me, and says not amen?   *35*
England hath long been mad, and scarr'd herself;
The brother blindly shed the brother's blood,
The father rashly slaughter'd his own son,
The son, compell'd, been butcher to the sire:
All this divided York and Lancaster,   *40*
Divided in their dire division,
O, now let Richmond and Elizabeth,
The true succeeders of each royal house,
By God's fair ordinance conjoin together;
And let their heirs—God, if thy will be so,—   *45*

Enrich the time to come with smooth-fac'd peace,
With smiling plenty, and fair prosperous days!
Abate the edge of traitors, gracious Lord,
That would reduce these bloody days again,
And make poor England weep in streams of blood!   *50*
Let them not live to taste this land's increase,
That would with treason wound this fair land's peace!
Now civil wounds are stopp'd, peace lives again:
That she may long live here, God say amen!   *Exeunt.*

❧ FINIS ❧

I.i.1. *winter . . . York.* Alluding to the cognizance of Edward IV, which was *a sun*, in memory of the *three suns*, which are said to have appeared at the battle which he gained over the Lancastrians at Mortimer's Cross, 1461. See *Holinshed*, iii. 660. There is also a quibble on 'son' and 'sun.' The early texts all have 'son'; modern editors adopt the emendation 'sun.'

I.i.12. *He capers.* I.e. War, first personified as a rough soldier, now 'capers.'

I.i.15. *amorous.* A looking-glass that reflects a face fond of itself (Schmidt). Cf. however, 'lascivious pleasing a lute' (13); that is, as Furness suggests, the looking-glass and the lute may be interpreted as active agents.

I.i.19. *feature.* Denoted the whole exterior personal appearance (Wright).
dissembling. Fraudful, deceitful (Johnson). There is some disagreement with his interpretation.

I.i.24. *week piping time of peace.* I.e. because in times of peace the loud, stirring strains of martial music are no longer heard. Cf. *Much Ado About Nothing*, II.iii.11–13: 'I have known, when there was no music with him but the drum and fife; and now had he rather hear the tabor and the pipe.'

I.i.29. *fair well-spoken days.* Cf. *Twelfth Night*, II.iv.6: 'Of these most brisk and giddy-paced times'; *Timon of Athens*, IV.iii.516: 'Strange times, that weep with laughing, not with weeping.'

I.i.30. *I am determined to prove a villain.* It is perhaps possible, as Charles Lamb suggests, that Richard uses villain here in the sense of 'churl' as opposed to 'courtier,' and not in our modern sense of 'wicked man.' On the other hand, cf. *3 Henry VI*, V, vi. 78, 79: 'Then, since the heavens have shap'd my body so, Let hell make crook'd my mind to answer it.' Lamb's suggestion is unnecessarily apologetic.

I.i.33. *By drunken prophecies.* I.e. by inventing prophecies for drunken men to spread abroad.

I.i.36. *true and just.* I.e. and therefore the less likely to entertain any suspicion (Wright).

I.i.39, 40. *About a prophecy, which says that G Of Edward's heirs the murtherer shall be.* '[Clarence's death] rose of a foolish prophesie which was, that, after K. Edward, one should reigne, whose first letter of his name should be a G.' *Holinshed*, iii. 703. *Halle*, 326.

I.i.44. *His majesty.* An anachronism. The title used by Edward IV was 'most high and mighty prince' (Bradley).

I.i.57. *cross-row.* Christ-cross-row. The alphabet was so called from the figure off the cross formerly prefixed to it (Murray: N.E.D.).

I.i.67. *tempers.* The reading of the Folio is 'That tempts him to this harsh extremity.' Most recent editors prefer here the reading of the Quarto. On the other hand Qq. 5-8 agree with the Folio in reading 'tempts.' 'Harsh' is found only in the Folio.

I.i.69. *Anthony Woodville*, Earl Rivers, eldest brother to the Queen of Edward IV, appointed governor to the Prince of Wales. See note on II.i.68.

I.i.74. *night-walking heralds.* Ironical description of the messengers busied with the king's illicit business (Furness).

I.i.75. *Mistress Shore.* Jane Shore was famous as the mistress of Edward IV. She was the daughter of a Cheapside mercer and the wife of a goldsmith in Lombard Street. She died in poverty c. 1527. See the tragedy by Nicholas Rowe, *Jane Shore*.

I.i.77. *Lord Hastings was for her delivery.* The Quarto reads 'Lord Hastings was to her for his delivery.' The Quarto reading here is more obvious, but feebler.

I.i.83. *The jealous o'erworn widow.* Elizabeth Woodville was born in 1437, so that her age at this time would be at least about forty. She had been married before she became Edward's wife, a fact which seems to intensify Richard's hate. Cf. line 94 below, which does not confirm the accusation of jealousy.

I.i.90. *an't.* Pope's modernization has been followed in preference to the 'and' of the early editions.

I.i.108. *abjects.* 'outcasts,' the more usual sense, is perhaps the meaning here. Cf. also *Henry VIII*. I.i.151, 152: 'and his eyes revil'd Me, as his abject object.'

I.i.111. *widow.* The word is used contemptuously, as in 83 above. I.e. the Widow Grey, whom King Edward IV has taken to wife.

I.i.117. *lie for you.* With probably a quibble on the other meaning of 'lie.'

I.i.136. *play.* The reading of the Quarto is 'prey.'

I.i.141. *Saint John.* Quarto, 'Saint Paul.' Elsewhere in the play Richard's favorite oath is by Saint Paul.

I.ii.1. *Anne.* The historical Lady Anne did not attend Henry VI's funeral; and the dialogue between her and Richard is Shakespeare's invention. 'The dead corps, on the Ascension euen [May 22, 1471], was conueied with billes and glaues pompouslie . . . from the Tower to the church of saint Paule, and there,

laid on a beire or coffen bare faced, the same in presence of the beholders did bleed: where it rested the space of one whole daie. From thense he was caried to the Blackfriers . . . : and, on the next daie after, it was conueied in a boat . . . vnto the monasterie of Chertseie. . . .' *Holinshed*, iii. 690. Richard married Anne in 1472.

I.ii.19. *wolves.* The reading of the Quarto is 'adders,' which some editors hold to be more consistent with the meaning of the passage.

I.ii.29. Chertsey is in Surrey.

I.ii.58. *Open their congeal'd mouths and bleed afresh.* Referring to the belief that a murdered body will bleed afresh in the presence of the murderer. See note on I.ii.1. above.

I.ii.78. *crimes.* The reading of the Quarto is 'evils.' Many editors adopt the Quarto reading to maintain the parallelism of lines 77-79 and 80-82.

I.ii.80. *diffus'd.* The Quarto reading of this line is 'defus'd infection of a man'; F1, 'defus'd infection of man'; F3, F4, 'diffus'd infection of a man.' There have been many conjectures concerning the exact meaning of 'defus'd.' See, however, *King Lear*, I.iv.2: 'That can my speech diffuse'; and *Merry Wives of Windsor*, IV.iv.55: 'With some diffused song.'

I.ii.96. *slain by Edward's hand.* Cf. *3 Henry VI*, V.v.38-40 in which the killing is portrayed; *Holinshed*, iii. 688.

I.ii.107. *hedge-hog.* Applied to Richard because of its hump-backed appearance, with a pun on Richard's heraldic emblem, the boar (hog).

I.ii.158. *poison on a fouler toad.* Toads were believed to be venomous.

I.ii.161. *basilisks.* Fabulous reptiles, also called *cockatrices*, alleged to be hatched by a serpent from a cock's eggs; ancient authors stated that their hissing drove away all other serpents, and that their breath, or even their look, was fatal (Murray. N. E. D.).

I.ii.168. *Rutland.* For an account of his murder see *3 Henry VI*, I. iii.

I.ii.224. *Crosby House* fronted on Bishopsgate Street Within. It was built by Sir John Crosby in 1466, and later Richard, when lord protector, was lodged there.

I.ii.240. *White-Friars.* According to Holinshed the body was conveyed to Blackfriars. See note on I.ii.1 above.

I.ii.241, 242. Cf. *Titus Andronicus*, II.i.86, 87: 'She is a woman, therefore may be woo'd; She is a woman, therefore may be won.'

I.ii.254. *three months since.* Tewkesbury was fought on May 4; Henry was buried on May 23, 1471.

I.iii.12. *the trust of Richard Glocester.* '. . . the duke of Gloucester bare him in open sight so reuerentlie to the prince . . . that at the councel next assembled he was made the onelie man, chosen and thought most meet to be protector of the king and his realme; so that (were it destinie or were it follie) the lambe was betaken to the woolfe to keepe.' *Holinshed*, iii. 716. *More*, 22/31. The historical date of Richard's appointment is April or May, 1483.

I.iii.15. *determin'd, not concluded yet.* I.e. it has been decided on, but has not yet been made official.

I.iii.S.d. *Derby.* Thomas, Lord Stanley, was not created Earl of Derby until 1485. Shakespeare has either confused this Lord Stanley with Sir William Stanley, or thought Thomas, Lord Stanley, later the Earl of Derby, two different men. In the Folio he is called Stanley during the third, fourth, and fifth acts.

I.iii.20. *Countess Richmond.* Margaret Beaufort, daughter of the Duke of Somerset. She married in 1455 Edmund Tudor, Earl of Richmond. She married next Lord Henry Stafford, and her third husband was Thomas, Lord Stanley. See preceding note.

I.iii.116–118. The Folio omits 114; the Quarto, 116.

I.iii.123. *Ere you were queen, ay, or your husband king.* Edward became king in 1460 when Richard was eight years old. The 2d and 3d parts of *Henry VI* similarly give him a prominent part in Edward's early struggles.

I.iii.131. *factious for the house of Lancaster.* Cf. *3 Henry VI*, III.ii.6, in which it is stated that Sir John Grey died 'in quarrel of the house of York.' The statement of Richard that Sir John was a Lancastrian is historically correct.

I.iii.133. *Margaret's battle.* Margaret was victorious at St. Albans in the battle of Bernard's Heath on Feb. 17, 1461. Some editors, however, believe that 'battle' here has the meaning of 'army.'

I.iii.164–166. The structure of these lines is confused. They may be paraphrased as follows: Which of you who looks at me does not tremble, if not because, as subjects, you bow before your queen, then since, as rebels, you quake before the sovereign you have deposed?

I.iii.171. Margaret fled into France in 1464 after the battle of Hexham. Edward issued a proclamation forbidding her to return. On April 14, 1471, she

landed at Weymouth. After the battle of Tewkesbury she was confined in the Tower until 1475. In 1476 she again went to France, after which time she did not return to England. She died in 1482. The historical time of the present scene in 1483, hence her introduction here is dramatic fiction.

I.iii.178. *The curse my noble father laid on thee.* Cf. *3 Henry VI*, I.iv.164–166: 'There, take the crown, and with the crown my curse, And in thy need such comfort come to thee As now I reap at thy too cruel hand!'

I.iii.191. *Northumberland.* Sir Henry Percy, third earl of Northumberland, killed at Towton, 1461. Cf. *3 Henry VI*, I.iv.150–151; 169–174.

I.iii.233. *elvish-mark'd.* A disfigurement given by the elves to a child at birth.
rooting hog. Richard's badge was a white boar. In the second year of Richard's reign, 1484, William Collingborne published the couplet:

'The Cat, the Rat, and Louell our dog,
Rule all England vnder an hog.

Meaning by the hog, the dreadfull wild boare, which was the kings cognisance.' *Holinshed*, iii. 746. *Halle*, 398. Collingborne was executed for this indiscretion.

I.iii.264. *Your fire-new stamp of honour is scarce current.* The figure of speech is from the art of coining or minting money. 'Fire-new' = newly coined. Dorset's title was granted him on April 18, 1475 (*Stow*, 713. *Holinshed*, iii. 702). He had therefore held this title for about eight years.

I.iii.285. *My charity is outrage, life my shame.* I.e. outrage is the only charity shown me, and my life is my shame.

I.iii.293, 294. *curses never pass The lips of those that breathe them in the air.* A possible reference to an old belief that curses to be efficacious should be uttered within walls. More probably the meaning is: 'curses never take effect outside the lips of those who utter them' (Tawney).

I.iii.330. The Quarto reading is 'you my noble Lord.' Capell's emendation 'you, my noble lords' is accepted by many editors.

I.iii.343. *Dorset.* In the Quarto the name appears as Vaughan. Spedding remarked (p. 85) that he could see no reason for the change. Pickersgill in reply (p. 11) points out that later it is upon Rivers, Vaughan, and Grey that Richard's vengeance falls. Nearly all editors accept the reading 'Vaughan.'

I.iii.363. *millstones.* Probably a proverbial expression. Cf. *Troilus and Cressida*, I.ii.138–140: 'Hecuba laughed that her eyes ran o'er.'—'With millstones.'

I.iv.S.d. In the Quarto Brakenbury and the Keeper are the same person. In the Folio Brakenbury does not enter until after line 75. It is possible that the Quarto text represents an acting version in which an extra character was omitted from economical reasons.

I.iv.10. *Burgundy.* Clarence, when a child, had resided under Burgundian protection at Utrecht, the Netherlands being then a part of the domains of the Dukes of Burgundy.

I.iv.45. *melancholy flood.* I.e. the river Styx, across which Charon, the 'sour ferryman,' conveys in his boat the souls of the newly dead into 'the kingdom of perpetual night,' i.e. Hades.

I.iv.49. *father-in-law.* Clarence married Isabel Neville, the elder daughter of Warwick.

I.iv.50. *What scourge for perjury.* Cf. *3 Henry VI*, V.i.107.

I.iv.53. *A shadow like an angel.* I.e. the ghost of Edward, Prince of Wales, son of Henry VI.

I.iv.56. *That stabb'd me in the field by Tewkesbury.* Cf. *3 Henry VI*, V.v.40, in which the killing is portrayed.

I.iv.147. *costard.* A species of large apple. The term was a vulgar colloquialism for the head.

I.iv.150. *sop.* A grim jest of the murderer. It was the custom to sop bread in wine. Probably there is also implied a quibble on 'milk-sop.'

I.iv.183. This line is omitted in the Folio. The preceding half line in the Quarto is 'to have redemption.' Probably the Folio omits the line in accordance with the statute of 1606 against blasphemy.

I.iv.214. *gallant-springing.* I.e. blooming Plantagenet; a prince in the spring of life (Johnson).

I.iv.238. *snow in harvest.* Cf. *Proverbs*, xxvi. 1: 'As snow in summer, and as rain in harvest, so honour is not seemly for a fool.'

I.iv.268. *malmsey-butt.* '. . . the duke was cast into the Tower, and therewith adiudged for a traitor, and priuilie drowned in a butt of malmesie, the eleuenth of March, in the beginning of the seuententh yeare of the kings reigne.' *Holinshed*, iii. 703. The earlier portion of this scene is Shakespeare's invention.

I.iv.271. *Pilate.* Cf. *Richard II*, IV.i.244: 'Though some of you with Pilate wash your hands.'

II.i.2. *united leauge.* 'But [King Edward], in his last sicknesse, when he perceiued his naturall strength so sore infeebled, that he despaired all recouerie . . . called some of them before him that were at variance, and in especiall the lord

marquesse Dorset, the queenes sonne by hir first husband. So did he also William the lord Hastings.' The lords, Holinshed then tells us, 'ech forgaue other, and ioined their hands togither; when (as it after appeared by their deeds) their hearts were farre asunder.' *Holinshed*, iii. 713, 714. *More*, 8/15.

II.i.7. *Rivers and Hastings.* The Folio has 'Dorset and Rivers,' but these two were nephew and uncle, both belonging to the queen's party. Line 25 below shows that the reading of the Quarto is, in this instance, the correct one. See also note on l. 70 below.

II.i.11. *So thrive I, as I truly smear the like.* I.e. May my fortune be in accordance with the truth of my oath. See also line 16 and line 24 below.

II.i.14, 15. *award Either of you to be the other's end.* I.e. cause each to die by the other's agency [either of you to suffer the other's end]. A prophetic warning. See III.iii.14.

II.i.68. *Of you, and you, Lord Rivers, and of Dorset.* The Quarto reading is: 'Of you, Lord Rivers, and Lord Grey, of you.' It is Grey later who is associated in death with Rivers.

II.i.70. *Lord Woodville, and Lord Scales.* The Quarto omits this line. Woodville was the Lord Rivers addressed in line 68, and he was also Lord Scales in right of his wife, the heir and daughter of Lord Scales. Shakespeare was apparently misled into thinking Rivers three separate persons by the passage in Halle, 347: 'The gouernance of this younge Prince was committed too lord Antony Wooduile erle Ryucrs and lord Scales, brother to the quene.' He was unaware that one person bore all three of these titles. See also *Holinshed*, iii. 714, a passage possible to misinterpret in the same way. See note on II.ii.150.

II.i.71–74. Cf. Milton's *Eikonoklastes* (1649), chap. 1, in which, in illustrating that 'the deepest policy of a tyrant hath been ever to counterfeit religious,' Milton states that the poets 'have been in this point so mindful of decorum, as to put never more pious words in the mouth of any person, than of a tyrant. I shall not instance an abstruse author . . . , but one whom we well know was the closest companion of these his [i.e., King Charles'] solitudes, William Shakespeare; who introduces the person of Richard the Third, speaking in as high a strain of piety and mortification as is uttered in any passage of this book [*Eikon Basilike*], and sometimes to the same sense and purpose with some words in this place: "I intended," saith he, "not only to oblige my friends, but my enemies." '

II.i.106. *give pardon to a slave.* '. . . although king Edward were consenting to his death, yet he much did both lament his infortunate chance, & repent his sudden execution: insomuch that, when anie person sued to him for the pardon of malefactors condemned to death, he would accustomablie saie, & openlie speake: "Oh infortunate brother, for whose life not one would make sute!" ' *Holinshed*, iii. 703. *Halle*, 362.

II.i.115. *Oxford.* John de Vere, thirteenth Earl of Oxford (1443–1513) fled to France before the battle of Tewkesbury was fought. Cf., however, *3 Henry VI*, V.v.2.

II.ii.6. *Castaways.* Persons lost or abandoned by Providence. Cf. *I Corinthians*, ix. 17: 'I myself should be a castaway.'

II.ii.24. For 'pitied me' the Quarto reads 'hugd me in his arme.'

II.ii.40. *Edward.* The Duchess and her grandchildren speak of Clarence's death (February, 1478) as recent. Queen Elizabeth next enters distracted with grief for the loss of King Edward (April 9, 1483).

II.ii.70. The precise meaning of this passage has been disputed. The general sense is as follows: Elizabeth says that so great have been her griefs that her eyes may be compared to the sea, governed by the influence of the moon, which receives back from the rivers the moisture which it gives forth.

II.ii.80. *The mother of these griefs.* I.e. by her years and position, the chief mourner of all.

II.ii.118. *broken rancour.* The structure of this passage is confused, but the general meaning clear. It may be paraphrased as follows: 'Your late quarrels, which, swollen high, had broken out in rancor, are now knit and joined together, and this healing of your quarrels must be preserved and cherished.'

II.ii.121. *little train.* '. . . the duke of Glocester, vnderstanding that the lords, which at that time were about the king, intended to bring him vp to his coronation accompanied with such power of their freends, that it should be hard for him to bring his purpose to passe, without the gathering and great assemblie of people and in maner of open warre, whereof the end (he wist) was doubtfull; and in which, the king being on their side, his part should haue the face and name of a rebellion: he secretlie therfore by diuers means caused the queene to be persuaded and brought in the mind, that it neither were need, and also should be ieopardous, the king to come vp strong.' *Holinshed*, iii. 714. *More*, 14/6.

II.ii.122. *Ludlow.* 'As soone as the king was departed, the noble prince his sonne drew toward London; which at the time of his decease kept his houshold at Ludlow in Wales. . . .' *Holinshed*, iii. 714. *More*, 12/6.

II.ii.150. *queen's proud kindred.* 'To the gouernance and ordering of this young prince, at his sending thither, was there appointed sir Anthonie Wooduile,

lord Riuers, and brother vnto the queene; a right honourable man, as valiant of hand as politike in counsell. Adioined were vnto him other of the same partie; and in effect euerie one as he was neerest of kin vnto the queene, so was he planted next about the prince. That drift by the queene now vnwiselie deuised, whereby hir bloud might of youth be rooted into the princes fauour, the duke of Glocester turned vnto their destruction; and vpon that ground set the foundation of all his vnhappie building.' *Holinshed*, iii. 714. *More*. 12/6.

II.iii.5. *seldom comes the better.* A proverbial saying. '. . . began there, here and there abouts, some maner of muttering among the people, as though all should not long be well, though they neither wist what they feared, nor wherefore: were it, that, before such great things, mens hearts of a secret instinct of nature misgiue them; as the sea without wind swelleth of himselfe sometime before a tempest. . . .' *Holinshed*, iii. 721. *More*, 43/19.

II.iii.13. *Woe is that land that's govern'd by a child.* Cf. *Ecclesiastes*, x, 16: 'Woe to thee, O land, when thy king is a child.'

II.iii.19. *nine months.* Henry VI was proclaimed king at Paris in October, 1422, when he was about a year old. His coronation at Paris did not take place until 1430, when he was about nine years old.

II.iv.1. *Stony-Stratford.* The Quarto reverses the order of the towns, putting Northampton first. The Prince was on his way from Ludlow to London. Stony-Stratford is nearer London than Northampton. The Folio reading, as pointed out by Pickersgill, is in accordance with Halle's *Chronicle.* The Prince was taken back to Northampton. See also *Holinshed*, iii. 715/1/48. *More*, 16/20; 18/7.

II.iv.28. *he could gnaw a crust at two hours old.* Cf. *3 Henry VI*, V.vi.53, 54: 'Teeth hadst thou in thy head when thou wast born. To signify thou cams 't to bite the world.'

II.iv.37. *Pitchers have ears.* A proverbial saying, 'small pitchers have great ears.' Cf. *Taming of the Shrew*, IV.iv.52: 'Pitchers have ears. . . .'

II.iv.S.d. The Quarto assigns the part of Messenger to Dorset, probably to avoid the introduction of another actor. The reception of the Messenger and the tone of his speeches indicate that the Folio is here correct.

II.iv.57. *map.* Possibly this word is here used in an astrological sense meaning a horoscope of future events.

II.iv.69. *we will to sanctuary.* Certain buildings belonging to ecclesiastical foundations, as well as churches, were privileged for criminals and other persons in danger of their lives. '[Queen Elizabeth] in great fright & heauinesse, bewailing her childes reigne, hir freends mischance, and hir owne infortune, damning the time that euer she dissuaded the gathering of power about the king, gat hir selfe in all the hast possible with hir yoonger sunne and hir daughters out of the palace of Westminster, (in which she then laie,) into the sanctuarie; lodging hir selfe and hir companie there in the abbats place.' *Holinshed*, iii. 715. *More*, 19/1.

III.i.S.d. *Cardinal.* According to *More*, 25/28 (Holinshed's authority), the Cardinal who undertook the mission of bringing the Duke of York out of sanctuary was Rotherham, Archbishop of York. In *Halle*, 352, the Cardinal of Act III, sc. i, is Bourchier, Archbiship of Canterbury. Critics are divided in opinion as to whether Shakespeare intended to present more than one personage.

III.i.16. ' "What my brother marquesse hath donne I cannot saie, but in good faith I dare well answer for mine vncle Riuers and my brother here, that they be innocent of anie such matter." ' *Holinshed*, iii. 715. *More*, 17/31.

III.i.S.d. 'When the king approched neere to the citie, Edmund Shaw, goldsmith, then maior, with William White, and Iohn Matthew, shiriffes, and all the other aldermen in scarlet, with fiue hundred horsse of the citizens, in violet, receiued him reuerentlie at Harnesie; and riding from thence accompanied him into the citie, which he entered the fourth daie of Maie, the first and last yeare of his reigne.' *Holinshed*, iii. 716. *More*, 22/24.

III.i.36. *pluck him perforce.* Richard, after advising that 'my lord cardinall' be sent to fetch the Duke of York out of sanctuary, added, 'And if she be percase so obstinate, and so preciselie set vpon hir owne will . . . then shall we, by mine aduise, by the kings authoritie, fetch him out of that prison. . . .' *Holinshed*. iii. 717. *More*, 24/25.

III.i.40, 41. *God [in heaven] forbid We should infringe the holy privilege Of blessed sanctuary.* 'God forbid that anie man should, for anie thing earthlie, enterprise to breake the immunitie & libertie of the sacred sanctuarie. . . .' *Holinshed*, iii. 717. *More*, 26/16. See also *Holinshed*, iii. 718, for the substance of the arguments used by Buckingham in ii. 48–56: Cf. 'And verilie, I haue often heard of sanctuarie men, but I neuer heard earst of sanctuarie children.' *Holinshed*, supra.

III.i.46. *Weigh it but with the grossness of this age.* The meaning seems to be that the present age is not one to stand on the mere technicalities of a situation when the person seeking sanctuary has no reason to claim it.

III.i.56. *children.* Buckingham sets up the presumption that children could

not commit crimes, and, therefore, could have no reason to seek sanctuary. See note on line 40 above.

III.i.66. *the Tower.* The Duke of York left sanctuary on June 16, 1483. *Excerpta Historica*, 16. 17. Edward V was already in the Tower on May 19. *Grants*, viii. 15. Shakespeare follows the account in *Holinshed*, iii. 721. *More*, 41/2.

III.i.70. *Did Julius Cæsar build that place.* The Tower is traditionally said to have been built by Julius Cæsar. The Norman Keep is to-day sometimes called Cæsar's Tower, although its official name is The White Tower, and it was built by William the Conqueror circa 1078. See Stow, *Survey*, ed. Morley, p. 73.

III.i.80. *So wise so young, they say, do never live long.* A proverbial saying. 'They be of short life who are of wit so pregnant' (Timothy Bright: *A Treatise of Melancholie*, 1586).

III.i.83. *the formal Vice, Iniquity.* A reference to the old morality plays in which the Vice (comic demon) was sometimes called Iniquity. Richard says that he will speak equivocally, like the Vice of the old play, and thus to one word give a double meaning. Fame may live long, but one person of whom he is thinking will not.

III.i.98. *dear.* This is probably a misprint for 'dread,' the reading of the Quarto.

III.i.133. *you should bear me on your shoulders.* The boy clearly is referring to Richard's deformity. Court jesters sometimes carried apes on their shoulders, and travelling showmen often led about with them at country fairs a bear and an ape, the ape on the bear's back. The speech, therefore, as Buckingham points out, is far from complimentary, in whatever sense the reference to the ape is meant. Cf. *Much Ado about Nothing*, II.i.32–34: 'I will even take sixpence in earnest of the bear-ward, and lead his apes into hell.' See also Autolycus' description of his imaginary robber, *Winter's Tale*, IV.iii.85.

III.i.143. The Quarto completes the line by reading 'needs will have it so.'

III.i.S.d. *Sennet.* A set flourish of trumpets, used to mark a royal progress.

III.i.173. *as it were far off, sound thou Lord Hastings.* '. . . the protector and the duke of Buckingham made veric good semblance vnto the lord Hastings. . . . And vndoubtedlie the protector loued him well, and loth was to haue lost him, sauing for feare least his life should haue quailed their purpose. For which cause he mooued, Catesbie to prooue with some words cast out a farre off, whether he could thinke it possible to win the lord Hastings vnto their part.' *Holinshed*, iii. 722. *More*, 45/3.

III.i.188. *Mistress Shore.* She became the mistress of Lord Hastings after the death of Edward IV.

III.i.198. *The earldom of Hereford, and all the moveables Whereof the king my brother was possess'd.* '. . . it was agreed that . . . the protector should grant him the quiet possession of the earldome of Hereford, which he claimed as his inheritance. . . . Besides these requests of the duke, the protector, of his owne mind, promised him a great quantitie of the kings treasure, and of his household stuffe.' *Holinshed*, iii. 721. *More*, 42/30.

III.ii.5. *stroke of four.* Dramatically, the next day after the action of the last scene. Historically, midnight of June 12-13, 1483.

III.ii.20. *separated council.* 'But the protector and the duke, after that they had sent the lord cardinall, the archbishop of Yorke, then lord chancellor, the bishop of Elie, the lord Stanleie, and the lord Hastings, then lord chamberleine, with manie other noble men, to common & deuise about the coronation in one place, as fast were they in an other place, contriuing the contrarie, and to make the protector king.' *Holinshed*, iii. 721. *More*, 43/6. Hastings' trust in Catesby and the latter's betrayal of the lord is described in *Holinshed*, iii. 722, and *More*, 44/8.

III.ii.26. *his dreams.* '. . . the selfe night next before his death, the lord Stanleie sent a trustie messenger vnto him [Hastings] at midnight in all the hast, requiring him to rise and ride awaie with him, for he was disposed vtterlie no longer to bide, he had so fearfull a dreame; in which him thought that a boare with his tuskes so rased them both by the heads, that the bloud ran about both their shoulders.' *Holinshed*, iii. 723. *More*, 48/19. Further, in the same passage, Hastings chides the messenger for his master's faith in dreams.

III.ii.70. *his head upon the bridge.* London Bridge, where the heads of traitors were exposed on a tower.

III.ii.88. *the day is spent.* The scene opens at four in the morning. The meaning, therefore, is that it is growing late, not that the day is over.

III.ii.99. *now we meet.* 'Vpon the verie Tower wharfe, so near the place where his head was off soone after, there met he [the lord Hastings] with one Hastings, a purseuant of his owne name. And, at their meeting in that place, he was put in remembrance of another time, in which it had happened them before to meet in like manner together in the same place. At which time the lord chamberleine had beene accused vnto king Edward by the Lord Riuers,

the queenes brother. . . .' See also the rest of the passage. *Holinshed*, iii. 723. *More*, 50/9.

III.ii.109. *Sir John.* Sir, a title formerly applied to priests and curates in general. The 'sir' has reference to the degree of bachelor of arts, being the usual English equivalent of the Latin *dominus*. Sir John was a common nickname for priests.

III.ii.113. *talking with a priest.* In Holinshed it is not Buckingham but a knight who is sent by Richard to accompany Hastings to the council. The knight finds Hastings in Tower Street, talking with a priest. ' "What, my lord, I pray you come on, whereto talke you so long with that priest? you haue no need of a priest yet." ' *Holinshed*, iii. 723. *More*, 49/26.

III.ii.115. *shriving.* Here used equivocally. Its religious meaning includes confessing and doing penance; its legal sense, imposing an obligation or penalty.

III.iii.S.d. The historical date of Rivers' execution could not have been earlier than June 23, 1483, for he made his will on that day. *Excerpta Historica*, 246, ed. 1831. Hastings was executed on June 13. Shakespeare assigns, dramatically, the execution of these two lords to the same day, June 13. In this he follows *Holinshed*, iii. 725, and *More*, 55/25.

III.iii.11. *Richard the Second here was hack'd to death.* Cf. *Richard II*, V.v.107–114.

III.iii.14. *Margaret's curse.* Margaret did not, as a matter of fact, 'exclaim on' Grey, but on Rivers, Dorset, and Hastings. See I.iii.225–229.

III.iv.26. *cue.* Words preceding each speech, learned by an actor when studying his part, to enable him to speak at the proper moment for his lines.

III.iv.32. *good strawberries.* '[Richard] said vnto the bishop of Elie: "My lord, you haue verie good strawberies at your garden in Holborn, I require you let vs haue a messe of them." "Gladlie, my lord" (quoth he) "would God I had some better thing as readie to your pleasure as that." ' *Holinshed*, iii. 722. *More*, 45/24.

III.iv.S.d. 'And soone . . . he returned into the chamber amongst them, all changed, with a woonderfull soure angrie countenance, knitting the browes, frowning, and fretting and gnawing on his lips . . . thus he began: "What were they worthie to haue that compasse and imagine the destruction of me, being so neere of bloud vnto the king, and protector of his roiall person and his realm? . . . Ye shall all see in what wise that sorceresse [the queene], and that other witch of hir councell, Shores wife, . . . by their sorcerie and witchcraft, wasted my bodie." ' *Holinshed*, iii. 722. *More*, 45/24.

III.iv.72. *blasted sapling.* Cf. *3 Henry VI*, III.ii.172, 173: 'She did corrupt frail nature with some bribe, To shrink mine arm up like a wither'd shrub.'

III.iv.77. *If.* '[Hastings] said: "Certeinlie, my lord, if they haue so heinouslie doone, they be worthie heinous punishment." "What" (quoth the protector) "thou seruest me, I weene, with 'ifs' and with 'ands': I tell thee they haue so doone, and that I will make good on thy bodie, traitor! . . . for, by saint Paule" (quoth he) "I will not to dinner till I see thy head off!" ' *Holinshed*, iii. 722. *More*, 45/24.

III.iv.87. *my foot-cloth horse did stumble.* The foot-cloth was a large, richly ornamented cloth laid over the back of a horse, and hanging down to the ground on each side. It was an old belief that the stumbling of a rider's horse was an omen of some great misfortune. 'Certeine is it also, that in riding towards the Tower, the same morning in which he was beheaded, his horse twise or thrise stumbled with him, almost to the falling.' *Holinshed*, iii. 723. *More*, 49/18.

III.iv.101. *air of your good looks.* I.e. favorable breeze of your good outward appearance (See 'air,' Murray, N.E.D.).

III.iv.102. *drunken sailor on a mast.* Cf. *Proverbs*, xxiii, 34: 'Yes, thou shalt be as he . . . that lieth upon the top of a mast.' The figure is repeated in *2 Henry IV*, III.i.18–25.

III.v.42. *Turks.* Elizabethan writers often used this term as a synonym for infidel. See *Prayer Book*, third collect for Good Friday: 'Turks, Infidels and Hereticks.'

III.v.51, 52. The Quarto assigns these two lines to the Mayor.

III.v.70. *too late of our intent.* I.e. too late to learn in advance of our purpose.

III.v.77. *a citizen.* For an account of Richard's reference see Boswell-Stone, *Shakespeare's Holinshed*, p. 375, note 2. The story is quoted by Halle and likewise is to be found in Grafton, ii. 107.

III.v.80. *sign.* Richard means that the citizen's shop was designated by a signboard with a crown painted on it.

III.v.86. *thus far come near my person.* I.e. thus far make intimate reference to me myself.

III.v.99. *Baynard's Castle.* On the Thames between Blackfriars and London Bridge. In Shakespeare's time the castle belonged to William Herbert, the Earl of Pembroke.

III.v.104. *Doctor Shaw.* 'John Shaw, clearke, brother to the maior.' *Holinshed*, iii. 725.

III.v.105. *Friar Penker.* 'frier Penker, prouinciall of the Augustine Friers.' *Holinshed*, iii. 725.

III.vii.5. *Lady Lucy.* The pre-contract was said to have been with Elizabeth Lucy, who was one of Edward's mistresses. '[Buckingham tells the citizens how Dr. Shaw] groundlie made open vnto you, the children of King Edward the fourth were neuer lawfullie begotten; forsomuch as the king (leauing his verie wife dame Elizabeth Lucie) was neuer lawfullie married vnto the queene their mother. . . .' *Holinshed*, iii. 720. *More*, 70/21. Buckingham also declared that 'the king's greedie appetite was insatiable, and euerie where ouer all the realme intollerable.' *Holinshed*, iii. 729. Buckingham likewise makes references to the things spoken of by Doctor Shaw 'as 'twere far off.'

III.vii.6. *contract by deputy.* See *3 Henry VI*, III.iii.49 ff. for an account of this. The lady was Bona, daughter of the Duke of Savoy, and sister of the French queen.

III.vii.15. *victories.* Richard commanded an expedition against Scotland in 1482, advancing as far as Edinburgh. Berwick was captured and ceded to England when peace was concluded.

III.vii.25. *statues.* 'When the duke had said, and looked that the people, whome he hoped that he maior had framed before, should, after this proposition made, haue cried, "King Richard, king Richard!" all was husht and mute, and not one word answered therevnto. . . .' *Holinshed*, 730. *More*, 72/16. Holinshed further describes Buckingham's efforts in substance as Shakespeare represents in this scene.

III.vii.46–249. The historical time of the rest of this scene is June 25, 1483, the day after Buckingham's speech at the Guildhall. Shakespeare makes one dramatic day of the whole scene. *More*'s order of events places Shaw's sermon on June 15 and Buckingham's speech on June 17. For an account of the Lord Mayor and his reception by Richard, see *Holinshed*, iii. 731, and *More*, 74/27. There is no historical authority for Richard's refusal of an audience on the ground of preoccupation with 'holy Exercise.'

III.vii.51. *maid's part.* I.e. with reference to the proverbial saying 'A Woman's nay doth stand for naught.' See *Two Gentlemen of Verona*, I.ii.56, 57: 'Since maids, in modesty, say "No" to that Which they would have the profferer construe "Ay." '

III.vii.143–175. Richard's reply is mainly Shakespeare's invention save for lines 151–153 and line 174, which are based on *Holinshed*, iii. 731; *More*, 75/20.

III.vii.168. *And much I need to help you, were there need.* 'I want much of the ability requisite to give you help, if help were needed' (Johnson); 'And much I ought to help you if you need help' (The Cowden-Clarkes). Dr. Johnson's paraphrase seems the more satisfactory.

III.vii.174. *happy stars.* A reference to the pseudo-science of astrology, meaning 'favorable conjunction of planets in his horoscope.'

III.vii.182. *a witness.* '[The Duchess of York] openlie obiected against his mariage, (as it were in discharge of hir conscience,) that the king was sure to dame Elizabeth Lucie and hir husband before God.' *Holinshed*, iii. 272. *More*, 61/31. For the rest of this scene, see *Holinshed*, iii. 731, *More*, 77/11.

III.vii.190. *pitch.* A technical term from falconry meaning the highest point in the flight of a falcon.

III.vii.191. *bigamy.* A statute in 4 Edw. I defined one aspect of bigamy as the marrying of a widow. Note that in the play Richard himself is guilty of 'bigamy,' if this definition be followed.

IV.i.35. *crowned.* The coronation was held in Westminster Abbey on July 6, 1483.

IV.i.45. *Richmond.* Dorset went with Queen Elizabeth into sanctuary at Westminster (*Polydore Vergil*, 540), and left it to join the rebellion raised by Buckingham in October, 1483 (*Holinshed*, iii. 743). After Buckingham's capture, Dorset succeeded in escaping by sea and 'arriued safelie in the duchie of Britaine.' *Holinshed*, iii. 743. *Halle*, 394.

IV.i.57. *cockatrice.* See note on 'basilisk,' I.ii.161.

IV.i.88. *Warwick.* Warwick was killed fighting on the Lancastrian side in the battle of Barnet, where Richard was one of the Yorkist generals.

IV.i.100. *Eighty odd.* The Duchess of York was born in 1415, and therefore was only sixty-eight in 1483.

IV.ii.9. *play the touch.* The touchstone was a black jasper from India used by Italian goldsmiths in testing the genuineness of gold (King). There are many references to touchstones in Elizabethan literature. Cf. *1 Henry IV*, IV.iv.9: 'To-morrow . . . is a day Wherein the fortune of ten thousand men Must bide the touch.'

IV.ii.45. *His name, my lord, is Tyrrell.* ' "Sir" (quoth his page) "there lieth one on your pallet without, that I dare well saie, to doo your grace pleasure, the thing were right hard that he would refuse." Meaning this by sir Iames Tirrell. . . .' *Holinshed*, iii. 734. *More*, 81/15. In the same passage Holinshed records

that when Richard broached the matter to Sir James 'he found him nothing strange.'

IV.ii.57. *grievous sick.* '[Richard] procured a common rumor (but he would not haue the author knowne) to be published and spred abroad among the common people, that the queene was dead; to the intent that she, taking some conceit of this strange fame, should fall into some sudden sicknesse or greeuous maladie....' (*Holinshed*, iii. 731. *Halle*, 407.

IV.ii.67. *brother's daughter.* *Stow* gives March 16, 1485, as the date of Anne's death. '[Richard] intended shortlie to marie the ladie Elizabeth, his brothers daughter.' *Holinshed*, iii. 751. *Halle*, 407.

IV.ii.100. *wife.* In 1484, according to Holinshed, there was surprise that the Lord Stanley had not been arrested as a reputed enemy of Richard, for Margaret, Stanley's wife, was mother to the Earl of Richmond. *Holinshed*, iii. 746. *Halle*, 398.

IV.ii.104. *prophesy.* This prophecy will be found in *Holinshed*, iii. 678.

IV.ii.107–126. This passage occurs only in the Quarto.

IV.ii.113. *Rougemont.* Richard visited Exeter in November, 1483. 'And during his abode here he went about the citie, & viewed the seat of the same, & at length he came to the castell; and, when he vnderstood that it was called Rugemont, suddenlie he fell into a dumpe, and (as one astonied) said: "Well, I see my daies be not long." He spake this of a prophesie told him, that, when he came once to Richmond, he should not long liue after....' *Holinshed*, iii. 746.

IV.ii.124. *Jack.* The figure which in old clocks struck the hour upon the bell. The word came to be a nickname for a busybody (Wright). Cf. *Richard II*, V.v.60: 'his Jack o' the clock.'

IV.ii.127. *resolve.* 'And, suerlie, the occasion of their variance is of diuerse men diuerslie reported. Some haue I heard say, that the duke [Buckingham], a little before his [Richard's] coronation, among other things, required of the protector the erle of Herefords lands, to the which he pretended himself iust inheritor.... [Richard] reiected the dukes request with manie spitefull and minatorie words.' *Holinshed*, iii. 736. *More*, 86/29.

IV.ii.132. *Brecknock.* A castle and property in Wales belonging to the Duke of Buckingham.

IV.iii.6. *flesh'd.* A term derived from hunting. Hounds were said to be fleshed when they ate of the first game which they killed. See note on lines 9, 10 below.

IV.iii.9, 10. *Dighton ... Forrest.* '... sir Iames Tirrell deuised, that they should be murthered in their beds. To the execution whereof, he appointed Miles Forrest, one of the foure that kept them, a fellow fleshed in murther before time. To him he ioined one Iohn Dighton, his owne horssekeeper, a big, broad square, and strong knaue.' *Holinshed*, iii. 735. *More*, 83/23. The qualms of the murderers are Shakespeare's own additions. According to Holinshed, in the same passage, Sir James would not admit to Richard that he knew the princes had been buried in 'so vile a corner' as under 'the stair foot, beneath a heap of stones.' See 1. 33.

IV.iii.40. *pent up.* Edward Plantagenet, Earl of Warwick, son of George Duke of Clarence 'had beene kept in prison within the Tower almost from his tender yeares.' *Holinshed*, iii. 787. *Halle*, 490.

IV.iii.41. *daughter.* Margaret Plantagenet, Countess of Salisbury, Clarence's daughter, was born August, 1473, and therefore was about twelve years old at Richard's death. Shakespeare has perhaps confused her with her first cousin. It was, according to Holinshed, the Lady Cicely, sister of Elizabeth, Richard's niece, that Richard planned to marry to a man of 'an vnknowne linage and familie.' *Holinshed*, iii. 752. *Halle*, 409.

IV.iii.42. *Abraham's bosom.* Cf. *St. Luke*, xvi, 22: 'And it came to pass, that the beggar died, and was carried by the angels into Abraham's bosom....'

IV.iii.44. *Britaine.* Richmond was in exile in Brittany.

IV.iii.S.d. *Ratcliff.* The quarto reading is 'Catesby,' and this has been generally accepted by subsequent editors.

IV.iii.50. *Morton.* '... sailed into Flanders, where he did the earle of Richmond good seruice.' *Holinshed*, iii. 741. *Halle*, 390.

IV.iii.52. *power.* The date of the beginning of Buckingham's revolt is October 18, 1483, according to the attainder of Buckingham, *Rotuli Parliamentorum*, vi. 245. For an account of Buckingham's march with his Welshmen, cf. *Holinshed*, iii. 743, *Halle*, 394.

IV.iii.59. *Jove's Mercury.* Mercury was the messenger who carried the commands of Jove.

IV.iv.6. *to France.* Actually, Margaret went to France in 1476, after which time she did not again return to England. See note, I.iii.171.

IV.iv.15. *right for right.* Justice answering to the claims of justice (Johnson).

IV.iv.28. *abstract.* Cf. *Hamlet*, II.ii.513, 514; 'for they are the abstracts and brief chronicles of the time.'

IV.iv.53, 54. These two lines are reversed in the Quarto, which makes a rather better sequence, though either can be defended. The Folio printer's eye may have been confused by three consecutive lines beginning with 'That.'

IV.iv.53. *galled eyes.* So too in *Hamlet*, I.ii.158ff.: 'Ere yet the salt of most unrighteous tears Had left the flushing in her galled eyes....'

IV.iv.87. *index ... pageant.* The 'index' was the written prologue sometimes distributed to the audience to explain the allegory in the 'pageant' or dumbshow (pantomimic action) to follow. The reference of course is to the representation of a play with a dumb-show. The 'index' here is said to have promised a happier conclusion than afterwards came to pass (Stevens; Wright).

IV.iv.90–92. These lines are obviously confused in the arrangement of the Quarto.

IV.iv.107. Cf. *Love's Labour's Lost*, IV. iii. 398: And justice always whirls in equal measure.'

IV.iv.131. *intestate.* The Folio reading is 'intestine.' There seems little doubt that 'intestine' is either a misprint or an attempted correction arising from a misunderstanding of the manuscript. The reading of Quarto has, therefore, been adopted in this text.

IV.iv.151. This line is omitted in the Quarto, and the query concerning Hastings is added to the preceding line of the Queen.

IV.iv.180. *Humphrey Hour.* No satisfactory explanation of this apparent sarcasm of Richard's has yet been made. Those who lacked the price of a meal were said to dine with Duke Humphrey, but how the saying is meant to be applied here is not clear.

IV.iv.212. *Elizabeth.* '[Richard] would rather take to wife his cousine and neece the ladie Elizabeth, than for lacke of that affinitie the whole realme should run to ruine.... Wherefore he sent to the queene (being in sanctuarie) diuerse and often messengers, which ... should so largelie promise promotions innumerable, and benefits, not onelie to hir, but also to hir sonne lord Thomas, Marquesse Dorset....' *Holinshed*, 750. *Halle*, 406. The passage further describes how the queen 'began somewhat to relent.'

IV.iv.224. *opposite.* According to the pseudoscience of astrology the 'opposition' of beneficent stars neutralised their good effects, turning them to evil aspects.

IV.iv.234. Cf. *Hamlet*, II.i.72: 'By indirections find directions out.'

IV.iv.244–247. *so thrive ...* I.e. May the success of my enterprise be as assured, as are my good intents toward you and yours in the future.

IV.iv.259. *Lethe.* A river of the Greek underworld whose waters produced forgetfulness in the souls who drank of it.

IV.iv.287. Cf. *3 Henry VI*, I.iv.79–83, and I.iii.178 above.

IV.iv.295. *conveyance.* Cf. *3 Henry VI*, III.iii.164: 'Thy sly conveyance and thy lord's false love.'

IV.iv.301. Richard repeats the argument he used to Anne in I.ii.121–130.

IV.iv.324. *Dorset.* Shakespeare ignores historical time here. Dorset first joined with Buckingham. That expedition failed in October, 1483. He then went abroad and joined Richmond, who set out on his successful expedition in August, 1485. (See, also, IV.i.44, 45, and IV.ii.51, 52 above.)

IV.iv.336. *love.* Theobald's emendation 'loan' has been generally accepted by modern editors.

IV.iv.345. Cf. Richard's earlier references: 'The deep-revolving, witty Buckingham,' IV.iv.45; 'High-reaching Buckingham,' IV.ii.34.

IV.iv.359. *king's King forbids.* The reference is to marriage within forbidden degrees of kinship. Cf. *Leviticus*, xviii. 14: 'Thou shalt not uncover the nakeness of thy father's brother, thou shalt not approach to his wife....'

IV.iv.377, 378. The Folio transposes these two lines. 378 is omitted in the Quartos from 2 through 8. It is probable, therefore, that in editing the Folio text an error occurred in the insertion of the missing line. The expression to 'harp on a string' was a common one.

IV.iv.379. *George.* An anachronism. The image of St. George on horseback, tilting at the dragon, was added to the collar of the badge of the Garter by Henry VIII (Ashmole).

IV.iv.387. In the Quarto this line follows 'thy life hath it dishonour'd.'

IV.iv.394. *God.* As elsewhere in the Folio text, the oaths have been modified to conform to the statute against blasphemy. The Folio here substitutes 'Heaven' for 'God.'

IV.iv.398. *brothers.* Earl Rivers is the only brother of Elizabeth introduced in the present play.

IV.iv.415. The Folio here reads 'repast.' Editors are agreed in regarding this as a misprint for the 'o'erpast' of the Quarto.

IV.iv.419. This line is omitted in the Quarto.

IV.iv.436. *found.* Many editors adopt the Quarto reading 'peevish-fond.'

IV.iv.443. Steevens notes here a reference to the fable on the phoenix.

IV.iv.457. *hull.* Literally, to float or be driven by the force of the wind or current on the hull alone; to drift to the wind with sails furled; to lie a-hull (Murray, *N.E.D.*).

IV.iv.459. *Norfolk.* On hearing of Richmond's landing, Richard 'sent to Iohn duke of Norffolke, ... and to other of his especiall & trustie friends of the

nobilitie, . . . willing them to muster and view all their seruants and tenants, . . . and with them to repaire to his presence with all speed and diligence.' *Holinshed*, iii. 754. *Halle*, 412.

IV.iv.465. *Ratcliff.* The Folio reading 'Catesby' (for Ratcliff) here is regarded by editors either as a misprint or an oversight.

Salisbury. Richmond was off the southwestern coast, close to Dorset. At Salisbury Richard would be able to prevent a junction with Buckingham's forces coming from Wales. '[Richard] tooke his iournie toward Salisburie, to the intent that in his iournie he might set on the dukes [Buckingham's] armie. . . .' *Holinshed*, iii. 743. *Halle*, 394.

IV.iv.500. *Welshman.* On his father's side. Richmond's father was the son of Owen Tudor and Katherine, widow of Henry V.

IV.iv.502. '[Richard] most mistrusted . . . Thomas lord Stanleie . . . For when the said lord Stanleie would haue departed into his countrie . . . the king in no wise would suffer him to depart, before he had left as an hostage in the court George Stanleie, lord Strange, his first begotten sonne and heire.' *Holinshed*, iii. 751. *Halle*, 408.

IV.iv.526. *Sir Edward Courtney.* Sir Edward Courtenay of Haccombe. He was created Earl of Devon on Henry VII's accession. For an account of these risings, see *Holinshed*, iii. 743. *Halle*, 393.

IV.iv.527. *Bishop of Exeter.* Shakespeare followed More's error in calling Peter Courtenay, Bishop of Exeter, brother of Sir Edward. Peter was the son of Sir Philip Courtenay of Powderham. The Bishop was the cousin of Sir Edward.

IV.iv.529. *The Guildfords.* The Guildfords were a distinguished family seated at Hempstead, near Cranbrook, Kent.

IV.iv.533. *owls! nothing but songs of death.* According to Pliny the cry of the screech-owl always betokened 'some heavy news.'

IV.iv.538. 'By this floud the passages were so closed, that neither the duke could come ouer Severn to his adherents or they to him. . . . The duke (being thus left almost post alone) was of necessitie compelled to flie. . . .' *Holinshed*, iii. 743. *Halle*, 394. on October 23, 1483, Richard 'made proclamation, that what person could shew and reueale where the duke of Buckingham was, should be highlie rewarded. . . .' *Holinshed*, iii. 744. *Halle*, 394.

IV.iv.549. *tempest.* Richmond sailed Oct. 12, 1483, and the same night the great storm arose that dispersed his fleet. The first ill-fated expedition is described in *Holinshed*, iii. 744. *Halle*, 396.

IV.iv.559. Buckingham was taken at Shrewsbury in October, 1483.

IV.iv.561. *landed.* Richmond, on his second expedition, landed at Milford Haven in August, 1485. Shakespeare has condensed, therefore, the history of two years in this scene.

IV.v.4. *If I revolt.* 'For the lord Stanleie was afraid, least, if he should seeme openlie to be a fautor or aider to the earle his sonne in law, before the day of the battell, that king Richard, (which yet vtterlie did not put him in diffidence and mistrust,) would put to some cruell death his sonne and heire apparent. . . .' *Holinshed*, iii. 753. *Halle*, 411.

IV.v.12–15. Sir Walter Herbert, created by Edward IV Baron Herbert; Sir Gilbert Talbot, uncle to the young Earl of Shrewsbury; Sir William Stanley, the brother of Richmond's step-father; redoubted Pembroke, Jasper Tudor, Richmond's uncle; Oxford and Sir James Blunt had come from France with Richmond; Rhys ap Thomas, a valiant Welsh leader from Carmarthenshire.

V.i.10. *All-Souls' day.* '[Buckingham] vpon All soules daie, without arreignment or iudgement . . . was at Salisburie, in the open market place, on a new scaffold, beheaded and put to death.' *Holinshed*, iii. 744. *Halle*, 395.

V.i.13. Cf. II.i.32–41.

V.i.19. *determin'd . . . wrongs.* I.e. the fixed period to which the punishment of my wrong-doing is postponed (Wright).

V.i.25. Cf. I.iii.307–311.

V.ii.8. Cf. *Psalm* lxxx: 'The wild boar out of the field doth root it [the vine] up: and the wild beasts of the field devour it.'

V.ii.20. *friends for fear.* 'Diuerse other noble personages, which inwardlie hated king Richard woorse than a tode or a serpent, did likewise resort to him with all their power and strength, wishing and working his destruction. . . .' *Holinshed*, iii. 745. *Halle*, 413.

V.iii.S.d. *Earl of Surrey.* This character is omitted in the quartos.

V.iii.12. *battalia.* '[Richmond's] whole number exceeded not fiue thousand men, beside the power of the Stanleies, whereof three thousand were in the field. . . .' *Holinshed*, iii. 755. *Halle*, 414.

V.iii.13. *tower.* Cf. *Proverbs*, xviii. 10: 'The name of the Lord is a strong tower.'

V.iii.S.d. *Dorset.* He was not at Bosworth Field, having been left behind in France by Richmond.

V.iii.69. *watch.* It is possible that 'watch' means here, as Doctor Johnson suggested, a watch-light or candle.

V.iii.102. *tender George.* Shakespeare seems to have been unaware that George Stanley was at this time a grown man. 'The child' of the chronicles is the same use of the word as in the ballad quoted in *King Lear*, III.iv.181, meaning 'young nobleman.'

V.iii.117. *bruising irons of wrath.* Cf. *Psalm* ii, 9: 'Thou shalt bruise them with a rod of iron.'

V.iii.125. *Richard's dream.* 'The fame went, that he had the same night a dreadfull and terrible dreame: for it seemed to him being asleepe, that he did see diuerse images like terrible diuels, which pulled and haled him, not suffering him to take anie quiet or rest. . . .' *Holinshed*, iii. 755. *Halle*, 414.

V.iii.156. *lance.* Some editors emend this line by the insertion of an adjective such as Collier's 'pointless' before 'lance.' As any such emendation rests upon no valid authority, the line should remain as it stands in the text.

V.iii.167. *laid.* Many editors prefer the reading 'lead' of the first Quarto. In all the Folios, however, and in the quartos from 2 through 8 the reading is 'laid' or 'layd.'

V.iii.191. *for hope.* Wright's paraphrase 'I died as regards hope' is probably correct, since it is confirmed by a passage in Greene's *James IV*, V.vi.(Dyce ed., p. 217). Steevens suggested 'I died for hoping to give you aid, before I could actually give it.'

V.iii.197. *coward conscience.* Cf. *Hamlet*, III.i.90: 'Thus conscience does make cowards of us all.'

V.iii.198. *lights burn blue.* There was an old superstition to the effect that spirits signified their presence by causing lights to become dim or to burn blue. Cf. *Julius Cæsar*, IV.iii.312: (at entrance of Ghost of Cæsar) 'How ill this taper burns!'

now. The 'not' of the Folio is probably a misprint. Cf. *Hamlet*, III.ii.386-388: ' 'Tis now the very witching time of night, When churchyards yawn, and hell itself breathes out Contagion to this world.'

V.iii.200. The punctuation off the line in the quarto deserves consideration: 'What do I feare? my selfe?'

V.iii.219. *shall.* The Quarto reading 'will' has been generally accepted.

V.iii.230–232. These lines are omitted in the Folio, by 'an accident of the press,' according to Spedding.

V.iii.240. *eaves-dropper.* The Folio 'ease-dropper' appears to be a misprint, although the same reading occurs in the quartos. The fourth Folio is the first text to make the emendation 'eaves-dropper.'

V.iii.250. *cried on.* An idiomatic expression. Cf. *Hamlet*, V.ii.376: 'This quarry cries on havoc'; *Othello*, V.i.51: 'whose noise is this that cries on murther?'

V.iii.256. For the substance of this oration, see *Holinshed*, iii. 757, 758. *Halle*, 417.

V.iii.274. *swear.* The Quarto 'sweat' is probably correct.

V.iii.326. *Jockey.* This couplet is in *Holinshed*, iii. 759, with the difference of 'Iacke' for 'Jockey.'

V.iii.336. For the substance of Richard's oration, see *Holinshed*, iii. 756, and *Halle*, 415.

V.iii.367. 'When king Richard was come to Bosworth, he sent a purseuant to the lord Stanleie, commanding him to aduance forward with his companie, and to come to his presence; which thing if he refused to doo, he sware, by Christes passion that he would strike off his sonnes head before he dined.' *Holinshed*, iii. 760. Halle, 420.

V.iii.368. *marsh.* 'Betweene both armies there was a great marish then . . . which the earle of Richmond left on his right hand; for this intent, that it should be on that side a defense for his part, and in so dooing he had the sunne at his backe, and in the faces of his enimies. When king Richard saw the earles companie was passed the marish, he did command with all hast to set vpon them.' *Holinshed*, iii. 758. *Halle*, 418.

V.iv.7. This line was imitated and parodied by several of Shakespeare's contemporaries. See Introduction.

V.iv.11. *six Richmonds.* It was not uncommon for a leader to have several of his knights dress like him. Cf. *1 Henry IV*, V.iii.1–29.

V.iv.17. *royalty.* The word is in the plural in the Folio.

V.iv.27. *Brandon.* Sir William Brandon was not slain at Bosworth.

V.iv.38, 39. Cf. *3 Henry VI*, II. v. Among the characters introduced are 'a Son that hath killed his Father' and 'a Father that hath killed his Son.'

V.iv.45. *their.* The reading of the Quarto. Folio, 'they.'

The Tragedy of King Richard the Second

Edited by
ROBERT T. PETERSSON

Dramatis Personae

KING RICHARD THE SECOND

JOHN OF GAUNT, *Duke of Lancaster* ⎫ *Uncles of*
EDMUND OF LANGLEY, *Duke of York* ⎬ *the King*

HENRY, *surnamed* BOLINGBROKE,
  Duke of Hereford, Son to John of Gaunt;
  afterward KING HENRY IV

DUKE OF AUMERLE, *Son to the Duke of York*

THOMAS MOWBRAY, *Duke of Norfolk*

DUKE OF SURREY

EARL OF SALISBURY

LORD BERKELEY

BUSHY ⎫
BAGOT ⎬ *Servants to King Richard*
GREEN ⎭

EARL OF NORTHUMBERLAND

HENRY PERCY, *surnamed* HOTSPUR, *his Son*

LORD ROSS

LORD WILLOUGHBY

LORD FITZWATER

BISHOP OF CARLISLE

ABBOT OF WESTMINSTER

LORD MARSHAL

SIR STEPHEN SCROOP

SIR PIERCE OF EXTON

CAPTAIN OF A BAND OF WELSHMEN

QUEEN *to King Richard*

DUCHESS OF YORK

DUCHESS OF GLOUCESTER

LADY ATTENDING ON THE QUEEN

LORDS, HERALDS, OFFICERS, SOLDIERS, TWO
  GARDENERS, KEEPER, MESSENGER, GROOM,
  AND OTHER ATTENDANTS

SCENE—*England and Wales.*

The Tragedy of King Richard the Second

INTRODUCTION

TEXT AND DATE

This, the fifth of Shakespeare's history plays, tells in highly ceremonious style the story of a king's fall—a fall which promised dramatic satisfaction both to King Richard himself in the 1390's and, less surprisingly, to London's playgoing public in the 1590's. The publisher, Andrew Wise, entered 'his copy' of *Richard II* in the Stationers' Register on August 29, 1597, and there is no reason to doubt that he acquired the play manuscript legitimately. Wise is thought to have purchased it from the Lord Chamberlain's Men, the company of players to which Shakespeare belonged, after Shakespeare had sold the company his rights to it. The absence of the playwright's name on the title page strongly suggests that Shakespeare had little reputation in 1597, but as the play sold well and had, according to Wilson, 'one of the most successful runs recorded for Elizabethan times,' his name appeared soon after, affixed to the two editions of 1598 and again to those of 1608 and 1615, which were the last before the First Folio of 1623.[1] It is the only play by Shakespeare which passed through three editions in less than two years.

The First Quarto of *Richard II* is classed as a 'good quarto' (as opposed to a 'bad quarto' or corrupt text of a play). On the basis of thorough and expert study—and the texts of very few Shakespearean plays have received as much attention—nearly all editors judge the First Quarto to have come from a playhouse manuscript in Shakespeare's (or a copyist's) hand, which was ultimately Shakespeare's own 'foul papers' or rough copy. The evidence for this rests mainly on the First Quarto's graphic but incomplete stage directions, its inconsistent designation of characters, and (according to some scholars) its punctuation.[2] It was, all in all, a very fine text which came from the printshop of Valentine Simmes in September of 1597 and went on sale at the Sign of the Angel, Wise's shop in Paul's Churchyard.

For reasons of political expediency, if not outright censorship, the First Quarto omits a crucial passage from the play, the so-called 'deposition scene' (IV.1.157–325). Therefore, this edition derives from a combination of the First Quarto of 1597 and, for the 'deposition scene,' the First Folio of 1623. While previous editors have almost without exception adopted this choice of texts, they have varied in the extent to which they have adhered to them. In accordance with the editorial policy for the series, the present edition makes as few departures as possible from its copy texts, fewer than are made in any other edition of the play.

Only about seventy departures from the First Quarto (hereafter called Q) and four departures from the 'deposition scene' in the First Folio (called F) have been deemed important enough to call for acknowledgment in the glosses or notes, although other categorical departures occur, shortly to be noted.

Q, regarded as a comparatively rare edition, is known to exist in four copies: the Huth (in the British Museum), the Capell (in Trinity College, Cambridge), and Petworth (in Petworth Castle), and the Devonshire (in the Huntington Library). Although no one of these copies is exactly like another,[3] the differences among them are, for the most part, of little significance to the general reader. In the ten or twelve cases where the differences are important they have been noted in the glosses. Nevertheless, the text of Q as it stands is by no means free from difficulties. As Pollard observes, 'on an average one error has been discovered on every page of the First Quarto, and . . . about once in every four pages there is a word or a phrase . . . for which no satisfactory solution can be discovered.'[4] For this reason, and for the purpose of bringing the reader into closer touch with Shakespeare's words, the glosses printed at the foot of each page in this edition are particularly full. (Meanings and usages to be found in *Webster's New Collegiate Dictionary* have nearly always been eliminated, however.)

The text of *Richard II* printed here follows Q, with the exception of (1) instances cited in the glosses or notes, and (2) certain departures made to assist the modern student in hearing and understanding the verse lines without doing violence to what Shakespeare wrote. The latter are as follows: archaic spellings which indicate nothing about Elizabethan pronunciation have been abandoned; stage directions have been added or enlarged (usually after F),[5] punctuation has been increased (since Q is underpunctuated) or altered (modern equivalents to the marks and capitals used in Elizabethan printing have been sought); and some changes in lineation have been made, for which F has often served as a valuable check. As in many other editions, elision is indicated not according to the copy texts but according to what the meter requires. (See the note to I.1.163.) Also, in some recurrent instances where F is more modern or more correct than Q, F has been followed without comment: *sit* (*Q set*), *thee* (*Q the*), *thine* (*Q thy*), *mine* (*Q my*) or the reverse, *my* (*Q mine*). Finally there is the troublesome problem of pronunciation. Although pronunciation is often problematical and one word may sometimes be pronounced in different ways, the intention in this edition is to preserve all copy-text spellings which indicate pronunciation. (For the special problem of past participles and verbs

---

1 For a summary description of the Qq and F, see the *New Variorum Edition of Shakespeare: The Life and Death of King Richard the Second*, ed. Matthew W. Black (Philadelphia, J. B. Lippincott, 1955), pp. 355–91.

2 Among the scanty stage directions in Q are such informal and vivid ones as: *He plucks it out of his bosoms and reades it* (V.2.) and *The murderers rush in* (V.5.). Speech-tags in Q are not consistent: Bolingbroke appears as *Bullingbrooke, Herford,* and *King;* Mowbray as both *Mowbray* and *Norfolk.* Q's punctuation is careful and dramatic in the set speeches, and especially there seems to show Shakespeare's hand.

3 A brief comparison of the copies of Q appears in the *New Variorum Edition,* pp. 357–9.

4 Alfred W. Pollard, *A New Shakespeare Quarto: The Tragedy of King Richard II* (London, Quaritch, 1916), pp. 33–34.

5 For the stage directions in this edition, see note to I.1.195SD.

in the past tense, see the note to I.2.30.) Pronunciation of proper names is no exception: wherever their spelling in the copy text indicates Elizabethan pronunciation (which may not be like that current today), the old forms are retained (e.g. *Bullingbrooke, Herford, Callice* for Calais, *Rainold* for Reginald). Although the spelling of unstressed syllables is not reproduced precisely as in Q, the forms of the names printed here are the forms which recur most frequent.

The particular attention given to pronunciation, lineation, and metrical values in this edition only recognizes that *Richard II*, together with *King John* and Parts 1 and 3 of *Henry VI*, is one of four Shakespearean plays written entirely in verse. Quite as much as it is a stage play, *Richard II* is a stately and stylized dramatic poem. Three-quarters of the lines are blank verse—more than in any major tragedy except *Anthony and Cleopatra*—and more pentameter rhymes occur in it than in any other plays except *Love's Labour's Lost* and *A Midsummer Night's Dream*.

After Q came the Second and Third Quartos in 1598. The Second (Q2) is in most respects poor. Printed from a copy of Q unlike any of the four surviving, it introduces more errors than it corrects, whereas Q3, which derives from it, was executed with great care and may well have been the printed source of F. Q4 and Q5, the latter being only a docile copy of the former, were printed in 1608 and 1615. In Q4 for the first time the 'deposition scene' was printed, though badly.

The First Folio text of *Richard II*, issued in 1623, is a well-edited work, but the question of its origin makes it the most controversial of the *Richard* texts. F is a thorough reworking of the play which succeeds in correcting about one-third of Q's original errors, about half of the new errors in Q2 and Q3, and nearly all the new errors in Q4 and Q5. And yet the number of fresh errors it introduces shows how difficult the text of *Richard II* is, even for the very capable editors of F.

F's text of the play shows signs of having been prepared for the theater as well as the private reader. As Wilson says, it bears 'all the stigmata of prompt-book.'[6] Not only do the playhouse cuts amount to fifty-one lines but the stage directions are greatly enlarged, the punctuation is far heavier, the verse lines are made more regular, the supernumeraries in III.4 clarified, and the speech-tags normalized.

Though the best opinions on the intricate question of F's origin are still unreconciled and the majority still favor Q5, the most recent authority, W. W. Greg, moves with Pollard[7] and Hasker toward the conclusion that Q3 was the primary textual source of F.[8] It is generally supposed that the quarto used—whichever it was—was collated with some independent authority originating in the theater. Some scholars judge the independent authority to have been a playhouse promptbook, but the matter is no more certain than the matter of whether the independent authority was printed or in manuscript. According to Greg, while the case for Q3 is 'virtually conclusive,'[9] the case for Q5 as basis

for the last 151 lines of the play (which were missing from the Q3 copy used for F) is a 'strong one, if less compelling.'

The 'deposition scene' printed in F is judged by Greg and others to come from a reputable playhouse manuscript, presumably a promptbook.[10] No one doubts that F took the scene from an authentic manuscript while Q4's scene came from a very inferior copy. Furthermore, almost no one doubts that the scene was, from the beginning, presented on the stage, even though it was not printed until 1608.

Plain and sure evidence for the dating of *Richard II* does not exist. We know that it cannot have been written later than the publication of Q in 1597 (or than the mention of the play in Meres' *Palladis Tamia* in 1598) and assume that it came somewhat earlier. Most scholars give 1597 as the approximate date, though a few, preferring not to fix it so exactly, merely include *Richard II* in the 'lyric group' of plays written between 1593 and 1596. Three kinds of 'evidence' are usually presented in support of the year 1595. The style, which is characteristically early and is similar to that of *Romeo and Juliet* and *King John*, shows such features as: a large number of rhymes (one-fifth of the play's 2,728 lines), quatrains in three places, and a strong inclination toward end-stopped lines. The other kinds of 'evidence' are: (1) passages in Daniel's *Civil Wars* (1595) believed to resemble parts of *Richard II*, and (2) a contemporary letter from Sir Richard Hoby to Sir Robert Cecil which mentions a performance of a play called *Richard II* in 1595. Although there are scholars who deny that Daniel is relevant or that Hoby's letter refers to a *Richard II* recently written by Shakespeare, the opinion of those willing to use these three arguments as evidence points, if inexactly, to 1595 as the date of composition.[11]

By now it is generally assumed that *Richard II* was first played during the fall season of 1595. Someone, perhaps Essex who very early took a fancy to the play, soon saw in it an application to current political affairs,[12] a consideration which led to the suppression of the 'deposition scene' during Queen Elizabeth's lifetime. But the exclusion of that climactic scene did not prevent the play from being performed. Even if Elizabeth, in her pique, was using the word 'forty' only as a round figure, she is said to have remarked, 'This tragedy was played forty times in open streets and houses.' We next hear of *Richard II* being presented, and for reasons now rather obscure, on the eve of the Essex Rebellion, February 24, 1601. Other performances occurred later on, like that recorded for 1607 on board the 'Dragon,' a vessel lying off Sierra Leone on its way to the East Indies. The more recent record of the play shows fifty major productions since 1900. The number of performances in that time has been enormous, including those by Maurice Evans who played the role of Richard about four hundred times between 1937 and 1940.[13]

Richard II has been studied by an incomparable group of Shakespearean scholars, and to them, as well as to the general editors of the present series, I owe a great debt of gratitude. All the important texts of the play have been thoroughly examined by one or another textual specialist—W. W. Greg, Richard E. Hasker, C. J. Sisson, and above all by A. W. Pollard in his

6 Wilson's New Cambridge edition, p. 111.

7 See W. W. Greg, *The Shakespeare First Folio* (Oxford, Oxford University Press, 1955), pp. 236–238; Pollard. *A New Shakespeare Quarto*, pp. 52–53; Richard E. Hasker, 'The Copy for the First Folio *Richard II*,' *Studies in Bibliography: Papers of the Bibliographical Society of the University of Virginia*, 5 (1952–53), [53]–72.

8 See Pollard, *A New Shakespeare Quarto*, pp. 51, 89, 98–99; Hasker, 'First Folio *Richard II*,' pp. 55–58, 70; also see Greg, *The Shakespeare First Folio*, pp. 237–238; and for his theory of a two-manuscript source, Wilson's New Cambridge edition, pp. 108–14.

9 Evidence in support of Q3 as source includes: *unpruind* for *unprund* (III.4.45); *mine for my* (IV.1.70); 97 errors in Q3 which were retained by F. Hasker, 'First Folio *Richard II*,' pp. 62–63, finds strong support for Q3 in the punctuation of F.

10 Greg, *The Shakespeare First Folio*, pp. 236–237.

11 See both Sir Edmund Chambers, 'The Date of Richard II,' *Review of English Studies*, 1 (1925), 75–76, and a summary of the evidence in the *New Variorum Edition*, pp. 393–395.

12 See Wilson's New Cambridge edition, pp. xvi–xxxiv, and Ure's New Arden edition, pp. lvii–lxii. (I have been unable to find the Papal Bull many editors refer to as having been issued in 1596 to stir Elizabeth's subjects against her and so depose her.)

13 See Harold Child's account of the stage history (in Wilson's New Cambridge edition, pp. lxxvii–xcii), and Matthew W. Black's in the *New Variorum Edition*, pp. 564–75.

exemplary introduction to Q3 published in 1916. Among the outstanding editions are those by Sir Edmund Chambers,[14] C. H. Herford, A. W. Verity, Sir Henry Newbolt, and more recently G. B. Harrison, G. L. Kittredge, J. Dover Wilson, and Peter Ure, of which I would single out for their particular excellence those of Chambers, Verity, and Wilson. And for its countless useful features, one welcomes the *New Variorum Edition* produced by Matthew W. Black.

SOURCES OF THE PLAY

While no one denies the truth of Wilson's statement that 'Holinshed furnishes the plain hempen warp upon which the colourful historical tapestry we call *Richard II* was woven,'[15] the other threads of the fabric have been endlessly woven and unwoven. Shakespeare's principal source for the play is the second edition (1587) of Raphael Holinshed's *Chronicles of England, Scotland, and Ireland,* and in addition eight other sources have been proposed, with more or less probability: five other chronicles, a verse history, and two early plays (one of them hypothetical). Before we turn to Holinshed it may be well to look briefly at these possible sources, remembering that new evidence might come along to buoy up the cases for some of them and sink others.

1. The 'Old Play.' The case for a hypothetical play, first presented in the 19th century and urged more recently by Chambers, Wilson, and Feuillerat (very emphatically by the latter two), has been carefully argued despite the lack of any proof for its existence. The play may well have existed, but until its exact nature is known and the many descriptions of it become one, the 'Old Play' shall continue to befog the issue of sources.[16]

2. Edward Hall, *The Union of the Two Noble and Illustrate Famelies of Lancastre & Yorke* (1548). Hall, the predecessor upon whom Holinshed chiefly depended for his Richard material, and occasionally even for his wording, is generally regarded as Shakespeare's direct source only in scenes 2 and 3 of the last act. These scenes, concerning Aumerle's complicity in the plot against Bolingbroke, bear close resemblance to both sources. (See Holinshed below, passage *b*.) Wilson believes the germ of another passage, Richard's famous abdication speech (III.3.146–162), to have come from Hall.[17]

3. French sources (a) 'Créton' or John Webb's *Translation of a French Metrical History of the Deposition of King Richard* (1399). (b) 'Traïson' or *Chronique de la Traïson et Mort de Richart Deux Roy Dengleterre* (?1412). (c) 'Jean Le Beau' or *La Chronique de Richard II* (between 1399 and 1449).[18] The use to which Shakespeare may have put these words, as well as their interrelation, are matters still very imperfectly understood, although some scholars consider 'Créton' and *Traïson* to be the same account, and 'Le Beau' to be a version of *Traïson*. In the opinions of Paul Reyher

and Wilson, Shakespeare consulted all three (see, e.g., the description of Gloucester's death by beheading, I.1.101–3 cf. n., which is unique to 'Le Beau'). Wilson believes the chief debt of Shakespeare to 'Le Beau' or *Traïson* to be in the conception of Richard's character after his downfall.[19]

4. 'Woodstock' or *The First Part of the Reign of King Richard the Second or Thomas of Woodstock* (c. 1591; Malone Society Reprints, 1929). Thorough and repeated study of this anonymous play reveals a large number of verbal parallels to Shakespeare's play. The prevailing opinion among scholars who assume that *Thomas of Woodstock* preceded Shakespeare's play is that Shakespeare knew it quite well and very frequently echoes its wording in the first two acts of *Richard II* (although Feuillerat is doubtful that Shakespeare ever read it). Some scholars judge the characterization of Gloucester as a 'plain well-meaning soul' to derive from *Thomas of Woodstock,* contrasting as it does with the unfavorable picture presented by Holinshed, Froissart, and Daniel.

5. Samuel Daniel, *The First Fowre Bookes of the Civile Wars Between the Two Houses of Lancaster and Yorke* (1595). The first two books of Daniel's work show constant and very close correspondence with Shakespeare's play, although indebtedness has not been proved finally. (Feuillerat believes that Shakespeare need not have known Daniel and that resemblances between them originate in the hypothetical 'Old Play.') The prevailing opinion now, however, moves toward the belief that Shakespeare was reading the poem as he composed. Daniel's influence has been felt in numerous passages,[20] among them V.4, where Exton explains the source of his murder motive.

6. *The Third and Fourthe Boke of Syr Johan Froissart of the Chronycles of Englande . . . Translated . . . By Johan Bourchier . . . Lord Berners* (1525). Recent scholars, beginning with Reyher, believe that Shakespeare's debt to Froissart is far greater than was suspected earlier. The most important contribution made by Froissart, according to Wilson, is in the characterization of John of Gaunt, especially Gaunt's attitude toward Richard, his deathbed scene, and his famous 'Methinks I am a prophet new inspir'd' as well as later speeches.[21]

7. Holinshed's *Chronicles*. None of Shakespeare's history plays, including *Henry V*, stays closer to Holinshed. The main departures from Holinshed's content are alterations in time, place, and characterization. Additions to Holinshed are, however, numerous: the conversation between Gaunt and the Duchess of Gloucester (I.2), Gaunt's deathbed scene (II.1), the meeting of Northumberland, Ross, and Willoughby (II.1), the appearances of the queen (especially II.1, III.4, V.1), Richard's presence in the deposition scene (IV.1), the Duchess of York's defense of Aumerle (V.2 and 3), and Exton's appearance with Richard's coffin (V.6). Also Richard's soliloquies were written independently of Holinshed and all other sources.

To understand the relationship between Shakespeare's play and its main source, one should read continuously that part of Holinshed's third volume covering the late years of Richard's reign (in the 1587 edition, pp. 486–519; in the Boswell-Stone edition, pp. 77–130). Here follow three passages from Holinshed, with the corresponding parts of Shakespeare's play in each case noted. For ease of comparison, the spelling and punctuation of the passages have been modernized.

14 Edmund K. Chambers; Falcon edition, London, Longmans, Green, 1895; C. H. Herford's Warwick Shakespeare, London, Blackie and Son, [1863]; A. W. Verity's Pitt Press Shakespeare, Cambridge, Cambridge University Press, 1899; Henry Newbolt's edition, Oxford, Clarendon Press, 1912; G. B. Harrison's *Shakespeare. Major Plays*, New York, Harcourt, Brace, 1948; George Lyman Kittredge's edition, Boston, Ginn & Co., 1941; J. Dover Wilson's New Cambridge edition, Cambridge, Cambridge University Press, 1939; and Peter Ure's New Arden edition, Cambridge, Harvard University Press, 1956.

15 New Cambridge edition, pp. li–lii.

16 See Wilson's New Cambridge edition, pp. lxiv–lxxv.

17 See p. 12 of the 1809 edition.

18 This is printed in Buchon's *Collection des Chroniques Nationales Françaises*, vol. 15, supplement 2, p. 10

19 See Wilson's whole argument, New Cambridge edition, pp. lviii–lxi, 211.

20 See Llewellyn M. Buell's Yale edition, pp. 126–127, and Wilson's New Cambridge edition, pp. xl–xliv, 156–157, 205, 235.

21 See Wilson's New Cambridge edition, pp. xliv–xlv, liv–lvii, 140, 199–200.

a. The death of Gaunt (compare II.1.150–217): 'The death of this duke gave occasion of increasing more hatred in the people of this realm toward the King; for he seized into his hands all the goods that belonged to him, and also received all the rents and revenues of his lands, which ought to have descended unto the Duke of Hereford by lawful inheritance, in revoking his letters-patent which he had granted to him before, by virtue whereof he might make his attorneys-general to sue livery for him of any manner of inheritances or possessions that might from thenceforth fall unto him, and that his homage might be respited, with making reasonable fine: whereby it was evident that the King meant his utter undoing.

'This hard dealing was much misliked of all nobility, and cried out against of the meaner sort. But, namely, the Duke of York was therefore sore moved, who before this time had borne things with so patient a mind as he could, though the same touched him very near, as the death of his brother the Duke of Gloucester, the banishment of his nephew the said Duke of Hereford, and other more injuries in great number, which, for the slippery youth of the King, he passed over for the time, and did forget as well as he might.'

b. The conspiracy against Bolingbroke (compare V.2.54–127 and V.3.23–152): 'At length, by the advice of the Earl of Huntington, it was devised that they should take upon them a solemn joust, to be enterprised between him and twenty on his part, and the Earl of Salisbury and twenty with him, at Oxford, to the which triumph King Henry should be desired; and when he should be most busily regarding the martial pastime, he suddenly should be slain and destroyed, and so by that means King Richard, who as yet lived, might be restored to liberty, and have his former estate and dignity. . . . This Earl of Rutland, departing before from Westminster to see his father, the Duke of York, as he sat at dinner had his counterpane [copy] of the indenture of the confederacy in his bosom.

'The father, espying it, would needs see what it was; and though the son humbly denied to show it, the father being more earnest to see it, by force took it out of his bosom, and perceiving the contents thereof, in a great rage caused his horses to be saddled out of hand and . . . incontinently mounted on horseback, to ride toward Windsor to the King, to declare to him the malicious intent of [his son and] his accomplices.

'The Earl of Rutland, seeing in what danger he stood, took his horse and rode another way to Windsor, in post, so that he got thither before his father; and when he was alighted at the castle gate, he caused the gates to be shut, saying that he must needs deliver the keys to the King. When he came before the King's presence, he kneeled down on his knees, beseeching him of mercy and forgiveness, and declaring the whole matter unto him in order as everything had passed, obtained pardon. Therewith came his father, and, being let in, delivered the indenture which he had taken from his son unto the King, who thereby perceiving his son's words to be true, changed his purpose for his going to Oxford.'

c. The death of King Richard (compare V.4 and V.5.96–120): 'Our writer, which seemeth to have great knowledge of King Richard's doings, saith that King Henry, sitting on a day at his table, sore sighing, said, "Have I no faithful friend which will deliver me of him whose life will be my death, and whose death will be the preservation of my life?" This saying was much noted of them which were present, and especially of one called Sir Piers of Exton. This knight incontinently departed from the court, with eight strong persons in his company, and came to Pomfret, commanding the esquire that was accustomed to sew and take the assay before King Richard, to do so no more, saying, "Let him eat now, for he shall not long eat." King Richard sat down to dinner, and was served without courtesy or assay, whereupon, much marveling at the sudden change, he demanded of the esquire why he did not his duty: "Sir (he said), I am otherwise commanded by Sir Piers of Exton, which is newly come from King Henry." When King Richard heard that word, he took the carving-knife in his hand, and struck the esquire on the head, saying, "The devil take Henry of Lancaster and you together!" And with that word Sir Piers entered the chamber, well armed, with eight tall men likewise armed, every of them having a bill in his hand.

'King Richard, perceiving this, put the table from him, and stepping to the foremost man, wrung the bill out of his hands, and so valiantly defended himself that he slew four of those that thus came to assail him. Sir Piers being half dismayed herewith, leapt into the chair where King Richard was wont to sit, while the other four persons fought with him, and chased him about the chamber. And in conclusion, as King Richard traversed his ground from one side of the chamber to another, and coming by the chair where Sir Piers stood, he was felled with a stroke of a pole-axe which Sir Piers gave him upon the head, and therewith rid him out of life, without giving him respite once to call to God for mercy of his passed offenses.'

In contrast to Wilson's view of Shakespeare's extreme indebtedness to his sources, see the sanely sceptical views of Peter Ure and Matthew W. Black.[22] The most comprehensive exposition of Shakespeare's possible sources is to be found in Black's *New Variorum Edition.*[23]

---

22 Ure's New Arden edition, pp. xxx–l, and Black's 'The Sources of Shakespeare's *Richard II*,' in *Joseph Quincy Adams Memorial Studies* (Washington, 1948), pp. 199–216.
23 Pp. 405–505.

ACT FIRST ❧ SCENE FIRST

Enter King Richard, John of Gaunt,
with other nobles and attendants.

King. Old John of Gaunt, time-honor'd Lancaster,
Hast thou, according to thy oath and band,
Brought hither Henry Herford, thy bold son,
Here to make good the boist'rous late appeal—
Which then our leisure would not let me hear—   *5*
Against the Duke of Norfolk, Thomas Mowbray?
  Gaunt. I have, my liege.
  King. Tell me, moreover, hast thou sounded him,
If he appeal the duke on ancient malice,
Or worthily, as a good subject should,   *10*
On some known ground of treachery in him?
  Gaunt. As near as I could sift him on that argument,
On some apparent danger seen in him
Aim'd at your highness, no inveterate malice.
  King. Then call them to our presence. Face to face,   *15*
And frowning brow to brow, ourselves will hear
The accuser and the accused freely speak.
High-stomach'd are they both, and full of ire,
In rage deaf as the sea, hasty as fire.

Enter Bullingbrooke and Mowbray.

  Bulling. Many years of happy days befall   *20*
My gracious sovereign, my most loving liege!
  Mowb. Each day still better others happiness,
Until the heavens, envying earth's good hap,
Add an immortal title to your crown!
  King. We thank you both. Yet one but flatters us,   *25*
As well appeareth by the cause you come;
Namely, to appeal each other of high treason.
Cousin of Herford, what dost thou object
Against the Duke of Norfolk, Thomas Mowbray?
  Bulling. First—heaven be the record to my speech!—   *30*
In the devotion of a subject's love,
Tend'ring the precious safety of my prince
And free from other misbegotten hate,
Come I appellant to this princely presence.
Now, Thomas Mowbray, do I turn to thee,   *35*
And mark my greeting well, for what I speak
My body shall make good upon this earth,
Or my divine soul answer it in heaven.
Thou art a traitor and a miscreant,
Too good to be so, and too bad to live,   *40*
Since the more fair and crystal is the sky,
The uglier seem the clouds that in it fly.
Once more, the more to aggravate the note,
With a foul traitor's name stuff I thy throat

And wish—so please my sovereign—ere I move,   *45*
What my tongue speaks, my right-drawn sword may prove.
  Mowb. Let not my cold words here accuse my zeal.
'Tis not the trial of a woman's war,
The bitter clamor of two eager tongues,
Can arbitrate this cause betwixt us twain.   *50*
The blood is hot that must be cool'd for this.
Yet can I not of such tame patience boast
As to be hush'd and naught at all to say.
First, the fair reverence of your highness curbs me
From giving reins and spurs to my free speech,   *55*
Which else would post until it had return'd
These terms of treason doubled down his throat.
Setting aside his high blood's royalty,
And let him be no kinsman to my liege,
I do defy him, and I spit at him,   *60*
Call him a slanderous coward and a villain;
Which to maintain I would allow him odds
And meet him, were I tied to run afoot
Even to the frozen ridges of the Alps,
Or any other ground inhabitable,   *65*
Where ever Englishman durst set his foot.
Meantime let this defend my loyalty—
By all my hopes most falsely doth he lie.
  Bulling. Pale trembling, coward, there I throw my gage,
Disclaiming here the kinred of the king,   *70*
And lay aside my high blood's royalty,
Which fear, not reverence, makes thee to except.
If guilty dread have left thee so much strength
As to take up mine honor's pawn, then stoop.
By that, and all the rites of knighthood else,   *75*
Will I make good against thee, arm to arm,
What I have spoke, or thou canst worse devise.
  Mowb. I take it up, and by that sword I swear
Which gently laid my knighthood on my shoulder,
I'll answer thee in any fair degree   *80*
Or chivalrous design of knightly trial;
And when I mount, alive may I not light,
If I be traitor or unjustly fight!
  King. What doth our cousin lay to Mowbray's charge?
It must be great that can inherit us   *85*
So much as of a thought of ill in him.
  Bulling. Look, what I speak, my life shall prove it true:
That Mowbray hath receiv'd eight thousand nobles
In name of lendings for your highness' soldiers,
The which he hath detain'd for lewd employments,   *90*
Like a false traitor and injurious villain.
Besides I say, and will in battle prove,
Or here or elsewhere to the furthest verge
That ever was survey'd by English eye,

ACT FIRST, SCENE FIRST; *cf. n.* **SD. King Richard**; *cf. n*   **1 John of Gaunt**; *cf. n.*   **2 band**: *bond*   **3 Herford**: *disyllabic* (read *'her-'* or *'har-'*); *cf. n.*   **4 late**: *six weeks previously* **appeal**: *accusation or challenge*   **9 appeal**: *accuse,* **on ancient malice**: *because of long-standing enmity*   **12 As near … argument**; *cf. n.* **sift**: *examine* **argument**: *subject*   **14 inveterate**: *trisyllabic*   **17 The accuser and the accused**: *read 'th' accuser and th' accuséd'*   **18 High-stomach'd**: *haughty*   **20 Bullingbrooke**: *Henry Bolingbroke, Duke of Hereford* (see I.l.3; *cf. n.*); *cf. n.* **Many … befall**; *cf. n.*   **22 better other's**: *make better the previous day's*   **23 heavens**: *monosyllabic* **envying**: *stressed — ⌣ —* (rhymes with 'replying')   **24 Add … crown**: *add immortality to kingship*   **27 to appeal**: *read 't' appeal'*   **32 Tend'ring**: *caring dearly for*   **34 appellant**; *cf. n.*   **40 good**: *i.e. high in rank*   **43 aggravate the note**: *increase the insult* **note**: *brand or stigma of disgrace* (from Latin *nota*).

46 right-drawn: *drawn in a rightful cause*   **47 accuse**: *cast doubt upon*   **49 eager**: *sharp, biting* (from French *aigre*)   **51 cool'd**: *i.e. by death*   **54 reverence of**: *respect for*   **56 post**: *speed*   **57 These terms of treason**: *i.e. traitor and miscreant* (l. 39). **doubled**: *F doubly.* (F refers throughout to the First Folio of 1623, F2 to the Second Folio, etc.).   **58 royalty**: *Bolingbroke was the king's first cousin*   **59 let him be**: *assuming that he is*   **63 tied**: *obliged, bound; cf. n.*   **64 Even**: *read 'e'en'* (as elsewhere)   **65 inhabitable**: *uninhabitable*   **67 this**: *i.e. the statement in l. 68*   **68 hopes**: *i.e. hopes of salvation*   **69 gage**: *pledge* (probably his iron glove or gauntlet).   **70 Disclaiming**: *renouncing* **kinred**: *old form of 'kindred'* **the king**: *other Qq, F a King*   **72 to except**: *take exception to, protest against*   **74 pawn**: *the gage* (l. 69).   **75 rites**: *F2 rights.* **else**: *besides this*   **77 thou … devise**; *cf. n.*   **80 in any fair degree**: *to any extent compatible with chivalric code*   **82 light**: *alight*   **85-86 inherit … thought**: *make us have as much as a thought*   **89 lendings**: *money advanced in lieu of regular pay*   **90 lewd**: *base, mean*   **91 injurious**: *pernicious*   **93 Or here or**: *either here or* **verge**: *boundary*

That all the treasons for these eighteen years   95
Complotted and contrived in this land
Fetch from false Mowbray their first head and spring.
Further I say, and further will maintain
Upon his bad life to make all this good,
That he did plot the Duke of Gloucester's death,   100
Suggest his soon-believing adversaries,
And consequently, like a traitor coward,
Sluic'd out his innocent soul through streams of blood,
Which blood, like sacrificing Abel's, cries,
Even from the tongueless caverns of the earth,   105
To me for justice and rough chastisement.
And by the glorious worth of my descent,
This arm shall do it, or this life be spent.
    King. How high a pitch his resolution soars!
Thomas of Norfolk, what say'st thou to this?   110
    Mowb. O, let my sovereign turn away his face,
And bid his ears a little while be deaf,
Till I have told this slander of his blood
How God and good men hate so foul a liar!
    King. Mowbray, impartial are our eyes and ears.   115
Were he my brother, nay, my kingdom's heir,
As he is but my father's brother's son,
Now, by my scepter's awe, I make a vow,
Such neighbor nearness to our sacred blood
Should nothing privilege him, nor partialize   120
The unstooping firmness of my upright soul.
He is our subject, Mowbray, so art thou.
Free speech and fearless I to thee allow.
    Mowb. Then, Bullingbrooke, as low as to thy heart,
Through the false passage of thy throat, thou liest!   125
Three parts of that receipt I had for Callice
Disburs'd I duly to his highness' soldiers.
The other part reserv'd I by consent,
For that my sovereign liege was in my debt
Upon remainder of a dear account   130
Since last I went to France to fetch his queen.
Now swallow down that lie! For Gloucester's death,
I slew him not, but to my own disgrace
Neglected my sworn duty in that case.
For you, my noble Lord of Lancaster,   135
The honorable father to my foe,
Once did I lay an ambush for your life—
A trespass that doth vex my grieved soul.
But ere I last receiv'd the sacrament
I did confess it, and exactly begg'd   140
Your grace's pardon, and I hope I had it.
This is my fault. As for the rest appeal'd,

It issues from the rancor of a villain,
A recreant and most degenerate traitor;
Which in myself I boldly will defend,   145
And interchangeably hurl down my gage
Upon this overweening traitor's foot,
To prove myself a loyal gentleman
Even in the best blood chamber'd in his bosom.
In haste whereof, most heartily I pray   150
Your highness to assign our trial day.
    King. Wrath-kindled gentlemen, he rul'd by me;
Let's purge this choler without letting blood.
This we prescribe, though no physician;
Deep malice makes too deep incision.   155
Forget, forgive, conclude and be agreed;
Our doctors say this is no month to bleed.
Good uncle, let this end where it begun;
We'll calm the Duke of Norfolk, you your son.
    Gaunt. To be a make-peace shall become my age.   160
Throw down, my son, the Duke of Norfolk's gage.
    King. And, Norfolk, throw down his.
    Gaunt.   When, Harry? When?
Obedience bids I should not bid again.
    King. Norfolk, thrown down, we bid. There is no boot.   165
    Mowb. Myself I throw, dread sovereign, at thy foot.
My life thou shalt command but not my shame.
The one my duty owes, but my fair name,
Despite of death that lives upon my grave,
To dark dishonor's use thou shalt not have.   170
I am disgrac'd, impeach'd, and baffled here;
Pierc'd to the soul with Slander's venom'd spear,
The which no balm can cure but his heart-blood
Which breath'd this poison.
    King.   Rage must be withstood.   175
Give me his gage; lions make leopards tame.
    Mowb. Yea, but not change his spots. Take but my shame,
And I resign my gage. My dear lord,
The purest treasure mortal times afford
Is spotless reputation. That away,   180
Men are but gilded loam or painted clay.
A jewel in a ten-times-barr'd-up chest
Is a bold spirit in a loyal breast.
Mine honor is my life, both grow in one;
Take honor from me and my life is done.   185
Then, dear my liege, mine honor let me try.
In that I live, and for that will I die.
    King. Cousin, throw up your gage. Do you begin.
    Bulling. O, God defend my soul from such deep sin!
Shall I seem crestfallen in my father's sight?   190
Or with pale beggar-fear impeach my height

---

95 **these eighteen years:** *i.e. since Wat Tyler's insurrection in 1381*   97 **Fetch:** *derive; other Qq Fetcht; F Fetch'd*   98 **maintain:** *undertake*   100 **Duke of Gloucester's death;** *cf. n.*
101–103 **Suggest ... blood;** *cf. n.*   101 **Suggest ... adversaries:** *did secretly incite his credulous enemies against him*   102 **consequently:** *subsequently*   106 **me:** *as Gaunt's eldest son and Gloucester's nephew*   107 **worth:** *honor*   108 **or:** *perhaps meaning 'before' (see I.I.77; cf. n.)*   109 **pitch:** *high point of a falcon's flight (a term in falconry)*   113 **this slander ... blood:** *i.e. this man (Hereford) who is a disgrace to his ancestry*   116 **my kingdom's:** *Four kingdomes*   118 **my:** *F; not in Qq*   **my scepter's awe:** *by the honor due my scepter*   119 **neighbor nearness;** *cf. n.*   **sacred blood;** *cf. n.*   120 **nothing:** *not at all*   **partialize:** *make partial*   124 **as low ... heart:** *from the bottom of your base heart*   126 **that receipt ... Callice:** *the money received from the Calais garrison*   **Callice:** *Calais (pronounced 'Cal'iss')*   129 **For that:** *because (as frequently)*   130 **Upon remainder ... account:** *as part balance of a heavy debt you owe me*   131 **last:** *lately*   **queen;** *cf. n.*   132 **For:** *as for (also in l. 135).*   135–141 **For you ... it;** *cf. n.*   139 **But:** *Q (Huth); F; Q (Devonshire, Capell, Petworth), Q2, Q3 Ah but; Q4, Q5 Ah, but (Q refers throughout to the First Quarto of 1597, Q2 to the Second Quarto, etc.)*   140 **exactly:** *explicitly*

144 **recreant:** *one false to his faith (or perhaps an adjective).*   **degenerate:** *(trisyllabic) degenerated from his race or blood*   145 **Which:** *i.e. the assertion of l.144*   **in myself:** *in my own person*   146 **interchangeably:** *in exchange for Bolingbroke's challenge*   150 **In haste whereof:** *to hasten which proof*   152 **gentleman:** *F Gentlemen*   153 **choler:** *anger; cf. n.*   154 **physician:** *four syllables (like incision in the next line)*   156 **conclude:** *come to terms*   157 **no month to bleed;** *cf. n.*   158 **begun:** *began*   164 **Obedience bids:** *Qq, F mistakenly print the words twice in ll. 163–164*   165 **no boot:** *no help, i.e. no use resisting*   169 **that:** *antecedent: name (l. 167)*   171 **impeach'd:** *accused*   **baffled:** *utterly dishonored*   174 **Which:** *who (antecedent: his, meaning 'of him').*   **breath'd:** *uttered*   176 **lions ... leopards;** *cf. n.*   177 **change his spots:** *see Jeremiah 13:23 (which Mowbray has in mind)*   178 **gage. My dear;** *cf. n.*   179 **mortal times:** *earthly life*   186 **try:** *test by combat*   188 **throw up:** *surrender the gage, give up the challenge; Qq; F throw downe; cf. n.*   189 **God:** *Qq; F heauen*   **deep:** *Qq; F foule*   191 **beggar-fear:** *fear befitting a miserable beggar; Q, F; other Qq beggr-face*   **impeach my height:** *call in question my high name and rank*

Before this outdar'd dastard? Ere my tongue
Shall wound my honor with such feeble wrong,
Or sound so base a parle, my teeth shall tear
The slavish motive of recanting fear   *195*
And spit it bleeding in his high disgrace,
Where shame doth harbor, even in Mowbray's face.

                                                        [Exit Gaunt.]

   King. We were not born to sue, but to command,
Which since we cannot do to make you friends,
Be ready, as your lives shall answer it,   *200*
At Coventry upon Saint Lambert's day.
There shall your swords and lances arbitrate
The swelling difference of your settled hate.
Since we cannot atone you, we shall see
Justice design the victor's chivalry.   *205*
Lord Marshal, command our officers at arms
Be ready to direct these home alarms.   *[Exeunt.]*

❧ Scene Second ❧

Enter John of Gaunt with the Duchess of Gloucester

   Gaunt. Alas, the part I had in Woodstock's blood
Doth more solicit me than your exclaims
To stir against the butchers of his life!
But since correction lieth in those hands
Which made the fault that we cannot correct,   *5*
Put we our quarrel to the will of heaven,
Who, when they see the hours ripe on earth,
Will rain hot vengeance of offenders' heads.
   Duch. Finds brotherhood in thee no sharper spur?
Hath love in thy old blood no living fire?   *10*
Edward's seven sons, whereof thyself art one,
Were as seven vials of his sacred blood,
Or seven fair branches springing from one root.
Some of those seven are dried by nature's course,
Some of the branches by the Destinies cut;   *15*
But Thomas, my dear lord, my life, my Gloucester,
One vial full of Edward's sacred blood,
One flourishing branch of his most royal root,
Is crack'd, and all the precious liquor split,
Is hack'd down, and his summer leaves all faded,   *20*
By Envy's hand and Murder's bloody ax.
Ah, Gaunt, his blood was thine! That bed, that womb,
That metal, that self-mold that fashioned thee
Made him a man; and though thou liv'st and breath'st,
Yet art thou slain in him. Thou dost consent   *25*
In some large measure to thy father's death
In that thou seest thy wretched brother die,
Who was the model of thy father's life.

Call it not patience, Gaunt; it is despair.
In suff'ring thus thy brother to be slaught'red,   *30*
Thou show'st the naked pathway to thy life,
Teaching stern Murder how to butcher thee.
That which in mean men we entitle patience
Is pale cold cowardice in noble breasts.
What shall I say? To safeguard thine own life,   *35*
The best way is to venge my Gloucester's death.
   Gaunt. God's is the quarrel; for God's substitute,
His deputy anointed in His sight,
Hath caus'd his death; the which if wrongfully,
Let heaven revenge; for I may never lift   *40*
An angry arm against His minister.
   Duch. Where then, alas, may I complain myself?
   Gaunt. To God, the widow's champion and defense.
   Duch. Why then, I will. Farewell, old Gaunt.
Thou goest to Coventry, there to behold   *45*
Our cousin Herford and fell Mowbray fight.
O, sit my husband's wrongs on Herford's spear,
That it may enter butcher Mowbray's breast!
Or if misfortune miss the first career,
Be Mowbray's sins so heavy in his bosom   *50*
That they may break his foaming courser's back
And throw the rider headlong in the lists,
A caitiff recreant to my cousin Herford!
Farewell, old Gaunt. Thy sometimes brother's wife
With her companion, Grief, must end her life.   *55*
   Gaunt. Sister, farewell; I must to Coventry.
As much good stay with thee, as go with me.
   Duch. Yet one word more. Grief boundeth where it falls,
Not with the empty hollowness, but weight.
I take my leave before I have begun,   *60*
For sorrow ends not when it seemeth done.
Commend me to thy brother, Edmund York.
Lo, this is all. Nay, yet depart not so.
Though this be all, do not so quickly go.
I shall remember more. Bid him—ah, what?—   *65*
With all good speed at Plashie visit me.
Alack, and what shall good old York there see
But empty lodgings and unfurnish'd walls,
Unpeopled offices, untrodden stones?
And what hear there for welcome but my groans?   *70*
Therefore commend me. Let him not come there
To seek out sorrow that dwells everywhere.
Desolate, desolate, will I hence and die.
The last leave of thee takes my weeping eye.   *Exeunt.*

---

193 feeble wrong: *i.e. of speaking in so weak and craven a tone*   **194 sound . . . parle;** *cf. n.*   **195 motive:** *instrument, i.e. the tongue*   **196 his:** *its* (or possibly Mowbray's) **SD. Exit Gaunt;** *cf. n.*   **201 Saint Lambert's day:** *September 17, celebrating the early 8th-century martyr*   **203 of:** *resulting from*   **204 atone:** *reconcile (make 'at one')* **we shall:** *Q; other Qq, F* you shall   **205 design . . . chivalry:** *designate the knight whose prowess will prevail*   **206 Marshal;** *cf. n.*   **207 home alarms:** *civil conflicts* (in contrast to the Irish rebellion perhaps hinted at here).   **1 the part . . . blood:** *my fraternal relationship to Woodstock* **Woodstock's:** *of Thomas of Woodstock, late Duke of Gloucester; F* Glousters blood; *cf. n.*   **2 solicit:** *rouse*   **4 those hands:** *i.e. Richard's*   **6 Put . . . to:** *let us entrust our cause to* **heaven:** *i.e. heavenly powers (frequently a plural in Shakespeare)*   **7 they:** *i.e. heaven (l. 6)*   **11 Edward's seven sons;** *cf. n.*   **14–21 Some . . . ax;** *cf. n.*   **14 Some . . . dried:** *some of the seven vials are empty, i.e. some of the sons are dead*   **21 Envy's hand:** *i.e. the hand of malice*   **23 self-mold:** *selfsame mold*

29 patience: *self-control*   **30 suff'ring:** *enduring* **slaught'red;** *cf. n.*   **31 naked:** *exposed, as to an enemy*   **33 mean:** *of low birth*   **37 God's substitute:** *i.e. Richard*   **38 anointed:** *with holy oil, in the coronation ceremony*   **40 may:** *can, must*   **42 Where:** *to whom* **then, alas, may:** *Q (Devonshire, Petworth); Q (Hush, Capell), other Qq, F then may; cf. n.*   **43 God:** *Qq; F* heauen (see I.i.187; *cf. n*)   **44 Why then . . . Gaunt;** *cf. n.*   **46 cousin:** *Hereford was her nephew and brother-in-law; cf. n.*   **49 misfortune:** *i.e. to Mowbray.* **career:** *charge (a technical term in jousting)*   **53 caitiff recreant to:** *a false and wretched coward vanquished by*   **54 sometimes:** *sometime, former*   **55 end:** *live out*   **58-59 Grief . . . weight;** *cf. n.*   **58 it:** *Q2; Q* is   **59 empty:** *Q (Devonshire, Petworth), other Qq; Q (Hugh, Capell), F* emptines   **60 begun:** *i.e. begun my lamenting*   **62 thy:** *other Qq, F* my   **66 Plashie:** *Qq, F; Pleshy, Gloucester's country residence in Essex*   **68 unfurnish'd:** *not hung with tapestries (or possibly without furniture)*   **70 hear:** *Q (Devonshire, Petworth), other Qq, F; Q (Huth, Capell)* cheere   **73 Desolate:** *disyllabic* **will I hence:** *I will hence*

❧ SCENE THIRD ❧

Enter the Lord Marshal and the Duke of Aumerle.

Mar. My lord Aumerle, is Harry Herford arm'd?
Aum. Yea, at all points, and longs to enter in.
Mar. The Duke of Norfolk, sprightfully and bold,
Stays but the summons of the appellant's trumpet.
 Aum. Why, then, the champions are prepar'd, and stay 5
For nothing but his majesty's approach.

The trumpets sound and the King enters with his nobles
[Gaunt, Bushy, Bagot, Green, and others]. When they are set,
enter [Mowbray,] the Duke of Norfolk in arms, defendant
[and herald].

 King. Marshal, demand of yonder champion
The cause of his arrival here in arms.
Ask him his name, and orderly proceed
To swear him in the justice of his cause. 10
 Mar. In God's name and the king's, say who thou art,
And why thou com'st thus knightly clad in arms,
Against what man thou com'st, and what thy quarrel.
Speak truly on thy knighthood and thy oath,
As so defend thee heaven and thy valor! 15
 Mowb. My name is Thomas Mowbray, Duke of Norfolk,
Who hither come engaged by my oath—
Which God defend a knight should violate!—
Both to defend my loyalty and truth
To God, my kind, and my succeeding issue 20
Against the Duke of Herford that appeals me;
And, by the grace of God and this mine arm,
To prove him, in defending of myself,
A traitor to my God, my king, and me.
And as I truly fight, defend me heaven! 25

The trumpets sound. Enter [Bullingbrooke,] the Duke of
Herford, appellant, in armor [, and herald].

 King. Marshal, ask yonder knight in arms
Both who he is and why he cometh hither
Thus plated in habiliments of war;
And formally according to our law,
Depose him in the justice of his cause. 30
 Mar. What is thy name? And wherefore com'st thou hither
Before King Richard in his royal lists?
Against whom comest thou? And what's thy quarrel?
Speak like a true knight, so defend thee heaven!
 Bulling. Harry of Herford, Lancaster, and Darby 35
Am I, who ready here do stand in arms
To prove, by God's grace and my body's valor,
In lists, on Thomas Mowbray, Duke of Norfolk,
That he is a traitor, foul and dangerous,
To God of heaven, King Richard, and to me. 40
And as I truly fight, defend me heaven.
 Mar. On pain of death, no person be so bold

Or daring-hardy as to touch the lists,
Except the Marshal and such officers
Appointed to direct these fair designs. 45
 Bulling. Lord Marshall, let me kiss my sovereign's hand
And bow my knee before his majesty;
For Mowbray and myself are like two men
That vow a long and weary pilgrimage.
Then let us take a ceremonious leave 50
And loving farewell of our several friends.
 Mar. The appellant in all duty greets your highness
And craves to kiss your hand and take his leave.
 King. We will descend and fold him in our arms.
Cousin of Herford, as they cause is right, 55
So be thy fortune in this royal fight!
Farewell, my blood, which if today thou shed,
Lament we may, but not revenge thee dead.
 Bulling. O, let no noble eye profane a tear
For me if I be gor'd with Mowbray's spear. 60
As confident as is the falcon's flight
Against a bird, do I with Mowbray fight.
My loving lord, I take my leave of you,
Of you, my noble cousin, Lord Aumerle;
Not sick, although I have to do with death, 65
But lusty, young, and cheerly drawing, breath.
Lo, as at English feasts, so I regreet
The daintiest last, to make the end most sweet.
O thou, the earthly author of my blood,
Whose youthful spirit, in me regenerate, 70
Doth with a twofold vigor lift me up
To reach at victory above my head,
Add proof unto mine armor with thy prayers,
And with thy blessings steel my lance's point,
That it may enter Mowbray's waxen coat 75
And furbish new the name of John a Gaunt
Even in the lusty havior of his son.
 Gaunt. God in thy good cause make thee prosperous!
Be swift like lightning in the execution,
And let thy blows, doubly redoubled, 80
Fall like amazing thunder on the casque
Of thy adverse pernicious enemy.
Rouse up thy youthful blood; be valiant and live.
 Bulling. Mine innocence and Saint George to thrive!
 Mowb. However God or fortune cast my lot, 85
There lives or dies, true to King Richard's throne,
A loyal, just, and upright gentleman.
Never did captive with a freer heart
Cast off his chains of bondage and embrace
His golden uncontroll'd enfranchisement, 90
More than my dancing soul doth celebrate
This feast of battle with mine adversary.
Most mighty liege, and my companion peers,
Take from my mouth the wish of happy years.
As gentle and as jocund as to jest 95

SD Marshal: *on this occasion, the Duke of Surrey, Aumerle on this occasion, High Constable of England*   **3 sprightfully and bold:** *with spirit and courage*   **4 the appellant's:** *read 'th' appellant's' (also in l. 52)*   **SD enter Mowbray:** *cf. n.*   **7 champion:** *trisyllabic*   **9 orderly:** *according to rule*   **10 swear him in:** *have him to take an oath as to*   **11 say who thou art;** *cf. n.*   **13 quarrel:** *complaint (a legal term)*   **15 As so defend;** *cf. n.*   **18 defend:** *forbid (compare French défendre)*   **20 my succeeding;** *cf. n.*   **28 plated:** *clad in plate armor; F placed*   **30 Depose:** *take his sworn statement (deposition)*   **33 comest:** *Q5; other Qq comes; F com'st*   **35 Darby:** *Derby (pronounced 'Darby')*   **39 he is:** *read 'he's' as F*

43 daring-hardy: *one of Shakespeare's compounded adjectives; Qq daring, hardy; F daring hardie*   **49 vow . . . pilgrimage:** *ironic prophecy of the double exile*   **51 several friends:** *friends one by one, or respective friends*   **57 blood:** *kinsman*   **66 cheerly:** *cheerily*   **67 regreet:** *greet*   **70 spirit:** *monosyllabic* **regenerate:** *regenerated*   **73 proof:** *capacity to resist weapons*   **75 waxen:** *i.e. easy to penetrate*   **76 furbish new:** *add new glory or luster to; F furnish new* **a Gaunt:** *(of) Gaunt*   **80 redoubled:** *four syllables*   **82 adverse:** *stressed* — *⌣́*; *F amaz'd (probably a printer's error)*   **83 Rouse . . . live:** *an alexandrine*   **84 Mine . . . George;** *cf. n.* **thrive:** *i.e. make me victorious*   **90 enfranchisement:** *release*   **95 gentle:** *calm* **jest:** *play, sport*

Go I to fight. Truth hath a quiet breast.

   King. Farewell, my lord. Securely I espy
Virtue with valor couched in thine eye.
Order the trial, Marshal, and begin.

   Mar. Harry of Herford, Lancaster, and Darby,   *100*
Receive thy lance, and God defend the right!

   Bulling. Strong as a tower in hope, I cry amen.

   Mar. Go bear this lance to Thomas, Duke of Norfolk.

   1. Herald. Harry of Herford, Lancaster, and Darby
Stands here for God, his sovereign, and himself,   *105*
On pain to be found false and recreant,
To prove the Duke of Norfolk, Thomas Mowbray,
A traitor to his God, his king, and him,
And dares him to set forward to the fight.

   2. Herald. Here standeth Thomas Mowbray, Duke   *110*
of Norfolk,
On pain to be found false and recreant,
Both to defend himself and to approve
Henry of Herford, Lancaster, and Darby
To God, his sovereign, and to him disloyal,   *115*
Courageously and with a free desire
Attending but the signal to begin.

   Mar. Sound trumpets and set forward combatants.

                    [A charge sounded.]
Stay! The king hath thrown his warder down.

   King. Let them lay by their helmets and their spears   *120*
And both return back to their chairs again.
Withdraw with us, and let the trumpets sound
While we return these dukes what we decree.

                     [A long flourish.]
Draw near,
And list what with our council we have done.   *125*
For that our kingdom's earth should not be soil'd
With that dear blood which it hath fostered;
And for our eyes do hate the dire aspect
Of civil wounds plough'd up with neighbors' sword;
And for we think the eagle-winged pride   *130*
Of sky-aspiring and ambitious thoughts
With rival-hating envy set on you
To wake our peace, which is in our country's cradle
Draws the sweet infant breath of gentle sleep;
Which so rous'd up with boist'rous untun'd drums,   *135*
With harsh-resounding trumpets' dreadful bray
And grating shock of wrathful iron arms,
Might from our quiet confines fright fair peace
And make us wade even in our kindred's blood;
Therefore we banish you our territories.   *140*
You, cousin Herford, upon pain of life,
Till twice five summers have enrich'd our fields,
Shall not regreet our fair dominions
But tread the stranger paths of banishment.

   Bulling. Your will be done. This must my comfort be— *145*
That sun that warms you here shall shine on me,

And those his golden beams to you here lent
Shall point on me and gild my banishment.

   King. Norfolk, for thee remains a heavier doom,
Which I with some unwillingness pronounce: *150*
The sly slow hours shall not determinate
The dateless limit of thy dear exile.
The hopeless word of 'never to return'
Breathe I against thee, upon pain of life.

   Mowb. A heavy sentence, my most sovereign liege,   *155*
And all unlook'd for from your highness' mouth.
A dearer merit, not so deep a maim
As to be cast forth in the common air,
Have I deserved at your highness' hands.
The language I have learnt these forty years,   *160*
My native English, now I must forgo;
And now my tongue's use is to me no more
Than an unstringed viol or a harp,
Or like a cunning instrument cas'd up
Or, being open, put into his hands   *165*
That knows no touch to tune the harmony.
Within my mouth you have enjail'd my tongue,
Doubly portcullis'd with my teeth and lips;
And dull, unfeeling, barren ignorance
Is made my jailer to attend on me.   *170*
I am too old to fawn upon a nurse,
Too far in years to be a pupil now.
What is thy sentence then but speechless death,
Which robs my tongue from breathing native breath?

   King. It boots thee not to be compassionate.   *175*
After our sentence plaining comes too late.

   Mowb. Then thus I turn me from my country's light
To dwell in solemn shades of endless night.

   King. Return again, and take an oath with thee.
Lay on our royal sword your banish'd hands,   *180*
Swear by the duty that you owe to God—
Our part therein we banish with yourselves—
To keep the oath that we administer:
You never shall, so help you truth and God,
Embrace each other's love in banishment;   *185*
Nor never look upon each other's face;
Nor never write, regreet, nor reconcile
This low'ring tempest of your home-bred hate;
Nor never by advised purpose meet
To plot, contrive, or complot any ill   *190*
'Gainst us, our state, our subjects, or our land.

   Bulling. I swear.

   Mowb. And I, to keep all this.

   Bulling. Norfolk, so far as to mine enemy:
By this time, had the king permitted us,   *195*
One of our souls had wand'red in the air,
Banish'd this frail sepulcher of our flesh
As now our flesh is banish'd from this land.
Confess thy treasons ere thou fly the realm.
Since thou hast far to go, bear not along   *200*
The clogging burthen of a guilty soul.

97 Securely: *confidently* (or possibly modifying *couched*).   **108 his God:** *Q (Devonshire, Petworth), other Qq, F; Q (Capell, Huth) God*   **113 approve:** *prove*   **119 warder:** *staff* **down:** *i.e. to stop the contest*   **123 While . . . decree:** *until I announce to these dukes my decision*   **124–125 Draw . . . list:** *one line in Q, F*   **124 Draw near:** *the short line gives the dukes time to approach*   **126 For that:** *in order that*   **128 for:** *because* **aspect:** *stressed — ─*   **129 civil:** *Q (Devonshire, Petworth), other Qq, F; Q (Huth, Capell) cruell*   **130–134 And for . . . sleep:** *not in F*   **132 envy:** *enmity* **set on you:** *set you on*   **133 wake:** *disturb*   **134 infant . . . sleep:** *i.e. peace of short duration*   **135 Which:** *antecedent: sleep* **untun'd:** *discordant*   **138 confines:** *territories*   **143 regreet:** *salute again (unlike l.3.67)* **dominions:** *four syllables*   **144 stranger:** *foreign*

149 doom: *sentence*   **151 determinate:** *set a limit to (a legal term)*   **152 dear:** *grievous* **exile:** *stressed — ─ (also in l. 219)*   **160 forty:** *a round figure (Mowbray is nearer thirty now)*   **164 cunning:** *i.e. made and played with skill*   **166 That:** *who*   **173 then:** *F; not in Qq*   **174 Which:** *antecedent: thy sentence*   **175 compassionate:** *appealing for pity*   **180 on . . . sword:** *i.e. on the cross hilt (also forms a Christian cross)*   **181 you owe:** *F; Qq y'owe*   **182 Our part therein:** *my share in your duty*   **194 so far . . . enemy:** *cf. n.*   **197 sepulcher:** *stressed — ─ —*   **201 burthen:** *burden*

Mowb. No, Bullingbrooke. If ever I were traitor,
My name be blotted from the book of life
And I from heaven banish'd as from hence!
But what thou art, God, thou, and I do know,   205
And all too soon, I fear, the king shall rue.
Farewell, my liege. Now no way can I stray.
Save back to England, all the world's my way.   *Exit.*
    King. Uncle, even in the glasses of thine eyes
I see thy grieved heart. Thy sad aspect   210
Hath from the number of this banish'd years
Pluck'd four away. *[To Bullingbrooke.]* Six frozen winters
   spent,
Return with welcome home from banishment.
    Bulling. How long a time lies in one little word!   215
Four lagging winters and four wanton springs
End in a word. Such is the breath of kings.
    Gaunt. I thank my liege that in regard of me
He shortens four years of my son's exile.
But little vantage shall I reap thereby,   220
For eare the six years that he hath to spend
Can change their moons and bring their times about,
My oil-dried lamp and time-bewasted light
Shall be extinct with age and endless night,
My inch of taper will be burnt and done,   225
And blindfold Death not let me see my son.
    King. Why, uncle, thou hast many years to live.
    Gaunt. But not a minute, king, that thou canst give.
Shorten my days thou canst with sullen sorrow
And pluck nights from me, but not lend a morrow.   230
Thou canst help time to furrow me with age,
But stop no wrinkle in his pilgrimage.
Thy word is current with him for my death,
But dead, thy kingdom cannot buy my breath.
    King. Thy son is banish'd upon good advice,   235
Whereto thy tongue a party-verdict gave.
Why at our justice seem'st thou then to lower?
    Gaunt. Things sweet to taste prove in digestion sour.
You urg'd me as a judge, but I had rather
You would have bid me argue like a father.   240
O, had it been a stranger, not my child,
To smooth his fault I should have been more mild.
A partial slander sought I to avoid,
And in the sentence my own life destroy'd.
Alas, I look'd when some of you should say   245
I was too strict to make mine own away,
But you gave leave to my unwilling tongue
Against my will to do myself this wrong.
    King. Cousin, farewell; and, uncle, bid him so.
Six years we banish him, and he shall go.   250
            [Flourish.] Exit [King Richard with train].
    Aum. Cousin, farewell. What presence must not know,
From where you do remain let paper show.
    Mar. My lord, no leave take I; for I will ride
As far as land will let me, by your side.

    Gaunt. O, to what purpose dost thou hoard thy words   255
That thou return'st no greeting to thy friends?
    Bulling. I have too few to take my leave of you,
When the tongue's office should be prodigal.
To breathe the abundant dolor of the heart.
    Gaunt. Thy grief is but thy absence for a time.   260
    Bulling. Joy absent, grief is present for that time.
    Gaunt. What is six winters? They are quickly gone.
    Bulling. To men in joy; but grief makes one hour ten.
    Gaunt. Call it a travel that thou tak'st for pleasure.
    Bulling. My heart will sigh when I miscall it so,   265
Which finds it an enforced pilgrimage.
    Gaunt. The sullen passage of thy weary steps
Esteem as foil wherein thou art to set
The precious jewel of thy home return.
    Bulling. Nay, rather every tedious stride I make   270
Will but remember me what a deal of world
I wander from the jewels that I love.
Must I not serve a long apprenticehood
To foreign passages, and in the end,
Having my freedom, boast of nothing else   275
But that I was a journeyman to grief?
    Gaunt. All places that the eye of heaven visits
And to a wise man ports and happy havens.
Teach thy necessity to reason thus:
There is no virtue like necessity.   280
Think not the king did banish thee,
But thou the king. Woe doth the heavier sit
Where it perceives it is but faintly borne.
Go, say I sent thee forth to purchase honor,
And not the king exil'd thee. Or suppose   285
Devouring pestilence hangs in our air
And thou art flying to a fresher clime.
Look what thy soul holds dear, imagine it
To lie that way thou goest, not whence thou com'st.
Suppose the singing birds musicians,   290
The grass whereon thou tread'st the presence strow'd,
The flowers fair ladies, and thy steps no more
Than a delightful measure or a dance;
For gnarling sorrow hath less power to bite
The man that mocks at it and sets it light.   295
    Bulling. O, who can hold a fire in his hand
By thinking on the frosty Caucasus?
Or cloy the hungry edge of appetite
By bare imagination of a feast?
Or wallow naked in December snow   300
By thinking on fantastic summer's heat?
O, no! The apprehension of the good
Gives but the greater feeling to the worse.
Fell Sorrow's tooth doth never rankle more
Than when he bites, but lanceth not the sore.   305
    Gaunt. Come, come, my son, I'll bring thee on thy way.
Had I thy youth and cause, I would not stay.

---

203 blotted . . . life: *compare Revelation 3:5*   **209 glasses:** *mirrors*   **210 aspect:** *stressed* — ́   **212 Pluck'd four away:** *cf. n.*   **216 wanton:** *luxuriant* (sportive, possibly)   **221 eare:** *e'er* (ever)   **222 bring their times about:** *cause their seasons to come around*   **224 night:** *Q4, F; Q* nightes   **233 is current:** *passes current, is valid*   **him:** *i.e. time*   **235 good advice:** *full consideration*   **236 party-verdict:** *assent*   **241–243 O . . . destroy'd:** *not in F*   **To smooth:** *in palliating*   **243 partial slander:** *charge of bias*   **sought:** *Q* (Devonshire, Huth), *Q 3–5; Q* (Capell, Petworth), *Q2* ought   **SD. Flourish . . . train:** *cf. n.*   **251–252 What . . . show:** *cf. n.*

259 the abundant: *read* 'th' abundant   **264 travel:** *F; Qq* trauaile (common Elizabethan spelling; here also a pun)   **266 Which finds:** *since it finds*   **267 sullen:** *slow and melancholy*   **268 foil:** *F* soyle (common confusion of *f* and long *s*) *cf. n.*   **270–295 Nay . . . light:** *not in F*   **271 remember . . . world:** *remind me how far*   **274 passages:** *wanderings*   **276 journeyman:** *artisan* (also a quibble for 'traveler' as 'journeyer')   **277–278 heaven . . . havens:** *a pun* (the words were pronounced alike)   **285 exil'd:** *stressed* — ́   **290 musicians:** *four syllables*   **291 strow'd:** *strewed cf. n.*   **293 measure:** *stately dance, or dancing figure*   **294 gnarling:** *snarling, growling*   **294 fire:** *disyllabic*   **301 fantastic:** *imaginary*   **303 greater . . . worse:** *greater poignancy to evil things*   **304 rankle:** *inflict a festering wound* (OED)   **305 he:** *other Qq, F* it

Bulling. Then, England's ground, farewell; sweet soil, adieu,
My mother, and my nurse, that bears me yet.
Where eare I wander, boast of this I can,   *310*
Though banish'd, yet a trueborn Englishman.   *Exeunt.*

❧ SCENE FOURTH ❧

*Enter the King with [Green and Bagot] at one door,
and the Lord Aumerle at another.*

King. We did observe. Cousin Aumerle,
How far brought you high Herford on his way?
Aum. I brought high Herford, if you call him so,
But to the next highway, and there I left him.
King. And say, what store of parting tears were shed?   *5*
Aum. Faith, none for me, except the northeast wind
Which then blew bitterly against our faces,
Awak'd the sleeping rheum, and so by chance
Did grace our hollow parting with a tear.
King. What said our cousin when you parted with him?   *10*
Aum. 'Farewell.'
And for my heart disdained that my tongue
Should so profane the word, that taught me craft
To counterfeit oppression of such grief
That words seem'd buried in my sorrow's grave.   *15*
Marry, would the word 'farewell' have length'ned hours
And added years to his short banishment,
He should have had a volume of farewells;
But since it would not, he had none of me.
King. He is our cousin, cousin; but 'tis doubt,   *20*
When time shall call him home from banishment,
Whether our kinsman come to see his friends.
Ourself and Bushy here, Bagot and Green,
Observ'd his courtship to the common people—
How he did seem to dive into their hearts   *25*
With humble and familiar courtesy;
What reverence he did throw away on slaves,
Wooing poor craftsmen with the craft of smiles
And patient underbearing of his fortune,
As 'twere to banish their affects with him.   *30*
Off goes his bonnet to an oyster-wench;
A brace of draymen did God speed him well
And had the tribute of his supple knee,
With 'Thanks, my countrymen, my loving friends,'
As were our England in reversion his,   *35*
And he our subjects' next degree in hope.
Green. Well, he is gone, and with him go these thoughts.
Now for the rebels which stand out in Ireland
Expedient manage must be made, my liege,
Ere further leisure yield them further means   *40*
For their advantage and your highness' loss.

King. We will ourself in person to this war;
And, for our coffers, with too great a court
And liberal largess, are grown somewhat light,
We are enforc'd to farm our royal realm,   *45*
The revenue whereof shall furnish us
For our affairs in hand. If that come short,
Our substitutes at home shall have blank charters,
Whereto, when they shall know what men are rich,
They shall subscribe them for large sums of gold   *50*
And send them after to supply our wants,
For we will make for Ireland presently.

Enter Bushy.

Bushy, what news?
Bushy. Old John of Gaunt is grievous sick, my lord,
Suddenly taken, and hath sent posthaste   *55*
To entreat your majesty to visit him.
King. Where lies he?
Bushy. At Ely House.
King. Now put it, God, in the physician's mind
To help him to his grave immediately!   *60*
The lining of his coffers shall make coats
To deck our soldiers for these Irish wars.
Come, gentlemen, let's all go visit him.
Pray God we may make haste, and come too late!
All. Amen.   *Exeunt*   *65*

ACT SECOND ❧ SCENE FIRST

Enter John of Gaunt, sick, with the Duke of York, etc.

Gaunt. Will the king come, that I may breathe my last
In wholesome counsel to his unstaid youth?
York. Vex not yourself, nor strive nor with your breath,
For all in vain comes counsel to his ear.
Gaunt. Oh, but they say the tongues of dying men   *5*
enforce attention like deep harmony.
Where words are scarce they are seldom spent in vain,
For they breathe truth that breathe their words in pain.
He that no more must say is listen'd more
Than they whom youth and ease have taught to glose.   *10*
More are men's ends mark'd than their lives before.
The setting sun, and music at the close,
As the last taste of sweets, is sweetest last,
Writ in remembrance more than things long past.
Though Richard my live's counsel would not hear,   *15*
My death's sad tale may yet undeaf his ear.
York. No, it is stopp'd with other flattering sounds,
As praises, of whose taste the wise are fond,
Lascivious meters, to whom venom sound
The open ear of youth doth always listen—   *20*

SD. Green and Bagot; *cf. n.*   **4 highway:** *a pun on high* (l. 3) *as 'proud' or 'main'*   **5 store:** *abundance*   **6 Faith:** *in faith*   **for me:** *for my part*   **7 blew:** F grew   **8 sleeping:** F sleepie   **rheum:** *tears*   **11–12 Farewell . . . tongue:** *one line in* Q, F   **12 for:** *because*   **13 that:** *i.e. my heart's disdain*   **16 Marry:** *indeed, to be sure* (originally an oath in the name of the Virgin Mary).   **19 of:** *from*   **20 cousin, cousin:** Q Coosens Coosin; F Cosin (Cosin)   **20–22 doubt . . . friends;** *cf. n.*   **23 Ourself . . . Green;** *cf. n.*   **27 What:** Q (Devonshire, Huth), F; Q (Capell, Petworth), *other Qq* With   **28 smiles:** F soules   **29 underbearing:** *endurance*   **30 their affects:** *i.e. the affection of the common people*   **35 reversion:** *right of future possession*   **36 next degree in hope:** *choice for heir presumptive*   **39 Expedient manage:** *expeditious arrangements*

43 great: *large and costly*   **43–44 court . . . largess;** *cf. n.*   **45 farm . . . realm;** *cf. n.*   **48 substitutes:** *deputies*   **50 subscribe them:** *fill in the amount to be paid* (see l. 45; *cf. n.*)   **51 them:** *i.e. large sums*   **52 presently:** *immediately*   **SD Enter Bushy:** Qq Enter Bushie with newes   **53 Bushy, what news;** *cf. n.*   **54 grievous:** F verie   **58 Ely House:** *Bishop of Ely's palace in London*   **61 coats:** *i.e. of mail*   **65 All:** *not in Qq.* F   **2 unstaid:** *stressed* — ∸   **9–12 He that . . . close:** *a quatrain*   **10 glose:** *speak flatteringly*   **12 close:** *final cadences*   **13 As:** *like*   **15 live's:** *old genitive form*   **16 My . . . tale:** *i.e. of Gaunt dying*   **17 flattering:** *disyllabic; hence* F flatt'ring   **18 of whose . . . fond;** *cf. n.*   **19 meters:** *songs*   **venom:** *venomous*

Report of fashions in proud Italy,
Whose manners still our tardy apish nation
Limps after in base imitation.
Where doth the world thrust forth a vanity—
So it be new, there's no respect how vile—   *25*
That is not quickly buzz'd into his ears?
Then all too late comes counsel to be heard
Where will doth mutiny with wit's regard.
Direct not him whose way himself will choose.
'Tis breath thou lack'st, and that breath wilt thou lose.   *30*
    Gaunt. Methinks I am a prophet new inspir'd
And thus expiring do foretell of him.
His rash fierce blaze of riot cannot last,
For violent fires soon burn out themselves;
Small showers last long, but sudden storms are short.   *35*
He tires betimes that spurs too fast betimes,
With eager feeding food doth choke the feeder.
Light vanity, insatiate cormorant,
Consuming means, soon preys upon itself.
This royal throne of kings, this scept'red isle,   *40*
This earth of majesty, this seat of Mars,
This other Eden, demiparadise,
This fortress built by Nature for herself.
Against infection and the hand of war,
This happy breed of men, this little world,   *45*
This precious stone set in the silver sea,
Which serves it in the office of a wall
Or as a moat defensive to a house
Against the envy of less happier lands;
This blessed plot, this earth, this realm, this England,   *50*
This nurse, this teeming womb of royal kings,
Fear'd by their breed and famous by their birth,
Renowned for their deeds as far from home,
For Christian service and true chivalry,
As is the sepulcher in stubborn Jewry   *55*
Of the world's ransom, blessed Mary's son;
This land of such dear souls, this dear dear land,
Dear for her reputation through the world,
Is now leas'd out—I die pronouncing it—
Like to a tenement or pelting farm.   *60*
England, bound in with the triumphant sea,
Whose rocky shore beats back the envious siege
Of wat'ry Neptune, is now bound in with shame,
With inky blots and rotten parchment bonds.
That England that was wont to conquer others   *65*
Hath made a shameful conquest of itself.
Ah, would the scandal vanish with my life,
How happy then were my ensuing death!

Enter King, Queen [, Aumerle, Bushy, Green, Bagot, Ross,
and Willoughby].

    York. The king is come. Deal mildly with his youth,
For young hot colts being rag'd do rage the more.   *70*
    Queen. How fares our noble uncle Lancaster?
    King. What comfort, man? How is't with aged Gaunt?
    Gaunt. O, how that name befits my composition!
Old Gaunt indeed, and gaunt in being old.
Within me Grief hath kept a tedious fast,   *75*
And who abstains from meat that is not gaunt?
For sleeping England long time have I watch'd;
Watching breeds leanness, leanness is all gaunt.
The pleasure that some fathers feed upon
Is my strict fast—I mean my children's looks—   *80*
And therein fasting hast thou made me gaunt.
Gaunt am I for the grave, gaunt as a grave,
Whose hollow womb inherits naught but bones.
    King. Can sick men play so nicely with their names?
    Gaunt. No, misery makes sport to mock itself.   *85*
Since thou dost seek to kill my name in me,
I mock my name, great king, to flatter thee.
    King. Should dying men flatter with those that live?
    Gaunt. No, no, men living flatter those that die.
    King. Thou, now a-dying, say'st thou flatter'st me.   *90*
    Gaunt. O, no! Thou diest, though I the sicker be.
    King. I am in health, I breathe, and see thee ill.
    Gaunt. Now He that made me knows I see thee ill—
Ill in myself to see, and in thee seeing ill.
Thy deathbed is no lesser than thy land,   *95*
Wherein thou liest in reputation sick;
And thou, too careless patient as thou art,
Committ'st thy anointed body to the cure
Of those physicians that first wounded thee.
A thousand flatterers sit within thy crown,   *100*
Whose compass is no bigger than thy head,
And yet, incaged in so small a verge,
The waste is no whit lesser than thy land.
O, had thy grandsire with a prophet's eye
Seen how his son's son should destroy his sons,   *105*
From forth thy reach he would have laid thy shame,
Deposing thee before thou wert possess'd,
Which art possess'd now to depose thyself.
Why, cousin, wert thou regent of the world,
It were a shame to let this land by lease;   *110*
But for thy world enjoying but this land,
Is it not more than shame to shame it so?
Landlord of England art thou now, not king.
Thy state of law is bondslave to the law,
And thou—   *115*
    King.   A lunatic lean-witted fool,
Presuming on an ague's privilege,

69 youth: *Richard was thirty-two*   **70 rag'd** *enraged; cf. n.*   **71 Queen:** *Richard's child-wife Isabelle*   **72 What comfort:** *i.e. 'do you feel better?'*   **73–83 O, how ... bones:** *a series of puns on gaunt; cf. n.*   **73 composition:** *bodily condition*   **77 watch'd:** *kept awake*   **81 therein fasting:** *modifies* me   **84 nicely:** *subtly, fancifully*   **86 to kill me:** *i.e. by banishing his son*   **89 those that die:** *i.e. Richard (see l. 95).*   **91 diest:** *monosyllabic*   **93 ill:** *evil and dimly*   **94 Ill ... ill:** *cf. n.*   **95–96: Thy ... sick:** *cf. n.*   **96 liest:** *monosyllabic*   **98 thy anointed:** *three syllables;* F thy' anointed   **99 those physicians:** *i.e. Richard's corrupt favorites*   **100–113 A thousand ... king:** *cf. n.*   **100 crown:** *both head and diadem*   **102 incaged:** F; Qq *inraged*   **verge:** *boundary (a legal term)*   **103 waste:** *destruction (here a legal term).*   **104 grandsire:** *Edward III*   **105 his son's:** *the Black Prince's.*   **his sons:** *Gloucester and Gaunt himself*   **107 possess'd:** *i.e. of the throne*   **108 Which:** *who*   **possess'd:** *i.e. by a mad impulse (originally by a devil).*   **depose thyself:** *i.e. be ruled by favorites*   **111 But ... land:** *cf. n.*   **113 now, not:** *other Qq* now not, not; Q5;f *now not, nor;* F *and not*   **114 state of law:** *legal status*   **115 And thou ... lunatic:** *cf. n.*   **116 lean-witted:** *gaunt-witted? (see l. 78)*

21 proud: *gorgeous, and corrupting*   **22 still:** *ever*   **tardy apish:** *unenterprising and imitative*   **23 imitation:** *five syllables*   **25 So:** *if, provided that* **there's no respect:** *it matters not*   **26 buzz'd:** *whispered (a contemptuous word).*   **28 with wit's regard:** *against good judgment*   **31–32 inspir'd ... expiring:** *a quibble*   **33 rash:** *fast kindled and fast burning* **riot:** *riotous living*   **34 violent fires:** *both disyllabic*   **35 showers:** *monosyllabic*   **36 betimes:** *soon, early*   **38 insatiate:** *insatiable*   **39 means:** *i.e. money*   **40–55 This royal ... Jewry;** *cf. n.*   **41 earth:** *England as an earth or world* (l. 45) *in itself*   **44 infection:** *pestilence (or possibly a moral word).*   **45 breed:** *race, or brood* **little world:** *Elizabethan microcosm*   **47 office:** *function*   **48 as a:** Q4, Q5, F; *other Qq* as   **49 envy:** *enmity*   **52 Fear'd:** *inspiring fear*   **54 For ... chivalry:** *almost parenthetical*   **55 stubborn:** *ruthless, or stubborn about accepting Christianity* **Jewry:** *Judea*   **56 Of the world's ransom:** *of the Savior who redeemed the world*   **60 tenement:** *real estate held by a tenant* **pelting:** *paltry*   **64 inky ... bonds:** *contemptuous expression for written deeds*   **SD. Enter ... Willoughby:** *cf. n.*

Dar'st with thy frozen admonition
Make pale our cheek, chasing the royal blood
With fury from his native residence.   *120*
Now, by my seat's right royal majesty,
Wert thou not brother to great Edward's son,
This tongue that runs so roundly in thy head
Should run thy head from thy unreverent shoulders.
    Gaunt. O, spare me not, my brother Edward's son,   *125*
For that I was his father Edward's son!
That blood already, like the pelican,
Hast thou tapp'd out and drunkenly carous'd.
My brother Gloucester, plain well-meaning soul—
Whom fair befall in heaven 'mongst happy souls!—   *130*
May be a precedent and witness good
That thou respect'st not spilling Edward's blood.
Join with the present sickness that I have,
And thy unkindness be like crooked age,
To crop at once a too long wither'd flower.   *135*
Live in thy shame, but die not shame with thee!
These words hereafter thy tormentors be!
Convey me to my bed, then to my grave.
Love they to live that love and honor have.
          Exit [borne off by his attendants.].
    King. And let them die that age and sullens have,   *140*
For both hast thou, and both become the grave.
    York. I do beseech your majesty, impute his words
To wayward sickliness and age in him.
He loves you, on my life, and holds you dear
As Harry Duke of Herford, were he here.   *145*
    King. Right, you say true. As Herford's love, so his;
As theirs, so mine; and all be as it is.

       [Enter Northumberland.]

    North. My liege, old Gaunt commends him to your majesty.
    King. What says he?
    North.   Nay, nothing; all is said.   *150*
His tongue is now a stringless instrument.
Words, life, and all, old Lancaster hath spent.
    York. Be York the next that must be bankrout so!
Though death be poor, it ends a mortal woe.
    King. The ripest fruit first falls, and so doth he.   *155*
His time is spent, our pilgrimage must be.
So much for that. Now for our Irish wars.
We must supplant those rough rug-headed kerns
Which live like venom where no venom else
But only they have privilege to live.   *160*
And for these great affairs do ask some charge,
Towards our assistance we do seize to us
The plate, coin, revenues, and moveables
Whereof our uncle Gaunt did stand possess'd.
    York. How long shall I be patient? Ah, how long   *165*
Shall tender duty make me suffer wrong?

Not Gloucester's death, nor Herford's banishment,
Nor Gaunt's rebukes, nor England's private wrongs,
Nor the prevention of poor Bullingbrooke
About his marriage, nor my own disgrace,   *170*
Have ever made me sour my patient cheek
Or bend one wrinkle on my sovereign's face.
I am the last of noble Edward's sons,
Of whom thy father, Prince of Wales, was first.
In war was never lion rag'd more fierce,   *175*
In peace was never gentle lamb more mild,
Than was that young and princely gentleman.
His face thou hast, for even so look'd he,
Accomplish'd with the number of thy hours.
But when he frown'd, it was against the French   *180*
And not against his friends. His noble hand
Did win what he did spend, and spent not that
Which his triumphant father's hand had won.
His hands were guilty of no kinred blood,
But bloody with the enemies of his kin.   *185*
O Richard! York is too far gone with grief,
Or else he never would compare between.
    King. Why, uncle, what the matter?
    York.   Oh my liege,
Pardon me, if you please; if not, I, pleas'd   *190*
Not to be pardon'd, am content withal.
Seek you to seize and gripe into your hands
The royalties and rights of banish'd Herford?
Is not Gaunt dead, and doth not Herford live?
Was not Gaunt just, and is not Harry true?   *195*
Did not the one deserve to have an heir?
Is not his heir a well-deserving son?
Take Herford's rights away, and take from time
His charters and his customary rights,
Let not tomorrow then ensue today.   *200*
Be not thyself; for how art thou a king
But by fair sequence and succession?
Now, afore God—God forbid I say true!—
If you do wrongfully seize Herford's rights,
Call in the letters-patents that he hath   *205*
By his attorney's general to sue
His livery, and deny his off'red homage,
You pluck a thousand dangers on your head,
You lose a thousand well-disposed hearts,
And prick my tender patience to those thoughts   *210*
Which honor and allegiance cannot think.
    King. Think what you will, we seize into our hands.
His plate, his goods, his money, and his lands.
    York. I'll not be by the while. My liege, farewell.
What will ensue hereof there's none can tell,   *215*
But by bad courses may be understood
That their events can never fall out good.   *Exit.*
    King. Go Bushy, to the Earl of Wiltshire straight.
Bid him repair to us to Ely House

118 admonition: *five syllables* **120 his:** *its* **123 roundly:** *glibly (also a pun)* **125 brother:** *other Qq; Q, F* brothers **127 like the pelican;** *cf. n.* **128 carous'd:** *drunk down in large drafts* **131 precedent:** *proof or example* **132 respect'st not:** *do not scruple about* **134 crooked:** *as with a sickle? (see l. 135)* **140 sullens:** *melancholy* **141 become:** *are fit, for* **146–147 As . . . mine;** *cf. n.* **148 Northumberland:** *i.e. Hotspur's father, Henry Percy, Earl of Northumberland* **him:** *himself* **150–217 Nay, nothing . . . good:** *for Holinshed's version see Appendix B* **151 tongue . . . instrument:** *compare I.3.162, 163* **153 bankrout:** *bankrupt; F* bankrupt **156 our pilgrimage must be:** *i.e. we must live on* **158 supplant:** *uproot, drive out* **rug-headed kerns:** *shaggy-haired Irish foot soldiers* **kerns:** *(which may be collective here)* **159–160 Which . . . live:** *refers to legend that St. Patrick rid Ireland of snakes* **161 for:** *because* **charge:** *outlay* **166 tender:** *scrupulous, perhaps excessively so*

168 Gaunt's: *i.e. given to Gaunt (objective genitive)* **private:** *suffered by private persons* **170 marriage . . . disgrace;** *cf. n.* **172 bend one wrinkle on:** *show one sign of criticism before* **174 Prince of Wales:** *Edward the Black Prince* **175 lion rag'd:** *lion that raged* **179 Accomplish'd . . . hours:** *when your age (i.e. thirty-two)* **the:** *F; Qq a* **187 compare between:** *draw comparisons (or perhaps the sentence is cut off)* **188–191 Why . . . withal;** *cf. n.* **192 gripe:** *grip* **193 royalties:** *privileges* **198 rights:** *i.e. of making the son heir to the father* **200 ensue:** *follow (here transitive)* **202 succession:** *four syllables* **205 letters-patents;** *cf. n.* **206–207 sue His livery:** *bring suit for delivery (of his property)* **210 patience:** *self-control* **216 by:** *concerning* **may:** *it may* **218 Earl of Wiltshire:** *Lord Treasurer of England*

To see this business. Tomorrow next 220
We will for Ireland; and 'tis time, I trow.
And we create, in absence of ourself,
Our uncle York Lord Governor of England,
For he is just and always lov'd us well.
Come on, our queen. Tomorrow must we part. 225
Be merry, for our time of stay is short.

     [Flourish.] Exeunt. Manent Northumberland
          [, Willoughby, and Ross].

 North. Well, lords, the Duke of Lancaster is dead.
 Ross. And living too, for now his son is duke.
 Wil. Barely in title, not in revenues.
 North. Richly in both, if justice had her right. 230
 Ross. My heart is great, but it must break with silence.
Ear't be disburden'd with a liberal tongue.
 North. Nay, speak thy mind, and let him nere speak more
That speaks thy words again to do thee harm!
 Wil. Tends that thou wouldst speak to the Duke of 235
Herford?
If it be so, out with it boldly, man.
Quick is mine ear to hear of good towards him.
 Ross. No good at all that I can do for him,
Unless you call it good to pity him, 240
Bereft and gelded of his patrimony.
 North. Now, afore God, 'tis shame such wrongs are borne
In him a royal prince and many mo
Of noble blood in this declining land.
The kind is not himself, but basely led 245
By flatterers. And what they will inform,
Merely in hate, 'gainst any of us all,
That will the king severely prosecute
'Gainst us, our lives, our children, and our heirs.
 Ross. The commons hath he pill'd with grievous taxes 250
And quite lost their hearts. The nobles hath, he fin'd
For ancient quarrels and quite lost their hearts.
 Wil. And daily new exactions are devis'd,
As blanks, benevolences, and I wot not what.
But what, a God's name, doth become of this? 255
 North. Wars hath not wasted it, for warr'd he hath not,
But basely yielded upon compromise
That which his noble ancestors achiev'd with blows.
More hath he spent in peace than they in wars.
 Ross. The Earl of Wiltshire hath the realm in farm. 260
 Wil. The king's grown bankrout like a broken man.
 North. Reproach and dissolution hangeth over him.
 Ross. He hath not money for these Irish wars,
His burthenous taxations notwithstanding,
But by the robbing of the banish'd duke. 265
 North. His noble kinsman. Most degenerate king!
But, lords, we hear this fearful tempest sing,
Yet seek no shelter to avoid the storm.
We see the wind sit sore upon our sails,
And yet we strike not, but securely perish. 270

 Ross. We see the very wrack that we must suffer,
And unavoided is the danger now
For suffering so the causes of our wrack.
 North. Not so. Even through the hollow eyes of death
I spy life peering, but I dare not say 275
How near the tidings of our comfort is.
 Wil. Nay, let us share thy thoughts as thou dost ours.
 Ross. Be confident to speak, Northumberland.
We three are but thyself, and, speaking so,
Thy words are but as thoughts. Therefore be bold. 280
 North. Then thus: I have from Le Port Blan, a bay
In Brittaine, receiv'd intelligence
That Harry Duke of Herford, Rainold Lord Cobham

    . . . . . .

That late broke from the Duke of Exeter, 285
His brother, Archbishop late of Canterbury,
Sir Thomas Erpingham, Sir John Ramston,
Sir John Norbery, Sir Robert Waterton, and Francis Quoint;
All these well furnish'd by the Duke of Brittaine
With eight tall ships, three thousand men of war, 290
Are making hither with all due expedience
And shortly mean to touch our northern shore.
Perhaps they had ere this, but that they stay
The first departing of the king for Ireland.
If then we shall shake off our slavish yoke, 295
Imp out our drooping country's broken wing,
Redeem from broking pawn the blemish'd crown,
Wipe off the dust that hides our scepter's gilt,
And make high majesty look like itself,
Away with me in post to Ravenspurgh. 300
But if you faint, as fearing to do so,
Stay and be secret, and myself will go.
 Ross. To horse, to horse! Urge doubts to them that fear.
 Wil. Hold out my horse, and I will first be there. *Exeunt.*

    ❧ SCENE SECOND ❧

    Enter the Queen, Bushy, Bagot.

 Bushy. Madam, your majesty is too much sad.
You promis'd, when you parted with the king,
To lay aside life-harming heaviness
And entertain a cheerful disposition.
 Queen. To please the king, I did; to please myself, 5
I cannot do it. Yet I know no cause
Why I should welcome such a guest as Grief,
Save bidding farewell to so sweet a guest
As my sweet Richard. Yet again, methinks
Some unborn sorrow, ripe in Fortune's womb, 10
Is coming towards me, and my inward soul
With nothing trembles. At something it grieves
More than with parting from my lord the king.

---

220 *see: see to* **business**: *trisyllabic* 232 **Ear't**: *before it* **liberal**: *disyllabic* 233 **nere**: *read 'ne'er' (never)* 235 **Tends … speak**: *does what you say refer?* 243 **In him**: *in his case (referring to wrongs)* **mo**: *more* 250 **pill'd**: *pillaged, plundered; F2; Qq pild; F pil'd* 254 **blanks**: *blank charters (see 1.4.48)* **benevolences**: *forced loans or gifts; read 'benev'lence'* 255 **a**: *in* **this**: *i.e. all this money* 256–258 **Wars … blows**; *cf. n.* 256 **hath**: *a southern plural* 258 **That … blows**: *an alexandrine* **noble**: *not in F* 260 **in farm**: *compare 1.4.45* 261 **king's**: *Q3; King; F Kings* 262 **dissolution**: *destruction* **hangeth over**: *read 'hang'th o'er'* 269 **sit sore**: *weigh heavily* 270 **strike not**: *lower not our sails (also a pun)* **securely**: *heedlessly*

273 **suffering**: *disyllabic* 276 **tidings**: *a singular* 279 **are but thyself**: *are of the same mind* 281 **Le Port Blan**; *cf. n.* 281–282 **a bay … intelligence**: *one line in Q, F* 282 **Brittaine**: *Q5, F Britaine; other Qq Brittanie* 283 **Rainold**: *Reginald* 283–285 **Cobham … Exeter**; *cf. n.* 287 **Sir John Ramston**: *more accurately, Sir Thomas Ramston* 288 **Quoint**; *cf. n.* 290 **men of war**: *soldiers* 295 **shall**: *mean to* 296 **Imp out**: *repair (a term in falconry)* 297 **broking pawn**: *pawn in the hands of brokers* 300 **in post**: *at full speed* **Ravenspurgh**: *once the main port on the Humber* 301 **faint**: *are fainthearted* **as**: *though* 303 **urge**: *mention* 304 **Hold out my horse**: *let my horse hold out* 3 **life-harming**: *Q3–5 halfe-harming; F selfe-harming* 4 **entertain**: *maintain* 12 **nothing**: *i.e. the sorrow yet unborn* **something**: *stressed — —*

Bushy. Each substance of a grief hath twenty shadows,
Which shows like grief itself but is not so; 15
For Sorrow's eye, glazed with blinding tears,
Divides one thing entire to many objects—
Like perspectives which, rightly gaz'd upon,
Show nothing but confusion, ey'd awry,
Distinguish form. So your sweet majesty, 20
Looking awry upon your lord's departure,
Find shapes of grief more than himself to wail,
Which, look'd on as it is, is naught but shadows
Of what it is not. Then, thrice-gracious queen.
More than your lord's departure weep not. More is not seen; 25
Or if it be, 'tis with false Sorrow's eye,
Which for things true weeps things imaginary.
Queen. It may be so, but yet my inward soul
Persuades me it is otherwise. Howere it be,
I cannot but be sad, so heavy sad 30
As, though on thinking on no thought I think,
Makes me with heavy nothing faint and shrink.
Bushy. 'Tis nothing but conceit, my gracious lady.
Queen. 'Tis nothing less. Conceit is still deriv'd
From some forefather grief. Mine is not so, 35
For nothing hath begot my something grief,
Or something hath the nothing that I grieve.
'Tis in reversion that I do possess;
But what it is, that is not yet known—what
I cannot name. 'Tis nameless woe, I wot. 40

[Enter Green.]

Green. God save your majesty! All well met, gentlemen.
I hope the king is not yet shipp'd for Ireland.
Queen. Why hop'st thou so? 'Tis better hope he is,
For his designs crave haste, his haste good hope.
Then wherefore dost thou hope he is not shipp'd? 45
Green. That he, our hope, might have retir'd his power
And driven into despair an enemy's hope
Who strongly hath set footing in this land.
The banish'd Bullingbrooke repeals himself
And with uplifted arms is safe arriv'd 50
At Ravenspurgh.
Queen. Now God in heaven forbid!
Green. Ah, madam, 'tis too true! And that is worse,
The Lord Northumberland, his son young Henry Percy,
The Lords of Ross, Beaumont, and Willoughby, 55
With all their powerful friends, are fled to him.
Bushy. Why have you not proclaim'd Northumberland
And all the rest revolted faction, traitors?
Green. We have; whereupon the Earl of Worcester
Hath broken his staff, resign'd his stewardship, 60
And all the household servants fled with him to Bullingbrooke.

Queen. So, Green, thou art the midwife to my woe,
And Bullingbrooke my sorrow's dismal heir.
Now hath my soul brought forth her prodigy,
And I, a gasping new-deliver'd mother, 65
Have woe to woe, sorrow to sorrow, join'd.
Bushy. Despair not, madam.
Queen. Who shall hinder me?
I will despair, and be at enmity
With cozening Hope. He is a flatterer,
A parasite, a keeper-back of Death, 70
Who gently would dissolve the bands of life
Which false Hope lingers in extremity.

[Enter York.]

Green. Here comes the Duke of York.
Queen. With signs of war about his aged neck. 75
O, full of careful business are his looks!
Uncle, for God's sake, speak comfortable words.
York. Should I do so, I should belie my thoughts.
Comfort's in heaven, and we are on the earth,
Where nothing lives but crosses, cares, and grief. 80
Your husband, he is gone to save far off
Whilst others come to make him lose at home.
Here am I left to underprop his land,
Who, weak with age, cannot support myself.
Now comes the sick hour that his surfeit made; 85
Now shall he try his friends that flatter'd him.

[Enter a servingman.]

Serv. My lord, your son was gone before I came.
York. He was? Why, so! Go all which way it will!
The nobles they are fled; the commons they are cold
And will, I fear, revolt on Herford's side. 90
Sirrah, get thee to Plashie to my sister Gloucester.
Bid her send me presently a thousand pound.
Hold, take my ring.
Serv. My lord, I had forgot to tell your lordship,
Today, as I came by, I called there— 95
But I shall grieve you to report the rest.
York. What is't, knave?
Serv. An hour before I came the duchess died.
York. God for his mercy! What a tide of woes
Comes rushing on this woeful land at once! 100
I know not what to do. I would to God—
So my untruth had not provok'd him to it—
The king had cut off my head with my brother's.
What, are there no posts dispatch'd for Ireland?
How shall we do for money for these wars? 105
Come, sister—cousin, I would say—pray pardon me.
Go, fellow, get thee home, provide some carts
And bring away the armor that is there. *[Exit servingman.]*
Gentlemen, will you go muster men?
If I know how or which way to order these affairs 110

---

14 shadows: *i.e. false images* **15 shows:** *a fairly common plural form* (see also II.3.5, III.3.171, V.3.94) **16 eye:** *F; Qq eyes* **18 perspectives:** *optical toys of various kinds; stressed* — — — — **rightly:** *from the front* (also a pun) **20 Distinguish form:** *show distinct shapes or designs* **22 himself:** *i.e. King Richard* **23 Which:** *i.e. the collection of apparent griefs* **25 More than . . . seen:** *an alexandrine; hence F more's* **33 conceit:** *fancy, imagination* **34 nothing less:** *anything but fancy* **35 forefather grief:** *i.e. former grief* **36 nothing:** *no real cause* **something:** *real, actual* **37 nothing:** *the unreal object of grief* **38 'Tis . . . possess;** *cf. n.* **46 That:** *demonstrative adjective* **49 repeals himself:** *recalls himself from exile* **50 uplifted:** *i.e. ready to fight* **55 Beaumont:** *Henry, fifth Baron Beaumont, an unimportant Yorkshire baron* **58 all the rest:** *other Qq, F the rest of the* **59 Earl of Worcester:** *Thomas Percy, Northumberland's brother* **60 broken:** *monosyllabic; hence other Qq, F broke* **61 to Bullingbrooke:** *a separate line in most editions*

63 dismal: *ill-omened* **64 prodigy:** *here a monstrous birth* **73 Hope lingers:** *F hopes linger* **lingers:** *causes to linger* **75 signs of war:** *armor* **76 careful:** *anxious* **78 Should . . . thoughts:** *not in F* **80 crosses:** *troubles, vexations* **85 surfeit:** *i.e. extravagant conduct* **87 son was gone:** *Aumerle joined Richard in Dublin* **89 The nobles . . . cold:** *an alexandrine* **91 Sirrah . . . Gloucester;** *cf. n.* **Sirrah:** *a condescending term of address* **Plashie:** (see I.2.66); *cf. n.* **99 God for:** *i.e. I pray God for* **102 untruth:** *disloyalty* **103 brother's:** *i.e. Gloucester's* **104 there no posts:** *F there postes* **106 sister:** *i.e. the Duchess of Gloucester*

Thus disorderly thrust into my hands,
Never believe me. Both are my kinsmen.
T' one is my sovereign, whom both my oath
And duty bids defend; t' other again
Is my kinsman, whom the king hath wrong'd, 115
Whom conscience and my kinred bids to right.
Well, somewhat we must do. Come, cousin,
I'll dispose of you. Gentlemen, go muster up your men
And meet me presently at Barkly.
I should to Plashie too, 120
But time will not permit. All is uneven,
And everything is left at six and seven. *Exeunt Duke, Queen.*
  Bushy. The wind sits fair for news to go for Ireland,
But none returns. For us to levy power
Proportionable to the enemy is all unpossible. 125
  Green. Besides, our nearness to the king in love
Is near the hate of those love not the king.
  Bagot. And that is the wavering commons, for their love
Lies in their purses, and whoso empties them
By so much fills their hearts with deadly hate. 130
  Bushy. Wherein the king stands generally condemn'd.
  Bagot. If judgment lie in them, then so do we,
Because we ever have been near the king.
  Green. Well, I will for refuge straight to Bristow Castle.
The Earl of Wiltshire is already there. 135
  Bushy. Thither will I with you, for little office
Will the hateful commons perform for us,
Except like curs to tear us all to pieces.
Will you go along with us?
  Bagot. No, I will to Ireland to his majesty. 140
Farewell. If heart's presages be not vain,
We three here part that nere shall meet again.
  Bushy. That's as York thrives to beat back Bullingbrooke.
  Green. Alas, poor duke! The task as he undertakes
Is numb'ring sands and drinking oceans dry. 145
Where one on his side fights, thousands will fly.
Farewell at once, for once, for all, and ever.
  Bushy. Well, we may meet again.
  Bagot.   I fear me, never.
                             [Exeunt.]

❧ Scene Third ❧

Enter [Bullingbrooke, the duke of] Herford, and Northumberland.

  Bulling. How far is it, my lord, to Barkly now?
  North. Believe me, noble lord,
I am a stranger here in Gloucestershire.
These high wild hills and rough uneven ways
Draws out of our miles and makes them wearisome, 5
And yet your fair discourse hath been as sugar,
Making the hard way sweet and delectable.
But I bethink me what a weary way

From Ravenspurgh to Cotshall will be found
In Ross and Willoughby, wanting your company, 10
Which, I protest, hath very much beguil'd
The tediousness and process of my travel.
But theirs is sweet'ned with the hope to have
The present benefit which I possess,
And hope to joy is little less in joy 15
Than hope enjoy'd. By this the weary lords
Shall make their way seem short as mine hath done
By sight of what I have, your noble company.
  Bulling. Of much less value is my company
Than your good words. But who comes here? 20

        Enter Harry Percy.

  North. It is my son, young Harry Percy,
Sent from my brother Worcester, whencesoever.
Harry, how fares your uncle?
  Percy. I had thought, my lord, to have learn'd his health
of you. 25
  North. Why, is he not with the queen?
  Percy. No, my good lord. He hath forsook the court,
Broken his staff of office, and dispers'd
The household of the king.
  North.   What was his reason? 30
He was not so resolv'd when last we spake togither.
  Percy. Because your lordship was proclaim'd traitor.
But he, my lord, is gone to Ravenspurgh
To offer service to the Duke of Herford,
And sent me over by Barkly to discover 35
What power the Duke of York had levied there,
Then with directions to repair to Ravenspurgh.
  North. Have you forgot the Duke of Herford, boy?
  Percy. No, my good lord, for that is not forgot
Which nere I did remember. To my knowledge, 40
I never in my life did look on him.
  North. Then learn to know him now. This is the duke.
  Percy. My gracious lord, I tender you my service,
Such as it is, being tender, raw, and young—
Which elder days shall ripen and confirm 45
To more approved service and desert.
  Bulling. I thank thee, gentle Percy, and be sure
I count myself in nothing else so happy
As in a soul rememb'ring my good friends.
And as my fortune ripens with thy love, 50
It shall be still thy true love's recompense.
My heart this covenant makes, my hand thus seals it.
  North. How far is it to Barkly? And what stir
Keeps good old York there with his men of war?
  Percy. There stands the castle by yon tuft of trees, 55
Mann'd with three hundred men, as I have heard,
And in it are the Lords of York, Barkly, and Seymer—
None else of name and noble estimate.

        [Enter Ross and Willoughby.]

  North. Here come the Lords of Ross and Willoughby,
Bloody with spurring, fiery red with haste. 60

---

111 disorderly thrust: *so Qq. Ff, but most editions read* thrust disorderly   **113 T' one:** *F* Th' one   **sovereign:** *trisyllabic*   **114 bids:** *singular with the collective subject* oath *and* duty   **t' other:** *F* th' other   **118 dispose of you:** *find you a safe place*   **119 presently:** *at once*   **Barkly:** *Berkeley* (pronounced 'Barkly')   **120–121 I . . . permit:** *one line in Q, F*   **123 for Ireland:** *F* to Ireland   **128 that is:** *read* 'that's' *as F*   **wavering:** (disyllabic) *fickle*   **131 Wherein:** *i.e. in emptying their purses*   **132 them:** *i.e. the hearts of the commons*   **so do we:** *i.e. stand condemned*   **134 I will:** *read* 'I'll' (also in l. 140)   **Bristow:** *cf. n.*   **136 office:** *service*   **137 hateful:** *full of hate*   **5 Draws:** *see II.2.15*   **6 your:** *F* our   **7 delectable:** *stressed* ´ — — ´ —

9 Cotshall: *Cotswold* (local pronunciation probably 'Cots'l')   **10 In:** *in the case of*   **12 tediousness and process:** *hendiadys*   **15 to joy:** *to enjoy*   **24 I had:** *read* 'I'd'   **to have:** *read* 't' have'   **30–31 What . . . resolv'd:** *F's lineation; one line in Q*   **35 over:** *read* 'o'er'   **38 Herford, boy:** *F; Q* Herfords boy   **43–44 tender, tender:** *both puns*   **46 approved:** *tested*   **52 covenant:** *disyllabic*   **57 Barkly:** *Thomas, Lord Berkeley*   **Seymer:** *Richard, Lord Seymour* (pronounced 'Seemer'); *other Qq, F* Seymour   **58 estimate:** *repute, estimation*

Bulling. Welcome, my lords. I wot your love pursues
A banish'd traitor. All my treasury
Is yet but unfelt thanks, which more enrich'd
Shall be your love and labor's recompense.

   Ross. Your presence makes us rich, most noble lord.   65
   Wil. And far surmounts our labor to attain it.
   Bulling. Evermore thanks, the exchequer of the poor,
Which, till my infant fortune comes to year,
Stands for my bounty. But who comes here?

              [Enter Barkly.]

   North. It is my Lord of Barkly, as I guess.   70
   Bark. My Lord of Herford, my message is to you.
   Bulling. My lord, my answer is—to Lancaster,
And I am come to seek that name in England,
And I must find that title in your tongue
Before I make reply to aught you say.   75
   Bark. Mistake me not, my lord. 'Tis not my meaning
To rase one title of your honor out.
To you, my lord, I come, what lord you will,
From the most gracious regent of this land,
The Duke of York, to know what pricks you on   80
To take advantage of the absent time
And fright our native peace with self-borne arms.

            [Enter York, attended.]

   Bulling. I shall not need transport my words by you.
Here comes his grace in person. My noble uncle!   *[Kneels.]*
   York. Show me thy humble heart, and not thy knee.   85
Whose duty is deceivable and false.
   Bulling. My gracious uncle!
   York. Tut, tut! Grace me no grace, nor uncle me no uncle.
I am no traitor's uncle, and that word 'grace'
In an ungracious mouth is but profane.   90
Why have those banish'd and forbidden legs
Dar'd once to touch a dust of England's ground?
But then more 'why?' Why have they dar'd to march
So many miles upon her peaceful bosom,
Frighting her pale-fac'd villages with war   95
And ostentation of despised arms?
Com'st thou because the anointed king is hence?
Why, foolish boy, the king is left behind,
And in my loyal bosom lies his power.
Were I but now the lord of such hot youth   100
As when brave Gaunt thy father and myself
Rescued the Black Prince, that young Mars of men,
From forth the ranks of many thousand French,
O, then how quickly should this arm of mine,
Now prisoner to the palsy, chastise thee   105
And minister correction to thy fault!
   Bulling. My gracious uncle, let me know my fault.
On what condition stands it and wherein?

   York. Even in condition of the worst degree,
In gross rebellion and detested treason.   110
Thou art a banish'd man and here art come,
Before the expiration of thy time,
In braving arms against thy sovereign.
   Bulling. As I was banish'd, I was banish'd Herford,
But as I come, I come for Lancaster.   115
And, noble uncle, I beseech your grace
Look on my wrongs with an indifferent eye.
You are my father, for methinks in you
I see old Gaunt alive. O, then, my father,
Will you permit that I shall stand condemn'd   120
A wandering vagabond, my rights and royalties
Pluck'd from my arms perforce, and given away
To upstart unthrifts? Wherefore was I born?
If that my cousin king be king in England,
It must be granted I am Duke of Lancaster.   125
You have a son, Aumerle, my noble cousin.
Had you first died, and he bin thus trod down,
He should have found his uncle Gaunt a father
To rouse his wrongs and chase them to the bay.
I am denied to sue my livery here,   130
And yet my letters-patents give me leave.
My father's goods are all distrain'd and sold,
And these, and all, are all amiss employ'd.
What would you have me do? I am a subject,
And I challenge law. Attorneys are denied me,   135
And therefore personally I lay my claim
To my inheritance of free descent.
   North. The noble duke hath been too much abus'd.
   Ross. It stands your grace upon to do him right.
   Wil. Base men by his endowments are made great.   140
   York. My lords of England, let me tell you this:
I have had feeling of my cousin's wrongs,
And labor'd all I could to do him right,
But in this kind to come, in braving arms,
Be his own carver and cut out his way   145
To find out right with wrong—it may not be.
And you that do abet him in this kind
Cherish rebellion and are rebels all.
   North. The noble duke hath sworn his coming is
But for his own, and for the right of that   150
We all have strongly sworn to give him aid,
And let him never see joy that breaks that oath!
   York. Well, well, I see the issue of these arms.
I cannot mend it, I must needs confess,
Because my power is weak and all ill left.   155
But if I could, by Him that gave me life
I would attach you all and make you stoop
Unto the sovereign mercy of the king.
But since I cannot, be it known unto you
I do remain as neuter. So fare you well—   160
Unless you please to enter in the castle
And there repose you for this night.

63 unfelt: *of no tangible worth* **which:** *i.e. treasury* **67 the exchequer:** *read 'th' exche-quer'* **72 my answer ... Lancaster;** *cf. n.* **74 title:** *a possible pun ('title' and 'tittle' were probably pronounced alike)* **78 what lord you will:** *whatever title you prefer* **79 gracious regent of:** *F glorious of* **81 absent time:** *i.e. time of Richard's absence* **82 self-borne:** *borne for himself (not the king); cf. n.* **86 duty:** *reverence* **88 Grace me no grace:** *call me not gracious* **no uncle:** *not in F* **92 a dust:** *a grain of dust* **93 But then 'why?':** *Q2–4 But more than why; Q5, F But more then why* **more 'why?':** *i.e. more questions to ask* **95 pale-fac'd:** *faces made pale from fright; proleptic* **97 anointed:** *read 'th' anointed'; see I.2.38* **hence:** *i.e. in Ireland* **100 the:** *F; not in Qq* **101–103 As when ... French:** *no historical basis is known for this* **105 prisoner:** *disyllabic* **palsy:** *paralysis* **chastise:** *stressed — —* **108 On what ... wherein;** *cf. n.*

113 braving: *defiant* **115 for Lancaster;** *cf. n.* **117 indifferent:** *impartial* **121 wandering:** *royalties both disyllabic* **124 in England:** *other Qq, F of England* **126 cousin:** *F Kinsman* **129 chase ... bay:** *put them at bay (a hunting expression)* **131 letters-patents:** *see II.1.205 cf. n.* **132 distrain'd:** *seized by writ* **135 I:** *not in F* **challenge law:** *claim my legal rights* **137 free:** *direct, legitimate* **139 stands your grace upon:** *is your grace's duty* **140 Base:** *low in rank* **endowments:** *revenues from lands* **143 labor'd all I could:** *i.e. by protesting to Richard* **144 kind:** *i.e. way of acting* **146 wrong:** *F Wrongs* **152 never:** *read 'ne'er'* **155 ill left:** *badly provided for* **157 attach:** *arrest*

Bulling. An offer, uncle, that we will accept.
But we must win your grace to go with us
To Bristow Castle, which they say is held   *165*
By Bushy, Bagot, and their complices,
The caterpillars of the commonwealth,
Which I have sworn to weed and pluck away.
 York. It may be I will go with you. But yet I'll pause,
For I am loath to break our country's laws.   *170*
Nor friends nor foes, to me welcome you are.
Things past redress are now with me past care.   *Exeunt.*

❧ SCENE FOURTH ❧

Enter the Earl of Salisbury and a Welsh captain.

 Captain. My Lord of Salisbury, we have stay'd ten days
And hardly kept our countrymen together,
And yet we hear no tidings from the king.
Therefore we will disperse ourselves. Farewell.
 Sal. Stay yet another day, thou trusty Welshman.   *5*
The king reposeth all his confidence in thee.
 Captain. 'Tis thought the king is dead. We will not stay.
The bay trees in our country are all wither'd,
And meteors fright the fixed stars of heaven.
The pale-fac'd moon looks bloody on the earth,   *10*
And lean-look'd prophets whisper fearful change.
Rich men look sad and ruffians dance and leap,
The one in fear to lose what they enjoy,
The other to enjoy by rage and war.
These signs forerun the death or fall of kings.   *15*
Farewell. Our countrymen are gone and fled,
As well assur'd Richard their king is dead.   *[Exit.]*
 Sal. Ah, Richard! With the eyes of heavy mind
I see thy glory like a shooting star
Fall to the base earth from the firmament.   *20*
Thy sun sets weeping in the lowly west,
Witnessing storms to come, woe, and unrest.
Thy friends are fled to wait upon thy foes,
And crossly to thy good all fortune goes.   *[Exit.]*

ACT THIRD ❧ SCENE FIRST

Enter [Bullingbrooke,] the Duke of Herford, York, Northumberland,
[Ross, Percy, Willoughby, with] Bushy and Green prisoners.

 Bulling. Bring forth these men.
Bushy and Green, I will not vex your souls—
Since presently your souls must part your bodies—
With too much urging your pernicious lives,
For 'twere no charity. Yet, to wash your blood   *5*
From off my hands, here in the view of men
I will unfold some causes of your deaths.
You have misled a prince, a royal king,
A happy gentleman in blood and lineaments,

By you unhappied and disfigur'd clean.   *10*
You have in manner with your sinful hours
Made a divorce betwixt his queen and him,
Broke the possession of a royal bed
And stain'd the beauty of a fair queen's cheeks
With tears drawn from her eyes by your foul wrongs.   *15*
Myself, a prince by fortune of my birth,
Near to the king in blood, and near in love
Till you did make him misinterpret me,
Have stoop'd my neck under your injuries
And sigh'd my English breath in foreign clouds,   *20*
Eating the bitter bread of banishment,
Whilst you have fed upon my signories,
Dispark'd my parks and fell'd my forest woods,
From my own windows torn my household coat,
Ras'd out my imprese, leaving me no sign,   *25*
Save men's opinions and my living blood,
To show the world I am a gentleman.
This and much more, much more than twice all this,
Condemns you to the death. See them deliver'd over
To execution and the hand of death.   *30*
 Bushy. More welcome is the stroke of death to me
Than Bullingbrooke to England. Lords, farewell.
 Green. My comfort is that heaven will take our souls
And plague injustice with the pains of hell.
 Bulling. My Lord Northumberland, see them dispatch'd. *35*
  [Exeunt Northumberland and others, with the prisoners.]
Uncle, you say the queen is at your house.
For God's sake, fairly let her be entreated.
Tell her I send to her my kind commends.
Take special care my greetings be deliver'd.
 York. A gentleman of mine I have dispatch'd   *40*
With letters of your love to her at large.
 Bulling. Thanks, gentle uncle. Come, lords, away,
To fight with Glendor and his complices.
Awhile to work, and after holiday.   *Exeunt.*

❧ SCENE SECOND ❧

[Drums. Flourish and colors.] Enter the King, Aumerle, [the Bishop
of] Carlisle [, and soldiers].

 King. Barkloughly Castle call they this at hand?
 Aum. Yea, my lord. How brooks your grace the air
After your late tossing on the breaking seas?
 King. Needs must I like it well. I weep for joy.
To stand upon my kingdom once again.   *5*
Dear earth, I do salute thee with my hand,
Though rebels wound thee with their horses' hoofs.
As a long-parted mother with her child
Plays fondly with her tears and smiles in meeting,
So weeping, smiling, greet I thee my earth,   *10*
And do thee favors with my royal hands.

167 caterpillars: *i.e. greedy parasites*   **171 welcome:** *stressed —́ ̲*   **1 Captain:** *F; Qq*
Welch[man] **Salisbury:** *disyllabic*   **2 hardly:** *with difficulty*   **6 The king . . . thee:** *an*
alexandrine   **8 are all:** *other Qq, F* all are   **11 lean-look'd:** *i.e. lean-faced*   **14 to:** *in*
hope to **rage:** *tumult*   **15 or fall:** *not in other Qq, F*   **18 the:** *not in other Qq, F*   **21**
weeping: *pathetic fallacy; also 'watery'*   **22 Witnessing:** *portending*   **24 crossly:** *ad-*
versely   **5 charity:** *(disyllabic) kindness*   **9 happy:** *fortunate*

10 clean: *completely*   **11 in manner:** *in a way* **sinful hours:** *i.e. of riotous living*   **13**
Broke . . . bed: *mentioned only in Holinshed* **Broke:** *interrupted*   **20 in:** *into*
22 signories: *estates, manors*   **23 Dispark'd:** *reduced to a common (a legal term).*   **24**
household coat: *coat of arms painted on the glass*   **25 imprese:** *crest or heraldic de-*
vice   **26 my living blood:** *myself while still living*   **32 Lords, farewell:** *not in F*   **36**
your house: *i.e. Langley*   **37 entreated:** *treated*   **41 at large:** *at great length*   **43**
Glendor: *Glendower; F* Glendoure; *cf. n.*   **1 Barkloughly Castle;** *cf. n.*   **2 brooks:**
endures, and also enjoys   **8 with:** *from*   **11 favors:** *F* fauor

Feed not thy sovereign's foe, my gentle earth,
Nor with thy sweets comfort his ravenous sense;
But let thy spiders that suck up thy venom,
And heavy-gaited toads, lie in their way,   15
Doing annoyance to the treacherous feet
Which with usurping steps do trample thee.
Yield stinging nettles to mine enemies,
And when they from thy bosom pluck a flower,
Guard it, I pray thee, with a lurking adder   20
Whose double tongue may with a mortal touch
Throw death upon thy sovereign's enemies.
Mock not my senseless conjuration, lords.
This earth shall have a feeling, and these stones
Prove armed soldiers ere her native king   25
Shall falter under foul rebellion's arms.
      Car. Fear not, my lord. That power that made you king
Hath power to keep you king in spite of all.
The means that heavens yield must be embrac'd,
And not neglected. Else if heaven would   30
And we will not, heaven's offer we refuse,
The proffer'd means of succors and redress.
      Aum. He means, my lord, that we are too remiss
Whilst Bullingbrooke, through our security,
Grows strong and great in substance and in power.   35
      King. Discomfortable cousin! Know'st thou not
That when the searching eye of heaven is hid
Behind the globe that lights the lower world,
Then thieves and robbers range abroad unseen
In murthers and in outrage boldly here;   40
But when from under this terrestrial ball
He fires the proud tops of the eastern pines
And darts his light through every guilty hole,
Then murthers, treasons, and detested sins,
The cloak of night being pluck'd from off their backs,   45
Stand bare and naked, trembling at themselves?
So when this thief, this traitor, Bullingbrooke,
Who all this while hath revel'd in the night
Whilst we were wand'ring with the antipodes,
Shall see us rising in our throne, the east,   50
His treasons will sit blushing in his face,
Not able to endure the sight of day,
But self-affrighted tremble at his sin.
Not all the water in the rough rude sea
Can wash the balm off from an anointed king.   55
The breath of worldly men cannot depose
The deputy elected by the Lord.
For every man that Bullingbrooke hath press'd
To lift shrewd steel against our golden crown,
God for his Richard hath in heavenly pay   60
A glorious angel. Then, if angels fight,
Weak men must fall, for heaven still guards the right.

Enter Salisbury.

Welcome, my lord. How far off lies your power?
      Sal. Nor near nor farther off, my gracious lord,
Than this weak arm. Discomfort guides my tongue   65
And bids me speak of nothing but despair.
One day too late, I fear me, noble lord,
Hath clouded all thy happy days on earth.
O, call back yesterday, bid time return,
And thou shalt have twelve thousand fighting men!   70
Today, today, unhappy day, too late,
Overthrows thy joys, friends, fortune, and thy state.
For all the Welshmen, hearing thou wert dead,
Are gone to Bullingbrooke, dispers'd, and fled.
      Aum. Comfort, my liege. Why looks your grace so pale? 75
      King. But now the blood of twenty thousand men
Did triumph in my face, and they are fled.
And till so much blood thither come again,
Have I not reason to look pale and dead?
All souls that will be safe, fly from my side,   80
For time hath set a blot upon my pride.
      Aum. Comfort, my liege. Remember who you are.
      King. I had forgot myself. Am I not king?
Awake, thou coward majesty! Thou sleep'st.
Is not the king's same twenty thousand names?   85
Arm, arm, my name! A puny subject strikes
At thy great glory. Look not to the ground,
Ye favorites of a king. Are we not high?
High be our thoughts. I know my uncle York
Hath power enough to serve our turn. But who comes here?   90

Enter Scroop.

      Scroop. More health and happiness betide my liege
Than can my care-tun'd tongue deliver him!
      King. Mine ear is open and my heart prepar'd.
The worst is wordly loss thou canst unfold.
Say, is my kingdom lost? Why, 'twas my care,   95
And what loss is it to be rid of care?
Strives Bullingbrooke to be as great as we?
Greater he shall not be. If he serve God,
We'll serve Him too and be his fellow so.
Revolt our subjects? That we cannot mend.   100
They break their faith to God as well as us.
Cry woe, destruction, ruin, and decay;
The worst is death, and death will have his day.
      Scroop. Glad am I that your highness is so arm'd
To bear the tidings of calamity.   105
Like an unreasonable stormy day
Which makes the silver rivers drown their shores
As if the world were all dissolv'd to tears,
So high above his limits swells the rage
Of Bullingbrooke, covering your fearful land   110
With hard bright steel and hearts harder than steel.
Whitebeards have arm'd their thin and hairless scalps

13 comfort: *stressed* — ⌣ — **15 heavy-gaited:** *slow-paced* **toads:** *thought to be poisonous* **16 annoyance:** *injury* **21 double:** *forked; cf. n.* **mortal:** *fatal* **22 Throw:** *spit, inflict* **23 senseless conjuration:** *conjuring of things that lack feeling* **25 native:** *lawful, natural* **29–32 The means . . . redress;** *cf. n.* **34 security:** *overconfidence, carelessness* **35 power:** F *friends; compare* II.3.36 **36 Discomfortable:** *discouraging* **37 eye of heaven:** *the sun cf. n.* **38 that:** *antecedent:* eye of heaven **lower world:** *i.e. the antipodes* **40 murthers:** *murders* **boldly:** Q *bouldy; other* Qq *bloudy;* F *bloody* **42 proud:** *lofty* **43 light:** F *Lightning* **guilty hole:** *where the guilty hide* **49 Whilst . . . antipodes:** *not in* F **the antipodes:** *read 'th' antipodes'; people on the opposite side of the earth* **55 balm:** *oil used to anoint a king* **off . . . anointed;** *cf. n.* **56 worldly:** *mortal* **59 shrewd:** *sharp and malicious*

64 near: *nearer* **67 One day too late:** *i.e. his arrival a day late* **70 twelve:** *forty, according to Holinshed* **72 Overthrows:** *read 'o'erthrows';* F *Orethrowes* **76–79 But now . . . dead:** *a quatrain* **76 But:** *just* **twenty:** *indefinite but large number* **84 coward:** F *sluggard* **85 twenty:** F *fortie* **SD Scroop:** *Sir Stephen Scroop, Wiltshire's elder brother* **91 More . . . betide:** *may more . . . befall* **99 be his fellow so:** *thus be Bolingbroke's equal* **102 destruction, ruin, and decay:** *synonyms* **and decay:** F *Losse, Decay* **109 his:** *its* **110 covering:** *disyllabic* **112 Whitebeards:** *old men* **arm'd:** *i.e. with helmets*

Against thy majesty. Boys with women's voices
Strive to speak big and clap their female joints
In stiff unwieldy arms against thy crown.   115
Thy very beadsmen learn to bend their bows
Of double-fatal yew against thy state.
Yea, distaff-women manage rusty bills
Against thy seat. Both young and old rebel,
And all goes worse than I have power to tell.   120
    King. Too well, too well thou tell'st a tale so ill.
Where is the Earl of Wiltshire? Where is Bagot?
What is become of Bushy? Where is Green?—
That they have let the dangerous enemy
Measure our confines with such peaceful steps?   125
If we prevail, their heads shall pay for it.
I warrant they have made peace with Bullingbrooke.
    Scroop. Peace have they made with him indeed, my lord.
    King. O villains, vipers, damn'd without redemption!
Dogs, easily won to fawn on any man!   130
Snakes, in my heart-blood warm'd, that sting my heart!
Three Judases, each one thrice worse than Judas!
Would they make peace? Terrible hell
Make war upon their spotted souls for this!
    Scroop. Sweet love, I see, changing his property,   135
Turns to the sourest and most deadly hate.
Again uncurse their souls. Their peace is made
With heads and not with hands. Those whom you curse
Have felt the worst of death's destroying wound
And lie full low, grav'd in the hollow ground.   140
    Aum. Is Bushy, Green, and the Earl of Wiltshire dead?
    Scroop. Ay, all of them at Bristow lost their heads.
    Aum. Where is the duke my father with his power?
    King. No matter where. Of comfort no man speak.
Let's talk of graves, of worms, and epitaphs,   145
Make dust our paper, and with rainy eyes
Write sorrow on the bosom of the earth.
Let's choose executors and talk of wills.
And yet not so, for what can we bequeath
Save our deposed bodies to the ground?   150
Our lands, our lives, and all are Bullingbrooke's,
And nothing can we call our own but death
And that small model of the barren earth
Which serves as paste and cover to our bones.
For God's sake, let us sit upon the ground   155
And tell sad stories of the death of kings—
How some have been depos'd, some slain in war,
Some haunted by the ghosts they have depos'd,
Some poison'd by their wives, some sleeping kill'd,
All murther'd. For within the hollow crown   160
That rounds the mortal temples of a king
Keeps Death his court, and there the antic sits,
Scoffing his state and grinning at his pomp,
Allowing him a breath, a little scene,
To monarchize, be fear'd, and kill with looks,   165

Infusing him with self and vain conceit,
As if this flesh which walls about our life
Were brass impregnable, and humor'd thus
Comes at the last and with a little pin
Bores through his castle wall, and farewell king!   170
Cover your heads and mock not flesh and blood
With solemn reverence. Throw away respect,
Tradition, form, and ceremonious duty,
For you have but mistook me all this while.
I live with bread like you, feel want,   175
Taste grief, need friends. Subjected thus,
How can you say to me I am a king?
    Car. My lord, wise men were nere sit and wail their woes,
But presently prevent the ways to wail.
To fear the foe, since fear oppresseth strength,   180
Gives in your weakness strength unto your foe,
And so your follies fight against yourself.
Fear, and be slain—no worse can come to fight.
And fight and die is death destroying death,
Where fearing dying pays death servile breath.   185
    Aum. My father hath a power. Inquire of him,
And learn to make a body of a limb.
    King. Thou chid'st me well. Proud Bullingbrooke, I come
To change blows with thee for our days of doom.
This ague fit of fear is overblown.   190
An easy task it is to win our own.
Say, Scroop, where lies our uncle with his power?
Speak sweetly, man, although thy looks be sour.
    Scroop. Men judge by the complexion of the sky
The state and inclination fo the day.   195
So may you by my dull and heavy eye:
My tongue hath but a heavier tale to say.
I play the torturer, by small and small
To lengthen out the worst that must be spoken.
Your uncle York is join'd with Bullingbrooke,   200
And all your northern castles yielded up,
And all your southern gentlemen in arms
Upon his party.
    King.   Thou hast said enough. *[To Aumerle.]* Beshrew
thee, cousin, which didst lead me forth   205
Of that sweet way I was in to despair!
What say you now? What comfort have we now?
By heaven, I'll hate him everlastingly
That bids me be of comfort any more.
Go to Flint Castle. There I'll pine away.   210
A king, woe's slave, shall kingly woe obey.
That power I have, discharge, and let them go
To ear the land that hath some hope to grow,
For I have none. Let no man speak again
To alter this, for counsel is but vain.   215
    Aum. My liege, one word.

---

114 **big:** *deeply* (like men) **female:** *i.e. weak*   115 **In:** *into*   116 **beadsmen:** *almsmen, old pensioners*   117 **double:** *both as poisonous berries and as deadly bows* **state:** *royalty*   118 **distaff-women:** *women who should only spin* **bills:** *a pike-battle-ax combination*   119 **seat:** *throne*   122 **Where is Bagot;** *cf. n.*   125 **Measure:** *traverse* **peaceful:** *unresisted*   127 **they have:** *read 'they've'*   130 **easily:** *disyllabic*   134 **Make war . . . this;** *cf. n.* **spotted:** *wicked* (not spotless)   135 **his property:** *its nature*   138 **heads:** *see l. 142* **hands:** *i.e. hands raised submissively*   139 **wound:** *F hand*   153 **model . . . earth:** *grave mound, or earthly body*   154 **paste and cover:** *like top crust on a pie; hendiadys*   158 **ghosts they:** *ghosts of those whom they*   162 **antic:** *Death as a grinning buffoon*   163 **Scoffing:** *sometimes transitive*

166 **self and vain conceit:** *vain self-conceit*   168 **humor'd thus:** *his humor satisfied (either Death's or the king's or both)*   169 **Comes:** *i.e. Death comes*   170 **his castle wall:** *i.e. his body* **wall:** *other Qq, F Walls*   171 **Cover your heads:** *even though in the royal presence*   178 **sit . . . woes:** *F waile their present woes*   179 **presently . . . wail:** *i.e. promptly cut off the causes of grief*   182 **And . . . yourself:** *not in F*   183 **to fight:** *in fighting*   185 **Where:** *whereas*   186 **My father:** *i.e. York* **power:** *army* **of:** *about*   187 **to make . . . limb:** *i.e. to make the best of what one has*   189 **for . . . doom:** *i.e. to see which one dies*   194–197 **Men judge . . . say:** *a quatrain*   199 **lengthen out:** *delay, defer; allusion to torture on the rack*   203 **Upon his party:** *on Bolingbroke's side* **party:** *F Faction*   204 **Beshrew:** *ill luck take (a mild curse)*   206 **Of:** *from*   210 **Flint Castle:** *near Chester, in Wales*   213 **ear:** *plow*

King.   He does me double wrong
That wounds me with the flatteries of his tongue.
Discharge my followers. Let them hence away,
From Richard's night to Bullingbrooke's fair day. *[Exeunt.]*

❧ SCENE THIRD ❧

*Enter [with drum and colors] Bullingbrooke, York, Northumberland.
[, attendants, and soldiers].*

Bulling. So that by this intelligence we learn
The Welshmen are dispers'd, and Salisbury
Is gone to meet the king, who lately landed
With some few private friends upon this coast.
 North. The news is very fair and good, my lord. *5*
Richard not far from hence hath hid his head.
 York. It would beseem the Lord Northumberland
To say 'King Richard.' Alack the heavy day
When such a sacred king should hide his head!
 North. Your grace mistakes. Only to be brief *10*
Left I his title out.
 York.   The time hath bin,
Would you have been so brief with him, he would
Have bin so brief with you to shorten you,
For taking so the head, your whole head's length. *15*
 Bulling. Mistake not, uncle, further than you should.
 York. Take not, good cousin, further than you should,
Lest you mistake. The heavens are over our heads.
 Bulling. I know it, uncle, and oppose not myself
Against their will. But who comes here? *20*

Enter Percy.

Welcome, Harry. What, will not this castle yield?
 Percy. The castle royally is mann'd, my lord,
Against thy entrance.
 Bulling. Royally!
Why, it contains no king? *25*
 Percy.   Yes, my good lord,
It doth contain a king. King Richard lies
Within the limits of yon lime and stone.
And with him are the Lord Aumerle, Lord Salisbury,
Sir Stephen Scroop, besides a clergyman *30*
Of holy reverence—who, I cannot learn.
 North. O, belike it is the Bishop of Carlisle.
 Bulling. Noble lords,
Go to the rude ribs of that ancient castle.
Through brazen trumpet send the breath of parle *35*
Into his ruin'd ears, and thus deliver:
Henry Bullingbrooke
On both his knees doth kiss King Richard's hand
And sends allegiance and true faith of heart
To his most royal person, hither come *40*
Even at his feet to lay my arms and power,

Provided that my banishment repeal'd
And lands restor'd again be freely granted.
If not, I'll use the advantage of my power
And lay the summer's dust with showers of blood *45*
Rain'd from the wounds of slaughter'd Englishmen.
The which, how far off from the mind of Bullingbrooke
It is, such crimson tempest should bedrench
The fresh green lap of fair King Richard's land,
My stooping duty tenderly shall show.
Go signify as much while here we march *50*
Upon the grassy carpet of this plain.
Let's march without the noise of threat'ning drum,
That from this castle's totter'd battlements
Our fair appointments may be well perus'd.
Methinks King Richard and myself should meet *55*
With no less terror than the elements
Of fire and water when their thund'ring shock
At meeting tears the cloudy cheeks of heaven.
Be he the fire, I'll be the yielding water.
The rage be his, whilst on the earth I rain *60*
My waters—on the earth, and not on him.
March on, and mark King Richard how he looks.

*[Parle without, and answer within; then a flourish. Enter,
on the walls, King Richard, the Bishop of Carlisle, Aumerle,
Scroop, Salisbury.]*

See, see, King Richard doth himself appear,
As doth the blushing discontented sun
From out the fiery portal of the east *65*
When he perceives the envious clouds are bent
To dim his glory and to stain the track
Of his bright passage to the occident.
 York. Yet looks he like a king. Behold his eye,
As bright as is the eagle's, lightens forth *70*
Controlling majesty. Alack, alack, for woe,
That any harm should stain so fair a show!
 King. [To Northumberland.] We are amaz'd, and thus long
have we stood
To watch the fearful bending of thy knee, *75*
Because we thought ourself thy lawful king.
And if we be, how dare thy joints forget
To pay their awful duty to our presence?
If we be not, show us the hand of God
That hath dismiss'd us from our stewardship; *80*
For well we know no hand of blood and bone
Can gripe the sacred handle of our scepter
Unless he do profane, steal, or usurp.
And though you think that all, as you have done,
Have torn their souls by turning them from us, *85*
And we are barren and bereft of friends,
Yet know my master, God omnipotent,
Is mustering in his clouds on our behalf
Armies of pestilence; and they shall strike
Your children yet unborn and unbegot *90*

10 mistakes: *perhaps to be read 'mistaketh,' to regularize the line* **12–14 The time ... shorten you:** *F's lineation (Q ends l. 12 with* him) **14 brief:** *unceremonious* **with you:** *F; not in Qq* **to shorten:** *as to shorten* **15 For ... head;** *cf. n.* **16 Mistake not:** *i.e. do not take amiss Northumberland's words* **17 cousin:** *nephew* **18 mistake:** *both 'mis-judge' and 'mis-take' (a quibble)* **mistake. The:** *Qq. F mistake the* **heavens:** *monosyllabic here and elsewhere* **over:** *read 'o'er'; F* ote **27 lies:** *dwells* **29 are:** *not in other Qq. F* **33 lords:** *Qq; F* lord **34 rude ribs:** *i.e. rough walls* **36 his ruin'd ears:** *i.e. its battered windows* **37–38 Henry ... hand:** *one line in Qq* **40 most:** *not in F* **41 Even:** *read 'e'en'* **my;** *cf. n.*

42, 43 Provided ... granted; *cf. n.* **44 the advantage:** *read 'th' advantage'* **45 showers:** *monosyllabic* **47 The which:** *antecedent: the whole threat (ll. 44–46)* **how:** *however* **49 stooping:** *reverential* **53 totter'd:** *variant spelling of 'tattered'* **54 fair appointments:** *splendid and terrible arms and armor* **perus'd:** *viewed* **57–59 elements ... heaven:** *an old explanation for thunder* **58 shock:** *F* smoake **SD Parle ... Salisbury;** *cf. n.* **68 track:** *F* tract **71, 72 lightens ... majesty:** *flashes with imperious majesty* **74 amaz'd:** *stunned, and in a maze* **76 fearful:** *timorous* **89 mustering:** *disyllabic*

That lift your vassal hands against my head
And threat the glory of my precious crown.
Tell Bullingbrooke—for yon methinks he stands—
That every stride he makes upon my land   95
Is dangerous treason. He is come to open
The purple testament of bleeding war.
But ere the crown he looks for live in peace,
Ten thousand bloody crowns of mother's sons
Shall ill become the flower of England's face,   100
Change the complexion of her maid-pale peace
To scarlet indignation, and bedew
Her pastors' grass with faithful English blood.
    North. The King of heaven forbid our lord the king
Should so with civil and uncivil arms   105
Be rush'd upon! Thy thrice-noble cousin
Harry Bullingbrooke doth humbly kiss thy hand.
And by the honorable tomb he swears
That stands upon your royal grandsire's bones,
And by the royalties of both your bloods—   110
Currents that spring from one most gracious head—
And by the buried hand of warlike Gaunt,
And by worth and honor of himself,
Comprising all that may be sworn or said,
His coming hither hath no further scope   115
Than for his lineal royalties, and to beg
Enfranchisement immediate on his knees.
Which on thy royal party granted once,
His glittering arms he will commend to rust,
His barbed steeds to stables, and his heart   120
To faithful service of your majesty.
This swears he, as he is a prince, is just.
And as I am a gentleman, I credit him.
    King. Northumberland, say thus the king returns:
His noble cousin is right welcome hither,   125
And all the number of his fair demands
Shall be accomplish'd without contradiction.
With all the gracious utterance thou hast,
Speak to his gentle hearing kind commends.
[To Aumerle.] We do debase ourselves, cousin, do we not, 130
To look so poorly and to speak so fair?
Shall we call back Northumberland and send
Defiance to the traitor, and so die?
    Aumerle. No, good my lord, let's fight with gentle words
Till time lend friends, and friends their helpful swords.   135
    King. O God, O God, that ere this tongue of mine
That laid the sentence of dread banishment
On yon proud man, should take it off again
With words of sooth! O that I were as great
As is my grief, or lesser than my name!   140
Or that I could forget what I have been!
Or not remember what I must be now!
Swell'st thou, proud heart? I'll give thee scope to beat,
Since foes have scope to beat both thee and me.

    Aumerle. Northumberland comes back from Bullingbrooke.
    King. What must the king do now? Must he submit?
The king shall do it. Must he be depos'd?
The king shall be contented. Must he lose
The name of king? A God's name, let it go!
I'll give my jewels for a set of beads,   150
My gorgeous palace for a hermitage,
My gay apparel for an almsman's gown,
My figur'd goblets for a dish of wood,
My scepter for a palmer's walking staff,
My subjects for a pair of carved saints,   155
And my large kingdom for a little grave,
A little little grave, an obscure grave.
Or I'll be buried in the king's highway,
Some way of common trade, where subjects' feet
May hourly trample on their sovereign's head;   160
For on my heart they tread now whilst I live,
And buried once, why not upon my head?
Aumerle, thou weep'st, my tender-hearted cousin.
We'll make foul weather with despised tears;
Our sighs and they shall lodge the summer corn   165
And make a dearth in this revolting land.
Or shall we play the wantons with our woes
And make some pretty match with shedding tears?
As thus—to drop them still upon one place
Till they have fretted us a pair of graves   170
Within the earth, and therein laid—there lies
Two kinsmen digg'd their graves with weeping eyes.
Would not this ill do well? Well, well, I see
I talk but idly, and you laugh at me.
Most mighty prince, my Lord Northumberland,   175
What says King Bullingbrooke? Will his majesty
Give Richard leave to live till Richard die?
You make a leg, and Bullingbrooke says aye.
    North. My lord, in the base court he doth attend
To speak with you, may it please you to come down.   180
    King. Down, down I come, like glist'ring Phaëton,
Wanting the manage of unruly jades.
In the base court? Base court, where kings grow base,
To come at traitors' calls and do them grace!
In the base court come down? Down, court! Down, king!   185
For night owls shriek where mounting larks should sing.
                                    [Exeunt from above.]

    Bulling. What says his majesty?
    North.   Sorrow and grief of heart
Makes him speak fondly, like a frantic man.
Yet he is come.   190

        [Enter King Richard and his attendants, below.]

    Bulling. Stand all apart
And show fair duty to his majesty.   *[He kneels down.]*
My gracious lord—
    King. Fair cousin, you debase your princely knee

92 That: *implied antecedent:* 'you' (in *your* of l. 91)   **96–97 He is … war:** *cf. n.*   **96 open:** F *ope*   **98–103 But ere … blood:** *a prophecy of the Wars of the Roses*   **100 ill … face:** *i.e. disfigure the beauty of the land's surface*   **103 pastors':** *pastures'* (the words were pronounced alike)   **105 civil and uncivil:** *domestic and barbarous*   **106 thrice-noble:** *cf. n.*   **109 grandsire's:** *Edward III's*   **110 royalties:** *royalty*   **116 royalties:** *disyllabic*   **117 Enfranchisement:** *restoration of rights, i.e. freedom* **immediate:** *trisyllabic*   **118 party:** *side, part*   **119 glittering:** *disyllabic* **commend:** *deliver up*   **120 barbed:** *armored*   **122 is a prince, is just:** *cf. n.* **just:** *true*   **124 returns:** *replies*   **126 demands:** *requests*   **130 ourselves:** F *our selfe*   **139 sooth:** *flattery*   **140 name:** *title*

149 A: *in*   **150 set of beads:** *rosary*   **153 figur'd:** *ornamented*   **157 obscure:** *stressed* **⌣ —**   **159 trade:** *traffic*   **162 buried once:** *once buried*   **164 despised:** *despicable*   **165 lodge:** *beat down*   **167 play the wantons:** *trifle*   **168 match:** *competition*   **170 fretted us:** *worn out for us*   **171, 172 there lies … eyes:** *a mock epitaph*   **172 digg'd:** *who dug*   **174 laugh:** F *mock*   **178 make a leg:** *make a bow*   **179 base court:** *lower courtyard*   **180 may it:** *read 'may't'*   **181 Phaëton:** *cf. n.*   **182 jades:** *vicious of worthless horses (here also men?)*   **184 grace:** *honor*   **186 night owls shriek:** *a death omen*   **188 Sorrow and grief:** *collective subject*   **191 Stand all apart:** *everyone stand back*

To make the base earth proud with kissing it.   *195*
Me rather had my heart might feel your love
Than my unpleas'd eye see your courtesy.
Up, cousin, up! Your heart is up, I know,
Thus high at least, although your knee be low.
    Bulling. My gracious lord, I come but for mine own.   *200*
    King. Your own is yours, and I am yours, and all.
    Bulling. So far be mine, my most redoubted lord,
As my true service shall deserve your love.
    King. Well you deserve. They well deserve to have
That know the strong'st and surest way to get.   *205*
Uncle, give me your hands. Nay, dry your eyes.
Tears show their love but want their remedies.
Cousin, I am too young to be your father,
Though you are old enough to be my heir.
What you will have, I'll give, and willing too,   *210*
For do we must what force will have us do.
Set on towards London. Cousin, is it so?
    Bulling. Yeah, my good lord.
    King.   Then I must not say no.
                                 [Flourish. Exeunt.]

❧ Scene Fourth ❧

Enter the Queen [and two ladies].

    Queen. What sport shall we devise here in this garden
To drive away the heavy thought of care?
    Lady. Madam, we'll play at bowls.
    Queen. 'Twill make me think the world is full of rubs
And that my fortune runs against the bias.   *5*
    Lady. Madam, we'll dance.
    Queen. My legs can keep no measure in delight
When my poor heart no measure keeps in grief.
Therefore no dancing, girl, some other sport.
    Lady. Madam, we'll tell tales.   *10*
    Queen. Of sorrow or of joy?
    Lady.   Of either, madam.
    Queen. Of neither, girl.
For if of joy, being altogether wanting,
It doth remember me the more of sorrow.   *15*
Or if of grief, being altogither had,
It adds more sorrow to my want of joy.
For what I have I need not to repeat,
And what I want it boots not to complain.
    Lady. Madam, I'll sing.   *20*
    Queen.   'Tis well that thou hast cause.
But thou shouldst please me better, wouldst thou weep.
    Lady. I could weep, madam, would it do you good.
    Queen. And I could sing, would weeping do me good,
And never borrow any tear of thee.   *25*

Enter [a gardener and two servants].

But stay, here come the gardeners.
Let's step into the shadow of these trees.
My wretchedness unto a row of pins,
They will talk of state, for everyone doth so
Against a change. Woe is forerun with woe.   *30*
                        [Queen and ladies step aside.]
    Gardener. Go bind thou up yon dangling apricocks,
Which, like unruly children, make their sire
Stoop with oppression of their prodigal weight.
Give some supportance to the bending twigs.
Go thou and, like an executioner,   *35*
Cut off the heads of too fast growing sprays
That look too lofty in your commonwealth.
All must be even in our government.
You thus employ'd, I will go root away
The noisome weeds which without profit suck   *40*
The soil's fertility from wholesome flowers.
    Servant. Why should we in the compass of a pale
Keep law and form and due proportion,
Showing, as in a model, our firm estate,
When our sea-walled garden, the whole land,   *45*
Is full of weeds, her fairest flowers chok'd up,
Her fruit trees all unprun'd, her hedges ruin'd,
Her knots disorder'd, and her wholesome herbs
Swarming with caterpillars?
    Gardener.   Hold thy peace.   *50*
He that hath suffer'd this disorder'd spring
Hath now himself met with the fall of leaf.
The weeds which his broad-spreading leaves did shelter,
That seem'd in eating him to hold him up,
Are pluck'd up root and all by Bullingbrooke—   *55*
I mean the Earl of Wiltshire, Bushy, Green.
    Servant. What, are they dead?
    Gardener.   They are, and Bullingbrooke
Hath seiz'd the wasteful king. O, what pity is it
That he had not so trimm'd and dress'd his land   *60*
As we this garden! We at time of year
Do wound the bark, the skin of our fruit trees,
Lest, being overproud in sap and blood,
With too much riches it confound itself.
Had he done so to great and growing men,   *65*
They might have liv'd to bear and he to taste
Their fruits of duty. Superfluous branches
We lop away, that bearing boughs may live.
Had he done so, himself had borne the crown
Which waste of idle hours hath quite thrown down.   *70*
    Servant. What, think you the king shall be depos'd?
    Gardener. Depress'd he is already, and depos'd
'Tis a doubt he will be. Letters came last night
To a dear friend of the good Duke of York's

28 My wretchedness . . . pins: *she will wager her misery against very little* (will give liberal odds) **pins:** *Qq* pines; *F* Pinnes   **29 They will:** *that they will; read 'they'll'; F* They'le **state:** *the country's condition*   **30 Against a change:** *in anticipation of revolution?*   **31 yon:** *other Qq; Q* yong; *F* yond   **apricocks:** *apricots; cf. n.*   **32–70 Which . . . thrown down:** *cf. n.*   **33 prodigal:** *disyllabic*   **35 thou:** *addressed to the other servant*   **38 even:** *neat*   **42 Servant:** *F; Qq* Man (*also in l.56*)   **pale:** *enclosure, walled garden*   **43 proportion:** *four syllables*   **44 in a model:** *in miniature*   **firm estate:** *condition of stability*   **48 knots:** *patterned flower beds*   **disorder'd:** *overgrown with weeds*   **52 fall of leaf:** *autumn*   **54 in eating him:** *while actually feeding on him*   **55 pluck'd:** *F* pull'd   **58–61 They are . . . year:** *cf. n.*   **61 garden! We at:** *Qq* garden at; *F* Garden, at   **time:** *proper time*   **62 Do:** *F* And   **63 overproud:** *too luxuriant*   **in:** *other Qq, F* with   **64 confound:** *destroy*   **67 Superfluous:** *stressed* ´– — — ´ —   **70 of:** *F* and   **72 Depress'd:** *humbled*   **73 doubt:** *perhaps a past participle (see I.4.20–22; cf. n.); F* doubted   **74 good:** *Q, Q2; not in other Qq, F*

196 Me . . . had: *I had rather*   **199 Thus high at least:** *here Richard touches his own head*   **200 mine own:** *what is rightfully mine*   **201 is yours:** *because he has taken it* **and all:** *i.e. and all is yours*   **202 redoubted:** *dread*   **206 Uncle:** *addressed to York* **hands:** *F* Hand   **207 want their remedies:** *offer no remedies*   **208 Cousin:** *again addressed to Bolingbroke*   **208, 209 too young . . . heir:** *cf. n.*   **212 is it so?:** *is that what you wish?*   **4 rubs:** *obstacles* (a bowling term)   **5 bias:** *the curve of the ball* (a bowling term); *cf. n.*   **7 measure:** *formal dance, or time to music*   **8 measure:** *limit* **grief:** *other Qq, F;* Q griefs   **11 joy:** *Qq. F* griefe   **16 had:** *i.e. present in me*   **19 want:** *lack*

That tell black tidings.   75
    Queen. O, I am press'd to death through want of speaking!
Thou, old Adam's likeness, set to dress this garden,
How dares thy harsh rude tongue sound this unpleasing news?
What Eve, what serpent, hath suggested thee
To make a second fall of cursed man?   80
Why dost thou say King Richard is depos'd?
Dar'st thou, thou little better thing than earth,
Divine his downfall? Say where, when, and how
Cam'st thou by this ill tidings? Speak, thou wretch.
    Gardener. Pardon me, madam. Little joy have I   85
To breathe this news, yet what I say is true.
King Richard, he is in the mighty hold
Of Bullingbrooke. Their fortunes both are weighed.
In your lord's scale is nothing but himself,
And some few vanities that make him light;   90
But in the balance of great Bullingbrooke,
Besides himself, are all the English peers,
And with that odds he weighs King Richard down.
Post you to London and you will find it so.
I speak no more than everyone doth know.   95
    Queen. Nimble Mischance, that art so light of foot,
Doth not thy embassage belong to me,
And am I last that knows it? O, thou think'st
To serve me last, that I may longest keep
Thy sorrow in my breast. Come, ladies, go   100
To meet at London London's king in woe.
What, was I born to this, that my sad look
Should grace the triumph of great Bullingbrooke?
Gard'ner, for telling me these news of woe,
Pray God the plants thou graft'st may never grow.   105
                            Exit [with ladies].
    Gardener. Poor queen, so that thy state might be no worse,
I would my skill were subject to thy curse.
Here did she fall a tear; here in this place
I'll set a bank of rue, sour herb of grace.
Rue, even for ruth, here shortly shall be seen,   110
In the remembrance of a weeping queen.   *Exeunt.*

ACT FOURTH ❧ SCENE FIRST

[Enter, as to the Parliament, Bullingbrooke, Aumerle, Northumber-
land, Percy, Fitzwater, Surrey, Bishop of Carlisle, Abbot of
Westminster, and another lord, herald, officers, and Bagot.]

    Bulling. Call forth Bagot.
Now, Bagot, freely speak thy mind:
What thou dost know of noble Gloucester's death,
Who wrought it with the king, and who perform'd
The bloody office of his timeless end.   5
    Bagot. Then set before my face the Lord Aumerle.
    Bulling. Cousin, stand forth, and look upon that man.

    Bagot. My Lord Aumerle, I know your daring tongue
Scorns to unsay what once it hath deliver'd.
In that dead time when Gloucester's death was plotted,   10
I heard you say, 'Is not my arm of length,
That reacheth from the restful English court
As far as Callice to mine uncle's head?'
Amongst much other talk that very time
I heard you say that you had rather refuse   15
The offer of an hundred thousand crowns
Than Bullingbrooke's return to England,
Adding withal, how blest this land would be
In this your cousin's death.
    Aum.   Princes and noble lords,   20
What answer shall I make to this base man?
Shall I so much dishonor my fair stars
On equal terms to give him chastisement?
Either I must, or have mine honor soil'd
With the attainder of his slanderous lips.   25
There is my gage, the manual seal of death
That marks thee out for hell. I say thou liest,
And will maintain what thou hast said is false
In thy heartblood, though being all too base
To stain the temper of my knightly sword.   30
    Bulling. Bagot, forbear. Thou shalt not take it up.
    Aum. Excepting one, I would he were the best
In all this presence that hath mov'd me so.
    Fitz. If that thy valor stand on sympathy,
There is my gage, Aumerle, in gage to thine.   35
By that fair sun which shows me where thou stand'st,
I heard thee say, and vauntingly thou spak'st it,
That thou wert cause of noble Gloucester's death.
If thou deniest it twenty times, thou liest.
And I will turn thy falsehood to thy heart,   40
Where it was forged, with my rapier's point.
    Aum. Thou dar'st not, coward, live to see that day.
    Fitz. Now, by my soul, I would it were this hour.
    Aum. Fitzwater, thou art damn'd to hell for this.
    Percy. Aumerle, thou liest. His honor is as true   45
In this appeal as thou art all unjust.
And that thou art so, there I throw my gage,
To prove it on thee to the extremest point
Of mortal breathing. Seize it, if thou dar'st.
    Aum. And if I do not, may my hands rot off   50
And never bandish more revengeful steel
Over the glittering helmet of my foe!
    Another Lord. I task the earth to the like, forsworn
Aumerle,
And spur thee on with full as many lies   55
As may be hollowed in thy treacherous ear
From sun to sun. There is my honor's pawn.

76 **press'd:** *a legal means of execution; also metaphorical*   77 **Adam's:** *the first garden-er's*   78 **How dares . . . news:** *an alexandrine*   79 **suggested:** *prompted, tempted*   80 **cursed man:** *see Genesis 3: 17–19*   84 **Cam'st:** *other Qq, F; Q Canst*   86 **this:** *other other Qq, F these*   94 **Post:** *travel posthaste*   **you will:** *read 'you'll'; F you'll*   97 **embas-sage:** *message*   **belong:** *pertain*   100 **Thy sorrow:** *the sorrow you report*   103 **triumph:** *triumphal procession*   **great:** *powerful*   104 **these:** *F this*   105 **Pray God:** *F I would*   106 **so:** *provided that*   **state:** *condition*   108 **fall:** *let fall; other Qq, F drop*   109, 110 **rue . . . ruth:** *cf. n.*   109 **sour:** *bitter*   4 **wrought it:** *worked it, i.e. persuaded the king to order it*   5 **timeless:** *untimely*

10 **dead:** *dark and sinister*   11 **of length:** *long*   12 **restful:** *peaceful*   13 **Callice:** *Calais (see I.1.126)*   15 **rather refuse:** *possibly to be read 'rath' refuse'*   17–19 **Than . . . lords;** *cf. n.*   17 **Than . . . return:** *than have Bolingbroke return*   **England:** *trisyllabic*   22 **fair stars:** *high birth and rank, as determined by the stars*   23 **to:** *as to*   **him:** *Q3, F: Q them; Q2 my*   25 **attainder:** *disgrace, stain*   **slanderous:** *disyllabic*   26 **manual seal:** *sealed warrant (a boast) cf. n.*   27 **I say:** *not in other Qq, F*   32 **one:** *i.e. Bolingbroke*   **best:** *noblest*   33 **mov'd:** *angered*   34 **Fitzwater:** *Walter Fitzwater (or Fitzwalter), fifth baron*   **stand on sympathy:** *insist on equality of rank*   35 **in gage to thine:** *mine against yours*   39 **deniest:** *disyllabic*   **liest:** *monosyl-labic*   41 **rapier's:** *not used in England before Shakespeare's day cf. n.*   42 **live:** *other Qq live I*   45 **Percy:** *F; Q L[ord] Per[cy]*   46 **appeal:** *accusation*   48, 49 **to the . . . breathing:** *to your last breath*   **the extremest:** *read 'th' extremest'*   52 **glittering:** *disyllabic*   53–61 **I task . . . as you:** *not in F*   53 **task the earth:** *cf. n.*   **to the like:** *read 't' th' like' (two syllables)*   55 **lies:** *i.e. charges of lying*   56 **As:** *Qq As it;*   **hollowed:** *shouted*   57 **sun to sun:** *Qq sinne to sinne*

Engage it to the trial, if thou dar'st.

   Aum. Who sets me else? By heaven, I'll throw at all!

I have a thousand spirits in one breast   60

To answer twenty thousand such as you.

   Surrey. My Lord Fitzwater, I do remember well

The very time Aumerle and you did talk.

   Fitz. 'Tis very true. You were in presence then,

And you can witness with me this is true.   65

   Surrey. As false, by heaven, as heaven itself is true!

   Fitz. Surry, thou liest.

   Surrey.   Dishonorable boy!

That lie shall lie so heavy on my sword

That it shall render vengeance and revenge   70

Till thou the lie-giver and that lie do lie

In earth as quiet as thy father's skull.

In proof whereof there is my honor's pawn.

Engage it to the trial, if thou dar'st.

   Fitz. How fondly dost thou spur a forward horse!   75

If I dare eat, or drink, or breathe, or live,

I dare meet Surrey in a wilderness,

And spit upon him whilst I say he lies,

And lies, and lies. There is my bond of faith

To tie thee to my strong correction.   80

As I intend to thrive in this new world,

Aumerle is guilty of my true appeal.

Besides, I heard the banish'd Norfolk say

That thou, Aumerle, didst send two of thy men

To execute the noble duke at Callice.   85

   Aum. Some honest Christian trust me with a gage

That Norfolk lies. Here do I throw down this,

If he may be repeal'd to try his honor.

   Bulling. These differences shall all rest under gage

Till Norfolk be repeal'd. Repeal'd he shall be   90

And, though mine enemy, restor'd again

To all his lands and signories. When he is return'd,

Against Aumerle we will enforce his trial.

   Car. That honorable day shall never be seen.

Many a time hath banish'd Norfolk fought   95

For Jesu Christ in glorious Christian field,

Streaming the ensign of the Christian cross

Against black pagans, Turks, and Saracens;

And toil'd with works of war, retir'd himself

To Italy, and there at Venice gave   100

His body to that pleasant country's earth

And his pure soul unto his captain's Christ,

Under whose colors he had fought so long.

   Bulling. Why, Bishop, is Norfolk dead?

   Car. As surely as I live, my lord.   105

   Bulling. Sweet peace conduct his sweet soul to the bosom

Of good old Abraham! Lords appellants,

Your differences shall all rest under gage

Till we assign you to your days of trial.

         Enter York [, attended].

   York. Great Duke of Lancaster, I come to thee   110

From plume-pluck'd Richard, who with willing soul

Adopts thee heir, and his high scepter yields

To the possession of thy royal hand.

Ascend his throne, descending now from him,

And long live Henry, fourth of that name!   115

   Bulling. In God's name, I'll ascend the regal throne.

   Car. Marry, God forbid!

Worst in this royal presence may I speak,

Yet best beseeming me to speak the truth.

Would God that any in this noble presence   120

Were enough noble to be upright judge

Of noble Richard! Then true noblesse would

Learn him forbearance from so foul a wrong.

What subject can give sentence on his king?

And who sits here that is not Richard's subject?   125

Thieves are not judg'd but they are by to hear,

Although apparent guilt be seen in them.

And shall the figure of God's majesty,

His captain, steward, deputy elect,

Anointed, crowned, planted many years,   130

Be judg'd by subject and inferior breath,

And he himself not present? O, forfend it God

That in a Christian climate souls refin'd

Should show no heinous, black, obscene a deed!

I speak to subjects, and a subject speaks,   135

Stirr'd up by God, thus boldly for his king.

My Lord of Herford here, whom you call king,

Is a foul traitor to proud Herford's king.

And if you crown him, let me prophesy,

The blood of English shall manure the ground   140

And future ages groan for this foul act.

Peace shall go sleep with Turks and infidels,

And in this seat of peace tumultuous wars

Shall kin with kin and kind with kind confound.

Disorder, horror, fear, and mutiny   145

Shall here inhabit, and this land be call'd

The field of Golgotha and dead men's skulls.

O, if you raise this house against this house,

It will the woefullest division prove

That ever fell upon this cursed earth.   150

Prevent it, resist it, let it not be so,

Lest child, child's children, cry against you 'woe!'

   North. Well have you argued, sir, and for your pains.

Of capital treason we arrest you here.

My Lord of Westminster, be it your charge   155

To keep him safely till his day of trial.

May it please you, lords, to grant the commons' suit?

   Bulling. Fetch hither Richard, that in common view

He may surrender. So we shall proceed

Without suspicion.   160

---

59 sets: *challenges* **throw at all:** *wager against all that is staked*   **62 Surrey;** *cf. n.*   **64 in presence:** *in our presence*   **67–69 Dishonorable . . . sword:** *F's lineation; one line in Qq*   **68 boy:** *actually Fitzwater was thirty-one*   **79 my bond:** *Q3, F; Q bond; Q2 the bond* **bond of faith:** *gage*   **80 correction:** *four syllables*   **81 new world:** *i.e. under Bolingbroke*   **87 this:** *a borrowed hood, according to Holinshed*   **88 repeal'd:** *recalled*   **89 differences:** *trisyllabic (also in l. 108)*   **92 signories:** *estates (compare III.1.22)* **he is:** *read 'he's'; F hee's*   **94 never:** *read 'ne'er'; F ne're*   **99 toil'd:** *exhausted* **retir'd himself:** *withdrew (compare French se retirer)*   **105 surely:** *other Qq, F sure*   **106, 107 bosom . . . Abraham:** *i.e. Paradise (see Luke 16:22)*   **107 Lords appellants:** *accusing lords*

111 plume-pluck'd: *broken in power and prestige (compare 'crestfallen')*   **114 descending . . . him:** *becoming now his heir*   **115 fourth of that name:** *F of that Name the Fourth* **Henry:** *read 'Henery'*   **117 Marry:** *see I.4.16*   **118 Worst:** *least in rank (or, possibly, least effective)*   **119 best:** *because of his sacred office*   **122 noblesse:** *other Qq, F Noblenesse*   **123 Learn:** *teach*   **126 but:** *unless*   **127 apparent:** *manifest*   **128 planted:** *established*   **132 forfend:** *F forbid*   **133 refin'd:** *i.e. by Christianity*   **134 obscene:** *odious (compare Latin obscenus)*   **138 Herford's king:** *i.e. King Richard*   **139–150 And if . . . earth:** *a prophecy of the Wars of the Roses*   **141 this:** *other Qq, F his*   **147 Golgotha:** *Calvary (see Matthew 27:33)*   **148 raise:** *rouse; F reare* **this house . . . house:** *see Matthew 12–25*   **151 Prevent:** *forestall* **let:** *other Qq, F and let*   **154 Of:** *on a charge of*   **157–325 May it please . . . king's fall:** *cf. n.*   **158–160 Fetch . . . suspicion:** *Q4, Q5 give the speech to Northumberland*   **159 surrender:** *abdicate*

York.   I will be his conduct.   [Exit.]
Bulling. Lords, you that here are under our arrest,
Procure your sureties for your days of answer.
Little are we beholding to your love,
And little look'd for at your helping hands.   *165*

[Re-enter York, with Richard, and officers bearing the regalia.]

King. Alack, why am I sent for to a king
Before I have shook off the real thoughts
Wherewith I reign'd? I hardly yet have learn'd
To insinuate, flatter, bow, and bend my knee.
Give Sorrow leave awhile to tutor me   *170*
To this submission. Yet I well remember
The favors of these men. Were they not mine?
Did they not sometime cry 'All hail!' to me?
So Judas did to Christ. But He in twelve
Found truth in all but one; I in twelve thousand, none.   *175*
God save the king! Will no man say amen?
Am I both priest and clark? Well then, amen.
God save the king, although I be not he;
And yet amen, if heaven do think him me.
To do what service am I sent for hither?   *180*
York. To do that office of thine own good will
Which tried majesty did make thee offer:
The resignation of thy state and crown
To Henry Bullingbrooke
King. Give me the crown. Here, cousin, seize the crown.   *185*
Here, cousin,
On this side my hand, and on that side thine.
Now is this golden crown like a deep well
That owes two buckets, filling one another,
The emptier ever dancing in the air,   *190*
The other down, unseen and full of water.
That bucket down and full of tears am I,
Drinking my griefs whilst you mount up on high.
Bulling. I thought you had been willing to resign.
King. My crown I am, but still my griefs are mine.   *195*
You may my glories and my state depose,
But not my griefs. Still am I king of those.
Bulling. Part of your cares you give me with your crown.
King. Your cares set up do not pluck my cares down.
My care is loss of care, by old care done.   *200*
Your care is gain of care, by new care won.
The cares I give I have, though given away.
They tend the crown, yet still with me they stay.
Bulling. Are you contented to resign the crown?
King. I, no—no, I, for I must nothing be.   *205*
Therefore no no, for I resign to thee.
Now mark me how I will undo myself.
I give this heavy weight from off my head
And this unwieldy scepter from my hand,
The pride of kingly sway from out my heart.   *210*
With mine own tears I wash away my balm,

With mine own hands I give away my crown,
With mine own tongue deny my sacred state,
With mine own breath release all duteous oaths.
All pomp and majesty I do forswear;   *215*
My manors, rents, revenues I forgo;
My acts, decrees, and statutes I deny.
God pardon all oaths that are broke to me!
God keep all vows unbroke are made to thee!
Make me, that nothing have, with nothing griev'd,   *220*
And thou with all pleas'd, that hast all achiev'd!
Long mayst thou live in Richard's seat to sit,
And soon lie Richard in an earthy pit!
God save King Henry, unking'd Richard says,
And send him many years of sunshine days!   *225*
What more remains?
North. No more, but that you read
These accusations and these grievous crimes
Committed by your person and your followers
Against the state and profit of this land,   *230*
That, by confessing them, the souls of men
May deem that you are worthily depos'd.
King. Must I do so? And must I ravel out
My weav'd-up follies? Gentle Northumberland,
If thy offenses were upon record,   *235*
Would it not shame thee in so fair a troop
To read a lecture of them? If thou wouldst,
There shouldst thou find one heinous article,
Containing the deposing of a king
And cracking the strong warrant of an oath,   *240*
Mark'd with a blot, damn'd in the book of heaven.
Nay, all of you that stand and look upon me
Whilst that my wretchedness doth bait myself,
Though some of you with Pilate wash your hands,
Showing an outward pity, yet you Pilates   *245*
Have here deliver'd me to my sour cross,
And water cannot wash away your sin.
North. My lord, dispatch. Read o're these articles.
King. Mine eyes are full of tears. I cannot see.
And yet salt water blinds them not so much   *250*
But they can see a sort of traitors here.
Nay, if I turn mine eyes upon myself,
I find myself a traitor with the rest;
For I have given here my soul's consent
T'undeck the pompous body of a king,   *255*
Made glory base and sovereignty a slave,
Proud majesty a subject, state a peasant.
North. My lord—
King. No lord of thine, thou haught insulting man,
Nor no man's lord. I have no name, no title;   *260*
No, not that name was given me at the font,
But 'tis usurp'd. Alack the heavy day,
That I have worn so many winters out
And know not now what name to call myself!
O, that I were a mockery king of snow,   *265*

161 conduct: *escort*   162 here are: *Q4, Q5 are heere, are*   163 sureties: *bail*   164
beholding: *beholden, indebted*   165 look'd: *Q4, Q5 looke*   169 To insinuate: *read 't'
insinuate'* knee: *Q4, Q5 limbes*   172 favors: *faces, features*   173 sometime: *once; Q4,
Q5 sometimes*   174 Judas: *see Matthew 26:49*   175 Found . . . none: *an alexandrine*   177 clark: *a parish clerk*   183 state: *kingship*   185 Give me . . . cousin: *not
in Q4, Q5*   186–187 Here . . . thine: *one line in Q4, Q5, F*   187 and: *Q4, Q5; not
in F*   187 owes: *owns*   199–203 Your cares . . . stay: *an extended pun on* care *as trouble
and sorrow*   205 I . . . I: *meaning 'aye' and 'aye' (a pun)*   206 no no: *adjective and
noun*   211 balm: *holy oil at the coronation*

215 pomp and majesty: *hendiadys*   216 revenues: *stressed* — ́ —   217 deny: *repeal*   221 thou: *i.e. thee*   232 worthily: *justly*   235 record: *stressed* — ́ —   236
so fair a troop: *such splendid company (sarcastic)*   237 read a lecture of: *i.e. deliver a
moral lesson from*   240 an oath: *i.e. Northumberland's oath of allegiance*   243 bait:
worry, harass; cf. n.   244 Pilate: *see Matthew 27:24–6*   246 sour: *bitter*   251 sort:
company, gang   255 pompous: *stately, splendid*   256 and: *Q4, Q5; F a*   260 Nor:
Q4, Q5; F No, nor   262 But 'tis usurp'd: *i.e. he has no name which is not usurped*   265
mockery: *(disyllabic) mock*

Standing before the sun of Bullingbrooke
To melt myself away in water drops!
Good king, great king, and yet not greatly good,
And if my word be sterling yet in England,
Let it command a mirror hither straight,   270
That it may show me what a face I have
Since it is bankrupt of his majesty.
 Bulling. Go some of you and fetch a looking glass.
          [Exit an attendant.]
 North. Read o'er this paper while the glass doth come.
 King. Fiend, thou torments me ere I come to hell!   275
 Bulling. Urge it no more, my Lord Northumberland.
 North. The commons will not then be satisfied.
 King. They shall be satisfied. I'll read enough.
When I do see the very book indeed
Where all my sins are writ, and that's myself.   280

   [Re-enter an attendant, with a glass.]

Give me that glass, and therein will I read.
No deeper wrinkles yet? Hath Sorrow struck
So many blows upon this face of mine
And made no deeper wounds? O flatt'ring glass,
Like to my followers in prosperity,   285
Thou dost beguile me! Was this face the face
That every day under his household roof
Did keep ten thousand men? Was this the face
That like the sun did make beholders wink?
Is this the face which fac'd so many follies,   290
That was at last outfac'd by Bullingbrooke?
A brittle glory shineth in this face—
As brittle as the glory is the face,
   [Dashes the glass against the ground.]
For there it is, crack'd in an hundred shivers.
Mark, silent king, the moral of this sport—   295
How soon my sorrow hath destroyed my face.
 Bulling. The shadow of your sorrow hath destroyed
The shadow of your face.
 King.   Say that again.
The shadow of my sorrow! Ha, let's see!   300
'Tis very true, my grief lies all within,
And these external manners of laments
Are merely shadows to the unseen grief
That swells with silence in the tortur'd soul.
There lies the substance, and I thank thee, king,   305
For thy great bounty, that not only giv'st
Me cause to wail, but teachest me the way
How to lament the cause. I'll beg one boon,
And then be gone and trouble you no more.
Shall I obtain it?   310
 Bulling. Name it, fair cousin.
 King. 'Fair cousin'? I am greater than a king.
For when I was a king, my flatterers
Were then but subjects; being now a subject,

I have a king here to my flatterer.   315
Being so great, I have no need to beg.
 Bulling. Yet ask.
 King. And shall I have?
 Bulling. You shall.
 King. Then give me leave to go.   320
 Bulling. Whither?
 King. Whither you will, so I were from your sights.
 Bulling. Go some of you, convey him to the Tower.
 King. O, good! Convey! Conveyers are you all
That rise thus nimbly by a true king's fall.   325
  [Exeunt King Richard, some lords, and a guard.]
 Bulling. On Wednesday next we solemnly set down
Our coronation. Lords, prepare yourselves.
  Exeunt. Manent [the Abbot of] Westminster, [the Bishop of]
           Carlisle, Aumerle.

 Abbot. A woeful pageant have we here beheld.
 Car. The woe's to come. The children yet unborn
Shall feel this day as sharp to them as thorn.   330
 Aum. You holy clergymen, is there no plot
To rid the realm of this pernicious blot?
 Abbot. My lord,
Before I freely speak my mind herein,
You shall not only take the sacrament   335
To bury mine intents, but also to effect
Whatever I shall happen to devise.
I see your brows are full of discontent,
Your hearts of sorrow, and your eyes of tears.
Come home with me to supper. I will lay   340
A plot shall show us all a merry day.   *Exeunt.*

ACT FIFTH ❧ SCENE FIRST

Enter the Queen with her attendants.

 Queen. This way the king will come. This is the way
To Julius Caesar's ill-erected tower,
To whose flint bosom my condemned lord
Is doom'd a prisoner by proud Bullingbrooke.
Here let us rest, if this rebellious earth   5
Have any resting for her true king's queen.

   Enter King Richard [and guard].

But soft, but see, or rather do not see,
My fair rose wither. Yet look up, behold,
That you in pity may dissolve to dew
And wash him fresh again with true-love tears.   10
Ah, thou the model where old Troy did stand,
Thou map of honor, thou King Richard's tomb,

315 to: *for, as* **318 have:** *Q4, Q5* have it **320 Then:** *Q4, Q5* Why then **322 sights:** *sight (referring to more than one person)* **324 Conveyers:** *thrives (a cant term)* **Exeunt . . . guard:** *not in Q4, Q5, F* **326–327 On . . . yourselves;** *cf. n.* **327 coronation;** *cf. n.* **328 pageant:** *spectacle* **329 woe's to come:** *another prophecy of the Wars of the Roses (see also III.3.98, IV.1.139)* **331 plot:** *plan* **333–336 My . . . herein:** *one line in Q, Q2* **My lord:** *not in F* **339 hearts:** *other Qq.* Heart **340–341 Come . . . plot:** *one line in Qq. F* Ile **341 merry:** *happy, fortunate* **1 Queen;** *cf. n.* **2 Caesar's . . . tower:** *legend says Caesar built the Tower of London* **7 soft:** *be silent a moment* **8 rose:** *i.e. Richard* **9 you:** *i.e. Isabelle herself* **12 map of honor:** *i.e. mere outline of former glory* **thou King . . . Richard:** *i.e. his body is the grave of his kingship*

267 To melt . . . drops; *cf. n.* **269 sterling:** *current, valuable* **272 his:** *its* **273 some:** *some one* **SD Exit . . . attendant:** *not in Q4, Q5, F* **275 torments:** *old form of 'tormentest'* **SD Re-enter . . . glass:** *F* Enter one with a Glasse **281–90 Give me . . . follies;** *cf. n.* **285 followers:** *disyllabic* **286–288 Was this . . . men:** *see l. 267 cf. n.* **289 wink:** *close their eyes* **290 fac'd:** *countenanced* **292 brittle:** *fragile* **SD Dashes . . . ground:** *not in Q4, Q5, F* **295 sport:** *play acting* **297 shadow:** *reflection* **destroyed:** *i.e. overshadowed* **298 shadow:** *image* **302 external . . . laments:** *outward signs of sorrow* **manners:** *Q4, Q5; F* manner **303 shadows:** *to appearances belonging to* **305 There . . . substance:** *not in Q4, Q5* **substance:** *reality, truth*

And not King Richard! Thou most beauteous inn,
Why should hard-favor'd grief be lodg'd in thee
When triumph is become an alehouse guest?   *15*

     King. Join not with grief, fair woman, do not so,
To make my end too sudden. Learn, good soul,
To think our former state a happy dream,
From which awak'd, the truth of what we are
Shows us but this. I am sworn brother, sweet,   *20*
To grim Necessity, and he and I
Will keep a league till death. Hie thee to France
And cloister thee in some religious house.
Our holy lives must win a new world's crown,
Which our profane hours here have thrown down.   *25*

     Queen. What, is my Richard both in shape and mind
Transform'd and weak'ned? Hath Bullingbrooke depos'd
Thine intellect? Hath he been in thy heart?
The lion dying thrusteth forth his paw
And wounds the earth, if nothing else, with rage   *30*
To be orepowr'd. And with thou, pupil-like,
Take thy correction, mildly kiss the rod,
And fawn on rage with base humility,
Which art a lion and the king of beasts?

     King. A king of beasts indeed. If aught but beasts,   *35*
I had been still a happy king of men.
Good sometime queen, prepare thee hence for France.
Think I am dead, and that even here thou tak'st,
As from my deathbed, thy last living leave.
In winter's tedious night sit by the fire   *40*
With good old folks, and let them tell thee tales
Of woeful ages long ago betid.
And ere thou bid good night, to quite their griefs
Tell thou the lamentable tale of me,
And send the hearers weeping to their beds.   *45*
For why, the senseless brands will sympathize
The heavy accent of thy moving tongue
And in compassion weep the fire out;
And some will mourn in ashes, some coal-black,
For the deposing of a rightful king.   *50*

     Enter Northumberland [, attended].

     North. My lord, the mind of Bullingbrooke is chang'd.
You must to Pomfret, not unto the Tower.
And, madam, there is order tane for you.
With all swift speed you must away to France.

     King. Northumberland, thou ladder wherewithal.   *55*
The mounting Bullingbrooke ascends my throne,
The time shall not be many hours of age
More than it is, ere foul sin gathering head
Shall break into corruption. Thou shalt think,
Though he divide the realm and give thee half,   *60*
It is too little, helping him to all.

He shall think that thou, which knowest the way
To plant unrightful kings, wilt know again,
Being nere so little urg'd, another way
To pluck him headlong from the usurped throne.   *65*
The love of wicked men converts to fear,
That fear to hate, and hate turns one or both
To worthy danger and deserved death.

     North. My guilt be on my head, and there an end.
Take leave and part, for you must part forthwith.   *70*

     King. Doubly divorc'd! Bad men, you violate
A twofold marriage—'twixt my crown and me,
And then betwixt me and my married wife.
Let me unkiss the oath 'twixt thee and me.
And yet not so, for with a kiss 'twas made.   *75*
Part us, Northumberland, I towards the north
Where shivering cold and sickness pines the clime,
My wife to France, from whence, set forth in pomp,
She came adorned hither like sweet May,
Sent back like Hallowmas or short'st of day.   *80*

     Queen. And must we be divided? Must we part?

     King. Aye, hand from hand, my love, and heart from heart.

     Queen. Banish us both, and send the king with me.

     North. That were some love, but little policy.

     Queen. Then whither he goes, thither let me go.   *85*

     King. So two, togither weeping, make one woe.
Weep thou for me in France, I for thee here.
Better far off than near, be nere the near.
Go, count thy way with sighs, I mine with groans.

     Queen. So longest way shall have the longest moans.   *90*

     King. Twice for one step I'll groan, the way being short,
And piece the way out with a heavy heart.
Come, come, in wooing sorrow let's be brief,
Since, wedding it, there is such length to grief.
One kiss shall stop our mouths, and dumbly part.   *95*
Thus give I mine, and thus take I thy heart.

     Queen. Give me mine own again. 'Twere no good part
To take on me to keep and kill thy heart.
So, now I have mine own again, be gone,
That I may strive to kill it with a groan.   *100*

     King. We make woe wanton with this fond delay.
Once more, adieu. The rest let sorrow say.   *Exeunt.*

❧ SCENE SECOND ❧

Enter the Duke of York and the Duchess.

     Duch. My lord, you told me you would tell the rest,
When weeping made you break the story off
Of our two cousins' coming into London.

     York. Where did I leave?

     Duch.   At that sad stop, my lord,   *5*

---

14 **hard-favor'd:** *ill-featured, ugly*   15 **alehouse:** *i.e. Bolingbroke (in contrast to Richard, the beauteous inn)*   20 **this:** *this wretched state* (condition)   25 **our:** *disyllabic* **profane:** (stressed ⏑ —) *earthly* **thrown:** *F* stricken   27 **Transform'd . . . Bullingbrooke:** *one line in Qq, F*   32 **thy:** *other Qq. F; Q* the   34 **Which:** *who* **the king:** *other Qq, F* a King   37 **sometime:** *other Qq, F; Q, Q2* sometimes   38 **even:** *read 'e'en'*   39 **thy:** *other Qq, F* my   42 **betid:** *happened; other Qq, F* betide   43 **quite:** *requite, give full return for; F* quit **griefs:** *other Qq, F* griefe   44 **tale:** *F* fall   46 **senseless brands:** *i.e. unfeeling logs on the fire* **sympathize:** *respond to; other Qq* sympathy   47 **moving:** *i.e. which moves others*   52 **Pomfret:** *the common pronunciation* (and occasional spelling) *of Pontefract Castle, Yorkshire*   53 **order tane:** *provision made.* **tane:** *taken*   54 **With . . . France;** *cf. n.*   55 **wherewithal:** *by means of which*   58 **gathering head:** *like a boil* **gathering:** *disyllabic*

62 **He:** *most editors print* And he (from Rowe) **knowest:** *F* know'st   65 **the usurped:** *read 'th' usurpèd'*   66 **men:** *F* friends   67–68 **turns . . . death:** *i.e. one wicked man destroys the other, or they destroy each other*   68 **worthy:** *merited*   70 **part . . . part:** *separate . . . depart*   74 **oath:** *marriage vow*   77 **pines the clime:** *afflicts the region*   78 **wife:** *F* Queene **pomp:** *splendor*   80 **Hallowmas:** *All Saints' Day* (November 1)   84 **Northumberland:** *F; Qq give the line to Richard* **policy:** *wisdom*   88 **Better . . . the near;** *cf. n.* **nere:** *read 'ne'er'* (never)   92 **piece the way out:** *lengthen the way*   94 **wedding:** *becoming attached to*   95 **dumbly part:** *i.e. shall part us without our saying good-by* **dumbly:** *other Qq* doubly   101 **wanton:** *frivolous* **fond:** *both loving and foolish*   3 **two cousins':** *i.e. Richard's and Bolingbroke's*

Where rude misgovern'd hands from windows' tops
Threw dust and rubbish on King Richard's head.

   York. Then, as I said, the duke, great Bullingbrooke,
Mounted upon a hot and fiery steed
Which his aspiring rider seem'd to know,   *10*
With slow but stately pace kept on his course,
Whilst all tongues cried 'God save thee, Bullingbrooke!'
You would have thought the very windows spake,
So many greedy looks of young and old
Through casements darted their desiring eyes   *15*
Upon his visage, and that all the walls
With painted imagery had said at once
'Jesu preserve thee! Welcome, Bullingbrooke!'
Whilst he, from the one side to the other turning,
Bareheaded, lower than his proud steed's neck,   *20*
Bespake them thus, 'I thank you, countrymen.'
And thus still doing, thus he pass'd along.

   Duch. Alack, poor Richard! Where rode he the whilst?

   York. As in a theater the eyes of men,
After a well-grac'd actor leaves the stage,   *25*
Are idly bent on him that enters next,
Thinking his prattle to be tedious,
Even so, or with much more contempt, men's eyes
Did scowl on gentle Richard. No man cried 'God save him!'
No joyful tongue gave him his welcome home,   *30*
But dust was thrown upon his sacred head,
Which with such gentle sorrow he shook off,
His face still combating with tears and smiles—
The badges of his grief and patience—
That had not God, for some strong purpose, steel'd   *35*
The hearts of men, they must perforce have melted
And barbarism itself have pitied him.
But heaven hath a hand in these events,
To whose high will we bound our calm contents.
To Bullingbrooke are we sworn subjects now,   *40*
Whose state and honor I for aye allow.

[Enter Aumerle.]

   Duch. Here comes my son Aumerle.

   York.   Aumerle that was,
But that is lost for being Richard's friend,
And, madam, you must call him Rutland now.   *45*
I am in parliament pledge for his truth
And lasting fealty to the new-made king.

   Duch. Welcome, my son. Who are the violets now
That strew the green lap of the new-come spring?

   Aum. Madam, I know not, nor I greatly care not.   *50*
God knows I had as lief be none as one.

   York. Well, bear you well in this new spring of time,
Lest you be cropp'd before you come to prime.
What news from Oxford? Do these justs and triumphs hold?

   Aum. For aught I know, my lord, they do.   *55*

   York. You will be there, I know.

   Aum. If God prevent not, I purpose so.

   York. What seal is that that hangs without thy bosom?
Yea, look'st thou pale? Let me see the writing.

   Aum. My lord, 'tis nothing.   *60*

   York.   No matter then who see it.
I will be satisfied. Let me see the writing.

   Aum. I do beseech your grace to pardon me.
It is a matter of small consequence
Which for some reasons I would not have seen.   *65*

   York. Which for some reasons, sir, I mean to see.
I fear, I fear—

   Duch.   What should you fear?
'Tis nothing but some band that he is ent'red into
For gay apparel 'gainst the triumph day.   *70*

   York. Bound to himself! What doth he with a bond
That he is bound to? Wife, thou art a fool.
Boy, let me see the writing.

   Aum. I do beseech you pardon me, I may not show it.

   York. I will be satisfied. Let me see it, I say.   *75*

He plucks it out of his bosom and reads it.

Treason! Foul treason! Villain! Traitor! Slave!

   Duch. What is the matter, my lord?

   York. Ho! Who is within there? Saddle my horse.
God for His mercy, what treachery is here!   *80*

   Duch. Why, what is it, my lord?

   York. Give me my boots, I say. Saddle my horse.
Now, by mine honor, by my life, by my troth,
I will appeach the villain.

   Duch.   What is the matter?   *85*

   York. Peace, foolish woman.

   Duch. I will not peace. What is the matter, Aumerle?

   Aum. Good mother, be content. It is no more
Than my poor life must answer.

   Duch.   Thy life answer?   *90*

   York. Bring me my boots! I will unto the king.

His man enters with his boots.

   Duch. Strike him, Aumerle. Poor boy, thou art amaz'd.
Hence, villain. Never more come in my sight.

   York. Give me my boots, I say!

   Duch. Why, York, what wilt thou do?   *95*
Wilt thou not hide the trespass of thine own?
Have we more sons? Or are we like to have?
Is not my teeming date drunk up with time?
And wilt thou pluck my fair son from mine age
And rob me of a happy mother's name?   *100*
Is he not like thee? Is he not thine own?

   York. Thou fond mad woman,
Wilt thou conceal this dark conspiracy?
A dozen of them here have tane the sacrament,
And interchangeably set down their hands,   *105*
To kill the king at Oxford.

6 windows' tops: *high windows, probably*   **7 Threw ... head:** *not in the known sources*   **10 Which:** *subject (not object) of* seem'd   **17 painted imagery:** *human figures on tapestry hangings*   **19 the one:** *probably to be read 'th' one';* F one   **20 lower:** *bending lower*   **23 Alack:** F Alas   **rode:** *other* Qq, F rides   **24 theater;** *cf. n.*   **26 idly:** *indifferently*   **28 Even:** *read 'e'en'*   **29 Did ... him:** *an alexandrine*   **gentle:** *not in* F   **34 patience:** *trisyllabic*   **37 barbarism itself:** *even barbarians*   **39 bound:** *submit*   **calm contents:** *proleptic*   **41 for aye allow:** *accept*   **42 son:** *stepson, historically*   **45 Rutland:** *his new, degraded title as Earl of Rutland*   **46 truth:** *loyalty*   **48 violets:** *i.e. court favorites*   **51 had as lief ... one:** *would be glad not to be one of them*   **53 cropp'd:** *both harvested and beheaded*   **54–127 What news ... gone:** *for Holinshed's version see Sources of the Play*   **54 Do ... hold:** F Hold those Iusts & Triumphs   **justs and triumphs:** *tilts (jousts) and tournaments (see ll. 67–68 cf. n.)*   **hold:** *take place*

58 seal ... hangs; *cf. n.*   **69 band:** *bond (see l. 71)*   **70 'gainst the triumph day:** *in anticipation of the festal day, here Epiphany (see ll. 71, 72 cf. n.);* F against the Triumph   **71, 72 Bound ... bound to;** *cf. n.*   **80 God ... mercy:** *I pray God for His mercy*   **83 by my life ... troth:** *other* Qq, F my life, my troth   **84 appeach:** *inform against*   **88 content:** *calm*   **89 answer:** *answer for*   **92 him:** *i.e. the servant*   **amaz'd:** *bewildered*   **97 more sons:** *historically, York had another son*   **98 teeming date drunk up:** *time for childbearing ended*   **104 here:** *York points to the bond*   **105 interchangeably set down:** *each man had a copy signed by all*

Duch.   He shall be none.
We'll keep him here. Then what is that to him?
     York. Away, fond woman! Were he twenty times my son,
I would appeach him.   *110*
     Duch.   Hadst thou groan'd for him
As I have done, thou wouldst be more pitiful.
But now I know my mind. Thou dost suspect
That I have been disloyal to thy bed
And that he is a bastard, not thy son.   *115*
Sweet York, sweet husband, be not of that mind.
He is as like thee as a man may be,
Not like to me, or any of my kin,
And yet I love him.
     York.   Make way, unruly woman!   *Exit. 120*
     Duch. After, Aumerle! Mount thee upon his horse,
Spur post and get before him to the king,
And beg thy pardon ere he do accuse thee.
I'll not be long behind. Though I be old,
I doubt not but to ride as fast as York.   *125*
And never will I rise up from the ground
Till Bullingbrooke have pardon'd thee. Away, be gone!

                                                              [Exeunt.]

❧ Scene Third ❧

[Enter Bullingbrooke, Percy, and other lords.]

     Bulling. Can no man tell me of my unthrifty son?
'Tis full three months since I did see him last.
If any plague hang over us, 'tis he.
I would to God, my lords, he might be found.
Inquire at London, 'mongst the taverns there,   *5*
For there, they say, he daily doth frequent,
With unrestrained loose companions,
Even such, they say, as stand in narrow lanes
And beat our watch and rob our passengers,
Which he, young wanton and effeminate boy,   *10*
Takes on the point of honor to support
So dissolute a crew.
     Percy. My lord, some two days since I saw the prince
And told him of those triumphs held at Oxford.
     Bulling. And what said the gallant?   *15*
     Percy. His answer was, he would unto the stews,
And from the common'st creature pluck a glove
And wear it as a favor, and with that
He would unhorse his lustiest challenger.
     Bulling. As dissolute as desperate, yet through both   *20*
I see some sparks of better hope which elder years
May happily bring forth. But who comes here?

Enter Aumerle, amazed.

     Aum. Where is the king?
     Bulling. What means our cousin, that he stares and looks
So wildly?   *25*
     Aum. Gad save your grace! I do beseech your majesty
To have some conference with your grace alone.
     Bulling. Withdraw yourselves and leave us here alone.
                                            [Exeunt Percy and lords.]
What is the matter with our cousin now?
     Aum. Forever may my knees grow to the earth,   *30*
My tongue cleave to my roof within my mouth,
Unless a pardon ere I rise or speak.
     Bulling. Intended or committed was this fault?
If on the first, how heinous ere it be,
To win thy after-love I pardon thee.   *35*
     Aum. Then give me leave that I may turn the key,
That no man enter till my tale be done.
     Bulling. Have thy desire.
               The Duke of York knocks at the door and crieth.
     York. My liege, beware! look to thyself!
Thou hast a traitor in thy presence there.   *40*
     Bulling. Villain, I'll make thee safe.   *[He draws.]*
     Aum. Stay thy revengeful hand. Thou hast no cause to fear.
     York. Open the door, secure foolhardy king!
Shall I for love speak treason to thy face?
Open the door, or I will break it open!   *45*

[Enter York.]

     Bulling. What is the matter, uncle? Speak.
Recover breath, tell us how near is danger,
That we may arm us to encounter it.
     York: Peruse this writing here and thou shalt know
The treason that my haste forbids me show.   *50*
     Aum. Remember, as thou read'st, thy promise pass'd.
I do repent me. Read not my name there.
My heart is not confederate with my hand.
     York. It was, villain, ere thy hand did set it down.
I tore it from the traitor's bosom, king.   *55*
Fear, and not love, begets his penitence.
Forget to pity him, lest thy pity prove
A serpent that will sting thee to the heart.
     Bulling. O heinous, strong, and bold conspiracy!
O loyal father of a treacherous son!   *60*
Thou sheer, immaculate, and silver fountain,
From whence this stream through muddy passages
Hath held his current and defil'd himself!
Thy overflow of good converts to bad,
And thy abundant goodness shall excuse   *65*
This deadly blot in thy digressing son.
     York. So shall my virtue be his vice's bawd,
And he shall spend mine honor with his shame,
As thriftless sons their scraping fathers' gold.
Mine honor lives when his dishonor dies.   *70*

107–108 He shall . . . here: *F's lineation; one line in Qq*   **107 be none:** *not be one of them*   **111–112 Hadst . . . done:** *one line in Qq*, F   **111 groan'd:** *i.e. in childbirth*   **112 thou would'st:** *read 'thou'dst'*   **pitiful:** *full of pity*   **117–118 a . . . any:** Q *(Devonshire, Capell, Petworth), other Qq, F;* Q *(Huth)* any . . . a   **121 his horse:** *one of his horse's perhaps; cf. n.*   **1 Bullingbrooke:** F; Q King H[enry] *(throughout the act)*   **me:** *not in* F   **son:** *Prince Hal, later Henry V (actually twelve at this time)*   **6 frequent:** *intransitive*   **7 companions:** *four syllables*   **9 beat . . . rob:** F rob . . . beat   **watch:** *watchmen*   **passengers:** *passers-by*   **10 wanton:** *probably a noun*   **effeminate:** *(trisyllabic) self-indulgent*   **11–12 Takes . . . crew:** *F's lineation; one line in Qq*   **11 Takes on the:** *makes of it a*   **12 So . . . crew:** *cf. n.*   **14 those:** F these   **held:** *to be held*   **16 stews:** *brothels*   **18 favor:** *i.e. mark of favor*   **that:** *i.e. the glove*   **19 lustiest:** *sturdiest and bravest*   **20 both:** *i.e. dissolute and desperate*   **21 I see . . . years:** *an alexandrine.*   **years:** F dayes   **22 happily:** *'happily' and 'haply'*

23–152 Where is . . . thee new: *for Holinshed's version see Appendix B*   **24–25 What . . . wildly:** *one line in Qq*   **27 conference:** *disyllabic*   **SD Exeunt . . . lords:** *not in* Q, F   **31 My tongue . . . mouth:** *compare Psalm 137:6*   **36 I may:** *other Qq, F;* Q May   **41 safe:** *i.e. harmless*   **SD He draws:** *not in* Q, F   **42 Stay . . . fear:** *an alexandrine*   **43 secure:** *heedless, overconfident*   **44 speak treason:** *i.e. abuse the king*   **46, 47 What . . . breath:** *one line in Qq,* F   **50 treason:** F reason   **haste forbids:** *i.e. York is breathless*   **53 confederate:** *(trisyllabic) a fellow conspirator with*   **57 to pity:** *to pardon*   **pity him:** *two syllables*   **58 serpent:** *cf. n.*   **59 strong:** *flagrant*   **61 sheer:** *pure and clear*   **63 held:** F had   **66 digressing:** *erring*   **70 lives:** *i.e. comes to life*

Or my sham'd life in his dishonor lies.
Thou kill'st me in his life. Giving him breath,
The traitor lives, the true man's put to death.
 Duch. [Within.] What ho, my liege! For God's sake
let me in!   *75*
 Bulling. What shrill-voic'd suppliant makes this eager cry?
 Duch. A woman, and thy aunt, great king. 'Tis I.
Speak with me, pity me, open the door!
A beggar begs that never begg'd before.
 Bulling. Our scene is alt'red from a serious thing, *80*
And now chang'd to 'The Beggar and the King.'
My dangerous cousin, let your mother in.
I know she is come to pray for your foul sin.
 York. If thou do pardon, whosoever pray,
More sins for this forgiveness prosper may.   *85*
This fest'red joint cut off, the rest rest sound,
This let alone will all the rest confound.

    [Enter Duchess.]

 Duch. O king, believe not this hard-hearted man!
Love loving not itself none other can.
 York. Thou frantic woman, what dost thou make here? *90*
Shall thy old dugs once more a traitor rear?
 Duch. Sweet York, be patient. Hear me, gentle liege.
 Bulling. Rise up, good aunt.
 Duch.   Not yet, I thee beseech.
Forever will I walk upon my knees,   *95*
And never see day that the happy sees,
Till thou give joy, until thou bid me joy
By pardoning Rutland, my transgressing boy.
 Aum. Unto my mother's prayers I bend my knee.
 York. Against them both my true joints bended be. *100*
Ill mayst thou thrive if thou grant any grace!
 Duch. Pleads he in earnest? Look upon his face.
His eyes do drop no tears, his prayers are in jest,
His words come from his mouth, ours from our breast.
He prays but faintly and would be denied,   *105*
We pray with heart and soul and all beside.
His weary joints would gladly rise, I know,
Our knees still kneel till to the ground they grow.
His prayers are full of false hypocrisy,
Ours of true zeal and deep integrity.   *110*
Our prayers do outpray his, then let them have
That mercy which true prayer ought to have.
 Bulling. Good aunt, stand up.
 Duch.   Nay, do not say, 'stand up.'
Say 'pardon' first, and afterwards 'stand up.' *115*
And if I were thy nurse, thy tongue to teach,
'Pardon' should be the first word of thy speech.
I never long'd to hear a word till now.
Say 'pardon,' king, let pity teach thee how.
The word is short, but not so short as sweet; *120*
No word like 'pardon' for kings' mouths so meet.

 York. Speak it in French, king. Say 'pardonne moy.'
 Duch. Dost thou teach pardon pardon to destroy?
Ah, my sour husband, my hard-hearted lord,
That sets the word itself against the word!   *125*
Speak 'pardon' as 'tis current in our land,
The chopping French we do not understand.
Thine eye begins to speak, set thy tongue there.
Or in thy piteous heart plant thou thine ear,
That hearing now our plaints and prayers do pierce, *130*
Pity may move thee 'pardon' to rehearse.
 Bulling. Good aunt, stand up.
 Duch.   I do not sue to stand.
Pardon is all the suit I have in hand.
 Bulling. I pardon him as God shall pardon me. *135*
 Duch. O happy vantage of a kneeling knee!
Yet am I sick for fear. Speak it again.
Twice saying 'pardon' doth not pardon twain,
But makes one pardon strong.
 Bulling. I pardon him with all my heart.   *140*
 Duch. A god on earth thou art.
 Bulling. But for our trusty brother-in-law and the Abbot,
With all the rest of that consorted crew,
Destruction straight shall dog them at the heels.
Good uncle, help to order several powers   *145*
To Oxford, or where ere these traitors are.
They shall not live within this world, I swear,
But I will have them, if I once know where.
Uncle, farewell; and cousin, adieu.
Your mother well hath pray'd, and prove you true. *150*
 Duch. Come, my old son. I pray God make thee new.
            Exeunt.

❧ Scene Fourth ❧

[Enter Exton and servant.]

 Exton. Didst thou not mark the king, what words he spake?
'Have I no friend will rid me of this living fear?'
Was it not so?
 Servant.   These were his very words.
 Exton. 'Have I no friend?' quoth he. He spake it twice *5*
And urg'd it twice togither, did he not?
 Servant. He did.
 Exton. And speaking it, he wishtly look'd on me,
As who should say, 'I would thou wert the man
That would divorce this terror from my heart,' *10*
Meaning the king at Pomfret. Come, let's go.
I am the king's friend, and will rid his foe. *[Exeunt.]*

122 pardonne moy: *expression of courteous refusal* **pardonne:** *trisyllabic* **124 sour:** *bitter* **126 Speak 'pardon':** *addressed to the king* **127 chopping French:** *mincing or jerky, such as to change meaning* **128 speak:** *i.e. express pity* **129 thy:** *Q* (Devonshire, Capell, Petworth), *other Qq, F; Q* (Huth) *this* **131 rehearse:** *speak, pronounce* **137 Yet:** *even now* (not 'nevertheless') **140 I . . . heart;** *cf. n.* **142 brother-in-law:** *the Earl of Huntingdon* (formerly Duke of Exeter) **and:** *not in F* **Abbot:** *the Abbot of Westminster* **143 the rest:** *about a dozen* (see V.2.104) **145 order several powers:** *make ready separate forces to be sent* **149 cousin:** *Qq, F; most editors print* cousin too *from Q6* (1634) **149–151 adieu . . . true . . . new:** *triple rhyme* (rare in Shakespeare, but see V.5.96–98) **SD Enter . . . servant;** *cf. n.* **1–12 Didst . . . foe:** *for Holinshed's version see "Sources of the Play"* **4 Servant:** *F; Q* Man (also in l. 7). **These:** *F* Those **8 wishtly:** *probably means 'longingly'* (compare 'wishly' and 'wishtly' in OED); *Q3, Q4, Q5, F* wistly, *closely, attentively* **9 As who:** *as one who*

71 in his dishonor lies: *depends on his dishonor* **76 voic'd:** *other Qq, F; Q, Q2* voice **eager:** *sharp* **81 Beggar . . . King:** *refers to the old ballad 'King Cophetua and the Beggar Maid'* **83 she is:** *read 'she's' as F* **86 rest rest:** *rest remains;* **F** rest rests **89 Love . . . itself:** *one* (i.e. York) *who loves not his own offspring* **90 make:** *do* **95 walk upon my knees:** *a form of penance.* **walk:** *F* kneele **98 Rutland:** *see V.2.43* **99 Unto:** *in addition to* **101 Ill . . . grace:** *not in F* **103 His eyes . . . jest:** *an alexandrine* **108 Our . . . grow:** *compare l. 30 above* **still kneel:** *shall continue to kneel; F* shall kneele **111 prayers:** *monosyllabic* **113 Bullingbrooke:** *F; Q* yorke **115 Say:** *F* But **116 And if:** *Qq, Ff; most editors print* An if (*old phrase for 'if'*)

❧ Scene Fifth ❧

Enter [King] Richard, alone.

King. I have been studying how I may compare
This prison where I live unto the world.
And for because the world is populous
And here is not a creature but myself,
I cannot do it. Yet I'll hammer it out.   *5*
My brain I'll prove the female of my soul,
My soul the father, and these two beget
A generation of still-breeding thoughts,
And these same thoughts people this little world
In humors like the people of this world,   *10*
For no thought is contented. The better sort,
As thoughts of things divine, are intermix'd
With scruples, and do set the word itself
Against the word,
As thus: 'Come, little ones,' and then again,   *15*
'It is as hard to come as for a camel
To thread the postern of a small needle's eye.'
Thoughts tending to ambition, they do plot
Unlikely wonders—how these vain weak nails
May tear a passage through the flinty ribs   *20*
Of this hard world, my ragged prison walls,
And, for they cannot, die in their own pride.
Thoughts tending to content flatter themselves
That they are not the first of fortune's slaves,
Nor shall not be the last, like seely beggars   *25*
Who sitting in the stocks refuge their shame,
That many have and others must sit there.
And in this thought they find a kind of ease,
Bearing their own misfortunes on the back
Of such as have before endur'd the like.   *30*
Thus play I in one person many people,
And none contented. Sometimes am I king,
Then treasons make me wish myself a beggar,
And so I am. Then crushing penury
Persuades me I was better when a king.   *35*
Then am I king'd again. And by and by
Think that I am unking'd by Bullingbrooke,
And straight am nothing. But what ere I be,
Nor I nor any man that but man is
With nothing shall be pleas'd till he be eas'd   *40*
With being nothing. Music do I hear?   *The music plays.*
Ha, ha! Keep time. How sour sweet music is
When time is broke and no proportion kept!
So is it in the music of men's lives.
And here have I the daintiness of ear   *45*
To check time broke in a disorder'd string,
But for the concord of my state and time

Had not an ear to hear my true time broke.
I wasted time, and now doth time waste me;
For now hath time made me his numb'ring clock.   *50*
My thoughts are minutes, and with sighs they jar
Their watches on unto mine eyes, the outward watch,
Whereto my finger, like a dial's point,
Is pointing still, in cleansing them from tears.
Now, sir, the sound that tells what hour it is   *55*
Are clamorous groans which strike upon my heart,
Which is the bell. So sighs and tears and groans
Show minutes, times, and hours. But my time
Runs posting on in Bullingbrooke's proud joy,
While I stand fooling here, his Jack of the clock.   *60*
This music mads me. Let it sound no more,
For though it have holp mad men to their wits,
In me it seems it will make wise men mad.
Yet blessing on his heart that gives it me!
For 'tis a sign of love, and love to Richard   *65*
Is a strange brooch in this all-hating world.

Enter a groom of the stable.

Groom. Hail, royal prince!
King.   Thanks, noble peer.
The cheapest of us is ten groats too dear.
What art thou? And how comest thou hither   *70*
Where no man never comes but that sad dog
That brings me food to make misfortune live?
Groom. I was a poor groom of thy stable, king,
When thou wert king, who, traveling towards York,
With much ado at length have gotten leave   *75*
To look upon my sometimes royal master's face.
O, how it ern'd my heart when I beheld
In London streets, that coronation day,
When Bullingbrooke rode on roan Barbary,
That horse that thou so often hast bestrid,   *80*
That horse that I so carefully have dress'd!
King. Rode he on Barbary? Tell me, gentle friend,
How went he under him?
Groom. So proudly as if he disdain'd the ground.
King. So proud that Bullingbrooke was on his back!   *85*
That jade hath eat bread from my royal hand,
This hand hath made him proud with clapping him.
Would he not stumble? Would he not fall down—
Since pride must have a fall—and break the neck
Of that proud man that did usurp his back?   *90*
Forgiveness, horse! Why do I rail on thee,
Since thou, created to be aw'd by man,
Wast born to bear? I was not made a horse,
And yet I bear a burthen like an ass,
Spurr'd, gall'd, and tir'd by jauncing Bullingbrooke.   *95*

---

1 I may: *other Qq. F* to   **3 for because:** *because (a reduplication).*   **5 hammer it:** *read 'hammer't' as F; worry it*   **8 still:** *constantly*   **9 this little world:** *both his microcosm (self) and his prison*   **10 humors:** *see I.1.153; cf. n.*   **13 scruples:** *doubts, difficulties*   **13–14 word . . . word:** *i.e. contradictions in Scripture;* F Faith . . . Faith   **14–15 Against . . . again:** *one line in Qq, F*   **15 Come, little ones:** *see Matthew 19:14*   **16–17 It is . . . eye:** *see Matthew 19:24*   **17 thread:** *Q5; other Qq* threed; *F* thred   **postern:** *small back gate, i.e. opening* **small:** *not in F.* **needle's** *monosyllabic (read 'neeld' or 'neel')*   **18 they:** *redundant*   **20–21 May tear . . . walls:** *compare III.3.34*   **21 ragged:** *rugged*   **22 for they cannot:** *since the nails cannot die* **in . . . pride:** *i.e. in their prime*   **25 seely:** *old form of 'silly,' or pitiful;* F silly   **26 refuge:** *stressed — ´* **refuge their shame:** *find refuge from their shame in the thought*   **29 misfortunes:** *F* misfortune   **31 person:** *other Qq, F* Prison   **33 treasons make:** *F* Treason makes   **34 so I am:** *so I become one (in my imagination)*   **36 king'd:** *Q2* king; *other Qq* a king   **38 be:** *F* am   **39 man is:** *is a man*   **41 being nothing:** *i.e. dying* **Sd The music:** *F* Music *(F's direction at l. 38)*   **43 proportion:** *rhythm*   **46 check:** *find fault with;* F heare   **47 time:** *life*

50–58 For now . . . hours: *cf. n.*   **50 numb'ring clock:** *clock that marks hours and minutes (not an hourglass)*   **51 jar:** *tick*   **52 Their . . . watch:** *an alexandrine* **watches:** *marks for minutes on a dial*   **53 dial's point:** *clock hand*   **56 which:** *F* that   **58 times:** *divisions of quarter- and half-hours* **times, and hours:** *F* Houres, and Times **hours:** *disyllabic*   **60 Jack of the clock:** *cf. n.*   **61, 62 This music . . . wits:** *an ancient cure (see Samuel 16:16, also* King Lear, *IV.7.31, 32)*   **62 holp:** *helped* **mad men:** *F* madmen   **66 brooch:** *ornament* **all-hating:** *i.e. which utterly hates Richard (or which hates all men).*   **67 royal, noble:** *puns; cf. n.*   **71 never:** *F* euer   **74 traveling towards:** *four syllables (read 'traveling tord' or 'trav'ling towards')*   **77 ern'd:** *grieved;* F yern'd, *moved to compassion*   **79 Barbary:** *part of northwest Africa famous for horses*   **80 bestrid:** *bestrode, mounted; F; Qq* bestride   **81 dress'd:** *groomed*   **84 he:** *F* he had   **86 jade:** *see III.3.182* **eat:** *eaten*   **87 clapping:** *patting*   **89 pride . . . fall:** *see Proverbs 16:18*   **95 Spurr'd, gall'd:** *F* Spur-gall'd   **jauncing:** *making the horse prance (participial adjective)*

[Enter keeper, with a dish.]

Keeper. Fellow, give place. Here is no longer stay.
King. If thou love me, 'tis time thou wert away.
Groom. What my tongue dares not, that my heart shall say.
                                        Exit groom.

Keeper. My lord, will't please you to fall to?
King. Taste of it first, as thou art wont to do.   *100*
Keeper. My lord, I dare not. Sir Pierce of Exton,
Who lately came from the king, commands the contrary.
King. The drivel take Henry of Lancaster, and thee!
Patience is stale, and I am weary of it.   *[Beats the keeper.]*
Keeper. Help, help, help!   *105*

[Exton and servants,] the murderers, rush in.

King. How now! What means Death in this rude assault?
Villain, thy own hand yields thy death's instrument.
Go thou and fill another room in hell.
                         Here Exton strikes him down.
That hand shall burn in never-quenching fire,   *110*
That staggers thus my person. Exton, thy fierce hand
Hath with the king's blood stain'd the king's own land.
Mount, mount, my soul! Thy seat is up on high,
Whilst my gross flesh sinks downward, here to die.   *[Dies.]*
Exton. As full of valor as of royal blood.   *115*
Both have I spill'd. O, would the deed were good!
For now the divel, that told me I did well,
Says that this deed is chronicl'd in hell.
This dead king to the living king I'll bear
Take hence the rest, and give them burial here.   *[Exeunt.]* *120*

❧ Scene Sixth ❧

[Flourish.] Enter Bullingbrooke with the Duke of York [, lords, and attendants].

Bulling. Kind uncle York, the latest news we hear
Is that the rebels have consum'd with fire
Our town of Ciceter in Gloucestershire,
But whether they be tane or slain we hear not.

Enter Northumberland.

Welcome, my lord. What is the news?   *5*
North. First, to thy sacred state wish I all happiness.
The next news is, I have to London sent
The heads of Oxford, Salisbury, Blunt, and Kent.
The manner of their taking may appear
At large discoursed in this paper here.   *10*
Bulling. We thank thee, gentle Percy, for thy pains,
And to thy worth will add right worthy gains.

Enter Lord Fitzwater.

Fitz. My lord, I have from Oxford sent to London
The heads of Broccas and Sir Bennet Seely,
Two of the dangerous consorted traitors   *15*
That sought at Oxford thy dire overthrow.
Bulling. Thy pains, Fitzwater, shall not be forgot.
Right noble is thy merit, well I wot.

Enter Henry Percy [and Carlisle].

Percy. The grand conspirator, Abbot of Westminster,
With clog of conscience and sour melancholy   *20*
Hath yielded up his body to the grave.
But here is Carlisle living, to abide
Thy kingly doom and sentence of his pride.
Bulling. Carlisle, this is your doom:
Choose out some secret place, some reverent room,   *25*
More than thou hast, and with it joy thy life.
So as thou liv'st in peace, die free from strife.
For though mine enemy thou hast ever been,
High sparks of honor in thee have I seen.

Enter Exton, with [attendants bearing] the coffin.

Exton. Great king, within this coffin I present   *30*
Thy buried fear. Herein all breathless lies
The mightiest of thy greatest enemies,
Richard of Bordeaux, by me hither brought.
Bulling. Exton, I thank thee not, for thou hast wrought
A deed of slander, with thy fatal hand,   *35*
Upon my head and all this famous land.
Exton. From your own mouth, my lord, did I this deed.
Bulling. They love not poison that do poison need,
Nor do I thee. Though I did wish him dead,
I hate the murtherer, love him murthered.   *40*
The guilt of conscience take thou for thy labor,
But neither my good word nor princely favor.
With Cain go wander through shades of night,
And never show thy head by day nor light.
Lords, I protest my soul is full of woe   *45*
That blood should sprinkle me to make me grow.
Come, mourn with me for what I do lament,
And put on sullen black incontinent.
I'll make a voyage to the Holy Land
To wash this blood off my guilty hand.   *50*
March sadly after, grace my mournings here
In weeping after this untimely bier.   *[Exeunt.]*

❧ Finis ❧

---

14 Broccas: *Holinshed: 'Sir Leonard [should be 'Bernard'] Brokas.'* **Seely:** *Holinshed: 'Sir Benet Cilie'* **20 clog:** *burden, weight* **22 abide:** *await* **23 doom:** *judgment* **of:** *on* **25 reverent room:** *sacred place; F reuerend, worthy of respect* **reverent:** *disyllabic* **29 High:** *noble* **SD attendants bearing:** *not in Q, F* **33 Bordeaux:** *stressed —́ —; Qq, F Burdeaux* **34–44 Exton ... light:** *this repudiation not in the known sources* **35 deed of slander:** *deed bringing censure and disgrace* **slander:** *other Qq, F slaughter* **40 murtherer:** *read 'murth'rer'* **him murthered:** *him who is murdered* **43 Cain:** *see Genesis 4:12, 14* **through:** *read 'thorough'* **shades:** *other Qq, F the shade* **48 sullen:** *mournful* **incontinent:** *at once* **49 voyage ... Land:** *links with 1 Henry IV, I.1.18–27* **51 sadly:** *solemnly* **grace:** *do honor to* **mournings:** *F mourning* **52 bier;** *cf. n.*

96–120 Fellow ... here: *for Holinshed's version see Appendix B* **96–98 stay ... away ... say:** *triple rhyme* **100 art:** *F wer't* **102 Who ... contrary:** *probably an alexandrine* **the king:** *F th' King* **103 divel:** *devil* **Sd Beats ... keeper:** *not in Q, F* **109 room:** *place, space* **114 die;** *cf. n.* **Sd Dies:** *not in Q, F* **116 spill'd:** *Holinshed says Exton wept bitterly* **120 burial:** *disyllabic* **1 latest news;** *cf. n.* **3 Ciceter:** *this (or Cicester) is the local pronunciation of Cirencester* **4 tane or slain:** *internal rhyme* **6 state:** *royalty* **8 Oxford ... Kent;** *cf. n.*

NOTES

I.i. Since no act or scene divisions appear in the Qq, they are (with the one exception noted at V.4.ISD) taken from F.

I.i.Sd. *King Richard.* Richard of Bordeaux (1367–1400), son of Edward the Black Prince. Although the play reaches back into earlier events, the action proper (which begins when Richard is just over thirty) covers only the last two years of his life. A decade earlier Richard had chosen five newly created peers as his favorites, which caused five established members of the nobility (Gloucester, Arundel, Warwick, Mowbray, and Bolingbroke) to accuse the favorites of treason. Overruling Richard, the parliament forthwith judged against his men, of whom two fled and three were put to death. But by 1397 Richard took firmer control and proceeded to arrest Gloucester, Arundel, and Warwick on old charges. All three were soon dead or banished. The remaining two lords, Mowbray and Bolingbroke, by now enjoying the titles of Duke of Norfolk and Duke of Hereford, were regaining some of their old eminence. But a quarrel then arose between them over the way Richard was treating his great nobles. According to Holinshed (whose generally accurate historical picture is closely followed by Shakespeare), Bolingbroke rose before the assembled parliament at Shrewsbury and accused Mowbray of treason. He charged that Mowbray, while riding with him from London to Brainford, spoke 'highlie to the kings dishonor.' Though Mowbray was not present when the charge was first made, he was later on hand to answer it before parliament. The action of the play begins in April 1398, several weeks after the episode at Shrewsbury. The two lords are being heard by Richard and the parliament at Windsor. Historically, Bolingbroke's accusation seems not to have involved questions of peculation, treasonous plots, and participation in Gloucester's murder, as it does here. But dramatically Shakespeare has designed to show Bolingbroke's action as his first move toward the crown in this drama of deposition, though just how deliberate that first move is, even within the play itself, is a matter of controversy.

I.i.1. *John of Gaunt.* John of Gaunt (corrupted from the French *Gand,* i.e. Ghent, were he was born) is fifty-eight and his brother York is fifty-seven. Above and beyond the Elizabethan inclination to view anyone over fifty as 'old,' Shakespeare makes a particularly sharp contrast between the age of these two figures and the 'youth' of the king (II.1.69).

I.i.3. *Herford.* Hereford (usually spelled *Herford* in Qq and F) was Henry Plantagenet (1367–1413), called Bolingbroke from the castle in Leicestershire where he was born, although he did not actually adopt this surname until his accession.

I.i.13. *As near . . . argument.* Although twelve-syllable lines may be read as alexandrines (six-stress lines), they are often more easily read with five stresses, not uncommonly with the final two syllables sounded very lightly. As a rule, alexandrine lines are few in the early plays—*Romeo and Juliet* has none at all—and quite numerous in the later. But this play, which has over thirty, is an exception.

I.i.20. *Bullingbrooke.* This, the usual spelling of Bolingbroke in Qq and F, indicates also the pronunciation of the name.

I.i.20. *Many . . . befall.* The line is metrically short, but omission of a weak opening syllable is a normal verse variation, perhaps sometimes allowing for an actor's expressive pause, and need not be filled in. (It should be remembered that while metrical regularity is usual in the play, variations are to be expected here as well as in other plays presumed to have been set directly from Shakespeare's own manuscript.)

I.i.34. *appellant.* 'Accuser' (noun) or 'bringing accusation' (adjective). If read as a noun, the word is almost a technical term for 'challenger' (see I.3.4, 52; IV.1.107).

I.i.63. *tied.* In order to indicate pronunciation in this edition, unaccented syllables concluding certain past tenses, past participles, and verbs inflected in the second-person singular of the present tense are printed with an apostrophe (e.g. *receiv'd time-honor'd, high-stomach'd, com'st, think'st*), regardless of their forms in the copy texts. Certain other verbs, however, and especially those ending in *-ied,* are printed in full because their final syllables are usually not accented (e.g. *tied, denied, lied;* also *baffled, rued, settled*).

I.i.77. *thou . . . devise.* So reads Q; Q2, F read *thou canst devise;* other Qq read *what thou canst devise.* Obviously after *worse* was dropped out in Q2, later versions attempted to make up the loss. Though the original meaning is not entirely clear, two interpretations at least are possible. *Or thou canst worse devise* may conclude the idea 'those treasonous acts that I say you have done, *or that you are capable of doing.'* On the other hand, if one agrees with H. H. Vaughan and Sir Edmund Chambers to take *or* to mean 'before,' the sense is 'before you can devise worse treasons.'

I.i.100. *Duke of Gloucester's death.* Thomas Woodstock, Duke of Gloucester, and youngest son of Edward III, was murdered when in the custody of Mowbray (then Earl of Nottingham) at Calais in 1397. Though proof is lacking, it was then assumed, and still is, that Richard gave orders for Mowbray to carry out the murder.

I.i.101–103. *Suggest . . . blood.* J. Dover Wilson asserts (though Peter Ure in the New Arden edition disagrees) that since Holinshed, Froissart, and the other French authorities say that Gloucester was strangled by towels and/or smothered in a featherbed, Shakespeare has followed 'Jean Le Beau' in *La Chronique de Richard II,* who says that Gloucester was beheaded. (See I.2.21, II.2.103, and "Sources of the Play.")

I.i.119. *neighbor nearness.* Though the F reading, *neighbour-neerenesse,* makes *neighbor* a noun, it may be an adjective. In Shakespeare's time the parts of speech were not treated so strictly as they were even later in the 17th century. Very frequently he uses adjectives as nouns, nouns as verbs, and so forth. Compare *exclaims* (I.2.2), *venom* (II.1.19), *ague* (III.2.190), *sooth* (III.3.139), *sunshine* (IV.1.225), *mockery* (IV.1.265), *true-love* (V.1.10), *triumph* (V.2.70), *peace* (V.2.87).

I.i.119. *sacred blood.* Here for the first time Richard strikes a note that rings throughout his speeches: divine right of kings, which in Richard's mind (as A. W. Verity observes in his edition, 1899) always refers not to the responsibilities but to the privileges of kingship.

I.i.131. *queen.* In 1395 a mission went to France to negotiate the marriage between Richard and Isabelle, the daughter of King Charles VI of France. Although she was only eight at the time, in the play she is treated as an adult.

I.i.135-41. *For you . . . it.* Here is one of the occasions on which Shakespeare has (except in l. 139) followed Holinshed very closely. Holinshed: 'True it is that once I laid an ambush to have slain the Duke of Lancaster that there sitteth; but nevertheless he hath pardoned me thereof, and there was good peace made betwixt us, for the which I yield him hearty thanks.' No other record of this incident has yet been discovered.

I.i.153. *choler.* Here the word seems also to have taken on its meaning as one of the four 'humors.' In ancient and medieval physiology and (what we now call) psychology, a man's health and temperament were thought to be determined by the relative amounts of the four fluids in his body: blood, melancholy (or black bile), choler (or yellow bile), and phlegm. These four, corresponding to the four elements in nature—air, earth, fire, and water—were thought to operate in such a way that an excess of air (blood) produced a sanguine man, of earth a melancholic man, of fire a choleric man, and of water a phlegmatic man.

I.i.157. *no month to bleed.* Elizabethan almanacs, e.g. *The Prognostycacion for ever of Erra Pater* (1602), explain, often in elaborate detail, what seasons are proper for the success of bleeding, pulling teeth, cutting hair, and more. April was a favorite month for bleeding, though evidently not in this case (which may be why the Ff read *time* and not *month* as in Qq).

I.i.176. *lions . . . leopards.* Basically the lion may be thought of as the emblem of English kings, and the golden leopard as the Mowbray crest. A more refined explanation is offered, however, in C. W. Scott-Giles, *Shakespeare's Heraldry* (London, Dutton, 1950), p. 75: 'In heraldic language, the lion rampant of Mowbray could not be called a leopard, but this term might be applied to the lion statant forming his crest, the lion in any attitude but rampant having been termed a leopard, or *lion leopardé,* in ancient heraldry. If, to point the king's words, it is decided to give Norfolk a crested helm for this scene, the beast forming the crest should be the stylized heraldic lion, not spotted or otherwise made to resemble the natural leopard.'

I.i.178. *gage. My dear.* Some variation in meaning is occasioned within this line by variations in punctuation. The punctuation printed here is from F; Q, Q4, and Q5 read *gage, my deare,* and Q2, Q3 read *gage my deare.*

I.i.188. *throw up.* Wilson thinks this means throw it up 'to the scaffold (upper stage) on which Ric[hard] and his nobles sit.' But most scholars (including C. J. Sisson, *New Readings in Shakespeare,* Cambridge, Cambridge University Press, 1956, 2, 15) prefer F's *throw downe.* (For descriptions of the different stages of various Elizabethan public theaters, see C. Walter Hodges, *The Globe Restored,* London, Ernest Benn, 1953.)

I.i.189. *God.* To comply with 'An Act to restrain the abuses of the Players' passed by James I in 1606, F nearly always substitutes *heaven* for Q's *God.*

I.i.194. *sound . . . parle.* A metaphor for sounding a trumpet (or beating a drum) to talk over terms—in this case, the terms of a shameful truce. (The form *parle* is taken from F; Qq read *parlee.*)

I.i.Sd. *Exit Gaunt.* This awkward exit (in F but not in Qq) is essential to Gaunt's entrance again at the opening of the next scene. (*Note:* Although stage directions for the present edition come mainly from Q, countless minor alterations

are made without being noted. However, since the directions in F are more numerous, more complete, and more accurate than those in Q, many of them have been adopted and are printed in square brackets. The exception to the adequacy of F's directions is the 'deposition scene' (IV.1.157–325), in which their absence or incompleteness has been compensated for from Capell and Lewis Theobald.)

I.i.206. *Marshal.* Thomas Holland, Duke of Surrey. The second syllable may be read lightly, or *Marshal* may be read as three syllables and the line as an alexandrine.

I.ii.1. *blood.* Here *blood* possibly means 'murder' since, as the argument runs in the edition of Henry Irving and Frank A. Marshall (1888–90), 'Lancaster was certainly privy to the proceedings against his brother,' as he was to those against his son.

I.ii.11. *Edward's seven sons.* Besides the Duchess' dead husband, Thomas of Woodstock, Duke of Gloucester (1355–97), they are: King Richard's father, Edward the Black Prince (1330–76); William of Hatfield (1336–44); Lionel of Antwerp, Duke of Clarence (1338–68); John of Gaunt (1340–99); Edmund of Langley, Duke of York (1341–1402); and William of Windsor, who died in infancy.

I.ii.14–21. *Some . . . ax.* Of the five dead sons, the Duchess is saying, four died of natural causes while the fifth, Gloucester, was murdered.

I.ii.30. *slaught'red.* There is some question about the pronunciation of several verbs which in Q show elision of the next to last syllable, as here, rather than the last. In this edition the Q forms have been preserved; the other instances in addition to *slaught'red* are: *wand'red* (I.3.196), *length'ned* (I.4.16), *off'red* (II.1.207), *sweet'ned* (II.3.13), *weak'ned* (V.1.27), *ent'red* (V.2.69), *alt'red* (V.3.81), and *fest'red* (V.3.87). For such forms see Helge Kökeritz, *Shakespeare's Pronunciation* (New Haven, Yale University Press, 1953), pp. 262–63, who argues convincingly that two alternative pronunciations existed in Shakespeare's time.

I.ii.42. *then, alas, may.* Significant variations within the four extant copies of Q, labeled Huth, Capell, Devonshire, and Petworth, are cited in the glosses. In all instances readings from the 'corrected' sheets precede those from the 'uncorrected.'

I.ii.44. *Why then . . . Gaunt.* Possibly this is a pentameter line whose shortness could be accounted for by prolonging *will* and reading *Farewell* as trisyllabic (it comes from 'fare ye well'). But probably the line is a tetrameter, of which Shakespeare wrote a good number when shifting to a new idea, especially at a speech's beginning or end.

I.ii.46. *cousin.* In Shakespeare the word indicates almost any sort of kindship except the closest (like father or brother).

I.ii.58–59. *Grief . . . weight.* Like a ball, her grief falls (subsides) only to rebound (surge up again), though not lightly like a ball.

I.iii.Sd. *enter Mowbray.* Strictly speaking, the appellant Bolingbroke (who is challenging) should appear in the lists first. (For deviations from the stage directions in Q, see I.1.Sd cf. n.)

I.iii.11. *say who thou art.* This formality was not altogether empty. Since a knight's crest might not be known and his beaver (visor) was down over his face, identification was sometimes necessary. Furthermore the question calls forth a statement of rank, and no knight was obliged to fight with anyone inferior in rank.

I.iii.15. *As so defend.* Some editors merely change *as* to *and*, although all Qq and Ff read *as*. It may be that before using the ordinary formula for oaths, which began with 'so' (see I.3.34), the Marshal first started out in a less usual way with *as*, or else that he used *as* in another sense, in effect ordering Richard to 'speak truly . . . in this fashion: so defend thee.'

I.iii.20. *my succeeding.* Sisson, *New Readings in Shakespeare, 2*, 16–17, regards F's *his succeeding* as a true correction since the usual oath is to God, the king, and the king's heirs and successors.

I.iii.84. *Mine . . . George.* This prayer to Saint George, patron saint of England, implies that a true patriot (Bolingbroke) is protecting his king and country against a traitor (Mowbray). Before *Mine* one must apply something like 'I pray.'

I.iii.194. *so far . . . enemy.* 'This much do I say to you my enemy.' But the line is obscure since Qq and F read *fare*, with *far* appearing only in the other Ff. Some editors follow George Tollet's explanation (Variorum edition, 1778): 'He only wishes him to *fare* like his enemy, and he disdains to say *fare* well.'

I.iii.212. *Pluck'd four away.* Holinshed says the sentence was reduced, but some weeks later, in Eltham. Anthony Steel, however, in *Richard II* (Cambridge, Cambridge University Press, 1941), p. 253, says that Richard, although not daring to ignore Bolingbroke's popularity on the occasion when he passed sentence, six months later increased the ten-year banishment to a sentence of life.

I.iii.Sd. *Flourish . . . train.* 'We have here an illustration how the absence of scenery on the Elizabethan stage affected the structure of plays. In a modern play, surely, this scene would end with the king's exit. The interview between Gaunt and Bolingbroke would be thrown into a fresh scene. For characters to remain behind and wind up a scene seems unnatural; it risks an anticlimax. But in the Elizabethan theatre, as there was no curtain to fall and practically no scenery to mark a change of scene, the tendency was to extend a scene instead of starting a fresh one: as if the playwright thought that certain characters might as well stay behind as go off and return' (A. W. Verity, Cambridge edition, 1899).

I.iii.251–252. *What . . . show.* 'What you cannot tell us in person, tell us by letter, wherever you may be' (although *presence* may mean, as Hardin Craig says in *Complete Works*, Chicago, Scott, Foresman, 1951, 'presence chamber at Court').

I.iii.268. *foil.* Refers to the gold leaf set behind a jewel to increase its brilliance.

I.iii.291. *strow'd.* It was an Elizabethan custom to strew the royal presence chamber with rushes (sometimes mixed with herbs).

I.iv.Sd. *Green and Bagot.* So F, while Q reads *with Bushie &c*, which is impossible since Bushy does not enter until l. 52.

I.iv.20–22. *doubt . . . friends.* Doubt may be a noun (meaning 'a matter of doubt') or a past participle (meaning 'suspected' or 'feared'). The sense of the lines seems to be that Richard expects Bolingbroke to return as an enemy, but more probably that Richard will see to it that he does not return.

I.iv.23. *Ourself . . . Green.* So reads F (though differently punctuated), but many editors reject both F and the shorter reading of the other Qq, *Our selfe and Bushie*, in favor of Q6 (1634): *Our selfe and Bushie, Bagot here and Greene.* Incidentally, the popular poetry of the period refers to the three as 'the Bush,' 'the Bag,' and 'the Green,' who do in 'the Swan' (Gloucester) and are then punished by 'the Eagle' (Bolingbroke). (For historical identifications see II.1.Sd cf. n.)

I.iv.43–44. *court . . . largess.* According to the chroniclers Richard's extravagance was notorious. It was said that he spent for his own purposes one third of the total national expenditure of £137,900. He himself boasts of keeping 10,000 retainers (IV.1.288); Holinshed writes that he wore 'a coat of gold and stone valued at 30,000 marks' (a possible error for 3,000); and a poem of the time (by Langland?), *On the Deposition of King Richard*, observes:

> *For where was ever any Christian king*
> *That held such an household by the half-deal*
> *As Richard in his realm, through misrule of others.*

Nevertheless, recent historians believe the records to show no such excess and abuse, and one of them draws quite another portrait of Richard as a tortured, melancholic, and highly neurotic figure (Anthony Steel, *Richard II*, pp. 173–175, 216, 278–279).

I.iv.45 *farm . . . realm.* As the lines following all but explain, bonds were issued which wealthy men were compelled to sign, *after* which the amount of money they were to pay the crown was filled in. Thus *subscribe them* (l. 50) means not writing in the names on the charters (as OED would have it), but rather (as in Ure, New Arden edition, p. 44) writing in the amount to be paid, on charters already signed. Evidently the 'loans' made for this scheme of collecting revenue were never repaid.

I.iv.53. *Bushy, what news.* So reads F (see I.4.SD cf. n.), while Q at this point has, instead of a speech, only the stage direction *Enter Bushie with newes*. Wilson and Sisson both take *Bushy* in this line to be an editorial addition to F and so spurious.

II.i.18. *of whose . . . fond.* So reads Q except that *fond* (from J. P. Collier) has been substituted for Q's *found* (which was doubtless taken over from the last word of that next line). Q2, by printing *state* for *taste* (*of whose state the wise are found*), began a series of odd readings: *of his state: then there are found,* in other Qq; *and of his state: then there are sound,* in F. although some editors think the sense of the words as printed here requires a negative or some other alteration (Wilson is inclined toward W. N. Lettsom's conjecture of *th' unwise* for *the wise*), they may well mean, 'like flattery, which even the wise (including Richard) have a fond taste for.'

II.i.40–55. *This royal . . . Jewry.* This highly eloquent and very famous speech on patriotism was so popular as to be included (except l. 50) in *England's Parnassus* (1600), although it was then mistakenly attributed to Michael Drayton. (A phonetic transcription of the speech, ll. 40–68, is printed in Kökeritz, *Shakespeare's Pronunciation*, pp. 358, 359). The ultimate source of the speech is Froissart.

II.i.Sd. *Enter . . . Willoughby.* Bushy is Sir John Bushy, Speaker of the House of Commons; *Green* Sir Henry Green, Justice of the King's Bench (under Edward III); *Bagot* Sir William Bagot, Sheriff of Leicestershire; *Ross* William, Lord ross, Lord Treasurer (under Henry IV); *Willoughby* William, Lord Willoughby, a Knight of the Garter. In Qq this direction appears after l. 70.

II.i.70. *rag'd.* Slightly altering Joseph Ritson's reading *rein'd*, Sisson reads *raynd* (i.e. 'reined,' or 'reined in') for Q's *ragde*, to correct what seems to him a pointless aphorism.

II.i.72–83. *O, how . . . bones.* Many have found Gaunt's punning ludicrously unsuited to a dying man, but Coleridge sees it otherwise: 'On a death-bed there is a feeling which may make all things appear but as puns and equivocations. And a passion there is that carries off its own excess by plays on words' (*Coleridge's Shakespearean Criticism*, ed. T. M. Raysor, 2 vols. Cambridge, Harvard University Press, 1930).

II.i.94. *Ill . . . ill.* A triple meaning: 'I who see you ill'; 'I am ill at what I see'; and 'what I see in you is ill (evil).' Usually the line is read as an alexandrine.

II.i.95–96. *Thy . . . sick.* Gaunt is comparing his own actual deathbed with the *deathbed* of the *sick* (i.e. evil) king, which is as broad as the whole nation.

II.i.100–113. *A thousand . . . king.* Lily B. Campbell, in *Shakespeare's 'Histories'* (San Marino, California, Huntington Library Publications, 1947), pp. 199–200, describes 'the sins which were brought up time after time when the fate of Richard II was pointed out to Elizabeth as a warning': being swayed by favorites, spilling the royal blood, and leasing out her kingdom (in the form of land grants and other special privileges).

II.i.111. *But . . . land.* 'But since your possessions are limited to this one country.'

II.i.115. *And thou . . . lunatic.* So read the Qq; F reads *And—/ Richard. And thou, a lunaticke.*

II.i.126. *like the pelican.* Young pelicans were fabled to feed on the heart's blood of the mother bird, just as Richard, according to Gaunt, has been draining and spilling the lifeblood of his royal family. In addition, the pelican is a Christian symbol for self-sacrifice. (See also *Hamlet*, IV.1.156–158.)

II.i.146–147. *As . . . mine.* Richard is purposely twisting York's words to make them mean: 'as Bolingbroke loves me, so does Gaunt; as they both love me, so I love them'—which is to say, not at all.

II.i.170. *marriage . . . disgrace.* The exiled Bolingbroke would have married the King of France's cousin had not Richard sent the Earl of Salisbury to prevent the match. The event is described in Holinshed, but the *disgrace* to which York refers is not explained there or in any other known source.

II.i.188–191. *Why . . . withal.* The pentameters are indicated by the present arrangement of lines, which differs from that in Q. The reading *withal* (from Q2; Q has *with all*) means here 'with not being pardoned.'

II.i.205. *letters-patents.* Open letters from the king by which certain rights were conferred. (The modern form would be 'letters patent.')

II.i.256–258. *Wars . . . blows.* The allusion is to the treaty Richard first made with Charles VI of France in 1393 and renewed in 1396 when he married Isabelle. The *compromise* refers to the cession of Brest by Richard to the Duke of Brittany in 1397.

II.i.281. *Le Port Blan.* Written *le Port Blan* in Qq, *Port le Blan* in F, and *Le port blanc* in Holinshed, this is a small port in Côtes du Nord.

II.i.283–285. *Cobham . . . Exeter.* Since Cobham had nothing to do with the Duke of Exeter, a line must be lost. Edmond Malone's edition of 1790 first supplies: 'The son of Richard, Earl of Arundel' (the *his* of l. 286 thus referring to the late earl).

II.i.288 *Quoint.* Although Qq read *Coines*, most editors print *Quoint*, following F, which is only another spelling of Holinshed's *Coint.*

II.ii.38. *'Tis . . . possess.* 'That which I feel is destined to be mine later on.' It is as though the grief is someone else's property which is to come to her in the future.

II.ii.91. *Sirrah . . . Gloucester.* As printed in Qq and F, some of York's lines (like this and ll. 118 and 121) are excessively long, while others (like ll. 93 and 109) are short. It seems likely that this irregularity, as well as the actual wording of York's speech, is Shakespeare's way of suggesting the aged, unsteady, and reticent condition of his character.

II.ii.91 *Plashie.* Actually York's sister died not in Pleshy but Barking, and later than this.

II.ii.134 *Bristow.* Here Qq read *Brist.* and F reads *Bristoll*, but elsewhere (II.3.165 and III.2.142) both Qq and F read *Bristow.* Since this latter spelling indicates pronunciation it is retained throughout.

II.iii.72. *my answer . . . Lancaster.* 'My answer is that I answer only to the title of Lancaster'—i.e. not to Hereford.

II.iii.82. *self-borne.* So read Qq, F, but since no Elizabethan distinction was made between the spellings *borne* and *born*, some editors adopt F3's *self-born*, meaning 'home-sprung,' i.e. productive of civil strife, and relate it to *native* nearby.

II.iii.108. *On what . . . wherein.* 'On what quality or fault of mine is it based, and in what does it consist?'

II.iii.115. *for Lancaster.* Which is to say that Bolingbroke comes either 'as Lancaster' or 'to claim the title and rights of the Duke of Lancaster.'

III.i.43. *Glendor.* Owen Glendower, Richard's squire and minstrel, did, historically speaking, escape to Wales but not until later. Verity and Wilson express

the possibility, and Sisson the certainty, that the 'Welsh Captain' in II.4 is Glendower himself.

III.ii.1. *Barkloughly Castle.* There is no such place. The name, written *Barclowlie* in Holinshed, is Holinshed's mistake for Harlech (i.e. Hertlowli) Castle in Wales.

III.ii.21. *double.* Shakespeare here falls into the popular misconception that a venomous snake poisons with its tongue rather than its fangs.

III.ii.29–32. *The means . . . redress.* This troublesome passage is printed here as it appears in all the Qq (F omits it), but with Pope's addition of *if* to complete both the meaning and meter of l. 30. Most editions follow Pope's other changes in the passage as well, but this seems like challenging the authority of all the Qq unnecessarily, since their version of the lines is acceptable in every other respect.

III.ii.37. *eye of heaven.* John Gower refers to Richard as 'Sol,' and Richard's tomb in Westminster Abbey bears the sign of the sun. Furthermore sun imagery is prominent through most of the play, for description of which see Paul Reyher, 'Le symbole du soleil dans la tragédie de "Richard II," ' *Revue de l'enseignement des langues vivantes*, 40 (1923), 254–60; Caroline Spurgeon, *Shakespeare's Imagery* (New York, Macmillan, 1935); W. H. Clemen, *The Development of Shakespeare's Imagery* (London, Methuen, 1951); and Samuel Kliger, 'The Sun Imagery in *Richard II*,' *Studies in Philology*, 45 (1948), 196–202.

III.ii.55. *off . . . anointed.* By omitting *off* F normalizes the meter, but since 'noint' was a common form of 'anoint' it does as well to read *an anointed* as three syllables.

III.ii.122. *Where is Bagot.* Since l. 132 mentions *three* traitors, since Aumerle does not mention Bagot in l. 141, and since we presume (from II.2.140) that Bagot has gone to join Richard in Ireland, most editors have taken the words *Where is Bagot?* to be either a corruption of the text or a lapse of memory on Shakespeare's part. But because Richard always associates the name of Bagot with the others and knows nothing of him at this time, it might seem queer if he did *not* mention Bagot. What Shakespeare knows is, in short, not identical with what Richard knows at this point. Had he chosen to, Shakespeare might have had someone (like Aumerle) explain to Richard that Bagot tried to join him in Ireland.

III.ii.134. *Make war . . . this.* So Q; F prints *make warre* with l. 133 and feebly ends the line with *this Offence* (Q has *this* alone).

III.iii.15. *For . . . head.* This almost parenthetical phrase probably means 'for omitting (i.e. taking away) his title,' but may mean 'for taking such liberties,' just as we speak of a frisky horse 'taking its head.'

III.iii.41. *my.* Here, as in a few other places, the speech shifts to the first person singular in order to avoid confusion for the playgoers.

III.iii.42, 43. *Provided . . . granted.* 'Provided that the repeal of my banishment and the restoration of my lands be freely granted.' Grammatically (the construction is Latin), the subject of the clause is *my banishment . . . again.*

III.iii.SD. *Parle . . . Salisbury.* In this direction taken from F (and slightly augmented), *Parle* refers to the trumpet call used to summon forces to parley. *On the walls* here no doubt indicates Richard's entrance on the upper stage.

III.iii.96, 97. *He is . . . war.* 'Bolingbroke has come to open the bloodstained will of war to claim its legacy.'

III.iii.106. *thrice-noble.* Perhaps *thrice* is merely emphatic, although it may have a definite meaning: Bolingbroke, already Duke of Hereford and Earl of Derby, is now claiming the title of Duke of Lancaster.

III.iii.122. *is a prince, is just.* Q and Q2 read *is princess iust*; other Qq read *is a Prince iust*; F reads *is a Prince, is iust.* Though these shifting readings are a sure sign of trouble, this edition and most others follow F. A recent interpretation by Sisson in *New Readings in Shakespeare, 2*, 24, is worth considering, however. He judges the compositor to have read 'prince & lust' in his copy as 'princes iust' instead of 'prince and just,' by mistaking the ampersand for an *s*, and then to have set 'princes,' quite naturally, as *princesse.* But this reading is not without difficulties: we cannot be sure how Shakespeare (or a copyist) wrote ampersands; there is no available proof that shakespeare (or the copyist) would have used the spelling 'princes' rather than 'princesse'; nor is Sisson able to complete the line using Q alone, since in the interest of meter and idiom he too must borrow the word *a* from Q3. The reading almost universally adopted from F is rougher and less idiomatic than Sisson's, but at least it is based on the revised readings of two critically reputable texts, Q3 and F.

III.iii.181. *Phaëton.* The son of Apollo who, because he lost control of the horses drawing the chariot of the Sun and drove so near the earth as almost to set it on fire, was hurled to the earth by a bolt of Zeus. Phaëton (knowledge of whom came chiefly from Ovid's *Metamorphoses*) was a favorite subject of Elizabethan emblem writers.

III.iii.208, 209. *too young . . . heir.* Although Richard and Bolingbroke were both thirty-three at this time, Shakespeare consistently suggests that Richard is young and Bolingbroke middle-aged.

III.iv.5. *bias.* OED indicates three meanings for the word: the way of rolling the ball, its course, and its construction. In this last sense *bias* is the lead weight inserted in one side of a bowling ball to make it 'run' in an arc so as to go around other balls lying in the path between the bowler and the jack (small white ball) he is trying to hit.

III.iv.31. *apricocks.* This reading from F gives the probable pronunciation (the Q spelling *Apricokes* is not significant). Apricots were not brought to England until the 14th century—another small anachronism.

III.iv.32–70. *Which . . . thrown down.* This conversation, developing a metaphorical comparison between kingship and gardening, reflects Shakespeare's love of gardens and their imaginative suggestions (compare *The Winter's Tale,* IV.4, and *Henry V,* V.2).

III.iv.58–61. *They are . . . year.* This lineation is Capell's. The lines in Qq and F end with *are, king, trimm'd,* and *year.*

III.iv.109–110. *rue . . . ruth.* A complex pun. The plant *rue* was also called 'herb of grace,' since *rue,* meaning 'repentance,' comes through God's grace. More than that, Shakespeare is also linking *rue* and *ruth,* both as they sound alike and as *rue* meaning 'repentance' resembles *ruth* meaning 'pity.'

IV.i.17–19. *Than . . . lords.* Capell's lineation, which is followed here, better preserves the pentameters than does that in Qq, F, which ends the lines with *withal* and *death.* L. 19 is an alexandrine.

IV.i.26. *manual seal.* A grim joke may be meant, turning on the reference of *manual* to a gage which is a glove (or gauntlet).

IV.i.41. *rapier.* For discussion of the rapier and other dueling matters, see Horace S. Craig, 'Dueling Scenes and Terms in Shakespeare's Plays,' *University of California Publications in English,* 9 (1940), 1–28.

IV.i.53. *task the earth.* So reads Q. Most editors interpret the phrase to mean 'charge the earth with bearing my gage too.' Chambers thinks the *task* is that of the earth serving as a field of combat; Capell sidesteps the difficulty by omitting *earth* and making *task thee* into a direct challenge to Aumerle. Still another possible meaning for the line derives from the reading in the other Qq, *take the earth:* 'I take the earth as my witness in returning the challenge to you, Aumerle.' In any case, as C. H. Herford properly observes (Warwick edition, 1893): 'the high-flown language is in keeping with the conventional tone of the challenge.'

IV.i.62. *Surrey.* Thomas Holland, third Earl of Kent, was created Duke of Surrey in 1397 and, as Richard's nephew, was naturally on Aumerle's side.

IV.i.157–325. *May it please . . . king's fall.* These celebrated lines comprising the so-called 'deposition scene' did not appear in the first three Qq of 1597, 1598, and 1598, while Queen Elizabeth was alive and sensitive to reports encouraging her own abdication. Though proof is lacking, the prevailing scholarly opinion is that the lines were written as an original part of the play, were regularly spoken on the stage, but were withheld from print for political reasons, or were actually censored. (The words *woeful pageant* in l. 328 reinforce the idea that the lines were spoken.) The passage was printed for the first time a few years after the queen's death—in Q4 (1608)— and has been printed as part of the play ever since. The present text is based on F, which in all but one or two details is superior to both Q4 and Q5 (1615). As a matter of historical fact Richard did not appear in person before the assembled parliament to make his resignation.

IV.i.243. *bait.* The figure is from sport, in which dogs charged and baited a bull or bear which was tied to a stake. Here *wretchedness* is one of the dogs.

IV.i.267. *To melt . . . drops.* The line echoes the close of Marlowe's *Doctor Faustus:* 'O soul, be changed into little water-drops, And fall into the ocean, ne'er be found,' just as ll. 286–91 below echo the famous passage earlier in Act V of *Faustus:* 'Was this the face that launch'd a thousand ships, And burnt the topless towers of Ilium?'

IV.i.281–290. *Give me . . . follies.* This arrangement of lines follows F. Because of three omissions in Q4 and Q5 (*and . . . read* in l. 281, *Thou dost . . . me* in l. 286, and *Was . . . winke* in ll. 288–89), the line arrangement is different there.

IV.i.326–227. *On . . . yourselves.* This reading is from F. The words in Q (which J. Dover Wilson in his edition calls 'a patch designed to cover the rent in the text made by the exclusion of the "Deposition" scene') reads:

Let it be so, and loe on wednesday next,
We solemnly proclaime our Coronation,
Lords be ready all.

Henry was crowned on Monday, October 13, 1399.

IV.i.327. *coronation.* 'It is significant for a study of Shakespeare's handling of history that he writes a deposition scene that is not in his sources, and omits a spectacular coronation that is' (Llewellyn M. Buell, Yale edition, 1921).

V.i.1. *Queen.* This scene of parting is not historical. The final separation occurred at Windsor, as represented in II.2.1–4.

V.i.54. *With . . . France.* The idea is not historical. Only after Bolingbroke had detained Isabelle at Sonning for several months did he allow her to return to France (in July 1401).

V.i.88. *Better . . . the near.* Which is to say, 'it is better that we be far apart than near yet not nearer'—since they will not be allowed to be together (the second *near* is comparative) even though Isabelle were to remain in England. Note the homonymic pun on *near* and *nere* (see Kökeritz, *Shakespeare's Pronunciation,* p. 131).

V.ii.24. *theater.* An anachronism in 1399, since the first mention of regular London theaters is around 1575. Other anachronisms are apricots (III.4.29) and the rapier (IV.1.40).

V.ii.58. *seal . . . hangs.* A seal was stamped on the lower end of a parchment strip whose other end was attached to the document. In this case the dangling seal hung outside the doublet.

V.ii.71, 72. *Bound . . . bound to.* Naturally the one to whom a debtor is *bound* would hold the bond, as in *The Merchant of Venice.* Thus Aumerle has not signed the usual bond to borrow money but was sworn to join in the conspiracy to kill the new king, which was to be disguised as a tourney on Epiphany Day, 1400. See York's query (l. 54) and Aumerle's remark (l. 57); the latter has a meaning quite unsuspected by York. Historically, the place agreed upon was not Oxford but Kingston, near Windsor.

V.ii.121. *his horse.* This odd reading in all Qq and Ff may have been influenced by Holinshed: 'The Earl of Rutland . . . took his horse.'

V.iii.12. *So . . . crew.* Since the *which* (i.e. whom) of l. 10 is the object of *support,* this line is left in the air, grammatically. It may be an afterthought.

V.iii.58. *serpent.* 'An allusion to the old fable of the man who warmed a half-frozen serpent by putting it in the bosom of his garment and was stung to death' (G.L. Kittredge's edition, 1941). Compare III.2.131, and *2 Henry VI,* III.1.344, 345.

V.iii.140. *I . . . heart.* So Qq and Ff, but there is excellent justification for transposing the two halves of the line and so preserving both rhyme and meter. Modern editors almost invariably make *With all my heart* end l. 140 and *I pardon him* begin l. 141.

V.iv.SD. *Enter . . . servant.* F prints the eleven lines of this scene as part of scene 3. Thus the two following scenes, which F prints as scenes 4 and 5, are printed in this and other editions as scenes 5 and 6.

V.v.50–58. *For now . . . hours.* 'There are three ways in which a clock notices the progress of time; viz., by the libration of the pendulum, the index on the dial, and the striking of the hour. To these the king, in his comparison, severally alludes; his sighs corresponding to the jarring of the pendulum, which, at the same time that it watches or numbers the seconds, marks also their progress in minutes on the dial or outward watch, to which the king compares his eyes; and their want of figures is supplied by a succession of tears, or, to use an expression of Milton [*Il Penseroso,* 130], *minute-drops:* his finger, by as regularly wiping these away, performs the office of the dial-point; his clamorous groans are the sounds that tell the hour' (Samuel Henley in Variorum edition of 1785). Note also the double sense of *watch* as wakefulness and as timepiece.

V.v.60. *Jack of the clock.* This mechanical figure (also called Jack-o'-th'-clock-house) was a little man in armor who struck the bell each quarter hour. Compare *Richard III,* IV.2.122.

V.v.67. *royal, noble.* Richard's pun (also said to have been made by Queen Elizabeth) is finished in l. 68. Since a *royal* or rose noble was a gold coin worth 10s. and the ordinary *noble* was worth 6s. 8d., the difference between them was ten groats (a groat being worth 4d.).

V.v.114. *die.* The approximate date was February 14, 1400. Richard's death at the hands of Exton is a tradition deriving from an anonymous French source which was eventually brought to England and so to Shakespeare. This version of the death does not sort with the appearance of Richard's remains exhumed in 1873 (which showed no clear signs of violence), nor with other more reputable reports of death by starvation, such as the rebel Percies' 'Letter of Defiance.' As Steel sums it up (*Richard II,* pp. 286–287), 'the Piers Exton story, which is of late and dubious origin, may therefore be rejected in favour of some form of starvation, whether self-inflicted or not, assisted possibly by smothering.' (For Holinshed's version see "Sources of the Play.")

V.vi.1. *latest news.* When the plot was discovered Bolingbroke decided against going to Oxford and remained at Windsor. The rebel *dukes* who marched there to surprise him found he had fled to London by night. After retreating to Cirencester the rebels were soon attacked, beaten, and confined to the abbey of Cirencester. A trick to assist their escape by firing houses in the neighborhood succeeded only in rousing the townsmen to retaliation. It was clear that Richard could not be allowed to live and that the resistance to Bolingbroke had lost its energy when two of the leading rebels taken after the fire, the Earls of Salisbury and Kent, were beheaded about sunset on January 7, 1400.

V.vi.8. *Oxford . . . Kent.* Since we have no record of a conspirator named

Oxford, the F reading is probably more accurate historically: *The heads of Salsbury, Spencer, Blunt, and Kent.* Thus *Spencer* would be Thomas Despencer (formerly Earl of Gloucester but degraded by Henry), and *Blunt* would be Sir Thomas Blunt or *Blount* (apparently no relation to Sir Walter Blunt of *Henry IV*).

V.vi.52. *bier.* Richard was buried in a common grave at Pontefract (or Pomfret). But afterward, when the false rumor spread abroad that Richard was still alive in Scotland, King Henry had the body disinterred and carried through the main cities of the realm to London. For two days it lay in Cheapside, and for a time in St. Paul's, before being carried to King's Langley where it was secluded in an 'obscure grave,' there to stay until Henry V (who was more chivalrous than his father) moved it to the beautiful tomb in Westminster Abbey, which Richard himself had built for his first wife, Anne of Bohemia. There the unfortunate king still lies, with the epitaph by Abbot Feckenham on the stone above him, serving as a motto to his character and this play: *Fuisse felicem miserrimum*—to have been fortunate was most wretched.

The Life and Death of King John

Edited by
Stanley T. Williams

Dramatis Personae

King John

Prince Henry, *Son to the King*

Arthur, *Duke of Britaine, Nephew to the King*

The Earl of Pembroke

The Earl of Essex

The Earl of Salisbury

The Lord Bigot

Hubert de Burgh

Robert Faulconbridge, *Son to Sir Robert Faulconbridge*

Philip the Bastard, *his Half-Brother*

James Gurney, *Servant to Lady Faulconbridge*

Peter of Pomfret, *a Prophet*

Philip, *King of France*

Lewis, *the Dauphin*

Lymoges, *Duke of Austria*

Cardinal Pandulph, *the Pope's Legate*

Melun, *a French Lord*

Chatillion, *Ambassador from France*

Queen Elinor, *Mother to King John*

Constance, *Mother to Arthur*

Blanch of Spain, *Niece to King John*

Lady Faulconbridge

Lords, Ladies, Citizens of Angiers, Sheriff, Heralds, Officers, Soldiers, Executioners, Messengers, and other Attendants

Scene—*Sometimes in England, and sometimes in France.*

The Life and Death of King John

INTRODUCTION

SOURCES OF THE PLAY

Kynge Johan, an old play on the subject of King John's quarrels with the Pope, was written by John Bale, Bishop of Ossory, probably between 1557 and 1563. No evidence exists that Shakespeare knew of this play, or that it affected another play which was unquestionably his source. This drama appeared first anonymously in London in 1591, printed 'for Sampson Clarke.' It was in two parts, each bearing a separate title: *The Troublesome Raigne of Iohn King of England, with the discouerie of King Richard Cordelions Base sonne (vulgarly named, The Bastard Fawconbridge): also the death of King Iohn at Swinstead Abbey. As it was (sundry times) publikely acted by the Queenes Maiesties Players, in the honourable Citie of London;* and, *The Second Part of the troublesome Raigne of King Iohn, conteining the death of Arthur Plantaginet, the landing of Lewes, and the poysning of King Iohn at Swinstead Abbey. As it was (sundry times) publikely acted by the Queenes Maiesties Players, in the honourable Citie of London.* In 1611 the first and second parts were reprinted together. This edition bore the inscription 'Written by W. Sh.,' and the third edition in 1622 had Shakespeare's name in full: 'Written by W. Shakespeare,'—obvious attempts to capitalize on the commercial value of the dramatist's name.

The facts concerning the authorship of *The Troublesome Raigne* are unknown. Although the theory that Shakespeare wrote it has had, at various times, the support of the critics Capell, Steevens, Tieck, Ulrici, there is no proof that this play was from his hand. Mr. Edward Rose in his *Shakespeare as an Adapter* even says: 'So entirely, indeed, has the dialogue been rewritten, that one can hardly imagine Shakespeare to have known the original play except by seeing it acted, and perhaps quickly reading it through.'[1] *The Troublesome Raigne*, produced in confessed rivalry with Marlowe's *Tamburlaine*, was written about 1589, just after the repulse of the Spanish armada. Fleay found in it hints of the work of Greene, Lodge, and Peele. The best modern opinion favors the authorship of the last-named poet. A main source was, of course, Holinshed's *Chronicles*, editions of which appeared in 1577 and 1587, but many dates and incidents in the old play are at variance with history.[2]

A study of *The Troublesome Raigne* reveals its creator's free use of history, and also its importance, scene by scene, as source material for Shakespeare. Although he constantly omitted and altered, *The Troublesome Raigne* and *King John* are so alike in theme and general plan that even the dramatic weaknesses of the older play persist in Shakespeare's version. In the former John inspires alternately our anger and our sympathy. He is domineering, murderous, and weak, yet he is the representative of England against papal tyranny. In *King John* he arouses similar

feelings. In the old play, too, are prefigurations of Shakespeare's characters: the tender, lovable Arthur, the queenly, despairing Constance, the manly, humorous, aggressive Bastard. *The Troublesome Raigne* is undistinguished by genius, but it must have seemed to Shakespeare, as it does now to us, potentially strong in characters and episodes of dramatic passion. Shakespeare uses only a few of the original lines; he cuts, emends, expands; but he bases his own tragedy on *The Troublesome Raigne*. There is indeed very little to suggest that he went behind this play for material, to Holinshed, Halle's *Chronicle*, or other sources.

Shakespeare's manipulation of the old play was characteristic. New dialogue, noble verse, different scenes, such as that between Hubert and Arthur, render King John a tragedy of character instead of a commonplace play on anti-Catholic issues. This ultra-Protestantism colors the whole of *The Troublesome Raigne*, obscuring character-portrayal. In this connection the following comments of Mr. Rose are suggestive concerning Shakespeare's use of *The Troublesome Raigne*: 'In reconstructing the play, the great want which struck Shakespeare seems to have been that of a strong central figure. He was attracted by the rough, powerful nature which he could see the Bastard's must have been; almost like a modern dramatist "writing up" a part for a star actor, he introduced Faulconbridge wherever it was possible, gave him the end of every act (except the third), and created, from a rude and inconsistent sketch, a character as strong, as complete, and as original as even he ever drew. Throughout a series of scenes, not otherwise very closely connected, this wonderfully real type of faulty, combative, not ignoble manhood is developed, a support and addition to the scenes in which he has least to say, a great power where he is prominent.

'This is the most striking example of his development of a character, but his treatment of Constance, Arthur, Hubert, Pandulph, and of some portions of the character of John himself, is very noticeable. The entire wonderful scene in which Constance laments the loss of her child is founded upon the seven lines:

> *"My tongue is tuned to story forth mishap;*
> *When did I breathe to tell a pleasing tale?*
> *Must Constance speak? Let tears prevent her talk.*
> *Must I discourse? Let Dido sigh, and say*
> *She weeps again to hear the wrack of Troy:*
> *Two words will serve, and then my tale is done—*
> *Eleanor's proud brat hath robbed me of my son!"*[3]

Thus Shakespeare breathes into the confused collection of incidents new life. He makes Pandulph, Salisbury, and Hubert human beings, and King John a subtle and somewhat baffling character. Although he actually omits four scenes and introduces no new ones, the total effect is enrichment. Some of the minor but significant changes are: at the time of the marriage contract between Lewis and Blanch, Constance does not appear; most of the attacks

---

1 *Macmillan's Magazine*, XXXIX, 69 ff., November, 1878.

2 Some examples of the substantial independence of *The Troublesome Raigne* from Holinshed are: the creation of the character of Philip out of a very short passage in the *Chronicles;* the story of Richard's slaying the lion; the identification of the Duke of Austria with the Viscount of Limoges; the connection of the capture and recapture of Angiers with the betrothal of Lewis and Blanch; the plunder of the Abbeys by the Bastard; and the chronology respecting Austria's death, the pilgrimage to Bury St. Edmunds, the King's resignation of his crown, and the wreck on Goodwin Sands.

3 Edward Rose (*op. cit.*), 71, 72.

on Rome are excised, and notably the scene in which Faulconbridge plunders the monasteries; the attitude of the Bastard towards his illegitimacy becomes definitely ironical; two long speeches of the Prophet, Peter of Pomfret, disappear; the death of Arthur is treated with more restraint, and the news of this is made concise and dramatic; the poisoning of the King takes place off the stage, and is unmotivated. A score of other alterations might be noted, but such characteristic changes will indicate Shakespeare's methods in wrestling from *The Troublesome Raigne* the elements for his own greater clarity, subtlety, and emotional strength.

THE HISTORY OF THE PLAY

Francis Meres mentions Shakespeare's tragedy of *King John* in *Palladis Tamia* (1598). There is no record of a performance between 1598 and 1642, the date of the closing of the theatres. Yet it doubtless was produced at the 'Theatre' or 'Curtain' playhouse, Shoreditch, in or about 1596, when *Romeo and Juliet* was acted. If so, it is credible that Shakespeare acted in the tragedy, since he was one of the actual players in the Chamberlain's Company from 1594 to 1603. There is no evidence that *King John* was revived during the Restoration. Pepys does not mention it, nor does Dryden.

Colley Cibber's adaptation of the tragedy, *Papal Tyranny in the Reign of King John,* written about 1736, was never formally acted because of protests against thus meddling with Shakespeare.[4] Later, however, Cibber brought forward a version at Covent Garden, on February 15, 1745. Both these incidents caused productions of Shakespeare's *King John*. The first known performance of this was at Covent Garden Theatre on February 26, 1737. Of it Davies remarked: 'So much was said, and with propriety, by the critics who wrote against Cibber in the public prints, in commendation of Shakespeare's K. John, that Mr. Rich very wisely determined to take the hint, and resolved to revive the long-forgotten tragedy. The principal parts, if I can trust my memory, were thus divided: King John, Mr. Delane; the Bastard, Tom Walker (the original Macheath); Hale acted the King of France, and Ryan Cardinal Pandulph; Lady Constance by Mrs. Hallam.... King John was acted several nights with great applause; but the king was not remarkably well represented by Delane; he could not easily assume the turbulent and gloomy passions of the character.[5] Walker's Faulconbridge, however, was considered excellent, even superior to the later interpretations of the character by such actors as Garrick, Sheridan, Delane, and Barry. On February 2, 1738, the play was again acted, this time with a fresh prologue. Genest records further performances of *King John* on March 2 and November 29 of this year; and also on March 8, 1739, October 22, 1739, and April 2, 1741, all at Covent Garden.

Garrick first appeared in the title-rôle of *King John* at Drury Lane on February 20, 1745. Others in the cast were Delane as the Bastard, Barry as Hubert, Macklin as Pandulph, and Mrs. Cibber as Constance. Garrick in the following season in Dublin acted the parts of John and Faulconbridge, alternating in these with T. Sheridan. *King John* was not among Garrick's most successful plays, but records of a few remarkable interpretations have

survived. Davies describes the scene (IV. ii) between the King and Hubert: 'When Hubert shewed him his warrant for the death of Arthur, saying to him, at the same time,

Here is your hand and seal for what I did,

Garrick snatched the warrant from his hand; and grasping it hard, in an agony of despair and horror, he threw his eyes to heaven, as if self-convicted of murder, and standing before the great Judge of the quick and dead to answer for the infringement of the divine command!'[6] Mrs. Cibber's portrayal of Constance has been declared by some critics to have been greater than that of even Mrs. Siddons: 'When going off the stage, in this scene [III. iv.], she uttered the words,

O Lord! my boy!

with such an emphatical scream of agony, as will never be forgotten by those who heard her.[7] On March 2, 1745, this cast of the play gave its eighth performance.

On March 16, 1747, at Drury Lane *King John* was produced by Delane as a benefit performance. It was again acted at Covent Garden on February 23, 1750, with Quin as the King, Barry as Faulconbridge, and Mrs. Cibber as Constance. At a performance at the same theatre on April 25, 1751, the part of Constance was taken by Mrs. Woffington. On January 23, 1754, *King John* was acted at Drury lane with Garrick playing the Bastard, and Mossop the King. In this rôle Garrick was unsuccessful. 'Various,' says Davies, 'have been the actors of this brave, generous, romantic, and humourous character, Faulconbridge: but, though Garrick, Sheridan, Delane, and Barry, have attempted it, they all fell short of the merits of Tom Walker. In him alone were the several requisites for the character: a strong and muscular person, a bold and intrepid look; manly deportment, vigorous action, and a humour which descended to an easy familiarity in conveying a jest or sarcasm with uncommon poignancy. Garrick had certainly much merit in the Bastard, but the want of the mechanical part was a deficiency not to be remedied by art.'[8] It may be said that *King John* was now definitely restored to the English stage. Prior to Kemble's representation in 1783, Genest and other historians of the theatre record numerous performances. Some of the more notable were those beginning at Drury Lane, on December 17, 1760, with the elder Sheridan and Garrick exchanging the rôles of King John and Faulconbridge; that on February 2, 1774, with Mrs. Barry as Constance; and that on November 29, 1777, with Henderson as King John.

The next significant appearance of *King John* was at Drury Lane on December 10, 1783, with J. P. Kemble and Mrs. Siddons, 'Their majesties,' says Boaden, 'being desirous of seeing the brother and sister together.'[9] Kemble studied the part of the King under the guidance of the older Sheridan. This was one of several remarkable performances in which the chief rôles were taken by the Kemble family. Mrs. Siddons again played Constance and Kemble the King at Drury Lane on March 1, 1792, and May 13, 1801, and at Covent Garden on February 14, 1804. In the last-named performance Charles Kemble acted Faulconbridge. These interpretations of the King and of Constance made a deep impression upon stage tradition. Various critics, among them Hazlitt, thought Kemble's acting of King John painfully artificial, but Boaden says of the scene with Hubert: 'The most cold-

---

4 'Colley [Cibber] ... went to the playhouse, and, without saying a word to any body, took the play from the prompter's desk, and marched off with it in his pocket. Pope, in his new edition of the Dunciad, ... hints at the cautious conduct of the poet-laureat: "King John in silence modestly expires."' Thomas Davies, *Dramatic Miscellanies*, London, 1785, I. 5.

5 Davies (*op cit*.), I, 5–9.

6 Davies (*op. cit.*), I, 69, 70.

7 *Ibid.*, I, 55, 56.

8 *Ibid.*, I, 15.

9 James Boaden, *Memoirs of the Life of John Philip Kemble*, Philadelphia, 1825, p. 76.

blooded, hesitating, cowardly and creeping villany, that ever abused the gift of speech, found in Mr. Kemble the only powers competent to give it utterance. And if I were to select a scene, in the whole compass of the drama, more appropriate to him than any other, I should, I think, fix upon this noiseless horror, this muttered suggestion of slaughterous thought, on which the midnight bell alone was fitted to break, by one solitary undulating sound, that added to the gloom.'[10]

Likewise, Mrs. Siddons' rendering of the part, which she herself called 'the majestic, the passionate, the tender,' evoked eloquent descriptions of her genius, especially in her pleas for vengeance and in her laments for Arthur.[11] One of the most memorable of these comments is her own, on her state of mind as she acted the part: 'Whenever I was called upon to personate the character of *Constance,* I never, from the beginning of the play to the end of my part in it, once suffered my dressing-room door to be closed, in order that my attention might be constantly fixed on those distressing events, which by this means, I could plainly hear going on upon the stage, the terrible effects of which progress were to be represented by me. Moreover, I never omitted to place myself, with *Arthur* in my hand, to hear the march, when, upon the reconciliation of England and France, they enter the gates of Angiers, to ratify the contract of marriage between the *Dauphin* and the *Lady Blanche:* because the sickening sounds of that march would usually cause the bitter tears of rage, disappointment, betrayed confidence, baffled ambition, and, above all, the agonizing feelings of maternal affection, to gush into my eyes. In short, the spirit of the whole drama took possession of my mind and frame, by my attention being incessantly riveted to the passing scene.'[12] We have also the testimony of Doran and Macready concerning the power of Charles Kemble's Faulconbridge.[13]

On December 3, 1816, Miss O'Neil appeared in *King John* as Constance. The Kembles continued to act in the tragedy during 1817, but the next distinctive performance was at Drury Lane on June 1, 1818. Edmund Kean played the King; Wallack, Faulconbridge; and Miss Macauley, Constance.[14] On March 3, 1823, at Covent Garden Macready took the rôle of John and Charles Kemble that of Faulconbridge. Macready's *Diary* describes his success in this part, which he repeated frequently before the close of 1842.

Two years later (1844) Samuel Phelps presented the play at Sadler's Wells, acting during this season the part of the King eighteen times. Marston was Faulconbridge and Mrs. Warner, Constance. Phelps and the younger Kean developed *King John* as a spectacle. 'In the year 1846,' says Cole, 'Charles Kean ventured on an experiment never before hazarded in America—the production of the two historical tragedies of "King John" and "Richard the Third," on a scale of splendour which no theatre in London or Paris could have surpassed.'[15] Cole estimates Charles Kean's interpre-

tation of King John as inferior only to his Hamlet, Lear, Wolsey, and Shylock. In this production Constance was played by Miss Ellen Tree, and Arthur by Miss Kate Terry. In the revival of 1858 Lacy acted Faulconbridge, Miss Kate Terry, Blanch; Miss Ellen Terry (then ten years old), Arthur, and Mr. Terry, King Philip.

Later English performances of *King John* have been rare. Osmond Tearle produced it at Stratford-on-Avon in February, 1890, and the Oxford University Dramatic Society in February, 1891. The most remarkable revival of these years was at the Haymarket Theatre on September 20, 1899. The cast included Mr. H. Beerbohm Tree as the King, Miss Julia Neilson as Constance, and Mr. Lewis Waller as Faulconbridge. The tragedy was compressed into three acts, and, besides considerable new stage business, two tableaux were added: the battle before Angiers and the signing of the Magna Charta. *The Saturday Review* of September 21 noted minor defects but praised the dialogues between John and Hubert. The Henry Talbot Dramatic Club acted the tragedy at the Athenaeum, at Glasgow, in May, 1907.[16] *King John* was presented again at Stratford in 1909, 1913, 1916, and once more in the spring of 1925. This version was acted ten times. Altogether there were nineteen performances of *King John* at Stratford between 1890 and 1925.[17]

King John was revived on Monday, September 4, 1926, at the Old Vic Theatre in London, with Duncan Yarrow as the King, Baliol Holloway as the Bastard, and Dorothy Massingham as Constance.[18]

Besides its vogue in England and America, *King John* had success on the Continent. In Germany an adaptation, *Arthur, Prinz von England,* was acted in Altona, and published about 1801. In 1835 the Schlegel-Tieck version was presented at Düsseldorf. Stuttgart witnessed in 1850 an acting of Schlegel's version, which in 1908 was performed at the Munich Hof-Theater. Since the first production in America at the Southwark Theatre, Philadelphia, on December 12, 1768, with Douglass as the King, the play has been acted at regular intervals. Among these representations were performances at the John Street Theatre, New York, in 1769; at the Baltimore Theatre on December 10, 1782, with Heard as King John; at the Park Theatre, New York, on various dates between 1798 and 1832. Associated with the play were such actors as T. A. Cooper, G. F. Cooke, Macready, and the Kembles. *King John* was produced at the Bowery Theatre, New York, on April 30, 1834, with J. B. Booth as John, and at the Park Theatre on November 16, 1846, with Charles Kean as the King. Other actors connected with American productions from 1856 to 1909 were E. L. Davenport, J. McCullough, and Robert Mantell.[19]

An American production of importance was Mantell's on March 8, 1909, at the New Amsterdam Theatre, New York. This *The Theatre* for April, 1909, though at variance with other criticisms, called 'a noble, impressive and adequate production.'[20]

10 *Ibid.,* pp. 77, 78.

11 See James Boaden, *Memoirs of Mrs. Siddons,* Philadelphia, 1827, pp. 218–220.

12 John William Cole, *The Life and Theatrical Times of Charles Kean,* London, 1859, II, 29.

13 See John Doran, *Annals of the English Stage,* London, 1888, III, 213, and *Macready's Reminiscences* (ed. S. F. Pollock), New York, 1875, p. 401.

14 See F. W. Hawkins, *The Life of Edmund Kean,* London, 1869, II, 50: 'His [Edmund Kean's] King John, without disturbing the impression which John Kemble had created by his performance of the character, was nobly represented. The absolute triumph was won, as might be expected, in the scene where he darkly intimated to Hubert his desire for Arthur's death. Churchill's lines on Sheridan possessed the full extent of their application here:
  ' "Behold him sound the depth of Hubert's soul,
    Whilst in his own contending passions roll;
    View the whole scene, with critic judgement scan,
    And then deny him merit if you can." '

15 Cole (*op. cit.*), I, 343, 344.

16 Portions of *King John* were acted by children of the London County Council Schools at the Shakespeare Exhibition, at the Whitechapel Art Gallery, in the autumn of 1910. For references to these three last-mentioned performances of *King John,* see *Review of English Studies,* III, No. 10, April, 1927.

17 See William Jaggard, *Shakespeare Memorial,* Stratford [1926], pp, 11, 17, 19, 21, 26.

18 See *The London Times,* September 6, 1926.

19 See G. O. Seilhamer, *History of the American Theatre,* Philadelphia, 1888, 1889, I, 242, 244, 249, 270, 317; II, 71, 77. On the American stage single scenes from *King John* were occasionally produced. See T. Allston Brown, *A History of the New York Stage,* New York, 1903, I, 15, 32, 36, 40, 42, 66, 124, 135, 212, 513; II, 429; III, 103. See also George C. D. Odell, *Annals of the New York Stage,* New York, 1927, I, 146; II, 176, 293, 317, 340, 366, 401, 477, 527, 555.

20 See also *The Independent,* March 25, 1909; *The Literary Digest,* March 20, 1909; *The Nation,* March 11, 1909; *The New York Tribune,* March 9, 1909.

ACT FIRST ❧ SCENE FIRST

[London. A Room of State in the Palace]
Enter King John, Queen Elinor, Pembroke, Essex, and Salisbury,
[and Others,] with the Chatillion of France.

K. John. Now, say, Chatillion, what would France with us?
Chat. Thus, after greeting, speaks the King of France,
In my behaviour, to the majesty,
The borrow'd majesty, of England here.
    Eli. A strange beginning: 'borrow'd majesty'!   *5*
    K. John. Silence, good mother; hear the embassy.
    Chat. Philip of France, in right and true behalf
Of thy deceased brother Geoffrey's son,
Arthur Plantagenet, lays most lawful claim
To this fair island and the territories,   *10*
To Ireland, Poitiers, Anjou, Touraine, Maine;
Desiring thee to lay aside the sword
Which sways usurpingly these several titles,
And put the same into young Arthur's hand,
Thy nephew and right royal sovereign.   *15*
    K. John. What follows if we disallow of this?
    Chat. The proud control of fierce and bloody war,
To enforce these rights so forcibly withheld.
    K. John. Here have we war for war, and blood for blood,
Controlment for controlment: so answer France.   *20*
    Chat. Then take my king's defiance from my mouth,
The farthest limit of my embassy.
    K. John. Bear mine to him, and so depart in peace:
Be thou as lightning in the eyes of France;
For ere thou canst report I will be there,   *25*
The thunder of my cannon shall be heard.
So, hence! Be thou the trumpet of our wrath,
And sullen presage of your own decay.
An honourable conduct let him have:
Pembroke, look to 't. Farewell, Chatillion.   *30*
         Exit Chat[illion] and Pem[broke].
    Eli. What now, my son! have I not ever said
How that ambitious Constance would not cease
Till she had kindled France and all the world
Upon the right and party of her son?
This might have been prevented and made whole   *35*
With very easy arguments of love,
Which now the manage of two kingdoms must
With fearful bloody issue arbitrate.
    K. John. Our strong possession, and our right, for us.
    Eli. Your strong possession much more than your right,   *40*
Or else it must go wrong with you and me:
So much my conscience whispers in your ear,
Which none but heaven, and you, and I, shall hear.

    Enter a Sheriff [who whispers to Essex].

    Essex. My liege, here is the strangest controversy,
Come from the country to be judg'd by you,   *45*

That e'er I heard: shall I produce the men?
    K. John. Let them approach.
Our abbeys and our priories shall pay
This expedition's charge.

    Enter Robert Faulconbridge, and Philip [his bastard brother].

          What men are you?   *50*
    Bast. Your faithful subject, I, a gentleman,
Born in Northamptonshire, and eldest son,
As I suppose, to Robert Faulconbridge,
A soldier, by the honour-giving hand
Of Cordelion knighted in the field.   *55*
    K. John. What art thou?
    Rob. The son and heir to that same Faulconbridge.
    K. John. Is that the elder, and art thou the heir?
You came not of one mother then, it seems.
    Bast. Most certain of one mother, mighty king,   *60*
That is well known; and, as I think, one father.
But for the certain knowledge of that truth
I put you o'er to heaven and to my mother:
Of that I doubt, as all men's children may.
    Eli. Out on thee, rude man! thou dost shame thy mother   *65*
And wound her honour with this diffidence.
    Bast. I, madam? no, I have no reason for it;
That is my brother's plea and none of mine;
The which if he can prove, a' pops me out
At least from fair five hundred pound a year: *70*
Heaven guard my mother's honour and my land!
    K. John. A good blunt fellow. Why, being younger born,
Doth he lay claim to thine inheritance?
    Bast. I know not why, except to get the land.
But once he slander'd me with bastardy: *75*
But whe'r I be as true-begot or no,
That still I lay upon my mother's head;
But that I am as well-begot, my liege,—
Fair fall the bones that took the pains for me!—
Compare our faces and be judge yourself.   *80*
If old Sir Robert did beget us both,
And were our father, and this son like him;
O old Sir Robert, father, on my knee
I give heaven thanks I was not like to thee!
    K. John. Why, what a madcap hath heaven lent us here!   *85*
    Eli. He hath a trick of Cordelion's face;
The ascent of his tongue affecteth him.
Do you not read some tokens of my son
In the large composition of this man?
    K. John. Mine eye hath well examined his parts,   *90*
And finds them perfect Richard. Sirrah, speak:
What doth move you to claim your brother's land?
    Bast. Because he hath a half-face, like my father.
With half that face would he have all my land;
A half-fac'd groat five hundred pound a year!   *95*
    Rob. My gracious liege, when that my father liv'd,
Your brother did employ my father much,—
    Bast. Well, sir, by this you cannot get my land:
Your tale must be how he employ'd my mother.

The Life and Death of King John; *cf. n.*   Scene One. SD the Chatillion of France;
cf. n.   **3 In my behaviour:** *as represented in my person and outward acts*   **6 embassy:**
ambassador's commission or message   **7 in ... behalf:** *for the benefit of*   **10 this fair
island;** *cf. n.*   **13** Cf. *n.*   **16 disallow of:** *refuse*   **20 Controlment:** *restraint*   **26
cannon;** *cf. n.*   **28 sullen:** *gloomy* **decay:** *ruin*   **29 conduct:** *escort*   **34 Upon:** *in
defense of* **party:** *cause*   **35 made whole:** *restored to health*   **36 easy:** *slight* **arguments:**
discussions   **37 manage:** *management*

48, 49 Our abbeys ... charge; *cf. n.*   **49 expedition's;** *cf.
n.*   **63 put ... o'er:** *refer*   **66 diffidence:** *distrust*   **69 a':** *he*   **75 once:** *once for
all*   **76 whe'r:** *whether*   **79 fall:** *befall*   **86 trick:** *peculiar or characteristic expression*   **87 affecteth:** *imitates*   **89 composition:** *constitution*   **93 half-face:** *thin
face*   **95 A half-fac'd groat;** *cf. n.*   **55 Cordelion;**

Rob. And once dispatch'd him in an embassy 100
To Germany, there with the emperor
To treat of high affairs touching that time.
Th' advantage of his absence took the king,
And in the mean time sojourn'd at my father's;
Where how he did prevail I shame to speak, 105
But truth is truth: large lengths of seas and shores
Between my father and my mother lay,—
As I have heard my father speak himself,—
When this same lusty gentleman was got.
Upon his death-bed he by will bequeath'd 110
His lands to me, and took it on his death
That this my mother's son was none of his;
And if he were, he came into the world
Full fourteen weeks before the course of time.
Then, good my liege, let me have what is mine, 115
My father's land, as was my father's will.
 K. John. Sirrah, your brother is legitimate;
Your father's wife did after wedlock bear him,
And if she did play false, the fault was hers;
Which fault lies on the hazards of all husbands 120
That marry wives. Tell me, how if my brother,
Who, as you say, took pains to get this son,
Had of your father claim'd this son for his?
In sooth, good friend, your father might have kept
This calf bred from his cow from all the world; 125
In sooth he might; then, if he were my brother's,
My brother might not claim him; nor your father,
Being none of his, refuse him: this concludes;
My mother's son did get your father's heir;
Your father's heir must have your father's land. 130
 Rob. Shall then my father's will be of no force
To dispossess that child which is not his?
 Bast. Of no more force to dispossess me, sir,
Than was this will to get me, as I think.
 Eli. Whether hadst thou rather be a Faulconbridge 135
And like thy brother, to enjoy thy land,
Or the reputed son of Cordelion,
Lord of thy presence and no land beside?
 Bast. Madam, and if my brother had my shape,
And I had his, Sir Robert's his, like him; 140
And if my legs were two such riding-rods,
My arms such eel-skins stuff'd, my face so thin
That in mine ear I durst not stick a rose
Lest men should say, 'Look, where three-farthings goes!'
And, to his shape, were heir to all this land, 145
Would I might never stir from off this place,
I would give it every foot to have this face;
I would not be Sir Nob in any case.
 Eli. I like thee well: wilt thou forsake thy fortune,
Bequeath thy land to him, and follow me? 150
I am a soldier and now bound to France.
 Bast. Brother, take you my land, I'll take my chance.
Your face hath got five hundred pound a year,
Yet sell your face for five pence and 'tis dear.

Madam, I'll follow you unto the death. 155
 Eli. Nay, I would have you go before me thither.
 Bast. Our country manners give our betters way.
 K. John. What is thy name?
 Bast. Philip, my liege, so is my name begun;
Philip, good old Sir Robert's wife's eldest son. 160
 K. John. From henceforth bear his name whose form thou
bearest:
Kneel thou down Philip, but rise more great;
Arise sir Richard, and Plantagenet.
 Bast. Brother by th' mother's side, give me your hand: 165
My father gave me honour, yours gave land.
Now blessed be the hour, by night or day,
When I was got, Sir Robert was away!
 Eli. The very spirit of Plantagenet!
I am thy grandam, Richard; call me so. 170
 Bast. Madam, by chance but not by truth; what though?
Something about, a little from the right,
 In at the window, or else o'er the hatch:
Who dares not stir by day must walk by night,
 And have is have, however men do catch. 175
Near or far off, well won is still well shot,
And I am I, howe'er I was begot.
 K. John. Go, Faulconbridge: now hast thou thy desire;
A landless knight makes thee a landed squire.
Come, madam, and come, Richard, we must speed 180
For France, for France, for it is more than need.
 Bast. Brother, adieu; good fortune come to thee!
For thou wast got i' th' way of honesty.

Exeunt all but Bastard.

A foot of honour better than I was;
But many a many foot of land the worse. 185
Well, now can I make any Joan a lady.
'Good den, Sir Richard!'—'God-a-mercy, fellow!'—
And if his name be George, I'll call him Peter;
For new-made honour doth forget men's names;
'Tis too respective and too sociable 190
For your conversion. Now your traveller,
He and his toothpick at my worship's mess,
And when my knightly stomach is suffic'd,
Why then I suck my teeth, and catechize
My picked man of countries: 'My dear sir,'— 195
Thus, leaning on mine elbow, I begin,—
'I shall beseech you,'—that is question now;
And then comes answer like an Absey-book:
'O, sir,' says answer, 'at your best command;
At your employment; at your service, sir'; 200
'No, sir,' says question, 'I, sweet sir, at yours';
And so, ere answer knows what question would,
Saving in dialogue of compliment,
And talking of the Alps and Apennines,
The Pyrenean and the river Po, 205
It draws toward supper in conclusion so.
But this is worshipful society,
And fits the mounting spirit like myself;

---

105 shame: *am ashamed* **109** lusty: *merry* got: *begotten* **111** took it on his death: *gave a strong assurance* **120** lies on the hazards: *is among the chances* **128** refuse: *disown* concludes: *settles the matter* **135** Whether ... rather: *wouldst thou rather; cf. n.* **138** presence: *person* **139** and if: *an if, if* **140** Sir Robert's his, like him; *cf. n.* **141** riding-rods: *switches* **143, 144** *Cf. n.* **145** to: *in addition to* **148** Sir Nob; *cf. n.* **150** Bequeath: *bestow* **151** bound: *intending to go*

163 *Cf. n.* **171** truth: *honesty* what though: *what does it matter?* **172** Something about: *somewhat circuitously* right: *straight road* **173** hatch: *half-door; cf. n.* **175** *Cf. n.* **179** *Cf. n.* **186** Joan: *peasant girl* **187** *Cf. n.* Good den: *good even* God-a-mercy: *God reward you* **190** respective: *considerate* **191** For your conversion; *for one who has undergone such a change of rank as you have* **191, 192** Now your traveller ... mess; *cf. n.* **195** picked: *refined* **198** Absey-book: *primer, horn-back* **205** Pyrenean: *Pyrenees*

For he is but a bastard to the time,
That doth not smack of observation;   210
And so am I, whether I smack or no;
And not alone in habit and device,
Exterior form, outward accoutrement,
But from the inward motion to deliver
Sweet, sweet, sweet poison for the age's tooth,   215
Which, though I will not practise to deceive,
Yet, to avoid deceit, I mean to learn;
For it shall strew the footsteps of my rising.
But who comes in such haste in riding-robes?
What woman-post is this? hath she no husband   220
That will take pains to blow a horn before her?

Enter Lady Faulconbridge and James Gurney.

O me! 'tis my mother. How now, good lady!
What brings you here to court so hastily?
    Lady F. Where is that slave, thy brother? where is he,
That holds in chase mine honour up and down?   225
    Bast. My brother Robert? old Sir Robert's son?
Colbrand the giant, that same mighty man?
Is it Sir Robert's son that you seek so?
    Lady F. Sir Robert's son! Ay, thou unreverend boy,
Sir Robert's son: why scorn'st thou at Sir Robert?   230
He is Sir Robert's son, and so art thou.
    Bast. James Gurney, wilt thou give us leave awhile?
    Gur. Good leave, good Philip.
    Bast.   Philip! sparrow! James,
There's toys abroad; anon I'll tell thee more.   235
                                                            Exit James.

Madam, I was not old Sir Robert's son:
Sir Robert might have eat his part in me
Upon Good Friday and ne'er broke his fast.
Sir Robert could do well: marry, to confess,
Could he get me? Sir Robert could not do it.   240
We know his handiwork; therefore, good mother,
To whom am I beholding for these limbs?
Sir Robert never holp to make this leg.
    Lady F. Hast thou conspired with thy brother too,
That for thine own gain shouldst defend mine honour?   245
What means this scorn, thou most untoward knave?
    Bast. Knight, knight, good mother, Basiliscolike.
What! I am dubb'd; I have it on my shoulder.
But, mother, I am not Sir Robert's son;
I have disclaim'd Sir Robert and my land;   250
Legitimation, name, and all is gone.
Then, good my mother, let me know my father;
Some proper man, I hope; who was it, mother?
    Lady F. Hast thou denied thyself a Faulconbridge?
    Bast. As faithfully as I deny the devil.   255
    Lady F. King Richard Cordelion was thy father:
By long and vehement suit I was seduc'd
To make room for him in my husband's bed.
Heaven lay not my transgression to my charge!

Thou art the issue of my dear offence,   260
Which was so strongly urg'd past my defence.
    Bast. Now, by this light, were I to get again,
Madam, I would not wish a better father.
Some sins do bear their privilege on earth,
And so doth yours; your fault was not your folly.   265
Needs must you lay your heart at his dispose,
Subjected tribute to commanding love,
Against whose fury and unmatched force
The aweless lion could not wage the fight,
Nor keep his princely heart from Richard's hand.   270
He that perforce robs lions of their hearts
May easily win a woman's. Ay, my mother,
With all my heart I thank thee for my father!
Who lives and dares but say thou didst not well
When I was got, I'll send his soul to hell.   275
Come, lady, I will show thee to my kin;
And they shall say, when Richard me begot,
If thou hadst said him nay, it had been sin;
Who says it was, he lies; I say 'twas not.

                                                            Exeunt.

ACT SECOND ❧ SCENE FIRST

[France. Before the Walls of Angiers]
Enter before Angiers, Philip, King of France, [and his Forces,] Lewis
[the] Dauphin, Austria [and his Forces], Constance, Arthur [and
Attendants].

    Lewis. Before Angiers well met, brave Austria.
Arthur, that great forerunner of thy blood,
Richard, that robb'd the lion of his heart
And fought the holy wars in Palestine,
By this grave duke came early to his grave;   5
And, for amends to his posterity,
At our importance hither is he come,
To spread his colours, boy, in thy behalf,
And to rebuke the usurpation
Of thy unnatural uncle, English John.   10
Embrace him, love him, give him welcome hither.
    Arth. God shall forgive you Cordelion's death
The rather that you give his offspring life,
Shadowing their right under your wings of war.
I give you welcome with a powerless hand,   15
But with a heart full of unstained love.
Welcome before the gates of Angiers, duke.
    Lewis. A noble boy! Who would not do thee right?
    Aust. Upon thy cheek lay I this zealous kiss,
As seal to this indenture of my love,   20
That to my home I will no more return
Till Angiers, and the right thou hast in France,
Together with that pale, that white-fac'd shore,
Whose foot spurns back the ocean's roaring tides
And coops from other lands her islanders,   25

209 bastard to the time: *no true son of the age*   **210 observation:** *obsequious-ness*   **211–217** *Cf. n.*   **212 habit:** *dress, bearing*   **device:** *shape*   **214 motion:** *impulse*   **217 deceit:** *being deceived*   **218** *Cf. n.*   **220 woman-post:** *woman-courier*   **221** *Cf. n.*   **227 Colbrand the giant;** *cf. n.*   **229 unreverend:** *irreverent*   **230 scorn'st:** *mock'st*   **232 give us leave:** *permit us to be alone*   **234 Philip! sparrow!;** *cf. n.*   **235 toys:** *rumors*   **abroad:** *about in the world*   **239 marry:** *indeed*   **240** *Cf. n.*   **242 beholding:** *indebted*   **243 holp:** *helped*   **246 untoward:** *unmannerly*   **247** *Cf. n.*   **248 dubb'd:** *made a knight*   **253 proper:** *handsome*

260 dear: *grievous*   **262 get:** *be begotten*   **264** *Cf. n.*   **266 dispose:** *disposal*   **267 Subjected:** *submissive*   **269 aweless:** *fearless*   **270** *Cf. n.*   **1 Lewis;** *cf. n.*   **2 fore-runner on thy blood;** *cf. n.*   **5** *Cf. n.*   **7 importance:** *importunity*   **9 rebuke:** *check*   **14 Shadowing:** *sheltering*   **20 indenture:** *contract*   **25 coops:** *encloses for protection or defense*

Even till that England, hedg'd in with the main,
That water-wall'd bulwark, still secure
And confident from foreign purposes,
Even till that utmost corner of the west
Salute thee for her king: till then, fair boy,   *30*
Will I not think of home, but follow arms.
    Const. O, take his mother's thanks, a widow's thanks,
Till your strong hand shall help to give him strength
To make a more requital to your love.
    Aust. The peace of heaven is theirs that lift their swords   *35*
In such a just and charitable war.
    K. Phil. Well then, to work our cannon shall be bent
Against the brows of this resisting town.
Call for our chiefest men of discipline,
To cull the plots of best advantages.   *40*
We'll lay before this town our royal bones,
Wade to the market-place in Frenchmen's blood,
But we will make it subject to this boy.
    Const. Stay for an answer to your embassy,
Lest unadvis'd you stain your swords with blood.   *45*
My Lord Chatillion may from England bring
That right in peace which here we urge in war;
And then we shall repent each drop of blood
That hot rash haste so indirectly shed.

          Enter Chatillion.

    K. Phil. A wonder, lady! lo, upon thy wish,   *50*
Our messenger, Chatillion, is arriv'd!
What England says, say briefly, gentle lord;
We coldly pause for thee; Chatillion, speak.
    Chat. Then turn your forces from this paltry siege
And stir them up against a mightier task.   *55*
England, impatient of your just demands,
Hath put himself in arms; the adverse winds,
Whose leisure I have stay'd, have given him time
To land his legions all as soon as I.
His marches are expedient to this town,   *60*
His forces strong, his soldiers confident.
With him along is come the mother-queen,
An Ate, stirring him to blood and strife;
With her her niece, the Lady Blanch of Spain;
With them a bastard of the king's deceas'd;   *65*
And all th' unsettled humours of the land,
Rash, inconsiderate, fiery voluntaries,
With ladies' faces and fierce dragons' spleens,
Have sold their fortunes at their native homes,
Bearing their birthrights proudly on their backs,   *70*
To make a hazard of new fortunes here.
In brief, a braver choice of dauntless spirits
Than now the English bottoms have waft o'er
Did never float upon the swelling tide,
To do offence and scathe in Christendom.   *75*
The interruption of their churlish drums
Cuts off more circumstance; they are at hand,   *Drum beats.*
To parley or to fight; therefore prepare.

    K. Phi. How much unlook'd for is this expedition!
    Aust. By how much unexpected, by so much   *80*
We must awake endeavour for defence,
For courage mounteth with occasion.
Let them be welcome then; we are prepar'd.

     Enter K[ing] of England, Bastard, Queen [Elinor], Blanch,
            Pembroke, and others.

    K. John. Peace be to France, if France in peace permit
Our just and lineal entrance to our own;   *85*
If not, bleed France, and peace ascend to heaven,
Whiles we, God's wrathful agent, do correct
Their proud contempt that beats his peace to heaven.
    K. Phi. Peace be to England, if that war return
From France to England, there to live in peace.   *90*
England we love; and, for that England's sake
With burden of our armour here we sweat.
This toil of ours should be a work of thine;
But thou from loving England art so far,
That thou hast under-wrought his lawful king,   *95*
Cut off the sequence of posterity,
Outfaced infant state, and done a rape
Upon the maiden virtue of the crown.
Look here upon thy brother Geoffrey's face;
These eyes, these brows, were moulded out of his;   *100*
This little abstract doth contain that large
Which died in Geoffrey, and the hand of time
Shall draw this brief into as huge a volume.
That Geoffrey was thy elder brother born,
And this his son; England was Geoffrey's right   *105*
And this is Geoffrey's in the name of God.
How comes it then that thou art call'd a king,
When living blood doth in these temples beat,
Which owe the crown that thou o'ermasterest?
    K. John. From whom hast thou this great commission,   *110*
France,
To draw my answer from thy articles?
    K. Phi. From that supernal judge, that stirs good
thoughts
In any breast of strong authority,   *115*
To look into the blots and stains of right.
That judge hath made me guardian to this boy,
Under whose warrant I impeach thy wrong
And by whose help I mean to chastise it.
    K. John. Alack! thou dost usurp authority.   *120*
    K. Phi. Excuse it is to beat usurping down.
    Eli. Who is it thou dost call usurper, France?
    Const. Let me make answer: thy usurping son.
    Eli. Out, insolent! thy bastard shall be king,
That thou mayst be a queen, and check the world!   *125*
    Const. My bed was ever to thy son as true
As thine was to thy husband, and this boy
Liker in feature to his father Geoffrey
Than thou and John in manners; being as like
As rain to water, or devil to his dam.   *130*

27 still: *always* **secure:** *free from care*   **34 more:** *greater*   **37 bent:** *aimed*   **39 discipline:** *military experience*   **40** *Cf. n.*   **43 But:** *if . . . not*   **45 unadvis'd:** *inconsiderately*   **49 indirectly:** *wrongly*   **53 coldly:** *calmly*   **58 stay'd:** *waited for*   **59 all:** *quite*   **60 expedient:** *expeditious*   **63 An Ate;** *cf. n.*   **64, 65 her niece . . . deceas'd;** *cf. n.*   **66 unsettled humours:** *men of unsettled*   **67 voluntaries:** *volunteers*   **68 spleens:** *the organ itself viewed as the seat of emotions and passions*   **72 choice:** *choice or picked company*   **73 bottoms:** *ships*   **waft:** *conveyed by water*   **75 scathe:** *harm*   **77 circumstance:** *details*

79 expedition: *speed*   **82 occasion:** *emergency*   **85 lineal:** *due by right of descent*   **87 Whiles:** *while*   **correct:** *punish*   **89 if that:** *if*   **95 under-wrought:** *undermined*   **his:** *its*   **96 sequence of posterity:** *hereditary succession*   **97 Outfaced:** *intimidated*   **infant state:** *state that belongs to an infant*   **101-103** *Cf. n.*   **109 owe:** *own*   **112 articles:** *heads or items in a list or document*   **114 supernal:** *heavenly*   **115, 116** *Cf. n.*   **118 impeach:** *call in question*   **121 Excuse;** *cf. n.*   **125 That thou mayst be a queen:** *cf. n.*   **check:** *curb*   **128 feature:** *shape*   **129** *Cf. n.*

My boy a bastard! By my soul I think
His father never was so true begot:
It cannot be and if thou wert his mother.
   Eli. There's a good mother, boy, that blots thy father.
   Const. There's a good grandam, boy, that would blot thee.   *135*
   Aust. Peace!
   Bast.   Hear the crier.
   Aust.   What the devil art thou?
   Bast. One that will play the devil, sir, with you,
And a' may catch your hide and you alone.   *140*
You are the hare of whom the proverb goes,
Whose valour plucks dead lions by the beard.
I'll smoke your skin-coat, and I catch you right.
Sirrah, look to 't; i' faith, I will, i' faith.
   Blanch. O well did he become that lion's robe,   *145*
That did disrobe the lion of that robe!
   Bast. It lies as sightly on the back of him.
As great Alcides' shoes upon an ass.
But, ass, I'll take that burthen from your back,
Or lay on that shall make your shoulders crack.   *150*
   Aust. What cracker is this same that deafs our ears
With this abundance of superfluous breath?
King Lewis, determine what we shall do straight.
   Lewis. Women and fools, break off your conference.
King John, this is the very sum of all: *155*
England and Ireland, Anjou, Touraine, Maine,
In right of Arthur do I claim of thee.
Wilt thou resign them and lay down thy arms?
   K. John. My life as soon! I do defy thee, France.
Arthur of Britaine, yield thee to my hand;   *160*
And out of my dear love I'll give thee more
Than e'er the coward hand of France can win.
Submit thee, boy.
   Eli.   Come to thy grandam, child.
   Const. Do, child, go to it grandam, child;   *165*
Give grandam kingdom, and it grandam will
Give it a plum, a cherry, and a fig;
There's a good grandam.
   Arth.   Good my mother, peace!
I would that I were low laid in my grave;   *170*
I am not worth this coil that's made for me.
   Eli. His mother shames him so, poor boy, he weeps.
   Const. Now shame upon you, whe'r she does or no!
His grandam's wrongs, and not his mother's shames,
Draws those heaven-moving pearls from his poor eyes,   *175*
Which heaven shall take in nature of a fee;
Ay, with these crystal beads heaven shall be brib'd
To do him justice and revenge on you.
   Eli. Thou monstrous slanderer of heaven and earth!
   Const. Thou monstrous injurer of heaven and earth!   *180*
Call not me slanderer; thou and thine usurp
The dominations, royalties, and rights
Of this oppressed boy. This is thy eldest son's son,
Infortunate in nothing but in thee:
Thy sins are visited in this poor child;   *185*
The canon of the law is laid on him,

Being but the second generation
Removed from thy sin-conceiving womb.
   K. John. Bedlam, have done.
   Const.   I have but this to say,   *190*
That he is not only plagued for her sin,
But God hath made her sin and her the plague
On this removed issue, plagu'd for her,
And with her plague; her sin his injury;
Her injury the beadle to her sin,   *195*
All punish'd in the person of this child,
And all for her, a plague upon her.
   Eli. Thou unadvised scold, I can produce
A will that bars the title of thy son.
   Const. Ay, who doubts that? a will! a wicked will;   *200*
A woman's will; a canker'd grandam's will!
   K. Phi. Peace, lady! pause, or be more temperate.
It ill beseems this presence to cry aim
To these ill-tuned repetitions.
Some trumpet summon hither to the walls   *205*
These men of Angiers; let us hear them speak
Whose title they admit, Arthur's or John's.

       Trumpet sounds. Enter a Citizen upon the walls.

   Cit. Who is it that hath warn'd us to the walls?
   K. Phi. 'Tis France, for England.
   K. John.   England for itself.   *210*
You mean of Angiers, and my loving subjects,—
   K. Phi. You loving men of Angiers, Arthur's subjects,
Our trumpet call'd you to this gentle parle,—
   K. John. For our advantage; therefore hear us first.
These flags of France, that are advanced here   *215*
Before the eye and prospect of your town,
Have hither march'd to your endamagement.
The cannons have their bowels full of wrath,
And ready mounted are they to spit forth
Their iron indignation 'gainst your walls: *220*
All preparation for a bloody siege
And merciless proceeding by these French
Confronts your city's eyes, your winking gates;
And but for our approach those sleeping stones,
That as a waist doth girdle you about,   *225*
By the compulsion of their ordinance
By this time from their fixed beds of lime
Had been dishabited, and wide havoc made
For bloody power to rush upon your peace.
But on the sight of us your lawful king.   *230*
Who painfully with much expedient march
Have brought a countercheck before your gates,
To save unscratch'd your city's threaten'd cheeks,
Behold, the French amaz'd vouchsafe a parle;
And now, instead of bullets wrapp'd in fire,   *235*
To make a shaking fever in your walls,
They shook but calm words folded up in smoke,
To make a faithless error in your ears:
Which trust accordingly, kind citizens,

132 true: *truly*   **133** *Cf. n.*   **and if:** *if*   **134 blots:** *calumniates*   **141 the proverb:** *cf. n.*   **143 smoke your skin-coat:** *give you a drubbing*   **right:** *properly*   **145, 146** *Cf. n.*   **145 become:** *adorn*   **148 Alcides' shoes;** *cf. n.*   **151 cracker:** *boaster*   **153 King Lewis;** *cf. n.*   **straight:** *immediately*   **154 Lewis;** *cf. n.*   **160 Britaine;** *cf. n.*   **161 dear:** *heartfelt*   **165 it:** *its*   **171** *Cf. n.*   **coil:** *disturbance*   **175 Draws:** *draw*   **183 eldest;** *cf. n.*   **185 visited:** *punished*   **186 The canon of the law;** *cf. n.*

189 Bedlam: *lunatic*   **192–197** *Cf. n.*   **198 unadvised:** *rash*   **199 A will;** *cf. n.*   **201 canker'd:** *malignant*   **203 cry aim:** *give encouragement*   **205 trumpet:** *trumpeter*   **208 warn'd:** *summoned*   **213 parle:** *parley*   **215 advanced:** *raised*   **216 prospect:** *range of vision*   **217 endamagement:** *injury*   **223 Confronts;** *cf. n.*   **winking:** *closed*   **225 doth:** *do*   **226 ordinance:** *ordnance, artillery*   **228 dishabited:** *dislodged*   **231 painfully:** *laboriously*   **expedient:** *speedy*   **232 countercheck:** *check*   **234 amaz'd:** *dumbfounded*   **238 faithless:** *disloyal*   **error:** *confusion*

And let us in, your king, whose labour'd spirits,   *240*
Forwearied in this action of swift speed,
Craves harbourage within your city walls.
   K. Phi. When I have said, make answer to us both.
Lo! in this right hand, whose protection
Is most divinely vow'd upon the right   *245*
Of him it holds, stands young Plantagenet,
Son to the elder brother of this man,
And king o'er him and all that he enjoys.
For this downtrodden equity, we tread
In warlike march these greens before your town,   *250*
Being no further enemy to you
Than the constraint of hospitable zeal,
In the relief of this oppressed child,
Religiously provokes. Be pleased then
To pay that duty which you truly owe   *255*
To him that owes it, namely, this young prince;
And then our arms, like to a muzzled bear,
Save in aspect, hath all offence seal'd up;
Our cannons' malice vainly shall be spent
Against th' invulnerable clouds of heaven;   *260*
And with a blessed and unvex'd retire,
With unhack'd swords and helmets all unbruis'd,
We will bear home that lusty blood again
Which here we came to sprout against your town,
And leave your children, wives, and you, in peace.   *265*
But if you fondly pass our proffer'd offer,
'Tis not the rounder of your old-fac'd walls
Can hide you from our messengers of war,
Though all these English and their discipline
Were harbour'd in their rude circumference.   *270*
Then tell us, shall your city call us lord,
In that behalf which we have challeng'd it?
Or shall we give the signal to our rage
And stalk in blood to our possession?
   Cit. In brief, we are the King of England's subjects: *275*
For him, and in his right, we hold this town.
   K. John. Acknowledge then the king, and let me in.
   Cit. That can we not; but he that proves the king,
To him will we prove loyal: till that time
Have we ramm'd up our gates against the world.   *280*
   K. John. Doth not the crown of England prove the king?
And if not that, I bring you witnesses,
Twice fifteen thousand hearts of England's breed,—
   Bast. Bastards, and else.
   K. John. To verify our title with their lives.   *285*
   K. Phi. As many and as well-born bloods as those,—
   Bast. Some bastards, too.
   K. Phi. Stand in his face to contradict his claim.
   Cit. Till you compound whose right is worthiest,
We for the worthiest hold the right from both.   *290*
   K. John. Then God forgive the sins of all those souls
That to their everlasting residence,
Before the dew of evening fall, shall fleet,
In dreadful trial of our kingdom's king!
   K. Phi. Amen, Amen! Mount, chevaliers! to arms!   *295*

   Bast. Saint George, that swing'd the dragon, and e'er since
Sits on's horseback at mine hostess' door,
Teach us some fence! *[To Austria.]* Sirrah, were I at home,
At your den, sirrah, with your lioness,
I would set an ox head to your lion's hide,   *300*
And make a monster of you.
   Aust.   Peace! no more.
   Bast. O! tremble, for you hear the lion roar.
   K. John. Up higher to the plain; where we'll set forth
In best appointment all our regiments.   *305*
   Bast. Speed then, to take advantage of the field.
   K. Phi. It shall be so; *[To Lewis]* and at the other hill
Command the rest to stand. God, and our right!

                                    Exeunt.

Here after excursions, Enter the Herald of France with Trumpets
to the gates.

   F. Her. You men of Angiers, open wide your gates,
And let young Arthur, Duke of Britaine, in,   *310*
Who by the hand of France this day hath made
Much work for tears in many an English mother,
Whose sons lie scatter'd on the bleeding ground;
Many a widow's husband grovelling lies,
Coldly embracing the discolour'd earth;   *315*
And victory, with little loss, doth play
Upon the dancing banners of the French,
Who are at hand, triumphantly display'd,
To enter conquerors and to proclaim
Arthur of Britaine England's king and yours.   *320*

Enter English Herald, with trumpet.

   E. Her. Rejoice, you men of Angiers, ring your bells;
King John, your king and England's, doth approach,
Commander of this hot malicious day.
Their armours, that march'd hence so silver-bright,
Hither return all gilt with Frenchmen's blood.   *325*
There stuck no plume in any English crest
That is removed by a staff of France;
Our colours do return in those same hands
That did display them when we first march'd forth;
And, like a jolly troop of huntsmen, come   *330*
Our lusty English, all with purpled hands
Dy'd in the dying slaughter of their foes.
Open your gates and give the victors way.
   Cit. Heralds, from off our towers we might behold,
From first to last, the onset and retire   *335*
Of both your armies, whose equality
By our best eyes cannot be censured.
Blood hath bought blood, and blows have answer'd blows;
Strength match'd with strength, and power confronted
power.   *340*
Both are alike; and both alike we like.
One must prove greatest. While they weigh so even,
We hold our town for neither, yet for both.

Enter the two Kings, with their powers, at several doors.

   K. John. France, hast thou yet more blood to cast away?
Say, shall the current of our right run on?   *345*

---

240 **labour'd:** *oppressed with labor*   241 **Forwearied:** *thoroughly exhausted*   242 **har-**
bourage: *shelter*   244 **in:** *held by*   245 **upon:** *on the side or party of*   250 **greens:**
turf   254 **Religiously:** *faithfully*   255 **owe;** *cf. n.*   261 **retire:** *return*   266 **fondly:**
foolishly   267 **rounder:** *roundure, circuit* **old-fac'd:** *venerable*   268 **messengers of**
war: *missiles*   284 **else:** *other kinds*   286 **bloods:** *men of mettle*   289 **compound:**
settle   290 *Cf. n.*   293 **fleet:** *pass away*

296 **swing'd:** *thrashed*   298 **fence:** *art of fencing*   300 **ox head;** *cf. n.*   323 **mali-**
cious: *violent*   325 **gilt:** *reddened*   327 **staff:** *shaft of a lance*   332 *Cf. n.*   334
Cit.; *cf. n.*   335 **retire:** *retreat*   337 **censured:** *estimated*

Whose passage, vex'd with thy impediment,
Shall leave his native channel and o'erswell
With course disturb'd even thy confining shores,
Unless thou let his silver water keep
A peaceful progress to the ocean.   350
    K. Phi. England, thou hast not sav'd one drop of blood,
In this hot trial, more than we of France;
Rather, lost more. And by this hand I swear,
That sways the earth this climate overlooks,
Before we will lay down our just-borne arms,   355
We'll put thee down, 'gainst whom these arms we bear,
Or add a royal number to the dead,
Gracing the scroll that tells of this war's loss
With slaughter coupled to the name of kings.
    Bast. Ha, majesty! how high thy glory towers   360
When the rich blood of kings is set on fire!
O now doth Death line his dead chaps with steel!
The swords of soldiers are his teeth, his fangs;
And now he feats, mousing the flesh of men,
In undetermin'd differences of kings.   365
Why stand these royal fronts amazed thus?
Cry 'havoc!' kings; back to the stained field,
You equal potents, fiery kindled spirits!
Then let confusion of one part confirm
The other's peace; till then, blows, blood, and death!   370
    K. John. Whose party do the townsmen yet admit?
    K. Phi. Speak, citizens, for England; who's your king?
    Cit. The King of England, when we know the king.
    K. Phi. Know him in us, that here hold up his right.
    K. John. In us, that are our own great deputy,   375
And bear possession of our person here,
Lord of our presence, Angiers, and of you.
    Cit. A greater power than we denies all this;
And, till it be undoubted, we do lock
Our former scruple in our strong-barr'd gates,   380
Kings of our fear; until our fears, resolv'd,
Be by some certain king purg'd and depos'd.
    Bast. By heaven, these scroyles of Angiers flout you, kings,
And stand securely on their battlements
As in a theatre, whence they gape and point   385
At your industrious scenes and acts of death.
Your royal presences be rul'd by me:
Do like the mutines of Jerusalem,
Be friends awhile and both conjointly bend
Your sharpest deeds of malice on this town.   390
By east and west let France and England mount
Their battering cannon charged to the mouths,
Till their soul-fearing clamours have brawl'd down
The flinty ribs of this contemptuous city.
I'd play incessantly upon these jades,   395
Even till unfenced desolation
Leave them as naked as the vulgar air.
That done, dissever your united strengths,

And part your mingled colours once again;
Turn face to face and bloody point to point;   400
Then, in a moment, Fortune shall cull forth
Out of one side her happy minion,
To whom in favour she shall give the day,
And kiss him with a glorious victory.
How like you this wild counsel, mighty states?   405
Smacks it not something of the policy?
    K. John. Now, by the sky that hangs above our heads,
I like it well. France, shall we knit our powers
And lay this Angiers even with the ground;
Then after fight who shall be king of it?   410
    Bast. And if thou hast the mettle of a king,
Being wrong'd as we are by this peevish town,
Turn thou the mouth of thy artillery,
As we will ours, against these saucy walls;
And when that we have dash'd them to the ground,   415
Why then defy each other, and, pell-mell,
Make work upon ourselves, for heaven or hell.
    K. Phi. Let it be so. Say, where will you assault?
    K. John. We from the west will send destruction
Into this city's bosom.   420
    Aust. I from the north.
    K. Phi.   Our thunder from the south
Shall rain their drift of bullets on this town.
    Bast. [*Aside.*] O prudent discipline! From north to south
Austria and France shoot in each other's mouth: 425
I'll stir them to it. Come, away, away!
    Cit. Hear us, great kings; vouchsafe a while to stay,
And I shall show you peace and fair-fac'd league.
Win you this city without stroke or wound;
Rescue those breathing lives to die in beds,   430
That here come sacrifices for the field.
Persever not, but hear me, mighty kings.
    K. John. Speak on with favour; we are bent to hear.
    Cit. That daughter there of Spain, the Lady Blanch,
Is near to England; look upon the years   435
Of Lewis the Dauphin and that lovely maid.
If lusty love should go in quest of beauty,
Where should he find it fairer than in Blanch?
If zealous love should go in search of virtue,
Where should he find it purer than in Blanch?   440
If love ambitions sought a match of birth,
Whose veins bound richer blood than Lady Blanch?
Such as she is, in beauty, virtue, birth,
Is the young Dauphin every way complete.
If not complete of, say he is not she;   445
And she again wants nothing, to name want,
If want it be not that she is not he.
He is the half part of a blessed man,
Left to be finished by such as she;
And she a fair divided excellence,   450
Whose fulness of perfection lies in him.
O! two such silver currents, when they join,
Do glorify the banks that bound them in;
And two such shores to two such streams made one,

Two such controlling bounds shall you be, kings,   455
To these two princes, if you marry them.
This union shall do more than battery can
To our fast-closed gates; for at this match,
With swifter spleen than powder can enforce,
The mouth of passage shall we fling wide ope,   460
And give you entrance; but without this match,
The sea enraged is not half so deaf,
Lions more confident, mountains and rocks
More free from motion, no, not death himself
In mortal fury half so peremptory,   465
As we to keep this city.
    Bast.   Here's a stay,
That shakes the rotten carcase of old Death
Out of his rags! Here's a large mouth, indeed,
That spits forth death and mountains, rocks and seas,   470
Talks as familiarly of roaring lions
As maids of thirteen do of puppy-dogs.
What cannoneer begot this lusty blood?
He speaks plain cannon fire, and smoke and bounce;
He gives the bastinado with his tongue;   475
Our ears are cudgell'd; not a word of his
But buffets better than a fist of France.
'Zounds! I was never so bethump'd with words
Since I first call'd my brother's father dad.
    Eli. [*Aside to King John.*] Son, list to this conjunction,   480
make this match;
Give with our niece a dowry large enough;
For by this knot thou shalt so surely tie
Thy now unsur'd assurance to the crown,
That yon green boy shall have no sun to ripe   485
The bloom that promiseth a mighty fruit.
I see a yielding in the looks of France;
Mark how they whisper: urge them while their souls
Are capable of this ambition,
Lest zeal, now melted by the windy breath   490
Of soft petitions, pity and remorse,
Cool and congeal again to what it was.
    Cit. Why answer not the double majesties
This friendly treaty of our threaten'd town?
    K. Phi. Speak England first, that hath been forward first   495
To speak unto this city: what say you?
    K. John. If that the Dauphin there, thy princely son,
Can in this book of beauty read 'I love,'
Her dowry shall weigh equal with a queen.
For Anjou and fair Touraine, Maine, Poitiers,   500
And all that we upon this side the sea,
Except this city now by us besieg'd,
Find liable to our crown and dignity,
Shall gild her bridal bed and make her rich
In titles, honours, and promotions,   505
As she in beauty, education, blood,
Holds hand with any princess of the world.
    K. Phi. What sayst thou, boy? look in the lady's face.
    Lew. I do, my lord; and in her eye I find
A wonder, or a wondrous miracle,   510

The shadow of myself form'd in her eye;
Which, being but the shadow of your son,
Becomes a sun, and makes your son a shadow.
I do protest I never lov'd myself
Till now infixed I beheld myself,   515
Drawn in the flattering table of her eye.

                     Whispers with Blanch.
    Bast. Drawn in the flattering table of her eye!
Hang'd in the frowning wrinkle of her brow!
And quarter'd in her heart! he doth espy
Himself love's traitor; this is pity now,   520
That hang'd and drawn and quarter'd, there should be
In such a love so vile a lout as he.
    Blanch. My uncle's will in this respect is mine:
If he see aught in you that makes him like,
That anything he sees, which moves his liking,   525
I can with ease translate it to my will;
Or if you will, to speak more properly,
I will enforce it easily to my love.
Further I will not flatter you, my lord,
That all I see in you is worthy love,   530
Than this: that nothing do I see in you,
Though churlish thoughts themselves should be your judge,
That I can find should merit any hate.
    K. John. What say these young ones? What say you, my
niece?   535
    Blanch. That she is bound in honour still to do
What you in wisdom still vouchsafe to say.
    K. John. Speak then, Prince Dauphin; can you love this
lady?
    Lew. Nay, ask me if I can refrain from love;   540
For I do love her most unfeignedly.
    K. John. Then do I give Volquessen, Touraine, Maine,
Poitiers, and Anjou, these five provinces,
With her to thee; and this addition more,
Full thirty thousand marks of English coin.   545
Philip of France, if thou be pleas'd withal,
Command thy son and daughter to join hands.
    K. Phi. It likes us well. Young princes, close your hands.
    Aust. And your lips too; for I am well assur'd
That I did so when I was first assur'd.   550
    K. Phi. Now, citizens of Angiers, ope your gates,
Let in that amity which you have made;
For at Saint Mary's chapel presently
The rites of marriage shall be solemniz'd.
Is not the Lady Constance in this troop?   555
I know she is not, for this match made up
Her presence would have interrupted much.
Where is she and her son? tell me, who knows.
    Lew. She is sad and passionate at your highness' tent.
    K. Phi. And, by my faith, this league that we have made   560
Will give her sadness very little cure.
Brother of England, how may we content
This widow lady? In her right we came;
Which we, God knows, have turn'd another way,
To our own vantage.   565

458 match: *cf. n.*   **459 spleen:** *energy* **enforce:** *compel*   **460 ope:** *open*   **465 pe-remptory:** *resolved*   **467 stay:** *hindrance*   **474 bounce:** *bang*   **475 bastinado:** *beating with a stick*   **478 'Zounds:** *God's wounds*   **480 list:** *listen*   **484 unsur'd:** *insecure*   **489 capable of:** *apt to be affected by*   **490–492** *Cf. n.*   **491 remorse:** *compassion*   **494 treaty:** *proposal tending to agreement*   **503 liable:** *subject*   **507 Holds hand with:** *matches*

516 table: *board or flat surface on which a picture is painted*   **522 so vile a lout:** *cf. n.*   **524 like:** *feel affection*   **526** *Cf. n.*   **527 properly:** *strictly*   **532 churlish:** *sparing of praise*   **542, 543** *Cf. n.*   **546 withal:** *with this*   **548 likes:** *pleases*   **550 assur'd:** *betrothed*   **552 that amity:** *those friends*   **553 presently:** *immediately*   **556 made up:** *which has been arranged*   **559 passionate:** *full of angry passion*

K. John.   We will heal up all;
For we'll create young Arthur Duke of Britaine
And Earl of Richmond; and this rich fair town
We make him lord of. Call the Lady Constance;
Some speedy messenger bid her repair   *570*
To our solemnity: I trust we shall,
If not fill up the measure of her will,
Yet in some measure satisfy her so,
That we shall stop her exclamation.
Go we, as well as haste will suffer us,   *575*
To this unlook'd for, unprepared pomp.
           Exeunt [all but the Bastard].
           [The Citizens retire from the walls.]

Bast. Mad world! mad kings! mad composition!
John, to stop Arthur's title in the whole,
Hath willingly departed with a part,   *580*
And France, whose armour conscience buckled on,
Whom zeal and charity brought to the field
As God's own soldier, rounded in the ear
With that same purpose-changer, that sly devil,
That broker, that still breaks the pate of faith,   *585*
That daily break-vow, he that wins of all,
Of kings, of beggars, old men, young men, maids,
Who, having no external thing to lose
But the word 'maid,' cheats the poor maid of that,
That smooth-fac'd gentleman, tickling Commodity,   *590*
Commodity, the bias of the world;
The world, who of itself is peized well,
Made to run even upon even ground,
Till this advantage, this vile-drawing bias,
This sway of motion, this Commodity,   *595*
Makes it take head from all indifferency,
From all direction, purpose, course, intent.
And this same bias, this Commodity,
This bawd, this broker, this all-changing word,
Clapp'd on the outward eye of fickle France,   *600*
Hath drawn him from his own determin'd aid,
From a resolv'd and honourable war,
To a most base and vile-concluded peace.
And why rail I on this Commodity?
But for because he hath not woo'd me yet.   *605*
Not that I have the power to clutch my hand
When his fair angels would salute my palm;
But for my hand, as unattempted yet,
Like a poor beggar, raileth on the rich.
Well, whiles I am a beggar, I will rail   *610*
And say there is no sin but to be rich;
And being rich, my virtue then shall be
To say there is no vice but beggary.
Since kings break faith upon Commodity,
Gain, be my lord, for I will worship thee!   *Exit.*   *615*

ACT THIRD ❧ SCENE FIRST

[Angiers. The French King's Pavilion]
Enter Constance, Arthur, and Salisbury.

Const. Gone to be married! gone to swear a peace!
False blood to false blood join'd! gone to be friends!
Shall Lewis have Blanch, and Blanch those provinces?
It is not so; thou hast misspoke, misheard;
Be well advis'd, tell o'er thy tale again;   *5*
It cannot be; thou dost but say 'tis so.
I trust I may not trust thee, for thy word
Is but the vain breath of a common man;
Believe me, I do not believe thee, man;
I have a king's oath to the contrary.   *10*
Thou shalt be punish'd for thus frighting me,
For I am sick and capable of fears;
Oppress'd with wrongs, and therefore full of fears;
A widow, husbandless, subject to fears;
A woman, naturally born to fears;   *15*
And though thou now confess thou didst but jest,
With my vex'd spirits I cannot take a truce,
But they will quake and tremble all this day.
What dost thou mean by shaking of thy head?
Why dost thou look so sadly on my son?   *20*
What means that hand upon that breast of thine?
Why holds thine eye that lamentable rheum,
Like a proud river peering o'er his bounds?
Be these sad signs confirmers of thy words?
Then speak again; not all thy former tale,   *25*
But this one word, whether thy tale be true.
Sal. As true as I believe you think them false
That give you cause to prove my saying true.
Const. O if thou teach me to believe this sorrow,
Teach thou this sorrow how to make me die!   *30*
And let belief and life encounter so
As doth the fury of two desperate men
Which in the very meeting fall and die.
Lewis marry Blanch! O boy! then where art thou?
France friend with England, what becomes of me?   *35*
Fellow, be gone! I cannot brook thy sight:
This news hath made thee a most ugly man.
Sal. What other harm have I, good lady, done,
But spoke the harm that is by others done?
Const. Which harm within itself so heinous is   *40*
As it makes harmful all that speak of it.
Arth. I do beseech you, madam, be content.
Const. If thou, that bid'st me be content, wert grim.
Ugly and slanderous to thy mother's womb,
Full of unpleasing blots and sightless stains,   *45*
Lame, foolish, crooked, swart, prodigious,
Patch'd with foul moles and eye-offending marks,
I would not care, I then would be content;
For then I should not love thee, no, nor thou
Become thy great birth, nor deserve a crown.   *50*
But thou art fair; and at thy birth, dear boy,
Nature and Fortune join'd to make thee great;

---

571 solemnity: *marriage ceremony*   **574 exclamation:** *loud complaint*   **577 composition:** *agreement*   **580 departed:** *parted*   **583 rounded:** *whispered*   **584 With:** *by*   **585 broker:** *go-between*   **586 break-vow:** *breaker of promises*   **588–591** *Cf. n.*   **590 tickling Commodity:** *flattering self-interest*   **592 peized:** *poised*   **594 vile-drawing:** *drawing into evil*   **595 sway:** *direction*   **596 take head:** *take power* **from all indifferency:** *out of all moderation*   **600 Clapp'd on the outward eye;** *cf. n.*   **602 resolv'd:** *determined upon*   **605 But for because:** *merely because*   **607 fair angels;** *cf. n.*   **608 for:** *because* **unattempted:** *untempted*   **614 upon:** *in consequence of*

17 spirits: *feelings* **take a truce:** *make peace*   **22 lamentable rheum:** *tears of sorrow*   **23 peering o'er:** *rising above*   **42 content:** *calm*   **44 slanderous:** *a disgrace*   **45 blots:** *blemishes* **sightless:** *unsightly* **stains:** *disfigurements*   **46 swart:** *swarthy* **prodigious:** *monstrous, misshapen*

Of Nature's gifts thou mayst with lilies boast
And with the half-blown rose. But Fortune, O!
She is corrupted, chang'd, and won from thee: 55
Sh' adulterates hourly with thine uncle John,
And with her golden hand hath pluck'd on France
To tread down fair respect of sovereignty,
And made his majesty the bawd to theirs.
France is a bawd to Fortune and King John,   60
That strumpet Fortune, that usurping John!
Tell me, thou fellow, is not France forsworn?
Envenom him with words, or get thee gone
And leave those woes alone which I alone
Am bound to underbear.   65
    Sal.   Pardon me, madam,
I may not go without you to the kings.
    Const. Thou mayst, thou shalt; I will not go with thee.
I will instruct my sorrows to be proud;
For grief is proud and makes his owner stoop.   70
To me and to the state of my great grief
Let kings assemble; for my grief's so great
That no supporter but the huge firm earth
Can hold it up: here I and sorrows sit;
Here is my throne, bid kings come bow to it,   75
                           [Seats herself on the ground.]

Enter King John, France [King Philip], Dauphin [Lewis], Blanch,
Elinor, Philip [the Bastard], Austria, Constance [and Attendants].

    K. Phi. 'Tis true, fair daughter, and this blessed day
Ever in France shall be kept festival;
To solemnize this day the glorious sun
Stays in his course and plays the alchemist,
Turning with splendour of his precious eye   80
The meagre cloddy earth to glittering gold;
The yearly course that brings this day about
Shall never see it but a holy day.
    Const. [Rising.] A wicked day, and not a holy day!
What hath this day deserv'd? what hath it done   85
That it in golden letters should be set
Among the high tides in the calendar?
Nay, rather turn this day out of the week,
This day of shame, oppression, perjury.
Or, if it must stand still, let wives with child   90
Pray that their burthens may not fall this day,
Lest that their hopes prodigiously be cross'd:
But on this day let seamen fear no wrack;
No bargains break that are not this day made;
This day all things begun come to ill end;   95
Yea, faith itself to hollow falsehood change!
    K. Phi. By heaven, lady, you shall have no cause
To curse the fair proceedings of this day:
Have I not pawn'd to you my majesty?
    Const. You have beguil'd me with a counterfeit   100
Resembling majesty, which, being touch'd and tried,
Proves valueless. You are forsworn, forsworn;

You came in arms to spill mine enemies' blood,
But now in arms you strengthen it with yours.
The grappling vigour and rough frown of war   105
Is cold in amity and painted peace,
And our oppression hath made up this league.
Arm, arm, you heavens, against these perjur'd kings!
A widow cries; be husband to me, heavens!
Let not the hours of this ungodly day   110
Wear out the day in peace; but, ere sunset,
Set armed discord 'twixt these perjur'd kings!
Hear me! O, hear me!
    Aust.   Lady Constance, peace!
    Const. War! war! no peace! peace is to me a war.   115
O, Lymoges! O, Austria! thou dost shame
That bloody spoil: thou slave, thou wretch, thou coward!
Thou little valiant, great in villainy!
Thou ever strong upon the stronger side!
Thou Fortune's champion, that dost never fight   120
But when her humorous ladyship is by
To teach thee safety! thou art perjur'd too,
And sooth'st up greatness. What a fool art thou,
A ramping fool, to brag, and stamp and swear
Upon my party! Thou cold-blooded slave,   125
Hast thou not spoke like thunder on my side?
Been sworn my soldier? bidding me depend
Upon thy stars, thy fortune, and thy strength?
And dost thou now fall over to my foes?
Thou wear a lion's hide! doff it for shame,   130
And hang a calfskin on those recreant limbs.
    Aust. O that a man should speak those words to me!
    Bast. And hang a calfskin on those recreant limbs.
    Aust. Thou dar'st not say so, villain, for thy life.
    Bast. And hang a calfskin on those recreant limbs.   135
    K. John. We like not this; thou dost forget thyself.

                    Enter Pandulph.

    K. Phi. Here comes the holy legate of the pope.
    Pand. Hail, you anointed deputies of heaven!
To thee, King John, my holy errand is.
I Pandulph, of fair Milan cardinal,   140
And from Pope Innocent the legate here,
Do in his name religiously demand
Why thou against the church, our holy mother,
So wilfully dost spurn; and, force perforce,
Keep Stephen Langton, chosen Archbishop   145
Of Canterbury, from that holy see?
This, in our foresaid holy father's name,
Pope Innocent, I do demand of thee.
    K. John. What earthy name to the interrogatories
Can task the free breath of a sacred king?   150
Thou canst not, cardinal, devise a name
So slight, unworthy and ridiculous,
To charge me to an answer, as the pope.
Tell him this tale; and from the mouth of England
Add thus much more: that no Italian priest   155

---

56 adulterates: *commits adultery*   **57 with her golden hand:** *by bribes*   **pluck'd on:**
incited   **59** *Cf. n.*   **63 Envenom:** *poison*   **65 underbear:** *endure*   **70–72 For grief
... assemble;** *cf. n.*   **71 state:** *seat of state*   **77 festival:** *like a feast-day*   **79 plays
the alchemist;** *cf. n.*   **81 meagre:** *barren*   **82 brings ... about:** *brings around*   **87
high tides:** *great festivals*   **90 stand still:** *still stand*   **92 prodigiously:** *by monstrous
births*   **93 But:** *except*   **wrack:** *wreck*   **99 pawn'd:** *pledged*   **100 counterfeit:** *false
coin*   **101 touch'd:** *tested as with the touchstone*

106 painted: *feigned*   **107 oppression:** *distress*   **121 humorous:** *fickle*   **123 sooth'st
up:** *flatterest*   **124 ramping:** *unrestrained*   **125 Upon my party:** *on my side*   **129 fall
over:** *desert*   **131 recreant:** *cowardly*   **142 religiously:** *solemnly*   **144 spurn:** *oppose
contemptuously*   **force perforce:** *by violent constraint*   **145 Stephen Langton;** *cf. n.*   **149**
Cf. n.   **150 task:** *compel*   **153 charge:** *command*

Shall tithe or toll in our dominions;
But as we under heaven are supreme head,
So under him that great supremacy,
Where we do reign, we will alone uphold,
Without th' assistance of a mortal hand.   *160*
So tell the pope, all reverence set apart
To him, and his usurp'd authority.
    K. Phi. Brother of England, you blaspheme in this.
    K. John. Though you and all the kings of Christendom
Are led so grossly by this meddling priest,   *165*
Dreading the curse that money may buy out;
And by the merit of vile gold, dross, dust,
Purchase corrupted pardon of a man,
Who in that sale sells pardon from himself;
Though you and all the rest, so grossly led,   *170*
This juggling witchcraft with revenue cherish;
Yet I alone, alone do me oppose
Against the pope, and count his friends my foes.
    Pand. Then, by the lawful power that I have,
Thou shalt stand curs'd and excommunicate;   *175*
And blessed shall he be that doth revolt
From his allegiance to a heretic;
And meritorious shall that hand be call'd,
Canonized and worshipp'd as a saint,
That takes away by any secret course   *180*
Thy hateful life.
    Const.   O lawful let it be
That I have room with Rome to curse awhile!
Good father cardinal, cry thou amen
To my keen curses; for without my wrong   *185*
There is no tongue hath power to curse him right.
    Pand. There's law and warrant, lady, for my curse.
    Const. And for mine too; when law can do me right,
Let it be lawful that law bar no wrong.
Law cannot give my child his kingdom here,   *190*
For he that holds his kingdom holds the law;
Therefore, since law itself is perfect wrong,
How can the law forbid my tongue to curse?
    Pand. Philip of France, on peril of a curse,
Let go the hand of that arch-heretic,   *195*
And raise the power of France upon his head,
Unless he do submit himself to Rome.
    Eli. Look'st thou pale, France? do not let go thy hand.
    Const. Look to that, devil, lest that France repent,
And by disjoining hands, hell lose a soul.   *200*
    Aust. King Philip, listen to the cardinal.
    Bast. And hang a calfskin on his recreant limbs.
    Aust. Well, ruffian, I must pocket up these wrongs,
Because—
    Bast. Your breeches best may carry them.   *205*
    K. John. Philip, what sayst thou to the cardinal?
    Const. What should he say, but as the cardinal?
    Lew. Bethink you, father; for the difference
Is purchase of a heavy curse from Rome,
Or the light loss of England for a friend: *210*
Forgo the easier.
    Blanch.   That's the curse of Rome.

    Const. O Lewis, stand fast! the devil tempts thee here,
In likeness of a new untrimmed bride.
    Blanch. The Lady Constance speaks not from her faith,   *215*
But from her need.
    Const.   O! if thou grant my need,
Which only lives but by the death of faith,
That need must needs infer this principle,
That faith would live again by death of need.   *220*
O then, tread down my need, and faith mounts up;
Keep my need up, and faith is trodden down!
    K. John. The king is mov'd, and answers not to this.
    Const. O be remov'd from him, and answer well!
    Aust. Do so, King Philip; hang no more in doubt.   *225*
    Bast. Hang nothing but a calfskin, most sweet lout.
    K. Phi. I am perplex'd, and know not what to say.
    Pand. What canst thou say but will perplex thee more,
If thou stand excommunicate and curs'd?
    K. Phi. Good reverend father, make my person yours,   *230*
And tell me how you would bestow yourself.
This royal hand and mine are newly knit,
And the conjunction of our inward souls
Married in league, coupled and link'd together
With all religious strength of sacred vows;   *235*
The latest breath that gave the sound of words
Was deep-sworn faith, peace, amity, true love
Between our kingdoms and our royal selves;
And even before this truce, but new before,
No longer than we well could wash our hands   *240*
To clap this royal bargain up of peace,
Heaven knows, they were besmear'd and overstain'd
With slaughter's pencil, where revenge did paint
The fearful difference of incensed kings:
And shall these hands, so lately purg'd of blood,   *245*
So newly join'd in love, so strong in both,
Unyoke this seizure and this kind regreet?
Play fast and loose with faith? so jest with heaven,
Make such unconstant children of ourselves,
As now again to snatch our palm from palm,   *250*
Unswear faith sworn, and on the marriage-bed
Of smiling peace to march a bloody host,
And make a riot on the gentle brow
Of true sincerity? O holy sir,
My reverend father, let it not be so!   *255*
Out of your grace, devise, ordain, impose
Some gentle order; and then we shall be bless'd
To do your pleasure and continue friends.
    Pand. All form is formless, order orderless,
Save what is opposite to England's love.   *260*
Therefore to arms! be champion of our church,
Or let the church, our mother, breathe her curse,
A mother's curse, on her revolting son.
France, thou mayst hold a serpent by the tongue,
A cased lion by the mortal paw,   *265*
A fasting tiger safer by the tooth,
Than keep in peace that hand which thou dost hold.

---

156 **tithe or toll:** *receive clerical revenues*   161 **set apart:** *discarded*   165 **grossly:** *stupidly*   166 **buy out:** *get rid of by a money payment*   168 **corrupted:** *bought by a bribe*   175 **excommunicate;** *cf. n.*   179 **Canonized:** *placed in the canon of saints*   196 **upon:** *against*   211 **Forgo the easier;** *cf. n.*

214 **new untrimmed bride;** *cf. n.*   217–222 *Cf. n.*   230 **make my person yours:** *put yourself in my place*   231 **bestow yourself:** *behave yourself*   236 **latest:** *most recently made* **breath:** *utterance*   237 **deep-sworn:** *solemnly sworn*   239 **new:** *recently*   239, 240 *Cf. n.*   241 **clap ... up:** *to strike hands reciprocally in token of a bargain*   244 **difference:** *quarrel*   247 **Unyoke:** *disjoin* **seizure:** *clasp* **regreet:** *greeting*   248 **Play fast and loose;** *cf. n.*   249 **unconstant:** *changeable*   256 **ordain:** *decree*   259 **form:** *orderly arrangement*   265 **A cased lion;** *cf.n.* **mortal:** *deadly*

K. Phi. I may disjoin my hand, but not my faith.

Pand. So mak'st thou faith an enemy to faith;
And like a civil war set'st oath to oath,   270
Thy tongue against thy tongue. O! let thy vow
First made to heaven, first be to heaven perform'd,
That is, to be the champion of our church.
What since thou swor'st is sworn against thyself
And may not be performed by thyself;   275
For that which thou hast sworn to do amiss
Is not amiss when it is truly done;
And being not done, where doing tends to ill,
The truth is then most done not doing it.
The better act of purposes mistook   280
Is to mistake again; though indirect,
Yet indirection thereby grows direct,
And falsehood falsehood cures, as fire cools fire
Within the scorched veins of one new burn'd.
It is religion that doth make vows kept,   285
But thou hast sworn against religion:
By what thou swear'st, against the thing thou swear'st,
And mak'st an oath the surety for thy truth
Against an oath; the truth thou art unsure
To swear, swears only not to be forsworn;   290
Else what a mockery should it be to swear!
But thou dost swear only to be forsworn;
And most forsworn, to keep what thou dost swear.
Therefore thy later vows against thy first
Is in thyself rebellion to thyself;   295
And better conquest never canst thou make
Than arm thy constant and thy nobler parts
Against these giddy loose suggestions:
Upon which better part our prayers come in,
If thou vouchsafe them. But, if not, then know   300
The peril of our curses light on thee
So heavy as thou shalt not shake them off,
But in despair die under their black weight.

Aust. Rebellion, flat rebellion!

Bast.   Will 't not be?   305
Will not a calfskin stop that mouth of thine?

Lew. Father, to arms!

Blanch.   Upon thy wedding-day?
Against the blood that thou hast married?
What! shall our feast be kept with slaughter'd men?   310
Shall braying trumpets and loud churlish drums,
Clamours of hell, be measures to our pomp?
O husband, hear me! ay, alack! how new
Is 'husband' in my mouth! Even for that name,
Which till this time my tongue did ne'er pronounce,   315
Upon my knee I beg, go not to arms
Against mine uncle.

Const.   O! upon my knee,
Made hard with kneeling, I do pray to thee,
Thou virtuous Dauphin, alter not the doom   320
Forethought by heaven.

Blanch. Now shall I see thy love: what motive may
Be stronger with thee than the name of wife?

Const. That which upholdeth him that thee upholds,
His honour. O thine honour, Lewis, thine honour!   325

Lew. I muse your majesty doth seem so cold,
When such profound respects do pull you on.

Pand. I will denounce a curse upon his head.

K. Phi. Thou shalt not need. England, I will fall from thee.

Const. O fair return of banish'd majesty!   330

Eli. O foul revolt of French inconstancy!

K. John. France, thou shalt rue this hour within this hour.

Bast. Old Time the clock-setter, that bald sexton Time,
Is it as he will? well then, France shall rue.

Blanch. The sun's o'ercast with blood; fair day, adieu!   335
Which is the side that I must go withal?
I am with both: each army hath a hand;
And in their rage, I having hold of both,
They whirl asunder and dismember me.
Husband, I cannot pray that thou mayst win;   340
Uncle, I needs must pray that thou mayst lose;
Father, I may not wish the fortune thine;
Grandam, I will not wish thy wishes thrive:
Whoever wins, on that side shall I lose;
Assured loss before the match be play'd.   345

Lew. Lady, with me, with me thy fortune lies.

Blanch. There where my fortune lives, where my life dies.

K. John. Cousin, go draw our puissance together.

                             [Exit Bastard.]

France, I am burn'd up with inflaming wrath;
A rage whose heat hath this condition,   350
That nothing can allay, nothing but blood,
The blood, and dearest-valu'd blood, of France.

K. Phi. Thy rage shall burn thee up, and thou shalt turn
To ashes, ere our blood shall quench that fire:
Look to thyself, thou art in jeopardy.   355

K. John. No more than he that threats. To arms let's hie!

                                    Exeunt.

❧ Scene Second ❧

[The Same. Plains near Angiers]
Alarums, excursions. Enter Bastard, with Austria's head.

Bast. Now, by my life, this day grows wondrous hot;
Some airy devil hovers in the sky
And pours down mischief. Austria's head lie there,
While Philip breathes.

Enter John, Arthur, Hubert.

K. John. Hubert, keep this boy. Philip, make up;   5
My mother is assailed in our tent,
And ta'en, I fear.

Bast.   My lord, I rescu'd her;
Her highness is in safety, fear you not.
But on, my liege; for very little pains   10
Will bring labour to a happy end.   *Exit.*

---

270 set'st ... to: *pittest ... against*   **276–279** *Cf. n.*   **280 act:** *execution*   **281, 282 though ... direct;** *cf. n.*   **282 indirection:** *irregular or unjust means*   **285–293** *Cf. n.*   **297 arm:** *by arming*   **298 suggestions:** *temptations*   **299 Upon which better part:** *in support of which better side*   **302 as:** *that*   **304 flat:** *downright*   **309 blood:** *blood-relationship*   **312 measures:** *melodies*   **320 doom:** *judgment*   **321 Forethought:** *predestined*   **322 motive:** *incitement to action*

326 muse: *wonder*   **327 profound respects:** *weighty considerations*   **328 denounce:** *proclaim*   **329 fall from:** *forsake*   **333 Old Time the clock-setter;** *cf. n.*   **336 withal:** *with*   **348 Cousin:** *kinsman*   **draw:** *gather*   **puissance:** *armed force*   **350 condition:** *quality*   **2 airy devil;** *cf. n.*   **4 breathes:** *takes breath*   **5 Philip;** *cf. n.*   **make up:** *push forward*

❧ Scene Third ❧

[The Same]

Alarums, excursions, retreat. Enter John, Elinor, Arthur, Bastard,
Hubert, Lords.

K. John. [To Elinor.] So shall it be; your grace shall stay
behind
So strongly guarded. *[To Arthur.]* Cousin, look not sad:
Thy grandam loves thee; and thy uncle will
As dear be to thee as thy father was.   *5*
    Arth. O this will make my mother die with grief!
    K. John. [To the Bastard.] Cousin, away for England! haste
before;
And, ere our coming, see thou shake the bags
Of hoarding abbots; imprison'd angels   *10*
Set at liberty; the fat ribs of peace
Must by the hungry now be fed upon;
Use our commission in his utmost force.
    Bast. Bell, book, and candle shall not drive me back,
When gold and silver becks me to come on.   *15*
I leave your highness. Grandam, I will pray,—
If ever I remember to be holy,—
For your fair safety; so I kiss your hand.
    Eli. Farewell, gentle cousin.
    K. John.   Coz, farewell.   *20*

                      [Exit Bastard.]

    Eli. Come hither, little kinsman; hark, a word.
                  [She takes Arthur aside.]
    K. John. Come hither, Hubert. O my gentle Hubert,
We owe thee much! within this wall of flesh
There is a soul counts thee her creditor,
And with advantage means to pay thy love;   *25*
And, my good friend, thy voluntary oath
Lives in this bosom, dearly cherished.
Give me thy hand. I had a thing to say,
But I will fit it with some better tune.
By heaven, Hubert, I am almost asham'd   *30*
To say what good respect I have of thee.
    Hub. I am much bounden to your majesty.
    K. John. Good friend, thou hast no cause to say so yet;
But thou shalt have; and creep time ne'er so slow,
Yet it shall come for me to do thee good.   *35*
I had a thing to say, but let it go.
The sun is in the heaven, and the proud day,
Attended with the pleasures of the world,
Is all too wanton and too full of gawds
To give me audience. If the midnight bell   *40*
Did, with his iron tongue and brazen mouth,
Sound on into the drowsy race of night;
If this same were a churchyard where we stand,
And thou possessed with a thousand wrongs;
Or if that surly spirit, melancholy,   *45*
Had bak'd thy blood and made it heavy, thick,
Which else runs tickling up and down the veins,
Making that idiot, laughter, keep men's eyes
And strain their cheeks to idle merriment,
A passion hateful to my purposes;   *50*

Or if that thou couldst see me without eyes,
Hear me without thine ears, and make reply
Without a tongue, using conceit alone,
Without eyes, ears, and harmful sound of words;
Then, in despite of brooded watchful day,   *55*
I would into thy bosom pour my thoughts.
But ah! I will not; yet I love thee well;
And, by my troth, I think thou lov'st me well.
    Hub. So well, that what you bid me undertake,
Though that my death were adjunct to my act,   *60*
By heaven, I would do it.
    K. John.   Do not I know thou wouldst?
Good Hubert! Hubert, Hubert, throw thine eye
On yon young boy: I'll tell thee what, my friend,
He is a very serpent in my way;   *65*
And whersoe'er this foot of mine doth tread
He lies before me. Dost thou understand me?
Thou art his keeper.
    Hub.   And I'll keep him so
That he shall not offend your majesty.   *70*
    K. John. Death.
    Hub.   My lord?
    K. John.   A grave.
    Hub.   He shall not live.
    K. John.   Enough.   *75*
I could be merry now. Hubert, I love thee;
Well, I'll not say what I intend for thee.
Remember. Madam, fare you well.
I'll send those powers o'er to your majesty.
    Eli. My blessing go with thee!   *80*
    K. John.   For England, cousin, go.
Hubert shall be your man, attend on you
With all true duty. On toward Calais, ho!   *Exeunt.*

❧ Scene Fourth ❧

[The Same. The French King's Tent]
Enter France, Dauphin, Pandulph, Attendants.

    K. Phi. So, by a roaring tempest on the flood,
A whole armado of convicted sail
Is scatter'd and disjoin'd from fellowship.
    Pand. Courage and comfort! all shall yet go well.
    K. Phi. What can go well when we have run so ill?   *5*
Are we not beaten? Is not Angiers lost?
Arthur ta'en prisoner? divers dear friends slain?
And bloody England into England gone,
O'erbearing interruption, spite of France?
    Lew. What he hath won that hath he fortified.   *10*
So hot a speed with such advice dispos'd,
Such temperate order in so fierce a cause,
Doth want example. Who hath read or heard
Of any kindred action like to this?
    K. Phi. Well could I bear that England had this praise,   *15*

---

8 **before:** *in front*   10, 11 **imprison'd . . . liberty;** *cf. n.*   14 **Bell, book, and candle;** *cf. n.*   15 **becks:** *beckons*   20 *Cf. n.*   25 **advantage:** *interest*   31 **respect:** *esteem*   32 **bounden:** *obliged*   39 **wanton:** *merry* **gawds:** *playthings*   42 *Cf. n.*   48 **keep:** *occupy*   50 **passion:** *an emotional state (mirth)*

53 **conceit:** *understanding*   55 **brooded:** *having a brood to watch over*   58 **troth:** *faith*   60 **adjunct to:** *connected with*   63 **throw:** *direct*   64 **what:** *something*   79 **powers:** *troops*   1 **flood:** *sea*   2 **armado:** *fleet of war* **convicted:** *defeated*   3 **fellowship:** *companionship*   6, 7 *Cf. n.*   9 **interruption:** *resistance* **spite of:** *in spite of*   11 **advice:** *consideration* **dispos'd:** *regulated*   13 **example:** *parallel case in the past*   14 **kindred:** *cognate*

So we could find some pattern of our shame.

Enter Constance.

Look, who comes here! a grave unto a soul,
Holding th' eternal spirit, against her will,
In the vile prison of afflicted breath.
I prithee, lady, go away with me.   20
    Const. Lo, now! now see the issue of your peace!
    K. Phi. Patience, good lady! comfort, gentle Constance!
    Const. No, I defy all counsel, all redress,
But that which ends all counsel, true redress,
Death, death; O, amiable, lovely death!   25
Thou odoriferous stench! sound rottenness!
Arise forth from the couch of lasting night,
Thou hate and terror to prosperity,
And I will kiss thy detestable bones,
And put my eyeballs in thy vaulty brows,   30
And ring these fingers with thy household worms,
And stop this gap of breath with fulsome dust,
And be a carrion monster like thyself.
Come, grin on me; and I will think thou smil'st
And buss thee as thy wife! Misery's love,   35
O, come to me!
    K. Phi.   O fair affliction, peace!
    Const. No, no, I will not, having breath to cry.
O that my tongue were in the thunder's mouth!
Then with a passion would I shake the world,   40
And rouse from sleep that fell anatomy
Which cannot hear a lady's feeble voice,
Which scorns a modern invocation.
    Pand. Lady, you utter madness and not sorrow.
    Const. Thou art [not] holy to belie me so;   45
I am not mad: this hair I tear is mine;
My name is Constance; I was Geoffrey's wife;
Young Arthur is my son, and he is lost!
I am not mad: I would to heaven I were!
For then 'tis like I should forget myself.   50
O, if I could, what grief should I forget!
Preach some philosophy to make me mad,
And thou shalt be canoniz'd, Cardinal.
For being not mad but sensible of grief,
My reasonable part produces reason   55
How I may be deliver'd of these woes,
And teaches me to kill or hang myself.
If I were mad, I should forget my son,
Or madly think a babe of clouts were he.
I am not mad: too well, too well I feel   60
The different plague of each calamity.
    K. Phi. Bind up those tresses. O! what love I note
In the fair multitude of those her hairs!
Where but by chance a silver drop hath fallen,
Even to that drop ten thousand wiry friends   65
Do glue themselves in sociable grief;
Like true, inseparable, faithful loves,
Sticking together in calamity.
    Const. To England, if you will.

    K. Phi.   Bind up your hairs.   70
    Const. Yes, that I will; and wherefore will I do it?
I tore them from their bonds, and cried aloud:
'O that these hands could so redeem my son,
As they have given these hairs their liberty!'
But now I envy at their liberty,   75
And will again commit them to their bonds,
Because my poor child is a prisoner.
And, Father Cardinal, I have heard you say
That we shall see and know our friends in heaven.
If that be true, I shall see my boy again;   80
For since the birth of Cain, the first male child,
To him that did but yesterday suspire,
There was not such a gracious creature born.
But now will canker-sorrow eat my bud
And chase the native beauty from his cheek,   85
And he will look as hollow as a ghost,
As dim and meagre as an ague's fit,
And so he'll die; and, rising so again,
When I shall meet him in the court of heaven
I shall not know him. Therefore never, never   90
Must I behold my pretty Arthur more.
    Pand. You hold too heinous a respect of grief.
    Const. He talks to me, that never had a son.
    K. Phi. You are as fond of grief as of your child.
    Const. Grief fills the room up of my absent child,   95
Lies in his bed, walks up and down with me,
Puts on his pretty looks, repeats his words,
Remembers me of all his gracious parts,
Stuffs out his vacant garments with his form:
Then have I reason to be fond of grief.   100
Fare you well: had you such a loss as I,
I could give better comfort than you do.
I will not keep this form upon my head,
When there is such disorder in my wit.
O Lord! my boy, my Arthur, my fair son!   105
My life, my joy, my food, my all the world!
My widow-comfort, and my sorrows' cure!   *Exit.*
    K. Phi. I fear some outrage, and I'll follow her.   *Exit.*
    Lew. There's nothing in this world can make me joy:
Life is as tedious as a twice-told tale,   110
Vexing the dull ear of a drowsy man;
And bitter shame hath spoil'd the sweet world's taste,
That it yields nought but shame and bitterness.
    Pand. Before the curing of a strong disease,
Even in the instant of repair and health,   115
The fit is strongest: evils that take leave,
On their departure most of all show evil.
What have you lost by losing of this day?
    Lew. All days of glory, joy, and happiness.
    Pand. If you had won it, certainly you had.   120
No, no; when Fortune means to men most good,
She looks upon them with a threat'ning eye.
'Tis strange to think how much King John hath lost
In this which he accounts so clearly won.
Are not you griev'd that Arthur is his prisoner?   125
    Lew. As heartily as he is glad he hath him.

---

16 So: *if* **pattern:** *precedent*   **19 breath:** *life*   **23 defy:** *reject*   **27 lasting:** *everlasting*   **30 vaulty:** *arched*   **32 gap of breath:** *mouth* **fulsome:** *physically disgusting*   **35 buss:** *kiss*   **41 fell anatomy:** *cruel skeleton*   **43 modern:** *everyday*   **45** *Cf. n.*   **50 like:** *probable*   **54 sensible of:** *capable of*   **59 babe of clouts:** *rag-doll*   **65 wiry friends;** *cf. n.*   **66 sociable:** *sympathetic*   **69 To England:** *cf. n.*

75 envy: *feel jealousy*   **82 suspire:** *draw breath*   **83 gracious:** *lovely*   **84 canker:** *like a canker worm*   **87 dim:** *lustreless*   **92 hold:** *entertain* **respect:** *opinion*   **94 fond:** *infatuated*   **98 Remembers:** *reminds*   **103 form:** *orderly arrangement*   **104 wit:** *mind*   **115 repair:** *restoration*   **118 day:** *day of battle*

Pand. Your mind is all as youthful as your blood.
Now hear me speak with a prophetic spirit;
For even the breath of what I mean to speak
Shall blow each dust, each straw, each little rub,   *130*
Out of the path which shall directly lead
Thy foot to England's throne; and therefore mark.
John hath seiz'd Arthur; and it cannot be,
That, whiles warm life plays in that infant's veins,
The misplac'd John should entertain an hour,   *135*
One minute, nay, one quiet breath of rest.
A sceptre snatch'd with an unruly hand
Must be as boisterously maintain'd as gain'd;
And he that stands upon a slippery place
Makes nice of no vile hold to stay him up: *140*
That John may stand, then Arthur needs must fall;
So be it, for it cannot be but so.
     Lew. But what shall I gain by young Arthur's fall?
     Pand. You, in the right of Lady Blanch your wife,
May then make all the claim that Arthur did.   *145*
     Lew. And lose it, life and all, as Arthur did.
     Pand. How green you are and fresh in this old world!
John lays you plots; the times conspire with you;
For he that steeps his safety in true blood
Shall find but bloody safety and untrue.   *150*
This act so evilly borne shall cool the hearts
Of all his people and freeze up their zeal,
That none so small advantage shall step forth
To check his reign, but they will cherish it;
No natural exhalation in the sky,   *155*
No scope of nature, no distemper'd day,
No common wind, no customed event,
But they will pluck away his natural cause
And call them meteors, prodigies, and signs,
Abortives, presages, and tongues of heaven,   *160*
Plainly denouncing vengeance upon John.
     Lew. May be he will not touch young Arthur's life,
But hold himself safe in his prisonment.
     Pand. O, sir, when he shall hear of your approach,
If that young Arthur be not gone already,   *165*
Even at that news he dies; and then the hearts
Of all his people shall revolt from him
And kiss the lips of unacquainted change,
And pick strong matter of revolt and wrath
Out of the bloody fingers' ends of John.   *170*
Methinks I see this hurly all on foot;
And, O! what better matter breeds for you
Than I have nam'd! The bastard Faulconbridge
Is now in England, ransacking the church,
Offending charity. If but a dozen French   *175*
Were there in arms, they would be as a call
To train ten thousand English to their side;
Or as a little snow, tumbled about,
Anon becomes a mountain. O noble Dauphin,

Go with me to the king. 'Tis wonderful   *180*
What may be wrought out of their discontent,
Now that their souls are topful of offence.
For England go; I will whet on the king.
     Lew. Strong reasons make strong actions. Let us go;
If you say ay, the king will not say not.   *Exeunt.*   *185*

ACT FOURTH ❧ SCENE FIRST

[Northampton. A Room in the Castle]
Enter Hubert and Executioners.

     Hub. Heat me these irons hot; and look thou stand
Within the arras. When I strike my foot
Upon the bosom of the ground, rush forth,
And bind the boy which you shall find with me
Fast to the chair. Be heedful. Hence, and watch.   *5*
     [1] Exec. I hope your warrant will bear out the deed.
     Hub. Uncleanly scruples! fear not you: look to 't.
                              [Exeunt Executioners.]
Young lad, come forth; I have to say with you.

Enter Arthur.

     Arth. Good morrow, Hubert.
     Hub.   Good morrow, little prince.   *10*
     Arth. As little prince, having so great a title
To be more prince, as may be. You are sad.
     Hub. Indeed, I have been merrier.
     Arth.   Mercy on me!
Methinks nobody should be sad but I.   *15*
Yet I remember, when I was in France,
Young gentlemen would be as sad as night,
Only for wantonness. By my christendom,
So I were out of prison and kept sheep,
I should be as merry as the day is long;   *20*
And so I would be here, but that I doubt
My uncle practises more harm to me.
He is afraid of me, and I of him.
Is it my fault that I was Geoffrey's son?
No, indeed, is 't not; and I would to heaven   *25*
I were your son, so you would love me, Hubert.
     Hub. [Aside.] If I talk to him, with his innocent prate
He will awake my mercy which lies dead;
Therefore I will be sudden and dispatch.
     Arth. Are you sick, Hubert? you look pale today.   *30*
In sooth, I would you were a little sick,
That I might sit all night and watch with you.
I warrant I love you more than you do me.
     Hub. [Aside.] His words do take possession of my
bosom.   *35*
Read here, young Arthur.   *[Showing a paper.]*
                         [Aside.] How now, foolish rheum!
Turning dispiteous torture out of door!
I must be brief, lest resolution drop

130 dust: *grain of dust* rub: *obstacle* 135 misplac'd: *usurping the place of another* entertain: *spend* 140 Makes nice of: *is scrupulous about* hold: *grasp* stay . . . up: *support* 147 green: *inexperienced* 148 you: *for your advantage* 149, 150 Cf. n. 151 so evilly borne: *carried through so wickedly* 153 advantage: *opportunity* 155 exhalation: *meteor* 156 scope of nature: *circumstance within the limits of nature's operations* distemper'd day: *day of bad weather* 157 customed: *customary* 158 his: *its* 160 Abortives: *untimely births* 163 prisonment: *captivity* 168 unacquainted: *unfamiliar* 169, 170 Cf. n. 171 hurly: *commotion* on foot: *started* 174 ransacking: *pillaging* 175 charity: *good will* 176 call: *decoy-bird* 177 train: *lure* 179 Anon: *straightway*

182 topful of offence: *brimful of displeasure* 183 whet on: *instigate* 2 arras: *cf. n.* 3 bosom: *surface* 6 bear out: *support* 7 fear not you: *do not be frightened* 18 wantonness: *sportiveness* christendom: *Christianity* 19 So: *provided that* 21 doubt: *fear* 22 practises: *schemes* 27 prate: *prattle* 29 sudden: *quick* dispatch: *make haste* 31 sooth: *truth* 38 dispiteous: *pitiless*

Out at mine eyes in tender womanish tears. 10
Can you not read it? is it not fair writ?

   Arth. Too fairly, Hubert, for so foul effect.
Must you with hot irons burn out both mine eyes?

   Hub. Young boy, I must.

   Arth.   And will you? 45

   Hub.   And I will.

   Arth. Have you the heart? When your head did but ache,
I knit my handkercher about your brows,—
The best I had, a princess wrought it me,—
And I did never ask it you again; 50
And with my hand at midnight held your head,
And like the watchful minutes to the hour,
Still and anon cheer'd up the heavy time,
Saying, 'What lack you?' and 'Where lies your grief?'
Or 'What good love may I perform for you?' 55
Many a poor man's son would have lien still,
And ne'er have spoke a loving word to you;
But you at your sick-service had a prince.
Nay, you may think my love was crafty love,
And call it cunning; do and if you will. 60
If heaven be pleas'd that you must use me ill,
Why then you must. Will you put out mine eyes?
These eyes that never did nor never shall
So much as frown on you?

   Hub.   I have sworn to do it; 65
And with hot irons must I burn them out.

   Arth. Ah! none but in this iron age would do it!
The iron of itself, though heat red-hot,
Approaching near these eyes, would drink my tears
And quench this fiery indignation 70
Even in the matter of mine innocence;
Nay, after that, consume away in rust,
But for containing fire to harm mine eye.
Are you more stubborn-hard than hammer'd iron?
And if an angel should have come to me 75
And told me Hubert should put out mine eyes,
I would not have believ'd him,—no tongue but Hubert's.

   Hub. [*Stamps.*] Come forth.

             [*Re-enter Executioners, with a cord, irons, &c.*]

Do as I bid you do.

   Arth. O! save me, Hubert, save me! my eyes are out 80
Even with the fierce looks of these bloody men.

   Hub. Give me the iron, I say, and bind him here.

   Arth. Alas! what need you be so boist'rous-rough?
I will not struggle; I will stand stone still.
For heaven sake, Hubert, let me not be bound! 85
Nay, hear me Hubert! Drive these men away,
And I will sit as quiet as a lamb;
I will not stir, nor wince, nor speak a word,
Nor look upon the iron angerly.
Thrust but these men away, and I'll forgive you, 90
Whatever torment you do put me to.

   Hub. Go, stand within; let me alone with him.

   [1] *Exec.* I am best pleas'd to be from such a deed.

                   [*Exeunt Executioners.*]

   Arth. Alas: I then have chid away my friend;
He hath a stern look, but a gentle heart. 95
Let him come back, that his compassion may
Give life to yours.

   Hub.   Come, boy, prepare yourself.

   Arth. Is there no remedy?

   Hub.   None, but to lose your eyes. 100

   Arth. O heaven! that there were but a moth in yours,
A grain, a dust, a gnat, a wandering hair,
Any annoyance in that precious sense.
Then feeling what small things are boisterous there,
Your vile intent must needs seem horrible. 105

   Hub. Is this your promise? go to, hold your tongue.

   Arth. Hubert, the utterance of a brace of tongues
Must needs want pleading for a pair of eyes.
Let me not hold my tongue; let me not, Hubert;
Or, Hubert, if you will, cut out my tongue, 110
So I may keep mine eyes. O! spare mine eyes,
Though to no one use but still to look on you!
Lo! by my troth, the instrument is cold
And would not harm me.

   Hub.   I can heat it, boy. 115

   Arth. No, in good sooth; the fire is dead with grief,
Being create for comfort, to be us'd
In undeserv'd extremes: see else yourself.
There is no malice in this burning coal;
The breath of heaven hath blown his spirit out 120
And strew'd repentant ashes on his head.

   Hub. But with my breath I can revive it, boy.

   Arth. And if you do, you will but make it blush
And glow with shame of your proceedings, Hubert.
Nay, it perchance will sparkle in your eyes; 125
And like a dog that is compell'd to fight,
Snatch at his master that doth tarre him on.
All things that you should use to do me wrong
Deny their office: only you do lack
That mercy which fierce fire and iron extends, 130
Creatures of note for mercy-lacking uses.

   Hub. Well, see to live; I will not touch thine eye
For all the treasure that thine uncle owes.
Yet am I sworn and I did purpose, boy,
With this same very iron to burn them out. 135

   Arth. O! now you look like Hubert; all this while
You were disguis'd.

   Hub.   Peace! no more. Adieu.
Your uncle must not know but you are dead;
I'll fill these dogged spies with false reports. 140
And, pretty child, sleep doubtless and secure,
That Hubert for the wealth of all the world
Will not offend thee.

   Arth.   O heaven! I thank you, Hubert.

   Hub. Silence! no more! go closely in with me: 145
Much danger do I undergo for thee.   *Exeunt.*

---

41 fair writ: *clearly written*   **42 effect:** *purpose*   **48 handkercher:** *handkerchief*   **49 wrought it me:** *worked it for me*   **52 watchful minutes to the hour:** *minutes that watch the progress of the hour*   **53 Still and anon:** *ever and anon*   **heavy:** *dreary*   **55 love:** *act of love*   **56 lien:** *lain*   **58 sick-service:** *service when sick*   **59 crafty:** *feigned*   **60 cunning:** *craft*   **67 iron:** *merciless*   **68 heat:** *heated*   **73 But:** *merely*   **for containing:** *because it contained*   **83 what:** *why*   **89 angerly:** *angrily*   **92 let . . . alone:** *trust*

93 from: *clear of*   **101 moth:** *minute particle of anything, a mote*   **104 boisterous:** *causing a great commotion*   **106 go to:** *come, no more*   **107, 108 Cf. n.**   **113 troth:** *faith*   **117 create:** *created*   **118 extremes:** *extremities*   **else:** *if it is not believed*   **120 spirit:** *vital energy*   **121 repentant:** *used in sign of repentance*   **125 sparkle:** *throw out sparks*   **127 tarre:** *provoke*   **129 Deny their office:** *refuse their proper function*   **130 extends:** *show*   **131 of note:** *noted*   **132 Well, see to live:** *cf. n.*   **139 but:** *that . . . not*   **141 doubtless:** *fearless*   **secure:** *without anxiety*   **145 closely:** *secretly*

❧ SCENE SECOND ❧

[The Same. A Room of State in the Palace]
Enter [King] John, [crowned], Pembroke, Salisbury, and other Lords.
[The King takes his state.]

K. John. Here once again we sit, once again crown'd,
And look'd upon, I hope, with cheerful eyes.
    Pem. This 'once again,' but that your highness pleas'd,
Was once superfluous: you were crown'd before,
And that high royalty was ne'er pluck'd off,   *5*
The faiths of men ne'er stained with revolt;
Fresh expectation troubled not the land
With any long'd for change or better state.
    Sal. Therefore, to be possess'd with double pomp,
To guard a title that was rich before,   *10*
To gild refined gold, to paint the lily,
To throw a perfume on the violet,
To smooth the ice, or add another hue
Unto the rainbow, or with taper-light
To seek the beauteous eye of heaven to garnish,   *15*
Is wasteful and ridiculous excess.
    Pem. But that your royal pleasure must be done,
This act is as an ancient tale new told,
And in the last repeating troublesome,
Being urged at a time unseasonable.   *20*
    Sal. In this the antique and well noted face
Of plain old form is much disfigured;
And, like a shifted wind unto a sail,
It makes the course of thoughts to fetch about,
Startles and frights consideration,   *25*
Makes sound opinion sick and truth suspected,
For putting on so new a fashion'd robe.
    Pem. When workmen strive to do better than well,
They do confound their skill in covetousness;
And oftentimes excusing of a fault   *30*
Doth make the fault the worse by the excuse:
As patches set upon a little breach
Discredit more in hiding of the fault
Than did the fault before it was so patch'd.
    Sal. To this effect, before you were new-crown'd,   *35*
We breath'd our counsel, but it pleas'd your highness
To overbear it, and we are all well pleas'd;
Since all and every part of what we would
Doth make a stand at what your highness will.
    K. John. Some reasons of this double coronation   *40*
I have possess'd you with and think them strong;
And more, more strong, when lesser is my fear,
I shall indue you with. Meantime but ask
What you would have reform'd that is not well,
And well shall you perceive how willingly   *45*
I will both hear and grant you your requests.
    Pem. Then I, as one that am the tongue of these
To sound the purposes of all their hearts,
Both for myself and them,—but, chief of all,
Your safety, for the which myself and them   *50*

Bend their best studies,—heartily request
Th' enfranchisement of Arthur; whose restraint
Doth move the murmuring lips of discontent
To break into this dangerous argument:
If what in rest you have in right you hold,   *55*
Why then your fears, which, as they say, attend
The steps of wrong, should move you to mew up
Your tender kinsman, and to choke his days
With barbarous ignorance, and deny his youth
The rich advantage of good exercise.   *60*
That the time's enemies may not have this
To grace occasions, let it be our suit
That you have bid us ask, his liberty;
Which for our goods we do no further ask
Than whereupon our weal, on you depending,   *65*
Counts it your weal he have his liberty.

Enter Hubert.

    K. John. Let it be so; I do commit his youth
To your direction. Hubert, what news with you?
            [Taking him apart.]
    Pem. This is the man should do the bloody deed;
He show'd his warrant to a friend of mine.   *70*
The image of a wicked heinous fault
Lives in his eye; that close aspect of his
Does show the mood of a much troubled breast;
And I do fearfully believe 'tis done,
What we so fear'd he had a charge to do.   *75*
    Sal. The colour of the king doth come and go
Between his purpose and his conscience,
Like heralds 'twixt two dreadful battles set:
His passion is so ripe it needs must break.
    Pem. And when it breaks, I fear will issue thence   *80*
The foul corruption of a sweet child's death.
    K. John. We cannot hold mortality's strong hand:
Good lords, although my will to give is living,
The suit which you demand is gone and dead:
He tells us Arthur is deceas'd to-night.   *85*
    Sal. Indeed we fear'd his sickness was past cure.
    Pem. Indeed we heard how near his death he was,
Before the child himself felt he was sick.
This must be answer'd, either here or hence.
    K. John. Why do you bend such solemn brows on me?   *90*
Think you I bear the shears of destiny?
Have I commandment on the pulse of life?
    Sal. It is apparent foul play; and 'tis shame
That greatness should so grossly offer it.
So thrive it in your game! and so, farewell.   *95*
    Pem. Stay yet, Lord Salisbury; I'll go with thee,
And find th' inheritance of this poor child,
His little kingdom of a forced grave.
That blood which ow'd the breadth of all this isle,

51 Bend: *direct* **studies:** *diligent endeavors*   **52 enfranchisement:** *release from prison*   **55** *If you rightfully hold what you are peaceably possessed of*   **57 mew up:** *shut up*   **60 exercise:** *training*   **61 time's:** *present state of affairs'*   **62 grace:** *lend credit to* **occasions:** *opportunities for fault-finding*   **64 goods:** *our own good*   **65 whereupon: in consequence of the fact that** **weal:** *welfare*   **71 image:** *semblance*   **72 Lives:** *is alive* **close aspect:** *secret expression*   **74 fearfully believe:** *fear and believe*   **75 charge: order**   **78 battles:** *armies arrayed for battle* **set:** *placed*   **79 break:** *break open (as a boil or tumor)*   **82 mortality's:** *death's*   **89 answer'd:** *atoned for* **hence:** *in the next world*   **90 bend . . . solemn brows:** *scowl*   **91 shears of destiny;** *cf. n.*   **94 grossly:** *flagrantly* **offer:** *venture*   **98 forced:** *violent*   **99 blood:** *life*

4 superfluous: *more than enough*   **6 stained:** *corrupted*   **7 expectation:** *excited craving*   **10 guard:** *ornament with borders, trim*   **15 eye of heaven:** *sun* **garnish: dress**   **23 a shifted wind:** *a change of wind*   **24 fetch about:** *alter their direction*   **25 consideration:** *thoughtfulness*   **29 confound:** *ruin*   **32 breach:** *rent*   **33 fault: defect**   **36 breath'd:** *spoke*   **37 overbear:** *overrule*   **39 made a stand at:** *no further than*   **41 possess'd you with:** *informed you of*   **43 indue:** *furnish*   **48 sound: utter**   **50 them:** *i.e. they*

Three foot of it doth hold; bad world the while!   *100*
This must not be thus borne; this will break out
To all our sorrows, and ere long, I doubt.

                       Exeunt [Lords].

   K. John. They burn in indignation. I repent.

         Enter Mes[senger].

There is no sure foundation set on blood,
No certain life achiev'd by others' death.   *105*
A fearful eye thou hast; where is that blood
That I have seen inhabit in those cheeks?
So foul a sky clears not without a storm:
Pour down thy weather. How goes all in France?
   Mess. From France to England. Never such a power   *110*
For any foreign preparation
Was levied in the body of a land.
The copy of your speed is learn'd by them;
For when you should be told they do prepare,
The tidings comes that they are all arriv'd.   *115*
   K. John. O! where hath our intelligence been drunk?
Where hath it slept? Where is my mother's care,
That such an army could be drawn in France,
And she not hear of it?
   Mess.   My liege, her ear   *120*
Is stopp'd with dust; the first of April died
Your noble mother; and, as I hear, my lord,
The Lady Constance in a frenzy died
Three days before. But this from rumour's tongue
I idly heard; if true or false I know not.   *125*
   K. John. Withhold thy speed, dreadful occasion!
O, make a league with me, till I have pleas'd
My discontented peers. What! mother dead!
How wildly then walks my estate in France!
Under whose conduct came those powers of France   *130*
That thou for truth giv'st out are landed here?
   Mess. Under the Dauphin.
   K. John.   Thou hast made me giddy
With these ill tidings.

    Enter Bastard, and Peter of Pomfret.

                 Now, what says the world   *135*
To your proceedings? do not seek to stuff
My head with more ill news, for it is full.
   Bast. But if you be afeard to hear the worst,
Then let the worst unheard fall on your head.
   K. John. Bear with me, cousin, for I was amaz'd   *140*
Under the tide; but now I breathe again
Aloft the flood, and can give audience
To any tongue, speak it of what it will.
   Bast. How I have sped among the clergymen,
The sums I have collected shall express.   *145*
But as I travail'd hither through the land,
I find the people strangely fantasied;
Possess'd with rumours, full of idle dreams,
Not knowing what they fear, but full of fear.

And here's a prophet that I brought with me   *150*
From forth the streets of Pomfret, whom I found
With many hundreds treading on his heels;
To whom he sung, in rude harsh-sounding rimes,
That, ere the next Ascension-day at noon,
Your highness should deliver up your crown.   *155*
   K. John. Thou idle dreamer, wherefore didst thou so?
   Peter. Foreknowing that the truth will fall out so.
   K. John. Hubert, away with him; imprison him;
And on that day at noon, whereon he says
I shall yield up my crown, let him be hang'd.   *160*
Deliver him to safety, and return,
For I must use thee.   *[Exit Hubert, with Peter.]*
         O my gentle cousin,
Hear'st thou the news abroad, who are arriv'd?
   Bast. The French, my lord; men's mouths are full of it.   *165*
Besides, I met Lord Bigot and Lord Salisbury,
With eyes as red as new-enkindled fire,
And others more, going to seek the grave
Of Arthur, whom they say is kill'd to-night
On your suggestion.   *170*
   K. John.   Gentle kinsman, go,
And thrust thyself into their companies.
I have a way to win their loves again;
Bring them before me.
   Bast.   I will seek them out.   *175*
   K. John. Nay, but make haste; the better foot before.
O, let me have no subject enemies,
When adverse foreigners affright my towns
With dreadful pomp of stout invasion.
Be Mercury, set feathers to thy heels,   *180*
And fly like thought from them to me again.
   Bast. The spirit of the time shall teach me speed.   *Exit.*
   K. John. Spoke like a sprightful noble gentleman.
Go after him; for he perhaps shall need
Some messenger betwixt me and the peers;   *185*
And be thou he.
   Mess.   With all my heart, my liege.   *[Exit.]*
   K. John. My mother dead!

         Enter Hubert.

   Hub. My lord, they say five moons were seen tonight;
Four fixed, and the fifth did whirl about   *190*
The other four in wondrous motion.
   K. John. Five moons!
   Hub.   Old men and beldams in the streets
Do prophesy upon it dangerously.
Young Arthur's death is common in their mouths;   *195*
And when they talk of him, they shake their heads
And whisper one another in the ear;
And he that speaks, doth gripe the hearer's wrist,
Whilst he that hears makes fearful action,
With wrinkled brows, with nods, with rolling eyes.   *200*
I saw a smith stand with his hammer, thus,
The whilst his iron did on the anvil cool,
With open mouth swallowing a tailor's news;
Who, with his shears and measure in his hand,

---

100 **bad world the while!:** *a bad world where such things happen!*   101 **borne:** *put up with*   102 **all our:** *of us all*   106 **fearful:** *full of fear*   109 **weather:** *tempest*   111 **preparation:** *expedition*   113 **copy:** *pattern*   115 **arriv'd:** *landed*   116 **intelligence:** *obtaining of secret information*   118 **drawn:** *assembled*   120–124 **My liege . . . before;** *cf. n.*   125 **idly:** *carelessly*   126 **occasion:** *course of events*   129 **estate:** *power*   130 **conduct:** *leadership*   140 **amaz'd:** *perplexed*   142 **Aloft:** *above*   144 **sped:** *fared*   147 **fantasied:** *possessed of fancies*

151 **forth:** *out*   156 **idle:** *foolish*   161 **safety:** *custody*   163 **gentle:** *noble*   170 **suggestion:** *secret incitement*   172 **companies:** *company*   179 **stout:** *bold*   183 **sprightful:** *spirited*   193 **beldams:** *hags*   194 **prophesy:** *make predictions*   199 **action:** *gesticulation*

Standing on slippers, which his nimble haste   *205*
Had falsely thrust upon contrary feet,
Told of a many thousand warlike French,
That were embattailed and rank'd in Kent.
Another lean unwash'd artificer
Cuts off his tale and talks of Arthur's death.   *210*
    K. John. Why seek'st thou to possess me with these fears?
Why urgest thou so oft young Arthur's death?
Thy hand hath murder'd him. I had a mighty cause
To wish him dead, but thou hadst none to kill him.
    Hub. No had, my lord? why, did you not provoke me?   *215*
    K. John. It is the curse of kings to be attended
By slaves that take their humours for a warrant
To break within the bloody house of life,
And on the winking of authority
To understand a law, to know the meaning   *220*
Of dangerous majesty, when, perchance, it frowns
More upon humour than advis'd respect.
    Hub. Here is your hand and seal for what I did.
    K. John. O, when the last accompt 'twixt heaven and earth
Is to be made, then shall this hand and seal   *225*
Witness against us to damnation!
How oft the sight of means to do ill deeds
Makes deeds ill done! Hadst not thou been by,
A fellow by the hand of nature mark'd,
Quoted and sign'd to do a deed of shame,   *230*
This murther had not come to my mind;
But taking note of thy abhorr'd aspect,
Finding thee fit for bloody villainy,
Apt, liable to be employ'd in danger,
I faintly broke with thee of Arthur's death;   *235*
And thou, to be endeared to a king,
Made it no conscience to destroy a prince.
    Hub. My lord,—
    K. John. Hadst thou but shook thy head or made a pause
When I spake darkly what I purposed,   *240*
Or turn'd an eye of doubt upon my face,
As bid me tell my tale in express words,
Deep shame had struck me dumb, made me break off,
And those thy fears might have wrought fears in me.
But thou didst understand me by my signs   *245*
And didst in signs again parley with sin;
Yea, without stop, didst let thy heart consent,
And consequently thy rude hand to act
The deed which both our tongues held vile to name.
Out of my sight, and never see me more!   *250*
My nobles leave me; and my state is brav'd,
Even at my gates, with ranks of foreign powers.
Nay, in the body of this fleshly land,
This kingdom, this confine of blood and breath,
Hostility and civil tumult reigns   *255*
Between my conscience and my cousin's death.
    Hub. Arm you against your other enemies:

I'll make a peace between your soul and you.
Young Arthur is alive: this hand of mine
Is yet a maiden and an innocent hand,   *260*
Not painted with the crimson spots of blood.
Within this bosom never enter'd yet
The dreadful motion of a murderous thought;
And you have slander'd nature in my form,
Which, howsoever rude exteriorly,   *265*
Is yet the cover of a fairer mind
Than to be butcher of an innocent child.
    K. John. Doth Arthur live? O, haste thee to the peers!
Throw this report on their incensed rage,
And make them tame to their obedience.   *270*
Forgive the comment that my passion made
Upon thy feature; for my rage was blind,
And foul imaginary eyes of blood
Presented thee more hideous than thou art.
O, answer not; but to my closet bring   *275*
The angry lords, with all expedient haste.
I conjure thee but slowly; run more fast.   *Exeunt.*

❧ SCENE THIRD ❧

[The Same. Before the Castle]
Enter Arthur, on the Walls.

    Arth. The wall is high; and yet will I leap down.
Good ground, be pitiful and hurt me not!
There's few or none do know me; if they did,
This ship-boy's semblance hath disguis'd me quite.
I am afraid; and yet I'll venture it.   *5*
If I get down, and do not break my limbs,
I'll find a thousand shifts to get away:
As good to die and go, as die and stay.

                                        [Leaps down.]

O me! my uncle's spirit is in these stones!
Heaven take my soul, and England keep my bones! *Dies.* *10*

Enter Pembroke, Salisbury, and Bigot.

    Sal. Lords, I will meet him at Saint Edmundsbury.
It is our safety, and we must embrace
This gentle offer of the perilous time.
    Pem. Who brought that letter from the cardinal?
    Sal. The Count Melun, a noble lord of France;   *15*
Whose private with me of the Dauphin's love
Is much more general than these lines import.
    Big. To-morrow morning let us meet him then.
    Sal. Or rather than set forward; for 'twill be
Two long days' journey, lords, or e'er we meet.   *20*

Enter Bastard.

    Bast. Once more to-day well met, distemper'd lords!
The king by me requests your presence straight.

206 **contrary:** *wrong*   208 **embattailed:** *set in order of battle*   215 **No had:** *had I not* **provoke:** *incite*   217 **humours:** *caprices*   218 **bloody:** *containing blood*   219–222 *Cf. n.*   224 **accompt:** *account*   230 **Quoted:** *set down in writing* **sign'd:** *marked out*   232 **abhorr'd:** *abominable* **aspect:** *appearance*   234 **Apt:** *ready* **liable:** *suitable*   235 **faintly:** *half-heartedly* **broke with thee:** *suggested the subject*   237 **no conscience:** *no matter of conscience*   240 **darkly:** *vaguely*   242 **As:** *as if to*   248 **consequently:** *by way of consequence*   251 **brav'd:** *defied*   253 **fleshly:** *consisting of flesh* **land:** *(applied to the human body)*   254 **confine:** *territory*   255 **civil tumult:** *internal war*

260 **maiden:** *bloodless*   263 **motion:** *impulse*   264 **form:** *image*   270 **make ... tame:** *subjugate*   271 **comment:** *criticism*   272 **feature:** *shape*   273 **imaginary:** *imaginative*   275 **closet:** *private room*   276 **expedient:** *expeditious*   277 **conjure:** *adjure*   4 **ship-boy's semblance:** *cf. n.*   7 **shifts:** *contrivances*   11 **him;** *cf. n.*   12 **safety:** *safeguard* **embrace:** *welcome*   16 **private:** *private communication* **love:** *friendship*   17 **general:** *far-reaching*   20 **or e'er:** *before*   21 **distemper'd:** *vexed*   22 **straight:** *immediately*

Sal. The king hath dispossess'd himself of us:
We will not line his thin bestained cloak
With our pure honours, nor attend the foot   *25*
That leaves the print of blood where'er it walks.
Return and tell him so: we know the worst.
    Bast. Whate'er you think, good words, I think, were best.
    Sal. Our griefs, and not our manners, reason now.
    Bast. But there is little reason in your grief;   *30*
Therefore 'twere reason you had manners now.
    Pem. Sir, sir, impatience hath his privilege.
    Bast. 'Tis true: to hurt his master, no man else.
    Sal. This is the prison.   *[Seeing Arthur.]*
                    What is he lies here?   *35*
    Pem. O death, made proud with pure and princely beauty!
The earth had not a hole to hide this deed.
    Sal. Murther, as hating what himself hath done,
Doth lay it open to urge on revenge.
    Big. Or when he doom'd this beauty to a grave,   *40*
Found it too precious princely for a grave.
    Sal. Sir Richard, what think you? You have beheld.
Or have you read or heard? or could you think
Or do you almost think, although you see,
That you do see? could thought, without this object,   *45*
Form such another? This is the very top,
The height, the crest, or crest unto the crest,
Of murther's arms; this is the bloodiest shame,
The wildest savagery, the vilest stroke,
That ever wall-eyed wrath or staring rage   *50*
Presented to the tears of soft remorse.
    Pem. All murthers past do stand excus'd in this:
And this, so sole and so unmatchable,
Shall give a holiness, a purity,
To the yet unbegotten sin of times;   *55*
And prove a deadly bloodshed but a jest,
Exampled by this heinous spectacle.
    Bast. It is a damned and a bloody work;
The graceless action of a heavy hand,
If that it be the work of any hand.   *60*
    Sal. If that it be the work of any hand!
We had a kind of light what would ensue.
It is the shameful work of Hubert's hand,
The practice and the purpose of the king,
From whose obedience I forbid my soul,   *65*
Kneeling before this ruin of sweet life,
And breathing to his breathless excellence
The incense of a vow, a holy vow,
Never to taste the pleasures of the world,
Never to be infected with delight,   *70*
Nor conversant with ease and idleness,
Till I have set a glory to this hand,
By giving it the worship of revenge.
    Pem. }
    Big. } Our souls religiously confirm thy words.

                    Enter Hubert.

    Hub. Lords, I am hot with haste in seeking you: *75*

Arthur doth live; the king hath sent for you.
    Sal. O! he is bold and blushes not at death.
Avaunt, thou hateful villain! get thee gone!
    Hub. I am no villain.
    Sal. [Drawing his sword.] Must I rob the law?   *80*
    Bast. Your sword is bright, sir; put it up again.
    Sal. Not till I sheathe it in a murtherer's skin.
    Hub. Stand back, Lord Salisbury, stand back, I say!
By heaven, I think my sword's as sharp as yours.
I would not have you, lord, forget yourself,   *85*
Nor tempt the danger of my true defence;
Lest I, by marking of your rage, forget
Your worth, your greatness, and nobility.
    Big. Out, dunghill! dar'st thou brave a nobleman?
    Hub. Not for my life; but yet I dare defend   *90*
My innocent life against an emperor.
    Sal. Thou art a murtherer.
    Hub.   Do not prove me so;
Yet I am none. Whose tongue soe'er speaks false,
Not truly speaks; who speaks not truly, lies.   *95*
    Pem. Cut him to pieces.
    Bast.   Keep the peace, I say.
    Sal. Stand by, or I shall gall you, Faulconbridge.
    Bast. Thou wert better gall the devil, Salisbury.
If thou but frown on me, or stir thy foot,   *100*
Or teach thy hasty spleen to do me shame,
I'll strike thee dead. Put up thy sword betime,
Or I'll so maul you and your toasting-iron,
That you shall think the devil is come from hell.
    Big. What wilt thou do, renowned Faulconbridge?   *105*
Second a villain and a murtherer?
    Hub. Lord Bigot, I am none.
    Big.   Who kill'd this prince?
    Hub. 'Tis not an hour since I left him well.
I honour'd him, I lov'd him; and will weep   *110*
My date of life out for his sweet life's loss.
    Sal. Trust not those cunning waters of his eyes,
For villainy is not without such rheum;
And he, long traded in it, makes it seem
Like rivers of remorse and innocency.   *115*
Away with me, all you whose souls abhor
Th' uncleanly savours of a slaughter-house,
For I am stifled with this smell of sin.
    Big. Away toward Bury, to the Dauphin there!
    Pem. There tell the king he may inquire us out.   *120*
                    Ex[eunt] Lords.
    Bast. Here's a good world! Knew you of this fair work?
Beyond infinite and boundless reach
Of mercy, if thou didst this deed of death,
Art thou damn'd, Hubert.
    Hub.   Do but hear me, sir.   *125*
    Bast. Ha! I'll tell thee what;
Thou'rt damn'd as black—nay, nothing is so black;
Thou art more deep damn'd than Prince Lucifer;
There is not yet so ugly a fiend of hell
As thou shalt be, if thou didst kill this child.   *130*
    Hub. Upon my soul,—
    Bast.   If thou didst but consent

---

29 **griefs:** *grievances* **reason:** *discourse* 50 **wall-eyed:** *glaring* **rage:** *madness* 51 **re-**
morse: *tenderness* 53 **sole:** *unique* 55 **times:** *future times* 56 **bloodshed:** *act of*
bloodshed 57 **Exampled:** *furnished a precedent* 59 **graceless:** *unchristian* **heavy:**
wicked 64 **practice:** *stratagem* 70 **infected:** *affected* 72 **this hand;** *cf. n.* 73
worship: *honor* 74 **religiously:** *under a solemn obligation*

78 **Avaunt:** *begone* 86 **true:** *just* 98 **Stand by:** *stand aside* **gall:** *make to*
smart 103 **toasting-iron:** *toasting fork (i.e. sword)* 109 *Cf. n.* 111 **date:** *term of*
existence 114 **traded:** *expert* 117 **savours:** *smells* 121 **good world:** *fine state of things*

To this most cruel act, do but despair;
And if thou want'st a cord, the smallest thread
That ever spider twisted from her womb   *135*
Will serve to strangle thee; a rush will be a beam
To hang thee on. Or wouldst thou drown thyself,
Put but a little water in a spoon,
And it shall be as all the ocean,
Enough to stifle such a villain up.   *140*
I do suspect thee very grievously.
    Hub. If I in act, consent, or sin of thought,
Be guilty of the stealing that sweet breath
Which was embounded in this beauteous clay,
Like hell want pains enough to torture me.   *145*
I left him well.
    Bast.   Go, bear him in thine arms.
I am amaz'd, methinks, and lose my way
Among the thorns and dangers of this world.
How easy dost thou take all England up!   *150*
From forth this morsel of dead royalty,
The life, the right and truth of all this realm
Is fled to heaven; and England now is left
To tug and scamble and to part by th' teeth
The unow'd interest of proud swelling state.   *155*
Now for the bare-pick'd bone of majesty
Doth dogged war bristle his angry crest,
And snarleth in the gentle eyes of peace.
Now powers from home and discontents at home
Meet in one line; and vast confusion waits,   *160*
As doth a raven on a sick-fallen beast,
The imminent decay of wrested pomp.
Now happy he whose cloak and center can
Hold out this tempest. Bear away that child,
And follow me with speed: I'll to the king: *165*
A thousand businesses are brief in hand,
And heaven itself doth frown upon the land.   *Exit.*

ACT FIFTH ❧ SCENE FIRST

[The Same. A room in the Palace]
Enter King John and Pandulph, [with the crown, and] Attendants.

    K. John. Thus have I yielded up into your hand
The circle of my glory.
    Pand. [Giving John the crown.] Take again
From this my hand, as holding of the pope,
Your sovereign greatness and authority.   *5*
    K. John. Now keep your holy word: go meet the French,
And from his holiness use all your power
To stop their marches 'fore we are enflam'd.
Our discontented counties do revolt;
Our people quarrel with obedience,   *10*
Swearing allegiance and the love of soul

To stranger blood, to foreign royalty.
This inundation of mistemper'd humour
Rests by you only to be qualified:
Then pause not; for the present time's so sick,   *15*
That present med'cine must be minister'd,
Or overthrow incurable ensues.
    Pand. It was my breath that blew this tempest up,
Upon your stubborn usage of the pope;
But since you are a gentle convertite,   *20*
My tongue shall hush again this storm of war
And make fair weather in your blust'ring land.
On this Ascension-day, remember well,
Upon your oath of service to the pope,
Go I to make the French lay down their arms.   *Exit.*   *25*
    K. John. Is this Ascension-day? Did not the prophet
Say that before Ascension-day at noon
My crown I should give off? Even so I have.
I did suppose it should be on constraint;
But, heaven be thank'd, it is but voluntary,   *30*

Enter Bastard.

    Bast. All Kent hath yielded; nothing there holds out
But Dover Castle; London hath receiv'd,
Like a kind host, the Dauphin and his powers.
Your nobles will not hear you, but are gone
To offer service to your enemy;   *35*
And wild amazement hurries up and down
The little number of your doubtful friends.
    K. John. Would not my lords return to me again
After they heard young Arthur was alive?
    Bast. They found him dead and cast into the streets,   *40*
An empty casket, where the jewel of life
By some damn'd hand was robb'd and ta'en away.
    K. John. That villain Hubert told me he did live.
    Bast. So, on my soul, he did, for aught he knew.
But wherefore do you droop? why look you sad?   *45*
Be great in act, as you have been in thought;
Let not the world see fear and sad distrust
Govern the motion of a kingly eye.
Be stirring as the time; be fire with fire;
Threaten the threat'ner, and outface the brow   *50*
Of bragging horror. So shall inferior eyes,
That borrow their behaviours from the great,
Grow great by your example and put on
The dauntless spirit of resolution.
Away! and glister like the god of war   *55*
When he intendeth to become the field:
Show boldness and aspiring confidence.
What! shall they seek the lion in his den
And fright him there? and make him tremble there?
O, let it not be said! Forage, and run   *60*
To meet displeasure farther from the doors,
And grapple with him ere he come so nigh.
    K. John. The legate of the pope hath been with me,
And I have made a happy peace with him;
And he hath promis'd to dismiss the powers   *65*
Led by the Dauphin.

141 grievously: *strongly*   144 embounded: *enclosed*   154 scamble: *scramble*   155
unow'd: *unowned* interest: *title, right*   157 dogged: *fierce*   159 discontents: *mutineers*   160 vast: *extending far and wide*   162 wrested pomp: *usurped majesty*   163
center: *girdle, ceinture*   166 brief in hand: *quickly to be undertaken*   2 circle:
crown   5 sovereign: *of supreme power or excellence*   8 'fore: *before* enflam'd: *set on
fire*   9 counties: *shires; or nobles*   10 quarrel with: *set themselves against*   11 love of
soul: *sincere love*

12 stranger: *strange*   13 mistemper'd: *disordered*   14 Rests by: *depends upon* qualified:
moderated   16 minister'd: *administered*   19 Upon: *in consequence of*   20 convertite:
convert   28 give off: *relinquish*   36 amazement: *distraction*   37 doubtful: *apprehensive*   50 outface: *stare down*   56 become: *adorn*   60 Forage: *range abroad for food*

Bast.   O inglorious league!
Shall we, upon the footing of our land,
Send fair-play orders and make compromise,
Insinuation, parley and base truce   *70*
To arms invasive? Shall a beardless boy,
A cocker'd silken wanton, brave our fields,
And flesh his spirit in a warlike soil,
Mocking the air with colours idly spread,
And find no check? Let us, my liege, to arms!   *75*
Perchance the cardinal cannot make your peace;
Or if he do, let it at least be said
They saw we had a purpose of defence.
   K. John. Have thou the ordering of this present time.
   Bast. Away then, with good courage! yet, I know,   *80*
Our party may well meet a prouder foe.   *Exeunt.*

❧ Scene Second ❧

[A Plain, near St. Edmundsbury. The French Camp]
Enter (in arms) Dauphin [Lewis], Salisbury, Melun, Pembroke,
Bigot, Soldiers.

   Lew. My Lord Melun, let this be copied out,
And keep it safe for our remembrance.
Return the precedent to those lords again;
That, having our fair order written down,
Both they and we, perusing o'er these notes,   *5*
May know wherefore we took the sacrament,
And keep our faiths firm and inviolable.
   Sal. Upon our sides it never shall be broken.
And, noble Dauphin, albeit we swear
A voluntary zeal, and an unurg'd faith   *10*
To your proceedings; yet, believe me, prince,
I am not glad that such a sore of time
Should seek a plaster by contemn'd revolt,
And heal the inveterate canker of one wound
By making many. O, it grieves my soul   *15*
That I must draw this metal from my side
To be a widow-maker! O! and there
Where honourable rescue and defence
Cries out upon the name of Salisbury.
But such is the infection of the time,   *20*
That, for the health and physic of our right,
We cannot deal but with the very hand
Of stern injustice and confused wrong.
And is 't not pity, O my grieved friends,
That we, the sons and children of this isle,   *25*
Were born to see so sad an hour as this;
Wherein we step after a stranger, march
Upon her gentle bosom, and fill up
Her enemies' ranks,—I must withdraw and weep
Upon the spot of this enforced cause,—   *30*
To grace the gentry of a land remote,

And follow unacquainted colours here?
What, here? O nation! that thou couldst remove!
That Neptune's arms, who clippeth thee about,
Would bear thee from the knowledge of thyself,   *35*
And gripple thee unto a pagan shore,
Where these two Christian armies might combine
The blood of malice in a vein of league,
And not to spend it so unneighbourly!
   Lew. A noble temper dost thou show in this;   *40*
And great affections wrastling in thy bosom
Doth make an earthquake of nobility.
O! what a noble combat hast [thou] fought
Between compulsion and a brave respect!
Let me wipe off this honourable dew,   *45*
That silverly doth progress on thy cheeks.
My heart hath melted at a lady's tears,
Being an ordinary inundation;
But this effusion of such manly drops,
This shower, blown up by tempest of the soul,   *50*
Startles mine eyes, and makes me more amaz'd
Than had I seen the vaulty top of heaven
Figur'd quite o'er with burning meteors.
Lift up thy brow, renowned Salisbury,
And with a great heart heave away this storm;   *55*
Commend these waters to those baby eyes
That never saw the giant world enrag'd,
Nor met with fortune other than at feasts,
Full warm of blood, of mirth, of gossiping.
Come, come; for thou shalt thrust thy hand as deep   *60*
Into the purse of rich prosperity
As Lewis himself; so, nobles, shall you all,
That knit your sinews to the strength of mine.

Enter Pandulph.

And even there, methinks, an angel spake:
Look, where the holy legate comes apace,   *65*
To give us warrant from the hand of heaven,
And on our actions set the name of right
With holy breath.
   Pand.   Hail, noble prince of France!
The next is this: King John hath reconcil'd   *70*
Himself to Rome; his spirit is come in
That so stood out against the holy church,
The great metropolis and see of Rome.
Therefore thy threat'ning colours now wind up,
And tame the savage spirit of wild war,   *75*
That, like a lion foster'd up at hand,
It may lie gently at the foot of peace,
And be no further harmful than in show.
   Lew. Your grace shall pardon me; I will not back.
I am too high-born to be propertied,   *80*
To be a secondary at control,
Or useful serving-man and instrument
To any sovereign state throughout the world.
Your breath first kindled the dead coal of wars

---

68 **footing:** *surface for the foot*   69 **fair-play orders:** *equitable conditions*   71 **invasive:** *invading*   72 **cocker'd silken wanton:** *spoilt or pampered child*   73 **flesh:** *initiate in bloodshed*   74 **idly:** *carelessly*   75 **liege:** *sovereign lord*   81 *Cf. n.*   3 **precedent:** *original draft of document*   4 **order:** *arrangement*   6 **took the sacrament;** *cf. n.*   13 **contemn'd:** *despicable*   14 **inveterate:** *of long standing* **canker:** *ulcer*   16 **metal:** *sword*   19 **Cries out upon:** *invokes*   21 **physic:** *cure*   22 **deal:** *act*   30 **spot:** *stain, disgrace* **enforced:** *involuntary*

32 **unacquainted:** *foreign*   34 **clippeth:** *embraceth*   35 **knowledge:** *consciousness*   36 **gripple:** *grapple; cf. n.*   38 **a vein of league;** *cf. n.*   40 **temper:** *condition of mind*   41 **affections:** *emotions* **wrastling:** *wrestling*   43, 44 *Cf. n.*   45 **dew:** *tears*   46 **silverly:** *with silvery brightness* **progress:** *move along*   52 **had I:** *if I had*   53 **Figur'd:** *figured as in a pattern*   56 **Commend:** *leave* **waters:** *tears*   59 **Full:** *exceedingly*   64 **an angel spake;** *cf. n.*   79 **shall:** *must* **back:** *go back*   80 **propertied:** *treated as a property*   81 **secondary:** *mere agent*

Between this chastis'd kingdom and myself,   *85*
And brought in matter that should feed this fire;
And now 'tis far too huge to be blown out
With that same weak wind which enkindled it.
You taught me how to know the face of right,
Acquainted me with interest to this land,   *90*
Yea, thrust this enterprise into my heart;
And come ye now to tell me John hath made
His peace with Rome? What is that peace to me?
I, by the honour of my marriage-bed,
After young Arthur, claim this land for mine;   *95*
And, now it is half-conquer'd, must I back
Because that John hath made his peace with Rome?
Am I Rome's slave? What penny hath Rome borne,
What men provided, what munition sent,
To underprop this action? Is 't not I   *100*
That undergo this change? Who else but I,
And such as to my claim are liable,
Sweat in this business and maintain this war?
Have I not heard these islanders shout out,
Vive le roy! as I have bank'd their towns?   *105*
Have I not here the best cards for the game
To win this easy match play'd for a crown?
And shall I now give o'er the yielded set?
No, no, on my soul, it never shall be said.
    Pand. You look but on the outside of this work.   *110*
    Lew. Outside or inside, I will not return
Till my attempt so much be glorified
As to my ample hope was promised
Before I drew this gallant head of war,
And cull'd these fiery spirits from the world,   *115*
To outlook conquest and to win renown
Even in the jaws of danger and of death.   *[Trumpet sounds.]*
What lusty trumpet thus doth summon us?

Enter Bastard.

    Bast. According to the fair play of the world,
Let me have audience; I am sent to speak.   *120*
My holy Lord of Milan, from the king
I come, to learn how you have dealt for him;
And, as you answer, I do know the scope
And warrant limited unto my tongue.
    Pand. The Dauphin is too wilful-opposite,   *125*
And will not temporize with my entreaties:
He flatly says he'll not lay down his arms.
    Bast. By all the blood that ever fury breath'd,
The youth says well. Now hear our English king;
For thus his royalty doth speak in me.   *130*
He is prepar'd, and reason too he should.
This apish and unmannerly approach,
This harness'd masque and unadvised revel,
This unheard sauciness and boyish troops,
The king doth smile at; and is well prepar'd   *135*
To whip this dwarfish war, these pigmy arms,
From out the circle of his territories.

That hand which had the strength, even at your door,
To cudgel you and make you take the hatch;
To dive, like buckets, in concealed wells;   *140*
To crouch in litter of your stable planks;
To lie like pawns lock'd up in chests and trunks;
To hug with swine; to seek sweet safety out
In vaults and prisons; and to thrill and shake,
Even at the crying of your nation's crow,   *145*
Thinking this voice an armed Englishman:
Shall that victorious hand be feebled here
That in your chambers gave you chastisement?
No! Know the gallant monarch is in arms,
And like an eagle o'er his aiery towers,   *150*
To souse annoyance that comes near his nest.
And you degenerate, you ingrate revolts,
You bloody Neroes, ripping up the womb
Of your dear mother England, blush for shame:
For your own ladies and pale-visag'd maids   *155*
Like Amazons come tripping after drums,
Their thimbles into armed gauntlets change,
Their needls to lances, and their gentle hearts
To fierce and bloody inclination.
    Lew. There end thy brave, and turn thy face in peace;   *160*
We grant thou canst outscold us. Fare thee well;
We hold our time too precious to be spent
With such a brabbler.
    Pond.   Give me leave to speak.
    Bast. No, I will speak.   *165*
    Lew.   We will attend to neither.
Strike up the drums; and let the tongue of war
Plead for our interest and our being here.
    Bast. Indeed, your drums, being beaten, will cry out;
And so shall you, being beaten. Do but start   *170*
An echo with the clamour of thy drum,
And even at hand a drum is ready brac'd
That shall reverberate all as loud as thine;
Sound but another, and another shall
As loud as thine rattle the welkin's ear   *175*
And mock the deep-mouth'd thunder. For at hand,—
Not trusting to this halting legate here,
Whom he hath us'd rather for sport than need,—
Is warlike John and in his forehead sits
A bare-ribb'd death, whose office is this day   *180*
To feast upon whole thousands of the French.
    Lew. Strike up our drums, to find this danger out.
    Bast. And thou shalt find it, Dauphin, do not doubt.

❧ SCENE THIRD ❧

[The Same. A Field of Battle]
Alarums. Enter [King] John and Hubert.
    K. John. How goes the day with us? O, tell me, Hubert!
    Hub. Badly, I fear. How fares your majesty?

---

86 matter: *fuel*   **90 interest:** *claim*   **94** Cf. n.   **100 underprop:** *maintain*   **102 liable:** *subject*   **105 bank'd:** *coasted*   **107 match:** *contest*   **108 set:** *game*   **114 head:** *armed force*   **116 outlook:** *stare down*   **118 lusty:** *vigorous*   **123 as:** *according as* **scope:** *latitude*   **124 limited:** *appointed*   **125 wilful-opposite:** *stubbornly hostile*   **126 temporize:** *come to terms*   **127 flatly:** *absolutely*   **132 apish:** *fantastic*   **133 harness'd:** *in armor* **unadvised:** *thoughtless*   **134 unheard:** *unheard of*   **137 circle:** *circuit*

139 take the hatch: *jump over the half-door, gate, or wicket*   **142 pawns:** *pledges*   **145 your nation's crow;** *cf. n.*   **150 aiery:** *broad (of an eagle)* **towers:** *soars*   **151 souse:** *swoop down upon* **annoyance:** *cause of hurt or pain*   **152 ingrate revolts:** *ungrateful rebels*   **155 maids:** *daughters*   **158 needls:** *needles*   **159 inclination:** *purpose*   **160 brave:** *bravado*   **163 brabbler:** *brawler*   **167 Strike up:** *beat loudly*   **172 brac'd:** *strung up, made tight*   **175 rattle:** *assail with a rattling noise* **welkin's:** *sky's*   **177 halting:** *ineffectual*   **180 office:** *function*

K. John. This fever, that hath troubled me so long,
Lies heavy on me: O, my heart is sick!

                Enter a Messenger.

   Mess. My lord, your valiant kinsman, Faulconbridge,   *5*
Desires your majesty to leave the field,
And send him word by men which way you go.
   K. John. Tell him, toward Swinstead, to the abbey
there.
   Mess. Be of good comfort: for the great supply   *10*
That was expected by the Dauphin here,
Are wrack'd three nights ago on Goodwin sands.
This news was brought to Richard but even now.
The French fight coldly, and retire themselves.
   K. John. Ay me! this tyrant fever burns me up,   *15*
And will not let me welcome this good news.
Set on toward Swinstead: to my litter straight;
Weakness possesseth me, and I am faint.   *Exeunt.*

❧ SCENE FOURTH ❧

[The Same. Another Part of the Same]
Enter Salisbury, Pembroke, and Bigot [and Others].

   Sal. I did not think the king so stor'd with friends.
   Pem. Up once again; but spirit in the French:
If they miscarry we miscarry too.
   Sal. That misbegotten devil, Faulconbridge,
In spite of spite, alone upholds the day.   *5*
   Pem. They say King John, sore sick, hath left the field.

      Enter Melun wounded [and led by Soldiers].

   Mel. Lead me to the revolts of England here.
   Sal. When we were happy we had other names.
   Pem. It is the Count Melun.
   Sal.   Wounded to death.   *10*
   Mel. Fly, noble English; you are bought and sold;
Unthread the rude eye of rebellion,
And welcome home again discarded faith.
Seek out King John and fall before his feet;
For if the French be lords of this loud day,   *15*
He means to recompense the pains you take
By cutting off your heads. Thus hath he sworn,
And I with him, and many moe with me,
Upon the altar at Saint Edmundsbury;
Even on that altar where we swore to you   *20*
Dear amity and everlasting love.
   Sal. May this be possible? may this be true?
   Mel. Have I not hideous death within my view,
Retaining but a quantity of life,
Which bleeds away, even as a form of wax   *25*
Resolveth from his figure 'gainst the fire?
What in the world should make me now deceive,
Since I must lose the use of all deceit?
Why should I then be false, since it is true

That I must die here and live hence by truth?   *30*
I say again, if Lewis do win the day,
He is forsworn, if e'er those eyes of yours
Behold another day break in the east.
But even this night, whose black contagious breath
Already smokes about the burning crest   *35*
Of the old, feeble, and day-wearied sun,
Even this ill night, your breathing shall expire,
Paying the fine of rated treachery
Even with a treacherous fine of all your lives,
If Lewis by your assistance win the day.   *40*
Commend me to one Hubert with your king;
The love of him, and this respect besides,
For that my grandsire was an Englishman,
Awakes my conscience to confess all this.
In lieu whereof, I pray you, bear me hence   *45*
From forth the noise and rumour of the field,
Where I may think the remnant of my thoughts
In peace, and part this body and my soul
With contemplation and devout desires.
   Sal. We do believe thee, and beshrew my soul   *50*
But I do love the favour and the form
Of this most fair occasion, by the which
We will untread the steps of damned flight,
And like a bated and retired flood,
Leaving our rankness and irregular course,   *55*
Stoop low within those bounds we have o'erlook'd,
And calmly run on in obedience,
Even to our ocean, to our great King John.
My arm shall give thee help to bear thee hence,
For I do see the cruel pangs of death   *60*
Right in thine eye. Away, my friends! New flight;
And happy newness, that intends old right.
            Exeunt [leading off Melun].

❧ SCENE FIFTH ❧

[The Same. The French Camp]
Enter Dauphin [Lewis], and his Train.

   Lew. The sun of heaven methought was loath to set,
But stay'd and made the western welkin blush,
When English measure backward their own ground
In faint retire. O, bravely came we off,
When with a volley of our needless shot,   *5*
After such bloody toil, we bid good night;
And wound our tott'ring colours clearly up,
Last in the field, and almost lords of it!

              Enter a Messenger.
   Mess. Where is my prince, the Dauphin?
   Lew.   Here: what news? *10*
   Mess. The Count Melun is slain; the English lords,

---

8 **Swinstead;** *cf. n.*   10 **supply:** *reinforcements*   12 **wrack'd:** *shipwrecked*   14 **coldly:** *without heat or passion*   15 **tyrant:** *pitiless*   1 **stor'd:** *provided*   3 **miscarry:** *come to grief*   5 **In spite of spite:** *notwithstanding anything*   6 **sore:** *grievously*   12 **Unthread the rude eye:** *retrace the rough path*   13 **home:** *to its right or proper place*   16 **He:** *i.e. the Dauphin*   18 **moe:** *more*   24 **quantity:** *fragment*   25 **a form of wax;** *cf. n.*   26 **Resolveth:** *dissolveth* **figure:** *shape*

34 **contagious:** *pestilential*   37 **breathing:** *life*   38 **rated:** *appraised*   39 **fine:** *end*   42 **respect:** *consideration*   43 **For that:** *because*   45 **In lieu whereof:** *in return for which*   46 **From forth:** *away* **rumour:** *confused noise*   48 **part:** *undergo the parting of*   50 **beshrew:** *a curse upon*   51 **But:** *if . . . not* **favour:** *appearance* **form:** *outward aspect*   53 **untread:** *retrace*   54 **bated:** *abated* **retired:** *subsided*   55 **Leaving:** *giving up* **rankness:** *fulness to overflowing*   56 **o'erlook'd:** *despised*   1 **methought:** *it seemed to me*   3 **English:** *Englishmen* **measure:** *traverse*   4 **faint:** *timid* **retire:** *retreat* **bravely:** *excellently*   7 **tott'ring:** *in rags; or swinging in the air* **clearly:** *stainlessly*

By his persuasion, are again fall'n off;
And your supply, which you have wish'd so long,
Are cast away and sunk, on Goodwin sands.

Lew. Ah, foul, shrewd news! Beshrew thy very heart!   *15*
I did not think to be so sad to-night
As this hath made me. Who was he that said
King John did fly an hour or two before
The stumbling night did part our weary powers?

Mess. Whoever spoke it, it is true, my lord.   *20*

Lew. Well; keep good quarter and good care tonight.
The day shall not be up so soon as I,
To try the fair adventure of to-morrow.   *Exeunt.*

❧ SCENE SIXTH ❧

[An open Place in the neighbourhood of Swinstead Abbey]
Enter Bastard and Hubert, severally.

Hub. Who's there? speak, ho! speak quickly, or I shoot.
Bast. A friend. What art thou?
Hub.   Of the part of England.
Bast. Whither dost thou go?
Hub. What's that to thee? Why may not I demand   *5*
Of thine affairs as well as thou of mine?
Bast. Hubert, I think?
Hub.   Thou hast a perfect thought.
I will upon all hazards well believe
Thou art my friend, that know'st my tongue so well.   *10*
Who art thou?
Bast.   Who thou wilt; and if thou please,
Thou mayst befriend me so much as to think
I come one way of the Plantagenets.
Hub. Unkind remembrance! thou and endless night   *15*
Have done me shame. Brave soldier, pardon me,
That any accent breaking from thy tongue
Should scape the true acquaintance of mine ear.
Bast. Come, come; sans compliment! What news abroad?
Hub. Why, here walk I in the black brow of night,   *20*
To find you out.
Bast.   Brief, then; and what's the news?
Hub. O! my sweet sir, news fitting to the night,
Black, fearful, comfortless, and horrible.
Bast. Show me the very wound of this ill news;   *25*
I am no woman; I'll not swound at it.
Hub. The king, I fear, is poison'd by a monk.
I left him almost speechless; and broke out
To acquaint you with this evil, that you might
The better arm you to the sudden time   *30*
Than if you had at leisure known of this.
Bast. How did he take it? who did taste to him?
Hub. A monk, I tell you; a resolved villain,
Whose bowels suddenly burst out. The king
Yet speaks, and peradventure may recover.   *35*
Bast. Whom didst thou leave to tend his majesty?
Hub. Why, know you not? The lords are all come back,

And brought Prince Henry in their company;
At whose request the king hath pardon'd them,
And they are all about his majesty.

Bast. Withhold thine indignation, mighty heaven,   *55*
And tempt us not to bear above our power!
I'll tell thee, Hubert, half my power this night,
Passing these flats, are taken by the tide;
These Lincoln Washes have devoured them;
Myself, well mounted, hardly have escap'd.   *60*
Away before! conduct me to the king;
I doubt he will be dead or ere I come.   *Exeunt.*

❧ SCENE SEVENTH ❧

[The Orchard in Swinstead Abbey]
Enter Prince Henry, Salisbury, and Bigot.

P. Hen. It is too late; the life of all his blood
Is touch'd corruptibly; and his pure brain,—
Which some suppose the soul's frail dwelling-house,—
Doth, by the idle comments that it makes,
Foretell the ending of mortality.   *5*

Enter Pembroke.

Pem. His highness yet doth speak, and holds belief
That, being brought into the open air,
It would allay the burning quality
Of that fell poison which assaileth him.
P. Hen. Let him be brought into the orchard here.   *10*
Doth he still rage: *[Exit Bigot.]*
Pem.   He is more patient
Than when you left him; even now he sung.
P. Hen. O, vanity of sickness! fierce extremes
In their continuance will not feel themselves.   *15*
Death, having prey'd upon the outward parts,
Leaves them invisible; and his siege is now
Against the mind, the which he pricks and wounds
With many legions of strange fantasies,
Which, in their throng and press to that last hold,   *20*
Confound themselves. 'Tis strange that death should sing.
I am the cygnet to this pale faint swan,
Who chants a doleful hymn to his own death,
And from the organ-pipe of frailty sings
His soul and body to their lasting rest.   *25*
Sal. Be of good comfort, prince; for you are born
To set a form upon that indigest
Which he hath left so shapeless and so rude.

[King] John brought in.

K. John. Ay, marry, now my soul hath elbowroom;
It would not out at windows, nor at doors.   *30*
There is so hot a summer in my bosom
That all my bowels crumble up to dust.
I am a scribbled form, drawn with a pen
Upon a parchment, and against this fire

12 are ... fall'n off: *have been faithless* 13 supply: *reinforcements* 14 cast away: *wrecked* 15 shrewd: *grievous* 19 stumbling: *causing to stumble* 21 quarter: *watch* 23 adventure: *chance* 3 part: *side* 8 perfect: *correct* 9 hazards: *perils* 15 Cf. n. endless: *infinite* 17 accent: *word* 19 sans: *without* 22 Brief: *briefly* 23 fitting to: *harmonizing with* 28 broke out: *rushed out* 30 sudden time: *emergency* 31 at leisure: *after delay* 32 taste: *act as taster* 33 resolved: *resolute*

42 tempt: *put to the test* 2 corruptibly: *so as to be corrupt* pure: *clear* 4 idle: *foolish* 5 mortality: *human life* 6 yet: *still* 9 fell: *fierce* 11 rage: *rave* 14 extremes: *extremities* 19 fantasies: *fanciful images* 20 hold: *stronghold* 21 Confound themselves: *mingle indistinguishably* 20, 21 Cf. n. 24 organ-pipe: *organ* 27 indigest: *shapeless mass* 33 form: *portrait*

Do I shrink up.   35

    P. Hen.   How fares your majesty?

    K. John. Poison'd, ill fare; dead, forsook, cast off;

And none of you will bid the winter come

To thrust his icy fingers in my maw;

Nor let my kingdom's rivers take their course   40

Through my burn'd bosom; nor entreat the north

To make his bleak winds kiss my parched lips

And comfort me with cold. I do not ask you much:

I beg cold comfort; and you are so strait

And so ingrateful you deny me that.   45

    P. Hen. O! that there were some virtue in my tears,

That might relieve you.

    K. John.   The salt in them is hot.

Within me is a hell; and there the poison

Is as a fiend confin'd to tyrannize   50

On unreprievable condemned blood.

Enter Bastard.

    Bast. O, I am scalded with my violent motion

And spleen of speed to see your majesty.

    K. John. O cousin, thou art come to set mine eye!

The tackle of my heart is crack'd and burnt,   55

And all the shrouds wherewith my life should sail

Are turned to one thread, one little hair;

My heart hath one poor string to stay it by,

Which holds but till thy news be uttered;

And then all this thou seest is but a clod   60

And module of confounded royalty.

    Bast. The Dauphin is preparing hitherward,

Where heaven he knows how we shall answer him:

For in a night the best part of my power,

As I upon advantage did remove,   65

Were in the Washes all unwarily

Devoured by the unexpected flood.   *[The King dies.]*

    Sal. You breathe these dead news in as dead an ear.

My liege! my lord! But now a king, now thus!

    P. Hen. Even so must I run on, and even so stop.   70

What surety of the world, what hope, what stay,

When this was now a king, and now is clay?

    Bast. Art thou gone so? I do but stay behind

To do the office for thee of revenge,

And then my soul shall wait on thee to heaven,   75

As it on earth hath been thy servant still.

Now, now, you stars, that move in your right spheres,

Where be your powers? Show now your mended faiths,

And instantly return with me again,

To push destruction and perpetual shame   80

Out of the weak door of our fainting land.

Straight let us seek, or straight we shall be sought:

The Dauphin rages at our very heels.

    Sal. It seems you know not, then, so much as we.

The Cardinal Pandulph is within at rest,   85

Who half an hour since came from the Dauphin,

And brings from him such offers of our peace

As we with honour and respect may take,

With purpose presently to leave this war.

    Bast. He will the rather do it when he sees   90

Ourselves well sinewed to our defence.

    Sal. Nay, 'tis in a manner done already;

For many carriages he hath dispatch'd

To the sea-side, and put his cause and quarrel

To the disposing of the cardinal: 95

With whom yourself, myself, and other lords,

If you think meet, this afternoon will post

To consummate this business happily.

    Bast. Let it be so. And you, my noble prince,

With other princes that may best be spar'd,   100

Shall wait upon your father's funeral.

    P. Hen. At Worcester must his body be interr'd,

For so he will'd it.

    Bast.   Thither shall it then.

And happily may your sweet self put on   105

The lineal state and glory of the land!

To whom, with all submission, on my knee,

I do bequeath my faithful services

And true subjection everlastingly.

    Sal. And the like tender of our love we make,   110

To rest without a spot for evermore.

    P. Hen. I have a kind soul that would give [you] thanks,

And knows not how to do it but with tears.

    Bast. O, let us pay the time but needful woe,

Since it hath been beforehand with our griefs.   115

This England never did, nor never shall,

Lie at the proud foot of a conqueror,

But when it first did help to wound itself.

Now these her princes are come home again,

Come the three corners of the world in arms,   120

And we shall shock them. Nought shall make us rue,

If England to itself do rest but true.   *Exeunt.*

❧ FINIS ❧

37 ill fare: *evil lot; cf. n.*   **39 maw:** *stomach*   **44 straight:** *niggardly*   **46 virtue:** *healing power*   **57 unreprievable:** *without possibility of a reprieve*   **53 spleen:** *eagerness*   **54 set:** *close*   **56 shrouds:** *sail-ropes*   **61 module:** *counterfeit* **confounded:** *ruined*   **63 heaven he knows;** *cf. n.*   **65 advantage:** *favorable opportunity*   **66 unwarily:** *unexpectedly*   **67 flood:** *flowing in of the tide*   **68 dead news:** *news of death*   **71 surety:** *certainty* **stay:** *prop*   **76 still:** *always*   **77 you stars;** *cf. n.*   **78 mended faiths:** *restored loyalty*

88 respect: *self-respect*   **91 sinewed:** *strengthened*   **93 carriages:** *vehicles*   **94 put:** *submitted*   **95 disposing:** *direction*   **108 bequeath:** *bestow*   **114, 115** *Cf. n.*   **121 shock:** *meet force with force*

The Life and Death of King John. This title is misleading. The action of the play begins in King John's thirty-fourth year and includes events during a period of about seventeen years.

I.i.S.d. *the Chatillion of France.* It is unlikely that this individual was a historical character, although he appears in *The Troublesome Raigne.* This reading, of the First Folio, seems to indicate that a title is meant, such as 'Chatelain,' or the name of a lord.

I.i.10. *this fair island.* In Holinshed's version King Philip of France lays no claim to the throne of England, but demands, in behalf of Arthur, the French possessions of the English kings. Arthur's right to Brittany was based on that of his father, Geoffrey Plantagenet, John's elder brother. Arthur, as Duke of Brittany, was subject to Philip Augustus, who received homage from him for Normandy, Maine, Anjou, Touraine, and Poitou. Philip, in turn, supported Arthur's claim to the English crown. Thus Philip, at the opening of the play, interferes for Arthur.

I.i.13. *Which sways usurpingly these several titles.* In history John's legal right to the crown was not questioned in England until towards the end of his reign.

I.i.26. *cannon.* Cannon were unknown in the time of King John. Similar anachronisms occur elsewhere in this play. Cf. II.i.37, 218, 473, 474.

I.i.48, 49. *Our abbeys and our priories shall pay This expedition's charge.* King John, as shown elsewhere in the play, is hostile to the clergy. This attitude is a survival from *The Troublesome Raigne,* in which it is an important issue.

I.i.49. *expedition's.* The reading of the First Folio is *expeditious.* This has generally been regarded as a misprint, and the spelling of the Second Folio has been adopted.

I.i.55. *Cordelion.* The reading of the First Folio. Folio spelling of 'Cœur de Lion,' the nickname of King Richard I.

I.i.95. *A half-fac'd groat.* The Bastard plays derisively on the phrase. He compares his brother's thin face to the profile on the coin, and, at the same time, uses the contemptuous Elizabethan epithet for thin-faced men. (Cf. 'This same half-faced fellow, Shadow,' *Henry IV, Part II,* III.ii.235.) The mention in *King John* of this coin, the groat, is an anachronism.

I.i.135–138. If Faulconbridge were the son of Richard Cœur-de-Lion, he would have rank but not the land.

I.i.140. *Sir Robert's his, like him.* A double genitive. The Bastard means: 'If I had my brother's shape, that is, Sir Robert's,—as he has.'

I.i.143, 144. *That in mine ear I durst not stick a rose Lest men should say, 'Look, where three-farthings goes!'* Queen Elizabeth coined in 1561 three-half-pence and three-farthing pieces of silver. The latter bore the queen's profile, with a rose behind the ear. Such silver coins were very thin, which is the point of the Bastard's taunt.

I.i.148. *Sir Nob.* Perhaps an early use of the cant word, *Nob,* for 'head'; or a nickname for 'Robert.'

I.i.163. *Kneel thou down Philip, but rise more great.* The First Folio reading, *rise,* which has been restored, creates a difficulty in the metre. This is removed by Steevens's reading *arise* or Pope's *rise up.*

I.i.173. *In at the window, or else o'er the hatch.* The Bastard's comparison is to surreptitious ways of entering a house. Cf.V.ii.139.

I.i.175. *And have is have, however men do catch.* The substance of the proverbs quoted by the Bastard is that after attaining an object the means of attainment is of little consequence.

I.i.179. *A landless knight makes thee a landed squire.* The Bastard, in achieving knighthood, has yielded claim to his brother's land.

I.i.187. *'Good den, Sir Richard!'—'God-a-mercy, fellow!'—.* In this line the Bastard begins to enact an imaginary conversation.

I.i.191, 192. *Now your traveller. He and his toothpick at my worship's mess.* The pronoun *your* is used in a general sense, 'a traveller.' The Bastard, in acting out these imaginary scenes, is ridiculing the foreign affectation, as it was then considered, of using toothpicks. He fancies himself, now a knight, addressed as 'your worship,' and in his proper place at a 'mess,' or dinner-party of four. In the succeeding lines he makes fun of courtly conversation.

I.i.211–217. *And so am I, whether I smack or no; And not alone in habit and device, Exterior form, outward accoutrement, But from the inward motion to deliver Sweet, sweet, sweet poison for the age's tooth, Which, though I will not practise to deceive, Yet, to avoid deceit, I mean to learn.* Faulconbridge declares that he, too, is *a bastard to the time,* that is, not a true son of the age. This is so, he says, in respect to his personal appearance and also in the absence in him of the impulse to practise flattery, though to avoid being deceived he means to learn this art.

I.i.218. *For it shall strew the footsteps of my rising.* 'As flowers are strewn in

the path of the great, so will this deceit make my way to success more easy and more pleasant.'

I.i.221. *That will take pains to blow a horn before her?* A play on the word *horn* as the symbol of the deluded husband. (Cf.II.i.300.) For some other instances in *King John* of the frequent plays on words, cf.II.i.332, 458, 512, 513, 607; III.i.183, 188–193, 217–222, 223, 224, 274–282, 285–293; and V.vii.36, 37.

I.i.227. *Colbrand the giant.* The Bastard alludes sarcastically to his brother's physical appearance. Colbrand, the Danish giant, was defeated by Guy of Warwick in the presence of King Athelstan. (Cf. *Henry VIII,* V.iv.21: 'I am not Samson, nor Sir Guy, nor Colbrand.') Michael Drayton describes the combat in his *Polyolbion* (1618, 1622), 'Twelfth Song,' ll. 216–235.

I.i.234. *Philip! sparrow!* From his chirp the sparrow was sometimes called Phip or Philip. Skelton's satirical poem, *Philip Sparrow,* had helped to popularize the phrase. The new-made knight objects jestingly to being called by his old, trivial name. He is now Sir Richard.

I.i.240. *Could he get me? Sir Robert could not do it.* The First Folio reads: *Could get me sir Robert could not doe it.* Modern texts inserted the pronoun *he* and the interrogation point.

I.i.247. *Knight, knight, good mother, Basilisco-like.* Theobald indicated the allusion here to the old play of *Soliman and Perseda,* supposedly by Kyd:

> 'Bas. *O, I swear, I swear . . .*
> *I, the aforesaid Basilisco—Knight, good fellow, knight, knight.*
> Piston. *Knave, good fellow, knave, knave.'*

In the same fashion Shakespeare makes the Bastard insist humorously on his title of knight.

I.i.264. *Some sins do bear their privilege on earth.* 'There are *sins* that whatever be determined of them above, are not much censured *on* earth' (Johnson).

I.i.270. *Nor keep his princely heart from Richard's hand.* Probably an allusion to the old metrical romance of *Richard Cœur-de-Lion.* Having killed with a blow of his fist the son of the Duke of Austria, Richard was given over to the fury of a lion. Undaunted, he tore out the lion's heart.

Act Second. This scene in the Folios is called I.ii. Lines 1–74 of the following scene (III.i.) form Act II, and III.i.75–end is III.i. In Act III, in the Folios, the second and third scenes make one scene (III.ii). Thus III.iv. in modern texts is in the Folios III.iii. In the last two acts the scene-division of the Folios is identical with that of later editions. All editions after Rowe's adhere to the modern arrangement.

Scene One. '. . . In spite of the fact that in the opening scene of the play Arthur's claim is represented as a just one and John as a usurper, the present scene by no means enlists sympathy on behalf of Arthur's supporters. The very words in which Philip introduces Austria as the cause of the early death of Richard Cordelion, are as a warning to the audience not to find their heroes here' (Moore-Smith).

II.i.1. *Lewis.* The Folio readings here and at line 18 have been restored. Many editors have substituted *King Philip* because of the seeming appropriateness of these speeches to his rôle and character in the play. A similar change has been made in this scene at line 154.

II.i.2. *forerunner of thy blood.* Richard was Arthur's uncle, being the brother of his father, Geoffrey.

II.i.5. *By this brave duke came early to his grave.* The old play, *The Troublesome Raigne,* caused this historical inaccuracy. Shakespeare has confused two enemies of Cœur-de-Lion: Austria and Vidomar, Viscount of Limoges. Richard was thrown into prison by the Duke of Austria (1192–1193), but was mortally wounded (1199) by an arrow before Vidomar's castle of Chaluz.

II.i.40. *To cull the plots of best advantages.* 'To select the stratagems that will be most to our advantage.'

II.i.63. *An Ate.* The allusion is to the goddess of revenge or mischief. (Cf. *Julius Cæsar,* III.i.290: 'With Ate by his side come hot from hell.')

II.i.64, 65. *her niece, the lady Blanch of Spain; With them a bastard of the king's deceas'd.* The word *niece* is used here as 'granddaughter.' Blanch was the daughter of Alphonso of Castile and Eleanor, the sister of King John, and the daughter of 'the mother-queen.' Line 65 is one of the few taken directly from *The Troublesome Raigne:* 'Next to them a Bastard of the King's deceast.'

II.i.101–103. *This little abstract doth contain that large Which died in Geoffrey, and the hand of time Shall draw this brief into as huge a volume.* At line 99 King Philip points to Arthur, calling King John's attention to the boy's resemblance to Geoffrey. He now compares Geoffrey to a book and Arthur to an abstract of

it. His metaphor likens Time to a writer who will gradually expand the abstract into a volume as large as the original.

II.i.115, 116. *In any breast of strong authority, To look into the blots and stains of right.* The reading in the First Folio for *breast* is *beast*. The passage means; 'In the breast of anyone possessing the authority to examine the blots and stains which deface or injure justice.'

II.i.121. *Excuse.* A noun, as in the First Folio, where there is no pause after the words. Most modern editors have added a mark of punctuation after *excuse*, rendering it a verb with the sense of 'pardon me.'

II.i.125. *That thou mayst be a queen.* A similar motive is ascribed to Constance in *The Troublesome Raigne.* Holinshed, likewise, says: Elinor 'saw, if he [Arthur] were king, how his mother Constance would looke to beare most rule within the realms of England, till hir sonne should come to lawfull age, to gouerne of himselfe.'

II.i.129. *Than thou and John in manners; being as like.* Constance goes on to say how Elinor and John are alike. Some texts place a comma after *John* and omit punctuation after *manners*.

II.i.133. *It cannot be and if thou wert his mother.* Constance sneers at Elinor's infidelity to her husband, Louis VII, from whom she was divorced. She later married King Henry II.

I.i.141. *the proverb.* The proverb alluded to is, 'Mortuo leoni et lepores insultant.' (Erasmus, *Adagia.*) 'A dead lion even hares insult.'

II.i.145, 146. *O well did he become that lion's robe, That did disrobe the lion of that robe!* In *The Troublesome Raigne* Blanch says:

'Ah joy betide his soule, to whom that spoile belong'd:
Ah Richard, how thy glorie here is wrong'd.'

II.i.148. *Alcides' shoes.* The Bastard thinks the sight of a lion's skin on Austria as ridiculous as that of Hercules' (*Alcides'*) shoes on the feet of an ass. The 'shoes of Hercules' appears frequently in the old comedies: '— Too draw the Lyons skin vpon Aesops Asse, or Hercules shoes on a childes feet . . .' (Gosson, *The School of Abuse,* 1579). Theobald offered, instead of *shoes, shows,* a noun, meaning the lion's skin worn by Hercules.

II.i.153. *King Lewis.* No very satisfactory reason can be given for Austria's reference to Lewis as *King.* The most plausible emendations of this reading of the First Folio are *King,—Lewis,* which makes Austria address both King Philip and the Dauphin; or the substitution of *Philip* for *Lewis.* Of this passage Moore-Smith writes: 'If this is what Shakespeare wrote, it was a strange slip to call the king of France here *Lewis* and not *Philip.* Many editors read "King Philip," but unfortunately the metre is against this change. While *Lewis* is generally a monosyllable in Shakespeare, *Philip* is never so.'

II.i.154. *Lewis.* Cf. note on II.i.1.

II.i.160. *Britaine.* Brittany or Bretagne.

II.i.171. *I am not worth this coil that's made for me.* A similar revelation of Arthur's character occurs in *The Troublesome Raigne:*

'Sweet Mother, cease these hastie madding fits;
For my sake let my Grandame haue her will.
O would she with her hands pull forth my heart,
I could affoord it to appease these broyles.'

II.i.183. *eldest.* Later readings have *eld'st* to make regular the metre in the latter half of this line.

II.i.186. *The canon of the law.* The Mosaic law (*Exodus* 20. 5): 'visiting the iniquity of the fathers upon the children unto the third and fourth generation . . .'

II.i.192–197. *But God hath made her sin and her the plague On this removed issue, plagu'd for her, And with her plague; her sin his injury; Her injury the beadle to her sin, All punish'd in the person of this child, And all for her, a plague upon her.* In the First Folio this passage reads:

But God hath made her sinne and her, the plague
On this remoued issue, plagued for her,
And with her plague her sinne: his iniury
Her iniurie the Beadle to her sinne,
All punish'd in the person of this childe,
And all for her, a plague vpon her.

The punctuation adopted for line 194 is that of Roby. There follows his explanation of the passage through line 196: 'God hath made her sin and herself to be a plague to this distant child, who is punished for her and with the punishment belonging to her: God has made her sin to be an injury to Arthur, and her injurious deeds to be the executioner to punish her sin; all which (viz., her first sin and her now injurious deeds) are punished in the person of this child.' Line 197 means: 'And all for her punishment, to be a curse upon her.'

II.i.199. *A will.* Elinor means 'testament' made by Richard, leaving the king-

dom to John. A statement to this effect occurs in Holinshed. Constance, in reply, quibbles on the word *will.* (Cf. *The Troublesome Raigne:*

'Q. El. *I can inferre a Will*
That barres the day he vrgeth by discent.
Const. *A Will indeede, a crabbed Womans will.*')

II.i.223. *Confronts.* The First Folio has *Comforts.* Editors who support this reading say that King John uses the word ironically.

II.i.255. *owe.* This word is used in its modern sense; *owes* in the next line has the meaning common in Shakespeare of 'owns.'

II.i.290. *We for the worthiest hold the right from both.* 'We keep from both sides the right which shall be reserved for that side which proves itself the most worthy.'

II.i.300. *ox head.* A reference to horns, as a sign of the deceived husband.

II.i.332. *Dy'd in the dying slaughter of their foes.* A play on the words, and an allusion to the savage custom of hunters dipping their hands in the blood of the slain animals.

II.i.334. *Cit.* In this line and in lines 373, 426, 435, 493, the Folio indicates the speaker as *Hubert,* an error explainable on the supposition that the same actor took the two parts of Hubert and the citizen. At line 378 the Folio wrongly assigns the citizen's speech to *Fra*[nce], i.e. King Philip.

II.i.362. *O now doth Death line his dead chaps with steel!* In this and in the two subsequent lines Death is conceived of as a skeleton. (Cf. III.iv.29–35, 41.)

II.i.367. *Cry 'havoc!' kings.* 'Command slaughter to proceed' (Johnson). (Cf. *Julius Caesar,* III.i.292): 'Cry, "Havoc!" and let slip the dogs of war.')

II.i.381. *Kings of our fear.* '. . . We shall trust to our strong barred gates as the protectors, or *Kings,* of our fear' (Staunton). Possibly the phrase means merely that the citizens have their fears under control. Many editors read 'Kings of ourselves.'

II.i.388. *mutines.* An allusion to the tale of John of Giscala and Simon bar Gioras, who gave up the war between themselves to unite against the Romans. The story occurs in Josephus, *Jewish War,* V. 6 §4. Malone thinks that Shakespeare might have known the version of this episode in *A Compendious and Most Marvellous History of the Latter Times of the Jewes Common-Weale,* . . . written in Hebrew by Joseph Ben Gorion, and translated into English by Peter Morwyng, in 1575.

II.i.436. *Dauphin.* Regularly spelled 'Dolphin' (occasionally 'Daulphin') in the Folio.

II.i.458. *match.* A play on the word 'marriage' and the 'match' which sets off a cannon.

II.i.490–492. *Lest zeal, now melted by the windy breath Of soft petitions, pity and remorse, Cool and congeal again to what it was.* Elinor compares zeal (i.e. King Philip's zeal in Arthur's cause) to ice which has temporarily been thawed by warm winds, but which, after they pass, will again freeze. (Cf. *The Two Gentlemen of Verona,* III.ii.6–10.)

II.i.522. *so vile a lout.* In history the marriage of Lewis and Blanch was fortunate. This speech is probably an echo from *The Troublesome Raigne,* in which the Bastard himself was promised the hand of Blanch. There is a pun in lines 517–521 on the legal penalty for treason, which was hanging, drawing, and quartering.

II.i.526. *I can with ease translate it to my will.* 'I can easily bring myself to desire it.'

II.i.542, 543. *Then do I give Volquessen, Touraine, Maine, Poitiers, and Anjou, these five provinces.* These lines are almost identical with two lines in *The Troublesome Raigne.* Volquessen was 'the ancient country of the Velocasses, whose capital was Rouen: divided in modern times into Vexin Normand and Vexin Français' (Wright).

II.i.588–591. *Who, having no external thing to lose but the word 'maid,' cheats the poor maid of that, That smooth-fac'd gentleman, tickling Commodity, Commodity, the bias of the world.* Who refers to maids, but at the word *cheats* the construction suddenly changes, making *Commodity,* in the next line, the subject of the figure of speech. In this the *world* is compared to the *bowl* in the game of bowls. Within the *bowl* is lead, which makes it turn, when rolled, towards this heavier side. The word *bias* is derived from the French 'biais.'

II.i.600. *Clapp'd on the outward eye.* 'Suddenly presented to the eye,—' (Moore-Smith). Possibly there is here another allusion to the game of bowls, since an aperture on one side of the bowl was called the eye.

II.i.607. *fair angels.* Coins valued at ten shillings each. Used here as a pun. (Cf. III.iii.10, 11; V.ii. 64.)

III.i.59. *And made his majesty the bawd to theirs.* 'France has played a dishonorable part in uniting their other majesties, Fortune and King John, and France has been bribed by Fortune to play this part' (Moore-Smith).

III.i.70–72. *For grief is proud and makes his owner stoop. To me and to the state of my great grief Let kings assemble.* Grief makes the sufferer humble and thus itself is proud. Constance's grief is so proud that the two kings must come to her.

III.i.79. *plays the alchemist.* Cf. Sonnet xxxiii:

'*Full many a glorious morning have I seen . . .*
Gilding pale streams with heavenly alchemy.'

III.i.145. *Stephen Langton.* It was King John's wish that John Gray, Bishop of Norwich, be elected, in 1205, Archbishop of Canterbury. The Pope prevented this choice. Holinshed describes how the Pope 'procured by his papall authoritie the moonks of Canturburie . . . to choose one Stephen Langton . . . whom John refused to acknowledge.'

III.i.149. *What earthy name to interrogatories.* 'What power on earth can force a king to answer questions put as to an accused person?'

III.i.175. *excommunicate.* Pandulph's speech would suggest to the Elizabethan audience the excommunication of Queen Elizabeth by Pope Pius V, in 1570.

III.i.211. *Forgo the easier.* 'To Blanch the curse of Rome seems the easier or lighter evil, because if Philip remains friendly with John, she will not be torn apart between her husband and her natural friends' (Moore-Smith).

III.i.213. *new untrimmed bride.* In this much-discussed passage *new* probably means 'newly' and *untrimmed* 'divested' of bridal clothes. It is possible, however, that reference is made to the bride appearing at the altar with flowing hair, that is, with tresses untrimmed.

III.i.217–222. *O! if thou grant my need, Which only lives but by the death of faith, That need must needs infer this principle, That faith would live again by death of need. O then, tread down my need, and faith mounts up; Keep my need up, and faith is trodden down!* 'O, if you will admit my need (distress), a need which exists merely because faith was not kept with me, that need is necessarily bound up with this principle, namely, that faith would once more live again, if my need were ended. O, then, if you will take away my need, faith will rise up, but if you continue my need, faith will still be trodden under foot.'

III.i.239, 240. *And even before this truce, but new before, No longer than we well could wash our hands.* 'The interval between our hostility and our friendship was hardly enough time in which to wash our hands.'

III.i.248. *Play fast and loose.* A gambling game, in which bets were made whether knots tied in a handkerchief or belt were fast or loose.

III.i.265. *A cased lion.* Other readings are *chased, caged, chafed.* A cased lion is a lion angered by confinement.

III.i.276–279. *For that which thou hast sworn to do amiss Is not amiss when it is truly done; And being not done, where doing tends to ill, The truth is then most done not doing it.* 'An act which you have sworn to commit unrighteously is not unrighteous if, after all, you perform it as truth requires; and in the case of an act which tends to evil, what truth requires is that it should not be performed at all' (Moore-Smith).

III.i.281, 282. *though indirect, Yet indirection thereby grows direct.* 'Though giving up an evil course in this way is an indirect way of so doing, yet such an indirect method brings one back into the right course.'

III.i.285–293. *It is religion that doth make vows kept, But thou hast sworn against religion: By what thou swear'st, against the thing thou swear'st, And mak'st an oath the surety for thy truth Against an oath; the truth thou art unsure. To swear, swears only not to be foresworn; Else what a mockery should it be to swear! But thou dost swear only to be forsworn; And most forsworn, to keep what thou dost swear.* The Folio punctuation of the first two lines has been restored. Line 287 may then be taken as in apposition with these two lines. A pause has been inserted in line 289, after *oath.* A paraphrase of the passage follows: 'Religion is the cause of keeping vows, but you have sworn against religion. By so doing you swear against the very thing by which you swear (namely, religion), and you make this oath a warrant of your truth as against the former oath. This later oath that you are so unreliable as to swear, is merely a promise that you will not forswear yourself. Without such a promise swearing would be a mockery. But you merely swear to forswear yourself, and so are most certainly forsworn in adhering to your oath.'

III.i. 333. *Old Time the clock-setter.* Time is compared to an old sexton, who regulates the clocks and digs the graves.

III.ii.2. *airy devil.* An allusion to the belief that certain evil spirits live in the air.

III.ii.5. *Philip.* Possibly an error. Philip Faulconbridge's name had been changed to Sir Richard Plantagenet (I.i.163).

III.iii.10, 11. *imprison'd angels Set at liberty.* Modern editors, following Sidney Walker, read *set at liberty Imprison'd angels.* (Cf. II.i.607; V.ii.64.) The restoration of the Folio reading renders the metre faulty.

III.iii.14. *Bell, book, and candle.* Used with reference to a form of excommunication which ended with the words: 'Do to the book, quench the candle, ring the bell!'

III.iii.20. *Come hither, little kinsman; hark, a word.* Elinor draws Arthur out of hearing, thus permitting King John to broach his plan to Hubert.

III.iii.42. *Sound on into the drowsy race of night.* Variant readings are: *one* for *on* and *ear* for *race.* The Folio reading, *race,* may mean 'course' or 'passage.'

III.iv.6, 7. *Are we not beaten? Is not Angiers lost? Arthur ta'en prisoner? divers dear friends slain?* These events occurred actually in different years. Arthur was captured and Elinor rescued at Mirabeau, in 1202. Angiers was conquered by King John in 1206.

III.iv.45. *Thou art not [holy] to belie me so.* The reading of the Fourth Folio. The First Folio has *thou art holy,* a reading which can only be justified as ironical.

III.iv.65. *wiry friends.* Rowe's correction of 'wiry fiends.'

III.iv.69. *To England.* Constance alludes perhaps to King Philip's invitation, in line 20.

III.iv.149, 150. *For he that steeps his safety in true blood Shall find but bloody safety and untrue.* 'He who to secure safety bathes himself in the blood of a true prince will find merely safety that is deceptive and that is productive of more bloodshed.'

III.iv.169, 170. *And pick strong matter of revolt and wrath Out of the bloody fingers' ends of John.* 'And find good reasons for revolt in the crimes in which John has participated.'

IV.i.2. *arras.* The hangings of the room, of tapestry, named from Arras in Picardy.

IV.i.107, 108. *Hubert, the utterance of a brace of tongues Must needs want pleading for a pair of eyes.* 'The words of two tongues would not be enough to plead for two eyes.'

IV.i.132. *Well, see to live.* ' "Well, live, and live with the means of seeing," that is, "with your eyes uninjured." ' (Malone).

IV.ii.91. *shears of destiny.* A reference to the myth of the Fates or Parcae. Atropos bore the shears and cut the thread of life.

IV.ii.120–124. *My liege, her ear Is stopp'd with dust; the first of April died Your noble mother; and, as I hear, my lord, The Lady Constance in a frenzy died Three days before.* According to history Elinor died in July, 1204, and Constance on August 31, 1201.

IV.ii.219. *And on the winking of authority To understand a law, to know the meaning Of dangerous majesty, when, perchance, it frowns More upon humour than advis'd respect.* 'When a person in authority winks, to interpret this as a command, to comprehend the meaning of a king in his darker moods, when, perhaps, he frowns more because of ill-temper than from deliberate consideration.'

IV.iii.4. *ship-boy's semblance.* Arthur is disguised as a sailor-boy.

IV.iii.11. *him.* Salisbury alludes to the Dauphin.

IV.iii.72. *this hand.* Salisbury lifts up his hand as he pronounces his vow.

IV.iii.109. *'Tis not an hour since I left him well.* Hubert apparently becomes aware now for the first time that Arthur is dead.

V.i.81. *Our party may well meet a prouder foe.* 'Our army may meet successfully even a prouder foe than the French.'

V.ii.6. *took the sacrament.* Solemnity was added to a covenant by having the parties to it take the eucharist together.

V.ii.36. *gripple.* The First Folio has *cripple,* which is seemingly a printer's error. *Gripple* is Pope's correction.

V.ii.38. *a vein of league.* A metaphor to describe the union of the two nations, forgetting their own quarrel for the new war. 'That is, make the angry blood of both flow, as it were, in one vein of alliance for crusading purposes' (Moberly).

V.ii.43, 44. *O! what a noble combat hast [thou] fought Between compulsion and a brave respect!* In the First, Second, and Third Folios the reading is *hast fought.* Lewis refers to the conflict in Salisbury's mind between the *compulsion* or necessity for acting as he has acted, and the love he bears his own country.

V.ii.64. *an angel spake.* Lewis thinks the appearance at this point of the pope's legate a divine sanction of his words. Possibly there is also a play on words connected with money: *purse* (line 61); *nobles* (line 62); and *angel* (line 64). An angel was the fee for the opinion of a lawyer. (Cf. the play *Sir Thomas More,* I.i.176; 'there spake an angel.') (Cf. also *King John,* II.i.607; III.iii.10.)

V.ii.94. *I, by the honour of my marriage-bed.* Lewis refers to his right to the lands by marriage, through his wife, Blanch, the niece of King John.

V.ii.145. *your nation's crow.* Probably an allusion to the gallic bird, the cock, with a derisive play on the two meanings of *crow;* and also to the flight of crows which dismayed the French at the battle of Poitiers. See the play *Edward III,* IV.vi.4, 5:

'*The amazed French*
Are quite distract with gazing on the crows.'

V.iii.8. *Swinstead.* An error, derived from the old play, for Swineshead, in Lincolnshire.

V.iv.25. *a form of wax.* An allusion to a tradition concerning witches: out of wax they made effigies of living persons. By piercing or burning these figures they could injure in the same way the individuals so represented. (Cf. Dante Gabriel Rossetti's ballad, *Sister Helen.*)

V.vi.15. *Unkind remembrance! thou and endless night.* Hubert blames himself for his faulty memory. This and the darkness have prevented recognition of his friend. An emendation of the Folio *endless* is *eyeless.*

V.vii.20, 21. *I am the cygnet to this pale faint swan, Who chants a doleful hymn to his own death.* An allusion to the well-known fable that the swan sang just before its death. (Cf. *Othello,* V.ii.293, 294: 'I will play the swan And die in music.')

V.vii.37. *ill fare.* Possibly a quibble on *fare* in the sense of food is intended. Cf. *Hamlet* III.ii.91–93.

V.vii.63. *heaven he knows.* The pronoun *he* refers to *heaven,* which has a personal sense, equivalent to 'God.' Cf. III.i.109: 'be husband to me, heavens.'

V.vii.77. *you stars.* Faulconbridge addresses the barons.

V.vii.114, 115. *O, let us pay the time but needful woe, Since it hath been beforehand with our griefs.* 'Let us indulge only in necessary mourning, since we have already paid in previous sorrows.'

THE TEXT OF THE PRESENT EDITION

The text of the present volume is, by permission of the Oxford University Press, that of the Oxford Shakespeare, edited by the late W. J. Craig. Craig's text has been carefully collated with the Shakespeare Folio of 1623, and the following deviations have been introduced:

1. The stage directions of the Folio have been restored. Speeches assigned by other editors to different characters have sometimes been ascribed again to the original speakers in the Folio, but in the case of two names for the same character, the modern name has ordinarily been retained (*e.g. Lewis* for *Dauphin, K. Phi.* for *France*). Necessary words and directions, omitted by the Folio, are added within square brackets.

2. Punctuation has been frequently altered, and spelling has been normalized to accord with modern English practice, e.g. Geoffrey, Poitiers, warlike, calfskin, villainy, fair play (instead of Geffrey, Poictiers, war-like, calf 's-skin, villany, fair-play). The form 'and if,' where it occurs in the Folio, has been restored in place of 'an if.' So burthen, murther, etc., for burden, murder, murderer. The Folio has also been followed in the use of 'Cordelion' for 'Cœur-de-Lion,' and in the indication of slurred vowels, e.g. th' unsettled, th' advantage.

3. The following changes of text have been introduced, usually in accordance with Folio authority. The readings of the present edition precede the colon, while Craig's readings follow it.

I.i.22	farthest F: furthest
51	subject, I, a gentleman F: subject I, a gentleman
135	Whether F: Whe'r
140	Sir Robert's his F: Sir Robert his
147	I would F: I'd
153	pound F: pounds
163	rise F: arise
165	th' mother's F: the mother's
222	'tis F: it is
II.i.37	to work our cannon F: to work: our cannon
106	Geoffrey's in the name of God. F: Geffrey's. In the name of God

121	Excuse it is F: Excuse; it is
148	shoes F: shows
153	King Lewis F: King,—Lewis
183	eldest F: eld'st
191	he is F: he's
194, 195	her plague; her sin his injury; Her injury the beadle to her sin: her plague, her sin; his injury Her injury, the beadle to her sin
197	And all for her, a plague upon her. F: And all for her. A plague upon her!
225	doth F: do
242	Craves F: Crave
258	hath F: have
267	rounder F: roundure
289	you F: thou
297	Sit's on's horseback F: Sits on his horse back
368	equal potents, fiery kindled F: equal-potents, fiery-kindled
381	Kings of our fear F: Kings of ourselves
449	as F: a
III.i.83	holy day F: holiday
149	earthy F: earthly
265	cased F: chafed
285, 286	kept, But thou hast sworn against religion: F: kept; But thou hast sworn against religion
300	them. But F: them; but
329	I will F: I'll
iii.10, 11	imprison'd angels Set at liberty F: set at liberty Imprisoned angels
29	tune F: time
42	on F: one
46	heavy, thick F: heavy-thick
IV.i.56	lien F: lain
85	heaven F: heaven's
101	moth F: mote
132	eye F: eyes
ii.97	th' inheritance F: the inheritance
115	comes F: come
146	travail'd F: travell'd
224	accompt F: account
228	deeds ill done F: ill deeds done
iii.42	You have F: Have you
163	center F: ceinture
V.i.61	farther F: further
62	come F: comes
ii.3	those F: these
10	zeal, and an F: zeal, an
27	stranger, march F: stranger march
41	wrastling F: wrestling
42	Doth F: Do
92	ye F: you
134	unheard F: unhair'd
v.3	When English measure F: when the English measur'd
vi.15	endless F: eyeless
vii.37	ill fare F: ill-fare
92	'tis F: it is

The First Part of King Henry the Fourth

Edited by TUCKER BROOKE

and

SAMUEL B. HEMINGWAY

Dramatis Personae

KING HENRY THE FOURTH

HENRY, PRINCE OF WALES

PRINCE JOHN OF LANCASTER } *his Sons*

RICHARD SCROOP, *Archbishop of York*

EDMUND MORTIMER, *Earl of March*

RALPH NEVILLE, *Earl of Westmorland*

HENRY PERCY, *Earl of Northumberland*

THOMAS PERCY, *Earl of Worcester, his Brother*

HENRY PERCY, *surnamed Hotspur,*
   Northumberland's Son

ARCHIBALD, *Earl of Douglas*

OWEN GLENDOWER, *a Welsh Chieftain*

SIR JOHN FALSTAFF

SIR WALTER BLUNT

SIR RICHARD VERNON

SIR MICHAEL, *Attendant on the Archbishop*
   of York

EDWARD POINS

PETO

GADSHILL

BARDOLPH
} *Companions of the Prince of*
Wales and Falstaff

FRANCIS, *a Tavern Drawer*

LADY KATE PERCY, *Wife of Hotspur and Sister*
   of Mortimer

LADY MORTIMER, *Wife of Mortimer and*
   Daughter of Glendower

MISTRESS QUICKLY, *Hostess of the Boar's Head*
   Tavern

LORDS, OFFICERS, SHERIFF OF LONDON,
   VINTNER, AN INN CHAMBERLAIN, TWO
   CARRIERS, TRAVELLERS, AND ATTENDANTS

SCENE—*Various parts of England and Wales.*

The First Part of King Henry the Fourth

INTRODUCTION

SOURCES OF THE PLAY

The sources of the serious plot of both parts of Shakespeare's *Henry IV* are (1) the 1587 edition of *The Chronicles of England, Scotland, and Ireland* by Raphael Holinshed 'of Bromecote in the County of Warr(wick)'; and (2) either Samuel Daniel's poem, *The Civile Wars between the two Houses of Lancaster and York* (1595) or some lost poem, play, or chronicle followed by both Daniel and Shakespeare.

The source of the comic plot is a crude and slight chronicle play called *The Famous Victories of Henry V*, acted as early as 1588 and entered for publication in 1594.

SELECTIONS FROM HOLINSHED'S ACCOUNT OF THE BATTLE OF SHREWSBURY[1]

The next day in the morning early, being the even of Mary Magdalene [21 July, 1403], they set their battles in order on both sides, and now, whilest the warriors looked when the token of battle should be given, the abbot of Shrewsbury, and one of the clerks of the privy seal, were sent from the king unto the Percies, to offer them pardon, if they would come to any reasonable agreement. By their persuasions, the lord Henry Percy began to give ear unto the king's offers, & so sent with them his uncle the Earl of Worcester, to declare unto the king the causes of those troubles....

It was reported for a truth, that now when the king had condescended unto all that was reasonable at his hands to be required, and seemed to humble himself more than was meet for his estate, the Earl of Worcester (upon his return to his nephew) made relation clean contrary to that the king had said, in such sort that he set his nephew's heart more in displeasure towards the king than ever it was before; driving him by that means to fight whether he would or not....

And forthwith the Lord Percy, as a captain of high courage, began to exhort the captains and soldiers to prepare themselves to battle, sith the matter was grown to that point, that by no means it could be avoided, 'so that,' said he, 'this day shall either bring us all to advancement & honor, or else if it shall chance us to be overcome, shall deliver us from the king's spiteful malice and cruel disdain: for playing the men (as we ought to do), better it is to die in battle for the commonwealth's cause, than through cowardlike fear to prolong life, which after shall be taken from us by the sentence of the enemy....'

Then suddenly blew the trumpets, the king's part crying, 'St. George! Upon them!' the adversaries cried *'Esperance! Percy!'* and so the two armies furiously joined....

The prince that day helped his father like a lusty young gentleman; for although he was hurt in the face with an arrow, so that

diverse noblemen that were about him would have conveyed him forth of the field, yet he would not suffer them so to do, lest his departure from amongst his men might happily have stricken some fear into their hearts: and so without regard of his hurt, he continued with his men, & never ceased either to fight where the battle was most hot, or to encourage his men where it seemed most need.

SELECTIONS FROM DANIEL'S CIVIL WARS (1595), BOOK III (THE BATTLE OF SHREWSBURY)

Stanza 100

And yet undaunted Hotspur, seeing the king
So near approach'd, leaving the work in hand ...
Brings a strong host of firm resolved might,
And plac'd his troops before the king in sight.

St. 101

'This day' (saith he), 'O faithful valiant friends,
Whatever it doth give, shall glory give:
This day with honor frees our state, or ends
Our misery with fame that still shall live.
And do but think how well this day he spends
That spends his blood his country to relieve:
Our holy cause, our freedom, and our right
Sufficient are to move good minds to fight.'

St. 107

But now begin these fury-moving sounds
The notes of wrath that music brought from hell,
The rattling drums which trumpet's voice confounds,
The cries, th'encouragements, the shouting shrell,
That all about the beaten air rebounds,
Thund'ring confused murmurs horrible ...

St. 110

There, lo that new-appearing glorious star,
Wonder of arms, the terror of the field,
Young Henry, laboring where the stoutest are,
And even the stoutest forces back to yield ...

St. 113

And dear it cost, and O much blood is shed
To purchase thee this losing victory,
O travailed King. Yet hast thou conquered
A doubtful day, a mighty enemy.
But O what wounds! what famous worth lies dead!
That makes the winner look with sorrowing eye:
Magnanimous Stafford lost, that much had wrought,
And valiant Shorly, who great glory got.

---

1 Spelling modernized.

St. 114
Such wrack of others' blood thou didst behold,
O furious Hotspur, ere thou lost thine own!
Which now once lost, that heat in thine waxt cold,
And soon became thy army overthrown.
And O that this great spirit, this courage bold,
Had in some good cause been rightly shown!
So had not we thus violently then
Have term'd that rage which valor should have been.

SELECTION FROM THE FAMOUS VICTORIES OF HENRY V[2]

The following is the first conversation[3] between Prince Hal and Falstaff (Sir John Oldcastle):

Enter Sir John Old-Castle.

Hen. 5. How now Sir John Old-Castle,
What news with you?

Joh. Old. I am glad to see your Grace at liberty,[4]
I was come, I, to visit you in prison.

Hen. 5. To visit me? Didst thou not know that I am a
Prince's son? . . . But I tell you, sirs, when I am king we will
have no such things. But, my lads, if the old king, my father,
were dead, we would all be kings.

Joh. Old. He is a good old man; God take him to his mercy
the sooner.

Hen. 5. But, Ned, so soon as I am king, the first thing I
will do, shall be to put my Lord Chief Justice out of office.
And thou shalt be my Lord Chief Justice of England.

Ned. Shall I be Lord Chief Justice? By gogs wounds, I'll be
the bravest Lord Chief Justice that ever was in England.

Hen. 5. Thou shalt hang none but pickpurses and horse-
stealers and such base-minded villains. But that fellow that will
stand by the highway side courageously with his sword and
buckler and take a purse, that fellow—give him commendations! Beside that, send him to me and I will give him an annual pension out of my Exchequer.

THE HISTORY OF THE PLAY

1 Henry IV was apparently written in the year 1597, when
Shakespeare completed his thirty-third year. He had probably
already produced ten or twelve successful plays, among them
Romeo and Juliet and *The Merchant of Venice.* The year 1596
had witnessed the English expedition to Spain and the capture
of the city of Cadiz; the year 1597 saw the 'Islands Voyage,'
another grandiose adventure under the command of the mercurial and Hotspur-like Earl of Essex. English patriotism never
found nobler expression than in the historical plays of Shakespeare written during these years of national trial and
endeavor.

In Shakespeare's first version of the play he evidently retained the name Oldcastle for the fat knight who attended the

---

2 For complete text see J. Q. Adams, *Chief Pre-Shakesperean Dramas*, pp. 667-690.
3 Spelling modernized. Compare Shakespeare's play, I. ii. 50 ff.
4 The Prince had just been committed to the Fleet Prison for striking the Lord Chief
Justice.

Prince. Hal's pun, 'my old lad of the castle' (I. ii. 37, 39)
probably bears witness to this, as does the metrical imperfection in the line

Away, good Ned. Falstaff sweats to death (II. ii. 107)

which would be corrected by the substitution of the word Oldcastle for Falstaff. In the first Quarto of *2 Henry IV,* the prefix
Old. is found instead of *Fal.* before Falstaff's speech in I. ii. 115,
and in the Epilogue to this play the author explicitly states that
the Falstaff of the play is not the Oldcastle who 'died a martyr.'
Despite this disclaimer, audiences seem long to have referred to
1 Henry IV as 'the play of Oldcastle.'

Oldcastle was a famous Lollard, and according to tradition
many Elizabethan Protestants (including Lord Cobham, the Lord
Chamberlain) protested against Shakespeare's degradation of an
honorable name, and 'some of that family being then remaining,
the Queen was pleased to command him to alter it.' It is at least
a singular coincidence that Shakespeare substituted the name of
a Lollard sympathizer, Sir John Fastolfe, in slightly disguised
form. The Falstaff of the play bears little resemblance, save in
name, to either Sir John Oldcastle, or Sir John Fastolfe.

Of the first performances and the first players of *Henry IV* no
records are extant; but the large number of contemporary references give testimony to the fact of the play's popularity. Ben
Jonson alludes to the fatness of Sir John Falstaff in the curtain-
line of his *Every Man out of his Humour* (1599), and in Beaumont
and Fletcher's *Knight of the Burning Pestle* (c. 1610), Ralph, the
apprentice, when asked to 'speak a huffing part,' declaims Hotspur's speech on honor, with variations. Shakespeare's chief rivals,
the Lord Admiral's players, in 1599 paid him the compliment
of producing two plays of their own on *The Life of Sir John
Oldcastle;* and even during the period of the Commonwealth,
Puritan legislation failed to prevent the clandestine performance
of a farcical abridgment of Shakespeare's play, known as *The
Bouncing Knight.* Professor Bentley has calculated that through
the whole seventeenth century Falstaff was the most popular of
all stage characters.[5]

John Lowin (1576-1659) is the earliest actor whose name is
associated with the play. James Wright in his *Historia Histrionica*
(1699) says that 'before the wars' Lowin acted Falstaff 'with
mighty applause.' Lowin seems to have joined Shakespeare's company in 1603, six or seven years after the probable date of the
first performance of *Henry IV.*

This play was one of the first to be revived publicly after
the Restoration. Pepys first saw it in December, 1660, and was
disappointed,—'my expectation being too great, . . . and my having a book I believe did spoil it a little.' The next spring, however, Pepys saw it again, and pronounced it 'a good play.' In
November, 1667, and September, 1668, Pepys attended performances again, and 'contrary to expectation was pleased in nothing
more than in Cartwright's speaking of Falstaff's speech about
"What is Honor?"'

During the 1670s John Lacey succeeded Cartwright in the
rôle of Falstaff; and in 1682, the year after Lacey's death, at the
time of the union of the King's and the Duke's players, the great
Thomas Betterton appeared as Hotspur. Eighteen years later, at
the age of sixty-five, Betterton appeared as Falstaff 'which drew
all the town more than any new play produced of late. . . . The

---

5 G. E. Bentley, *Shakespeare and Jonson: Their Reputations in the Seventeenth Century
Compared* (1945).

critics allow that Betterton has hit the humor of Falstaff better than any that have aimed at it before, . . . though he lacks the waggery of Estcourt, the drollery of Harper, and the salaciousness of Jack Evans.' (Genest, II, 381; V. 596). Six notable Falstaffs in one generation is a record of which the seventeenth century may be proud.

Betterton's acting version of the play was published in 1700. Genest notes that he 'judiciously retains' the conversation of Falstaff and the Prince in Act Second, and also the first scene in Act Third, although he omits the character of Lady Mortimer. The obvious inference to be drawn from Genest's opening remark is indeed astounding, namely, that it had been the custom, before Betterton's time, to cut the great Boar's Head Tavern scene. But it was after Betterton's time that, according to Genest, a 'happy (*sic*) addition' was made to Falstaff's speech which begins 'By the Lord, I knew ye as well as he that made ye' by prefixing the question 'Do ye think that I did not know ye?' This singularly infelicitous addition to Shakespeare's text was retained by Sir Herbert Tree in his performance of the Boar's Head Tavern scene at the Shakespeare Tercentenary Festival in the New Amsterdam Theatre, New York, in April, 1916.

Verbruggen was Betterton's Hotspur, and according to Genest (II. 381) he was 'nature without extravagance, and freedom without licentiousness,—he was vociferous without bellowing.' The inference to be drawn with respect to former performances is again interesting.

Twenty other actors are known to have played Falstaff between 1700 and 1750, and the play-bills of twenty performances of *1 Henry IV* between 1706 and 1826 are in existence. Six of these performances were at the Haymarket, seven at Drury Lane, two at Lincoln's Inn Fields, and five at Covent Garden.

Garrick first appeared as Hotspur at the Covent Garden performance in 1746, his rival, Quin, appearing as Falstaff, a rôle in which he had made himself a name eight years before. We are told that 'the advantage was greatly on Quin's side, as the part of Hotspur was not suited to Garrick's figure or style of acting.'

Henderson was the great Falstaff of the latter half of the eighteenth century, and played at the Haymarket, Drury Lane, and Covent Garden. He is said to have made Falstaff 'neither very vulgar nor very polite.' An entirely unique performance must have been that of 1786 when Mrs. Webb appeared as Falstaff in a 'benefit' for herself.

In 1818 William Charles Macready (1793-1873) succeeded the aging and long famous John Philip Kemble as Hotspur at the Drury Lane Theatre; while Kemble's younger brother, Charles, appeared as Falstaff in the 1824 production at Covent Garden. 'He endeavored to rescue the part from coarseness. In the presence of the king and in the conversation with Westmorland, he invested it with gentility and courtly bearing.'

Another popular Falstaff of the early nineteenth century was George Bartley, who made his first appearance in the rôle in 1815. 'His success was equal to his most sanguine expectations, and richly merited.' Bartley made a triumphal tour of America in 1818-1819, and gave instruction in reading and elocution in many American colleges. In 'Hertford,' the capital of Connecticut, he and his accomplished wife were arrested for indulging in dramatic readings, one Ebenezer Huntington, a puritanical Attorney General, having resurrected one of Connecticut's famous blue laws for this purpose.

After Bartley's farewell performance in 1852, there were few revivals of Henry IV, and the play, which for two centuries had been almost continuously acted, nearly disappeared from the stage, except for the sterling productions of Samuel Phelps (1804-1878) and later of the Old Vic company, and in America of Otis Skinner (1858-1942). One may perhaps hold the 'Shakespeare idolaters' of the school of Lamb and Hazlitt partly to blame. In their transcendental enthusiasm they insisted upon a Falstaff as huge in mind as in body, and they ended by pushing him over the whole play and beyond the grasp of the mere actor. The inclusion of *1 Henry IV* in the repertoires of Sir Herbert Tree and of Sir Francis Benson's company at the Stratford Memorial Theatre did little for its fame; and Julia Marlowe's production in 1896 drew from New York critics the opinion that the play is inherently 'unactable.' But there are clear signs that it is returning to the boards. The Margaret Webster arrangement in 1939, with Maurice Evans as Falstaff and with some intrusions from *Part Two*, ran for seventy-four performances in New York, and the full-length production of both parts in 1945 by Laurence Olivier and the Old Vic company (on visit from London) was one of the most unquestioned successes that Shakespeare had had on the New York stage.

ACT FIRST ❧ SCENE FIRST

[Westminster. The King's Palace]
Enter the King, Lord John of Lancaster, Earl of Westmorland, with
others.

King. So shaken as we are, so wan with care,
Find we a time for frighted peace to pant,
And breathe short-winded accents of new broils
To be commenc'd in stronds afar remote.
No more the thirsty entrance of this soil   5
Shall daub her lips with her own children's blood,
No more shall trenching war channel her fields,
Nor bruise her flowerets with the armed hoofs
Of hostile paces. Those opposed eyes,
Which like the meteors of a troubled heaven,   10
All of one nature, of one substance bred,
Did lately meet in the intestine shock
And furious close of civil butchery,
Shall now in mutual well-beseeming ranks
March all one way, and be no more oppos'd   15
Against acquaintance, kindred, and allies.
The edge of war, like an ill-sheathed knife,
No more shall cut his master. Therefore, friends,
As far as to the sepulcher of Christ—
Whose soldier now, under whose blessed cross   20
We are impressed and engag'd to fight—
Forthwith a power of English shall we levy,
Whose arms were moulded in their mothers' womb,
To chase these pagans in those holy fields,
Over whose acres walk'd those blessed feet   25
Which fourteen hundred years ago were nail'd
For our advantage on the bitter cross.
But this our purpose now is twelve month old,
And bootless 'tis to tell you we will go.
Therefore we meet not now. Then let me hear   30
Of you, my gentle cousin Westmorland,
What yesternight our council did decree
In forwarding this dear expedience.

West. My liege, this haste was hot in question,
And many limits of the charge set down   35
But yesternight, when all athwart there came
A post from Wales, loaden with heavy news,
Whose worst was that the noble Mortimer,
Leading the men of Herefordshire to fight
Against the irregular and wild Glendower,   40
Was by the rude hands of that Welshman taken,
A thousand of his people butchered,
Upon whose dead corpes there was such misuse,
Such beastly shameless transformation
By those Welshwomen done, as may not be   45
(Without much shame) re-told or spoken of.

King. It seems then that the tidings of this broil
Brake off our business for the Holy Land.

West. This match'd with other did, my gracious lord,

For more uneven and unwelcome news
Came from the North, and thus it did import:
On Holy-rood day, the gallant Hotspur there,
Young Harry Percy, and brave Archibold,
That ever-valiant and approved Scot,
At Holmedon met,   55
Where they did spend a sad and bloody hour,
As by discharge of their artillery
And shape of likelihood the news was told;
For he that brought them in the very heat
And pride of their contention did take horse,   60
Uncertain of the issue any way.

King. Here is a dear, a true, industrious friend,
Sir Walter Blunt, new lighted from his horse,
Stain'd with the variation of each soil
Betwixt that Holmedon and this seat of ours;   65
And he hath brought us smooth and welcome news.
The Earl of Douglas is discomfited,
Ten thousand bold Scots, two and twenty knights,
Balk'd in their own blood did Sir Walter see
On Holmedon's plains. Of prisoners Hotspur took   70
Mordake Earl of Fife, and eldest son
To beaten Douglas, and the Earl of Athol,
Of Murray, Angus, and Menteith.
And is not this an honorable spoil?
A gallant prize? ha, cousin, is it not?   75
    West. In faith,
It is a conquest for a prince to boast of.

King. Yea, there thou mak'st me sad, and mak'st
me sin
In envy, that my Lord Northumberland   80
Should be the father to so blest a son,
A son who is the theme of honor's tongue,
Amongst a grove the very straightest plant,
Who is sweet Fortune's minion and her pride;
Whilst I by looking on the praise of him   85
See riot and dishonor stain the brow
Of my young Harry. O that it could be prov'd
That some night-tripping fairy had exchang'd
In cradle-clothes our children where they lay,
And call'd mine Percy, his Plantagenet.   90
Then would I have his Harry, and he mine.
But let him from my thoughts. What think you, coz,
Of this young Percy's pride? The prisoners
Which he in this adventure hath surpris'd
To his own use he keeps, and sends me word   95
I shall have none but Mordake Earl of Fife.

West. This is his uncle's teaching. This is Worcester,
Malevolent to you in all aspécts,
Which makes him prune himself, and bristle up
The crest of youth against your dignity.   100

King. But I have sent for him to answer this.
And for this cause a while we must neglect
Our holy purpose to Jerusalem.
Cousin, on Wednesday next our council we
Will hold at Windsor. So inform the lords: 105
But come yourself with speed to us again,

4 stronds: *coasts; cf. n.*   **5** *Cf. n.*   **7 trenching:** *trench-digging*   **channel:** *make channels in*   **12 intestine:** *internal, civil*   **13 close:** *grapple*   **14 mutual well-beseeming ranks:** *ranks which have, most properly, a common interest*   **21 impressed:** *compelled into service*   **26** *Cf. n.*   **28** *Cf. n.*   **29 bootless:** *useless*   **33 dear expedience:** *important expedition*   **34 hot in question:** *in hot debate*   **35 limits of the charge:** *implementing provisions*   **36 athwart:** *crossing this plan*   **38 Mortimer;** *cf. n.*   **40 irregular:** *lawless*   **43 corpes:** *bodies*   **49 match'd:** *joined*

50 uneven: *disconcerting*   **52 Holy-rood day;** *cf. n.*   **53 Young Harry Percy;** *cf. n.*   **54 approved:** *well-tried*   **57, 58** *Cf. n.*   **69 Balk'd:** *piled up*   **71 Mordake;** *cf. n.*   **84 minion:** *darling*   **92 coz:** *cousin, used by the sovereign in addressing any nobleman*   **92–96** *Cf. n.*   **98** *Cf. n.*   **99 Which:** *who*

For more is to be said and to be done
Than out of anger can be uttered.

  West. I will, my liege.   *Exeunt.*

❧ SCENE SECOND ❧

[Westminster. A Public Waiting Room at Court]
Enter Prince of Wales and Sir John Falstaff.

Fal. Now Hal, what time of day is it, lad?

Prince. Thou art so fat-witted with drinking of old sack, and unbuttoning thee after supper, and sleeping upon benches after noon, that thou hast forgotten to demand that truly which thou wouldst truly know. What a devil hast thou to do with 5 the time of the day? Unless hours were cups of sack, and minutes capons, and clocks the tongues of bawds, and dials the signs of leaping-houses, and the blessed sun himself a fair hot wench in flame-color'd taffeta, I see no reason why thou shouldst be so superfluous to demand the time of the day. 10

Fal. Indeed you come near me now, Hal; for we that take purses go by the moon and the seven stars, and not by Phœbus, he, 'that wandering knight so fair.' And I prithee, sweet wag, when thou art a king, as God save thy Grace— Majesty I should say, for grace thou wilt have none— 15

Prince. What, none?

Fal. No, by my troth; not so much as will serve to be prologue to an egg and butter.

Prince. Well, how then? come roundly, roundly.

Fal. Marry then, sweet wag, when thou art king let not 20 us that are squires of the night's body be called thieves of the day's beauty. Let us be Diana's foresters, gentlemen of the shade, minions of the moon; and let men say we be men of good government, being governed as the sea is, by our noble and chaste mistress the moon, under whose countenance we 25 steal.

Prince. Thou sayest well, and it holds well too; for the fortune of us that are the moon's men doth ebb and flow like the sea, being governed as the sea is by the moon. As for proof now: a purse of gold most resolutely snatched on Monday 30 night and most dissolutely spent on Tuesday morning; got with swearing 'Lay by!' and spent with crying 'Bring in!' now in as low an ebb as the foot of the ladder, and by and by in as high a flow as the ridge of the gallows.

Fal. By the Lord thou sayest true, lad. And is not my 35 hostess of the tavern a most sweet wench?

Prince. As the honey of Hybla, my old lad of the castle. And is not a buff jerkin a most sweet robe of durance?

Fal. How now, how now, mad wag! what, in thy quips and thy quiddities? what a plague have I to do with a buff jerkin? 40

Prince. Why, what a pox have I to do with my hostess of the tavern?

Fal. Well, thou hast called her to a reckoning many a time and oft.

Prince. Did I ever call for thee to pay thy part? 45

Fal. No, I'll give thee thy due, thou hast paid all there.

Prince. Yea, and elsewhere, so far as my coin would stretch; and where it would not, I have used my credit.

Fal. Yea, and so used it that were it not here apparent that thou art heir-apparent—but I prithee sweet wag, shall there 50 be gallows standing in England when thou art king and resolution thus fubbed as it is with the rusty curb of old Father Antic the Law? Do not thou, when thou art king, hang a thief.

Prince. No, thou shalt.

Fal. Shall I? O rare! By the Lord I'll be a brave judge. 55

Prince. Thou judgest false already. I mean thou shalt have the hanging of the thieves, and so become a rare hangman.

Fal. Well, Hal, well; and in some sort it jumps with my humor as well as waiting in the court, I can tell you.

Prince. For obtaining of suits? 60

Fal. Yea, for obtaining of suits, whereof the hangman hath no lean wardrobe. 'Sblood I am as melancholy as a gib cat, or a lugged bear.

Prince. Or an old lion, or a lover's lute.

Fal. Yea, or the drone of a Lincolnshire bagpipe. 65

Prince. What sayest thou to a hare, or the melancholy of Moorditch?

Fal. Thou hast the most unsavory similes, and art indeed the most comparative, rascalliest, sweet young prince! But Hal, I prithee trouble me no more with vanity. I would to God 70 thou and I knew where a commodity of good names were to be bought. An old lord of the council rated me the other day in the street about you, sir, but I marked him not; and yet he talked very wisely, but I regarded him not; and yet he talked wisely, and in the street too. 75

Prince. Thou didst well, for wisdom cries out in the streets and no man regards it.

Fal. O thou hast damnable iteration, and art indeed able to corrupt a saint. Thou hast done much harm upon me, Hal, God forgive thee for it! Before I knew thee, Hal, I knew 80 nothing, and now am I, if a man should speak truly, little better than one of the wicked. I must give over this life, and I will give it over. By the Lord, an I do not, I am a villain. I'll be damned for never a king's son in Christendom.

Prince. Where shall we take a purse tomorrow, Jack? 85

Fal. 'Zounds! where thou wilt, lad, I'll make one. An I do not, call me villain and baffle me.

Prince. I see a good amendment of life in thee: from praying to purse-taking.

Fal. Why, Hal, 'tis my vocation, Hal. 'Tis no sin for a 90 man to labor in his vocation.

Enter Poins.

Poins! Now shall we know if Gadshill have set a match. O, if men were to be saved by merit, what hole in hell were hot enough for him? This is the most omnipotent villain that ever cried 'Stand!' to a true man. 95

Prince. Good morrow, Ned.

Poins. Good morrow, sweet Hal. What says Monsieur Re-

---

108 uttered; *cf. n.* **SCENE SECOND S. d.;** *cf. n.* **2 sack:** *sweet Spanish wine* **8 leaping-houses:** *brothels* **10 superfluous:** *supererogatory* **12** *Cf. n.* **13 wandering knight;** *cf. n.* **14–26** *Cf. n.* **18 egg and butter:** *scrambled egg* **19 roundly:** *plainly, to the point* **20 Marry:** *well* (originally an oath) **22 Diana's:** *the moon's* **23 minions:** *favorites* **32 'Lay by':** *address of highwaymen to their victims* **'Bring in':** *a call for wine* **37 honey of Hybla:** *Sicilian honey* **lad of the castle;** *cf. "History of the Play"* **38 buff jerkin . . . durance;** *cf. n.* **durance:** *a stuff noted for its durability* **39 quips:** *jests* **quiddities:** *subtleties, puns*

51 resolution: *enterprise* **fubbed:** *hampered* **52 Antic:** *buffoon* **55 brave:** *fine* **58 jumps:** *agrees* **59 humor:** *inclination* **61 obtaining of suits:** *the clothes of the criminal were the hangman's perquisite* **62 'Sblood:** *God's blood* **gib cat:** *tom cat* **63 lugged bear:** *bear led by a rope* **66 hare;** *cf. n.* **67 Moorditch;** *cf. n.* **69 comparative: witty, critical** **71 commodity:** *second-hand supply* **78 damnable iteration;** *cf. n.* **86 'Zounds:** *God's wounds* **87 baffle:** *hang by the heels* (a punishment inflicted on recreant knights) **92 Gadshill;** *cf. n.* **set a match:** *planned a robbery*

morse? What says Sir John Sack-and-Sugar, Jack? How agrees the devil and thee about thy soul, that thou soldest him on Good-Friday last for a cup of Madeira and a cold capon's leg?

Prince. Sir John stands to his word. The devil shall have his bargain, for he was never yet a breaker of proverbs. He will give the devil his due.

Poins. Then art thou damned for keeping thy word with the devil. *105*

Prince. Else he had been damned for cozening the devil.

Poins. But my lads, my lads, to-morrow morning, by four o'clock early at Gadshill there are pilgrims going to Canterbury with rich offerings, and traders riding to London with fat purses. I have vizards for you all, you have horses for your- *110* selves. Gadshill lies to-night in Rochester, I have bespoke supper to-morrow night in Eastcheap; we may do it as secure as sleep. If you will go, I will stuff your purses full of crowns. If you will not, tarry at home and be hanged.

Fal. Hear ye, Yedward, if I tarry at home and go not, *115* I'll hang you for going.

Poins. You will, chops?

Fal. Hal, wilt thou make one?

Prince. Who, I rob? I a thief? Not I, by my faith.

Fal. There's neither honesty, manhood, nor good fellow- *120* ship in thee, nor thou cam'st not of the blood royal, if thou darest not stand for ten shillings.

Prince. Well then, once in my days I'll be a madcap.

Fal. Why, that's well said.

Prince. Well, come what will, I'll tarry at home. *125*

Fal. By the Lord, I'll be a traitor then, when thou art king.

Prince. I care not.

Poins. Sir John, I prithee leave the prince and me alone. I will lay him down such reasons for this adventure that he shall go. *130*

Fal. Well God give thee the spirit of persuasion and him the ears of profiting, that what thou speakest may move, and what he hears may be believed, that the true prince may (for recreation sake) prove a false thief, for the poor abuses of the time want countenance. Farewell. You shall find me in *135* Eastcheap.

Prince. Farewell the latter spring! Farewell All-hallown summer! *[Exit Falstaff.]*

Poins. Now my good sweet honey lord, ride with us to-mor-row. I have a jest to execute, that I cannot manage alone. *140* Falstaff, Bardolph, Peto, and Gadshill shall rob those men that we have already waylaid. Yourself and I will not be there. And when they have the booty, if you and I do not rob them, cut this head off from my shoulders.

Prince. How shall we part with them in setting forth?

Poins. Why, we will set forth before or after them, and ap-point them a place of meeting, wherein it is at our pleasure *145* to fail; and then will they adventure upon the exploit them-selves, which they shall have no sooner achieved but we'll set upon them.

Prince. Yea but 'tis like that they will know us by our horses, by our habits, and by every other appointment to *150* be ourselves.

Poins. Tut! our horses they shall not see, I'll tie them in the wood. Our vizards we will change after we leave them. *155* And sirrah, I have cases of buckram for the nonce, to immask our noted outward garments.

Prince. Yea, but I doubt they will be too hard for us.

Poins. Well, for two of them, I know them to be as true-bred cowards as ever turned back; and for the third, if he *160* fight longer than he sees reason, I'll forswear arms. The virtue of this jest will be the incomprehensible lies that this same fat rogue will tell us when we meet at supper: how thirty at least he fought with, what wards, what blows, what extremities he endured, and in the reproof of this lies the jest. *165*

Prince. Well, I'll go with thee. Provide us all things neces-sary, and meet me to-morrow night in Eastcheap. There I'll sup. Farewell.

Poins. Farewell, my lord. *Exit Poins.*

Prince. I know you all, and will awhile uphold *170*
The unyok'd humor of your idleness.
Yet herein will I imitate the sun,
Who doth permit the base contagious clouds
To smother up his beauty from the world,
That when he please again to be himself, *175*
Being wanted, he may be more wonder'd at
By breaking through the foul and ugly mists
Of vapors that did seem to strangle him.
If all the year were playing-holidays,
To sport would be as tedious as to work; *180*
But when they seldom come, they wish'd for come,
And nothing pleaseth but rare accidents.
So when this loose behavior I throw off,
And pay the debt I never promised,
By how much better than my word I am, *185*
By so much shall I falsify men's hopes,
And like bright metal on a sullen ground,
My reformation, glittering o'er my fault,
Shall show more goodly, and attract more eyes,
Than that which hath no foil to set it off. *190*
I'll so offend, to make offence a skill,
Redeeming time when men think least I will. *Exit.*

❧ Scene Third ❧

[Windsor Castle].
Enter the King, Northumberland, Worcester, Hotspur, Sir Walter Blunt, with others.

King. My blood hath been too cold and temperate,
Unapt to stir at these indignities,
And you have found me; for accordingly
You tread upon my patience. But be sure
I will from henceforth rather be myself, *5*
Mighty, and to be fear'd, than my condition,
Which hath been smooth as oil, soft as young down,

---

100 *Cf. n.* 106 cozening: *cheating* 108 pilgrims; *cf. n.* 110 vizards: *masks* 112 Eastcheap; *cf. n.* 117 chops: *fat face* 122 stand for ten shillings; *cf. n.* 123 Well then, etc.; *cf. n.* 137 the latter spring; *cf. n.* 137–38 Allhallown summer: *All Saints' summer; cf. n.* 141 Bardolph, Peto; *cf. n.* 142 waylaid: *lain in wait for, snared* 150 habits: *clothes* appointment: *equipment*

156 sirrah; *cf. n.* cases of buckram: *cloaks of coarse linen* for the nonce: *for the occa-sion* noted: *well-known* 160 the third; *cf. n.* 162 incomprehensible: *lim-itless* 164 wards: *guards in fencing* 165 reproof: *refutation* 170–172 *Cf. n.* 171 unyok'd humor: *unrestrained caprice* 173 contagious: *pestilential* 182 accidents: *events not arising from routine* 187 sullen: *dull* Scene Third Windsor Castle; *cf. n.* 3 found me: *guessed my character* 6 condition: *natural disposition*

And therefore lost that title of respect,
Which the proud soul ne'er pays but to the proud.
   Wor. Our house, my sovereign liege, little deserves   *10*
The scourge of greatness to be us'd on it,
And that same greatness too, which our own hands
Have holp to make so portly.
   North. My lord—
   King. Worcester, get thee gone, for I do see   *15*
Danger and disobedience in thine eye.
O sir, your presence is too bold and peremptory,
And majesty might never yet endure
The moody frontier of a servant brow.
You have good leave to leave us. When we need   *20*
Your use and counsel we shall send for you.   *Exit Worcester.*
[*To Northumberland.*] You were about to speak.
   North.   Yea my good lord.
Those prisoners in your highness' name demanded,
Which Harry Percy here at Holmedon took,   *25*
Were, as he says, not with such strength denied
As is deliver'd to your majesty.
Either envy therefore, or misprision,
Is guilty of this fault, and not my son.
   Hot. My liege, I did deny no prisoners.   *30*
But I remember when the fight was done,
When I was dry with rage, and extreme toil,
Breathless and faint, leaning upon my sword,
Came there a certain lord, neat and trimly dress'd,
Fresh as a bridegroom, and his chin, new reap'd,   *35*
Show'd like a stubble-land at harvest-home.
He was perfumed like a milliner,
And 'twixt his finger and his thumb he held
A pouncet-box, which ever and anon
He gave his nose, and took't away again,   *40*
Who therewith angry, when it next came there
Took it in snuff, and still he smil'd and talk'd.
And as the soldiers bore dead bodies by,
He call'd them untaught knaves, unmannerly,
To bring a slovenly unhandsome corse   *45*
Betwixt the wind and his nobility.
With many holiday and lady terms
He question'd me, amongst the rest demanded
My prisoners in your majesty's behalf.
I then, all smarting with my wounds being cold,   *50*
To be so pester'd with a popinjay,
Out of my grief and my impatience
Answer'd neglectingly, I know not what,
He should, or he should not, for he made me mad
To see him shine so brisk, and smell so sweet,   *55*
And talk so like a waiting-gentlewoman,
Of guns, and drums, and wounds—God save the mark!—
And telling me the sovereign'st thing on earth
Was parmaceti, for an inward bruise;
And that it was great pity, so it was,   *60*
This villainous saltpeter should be digg'd

Out of the bowels of the harmless earth,
Which many a good tall fellow had destroy'd
So cowardly, and but for these vile guns
He would himself have been a soldier.   *65*
This bald unjointed chat of his, my lord,
I answer'd indirectly, as I said,
And I beseech you, let not his report
Come current for an accusation
Betwixt my love and your high majesty.   *70*
   Blunt. The circumstance consider'd, good my lord,
What e'er Lord Harry Percy then had said
To such a person, and in such a place,
At such a time, with all the rest re-told,
May reasonably die, and never rise   *75*
To do him wrong, or any way impeach
What then he said, so he unsay it now.
   King. Why yet he doth deny his prisoners,
But with proviso and exception,
That we at our own charge shall ransom straight   *80*
His brother-in-law, the foolish Mortimer,
Who, on my soul, hath wilfully betray'd
The lives of those that he did lead to fight
Against that great magician, damn'd Glendower,
Whose daughter, as we hear, that Earl of March   *85*
Hath lately married. Shall our coffers then
Be emptied, to redeem a traitor home?
Shall we buy treason, and indent with fears,
When they have lost and forfeited themselves?
No, on the barren mountains let him starve;   *90*
For I shall never hold that man my friend,
Whose tongue shall ask me for one penny cost
To ransom home revolted Mortimer.
   Hot. Revolted Mortimer!
He never did fall off, my sovereign liege,   *95*
But by the chance of war. To prove that true
Needs no more but one tongue for all those wounds,
Those mouthed wounds which valiantly he took,
When on the gentle Severn's sedgy bank,
In single opposition hand to hand,   *100*
He did confound the best part of an hour
In changing hardiment with great Glendower.
Three times they breath'd and three times did they drink,
Upon agreement, of swift Severn's flood,
Who then affrighted with their bloody looks,   *105*
Ran fearfully among the trembling reeds,
And hid his crisp head in the hollow bank,
Blood-stained with these valiant combatants.
Never did base and rotten policy
Color her working with such deadly wounds,   *110*
Nor never could the noble Mortimer
Receive so many, and all willingly.
Then let not him be slander'd with revolt.
   King. Thou dost belie him, Percy, thou dost belie him.
He never did encounter with Glendower.   *115*
I tell thee,
He durst as well have met the devil alone

---

8 lost: *hath lost*   **13 portly:** *stately*   **19 moody:** *angry* **frontier:** *outworks of a fort* (used figuratively)   **27 deliver'd:** *reported*   **28 misprision:** *misapprehension*   **37 milliner;** *cf. n.*   **38 pouncet-box:** *a perforated box for perfumes*   **41 in snuff:** *as an offence* (with play on the word *snuff)*   **47 holiday and lady terms:** *choice and ladylike expressions*   **48 question'd:** *chatted with*   **51 popinjay:** *parrot*   **52 grief:** *pain*   **57 God save the mark;** *cf. n.*   **58 sovereign'st:** *of supreme excellence*   **59 parmaceti:** *spermaceti, a substance found in whales*

63 tall: *valiant*   **74 re-told:** *that he has told over*   **76 impeach:** *call in question*   **81 brother-in-law;** *cf. n. on lines 147, 148*   **85 Earl of March:** *Mortimer*   **88 indent:** *bargain*   **95 fall off:** *desert*   **98 mouthed wounds:** *wounds that speak aloud*   **101 confound:** *consume*   **102 changing hardiment:** *exchanging valor*   **107 crisp:** *curled, i.e., rippled*   **110 Color:** *disguise*

As Owen Glendower for an enemy.
Art thou not asham'd? But sirrah, hénceforth
Let me not hear you speak of Mortimer.   *120*
Send me your prisoners with the speediest means,
Or you shall hear in such a kind from me
As will displease you. My Lord Northumberland,
We license your departure with your son.
Send us your prisoners, or you will hear of it.   *125*
            Exit King [with Blunt and train].
    Hot. And if the devil come and roar for them
I will not send them. I will after straight
And tell him so, for I will ease my heart,
Albeit I make a hazard of my head.
    North. What? drunk with choler? stay, and pause awhile.   *130*
Here comes your uncle.

          Enter Worcester.

    Hot.   Speak of Mortimer?
'Zounds I will speak of him! and let my soul
Want mercy if I do not join with him.
Yea on his part I'll empty all these veins,   *135*
And shed my dear blood, drop by drop in the dust,
But I will lift the down-trod Mortimer
As high in the air as this unthankful king,
As this ingrate and canker'd Bolingbroke.
    North. Brother, the king hath made your nephew mad.   *140*
    Wor. Who struck this heat up after I was gone?
    Hot. He will, forsooth, have all my prisoners.
And when I urg'd the ransom once again
Of my wife's brother, then his cheek look'd pale,
And on my face he turn'd an eye of death,   *145*
Trembling even at the name of Mortimer.
    Wor. I cannot blame him. Was not he proclaim'd
By Richard that dead is, the next of blood?
    North. He was. I heard the proclamation.
And then it was, when the unhappy king   *150*
(Whose wrongs in us God pardon) did set forth
Upon his Irish expedition;
From whence he, intercepted, did return
To be depos'd, and shortly murdered.
    Wor. And for whose death, we in the world's wide mouth   *155*
Live scandaliz'd and foully spoken of.
    Hot. But soft, I pray you, did King Richard then
Proclaim my brother Edmund Mortimer
Heir to the crown?
    North.   He did; myself did hear it.   *160*
    Hot. Nay, then I cannot blame his cousin king,
That wish'd him on the barren mountains starve.
But shall it be that you that set the crown
Upon the head of this forgetful man,
And for his sake wear the detested blot   *165*
Of murtherous subornation—shall it be,
That you a world of curses undergo,
Being the agents, or base second means,
The cords, the ladder, or the hangman rather—
O pardon me that I descend so low,   *170*
To show the line and the predicament

Wherein you range under this subtle king!—
Shall it for shame be spoken in these days,
Or fill up chronicles in time to come,
That men of your nobility and power   *175*
Did gage them both in an unjust behalf
(As both of you, God pardon it, have done)
To put down Richard, that sweet lovely rose,
And plant this thorn, this canker Bolingbroke?
And shall it in more shame be further spoken,   *180*
That you are fool'd, discarded, and shook off
By him, for whom these shames ye underwent?
No. Yet time serves wherein you may redeem
Your banish'd honors and restore yourselves
Into the good thoughts of the world again.   *185*
Revenge the jeering and disdain'd contempt
Of this proud king, who studies day and night
To answer all the debt he owes to you,
Even with the bloody payment of your deaths.
Therefore I say—   *190*
    Wor.   Peace cousin, say no more.
And now I will unclasp a secret book,
And to your quick-conceiving discontents
I'll read you matter deep and dangerous,
As full of peril and adventurous spirit   *195*
As to o'er-walk a current roaring loud
On the unsteadfast footing of a spear.
    Hot. If he fall in, good night. Or sink, or swim!
Send danger from the east unto the west,
So honor cross it, from the north to south,   *200*
And let them grapple! O the blood more stirs
To rouse a lion than to start a hare.
    North. Imagination of some great exploit
Drives him beyond the bounds of patience.
    Hot. By heaven methinks it were an easy leap   *205*
To pluck bright honor from the pale-fac'd moon,
Or dive into the bottom of the deep,
Where fadom-line could never touch the ground,
And pluck up drowned honor by the locks,
So he that doth redeem her thence might wear   *210*
Without corrival all her dignities.
But out upon this half-fac'd fellowship!
    Wor. He apprehends a world of figures here,
But not the form of what he should attend.
Good cousin, give me audience for a while.   *215*
    Hot. I cry you mercy.
    Wor.   Those same noble Scots
That are your prisoners—
    Hot.   I'll keep them all
By God he shall not have a Scot of them,   *220*
No, if a Scot would save his soul he shall not.
I'll keep them, by this hand.
    Wor.   You start away,
And lend no ear unto my purposes.
Those prisoners you shall keep.   *225*
    Hot.   Nay, I will; that's flat!
He said he would not ransom Mortimer,

---

122 kind: *way*   **126 And if:** *Even if*   **127 straight:** *immediately*   **129 Albeit ...**
hazard: *though at the risk*   **130 choler:** *anger*   **139 canker'd:** *malignant*   **Bolingbroke;**
cf. n.   **147, 148** *Cf. n.*   **151 in us:** *at our hands*   **166 murtherous subornation:**
secret prompting to murder   **171 line:** *rank*   **predicament:** *situation, classification*

172 range: *stand*   **176 gage them:** *pledge themselves*   **179 canker:** *dog-rose*   **186 disdain'd:** *disdainful*   **198 good night:** *so be it*   **Or ... swim:** *let him take his chance, either to sink or swim*   **208 fadom-line:** *sounding-rope, measured in fathoms*   **210 So:** *provided that*   **211 corrival:** *partner*   **212 half-fac'd:** *one-sided*   **213 apprehends:** *imagines*   **figures:** *unpractical fancies*   **216 cry you mercy:** *beg your pardon*

Forbade my tongue to speak of Mortimer.
But I will find him when he lies asleep,
And in his ear I'll holla 'Mortimer!'   230
Nay,
I'll have a starling shall be taught to speak
Nothing but 'Mortimer,' and give it him
To keep his anger still in motion.
    Wor. Hear you, cousin; a word.   235
    Hot. All studies here I solemnly defy,
Save how to gall and pinch this Bolingbroke.
And that same sword-and-buckler Prince of Wales,
But that I think his father loves him not,
And would be glad he met with some mischance,   240
I would have him poison'd with a pot of ale.
    Wor. Farewell, kinsman. I will talk to you
When you are better temper'd to attend.
    North. Why, what a wasp-sting and impatient fool
Art thou, to break into this woman's mood,   245
Tying thine ear to no tongue but thine own!
    Hot. Why, look you, I am whipp'd and scourg'd with rods,
Nettled, and stung with pismires, when I hear
Of this vile politician Bolingbroke.
In Richard's time—what do you call the place?—   250
A plague upon't, it is in Gloucestershire—
'Twas where the madcap duke his uncle kept,
His uncle York—where I first bow'd my knee
Unto this king of smiles, this Bolingbroke—
'Sblood!   255
When you and he came back from Ravenspurgh.
    North. At Berkeley Castle.
    Hot.   You say true.
Why, what a candy deal of courtesy
This fawning greyhound then did proffer me: 260
'Look when his infant fortune came to age,'
And 'gentle Harry Percy,' and 'kind cousin.'
O, the devil take such cozeners. God forgive me!
Good uncle, tell your tale, I have done.
    Wor. Nay, if you have not, to it again.   265
We'll stay your leisure.
    Hot.   I have done, i' faith.
    Wor. Then once more to your Scottish prisoners.
Deliver them up without their ransom straight,
And make the Douglas' son your only mean   270
For powers in Scotland, which for divers reasons
Which I shall send you written, be assur'd
Will easily be granted. *[To Northumberland.]* You, my lord,
Your son in Scotland being thus employ'd,
Shall secretly into the bosom creep   275
Of that same noble prelate wellbelov'd,
The Archbishop.
    Hot. Of York, is it not?
    Wor.   True; who bears hard
His brother's death at Bristow, the Lord Scroop.   280
I speak not this in estimation,
As what I think might be, but what I know
Is ruminated, plotted, and set down,

And only stays but to behold the face
Of that occasion that shall bring it on.   285
    Hot. I smell 't! Upon my life it will do well!
    North. Before the game's afoot thou still lett'st slip.
    Hot. Why, it cannot choose but be a noble plot!
And then the power of Scotland, and of York,
To join with Mortimer, ha?   290
    Wor.   And so they shall.
    Hot. In faith, it is exceedingly well aim'd.
    Wor. And 'tis no little reason bids us speed,
To save our heads by raising of a head.
For bear ourselves as even as we can,   295
The king will always think him in our debt,
And think we think ourselves unsatisfied,
Till he hath found a time to pay us home.
And see already how he doth begin
To make us strangers to his looks of love.   300
    Hot. He does, he does! We'll be reveng'd on him.
    Wor. Cousin, farewell. No further go in this,
Than I by letters shall direct your course
When time is ripe, which will be suddenly.
I'll steal to Glendower and Lord Mortimer,   305
Where you and Douglas, and our powers at once,
As I will fashion it, shall happily meet,
To bear our fortunes in our own strong arms,
Which now we hold at much uncertainty.
    North. Farewell, good brother. We shall thrive, I trust.   310
    Hot. Uncle, adieu. O let the hours be short,
Till fields, and blows, and groans, applaud our sport!   *Exeunt.*

Act Second ❧ Scene First

[Rochester. The Yard of a Carriers' Inn]
Enter a Carrier with a lantern in his hand.

    1. Car. Heigh-ho! An it be not four by the day I'll be
hanged. Charles' Wain is over the new chimney, and yet our
horse not packed. What, ostler!
    Ost. [within]. Anon, anon.
    1. Car. I prithee, Tom, beat Cut's saddle, put a few flocks   5
in the point. Poor jade is wrung in the withers, out of all cess.

Enter another Carrier.

    2. Car. Peas and beans are as dank here as a dog, and that
is the next way to give poor jades the bots. This house is
turned upside down since Robin Ostler died.
    1. Car. Poor fellow never joyed since the price of oats   10
rose. It was the death of him.
    2. Car. I think this be the most villainous house in all
London road for fleas. I am stung like a tench.
    1. Car. Like a tench! by the mass there is ne'er a king christen
could be better bit than I have been since the first cock.   15

---

232 **starling:** *a bird with remarkable powers of mimicry*   236 **defy:** *renounce*   238 **sword-and-buckler:** *swashbuckler, ruffianly*   248 **pismires:** *ants*   252 **kept:** *stayed*   253 **York;** *cf. n.*   259 **candy deal:** *sugary lot*   259 **Look when:** *whenever; cf. n.*   263 **cozeners:** *swindlers*   266 **stay:** *await*   280 **Bristow:** *Bristol*   **Scroop;** *cf. n.*   281 **estimation:** *conjecture*

287 **still:** *always*   **lett'st slip:** *art letting the hounds loose from the leash*   294 **head: army**   295 **even:** *prudently*   302 **Cousin:** *kinsman*   304 **suddenly:** *very soon*   307 **happily:** *perchance, if all goes well*   **Scene First. S. d.;** *cf. n.*   2 **Charles' Wain;** *cf. n.*   5 **Cut:** *slang name for a horse with a docked tail*   **flocks:** *tufts of wool*   6 **point:** *head of the saddle*   **wrung:** *galled*   **withers:** *neck*   **out of all cess:** *beyond all reckoning*   7 **dank:** *moldy*   8 **next:** *most direct, surest*   **bots:** *disease of horses caused by worms*   13 **tench;** *cf. n.*   14 **king christen:** *Christian king*

2. Car. Why, they will allow us ne'er a jordan, and then we leak in your chimney, and your chamber-lie breeds fleas like a loach.

1. Car. What, ostler, come away and be hanged, come away!

2. Car. I have a gammon of bacon, and two razes of   20 ginger, to be delivered as far as Charing Cross.

1. Car. Godsbody! the turkeys in my pannier are quite starved. What, ostler? A plague on thee, hast thou never an eye in thy head? canst not hear? An 'twere not as good deed as drink to break the pate on thee, I am a very villain.   25 Come and be hanged! hast no faith in thee?

Enter Gadshill.

Gads. Good morrow carriers. What's o'clock?

1. Car. I think it be two o'clock.

Gads. I prithee lend me thy lantern, to see my gelding in the stable.   30

1. Car. Nay, by God, soft! I know a trick worth two of that, i' faith.

Gads. I pray thee lend me thine.

2. Car. Ay, when, canst tell? Lend me thy lantern, quoth he! Marry I'll see thee hanged first.   35

Gads. Sirrah carrier, what time do you mean to come to London?

2. Car. Time enough to go to bed with a candle, I warrant thee. Come neighbor Mugs, we'll call up the gentlemen. They will along with company, for they have great charge.   40

Exeunt [Carriers].

Enter Chamberlain.

Gads. What ho, chamberlain?

Cham. 'At hand, quoth pickpurse.'

Gads. That's even as fair as 'at hand, quoth the chamberlain.' For thou variest no more from picking of purses, than giving direction doth from laboring. Thou layest the plot how.   45

Cham. Good morrow, Master Gadshill. It holds current that I told you yesternight. There's a franklin in the wild of Kent hath brought three hundred marks with him in gold. I heard him tell it to one of his company last night at supper—a kind of auditor, one that hath abundance of charge too, God   50 knows what. They are up already, and call for eggs and butter. They will away presently.

Gads. Sirrah, if they meet not with Saint Nicholas' clerks, I'll give thee this neck.

Cham. No, I'll none of it. I pray thee keep that for the   55 hangman, for I know thou worshippest Saint Nicholas as truly as a man of falsehood may.

Gads. What talkest thou to me of the hangman? If I hang, I'll make a fat pair of gallows. For if I hang, old Sir John hangs with me, and thou knowest he is no starveling. Tut,   60 there are other Trojans that thou dream'st not of, the which for sport sake are content to do the profession some grace, that would (if matters should be looked into) for their own credit

sake make all whole. I am joined with no foot land-rakers, no long-staff sixpenny strikers, none of these mad mustachio-   65 purple-hued malt worms, but with nobility, and tranquillity, burgo-masters and great oneyers, such as can hold in, such as will strike sooner than speak, and speak sooner than drink, and drink sooner than pray. And yet, zounds, I lie, for they pray continually to their saint the commonwealth; or rather not   70 pray to her, but prey on her, for they ride up and down on her, and make her their boots.

Cham. What, the commonwealth their boots? will she hold out water in foul way?

Gads. She will, she will, justice hath liquored her. We   75 steal as in a castle, cock-sure. We have the receipt of fernseed, we walk invisible.

Cham. Nay by my faith, I think you are more beholding to the night than to fernseed for your walking invisible.

Gads. Give me thy hand. Thou shalt have a share in our   80 purchase, as I am a true man.

Cham. Nay, rather let me have it, as you are a false thief.

Gads. Go to, *homo* is a common name to all men. Bid the ostler bring my gelding out of the stable. Farewell, you muddy knave.   *Exeunt.* 85

❧ Scene Second ❧

[Gadshill. On the London-Canterbury Road]
Enter Prince, Poins, and Peto, &c.

Poins. Come, shelter, shelter! I have removed Falstaff's horse, and he frets like a gummed velvet.

Prince. Stand close.

Enter Falstaff.

Fal. Poins! Poins, and be hanged! Poins!

Prince. Peace, ye fat-kidneyed rascal! What a brawling   5 dost thou keep!

Fal. Where's Poins, Hal?

Prince. He is walked up to the top of the hill. I'll go seek him.   *[Withdraws.]*

Fal. I am accursed to rob in that thief's company. The   10 rascal hath removed my horse, and tied him I know not where. If I travel but four foot by the squire further afoot, I shall break my wind. Well, I doubt not but to die a fair death for all this, if I 'scape hanging for killing that rogue. I have forsworn his company hourly any time this two and twenty years,   15 and yet I am bewitched with the rogue's company. If the rascal have not given me medicines to make me love him, I'll be hanged. It could not be else. I have drunk medicines. Poins! Hal! a plague upon you both! Bardolph! Peto! I'll starve ere I'll rob a foot further. An 'twere not as good a deed as drink   20 to turn true man, and to leave these rogues, I am the veriest varlet that ever chewed with a tooth. Eight yards of uneven ground is threescore and ten miles afoot with me, and the stony-hearted villains know it well enough. A plague upon it when thieves can not be true one to another!   *They whistle.* 25

16 jordan: *chamber-pot* 17 your ... your: *colloquialism for 'any'* chamber-lie: *urine* 18 loach: *a fish that breeds several times a year* 20 razes: *roots* 21 Charing Cross; *cf. n.* 23 starved: *perishing of cold, probably* 28 two o'clock; *cf. n.* 40 charge: *baggage* 41 chamberlain: *servant in charge of guests' rooms* 46 holds current: *proves true* 47 franklin: *freeholder* wild: *'Weald,' an agricultural section, once wooded* 48 mark: *13s. 4d., two-thirds of a pound sterling* 53 St. Nicholas' clerks: *thieves; cf. n.* 61 Trojans: *a cant name for rioters*

64 foot land-rakers, etc.; *cf. n.* 72 boots: *booty* 75 liquored; *cf. n.* 76 as in a castle: *in perfect security* receipt of fernseed; *cf. n.* 78 beholding: *obliged* 81 purchase: *plunder* 83 homo; *cf. n.* 2 gummed velvet; *cf. n.* 3 close: *out of sight* 12 squire: *foot-rule* 17 medicines: *love potions (cf. Othello I. iii. 61)*

Whew! A plague upon you all! Give me my horse, you rogues! give me my horse and be hanged.

Prince [coming forward]. Peace, ye fatguts! Lie down, lay thine ear close to the ground, and list if thou canst hear the tread of travellers.   30

Fal. Have you any levers to lift me up again being down? 'Sblood! I'll not bear mine own flesh so far afoot again for all the coin in thy father's exchequer. What a plague mean ye to colt me thus?

Prince. Thou liest. Thou art not colted, thou art uncolted.

Fal. I prithee, good Prince, Hal, help me to my horse, good king's son.

Prince. Out, ye rogue! shall I be your ostler?

Fal. Hang thyself in thine own heir-apparent garters! If I be ta'en, I'll peach for this. An I have not ballads made on you   40 all, and sung to filthy tunes, let a cup of sack be my poison. When a jest is so forward, and afoot too, I hate it.

Enter Gadshill [and Bardolph].

Gads. Stand.

Fal. So I do, against my will.

Poins. O 'tis our setter. I know his voice. Bardolph, what   45 news?

Bard. Case ye, case ye! on with your vizards! There's money of the king's coming down the hill. 'Tis going to the king's exchequer.

Fal. You lie, ye rogue, 'tis going to the king's tavern.   50

Gads. There's enough to make us all.

Fal. To be hanged.

Prince. Sirs, you four shall front them in the narrow lane. Ned Poins and I will walk lower. If they 'scape from your encounter, then they light on us.   55

Peto. How many be there of them?

Gads. Some eight or ten.

Fal. 'Zounds! will they not rob us?

Prince. What, a coward, Sir John Paunch?

Fal. Indeed I am not John of Gaunt your grandfather,   60 but yet no coward, Hal.

Prince. Well, we leave that to the proof.

Poins. Sirrah Jack, thy horse stands behind the hedge. When thou needst him, there thou shalt find him. Farewell, and stand fast.

Fal. Now can not I strike him if I should be hanged.   65

Prince. Ned, where are our disguises?

Poins. Here, hard by. Stand close.

                                        [Prince and Poins withdraw.]

Fal. Now my masters, happy man be his dole, say I. Every man to his business.

Enter the Travellers.

Trav. Come, neighbor, the boy shall lead our horses   70 down the hill. We'll walk afoot awhile and ease our legs.

Thieves. Stand!

Trav. Jesus bless us!

Fal. Strike! down with them! cut the villains' throats! Ah, whoreson caterpillars, bacon-fed knaves, they hate us youth.   75 Down with them! fleece them!

Trav. O we are undone, both we and ours for ever!

Fal. Hang ye, gorbellied knaves, are ye undone? No, ye fat chuffs, I would your store were here! On, bacons, on! What,   80 ye knaves, young men must live. You are grand-jurors, are ye? We'll jure ye, i' faith.

                              Here they rob them and bind them. Exeunt.

Enter the Prince and Poins.

Prince. The thieves have bound the true men. Now could thou and I rob the thieves, and go merrily to London, it would be argument for a week, laughter for a month, and   85 a good jest for ever.

Poins. Stand close. I hear them coming.

Enter the thieves again.

Fal. Come my masters, let us share, and then to horse before day. An the Prince and Poins be not two arrant cowards there's no equity stirring. There's no more valor in that   90 Poins, than in a wild duck.

Prince. Your money!

Poins. Villains!

As they are sharing, the Prince and Poins set upon them. They all run away, and Falstaff after a blow or two runs away too, leaving the booty behind them.

Prince. Got with much ease. Now merrily to horse. The thieves are all scatter'd, and possess'd with fear   95 So strongly, that they dare not meet each other. Each takes his fellow for an officer. Away, good Ned. Falstaff sweats to death And lards the lean earth as he walks along. Were 't not for laughing I should pity him.   100

Poins. How the fat rogue roar'd!   *Exeunt.*

❧ Scene Third ❧

[Warkworth Castle, Northumberland]
Enter Hotspur, solus, reading a letter.

But for mine own part, my lord, I could be well contented to be there, in respect of the love I bear your house.

He could be contented! Why is he not then? In the respect of the love he bears our house! He shows in this, he loves his own barn better than he loves our house. Let me see some more.

The purpose you undertake is dangerous—

Why, that's certain. 'Tis dangerous to take a cold, to sleep,   5 to drink. But I tell you, my lord fool, out of this nettle danger, we pluck this flower safety.

The purpose you undertake is dangerous, the friends you have named uncertain, the time itself unsorted, and your whole plot too light, for the counterpoise of so great an opposition.

Say you so? say you so? I say unto you again, you are a shallow cowardly hind, and you lie. What a lack-brain is this! By the Lord our plot is a good plot as ever was laid, our friends true and

35 **colt:** *make a fool of*   39 **heir-apparent garters;** *cf. n.*   40 **peach:** *turn informer*   42 **forward:** *bold*   45 **setter:** *the one who set the match; cf. I. ii. 92*   47 **Case ye:** *put on your masks*   60 **John of Gaunt;** *cf. n.*   62 **proof:** *test*   68 **happy man be his dole:** *happiness be his portion, or, luck be with us*   75 **whoreson:** *miserable*

79 **gorbellied:** *fat-paunched*   80 **chuffs:** *misers* **bacons:** *rustics*   82 **jure:** *a verb of Falstaff's own making*   85 **argument:** *subject for conversation*   90 **no equity stirring:** *no such thing as fair judgment* **SCENE THIRD. S.d.;** *cf. n.*   9 **unsorted:** *ill-chosen*   12 **hind:** *servant, slave*

constant! a good plot, good friends, and full of expectation! an excellent plot, very good friends! What a frosty-spirited rogue is this! Why, my lord of York commends the plot, and the general course of the action. 'Zounds! an I were now by this rascal I could brain him with his lady's fan. Is there not my father, my uncle, and myself? Lord Edmund Mortimer, my lord of York, and Owen Glendower? Is there not besides the Douglas? Have I not all their letters to meet me in arms by the ninth of the next month, and are they not some of them set forward already? What a pagan rascal is this, an infidel! Ha! You shall see now in very sincerity of fear and cold heart will he to the king and lay open all our proceedings. O, I could divide myself, and go to buffets, for moving such a dish of skim milk with so honorable an action. Hang him, let him tell the king! We are prepared. I will set forward to-night.

Enter his Lady.

How now, Kate! I must leave you within these two hours.
 Lady P. O my good lord, why are you thus alone?
For what offence have I this fortnight been
A banish'd woman from my Harry's bed?   *30*
Tell me sweet lord, what is't that takes from thee
Thy stomach, pleasure, and thy golden sleep?
Why dost thou bend thine eyes upon the earth,
And start so often when thou sitt'st alone?
Why hast thou lost the fresh blood in thy cheeks,   *35*
And given my treasures and my rights of thee
To thick-eyed musing, and curst melancholy?
In thy faint slumbers I by thee have watch'd,
And heard thee murmur tales of iron wars,
Speak terms of manage to thy bounding steed,   *40*
Cry 'Courage! to the field!' And thou hast talk'd
Of sallies and retires, of trenches, tents,
Of palisadoes, frontiers, parapets,
Of basilisks, of cannon, culverin,
Of prisoners' ransom, and of soldiers slain,   *45*
And all the currents of a heady fight.
Thy spirit within thee hath been so at war,
And thus hath so bestirr'd thee in thy sleep,
That beads of sweat have stood upon thy brow
Like bubbles in a late-disturbed stream;   *50*
And in thy face strange motions have appear'd,
Such as we see when men restrain their breath,
On some great sudden hest. O what portents are these?
Some heavy business hath my lord in hand,
And I must know it. Else he loves me not.   *55*
 Hot. What ho! *[Enter Servant.]* Is Gilliams with the packet gone?
 Serv. He is, my lord, an hour ago.
 Hot. Hath Butler brought those horses from the sheriff?
 Serv. One horse, my lord, he brought even now.   *60*
 Hot. What horse? a roan? a crop-ear is it not?
 Serv. It is, my lord.
 Hot.   That roan shall be my throne.
Well, I will back him straight. O, *Esperance!*

Bid Butler lead him forth into the park. *[Exit Servant.]* *65*
 Lady P. But hear you, my lord.
 Hot. What sayst thou, my lady?
 Lady P. What is it carries you away?
 Hot. Why, my horse (my love), my horse.
 Lady P. Out, you mad-headed ape!   *70*
A weasel hath not such a deal of spleen
As you are toss'd with. In faith
I'll know your business, Harry, that I will.
I fear my brother Mortimer doth stir
About his title, and hath sent for you   *75*
To line his enterprise. But if you go—
 Hot. So far afoot, I shall be weary, love.
 Lady P. Come, come, you paraquito! answer me
Directly unto this question that I ask.
In faith I'll break thy little finger, Harry,   *80*
An if thou wilt not tell me all things true.
 Hot. Away,
Away, you trifler! Love, I love thee not.
I care not for thee, Kate. This is no world
To play with mammets and to tilt with lips.   *85*
We must have bloody noses, and crack'd crowns,
And pass them current too. God's me, my horse!
What sayst thou, Kate? what wouldst thou have with me?
 Lady P. Do you not love me? do you not indeed?
Well, do not then, for since you love me not   *90*
I will not love myself. Do you not love me?
Nay, tell me if you speak in jest or no.
 Hot. Come, wilt thou see me ride?
And when I am o' horseback I will swear
I love thee infinitely. But hark you Kate,   *95*
I must not have you henceforth question me
Whither I go, nor reason whereabout.
Whither I must, I must. And to conclude,
This evening must I leave you, gentle Kate.
I know you wise, but yet no farther wise   *100*
Than Harry Percy's wife. Constant you are,
But yet a woman; and for secrecy
No lady closer, for I well believe
Thou wilt not utter what thou dost not know,
And so far will I trust thee, gentle Kate.   *105*
 Lady P. How! so far?
 Hot. Not an inch further. But hark you Kate;
Whither I go, thither shall you go too.
To-day will I set forth, to-morrow you.
Will this content you, Kate?   *110*
 Lady P.   It must, of force. *Exeunt.*

❧ Scene Fourth ❧

[The Boar's Head Tavern, Eastcheap, London]
Enter Prince and Poins.

 Prince. Ned, prithee come out of that fat room, and lend me thy hand to laugh a little.
 Poins. Where hast been, Hal?
 Prince. With three or four loggerheads, amongst three or

---

23 **divide myself;** *cf. n.* 27 **Kate;** *cf. n.* 32 **stomach:** *appetite* 36, 37 *Cf. n.* 37 **curst:** *perverse* 40 **manage:** *direction* 42 **retires:** *retreats* 43 **palisadoes:** *sharp stakes driven into the ground as defence against cavalry* **frontiers:** *outworks; cf. I. iii. 19* 44 **basilisks;** *cf. n.* 46 **currents:** *drifts, movements* **heady:** *headlong* 53 **hest:** *command* 64 **Esperance:** *the motto of the Percy family*

71 **spleen:** *caprice* 76 **line:** *strengthen* 85 **mammets:** *dolls* 86 **crack'd crowns;** *cf. n.* 1 **fat:** *close, stuffy; cf. n.*

four score hogsheads. I have sounded the very bass-string of   5
humility. Sirrah, I am sworn brother to a leash of drawers, and
can call them all by their christen names, as Tom, Dick, and
Francis. They take it already upon their salvation, that though
I be but Prince of Wales, yet I am the king of courtesy, and
tell me flatly I am no proud Jack like Falstaff, but a Corin-   10
thian, a lad of mettle, a good boy (by the Lord so they call
me), and when I am King of England I shall command all the
good lads in Eastcheap. They call drinking deep 'dyeing scarlet,' and when you breathe in your watering they cry 'hem!'
and bid you play it off. To conclude, I am so good a profi-   15
cient in one quarter of an hour that I can drink with any tinker in his own language, during my life. I tell thee, Ned, thou
hast lost much honor, that thou wert not with me in this action. But sweet Ned—to sweeten which name of Ned, I give
thee this pennyworth of sugar, clapped even now into my   20
hand by an underskinker, one that never spake other English
in his life than 'Eight shillings and six-pence,' and 'You are welcome,' with this shrill addition, 'Anon, anon, sir!' 'Score a pint
of bastard in the Half-moon,' or so. But Ned, to drive away
the time till Falstaff come, I prithee do thou stand in some   25
by-room, while I question my puny drawer to what end he
gave me the sugar, and do thou never leave calling 'Francis!'
that his tale to me may be nothing but 'Anon.' Step aside and
I'll show thee a precedent.

Poins. Francis!   30

Prince. Thou art perfect.— *[Exit Poins.]* Francis!

Enter Drawer [Francis].

Fran. Anon, anon, sir. Look down into the Pomgarnet,
Ralph.

Prince. Come hither, Francis.

Fran. My lord.   35

Prince. How long hast thou to serve, Francis?

Fran. Forsooth, five years, and as much as to—

Poins [within]. Francis!

Fran. Anon, anon, sir.

Prince. Five years! by'r lady a long lease for the clinking   40
of pewter; but Francis, darest thou be so valiant, as to play
the coward with thy indenture, and show it a fair pair of
heels, and run from it?

Fran. O Lord, sir! I'll be sworn upon all the books in
England, I could find in my heart—   45

Poins [within]. Francis!

Fran. Anon, sir.

Prince. How old art thou, Francis?

Fran. Let me see—about Michaelmas next I shall be—

Poins [within]. Francis!   50

Fran. Anon, sir. Pray stay a little, my lord.

Prince. Nay but hark you, Francis. For the sugar thou
gavest me—'twas a pennyworth, was't not?

Fran. O Lord, I would it had been two.

Prince. I will give thee for it a thousand pound. Ask me   55
when thou wilt, and thou shalt have it.

Poins [within]. Francis!

Fran. Anon, anon.

Prince. Anon, Francis? No, Francis, but to-morrow, Francis.
Or, Francis, o' Thursday. Or indeed, Francis, when thou   60
wilt. But Francis!

Fran. My lord?

Prince. Wilt thou rob this leathern-jerkin, crystal-button,
not-pated, agate-ring, puke-stocking, caddis-garter, smooth-
tongue, Spanish-pouch—   65

Fran. O Lord sir, who do you mean?

Prince. Why then, your brown bastard is your only drink.
For look you, Francis, your white canvas doublet will sully.
In Barbary, sir, it cannot come to so much.

Fran. What, sir?   70

Poins [within]. Francis!

Prince. Away, you rogue! Dost thou not hear them call?

*Here they both call him. The Drawer stands amazed, not
knowing which way to go.*

Enter Vintner.

Vint. What! stand'st thou still, and hear'st such a calling?
Look to the guests within.   *[Exit Francis.]*
My lord, old Sir John with half a dozen more are at the   75
door. Shall I let them in?

Prince. Let them alone awhile, and then open the door.
[Exit Vintner.] Poins!

Poins [within]. Anon, anon, sir.

Enter Poins.

Prince. Sirrah, Falstaff and the rest of the thieves are at   80
the door. Shall we be merry?

Poins. As merry as crickets, my lad. But hark ye, what cunning match have you made with this jest of the drawer? Come,
what's the issue?

Prince. I am now of all humors, that have showed them-   85
selves humors since the old days of goodman Adam to the
pupil age of this present twelve o'clock at midnight. *[Francis
crosses the stage.]* What's o'clock, Francis?

Fran. Anon, anon, sir.   *[Exit.]*

Prince. That ever this fellow should have fewer words   90
than a parrot, and yet the son of a woman! His industry is up-
stairs and down-stairs, his eloquence the parcel of a reckoning.
I am not yet of Percy's mind, the Hotspur of the North, he
that kills me some six or seven dozen of Scots at a breakfast,
washes his hands, and says to his wife, 'Fie upon this quiet   95
life! I want work.' 'O my sweet Harry,' says she, 'how many
hast thou killed to-day?' 'Give my roan horse a drench,' says
he, and answers, 'Some fourteen,' and hour after, 'a trifle, a trifle.' I prithee call in Falstaff. I'll play Percy, and that damned
brawn shall play Dame Mortimer his wife. 'Rivo!' says the   100
drunkard. Call in Ribs, call in Tallow.

*Enter Falstaff, [Bardolph, Peto, and Gadshill. The Drawer follows
with wine].*

Poins. Welcome, Jack! Where hast thou been?

Fal. A plague of all cowards I say, and a vengeance too!

---

6 **leash:** *three on a string* **drawers:** *waiters*   8 **take it . . . upon:** *swear by*   10, 11
Corinthian: *gay fellow*   14 **breathe . . . watering:** *stop to breathe while drinking*   15
play: *toss*   16, 17 **tinker;** *cf. n.*   21 **underskinker:** *under-tapster*   24 **bastard:** *sweet
Spanish wine* **Half-moon:** *name of a room in the inn*   29 **precedent:** *example*   32
Pomgarnet: *'Pomegranate,' a room in the inn*   36 **to serve:** *i.e., as apprentice to the Vint-
ner*   42 **indenture:** *contract*   49 **Michaelmas;** *cf. n.*

64 **not-pated:** *nut-pated, with closely cropped head* **puke:** *dark-colored and woolen* **caddis:**
cheap yarn   67 **ff.;** *cf. n.*   83 **match:** *game*   87 **pupil age:** *mere child's age*   92
parcel of a reckoning: *an item on a bill*   93 **not yet of Percy's mind;** *cf. n.*   97
drench: *bran and water*   100 **brawn:** *fattened pig* **'Rivo':** *a Spanish (?). exclamation of
drunkards*

marry and amen! Give me a cup of sack, boy. Ere I lead this
life long I'll sew nether-stocks and mend them, and foot   105
them too. A plague of all cowards! Give me a cup of sack,
rogue.—Is there no virtue extant?   *He drinketh.*

Prince. Didst thou never see Titan kiss a dish of butter—
pitiful-hearted Titan—that melted at the sweet tale of the
sun's? If thou didst, then behold that compound.   110

Fal. You rogue, here's lime in this sack too. There is
nothing but roguery to be found in villainous man. Yet a
coward is worse than a cup of sack with lime in it, a villainous coward! Go thy ways, old Jack; die when thou wilt. If
manhood, good manhood, be not forgot upon the face of
the earth, then am I a shotten herring. There lives not three
good men unhanged in England, and one of them is fat,
and grows old. God help the while! a bad world I say. I
would I were a weaver. I could sing psalms, or anything.
A plague of all cowards I say still.   120

Prince. How now wool-sack! what mutter you?

Fal. A king's son! If I do not beat thee out of thy kingdom
with a dagger of lath, and drive all thy subjects afore thee like
a flock of wild geese, I'll never wear hair on my face more.
You Prince of Wales!   125

Prince. Why you whoreson round man, what's the matter?

Fal. Are not you a coward? Answer me to that. And Poins
there?

Poins. 'Zounds ye fat paunch, an ye call me coward, by
the Lord I'll stab thee.   130

Fal. I call thee coward? I'll see thee damned ere I call thee
coward, but I would give a thousand pound I could run as fast
as thou canst. You are straight enough in the shoulders, you care
not who sees your back. Call you that backing of your friends? A
plague upon such backing! give me them that will face me.   135
Give me a cup of sack. I am a rogue if I drunk to-day.

Prince. O villain! thy lips are scarce wiped since thou
drunk'st last.

Fal. All is one for that. A plague of all cowards, still say I.
          He drinketh.

Prince. What's the matter?   140

Fal. What's the matter? there be four of us here have ta'en
a thousand pound this day morning.

Prince. Where is it, Jack? where is it?

Fal. Where is it? Taken from us it is. A hundred upon
poor four of us.   145

Prince. What, a hundred, man?

Fal. I am a rogue if I were not at half-sword with a dozen
of them two hours together. I have 'scap'd by miracle. I am
eight times thrust through the doublet, four through the hose,
my buckler cut through and through, my sword hacked like
a handsaw: *ecce signum!* I never dealt better since I was a man.
All would not do. A plague of all cowards! Let them speak. If
they speak more or less than truth, they are villains, and the
sons of darkness.

Prince. Speak, sirs. How was it?   155

Gads. We four set upon some dozen—

Fal. Sixteen at least, my lord.

Gads. And bound them.

Peto. No, no, they were not bound.

Fal. You rogue, they were bound, every man of them,   160
or I am a Jew else, an Ebrew Jew.

Gads. As we were sharing, some six or seven fresh men
set upon us—

Fal. And unbound the rest, and then come in the other.

Prince. What, fought you with them all?   165

Fal. All? I know not what you call all, but if I fought not
with fifty of them I am a bunch of radish. If there were not
two or three and fifty upon poor old Jack, then am I no
two-legg'd creature.

Prince. Pray God you have not murdered some of them.   170

Fal. Nay, that's past praying for. I have peppered two of
them. Two I am sure I have paid, two rogues in buckram
suits. I tell thee what, Hal, if I tell thee a lie, spit in my face,
call me horse. Thou knowest my old ward. Here I lay, and
thus I bore my point. Four rogues in buckram let drive at   175
me—

Prince. What, four? Thou saidst but two even now.

Fal. Four, Hal. I told thee four.

Poins. Ay, ay, he said four.

Fal. These four came all a-front, and mainly thrust at   180
me. I made me no more ado, but took all their seven points
in my target, thus.

Prince. Seven? Why, there were but four even now.

Fal. In buckram?

Poins. Ay, four in buckram suits.   185

Fal. Seven, by these hilts, or I am a villain else.

Prince. Prithee let him alone. We shall have more anon.

Fal. Dost thou hear me, Hal?

Prince. Ay, and mark thee too, Jack.

Fal. Do so, for it is worth the listening to. These nine   190
in buckram that I told thee of—

Prince. So, two more already.

Fal. Their points being broken—

Poins. Down fell their hose.

Fal. Began to give me ground. But I followed me close,   195
came in, foot and hand, and with a thought, seven of the
eleven I paid.

Prince. O monstrous! Eleven buckram men grown out of
two.

Fal. But as the devil would have it, three misbegotten   200
knaves in Kendal green came at my back, and let drive at
me—for it was so dark, Hal, that thou couldst not see thy
hand.

Prince. These lies are like their father that begets them,
gross as a mountain, open, palpable. Why thou clay-brained
guts, thou knotty-pated fool, thou whoreson obscene greasy
tallow-catch—

Fal. What, art thou mad? art thou mad? Is not the truth
the truth?

Prince. Why, how couldst thou know these men in Kendal
green, when it was so dark thou couldst not see thy hand?
Come, tell us your reason. What sayest thou to this?

Poins. Come, your reason, Jack, your reason.

Fal. What, upon compulsion? 'Zounds! an I were at the
strappado, or all the racks in the world, I would not tell   215

104 **nether-stocks:** *stockings*   107 **virtue:** *courage*   109 **Titan, etc.;** *cf. n.*   109–10
sweet . . . sun's; *cf. n.*   116 **shotten herring:** *a herring that has cast its roe*   119 **weaver;**
cf. n.   147 **at half-sword:** *at close quarters*   151 **ecce signum:** *behold the
proof*   155–63 *Cf. n.*

164 **other:** *others*   172 **paid:** *killed*   174 **ward:** *fencer's posture of defence*   180 **mainly:**
strongly (cf. might and main)   182 **target:** *shield*   186 **these hilts:** *the cross-hilt of his
sword*   193 **points;** *cf. n.*   201 **Kendal green;** *cf. n.*   206 **knotty-pated:** *thick-
headed*   206–07 **tallow-catch:** *lump of tallow* (tallow-keech)? *tub of tallow* (tallow-
ketch)?   215 **strappado;** *cf. n.*

you on compulsion. Give you a reason on compulsion?
If reasons were as plentiful as blackberries, I would give no
man a reason upon compulsion, I.

Prince. I'll be no longer guilty of this sin. This sanguine
coward, this bed-presser, this horse-backbreaker, this huge   220
hill of flesh—

Fal. 'Sblood, you starveling, you elf-skin, you dried neat's-
tongue, you bull's pizzle, you stockfish! O for breath to utter
what is like thee, you tailor's yard, you sheath, you bowcase,
you vile standing-tuck—   225

Prince. Well, breathe awhile, and then to it again, and
when thou hast tired thyself in base comparisons, hear me
speak but this.

Poins. Mark, Jack.

Prince. We two saw you four set on four, and [you] bound
them and were masters of their wealth. Mark now how a plain
tale shall put you down. Then did we two set on you four
and, with a word, outfaced you from your prize, and have it,
yea, and can show it you here in the house. And Falstaff, you
carried your guts away as nimbly, with as quick dexterity, and
roared for mercy, and still run and roared, as ever I heard bullcalf. What a slave art thou to hack thy sword as thou hast
done, and then say it was in fight! What trick, what device,
what starting-hole canst thou now find out, to hide thee from
this open and apparent shame?   240

Poins. Come, let's hear, Jack. What trick hast thou now?

Fal. By the Lord, I knew ye as well as he that made ye.
Why, hear you, my masters. Was it for me to kill the heir-
apparent? Should I turn upon the true prince? Why, thou
knowest I am as valiant as Hercules: but beware instinct,   245
the lion will not touch the true prince. Instinct is a great matter. I was now a coward on instinct. I shall think the better of
myself and thee during my life; I for a valiant lion, and thou
for a true prince. But by the Lord, lads, I am glad you have
the money. Hostess, clap to the doors, watch to-night, pray   250
to-morrow. Gallants, lads, boys, hearts of gold, all the titles of
good fellowship come to you! What, shall we be merry? shall
we have a play extempore?

Prince. Content. And the argument shall be thy running
away.   255

Fal. Ah! no more of that, Hal, an thou lovest me!

Enter Hostess.

Host. O Jesu, my lord the prince!

Prince. How now my lady the hostess! what say'st thou
to me?

Host. Marry my lord, there is a nobleman of the court   260
at door would speak with you. He says he comes from your
father.

Prince. Give him as much as will make him a royal man,
and send him back again to my mother.

Fal. What manner of man is he?   265

Host. An old man.

Fal. What doth gravity out of his bed at midnight? Shall
I give him his answer?

Prince. Prithee do, Jack.

Fal. Faith, and I'll send him packing.   *Exit.* 270

Prince. Now sirs, by'r lady you fought fair. So did you,
Peto, so did you, Bardolph. You are lions too, you ran away
upon instinct, you will not touch the true prince; no, fie!

Bard. Faith, I ran when I saw others run.

Prince. Faith, tell me now in earnest, how came   275
Falstaff's sword so hacked?

Peto. Why, he hacked it with his dagger, and said he would
swear truth out of England, but he would make you believe it
was done in fight, and persuaded us to do the like.

Bard. Yea, and to tickle our noses with speargrass, to make
them bleed, and then to beslubber our garments with it, and
swear it was the blood of true men. I did that I did not this
seven year before, I blushed to hear his monstrous devices.

Prince. O villain! thou stolest a cup of sack eighteen years
ago and wert taken with the manner, and ever since thou hast
blushed extempore. Thou hadst fire and sword on thy side,
and yet thou ranst away; what instinct hadst thou for it?

Bard. [*pointing to his own face*]. My lord, do you see these
meteors? Do you behold these exhalations?

Prince. I do.   290

Bard. What think you they portend?

Prince. Hot livers, and cold purses.

Bard. Choler, my lord, if rightly taken.

Prince. No, if rightly taken, halter.

Enter Falstaff.

Here comes lean Jack, here comes Barebone. How now   295
my sweet creature of bombast! How long is't ago, Jack, since
thou sawest thine own knee?

Fal. My own knee! When I was about thy years, Hal, I was
not an eagle's talon in the waist. I could have crept into any
alderman's thumb-ring. A plague of sighing and grief! it blows
a man up like a bladder. There's villainous news abroad. Here
was Sir John Bracy from your father. You must to the court in
the morning. That same mad fellow of the North, Percy, and
he of Wales that gave Amamon the bastinado and made Lucifer cuckold, and swore the devil his true liegeman upon   305
the cross of a Welsh hook—what a plague call you him?

Poins. O, Glendower.

Fal. Owen, Owen, the same; and his son-in-law Mortimer,
and old Northumberland, and that sprightly Scot of Scots,
Douglas, that runs a-horseback up a hill perpendicular.   310

Prince. He that rides at high speed, and with his pistol
kills a sparrow flying.

Fal. You have hit it.

Prince. So did he never the sparrow.

Fal. Well, that rascal hath good mettle in him. He will   315
not run.

Prince. Why, what a rascal art thou then, to praise him
so for running!

Fal. A-horseback, ye cuckoo; but afoot he will not budge
a foot.   320

Prince. Yes, Jack, upon instinct.

Fal. I grant ye, upon instinct. Well, he is there too, and one
Mordake, and a thousand bluecaps more. Worcester is stolen
away to-night. Thy father's beard is turned white with the news.
You may buy land now as cheap as stinking mackerel.   325

---

216 reasons: *cf. n.*   **219 sanguine:** *red-faced*   **222–23 neat's-tongue:** *ox tongue*   **223
stockfish:** *dried cod*   **225 standing-tuck:** *small rapier standing on end*   **233 outfaced:** *frightened*   **239 starting-hole:** *subterfuge* (hunted animal's shelter)   **242 I knew ye:** *cf. n.*   **263
royal:** *cf. n.*

285 taken … manner: *taken in the act*   **288–94** *Cf. n.*   **289 exhalations:** *meteors*   **293
rightly taken:** *correctly diagnosed*   **294 rightly taken:** *justly arrested*   **296 bombast:** *cotton
stuffing*   **304 Amamon:** *a devil; cf. n.*   **bastinado:** *a cudgelling*   **306 Welsh hook:** *weapon
resembling a halberd*   **323 bluecaps:** *Scots* (so called from their blue bonnets)

Prince. Why then, it is like if there come a hot June, and this civil buffeting hold, we shall buy maidenheads as they buy hobnails, by the hundreds.

Fal. By the mass, lad, thou sayest true. It is like we shall 330 have good trading that way. But tell me, Hal, art not thou horrible afeard? Thou being heir-apparent, could the world pick thee out three such enemies again as that fiend Douglas, that spirit Percy, and that devil Glendower? Art thou not horribly afraid? doth not thy blood thrill at it? 335

Prince. Not a whit, i' faith. I lack some of thy instinct.

Fal. Well, thou wilt be horribly chid to-morrow when thou comest to thy father. If thou love me, practise an answer.

Prince. Do thou stand for my father and examine me upon the particulars of my life. 340

Fal. Shall I? Content. This chair shall be my state, this dagger my scepter, and this cushion my crown.

Prince. Thy state is taken for a joined-stool, thy golden scepter for a leaden dagger, and thy precious rich crown for a pitiful bald crown. 345

Fal. Well, an the fire of grace be not quite out of thee, now shalt thou be moved. Give me a cup of sack to make my eyes look red, that it may be thought I have wept, for I must speak in passion, and I will do it in King Cambyses' vein.

Prince. Well, here is my leg. 350

Fal. And here is my speech. Stand aside, nobility.

Host. O Jesu! This is excellent sport, i' faith!

Fal. Weep not, sweet queen, for trickling tears are vain.

Host. O, the father! how he holds his countenance!

Fal. For God's sake, lords, convey my tristful queen, 355
For tears do stop the floodgates of her eyes.

Host. O Jesu, he doth it as like one of these harlotry players as ever I see!

Fal. Peace, good pintpot, peace, good tickle-brain.

[Bardolph conveys the Hostess from the stage.]

— Harry, I do not only marvel where thou spendest thy time, but also how thou are accompanied. For though the camomile, the more it is trodden on, the faster it grows, yet youth, the more it is wasted, the sooner it wears. That thou art my son, I have partly thy mother's word, partly my own opinion, but chiefly a villainous trick of thine eye, and a foolish hanging 365 of thy nether lip, that doth warrant me. If then thou be son to me, here lies the point: why, being son to me, art thou so pointed at? Shall the blessed sun of heaven prove a micher, and eat blackberries? A question not to be asked. Shall the son of England prove a thief, and take purses? A question to be asked. There is a thing, Harry, which thou hast often heard of, and it is known to many in our land by the name of pitch. This pitch (as ancient writers do report) doth defile; so doth the company thou keepest. For, Harry, now I do not speak to thee in drink, but in tears; not in pleasure, but in passion; 375 not in words only, but in woes also. And yet there is a virtuous man, whom I have often noted in thy company, but I know not his name.

Prince. What manner of man, an it like your Majesty?

Fal. A goodly portly man, i' faith, and a corpulent; of a 380 cheerful look, a pleasing eye, and a most noble carriage; and as I think, his age some fifty, or by'r lady inclining to threescore. And now I remember me, his name is Falstaff. If that man should be lewdly given, he deceiveth me. For, Harry, I see virtue in his looks. If then the tree may be known by the fruit, as the fruit by the tree, then peremptorily I speak it, there is virtue in that Falstaff. Him keep with, the rest banish. And tell me now thou naughty varlet, tell me where hast thou been this month?

Prince. Dost thou speak like a king? Do thou stand for me, and I'll play my father. 390

Fal. Depose me? If thou dost it half so gravely, so majestically, both in word and matter, hang me up by the heels for a rabbit-sucker, or a poulter's hare.

Prince. Well, here I am set.

Fal. And here I stand. Judge, my masters. 395

Prince. Now Harry, whence come you?

Fal. My noble lord, from Eastcheap.

Prince. The complaints I hear of thee are grievous.

Fal. 'Sblood, my lord, they are false! *[Aside to Prince.]*
Nay, I'll tickle ye for a young prince, i' faith. 400

Prince. Swearest thou, ungracious boy? Henceforth ne'er look on me. Thou art violently carried away from grace. There is a devil haunts thee in the likeness of an old fat man, a tun of man is thy companion. Why dost thou converse with that trunk of humors, that bolting-hutch of beastliness, that 405 swoln parcel of dropsies, that huge bombard of sack, that stuffed cloak-bag of guts, that roasted Manningtree ox with the pudding in his belly, that reverend vice, that grey iniquity, that father ruffian, that vanity in years? Wherein is he good, but to taste sack and drink it? wherein neat and cleanly, but to 410 carve a capon and eat it? wherein cunning, but in craft? wherein crafty, but in villainy? wherein villainous, but in all things? wherein worthy, but in nothing?

Fal. I would your Grace would take me with you. Whom means your Grace? 415

Prince. That villainous abominable misleader of youth, Falstaff, that old white-bearded Satan.

Fal. My lord, the man I know.

Prince. I know thou dost.

Fal. But to say I know more harm in him than in myself, were to say more than I know. That he is old, the more the pity, his white hairs do witness it; but that he is (saving your reverence) a whoremaster, that I utterly deny. If sack and sugar be a fault, God help the wicked! If to be old and merry be a sin, then many an old host that I know is damned. If to 425 be fat be to be hated, then Pharaoh's lean kine are to be loved. No, my good lord, banish Peto, banish Bardolph, banish Poins; but for sweet Jack Falstaff, kind Jack Falstaff, true Jack Falstaff, valiant Jack Falstaff, and therefore more valiant, being, as he is, old Jack Falstaff—banish not him thy Harry's company, 430 banish not him thy Harry's company. Banish plump Jack, and banish all the world.

Prince. I do, I will.

Enter Bardolph running.

Bard. O my lord, my lord! the sheriff with a most monstrous watch is at the door. 435

---

341 state: *throne of state*   **349 passion:** *deep feeling*   **Cambyses':** *cf. n.*   **350 leg:** *bow*   **354 the father:** *i.e., Falstaff in the role of father*   **355 tristful:** *sorrowful*   **357 harlotry:** *rascally*   **359 tickle-brain:** *a strong liquor; cf. n.*   **360 ff.;** *Cf. n.*   **361 camomile:** *a strong-scented herb*   **366 nether:** *lower*   **368 micher:** *truant*

393 *Cf. n.*   **400** *Cf. n.*   **401 Henceforth, etc.;** *cf. n.*   **405 trunk of humors:** *chest full of infirmities* **bolting-hutch:** *bin for sifting meal*   **406 bombard:** *large leather vessel for holding liquor*   **407 cloak-bag:** *portmanteau* **Manningtree:** *cf. n.*   **414 take me with you:** *let me follow your meaning*   **422–23 saving . . . reverence:** *an apologetic phrase introducing a remark that might offend the hearer*   **426 Pharaoh's lean kine;** *cf. n.*   **430 banish not him, etc.;** *cf. n.*

Fal. Out ye rogue! Play out the play. I have much
to say in the behalf of that Falstaff.

               Enter the Hostess.

    Host. O Jesu, my lord, my lord!
    Prince. Heigh, heigh! the devil rides upon a fiddlestick.
What's the matter?   *440*
    Host. The sheriff and all the watch are at the door.
They are come to search the house. Shall I let them in?
    Fal. Dost thou hear, Hal? Never call a true piece of gold a
counterfeit. Thou art essentially mad without seeming so.
    Prince. And thou a natural coward without instinct.   *445*
    Fal. I deny your major. If you will deny the sheriff, so;
if not, let him enter. If I become not a cart as well as another
man, a plague on my bringing up! I hope I shall as soon be
strangled with a halter as another.
    Prince. Go hide thee behind the arras. The rest walk up   *450*
above. Now my masters, for a true face and good conscience.
    Fal. Both which I have had, but their date is out, and
therefore I'll hide me.   *Exit.*
    Prince. Call in the sheriff.

         Enter Sheriff and the Carrier.

Now master sheriff, what is your will with me?   *455*
    Sher. First pardon me, my lord. A hue and cry
Hath follow'd certain men unto this house.
    Prince. What men?
    Sher. One of them is well known, my gracious lord,
A gross fat man.   *460*
    Car.   As fat as butter.
    Prince. The man, I do assure you, is not here,
For I myself at this time have employ'd him.
And sheriff, I will engage my word to thee,
That I will by to-morrow dinner-time   *465*
Send him to answer thee or any man,
For anything he shall be charg'd withal.
And so let me entreat you leave the house.
    Sher. I will, my lord. There are two gentlemen
Have in this robbery lost three hundred marks.   *470*
    Prince. It may be so. If he have robb'd these men
He shall be answerable. And so farewell.
    Sher. Good night, my noble lord.
    Prince. I think it is good morrow, is it not?
    Sher. Indeed, my lord, I think it be two o'clock.   *475*
                           Exit [with Carrier].
    Prince. This oily rascal is known as well as Paul's.
Go call him forth.
    Peto. Falstaff!—Fast asleep behind the arras, and snorting
like a horse.
    Prince. Hark, how hard he fetches breath. Search his   *480*
pockets.

    He searcheth his pocket, and findeth certain papers.

What hast thou found?
    Peto. Nothing but papers, my lord.
    Prince. Let's see what they be. Read them.

    Peto.   *485*

Item, a capon	2s.	2d.
Item, sauce		4d.
Item, sack, two gallons	5s.	8d.
Item, anchovies and sack after supper	2s.	6d.
Item, bread		ob.

    Prince. O monstrous! but one halfpenny-worth of   *490*
bread to this intolerable deal of sack? What there is else, keep
close. We'll read it at more advantage. There let him sleep till
day. I'll to the court in the morning. We must all to the wars,
and thy place shall be honorable. I'll procure this fat rogue a
charge of foot, and I know his death will be a march of   *495*
twelve score. The money shall be paid back again with advantage.
Be with me betimes in the morning. And so good morrow, Peto.
    Peto. Good morrow, good my lord.   *Exeunt.*

ACT THIRD ❧ SCENE FIRST

[Glendower's Castle in North Wales]
Enter Hotspur, Worcester, Lord Mortimer, Owen Glendower.

    Mort. These promises are fair, the parties sure,
And our induction full of prosperous hope.
    Hot. Lord Mortimer, and Cousin Glendower,
Will you sit down?
And Uncle Worcester? A plague upon it,
I have forgot the map.   *5*
    Glend.   No, here it is.
Sit, Cousin Percy, sit, good Cousin Hotspur,
For by that name as oft as Lancaster
Doth speak of you, his cheek looks pale, and with
A rising sigh he wisheth you in heaven.   *10*
    Hot. And you in hell, as often as he hears
Owen Glendower spoke of.
    Glend. I cannot blame him; at my nativity
The front of heaven was full of fiery shapes,
Of burning cressets, and at my birth   *15*
The frame and huge foundation of the earth
Shak'd like a coward.
    Hot. Why so it would have done at the same season if your
mother's cat had but kittened, though yourself had never
been born.   *20*
    Glend. I say the earth did shake when I was born.
    Hot. And I say the earth was not of my mind,
If you suppose as fearing you it shook.
    Glend. The heavens were all on fire, the earth did tremble.
    Hot. O then th' earth shook to see the heavens on fire,   *25*
And not in fear of your nativity.
Diseased nature oftentimes breaks forth
In strange eruptions. Oft the teeming earth
Is with a kind of colic pinch'd and vex'd,
By the imprisoning of unruly wind   *30*
Within her womb, which for enlargement striving
Shakes the old beldam earth, and topples down
Steeples and mossgrown towers. At your birth

443, 444 *Cf. n.*   **446 major:** *major premise; cf. n.*   **447 cart:** *cart used for taking criminals to the gallows*   **450 arras:** *hanging screen of tapestry placed around the walls of a room*   **450, 451** *Cf. n.*   **462, 463** *Cf. n.*   **476 Paul's:** *St. Paul's Cathedral*

489 ob.: *obolus = half-penny*   **495 charge of foot:** *command of infantry*   **496 twelve score:** *240 yards of common archery range (cf. 2 Henry IV, III. ii. 43)*   **advantage:** *interest*   **2 induction:** *beginning*   **8 Lancaster:** *the king*   **15 cressets:** *beacon lights*   **31 enlargement:** *release*   **32 beldam:** *grandmother*

Our grandam earth, having this distemperature,   *35*
In passion shook.
   Glend.   Cousin, of many men
I do not bear these crossings. Give me leave
To tell you once again that at my birth
The front of heaven was full of fiery shapes,   *40*
The goats ran from the mountains, and the herds
Were strangely clamorous to the frighted fields.
These signs have mark'd me extraordinary,
And all the courses of my life do show
I am not in the roll of common men.   *45*
Where is he living, clipt in with the sea
That chides the banks of England, Scotland, Wales,
Which calls me pupil or hath read to me?
And bring him out that is but woman's son
Can trace me in the tedious ways of art,   *50*
And hold me pace in deep experiments.
   Hot. I think there's no man speaks better Welsh.
I'll to dinner.
   Mort. Peace, Cousin Percy, you will make him mad.
   Glend. I can call spirits from the vasty deep.   *55*
   Hot. Why so can I, or so can any man,
But will they come when you do call for them?
   Glend. Why I can teach you, cousin, to command
The devil.
   Hot. And I can teach thee, coz, to shame the devil,   *60*
By telling truth. Tell truth and shame the devil.
If thou have power to raise him bring him hither,
And I'll be sworn I have power to shame him hence.
O while you live tell truth and shame the devil!
   Mort. Come, come,   *65*
No more of this unprofitable chat.
   Glend. Three times hath Henry Bolingbroke made head
Against my power. Thrice from the banks of Wye
And sandy-bottom'd Severn have I sent him
Bootless home, and weather-beaten back.   *70*
   Hot. Home without boots, and in foul weather too,
How 'scapes he agues, in the devil's name?
   Glend. Come, here's the map. Shall we divide our right,
According to our threefold order ta'en?
   Mort. The archdeacon hath divided it   *75*
Into three limits very equally.
England, from Trent and Severn hitherto,
By south and east, is to my part assign'd;
All westward, Wales beyond the Severn shore,
And all the fertile land within that bound   *80*
To Owen Glendower; and, dear coz, to you
The remnant northward, lying off from Trent.
And our indentures tripartite are drawn,
Which being sealed interchangeably,
A business that this night may execute,   *85*
To-morrow, Cousin Percy, you and I
And my good Lord of Worcester will set forth
To meet your father and the Scottish power,
As is appointed us, at Shrewsbury.
My father Glendower is not ready yet,   *90*

Nor shall we need his help these fourteen days.
[To Glendower.]
Within that space you may have drawn together
Your tenants, friends, and neighboring gentlemen.
   Glend. A shorter time shall send me to you, lords,   *95*
And in my conduct shall your ladies come,
From whom you now must steal and take no leave,
For there will be a world of water shed,
Upon the parting of your wives and you.
   Hot. Methinks my moiety, north from Burton here,   *100*
In quantity equals not one of yours.
See how this river comes me cranking in,
And cuts me from the best of all my land,
A huge half-moon, a monstrous cantle out.
I'll have the current in this place damm'd up,   *105*
And here the smug and silver Trent shall run
In a new channel, fair and evenly.
It shall not wind with such a deep indent,
To rob me of so rich a bottom here.
   Glend. Not wind? it shall! it must! You see it doth.   *110*
   Mort. Yea, but
Mark how he bears his course, and runs me up
With like advantage on the other side,
Gelding the opposed continent as much
As on the other side it takes from you.   *115*
   Wor. Yea, but a little charge will trench him here,
And on this north side win this cape of land,
And then he runs straight and even.
   Hot. I'll have it so. A little charge will do it.
   Glend. I'll not have it alter'd.   *120*
   Hot.   Will not you?
   Glend. No, nor you shall not.
   Hot.   Who shall say me nay?
   Glend. Why that will I.
   Hot.   Let me not understand you then.
Speak it in Welsh.
   Glend. I can speak English, lord, as well as you,
For I was train'd up in the English court,
Where, being but young, I framed to the harp
Many an English ditty lovely well,   *130*
And gave the tongue a helpful ornament,
A virtue that was never seen in you.
   Hot. Marry,
And I am glad of it with all my heart.
I had rather be a kitten and cry mew,   *135*
Than one of these same meter ballet-mongers.
I had rather hear a brazen canstick turn'd,
Or a dry wheel grate on the axletree,
And that would set my teeth nothing on edge,
Nothing so much as mincing poetry;   *140*
'Tis like the forc'd gait of a shuffling nag.
   Glend. Come, you shall have Trent turn'd.
   Hot. I do not care. I'll give thrice so much land
To any well-deserving friend.
But in the way of bargain, mark ye me,   *145*
I'll cavil on the ninth part of a hair.
Are the indentures drawn? Shall we be gone?

---

36 passion: *pain*   **46 clipt in with:** *surrounded by*   **47 chides:** *lashes*   **48 read to:**
instructed   **50 trace:** *follow*   **art:** *magic*   **70 Bootless:** *without advantage; cf. I. i. 29*   **75
The archdeacon;** *cf. n.*   **77 hitherto:** *in this direction (i.e., south and east)*   **83 indentures
tripartite:** *agreements between three parties*   **84 interchangeably:** *each party signing each copy*

96 conduct: *escort*   **100 moiety:** *portion*   **102 cranking:** *winding*   **103 the best of
all my land;** *cf. n.*   **104 cantle:** *piece*   **106 smug:** *neat, trim*   **109 bottom:** *low,
rich land*   **114 Gelding:** *cutting*   **opposed continent:** *country opposite*   **116 charge:**
expense   **131** *Cf. n.*   **137 canstick:** *candlestick*   **140 mincing:** *affected*

Glend. The moon shines fair. You may away by night.
I'll haste the writer, and withal
Break with your wives of your departure hence.　　　　*150*
I am afraid my daughter will run mad,
So much she doteth on her Mortimer.　　　　*Exit.*

　　Mort. Fie, Cousin Percy, how you cross my father!

　　Hot. I cannot choose. Sometime he angers me
With telling me of the moldwarp and the ant,　　　　*155*
Of the dreamer Merlin and his prophecies,
And of a dragon and a finless fish,
A clip-wing'd griffin and a moulten raven,
A couching lion and a ramping cat,
And such a deal of skimble-skamble stuff,　　　　*160*
As puts me from my faith. I tell you what;
He held me last night at least nine hours
In reckoning up the several devils' names
That were his lackeys. I cried 'hum!' and 'Well, go to,'
But mark'd him not a word. O he is as tedious　　　　*165*
As a tired horse, a railing wife,
Worse than a smoky house. I had rather live
With cheese and garlic in a windmill, far,
Than feed on cates and have him talk to me,
In any summer-house in Christendom.　　　　*170*

　　Mort. In faith he is a worthy gentleman,
Exceedingly well read and profited
In strange concealments, valiant as a lion,
And wondrous affable; and as bountiful
As mines of India. Shall I tell you, cousin,　　　　*175*
He holds your temper in a high respect,
And curbs himself even of his natural scope
When you come cross his humor; faith he does.
I warrant you that man is not alive
Might so have tempted him as you have done　　　　*180*
Without the taste of danger and reproof.
But do not use it oft, let me entreat you.

　　Wor. In faith, my lord, you are too wilful-blame,
And since your coming hither have done enough
To put him quite besides his patience.　　　　*185*
You must needs learn, lord, to amend this fault.
Though sometimes it show greatness, courage, blood,
And that's the dearest grace it renders you,
Yet often times it doth present harsh rage,
Defect of manners, want of government,　　　　*190*
Pride, haughtiness, opinion, and disdain—
The least of which haunting a nobleman
Loseth men's hearts and leaves behind a stain
Upon the beauty of all parts besides,
Beguiling them of commendation.　　　　*195*

　　Hot. Well, I am school'd. Good manners be your speed!
Here come our wives, and let us take our leave.

Enter Glendower with the Ladies.

　　Mort. This is the deadly spite that angers me,
My wife can speak no English, I no Welsh.

　　Glend. My daughter weeps. She'll not part with you.　　　　*200*

She'll be a soldier too, she'll to the wars.

　　Mort. Good father, tell her that she and my Aunt Percy
Shall follow in your conduct speedily.

　　　　*Glendower speaks to her in Welsh, and she
　　　　　　　　　answers him in the same.*

　　Glend. She is desperate here, a peevish self-will'd harlotry,
one that no persuasion can do good upon.　　　　*205*

　　　　　　The lady speaks in Welsh.

　　Mort. I understand thy looks. That pretty Welsh
Which thou pour'st down from these swelling heavens
I am too perfect in, and but for shame,
In such a parley should I answer thee.

　　　　　　The lady again in Welsh.

I understand thy kisses, and thou mine,　　　　*210*
And that's a feeling disputation.
But I will never be a truant, love,
Till I have learnt thy language, for thy tongue
Makes Welsh as sweet as ditties highly penn'd,
Sung by a fair queen in a summer's bower,　　　　*215*
With ravishing division, to her lute.

　　Glend. Nay, if you melt, then will she run mad.

　　　　　　The lady speaks again in Welsh.

　　Mort. O I am ignorance itself in this.

　　Glend. She bids you
On the wanton rushes lay you down,　　　　*220*
And rest your gentle head upon her lap,
And she will sing the song that pleaseth you,
And on your eyelids crown the god of sleep,
Charming your blood with pleasing heaviness,
Making such difference 'twixt wake and sleep,　　　　*225*
As is the difference betwixt day and night,
The hour before the heavenly-harness'd team
Begins his golden progress in the east.

　　Mort. With all my heart I'll sit and hear her sing.
By that time will our book, I think, be drawn.　　　　*230*

　　Glend. Do so,
And those musicians that shall play to you
Hang in the air a thousand leagues from hence,
And straight they shall be here. Sit, and attend.

　　Hot. Come, Kate, thou art perfect in lying down.　　　　*235*
Come, quick, quick, that I may lay my head in thy lap.

　　Lady P. Go, ye giddy goose.　　　　*The music plays.*

　　Hot. Now I perceive the devil understands Welsh,
And 'tis no marvel he is so humorous.
By'r lady, he's a good musician.　　　　*240*

　　Lady P. Then should you be nothing but musical, for you
are altogether governed by humors. Lie still, ye thief, and hear
the lady sing in Welsh.

　　Hot. I had rather hear Lady my brach howl in Irish.

　　Lady P. Wouldst thou have thy head broken?　　　　*245*

　　Hot. No.

　　Lady P. Then be still.

　　Hot. Neither; 'tis a woman's fault.

　　Lady P. Now God help thee!

　　Hot. To the Welsh lady's bed.　　　　*250*

　　Lady P. What's that?

---

150 Break with: *inform*　　**154 cannot choose:** *have no choice*　　**155–159** *Cf. n.*　　**160 skimble-skamble:** *nonsensical*　　**169 cates:** *dainties*　　**170 summer-house:** *country pleasure-house*　　**172 profited:** *proficient*　　**173 concealments:** *mysteries*　　**177 scope:** *tendencies*　　**183 too wilful-blame:** *to be blamed for too great wilfulness*　　**185 quite besides:** *completely out of*　　**187 blood:** *spirit*　　**188 dearest:** *most valuable*　　**189 present:** *indicate*　　**190 government:** *self-control*　　**191 opinion:** *arrogance*　　**195 Beguiling:** *cheating*　　**196 be your speed:** *bring you good fortune*

202 Aunt; *cf. n. on I. iii. 147, 148*　　**204 harlotry:** *silly girl*　　**206–209** *Cf. n.*　　**211 disputation:** *conversation*　　**214 highly penn'd:** *written in high style*　　**216 division:** *modulation*　　**220 wanton:** *soft, luxurious*　　**230 book:** *document, indentures*　　**236 head . . . lap;** *cf. Hamlet III. ii. 108-110*　　**239 he:** *because he* **humorous:** *capricious, queer*　　**244 brach:** *a bitch-hound*

Hot. Peace, she sings.   *Here the lady sings a Welsh song.*

Hot. Come, Kate, I'll have your song too.

Lady P. Not mine, in good sooth.

Hot. Not yours, 'in good sooth!' Heart, you swear like a   *255*
comfit-maker's wife. 'Not you in good sooth,' and 'as true as I
live,' and 'as God shall mend me,' and 'as sure as day': and
giv'st such sarcenet surety for thy oaths, as if thou never
walk'st further than Finsbury. Swear me, Kate, like a lady as
thou art, a good mouth-filling oath, and leave 'in sooth,'   *260*
and such protest of pepper-gingerbread, to velvet-guards and
Sunday-citizens. Come, sing.

Lady P. I will not sing.

Hot. 'Tis the next way to turn tailor, or be redbreast-
teacher. An the indentures be drawn, I'll away within these   *265*
two hours, and so, come in when ye will.   *Exit.*

Glend. Come, come, Lord Mortimer. You are as slow
As hot Lord Percy is on fire to go.
By this our book is drawn. We'll but seal, and then to horse
immediately.   *270*

Mort. With all my heart.   *Exeunt.*

❧ Scene Second ❧

[Westminster. The Palace.]
Enter the King, Prince of Wales, and others.

King. Lords, give us leave. The Prince of Wales and I
Must have some private conference. But be near at hand,
For we shall presently have need of you.   *Exeunt Lords.*
I know not whether God will have it so,
For some displeasing service I have done,   *5*
That in his secret doom out of my blood
He'll breed revengement and a scourge for me.
But thou dost in thy passages of life,
Make me believe that thou art only mark'd
For the hot vengeance, and the rod of heaven,   *10*
To punish my mistreadings. Tell me else,
Could such inordinate and low desires,
Such poor, such bare, such lewd, such mean attempts,
Such barren pleasures, rude society,
As thou art match'd withal, and grafted to,   *15*
Accompany the greatness of thy blood,
And hold their level with thy princely heart?

Prince. So please your majesty, I would I could
Quit all offences with as clear excuse,
As well, as I am doubtless I can purge   *20*
Myself of many I am charg'd withal.
Yet such extenuation let me beg,
As in reproof of many tales devis'd,
Which oft the ear of greatness needs must hear
By smiling pickthanks and base newsmongers,   *25*
I may, for some things true, wherein my youth
Hath faulty wander'd, and irregular,
Find pardon on my true submission.

King. God pardon thee! yet let me wonder, Harry,
At thy affections, which do hold a wing   *30*
Quite from the flight of all thy ancestors.
Thy place in council thou hast rudely lost,
Which by thy younger brother is supplied,
And art almost an alien to the hearts
Of all the court and princes of my blood.   *35*
The hope and expectation of thy time
Is ruin'd, and the soul of every man
Prophetically do forethink thy fall.
Had I so lavish of my presence been,
So common-hackney'd in the eyes of men,   *40*
So stale and cheap to vulgar company,
Opinion, that did help me to the crown,
Had still kept loyal to possession,
And left me in reputeless banishment,
A fellow of no mark nor likelihood.   *45*
By being seldom seen, I could not stir
But like a comet I was wonder'd at;
That men would tell their children 'This is he.'
Others would say, 'Where? which is Bolingbroke?'
And then I stole all courtesy from heaven,   *50*
And dress'd myself in such humility
That I did pluck allegiance from men's hearts,
Loud shouts, and salutations from their mouths,
Even in the presence of the crowned king.
Thus did I keep my person fresh and new,   *55*
My presence like a robe pontifical,
Ne'er seen but wonder'd at; and so my state,
Seldom, but sumptuous, showed like a feast,
And wan by rareness such solemnity.
The skipping king, he ambled up and down,   *60*
With shallow jesters, and rash bavin wits,
Soon kindled, and soon burnt, carded his state,
Mingled his royalty with cap'ring fools,
Had his great name profaned with their scorns,
And gave his countenance, against his name,   *65*
To laugh at gibing boys, and stand the push
Of every beardless vain comparative,
Grew a companion to the common streets,
Enfeoff'd himself to popularity,
That being daily swallow'd by men's eyes,   *70*
They surfeited with honey, and began
To loathe the taste of sweetness, whereof a little
More than a little is by much too much.
So when he had occasion to be seen,
He was but as the cuckoo is in June,   *75*
Heard, not regarded; seen, but with such eyes
As, sick and blunted with community,
Afford no extraordinary gaze,
Such as is bent on sun-like majesty,
When it shines seldom in admiring eyes,   *80*
But rather drows'd, and hung their eyelids down,
Slept in his face, and render'd such aspéct
As cloudy men use to their adversaries,
Being with his presence glutted, gorg'd, and full.

---

256 comfit-maker: *confectioner*   **258 sarcenet:** *flimsy*   **259 Finsbury;** *cf. n.*   **261 velvet-guards;** *cf. n.*   **264 tailor;** *cf. n.*   **redbreast-teacher:** *trainer of singing-birds*   **1 give
us leave:** *leave us*   **3 presently:** *immediately*   **6 doom:** *judgment*   **8 thy passages of
life:** *the actions of thy life*   **19 Quit:** *clear myself of*   **20 As well:** *and as well*   **doubtless:**
positive, without doubt   **22 extenuation:** *mitigation of censure*   **23-28** *Cf. n.*

30 affections: *tastes*   **hold a wing:** *take a course*   **31 from the flight:** *unlike the direction*   **36 time:** *age, reign*   **42 Opinion:** *public opinion*   **43 to possession:** *to the
possessor, i.e., King Richard*   **48, 70 That:** *so that*   **50 stole, etc.;** *cf. n.*   **59 wan:**
won   **61 bavin:** *brushwood, which soon burns out*   **62 carded;** *cf. n.*   **65 against his
name:** *contrary to his dignity*   **66 stand the push:** *face the competition*   **67 comparative:**
one who affects wit; cf. I. ii. 69   **69 Enfeoff'd himself:** *gave himself up entirely*   **popularity:** *low company*   **77 community:** *commonness*   **83 cloudy:** *sullen*

And in that very line, Harry, standest thou,   *85*
For thou hast lost thy princely privilege
With vile participation. Not an eye
But is aweary of thy common sight,
Save mine, which hath desir'd to see thee more—
Which now doth that I would not have it do,   *90*
Make blind itself with foolish tenderness.
     Prince. I shall hereafter, my thrice gracious lord,
Be more myself.
     King.   For all the world,
As thou art to this hour was Richard then,   *95*
When I from France set foot at Ravenspurgh,
And even as I was then, is Percy now.
Now, by my scepter, and my soul to boot,
He hath more worthy interest to the state
Than thou the shadow of succession.   *100*
For of no right, nor color like to right,
He doth fill fields with harness in the realm,
Turns head against the lion's armed jaws,
And, being no more in debt to years than thou,
Leads ancient lords and reverend bishops on   *105*
To bloody battles, and to bruising arms.
What never-dying honor hath he got
Against renowned Douglas! whose high deeds,
Whose hot incursions, and great name in arms,
Holds from all soldiers chief majority   *110*
And military title capital
Through all the kingdoms that acknowledge Christ.
Thrice hath this Hotspur, Mars in swathling clothes,
This infant warrior, in his enterprises
Discomfited great Douglas, ta'en him once,   *115*
Enlarged him, and made a friend of him,
To fill the mouth of deep defiance up,
And shake the peace and safety of our throne.
And what say you to this? Percy, Northumberland,
The Archbishop's Grace of York, Douglas, Mortimer,   *120*
Capitulate against us, and are up.
But wherefore do I tell these news to thee?
Why, Harry, do I tell thee of my foes,
Which art my near'st and dearest enemy?
Thou that art like enough through vassal fear,   *125*
Base inclination, and the start of spleen,
To fight against me under Percy's pay,
To dog his heels, and curtsy at his frowns,
To show how much thou art degenerate.
     Prince. Do not think so. You shall not find it so.   *130*
And God forgive them that so much have sway'd
Your majesty's good thoughts away from me.
I will redeem all this on Percy's head,
And in the closing of some glorious day
Be bold to tell you that I am your son,   *135*
When I will wear a garment all of blood,
And stain my favors in a bloody mask,
Which, wash'd away, shall scour my shame with it.
And that shall be the day, whene'er it lights,
That this same child of honor and renown,   *140*

This gallant Hotspur, this all-praised knight,
And your unthought-of Harry chance to meet.
For every honor sitting on his helm,
Would they were multitudes, and on my head
My shames redoubled. For the time will come   *145*
That I shall make this Northern youth exchange
His glorious deeds for my indignities.
Percy is but my factor, good my lord,
To engross up glorious deeds on my behalf.
And I will call him to so strict account,   *150*
That he shall render every glory up,
Yea, even the slightest worship of his time,
Or I will tear the reckoning from his heart.
This in the name of God I promise here,
The which if he be pleas'd I shall perform,   *155*
I do beseech your majesty may salve
The long-grown wounds of my intemperance.
If not, the end of life cancels all bands,
And I will die a hundred thousand deaths
Ere break the smallest parcel of this vow.   *160*
     King. A hundred thousand rebels die in this.
Thou shalt have charge and sovereign trust herein.

               Enter Blunt.

How now, good Blunt! Thy looks are full of speed.
     Blunt. So hath the business that I come to speak of.
Lord Mortimer of Scotland hath sent word,   *165*
That Douglas and the English rebels met
The eleventh of this month at Shrewsbury.
A mighty and a fearful head they are,
If promises be kept on every hand,
As ever offer'd foul play in a state.   *170*
     King. The Earl of Westmorland set forth to-day,
With him my son, Lord John of Lancaster,
For this advertisement is five days old.
On Wednesday next, Harry, you shall set forward.
On Thursday we ourselves will march. Our meeting   *175*
Is Bridgenorth, and Harry, you shall march
Through Gloucestershire, by which account,
Our business valued, some twelve days hence
Our general forces at Bridgenorth shall meet.
Our hands are full of business, let's away.   *180*
Advantage feeds him fat while men delay.   *Exeunt.*

❧ Scene Third ❧

[Eastcheap. The Boar's Head Tavern.]
Enter Falstaff and Bardolph.

     Fal. Bardolph, am I not fallen away vilely since this last action? Do I not bate? Do I not dwindle? Why, my skin hangs about me like an old lady's loose gown. I am withered like an old apple-john. Well, I'll repent, and that suddenly, while I am in some liking. I shall be out of heart shortly, and then I   *5*
shall have no strength to repent. An I have not forgotten what

---

87 vile participation: *base companionship*   **99 interest:** *claim*   **100 shadow of succession;** *cf. n.*   **101 color:** *pretext*   **102 harness:** *armed men*   **104** *Cf. n.*   **110 majority:** *pre-eminence*   **111 capital:** *chief*   **116 Enlarged:** *released*   **121 Capitulate:** *form a league*   **125 vassal:** *slavish*   **126 start of spleen:** *impulse of ill temper*   **137 favors:** *features*

148 factor: *agent*   **149 engross up:** *buy up*   **152 worship:** *distinction*   **158 bands:** *bonds*   **165 Lord Mortimer of Scotland;** *cf. n.*   **173 advertisement:** *information*   **175 meeting:** *rendezvous*   **178 valued:** *taken into consideration*   **2 bate:** *fall off, grow thin*   **4 apple-john:** *an apple that keeps well but becomes very shrivelled*   **5 liking:** *(good) bodily condition*

the inside of a church is made of, I am a peppercorn, a brewer's horse. The inside of a church? Company, villainous company, hath been the spoil of me.

Bard. Sir John, you are so fretful you cannot live long.   10

Fal. Why, there is it! Come sing me a bawdy song, make
me merry. I was as virtuously given as a gentleman need to be;
virtuous enough, swore little, diced not above seven times a
week, went to a bawdy-house not above once in a quarter—of
an hour, paid money that I borrowed—three or four times,   15
lived well, and in good compass. And now I live out of all
order, out of all compass.

Bard. Why, you are so fat, Sir John, that you must needs
be out of all compass; out of all reasonable compass, Sir John.

Fal. Do thou amend thy face, and I'll amend my life.   20
Thou art our admiral, thou bearest the lantern in the poop,
but 'tis in the nose of thee. Thou art the Knight of the Burning Lamp.

Bard. Why, Sir John, my face does you no harm.

Fal. No, I'll be sworn. I make as good use of it as many   25
a man doth of a death's head, or a *memento mori.* I never see
thy face, but I think upon hell-fire, and Dives that lived in
purple: for there he is in his robes, burning, burning. If thou
wert any way given to virtue, I would swear by thy face: my
oath should be, 'By this fire that's God's angel.' But thou   30
art altogether given over: and wert indeed, but for the light in
thy face, the son of utter darkness. When thou ran'st up Gadshill in the night to catch my horse, if I did not think thou
hadst been an *ignis fatuus,* or a ball of wildfire, there's no purchase in money. O thou art a perpetual triumph, an   35
everlasting bonfire-light! Thou hast saved me a thousand marks
in links and torches, walking with thee in the night betwixt tavern and tavern; but the sack that thou hast drunk me would
have bought me lights as good cheap at the dearest chandler's
in Europe. I have maintained that salamander of yours with   40
fire any time this two and thirty years, God reward me for it!

Bard. 'Sblood, I would my face were in your belly.

Fal. God-a-mercy! so should I be sure to be heart-burned.

Enter Hostess.

How now, Dame Partlet the hen! Have you inquired yet
who picked my pocket?   45

Host. Why Sir John, what do you think, Sir John? Do you
think I keep thieves in my house? I have searched, I have inquired, so has my husband, man by man, boy by boy, servant by
servant. The tithe of a hair was never lost in my house before.

Fal. Ye lie, hostess. Bardolph was shaved, and lost many   50
a hair, and I'll be sworn my pocket was picked. Go to, you
are a woman! Go.

Host. Who, I? No. I defy thee. God's light! I was never
called so in mine own house before.

Fal. Go to! I know you well enough.   55

Host. No, Sir John, you do not know me, Sir John. I know
you, Sir John. You owe me money, Sir John, and now you
pick a quarrel to beguile me of it. I bought you a dozen of
shirts to your back.

Fal. Dowlas, filthy dowlas. I have given them away to   60
bakers' wives, and they have made bolters of them.

Host. Now as I am a true woman, holland of eight shillings an
ell! You owe money here besides, Sir John, for your diet, and by-
drinkings, and money lent you, four and twenty pound.

Fal. He had his part of it. Let him pay.   65

Host. He? alas! he is poor. He hath nothing.

Fal. How? poor? Look upon his face. What call you rich?
Let them coin his nose, let them coin his cheeks. I'll not pay a
denier. What? will you make a younker of me? Shall I not take
mine ease in mine inn, but I shall have my pocket picked?   70
I have lost a seal-ring of my grandfather's worth forty mark.

Host. O Jesu, I have heard the prince tell him, I know not
how oft, that that ring was copper.

Fal. How? the prince is a Jack, a sneak-up, 'Sblood! an he
were here, I would cudgel him like a dog if he would say so.   75

Enter the Prince marching [with Peto], and Falstaff meets him,
playing upon his truncheon like a fife.

Fal. How now, lad? is the wind in that door, i' faith? Must
we all march?

Bard. Yea, two and two, Newgate fashion.

Host. My lord, I pray you hear me.

Prince. What sayest thou, Mistress Quickly? How doth thy   80
husband? I love him well. He is an honest man.

Host. Good my lord, hear me.

Fal. Prithee let her alone, and list to me.

Prince. What say'st thou, Jack?

Fal. The other night I fell asleep here, behind the arras,   85
and had my pocket picked. This house is turned bawdy-house,
they pick pockets.

Prince. What didst thou lose, Jack?

Fal. Wilt thou believe me, Hal? Three or four bonds of
forty pound apiece, and a seal-ring of my grandfather's.   90

Prince. A trifle. Some eightpenny matter.

Host. So I told him, my lord, and I said I heard your Grace
say so. And, my lord, he speaks most vilely of you, like a foul-
mouthed man as he is, and said he would cudgel you.

Prince. What? he did not!   95

Host. There's neither faith, truth, nor womanhood in me
else.

Fal. There's no more faith in thee than in a stewed prune,
nor no more truth in thee than in a drawn fox, and for womanhood, Maid Marian may be the deputy's wife of the   100
ward to thee. Go, you thing, go!

Host. Say, what thing? what thing?

Fal. What thing? Why, a thing to thank God on.

Host. I am no thing to thank God on, I would thou
shouldst know it! I am an honest man's wife, and setting   105
thy knighthood aside, thou art a knave to call me so.

Fal. Setting thy womanhood aside, thou art a beast to say
otherwise.

Host. Say, what beast, thou knave thou?

Fal. What beast? Why, an otter.   110

Prince. An otter, Sir John? why an otter?

Fal. Why? She's neither fish nor flesh; a man knows not
where to have her.

7 peppercorn: *the dried berry from which pepper is ground* **brewer's horse;** *cf. n.*   **21**
admiral: *flagship*   **26 memento mori;** *cf. n.*   **27 Dives;** *cf. n.*   **30 God's angel;**
cf. n.   **34 ignis fatuus:** *will o' the wisp*   **35 triumph:** *festive celebration*   **36 links:**
street lights   **39 as good cheap:** *at as good a bargain*   **40 salamander:** *mythical animal*
supposed to live in fire   **44 Partlet;** *cf. n.*   **49 tithe:** *tenth part; cf. n.*

60 dowlas: *coarse linen*   **61 bolters:** *sieves*   **62 holland:** *fine linen*   **63 ell:** *yard and a*
quarter   **69 denier:** *the tenth part of a penny*   **younker:** *young greenhorn*   **74 sneak-up:**
shirker   **S. d. truncheon:** *officer's baton*   **78 Newgate:** *a prison*   **99 drawn fox:** *a fox driven*
from cover and tricky in his attempts to get back   **100 Cf. n.**

Host. Thou art an unjust man in saying so. Thou or any man knows where to have me, thou knave thou!   *115*

Prince. Thou say'st true, hostess, and he slanders thee most grossly.

Host. So he doth you, my lord, and said this other day you ought him a thousand pound.

Prince. Sirrah, do I owe you a thousand pound?   *120*

Fal. A thousand pound, Hal? a million. Thy love is worth a million. Thou owest me thy love.

Host. Nay my lord, he called you Jack, and said he would cudgel you.

Fal. Did I, Bardolph?   *125*

Bard. Indeed, Sir John, you said so.

Fal. Yea, if he said my ring was copper.

Prince. I say 'tis copper. Darest thou be as good as thy word now?

Fal. Why, Hal, thou knowest, as thou art but man, I   *130* dare. But as thou art prince, I fear thee as I fear the roaring of the lion's whelp.

Prince. And why not as the lion?

Fal. The king himself is to be feared as the lion. Dost thou think I'll fear thee as I fear thy father? Nay an I do,   *135* I pray God my girdle break.

Prince. O, if it should, how would thy guts fall about thy knees! But sirrah, there's no room for faith, truth, nor honesty, in this bosom of thine. It is all filled up with guts and midriff. Charge an honest woman with picking thy pocket!   *140* Why, thou whoreson, impudent, embossed rascal, if there were anything in thy pocket but tavern reckonings, memorandums of bawdy-houses, and one poor pennyworth of sugar-candy to make thee long-winded—if thy pocket were enriched with any other injuries but these, I am a villain.   *145* And yet you will stand to it, you will not pocket up wrong. Art thou not ashamed?

Fal. Dost thou hear, Hal? Thou knowest in the state of innocency Adam fell, and what should poor Jack Falstaff do in the days of villainy? Thou seest I have more flesh than another man, and   *150* therefore more frailty. You confess then you picked my pocket?

Prince. It appears so by the story.

Fal. Hostess, I forgive thee. Go make ready breakfast, love thy husband, look to thy servants, cherish thy guests. Thou shalt find me tractable to any honest reason. Thou seest I   *155* am pacified still. Nay, prithee be gone.   *Exit Hostess.* Now Hal, to the news at court. For the robbery, lad? How is that answered?

Prince. O my sweet beef, I must still be good angel to thee. The money is paid back again.   *160*

Fal. O I do not like that paying back. 'Tis a double labor.

Prince. I am good friends with my father and may do anything.

Fal. Rob me the exchequer the first thing thou dost, and do it with unwashed hands too.   *165*

Bard. Do, my lord!

Prince. I have procured thee, Jack, a charge of foot.

Fal. I would it had been of horse. Where shall I find one that can steal well? O for a fine thief of the age of two and twenty or thereabouts! I am heinously unprovided. Well,   *170* God be thanked for these rebels. They offend none but the virtuous. I laud them, I praise them.

Prince. Bardolph!

Bard. My lord?

Prince. Go bear this letter to Lord John of Lancaster, to   *175* my brother John; this to my Lord of Westmorland. Go, Peto, to horse, to horse! for thou and I have thirty miles to ride yet ere dinner-time. Jack, meet me to-morrow in the Temple-hall at two o'clock in the afternoon. There shalt thou know thy charge, and there receive money and order for their furniture.   *180* The land is burning, Percy stands on high, And either we or they must lower lie.

Fal. Rare words! brave world! Hostess, my breakfast; come! O, I could wish this tavern were my drum.   *Exeunt omnes.*

ACT FOURTH ❧ SCENE FIRST

[The Rebel Camp near Shrewsbury]
Enter Harry Hotspur, Worcester, and Douglas.

Hot. Well said, my noble Scot! If speaking truth
In this fine age were not thought flattery,
Such attribution should the Douglas have
As not a soldier of this season's stamp
Should go so general current through the world.   *5*
By God, I cannot flatter. I do defy
The tongues of soothers. But a braver place
In my heart's love hath no man than yourself.
Nay, task me to my word. Approve me, lord.

Doug. Thou art the king of honor.   *10*
No man so potent breathes upon the ground
But I will beard him.

Hot.   Do so, and 'tis well—

Enter one with letters.

What letters hast thou there?— *[To Doug.]* I can but thank you.   *15*

Messenger. These letters come from your father.

Hot. Letters from him? Why comes he not himself?

Mess. He cannot come, my lord. He is grievous sick.

Hot. 'Zounds! how has he the leisure to be sick
In such a justling time? Who leads his power?   *20*
Under whose government come they along?

Mess. His letters bears his mind, not I, my lord.

Wor. I prithee tell me, doth he keep his bed?

Mess. He did, my lord, four days ere I set forth,
And at the time of my departure thence   *25*
He was much fear'd by his physicians.

Wor. I would the state of time had first been whole
Ere he by sickness had been visited.
His health was never better worth than now.

Hot. Sick now? droop now? This sickness doth infect   *30*
The very life-blood of our enterprise.
'Tis catching hither, even to our camp.
He writes me here that inward sickness—
And that his friends by deputation could not
So soon be drawn, nor did he think it meet   *35*
To lay so dangerous and dear a trust
On any soul remov'd but on his own—

---

119 ought: *owed*   **141 embossed:** *swollen*   **145 injuries;** *cf. n.*   **165 unwashed hands;** *cf. n.*

180 furniture: *equipment*   **184 drum;** *cf. n.*   **2 fine:** *sophisticated*   **3 attribution:** *credit*   **4, 5** *Cf. n.*   **6 defy:** *despise*   **7 soothers:** *flatterers*   **9 task me to my word:** *challenge me to make good my word* **Approve:** *test*   **20 justling:** *busy*

Yet doth he give us bold advertisement,
That with our small conjunction we should on,
To see how fortune is dispos'd to us;　　　　　　　40
For, as he writes, there is no quailing now,
Because the king is certainly possess'd
Of all our purposes. What say you to it?
　　Wor. Your father's sickness is a maim to us.
　　Hot. A perilous gash, a very limb lopp'd off.　　45
And yet, in faith, it is not. His present want
Seems more than we shall find it. Were it good
To set the éxact wealth of all our states
All at one cast? to set so rich a main
On the nice hazard of one doubtful hour?　　　　　50
It were not good, for therein should we read
The very bottom and the soul of hope,
The very list, the very utmost bound
Of all our fortunes.
　　Doug. Faith, and so we should, where now remains　　55
A sweet reversion. We may boldly spend
Upon the hope of what is to come in.
A comfort of retirement lives in this.
　　Hot. A rendezvous, a home to fly unto,
If that the devil and mischance look big　　　　　60
Upon the maidenhead of our affairs.
　　Wor. But yet I would your father had been here.
The quality and hair of our attempt
Brooks no division. It will be thought
By some that know not why he is away,　　　　　65
That wisdom, loyalty, and mere dislike
Of our proceedings kept the earl from hence.
And think how such an apprehension
May turn the tide of fearful faction,
And breed a kind of question in our cause.　　　　70
For well you know we of the offering side
Must keep aloof from strict arbitrement,
And stop all sight-holes, every loop from whence
The eye of reason may pry in upon us.
This absence of your father's draws a curtain,　　75
That shows the ignorant a kind of fear
Before not dreamt of.
　　Hot.　　　　　　　　You strain too far.
I rather of his absence make this use:
It lends a lustre and more great opinion,　　　　80
A larger dare to our great enterprise,
Than if the earl were here. For men must think,
If we without his help can make a head
To push against a kingdom, with his help
We shall o'erturn it topsy-turvy down.　　　　　85
Yet all goes well, yet all our joints are whole.
　　Doug. As heart can think! There is not such a word
Spoke of in Scotland as this term of fear.

　　　　　　　Enter Sir Richard Vernon.

　　Hot. My cousin Vernon! Welcome, by my soul.
　　Ver. Pray God my news be worth a welcome, lord.　　90

The Earl of Westmorland, seven thousand strong,
Is marching hitherwards, with him Prince John.
　　Hot. No harm. What more?
　　Ver.　　　　　　　　And further I have learn'd,
The king himself in person is set forth,　　　　95
Or hitherwards intended speedily
With strong and mighty preparation.
　　Hot. He shall be welcome too. Where is his son,
The nimble-footed madcap Prince of Wales,
And his comrádes that daff'd the world aside　　100
And bid it pass?
　　Ver.　　　　All furnish'd, all in arms,
All plum'd like estridges that woo the wind;
Bating like eagles having lately bath'd,
Glittering in golden coats like images,　　　　105
As full of spirit as the month of May,
And gorgeous as the sun at midsummer:
Wanton as youthful goats, wild as young bulls.
I saw young Harry with his beaver on,
His cushes on his thighs, gallantly arm'd,　　　110
Rise from the ground like feather'd Mercury,
And vaulted with such ease into his seat,
As if an angel dropp'd down from the clouds,
To turn and wind a fiery Pegasus,
And witch the world with noble horsemanship.　　115
　　Hot. No more, no more. Worse than the sun in March
This praise doth nourish agues. Let them come!
They come like sacrifices in their trim,
And to the fire-ey'd maid of smoky war,
All hot and bleeding will we offer them.　　　　120
The mailed Mars shall on his altar sit
Up to the ears in blood. I am on fire
To hear this rich reprisal is so nigh,
And yet not ours. Come let me taste my horse,
Who is to bear me like a thunderbolt　　　　　125
Against the bosom of the Prince of Wales.
Harry to Harry shall, hot horse to horse,
Meet and ne'er part till one drop down a corse.
O that Glendower were come!
　　Ver.　　　　　　　There is more news.　　130
I learn'd in Worcester as I rode along,
He cannot draw his power this fourteen days.
　　Doug. That's the worst tidings that I hear of yet.
　　Wor. Ay by my faith, that bears a frosty sound.
　　Hot. What may the king's whole battle reach unto?　　135
　　Ver. To thirty thousand.
　　Hot.　　　　　　　Forty let it be.
My father and Glendower being both away,
The powers of us may serve so great a day.
Come let us take a muster speedily.　　　　　140
Doomsday is near, die all, die merrily.
　　Doug. Talk not of dying. I am out of fear
Of death or death's hand for this one half-year.

　　　　　　　　　　　　　Exeunt omnes.

---

38 **advertisement:** *advice*　39 **conjunction:** *united forces*　42 **possess'd:** *informed*　46 **His present want:** *his absence now*　49 **main:** *stake*　50 **nice:** *slender, precarious*　52 **soul:** *final essence*　53 **list:** *limit*　56 **reversion:** *right of future possession*　58 *Cf. n.*　60 **big:** *threateningly*　63 **hair:** *nature*　69 **fearful:** *timid*　71 **the offering side:** *the offensive*　72 **arbitrement:** *judicial inquiry*　73 **loop:** *loophole*　75 **draws:** *draws aside*　80 **opinion:** *prestige*

100 **daff'd:** *thrust*　102 **furnish'd:** *equipped*　103 **estridges:** *ostriches; cf. n.*　104 **Bating:** *flapping their wings (falconry term); cf. n.*　105 *Cf. n.*　106 *Cf. n.*　109 **beaver:** *helmet*　110 **cushes:** *cuisses, thigh-armor*　114 **wind:** *wheel round*　111, 112 *Cf. n.*　113 **trim:** *trappings*　119 **fire-ey'd maid;** *cf. n.*　123 **reprisal:** *prize*

❧ Scene Second ❧

[Warwickshire. A Road near Coventry]
Enter Falstaff and Bardolph.

Fal. Bardolph, get thee before to Coventry. Fill me a bottle
of sack. Our soldiers shall march through. We'll to Sutton
Cophill to-night.

Bard. Will you give me money, captain?

Fal. Lay out, lay out.   5

Bard. This bottle makes an angel.

Fal. And if it do, take it for thy labor. And if it make
twenty take them all; I'll answer the coinage. Bid my lieutenant Peto meet me at town's end.

Bard. I will, captain. Farewell.   *Exit.* 10

Fal. If I be not ashamed of my soldiers, I am a soused gurnet. I
have misused the king's press damnably. I have got, in exchange
of a hundred and fifty soldiers, three hundred and odd pounds. I
press me none but good householders, yeomen's sons; inquire me
out contracted bachelors, such as had been asked twice on the   15
banes—such a commodity of warm slaves, as had as lief hear the
devil as a drum, such as fear the report of a caliver worse than a
struck fowl or a hurt wild duck. I pressed me none but such toasts-
and-butter, with hearts in their bellies no bigger than pins' heads,
and they have bought out their services, and now my whole   20
charge consists of ancients, corporals, lieutenants, gentlemen of
companies: slaves as ragged as Lazarus in the painted cloth,
where the glutton's dogs licked his sores, and such as indeed were
never soldiers, but discarded, unjust serving-men, younger sons
to younger brothers, revolted tapsters and ostlers trade-fallen,
the cankers of a calm world and a long peace, ten times   25
more dishonorable ragged than an old faz'd ancient. And
such have I to fill up the rooms of them as have bought out
their services, that you would think that I had a hundred
and fifty tottered prodigals, lately come from swine-keeping,
from eating draff and husks. A mad fellow met me on   30
the way, and told me I had unloaded all the gibbets, and
pressed the dead bodies. No eye hath seen such scarecrows.
I'll not march through Coventry with them, that's flat. Nay,
and the villains march wide betwixt the legs, as if they had gyves
on, for indeed I had the most of them out of prison.   35
There's but a shirt and a half in all my company, and the half
shirt is two napkins tacked together, and thrown over the
shoulders like a herald's coat without sleeves, and the shirt,
to say the truth, stolen from my host at Saint Alban's, or
the red-nose inn-keeper of Daventry. But that's all one,   40
they'll find linen enough on every hedge.

Enter the Prince, and the Lord of Westmorland.

Prince. How now, blown Jack? how now, quilt?

Fal. What, Hal? How now, mad wag? What a devil dost thou in
Warwickshire? My good Lord of Westmorland, I cry you mercy. I
thought your honor had already been at Shrewsbury.   45

West. Faith, Sir John, 'tis more than time that I were there,
and you too, but my powers are there already. The king, I can
tell you, looks for us all. We must away all night.

Fal. Tut, never fear me. I am as vigilant as a cat to steal   50
cream.

Prince. I think to steal cream indeed, for thy theft hath
already made thee butter. But tell me, Jack, whose fellows
are these that come after?

Fal. Mine, Hal, mine.

Prince. I did never see such pitiful rascals.   55

Fal. Tut, tut! Good enough to toss, food for powder,
food for powder. They'll fill a pit as well as better; tush,
man, mortal men, mortal men.

West. Ay, but Sir John, methinks they are exceeding poor
and bare, too beggarly.   60

Fal. Faith, for their poverty I know not where they had
that, and for their bareness I am sure they never learned that
of me.

Prince. No, I'll be sworn, unless you call three fingers in the
ribs bare. But sirrah, make haste. Percy is already in the field.   65

Fal. What, is the king encamped?

West. He is, Sir John. I fear we shall stay too long.

Fal. Well, to the latter end of a fray, and the beginning
of a feast, fits a dull fighter and a keen guest.   *Exeunt.*

❧ Scene Third ❧

[The Rebel Camp near Shrewsbury]
Enter Hotspur, Worcester, Douglas, and Vernon.

Hot. We'll fight with him to-night.

Wor.   It may not be.

Doug. You give him then advantage.

Ver.   Not a whit.

Hot. Why say you so? Looks he not for supply?   5

Ver. So do we.

Hot.   His is certain, ours is doubtful.

Wor. Good cousin, be advis'd. Stir not to-night.

Ver. Do not, my lord.

Doug.   You do not counsel well.   10
You speak it out of fear, and cold heart.

Ver. Do me no slander, Douglas. By my life—
And I dare well maintain it with my life—
If well-respected honor bid me on,
I hold as little counsel with weak fear   15
As you, my lord, or any Scot that this day lives.
Let it be seen to-morrow in the battle
Which of us fears.

Doug.   Yea, or to-night.

Ver.   Content.   20

Hot. To-night, say I.

Ver. Come, come, it may not be. I wonder much,
Being men of such great leading as you are,
That you foresee not what impediments
Drag back our expedition. Certain horse   25
Of my cousin Vernon's are not yet come up.
Your uncle Worcester's horses came but to-day,
And now their pride and mettle is asleep,
Their courage with hard labor tame and dull,
That not a horse is half the half himself.   30

Hot. So are the horses of the enemy

2 **Sutton Cophill**; *cf. n.*   6 **makes an angel**; *cf. n.*   8 **answer the coinage**; *cf. n.*   11
soused gurnet: *pickled fish*   12 **king's press**: *royal warrant for conscripting troops;*
cf. n.   14 **yeomen's**: *small freeholders*   15 **banes**: *marriage banns* **warm**: *luxury-lov-*
ing   17 **caliver**: *musket*   21 **ancients**: *ensigns*   22 **Lazarus**; *cf. III. iii. 27, n.*
painted cloth: *hanging decorated with figures*   25 **cankers**: *caterpillars*   26 **faz'd**: *feazed,*
unraveled **ancient**: *flag*   27 **as**: *who*   29 **tottered**: *tattered* **prodigals**; *cf. n.*
30 **draff**: *pig-wash*   34 **gyves**: *fetters*   36 **but**; *cf. n.*   42 **blown**: *swollen*

56 **to toss**: *i.e., upon a pike*   67 **stay**: *linger*   14 **well-respected**: *well-considered, reason-*
able   23 **leading**: *generalship*   30 **half himself**; *cf. n.*

In general journey-bated and brought low.
The better part of ours are full of rest.

Wor. The number of the king exceedeth ours.
For God's sake, cousin, stay till all come in. 35

The trumpet sounds a parley.

Enter Sir Walter Blunt.

Blunt. I come with gracious offers from the king,
If you vouchsafe me hearing, and respect.

Hot. Welcome, Sir Walter Blunt! and would to God
You were of our determination.
Some of us love you well, and even those some 40
Envy your great deservings and good name,
Because you are not of our quality,
But stand against us like an enemy.

Blunt. And God defend but still I should stand so,
So long as out of limit and true rule 45
You stand against anointed majesty.
But to my charge. The king hath sent to know
The nature of your griefs, and whereupon
You conjure from the breast of civil peace
Such bold hostility, teaching his duteous land 50
Audacious cruelty. If that the king
Have any way your good deserts forgot,
Which he confesseth to be manifold,
He bids you name your griefs, and with all speed
You shall have your desires with interest, 55
And pardon absolute for yourself, and these
Herein misled by your suggestion.

Hot. The king is kind, and well we know the king
Knows at what time to promise, when to pay.
My father, and my uncle, and myself, 60
Did give him that same royalty he wears.
And when he was not six and twenty strong,
Sick in the world's regard, wretched and low,
A poor unminded outlaw sneaking home,
My father gave him welcome to the shore. 65
And when he heard him swear and vow to God,
He came but to be Duke of Lancaster,
To sue his livery, and beg his peace
With tears of innocency, and terms of zeal,
My father, in kind heart and pity mov'd, 70
Swore him assistance, and perform'd it too.
Now when the lords and barons of the realm
Perceiv'd Northumberland did lean to him,
The more and less came in with cap and knee,
Met him in boroughs, cities, villages, 75
Attended him on bridges, stood in lanes,
Laid gifts before him, proffer'd him their oaths,
Gave him their heirs as pages, follow'd him,
Even at the heels, in golden multitudes.
He presently, as greatness knows itself, 80
Steps me a little higher than his vow
Made to my father while his blood was poor
Upon the naked shore at Ravenspurgh,
And now, forsooth, takes on him to reform
Some certain edicts, and some strait decrees, 85

That lie too heavy on the commonwealth,
Cries out upon abuses, seems to weep
Over his country's wrongs, and by this face,
This seeming brow of justice, did he win
The hearts of all that he did angle for: 90
Proceeded further, cut me off the heads
Of all the favorites that the absent king
In deputation left behind him here,
When he was personal in the Irish war.

Blunt. Tut! I came not to hear this. 95
Hot. Then to the point.
In short time after, he depos'd the king,
Soon after that depriv'd him of his life,
And in the neck of that task'd the whole state,
To make that worse, suffer'd his kinsman March 100
(Who is, if every owner were well plac'd,
Indeed his king) to be engag'd in Wales,
There without ransom to lie forfeited,
Disgrac'd me in my happy victories,
Sought to entrap me by intelligence, 105
Rated mine uncle from the council-board,
In rage dismiss'd my father from the court,
Broke oath on oath, committed wrong on wrong,
And in conclusion drove us to seek out
This head of safety, and withal to pry 110
Into his title, the which we find
Too indirect for long continuance.

Blunt. Shall I return this answer to the king?
Hot. Not so, Sir Walter. We'll withdraw awhile.
Go to the king, and let there be impawn'd 115
Some surety for a safe return again,
And in the morning early shall mine uncle
Bring him our purposes. And so farewell.

Blunt. I would you would accept of grace and love.
Hot. And may be so we shall. 120
Blunt. Pray God you do. *Exeunt.*

❧ SCENE FOURTH ❧

[York. The Archbishop's Palace]
Enter the Archbishop of York and Sir Michael.

Arch. Hie, good Sir Michael, bear this sealed brief
With winged haste to the lord marshal,
This to my cousin Scroop, and all the rest
To whom they are directed. If you knew
How much they do import, you would make haste. 5
Sir M. My good lord,
I guess their tenor.
Arch. Like enough you do.
To-morrow, good Sir Michael, is a day,
Wherein the fortune of ten thousand men 10
Must bide the touch. For sir, at Shrewsbury,
As I am truly given to understand,
The king with mighty and quick-raised power
Meets with Lord Harry. And I fear, Sir Michael,

---

32 journey-bated: *wearied with travel* **37 respect:** *deference as the king's spokesman* **42 quality:** *profession, party* **44 defend:** *forbid* **57 suggestion:** *instigation* **68 sue his livery:** *bring suit for the delivery of his lands* **74 more and less:** *great and small* **76 Attended:** *awaited* **85 strait:** *strict*

94 personal: *in person* **99 in the neck:** *'on the heels'* **task'd:** *taxed* **102 engag'd:** *held as hostage* **105 intelligence:** *information obtained through spies* **106 Rated:** *drove away by chiding* **110 head of safety:** *army for protection* **112 indirect:** *crooked* **1 brief:** *letter* **11 bide the touch:** *be put to the test*

What with the sickness of Northumberland,   *15*
Whose power was in the first proportion,
And what with Owen Glendower's absence thence,
Who with them was a rated sinew too—
And comes not in, o'er-rul'd by prophecies—
I fear the power of Percy is too weak   *20*
To wage an instant trial with the king.
    Sir M. Why my good lord, you need not fear. There is
Douglas, and Lord Mortimer.
    Arch. No, Mortimer is not there.
    Sir M. But there is Mordake, Vernon, Lord Harry Percy,   *25*
And there is my Lord of Worcester, and a head
Of gallant warriors, noble gentlemen.
    Arch. And so there is. But yet the king hath drawn
The special head of all the land together:
The Prince of Wales, Lord John of Lancaster,   *30*
The noble Westmorland, and warlike Blunt,
And many mo corrivals and dear men
Of estimation and command in arms.
    Sir M. Doubt not, my lord, they shall be well oppos'd.
    Arch. I hope no less; yet needful 'tis to fear.   *35*
And to prevent the worst, Sir Michael, speed.
For if Lord Percy thrive not, ere the king
Dismiss his power, he means to visit us,
For he hath heard of our confederacy,
And 'tis but wisdom to make strong against him.   *40*
Therefore make haste. I must go write again
To other friends, and so farewell, Sir Michael.   *Exeunt.*

ACT FIFTH ⅌ Scene First

[Shrewsbury. The King's Camp]
Enter the King, Prince of Wales, Lord John of Lancaster, Sir Walter
Blunt, and Falstaff.

    King. How bloodily the sun begins to peer
Above yon busky hill! The day looks pale
At his distemperature.
    Prince.   The southern wind
Doth play the trumpet to his purposes,   *5*
And by his hollow whistling in the leaves
Foretells a tempest and a blustering day.
    King. Then with the losers let it sympathize,
For nothing can seem foul to those that win.
                The trumpet sounds.

Enter Worcester [and Vernon].

How now, my Lord of Worcester? 'Tis not well,   *10*
That you and I should meet upon such terms
As now we meet. You have deceiv'd our trust,
And made us doff our easy robes of peace,
To crush our old limbs in ungentle steel.
This is not well, my lord, this is not well.   *15*
What say you to it? Will you again unknit
This churlish knot of all-abhorred war,

And move in that obedient orb again,
Where you did give a fair and natural light,
And be no more an éxhal'd meteor,   *20*
A prodigy of fear, and a portent
Of broached mischief to the unborn times?
    Wor. Hear me, my liege.
For mine own part I could be well content,
To entertain the lag-end of my life   *25*
With quiet hours. For I do protest
I have not sought the day of this dislike.
    King. You have not sought it! How comes it then?
    Fal. Rebellion lay in his way, and he found it.
    Prince. Peace, chewet, peace!   *30*
    Wor. It pleas'd your majesty to turn your looks
Of favor from myself, and all our house,
And yet I must remember you, my lord,
We were the first and dearest of your friends.
For you my staff of office did I break   *35*
In Richard's time, and posted day and night
To meet you on the way, and kiss your hand,
When yet you were in place and in account
Nothing so strong and fortunate as I.
It was myself, my brother and his son,   *40*
That brought you home, and boldly did outdare
The dangers of the time. You swore to us,
And you did swear that oath at Doncaster,
That you did nothing purpose 'gainst the state,
Nor claim no further than your new-fall'n right,   *45*
The seat of Gaunt, dukedom of Lancaster.
To this we swore our aid: but in short space
It rain'd down fortune show'ring on your head,
And such a flood of greatness fell on you,
What with our help, what with the absent king,   *50*
What with the injuries of a wanton time,
The seeming sufferances that you had borne,
And the contrarious winds that held the king
So long in his unlucky Irish wars,
That all in England did repute him dead—   *55*
And from this swarm of fair advantages,
You took occasion to be quickly woo'd
To gripe the general sway into your hand,
Forgot your oath to us at Doncaster,
And being fed by us, you us'd us so   *60*
As that ungentle gull, the cuckoo's bird,
Useth the sparrow: did oppress our nest,
Grew by our feeding to so great a bulk,
That even our love durst not come near your sight,
For fear of swallowing: but with nimble wing   *65*
We were enforc'd for safety's sake to fly
Out of your sight, and raise this present head,
Whereby we stand opposed by such means
As you yourself have forg'd against yourself
By unkind usage, dangerous countenance,   *70*
And violation of all faith and troth,
Sworn to us in your younger enterprise.
    King. These things, indeed, you have articulate,
Proclaim'd at market-crosses, read in churches,

---

18 rated sinew: *strength on which they counted*   **32 mo:** *more* **dear:** *valued*   **33 estimation:** *reputation* **S. d.;** *cf. n.*   **2 busky:** *bushy* **3 his distemperature:** *the sun's inclemency*   **5 his purposes:** *'that which the sun portends' (Johnson)*   **14 old limbs;** *cf. n.*

18 obedient orb: *sphere of obedience*   **20 éxhal'd:** *drawn forth; especially vapors drawn forth by the sun and producing meteors*   **22 broached:** *begun*   **30 chewet:** *jackdaw (?)*   **51 wanton time:** *frivolous reign*   **52 sufferances:** *sufferings*   **61 gull:** *an unfledged nestling; cf. n.*   **70 dangerous:** *threatening*   **73 articulate:** *set forth in articles*

To face the garment of rebellion   75
With some fine color that may please the eye
Of fickle changelings and poor discontents,
Which gape and rub the elbow at the news
Of hurlyburly innovation.
And never yet did insurrection want   80
Such water-colors to impaint his cause,
Nor moody beggars, starving for a time
Of pell-mell havoc and confusion.
   Prince. In both your armies there is many a soul
Shall pay full dearly for this encounter,   85
If once they join in trial. Tell your nephew,
The Prince of Wales doth join with all the world
In praise of Henry Percy. By my hopes,
This present enterprise set off his head,
I do not think a braver gentleman,   90
More active-valiant, or more valiant-young,
More daring, or more bold, is now alive
To grace this latter age with noble deeds.
For my part, I may speak it to my shame,
I have a truant been to chivalry,   95
And so I hear he doth account me too.
Yet this before my father's majesty—
I am content that he shall take the odds
Of his great name and estimation,
And will, to save the blood on either side,   100
Try fortune with him in a single fight.
   King. And Prince of Wales, so dare we venture thee,
Albeit, considerations infinite
Do make against it. No, good Worcester, no.
We love our people well, even those we love   105
That are misled upon your cousin's part.
And, will they take the offer of our grace,
Both he, and they, and you, yea every man
Shall be my friend again, and I'll be his.
So tell your cousin, and bring me word   110
What he will do. But if he will not yield,
Rebuke and dread correction wait on us,
And they shall do their office. So be gone.
We will not now be troubled with reply.
We offer fair, take it advisedly. *Exit Worcester [with Vernon].* 115
   Prince. It will not be accepted, on my life.
The Douglas and the Hotspur both together
Are confident against the world in arms.
   King. Hence, therefore, every leader to his charge,
For on their answer will we set on them,   120
And God befriend us as our cause is just!
            Exeunt. Manent Prince and Falstaff.
   Fal. Hal, if thou see me down in the battle, and bestride
me, so; 'tis a point of friendship.
   Prince. Nothing but a colossus can do thee that friendship.
Say thy prayers, and farewell.   125
   Fal. I would it were bedtime, Hal, and all well.
   Prince. Why, thou owest God a death.
   Fal. 'Tis not due yet. I would be loath to pay him before

his day. What need I be so forward with him that calls not on
me? *[Exit Prince.]* Well, 'tis no matter. Honor pricks me   130
on. Yea, but how if honor prick me off when I come on? how
then? Can honor set to a leg? No. Or an arm? No. Or take away
the grief of a wound? No. Honor hath no skill in surgery then?
No. What is honor? A word. What is that word honor? Air. A
trim reckoning! Who hath it? He that died o' Wednesday.   135
Doth he feel it? No. Doth he hear it? No. 'Tis insensible then?
Yea, to the dead. But will it not live with the living? No.
Why? Detraction will not suffer it. Therefore I'll none of it.
Honor is a mere scutcheon, and so ends my catechism.
                      Exit.

❧ Scene Second ❧

[Shrewsbury. The Rebel Camp]
Enter Worcester and Sir Richard Vernon.

   Wor. O no, my nephew must not know, Sir Richard,
The liberal and kind offer of the king.
   Ver. 'Twere best he did.
   Wor.   Then are we all undone.
It is not possible, it cannot be   5
The king should keep his word in loving us.
He will suspect us still, and find a time
To punish this offence in other faults.
Suspicion all our lives shall be stuck full of eyes,
For treason is but trusted like the fox,   10
Who, never so tame, so cherish'd and lock'd up,
Will have a wild trick of his ancestors.
Look how we can, or sad or merrily,
Interpretation will misquote our looks,
And we shall feed like oxen at a stall,   15
The better cherish'd still the nearer death.
My nephew's trespass may be well forgot—
It hath the excuse of youth and heat of blood,
And an adopted name of privilege—
A hare-brain'd Hotspur, govern'd by a spleen.   20
All his offences live upon my head
And on his father's. We did train him on,
And his corruption being ta'en from us,
We as the spring of all shall pay for all.
Therefore, good cousin, let not Harry know   25
In any case the offer of the king.
   Ver. Deliver what you will, I'll say 'tis so.
Here comes your cousin.

Enter Hotspur [and Douglas].

   Hot. My uncle is return'd. Deliver up
My Lord of Westmorland. Uncle, what news?   30
   Wor. The king will bid you battle presently.
   Doug. Defy him by the Lord of Westmorland.
   Hot. Lord Douglas, go you and tell him so.
   Doug. Marry and shall, and very willingly!   *Exit Douglas.*
   Wor. There is no seeming mercy in the king.   35
   Hot. Did you beg any? God forbid!
   Wor. I told him gently of our grievances,

75 **face:** *trim*   77 **discontents:** *malcontents*   79 **innovation:** *revolution*   81 **water-colors:** *temporary dyes (pretexts)*   83 **pell-mell havoc:** *indiscriminate plunder*   89 **set off his head:** *taken from his account*   102 **dare we:** *we would dare (in other circumstances)*   112 **wait on us:** *are in our service*   116 **It:** *i.e., the king's 'offer of grace'* (line 107)   **S.d. Manent:** *remain on the stage*   122 **bestride:** *stand over* **so:** *very well* 127, 128 *Cf. n.*

139 **scutcheon:** *shield with armorial bearings, carried in funeral processions*   9 **Suspicion;** *cf. n.*   13 **or . . . or:** *either . . . or*   19 **adopted name of privilege:** *nickname which carries certain privileges with it*   27 **Deliver:** *report*   29 **Deliver up:** *release*

Of his oath-breaking, which he mended thus,
By now forswearing that he is forsworn.
He calls us rebels, traitors, and will scourge   40
With haughty arms this hateful name in us.

Enter Douglas.

Doug. Arm, gentlemen! To arms! for I have thrown
A brave defiance in King Henry's teeth,
And Westmorland, that was engag'd, did bear it,
Which cannot choose but bring him quickly on.   45
Wor. The Prince of Wales stepp'd forth before the king,
And, nephew, challeng'd you to single fight.
Hot. O would the quarrel lay upon our heads,
And that no man might draw short breath to-day
But I and Harry Monmouth! Tell me, tell me,   50
How show'd his tasking? seem'd it in contempt?
Ver. No, by my soul, I never in my life
Did hear a challenge urg'd more modestly,
Unless a brother should a brother dare
To gentle exercise and proof of arms.   55
He gave you all the duties of a man,
Trimm'd up your praises with a princely tongue,
Spoke your deservings like a chronicle,
Making you ever better than his praise,
By still dispraising praise valu'd with you: 60
And, which became him like a prince indeed,
He made a blushing cital of himself,
And chid his truant youth with such a grace
As if he master'd there a double spirit
Of teaching and of learning instantly.   65
There did he pause. But let me tell the world,
If he outlive the envy of this day,
England did never owe so sweet a hope,
So much misconstru'd in his wantonness.
Hot. Cousin, I think thou art enamored   70
On his follies. Never did I hear
Of any prince so wild a libertine.
But be he as he will, yet once ere night
I will embrace him with a soldier's arm,
That he shall shrink under my courtesy.   75
Arm, arm with speed! And fellows, soldiers, friends,
Better consider what you have to do,
Than I, that have not well the gift of tongue,
Can lift your blood up with persuasion.

Enter a Messenger.

Mess. My lord, here are letters for you.   80
Hot. I cannot read them now.
O gentlemen, the time of life is short.
To spend that shortness basely were too long,
If life did ride upon a dial's point,
Still ending at the arrival of an hour.   85
And if we live, we live to tread on kings,
If die, brave death, when princes die with us!
Now, for our consciences, the arms are fair
When the intent of bearing them is just.

Enter another Messenger.

Mess. My lord, prepare! The king comes on apace.   90
Hot. I thank him that he cuts me from my tale,
For I profess not talking. Only this—
Let each man do his best. And here draw I
A sword, whose temper I intend to stain
With the best blood that I can meet withal   95
In the adventure of this perilous day.
Now, *Esperance!* Percy! and set on.
Sound all the lofty instruments of war,
And by that music let us all embrace,
For, heaven to earth, some of us never shall   100
A second time do such a courtesy.

*Here they embrace. The trumpets sound. The King enters with
his power. Alarm to the battle. Then enter Douglas and Sir
Walter Blunt.*

Blunt. What is thy name, that in battle thus
Thou crossest me? What honor dost thou seek   105
Upon my head?
Doug.   Know then, my name is Douglas,
And I do haunt thee in the battle thus
Because some tell me that thou art a king.
Blunt. They tell thee true.   110
Doug. The Lord of Stafford dear to-day hath bought
Thy likeness, for instead of thee, King Harry,
This sword hath ended him. So shall it thee
Unless thou yield thee as my prisoner.
Blunt. I was not born a yielder, thou proud Scot,   115
And thou shalt find a king that will revenge
Lord Stafford's death.

They fight. Douglas kills Blunt.

Then enter Hotspur.

Hot. O Douglas, hadst thou fought at Holmedon thus I
never had triúmph'd upon a Scot.   120
Doug. All's done, all's won! Here breathless lies the king.
Hot. Where?
Doug. Here.
Hot. This, Douglas? No. I know this face full well.
A gallant knight he was—his name was Blunt—   125
Semblably furnish'd like the king himself.
Doug. Ah, 'fool' go with thy soul whither it goes!
A borrow'd title hast thou bought too dear.
Why didst thou tell me that thou wert a king?
Hot. The king hath many marching in his coats.   130
Doug. Now by my sword, I will kill all his coats.
I'll murder all his wardrobe, piece by piece,
Until I meet the king.
Hot.   Up, and away!
Our soldiers stand full fairly for the day.   *Exeunt.*   135

Alarm. Enter Falstaff solus.

Fal. Though I could 'scape shot-free at London, I fear the
shot here. Here's no scoring but upon the pate. Soft! who are
you? Sir Walter Blunt! There's honor for you. Here's no vanity! I
am as hot as molten lead, and as heavy too. God keep lead out
of me! I need no more weight than mine own bowels.   140
I have led my ragamuffins where they are peppered. There's

39 forswearing: *denying on oath* **forsworn:** *perjured* **51 tasking:** *challenge* **56 all the duties of a man:** *all that one man owes another* **62 cital of:** *reference to* **68 owe:** *own* **72 libertine;** *cf. n.* **84 dial's point:** *hand of a clock*

S.d.; *cf. n.* **104** *Cf. n.* **125** *Cf. n.* **126 Semblably furnish'd:** *dressed to resemble* **127 'fool' go with thy soul;** *cf. n.* **136 shot-free:** *without having to pay*

not three of my hundred and fifty left alive, and they are for the town's end, to beg during life. But who comes here?

Enter the Prince.

Prince. What, stand'st thou idle here? Lend me thy sword.
Many a nobleman lies stark and stiff   *145*
Under the hoofs of vaunting enemies,
Whose deaths are yet unreveng'd. I prithee lend me thy sword.

Fal. O Hal, I prithee give me leave to breathe awhile. Turk Gregory never did such deeds in arms as I have done this day. I have paid Percy, I have made him sure.   *150*

Prince. He is indeed, and living to kill thee. I prithee lend me thy sword.

Fal. Nay, before God, Hal, if Percy be alive thou gett'st not my sword, but take my pistol if thou wilt.

Prince. Give it me. What? Is it in the case?   *155*

Fal. Ay, Hal, 'tis hot, 'tis hot. There's that will sack a city.

The Prince draws it out, and finds it to be a bottle of sack.

Prince. What, is it a time to jest and dally now?
                        He throws the bottle at him. Exit.

Fal. Well, if Percy be alive, I'll pierce him. If he do come in my way, so. If he do not, if I come in his willingly, let him make a carbonado of me. I like not such grinning honor   *160* as Sir Walter hath. Give me life! which if I can save, so: if not, honor comes unlooked for, and there's an end.   *Exit.*

❧ Scene Third ❧

[Another Part of the Battle Field. The King's Post]
Alarm. Excursions. Enter the King, the Prince, Lord John of Lancaster, Earl of Westmorland.

King. I prithee, Harry, withdraw thyself. Thou bleedest too much. Lord John of Lancaster, go you with him.

John. Not I, my lord, unless I did bleed too.

Prince. I beseech your majesty make up,
Lest your retirement do amaze your friends.   *5*

King. I will do so. My lord of Westmorland, lead him to his tent.

West. Come, my lord, I'll lead you to your tent.

Prince. Lead me, my lord? I do not need your help,
And God forbid a shallow scratch should drive   *10*
The Prince of Wales from such a field as this,
Where stain'd nobility lies trodden on,
And rebels' arms triúmph in massacres!

John. We breathe too long. Come, Cousin Westmorland,
Our duty this way lies. For God's sake, come.   *15*
                        [Exeunt Lord John and Westmorland.]

Prince. By God, thou hast deceiv'd me, Lancaster.
I did not think thee lord of such a spirit.
Before, I lov'd thee as a brother, John,
But now I do respect thee as my soul.   *20*

King. I saw him hold Lord Percy at the point,
With lustier maintenance than I did look for
Of such an ungrown warrior.

Prince.   O this boy

Lends mettle to us all.   *Exit.* *25*

Enter Douglas.

Doug. Another king? They grow like Hydra's heads.
I am the Douglas, fatal to all those
That wear those colors on them. What art thou
That counterfeit'st the person of a king?

King. The king himself, who, Douglas, grieves at heart   *30*
So many of his shadows thou hast met
And not the very king. I have two boys
Seek Percy and thyself about the field,
But seeing thou fall'st on me so luckily
I will assay thee. So defend thyself.   *35*

Doug. I fear thou art another counterfeit.
And yet, in faith, thou bear'st thee like a king.
But mine I am sure thou art whoe'er thou be,
And thus I win thee.   *They fight, the king being in danger,*

Enter Prince of Wales.

Prince. Hold up thy head, vile Scot, or thou art like   *40*
Never to hold it up again! the spirits
Of valiant Shirley, Stafford, Blunt are in my arms.
It is the Prince of Wales that threatens thee,
Who never promiseth but he means to pay.
                        They fight. Douglas flieth.   *45*
Cheerly, my lord! How fares your Grace?
Sir Nicholas Gawsey hath for succor sent,
And so hath Clifton. I'll to Clifton straight.

King. Stay and breathe awhile.
Thou hast redeem'd thy lost opinion,   *50*
And show'd thou mak'st some tender of my life,
In this fair rescue thou hast brought to me.

Prince. O God! they did me too much injury,
That ever said I hearken'd for your death.
If it were so, I might have let alone   *55*
The insulting hand of Douglas over you,
Which would have been as speedy in your end
As all the poisonous potions in the world,
And sav'd the treacherous labor of your son.

King. Make up to Clifton. I'll to Sir Nicholas Gawsey.   *60*
                                                        Exit.

Enter Hotspur.

Hot. If I mistake not, thou art Harry Monmouth.

Prince. Thou speak'st as if I would deny my name.

Hot. My name is Harry Percy.

Prince.   Why then I see   *65*
A very valiant rebel of the name.
I am the Prince of Wales, and think not, Percy,
To share with me in glory any more.
Two stars keep not their motion in one sphere,
Nor can one England brook a double reign   *70*
Of Harry Percy and the Prince of Wales.

Hot. Nor shall it, Harry, for the hour is come
To end the one of us, and would to God
Thy name in arms were now as great as mine.

Prince. I'll make it greater ere I part from thee,   *75*
And all the budding honors on thy crest

148–149 Turk Gregory; *cf. n.*   **158 pierce;** *cf. n.*   **160 carbonado:** *a piece of meat slashed for broiling*   **4 make up:** *go forward*   **5 amaze:** *alarm*   **22 lustier maintenance:** *more vigorous bearing*

26 Hydra: *a fabled monster, whose heads grew again as they were cut off*   **33 Seek:** *who seek*   **44 but:** *unless*   **51 mak'st some tender:** *hast some regard for*   **54 hearken'd for:** *watched for, desired*   **69** *Cf. n.*

I'll crop to make a garland for my head.

Hot. I can no longer brook thy vanities.   *They fight.*

Enter Falstaff.

Fal. Well said, Hal! to it, Hal! Nay, you shall find no boy's
play here, I can tell you.   80

*Enter Douglas. He fighteth with Falstaff. He [i.e., Falstaff] falls
down as if he were dead. [Exit Douglas.] The Prince killeth Percy.*

Hot. O Harry, thou hast robb'd me of my youth.
I better brook the loss of brittle life
Than those proud titles thou hast won of me.
They wound my thoughts worse than thy sword my flesh.
But thoughts (the slaves of life) and life (time's fool)   85
And time, that takes survey of all the world,
Must have a stop. O, I could prophesy,
But that the earthy and cold hand of death
Lies on my tongue. No, Percy, thou art dust,
And food for—   *[Dies.]* 90

Prince. For worms, brave Percy. Fare thee well, great heart!
Ill-weav'd ambition, how much art thou shrunk!
When that this body did contain a spirit,
A kingdom for it was too small a bound,
But now two paces of the vilest earth   95
Is room enough. This earth, that bears thee dead,
Bears not alive so stout a gentleman.
If thou wert sensible of courtesy,
I should not make so dear a show of zeal.
But let my favors hide thy mangled face,   100
And even in thy behalf I'll thank myself,
For doing these fair rites of tenderness.
Adieu, and take thy praise with thee to heaven!
Thy ignominy sleep with thee in the grave,
But not remember'd in thy epitaph!   105

He spieth Falstaff on the ground.

What, old acquaintance! Could not all this flesh
Keep in a little life? Poor Jack, farewell!
I could have better spar'd a better man.
O I should have a heavy miss of thee,   110
If I were much in love with vanity.
Death hath not struck so fat a deer to-day,
Though many dearer, in this bloody fray.
Embowell'd will I see thee by and by.
Till then in blood by noble Percy lie.   *Exit.* 115

Falstaff riseth up.

Fal. Embowelled? if thou embowel me to-day, I'll give you
leave to powder me and eat me too to-morrow. 'Sblood! 'twas
time to counterfeit, or that hot termagant Scot had paid me
scot and lot too. Counterfeit? I lie, I am no counterfeit. To
die is to be a counterfeit, for he is but the counterfeit of a   120
man, who hath not the life of a man: but to counterfeit dying,
when a man thereby liveth, is to be no counterfeit, but the
true and perfect image of life indeed. The better part of valor
is discretion, in the which better part I have saved my life.
'Zounds! I am afraid of this gunpowder Percy, though he   125
be dead. How if he should counterfeit too and rise? By my

faith, I am afraid he would prove the better counterfeit. Therefore I'll make him sure: yea, and I'll swear I killed him. Why
may not he rise as well as I? Nothing confutes me but eyes,
and nobody sees me. Therefore, sirrah, with a new wound   130
in your thigh, come you along with me.

He takes up Hotspur on his back.

Enter Prince and John of Lancaster.

Prince. Come, brother John, full bravely hast thou flesh'd
Thy maiden sword.

John.   But soft! Whom have we here?   135
Did you not tell me this fat man was dead?

Prince. I did. I saw him dead, breathless and bleeding
On the ground.—Art thou alive? or is it
Fantasy that plays upon our eyesight?
I prithee speak. We will not trust our eyes   140
Without our ears. Thou art not what thou seem'st.

Fal. No, that's certain. I am not a double man: but if I be
not Jack Falstaff, then am I a Jack. There is Percy *[throwing
down the body]*. If your father will do me any honor, so: if
not, let him kill the next Percy himself. I look to be either   145
earl or duke, I can assure you.

Prince. Why, Percy I killed myself, and saw thee dead.

Fal. Didst thou? Lord, Lord, how this world is given to
lying! I grant you I was down, and out of breath, and so was
he, but we rose both at an instant, and fought a long hour   150
by Shrewsbury clock. If I may be believed, so: if not, let them
that should reward valor bear the sin upon their own heads.
I'll take it upon my death, I gave him this wound in the
thigh. If the man were alive, and would deny it, 'zounds, I
would make him eat a piece of my sword.   155

John. This is the strangest tale that ever I heard.

Prince. This is the strangest fellow, brother John.
Come, bring your luggage nobly on your back.
For my part, if a lie may do thee grace,
I'll gild it with the happiest terms I have.   160

A retreat is sounded.

The trumpet sounds retreat, the day is ours.
Come brother, let us to the highest of the field,
To see what friends are living, who are dead.   *Exeunt.*

Fal. I'll follow, as they say, for reward. He that rewards   165
me, God reward him! If I do grow great, I'll grow less, for
I'll purge and leave sack, and live cleanly as a nobleman
should do.   *Exit.*

❧ SCENE FOURTH ❧

[The Battle Field]
*The trumpets sound. Enter the King, Prince of Wales, Lord John
of Lancaster, Earl of Westmorland, with Worcester and
Vernon prisoners.*

King. Thus ever did rebellion find rebuke.
Ill-spirited Worcester, did not we send grace,
Pardon, and terms of love to all of you?
And wouldst thou turn our offers contrary?
Misuse the tenor of thy kinsman's trust?   5
Three knights upon our party slain to-day,
A noble earl, and many a creature else,

79 Well said: *well tried, well done*   **84 They:** *i.e., the titles lost*   **97 stout:** *valiant*   **99
dear:** *affectionate*   **100 favors;** *cf. n.*   **114 Embowell'd:** *disembowelled for em-
balming*   **117 powder:** *salt*   **118 termagant:** *violent; cf. n.*   **119 scot and lot:** *a tax
paid according to one's ability and resources*

162 highest: *highest ground, best viewpoint; cf. n.*   **165 I'll follow;** *cf. n.*

Had been alive this hour,
If like a Christian thou hadst truly borne
Betwixt our armies true intelligence.   10
    Wor. What I have done my safety urg'd me to:
And I embrace this fortune patiently,
Since not to be avoided it falls on me.
    King. Bear Worcester to the death and Vernon too.
Other offenders we will pause upon.   15
                      Exit Worcester and Vernon [guarded].
How goes the field?
    Prince. The noble Scot, Lord Douglas, when he saw
The fortune of the day quite turn'd from him,
The noble Percy slain, and all his men   20
Upon the foot of fear, fled with the rest,
And falling from a hill, he was so bruis'd
That the pursuers took him. At my tent
The Douglas is, and I beseech your Grace
I may dispose of him.   25
    King.   With all my heart.
    Prince. Then, brother John of Lancaster, to you
This honorable bounty shall belong.
Go to the Douglas, and deliver him

Up to his pleasure, ransomless and free.   30
His valors shown upon our crests to-day
Have taught us how to cherish such high deeds,
Even in the bosom of our adversaries.
    John. I thank your Grace for this high courtesy,
Which I shall give away immediately.   35
    King. Then this remains, that we divide our power.
You, son John, and my cousin Westmorland
Towards York shall bend you, with your dearest speed,
To meet Northumberland and the prelate Scroop,
Who, as we hear, are busily in arms.   40
Myself and you, son Harry, will towards Wales,
To fight with Glendower and the Earl of March.
Rebellion in this land shall loose his sway,
Meeting the check of such another day,
And since this business so fair is done,   45
Let us not leave till all our own be won.   *Exeunt.*

⁂ FINIS ⁂

---

21 **Upon the foot of fear:** *flying in fear*   31 **valors:** *acts of prowess*   38 **dearest:** *best*   46 **leave:** *leave off*

NOTES

At the time of his sudden death in June of 1946, Professor Brooke had completed his work on the text, notes, and glosses for Hamlet, King Lear, Othello, *and* I Henry IV. *The editorial tasks which he left unfinished—preparation of some of the final copy for the press, reading of the proofs, compilation of the* Indexes of Words Glossed, *decisions as to certain matters of style and format, and, in the case of* I Henry IV, *the rescuing of the text from the prescriptive punctuation of the eighteenth-century editors—have been undertaken by Professor Benjamin Nangle.*

Textual Note. The differences between the Quarto text of this play, first printed in 1598, and the Folio text published in 1623 are unusually small. The Folio here has little or no independent authority. It appears to have been set up from a copy of the Quarto of 1613 (the fifth in sequence from the *editio princeps* of 1598) and it passed on, with additions of its own, the great body of small textual errors which this popular play had picked up in the course of rapid quarto printing. Even in the matter of stage directions the Folio has little new to offer; it usually reprints the quarto directions with only casual changes of wording. It did, however, divide the play into acts and scenes, something not attempted in the quartos, and did this with completeness and accuracy. In the present edition no changes have been made in the Folio act and scene headings except to translate them out of their Latin style: 'Actus Primus. Scaena Prima.,' etc. The stage directions reproduce usually those of the 1598 Quarto, sometimes those of the Folio. Necessary amplifications and other essential matter omitted in the original editions are supplied within square brackets.

The present text is based mainly on that of the extant 1598 edition, usually referred to as the First Quarto. There was, however, an earlier edition, probably printed a few months before, of which one single sheet of four leaves is preserved in the Folger Shakespeare Library. It enables us to recover a word that Shakespeare almost certainly wrote, the word *fat* in II.ii.101.

In Shakespeare's usage it was optional to give full syllabic value to the ending *-ed* of past verbal forms or (as is generally done now) to contract this ending with the preceding syllable. In the present text final *-ed* must always be pronounced as a separate syllable in order to preserve the original rhythm of the verse. Where rhythm requires the contracted form, the spelling *-'d* is used.

Shakespeare accented a number of words on syllables which do not now bear the accent, and sometimes his practice in this matter was inconsistent. Where an unusual accentuation is required, it is indicated by an acute mark over the stressed vowel, as in *éxact*.

Obsolete words and words employed in now unusual senses are explained in footnotes the first time they occur in the text. Repetitions are not noted and when they occur can be found in the *Index of Words Glossed* at the end of the volume.

The critical and general notes in the present section are announced by the symbol, *cf. n.*, at the bottom of the page of text to which each has relevance. A name at the end of a note (in parentheses) indicates the authority; but no special effort is made to give credit for material which is common property or which is, so far as known, new in the present edition.

I.i.4. *stronds afar remote.* The idea of pilgrimage reminds Shakespeare of the opening of Chaucer's *Canterbury Tales*, with its allusion to palmers seeking 'straunge strondes.'

I.i.5. *entrance of this soil.* The earth is personified, and the dry surface is called her mouth.

I.i.26. *fourteen hundred years ago.* The purpose is to give the audience the historical date, which was 1402. The figure, however, is about thirty years in error, because the Christian era is reckoned from Christ's birth, not his crucifixion.

I.i.28. Cf. the last lines of Shakespeare's *Richard II*, King Henry's speech when news is brought him that, at his suggestion, King Richard, his predecessor whose throne he has usurped, has been murdered:

> *Lords, I protest, my soul is full of woe*
> *That blood should sprinkle me to make me grow:*
> *Come, mourn with me for that I do lament*
> *And put on sullen black incontinent:*
> *I'll make a journey to the Holy Land*
> *To wash this blood from off my guilty hand.*

During the year (actually two and a half years) which has intervened, civil wars have prevented the fulfilment of this vow.

I.i.38. *Mortimer.* Earl of March, rightful heir to the throne of England (see genealogical table in note on I.iii.147,148), now (according to the play) in command of King Henry's forces on the western front.

I.i.52. *Holy-rood day.* Holy Cross Day, 14 September.

I.i.53. *Young Harry Percy.* The youngest member of the great Percy family, now in command of the king's forces on the northern front. The Percies had been King Henry's chief supporters in his usurpation of the throne.

I.i.57, 58. *As . . . the news was told.* As we learned by the sound of their artillery and by probable conjecture.

I.i.71. *Mordake* (i.e. Murdoch Stuart), *Earl of Fife.* He was not son to beaten Douglas, but to the Duke of Albany, regent of Scotland. Shakespeare's error is due to a mistake in punctuation in Holinshed's list of Hotspur's prisoners, which reads: 'Mordacke earle of Fife, son to the governour Archembald earle Dowglas,' etc. A comma was omitted after 'governour,' and Shakespeare understood that 'Archembald' was 'governour.'

I.i.92-96. By the law of arms, the king might claim only such prisoners as were of royal blood, and the historical Hotspur was therefore within his rights in refusing to send to the king any prisoners except Mordake. But Shakespeare did not know that Mordake was of royal blood (see preceding note) and he was apparently ignorant of the law of arms which gave Hotspur the right to keep the rest of the prisoners. No attempt is made to explain why Shakespeare's Hotspur sent Mordake to the king—Shakespeare merely follows the facts as set down in Holinshed. The indignation of King Henry and Westmorland, in this scene, at 'young Percy's pride'; Hotspur's conciliatory tone and his explanations when he appears at court (I.iii.); and the fact that neither Hotspur nor his uncle, Worcester, the experienced diplomat, ever suggests that Hotspur has a legal right to his prisoners; all these things indicate that Shakespeare's Hotspur is not within his rights in keeping the prisoners. His refusal was, at first, a thoughtless and impetuous act; and the refusal once made, the shrewd Worcester saw reasons for influencing his nephew to stand by this first hasty reply to the king's demand.

I.i.98. *Malevolent to you in all aspects.* An astrological allusion, referring to the supposed good and evil influences of the planets. The king uses another astrological figure in his address to Worcester in V.i.18-22.

I.i.108. *uttered.* Used here in its peculiar Elizabethan sense, namely, to put into circulation or to offer to the public. The substance of the king's speech is: 'Dismiss the lords until Wednesday next, but you yourself return to me at once, for more is to be said and done, than I can say or do in public in my present angry condition.'

I.ii.S.d. *Enter Prince of Wales and Sir John Falstaff.* They do not come in together. Falstaff is asleep on a bench and the Prince is awaking him as the scene opens.

I.ii.12. *seven stars.* The Pleiades.

I.ii.13. *wandering knight.* El Donzel del Febo, Knight of the Sun (or Phœbus), hero of a popular Spanish romance. This quotation is perhaps from some contemporary ballad founded on the romance.

I.ii.14-26. Falstaff plays on the word Grace, using it first as a title, then in reference to the spiritual state of grace, and finally as 'grace before meat.' From this simple pun he proceeds to a more complicated play on words. There is the obvious play on *night* and *knight* in line 21, followed in lines 21,22 by the play on the words *body, beauty,* and *booty,* in each of which the vowel sound, in Shakespeare's day, approximated the round *o* sound, as in *note.* Finally there is the play on the phrase *under whose countenance.*

I.ii.38. *buff jerkin . . . durance.* A buff jerkin, the jacket of heavy yellowish leather regularly worn by a sheriff's officer, is certainly durable and perhaps both confining in itself and a symbol of confinement (durance vile) for offenders; but the phrase *robe of durance* seems, when naturally interpreted, to introduce an illogical shift from the costume of the officer to that of his prisoner. Perhaps Hal's lack of logic is intentional, since if the hostess can be called a most sweet wench, all distinctions are lost.

I.ii.66. Eating the flesh of a hare was supposed to generate melancholy.

I.ii.67. *Moorditch.* A stagnant ditch and morass outside the north wall of London. The Theatre and Curtain playhouses were close by.

I.ii.78. *damnable iteration.* A damnable trick of quoting and misapplying. Falstaff and the Prince have both been parodying the first chapter of *Proverbs* (verse 20 ff.): 'Wisdom crieth without; she uttereth her voice in the streets. She crieth in the chief place of concourse . . . "I have stretched out my hand, and no man regarded; but ye have set at naught all my counsel, and would none of my reproof." '

I.ii.92. *Gadshill.* The *nom de guerre* of one of the robbers and the scene of his exploits.

I.ii.100. *a cup of Madeira and a cold capon's leg.* The keeping of Lent was strenuously demanded in the Anglican as well as the Catholic Church.

I.ii.108. *There are pilgrims going to Canterbury.* Perhaps another Chaucer allusion (cf. n. on I.i.4). The pilgrims are not again mentioned, and they are the only element in this part of the play that is not contemporary Elizabethan.

I.ii.112. *Eastcheap.* The district in central London where the Boar's Head Tavern, the rendezvous of Hal and Falstaff, was situated.

I.ii.122. *stand for ten shillings.* Primarily, take your stand as a highwayman for a profit of that amount; but Falstaff is also quibbling on the name of the gold coin, 'royal,' which stood for (had the value of) ten shillings.

I.ii.123. *Well, then,* etc. The Prince is teasing Falstaff. He has no idea of going, as line 125 shows.

I.ii.137. *the latter spring.* Good Elizabethan idiom. Pope emended it to 'thou latter spring.'

I.ii.137,138. *Allhallown summer.* The warm weather which comes at about the time of All Saints' Day, 1 November; called in America Indian Summer. The reference is to Falstaff's youthful spirit in his old age.

I.ii.141. *Bardolph, Peto.* In all the early texts these names are here replaced by 'Harvey, Rossill.' The characters were probably so called, when Falstaff was called 'Oldcastle,' and later given new names. (In the Quarto text Bardolph is regularly called 'Bardoll.')

I.ii.156. *sirrah.* The ordinary form of address to children and servants; here, a sign of Poins's undue familiarity with the Prince.

I.ii.160. *the third.* Falstaff. Shakespeare's inaccuracy in unimportant details is well illustrated here. He has just mentioned four robbers (line 141), and now implies, at least, that there are to be but three.

I.ii.170-192. One interpretation of the Prince's speech is that it is a striking example of the use of soliloquy in a choral function, to give the audience information uncolored by the personality of the speaker; and that Shakespeare is here describing the Prince's character and expects us to accept the description at face value without imputing vanity or insincerity to his mouthpiece, who has ceased to speak in his own person. See L. L. Schücking, *Character Problems in Shakespeare's Plays,* 1922, 217-221. Another school of critics sees in this speech the first indication of the cool and calculating nature of the Prince.

I.iii.S.d. *Windsor Castle.* The scene is stated by Holinshed. Cf.I.i.104.

I.iii.37. *milliner.* In Shakespeare's time, milliners, i.e., dealers in women's clothes from Milan, were for the most part men.

I.iii.57. *God save the mark.* An expression of impatient scorn (O.E.D.).

I.iii.139. *Bolingbroke.* King Henry is referred to by several names during the course of the play. Before his accession he was commonly known as Henry of Bolingbroke, from the fact that he was born in Bolingbroke Castle in Lincolnshire. He also bore the titles Earl of Derby, Duke of Hereford, and, after his father's death, Duke of Lancaster.

I.iii.147, 148. The following genealogical table will help to make clear this question of the succession to the English throne:

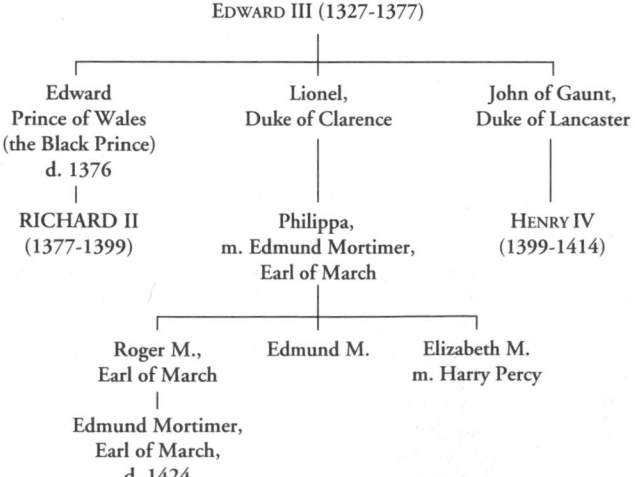

EDWARD III (1327-1377)

Edward	Lionel,	John of Gaunt,
Prince of Wales	Duke of Clarence	Duke of Lancaster
(the Black Prince)		
d. 1376		

RICHARD II	Philippa,	HENRY IV
(1377-1399)	m. Edmund Mortimer,	(1399-1414)
	Earl of March	

| Roger M., | Edmund M. | Elizabeth M. |
| Earl of March | | m. Harry Percy |

Edmund Mortimer,
Earl of March,
d. 1424

Shakespeare follows the chroniclers in confusing Edmund Mortimer, the son of Philippa, with Edmund Mortimer, the son of Roger. It was Roger Mortimer who was King Richard's heir, and was so proclaimed in the October Parliament of 1385. At his death in 1398, one year before King Richard's, his seven-year-old son succeeded to his claim. But it was the elder Edmund, brother to Roger, who fought Glendower and married his daughter. Hotspur's brother-in-law, therefore, was not heir to the throne. The heir, as the table shows, was the nephew of Lady Percy, and in III.i.202, Mortimer refers to Lady Percy as 'my aunt Percy.' Here (line 159), and in line 81, Mortimer is represented as Hotspur's brother-in-law.

I.iii.253. *York.* Edmund of Langley, Duke of York, younger brother to John of Gaunt, uncle to King Richard and King Henry. Richard had appointed York regent of England during the king's absence in Ireland. Richard had previously exiled Henry, and the latter chose this period of the king's absence from his realm to return and claim his father's estates, which had been unjustly confiscated by Richard to pay for this same Irish expedition. Henry was met at Ravenspurgh, on the coast of Yorkshire, by Northumberland; at Doncaster, in southern Yorkshire, by Worcester; and finally at Berkeley Castle, in Gloucestershire, by Hotspur. The interview between Hotspur and Henry, from which Hotspur quotes in his next speech, is presented in Shakespeare's *Richard II,* II.iii.

I.iii.259. *Look when.* A remarkable localism, used frequently by Shakespeare in his earlier works. See Mark Eccles, 'Shakespeare's Use of *Look How* and similar Idioms' (*J.E.G.P.,* July, 1943).

I.iii.280. *the Lord Scroop.* The Earl of Wiltshire, one of the adherents of King Richard, executed by order of Henry; see *Richard II,* III.ii.141 ff. He was not the brother of the archbishop, as Holinshed states, but of an allied family.

II.i.S.d. *The Yard of a Carriers' Inn.* The carriers transported produce and other merchandise between London and the country, using the appointed inn-yards for loading and unloading. The companies of actors employed the same inn-yards for plays when regular playhouses were not available. The scene here presented is doubtless based on what Shakespeare would have observed at the Cross Keys Inn in London, where his company acted in 1594.

II.i.2. *Charles' Wain.* Probably a corruption of 'churl's wain' or 'countryman's wagon,' a name for the constellation now known as the Great Bear.

II.i.13. There is an old superstition, referred to in Pliny's *Natural History,* ix.47, that fishes are infested with fleas. Cf. line 18.

II.i.21. *Charing Cross.* In Shakespeare's time a village on the road from London to Westminster; now in the heart of Greater London.

II.i.28. *two o'clock.* Compare line 1 above. The carriers suspect Gadshill and refuse to co-operate (Steevens).

II.i.53. *Saint Nicholas.* A popular saint in the Roman and Russian Churches, now familiarly known as Santa Claus. He was the patron saint of scholars, children, parish clerks, travellers, sailors, and pawn-brokers. His aid was invoked by travellers to protect them from perils of the road, especially from robbers. But here the allusion is to his opposite, 'Old Nick,' the devil.

II.i.64 ff. *foot land-rakers,* foot-pads; *long-staff sixpenny strikers,* fellows who would knock a man down to get sixpence from him; *mustachio-purple-hued malt worms,* fellows whose moustaches are so constantly immersed in ale that they have become purple; *tranquillity,* people who live at ease; *great oneyers,* great ones (with a play on the words *one* and *own* which were pronounced alike); *such as can hold in,* such as can keep their own counsel (an accomplishment which Gadshill seems to find it difficult to imitate).

II.i.75. Greasing of boots to make them waterproof was called 'liquoring' them.

II.i.76. *receipt of fernseed.* The seeding of ferns was a mystery to early botanists. According to popular superstition, fernseed was visible only on Saint John's Eve (23 June), and those who gathered it then, according to a certain rite, were themselves rendered invisible.

II.i.83. *homo is a common name to all men.* Even a false thief is a true *homo.* A small joke out of Lily's Latin grammar.

II.ii.2. *frets like a gummed velvet.* Velvet stiffened with gum very soon chafed.

II.ii.39. *heir-apparent garters.* 'Alluding to the Order of the Garter, in which he was enrolled as heir-apparent' (Johnson).

II.ii.60. *John of Gaunt.* There is a pun, as if on 'John o' Gaunt' and 'John o' Paunch' (Kittredge).

II.iii.S.d. The writer of this letter is not specified.

II.iii.26. I could divide myself into two parts and then fight with myself.

II.iii.30. *Kate.* The actual name of Hotspur's wife was Elizabeth, not Kate; cf. genealogical table left. Shakespeare seems to have had a peculiar fondness for the name Kate.

II.iii.39, 40. Why have you allowed musing and melancholy, which have made you *thick-eyed,* i.e., blind to all outward things, to make you forget your attention to me, which is my *treasure?*

II.iii.47. The basilisk cannon was named from the fabulous monster whose look was reputed to kill. The culverin is also named from a serpent.

II.iii.89. *crowns.* Used quibblingly: broken heads, or damaged coin, still in circulation, 'passing current.' Behind this is the idea of the crown of the kingdom at which Hotspur means to have a crack.

II.iv.1. *fat room.* Certainly not 'vat-room,' as sometimes explained. It is the Prince, not Poins, who has been in the latter.

II.iv.17. *tinker.* Tinkers were famous for their capacity for strong drink and for their picturesque vocabulary.

II.iv.49. *Michaelmas.* The feast of St. Michael, 29 September; one of the four quarter days of the English business year.

II.iv.67. ff. Hal here talks nonsense, with the express purpose of confusing Francis still more. A vague meaning can be found. Francis was doubtless wearing a white canvas doublet, and the price of sugar (cf. line 53) would be less in Barbary, whence it was originally imported.

II.iv.93. *I am not yet of Percy's mind.* The Prince returns to his previous remark, 'I am now of all humors' (85) and qualifies it. The sudden transition from Francis to Hotspur in line 93 is surprising. It is perhaps the feverish activity of the drawer Francis, who is rushing up and down stairs, crying 'anon' in reply to all questions, that reminds the Prince of a similar nervous activity in Hotspur. Shakespeare loses no opportunity of bringing Hal and Hotspur into contrast.

II.iv.109. *Titan.* The sun. Mispunctuation has made this speech obscure in most editions. The phrase 'pitiful-hearted Titan' is parenthetical, as Warburton first suggested, and the clause beginning 'that melted' refers to 'butter.'

II.iv.109-110. *the sweet tale of the sun's.* The sun's sweet tale. Modern idiom would require 'this sweet tale,' etc.

II.iv.119. *weaver.* Elizabethan weavers were, in large part, 'psalm-singing Puritans,' who had fled to England from the religious persecutions in the Low Countries.

II.iv.155-163. On the confusion of speakers here in the early texts compare note on I.ii.141 and B. H. Bronson, 'A Note on Gadshill, our Setter,' *PMLA*, 1930, pp. 749-753.

II.iv.193. *points.* Falstaff refers to the points of swords. Poins, in his reply, quibblingly interprets points in another sense, namely laces for garments.

II.iv.201. *Kendal green.* A dark green woolen cloth made at Kendal in Westmorland; the traditional costume of Robin Hood.

II.iv.215. *strappado.* A military punishment which consisted of fastening a rope under the arms of the offender, drawing him up by a pulley to the top of a high beam and then suddenly letting him down with a jerk.

II.iv.216. *reasons.* A play on the words *reasons* and *raisins*, which were pronounced alike.

II.iv.242. *By the Lord, I knew ye.* The truth seems to be that whether or not Falstaff recognized the Prince and Poins in their disguise and fled with conviction from the scene of the robbery, in the twelve hours or more during which he was conducting the retreat of his followers from Gadshill to the Boar's Head, he has come to a clear idea of what happened. He therefore enters the inn in the present scene aware of the trick that has been played upon him and prepared with a careful plan for turning the situation to the advantage of his own quick wit. Thus he lures Hal and Poins on with Gargantuan lies and evades them with blithe sophistry when they think they have him cornered.

II.iv.263. *royal.* A royal was 10s.; a noble 6s. 8d. Cf. I.ii.122.

II.iv.288-294. Bardolph becomes angry and adopts a threatening attitude. 'My red face,' he implies, 'portends *choler* (anger).' Hal finds it merely a sign of a *hot liver* (caused by drinking) and an empty purse (also caused by drink). When Bardolph insists that it is *choler*, Hal quibblingly interprets *choler* as collar, the hangman's noose or *halter*.

II.iv.304, 305. *Amamon . . . Lucifer.* Amaymon was a king of devils, mentioned in Reginald Scot's popular *Discovery of Witchcraft* (1584). *Made Lucifer cuckold* is Falstaff's way of saying that Glendower provided him with his well-known horns (J. Q. Adams).

II.iv.349. *King Cambyses.* A ranting bombastic tragedy by Thomas Preston (1570). Line 353 shows that Falstaff knew more than the name of the play, one line of which reads: '(At this tale tolde let the Queene weep.)

Queene: These wordes to hear makes stilling teares issue from christal eyes.'

II.iv.359. Falstaff may be referring to the Hostess as a pintpot always well filled with tickle-brain, or he may be using tickle-brain not in its technical sense, but merely as an appropriate word for describing the flighty character of the Hostess.

II.iv.360. ff. Falstaff is here burlesquing the somewhat pompous and artificial style of King Henry, and Shakespeare is, at the same time, burlesquing the fashionable and artificial prose style of his own contemporaries, known as Euphuism. This style was exemplified in John Lyly's *Euphues* (1578-1580), and its chief characteristics are: (1) The constant use of antithesis, (2) The use of alliteration to emphasize the antithetic clauses, (3) The frequent use of a long string of similes all relating to the same subject, often taken from the fabulous qualities ascribed to plants, animals, and minerals, (4) The constant use of rhetorical questions, (5) Frequent quotation of proverbs. Falstaff's first figure is taken directly from *Euphues* (ed. Bond, vol. I, p. 196): 'Though the Camomill the more it is trodden and pressed downe, the more it spreadeth, yet the Violet the oftner

it is handeled and touched, the sooner it withereth and decayeth.' The following passages are good examples of Euphuism: 'Though thou haue eaten the seedes of Rockatte which breede incontinencie, yet haue I chewed the leafe Cresse which mainteineth modestie. Though thou beare in thy bosome the hearbe Araxa most noisome to virginitie, yet haue I the stone that groweth in the mounte Tmolus, the vpholder of chastitie' (Bond, I.222). 'Well doth he know that the glass once crased will with the least clappe be cracked. . . . But can Euphues conuince me of fleetinge, seeing for his sake I breake my fidelitie? Can he condemne me of disloyaltie, when he is the only cause of my dislyking? May he condemn me of trecherye, who hath this testimony as tryall of my good will? Doth he not remember that . . . though the Spyder poyson the Flye, she cannot infect the Bee? That though I have bene light to Philautus, yet I may be louely to Euphues?' (Bond. I. 205-206.)

II.iv.393. Falstaff is comparing himself with the thinnest things he can think of, a young sucking rabbit, or a hare hung up in a poulterer's shop.

II.iv.400. *I'll tickle ye,* etc. This is obviously an aside to Hal, and not part of Falstaff's speech in his rôle as Prince. As he begins his performance, he whispers to Hal, 'My acting of the part of a young prince will tickle you, i' faith.'

II.iv.401. *Henceforth ne'er look on me.* Here Hal speaks the words Falstaff dreads. See note on line 430 below.

II.iv.407. *Manningtree ox.* Manningtree is a town in Essex, famous for its fairs at which oxen were roasted whole.

II.iv.426. *Pharaoh's lean kine.* Cf. Genesis 41. 19.

II.iv.430. *banish not him thy Harry's company,* etc. This redoubled cry underlines the great fear which lends pathos to Falstaff's effort to make himself an indispensable clown and gives him a kinship with the poet of the Sonnets. Cf. Sonnet 87,

Farewell! Thou art too dear for my possessing,
And like enough thou know'st thy estimate.

II.iv.443, 444. As in lines 435 ff., Falstaff is loath, even in the face of peril, to forgo his spirited defence of himself (cf. 420-432). He has been hurt by Hal's drastic abuse of him in 399-413, and as the sheriff approaches he makes a last appeal: 'Never miscall one who, like me, is true gold.' 'You, too,' he adds, 'sober though you seem, are essentially a madcap.' (That is, we are brothers under the skin.)

II.iv.446. *I deny your major.* The syllogism that Falstaff has in mind may run thus:—Major premise: All who run away are natural cowards. Minor premise: Falstaff ran away. Conclusion (stated by Prince): Therefore, Falstaff is a natural coward. Elizabethan schoolboys were well trained in this exercise, and an average audience could probably supply the missing terms. There is also a pun on *major* as here used and major, the mayor of a town, the officer next in rank above the sheriff.

II.iv.450, 451. Falstaff hides behind the curtain which divided the outer from the inner stage in the Elizabethan theatre; the others *walk above*, i.e., on the balcony above the inner stage.

II.iv.462, 463. *The man, I do assure you, is not here.* Truth is considerably strained. The man, says the prince, is not here immediately in presence, for I have sent him on a mission behind the arras.

III.i.75. *The archdeacon hath divided it.* Shakespeare found in Holinshed's Chronicle the statement that the deputies of the conspirators divided the realm 'in the house of the Archdeacon of Bangor.' This led Theobald to the quaint idea that the present scene takes place in the Archdeacon of Bangor's house. Shakespeare, who handles the historical situation very freely (the division was not projected till after the deaths of Hotspur and Worcester), evidently assumes the scene to occur in one of Glendower's castles, possibly Penrhyn or Carnarvon, which are both close to Bangor. The value of the archdeacon was that as a clerk he could draw up formal papers and phrase them in Latin.

III.i.103. *the best of all my land.* All Lincolnshire and part of Nottinghamshire. Hotspur's proposal to divert the Trent River is entirely unhistoric. It may have been suggested to Shakespeare by a contemporary disturbance which made a good deal of noise. Sir Thomas Stanhope of Nottinghamshire maintained a weir at Shelford for the purpose of diverting the water of the Trent. On Easter Eve, 1593, 'a great and unlawful assembly of a multitude of persons' gathered together 'in tumultuous and riotous manner' to pull down the weir, and the resulting disorders kept Queen Elizabeth's Privy Council apprehensive for four months. See J. R. Dasent, *Acts of the Privy Council*, New Series, vol. xxiv, pp. 201 ff.

III.i.131. *gave the tongue a helpful ornament.* That is, by learning to sing English poetry to the harp I made my use of the language both effective and graceful.

III.i.155-159. The division of the kingdom was made by the conspirators, according to Holinshed, 'through a foolish credit given to a vain prophecy' that Henry was a moldwarp (a mole) whose kingdom should be divided among a wolf, a dragon, and a lion. This cryptic prophecy was attributed to Merlin, and is referred to in *The Mirror for Magistrates* (1559):

> And for to set us hereon more agog,
> A prophet came (a vengeaunce take them all)
> Affirming Henry to be Gog-magog,
> Whom Merlin doth a mouldwarp ever call,
> Accursed of God, that must be brought in thrall
> By a wulf, a dragon, and a lyon strong,
> Which shuld devide his kingdome them amonge.

Hotspur evidently has not shared in the 'foolish credit' given to the 'vain prophecy' and his only memory of the discussion is that Glendower talked a lot of Celtic nonsense.

III.i.206-209. Mortimer seems to be trying to say that though he does not understand his wife's speech, he understands her looks, and that he is *too perfect* in the language of tears (i.e., *that pretty Welsh* which she pours down from her swollen eyes). So near to tears is the bridegroom himself that shame alone prevents his answering his wife's tears with tears.

III.i.259. *Finsbury.* Archery grounds just outside London, a favorite resort of respectable middle-class citizens.

III.i.261. *velvet-guards.* Velvet trimmings; hence women that wear such finery, notably wives of aldermen.

III.i.264. *tailor.* Tailors, like weavers (cf. II.iv.119n.), were noted for singing at their work.

III.ii.23-28. *As, in reproof,* etc. That, in rebuke of the many falsehoods alleged against me, I may, on showing penitence, find pardon for some real faults of my youth.

III.ii.50. I assumed, or took upon myself, a heavenly graciousness of bearing.

III.ii.62. *carded.* To card was to mix different kinds of drink; so King Richard mixed his high state and dignity with baseness.

III.ii.100. Hal's claim to the crown is shadowy compared with Hotspur's, for Hal's claim is that of inheritance from a usurper who has been rewarded with the crown for his services to the state; whereas Hotspur's claim is that of efficient public service, performed by himself.

III.ii.104. *being no more in debt to years than thou.* Shakespeare's unhistorical assumption for dramatic effect. Hotspur was actually of King Henry's age.

III.ii.165. *Lord Mortimer of Scotland.* Shakespeare's error for George Dunbar, whom Holinshed calls 'the Scot, the Earl of March.' In England, but not in Scotland, the title, Earl of March, ran in the Mortimer family.

III.iii.7, 8. *brewer's horse.* The point of this comparison lies probably in the fact that a brewer's horse carries good liquor on his back, instead of in his belly. They were the lowest of the horse kind.

III.iii.26. It was the fashion to wear, as a *memento mori,* reminder of death, a ring or pin on the stone of which was engraved a skull and cross-bones.

III.iii.27. *Dives that lived in purple.* See St. Luke's Gospel, 16. 19-31.

III.iii.30. Cf. Psalm 104. 4: 'Who maketh his angels spirits; his ministers a flaming fire.'

III.iii.44. *Partlet.* The name of the hen in the famous story of the Cock and the Fox; cf. Chaucer's *Nonnes Preestes Tale.* The hen-like characteristics of the Hostess are apparent in the conversation immediately following.

III.iii.49. *tithe.* Lewis Theobald's emendation for 'tight.'

III.iii.100. *Maid Marian.* The mistress of Robin Hood, often impersonated by a man in the morris-dances, in which she was traditionally a rather disreputable person. 'As regards womanliness,' says Falstaff to the Hostess, 'in comparison with you, Maid Marian is as respectable a person as the wife of the deputy-alderman of this ward.'

III.iii.145. *injuries.* 'As the pocketing of injuries was a common phrase, I suppose the Prince calls the contents of Falstaff's pockets injuries' (Steevens). Cf. 147,148. Hal is sardonically implying that the alleged riches of Falstaff's pockets are all things he is better without.

III.iii.165. *unwashed hands.* Without stopping to wash your hands, i.e., at once; or, possibly, without any over-fastidious scruples.

III.iii.184. *drum.* Used here in the sense of rallying-point or recruiting station.

IV.i.4, 5. Another figurative expression referring to coinage; 'Your fame would circulate more widely than that of any soldier of this season's coinage.'

IV.i.58. 'The comfort of having something to fall back upon.'

IV.i.103. *estridges that woo the wind.* Ostriches increase their speed on ground by receiving the wind into their open wings. The early editions all read 'with'

instead of *woo.* The assumption behind the present emendation is that the original printer did not understand the image and misread the verb as the preposition, which was often written 'wth.' Ostrich feathers are (and were) the Prince of Wales's cognizance.

IV.i.104. *Bating.* Again the early editions agree in a senseless form, 'Baited' or 'Bayted.' The printer seems to have been misled by the past participles he had set up in the previous lines and by the following one in *bath'd.* Note that the shift to the present participle is continued in *Glittering* (line 105), and that 'Baited . . . bath'd' would make a very inharmonious verse.

IV.i.105. *images.* The reference is probably to the gilded robes which adorn the images of the saints in churches.

IV.i.106. *As full of spirit as the month of May.* It is hard not to believe that Shakespeare is again consciously remembering Chaucer's Prologue. Compare the latter's description of his Squire (*Prol.* 92),

> He was as fresshe as is the month of May.

IV.i.111, 112. 'Your praise of him causes me greater fever than the ague in spring.'

IV.i.119. *fire-ey'd maid.* Bellona, goddess of war.

IV.ii.2. *Sutton Cophill.* Sutton Coldfield, a town twenty-four miles northwest of Coventry.

IV.ii.6. 'makes an angel, or ten shillings, that I have spent.'

IV.ii.8. *answer the coinage.* Guarantee that they are not counterfeit (as of course they would not be, being figments of Falstaff's imagination).

IV.ii.12. *I have misused the king's press damnably.* An epidemic of graft in connection with the enlistment of troops for service in France and Ireland gave this scene contemporary topical value. For Captain Joshua Hilliard's peculations from one hundred and fifty men levied in Gloucestershire in 1593 see G. B. Harrison, *An Elizabethan Journal*, vol. i, p. 231 f. Falstaff is here not merely exposing his original sin; he is acting as a humorous commentator on the news.

IV.ii.29. St. Luke's Gospel, 15. 15, 16.

IV.ii.36. *but a shirt.* An emendation of Nicholas Rowe, Shakespeare's first editor (1674-1718). The early texts have 'not a shirt.'

IV.iii.30. *half himself.* Emended by George Steevens (1736-1800). Nearly all texts have 'half of himself,' which destroys the line.

V.i.S.d. The early texts include among the characters in this scene the Earl of Westmorland, who, according to V.ii.29,30, cannot be there.

V.i.14. *old limbs.* The historical King Henry was thirty-seven years old at the time of the battle of Shrewsbury; the historical Hotspur was about forty; and the historical Prince Hal seventeen. The King of Shakespeare's play is, however, an elderly man, and Hotspur and Hal are both young. I.i.88-91 shows that Shakespeare regarded his two youthful heroes as of the same age; and III.ii.113,114 would indicate that they were very young.

V.i.61, 62. The cuckoo frequently lays her eggs in the hedge-sparrow's nest; and the hedge-sparrow brings up the young cuckoos, until they have grown 'to such a bulk' that they destroy their foster-parents. Cf. *Lear*, I.iv.204, 205:

> The hedge-sparrow fed the cuckoo so long
> That it's had it head bit off by it young.

V.i.127, 128. There is probably a pun here on the words death and debt which were pronounced similarly.

V.ii.9. *Suspicion.* Another emendation of Rowe (1714) for 'Supposition' in all the early copies. As emended the line is an impressive alexandrine, well suited to emphasize the gravity of Worcester's warning. The immediate source of the image in this line is Spenser's *Faerie Queene* (I.iv.31), where Envy is 'ypainted full of eyes.'

V.ii.72. *a libertine.* Emendation of Edward Capell (1713-1781). The first Quarto has 'a libertie'; the fifth Quarto and Folio 'at libertie.'

V.ii.S.d. At this point modern editors, mistakenly, begin a new scene. The stage direction shows Shakespeare's intention. The spectacle of Hotspur's army embracing merges with the other spectacle of the entrance of the king's army. For a time the stage is crowded with fighting figures, who gradually disappear as in a dance movement. Then, immediately, Douglas and Blunt return to face each other on the empty stage.

V.ii.104. *What is thy name, that in battle thus?* The line lacks a syllable, but is probably as Shakespeare wrote it. He sometimes uses trochaic rhythms to give the sense of brusque or violent movement, as in the opening lines of the witches in *Macbeth.*

V.ii.125. *his name was Blunt.* It is perhaps surprising that Hotspur does not remember introducing Sir Walter Blunt to Douglas on the day before. See IV.iii.38.

V.ii.127. *'fool' go with thy soul.* May that epithet accompany you to the next world.

V.ii.148-149. *Turk Gregory.* Editors all agree that Falstaff here refers to Pope Gregory VII, Hildebrand, who, as a friar, was famous for violent exploits. Attempts to explain the appellation Turk are not very satisfactory. Falstaff perhaps has in mind the phrase 'to fight like a Turk.'

V.ii.158. Another pun. The -ie- of pierce was pronounced like the -e- of Percy.

V.iii.69. A reference to Ptolemaic astronomy, according to which each planet was fixed in a crystal sphere with which it revolved.

V.iii.100. *favors.* Here probably used for the Prince's ostrich feathers, the badge of his rank, which he removes from his helmet. See H. Hartman, 'Prince Hal's "Shew of Zeale",' *PMLA,* 1931, pp. 720-723.

V.iii.118. *termagant.* Name of one of the fabled idols worshipped by Mohammedans, according to mediæval romance.

V.iii.162. *Come, brother, let us to the highest of the field.* The word *brother* is 'extra-metrical'; that is, the verse line is complete without it. The addition of such words, normally words of direct address, was one of the allowable variations in dramatic blank verse.

V.iii.165. *I'll follow, as they say, for reward.* Falstaff returns, with better expectations, to the vocation in which we first see him (I.ii), that of suitor for court patronage.

The Second Part of King Henry the Fourth

Edited by
SAMUEL B. HEMINGWAY

Dramatis Personae

RUMOUR, *the Presenter*
KING HENRY THE FOURTH
PRINCE HENRY, *afterwards crowned King Henry the Fifth*
PRINCE JOHN OF LANCASTER ⎫ *Sons to Henry the Fourth,*
HUMPHREY OF GLOUCESTER ⎬ *and brethren to Henry*
THOMAS OF CLARENCE ⎭ *the Fifth*
NORTHUMBERLAND ⎫
THE ARCHBISHOP OF YORK ⎪
MOWBRAY ⎪
HASTINGS ⎪ *Opposites against King*
LORD BARDOLPH ⎬ *Henry the Fourth*
TRAVERS ⎪
MORTON ⎪
COLEVILE ⎭
WARWICK ⎫
WESTMORELAND ⎪
SURREY ⎪
GOWER ⎬ *of the King's Party*
HARCOURT ⎪
[BLUNT] ⎪
LORD CHIEF JUSTICE ⎭

[*Servant to the Lord Chief Justice*]
POINS, FALSTAFF, BARDOLPH, PISTOL, PETO, PAGE,
    Irregular Humorists
SHALLOW AND SILENCE, *Both Country Justices*
DAVY, *Servant to Shallow*
FANG AND SNARE, *two Sergeants*
MOULDY, SHADOW, WART, FEEBLE, BULLCALF,
    Country Soldiers
[PORTER AT WARKWORTH CASTLE]
[FRANCIS, *a Drawer*]
Drawers, Beadles, Grooms
[Lords and Attendants, Officers and Soldiers]

NORTHUMBERLAND'S WIFE
PERCY'S WIDOW
HOSTESS QUICKLY
DOLL TEARSHEET
EPILOGUE

The Second Part of King Henry the Fourth

INTRODUCTION

SOURCES OF THE PLAY

The principal source of the main plot of this play is the 1587 edition of *The Chronicles of England, Scotland, and Ireland,* by Raphael Holinshed. Samuel Daniel's poem, *The Civill Wars of England* (1595), or its source, may well have had some influence. Several incidents in the comic plot are taken, apparently, from the play *The Famous Victories of Henry V,* first acted in 1588, licensed in 1594, and published in 1598.

HOLINSHED'S CHRONICLE

According to Holinshed, the Earl of Northumberland was pardoned by the king after the battle of Shrewsbury in 1403. But in 1405 when 'the king was minded to haue gone into Wales against the rebels that vnder their cheeftane Owen Glendower ceassed not to doo much mischeef against the English subjects,' he was 'further disquieted' by a 'conspiracie put in practise against him at home by the Earle of Northumberland who had conspired with Richard Scroope, Archbishop of Yorke, Thomas Mowbraie earle marshall,' and others. 'The King aduertised of these matters left his iournie into Wales and marched with all speed toward the north parts. Also Rafe Neuill earl of Westmerland, that was not farre off, together with the lord Iohn of Lancaster, the king's sonne, being informed of this rebellious attempt, assembled togither such power as they might make . . . made forward against the rebels, and coming into a plaine within the forrest of Galtree caused their standards to be pitched downe in the like sort as the Archbishop had pitched his ouer against them, being farre stronger in number of people than the other, for as some write there were of the rebels at least twentie thousand men.'

Shakespeare follows Holinshed closely in describing the 'subtill policie' whereby the rebels are disposed of; but he transfers the odium attaching to this action from the earl of Westmoreland to Lord John of Lancaster.

The events of the next eight years, as related by Holinshed, are unnoticed in the play. Shakespeare proceeds immediately to the death of the king, and again follows the Chronicle closely. '1413. The morrow after Candlemas daie began a parlement which the king had called at London, but he departed this life before the same parlement was ended; for now that his prouisions were readie and that he was furnished with sufficient treasure, soldiers, capteins, vittels, munitions, tall ships, strong gallies, and all things necessarie for such a roiall iournie as he pretended to take into the holie land, he was eftsoones taken with a sore sicknesse, which was not a leprosie striken by the hand of God, as foolish friars imagined, but a verie apoplexie. . . . During this sicknesse he caused his crowne to be set on a pillow at his bed's head, and suddenlie his pangs so sore troubled him that he laie as though all his vitall spirits had beene from him departed. Such as were about him couered his face with a linen cloth. The prince, his sonne, being hereof aduertised, entered into the chamber, tooke awaie the crowne, and departed. The father being suddenlie reuiued out of that trance quicklie perceiued the lacke of his crowne; and hauing knowledge that the prince his sonne had taken it awaie caused him to come before his presence requiring of him what he meant so to misuse himself. The prince with a good audacitie answered, Sir, to mine and all mens iudgements you seemed dead in this world, wherefore I as youre next heire apparent tooke that as mine owne, and not as yours. Well, faire sonne, said the king with a great sigh, what right I had to it God knoweth. Well, said the prince, if you die king, I will haue the garland and trust to keepe it with the sword against all mine enemies as you haue done. Then said the king, I commit all to God, and remember you to doo well. With that he turned himself in his bed and shortlie after departed to God in a chamber of the abbats of Westminster called Ierusalem, . . . when he had reigned thirteene yeares in great perplexitie and little pleasure.'

Holinshed then tells us that 'king Henrie the fift was crowned the ninth of Aprill, being Passion Sundaie, which was a sore, ruggie, and tempestuous daie, with wind, snow, and sleet, that men greatlie maruelled thereat, making diuerse interpretations what that might signifie. But this king, to show that in his person princelie honors should change publike manners, he determined to put on him the shape of a new man. For whereas aforetime he had made himself a companion unto misrulie mates of dissolute order and life, he now banished them all from his presence, but not unrewarded or else unpreferred, inhibiting them upon a great paine not once to approach, lodge, or soiourne within ten miles of his court or presence: and in their places he chose men of grauitie, wit, and high policie, by whose wise councel he might at all times rule to his honor and dignity; calling to mind how once to hie offence of the king his father he had with his fist striken the cheefe iustice for sending one of his minions, upon desert, to prison, when the iustice stoutlie commanded himself also streict to ward, and the prince obeied.'

DANIEL'S CIVILL WARS

In the fourth book of his *Civill Wars,* Daniel condenses history even more radically than Shakespeare. The king falls sick immediately after his victory at Shrewsbury, and is afflicted by spectres of Conscience and Death. He commands

> 'some that attending were
> To fetch the crowne and set it in his sight;
> On which with fixed eye and heauie cheere
> Casting a looke, O God, sayeth he, what right
> I had to thee my soule doth now conceiue,—

Thee which with blood I got, with horror leave.'

Horror so overwhelms the king that he swoons—

'When loe his Sonne comes in and takes away
The fatall crowne from thence and out he goes
As if unwilling longer time to lose.'

The king revives, summons the prince, and says:

'O sonne, what needes thee make such speed
Vnto that care where feare exceedes thy right,
And when his sinne whom thou shalt now succeed
Shall still upbraide thy inheritance of might?
And if thou canst liue, and liue great, from woe,
Without this carefull trauaille, let it goe.'

The prince replies:

'What wrong hath not continuance quite outworne?
Yeeres make that right which neuer was so borne.'

The king dies praying that virtuous deeds and the holy wars of
his son may atone for his own sins.

THE FAMOUS VICTORIES OF HENRY V

In this crude play Prince Hal is twice committed to prison,
once by the Lord Mayor for rioting in the streets after a merry
evening at the tavern in Eastcheap, and once by the Lord Chief
Justice for giving him 'a box on the ear' upon his refusal to
pardon one of the prince's companions who has been convicted
of highway robbery.

The following are characteristic selections:

Enter Henry the fourth, with the earle of Exeter and the
earle of Oxford.

Oxf. Please your maiestie, heere is my Lord maior and the sheriffe
of London.
King Hen. 4. *Admit them to our presence.*

Enter the Maior and the Sheriffe.

    Now, my good Lord Maior of London, the cause of
my sending to you at this time is to tel you of a matter which I
have learned of my councell: Herein I understand that you haue
committed my sonne to prison without our leaue and license. What
although he be a rude youth and likely to give occasion, yet you
might haue considered that he is a Prince and my sonne, and not
to be halled to prison by euery subject.
Maior. *May it please your maiestie to give us leaue to tell our*
tale.
King Hen. 4. *Or else God forbid, otherwise you might think me*
an vnequall Iudge, hauing more affection to my sonne then to any
rightfull iudgement.
Maior. *Then if it please your Maiestie, this night betwixt two*
and three of the clocke of the morning, my Lord the young Prince
with a very disordered companie, came to the olde Tauerne in East-
cheape, and whether it was that their Musicke liked them not, or
whether they were ouercome with wine, I know not, but they drew
their swords and into the street they went, and some toke my Lord
the young Princes part, and some tooke the other, but betwixt them
there was such a bloodie fray for the space of half an houre, that
neither watchmen nor any other could stay them, till my brother the
Sheriffe of London and I were sent for, and at the laste with much

adoo we staied them, but it was long first, which was a great
disquieting to all your louing subiects thereabouts: and then my good
Lord, we knew not whether your grace had sent them to trie vs,
whether we would doe iustice, or whether it were of their owne
voluntarie will or not, we cannot tell, and therefore for our owne
safegard we sent him to ward where he wanteth nothing that is fit
for his grace.
King Hen. 4. *Stand aside vntill we haue further deliberated on*
your answere.   Exit Maior.
  Hen. 4. *Ah Harry, Harry, now thrice accursed Harry,*
    That hath gotten a sonne which with greefe
    Will end his fathers dayes.
    Oh my sonne, a Prince thou art, I a Prince indeed,
    And to deserue punishment
    And well haue they done, and like faithfull subiects:
    Discharge them and let them go.   Exit omnes.

•   •   •   •   •   •   •   •

A little later the Lord Chief Justice is conducting the trial of
one Cuthbert Cutter, a follower of Prince Hal's, for having
robbed 'a poore Carrier vpon Gads hill in Kent.' The Prince
enters, with 'Ned and Tom,' and demands the release of his man
who has but robbed 'in iest.' The Chief Justice is courteous but
resolute.

  Hen. 5. *Tell me, my lord, shall I haue my man?*
  Iudge. *I cannot, my lord.*
  Hen. 5. *But will you not let him go?*
  Iudge. *I am sorrie his case is so ill.*
  Hen. 5. *Tush, case me no casings, shall I haue my man?*
  Iudge. *I cannot, nor I may not, my lord.*
  Hen. 5. *No: then I will haue him.*
              He giueth him a box on the eare.
  Ned. *Gogs wounds, my lord, shal I cut off his head?*
  Hen. 5. *No, I charge you draw not your swords,*
    But get you hence, prouyde a noyse of Musitians,
    Away, be gone.   Exeunt the Theefe.
  Iudge. *Well, my Lord, I am content to take it at your hands.*
  Hen. 5. *Nay, and you be not you shall haue more.*
  Iudge. *Why, I pray you, my Lord, who am I?*
  Hen. 5. *You, who knowes not you?*
    Why man, you are the Lord chiefe Justice of England.
  Iudge. *Your grace hath said truth, therefore in striking me*
in this place, you greatly abuse me, and not me onely but also
your father: whose liuely person here in this place I doo represent.
And therefore to teach you what prerogatiues meane, I commit
you to the Fleete, Vntill we haue spoken to your father.
  Hen. 5. *Why then belike you meane to send me to the Fleete?*
  Iudge. *I, indeed, and therefore carry him away.*
        Exeunt Hen. 5. with the Officers.

The scene of the Prince's repentance and reconciliation with
his father, which Shakespeare uses in *1 Henry IV*, the *The Famous*
Victories immediately precedes the following scene in the King's
deathchamber. The King is sleeping.

Enter Lord of Exeter and Oxford.

  Exe. *Come easily, my Lord, for waking of the King.*
  Hen. 4. *Now, my Lords.*
  Oxf. *How doth your Grace feele yourselfe?*
  Hen. 4. *Somewhat better after my sleepe,*
    But good my lords take off my crowne,

Remove my chair a little backe, and set me right.
Ambo. *And please your grace, the crowne is taken away.*
Hen. 4. *The Crowne taken away,*
  Good my lord of Oxford, go see who hath done this deed:
  No doubt tis some vilde traitor that hath done it,
  To depriue my sonne. They that would do it now
  Would seeke to scrape and scrawle for it after my death.

Enter Lord of Oxford with the Prince.

Oxf. *Here and please your Grace,*
  Is my Lord the yong Prince with the Crowne.

Hen. 4. *Why how now my sonne?*
  I had thought the last time I had you in schooling,
  And do you now begin againe?
  Doest thou thinke the time so long
  That thou wouldest haue it before the
  Breath be out of my mouth?

Hen. 5. *Most soueraign Lord, and welbeloued father,*
  I came into your Chamber to comfort the melancholy
  Soule of your bodie, and finding you at that time
  Past all recouerie, and dead to my thinking,
  God is my witness: and what should I doo
  But with weeping tears lament the death of you my father,
  And after that seeing the Crowne I tooke it:
  And tell me my father, who might better take it then I,
  After your death? But seeing you liue
  I most humbly render it into your Maiesties hands
  And the happiest man aliue, that my father liue:
  And liue my Lord and Father for euer.

Hen. 4. *Stand vp my sonne,*
  Thine answere hath sounded wel in mine eares,
  For I must nedes confesse that I was in a very sound sleepe.
  But come neare my sonne,
  And let me put thee in possession whilst I liue.

Hen. 5. *Well may I take it at your maiesties hands,*
  But it shall neuer touch my head so long as my father liues.

He taketh the crowne.

The King blesses his son, prophesies a glorious reign, calls for music, draws the curtains of his bed, and dies. After the coronation of the new King there is a conversation between the King and three of his old followers, Ned, Tom, and Iockey, who accost him as he appears in state with the Archbishop of Canterbury, and remind him of his promise to make Ned Lord Chief Justice.

Hen. 5. *I prethee Ned, mend thy manners,*
  And be more modester in thy tearmes,
  For my vnfeigned greefe is not to be ruled by thy flattering
  And dissembling talke. Thou saiest I am chaunged,
  So I am indeed, and so must thou be and that quickly,
  Or else I must cause thee to be chaunged.

Tom. *I trust we haue not offended your grace no way.*

Hen. 5. *Ah, Tom, your former life greeues me,*
  And makes me to abandon and abolish your company for euer.
  And therefore not vpon paine of deeth to approch my presence
  By ten miles space. Then if I heare wel of you,
  It may be I will do somewhat for you,
  Otherwise looke for no more fauour at my hands
  Then at any other mans. And therefore be gone,
  We haue other matters to talke on.   *Exeunt Knights.*

THE HISTORY OF THE PLAY

The success of *Henry IV, Part I*, led Shakespeare, apparently, to write the second part as a sequel. The date of its composition may be definitely stated as lying somewhere between 1596 and 1599. The death of Amurath III, to which reference is made in V. ii. 48, occurred in 1596; and in Ben Jonson's *Every Man out of his Humour* (Act V. sc. ii.), written in 1599, reference is made to Justice Silence. That *Henry IV, Part II*, was written before *Henry V* is evidenced by the unfulfilled promise in the Epilogue of the present play (see the note on that passage).

An acting version of the play, the only known contemporary Quarto edition, was printed in 1600 and entered on the Stationers' Register on August 23 of that year. The full text of the play appeared for the first time in the First Folio in 1623. Of the many contemporary allusions to the play of *Henry IV* and the characters of the play, the following refer unquestionably to *Part II*.

(1) Sir Charles Percy, third son of the twentieth Earl of Northumberland, Lord of Dumbleton in Gloucestershire, a follower of the Earl of Essex, and an admirer, perhaps a friend, of Shakespeare's, writes in a letter dated December 27, 1600 (?): "I am here so pestered with country business that I shall not be able as yet to come to London. If I stay here long in this fashion, at my return you will find me so dull that I shall be taken for Justice Shallow or Justice Silence."

(2) Dekker in *Satiromastix* (1602), *Ad Lectorem*, refers to Master Justice Shallow.

(3) Ben Jonson in *Epicœne* (1609), II. v., refers to Doll Tearsheet.

Of early performances and players of *Henry IV, Part II*, there are even fewer records than there are of *Part I*. James Wright in his *Historia Histrionica* (1699) says that 'before the wars' Lowin acted Falstaff 'with mighty applause.' Pepys, who attended at least three revivals of the first part of the play between 1660 and 1668, makes no mention of any Restoration revival of the second part. In 1700 Betterton, after a triumphant revival of *Part I*, undertook a revision and revival of *Part II*. His version held the stage for many years, and is reprinted in Lacy's *Acting Edition of Old Plays*. Chetwood tells an amusing anecdote concerning Betterton's interpretation of the part of Falstaff in *Part II*. Johnson, an actor, while playing in Dublin, had seen Baker, a master-pavior, play Falstaff. Upon his return to England he gave Mr. Betterton the manner of Baker's playing, which the great actor not only approved of, but imitated, and allowed that it was better than his own.

Betterton's arrangement of the play was as follows:

Act I begins with I. ii.; then follows the scenes at the Archbishop's, and the arrest of Falstaff from Act II.

Act II contains the rest of Shakespeare's Act II, with the Warkworth Castle scenes omitted.

Act III begins with the scene at Shallow's house, but the rest of the act follows Shakespeare.

Act IV begins with the King's soliloquy on sleep, taken from Act III; then comes the scene of the King's death, followed by the scene in which Silence sings; and the act closes with the interview between the Lord Chief Justice and King Henry V.

In Act V, Betterton omits the comic scenes (i. and iv.), and opens the act with the King's progress *to* Westminster Abbey. Falstaff is rebuked, but is not sent to the Fleet, and the play concludes with an abridgment of the first Act of *Henry V*.

Betterton had the good taste not to tamper with Shakespeare's wording to any great extent.

On December 17, 1720, at Drury Lane, the play was revived again. It was acted five nights successively and once afterwards. It was in this revival that Cibber first appeared as Justice Shallow and made 'one of the great successes of the day.' Mills was Falstaff, and Wilks the Prince. Eleven years later (1731) came another Drury Lane revival, with Mills as the Prince, Harper as Falstaff, and Cibber still playing Shallow. Five years later (1736) the same company, with the exception of Harper, produced the play again at Drury Lane for the benefit of the great Quin, who played Falstaff. In 1744 and 1749 there were revivals at the Covent Garden Theatre, Quin again playing Falstaff.

A performance at Drury Lane in 1758 was made notable by Garrick's first appearance in the rôle of the King. He had appeared as Hotspur in *Part I* twelve years before, but had not achieved great success in that rôle. As the King in *Part II* 'his figure did not assist him, but the forcible expression of his countenance, and his energy of utterance, made ample amends for the defect of person.'

On December 11, 1761, and for twenty-two consecutive days, *King Henry IV, Part II,* was presented at Covent Garden in honor of the coronation of King George III. For this performance an elaborate coronation pageant was devised which was used again in 1821 by Macready at the time of the coronation of William IV. Other revivals occured at Drury Lane in 1764 and 1777, and at Covent Garden in 1773, 1784, and 1804. A sensational feature of the 1773 performance was the appearance of an anonymous 'Gentleman' as the King, 'his first performance on any stage,' and of Mrs. Lessingham, for whose benefit the play was given, as Prince Hal. In the 1804 production John Philip Kemble played the King, and Charles Kemble the Prince. Charles Kemble again appeared as the Prince in Macready's production in June, July, and August, 1821.

Of Macready's performance he himself writes in his *Reminiscences;* 'Kemble had revived the play in 1804, but produced little effect. Garrick had not given the prominence he had expected to the part of the King, and for these reasons I begged to be excused from appearing in it. But my objections were set aside.... To every line of it I gave the most deliberate attention, and felt the full power of its pathos. The audience hung intently on every word. The admission of the perfect success of the performance was without dissent. The revival rewarded the managers with houses crowded to the ceiling for many nights, nor was this attributable to the pageant only, for the acting was of the highest order. Fawcett was the best Falstaff then upon the stage, but he more excelled in other parts.' The perfection of Macready's success was not, however, 'without dissent.' 'An old playgoer,' in a letter to Tallis's *Dramatic Magazine* for April, 1851, says of Macready's Henry IV: "In this rôle he approached nearest to an elocutionist, but generally the effect of his declamation was unpleasant, harsh, and grating. Kemble's poses were studied but graceful, not like the stiff upright *posés* of Macready wherein I have often wondered how he could preserve his equilibrium."

On March 17, 1853, in his ninth season at Sadler's Wells, Samuel Phelps produced *King Henry IV, Part II,* he himself playing the double rôle of the King and Justice Shallow. Contemporary reviews speak of his complete triumph, and say that sceptical critics are now converted to this as a stage play. Phelps used Betterton's version, and revived the play again in London in 1864 and in 1874. In the 1874 production Forbes-Robertson, aged 21, appeared as Prince Hal. William Winter records an interesting anecdote of the first rehearsal. Phelps, after watching Forbes-Robertson for a time, said: 'Young man, I see that you know nothing about this. Come to my room tonight.'

The play had been practically unknown on the American stage. There were twenty-six revivals of *Part I* in America in the eighteenth century, but apparently none of *Part II.* In the nineteenth century the American comedian, James H. Hackett, played the part of Falstaff almost annually from 1830 to 1870, in both England and America, but it was the Falstaff of *Part I* and of *The Merry Wives.* In 1895-1896 Miss Julia Marlowe played the part of Prince Hal in an abridged version of the two parts of the play; and in 1896-1897 Daly planned a revival which never got beyond rehearsal. Miss Ada Rehan was to play Prince Hal, and James Lewis, Falstaff. The Delta Psi Dramatic Club of Harvard University gave a creditable amateur performance of *Part II* in the winter of 1915-1916.

INDUCTION

[Warkworth. Before Northumberland's Castle]
Enter Rumour, painted full of tongues.

Rum. Open your ears; for which of you will stop
The vent of hearing when loud Rumour speaks?
I, from the orient to the drooping west,
Making the wind my post-horse, still unfold
The acts commenced on this ball of earth: 5
Upon my tongues continual slanders ride,
The which in every language I pronounce,
Stuffing the ears of men with false reports.
I speak of peace, while covert enmity
Under the smile of safety wounds the world: 10
And who but Rumour, who but only I,
Make fearful musters and prepar'd defence,
Whilst the big year, swoln with some other grief,
Is thought with child by the stern tyrant war,
And no such matter? Rumour is a pipe 15
Blown by surmises, jealousies, conjectures,
And of so easy and so plain a stop
That the blunt monster with uncounted heads,
The still-discordant wavering multitude,
Can play upon it. But what need I thus 20
My well-known body to anatomize
Among my household? Why is Rumour here?
I run before King Harry's victory;
Who in a bloody field by Shrewsbury
Hath beaten down young Hotspur and his troops, 25
Quenching the flame of bold rebellion
Even with the rebels' blood. But what mean I
To speak so true at first? my office is
To noise abroad that Harry Monmouth fell
Under the wrath of noble Hotspur's sword, 30
And that the king before the Douglas' rage
Stoop'd his anointed head as low as death.
This have I rumour'd through the peasant towns
Between the royal field of Shrewsbury
And this worm-eaten hole of ragged stone, 35
Where Hotspur's father, old Northumberland,
Lies crafty-sick. The posts come tiring on,
And not a man of them brings other news
Than they have learn'd of me: from Rumour's tongues
They bring smooth comforts false, worse than true wrongs. 40
Exit.

ACT FIRST ❧ SCENE FIRST

[The Same]
Enter Lord Bardolph, at one door.

L. Bard. Who keeps the gate here? ho!

[Enter the Porter above.]

Where is the earl?

Port. What shall I say you are?
L. Bard. Tell thou the earl
That the Lord Bardolph doth attend him here. 5
Port. His Lordship is walk'd forth into the orchard:
Please it your honour knock but at the gate,
And he himself will answer.

Enter Northumberland.

L. Bard. Here comes the earl.
North. What news, Lord Bardolph? every minute now 10
Should be the father of some stratagem.
The times are wild; contention, like a horse
Full of high feeding, madly hath broke loose
And bears down all before him.
L. Bard. Noble earl, 15
I bring you certain news from Shrewsbury.
North. Good, an God will!
L. Bard. As good as heart can wish.
The king is almost wounded to the death;
And, in the fortune of my lord your son, 20
Prince Harry slain outright; and both the Blunts
Kill'd by the hand of Douglas; young Prince John
And Westmoreland and Stafford fled the field;
And Harry Monmouth's brawn, the hulk Sir John,
Is prisoner to your son: O! such a day, 25
So fought, so follow'd, and so fairly won,
Came not till now to dignify the times
Since Cæsar's fortunes.
North. How is this deriv'd?
Saw you the field? came you from Shrewsbury? 30
L. Bard. I spake with one, my lord, that came from thence;
A gentleman well bred and of good name,
That freely render'd me these news for true.
North. Here comes my servant Travers, whom I sent
On Tuesday last to listen after news. 35
L. Bard. My lord, I over-rode him on the way;
And he is furnish'd with no certainties
More than he haply may retail from me.

Enter Travers.

North. Now, Travers, what good tidings comes with you?
Tra. My lord, Sir John Umfrevile turn'd me back 40
With joyful tidings; and, being better hors'd,
Out-rode me. After him came spurring hard
A gentleman, almost forspent with speed,
That stopp'd by me to breathe his bloodied horse.
He ask'd the way to Chester; and of him 45
I did demand what news from Shrewsbury.
He told me that rebellion had bad luck,
And that young Harry Percy's spur was cold.
With that he gave his able horse the head,
And, bending forward, struck his armed heels 50
Against the panting sides of his poor jade
Up to the rowel-head, and, starting so,
He seem'd in running to devour the way,
Staying no longer question.

S.d. Enter Rumour, etc.; *cf. n.* 2 vent: *aperture* 4 still: *always* 17 stop: *hole in wind instrument by which difference of pitch is obtained* 24 Shrewsbury; *cf. n.* 29 Harry Monmouth; *cf. n.* 33 peasant: *provincial* 35 hole; *cf. n.* 37 crafty- sick: *feigning sickness* tiring: *riding until they are tired*

3 What: *who* 5 attend: *await* 6 orchard: *garden* 17 an: *if* 24 brawn: *the fleshy part of the body, especially the buttocks or the calf of the leg* 26 follow'd: *carried through* 36 over-rode: *passed* 43 forspent: *exhausted* 49 able: *active* 54 Staying: *awaiting* question: *talk*

North.   Ha! Again: 55
Said he young Harry Percy's spur was cold?
Of Hotspur, Coldspur? that rebellion
Had met ill luck?
   L. Bard.   My lord, I'll tell you what:
If my young lord your son have not the day,   60
Upon mine honour, for a silken point
I'll give my barony: never talk of it.
   North. Why should the gentleman that rode by Travers
Give then such instances of loss?
   L. Bard.   Who, he?   65
He was some hilding fellow that had stolen
The horse he rode on, and, upon my life,
Spoke at a venture. Look, here comes more news.

Enter Morton.

   North. Yea, this man's brow, like to a title-leaf,
Foretells the nature of a tragic volume: 70
So looks the strond, whereon the imperious flood
Hath left a witness'd usurpation.
Say, Morton, didst thou come from Shrewsbury?
   Mor. I ran from Shrewsbury, my noble lord;
Where hateful death put on his ugliest mask   75
To fright our party.
   North.   How doth my son, and brother?
Thou tremblest, and the whiteness in the cheek
Is apter than thy tongue to tell thy errand.
Even such a man, so faint, so spiritless,   80
So dull, so dead in look, so woe-begone,
Drew Priam's curtain in the dead of night,
And would have told him half his Troy was burn'd;
But Priam found the fire ere he his tongue,
And I my Percy's death ere thou report'st it.   85
This thou wouldst say, 'Your son did thus and thus;
Your brother thus; so fought the noble Douglas';
Stopping my greedy ear with their bold deeds:
But in the end, to stop mine ear indeed,
Thou hast a sigh to blow away this praise,   90
Ending with 'Brother, son, and all are dead.'
   Mor. Douglas is living, and your brother, yet;
But, for my lord your son,—
   North.   Why, he is dead.—
See, what a ready tongue suspicion hath!   95
He that but fears the thing he would not know
Hath by instinct knowledge from others' eyes
That what he fear'd is chanced. Yet speak, Morton:
Tell thou thy earl his divination lies,
And I will take it as a sweet disgrace   100
And make thee rich for doing me such wrong.
   Mor. You are too great to be by me gainsaid;
Your spirit is too true, your fears too certain.
   North. Yet, for all this, say not that Percy's dead.
I see a strange confession in thine eye: 105
Thou shak'st thy head, and hold'st it fear or sin
To speak a truth. If he be slain, say so;
The tongue offends not that reports his death:
And he doth sin that doth belie the dead,
Not he which says the dead is not alive.   110

Yet the first bringer of unwelcome news
Hath but a losing office, and his tongue
Sounds ever after as a sullen bell,
Remember'd knolling a departing friend.
   L. Bard. I cannot think, my lord, your son is dead.   115
   Mor. I am sorry I should force you to believe
That which I would to God I had not seen;
But these mine eyes saw him in bloody state,
Rendering faint quittance, wearied and out-breath'd,
To Harry Monmouth; whose swift wrath beat down   120
The never-daunted Percy to the earth,
From whence with life he never more sprung up.
In few, his death,—whose spirit lent a fire
Even to the dullest peasant in his camp,—
Being bruited once, took fire and heat away   125
From the best-temper'd courage in his troops;
For from his metal was his party steel'd;
Which once in him abated, all the rest
Turn'd on themselves, like dull and heavy lead:
And as the thing that's heavy in itself,   130
Upon enforcement flies with greatest speed,
So did our men, heavy in Hotspur's loss,
Lend to this weight such lightness with their fear
That arrows fled not swifter toward their aim
Than did our soldiers, aiming at their safety,   135
Fly from the field. Then was that noble Worcester
Too soon ta'en prisoner; and that furious Scot,
The bloody Douglas, whose well-labouring sword
Had three times slain the appearance of the king,
'Gan vail his stomach, and did grace the shame   140
Of those that turn'd their backs; and in his flight,
Stumbling in fear, was took. The sum of all
Is, that the king hath won, and hath sent out
A speedy power to encounter you, my lord,
Under the conduct of young Lancaster   145
And Westmoreland. This is the news at full.
   North. For this I shall have time enough to mourn.
In poison there is physic; and these news,
Having been well, that would have made me sick,
Being sick, have in some measure made me well: 150
And as the wretch, whose fever-weaken'd joints,
Like strengthless hinges, buckle under life,
Impatient of his fit, breaks like a fire
Out of his keeper's arms, even so my limbs,
Weaken'd with grief, being now enrag'd with grief,   155
Are thrice themselves. Hence, therefore, thou nice crutch!
A scaly gauntlet now, with joints of steel
Must glove this hand: and hence, thou sickly quoif!
Thou art a guard too wanton for the head
Which princes, flesh'd with conquest, aim to hit.   160
Now bind my brows with iron; and approach
The ragged'st hour that time and spite dare bring
To frown upon the enrag'd Northumberland!
Let heaven kiss earth! now let not nature's hand
Keep the wild flood confin'd! let order die!   165

---

119 quittance: *return of blows*   **123** In few: *in short*   **125** bruited: *rumored*   **127–129** Cf. n.   **139** Cf. n.   **140** 'Gan vail his stomach: *began to lower his arrogant spirit*   did grace: *reflected credit on, set in a good light*   **152** buckle: *bend*   **155** grief: *suffering* grief: *sorrow*   **156** nice: *dainty, effeminate*   **158** sickly quoif: *sick man's hood*   **159** wanton: *effeminate*   **160** flesh'd: *made fierce by combat as a dog fed only on flesh*   **162** ragged'st: *roughest*

---

61 point: *lacing, garter*   **66** hilding: *worthless*   **71** strond: *shore*   **72** witness'd usurpation: *traces of its usurpation*   **79** apter: *more ready*   **98** is chanced: *has happened*

And let this world no longer be a stage
To feed contention in a lingering act;
But let one spirit of the first-born Cain
Reign in all bosoms, that, each heart being set
On bloody courses, the rude scene may end,   170
And darkness be the burier of the dead!

    Tra. This strained passion doth you wrong, my lord.
    L. Bard. Sweet earl, divorce not wisdom from your honour.
    Mor. The lives of all your loving complices
Lean on your health; the which, if you give o'er   175
To stormy passion, must perforce decay.
You cast the event of war, my noble lord,
And summ'd the account of chance, before you said,
'Let us make head.' It was your presurmise
That in the dole of blows your son might drop: 180
You knew he walk'd o'er perils, on an edge,
More likely to fall in than to get o'er;
You were advis'd his flesh was capable
Of wounds and scars, and that his forward spirit
Would lift him where most trade of danger rang'd: 185
Yet did you say, 'Go forth'; and none of this,
Though strongly apprehended, could restrain
The stiff-borne action: what hath then befallen,
Or what hath this bold enterprise brought forth,
More than that being which was like to be?   190

    L. Bard. We all that are engaged to this loss
Knew that we ventur'd on such dangerous seas
That if we wrought out life 'twas ten to one;
And yet we ventur'd, for the gain propos'd
Chok'd the respect of likely peril fear'd;   195
And since we are o'erset, venture again.
Come, we will all put forth, body and goods.

    Mor. 'Tis more than time: and, my most noble lord,
I hear for certain, and do speak the truth,
The gentle Archbishop of York is up,   200
With well-appointed powers: he is a man
Who with a double surety binds his followers.
My lord your son had only but the corpse,
But shadows and the shows of men to fight;
For that same word, rebellion, did divide   205
The action of their bodies from their souls;
And they did fight with queasiness, constrain'd,
As men drink potions, that their weapons only
Seem'd on our side: but, for their spirits and souls,
This word, rebellion, it had froze them up,   210
As fish are in a pond. But now the bishop
Turns insurrection to religion:
Suppos'd sincere and holy in his thoughts,
He's follow'd both with body and with mind,
And doth enlarge his rising with the blood   215
Of fair King Richard, scrap'd from Pomfret stones;
Derives from heaven his quarrel and his cause;
Tells them he doth bestride a bleeding land,
Gasping for life under great Bolingbroke;
And more and less do flock to follow him.   220

    North. I knew of this before; but, to speak truth,
This present grief had wip'd it from my mind.
Go in with me; and counsel every man
The aptest way for safety and revenge:
Get posts and letters, and make friends with speed: 225
Never so few, and never yet more need.   *Exeunt.*

❧ SCENE SECOND ❧

[London. A Street]
Enter Sir John [Falstaff,] with his Page bearing his sword
and buckler.

    Fal. Sirrah, you giant, what says the doctor to my water?
    Page. He said, sir, the water itself was a good healthy water;
but, for the party that owed it, he might have moe diseases
than he knew for.
    Fal. Men of all sorts take a pride to gird at me: the brain   5
of this foolish-compounded clay, man, is not able to invent
anything that tends to laughter, more than I invent or is invented on me: I am not only witty in myself, but the cause
that wit is in other men. I do here walk before thee like a sow
that hath overwhelmed all her litter but one. If the prince   10
put thee into my service for any other reason than to set me
off, why then I have no judgment. Thou whoreson mandrake,
thou art fitter to be worn in my cap than to wait at my heels.
I was never manned with an agate till now; but I will set you
neither in gold nor silver, but in vile apparel, and send you   15
back again to your master, for a jewel; the juvenal, the prince
your master, whose chin is not yet fledged. I will sooner have
a beard grow in the palm of my hand than he shall get one on
his cheek; and yet he will not stick to say, his face is a face-
royal: God may finish it when he will, it is not a hair amiss   20
yet: he may keep it still as a face-royal, for a barber shall never
earn sixpence out of it; and yet he'll be crowing as if he had
writ man ever since his father was a bachelor. He may keep his
own grace, but he is almost out of mine, I can assure him.
What said Master Dombledon about the satin for my short   25
cloak and my slops?
    Page. He said, sir, you should procure him better assurance
than Bardolph; he would not take his bond and yours: he
liked not the security.
    Fal. Let him be damned like the glutton! Pray God his   30
tongue be hotter! A whoreson Achitophel! a rascally yea-forsooth knave! to bear a gentleman in hand, and then stand
upon security. The whoreson smooth-pates do now wear nothing but high shoes, and bunches of keys at their girdles; and if
a man is through with them in honest taking up, then they   35
must stand upon security. I had as lief they would put ratsbane
in my mouth as offer to stop it with security. I looked a' should
have sent me two and twenty yards of satin, as I am a true
knight, and he sends me security. Well, he may sleep in security; for he hath the horn of abundance, and the lightness   40

172 **strained passion:** *exaggerated emotion*   174 **complices:** *allies*   177–190;
Cf. n.   177 **cast the event:** *considered the outcome*   179 **make head:** *raise an
army*   180 **dole:** *distribution*   181 **edge:** *dangerous path*   183 **advis'd:** *aware*   188
stiff-borne: *obstinately carried out*   191 **engaged to:** *involved in*   195 **respect:** *consideration*   201 **well-appointed:** *well-equipped*   207 **queasiness:** *squeamishness*   215, 216
Cf. n.   215 **enlarge:** *widen the scope or appeal*   219 **Bolingbroke;** *cf. n.*   220 **more
and less:** *high and low*

225 **make:** *collect*   3 **owed:** *owned*   5 **gird:** *jeer*   12 **whoreson:** *a coarse term of
endearment (as here) or of contempt (as in l. 33)*   12 **mandrake:** *a poisonous plant whose
forked root was supposed to resemble the human form*   14 **manned with an agate:**
cf. n.   16 **juvenal:** *used focularly for 'youth'*   21 **face-royal;** *cf. n.*   22 **writ man:**
enrolled himself a man   26 **slops:** *loose breeches*   30 **glutton;** *cf. n.*   31 **Achitophel;**
cf. n.   31, 32 **yea-forsooth knave;** *cf. n.*   32 **bear … in hand:** *delude with false
hopes*   33 **smooth-pates:** *round-heads, or Puritanical citizen class*   35 **through:** *serious*   **taking up:** *obtaining goods on trust*   37 **a':** *he*   40–42; *Cf. n.*

of his wife shines through it: and yet cannot he see, though he have his own lanthorn to light him. Where's Bardolph?

Page. He's gone into Smithfield to buy your worship a horse.

Fal. I bought him in Paul's, and he'll buy me a horse in 45 Smithfield: an I could get me but a wife in the stews, I were manned, horsed, and wived.

Enter Chief Justice and Servant.

Page. Sir, here comes the nobleman that committed the prince for striking him about Bardolph.

Fal. Wait close; I will not see him. 50

Ch. Just. What's he that goes there?

Ser. Falstaff, an 't please your lordship.

Ch. Just. He that was in question for the robbery?

Ser. He, my lord; but he hath since done good service at Shrewsbury, and, as I hear, is now going with some charge 55 to the Lord John of Lancaster.

Ch. Just. What, to York? Call him back again.

Ser. Sir John Falstaff!

Fal. Boy, tell him I am deaf.

Page. You must speak louder, my master is deaf. 60

Ch. Just. I am sure he is, to the hearing of anything good. Go, pluck him by the elbow; I must speak with him.

Ser. Sir John!

Fal. What! a young knave, and beg! Is there not wars? is there not employment? doth not the king lack subjects? do 65 not the rebels want soldiers? Though it be a shame to be on any side but one, it is worse shame to beg than to be on the worst side, were it worse than the name of rebellion can tell how to make it.

Ser. You mistake me, sir. 70

Fal. Why, sir, did I say you were an honest man? setting my knighthood and my soldiership aside, I had lied in my throat if I had said so.

Ser. I pray you, sir, then set your knighthood and your soldiership aside, and give me leave to tell you you lie in 75 your throat if you say I am any other than an honest man.

Fal. I give thee leave to tell me so! I lay aside that which grows to me! If thou gett'st any leave of me, hang me: if thou takest leave, thou wert better be hanged. You hunt counter: hence! avaunt! 80

Ser. Sir, my lord would speak with you.

Ch. Just. Sir John Falstaff, a word with you.

Fal. My good lord! God give your lordship good time of day. I am glad to see your lordship abroad; I heard say your lordship was sick: I hope your lordship goes abroad by advice. 85 Your lordship, though not clean past your youth, hath yet some smack of age in you, some relish of the saltness of time; and I most humbly beseech your lordship to have a reverend care of your health.

Ch. Just. Sir John, I sent for you before your expedition 90 to Shrewsbury.

Fal. An 't please your lordship, I hear his majesty is returned with some discomfort from Wales.

Ch. Just. I talk not of his majesty. You would not come when I sent for you. 95

Fal. And I hear, moreover, his highness is fallen into this same whoreson apoplexy.

Ch. Just. Well, God mend him! I pray you, let me speak with you.

Fal. This apoplexy is, as I take it, a kind of lethargy, 100 an 't please your lordship; a kind of sleeping in the blood, a whoreson tingling.

Ch. Just. What tell you me of it? be it as it is.

Fal. It hath it original from much grief, from study and perturbation of the brain. I have read the cause of his 105 effects in Galen: it is a kind of deafness.

Ch. Just. I think you are fallen into the disease, for you hear not what I say to you.

Fal. Very well, my lord, very well: rather, an 't please you, it is the disease of not listening, the malady of not marking, 110 that I am troubled withal.

Ch. Just. To punish you by the heels would amend the attention of your ears; and I care not if I do become your physician.

Fal. I am as poor as Job, my lord, but not so patient: 115 your lordship may minister the potion of imprisonment to me in respect of poverty; but how I should be your patient to follow your prescriptions, the wise may make some dram of a scruple, or indeed a scruple itself.

Ch. Just. I sent for you, when there were matters against 120 you for your life, to come speak with me.

Fal. As I was then advised by my learned counsel in the laws of this land-service, I did not come.

Ch. Just. Well, the truth is, Sir John, you live in great infamy. 125

Fal. He that buckles him in my belt cannot live in less.

Ch. Just. Your means are very slender, and your waste is great.

Fal. I would it were otherwise: I would my means were greater and my waist slenderer. 130

Ch. Just. You have misled the youthful prince.

Fal. The young prince hath misled me: I am the fellow with the great belly, and he my dog.

Ch. Just. Well, I am loath to gall a new-healed wound: your day's service at Shrewsbury hath a little gilded over 135 your night's exploit on Gadshill: you may thank the unquiet time for your quiet o'er-posting that action.

Fal. My lord!

Ch. Just. But since all is well, keep it so: wake not a sleeping wolf. 140

Fal. To wake a wolf is as bad as to smell a fox.

Ch. Just. What! you are as a candle, the better part burnt out.

Fal. A wassail candle, my lord; all tallow: if I did say of wax, my growth would approve the truth. 145

Ch. Just. There is not a white hair on your face but should have his effect of gravity.

Fal. His effect of gravy, gravy, gravy.

Ch. Just. You follow the young prince up and down, like his ill angel. 150

Fal. Not so, my lord; your ill angel is light, but I hope he that looks upon me will take me without weighing: and yet, in some respects, I grant, I cannot go, I cannot tell. Virtue is of

---

103 What: *why*   **104 it:** *its*   **105 his:** *its*   **112 punish by the heels:** *commit to prison; originally, to the stocks*   **117 in respect of:** *on account of*   **123 land-service:** *military service*   **132, 133:** *Cf. n.*   **137 o'er-posting:** *getting over rapidly*   **144 wassail candle:** *large candle used at a feast*   **145 wax;** *cf. n.* **approve:** *prove*   **151 ill:** *evil*   **151–153;** *Cf. n.*

45 Paul's; *cf. n.*   **49, 50** *Cf. n.*   **55 charge:** *military command*   **79 hunt counter; cf. n.**

so little regard in these costermonger times that true valour is turned bear-herd: pregnancy is made a tapster, and hath his quick wit wasted in giving reckonings: all the other gifts apper-tinent to man, as the malice of this age shapes them, are not worth a gooseberry. You that are old consider not the capacit-ies of us that are young; you measure the heat of our livers with the bitterness of your galls; and we that are in the *160* vaward of our youth, I must confess, are wags too.

Ch. Just. Do you set down your name in the scroll of youth, that are written down old with all the characters of age? Have you not a moist eye, a dry hand, a yellow cheek, a white beard, a decreasing leg, an increasing belly? Is not your *165* voice broken, your wind short, your chin double, your wit single, and every part about you blasted with antiquity, and will you yet call yourself young? Fie, fie, fie, Sir John!

Fal. My lord, I was born about three of the clock in the afternoon, with a white head, and something a round belly. For my voice, I have lost it with hollaing, and singing of an-thems. To approve my youth further, I will not: the truth is, I am only old in judgment and understanding; and he that will caper with me for a thousand marks, let him lend me the money, and have at him! For the box o' the ear that the *175* prince gave you, he gave it like a rude prince, and you took it like a sensible lord. I have checked him for it, and the young lion repents; marry, not in ashes and sackcloth, but in new silk and old sack.

Ch. Just. Well, God send the prince a better companion! *180*

Fal. God send the companion a better prince! I cannot rid my hands of him.

Ch. Just. Well, the king hath severed you and Prince Harry. I hear you are going with Lord John of Lancaster against the archbishop and the Earl of Northumberland. *185*

Fal. Yea; I thank your pretty sweet wit for it. But look you pray, all you that kiss my lady Peace at home, that our armies join not in a hot day; for, by the Lord, I take but two shirts out with me, and I mean not to sweat extraordinarily: if it be a hot day, and I brandish anything but my bottle, I would *190* I might never spit white again. There is not a dangerous action can peep out his head but I am thrust upon it. Well, I cannot last ever. But it was always yet the trick of our English nation, if they have a good thing, to make it too common. If you will needs say I am an old man, you should give me rest. I *195* would to God my name were not so terrible to the enemy as it is: I were better to be eaten to death with rust than to be scoured to nothing with perpetual motion.

Ch. Just. Well, be honest, be honest; and God bless your expedition. *200*

Fal. Will your lordship lend me a thousand pound to furnish me forth?

Ch. Just. Not a penny; not a penny; you are too impatient to bear crosses. Fare you well: commend me to my cousin Westmoreland. *[Exeunt Chief Justice and Servant.]* *205*

Fal. If I do, fillip me with a three-man beetle. A man can no more separate age and covetousness than a' can part young limbs and lechery; but the gout galls the one, and the pox pinches the other; and so both the degrees prevent my curses. Boy! *210*

Page. Sir!

Fal. What money is in my purse?

Page. Seven groats and twopence.

Fal. I can get no remedy against this consumption of the purse: borrowing only lingers and lingers it out, but the *215* disease is incurable. Go bear this letter to my Lord of Lancas-ter; this to the prince; this to the Earl of Westmoreland; and this to old Mistress Ursula, whom I have weekly sworn to marry since I perceived the first white hair on my chin. About it: you know where to find me. A pox of this gout! or, a gout *220* of this pox! for the one or the other plays the rogue with my great toe. 'Tis no matter if I do halt; I have the wars for my col-our, and my pension shall seem the more reasonable. A good wit will make use of anything; I will turn diseases to commodity.

Exeunt.

❧ SCENE THIRD ❧

[York. The Archbishop's Palace]
Enter Archbishop, Hastings, Mowbray, and Lord Bardolph.

Arch. Thus have you heard our cause and known our means;
And, my most noble friends, I pray you all,
Speak plainly your opinions of our hopes:
And first, Lord Marshal, what say you to it? *5*

Mowb. I well allow the occasion of our arms;
But gladly would be better satisfied
How in our means we should advance ourselves
To look with forehead bold and big enough
Upon the power and puissance of the king. *10*

Hast. Our present musters grow upon the file
To five-and-twenty thousand men of choice;
And our supplies live largely in the hope
Of great Northumberland, whose bosom burns
With an incensed fire of injuries. *15*

L. Bard. The question, then, Lord Hastings, standeth thus:
Whether our present five-and-twenty thousand
May hold up head without Northumberland.

Hast. With him, we may.

L. Bard.   Ay, marry, there's the point: *20*
But if without him we be thought too feeble,
My judgment is, we should not step too far
Till we had his assistance by the hand;
For in a theme so bloody-fac'd as this,
Conjecture, expectation, and surmise *25*
Of aids incertain should not be admitted.

Arch. 'Tis very true, Lord Bardolph; for, indeed
It was young Hotspur's case at Shrewsbury.

L. Bard. It was, my lord; who lin'd himself with hope,
Eating the air on promise of supply, *30*
Flattering himself with project of a power
Much smaller than the smallest of his thoughts;
And so, with great imagination
Proper to madmen, led his powers to death,

---

154 **costermonger:** *commercial*   155 **bear-herd:** *one who leads about a tame bear* **pregnancy:** *readiness of wit*   156 **reckonings:** *bills*   161 **vaward:** *vanguard*   167 **single:** *thin*   174 **marks:** *a mark was worth about thirteen shillings*   179 **sack:** *Spanish wine*   191 **spit white;** *cf. n.*   203, 204; *Cf. n.*   206; *Cf. n.*   209 **prevent:** *anticipate*

213 **groat:** *a coin worth fourpence*   222 **halt:** *limp* **colour:** *excuse*   224 **commodity:** *merchandise to be sold at a profit*   11 **file:** *muster roll*   13 **supplies:** *reinforcements*   29 **lin'd:** *strengthened*   31, 32 **project … smaller:** *anticipation of an army actually much smaller*

And winking leap'd into destruction. 35

    Hast. But, by your leave, it never yet did hurt
To lay down likelihoods and forms of hope.

    L. Bard. Yes, if this present quality of war,—
Indeed the instant action,—a cause on foot,
Lives so in hope, as in an early spring 40
We see the appearing buds; which, to prove fruit,
Hope gives not so much warrant as despair
That frosts will bite them. When we mean to build,
We first survey the plot, then draw the model;
And when we see the figure of the house, 45
Then must we rate the cost of the erection;
Which if we find outweighs ability,
What do we then but draw anew the model
In fewer offices, or at last desist
To build at all? Much more, in this great work,— 50
Which is almost to pluck a kingdom down
And set another up,—should we survey
The plot of situation and the model,
Consent upon a sure foundation,
Question surveyors, know our own estate, 55
How able such a work to undergo,
To weigh against his opposite; or else,
We fortify in paper, and in figures,
Using the names of men instead of men:
Like one that draws the model of a house 60
Beyond his power to build it; who, half through,
Gives o'er and leaves his part-created cost
A naked subject to the weeping clouds,
And waste for churlish winter's tyranny.

    Hast. Grant that our hopes, yet likely of fair birth, 65
Should be still-born, and that we now possess'd
The utmost man of expectation;
I think we are a body strong enough,
Even as we are, to equal with the king.

    L. Bard. What! is the king but five-and-twenty thousand? 70

    Hast. To us no more; nay, not so much, Lord Bardolph.
For his divisions, as the times do brawl,
Are in three heads: one power against the French,
And one against Glendower; perforce, a third
Must take up us: so is the unfirm king 75
In three divided, and his coffers sound
With hollow poverty and emptiness.

    Arch. That he should draw his several strengths together
And come against us in full puissance,
Need not be dreaded. 80

    Hast. If he should do so,
He leaves his back unarm'd, the French and Welsh
Baying him at the heels: never fear that.

    L. Bard. Who is it like should lead his forces hither?

    Hast. The Duke of Lancaster and Westmoreland; 85
Against the Welsh, himself and Harry Monmouth:
But who is substituted 'gainst the French
I have no certain notice.

    Arch. Let us on
And publish the occasion of our arms.
The commonwealth is sick of their own choice; 90

Their over-greedy love hath surfeited.
A habitation giddy and unsure
Hath he that buildeth on the vulgar heart.
O thou fond many! with what loud applause 95
Didst thou beat heaven with blessing Bolingbroke
Before he was what thou wouldst have him be:
And being now trimm'd in thine own desires,
Thou, beastly feeder, art so full of him
That thou provok'st thyself to cast him up. 100
So, so, thou common dog, didst thou disgorge
Thy glutton bosom of the royal Richard,
And now thou wouldst eat thy dead vomit up,
And howl'st to find it. What trust is in these times?
They that, when Richard liv'd, would have him die, 105
Are now become enamour'd on his grave:
Thou, that threw'st dust upon his goodly head,
When through proud London he came sighing on
After the admired heels of Bolingbroke,
Cry'st now, 'O earth! yield us that king again, 110
And take thou this!' O, thoughts of men accurst!
Past and to come seem best; things present worst.

    Mowb. Shall we go draw our numbers and set on?

    Hast. We are time's subjects, and time bids be gone. *[Exeunt.]*

Act Second ❧ Scene First

[London. A Street]
Enter Hostess [Quickly of the Tavern], with two Officers,
Fang and Snare.

    Host. Master Fang, have you entered the action?

    Fang. It is entered.

    Host. Where's your yeoman? Is 't a lusty yeoman? will a'
stand to 't?

    Fang. Sirrah!—where's Snare? 5

    Host. O Lord, ay! good Master Snare.

    Snare. Here, here.

    Fang. Snare, we must arrest Sir John Falstaff.

    Host. Yea, good Master Snare; I have entered him and all.

    Snare. It may chance cost some of us our lives, for he 10
will stab.

    Host. Alas the day! take heed of him: he stabbed me in
mine own house, and that most beastly. In good faith, a' cares
not what mischief he doth if his weapon be out: he will foin
like any devil; he will spare neither man, woman, nor child. 15

    Fang. If I can close with him I care not for his thrust.

    Host. No, nor I neither: I'll be at your elbow.

    Fang. An I but fist him once; an a' come but within my
vice,—

    Host. I am undone by his going; I warrant you, he's an 20
infinitive thing upon my score. Good Master Fang, hold him
sure: good Master Snare, let him not 'scape. A' comes continu-
antly to Pie-corner—saving your manhoods—to buy a saddle;
and he's indited to dinner to the Lubber's Head in Lumbert
Street, to Master Smooth's the silkman: I pray ye, since my 25

---

35 winking: *with eyes closed*   **38–43;** *Cf. n.*   **45 figure:** *plan*   **49 offices:** *domestic quarters*   **55–57;** *Cf. n.*   **62 part-created cost:** *costly fragment*   **64 churlish:** *rough*   **72 as . . . brawl:** *as the turbulent times dictate*   **84 like:** *probable*

95 fond many: *foolish multitude*   **98 trimm'd . . . desires:** *supplied with what thou didst desire*   **114 draw:** *assemble*   **3 yeoman:** *sheriff's officer*   **14 foin:** *thrust (in fencing)*   **19 vice:** *figuratively, grip*   **21 infinitive:** *infinite (Dame Quickly's more obvious errors in speech are not, hereafter, glossed)*   **upon my score:** *in my debt*   **24, 25 Lubber's . . . Street:** *Libbard's, i.e., Leopard's Head Inn, in Lombard Street*

exion is entered, and my case so openly known to the world,
let him be brought in to his answer. A hundred mark is a long
one for a poor lone woman to bear; and I have borne, and
borne, and borne; and have been fubbed off, and fubbed off,
and fubbed off, from this day to that day, that it is a shame *30*
to be thought on. There is no honesty in such dealing; unless
a woman should be made an ass, and a beast, to bear every
knave's wrong. Yonder he comes; and that arrant malmsey-nose
knave, Bardolph, with him. Do your offices, do your offices,
Master Fang and Master Snare; do me, do me, do me your *35*
offices.

Enter Falstaff, and Bardolph.

Fal. How now! whose mare's dead? what's the matter?
Fang. Sir John, I arrest you at the suit of Mistress Quickly.
Fal. Away, varlets! Draw, Bardolph: cut me off the villain's
head; throw the quean in the channel. *40*
Host. Throw me in the channel! I'll throw thee in the chan-
nel. Wilt thou? wilt thou? thou bastardly rogue! Murder, mur-
der! Ah, thou honey-suckle villain! wilt thou kill God's officers
and the king's? Ah, thou honey-seed rogue! thou art a honey-
seed, a man-queller, and a woman-queller. *45*
Fal. Keep them off, Bardolph.
Fang. A rescue! a rescue!
Host. Good people, bring a rescue or two! Thou wo't, wo't
thou? thou wo't, wo't ta? do, do, thou rogue! do, thou hemp-
seed! *50*
Fal. Away, you scullion! you rampallian! you fustilarian!
I'll tickle your catastrophe.

Enter Chief Justice.

Ch. Just. What is the matter? keep the peace here, ho!
Host. Good my lord, be good to me! I beseech you, stand
to me! *55*
Ch. Just. How now, Sir John! what! are you brawling here?
Doth this become your place, your time and business?
You should have been well on your way to York.
Stand from him, fellow: wherefore hang'st upon him?
Host. O, my most worshipful lord, an 't please your grace, *60*
I am a poor widow of Eastcheap, and he is arrested at my suit.
Ch. Just. For what sum?
Host. It is more than for some, my lord; it is for all I have.
He hath eaten me out of house and home; he hath put all my
substance into that fat belly of his: but I will have some of *65*
it out again, or I will ride thee o' nights like the mare.
Fal. I think I am as like to ride the mare if I have any
vantage of ground to get up.
Ch. Just. How comes this, Sir John? Fie! what man of good
temper would endure this tempest of exclamation? Are you *70*
not ashamed to enforce a poor widow to so rough a course to
come by her own?
Fal. What is the gross sum that I owe thee?
Host. Marry, if thou wert an honest man, thyself and the
money too. Thou didst swear to me upon a parcel-gilt *75*
goblet, sitting in my Dolphin-chamber, at the round table, by

a sea-coal fire, upon Wednesday in Wheeson week, when the
prince broke thy head for liking his father to a singing-man of
Windsor, thou didst swear to me then, as I was washing thy
wound, to marry me and make me my lady thy wife. Canst *80*
thou deny it? Did not goodwife Keech, the butcher's wife,
come in then and call me gossip Quickly? coming in to borrow a
mess of vinegar; telling us she had a good dish of prawns;
whereby thou didst desire to eat some, whereby I told thee they
were ill for a green wound? And didst thou not, when she was *85*
gone down stairs, desire me to be no more so familiarity with
such poor people; saying that ere long they should call me
madam? And dist thou not kiss me and bid me fetch thee thirty
shillings? I put thee now to thy book-oath: deny it if thou canst.
Fal. My lord, this is a poor mad soul; and she says up *90*
and down the town that her eldest son is like you. She hath
been in good case, and the truth is, poverty hath distracted
her. But for those foolish officers, I beseech you I may have
redress against them.
Ch. Just. Sir John, Sir John, I am well acquainted with *95*
your manner of wrenching the true cause the false way. It is
not a confident brow, nor the throng of words that come with
such more than impudent sauciness from you, can thrust me
from a level consideration; you have, as it appears to me, practised upon the easy-yielding spirit of this woman, and made
her serve your uses both in purse and in person.
Host. Yea, in troth, my lord.
Ch. Just. Prithee, peace. Pay her the debt you owe her, and
unpay the villainy you have done her: the one you may do
with sterling money, and the other with current repentance. *105*
Fal. My lord, I will not undergo this sneap without reply.
You call honourable boldness impudent sauciness: if a man will
make curtsy, and say nothing, he is virtuous. No, my lord, my
humble duty remembered, I will not be your suitor: I say to
you, I do desire deliverance from these officers, being upon *110*
hasty employment in the king's affairs.
Ch. Just. You speak as having power to do wrong: but answer in the effect of your reputation, and satisfy the poor
woman.
Fal. Come hither, hostess.   *[Taking her aside.] 115*

Enter Master Gower.

Ch. Just. Now, Master Gower! what news?
Gow. The king, my lord, and Harry Prince of Wales
Are near at hand: the rest the paper tells.   *[Gives a letter.]*
Fal. As I am a gentleman.
Host. Faith, you said so before. *120*
Fal. As I am a gentleman. Come, no more words of it.
Host. By this heavenly ground I tread on, I must be fain to
pawn both my plate and the tapestry of my dining-chambers.
Fal. Glasses, glasses, is the only drinking: and for thy walls,
a pretty slight drollery, or the story of the Prodigal, or the *125*
German hunting in water-work, is worth a thousand of these
bed-hangings and these fly-bitten tapestries. Let it be ten pound if
thou canst. Come, an it were not for thy humours, there's not a
better wench in England. Go, wash thy face, and draw the action.

---

26 exion: *Dame Quickly's error for 'action'*   **28 one;** *cf. n.*   **29 fubbed:** *fobbed, i.e., put off deceitfully*   **33 malmsey-nose:** *red-nosed*   **40 quean:** *hussy*   **41 channel:** *kennel, i.e., gutter*   **43 honey-suckle:** *Dame Quickly's error for 'homicidal'*   **44 honey-seed:** *homicide*   **45 man-queller:** *man-killer*   **49 wo't:** *wouldst* **ta:** *thou* **51, 52; Cf. n.**   **66 mare:** *nightmare*   **70 temper:** *character*   **75 parcel-gilt:** *partly gilded*

77 sea-coal: *mineral coal* (brought by boat from newcastle)   **Wheeson:** *Whitsun* **81**   **Keech:** *literally 'a lump of fat'*   **85 green:** *fresh*   **91 case:** *circumstances*   **99 level: steady*   **105 current:** *genuine, with pun upon 'sterling'*   **106 sneap:** *snub*   **112; Cf. n.** **114 in the effect of:** *in a manner suitable to*   **124; Cf. n.*   **125 drollery:** *humorous painting*   **126 German hunting:** *German hunting-scene* **water-work:** *water colors* **128 humours:** *caprices*   **129 draw:** *withdraw*

Come, thou must not be in this humour with me; dost not   *130*
know me? Come, come, I know thou wast set on to this.

Host. Prithee, Sir John, let it be but twenty nobles: i' faith,
I am loath to pawn my plate, so God save me, la!

Fal. Let it alone; I'll make other shift: you'll be a fool still.

Host. Well, you shall have it, though I pawn my gown.   *135*
I hope you'll come to supper. You'll pay me all together?

Fal. Will I live? *[To Bardolph.]* Go, with her, with her;
hook on, hook on.

Host. Will you have Doll Tearsheet meet you at supper?

Fal. No more words; let's have her.   *140*

   Exeunt Hostess, [Bardolph, Page,] and Sergeant[s].

Ch. Just. I have heard better news.

Fal. What's the news, my lord?

Ch. Just. Where lay the king last night?

Gow. At Basingstoke, my lord.

Fal. I hope, my lord, all's well: what is the news, my lord?   *145*

Ch. Just. Come all his forces back?

Gow. No; fifteen hundred foot, five hundred horse,
Are march'd up to my Lord of Lancaster,
Against Northumberland and the archbishop.

Fal. Comes the king back from Wales, my noble lord?   *150*

Ch. Just. You shall have letters of me presently. Come,
go along with me, good Master Gower.

Fal. My lord!

Ch. Just. What's the matter?

Fal. Master Gower, shall I entreat you with me to dinner?   *155*

Gow. I must wait upon my good lord here; I thank you,
good Sir John.

Ch. Just. Sir John, you loiter here too long, being you are
to take soldiers up in counties as you go.

Fal. Will you sup with me, Master Gower?   *160*

Ch. Just. What foolish master taught you these manners,
Sir John?

Fal. Master Gower, if they become me not, he was a
fool that taught them me. This is the right fencing grace,
my lord; tap for tap, and so part fair.   *165*

Ch. Just. Now the Lord lighten thee! thou art a great fool.

   Exeunt.

❧ SCENE SECOND ❧

[The Same]
Enter Prince Henry [and] Poins.

Prince. Before God, I am exceeding weary.

Poins. Is 't come to that? I had thought weariness durst not
have attached one of so high blood.

Prince. Faith, it does me, though it discolours the complexion of my greatness to acknowledge it. Doth it not show   *5*
vilely in me to desire small beer?

Poins. Why, a prince should not be so loosely studied as to
remember so weak a composition.

Prince. Belike then my appetite was not princely got; for, by
my troth, I do now remember the poor creature, small beer.   *10*
But, indeed, these humble considerations make me out of love
with my greatness. What a disgrace is it to me to remember
thy name, or to know thy face to-morrow! or to take note

how many pair of silk stockings thou hast; *viz.* these, and
those that were thy peach-coloured ones! or to bear the   *15*
inventory of thy shirts; as, one for superfluity, and another for
use! But that the tennis-court-keeper knows better than I, for it
is a low ebb of linen with thee when thou keepest not racket
there; as thou hast not done a great while, because the rest of
thy low-countries have made a shift to eat up thy holland: *20*
and God knows whether those that bawl out the ruins of thy
linen shall inherit his kingdom; but the midwives say the children are not in the fault; whereupon the world increases, and
kindreds are mightily strengthened.

Poins. How ill it follows, after you have laboured so hard,   *25*
you should talk so idly! Tell me, how many good young
princes would do so, their fathers being so sick as yours at
this time is?

Prince. Shall I tell thee one thing, Poins?

Poins. Yes, faith, and let it be an excellent good thing.   *30*

Prince. It shall serve among wits of no higher breeding
than thine.

Poins. Go to; I stand the push of your one thing that you
will tell.

Prince. Marry, I tell thee, it is not meet that I should be   *35*
sad, now my father is sick: albeit I could tell to thee,—as to
one it pleases me, for fault of a better, to call my friend,—I
could be sad, and sad indeed too.

Poins. Very hardly upon such a subject.

Prince. By this hand, thou thinkest me as far in the devil's   *40*
book as thou and Falstaff for obduracy and persistency: Let the
end try the man. But I tell thee my heart bleeds inwardly that
my father is so sick; and keeping such vile company as thou
art hath in reason taken from me all ostentation of sorrow.

Poins. The reason?   *45*

Prince. What wouldst thou think of me if I should weep?

Poins. I would think thee a most princely hypocrite.

Prince. It would be every man's thought; and thou art a
blessed fellow to think as every man thinks: never a man's
thought in the world keeps the road-way better than thine: *50*
every man would think me an hypocrite indeed. And what
accites your most worshipful thought to think so?

Poins. Why, because you have been so lewd and so much
engraffed to Falstaff.

Prince. And to thee.   *55*

Poins. By this light, I am well spoke on; I can hear it with
mine own ears: the worst that they can say of me is that I am
a second brother and that I am a proper fellow of my hands;
and those two things I confess I cannot help. By the mass,
here comes Bardolph.   *60*

   Enter Bardolph and Page.

Prince. And the boy that I gave Falstaff: a' had him from
me Christian; and look, if the fat villain have not transformed
him ape.

Bard. God save your Grace!

Prince. And yours, most noble Bardolph.   *65*

Poins. *[To the Page.]* Come, you virtuous ass, you bashful
fool, must you be blushing? wherefore blush you now? What a
maidenly man-at-arms are you become! Is 't such a matter to
get a pottle-pot's maidenhead?

132 **nobles:** *gold coins worth about six shillings*   151 **presently:** *immediately*   164;
Cf. n.   166 **lighten:** *enlighten, used quibblingly*   3 **attached:** *seized*   4 **discolours the**
complexion of my greatness: *makes me blush*   7 **studied:** *inclined*   19–24; **Cf. n.**   33 **push:** *thrust*   52 **accites:** *invites*   53 **lewd:** *worthless* **much en-**
graffed: *closely attached*   58 **second brother:** *younger son* **proper fellow of my hands:**
good fellow with my fists   69 **pottle-pot:** *two-quart tankard*

Page. A' calls me even now, my lord, through a red lattice,   70
and I could discern no part of his face from the window: at
last, I spied his eyes, and methought he had made two holes
in the ale-wife's new petticoat, and peeped through.

Prince. Hath not the boy profited?

Bard. Away, you whoreson upright rabbit, away!   75

Page. Away, you rascally Althea's dream, away!

Prince. Instruct us, boy; what dream, boy?

Page. Marry, my lord, Althea dreamed she was delivered
of a firebrand; and therefore I call him her dream.

Prince. A crown's worth of good interpretation. There   80
'tis, boy.   *[Gives him money.]*

Poins. O! that this good blossom could be kept from cankers. Well, there is sixpence to preserve thee.

Bard. An you do not make him be hanged among you,
the gallows shall have wrong.   85

Prince. And how doth thy master, Bardolph?

Bard. Well, my lord. He heard of your Grace's coming to
town: there's a letter for you.

Poins. Delivered with good respect. And how doth the
martlemas, your master?   90

Bard. In bodily health, sir.

Poins. Marry, the immortal part needs a physician; but that
moves not him: though that be sick, it dies not.

Prince. I do allow this wen to be as familiar with me as my
dog; and he holds his place, for look you how he writes.   95

Poins. *[looking over the Prince's shoulder.]* 'John Falstaff,
knight,'—every man must know that, as oft as he has occasion
to name himself: even like those that are kin to the king, for
they never prick their finger but they say, 'There's some of the
king's blood spilt.' 'How comes that?' says he that takes   100
upon him not to conceive. The answer is as ready as a
borrower's cap, 'I am the king's poor cousin, sir.'

Prince. Nay, they will be kin to us, or they will fetch it
from Japhet. But to the letter: 'Sir John Falstaff, knight, to the
son of the king nearest his father, Harry Prince of Wales,   105
greeting.'

Poins. Why, this is a certificate.

Prince. Peace! 'I will imitate the honourable Romans in
brevity:'

Poins. He sure means brevity in breath, short-winded.   110

Prince. 'I commend me to thee, I commend thee, and I
leave thee. Be not too familiar with Poins; for he misuses thy
favours so much that he swears thou art to marry his sister
Nell. Repent at idle times as thou mayest, and so farewell.

　　　　　　　'Thine, by yea and no,—which is as   115
　　　　　　　much as to say, as thou usest him,
　　　　　　　Jack Falstaff, with my familiars;
　　　　　　　John, with my brothers and sisters,
　　　　　　　and *Sir John* with all Europe.'

Poins. My lord, I'll steep this letter in sack and make   120
him eat it.

Prince. That's to make him eat twenty of his words. But
do you use me thus, Ned? must I marry your sister?

Poins. God send the wench no worse fortune!—but I
never said so.   125

Prince. Well, thus we play the fools with the time, and

the spirits of the wise sit in the clouds and mock us. Is your
master here in London?

Bard. Yea, my lord.

Prince. Where sups he? doth the old board feed in the   130
old frank?

Bard. At the old place, my lord, in Eastcheap.

Prince. What company?

Page. Ephesians, my lord, of the old church.

Prince. Sup any women with him?   135

Page. None, my lord, but old Mistress Quickly and
Mistress Doll Tearsheet.

Prince. What pagan may that be?

Page. A proper gentlewoman, sir, and a kinswoman of
my master's.   140

Prince. Even such kin as the parish heifers are to the
town bull. Shall we steal upon them, Ned, at supper?

Poins. I am your shadow, my lord; I'll follow you.

Prince. Sirrah, you boy, and Bardolph; no word to your
master that I am yet come to town: there's for your silence.

　　　　　　　　　　　　　　[Gives money.]

Bard. I have no tongue, sir.

Page. And for mine, sir, I will govern it.

Prince. Fare ye well; go. *[Exeunt Bardolph and Page.]* This
Doll Tearsheet should be some road.   150

Poins. I warrant you, as common as the way between Saint
Albans and London.

Prince. How might we see Falstaff bestow himself to-night
in his true colours, and not ourselves be seen?

Poins. Put on two leathern jerkins and aprons, and wait   155
upon him at his table as drawers.

Prince. From a god to a bull a heavy descension! it was
Jove's case. From a prince to a prentice! a low transformation!
that shall be mine; for in every thing the purpose must weigh
with the folly. Follow me, Ned.   *Exeunt.* 160

❧ SCENE THIRD ❧

[Warkworth. Before Northumberland's Castle]
Enter Northumberland, his wife, and the wife to Harry Percy.

North. I pray thee, loving wife, and gentle daughter,
Give even way unto my rough affairs:
Put not you on the visage of the times,
And be like them to Percy troublesome.

Lady N. I have given over, I will speak no more: 5
Do what you will; your wisdom be your guide.

North. Alas! sweet wife, my honour is at pawn;
And, but my going, nothing can redeem it.

Lady P. O! yet for God's sake, go not to these wars.
The time was, father, that you broke your word   10
When you were more endear'd to it than now;
When your own Percy, when my heart's dear Harry,
Threw many a northward look to see his father
Bring up his powers; but he did long in vain.
Who then persuaded you to stay at home?   15
There were two honours lost, yours and your son's:
For yours, the God of heaven brighten it!
For his, it stuck upon him as the sun
In the grey vault of heaven; and by his light

---

70 red lattice: *ale-house window*   **76–79;** *Cf. n.*   **82, 83 cankers:** *canker-worms*   **90
martlemas;** *cf. n.*   **94 wen:** *swelling, i.e., Falstaff*   **100 takes upon him:** *pretends
conceive: understand*   **101, 102 borrower's cap;** *cf. n.*   **103 fetch it from Japhet:** *trace
kingship through Japhet, the son of Noah*   **103 ff.; Cf. n.**

131 frank: *sty*   **134 Ephesians:** *slang term for jolly fellow*   **153 bestow:** *behave*   **157,
158; Cf. n.**   **11 endear'd:** *bound*

Did all the chivalry of England move   20
To do brave acts: he was indeed the glass
Wherein the noble youth did dress themselves:
He had no legs, that practis'd not his gait;
And speaking thick, which nature made his blemish,
Became the accents of the valiant;   25
For those that could speak low and tardily,
Would turn their own perfection to abuse,
To seem like him: so that, in speech, in gait,
In diet, in affections of delight,
In military rules, humours of blood,   30
He was the mark and glass, copy and book,
That fashion'd others. And him, O wondrous him!
O miracle of men! him did you leave,—
Second to none, unseconded by you,—
To look upon the hideous god of war   35
In disadvantage; to abide a field
Where nothing but the sound of Hotspur's name
Did seem defensible: so you left him.
Never, O! never, do his ghost the wrong
To hold your honour more precise and nice   40
With others than with him: let them alone.
The marshal and the archbishop are strong:
Had my sweet Harry had but half their numbers,
To-day might I, hanging on Hotspur's neck,
Have talk'd of Monmouth's grave.   45
    North.   Beshrew your heart,
Fair daughter! you do draw my spirits from me
With new lamenting ancient oversights.
But I must go and meet with danger there,
Or it will seek me in another place,   50
And find me worse provided.
    Lady N.   O! fly to Scotland,
Till that the nobles and the armed commons
Have of their puissance made a little taste.
    Lady P. If they get ground and vantage of the king,   55
Then join you with them, like a rib of steel,
To make strength stronger; but, for all our loves,
First let them try themselves. So did your son;
He was so suffer'd: so came I a widow;
And never shall have length of life enough   60
To rain upon remembrance with mine eyes,
That it may grow and sprout as high as heaven,
For recordation to my noble husband.
    North. Come, come, go in with me. 'Tis with my mind
As with the tide swell'd up unto his height,   65
That makes a still-stand, running neither way:
Fain would I go to meet the archbishop,
But many thousand reasons hold me back.
I will resolve for Scotland: there am I,
Till time and vantage crave my company.   *Exeunt.*   70

❧ SCENE FOURTH ❧

[London. A Room in the Boar's Head Tavern, in Eastcheap]
Enter two Drawers [Francis and another].

First Draw. What the devil hast thou brought there? apple-johns? thou knowest Sir John cannot endure an apple-john.

Sec. Draw. Mass, thou sayst true. The prince once set a dish of apple-johns before him, and told him there were five more Sir Johns; and, putting off his hat, said, 'I will now take my   5 leave of these six dry, round, old withered knights.' It angered him to the heart; but he hath forgot that.

First Draw. Why then, cover, and set them down: and see if thou canst find out Sneak's noise; Mistress Tearsheet would fain hear some music. Dispatch: the room where they supped   10 is too hot; they'll come in straight.

Sec. Draw. Sirrah, here will be the prince and Master Poins anon; and they will put on two of our jerkins and aprons; and Sir John must not know of it: Bardolph hath brought word.

First Draw. By the mass, here will be old utis: it will   15 be an excellent stratagem.

Sec. Draw. I'll see if I can find out Sneak.   *Exit.*

Enter Hostess and Doll.

Host. I' faith, sweetheart, methinks now you are in an excellent good temperality: your pulsidge beats as extraordinarily as heart would desire; and your colour, I warrant you, is as red   20 as any rose; in good truth, la! But, i' faith, you have drunk too much canaries, and that's a marvellous searching wine, and it perfumes the blood ere one can say, What's this? How do you now?

Dol. Better than I was: hem!   25

Host. Why, that's well said; a good heart's worth gold. Lo! here comes Sir John.

Enter Falstaff [singing].

Fal. 'When Arthur first in court'—Empty the jordan.—*[Exit Drawer.]*—'And was a worthy king.' How now, Mistress Doll!

Host. Sick of a calm: yea, good faith.   30

Fal. So is all her sect; an they be once in a calm they are sick.

Dol. A pox damn you, you muddy rascal, is that all the comfort you give me?

Fal. You make fat rascals, Mistress Doll.   35

Dol. I make them! gluttony and diseases make them; I make them not.

Fal. If the cook help to make the gluttony, you help to make the diseases, Doll: we catch of you, Doll, we catch of you; grant that, my poor virtue, grant that.   40

Dol. Yea, joy, our chains and our jewels.

Fal. 'Your brooches, pearls, and owches':—for to serve bravely is to come halting off, you know: to come off the breach with his pike bent bravely, and to surgery bravely; to venture upon the charged chambers bravely,—   45

Dol. Hang yourself, you muddy conger, hang yourself!

Host. By my troth, this is the old fashion; you two never meet but you fall to some discord: you are both, i' good truth,

---

24 thick: *fast*   **29 affections of delight:** *favorite pastimes*   **30 blood:** *disposition*   **38 defensible:** *able to furnish defense*   **40 nice:** *scrupulous*   **63 For recordation to:** *in memory of*

2 apple-johns: *apples that keep well but become very much shriveled*   **8 cover:** *set the table*   **9 noise:** *band of musicians*   **15 old utis:** *rare sport*   **28;** *Cf. n.*   **jordan:** *chamber-pot*   **30 calm:** *mistake for 'qualm'*   **31 sect:** *sex*   **42;** *Cf. n.*   **owches:** *jewels*   **45 chambers:** *small cannon*   **46 conger:** *eel*

as rheumatic as two dry toasts; you cannot one bear with
another's confirmities. What the good-year! one must bear,   *50*
and that must be you: you are the weaker vessel, as they
say, the emptier vessel.

Dol. Can a weak empty vessel bear such a huge full hogshead? there's a whole merchant's venture of Bordeaux stuff in
him: you have not seen a hulk better stuffed in the hold.   *55*
Come, I'll be friends with thee, Jack: thou art going to the
wars; and whether I shall ever see thee again or no, there is
nobody cares.

Enter Drawer [Francis].

Fran. Sir, Ancient Pistol's below, and would speak with you.

Dol. Hang him, swaggering rascal! let him not come   *60*
hither: it is the foul-mouthedest rogue in England.

Host. If he swagger, let him not come here: no, by my faith;
I must live among my neighbours; I'll no swaggerers: I am in
good name and fame with the very best. Shut the door; there
comes no swaggerers here: I have not lived all this while to   *65*
have swaggering now: shut the door, I pray you.

Fal. Dost thou hear, hostess?

Host. Pray ye, pacify yourself, Sir John: there comes no
swaggerers here.

Fal. Dost thou hear? it is mine ancient.   *70*

Host. Tilly-fally, Sir John, ne'er tell me: your ancient swaggerer comes not in my doors. I was before Master Tisick, the
debuty, t'other day; and, as he said to me,—'twas no longer
ago than Wedesday last,—'I' good faith, neighbor Quickly,'
says he;—Master Dumbe, our minister, was by then;—   *75*
'Neighbour Quickly,' says he, 'receive those that are civil, for,'
said he, 'you are in an illname'; now, a' said so, I can tell
whereupon; 'for,' says he, 'you are an honest woman, and well
thought on; therefore take heed what guests you receive: receive,' says he, 'no swaggering companions.' There comes   *80*
none here:—you would bless you to hear what he said. No,
I'll no swaggerers.

Fal. He's no swaggerer, hostess; a tame cheater, i' faith; you
may stroke him as gently as a puppy greyhound: he'll not swagger with a Barbary hen if her feathers turn back in any show   *85*
of resistance. Call him up, drawer.   *[Exit Francis.]*

Host. Cheater, call you him? I will bar no honest man my
house, nor no cheater; but I do not love swaggering, by my
troth; I am the worse, when one says swagger. Feel, masters,
how I shake; look you, I warrant you.   *90*

Dol. So you do, hostess.

Host. Do I? yea, in very truth, do I, an 'twere an aspen leaf:
I cannot abide swaggerers.

Enter Ancient Pistol, and Bardolph and his boy.

Pist. God save you, Sir John!

Fal. Welcome, Ancient Pistol. Here, Pistol, I charge you   *95*
with a cup of sack: do you discharge upon mine hostess.

Pist. I will discharge upon her, Sir John, with two bullets.

Fal. She is pistol-proof, sir; you shall hardly offend her.

Host. Come, I'll drink no proofs nor no bullets: I'll drink
no more than will do me good, for no man's pleasure, I.   *100*

Pist. Then to you, Mistress Dorothy; I will charge you.

Dol. Charge me! I scorn you, scurvy companion. What! you
poor, base, rascally, cheating, lack-linen mate! Away, you
mouldy rogue, away! I am meat for your master.

Pist. I know you, Mistress Dorothy.   *105*

Dol. Away, you cut-purse rascal! you filthy bung, away! By
this wine, I'll thrust my knife in your mouldy chaps an you
play the saucy cuttle with me. Away, you bottle-ale rascal! you
basket-hilt stale juggler, you! Since when, I pray you, sir?
God's light! with two points on your shoulder? much!   *110*

Pist. God let me not live but I will murder your ruff for
this!   *[Attacking her, and tearing her ruff.]*

Fal. No more, Pistol: I would not have you go off here. Discharge yourself of our company, Pistol.

Host. No, good captain Pistol; not here, sweet captain.   *115*

Dol. Captain! thou abominable damned cheater, art thou
not ashamed to be called captain? An captains were of my
mind, they would truncheon you out for taking their names
upon you before you have earned them. You a captain, you
slave! for what? for tearing a poor whore's ruff in a bawdy-   *120*
house? He a captain! Hang him, rogue! He lives upon mouldy
stewed prunes and dried cakes. A captain! God's light, these
villains will make the word captain as odious as the word
'occupy,' which was an excellent good word before it was ill
sorted: therefore captains had need look to 't.   *125*

Bard. Pray thee, go down, good ancient.

Fal. Hark thee hither, Mistress Doll.

Pist. Not I; I tell thee what, Corporal Bardolph; I could
tear her. I'll be revenged of her.

Page. Pray thee, go down.   *130*

Pist. I'll see her damned first; to Pluto's damned lake, by
this hand, to the infernal deep, with Erebus and tortures vile
also. Hold hook and line, say I. Down, down, dogs! down
faitors. Have we not Hiren here?

Host. Good Captain Peesel, be quiet; 'tis very late, i'   *135*
faith. I beseek you now, aggravate your choler.

Pist. These be good humours, indeed! Shall pack-horses,
And hollow pamper'd jades of Asia,
Which cannot go but thirty mile a day,
Compare with Cæsars, and with Cannibals,   *140*
And Trojan Greeks? nay, rather damn them with
King Cerberus; and let the welkin roar.
Shall we fall foul for toys?

Host. By my troth, captain, these are very bitter words.

Bard. Be gone, good ancient: this will grow to a brawl   *145*
anon.

Pist. Die men like dogs! give crowns like pins! Have we
not Hiren here?

Host. O' my word, captain, there's none such here. What
the good-year! do you think I would deny her? for God's   *150*
sake! be quiet.

Pist. Then feed, and be fat, my fair Calipolis.
Come, give's some sack.
Si fortune me tormente, sperato me contento.
Fear we broadsides? no, let the fiend give fire: *155*

102 companion: *a term of contempt*   **103 mate:** *fellow, 'chap'*   **106 bung:** *slang for*
'sharper'   **107 chaps:** *jaws*   **108 cuttle:** *slang for 'cutpurse'*   **109 basket-hilt:** *referring*
to the basket-shaped steel hand-guard on the hilt of Pistol's sword   **juggler:** *trickster*   **Since**
when, etc.: *a cant exclamation of scorn*   **110 two points:** *shoulder tags, mark of an*
army commission   **124 occupy;** *cf. n.*   **134 faitors:** *imposters*   **Hiren;** *cf. n.*   **138, 139;**
Cf. n.   **140 Cannibals:** *blunder for 'Hannibals'*   **143 toys:** *trifles*   **152;** *Cf. n.*
154; *Cf. n.*

49 rheumatic: *error for 'splenetic' (?)*   **50 good-year:** *corruption of French 'goujere,' 'the*
pox'   **59 Ancient:** *ensign or second lieutenant, Peto being Captain Falstaff's first lieuten-*
ant   **63 swaggerers:** *bullies*   **73 debuty;** *cf. n.*   **83 tame cheater;** *cf. n.*   **85 Bar-**
bary hen: *a hen whose feathers naturally turn back*

Give me some sack; and, sweetheart, lie thou there.

                                     [Laying down his sword.]

Come we to full points here, and are *et ceteras* nothing?

Fal. Pistol, I would be quiet.

Pist. Sweet knight, I kiss thy neif. What! we have seen
the seven stars.   *160*

Dol. For God's sake, thrust him down stairs! I cannot
endure such a fustian rascal.

Pist. 'Thrust him down stairs!' know we not Galloway nags?

Fal. Quoit him down, Bardolph, like a shove-groat shilling:
nay, an a' do nothing but speak nothing, a' shall be nothing   *165*
here.

Bard. Come, get you down stairs.

Pist. What! shall we have incision? Shall we imbrue?

                                  [Snatching up his sword.]

Then death rock me asleep, abridge my doleful days!
Why then, let grievous, ghastly, gaping wounds   *170*
Untwine the Sisters Three! Come, Atropos, I say!

Host. Here's goodly stuff toward!

Fal. Give me my rapier, boy.

Dol. I pray thee, Jack, I pray thee, do not draw.

Fal. Get you down stairs.   *[Drawing.]* *175*

Host. Here's a goodly tumult! I'll forswear keeping house,
afore I'll be in these tirrits and frights. So; murder, I warrant
now. Alas, alas! put up your naked weapons; put up your
naked weapons.   *[Exeunt Bardolph and Pistol.]*

Dol. I pray thee, Jack, be quiet; the rascal's gone. Ah!   *180*
you whoreson little valiant villain, you!

Host. Are you not hurt i' the groin? methought a' made a
shrewd thrust at your belly.

[Enter Bardolph.]

Fal. Have you turned him out o' doors?

Bard. Yea, sir: the rascal's drunk. You have hurt him,   *185*
sir, i' the shoulder.

Fal. A rascal, to brave me!

Dol. Ah, you sweet little rogue, you! Alas, poor ape, how
thou sweatest! Come, let me wipe thy face; come on, you
whoreson chops. Ah, rogue! i' faith, I love thee. Thou art   *190*
as valorous as Hector of Troy, worth five of Agamemnon,
and ten times better than the Nine Worthies. Ah, villain!

Fal. A rascally slave! I will toss the rogue in a blanket.

Dol. Do, an thou darest for thy heart: an thou dost, I'll
canvass thee between a pair of sheets.   *195*

Enter Music.

Page. The music is come, sir.

Fal. Let them play. Play, sirs. Sit on my knee, Doll. A
rascal bragging slave! the rogue fled from me like quicksilver.

Dol. I' faith, and thou followedst him like a church. Thou
whoreson little tidy Bartholomew boar-pig, when wilt thou   *200*
leave fighting o' days, and foining o' nights, and begin to
patch up thine old body for heaven?

Enter [behind] the Prince and Poins, disguised [like Drawers].

Fal. Peace, good Doll! do not speak like a death's head:
do not bid me remember mine end.

Dol. Sirrah, what humour's the prince of?   *205*

Fal. A good shallow young fellow: a' would have made
a good pantler, a' would have chipped bread well.

Dol. They say, Poins has a good wit.

Fal. He a good wit! hang him, baboon! his wit is as thick
as Tewksbury mustard: there is no more conceit in him   *210*
than is in a mallet.

Dol. Why does the prince love him so, then?

Fal. Because their legs are both of a bigness, and a' plays at
quoits well, and eats conger and fennel, and drinks off candles'
ends for flapdragons, and rides the wild mare with the boys,   *215*
and jumps on joint-stools, and swears with a good grace, and
wears his boots very smooth, like unto the sign of the leg, and
breeds no bate with telling of discreet stories; and such other
gambol faculties a' has, that show a weak mind and an able
body, for the which the prince admits him: for the prince   *220*
himself is such another; the weight of a hair will turn the
scales between their avoirdupois.

Prince. Would not this nave of a wheel have his ears cut
off?

Poins. Let's beat him before his whore.   *225*

Prince. Look, whether the withered elder hath not his
poll clawed like a parrot.

Poins. Is it not strange that desire should so many years
outlive performance?

Fal. Kiss me, Doll.   *230*

Prince. Saturn and Venus this year in conjunction! what
says the almanack to that?

Poins. And, look, whether the fiery Trigon, his man, be not
lisping to his master's old tables, his note-book, his counsel-
keeper.   *235*

Fal. Thou dost give me flattering busses.

Dol. By my troth, I kiss thee with a most constant heart.

Fal. I am old, I am old.

Dol. I love thee better than I love e'er a scurvy young
boy of them all.   *240*

Fal. What stuff wilt have a kirtle of? I shall receive money
o' Thursday; shalt have a cap to-morrow. A merry song! come:
it grows late; we'll to bed. Thou'lt forget me when I am gone.

Dol. By my troth, thou'lt set me a-weeping an thou sayst
so: prove that ever I dress myself handsome till thy return.   *245*
Well, hearken at the end.

Fal. Some sack, Francis!

Prince. }
Poins.   } *[Coming forward.]* Anon, anon, sir.

Fal. Ha! a bastard son of the king's? And art not thou   *250*
Poins his brother?

Prince. Why, thou globe of sinful continents, what a life
dost thou lead!

Fal. A better than thou: I am a gentleman; thou art a
drawer.   *255*

Prince. Very true, sir; and I come to draw you out by
the ears.

157 full points: *a full stop*   **159 neif:** *fist*   **160 seven stars:** *the Pleiades*   **162 fustian:**
nonsensical   **163 Galloway nags:** *small and inferior breed of horses*   **164 Quoit:**
pitch **shove-groat;** *cf. n.*   **168 imbrue:** *draw blood*   **171 Sisters Three:** *the Fates,
Clotho, Lachesis, and Atropos*   **172 toward:** *at hand*   **177 tirrits:** *blunder for terrors
(?)*   **190 chops:** *fat-face*   **200 Bartholomew boar-pig:** *roast pig, a favorite dish at Bartholomew Fair*

207 pantler: *servant in charge of the pantry*   **210 conceit:** *imagination*   **214, 215 drinks
. . . flapdragons;** *cf. n.*   **215 rides . . . mare:** *plays see-saw*   **216 joint-stools:** *stools made by
a joiner, as distinguished from those of rough make*   **217 sign of the leg:** *a shoemaker's
sign*   **218 breeds no bate:** *causes no strife*   **219 gambol:** *sportive*   **223 nave of a wheel:**
Falstaff's knavery and rotundity are both included in this phrase   **227 poll:** *head*   **231;**
Cf. n.   **233 fiery Trigon:** *Bardolph; cf. n.*   **234 lisping:** *making love*   **old tables:** *old account
book, i.e., the hostess*   **241 kirtle:** *waist or skirt or both*   **246 hearken at:** *watch*

Host. O! the Lord preserve thy good Grace; by my troth, welcome to London. Now, the Lord bless that sweet face of thine! O Jesu! are you come from Wales? 260

Fal. Thou whoreson mad compound of majesty, by this light flesh and corrupt blood *[pointing at Doll]*, thou art welcome.

Dol. How, you fat fool! I scorn you.

Poins. My lord, he will drive you out of your revenge 265 and turn all to a merriment, if you take not the heat.

Prince. You whoreson candle-mine, you, how vilely did you speak of me even now before this honest, virtuous, civil gentlewoman!

Host. God's blessing of your good heart! and so she is, 270 by my troth.

Fal. Didst thou hear me?

Prince. Yea; and you knew me, as you did when you ran away by Gadshill: you knew I was at your back, and spoke it on purpose to try my patience. 275

Fal. No, no, no; not so; I did not think thou wast within hearing.

Prince. I shall drive you then to confess the wilful abuse; and then I know how to handle you.

Fal. No abuse, Hal, o' mine honour; no abuse. 280

Prince. Not to dispraise me, and call me pantler and bread-chipper and I know not what?

Fal. No abuse, Hal.

Poins. No abuse!

Fal. No abuse, Ned, in the world; honest Ned, none. I 285 dispraised him before the wicked, that the wicked might not fall in love with him; in which doing I have done the part of a careful friend and a true subject, and thy father is to give me thanks for it. No abuse, Hal; none, Ned, none: no, faith, boys, none. 290

Prince. See now, whether pure fear and entire cowardice doth not make thee wrong this virtuous gentlewoman to close with us? Is she of the wicked? Is thine hostess here of the wicked? Or is thy boy of the wicked? Or honest Bardolph, whose zeal burns in his nose, of the wicked? 295

Poins. Answer, thou dead elm, answer.

Fal. The fiend hath pricked down Bardolph irrecoverable; and his face is Lucifer's privy-kitchen, where he doth nothing but roast malt-worms. For the boy, there is a good angel about him; but the devil outbids him too. 300

Prince. For the women?

Fal. For one of them, she is in hell already, and burns poor souls. For the other, I owe her money; and whether she be damned for that, I know not.

Host. No, I warrant you. 305

Fal. No, I think thou art not; I think thou art quit for that. Marry, there is another indictment upon thee, for suffering flesh to be eaten in thy house, contrary to the law; for the which I think thou wilt howl.

Host. All victuallers do so: what's a joint of mutton or 310 two in a whole Lent?

Prince. You, gentlewoman,—

Dol. What says your Grace?

Fal. His Grace says that which his flesh rebels against.

Peto knocks at door.

Host. Who knocks so loud at door? Look to the door 315 there, Francis.

Enter Peto.

Prince. Peto, how now! what news?

Peto. The king your father is at Westminster; And there are twenty weak and wearied posts Come from the north: and as I came along, 320 I met and overtook a dozen captains, Bare-headed, sweating, knocking at the taverns, And asking every one for Sir John Falstaff.

Prince. By heaven, Poins, I feel me much to blame, So idly to profane the precious time, 325 When tempest of commotion, like the south, Borne with black vapour, doth begin to melt And drop upon our bare unarmed heads. Give me my sword and cloak. Falstaff, good night.

Exeunt Prince and Poins [Bardolph and Peto].

Fal. Now comes in the sweetest morsel of the night, and we must hence and leave it unpicked. *[Knocking within.]* More knocking at the door!

[Enter Bardolph.]

How now! what's the matter?

Bard. You must away to court, sir, presently; A dozen captains stay at door for you. 335

Fal. [To the Page]. Pay the musicians, sirrah. Farewell, hostess, farewell, Doll. You see, my good wenches, how men of merit are sought after: the undeserver may sleep when the man of action is called on. Farewell, good wenches. If I be not sent away post, I will see you again ere I go. 340

Dol. I cannot speak; if my heart be not ready to burst,— well, sweet Jack, have a care of thyself.

Fal. Farewell, farewell. *Exit [Falstaff, with Bardolph].*

Host. Well, fare thee well: I have known thee these twenty-nine years, come peascod-time; but an honester, and truer- 345 hearted man,—well, fare thee well.

Bard. [Within.] Mistress Tearsheet!

Host. What's the matter?

Bard. [Within.] Bid Mistress Tearsheet come to my master.

Host. O! run, Doll, run; run, good Doll. Come! 350

She comes blubbered.

Yea, will you come, Doll? *Exeunt.*

ACT THIRD ❧ SCENE FIRST

[Westminster. The Palace]
Enter the King in his night-gown, with a Page.

King. Go, call the Earls of Surrey and of Warwick; But, ere they come, bid them o'er-read these letters, And well consider of them. Make good speed.

[Exit Page.]

How many thousand of my poorest subjects Are at this hour asleep! O sleep! O gentle sleep! 5 Nature's soft nurse, how have I frighted thee, That thou no more wilt weigh my eyelids down

266 take . . . the heat: *strike while the iron's hot* 268 candle-mine: *mine of tallow* 292 close: *make peace* 296 dead elm; *cf. n.* 297 pricked down: *marked down* 299 malt-worms: *ale-topers* 306 quit: *absolved*

319 posts: *couriers* 326 south: *south wind* 340 post: *in haste* S.d. blubbered: *in tears* S.d. night-gown: *dressing gown*

And steep my senses in forgetfulness?
Why rather, sleep, liest thou in smoky cribs,
Upon uneasy pallets stretching thee,   10
And hush'd with buzzing night-flies to thy slumber,
Than in the perfum'd chambers of the great,
Under the canopies of costly state,
And lull'd with sound of sweetest melody?
O thou dull god! why liest thou with the vile   15
In loathsome beds, and leav'st the kingly couch
A watch-case or a common 'larum bell?
Wilt thou upon the high and giddy mast
Seel up the ship-boy's eyes, and rock his brains
In cradle of the rude imperious surge,   20
And in the visitation of the winds,
Who take the ruffian billows by the top,
Curling their monstrous heads, and hanging them
With deaf'ning clamour in the slippery clouds
That with the hurly death itself awakes?   25
Canst thou, O partial sleep! give thy repose
To the wet sea-boy in an hour so rude,
And in the calmest and most stillest night,
With all appliances and means to boot,
Deny it to a king? Then, happy low, lie down!   30
Uneasy lies the head that wears a crown.

Enter Warwick and Surrey.

War. Many good morrows to your majesty!
King. Is it good morrow, lords?
War. 'Tis one o'clock, and past.
King. Why then, good morrow to you all, my lords.   35
Have you read o'er the letters that I sent you?
War. We have, my liege.
King. Then you perceive the body of our kingdom,
How foul it is; what rank diseases grow,
And with what danger, near the heart of it.   40
War. It is but as a body, yet distemper'd,
Which to his former strength may be restor'd
With good advice and little medicine:
My Lord Northumberland will soon be cool'd.
King. O God! that one might read the book of fate,   45
And see the revolution of the times
Make mountains level, and the continent,—
Weary of solid firmness,—melt itself
Into the sea! and, other times, to see
The beachy girdle of the ocean   50
Too wide for Neptune's hips; how chances mock,
And changes fill the cup of alteration
With divers liquors! O! if this were seen,
The happiest youth, viewing his progress through,
What perils past, what crosses to ensue.   55
Would shut the book, and sit him down and die.
'Tis not ten years gone
Since Richard and Northumberland, great friends,
Did feast together, and in two years after
Were they at wars: it is but eight years since   60
This Percy was the man nearest my soul,
Who like a brother toil'd in my affairs
And laid his love and life under my foot;
Yea, for my sake, even to the eyes of Richard

Gave him defiance. But which of you was by,—   65
[*To Warwick.*] You, cousin Nevil, as I may remember,—
When Richard, with his eye brimful of tears,
Then check'd and rated by Northumberland,
Did speak these words, now prov'd a prophecy?
'Northumberland, thou ladder, by the which   70
My cousin Bolingbroke ascends my throne';
Though then, God knows, I had no such intent,
But that necessity so bow'd the state
That I and greatness were compelled to kiss:
'The time shall come,' thus did he follow it,   75
'The time will come, that foul sin, gathering head,
Shall break into corruption':—so went on,
Foretelling this same time's condition
And the division of our amity.
War. There is a history in all men's lives,   80
Figuring the nature of the times deceas'd;
The which observ'd, a man may prophesy,
With a near aim, of the main chance of things
As yet not come to life, which in their seeds
And weak beginnings lie intreasured.   85
Such things become the hatch and brood of time;
And by the necessary form of this
King Richard might create a perfect guess
That great Northumberland, then false to him,
Would of that seed grow to a greater falseness,   90
Which should not find a ground to root upon,
Unless on you.
King.   Are these things then necessities?
Then let us meet them like necessities;
And that same word even now cries out on us.   95
They say the bishop and Northumberland
Are fifty thousand strong.
War.   It cannot be, my lord!
Rumour doth double, like the voice and echo,
The numbers of the fear'd. Please it your Grace   100
To go to bed: upon my soul, my lord,
The powers that you already have sent forth
Shall bring this prize in very easily.
To comfort you the more, I have receiv'd
A certain instance that Glendower is dead.   105
Your majesty hath been this fortnight ill,
And these unseason'd hours perforce must add
Unto your sickness.
King.   I will take your counsel:
And were these inward wars once out of hand,   110
We would, dear lords, unto the Holy Land.   *Exeunt.*

❧ SCENE SECOND ❧

[*Before Justice Shallow's House in Gloucestershire*]
Enter Shallow and Silence, with Mouldy, Shadow, Wart, Feeble,
Bullcalf [and Servants].

Shal. Come on, come on, come on, sir; give me your hand,
sir, give me your hand, sir: an early stirrer, by the rood! And
how doth my good cousin Silence?
Sil. Good morrow, good cousin Shallow.
Shal. And how doth my cousin, your bedfellow? and your   5
fairest daughter and mine, my god-daughter Ellen?

---

17 watch-case: *sentry-box*   **19 Seel:** *sew together* (a hawking term)   **25 hurly:** *tumult*
68 check'd: *rebuked*   **81 Figuring:** *symbolizing*   **87 necessary form:** *logical neces-*
sity   **105 instance:** *proof*   **107 unseason'd:** *unseasonable*   **2 rood:** *cross*

Sil. Alas! a black ousel, cousin Shallow!

Shal. By yea and nay, sir, I dare say my cousin William is become a good scholar. He is at Oxford still, is he not?

Sil. Indeed, sir, to my cost.   *10*

Shal. A' must, then, to the inns o' court shortly. I was once of Clement's Inn; where I think they will talk of mad Shallow yet.

Sil. You were called 'lusty Shallow' then, cousin.

Shal. By the mass, I was called anything; and I would   *15* have done anything indeed too, and roundly too. There was I, and Little John Doit of Staffordshire, and black George Barnes, and Francis Pickbone, and Will Squele a Cotswold man; you had not four such swinge-bucklers in all the inns o' court again: and, I may say to you, we knew where the *bona-robas* *20* were, and had the best of them all at commandment. Then was Jack Falstaff, now Sir John, a boy, and page to Thomas Mowbray, Duke of Norfolk.

Sil. This Sir John, cousin, that comes hither anon about soldiers?   *25*

Shal. The same Sir John, the very same. I see him break Skogan's head at the court gate, when a' was a crack not thus high: and the very same day did I fight with one Sampson Stockfish, a fruiterer, behind Gray's Inn. Jesu! Jesu! the mad days that I have spent; and to see how many of my old   *30* acquaintance are dead!

Sil. We shall all follow, cousin.

Shal. Certain, 'tis certain; very sure, very sure: death, as the Psalmist saith, is certain to all; all shall die. How a good yoke of bullocks at Stamford fair?   *35*

Sil. By my troth, I was not there.

Shal. Death is certain. Is old Double of your town living yet?

Sil. Dead, sir.

Shal. Jesu! Jesu! dead! a' drew a good bow; and dead! a'   *40* shot a fine shoot: John a Gaunt loved him well, and betted much money on his head. Dead! a' would have clapped i' the clout at twelve score; and carried you a forehand shaft a fourteen and fourteen and a half, that it would have done a man's heart good to see. How a score of ewes now?   *45*

Sil. Thereafter as they be: a score of good ewes may be worth ten pounds.

Shal. And is old Double dead?

Sil. Here come two of Sir John Falstaff's men, as I think.

Enter Bardolph, and his Boy.

Shal. Good morrow, honest gentlemen.   *50*

Bard. I beseech you, which is Justice Shallow?

Shal. I am Robert Shallow, sir; a poor esquire of this county, and one of the king's justices of the peace: what is your good pleasure with me?

Bard. My captain, sir, commends him to you; my captain,   *55* Sir John Falstaff: a tall gentleman, by heaven, and a most gallant leader.

Shal. He greets me well, sir. I knew him a good backsword man. How doth the good knight? may I ask how my lady his wife doth?   *60*

Bard. Sir, pardon; a soldier is better accommodated than with a wife.

Shal. It is well said, in faith, sir; and it is well said indeed too. 'Better accommodated!' it is good; yea indeed, is it: good phrases are surely and ever were, very commendable. Accom-   *65* modated! it comes of *accommodo*: very good; a good phrase.

Bard. Pardon me, sir; I have heard the word. 'Phrase,' call you it? By this good day, I know not the phrase; but I will maintain the word with my sword to be a soldier-like word, and a word of exceeding good command, by heaven. Accom-   *70* modated; that is, when a man is, as they say, accommodated; or, when a man is, being, whereby, a' may be thought to be accommodated, which is an excellent thing.

Enter Falstaff.

Shal. It is very just. Look, here comes good Sir John. Give me your good hand, give me your worship's good hand. By   *75* my troth, you look well and bear your years very well: welcome, good Sir John.

Fal. I am glad to see you well, good Master Robert Shallow. Master Surecard, as I think.

Shal. No, Sir John; it is my cousin, Silence, in commission   *80* with me.

Fal. Good Master Silence, it well befits you should be of the peace.

Sil. Your good worship is welcome.

Fal. Fie! this is hot weather, gentlemen. Have you provided   *85* me here half a dozen sufficient men?

Shal. Marry, have we, sir. Will you sit?

Fal. Let me see them, I beseech you.

Shal. Where's the roll? where's the roll? where's the roll? Let me see, let me see, So, so, so, so, so, so, so: yea, marry, sir: *90* Ralph Mouldy! let them appear as I call; let them do so, let them do so. Let me see; where is Mouldy?

Moul. Here, an 't please you.

Shal. What think you, Sir John? a good-limbed fellow; young, strong, and of good friends.   *95*

Fal. Is thy name Mouldy?

Moul. Yea, an 't please you.

Fal. 'Tis the more time thou wert used.

Shal. Ha, ha, ha! most excellent, i' faith! things that are mouldy lack use: very singular good. In faith, well said, Sir   *100* John; very well said.

Fal. Prick him.

Moul. I was pricked well enough before, an you could have let me alone: my old dame will be undone now for one to do her husbandry and her drudgery: you need not to have   *105* pricked me; there are other men fitter to go out than I.

Fal. Go to: peace, Mouldy! you shall go. Mouldy, it is time you were spent.

Moul. Spent!

Shal. Peace, fellow, peace! stand aside: know you where   *110* you are? For the other, Sir John: let me see. Simon Shadow!

Fal. Yea, marry, let me have him to sit under: he's like to be a cold soldier.

Shal. Where's Shadow?

Shad. Here, sir.   *115*

Fal. Shadow, whose son art thou?

---

7 ousel: *blackbird*   **11 inns o' court:** *colleges of law*   **16 roundly:** *thoroughly*   **19 swinge-bucklers:** *roisterers*   **20 bona-robas:** *showy harlots*   **21–23** *Cf. n.*   **27 Skogan;** *cf. n.*   **crack:** *lively youngster*   **34 How:** *what price*   **42, 43 clapped i' the clout:** *hit the white mark in the target*   **43 at twelve score:** *at twelve score yards*   **forehand shaft:** *arrow made for shooting straight forward*   **a fourteen, etc.:** *fourteen score yards*   **56 tall:** *doughty*   **58, 59 backsword man:** *fighter at single-sticks*

61 accommodated; *cf. n.*   **79 Surecard:** *the name signifies 'boon companion'*   **80 commission:** *office*   **86 sufficient:** *fit*   **102 Prick:** *mark down*

Shad. My mother's son, sir.

Fal. Thy mother's son! like enough, and thy father's shadow: so the son of the female is the shadow of the male: it is often so, indeed; but not of the father's substance.   *120*

Shal. Do you like him, Sir John?

Fal. Shadow will serve for summer; prick him, for we have a number of shadows to fill up the muster-book.

Shal. Thomas Wart?

Fal. Where's he?   *125*

Wart. Here, sir.

Fal. Is thy name Wart?

Wart. Yea, sir.

Fal. Thou art a very ragged wart.

Shal. Shall I prick him, Sir John?   *130*

Fal. It were superfluous; for his apparel is built upon his back, and the whole frame stands upon pins: prick him no more.

Shal. Ha, ha, ha! you can do it, sir; you can do it: I commend you well. Francis Feeble!

Fee. Here, sir.   *135*

Fal. What trade art thou, Feeble?

Fee. A woman's tailor, sir.

Shal. Shall I prick him, sir?

Fal. You may; but if he had been a man's tailor he'd have pricked you. Wilt thou make as many holes in an enemy's   *140* battle as thou hast done in a woman's petticoat?

Fee. I will do my good will, sir: you can have no more.

Fal. Well said, good woman's tailor! well said, courageous Feeble! Thou wilt be as valiant as the wrathful dove or most magnanimous mouse. Prick the woman's tailor; well, Master *145* Shallow; deep, Master Shallow.

Fee. I would Wart might have gone, sir.

Fal. I would thou wert a man's tailor, that thou mightst mend him, and make him fit to go. I cannot put him to a private soldier that is the leader of so many thousands: *150* let that suffice, most forcible Feeble.

Fee. It shall suffice, sir.

Fal. I am bound to thee, reverend Feeble. Who is next?

Shal. Peter Bullcalf o' the green!

Fal. Yea, marry, let's see Bullcalf.   *155*

Bull. Here, sir.

Fal. 'Fore God, a likely fellow! Come, prick me Bullcalf till he roar again.

Bull. O Lord! good my lord captain,—

Fal. What! dost thou roar before thou art pricked?   *160*

Bull. O Lord, sir! I am a diseased man.

Fal. What disease hast thou?

Bull. A whoreson cold, sir; a cough, sir, which I caught with ringing in the king's affairs upon his coronation day, sir.

Fal. Come, thou shalt go to the wars in a gown; we will *165* have away thy cold; and I will take such order that thy friends shall ring for thee. Is here all?

Shal. Here is two more called than your number; you must have but four here, sir: and so, I pray you, go in with me to dinner.   *170*

Fal. Come, I will go drink with you, but I cannot tarry dinner. I am glad to see you, by my troth, Master Shallow.

Shal. O, Sir John, do you remember since we lay all night in the windmill in Saint George's field?

Fal. No more of that, good Master Shallow, no more of *175* that.

Shal. Ha! 'twas a merry night. And is Jane Nightwork alive?

Fal. She lives, Master Shallow.

Shal. She never could away with me.

Fal. Never, never; she would always say she could not *180* abide Master Shallow.

Shal. By the mass, I could anger her to the heart. She was then a *bona-roba.* Doth she hold her own well?

Fal. Old, old, Master Shallow.

Shal. Nay, she must be old; she cannot choose but be *185* old; certain she's old; and had Robin Nightwork by old Nightwork before I came to Clement's Inn.

Sil. That's fifty-five years ago.

Shal. Ha! cousin Silence, that thou hadst seen that that this knight and I have seen. Ha! Sir John, said I well?   *190*

Fal. We have heard the chimes at midnight, Master Shallow.

Shal. That we have, that we have, that we have; in faith, Sir John, we have. Our watchword was, 'Hem boys!' Come, let's to dinner; come, let's to dinner. Jesus, the days that we have seen! Come, come.   *Exeunt [Falstaff, Shallow, and Silence].* *195*

Bull. Good Master Corporate Bardolph, stand my friend, and here's four Harry ten shillings in French crowns for you. In very truth, sir, I had as lief be hanged, sir, as go: and yet, for mine own part, sir, I do not care; but rather, because I am unwilling, and, for mine own part, have a desire to stay *200* with my friends: else, sir, I did not care, for mine own part, so much.

Bard. Go to; stand aside.

Moul. And, good Master corporal captain, for my old dame's sake, stand my friend: she has nobody to do any- *205* thing about her, when I am gone; and she is old, and cannot help herself. You shall have forty, sir.

Bard. Go to; stand aside.

Fee. By my troth, I care not; a man can die but once; we owe God a death. I'll ne'er bear a base mind: an 't be my *210* destiny, so; an 't be not, so. No man's too good to serve's prince; and let it go which way it will, he that dies this year is quit for the next.

Bard. Well said; thou'rt a good fellow.

Fee. Faith, I'll bear no base mind.   *215*

Enter Falstaff and the Justices.

Fal. Come, sir, which men shall I have?

Shal. Four, of which you please.

Bard. [*To Falstaff.*] Sir, a word with you. I have three pound to free Mouldy and Bullcalf.

Fal. [*Aside to Bardolph.*] Go to; well.   *220*

Shal. Come, Sir John, which four will you have?

Fal. Do you choose for me.

Shal. Marry, then, Mouldy, Bullcalf, Feeble, and Shadow.

Fal. Mouldy, and Bullcalf: for you, Mouldy, stay at home till you are past service: and for your part, Bullcalf, grow *225* till you come unto it: I will none of you.

Shal. Sir John, Sir John, do not yourself wrong: they are your likeliest men, and I would have you served with the best.

Fal. Will you tell me, Master Shallow, how to choose a man? Care I for the limb, the thewes, the stature, bulk, and *230*

---

123 shadows: *names, for which we receive pay, though we have not the men*   141 battle: *army*   150 thousands: *i.e., vermin*   166 such order: *such measures*

179 away with: *endure*   196 Corporate: *blunder for 'Corporal'*   197 Harry ten shillings; *cf. n.*   218, 219 three pound; *cf. n.*

big assemblance of a man! Give me the spirit, Master Shallow.
Here's Wart; you see what a ragged appearance it is: a' shall
charge you and discharge you with the motion of a pewterer's
hammer, come off and on swifter than he that gibbets on the
brewer's bucket. And this same half-faced fellow, Shadow,   *235*
give me this man: he presents no mark to the enemy; the foeman may with as great aim level at the edge of a penknife.
And, for a retreat; how swiftly will this Feeble the woman's
tailor run off! O! give me the spare men, and spare me the
great ones. Put me a caliver into Wart's hand, Bardolph.   *240*

   Bard. Hold, Wart, traverse; thus, thus, thus.

   Fal. Come, manage me your caliver. So: very well: go to:
very good: exceeding good. O, give me always a little, lean,
old, chopp'd, bald shot. Well said, i' faith, Wart; thou'rt a
good scab: hold, there's a tester for thee.   *245*

   Shal. He is not his craft's master, he doth not do it right. I
remember at Mile-end Green, when I lay at Clement's Inn,—
I was then Sir Dagonet in Arthur's show,—there was a little
quiver fellow, and a' would manage you his piece thus: and a'
would about and about, and come you in, and come you   *250*
in; 'rah, tah, tah,' would a' say; 'bounce,' would a' say; and
away again would a' go, and again would a' come: I shall
never see such a fellow.

   Fal. These fellows will do well, Master Shallow. God keep
you, Master Silence: I will not use many words with you.   *255*
Fare you well, gentlemen both: I thank you: I must a dozen
mile to-night. Bardolph, give the soldiers coats.

   Shal. Sir John, the Lord bless you! God prosper your affairs!
God send us peace! At your return visit our house; let our old
acquaintance be renewed: peradventure I will with ye to the   *260*
court.

   Fal. 'Fore God I would you would, Master Shallow.

   Shal. Go to; I have spoke at a word. God keep you.

   Fal. Fare you well, gentle gentlemen.

                            Exit [Shallow, with Silence].
On, Bardolph; lead the men away.   *265*

                            [Exit Bardolph, with recruits.]
As I return, I will fetch off these justices: I do see the bottom
of Justice Shallow. Lord, Lord! how subject we old men are to
this vice of lying. This same starved justice hath done nothing
but prate to me of the wildness of his youth and the feats he
hath done about Turnbull Street; and every third word a lie,   *270*
duer paid to the hearer than the Turk's tribute. I do remember
him at Clement's Inn like a man made after supper of a
cheese-paring: when a' was naked he was for all the world like
a forked radish, with a head fantastically carved upon it with a
knife: a' was so forlorn that his dimensions to any thick sight
were invisible: a' was the very genius of famine; yet lecherous
as a monkey, and the whores called him mandrake: a' came
ever in the rearward of the fashion and sung those tunes to the
over-scutched huswives that he heard the carmen whistle, and
sware they were his fancies or his good-nights. And now is   *280*
this Vice's dagger become a squire, and talks as familiarly of
John a Gaunt as if he had been sworn brother to him; and I'll
be sworn a' never saw him but once in the Tilt-yard, and then

he burst his head for crowding among the marshal's men. I
saw it and told John a Gaunt he beat his own name; for you
might have thrust him and all his apparel into an eel-skin; the
case of a treble hautboy was a mansion for him, a court; and
now has he land and beefs. Well, I'll be acquainted with him,
if I return; and it shall go hard but I'll make him a philosopher's two stones to me. If the young dace be a bait for the   *290*
old pike, I see no reason in the law of nature but I may snap
at him. Let time shape, and there an end.   *Exit.*

ACT FOURTH ❧ Scene First

*Enter the Archbishop, Mowbray, [Lord] Bardolph, Hastings, within
the Forest of Gaultree.*

   Arch. What is this forest call'd?
   Hast. 'Tis Gaultree Forest, an 't shall please your Grace.
   Arch. Here stand, my lords, and send discoverers forth,
To know the numbers of our enemies.
   Hast. We have sent forth already.   *5*
   Arch.   'Tis well done.
My friends and brethren in these great affairs,
I must acquaint you that I have receiv'd
New-dated letters from Northumberland;
Their cold intent, tenour and substance, thus: *10*
Here doth he wish his person, with such powers
As might hold sortance with his quality;
The which he could not levy; whereupon
He is retir'd, to ripe his growing fortunes,
To Scotland; and concludes in hearty prayers   *15*
That your attempts may overlive the hazard
And fearful meeting of their opposite.
   Mowb. Thus do the hopes we have in him touch ground
And dash themselves to pieces.

                 Enter a Messenger.

   Hast.   Now, what news?   *20*
   Mess. West of this forest, scarcely off a mile,
In goodly form comes on the enemy;
And, by the ground they hide, I judge their number
Upon or near the rate of thirty thousand.
   Mowb. The just proportion that we gave them out.   *25*
Let us sway on and face them in the field.

                 Enter Westmoreland.

   Arch. What well-appointed leader fronts us here?
   Mowb. I think it is my Lord of Westmoreland.
   West. Health and fair greeting from our general,
The Prince, Lord John and Duke of Lancaster.   *30*
   Arch. Say on, my Lord of Westmoreland, in peace,
What doth concern your coming.
   West.   Then, my lord,
Unto your Grace do I in chief address
The substance of my speech. If that rebellion   *35*
Came like itself, in base and abject routs,
Led on by bloody youth, guarded with rags,

231 assemblance: *appearance*   **234 gibbets;** *cf. n.*   **240 caliver:** *light musket*   **241
traverse:** *march*   **244 chopp'd:** *chapped*   **245 tester:** *sixpence*   **246–248** *Cf. n.*
249 quiver: *nimble*   **250 come you in:** *make a home thrust*   **251 bounce:**
bang   **263 at a word:** *briefly but sincerely*   **266 fetch off:** *get the better of, 'take
in'*   **271 duer:** *more duly*   **279 over-scutched huswives:** *cant term for 'harlots'* **carmen:** *teamsters*   **280 fancies . . . good-nights:** *common names for little poems*   **281
Vice's dagger;** *cf. n.*

287 hautboy: *slender reed instrument, oboe*   **289, 290 philosopher's two stones;** *cf. n.*   **12
hold sortance:** *be in accord* **quality:** *rank*   **22 form:** *formation*   **25 just proportion:** *exact
size* **gave them out:** *described them*   **36 routs:** *gangs*   **37 guarded:** *decked*

And countenanc'd by boys and beggary;
I say, if damn'd commotion so appear'd,
In his true, native, and most proper shape,   40
You, reverend father, and these noble lords
Had not been here, to dress the ugly form
Of base and bloody insurrection
With your fair honours. You, lord archbishop,
Whose see is by a civil peace maintain'd,   45
Whose beard the silver hand of peace hath touch'd,
Whose learning and good letters peace hath tutor'd,
Whose white investments figure innocence,
The dove and very blessed spirit of peace,
Wherefore do you so ill translate yourself   50
Out of the speech of peace that bears such grace
Into the harsh and boisterous tongue of war;
Turning your books to greaves, your ink to blood,
Your pens to lances, and your tongue divine
To a loud trumpet and a point of war?   55
    Arch. Wherefore do I this? so the question stands.
Briefly to this end: we are all diseas'd;
And, with our surfeiting and wanton hours
Have brought ourselves into a burning fever,
And we must bleed for it: of which disease   60
Our late king, Richard, being infected, died.
But, my most noble Lord of Westmoreland,
I take not on me here as a physician,
Nor do I as an enemy to peace
Troop in the throngs of military men;   65
But rather show a while like fearful war,
To diet rank minds sick of happiness
And purge the obstructions which begin to stop
Our very veins of life. Hear me more plainly:
I have in equal balance justly weigh'd   70
What wrongs our arms may do, what wrongs we suffer,
And find our griefs heavier than our offences.
We see which way the stream of time doth run
And are enforc'd from our most quiet sphere
By the rough torrent of occasion;   75
And have the summary of all our griefs,
When time shall serve, to show in articles,
Which long ere this we offer'd to the king,
And might by no suit gain our audience.
When we are wrong'd and would unfold our griefs,   80
We are denied access unto his person
Even by those men that most have done us wrong.
The dangers of the days but newly gone,—
Whose memory is written on the earth
With yet appearing blood,—and the examples   85
Of every minute's instance, present now,
Have put us in these ill-beseeming arms;
Not to break peace, or any branch of it,
But to establish here a peace indeed,
Concurring both in name and quality.   90
    West. When ever yet was your appeal denied?
Wherein have you been galled by the king?
What peer hath been suborn'd to grate on you,
That you should seal this lawless bloody book
Of forg'd rebellion with a seal divine,   95
And consecrate commotion's bitter edge?

    Arch. My brother general, the commonwealth,
To brother born an household cruelty,
I make my quarrel in particular.
    West. There is no need of any such redress;   100
Or if there were, it not belongs to you.
    Mowb. Why not to him in part, and to us all
That feel the bruises of the days before,
And suffer the condition of these times
To lay a heavy and unequal hand   105
Upon our honours?
    West.   O! my good Lord Mowbray,
Construe the times to their necessities,
And you shall say indeed, it is the time,
And not the king, that doth you injuries.   110
Yet, for your part, it not appears to me
Either from the king or in the present time
That you should have an inch of any ground
To build a grief on: were you not restor'd
To all the Duke of Norfolk's signories,   115
Your noble and right well-remember'd father's?
    Mowb. What thing, in honour, had my father lost,
That need to be reviv'd and breath'd in me?
The king that lov'd him as the state stood then,
Was force perforce compell'd to banish him: 120
And then that Harry Bolingbroke and he,
Being mounted and both roused in their seats,
Their neighing coursers daring of the spur,
Their armed staves in charge, their beavers down,
Their eyes of fire sparkling through sights of steel,   125
And the loud trumpet blowing them together,
Then, then when there was nothing could have stay'd
My father from the breast of Bolingbroke,
O! when the king did throw his warder down,
His own life hung upon the staff he threw;   130
Then threw he down himself and all their lives
That by indictment and by dint of sword
Have since miscarried under Bolingbroke.
    West. You speak, Lord Mowbray, now you know not what.
The Earl of Hereford was reputed then   135
In England the most valiant gentleman:
Who knows on whom Fortune would then have smil'd?
But if your father had been victor there,
He ne'er had borne it out of Coventry;
For all the country in a general voice   140
Cried hate upon him; and all their prayers and love
Were set on Hereford, whom they doted on
And bless'd and grac'd indeed, more than the king.
But this is mere digression from my purpose.
Here come I from our princely general   145
To know your griefs; to tell you from his Grace
That he will give you audience; and wherein
It shall appear that your demands are just,
You shall enjoy them; everything set off
That might so much as think you enemies.   150
    Mowb. But he hath forc'd us to compel this offer,
And it proceeds from policy, not love.

---

55 **point:** *trumpet signal*   72 **griefs:** *grievances*   96 **commotion's:** *insurrection's*

97–99 *Cf. n.*   108 **to:** *according to*   118 **breath'd:** *given breath of life*   121 **ff.**
Cf. n.   124 **armed staves:** *lances* **in charge:** *in rest for the charge* **beavers:** *movable fronts
of the helmets*   125 **sights:** *eyeholes of the helmet*   129 **warder:** *staff of command*   133
miscarried: *perished*   135 **Earl of Hereford:** *King Henry, actually Duke of Hereford at the
time of his banishment (cf. Richard II, I. iii. 21)*   149 **set off:** *ignored*

West. Mowbray, you overween to take it so.
This offer comes from mercy, not from fear:
For, lo! within a ken our army lies   155
Upon mine honour, all too confident
To give admittance to a thought of fear.
Our battle is more full of names than yours,
Our men more perfect in the use of arms,
Our armour all as strong, our cause the best;   160
Then reason will our hearts should be as good:
Say you not then our offer is compell'd.
   Mowb. Well, by my will we shall admit no parley.
   West. That argues but the shame of your offence:
A rotten case abides no handling.   165
   Hast. Hath the Prince John a full commission,
In very ample virtue of his father,
To hear and absolutely to determine
Of what conditions we shall stand upon?
   West. That is intended in the general's name.   170
I muse you make so slight a question.
   Arch. Then take, my Lord of Westmoreland, this schedule,
For this contains our general grievances:
Each several article herein redress'd;
All members of our cause, both here and hence,   175
That are insinew'd to this action,
Acquitted by a true substantial form;
And present execution of our wills
To us and to our purposes consign'd;
We come within our awful banks again   180
And knit our powers to the arm of peace.
   West. This will I show the general. Please you, lords,
In sight of both our battles we may meet;
And either end in peace, which God so frame!
Or to the place of difference call the swords   185
Which must decide it.
   Arch.   My lord, we will do so.
                                  Exit Westmoreland.
   Mowb. There is a thing within my bosom tells me
That no conditions of our peace can stand.
   Hast. Fear you not that: if we can make our peace   190
Upon such large terms, and so absolute
As our conditions shall consist upon,
Our peace shall stand as firm as rocky mountains.
   Mowb. Yea, but our valuation shall be such
That every slight and false-derived cause,   195
Yea, every idle, nice, and wanton reason
Shall to the king taste of this action;
That, were our royal faiths martyrs in love,
We shall be winnow'd with so rough a wind
That even our corn shall seem as light as chaff   200
And good from bad find no partition.
   Arch. No, no, my lord. Note this; the king is weary
Of dainty and such picking grievances:
For he hath found to end one doubt by death
Revives two greater in the heirs of life;   205
And therefore will he wipe his tables clean,
And keep no tell-tale to his memory

That may repeat and history his loss
To new remembrance; for full well he knows
He cannot so precisely weed this land   210
As his misdoubts present occasion:
His foes are so enrooted with his friends
That, plucking to unfix an enemy,
He doth unfasten so and shake a friend.
So that this land, like an offensive wife,   215
That hath enrag'd him on to offer strokes,
As he is striking, holds his infant up
And hangs resolv'd correction in the arm
That was uprear'd to execution.
   Hast. Besides, the king hath wasted all his rods   220
On late offenders, that he now doth lack
The very instruments of chastisement;
So that his power, like to a fangless lion,
May offer, but not hold.
   Arch.   'Tis very true: 225
And therefore be assur'd, my good lord marshal,
If we do now make our atonement well,
Our peace will, like a broken limb united,
Grow stronger for the breaking.
   Mowb.   Be it so.   230
Here is return'd my Lord of Westmoreland.

Enter Westmoreland.

   West. The prince is here at hand: pleaseth your lordship,
To meet his Grace just distance 'tween our armies?
   Mowb. Your Grace of York, in God's name then, set
forward.   235
   Arch. Before, and greet his Grace: my lord, we come.

❧ SCENE SECOND ❧

[The Same]
Enter Prince John of Lancaster and his army.

   Lanc. You are well encounter'd here, my cousin Mowbray:
Good day to you, gentle lord archbishop;
And so to you, Lord Hastings, and to all.
My Lord of York, it better show'd with you.
When that your flock, assembled by the bell,   5
Encircled you to hear with reverence
Your exposition on the holy text
Than now to see you here an iron man,
Cheering a rout of rebels with your drum,
Turning the word to sword and life to death.   10
That man that sits within a monarch's heart
And ripens in the sunshine of his favour,
Would he abuse the countenance of the king,
Alack! what mischiefs might he set abroach
In shadow of such greatness. With you, lord bishop,   15
It is even so. Who hath not heard it spoken
How deep you were within the books of God?
To us the speaker in his parliament;
To us the imagin'd voice of God himself;

---

153 **overween:** *are arrogant*   155 **within a ken:** *within seeing distance*   158 **names:** *noble and soldierly names*   167 **In . . . virtue:** *by complete authority*   170 **intended:** *implied*   171 **muse:** *wonder* **slight:** *trivial*   176 **insinew'd:** *joined as by sinews*   179 **consign'd;** *cf. n.*   180 **awful:** *respectful, reverential*   194 **our valuation:** *the king's estimation of us*   196 **nice:** *trivial*   203 **picking:** *fastidious*

211 **misdoubts:** *suspicions*   218 **hangs:** *suspends* **resolv'd correction:** *chastisement which had been determined upon*   224 **offer:** *attach*   227 **atonement:** *reconciliation*   236 **Before:** *go before me* **Scene Second;** *cf. n.*

The very opener and intelligencer *20*
Between the grace, the sanctities of heaven,
And our dull workings. O! who shall believe
But you misuse the reverence of your place,
Employ the coutenance and grace of heaven,
As a false favourite doth his prince's name, *25*
In deeds dishonourable? You have taken up,
Under the counterfeited zeal of God,
The subjects of his substitute, my father;
And both against the peace of heaven and him
Have here upswarm'd them. *30*
 Arch.   Good my Lord of Lancaster,
I am not here against your father's peace;
But, as I told my Lord of Westmoreland,
The time misorder'd doth, in common sense,
Crowd us and crush us to this monstrous form, *35*
To hold our safety up. I sent your Grace
The parcels and particulars of our grief,—
The which hath been with scorn shov'd from the court,—
Whereon this Hydra son of war is born;
Whose dangerous eyes may well be charm'd asleep *40*
With grant of our most just and right desires,
And true obedience, of this madness cur'd,
Stoop tamely to the foot of majesty.
 Mowb. If not, we ready are to try our fortunes
To the last man. *45*
 Hast. And though we here fall down,
We have supplies to second our attempt:
If they miscarry, theirs shall second them;
And so success of mischief shall be born,
And heir from heir shall hold this quarrel up *50*
Whiles England shall have generation.
 Lanc. You are too shallow, Hastings, much too shallow,
To sound the bottom. of the after-times.
 West. Pleaseth your Grace, to answer them directly
How far forth you do like their articles. *55*
 Lanc. I like them all, and do allow them well;
And swear here, by the honour of my blood,
My father's purposes have been mistook,
And some about him have too lavishly
Wrested his meaning and authority. *60*
My lord, these griefs shall be with speed redress'd;
Upon my soul, they shall. If this may please you,
Discharge your powers unto their several counties,
As we will ours: and here between the armies
Let's drink together friendly and embrace, *65*
That all their eyes may bear those tokens home
Of our restored love and amity.
 Arch. I take your princely word for these redresses.
 Lanc. I give it you, and will maintain my word:
And thereupon I drink unto your Grace. *70*
 Hast. [*To an Officer.*] Go, captain, and deliver to the army
This news of peace: let them have pay, and part:
I know it will well please them: hie thee, captain.
          Exit [*Officer*].
 Arch. To you, my noble Lord of Westmoreland.
 West. I pledge your Grace: and, if you knew what pains *75*
I have bestow'd to breed this present peace,

You would drink freely; but my love to you
Shall show itself more openly hereafter.
 Arch. I do not doubt you.
 West.   I am glad of it. *80*
Health to my lord and gentle cousin, Mowbray.
 Mowb. You wish me health in very happy season;
For I am, on the sudden, something ill.
 Arch. Against ill chances men are ever merry,
But heaviness foreruns the good event. *85*
 West. Therefore be merry, coz; since sudden sorrow
Serves to say thus, Some good thing comes to-morrow.
 Arch. Believe me, I am passing light in spirit.
 Mowb. So much the worse if your own rule be true.
         Shout [*within*].
 Lanc. The word of peace is render'd: hark, how they shout!
 Mowb. This had been cheerful, after victory.
 Arch. A peace is of the nature of a conquest;
For then both parties nobly are subdu'd,
And neither party loser.
 Lanc.   Go, my lord, *95*
And let our army be discharged too. *Exit* [*Westmoreland*].
And, good my lord, so please you, let our trains
March by us, that we may peruse the men
We should have cop'd withal.
 Arch. Go, good Lord Hastings, *100*
And, ere they be dismiss'd, let them march by.
         Exit [*Hastings*].
 Lanc. I trust, lords, we shall lie to-night together.

     Enter Westmoreland.

Now, cousin, wherefore stands our army still?
 West. The leaders, having charge from you to stand,
Will not go off until they hear you speak. *105*
 Lanc. They know their duties.

     Enter Hastings.

 Hast. My lord, our army is dispers'd already:
Like youthful steers unyok'd, they take their courses
East, west, north, south; or, like a school broke up,
Each hurries toward his home and sporting-place. *110*
 West. Good tidings, my Lord Hastings; for the which
I do arrest thee, traitor, of high treason:
And you, lord archbishop, and you, Lord Mowbray,
Of capital treason I attach you both.
 Mowb. Is this proceeding just and honourable? *115*
 West. Is your assembly so?
 Arch. Will you thus break your faith?
 Lanc.   I pawn'd thee none.
I promis'd you redress of these same grievances
Whereof you did complain; which, by mine honour, *120*
I will perform with a most Christian care.
But for you, rebels, look to taste the due
Meet for rebellion and such acts as yours.
Most shallowly did you these arms commence,
Fondly brought here and foolishly sent hence. *125*
Strike up our drums! pursue the scatter'd stray:
God, and not we, hath safely fought to-day.

---

20 intelligencer: *interpreter* **22 workings:** *actions* **26 taken up:** *levied* **49 success:** *succession* **72 part:** *depart*

84 Against: *when about to face* **85 heaviness:** *depression* **88 passing:** *exceedingly* **90 render'd:** *reported* **97 peruse:** *inspect* **118 pawn'd:** *pledged* **124 shallowly:** *thoughtlessly* **125 Fondly:** *foolishly*

Some guard these traitors to the block of death;
Treason's true bed, and yielder up of breath.   *Exeunt.*

❧ SCENE THIRD ❧

[Another Part of the Forest]
Alarums. Excursions. Enter Falstaff and Colevile.

Fal. What's your name, sir? of what condition are you, and
of what place, I pray?

Cole. I am a knight, sir; and my name is Colevile of the
dale.

Fal. Well then, Colevile is your name, a knight is your   5
degree, and your place the dale: Colevile shall be still your
name, a traitor your degree, and the dungeon your place, a
place deep enough; so shall you be still Colevile of the dale.

Cole. Are not you Sir John Falstaff?

Fal. As good a man as he, sir, whoe'er I am. Do ye yield,   10
sir, or shall I sweat for you? If I do sweat, they are the drops
of thy lovers, and they weep for thy death: therefore rouse up
fear and trembling, and do observance to my mercy.

Cole. I think you are Sir John Falstaff, and in that thought
yield me.   15

Fal. I have a whole school of tongues in this belly of mine,
and not a tongue of them all speaks any other word but my
name. An I had but a belly of any indifferency, I were simply
the most active fellow in Europe: my womb, my womb, my
womb undoes me. Here comes our general.   20

Enter Prince John, Westmoreland and the rest.

Lanc. The heat is past, follow no further now. Call in the
powers, good cousin Westmoreland.   *[Exit Westmoreland.]*
Now, Falstaff, where have you been all this while?
When everything is ended, then you come:
These tardy tricks of yours will, on my life,   25
One time or other break some gallows' back.

Fal. I would be sorry, my lord, but it should be thus: I
never knew yet but rebuke and check was the reward of valour. Do you think me a swallow, an arrow, or a bullet? have
I, in my poor and old motion, the expedition of thought? I   30
have speeded hither with the very extremest inch of possibility;
I have foundered nine score and odd posts; and here, travel-
tainted as I am, have, in my pure and immaculate valour,
taken Sir John Colevile of the dale, a most furious knight and
valorous enemy. But what of that? he saw me, and yielded;   35
that I may justly say with the hook-nosed fellow of Rome,
'I came, saw, and overcame.'

Lanc. It was more of his courtesy than your deserving.

Fal. I know not: here he is, and here I yield him; and I beseech your Grace, let it be booked with the rest of this day's   40
deeds; or, by the Lord, I will have it in a particular ballad else,
with mine own picture on the top on 't, Colevile kissing my
foot. To the which course if I be enforced, if you do not all
show like gilt two-pences to me, and I in the clear sky of fame
o'ershine you as much as the full moon doth the cinders of   45
the element, which show like pins' heads to her, believe not

the word of the noble. Therefore let me have right, and let desert mount.

Lanc. Thine's too heavy to mount.

Fal. Let it shine then.   50

Lanc. Thine's too thick to shine.

Fal. Let it do something, my good lord, that may do me
good, and call it what you will.

Lanc. Is thy name Colevile?

Cole. It is, my lord.   55

Lanc. A famous rebel art thou, Colevile.

Fal. And a famous true subject took him.

Cole. I am, my lord, but as my betters are
That led me hither: had they been rul'd by me
You should have won them dearer than you have.   60

Fal. I know not how they sold themselves: but thou, like a
kind fellow, gavest thyself away gratis, and I thank thee for
thee.

Enter Westmoreland.

Lanc. Now, have you left pursuit?

West. Retreat is made and execution stay'd.   65

Lanc. Send Colevile with his confederates
To York, to present execution.
Blunt, lead him hence, and see you guard him sure.
          Exit [Blunt] with Colevile.
And now dispatch we toward the court, my lords:
I hear, the king my father is sore sick: 70
Our news shall go before us to his majesty,
Which, cousin *[addressing Westmoreland]*, you shall bear, to
comfort him;
And we with sober speed will follow you.

Fal. My lord, I beseech you, give me leave to go,   75
Through Gloucestershire, and when you come to court
Stand my good lord, pray, in your good report.

Lanc. Fare you well, Falstaff: I, in my condition,
Shall better speak of you than you deserve.
          [Exeunt all but Falstaff.]

Fal. I would you had but the wit: 'twere better than your   80
dukedom. Good faith, this same young sober-blooded boy doth
not love me; nor a man cannot make him laugh; but that's no
marvel, he drinks no wine. There's never none of these demure
boys come to any proof; for thin drink doth so over-cool their
blood, and making many fish-meals, that they fall into a   85
kind of male green-sickness; and then, when they marry, they
get wenches. They are generally fools and cowards, which some
of us should be too but for inflammation. A good sherris-sack
hath a two-fold operation in it. It ascends me into the brain;
dries me there all the foolish and dull and crudy vapours   90
which environ it; makes it apprehensive, quick, forgetive, full
of nimble, fiery and delectable shapes; which, deliver'd o'er to
the voice, the tongue, which is the birth, becomes excellent wit.
The second property of your excellent sherris is, the warming
of the blood; which, before cold and settled, left the liver   95
white and pale, which is the badge of pusillanimity and cowardice: but the sherris warms it and makes it course from the inwards to the parts extreme. It illumineth the face, which, as a
beacon, gives warning to all the rest of this little kingdom,

---

1 condition: *rank*   **13 observance:** *homage*   **18 indifferency:** *moderate size*   **21 heat:**
race, pursuit   **28 check:** *reproof*   **30 expedition:** *speed*   **32 posts:** *post-horses*   **45**
cinders: *glowing coals, stars*   **46 element:** *sky*

67 present: *immediate*   **69 dispatch we:** *let us hasten*   **77 Stand my good lord:** *be*
my kind patron   **78 condition:** *official capacity*   **84 come to any proof:** *turn out*
well   **87 get wenches:** *beget girls*   **78 sherris-sack:** *sherry*   **90 crudy:** *crude,*
raw   **91 forgetive:** *inventive*

man, to arm; and then the vital commoners and inland   *100*
petty spirits muster me all to their captain, the heart, who,
great and puffed up with this retinue, doth any deed of
courage; and this valour comes of sherris. So that skill in
the weapon is nothing without sack, for that sets it a-work;
and learning, a mere hoard of gold kept by a devil till   *105*
sack commences it and sets it in act and use. Hereof comes it
that Prince Harry is valiant; for the cold blood he did naturally
inherit of his father, he hath, like lean, sterile, and bare land,
manured, husbanded, and tilled, with excellent endeavour of
drinking good and good store of fertile sherris, that he is   *110*
become very hot and valiant. If I had a thousand sons, the first
human principle I would teach them should be, to forswear
thin potations and to addict themselves to sack.

Enter Bardolph.

How now, Bardolph?

    Bard. The army is discharged all and gone.   *115*

    Fal. Let them go. I'll through Gloucestershire; and there will
I visit Master Robert Shallow, esquire: I have him already tempering between my finger and my thumb, and shortly will I
seal with him. Come away.   *Exeunt.*

❧ SCENE FOURTH ❦

[Westminster. The Jerusalem Chamber]
Enter the King, Warwick, Thomas Duke of Clarence, Humphrey of
Gloucester [and others].

    King. Now, lords, if God doth give successful end
To this debate that bleedeth at our doors,
We will our youth lead on to higher fields
And draw no swords, but what are sanctified.
Our navy is address'd, our power collected,   *5*
Our substitutes in absence well invested,
And everything lies level to our wish:
Only, we want a little personal strength;
And pause us, till these rebels, now afoot,
Come underneath the yoke of government.   *10*

    War. Both which we doubt not but your majesty
Shall soon enjoy.

    King.   Humphrey, my son of Gloucester,
Where is the prince your brother?

    Glo. I think he's gone to hunt, my lord, at Windsor.   *15*

    King. And how accompanied?

    Glo.   I do not know, my lord.

    King. Is not his brother Thomas of Clarence with him?

    Glo. No, my good lord; he is in presence here.

    Cla. What would my lord and father?   *20*

    King. Nothing but well to thee, Thomas of Clarence.
How chance thou art not with the prince thy brother?
He loves thee, and thou dost neglect him, Thomas;
Thou hast a better place in his affection
Than all thy brothers: cherish it, my boy,   *25*
And noble offices thou mayst effect
Of mediation, after I am dead,
Between his greatness and thy other brethren:

Therefore omit him not; blunt not his love,
Nor lose the good advantage of his grace   *30*
By seeming cold or careless of his will;
For he is gracious, if he be observ'd:
He hath a tear for pity and a hand
Open as day for melting charity;
Yet, notwithstanding, being incens'd, he's flint;   *35*
As humorous as winter, and as sudden
As flaws congealed in the spring of day.
His temper therefore must be well observ'd:
Chide him for faults, and do it reverently,
When you perceive his blood inclin'd to mirth;   *40*
But, being moody, give him line and scope,
Till that his passions, like a whale on ground,
Confound themselves with working. Learn this, Thomas,
And thou shalt prove a shelter to thy friends,
A hoop of gold to bind thy brothers in,   *45*
That the united vessel of their blood,
Mingled with venom of suggestion—
As, force perforce, the age will pour it in—
Shall never leak, though it do work as strong
As aconitum or rash gunpowder.   *50*

    Cla. I shall observe him with all care and love.

    King. Why art thou not at Windsor with him, Thomas?

    Cla. He is not there to-day; he dines in London.

    King. And how accompanied? canst thou tell that?

    Cla. With Poins and other his continual followers.   *55*

    King. Most subject is the fattest soil to weeds;
And he, the noble image of my youth,
Is overspread with them: therefore my grief
Stretches itself beyond the hour of death:
The blood weeps from my heart when I do shape   *60*
In forms imaginary the unguided days
And rotten times that you shall look upon
When I am sleeping with my ancestors.
For when his headstrong riot hath no curb,
When rage and hot blood are his counsellors,   *65*
When means and lavish manners meet together,
O! with what wings shall his affections fly
Towards fronting peril and oppos'd decay.

    War. My gracious lord, you look beyond him quite:
The prince but studies his companions   *70*
Like a strange tongue, wherein, to gain the language,
'Tis needful that the most immodest word
Be look'd upon, and learn'd; which once attain'd,
Your highness knows, comes to no further use
But to be known and hated. So, like gross terms,   *75*
The prince will in the perfectness of time
Cast off his followers; and their memory
Shall as a pattern or a measure live,
By which his Grace must mete the lives of others,
Turning past evils to advantages.   *80*

    King. 'Tis seldom when the bee doth leave her comb
In the dead carrion.

Enter Westmoreland.

                                Who's here? Westmoreland!

    West. Health to my sovereign, and new happiness

104, 105 *Cf. n.*   **117–119** tempering . . . seal: *the allusion is to sealing-wax*   **S.d. Jerusa-**
lem Chamber; *cf. n.*   **5** address'd: *prepared*   **6** invested: *invested with authority*

29 omit: *neglect*   **32** observ'd: *humored*   **35–37** *Cf. n.*   **43** Confound: *ex-*
haust   **46–50** *Cf. n.*   **67** affections: *inclinations*   **69** look beyond: *misjudge*   **79**
mete: *measure*   **81–83** *Cf. n.*

Added to that that I am to deliver!   85
Prince John your son doth kiss your Grace's hand:
Mowbray, the Bishop Scroop, Hastings and all
Are brought to the correction of your law.
There is not now a rebel's sword unsheath'd,
But Peace puts forth her olive everywhere.   90
The manner how this action hath been borne
Here at more leisure may your highness read,
With every course in his particular.
 King. O Westmoreland! thou art a summer bird,
Which ever in the haunch of winter sings   95
The lifting up of day.

      Enter Harcourt.

     Look! here's more news.
 Har. From enemies heaven keep your majesty;
And, when they stand against you, may they fall
As those that I am come to tell you of!   100
The Earl Northumberland, and the Lord Bardolph,
With a great power of English and of Scots,
Are by the sheriff of Yorkshire overthrown.
The manner and true order of the fight
This packet, please it you, contains at large.   105
 King. And wherefore should these good news make me sick?
Will Fortune never come with both hands full
But write her fair words still in foulest letters?
She either gives a stomach and no food:
Such are the poor, in health; or else a feast   110
And takes away the stomach; such are the rich,
That have abundance and enjoy it not.
I should rejoice now at this happy news,
And now my sight fails, and my brain is giddy.
O me! come near me, now I am much ill.   115
 Glo. Comfort, your majesty!
 Cla.   O my royal father!
 West. My sovereign lord, cheer up yourself: look up!
 War. Be patient, princes: you do know these fits
Are with his highness very ordinary: 120
Stand from him, give him air; he'll straight be well.
 Cla. No, no; he cannot long hold out these pangs:
The incessant care and labour of his mind
Hath wrought the mure that should confine it in
So thin, that life looks through and will break out.   125
 Glo. The people fear me; for they do observe
Unfather'd heirs and loathly births of nature:
The seasons change their manners, as the year
Had found some months asleep and leap'd them over.
 Cla. The river hath thrice flow'd, no ebb between;   130
And the old folk, time's doting chronicles,
Say it did so a little time before
That our great-grandsire, Edward, sick'd and died.
 War. Speak lower, princes, for the king recovers.
 Glo. This apoplexy will certain be his end.   135
 King. I pray you take me up, and bear me hence
Into some other chamber: softly, pray.
  [Attendants and Lords take the King up, convey him into an
      inner room, and lay him upon a bed.]

     🙟 Scene Fifth 🙝

     [Another Chamber
King Henry lying on a bed: Clarence, Gloucester, Warwick, and
     Others in attendance.]

 King. Let there be no noise made, my gentle friends;
Unless some dull and favourable hand
Will whisper music to my weary spirit.
 War. Call for the music in the other room.
 King. Set me the crown upon my pillow here.   5
 Cla. His eye is hollow, and he changes much.
 War. Less noise, less noise!

     Enter Prince Henry.

 Prince.   Who saw the Duke of Clarence?
 Cla. I am here, brother, full of heaviness.
 Prince. How now! rain within doors, and none abroad!   10
How doth the king?
 Glo.   Exceeding ill.
 Prince.   Heard he the good news yet?
Tell it him.
 Glo. He alter'd much upon the hearing it.   15
 Prince. If he be sick with joy, he'll recover without physic.
 War. Not so much noise, my lords. Sweet prince, speak low;
The king your father is dispos'd to sleep.
 Cla. Let us withdraw into the other room.
 War. Will 't please your Grace to go along with us?   20
 Prince. No; I will sit and watch here by the king.
      [Exeunt all but the Prince.]
Why doth the crown lie there upon his pillow,
Being so troublesome a bedfellow?
O polish'd perturbation! golden care!
That keep'st the ports of slumber open wide   25
To many a watchful night! Sleep with it now!
Yet not so sound, and half so deeply sweet
As he whose brow with homely biggin bound
Snores out the watch of night. O majesty!
When thou dost pinch thy bearer, thou dost sit   30
Like a rich armour worn in heat of day,
That scalds with safety. By his gates of breath
There lies a downy feather which stirs not:
Did he suspire, that light and weightless down
Perforce must move. My gracious lord! my father!   35
This sleep is sound indeed; this is a sleep
That from this golden rigol hath divorc'd
So many English kings. Thy due from me
Is tears and heavy sorrows of the blood,
Which nature, love, and filial tenderness   40
Shall, O dear father! pay thee plenteously:
My due from thee is this imperial crown,
Which, as immediate from thy place and blood,
Derives itself to me. Lo! here it sits,   *[Putting it on his head.]*
Which God shall guard; and put the world's whole strength 45
Into one giant arm, it shall not force
This lineal honour from me. This from thee
Will I to mine leave, as 'tis left to me.   *Exit.*
 King. [Waking.] Warwick! Gloucester! Clarence!

  Enter Warwick, Gloucester, Clarence [and the rest].

---

93 particular: *detail* **95 haunch:** *end* **109 stomach:** *appetite* **124 wrought the mure:** *worn the wall* **126 fear:** *frighten* **127** (Such portents as) *creatures born without parents and other monstrosities* **128 as:** *as if*

9 full: *soothing, drowsy* **25 ports:** *gates* **28 biggin:** *nightcap* **32 with safety:** *while it gives safety* **34 suspire:** *breathe* **37 rigol:** *circle, crown* **43 immediate:** *next in line*

Cla.   Doth the king call?   50
War. What would your majesty? How fares your Grace?
King. Why did you leave me here alone, my lords?
Cla. We left the prince my brother here, my liege,
Who undertook to sit and watch by you.
 King. The Prince of Wales! Where is he? let me see him: 55
He is not here.
 War. This door is open; he is gone this way.
 Glo. He came not through the chamber where we stay'd.
 King. Where is the crown? who took it from my pillow?
 War. When we withdrew, my liege, we left it here.   60
 King. The prince hath ta'en it hence: go, seek him out.
Is he so hasty that he doth suppose
My sleep my death?
Find him, my Lord of Warwick; chide him hither.
        [Exit Warwick.]
This part of his conjoins with my disease,   65
And helps to end me. See, sons, what things you are!
How quickly nature falls into revolt
When gold becomes her object!
For this the foolish over-careful fathers
Have broke their sleep with thoughts,   70
Their brains with care, their bones with industry;
For this they have engrossed and pil'd up
The canker'd heaps of strange-achieved gold;
For this they have been thoughtful to invest
Their sons with arts and martial exercises: 75
When, like the bee, culling from every flower
The virtuous sweets,
Our thighs packed with wax, our mouths with honey,
We bring it to the hive, and like the bees,
Are murder'd for our pains. This bitter taste   80
Yield his engrossments to the ending father.

     Enter Warwick.

Now, where is he that will not stay so long
Till his friend sickness hath determin'd me?
 War. My lord, I found the prince in the next room,
Washing with kindly tears his gentle cheeks,   85
With such a deep demeanour in great sorrow
That tyranny, which never quaff'd but blood,
Would, by beholding him, have wash'd his knife
With gentle eye-drops. He is coming hither.
 King. But wherefore did he take away the crown?   90

     Enter Prince Henry.

Lo, where he comes. Come hither to me, Harry.
Depart the chamber, leave us here alone.
     Exeunt [Warwick, and the rest].
 Prince. I never thought to hear you speak again.
 King. Thy wish was father, Harry, to that thought:
I stay too long by thee, I weary thee.   95
Dost thou so hunger for mine empty chair
That thou wilt needs invest thee with my honours
Before thy hour be ripe? O foolish youth!
Thou seek'st the greatness that will overwhelm thee.
Stay but a little; for my cloud of dignity   100
Is held from falling with so weak a wind

That it will quickly drop: my day is dim.
Thou hast stol'n that which after some few hours
Were thine without offence; and at my death
Thou hast seal'd up my expectation: 105
Thy life did manifest thou lov'dst me not,
And thou wilt have me die assur'd of it.
Thou hid'st a thousand daggers in thy thoughts,
Which thou hast whetted on thy stony heart,
To stab at half an hour of my life.   110
What! canst thou not forbear me half an hour?
Then get thee gone and dig my grave thyself,
And bid the merry bells ring to thine ear
That thou art crowned, not that I am dead.
Let all the tears that should bedew my hearse   115
Be drops of balm to sanctify thy head:
Only compound me with forgotten dust;
Give that which gave thee life unto the worms.
Pluck down my officers, break my decrees;
For now a time is come to mock at form.   120
Harry the Fifth is crown'd! Up, vanity!
Down, royal state! all you sage counsellors, hence!
And to the English court assemble now,
From every region, apes of idleness!
Now, neighbour confines, purge you of your scum: 125
Have you a ruffian that will swear, drink, dance,
Revel the night, rob, murder, and commit
The oldest sins the newest kind of ways?
Be happy, he will trouble you no more:
England shall double gild his treble guilt.   130
England shall give him office, honour, might;
For the fifth Harry from curb'd licence plucks
The muzzle of restraint, and the wild dog
Shall flesh his tooth in every innocent.
O my poor kingdom! sick with civil blows,   135
When that my care could not withhold thy riots,
What wilt thou do when riot is thy care?
O! thou wilt be a wilderness again,
Peopled with wolves, thy old inhabitants.
 Prince. O! pardon me, my liege; but for my tears,   140
The moist impediments unto my speech,
I had forestall'd this dear and deep rebuke
Ere you with grief had spoke and I had heard
The course of it so far. There is your crown;
And he that wears the crown immortally   145
Long guard it yours! If I affect it more
Than as your honour and as your renown,
Let me no more from this obedience rise,—
Which my most inward, true, and duteous spirit
Teacheth,—this prostrate and exterior bending.   150
God witness with me, when I here came in,
And found no course of breath within your majesty,
How cold it struck my heart! if I do feign,
O! let me in my present wildness die
And never live to show the incredulous world   155
The noble change that I have purposed.
Coming to look on you, thinking you dead,
And dead almost, my liege, to think you were,
I spake unto the crown as having sense,
And thus upbraided it: 'The care on thee depending   160

65 part: *act*   **72 engrossed:** *amassed*   **73 canker'd:** *tarnished*   **strange-achieved:** *gained in foreign lands*   **77 virtuous:** *beneficial*   **83 determin'd:** *ended*   **85 kindly:** *natural*   **105 seal'd up:** *confirmed fully*   **120 form:** *order*   **121 vanity:** *folly*   **137 care:** *special study*   **142 dear:** *earnest*   **146 affect:** *aspire to*

Hath fed upon the body of my father;
Therefore, thou best of gold art worst of gold:
Other, less fine in carat, is more precious,
Preserving life in medicine potable:
But thou most fine, most honour'd, most renown'd,   165
Hast eat thy bearer up.' Thus, my most royal liege,
Accusing it, I put it on my head,
To try with it, as with an enemy
That had before my face murder'd my father,
The quarrel of a true inheritor.   170
But if it did infect my blood with joy,
Or swell my thoughts to any strain of pride;
If any rebel or vain spirit of mine
Did with the least affection of a welcome
Give entertainment to the might of it,   175
Let God for ever keep it from my head,
And make me as the poorest vassal is
That doth with awe and terror kneel to it!
    King. O my son!
God put it in thy mind to take it hence,   180
That thou mightst win the more thy father's love,
Pleading so wisely in excuse of it.
Come hither, Harry: sit thou by my bed;
And hear, I think, the very latest counsel
That ever I shall breathe. God knows, my son,   185
By what by-paths and indirect crook'd ways
I met this crown; and I myself know well
How troublesome it sat upon my head:
To thee it shall descend with better quiet,
Better opinion, better confirmation;   190
For all the soil of the achievement goes
With me into the earth. It seem'd in me
But as an honour snatch'd with boisterous hand,
And I had many living to upbraid
My gain of it by their assistances;   195
Which daily grew to quarrel and to bloodshed,
Wounding supposed peace. All these bold fears
Thou seest with peril I have answered;
For all my reign hath been but as a scene
Acting that argument; and now my death   200
Changes the mode: for what in me was purchas'd,
Falls upon thee in a more fairer sort;
So thou the garment wear'st successively.
Yet, though thou stand'st more sure than I could do,
Thou art not firm enough, since griefs are green;   205
And all my friends, which thou must make thy friends,
Have but their stings and teeth newly ta'en out;
By whose fell working I was first advanc'd,
And by whose power I well might lodge a fear
To be again displac'd: which to avoid,   210
I cut them off; and had a purpose now
To lead out many to the Holy Land,
Lest rest and lying still might make them look
Too near unto my state. Therefore, my Harry,
Be it thy course to busy giddy minds   215
With foreign quarrels; that action, hence borne out,
May waste the memory of the former days.
More would I, but my lungs are wasted so

That strength of speech is utterly denied me.
How I came by the crown, O God, forgive!   220
And grant it may with thee in true peace live.
    Prince. My gracious liege,
You won it, wore it, kept it, gave it me;
Then plain and right must my possession be:
Which I with more than with a common pain   225
'Gainst all the world will rightfully maintain.

            Enter Lord John of Lancaster, and Warwick.

    King. Look, look, here comes my John of Lancaster.
    Lanc. Health, peace, and happiness to my royal father!
    King. Thou bring'st me happiness and peace, son John;
But health, alack, with youthful wings is flown   230
From this bare wither'd trunk: upon thy sight
My worldly business makes a period.
Where is my Lord of Warwick?
    Prince.   My Lord of Warwick!

            [Warwick comes forward.]

    King. Doth any name particular belong   235
Unto the lodging where I first did swound?
    War. 'Tis call'd Jerusalem, my noble lord.
    King. Laud be to God! even there my life must end.
It hath been prophesied to me many years
I should not die but in Jerusalem,   240
Which vainly I suppos'd the Holy Land.
But bear me to that chamber; there I'll lie:
In that Jerusalem shall Harry die.   *Exeunt.*

ACT FIFTH ❧ SCENE FIRST

[Justice Shallow's House in Gloucestershire]
Enter Shallow, Falstaff, Bardolph [and Bardolph's boy].

    Shal. By cock and pie, sir, you shall not away to-night.
What! Davy, I say.
    Fal. You must excuse me, Master Robert Shallow.
    Shal. I will not excuse you; you shall not be excused; excuses shall not be admitted; there is no excuse shall serve;   5
you shall not be excused. Why, Davy!

            Enter Davy.

    Davy. Here, sir.
    Shal. Davy, Davy, Davy, Davy, let me see, Davy; let me see:
yea, marry, William cook, bid him come hither. Sir John, you
shall not be excused.   10
    Davy. Marry, sir, thus; those precepts cannot be served:
and again, sir, shall we sow the headland with wheat?
    Shal. With red wheat, Davy. But for William cook: are
there no young pigeons?
    Davy. Yes, sir. Here is now the smith's note for shoeing   15
and plough-irons.
    Shal. Let it be cast and paid. Sir John, you shall not be
excused.
    Davy. Now, sir, a new link to the bucket must needs be

---

164 medicine potable; *cf. n.*   **191 soil:** *pollution*   **200 argument:** *story*   **201 mode;**
cf. n. **purchas'd:** *acquired by my own act, not inherited*   **203 successively:** *by right of*
succession   **216 hence:** *in other lands*   **217 waste:** *consume*

1 cock and pie; *cf. n.*   **11 precepts:** *summonses*   **17 cast:** *reckoned*

had: and, sir, do you mean to stop any of William's wages,   20
about the sack he lost the other day at Hinckley fair?

Shal. A' shall answer it. Some pigeons, Davy, a couple of
short-legged hens, a joint of mutton, and any petty little tiny
kickshaws, tell William cook.

Davy. Doth the man of war stay all night, sir?   25

Shal. Yea, Davy. I will use him well. A friend i' the court is
better than a penny in purse. Use his men well, Davy, for they
are arrant knaves, and will backbite.

Davy. No worse than they are back-bitten, sir; for they have
marvellous foul linen.   30

Shal. Well conceited, Davy: about thy business, Davy.

Davy. I beseech you, sir, to countenance William Visor of
Wincot against Clement Perkes o' the hill.

Shal. There is many complaints, Davy, against that Visor:
that Visor is an arrant knave, on my knowledge.   35

Davy. I grant your worship that he is a knave, sir; but yet,
God forbid, sir, but a knave should have some countenance at
his friend's request. An honest man, sir, is able to speak for
himself, when a knave is not. I have served your worship truly,
sir, this eight years; and if I cannot once or twice in a quarter
bear out a knave against an honest man, I have but a very little credit with your worship. The knave is mine honest friend,
sir; therefore, I beseech your worship, let him be countenanced.

Shal. Go to; I say he shall have no wrong. Look about, Davy.
[Exit Davy.] Where are you, Sir John? Come, come, come; off   45
with your boots. Give me your hand, Master Bardolph.

Bard. I am glad to see your worship.

Shal. I thank thee with all my heart, kind Master Bardolph:— *[To the Page.]* and welcome, my tall fellow. Come,
Sir John.   50

Fal. I'll follow you, good Master Robert Shallow. *[Exit Shallow.]* Bardolph, look to our horses. *[Exeunt Bardolph and Page.]*
If I were sawed into quantities, I should make four dozen of
such bearded hermit's staves as Master Shallow. It is a wonderful thing to see the semblable coherence of his men's spirits   55
and his: they, by observing him, do bear themselves like foolish
justices; he, by conversing with them, is turned into a justice-
like serving-man. Their spirits are so married in conjunction
with the participation of society that they flock together in consent, like so many wild-geese. If I had a suit to Master Shal-   60
low, I would humour his men with the imputation of being
near their master: if to his men, I would curry with Master
Shallow that no man could better command his servants. It is
certain that either wise bearing or ignorant carriage is caught,
as men take diseases, one of another: therefore let men take   65
heed of their company. I will devise matter enough out of this
Shallow to keep Prince Harry in continual laughter the wearing
out of six fashions,—which is four terms, or two actions,—and
a' shall laugh without intervallums. O! it is much that a lie
with a slight oath and a jest with a sad brow will do with a   70
fellow that never had the ache in his shoulders. O! you shall
see him laugh till his face be like a wet cloak ill laid up!

Shal. [Within.] Sir John!

Fal. I come, Master Shallow: I come, Master Shallow.

                                           [Exit.]

24 **kickshaws:** *fancy dishes*   31 **Well conceited:** *cleverly put*   32 **countenance:**
favor   53 **quantities:** *small pieces*   55 **semblable coherence:** *approach to likeness*   60
consent: *agreement*   68 **terms:** *i.e., of court*   **actions:** *legal actions for debt*   69 **inter-**
vallums: *intervals*   70 **sad:** *sober*   72 **ill laid up:** *carelessly put away*

❧ SCENE SECOND ❧

[Westminster. The Palace]
Enter the Earl of Warwick and the Lord Chief Justice.

War. How now, my Lord Chief Justice! whither away?
Ch. Just. How doth the king?
War. Exceeding well: his cares are now all ended.
Ch. Just. I hope not dead.
War.   He's walk'd the way of nature;   5
And to our purposes he lives no more.
Ch. Just. I would his majesty had call'd me with him:
The service that I truly did his life
Hath left me open to all injuries.
War. Indeed I think the young king loves you not.   10
Ch. Just. I know he doth not, and do arm myself
To welcome the condition of the time,
Which cannot look more hideously upon me
Than I have drawn it in my fantasy.

*Enter John of Lancaster, Gloucester, Clarence [Westmoreland,
and others].*

War. Here come the heavy issue of dead Harry: 15
O! that the living Harry had the temper
Of him, the worst of these three gentlemen.
How many nobles then should hold their places,
That must strike sail to spirits of vile sort!
Ch. Just. O God! I fear all will be overturn'd.   20
Lanc. Good morrow, cousin Warwick, good morrow.
Glo. ⎱
Cla. ⎰ Good morrow, cousin.
Lanc. We meet like men that had forgot to speak.
War. We do remember; but our argument   25
Is all too heavy to admit much talk.
Lanc. Well, peace be with him that hath made us heavy!
Ch. Just. Peace be with us, lest we be heavier!
Glo. O! good my lord, you have lost a friend indeed;
And I dare swear you borrow not that face   30
Of seeming sorrow; it is sure your own.
Lanc. Though no man be assur'd what grace to find,
You stand in coldest expectation.
I am the sorrier; would 'twere otherwise.
Cla. Well, you must now speak Sir John Falstaff fair,   35
Which swims against your stream of quality.
Ch. Just. Sweet princes, what I did, I did in honour,
Led by the impartial conduct of my soul;
And never shall you see that I will beg
A ragged and forestall'd remission.   40
If truth and upright innocency fail me,
I'll to the king my master that is dead,
And tell him who hath sent me after him.
War. Here comes the prince.

Enter the Prince and Blunt.

Ch. Just. Good morrow, and God save your majesty!   45
Prince. This new and gorgeous garment, majesty,
Sits not so easy on me as you think.
Brothers, you mix your sadness with some fear:
This is the English, not the Turkish court;

15 **heavy:** *sorrowful*   25 **argument:** *subject of conversation*   33 **coldest:** *most hope-*
less   36 *Cf. n.*   40 **ragged:** *beggarly*   **forestalled remission:** *pardon that is sure not to*
be granted

Not Amurath an Amurath succeeds,   50
But Harry Harry. Yet be sad, good brothers,
For, by my faith, it very well becomes you:
Sorrow so royally in you appears
That I will deeply put the fashion on
And wear it in my heart. Why then, be sad;   55
But entertain no more of it, good brothers,
Than a joint burden laid upon us all.
For me, by heaven, I bid you be assur'd,
I'll be your father and your brother too;
Let me but bear your love, I'll bear your cares: 60
Yet weep that Harry's dead, and so will I;
But Harry lives that shall convert those tears
By number into hours of happiness.
    Brothers. We hope no other from your majesty.
    Prince. You all look strangely on me: [*To the Chief Justice.*]   65
and you most;
You are, I think, assur'd I love you not.
    Ch. Just. I am assur'd, if I be measur'd rightly,
Your majesty hath no just cause to hate me.
    Prince. No?   70
How might a prince of my great hopes forget
So great indignities you laid upon me?
What! rate, rebuke, and roughly send to prison
The immediate heir of England! Was this easy?
May this be wash'd in Lethe, and forgotten?   75
    Ch. Just. I then did use the person of your father;
The image of his power lay then in me:
And, in the administration of his law,
Whiles I was busy for the commonwealth,
Your highness pleased to forget my place,   80
The majesty and power of law and justice,
The image of the king whom I presented,
And struck me in my very seat of judgment;
Whereon, as an offender to your father,
I gave bold way to my authority,   85
And did commit you. If the deed were ill,
Be you contented, wearing now the garland,
To have a son set your decrees at nought,
To pluck down justice from your awful bench,
To trip the course of law, and blunt the sword   90
That guards the peace and safety of your person;
Nay, more, to spurn at your most royal image
And mock your workings in a second body.
Question your royal thoughts, make the case yours;
Be now the father and propose a son,   95
Hear your own dignity so much profan'd,
See your most dreadful laws so loosely slighted,
Behold yourself so by a son disdain'd;
And then imagine me taking your part,
And in your power soft silencing your son: 100
After this cold considerance, sentence me;
And, as you are a king, speak in your state
What I have done that misbecame my place,
My person, or my liege's sovereignty.
    Prince. You are right, justice; and you weigh this well;   105
Therefore still bear the balance and the sword:

And I do wish your honours may increase
Till you do live to see a son of mine
Offend you and obey you, as I did.
So shall I live to speak my father's words: 110
'Happy am I, that have a man so bold
That dares do justice on my proper son;
And not less happy, having such a son,
That would deliver up his greatness so
Into the hands of justice.' You did commit me: 115
For which, I do commit into your hand
The unstained sword that you have us'd to bear;
With this remembrance, that you use the same
With the like bold, just, and impartial spirit
As you have done 'gainst me. There is my hand: 120
You shall be as a father to my youth;
My voice shall sound as you do prompt mine ear,
And I will stoop and humble my intents
To your well-practis'd wise directions.
And, princes all, believe me, I beseech you;   125
My father is gone wild into his grave,
For in his tomb lie my affections;
And with his spirit sadly I survive,
To mock the expectation of the world,
To frustrate prophecies, and to raze out   130
Rotten opinion, who hath writ me down
After my seeming. The tide of blood in me
Hath proudly flow'd in vanity till now:
Now doth it turn and ebb back to the sea,
Where it shall mingle with the state of floods   135
And flow henceforth in formal majesty.
Now call we our high court of parliament;
And let us choose such limbs of noble counsel,
That the great body of our state may go
In equal rank with the best govern'd nation;   140
That war or peace, or both at once, may be
As things acquainted and familiar to us;
In which you, father, shall have foremost hand.
Our coronation done, we will accite,
As I before remember'd, all our state: 145
And, God consigning to my good intents,
No prince nor peer shall have just cause to say,
God shorten Harry's happy life one day.   *Exeunt.*

❧ SCENE THIRD ❧

[The Garden of Justice Shallow's House in Gloucestershire]
Enter Sir John, Shallow, Silence, Davy, Bardolph, Page.

    Shal. Nay, you shall see my orchard, where, in an arbour,
we will eat a last year's pippin of mine own graffing, with a
dish of caraways, and so forth; come, cousin Silence; and then
to bed.
    Fal. 'Fore God, you have here a goodly dwelling, and a   5
rich.
    Shal. Barren, barren, barren; beggars all, beggars all, Sir
John: marry, good air. Spread, Davy; spread: well said, Davy.

50 *Cf. n.*   **74 easy:** *trivial*   **75 Lethe:** *the river of oblivion*   **76 use the person:** *make use of my position as personal representative*   **82 presented:** *represented*   **87 garland: crown*   **93 second body:** *deputy*   **95 propose:** *imagine*   **101 considerance:** *consideration*   **106 balance and the sword:** *emblems of Justice*

112 proper: *own*   **118 remembrance:** *admonition*   **126, 127** *Cf. n.*   **128 sadly:** *soberly*   **132 After my seeming:** *according to appearances*   **135 state of floods:** *majesty of the ocean*   **140 In equal rank:** *step by step*   **144 accite:** *summon*   **145 remember'd: mentioned*   **146 consigning to:** *confirming*   **2 graffing:** *grafting*   **3 caraways:** *confection made with caraway seeds*   **8 said:** *done*

Fal. This Davy serves you for good uses; he is your serving-man and your husband.   *10*

Shal. A good varlet, a good varlet, a very good varlet, Sir John: by the mass, I have drunk too much sack at supper: a good varlet. Now sit down, now sit down. Come, cousin.

Sil. Ah, sirrah! quoth a', we shall

     'Do nothing but eat, and make good cheer,   *15*
     And praise God for the merry year;
     When flesh is cheap and females dear,
     And lusty lads roam here and there,
         So merrily.
     And ever among so merrily.'   *20*

Fal. There's a merry heart! Good Master Silence, I'll give you a health for that anon.

Shal. Give Master Bardolph some wine, Davy.

Davy. Sweet sir, sit; I'll be with you anon: most sweet sir, sit. Master page, good master page, sit. Proface! What you   *25* want in meat we'll have in drink: but you must bear: the heart's all.   *[Exit.]*

Shal. Be merry, Master Bardolph; and my little soldier there, be merry.

Sil. 'Be merry, be merry, my wife has all;   *30*
     For women are shrews, both short and tall:
     'Tis merry in hall when beards wag all,
         And welcome merry Shrove-tide.
     Be merry, be merry.'

Fal. I did not think Master Silence had been a man of   *35* this mettle.

Sil. Who, I? I have been merry twice and once ere now.

[Enter Davy.]

Davy. There's a dish of leather-coats for you.
             [Setting them before Bardolph.]

Shal. Davy!

Davy. Your worship! I'll be with you straight.   *40* A cup of wine, sir?

Sil. 'A cup of wine that's brisk and fine
And drink unto the leman mine;
And a merry heart lives long-a.'

Fal. Well said, Master Silence.   *45*

Sil. And we shall be merry, now comes in the sweet o' the night.

Fal. Health and long life to you, Master Silence.

Sil. 'Fill the cup, and let it come;
I'll pledge you a mile to the bottom.'   *50*

Shal. Honest Bardolph, welcome: if thou wantest anything and wilt not call, beshrew thy heart. *[To the Page.]* Welcome, my little tiny thief; and welcome indeed too. I'll drink to Master Bardolph and to all the cavaleros about London.

Davy. I hope to see London once ere I die.   *55*

Bard. An I might see you there, Davy,—

Shal. By the mass, you'll crack a quart together: ha! will you not, Master Bardolph?

Bard. Yea, sir, in a pottle-pot.

Shal. By God's liggens, I thank thee. The knave will stick   *60* by thee, I can assure thee that: a' will not out; he is true bred.

Bard. And I'll stick by him, sir.

Shal. Why, there spoke a king. Lack nothing: be merry.
            [One knocks at the door.]
Look who's at door there. Ho! who knocks?   *[Exit Davy.]*

Fal. [To Silence, who drinks a bumper.] Why, now you   *65* have done me right.

Sil.   'Do me right,
         And dub me knight:
            Samingo.'

Is 't not so?   *70*

Fal. 'Tis so.

Sil. Is 't so? Why, then, say an old man can do somewhat.

[Enter Davy.]

Davy. An 't please your worship, there's one Pistol come from the court with news.

Fal. From the court! let him come in.   *75*

Enter Pistol.

How now, Pistol!

Pist. Sir John, God save you, sir!

Fal. What wind blew you hither, Pistol?

Pist. Not the ill wind which blows no man to good. Sweet knight, thou art now one of the greatest men in this   *80* realm.

Sil. By 'r lady, I think a' be, but goodman Puff of Barson.

Pist. Puff!
Puff in thy teeth, most recreant coward base!
Sir John, I am thy Pistol and thy friend,   *85*
And helter-skelter have I rode to thee,
And tidings do I bring and lucky joys
And golden times and happy news of price.

Fal. I prithee now, deliver them like a man of this world.

Pist. A foutra for the world and worldlings base!   *90*
I speak of Africa and golden joys.

Fal. O base Assyrian knight, what is thy news?
Let King Cophetua know the truth thereof.

Sil. 'And Robin Hood, Scarlet, and John.'

Pist. Shall dunghill curs confront the Helicons?   *95*
And shall good news be baffled?
Then, Pistol, lay thy head in Furies' lap.

Shal. Honest gentlemen, I know not your breeding.

Pist. Why then, lament therefore.

Shal. Give me pardon, sir: if, sir, you come with news   *100* from the court, I take it there's but two ways: either to utter them, or to conceal them. I am sir, under the king, in some authority.

Pist. Under which king, Bezonian? speak, or die.

Shal. Under King Harry.   *105*

Pist.   Harry the Fourth? or Fifth?

Shal. Harry the Fourth.

Pist.   A foutra for thine office!
Sir John, thy tender lambkin now is king;
Harry the Fifth's the man. I speak the truth: *110*
When Pistol lies, do this; and fig me, like

---

10 **husband:** *husbandman*   20 **ever among:** *all the while*   25 **Proface:** *may it do you good (Italian 'prò vi faccia')*   27 **heart:** *intention*   33 **Shrove-tide:** *a time of special merriment at the close of the carnival*   39 **leather-coats:** *russet apples*   43 **leman:** *sweetheart*   54 **cavaleros:** *cavaliers*   60 **liggens:** *an original oath of Shallow's*   61 **will not out:** *will not fail (sporting term)*

66 **done me right:** *a common expression in drinking healths*   68 **dub me knight:** *cf. n.*   69 **Samingo:** *San Domingo, a common refrain in drinking songs*   82 **but:** *except*   **Barson:** *Barston in Warwickshire*   88 **price:** *value*   90 **foutra:** *exclamation of contempt*   93, 94 *These lines refer to popular ballads*   95 *Cf. n.*   104 **Bezonian:** *base beggar*   111 **fig:** *to thrust the thumb between two closed fingers, or into the mouth, a vulgar insult, imported from Spain*

The bragging Spaniard.

Fal. What! is the old king dead?

Pist. As nail in door: the things I speak are just.

Fal. Away, Bardolph! saddle my horse. Master Robert   *115*
Shallow, choose what office thou wilt in the land, 'tis thine.
Pistol, I will double charge thee with dignities.

Bard. O joyful day!
I would not take a knighthood for my fortune.

Pist. What! I do bring good news.   *120*

Fal. Carry Master Silence to bed. Master Shallow, my Lord
Shallow, be what thou wilt, I am Fortune's steward. Get on
thy boots: we'll ride all night. O sweet Pistol! Away, Bardolph!
[*Exit Bardolph.*] Come, Pistol, utter more to me; and withal
devise something to do thyself good. Boot, boot, Master   *125*
Shallow: I know the young king is sick for me. Let us take
any man's horses; the laws of England are at my commandment. Blessed are they which have been my friends, and woe
to my lord chief justice!

Pist. Let vultures vile seize on his lungs also!   *130*
'Where is the life that late I led?' say they:
Why, here it is: welcome these pleasant days!   *Exeunt.*

❧ SCENE FOURTH ❧

[London. A Street]
Enter Hostess Quickly, Doll Tearsheet, and Beadles.

Host. No, thou arrant knave: I would to God that I might
die that I might have thee hanged; thou hast drawn my shoulder out of joint.

First Bead. The constables have delivered her over to me,
and she shall have whipping-cheer enough, I warrant her: *5*
there hath been a man or two lately killed about her.

Dol. Nut-hook, nut-hook, you lie. Come on; I'll tell thee
what, thou damned tripe-visaged rascal, an the child I now go
with do miscarry, thou wert better thou hadst struck thy
mother, thou paper-faced villain.   *10*

Host. O the Lord! that Sir John were come; he would make
this a bloody day to somebody. But I pray God the fruit of
her womb miscarry!

First Bead. If it do, you shall have a dozen of cushions again;
you have but eleven now. Come, I charge you both go with   *15*
me; for the man is dead that you and Pistol beat amongst you.

Dol. I'll tell you what, you thin man in a censer, I will have
you as soundly swinged for this, you blue-bottle rogue! you
filthy famished correctioner! if you be not swinged, I'll forswear
half-kirtles.   *20*

First Bead. Come, come, you she knight-errant, come.

Host. O God, that right should thus overcome might! Well,
of sufferance comes ease.

Dol. Come, you rogue, come: bring me to a justice.

Host. Ay; come, you starved blood-hound.   *25*

Dol. Goodman death! goodman bones!

Host. Thou atomy, thou!

Dol. Come, you thin thing; come, you rascal!

First Bead. Very well.   *Exeunt.*

114 **just:** *correct*   131 *Quotation from another ballad*   7 **nut-hook:** *slang for beadle; cf.*
catchpole   17 **in a censer:** *i.e., a figure embossed on a censer*   18 **swinged:** *whipped* **blue-**
bottle: *the reference is to the beadle's blue livery*   20 **half-kirtles:** *waists or skirts*   23 **of**
sufferance: *out of suffering*   27 **atomy:** *Dame Quickly's confusion of 'atom' with 'anatomy' =*
skeleton

❧ SCENE FIFTH ❧

[A public Place near Westminster Abbey]
Enter two Grooms, strewers of rushes.

First Groom. More rushes, more rushes.

Sec. Groom. The trumpets have sounded twice.

First Groom. 'Twill be two o'clock ere they come from the
coronation. Dispatch, dispatch.   *Exeunt Grooms.*

Trumpets sound, and the King and his train pass over the stage.
After them, enter Falstaff, Shallow, Pistol, Bardolph, and the Boy.

Fal. Stand here by me, Master Robert Shallow; I will   *5*
make the king do you grace. I will leer upon him, as a' comes
by; and do but mark the countenance that he will give me.

Pist. God bless thy lungs, good knight.

Fal. Come here, Pistol; stand behind me. O! if I had had
time to have made new liveries, I would have bestowed the   *10*
thousand pound I borrowed of you. But 'tis no matter; this
poor show doth better: this doth infer the zeal I had to see
him.

Shal. It doth so.

Fal. It shows my earnestness of affection.   *15*

Shal. It doth so.

Fal. My devotion.

Shal. It doth, it doth, it doth.

Fal. As it were, to ride day and night; and not to deliberate,
not to remember, not to have patience to shift me.   *20*

Shal. It is best, certain.

Fal. But to stand stained with travel, and sweating with desire to see him; thinking of nothing else; putting all affairs else
in oblivion, as if there were nothing else to be done but to see
him.   *25*

Pist. 'Tis *semper idem,* for *absque hoc nihil est:* 'Tis all in
every part.

Shal. 'Tis so, indeed.

Pist. My knight, I will inflame thy noble liver,
And make thee rage.   *30*
Thy Doll, and Helen of thy noble thoughts,
Is in base durance and contagious prison;
Hal'd thither
By most mechanical and dirty hand:
Rouse up revenge from ebon den with fell Alecto's snake,   *35*
For Doll is in: Pistol speaks nought but truth.

Fal. I will deliver her.   [*Shouts within and trumpets sound.*]

Pist. There roar'd the sea, and trumpet-clangour sounds.

The trumpets sound. Enter King Henry the Fifth, Brothers, Lord
Chief Justice.

Fal. God save thy grace, King Hal! my royal Hal!

Pist. The heavens thee guard and keep, most royal imp   *40*
of fame!

Fal. God save thee, my sweet boy!

K. Hen. V. My lord chief justice, speak to that vain man.

Ch. Just. Have you your wits? know you what 'tis you
speak?   *45*

Fal. My king! my Jove! I speak to thee, my heart!

K. Hen. V. I know thee not, old man: fall to thy prayers;
How ill white hairs become a fool and jester!

26, 27 *Cf. n.*   34 **mechanical:** *common, vulgar*   35 **ebon:** *black* **Alecto:** *one of the*
Furies   40 **imp:** *child*   43 **vain:** *foolish*

I have long dream'd of such a kind of man,
So surfeit-swell'd, so old, and so profane; 50
But, being awak'd, I do despise my dream.
Make less thy body hence, and more thy grace;
Leave gormandising; know the grave doth gape
For thee thrice wider than for other men.
Reply not to me with a fool-born jest: 55
Presume not that I am the thing I was;
For God doth know, so shall the world perceive,
That I have turn'd away my former self;
So will I those that kept me company.
When thou dost hear I am as I have been, 60
Approach me, and thou shalt be as thou wast,
The tutor and the feeder of my riots:
Till then, I banish thee, on pain of death,
As I have done the rest of my misleaders,
Not to come near our person by ten mile. 65
For competence of life I will allow you,
That lack of means enforce you not to evil:
And, as we hear you do reform yourselves,
We will, according to your strength and qualities,
Give you advancement. Be it your charge, my lord, 70
To see perform'd the tenour of our word.
Set on. *Exit the King [with his Train].*

Fal. Master Shallow, I owe you a thousand pound.

Shal. Yea, marry, Sir John; which I beseech you to let me
have home with me. 75

Fal. That can hardly be, Master Shallow. Do not you grieve
at this: I shall be sent for in private to him. Look you, he
must seem thus to the world. Fear not your advancements; I
will be the man yet that shall make you great.

Shal. I cannot perceive how, unless you give me your 80
doublet and stuff me out with straw. I beseech you, good Sir
John, let me have five hundred of my thousand.

Fal. Sir, I will be as good as my word: this that you heard
was but a colour.

Shal. A colour that I fear you will die in, Sir John. 85

Fal. Fear no colours: go with me to dinner.
Come, Lieutenant Pistol; come, Bardolph: I shall be sent for
soon at night.

Enter Justice and Prince John.

Ch. Just. Go, carry Sir John Falstaff to the Fleet;
Take all his company along with him. 90

Fal. My lord, my lord!

Ch. Just. I cannot now speak: I will hear you soon.
Take them away.

Pist. Si fortuna me tormenta, spero contenta.

Exeunt. Mane[n]t [Prince John of] Lancaster and Chief Justice.

Lanc. I like this fair proceeding of the king's. 95
He hath intent his wonted followers
Shall all be very well provided for;
But all are banish'd till their conversations
Appear more wise and modest to the world.

Ch. Just. And so they are. 100

Lanc. The king hath call'd his parliament, my lord.

Ch. Just. He hath.

Lanc. I will lay odds, that, ere this year expire,
We bear our civil swords and native fire
As far as France. I heard a bird so sing, 105
Whose music, to my thinking, pleas'd the king.
Come, will you hence? *Exeunt.*

❧ EPILOGUE ❧

[Spoken by a Dancer.]

First, my fear; then, my curtsy; last my speech. My fear is, your
displeasure, my curtsy, my duty, and my speech, to beg your pardon. If you look for a good speech now, you undo me; for what I
have to say is of mine own making; and what indeed I should say
will, I doubt, prove mine own marring. But to the purpose, and 5
so to the venture. Be it known to you,—as it is very well,—I was
lately here in the end of a displeasing play, to pray your patience
for it and to promise you a better. I did mean indeed to pay you
with this; which, if like an ill venture it come unluckily home, I
break, and you, my gentle creditors, lose. Here, I promised you 10
I would be, and here I commit my body to your mercies: bate me
some and I will pay you some; and, as most debtors do, promise
you infinitely.

If my tongue cannot entreat you to acquit me, will you command me to use my legs? and yet that were but light payment, 15
to dance out of your debt. But a good conscience will make any
possible satisfaction, and so will I. All the gentlewomen here have
forgiven me: if the gentlemen will not, then the gentlemen do not
agree with the gentlewomen, which was never seen before in such
an assembly. 20

One word more, I beseech you. If you be not too much cloyed
with fat meat, our humble author will continue the story, with Sir
John in it, and make you merry with fair Katharine of France:
where, for anything I know, Falstaff shall die of a sweat, unless
already a' be killed with your hard opinions; for Oldcastle 25
died a martyr, and this is not the man. My tongue is weary;
when my legs are too, I will bid you good night: and so kneel
down before you; but, indeed, to pray for the queen.

❧ FINIS ❧

---

85 colour: *pun on collar, halter*　　86 Fear no colours: *have no fear; originally, fear no
enemy*　　89 the Fleet: *a London prison*　　　　98 conversations: *habits*　　Epilogue; *cf. n.*　　5 doubt: *fear*　　9 break: *became bankrupt*　　11 bate: *remit*　　28 to pray for the queen; *cf. n.*

NOTES

Ind. S.d. *Rumour, painted full of tongues.* Vergil (*Æneid* iv. 174) describes Fame, or Rumour, as covered with ears, eyes, and tongues. Cf. also Chaucer, *Hous of Fame*, 1389-90.

Ind.24. *Shrewsbury.* The last act of Shakespeare's *Henry IV, Part I*, is devoted to the battle of Shrewsbury, in which the King and his armies overcome the rebel forces under young Harry Percy (Hotspur); his uncle, the Earl of Worcester; and the Scottish Earl of Douglas.

Ind.29. *Harry Monmouth.* Henry, Prince of Wales, who, according to Shakespeare, killed Hotspur in single combat at the battle of Shrewsbury. Monmouth was the place of his birth.

Ind.35. *hole.* Shakespeare is obviously playing on the words *hole* and *hold*. Most modern editors have spoiled the rather poor pun by substituting the word *hold* for *hole*.

I.i.128-130. 'By his spirit was his party inspired, i.e., made keen and sharp as steel; but, when once his spirit was brought down (technically, reduced to a lower temper) all his followers became dull and heavy as lead.'

I.i.140. In *1 Henry IV*, V. iii., Douglas kills Sir Walter Blunt, who was dressed to resemble the King, and tells us that he has already killed the Lord of Stafford in the king's 'likeness.' When, later, Prince Hal challenges Douglas to single combat, he says:

> 'the spirits
> Of valiant Shirley, Stafford, Blunt, are in my arms.'

I.i.178-191. These lines are the first of a series of passages omitted in the Quarto texts of the play and added by the Folio. The other important Folio additions are the following: I.i.201-221; I.iii.22-25; I.iii.38-57; I.iii.87-113; II.iii.23-45; IV.i.58-82; Epilogue 27, 28 (and so kneel . . . queen). Furthermore, the whole of III.i., containing the King's famous soliloquy on sleep, is omitted in certain Quarto copies, though added in others. On the other hand, certain passages, usually shorter and belonging to the prose scenes, are omitted in the Folio version; viz., I.ii.193-198 (But it was . . . motion); II.ii.20-24 (and God . . . strengthened); II.iv.10, 11 (Dispatch . . . straight); II.iv.113-114; II.iv.350 f. (Come! . . . come, Doll?); III.i.53-56 (O! . . . die); III.ii.277, 278 (yet lecherous . . . mandrake); III.ii.278-280 (and sung . . . good-nights); IV.i.96; IV.i.98.

I.i.216, 217. According to Shakespeare, King Richard II, predecessor and cousin of Henry IV, was murdered in Pomfret castle at Henry's hint, after the latter had forced Richard's abdication. Cf. Shakespeare's *Richard II*. Richard Scroop, Archbishop of York, belonged to a family which was firmly attached to the cause of Richard.

I.i.220. *Bolingbroke.* King Henry, born in Bolingbroke castle, Lincolnshire.

I.ii.14. *manned with an agate.* Attended by a servant as small as a figure cut in an agate.

I.ii.21. *face-royal.* A royal was a gold coin worth ten shillings. Falstaff is here playing on the double sense of a 'royal face' and the face stamped on the coin.

I.ii.30. *glutton.* The parable of Dives and Lazarus (St. Luke 16. 19-31) is frequently referred to by Falstaff, possibly because Dives, 'the glutton,' who 'fared sumptuously every day,' but who went to hell and called out for the poor man Lazarus to 'dip the tip of his finger in water and cool my tongue,' reminds Falstaff of his own manner of life and probable fate.

I.ii.31. *Achitophel.* The counsellor of Absalom (II Samuel 15-17) who was cursed by David, and who 'gat him home to his house and hanged himself' after Absalom rejected his counsel.

I.ii.31, 32. *yea-forsooth knave.* The reference is to the mild oaths employed by the Puritanical middle-class tradespeople of Shakespeare's own day. Cf. Hotspur's ridicule of this same trait in *1 Henry IV*, III.i.254 ff.

I.ii.40-42. Falstaff is here playing with the ancient jest that deceived husbands wear invisible horns. Lightness is obviously used in a double sense, and the old spelling of lanthorn, which emphasizes the horn sides of an Elizabethan lantern, carries out the jest.

I.ii.45. *Paul's.* The nave of St. Paul's Cathedral was in Shakespeare's day the business center of London. From eleven to twelve, and three to six, daily, men of all professions and trades congregated there. Men out of work, and masters looking for servants, posted their advertisements on the pillars of the nave. Falstaff is probably referring here to a popular saying, quoted in *The Choice of Change*, 1598: 'A man must not make choice of three things in three places: of a wife in Westminster, of a servant in Paul's, of a horse in Smithfield; lest he choose a quean, a knave, or a jade.' Smithfield is the great cattle market of London.

I.ii.49, 50. This episode from *The Famous Victories of Henry V* is reprinted in the Introduction.

I.ii.79. *hunt counter.* A hunting term meaning to follow the trail in a direction opposite to that which the game has taken. There is also perhaps here a pun on the two Compters, or debtors', prisons in London.

I.ii.132, 133. Blind beggars often had dogs to lead them through the streets.

I.ii.145. *wax.* 'A poor quibble on the word wax, which signifies increase as well as the matter of the honey-comb.' Johnson.

I.ii.151-153. An angel was a gold coin, worth upwards of six shillings, which took its name from its device, the archangel Michael. Falstaff is here punning on the word, and in the phrases *cannot go* and *cannot tell*, he is perhaps using terms which refer to the circulation of money, meaning 'I cannot pass current. I cannot count as good coin.'

I.ii.191. *spit white.* Furnivall quotes *Batman uppon Bartholome* (1582): 'If the spettle be white viscus, the sicknesse cometh of fleame; if black, of melancholy;—the white spettle not knottie, signifieth health.'

I.ii.203, 204. *bear crosses.* Another quibble on coins, many of which were marked with crosses.

I.ii.206. A three-man beetle is a mallet so heavy that it requires three men to swing it. *Filliping the load*, according to Steevens, is a Warwickshire game, in which a toad is placed on the end of a short board placed across a log; the other end of the board is then struck with a mallet, and the toad thrown into the air. If Falstaff took the part of the toad in this game, it would, he implies, require a three-man beetle to fillip one of his size.

I.iii.38-43. Many emendations have been suggested for this apparently corrupt passage. It is probable that a line has been lost here, but it is possible to understand Lord Bardolph's speech without changing the text. Lord Hastings has just been remonstrating with Lord Bardolph for his pessimism, saying that hope never injured any cause. Lord Bardolph replies: 'Yes, it does,—if, for example, this present business of war (indeed this very action now contemplated, this cause that is now on foot), lives merely on such desperate hopes as buds which appear too early in the spring; for hope gives less warrant that these buds will become fruit than despair gives that the frosts will destroy them.'

I.iii.55-57. 'Know how well able our estate is to undergo such a work, and how well able it is to balance the power of our opponent.'

II.i.26, 27. When Dame Quickly says, 'A hundred mark is a long one,' i.e., a long mark, score, or reckoning, she puns on a hundred marks as a debt and a hundred yard mark at archery.

II.i.51, 52. *rampallian.* Elizabethan slang, rascal, rapscallion; used also by Beaumont and Fletcher. *Fustilarian*, a word coined by Falstaff, suggested by the word *fustilugs*, a fat, frowsy woman. *Catastrophe*, in the sense of conclusion, end; used jocularly here for the posteriors.

II.i.112. Falstaff has the legal right to demand protection against the just claims of Mistress Quickly, as he is about to set forth for the north on the King's business. The Chief Justice admits his 'power to do wrong' in this matter, but urges him to answer the poor woman's suit in a manner suitable to his reputation as a gentleman and soldier.

II.i.124. Falstaff tries to comfort Mistress Quickly for the loss of her plate by assuring her that glasses are much more fashionable and pleasanter to drink from than silver goblets.

II.i.164. 'This is the proper behaviour in fencing.' Falstaff refers to his inattention to the Justice's remarks as a retaliation for the Justice's inattention to his questions in ll. 143 ff.

II.ii.19-24. Shirts were made of holland linen (worth 'eight shillings an ell,' cf. *1 Henry IV*, III.iii.62, 63). The play on the words holland and low-countries is apparent. The Prince proceeds to assume that Poins's shortage in shirts is due to the fact that his old shirts are serving as garments for his illegitimate children, who 'bawl out' from 'the ruins of his linen.'

II.ii.76-79. Either Shakespeare or the Page confuses the dream of Hecuba with that of Althea. Althea dreamed that the Fates told her that her newborn son would live only so long as a burning brand on the hearth remained unconsumed. Althea snatched the brand from the hearth, extinguished the fire, and prolonged her son's life.

II.ii.90. *martlemas.* Corrupted form of Martinmas, or the Feast of St. Martin, November 11. This day was considered the last day of autumn, and was also the day for salting and hanging the winter's supply of beef. The reference is obviously to Falstaff's hearty old age (cf. *All-hallown summer, 1 Henry IV*, I.ii.137, 138, note), or to Falstaff as a 'martlemas beef.'

II.ii.101, 102. *borrower's cap.* A man asking for a loan is always very ready to take off his cap.

II.ii.103ff. Most modern editors have rearranged the following speeches, giving to Poins the reading of Falstaff's letter to Hal. The Quarto and Folio arrangement, followed with one exception (cf. Introduction) in this text, seems more natural. In lines 87, 88 Bardolph evidently gives the letter to the Prince, not to Poins. In line 95 the Prince shows the letter to Poins, but does not necessarily give it to him.

II.ii.158. The parallel is not striking. Jove took the form of a bull to woo Europa. Hal disguises himself as a waiter to spy upon Falstaff. The leather jerkins are the only connecting link.

II.iv.28. The ballad sung by Falstaff has been preserved in Percy's *Reliques.*

II.iv.42. Another scrap of an old ballad.

II.iv.73. *debuty.* Mistress Quickly's pronunciation of deputy, and of Wednesday in line 74, both of which are corrected in the Folio text, indicates that she has a cold in her head.

II.iv.83. *tame cheater.* A cant term for a low gamester, especially for a gamester's decoy. Mistress Quickly understands the word in the sense of escheator, or officer of the exchequer. The Cambridge editors suggest the emendation *chetah,* the hunting leopard, known in Europe as early as the fifteenth century. The sentence, *you may stroke him as gently as a puppy greyhound,* would indicate at least that Falstaff is playing on the two words *cheater* and *chetah.* One would hardly speak of stroking a gamester's decoy.

II.iv.124. *occupy.* This word was used only in an obscene sense in Shakespeare's day. From the sixteenth to the nineteenth century it seldom appears in literature.

II.iv.134. *Have we not Hiren here?* This phrase, which became proverbial in Elizabethan drama, probably originated in a lost play by George Peele, entitled, *The Turkish Mahomet and Hyren* (Irene) *the Fair Greek.* Pistol applies the name to his sword. Mistress Quickly (ll. 148) thinks he is inquiring for some woman.

II.iv.138, 139. Pistol misquotes from Marlowe's *Tamburlaine the Great, Pt. II,* IV, iv:

'Holla, ye pamper'd jades of Asia!
What! can ye draw but twenty miles a day?'

II.iv.152. Another burlesque of contemporary drama. This time Shakespeare puts into Pistol's mouth a reference to Peele's *Battle of Alcazar,* printed in 1594, in which Muley Mahomet enters with lion's flesh on his sword, which he offers to his wife with the words,

'Feed then and faint not, my fair Calypolis.'

II.iv.154. Most editors assume that Pistol is speaking bad Italian. The Cambridge editors suggest that it is perhaps bad Spanish, and that he is reading the motto on his Toledo blade. Douce gives an illustration of a sword with a French version of this motto inscribed upon it. Farmer says: 'Pistol is only a copy of Hannibal Gonsaga who vaunted on yielding himself a prisoner, as you may read in an old collection of tales called *Wits, Fits, Fancies:*

'Si Fortuna me tormenta
Il speranza me contenta.'

Whatever the language, the meaning of Pistol's motto is, If Fortune torments me, Hope contents me.

II.iv.164. *shove-groat shilling.* Shove-groat was a game which was a cross between shuffle-board and 'pitching pennies.' It was played on a board three feet long and a foot wide, and the object of the players was to shove coins into numbered spaces at the far end of the board.

II.iv.214, 215. *drinks . . . flapdragons.* Flapdragon or snapdragon is a sport which consists in snapping raisins or grapes from burning brandy and eating them.

II.iv.231. An impossible conjunction of planets.

II.iv.233. *fiery Trigon.* Poins continues the astrological figure by referring to the red-nosed Bardolph as the fiery Trigon. When the three superior planets were in that division of the zodiac which consisted of the three so-called fiery signs, Aries, Leo, and Sagittarius, they were said to be in the fiery Trigon, or triangle; when they were in Cancer, Scorpio, and Pisces, they were in the watery Trigon, etc.

II.iv.296. *dead elm.* Shakespeare mentions elms three times,—here and in *The Comedy of Errors,* II.ii.175, and in *A Midsummer Night's Dream,* IV.i.42. In both *C. of E.* and *M. N. D.* the reference is to the practice of training ivy on elm trees, illustrating the relation of woman to man. Poins is therefore probably referring to the posture of Falstaff and Doll.

III.ii.21-23. Sir John Oldcastle and Sir John Fastolfe, with both of whom Falstaff has been identified (cf. *1 Henry IV,* Introduction), were both pages to the Duke of Norfolk in their youth.

III.ii.27. *Skogan.* Shakespeare probably took the name from a jest book published in 1565, called *Scogin's Jests.* This Scogin was the court fool of King Edward IV. It is possible, however, that the reference is to Chaucer's friend, Henry Scogan, described by Ben Jonson in *The Fortunate Isles* as 'a fine gentleman, and master of arts, of Henry the Fourth's time.'

III.ii.61. *accommodated.* This is one of the words which Ben Jonson (*Discoveries*) refers to as one of 'the perfumed terms of the time.' Bardolph is giving himself airs and imitating the affectations of fashionable gallants.

III.ii.197. Bull calf means to say: 'Here, in French crowns, is the equivalent of four English ten-shilling pieces, or ten-shilling pieces with King Henry's head on them.' As a matter of fact Henry VII was the first English king whose head appeared on ten shilling pieces.

III.ii.219. *three pound.* Falstaff's followers adopt his own methods. Bardolph has collected four pounds, forty shillings from each of the two men, but decides to keep a commission of twenty-five per cent.

III.ii.234. *gibbets.* A brewer's gibbet was the yoke worn across the shoulders for carrying buckets of beer from the vat to the barrels. Falstaff refers to the dexterity with which brewers' men swing the buckets on to the gibbet.

III.ii.246-248. Sir Dagonet was King Arthur's fool. Arthur's show was an exhibition of archery held annually at Mile-end Green by a society called The Auncient Order, Societie, and Unitie laudable of Prince Arthur and his Knightly Armoury of the Round Table. There were fifty-eight members and each took the name of one of the knights in the old romances.

III.ii.281. *Vice's dagger.* The Vice, a character in the old Morality plays, carried a thin wooden dagger.

III.ii.289, 290. *philosopher's two stones.* The philosophers' stone is the reputed stone of the alchemists which transmutes base metals into gold. Falstaff decides that Justice Shallow will be as valuable to him as two philosophers' stones!

IV.i.97-99. This passage is obviously corrupt. The archbishop means in general: 'I make this my quarrel on both public and private grounds, that is, because of the sufferings of the commonwealth and of my own. family at the hands of King Henry.' The Archbishop's brother, an adherent of King Richard, had been executed by King Henry's order; cf. *1 Henry IV,* I.iii.279, 280.

IV.i.121 ff. This contest is described in the first act of Shakespeare's *Richard II.*

IV.i.179. *consign'd.* The Quarto and Folio read confin'd; consign'd is Johnson's emendation. The meaning seems to be that the terms of surrender include the stipulation that the execution of the wishes of the rebels shall be consigned to their own hands.

IV.ii. Shakespeare evidently had no thought of a change of scene, or of pause in action, here. Even the first Folio has no stage direction of exeunt at the end of Scene i., and no indication of scene division. I have kept the conventional modern arrangement for convenience of reference; but the reader should remember that the Archbishop and his party do not leave the stage,—they merely step forward to greet Prince John as he enters.

IV.iii.104, 105. *a mere hoard of gold kept by a devil.* Falstaff refers to the old superstition that gold mines were guarded by devils.

IV.iv.S.d. *The Jerusalem Chamber.* An apartment adjoining the southwest tower of Westminster Abbey, built in the fourteenth century as a guest-chamber, and deriving its name from the tapestries depicting the history of Jerusalem with which it was hung. Since the seventeenth century it has been used as a council chamber.

IV.iv.35-37. 'Nevertheless when he is incensed he breaks out in fiery fashion like flint; he abounds in caprices as winter abounds in moisture; and he changes his moods as suddenly as water freezes and melts at the edge of a pond at daybreak.' *Flaws* are the blades of ice seen on the edges of water on winter mornings.

IV.iv.46-50. 'That the vessel of their united blood may never leak, even though that blood should be mingled with the venom caused by hints and suggestions tending toward discord, which in this age will be sure to be poured in; and even though this venom should work with the strength of aconite or gunpowder.'

IV.iv.81, 83. 'It seldom happens that the bee, having deposited her comb in dead carrion, leaves the comb and the carrion.' The application is to the Prince and his low company.

IV.v.164. *medicine potable.* 'There has long prevailed an opinion that a solution of gold has great medicinal virtues, and that the incorruptibility of gold might be communicated to the body impregnated with it.' Johnson.

IV.v.201. *mode.* The key in which music is written, used figuratively and associated with 'mood' in the sense of state of mind.

V.i.1. *cock and pie.* The origin of this common Elizabethan oath is obscure. Cock is probably a corruption of God, as in the oath Cock's wounds; and pie is perhaps the Roman service book which was sometimes so called, though the word pie applies more properly to the index of the service book. By Shakespeare's time the meaning of the oath was forgotten, and Justice Shallow doubtless thinks he is swearing by a cock and a magpie.

V.ii.36. 'Which goes against the grain with one in your position.'

V.ii.50. This allusion helps to fix the date of the play. Amurath the Fourth succeeded his father on the Turkish throne in 1596. Upon his accession he invited his brothers to dinner and had them all strangled.

V.ii.126, 127. This strange remark of the Prince seems to mean that inasmuch as his own wild affections and desires died at the moment of his father's death, they are now, as it were, buried with his father. Hence his father may be said to be buried with wild affections, or to have 'gone wild into his grave.'

V.iii.69. *dub me knight.* The reference is to the Elizabethan custom of giving the title of knight for the evening to a man who, kneeling to his mistress, drained a mighty bumper to her health.

V.iii.96. Helicon was the abode of the Muses. Pistol resents having such low fellows as Robin Hood and his men brought into this very grandiloquent literary conversation.

V.v.26, 27. Pistol quotes two Latin phrases which have no significance here, and then proceeds to mistranslate them. The Latin means literally: it is always the same, for without this there is nothing.

Epil. Shakespeare's authorship of this epilogue has been questioned. The dancer says it is of his own making, but he speaks for the author in promising a continuation of the play and in assuring the audience that Falstaff is not Sir John Oldcastle (cf. note on III.ii.21-23, and Introduction to *1 Henry IV*, in the present edition). It is interesting to note that Shakespeare's original intention was to continue the Falstaff plot through the play of *Henry V*; but, as Coleridge remarks, 'Agincourt is not the place for the splendid mendacity of Falstaff. With the coronation of Henry V opens a new period of glorious enthusiasm and patriotic fervor. There is no longer any place for Falstaff on earth; he must find refuge in "Arthur's bosom." '

Epil. 28. *pray for the queen.* It was the custom to end plays with a prayer for the sovereign. This custom originated in the interludes.

The Text of the Present Edition

The text of the present edition is, in the main, by permission of the Oxford University Press, that of the Oxford Shakespeare, edited by the late W. J. Craig. Stage directions, when not bracketed, are from either the First Quarto or the First Folio or both; bracketed stage directions are modern. The title of the play is from the First Quarto.

In II.ii.104-121 the present editor has substituted the original assignment of speeches, in ll. 104, 109, as found in both Quarto and Folio, for Craig's assignment, as there seems to be no sufficient reason for emendations. He has also assigned ll. 110-120 to the Prince. Craig divides as follows:

104-107 Poins. Sir John . . . certificate.
108   Prince. Peace.
108-121 Poins. I will . . . eat it.

Many minor departures from the Oxford text have been made in this edition in an attempt to arrive at a consistent text. The Oxford editor has in the majority of cases followed the readings of the First Quarto, but in about fifty instances he has adopted the slightly different expressions used in the more formal and less colloquial Folio text. For example, in the scenes of low comedy, *he* in the Folio is almost invariably *a'* in the Quarto; *is it* is *is 't; it is* is *'tis;* etc. The Oxford editor has used sometimes the formal, sometimes the informal expression. He sometimes follows the Folio in correcting the grammar and the mispronunciations of Mistress Quickly and Justice Shallow, and sometimes does not; he frequently omits the oaths found in the Quarto and expurgated in the Folio, but more frequently includes them. The present editor has not thought it wise to burden his pages with a long list of the minor changes he has made in the Oxford text. His policy has been to follow, in general, the more colloquial Quarto text.

In the following list of other variants the readings of the present edition precede the colon, Craig's readings follow it, and the Quarto or Folio authority is given wherever involved:

Ind. 35	hole QF: hold	
I.i.40	comes QF: come	
ii.3	moe Q: more F	
35	through QF: thorough	
104	it QF: its	
II.i.1	action QF: exion	
5	Sirrah!—: Sirrah, QF	
63	all I have Q: all, all I have F	
142	my lord Q: my good lord F	
ii.16	another Q: one other F	
51	an QF: a	
59	those QF: these	
66	*Poins* QF: *Bard.*	
98	kin QF: akin	
110	he sure Q: sure he F	
iii.65	his QF: its	
iv.33	a pox damn you Q: omit F	
41	Yea, joy Q: Ay, marry F	
73	debuty Q: deputy F	
74	Wedesday Q: Wednesday F	
111	but I will Q: I will (passage omitted in F)	
134	faitors (faters Q): fates F	
154	fortune Q: fortuna F	
242	shalt have Q: thou shalt have F	
351-352	Come! *(She comes blubbered.)* Yea, will you come, Doll? Q: omit F	
III.ii.174	field QF: fields	
276	invisible: invincible QF	
IV.ii.14	mischiefs QF: mischief	
v. 149	inward, true, and Q: true and inward F	
V.iii.128	Blessed Q: Happy F	
129	to Q: unto F	
iv. 1, 2	that I might die Q: I might die F	
9	wert Q: hadst F	
v. 21	best, Q: most F	

The Life of Henry the Fifth

Edited by
R. J. DORIUS

Dramatis Personae

KING HENRY THE FIFTH
DUKE OF GLOUCESTER ⎫
DUKE OF BEDFORD ⎬ *Brothers to the King*
DUKE OF CLARENCE ⎭
DUKE OF EXETER, *Uncle to the King*
DUKE OF YORK, *Cousin to the King*
EARL OF SALISBURY
EARL OF WESTMORELAND
EARL OF WARWICK
ARCHBISHOP OF CANTERBURY
BISHOP OF ELY
EARL OF CAMBRIDGE
LORD SCROOP
SIR THOMAS GREY
SIR THOMAS ERPINGHAM ⎫
GOWER, *an English Captain* ⎪ *Officers in King*
FLUELLEN, *a Welsh Captain* ⎬ *Henry's army*
MACMORRIS, *an Irish Captain* ⎪
JAMY, *a Scottish Captain* ⎭
JOHN BATES ⎫
ALEXANDER COURT ⎬ *Soldiers in the same*
MICHAEL WILLIAMS ⎭
PISTOL
NYM
BARDOLPH
BOY
A HERALD

CHORUS

CHARLES THE SIXTH, *King of France*
LEWIS, *the Dauphin*
DUKE OF BURGUNDY
DUKE OF ORLEANS
DUKE OF BERRI
DUKE OF BRITAINE
DUKE OF BOURBON
THE CONSTABLE OF FRANCE
RAMBURES ⎫
GRANDPRÉ ⎬ *French Lords*
BEAUMONT ⎭
GOVERNOR OF HARFLEUR
MONTJOY, *a French Herald*
AMBASSADORS TO THE KING OF ENGLAND

ISABEL, *Queen of France*
KATHARINE, *Daughter to Charles and Isabel*
ALICE, *a Lady attending on her*
HOSTESS OF THE BOAR'S HEAD TAVERN IN EASTCHEAP
  (FORMERLY MISTRESSS QUICKLY, NOW MARRIED
  TO PISTOL)

LORDS, LADIES, OFFICERS, FRENCH AND ENGLISH
  SOLDIERS, CITIZENS, MESSENGERS, AND ATTENDANTS

SCENE—*England and France.*

The Life of Henry the Fifth

INTRODUCTION

TEXT AND DATE

Problems of text and date relating to *Henry V* are, when compared with the complexity of these matters for many of the plays, relatively simple. Shakespeare rarely refers to clearly datable historical events within his lifetime, but this play contains the only such reference which establishes at once the dates after which and before which the play was probably written. Lines 29–34 in the Prologue to Act V compare the glorious return from France of England's 'conqu'ring Caesar,' King Henry, with that of 'the general of our gracious empress' from Ireland, 'Bringing rebellion broached on his sword.' This general has long been identified with Essex, who left England to establish firmly England's supremacy over Ireland in March 1599 and returned in disgrace the following September. Since public expectation concerning this venture began to wane by June of that year, Shakespeare's high-spirited parallel must have been penned by mid-summer. A little earlier the now famous list of plays given by Meres in his *Palladis Tamia* (September 1598) mentions *Henry IV* but not *Henry V*.

We know that *Henry V* was acted by the Chamberlain's men (Shakespeare's company) in 1599. It was printed in 1600 in the small quarto form in which single plays were published, and in two later quartos, derived from the first, in 1602 and again in 1619 (marked 1608). The first of these (Q) is probably a radical abridgment of an acting version of the play, possibly memorized or 'reported' by a pirate actor or actors and sold to a printer for ready money. It is one of the 'Bad' Quartos, shorter than the Folio text by some 1700 lines, and it omits all of the choruses and the Epilogue, three entire scenes (I.1, III.1, and IV.2), and eleven other passages of from about twenty to eighty lines. Except in a few speeches it is so garbled (setting many passages of prose as absurdly irregular verse) that it is useful only in corroborating readings of the Folio or in supplying an occasional word or phrase where the Folio reading is doubtful.

The First Folio (F) of 1623 offers us the only good text of this play. It is probably taken from a manuscript in Shakespeare's hand (his 'foul' papers), from a scribal copy of such a manuscript, or possibly from both. Though several of its proper names are confused (Henry is once called 'Ireland'), though Pistol's speeches are printed as prose, and the French is often almost unintelligible, F affords us a commendable and interesting copy text, in a form (with or without revisions by the author) very similar to that which Shakespeare probably handed his players. Scene divisions are not indicated, and although act divisions are marked carelessly, the position of the five choruses relieves us of all doubt concerning this matter. Lineation is often clearly wrong (most of Pistol's speeches) and sometimes doubtful, but punctuation is as thorough as it is for any of the other plays in F. Pointing is, nevertheless, by modern standards, frequently erratic and excessive, and in this text, except in several passages of colorful prose, it is considerably simplified. By and large (though with many exceptions) the numerous colons in F are here given as periods and the semicolons as commas; many commas are dropped entirely.

The presence in this play of the dialect forms of Fluellen and the other captains (most of which are retained) and of a puzzling version of 16th-century French (here normalized) renders problems of orthography in *Henry V* especially interesting. The glosses call attention to the pronunciation of many words, and many spellings which indicate pronunciation different from our own have been retained, e.g. *Callice* for Calais, *Harflew* for Harfleur, *Dolphin* for Dauphin, *bankrout* for bankrupt, *creeple* for cripple, *perfit* for perfect, *shrowdly* for shrewdly, *venter* for venture, *divel* (also *devil*), *doo'st, farwell, huswife, mervailous, murther, vawting, wrack*, and all significant forms in the dialects of the four captains. The F spellings of other words (like *vp-peer'd*) are indicated in the notes or glosses when important for the meaning or meter of a particular passage. Among the forms not usually noted are *I* for ay, *Ile* for I'll, *wee'l* for we'll, *ore* for o'er, *onely* for only, *shew* for show, and archaic spellings like *howre, yeeres, Iland, Soueraign,* and *Souldiers*. Spellings that for the Elizabethans were completely interchangeable are also not usually indicated: *an, and; loose, lose; than, then,* and *to, too*. Many other interesting spellings (often phonetic) have not ordinarily been retained or glossed; *atchieve, basterd, batcheler, begger, fierie* and *Squier, Gloster, Humfrey, Lyms* (limbs), *perswaded, Reyne* (reign), *shoo* (shoe), *Syens* (scions), and *Marshall* for martial and *Rights* for rites. Problems connected with the French of F are discussed briefly in the notes to III.4, and the original French of this scene is reproduced at the end of this Appendix.

In recent years several irregularities in the F text of *Henry V* have been considered as composite evidence for Shakespeare's working over parts of the original text of the play at a later date, with some specific purpose in mind. The most interesting of the explanations put forth for revision revolves about the possible presence of Falstaff in the first version of the play. Proponents of this theory maintain that Shakespeare then cut the fat knight out for one of several reasons and substituted for him several new scenes or parts of scenes. The passages in question involve II.1 and 3, III.2, and several lines in III.6, in IV.1 and 7–8, and in V.1. Some of the evidence for alteration within these scenes is given in the notes. The Prologue of Act II, for example, prepares us for King Henry's unmasking of the traitors in Southampton and then for scenes in France. But the last two lines of the Prologue seem introduced, rather awkwardly, to account for scenes 1 and 3, which are laid instead in London. These scenes present the merry interchanges of Nym, Bardolph, and Pistol, and culminate in Mistress Quickly's famous description of Falstaff's death. In III.2., furthermore, the Boy's soliloquy (11. 27–49) and the curiously independent episode of the four captains 11.50ff.) show possible signs of having been altered or added to the original text. Similarly, in IV.1 the speeches of Pistol (as everywhere in the play), the discussion between Henry and the three soldiers about war, the episode of Williams' glove, Henry's famous first soliloquy before Agincourt (11. 207–261); in IV.7 and 8 the continuation of the glove episode; and in V.1 the capping of the quarrel between Pistol and Fluellen—all may have been altered by Shakespeare.

It is possible that the promise in the Epilogue to 2 *Henry IV* to 'continue the story with Sir John [Falstaff] in it' was originally fulfilled. Then, because of the permanent absence from the Chamberlain's men of the actor who played the part of Falstaff (Will Kemp), or, more probably, because the Master of the Revels deleted the role out of deference to Lord Cobham (who saw in the part an insult to his family name), or for some other reason, Falstaff was dropped and new material added to the play. In the version handed down to us Pistol may have taken over much of the role of Falstaff, and Shakespeare may have expanded the part of Fluellen and the subplot generally to make up for the loss of his overwhelmingly popular character. In the present form the play is very long—nearly 3,400 lines.

Despite the evidence for major revision in the F text summarized briefly here and in the notes, however, the nature and extent of such revision, and the reasons for it, are still far from clear. Theories about the possible presence of Falstaff in an earlier version of the play raise serious problems about the nature of *Henry V* and its immediate predecessor in the series. After the dramatic rightness of the rejection of Falstaff at the end of 2 *Henry IV*, it is difficult to imagine his being revived to play a role very different from that assigned the buffoon Sir John in *The Merry Wives*. Certainly the presence of the old Falstaff in the world of the reformed and heroic Henry V would greatly alter the nature of this play. If the aging knight once joined the other irregular humorists on the fields of France, clear traces of his presence, in the kinds of recurring themes and images which relate him so profoundly to the two parts of *Henry IV*, have disappeared.

The editor of this edition of *Henry V* is deeply indebted to the careful scholarship of many students of the play. The arguments for revision given above have been developed by Alfred Pollard, Dover Wilson, and G. I. Duthie, and further supported by the detailed evidence of Allan Wilkinson and (especially) J. H. Walter. Of the editions of the play consulted, those by Dover Wilson (Cambridge), G. B. Harrison (Harcourt, Brace), G. L. Kittredge (Ginn), G. C. Moore Smith (Heath), and J. H. Walter (Methuen) have proved to be most helpful. The general editors of the Yale Shakespeare have offered many valuable suggestions.

ACT III, SCENE 4, IN THE FRENCH OF THE FIRST FOLIO

Enter Katherine and an old Gentlewoman.

Kathe. *Alice, tu as este en Angleterre, & tu bien parlas le Language.*

Alice. *En peu Madame.*

Kath. *Ie te prie m'ensigniez, il faut que ie apprend a parlen: Comient appelle vous le main en Anglois?*

Alice. *Le main il & appelle de Hand.*

Kath. *De Hand.*

Alice. *E. le doyts.*

Kat. *Le doyts, ma foy Ie oublie, e doyt mays, ie me souemeray le doyts ie pense qu'ils ont appelle de fingres, ou de fingres.*

Alice. *Le main de Hand, le doyts le Fingres, ie pense que ie suis le bon escholier.*

Kath. *I'ay gaynie diux mots d'Anglois vistement, coment appelle vous le ongles?*

Alice. *Le ongles, les appellons de Nayles.*

Kath. *De Nayles escoute: dites moy, sie ie parle bien: de Hand, de Fingres, e de Nayles.*

Alice. *C'est bien dict Madame, il & fort bon Anglois.*

Kath. *Dites moy l'Anglois pour le bras.*

Alice. *De Arme, Madame.*

Kath. *E de coudee.*

Alice. *D'Elbow.*

Kath. *D'Elbow; Ie men fay le repiticio de touts les mots que vous maves, apprins des a present.*

Alice. *Il & trop difficile Madame, comme Ie pense.*

Kath. *Excuse moy Alice escoute, d'Hand, de Fingre, de Nayles, d'Arma, de Bilbow.*

Alice. *D'Elbow, Madame.*

Kath. *O Seigneur Dieu, ie men oublie d'Elbow, coment appelle vous le col.*

Alice. *De Nick, Madame.*

Kath. *De Nick, e le menton.*

Alice. *De Chin.*

Kath. *De Sin: le col de Nick, le menton de Sin.*

Alice. *Ouy. Sauf vostre honneur en verite vous prononcies les mots ausi droict, que le Natifs d'Angleterre.*

Kath. *Ie ne doute point d'apprendre par de grace de Dieu, & en peu de temps.*

Alice. *N'aue vos y desia oublie ce que ie vous a ensignie.*

Kath. *Nome ie recitera a vous promptement, d'Hand, de Fingre, de Maylees.*

Alice. *De Nayles, Madame.*

Kath. *De Nayles, de Arme, de Ilbow.*

Alice. *Sans vostre honeus d'Elbow.*

Kath. *Ainsi de ie d'Elbow, de Nick, & de Sin: coment appelle vous les pied & de roba.*

Alice. *Le Foot Madame, & le Count.*

Kath. *Le Foot, & le Count: O Seignieur Dieu, il sont le mots de son mauvais corruptible grosse & impudique, & non pour le Dames de Honeur d'vser: Ie ne voudray pronouncer ce mots deuant le Seigneurs de France, pour toute le monde, fo le Foot & le Count neant moys, Ie recitera vn autrefoys ma lecon ensembe, d'Hand, de Fingre, de Nayles, d'Arme, d'Elbow, de Nick, de Sin, de Foot, le Count.*

Alice. *Excellent, Madame.*

Kath. *C'est asses pour vne foyes, alons nous a diner.*

                                Exit.

SOURCES OF THE PLAY

Henry V is the ninth and last (if we do not include *Henry VIII*) of the unified series of plays in which Shakespeare dramatizes a memorable succession of events in English history, primarily (*King John* excepted) of the late 14th and the 15th centuries. For it, as for the earlier plays, Shakespeare turned chiefly to the second edition (1587) of Raphael Holinshed's *Chronicles of England, Scotland, and Ireland*. He seems to follow his source more closely for this play than for any of the others—in some places, as in the prolonged airing of Henry's claims to the French throne in I.2, or the listing of the dead after Agincourt in IV.8, versifying Holinshed, phrase by phrase, for many lines at a time. Many of the major scenes of the play—the conspiracy at Southampton, the siege of Harfleur, interchanges at the French court, speeches of Henry to the French herald and to his soldiers, and others—are very close in particular passages to Holinshed's narrative. The selections from the *Chronicles* given in the notes of this edition, however, cannot suggest the unrelaxing alertness of Shakespeare in selecting and organizing details from his source, and the student is urged to consult the full narrative of Henry's reign for himself. Two-thirds of Holinshed's account is concerned with events following Agincourt, but the Prologue to Act

V of *Henry V* leaps from 1415 to 1420, across later campaigns in France, to the negotiations at Troyes, where Shakespeare makes us 'merry with fair Katharine of France,' as the Epilogue of 2 *Henry IV* had promised. Nearly all of the central and varied scene before Agincourt (IV.1) is Shakespeare's invention, and so, of course, are Pistol and his crew (inherited—all but Nym—from *Henry IV*), the four captains fighting under Henry, and, throughout, the dramatic heightening and structuring that have shaped from the stuff of history a work of art.

Holinshed's account is largely based upon Edward Hall's *The Union of the Two Noble and Illustre Families of Lancaster and York*, 1548. Since Holinshed reproduces many entire passages from Hall with scarcely the change of a word, it is frequently impossible to know when Shakespeare is reading directly from the earlier chronicle. But the passage in which the nobles persuade Henry to go to war (I.2), that in which the Constable describes the English soldiers (IV.2), and several other single words, phrases, or lines seem clearly derived from Hall. More important for Shakespeare than these details, however, was Hall's conception of history, which is far more unified and imaginative than that of Holinshed. Hall's viewing of the course of history from the deposition of Richard II through the victories of Henry V, and beyond, as a single movement, involving divine vengeance and human retribution on a grand scale, doubtless aided Shakespeare greatly in his organizing of the diverse materials that lie behind this related series of plays.

At least three incidents in *Henry V*—the gift of the tennis balls, Pistol's capture of the French soldier, and Henry's wooing of Katharine—are possibly indebted to an old play on the life of Henry, surviving in a corrupted form as *The Famous Victories of Henry the Fift*, registered in 1594. A selection from the wooing scene of this play is given below. It is quite possible that Shakespeare consulted a biography of Henry (the *Gesta Henrici Quinti*) written by a chaplain who accompanied him on his first campaign, and another biography with almost the same title written (by the 'Pseudo-Elmham') about thirty years after his death. Shakespeare's possible further indebtedness to the *Brut*, to the Italian chronicler Tito Livio, the French Le Fèvre or Monstrelet, or the English Fabyan is difficult to prove.

A PORTION OF THE WOOING SCENE FROM 'THE FAMOUS VICTORIES OF HENRY THE FIFT.'

Katheren. *And it please your Maiestie,*
   My father sent me to know if you will debate any of these
   Vnreasonable demands which you require:

Hen. 5. *Now trust me Kate,*
   I commend thy fathers wit greatly in this,
   For none in the world could sooner haue made me debate it
   If it were possible:
   But tell me sweete Kate, canst thou tell me how to loue?
Kate. *I cannot hate my good Lord,*
   Therefore far vnfit were it for me to loue.
Hen. 5. *Tush Kate, but tell me in plaine termes,*
   Canst thou loue the King of England?
   I cannot do as these Countries do,
   That spend halfe their time in woing:
   Tush wench, I am none such,
   But wilt thou go ouer to England?
Kate. *I would to God, that I had your Maiestie,*
   As fast in loue, as you haue my father in warres,
   I would not vouchsafe so much as one looke,
   Until you had related all these vnreasonable demands.
Hen. 5. *Tush Kate, I know thou wouldst not vse me so*
   Hardly: but tell me, canst thou loue the king of England?
Kate. *How should I loue him, that hath dealt so hardly*
   With my father.
Hen. 5. *But ile deale as easily with thee,*
   As thy heart can imagine, or tongue can require,
   How saist thou, what will it be?
Kate. *If I were of my owne direction,*
   I could giue you answere;
   But seeing I stand at my fathers direction,
   I must first know his will.
Hen. 5. *But shal I have thy good wil in the mean season?*
Kate. *Whereas I can put your grace in no assurance,*
   I would be loth to put in any dispaire.
Hen. 5. *Now before God, it is a sweete wench.*
                          She goes aside and speaks as followeth
Kat. *I may thinke my selfe the happiest in the world,*
   That is beloued of the mightie King of England.
Hen. 5. *Well Kate, are you at hoast with me?*
   Sweete Kate, tel thy father from me,
   That none in the world could sooner haue perswaded me to
   It then thou, and so tel thy father from me.
Kat. *God keepe your Maiestie in good health.*
                                  Exit KAT.
Hen. 5. *Farwel sweet Kate, in faith, it is a sweet wench,*
   But if I knew I could not haue her fathers good wil,
   I would so rowse the Towers ouer his eares,
   That I would make him be glad to bring her me,
   Upon his hands and knees.
                                Exit KING.

ENTER PROLOGUE

O for a Muse of fire, that would ascend
The brightest heaven of invention,
A kingdom for a stage, princes to act,
And monarchs to behold the swelling scene!
Then should the warlike Harry, like himself,   5
Assume the port of Mars, and at his heels,
Leash'd in like hounds, should famine, sword, and fire
Crouch for employment. But pardon, gentles all,
The flat unraised spirits that hath dar'd
On this unworthy scaffold to bring forth   10
So great an object. Can this cockpit hold
The vasty fields of France? Or may we cram
Within this wooden O the very casques
That did affright the air at Agincourt?
O, pardon! since a crooked figure may   15
Attest in little place a million,
And let us, ciphers to this great accompt,
On your imaginary forces work.
Suppose within the girdle of these walls
Are now confin'd two mighty monarchies,   20
Whose high upreared and abutting fronts
The perilous narrow ocean parts asunder.
Piece out our imperfections with your thoughts.
Into a thousand parts divide one man,
And make imaginary puissance.   25
Think when we talk of horses that you see them
Printing their proud hoofs i' th' receiving earth.
For 'tis your thoughts that now must deck our kings,
Carry them here and there, jumping o'er times,
Turning th' accomplishment of many years   30
Into an hourglass. For the which supply,
Admit me Chorus to this history,
Who prologue-like your humble patience pray
Gently to hear, kindly to judge, our play.   *Exit.*

ACT FIRST ❧ SCENE FIRST

Enter the two Bishops—[the Archbishop] of Canterbury and
[the Bishop of] Ely.

Cant. My lord, I'll tell you. That self bill is urg'd
Which in th' eleventh year of the last king's reign
Was like, and had indeed against us pass'd,
But that the scambling and unquiet time
Did push it out of farther question.   5
    Ely. But how, my lord, shall we resist it now?
    Cant. It must be thought on. If it pass against us,
We lose the better half of our possession.

For all the temporal lands which men devout
By testament have given to the Church   10
Would they strip from us—being valu'd thus:
As much as would maintain to the king's honor
Full fifteen earls and fifteen hundred knights,
Six thousand and two hundred good esquires;
And, to relief of lazars and weak age,   15
Of indigent faint souls past corporal toil,
A hundred almshouses right well supplied;
And to the coffers of the king beside,
A thousand pounds by th' year. Thus runs the bill.
    Ely. This would drink deep.   20
    Cant.   'Twould drink the cup and all.
    Ely. But what prevention?
    Cant. The king is full of grace and fair regard.
    Ely. And a true lover of the holy Church.
    Cant. The courses of his youth promis'd it not.   25
The breath no sooner left his father's body,
But that his wildness, mortified in him,
Seem'd to die too. Yea, at that very moment,
Consideration like an angel came
And whipp'd th' offending Adam out of him,   30
Leaving his body as a paradise
T' envelop and contain celestial spirits.
Never was such a sudden scholar made;
Never came reformation in a flood
With such a heady currance, scouring faults,   35
Nor never Hydra-headed willfulness
So soon did lose his seat, and all at once,
As in this king.
    Ely.   We are blessed in the change.
    Cant. Hear him but reason in divinity,   40
And, all-admiring, with an inward wish
You would desire the king were made a prelate.
Hear him debate of commonwealth affairs,
You would say it hath been all in all his study.
List his discourse of war, and you shall hear   45
A fearful battle rend'red you in music.
Turn him to any cause of policy,
The Gordian knot of it he will unloose,
Familiar as his garter; that, when he speaks,
The air, a charter'd libertine, is still,   50
And the mute wonder lurketh in men's ears
To steal his sweet and honey'd sentences.
So that the art and practic part of life
Must be the mistress to this theoric;
Which is a wonder how his grace should glean it,   55
Since his addiction was to courses vain,
His companies unletter'd, rude, and shallow,
His hours fill'd up with riots, banquets, sports,
And never noted in him any study,
Any retirement, any sequestration   60

SD Prologue; *cf. n.*   **2 invention:** *poetic creation; -ion is frequently dissyllabic, as in 1. 16*   **6 port:** *bearing*   **8 gentles:** *gentle audience*   **9 unraised:** *uninspired* **spirits . . . hath;** *cf. n.*   **10 scaffold:** *stage*   **11 cockpit;** *cf. n.*   **12 vasty:** *vast*   **13 wooden O:** *wooden circle; cf. n.* **casques:** *helmets*   **15 crooked figure;** *cf. n.*   **16 Attest:** *stand for*   **17 accompt:** *means and is pronounced 'account'*   **18 imaginary forces:** *powers of imagination*   **21 abutting fronts** *i.e coasts of Dover and Calais*   **22 perilous** *dissyllabic, and often written 'parlous.'*   **23 Piece out** *supplement*   **25 puissance** *forces, troops (here a trisyllable).*   **27 proud** *spirited*   **28 deck** *equip*   **29 jumping o'er times** *the historical period of the play is 1414–20*   **31 supply** *service*   **1 self:** *same*   **2 eleventh year:** *1410*   **3 like:** *likely (to pass).*   **4 scambling:** *turbulent*   **5 question:** *consideration*   **7–19 It must . . . the bill;** *cf. n.*

9 temporal: *i.e. not used for religious purposes*   **15 lazars:** *diseased beggars, especially lepers*   **16 corporal:** *read 'corp'ral'; cf. n.*   **17 supplied;** *cf. n.*   **23 fair regard:** *kind consideration*   **25 courses . . . youth;** *cf. n.*   **27 mortified:** *killed*   **29 Consideration:** *reflection, spiritual contemplation*   **30 offending Adam;** *cf. n.*   **34 flood;** *cf. n.*   **35 heady currance:** *headlong current*   **36 Hydra-headed:** *the Hydra was a many-headed monster killed by Hercules*   **37 his seat:** *its power*   **40 divinity:** *theology*   **45 List:** *listen to*   **47 cause of policy:** *problem of statecraft*   **49 Familiar:** *as though it were as familiar that: so that*   **50 charter'd libertine:** *one privileged to have freedom*   **51 wonder:** *wonderer*   **52 sentences:** *wise sayings*   **53, 54 art . . . theoric:** *i.e. experience must have taught him theory*   **56 vain:** *idle*   **57 companies:** *companions* **rude:** *uncultivated*   **60 sequestration:** *withdrawal, seclusion*

From open haunts and popularity.

Ely. The strawberry grows underneath the nettle,
And wholesome berries thrive and ripen best
Neighbor'd by fruit of baser quality.
And so the prince obscur'd his contemplation   65
Under the veil of wildness, which, no doubt,
Grew like the summer grass, fastest by night,
Unseen, yet crescive in his faculty.

Cant. It must be so, for miracles are ceas'd,
And therefore we must needs admit the means   70
How things are perfected.

Ely.   But, my good lord,
How now for mitigation of this bill
Urg'd by the Commons? Doth his majesty
Incline to it, or no?   75

Cant.   He seems indifferent,
Or rather swaying more upon our part
Than cherishing th' exhibiters against us.
For I have made an offer to his majesty,
Upon our spiritual convocation   80
And in regard of causes now in hand,
Which I have open'd to his grace at large,
As touching France, to give a greater sum
Than ever at one time the clergy yet
Did to his predecessors part withal.   85

Ely. How did this offer seem receiv'd, my lord?

Cant. With good acceptance of his majesty,
Save that there was not time enough to hear,
As I perceiv'd his grace would fain have done,
The severals and unhidden passages   90
Of his true titles to some certain dukedoms,
And generally to the crown and seat of France,
Deriv'd from Edward, his great-grandfather.

Ely. What was th' impediment that broke this off?

Cant. The French ambassador upon that instant   95
Crav'd audience, and the hour I think is come
To give him hearing. Is it four o'clock?

Ely. It is.

Cant. Then go we in to know his embassy,
Which I could with a ready guess declare   100
Before the Frenchman speak a word of it.

Ely. I'll wait upon you, and I long to hear it.   *Exeunt.*

❧ SCENE SECOND ❧

*Enter the King, Humphrey [Duke of Gloucester], Bedford, Clarence,
Warwick, Westmoreland, and Exeter [with Attendants].*

King. Where is my gracious Lord of Canterbury?

Exe. Not here in presence.

King.   Send for him, good uncle.

West. Shall we call in th' ambassador, my liege?

King. Not yet, my cousin. We would be resolv'd   5

Before we hear him of some things of weight
That task our thoughts, concerning us and France.

*Enter two Bishops [the Archbishop of Canterbury and the Bishop
of Ely].*

Cant. God and his angels guard your sacred throne
And make you long become it!

King.   Sure we thank you.   10
My learned lord, we pray you to proceed
And justly and religiously unfold
Why the law Salic that they have in France
Or should or should not bar us in our claim.
And God forbid, my dear and faithful lord,   15
That you should fashion, wrest, or bow your reading,
Or nicely charge your understanding soul
With opening titles miscreate, whose right
Suits not in native colors with the truth.
For God doth know how many now in health   20
Shall drop their blood in approbation
Of what your reverence shall incite us to.
Therefore take heed how you impawn our person,
How you awake our sleeping sword of war.
We charge you, in the name of God, take heed.   25
For never two such kingdoms did contend
Without much fall of blood, whose guiltless drops
Are every one a woe, a sore complaint
'Gainst him whose wrongs gives edge unto the swords
That makes such waste in brief mortality.   30
Under this conjuration, speak, my lord,
For we will hear, note, and believe in heart
That what you speak is in your conscience wash'd
As pure as sin with baptism.

Cant. Then hear me, gracious sovereign, and you peers,   35
That owe yourselves, your lives, and services
To this imperial throne. There is no bar
To make against your highness' claim to France
But this which they produce from Pharamond:
In terram Salicam mulieres ne succedant—   40
'No woman shall succeed in Salic land.'
Which Salic land the French unjustly gloze
To be the realm of France, and Pharamond
The founder of this law and female bar.
Yet their own authors faithfully affirm   45
That the land Salic is in Germany,
Between the floods of Sala and of Elbe,
Where Charles the Great, having subdu'd the Saxons,
There left behind and settled certain French,
Who, holding in disdain the German women   50
For some dishonest manners of their life,
Establish'd then this law: to wit, no female
Should be inheritrix in Salic land.
Which Salic, as I said, 'twixt Elbe and Sala,
Is at this day in Germany call'd Meissen.   55
Then doth it well appear the Salic law
Was not devised for the realm of France,

---

61 **popularity:** *low company*   65 **contemplation:** *thoughtfulness*   66 **which:** *i.e. his contemplation*   68 **crescive ... faculty:** *increasing in its natural power*   71 **perfected:** *stressed* ‿‒‿   76 **indifferent:** *impartial*   78 **exhibiters:** *i.e. those who sponsored the bill in Parliament*   80 **Upon:** *as a result of*   81 **causes:** *issues*   82 **open'd ... at large:** *set forth in full*   85 **withal:** *with*   90 **severals ... passages:** *details and clear lines of descent*   92 **seat:** *throne*   93 **Edward:** *cf. n.*   94 **impediment:** *interruption*   **SD Clarence:** *does not speak, and appears here only*   **Westmoreland:** *F Westmerland suggests pronunciation.* (F refers throughout to the First Folio of 1623, F2 to the Second Folio, etc.).   5 **cousin:** *Westmoreland married Henry's cousin*   **resolved ... of:** *satisfied about*

7 **task:** *trouble, occupy*   13 **law Salic:** *cf. n.*   14 **Or ... or:** *either ... or*   17 **nicely charge:** *burden with excessive ingenuity*   18 **opening:** *setting forth*   **miscreate:** *falsely fabricated*   19 **in... colors:** *in their essential nature*   21, 22 **in approbation Of:** *in proving the justice of*   23 **impawn:** *pledge*   29 **wrongs:** *wrongful acts*   29, 30 **gives ... makes:** *cf. n.*   30 **mortality:** *human life*   31 **conjuration:** *solemn appeal*   34 **sin:** *original sin*   39 **Pharamond:** *legendary Frankish king*   42 **gloze:** *gloss, interpret*   44 **female bar:** *bar against females*   48 **Charles the Great:** *Charlemagne; cf. n.*   51 **dishonest:** *unchaste*

Nor did the French possess the Salic land
Until four hundred one and twenty years
After defunction of King Pharamond,   *60*
Idly suppos'd the founder of this law,
Who died within the year of our redemption,
Four hundred twenty-six; and Charles the Great
Subdu'd the Saxons and did seat the French
Beyond the River Sala in the year   *65*
Eight hundred five. Besides, their writers say,
King Pepin, which deposed Childeric,
Did, as heir general, being descended
Of Blithild, which was daughter to King Clothair,
Make claim and title to the crown of France.   *70*
Hugh Capet also—who usurp'd the crown
Of Charles the Duke of Lorraine, sole heir male
Of the true line and stock of Charles the Great—
To find his title with some shows of truth,
Though in pure truth it was corrupt and naught,   *75*
Convey'd himself as th' heir to th' Lady Lingare,
Daughter to Charlemagne, who was the son
To Lewis the emperor, and Lewis the son
Of Charles the Great. Also King Lewis the Tenth,
Who was sole heir to the usurper Capet,   *80*
Could not keep quiet in his conscience,
Wearing the crown of France, till satisfied
That fair Queen Isabel, his grandmother,
Was lineal of the Lady Ermengare,
Daughter to Charles the foresaid Duke of Lorraine;   *85*
By which marriage the line of Charles the Great
Was reunited to the crown of France.
So that, as clear as is the summer's sun,
King Pepin's title and Hugh Capet's claim,
King Lewis his satisfaction, all appear   *90*
To hold in right and title of the female.
So do the kings of France unto this day,
Howbeit they would hold up this Salic law
To bar your highness claiming from the female,
And rather choose to hide them in a net   *95*
Than amply to imbare their crooked titles,
Usurp'd from you and your progenitors.
     King. May I with right and conscience make this claim?
     Cant. The sin upon my head, dread sovereign!
For in the Book of Numbers is it writ: *100*
When the man dies, let the inheritance
Descend unto the daughter. Gracious lord,
Stand for your own, unwind your bloody flag,
Look back into your mighty ancestors.
Go, my dread lord, to your great-grandsire's tomb,   *105*
From whom you claim. Invoke his warlike spirit,
And your great-uncle's, Edward the Black Prince,
Who on the French ground play'd a tragedy,
Making defeat on the full power of France,
Whiles his most mighty father on a hill   *110*

Stood smiling to behold his lion's whelp
Forage in blood of French nobility.
O noble English, that could entertain
With half their forces the full pride of France
And let another half stand laughing by,   *115*
All out of work and cold for action!
     Ely. Awake remembrance of these valiant dead,
And with your puissant arm renew their feats.
You are their heir, you sit upon their throne.
The blood and courage that renowned them   *120*
Runs in your veins. And my thrice-puissant liege
Is in the very May morn of his youth,
Ripe for exploits and mighty enterprises.
     Exe. Your brother kings and monarchs of the earth
Do all expect that you should rouse yourself,   *125*
As did the former lions of your blood.
     West. They know your grace hath cause and means and might;
So hath your highness. Never King of England
Had nobles richer and more loyal subjects,   *130*
Whose hearts have left their bodies here in England
And lie pavilion'd in the fields of France.
     Cant. O, let their bodies follow, my dear liege,
With blood and sword and fire to win your right!
In aid whereof we of the spirituality   *135*
Will raise your highness such a mighty sum
As never did the clergy at one time
Bring in to any of your ancestors.
     King. We must not only arm t' invade the French,
But lay down our proportions to defend   *140*
Against the Scot, who will make road upon us
With all advantages.
     Cant. They of those marches, gracious sovereign,
Shall be a wall sufficient to defend
Our inland from the pilfering borderers.   *145*
     King. We do not mean the coursing snatchers only,
But fear the main intendment of the Scot,
Who hath been still a giddy neighbor to us.
For you shall read that my great-grandfather
Never went with his forces into France   *150*
But that the Scot on his unfurnish'd kingdom
Came pouring like the tide into a breach,
With ample and brim fullness of his force,
Galling the gleaned land with hot assays,
Girding with grievous siege castles and towns;   *155*
That England, being empty of defense,
Hath shook and trembled at th' ill neighborhood.
     Cant. She hath been then more fear'd than harm'd, my liege.
For hear her but exampled by herself:
When all her chivalry hath been in France   *160*
And she a mourning widow of her nobles,
She hath herself not only well defended
But taken and impounded as a stray

---

60 defunction: *death*   **68 heir general:** *male or female legal heir*   **74 find:** *provide; Q fine, furbish.* (Q refers throughout to the First Quarto of 1600, Q2 to the Second Quarto, etc.). **shows:** *appearance*   **76 Convey'd:** *falsely represented*   **77 Charlemagne:** *historically Charles the Bald*   **79 Lewis the Tenth:** *read 'Lews'; cf. n.*   **81 conscience:** *trisyllabic*   **84 lineal:** *direct descendant*   **88–104 So that . . . ancestors;** *cf. n.*   **90 Lewis his:** *Lewis'*   **95 hide . . . net:** *hide themselves in transparent deceits or contradictions*   **96 amply to imbare:** *to lay bare completely; cf. n.*   **100 Numbers:** *see Numbers 27:8*   **106 claim:** *i.e. your right*   **109 defeat:** *destruction, at the Battle of Crécy, 1346*

112 Forage in: *prey on*   **113 entertain:** *occupy*   **116 for:** *for want of*   **118 puissant:** *powerful*   **129 hath:** *accented word*   **132 pavilion'd:** *encamped*   **135 spiritualty:** *clergy* (trisyllabic)   **140 lay . . . proportions:** *estimate the required number of troops*   **141 road:** *inroad*   **142 all advantages:** *every favorable opportunity*   **143 marches:** *borders*   **146 coursing snatchers:** *mounted raiders*   **147 intendment:** *intention*   **148 still:** *always* **giddy:** *unstable*   **151 unfurnish'd:** *unprotected*   **154 Galling:** *blistering* **gleaned:** *stripped of its defenders* **assays:** *attacks*   **156 That:** *so that*   **158 fear'd:** *frightened*   **159 exampled by:** *setting a precedent for*   **163 impounded . . . stray:** *put in a pound like a stray animal*

The King of Scots, whom she did send to France
To fill King Edward's fame with prisoner kings   165
And make her chronicle as rich with praise
As is the ooze and bottom of the sea
With sunken wrack and sumless treasuries.

    Ely. But there's a saying very old and true:

    'If that you will France win,   170
    Then with Scotland first begin.'

For once the eagle England being in prey,
To her unguarded nest the weasel Scot
Comes sneaking, and so sucks her princely eggs,
Playing the mouse in absence of the cat,   175
To tame and havoc more than she can eat.

    Exe. It follows then the cat must stay at home.
Yet that is but a crush'd necessity,
Since we have locks to safeguard necessaries
And pretty traps to catch the petty thieves.   180
While that the armed hand doth fight abroad,
Th' advised head defends itself at home.
For government, though high and low and lower,
Put into parts, doth keep in one consent,
Congreeing in a full and natural close,   185
Like music.

    Cant. Therefore doth heaven divide
The state of man in divers functions,
Setting endeavor in continual motion,
To which is fixed as an aim or butt   190
Obedience. For so work the honeybees,
Creatures that by a rule in nature teach
The act of order to a peopled kingdom.
They have a king, and officers of sorts,
Where some like magistrates correct at home,   195
Others like merchants venter trade abroad,
Others like soldiers armed in their stings
Make boot upon the summer's velvet buds,
Which pillage they with merry march bring home
To the tent royal of their emperor;   200
Who, busied in his majesty, surveys
The singing masons building roofs of gold,
The civil citizens kneading up the honey,
The poor mechanic porters crowding in
Their heavy burthens at his narrow gate,   205
The sad-ey'd justice with his surly hum,
Delivering o'er to executors pale
The lazy yawning drone. I this infer,
That many things having full reference
To one consent may work contrariously: 210
As many arrows loosed several ways
Come to one mark; as many ways meet in one town;
As many fresh streams meet in one salt sea;

As many lines close in the dial's center—
So may a thousand actions, once afoot,   215
End in one purpose, and be all well borne
Without defeat. Therefore to France, my liege!
Divide your happy England into four,
Whereof take you one quarter into France,
And you withal shall make all Gallia shake.   220
If we with thrice such powers left at home
Cannot defend our own doors from the dog,
Let us be worried and our nation lose
The name of hardiness and policy.

    King. Call in the messengers sent from the Dolphin.   225

                   [Exeunt some Attendants.]
Now are we well resolv'd, and by God's help
And yours, the noble sinews of our power,
France being ours, we'll bend it to our awe
Or break it all to pieces. Or there we'll sit,
Ruling in large and ample empery   230
O'er France and all her almost kingly dukedoms,
Or lay these bones in an unworthy urn,
Tombless, with no remembrance over them.
Either our history shall with full mouth
Speak freely of our acts, or else our grave,   235
Like Turkish mute, shall have a tongueless mouth,
Not worship'd with a waxen epitaph.

             Enter Ambassadors of France.

Now are we well prepar'd to know the pleasure
Of our fair cousin Dolphin, for we hear
Your greeting is from him, not from the king.   240

    Amb. May't please your majesty to give us leave
Freely to render what we have in charge,
Or shall we sparingly show you far off
The Dolphin's meaning and our embassy?

    King. We are no tyrant, but a Christian king,   245
Unto whose grace our passion is as subject
As is our wretches fett'red in our prisons.
Therefore with frank and with uncurbed plainness
Tell us the Dolphin's mind.

    Amb.   Thus, then, in few: 250
Your highness, lately sending into France,
Did claim some certain dukedoms in the right
Of your great predecessor, King Edward the Third.
In answer of which claim, the prince our master
Says that you savor too much of your youth,   255
And bids you be advis'd. There's nought in France
That can be with a nimble galliard won.
You cannot revel into dukedoms there.
He therefore sends you, meeter for your spirit,
This tun of treasure, and, in lieu of this,   260
Desires you let the dukedoms that you claim
Hear no more of you. This the Dolphin speaks.

    King. What treasure, uncle?

    Exeter.   Tennis balls, my liege.

---

164 King of Scots: *David Bruce*   **166 her:** *F their*   **168 wrack:** *wreck* **sumless:** *inestimable*   **170 France:** *probably dissyllabic*   **172 in prey:** *in search of prey*   **176 tame:** *broach, break into; cf. n.* **havoc:** *destroy*   **177 then:** *F theu*   **178 crush'd:** *forced; Q curst*   **180 pretty:** *good, ingenious; may rhyme with* petty   **181 advised:** *thoughtful*   **184, 185 parts . . . close:** *terms referring to both government and music*   **184 consent:** *harmony (cf. 'concent').*   **185 Congreeing:** *agreeing, harmonizing* **natural:** *read 'nat'ral'* **close:** *cadence*   **188 state of man:** *human life*   **190 butt:** *end, target*   **191 honeybees;** *cf. n.*   **192 rule:** *precept*   **193 act:** *operation*   **194 sorts:** *various ranks*   **195 correct:** *inflict punishment*   **196 venter trade:** *venture upon, speculate in trade*   **198 Make . . . upon:** *plunder*   **203 civil:** *well-behaved*   **206 sad-ey'd:** *sober-looking*   **207 executors:** *executioners; stressed ´ — — ´ —*   **211 loosed . . . ways:** *shot from different directions*

214 dial's: *sundial's*   **216 End:** *Q; F And* **borne:** *carried out*   **220 withal:** *therewith* **Gallia:** *Latin name for France*   **221 powers:** *forces*   **224 policy:** *statesmanship*   **225 Dolphin:** *Dauphin; cf. n.*   **229 Or:** *either*   **230 empery:** *sovereignty*   **232 urn:** *grave*   **236 Turkish mute;** *cf. n.*   **237 worship'd:** *honored* **with . . . epitaph:** *even with an epitaph made out of wax*   **242 render:** *report* **grace:** *merciful disposition*   **247 is:** *see I. Pro. 9; cf. n.*   **250 in few:** *in brief*   **256 be advis'd:** *consider*   **257 galliard:** *a lively dance*   **259 meeter:** *more fitting*   **260 tun:** *cask* **in lieu of:** *in return for*   **264-272 Tennis . . . chases;** *cf. n.*

King. We are glad the Dolphin is so pleasant with us.   265
His present and your pains we thank you for.
When we have match'd our rackets to these balls,
We will in France, by God's grace, play a set
Shall strike his father's crown into the hazard.
Tell him he hath made a match with such a wrangler   270
That all the courts of France will be disturb'd
With chases. And we understand him well,
How he comes o'er us with our wilder days,
Not measuring what use we made of them.
We never valu'd this poor seat of England,   275
And therefore, living hence, did give ourself
To barbarous license, as 'tis ever common
That men are merriest when they are from home.
But tell the Dolphin I will keep my state,
Be like a king, and show my sail of greatness,   280
When I do rouse me in my throne of France.
For that I have laid by my majesty
And plodded like a man for working days.
But I will rise there with so full a glory
That I will dazzle all the eyes of France—   285
Yea, strike the Dolphin blind to look on us.
And tell the pleasant prince this mock of his
Hath turn'd his balls to gunstones, and his soul
Shall stand sore charged for the wasteful vengeance
That shall fly with them. For many a thousand widows   290
Shall this his mock mock out of their dear husbands,
Mock mothers from their sons, mock castles down.
And some are yet ungotten and unborn
That shall have cause to curse the Dolphin's scorn.
But this lies all within the will of God,   295
To whom I do appeal and in whose name,
Tell you the Dolphin, I am coming on,
To venge me as I may and to put forth
My rightful hand in a well-hallow'd cause.
So get you hence in peace. And tell the Dolphin   300
His jest will savor but of shallow wit
When thousands weep more than did laugh at it.
Convey them with safe conduct. Fare you well.

                              Exeunt Ambassadors.

Exeter. This was a merry message.
King. We hope to make the sender blush at it.   305
Therefore, my lords, omit no happy hour
That may give furth'rance to our expedition.
For we have now no thought in us but France,
Save those to God, that run before our business.
Therefore let our proportions for these wars   310
Be soon collected, and all things thought upon
That may with reasonable swiftness add
More feathers to our wings. For, God before,
We'll chide this Dolphin at his father's door.
Therefore let every man now task his thought,   315
That this fair action may on foot be brought.

                              Exeunt.

ACT SECOND ❧

Flourish. Enter Chorus.

Now all the youth of England are on fire,
And silken dalliance in the wardrobe lies.
Now thrive the armorers, and honor's thought
Reigns solely in the breast of every man.
They sell the pasture now to buy the horse,   5
Following the mirror of all Christian kings
With winged heels, as English Mercuries.
For now sits Expectation in the air
And hides a sword from hilts unto the point
With crowns imperial, crowns and coronets,   10
Promis'd to Harry and his followers.
The French, advis'd by good intelligence
Of this most dreadful preparation,
Shake in their fear and with pale policy
Seek to divert the English purposes.   15
O England! model to thy inward greatness,
Like little body with a mighty heart,
What mightst thou do that honor would thee do,
Were all thy children kind and natural!
But see, thy fault France hath in thee found out,   20
A nest of hollow bosoms, which he fills
With treacherous crowns. And three corrupted men—
One, Richard Earl of Cambridge, and the second,
Henry Lord Scroop of Masham, and the third,
Sir Thomas Grey, knight, of Northumberland—   25
Have, for the gilt of France—O, guilt indeed!—
Confirm'd conspiracy with fearful France.
And by their hands this grace of kings must die,
If hell and treason hold their promises,
Ere he take ship for France, and in Southampton.   30
Linger your patience on, and we'll digest
Th' abuse of distance, force a play.
The sum is paid, the traitors are agreed,
The king is set from London, and the scene
Is not transported, gentles, to Southampton.   35
There is the playhouse now, there must you sit,
And thence to France shall we convey you safe
And bring you back, charming the narrow seas
To give you gentle pass. For, if we may,
We'll not offend one stomach with our play.   40
But till the king come forth, and not till then,
Unto Southampton do we shift our scene.   *Exit.*

---

265 **pleasant:** *facetious*   268–272 **set . . . chases;** *cf. n.*   270 **he hath:** *read 'he'th'*   273 **comes o'er:** *taunts*   275 **seat:** *throne*   276 **hence:** *away from the court*   279 **state:** *chair of state, dignity*   282 **For that:** *to that end*   288 **gunstones:** *cannon balls, originally*   289 **wasteful:** *devastating*   293 **ungotten:** *unbegotten*   298 **venge me:** *avenge myself*   303 **Convey:** *escort*   306 **omit:** *neglect* **happy:** *favorable*   310 **proportions:** *forces*   313 **God before:** *God leading us*   315 **task his thought:** *take careful thought*

SD Flourish *music of trumpets; cf. n.*   2 **silken dalliance:** *the clothes and manners of society*   6 **mirror:** *perfect pattern*   7 **winged . . . Mercuries;** *cf. n.*   9 **hilts:** *crosspiece protecting the handle*   12 **intelligence:** *espionage*   14 **pale policy:** *diplomacy directed by fear*   16 **model to:** *small replica of*   18 **would thee do:** *would have thee do*   19 **kind:** *showing filial love*   20 **see . . . hath:** *many editors read 'see thy fault! France hath'* **France:** *King of France*   22 **crowns:** *crown pieces, gold*   26 **gilt . . . guilt;** *common pun in Shakespeare, gilt meaning 'gold'*   28 **grace of kings:** *one who dignifies the role of kingship*   31-2 **digest . . . abuse:** *overcome the problem*   32 **force:** *stuff out, or make a play in spite of difficulties*   39 **pass:** *passage*   39-40 **For . . . play;** *cf. n.*   39 **may:** *can help it*   40 **offend one stomach:** *offend anyone's taste, or make anyone seasick*   41-2 **But . . . scene:** *the scene will be shifted to Southampton when the king comes forth (scene 2).*

❧ SCENE FIRST ❧

Enter Corporal Nym and Lieutenant Bardolph

Bard. Well met, Corporal Nym.

Nym. Good morrow, Lieutenant Bardolph.

Bard. What, are Ancient Pistol and you friends yet?

Nym. For my part, I care not. I say little. But when time
shall serve, there shall be smiles—but that shall be as it　　5
may. I dare not fight, but I will wink and hold out mine
iron. It is a simple one, but what though? It will toast
cheese, and it will endure cold, as another man's sword will,
and there's an end.

Bard. I will bestow a breakfast to make you friends, and　10
we'll be all three sworn brothers to France. Let's be so, good
Corporal Nym.

Nym. Faith, I will live so long as I may, that's the certain of
it. And when I cannot live any longer, I will do as I may.
That is my rest, that is the rendezvous of it.　　15

Bard. It is certain, corporal, that he is married to Nell
Quickly, and certainly she did you wrong, for you were troth-
plight to her.

Nym. I cannot tell. Things must be as they may. Men may
sleep, and they may have their throats about them at that　20
time, and some say knives have edges. It must be as it may.
Though patience be a tired mare, yet she will plod. There
must be conclusions. Well, I cannot tell.

Enter Pistol and [Hostess] Quickly.

Bard. Here comes Ancient Pistol and his wife. Good corporal, be patient here. How now, mine host Pistol?　　25

Pist: Base tyke, call'st thou me host?
Now by this hand I swear I scorn the term,
Nor shall my Nell keep lodgers.

Host. No, by my troth, not long. For we cannot lodge and
board a dozen or fourteen gentlewomen that live honestly by　30
the prick of their needles, but it will be thought we keep a
bawdy house straight. *[Nym and Pistol draw.]* O welladay,
Lady! If he be not hewn now, we shall see willful adultery and
murther committed.

Bard. Good lieutenant! Good corporal! Offer nothing here.　35

Nym. Pish!

Pist. Pish for thee, Iceland dog! Thou prick-ear'd cur of
Iceland!

Host. Good Corporal Nym, show thy valor, and put up
your sword.　　40

Nym. Will you shog off? I would have you solus.

Pist. 'Solus,' egregious dog? O viper vile!
The 'solus' in thy most mervailous face,
The 'solus' in thy teeth, and in thy throat,
And in thy hateful lungs—yea, in thy maw, perdy,　　45
And, which is worse, within thy nasty mouth!
I do retort the 'solus' in thy bowels,

For I can take, and Pistol's cock is up,
And flashing fire will follow.

Nym. I am not Barbason; you cannot conjure me. I　　50
have an humor to knock you indifferently well. If you grow
foul with me, Pistol, I will scour you with my rapier, as I
may, in fair terms. If you would walk off, I would prick
your guts a little, in good terms, as I may, and that's the
humor of it.　　55

Pist. O braggart vile, and damned furious wight!
The grave doth gape and doting death is near.
Therefore exhale.

Bard. Hear me, hear me what I say. He that strikes the first
stroke, I'll run him up to the hilts, as I am a soldier.　　60

[Draws.]

Pist. An oath of mickle might, and fury shall abate.
Give me thy fist, thy forefoot to me give.
Thy spirits are most tall.

Nym. I will cut thy throat one time or other in fair terms,
that is the humor of it.　　65

Pist. 'Couple a gorge!'
That is the word. I thee defy again.
O hound of Crete, think'st thou my spouse to get?
No, to the spital go,
And from the powd'ring tub of infamy　　70
Fetch forth the lazar kite of Cressid's kind,
Doll Tearsheet, she by name, and her espouse.
I have, and I will hold, the quondam Quickly
For the only she, and—pauca, there's enough.
Go to!　　75

Enter the Boy.

Boy. Mine host Pistol, you must come to my master, and
your hostess. He is very sick and would to bed. Good Bardolph, put thy face between his sheets and do the office of a
warming pan. Faith, he's very ill.

Bard. Away, you rogue!　　80

Host. By my troth, he'll yield the crow a pudding one of
these days. The king has kill'd his heart. Good husband, come
home presently.　　　　　　　　　　　　　　　*Exit [with Boy].*

Bard. Come, shall I make you two friends? We must to
France together. Why the divel should we keep knives to cut　85
one another's throats?

Pist. Let floods o'erswell, and fiends for food howl on!

Nym. You'll pay me the eight shillings I won of you at
betting?

Pist. Base is the slave that pays.　　90

Nym. That now I will have. That's the humor of it.

Pist. As manhood shall compound. Push home.

[They] draw.

Bard. By this sword, he that makes the first thrust, I'll kill
him! By this sword, I will.

---

1 Nym: *the name means 'steal and 'thief'*　**3 Ancient:** *ensign, second lieutenant*　**6 wink:**
keep my eyes closed　**iron:** *sword*　**11 sworn brothers:** *comical allusion to knightly brethren
in arms*　**13 may:** *can*　**15 rest:** *resolve*　**rendezvous:** *refuge, last resort*　**16, 17 Nell
Quickly;** *cf. n.*　**17, 18 trothplight:** *formally bethrothed*　**22 Though . . . plod;**
cf. n.　**mare:** *Q; F name*　**26 tyke:** *cur; cf. n.*　**host:** *tavernkeeper*　**30 honestly:**
chastely　**32 Nym . . . draw:** *perhaps only Nym draws here*　**welladay:** *wellaway*　**Lady:** *by
Our Lady*　**33 hewn:** *cut down; many editors read* drawn　**37 Iceland . . . cur:** *lap dogs
with sharp erect ears*　**41 shog off:** *move off*　**solus:** *alone (Pistol thinks it an insult and
rants like a conjuror).*　**42 egregious:** *in the highest degree*　**43 mervailous;** *marvelous;
here stressed —́—*　**45 maw:** *stomach*　**perdy:** *by God, indeed*

48 take: *strike; catch fire; bewitch*　**Pistol's cock:** *lever on a gun; cf. n.*　**50 I am . . . me
I:** *cannot be called up and dismissed like a fiend*　**51 indifferently:** *fairly*　**52 scour:**
thrash; clean out a pistol　**53 in fair terms:** *in good style*　**55 humor;** *cf. n.*　**58
exhale:** *draw your sword; die*　**SD Draws:** *Q They drawe*　**61 mickle:** *great*　**63 tall:**
courageous　**66 Couple a gorge:** *Pistol's French for* couper la gorge, *'to cut the throat'*　**67
thee defy:** *Q; F* defie thee　**69-73 No . . . espouse;** *cf. n.*　**69 spital:** *hospital*　**70
powd'ring tub:** *i.e. for curing venereal diseases by sweating*　**71 lazar . . . kind;** *cf. n.*　**73
quondam:** *former (now Mistress Pistol).*　**74 only she:** *only woman for me*　**pauca:** *in
few words*　**74, 75 enough. Go to:** *F* enough to go to　**77 your many editors read*
you,　**78, 79 face . . . pan;** *cf. n.*　**81 he'll . . . pudding:** *the boy will be hanged and
devoured by crows (proverbial).*　**82 kill'd his heart;** *cf. n.*　**83 presently:** *immediately*　**85 divel;** *cf. n.*　**92 compound:** *come to terms*

Pist. 'Sword' is an oath, and oaths must have their course.   *95*

Bard. Corporal Nym, an thou wilt be friends, be friends. An thou wilt not, why then be enemies with me too. Prithee put up.

[*Nym.* I shall have my eight shillings I won of you at betting?]   *100*

Pist. A noble shalt thou have, and present pay,
And liquor likewise will I give to thee,
And friendship shall combine, and brotherhood.
I'll live by Nym, and Nym shall live by me.
Is not this just? For I shall sutler be   *105*
Unto the camp, and profits will accrue.
Give me thy hand.

Nym. I shall have my noble?

Pist. In cash, most justly paid.

Nym. Well then, that's the humor of't.   *110*

Enter Hostess.

Host. As ever you come of women, come in quickly to Sir John. Ah, poor heart! he is so shak'd of a burning quotidian tertian that it is most lamentable to behold. Sweet men, come to him.

Nym. The king hath run bad humors on the knight, that's   *115*
the even of it.

Pist. Nym, thou hast spoke the right.
His heart is fracted and corroborate.

Nym. The king is a good king, but it must be as it may.
He passes some humors and careers.   *120*

Pist. Let us condole the knight, for, lambkins, we will live.

[Exeunt.]

❧ Scene Second ❧

Enter Exeter, Bedford, and Westmoreland.

Bedford. 'Fore God, his grace is bold to trust these traitors.

Exe. They shall be apprehended by and by.

West. How smooth and even they do bear themselves,
As if allegiance in their bosoms sat,
Crowned with faith and constant loyalty!   *5*

Bedford. The king hath note of all that they intend,
By interception which they dream not of.

Exe. Nay, but the man that was his bedfellow,
Whom he hath dull'd and cloy'd with gracious favors—
That he should for a foreign purse so sell   *10*
His sovereign's life to death and treachery!

Sound trumpets. Enter the King, Scroop, Cambridge, and Grey [with Attendants].

King. Now sits the wind fair, and we will aboard.
My Lord of Cambridge, and my kind Lord of Masham,
And you, my gentle knight, give me your thoughts.
Think you not that the pow'rs we bear with us   *15*
Will cut their passage through the force of France,

Doing the execution and the act
For which we have in head assembled them?

Scroop. No doubt, my liege, if each man do his best.

King. I doubt not that, since we are well persuaded   *20*
We carry not a heart with us from hence
That grows not in a fair consent with ours,
Nor leave not one behind that doth not wish
Success and conquest to attend on us.

Cam. Never was monarch better fear'd and lov'd   *25*
Than is your majesty. There's not, I think, a subject
That sits in heart-grief and uneasiness
Under the sweet shade of your government.

Grey. True. Those that were your father's enemies
Have steep'd their galls in honey and do serve you   *30*
With hearts create of duty and of zeal.

King. We therefore have great cause of thankfulness
And shall forget the office of our hand
Sooner than quittance of desert and merit
According to the weight and worthiness.   *35*

Scroop. So service shall with steeled sinews toil,
And labor shall refresh itself with hope
To do your grace incessant services.

King. We judge no less. Uncle of Exeter,
Enlarge the man committed yesterday   *40*
That rail'd against our person. We consider
It was excess of wine that set him on,
And on his more advice we pardon him.

Scroop. That's mercy, but too much security.
Let him be punish'd, sovereign, lest example   *45*
Breed, by his sufferance, more of such a kind.

King. O, let us yet be merciful!

Cam. So may your highness, and yet punish too.

Grey. Sir,
You show great mercy if you give him life,   *50*
After the taste of much correction.

King. Alas, your too much love and care of me
Are heavy orisons 'gainst this poor wretch!
If little faults, proceeding on distemper,
Shall not be wink'd at, how shall we stretch our eye   *55*
When capital crimes, chew'd, swallow'd, and digested,
Appear before us? We'll yet enlarge that man,
Though Cambridge, Scroop, and Grey, in their dear care
And tender preservation of our person,
Would have him punish'd. And now to our French causes.   *60*
Who are the late commissioners?

Cam. I one, my lord.
Your highness bade me ask for it today.

Scroop. So did you me, my liege.

Grey. And I, my royal sovereign.   *65*

King. Then, Richard Earl of Cambridge, there is yours,
There yours, Lord Scroop of Masham, and, Sir Knight,
Grey of Northumberland, this same is yours.
Read them, and know I know your worthiness.
My Lord of Westmoreland and Uncle Exeter,   *70*

95 an: *if;* F (frequently) &   97, 98 put up: *sheathe your sword*   99, 100 I ... betting: Q: *not in* F   101 noble; *cf. n.*   104 by Nym: *i.e. by thievery*   105 sutler: *one who sells provisions and liquor to an army*   110 that's: F *that*   112, 113 quotidian tertian; *cf. n.*   115 run ... humors: *vented his ill humor*   118 fracted: *broken; cf. n.*   120 passes ... careers; *cf. n.*   2 apprehended ... by: *arrested: very soon*   7 interception: *i.e. by intercepting their communications*   8 bedfellow: *bosom friend* (Scroop).   15 pow'rs: *forces;* F powres

18 in head: *in an armed force*   22 grows ... consent: *is not in agreement*   29 Grey: F Kni [ght]   30 galls: *bitterness, resentment*   31 create: *made*   33 office: *use*   34 quittance of: *recompense for*   40 Enlarge: *release*   43 his more advice: *his thinking better of it, or our further consideration about him.*   44 security: *carelessness, overconfidence*   46 his sufferance: *i.e. letting him go without punishment*   49 Sir: F prints with l. 50   53 orisons: *prayers*   54 distemper: *i.e. drunkenness*   55 wink'd at: *overlooked*   stretch our eye: *open our eyes sufficiently wide*   57 yet: *nevertheless*   61 late: *lately appointed*   63 it: *i.e. an appointment as commissioner*

We will aboard tonight. Why, how now, gentlemen!
What see you in those papers that you lose
So much complexion? Look ye how they change!
Their cheeks are paper. Why, what read you there,
That have so cowarded and chas'd your blood   75
Out of appearance?
    Cam.   I do confess my fault,
And do submit me to your highness' mercy.
    Grey, Scroop. To which we all appeal.
    King. The mercy that was quick in us but late   80
By your own counsel is suppress'd and kill'd.
You must not dare, for shame, to talk of mercy,
For your own reasons turn into your bosoms
As dogs upon their masters, worrying you.
See you, my princes and my noble peers,   85
These English monsters! My Lord of Cambridge here,
You know how apt our love was to accord
To furnish him with all appertinents
Belonging to his honor. And this man
Hath, for a few light crowns, lightly conspir'd   90
And sworn unto the practices of France
To kill us here in Hampton. To the which
This knight, no less for bounty bound to us
Than Cambridge is, hath likewise sworn. But O,
What shall I say to thee, Lord Scroop—thou cruel,   95
Ingrateful, savage, and inhuman creature?
Thou that didst bear the key of all my counsels,
That knew'st the very bottom of my soul,
That almost mightst have coin'd me into gold—
Wouldst thou have practic'd on me for thy use?   100
May it be possible that foreign hire
Could out of thee extract one spark of evil
That might annoy my finger? 'Tis so strange
That, though the truth of it stands off as gross
As black and white, my eye will scarcely see it.   105
Treason and murther ever kept together,
As two yoke-divels sworn to either's purpose,
Working so grossly in a natural cause
That admiration did not whoop at them.
But thou, 'gainst all proportion, didst bring in   110
Wonder to wait on treason and on murther.
And whatsoever cunning fiend it was
That wrought upon thee so preposterously
Hath got the voice in hell for excellence.
All other divels that suggest by treasons   115
Do botch and bungle up damnation
With patches, colors, and with forms being fetch'd
From glist'ring semblances of piety.
But he that temper'd thee bade thee stand up,
Gave thee no instance why thou shouldst do treason,   120
Unless to dub thee with the name of traitor.
If that same demon that hath gull'd thee thus

Should with his lion gait walk the whole world,
He might return to vasty Tartar back
And tell the legions 'I can never win   125
A soul so easy as that Englishman's.'
O, how hast thou with jealousy infected
The sweetness of affiance! Show men dutiful?
Why, so didst thou. Seem they grave and learned?
Why, so didst thou. Come they of noble family?   130
Why, so didst thou. Seem they religious?
Why, so didst thou. Or are they spare in diet,
Free from gross passion or of mirth or anger,
Constant in spirit, not swerving with the blood;
Garnish'd and deck'd in modest complement,   135
Not working with the eye without the ear,
And but in purged judgment trusting neither?
Such and so finely bolted didst thou seem.
And thus thy fall hath left a kind of blot
To mark the full-fraught man and best indu'd   140
With some suspicion. I will weep for thee.
For this revolt of thine, methinks, is like
Another fall of man. Their faults are open.
Arrest them to the answer of the law,
And God acquit them of their practices!   145
    Exe. I arrest thee of high treason, by the name of Richard
Earl of Cambridge.
I arrest thee of high treason, by the name of Henry Lord
Scroop of Masham.
I arrest thee of high treason, by the name of Thomas Grey,   150
knight, of Northumberland.
    Scroop. Our purposes God justly hath discover'd,
And I repent my fault more than my death,
Which I beseech your highness to forgive,
Although my body pay the price of it.   155
    Cam. For me, the gold of France did not seduce,
Although I did admit it as a motive,
The sooner to effect what I intended.
But God be thanked for prevention,
Which I in sufferance heartily will rejoice,   160
Beseeching God and you to pardon me.
    Grey. Never did faithful subject more rejoice
At the discovery of most dangerous treason
Than I do at this hour joy o'er myself,
Prevented from a damned enterprise.   165
My fault, but not my body, pardon, sovereign.
    King. God quit you in his mercy! Hear your sentence.
You have conspir'd against our royal person,
Join'd with an enemy proclaim'd, and from his coffers
Receiv'd the golden earnest of our death.   170
Wherein you would have sold your king to slaughter,
His princes and his peers to servitude,
His subjects to oppression and contempt,
And his whole kingdom into desolation.
Touching our person, seek we no revenge,   175

---

80 quick: *alive* **83 reasons:** *arguments* **87 accord:** *consent* **88 him:** *F2; not in F* **appertinents:** *appurtenances* **90 lightly:** *thoughtlessly, easily* **91 practices:** *plots* **92 Hampton:** *Southampton* **93 for bounty:** *i.e. for our bounty to him* **97 counsels:** *secrets* **100 practic'd . . . use:** *used me for your own purposes (Scroop had been treasurer).* **101 May:** *can* **103 annoy my finger:** *hurt even my finger* **104 gross:** *obvious, flagrant* **108 Working . . . cause:** *working together so obviously in a cause natural for them* **109 admiration:** *wonder,* **whoop:** *cry out; F* hoope **110 proportion:** *natural order* **113 preposterously:** *monstrously, unnaturally* **114 voice:** *vote* **115 All:** *F* And **115-118 suggest . . . piety;** *cf. n.* **119 temper'd:** *molded* **stand up:** *i.e. take up treason boldly* **121 dub:** *confer knighthood upon (ironical).* **122 gull'd:** *deceived*

123 lion gait: *see 1 Peter 5:8* **124 Tartar:** *Tartarus, hell* **127 jealousy:** *suspicion* **128 affiance:** *trust, allegiance* **Show:** *appear* **128-141 Show . . . suspicion;** *cf. n.* **131 religious:** *(four syllables).* **133 or . . . or:** *either . . . or* **134 blood:** *passions* **135 modest complement:** *outward appearance of modesty* **137 purged:** *free from whim or partiality* **138 bolted:** *sifted, like flower from bran* **140 mark the:** *F* make thee **full-fraught:** *fully furnished* **indu'd:** *endowed* **148 Henry:** *Q; F* Thomas **149 Masham:** *F.* Marsham **159 prevention:** *forestallment (four syllables).* **160 I:** *F2; not in F* **sufferance:** *suffering (death); cf. n.* **167 quit:** *absolve* **168–182 You have . . . hence;** *cf. n.* **170 earnest:** *partial payment given on account of services to be rendered*

But we our kingdom's safety must so tender,
Whose ruin you have sought, that to her laws
We do deliver you. Get you therefore hence,
Poor miserable wretches, to your death,
The taste whereof God of his mercy give   *180*
You patience to endure and true repentance
Of all your dear offenses! Bear them hence.

      Exeunt [Scroop, Cambridge, and Grey, guarded].

Now, lords, for France, the enterprise whereof
Shall be to you as us, like glorious.   *185*
We doubt not of a fair and lucky war,
Since God so graciously hath brought to light
This dangerous treason lurking in our way
To hinder our beginnings. We doubt not now
But every rub is smoothed on our way.   *190*
Then forth, dear countrymen. Let us deliver
Our puissance into the hand of God,
Putting it straight in expedition.
Cheerly to sea, the signs of war advance!
No King of England, if not King of France!   *195*

        Flourish. [Exeunt.]

❧ SCENE THIRD ❧

Enter Pistol, Nym, Bardolph, Boy, and Hostess.

Host. Prithee, honey-sweet husband, let me bring thee to
Staines.

Pist. No, for my manly heart doth earn.
Bardolph, be blithe. Nym, rouse thy vaunting veins. Boy, bristle thy courage up; for Falstaff he is dead, And we must *5*
earn therefore.

Bard. Would I were with him, wheresome'er he is, either in
heaven or in hell!

Host. Nay, sure, he's not in hell. He's in Arthur's bosom, if
ever man went to Arthur's bosom. A' made a finer end, *10*
and went away an it had been any christome child. A' parted
ev'n just between twelve and one, ev'n at the turning o' th'
tide. For after I saw him fumble with the sheets, and play with
flowers, and smile upon his finger's end, I knew there was but
one way. For his nose was as sharp as a pen, and a' babbled *15*
of green fields. 'How now, Sir John!' quoth I. 'What, man! Be
o' good cheer.' So a' cried out 'God, God, God!' three or four
times. Now I, to comfort him, bid him a' should not think of
God; I hop'd there was no need to trouble himself with any
such thoughts yet. So a' bade me lay more clothes on his *20*
feet. I put my hand into the bed and felt them, and they were
as cold as any stone. Then I felt to his knees, and so upward
and upward, and all was as cold as any stone.

Nym. They say he cried out of sack.

Host. Ay, that a' did. *25*

Bard. And of women.

Host. Nay, that a' did not.

Boy. Yes, that a' did, and said they were devils incarnate.

Host. A' could never abide carnation. 'Twas a color he never
lik'd. *30*

Boy. A' said once the devil would have him about women.

Host. A' did in some sort, indeed, handle women; but then
he was rheumatic, and talk'd of the whore of Babylon.

Boy. Do you not remember a' saw a flea stick upon Bardolph's nose, and a' said it was a black soul burning in hell? *35*

Bard. Well, the fuel is gone that maintain'd that fire. That's
all the riches I got in his service.

Nym. Shall we shog? The king will be gone from
Southampton.

Pist. Come, let's away. My love, give me thy lips. *40*
Look to my chattels and my movables.
Let senses rule. The word is 'Pitch and pay.'
Trust none;
For oaths are straws, men's faiths are wafer cakes,
And hold-fast is the only dog, my duck. *45*
Therefore Caveto be thy counselor.
Go, clear thy crystals. Yoke-fellows in arms,
Let us to France, like horseleeches, my boys,
To suck, to suck, the very blood to suck!

Boy. And that's but unwholesome food, they say. *50*

Pist. Touch her soft mouth, and march.

Bard. Farewell, Hostess.   *[Kissing her.]*

Nym. I cannot kiss, that is the humor of it. But adieu.

Pist. Let huswifery appear. Keep close, I thee command.

Host. Farewell, adieu.   *Exeunt.* *55*

❧ SCENE FOURTH ❧

*Flourish. Enter the French King, the Dolphin, the Dukes of Berri
and Britaine [, the Constable, and others].*

King. Thus comes the English with full pow'r upon us,
And more than carefully it us concerns
To answer royally in our defenses.
Therefore the Dukes of Berri and of Britaine,
Of Brabant and of Orleans, shall make forth, *5*
And you, Prince Dolphin, with all swift dispatch,
To line and new repair our towns of war
With men of courage and with means defendant.
For England his approaches makes as fierce
As waters to the sucking of a gulf. *10*
It fits us then to be as provident
As fear may teach us out of late examples
Left by the fatal and neglected English
Upon our fields.

Dol.   My most redoubted father, *15*
It is most meet we arm us 'gainst the foe,
For peace itself should not so dull a kingdom,

176 tender: *cherish* **177 have:** *Q; not in F* **182 dear:** *often an intensive, 'serious'* **185
like:** *alike* **186 fair:** *fortunate* **190 rub:** *obstacle (figure from bowling)* **192 puissance:** *forces (trisyllabic)* **193 straight in expedition:** *immediately in motion* **expedition:**
five syllables **194 signs:** *standards* **2 Staines:** *commonly the first stop on the road to
Southampton* **3-6 No . . . therefore:** *F prints this and ll. 40-49 as prose* **6 earn:**
grieve **9 Arthur's bosom:** *The Hostess mistakes Arthur's bosom for Abraham's (heaven); see
Luke 16:22* **10 A':** *he cf. n.* **11 an:** *as if* **christome:** *chrisom, just christened, entirely
innocent; cf.n.* **14 finger's end:** *F* fingers end; *most editors read* fingers' end *or* ends
(Q) **15 a' babbled . . . fields;** *cf.n.* **22 knees:** *Q adds* 'and they were as cold as any
stone' **upward:** *F.* vp-peer'd, *and* vpward, *suggests pronunciation* **26 of:** *against* **sack:**
a white wine; cf. n.

33 rheumatic: *probably she means 'lunatic'; F* rumatique; *stressed* ́ — — **whore of Babylon:** *the 'scarlet woman' of Revelations 17; the Church of Rome (Romeatic)* **38 shog:** *move
on* **41 movables:** *furniture, possessions* **42 senses:** *common sense* **word:** *Q; F*
world **Pitch and pay:** *i.e. cash down* **45 hold-fast:** *from the old proverb 'Brag is a good
dog, but Hold-fast is better'* **46 Caveto:** *caution; Q* cophetua **47 crystals:** *eyes* **52
Farwell:** *farewell* **54 huswifery:** *housewifery, good management (pronounced 'húzzifry')*
Keep: *close stay at home* **SD Flourish:** *trumpet fanfare* **Constable:** *here the chief military
officer of France* **7 line:** *strengthen* **8 means defendant:** *means of defense* **10 gulf:**
whirlpool **12 late examples:** *battles at Crécy and Poitiers See ll. 56-67 below* **13 fatal
and neglected:** *fatally underrated* **15 redoubted:** *feared*

Though war nor no known quarrel were in question,
But that defenses, musters, preparations
Should be maintain'd, assembled, and collected   20
As were a war in expectation.
Therefore I say 'tis meet we all go forth
To view the sick and feeble parts of France.
And let us do it with no show of fear—
No, with no more than if we heard that England   25
Were busied with a Whitsun morris dance.
For, my good liege, she is so idly king'd,
Her scepter so fantastically borne,
By a vain, giddy, shallow, humorous youth,
That fear attends her not.   30
     Con.   O, peace, Prince Dolphin!
You are too much mistaken in this king.
Question your grace the late ambassadors,
With what great state he heard their embassy,
How well supplied with noble councilors,   35
How modest in exception, and withal
How terrible in constant resolution,
And you shall find his vanities forespent
Were but the outside of the Roman Brutus,
Covering discretion with a coat of folly,   40
As gardeners do with ordure hide those roots
That shall first spring and be most delicate.
     Dol. Well, 'tis not so, my Lord High Constable,
But though we think it so, it is no matter.
In cases of defense 'tis best to weigh   45
The enemy more mighty than he seems.
So the proportions of defense are fill'd,
Which of a weak and niggardly projection
Doth like a miser spoil his coat with scanting
A little cloth.   50
     King.   Think we King Harry strong,
And, princes, look you strongly arm to meet him.
The kindred of him hath been flesh'd upon us,
And he is bred out of that bloody strain
That haunted us in our familiar paths.   55
Witness our too much memorable shame
When Cressy battle fatally was struck,
And all our princes captiv'd by the hand
Of that black name, Edward, Black Prince of Wales,
Whiles that his mountain sire, on mountain standing,   60
Up in the air, crown'd with the golden sun,
Saw his heroical seed, and smil'd to see him
Mangle the work of nature and deface
The patterns that by God and by French fathers
Had twenty years been made. This is a stem   65
Of that victorious stock, and let us fear
The native mightiness and fate of him.

Enter a Messenger.

     Mess. Ambassadors from Harry King of England
Do crave admittance to your majesty.

     King. We'll give them present audience. Go, and bring   70
them.   *[Exeunt Messenger and certain Lords.]*
You see this chase is hotly follow'd, friends.
     Dol. Turn head and stop pursuit. For coward dogs
Most spend their mouths when what they seem to threaten
Runs far before them. Good my sovereign,   75
Take up the English short, and let them know
Of what a monarchy you are the head.
Self-love, my liege, is not so vile a sin
As self-neglecting.

Enter [Lords, with] Exeter [and train].

     King.   From our brother of England?   80
     Exe. From him, and thus he greets your majesty:
He wills you, in the name of God Almighty,
That you divest yourself and lay apart
The borrow'd glories that by gift of heaven,
By law of nature and of nations, 'longs   85
To him and to his heirs—namely, the crown
And all wide-stretched honors that pertain
By custom and the ordinance of times
Unto the crown of France. That you may know
'Tis no sinister nor no awkward claim,   90
Pick'd from the wormholes of long-vanish'd days,
Nor from the dust of old oblivion rak'd,
He sends you this most memorable line,
In every branch truly demonstrative,
Willing you overlook this pedigree.   95
And when you find him evenly deriv'd
From his most fam'd of famous ancestors,
Edward the Third, he bids you then resign
Your crown and kingdom, indirectly held
From him, the native and true challenger.   100
     King. Or else what follows?
     Exe. Bloody constraint, for if you hide the crown
Even in your hearts, there will he rake for it.
Therefore in fierce tempest is he coming,
In thunder and in earthquake, like a Jove,   105
That, if requiring fail, he will compel.
And bids you, in the bowels of the Lord,
Deliver up the crown, and to take mercy
On the poor souls for whom this hungry war
Opens his vasty jaws, and on your head   110
Turning the widows' tears, the orphans' cries,
The dead men's blood, the pining maidens' groans,
For husbands, fathers, and betrothed lovers
That shall be swallow'd in this controversy.
This is his claim, his threat'ning, and my message,   115
Unless the Dolphin be in presence here,
To whom expressly I bring greeting too.
     King. For us, we will consider of this further.
Tomorrow shall you bear our full intent
Back to our brother of England.   120

---

21 **expectation:** *five syllables*   26 **Whitsun . . . dance;** *cf. n.*   27 **idly king'd:** *i.e. has so frivolous a king*   29 **humorous:** *capricious*   36 **exception:** *disagreement*   37 **constant:** *firm*   38 **forespent:** *former*   39 **Brutus;** *cf. n.*   41 **ordure:** *manure*   47 **proportions . . . fill'd:** *numbers necessary for defense are completed*   48 **of a weak . . . projection:** *if they are estimated on too small a scale*   53 **flesh'd:** *aroused by the first taste of blood, or initiated in fighting* (against us).   57 **Cressy battle:** *the victory of Edward III over the French at Crécy in 1346; cf. n.* **struck:** *fought*   60 **mountain sire:** *mighty sire* (or born among the mountains), *Edward III*   67 **native . . . fate:** *powerful inherited destiny*

70 **present:** *immediate*   73 **Turn head:** *stand at bay* (from hunting).   74 **spend their mouths:** *bark*   76 **Take up . . . short:** *answer curtly*   88 **ordinance of times:** *usage of past ages*   90 **sinister:** *irregular; stressed* — ´—   **awkward:** *indirect, perverse*   93 **memorable line:** *noteworthy pedigree*   94 **demonstrative:** *proving his claims*   95 **overlook:** *look over*   96 **evenly:** *directly*   99 **indirectly:** *not in a direct line of descent*   100 **challenger:** *claimant*   102 **constraint:** *force*   103 **Even:** *here and in l. 144 read 'e'en'*   104 **fierce;** *cf. n.*   106 **That:** *so that* **requiring:** *requesting*   107 **in the bowels:** *'by the mercy,' a phrase from Holinshed* (after Philippians 1:8).   110 **vasty:** *vast*   112 **pining:** *Q: F priuy*   118 **For us:** *for my part*

Dol.   For the Dolphin,
I stand here for him. What to him from England?

    Exe. Scorn and defiance, slight regard, contempt,
And anything that may not misbecome
The mighty sender, doth he prize you at.   *125*
Thus says my king. An if your father's highness
Do not, in grant of all demands at large,
Sweeten the bitter mock you sent his majesty,
He'll call you to so hot an answer of it
That caves and womby vaultages of France   *130*
Shall chide your trespass and return your mock
In second accent of his ordinance.

    Dol. Say, if my father render fair return,
It is against my will, for I desire
Nothing but odds with England. To that end,   *135*
As matching to his youth and vanity,
I did present him with the Paris balls.

    Exe. He'll make your Paris Louvre shake for it,
Were it the mistress court of mighty Europe.
And be assur'd you'll find a difference,   *140*
As we his subjects have in wonder found,
Between the promise of his greener days
And these he masters now. Now he weighs time
Even to the utmost grain. That you shall read
In your own losses, if he stay in France.   *145*

    King. Tomorrow shall you know our mind at full.   *Flourish.*

    Exe. Dispatch us with all speed, lest that our king
Come here himself to question our delay,
For he is footed in this land already.

    King. You shall be soon dispatch'd with fair conditions.   *150*
A night is but small breath and little pause
To answer matters of this consequence.   *Exeunt.*

ACT THIRD ❧

Flourish. Enter Chorus.

Thus with imagin'd wing our swift scene flies
In motion of no less celerity
Than that of thought. Suppose that you have seen
The well-appointed king at Hampton pier
Embark his royalty, and his brave fleet   *5*
With silken streamers the young Phoebus fanning.
Play with your fancies, and in them behold
Upon the hempen tackle ship boys climbing.
Hear the shrill whistle which doth order give
To sounds confus'd. Behold the threaden sails,   *10*
Borne with th' invisible and creeping wind,
Draw the huge bottoms through the furrow'd sea,
Breasting the lofty surge. O, do but think
You stand upon the rivage and behold
A city on th' inconstant billows dancing,   *15*

For so appears this fleet majestical,
Holding due course to Harflew. Follow, follow!
Grapple your minds to sternage of this navy,
And leave your England as dead midnight still,
Guarded with grandsires, babies, and old women,   *20*
Either past or not arriv'd to pith and puissance.
For who is he whose chin is but enrich'd
With one appearing hair that will not follow
These cull'd and choice-drawn cavaliers to France?
Work, work your thoughts, and therein see a siege.   *25*
Behold the ordinance on their carriages,
With fatal mouths gaping on girded Harflew.
Suppose th' ambassador from the French comes back,
Tells Harry that the king doth offer him
Katharine his daughter, and with her, to dowry,   *30*
Some petty and unprofitable dukedoms.
The offer likes not. And the nimble gunner
With linstock now the divelish cannon touches,

                   Alarum, and chambers go off.
And down goes all before them. Still be kind,   *35*
And eche out our performance with your mind.   *Exit.*

❧ SCENE FIRST ❧

*Alarum. Enter the King, Exeter, Bedford, and Gloucester
[and Soldiers, with] scaling ladders at Harflew.*

    King. Once more unto the breach, dear friends, once more,
Or close the wall up with our English dead.
In peace there's nothing so becomes a man
As modest stillness and humility.
But when the blast of war blows in our ears,   *5*
Then imitate the action of the tiger.
Stiffen the sinews, summon up the blood,
Disguise fair nature with hard-favor'd rage.
Then lend the eye a terrible aspect;
Let it pry through the portage of the head   *10*
Like the brass cannon. Let the brow o'erwhelm it
As fearfully as doth a galled rock
O'erhang and jutty his confounded base,
Swill'd with the wild and wasteful ocean.
Now set the teeth and stretch the nostril wide,   *15*
Hold hard the breath and bend up every spirit
To his full height. On, on, you noblest English,
Whose blood is fet from fathers of war proof!
Fathers that like so many Alexanders
Have in these parts from morn till even fought   *20*
And sheath'd their swords for lack of argument.
Dishonor not your mothers. Now attest
That those whom you call'd fathers did beget you.
Be copy now to men of grosser blood
And teach them how to war. And you, good yeomen,   *25*
Whose limbs were made in England, show us here

The mettle of your pasture. Let us swear
That you are worth your breeding, which I doubt not,
For there is none of you so mean and base
That hath not noble luster in your eyes.   30
I see you stand like greyhounds in the slips,
Straining upon the start. The game's afoot!
Follow your spirit, and upon this charge
Cry 'God for Harry, England, and St. George!'

                    [Exeunt.] Alarum, and chambers go off.

❧ SCENE SECOND ❧

Enter Nym, Bardolph, Pistol, and Boy

Bard. On, on, on, on, on! to the breach, to the breach!
Nym. Pray thee, corporal, stay. The knocks are too hot, and,
for mine own part, I have not a case of lives. The humor of it
is too hot, that is the very plain song of it.
Pist. The plain song is most just, for humors do abound: 5

  Knocks go and come, God's vassals drop and die,
          And sword and shield
              In bloody field
          Doth win immortal fame.

Boy. Would I were in an alehouse in London! I would   10
give all my fame for a pot of ale and safety.
Pistol. and I:

  If wishes would prevail with me,
  My purpose should not fail with me,
          But thither would I hie.   15

Boy:

  As duly,
      But not as truly,
          As bird doth sing on bough.

                    Enter Fluellen   20

Flu. Up to the breach, you dogs! Avaunt, you cullions!
                            Driving them forward.]
Pist. Be merciful, great duke, to men of mold.
Abate they rage, abate thy manly rage,
Abate thy rage, great duke!
Good bawcock, bate thy rage! Use lenity, sweet chuck!   25
Nym. These be good humors! Your honor wins bad humors.
                            Exeunt [all but Boy].
Boy. As young as I am, I have observ'd these three swashers.
I am boy to them all three, but all they three, though they
would serve me, could not be man to me; for indeed three
such antics do not amount to a man. For Bardolph, he is   30
white-liver'd and red-fac'd, by the means whereof a' faces it
out, but fights not. For Pistol, he hath a killing tongue and a
quiet sword, by the means whereof a' breaks words and keeps

whole weapons. For Nym, he hath heard that men of few
words are the best men, and therefore he scorns to say his pray- 35
ers, lest a' should be thought a coward. But his few bad words
are match'd with as few good deeds, for a' never broke any
man's head but his own, and that was against a post when he
was drunk. They will steal anything, and call it purchase. Bardolph stole a lute case, bore it twelve leagues, and sold it for 40
three halfpence. Nym and Bardolph are sworn brothers in
filching, and in Callice they stole a fire shovel. I knew by that
piece of service the men would carry coals. They would have
me as familiar with men's pockets as their gloves or their handkerchers, which makes much against my manhood, if I should   45
take from another's pocket to put into mine; for it is plain
pocketing up of wrongs. I must leave them and seek some better service. Their villainy goes against my weak stomach, and
therefore I must cast it up.   *Exit.*

Enter Gower [and Fluellen.]

Gow. Captain Fluellen, you must come presently to the   50
mines. The Duke of Gloucester would speak with you.
Flu. To the mines? Tell you the duke, it is not so good to
come to the mines. For look you, the mines is not according
to the disciplines of the war; the concavities of it is not sufficient. For look you, th' athversary, you may discuss unto   55
the duke, look you, is digt himself four yard under the count-
ermines. By Cheshu, I think a' will plow up all, if there is not
better directions.
Gow. The Duke of Gloucester, to whom the order of the
siege is given, is altogether directed by an Irishman, a very   60
valiant gentleman, i' faith.
Flu: It is Captain Macmorris, is it not?
Gow. I think it be.
Flu. By Cheshu, he is an ass, as in the world! I will verify
as much in his beard. He has no more directions in the   65
true disciplines of the wars, look you, of the Roman disciplines, than is a puppy dog.

Enter Macmorris and Captain Jamy.

Gow. Here a' comes, and the Scots captain, Captain Jamy,
with him.
Flu. Captain Jamy is a marvelous falorous gentleman, that   70
is certain, and of great expedition and knowledge in th' aunchi-
ant wars, upon my particular knowledge of his directions. By
Cheshu, he will maintain his argument as well as any military
man in the world, in the disciplines of the pristine wars of the
Romans.   75
Jamy. I say gud day, Captain Fluellen.
Flu. God-den to your worship, good Captain James.
Gow. How now, Captain Macmorris! Have you quit the
mines? Have the pioners given o'er?
Mac. By Chrish, la, tish ill done! The work ish give over,   80
the trompet sound the retreat. By my hand, I swear, and my
father's soul, the work ish ill done! It ish give over. I would

---

27 mettle . . . pasture: *the quality of your breeding; cf. n.*   **31 slips:** *leashes; collar, quickly released*   **32 Straining:** *F Straying*   **34 St. George:** *patron saint of England*   **3 case:** *set*   **5 plain song:** *simple truth* (simple melody without variations)   **just:** *correct*   **6-9 Knocks . . . fame:** *cf. n.*   **17 duly:** *surely*   **18 truly:** 'in tune' and 'faithfully'   **21 cullions:** *rascals; cf. n.*   **22 men of mold:** *men of earth, mortal men*   **25 bawcock:** *fine fellow* (French *beau coq*)   **chuck:** *chick*   **27 swashers:** *swaggerers*   **29 man:** 'man' and 'servant'   **30 antics:** *buffoons; F Antiques*   **For:** *as for*   **31 white-liver'd:** *cowardly*   **31, 32 faces it out:** *puts a good face on it*   **33 breaks words:** 'mistakes his words' and 'breaks promises'

35 best: *bravest*   **37 broke:** *bruised, drew blood from*   **39 purchase:** *booty*   **42 Callice:** *Calais; stressed --́ —*   **43 piece of service:** *warlike deed*   **carry coals:** *put up with insults; do the dirty work*   **45 makes:** *goes*   **47 pocketing . . . wrongs:** *pun* ('stealing' and 'bearing insults')   **49 cast it up:** *pun* (throw it up)   **50 presently:** *immediately*   **51 mines:** *i.e. under the enemy's walls*   **Gloucester;** *cf. n.*   **54 disciplines . . . war:** *military science*   **57 Cheshu:** *Jesu*   **58 directions:** 'management,' or 'instructions to this troops'   **62 Fluellen;** *cf. n.*   **65 in . . . beard:** *to his face*   **70 falorous:** *valorous*   **71 expedition:** *readiness in argument*   **aunchiant:** *ancient*   **76 Jamy;** *cf. n.*   **77 God-den:** *good evening* (commonly used in the afternoon)   **79 pioners:** *engineering troops, sappers.*   **given o'er:** *given up*

have blowed up the town, so Chrish save me, la! in an hour.
O, tish ill done, tish ill done! By my hand, tish ill done!

Flu. Captain Macmorris, I beseech you now, will you   85
voutsafe me, look you, a few disputations with you, as partly
touching or concerning the disciplines of the war, the Roman
wars, in the way of argument, look you, and friendly communication—partly to satisfy my opinion and partly for the satisfaction, look you, of my mind, as touching the direction of the   90
military discipline. That is the point.

Jamy. It sall be vary gud, gud feith, gud captens bath, and I
sall quit you with gud leve, as I may pick occasion. That sall I,
mary.

Mac. It is no time to discourse, so Chrish save me! The   95
day is hot, and the weather, and the wars, and the king, and
the dukes. It is no time to discourse. The town is beseech'd,
and the trumpet call us to the breach, and we talk, and, be
Chrish, do nothing! 'Tis shame for us all. So God sa' me, 'tis
shame to stand still, it is shame, by my hand! And there is   100
throats to be cut, and works to be done, and there ish nothing
done, so Chrish sa' me, la!

Jamy. By the mess, ere theise eyes of mine take themselves
to slomber, ay'll de gud service, or I'll lig i' th' grund for it.
Ay, or go to death! And I'll pay't as valorously as I may,   105
that sall I suerly do, that is the breff and the long. Mary, I
wad full fain heard some question 'tween you tway.

Flu. Captain Macmorris, I think, look you, under your correction, there is not many of your nation—

Mac. Of my nation! What ish my nation? Ish a villain,   110
and a bastard, and a knave, and a rascal. What ish my nation?
Who talks of my nation?

Flu. Look you, if you take the matter otherwise than is
meant, Captain Macmorris, peradventure I shall think you do
not use me with that affability as in discretion you ought   115
to use me, look you, being as good a man as yourself, both in
the disciplines of war, and in the derivation of my birth, and
in other particularities.

Mac. I do not know you so good a man as myself. So
Chrish save me, I will cut off your head!   120

Gow. Gentlemen both, you will mistake each other.

Jamy. Ah, that's a foul fault!   *A parley [sounded].*

Gow. The town sounds a parley.

Flu. Captain Macmorris, when there is more better opportunity to be required, look you, I will be so bold as to tell you   125
I know the disciplines of war. And there is an end.   *Exeunt.*

❧ SCENE THIRD ❧

*[Enter the Governor and some Citizens on the walls.] Enter the
King [Henry] and all his train before the gates.*

King. How yet resolves the governor of the town?
This is the latest parle we will admit.
Therefore to our best mercy give yourselves,
Or like to men proud of destruction
Defy us to our worst. For, as I am a soldier,   5

A name that in my thoughts becomes me best,
If I begin the batt'ry once again,
I will not leave the half-achiev'd Harflew
Till in her ashes she lie buried.
The gates of mercy shall be all shut up,   10
And the flesh'd soldier, rough and hard of heart,
In liberty of bloody hand shall range
With conscience wide as hell, mowing like grass
Your fresh fair virgins and your flow'ring infants.
What is it then to me if impious War,   15
Array'd in flames like to the prince of fiends,
Do with his smirch'd complexion all fell feats
Enlink'd to waste and desolation?
What is't to me, when you yourselves are cause,
If your pure maidens fall into the hand   20
Of hot and forcing violation?
What rein can hold licentious wickedness
When down the hill he holds his fierce career?
We may as bootless spend our vain command
Upon th' enraged soldiers in their spoil   25
As send precepts to the leviathan
To come ashore. Therefore, you men of Harflew,
Take pity of your town and of your people
Whiles yet my soldiers are in my command,
Whiles yet the cool and temperate wind of grace   30
O'erblows the filthy and contagious clouds
Of heady murther, spoil, and villainy.
If not—why, in a moment look to see
The blind and bloody soldier with foul hand
Defile the locks of your shrill-shrieking daughters,   35
Your fathers taken by the silver beards
And their most reverend heads dash'd to the walls,
Your naked infants spitted upon pikes
Whiles the mad mothers with their howls confus'd
Do break the clouds, as did the wives of Jewry   40
At Herod's bloody-hunting slaughtermen.
What say you? Will you yield, and this avoid,
Or, guilty in defense, be thus destroy'd?

Governor. Our expectation hath this day an end.
The Dolphin, whom of succors we entreated,   45
Returns us that his pow'rs are yet not ready
To raise so great a siege. Therefore, great king,
We yield our town and lives to thy soft mercy.
Enter our gates, dispose of us and ours,
For we no longer are defensible.   50

King. Open your gates. Come, Uncle Exeter,
Go you and enter Harflew. There remain,
And fortify it strongly 'gainst the French.
Use mercy to them all. For us, dear uncle,
The winter coming on, and sickness growing   55
Upon our soldiers, we will retire to Callice.

92, 93 **bath:** *both* **quit . . . leve:** *answer you with your permission*   97 **beseech'd:** *besieged*   103 **mess:** *Mass.* **theise:** *these*   104 **de:** *do* **lig:** *lie*   107 **tway:** *two*   108,
109 **under . . . correction:** *correct me if I'm wrong*   123 **parley:** *trumpet summons to a
parley*   125 **required:** *probably 'found'*   **SD gates:** *the gates of Harfleur; in F the Governor
enters at l. 43*   2 **latest parle:** *last parley; cf. n.*   4 **proud of destruction:** *proudly headed
toward self-destruction*

8 **half-achiev'd:** *half won* **Harflew:** *Harfleur*   11 **flesh'd:** *made fierce by the taste of
blood*   12 **liberty:** *license*   17 **fell:** *cruel*   18 **Enlink'd to:** *associated with*   23 **career:** *swift course*   24 **bootless:** *vainly*   26 **precepts:** *summons (a legal term); stressed
— ‿ —* **leviathan:** *whale*   27 **ashore:** *F ends l. 26 here*   30 **temperate:** *read 'temp'rate'*
grace: *mercy*   31 **O'erblows:** *blows away* **contagious:** *clouds and mists were thought to
carry contagion*   32 **heady:** *headstrong, violent; F heady*   35 **Defile:** *F Desire*   40
break: *pierce*   41 **slaughtermen:** *i.e. the Slaughter of the Innocents (see Matthew 2:16-
18)*   44 **expectation:** *hope*   45 **of:** *for*   50 **defensible:** *capable of defending ourselves*   54 **all. For us:** *F all for vs*   56 **Callice:** *Calais*

Tonight in Harflew will we be your guest;
Tomorrow for the march are we address'd.

Flourish, and enter the town.

❧ SCENE FOURTH ❧

Enter Katharine and [Alice,] an old gentlewoman.

Kath. Alice, tu as été en Angleterre, et tu parles bien le language.

Alice. Un peu, madame.

Kath. Je te prie, m'enseignez. Il faut que j'apprenne à parler. Comment appelez-vous la main en anglais?   5

Alice. La main? Elle est appelée de hand.

Kath. De hand. Et les doigts?

Alice. Les doigts? Ma foi, j'oublie les doigts, mais je me souviendrai. Les doigts? Je pense qu'ils sont appelés de fingres— oui, de fingres.   10

Kath. La main, de hand; les doigts, de fingres. Je pense que je suis le bon écolier. J'ai gagné deux mots d'anglais vitement. Comment appelez-vous les ongles?

Alice. Les ongles? Nous les appelons de nayles.

Kath. De nayles. Écoutez. Dites-moi si je parle bien: de   15 hand, de fingres, et de nayles.

Alice. C'est bien dit, madame; il est fort bon anglais.

Kath. Dites-moi l'anglais pour le bras.

Alice. De arm, madame.

Kath. Et le coude?   20

Alice. D' elbow.

Kath. D' elbow. Je m'en fais la répétition de tous les mots que vous m'avez appris dès à présent.

Alice. Il est trop difficile, madame, comme je pense.

Kath. Excusez-moi, Alice. Écoutez: d' hand, de fingre, de   25 nayles, d' arma, de bilbow.

Alice. D' elbow, madame.

Kath. O, Seigneur Dieu, je m'en oublie! D' elbow. Comment appelez-vous le col?

Alice. De nick, madame.   30

Kath. De nick. Et le menton?

Alice. De chin.

Kath. De sin. Le col, de nick; le menton, de sin.

Alice. Oui. Sauf votre honneur, en vérité, vous prononcez les mots aussi droit que les natifs d'Angleterre.   35

Kath. Je ne doute point d'apprendre, par la grâce de Dieu, et en peu de temps.

Alice. N'avez-vous pas déjà oublié ce que je vous ai enseigné?

Kath. Non, je réciterai à vous promptement: d' hand, de   40 fingre, de maylees—

Alice. De nayles, madame.

Kath. De nayles, de arm, de ilbow.

Alice. Sauf votre honneur, d' elbow.

Kath. Ainsi dis-je: d' elbow, de nick, et de sin. Comment   45 appelez-vous le pied et la robe?

Alice. Le foot, madame, et le count.

Kath. Le foot et le count! O, Seigneur Dieu! ils sont les mots de son mauvais, corruptible, gros, et impudique, et non pour les dames d'honneur d'user. Je ne voudrais prononcer ces mots devant les seigneurs de France pour tout le monde. Foh! Le foot et le count! Néanmoins, je réciterai une autre fois ma leçon ensemble: d' hand, de fingre, de nayles, d 'arm, d' elbow, de nick, de sin, de foot, le count.

Alice. Excellent, madame!   55

Kath. C'est assez pour une fois. Allons-nous à dîner.

Exeunt.

❧ SCENE FIFTH ❧

Enter the King of France, the Dolphin, [the Duke of Britaine,] the Constable of France, and others.

King: 'Tis certain he hath pass'd the river Somme.

Con. And if he be not fought withal, my lord,
Let us not live in France. Let us quit all
And give our vineyards to a barbarous people.

Dol. O, Dieu vivant! Shall a few sprays of us,   5
The emptying of our fathers' luxury,
Our scions, put in wild and savage stock,
Spurt up so suddenly into the clouds
And overlook their grafters?

Brit. Normans, but bastard Normans, Norman bastards!   10

58 address'd: *prepared*   3 Un peu: *see Introduction; cf. n.*   7 Et les doigts; *cf. n.*
Translation.
Kath. Alice, you have been in England and speak the language well.
Alice. A little, my lady.
Kath. I pray you, teach me. I must learn to speak it. What do you call la main in English?
Alice. La main? It is called de hand.
Kath. De hand. And les doigts?
Alice. Les doigts? Dear me, I forget les doigts, but I shall remember. Les doigts? I think that they are called de fingres—yes, de fingres.
Kath. La main, de hand; les doigts, de fingres. I think that I am a good scholar. I have acquired two words of English quickly. What do you call les ongles?
Alice. Les ongles? We call them de nayles.
Kath. De nayles. Listen. Tell me whether or not I speak correctly: de hand, de fingres, and de nayles.
Alice. That is correct, my lady; it is very good English.
Kath. Tell me the English for le bras.
Alice. De arm, my lady.
Kath. And le coude?
Alice. D' elbow.
Kath. D' elbow. I am going to repeat all the words you have taught me up to now.
Alice. It is too difficult, my lady, I think.
Kath. Pardon me, Alice. Listen: d' hand, de fingre, de nayles, d' arma, de bilbow.
Alice. D' elbow, my lady.
Kath. O, Lord, I forget! D' elbow. What do you call le col?
Alice. De nick, my lady.
Kath. De nick. And le menton?

Alice. De chin.
Kath. De sin. Le col, de nick; le menton, de sin.
Alice. Yes. Saving your grace, in truth you pronounce the words as well as the people of England [do].
Kath. I don't doubt that I shall learn, with God's help, and in a short time.
Alice. Haven't you already forgotten what I have taught you?
Kath. No, I shall recite to you at once: d' hand, de fingre, de maylees—
Alice. De nayles, my lady.
Kath. De nayles, de arm, de ilbow.
Alice. Saving your grace, d' elbow.
Kath. That's what I said; d' elbow, de nick, and de sin. What do you call le pied and la robe?
Alice. Le foot, my lady, and le count.
Kath. Le foot and le count! O, Lord! those are naughty words, wicked, coarse, and immodest and [are] not for fine ladies to use. I wouldn't pronounce these words before the lords of France for the whole world. Fie! le foot and le count! Nevertheless, I shall recite my whole lesson once more: d' hand, de fingre, de nayles, d' arm, d' elbow, de nick, de sin, de foot, le count.
Alice. Excellent, my lady.
Kath. That's enough for one time. Let's go to dinner.
SD Britaine; *cf. n.*   2 withal: *with*   5 sprays: *offshoots*   6 luxury: *lust*   9 overlook ... grafters; *cf. n.*

Mort Dieu! ma vie! if they march along
Unfought withal, but I will sell my dukedom
To buy a slobb'ry and a dirty farm
In that nook-shotten isle of Albion.

   Con. Dieu de batailles! Where have they this mettle?   *15*
Is not their climate foggy, raw, and dull,
On whom, as in despite, the sun looks pale,
Killing their fruit with frowns? Can sodden water,
A drench for sur-rein'd jades, their barley broth,
Decoct their cold blood to such valiant heat?   *20*
And shall our quick blood, spirited with wine,
Seem frosty? O, for honor of our land,
Let us not hang like roping icicles
Upon our houses' thatch, whiles a more frosty people
Sweat drops of gallant youth in our rich fields!   *25*
Poor we may call them in their native lords.

   Dol. By faith and honor,
Our madams mock at us and plainly say
Our mettle is bred out, and they will give
Their bodies to the lust of English youth   *30*
To new-store France with bastard warriors.

   Brit. They bid us to the English dancing schools
And teach lavoltas high and swift corantos,
Saying our grace is only in our heels
And that we are most lofty runaways.   *35*

   King. Where is Montjoy the herald? Speed him hence.
Let him greet England with our sharp defiance.
Up, princes, and, with spirit of honor edg'd
More sharper than your swords, hie to the field.
Charles Delabreth, High Constable of France,   *40*
You Dukes of Orleans, Bourbon, and of Berri,
Alençon, Brabant, Bar, and Burgundy,
Jaques Chatillon, Rambures, Vaudemont,
Beaumont, Grandpré, Roussi, and Faulconbridge,
Foix, Lestrake, Bouciqualt, and Charolois—   *45*
High dukes, great princes, barons, lords, and knights,
For your great seats now quit you of great shames.
Bar Harry England, that sweeps through our land
With pennons painted in the blood of Harflew.
Rush on his host as doth the melted snow   *50*
Upon the valleys, whose low vassal seat
The Alps doth spit and void his rheum upon.
Go down upon him—you have power enough—
And in a captive chariot into Roan
Bring him our prisoner.   *55*

   Con.   This becomes the great.
Sorry am I his numbers are so few,
His soldiers sick and famish'd in their march.
For I am sure, when he shall see our army,
He'll drop his heart into the sink of fear   *60*
And for achievement offer us his ransom.

   King. Therefore, Lord Constable, haste on Montjoy,
And let him say to England that we send
To know what willing ransom he will give.
Prince Dolphin, you shall stay with us in Roan.   *65*

   Dol. Not so, I do beseech your majesty.

   King. Be patient, for you shall remain with us.
Now forth, Lord Constable and princes all,
And quickly bring us word of England's fall.   *Exeunt.*

❧ SCENE SIXTH ❧

Enter Captains, English and Welsh: Gower and Fluellen.

   Gow. How now, Captain Fluellen! Come you from the
bridge?

   Flu. I assure you there is very excellent services committed
at the bridge.

   Gow. Is the Duke of Exeter safe?   *5*

   Flu. The Duke of Exeter is as magnanimous as Agamemnon, and a man that I love and honor with my soul, and my
heart, and my duty, and my live, and my living, and my uttermost power. He is not—God be praised and blessed!—any
hurt in the world, but keeps the bridge most valiantly, with   *10*
excellent discipline. There is an aunchient lieutenant there at
the pridge, I think in my very conscience he is as valiant a
man as Mark Antony, and he is a man of no estimation in the
world, but I did see him do as gallant service.

   Gow. What do you call him?   *15*

   Flu. He is call'd Aunchient Pistol.

   Gow. I know him not.

Enter Pistol.

   Flu. Here is the man.

   Pist. Captain, I thee beseech to do me favors.
The duke of Exeter doth love thee well.   *20*

   Flu. Ay, I praise God, and I have merited some love at his
hands.

   Pist. Bardolph, a soldier firm and sound of heart,
And of buxom valor, hath by cruel fate.
And giddy Fortune's furious fickle wheel,   *25*
That goddess blind,
That stands upon the rolling restless stone—

   Flu. By your patience, Aunchient Pistol. Fortune is painted
blind, with a muffler afore his eyes, to signify to you, that Fortune is blind. And she is painted also with a wheel, to signify   *30*
to you, which is the moral of it, that she is turning and inconstant, and mutability, and variation. And her foot, look you, is
fixed upon a spherical stone, which rolls, and rolls, and rolls.
In good truth, the poet makes a most excellent description of
it. Fortune is an excellent moral.   *35*

   Pist. Fortune is Bardolph's foe, and frowns on him,
For he hath stol'n a pax, and hanged must a' be—
A damned death!
Let gallows gape for dog, let man go free,
And let not hemp his windpipe suffocate.   *40*

11 Mort . . . vie: *F* Mort du ma vie *and most editors read* Mort de ma vie   **13 slobb'ry:**
muddy   **14 nook-shotten:** *running out into corners or angles*   **15 batailles:** *trisyllabic*
Where: *whence*   **mettle:** *stuff, courage*   **17 despite:** *spite*   **18 sodden:** *boiled*   **19**
drench: *medicinal draught*   **sur-rein'd:** *overridden*   **jades:** *horses* (contemptuous).   **20 De-**
coct: *warm up*   **23 roping:** *hanging down like ropes*   **26 Poor . . . lords:** *i.e. their*
fields have bred leaders of poor quality   **may:** *F2; not in F*   **33 lavoltas:** *high jumping*
dances   **corantos:** *rapid sliding dances*   **36 Montjoy:** *title of the chief herald or king-at-*
arms of France   **38 spirit:** *here and elsewhere read 'sprite' or 'spir't'*   **40–45 Charles . . .**
Charolois: *all these names are taken from Holinshed*   **44 Faulconbridge;** *cf. n.*   **46**
knights: *F Kings*   **47 seats:** *estates, fiefs*   **quit you:** *absolve yourselves*   **52 void his**
rheum: *spit*   **54 Roan:** *Rouen*   **61 for achievement:** *i.e. instead of victory*

SD English and Welsh; *cf. n.*   **6 Agamemnon:** *general of the Greek forces that besieged*
Troy   **8 live . . . living;** *cf. n.*   **11 discipline:** *military science*   **aunchient lieutenant:**
two ridiculously juxtaposed titles; perhaps 'sublieutenant'   **aunchient;** *ancient (ensign)*   **13**
estimation: *reputation*   **19, 20 Captain . . well:** *F prints all of Pistol's speeches in this scene*
as prose   **24 buxom:** *lively*   **25 furious:** *cruel*   **29 his:** *F; often emended to her*   **35**
moral: *a symbolical figure*   **37 pax;** *cf. n.*

But Exeter hath given the doom of death
For pax of little price.
Therefore go speak—the duke will hear thy voice,
And let not Bardolph's vital thread be cut
With edge of penny cord and vile reproach.   45
Speak, captain, for his life, and I will thee requite.
    Flu. Aunchient Pistol, I do partly understand your meaning.
    Pist. Why, then, rejoice therefore.
    Flu. Certainly, aunchient, it is not a thing to rejoice at. For
if, look you, he were my brother, I would desire the duke to   50
use his good pleasure and put him to execution, for discipline
ought to be used.
    Pist. Die and be damn'd! and figo for thy friendship!
    Flu. It is well.
    Pist. The fig of Spain!   *Exit.*   55
    Flu. Very good.
    Gow. Why, this is an arrant counterfeit rascal. I remember
him now—a bawd, a cutpurse.
    Flu. I'll assure you, a' utt'red as prave words at the pridge as
you shall see in a summer's day. But it is very well. What   60
he has spoke to me, that is well, I warrant you, when time is
serve.
    Gow. Why, 'tis a gull, a fool, a rogue, that now and then
goes to the wars to grace himself, at his return into London,
under the form of a soldier. And such fellows are perfit in   65
the great commanders' names, and they will learn you by rote
where services were done—at such and such a sconce, at such
a breach, at such a convoy; who came off bravely, who was
shot, who disgrac'd, what terms the enemy stood on. And this
they con perfitly in the phrase of war, which they trick up   70
with new-tuned oaths. And what a beard of the general's cut
and a horrid suit of the camp will do among foaming bottles
and ale-wash'd wits is wonderful to be thought on. But you
must learn to know such slanders of the age, or else you may
be marvelously mistook.   75
    Flu. I tell you what, Captain Gower. I do perceive he is not
the man that he would gladly make show to the world he is.
If I find a hole in his coat, I will tell him my mind. [*Drum
within.*] Hark you, the king is coming, and I must speak with
him from the pridge.   80

*Drum and colors. Enter the King [Henry] and his poor Soldiers
[and Gloucester].*

    Flu. God pless your majesty!
    King. How now, Fluellen! Cam'st thou from the bridge?
    Flu. Ay, so please your majesty. The Duke of Exeter has
very gallantly maintain'd the pridge. The French is gone off,
look you, and there is gallant and most prave passages.   85
Marry, th' athversary was have possession of the pridge, but he
is enforced to retire, and the Duke of Exeter is master of the
pridge. I can tell your majesty, the duke is a prave man.
    King. What men have you lost, Fluellen?
    Flu. The perdition of th' athversary hath been very great, 90
reasonable great. Marry, for my part, I think the duke hath
lost never a man but one that is like to be executed for rob-

bing a church—one Bardolph, if your majesty know the man.
His face is all bubukles and whelks, and knobs, and flames o'
fire, and his lips blows at his nose, and it is like a coal of   95
fire, sometimes plue, and sometimes red; but his nose is executed, and his fire's out.
    King. We would have all such offenders so cut off. And we
give express charge that in our marches through the country
there be nothing compell'd from the villages, nothing taken   100
but paid for, none of the French upbraided or abused in disdainful language. For when lenity and cruelty play for a kingdom, the gentler gamester is the soonest winner.

                    Tucket. Enter Montjoy.

    Mont. You know me by my habit,
    King. Well then, I know thee. What shall I know of thee? 105
    Mont. My master's mind.
    King. Unfold it.
    Mont. Thus says my king: Say thou to Harry of England:
Though we seem'd dead, we did but sleep. Advantage is a better soldier than rashness. Tell him we could have rebuk'd him 110
at Harflew, but that we thought not good to bruise an injury
till it were full ripe. Now we speak upon our cue, and our
voice is imperial. England shall repent his folly, see his weakness, and admire our sufferance. Bid him therefore consider of
his ransom, which must proportion the losses we have   115
borne, the subjects we have lost, the disgrace we have digested;
which in weight to reanswer, his pettiness would bow under.
For our losses, his exchequer is too poor. For th' effusion of
our blood, the muster of his kingdom too faint a number. And
for our disgrace, his own person kneeling at our feet but a   120
weak and worthless satisfaction. To this add defiance, and tell
him, for conclusion, he hath betrayed his followers, whose condemnation is pronounc'd. So far my king and master; so much
my office.
    King. What is thy name? I know thy quality.   125
    Mont. Montjoy.
    King. Thou dost thy office fairly. Turn thee back,
And tell thy king I do not seek him now,
But could be willing to march on to Callice
Without impeachment. For, to say the sooth,   130
Though 'tis no wisdom to confess so much
Unto an enemy of craft and vantage,
My people are with sickness much enfeebl'd,
My numbers lessen'd, and those few I have
Almost no better than so many French;   135
Who when they were in health, I tell thee, herald,
I thought upon one pair of English legs
Did march three Frenchmen. Yet forgive me, God,
That I do brag thus! This your air of France
Hath blown that vice in me. I must repent.   140
Go therefore, tell thy master here I am.
My ransom is this frail and worthless trunk;
My army but a weak and sickly guard.

94 bubukles: *Fluellen's word for 'carbuncles.'* **whelks:** *boils*   **100 compell'd:**
forced   **102 lenity:** *Q; F Leuitie*   **SD Tucket:** *trumpet signal*   **104 habit:** *i.e. his herald's
tabard coat*   **109 Advantage:** *cautions, awaiting a favorable opportunity*   **111 bruise:**
squeeze (as in squeezing a boil).   **112 upon . . . cue:** *at the right moment*   **113 England:**
i.e. Henry   **114 admire . . . sufferance:** *wonder at our forbearance*   **115 proportion:** *be
in proportion to*   **117 in weight . . . under:** *i.e. his public resources would collapse under
any attempt to compensate fully*   **125 quality:** *profession*   **127 dost:** *F doo'st; see IV.7.162*
fairly: *splendidly*   **129 Callice:** *Calais*   **130 impeachment:** *hindrance*   **132 of . . .
vantage:** *who is cunning and has the advantage*   **140 blown:** *puffed up*

53 figo; *cf. n.*   **57 arrant:** *out-and-out*   **58 bawd:** *pander*   **59 prave:** *brave, i.e.
fine*   **60 is serve:** *i.e. shall serve*   **62 gull:** *simpleton*   **65 perfit:** *perfect*   **66 learn:**
teach   **67 sconce:** *fortification*   **69 stood:** *insisted*   **70 con:** *learn by heart*   **71
new-tuned:** *newly composed*   **74 slanders:** *scandals, abuses*   **78 hole . . . coat:** *i.e. some
weak spot in his record*   **80 from:** *about, or with news from*   **85 passages:** *deeds*   **90
perdition:** *loss*

Yet, God before, tell him we will come on,
Though France himself and such another neighbor   145
Stand in our way. There's for thy labor, Montjoy.
Go bid thy master well advise himself.
If we may pass, we will. If we be hind'red,
We shall your tawny ground with your red blood
Discolor. And so, Montjoy, fare you well.   150
The sum of all our answer is but this:
We would not seek a battle as we are,
Nor, as we are, we say we will not shun it.
So tell your master.
    Mont. I shall deliver so. Thanks to your highness.   *[Exit.]*
    Glouc. I hope they will not come upon us now.
    King. We are in God's hand, brother, not in theirs.
March to the bridge. It now draws toward night.
Beyond the river we'll encamp ourselves,
And on tomorrow bid them march away.   *Exeunt.*   160

❧ SCENE SEVENTH ❧

Enter the Constable of France, the Lord Rambures, Orleans,
Dolphin, with others.

    Con. Tut, I have the best armor of the world. Would it
were day!
    Orl. You have an excellent armor, but let my horse have his
due.
    Con. It is the best horse of Europe.   5
    Orl. Will it never be morning?
    Dol. My lord of Orleans, and my Lord High Constable, you
talk of horse and armor?
    Orl. You are as well provided of both as any prince in the
world.   10
    Dol. What a long night is this! I will not change my horse
with any that treads but on four pasterns. Ça, ha! he bounds
from the earth as if his entrails were hairs: le cheval volant, the
Pegasus, chez les narines de feu! When I bestride him, I soar, I
am a hawk. He trots the air. The earth sings when he   15
touches it. The basest horn of his hoof is more musical than
the pipe of Hermes.
    Orl. He's of the color of the nutmeg.
    Dol. And of the heat of the ginger. It is a beast for Perseus:
he is pure air and fire, and the dull elements of earth and   20
water never appear in him, but only in patient stillness while
his rider mounts him. He is indeed a horse, and all other jades
you may call beasts.
    Con. Indeed, my lord, it is a most absolute and excellent
horse.   25
    Dol. It is the prince of palfreys His neigh is like the bidding
of a monarch, and his countenance enforces homage.
    Orl. No more, cousin.
    Dol. Nay, the man hath no wit that cannot from the rising
of the lark to the lodging of the lamb vary deserved praise   30

on my palfrey. It is a theme as fluent as the sea. Turn the
sands into eloquent tongues, and my horse is argument for
them all. 'Tis a subject for a sovereign to reason on, and for a
sovereign's sovereign to ride on, and for the world, familiar to
us and unknown, to lay apart their particular functions and   35
wonder at him. I once writ a sonnet in his praise, and began
thus, 'Wonder of nature—'
    Orl. I have heard a sonnet begin so to one's mistress.
    Dol. Then did they imitate that which I compos'd to my
courser, for my horse is my mistress.   40
    Orl. Your mistress bears well.
    Dol. Me well, which is the prescript praise and perfection of
a good and particular mistress.
    Con. Nay, for methought yesterday your mistress shrewdly
shook your back.   45
    Dol. So perhaps did yours.
    Con. Mine was not bridled.
    Dol. O, then belike she was old and gentle, and you rode
like a kern of Ireland, your French hose off and in your strait
strossers.   50
    Con. You have good judgment in horsemanship.
    Dol. Be warn'd by me then. They that ride so, and ride not
warily, fall into foul bogs. I had rather have my horse to my
mistress.
    Con. I had as live have my mistress a jade.   55
    Dol. I tell thee, Constable, my mistress wears his own hair.
    Con. I could make as true a boast as that if I had a sow to
my mistress.
    Dol. 'Le chien est retourné à son propre vomissement, et la
truie lavée au bourbier.' Thou mak'st use of anything.   60
    Con. Yet do I not use my horse for my mistress, or any
such proverb so little kin to the purpose.
    Rambures. My Lord Constable, the armor that I saw in your
tent tonight—are those stars or suns upon it?
    Con. Stars, my lord.   65
    Dol. Some of them will fall tomorrow, I hope.
    Con. And yet my sky shall not want.
    Dol. That may be, for you bear a many superfluously, and
'twere more honor some were away.
    Con. Ev'n as your horse bears your praises, who would   70
trot as well were some of your brags dismounted.
    Dol. Would I were able to load him with his desert! Will it
never be day? I will trot tomorrow a mile, and my way shall
be paved with English faces.
    Con. I will not say so for fear I should be fac'd out of   75
my way. But I would it were morning, for I would fain be
about the ears of the English.
    Rambures. Who will go to hazard with me for twenty
prisoners?
    Con. You must first go yourself to hazard ere you have   80
them.
    Dol. 'Tis midnight. I'll go arm myself.   *Exit.*
    Orl. The Dolphin longs for morning.
    Rambures. He longs to eat the English.
    Con. I think he will eat all he kills.   85
    Orl. By the white hand of my lady, he's a gallant prince.

---

146 There's . . . labor: *he gives the herald a purse of some valuable*   **148-150 If we . . .
Discolor;** *cf. n.*   **149 tawny:** *yellow*   **SD Dolphin;** *cf. n.*   **12 pasterns:** *the part of
a horse's leg between hoof and fetlock; F2; F* postures   **13 as if . . . hairs:** *i.e. as if he were
stuffed with hair (like a tennis ball); cf. n.*   **13, 14 le cheval . .. feu:** *Pegasus, the flying
horse with nostrils of fire*   **16 basest horn:** *note pun*   **17 Hermes:** *who charmed Argus
to sleep by playing on his pipe*   **19 Perseus:** *the Greek hero who rode on Pegasus*   **22
jades;** *cf. n.*   **24 absolute:** *perfect*   **26 palfreys:** *saddle horses, usually for ladies*   **30
lodging:** *lying down*

32 argument: *subject*   **33 reason:** *discourse*   **42 prescript:** *prescribed*   **43 particular:**
belonging only to one lover   **44 shrewdly:** *viciously*   **49 kern:** *Irish foot soldier* **French
hose:** *baggy breeches*   **49, 50 strait strossers:** *tight trousers, i.e. bare-legged or in under-
pants*   **55 live:** *lief*   **57 to:** *as*   **59, 60 Le ... bourbier;** *cf. n.*   **60 Thou ...
anything:** *i.e. to win an argument*   **75 fac'd .. way:** *outfaced, put to shame; driven
off*   **80 go to hazard:** *play craps*

Con. Swear by her foot, that she may tread out the oath.

Orl. He is simply the most active gentleman of France.

Con. Doing is activity, and he will still be doing.

Orl. He never did harm that I heard of.   90

Con. Nor will do none tomorrow. He will keep that good name still.

Orl. I know him to be valiant.

Con. I was told that by one that knows him better than you.   95

Orl. What's he?

Con. Marry, he told me so himself, and he said he car'd not who knew it.

Orl. He needs not. It is no hidden virtue in him.

Con. By my faith, sir, but it is. Never anybody saw it   100 but his lackey 'Tis a hooded valor, and when it appears it will bate.

Orl. 'Ill will never said well.'

Con. I will cap that proverb with 'There is flattery in friendship.'   105

Orl. And I will take up that with 'Give the devil his due.'

Con. Well plac'd. There stands your friend for the devil. Have at the very eye of that proverb with 'A pox of the devil!'

Orl. You are the better at proverbs, by how much 'A fool's bolt is soon shot.'   110

Con. You have shot over.

Orl. *'Tis not the first time you were overshot.*

Enter a Messenger.

Mes. My Lord High Constable, the English lie within fifteen hundred paces of your tents.

Con. Who hath measur'd the ground?   115

Mess. The Lord Grandpré.

Con. A valiant and most expert gentleman. Would it were day! Alas, poor Harry of England! He longs not for the dawning as we do.

Orl. What a wretched and peevish fellow is this King of   120 England, to mope with his fat-brain'd followers so far out of his knowledge!

Con. If the English had any apprehension, they would run away.

Orl. That they lack, for if their heads had any intellectual   125 armor, they could never wear such heavy headpieces.

Rambures. That island of England breeds very valiant creatures. Their mastiffs are of unmatchable courage.

Orl. Foolish curs, that run winking into the mouth of a Russian bear and have their heads crush'd like rotten apples!   130 You may as well say that's a valiant flea that dare eat his breakfast on the lip of a lion.

Con. Just, just. And the men do sympathize with the mastiffs in robustious and rough coming on, leaving their wits with their wives. And then give them great meals of beef and iron and   135 steel, they will eat like wolves and fight like devils.

Orl. Ay, but these English are shrowdly out of beef.

Con. Then shall we find tomorrow they have only stomachs to eat and none to fight. Now is it time to arm. Come, shall we about it?   140

Orl. It is now two o'clock. But let me see, by ten We shall have each a hundred Englishmen.   *Exeunt.*

ACT FOURTH

[Enter] Chorus.

Now entertain conjecture of a time
When creeping murmur and the poring dark
Fills the wide vessel of the universe.
From camp to camp through the foul womb of night
The hum of either army stilly sounds,   5
That the fix'd sentinels almost receive
The secret whispers of each other's watch.
Fire answers fire, and through their paly flames
Each battle sees the other's umber'd face.
Steed threatens steed, in high and boastful neighs   10
Piercing the night's dull ear. And from the tents
The armorers, accomplishing the knights,
With busy hammers closing rivets up,
Give dreadful note of preparation.
The country cocks do crow, the clocks do toll,   15
And the third hour of drowsy morning name.
Proud of their numbers and secure in soul,
The confident and overlusty French
Do the low-rated English play at dice,
And chide the creeple tardy-gaited night   20
Who like a foul and ugly witch doth limp
So tediously away. The poor condemned English,
Like sacrifices, by their watchful fires
Sit patiently and inly ruminate
The morning's danger. And their gesture sad,   25
Investing lank-lean cheeks and war-worn coats,
Presenteth them unto the gazing moon
So many horrid ghosts. O, now, who will behold
The royal captain of this ruin'd band
Walking from watch to watch, from tent to tent,   30
Let him cry 'Praise and glory on his head!'
For forth he goes and visits all his host,
Bids them good morrow with a modest smile,
And calls them brothers, friends, and countrymen.
Upon his royal face there is no note   35
How dread an army hath enrounded him,
Nor doth he dedicate one jot of color
Unto the weary and all-watched night,
But freshly looks and overbears attaint
With cheerful semblance and sweet majesty,   40

87 tread out: *treat with contempt*   **89 still:** *always*   **101 lackey:** *a running footman* **servant:** *(the only person he has stood up to).*   **101, 102 hooded ... bate:** *cf. n.* **103-110 Ill will ... shot:** *in this game of 'capping proverbs' the one who has the last word wins*   **109 how much:** *as much as*   **110 bolt:** *arrow*   **111 shot over:** *missed the target*   **112 overshot:** *outshot*   **120 peevish:** *foolish*   **121 fat-brain'd:** *fat-headed*   **121, 122 out ... knowledge:** *beyond his experience or understanding*   **123 apprehension:** *common sense (pun on 'fear').*   **128 mastiffs:** *well known throughout Europe for their bull-and-bear-baiting*   **129 winking:** *with their eyes shut*   **129-130 Russian bear:** *highly prized in bear-baiting*   **133 Just, just:** *exactly so*   **sympathize with:** *resemble*   **134 robustious:** *violent*   **coming on:** *attack*   **135, 136 give ... devils:** *cf. n.*

137 shrowdly: *shrewdly, grievously*   **138 stomachs:** *inclinations*   **1 entertain conjecture:** *imagine*   **2 poring:** *eye-straining*   **5 stilly:** *quietly*   **6 That:** *so that*   **8 paly:** *pale*   **9 battle:** *army*   **umber'd:** *dark brown, i.e. shadowy*   **12 accomplishing:** *completing the equipment of*   **13 rivets:** *cf. n.*   **16 name:** *F* nam'd   **17 secure:** *carefree, overconfident*   **18 overlusty:** *too merry*   **19 play at dice:** *i.e. play for their lives*   **20 creeple:** *cripple*   **24 inly:** *inwardly*   **25 gesture sad:** *serious bearing*   **26 Investing:** *clothing with dignity*   **27 Presenteth:** *F* Presented   **33 good morrow:** *good morning*   **35 note:** *sign*   **37 dedicate:** *sacrifice*   **38 all-watched:** *sleepless throughout*   **39 overbears attaint:** *conquers any sign of fatigue and fear*   **40 semblance:** *appearance*

That every wretch, pining and pale before,
Beholding him, plucks comfort form his looks.
A largess universal like the sun
His liberal eye doth give to every one,
Thawing cold fear; that mean and gentle all   45
Behold, as may unworthiness define,
A little touch of Harry in the night.
And so our scene must to the battle fly,
Where—O, for pity!—we shall much disgrace
With four or five most vile and ragged foils,   50
Right ill-dispos'd in brawl ridiculous,
The name of Agincourt. Yet sit and see,
Minding true things by what their mock'ries be.   *Exit.*

❧ SCENE FIRST ❧

Enter the King [Henry], Bedford, and Gloucester.

King. Gloucester, 'tis true that we are in great danger;
The greater therefore should our courage be.
Good morrow, brother Bedford. God Almighty!
There is some soul of goodness in things evil,
Would men observingly distill it out.   5
For our bad neighbor makes us early stirrers,
Which is both healthful and good husbandry.
Besides, they are our outward consciences
And preachers to us all, admonishing
That we should dress us fairly for our end.   10
Thus may we gather honey from the weed
And make a moral of the divel himself.

Enter Erpingham.

Good morrow, old Sir Thomas Erpingham.
A good soft pillow for that good white head
Were better than a churlish turf of France.   15
Erp. Not so, my liege. This lodging likes me better,
Since I may say 'Now lie I like a king.'
King. 'Tis good for men to love their present pains
Upon example; so the spirit is eas'd.
And when the mind is quick'ned, out of doubt   20
The organs, though defunct and dead before,
Break up their drowsy grave and newly move
With casted slough and fresh legerity.
Lend me thy cloak, Sir Thomas. Brothers both,
Commend me to the princes in our camp.   25
Do my good morrow to them, and anon
Desire them all to my pavilion.
Glouc. We shall, my liege.
Erp. Shall I attend your grace?
King.   No, my good knight.   30
Go with my brothers to my lords of England.
I and my bosom must debate awhile,
And then I would no other company.

Erp. The Lord in heaven bless thee, noble Harry!
Exeunt [all but the King].
King. God-a-mercy, old heart! Thou speak'st cheerfully.   35

Enter Pistol.

Pist. Qui va là?
King. A friend.
Pist. Discuss unto me, art thou officer,
Or art thou base, common, and popular?
King. I am a gentleman of a company.   40
Pist. Trail'st thou the puissant pike?
King. Even so. What are you?
Pist. As good a gentleman as the emperor.
King. Then you are a better than the king.
Pist. The king's a bawcock and a heart of gold,   45
A lad of life, an imp of fame,
Of parents good, of fist most valiant.
I kiss his dirty shoe, and from heartstring
I love the lovely bully. What is thy name?
King. Harry le Roy.   50
Pist. Le Roy? A Cornish name. Art thou of Cornish crew?
King. No, I am a Welshman.
Pist. Know'st thou Fluellen?
King. Yes.
Pist. Tell him I'll knock his leek about his pate   55
Upon Saint Davy's day.
King. Do not you wear your dagger in your cap that day,
lest he knock that about yours.
Pist. Art thou his friend?
King. And his kinsman too.   60
Pist. The figo for thee then!
King. I thank you. God be with you!
Pist. My name is Pistol call'd.   *Exit. Manet King.*
King. It sorts well with your fierceness.

Enter Fluellen and Gower.

Gow. Captain Fluellen!   65
Flu. So! in the name of Jesu Christ, speak fewer! It is the greatest admiration in the universal world, when the true and aunchient prerogatifes and laws of the wars is not kept. If you would
take the pains but to examine the wars of Pompey the Great, you
shall find, I warrant you, that there is no tiddle-taddle nor   70
pibble-pabble in Pompey's camp. I warrant you, you shall find
the ceremonies of the wars, and the cares of it, and the forms of
it, and the sobriety of it, and the modesty of it, to be otherwise.
Gow. Why, the enemy is loud. Your hear him all night.
Flu. If the enemy is an ass and a fool and a prating cox-   75
comb, is it meet, think you, that we should also, look you, be
an ass and a fool and a prating coxcomb, in your own conscience now?
Gow. I will speak lower.
Flu. I pray you and beseech you that you will.   80
Exeunt [Gower and Fluellen].

---

41 **That:** *so that*   43 **like the sun;** *cf. n.*   45 **mean and gentle:** *those of low birth and gentlemen*   46 **as ... define:** *so far as our poor abilities can depict it*   47 **touch:** *glimpse*   50-2 **With ... Agincourt;** *cf. n.*   50 **foils:** *rapiers*   51 **dispos'd:** *set forth*   53 **Minding:** *imagining*   3 **Good:** *F God; cf. n.*   7 **husbandry:** *economy, management*   8 **they:** *things evil (1. 4) or the French*   10 **dress us fairly:** *prepare ourselves properly*   12 **make ... of:** *find a moral lesson in*   **SD Erpingham;** *cf. n.*   15 **churlish:** *niggardly, rough*   16 **likes:** *pleases*   19 **Upon example:** *i.e. knowing others have endured the same troubles*   23 **casted slough:** *skin cast off*   **legerity:** *nimbleness*   26 **Do:** *convey*   **anon:** *immediately*   27 **pavilion:** *four syllables*

35 **God-a-mercy:** *many thanks*   36 **Qui va là:** *who goes there? cf. n.*   39 **popular:** *one of the common people*   40 **gentleman ... company:** *a gentleman volunteer, or a soldier on probation for promotion*   41 **Trail'st ... pike:** *are you in the infantry?*   **puissant:** *powerful pike: long, heavy lance*   45 **bawcock:** *fine fellow*   46 **imp:** *child, scion*   52 **Welshman:** *the king was born at Monmouth, on the Welsh border*   55 **leek:** *vegetable related to the onion; the national emblem of the Welsh*   61 **figo:** *see III.6.53; cf. n.*   64 **sorts:** *fits*   66 **fewer:** *F; many editors give lower (Q3). Q lower*   67 **admiration:** *wonder*   **prerogatifes:** *prerogatives, laws*   71 **Pompey's camp;** *cf. n.*   73 **modesty:** *moderation*

King. Though it appear a little out of fashion,
There is much care and valor in this Welshman.

Enter three Soldiers, John Bates, Alexander Court, and Michael
Williams.

Court. Brother John Bates, is not that the morning which
breaks yonder?

Bates. I think it be, but we have no great cause to desire 85
the approach of day.

Will. We see yonder the beginning of the day, but I think
we shall never see the end of it. Who goes there?

King. A friend.

Will. Under what captain serve you? 90

King. Under Sir Thomas Erpingham.

Will. A good old commander and a most kind gentleman. I
pray you, what thinks he of our estate?

King. Even as men wrack'd upon a sand, that look to be
wash'd off the next tide. 95

Bates. He hath not told his thought to the king?

King. No, nor it is not meet he should. For though I speak
it to you, I think the king is but a man, as I am. The violet
smells to him as it doth to me; the element shows to him as it
doth to me; all his senses have but human conditions. His 100
ceremonies laid by, in his nakedness he appears but a man. And
though his affections are higher mounted than ours, yet when
they stoop, they stoop with the like wing. Therefore, when he
sees reason of fears, as we do, his fears, out of doubt, be of the
same relish as ours are. Yet in reason no man should possess 105
him with any appearance of fear, lest he, by showing it, should
dishearten his army.

Bates. He may show what outward courage he will, but I believe, as cold a night as 'tis, he could wish himself in Thames
up to the neck. And so I would he were, and I by him, at 110
all adventures, so we were quit here.

King. By my troth, I will speak my conscience of the king. I
think he would not wish himself anywhere but where he is.

Bates. Then I would he were here alone. So should he be
sure to be ransomed, and a many poor men's lives saved. 115

King. I dare say you love him not so ill to wish him here
alone, howsoever you speak this to feel other men's minds. Methinks I could not die anywhere so contented as in the king's
company, his cause being just and his quarrel honorable.

Will. That's more than we know. 120

Bates. Ay, or more than we should seek after, for we know
enough if we know we are the king's subjects. If his cause be
wrong, our obedience to the king wipes the crime of it out of
us.

Will. But if the cause be not good, the king himself hath 125
a heavy reckoning to make when all those legs and arms and
heads chopp'd off in a battle shall join together at the latter
day and cry all 'We died at such a place'—some swearing,
some crying for a surgeon, some upon their wives left poor behind them, some upon the debts they owe, some upon their 130

children rawly left. I am afeard there are few die well that die
in a battle, for how can they charitably dispose of anything
when blood is their argument? Now if these men do not die
well, it will be a black matter for the king that led them to it,
who to disobey were against all proportion of subjection. 135

King. So, if a son that is by his father sent about merchandise do sinfully miscarry upon the sea, the imputation of his
wickedness, by your rule, should be imposed upon his father
that sent him. Or if a servant under his master's command
transporting a sum of money be assailed by robbers and die 140
in many irreconcil'd iniquities, you may call the business of the
master the author of the servant's damnation. But this is not
so. The king is not bound to answer the particular endings of
his soldiers, the father of his son, nor the master of his servant.
For they purpose not their death when they purpose their 145
services. Besides, there is no king, be his cause never so spotless,
if it come to the arbitrement of swords, can try it out with all
unspotted soldiers. Some peradventure have on them the guilt
of premeditated and contrived murther; some, of beguiling virgins with the broken seals of perjury; some, making the 150
wars their bulwark, that have before gored the gentle bosom of
peace with pillage and robbery. Now if these men have defeated the law and outrun native punishment, though they can
outstrip men, they have no wings to fly from God. War is his
beadle, war is his vengeance, so that here men are punish'd 155
for before-breach of the king's laws in now the king's quarrel.
Where they feared the death, they have borne life away, and
where they would be safe, they perish. Then if they die unprovided, no more is the king guilty of their damnation than he
was before guilty of those impieties for the which they are 160
now visited. Every subject's duty is the king's, but every subject's
soul is his own. Therefore should every soldier in the wars do
as every sick man in his bed—wash every mote out of his conscience. And dying so, death is to him advantage, or not
dying, the time was blessedly lost wherein such preparation 165
was gained. And in him that escapes, it were not sin to think
that, making God so free an offer, he let him outlive that day to
see his greatness and to teach others how they should prepare.

Will. 'Tis certain every man that dies ill, the ill upon his
own head—the king is not to answer it. 170

Bates. I do not desire he should answer for me, and yet I determine to fight lustily for him.

King. I myself heard the king say he would not be ransom'd.

Will. Ay, he said so to make us fight cheerfully. But when our
throats are cut, he may be ransom'd and we ne'er the wiser. 175

King. If I live to see it, I will never trust his word after.

Will. You pay him then! That's a perilous shot out of an elder-gun, that a poor and a private displeasure can do against a
monarch! You may as well go about to turn the sun to ice
with fanning in his face with a peacock's feather. You'll never 180
trust his word after! Come, 'tis a foolish saying.

---

81 **out of fashion:** *out of the ordinary, quaint* 91 **Thomas:** *F Iohn* 93 **estate:** *condi-*
tion 94 **wrack'd:** *wrecked* **sand:** *sand bar* 97 **meet:** *fitting* 99 **element shows:**
sky appears 100 **conditions:** *characteristics* 101 **ceremonies:** *symbols of state* 102
affections . . . mounted: *desires soar higher* 103 **stoop:** *sweep down (image from fal-*
conry). 104 **out of doubt:** *without doubt* 104, 105 **be . . relish:** *i.e. taste the*
same 105, 106 **possess him:** *take possession of him* 110, 111 **at all adventures:** *at*
all hazards 111 **quit:** *finished with this job* 112 **conscience:** *inner thoughts* 117
feel: *test* 127, 128 **latter day:** *judgment day* 129 **some upon:** *i.e. crying out the*
names of

131 **rawly left:** *poorly provided for* **die well:** *i.e. who die a Christian death.* 132 **charitably**
. . . anything: *settle anything in a spirit of charity* 135 **proportion of subjection:** *proper*
behavior for subjects 136, 137 **about merchandise:** *on a trading voyage* 137 **sinfully**
miscarry: *die in his sins* 141 **irreconcil'd iniquities:** *sins not confessed and atoned*
for 143 **answer:** *answer for* 147 **arbitrement:** *decision:* 148 **unspotted:** *sin-*
less 149 **contrived:** *deliberately planned* 151 **bulwark:** *defense; excuse for plunder-*
ing 153 **outrun . . . punishment:** *escaped punishment in their own country* 155 **beadle:**
parish officer who arrested and administered punishment 156 **before-. . . now:** *previous . . .*
what is now 157, 158 **Where . . . perish:** *see Matthew 16:25* 158, 159 **unprovided:**
unprepared for death 161 **visited:** *i.e. with punishment from God* 163 **mote:** *tiniest spot;*
F Moth 167 **offer:** *i.e. of his soul* 172 **lustily:** *vigorously* 177 **pay him:** *give him*
what he deserves 177, 178 **elder-gun:** *popgun:*

King. Your reproof is something too round. I should be
angry with you if the time were convenient.

Will. Let it be a quarrel between us if you live.

King. I embrace it.   *185*

Will. How shall I know thee again?

King. Give me any gage of thine, and I will wear it in my
bonnet. Then if ever thou dar'st acknowledge it, I will make it
my quarrel.

Will. Here's my glove. Give me another of thine.   *190*

King. There.

Will. This will I also wear in my cap. If ever thou come to
me and say, after tomorrow, 'this is my glove,' by this hand, I
will take thee a box on the ear.

King. If ever I live to see it, I will challenge it.   *195*

Will. Thou dar'st as well be hang'd.

King. Well, I will do it, though I take thee in the king's
company.

Will. Keep thy word. Fare thee well.

Bates. Be friends, you English fools, be friends. We have   *200*
French quarrels enow, if you could tell how to reckon.

King. Indeed, the French may lay twenty French crowns to
one they will beat us, for they bear them on their shoulders. But
it is no English treason to cut French crowns, and tomorrow
the king himself will be a clipper.   *Exeunt Soldiers.*   *205*
Upon the king! Let us our lives, our souls,
Our debts, our careful wives,
Our children, and our sins lay on the king!
We must bear all. O, hard condition,
Twin-born with greatness, subject to the breath   *210*
Of every fool, whose sense no more can feel
But his own wringing! what infinite heartsease
Must kings neglect that private men enjoy!
And what have kings that privates have not too,
Save ceremony, save general ceremony?   *215*
And what art thou, thou idol Ceremony?
What kind of god art thou, that suffer'st more
Of mortal griefs than do they worshipers?
What are thy rents? What are thy comings-in?
O Ceremony, show me but thy worth!   *220*
What is thy soul of adoration?
Art thou ought else but place, degree, and form,
Creating awe and fear in other men?
Wherein thou art less happy being fear'd
Than they in fearing.   *225*
What drink'st thou oft instead of homage sweet
But poison'd flattery? O, be sick, great greatness,
And bid thy ceremony give thee cure!
Think'st thou the fiery fever will go out
With titles blown from adulation?   *230*
Will it give place to flexure and low bending?
Canst thou, when thou command'st the beggar's knee,
Command the health of it? No, thou proud dream,
That play'st so subtly with a king's repose.
I am a king that find thee, and I know   *235*

'Tis not the balm, the scepter, and the ball,
The sword, the mace, the crown imperial,
The intertissu'd robe of gold and pearl,
The farced title running 'fore the king,
The throne he sits on, nor the tide of pomp   *240*
That beats upon the high shore of this world—
No, not all these, thrice-gorgeous Ceremony,
Not all these, laid in bed majestical,
Can sleep so soundly as the wretched slave
Who, with a body fill'd and vacant mind,   *245*
Gets him to rest cramm'd with distressful bread,
Never sees horrid night, the child of hell,
But like a lackey, from the rise to set,
Sweats in the eye of Phoebus, and all night
Sleeps in Elysium. Next day after dawn,   *250*
Doth rise and help Hyperion to his horse
And follows so the ever-running year
With profitable labor to his grave.
And, but for ceremony, such a wretch,
Winding up days with toil and nights with sleep,   *255*
Had the forehand and vantage of a king.
The slave, a member of the country's peace,
Enjoys it, but in gross brain little wots
What watch the king keeps to maintain the peace,
Whose hours the peasant best advantages.   *260*

Enter Erpingham.

Erp. My lord, your nobles, jealous of your absence,
Seek through your camp to find you.

King.   Good old knight,
Collect them all together at my tent.
I'll be before thee.   *265*

Erp.   I shall do't, my lord.   *Exit.*

King. O God of battles, steel my soldiers' hearts,
Possess them not with fear! Take from them now
The sense of reck'ning, if th' opposed numbers
Pluck their hearts from them. Not today, O Lord,   *270*
O, not today, think not upon the fault
My father made in compassing the crown!
I Richard's body have interred new
And on it have bestow'd more contrite tears
Than from it issu'd forced drops of blood.   *275*
Five hundred poor I have in yearly pay,
Who twice a day their wither'd hands hold up
Toward heaven, to pardon blood. And I have built
Two chantries where the sad and solemn priests
Sing still for Richard's soul. More will I do,   *280*
Though all that I can do is nothing worth,
Since that my penitence comes after all,
Imploring pardon.

Enter Gloucester.

Glouc. My liege!

182 round: *outspoken*   **187 gage:** *pledge*   **194 take:** *give*   **201 enow:** *enough*   **202-
205 Indeed ... clipper;** *cf. n.*   SD **Exeunt Soldiers:** *F puts after l. 228*   **207 careful:**
full of care   **209-213 We must ... enjoy;** *cf. n.*   **211 sense:** *sensibility*   **212 wringing:**
suffering   **213 neglect:** *forego*   **215 ceremony:** *accessory or symbol of state*   **219 comings-in:** *income*   **221 soul of adoration:** *that central virtue which makes people adore thee;
cf. n.*   **222 form:** *formality*   **229, 230 Think'st ... adulation:** *Can the empty titles of
flattery blow out the fire of a fever?*   **231 give place to:** *retire before*   **flexure:** *bending the
knee*   **235 find thee:** *find thee out*

236 balm: *holy oil with which kings are anointed*   **scepter:** *golden rod held by a king*   **ball:**
the globe carried as a sign of sovereignty   **237 mace:** *symbolizes the power to strike down
offenders*   **238 intertissu'd:** *interwoven*   **239 farced:** *stuffed* (with pompous
phrases)   **246 distressful:** *hard-earned*   **249 Phoebus:** *the sun*   **250 Elysium:** *Paradise*   **251 Hyperion:** *the sun*   **255 Winding up:** *occupying and crowing*   **256 forehand:** *upper hand*   **257 member:** *sharer*   **258 gross:** *dull*   **wots:** *knows*   **260 best
advantages:** *turns to the greatest profit*   **261 jealous:** *of apprehensive about*   **269 sense
of:** *faculty for*   **reck'ning, if;** *cf. n.*   **270-283 Not today ... pardon;** *cf. n.*   **272
compassing:** *getting possession of*   **279 chantries:** *chapels where priests sing masses for the
dead*   **sad:** *grave*   **280 still:** *continuously*

King. My brother Gloucester's voice? Ay.   285
I know thy errand, I will go with thee.
The day, my friends, and all things stay for me.

                                   Exeunt.

❧ Scene Second ❧

Enter the Dolphin, Orleans, Rambures, and Beaumont.

Orl. The sun doth gild our armor. Up, my lords!
Dol. Montez à cheval! My horse! Varlet! Laquais! Ha!
Orl. O brave spirit!
Dol. Via! les eaux et la terre.
Orl. Rien puis? L'air et le feu.   5
Dol. Ciel! Cousin Orleans.

Enter Constable.

Now, my Lord Constable?
  Con. Hark how our steeds for present service neigh!
  Dol. Mount them and make incision in their hides,
That their hot blood may spin in English eyes   10
And dout them with superfluous courage, ha!
Rambures. What, will you have them weep our horses' blood?
How shall we then behold their natural tears?

Enter Messenger.

Mess. The English are embattl'd, you French peers.
  Con. To horse, you gallant princes, straight to horse!   15
Do but behold yon poor and starved band,
And your fair show shall suck away their souls,
Leaving them but the shales and husks of men.
There is not work enough for all our hands,
Scarce blood enough in all their sickly veins   20
To give each naked curtal ax a stain,
That our French gallants shall today draw out
And sheathe for lack of sport. Let us but blow on them,
The vapor of our valor will o'erturn them.
'Tis positive 'gainst all exceptions, lords,   25
That our superfluous lackeys and our peasants,
Who in unnecessary action swarm
About our squares of battle, were enow
To purge this field of such a hilding foe,
Though we upon this mountain's basis by   30
Took stand for idle speculation.
But that our honors must not. What's to say?
A very little little let us do,
And all is done. Then let the trumpets sound
The tucket sonance and the note to mount,   35
For our approach shall so much dare the field
That England shall couch down in fear and yield.

Enter Grandpré.

Grand. Why do you stay so long, my lords of France?
Yon island carrions, desperate of their bones,
Ill-favoredly become the morning field.   40
Their ragged curtains poorly are let loose,
And our air shakes them passing scornfully.
Big Mars seems bankrout in their beggar'd host
And faintly through a rusty beaver peeps.
The horsemen sit like fixed candlesticks   45
With torch staves in their hand, and their poor jades
Lob down their heads, dropping the hides and hips,
The gum down-roping from their pale-dead eyes,
And in their pale dull mouths the gimmal'd bit
Lies foul with chaw'd grass, still and motionless.   50
And their executors, the knavish crows,
Fly o'er them all, impatient for their hour.
Description cannot suit itself in words
To demonstrate the life of such a battle
In life so liveless as it shows itself.   55
  Con. They have said their prayers, and they stay for death.
  Dol. Shall we go send them dinners and fresh suits
And give their fasting horses provender,
And after fight with them?
  Con. I stay but for my guidon. To the field!   60
I will the banner from a trumpet take
And use it for my haste. Come, come away!
The sun is high, and we outwear the day.   *Exeunt.*

❧ Scene Third ❧

*Enter Gloucester, Bedford, Exeter, Erpingham with all his host,
Salisbury, and Westmoreland.*

Glouc. Where is the king?
Bedford: The king himself is rode to view their battle.
West. Of fighting men they have full three-score thousand.
Exe. There's five to one; besides, they all are fresh.
Sal. God's arm strike with us! 'Tis a fearful odds.   5
God bye you, princes all. I'll to my charge.
If we no more meet till we meet in heaven,
Then joyfully, my noble Lord of Bedford,
My dear Lord Gloucester, and my good Lord Exeter,
And my kind kinsman, warriors all, adieu!   10
  Bedford. Farwell, good Salisbury, and good luck go with
thee!
  Exe. Farwell, kind lord. Fight valiantly today.
And yet I do thee wrong to mind thee of it,
For thou art fram'd of the firm truth of valor.   15

                          [Exit Salisbury.]

  Bedford. He is as full of valor as of kindness,
Princely in both.

---

287 friends: *F* friend   **SD Beaumont:** *does not speak, and appears here only*   **1 armor. Up:** *F* Armour vp   **2 Montez à cheval:** *To horse!* **Varlet:** *valet; F* Verlot **Laquais:** *lackey, servant*   **4-6 Via … Ciel:** *Away, water and earth./Nothing more? Air and fire./-Heavens!*   **8 present:** *immediate*   **9 make incision:** *i.e. with spurs*   **10 spin in:** *gush forth into*   **11 dout:** *put out; F* doubt **courage:** *thought to reside in the blood*   **14 embattl'd:** *drawn up in battle formation*   **17 fair show:** *splendid appearance*   **18 shales:** *shells*   **21 curtal ax:** *cutlass, short curved sword used by horsemen when the lance is broken*   **25 positive … exceptions:** *certain against all objections* **'gainst:** *F* against   **28 enow:** *enough*   **29 hilding:** *worthless*   **31 for … speculation:** *as idle onlookers*   **35 tucket sonance:** *trumpet call*   **36 dare:** *dazzle, frighten*   **37 couch:** *crouch*

39 carrions: *carcasses* **desperate of:** *without hope of saving*   **40 Ill-favoredly become:** *are ugly or incongruous upon*   **41 curtains:** *banners*   **42 passing:** *very*   **43 bankrout:** *bankrupt*   **44 beaver:** *the movable part of the helmet*   **45 candlesticks:** *figures of men on ornamental candlesticks*   **47 Lob:** *hang*   **48 down-roping:** *dangling down like rope*   **49 gimmal'd:** *jointed; often read* gimmal; *F* Iymold   **51 executors:** *i.e. those who will have the disposal of what is left of their bodies*   **52 them all, impatient:** *F; many editors read* them, all impatient   **53 suit … words:** *clothe itself in adequate language*   **54 demonstrate … battle:** *depict such an army to the life*   **55 liveless:** *lifeless; see III.6.8-9; cf. n.*   **60 guidon:** *standard; F* Guard:on   **61 banner:** *streamer fastened to a trumpet*   **63 outwear:** *wear out*   **2 battle:** *army lines*   **3-4 threescore … to one:** *from Holinshed, who says 'six times as manie.'*   **6 God … you:** *most editors read* God be wi' you; *F* God buy you **charge:** *command*   **11-15 farewell … valor:** *farewell, etc.; cf. n.*   **14 mind:** *remind*   **15 fram'd:** *made*

Enter the king.

West. O, that we now had here
But one ten thousand of those men in England
That do no work today!
    King.   What's he that wishes so?   20
My cousin Westmoreland? No, my fair cousin.
If we are mark'd to die, we are enow
To do our country loss, and if to live,
The fewer men, the greater share of honor.   25
God's will! I pray thee wish not one man more.
By Jove, I am not covetous for gold,
Nor care I who doth feed upon my cost.
It yearns me not if men my garments wear;
Such outward things dwell not in my desires.   30
But if it be a sin to covet honor,
I am the most offending soul alive.
No, faith, my coz, wish not a man from England.
God's peace! I would not lose so great an honor
As one man more, methinks, would share from me   35
For the best hope I have. O, do not wish one more!
Rather proclaim it, Westmoreland, through my host
That he which hath no stomach to this fight,
Let him depart. His passport shall be made
And crowns for convoy put into his purse.   40
We would not die in that man's company
That fears his fellowship to die with us.
This day is call'd the feast of Crispian.
He that outlives this day and comes safe home
Will stand a-tiptoe when this day is nam'd   45
And rouse him at the name of Crispian
He that shall see this day and live old age
Will yearly on the vigil feast his neighbors
And say 'Tomorrow is Saint Crispian.'
Then will he strip his sleeve and show his scars,   50
[And say 'These wounds I had on Crispin's day.']
Old men forget; yet all shall be forgot,
But he'll remember with advantages
What feats he did that day. Then shall our names,
Familiar in this mouth as household words—   55
Harry the King, Bedford and Exeter,
Warwick and Talbot, Salisbury and Gloucester—
Be in their flowing cups freshly rememb'red.
This story shall the good man teach his son.
And Crispin Crispian shall ne'er go by   60
From this day to the ending of the world,
But we in it shall be remembered—
We few, we happy few, we band of brothers.
For he today that sheds his blood with me
Shall be my brother. Be he ne'er so vile,   65
This day shall gentle his condition.
And gentlemen in England now abed
Shall think themselves accurs'd they were not here,
And hold their manhoods cheap whiles any speaks
That fought with us upon Saint Crispin's day.   70

Enter Salisbury.

Sal. My sovereign lord, bestow yourself with speed.
The French are bravely in their battles set
And will with all expedience charge on us.
    King. All things are ready if our minds be so.
    West. Perish the man whose mind is backward now!   75
    King. Thou dost not wish more help from England, coz?
    West. God's will, my liege! Would you and I alone
Without more help, could fight this royal battle!
    King. Why, now thou hast unwish'd five thousand men,
Which likes me better than to wish us one.   80
You know your places. God be with you all!

Tucket. Enter Montjoy.

    Mont. Once more I come to know of thee, King Harry,
If for thy ransom thou wilt now compound
Before thy most assured overthrow.
For certainly thou art so near the gulf   85
Thou needs must be englutted. Besides, in mercy,
The Constable desires thee thou wilt mind
Thy followers of repentance, that their souls
May make a peaceful and a sweet retire
From off these fields, where, wretches, their poor bodies   90
Must lie and fester.
    King.   Who hath sent thee now?
    Mont. The Constable of France.
    King. I pray thee bear my former answer back.
Bid them achieve me and then sell my bones.   95
Good God! Why should they mock poor fellows thus?
The man that once did sell the lion's skin
While the beast liv'd was kill'd with hunting him.
A many of our bodies shall no doubt
Find native graves, upon the which, I trust,   100
Shall witness live in brass of this day's work.
And those that leave their valiant bones in France,
Dying like men, though buried in your dunghills,
They shall be fam'd. For there the sun shall greet them
And draw their honors reeking up to heaven,   105
Leaving their earthly parts to choke your clime,
The smell whereof shall breed a plague in France.
Mark then abounding valor in our English,
That being dead, like to the bullet's crasing,
Break out into a second course of mischief,   110
Killing in relapse of mortality.
Let me speak proudly. Tell the Constable
We are but warriors for the working day.
Our gayness and our gilt are all besmirch'd
With rainy marching in the painful field.   115
There's not a piece of feather in our host—
Good argument, I hope, we will not fly—
And time hath worn us into slovenry.
But, by the mass, our hearts are in the trim,
And my poor soldiers tell me, yet ere night   120
They'll be in fresher robes, or they will pluck
The gay new coats o'er the French soldiers' heads

18-20 O . . . today; *cf. n.*   28 upon: *at*   29 yearns: *grieves*   31, 32 But if . . . alive;
cf. n.   40 convoy: *traveling expenses*   42 fears . . . us: *fears to share death with us.*   43
Crispian; *cf. n.*   47 live: F; live to; *cf. n.*   48 vigil: *eve of a Christian festival*   51
And say . . . day: Q: *not in F*   53 advantages: *exaggerations*   65 vile: *of low
birth*   66 gentle . . . condition: *give him the rank of a gentleman*

71 bestow yourself: *take up your position*   72 bravely: *in splendid array* battles:: *lines of
battle* 73 expedience: *haste* 80 likes: *pleases* 83 compound: *make terms* 85
gulf: *whirlpool* 86 englutted: *swallowed up* 87 mind: *remind* 95 achieve: *capture,
kill* 100 native: *i.e. in England* 101 in brass: *i.e. a memorial table in a church* 109
crasing: *variant form of 'grazing,' rebounding* 111 relapse of mortality: *renewed power to
kill; decomposition* 113 working day: *i.e. strictly for business* 116 feather: *i.e. in plumes
on the helmets* 117 argument: *proof*

And turn them out of service. If they do this—
As, if God please, they shall—my ransom then
Will soon be levied. Herald, save thou thy labor.   *125*
Come thou no more for ransom, gentle herald.
They shall have none, I swear, but these my joints,
Which if they have as I will leave 'em them,
Shall yield them little, tell the Constable.
    Mont. I shall, King Harry. And so fare thee well.   *130*
Thou never shalt hear herald any more.   *Exit.*
    King. I fear thou wilt once more come again for a ransom.

            Enter York.

    York. My lord, most humbly on my knee I beg
The leading of the vaward.
    King. Take it, brave York. Now, soldiers, march away,   *135*
And how thou pleasest, God, dispose the day!   *Exeunt.*

        ❧ SCENE FOURTH ❧

    Alarum. Excursions. Enter Pistol, French Soldier, Boy.

    Pist. Yield, cur!
    French. Je pense que vous êtes le gentilhomme de bonne
qualité.
    Pist. Qualtitie calmie custure me! Art thou a gentleman?
What is thy name? Discuss.   *5*
    French. O Seigneur Dieu!
    Pist. O Signieur Dew should be a gentleman.
Perpend my words, O Signieur Dew, and mark.
O Signieur Dew, thou diest on point of fox,
Except, O Signieur, thou do give to me   *10*
Egregious ransom.
    French. O, prenez miséricorde! Ayez pitié de moi!
    Pist. Moy shall not serve, I will have forty moys,
Or I will fetch thy rim out at thy throat
In drops of crimson blood.   *15*
    French. Est-il impossible d'échapper la force de ton bras?
    Pist. Brass, cur?
Thou damned and luxurious mountain goat,
Offer'st me brass?
    French. O, pardonnez-moi!   *20*
    Pist. Say'st thou me so? Is that a ton of moys?
Come hither, boy. Ask me this slave in French
What is his name.
    Boy. Ecoutez. Comment êtes-vous appelé?
    French. Monsieur le Fer.   *25*
    Boy. He says his name is Master Fer.
    Pist. Master Fer! I'll fer him, and firk him, and ferret him!
Discuss the same in French unto him.
    Boy. I do not know the French for fer, and ferret, and firk.

    Pist. Bid him prepare, for I will cut his throat.   *30*
    French. Que dit-il, monsieur?
    Boy. Il me commande à vous dire que vous faites vous prêt,
car ce soldat ici est disposé tout à cette heure de couper votre
gorge.
    Pist. Owy, cuppele gorge, permafoy,   *35*
Peasant, unless thou give me crowns, brave crowns,
Or mangled shalt thou be by this my sword.
    French. O, je vous supplie, pour l'amour de Dieu, me par-
donner! Je suis le gentilhomme de bonne maison. Gardez ma
vie, et je vous donnerai deux cents écus.   *40*
    Pist. What are his words?
    Boy. He prays you to save his life. He is a gentleman of a
good house, and for his ransom he will give you two hundred
crowns.
    Pist. Tell him my fury shall abate, and I   *45*
The crowns will take.
    French. Petit monsieur, que dit-il?
    Boy. Encore qu'il est contre son jurement de pardonner
aucun prisonnier; néanmoins, pour les écus que vous l'avez promis, il est content de vous donner la liberté, le franshisement.
    French. Sur mes genoux je vous donne mille remercîments,
et je m'estime heureux que je suis tombé entre les mains d'un
chevalier, je pense, le plus brave, vaillant, et très distingué seigneur d'Angleterre.
    Pist. Expound unto me, boy.   *55*
    Boy. He gives you upon his knees a thousand thanks, and
he esteems himself happy that he hath fall'n into the hands of
one (as he thinks) the most brave, valorous, and thrice-worthy
signieur of England.
    Pist. As I suck blood, I will some mercy show!   *60*
Follow me.
    Boy. Suivez-vous le grand capitaine.

        [Exeunt Pistol and French Soldier.]
I did never know so full a voice issue from so empty a heart.
But the saying is true: 'The empty vessel makes the greatest
sound.' Bardolph and Nym had ten times more valor than   *65*
this roaring divel i' th' old play, that everyone may pare his
nails with a wooden dagger, and they are both hang'd. And so
would this be, if he durst steal anything adventurously. I must
stay with the lackeys, with the luggage of our camp. The
French might have a good prey of us, if he knew of it, for   *70*
there is none to guard it but boys.   *Exit.*

        ❧ SCENE FIFTH ❧

    Enter Constable, Orleans, Bourbon, Dolphin, and Rambures.

    Con. O diable!
    Orl. O Seigneur! le jour est perdu, tout est perdu!

---

123 turn . . . service: *deprive them of their coats as if they wer servants wearing their master's livery* **128 'em:** *F* vm **132 thou wilt:** *read 'thou'lt'* **134 vaward:** *vanguard* **SD Alarum:** *trumpet call to arms* **Excursions:** *sallies across the stage as if in battle; cf. n.* **2-3 Je . . . qualité:** *I think that you are a gentleman of high rank* **4 Qualtitie . . . me;** *cf. n.* **7-11 O . . . ransom;** *cf. n.* **8 Perpend:** *ponder* **9 fox:** *sword* **11 Egregious:** *enormous* **12 O . . . moi:** *O, have mercy! Have pity on me! (moi was pronounced 'moy').* **13 Moy:** *Pistol perhaps thinks that the Frenchman speaks of a coin, or unit of measure* **14 Or:** *F for* **rim:** *diaphragm* **16 Est-il . . . bras:** *Is it impossible to escape the strength of your arm?* **17 Brass:** *the s in bras was sounded in French of this period* **18 luxurious:** *lascivious* **20, 21 pardonnez . . . a ton of:** *most of Pistol's echoes are of this sort* **24 Ecoutez . . . appelé:** *Listen What is your name?* **27 firk:** *beat* **29 ferret:** *worry*

31-34 Que . . . gorge: *What doe she say, sir?* Boy. *He bids me tell you that you prepare yourself, because this soldier is inclined to cut your throat at once* **33 à cette heure;** *cf. n.* **35 Owy . . . permafoy:** *Yes, cut your throat, in faith cf. n.* **36 brave:** *fine* **38-40 O . . . écus:** *O, I beseech you, for the love of God, to pardon me! I am a gentleman of a good house. Save my life, and I shall give you two hundred crowns* **47-54 Petit . . . d'Angleterre:** *Little sir, what does he say?* Boy. [I say] *again that it is against his oath to pardon any prisoner; nevertheless, for the crowns which you have promised, he is willing to give you your liberty, your freedom.* Frenchman. *On my knees I give you a thousand thanks, and I consider myself happy that I have fallen into the hands of a knight, I think the bravest, the most valiant and distinguished nobleman in England* **62 Suivez-vous . . . capitaine:** *Follow the great captain* **63 heart:** *the seat of courage* **66, 67 roaring . . . dagger;** *cf. n.* **66 that . . . his:** *whose* **2 O . . . perdu:** *O Lord! the day is lost, all is lost!*

Dol. Mort Dieu! ma vie! all is confounded, all!
Reproach and everlasting shame
Sits mocking in our plumes.   *A short alarum.*   5
O méchante fortune! Do not run away.
   Con. Why, all our ranks are broke.
   Dol. O, perdurable shame! Let's stab ourselves.
Be these the wretches that we play'd at dice for?
   Orl. Is this the king we sent to for his ransom?   10
   Bourbon. Shame, and eternal shame, nothing but shame!
Let us die in honor. Once more back again!
And he that will not follow Bourbon now,
Let him go hence, and with his cap in hand,
Like a base pander hold the chamber door   15
Whilst by a slave no gentler than my dog
His fairest daughter is contaminated.
   Con. Disorder that hath spoil'd us, friend us now!
Let us on heaps go offer up our lives.
   Orl. We are enow yet living in the field   20
To smother up the English in our throngs,
If any order might be thought upon.
   Bourbon. The divel take order now! I'll to the throng.
Let life be short, else shame will be too long.

                                          Exeunt.

❧ SCENE SIXTH ❧

Alarum. Enter the King and his train, [Exeter, and others,]
with Prisoners.

   King. Well have we done, thrice valiant countrymen!
But all's not done; yet keep the French the field.
   Exe. The Duke of York commends him to your majesty.
   King. Lives he, good uncle? Thrice within this hour
I saw him down, thrice up again and fighting.   5
From helmet to the spur all blood he was.
   Exe. In which array, brave soldier, doth he lie
Larding the plain, and by his bloody side,
Yoke-fellow to his honor-owing wounds,
The noble Earl of Suffolk also lies.   10
Suffolk first died, and York, all haggled over,
Comes to him where in gore he lay insteep'd,
And takes him by the beard, kisses the gashes
That bloodily did yawn upon his face,
And cries aloud 'Tarry, my cousin Suffolk!   15
My soul shall thine keep company to heaven.
Tarry, sweet soul, for mine, then fly abreast,
As in this glorious and well-foughten field
We kept together in our chivalry.'
Upon these words I came and cheer'd him up.   20
He smil'd me in the face, raught me his hand,
And with a feeble gripe says 'Dear my lord,
Commend my service to my sovereign.'
So did he turn, and over Suffolk's neck
He threw his wounded arm and kiss'd his lips,   25
And so espous'd to death, with blood he seal'd

A testament of noble-ending love.
The pretty and sweet manner of it forc'd
Those waters from me which I would have stopp'd.
But I had not so much of man in me,   30
And all my mother came into mine eyes
And gave me up to tears.
   King.   I blame you not,
For, hearing this, I must perforce compound
With mistful eyes, or they will issue too.   *Alarum.*   35
But hark! What new alarum is this same?
The French have reinforc'd their scatter'd men.
Then every soldier kill his prisoners.
Give the word through.   *Exeunt.*

❧ SCENE SEVENTH ❧

Enter Fluellen and Gower.

   Flu. Kill the poys and the luggage! 'Tis expressly against the
law of arms. 'Tis as arrant a piece of knavery, mark you now,
as can be offert. In your conscience, now, is it not?
   Gow. 'Tis certain there's not a boy left alive, and the cowardly rascals that ran form the battle ha' done this slaughter.   5
Besides, they have burned and carried away all that was in the
king's tent, wherefore the king most worthily hath caus'd every
soldier to cut his prisoner's throat. O, 'tis a gallant king!
   Flu. Ay, he was porn at Monmouth, Captain Gower. What
call you the town's name where Alexander the Pig was born?   10
   Gow. Alexander the Great.
   Flu. Why, I pray you, is not 'pig' great? The pig, or the
great, or the mighty, or the huge, or the magnanimous are all
one reckonings, save the phrase is a little variations.
   Gow. I think Alexander the Great was born in Macedon.   15
His father was called Philip of Macedon, as I take it.
   Flu. I think it is Macedon where Alexander is porn. I tell
you, captain, if you look in the maps of the 'orld, I warrant
you sall find, in the comparisons between Macedon and Monmouth, that the situations, look you, is both alike. There is a   20
river in Macedon, and there is also moreover a river at Monmouth. It is call'd Wye at Monmouth, but it is out of my
prains what is the name of the other river. But 'tis all one; 'tis
alike as my fingers is to my fingers, and there is salmons in
both. If you mark Alexander's life well, Harry of Mon-   25
mouth's life is come after it indifferent well, for there is figures
in all things. Alexander, God knows, and you know, in his
rages, and his furies, and his wraths, and his cholers, and his
moods, and his displeasures, and his indignations, and also
being a little intoxicates in his prains, did in his ales and   30
his angers, look you, kill his best friend, Cleitus.
   Gow. Our king is not like him in that. He never kill'd any
of his friends.
   Flu. It is not well done, mark you now, to take the tales
out of my mouth, ere it is made and finished. I speak but in   35
the figures and comparisons of it. As Alexander kill'd his friend
Cleitus, being in his ales and his cups, so also Harry Mon-

3 Mort … vie: *F* Mor Dieu ma vie; *see III.5.11.*   **confounded:** *ruined*   **6 méchante:**
wicked, spiteful   **8 perdurable:** *everlasting*   **9 Be:** *are*   **12 die in honor. Once;**
cf. n.   **16 by a slave:** *O; F* a base slaue   **18 spoil'd:** *ruined*   **friend:** *befriend*   **19**
on heaps: *in crowds*   **3 commends him:** *sends his respects*   **8 Larding:** *enriching*   **9**
honor-owing: *possessing honor, honorable*   **11 haggled:** *hacked*   **12 insteep'd:**
stained   **14, 15 face, And:** *Q; F* face. He   **21 raught:** *reached*   **22 gripe:** *grip*

28 pretty: *lovely*   **31 mother:** *the more tender part of me*   **34 compound:** *come to*
terms   **35 issue:** *flow*   **Alarum:** *trumpet call to arms*   **38 kill his prisoners:** *i.e. so that*
the prisoners could not revolt and kill their captors; cf. n.   **IV.7** *F wrongly heads this* Actus
Quartus   **13 magnanimous:** *great souled*   **26 is … well:** *takes after it fairly well* **fi-**
gures: *prototypes, analogies, significance*   **31 Cleitus:** *one of the generals of Alexander the*
Great

mouth, being in his right wits and his good judgments, turn'd away the fat knight with the great-belly doublet. He was full of jests, and gipes, and knaveries, and mocks. I have forgot his 40 name.

Gow. Sir John Falstaff.

Flu. That is he. I'll tell you, there is good men porn at Monmouth.

Gow. Here comes his majesty.   45

Alarum. Enter King Harry and Bourbon with Prisoners, [Warwick, Gloucester, Exeter, and others]. Flourish.

King. I was not angry since I came to France
Until this instant. Take a trumpet, herald.
Ride thou unto the horsemen on yon hill.
If they will fight with us, bid them come down,
Or void the field. They do offend our sight.   50
If they'll do neither, we will come to them
And make them skirr away as swift as stones
Enforced from the old Assyrian slings.
Besides, we'll cut the throats of those we have,
And not a man of them that we shall take   55
Shall taste our mercy. Go and tell them so.

Enter Montjoy.

Exe. Here comes the herald of the French, my liege.
Glou. His eyes are humbler than they us'd to be.
King. How now! What means this, herald? Know'st thou not   60
That I have fin'd these bones of mine for ransom?
Com'st thou again for ransom?

Mont.   No, great king.
I come to thee for charitable license,
That we may wander o'er this bloody field   65
To book our dead, and then to bury them,
To sort our nobles from our common men.
For many of our princes—woe the while!—
Lie drown'd and soak'd in mercenary blood.
So do our vulgar drench their peasant limbs   70
In blood of princes, and their wounded steeds
Fret fetlock-deep in gore and with wild rage
Yerk out their armed heels at their dead masters,
Killing them twice. O, give us leave, great king,
To view the field in safety and dispose   75
Of their dead bodies!

King.   I tell thee truly, herald,
I know not if the day be ours or no,
For yet a many of your horsemen peer
And gallop o'er the field.   80

Mont.   The day is yours.
King. Prais'd be God and not our strength for it!
What is this castle call'd that stands hard by?

Mont. They call it Agincourt.

King. Then call we this the field of Agincourt,   85
Fought on the day of Crispin Crispianus.

Flu. Your grandfather of famous memory, an't please your majesty, and your great-uncle Edward the Plack Prince of Wales, as I have read in the chronicles, fought a most prave pattle here in France.   90

King. They did, Fluellen.

Flu. Your majesty says very true. If your majesties is rememb'red of it, the Welshmen did good service in a garden where leeks did grow, wearing leeks in their Monmouth caps, which your majesty know to this hour is an honorable badge of   95
the service. And I do believe your majesty takes no scorn to wear the leek upon Saint Tavy's Day.

King. I wear it for a memorable honor,
For I am Welsh, you know, good countryman.

Flu. All the water in Wye cannot wash your majesty's Welsh   100
plood out of your pody, I can tell you that. God pless it, and preserve it, as long as it pleases his grace, and his majesty too!

King. Thanks, good my countryman.

Flu. By Jeshu, I am your majesty's countryman, I care not who know it! I will confess it to all the 'orld. I need not   105
to be ashamed of your majesty, praised be God, so long as your majesty is an honest man.

King. God keep me so!

Enter Williams.

Our heralds go with him.
Bring me just notice of the numbers dead   110
On both our parts.   *[Exeunt Heralds with Montjoy.]*
Call yonder fellow hither.

Exe. Soldier, you must come to the king.

King. Soldier, why wear'st thou that glove in thy cap?

Will. An't please your majesty, 'tis the gage of one that   115
I should fight withal, if he be alive.

King. An Englishman?

Will. An't please your majesty, a rascal that swagger'd with me last night, who, if alive and ever dare to challenge this glove, I have sworn to take him a box o' th' ear. Or if I   120
can see my glove in his cap—which he swore as he was a soldier he would wear, if alive—I will strike it out soundly.

King. What think you, captain Fluellen? Is it fit this soldier keep his oath?

Flu. He is a craven and a villain else, an't please your   125
majesty, in my conscience.

King. It may be his enemy is a gentleman of great sort, quite from the answer of his degree.

Flu. Though he be as good a gentleman as the divel is, as Lucifer and Belzebub himself, it is necessary, look your   130
grace, that he keep his vow and his oath. If he be perjur'd, see you now, his reputation is as arrant a villain and a Jacksauce as ever his black shoe trod upon God's ground, and his earth, in my conscience, la!

King. Then keep thy vow, sirrah, when thou meet'st   135
the fellow.

Will. So I will, my liege, as I live.

39 **great-belly doublet:** *a long waistcoat*   40 **gipes:** *jibes*   42 **Falstaff:** *see the famous rejection scene (2 Henry IV, V.5).*   **SD Bourbon;** *cf. n.*   46-56 **I was . . . them so;** *cf. n.*   47 **trumpet:** *trumpeter*   50 **void:** *abandon*   52 **skirr:** *scurry*   53 **Assyrian slings:** *see Judith 9:7*   54-56 **we'll cut . . . mercy:** *Gower said (11. 7, 8) that the order given at IV.6.38 was already carried out*   57-84 **Here comes . . . Agincourt;** *cf. n.*   61 **fin'd:** *reserved as a fine, fixed as the price to be paid*   66 **book:** *register*   69 **mercenary blood:** *blood of average soldiers, who, unlike the nobles, fight for wages*   70 **vulgar:** *common soldiers*   71 **and their:** *F and with*   72 **Fret:** *chafe*   73 **Yerk:** *kick*   **armed:** *spiked*   79 **Peer:** *appear*

87 **grandfather:** *great-grandfather (if Edward III is meant).*   90 **pattle:** *The Battle of Crécy*   93, 94 **Welshmen . . . caps;** *cf. n.*   98 **memorable honor:** *honorable memorial*   100, 101 **Welsh plood;** *cf. n.*   108 **God:** *F Good*   110, 111 **Bring . . . parts;** *cf. n.*   110 **just:** *exact*   119 **alive:** *F; many editors read a' live*   120 **take:** *give*   128 **quite . . . degree:** *too far above Williams' rank to accept any challenge from him*   132 **Jacksauce:** *saucy knave*   133 **his . . . shoe:** *anyone whose dirty foot*

King. Who serv'st thou under?

Will. Under Captain Gower, my liege.

Flu. Gower is a good captain, and is good knowledge   *140*
and literatured in the wars.

King. Call him hither to me, soldier.

Will. I will, my liege.

King. Here, Fluellen, wear thou this favor for me and stick
it in thy cap. When Alençon and myself were down together, I
pluck'd this glove from his helm. If any man challenge this, he
is a friend to Alençon and an enemy to our person. If thou encounter any such, apprehend him, an thou dost me love.

Flu. Your grace doo's me as great honors as can be desir'd
in the hearts of his subjects. I would fain see the man, that   *150*
has but two legs, that shall find himself aggrief'd at this glove,
that is all. But I would fain see it once, an please god of his
grace that I might see.

King. Know'st thou Gower?

Flue. He is my dear friend, an please you.   *155*

King. Pray thee, go seek him and bring him to my tent.

Flu. I will fetch him.   *Exit.*

King. My Lord of Warwick, and my brother Gloucester,
Follow Fluellen closely at the heels.
The glove which I have given him for a favor   *160*
May haply purchase him a box o' th' ear.
It is the soldier's. I by bargain should
Wear it myself. Follow, good cousin Warwick.
If that the soldier strike him, as I judge
By his blunt bearing he will keep his word,   *165*
Some sudden mischief may arise of it.
For I do know Fluellen valiant.
And, touch'd with choler, hot as gunpowder,
And quickly will return an injury.
Follow, and see there be no harm between them.   *170*
Go you with me, uncle of Exeter.   *Exeunt.*

❧ SCENE EIGHTH ❧

Enter Gower and Williams.

Will. I warrant it is to knight you, captain.

Enter Fluellen

Flu. God's will and his pleasure, captain, I beseech you
now, come apace to the king. there is more good toward you
peradventure than is in your knowledge to dream of.

Will. Sir, know you this glove?   *5*

Flu. Know the glove! I know the glove is a glove.

Will. I know this, and thus I challenge it.

Strikes him.

Flu. 'Sblood! an arrant traitor as any is in the universal
world, or in France, or in England!

Gow. How now, sir! You villain!   *10*

Will. Do you think I'll be forsworn?

Flu. Stand away, Captain Gower. I will give treason his payment into plows, I warrant you.

Will. I am no traitor.

Flu. That's a lie in thy throat! I charge you in his majesty's   *15*
name, apprehend him. He's a friend of the Duke Alençon's.

Enter Warwick and Gloucester.

War. How now, how now! What's the matter?

Flu. My Lord of Warwick, here is—praised be God for
it!—a most contagious treason come to light, look you, as you
shall desire in a summer's day. Here is his majesty.   *20*

Enter King and Exeter.

King. How now! What's the matter?

Flu. My liege, here is a villain and a traitor that, look your
grace, has struck the glove which your majesty is take out of
the helmet of Alençon.

Will. My liege, this was my glove, here is the fellow of it.   *25*
And he that I gave it to in change promis'd to wear it in his
cap. I promis'd to strike him if he did. I met this man with
my glove in his cap, and I have been as good as my word.

Flu. Your majesty hear now, saving your majesty's manhood,
what an arrant, rascally, beggarly, lousy knave it is. I hope   *30*
your majesty is pear me testimony and witness, and will
avouchment, that this is the glove of Alençon that your majesty is give me, in your conscience now.

King. Give me thy glove, soldier. Look, here is the fellow of it.
'Twas I indeed thou promised'st to strike,   *35*
And thou hast given me most bitter terms.

Flu. An please your majesty, let his neck answer for it, if
there is any martial law in the world.

King. How canst thou make me satisfaction?

Will. All offenses, my lord, come from the heart. Never   *40*
came any from mine that might offend your majesty.

King. It was ourself thou didst abuse.

Will. Your majesty came not like yourself. You appear'd to
me but as a common man. Witness the night, your garments,
your lowliness. And what your highness suffer'd under that   *45*
shape, I beseech you take it for your own fault, and not mine.
For had you been as I took you for, I made no offense. Therefore I beseech your highness pardon me.

King. Here, uncle Exeter, fill this glove with crowns
And give it to this fellow. Keep it, fellow,   *50*
And wear it for an honor in thy cap
Till I do challenge it. Give him the crowns,
And, captain, you must needs be friends with him.

Flu. By this day and this light, the fellow has mettle enough
in his belly. Hold, there is twelve pence for you, and I pray   *55*
you to serve God, and keep you out of prawls and prabbles,
and quarrels, and dissentions, and I warrant you it is the better
for you.

Will. I will none of your money.

Flu. It is with a good will. I can tell you it will serve   *60*
you to mend your shoes. Come, wherefore should you be so
pashful? Your shoes is not so good. 'Tis a good silling, I warrant you, or I will change it.

Enter [an English] Herald.

King. Now, herald, are the dead numb'red?

Herald. Here is the number of the slaught'red French.   *65*

[Gives a paper.]

---

148 apprehend: *arrest* an: *if*   149 doo's: *does; cf. n.*   168 choler: *anger*   169 injury: *insult*   8 'Sblood: *by God's blood* any is: *F anyes*   11 be forsworn: *break my
oath*

26 change: *exchange*   32 avouchment: *certify*   36 terms: *words*   37 An: *if it*   38
martial: *F Marshall*   56 prabbles: *quarrels*   62 silling: *shilling*

King. What prisoners of good sort are taken, uncle?

Exe. Charles Duke of Orleans, nephew to the king,
John Duke of Bourbon and Lord Bouciqualt.
Of other lords and barons, knights and squires,
Full fifteen hundred, besides common men.   70

King. This note doth tell me of ten thousand French
That in the field lie slain. Of princes in this number,
And nobles bearing banners, there lie dead
One hundred twenty-six. Added to these,
Of knights, esquires, and gallant gentlemen,   75
Eight thousand and four hundred, of the which
Five hundred were but yesterday dubb'd knights.
So that in these ten thousand they have lost
There are but sixteen hundred mercenaries.
The rest are princes, barons, lords, knights, squires,   80
And gentlemen of blood and quality.
The names of those their nobles that lie dead:
Charles Delabreth, High Constable of France,
Jaques of Chatillon, Admiral of France,
The master of the crossbows, Lord Rambures,   85
Great Master of France, the brave Sir Guichard Dolphin,
John Duke of Alençon, Anthony Duke of Brabant,
The brother to the Duke of Burgundy,
And Edward Duke of Bar. Of lusty earls,
Grandpré and Roussi, Faulconbridge and Foix,   90
Beaumont and Marle, Vaudemont and Lestrake.
Here was a royal fellowship of death!
Where is the number of our English dead?

[Herald gives another paper.]

Edward the Duke of York, the Earl of Suffolk,
Sir Richard Kikely, Davy Gam, esquire.   95
None else of name, and of all other men,
But five and twenty. O God, thy arm was here!
And not to us, but to thy arm alone
Ascribe we all. When, without stratagem,
But in plain shock and even play of battle,   100
Was ever known so great and little loss
On one part and on th' other? Take it, God,
For it is none but thine!

Exe.   'Tis wonderful!

King. Come, go we in procession to the village.   105
And be it death proclaimed through our host
To boast of this, or take that praise from God
Which is his only.

Flu. Is it not lawful, an please your majesty, to tell how
many is kill'd?   110

King. Yes, captain, but with this acknowledgment,
That God fought for us.

Flu. Yes, my conscience, he did us great good.

King. Do we all holy rites.
Let there be sung *Non nobis* and *Te Deum,*   115
The dead with charity enclos'd in clay.
And then to Callice, and to England then,
Where ne'er from France arriv'd more happy men.   *Exeunt.*

ACT FIFTH

Enter Chorus.

Vouchsafe to those that have not read the story
That I may prompt them. And of such as have,
I humbly pray them to admit th' excuse
Of time, of numbers, and due course of things
Which cannot in their huge and proper life   5
Be here presented. Now we bear the king
Toward Callice. Grant him there. There seen,
Heave him away upon your winged thoughts
Athwart the sea. Behold, the English beach
Pales in the flood with men, with wives and boys,   10
Whose shouts and claps outvoice the deep-mouth'd sea,
Which like a mighty whiffler 'fore the king
Seems to prepare his way. So let him land
And solemnly see him set on to London.
So swift a pace hath thought that even now   15
You may imagine him upon Blackheath,
Where that his lords desire him to have borne
His bruised helmet and his bended sword
Before him through the city. He forbids it,
Being free from vainness and self-glorious pride,   20
Giving full trophy, signal, and ostent
Quite from himself to God. But now behold,
In the quick forge and working house of thought,
How London doth pour out her citizens!
The mayor and all his brethren in best sort,   25
Like to the senators of th' antique Rome,
With the plebeians swarming at their heels,
Go forth and fetch their conqu'ring Caesar in;
As, by a lower but loving likelihood,
Were now the general of our gracious empress,   30
As in good time he may, from Ireland coming,
Bringing rebellion broached on his sword,
How many would the peaceful city quit
To welcome him! Much more, and much more cause,
Did they this Harry. Now in London place him—   35
As yet the lamentation of the French
Invites the King of England's stay at home;
The emperor's coming in behalf of France
To order peace between them—and omit
All the occurrences, whatever chanc'd,   40
Till Harry's back return again to France.
There must we bring him, and myself have play'd
The interim, by rememb'ring you 'tis past.
Then brook abridgment, and your eyes advance,
After your thoughts, straight back again to France.   *Exit.*   45

---

66 sort: *rank*   **67-97 Charles . . . twenty:** *both names and phrasing (except l. 91) are taken from Holinshed*   **68 Bouciqualt:** *F* Bouchiquald   **71 note:** *list*   **73 bearing banners:** *i.e. indicating their coats of arms*   **79 mercenaries:** *common soldiers*   **90 Faulconbridge:** *F* Fauconbridge and Foyes; *see III.5.44; cf. n.*   **91 Lestrake:** *Holinshed; F* Lestrale   **95 Kikely:** *Holinshed; F* Ketly   **96 name:** *rank*   **97 But . . . twenty;** *cf. n.*   **105 we:** *F* me   **114 rites:** *F* Rights; *passage is close to Holinshed*   **115 Non . . . Deum:** *well known psalms*   **116 charity . . . clay:** *full Christian burial*

3 excuse: *omission or scanting of; cf. n.*   **10 Pales in:** *surrounds, bounds with wives F2; with not in F*   **12 whiffler:** *an officer who goes before a procession to clear the way*   **14 solemnly:** *in state*   **16 Blackheath:** *district south of London*   **17 Where that:** *where*   **17-22 Where . . . God;** *cf. n.*   **21 trophy:** *tokens of victory*   **signal:** *sign of victory*   **ostent:** *triumphal show*   **25 in best sort:** *in finest array*   **26 antique:** *stressed ━ ─*   **29 loving likelihood:** *affectionate probability; F by louing*   **30 general;** *cf. n.*   **32 broached:** *stuck on a spit, transfixed*   **38 emperor's coming;** *cf. n.*   **42, 43 myself . . . interim:** *i.e. I have told all that has happened between Acts IV (1415) and V (1420)*   **43 rememb'ring:** *reminding*   **44 brook abridgment:** *put up with our cutting down the story*

❧ SCENE FIRST ❧

Enter Fluellen and Gower.

Gow. Nay, that's right. But why wear you your leek today?
Saint Davy's Day is past.

Flu. There is occasions and causes why and wherefore in all
things. I will tell you asse my friend, Captain Gower. The rascally, scauld, beggarly, lousy, pragging knave Pistol—which   5
you and yourself, and all the world, know to be no petter
than a fellow, look you now, of no merits—he is come to me,
and prings me pread and salt yesterday, look you, and bid me
eat my leek. It was in a place where I could not breed no
contention with him. But I will be so bold as to wear it in   10
my cap till I see him once again, and then I will tell him a
little piece of my desires.

Enter Pistol.

Gow. Why, here he comes, swelling like a turkey cock

Flu. 'tis no matter for his swellings, nor his turkey cocks.
God pless you, Aunchient Pistol! You scurvy, lousy knave,   15
God pless you!

Pist. Ha! art thou bedlam? Dost thou thirst, base Trojan,
To have me fold up Parca's fatal web?
Hence! I am qualmish at the smell of leek.

Flu. I peseech you heartily, scurvy, lousy knave, at my   20
desires, and my requests, and my petitions, to eat, look you,
this leek. Because, look you, you do not love it, nor your affections, and your appetites and your digestions doo's not agree
with it, I would desire you to eat it.

Pist. Not for Cadwallader and all his goats.   25

Flu. There is one goat for you. *Strikes him*
Will you be so good, scauld knave, as eat it?

Pist. Base Trojan, thou shalt die!

Flu. You say very true, scauld knave, when God's will is.
I will desire you to live in the meantime, and eat your   30
victuals. Come, there is sauce for it. [*Strikes him.*] You
call'd me yesterday mountain squire, but I will make you
today a squire of low degree. I pray you fall to. If you can
mock a leek, you can eat a leek.

Gow. Enough, captain. You have astonish'd him.   35

Flu. I say, I will make him eat some part of my leek, or I
will peat his pate four days. Bite, I pray you. It is good for
your green wound and your bloody coxcomb.

Pist. Must I bite?

Flu. Yes, certainly, and out of doubt and out of question   40
too, and ambiguities.

Pist. By this leek, I will most horribly revenge! I eat and eat,
I swear—

Flu. Eat, I pray you. Will you have some more sauce to
your leek? There is not enough leek to swear by.   45

Pist. Quiet thy cudgel. Thou dost see I eat.

Flu. Much good do you, scauld knave, heartily. Nay, pray
you throw none away. The skin is good for your broken coxcomb. When you take occasions to see leeks hereafter, I pray
you mock at 'em, that is all.   50

Pist. Good.

Flu. Ay, leeks is good. Hold you, there is a groat to heal
your pate.

Pist. Me a groat!

Flu. Yes, verily, and in truth you shall take it, or I have   55
another leek in my pocket, which you shall eat.

Pist. I take thy groat in earnest of revenge.

Flu. If I owe you anything, I will pay you in cudgels. You
shall be a woodmonger, and buy nothing of me but cudgels.
God bye you, and keep you, and heal your pate.   60

Exit.

Pist. All hell shall stir for this!

Gow. Go, go. You are a counterfeit cowardly knave. Will
you mock at an ancient tradition, begun upon an honorable respect and worn as a memorable trophy of predeceased valor,
and dare not avouch in your deeds any of your words? I   65
have seen you gleeking and galling at this gentleman twice or
thrice. You thought because he could not speak English in the
native garb he could not therefore handle an English cudgel.
You find it otherwise, and henceforth let a Welsh correction
teach you a good English condition. Fare ye well.   *Exit.*   70

Pist. Doth Fortune play the huswife with me now?
News have I that my Doll is dead i' th' spital
Of malady of France,
And there my rendezvous is quite cut off.
Old I do wax, and from my weary limbs   75
Honor is cudgel'd. Well, bawd I'll turn
And something lean to cutpurse of quick hand.
To England will I steal, and there I'll steal.
And patches will I get unto these cudgel'd scars
And swear I got them in the Gallia wars.   *Exit.*   80

❧ SCENE SECOND ❧

*Enter, at one door, King Henry, Exeter, Bedford, [Gloucester] War-
wick, [Westmoreland,] and other Lords; at another, Queen Isabel,
the [French] King, [the Princess Katharine, Alice, and other Ladies;]
the Duke of Burgundy, and other French.*

King H. Peace to this meeting, wherefore we are met!
Unto our brother France, and to our sister,
Health and fair time of day. Joy and good wishes
To our most fair and princely cousin Katharine.
And as a branch and member of this royalty,   5
By whom this great assembly is contriv'd,
We do salute you, Duke of Burgundy.
And, princes French, and peers, health to you all!

France. Right joyous are we to behold your face,
Most worthy brother England, fairly met.   10
So are you, princes English, every one.

---

5 scauld: *scabby, scurvy*   **8 yesterday:** *i.e. Saint Davy's Day*   **17-19 Ha . . . leek:** *F
prints as prose*   **17 bedlam:** *lunatic*   **Trojan:** *a dissolute fellow*   **18 fold . . . web:** *cut
the thread of your life; the Parcae were the Roman Fates*   **19 am qualmish:** *feel sick*   **25
Cadwallader:** *the last of the Welsh kings*   **32 mountain squire:** *i.e. poor Welshman*   **32,
33 make . . . degree:** *i.e. cut you down to size (the allusion is to a popular metrical romance*   **35 astonish'd:** *dismayed, stunned*   **38 green:** *fresh, raw*   **coxcomb:** *head*   **47
do:** *may it do*

51 Good: *very well*   **54 groat:** *fourpence*   **57 in earnest:** *as payment on account*   **59
woodmonger:** *dealer in wood*   **60 bye:** *be with; F bu'y*   **63 begun:** *F began*   **63,
64 upon . . . respect:** *for an honourable reason*   **64 memorable:** *commemorative*   **predeceased:** *long since dead*   **65 avouch:** *support*   **66 gleeking:** *mocking*   **galling:** *annoying,
scoffing*   **68 garb:** *fashion*   **70 condition:** *disposition, character*   **71-78 Doth . . .
steal:** *F prints as prose*   **71-80 Doth . . . wars;** *cf. n.*   **71 huswife:** *hussy, i.e. jilt; probably
pronounced 'hussif,'*   **72 spital:** *hospital*   **73 Of malady of France:** *venereal disease; F of
a*   **76 bawd:** *pander*   **77 something . . . to:** *to some extent turn to*   **78 steal;**
cf. n.   **80 swear:** *F swore*   **SD Burgundy:** *F Bourgongne.*   **1 wherefore:** *for
which*   **5 royalty:** *royal family*   **6 contriv'd:** *arranged*   **9 France:** *the French king; F
indicates Henry (below) by England*

Queen. So happy be the issue, brother England,
Of this good day and of this gracious meeting
As we are now glad to behold your eyes—
Your eyes which hitherto have borne in them   *15*
Against the French, that met them in their bent,
The fatal balls of murthering basilisks.
The venom of such looks, we fairly hope,
Have lost their quality, and that this day
Shall change all griefs and quarrels into love.   *20*
   King H. To cry amen to that, thus we appear.
   Queen. You English princes all, I do salute you.
   Burg. My duty to you both, on equal love,
Great Kings of France and England! That I have labor'd
With all my wits, my pains, and strong endeavors   *25*
To bring your most imperial majesties
Unto this bar and royal interview,
Your mightiness on both parts best can witness.
Since then my office hath so far prevail'd
That face to face and royal eye to eye   *30*
You have congreeted, let it not disgrace me
If I demand before this royal view
What rub or what impediment there is
Why that the naked, poor, and mangled Peace,
Dear nurse of arts, plenties, and joyful births,   *35*
Should not in this best garden of the world,
Our fertile France, put up her lovely visage?
Alas, she hath from France too long been chas'd,
And all her husbandry doth lie on heaps,
Corrupting in it own fertility.   *40*
Her vine, the merry cheerer of the heart,
Unpruned dies. Her hedges even-pleach'd,
Like prisoners wildly overgrown with hair,
Put forth disorder'd twigs. Her fallow leas
The darnel, hemlock, and rank fumitory   *45*
Doth root upon, while that the colter rusts
That should deracinate such savagery.
The even mead, that erst brought sweetly forth
The freckled cowslip, burnet, and green clover,
Wanting the scythe, all uncorrected, rank,   *50*
Conceives by idleness, and nothing teems
But hateful docks, rough thistles, kecksies, burrs,
Losing both beauty and utility.
And as our vineyards, fallows, meads, and hedges,
Defective in their natures, grow to wildness,   *55*
Even so our houses and ourselves and children
Have lost, or do not learn for want of time,
The sciences that should become our country,
But grow like savages—as soldiers will
That nothing do but meditate on blood—   *60*
To swearing and stern looks, defus'd attire,
And everything that seems unnatural.

Which to reduce into our former favor
You are assembled. And my speech entreats
That I may know the let why gentle Peace   *65*
Should not expel these inconveniences
And bless us with her former qualities.
   King H. If, Duke of Burgundy, you would the peace
Whose want gives growth to th' imperfections
Which you have cited, you must buy that peace   *70*
With full accord to all our just demands,
Whose tenors and particular effects
You have, enschedul'd briefly, in your hands.
   Burg. The king hath heard them, to the which as yet.
There is no answer made.   *75*
   King H.   Well then, the peace
Which you before so urg'd lies in his answer.
   France. I have but with a cursitory eye
O'erglanc'd the articles. Pleaseth your grace
To appoint some of your council presently   *80*
To sit with us once more, with better heed
To resurvey them, we will suddenly
Pass our accept and peremptory answer.
   King H. Brother, we shall. Go, uncle Exeter,
And brother Clarence, and you, brother Gloucester,   *85*
Warwick, and Huntingdon, go with the king.
And take with you free power to ratify,
Augment, or alter, as your wisdoms best
Shall see advantageable for our dignity,
Anything in or out of our demands,   *90*
And we'll consign thereto. Will you, fair sister,
Go with the princes or stay here with us?
   Queen. Our gracious brother, I will go with them.
Happily a woman's voice may do some good
When articles too nicely urg'd be stood on.   *95*
   King H. Yet leave our cousin Katharine here with us.
She is our capital demand, compris'd
Within the forerank of our articles.
   Queen. She hath good leave.

     Exeunt. Manent King [Henry] and Katharine [and Alice].

   King H.   Fair Katharine, and most fair,   *100*
Will you vouchsafe to teach a soldier terms
Such as will enter at a lady's ear
And plead his love suit to her gentle heart?
   Kath. Your majesty shall mock at me. I cannot speak your
England.   *105*
   King H. O fair Katharine, if you will love me soundly with
your French heart, I will be glad to hear you confess it bro-
kenly with your English tongue. Do you like me, Kate?
   Kath. Pardonnez-moi, I cannot tell vat is 'like me.'
   King H. An angel is like you, Kate, and you are like an   *110*
angel.
   Kath. Que dit-il? Que je suis semblable à les anges?

Alice. Oui, vraiment, sauf votre grâce, ainsi dit-il.

King H. I said so, dear Katharine, and I must not blush to
affirm it.   *115*

Kath. O bon Dieu! Les langues des hommes sont pleines de
tromperies.

King H. What says she, fair one? That the tongues of men
are full of deceits?

Alice. Oui, dat de tongues of de mans is be full of   *120*
deceits. Dat is de princess.

King. The princess is the better Englishwoman. I' faith,
Kate, my wooing is fit for thy understanding. I am glad thou
canst speak no better English, for if thou couldst, thou wouldst
find me such a plain king that thou wouldst think I had   *125*
sold my farm to buy my crown. I know no ways to mince it
in love, but directly to say 'I love you.' Then if you urge me
farther than to say 'Do you in faith?' I wear out my suit. Give
me your answer, i' faith, do, and so clap hands and a bargain.
How say you, lady?   *130*

Kath. Sauf votre honneur, me understand vell.

King H. Marry, if you would put me to verses, or to dance
for your sake, Kate, why, you undid me. For the one I have
neither words nor measure, and for the other I have no
strength in measure, yet a reasonable measure in strength. If *135*
I could win a lady at leapfrog, or by vawting into my saddle
with my armor on my back, under the correction of bragging
be it spoken, I should quickly leap into a wife. Or if I might
buffet for my love, or bound my horse for her favors, I could
lay on like a butcher and sit like a jackanapes, never off.   *140*
But before God, Kate, I cannot look greenly not gasp out my
eloquence, nor I have no cunning in protestation—only downright oaths, which I never use till urg'd, nor never break for
urging. If thou canst love a fellow of this temper, Kate, whose
face is not worth sunburning, that never looks in his glass *145*
for love of anything he sees there, let thine eye be thy cook. I
speak to thee plain soldier. If thou canst love me for this, take
me. If not, to say to thee that I shall die, is true—but for thy
love, by the Lord, no. Yet I love thee too. And while thou
liv'st, dear Kate, take a fellow of plain and uncoined   *150*
constancy, for he perforce must do thee right, because he hath
not the gift to woo in other places. For these fellows of infinite
tongue that can rhyme themselves into ladies' favors, they do always reason themselves out again. What! A speaker is but a
prater, a rhyme is but a ballad. A good leg will fall, a straight *155*
back will stoop, a black beard will turn white, a curl'd pate
will grow bald, a fair face will wither, a full eye will wax hollow. But a good heart, Kate, is the sun and the moon, or
rather the sun and not the moon, for it shines bright and
never changes, but keeps his course truly. If thou would have *160*
such a one, take me. And take me, take a soldier; take a soldier, take a king. And what say'st thou then to my love?
Speak, my fair, and fairly, I pray thee.

Kath. Is it possible dat I sould love de enemy of France?

King H. No, it is not possible you should love the   *165*
enemy of France, Kate. But in loving me you should love the
friend of France, for I love France so well that I will not part
with a village of it. I will have it all mine. And, Kate, when
France is mine and I am yours, then yours is France and you
are mine.   *170*

Kath. I cannot tell vat is dat.

King H. No, Kate? I will tell thee in French, which I am
sure will hang upon my tongue like a new-married wife about
her husband's neck, hardly to be shook off. Je quand sur le
possession de France, et quand vous avez le possession de   *175*
moi—let me see, what then? Saint Denis be my speed!—donc
votre est France, et vous êtes mienne. It is as easy for me,
Kate, to conquer the kingdom as to speak so much more
French. I shall never move thee in French, unless it be to
laugh at me.   *180*

Kath. Sauf votre honneur, le français que vous parlez, il est
meilleur que l'anglais lequel je parle.

King H. No, faith, is't not, Kate. But thy speaking of my
tongue, and I thine, most truly-falsely, must needs be granted
to be much at one. But, Kate, dost thou understand thus   *185*
much English? Canst thou love me?

Kath. I cannot tell.

King H. Can any of your neighbors tell, Kate? I'll ask them.
Come, I know thou lovest me, and at night, when you come
into your closet, you'll question this gentlewoman about   *190*
me. and I know, Kate, you will to her dispraise those parts in
me that you love with your heart. But, good Kate, mock me
mercifully, the rather, gentle princess, because I love thee cruelly. If ever thou beest mind, Kate, as I have a saving faith
within me tells me thou shalt, I get thee with scambling,   *195*
and thou must therefore needs prove a good soldier-breeder.
Shall not thou and I, between Saint Denis and Saint George,
compound a boy, half French, half English, that shall go to
Constantinople and take the Turk by the beard? Shall we not?
What say'st thou, my fair flower-de-luce?   *200*

Kath. I do not know dat.

King H. No 'tis hereafter to know, but now to promise. Do
but now promise, Kate, you will endeavor for your French part
of such a boy, and for my English moiety take the word of a
king and a bachelor. How answer you, la plus belle   *205*
Katharine du monde, mon très cher et divin déesse?

Kath. Your majestee 'ave fausse French enough to deceive de
most sage damoiselle dat is en France.

King H. Now, fie upon my false French! By mine honor, in
true English, I love thee, Kate; by which honor I dare not   *210*
swear thou lovest me. Yet my blood begins to flatter me that
thou dost, notwithstanding the poor and untempering effect of
my visage. Now beshrew my father's ambition! He was thinking of civil wars when he got me; therefore was I created with
a stubborn outside, with an aspect of iron, that when I come   *215*
to woo ladies, I fright them. But in faith, Kate, the elder I
wax, the better I shall appear. My comfort is that old age, that
ill layer-up of beauty, can do no more spoil upon my face.

---

126 mince it: *speak affectedly*   **128 wear . . . suit:** *exhaust my petition* (quibble).   **129
clap:** *clasp*   **133 undid:** *would undo*   **134, 135 measure . . . measure:** *triple pun: 'meter'
. . . 'stately court dance' . . . 'amount'*   **136 vawting:** *vaulting; cf. n.*   **137 under . . . of:**
subject to correction for   **139 buffet:** *box* **bound my horse:** *make my horse prance*   **140
jackanapes:** *monkey*   **141 greenly:** *foolishly*   **142 cunning:** *skill* **protestation:** *protesting* (his love).   **144 temper:** *disposition*   **145 not . . . sunburning:** *i.e. already as
brown as possible*   **146 let . . . cook:** *let your eye dress this plain dish as it wishes*   **150
uncoined:** *genuine; not minted nor passing current*   **155 ballad:** *doggerel* **fall:** *shrink* **160
his:** *its*

174-177 Je . . . mienne: *When I [have] possession of France, and when you have possession of
me . . . then France is yours and you are mine*   **176 Saint Denis:** *patron saint of
France*   **181-182 Sauf . . . parle:** *Saving your honor, the French that you speak is better than
the English that I speak*   **185 at one:** *alike*   **190 closet:** *private apartment*   **195 with
scambling:** *by scuffling, fighting*   **199 the Turk:** *the Grand Turk, the Sultan*   **200 flower-de-luce:** *fleur-de-lis, the emblem of France*   **204 moiety:** *share*   **205 bachelor:** *young
knight*   **205, 206 la plus . . . déesse:** *the most beautiful Katharine in the world, my very
dear and divine goddess*   **211 blood:** *natural impulse*   **212 untempering:** *unsoftening,
unattractive*   **213 beshrew:** *confound*   **214 got:** *begot*   **215 stubborn:** *rude, rough*

Thou hast me, if thou hast me, at the worst, and thou shalt
wear me, if thou wear me, better and better. And therefore   220
tell me, most fair Katharine, will you have me? Put off your
maiden blushes, avouch the thoughts of your heart with the
looks of an empress, take me by the hand, and say 'Harry of
England, I am thine.' Which word thou shalt no sooner bless
mine ear withal but I will tell thee aloud 'England is thine,   225
Ireland is thine, France is thine, and Henry Plantagenet is
thine'—who, though I speak it before his face, if he be not fellow with the best king, thou shalt find the best king of good
fellows. Come, your answer in broken music, for thy voice is
music, and thy English broken. Therefore, queen of all,   230
Katharine, break thy mind to me in broken English. Wilt
thou have me?

Kath. Dat is as it sall please de roi mon père.

King H. Nay, it will please him well, Kate. It shall please
him, Kate.   235

Kath. Den it sall also content me.

King H. Upon that I kiss your hand, and I call you my
queen.

Kath. Laissez, mon seigneur, laissez, laissez! Ma foi, je ne
veux point que vous abaissiez votre grandeur en baisant la   240
main d'une de votre seigneurie indigne serviteur. Excusez-
moi, je vous supplie, mon très-puissant seigneur.

King H. Then I will kiss your lips, Kate.

Kath. Les dames et damoiselles pour être baisées devant leur
noces, il n'est pas la coutume de France.   245

King H. Madam my interpreter, what says she?

Alice. Dat it is not be de fashon pour les ladies of France—I
cannot tell vat is 'baiser' en Anglish.

King H. To kiss.

Alice. Your majestee entendre bettre que moi.   250

King H. It is not a fashion for the maids in France to
kiss before they are married, would she say?

Alice. Oui, vraiment.

King H. O Kate, nice customs cursy to great kings. Dear
Kate, you and I cannot be confin'd within the weak list of   255
a country's fashion. We are the makers of manners, Kate,
and the liberty that follows our places stops the mouth of all
find-faults, as I will do yours for upholding the nice fashion
of your country in denying me a kiss. Therefore, patiently
and yielding. *[Kisses her.]* You have witchcraft in your lips,   260
Kate. There is more eloquence in a sugar touch of them than
in the tongues of the French council, and they should sooner
persuade Harry of England than a general petition of
monarchs. Here comes your father.

*Enter the French Power, [the French King and Queen, Burgundy,]
and the English Lords.*

Burg. God save your majesty! My royal cousin, teach you   265
our princess English?

King H. I would have her learn, my fair cousin, how perfectly I love her, and that is good English.

Burg. Is she not apt?

King H. Our tongue is rough, coz, and my condition is   270
not smooth; so that, having neither the voice nor the heart of
flattery about me, I cannot so conjure up the spirit of love in
her that he will appear in his true likeness.

Burg. Pardon the frankness of my mirth if I answer you for
that. If you would conjure in her, you must make a circle;   275
if conjure up love in her in his true likeness, he must appear
naked and blind. Can you blame her, then, being a maid yet
ros'd over with the virgin crimson of modesty, if she deny the
appearance of a naked blind boy in her naked seeing self? It
were, my lord, a hard condition for a maid to consign to.   280

King H. Yet they do wink and yield, as love is blind
and enforces.

Burg. They are then excus'd, my lord, when they see not
what they do.

King. H. Then, good my lord, teach your cousin to   285
consent winking.

Burg. I will wink on her to consent, my lord, if you will
teach her to know my meaning. For maids well summer'd and
warm kept are like flies at Bartholomewtide, blind, though they
have their eyes. And then they will endure handling, which   290
before would not abide looking on.

King H. This moral ties me over to time and a hot summer.
And so I shall catch the fly, your cousin, in the latter end, and
she must be blind too.

Burg. As love is, my lord, before it loves.   295

King H. It is so. And you may, some of you, thank love
for my blindness, who cannot see many a fair French city for
one fair French maid that stands in my way.

French King. Yes, my lord, you see them perspectively—the
cities turn'd into a maid, for they are all girdled with   300
maiden walls that war hath never ent'red.

King H. Shall Kate be my wife?

French King. So please you.

King H. I am content, so the maiden cities you talk of may
wait on her. So the maid that stood in the way for my   305
wish shall show me the way to my will.

French King. We have consented to all terms of reason.

King H. Is't so, my lords of England?

West. The king hath granted every article:
His daughter first, and then in sequel all,   310
According to their firm proposed natures.

Exe. Only he hath not yet subscribed this: Where your majesty demands that the King of France, having any occasion to
write for matter of grant, shall name your highness in this
form and with this addition, in French, 'Notre très-cher   315
fils Henri, Roi d'Angleterre, Héritier de France'; and thus
in Latin, 'Praeclarissimus filius noster Henricus, Rex Angliae
et Haeres Franciae.'

French King. Nor this I have not, brother, so denied,
But your request shall make me let it pass.   320

King H. I pray you, then, in love and dear alliance,
Let that one article rank with the rest,

---

222 avouch: *declare*   **229 broken music:** *garbled English; music arranged for parts*   **231
break:** *reveal*   **233 roi mon père:** *king my father*   **239-242 Laissez . . . seigneur:** *Don't,
my lord, don't, don't! I do not wish you to lower your greatness by kissing the hand of your
unworthy servant. Excuse me, I beg you, my most powerful lord*   **244, 245 Les dames . . .
France:** *For ladies and young girls to be kissed before their marriage—it is not the custom in
France*   **250 Your . . . moi:** *Your majesty understands better than I*   **253 Oui, vraiment:**
Yes, truly   **254 nice:** *fastidious*, **cursy:** *curtsy, bow*   **255 list:** *boundary*   **257 follows
. . . places:** *goes with our position*

270 condition: *disposition*   **281 wink:** *shut the eyes*   **288 summer'd:** *nurtured*   **289
flies . . . Bartholomewtide:** *i.e. August 24, when flies are torpid in the late summer*   **292
This moral:** *i.e. the moral to be drawn from this*   **299 perspectively:** *as though seen through
a 'perspective,' a glass which produces optical illusions*   **301 never:** *not in F*   **304 so:** *so
long as*   **305 wait on:** *accompany (as dowry)*   **306 will:** *desire*   **310 then:** *F2; F and
in sequel.*   **311 firm . . natures:** *the definite character of the terms proposed*   **312 subscribed:** *signed, assented to* **Where:** *whereas*   **314 matter of grant:** *i.e. documents conferring
lands or titles*   **315 addition:** *title*   **317 Praeclarissimus:** *most renowned;
cf. n.*

And thereupon give me your daughter.

French King. Take her, fair son, and from her blood raise up
Issue to me, that the contending kingdoms   325
Of France and England, whose very shores look pale
With envy of each other's happiness,
May cease their hatred, and this dear conjunction
Plant neighborhood and Christianlike accord
In their sweet bosoms, that never war advance   330
His bleeding sword 'twist England and fair France.

Lords. Amen!

King H. Now welcome, Kate. And bear me witness all
That here I kiss her as my sovereign queen. *Flourish.*

Queen. God, the best maker of all marriages,   335
Combine your hearts in one, your realms in one!
As man and wife, being two, are one in love,
So be there 'twixt your kingdoms such a spousal
That never may ill office or fell jealousy,
Which troubles oft the bed of blessed marriage,   340
Thrust in between the paction of these kingdoms
To make divorce of their incorporate league;
That English may as French, French Englishmen,
Receive each other. God speak this Amen!

All. Amen!   345

King H. Prepare we for our marriage, on which day,
My Lord of Burgundy, we'll take your oath

And all the peers', for surety of our leagues.
Then shall I swear to Kate, and you to me,
And may our oaths well kept and prosp'rous be!   350

Sennet. Exeunt.

❧ EPILOGUE ❧

[Enter Chorus]

Thus far, with rough and all-unable pen,
Our bending author hath pursu'd the story,
In little room confining mighty men,
Mangling by starts the full course of their glory.
Small time, but in that small most greatly liv'd   5
This star of England. Fortune made his sword,
By which the world's best garden he achiev'd,
And of it left his son imperial lord.
Henry the Sixth, in infant bands crown'd King
Of France and England, did this king succeed,   10
Whose state so many had the managing
That they lost France and made his England bleed.
Which oft our stage hath shown, and for their sake
In your fair minds let this acceptance take.   *[Exit.]*

❧ FINIS ❧

---

328 **conjunction:** *union*   338 **spousal:** *marriage*   339 **ill office:** *any hostile act*   341 **paction:** *alliance; F Pation*

348 **surety:** *ratification*   **SD Sennet:** *set of notes on a trumpet*   **Epilogue:** *a sonnet*   2 **bending:** *i.e. under the weight of his task; bowing*   4 **Mangling by starts:** *marring by telling it in fits and starts*   7 **achiev'd:** *won*   9 **infant bands:** *swaddling clothes*   13 **oft ... shown:** *clear proof of the popularity of the three parts of* King Henry VI   14 **let ... take:** *may this receive your favor*

NOTES

The Actors' Names *King Henry the Fifth:* born 1387, became king 1413, died 1422; eldest son of Henry IV. His campaigns in France and his marriage to Princess Katharine mark the high point of Lancastrian rule in England.

Duke of Gloucester (1391–1447): Humphrey, youngest son of Henry IV and possibly the only one of Henry's brothers actually present at Agincourt; after Henry's death deputy-protector of England; patron of Lydgate (see 2 *Henry IV* and 1, 2 *Henry VI*).

Duke of Bedford (1389–1435): John of Lancaster, third son of Henry IV; left in England as lieutenant of the kingdom during the Agincourt campaign; later regent of France and protector of England under Henry VI; famous for his role in the burning of Joan of Arc (see 1, 2 *Henry IV* and 1 *Henry VI*).

Duke of Exeter: Thomas Beaufort, youngest son of John of Gaunt by Catherine Swynford; probably left by Henry in command at Harfleur, though in Shakespeare's sources Exeter leaves Sir John Fastolfe at Harfleur and rejoins the king (see 1 *Henry VI*).

Duke of York: son of Edmund, fifth son of Edward III; called 'Aumerle' in *Richard II*. After his death at Agincourt his title passed to the son of his brother Richard, Earl of Cambridge (see below). This son's claim to the throne in the next reign initiated the wars of York and Lancaster.

Earl of Salisbury: Thomas Montacute; slain at the siege of Orleans, 1428 (see 1 *Henry VI*).

Earl of Westmoreland: Ralph Neville, Warden of the Scotch Marches; supporter of Bolingbroke against Richard II (see 1, 2 *Henry IV*).

Earl of Warwick: a governor of the young king Henry VI (see 2 *Henry IV* and 1, 2 *Henry VI*).

Archbishop of Canterbury: Henry Chichele, founder of All Soul's College, Oxford; an opponent of Wycliffe and a warm advocate of the war in France.

Bishop of Ely: John Fordham, once the secretary of Richard II.

Earl of Cambridge: Richard, second son of Edmund, Duke of York (see *Richard II*); executed in 1415 for plotting to put the Earl of March on the throne; father of Richard, Duke of York (slain at Wakefield in 1460), whose youngest son became Richard III.

Lord Scroop: eldest son of Sir Stephen Scroop (see *Richard II*) and nephew of the Archbishop in the *Henry IV* plays; beheaded 1415.

Sir Thomas Grey: son-in-law of the Earl of Westmoreland; executed 1415.

Sir Thomas Erpingham: steward of the king's house; mentioned in Drayton's 'Ballad of Agincourt' as commander of the English archers.

Charles the Sixth, King of France: born 1368, became king 1380, died 1422. Since he survived Henry by two months, Henry never became King of France. His eldest daughter, Isabella, was the second queen of Richard II, and his youngest, Katharine the Fair, appears in this play. He was subject to prolonged fits of insanity and was present neither at Agincourt nor at Troyes, at the betrothal of his daughter.

Lewis, the Dauphin: His brother became Charles VII, who died in 1461. Actually there were three Dauphins during the period of this play.

Duke of Burgundy: in III.5.42 and IV.8.87 John the Fearless; in V.2 Philip the Good. After the murder of his father by adherents of the Dauphin Charles, Philip brought about the peace between Charles VI and Henry V, thus excluding the Dauphin from the succession.

Duke of Orleans: imprisoned in England for twenty-five years after Agincourt, where he wrote some of the finest French poetry of the century.

The Constable of France: Charles de la Bret, half-brother of Henry V; commanded the French army at Agincourt and was killed there.

Isabel, Queen of France: daughter of Stephen II of Bavaria. Unable to control the two parties fighting for power in France, led by the Duke of Burgundy and the Duke of Orleans (the Armagnacs), she consented to the treaty of Troyes, in which Henry V became heir to the French throne.

Katharine: married Henry V in 1420 and became the mother of Henry VI; by her second husband, Owen Tudor, grandmother of Henry VII of England.

Prologue. SD. This is a single figure, the 'chorus' of the play, who speaks a prologue before each of the acts. Nowhere else does Shakespeare employ the chorus so consistently as in this play.

Prologue. 9. *spirits . . . hath.* Shakespeare frequently employs singular forms of verbs with plural subjects.

Prologue. 11 *cockpit.* The round or octagonal theater was similar to the pits in which cockfights were held.

Prologue. 13. *wooden O.* Probably the Curtain (rather than the Globe) theater, where the play was performed.

Prologue 15. *crooked figure.* Curved, like a naught, which in the unit's place and along with other figures may represent a million.

I.i.7-19. *It must . . the bill.* The following passage from Shakespeare's principal source, Holinshed's *Chronicles* (see Sources), suggests the detailed nature of his borrowing. Shakespeare underplays (11 7-8, 79-85) the clergy's motive for wanting war. The bill recommended

> *that the temporall lands deuoutlie giuen, and disordinatlie spent by religious, and other spirituall persons, should be seized into the kings hands, sith the same might suffice to mainteine, to the honor of the king, and defense of the realme, fifteene earles, fifteen hundred knights, six thousand and two hundred esquiers, and a hundred almessehouses, for reliefe onelie of the poore, impotent, and needie persons, and the king to haue cleerelie to his coffers twentie thousand pounds, with manie other prouisions and values of religious houses, which I passe ouer.*
>
> *This bill was much noted, and more feared among the religious sort, whom suerlie it touched verie neere, and therefore to find remedie against it, they determined to assaie all waies to put by and ouerthrow this bill: wherein they thought best to trie if they might mooue the kings mood with some sharpe inuention, that he should not regard the importunate petitions of the commons.*

On his deathbed, Henry's father had advised his son to 'busy giddy minds With foreign quarrels' (2 *Henry IV*, IV.5.215-216), in order to lessen the civil strife that had so shaken the previous reign. Shakespeare does not mention this reason for war in the next scene, nor does he render it easy for us to decide to what degree this king is like the 'politician,' his father. See the two long interviews between Henry IV and Prince Hal (1 *Henry IV*, III.2 and 2 *Henry IV*, IV.5).

I.i.16. *corporal.* As in rapid modern speech, the following three-syllable words (among others) probably had the value of dissyllables: *opening* (I.2.18), *reverence* (I.2.22), *pilfering* (I.2.145), *prisoner* (I.2.165), *natural* (I.2.185 and II.2.108), *barbarous* (I.2.277), *treacherous* (II.Pro.22), *Covering* (II.4.40), *reverend* (III.3.37), and so on. Similarly *You would* in 1. 42 is probably 'You'd.'

I.i.17. *supplied.* To prevent misreading, this text does not indicate elision in *ied* endings, e.g. *mortified* and *satisfied.*

I.i.25. *courses . . . youth.* In the two parts of *Henry IV*, the young prince is a drinking companion of Falstaff and the despair of his father the king. (See II.4.143; cf. n.)

I.i.30. *offending Adam.* This allusion to original sin, to sinfulness inherited from Adam, parallels closely the baptismal service from the *Book of Common Prayer.* Compare also Genesis 3:23-4.

I.i.34 *flood.* Probably an allusion to Hercules' cleansing of the Augean stables by turning a river through them.

I.i.93. *Edward.* Edward III of England, son of Isabella, the daughter of Philip IV of France. When Isabella, after the death of her brothers, claimed the throne of France for her son Edward, an assembly of French peers and barons barred inheritance through the female.

I.ii.13. *law Salic.* The Salic law forbade the succession of a woman to the French throne, as Canterbury explains below. (See I.1.93; cf. n.)

I.ii.29, 30. *gives . . . makes.* Another instance of the apparent lack of agreement between subject and verb. Compare *is . . . wretches*, 1. 247.

I.ii.48. *Charles the Great.* L1. 37-102 are taken almost line by line from Holinshed. For closeness to the source they are probably unique in Shakespeare. The dates of the reigns of the sovereigns mentioned, in chronological order, are as follows: Clothair I, 558-61; Childeric III, 742-51 (last of the Merovingian kings, deposed by Pepin); Pepin, 752-68 (son of Charles Martel and founder of the Carlovingian dynasty); Charles the Great (Charlemagne), 768-814 (son of Pepin); Louis I, *le Débonnaire*, 814-40 (son of Charlemagne); Charles I, the Bald (called Charlemagne, 1. 75), 840-77; Hugh Capet, 987-96 (defeated Charles, Duke of Lorraine; was elected to the throne after the death of Louis V, and founded the dynasty which bears his name.); Louis IX (called Lewis the Tenth, 1. 79), 1226-70, Saint Louis.

I.ii.79. *Lewis the Tenth.* Actually Louis IX. Throughout this passage, as elsewhere in the play, Shakespeare is following Holinshed's *Chronicles* so closely that he reproduces entire phrases and several of Holinshed's errors.

I.ii.88-104. *So that . . . ancestors.* Compare simile, proper names, and phrasing (see 1. 133 ff.) with the following passage from Holinshed:

> *. . . so that more cleere than the sunne it openlie appeareth, that the title of king Pepin, the claime of High Capet, the possession of Lewes, yea and the French kings to this daie, are deriued and conueied from the heire female, though they*

would vnder the colour of such a fained law, barre the kings and princes of this realme of England of their right and lawfull inheritance.

The archbishop further alledged out of the booke of Numbers this saieng: When a man dieth without a sonne, let the inheritance descend to his daughter. At length, hauing said sufficientlie for the proofe of the kings iust and lawfull title to the crowne of France, he exhorted him to aduance foorth his banner to fight for his right, to conquer his inheritance, to spare neither bloud, sword, nor fire, sith his warre was iust, his cause good, and his claime true.

I.ii.96. *amply to imbare.* Many editors follow *imbar* (F3), a variant of 'embar,' interpreting it variously to mean 'bar in,' 'secure,' 'exclude,' etc. The form *imbar* may be supported by the three occurrences of the word *bar* in the Archbishop's speech (Walter). F reads *imbarre.*

I.ii.176. *tame.* Many editors read *tear* (after Rowe); Q *spoyle.*

I.ii.191. *honeybees.* This was a familiar parallel in Shakespeare's day and is found among other places in Lyly's *Euphues.*

I.ii.225. *Dolphin.* The heir apparent to the French throne. The F spelling is retained throughout.

I.ii.236. *Turkish mute.* A slave whose tongue is removed to prevent his betraying royal secrets.

I.ii.264-272. *Tennis . . . chases.* This extended figure (and 11.255-257 above) is derived from Holinshed. The ambassadors

. . . brought with them a barrell of Paris balles, which from their maister they presented to him for a token that was taken in verie ill part, as sent in scorne, to signifie, that it was more meet for the king to passe the time with such childish exercise, than to attempt any worthie exploit. Wherefore the K. wrote to him, that yer ought long, he would tosse him some London balles that perchance should shake the walles of the best court in France.

I.ii.268-272. *set . . . chases.* These are terms from the popular court tennis of the day: *hazard,* places from which the ball cannot be returned; *wrangler,* opponent; *chases,* second bounds of the ball, a missed return.

II. Prologue. SD. *Flourish.* Act II is not indicated here in F. Act III is marked *Secundus* and Act IV *Tertius.* The F *Flourish* here and at the entry of the chorus before Act III possibly belongs with the final lines of Acts I and II.

II. Prologue. 7. *winged . . . Mercuries.* The herald and messenger of the gods, Mercury or Hermes, is represented as wearing winged sandals and a winged cap.

II. Prologue. 39-40. *For . . . play.* The original Prologue may have ended with this couplet. Ll. 41-2 may prepare for the later addition of scenes 1 and 3. (See Sources.)

II.i.16, 17. *Nell Quickly.* Hostess of Falstaff's favorite tavern, the Boar's Head, in Eastcheap. In *Quickly, -ly* rhymes with 'lie.'

II.i.22. *Through . . . plod.* 'To be patient is fatiguing, but it will achieve its object in the end.' F reads 'may, though . . . plodde, there' Many sentences in the prose of F are separated only by commas.

II.i.26. *tyke.* All of Pistol's following speeches (except ll. 61-63) are printed as prose in F.

II.i.48. *Pistol's cock.* The 16th-century pistol was a small, noisy, inaccurate weapon. A *pistólfo* was a rogue who lived by his wits.

II.i.55. *humor.* Humor could mean anything from 'temperament' to 'whim.' Through Nym's repetitions of this word and other phrases, Shakespeare seems to be parodying their excessive use in his day.

II.i.69-73. *No . . . espouse.* Doll is Falstaff's girl in *2 Henry IV,* and the Hostess once disliked her present husband. These are possible signs that this scene and II.3 were added later. (See II.3.10; cf. n.) A 'tear sheet' was a sheet of high quality (quibble).

II.i.71. *lazar . . . kind.* Cressida, proverbial after (though not in) Chaucer as a prostitute, was frequently referred to in such terms as *lazar* (beggar, leper) and *kite* (a bird of prey) or *kit* (Kate, a loose woman). Doll was sent to prison in *2 Henry IV,* V.4.

II.i.78, 79. *face . . . pan.* See *1 Henry IV,* III.3.26-55, for Bardolph's fiery face.

II.i.82. *kill'd his heart.* See the famous rejection of Falstaff in *2 Henry IV,* V.5.39 ff.

II.i.85. *divel.* The spellings *deuil, diuel,* and *deule* are used interchangeably in F.

II.i.101. *noble.* A third of a pound (6s. 8d.), less than the eight shillings Nym asked for, because this is to be cash payment.

II.i.112, 113. *quotidian tertian.* The Hostess is as usual confused. The fever called the *quotidian* recurs daily, the *tertian* every other day. The Q *tashan contigian* suggests Mrs. Quickly's pronunciation.

II.i.118. *fracted.* Pistol's flair for high-sounding terms prompts him to give such words meanings of his own. The two words here may mean 'broken and contrite' (or 'corrupted'), or 'humbled and full of grace' (Walter).

II.i.120. *passes . . . careers.* He gives his temperament free reign. *Passes* means 'indulges in.' A *career* is a short fast gallop.

II.ii.115-118. *suggest . . . piety.* Tempt to damnable acts with a patchwork of arguments, to give a deceptive appearance of righteousness.

II.ii.128-141. *Show . . . suspicion.* Compare this portrait of (what Henry thought to be) a kind of ideal man with the terms in which Shakespeare characterizes Richard II's folly, Henry IV's policy, Falstaff's fatness and rioting, John of Gaunt's leanness and sense of responsibility, and the virtues of the 'mirror' of kings, Henry V.

II.ii.160. *sufferance.* This word and *heartily* here and *dangerous* in ll. 163 and 188 are probably dissyllabic. Also read 'discov'ry' in l. 163.

II.ii.168-182. *You have . . . hence.* Holinshed gives Henry's speech this form:

Having thus conspired the death and destruction of me, which am the head of the realme and gouernour of the people, it maie be (no doubt) but that you likewise haue sworne the confusion of all that are here with me, and also the desolation of your owne countrie. to what horror (O Lord) for any true English hart to consider, that such an execrable iniquitie should euer so bewrap you, as for pleasing of a forren enemie to imbrue your hands in your bloud, and to ruine your owne natiue soile. Reuenge herein touching my person, though I seek not; yet for the safegard of you my deere freends, & for due preseruation of all sorts, I am by office to cause example to be shewed. Get ye hence therefore ye poore miserable wretches to the receiuing of your iust reward, wherein Gods maiestie giue you grace of his mercie and repentance of your heinous offenses.

II.iii.10. *A'.* The frequency of the occurence of this form of 'he' (fourteen times) and the appearance of other characteristic Shakespearean colloquialisms and spellings in this scene in F (e g. *brissle, vp-peer'd, Deules, rumatique, shogg*) suggest that the scene (and others) may have been added in Shakespeare's hand to an earlier manuscript of the play copied out by a scribe (Walter; see Introduction).

II.iii.11-12. *christome.* This word is probably a fusion of 'chrisomchild' and 'christened child' (Kökeritz). Q reads *crysombd.*

II.iii.15. *a' babbled . . . fields.* F prints 'a Table of greene fields.' Theobald's emendation given here is perhaps the most famous ever made on a Shakespearean test. *Table* is probably, however, a misprint for 'talke' (Harrison) or 'talkt' (Prouty). Q reads 'And talk of floures.'

II.iii.24. *sack.* Falstaff's favorite drink. See *2 Henry IV,* IV.3.88-113.

II.iv.26. *Whitsun . . . dance.* Whitsuntide in the spring was an occasion for festivities and open-air folk dancing.

II.iv.39. *Brutus.* Brutus the Liberator planned to drive King Tarquin out of Rome, while pretending to be an idiot.

II.iv.57. *Cressy battle.* The spelling in F of several French proper names (*Harflew, Callice, Roan*) is retained throughout this text.

II.iv.104. *fierce.* This reading of F and Q may be a printer's error for 'fierie.' The word *fierce* is probably dissyllabic here.

II.iv.138. *Louvre.* The F *Louer* suggests pronunciation and the point of the next line. See I.2.258-66; cf. n.

II.iv.143. *weighs time.* The significance of Henry's weighing of time should be seen in the light of the many earlier references to Prince Hal's need to 'redeem' the time he wasted in his youth (*1 Henry IV,* I.2.187 ff., III.2.130 ff., V.3.50 ff.; *2 Henry IV,* II.4.319 ff., V.2.129 ff., etc.). See also Warwick's defense of the Prince's idling (*2 Henry IV,* IV.4.70 ff.), partly echoed by the two bishops in the first scene of this play. Passages which suggest the relationship between time and Richard II (*Richard II,* II.1.198 ff., V.5.45 ff., etc.), Hotspur (*1 Henry IV,* V.2.82 ff., and V.3.81 ff.), and Falstaff are especially illuminating.

II.iv.SD. *Flourish.* In F. This SD is transferred to the end of the scene by most editors, but the king may rise here, thus dismissing the embassy.

III.i.7. *summon.* The Arden edition suggests that the generally accepted *summon* is a far less likely emendation for the F *commune* than the more probable 'coniure' or 'conjure' (see V.2.271, 274, 275).

III.i.25. *yeomen.* The longbowmen drawn from these freeholders were unbeatable at Crécy, Poitiers, and Agincourt.

III.i.27. *mettle . . . pasture.* The F *mettell* brings both 'mettle' and 'metal' to life in this word. This play is especially rich in puns and equivocations of this kind, only a few of which can be indicated in the glosses.

III.ii.9-12. *Knocks . . . fame.* F prints these lines and 11. 13-19 and 22-25 below as prose.

III.ii.21. *cullions.* The strangeness of this speech in Fluellen's mouth and Pistol's replying with *great duke,* the infrequency of Fluellen's substituting *p*'s for *b*'s (only in *Plow,* perhaps, 1. 57), the unusual number of oaths (nine by *Cheshu* or *Chrish,* from 1. 72 to 1.120), and the speech headings in F (*Welch, Scot, Irish*)—all may suggest that this independent scene is a later addition to the play. (See Introduction.)

III.ii.51. *Gloucester.* Holinshed records that

> ... the duke of Glocester, to whome the order of the siege was committed, made three mines vnder the ground, and approaching to the wals with his engins and ordinance, would not suffer them within to take anie rest. For although they with their countermining som what disappointed the Englishmen, & came to fight with them hand to hand within the mines, so that they went no further forward with that worke; yet they were so inclosed on ech side, as well by water as land, that succour they saw could none come to them.

III.ii.62. *Fluellen.* F reads *Welch.* Throughout this scene for *Jamy* F reads *Scot,* and for Macmorris F reads *Irish.* (See III.6.SD; cf. n.)

III.ii.76. *Jamy* Jamy's speech gives us a good example of the Scots employed in plays of Shakespeare's time.

III.iii.2. *latest parle.* This passage and a few others in the play (see IV.6.38; cf. n.) probably prompted Yeats to say what others have said in varying ways, that Henry 'has the gross vices, the coarse nerves, of one who is to rule among violent people.... He is as remorseless and undistinguished as some natural force.' The king of this scene must be viewed, however, with the Henry of the choruses and of IV.1.

III.iv.3. *Un peu.* F *En peu.* The curious French of F has been clarified and normalized by many editors. Some of the F forms, like this one, perhaps, suggest attempts at phonetic spelling. A great many represent older French (frequently provincial) forms: *este* for *êtes, parlas* for *parles, doyts* for *doights, escholier* for *écolier, dict* for *dites, apprins* for *appris, vostre* for *vôtre, desia* for *deja, Anglois* for *anglais,* and so on. Many other odd forms in F are attributable too Shakespeare's handwriting and to the compositor's ignorance of French. This scene is reproduced in full in the French of F at the end of Introduction.

III.iv.8. *Et les doigts.* F assigns these words to Alice, the following speech to Katharine, and part of the next ('La main ... écolier') to Alice. Much of the humor of this scene derives from the sound in French of several of the English words—*foot (foutre),* and *count (con[t])* for 'gown'— and form translations like *nick* (pudendum) for 'neck' and *sin* for 'chin.'

III.v.SD. *Britaine.* Not in F. Most editors give the Q *Burbon* here, but the following relevant speeches are headed *Brit.* in F, and Holinshed names Britaine, not Bourbon, as of the king's council.

III.v.9. *overlook ... grafters.* Shall slips (scions) taken from French stock overtop the parent trees? The Dauphin is referring to the uniting of Norman French and native Anglo-Saxon blood after 1066.

III.v.44. *Faulconbridge.* Often given as *Fauconbridge* or *Fauconberg.* Holinshed suggests the correct forms of F *Loys* and *Lestrale* in the next line. (See IV.8.89.)

III.vi.SD. *English and Welsh.* By such tags Shakespeare points up the national characteristics of the leaders united under Henry. However, the duplication in this entry notice (*Welsh ... Fluellen*), and the substitution in Fluellen's speeches here of *p* for *b* only once (*pride,* l. 12) suggest possible revision of the first part of this scene. After Pistol leaves the stage at l. 55 there are ten such substitutions. (See Introduction.) The *bridge* in l. 2 is over the little river Ternoise at Blangy. Henry and his army crossed it on October 24, 1415, the night before the battle of Agincourt.

III.vi.8. *live ... living.* The first word may be an anticipation of the second, but *live* occurs at III.7.55 for 'lief' and *liveless* at IV.2.55 for 'lifeless.'

III.vi.41. *pax.* A plate stamped with a picture of Christ, the Virgin, or a saint. Holinshed mentions the stealing of a pyx, the vessel containing the consecrated wafer, by an unnamed soldier: 'Yet in this great necessitie, the poore people of the countrie were not spoiled, nor anie thing taken from them without paiment, nor anie outrage or offense doone by the Englishmen, except one, which was, that a souldiour took a pix out of a church, for which he was apprehended, & the king not once remooued till the box was restored, and the offender strangled.'

III.vi.53. *figo.* The accompanying insulting gesture is made by inserting the thumb between two closed fingers or into the mouth. The gesture is repeated with 'fig of Spain,' at l. 55.

III.vi.148-150. *If we ... Discolor.* This phrasing is directly from Holinshed. Henry says 'If anie of your nation attempt once to stop me in my iournie now towards Calis, at their ieopardie be it; and yet wish I not anie of you so vnaduised, as to be the occasion that I die your tawnie ground with your red bloud.'

III.vii.SD. *Dolphin.* In III.5.65, 67 the French king requests that the Dauphin not go to battle.

III.vii.13. *as if ... hairs.* The word may be 'hares' (F *hayres*). This passage, like several in French in this play, is very similar to one in John Eliot's lively English and French conversation manual, *Ortho-epia Gallica,* 1593.

III.vii.22. *jades.* Many of the words in this passage have double meanings— e.g. *jade* (a term of contempt for a woman or a horse), and *horse*-whores. (See III.4.7; cf. n.)

III.vii.59, 60. *Le ... bourbier.* 'The dog is turned to his own vomit again, and the sow that was washed to her wallowing in the mire.' (2 Peter 2:22.)

III.vii.101, 102. *hooded ... bate.* 'It is never very apparent, and when it does appear it rapidly diminishes.' The metaphor is from falconry. The hawk was carried with a hood over its head, and when this was removed it would *bate,* i.e. flap its wings before flight. But *bate* here also means 'abate,' 'diminish.'

III.vii.135, 136. *give ... devils.* The claim that Shakespeare consulted Edward Hall's chronicle (1548) in writing this play is supported by parallels like the following (not in Holinshed). Hall's Constable says '... keepe an Englishman one moneth from his warme bed, fat befe and stale drynke, and let him that season tast colde and suffre hunger, you then shall se his courage abated.'

IV. Prologue. 13. *rivets.* Knights were literally riveted into parts of their armor and could not get out without help.

IV. Prologue. 43. *like the sun.* See Prince Hal's comparing of himself with the sun (1 *Henry IV,* I.2.172 ff.) and the use of sun imagery to characterize Richard II.

IV. Prologue. 50-2. *With ... Agincourt.* Unless Shakespeare (improbably) is referring to Pistol and the Frenchman (IV.4) or Fluellen and Williams (IV.8), we do not see these *foils* or this *brawl.* Perhaps some encounter has been omitted.

IV.i.3. *Good.* Though the choruses and his friends pay Henry unqualified and convincing personal tribute from the beginning, the following scene affords us the first sustained inward view of the king as man and soldier in the play. Compare the tone of the king's speeches here with that of his soliloquies as prince (1 *Henry IV,* I.2.201 ff. and 2 *Henry IV,* IV.5.22 ff.).

IV.i.SD. *Erpingham.* The king's request to Sir Thomas to assemble the nobles at his tent is repeated twice (ll. 27 and 264), and ll. 32, 33 prepare us for a soliloquy which is delayed until l. 207. Since this first soliloquy is closely related to the previous conversation, it may have been that only the second (ll. 267-284, after Erpingham's return) appeared in a possible first form of the play. (See Sources.)

IV.i.36. *Qui va là.* F *Che vous la?*; O *Ke ve la?* 'Kivala' was Elizabethan thieves' argot for 'Who goes there?' (See III.7.112; cf. n.) F prints Pistol's speeches as prose.

IV.i.71. *Pompey's camp.* Fluellen is mistaken, for Pompey's camp before Pharsalia was notoriously undisciplined.

IV.i.202-205. *Indeed ... clipper.* Crowns means both 'heads' and 'coins.' The French, outnumbering the English, *may lay* ('bet') more crowns on their victory. But it's not treason for an Englishman to 'clip' (cut off) French crowns. 'Clipping' (cutting off the edges of) English crowns (coins) was punishable by death, because it made them lighter and debased their value.

IV.i.209-213. *We must ... enjoy.* F 'We ... all./O ... Greatnesse,/Subiect ... sence/No ... wringing./What ... neglect,/That ... enioy?'

IV.i.221. *soul of adoration.* F 'What? is thy Soule of Odoration?' (*adoration* has five syllables and *condition,* l. 210, has four.)

IV.i.269. *reck'ning. if* Possibly 'reck'ning or'; F 'reckning of'; Q 'rekconing,/That ... May not appall their courage.'

IV.i.270-283. *Not today ... pardon.* See 2 *Henry IV,* IV.5.187-221. Henry's father was a usurper and responsible for the murder of Richard II. With this prayer, Henry seems to free England at least temporarily from the blight prophesied by the Bishop of Carlisle (*Richard II,* IV.1.117 ff.). Holinshed writes that Henry 'caused the bodie of king Richard to be remooued with all funerall dignitie conuenient for his estate, from Langlie to Westminster, where he was honorablie interred with queene Anne his first wife, in a solemne toome erected and set vp at the charges of this king.'

IV.iii.11-14. *Farwell ... valor.* In F ll. 13-14 follow l. 11, and all are attributed to Bedford. Then follows l. 12, which is given to Exeter.

IV.iii.16-18. *O ... today.* Shakespeare heightens a passage in Holinshed:

> It is said, that as he heard one of the host vtter his wish to another thus: I would to god there were with vs now so manie good soldiers as are at this houre within England! the king answered: I would not wish a man more then I haue ... But let no man ascribe victorie to our owne strength and might, but onelie to Gods assistance, to whome I haue no doubt we shall worthilie haue cause to giue thanks therefore. And if so be that for our offenses sakes we shall be deliuered into the hands of our enimies, the lesse number we be, the lesse damage shall the realme of England susteine.

IV.iii.28-9. *But if ... alive.* Compare with this speech Hotspur and Falstaff on honor (1 *Henry IV,* I.3.205-212 and V.1.132-139).

IV.iii.40. *Crispian.* Crispinus and Crispianus, patron saints of shoemakers were martyred 287 A.D. Their day and that of the battle of Agincourt fell on October 25.

IV.iii.44. *live.* Most editors, following Pope, transpose *see* and *live.* Greg and others suggest 'live t' old.'

IV.iv.SD. *Excursions.* In Q the order of IV.4 and IV.5 is reversed. Compare Pistol's capturing the Frenchman in this scene and the showing up of Pistol in V.1 with Falstaff's claiming the victory over Hotspur (1 *Henry IV*, V.4) or his capturing Colevile (2 *Henry IV*, IV.3) and the attempts to show up Falstaff (1 *Henry IV*, II.4 and III.3 and so on). Shakespeare patterned Part 2 of *Henry IV* very closely after Part 1, and he repeated some of the patterns of both in this play.

IV.iv.4. *Qualtitie . . . me.* Thus the F. Possibly 'Calen o custure me' (Malone) or 'Callino, castore me' (Boswell). Probably the Irish refrain to a popular Elizabethan song, recited by Pistol to mock the Frenchman.

IV.iv.7-11. *O . . . ransom.* F prints these lines and the following speeches of Pistol as prose: ll 13-15, 17-19, 21-23, 35-37, 45, 46, 60-61.

IV.iv.33. *à cette heure.* The spelling in F (*asture*) was a frequent English form of the French phrase. (See III.7.13-14; cf. n.)

IV.iv.35. *Owy . . . permafoy.* See 'Couple a gorge!' at II.1.73.

IV.iv.36, 37. *roaring . . . dagger.* Pistol is like the bragging but cowardly Devil of the old morality plays, whose nails the Vice or clown insultingly offered to pare with a wooden dagger.

IV.v.12. *die in honor.* Once F reads 'dye in once'; Q 'Lets dye with honour.' *Honor* is the word most frequently adopted (after Q) to supply F's missing word. Wilson suggests the more idiomatic 'in harness'; Mason and Walter read 'in arms.'

IV.vi.38. *kill his prisoners.* The sudden attack of the French and Henry's orders are historical, and Henry's severity has been variously defended in the light of military codes of the day. Note the reasons for this order given in the following scene, ll. 1-11 and 46-56. Holinshed writes that:

> *certeine Frenchmen on horssebacke . . . to the number of six hundred horssemen, which were the first that fled, hearing that the English tents & pauilions were a good waie distant from the armie, without anie sufficient gard to defend the same . . . entred vpon the kings campe and there spoiled the hails, robbed the tents, brake vp chests, and carried away caskets and slue such seruants as they found to make anie resistance. . . . But when the outcrie of the lackies and boies which ran away for feare of the Frenchmen thus spoiling the campe, came to the kings eares, he doubting least his enimies should gather togither againe, and begin a new field; and mistrusting further that the prisoners would be an aid to his enimies . . . contrarie to his accustomed gentlenes, commanded by sound of trumpet that euerie man (vpon paine of death) should incontinentlie slaie his prisoner.*

IV.vii.SD. *Bourbon.* This appears in F. He does not speak (but neither do several of those who enter at V.2 and elsewhere), and most editors omit his name.

IV.vii.46-56. *I was . . . them so.* This appears in Holinshed but not in Hall:

> *Some write, that the king perceiuing his enimies in one part to assemble togither, as though they meant to giue a new battell for preseruation of the prisoners, sent to them an herald, commanding them either to depart out of his sight, or else to come forward at once, and give battell: promising herewith, that if they did offer to fight againe, not onelie those prisoners which his people alreadie had taken; but also so manie of them as in this new conflict, which they thus attempted should fall into his hands, should die the death without redemption.*

IV.vii.57-84. *Here comes . . . Agincourt.* Shakespeare is here very close to Holinshed:

> *In the morning, Montioie king at armes and foure other French heralds came to the K. to know the number of prisoners, and to desire buriall for the dead. Before he made them answer (to vnderstand what they would saie) he demanded of them whie they made to him that request, considering that he knew not whether the victorie was his or theirs? When Montioie by true and iust confession had cleered that doubt to the high praise of the king, he desired of Montioie to vnderstand the name of the castell neere adioining: when they had told him that it was called Agincourt, he said, Then shall this conflict be called the battell of Agincourt.*

IV.vii.93-94. *Welshmen . . . caps.* Nothing else is known of this incident nor of the Welsh custom of wearing leeks in these round, brimless, high-crowned

caps. The custom is supposed to commemorate a victory of the Welsh over the Saxons on St. David's Day, March 1, 540. David (*Tavy*) is the patron saint of Wales.

IV.viii.100, 101. *Welsh plood.* Henry's great-grandmother was a Welsh princess. queen Elizabeth herself was descended from Owen Tudor, a Welshman who married Queen Katharine, Henry's widow.

IV.vii.110-111. *Bring . . . parts.* The king's request is not satisfied until sc. 8, l. 64, when a herald returns with the information. Since the intervening 135 lines complete the episode of the glove, which may have been added later, it is possible that this scene also underwent revision. Fluellen's apparent failure to recognize Williams at sc. 8, l. 10, after he had confronted him at ll. 123 ff., and the king's sending twice for Gower (at l. 142 and l. 154—thus, however, enabling Fluellen and Williams to meet) may indicate alterations.

IV.vii.149. *doo's.* This form (perhaps suggesting pronunciation) is not peculiar to Fluellen's speech, for the king (also Welsh) uses it at III.6.127 and V.2.185 and 211.

IV.viii.97. *But . . . twenty.* Historically the differences between the French and English losses were apparently staggering. Through their failure to adapt their techniques of conducting mass charges in full armor to the English defensive lines of protected archers, the French, according to Hall and Holinshed, lost 10,000 men (though the latest estimate is 7,000), against a recently estimated English loss of from 400 to 500.

V. Prologue. 3. *excuse.* Between Agincourt and the Treaty of Troyes (1420) five years have elapsed, during which Henry has conducted a second campaign in France.

V. Prologue. 17-22. *Where . . . God.* This appears as follows in Holinshed: 'The king like a graue and sober personage, and as one remembering from whom all victories are sent, seemed little to regard such vaine [six] pompe and shewes as were in triumphant sort deuised for his welcoming home from so prosperous a iournie, in so much that he would not suffer his helmet to be carried with him, whereby might haue appeared to the people the blowes and dints that were to be seene in the same.'

V. Prologue. 30. *general.* The Earl of Essex left London on March 27, 1599, and returned, his attempt to suppress Tyrone's rebellion a failure, on the following September 28. (See Introduction.)

V. Prologue. 38. *emperor's coming.* In May 1416 the Holy Roman Emperor, Sigismund, came to England to negotiate between the French king and Henry.

V.i.71-88. *Doth . . . wars.* Pistol refers to Nell Quickly (see II.1.16, 17) as *Doll* here (in both F and O), and much in this speech may suggest Falstaff. A 'doll' was, however, a woman of easy virtue. (See Introduction.)

V.i.78. *steal.* Pronounced 'stale,' with probable puns on 'urinate' and 'prostitute.' See III.2.39.

V.ii.17. *balls . . . basilisks.* A double pun: *balls* refers to both eyeballs and cannon balls, and *basilisks* to large cannon and fabulous serpents, whose glance means death.

V.ii.36. *best garden.* Compare the following portrait of a disordered garden with two others in *Richard II*—Gaunt's picture of England, the 'other Eden' (II.1), and the Gardener's exact parallel between the commonwealth and nature (III.4).

V.ii.136. *vawting.* Many of the words in the following passages have double meanings—e.g. *uncoined constancy, tongue, rhyme, reason, wear,* and later *conjure up, circle, hard,* and so on.

V.ii.317. *Praeclarissimus:* Shakespeare copied a misprint in Holinshed. The French *très-cher* should be paralleled by *praecarissimus,* 'very dear' Holinshed places this meeting between the French and the English in St. Peter's Church, 'where was a verie ioious meeting betwixt them (and this was on the twentith daie of Maie) and there the king of England, and the ladie Katharine were affianced. After this, the two kings and their councell assembled togither diuerse daies, wherein the first concluded agreement was in diuerse points altered and brought to a certeintie.'

The Life of King Henry the Eighth

Edited by JOHN M. BERDAN

and

TUCKER BROOKE

Dramatis Personae

KING HENRY THE EIGHTH
CARDINAL WOLSEY
CARDINAL CAMPEIUS
CAPUCIUS, *Ambassador from the Emperor Charles V*
CRANMER, *Archbishop of Canterbury*
DUKE OF NORFOLK
DUKE OF SUFFOLK
DUKE OF BUCKINGHAM
EARL OF SURREY
LORD CHANCELLOR
LORD CHAMBERLAIN
GARDINER, *Bishop of Winchester*
BISHOP OF LINCOLN
LORD ABERGAVENNY
LORD SANDYS
SIR THOMAS LOVELL
SIR HENRY GUILFORD
SIR ANTHONY DENNY
SIR NICHOLAS VAUX

CROMWELL, *Servant to Wolsey*
GRIFFITH, *Gentleman-Usher to Queen Katharine*
DOCTOR BUTTS, *Physician to the King*
BRANDON, AND A SERGEANT-AT-ARMS
QUEEN KATHARINE, *Wife to King Henry*
ANNE BULLEN, *her Maid of Honour; later Queen*
AN OLD LADY, *Friend to Anne Bullen*
PATIENCE, *Woman to Queen Katharine*

SECRETARIES TO WOLSEY; THREE GENTLEMEN;
GARTER KING-AT-ARMS; SURVEYOR TO THE DUKE OF
BUCKINGHAM; DOOR-KEEPER OF THE COUNCIL
CHAMBER; PORTER, AND HIS MAN; PAGE TO GARDINER;
A CRIER; SEVERAL LORDS AND LADIES IN THE DUMB
SHOWS; WOMEN ATTENDING UPON THE QUEEN;
SPIRITS WHICH APPEAR TO HER; SCRIBES, OFFICERS,
GUARDS, ETC.

SCENE—*London and Westminster; once at Kimbolton.*

The Life of King Henry the Eighth

INTRODUCTION

SOURCES OF THE PLAY

The sources of *Henry VIII* are Holinshed's *Chronicle* for the first four acts and the last scene of the fifth act, and Foxe's *Book of Martyrs* for the first four scenes of the fifth act. Mr. Chambers[1] posits an earlier version of the play called by the name of Buckingham. This does not seem probable because Holinshed is not the 'source' in the rather vague sense applicable to the other plays. Here much of the play is merely Holinshed's scenes dramatized and his words put into blank verse. A fair illustration is the speech of the First Gentleman, II.i.173–177.

> Yes, but it held not;
> For when the king once heard it, out of anger
> He sent command to the lord mayor straight
> To stop the rumour, and allay those tongues
> That durst disperse it.

Compare this passage with Holinshed:

'The king was offended with those tales, and sent for Sir Thomas Seimor maior of the citie of London, secretlie charging him to see that the people ceased from such talke.'

But as the play covers a period of twenty-four years, over a hundred folio pages in Holinshed, the playwrights selected passages to dramatize. From this condition three criticisms follow:

(1) The chronology is hopelessly confused, as the action is compressed into six or seven days. This confusion is partly unavoidable; the changes which occur during a quarter of a century must be ignored. The characters of the first act would have actually been old men or have died at the time the last must be dated. But also the playwrights did not care about the actual sequence of events, and the historical order of events is unnecessarily disarranged in the play.

(2) The characters neither develop, nor are they consistent. An illustration of the first point may be found in the treatment of the character of Henry himself. In 1520, the date of the opening of the play, he was twenty-nine years old, in the full vigor of his young manhood, athletic, fond of pleasure, and still tricked by the external; in 1544, the latest date in the play, he was old, sick, with an indomitable will and a shrewd sense that made him the most powerful personality in Europe. But the King Henry of the play is the same from the first act to the fifth. This may be due to the fact that the writers are frankly disregarding the lapse of time. The explanation for the inconsistency of the characters is quite different. The best illustration of this is to be found in the character of Wolsey. The fallen Wolsey of Act III has little in common with the arrogant prelate that plotted the fall of Buckingham. In Act III he is a heroic character with whose misfortunes the audience sympathizes; in Act I he is a tyrant,

and there is no attempt to bridge this gap. These opposing interpretations of the same person are to be found in the original authority. Holinshed's work is not a history in the modern sense. A modern historian studies the period, determines the relative values of the various incidents, and presents us with a unified interpretation of the events. But this is not the method of the old chroniclers. Holinshed copies previous writers, stating the fact in the margin, but he makes no attempt to reconcile them. For the character of Wolsey he relies first upon the narrative of Polydore Vergil. The latter was an Italian who came to England about 1501. He got into trouble with Wolsey and was put into prison by the latter. Consequently when he wrote his history of England, he gave an unfavorable account of Wolsey and imputed base motives for his actions. This account Holinshed followed. But toward the end of his account he ran into the life of Wolsey written by George Cavendish, who had been Wolsey's gentleman usher. Naturally to Cavendish Wolsey was ideal magnificence personified. Consequently when Holinshed grafted Cavendish's opinion of Wolsey's character upon the narrative of Polydore Vergil it formed an unexpected conclusion. In one scene of the play the two points of view are brought into sharp contrast. In Act IV, scene ii, Katharine is giving vent to ideas of Polydore Vergil, whereas Griffith replies by talking Cavendish.

(3) In any drama the scenes should have an organic relation, the succeeding scene should develop from those preceding, until in the last act the audience perceives the drama as a unified whole. That is far from the case here. The leading personage of the first part is Buckingham; then Wolsey takes the stage, then Katharine, and we end with Cranmer and the christening of Elizabeth. Thus the drama is not a drama at all; it is a series of almost unrelated scenes, describing events that occurred in the reign of Henry VIII, and with him as vaguely felt center. This again is due to the writers' dependence upon Holinshed. He had no philosophical conception of the reign, and they did little more than dramatize selected scenes as they came to them. According to the statements in the Prologue they regarded this dependence as a virtue. That is the obvious meaning of the line

'To make that only true we now intend,'

and the emphasis upon truth in line 9. In other words, they felt that they were following Holinshed as carefully as possible.

THE HISTORY OF THE PLAY

On June 29, 1613, the Globe Theatre, the theatre with which Shakespeare was connected, burned to the ground, 'the house being filled with people to behold the play, viz. of Henry the

---

1 E. K. Chambers, *The Elizabethan Stage*, Vol. 2, p. 202.

Eighth.' Such is Stowe's brief account. The day following Thomas Lorkin wrote to Sir Thomas Puckering:

'No longer since than yesterday, while Burbage's company were acting at the Globe the play of Henry VIII, and there shooting off certain chambers [cannon] in way of triumph, the fire catched and fastened upon the thatch of the house, and there burned so furiously, as it consumed the whole house, all in less than two hours, the people having enough to do to save themselves.'

The most famous account is that written on July 2 by Sir Henry Wotton to his nephew:

'Now, to let matters of state sleep, I will entertain you at the present with what has happened this week at the Bankside. The King's players had a new play, called *All is True,* representing some principal pieces of the reign of Henry VIII, which was set forth with many extraordinary circumstances of pomp and majesty, even to the matting of the stage; the Knights of the Order with their Georges and garters, the Guards with their embroidered coats, and the like: sufficient in truth within a while to make greatness very familiar, if not ridiculous. Now, King Henry making a masque at the Cardinal Wolsey's house, and certain chambers being shot off at his entry, some of the paper, or other stuff, wherewith one of them was stopped, did light on the thatch, where being thought at first but an idle smoke, and their eyes more attentive to the show, it kindled inwardly, and ran round like a train, consuming within less than an hour the whole house to the very grounds. This was the fatal period of that virtuous fabric, wherein yet nothing did perish but wood and straw, and a few forsaken cloaks; only one man had his breeches set on fire, that would perhaps have broiled him, if he had not by the benefit of a provident wit put it out with bottle ale.'

There are other contemporary allusions to the famous fire, but the foregoing are the most precise. Thus there is no question that the Globe was set on fire during the performance of a play dealing with the reign of Henry VIII. Although there were other plays centering around Henry VIII at this time, the probability is that the particular play is, certainly for the most part, the one we have. Contemporary verses mention both Heminges and Condell as being the actors in it; and Heminges and Condell ten years later printed our play as belonging to the Shakespearean repertoire. In 1623 they could scarcely have forgotten the play that had proved so disastrous to them. If this is the play, either Sir Henry Wotton was mistaken about the title, or it was advertised under an alternative title *All is True,* and the lines of the Prologue may allude to this alternative title. There are two slight corroborative details. In Act I, scene iv, a stage direction reads 'chambers discharged'; the Globe would seem, then, to have burned at the end of the first act. And the 'business' of the part of King Henry was said after the Restoration to have been handed down from Shakespeare himself.

The suggestion of Chambers and others that it was an old play revamped does not seem probable. Sir Henry Wotton speaks of it as a 'new play.' This seems borne out by internal evidence. The play apparently was thrown together hurriedly, without much planning, to meet some emergency. What that emergency was it is impossible to tell at this late date. It has been suggested that the play was written to celebrate the marriage of the Princess Elizabeth with the Elector Palatine, which took place on the fourteenth of February, 1613. But as runs were very brief in that age, it is questionable whether Wotton would have described it

four months later as 'new' if that had been the case. There is no need for positing a great ceremonial, or an affair of state, to call for the play. The emergency may equally well have been purely theatrical: that the manager was disappointed in a play for which he had contracted, or that the play he had intended to produce was unavailable for one of a hundred reasons, and a new play had to be substituted. At least, *Henry VIII* shows signs of hurried work. As we do not have the manuscript, it is always possible that the obvious errors in the text are due to the mistakes of the typesetter. That is not true in some cases here. The authors themselves must be held responsible for imprisoning Wolsey in Asher House, the residence of the Bishop of Winchester, when Wolsey was himself Bishop of Winchester. Such a slip can mean only that the authors had read their Holinshed rapidly. The banquet after the coronation is plainly stated to have been held in Westminster Hall; on a preceding page, following the account of a previous procession, Holinshed tells us that Anne retired to Whitehall. Presumably the authors lost the place in the chronicle and they have put the coronation banquet in Whitehall. Sandys, who was 'Lord' Sandys in Act I, is degraded to mere knighthood in Act II. Such mistakes as these are not due to an ignorant typesetter; they are due to a writer that cares vastly more for the theatrical significance of the scene than for historical accuracy. Other errors, while possibly typographical, are probably due to careless composition. Reading the black letter of Holinshed hastily, the authors transformed his phrase 'bottom of my conscience' into 'bosom of my conscience' (II.iv.195) and his noun chattels, which he spells 'cattels,' into 'castles' (III.ii.406). Slips like these all favor the assumption that for some reason a new play was required and authors set to work at full speed to produce one. It was written to be played, not to be read, and such errors as the foregoing, are, from the point of view of the audience, immaterial. The wonder is, not that the play is so poor, but that it is so good. The authors have succeeded in constructing a drama with pageant-like scenes and a few opportunities for good actors. These were the characteristics of it from the very beginning. According to contemporary accounts Burbage himself played in it, and Wotton stresses the elaborateness of the costumes. And these are the characteristics that have caused it to be revived over and over again. Pepys saw the great production in 1664, when Betterton played the King; Harris, Wolsey; Smith, Buckingham; and Mrs. Betterton, Queen Katharine. His comment is unfavorable:

'But my wife and I rose from table, pretending business, and went to the Duke's house (Lincoln's Inn Fields), the first play I have been at these six months, according to my last vowe, and here saw the so much cried-up play of "Henry the Eighth"; which, though I went with resolution to like it, is so simple a thing made up of a great many patches, that, besides the shows and procession in it, there is nothing in the world good or well done. Thence mightily dissatisfied back at night to my uncle Wight's....'

Four years later, however, he is not so fastidious.

'After dinner, my wife and I to the Duke's playhouse, and there did see "King Harry the Eighth"; and was mightily pleased, better than I ever expected, with the history and the shows of it.'

There were at least twelve revivals in the eighteenth century. In 1727 was the famous one at Drury Lane, at which the management spent £1000 on the coronation scene alone. Most of the great actors and actresses are associated with it, and theatrical

anecdote concerning the business used by them is still current. When Colley Cibber declaimed the lines

> *This candle burns not clear; 'tis I must snuff it;*
> *Then out it goes . . . (III.ii.127–128)*

he imitated snuffing a candle with a pair of snuffers!

The same popularity continued in the nineteenth century; Kemble, Kean and Macready starred in it, and Mrs. Siddons made a traditionally great Queen Katharine. In more recent times Irving gave a great production of it in 1892 at the Lyceum; he himself played Wolsey; Ellen Terry, Katharine; and Forbes Robertson, Buckingham. And it was *Henry VIII* that Beerbohm Tree brought to New York to celebrate Shakespeare's tercentenary in 1916, a choice that must have made Shakespeare turn in his grave! This production, also, stressed the scenic values of the play, more than the acting.

AUTHORSHIP OF THE PLAY

The question of the authorship of *Henry VIII* is still partly unsolved. It is assigned to Shakespeare chiefly because it appears in the First Folio of 1623. That was edited by Heminges and Condell, two actors who had been in Shakespeare's company and who, by contemporary reports, had had parts in this particular play. The assumption is that when it is classed by them among Shakespeare's plays, they knew what they were talking about. On the other hand, it has been pointed out that the publication of the First Folio was a commercial venture, involving separate copyrights, and that, while the play, *Henry VIII,* was undoubtedly played by Shakespeare's company, it does not necessarily follow that he wrote the whole of it, the major part of it, or even any of it at all. As early as 1758 it was remarked that certain parts of the play have metrical peculiarities unlike Shakespeare's style. But it was not until a hundred years later that James Spedding, led by a remark of the poet Tennyson, made a careful investigation, and published his results in the *Gentleman's Magazine,* in 1850. Aside from subtler criteria, the great test is the proportionately large use of the eleven syllable line, the so-called feminine ending. As an example chosen at random, take the Chamberlain's speech in I.iii. The extra syllables are italicized.

> '*As far as I can see, all the good our Eng*li*sh*
> *Have got by the late voyage is but mere*l*y*
> *A fit or two o' the face; but they are shrewd ones;*
> *For when they hold 'em, you would swear direct*l*y*
> *Their very noses had been counsellors*
> *To Pepin or Clotharius, they keep state so.*'

It is easy to rewrite this without many such endings.

> '*As far as I can see, all the good our Eng*li*sh*
> *Have got by the late voyage is but slight,*
> *A fit or two o' the face; but they are shrewd;*
> *For when they hold 'em, you would swear at once*
> *Their very noses had been counsellors*
> *To Pepin or Clotharius, they so keep state.*'

It is not the question whether one type of verse is better than the other,—in the passage selected, neither is particularly good,—the point is that whereas Shakespeare in his known works uses this extra syllable comparatively rarely, such frequent use of the extra syllable is the characteristic of the style of Shakespeare's great contemporary dramatist, John Fletcher. The reader can amuse himself by testing the lines. Spedding drew up the following table from his edition:

Act	Scene	Lines	Red. Syll.	Proportion	Author
1	1	225	63	1 to 3.5	Shakespeare
	2	215	74	1 to 2.9	Shakespeare
	3 & 4	172	100	1 to 1.7	Fletcher
2	1	164	97	1 to 1.6	Fletcher
	2	129	77	1 to 1.6	Fletcher
	3	107	41	1 to 2.6	Shakespeare
	4	230	72	1 to 3.1	Shakespeare
3	1	166	119	1 to 1.3	Fletcher
	2 (to King's exit)	193	62	1 to 3	Shakespeare
	3	257	152	1 to 1.6	Fletcher
4	1	116	57	1 to 2	Fletcher
	2	80	51	1 to 1.5	Fletcher
	3	93	51	1 to 1.8	Fletcher
5	1	176	68	1 to 2.5	Shakespeare (altered)
	2	217	115	1 to 1.8	Fletcher
	3 almost all prose				Fletcher
	4	73	44	1 to 1.6	Fletcher

To account for the conditions as shown in the table above there are only three possible explanations. (1) Shakespeare wrote the whole play but for some unaccountable reason in many of the scenes imitated the style of Fletcher. This is the explanation given by Sir Sidney Lee. (2) Shakespeare and Fletcher collaborated. Collaboration between two or more playwrights was very common in the Elizabethan age. But here almost every great scene is written by Fletcher. If *Henry VIII* was a 'new' play in 1613, Shakespeare had already written *Macbeth, Hamlet,* and *Lear;* he was a veteran dramatist with an established reputation. The question consequently arises why under these circumstances the younger writer should take all the great opportunities and the older do merely the filling in. (3) Shakespeare had no hand in the play whatever; it was merely played under his direction. The non-Fletcherian scenes are not by Shakespeare, but by Massinger. This explanation was suggested in the 1880s by Mr. Robert Boyle. It was later argued by Mr. H. Dugdale Sykes, largely on the ground of coincidences of phrasing between *Henry VIII* and Massinger's known plays. It may be interesting to compare the table made by Mr. Sykes with the table of Spedding.

Prologue		Fletcher
Act 1, Sc. 1		Massinger
2		Massinger
3		Massinger & Fletcher
4		Massinger & Fletcher
Act 2, Sc. 1		Massinger & Fletcher
2		Fletcher
3		Massinger
4		Massinger
Act 3, Sc. 1		Massinger & Fletcher
2	(to exit of King)	Massinger
	(from exit of King)	Fletcher
Act 4, Sc. 1		Massinger
2		Massinger & Fletcher
Act 5, Sc. 1		Massinger
2		Fletcher
3		Massinger & Fletcher
4		Fletcher
5		Fletcher
Epilogue		Massinger

As a possible explanation of the peculiarities fo the play and its passing under Shakespeare's name, Mr. Leicester Bradner suggests that Shakespeare's company suddenly required a play on the general subject of Henry VIII to balance the successful performance of Rowley's *When You See Me, You Know Me* at a rival theatre. This is, of course, only guesswork.

In conclusion: The play was hastily thrown together. It shows no one creative mind. It is a series of scenes, taken from well-known books, scenes which have little relation, even chronological, between them. It has no development of character. And its versification is, in the main, non-Shakespearean. Therefore the conclusion seems inevitable that whatever Shakespeare's share may have been in its composition, it was the minimum amount necessary to have it included by his first editors among his works.

THE PROLOGUE

I come no more to make you laugh: things now,
That bear a weighty and a serious brow,
Sad, high, and working, full of state and woe,
Such noble scenes as draw the eye to flow,
We now present. Those that can pity here   5
May, if they think it well, let fall a tear;
The subject will deserve it. Such as give
Their money out of hope they may believe,
May here find truth too. Those that come to see
Only a show or two, and so agree   10
The play may pass, if they be still and willing,
I'll undertake may see away their shilling
Richly in two short hours. Only they
That come to hear a merry, bawdy play,
A noise of targets, or to see a fellow   15
In a long motley coat guarded with yellow,
Will be deceiv'd; for, gentle hearers, know,
To rank our chosen truth with such a show
As fool and fight is, besides forfeiting
Our own brains, and the opinion that we bring,   20
To make that only true we now intend,
Will leave us never an understanding friend.
Therefore, for goodness' sake, and as you are known
The first and happiest hearers of the town,
Be sad, as we would make ye: think ye see   25
The very persons of our noble story
As they were living; think you see them great,
And follow'd with the general throng and sweat
Of thousand friends; then in a moment see
How soon this mightiness meets misery: 30
And if you can be merry then, I'll say
A man may weep upon his wedding day.

ACT FIRST ❧ SCENE FIRST

[London. An Antechamber in the Palace]
*Enter the Duke of Norfolk at one door; at the other, the Duke of
Buckingham and the Lord Abergavenny.*

Buck. Good morrow, and well met. How have you done,
Since last we saw in France?
    Nor.   I thank your Grace,
Healthful; and ever since a fresh admirer
Of what I saw there.
    Buck.   An untimely ague   5
Stay'd me a prisoner in my chamber, when
Those suns of glory, those two lights of men,
Met in the vale of Andren.
    Nor.   'Twixt Guynes and Arde: 10
I was then present, saw them salute on horseback;
Beheld them, when they lighted, how they clung

In their embracement, as they grew together;
Which had they, what four thron'd ones could have weigh'd
Such a compounded one?   15
    Buck.   All the whole time
I was my chamber's prisoner.
    Nor.   Then you lost
The view of earthly glory: men might say,
Till this time pomp was single, but now married   20
To one above itself. Each following day
Became the next day's master, till the last
Made former wonders its. To-day the French
All clinquant, all in gold, lie heathen gods,
Shone down the English; and to-morrow they   25
Made Britain India: every man that stood
Show'd like a mine. Their dwarfish pages were
As cherubins, all gilt: the madams, too,
Not us'd to toil, did almost sweat to bear
The pride upon them, that their very labour   30
Was to them as a painting. Now this masque
Was cried incomparable; and the ensuing night
Made it a fool and beggar. The two kings,
Equal in lustre, were now best, now worst,
As presence did present them; him in eye   35
Still him in praise; and, being present both,
'Twas said they saw but one; and no discerner
Durst wag his tongue in censure. When these suns—
For so they phrase 'em—by their heralds challeng'd
The noble spirits to arms, they did perform   40
Beyond thought's compass; that former fabulous story,
Being now seen possible enough, got credit,
That Bevis was believ'd.
    Buck.   O, you go far!
    Nor. As I belong to worship, and affect   45
In honour honesty, the tract of everything
Would by a good discourser lose some life,
Which action's self was tongue to.
    Buck.   All was royal;
To the disposing of it nought rebell'd,   50
Order gave each thing view; the office did
Distinctly his full function. Who did guide,
I mean, who set the body and the limbs
Of this great sport together?
    Nor.   As you guess.   55
One certes, that promises no element
In such a business.
    Buck.   I pray you, who, my lord?
    Nor. All this was order'd by the good discretion
Of the right reverend Cardinal of York.   60
    Buck. The devil speed him! no man's pie is freed
From his ambitious finger. What had he
To do in these fierce vanities? I wonder
That such a keech can with his very bulk
Take up the rays o' the beneficial sun,   65
And keep it from the earth.
    Nor.   Surely, sir,
There's in him stuff that puts him to these ends;

The Prologue; *cf. n.*   **3 Sad:** *serious* **working:** *full of pathos* **state:** *dignity*   **9 truth;** *cf. n.*   **12 shilling;** *cf. n.*   **16 In . . . coat;** *cf. n.* **guarded:** *trimmed*   **19 As fool and fight is;** *cf. n.*   **20 opinion:** *reputation, intention* **21 intend:** *undertake*   **22 Will leave us;** *cf. n.*   **25, 26** *Cf. n.*   **Scene First** S. d. Duke of Norfolk, Duke of Buckingham, Lord Abergavenny; *cf. n.*   **2 saw:** *met*   **8 Those suns of glory;** *cf. n.*   **9 vale of Andren;** *cf. n.*

16 All the whole time; *cf. n.*   **23 its;** *cf. n.*   **24 clinquant:** *glittering*   **35 him in eye:** *the one present* **43 That:** *so that* **Bevis:** *cf. n.*   **45 worship:** *noble rank* **46 tract:** *course*   **47, 48 Would . . . tongue to:** *could not be presented even by a skilful narrator with the vividness which the reality expressed* **48–54** *Cf. n.*   **63 fierce:** *extravagant* **64 keech:** *lump of fat*

For, being not propp'd by ancestry, whose grace
Chalks successors their way, nor call'd upon   70
For high feats done to the crown; neither allied
To eminent assistants; but, spider-like,
Out of his self-drawing web, a' gives us note,
The force of his own merit makes his way;
A gift that heaven gives for him, which buys   75
A place next to the king.
  Aber.   I cannot tell
What heaven hath given him: let some graver eye
Pierce into that; but I can see his pride
Peep through each part of him: whence has he that?   80
If not from hell, the devil is a niggard,
Or has given all before, and he begins
A new hell in himself.
  Buck.   Why the devil,
Upon this French going-out, took he upon him,   85
Without the privity o' the king, to appoint
Who should attend on him? He makes up the file
Of all the gentry; for the most part such
To whom as great a charge as little honour
He meant to lay upon,—and his own letter   90
(The honourable board of council out)
Must fetch him in,—he papers.
  Aber.   I do know
Kinsmen of mine, three at the least, that have
By this so sicken'd their estates, that never   95
They shall abound as formerly.
  Buck.   O, many
Have broke their backs with laying manors on 'em
For this great journey. What did this vanity
But minister communication of   100
A most poor issue?
  Nor.   Grievingly I think,
The peace between the French and us not values
The cost that did conclude it.
  Buck.   Every man,   105
After the hideous storm that follow'd, was
A thing inspir'd; and, not consulting, broke
Into a general prophecy: That this tempest,
Dashing the garment of this peace, aboded
The sudden breach on 't.   110
  Nor.   Which is budded out;
For France hath flaw'd the league, and hath attach'd
Our merchants' goods at Bordeaux.
  Aber.   Is it therefore
Th' ambassador is silenc'd?   115
  Nor.   Marry, is 't.
  Aber. A proper title of a peace; and purchas'd
At a superfluous rate!
  Buck.   Why, all this business
Our reverend cardinal carried.   120
  Nor.   Like it your Grace,
The state takes notice of the private difference
Betwixt you and the cardinal. I advise you,—
And take it from a heart that wishes towards you

Honour and plenteous safety,—that you read   125
The cardinal's malice and his potency
Together; to consider further that
What his high hatred would effect wants not
A minister in his power. You know his nature,
That he's revengeful; and I know his sword   130
Hath a sharp edge: it's long, and 't may be said,
It reaches far; and where 'twill not extend,
Thither he darts it. Bosom up my counsel,
You'll find it wholesome. Lo where comes that rock
That I advise your shunning.   135

*Enter Cardinal Wolsey,—the Purse borne before him,—certain of
the Guard, and two Secretaries with papers. The Cardinal in his
passage fixeth his eye on Buckingham, and Buckingham on
him, both full of disdain.*

  Car. The Duke of Buckingham's surveyor, ha?
Where's his examination?
  Secr.   Here, so please you.
  Car. Is he in person ready?
  Secr.   Ay, please your Grace.   140
  Car. Well, we shall then know more; and Buckingham
Shall lessen this big look. *[Exeunt Cardinal and his Train.]*
  Buck. This butcher's cur is venom'd-mouth'd, and I
Have not the power to muzzle him; therefore best
Not wake him in his slumber. A beggar's book   145
Outworths a noble's blood.
  Nor.   What! are you chaf'd?
Ask God for temperance; that's th' appliance only
Which your disease requires.
  Buck.   I read in's looks   150
Matter against me; and his eye revil'd
Me as his abject object: at this instant
He bores me with some trick. He's gone to the king:
I'll follow, and outstare him.
  Nor.   Stay, my lord,   155
And let your reason with your choler question
What 'tis you go about. To climb steep hills
Requires slow pace at first: anger is like
A full hot horse, who being allow'd his way,
Self-mettle tires him. Not a man in England   160
Can advise me like you: be to yourself
As you would to your friend.
  Buck.   I'll to the king;
And from a mouth of honour quite cry down
This Ipswich fellow's insolence, or proclaim   165
There's difference in no persons.
  Nor.   Be advis'd;
Heat not a furnace for your foe so hot
That it do singe yourself. We may outrun
By violent swiftness that which we run at,   170
And lose by overrunning. Know you not,
The fire that mounts the liquor till 't run o'er,
In seeming to augment it wastes it? Be advis'd:
I say again, there is no English soul
More stronger to direct you than yourself,   175
If with the sap of reason you would quench,
Or but allay, the fire of passion.

73 **Out . . . web**; *cf. n.* **a':** *he* 86 **privity:** *knowledge* 88–92 *Cf. n.* 92 **fetch him in:** *cheat* **papers:** *lists* 98 **with . . . on 'em:** *by selling manorial estates in order to buy personal equipment* 100 **minister communication**; *cf. n.* 106 **hideous storm**; *cf. n.* 112 **For . . . league**; *cf. n.* 115 **Th' ambassador is silenc'd**; *cf. n.* 121 **Like . . . Grace:** *may it please your Grace*

137 *Cf. n.* 143 **This butcher's cur**; *cf. n.* **venom'd:** *venomous* 145 **book:** *learning* 148 **temperance:** *moderation* **appliance:** *remedy* 152 **abject object:** *object of his contempt* 153 **bores:** *cheats* 165 **Ipswich**; *cf. n.*

Buck.   Sir,
I am thankful to you, and I'll go along
By your prescription: but this top-proud fellow   *180*
Whom from the flow of gall I name not, but
From sincere motions,—by intelligence,
And proofs as clear as founts in July, when
We see each grain of gravel,—I do know
To be corrupt and treasonous.   *185*
     Nor.   Say not 'treasonous.'
     Buck. To the king I'll say 't; and make my vouch as strong
As shore of rock. Attend. This holy fox,
Or wolf, or both,—for he is equal ravenous
As he is subtle, and as prone to mischief   *190*
As able to perform 't, his mind and place
Infecting one another, yea, reciprocally,—
Only to show his pomp as well in France
As here at home, suggests the king our master
To this last costly treaty: th' interview,   *195*
That swallow'd so much treasure, and like a glass
Did break i' the rinsing.
     Nor.   Faith, and so it did.
     Buck. Pray give me favour, sir. This cunning cardinal
The articles o' the combination drew   *200*
As himself pleas'd; and they were ratified
As he cried, 'Thus let be,' to as much end
As give a crutch to the dead. But out count-cardinal
Has done this, and 'tis well; for worthy Wolsey,
Who cannot err, he did it. Now this follows,—   *205*
Which, as I take it, is a kind of puppy
To the old dam, treason,—Charles the emperor,
Under pretence to see the queen his aunt,
For 'twas indeed his colour, but he came
To whisper Wolsey,—here makes visitation: *210*
His fears were that the interview betwixt
England and France might, through their amity,
Breed him some prejudice; for from this league
Peep'd harms that menac'd him. He privily
Deals with our cardinal, and, as I trow,—   *215*
Which I do well; for I am sure the emperor
Paid ere he promis'd, whereby his suit was granted
Ere it was ask'd;—but when the way was made,
And pav'd with gold, the emperor thus desir'd:
That he would please to alter the king's course,   *220*
And break the foresaid peace. Let the king know—
As soon he shall by me—that thus the cardinal
Does buy and sell his honour as he pleases,
And for his own advantage.
     Nor.   I am sorry   *225*
To hear this of him; and could wish he were
Something mistaken in 't.
     Buck.   No, not a syllable:
I do pronounce him in that very shape
He shall appear in proof.   *230*

*Enter Brandon; a Sergeant-at-Arms before him, and two or three
of the Guard.*

     Bran. Your office, sergeant; execute it.

     Serg.   Sir,
My Lord the Duke of Buckingham, and Earl
Of Hereford, Stafford, and Northampton, I
Arrest thee of high treason, in the name   *235*
Of our most sovereign king.
     Buck.   Lo you, my lord,
The net has fall'n upon me! I shall perish
Under device and practice.
     Bran.   I am sorry   *240*
To see you ta'en from liberty, to look on
The business present. 'Tis his highness' pleasure
You shall to the Tower.
     Buck.   It will help me nothing
To plead mine innocence, for that dye is on me   *245*
Which makes my whit'st part black. The will of heaven
Be done in this and all things! I obey.
O, my Lord Abergavenny, fare you well!
     Bran. Nay, he must bear you company. [*To Abergavenny.*]
The King   *250*
Is pleas'd you shall to the Tower, till you know
How he determines further.
     Aber.   As the duke said,
The will of heaven be done, and the king's pleasure
By me obey'd!   *255*
     Bran.   Here is a warrant from
The king t' attach Lord Montacute; and the bodies
Of the duke's confessor, John de la Car,
One Gilbert Peck, his chancellor,—
     Buck.   So, so;   *260*
These are the limbs o' the plot: no more, I hope.
     Bran. A monk o' the Chartreux.
     Buck.   O! Nicholas Hopkins?
     Bran.   He.
     Buck. My surveyor is false; the o'er-great cardinal   *265*
Hath show'd him gold. My life is spann'd already:
I am the shadow of poor Buckingham,
Whose figure even this instant cloud puts on,
By dark'ning my clear sun. My lord, farewell.   *Exeunt.*

❧ SCENE SECOND ❧

[*The Council Chamber*]
*Cornets. Enter King Henry, leaning on the Cardinal's shoulder, the
nobles and Sir Thomas Lovell; the Cardinal places himself under
the King's feet on his right side.*

     King. My life itself, and the best heart of it,
Thanks you for this great care: I stood i' the level
Of a full-charg'd confederacy, and give thanks
To you that chok'd it. Let be call'd before us
That gentleman of Buckingham's; in person   *5*
I'll hear him his confessions justify;
And point by point the treasons of his master
He shall again relate.

---

180 **top-proud:** *supremely insolent*   182 **motions:** *motives*   187 **vouch:** *proof*   194
suggests: *tempts*   200 **combination:** *agreement*   203 **count-cardinal;** *cf. n.*   207
Charles the emperor; *cf. n.*   209 **colour:** *excuse*   214 **He privily;** *cf. n.*   227
mistaken: *misjudged*   S. d. **Enter Brandon;** *cf. n.*

234 **Hereford;** *cf. n.*   237 **Lo you:** *behold!*   239 **device and practice:** *plot and
trick*   240–242 **I am sorry,** *etc; cf. n.*   248 **Lord Abergavenny;** *cf. n.*   258 **John
de la Car;** *cf. n.*   259 **Gilbert Peck, his chancellor;** *cf. n.*   263 **Nicholas Hopkins;**
cf. n.   268 **instant:** *moment; cf. n.*   269 **My lord;** *cf. n.*   Scene Second S. d.
Cf. n.   2 **level:** *range, aim*   3 **confederacy:** *conspiracy*   5 **That . . . Buckingham's:**
the surveyor

A noise within, crying, 'Room for the Queen, ushered by the Duke
of Norfolk.' Enter the Queen, Norfolk and Suffolk: she kneels.
King riseth from his state, takes her up, kisses, and placeth
her by him.

Queen. Nay, we must longer kneel: I am a suitor.
King. Arise, and take place by us: half your suit   *10*
Never name to us; you have half our power:
The other moiety, ere you ask, is given;
Repeat your will, and take it.
Queen.   Thank your majesty.
That you would love yourself, and in that love   *15*
Not unconsider'd leave your honour nor
The dignity of your office, is the point
Of my petition.
King.   Lady mine, proceed.
Queen. I am solicited, not by a few,   *20*
And those of true condition, that your subjects
Are in great grievance: there have been commissions
Sent down among 'em, which hath flaw'd the heart
Of all their loyalties: wherein, although,
My good Lord Cardinal, they vent reproaches   *25*
Most bitterly on you, as putter-on
Of these exactions, yet the king our master,—
Whose honour heaven shield from soil!—even he escapes not
Language unmannerly; yea, such which breaks
The sides of loyalty, and almost appears   *30*
In loud rebellion.
Nor.   Not almost appears,
It doth appear; for, upon these taxations,
The clothiers all, not able to maintain
The many to them longing, have put off   *35*
The spinsters, carders, fullers, weavers, who,
Unfit for other life, compell'd by hunger
And lack of other means, in desperate manner
Daring th' event to the teeth, are all in uproar,
And danger serves among them.   *40*
King.   Taxation?
Wherein? and what taxation? My Lord Cardinal,
You that are blam'd for it alike with us,
Know you of this taxation?
Car.   Please you, sir,   *45*
I know but of a single part in aught
Pertains to the state; and front but in that file
Where others tell steps with me.
Queen.   No, my lord?
You know no more than others; but you frame   *50*
Things that are known alike; which are not wholesome
To those which would not know them, and yet must
Perforce be their acquaintance. These exactions,
Whereof my sovereign would have note, they are
Most pestilent to the hearing; and to bear 'em,   *55*
The back is sacrifice to the load. They say
They are devis'd by you, or else you suffer
Too hard an exclamation.
King.   Still exaction!
The nature of it? In what kind, let's know,   *60*
Is this exaction?

Queen.   I am much too venturous
In tempting of your patience; but am bolden'd
Under your promis'd pardon. The subjects' grief
Comes through commissions, which compels from each   *65*
The sixth part of his substance, to be levied
Without delay; and the pretence for this
Is nam'd, your wars in France. This makes bold mouths:
Tongues spit their duties out, and cold hearts freeze
Allegiance in them; their curses now   *70*
Live where their prayers did; and it's come to pass,
This tractable obedience is a slave
To each incensed will. I would your highness
Would give it quick consideration, for
There is no primer business.   *75*
King.   By my life,
This is against our pleasure.
Car.   And for me,
I have no further gone in this than by
A single voice, and that not pass'd me but   *80*
By learned approbation of the judges. If I am
Traduc'd by ignorant tongues, which neither know
My faculties nor person, yet will be
The chronicles of my doing, let me say
'Tis but the fate of place, and the rough brake   *85*
That virtue must go through. We must not stint
Our necessary actions, in the fear
To cope malicious censurers; which ever,
As ravenous fishes, do a vessel follow
That is new-trimm'd, but benefit no further   *90*
Than vainly longing. What we oft do best,
By sick interpreters, once weak ones, is
Not ours, or not allow'd; what worst, as oft,
Hitting a grosser quality, is cried up
For our best act. If we shall stand still,   *95*
In fear our motion will be mock'd or carp'd at,
We should take root here where we sit, or sit
State-statues only.
King.   Things done well,
And with a care, exempt themselves from fear;   *100*
Things done without example in their issue
Are to be fear'd. Have you a precedent
Of this commission? I believe, not any.
We must not rend our subjects from our laws,
And stick them in our will. Sixth part of each?   *105*
A trembling contribution! Why, we take
From every tree, lop, bark, and part o' the timber;
And though we leave it with a root, thus hack'd,
The air will drink the sap. To every county
Where this is question'd, send our letters, with   *110*
Free pardon to each man that has denied
The force of this commission. Pray, look to 't;
I put it to your care.
Car. [*To the Secretary.*] A word with you.
Let there be letters writ to every shire,   *115*
Of the king's grace and pardon. The griev'd commons
Hardly conceive of me; let it be nois'd
That through our intercession this revokement

S. d. Suffolk; *cf. n.* state; *cf. n.*   12 moiety: *half*   13 Repeat your will: *say what you*
desire   22 commissions; *cf. n.*   35 longing: *belonging*   47 front but in that file:
only march in the front rank   58 exclamation: *reproach*

83, 84 yet . . . doing: *yet presume to know all that I do*   88 cope: *encounter*   92 sick:
envious of us   93 allow'd: *approved*   101 example: *precedent* issue: *conse-*
quences   105 stick . . . in: *make dependent upon* will: *arbitrary caprice*   106 trembling:
tremendous, fearful   107 lop: *branches*   117 Hardly conceive: *think hardly*

And pardon comes: I shall anon advise you
Further in the proceeding.   *Exit Secretary.*   *120*

Enter Surveyor.

  Queen. I am sorry that the Duke of Buckingham
Is run in your displeasure.
  King.   It grieves many:
The gentleman is learn'd, and a most rare speaker,
To nature none more bound; his training such   *125*
That he may furnish and instruct great teachers,
And never seek for aid out of himself. Yet see,
When these so noble benefits shall prove
Not well dispos'd, the mind growing once corrupt,
They turn to vicious forms, ten times more ugly   *130*
Than ever they were fair. This man so complete,
Who was enroll'd 'mongst wonders, and when we,
Almost with ravish'd listening, could not find
His hour of speech a minute; he, my lady,
Hath into monstrous habits put the graces   *135*
That once were his, and is become as black
As if besmear'd in hell. Sit by us; you shall hear—
This was his gentleman in trust—of him
Things to strike honour sad. Bid him recount
The fore-recited practices, whereof   *140*
We cannot feel too little, hear too much.
  Car. Stand forth; and with bold spirit relate what you,
Most like a careful subject, have collected
Out of the Duke of Buckingham.
  King.   Speak freely.   *145*
  Surv. First, it was usual with him,—every day
It would infect his speech,—that if the king
Should without issue die, he'd carry it so
To make the sceptre his. These very words
I've heard him utter to his son-in-law,   *150*
Lord Abergavenny, to whom by oath he menac'd
Revenge upon the cardinal.
  Car.   Please your highness, note
This dangerous conception in this point.
Not friended by his wish, to your high person   *155*
His will is most malignant; and it stretches
Beyond you, to your friends.
  Queen.   My learn'd Lord Cardinal,
Deliver all with charity.
  King.   Speak on: *160*
How grounded he his title to the crown
Upon our fail? to this point hast thou heard him
At any time speak aught?
  Surv.   He was brought to this
By a vain prophecy of Nicholas Henton.   *165*
  King. What was that Henton?
  Surv.   Sir, a Chartreux friar,
His confessor, who fed him every minute
With words of sovereignty.
  King.   How know'st thou this?   *170*
  Surv. Not long before your highness sped to France,
The duke being at the Rose, within the parish
Saint Lawrence Poultney, did of me demand
What was the speech among the Londoners

Concerning the French journey: I replied,   *175*
Men fear'd the French would prove perfidious,
To the king's danger. Presently the duke
Said, 'twas the fear, indeed; and that he doubted
'Twould prove the verity of certain words
Spoke by a holy monk; 'that oft,' says he,   *180*
'Hath sent to me, wishing me to permit
John de la Car, my chaplain, a choice hour
To hear from him a matter of some moment:
Whom after under the confession's seal
He solemnly had sworn, that what he spoke,   *185*
My chaplain to no creature living but
To me should utter, with demure confidence
This pausingly ensu'd: neither the king nor 's heirs—
Tell you the duke—shall prosper: bid him strive
To [gain] the love o' the commonalty: the duke   *190*
Shall govern England.'
  Queen.   If I know you well,
You were the duke's surveyor, and lost your office
On the complaint o' the tenants: take good heed
You charge not in your spleen a noble person,   *195*
And spoil your nobler soul. I say, take heed;
Yes, heartily beseech you.
  King.   Let him on.
Go forward.
  Surv.   On my soul, I'll speak but truth.   *200*
I told my lord the duke, by the devil's illusions
The monk might be deceiv'd; and that 'twas dangerous
for him
To ruminate on this so far, until
It forg'd him some design, which, being believ'd,   *205*
It was much like to do. He answer'd, 'Tush!
It can do me no damage'; adding further,
That had the king in his last sickness fail'd,
The cardinal's and Sir Thomas Lovell's heads
Should have gone off.   *210*
  King.   Ha! what, so rank? Ah, ha!
There's mischief in this man. Canst thou say further?
  Surv. I can, my liege.
  King.   Proceed.
  Surv.   Being at Greenwich,   *215*
After your highness had reprov'd the duke
About Sir William Bulmer,—
  King.   I remember
Of such a time: being my sworn servant,
The duke retain'd him his. But on; what hence?   *220*
  Surv. 'If,' quoth he, 'I for this had been committed,
As, to the Tower, I thought, I would have play'd
The part my father meant to act upon
Th' usurper Richard; who, being at Salisbury,
Made suit to come in's presence; which if granted,   *225*
As he made semblance of his duty, would
Have put his knife into him.'
  King.   A giant traitor!
  Car. Now, madam, may his highness live in freedom,
And this man out of prison?   *230*
  Queen.   God mend all!

---

125 To . . . bound: *no one more gifted by nature*   129 dispos'd: *directed*   140 practices:
plots   142 Stand forth; *cf. n.*   148 carry it so: *so arrange matters as*   162 Upon
our fail: *if we should die*   165 Henton; *cf. n.*   171–191 *Cf. n.*

177 Presently: *at once*   184 confession's seal; *cf. n.*   190 To gain; *cf. n.*   193 You
were the duke's surveyor; *cf. n.*   195 spleen: *malice*   200–210 *Cf. n.*   203 for
him; *cf. n.*   217 Bulmer; *cf. n.*   222 As . . . thought: *to the Tower, as I thought I
should be*   226 would: *i.e. my father would*

King. There's something more would out of thee? what
sayst?

    Surv. After 'the duke his father,' with 'the knife,'
He stretch'd him, and, with one hand on his dagger,   *235*
Another spread on's breast, mounting his eyes,
He did discharge a horrible oath; whose tenour
Was, were he evil us'd, he would outgo
His father by as much as a performance
Does an irresolute purpose.   *240*
    King.   There's his period:
To sheathe his knife in us. He is attach'd;
Call him to present trial: if he may
Find mercy in the law, 'tis his; if none,
Let him not seek 't of us: by day and night!   *245*
He's traitor to the height.   *Exeunt.*

❦ Scene Third ❦

[A Room in the Palace]
Enter Lord Chamberlain and Lord Sandys.

    L. Ch. Is 't possible the spells of France should juggle
Men into such strange mysteries?
    L. San.   New customs,
Though they be never so ridiculous,
Nay, let 'em be unmanly, yet are follow'd.   *5*
    L. Ch. As far as I see, all the good our English
Have got by the late voyage is but merely
A fit or two o' the face; but they are shrewd ones;
For when they hold 'em, you would swear directly
Their very noses had been counsellors   *10*
To Pepin or Clotharius, they keep state so.
    L. San. They have all new legs, and lame ones: one would
take it,
That never saw 'em pace before, the spavin
Or springhalt reign'd among 'em.   *15*
    L. Ch.   Death! my lord
Their clothes are after such a pagan cut too,
That, sure, they've worn out Christendom.

Enter Sir Thomas Lovell.

                How now!
What news, Sir Thomas Lovell?   *20*
    Lov.   Faith, my lord,
I hear of none but the new proclamation
That's clapp'd upon the court-gate.
    L. Ch.   What is 't for?
    Lov. The reformation of our travell'd gallants,   *25*
That fill the court with quarrels, talk, and tailors.
    L. Ch. I'm glad 'tis there: now I would pray our monsieurs
To think an English courtier may be wise,
And never see the Louvre.
    Lov.   They must either—   *30*
For so run the conditions—leave those remnants
Of fool and feather that they got in France,
With all their honourable points of ignorance

Pertaining thereunto,—as fights and fireworks;
Abusing better men than they can be,   *35*
Out of a foreign wisdom;—renouncing clean
The faith they have in tennis and tall stockings,
Short blister'd breeches, and those types of travel,
And understand again like honest men;
Or pack to their old playfellows: there, I take it,   *40*
They may, *cum privilegio,* wear away
The lag end of their lewdness, and be laugh'd at.
    L. San. 'Tis time to give 'em physic, their diseases
Are grown so catching.
    L. Ch.   What a loss our ladies   *45*
Will have of these trim vanities!
    Lov.   Ay, marry,
There will be woe indeed, lords: the sly whoresons
Have got a speeding trick to lay down ladies;
A French song and a fiddle has no fellow.   *50*
    L. San. The devil fiddle 'em! I am glad they're going:
For, sure, there's no converting of 'em: now
An honest country lord, as I am, beaten
A long time out of play, may bring his plainsong
And have an hour of hearing; and, by 'r lady,   *55*
Held current music too.
    L. Ch.   Well said, Lord Sandys;
Your colt's tooth is not cast yet.
    L. San.   No, my lord;
Nor shall not, while I have a stump.   *60*
    L. Ch.   Sir Thomas,
Whither were you a-going?
    Lov.   To the cardinal's:
Your lordship is a guest too.
    L. Ch.   O! 'tis true: *65*
This night he makes a supper, and a great one,
To many lords and ladies; there will be
The beauty of this kingdom, I'll assure you.
    Lov. That churchman bears a bounteous mind indeed,
A hand as fruitful as the land that feeds us;   *70*
His dews fall everywhere.
    L. Ch.   No doubt he's noble;
He had a black mouth that said other of him.
    L. San. He may, my lord; h'as wherewithal: in him
Sparing would show a worse sin than ill doctrine: *75*
Men of his way should be most liberal;
They are set here for examples.
    L. Ch.   True, they are so;
But few now give so great ones. My barge stays;
Your lordship shall along. Come, good Sir Thomas,   *80*
We shall be late else; which I would not be,
For I was spoke to, with Sir Henry Guilford,
This night to be comptrollers.
    L. San.   I am your lordship's.
                              Exeunt.

---

34 fireworks; *cf. n.*   **37 tall stockings;** *cf. n.*   **38 blister'd:** *swollen, puffy*   **39 understand:** *an obvious pun*   **41 cum privilegio:** *by special privilege*   **53, 54 beaten ... play:** *long ignored*   **54 plainsong:** *homely ditty, simple wooing*   **56 Held current music:** *be held fashionable*   **58 colt's tooth:** *youthful wildness*   **66 makes:** *gives*   **73 had:** *would have*   **74 h'as:** *he has*   **79 My barge stays;** *cf. n.*   **83 comptrollers:** *masters of ceremonies*

---

241 period: *ultimate purpose*   **245 by day and night;** *cf. n.*   **Scene Third;** *cf. n.*   **8 A fit ... face:** *a grimace or two*   **11 Pepin or Clotharius:** *early French kings*   **14, 15 spavin ... springhalt;** *cf. n.*   **32 fool and feather:** *light-brained folly; cf. n.*

❧ SCENE FOURTH ❧

[The Presence-chamber in York-Place]
Hautboys. A small table under a state for the Cardinal, a
longer table for the guests. Then enter Anne Bullen, and divers
other ladies and gentlemen, as guests, at one door; at another
door enter Sir. Henry Guilford.

Guil. Ladies, a general welcome from his Grace
Salutes ye all; this night he dedicates
To fair content and you. None here, he hopes,
In all this noble bevy, has brought with her
One care abroad; he would have all as merry   5
As, first, good company, good wine, good welcome
Can make good people.

Enter Lord Chamberlain, Lord Sandys, and Lovell.

O, my lord, y' are tardy!
The very thought of this fair company
Clapp'd wings to me.   10
   L. Ch. You are young, Sir Harry Guilford.
   L. San. Sir Thomas Lovell, had the cardinal
But half my lay-thoughts in him, some of these
Should find a running banquet ere they rested,
I think would better please 'em: by my life,   15
They are a sweet society of fair ones.
   Lov. O that your lordship were but now confessor
To one or two of these!
   L. San.   I would I were;
They should find easy penance.   20
   Lov.   Faith, how easy?
   L. San. As easy as a down-bed would afford it.
   L. Ch. Sweet ladies, will it please you sit? Sir Harry,
Place you that side, I'll take the charge of this;
His Grace is entering. Nay you must not freeze;   25
Two women plac'd together makes cold weather:
My Lord Sandys, you are one will keep 'em waking;
Pray, sit between these ladies.
   L. San.   By my faith,
And thank your lordship. By your leave, sweet ladies   30
If I chance to talk a little wild, forgive me;
I had it from my father.
   Anne.   Was he mad, sir?
   L. San. O very mad, exceeding mad; in love too:
But he would bite none; just as I do now,   35
He would kiss you twenty with a breath.   *[Kisses her.]*
   L. Ch.   Well said, my lord.
So, now y' are fairly seated. Gentlemen,
The penance lies on you, if these fair ladies
Pass away frowning.   40
   L. San.   For my little cure,
Let me alone.

Hautboys. Enter Cardinal Wolsey and takes his state.

   Car. Y' are welcome, my fair guests: that noble lady,
Or gentleman, that is not freely merry,
Is not my friend. This, to confirm my welcome;   45
And to you all, good health.   *[Drinks.]*
   L. San.   Your Grace is noble:

Let me have such a bowl may hold my thanks,
And save me so much talking.
   Car.   My lord Sandys,   50
I am beholding to you: cheer your neighbours.
Ladies, you are not merry: gentlemen,
Whose fault is this?
   L. San.   The red wine first must rise
In their fair cheeks, my lord; then we shall have 'em   55
Talk us to silence.
   Anne.   You are a merry gamester,
My Lord Sandys.
   L. San.   Yes, if I make my play.
Here's to your ladyship; and pledge it, madam,   60
For 'tis to such a thing,—
   Anne.   You cannot show me.
   L. San. I told your Grace they would talk anon.
                Drum and trumpet; chambers discharged.
   Car.   What's that?
   L. Ch. Look out there, some of ye.   65
   Car.   What warlike voice,
And to what end, is this? Nay, ladies, fear not;
By all the laws of war y' are privileg'd.

Enter a servant.

   L. Ch. How now, what is 't?
   Serv.   A noble troop of strangers;   70
For so they seem: they've left their barge and landed;
And hither make, as great ambassadors
From foreign princes.
   Car.   Good Lord Chamberlain,
Go, give 'em welcome; you can speak the French tongue;   75
And, pray, receive 'em nobly, and conduct 'em
Into our presence, where this heaven of beauty
Shall shine at full upon them. Some attend him.
                All rise, and tables removed.
You have now a broken banquet; but we'll mend it.
A good digestion to you all; and once more   80
I shower a welcome on ye; welcome all.

Hautboys. Enter King, and Others, as masquers, habited like shep-
herds, ushered by the Lord Chamberlain. They pass directly
before the Cardinal, and gracefully salute him.

A noble company! what are their pleasures?
   L. Ch. Because they speak no English, thus they pray'd
To tell your Grace: that, having heard by fame
Of this so noble and so fair assembly   85
This night to meet here, they could do no less,
Out of the great respect they bear to beauty,
But leave their flocks; and, under your fair conduct,
Crave leave to view these ladies, and entreat
An hour of revels with 'em   90
   Car.   Say, Lord Chamberlain,
They have done my poor house grace; for which I pay 'em
A thousand thanks, and pray 'em take their pleasures.
                Choose ladies. The King and Anne Bullen.
   King. The fairest hand I ever touch'd! O beauty,
Till now I never knew thee!   *Music. Dance.*
   Car. My lord.

Scene Fourth; *cf. n.*   14 running banquet: *slight repast, but with a pun*   37 Well said:
that's right   41 cure: *remedy (?); charge (?)*

48 may: *as may be large enough to*   51 beholding: *indebted*   59 make my play:
win   S. d. chambers discharged: *small cannon fired; cf. n.*   94 The fairest hand;
cf. n.

L. Ch.   Your Grace?

Car.   Pray tell 'em thus much from me:
There should be one amongst 'em, by his person,
More worthy this place than myself; to whom,   *100*
If I but knew him, with my love and duty
I would surrender it.

L. Ch.   I will, my lord.   *Whisper.*

Car. What say they?

L. Ch.   Such a one, they all confess,   *105*
There is indeed; which they would have your Grace
Find out, and he will take it.

Car.   Let me see then.
By all your good leaves, gentlemen, here I'll make
My royal choice.   *110*

King.   Ye have found him, cardinal.
You hold a fair assembly; you do well, lord:
You are a churchman, or, I'll tell you, cardinal,
I should judge now unhappily.

Car.   I am glad   *115*
Your Grace is grown so pleasant.

King.   My Lord Chamberlain,
Prithee, come hither. What fair lady's that?

L. Ch. An 't please your Grace, Sir Thomas Bullen's
daughter,   *120*
The Viscount Rochford, one of her highness' women.

King. By heaven, she is a dainty one. Sweetheart,
I were unmannerly to take you out,
And not to kiss you. A health, gentlemen!
Let it go round.   *125*

Car. Sir Thomas Lovell, is the banquet ready
I' the privy chamber?

Lov.   Yes, my lord.

Car.   Your Grace,
I fear, with dancing is a little heated.   *130*

King. I fear, too much.

Car.   There's fresher air, my lord,
In the next chamber.

King. Lead in your ladies, every one. Sweet partner,
I must not yet forsake you. Let's be merry: *135*
Good my Lord Cardinal, I have half a dozen healths
To drink to these fair ladies, and a measure
To lead 'em once again; and then let's dream
Who's best in favour. Let the music knock it.

                         Exeunt with trumpets.

ACT SECOND ❧ SCENE FIRST

[Westminster. A Street]
Enter two Gentlemen at several doors.

1. Gent. Whither away so fast?

2. Gent.   O! God save ye.
E'en to the hall, to hear what shall become
Of the great Duke of Buckingham.

1. Gent.   I'll save you   *5*

That labour, sir. All's now done but the ceremony
Of bringing back the prisoner.

2. Gent.   Were you there?

1. Gent. Yes, indeed, was I.

2. Gent.   Pray speak what has   *10*
happen'd.

1. Gent. You may guess quickly what.

2. Gent.   Is he found guilty?

1. Gent. Yes, truly is he, and condemn'd upon 't.

2. Gent. I am sorry for 't.   *15*

1. Gent.   So are a number more.

2. Gent. But, pray, how pass'd it?

1. Gent. I'll tell you in a little. The great duke
Came to the bar; where to his accusations
He pleaded still not guilty, and alleg'd   *20*
Many sharp reasons to defeat the law.
The king's attorney on the contrary
Urg'd on the examinations, proofs, confessions
Of divers witnesses, which the duke desir'd
To have brought, *vivâ voce,* to his face: *25*
At which appear'd against him his surveyor;
Sir Gilbert Peck, his chancellor; and John Car,
Confessor to him; with that devil-monk,
Hopkins, that made this mischief.

2. Gent.   That was he   *30*
That fed him with his prophecies?

1. Gent.   The same.
All these accus'd him strongly; which he fain
Would have flung from him, but, indeed, he could not:
And so his peers, upon this evidence,   *35*
Have found him guilty of high treason. Much
He spoke, and learnedly, for life; but all
Was either pitied in him or forgotten.

2. Gent. After all this how did he bear himself?

1. Gent. When he was brought again to the bar, to hear *40*
His knell rung out, his judgment, he was stirr'd
With such an agony, he sweat extremely,
And something spoke in choler, ill and hasty:
But he fell to himself again, and sweetly
In all the rest show'd a most noble patience.   *45*

2. Gent. I do not think he fears death.

1. Gent.   Sure, he does not;
He never was so womanish; the cause
He may a little grieve at.

2. Gent.   Certainly   *50*
The cardinal is the end of this.

1. Gent.   'Tis likely
By all conjectures: first, Kildare's attainder,
Then deputy of Ireland; who remov'd,
Earl Surrey was sent thither, and in haste too,   *55*
Lest he should help his father.

2. Gent.   That trick of state
Was a deep envious one.

1. Gent.   At his return,
No doubt he will requite it. This is noted,   *60*
And generally, whoever the king favours,
The cardinal instantly will find employment,
And far enough from court too.

2. Gent.   All the commons

---

114 *unhappily: censoriously; i.e. I should think you flirtatious*   **116** *pleasant: light-hearted, humorous*   **119–121** *Sir Thomas ... Rochford: daughter of Sir Thomas Bullen, Viscount Rochford*   **123** *take you out: choose you as dancing partner*   **124 And ... kiss you;** *cf. n.*   **137** *measure: stately dance*   **139 knock it:** *strike up*   **Scene First;** *cf. n.* **S. d. several:** *different*

14 upon 't: *upon the verdict*   **22 on the contrary:** *on the opposite side*   **25 To have brought;** *cf. n.*   **55, 56 Earl Surrey ... his father;** *cf. n.*   **58 envious:** *malicious*

Hate him perniciously, and o' my conscience,   *65*
Wish him ten fathom deep: this duke as much
They love and dote on; call him bounteous Buckingham,
The mirror of all courtesy—

Enter Buckingham from his arraignment—Tipstaves before him;
the axe with the edge towards him; halberds on each
side—accompanied with Sir Thomas Lovell, Sir Nicholas Vaux,
Sir William Sandys, and common people, etc.

    1. Gent.   Stay there, sir,
And see the noble ruin'd man you speak of.   *70*
    2. Gent. Let's stand close, and behold him.
    Buck.   All good people,
You that thus far have come to pity me,
Hear what I say, and then go home and lose me.
I have this day receiv'd a traitor's judgment,   *75*
And by that name must die: yet heaven bear witness,
And if I have a conscience, let it sink me,
Even as the axe falls, if I be not faithful!
The law I bear no malice for my death,
'T has done upon the premises but justice;   *80*
But those that sought it I could wish more Christians:
Be what they will, I heartily forgive 'em.
Yet let 'em look they glory not in mischief,
Nor build their evils on the graves of great men;
For then my guiltless blood must cry against 'em.   *85*
For further life in this world I ne'er hope,
Nor will I sue, although the king have mercies
More than I dare make faults. You few that lov'd me,
And dare be bold to weep for Buckingham,
His noble friends and fellows, whom to leave   *90*
Is only bitter to him, only dying,
Go with me, like good angels, to my end;
And as the long divorce of steel falls on me,
Make of your prayers one sweet sacrifice,
And lift my soul to heaven. Lead on, o' God's name.   *95*
    Lov. I do beseech your Grace, for charity,
If ever any malice in your heart
Were hid against me, now to forgive me frankly.
    Buck. Sir Thomas Lovell, I as free forgive you
As I would be forgiven: I forgive all.   *100*
There cannot be those numberless offences
'Gainst me that I cannot take peace with: no black envy
Shall make my grave. Commend me to his Grace;
And if he speak of Buckingham, pray, tell him
You met him half in heaven. My vows and prayers   *105*
Yet are the king's; and, till my soul forsake,
Shall cry for blessings on him: may he live
Longer than I have time to tell his years!
Ever belov'd and loving may his rule be!
And when old time shall lead him to his end,   *110*
Goodness and he fill up one monument!
    Lov. To the water side I must conduct your Grace;
Then give my charge up to Sir. Nicholas Vaux,
Who undertakes you to your end.
    Vaux.   Prepare there!   *115*
The duke is coming. See the barge be ready;
And fit it with such furniture as suits

The greatness of his person.
    Buck.   Nay, Sir Nicholas,
Let it alone; my state now will but mock me.   *120*
When I came hither, I was Lord High Constable,
And Duke of Buckingham; now poor Edward Bohun:
Yet I am richer than my base accusers,
That never knew what truth meant: I now seal it;
And with that blood will make 'em one day groan for 't.   *125*
My noble father, Henry of Buckingham,
Who first raised head against usurping Richard,
Flying for succour to his servant Banister,
Being distress'd, was by that wretch betray'd,
And without trial fell: God's peace be with him!   *130*
Henry the Seventh succeeding, truly pitying
My father's loss, like a most royal prince,
Restor'd me to my honours, and, out of ruins,
Made my name once more noble. Now his son,
Henry the Eighth, life, honour, name, and all   *135*
That made me happy, at one stroke has taken
For ever from the world. I had my trial,
And must needs say, a noble one; which makes me
A little happier than my wretched father:
Yet thus far we are one in fortunes; both   *140*
Fell by our servants, by those men we lov'd most:
A most unnatural and faithless service!
Heaven has an end in all; yet, you that hear me,
This from a dying man receive as certain:
Where you are liberal of your loves and counsels   *145*
Be sure you be not loose; for those you make friends
And give your hearts to, when they once perceive
The least rub in your fortunes, fall away
Like water from ye, never found again
But where they mean to sink ye. All good people,   *150*
Pray for me! I must now forsake ye: the last hour
Of my long weary life is come upon me.
Farewell:
And when you would say something that is sad,
Speak how I fell. I have done; and God forgive me!   *155*
         Exeunt Duke and Train.
    1. Gent. O this is full of pity! Sir, it calls,
I fear, too many curses on their heads
That were the authors.
    2. Gent.   If the duke be guiltless,
'Tis full of woe; yet I can give you inkling   *160*
Of an ensuing evil, if it fall,
Greater than this.
    1. Gent.   Good angels keep it from us!
What may it be? You do not doubt my faith, sir?
    2. Gent. This secret is so weighty, 'twill require   *165*
A strong faith to conceal it.
    1. Gent.   Let me have it;
I do not talk much.
    2. Gent.   I am confident:
You shall, sir. Did you not of late days hear   *170*
A buzzing of a separation
Between the king and Katharine?
    1. Gent.   Yes, but it held not;
For when the king once heard it, out of anger

He sent command to the lord mayor straight   175
To stop the rumour, and allay those tongues
That durst disperse it.
    2. Gent.   But that slander, sir,
Is found a truth now; for it grows again
Fresher than e'er it was; and held for certain   180
The king will venture at it. Either the cardinal,
Or some about him near, have, out of malice
To the good queen, possess'd him with a scruple
That will undo her. To confirm this too,
Cardinal Campeius is arriv'd, and lately;   185
As all think, for this business.
    1. Gent.   'Tis the cardinal;
And merely to revenge him on the emperor
For not bestowing on him, at his asking,
The archbishopric of Toledo, this is purpos'd.   190
    2. Gent. I think you have hit the mark: but is 't not cruel
That she should feel the smart of this? The cardinal
Will have his will, and she must fall.
    1. Gent.   'Tis woeful.
We are too open here to argue this!   195
Let's think in private more.   *Exeunt.*

❧ Scene Second ❧

[An antechamber in the Palace]
Enter Lord Chamberlain, reading this letter.

L. Ch. 'My lord, The horses your lordship sent for, with all
the care I had, I saw well chosen, ridden, and furnished. They
were young and handsome, and of the best breed in the north.
When they were ready to set out for London, a man of my
Lord Cardinal's, by commission and main power, took 'em   5
from me; with this reason: His master would be served before
a subject, if not before the king; which stopped our mouths, sir.'
I fear he will indeed. Well, let him have them:
He will have all, I think.

Enter to the Lord Chamberlain the Dukes of Norfolk and Suffolk.

    Nor. Well met, my Lord Chamberlain.   10
    L. Ch. Good day to both your Graces.
    Suf. How is the king employ'd?
    L. Ch.   I left him private,
Full of sad thoughts and troubles.
    Nor.   What's the cause?   15
    L. Ch. It seems the marriage with his brother's wife
Has crept too near his conscience.
    Suf.   No; his conscience
Has crept too near another lady.
    Nor.   'Tis so: 20
This is the cardinal's doing: the king-cardinal,
That blind priest, like the eldest son of Fortune,
Turns what he list. The king will know him one day.
    Suf. Pray God he do! he'll never know himself else.
    Nor. How holily he works in all his business,   25
And with what zeal! for, now he has crack's the league
Between us and the emperor, the queen's great nephew,
He dives into the king's soul, and there scatters

Dangers, doubts, wringing of the conscience,
Fears, and despairs; and all these for his marriage: 30
And out of all these, to restore the king,
He counsels a divorce; a loss of her,
That like a jewel has hung twenty years
About his neck, yet never lost her lustre;
Of her that loves him with that excellence   35
That angels love good men with; even of her,
That, when the greatest stroke of fortune falls,
Will bless the king: and is not his course pious?
    L. Ch. Heaven keep me from such counsel! 'Tis most
true   40
These news are everywhere; every tongue speaks 'em,
And every true heart weeps of 't. All that dare
Look into these affairs see his main end,
The French king's sister. Heaven will one day open
The king's eyes, that so long have slept upon   45
This bold bad man.
    Suf.   And free us from his slavery.
    Nor. We had need pray,
And heartily, for our deliverance;
Or this imperious man will work us all   50
From princes into pages. All men's honours
Lie like one lump before him, to be fashion'd
Into what pitch he please.
    Suf.   For me, my lords,
I love him not, nor fear him; there's my creed.   55
As I am made without him, so I'll stand,
If the king please; his curses and his blessings
Touch me alike, they're breath I not believe in.
I knew him, and I know him; so I leave him
To him that made him proud, the pope.   60
    Nor.   Let's in;
And with some other business put the king
From these sad thoughts, that work too much upon him.
My lord, you'll bear us company?
    L. Ch.   Excuse me;   65
The king has sent me otherwhere: besides,
You'll find a most unfit time to disturb him:
Health to your lordships.
    Nor.   Thanks, my good Lord
Chamberlain.   70

Exit Lord Chamberlain, and the King draws
the curtain and sits reading pensively.

    Suf. How sad he looks! sure, he is much afflicted.
    King. Who's there? Ha?
    Nor.   Pray God he be not angry.
    King. Who's there, I say? How dare you thrust yourselves
Into my private meditations?   75
Who am I? Ha?
    Nor. A gracious king that pardons all offences
Malice ne'er meant: our breach of duty this way
Is business of estate; in which we come
To know your royal pleasure.   80
    King.   Ye are too bold.
Go to; I'll make ye know your times of business.
Is this an hour for temporal affairs? Ha?

Enter Wolsey and Campeius with a commission.

176 allay: *quiet* 185 Cardinal Campeius; *cf. n.* 190 The archbishopric of Toledo;
cf. n. 18, 19 No ... lady; *cf. n.* 22 blind; *cf. n.*

53 pitch: *height* (?), *black defilement* (?)   S. d.; *Cf. n.*   79 estate: *state*

Who's there? my good Lord Cardinal? O, my Wolsey,
The quiet of my wounded conscience!   85
Thou art a cure fit for a king. *[To Campeius.]* You're welcome,
Most learned reverend sir, into our kingdom:
Use us, and it. *[To Wolsey.]* My good lord, have great care
I be not found a talker.
    Wol.   Sir, you cannot.   90
I would your Grace would give us but an hour
Or private conference.
    King. [To Norfolk and Suffolk.] We are busy: go.
    Nor. [Aside to Suffolk.] This priest has no pride in him!
    Suf. [Aside to Norfolk.]   Not to speak of;
I would not be so sick though for his place:
But this cannot continue.
    Nor. [Aside to Suffolk.] If it do,
I'll venture one have-at-him.
    Suf. [Aside to Norfolk.] I another.   100
                        Exeunt Norfolk and Suffolk.
    Wol. Your Grace has given a precedent of wisdom
Above all princes, in committing freely
Your scruple to the voice of Christendom.
Who can be angry now? what envy reach you?
The Spaniard, tied by blood and favour to her,   105
Must now confess, if they have any goodness,
The trial just and noble. All the clerks,
I mean the learned ones, in Christian kingdoms
Have their free voices. Rome, the nurse of judgment,
Invited by your noble self, hath sent   110
One general tongue unto us, this good man,
This just and learned priest, Cardinal Campeius;
Whom once more I present unto your highness.
    King. And once more in mine arms I bid him
welcome,   115
And thank the holy conclave for their loves:
They have sent me such a man I would have wish'd for.
    Cam. Your Grace must needs deserve all strangers' loves,
You are so noble. To your highness' hand
I tender my commission, by whose virtue,—   120
The court of Rome commanding,—you, my Lord
Cardinal of York, are join'd with me, their servant,
In the unpartial judging of this business.
    King. Two equal men. The queen shall be acquainted
Forthwith for what you come. Where's Gardiner?   125
    Wol. I know your majesty has always lov'd her
So dear in heart, not to deny her that
A woman of less place might ask by law:
Scholars, allow'd freely to argue for her.
    King. Ay, and the best she shall have; and my favour   130
To him that does best: God forbid else. Cardinal,
Prithee, call Gardiner to me, my new secretary:
I find him a fit fellow.

                        Enter Gardiner.

    Wol. [Aside to Gardiner.] Give me your hand; much joy and
favour to you;   135
You are the king's now.
    Gard. [Aside to Wolsey.] But to be commanded
For ever by your Grace, whose hand has rais'd me.

    King. Come hither, Gardiner.
                        Walks and whispers [with Gardiner].
    Cam. My Lord of York, was not one Doctor Pace   140
In this man's place before him?
    Wol.   Yes, he was.
    Cam. Was he not held a learned man?
    Wol.   Yes, surely.
    Cam. Believe me, there's an ill opinion spread then   145
Even of yourself, Lord Cardinal.
    Wol.   How? of me?
    Cam. They will not stick to say, you envied him,
And fearing he would rise, he was so virtuous,
Kept him a foreign man still, which so griev'd him   150
That he ran mad and died.
    Wol.   Heaven's peace be with him!
That's Christian care enough: for living murmurers
There's places of rebuke. He was a fool,
For he would needs be virtuous. That good fellow,   155
If I command him, follows my appointment:
I will have none so near else. Learn this, brother,
We live not to be grip'd by meaner persons.
    King. Deliver this with modesty to the queen.
                                                    Exit Gardiner.
The most convenient place that I can think of   160
For such receipt of learning is Blackfriars;
There ye shall meet about this weighty business.
My Wolsey, see it furnished. O my lord!
Would it not grieve an able man to leave
So sweet a bedfellow? But, conscience, conscience!   165
O 'tis a tender place, and I must leave her.   *Exeunt.*

❦ SCENE THIRD ❦

[An Antechamber in the Queen's Apartments]
Enter Anne Bullen and an Old Lady.

    Anne. Not for that neither: here's the pang that pinches:
His highness having liv'd so long with her, and she
So good a lady that no tongue could ever
Pronounce dishonour of her—by my life,
She never knew harm-doing—O! now, after   5
So many courses of the sun enthroned,
Still growing in a majesty and pomp, the which
To leave a thousand-fold more bitter than
'Tis sweet at first t' acquire: after this process
To give her the avaunt, it is a pity   10
Would move a monster.
    Old La.   Hearts of most hard temper
Melt and lament for her.
    Anne.   O God's will! much better
She ne'er had known pomp: through 't be temporal,   15
Yet if that quarrel, Fortune, do divorce
It from the bearer, 'tis a sufferance panging
As soul and body's severing.
    Old La.   Alas! poor lady,
She's a stranger now again.   20

89 **talker:** *boaster, i.e. he means what he says*   96 **sick:** *sick with pride*   99 **have-at-him;** *cf. n.*   116 **holy conclave:** *the college of Cardinals*   123 **unpartial:** *impartial*   124 **equal:** *just*   125 **Gardiner;** *cf. n.*   128 *Cf. n.*

140 **Doctor Pace;** *cf. n.*   153 **Christian care:** *to wish him peace is all a Christian need do*   157 **none . . . else:** *no others so near the king*   161 **Blackfriars;** *cf. n.*   **Scene Third;** *cf. n.*   1-11 *Cf. n.*   10 **the avaunt:** *the order to be off*   16 **quarrel:** *quarreler, the abstract for the concrete*   17 **sufferance:** *suffering*   **panging:** *causing pangs*

Anne.   So much the more
Must pity drop upon her. Verily,
I swear, 'tis better to be lowly born,
And range with humble livers in content,
Than to be perk'd up in a glist'ring grief   25
And wear a golden sorrow.
    Old La.   Our content
Is our best having.
    Anne.   By my troth and maidenhead
I would not be a queen.   30
    Old La.   Beshrew me, I would,
And venture maidenhead for 't; and so would you,
For all this spice of your hypocrisy.
You, that have so fair parts of woman on you,
Have too a woman's heart; which ever yet   35
Affected eminence, wealth, sovereignty:
Which, to say sooth, are blessings, and which gifts—
Saving your mincing—the capacity
Of your soft cheveril conscience would receive,
If you might please to stretch it.   40
    Anne.   Nay, good troth.
    Old La. Yes, troth, and troth; you would not be a queen?
    Anne. No, not for all the riches under heaven.
    Old La. 'Tis strange: a three-pence bow'd would hire me,
Old as I am, to queen it. But, I pray you,   45
What think you of a duchess? have you limbs
To bear that load of title?
    Anne.   No, in truth.
    Old La. Then you are weakly made. Pluck off a little:
I would not be a young count in your way,   50
For more than blushing comes to: if your back
Cannot vouchsafe this burthen, 'tis too weak
Ever to get a boy.
    Anne.   How you do talk!
I swear again, I would not be a queen   55
For all the world.
    Old La.   In faith, for little England
You'd venture an emballing: I myself
Would for Carnarvonshire, although there 'long'd
No more to the crown but that. Lo! who comes here?   60

         Enter Lord Chamberlain.

    L. Ch. Good morrow, ladies. What were 't worth to know
The secret of your conference?
    Anne.   My good lord,
Not your demand; it values not your asking:
Our mistress' sorrows we were pitying.   65
    L. Ch. It was a gentle business, and becoming
The action of good women: there is hope
All will be well.
    Anne.   Now, I pray God, amen!
    L. Ch. You bear a gentle mind, and heavenly blessings   70
Follow such creatures. That you may, fair lady,
Perceive I speak sincerely, and high note's
Ta'en of your many virtues, the king's majesty

Commends his good opinion of you, and
Does purpose honour to you no less flowing   75
Than Marchioness of Pembroke; to which title
A thousand pound a year, annual support,
Out of his grace he adds.
    Anne.   I do not know
What kind of my obedience I should tender.   80
More than my all is nothing, nor my prayers
Are not words duly hallow'd, nor my wishes
More worth than empty vanities; yet prayers and wishes
Are all I can return. Beseech your lordship,
Vouchsafe to speak my thanks and my obedience,   85
As from a blushing handmaid, to his highness,
Whose health and royalty I pray for.
    L. Ch.   Lady,
I shall not fail t' approve the fair conceit
The king hath of you. *[Aside.]* I have perus'd her well;   90
Beauty and honour in her are so mingled
That they have caught the king; and who knows yet
But from this lady may proceed a gem
To lighten all this isle? *[To her.]* I'll to the king,
And say I spoke with you.   95
    Anne.   My honour'd lord.
                Exit Lord Chamberlain.

    Old La. Why, this it is; see, see!
I have been begging sixteen years in court,
Am yet a courtier beggarly, nor could
Come pat betwixt too early and too late   100
For any suit of pounds; and you, O fate!
A very fresh-fish here—fie, fie, upon
This compell'd fortune!—have your mouth fill'd up
Before you open it.
    Anne.   This is strange to me.   105
    Old La. How tastes it? is it bitter? forty pence, no.
There was a lady once,—'tis an old story,—
That would not be a queen, that would she not
For all the mud in Egypt: have you heard it?
    Anne. Come, you are pleasant.   110
    Old La.   With your theme I could
O'ermount the lark. The Marchioness of Pembroke!
A thousand pounds a year, for pure respect!
No other obligation! By my life,
That promises moe thousands: honour's train   115
Is longer than his fore-skirt. By this time
I know your back will bear a duchess. Say,
Are you not stronger than you were?
    Anne.   Good lady,
Make yourself mirth with your particular fancy,   120
And leave me out on 't. Would I had no being,
If this salute my blood a jot: it faints me,
To think what follows.
The queen is comfortless, and we forgetful
In our long absence. Pray, do not deliver   125
What here you've heard to her.
    Old La.   What do you think me? *Exeunt.*

---

25 perk'd up: *trimmed out*   **28 having:** *possession*   **39 cheveril:** *kid-leather, a type of flexibility*   **44 bow'd:** *made crooked, worthless; cf. n.*   **49 Pluck off a little:** *come down to a lower rank*   **52 vouchsafe:** *be willing to accept*   **53 Ever to get a boy;** *cf. n.*   **57 little England;** *cf. n.*   **58 emballing;** *cf. n.*   **59 Carnarvonshire;** *cf. n.*   **64 Not your demand:** *not worth your question*

74 Commends: *sends to you; cf. n.*   **76 Marchioness of Pembroke;** *cf. n.*   **81, 82 nor ... not:** *the usual double negative*   **84 Beseech:** *I beseech*   **89 conceit:** *opinion*   **93 a gem;** *cf. n.*   **101 suit of pounds:** *petition for money*   **102 Cf. n.**   **103 compell'd:** *unsought, violent*   **106 forty pence:** *a customary amount for a wager*   **109 mud in Egypt; cf. n.**   **115 moe:** *other, more*   **116 fore-skirt:** *front of gown*   **122 salute:** *affect*   **it faints me:** *I am depressed*

❧ SCENE FOURTH ❧

[A Hall in Blackfriars]

Trumpets, sennet, and cornets. Enter two Vergers, with short silver wands; next them, two Scribes, in the habit of doctors; after them, the Bishop of Canterbury, alone; after him, the Bishops of Lincoln, Ely, Rochester, and Saint Asaph; next them, with some small distance, follows a Gentleman bearing the purse, with the great seal, and a cardinal's hat; then two Priests, bearing each a silver cross; then a Gentleman-Usher bare-headed, accompanied with a Sergeant-at-Arms, bearing a silver mace; then two Gentlemen, bearing two great silver pillars; after them, side by side, the two Cardinals; two Noblemen with the sword and mace. The King takes place under the cloth of state; the two Cardinals sit under him as judges. The Queen takes place some distance from the King. The Bishops place themselves on each side the court, in manner of a consistory; below them, the Scribes. The Lords sit next the Bishops. The rest of the Attendants stand in convenient order about the stage.

Wol. Whilst our commission from Rome is read,
Let silence be commanded.
 King.   What's the need?
It hath already publicly been read,
And on all sides th' authority allow'd;   *5*
You may then spare that time.
 Wol.   Be 't so. Proceed.
Scribe. Say, Henry King of England, come into the court.
Crier. Henry King of England, &c.
King. Here.   *10*
Scribe. Say, Katharine Queen of England, come into the court.
Crier. Katharine Queen of England, &c.

The Queen makes no answer, rises out of her chair, goes about the court, comes to the King, and kneels at his feet; then speaks.

 Queen. Sir, I desire you do me right and justice;
And to bestow your pity on me; for   *15*
I am a most poor woman, and a stranger,
Born out of your dominions; having here
No judge indifferent, nor no more assurance
Of equal friendship and proceeding. Alas, sir,
In what have I offended you? What cause   *20*
Hath my behaviour given to your displeasure,
That thus you should proceed to put me off
And take your good grace from me? Heaven witness,
I have been to you a true and humble wife,
At all times to your will conformable;   *25*
Ever in fear to kindle your dislike,
Yea, subject to your countenance, glad or sorry
As I saw it inclin'd. When was the hour
I ever contradicted your desire,
Or made it not mine too? Or which of your friends   *30*
Have I not strove to love, although I knew
He were mine enemy? What friend of mine,
That had to him deriv'd your anger, did I
Continue in my liking? nay, gave notice
He was from thence discharg'd. Sir, call to mind   *35*
That I have been your wife, in this obedience

Upward of twenty years, and have been blest
With many children by you. If, in the course
And process of this time, you can report,
And prove it too, against mine honour aught,   *40*
My bond to wedlock, or my love and duty,
Against your sacred person, in God's name
Turn me away; and let the foul'st contempt
Shut door upon me, and so give me up
To the sharp'st kind of justice. Please you, sir,   *45*
The king, your father, was reputed for
A prince most prudent, of an excellent
And unmatch'd wit and judgment. Ferdinand,
My father, King of Spain, was reckon'd one
The wisest prince that there had reign'd by many   *50*
A year before. It is not to be question'd
That they had gather'd a wise council to them
Of every realm, that did debate this business,
Who deem'd our marriage lawful. Wherefore I humbly
Beseech you, sir, to spare me, till I may   *55*
Be by my friends in Spain advis'd, whose counsel
I will implore. If not, i' the name of God,
Your pleasure be fulfill'd!
 Wol.   You have here, lady,—
And of your choice,—these reverend fathers; men   *60*
Of singular integrity and learning,
Yea, the elect o' the land, who are assembled
To plead your cause. It shall be therefore bootless
That longer you desire the court, as well
For your own quiet, as to rectify   *65*
What is unsettled in the king.
 Camp.   His Grace
Hath spoken well and justly. Therefore, madam,
It's fit this royal session do proceed,
And that, without delay, their arguments   *70*
Be now produc'd and heard.
 Queen.   Lord Cardinal,
To you I speak.
 Wol.   Your pleasure, madam?
 Queen.   Sir,   *75*
I am about to weep; but, thinking that
We are a queen,—or long have dream'd so,—certain
The daughter of a king, my drops of tears
I'll turn to sparks of fire.
 Wol.   Be patient yet.   *80*
 Queen. I will, when you are humble; nay, before,
Or God will punish me. I do believe,
Induc'd by potent circumstances, that
You are mine enemy; and make my challenge
You shall not be my judge; for it is you   *85*
Have blown this coal betwixt my lord and me,
Which God's dew quench! Therefore I say again,
I utterly abhor, yea, from my soul
Refuse you for my judge, whom, yet once more,
I hold my most malicious foe, and think not   *90*
At all a friend to truth.
 Wol.   I do profess
You speak not like yourself; who ever yet

Scene Fourth S. d.; *cf.* n.   **8 &c.:** *i.e. the Crier recites the formal summons*   **14 Sir, I desire;** *cf.* n.   **18 indifferent:** *impartial*   **33 to him deriv'd:** *drawn upon himself*

38 many children; *cf.* n.   **50 by:** *in the course of*   **64 That . . . court:** *i.e. that you request the court to delay its proceedings*   **83 potent circumstances:** *strong evidences*   **84 challenge:** *a law term still used in claiming an objection to a juryman*   **87 God's dew:** *i.e. of mercy*   **88 abhor:** *protest against*

Have stood to charity, and display'd th' effects
Of disposition gentle, and of wisdom   *95*
O'ertopping woman's power. Madam, you do me wrong:
I have no spleen against you; nor injustice
For you or any: how far I have proceeded,
Or how far further shall, is warranted
By a commission from consistory,   *100*
Yea, the whole consistory of Rome. You charge me
That I have blown this coal: I do deny it.
The king is present: if it be known to him
That I gainsay my deed, how may he wound,
And worthily, my falsehood; yea, as much   *105*
As you have done my truth. If he know
That I am free of your report, he knows
I am not of your wrong. Therefore in him
It lies to cure me; and the cure is to
Remove these thoughts from you: the which before   *110*
His highness shall speak in, I do beseech
You, gracious madam, to unthink your speaking,
And to say so no more.
    Queen.   My lord, my lord,
I am a simple woman, much too weak   *115*
To oppose your cunning. Y' are meek and humble-mouth'd;
You sign your place and calling, in full seeming,
With meekness and humility; but your heart
Is cramm'd with arrogancy, spleen, and pride.
You have, by fortune and his highness' favours,   *120*
Gone slightly o'er low steps, and now are mounted
Where powers are your retainers, and your words,
Domestics to you, serve your will as 't please
Yourself pronounce their office. I must tell you,
You tender more your person's honour than   *125*
Your high profession spiritual; that again
I do refuse you for my judge; and here,
Before you all, appeal unto the pope,
To bring my whole cause 'fore his holiness,
And to be judg'd by him.   *130*
                   She curtsies to the King, and offers to depart.
    Camp.   The queen is obstinate,
Stubborn to justice, apt to accuse it, and
Disdainful to be tried by 't: 'tis not well.
She's going away.
    King. Call her again.   *135*
    Crier. Katharine Queen of England, come into the court.
    Gent. Ush. Madam, you are call'd back.
    Queen. What need you note it? pray you, keep your way:
When you are call'd, return. Now, the Lord help!
They vex me past my patience. Pray you, pass on: *140*
I will not tarry; no, nor ever more
Upon this business my appearance make
In any of their courts.   *Exeunt Queen, and her Attendants.*
    King.   Go thy ways, Kate:
That man i' the world who shall report he has   *145*
A better wife, let him in nought be trusted,
For speaking false in that: thou art, alone,—
If thy rare qualities, sweet gentleness,

Thy meekness saintlike, wifelike government,
Obeying in commanding, and thy parts   *150*
Sovereign and pious else, could speak thee out,—
The queen of earthly queens. She's noble born;
And, like her true nobility, she has
Carried herself towards me.
    Wol.   Most gracious sir,   *155*
In humblest manner I require your highness,
That it shall please you to declare, in hearing
Of all these ears,—for where I am robb'd and bound
There must I be unloos'd, although not there
At once and fully satisfied,—whether ever I   *160*
Did broach this business to your highness, or
Laid any scruple in your way, which might
Induce you to the question on 't? or ever
Have to you, but with thanks to God for such
A royal lady, spake one the least word that might   *165*
Be to the prejudice of her present state,
Or touch of her good person?
    King.   My Lord Cardinal,
I do excuse you; yea, upon mine honour,
I free you from 't. You are not to be taught   *170*
That you have many enemies, that know not
Why they are so, but, like to village curs,
Bark when their fellows do. By some of these
The queen is put in anger. Y' are excus'd:
But will you be more justified? You ever   *175*
Have wish'd the sleeping of this business; never
Desir'd it to be stirr'd; but oft have hinder'd, oft,
The passages made toward it. On my honour,
I speak my good lord Cardinal to this point,
And thus far clear him. Now, what mov'd me to 't,   *180*
I will be bold with time and your attention:
Then mark th' inducement. Thus it came; give heed to 't:
My conscience first receiv'd a tenderness,
Scruple, and prick, on certain speeches utter'd
By the Bishop of Bayonne, then French ambassador,   *185*
Who had been hither sent on the debating
A marriage 'twixt the Duke of Orleans and
Our daughter Mary. I' the progress of this business,
Ere a determinate resolution, he—
I mean, the bishop—did require a respite,   *190*
Wherein he might the king his lord advertise
Whether our daughter were legitimate,
Respecting this our marriage with the dowager,
Sometimes our brother's wife. This respite shook
The bosom of my conscience, enter'd me,   *195*
Yea, with a splitting power, and made to tremble
The region of my breast; which forc'd such way,
That many-maz'd considerings did throng,
And press'd in with this caution. First, methought
I stood not in the smile of heaven, who had   *200*
Commanded nature, that my lady's womb,
If it conceiv'd a male child by me, should
Do no more offices of life to 't than
The grave does to the dead; for her male issue
Or died where they were made, or shortly after   *205*

---

94 stood to: *taken the side of*   **111 in:** *in reference to, upon*   **112 unthink your speaking:**
disabuse your mind of what you have said   **117 sign:** *mark* **seeming:** *feigning*   **121**
slightly: *easily*   **111 powers:** *powers incidental to your high offices*   **122–124 your words**
. . . office; *cf. n.*   **125 tender:** *regard*   **132 apt:** *readily inclined*   **137 Gent. Ush.;**
cf. n.

149 government: *behavior*   **167 touch . . . person:** *sullying of her good reputation*   **179**
speak: *bear witness in favor of*   **181** *I ask time and your attention while I explain*   **185**
Bishop of Bayonne; *cf. n.*   **191 advertise:** *inform*   **194 Sometimes:** *sometime, for-*
merly   **195 bosom of my conscience;** *cf. n.*   **198 many-maz'd:** *intricate*

This world had air'd them. Hence I took a thought,
This was a judgment on me; that my kingdom,
Well worthy the best heir o' the world, should not
Be gladded in 't by me. Then follows that
I weigh'd the danger which my realms stood in   *210*
By this my issue's fail; and that gave to me
Many a groaning throe. Thus hulling in
The wild sea of my conscience, I did steer
Toward this remedy, whereupon we are
Now present here together; that's to say,   *215*
I meant to rectify my conscience, which
I then did feel full sick, and yet not well,
By all the reverend fathers of the land
And doctors learn'd. First, I began in private
With you, my Lord of Lincoln; you remember   *220*
How under my oppression I did reek,
When I first mov'd you.
     Lin.   Very well, my liege.
     King. I have spoke long: be please'd yourself to say
How far you satisfied me.   *225*
     Lin.   So please your highness,
The question did at first so stagger me,
Bearing a state of mighty moment in 't,
And consequence of dread, that I committed
The daring'st counsel that I had to doubt,   *230*
And did entreat your highness to this course
Which you are running here.
     King.   I then mov'd you,
My Lord of Canterbury, and got your leave
To make this present summons. Unsolicited   *235*
I left no reverend person in this court;
But by particular consent proceeded
Under your hands and seals; therefore go on,
For no dislike i' the world against the person
Of the good queen; but the sharp thorny points   *240*
Of my alleged reasons drives this forward.
Prove but our marriage lawful, by my life
And kingly dignity, we are contented
To wear our mortal state to come with her,
Katharine our queen, before the primest creature   *245*
That's paragon'd o' the world.
     Camp.   So please your highness,
The queen being absent, 'tis a needful fitness
That we adjourn this court till further day:
Meanwhile must be an earnest motion   *250*
Made to the queen, to call back her appeal
She intends unto his holiness.
     King.   *[Aside.]*   I may perceive
These cardinals trifle with me: I abhor
This dilatory sloth and tricks of Rome.   *255*
My learn'd and well-beloved servant Cranmer,
Prithee, return: with thy approach, I know,
My comfort comes along. Break up the court:
I say, set on.   *Exeunt, in manner as they entered.*

ACT THIRD ❧ SCENE FIRST

[The Palace at Bridewell. A Room in the Queen's Apartment]
Enter the Queen and her women as at work.

     Queen. Take thy lute, wench; my soul grows sad with troubles;
Sing and disperse 'em, if thou canst. Leave working.

           Song
   'Orpheus with his lute made trees,   *5*
   And the mountain tops that freeze,
      Bow themselves, when he did sing:
   To his music plants and flowers
   Ever sprung, as sun and showers
      There had made a lasting spring.   *10*

   'Every thing that heard him play,
   Even the billows of the sea,
      Hung their heads, and then lay by.
   In sweet music is such art,
   Killing care and grief of heart   *15*
      Fall asleep or, hearing, die.'

         Enter a Gentleman.

     Queen. How now!
     Gent. An 't please your Grace, the two great cardinals
Wait in the presence.
     Queen.   Would they speak with me?   *20*
     Gent. They will'd me say so, Madam.
     Queen.   Pray their Graces
To come near. *[Exit Gentleman.]* What can be their business
With me, a poor weak woman, fall'n from favour?
I do not like their coming, now I think on 't.   *25*
They should be good men, their affairs as righteous;
But all hoods make not monks.

     Enter the two Cardinals, Wolsey and Campeius.

     Wol.   Peace to your highness!
     Queen. Your Graces find me here part of a housewife,
I would be all, against the worst may happen.   *30*
What are your pleasures with me, reverend lords?
     Wol. May it please you, noble madam, to withdraw
Into your private chamber, we shall give you
The full cause of our coming.
     Queen.   Speak it here.   *35*
There's nothing I have done yet, o' my conscience,
Deserves a corner: would all other women
Could speak this with as free a soul as I do!
My lords, I care not—so much I am happy
Above a number—if my actions   *40*
Were tried by every tongue, every eye saw 'em,
Envy and base opinion set against 'em,
I know my life so even. If your business
Seek me out, and that way I am wife in,
Out with it boldly: truth loves open dealing.   *45*
     Wol. Tanta est erga te mentis integritas, regina
serenissima,—
     Queen. O, good my lord, no Latin!

---

212 **hulling:** *drifting without sail at the mercy of the waves*   228 **state:** *political issue*   241
drives: *drive; cf. n.*   246 **paragon'd:** *set forth as a model*   256 **Cranmer;** *cf. n.*

Scene First; *cf. n.*   9 **as:** *as if*   18 **An't:** *if it*   19 **presence:** *presence-chamber*   27
all ... monks; *cf. n.*   29 **part of:** *in part*   32 **May it:** *if it may*   44 **that way I
am wife in:** *i.e. how I behave as a wife*   46–47 *Cf. n.*

I am not such a truant since my coming
As not to know the language I have liv'd in: 50
A strange tongue makes my cause more strange, suspicious;
Pray, speak in English: here are some will thank you,
If you speak truth, for their poor mistress' sake:
Believe me, she has had much wrong. Lord Cardinal,
The willing'st sin I ever yet committed   55
May be absolv'd in English.
    Wol.   Noble lady,
I am sorry my integrity should breed,—
And service to his majesty and you,—
So deep suspicion, where all faith was meant.   60
We come not by the way of accusation,
To taint that honour every good tongue blesses,
Nor to betray you any way to sorrow;—
You have too much, good lady: but to know
How you stand minded in the weighty difference   65
Between the king and you; and to deliver,
Like free and honest men, our just opinions
And comforts to your cause.
    Camp.   Most honour'd madam,
My Lord of York, out of his noble nature,   70
Zeal and obedience he still bore your Grace,
Forgetting, like a good man, your late censure
Both of his truth and him,—which was too far,—
Offers, as I do, in a sign of peace,
His service and his counsel.   75
    Queen.   [*Aside.*]   To betray me.
My lords, I thank you both for your good wills;
Ye speak like honest men,—pray God, ye prove so!—
But how to make ye suddenly an answer
In such a point of weight, so near mine honour,—   80
More near my life, I fear,—with my weak wit,
And to such men of gravity and learning,
In truth I know not. I was set at work
Among my maids; full little, God knows, looking
Either for such men or such business.   85
For her sake that I have been,—for I feel
The last fit of my greatness,—good your Graces,
Let me have time and counsel for my cause:
Alas! I am a woman, friendless, hopeless.
    Wol. Madam, you wrong the king's love with these fears: 90
Your hopes and friends are infinite.
    Queen.   In England
But little for my profit. Can you think, lords,
That any Englishman dare give me counsel?
Or be a known friend, 'gainst his highness' pleasure,—   95
Though he be grown so desperate to be honest,—
And live a subject? Nay, forsooth, my friends,
They that must weigh out my afflictions,
They that my trust must grow to, live not here:
They are, as all my other comforts, far hence   100
In mine own country, lords.
    Camp.   I would your Grace
Would leave your griefs, and take my counsel.
    Queen.   How, sir?
    Camp. Put your main cause into the king's protection;   105
He's loving and most gracious: 'twill be much
Both for your honour better and your cause;

For if the trial of the law o'ertake ye,
You'll part away disgrac'd.
    Wol.   He tells you rightly.   110
    Queen. Ye tell me what ye wish for both: my ruin.
Is this your Christian counsel? out upon ye!
Heaven is above all yet; there sits a judge
That no king can corrupt.
    Camp.   Your rage mistakes us.   115
    Queen. The more shame for ye! holy men I thought ye,
Upon my soul, two reverend cardinal virtues;
But cardinal sins and hollow hearts I fear ye.
Mend 'em, for shame, my lords. Is this your comfort?
The cordial that ye bring a wretched lady,   120
A woman lost among ye, laugh'd at, scorn'd?
I will not wish ye half my miseries,
I have more charity; but say, I warn'd ye:
Take heed, for heaven's sake, take heed, lest at once
The burthen of my sorrows fall upon ye.   125
    Wol. Madam, this is a mere distraction;
You turn the good we offer into envy.
    Queen. Ye turn me into nothing: woe upon ye,
And all such false professors! Would you have me—
If you have any justice, any pity;   130
If ye be anything but churchmen's habits—
Put my sick cause into his hands that hates me?
Alas! h'as banish'd me his bed already,
His love too long ago! I am old, my lords,
And all the fellowship I hold now with him   135
Is only my obedience. What can happen
To me above this wretchedness? all your studies
Make me a curse like this.
    Camp.   Your fears are worse.
    Queen. Have I liv'd thus long—let me speak myself,   140
Since virtue finds no friends—a wife, a true one?
A woman, I dare say without vainglory,
Never yet branded with suspicion?
Have I with all my full affections
Still met the king? lov'd him next heaven? obey'd him?   145
Been, out of fondness, superstitious to him?
Almost forgot my prayers to content him?
And am I thus rewarded? 'Tis not well, lords.
Bring me a constant woman to her husband,
One that ne'er dreamed a joy beyond his pleasure,   150
And to that woman, when she has done most,
Yet will I add an honour, a great patience.
    Wol. Madam, you wander from the good we aim at.
    Queen. My lord, I dare not make myself so guilty,
To give up willingly that noble title   155
Your master wed me to: nothing but death
Shall e'er divorce my dignities.
    Wol.   Pray hear me.
    Queen. Would I had never trod this English earth,
Or felt the flatteries that grow upon it!   160
Ye have angels' faces, but heaven knows your hearts.
What will become of me now, wretched lady?
I am the most unhappy woman living.
[*To her women.*] Alas! poor wenches, where are now your
fortunes?   165
Shipwrack'd upon a kingdom, where no pity,

---

68 **your cause**; *cf. n.*   83 **was set**: *was sitting*   96 **so .. honest**: *so reckless as to be honest*   98 **weigh out**: *outweigh (?), ponder (?)*

127 **envy**: *malice*   140 **speak myself**, *cf. II.iv179*   149 **a constant ... husband**: *a woman constant to her husband*   161 **angel's faces**; *cf. n.*

No friends, no hope; no kindred weep for me;
Almost no grave allow'd me. Like the lily,
That once was mistress of the field and flourish'd,
I'll hang my head and perish.   *170*
   Wol.   If your Grace
Could but be brought to know our ends are honest,
You'd feel more comfort. Why should we, good lady,
Upon what cause, wrong you? alas! our places,
The way of our profession is against it: *175*
We are to cure such sorrows, not to sow 'em.
For goodness' sake, consider what you do;
How you may hurt yourself, ay, utterly
Grow from the king's acquaintance, by this carriage.
The hearts of princes kiss obedience,   *180*
So much they love it; but to stubborn spirits
They swell, and grow as terrible as storms.
I know you have a gentle, noble temper,
A soul as even as a calm: pray think us
Those we profess, peace-makers, friends, and servants.   *185*
   Camp. Madam, you'll find it so. You wrong your
virtues
With these weak women's fears: a noble spirit,
As yours was put into you, ever casts
Such doubts, as false coin, from it. The king loves you;   *190*
Beware you lose it not: for us, if you please
To trust us in your business, we are ready
To use our utmost studies in your service.
   Queen. Do what ye will, my lords: and, pray, forgive me,
If I have us'd myself unmannerly.   *195*
You know I am a woman, lacking wit
To make a seemly answer to such persons.
Pray do my service to his majesty:
He has my heart yet; and shall have my prayers
While I shall have my life. Come, reverend fathers,   *200*
Bestow your counsels on me. She now begs
That little thought, when she set footing here,
She should have bought her dignities so dear.   *Exeunt.*

❧ Scene Second ❧

[Antechamber to the King's Apartment]
Enter the Duke of Norfolk, Duke of Suffolk, Lord Surrey, and
Lord Chamberlain.

   Nor. If you will now unite in your complaints,
And force them with a constancy, the cardinal
Cannot stand under them. If you omit
The offer of this time, I cannot promise
But that you shall sustain moe new disgraces   *5*
With these you bear already.
   Sur.   I am joyful
To meet the least occasion that may give me
Remembrance of my father-in-law, the duke,
To be reveng'd on him.   *10*
   Suf.   Which of the peers
Have uncontemn'd gone by him, or at least
Strangely neglected? When did he regard

The stamp of nobleness in any person,
Out of himself?   *15*
   L. Ch.   My lords, you speak your pleasures:
What he deserves of you and me, I know;
What we can do to him,—though now the time
Gives way to us,—I much fear. If you cannot
Bar his access to the king, never attempt   *20*
Anything on him, for he hath a witchcraft
Over the king in's tongue.
   Nor.   O fear him not!
His spell in that is out: the king hath found
Matter against him that for ever mars   *25*
The honey of his language. No, he's settled,
Not to come off, in his displeasure.
   Sur.   Sir,
I should be glad to hear such news as this
Once every hour.   *30*
   Nor.   Believe it, this is true.
In the divorce his contrary proceedings
Are all unfolded; wherein he appears
As I would wish mine enemy.
   Sur.   How came   *35*
His practices to light?
   Suf.   Most strangely.
   Sur.   O how? how?
   Suf. The cardinal's letters to the pope miscarried,
And came to th' eye o' the king; wherein was read,   *40*
How that the cardinal did entreat his holiness
To stay the judgment o' the divorce; for if
It did take place, 'I do,' quoth he, 'perceive
My king is tangled in affection to
A creature of the queen's, Lady Anne Bullen.'   *45*
   Sur. Has the king this?
   Suf.   Believe it.
   Sur.   Will this work?
   L. Ch. The king in this perceives him, how he coasts
And hedges his own way. But in this point   *50*
All his tricks founder, and he brings his physic
After his patient's death: the king already
Hath married the fair lady.
   Sur.   Would he had!
   Suf. May you be happy in your wish, my lord!   *55*
For I profess, you have it.
   Sur.   Now all my joy
Trace the conjunction!
   Suf.   My amen to 't!
   Nor.   All men's.   *60*
   Suf. There's order given for her coronation:
Marry, this is yet but young, and may be left
To some ears unrecounted. But, my lords,
She is a gallant creature, and complete
In mind and feature: I persuade me, from her   *65*
Will fall some blessing to this land, which shall
In it be memoriz'd.
   Sur.   But will the king
Digest this letter of the cardinal's?
The Lord forbid!   *70*
   Nor.   Marry, amen!

179 carriage: *behavior*   185 Those we profess: *what we profess to be*   195 us'd: *behaved*
Scene Second; *cf. n.*   2 force: *urge*   9 my father-in-law, the duke: *i.e. the Duke of*
Buckingham

15 Out of: *except*   19 Gives way to us: *favors us*   27 Not to come off; *cf. n.*   32
contrary: *inconsistent, devious*   39 *Cf. n.*   54 Would he had; *cf. n.*   58 Trace:
follow   66 some blessing; *cf. n.*   69 Digest: *put up with*

Suf.   No, no;
There be moe wasps that buzz about his nose
Will make this sting the sooner. Cardinal Campeius
Is stol'n away to Rome; hath ta'en no leave;   75
Has left the cause o' the king unhandled; and
Is posted, as the agent of our cardinal,
To second all his plot. I do assure you
The king cried 'Ha!' at this.
    L. Ch.   Now, God incense him,   80
And let him cry 'Ha!' louder.
    Nor.   But, my lord,
When returns Cranmer?
    Suf. He is return'd in his opinions, which
Have satisfied the king for his divorce,   85
Together with all famous colleges
Almost in Christendom. Shortly, I believe,
His second marriage shall be publish'd, and
Her coronation. Katharine no more
Shall be call'd queen, but princess dowager,   90
And widow to Prince Arthur.
    Nor.   This same Cranmer's
A worthy fellow, and hath ta'en much pain
In the king's business.
    Suf.   He has; and we shall see him   95
For it an archbishop.
    Nor.   So I hear.
    Suf.   'Tis so.

Enter Wolsey and Cromwell.

The cardinal!
    Nor.   Observe, observe; he's moody.   100
    Car. The packet, Cromwell,
Gave 't you the king?
    Crom. To his own hand, in's bedchamber.
    Car. Look'd he o' th' inside of the paper?
    Crom.   Presently   105
He did unseal them; and the first he view'd,
He did it with a serious mind; a heed
Was in his countenance. You he bade
Attend him here this morning.
    Car.   Is he ready   110
To come abroad?
    Crom.   I think, by this he is.
    Car. Leave me awhile.   *Exit Cromwell.*
[*Aside.*] It shall be to the Duchess of Alençon,
The French King's sister; he shall marry her.   115
Anne Bullen! No; I'll no Anne Bullens for him:
There's more in 't than fair visage. Bullen!
No, we'll no Bullens. Speedily I wish
To hear from Rome. The Marchioness of Pembroke!
    Nor. He's discontented.   120
    Suf.   May be he hears the king
Does whet his anger to him.
    Sur.   Sharp enough,
Lord, for thy justice!
    Car. The late queen's gentlewoman, a knight's daughter,   125
To be her mistress' mistress! the queen's queen!
This candle burns not clear: 'tis I must snuff it;

Then, out it goes. What though I know her virtuous
And well deserving? yet I know her for
A spleeny Lutheran; and not wholesome to   130
Our cause, that she should lie i' the bosom of
Our hard-rul'd king. Again, there is sprung up
An heretic, an arch one, Cranmer; one
Hath crawl'd into the favour of the king,
And is his oracle.   135
    Nor.   He is vex'd at something.
    Sur. I would 'twere something that would fret the string,
The master-cord on's heart!

Enter King, reading of a schedule.

    Suf.   The king, the king!
    King. What piles of wealth hath he accumulated   140
To his own portion! and what expense by the hour
Seems to flow from him! How, i' the name of thrift,
Does he rake this together? Now, my lords,
Saw you the cardinal?
    Nor.   My lord, we have   145
Stood here observing him. Some strange commotion
Is in his brain: he bites his lip, and starts;
Stops on a sudden, looks upon the ground,
Then lays his finger on his temple; straight
Springs out into fast gait; then stops again,   150
Strikes his breast hard; and anon he casts
His eye against the moon: in most strange postures
We have seen him set himself.
    King.   It may well be,
There is a mutiny in's mind. This morning   155
Papers of state he sent me to peruse,
As I requir'd; and wot you what I found
There, on my conscience, put unwittingly?
Forsooth, an inventory, thus importing:
The several parcels of his plate, his treasure,   160
Rich stuffs and ornaments of household, which
I find at such proud rate that it out-speaks
Possession of a subject.
    Nor.   It's heaven's will:
Some spirit put this paper in the packet   165
To bless your eye withal.
    King.   If we did think
His contemplation were above the earth,
And fix'd on spiritual object, he should still
Dwell in his musings: but I am afraid   170
His thinkings are below the moon, not worth
His serious considering.

King takes his seat, whispers Lovell,
who goes to the Cardinal.

    Car.   Heaven forgive me!
Ever God bless your highness!
    King.   Good my lord,   175
You are full of heavenly stuff, and bear the inventory
Of your best graces in your mind, the which
You were now running o'er: you have scarce time
To steal from spiritual leisure a brief span
To keep your earthly audit: sure, in that   180

74 **Cardinal Campeius**; *cf. n.*   84 **return'd in his opinions**: *i.e. having forwarded the opinions of universities he was sent to get*   89–91 **Katharine … Arthur**; *cf. n.*   114 **Duchess of Alençon**; *cf. n.*

130 **A spleeny Lutheran**; *cf. n.*   134 **Hath**: *who hath*   S. d.; *cf. n.*   162, 163 **outspeaks … subject**: *indicates more than a subject should possess*   166 **withal**: *therewith*

I deem you an ill husband, and am glad
To have you therein my companion.
   Car.   Sir,
For holy offices I have a time; a time
To think upon the part of business which   185
I bear i' the state; and nature does require
Her times of preservation, which perforce
I, her frail son, amongst my brethren mortal,
Must give my tendance to.
   King.   You have said well.   190
   Car. And ever may your highness yoke together,
As I will lend you cause, my doing well
With my well saying.
   King.   'Tis well said again;
And 'tis a kind of good deed to say well: 195
And yet words are no deeds. My father lov'd you:
He said he did, and with his deed did crown
His word upon you. Since I had my office,
I have kept next my heart; have not alone
Employ'd you where high profits might come home,   200
But par'd my present havings, to bestow
My bounties upon you.
   Car.   [*Aside.*] What should this mean?
   Sur. [*Aside.*] The Lord increase this business!
   King.   Have I not made you
The prime man of the state? I pray you, tell me
If what I now pronounce you have found true;
And if you may confess it, say withal,
If you are bound to us or no. What say you?
   Car. My sovereign, I confess your royal graces,   210
Shower'd on me daily, have been more than could
My studied purposes requite; which went
Beyond all man's endeavours. My endeavours
Have ever come too short of my desires,
Yet fil'd with my abilities. Mine own ends   215
Have been mine so, that evermore they pointed
To the good of your most sacred person and
The profit of the state. For your great graces
Heap'd upon me, poor undeserver, I
Can nothing render but allegiant thanks,   220
My prayers to heaven for you, my loyalty,
Which ever has and ever shall be growing,
Till death, that winter, kill it.
   King.   Fairly answer'd:
A loyal and obedient subject is   225
Therein illustrated; the honour of it
Does pay the act of it, as i' the contrary
The foulness is the punishment. I presume
That as my hand has open'd bounty to you,
My heart dropp'd love, my power rain'd honour, more   230
On you than any; so your hand and heart,
Your brain, and every function of your power,
Should, notwithstanding that your bond of duty,
As 'twere in love's particular, be more
To me, your friend, than any.   235
   Car.   I do profess,

That for your highness' good I ever labour'd
More than mine own; that am, have, and will be.
Though all the world should crack their duty to you,
And throw it from their soul; though perils did   240
Abound as thick as thought could make 'em, and
Appear in forms more horrid, yet my duty,
As doth a rock against the chiding flood,
Should the approach of this wild river break,
And stand unshaken yours.   245
   King.   'Tis nobly spoken.
Take notice, lords, he has a loyal breast,
For you have seen him open 't. Read o'er this;
                          [*Giving him papers.*]
And after, this: and then to breakfast with
What appetite you have.   250

       Exit King, frowning upon the Cardinal; the nobles
            throng after him, smiling and whispering.

   Car.   What should this mean?
What sudden anger's this? how have I reap'd it?
He parted frowning from me, as if ruin
Leap'd from his eyes. So looks the chafed lion
Upon the daring huntsman that has gall'd him: 255
Then makes him nothing. I must read this paper;
I fear, the story of his anger. 'Tis so:
This paper has undone me! 'Tis th' account
Of all that world of wealth I have drawn together
For mine own ends; indeed, to gain the popedom,   260
And fee my friends in Rome. O negligence!
Fit for a fool to fall by: what cross devil
Made me put this main secret in the packet
I sent the king? Is there no way to cure this?
No new device to beat this from his brains?   265
I know 'twill stir him strongly; yet I know
A way, if it take right, in spite of fortune
Will bring me off again. What's this?—'To the Pope!'
The letter, as I live, with all the business
I writ to's holiness. Nay then, farewell!   270
I have touch'd the highest point of all my greatness;
And from that full meridian of my glory,
I haste now to my setting. I shall fall
Like a bright exhalation in the evening,
And no man see me more.   275

       Enter to Wolsey the Dukes of Norfolk and Suffolk, the Earl of
            Surrey, and the Lord Chamberlain.

   Nor. Hear the king's pleasure, cardinal: who commands you
To render up the great seal presently
Into our hands; and to confine yourself
To Asher-house, my Lord of Winchester's,
Till you hear further from his highness.   280
   Car.   Stay:
Where's your commission, lords? words cannot carry
Authority so weighty.
   Suf.   Who dare cross 'em,
Bearing the king's will from his mouth expressly?   285
   Car. Till I find more than will or words to do it,—
I mean your malice,—know, officious lords,

181 an ill husband: *a bad manager*   **201 par'd ... havings:** *diminished my present posses-*
sions   **210–215** *Cf. n.*   **215 fil'd:** *kept pace with*   **216 so:** *in this sense only*   **220**
allegiant: *loyal*   **226, 227 the honour ... act of it:** *a loyal subject's nobility of character*
rewards him for his actions   **227 the contrary:** *a character of the opposite nature*   **233–235**
Should ... any; *cf. n.*

238 that am, have, and will be; *cf. n.*   **262 cross:** *perverse*   **263 main:** *chief*   **274**
exhalation: *falling star*   **279 Asher-house;** *cf. n.*

I dare and must deny it. Now I feel
Of what coarse metal ye are moulded, envy:
How eagerly ye follow my disgraces,   290
As if it fed ye! and how sleek and wanton
Ye appear in everything may bring my ruin!
Follow your envious courses, men of malice;
You have Christian warrant for 'em, and, no doubt,
In time will find their fit rewards. That seal   295
You ask with such a violence, the king—
Mine and your master—with his own hand gave me;
Bade me enjoy it with the place and honours
During my life; and to confirm his goodness,
Tied it by letters-patents. Now who'll take it?   300
   Sur. The king, that gave it.
   Car.   It must be himself then.
   Sur. Thou art a proud traitor, priest.
   Car.   Proud lord, thou liest:
Within these forty hours Surrey durst better   305
Have burnt that tongue than said so.
   Sur.   Thy ambition,
Thou scarlet sin, robb'd this bewailing land
Of noble Buckingham, my father-in-law:
The heads of all thy brother cardinals—   310
With thee and all thy best parts bound together—
Weigh'd not a hair of his. Plague of your policy!
You sent me deputy for Ireland,
Far from his succour, from the king, from all
That might have mercy on the fault thou gave'st him;   315
Whilst your great goodness, out of holy pity,
Absolv'd him with an axe.
   Car.   This and all else
This talking lord can lay upon my credit,
I answer is most false. The duke by law   320
Found his deserts: how innocent I was
From any private malice in his end,
His noble jury and foul cause can witness.
If I lov'd many words, lord, I should tell you,
You have as little honesty as honour,   325
That in the way of loyalty and truth
Toward the king, my ever royal master,
Dare mate a sounder man than Surrey can be,
And all that love his follies.
   Sur.   By my soul,   330
Your long coat, priest, protects you; thou shouldst feel
My sword i' the life-blood of thee else. My lords,
Can ye endure to hear this arrogance?
And from this fellow? If we live thus tamely,
To be thus jaded by a piece of scarlet,   335
Farewell nobility; let his Grace go forward,
And dare us with his cap like larks.
   Car.   All goodness
Is poison to thy stomach.
   Sur.   Yes, that goodness   340
Of gleaning all the land's wealth into one,
Into your own hands, cardinal, by extortion:
The goodness of your intercepted packets,
You writ to the pope against the king: your goodness,
Since you provoke me, shall be most notorious.   345
My Lord of Norfolk, as you are truly noble,

As you respect the common good, the state
Of our despis'd nobility, our issues,
Who, if he live, will scarce be gentlemen,
Produce the grand sum of his sins, the articles   350
Collected from his life. I'll startle you
Worse than the sacring bell, when the brown wench
Lay kissing in your arms, Lord Cardinal.
   Car. How much, methinks, I could despise this man,
But that I am bound in charity against it!   355
   Nor. Those articles, my lord, are in the king's hand;
But, thus much, they are foul ones.
   Car.   So much fairer
And spotless shall mine innocence arise
When the king knows my truth.   360
   Sur.   This cannot save you:
I thank my memory, I yet remember
Some of these articles; and out they shall.
Now, if you can blush, and cry 'guilty,' cardinal,
You'll show a little honesty.   365
   Car.   Speak on, sir;
I dare your worst objections. If I blush,
It is to see a nobleman want manners.
   Sur. I had rather want those than my head. Have at you!
First, that, without the king's assent or knowledge,   370
You wrought to be a legate, by which power
You maim'd the jurisdiction of all bishops.
   Nor. Then, that in all you writ to Rome, or else
To foreign princes, *Ego et Rex meus*
Was still inscrib'd; in which you brought the king   375
To be your servant.
   Suf.   Then, that without the knowledge
Either of king or council, when you went
Ambassador to the emperor, you made bold
To carry into Flanders the great seal.   380
   Sur. Item, you sent a large commission
To Gregory de Cassado, to conclude,
Without the king's will or the state's allowance,
A league between his highness and Ferrara.
   Suf. That, out of mere ambition, you have caus'd   385
Your holy hat to be stamp'd on the king's coin.
   Sur. Then, that you have sent innumerable substance,—
By what means got, I leave to your own conscience,—
To furnish Rome, and to prepare the ways
You have for dignities; to the mere undoing   390
Of all the kingdom. Many more there are,
Which, since they are of you, and odious,
I will not taint my mouth with.
   L. Ch.   O my lord!
Press not a falling man too far; 'tis virtue: 395
His faults lie open to the laws; let them,
Not you, correct him. My heart weeps to see him
So little of his great self.
   Sur.   I forgive him.
   Suf. Lord Cardinal, the king's further pleasure is,   400
Because all those things you have done of late,
By your power legatine within this kingdom,
Fall into the compass of a *præmunire*:

---

348 issues: *children*   **352 sacring bell;** *cf. n.*   **356 hand:** *possession*   **367 objections:** *accusations*   **370 First, that;** *cf. n.*   **371 wrought:** *contrived*   **381 Item:** *likewise*   **390 mere:** *absolute*   **403 præmunire:** *the accusation of maintaining the papal power in England*

289 envy: *namely, of envy*   **300 letters-patents:** *legal documents*   **328 Dare mate:** *I dare rival*   **335 jaded:** *befooled*   **337 dare:** *dazzle birds with a piece of scarlet cloth, to catch them*

That therefore such a writ be su'd against you,
To forfeit all your goods, lands, tenements,   *405*
Chattels, and whatsoever, and to be
Out of the king's protection. This is my charge.

    Nor. And so we'll leave you to your meditations
How to live better. For your stubborn answer
About the giving back the great seal to us,   *410*
The king shall know it, and, no doubt, shall thank you.
So fare you well, my little good Lord Cardinal.

                          Exeunt all but Wolsey.

    Car. So farewell to the little good you bear me.
Farewell! a long farewell, to all my greatness!
This is the state of man: to-day he puts forth   *415*
The tender leaves of hopes; to-morrow blossoms,
And bears his blushing honours thick upon him;
The third day comes a frost, a killing frost,
And when he thinks, good easy man, full surely
His greatness is a-ripening, nips his root,   *420*
And then he falls, as I do. I have ventur'd,
Like little wanton boys that swim on bladders,
This many summers in a sea of glory,
But far beyond my depth: my high-blown pride
At length broke under me, and now has left me,   *425*
Weary and old with service, to the mercy
Of a rude stream, that must for ever hide me.
Vain pomp and glory of this world, I hate ye.
I feel my heart now open'd. O how wretched
Is that poor man that hangs on princes' favours!   *430*
There is, betwixt that smile we would aspire to,
That sweet aspect of princes, and their ruin,
More pangs and fears than wars or women have;
And when he falls, he falls like Lucifer,
Never to hope again.   *435*

         Enter Cromwell, standing amazed.

            Why, how now, Cromwell!
    Crom. I have no power to speak, sir.
    Car.   What! amaz'd
At my misfortunes? Can thy spirit wonder
A great man should decline? Nay, an you weep,   *440*
I am fall'n indeed.
    Crom.   How does your Grace?
    Car.   Why, well:
Never so truly happy, my good Cromwell.
I know myself now; and I feel within me   *445*
A peace above all earthly dignities,
A still and quiet conscience. The king has cur'd me,
I humbly thank his Grace; and from these shoulders,
These ruin'd pillars, out of pity taken
A load would sink a navy, too much honour.   *450*
O, 'tis a burden, Cromwell, 'tis a burden
Too heavy for a man that hopes for heaven!
    Crom. I am glad your Grace has made that right use of it.
    Car. I hope I have: I am able now, methinks,—
Out of a fortitude of soul I feel,—   *455*
To endure more miseries and greater far
Than my weak-hearted enemies dare offer.
What news abroad?

    Crom.   The heaviest, and the worst,
Is your displeasure with the king.   *460*
    Car.   God bless him!
    Crom. The next is, that Sir Thomas More is chosen
Lord Chancellor in your place.
    Car.   That's somewhat sudden:
But he's a learned man. May he continue   *465*
Long in his highness' favour, and do justice
For truth's sake and his conscience; that his bones,
When he has run his course and sleeps in blessings,
May have a tomb of orphans' tears wept on him!
What more?   *470*
    Crom.   That Cranmer is return'd with welcome,
Install'd Lord Archbishop of Canterbury.
    Car. That's news indeed.
    Crom.   Last, that the Lady Anne,
Whom the king hath in secrecy long married,   *475*
This day was view'd in open as his queen,
Going to chapel; and the voice is now
Only about her coronation.
    Car. There was the weight that pull'd me down. O
Cromwell!   *480*
The king has gone beyond me: all my glories
In that one woman I have lost for ever.
No sun shall ever usher forth mine honours,
Or gild again the noble troops that waited
Upon my smiles. Go, get thee from me, Cromwell;   *485*
I am a poor fall'n man, unworthy now
To be thy lord and master. Seek the king;—
That sun, I pray, may never set!—I have told him
What, and how true thou art: he will advance thee.
Some little memory of me will stir him—   *490*
I know his noble nature—not to let
Thy hopeful service perish too. Good Cromwell,
Neglect him not; make use now, and provide
For thine own future safety.
    Crom.   O my lord!   *495*
Must I then leave you? must I needs forgo
So good, so noble, and so true a master?
Bear witness all that have not hearts of iron,
With what a sorrow Cromwell leaves his lord.
The king shall have my service; but my prayers   *500*
For ever and for ever shall be yours.
    Car. Cromwell, I did not think to shed a tear
In all my miseries: but thou hast forc'd me,
Out of thy honest truth, to play the woman.
Let's dry our eyes: and thus far hear me, Cromwell;   *505*
And when I am forgotten, as I shall be,
And sleep in dull cold marble, where no mention
Of me more must be heard of, say, I taught thee:
Say, Wolsey, that once trod the ways of glory,
And sounded all the depths and shoals of honour,   *510*
Found thee a way, out of his wrack, to rise in;
A sure and safe one, though thy master miss'd it.
Mark but my fall, and that that ruin'd me.
Cromwell, I charge thee, fling away ambition.
By that sin fell the angels: how can man then,   *515*
The image of his Maker, hope to win by it?
Love thyself last: cherish those hearts that hate thee;

---

406 Chattels; *cf. n.*   **432 their ruin:** *i.e. the ruin they cause*   **434 Lucifer;** *cf. n.*   **440**
an: *if*

476 in open: *publicly*

Corruption wins not more than honesty.
Still in thy right hand carry gentle peace,
To silence envious tongues. Be just, and fear not: *520*
Let all the ends thou aim'st at be thy country's,
Thy God's, and truth's. Then if thou fall'st, O Cromwell,
Thou fall'st a blessed martyr. Serve the king;
And,—prithee, lead me in:
There take an inventory of all I have,   *525*
To the last penny: 'tis the king's. My robe,
And my integrity to heaven is all
I dare now call mine own. O Cromwell, Cromwell!
Had I but serv'd my God with half the zeal
I serv'd my king, he would not in mine age   *530*
Have left me naked to mine enemies.
    Crom. Good sir, have patience.
    Car.   So I have. Farewell
The hopes of court! my hopes in heaven do dwell.   *Exeunt.*

ACT FOURTH ❧ SCENE FIRST

[A Street in Westminster]
Enter two Gentlemen, meeting one another.

    1. Gent. Y' are well met once again.
    2. Gent.   So are you.
    1. Gent. You come to take your stand here, and behold
The Lady Anne pass from her coronation?
    2. Gent. 'Tis all my business. At our last encounter   *5*
The Duke of Buckingham came from his trial.
    1. Gent. 'Tis very true: but that time offer'd sorrow;
This, general joy.
    2. Gent.   'Tis well: the citizens,
I am sure, have shown at full their royal minds,   *10*
As, let 'em have their rights, they are ever forward,
In celebration of this day with shows,
Pageants, and sights of honour.
    1. Gent.   Never greater;
Nor, I'll assure you, better taken, sir.   *15*
    2. Gent. May I be bold to ask what that contains,
That paper in your hand?
    1. Gent.   Yes; 'tis the list
Of those that claim their offices this day
By custom of the coronation.   *20*
The Duke of Suffolk is the first, and claims
To be high-steward; next, the Duke of Norfolk,
He to be earl marshal: you may read the rest.
    2. Gent. I thank you, sir: had I not known those customs,
I should have been beholding to your paper.   *25*
But, I beseech you, what's become of Katharine,
The princess dowager? How goes her business?
    1. Gent. That I can tell you too. The Archbishop
Of Canterbury, accompanied with other
Learned and reverend fathers of his order,   *30*
Held a late court at Dunstable, six miles off
From Ampthill, where the princess lay; to which
She was often cited by them, but appear'd not:

And, to be sort, for not appearance and
The king's late scruple, by the main assent   *35*
Of all these learned men was was divorc'd,
And the late marriage made of none effect:
Since which she was remov'd to Kimbolton,
Where she remains now sick.
    2. Gent.   Alas! good lady!   *40*
                          [Trumpets.]
The trumpets sound: stand close, the queen is coming.
                         Hautboys.

THE ORDER OF THE CORONATION

1. *A lively flourish of trumpets.*
2. *Then, two Judges.*
3. Lord Chancellor, *with purse and mace before him.*
4. Choristers, *singing.*   *Music.*
5. Mayor of London, *bearing the mace. Then* Garter, *in his coat of arms, and on his head he wore a gilt copper crown.*
6. Marquess Dorset, *bearing a sceptre of gold, on his head a demi-coronal of gold. With him, the* Earl of Surrey, *bearing the rod of silver with the dove, crowned with an earl's coronet. Collars of Esses.*
7. Duke of Suffolk, *in his robe of estate, his coronet on his head, bearing a long white wand, as high-steward. With him, the* Duke of Norfolk, *with the rod of marshalship, a coronet on his head. Collars of Esses.*
8. *A canopy borne by four of the Cinque-ports; under it, the* Queen *in her robe; in her hair, richly adorned with pearl, crowned. On each side her, the* Bishops of London *and* Winchester.
9. *The old* Duchess of Norfolk, *in a coronal of gold, wrought with flowers, bearing the Queen's train.*
10. *Certain Ladies or Countesses, with plain circlets of gold, without flowers.*

    Exeunt, first passing over the stage in order and state,
                and then, a great flourish of trumpets.

    2. Gent. A royal train, believe me. These I know;
Who's that that bears the sceptre?
    1. Gent.   Marquess Dorset:
And that the Earl of Surrey with the rod.   *45*
    2. Gent. A bold brave gentleman. That should be
The Duke of Suffolk?
    1. Gent.   'Tis the same: high-steward.
    2. Gent. And that my Lord of Norfolk?
    1. Gent.   Yes.   *50*
    2. Gent. *[Looking on the Queen.]* Heaven bless thee!
Thou hast the sweetest face I ever look'd on.
Sir, as I have a soul, she is an angel;
Our king has all the Indies in his arms,
And more and richer, when he strains that lady: *55*
I cannot blame his conscience.
    1. Gent.   They that bear
The cloth of honour over her, are four barons
Of the Cinque-ports.
    2. Gent. Those men are happy; and so are all are near her.
I take it, she that carries up the train

523 Thou ... martyr; *cf. n.*   529–531 Cf. n.   Scene First; *cf. n.*   5 last encounter;
cf. n.   19 Of those that claim; *cf. n.*   31 Dunstable; *cf. n.*

38 Kimbolton; *cf. n.*   S. d. The Order of the Coronation; *cf. n.*   Collars of Esses;
cf. n.   in her hair: *with flowing hair*

Is that old noble lady, Duchess of Norfolk.
  1. Gent. It is; and all the rest are countesses.
  2. Gent. Their coronets say so. These are stars indeed;
And sometimes falling ones.   *65*
  1. Gent.   No more of that.

Enter a third Gentleman.

God save you, sir! Where have you been broiling?
  3. Gent. Among the crowd i' the Abbey; where a finger
Could not be wedg'd in more: I am stifled
With the mere rankness of their joy.   *70*
  2. Gent.   You saw
The ceremony?
  3. Gent.   That I did.
  1. Gent.   How was it?
  3. Gent. Well worth the seeing.   *75*
  2. Gent.   Good sir, speak it to us.
  3. Gent. As well as I am able. The rich stream
Of lords and ladies, having brought the queen
To a prepar'd place in the choir, fell off
A distance from her; while her Grace sat down   *80*
To rest awhile, some half an hour or so,
In a rich chair of state, opposing freely
The beauty of her person to the people.
Believe me, sir, she is the goodliest woman
That ever lay by man: which when the people   *85*
Had the full view of, such a noise arose
As the shrouds make at sea in a stiff tempest,
As loud, and to as many tunes. Hats, cloaks,—
Doublets, I think,—flew up; and had their faces
Been loose, this day they had been lost. Such joy   *90*
I never saw before. Great-bellied women,
That had not half a week to go, like rams
In the old time of war, would shake the press,
And make 'em reel before 'em. No man living
Could say, 'This is my wife,' there; all were woven   *95*
So strangely in one piece.
  2. Gent.   But, what follow'd?
  3. Gent. At length her Grace rose, and with modest paces
Came to the altar; where she kneel'd, and, saintlike,
Cast her fair eyes to heaven and pray'd devoutly.   *100*
Then rose again and bow'd her to the people:
When by the Archbishop of Canterbury
She had all the royal makings of a queen,
As holy oil, Edward Confessor's crown,
The rod, and bird of peace, and all such emblems   *105*
Laid nobly on her: which perform'd, the choir,
With all the choicest music of the kingdom,
Together sung *Te Deum.* So she parted,
And with the same full state pac'd back again
To York-place, where the feast is held.   *110*
  1. Gent.   Sir,
You must no more call it York-place, that's past;
For since the cardinal fell, that title's lost:
'Tis now the king's, and call'd Whitehall.
  3. Gent.   I know it;   *115*
But 'tis so lately alter'd that the old name
Is fresh about me.

  2. Gent.   What two reverend bishops
Were those that went on each side of the queen?
  3. Gent. Stokesly and Gardiner; the one of   *120*
Winchester,—
Newly preferr'd from the king's secretary,—
The other, London.
  2. Gent.   He of Winchester
Is held no great good lover of the archbishop's,   *125*
The virtuous Cranmer.
  3. Gent.   All the land knows that:
However, yet there's no great breach; when it comes,
Cranmer will find a friend will not shrink from him.
  2. Gent. Who may that be, I pray you?   *130*
  3. Gent.   Thomas Cromwell:
A man in much esteem with the king, and truly
A worthy friend. The king
Has made him master o' the jewel house,
And one already of the privy-council.   *135*
  2. Gent. He will deserve more.
  3. Gent.   Yes, without all doubt.
Come, gentlemen, ye shall go my way, which
Is to the court, and there ye shall be my guests:
Something I can command. As I walk thither,   *140*
I'll tell ye more.
  Both.   You may command us, sir.   *Exeunt.*

❧ SCENE SECOND ❧

[Kimbolton]
Enter Katharine, Dowager, sick: led between Griffith her gentleman-
usher and Patience her woman.

  Grif. How does your Grace?
  Kath.   O Griffith! sick to death!
My legs, like loaden branches, bow to the earth,
Willing to leave their burthen. Reach a chair:
So; now, methinks, I feel a little ease.   *5*
Didst thou not tell me, Griffith, as thou led'st me,
That the great child of honour, Cardinal Wolsey,
Was dead?
  Grif.   Yes, madam; but I think your Grace,
Out of the pain you suffer'd, gave no ear to 't.   *10*
  Kath. Prithee, good Griffith, tell me how he died:
If well, he stepp'd before me, happily,
For my example.
  Grif.   Well, the voice goes, madam:
For after the stout Earl Northumberland   *15*
Arrested him at York, and brought him forward,
As a man sorely tainted, to his answer,
He fell sick suddenly, and grew so ill
He could not sit his mule.
  Kath.   Alas! poor man.   *20*
  Grif. At last, with easy roads, he came to Leicester;
Lodg'd in the abbey, where the reverend abbot,
With all his covent, honourably receiv'd him;
To whom he gave these words: 'O father abbot,

---

70 **rankness:** *exuberance* 76 **ff.** *Cf. n.* 82 **opposing:** *exposing* 87 **shrouds:** *sail-*
ropes 110 **York-place;** *cf. n.*

120 **Stokesly and Gardiner;** *cf. n.* 131 **Thomas Cromwell;** *cf. n.* 140 **Something I**
can command: *I can order refreshments* 7, 8 **Cardinal Wolsey, Was dead;** *cf. n.* 11
tell me how he died; *cf. n.* 12 **happily:** *by good chance* 21 **roads:** *stages* 23
covent: *convent, body of monks*

An old man, broken with the storms of state,   *25*
Is come to lay his weary bones among ye:
Give him a little earth for charity.'
So went to bed, where eagerly his sickness
Pursu'd him still; and three nights after this,
About the hour of eight,—which he himself   *30*
Foretold should be his last,—full of repentance,
Continual meditations, tears, and sorrows,
He gave his honours to the world again,
His blessed part to heaven, and slept in peace.
    Kath. So may he rest; his faults lie gently on him!   *35*
Yet thus far, Griffith, give me leave to speak him,
And yet with charity. He was a man
Of an unbounded stomach, ever ranking
Himself with princes; one that by suggestion
Tied all the kingdom. Simony was fair-play.   *40*
His own opinion was his law; i' the presence
He would say untruth, and be ever double
Both in his words and meaning. He was never,
But where he meant to ruin, pitiful.
His promises were, as he then was, mighty;   *45*
But his performance, as he is now, nothing:
Of his own body he was ill, and gave
The clergy ill example.
    Grif.   Noble madam,
Men's evil manners live in brass; their virtues   *50*
We write in water. May it please your highness
To hear me speak his good now?
    Kath.   Yes, good Griffith,
I were malicious else.
    Grif.   This cardinal,   *55*
Though from an humble stock, undoubtedly
Was fashion'd to much honour. From his cradle
He was a scholar, and a ripe and good one:
Exceeding wise, fair-spoken, and persuading;
Lofty and sour to them that lov'd him not,   *60*
But to those men that sought him sweet as summer.
And though he were unsatisfied in getting,—
Which was a sin,—yet in bestowing, madam,
He was most princely. Ever witness for him
Those twins of learning that he rais'd in you,   *65*
Ipswich, and Oxford! one of which fell with him,
Unwilling to outlive the good that did it;
The other though unfinish'd, yet so famous,
So excellent in art, and still so rising,
That Christendom shall ever speak his virtue.   *70*
His overthrow heap'd happiness upon him;
For then, and not till then, he felt himself,
And found the blessedness of being little.
And, to add greater honours to his age
Than man could give him, he died fearing God.   *75*
    Kath. After my death I wish no other herald,
No other speaker of my living actions,
To keep mine honour from corruption,
But such an honest chronicler as Griffith.
Whom I most hated living, thou hast made me,   *80*

With thy religious truth and modesty,
Now in his ashes honour. Peace be with him!
Patience, be near me still, and set me lower:
I have not long to trouble thee. Good Griffith,
Cause the musicians play me that sad note   *85*
I nam'd my knell, whilst I sit meditating
On that celestial harmony I go to.
                     Sad and solemn music.
    Grif. She is asleep: good wench, let's sit down quiet,
For fear we wake her. Softly, gentle Patience.

THE VISION

Enter, solemnly tripping one after another, six Personages, clad in white robes, wearing on their heads garlands of bays, and golden vizards on their faces; branches of bays or palm in their hands. They first congee unto her, then dance; and, at certain changes, the first two hold a spare garland over her head; at which, the other four make reverend curtsies. Then, the two that held the garland deliver the same to the other next two, who observe the same order in their changes, and holding the garland over her head: which done, they deliver the same garland to the last two, who likewise observe the same order, at which,—as it were by inspiration,—she makes in her sleep signs of rejoicing, and holdeth up her hands to heaven: and so in their dancing vanish, carrying the garland with them. The music continues.

    Kath. Spirits of peace, where are ye? Are ye all gone,   *90*
And leave me here in wretchedness behind ye?
    Grif. Madam, we are here.
    Kath.   It is not you I call for:
Saw ye none enter since I slept?
    Grif.   None, madam.   *95*
    Kath. No? Saw you not even now a blessed troop
Invite me to a banquet; whose bright faces
Cast thousand beams upon me, like the sun?
They promis'd me eternal happiness,
And brought me garlands, Griffith, which I feel   *100*
I am not worthy yet to wear: I shall assuredly.
    Grif. I am most joyful, madam, such good dreams
Possess your fancy.
    Kath.   Bid the music leave.
They are harsh and heavy to me.   *Music ceases.*
    Pat.   Do you note
How much her Grace is alter'd on the sudden?
How long her face is drawn? How pale she looks,
And of an earthy cold? Mark her eyes!
    Grif. She is going, wench. Pray, pray.   *110*
    Pat. Heaven comfort her!

Enter a Messenger.

    Mess. An 't like your Grace,—
    Kath.   You are a saucy fellow:
Deserve we no more reverence?
    Grif.   You are to blame,   *115*
Knowing she will not lose her wonted greatness,
To use so rude behaviour; go to, kneel.
    Mess. I humbly do entreat your highness' pardon;
My haste made me unmannerly. There is staying

35 So may he rest, etc.; *cf. n.*   **36 speak him:** *describe him; cf. II.iv.179; III.i.140*   **38
stomach:** *pride*   **39, 40 by suggestion Tied:** *by trickery restricted the liberties of*   **40
Simony:** *the selling of positions in the church*   **41 i' the presence:** *before the king*   **55
This cardinal;** *cf. n.*   **57 From his cradle;** *cf. n.*   **66 Ipswich, and Oxford;**
cf. n.   **67 did:** *i.e. founded*

S. d. congee: *bow*   **changes:** *movements of the dance*   **101 shall:** *shall be worthy*   **104
music:** *musicians*   **leave:** *leave off*

A gentleman, sent from the king, to see you.   *120*
 Kath. Admit him entrance, Griffith: but this fellow
Let me ne'er see again.   *Exit Messenger.*

    Enter Lord Capucius.

     If my sight fail not,
You should be lord ambassador from the emperor,
My royal nephew, and your name Capucius.   *125*
 Cap. Madam, the same; your servant.
 Kath.   O, my lord,
The times and titles now are alter'd strangely
With me, since first you knew me. But, I pray you,
What is your pleasure with me?   *130*
 Cap.   Noble lady,
First, mine own service to your Grace; the next,
The king's request that I would visit you,
Who grieves much for your weakness, and by me
Sends you his princely commendations,   *135*
And heartily entreats you take good comfort.
 Kath. O, my good lord, that comfort comes too late!
'Tis like a pardon after execution:
That gentle physic, given in time, had cur'd me;
But now I am past all comforts here but prayers.   *140*
How does his highness?
 Cap.   Madam, in good health.
 Kath. So may he ever do, and ever flourish,
When I shall dwell with worms, and my poor name
Banish'd the kingdom. Patience, is that letter   *145*
I cause'd you write, yet sent away?
 Pat.   No, madam.
     [Giving it to Katharine.]
 Kath. Sir, I most humbly pray you to deliver
This to my lord the king.
 Cap.   Most willing, madam.   *150*
 Kath. In which I have commended to his goodness
The model of our chaste loves, his young daughter:
The dews of heaven fall thick in blessings on her!
Beseeching him to give her virtuous breeding,—
She is young, and of a noble modest nature,   *155*
I hope she will deserve well,—and a little
To love her for her mother's sake, that lov'd him,
Heaven knows how dearly. My next poor petition
Is, that his noble Grace would have some pity
Upon my wretched women, that so long   *160*
Have follow'd both my fortunes faithfully:
Of which there is not one, I dare avow,—
And now I should not lie,—but will deserve,
For virtue, and true beauty of the soul,
For honesty and decent carriage,   *165*
A right good husband, let him be a noble;
And, sure, those men are happy that shall have 'em.
The last is, for my men: they are the poorest,
But poverty could never draw 'em from me;
That they may have their wages duly paid 'em,   *170*
And something over to remember me by.
If heaven had pleas'd to have given me longer life
And able means, we had not parted thus.
These are the whole contents: and, good my lord,

By that you love the dearest in this world,   *175*
As you wish Christian peace to souls departed,
Stand these poor people's friend, and urge the king
To do me this last right.
 Cap.   By heaven, I will,
Or let me lose the fashion of a man!   *180*
 Kath. I thank you, honest lord. Remember me
In all humility unto his highness:
Say his long trouble now is passing
Out of this world. Tell him, in death I bless'd him,
For so I will. Mine eyes grow dim. Farewell,   *185*
My lord. Griffith, farewell. Nay, Patience,
You must not leave me yet. I must to bed;
Call in more women. When I am dead, good wench,
Let me be us'd with honour: strew me over
With maiden flowers, that all the world may know   *190*
I was a chaste wife to my grave. Embalm me,
Then lay me forth: although unqueen'd, yet like
A queen, and daughter to a king, inter me.
I can no more.   *Exeunt, leading Katharine.*

ACT FIFTH   SCENE FIRST

[London. A Gallery in the Palace]
*Enter Gardiner, Bishop of Winchester, a Page with a torch before
him, met by Sir Thomas Lovell.*

 Gar. It's one o'clock, boy, is 't not?
 Boy.   It hath struck.
 Gar. These should be hours for necessities,
Not for delights: times to repair our nature
With comforting repose, and not for us   *5*
To waste these times. Good hour of night, Sir Thomas!
Whither so late?
 Lov.   Came you from the king, my lord?
 Gar. I did, Sir Thomas; and left him at primero
With the Duke of Suffolk.   *10*
 Lov.   I must to him too,
Before he go to bed. I'll take my leave.
 Gar. Not yet, Sir Thomas Lovell. What's the matter?
It seems you are in haste: and if there be
No great offence belongs to 't, give your friend   *15*
Some touch of your late business. Affairs, that walk—
As they say spirits do—at midnight, have
In them a wilder nature than the business
That seeks dispatch by day.
 Lov.   My lord, I love you,   *20*
And durst commend a secret to your ear
Much weightier than this work. The queen's in labour,
They say, in great extremity; and fear'd
She'll with the labour end.
 Gar.   The fruit she goes with   *25*
I pray for heartily, that it may find
Good time, and live: but for the stock, Sir Thomas,
I wish it grubb'd up now.
 Lov.   Methinks I could
Cry the amen; and yet my conscience says   *30*

125 Capucius; *cf. n.* **152** model: *memorial* **his young daughter:** *Mary Tudor* **161**
both my fortunes: *prosperity and adversity*

180 fashion: *shape* **Act Fifth;** *cf. n.* **9** primero: *a game of cards* **16** touch: *hint*
late: *i.e. nocturnal* **23** fear'd: *it is feared*

She's a good creature, and, sweet lady, does
Deserve our better wishes.
 Gar.   But, sir, sir,
Hear me, Sir Thomas: y' are a gentleman
Of mine own way. I know you wise, religious;   *35*
And, let me tell you, it will ne'er be well,
'Twill not, Sir Thomas Lovell, take 't of me,
Till Cranmer, Cromwell, her two hands, and she,
Sleep in their graves.
 Lov.   Now, sir, you speak of two *40*
The most remark'd i' the kingdom. As for Cromwell,
Beside that of the jewel-house, is made master
O' the rolls, and the king's secretary; further, sir,
Stands in the gap and trade of moe preferments,
With which the time will load him. Th' archbishop *45*
Is the king's hand and tongue; and who dare speak
One syllable against him?
 Gar.   Yes, yes, Sir Thomas,
There are that dare; and I myself have ventur'd
To speak my mind of him: and indeed this day, *50*
—Sir, I may tell it you,—I think I have
Incens'd the lords o' the council that he is—
For so I know he is, they know he is—
A most arch heretic, a pestilence
That does infect the land: with which they mov'd *55*
Have broken with the king, who hath so far
Given ear to our complaint,—of his great grace
And princely care, foreseeing those fell mischiefs
Our reasons laid before him,—hath commanded
To-morrow morning to the council-board *60*
He be convented. He's a rank weed, Sir Thomas,
And we must root him out. From your affairs
I hinder you too long: good-night, Sir Thomas!
 Lov. Many good-nights, my lord. I rest your servant.
        Exeunt Gardiner and Page.

      Enter King and Suffolk.

 King. Charles, I will play no more to-night; *65*
My mind's not on 't; you are too hard for me.
 Suf. Sir, I did never win of you before.
 King. But little, Charles;
Nor shall not when my fancy's on my play.
Now, Lovell, from the queen what is the news? *70*
 Lov. I could not personally deliver to her
What you commanded me, but by her woman
I sent your message; who return'd her thanks
In the great'st humbleness, and desir'd your highness
Most heartily to pray for her. *75*
 King.   What sayst thou? Ha?
To pray for her? what, is she crying out?
 Lov. So said her woman; and that her sufferance made
Almost each pang a death.
 King.   Alas! good lady. *80*
 Suf. God safely quit her of her burthen, and
With gentle travail, to the gladding of
Your highness with an heir!
 King.   'Tis midnight, Charles;

Prithee, to bed; and in thy prayers remember *85*
Th' estate of my poor queen. Leave me alone;
For I must think of that which company
Would not be friendly to.
 Suf.   I wish your highness
A quiet night, and my good mistress will *90*
Remember in my prayers.
 King.   Charles, good-night.
          Exit Suffolk.

   Enter Sir Anthony Denny.

Well, sir, what follows?
 Den. Sir, I have brought my lord the archbishop,
As you commanded me. *95*
 King.   Ha! Canterbury?
 Den. Ay, my good lord.
 King.   'Tis true: where is he, Denny?
 Den. He attends your highness' pleasure.
 King.   Bring him to us.
         [Exit Denny.]
 Lov. *[Aside.]* This is about that which the bishop spake:
I am happily come hither.

    Enter Cranmer and Denny.

 King.   Avoid the gallery.
        Lovell seems to stay.
Ha! I have said. Begone.
What!—   *Exeunt Lovell and Denny.* *105*
 Cran. I am fearful. Wherefore frowns he thus?
'Tis his aspect of terror. All's not well.
 King. How now, my lord! You do desire to know
Wherefore I sent for you.
 Cran.   *[Kneeling.]* It is my duty *110*
T' attend your highness' pleasure.
 King.   Pray you, arise,
My good and gracious Lord of Canterbury.
Come, you and I must walk a turn together:
I have news to tell you. Come, come, give me your hand. *115*
Ah! my good lord, I grieve at what I speak,
And am right sorry to repeat what follows.
I have, and most unwillingly, of late
Heard many grievous, I do say, my lord,
Grievous complaints of you; which, being consider'd, *120*
Have mov'd us and our council, that you shall
This morning come before us; where, I know,
You cannot with such freedom purge yourself,
But that, till further trial in those charges
Which will require your answer, you must take *125*
Your patience to you, and be well contented
To make your house our Tower: you, a brother of us,
It fits we thus proceed, or else no witness
Would come against you.
 Cran.   *[Kneeling.]* I humbly thank your highness;
And am right glad to catch this good occasion
Most thoroughly to be winnow'd, where my chaff
And corn shall fly asunder; for I know
There's none stands under more calumnious tongues
Than I myself, poor man. *135*

---

35 way: *way of thinking* **42 that:** *the mastership; cf. IV.i.134* **is:** *he is* **44 gap and trade:** *the opening and track by which preferments come* **52 Incens'd:** *impressed upon* **55 with which they mov'd:** *moved by which they* **56 broken with:** *communicated with* **61 convented:** *summoned*

86 estate: *condition* **102 happily:** *fortunately* **Avoid:** *go out from* **127 you ... us:** *since you are of nearly royal rank* (as head of the church)

King.   Stand up, good Canterbury:
Thy truth and thy integrity is rooted
In us, thy friend. Give me thy hand, stand up:
Prithee, let's walk. Now, by my holidame,
What manner of man are you? My lord, I look'd   *140*
You would have given me your petition, that
I should have ta'en some pains to bring together
Yourself and your accusers; and to have heard you,
Without indurance, further.
    Cran.   Most dread liege,   *145*
The good I stand on is my truth and honesty:
If they shall fail, I, with mine enemies,
Will triumph o'er my person, which I weigh not,
Being of those virtues vacant. I fear nothing
What can be said against me.   *150*
    King.   Know you not
How your state stands i' the world, with the whole
world?
Your enemies are many, and not small; their practices
Must bear the same proportion; and not ever   *155*
The justice and the truth o' the question carries
The due o' the verdict with it. At what ease
Might corrupt minds procure knaves as corrupt
To swear against you? Such things have been done.
You are potently oppos'd, and with a malice   *160*
Of as great size. Ween you of better luck,
I mean in perjur'd witness, than your Master,
Whose minister you are, whiles here he liv'd
Upon this naughty earth? Go to, go to;
You take a precipice for no leap of danger,   *165*
And woo your own destruction.
    Cran.   God and your majesty
Protect mine innocence! or I fall into
The trap is laid for me!
    King.   Be of good cheer;   *170*
They shall no more prevail than we give way to.
Keep comfort to you; and this morning see
You do appear before them. If they shall chance,
In charging you with matters, to commit you,
The best persuasions to the contrary   *175*
Fail not to use, and with what vehemency
Th' occasion shall instruct you. If entreaties
Will render you no remedy, this ring
Deliver them, and your appeal to us
There make before them. Look! the good man weeps: *180*
He's honest, on mine honour. God's blest mother!
I swear he is true-hearted; and a soul
None better in my kingdom. Get you gone,
And do as I have bid you.   *Exit Cranmer.*
                    He has strangled   *185*
His language in his tears.

                    Enter Old Lady.

    Gent. within. Come back: what mean you?
    Lady. I'll not come back; the tidings that I bring
Will make my boldness manners. Now, good angels

Fly o'er thy royal head, and shade thy person   *190*
Under their blessed wings!
    King.   Now, by thy looks
I guess thy message. Is the queen deliver'd?
Say, ay; and of a boy.
    Lady.   Ay, ay, my liege;   *195*
And of a lovely boy: the God of heaven
Both now and ever bless her! 'Tis a girl,
Promises boys hereafter. Sir, your queen
Desires your visitation, and to be
Acquainted with this stranger: 'tis as like you   *200*
As cherry is to cherry.
    King.   Lovell!

                    [Enter Lovell.]

    Lov.   Sir!
    King. Give her an hundred marks. I'll to the queen.
                    Exit King.
    Lady. An hundred marks! By this light, I'll ha' more.   *205*
An ordinary groom is for such payment.
I will have more, or scold it out of him.
Said I for this, the girl was like to him?
I will have more, or else unsay't; and now,
While it is hot, I'll put it to the issue.   *210*
                    Exit Lady [with Lovell].

❦ SCENE SECOND ❦

[The Lobby before the Council-Chamber]
Enter Cranmer, Archbishop of Canterbury.

    Cran. I hope I am not too late; and yet the gentleman,
That was sent to me from the council, pray'd me
To make great haste. All fast? what means this? Ho!
Who waits there?

                    Enter Keeper.

                    Sure, you know me?   *5*
    Keep.   Yes, my lord;
But yet I cannot help you.
    Cran.   Why?
    Keep. Your Grace must wait till you be call'd for.

                    Enter Doctor Butts.

    Cran.   So.   *10*
    Butts. [Aside.] This is a piece of malice. I am glad
I came this way so happily. The king
Shall understand it presently.
    Cran.   [Aside.] 'Tis Butts,
The king's physician. As he pass'd along,   *15*
How earnestly he cast his eyes upon me.
Pray heaven he sound not my disgrace! For certain,
This is of purpose laid by some that hate me,—
God turn their hearts! I never sought their malice,—
To quench mine honour: they would shame to make me   *20*
Wait else at door, a fellow-counsellor

---

139 holidame: *halidom, a customary oath*   **144 indurance:** *imprisonment*   **146 The good I stand on:** *my defense*   **148 my person ... weigh not:** *my body which I do not value*   **149 Being:** *if it be*   **nothing:** *not at all*   **154 practices:** *plots*   **155 bear ... proportion:** *likewise be many and not small*   **ever:** *in every case*   **161 Ween:** *dream*   **169 is:** *which is*

17 sound: *penetrate, discover*

'Mong boys, grooms, and lackeys. But their pleasures
Must be fulfill'd, and I attend with patience.

Enter the King and Butts at a window above.

Butts. I'll show your Grace the strangest sight,—
King.   What's that, Butts?   *25*
Butts. I think your highness saw this many a day.
King. Body o' me, where is it?
Butts.   There, my lord:
The high promotion of his Grace of Canterbury,
Who holds his state at door 'mongst pursuivants,   *30*
Pages, and footboys
King.   Ha! 'Tis he, indeed.
Is this the honour they do one another?
'Tis well there's one above 'em yet. I had thought
They had parted so much honesty among 'em,—   *35*
At least, good manners,—as not thus to suffer
A man of his place, and so near our favour,
To dance attendance on their lordship's pleasures,
And at the door too, like a post with packets.
By holy Mary, Butts, there's knavery: *40*
Let 'em alone, and draw the curtain close;
We shall hear more anon.   *[Exeunt above.]*

❧ SCENE THIRD ❧

[The Council-Chamber]
*A council-table brought in with chairs and stoves, and placed
under the state. Enter Lord Chancellor, places himself at the upper
end of the table on the left hand; a seat being left void above
him, as for Canterbury's seat; Duke of Suffolk, Duke of Norfolk,
Surrey, Lord Chamberlain, Gardiner seat themselves in order on
each side; Cromwell at lower end as Secretary.*

Chan. Speak to the business, Master Secretary:
Why are we met in council?
Crom.   Please your honours,
The chief cause concerns his Grace of Canterbury.
Gar. Has he had knowledge of it?   *5*
Crom.   Yes.
Nor.   Who waits there?
Keep. Without, my noble lords?
Gar.   Yes.
Keep.   My lord archbishop: *10*
And has done half an hour, to know your pleasures.
Chan. Let him come in.
Keep.   Your Grace may enter now.
                    Cranmer approaches the council-table.
Chan. My good lord archbishop, I'm very sorry
To sit here at this present and behold   *15*
That chair stand empty: but we all are men,
In our own natures frail, and capable
Of our flesh; few are angels: out of which frailty
And want of wisdom, you, that best should teach us,
Have misdemean'd yourself, and not a little: *20*
Toward the king first, then his laws, in filling

The whole realm, by your teaching and your chaplains,—
For so we are inform'd,—with new opinions,
Divers and dangerous, which are heresies,
And, not reform'd, may prove pernicious.   *25*
Gar. Which reformation must be sudden too,
My noble lords; for those that tame wild horses
Pace 'em not in their hands to make 'em gentle,
But stop their mouths with stubborn bits, and spur 'em,
Till they obey the manage. If we suffer—   *30*
Out of our easiness and childish pity
To one man's honour—this contagious sickness,
Farewell all physic: and what follows then?
Commotions, uproars, with a general taint
Of the whole state: as, of late days, our neighbours, *35*
The upper Germany, can dearly witness,
Yet freshly pitied in our memories.
Cran. My good lords, hitherto in all the progress
Both of my life and office, I have labour'd,
And with no little study, that my teaching   *40*
And the strong course of my authority
Might go one way, and safely; and the end
Was ever, to do well: nor is there living,—
I speak it with a single heart, my lords,—
A man that more detests, more stirs against,   *45*
Both in his private conscience and his place,
Defacers of a public peace, than I do.
Pray heaven the king may never find a heart
With less allegiance in it! Men that make
Envy and crooked malice nourishment   *50*
Dare bit the best. I do beseech your lordships
That, in this case of justice, my accusers,
Be what they will, may stand forth face to face,
And freely urge against me.
Suf.   Nay, my lord,   *55*
That cannot be: you are a counsellor,
And by that virtue no man dare accuse you.
Gar. My lord, because we have business of more
moment,
We will be short with you. 'Tis his highness' pleasure, *60*
And our consent, for better trial of you,
From hence you be committed to the Tower;
Where, being but a private man again,
You shall know many dare accuse you boldly,
More than, I fear, you are provided for.   *65*
Cran. Ah, my good Lord of Winchester, I thank you!
You are always my good friend: if your will pass,
I shall both find your lordship judge and juror,
You are so merciful. I see your end;
'Tis my undoing. Love and meekness, lord,   *70*
Become a churchman better than ambition:
Win straying souls with modesty again,
Cast none away. That I shall clear myself,
Lay all the weight ye can upon my patience,
I make as little doubt as you do conscience   *75*
In doing daily wrongs. I could say more,
But reverence to your calling makes me modest.
Gar. My lord, my lord, you are a sectary;
That's the plain truth: your painted gloss discovers,

S. d. *at a window above; cf. n.*   **30 pursuivants:** *minor officers attendant upon heralds*   **35 parted:** *divided*   **39 post with packets:** *a messenger with letters*   **17, 18
capable ... flesh:** *susceptible of being influenced by our fleshly nature*

25 not: *if not*   **30 manage:** *rider's control*   **35-37 as, of late days, etc.; cf. n.*   **74
Lay:** *though you lay*   **77 modest:** *moderate*   **78 sectary:** *a member of a religious sect,
therefore hostile to the Church*   **79 discovers:** *reveals*

To men that understand you, words and weakness. *80*
 Crom. My Lord of Winchester, y' are a little,
By your good favour, too sharp; men so noble,
However faulty, yet should find respect
For what they have been: 'tis a cruelty
To load a falling man. *85*
 Gar.   Good Master Secretary,
I cry your honour mercy; you may worst
Of all this table say so.
 Crom.   Why, my lord?
 Gar. Do not I know you for a favourer *90*
Of this new sect? ye are not sound.
 Crom.   Not sound?
 Gar. Not sound, I say.
 Crom.   Would you were half so honest!
Men's prayers then would seek you, not their fears. *95*
 Gar. I shall remember this bold language.
 Crom.   Do.
Remember your bold life too.
 Chan.   This is too much;
Forbear, for shame, my lords. *100*
 Gar.   I have done.
 Crom.   And I.
 Chan. Then thus for you, my lord: it stands agreed,
I take it, by all voices, that forthwith
You be convey'd to the Tower a prisoner; *105*
There to remain till the king's further pleasure
Be known unto us. Are you all agreed, lords?
 All. We are.
 Cran. Is there no other way of mercy,
But I must needs to the Tower, my lords? *110*
 Gar.   What other
Would you expect? You are strangely troublesome.
Let some o' the guard be ready there.

    Enter the Guard.

 Cran.   For me?
Must I go like a traitor thither? *115*
 Gar.   Receive him,
And see him safe i' the Tower.
 Cran.   Stay, good my lords;
I have a little yet to say. Look there, my lords;
By virtue of that ring I take my cause *120*
Out of the gripes of cruel men, and give it
To a most noble judge, the king my master.
 Chan. This is the king's ring.
 Sur.   'Tis no counterfeit?
 Suf. 'Tis the right ring, by heaven! I told ye all, *125*
When we first put this dangerous stone a-rolling,
'Twould fall upon ourselves.
 Nor.   Do you think my lords,
The king will suffer but the little finger
Of this man to be vex'd? *130*
 Chan.   'Tis now too certain:
How much more is his life in value with him?
Would I were fairly out on 't.
 Crom.   My mind gave me,
In seeking tales and informations *135*

Against this man—whose honesty the devil
And his disciples only envy at—
Ye blew the fire that burns ye: now have at ye!

  Enter King, frowning on them: takes his seat.

 Gar. Dread sovereign, how much are we bound to heaven
In daily thanks, that gave us such a prince, *140*
Not only good and wise, but most religious:
One that in all obedience makes the Church
The chief aim of his honour; and to strengthen
That holy duty, out of dear respect,
His royal self in judgment comes to hear *145*
The cause betwixt her and this great offender.
 King. You were ever good at sudden commendations,
Bishop of Winchester; but know, I come not
To hear such flattery now, and in my presence
They are too thin and base to hide offences. *150*
To me you cannot reach; you play the spaniel,
And think with wagging of your tongue to win me;
But, whatsoe'er thou tak'st me for, I'm sure
Thou hast a cruel nature and a bloody.
[*To Cranmer.*] Good man, sit down. Now let me see the *155*
  proudest
He, that dares most, but wag his finger at thee.
By all that's holy, he had better starve
Than but once think his place becomes thee not.
 Sur. May it please your Grace,— *160*
 King.   No, sir, it does not please me.
I had thought I had had men of some understanding
And wisdom of my council; but I find none.
Was it discretion, lords, to let this man,
This good man—few of you deserve that title,— *165*
This honest man, wait like a lousy footboy
At chamber-door? and one as great as you are?
Why, what a shame was this! Did my commission
Bid ye so far forget yourselves? I gave ye
Power as he was a counsellor to try him, *170*
Not as a groom. There's some of ye, I see,
More out of malice than integrity,
Would try him to the utmost, had ye mean;
Which ye shall never have while I live.
 Chan.   Thus far, *175*
My most dread sovereign, may it like your Grace
To let my tongue excuse all. What was purpos'd
Concerning his imprisonment was rather—
If there be faith in men—meant for his trial
And fair purgation to the world, than malice,— *180*
I'm sure, in me.
 King.   Well, well, my lords, respect him;
Take him, and use him well; he's worthy of it.
I will say thus much for him: if a prince
May be beholding to a subject, I *185*
Am, for his love and service, so to him.
Make me no more ado, but all embrace him:
Be friends, for shame, my lords! My Lord of Canterbury,
I have a suit which you must not deny me;
That is, a fair young maid that yet wants baptism: *190*
You must be godfather, and answer for her.
 Cran. The greatest monarch now alive may glory

---

80 words and weakness: *weak verbosity* **99 This is too much;** *cf. n.* **125 right:**
genuine **134 My mind gave me:** *I suspected*   **159 his place;** *cf. n.* **163 of:** *as members of* **173 mean:** *opportunity*

In such an honour: how may I deserve it,
That am a poor and humble subject to you?

    King. Come, come, my lord, you'd spare your spoons.   *195*
You shall have two noble partners with you: the old Duchess
of Norfolk, and Lady Marquess Dorset. Will these please you?
Once more, my Lord of Winchester, I charge you,
Embrace and love this man.

    Gar.   With a true heart   *200*
And brother-love I do it.

    Cran.   And let heaven
Witness, how dear I hold this confirmation.

    King. Good man! those joyful tears show thy true heart.
The common voice, I see, is verified   *205*
Of thee, which say thus: 'Do my Lord of Canterbury
A shrewd turn, and he's your friend for ever.'
Come, lords, we trifle time away: I long
To have this young one made a Christian.
As I have made ye one, lords, one remain;   *210*
So I grow stronger, you more honour gain.   *Exeunt.*

❧ SCENE FOURTH ❧

[The Palace-Yard]
Noise and tumult within. Enter Porter and his Man.

    Port. You'll leave your noise anon, ye rascals. Do you take
the court for Parish-garden? ye rude slaves, leave your
gaping.

    [Voice] Within. Good Master Porter, I belong to the larder.

    Port. Belong to the gallows, and be hanged, ye rogue! Is   *5*
this a place to roar in? Fetch me a dozen crab-tree staves, and
strong ones: these are but switches to 'em. I'll scratch your
heads: you must be seeing christenings! Do you look for ale
and cakes here, you rude rascals?

    Man. Pray, sir, be patient: 'tis as much impossible—   *10*
Unless we sweep 'em from the doors with cannons—
To scatter 'em, as 'tis to make 'em sleep
On May-day morning; which will never be.
We may as well push against Paul's as stir 'em.

    Port. How got they in, and be hang'd?   *15*

    Man. Alas, I know not; how gets the tide in?
As much as one sound cudgel of four foot—
You see the poor remainder—could distribute,
I made no spare, sir.

    Port.   You did nothing, sir.   *20*

    Man. I am not Samson, nor Sir Guy, nor Colbrand,
To mow 'em down before me; but if I spar'd any
That had a head to hit, either young or old,
He or she, cuckold or cuckold-maker,
Let me ne'er hope to see a chine again;   *25*
And that I would not for a cow, God save her!

    Within. Do you hear, Master Porter?

    Port. I shall be with you presently, good Master puppy.
Keep the door close, sirrah.

    Man. What would you have me do?   *30*

    Port. What should you do, but knock 'em down by the

dozens? Is this Moorfields to muster in? or have we some
strange Indian with the great tool come to court, the women
so besiege us? Bless me, what a fry of fornication is at door!
On my Christian conscience, this one christening will beget   *35*
a thousand: here will be father, godfather, and all together.

    Man. The spoons will be the bigger, sir. There is a fellow
somewhat near the door, he should be a brazier by his face,
for, o' my conscience, twenty of the dog days now reign in's
nose: all that stand about him are under the line, they need   *40*
no other penance. That fire-drake did I hit three times on the
head, and three times was his nose discharged against me: he
stands there, like a mortar-piece, to blow us. There was a haberdasher's wife of small wit near him, that railed upon me till
her pinked porringer fell off her head, for kindling such a   *45*
combustion in the state. I missed the meteor once, and hit
that woman, who cried out, 'Clubs!' when I might see from far
some forty truncheoners draw to her succour, which were the
hope o' the Strand, where she was quartered. They fell on; I
made good my place; at length they came to the broomstaff   *50*
to me; I defied 'em still; when suddenly a file of boys behind
'em, loose shot, delivered such a shower of pebbles, that I was
fain to draw mine honour in, and let 'em win the work. The
devil was amongst 'em, I think, surely.

    Port. These are the youths that thunder at a playhouse,   *55*
and fight for bitten apples; that no audience, but the Tribulation of Tower-hill, or the Limbs of Limehouse, their dear brothers, are able to endure. I have some of 'em in *Limbo Patrum,*
and there they are like to dance these three days; besides the
running banquet of two beadles, that is to come.   *60*

Enter Lord Chamberlain.

    L. Ch. Mercy o' me, what a multitude are here!
They grow still too, from all parts they are coming,
As if we kept a fair here! Where are these porters,
These lazy knaves? Y' have made a fine hand, fellows:
There's a trim rabble let in. Are all these   *65*
Your faithful friends o' the suburbs? We shall have
Great store of room, no doubt, left for the ladies,
When they pass back from the christening.

    Port.   An 't please your honour,
We are but men; and what so many may do,   *70*
Not being torn a-pieces, we have done:
An army cannot rule 'em.

    L. Ch.   As I live,
If the king blame me for 't, I'll lay ye all
By th' heels, and suddenly; and on your heads   *75*
Clap round fines for neglect: y' are lazy knaves;
And here ye lie baiting of bombards, when
Ye should do service. Hark! the trumpets sound;
They're come already from the christening.
Go, break among the press, and find a way out   *80*
To let the troop pass fairly, or I'll find
A Marshalsea shall hold ye play these two months.

    Port. Make way there for the princess.

---

195 spare your spoons: *save christening presents*   **203 confirmation:** *assurance*   **207
shrewd:** *malicious (i.e. he returns good for evil)*   **2 Parish-garden;** *cf. n.*   **4 larder:**
the pantry (therefore he had the right to enter)   **13 May-day morning;** *cf. n.*   **14
Paul's:** *St. Paul's Cathedral*   **21** *Cf. n.*   **25 chine:** *roast of beef*   **26 for a cow;** *cf. n.*

32 Moorfields; *cf. n.*   **33 strange Indian;** *cf. n.*   **37 The spoons;** *cf. n.*   **38 brazier:**
worker in brass   **40 under the line:** *under the equator (where it is hot)*   **41 fire-drake:**
fiery dragon (the man with the red nose)   **43 mortar-piece:** *small cannon*   **45 pinked
porringer:** *a bowl-shaped hat slashed with holes*   **47 Clubs;** *cf. n.*   **49 Strand:** *street in
London*   **53 work:** *outwork*   **56, 57 Tribulation . . . Limehouse;** *cf. n.*   **58 Limbo
Patrum:** *i.e. jail*   **60 running banquet;** *cf. n.*   **64 fine hand:** *pretty business*   **70, 71
what . . . a-pieces:** *what our number may do without being torn to pieces*   **76 round:**
heavy   **77 baiting of bombards:** *drinking deep*   **82 Marshalsea:** *a prison*

Man. You great fellow,
Stand close up, or I'll make your head ache. 85
Port. You i' the camlet, get up o' the rail:
I'll pick you o'er the pales else. *Exeunt.*

❧ Scene Fifth ❧

[The Palace]

*Enter trumpets, sounding; then two Aldermen, Lord Mayor,
Garter, Cranmer, Duke of Norfolk, with his marshal's staff,
Duke of Suffolk, two Noblemen bearing great standing-bowls
for the christening gifts: then four Noblemen bearing a canopy,
under which the Duchess of Norfolk, godmother, bearing the
child, richly habited in a mantle, &c., train borne by a Lady:
then follows the Marchioness Dorset, the other godmother, and
ladies. The troop pass once about the stage, and Garter speaks.*

Gart. Heaven, from thy endless goodness, send prosperous
life, long, and ever happy, to the high and mighty Princess of
England, Elizabeth!

Flourish. Enter King and Guard.

Cran. [*Kneeling.*] And to your royal Grace, and the good
queen, 5
My noble partners and myself thus pray:
All comfort, joy, in this most gracious lady,
Heaven ever laid up to make parents happy,
May hourly fall upon ye!
King. Thank you, good lord archbishop: 10
What is her name?
Cran. Elizabeth.
King. Stand up, lord.
[The King kisses the Child.]
With this kiss take my blessing; God protect thee!
Into whose hand I give thy life. 15
Cran. Amen.
King. My noble gossips, y' have been too prodigal:
I thank ye heartily: so shall this lady
When she has so much English.
Cran. Let me speak, sir, 20
For heaven now bids me; and the words I utter
Let none think flattery, for they'll find 'em truth.
This royal infant,—heaven still move about her!—
Though in her cradle, yet now promises
Upon this land a thousand thousand blessings, 25
Which time shall bring to ripeness. She shall be—
But few now living can behold that goodness—
A pattern to all princes living with her,
And all that shall succeed: Saba was never
More covetous of wisdom and fair virtue 30
Than this pure soul shall be: all princely graces,
That mould up such a mighty piece as this is,
With all the virtues that attend the good,
Shall still be doubled on her; truth shall nurse her;
Holy and heavenly thoughts still counsel her; 35
She shall be lov'd and fear'd. Her own shall bless her;
Her foes shake like a field of beaten corn,

And hang their heads with sorrow. Good grows with her.
In her days every man shall eat in safety
Under his own vine what he plants; and sing 40
The merry songs of peace to all his neighbours.
God shall be truly known; and those about her
From her shall read the perfect ways of honour,
And by those claim their greatness, not by blood.
Nor shall this peace sleep with her; but as when 45
The bird of wonder dies, the maiden phœnix,
Her ashes new-create another heir
As great in admiration as herself,
So shall she leave her blessedness to one,—
When heaven shall call her from this cloud of darkness,— 50
Who, from the sacred ashes of her honour,
Shall star-like rise, as great in fame as she was,
And so stand fix'd. Peace, plenty, love, truth, terror,
That were the servants to this chosen infant,
Shall then be his, and like a vine grow to him: 55
Wherever the bright sun of heaven shall shine,
His honour and the greatness of his name
Shall be, and make new nations. He shall flourish,
And, like a mountain cedar, reach his branches
To all the plains about him. Our children's children 60
Shall see this, and bless heaven.
King. Thou speakest wonders.
Cran. She shall be, to the happiness of England,
An aged princess; many days shall see her,
And yet no day without a deed to crown it. 65
Would I had known no more! but she must die,
She must, the saints must have her; yet a virgin,
A most unspotted lily shall she pass
To the ground, and all the world shall mourn her.
King. O lord archbishop! 70
Thou hast made me now a man: never, before
This happy child, did I get anything.
This oracle of comfort has so pleas'd me,
That when I am in heaven, I shall desire
To see what this child does, and praise my Maker. 75
I thank ye all. To you, my good Lord Mayor,
And your good brethren, I am much beholding;
I have receiv'd much honour by your presence,
And ye shall find me thankful. Lead the way, lords:
Ye must all see the queen, and she must thank ye; 80
She will be sick else. This day, no man think
H'as business at his house; for all shall stay:
This little one shall make it holiday. *Exeunt.*

❧ The Epilogue ❧

*'Tis ten to one, this play can never please
All that are here. Some come to take their ease
And sleep an act or two; but those, we fear,
We've frightened with our trumpets; so, 'tis clear
They'll say 'tis naught: others, to hear the city 5
Abus'd extremely, and to cry, 'That's witty!'
Which we have not done neither: that, I fear,
All the expected good we're like to hear*

---

86 i' the camlet: *in the woolen suit* **87 pick:** *pitch* **pales:** *palisade* **Scene Fifth;**
cf. n. **S. d. Garter:** *the chief herald* **6 My noble partners:** *the other sponsors* 17
prodigal: *generous* **29 Saba:** *the Queen of Sheba*

48 great in admiration: *admirable* **49 to one:** *James I, the successor of Elizabeth* 7
that: *so that*

For this play at this time is only in
The merciful construction of good women; 10
For such a one we show'd 'em: if they smile,

And say 'twill do, I know within a while
All the best men are ours; for 'tis ill hap
If they hold when their ladies bid 'em clap.

❧ FINIS ❧

Notes

Dramatis Personæ, omitted in the Folio, were first supplied by Rowe in 1709.

The Prologue. For general discussion of authorship, see Authorship of the Play. It may be well, however, to state here that the question of the authorship of many parts of this play is undecided. For 150 years Shakespeare's authorship of the *Prologue* was denied. In the eighteenth century Dr. Samuel Johnson attributed it to Fletcher; in the nineteenth, it was given to Ben Johnson, and to Chapman; in the twentieth, to Massinger. Besides the *Induction* to *2 Henry IV* there are only three other prologues in Shakespeare's works, those to *Troilus and Cressida, Romeo and Juliet* and *Henry V*. In each case the prologue serves to explain the play. Here it is actually misleading, since the last lines of the *Prologue* promise as a tragedy and the Fifth Act is far from tragic. And the tone of this *Prologue* is curiously apologetic.

Pro. 9. *May here find truth too.* The play of Henry VIII in 1613 had, as an alternative title, *All is True.* (See quotation from Sir Henry Wotton, The History of the Play.) Some critics find here and in

'To rank our chosen truth with such a snow' (l. 18) and
'To make that only true we now intend' (l. 21)

allusions to that title. If these lines contain allusions to that title, the question of the date is settled.

Pro. 12. *shilling.* The price of admission to the best seats in the theatre. It must be remembered, however, that the purchasing power of a shilling was over eight times that at present.

Pro. 16. *In a long motley coat.* The customary costume of the stage fool.

Pro. 19. *As fool and fight is.* Dr. Johnson and later critics have regarded this gratuitous attack upon the stage fool and the stage battle as decisive evidence of the non-Shakespearean authorship of the *Prologue*, because both fools and fights are very often used by Shakespeare. It is possible that the lines, 14-16, may be an attack upon Samuel Rowley's *When you see me you know me.* (See History of the Play.)

Pro. 22. *Will leave us.* Awkward construction. The whole line, 21, is in apposition with *opinion.* The passage, 17-22, may then be paraphrased: gentle hearers, you must understand that to rank our play with a foolish comedy is, besides forfeiting our intelligence and our reputation for presenting historical truth, to lose us our friends.

Pro. 25, 26. *think ye see. see—story* are bad rimes. Theobald emends *think before ye—story*; Heath, *think ye see—history.* Actually, these rimes indicate merely that the Prologue was written hastily, not that there was an error in the printing.

I.i. S.d. *London. An Antechamber in the Palace.* The Folio, here as elsewhere, omits any indication of place. Unlike our modern stage with its elaborate sets of scenery, the Shakespearean stage was comparatively bare, with an apron projecting out into the pit. In all probability the authors had no particular place here in mind. If a particular palace must be mentioned, it was presumably that at Greenwich, to which the King, according to Holinshed, returned after the Field of the Cloth of Gold, June, 1520. It could not have been Bridewell, as has been suggested, because that palace was not built until two years later. The question is of no importance.

I.i. S.d. *Enter the Duke of Norfolk.* Thomas Howard (1448-1524), was created Duke of Norfolk in 1514 in recognition of his having won the Battle of Flodden Field. His son, the father of the poet Surrey, married Elizabeth, the eldest daughter of the Duke of Buckingham in 1513. Thus there was a close tie between the Duke of Norfolk and the Duck of Buckingham, in spite of which it was Norfolk who presided at Buckingham's trial and received as recompense part of the latter's sequestered estates. The authors seem unaware of this connection between the two noblemen: Norfolk's part in Buckingham's trial is ignored, and they seem unconscious of the difference of thirty-five years between the two speakers. Norfolk is an old man, seventy-seven, and as he died in 1524 his appearance in III.ii. is an anachronism. Historically it was Buckingham, not Norfolk, that accompanied Henry to France.

I.i. S.d. *Duke of Buckingham.* Edward Stafford (1478-1521), third Duke of Buckingham. The authors follow Holinshed in attributing Buckingham's fall to the hatred of Wolsey; there is slight foundation for this idea.

I.i. S.d. *Lord Abergavenny.* George Neville (1471-1535) was a son-in-law of the Duke of Buckingham. He was imprisoned in 1521 for complicity in Buckingham's treason, but was pardoned in March, 1522.

I.i.8. *Those suns of glory.* Francis I, King of Franc, and Henry VIII, King of England.

I.i.9. *vale of Andren.* Altered in the Second Folio to Vale of Arde, but Andren is copied from Holinshed. It is the valley separating Guynes, a town in Picardy which then belonged to the English, from Arde (or Ardres), a town also in Picardy belonging to the French. It was the locality selected for the interview between the two kings, from the seventh to the fourteenth of June, 1520, called from the magnificence of the appointments the 'Field of the Cloth of Gold.' The interview had little political significance. The time of this scene is approximately the fall of 1520.

I.i.16. *All the whole time.* Incorrect. Buckingham was present at the Field of the Cloth of Gold; it was Norfolk that remained behind in England.

I.i.23. *its.* Both the First and Second Folios read *it's.* The neuter possessive pronoun *its* was at this time slowly replacing the older neuter pronoun *his,* as used, for example, in l. 52 of this scene. This is the only case in Shakespeare's works where *its* is used absolutely.

I.i.43. *Bevis.* The hero of the old tale *Bevis of Hamptoun,* a person that performs miraculous feats.

I.i.48–54. *All was royal.* The assignment of speeches here is that of the Folio. Since Theobald, every editor has accepted his change which gives *All was royal ... function* to Norfolk and *As you guess* to Buckingham. The Folio reading is restored on the general principle that unnecessary tampering with the text as given is unjustifiable. In addition, there is a gain in the original reading. Buckingham's emphasis on *royal* gives the actor his first opportunity to show the character's love of rank. Buckingham's speech is, then, one of acquiescence; the performance has been carried out as it should have been. On the other hand, Norfolk, who knows of Buckingham's hatred to Wolsey, to this expressed approval replies maliciously 'As you would suppose when you consider you planned it.' The Folio reading consequently makes a more dramatic scene.

I.i.73. *Out of his self-drawing web.* The Folio here reads:

Out of his self-drawing web. O gives us note.

Capell's emendation is here followed. *A' gives us note* means that he himself tells us that, spider-like, he has created his own greatness.

I.i.88–92. *for the most part such, etc.* This speech is marked by the incoherence of anger. *Such* is the object of the verb *papers; letter* is the subject of the verb *must fetch; such* is the antecedent of *him.* The meaning is: generally he lists (papers) such persons as he both wishes to tax heavily and at the same time give little honor to, and his own handwriting (letter) cheats them into incurring this expense, now that the Board of the Council is out of the way. By putting this passage into blank verse the authors cannot be said to have improved upon the clarity of Holinshed:

'The peeres of the realme receiuing letters to prepare themselues to attend the king in this iournie, and no necessarie cause expressed, why nor wherefore; seemed to grudge, that such a costlie iournie should be taken in hand to their importunate charges and expenses, without consent of the whole boord of the councell.' Holinshed (1587), p. 855.

I.i.100. *minister communication.* These speeches of Buckingham seem to be derived from the passage from Holinshed continuing that quoted in the preceding note:

'But namelie the duke of Buckingham, being a man of a loftie courage, but not most liberall, sore repined that he should be at so great charges for his furniture foorth at this time, saieng; that he knew not for what cause so much monie should be spent about the sight of a vaine talke to be had, and communication to be ministred of things of no importance. Wherefore he sticked not to saie, that it was an intollerable matter to obeie such a vile and importunate person.'

I.i.106. *hideous storm.* Holinshed (1587), p. 860: 'On Mondaie, the eighteenth of June, was such an hideous storme of wind and weather, that manie coniectured it did prognosticate trouble and hatred shortlie after to follow between princes.'

I.i.112. *For France hath flaw'd the league.* Holinshed (1587), p. 872: 'Many complaints were made by the merchants to the king and his councell of the Frenchmen, which spoiled them by sea of their goods.... The sixt of March, the French king commanded all Englishmens goods being in Burdeaux to be attached, and put under arrest.... The king, understanding how his subiects were handled at Burdeaux by the French kings commandement, in breach of the league, the French ambassadour was called before the councell....' As this was March, 1522, and Buckingham was executed on Friday, May 17, 1521, the authors of the play have muddled their dates.

I.i.115. *Th' ambassador is silenc'd.* Holinshed (1587), p. 873: 'The ambassadour in words so well as he could excused his master, but in the end hee was commanded to keepe his house.'

I.i.137. *The Duke of Buckingham's surveyor.* Holinshed (1587), p. 862:
'. . . The cardinall boiling in hatred against the duke of Buckingham, and thirsting for his bloud, deuised to make Charles Kneuet, that had beene the dukes surueior, and put from him (as ye haue heard) an instrument to bring the duke to destruction.'

Holinshed borrowed this explanation of Buckingham's fall from Polydore Vergil, a personal enemy of Wolsey. Modern investigation has shown that Wolsey's hatred was not the chief cause of the tragedy.

I.i.143. *This butcher's cur.* Wolsey's father sold meat among other things. His will shows him to have been a successful retail grocer and butcher, and the Ipswich town records prove that he was not over-scrupulous. Wolsey was often taunted with his lowly origin.

> 'How be it the primordyall
> Of his wretched originall,
> And his base progeny,
> And his gresy genealogy,
> He came of the sank royall (royal blood),
> That was the cast out of a bochers stall.'
>
>   Skelton's *Why Come Ye not to Court.*

I.i.165. *Ipswich.* Ipswich was Wolsey's birthplace.

I.i.172. *count-cardinal.* The title is hyphenated because a secular title is joined to an ecclesiastical one. Wolsey was both Archbishop of York and Count of Hexamshire.

I.i.207. *Charles the emperor.* Charles V, Emperor of the Holy Roman Empire and King of Spain. His mother, Joanna, was a sister of Katharine of Aragon, wife of Henry VIII. He landed at Dover, May 26, 1520. The real and pretended motives for this visit are taken form Holinshed.

I.i.214. *He privily.* He was omitted in the First Folio, but supplied in the Second.

I.i. S.d. *Enter Brandon.* A Sir Thomas Brandon is mentioned by Holinshed as Master of the King's Horse. Yet, according to Holinshed, the arrest was made by Sir Henry Marny, Captain of the King's Guard. There is no dramatic reason for this change of persons; it merely shows that the dramatists worked up the material for the play rapidly.

I.i.234. *Hereford.* The Folio misprints Hertford.

I.i.240–242. *I am sorry, etc.* Two coördinate clauses. I am sorry to see that you are taken prisoner and to be an eye-witness to the event.

I.i.248. *Lord Abergavenny.* The Folio spells the name Aburgany, a spelling that indicates the pronunciation. The fact of the arrest is taken from Holinshed, 'and so likewise was lord Montacute, and both led to the Tower.'

I.i.258. *John de la Car.* Taken from Holinshed, maister John de la Car alias de la Court.' John Delacourt acted as the intermediary between the Duke and Nicholas Hopkins, the Carthusian monk. Cf. n. on I.i.263.

I.i.259. *One Gilbert Peck, his chancellor.* Both Folios here read 'councel-lour.' This was corrected by Theobald from Holinshed. But there was a double error, since the name of the Duke's chancellor given by Holinshed is Gilbert Perke. Apparently 'Peck' is a misprint for Perk. Really the chancellor was Robert Gilbert. This mistake probably arose from the fact that in one of the state papers he is called 'Robert Gilbert clerk, then his chancellor.' Hall mistook 'clerk' for a name, and misprinted it Perke. Holinshed copied Hall, and the dramatists followed Holinshed. But a few paragraphs farther on. Holinshed gives both the name and title correctly: 'the said duke had sent his chancellour Robert Gilbert chapleine.' This is another indication that the dramatists had not read Holinshed carefully.

I.i.263. *Nicholas Hopkins.* The Folios read Michaell. Theobald corrected this to Nicholas, following Holinshed. Hopkins, a monk of the Charterhouse at Henton, was a religious enthusiast, with gift of prophecy. Unintentionally he brought the Duke into danger and died broken-hearted.

I.i.268. *instant.* These lines, 267–269, develop an elaborate meteorological figure. This very instant, eclipsing the clear sun of my prosperity, throws a cloud upon my figure and makes me only the shadow of what I was.

I.i.269. *My lord.* The Folio, which reads *lords,* is obviously incorrect, because, as Abergavenny is arrested with him and Brandon accompanies him, there is only one person, Norfolk, left on the stage.

I.ii. S.d. *The Council Chamber.* These locations of the scenes are later additions. On the Elizabethan stage there was no front curtain and ordinarily no intermission. As Buckingham and Abergavenny are led off at one side, with Norfolk following, trumpets are heard and the King enters from the other side. Sir Thomas Lovell was the Constable of the Tower. The scene follows the long account of the charges against Buckingham as given in Holinshed, with the important exception that the petition of Katharine and her attack upon Wolsey are the creation of the dramatists.

I.ii. S.d. *Suffolk.* Charles Brandon, created Duke of Suffolk in 1514, married Mary Tudor, Henry's sister, the dowager Queen of France.

I.ii. S.d. *King riseth from his state.* The 'state' was a raised throne with a canopy. This had been brought on by stage hands after the end of the first scene.

I.ii.22. *there have been commissions.* This account is taken from Holinshed (1587), p. 891. But the chronology is confused. The commissions were sent in March, 1525, four years after Buckingham's death. But for this there is the dramatic reason that antedating these events enables Katharine to plead both for the people and for Buckingham, and by so doing to intensify Wolsey's dislike of her.

I.ii.142. *Stand forth.* J. S. Brewer comments on this scene as follows:

> 'It will be remembered that in Shakespeare's play the Duke is declared guilty by the King at a meeting of the Privy Council, even before his regular trial had taken place;—a process altogether informal. In the Council Chamber in which Queen Katharine and Wolsey are present, the King is represented as conducting the examination of the Duke's surveyor, Charles Knyvet, in person. The Duke has no one there to defend him; the witnesses are not subjected to cross-examination, nor is any attempt made to ascertain the accuracy of their charges, or to test their honesty and good faith by the methods now adopted in similar cases. The Duke's guilt is assumed upon their unsupported assertions. In this travesty of justice, the Queen is the only person who appears to retain any sense of what is due to reason and equity; but she is too feeble an advocate, too much bewildered by the sophistry which she feels, but is unable to unravel, to render the accused any effectual help. Besides, when kings sit in council, who shall contradict them? When their minds are already made up, "God mend all," is the natural and sole reflection which presents itself to the thoughts of inferiors. Strange as this proceeding may appear, it is not due merely to the poet's imagination. It presents us with a general likeness of State prosecutions in the Tudor times. The presumption that men are innocent until they are legally proved to be guilty, the facilities granted to the accused for substantiating his innocence by retaining the ablest advocate, the methods for sifting evidence now in use, had no existence then. In crimes against the sovereign, real or supposed, men were presumed to be guilty until they proved themselves to be innocent, and that proof was involved in endless difficulties. What advocate or what witness would have ventured to brave the displeasure of a Tudor king, by appearing in defense of a criminal, on whose guilt the King had pronounced already? With the exception of making Wolsey present at the examination of the Duke's servants and surveyor, Shakespeare has strictly adhered to facts in this preliminary examination of the Duke's servants.'
>
>   (J. S. Brewer, *The Reign of Henry VIII,* I. 383.)

I.ii.165. *Henton.* This, the Folio reading, was altered by Theobald to 'Hopkins.' But as he was often called Henton from the monastery to which he belonged, 'there is no need to amend the text.' (Gollancz.) Cf. I.i.263 and note.

I.ii.171–191. These twenty lines are merely Holinshed (1587), p. 864, in blank verse.

I.ii.184. *confession's seal.* Theobald's emendation of the Folio's reading *Commissions seal.* It comes from Holinshed, 'under the seal of confession.'

I.ii.190. *To gain.* The word *gain* was added in the Fourth Folio to complete the meter.

I.ii.193. *You were the duke's surveyor.* The accusation against Knyvet is taken from Holinshed.

I.ii.200–210. This speech is versified Holinshed.

I.ii.203. *for him.* Capell's emendation for the *for this* of the Folio.

I.ii.217. *Bulmer.* The Folio printer transposed the letters, so that the name reads *Blumer.*

I.ii.245. *by day and night.* An exclamation. Cf. *Hamlet,* I.v.182, 'O day and night, but this is wondrous strange!'

I.iii. The third scene, which serves only as a prelude to the fourth, is typical of Fletcher's style. It has been explained by some commentators as being an attack upon the courtiers of James I. Although there is no dramatic reason for its existence, it is an expansion of one paragraph of Holinshed (1587), p. 850, and of another on p. 852. Owing to the fact that the dramatists skipped back and forth in versifying the passages from Holinshed, the chronology is hopeless. This scene was in 1519. At this time the Lord Chamberlain was Charles Somerset, Earl of Worcester, and Sir William Sands (or Sandys) had not been raised to the nobility.

I.iii.14,15. *spavin Or springhalt.* Verplanck's emendation for the Folio,

> . . . the Spauen
> A Spring-halt . . .

because the two diseases are different, although each causes lameness in a horse.

I.iii.32. *Of fool and feather.* Alluding to the long feathers worn in the hats.

I.iii.34. *as fights and fireworks.* There had been jousting at the Field of the Cloth of Gold, and the interview had ended with a display of fireworks.

I.iii.37. *tall stockings.* The extreme of the fashion was very short puffed trousers and long stockings, reaching above the knee.

I.iii.79. *My barge stays.* Before the Victoria Embankment was built, the palaces along the river front had steps leading down to the river, because the ordinary means of travel was by boat.

I.iv. This scene, also by Fletcher, is a dramatization of the passage from Holinshed (1587), pp. 921 ff. But Holinshed's *Chronicle* is itself a compilation from a number of previous works. this particular passage is an almost verbatim reprint from George Cavendish's *Life of Cardinal Wolsey.* According to Hall, the entertainment took place January 3, 1527. Consequently chronological order in the play is incorrect in placing it before Buckingham's death. This error arose from the fact that Holinshed, after he had finished a year-by-year account of Wolsey's career, summarized his character, drawing from Cavendish. Consequently in this part of Holinshed no dates are given to the events described. This error in dating causes another, namely, that in 1527 the Lord Chamberlain and Lord Sandys were not different persons, as Sandys had become Lord Chamberlain the year before. Sir. Henry Guilford was Master of Horse.

York Place, then the residence of Wolsey, later became Whitehall, the royal palace. Cf. IV.i.112–114.

I.iv. S.d. *Chambers discharged.* This appears to have been the occasion of the conflagration which destroyed the Globe Theatre. See History of the Play.

I.iv. 94. *The fairest hand.* Anne Boleyn's presence at this entertainment is an invention of the dramatists. There is no indication in Holinshed that she was there.

I.iv.124. *And not to kiss you.* Kissing before the dance was the custom. If he had not kissed her, he would have been 'unmannerly.'

II.i. This scene (by Fletcher), while scarcely advancing the action of the drama, is yet finely effective, taken by itself. It is a close dramatization from Holinshed (1587), p. 865, even to the extent of keeping many of the original phrases.

II.i.25. *To have brought.* The first three Folios read *To him brought;* the correction was made in the Fourth.

II.i.55, 56. *Earl Surrey was sent thither, and in haste too, Lest he should help his father.* Thomas Howard, Earl of Surrey and in 1524 Duke of Norfolk, had married Elizabeth Stafford, the eldest daughter of the Duke of Buckingham.

II.i.68. *The mirror of all courtesy.* 'He is tearmed in the books of the law in the said thirteenth yeare of Henrie the eight (where his arreignement is liberallie set downe) to be the floure and mirror of all courtesie.' Holinshed (1587), p. 870.

II.i. S.d. *the axe with the edge towards him.* This indicated that the prisoner had been condemned.

II.i. S.d. *Sir William Sandys.* The same character that has figured in Act I as Lord Sandys, only here his title is correctly given. Theobald corrected the Folio, which reads *Walter.*

II.i.84. *evils.* Some commentators have wished to take *evils* in this passage and in *Measure for Measure,* II.ii.209, in the Elizabethan sense of *privy* or *outhouse.* This meaning at best is doubtful. Here, however, where the style is both elliptical and metaphorical, the usual sense of *crimes* seems the simpler reading.

II.i.122. *Edward Bohun.* Buckingham's surname was Stafford, although he was a remote descendant of the Bohun family. The mistake, however, is in Holinshed.

II.i.126. *My noble father.* Henry Stafford, High Constable of England and Duke of Buckingham, raised a revolt against Richard III, was betrayed by his servant, Humphrey Banaster, and beheaded in 1483, 'without arreignement or iudgement.'

II.i.171-177. This passage is versified Holinshed (1587), p. 897.

II.i.160. *Cardinal Campeius.* Cardinal Lorenzo Campeggio was sent by the Pope, Clement VII, to judge the question jointly with Wolsey. As the Pope had withheld the power to make a decision, the trial was necessarily adjourned.

II.i.190. *The archbishopric of Toledo.* This motivation of Wolsey's conduct is taken from Holinshed.

II.ii.18, 19. *No; his conscience Has crept too near another lady.* As has been pointed out by Mr. Vaughan, this speech of Suffolk is an aside, and Norfolk's ' 'Tis so' is in agreement with the opinion of the Chamberlain. This speech is incongruous coming from the mouth of the historical Duke of Suffolk!

II.ii.22. *That blind priest.* Reckless, because he cannot see. But the adjective suggests the familiar figure of Fortune, with her wheel.

II.ii. S.d. At the back of the Elizabethan stage there was a gallery. Under the gallery was a recess, screened by curtains. This recess here is used as the King's study. And it is upon the gallery that the King and Butts play in Act V.ii.

II.ii.99. *have-at-him.* A thrust. This is Dyce's emendation of the Folio 'If it doe; Ile venture one; haue at him.'

II.ii.125. *Gardiner.* Stephen Gardiner (1483-1555), Trinity College, Cambridge, early distinguished himself as a student in Civil and Canon Law. As such, he was employed by Henry as an agent in the divorce proceedings. After Wolsey's death he was rewarded by being made Bishop of Winchester (1531). He later became an opponent of Cranmer and the Reformation, was imprisoned throughout the reign of Edward VI, and was one of the chief counsellors of Mary. Since it was in her reign that the Protestants were persecuted, Gardiner was popularly held responsible and generally hated.

II.ii.128. Taken from Holinshed.

II.ii.140. *Doctor Pace.* Richard Pace (1482?-1536), a celebrated scholar and writer, succeeded the famous John Colet as Dean of St. Paul's. He was also Dean of Exeter and of Salisbury. He had been sent on many embassies, but in 1525 he was forced to return to England owing to mental derangement. Holinshed is reporting popular gossip in crediting this insanity to the persecutions of the Cardinal, but an examination of the state papers does not justify such a conclusion.

II.ii.161. *Blackfriars.* Before the Reformation the monastic establishment of the Dominicans, between Ludgate Hill and the Thames. The locality is still marked by Blackfriars Bridge.

II.iii. This scene, which has no structural importance in the play, is used to characterize Anne Boleyn. Except for the brief conversation in I.iv. and her appearance in the procession in IV.i., this is her only scene. The contrast between the dramatic importance given to Katharine by the dramatist and that given to Anne, the mother of Queen Elizabeth, is curious.

II.iii.1-11. The ejaculatory form of Anne's speech expresses her emotion, and also marks the reappearance of Shakespeare's style.

II.iii.44. *three-pence.* This is an anachronism, because 'the first large and regular coinage of three-pence took place in the reign of Elizabeth' (Fairholt).

II.iii.53. *Ever to get a boy.* An allusion to Henry's desire for a male heir.

II.iii.46. *little England.* Steevens suggested that 'little England' may be Pembrokeshire. This interpretation is over-subtle as the Old Lady is not supposed to know that Anne was about to be created Marchioness of Pembroke and certainly the audience does not know it.

II.iii.58. *emballing.* Explained by commentators as a reference to the ball, the symbol of power, place in the hand of the sovereign at the coronation. It was not used at the coronation of a queen-consort; Anne was given a dove upon an ivory staff. Merely an indelicate joke.

II.iii.59. *Carnarvonshire.* A barren county in Wales, in contrast to fertile England.

II.iii.74. *of you.* The Folio reads

'Commends his good opinion of you, to you;'

Presumably the 'to you' is an error of the typesetter, although the verse of this play is so ragged that the dramatists may have written it so.

II.ii.76. *Marchioness of Pembroke.* Taken from Holinshed.

II.iii.93. *a gem.* An allusion to Queen Elizabeth.

II.iii.102. *fie, fie.* The Folio gives three *fie's;* but the third is an extra syllable in the line.

II.iii.109. *mud in Egypt.* The wealth of Egypt is due to the mud deposited by the overflowing Nile.

II.iv. S.d. The location of this scene is taken from Holinshed. Bishop of Canterbury is an obvious error for Archbishop of Canterbury. At this time, June 21, 1529, the Archbishop of Canterbury was William Warham; the Bishop of Lincoln, John Longland; the Bishop of Ely, Nicholas West; the Bishop of Rochester, John Fisher; and the Bishop of Saint Asaph was Henry Standish. The details of this procession are taken from Holinshed. In an uneducated age, the meaning of events was explained to the crowd by symbols. The *purse* was carried to represent the Treasury; the *great seal* signified that Wolsey was Lord Chancellor; the *hat,* that he was a cardinal; the *two crosses* represented his archbishopric and his commission from the Pope as legate; the *silver mace* was the emblem of authority; the *two pillars,* the insignia of a cardinal. The procession, then, was a visible representation of Wolsey's position in the Church and in the State. The scene is a dramatization of Holinshed (1587), pp. 907, 908; the speeches are little more than a versifying of Holinshed's prose.

II.iv.14. *Sir, I desire.* Compare this speech with Holinshed: 'Sir (quoth she) I desire you to doo me justice and right, and take some pitie upon me, for I am a poore woman, and a stranger, borne out of your dominion, having here no indifferent counsell, and assurance of freendship. Alas sir, what have I offended you, or what occasion of displeasure have I shewed you, intending thus to put me from you after this sort? I take God to my judge, I have beene to you a true and humble wife, ever conformable to your will and pleasure, that never contrar-

ied or gainesaid any thing thereof, and being alwaies contented with all things wherein you had any delight, whether little or much, without grudge or displeasure, I loved for your sake all them whom you loved, whether they were my freends or enimies,' etc., etc. The other speeches are equally close.

II.iv.38. *many children.* Of the five children that Katharine had borne, only one survived, Mary. She succeeded her half-brother, Edward VI, on the throne.

II.iv.122–124. *your words, Domestics to you, etc.* Your words, like household servants, perform any service that your will desires.

II.iv.137. *Gent. Ush.* From Holinshed, the name of the gentleman usher is Griffith. He appears again in IV.ii.

II.iv.185. *Bishop of Bayonne.* As a matter of fact, Cavendish, who is Holinshed's authority here, was mistaken; it was not Du Bellay, Bishop of Bayonne, but Grammont, Bishop of Tarbes, that came on this embassy.

II.iv.195. *bosom of my conscience.* Holinshed's phrase is 'bottom of my conscience.'

II.iv.241. *drives.* The old Northern English plural, common in Shakespeare. Compare 'compels' in I.ii.65.

II.iv.256. *Cranmer.* Cranmer was then abroad, collecting opinions concerning the validity of the King's marriage.

III.i. The location of this scene is taken from Holinshed, and is dramatized from the account there given.

III.i.27. *But all hoods make not monks.* The Latin form of this proverb, *cucullus non facit monachum*, is quoted also in *Measure for Measure* and in *Twelfth Night.*

III.i.46–47. *Tanta est erga te, etc.* 'So great is the honesty of our purpose toward you, most noble Queen.' As Holinshed says only that they started to speak Latin, these words are the creation of the dramatists.

III.i.68. *your cause.* The Second Folio corrects the First, which reads *our cause.*

III.i.161. *Ye have angels' faces.* Katharine is a Spaniard. She is here alluding to Pope Gregory's famous exclamation, *Non Angli sed angeli.*

III.ii. This scene, with the possible exception of the death of Katharine, IV. ii, is the most famous one in the play. Nichol Smith divides it into: (1) the interview between the King and Wolsey; (2) the interview between the nobles and Wolsey; (3) the interview between Wolsey and Cromwell. Of these three only the second is taken directly from Holinshed, but details in the first and third are from Holinshed's summary of Wolsey's character.

The chronology is hopelessly confused. 'Lord' Surrey, the Earl of Surrey, was after 1524 the poet Surrey, because his grandfather, the Norfolk of the First Act, had died in that year and transmitted the ducal title to the poet's father, the Norfolk of this scene. More's appointment as Chancellor followed Wolsey's death, and Cranmer was consecrated Archbishop of Canterbury, March 30, 1533. For dramatic effect events thus separated by years are condensed into one scene.

III.ii.27. *Not to come off.* In the speech, the pronouns are ambiguous. No, he (Wolsey) is settled in his (the King's) displeasure, not to escape.

III.ii.39. *The cardinal's letters.* Holinshed (1587), p. 909: 'he required the pope by letters and secret messengers, that in anie wise he should defer the iudgement of the diuorce, till he might frame the kings mind to his purpose.'

III.ii.54. *Would he had!* As Anne Boleyn was the niece of the 'Lord Surrey' of the play, the exclamation is natural enough. The dramatists, however, show no knowledge of this relationship. Apparently the only value of the information is its relation to the fall of Wolsey.

III.ii.66. *Will fall some blessing.* An obvious allusion to Queen Elizabeth.

III.ii.74. *Cardinal Campeius.* The dramatists here abandon Holinshed, who expressly states that Campeggio took a formal leave of the King. Boswell-Stone suggests that this idea comes from Foxe, according to whose account Campeggio 'craftily shifted hym self out of the realme before the day came appointed for determination, leauing his suttle felow behynd hym to wey with the king in the meane time.'

III.ii.89–91. *Katharine no more Shall be call'd queen, etc.* Holinshed (1587), p. 929: 'It was also enacted the same time that queene Katharine should no more be called queene, but princesse Dowager, as the widow of prince Arthur.'

III.ii.114. *Duchess of Alençon.* This is an anachronism, since Margaret, Duchess of Alençon, was married to Henry d'Albret, King of Navarre, January, 1527.

III.ii.130. *A spleeny Lutheran.* According to Foxe, and the Elizabethan tradition, Anne Boleyn was an enthusiastic champion of the Protestant Reformation.

III.ii. S.d. *Enter King, reading of a schedule.* This incident never happened to Wolsey, but, as Steevens first pointed out, Holinshed chronicles one like it that did happen to the Bishop of Durham in 1523. After Wolsey's fall, however, an elaborate inventory of the contents of Hampton Court was made by the King's order.

III.ii.210–215. *My sovereign, etc.* The English here is careless, but the meaning

is obvious. My sovereign, I confess that your royal favors, which were showered upon me daily, have been more than my earnest efforts could requite; your favors went beyond any man's endeavors; my endeavors have always come short of my desires, but they have kept pace with my ability.

III.ii.233–235. Should, not from duty, but from a supreme love, belong to me above all men.

III.ii.238. *that am, have, and will be.* This, the reading of the Folio, has been the cause of more emendation than any line of the play. Yet in all probability the line is as the authors wrote it. The expression is elliptical with the forms of the verb 'labour' omitted. The passage in full means: 'I do profess, that for your highness' good I ever laboured more than for my own good: that I am labouring, have laboured, and will be labouring.'

III.ii.279. *Asher-house.* A curious error, because Asher (or Esher) House was the official residence of the Bishop of Winchester and at this time the Bishop of Winchester was Wolsey himself. Of course, the authors meant by 'Bishop of Winchester' Stephen Gardiner, but he did not become Bishop until 1531, after Wolsey's death. Wolsey did go to Asher, according to Holinshed.

III.ii.352. *Worse than the sacring bell.* In the Roman Catholic service, the sacring bell is rung at the elevation of the Host during the Mass, or before the Sacraments when they are carried through the streets. There is no historical truth to this particular accusation, although Wolsey's life was not chaste.

III.ii.370. *First, that, etc.* This list of accusations is taken from Holinshed.

III.ii.406. *Chattels.* Theobald's emendation for the Folio reading, *Castles,* taken from Holinshed's enumeration: 'to forfeit all his lands, tenements, goods, and cattels.'

III.ii.434. *he falls like Lucifer.* Isaiah 14. 12: 'How art thou fallen from heaven, O Lucifer, son of the morning!'

III.ii.523. *Thou fall'st a blessed martyr.* This line is prophecy, after the event. Cromwell, who from his suppression of the monasteries was considered to be a supporter of the Reformation, was executed in 1540.

III.ii.529–531. *Had I but serv'd my God, etc.* This, the most quoted passage in the play, is adapted from Holinshed (1587, p. 917): 'Master Kinston (quoth the cardinall) I see the matter how it is framed: but if I had serued God as diligentlie as I haue doone the king, he would not haue giuen me ouer in my greie haires.'

IV.i. The locality of this scene is inferred from the scene itself. The coronation took place June 1, 1533.

IV.i.5. *At our last encounter.* The two gentlemen last appeared in II.i., when Buckingham came forth after his trial. Historically twelve years separated these two events.

IV.i.19. *Of those that claim.* By long custom the right to perform the various services is vested in certain families. Holinshed (1587), p. 930:

> 'In the beginning of Maie, the king caused open proclamations to be made, that all men that claimed to doo anie seruice, or execute anie office at the solemne feast of the coronation by the waie of tenure, grant, or prescription, should put their grant three weeks after Easter in the Starre-chamber before Charles duke of Suffolke, for that time high steward of England, and the lord chancellor and other commissioners. The duke of Norfolke claimed to be erle mershall, and to exercise his office at that feast; the erle of Arundell claimed to be high butler, and to exercise the same; the erle of Oxford claimed to be chamberlain; the viscount Lisle claimed to be pantler; the lord Aburgauennie to be chief larderer; and the lord Braie claimed to be almoner, and sir Henrie Wiat knight claimed to be ewrer. All these noble personages desired their offices with their fees.
> 'Beside these, the maior of London claimed to serue the queene with a cup of gold, and a cup of assaie of the same, and that twelve citizens should attend on the cupboard, and the maior to have the cup and cup of assaie for his labor: which petition was allowed. The five ports claimed to beare a canopie ouer the queens head the daie of the coronation with foure guilt belles, and to haue the same for a reward, which to them was allowed. Diuerse other put in petie claimes which were not allowed, bicause they seemed onlie to be doone at the kings coronation.'

IV.i.31. *Dunstable.* The court was held at Dunstable Priory, in Bedfordshire, six miles from Ampthill Castle, a royal residence.

IV.i.48. *Kimbolton.* In the fall of 1535 Katharine at her own request had been removed to Kimbolton Castle in Huntingdonshire, then belonging to the Wingfield family. The Folio spells the word 'Kymmalton.'

IV.i. S.d. *The Order of the Coronation.* The details of this procession, which is the reason for the scene, are taken from Holinshed. But they are somewhat changed to suit the stage. Thus the Earl of Surrey carries the rod with the dove, instead of the Earl of Arundell, and the Duke of Norfolk the staff of marshalship, instead of Sir William Howard, probably, as Wright suggests, to avoid introduc-

ing two new characters. Possibly to avoid confusion in the personages, the Earl of Oxford, then High Chamberlain, who carries the crown on a cushion, is also omitted.

The 'Collars of Esses' were so called because the links in the chains were in the shape of the letter S.

The 'Cinque-ports,' Dover, Hastings, Romney, Hythe and Sandwich, have the privilege of sending representatives to carry the canopy at the coronation. Cf. note on IV.i.19.

IV.i.76 ff. The 'third Gentleman' is obviously introduced to give an account of the coronation to the audience. The details of the scene follow Holinshed, as usual.

IV.i.110. *York-place, where the feast is held.* After Wolsey's fall, York-place, the official residence of Wolsey as Archbishop of York, was annexed to the property of the Crown, and became the royal palace of Whitehall. It served as a royal residence until it burned in 1697. Only the banqueting hall remained. The coronation feast, however, was not held in Whitehall; as Holinshed correctly states, it was held in Westminster Hall. The confusion in the play may have arisen from the fact that in Holinshed there is also a long detailed account of the procession escorting the Queen from the Tower to Westminster. At the end of that, the first procession, he states that Anne 'withdrew herself with a few ladies to the Whitehall and so to her chamber.'

IV.i.120. *Stokesly and Gardiner.* John Stokesly was made Bishop of London in 1530; Stephen Gardiner, Bishop of Winchester in 1531. As Gardiner was considered an enemy of the Reformation, he was 'no great good lover' of Cranmer. Thus l. 125 prepares for the first scene in Act V.

IV.i.131. *Thomas Cromwell.* Cromwell was made a member of the Privy Council in 1531 and Master of the Jewel House in 1532.

IV.ii.7, 8. *Cardinal Wolsey, Was dead.* For dramatic reasons the death of Wolsey precedes that of Katharine by only a short interval. Historically, Wolsey died November 29, 1530, whereas this scene would have occurred in January, 1536.

IV.ii.11. *tell me how he died.* This account is condensed from Holinshed (1587), p. 917.

IV.ii.35. *So may he rest, etc.* Katharine's characterization of Wolsey is, point by point, taken from Holinshed (1587), p. 922. 'This cardinall (as you may perceive in this storie) was of a great stomach, for he compted himselfe equall with princes, & by craftie suggestion gat into his hands innumerable treasure: he forced little on simonie, and was not pittifull, and stood affectionate in his owne opinion: in open presence he would lie and saie untruth, and was double both in speach and meaning: he would promise much and performe little: he was vicious of his bodie, & gaue the clergie euill example. . . .'

IV.ii.55 ff. Griffith's commendation of Wolsey is equally taken from Holinshed (1587), p. 917: 'This cardinall (as Edward Campian in his historie of Ireland describeth him) was a man undoubtedly borne to honor: I thinke (saith he) some princes bastard, no butchers sonne, exceeding wise, faire spoken, high minded, full of reuenge, vitious of his bodie, loftie to his enemies, were they neuer so big, to those that accepted and sought his freendship woonderfull courteous, a ripe schooleman, thrall to affections, brought a bed with flatterie, insatiable to get, and more princelie in bestowing, as appeareth by his two colleges at Ipswich and Oxenford, the one ouerthrowne with his fall, the other unfinished, and yet as it lieth as an house for students, considering all the appurtenances incomparable thorough Christendome, whereof Henrie the eight is now called founder, bicause he let it stand . . . neuer happie till this his ouerthrow. Wherein he shewed such moderation, and ended so perfectlie, that the houre of his death did him more honor, than all the pompe of his life passed.'

IV.ii.57. *From his cradle.* Many editors prefer Theobald's punctuation, which puts a period after 'cradle' instead of after 'honour.'

IV.ii.66. *Ipswich, and Oxford.* The college founded by Wolsey at Ipswich remains only in a gatehouse; Christ Church at Oxford was founded by Wolsey and originally called Cardinal College.

IV.ii.125. *Capucius.* Holinshed (1587), p. 939: 'The princesse Dowager lieng at Kimbolton, fell into hir last sicknesse, whereof the king being aduertised, appointed the emperors ambassador that was legier here with him named Caputius, to go to visit hir, and to do his commendations to hir, and will hir to be of good comfort.'

V. The first four scenes of this act dramatize an anecdote told by Foxe in his *Acts and Monuments of Martyrs* (usually called briefly the *Book of Martyrs*) (1583), pp. 1866 and 1867. The fifth scene is taken from Holinshed (1587), pp. 934-935.

There is no attempt at chronology. Sir Thomas Lovell died in 1524; Elizabeth was born 1533; Cromwell was executed in 1540; and the scene with Cranmer must have been in 1544 or 1545.

V.ii. S.d. *Enter the King and Butts at a window above.* In the Folio there is no division between this scene and the one following. This was unfortunately introduced by White to conform to our modern stage conventions. The King and Butts appeared upon the gallery across the back of the Elizabethan stage. Then, with them in full view of the audience but out of the sight of the actors upon the stage, the council assembled below.

V.iii.35-37. Doubtless as allusion to the Anabaptist rising in Münster under John of Leyden, 1534-1535.

V.iii.99. *This is too much.* The Folio gives all the speeches in this scene, here assigned to the Lord Chancellor, to the Lord Chamberlain. As was pointed out by Capell, they belong rather to the Lord Chancellor because he was the presiding officer. The error was probably due to a misreading of the abbreviation Chan. into Cham. Some modern editors, however, assign one of the seven speeches to the Lord Chamberlain, since otherwise he would be silent.

V.iii.159. *his place.* This is the reading of the Folio. Paraphrased, it means: now let the proudest deny that thou art his equal, that his position becomes thee. Some modern editors, however, follow Rowe's emendation, 'this place.'

V.iv.2. *Parish-garden.* The corrupt pronunciation for Paris-garden, a place of unruly entertainment near the site of the Globe Theatre.

V.iv.13. *May-day morning.* On the first of May it was customary to go out early into the fields to gather flowers and dew, which was considered good for the complexion.

V.iv.21. *I am not Samson, etc.* The allusion to the proverbial strength of Samson as told in the Old Testament story is obvious. Sir Guy of Warwick is the hero of the medieval romance of the same name; one of his adventures is the killing of the giant Colbrand.

V.iv.26. *for a cow.* A proverbial expression, still in use, it is said.

V.iv.32. *Moorfields.* The exercising ground of the London militia.

V.iv.33. *strange Indian.* It was the Jacobean custom to exhibit Indians, much as we do Hottentots. If the date of exhibition of such an Indian could be ascertained, it would be a clue to the troubled question of the date of the play. Compare *The Tempest*, II.ii.28-34.

V.iv.37. *The spoons will be the bigger.* Spoons were favorite gifts at christenings. See V.iii.195.

V.iv.47. *Clubs.* 'Clubs' was the rallying cry of the London apprentices.

V.iv.56, 57. *Tribulation of Tower-hill, or the Limbs of Limehouse.* These are fanciful names, alluding to unruly districts of London.

V.iv.60. *running banquet.* The two beadles (officers of the law) will chase them, whipping them, after the prison term of three days has expired.

V.v. Elizabeth was christened September 10, 1533.

THE TEXT OF THE PRESENT EDITION

The text of the present volume is based, by permission of the Oxford University Press, upon that of the Oxford Shakespeare, edited by the late W. J. Craig. Craig's text has been carefully collated with the Shakespeare Folio of 1623, and the following deviations have been introduced:

1. The stage directions of the Folio have been restored. Necessary words and directions, omitted by the Folio, are added within square brackets.

2. Spelling has been normalized to accord with modern English practice; e.g., Blackfriars, Sandys, everywhere, warlike, vainglory, reverend, sovereign (instead of Black-Friars, Sands, every where, war-like, vain-glory, rev'rend, sov'reign). The punctuation has been largely revised, and a number of old-fashioned Folio forms restored; e.g., th' effects, t' aspire, y' are (you're), burthen (burden).

3. The following changes of text have been introduced, usually in accordance with Folio authority. The readings of the present edition precede the colon, while Craig's readings follow it.

> I.i.49–52 All was royal . . . his full function (assigned to Buckingham F): (assigned to Norfolk)
> 55 As you guess (assigned to Norfolk F): (assigned to Buck.)
> 73 a' (O F): he
> 90 upon,—: upon;
> 92 in,—: in
> 143 venom'd-mouth'd F: venom-mouth'd
> 172 till 't F: till it
> ii.35 longing F: 'longing
> 65 compels F: compel
> 165, 166 Henton F: Hopkins
> 217 Bulmer: Blumer F
> iii.74 h'as (Ha's F): he has

iv.93 'em F: them

111 Ye F: You

II.i. S.d. (Follows line 69 in Craig)

125 'em F: them

ii.5 'em F: them

66 has (ha's F): hath

72 Who's F: Who is

114 mine F: my

123 unpartial F: impartial

iii.115 moe (mo F): more

iv.137 Gent. Ush. F: Grif.

198 many-maz'd: many maz'd F

233 I then F: Then I

241 drives F: drive

III.i.74 in a F: in

129, 130 you F: ye

133 h'as (ha's F): he has

176 'em F: them

ii.39 letters F: letter

41 How that F: That

103 in's F: in his

133 An F: A

282 lords F: lord

469 him F: 'em

516 by it F: by 't

IV.i.94 before 'em F: before them

ii.56 an humble F: a humble

57 honour. From F: honour from

V.i.14 and F: an

204 an F: a

iii.81 y' are F: you are

131 Chan.: Cham. F

159 his F: this

207 he's F: he is

iv.2 Parish-garden (Parish Garden F): Paris-garden

5 ye F: you

76 y' are F: ye' re

v.82 H'as ('Has F): He has

The Tragedy of Titus Andronicus

Edited by
A. M. WITHERSPOON

Dramatis Personae

SATURNINUS, *Son to the late Emperor of Rome, and afterwards declared Emperor*

BASSIANUS, *Brother to Saturninus, in love with Lavinia*

TITUS ANDRONICUS, *a Roman, General against the Goths*

MARCUS ANDRONICUS, *Tribune of the People, and Brother to Titus*

LUCIUS
QUINTUS
MARTIUS   } *Sons to Titus Andronicus*
MUTIUS

YOUNG LUCIUS, *a Boy, Son to Lucius*

PUBLIUS, *Son to Marcus Andronicus*

SEMPRONIUS
CAIUS   } *Kinsmen to Titus*
VALENTINE

AEMILIUS, *a noble Roman*

ALARBUS
DEMETRIUS } *Sons to Tamora*
CHIRON

AARON, *a Moor, beloved by Tamora*

A CLOWN

TAMORA, *Queen of the Goths*

LAVINIA, *Daughter to Titus Andronicus*

A NURSE, AND A BLACK CHILD

SENATORS, TRIBUNES, OFFICERS, SOLDIERS, AND ATTENDANTS

SCENE—*Rome, and the Country near it.*

The Tragedy of Titus Andronicus

INTRODUCTION

SOURCES OF THE PLAY

No single and direct source of the story of *Titus Andronicus* has ever been discovered. It is probable that the play as we have it was based on an older play, but there is no conclusive evidence of the existence of any version, English or foreign, prior to the text that we now have. The plot seems, however, to combine many themes and incidents found in other forms of literature. The story proper is apparently without any historical basis, and is curiously anachronistic in arrangement. A Roman emperor and a tribune are made contemporary; the emperor is engaged, as no Roman emperor ever was, in warring upon the Goths; and the Rome in which the scene is laid is, according to Aaron the Moor, the seat of 'Popish ceremonies.' As for the surname, Andronicus, no Roman emperor ever bore it, although there was a Byzantine emperor, Andronicus Comnenus, of the twelfth century A.D., and it is not without significance that he is represented by Nicetas Choniata as having shot arrows with certain devices attached in the siege of Prusa. It may be worth noting, too, that after the removal of the empire to Byzantium in the fourth century there were wars with the Goths, and thus a remote historical background for some of the incidents of the play may be postulated. Finally, the similarity of the name Tamora to that of Tomyris, the vengeful queen of the Getæ, has been pointed out.

Baildon (Arden ed.) suggests an Oriental origin for the story, in view of its peculiar cruelty and lavish bloodshed, and the presence in it of those two Bashibazouks, Chiron and Demetrius. But if the story came from the Orient, it has undergone many modifications in transit.

The different threads of the plot of *Titus Andronicus* bear striking resemblance to other well-known themes and legends. The author frequently likens Lavinia's fate to that of Philomela, which Ovid's *Metamorphoses* had made known to England. The cruelty and villainy of Aaron suggest at once the deeds of Barabas and Ithamore in Marlowe's *Jew of Malta*. There is, furthermore, in Evans's *Old Ballads* and in the *Roxburghe Ballads,* a poem of about 1570 entitled, *'A Lamentable Ballad of the Tragical End of a Gallant Lord and of his Beautiful Lady, with the untimely death of their children, wickedly performed by a heathen Blackamore, their servant: The like seldom heard before.'* The theme of the 'heathen blackamore' was very popular. Professor Koeppel (in *Englische Studien*, 16. 370) points out several other versions of it: a Latin version by Pontano, an adaptation by Bandello in the twenty-first novel of his third book, a French paraphrase by Belleforest in the second volume of his *Histoires Tragiques*. And there are other versions in other languages.

When *Titus Andronicus* was entered on the Stationers' Register on February 6, 1593-4, there was entered also 'by warrant from Mr. Woodcock, the ballad thereof.' It is now generally agreed that this ballad is the same as that reprinted in Percy's *Reliques,* entitled *Titus Andronicus's Complaint,* and that it is not a source of the play but instead is based on the play. It cannot, according to Chappell, be earlier, in its extant form, than 1600.

In connection with the question of the sources of the play, several other facts now enter. Henslowe in his Diary records a play, 'tittus & vespacia' (which he calls elsewhere 'tittus') as having been performed by Strange's men on April 11, 1592, and frequently thereafter. No copy of this play now exists. There is, furthermore, a volume, *Englische Comedien und Tragedien,* 1620, which comprises the repertory of a group of English comedians acting in Germany in the early seventeenth century, and which contains a play entitled *Eine sehr Klägliche Tragœdia von Tito Andronico und der hoffertigen Kayserin.*[1] In this play Titus's son is called Vespasianus instead of Lucius. It has been assumed, therefore, in some quarters that Henslowe's 'tittus & vespacia' was the original of the German play and at the same time an earlier version of our English *Titus Andronicus.*[2] But such assumptions are more or less gratuitous. There may have been an earlier play than our *Titus Andronicus* on the same subject. But in all probability the 'tittus & vespacia' of Henslowe had nothing to do with the play recorded elsewhere by him as 'titus & ondronicus' (our *Titus Andronicus*), but dealt instead with the heroic theme of the destruction of Jerusalem by Titus Vespasian, the second of the Flavian emperors, and the hero of later tragedies by Corneille and Racine. The German play is quite certainly a translation, albeit a very free one, of our *Titus Andronicus.* The fact that Titus's son, Lucius, is given the name Vespasian in the German play can be easily explained, as Mr. R. Crompton Rhodes points out (*Times Literary Supplement,* May 22, 1924): Lucius is the son of Titus and an emperor of Rome, and the mental association of his name with Vespasian is explicable. The other changes of name in the German play have similarly associative reasons. Aaron the Moor becomes Morion, and Lavinia becomes Andronica.

About a quarter of a century ago there were numerous lengthy and learned discussions as to the existence of earlier versions and editions of *Titus Andronicus,* and the interrelations of the English, German, and Dutch versions of plays on similar themes. They were occasioned largely by the fact that until 1904 no copy of *Titus Andronicus* earlier than the Quarto of 1600 was known, and editors and commentators were much exercised to explain the identity of the 'titus & ondronicus' mentioned in Henslowe's

---

1 Reprinted in Cohn's *Shakespeare in Germany,* 1865, pp. 156-235.

2 There are extant also a Dutch play, *Aran en Titus,* by Jan Vos, printed first in 1642, and a program of a German play acted at Linz in 1699 which agrees substantially with the Dutch play. The connections and relations between these two plays, and the whole question of the relationship of the Shakespearean *Titus Andronicus* to continental plays on similar themes, is discussed at length by H. de W. Fuller and G. P. Baker in *Pub. Mod. Lang. Assn.,* 16. 1-76, 1901.

Diary under the date of January 23, 1594. Fortunately in 1904 a copy of the 1594 Quarto, the first edition of the play, came to light, settling many vexatious questions. It is now generally conceded that this 1594 edition of *Titus Andronicus* is the play recorded in Henslowe's Diary as 'titus & ondronicus' and that it is also identical with the 'Titus and Andronicus' and 'Tytus Andronicus' of the Stationers' Register.

The History of the Play

The earliest known mention of a work with the title of *Titus Andronicus* is contained in an entry in the Stationers' Register on February 6, 1593-4: 'John Danter. A booke entitled A noble Roman historye of Tytus Andronicus.' Philip Henslowe's Diary, under the dates of January 23 and 28, and February 6 of the same year, records a new play, 'titus & ondronicus,' as having been acted by 'the earle of susex his men.' Two later entries, made on June 5 and June 12, 1594, note the performance of a play called 'andronicous' by the Lord Admiral's and the Lord Chamberlain's men. Finally, in this same year, there was printed at London a quarto edition[3] of the play now known as *Titus Andronicus*, bearing the following title-page: 'The Most Lamentable Romaine Tragedie of Titus Andronicus: As it was Plaide by the Right Honourable the Earle of Darbie, Earle of Pembrooke, and Earle of Sussex their Servants. . . . London, Printed by Iohn Danter . . . 1594.'

A second quarto, based on the 1594 edition, was published in 1600, and contains only slight changes in the text. One passage of six lines is omitted from the first scene of the 1600 edition, and another of five lines is omitted from the last scene of the play (cf. notes on I.i.35 and V.iii.166), while the last four lines of the 1600 edition are not found in the First Quarto. On the title-page of the Second Quarto the name of the Lord Chamberlain's company is added to those of the three companies mentioned on the title-page of the First Quarto.

A third quarto, of which the 1600 edition was the original, was printed in 1611. Fourteen copies of the Third Quarto are known, one of which is in the Elizabethan Club at Yale.

The text of the First Folio of 1623 was printed from the Third Quarto with MS. additions, and contains one scene (III. ii.) which does not appear in any of the Quartos.

The history of Titus and Aaron on the stage falls into two general divisions: the period of about a quarter of a century after its composition until the death of Shakespeare, and the three centuries since that time. During the first three decades of its existence, *Titus* was one of the most popular of all the plays attributed to Shakespeare; for the last three hundred years it has had almost the scantiest stage-history of them all. The First Quarto bears the motto, *Aut nunc aut nunquam*, and never was a more appropriate motto affixed to a play. There was only one period in the history of the English stage when *Titus Andronicus* ever could have been popular, and popular it was then beyond all precedent.

The title-page of the Third Quarto assures us that the trag-

edy had 'sundry times beene plaide by the Kings Majesties Servants,' and from the other title-pages and Henslowe's Diary we learn that three different companies continued to play it, two of which changed their names at two different periods of their career; but under whatever name or sovereign, they continued to play *Titus*. The play is entered in Henslowe's Diary no less than fifteen times, if we may assume that all the Titus and Andronicus plays which he records are identical. Numerous other contemporary allusions also attest its popularity. The events with which the first act of *Titus* concerns itself were familiar enough to furnish a simile for the author of the play, *A Merry Knack to Know a Knave*, which was published anonymously in 1594:

> '*Osrick. My gracious lord, as welcome shall you be,*
> *To me, my daughter, and my son-in-law,*
> *As Titus was unto the Roman senators,*
> *When he had made a conquest on the Goths;*
> *That, in requital of his service done,*
> *Did offer him the imperial diadem.*
> *As they in Titus, we in your grace, still find*
> *The perfect figure of a princely mind.*[4]

In 1614, twenty years after the First Quarto, Ben Jonson takes occasion in the Induction to his *Bartholomew Fair* to censure those (of whom there were presumably a goodly number) who still 'swear that Jeronimo or Andronicus are the best plays yet.' Whether Jonson is referring to our *Titus Andronicus* or not, the vogue of *Titus* would thus seem to have passed by this time with men of Jonson's tastes, but the contemptuous tone of his statement testifies that there were those to whom such blood-and-thunder plays still appealed. The *Shakspere Allusion-Book* records other references to the play from time to time. At the middle of the century strands of its gory locks were still in evidence. In 1648 an anonymous writer, J. S., issued a compilation of 'wise and learned sentences and phrases' from favorite authors under the title, *Wit's Labyrinth*. Of the half-dozen or more Shakespearean plays from which the compiler culled his phrases, only *Titus Andronicus* is honored by having as many as three sentences quoted.

As the century wore on, however, the performances of Titus grew fewer and fewer. In 1678, 'about the time of the Popishplot,' says Gerard Langbaine, the play was 'revived' and refurbished to suit the tastes and exigencies of the stage, and produced by Edward Ravenscroft. This revised version of the tragedy was published in 1687 with the following title: *Titus Andronicus or the Rape of Lavinia. Acted at the Theatre Royall, A Tragedy Alter'd from Mr. Shakespear's Works*. In his introduction, Ravenscroft speaks of the success which had *matched* the labor of revising the play, a process which left *Titus* with 'the language not only refin'd, but many scenes entirely new: besides most of the principal characters heighten'd and the plot much encreas'd.' It is instructive to see in what manner the characters were 'heightened.' As if the original play were not horrible enough, Ravenscroft adds infanticide to Tamora's crimes, and has Aaron offer to eat his dead child's body. The Moor is tortured and finally burned to death on the stage.

Ravenscroft's revision was still the accepted version at the close of the century, according to the list of Shakespeare's plays given by Charles Gildon in 1698 in his continuation of Langbaine's

---

3 The 1594 Quarto of *Titus* was recorded by Gerard Langbaine in 1691 in the list of Shakespeare's plays in his *Account of the English Dramatick Poets*, but no copy of the edition seems to have been known during the next two hundred years, and Langbaine's testimony was generally discredited. At last, in 1904, a copy was discovered in Lund, Sweden, vindicating Langbaine, and settling various disputes.

4 Dodsley's *Old English Plays*, ed. Hazlitt, 1874, 6. 572.

work, previously mentioned. After the turn of the century we first hear definitely of a performance of *Titus* in 1717. There were at least three performances, on August 13, 20, and 23, of that year, at Drury Lane. The advertisement in the *Daily Courant* of the 20th states that the play had been given 'but twice these fifteen years.' The most interesting fact recorded in the notice is that the part of Aaron was taken by the celebrated James Quin, who repeated the performance again in 1720 and 1721, at Lincoln's Inn Fields. The version of Ravenscroft still obtained, the play being announced in all cases as 'Titus Andronicus with the Rape of Lavinia, alter'd from Shakspeare.'

A century and a quarter elapsed before Titus and Aaron again walked the boards. Another much-altered version of the text was used, prepared for the occasion by C. A. Somerset, the author of *Shakespeare's Early Days,* a popular work of the time. The play was performed at the Britannia Theatre in London, the opening performance taking place on March 15, 1852. In this new version, the tragedy was given intermittently for some five years, with performances both in London and Dublin. The rôle of Aaron was taken by the famous negro tragedian, Ira Aldridge, 'the African Roscius.' Into the version employed by Aldridge there was incorporated a scene from a play called *Zaraffa, the Slave King,* which had been written especially for Aldridge.

It is significant with regard to the tastes of the audiences of the times that both in 1717 and in 1852 the producers of *Titus* felt it necessary to follow the performance of the tragedy with a farce. In 1717, 'by the desire of some Persons of Quality,' so the stage-bill informs us, Farquhar's one-act farce, *The Stage-Coach,* was added. In 1852 Aldridge offered a farce entitled 'Mummy' and some negro songs which he had brought from his native Maryland.

After 1857 it was sixty-six years before any producer had the desire or the hardihood to present the lamentable Roman tragedy. Under the management of Miss Lilian Baylis, the entire cycle of Shakespeare's plays was given between 1914 and 1924 at the Old Vic Theatre on the Surrey side of the Thames, an achievement which had not been accomplished since the days of Shakespeare. *Titus Andronicus* was produced here by Mr. Robert Atkins on October 8, 1923, the thirty-fifth of the cycle of Shakespeare's thirty-seven plays. That *Titus* should have been included in the repertory is due, of course, not to any inherent virtues in the play itself, but to Miss Baylis's ambition to make the Shakespearean wheel, for once at least, come full circle. A large audience was drawn to the Old Vic through curiosity, and the comments of the spectators and the newspapers were at one in declaring the play impossibly bad. The *Times* mentioned among the qualities which make it tolerable at all the swiftness and firmness of the telling, and the extraordinary dexterity with which the plot moves from death to death. 'It could never have appealed to the cultured classes,' said the *Morning Post,* 'but had all the elements of popular success. . . . It is very repulsive, but workmanlike.' The text used was the original version of the First Folio, with one noteworthy and very effective emendation: a laughing-scene for Aaron was introduced in Act III just before his exit, after he has cut off Titus's hand. The Moor's satanic laughter is not specifically referred to in the text, but is justified by his remarks. (Cf. V.i.113-115.) A very fine stage-setting by Hubert Hine was used in the production at the Old Vic.

Titus has been produced only once in America. It was performed by the Yale Chapter of the Fraternity of Alpha Delta Phi,

in New Haven, on April 14 and 15, 1924, under the direction of Mr. E. M. Woolley and Professor J. M. Berdan. The production was the annual performance of a series of Elizabethan plays, given in the Elizabethan manner, with the original text.

The Prinzregententheater in Munich was the scene of the latest performance of *Titus,* on October 15, 1924. The German version used was the translation of Nicolaus Delius, and very elaborate scenery by Eugen Keller was employed.

Titus Andronicus is the only play of the Shakespearean canon that has not been performed at the Shakespeare Memorial Theatre in Stratford.

THE AUTHORSHIP OF THE PLAY

The external evidence for the Shakespearean authorship of *Titus Andronicus* rests on its inclusion in the Folio of 1623 by Heminges and Condell, friends and fellow actors of Shakespeare, and its mention by Francis Meres in a list of Shakespeare's plays in his *Palladis Tamia* in 1598, four years after the appearance of the First Quarto. It is again listed as Shakespeare's by Gerard Langbaine[5] in 1691. Such evidence is not easily contestable, especially in view of the close connection between Shakespeare and the editors of the Folio, and the fact that Meres seems to have been sufficiently familiar with Shakespeare to have known of his privately circulated sonnets some eleven years before they were first printed. But in spite of these facts, the play, largely because of its repulsive theme, the crudeness of workmanship displayed throughout, the un-Shakespearean quality of many of its lines, and the presence in the text of numerous traces of the work of other authors, has been a storm-centre in Shakespearean criticism for over two centuries, and to-day it finds itself rejected, either partially or wholly, by far the greater number of editors and critics.

The first doubt as to Shakespeare's authorship of which we have any record is contained in the preface to Edward Ravenscroft's revision of the play in 1687, wherein he says: 'I have been told by some anciently conversant with the stage that it was not originally his, but brought by a private author to be acted, and he only gave some master-touches to one or two of the principal parts or characters; this I am apt to believe, because 't is the most incorrect and indigested piece in all his works. It seems rather a heap of rubbish than a structure.'

The integrity of Ravenscroft is discredited by Langbaine, who intimates that Ravenscroft was merely trying to belittle Shakespeare in order to exalt himself. He quotes part of the prologue which Ravenscroft originally prefixed to his revision of *Titus* in 1678, in which he called the play Shakespeare's and produced it as such, saying of his own part in it that he had

'but winnow'd Shakespeare's corn,
So far he was from robbing him of 's treasure,
That he did add his own, to make full measure.'

Ravenscroft's statement is, however, accepted in substance by the majority of critics since his day.

External evidence against Shakespeare's authorship of *Titus* has been found in the absence of his name from all three Quartos

---

5 In the work referred to in the History of the Play.

of the play. The conclusiveness of this evidence is impaired, however, by the fact that the poet's name does not appear on any of the Quartos of *Henry V,* or on any of the first three Quartos of *Romeo and Juliet.*

Eighteenth-century critics and editors, with the exception of Capell, denied the Shakespearean authorship of the play. Theobald thought Shakespeare might have added 'a few fine touches' to the play. Johnson, Farmer, and Steevens, reject the Shakespearean theory entirely. Johnson says of it: 'All the editors and critics agree in supposing this play spurious. I see no reason for differing from them; for the colour of the style is wholly different from that of the other plays, and there is an attempt at regular versification, and artificial closes, not always inelegant, yet seldom pleasing. The barbarity of the spectacles and the general massacre, which are here exhibited, can scarcely be conceived tolerable to any audience, yet we are told by Jonson that they were not only borne but praised. That Shakespeare wrote any part of it, though Theobald declares it *incontestable,* I see no reason for believing. . . . I do not find Shakespeare's touches very discernible.' Malone thought that Shakespeare might have written a few lines in the play, or perhaps have given some assistance to the author in revising it.

In the nineteenth century, critics were more widely divided in their opinions. Seymour, Drake, Singer, the Coleridges, Hallam, Dyce, Fleay, and others denied that Shakespeare had any part in its composition. Furnivall (Introduction to *Leopold Shakspere*), Ingleby (*Shakespeare: The Man and the Book*), Dowden (*Shakspere: His Mind and Art*), Herford (Introduction to *Eversley Shakespeare*), Hudson, and Rolfe, agreed that very little of the play could have been written by Shakespeare. On the other hand, a group of critics of whom we may name Collier (*Annals of the Stage,* 1831), Verplanck (*Illustrated Shakespeare,* 1847), Knight (*Pictorial Shakespeare,* 1867), Appleton Morgan (*Bankside Shakespeare,* 1890), and Crawford ('The Date and Authenticity of "Titus Andronicus,"' *Shakespeare Jahrbuch,* 1900), considered the play the work of Shakespeare, his earliest and crudest composition, produced when he was still under the influence of his predecessors. The latter view was concurred in almost unanimously by the German school: Schlegel, Delius, Bodenstedt, Franz Horn, Ulrici, Kurz, Sarrazin, Brandl, Creizenach, and Schröer. Gervinus, as in other matters of Shakespearean criticism, dissented from the opinion of his countrymen, and sided with the British school which denied Shakespeare's authorship of *Titus.*

The twentieth century brought with it the discovery of the First Quarto of *Titus,* and consequent fresh and lengthy discussions as to its authorship. There was a revival in certain quarters of the tendency to consider the play a work of Shakespeare's earlier days, and among the adherents of this opinion were Collins, Boas, Saintsbury, McCallum, and Raleigh. Courthope, in the appendix, 'On the Authenticity of Some of the Early Plays Assigned to Shakespeare, and their Relationship to the Development of his Dramatic Genius,' to his *History of English Poetry,* vol. iv, 1903, espouses the theory of the Shakespearean authorship of *Titus.* His formal conclusion is 'That there are no sufficient internal reasons to warrant us in resisting the testimony of the folio of 1623 that *Titus Andronicus* and *King Henry VI.* are the work of Shakespeare.' Greg, in his edition of Henslowe's Diary (II. 161), gives his opinion of the circumstances of Shakespeare's connection with *Titus:* 'I fail to discover any clear internal evidence of Shakespeare having touched the play at all, though there are a few lines whose Shakespearian authorship I do not think

impossible. . . . The Chamberlain's men, following their practice in the case of the other Pembroke's plays, *Hamlet* and the *Taming of a Shrew,* caused *Titus* to be worked over by a young member of their company named William Shakespeare. Thus revised the piece achieved sufficient success to call for notice by Francis Meres in 1598, and thenceforth passed as one of the "works" of the favourite playwright-actor. This MS. perished in the fire at the Globe in 1613. Wishing to replace their prompt copy the King's men procured a copy of the printed edition (1611), a device to which they certainly resorted in other cases too. In this they made certain alterations in the stage directions, and in doing so noticed the absence of one scene at least (III.ii.) which they were in the habit of acting and which had proved popular. This the actors were able to reconstruct from memory, and a manuscript insertion of some 85 lines was made in the quarto. Ten years later this doctored prompt copy was sent to press for the text of the collected folio.'

So far as there may be said to be a prevailing theory among American students, it is that Shakespeare is the reviser, to some extent, of an older play. But as to the author or authors of the original work, and as to the nature and extent of the revision, there is considerable latitude of opinion. Among American students of the play there are to be mentioned Schelling, Fuller, Baker, Wendell, Stoll, H. D. Gray, and Parrott. J. Q. Adams, in his *Life of Shakespeare,* 1923 (p. 134), pictures Shakespeare shortly after the death of Marlowe 'exercising his skill in touching up several of the old stock pieces belonging to the company, plays, no doubt, in which he himself had been called upon to act. Perhaps one of these was *Titus Andronicus,* mainly, if not entirely, by George Peele. . . . Shakespeare could hardly have had a genuine artistic interest in the bloody *Titus,* but his business shrewdness showed him the opportunity of turning it into a great money-maker for his company.'

The two lengthiest recent discussions of the authorship of the play are by H. B. Baildon (*Arden Shakespeare,* 1904), who believes the play to be substantially and essentially the work of Shakespeare, and J. M. Robertson, whose elaborate study, *Did Shakespeare Write 'Titus Andronicus'?,* 1905, revised in 1924 as *An Introduction to the Study of the Shakespeare Canon, Proceeding on the Problem of 'Titus Andronicus,'* rejects *in toto* the theory that the play is the work of Shakespeare.

The arguments concerning the Shakespearean authorship of *Titus* turn largely on the consideration of questions of the metrical construction, versification, vocabulary, characters, theme, and general style of the play. Few hard and fast conclusions can be drawn from all the evidence produced, however, as there is little agreement among critics as to its proper interpretation. Studies of the metre of the play, with special attention to the number of double and triple endings, riming lines, and the quality of the blank verse employed in it, have been made in endeavors to throw light on the question of authorship, but nothing definitely conclusive has come of it, so varied are the constructions placed upon the data obtained. Again, the elaborate investigations of the style of the play and the innumerable similarities of idea and expression between *Titus* and other Elizabethan plays have resulted in the discovery of much valuable information as to the wholesale borrowings of the writers of the time, but the findings are construed in widely different ways. What seems to one critic or school convincing evidence of Shakespearean workmanship, is often quite as convincing to another that Shakespeare had nothing to do with the play. Flügel, for instance, thought Aaron as

un-Shakespearean as could be, whereas Saintsbury, Collins, Parrott, and others have found him genuinely Shakespearean. Schröer and Parrott, again, consider the classical allusions quite in Shakespeare's manner; but, says Robertson, who finds the classical allusions thoroughly pre-Shakespearean, 'what is obviously non-Shakespearean is the classicism of the play.' Not only are the critics in disagreement with one another, but they are not consistent with themselves. Schröer, whose study, *Über Titus Andronicus*, 1891, is the most comprehensive of the German arguments advocating Shakespeare's authorship of the play, contends, as Robertson notes, that 'verbal coincidence between two poems speaks rather against than for identity of authorship—' (p. 73), and yet some fifty-two pages later he argues that Aaron's praise of blackness (IV.ii.74, 102) is a favorite idea with Shakespeare, because we have it again in *Love's Labour's Lost* (V.ii.20, 41).

The attempts at choosing what in the play is genuinely Shakespearean, as distinguished from what may be considered the work of his supposed collaborators, have not met with any greater success. Almost every editor who accepts in part the Shakespearean hypothesis has his favorite list of selections which he believes authentic. Such passages consist in most cases of the more lyrical sections, and include, of course, all the better lines of the tragedy. But there is a remarkable disagreement among them, and such selections, if put together properly, would constitute almost the whole of the play. Coleridge, from a poet's point of view, considered as worthy of Shakespeare only some forty lines from the 'Revenge' scene (V.ii.21-60), whereas Swinburne, from another poet's point of view, disregarded all but the 'Clown' scene (IV.iii.). The one scene on which there has been more general agreement, perhaps, than on any other, is the second scene of Act III, which appeared for the first time in the Folio, and therefore attracts attention to itself as having perhaps come from Shakespeare's own copy or his MSS. The whole process of picking and choosing must be considered futile, however, and especially since half of the passages tagged as certainly Shakespearean have been shown to be similar to, or identical with, passages in Peele, Greene, Marlowe, and others.

Nor do we find any grounds for more definite conclusions when we examine the passages in *Titus* which are most strikingly suggestive of lines and scenes in Shakespeare's authenticated works. The theme of *Lucrece* is similar to that of the plot in which Lavinia figures, but we cannot therefore conclude that Shakespeare is necessarily the author of *Titus* because he is the author of *Lucrece*. The poem may, indeed, have been suggested by the play, or the play by the poem, but identity of authorship is no more requisite in such a supposition than it is if we suppose the plot of Shylock to have been suggested by Marlowe's *Jew of Malta*. It must be admitted that Aaron's lines (IV.ii.104, 105),

> 'For all the water in the ocean
> Can never turn the swan's black legs to white,'

suggest those of *Richard II* (III.ii.54, 55),

> 'Not all the water in the rough rude sea
> Can wash the balm off from an anointed king,'

and still further the cry of Lady Macbeth (*Macbeth*, II.ii.60, 61),

> 'Will all great Neptune's ocean wash this blood
> Clean from my hand?'

But we are not justified in concluding that the author of the two later passages is necessarily the author of the first. Shakespeare was as imitative as he was repetitive, even if we assume that he had Aaron's lines in mind when he was composing the two later passages.

There is a clear verbal parallel between lines in Tamora's speech (II.iii.17-19),

> 'And, whilst the babbling echo mocks the hounds,
> Replying shrilly to the well-tun'd horns,
> As if a double hunt were heard at once, . . .'

and two lines (695, 696) of *Venus and Adonis*,

> 'Thus do they [the hounds] spend their mouths:
> Echo replies
> As if another chase were in the skies.'

As Parrott points out,[6] these parallels, and others which he gives, are unmistakable, and he accordingly assigns the paralleled lines and Tamora's speech to Shakespeare; but, as Robertson observes, it does not follow necessarily that Shakespeare must himself have written Tamora's speech. Any of his contemporaries would have copied such a fine passage without scruple if he had wished to do so.

The studies of the characters of the play in relation to those of others of Shakespeare's plays have been no more conclusive in their results. Aaron, for example, is quite generally considered, by all who uphold Shakespeare's intimate connection with the play, as a first draft and prototype of Shylock, Iago, Richard III, Edmund, and most of Shakespeare's villains. It is by external and superficial implications, however, rather than by inherent likenesses that he is connected with them. He is a Moor, and the tragedy of *Othello the Moor* is at once suggested, wherein, as it happens, there is Iago, a villain in the popular sense, and certain similarities in the characters of Iago and Aaron begin to appear. But fundamentally and essentially Aaron and Iago are not of the same stripe. Aaron is pre-Shakespearean rather than Shakespearean, and belongs to the tribe of Tamburlaine, Barabas, Ithamore, Eleazar, and Peele's Moor, Muly Muhamet, rather than to that of Iago. His melodramatic rant and braggadocio, and his comic-opera frenzy for evil-doing, form a striking contrast to the tragically sinister and motiveless malignity of Iago. As for his relation to Shylock, is not the apparent connection between them based subconsciously on the circumstance of their being members respectively of races alike alien and despised from the Elizabethan point of view? Similarities and parallels between Tamora, and the Margaret of the *Henry VI* trilogy (who is fundamentally non-Shakespearean), on the one hand, and Lady Macbeth on the other, seem equally superficial. The three have little in common but their imperiousness. The treatment of the character of Titus certainly does not suggest Shakespeare's handling of the characters of Lear, Othello, and Macbeth. Nor does young Lucius seem to have more than his tender years in common with Prince Arthur and the young princes of *Richard III*. There is, however, one character, the Clown, in *Titus*, who is quite in the manner and tradition of Shakespeare, but even he is not distinctively and exclusively Shakespearean. Elizabethan and Tudor drama have clowns and to spare, and the clown of *Titus* is not more like the clowns of Shakespeare than he is like those of his contemporaries. But he is the one typically Shakespearean thing in the entire play, and he may very well be conceded to Shakespeare as being of a piece with Launce, Launcelot Gobbo, and Elbow, and as

---

6 'Shakespeare's Revision of "Titus Andronicus,"' *Mod. Lang. Rev.*, xiv. 27, 28.

constituting one of the 'master-touches' which Ravenscroft represents Shakespeare as imparting to the play.

Previous study of characters, metre, phrasing, and general stylistic qualities cannot, therefore, be said to have produced any conclusive or convincing reasons for considering *Titus* Shakespeare's. The work of critics, ranging from the early observations of Steevens and Malone down to the exhaustive researches of Robertson, have proved that the play is a collection of materials drawn from a common stock used by all Elizabethan dramatists, and that, in particular, it is a tissue of words, phrases, and sentiments taken largely from Peele, Greene, Kyd, Marlowe, and Lodge. The author, or authors, of *Titus Andronicus,* whoever they were, simply followed the common habit of turning to other authors and similar works: what they thought they might require, they went and took to furnish out a lamentable Roman tragedy.

Close examination of the text of *Titus,* therefore, reveals no more reason for including it in the canon of Shakespeare's plays than could be found for including many of those pre-Shakespearean plays with which it is organically and spiritually connected—the *Spanish Tragedy, Lust's Dominion, Selimus,* the *Battle of Alcazar,* the *Troublesome Reign,* the *Chronicle History of King Leir,* and others.

But it is not merely or chiefly the negative argument—that *Titus* is lacking in distinctive and convincing Shakespearean characteristics—that justifies the rejection of the play as Shakespeare's, but the more fundamental and positive fact that it contains much that is certainly not Shakespeare's and that is as certainly the work of other Elizabethans. That the version of the play which was printed in the 1594 Quarto could not have been completed earlier than the middle of the year 1593 is proved by the fact that it copies directly or indirectly many phrases and passages of Peele's *Honour of the Garter,* which was written to celebrate an event that occurred on June 26, 1593; and yet the language, the metre, and the style of *Titus* is noticeably different from that of the works which Shakespeare had already written and was writing during this particular period—the *Comedy of Errors, Love's Labour's Lost, Two Gentlemen of Verona, Richard III,* and *A Midsummer Night's Dream,* and the poems, *Venus and Adonis* and *Lucrece.* As late as 1593 he would hardly have written such bad lines or constructed so poor a play. If he had written it as early as 1589 or 1590, he could hardly have written in a style so wholly unlike that of the *Comedy of Errors* and *Love's Labour's Lost,* which he was presumably engaged in composing at that time.

Moreover, the language of *Titus* is shot through with words and expressions which Shakespeare did not use in any of his unquestioned works. A list of these words peculiar to *Titus,* first begun by Fleay, and corrected and added to by Grosart, Verity, and latterly by Robertson, contains upwards of a hundred terms which are the common property of Peele, Greene, and Kyd, respectively, but are never used by Shakespeare. If to these be added the host of classical allusions and tags found in *Titus* and in no other Shakespearean work, the linguistic medium of the play becomes a thing apart in the language of the Shakespearean canon.

But more fundamental than all these considerations of style, metre, vocabulary, and characterization, is the fact that the theme and the author's handling of it, and the general atmosphere and spirit of *Titus Andronicus,* are wholly unlike and utterly alien to anything we have of Shakespeare, or could expect from him. A theme of such unmitigated horror never appealed to Shakespeare

in his later career as a dramatist, and least of all could it have appealed to the young Shakespeare of *Love's Labour's Lost* and the *Midsummer Night's Dream.* He came closest to such themes in *Romeo and Juliet* in the year following the first publication of *Titus,* and in *Hamlet,* a few years later, and his method of handling them in those plays is the best evidence of what he could do and would do with the type of tragedy bequeathed to him by Seneca and Kyd. In none of his tragedies does he deal with blood for blood's sake, but in *Titus* there is no relief from bloodletting, either by the inevitable Shakespearean interspersion of comic scenes, or by the interjection of another and more romantic plot. Horrors are heaped on horrors in a way that would have sickened the sentimental author of Shakespeare's early plays, and would have disgusted the author of *Othello* and *King Lear.* And all to no purpose. In *Romeo and Juliet,* the tragedy and the bloodshed result in the burying of the parents' strife; in *Othello,* it is the cause which leads a man great of heart to slay Desdemona, not without recognizing the pity of it; in *King Lear,* the evil consumes itself, and a clear morning follows the storm of passion and tragedy. But in *Titus Andronicus* it is all

> *'Irrecoverably dark, total eclipse*
> *Without all hope of day.'*

The tragic energy all goes for nothing; Titus's madness is without any redeeming element. Shakespeare might have been capable of producing the bad lines of the play, its crude construction, its feeble characterization, and its poor workmanship in general, but that he could have written at any time a play so wholly unlike any of his other work seems incredible. If *Titus Andronicus* be Shakespeare's, we shall have to posit a complete change in his mental, spiritual, and artistic processes and attitudes between the time of its composition and the date when he began to produce his other dramatic work.

If Shakespeare, then, did not write *Titus,* who was the author of the piece? Any one of a half-dozen of his contemporaries is a more likely candidate for the questionable honor. Its Senecanism and melodrama it has in common with a score of other tragedies of the time. Its mannerisms of style, versification, and vocabulary are those of Kyd, Marlowe, Greene, Peele, and Lodge. Accordingly, four at least of these have been suggested as its possible author, and none of them has wanted defenders among the critics to make good his claim.

In the process of looking for specific traces of different hands in the play, however, many difficulties present themselves. Some idea of the general state of criticism with regard to this particular matter may be gained from a glance at the various interpretations placed on a single passage from Aaron's speech (II.i.1-9):

> *'Now climbeth Tamora Olympus' top,*
> *Safe out of Fortune's shot; and sits aloft,*
> *Secure of thunder's crack or lightning flash,*
> *Advanc'd above pale envy's threat'ning reach.*
> *As when the golden sun salutes the morn,*
> *And, having gilt the ocean with his beams,*
> *Gallops the zodiac in his glistering coach,*
> *And overlooks the highest-peering hills;*
> *So Tamora.'*

Bullen, in his edition of Marlowe's plays, was of the opinion that this passage was written by Marlowe, in view of Marlowe's having written, in the third chorus of Act III of *Faustus,* the line,

'Did mount himself to scale Olympus' top.'

Appleton Morgan (*Bankside Shakespeare*) thinks the passage Shakespeare's without question, and considers it a remarkably good imitation of Marlowe's style. Crawford, however, sees in lines 3-5 of the passage an echo of Peele's *Honour of the Garter* (line 410),

> *'Out of Oblivion's reach or Envy's shot,'*

while Robertson finds in line 7 a direct echo of a line from Peele's *Anglorum Feriæ,*

> *'Gallops the zodiac in his fiery wain,'*

and notes other lines from Peele's *David and Bethsabe* strikingly parallel in structure and abounding in verbal coincidences. Such resemblances are, indeed, very striking, but do they definitely prove more than that there was a singular community of thought and similarity of expression, and no little amount of imitation, among Elizabethan poets? And what, to give only one instance, shall be said of the lines in the *Merchant of Venice* (IV.i.10, 11),

> *'no lawful means can carry me*
> *Out of his envy's reach'?*

That they are Shakespeare's has never been questioned, but if they had occurred in *Titus,* would they not certainly be catalogued as Peele's or Marlowe's by just such reasoning? If mere similarity or identity of thought or expression is to be accepted as a criterion of authorship, then almost any Elizabethan dramatist may be proved to have written parts of almost any play of the time.

The play is so patently of the same species as the *Spanish Tragedy,* that Kyd was early suggested by Farmer as author of *Titus.* Hartley Coleridge concurred in this, and Fleay, Sir Sidney Lee, Parrott, and Robertson have since thought Kyd a probable first draftsman of the play. Boswell preferred to consider Marlowe, and Fleay also inclined to this opinion. The character of Aaron is by almost all critics conceded to be modeled on Marlowe's Barabas and Ithamore. Much of the verse also, if not Marlowe's, is close imitation of that poet's lines. The share of Robert Greene in *Titus* has received more attention than that of any other of the possible authors except Peele. In a long and scholarly article[7] Grosart set forth his many claims to the authorship, and he has received the serious consideration of every critic since. The play unquestionably contains much that was written by Greene, but whether his passages got into it by his own pen, or whether his imitators put them there is a problem that cannot be solved. Parrott and Robertson agree substantially in conceding to Greene's authorship the first scene of Act II, and traces of his manner are not wanting throughout the play. Grant White thought *Titus* was written by Greene, Marlowe, and Shakespeare, and later revised by Shakespeare.

But of all those for whom the authorship of *Titus* is claimed, George Peele is the foremost. His influence and his mannerisms are evident throughout the play, which is as Peelean in spirit as it is non-Shakespearean. Indeed, if the play were not specially credited to Shakespeare, there can be little doubt that it would be readily assigned to Peele by the majority of students of Elizabethan drama. 'Almost every page,' says Dugdale Sykes, 'exhibits

traces of Peele's vocabulary and phrasing.[8] At least one third of the entire play has been shown to be directly or indirectly copied from his works. The most important developments in the study and criticism of *Titus* during the present century have centered in the question of Peele's connection with the play, and to the earlier proofs of Fleay, Verity, and Crawford of his great share in its text, abundant evidence has been added by the exhaustive researches of Sykes and Robertson. J. Q. Adams adheres to the theory of Peele's authorship of the play in his *Life,* and it is not unreasonable to expect that future critics may consider the evidence sufficient to establish his claim to the play. When all allowances are made for the Elizabethan tendency toward imitation of other works, the play still remains characteristically Peelean, exhibiting all his sentimentality, his weakness for rodomontade, his fondness for the historical background in tragedy, his peculiar interest in Oriental themes, his love of martial exploits and exploiters, and his glorification of the fatherland, identical here with Rome, as it is in *David and Bethsabe* with Judæa. Surely there was no one so likely as Peele to have chosen such a subject for a tragedy, and, given the theme here found, there can be little doubt that he would have written substantially what we have in *Titus Andronicus.*

What conclusions, then, are to be drawn from all the mass of critical discussion on the authorship of *Titus Andronicus,* and the scores of conflicting interpretations and opinions of the play which have arisen during the two centuries and a half since Ravenscroft gave to the world the story of the 'private author'? There are certain general conclusions that do no violence to such facts as we have, and can be brought into reasonable conformity with the evidence available. First, the tragedy as it stands in the Folio of 1623 does not seem at all Shakespearean in substance, or treatment, or spirit. What we know of the mind and the tastes of Shakespeare forbids the ascription of this play to his pen, even as its earliest and crudest production. Secondly, from what is known of the manner, tastes, and workmanship of his contemporaries, the presumption is that George Peele is substantially the author of *Titus Andronicus,* with assistance, perhaps, from Robert Greene. Thirdly, the fact that the play was listed as Shakespeare's by Meres, and was printed as Shakespeare's in the Folio by Heminges and Condell, warrants the conclusion that Shakespeare retouched it to some extent. And thus we arrive, by a most circuitous process of reasoning, exactly where the controversy started, with Ravenscroft's statement in 1687. The most that Shakespeare could have had to do with *Titus Andronicus* is, we must believe, no more than what those 'anciently conversant with the stage' gave as their testimony—'he only gave some master-touches to one or two of the principal parts or characters.'

THE BALLAD OF TITUS ANDRONICUS'S COMPLAINT

The following ballad, referred to in Sources of the Play, is found in Book II of the first volume of Percy's *Reliques.* 'Throughout the ballad,' says Grant White, 'there is evident effort to compress all the incidents of the story within as brief a relation as possible; and this is not the style of a ballad written for the ballad's sake.'

7 'Was Robert Greene Substantially the Author of "Titus Andronicus"?' *Englische Studien,* xxii. 389-436.

8 *Sidelights on Shakespeare,* 1919, p. 125.

TITUS ANDRONICUS'S COMPLAINT

You noble minds, and famous martiall wights,
That in defence of native country fights,
Give eare to me, that ten yeeres fought for Rome,
Yet reapt disgrace at my returning home.

In Rome I lived in fame fulle threescore yeeres,
My name beloved was of all my peeres;
Full five and twenty valiant sonnes I had,
Whose forwarde vertues made their father glad.

For when Rome's foes their warlike forces bent,
Against them stille my sonnes and I were sent;
Against the Goths full ten yeeres weary warre
We spent, receiving many a bloudy scarre.

Just two and twenty of my sonnes were slaine
Before we did returne to Rome againe:
Of five and twenty sonnes, I brought but three
Alive, the stately towers of Rome to see.

When wars were done, I conquest home did bring,
And did present my prisoners to the king,
The queene of Goths, her sons, and eke a moore,
Which did such murders, like was nere before.

The emperour did make this queene his wife,
Which bred in Rome debate and deadlie strife;
The moore, with her two sonnes did growe soe proud,
That none like them in Rome might bee allowd.

The moore soe pleas'd this new-made empress' eie,
That she consented to him secretlye
For to abuse her husbands marriage bed,
And soe in time a blackamore she bred.

Then she, whose thoughts to murder were inclinde,
Consented with the moore of bloody minde
Against myselfe, my kin, and all my friendes,
In cruell sort to bring them to their endes.

Soe when in age I thought to live in peace,
Both care and griefe began then to increase:
Amongst my sonnes I had one daughter bright,
Which joy'd, and pleased best my aged sight:

My deare Lavinia was betrothed than
To Cesars sonne, a young and noble man:
Who in a hunting by the emperours wife
And her two sonnes, bereaved was of life.

He being slaine, was cast in cruel wise,
Into a darksome den from light of skies:
The cruell moore did come that way as then
With my three sonnes, who fell into the den.

The moore then fetcht the emperour with speed,
For to accuse them of that murderous deed;
And when my sonnes within the den were found,
In wrongfull prison they were cast and bound.

But nowe, behold! what wounded most my mind,
The empresses two sonnes of savage kind
My daughter ravished without remorse,
And took away her honour, quite perforce.

When they had tasted of soe sweete a flowre,
Fearing this sweete should shortly turn to sowre,
They cutt her tongue, whereby she could not tell
How that dishonoure unto her befell.

Then both her hands they basely cutt off quite,
Whereby their wickednesse she could not write;
Nor with her needle on her sampler sowe
The bloudye workers of her direfull woe.

My brother Marcus found her in the wood,
Staining the grassie ground with purple bloud,
That trickled from her stumpes, and bloudlesse armes:
Noe tongue at all she had to tell her harmes.

But when I sawe her in that woefull case,
With teares of bloud I wet mine aged face:
For my Lavinia I lamented more
Then for my two and twenty sonnes before.

When as I sawe she could not write nor speake,
With grief mine aged heart began to breake;
We spred an heape of sand upon the ground,
Whereby those bloudy tyrants out we found.

For with a staffe, without the helpe of hand,
She writt these wordes upon the plat of sand:
"The lustfull sonnes of the proud emperesse
Are doers of this hateful wickednesse."

I tore the milk-white hairs from off mine head,
I curst the houre wherein I first was bred,
I wisht this hand, that fought for countrie's fame,
In cradle rockt, had first been stroken lame.

The moore delighting still in villainy
Did say, to sett my sonnes from prison free
I should unto the king my right hand give,
And then my three imprisoned sonnes should live.

The moore I caused to strike it off with speede,
Whereat I grieved not to see it bleed,
But for my sonnes would willingly impart,
And for their ransome send my bleeding heart.

But as my life did linger thus in paine,
They sent to me my bootlesse hand againe,
And therewithal the heades of my three sonnes,
Which filld my dying heart with fresher moanes.

Then past reliefe I upp and downe did goe,
And with my teares writ in the dust my woe:
I shot my arrowes towards heaven hie,
And for revenge to hell often did crye.

The empresse then, thinking that I was mad,
Like Furies she and both her sonnes were clad,
(She nam'd Revenge, and Rape and Murder they)
To undermine and heare what I would say.

I fed their foolish veines a certaine space,
Untill my friendes did find a secret place,
Where both her sonnes unto a post were bound,
And just revenge in cruell sort was found.

I cut their throates, my daughter held the pan
Betwixt her stumpes, wherein the bloud it ran:
And then I ground their bones to powder small,
And made a paste for pyes streight therewithall.

Then withe their fleshe I made two mighty pyes,
And at a banquet served in stately wise:
Before the empresse set this lothsome meat;
So of her sonnes own flesh she well did eat.

Myself bereav'd my daughter then of life,
The empresse then I slewe with bloudy knife,
And stabb'd the emperour immediatelie,
And then myself: even soe did Titus die.

Then this revenge against the moore was found,
Alive they sett him halfe into the ground,
Whereas he stood untill such time he starv'd.
And soe God send all murderers may be serv'd.

ACT FIRST ❧ SCENE FIRST

[Rome. Before the Capitol. The Tomb of the Andronici appearing]
Flourish. Enter the Tribunes and Senators aloft; and then enter
Saturninus and his Followers at one door, and Bassianus and his
Followers at the other, with drum and colours.

Sat. Noble patricians, patrons of my right,
Defend the justice of my cause with arms;
And, countrymen, my loving followers,
Plead my successive title with your swords:
I am his first-born son that was the last   5
That wore the imperial diadem of Rome;
Then let my father's honours live in me,
Nor wrong mine age with this indignity.

Bas. Romans, friends, followers, favourers of my right,
If ever Bassianus, Cæsar's son,   10
Were gracious in the eyes of royal Rome,
Keep then this passage to the Capitol,
And suffer not dishonour to approach
The imperial seat, to virtue consecrate,
To justice, continence, and nobility;   15
But let desert in pure election shine,
And, Romans, fight for freedom in your choice.

Enter Marcus Andronicus, aloft, with the crown.

Mar. Princes, that strive by factions and by friends
Ambitiously for rule and empery,
Know that the people of Rome, for whom we stand   20
A special party, have, by common voice,
In election for the Roman empery,
Chosen Andronicus, surnamed Pius,
For many good and great deserts to Rome;
A nobler man, a braver warrior,   25
Lives not this day within the city walls;
He by the senate is accited home
From weary wars against the barbarous Goths;
That, with his sons, a terror to our foes,
Hath yok'd a nation, strong, train'd up in arms.   30
Ten years are spent since first he undertook
This cause of Rome, and chastised with arms
Our enemies' pride: five times he hath return'd
Bleeding to Rome, bearing his valiant sons
In coffins from the field;   35
And now at last, laden with honour's spoils,
Returns the good Andronicus to Rome,
Renowned Titus, flourishing in arms.
Let us entreat, by honour of his name,
Whom worthily you would have now succeed,   40
And in the Capitol and senate's right,
Whom you pretend to honour and adore,
That you withdraw you and abate your strength;
Dismiss your followers, and, as suitors should,
Plead your deserts in peace and humbleness.   45

Sat. How fair the tribune speaks to calm my thoughts!

Bas. Marcus Andronicus, so I do affy
In thy uprightness and integrity,

And so I love and honour thee and thine,
Thy noble brother Titus and his sons,   50
And her to whom my thoughts are humbled all,
Gracious Lavinia, Rome's rich ornament,
That I will here dismiss my loving friends,
And to my fortunes and the people's favour
Commit my cause in balance to be weigh'd.   55

Exeunt Soldiers [of Bassianus].

Sat. Friends, that have been thus forward in my right,
I thank you all and here dismiss you all;
And to the love and favour of my country
Commit myself, my person, and the cause.

[Exeunt Soldiers of Saturninus.]

Rome, be as just and gracious unto me   60
As I am confident and kind to thee.
Open the gates, and let me in.

Bas. Tribunes, and me, a poor competitor.

Flourish. They go up into the Senate-house.

Enter a Captain.

Cap. Romans, make way! the good Andronicus,
Patron of virtue, Rome's best champion,   65
Successful in the battles that he fights,
With honour and with fortune is return'd
From where he circumscribed with his sword,
And brought to yoke, the enemies of Rome.

Sound drums and trumpets, and then enter two of Titus's Sons
[Martius and Mutius]; after them two Men bearing a Coffin
covered with black; then two other Sons [Lucius and Quintus].
After them, Titus Andronicus; and then Tamora, the Queen of
Goths, and her three Sons, [Alarbus,] Chiron, and Demetrius,
with Aaron the Moor, and Others, [Prisoners,] as many as can
be. They set down the Coffin, and Titus speaks.

Tit. Hail, Rome, victorious in thy mourning weeds!   70
Lo! as the bark, that hath discharg'd her fraught,
Returns with precious lading to the bay
From whence at first she weigh'd her anchorage,
Cometh Andronicus, bound with laurel boughs,
To re-salute his country with his tears,   75
Tears of true joy for his return to Rome.
Thou great defender of this Capitol,
Stand gracious to the rites that we intend!
Romans, of five-and-twenty valiant sons,
Half of the number that King Priam had,   80
Behold the poor remains, alive, and dead!
These that survive, let Rome reward with love;
These that I bring unto their latest home,
With burial among their ancestors.
Here Goths have given me leave to sheathe my sword.   85
Titus, unkind and careless of thine own,
Why suffer'st thou thy sons, unburied yet,
To hover on the dreadful shore of Styx?
Make way to lay them by their brethren.   *They open the tomb.*
There greet in silence, as the dead are wont,   90
And sleep in peace, slain in your country's wars!
O sacred receptacle of my joys,
Sweet cell of virtue and nobility,

Scene One, S. d. **aloft:** *cf. n.*   **4 successive title:** *title to the succession*   **8 age:** *senior-ity*   **9 Romans:** *cf. n.*   **16 pure election:** *free choice*   **19 empery:** *imperial power*   **22 election:** *nomination*   **27 accited:** *summoned*   **35 In coffins from the field:** *cf. n.*   **42 pretend:** *profess*   **47 affy:** *have faith*

64 *Cf. n.*   **68 circumscribed:** *restrained*   **70 weeds:** *garments*   **71 fraught:** *freight*   **73 anchorage:** *anchor*   **77 great defender:** *Jupiter Capitolinus, to whom the Capitol was sacred*

How many sons of mine hast thou in store,
That thou wilt never render to me more!   *95*

Luc. Give us the proudest prisoner of the Goths,
That we may hew his limbs, and on a pile
Ad manes fratrum sacrifice his flesh,
Before this earthy prison of their bones;
That so the shadows be not unappeas'd,   *100*
Nor we disturb'd with prodigies on earth.

Tit. I give him you, the noblest that survives,
The eldest son of this distressed queen.

Tam. Stay, Roman brethren! Gracious conqueror,
Victorious Titus, rue the tears I shed,   *105*
A mother's tears in passion for her son:
And if thy sons were ever dear to thee,
O! think my sons to be as dear to me.
Sufficeth not that we are brought to Rome,
To beautify thy triumphs and return,   *110*
Captive to thee and to thy Roman yoke,
But must my sons be slaughter'd in the streets,
For valiant doings in their country's cause?
O! if to fight for king and commonweal
Were piety in thine, it is in these.   *115*
Andronicus, stain not thy tomb with blood!
Wilt thou draw near the nature of the gods?
Draw near them then in being merciful;
Sweet mercy is nobility's true badge:
Thrice-noble Titus, spare my first-born son!   *120*

Tit. Patient yourself, madam, and pardon me.
These are their brethren, whom your Goths beheld
Alive and dead, and for their brethren slain
Religiously they ask a sacrifice:
To this your son is mark'd, and die he must,   *125*
T'appease their groaning shadows that are gone.

Luc. Away with him! and make a fire straight;
And with our swords, upon a pile of wood,
Let's hew his limbs till they be clean consum'd.

                Exeunt [Titus's] Sons with Alarbus.

Tam. O cruel, irreligious piety!   *130*

Chi. Was ever Scythia half so barbarous?

Dem. Oppose not Scythia to ambitious Rome.
Alarbus goes to rest, and we survive
To tremble under Titus' threatening look.
Then, madam, stand resolv'd; but hope withal   *135*
The self-same gods, that arm'd the Queen of Troy
With opportunity of sharp revenge
Upon the Thracian tyrant in his tent,
May favour Tamora, the Queen of Goths—
When Goths were Goths, and Tamora was queen—   *140*
To quit the bloody wrongs upon her foes.

         Enter the Sons of Andronicus again.

Luc. See, lord and father, how we have perform'd
Our Roman rites. Alarbus' limbs are lopp'd,
And entrails feed the sacrificing fire,
Whose smoke, like incense, doth perfume the sky.   *145*
Remaineth nought but to inter our brethren,
And with loud 'larums welcome them to Rome.

Tit. Let it be so; and let Andronicus

Make this his latest farewell to their souls.

           Flourish. Then sound trumpets, and lay
                   the coffin in the tomb.

In peace and honour rest you here, my sons;   *150*
Rome's readiest champions, repose you here in rest,
Secure from worldly chances and mishaps!
Here lurks no treason, here no envy swells,
Here grow no damned grudges, here are no storms,
No noise, but silence and eternal sleep: *155*
In peace and honour rest you here, my sons!

                Enter Lavinia.

Lav. In peace and honour live Lord Titus long;
My noble lord and father, live in fame!
Lo! at this tomb my tributary tears
I render for my brethren's obsequies;   *160*
And at thy feet I kneel, with tears of joy
Shed on the earth for thy return to Rome.
O! bless me here with thy victorious hand,
Whose fortunes Rome's best citizens applaud.

Tit. Kind Rome, that hast thus lovingly reserv'd   *165*
The cordial of mine age to glad my heart!
Lavinia, live; outlive thy father's days,
And fame's eternal date, for virtue's praise!

    [Enter, below, Marcus Andronicus and Tribunes; re-enter
          Saturninus, Bassianus, and Others.]

Mar. Long live Lord Titus, my beloved brother,
Gracious triumpher in the eyes of Rome!   *170*

Tit. Thanks, gentle Tribune, noble brother Marcus.

Mar. And welcome, nephews, from successful wars,
You that survive, and you that sleep in fame!
Fair lords, your fortunes are alike in all,
That in your country's service drew your swords;   *175*
But safer triumph is this funeral pomp,
That hath aspir'd to Solon's happiness,
And triumphs over chance in honour's bed.
Titus Andronicus, the people of Rome,
Whose friend in justice thou hast ever been,   *180*
Send thee by me, their tribune and their trust,
This palliament of white and spotless hue;
And name thee in election for the empire,
With these our late-deceased emperor's sons:
Be *candidatus* then, and put it on,   *185*
And help to set a head on headless Rome.

Tit. A better head her glorious body fits
Than his that shakes for age and feebleness.
What should I don this robe, and trouble you?
Be chosen with proclamations to-day,   *190*
To-morrow yield up rule, resign my life,
And set abroad new business for you all?
Rome, I have been thy soldier forty years,
And led my country's strength successfully,
And buried one-and-twenty valiant sons,   *195*
Knighted in field, slain manfully in arms,
In right and service of their noble country.
Give me a staff of honour for mine age,
But not a sceptre to control the world:

---

98 **Ad manes fratrum:** *to the shades of [our] brothers; cf. n.*   106 **passion:** *suffering*   117-
119 *Cf. n.*   121 **Patient:** *quiet*   131 **Scythia;** *cf. n.*   132 **Oppose:** *compare*   136
Queen of Troy: *Hecuba*   138 **Thracian tyrant;** *cf. n.*   141 **quit:** *requite*

154 **grudges;** *cf. n.*   165 **reserv'd:** *preserved*   168 **date:** *duration; cf. n.*   177 **Solon's
happiness;** *cf. n.*   182 **palliament:** *cloak (Lat. pallium), Roman robe of state*   183 **name
thee in election:** *nominate thee*   185 **candidatus:** *a candidate*   189 **What:** *why*

Upright he held it, lords, that held it last.   *200*

    Mar. Titus, thou shalt obtain and ask the empery.

    Sat. Proud and ambitious tribune, canst thou tell?—

    Tit. Patience, Prince Saturninus.

    Sat.   Romans, do me right:

Patricians, draw your swords, and sheathe them not   *205*

Till Saturninus be Rome's emperor.

Andronicus, would thou wert shipp'd to hell,

Rather than rob me of the people's hearts!

    Luc. Proud Saturnine, interrupter of the good

That noble-minded Titus means to thee!   *210*

    Tit. Content thee, prince; I will restore to thee

The people's hearts, and wean them from themselves.

    Bas. Andronicus, I do not flatter thee,

But honour thee, and will do till I die;

My faction if thou strengthen with thy friends,   *215*

I will most thankful be; and thanks to men

Of noble minds is honourable meed.

    Tit. People of Rome, and people's tribunes here,

I ask your voices and your suffrages:

Will you bestow them friendly on Andronicus?   *220*

    Tribunes. To gratify the good Andronicus,

And gratulate his safe return to Rome,

The people will accept whom he admits.

    Tit. Tribunes, I thank you; and this suit I make,

That you create your emperor's eldest son,   *225*

Lord Saturnine; whose virtues will, I hope,

Reflect on Rome as Titan's rays on earth,

And ripen justice in this commonweal:

Then, if you will elect by my advice,

Crown him, and say, 'Long live our emperor!'   *230*

    Mar. With voices and applause of every sort,

Patricians and plebeians, we create

Lord Saturninus Rome's great emperor,

And say, 'Long live our Emperor Saturnine!'

                    A long flourish till they come down.

    Sat. Titus Andronicus, for thy favours done   *235*

To us in our election this day,

I give thee thanks in part of thy deserts,

And will with deeds requite thy gentleness:

And, for an onset, Titus, to advance

Thy name and honourable family,   *240*

Lavinia will I make my empress,

Rome's royal mistress, mistress of my heart,

And in the sacred Pantheon her espouse.

Tell me, Andronicus, doth this motion please thee?

    Tit. It doth, my worthy lord; and in this match   *245*

I hold me highly honour'd of your Grace:

And here in sight of Rome to Saturnine,

King and commander of our commonweal,

The wide world's emperor, do I consecrate

My sword, my chariot, and my prisoners;   *250*

Presents well worthy Rome's imperious lord:

Receive them then, the tribute that I owe,

Mine honour's ensigns humbled at thy feet.

    Sat. Thanks, noble Titus, father of my life!

How proud I am of thee and of thy gifts   *255*

Rome shall record, and, when I do forget

The least of these unspeakable deserts,

Romans, forget your fealty to me.

    Tit. [*To Tamora.*] Now, madam, are you prisoner to

an emperor;   *260*

To him that, for your honour and your state,

Will use you nobly and your followers.

    Sat. [*Aside.*] A goodly lady, trust me; of the hue

That I would choose, were I to choose anew.

[*To Tamora.*] Clear up, fair queen, that cloudy countenance: *265*

Though chance of war hath wrought this change of cheer,

Thou com'st not to be made a scorn in Rome:

Princely shall be thy usage every way.

Rest on my word, and let not discontent

Daunt all your hopes: madam, he comforts you   *270*

Can make you greater than the Queen of Goths.

Lavinia, you are not displeas'd with this?

    Lav. Not I, my lord; sith true nobility

Warrants these words in princely courtesy.

    Sat. Thanks, sweet Lavinia. Romans, let us go;   *275*

Ransomless here we set our prisoners free:

Proclaim our honours, lords, with trump and drum.

           [Flourish. Saturninus courts Tamora

                   in dumb show.]

    Bas. [*Seizing Lavinia.*] Lord Titus, by your leave,

this maid is mine.

    Tit. How, sir! Are you in earnest then, my lord?   *280*

    Bas. Ay, noble Titus; and resolv'd withal

To do myself this reason and this right.

    Mar. *Suum cuique* is our Roman justice:

This prince in justice seizeth but his own.

    Luc. And that he will, and shall, if Lucius live.   *285*

    Tit. Traitors, avaunt! Where is the emperor's guard?

Treason, my lord! Lavinia is surpris'd.

    Sat. Surpris'd! By whom?

    Bas.   By him that justly may

Bear his betroth'd from all the world away.   *290*

               [Exeunt Marcus and Bassianus

                   with Lavinia.]

    Mut. Brothers, help to convey her hence away,

And with my sword I'll keep this door safe.

           [Exeunt Lucius, Quintus, and Martius.]

    Tit. Follow, my lord, and I'll soon bring her back.

    Mut. My lord, you pass not here.

    Tit.   What! villain boy;   *295*

Barr'st me my way in Rome?   *He kills him.*

    Mut.   Help, Lucius, help!

[Exeunt, during the fray, Saturninus, Tamora, Demetrius, Chiron,
and Aaron. Re-enter Lucius.]

    Luc. My lord, you are unjust; and, more than so,

In wrongful quarrel you have slain your son.

    Tit. Nor thou, nor he, are any sons of mine;   *300*

My sons would never so dishonour me.

Traitor, restore Lavinia to the emperor.

    Luc. Dead, if you will; but not to be his wife

That is another's lawful promis'd love.   *[Exit.]*

Enter, aloft, the Emperor with Tamora and her two Sons, and
Aaron the Moor.

201 obtain and ask: *obtain by merely asking*   **218 people's tribunes;** *cf. n.*   **222 gratulate:** *celebrate*   **225 create:** *elect*   **227 Titan's:** *the sun god's*   **238 gentleness:** *noble conduct*   **239 onset:** *beginning*

266 cheer: *countenance*   **271 Can:** *who can*   **273 sith:** *since*   **283 Suum cuique:** *to every man his due*

Sat. No, Titus, no; the emperor needs her not,   *305*
Nor her, nor thee, nor any of thy stock:
I'll trust, by leisure, him that mocks me once;
Thee never, nor thy traitorous haughty sons,
Confederates all thus to dishonour me.
Was none in Rome to make a stale   *310*
But Saturnine? Full well, Andronicus,
Agreed these deeds with that proud brag of thine,
That saidst I begg'd the empire at thy hands.
   Tit. O monstrous! what reproachful words are these!
   Sat. But go thy ways; go, give that changing piece   *315*
To him that flourish'd for her with his sword.
A valiant son-in-law thou shalt enjoy;
One fit to bandy with thy lawless sons,
To ruffle in the commonwealth of Rome.
   Tit. These words are razors to my wounded heart.   *320*
   Sat. And therefore, lovely Tamora, Queen of Goths,
That like the stately Phœbe 'mongst her nymphs,
Dost overshine the gallant'st dames of Rome,
If thou be pleas'd with this my sudden choice,
Behold, I choose thee, Tamora, for my bride,   *325*
And will create thee Empress of Rome.
Speak, Queen of Goths, dost thou applaud my choice?
And here I swear by all the Roman gods,
Sith priest and holy water are so near,
And tapers burn so bright, and everything   *330*
In readiness for Hymenæus stand,
I will not re-salute the streets of Rome,
Or climb my palace, till from forth this place
I lead espous'd my bride along with me.
   Tam. And here, in sight of heaven, to Rome I swear,   *335*
If Saturnine advance the Queen of Goths,
She will a handmaid be to his desires,
A loving nurse, a mother to his youth.
   Sat. Ascend, fair queen, Pantheon. Lords, accompany
Your noble emperor, and his lovely bride,   *340*
Sent by the heavens for Prince Saturnine,
Whose wisdom hath her fortune conquered:
There shall we consummate our spousal rights.

                          Exeunt omnes [but Titus].

   Tit. I am not bid to wait upon this bride.
Titus, when wert thou wont to walk alone,   *345*
Dishonour'd thus, and challenged of wrongs?

        Enter Marcus and Titus's Sons.

   Mar. O Titus, see! O, see what thou hast done!
In a bad quarrel slain a virtuous son.
   Tit. No, foolish tribune, no; no son of mine,
Nor thou, nor these, confederates in the deed   *350*
That hath dishonour'd all our family:
Unworthy brother, and unworthy sons!
   Luc. But let us give him burial, as becomes;
Give Mutius burial with our brethren.
   Tit. Traitors, away! he rests not in this tomb.   *355*
This monument five hundred years hath stood,
Which I have sumptuously re-edified:
Here none but soldiers and Rome's servitors

Repose in fame; none basely slain in brawls.
Bury him where you can; he comes not here.   *360*
   Mar. My lord, this is impiety in you.
My nephew Mutius' deeds do plead for him;
He must be buried with his brethren.

                  Titus's two Sons speak.

 [Quin.] }
 [Mart.] } And shall, or him we will accompany.   *365*
   Tit. And shall! What villain was it spake that word?

              Titus's Son [Quintus] speaks.

 [Quin.] He that would vouch it in any place but here.
   Tit. What! would you bury him in my despite?
   Mar. No, noble Titus; but entreat of thee
To pardon Mutius, and to bury him.   *370*
   Tit. Marcus, even thou hast struck upon my crest,
And, with these boys, mine honour thou hast wounded:
My foes I do repute you every one;
So trouble me no more, but get you gone.
   1. Son [Mart.] He is not with himself; let us withdraw.   *375*
   2. Son [Quin.] Not I, till Mutius' bones be buried.

              The Brother and the Sons kneel.

   Mar. Brother, for in that name doth nature plead,—
   2. Son. Father, and in that name doth nature speak,—
   Tit. Speak thou no more, if all the rest will speed.
   Mar. Renowned Titus, more than half my soul,—   *380*
   Luc. Dear father, soul and substance of us all,—
   Mar. Suffer thy brother Marcus to inter
His noble nephew here in virtue's nest,
That died in honour and Lavinia's cause.
Thou art a Roman; be not barbarous: *385*
The Greeks upon advice did bury Ajax
That slew himself; and wise Laertes' son
Did graciously plead for his funerals.
Let not young Mutius, then, that was thy joy,
Be barr'd his entrance here.   *390*
   Tit.   Rise, Marcus, rise.
The dismal'st day is this that e'er I saw,
To be dishonour'd by my sons in Rome!
Well, bury him, and bury me the next.

              They put him in the tomb.

   Luc. There lie thy bones, sweet Mutius, with thy friends,   *395*
Till we with trophies do adorn thy tomb.

              They all kneel and say,

 [All.] No man shed tears for noble Mutius;
He lives in fame that died in virtue's cause.

          [Exeunt all but Marcus and Titus.]

   Mar. My lord,—to step out of these dreary dumps,—
How comes it that the subtle Queen of Goths   *400*
Is of a sudden thus advanc'd in Rome?
   Tit. I know not, Marcus; but I know it is;
Whether by device or no, the heavens can tell.
Is she not, then, beholding to the man
That brought her for this high good turn so far?   *405*
   [Mar.] Yes, and will nobly him remunerate.

Flourish. Enter the Emperor, Tamora and her two Sons, with the
   Moor, at one door. Enter, at the other door, Bassianus and
           Lavinia, with Others.

---

307 I'll . . . leisure: *I'll be in no hurry to trust*   **310 stale:** *laughing-stock*   **315 piece:** *wench*   **318 bandy:** *contend; cf. n.*   **319 ruffle:** *be disorderly*   **329 priest and holy water;** *cf. n.*   **331 Hymenæus:** *Hymen, the god of marriage*   **344 bid:** *invited*   **346 challenged:** *accused*   **357 re-edified:** *restored*

375 not with himself: *beside himself*   **379 will speed:** *wish to succeed*   **Ajax;** *cf. n.*   **386 upon advice:** *after deliberation*   **387 Laertes' son:** *Ulysses*   **388 funerals:** *obsequies*   **399 dumps:** *low spirits*   **403 device:** *scheming*   **404 beholding:** *beholden*

Sat. So, Bassianus, you have play'd your prize:
God give you joy, sir, of your gallant bride.

   Bas. And you of yours, my lord! I say no more,
Nor wish no less; and so I take my leave.   *410*

   Sat. Traitor, if Rome have law or we have power,
Thou and thy faction shall repent this rape.

   Bas. Rape call you it, my lord, to seize my own,
My true-betrothed love and now my wife?
But let the laws of Rome determine all;   *415*
Meanwhile, I am possess'd of that is mine.

   Sat. 'Tis good, sir: you are very short with us;
But, if we live, we'll be as sharp with you.

   Bas. My lord, what I have done, as best I may,
Answer I must and shall do with my life.   *420*
Only thus much I give your Grace to know:
By all the duties that I owe to Rome,
This noble gentleman, Lord Titus here,
Is in opinion and in honour wrong'd;
That, in the rescue of Lavinia,   *425*
With his own hand did slay his youngest son,
In zeal to you and highly mov'd to wrath
To be controll'd in that he frankly gave:
Receive him, then, to favour, Saturnine,
That hath express'd himself in all his deeds   *430*
A father and a friend to thee and Rome.

   Tit. Prince Bassianus, leave to plead my deeds:
'Tis thou and those that have dishonour'd me.
Rome and the righteous heavens by my judge,
How I have lov'd and honour'd Saturnine!   *435*

   Tam. My worthy lord, if ever Tamora
Were gracious in those princely eyes of thine,
Then hear me speak indifferently for all;
And at my suit, sweet, pardon what is past.

   Sat. What, madam! be dishonour'd openly,   *440*
And basely put it up without revenge?

   Tam. Not so, my lord; the gods of Rome forfend
I should be author to dishonour you!
But on mine honour dare I undertake
For good Lord Titus' innocence in all,   *445*
Whose fury not dissembled speaks his griefs.
Then, at my suit, look graciously on him;
Lose not so noble a friend on vain suppose,
Nor with sour looks afflict his gentle heart.
[*Aside to Saturninus.*] My lord, be rul'd by me, be won at last;
Dissemble all your griefs and discontents:
You are but newly planted in your throne;
Lest, then, the people, and patricians too,
Upon a just survey, take Titus' part,
And so supplant you for ingratitude,   *455*
Which Rome reputes to be a heinous sin,
Yield at entreats, and then let me alone,
I'll find a day to massacre them all,
And raze their faction and their family,
The cruel father, and his traitorous sons,   *460*
To whom I sued for my dear son's life;
And make them know what 'tis to let a queen

Kneel in the streets and beg for grace in vain.
[*Aloud.*] Come, come, sweet emperor—come, Andronicus—
Take up this good old man, and cheer the heart   *465*
That dies in tempest of thy angry frown.

   Sat. Rise, Titus, rise; my empress hath prevail'd.

   Tit. I thank your majesty, and her, my lord.
These words, these looks, infuse new life in me.

   Tam. Titus, I am incorporate in Rome,   *470*
A Roman now adopted happily,
And must advise the emperor for his good.
This day all quarrels die, Andronicus;
And let it be mine honour, good my lord,
That I have reconcil'd your friends and you.   *475*
For you, Prince Bassianus, I have pass'd
My word and promise to the emperor,
That you will be more mild and tractable.
And fear not, lords, and you, Lavinia:
By my advice, all humbled on your knees,   *480*
You shall ask pardon of his majesty.
           [*Marcus, Lavinia, and the Sons of Titus kneel.*]

   Luc. We do; and vow to heaven and to his highness,
That what we did was mildly as we might,
Tend'ring our sister's honour and our own.

   Mar. That, on mine honour, here I do protest.   *485*

   Sat. Away, and talk not; trouble us no more.

   Tam. Nay, nay, sweet emperor, we must all be friends:
The tribune and his nephews kneel for grace;
I will not be denied: sweetheart, look back.

   Sat. Marcus, for thy sake, and thy brother's here,   *490*
And at my lovely Tamora's entreats,
I do remit these young men's heinous faults:
Stand up.
           [*Marcus, Lavinia, and the Others rise.*]
Lavinia, though you left me like a churl,
I found a friend, and sure as death I sware   *495*
I would not part a bachelor from the priest.
Come; if the emperor's court can feast two brides,
You are my guest, Lavinia, and your friends.
This day shall be a love-day, Tamora.

   Tit. To-morrow, an it please your majesty   *500*
To hunt the panther and the hart with me,
With horn and hound we'll give your Grace *bon jour.*

   Sat. Be it so, Titus, and gramercy too.   *Exeunt.*

ACT SECOND ❦ SCENE FIRST

[Rome. Before the Palace]
Flourish. Enter Aaron alone.

   Aar. Now climbeth Tamora Olympus' top,
Safe out of Fortune's shot; and sits aloft,
Secure of thunder's crack or lightning flash,
Advanc'd above pale envy's threat'ning reach.
As when the golden sun salutes the morn,   *5*
And, having gilt the ocean with his beams,

---

407 **play'd your prize**; *cf. n.*   424 **opinion**: *reputation*   428 **controll'd**: *restrained, hindered* **frankly**: *freely*   432 **leave**: *cease*   438 **indifferently**: *impartially*   441 **put it up**: *put up with it*   442 **forfend**: *forbid*   443 **author . . . you**: *author of your dishonor*   444 **undertake**: *vouch*   448 **suppose**: *supposition*   457 **at entreats**: *to entreaties* **let me alone**: *leave everything to me*

470 **incorporate**: *incorporated, established*   483 **mildly as we might**: *as gently as possible*   484 **Tend'ring**: *having a tender regard for*   493 **Stand up**; *cf. n.*   494 **churl**: *a mean, worthless person*   496 **part**: *depart*   499 **love-day**; *cf. n.*   501 **To hunt the panther**; *cf. n.*   502 **bon jour**: *good morning*   503 **gramercy**: *many thanks* (Fr. grand merci)   3 **Secure of**: *safe from*

Gallops the zodiac in his glistering coach,
And overlooks the highest-peering hills;
So Tamora.
Upon her wit doth earthly honour wait   10
And virtue stoops and trembles at her frown.
Then, Aaron, arm thy heart, and fit thy thoughts
To mount aloft with thy imperial mistress,
And mount her pitch, whom thou in triumph long
Hast prisoner held, fetter'd in amorous chains,   15
And faster bound to Aaron's charming eyes
Than is Prometheus tied to Caucasus.
Away with slavish weeds and servile thoughts!
I will be bright, and shine in pearl and gold,
To wait upon this new-made empress.   20
To wait, said I? to wanton with this queen,
This goddess, this Semiramis, this nymph,
This siren, that will charm Rome's Saturnine,
And see his shipwrack and his commonweal's.
Hollo! what storm is this?   25

Enter Chiron and Demetrius, braving.

Dem. Chiron, thy years want wit, thy wit wants edge
And manners, to intrude where I am grac'd,
And may, for aught thou know'st, affected be.
  Chi. Demetrius, thou dost overween in all
And so in this, to bear me down with braves.   30
'Tis not the difference of a year or two
Makes me less gracious or thee more fortunate:
I am as able and as fit as thou
To serve, and to deserve, my mistress' grace;
And that my sword upon thee shall approve,   35
And plead my passions for Lavinia's love.
  Aar. Clubs, clubs! these lovers will not keep the peace.
  Dem. Why, boy, although our mother, unadvis'd,
Gave you a dancing-rapier by your side
Are you so desperate grown, to threat your friends?   40
Go to; have your lath glu'd within your sheath
Till you know better how to handle it.
  Chi. Meanwhile, sir, with the little skill I have,
Full well shalt thou perceive how much I dare.
  Dem. Ay, boy, grow ye so brave?   *They draw.*
  Aar.   Why, how now, lords!
So near the emperor's palace dare you draw,
And maintain such a quarrel openly?
Full well I wot the ground of all this grudge:
I would not for a million of gold   50
The cause were known to them it most concerns;
Nor would your noble mother for much more
Be so dishonour'd in the court of Rome.
For shame, put up.
  Dem.   Not I, till I have sheath'd   55
My rapier in his bosom, and withal
Thrust those reproachful speeches down his throat
That he hath breath'd in my dishonour here.

Chi. For that I am prepar'd and full resolv'd,
Foul-spoken coward, that thunder'st with thy tongue,   60
And with thy weapon nothing dar'st perform!
  Aar. Away, I say!
Now, by the gods that warlike Goths adore,
This petty brabble will undo us all.
Why, lords, and think you not how dangerous   65
It is to jet upon a prince's right?
What! is Lavinia then become so loose,
Or Bassianus so degenerate,
That for her love such quarrels may be broach'd
Without controlment, justice, or revenge?   70
Young lords, beware! an should the empress know
This discord's ground, the music would not please.
  Chi. I care not, I, knew she and all the world:
I love Lavinia more than all the world.
  Dem. Youngling, learn thou to make some meaner choice: 75
Lavinia is thine elder brother's hope.
  Aar. Why, are ye mad? or know ye not in Rome
How furious and impatient they be,
And cannot brook competitors in love?
I tell you, lords, you do but plot your deaths   80
By this device.
  Chi.   Aaron, a thousand deaths
Would I propose, to achieve her whom I love.
  Aar. To achieve her! how?
  Dem.   Why mak'st thou it so strange? 85
She is a woman, therefore may be woo'd;
She is a woman, therefore may be won;
She is Lavinia, therefore must be lov'd.
What, man! more water glideth by the mill
Than wots the miller of; and easy it is   90
Of a cut loaf to steal a shive, we know:
Though Bassianus be the emperor's brother,
Better than he have worn Vulcan's badge.
  Aar. [*Aside.*] Ay, and as good as Saturninus may.
  Dem. Then why should he despair that knows to court it. 95
With words, fair looks, and liberality?
What! hast thou not full often struck a doe,
And borne her cleanly by the keeper's nose?
  Aar. Why, then, it seems, some certain snatch or so
Would serve your turns.   100
  Chi   Ay, so the turn were serv'd.
  Dem. Aaron, thou hast hit it.
  Aar.   Would you had hit it too!
Then should not we be tir'd with this ado.
Why, hark ye, hark ye! and are you such fools   105
To square for this? Would it offend you, then,
That both should speed?
  Chi.   Faith, not me.
  Dem. Nor me, so I were one.
  Aar. For shame, be friends, and join for that you jar: 110
'Tis policy and stratagem must do
That you affect; and so must you resolve
That what you cannot as you would achieve,
You must perforce accomplish as you may.

7 **Gallops:** *gallops over*   8 **overlooks:** *looks down on*   14 **pitch;** *cf. n.*   16 **charming:** *having power to charm, or cast a spell*   17 **Prometheus;** *cf. n.*   18 **weeds:** *garments*   22 **Semiramis;** *cf. n.*   **S. d. braving:** *defying each other*   27 **grac'd:** *favored*   28 **affected:** *loved*   29 **dost overween:** *art presumptuous*   30 **braves:** *brags*   35 **approve:** *prove*   37 **Clubs, clubs!;** *cf. n.*   38 **unadvis'd:** *thoughtlessly, rashly*   39 **dancing-rapier:** *a sword worn only for ornament*   41 **lath:** *contemptuous term for sword; cf. n.*   49 **wot:** *know*   54 **put up:** *sheathe your swords*   55 **Not I;** *cf. n.*

64 **brabble:** *squabble, brawl*   66 **jet:** *encroach*   72 **ground;** *cf. n.*   83 **propose:** *risk, undertake*   **achieve:** *win*   86 **She is a woman;** *cf. n.*   89 **water glideth by the mill;** *cf. n.*   91 **shive:** *slice*   93 **Vulcan's badge;** *cf. n.*   106 **square:** *put oneself in a boxing attitude, quarrel*   110 **that you jar:** *that which you are quarreling about*   112 **affect:** *desire*

Take this of me: Lucrece was not more chaste   *115*
Than this Lavinia, Bassianus' love.
A speedier course than ling'ring languishment
Must we pursue, and I have found the path.
My lords, a solemn hunting is in hand;
There will the lovely Roman ladies troop: *120*
The forest walks are wide and spacious,
And many unfrequented plots there are
Fitted by kind for rape and villainy:
Single you thither, then, this dainty doe,
And strike her home by force, if not by words: *125*
This way, or not at all, stand you in hope.
Come, come, our empress, with her sacred wit
To villainy and vengeance consecrate,
Will we acquaint with all that we intend;
And she shall file our engines with advice,   *130*
That will not suffer you to square yourselves,
But to your wishes' height advance you both.
The emperor's court is like the house of Fame;
The palace full of tongues, of eyes, and ears:
The woods are ruthless, dreadful, deaf, and dull;   *135*
There speak, and strike, brave boys, and take your turns;
There serve your lusts, shadow'd from heaven's eye,
And revel in Lavinia's treasury.
    Chi. Thy counsel, lad, smells of no cowardice.
    Dem. Sit fas aut nefas, till I find the stream   *140*
To cool this heat, a charm to calm these fits,
Per Styga, per manes vehor.   *Exeunt.*

❧ Scene Second ❧

[A Forest near Rome]
Enter Titus Andronicus and his three Sons, making a noise with
hounds and horns, and Marcus.

    Tit. The hunt is up, the morn is bright and grey,
The fields are fragrant and the woods are green.
Uncouple here and let us make a bay,
And wake the emperor and his lovely bride,
And rouse the prince and ring a hunter's peal,   *5*
That all the court may echo with the noise.
Sons, let it be your charge, as it is ours,
To attend the emperor's person carefully:
I have been troubled in my sleep this night,
But dawning day new comfort hath inspir'd.   *Wind horns.*

Here a cry of hounds, and wind horns in a peal, then enter
Saturninus, Tamora, Bassianus, Lavinia, Chiron, Demetrius,
and their Attendants.

Many good morrows to your majesty;
Madam, to you as many and as good;
I promised your Grace a hunter's peal.
    Sat. And you have rung it lustily, my lord;
Somewhat too early for new-married ladies.   *15*

    Bas. Lavinia, how say you?
    Lav.   I say, no;
I have been broad awake two hours and more.
    Sat. Come on, then; horse and chariots let us have,
And to our sport.—*[To Tamora.]* Madam, now shall ye see   *20*
Our Roman hunting.
    Mar.   I have dogs, my lord,
Will rouse the proudest panther in the chase,
And climb the highest promontory top.
    Tit. And I have horse will follow where the game   *25*
Makes way, and run like swallows o'er the plain.
    Dem. [Aside.] Chiron, we hunt not, we, with horse nor
    hound,
But hope to pluck a dainty doe to ground.   *Exeunt.*

❧ Scene Third ❧

[A lonely part of the Forest]
Enter Aaron alone [with a bag of gold].

    Aar. He that had wit would think that I had none,
To bury so much gold under a tree,
And never after to inherit it.
Let him that thinks of me so abjectly
Know that this gold must coin a stratagem,   *5*
Which, cunningly effected, will beget
A very excellent piece of villainy:
And so repose, sweet gold, for their unrest
That have their alms out of the empress' chest.

[Hides the gold.]

Enter Tamora to the Moor.

    Tam. My lovely Aaron, wherefore look'st thou sad,   *10*
When everything doth make a gleeful boast?
The birds chant melody on every bush,
The snake lies rolled in the cheerful sun,
The green leaves quiver with the cooling wind,
And make a chequer'd shadow on the ground.   *15*
Under their sweet shade, Aaron, let us sit,
And, whilst the babbling echo mocks the hounds,
Replying shrilly to the well-tun'd horns,
As if a double hunt were heard at once,
Let us sit down and mark their yelping noise;   *20*
And after conflict, such as was suppos'd
The wandering prince and Dido once enjoy'd,
When with a happy storm they were surpris'd,
And curtain'd with a counsel-keeping cave,
We may, each wreathed in the other's arms,
Our pastimes done, possess a golden slumber;
Whiles hounds and horns and sweet melodious birds
Be unto us as is a nurse's song   *25*
Of lullaby to bring her babe asleep.
    Aar. Madam, though Venus govern your desires,
Saturn is dominator over mine:
What signifies my deadly-standing eye,
My silence and my cloudy melancholy,   *30*

115 Lucrece: *cf. n.*   117 ling'ring languishment: *a long-drawn-out courtship*   119 sol-emn: *formal, grand*   123 by kind: *by nature*   127 sacred; *cf. n.*   130 file our en-gines: *sharpen, or finish off, our designs*   131 square yourselves: *settle it between yourselves*   133 house of Fame; *cf. n.*   140 Sit fas aut nefas: *Be it right or wrong*   142 Per Styga, per manes vehor: *I am borne across the Styx, and among the shades of the dead; cf. n.*   1 grey; *cf. n.*   3 Uncouple here; *cf. n.*   bay: *barking*   9 I have been trou-bled; *cf. n.*

25 horse: *horses*   26 Makes way: *opens up a passage*   3 inherit: *possess*   9 alms . . . chest; *cf. n.*   17 echo mocks the hounds, etc.; *cf. n.*   22 The wandering prince: *Æneas* (cf. Vergil, *Æneid* 4. 165 ff.)   23 happy: *lucky*   31 Saturn is dominator; *cf. n.*   32 deadly-standing: *fixedly staring like that of the dead*

My fleece of woolly hair that now uncurls
Even as an adder when she doth unroll   35
To do some fatal execution?
No, madam, these are no venereal signs:
Vengeance is in my heart, death in my hand,
Blood and revenge are hammering in my head.
Hark, Tamora, the empress of my soul,   40
Which never hopes more heaven than rests in thee:
This is the day of doom for Bassianus;
His Philomel must lose her tongue to-day,
Thy sons make pillage of her chastity,
And wash their hands in Bassianus' blood.   45
Seest thou this letter? take it up, I pray thee,
And give the king this fatal-plotted scroll.
Now question me no more; we are espied;
Here comes a parcel of our hopeful booty,
Which dreads not yet their lives' destruction.   50

Enter Bassianus and Lavinia.

    Tam. Ah! my sweet Moor, sweeter to me than life!
    Aar. No more, great empress; Bassianus comes:
Be cross with him; and I'll go fetch thy sons
To back thy quarrels, whatsoe'er they be.   *[Exit.]*
    Bas. Whom have we here? Rome's royal empress,   55
Unfurnish'd of her well-beseeming troop?
Or is it Dian, habited like her,
Who hath abandoned her holy groves,
To see the general hunting in this forest?
    Tam. Saucy controller of our private steps!   60
Had I the power that some say Dian had,
Thy temples should be planted presently
With horns, as was Actæon's; and the hounds
Should drive upon thy new-transformed limbs,
Unmannerly intruder as thou art!   65
    Lav. Under your patience, gentle empress,
'Tis thought you have a goodly gift in horning;
And to be doubted that your Moor and you
Are singled forth to try experiments.
Jove shield your husband from his hounds to-day!   70
'Tis pity they should take him for a stag.
    Bas. Believe me, queen, your swarth Cimmerian
Doth make your honour of his body's hue,
Spotted, detested, and abominable.
Why are you sequester'd from all your train,   75
Dismounted from your snow-white goodly steed,
And wander'd hither to an obscure plot,
Accompanied but with a barbarous Moor,
If foul desire had not conducted you?
    Lav. And, being intercepted in your sport,   80
Great reason that my noble lord be rated
For sauciness. I pray you, let us hence,
And let her joy her raven-colour'd love;
This valley fits the purpose passing well.
    Bas. The king my brother shall have note of this.   85
    Lav. Ay, for these slips have made him noted long:
Good king, to be so mightily abus'd!
    Tam. Why have I patience to endure all this?

Enter Chiron and Demetrius.

    Dem. How now, dear sovereign, and our gracious mother!
Why doth your highness look so pale and wan?   90
    Tam. Have I not reason, think you, to look pale?
These two have 'tic'd me hither to this place:
A barren detested vale, you see, it is;
The trees, though summer, yet forlorn and lean,
O'ercome with moss and baleful mistletoe: 95
Here never shines the sun; here nothing breeds,
Unless the nightly owl or fatal raven:
And when they show'd me this abhorred pit,
They told me, here, at dead time of the night,
A thousand fiends, a thousand hissing snakes,   100
Ten thousand swelling toads, as many urchins,
Would make such fearful and confused cries,
As any mortal body hearing it
Should straight fall mad, or else die suddenly.
No sooner had they told this hellish tale,   105
But straight they told me they would bind me here
Unto the body of a dismal yew,
And leave me to this miserable death:
And then they call'd me foul adulteress,
Lascivious Goth, and all the bitterest terms   110
That ever ear did hear to such effect;
And, had you not by wondrous fortune come,
This vengeance on me had they executed.
Revenge it, as you love your mother's life,
Or be ye not henceforth call'd my children.   115
    Dem. This is a witness that I am thy son.
             Stabs him [i.e. Bassianus].
    Chi. And this for me, struck home to show my strength.
          [Also stabs Bassianus, who dies.]
    Lav. Ay, come, Semiramis, nay, barbarous Tamora;
For no name fits thy nature but thy own.
    Tam. Give me thy poniard; you shall know, my boys,   120
Your mother's hand shall right your mother's wrong.
    Dem. Stay, madam; here is more belongs to her:
First thrash the corn, then after burn the straw.
This minion stood upon her chastity,
Upon her nuptial vow, her loyalty,   125
And with that painted hope braves your mightiness:
And shall she carry this unto her grave?
    Chi. An if she do, I would I were an eunuch.
Drag hence her husband to some secret hole,
And make his dead trunk pillow to our lust.   130
    Tam. But when ye have the honey ye desire,
Let not this wasp outlive, us both to sting.
    Chi. I warrant you, madam, we will make that sure.
Come, mistress, now perforce we will enjoy
That nice-preserved honesty of yours.   135
    Lav. O Tamora! thou bear'st a woman's face,—
    Tam. I will not hear her speak; away with her!
    Lav. Sweet lords, entreat her hear me but a word.
    Dem. Listen, fair madam: let it be your glory
To see her tears; but be your heart to them   140
As unrelenting flint to drops of rain.
    Lav. When did the tiger's young ones teach the dam?

---

37 venereal: *erotic*   **43 Philomel:** *cf. n.*   **49 parcel:** *part*   **56 well-beseeming troop:** *the guard of honor suitable to an empress*   **62 presently:** *immediately*   **63 horns . . . Actæon's:** *cf. n.*   **64 drive upon:** *rush upon*   **72 Cimmerian:** *cf. n.*   **83 joy:** *enjoy*   **86 slips:** *offences; cf. n.*   **87 abus'd:** *deceived*

92 'tic'd: *enticed*   **93 barren detested vale;** *cf. n.*   **97 fatal:** *evil-omened*   **101 urchins:** *hedgehogs*   **110 Lascivious Goth;** *cf. n.*   **124 minion:** *saucy person*   **stood:** *prided herself*   **126 painted:** *unreal, false (?); cf. n.*   **135 nice-preserved:** *prudishly preserved*

O! do not learn her wrath; she taught it thee;
The milk thou suck'dst from her did turn to marble;
Even at thy teat thou hadst thy tyranny.   *145*
Yet every mother breeds not sons alike:
[*To Chiron.*] Do thou entreat her show a woman pity.
    Chi. What! wouldst thou have me prove myself a bastard?
    Lav. 'Tis true! the raven doth not hatch a lark:
Yet have I heard—O could I find it now!—   *150*
The lion mov'd with pity did endure
To have his princely paws par'd all away.
Some say that ravens foster forlorn children,
The whilst their own birds famish in their nests:
O, be to me, though thy hard heart say no,   *155*
Nothing so kind, but something pitiful!
    Tam. I know not what it means; away with her!
    Lav. O, let me teach thee! for my father's sake,
That gave thee life when well he might have slain thee,
Be not obdurate, open thy deaf ears.   *160*
    Tam. Hadst thou in person ne'er offended me,
Even for his sake am I pitiless.
Remember, boys, I pour'd forth tears in vain
To save your brother from the sacrifice;
But fierce Andronicus would not relent: *165*
Therefore, away with her, and use her as you will:
The worse to her, the better lov'd of me.
    Lav. O Tamora! be call'd a gentle queen,
And with thine own hands kill me in this place;
For 'tis not life that I have begg'd so long;   *170*
Poor I was slain when Bassianus died.
    Tam. What begg'st thou, then? fond woman, let me go.
    Lav. 'Tis present death I beg; and one thing more
That womanhood denies my tongue to tell.
O keep me from their worse than killing lust,   *175*
And tumble me into some loathsome pit,
Where never man's eye may behold my body!
Do this, and be a charitable murderer.
    Tam. So should I rob my sweet sons of their fee:
No, let them satisfy their lust on thee.   *180*
    Dem. Away! for thou hast stay'd us here too long.
    Lav. No grace! no womanhood! Ah, beastly creature,
The blot and enemy to our general name.
Confusion fall—
    Chi. Nay, then I'll stop your mouth. Bring thou her   *185*
husband:
This is the hole where Aaron bid us hide him.

[*Demetrius throws the body of Bassianus into the pit; then exeunt
    Demetrius and Chiron, dragging off Lavinia.*]

    Tam. Farewell, my sons: see that you make her sure.
Ne'er let my heart know merry cheer indeed
Till all the Andronici be made away.   *190*
Now will I hence to seek my lovely Moor,
And let my spleenful sons this trull deflower.   *Exit.*

Enter Aaron, with [Quintus and Martius,] two of Titus's Sons.

    Aar. Come on, my lords, the better foot before:
Straight will I bring you to the loathsome pit
Where I espied the panther fast asleep.   *195*

    Quin. My sight is very dull, whate'er it bodes.
    Mart. And mine, I promise you: were 't not for shame,
Well could I leave our sport to sleep awhile.
                                        [*Falls into the pit.*]
    Quin. What! art thou fall'n? What subtle hole is this,
Whose mouth is cover'd with rude-growing briers,   *200*
Upon whose leaves are drops of new-shed blood
As fresh as morning's dew distill'd on flowers?
A very fatal place it seems to me.
Speak, brother, hast thou hurt thee with the fall?
    Mart. O brother! with the dismal'st object hurt   *205*
That ever eye with sight made heart lament.
    Aar. [*Aside.*] Now will I fetch the king to find them here,
That he thereby may give a likely guess
How these were they that made away his brother.
                                        Exit Aaron.
    Mart. Why dost not comfort me, and help me out   *210*
From this unhallow'd and blood-stained hole?
    Quin. I am surprised with an uncouth fear;
A chilling sweat o'erruns my trembling joints:
My heart suspects more than mine eye can see.
    Mart. To prove thou hast a true-divining heart,   *215*
Aaron and thou look down into this den,
And see a fearful sight of blood and death.
    Quin. Aaron is gone; and my compassionate heart
Will not permit mine eyes once to behold
The thing whereat it trembles by surmise.   *220*
O tell me how it is! for ne'er till now
Was I a child, to fear I know not what.
    Mart. Lord Bassianus lies embrewed here,
All on a heap, like to a slaughter'd lamb,
In this detested, dark, blood-drinking pit.   *225*
    Quin. If it be dark, how dost thou know 'tis he?
    Mart. Upon his bloody finger he doth wear
A precious ring, that lightens all the hole,
Which, like a taper in some monument,
Doth shine upon the dead man's earthy cheeks,   *230*
And shows the ragged entrails of the pit:
So pale did shine the moon on Pyramus
When he by night lay bath'd in maiden blood.
O brother! help me with thy fainting hand—
If fear hath made thee faint, as me it hath—   *235*
Out of this fell devouring receptacle,
As hateful as Cocytus' misty mouth.
    Quin. Reach me thy hand, that I may help thee out;
Or, wanting strength to do thee so much good,
I may be pluck'd into the swallowing womb   *240*
Of this deep pit, poor Bassianus' grave.
I have no strength to pluck thee to the brink.
    Mart. Nor I no strength to climb without thy help.
    Quin. Thy hand once more; I will not loose again,
Till thou art here aloft, or I below.   *245*
Thou canst not come to me: I come to thee.   *Both fall in.*

Enter the Emperor, [with] Aaron the Moor.

    Sat. Along with me: I'll see what hole is here,
And what he is that now is leap'd into it.
Say, who art thou that lately didst descend

---

143 **learn:** *teach*   152 **paws:** *i.e. claws; cf. n.*   153 **ravens ... children;** *cf. n.*   172
fond: *foolish*   173 **present:** *instant*   183 **blot ... name:** *a blot on, and enemy to, the good name of women in general*   192 **spleenful:** *hot, eager*   **trull:** *loose woman*

212 **uncouth:** *strange, horrible*   223 **embrewed:** *soaked in blood*   224 **on a heap:** *in a heap*   228 **A precious ring;** *cf. n.*   232 **Pyramus;** *cf. n.*   237 **Cocytus:** *the river of lamentation in Hades*   244 **loose:** *loose my hold*

Into this gaping hollow of the earth? 250
   Mart. The unhappy son of old Andronicus;
Brought hither in a most unlucky hour,
To find thy brother Bassianus dead.
   Sat. My brother dead! I know thou dost but jest:
He and his lady both are at the lodge, 255
Upon the north side of this pleasant chase;
'Tis not an hour since I left him there.
   Mart. We know not where you left him all alive;
But, out alas! here have we found him dead.

Enter Tamora [with Attendants], [Titus] Andronicus, and Lucius.

   Tam. Where is my lord, the king? 260
   Sat. Here, Tamora; though griev'd with killing grief.
   Tam. Where is thy brother Bassianus?
   Sat. Now to the bottom dost thou search my wound:
Poor Bassianus here lies murthered.
   Tam. Then all too late I bring this fatal writ, 265
The complot of this timeless tragedy;
And wonder greatly that man's face can fold
In pleasing smiles such murderous tyranny.
                She giveth Saturnine a letter. Saturninus
                           reads the letter.
   Sat. 'And if we miss to meet him handsomely,
Sweet huntsman, Bassianus 'tis we mean, 270
Do thou so much as dig the grave for him:
Thou know'st our meaning. Look for thy reward
Among the nettles at the elder-tree
Which overshades the mouth of that same pit
Where we decreed to bury Bassianus: 275
Do this, and purchase us thy lasting friends.'
O Tamora! was ever heard the like?
This is the pit, and this the elder-tree.
Look, sirs, if you can find the huntsman out
That should have murther'd Bassianus here. 280
   Aar. My gracious lord, here is the bag of gold.
   Sat. [To Titus.] Two of thy whelps, fell curs of
     bloody kind,
Have here bereft my brother of his life.
Sirs, drag them from the pit unto the prison: 285
There let them bide until we have devis'd
Some never-heard-of torturing pain for them.
   Tam. What! are they in this pit? O wondrous thing!
How easily murder is discovered!
   Tit. High emperor, upon my feeble knee 290
I beg this boon with tears not lightly shed;
That this fell fault of my accursed sons,
Accursed, if the fault be prov'd in them,—
   Sat. If it be prov'd! you see it is apparent.
Who found this letter? Tamora, was it you? 295
   Tam. Andronicus himself did take it up.
   Tit. I did, my lord: yet let me be their bail;
For, by my father's reverend tomb, I vow
They shall be ready at your highness' will
To answer their suspicion with their lives. 300
   Sat. Thou shalt not bail them: see thou follow me.
Some bring the murther'd body, some the murtherers:
Let them not speak a word; the guilt is plain;

For, by my soul, were there worse end than death,
That end upon them should be executed. 305
   Tam. Andronicus, I will entreat the king:
Fear not thy sons, they shall do well enough.
   Tit. Come, Lucius, come; stay not to talk with them.
                                   Exeunt.

❧ SCENE FOURTH ❧

[Another part of the Forest]
Enter the Empress's Sons, with Lavinia, her hands cut off, and her
tongue cut out, and ravished.

   Dem. So, now go tell, an if thy tongue can speak,
Who 'twas that cut thy tongue and ravish'd thee.
   Chi. Write down thy mind, bewray thy meaning so;
An if thy stumps will let thee play the scribe.
   Dem. See, how with signs and tokens she can scrowl. 5
   Chi. Go home, call for sweet water, wash thy hands.
   Dem. She hath no tongue to call, nor hands to wash;
And so let's leave her to her silent walks.
   Chi. An 'twere my case, I should go hang myself.
   Dem. If thou hadst hands to help thee knit the cord. 10
                  Exeunt [Demetrius and Chiron].
                           Wind horns.

Enter Marcus, from hunting, to Lavinia.

   Mar. Who's this? my niece, that flies away so fast?
Cousin, a word; where is your husband?
If I do dream, would all my wealth would wake me!
If I do wake, some planet strike me down,
That I may slumber in eternal sleep! 15
Speak, gentle niece, what stern ungentle hands
Hath lopp'd and hew'd and made thy body bare
Of her two branches, those sweet ornaments,
Whose circling shadows kings have sought to sleep in,
And might not gain so great a happiness 20
As have thy love? Why dost not speak to me?
Alas! a crimson river of warm blood,
Like to a bubbling fountain stirr'd with wind,
Doth rise and fall between thy rosed lips,
Coming and going with thy honey breath. 25
But, sure, some Tereus hath deflower'd thee,
And, lest thou shouldst detect him, cut they tongue.
Ah! now thou turn'st away thy face for shame;
And, notwithstanding all this loss of blood,
As from a conduit with three issuing spouts, 30
Yet do thy cheeks look red as Titan's face
Blushing to be encounter'd with a cloud.
Shall I speak for thee? shall I say 'tis so?
O that I knew thy heart! and knew the beast,
That I might rail at him to ease my mind. 35
Sorrow conceal'd, like to an oven stopp'd,
Doth burn the heart to cinders where it is.
Fair Philomela, she but lost her tongue,
And in a tedious sampler sew'd her mind:
But, lovely niece, that mean is cut from thee; 40

256 chase: *hunting-ground*   **263 search:** *probe*   **266 complot:** *plot* **timeless:** *un-timely*   **275 decreed:** *determined*

307 Fear not: *fear not for*   **5 scrowl:** *scrawl (?); cf. n.*   **6 sweet:** *perfumed*   **12 Cousin:** *near relation, of either sex*   **17 Hath:** *have*   **26 Tereus;** *cf. n.*   **31 Titan's:** *the sun's*   **34 thy heart:** *what is in thy mind*   **39 mind:** *meaning; cf. n.*   **40 mean:** *means*

A craftier Tereus hast thou met withal,
And he hath cut those pretty fingers off,
That could have better sew'd than Philomel.
O! had the monster seen those lily hands
Tremble, like aspen-leaves, upon a lute,   45
And make the silken strings delight to kiss them,
He would not, then, have touch'd them for his life;
Or had he heard the heavenly harmony
Which that sweet tongue hath made,
He would have dropp'd his knife, and fell asleep,   50
As Cerberus at the Thracian poet's feet.
Come, let us go, and make thy father blind;
For such a sight will blind a father's eye:
One hour's storm will drown the fragrant meads;
What will whole months of tears thy father's eyes?   55
Do not draw back, for we will mourn with thee:
O could our mourning ease thy misery!   *Exeunt.*

ACT THIRD ❧ SCENE FIRST

[Rome. A Street]
Enter the Judges and Senators [and Tribunes], with Titus's two Sons,
bound, passing on the Stage to the place of execution;
and Titus going before, pleading.

Tit. Hear me, grave fathers! noble tribunes, stay!
For pity of mine age, whose youth was spent
In dangerous wars, whilst you securely slept;
For all my blood in Rome's great quarrel shed;
For all the frosty nights that I have watch'd;   5
And for these bitter tears, which now you see
Filling the aged wrinkles in my cheeks:
Be pitiful to my condemned sons,
Whose souls are not corrupted as 'tis thought.
For two-and-twenty sons I never wept,   10
Because they died in honour's lofty bed.
For these, tribunes, in the dust I write

       Andronicus lieth down, and the Judges
             pass by him [and exeunt].

My heart's deep languor and my soul's sad tears.
Let my tears stanch the earth's dry appetite;
My sons' sweet blood will make it shame and blush.   15

       Exeunt [Senators, Tribunes, and the
             Others, with the Prisoners].

O earth! I will befriend thee more with rain,
That shall distil from these two ancient urns,
Than youthful April shall with all his showers:
In summer's drought I'll drop upon thee still;
In winter with warm tears I'll melt the snow,   20
And keep eternal spring-time on thy face,
So thou refuse to drink my dear sons' blood.

Enter Lucius, with his weapon drawn.

O reverend tribunes! O gentle, aged men!
Unbind my sons, reverse the doom of death:
And let me say, that never wept before,   25
My tears are now prevailing orators.
   Luc. O noble father, you lament in vain:

The tribunes hear you not, no man is by;
And you recount your sorrows to a stone.
   Tit. Ah, Lucius, for thy brothers let me plead!   30
Grave tribunes, once more I entreat of you,—
   Luc. My gracious lord, no tribune hears you speak.
   Tit. Why, 'tis no matter, man: if they did hear,
They would not mark me, or if they did mark,
They would not pity me, yet plead I must,   35
And bootless, unto them.
Therefore I tell my sorrows to the stones,
Who, though they cannot answer my distress,
Yet in some sort they are better than the tribunes,
For that they will not intercept my tale.   40
When I do weep, they humbly at my feet
Receive my tears, and seem to weep with me;
And, were they but attired in grave weeds,
Rome could afford no tribune like to these.
A stone is as soft wax, tribunes more hard than stones;   45
A stone is silent, and offendeth not,
And tribunes with their tongues doom men to death.   *[Rises.]*
But wherefore stand'st thou with thy weapon drawn?
   Luc. To rescue my two brothers from their death;
For which attempt the judges have pronounc'd   50
My everlasting doom of banishment.
   Tit. O happy man! they have befriended thee.
Why, foolish Lucius, dost thou not perceive
That Rome is but a wilderness of tigers?
Tigers must prey; and Rome affords no prey   55
But me and mine: how happy art thou then,
From these devourers to be banished!
But who comes with our brother Marcus here?

Enter Marcus and Lavinia.

   Mar. Titus, prepare thy aged eyes to weep;
Or, if not so, thy noble heart to break: 60
I bring consuming sorrow to thine age.
   Tit. Will it consume me? let me see it then.
   Mar. This was thy daughter.
   Tit. Why, Marcus, so she is.
   Luc. Ay me! this object kills me.   65
   Tit. Faint-hearted boy, arise, and look upon her.
Speak, Lavinia, what accursed hand
Hath made thee handless in thy father's sight?
What fool hath added water to the sea,
Or brought a faggot to bright-burning Troy?   70
My grief was at the height before thou cam'st;
And now, like Nilus, it disdaineth bounds.
Give me a sword, I'll chop off my hands too;
For they have fought for Rome, and all in vain;
And they have nurs'd this woe, in feeding life;   75
In bootless prayer have they been held up,
And they have serv'd me to effectless use:
Now all the service I require of them
Is that the one will help to cut the other.
'Tis well, Lavinia, that thou hast no hands,   80
For hands, to do Rome service, are but vain.
   Luc. Speak, gentle sister, who hath martyr'd thee?
   Mar. O! that delightful engine of her thoughts,

---

51 Cerberus . . . feet; *cf. n.*   **10 two-and-twenty sons;** *cf. n.*

34-37 *Cf. n.*   **72 Nilus:** *the river Nile*   **77 effectless:** *ineffectual*   **83 engine:** *instrument*

That blabb'd them with such pleasing eloquence,
Is torn from forth that pretty hollow cage,   85
Where, like a sweet melodious bird, it sung
Sweet varied notes, enchanting every ear.

    Luc. O! say thou for her, who hath done this deed?

    Mar. O! thus I found her straying in the park,
Seeking to hide herself, as doth the deer,   90
That hath receiv'd some unrecuring wound.

    Tit. It was my dear; and he that wounded her
Hath hurt me more than had he kill'd me dead:
For now I stand as one upon a rock
Environ'd with a wilderness of sea,   95
Who marks the waxing tide grow wave by wave,
Expecting ever when some envious surge
Will in his brinish bowels swallow him.
This way to death my wretched sons are gone;
Here stands my other son, a banish'd man,   100
And here my brother, weeping at my woes:
But that which gives my soul the greatest spurn,
Is dear Lavinia, dearer than my soul.
Had I but seen thy picture in this plight
It would have madded me: what shall I do   105
Now I behold thy lively body so?
Thou hast no hands to wipe away thy tears,
Nor tongue to tell me who hath martyr'd thee:
Thy husband he is dead, and for his death
Thy brothers are condemn'd, and dead by this.   110
Look, Marcus! ah! son Lucius, look on her:
When I did name her brothers, then fresh tears
Stood on her cheeks, as doth the honey-dew
Upon a gather'd lily almost wither'd.

    Mar. Perchance she weeps because they kill'd her husband;
Perchance because she knows them innocent.

    Tit. If they did kill thy husband, then be joyful,
Because the law hath ta'en revenge on them.
No, no, they would not do so foul a deed;
Witness the sorrow that their sister makes.   120
Gentle Lavinia, let me kiss thy lips;
Or make some sign how I may do thee ease.
Shall thy good uncle, and thy brother Lucius,
And thou, and I, sit round about some fountain,
Looking all downwards, to behold our cheeks   125
How they are stain'd, like meadows yet not dry,
With miry slime left on them by a flood?
And in the fountain shall we gaze so long
Till the fresh taste be taken from that clearness,
And made a brine-pit with our bitter tears?   130
Or shall we cut away our hands, like thine?
Or shall we bite our tongues, and in dumb shows
Pass the remainder of our hateful days?
What shall we do? let us, that have our tongues,
Plot some device of further misery,   135
To make us wonder'd at in time to come.

    Luc. Sweet father, cease your tears; for at your grief
See how my wretched sister sobs and weeps.

    Mar. Patience, dear niece. Good Titus, dry thine eyes.

    Tit. Ah, Marcus, Marcus, brother! well I wot   140
Thy napkin cannot drink a tear of mine,
For thou, poor man, hast drown'd it with thine own.

    Luc. Ah, my Lavinia, I will wipe thy cheeks.

    Tit. Mark, Marcus, mark! I understand her signs:
Had she a tongue to speak, now would she say   145
That to her brother which I said to thee:
His napkin, with his true tears all bewet,
Can do no service on her sorrowful cheeks.
O what a sympathy of woe is this!
As far from help as limbo is from bliss.   150

           Enter Aaron the Moor, alone.

    Aar. Titus Andronicus, my lord the emperor
Sends thee this word: that, if thou love thy sons,
Let Marcus, Lucius, or thyself, old Titus,
Or any one of you, chop off your hand,
And send it to the king: he for the same   155
Will send thee hither both thy sons alive;
And that shall be the ransom for their fault.

    Tit. O gracious emperor! O gentle Aaron!
Did ever raven sing so like a lark,
That gives sweet tidings of the sun's uprise?   160
With all my heart, I'll send the emperor my hand:
Good Aaron, wilt thou help to chop it off?

    Luc. Stay, father! for that noble hand of thine,
That hath thrown down so many enemies,
Shall not be sent; my hand will serve the turn: 165
My youth can better spare my blood than you;
And therefore mine shall save my brothers' lives.

    Mar. Which of your hands hath not defended Rome,
And rear'd aloft the bloody battle-axe,
Writing destruction on the enemy's castle?   170
O! none of both but are of high desert:
My hand hath been but idle; let it serve
To ransom my two nephews from their death;
Then have I kept it to a worthy end.

    Aar. Nay, come, agree whose hand shall go along,   175
For fear they die before their pardon come.

    Mar. My hand shall go.

    Luc.   By heaven, it shall not go!

    Tit. Sirs, strive no more: such wither'd herbs as these
Are meet for plucking up, and therefore mine.   180

    Luc. Sweet father, if I shall be thought thy son,
Let me redeem my brothers both from death.

    Mar. And for our father's sake, and mother's care,
Now let me show a brother's love to thee.

    Tit. Agree between you; I will spare my hand.   185

    Luc. Then I'll go fetch an axe.

    Mar.   But I will use the axe.

            Exeunt [Lucius and Marcus].

    Tit. Come hither, Aaron; I'll deceive them both:
Lend me thy hand, and I will give thee mine.

    Aar. [*Aside.*] If that be call'd deceit, I will be honest,   190
And never, whilst I live, deceive men so:
But I'll deceive you in another sort,
And that you'll say, ere half an hour pass.

           He cuts off Titus's hand.

          Enter Lucius and Marcus again.

    Tit. Now stay your strife: what shall be is dispatch'd.
Good Aaron, give his majesty my hand: 195

---

91 unrecuring: *incurable*   **97 envious:** *malignant*   **98 his:** *its*   **102 spurn:**
pang   **141 napkin:** *handkerchief*

150 limbo: *i.e. hell; cf. n.*   **170 the enemy's castle;** *cf. n.*   **171 both:** *both of you*   **192
sort:** *fashion*

Tell him it was a hand that warded him
From thousand dangers; bid him bury it:
More hath it merited; that let if have.
As for my sons, say I account of them
As jewels purchas'd at an easy price; 200
And yet dear too, because I bought mine own.

Aar. I go, Andronicus; and for thy hand,
Look by and by to have thy sons with thee.
[Aside.] Their heads, I mean. O how this villainy
Doth fat me with the very thoughts of it! 205
Let fools do good, and fair men call for grace,
Aaron will have his soul black like his face. *Exit.*

Tit. O! here I lift this one hand up to heaven,
And bow this feeble ruin to the earth:
If any power pities wretched tears, 210
To that I call!—*[To Lavinia.]*—What! wilt thou kneel
with me?
Do, then dear heart; for heaven shall hear our prayers,
Or with our sighs we'll breathe the welkin dim,
And stain the sun with fog, as sometime clouds 215
When they do hug him in their melting bosoms.

Mar. O brother, speak with possibilities,
And do not break into these deep extremes.

Tit. Is not my sorrow deep, having no bottom?
Then be my passions bottomless with them. 220

Mar. But yet let reason govern thy lament.

Tit. If there were reason for these miseries,
Then into limits could I bind my woes.
When heaven doth weep, doth not the earth o'erflow?
If the winds rage, doth not the sea wax mad, 225
Threat'ning the welkin with his big-swoll'n face?
And wilt thou have a reason for this coil?
I am the sea; hark how her sighs do flow!
She is the weeping welkin, I the earth:
Then must my sea be moved with her sighs; 230
Then must my earth with her continual tears
Become a deluge, overflow'd and drown'd;
For why my bowels cannot hide her woes,
But like a drunkard must I vomit them.
Then give me leave, for losers will have leave 235
To ease their stomachs with their bitter tongues.

Enter a Messenger with two heads and a hand.

Mess. Worthy Andronicus, ill art thou repaid
For that good hand thou sent'st the emperor.
Here are the heads of thy two noble sons,
And here's thy hand, in scorn to thee sent back: 240
Thy griefs their sports, thy resolution mock'd;
That woe is me to think upon thy woes,
More than remembrance of my father's death. *Exit.*

Mar. Now let hot Ætna cool in Sicily,
And be my heart an ever-burning hell! 245
These miseries are more than may be borne.
To weep with them that weep doth ease some deal,
But sorrow flouted at is double death.

Luc. Ah! that this sight should make so deep a wound,
And yet destested life not shrink thereat! 250
That ever death should let life bear his name,

Where life hath no more interest but to breathe!
[Lavinia kisses Titus.]

Mar. Alas! poor heart; that kiss is comfortless
As frozen water to a starved snake.

Tit. When will this fearful slumber have an end? 255

Mar. Now, farewell, flattery: die, Andronicus;
Thou dost not slumber: see, thy two sons' heads,
Thy warlike hand, thy mangled daughter here;
Thy other banish'd son, with this dear sight
Struck pale and bloodless; and thy brother, I, 260
Even like a stony image, cold and numb.
Ah! now no more will I control my griefs.
Rent off thy silver hair, thy other hand
Gnawing with thy teeth; and be this dismal sight
The closing up of our most wretched eyes! 265
Now is a time to storm; why art thou still?

Tit. Ha, ha, ha!

Mar. Why dost thou laugh? it fits not with this hour.

Tit. Why, I have not another tear to shed:
Besides, this sorrow is an enemy, 270
And would usurp upon my watery eyes,
And make them blind with tributary tears:
Then which way shall I find Revenge's cave?
For these two heads do seem to speak to me,
And threat me I shall never come to bliss 275
Till all these mischiefs be return'd again
Even in their throats that have committed them.
Come, let me see what task I have to do.
You heavy people, circle me about,
That I may turn me to each one of you, 280
And swear unto my soul to right your wrongs.
The vow is made. Come, brother, take a head;
And in this hand the other will I bear.
Lavinia, thou shalt be employ'd in these things:
Bear thou my hand, sweet wench, between thy teeth. 285
As for thee, boy, go get thee from my sight;
Thou art an exile, and thou must not stay:
Hie to the Goths and raise an army there:
And if you love me, as I think you do,
Let's kiss and part, for we have much to do. 290
Exeunt. Manet Lucius.

Luc. Farewell, Andronicus, my noble father;
The woefull'st man that ever liv'd in Rome:
Farewell, proud Rome; till Lucius come again,
He leaves his pledges dearer than his life.
Farewell, Lavinia, my noble sister; 295
O would thou wert as thou tofore hast been!
But now nor Lucius nor Lavinia lives
But in oblivion and hateful griefs.
If Lucius live, he will requite your wrongs,
And make proud Saturnine and his empress 300
Beg at the gates like Tarquin and his queen.
Now will I to the Goths, and raise a power,
Too be reveng'd on Rome and Saturnine. *Exit Lucius.*

---

214 welkin: *sky* **217 with:** *within the range of* **227 coil:** *confusion* **233 For why:**
because **242 That:** *so that* **247 some deal:** *somewhat; cf. n.*

254 starved: *benumbed with cold* **259 dear sight:** *a sight that touches him very
closely* **263 Rent:** *rend* **279 heavy:** *sorrowful* **296 tofore:** *heretofore* **302
power:** *army*

❧ Scene Second ❧

[The Same. A Room in Titus's House] A Banquet [set out]
Enter Andronicus, Marcus, Lavinia, and the Boy [young Lucius].

Tit. So, so; now sit; and look you eat no more
Than will preserve just so much strength in us
As will revenge these bitter woes of ours.
Marcus, unknit that sorrow-wreathen knot:
Thy niece and I, poor creatures, want our hands,   *5*
And cannot passionate our ten-fold grief
With folded arms. This poor right hand of mine
Is left to tyrannize upon my breast;
Who, when my heart, all mad with misery,
Beats in this hollow prison of my flesh,   *10*
Then thus I thump it down.
[To Lavinia.] Thou map of woe, that thus dost talk in signs!
When thy poor heart beats with outrageous beating
Thou canst not strike it thus to make it still.
Wound it with sighing, girl, kill it with groans;   *15*
Or get some little knife between thy teeth,
And just against thy heart make thou a hole;
That all the tears that thy poor eyes let fall
May run into that sink, and, soaking in,
Drown the lamenting fool in sea-salt tears.   *20*
Mar. Fie, brother, fie! teach her not thus to lay
Such violent hands upon her tender life.
Tit. How now! has sorrow made thee dote already?
Why, Marcus, no man should be mad but I.
What violent hands can she lay on her life?   *25*
Ah! wherefore dost thou urge the name of hands?
To bid Æneas tell the tale twice o'er,
How Troy was burnt and he made miserable?
O handle not the theme, to talk of hands,
Lest we remember still that we have none!   *30*
Fie, fie! how franticly I square my talk,
As if we should forget we had no hands,
If Marcus did not name the word of hands.
Come, let's fall to; and, gentle girl, eat this:
Here is no drink. Hark, Marcus, what she says;   *35*
I can interpret all her martyr'd signs:
She says she drinks no other drink but tears,
Brew'd with her sorrow, mash'd upon her cheeks.
Speechless complainer, I will learn thy thought;
In thy dumb action will I be as perfect   *40*
As begging hermits in their holy prayers:
Thou shalt not sigh, nor hold thy stumps to heaven,
Nor wink, nor nod, nor kneel, nor make a sign,
But I of these will wrest an alphabet,
And by still practice learn to know thy meaning.   *45*
Boy. Good grandsire, leave these bitter deep laments:
Make my aunt merry with some pleasing tale.
Mar. Alas! the tender boy, in passion mov'd,
Doth weep to see his grandsire's heaviness.
Tit. Peace, tender sapling; thou art made of tears,   *50*
And tears will quickly melt thy life away.
             Marcus strikes the dish with a knife.
What dost thou strike at, Marcus, with thy knife?

Mar. At that that I have kill'd, my lord,—a fly.
Tit. Out on thee, murderer! thou kill'st my heart;
Mine eyes are cloy'd with view of tyranny: *55*
A deed of death, done on the innocent,
Becomes not Titus' brother. Get thee gone;
I see thou art not for my company.
Mar. Alas! my lord, I have but kill'd a fly.
Tit. 'But!' How, if that fly had a father and mother?   *60*
How would he hang his slender gilded wings
And buzz lamenting doings in the air!
Poor harmless fly,
That, with his pretty buzzing melody,
Came here to make us merry! and thou hast kill'd him.   *65*
Mar. Pardon me, sir; it was a black ill-favour'd fly,
Like to the empress' Moor; therefore I kill'd him.
Tit. O, O, O!
Then pardon me for reprehending thee,
For thou hast done a charitable deed.   *70*
Give me thy knife, I will insult on him;
Flattering myself, as if it were the Moor
Come hither purposely to poison me.
There's for thyself, and that's for Tamora.
Ah, sirrah!   *75*
Yet I think we are not brought so low,
But that between us we can kill a fly
That comes in likeness of a coal-black Moor.
Mar. Alas, poor man! grief has so wrought on him,
He takes false shadows for true substances.   *80*
Tit. Come, take away. Lavinia, go with me:
I'll to thy closet; and go read with thee
Sad stories chanced in the times of old.
Come, boy, and go with me: thy sight is young,
And thou shalt read when mine begin to dazzle.   *Exeunt.* *85*

ACT FOURTH ❧ Scene First

[Rome. Titus's Garden]
Enter young Lucius, and Lavinia running after him, and the Boy
flies from her, with his books under his arm. [Then] enter
Titus and Marcus.

Boy. Help, grandsire, help! my aunt Lavinia
Follows me everywhere, I know not why.
Good uncle Marcus, see how swift she comes:
Alas, sweet aunt! I know not what you mean.
Mar. Stand by me, Lucius; do not fear thine aunt.   *5*
Tit. She loves thee, boy, too well to do thee harm.
Boy. Ay, when my father was in Rome, she did.
Mar. What means my niece Lavinia by these signs?
Tit. Fear her not, Lucius: somewhat doth she mean.
See, Lucius, see how much she makes of thee;   *10*
Somewhither would she have thee go with her.
Ah, boy! Cornelia never with more care
Read to her sons, than she hath read to thee
Sweet poetry and Tully's Orator.

Scene Two: *cf. n.*   **4 sorrow-wreathen knot:** *cf. n.*   **12 map:** *picture*   **15 Wound it with sighing;** *cf. n.*   **31 square:** *shape, fashion*   **36 martyr'd signs:** *signs of her martyrdom*   **38 Brew'd ... mash'd;** *cf. n.*   **40 be as perfect:** *show as perfect an understanding*   **44 of these:** *from these*   **45 still:** *constant*

62 lamenting doings: *stories of lamentable deeds*   **71 insult on:** *exult over*   **76 Yet ... low:** *we are not yet brought so low*   **81 take away:** *clear the table*   **85 mine:** *mine eyes*   **12 Cornelia:** *the mother of the Gracchi*   **14 Tully's Orator:** *Cicero's De Oratore*

[Mar.] Canst thou not guess wherefore she plies thee thus?

Boy. My lord, I know not, I, nor can I guess,
Unless some fit or frenzy do possess her;
For I have heard my grandsire say full oft,
Extremity of griefs would make men mad;
And I have read that Hecuba of Troy   20
Ran mad through sorrow; that made me to fear,
Although, my lord, I know my noble aunt
Loves me as dear as e'er my mother did,
And would not, but in fury, fright my youth;
Which made me down to throw my books and fly,   25
Causeless, perhaps. But pardon me, sweet aunt;
And, madam, if my uncle Marcus go,
I will most willingly attend your ladyship.

Mar. Lucius, I will.
                              *[Lavinia turns over with her stumps the
                              books which Lucius has let fall.]*

Tit. How now, Lavinia! Marcus, what means this?   30
Some book there is that she desires to see.
Which is it, girl, of these? Open them, boy.
But thou art deeper read, and better skill'd;
Come, and take choice of all my library,
And so beguile thy sorrow, till the heavens   35
Reveal the damn'd contriver of this deed.
Why lifts she up her arms in sequence thus?

Mar. I think she means that there was more than one.
Confederate in the fact: ay, more there was;
Or else to heaven she heaves them for revenge.   40

Tit. Lucius, what book is that she tosseth so?

Boy. Grandsire, 'tis Ovid's Metamorphoses;
My mother gave it me.

Mar.   For love of her that's gone,
Perhaps, she cull'd it from among the rest.   45

Tit. Soft! so busily she turns the leaves! Help her.
What would she find? Lavinia, shall I read?
This is the tragic tale of Philomel,
And treats of Tereus' treason and his rape;
And rape, I fear, was root of thine annoy.   50

Mar. See, brother, see! note how she quotes the leaves.

Tit. Lavinia, wert thou thus surpris'd, sweet girl,
Ravish'd and wrong'd, as Philomela was,
Forc'd in the ruthless, vast, and gloomy woods?
See, see!   55
Ay, such a place there is, where we did hunt,—
O had we never, never hunted there!—
Pattern'd by that the poet here describes,
By nature made for murthers and for rapes.

Mar. O! why should nature build so foul a den,   60
Unless the gods delight in tragedies?

Tit. Give signs, sweet girl, for here are none but friends,
What Roman lord it was durst do the deed:
Or slunk not Saturnine, as Tarquin erst,
That left the camp to sin in Lucrece' bed?   65

Mar. Sit down, sweet niece: brother, sit down by me.
Apollo, Pallas, Jove, or Mercury,
Inspire me, that I may this treason find!
My lord, look here; look here, Lavinia:

This sandy plot is plain; guide, if thou canst,   70
This after me.
                              *He writes his name with his staff, and
                              guides it with feet and mouth.*
          I have writ my name
Without the help of any hand at all.
Curs'd be that heart that forc'd us to this shift!
Write thou, good niece, and here display at last   75
What God will have discover'd for revenge.
Heaven guide thy pen to print thy sorrows plain,
That we may know the traitors and the truth!
                              *She takes the staff in her mouth, and
                              guides it with her stumps, and writes.*

Tit. O! do ye read, my lord, what she hath writ?
'Stuprum, Chiron, Demetrius.'   80

Mar. What, what! the lustful sons of Tamora
Performers of this heinous, bloody deed?

*Tit. Magni dominator poli,
Tam lentus audis scelera? tam lentus vides?*

Mar. O calm thee, gentle lord! although I know   85
There is enough written upon this earth
To stir a mutiny in the mildest thoughts
And arm the minds of infants to exclaims.
My lord, kneel down with me; Lavinia, kneel;
And kneel, sweet boy, the Roman Hector's hope;   90
And swear with me, as, with the woeful fere
And father of that chaste dishonour'd dame,
Lord Junius Brutus sware for Lucrece' rape,
That we will prosecute by good advice
Mortal revenge upon these traitorous Goths,   95
And see their blood, or die with this reproach.

Tit. 'Tis sure enough, an you knew how;
But if you hunt these bear-whelps, then beware:
The dam will wake, an if she wind you once:
She's with the lion deeply still in league,   100
And lulls him whilst she playeth on her back,
And when he sleeps will she do what she list.
You're a young huntsman, Marcus; let it alone;
And, come, I will go get a leaf of brass,
And with a gad of steel will write these words,   105
And lay it by: the angry northern wind
Will blow these sands like Sibyl's leaves abroad,
And where's your lesson then? Boy, what say you?

Boy. I say, my lord, that if I were a man,
Their mother's bed-chamber should not be safe   110
For these bad bondmen to the yoke of Rome.

Mar. Ay, that's my boy! thy father hath full oft
For his ungrateful country done the like.

Boy. And, uncle, so will I, an if I live.

Tit. Come, go with me into mine armoury: 115
Lucius, I'll fit thee; and withal my boy
Shall carry from me to the empress' sons
Presents that I intend to send them both:
Come, come! thou'lt do thy message, wilt thou not?

Boy. Ay, with my dagger in their bosoms, grandsire. 120

Tit. No, boy, not so; I'll teach thee another course.
Lavinia, come. Marcus, look to my house;

---

15 plies: *importunes*   **20, 21** Hecuba … sorrow; *cf. n.*   **24** fury: *madness*   **37** in sequence: *one after the other; cf. n.*   **39** fact: *deed*   **48** Philomel; *cf. n. on II.iii. 43*   **49** annoy: *suffering*   **51** quotes: *examines*   **58** Pattern'd by: *fashioned after*   **64** erst: *formerly*

80 Stuprum: *rape*   **83** Magni dominator, etc.: *Ruler of the great heaven, dost thou so calmly hear crimes, so calmly look upon them? Cf. n.*   **88** exclaims: *exclamations*   **89–93** My lord, kneel down, etc.; *cf. n.*   **91** fere: *mate*   **99** wind: *scent*   **105** gad: *point*   **107** Sibyl's leaves; *cf. n.*

Lucius and I'll go brave it at the court:
Ay, marry, will we, sir; and we'll be waited on.
Exeunt [Titus, Lavinia, and young Lucius].

   Mar. O heavens! can you hear a good man groan,   *125*
And not relent or not compassion him?
Marcus, attend him in his ecstasy,
That hath more scars of sorrow in his heart
Than foemen's marks upon his batter'd shield;
But yet so just that he will not revenge.   *130*
Revenge the heavens for old Andronicus!   *Exit.*

❧ SCENE SECOND ❧

[The same. A Room in the Palace]
Enter Aaron, Chiron, and Demetrius at one door; and at another
door young Lucius and another, with a bundle of weapons,
and verses writ upon them.

   Chi. Demetrius, here's the son of Lucius;
He hath some message to deliver us.
   Aar. Ay, some mad message from his mad grandfather.
   Boy. My lords, with all the humbleness I may,
I greet your honours from Andronicus;   *5*
[Aside.] And pray the Roman gods, confound you both!
   Dem. Gramercy, lovely Lucius: what's the news?
   Boy. *[Aside.]* That you are both decipher'd, that's the news,
For villains mark'd with rape. *[Aloud.]* May it please you,
My grandsire, well advis'd, hath sent by me   *10*
The goodliest weapons of his armoury,
To gratify your honourable youth,
The hope of Rome, for so he bade me say;
And so I do, and with his gifts present
Your lordships, that whenever you have need,   *15*
You may be armed and appointed well.
And so I leave you both: *[Aside.]* like bloody villains.
Exit [with Attendant].

   Dem. What's here? A scroll, and written round about?
Let's see:—
[Reads.] 'Integer vitæ, scelerisque purus,   *20*
Non eget Mauri jaculis, nec arcu.'
   Chi. O! 'tis a verse in Horace; I know it well:
I read it in the grammar long ago.
   Aar. Ay, just, a verse in Horace; right, you have it.
[Aside.] Now, what a thing it is to be an ass!   *25*
Here's no sound jest! the old man hath found their guilt
And sends them weapons wrapp'd about with lines,
That wound, beyond their feeling, to the quick;
But were our witty empress well afoot,
She would applaud Andronicus' conceit: *30*
But let her rest in her unrest awhile.
[To them.] And now, young lords, was't not a happy star
Led us to Rome, strangers and more than so,
Captives, to be advanced to this height?
It did me good before the palace gate   *35*
To brave the tribune in his brother's hearing.
   Dem. But me more good, to see so great a lord
Basely insinuate and send us gifts.

   Aar. Had he not reason, Lord Demetrius?
Did you not use his daughter very friendly?   *40*
   Dem. I would we had a thousand Roman dames
At such a bay, by turn to serve our lust.
   Chi. A charitable wish and full of love.
   Aar. Here lacks but your mother for to say amen.
   Chi. And that would she for twenty thousand more.   *45*
   Dem. Come, let us go and pray to all the gods
For our beloved mother in her pains.
   Aar. *[Aside.]* Pray to the devils; the gods have
given us over.   *Flourish [within].*
   Dem. Why do the emperor's trumpets flourish thus?   *50*
   Chi. Belike, for joy the emperor hath a son.
   Dem. Soft! who comes here?

Enter Nurse with a blackamoor Child.

   Nur. Good morrow, lords. O! tell me, did you see
Aaron the Moor?
   Aar. Well, more or less, or ne'er a whit at all,   *55*
Here Aaron is; and what with Aaron now?
   Nur. O gentle Aaron! we are all undone.
Now help, or woe betide thee evermore!
   Aar. Why, what a caterwauling dost thou keep!
What dost thou wrap and fumble in thine arms?   *60*
   Nur. O! that which I would hide from heaven's eye,
Our empress' shame, and stately Rome's disgrace!
She is deliver'd, lords, she is deliver'd.
   Aar. To whom?
   Nur.   I mean, she is brought a-bed.   *65*
   Aar. Well, God give her good rest! What hath he sent her?
   Nur. A devil.
   Aar. Why, then she's the devil's dam: a joyful issue.
   Nur. A joyless, dismal, black, and sorrowful issue.
Here is the babe, as loathsome as a toad   *70*
Amongst the fairest breeders of our clime.
The empress sends it thee, thy stamp, thy seal,
And bids thee christen it with thy dagger's point.
   Aar. 'Zounds, ye whore! is black so base a hue?
Sweet blowse, you are a beauteous blossom, sure.   *75*
   Dem. Villain, what hast thou done?
   Aar. That which thou canst not undo.
   Chi. Thou hast undone our mother.
   [Aar. Villain, I have done thy mother.]
   Dem. And therein, hellish dog, thou hast undone.   *80*
Woe to her chance, and damn'd her loathed choice!
Accurs'd the offspring of so foul a fiend!
   Chi. It shall not live.
   Aar. It shall not die.
   Nur. Aaron, it must; the mother wills it so.   *85*
   Aar. What! must it, nurse? then let no man but I
Do execution on my flesh and blood.
   Dem. I'll broach the tadpole on my rapier's point:
Nurse, give it me; my sword shall soon dispatch it.
   Aar. Sooner this sword shall plough thy bowels up.   *90*
[Takes the Child from the Nurse, and draws.]
Stay, murtherous villains! will you kill your brother?
Now, by the burning tapers of the sky,
That shone so brightly when this boy was got,

126 compassion: *have compassion on*   127 ecstasy: *frenzy*   10 well-advis'd: *in his right mind*   16 appointed: *equipped*   20 Integer vitæ, etc.: *cf. n.*   24 just: *just so*   26 sound jest: *cf. n.*

42 At such a bay: *under such circumstances*   51 Belike: *probably*   74 'Zounds: *cf. n.*   75 blowse: *cf. n.*   88 broach: *spit*

He dies upon my scimitar's sharp point
That touches this my first-born son and heir.   *95*
I tell you, younglings, not Enceladus,
With all his threat'ning band of Typhon's brood,
Nor great Alcides, not the god of war,
Shall seize this prey out of his father's hands.
What, what, ye sanguine, shallow-hearted boys!   *100*
Ye white-lim'd walls! ye alehouse painted signs!
Coal-black is better than another hue,
In that it scorns to bear another hue;
For all the water in the ocean
Can never turn the swan's black legs to white,   *105*
Although she lave them hourly in the flood.
Tell the empress from me, I am of age
To keep mine own, excuse it how she can.
 Dem. Wilt thou betray thy noble mistress thus?
 Aar. My mistress is my mistress; this myself;   *110*
The vigour, and the picture of my youth:
This before all the world do I prefer;
This maugre all the world will I keep safe,
Or some of you shall smoke for it in Rome.
 Dem. By this our mother is for ever sham'd.   *115*
 Chi. Rome will despise her for this foul escape.
 Nur. The emperor in his rage will doom her death.
 Chi. I blush to think upon this ignomy.
 Aar. Why, there's the privilege your beauty bears.
Fie, treacherous hue! that will betray with blushing   *120*
The close enacts and counsels of the heart.
Here's a young lad fram'd of another leer:
Look how the black slave smiles upon the father,
As who should say, 'Old lad, I am thine own.'
He is your brother, lords, sensibly fed   *125*
Of that self blood that first gave life to you;
And from that womb where you imprison'd were
He is enfranchised and come to light:
Nay, he is your brother by the surer side,
Although my seal be stamped in his face.   *130*
 Nur. Aaron, what shall I say unto the empress?
 Dem. Advise thee, Aaron, what is to be done,
And we will all subscribe to thy advice:
Save thou the child, so we may all be safe.
 Aar. Then sit we down, and let us all consult.   *135*
My son and I will have the wind of you:
Keep there; now talk at pleasure of your safety.   *[They sit.]*
 Dem. How many women saw this child of his?
 Aar. Why, so, brave lords! when we join in league,
I am a lamb; but if you brave the Moor,   *140*
The chafed boar, the mountain lioness,
The ocean swells not so as Aaron storms.
But say, again, how many saw the child?
 Nur. Cornelia the midwife, and myself,
And no one else but the deliver'd empress.   *145*
 Aar. The empress, the midwife, and yourself:
Two may keep counsel when the third's away.
Go to the empress; tell her this I said:

          He kills her.

'Weke, weke!'
So cries a pig prepared to the spit.   *150*
 Dem. What mean'st thou, Aaron? Wherefore didst thou this?
 Aar. O Lord, sir, 'tis a deed of policy:
Shall she live to betray this guilt of ours,
A long-tongu'd babbling gossip? no, lords, no.
And now be it known to you my full intent.   *155*
Not far, one Muli lives, my countryman;
His wife but yesternight was brought to bed.
His child is like to her, fair as you are:
Go pack with him, and give the mother gold,
And tell them both the circumstance of all,   *160*
And how by this their child shall be advanc'd,
And be received for the emperor's heir,
And substituted in the place of mine,
To calm this tempest whirling in the court;
And let the emperor dandle him for his own.   *165*
Hark ye, lords; ye see, I have given her physic,

          [Pointing to the Nurse.]

And you must needs bestow her funeral;
The fields are near, and you are gallant grooms.
This done, see that you take no longer days,
But send the midwife presently to me.   *170*
The midwife and the nurse well made away,
Then let the ladies tattle what they please.
 Chi. Aaron, I see thou wilt not trust the air
With secrets.
 Dem.   For this care of Tamora,   *175*
Herself and hers are highly bound to thee.

    Exeunt [Demetrius and Chiron, bearing
         off the Nurse's body].

 Aar. Now to the Goths, as swift as swallow flies:
There to dispose this treasure in mine arms,
And secretly to greet the empress' friends.
Come on, you thick-lipp'd slave, I'll bear you hence;   *180*
For it is you that puts us to our shifts:
I'll make you feed on berries and on roots,
And feed on curds and whey, and suck the goat,
And cabin in a cave, and bring you up
To be a warrior, and command a camp.   *Exit. 185*

❧ SCENE THIRD ❧

[The same. A Public Place]
Enter Titus, old Marcus, young Lucius, and other gentlemen,
[Publius, Sempronius, and Caius] with bows; and Titus
bears the arrows, with letters on the ends of them.

 Tit. Come, Marcus, come; kinsmen, this is the way.
Sir boy, let me see your archery:
Look ye draw home enough, and 'tis there straight.
Terras Astræa reliquit:
Be you remember'd, Marcus, she's gone, she's fled.   *5*
Sirs, take you to your tools. You, cousins, shall
Go sound the ocean, and cast your nets;
Haply you may find her in the sea;

---

96 Enceladus: *one of the Titans confined under Mt. Ætna* **97 Typhon's brood;** *cf. n.*
98 Alcides: *Hercules* **100 sanguine:** *blood-colored* **101 white-lim'd:** *white-washed* **106 lave:** *wash* **113 maugre:** *in spite of* **116 escape:** *escapade* **118 ignomy:** *ignominy* **121 enacts:** *workings* **122 leer:** *complexion* **125 sensibly:** *manifestly* **126 self:** *selfsame* **132 Advise thee:** *consider* **136 have the wind of you:** *keep an eye upon you*

156 one Muli lives; *cf. n.* **159 pack:** *plot* **160 circumstance of all:** *all the details* **167 bestow her funeral:** *give her burial* **169 no longer days:** *no more time* **170 presently:** *instantly* **178 dispose:** *dispose of* **4 Terras Astræa reliquit:** *Astræa has left the earth; cf. n.* **5 Be you remember'd:** *be mindful*

Yet there's as little justice as at land.
No; Publius and Sempronius, you must do it;   *10*
'Tis you must dig with mattock and with spade,
And pierce the inmost centre of the earth:
Then, when you come to Pluto's region,
I pray you, deliver him this petition;
Tell him, it is for justice and for aid,   *15*
And that it comes from old Andronicus,
Shaken with sorrows in ungrateful Rome.
Ah, Rome! Well, well; I made thee miserable
What time I threw the people's suffrages
On him that thus doth tyrannize o'er me.   *20*
Go, get you gone; and pray be careful all,
And leave you not a man-of-war unsearch'd:
This wicked emperor may have shipp'd her hence;
And, kinsmen, then we may go pipe for justice.
    Mar. O Publius! is not this a heavy case,   *25*
To see thy noble uncle thus distract?
    Pub. Therefore, my lord, it highly us concerns
By day and night to attend him carefully,
And feed his humour kindly as we may,
Till time beget some careful remedy.   *30*
    Mar. Kinsmen, his sorrows are past remedy.
John with the Goths, and with revengeful war
Take wreak on Rome for this ingratitude,
And vengeance on the traitor Saturnine.
    Tit. Publius, how now! how now, my masters!   *35*
What! have you met with her?
    Pub. No, my good lord; but Pluto sends you word,
If you will have Revenge from hell, you shall:
Marry, for Justice, she is so employ'd,
He thinks, with Jove in heaven, or somewhere else,   *40*
So that perforce you must needs stay a time.
    Tit. He doth me wrong to feed me with delays.
I'll dive into the burning lake below,
And pull her out of Acheron by the heels.
Marcus, we are but shrubs, no cedars we;   *45*
No big-bon'd men fram'd of the Cyclops' size;
But metal, Marcus, steel to the very back,
Yet wrung with wrongs more than our backs can bear:
And sith there's no justice in earth nor hell,
We will solicit heaven and move the gods   *50*
To send down Justice for to wreak our wrongs.
Come, to this gear. You are a good archer, Marcus.
                        He gives them the arrows.
Ad Jovem, that's for you: here, *ad Apollinem:*
Ad Martem, that's for myself:
Here, boy, to Pallas: here, to Mercury: *55*
To Saturn, Caius, not to Saturnine;
You were as good to shoot against the wind.
To it, boy! Marcus, loose when I bid.
Of my word, I have written to effect;
There's not a god left unsolicited.   *60*
    Mar. Kinsmen, shoot all your shafts into the court:
We will afflict the emperor in his pride.
    Tit. Now, masters, draw. *[They shoot.]* O! well said, Lucius!

Good boy, in Virgo's lap: give it Pallas.
    Mar. My lord, I aim a mile beyond the moon;   *65*
Your letter is with Jupiter by this.
    Tit. Ha, ha! Publius, Publius, what hast thou done?
See, see! thou hast shot off one of Taurus' horns.
    Mar. This was the sport, my lord: when Publius shot,
The Bull, being gall'd, gave Aries such a knock   *70*
That down fell both the Ram's horns in the court;
And who should find them but the empress' villain?
She laugh'd, and told the Moor, he should not choose
But give them to his master for a present.
    Tit. Why, there it goes: God give his lordship joy!   *75*

    Enter the Clown, with a basket, and two pigeons in it.

News! news from heaven! Marcus, the post is come.
Sirrah, what tidings? have you any letters?
Shall I have justice? what says Jupiter?
    Clo. O! the gibbet-maker? He says that he hath taken
them down again, for the man must not be hanged till the   *80*
next week.
    Tit. But what says Jupiter, I ask thee?
    Clo. Alas! sir, I know not Jupiter; I never drank with
him in all my life.
    Tit. Why, villain, art not thou the carrier?   *85*
    Clo. Ay, of my pigeons, sir; nothing else.
    Tit. Why, didst thou not come from heaven?
    Clo. From heaven! alas! sir, I never came there. God
forbid I should be so bold to press to heaven in my young
days. Why, I am going with my pigeons to the tribunal plebs,
to take up a matter of brawl betwixt my uncle and one of
the emperial's men.
    Mar. Why, sir, that is as fit as can be to serve for your
oration; and let him deliver the pigeons to the emperor
from you.   *95*
    Tit. Tell me, can you deliver an oration to the emperor
with a grace?
    Clo. Nay, truly, sir, I could never say grace in all my life.
    Tit. Sirrah, come hither: make no more ado,
But give your pigeons to the emperor: *100*
By me thou shalt have justice at his hands.
Hold, hold; meanwhile, here's money for thy charges.
Give me pen and ink.
Sirrah, can you with a grace deliver a supplication?
    Clo. Ay, sir.   *105*
    Tit. Then here is a supplication for you. And when you
come to him, at the first approach you must kneel; then kiss
his foot; then deliver up your pigeons; and then look for your
reward. I'll be at hand, sir; see you do it bravely.
    Clo. I warrant you, sir; let me alone.   *110*
    Tit. Sirrah, hast thou a knife? Come, let me see it.
Here, Marcus, fold it in the oration;
For thou hast made it like an humble suppliant:
And when thou hast given it the emperor,
Knock at my door, and tell me what he says.   *115*
    Clo. God be with you, sir; I will.   *Exit.*
    Tit. Come, Marcus, let us go. Publius, follow me.   *Exeunt.*

---

13 Pluto's region: *the infernal regions*   **24 pipe:** *whistle*   **30 careful remedy:** *remedy obtained through the exercise of care (?).*   **33 wreak:** *revenge*   **39 for:** *as for*   **43, 44 burning lake … Acheron;** *cf. n.*   **46 Cyclops:** *giants, servants of Vulcan*   **51 wreak:** *revenge*   **52 gear:** *business*   **53, 54 Ad Jovem, etc.:** *to Jupiter, to Apollo, to Mars*   **58 loose:** *shoot*   **59 Of my word:** *upon my word* **to effect:** *to the purpose*   **63 well said:** *well done*

64-70 Virgo … Taurus … Aries: *constellations; cf. n.*   **90 tribunal plebs:** *tribune of the people (properly, tribunus plebis)*   **91 take up:** *make up*   **92 emperial's:** *emperor's*   **109 bravely:** *in good style*

❧ SCENE FOURTH ❧

[The Same. Before the Palace]
Enter the Emperor and Empress, and her two Sons [Lords and
Others]. The Emperor brings the arrows in his hand
that Titus shot at him.

Sat. Why, lords, what wrongs are these! Was ever seen
An emperor in Rome thus overborne,
Troubled, confronted thus; and, for the extent
Of egal justice, us'd in such contempt?
My lords, you know, [as do] the mightful gods,— 5
However these disturbers of our peace
Buzz in the people's ears,—there nought hath pass'd,
But even with law, against the wilful sons
Of old Andronicus. And what an if
His sorrows have so overwhelm'd his wits, 10
Shall we be thus afflicted in his wreaks,
His fits, his frenzy, and his bitterness?
And now he writes to heaven for his redress:
See, here's to Jove, and this to Mercury;
This to Apollo; this to the god of war; 15
Sweet scrolls to fly about the streets of Rome!
What's this but libelling against the senate,
And blazoning our injustice everywhere?
A goodly humour, is it not, my lords?
As who would say, in Rome no justice were. 20
But if I live, his feigned ecstasies
Shall be no shelter to these outrages;
But he and his shall know that justice lives
In Saturninus' health; whom, if she sleep,
He'll so awake, as she in fury shall 25
Cut off the proud'st conspirator that lives.
 Tam. My gracious lord, my lovely Saturnine,
Lord of my life, commander of my thoughts,
Calm thee, and bear the faults of Titus' age,
Th' effects of sorrow for his valiant sons, 30
Whose loss hath pierc'd him deep and scarr'd his heart;
And rather comfort his distressed plight
Than prosecute the meanest or the best
For these contempts.—*[Aside.]* Why, thus it shall become
High-witted Tamora to gloze with all: 35
But, Titus, I have touch'd thee to the quick,
Thy life-blood out: if Aaron now be wise,
Then is all safe, the anchor's in the port.

Enter Clown.

How now, good fellow! wouldst thou speak with us?
 Clo. Yea, forsooth, an your mistership be emperial. 40
 Tam. Empress I am, but yonder sits the emperor.
 Clo. 'Tis he. God and Saint Stephen give you good den.
I have brought you a letter and a couple of pigeons here.
    He [Saturninus] reads the letter.
 Sat. Go, take him away, and hang him presently.
 Clo. How much money must I have? 45
 Tam. Come, sirrah, you must be hanged.
 Clo. Hanged! By'r lady, then I have brought up a neck to a
fair end.   *Exit [guarded].*

Sat. Despiteful and intolerable wrongs!
Shall I endure this monstrous villainy? 50
I know from whence this same device proceeds:
May this be borne? As if his trait'rous sons,
That died by law for murther of our brother,
Have by my means been butcher'd wrongfully!
Go, drag the villain hither by the hair; 55
Nor age nor honour shall shape privilege.
For this proud mock I'll be thy slaughterman,
Sly frantic wretch, that holp'st to make me great,
In hope thyself should govern Rome and me.

Enter Nuntius Æmilius.

What news with thee, Æmilius? 60
 Æmil. Arm, my lords! Rome never had more cause.
The Goths have gather'd head, and with a power
Of high-resolved men, bent to the spoil,
They hither march amain, under conduct
Of Lucius, son to old Andronicus; 65
Who threats, in course of this revenge, to do
As much as ever Coriolanus did.
 Sat. Is warlike Lucius general of the Goths?
These tidings nip me, and I hang the head
As flowers with frost or grass beat down with storms. 70
Ay, now begins our sorrows to approach:
'Tis he the common people love so much.
Myself hath often heard them say,
When I have walked like a private man,
That Lucius' banishment was wrongfully, 75
And they have wish'd that Lucius were their emperor.
 Tam. Why should you fear? is not your city strong?
 Sat. Ay, but the citizens favour Lucius,
And will revolt from me to succour him.
 Tam. King, be thy thoughts imperious, like thy name. 80
Is the sun dimm'd, that gnats do fly in it?
The eagle suffers little birds to sing,
And is not careful what they mean thereby,
Knowing that with the shadow of his wings
He can at pleasure stint their melody; 85
Even so mayst thou the giddy men of Rome.
Then cheer thy spirit; for know, thou emperor,
I will enchant the old Andronicus
With words more sweet, and yet more dangerous,
Than baits to fish, or honey-stalks to sheep, 90
Whenas the one is wounded with the bait,
The other rotted with delicious food.
 Sat. But he will not entreat his son for us.
 Tam. If Tamora entreat him, then he will:
For I can smooth and fill his aged ear 95
With golden promises, that, were his heart
Almost impregnable, his old ears deaf,
Yet should both ear and heart obey my tongue.
[To Æmilius.] Go thou before, be our ambassador:
Say that the emperor requests a parley 100
Of warlike Lucius, and appoint the meeting,
Even at his father's house, the old Andronicus.
 Sat. Æmilius, do this message honourably:
And if he stand on hostage for his safety,

3, 4, extent Of egal justice: *maintenance of equal justice* **7 Buzz:** *whisper* **8 even with:** *in accord with* **11 wreaks:** *revenges* **21 ecstasies:** *insanity* **25 as:** *that* **35 High-witted:** *cunning* **gloze:** *beguile* **40 mistership:** *the clown's attempt at 'mistress-ship'* **42 good den:** *good evening*

56 shape privilege: *constitute exemption from punishment* **66 in course of:** *in carrying out* **67 Coriolanus;** *cf. n.* **71 begins:** *begin* **85 stint:** *stop* **90 honey-stalks;** *cf. n.* **91 Whenas:** *when* **95 smooth:** *flatter* **104 stand on hostage:** *demand hostages*

Bid him demand what pledge will please him best.   *105*
  Æmil. Your bidding shall I do effectually.   *Exit.*
  Tam. Now will I to that old Andronicus,
And temper him with all the art I have,
To pluck proud Lucius from the warlike Goths.
And now, sweet emperor, be blithe again,   *110*
And bury all thy fear in my devices.
  Sat. Then go successantly, and plead to him.   *Exeunt.*

ACT FIFTH ❧ SCENE FIRST

[Plains near Rome]
Flourish. Enter Lucius with an Army of Goths,
with drum and colours.

  Luc. Approved warriors, and my faithful friends,
I have received letters from great Rome,
Which signify what hate they bear their emperor,
And how desirous of our sight they are.
Therefore, great lords, be, as your titles witness,   *5*
Imperious and impatient of your wrongs;
And wherein Rome hath done you any scath,
Let him make treble satisfaction.
  [1.] Goth. Brave slip, sprung from the great Andronicus,
Whose name was once our terror, now our comfort;   *10*
Whose high exploits and honourable deeds
Ingrateful Rome requites with foul contempt;
Be bold in us: we'll follow where thou lead'st,
Like stinging bees in hottest summer's day
Led by their master to the flower'd fields,   *15*
And be aveng'd on cursed Tamora.
  [All the Goths.] And, as he saith, so say we all with him.
  Luc. I humbly thank him, and I thank you all.
But who comes here, led by a lusty Goth?

Enter a Goth, leading of Aaron, with his Child in his arms.

  [2.] Goth. Renowned Lucius, from our troops I stray'd,   *20*
To gaze upon a ruinous monastery;
And as I earnestly did fix mine eye
Upon the wasted building, suddenly
I heard a child cry underneath a wall.
I made unto the noise; when soon I heard   *25*
The crying babe controll'd with this discourse:
'Peace, tawny slave, half me and half thy dam!
Did not thy hue bewray whose brat thou art,
Had nature lent thee but thy mother's look,
Villain, thou mightst have been an emperor: *30*
But where the bull and cow are both milk-white,
They never do beget a coal-black calf.
Peace, villain, peace!'—even thus he rates the babe—
'For I must bear thee to a trusty Goth;
Who, when he knows thou art the empress' babe,   *35*
Will hold thee dearly for thy mother's sake.'
With this, my weapon drawn, I rush'd upon him,
Surpris'd him suddenly, and brought him hither,
To use as you think needful of the man.

  Luc. O worthy Goth, this is the incarnate devil   *40*
That robb'd Andronicus of his good hand:
This is the pearl that pleas'd your empress' eye,
And here's the base fruit of his burning lust.
Say, wall-ey'd slave, whither wouldst thou convey
This growing image of thy fiend-like face?   *45*
Why dost not speak? What! deaf? not a word?
A halter, soldiers! hang him on this tree,
And by his side his fruit of bastardy.
  Aar. Touch not the boy; he is of royal blood.
  Luc. Too like the sire for ever being good.   *50*
First hang the child, that he may see it sprawl;
A sight to vex the father's soul withal.
Get me a ladder.

*[A ladder is brought, which Aaron
is made to ascend.]*

  Aar.   Lucius, save the child;
And bear it from me to the empress.   *55*
If thou do this, I'll show thee wondrous things,
That highly may advantage thee to hear:
If thou wilt not, befall what may befall,
I'll speak no more but 'Vengeance rot you all!'
  Luc. Say on; and if it please me which thou speak'st,   *60*
Thy child shall live, and I will see it nourish'd.
  Aar. And if it please thee! why, assure thee, Lucius,
'Twill vex thy soul to hear what I shall speak;
For I must talk of murthers, rapes, and massacres,
Acts of black night, abominable deeds,   *65*
Complots of mischief, treason, villainies
Ruthful to hear, yet piteously perform'd:
And this shall all be buried by my death,
Unless thou swear to me my child shall live.
  Luc. Tell on thy mind: I say, thy child shall live.   *70*
  Aar. Swear that he shall, and then I will begin.
  Luc. Who should I swear by? thou believ'st no god:
That granted, how canst thou believe an oath?
  Aar. What if I do not? as, indeed, I do not;
Yet, for I know thou art religious,   *75*
And hast a thing within thee called conscience,
With twenty popish tricks and ceremonies,
Which I have seen thee careful to observe,
Therefore I urge thy oath; for that I know
An idiot holds his bauble for a god,   *80*
And keeps the oath which by that god he swears,
To that I'll urge him: therefore thou shalt vow
By that same god, what god soe'er it be,
That thou ador'st and hast in reverence,
To save my boy, to nourish and bring him up: *85*
Or else I will discover nought to thee.
  Luc. Even by my god I sear to thee I will.
  Aar. First, know thou, I begot him on the empress.
  Luc. O most insatiate, luxurious woman!
  Aar. Tut! Lucius, this was but a deed of charity   *90*
To that which thou shalt hear of me anon.
'Twas her two sons that murder'd Bassianus;
They cut thy sister's tongue and ravish'd her,
And cut her hands and trimm'd her as thou saw'st.
  Luc. O detestable villain! call'st thou that trimming?   *95*

---

108 temper: *influence*   **112 successantly:** *in succession* (?).   **I Approved:** *tried*   **7
scath:** *harm*   **9 slip:** *scion*   **26 controll'd:** *restrained*   **33 rates:** *scolds*

42 pearl … eye; *cf. n.*   **44 wall-ey'd:** *white-eyed*   **50 for ever being:** *ever to be*   **67
piteously:** *pitiably*   **75 for:** *because*   **79 urge:** *insist upon*   **80 idiot … bauble;**
cf. n.   **89 luxurious:** *lustful*

Aar. Why, she was wash'd, and cut, and trimm'd, and
'twas
Trim sport for them that had the doing of it.
     Luc. O barbarous, beastly villains, like thyself!
     Aar. Indeed, I was their tutor to instruct them.   *100*
That codding spirit had they from their mother,
As sure a card as ever won the set;
That bloody mind, I think, they learn'd of me,
As true a dog as ever fought at head.
Well, let my deeds be witness of my worth.   *105*
I train'd thy brethren to that guileful hole
Where the dead corpse of Bassianus lay;
I wrote the letter that thy father found,
And hid the gold within the letter mention'd,
Confederate with the queen and her two sons: *110*
And what not done, that thou hast cause to rue,
Wherein I had no stroke of mischief in it?
I play'd the cheater for thy father's hand,
And, when I had it, drew myself apart,
And almost broke my heart with extreme laughter.   *115*
I pry'd me through the crevice of a wall
When, for his hand, he had his two sons' heads;
Beheld his tears, and laugh'd so heartily,
That both mine eyes were rainy like to his:
And when I told the empress of this sport,   *120*
She sounded almost at my pleasing tale,
And for my tidings gave me twenty kisses.
     [1.] Goth. What! canst thou say all this, and never blush?
     Aar. Ay, like a black dog, as the saying is.
     Luc. Art thou not sorry for these heinous deeds?   *125*
     Aar. Ay, that I had not done a thousand more.
Even now I curse the day, and yet, I think,
Few come within the compass of my curse,
Wherein I did not some notorious ill:
As kill a man, or else devise his death;   *130*
Ravish a maid, or plot the way to do it;
Accuse some innocent, and forswear myself;
Set deadly enmity between two friends;
Make poor men's cattle break their necks;
Set fire on barns and hay-stacks in the night,   *135*
And bid the owners quench them with their tears.
Oft have I digg'd up dead men from their graves,
And set them upright at their dear friends' doors,
Even when their sorrows almost were forgot;
And on their skins, as on the bark of trees,   *140*
Have with my knife carved in Roman letters,
'Let not your sorrow die, though I am dead.'
Tut! I have done a thousand dreadful things
As willingly as one would kill a fly,
And nothing grieves me heartily indeed   *145*
But that I cannot do ten thousand more.
     Luc. Bring down the devil, for he must not die
So sweet a death as hanging presently.
     Aar. If there be devils, would I were a devil,
To live and burn in everlasting fire,   *150*
So I might have your company in hell,
But to torment you with my bitter tongue!
     Luc. Sirs, stop his mouth, and let him speak no more.

[Enter a Goth.]

     Goth. My lord, there is a messenger from Rome
Desires to be admitted to your presence.   *155*
     Luc. Let him come near.

Enter Æmilius.

Welcome, Æmilius! what's the news from Rome?
     Æmil. Lord Lucius, and you princes of the Goths,
The Roman emperor greets you all by me;
And, for he understands you are in arms,   *160*
He craves a parley at your father's house,
Willing you to demand your hostages,
And they shall be immediately deliver'd.
     [1.] Goth. What says our general?
     Luc. Æmilius, let the emperor give his pledges   *165*
Unto my father and my uncle Marcus,
And we will come. March away.   *Flourish. Exeunt.*

❧ SCENE SECOND ❧

[Rome. Before Titus's House]
Enter Tamora and her two Sons, disguised.

     Tam. Thus, in this strange and sad habiliment,
I will encounter with Andronicus,
And say I am Revenge, sent from below
To join with him and right his heinous wrongs.
Knock at his study, where, they say, he keeps,   *5*
To ruminate strange plots of dire revenge;
Tell him, Revenge is come to join with him,
And work confusion on his enemies.
               They knock. Titus opens his study door [above].
     Tit. Who doth molest my contemplation?
Is it your trick to make me ope the door,   *10*
That so my sad decrees may fly away,
And all my study be to no effect?
You are deceiv'd; for what I mean to do,
See here, in bloody lines I have set down;
And what is written shall be executed.   *15*
     Tam. Titus, I am come to talk with thee.
     Tit. No, not a word; how can I grace my talk,
Wanting a hand to give it action?
Thou hast the odds of me; therefore no more.
     Tam. If thou didst know me, thou wouldst talk with me. *20*
     Tit. I am not mad; I know thee well enough:
Witness this wretched stump, witness these crimson lines;
Witness these trenches made by grief and care;
Witness the tiring day and heavy night;
Witness all sorrow, that I know thee well   *25*
For our proud empress, mighty Tamora.
Is not thy coming for my other hand?
     Tam. Know, thou sad man, I am not Tamora;
She is thy enemy, and I thy friend:
I am Revenge, sent from th' infernal kingdom,   *30*
To ease the gnawing vulture of thy mind,
By working wreakful vengeance on thy foes.
Come down, and welcome me to this world's light;

101 **codding:** *lecherous*   106 **train'd:** *enticed*   111 **what not done:** *what was not done*   121 **sounded:** *swooned*   124 **like a black dog;** *cf. n.*   126 ff. *Cf. n.*   147 **Bring down the devil;** *cf. n.*

162 **Willing:** *desiring*   2 **encounter with:** *meet*   11 **sad decrees:** *serious resolutions*   32 **wreakful:** *wrathful*

Confer with me of murder and of death.
There's not a hollow cave or lurking-place,   35
No vast obscurity or misty vale,
Where bloody murther or detested rape
Can couch for fear, but I will find them out;
And in their ears tell them my dreadful name,
Revenge, which makes the foul offenders quake.   40
    Tit. Art thou Revenge? and art thou sent to me,
To be a torment to mine enemies?
    Tam. I am; therefore come down, and welcome me.
    Tit. Do me some service ere I come to thee.
Lo, by thy side where Rape and Murder stands;   45
Now give some surance that thou art Revenge:
Stab them, or tear them on thy chariot-wheels,
And then I'll come and be thy waggoner,
And whirl along with thee about the globes.
Provide thee two proper palfreys, black as jet,   50
To hale thy vengeful waggon swift away,
And find out murtherers in their guilty caves:
And when thy car is loaden with their heads,
I will dismount, and by the waggon-wheel
Trot like a servile footman all day long,   55
Even from Hyperion's rising in the east
Until his very downfall in the sea:
And day by day I'll do this heavy task,
So thou destroy Rapine and Murder there.
    Tam. These are my ministers, and come with me.   60
    Tit. Are these thy ministers? what are they call'd?
    Tam. Rape and Murder; therefore called so,
'Cause they take vengeance of such kind of men.
    Tit. Good Lord, how like the empress' sons they are,
And you the empress! but we worldly men   65
Have miserable, mad, mistaking eyes.
O sweet Revenge! now do I come to thee;
And, if one arm's embracement will content thee,
I will embrace thee in it by and by.   *[Exit above.]*
    Tam. This closing with him fits his lunacy.   70
Whate'er I forge to feed his brain-sick fits,
Do you uphold and maintain in your speeches,
For now he firmly takes me for Revenge;
And, being credulous in this mad thought,
I'll make him send for Lucius his son;   75
And, whilst I at a banquet hold him sure,
I'll find some cunning practice out of hand
To scatter and disperse the giddy Goths,
Or, at the least, make them his enemies.
See, here he comes, and I must ply my theme.   80

[Enter Titus, below.]

    Tit. Long have I been forlorn, and all for thee:
Welcome, dread Fury, to my woeful house:
Rapine and Murther, you are welcome too.
How like the empress and her sons you are!
Well are you fitted had you but a Moor: 85
Could not all hell afford you such a devil?
For well I wot the empress never wags
But in her company there is a Moor;
And would you represent our queen aright,

It were convenient you had such a devil.   90
But welcome, as you are. What shall we do?
    Tam. What wouldst thou have us do, Andronicus?
    Dem. Show me a murtherer, I'll deal with him.
    Chi. Show me a villain that hath done a rape,
And I am sent to be reveng'd on him.   95
    Tam. Show me a thousand that have done thee wrong,
And I will be revenged on them all.
    Tit. Look round about the wicked streets of Rome,
And when thou find'st a man that's like thyself,
Good Murder, stab him; he's a murtherer.   100
Go thou with him; and when it is thy hap
To find another that is like to thee,
Good Rapine, stab him; he's a ravisher.
Go thou with them; and in the emperor's court
There is a queen attended by a Moor;   105
Well mayst thou know her by thy own proportion,
For up and down she doth resemble thee:
I pray thee, do on them some violent death;
They have been violent to me and mine.
    Tam. Well hast thou lesson'd us; this shall we do.   110
But would it please thee, good Andronicus,
To send for Lucius, thy thrice-valiant son,
Who leads towards Rome a band of warlike Goths,
And bid him come and banquet at thy house:
When he is here, even at thy solemn feast,   115
I will bring in the empress and her sons,
The emperor himself, and all thy foes,
And at thy mercy shall they stoop and kneel,
And on them shalt thou ease thy angry heart.
What says Andronicus to this device?   120
    Tit. Marcus, my brother! 'tis sad Titus calls.

Enter Marcus.

Go, gentle Marcus, to thy nephew Lucius;
Thou shalt inquire him out among the Goths:
Bid him repair to me, and bring with him
Some of the chiefest princes of the Goths;   125
Bid him encamp his soldiers where they are:
Tell him, the emperor and the empress too
Feast at my house, and he shall feast with them.
This do thou for my love; and so let him,
As he regards his aged father's life.   130
    Mar. This will I do, and soon return again.   *[Exit.]*
    Tam. Now will I hence about thy business,
And take my ministers along with me.
    Tit. Nay, nay, let Rape and Murder stay with me;
Or else I'll call my brother back again,   135
And cleave to no revenge but Lucius.
    Tam. [Aside to her sons.] What say you, boys? will
you bide with him,
Whiles I go tell my lord the emperor
How I have govern'd our determin'd jest?   140
Yield to his humour, smooth, and speak him fair,
And tarry with him till I turn again.
    Tit. [Aside.] I know them all, though they suppose me mad;
And will o'erreach them in their own devices:
A pair of cursed hell-hounds and their dam.   145

---

36 **obscurity:** *obscure place*   46 **surance:** *assurance*   56 **Hyperion:** *the old sun-
god*   59 **Rapine:** *rape*   65 **worldly:** *living in the world*   70 **closing:** *agreeing*   77
practice: *stratagem*

107 **up and down:** *completely*   140 **govern'd ... jest:** *managed our proposed deception*   142 **turn:** *return*

Dem. [*Aside to Tamora.*] Madam, depart at pleasure; leave us here.

Tam. Farewell, Andronicus: Revenge now goes
To lay a complot to betray thy foes.   [*Exit Tamora.*]

Tit. I know thou dost; and, sweet Revenge, farewell.   *150*

Chi. Tell us, old man, how shall we be employ'd?

Tit. Tut! I have work enough for you to do.
Publius, come hither, Caius and Valentine!

[*Enter Publius and Others.*]

Pub. What is your will?

Tit. Know you these two?   *155*

Pub. The empress' sons,
I take them, Chiron [and] Demetrius.

Tit. Fie, Publius, fie! thou art too much deceiv'd;
The one is Murder, Rape is the other's name;
And therefore bind them, gentle Publius;   *160*
Caius and Valentine, lay hands on them;
Oft have you heard me wish for such an hour,
And now I find it: therefore bind them sure,
[And stop their mouths, if they begin to cry.]

[*Exit. Publius and the Others lay
hold on Chiron and Demetrius.*]

Chi. Villians, forbear! we are the empress' sons.   *165*

Pub. And therefore do we what we are commanded.
Stop close their mouths, let them not speak a word.
Is he sure bound? look that you bind them fast.

Enter Titus Andronicus with a knife, and Lavinia with a basin.

Tit. Come, come, Lavinia; look, thy foes are bound.
Sirs, stop their mouths, let them not speak to me,   *170*
But let them hear what fearful words I utter.
O villains, Chiron and Demetrius!
Here stands the spring whom you have stain'd with mud,
This goodly summer with your winter mix'd.
You kill'd her husband, and for that vile fault   *175*
Two of her brothers were condemn'd to death,
My hand cut off and made a merry jest:
Both her sweet hands, her tongue, and that more dear
Than hands or tongue, her spotless chastity,
Inhuman traitors, you constrain'd and forc'd.   *180*
What would you say if I should let you speak?
Villains! for shame you could not beg for grace.
Hark, wretches! how I mean to martyr you.
This one hand yet is left to cut your throats,
Whilst that Lavinia 'tween her stumps doth hold   *185*
The basin that receives your guilty blood.
You know your mother means to feast with me,
And calls herself Revenge, and thinks me mad.
Hark! villains, I will grind your bones to dust,
And with your blood and it I'll make a paste;
And of the paste a coffin I will rear,   *190*
And make two pasties of your shameful heads;
And bid that strumpet, your unhallow'd dam,
Like to the earth swallow her own increase.
This is the feast that I have bid her to,
And this the banquet she shall surfeit on;   *195*
For worse than Philomel you us'd my daughter,

And worse than Progne I will be reveng'd.
And now prepare your throats. Lavinia, come.
Receive the blood: and when that they are dead,   *200*
Let me go grind their bones to powder small,
And with this hateful liquor temper it;
And in that paste let their vile heads be bak'd.
Come, come, be every one officious
To make this banquet, which I wish might prove   *205*
More stern and bloody than the Centaurs' feast.

He cuts their throats.

So, now bring them in, for I'll play the cook,
And see them ready 'gainst their mother comes.

Exeunt [bearing the dead bodies].

❧ SCENE THIRD ❧

*[The Same. The Court of Titus's House]
Enter Lucius, Marcus, and the Goths [with Aaron prisoner].*

Luc. Uncle Marcus, since 'tis my father's mind
That I repair to Rome, I am content.

[1.] Goth. And ours with thine, befall what fortune will.

Luc. Good uncle, take you in this barbarous Moor,
This ravenous tiger, this accursed devil;   *5*
Let him receive no sustenance, fetter him,
Till he be brought unto the empress' face,
For testimony of her foul proceedings:
And see the ambush of our friends be strong;
I fear the emperor means no good to us.   *10*

Aar. Some devil whisper curses in my ear,
And prompt me, that my tongue may utter forth
The venomous malice of my swelling heart!

Luc. Away, inhuman dog! unhallow'd slave!
Sirs, help our uncle to convey him in.   *15*

*[Exeunt Goths, with Aaron.] Flourish
[within].*

The trumpets show the emperor is at hand.

*Sound trumpets. Enter Emperor and Empress, with [Æmilius,]
Tribunes, [Senators,] and Others.*

Sat. What! hath the firmament more suns than one?

Luc. What boots it thee, to call thyself a sun?

Mar. Rome's emperor, and nephew, break the parle;
These quarrels must be quietly debated.   *20*
The feast is ready which the careful Titus
Hath ordain'd to an honourable end,
For peace, for love, for league, and good to Rome:
Please you, therefore, draw nigh, and take your places.

Sat. Marcus, we will.   *Hautboys.*

*A table brought in. [The Company sit down at table.] Enter
Titus, like a Cook, placing the meat on the table; and Lavinia
with a veil over her face [and young Lucius with Others].*

Tit. Welcome, my gracious lord; welcome, dread queen;
Welcome, ye warlike Goths; welcome, Lucius;
And welcome, all. Although the cheer be poor,

---

191 coffin: *pie-crust; cf. n.*   **194 increase:** *offspring*

198 worse than Progne; *cf. n.*   **202 temper:** *mix*   **204 officious:** *active*   **206 Centaurs' feast;** *cf. n.*   **3 ours with thine:** *our will is one with thine*   **19 break the parle:** *stop the parley*

'Twill fill your stomachs, please you eat of it.

   Sat. Why art thou thus attir'd, Andronicus?   30

   Tit. Because I would be sure to have all well

To entertain your highness, and your empress.

   Tam. We are beholding to you, good Andronicus.

   Tit. An if your highness knew my heart, you were.

My lord the emperor, resolve me this: 35

Was it well done of rash Virginius

To slay his daughter with his own right hand,

Because she was enforc'd, stain'd, and deflower'd?

   Sat. It was, Andronicus.

   Tit. Your reason, mighty lord?   40

   Sat. Because the girl should not survive her shame,

And by her presence still renew his sorrows.

   Tit. A reason mighty, strong, and effectual;

A pattern, precedent, and lively warrant,

For me most wretched, to perform the like.   45

Die, die, Lavinia, and thy shame with thee;

And with thy shame thy father's sorrow die!   *He kills her.*

   Sat. What hast done, unnatural and unkind?

   Tit. Kill'd her, for whom my tears have made me blind.

I am as woeful as Virginius was,   50

And have a thousand times more cause than he

[To do this outrage: and it now is done.]

   Sat. What! was she ravish'd? tell who did the deed.

   Tit. Will 't please you eat? will 't please your highness feed?

   Tam. Why hast thou slain thine only daughter thus?   55

   Tit. Not I; 'twas Chiron and Demetrius:

They ravish'd her, and cut away her tongue:

And they, 'twas they, that did her all this wrong.

   Sat. Go fetch them hither to us presently.

   Tit. Why, there they are both, baked in that pie;   60

Whereof their mother daintily hath fed,

Eating the flesh that she herself hath bred.

'Tis true, 'tis true; witness my knife's sharp point.

                 He stabs the Empress.

   Sat. Die, frantic wretch, for this accursed deed!

                 [Kills Titus.]

   Luc. Can the son's eye behold his father bleed?   65

There's meed for meed, death for a deadly deed!

       [Kills Saturninus. A great tumult. The

       people in confusion disperse. Marcus,

       Lucius, and their partisans go up

       into the balcony.]

   Mar. You sad-fac'd men, people and sons of Rome,

By uproars sever'd, like a flight of fowl

Scatter'd by winds and high tempestuous gusts,

O! let me teach you how to knit again   70

This scatter'd corn into one mutual sheaf,

These broken limbs again into one body;

Lest Rome herself be bane unto herself,

And she whom mighty kingdoms curtsy to,

Like a forlorn and desperate castaway,   75

Do shameful execution on herself.

But if my frosty signs and chaps of age,

Grave witnesses of true experience,

Cannot induce you to attend my words,

[To Lucius.] Speak, Rome's dear friend, as erst our ancestor,   80

When with his solemn tongue he did discourse

To love-sick Dido's sad attending ear

The story of that baleful burning night

When subtle Greeks surpris'd King Priam's Troy;

Tell us what Sinon hath bewitch'd our ears,   85

Or who hath brought the fatal engine in

That gives our Troy, our Rome, the civil wound.

My heart is not compact of flint nor steel,

Nor can I utter all our bitter grief,

But floods of tears will drown my oratory,   90

And break my very utterance, even in the time

When it should move you to attend me most,

Lending your kind commiseration.

Here is a captain, let him tell the tale;

Your hearts will throb and weep to hear him speak.   95

   Luc. This, noble auditory, be it known to you,

That cursed Chiron and Demetrius

Were they that murdered our emperor's brother;

And they it was that ravished our sister.

For their fell faults our brothers were beheaded,   100

Our father's tears despis'd, and basely cozen'd

Of that true hand that fought Rome's quarrel out,

And sent her enemies unto the grave:

Lastly, myself unkindly banished,

The gates shut on me, and turn'd weeping out,   105

To beg relief among Rome's enemies;

Who drown'd their enmity in my true tears,

And op'd their arms to embrace me as a friend:

And I am turn'd forth, be it known to you,

That have preserv'd her welfare in my blood,   110

And from her bosom took the enemy's point,

Sheathing the steel in my adventurous body.

Alas! you know I am no vaunter, I;

My scars can witness, dumb although they are,

That my report is just and full of truth.   115

But, soft! methinks I do digress too much,

Citing my worthless praise: O, pardon me!

For when no friends are by, men praise themselves.

   Mar. Now is my turn to speak. Behold this child;

       [Pointing to the Child in the arms

       of an Attendant.]

Of this was Tamora delivered,   120

The issue of an irreligious Moor,

Chief architect and plotter of these woes.

The villain is alive in Titus' house,

Damn'd as he is, to witness this is true.

Now judge what cause had Titus to revenge   125

These wrongs, unspeakable, past patience,

Or more than any living man could bear.

Now you have heard the truth, what say you Romans?

Have we done aught amiss, show us wherein,

And, from the place where you behold us now,   130

The poor remainder of Andronici

Will, hand in hand, all headlong cast us down,

And on the ragged stones beat forth our brains,

And make a mutual closure of our house.

Speak, Romans, speak! and if you say we shall,   135

Lo! hand in hand, Lucius and I will fall.

   Æmil. Come, come, thou reverend man of Rome,

---

33 **beholding:** *beholden*   35 **resolve me:** *tell me*   36, 37 **rash Virginius . . . his daughter;** *cf. n.*   38 **enforc'd:** *violated*   66 **meed for meed:** *measure for measure*   71 **mutual:** *united*   77 **chaps:** *wrinkles*   80 **our ancestor:** *Æneas*

85 **Sinon;** *cf. n.*   88 **compact:** *composed*   93-97 *Cf. n.*   100 **fell:** *cruel*   101 **and basely cozen'd:** *and [he] basely cheated*   124 **Damn'd as he is;** *cf. n.*   134 **closure:** *end*

And bring our emperor gently in thy hand,
Lucius, our emperor; for well I know
The common voice do cry it shall be so.   140
　　[*Romans.*] Lucius, all hail! Rome's royal emperor!
　　Mar. [*To Attendants.*] Go, go into old Titus' sorrowful
house,
And hither hale that misbelieving Moor,
To be adjudg'd some direful slaughtering death,   145
As punishment for his most wicked life.
　　　　　　　　　　　　　　[*Exeunt Attendants.*]
　　　　　　　　[*Lucius, Marcus, and the Others descend.*]
　　[*Romans.*] Lucius, all hail! Rome's gracious governor!
　　Luc. Thanks, gentle Romans: may I govern so,
To heal Rome's harms, and wipe away her woe!
But, gentle people, give me aim awhile,   150
For nature puts me to a heavy task.
Stand all aloof; but, uncle, draw you near,
To shed obsequious tears upon this trunk.
O! take this warm kiss on thy pale cold lips,

　　　　　　　　　　　　　　　[*Kisses Titus.*]

These sorrowful drops upon thy blood-stain'd face,   155
The last true duties of thy noble son!
　　Mar. Tear for tear, and loving kiss for kiss,
Thy brother Marcus tenders on thy lips:
O! were the sum of these that I should pay
Countless and infinite, yet would I pay them.   160
　　Luc. Come hither, boy; come, come, and learn of us
To melt in showers: thy grandsire lov'd thee well:
Many a time he danc'd thee on his knee,
Sung thee asleep, his loving breast thy pillow;
Many a matter hath he told to thee,   165
Meet and agreeing with thine infancy;
In that respect, then, like a loving child,
Shed yet some small drops from thy tender spring,
Because kind nature doth require it so:
Friends should associate friends in grief and woe.   170
Bid him farewell; commit him to the grave;
Do him that kindness, and take leave of him.

　　Boy. O grandsire, grandsire! even with all my heart
Would I were dead, so you did live again.
O Lord! I cannot speak to him for weeping;   175
My tears will choke me if I ope my mouth.

　　　　　　　[*Re-enter Attendants with Aaron.*]

　　[*1.*] *Roman.* You sad Andronici, have done with woes:
Give sentence on this execrable wretch,
That hath been breeder of these dire events.
　　Luc. Set him breast-deep in earth, and famish him;   180
There let him stand, and rave, and cry for food:
If any one relieves or pities him,
For the offence he dies. This is our doom:
Some stay to see him fasten'd in the earth.
　　Aar. O, why should wrath be mute, and fury dumb?   185
I am no baby, I, that with base prayers
I should repent the evils I have done.
Ten thousand worse than ever yet I did
Would I perform, if I might have my will:
If one good deed in all my life I did,   190
I do repent it from my very soul.
　　Luc. Some loving friends convey the emperor hence,
And give him burial in his father's grave.
My father and Lavinia shall forthwith
Be closed in our household's monument.   195
As for that heinous tiger, Tamora,
No funeral rite, nor man in mournful weeds!
No mournful bell shall ring her burial;
But throw her forth to beasts and birds of prey.
Her life was beast-like, and devoid of pity;   200
And, being so, shall have like want of pity.
See justice done on Aaron, that damn'd Moor,
By whom our heavy haps had their beginning:
Then, afterwards, to order well the state,
That like events may ne'er it ruinate.   *Exeunt omnes.*

　　　　　　　　　　❧　FINIS　❧

150 give me aim; *cf. n.*　　**153 obsequious tears:** *tears befitting a funeral*　　**166–170** *Cf. n.*
170 associate: *accompany*　　　　　　　　**201** *Cf. n.*

NOTES

Dramatis Personæ. A list of characters was first given in Rowe's edition of 1709. The First Folio divides the play into acts, of which the first is headed *Actus Primus. Scœna Prima.* There is no further division into scenes.

I.i.S.d. *aloft.* The tribunes and senators enter on the gallery which was situated at the back of the Elizabethan stage, and served a variety of purposes. It was, e.g., the balcony from which Juliet speaks to Romeo in *Romeo and Juliet,* and in *The Taming of the Shrew* it served as the gallery from which Christopher Sly and his attendants watch the play performed on the lower stage. Cf. also below, I.i. 304 and V.ii.8.

I.i.9. *Romans.* 'As a matter of orthoepy, it is perhaps worthy of notice that throughout this play, and generally in English books printed before the middle of the seventeenth century, this word is spelled *Romaines* or *Romanes.* "Romaine" could hardly have been pronounced *Roman.*' (White.)

I.i.35. *In coffins from the field.* After these words in the Quarto of 1594, there is a passage of three and a half lines which was omitted from the later texts. Lines 35-38 in the 1594 Quarto read as follows:

> 'In coffins from the field, and at this day
> To the Monument of that Andronici
> Done sacrifice of expiation
> And slaine the Noblest prisoner of the Gothes.'

I.i.64. Because of the fact that there is a distinct break here between the action that has just finished and that now commencing, Pope, Capell, Malone, and other editors begin a new scene with line 64. There is no change of place, however, and later editors prefer to make no change in the scene.

I.i.98. *Ad manes fratrum sacrifice his flesh.* Human sacrifices to propitiate the shades of the dead were, of course, unknown in Rome, but neither the author nor his audience was scrupulous with respect to historical or geographical accuracy. Cf. note on I.i.329.

I.i.117-119. *Wilt thou draw near . . . nobility's true badge.* It is hardly necessary to mention the resemblance between this sentiment of Tamora's and that expressed by Portia, *Merchant of Venice,* IV.i.88-106.

I.i.131. *Was ever Scythia half so barbarous?* Cf. *King Lear,* I.i.118-120:

> 'The barbarous Scythian
> Or he that makes his generation messes
> To gorge his appetite.'

I.i.138. *the Thracian tyrant.* Polymnestor, upon whom Hecuba, Queen of Troy, took vengeance for the death of her son, Polydorus. It was not in *his* tent, however, but in her own, to which she had induced Polymnestor to come, that she made the 'opportunity of sharp revenge.' The allusion is to the *Hecuba* of Euripides, which had not been translated into English in Shakespeare's time.

I.i.154. *grudges.* The Quarto of 1600 has *drugs,* but the Quarto of 1611 and the First Folio have *grudges,* a word which seems to be more in keeping with the sense of the preceding line.

I.i.168. *fame's eternal date.* Cf. *Sonnets,* 18.4:

> 'And summer's lease hath all too short a date.'

Dr. Johnson remarks: 'To *outlive an eternal date* is, though not philosophical, yet poetical sense. He wishes that her life may be longer than his, and her praise longer than fame.'

I.i.177. *Solon's happiness.* Alluding to the remarks of the philosopher Solon to Crœsus, king of Lydia, to the effect that true happiness is dependent on honor, and that no man can be finally adjudged happy until after his death. Cf. *Herodotus,* 1.32.

I.i.218. *people's tribunes.* The First Folio has 'noble tribunes.' It may be that it was originally written 'people's,' and changed to 'noble' when the play was acted, as the latter word is somewhat more sonorous.

I.i.318. *bandy.* A term from the game of tennis, meaning to strike the ball to and fro.

I.i.329. *priest and holy water.* Such references to Christian ritual are, of course, anachronistic, but in the true Shakespearean manner. Cf. the 'popish tricks and ceremonies' of V.i.77 below.

I.i.386. *Ajax.* This seems to be an allusion to the *Ajax* of Sophocles, in which Ulysses pleads with Agamemnon for permission to bury the body of Ajax. So far as is known the *Ajax* had not been translated into English in Shakespeare's day.

I.i.407. *you have play'd your prize.* Won what you were competing for. 'A metaphor borrowed from the fencing schools, prizes being played for certain

degrees in the schools where the art of defence was taught—degrees of Master, Provost, and Scholar.' (Dyce's *Glossary.*)

I.i.493. *Stand up.* These two words were regarded as stage directions by Pope and by several editors after him. In the quartos and folios, they form the first part of what in our text is line 494.

I.i.499. *love-day.* A day appointed by the Church for the settlement of disputes amicably out of court, by an umpire. Cf. Gower, *Confessio Amantis,* I.39.

> 'Hell is full of such discord
> That there may be no loveday.'

I.i.501. *To hunt the panther.* The same type of imagination which infested the Roman forest with panthers introduced the lioness to the forest of Arden, and brought the bear to the seacoast of Bohemia and to the woods of Crete.

II.i.14. *mount her pitch.* Pitch = point. A technical expression in falconry denoting the height to which a falcon soars before attacking the prey. Cf. Romeo's remarks, *Romeo and Juliet,* I.iv.19ff.

> 'I am too sore enpierced with his shaft,
> To soar with his light feathers; and so bound,
> I cannot bound a pitch above dull woe.'

Aaron means that he will soar to whatever height Tamora attains.

II.i.17. *Prometheus tied to Caucasus.* No other play of Shakespeare's is so full of allusions to classical mythology, or contains so many Latin expressions and Latinized forms as *Titus Andronicus.*

II.i.22. *Semiramis.* This legendary queen of Assyria was famous alike for her cruelty and her voluptuousness.

II.i.37. *Clubs, clubs!* A call for men armed with clubs to put down a disturbance. It was a familiar cry in the streets of Elizabethan London. Originally the rallying cry of the apprentices, it became later the regular call for the policemen.

II.i.41. *lath.* The stage sword or dagger used by the Vice in the old moralities was made of a lath, and the latter term came quite naturally to be used for an ineffective weapon. Cf. *Twelfth Night,* IV.ii.119 ff.

II.i.55. *Not I.* Warburton suggested that this speech be given to Chiron, and the following to Demetrius, on the not very plausible ground that it is Chiron who has made the 'reproachful speeches.'

II.i.72. *This discord's ground.* 'There is a play upon the musical sense of *ground* (="plain-song" or theme).' (Rolfe.)

II.i.86. *She is a woman, etc.* A quasi-proverbial expression found in several plays of Shakespeare, as well as elsewhere. Cf. *1 Henry VI,* V.iii.78, 79:

> 'She's beautiful and therefore to be woo'd,
> She is a woman, therefore to be won.'

II.i.89-91. *more water glideth by the mill, Than wots the miller of; and easy it is Of a cut loaf to steal a shive.* Collier noted the fact that both of these proverbs occur within a page of each other in *The Cobler of Canterburie,* 1590: 'Much water runnes by the mill that the miller wots not on. . . . The Prior perceived that the scull had cut a shive on his loafe.' (Cf. Ouvry's reprint, London, 1862, pp. 12 ff.) Both *The Cobler of Canterburie* and *Titus Andronicus* have been attributed to Greene. Cf. Authorship of the Play. Rolfe quotes the Scottish proverb, 'Mickle water goes by the miller when he sleeps.'

II.i.93. *Vulcan's badge.* The cuckold's horns. The allusion is to the intrigue of Mars and Venus, the wife of Vulcan.

II.i.115. *Lucrece was not more chaste.* The story of Tarquin's rape of Lucrece seems to have been much in the mind of the author at this time. Cf. below IV. i.64, 91 ff. Shakespeare's *Rape of Lucrece* was printed first in 1594, the date also of the first Quarto of *Titus Andronicus.* On the similarities between the two works, see Authorship of the Play.

II.i.127. *sacred wit.* Although sacred is usually taken here as a Latinism meaning *accursed,* there is, as has been noted in some quarters, an ironical sound about the word in this connection which accords well with Aaron's character.

II.i.133. *house of Fame.* An obvious allusion to Chaucer's *Hous of Fame,* III. 291-300. A still earlier version, of course, is that of Vergil; cf. *Æneid,* Iv. 183 ff.

II.i.142. *Per Styga,* etc. The poet is apparently quoting from memory a line from Seneca, with whose tragedies he was undoubtedly familiar. In this connection, cf. Seneca's *Hippolytus,* 1180:

'Per Styga, per amnes igneos amens sequar,'

and *Hercules Furens*, 90, 91:

'I am Styga et manes feros
Fugisse credis?'

II.ii.1. *the morn is bright and grey.* Much pedantic discussion has taken place as to the precise meaning of the term *grey*, which Shakespeare uses constantly in describing the morning sky. But from the context here and elsewhere, there seems no reason for thinking that it means anything but *bright*, and that in the expression in our text, as in the other cases, it is not synonymous with the word *bright*. Cf. *Much Ado About Nothing*, V.iii.25 ff.:

'the gentle day . . .
Dapples the drowsy east with spots of grey.'

By the same token, the *grey-ey'd* morn of *Romeo and Juliet*, II.i.247, is the *bright-eyed* morn.

II.ii.3. *Uncouple here.* Loose the hounds. This passage with its reference to hunting and the joy of being in the open is strikingly suggestive of the descriptions of the hunt in *Venus and Adonis*. The latter was printed in 1593, one year before the publication of *Titus Andronicus*, and a date not so far removed from Shakespeare's own hunting days in Warwickshire. Cf. below, II.iii.17–19.

II.ii.9. *I have been troubled.* There is nothing more suggestive of the Shakespearean authorship of the play than these presentiments of evil, of which the poet constantly makes use in all his tragedies. Cf. below, II.iii.196 ff.

II.iii.9. *alms out of the empress' chest.* Rather obscure, but apparently meaning, as Stoll suggests, that Aaron has taken the gold from Tamora's chest.

II.iii.17-19. *babbling echo mocks the hounds . . . a double hunt were heard at once.* Cf. the strikingly similar lines in *Venus and Adonis*, 695, 696:

'Then do they spend their mouths: Echo replies,
As if another chase were in the skies.'

For other similarities between this play and *Venus and Adonis*, cf. Introduction.

II.iii.31. *Saturn is dominator.* According to the mediæval theory, persons born under the domination of the planet Saturn were of a morose, or *saturnine*, disposition. Collins quotes Greene, *Planetomachia*, 1585: 'The star of Saturn is especially cooling.' The planet Venus, which, according to Aaron, governs Tamora's disposition, has an entirely different influence.

II.iii.43. *Philomel.* Philomela, daughter of Pandion, was ravished by Tereus, king of Thrace, who was the husband of her sister, Progne. Tereus then cut out her tongue to prevent her exposing him. That the story had made a deep impression on the poet's mind is witnessed by the frequent allusions to it in this play (cf. below, II.iv.43, IV.i.48 ff., and V.ii.197). Cf. also in this connection the *Rape of Lucrece*, 1128-1134.

II.iii.63. *With horns, as was Actæon's.* Actæon, a Theban prince, while hunting, accidentally saw Diana bathing, and was transformed by her into a stag, to be slain immediately by his dogs. The 'horns' which Tamora would fain see on Bassianus' temples are, of course, those of the cuckold.

II.iii.72. *swarth Cimmerian.* Homer (cf. *Odyssey*, XI.14) describes the Cimmerians as dwelling on the confines of the earth, 'shrouded in mist and darkness . . . and never does the shining sun look down on them.' Cf. Milton's 'dark Cimmerian desert' (*L'Allegro*, 10).

II.iii.86. *these slips have made him noted long.* Dr. Johnson points out the fact that Tamora and Saturninus have presumably been married but one night.

II.iii.93. *barren detested vale.* Tamora's description of this place here and in the lines immediately following is rather at variance with her description of it above (II.iii.12-16). Or are we to assume that the scene has changed during the action?

II.iii.110. *Lascivious Goth.* The Elizabethans pronounced *Goth* to sound like *goat*, and Shakespeare frequently quibbles on the word. Cf. *As You Like It*, III.iii. 5, 6: 'I am here with thee and thy goats, as the most capricious poet, honest Ovid, was among the Goths.' (*Capricious* is from the Latin *capra*, goat.)

II.iii.126. *And with that painted hope braves your mightiness.* The line stands thus in all the quartos and in the First Folio. The second, third, and fourth folios insert 'she' before 'braves.' It presents a crux as famous as any in Shakespeare. Various emendations have been suggested, and White suggests with reservations the reading, 'And with that faint hope braves, etc.' C. D. Stewart, in *Some Textual Difficulties in Shakespeare*, p. 156, offers the following interpretation: 'A painting occupies a position half way between the unsubstantial, uncertain, self-supported vision of a thing and the thing itself. Now when Lavinia gave him [Demetrius] such refusals his *hope* of success became more vivid. When she spoke of her chastity and gave excuses that were no real excuses to him, she only aggravated his passion and seemed to be artfully drawing him on; and only to refuse him. It was as if she had painted the picture of his success with her own hands, or in

her own person, and held it up before him. She made herself a "painted hope." This is simply a hope whose pictures are more vivid, more real, than the uncertain visions of hope unassisted.'

II.iii.151,152. *The lion, mov'd with pity, did endure To have his princely paws par'd all away.* Probably an allusion to the story of Androclus and the lion.

II.iii.153. *Some say that ravens foster forlorn children.* Doubtless a bit of folk-lore. Cf. *The Winter's Tale*, II.iii.219, 220:

'Some powerful spirit instruct the kites and ravens
To be thy nurses.'

The Biblical story of the feeding of Elijah by ravens may have given rise to it. Cf. 1 Kings 17. 3-6.

II.iii.228. *A precious ring, that lightens all the hole.* Probably an allusion to the carbuncle, formerly believed to emit radiance of its own in the dark.

II.iii.232. *So pale did shine the moon on Pyramus.* Cf. *Midsummer Night's Dream*, III.i.43 ff.

II.iv.5. *See, how with signs and tokens she can scrowl.* Ironically enough, Demetrius here suggests the very means by which Lavinia later exposes his crime, thus inciting her father to kill him. Cf. *King Lear*, III.vii.64-66, where Gloucester unwittingly pictures to Regan, in speaking of her treatment of Lear, the torture which Cornwall and she are to inflict upon him immediately afterward.

II.iv.26. *some Tereus hath deflower'd thee.* Cf. note on II.iii.43.

II.iv.39. *in a tedious sampler sew'd her mind.* Philomela, after being ravished and mutilated by Tereus, made known her condition by working a sampler on which she told the story.

II.iv.51. *Cerberus at the Thracian poet's feet.* Orpheus, when he descended into Hades to seek his wife, Eurydice, was able by his music to charm Cerberus, the triple-headed watch-dog of the infernal regions.

III.i.10. *two-and-twenty sons.* Is Titus here including among the two-and-twenty who died 'in honour's lofty bed' his son Mutius, whom he has slain (cf. I.i.296) for what he considered a dishonorable deed? If not, he was the father of twenty-six sons instead of the five-and-twenty of I.i.79. Baildon suggests (*Arden Shakespeare*) that 'Shakespeare had invented the Mutius episode and forgotten to alter the original number.'

III.i.34-37. *They would mot mark me . . . tell my sorrows to the stones.* This passage as it stands in the First Folio is manifestly corrupt, reading as follows:

'if they did heare
They would not marke me: oh if they did heare
They would not pitty me.
Therefore I tell my sorrowes bootles to the stones.'

The reading in our text is from the Quarto of 1600, and although perhaps slightly corrupt, seems the most nearly satisfactory of the various readings.

III.i.150. *limbo.* Popularly used for hell, but, in the strict sense of the term, *limbo* is not hell or any place of punishment, but, according to mediæval theology, a region bordering hell, where dwelt the patriarchs, who died before the resurrection of Christ. They were believed to have been carried to heaven with our Lord at his ascension. The souls of unbaptized infants are, according to other theories, also assigned to limbo.

III.i.170. *Writing destruction on the enemy's castle.* This line, as might be expected from the unusual expression, has caused much trouble to commentators. Nares explains the word *castle* as meaning a kind of helmet, quoting unconvincingly from *Troilus and Cressida* (V.ii.212):

'Stand fast, and wear a castle on thy head.'

III.i.247. *some deal.* Deal is from the O. E. *Dæl*, part. Cf. Chaucer, *Legend of Good Women*, 1182, 1183:

'Her suster Anne, as she that coude her good,
Seide as her thoughte, and somdel hit withstood.'

The word survives to-day in such expressions as *a good deal*, etc.

III.ii. This scene appears for the first time in the First Folio.

III.ii.4. *sorrow-wreathen knot.* Marcus' arms, which are crossed on his breast in an attitude of profound grief. Cf. *The Tempest*, I.ii.261, 'His arms in this sad knot.'

III.ii.15. *Wound it with sighing, girl, kill it with groans.* It was formerly thought that a heavy sigh draws a drop of blood from the heart. Cf. *Midsummer Night's Dream*, III.ii.97, 98:

'All fancy-sick she is and pale of cheer,
With sighs of love, that costs the fresh blood dear.'

III.ii.38. *Brew'd with her sorrow, mash'd upon her cheeks.* A rather prosaic allusion to the mash-tub and the operations of the brewing-house.

IV.i.20,21. *Hecuba of Troy Ran mad through sorrow.* After avenging the death of her son, Polydorus, Hecuba, wife of Priam, ran mad. Cf. above, note on I.i.138.

IV.i.37. Immediately before this line in the Folio occur the words, 'What booke?' Most modern editors omit them from the text, concurring in Dyce's opinion that 'the transcriber had inadvertently passed on to the line, *Lucius, what book,* etc., and when he afterwards perceived his mistake, and drew his pen through the misplaced line, he may have left two words of it not fully blotted out.'

IV.i.83, 84. *Magni dominator poli,* etc. Cf. Seneca's *Hippolytus,* 671, 672:

> *'Magne regnator deum,*
> *Tam lentus audis scelera? Tam lentus vides?'*

The poet is probably trying to quote from memory, and gets his terms confused. Seneca's tragedies abound in such similar epithets as *regnator deum, dominator poli, gubernator poli,* etc.

IV.i.89–93. *My lord, kneel down ... Lord Junius Brutus sware for Lucrece' rape.* Cf. the very similar lines in the *Rape of Lucrece* (1846-1848):

> *'Then jointly to the ground their knees they bow;*
> *And that deep vow, which Brutus made before,*
> *He doth again repeat, and that they swore.'*

IV.i.107. *Sibyl's leaves.* The leaves of the prophetic books of the Cumæan Sibyl, a woman of oracular powers, who, in classical mythology, appeared before Tarquin the Proud, offering him her nine books for three hundred pieces of gold. He refused to buy them, whereupon she burned three of the books and then returned, offering the remaining six for the original price. Tarquin again refused. The Sibyl again burned three books, and returned with a final offer of the remaining three for the price of the original nine. Tarquin, advised by his augur, then paid the three hundred pieces of gold for the three books, and the Sibyl disappeared. In times of political trouble, the Romans used to consult the Sibylline books. Cf. *Æneid,* VI.1-75.

IV.ii.20, 21. *Integer vitæ,* etc. The beginning of the famous twenty-second ode of the first book of Horace. 'He who is pure in life and unstained from sin, needs not the darts of the Moor, nor the bow.' Shakespeare is much more likely than Chiron to have 'read it in the grammar long ago.'

IV.ii.26. *no sound jest.* 'No joking matter.' The quartos have *found,* which Theobald considered a misprint for *fond.*

IV.ii.74. *'Zounds.* The oath, 'Zounds ('God's wounds'), which is found in all the quartos, is replaced in the First Folio by the expression 'Out!' because of the statute of 1606 forbidding swearing, blasphemy, etc., on the stage.

IV.ii.75. *blowse.* 'If "blowsy" mean ruddy and fat-faced, which it seems to do, the substantive would seem not correctly applied to a new-born black-a-moor child. Perhaps it had passed into a familiar term of jocose endearment for a child.' (White.)

IV.ii.97. *Typhon's brood.* Typhon, or Typheus, one of the Titans, who, with his brood, dwelt in the infernal regions and waged war against Zeus and the other Olympian gods.

IV.ii.156. *Not far, one Muli lives.* Steevens was the first to correct the reading of the old editions, 'Not far, one Muliteus.'

IV.iii.4. *Terras Astræa reliquit.* Cf. Ovid, *Metamorphoses,* I.150. Astræa, the goddess of justice, was the last of all the gods to forsake mankind.

IV.iii.43, 44. *I'll dive into the burning lake below, And pull her out of Acheron by the heels.* Acheron, the river of woe in Hades, is here referred to as a burning lake, doubtless by confusion with the Christian lake of fire and brimstone. Titus' rant reminds the reader at once of Hotspur's intention (*1 Henry IV,* I.iii.203 ff.) to

> *'dive into the bottom of the deep, ...*
> *And pluck up drowned honour by the locks.'*

IV.iii.64-70. *Virgo ... Taurus ... Aries.* The constellation *Virgo* (the Virgin) was supposed to represent Astræa after she had left the earth (cf. IV.iii.4). *Taurus* (the Bull) and *Aries* (the Ram) are also zodiacal constellations.

IV.iv.67. *Coriolanus.* This is the theme of Shakespeare's last tragedy, *Coriolanus,* which was written about 1608 or 1609.

IV.iv.90. *honey-stalks.* According to Dr. Johnson, honey-stalks are sweet-clover flowers.

V.i.42. *The pearl that pleas'd your empress' eye.* Alluding to an old proverb, which Shakespeare uses in *Two Gentlemen of Verona* (V.ii.11, 12),

> *'the old saying is,*
> *Black men are pearls in beauteous ladies' eyes.'*

V.i.80. *An idiot holds his bauble for a god.* The bauble was the carved head with asses' ears that surmounted the baton which was carried by the court fool as a mock emblem of his office.

V.i.124. *like a black dog, as the saying is.* 'To blush like a black dog' is one of the old proverbs in Ray's collection.

V.i.126 ff. Aaron's circumstantial account of his misdeeds suggests at once the similar list of offences for which Barabas claims credit in Marlowe's *Jew of Malta* (II.iii.177 ff.).

V.i.147. *Bring down the devil.* Aaron's speech has evidently just been made from the top of the ladder on which he was to be hanged.

V.ii.191. *of the paste a coffin I will rear.* In early English cookery books the crust of a pie was always known as the coffin. According to Selden (cf. *Table-Talk,* under *Christmas*), Christmas pies were baked originally in a long coffin-shaped crust, in imitation of the manger in which our Lord was laid at his birth.

V.ii.198. *worse than Progne I will be reveng'd.* The author's absorbing interest in the story of the ravishment and mutilation of Philomela by Tereus has been mentioned (cf. note on II.iii.43). After Tereus had cut out her tongue, Philomela embroidered the story of her wrongs on a sampler, which she sent to her sister, Progne, wife of Tereus. The two sisters then revenged themselves on the guilty husband by murdering his son, Itylus, and serving his body at a banquet to his father. As a result of the horrible affair, Philomela was changed into a nightingale, Progne into a swallow, and Tereus into a hawk.

V.ii.206. *the Centaurs' feast.* A reference to the story in classical mythology (told by Ovid in the twelfth book of the *Metamorphoses*) of the battle between the Centaurs and the Lapithæ, at the wedding-feast of Hippodamia and Pirithous. Cf. *Midsummer Night's Dream,* V.i.44.

V.iii.36-38. *Was it well done of rash Virginius To slay his daughter ... stain'd and deflower'd?* In 449 B.C., Virginius, a centurion, slew his daughter, Virginia, to save her from Appius Claudius, the decemvir, who had attempted to violate her. The story was a favorite with the Elizabethans, and a drama on the subject, *The Tragicall Comedie of Apius and Virginia,* appeared about 1563. See Macaulay's *Lays of Ancient Rome.* The story is incorrectly given in the text.

V.iii.85. *Sinon.* The Greek who persuaded the Trojans to admit the wooden horse into Toy.

V.iii.93-97. In the 1594 Quarto these lines read as follows:

> *'And force you to commiseration,*
> *Here's Rome's young captain, let him tell the tale,*
> *While I stand by and weep to hear him speak.*
>   Lucius. *then, gracious auditory, be it known to*
>   *you,*
> *That Chiron and the damn'd Demetrius,'* etc.

V.iii.124. *Damn'd as he is.* The quartos and folios have *And as he is,* which Theobald emended to the reading given in the text. Cf. Brabantio's remark (*Othello,* I.ii.63),

> *'Damn'd as thou art, thou hast enchanted her.'*

V.iii.150. *give me aim awhile.* Stand by and observe the result of my efforts. A figure from archery. The person who 'gave aim' stood near the target and reported the success of the shots. White suggests, 'Give me air awhile.' Schmidt, retaining the original reading, paraphrases, 'Give room and scope to my thoughts.'

V.iii.166-170. These lines appear for the first time in the Quarto of 1600. In their place, the Quarto of 1594 has the following five lines:

> *'And bid thee bear his pretty tales in mind,*
> *And talk of them when he was dead and gone.*
>   Mar. *How many thousand times hath these poor lips,*
> *When they were living, warmed themselves on thine!*
> *O now, sweet boy, give them their latest kiss;'* etc.

V.iii.201. In the Quarto of 1594 this line reads,

> *'And being dead let birds on her take pity.'*

THE TEXT OF THE PRESENT EDITION

The text of the present volume is, by permission of the Oxford University Press, that of the Oxford Shakespeare, edited by the late W. J. Craig, except for the following deviations:

1. The stage directions of the First Folio have been restored, necessary modern additions being enclosed in square brackets. Passages of text for which the Folio offers no equivalent are similarly bracketed.

2. Many minor changes in punctuation have been made, and the spelling of certain words normalized in accordance with English usage; e.g. everything, swoll'n, villainy. The old forms, murther, murtherer, etc., which occur in the Folio beside murder, murderer, etc., have been retained.

3. The following alterations, most of them reversions to the readings of the First Folio, have been made in the text, the reading of the present text preceding the colon, and that of Craig following it:

I.i.108   sons F: son
   126   T'appease F: to appease
   154   grudges F: drugs
   495   sware F: swore
II.i.25   Hollo! F: Holla!
 iii.55   whom F: who
   126   braves F: she braves
 iv.17   Hath F: have
III.i.12   these, tribunes F: these, these, tribunes
    36   And bootless,: All bootless
   228   flow F: blow
   262   my F: thy
  ii.9   Who, when F: And when
   60   'But!' How, if that fly had a father and
          mother? F: But how if that fly had a
          father and a mother?
   85   begin F: begins
IV.i.46   so busily she turns the leaves! Help her. F:
         see how busily she turns the leaves!
         [Helping her.
   79   ye F: you
  131   Revenge the heavens F: Revenge, ye
         heavens,
 ii.65   she is F: she's

   152   Lord F: lord
   166   ye F: you
 iii.2   let me see F: now let me see
    8   Haply F: Happily
   67   Ha, ha! F: Ha!
  113   an humble suppliant F: a humble suppliant
  114   given it the emperor F: given it to the emperor
 iv.2   emperor in Rome F: emperor of Rome
   30   Th'effects F: The effects
   61   Arm, my lords. F: Arm, arm, my lord.
   71   begins F: begin
   92   food F: feed
V.i.62   And if F: An if
   89   luxurious F: luxurious and
  121   sounded F: swounded
 ii.30   th'infernal F: the infernal
   40   offenders F: offender
   49   globes F: globe
   50   Provide thee F: Provide
   62   Rape F: Rapine
  137   bide F: abide
  198   Progne F: Procne
  205   might F: may
  207   I'll F: I will
 iii.1   'tis F: it is
   11   my F: mine
   38   enforc'd F: enforced
   48   hast F: hast thou
   52   now is F: is now
   68   uproars F: uproar
   96   This F: then
  109   I am turn'd forth F: I am the turn'd forth

The Tragedy of Romeo and Juliet

Edited by

RICHARD HOSLEY

Dramatis Personae

ESCALUS, *Prince of Verona*

PARIS, *a young Nobleman, Kinsman to the Prince*

MONTAGUE } *Heads of two opposed Houses*
CAPULET }

2. CAPULET, *Cousin to Capulet*

ROMEO, *Son to Montague*

MERCUTIO, *Kinsman to the Prince* } *Friends*
BENVOLIO, *Nephew to Montague* } *to Romeo*

TYBALT, *Nephew to Capulet's Wife*

FRIAR LAWRENCE } *Franciscans*
FRIAR JOHN }

BALTHASAR, *Servant to Romeo*

ABRAM, *Servant to Montague*

SAMPSON } *Servants to Capulet*
GREGORY }

PETER, *Servant to Juliet's nurse*

AN APOTHECARY

THREE MUSICIANS

PAGE TO PARIS

CHIEF WATCHMAN

CHORUS

MONTAGUE'S WIFE

CAPULET'S WIFE

JULIET, *Daughter to Capulet*

NURSE TO JULIET

CITIZENS OF VERONA, KINSFOLK OF BOTH
HOUSES, MASKERS, SERVINGMEN, PAGES,
WATCHMEN, AND THE PRINCE'S TRAIN

The Tragedy of Romeo and Juliet

INTRODUCTION

TEXT AND DATE

The most authoritative source of the text of *Romeo and Juliet* is the 'good' Second Quarto, printed 'by Thomas Creede for Cuthbert Burby' in 1599.[1] That the copy consisted mainly of Shakespeare's 'foul papers' (working manuscript) is in part suggested by the inconsistent designation of characters in speech headings, for it seems likely that a character's dramatic function rather than his proper name would occasionally suggest itself to the author as he wrote out his manuscript.[2] Capulet's Wife, for example, is designated by such various speech headings as Wife, Mother, Old Lady, and Lady; and on the two occasions when Capulet speaks to Juliet his normal heading changes to Father. In a promptbook, on the other hand, such irregularities of designation would necessarily have been normalized in order to simplify the book-keeper's task of regulating performances. Additional evidence that Shakespeare's foul papers served as copy for Q2 is provided by a number of duplicate versions of individual words, phrases, and passages throughout the 'text proper' of the play. In each case one version appears to be the author's revision of the other, which he had not (or had not clearly) deleted from his manuscript and which was therefore set up along with its revision by the Q2 compositor. An example of 'revisional duplication' is the phrase 'I will believe,' printed in Q2 immediately before the 'Shall I believe' which the context demands and which editors customarily print as the revision, after deleting Shakespeare's first thought (V.3.103). Since the book-keeper or his scribe would recognize such duplications as stigmata of the author's composition, it is unlikely that the revisional duplications would have been reproduced in the promptbook.[3] Another kind of Q2 duplication, chiefly in stage directions but also in speech headings, suggests that the book-keeper, in preparation for transcribing the promptbook, had looked over Shakespeare's foul papers and added to them occasional notes clarifying the location of entrances and the designation of characters, without however deleting Shakespeare's original notation. Examples are afforded by the duplication of directions for the Friar's entrance at the beginning of V. 2, and by the speech heading 'M. Wife. 2.' at I.1.76. Thus the copy for Q2 appears to have been a text of *Romeo and Juliet* from which the promptbook was subsequently derived, either by direct transcription of the foul papers or by transcription of a 'fair copy' itself transcribed from the foul papers. The statement on the title page of Q2 that the text in that edition is 'newly corrected, augmented, and amended' does not mean that Q2 is the revision of an earlier version of *Romeo and Juliet* but rather that the authentic text is now being published to replace the pirated edition of 1597. The title page of Q2 also records that *Romeo and Juliet* had been 'sundry times publicly acted by the right Honorable the Lord Chamberlain his Servants.' Neither Q2 nor the 1597 Quarto was entered in the Stationers' Register.

The debased state of the text in the 'bad' First Quarto of *Romeo and Juliet*, printed 'by John Danter' in 1597,[4] suggests that this edition is one of the 'stolen and surreptitious copies' mentioned by Heminge and Condell in their epistle to the reader of the First Folio (1623). Although in the 18th century Q1 was thought to be an early draft of *Romeo and Juliet*, during the following century the view gradually prevailed that Q1 is a stenographic or memorial report; and the theory is now generally accepted that Q1 is a memorial reconstruction of Shakespeare's *Romeo and Juliet*, made by players who were familiar with the promptbook version of Shakespeare's company. (Although there were probably at least two reporters, for convenience they will be here referred to collectively as the Q1 reporter.) Because of gaps in the Q1 text and cuts in the number of necessary players, it has been suggested that Q1 is a memorial report of an abbreviated acting version made by Shakespeare's company from their promptbook.[5] Such a shortened version might well have been prepared for performance in the provinces, and if *Romeo and Juliet* was indeed written by 1592, Shakespeare's company may have performed it there during the period from 1592 to 1594 when the London theaters were closed because of plague. However, it is also possible that many of the lacunae observable in Q1 are memorial errors and that others are cuts stemming from the theatrical use to which the reconstruction itself may have been put, whether in London or the provinces is not clear. The uncertainty is complicated by our ignorance of the purpose for which the text of Q1 was reconstructed. The report may have been made for the specific purpose of providing printer's copy, but since we do not know the price an Elizabethan publisher would pay for a dramatic manuscript, we can only speculate on whether reporting for publication would have been profitable. Or, on the other hand, the report may have been made in order that a group of players without access to a Shakespearian manuscript might give performances of *Romeo and Juliet*, in which case the copy for Q1 may originally have been a promptbook or the foul papers of one. The latter explanation seems perhaps the more probable, but one cannot dogmatize; and difficult as they are, the problems posed by Q1 are only part of the more difficult larger question of Elizabethan bad quartos in general. In any case, Q1, although it was printed two years earlier than Q2, is derived from the promptbook version and therefore represents the text of *Romeo and Juliet* at a later rather than an earlier stage of its

---

1 *Romeo and Juliet, Second Quarto, 1599*, London, 1949 (fac. ed.).

2 See R. B. McKerrow, 'A Suggestion Regarding Shakespeare's Manuscripts,' *The Review of English Studies, 11* (1935), 459-65.

3 The revisional duplications are briefly discussed in the notes to II.1.247-250 and V.3.103; and a full discussion appears in the present writer's article, 'The Corrupting Influence of the Bad Quarto on the Received Text of *Romeo and Juliet*,' *Shakespeare Quarterly, 4* (1953), 28-32 (hereafter referred to as 'The Received Text').

4 *Romeo and Juliet by William Shakspere, the First Quarto, 1597*, London, 1886 (fac. ed.).

5 H. R. Hoppe, *The Bad Quarto of Romeo and Juliet*, Cornell University Press, 1948.

history than does Q2.[6] Moreover, the text of Q1, deriving as it does from actual performances, reflects in considerable detail the staging and stage business of a contemporary production in an Elizabethan public playhouse.[7] It is, of course, not the reported Q1 version but rather the promptbook version of Shakespeare's company which is referred to on the title page of Q1, in the statement that *Romeo and Juliet* had been 'often (with great applause) played publicly by the right Honorable the Lord of Hunsdon his Servants,' for the Chamberlain's Men were so styled from July 1596 to April 1597.

The general nature of the variations between Q1 and Q2 can be only briefly illustrated here. The text of Mercutio's death speech, for example, corresponding to III.1.86–105 in Q2 and the present edition, reads in Q1 as follows:

> *Tybalt under Romeo's arm thrusts Mercutio in, and flies.*
>
> Mercutio. *Is he gone? hath he nothing? A pox on your houses.*
> Romeo. *What! art thou hurt, man? The wound is not deep.*
> Mercutio. *No, not so deep as a well, not so wide as a barn door—but it will serve, I warrant. What meant you to come between us? I was hurt under your arm.*
> Romeo. *I did all for the best.*
> Mercutio. *A pox of your houses, I am fairly dress'd. Sirrah, go fetch me a surgeon.*
> Boy. *I go, my lord.*
> Mercutio. *I am pepper'd for this world, I am sped. I' faith, he hath made worms' meat of me. And ye ask for me tomorrow, you shall find me a grave man. A pox of your houses! I shall be fairly mounted upon four men's shoulders— For your house of the Montagues and the Capulets! And then some peasantly rogue, some sexton, some base slave shall write my epitaph— that Tybalt came and broke the Prince's laws, and Mercutio was slain for the first and second cause. Where's the surgeon?*
> Boy. *He's come, sir.*
> Mercutio. *Now he'll keep a mumbling in my guts on the other side. come Benvolio, lend me thy hand. A pox of your houses!*
>
> *Exeunt.*

Although this passage varies considerably from Q2, one feels that the Q1 reporter here imitated at least the spirit if not the letter of Shakespeare's words; but elsewhere, and as a rule, the reporter grossly mistakes or subtly debases Shakespeare's original text. Two further examples will suffice to illustrate these effects of memorial transmission. One is the substitution in Q1 of the name Francis for Lawrence, obviously suggested by the Friar's invocations of the founder of his order (II.2 SD); and the other is the garbling of 'Mercy but murders, pardoning those that kill,' which appears in Q1 as 'Mercy to all but murd'rers, pardoning none that kill'

(III.1.198). Other examples may be culled at random from one of the parallel-text editions.[8]

Q2 and Q1 are both 'substantive' editions in the sense that each was printed from a manuscript, and all other editions are 'derivative' from these two.[9] However, Q2 may be more precisely described as a 'mixed' text,[10] since in the course of printing it suffered 'contamination' by Q1. That is, in addition to Shakespeare's foul papers, an exemplar of Q1 was in part used as copy for Q2, as is evident from sporadic 'bibliographical links' between the two editions.[11] The most striking of these are common typographical peculiarities such as italic print for the Nurse's speeches in I.3 and identical turnovers in prose lineation at I.3.4 and 16. In fact, the 85-line passage from I.2.55 to I.3.32 appears to have been printed directly from Q1 without editorial correction, for, in addition to the bibliographical links between them, the two editions here vary in only four trivial readings. But the contamination is not limited to this passage. In other sections of the text, although Q2 additions and extensive textual variants suggest that the Q2 compositor worked chiefly from Shakespeare's manuscript, bibliographical links occasionally reveal the influence of Q1. Two hypotheses have been suggested in explanation of this contamination. One is that an edited exemplar of Q1 served in part as copy for Q2, and the other is that an unedited exemplar of Q1 was occasionally consulted by the Q2 compositor. The hypothesis of an 'edited quarto' assumes that an editor was given Shakespeare's foul papers, an exemplar of Q1, and the task of preparing copy for Q2. According to a tentatively proposed form of the hypothesis, the editor tore occasional 'good' leaves out of his First Quarto, corrected them with pen and ink so as to bring their text into conformity with that of Shakespeare's manuscript, and interleaved them with manuscript leaves transcribed from that manuscript.[12] Elsewhere the present writer has advanced objections to this hypothesis of 'composite' copy and in its place developed the hypothesis of 'occasional consultation.'[13] This hypothesis, which has been adopted in the present edition, abandons the postulate of an editor. It assumes, rather, that the Q2 compositor was provided with Shakespeare's foul papers and (because of a defect in them) with an uncorrected exemplar of Q1. The compositor set most of his text from the foul papers, but because of a defective or missing leaf in that manuscript he set up the 85-line passage from I.2.55 to I.3.32 directly from Q1. (If we assume that Shakespeare's foul papers contained about fifty lines to a page, or a hundred to a leaf,[14] the passage in question may have been written on the fourth leaf of Shakespeare's manuscript, since the preceding text of the play amounts to about three hundred lines.) Having therefore an exemplar of Q1 at hand, in other parts of the text the Q2 compositor occasionally consulted Q1, either to verify a difficult reading in Shakespeare's foul papers (such as *Rosaline* at II.3.5) or to derive from Q1 a stage direction absent from the foul papers (such as that at II.3.88). Then, wishing to avoid the unnecessary labor of immediately returning to his manuscript copy only to locate the same

---

6 This view, a corollary to the memorial-reconstruction theory, is supported by a comparison of the revisional duplications in Q2 with their corresponding passages in Q1, for in each of the three longer examples it is substantially the revised version which appears in Q1 (II.1.247-250, III.3.41-44, and V.3.109-121). This situation apparently came about because the revisions (rather than the original versions) were incorporated in the promptbook when it was transcribed from the foul papers which later became the copy for Q2; and accordingly the revisions, having been used in the theater, were substantially reproduced in the copy for Q1 by a reporter familiar with performances. The evidence of the revisional duplications thus disproves the theory that Q1 represents an early draft of Q2, for Shakespeare, in writing out the manuscript which later became the copy for Q2, would not in three separate instances have revised a passage in a source-manuscript (which later became the copy for Q1) and then have made of his first revision a second revision in which he returned substantially to the original text of his source.

7 See Richard Hosley, 'The Use of the Upper Stage in *Romeo and Juliet*,' *Shakespeare Quarterly*, 5 (1954).

8 *Romeo and Juliet, Parallel Texts of the First Two Quartos*, ed. P. A. Daniel, London, 1874, or *Shakespeare's Romeo and Julia*,' ed. Tycho Mommsen, Oldenburg. 1859.

9 See R. B. McKerrow, *Prolegomena for the Oxford Shakespeare*, Oxford, 1939, p. 8.

10 See Sir Walter Greg, *The Editorial Problem in Shakespeare*, Oxford, 1942, pp. xiv-xvii.

11 Sidney Thomas, 'The Bibliographical Links Between the First Two Quartos of *Romeo and Juliet*,' *The Review of English Studies*, 25 (1949), 110-14.

12 G. I. Duthie, 'The Text of Shakespeare's *Romeo and Juliet*,' *Studies in Bibliography*, 4 (1952), 3-18.

13 'The Received Text,' pp. 12-16.

14 See Greg, *The Editorial Problem in Shakespeare*, p. 24.

place he had just found in his quarto copy, the compositor set up directly from Q1 the line or two he could carry in his head; and when, after doing so, he again needed to consult copy, he returned to his chief copy, Shakespeare's foul papers. Thus the Q2 compositor occasionally reproduced, in the text which he was setting mainly from manuscript, certain of Q1's typographical peculiarities and perhaps some of its textual readings.

The first of the early 'derivative' editions was Q3, printed from Q2 in 1609 with a scattering of corrections. It seems likely that the editor was the Q3 compositor since he generally emended only misprints and of Q2's larger errors only corrected one, the omission of a speech heading at II.1.243. Q3 served as copy for the First Folio (1623), where the text was further corrected but carelessly printed.[15] The F1 editor's corrections appear to be conjectural emendations without Shakespearian or playhouse authority. F1 in turn served as copy for F2 (1632), whose editor made 114 deliberate editorial changes in the text, more than in any other play in the First Folio.[16] Again it seems clear that the corrections have no substantive authority. The F2 editor's emendations initiated an editorial tradition which passed more or less unchanged through F3 (1663) and F4 (1685) to Rowe's edition of 1709. None of these editions was contaminated by Q1. On the other hand, the editor of the undated Q4 (printed from Q3 between 1609 and 1637) occasionally consulted Q1 and on its authority vigorously emended the text.[17] Thus he also established an editorial tradition, which passed to Q5 (1637) and to Pope's edition of 1723. Considering that it is a derivative edition, Q4 has had an unusually great influence on the received text through the use made of it by Pope, who, presumably being ignorant of its derivation from Q3, may well have assumed it to be earlier than Q1, with which it agrees in many important particulars to the exclusion of Q2. Pope consulted Q1 as well as Q4, and, since in any case he appears to have considered Q2's variations from Q1 to be spurious changes and additions by the players,[18] he not surprisingly omitted from his edition some sections of the text originating with Q2 and freely introduced to it attractive Q1 variants and the assignment of speeches in Q1 and Q4. An example of Pope's eclecticism is the Q1 variant *name*, traditionally substituted for Q2's *word* in 'a rose By any other word would smell as sweet' (II.1.90, 91). This eclecticism was somewhat curbed by Theobald (1733) and succeeding editors, and in the 19th and 20th centuries editors have tended to use fewer and fewer Q1 variants. However, the text was finally purged of such subjective eclecticism only in an edition of 1947,[19] and the present edition is the first to challenge Pope's assignment of a number of speeches. Examples of Pope's considerable influence on the modern editorial tradition are discussed in the notes to II.1. 242-246 and 247-250.

The interrelationship of the various early editions of *Romeo and Juliet* is summarized by the following stemma, in which an asterisk indicates a lost manuscript (hypothetical in the case of the promptbook), a solid line direct transmission, a double line memorial transmission, and a broken line contamination:

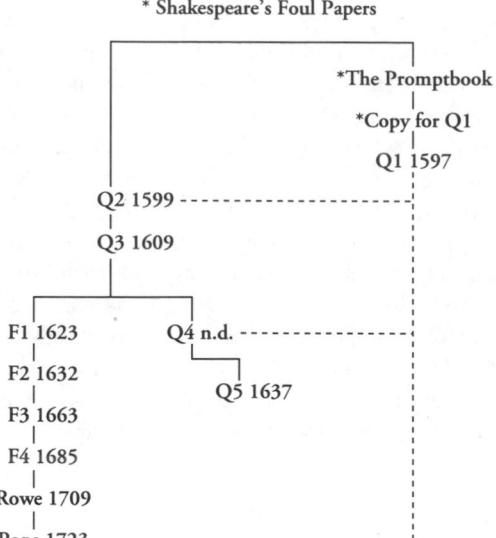

In preparing the present edition, the editor has used Q2 as copy text. Compositor's errors and corruptions originating with Shakespeare's foul papers are corrected, silently where obvious but with a footnote where the change affects the substance of the reading. Abbreviations are expanded. The designation of characters is generally normalized in speech headings and stage directions, and the punctuation and spelling are modernized, except for occasional forms like *umpeer* which reflect an Elizabethan pronunciation (IV.1.65). The passage from I.2.55 to I.3.32 is reprinted from Q1, the only substantive source of this section of the text.[20] Two lines omitted from Q2 are supplied from Q1 (I.4.7-8). The Q1 stage directions are generally incorporated in the present text, enclosed however in angle brackets in order to remind the reader that, while most of them probably indicate the action and stage business of Shakespeare's company, some of them may have originated with another group of players. The editor has not hesitated to emend a reading common to the two substantive editions where Q1 appears to be corrupt and Q2 to have been contaminated by Q1; but where a good Q2 reading varies from Q1 he has generally assumed that Q2 reproduces the reading of Shakespeare's foul papers and Q1 the reporter's memorial error. About forty Q1 variants are used, in each case the debt to Q1 being recorded in a note at the foot of the page. This eclecticism is, however, deliberately limited to the use of Q1 variants where Q2 is corrupt; and where both editions appear to be corrupt although variant, the editor has conjecturally emended the Q2 reading to a third reading, without regard to Q1.[21] Examples of the principle of Q2 emendation without reference to Q1 are discussed in the notes to II.1.40, 242-246, and 247-250.

There is no external evidence for the date of composition of *Romeo and Juliet*. It had undoubtedly been written by 1596, for the title page of Q1 records that *Romeo and Juliet* had been 'often' played by Lord Hunsdon's Men—a designation of Shakespeare's company which was superseded in April 1597. It is usually assigned to 1595, on the evidence of stylistic resemblances to the sonnets and to plays traditionally dated between 1594 and 1596: *The Two Gentlemen of Verona, Love's Labour's Lost, Richard II,* and *A Midsummer Night's Dream.* However, the dating of

15 Charlton Hinman, 'The Proof-Reading of the First Folio Text of *Romeo and Juliet,' Studies in Bibliography, 6 (1954),* 61-70.

16 M. W. Black and M. A. Shaaber, *Shakespeare's Seventeenth-Century Editors 1632-1685,* New York, 1937, p.32.

17 *Romeo and Juliet by William Shakspere, the Undated Quarto,* London, 1887 (fac.ed.) Examples of individual Q1 readings which the Q4 editor substituted for those of Q2 and Q3 are *agill* for *aged* (III.1.166), *thou* for *then* (III.3.53), *pronounce* for *prouaunt* (II.1.12), *doue* for *day* (II.1.12), and *open Et cætera* for *open* (II.1.40).

18 *The Works of Shakespeare,* 6 vols., London, 1723-25, *1,* xvi.

19 *The Tragedy of Romeo and Juliet,* ed. H. R. Hoppe, Crofts Classics, New York, 1947.

20 Duthie, 'The Text of Shakespeare's *Romeo and Juliet,'* pp. 22-3.

21 See 'The Received Text,' pp. 20-1.

some of these works is equally conjectural as that of *Romeo and Juliet*, and the argument of style is inconclusive, since it could also be maintained that parts of *Romeo and Juliet* resemble Shakespeare's earliest work, traditionally dated in the opening years of the 1590s. If in the future Shakespeare's sonnets and first few plays are redated somewhat earlier, more respect may be accorded the date of 1591 which, since there was an earthquake in England in 1580, is suggested by the Nurse's statement that Juliet's weaning is 'since the earthquake now eleven years' (I.3.23). The implication of this topical allusion is usually rejected, in part because *Romeo and Juliet* was a popular play and there are no extant references to it before 1598. However, if the play was written in 1591 or 1592, it might have been performed only a few times before the plague closed London theaters in 1592,[22] and thus its popularity may date from the reopening of theaters in 1594. A conservative conjecture for the date of composition is 1591 or 1592.

SOURCES OF THE PLAY

Although 'separation' and 'potion' romances analogous to *Romeo and Juliet* can be traced back to Ovid and the early Christian Xenophon of Ephesus, the essential features of Shakespeare's plot first appear in the thirty-third story of Masuccio Salernitano's *Novellino*, published at Naples in 1476.[23] In Masuccio, however, there is no mention of rival families, so that the secrecy of the lovers' marriage is unmotivated. Mariotto is banished from Siena for killing a fellow citizen, and by means of a friar's potion Giannozza escapes being forced into a second marriage. After the friar restores her to consciousness, Giannozza follows Mariotto to Alexandria; but in the meanwhile Mariotto, ignorant of her action, has returned to Siena, only to be apprehended and executed. Giannozza retires to a convent where she dies of grief.

Directly or indirectly, Masuccio's story of Mariotto and Giannozza became the source of over a dozen versions of the legend of Romeo and Juliet in half a dozen languages of Renaissance Europe.[24] It is the direct source of Luigi da Porto's *Historia novellamente ritrovata di due nobili amanti, con la lor pietosa morte*, published at Venice around 1530.[25] Here the lovers are first called Romeo and Giulietta, and fiction is first confounded with history by da Porto's associating their families with the historical Montecchi and Cappelletti, mentioned as examples of civil dissension by Dante in the *Purgatorio* (VI. 106). (The Montecchi appear to have been a 13th-century faction in Verona and the Cappelletti a party in Cremona during the same century. The erroneous conception of the two unrelated political groups as opposed Veronese families originates with late 14th-century commentators on Dante.) Since da Porto asserts that the events of his story occurred in Verona during the reign of Bartolommeo della Scala (Shakespeare's Prince Escalus), the legend of Romeo and Juliet came ultimately to be accepted as history. Thus a Renaissance historian of Verona recorded that the lovers died in the year

1303, and the tourist in Verona will still be shown the alleged tomb of Giulietta.

Shakespeare may or may not have read da Porto's novella, but in any case it initiated a tradition which culminates in Shakespeare's direct source. In addition to naming the lovers Romeo and Giulietta and setting them against a background of civil strife, da Porto names the Friar Lorenzo; invents the characters of Marcuccio, Tebaldo, and the Conte di Lodrone (Shakespeare's Mercutio, Tybalt, and Paris); develops the characters of Giulietta's mother and father; introduces the meeting of the lovers at a Cappelletti ball which Romeo attends in disguise; considerably develops the psychology, dialogue, and actions of the lovers beyond Masuccio; and, possibly under the influence of Ovid's story of Pyramus and Thisbe (*Metamorphoses*, IV. 55-166), substitutes for Masuccio's ending substantially Shakespeare's, except that Giulietta's suitor does not appear at the tomb and that Giulietta awakens before Romeo dies of poison and herself commits suicide by holding her breath.

Da Porto's novella is in turn the source of one of Matteo Bandello's *Novelle* (1554), 'La Sfortunata Morte di due infelicissimi amanti, che l'uno di veleno e l'altro di dolore morirono.'[26] Bandello's story is essentially da Porto's, but he adds to the tradition many details which occur in Shakespeare: the name Paris di Lodrone; an unnamed character corresponding to Benvolio; the character of the Nurse, who takes over the plot functions of Giulietta's maid and her servant Pietro in da Porto; the window scene and the rope ladder; and the character of Fra Anselmo (Shakespeare's Friar John) who, being quarantined for plague, fails to inform Romeo of the potion plot. Bandello also makes the Cappelletti the aggressors in the fight in which Romeo kills Tebaldo, and he amplifies the love scenes, probably under the influence of an earlier Italian version by Gerardo Boldieri (1553).

In 1559 Bandello's novella was translated into French with a few significant variations by Pierre Boisteau as the third of his *Histoires Tragiques*, 'L'Histoire de deux amants, dont l'un mourut de venin, l'autre de tristesse.' Boisteau derives the character of the apothecary from an earlier French version by Adrien Sevin (1542), and he changes Bandello's ending by causing Rhomeo to die before Juliette awakens and Juliette to kill herself with Rhomeo's knife. In 1562 Boisteau's *histoire* was adapted into English by Arthur Brooke as a long poem in poulter's measure entitled *The Tragical History of Romeus and Juliet, written first in Italian by Bandell, and now in English by Ar. Br.*[27] This appears to be Shakespeare's immediate and only source. Brooke invents the name of Friar John, adds much description and dialogue, develops the idea of Fortune as arbitress of the lovers' destiny, and introduces the conception of the Nurse as a garrulous old woman. Brooke was probably influenced by a lost play on Romeo and Juliet, for, in his rabidly Protestant preface (where he interprets his theme as filial disobedience), he says that he recently saw 'the same argument' as that of his poem 'set forth on stage' with more commendation than he can look for. This tantalizing reference may be to a French *Roméo et Juliette* which was apparently in existence around 1560. Such a play would probably not, however, have come to Shakespeare's attention; and even if the piece to which Brooke alludes was English, its early date and the

22 James G. McManaway, 'Recent Studies in Shakespeare's Chronology,' *Shakespeare Survey, 3* (1950), 25-6.

23 *The Novellino of Masuccio*, tr, W. G. Waters, 2 vols., London, 1895, *2*, 155-65.

24 Olin H. Moore, *The Legend of Romeo and Juliet*, The Ohio State University Press, 1950.

25 'The recently discovered story of two noble lovers, with their pitiable death,' *The Original Story of Romeo and Juliet by Luigi da Porto*, tr. G. Pace-Sanfelice, Cambridge, 1868.

26 'The unfortunate death of two most unhappy lovers, one of whom died of poison and the other of grief,' *Novellieri Italiani: Matteo Bandello, Twelve Stories*, tr. Percy Pinkerton, London, 1895, pp. 169-233.

27 *Romeus and Juliet*, ed. P. A. Daniel, London, 1875, or *Brooke's Romeus and Juliet*, ed. J. J. Munro, London, 1908.

absence of evidence that it was ever printed suggest that it probably did not influence Shakespeare, except perhaps indirectly through Brooke's poem. In 1567 Boisteau's version of Bandello was literally translated into English prose by William Painter as the twenty-fifth novel in the second volume of his *Palace of Pleasure,* 'The Goodly History of the True and Constant Love between Rhomeo and Julietta.'[28] Shakespeare had probably read Painter's novella, but he appears not to have made direct use of it. Other versions of the legend, such as a tragi-comedy by Lope de Vega entitled *Los Castelvines y Monteses,* have no bearing on Shakespeare's play.

Shakespeare follows Brooke closely in the details of his plot, but the stage required him to make several shifts of emphasis in structure and character delineation.[29] He unifies the action and gives it a sense of urgency by compressing its duration from months to less than four days, and unlike Brooke and earlier writers he introduces most of his minor characters immediately. Thus the audience is prepared first for Tybalt's death (the cause of the lovers' separation) by his ominous appearances in the opening scene and again at the Capulets' feast, and secondly for the projected marriage with Paris (the cause of Juliet's drinking the potion) by his appearance in the second scene as Juliet's suitor. The death of Paris at Juliet's tomb is also Shakespeare's innovation. Shakespeare keeps his political theme in the audience's mind from beginning to end by thrice staging the crescendo of a fight followed by entrances of the higher ranks of both houses, a mob of outraged Citizens, and the Prince, symbol of civil authority and order. He gives the Friar a sympathetic character and a homiletic fondness for analogies between the soul of man and the external world of nature. He develops Brooke's portrait of the Nurse by heightening her vulgarity, and he creates the comic character of the pompous but tetchy old Capulet. He invents the name of Benvolio the well-wisher, and from a hint in Brooke he

creates the character of Mercutio the realist, forever running atilt at such worshipers of convention as Tybalt the honor-mongering duelist and Rosaline's posturing lover Romeo. In Brooke's poem Mercutio is only briefly characterized (after da Porto's original conception) as

> *A courtier that each where was highly had in price,*
> *For he was courteous of his speech, and pleasant of device.*
> *Even as a lion would among the lambs be bold,*
> *Such was among the bashful maids Mercutio to behold.*
> *With friendly gripe he seized fair Juliet's snowish hand:*
> *A gift he had that Nature gave him in his swathing band,*
> *That frozen mountain ice was never half so cold,*
> *As were his hands, though ne'er so near the fire he did them hold.*
>
> (*Romeus and Juliet, ll. 255-262*)

After this single incident at the Capulets' feast Brooke's Mercutio does not reappear. Shakespeare's Mercutio, however, is almost as central a character as Juliet or Romeo, for his death is the keystone of the plot's structure and his satirical thrusts at Romeo's Petrarchan love and Tybalt's meticulous fencing help to define Shakespeare's chief contributions to the legend, the full-bodied and closely related themes of love and civil disorder. Certainly Shakespeare's play is the tragedy of 'star-cross'd lovers,' but certainly also the members of Shakespeare's audience, endowed with a Tudor abhorrence of civil war, were aware of the Prince's errors of policy in permitting rival factions to exist within the state; and the Prince himself, echoing Machiavelli's condemnation of misguided clemency, belatedly recognizes that 'Mercy but murders, pardoning those that kill' (III.1.198). Thus Shakespeare leavens his love story with a commonplace theme of Renaissance political theory.

---

28 *Rhomeo and Julietta,* ed. P. A. Daniel, London, 1875.
29 R. A. Law, 'On Shakespeare's Changes of his Source Material in *Romeo and Juliet,*' University of Texas *Studies in English, 9* (1929), 86-102.

The Prologue

[Enter Chorus.]

CHORUS. *Two households both alike in dignity*
(In fair Verona where we lay our scene)
From ancient grudge break to new mutiny,
Where civil blood makes civil hands unclean.
From forth the fatal loins of these two foes   *5*
A pair of star-cross'd lovers take their life,
Whose misadventur'd piteous overthrows
Doth with their death bury their parents' strife.
The fearful passage of their death-mark'd love
And the continuance of their parents' rage   *10*
(Which but their children's end nought could remove)
Is now the two hours' traffic of our stage,
The which if you with patient ears attend
What here shall miss our toil shall strive to mend. *[Exit.]*

ACT FIRST ❧ SCENE FIRST

Enter Sampson and Gregory with swords and bucklers, of the
House of Capulet.

Sampson. Gregory, on my word we 'll not carry coals.
Gregory. No, for then we should be colliers.
Sampson. I mean, and we be in choler we 'll draw.
Gregory. Ay, while you live draw your neck out of collar.
Sampson. I strike quickly, being moved.   *5*
Gregory. But thou art not quickly moved to strike.
Sampson. A dog of the house of Montague moves me.
Gregory. To move is to stir, and to be valiant is to stand.
Therefore if thou art moved thou run'st away.
Sampson. A dog of that house shall move me to stand. *10*
I will take the wall of any man or maid of Montague's.
Gregory. That shows thee a weak slave, for the weakest
goes to the wall.
Sampson. 'Tis true, and therefore women, being the weaker
vessels, are ever thrust to the wall. Therefore I will push *15*
Montague's men from the wall and thrust his maids to the wall.
Gregory. The quarrel is between our masters and us their
men.
Sampson. 'Tis all one, I will show myself a tyrant. When I
have fought with the men I will be civil with the maids—I *20*
will cut off their heads.
Gregory. The heads of the maids?
Sampson. Ay, the heads of the maids or their maidenheads.
Take it in what sense thou wilt.
Gregory. They must take it in sense that feel it.   *25*
Sampson. Me they shall feel while I am able to stand,
and 'tis known I am a pretty piece of flesh.
Gregory. 'Tis well thou art not fish—if thou hadst, thou

hadst been poor-john. Draw thy tool! Here comes two of
the house of Montagues.   *30*

Enter two Servingmen ⟨of the Montagues⟩.

Sampson. My naked weapon is out. Quarrel, I will back
thee.
Gregory. How? turn thy back and run?
Sampson. Fear me not.
Gregory. No marry, I fear thee!   *35*
Sampson. Let us take the law of our sides—let them begin.
Gregory. I will frown as I pass by, and let them take it as
they list.
Sampson. Nay, as they dare. I will bite my thumb at them,
which is disgrace to them if they bear it.   *40*
Abram. Do you bite your thumb at us, sir?
Sampson. I do bite my thumb, sir.
Abram. Do you bite your thumb at us, sir?
Sampson. Is the law of our side if I say 'ay'?
Gregory. No.   *45*
Sampson. No sir, I do not bite my thumb at you, sir.
But I bite my thumb, sir.
Gregory. Do you quarrel, sir?
Abram. Quarrel, sir? No sir.
Sampson. But if you do, sir, I am for you. I serve as *50*
good a man as you.
Abram. No better.
Sampson. Well, sir.

Enter Benvolio.

Gregory. Say 'better,' here comes one of my master's
kinsmen.   *55*
Sampson. Yes, better, sir.
Abram. You lie.
Sampson. Draw, if you be men. Gregory, remember thy
washing blow.   *They fight.*
Benvolio. Part, fools!   *60*
Put up your swords, you know not what you do.

Enter Tybalt.

Tybalt. What! art thou drawn among these heartless hinds?
Turn thee, Benvolio, look upon thy death.
Benvolio. I do but keep the peace—put up thy sword
Or manage it to part these men with me.   *65*
Tybalt. What! drawn and talk of peace? I hate the word,
As I hate hell, all Montagues and thee.
Have at thee, coward.   *[They fight.]*

Enter three or four Citizens with clubs or partisans.

Citizens. Clubs, bills and partisans! Strike! Beat them down!
Down with the Capulets! Down with the Montagues! *70*

Enter old Capulet in his gown, and his Wife.

---

29 poor-john: *dried salt cod* **two:** *Q1, Q2 omits* **SD two** *So Q1; Q2 two other* ⟨of the Montagues⟩ **31 back:** *support (but Gregory quibbles)* **34 Fear me not:** *don't worry about me (Gregory quibbles)* **35 marry:** *indeed (by the Virgin Mary)* **38 list:** *please* **39 bite my thumb:** *an insult; cf. n.* **41 Abram:** *one of the Montague Servingmen* Sd **Benvolio;** *cf. n.* **54 one:** *Tybalt, whom Gregory sees approaching* **56–76 Yes, better, sir . . . seek a foe;** *cf. n.* **59 washing:** *swashing, swashbuckling* **washing blow:** *of sword against buckler (see II.3.24; cf. n.)* **62 heartless:** *cowardly (pun on 'hart,' stag)* **hinds:** *menials (quibble on 'female deer')* **64 put up:** *sheathe* **SD partisans:** *broad-bladed pikes* **69 Citizens:** *Q2 Offi. cf. n.* **Clubs . . . partisans:** *a rallying cry of London apprentices,* **bills:** *ax-headed spears* **SD gown:** *dressing gown*

The Prologue; *cf. n.* **1 dignity:** *rank* **3 mutiny:** *strife* **4 civil:** *of citizens* **6 star-cross'd:** *predestined to be thwarted* **9 passage:** *course.* **12 two hours;** *cf. n.* **14 miss:** *be lacking* **Act I, Scene 1;** *cf. n.* **1 carry coals:** *do dirty work, be imposed upon* **1–8 coals . . . move;** *cf. n.* **2 colliers:** *coal-dealers* **3 and if choler:** *that one of the four humors which produces anger* **11 take the wall;** *cf. n.* **12, 13 goes to the wall:** *is thrust out of the way (proverbial)* **14, 15 weaker vessels:** *see 1 Peter 3:7* **18 men:** *servants* **20 civil:** *orderly, well-governed (quibble on 'polite')* **25 in:** *Q1, Q2 omits* **sense:** *physical sensation*

Capulet. What noise is this? give me my long sword, ho!
Wife. A crutch, a crutch! why call you for a sword?

        Enter old Montague and his Wife.

Capulet. My sword, I say, old Montague is come
And flourishes his blade in spite of me.
   Montague. Thou villain Capulet! Hold me not, let me go.   *75*
   Montague's Wife. Thou shalt not stir one foot to seek a foe.

        Enter Prince Escalus with his Train.

   Prince. Rebellious subjects, enemies to peace,
Profaners of this neighbor-stained steel—
Will they not hear? What ho! you men, you beasts,
That quench the fire of your pernicious rage   *80*
With purple fountains issuing from your veins—
On pain of torture, from those bloody hands
Throw your mistemper'd weapons to the ground
And hear the sentence of your moved Prince.
Three civil brawls, bred of an airy word,   *85*
By thee, old Capulet and Montague,
Have thrice disturb'd the quiet of our streets
And made Verona's ancient citizens
Cast by their grave beseeming ornaments
To wield old partisans, in hands as old,   *90*
Canker'd with peace, to part your canker'd hate.
If ever you disturb our streets again
Your lives shall pay the forfeit of the peace.
For this time all the rest depart away.
You Capulet, shall go along with me.   *95*
And Montague, come you this afternoon
To know our farther pleasure in this case
To old Freetown, our common judgment place.
Once more, on pain of death, all men depart.

     Exeunt [all but Montague, his Wife and Benvolio].

   Montague. Who set this ancient quarrel new abroach?   *100*
Speak nephew, were you by when it began?
   Benvolio. Here were the servants of your adversary
And yours, close fighting ere I did approach.
I drew to part them. In the instant came
The fiery Tybalt with his sword prepar'd,   *105*
Which as he breath'd defiance to my ears
He swung about his head and cut the winds,
Who, nothing hurt withal, hiss'd him in scorn.
While we were interchanging thrusts and blows,
Came more and more, and fought on part and part   *110*
Till the Prince came, who parted either part.
   Montague's Wife. O where is Romeo? saw you him today?
Right glad I am he was not at this fray.
   Benvolio. Madam, an hour before the worship'd Sun
Peer'd forth the golden window of the East.   *115*
A troubled mind drove me to walk abroad,
Where underneath the grove of sycamore

That westward rooteth from this city side,
So early walking did I see your son.
Towards him I made, but he was ware of me.   *120*
And stole into the covert of the wood.
I, measuring his affections by my own,
(Which then most sought where most might not be found,
Being one too many by my weary self)
Pursu'd my humor, not pursuing his,   *125*
And gladly shunn'd who gladly fled from me.
   Montague. Many a morning hath he there been seen,
With tears augmenting the fresh morning's dew,
Adding to clouds more clouds with his deep sighs;
But all so soon as the all-cheering Sun   *130*
Should in the farthest East begin to draw
The shady curtains from Aurora's bed,
Away from light steals home my heavy son
And private in his chamber pens himself,
Shuts up his windows, locks fair daylight out   *135*
And makes himself an artificial night.
Black and portentous must this humor prove
Unless good counsel may the cause remove.
   Benvolio. My noble uncle, do you know the cause?
   Montague. I neither know it nor can learn of him.   *140*
   Benvolio. Have you importun'd him by any means?
   Montague. Both by myself and many other friends.
But he, his own affections' counselor,
Is to himself—I will not say how true—
But to himself so secret and so close,   *145*
So far from sounding and discovery,
As is the bud bit with an envious worm
Ere he can spread his sweet leaves to the air
Or dedicate his beauty to the sun.
Could we but learn from whence his sorrows grow,   *150*
We would as willingly give cure as know.

        Enter Romeo.

   Benvolio. See where he comes. So please you, step aside,
I'll know his grievance or be much denied.
   Montague. I would thou wert so happy by thy stay
To hear true shrift. Come madam, let's away.   *155*
       Exeunt [Montague and his Wife].
   Benvolio. Good morrow, cousin.
   Romeo.   Is the day so young?
   Benvolio. But new struck nine.
   Romeo.   Ay me, sad hours seem long.
Was that my father that went hence so fast?   *160*
   Benvolio. It was. What sadness lengthens Romeo's hours?
   Romeo. Not having that which, having, makes them short.
   Benvolio. In love!
   Romeo. Out—
   Benvolio. Of love?   *165*
   Romeo. Out of her favor where I am in love.
   Benvolio. Alas that Love, so gentle in his view,

---

71 **long sword;** *cf. n.* **SD Enter old Montague ... Wife;** *cf. n.*   74 **spite:** *defiance*   78 **neighbor-stained:** *stained with neighbors' blood*   83 **mistemper'd:** *tempered for evil* (quibble on 'ill-tempered')   84 **sentence:** *decree* **moved:** *angered*   85 **airy:** *light, trifling*   91 **Canker'd ... canker'd:** *corroded ... malignant*   92, 93 **If ever you disturb ... the peace;** *cf. n.*   93 **forfeit:** *penalty for the breach*   98 **Freetown:** *Brooke's translation of the Italian* Villa Franca   100 **new:** *again* **abroach:** *broached and left running* (like beer from a cask); *compare I.4.203; cf. n.*   108 **withal:** *thereby*   110 **part and part:** *either side*   111 **either part:** *both parties*   116 **drove:** Q2 *drive* **abroad:** *away from home*

122 **affections:** *feelings*   123 **where:** *a place where* **most:** *most people*   125 **humor:** *inclination* (for solitude)   126 **who:** *him who*   127–138 **Many a morning ... remove;** *cf. n.*   132 **Aurora:** *goddess of the dawn*   133 **heavy:** *melancholy*   141 **importun'd:** *questioned insistently* (stressed — ´ —)   143 **his ... counselor:** *who keeps his own feelings secret*   145 **so secret and so close;** *cf. n.* **close:** *reticent*   146 **sounding:** *fathoming*   147 **envious:** *malicious*   149 **sun:** Q2 *same*   154 **happy:** *fortunate*   155 **shrift:** *confession*   156 **Good morrow:** *good morning*   158 **new:** *recently*   162 **having, makes:** *if I had it* **would:** *make*   167 **Love:** *Cupid, view appearance*

Should be so tyrannous and rough in proof.

Romeo. Alas that Love, whose view is muffled still,
Should without eyes see pathways to his will.   *170*
Where shall we dine?—O me! what fray was here?
Yet tell me not, for I have heard it all,
Here's much to do with hate but more with love.
Why then, O brawling love, O loving hate,
O anything of nothing first created,   *175*
O heavy lightness, serious vanity,
Misshapen Chaos of well-seeming forms,
Feather of lead, bright smoke, cold fire, sick health,
Still-waking sleep that is not what it is—
This love feel I that feel no love in this.   *180*
Dost thou not laugh?

Benvolio.   No coz, I rather weep.

Romeo. Good heart, at what?

Benvolio.   At thy good heart's oppression.

Romeo. Why, such is love's transgression.   *185*
Griefs of mine own lie heavy in my breast,
Which thou wilt propagate to have it press'd
With more of thine. This love that thou hast shown
Doth add more grief to too much of mine own.
Love is a smoke made with the fume of sighs,   *190*
Being purg'd a fire sparkling in lovers' eyes,
Being vex'd a sea nourish'd with loving tears.
What is it else? a madness most discreet,
A choking gall and a preserving sweet.
Farewell, my coz.   *195*

Benvolio.   Soft, I will go along,
And if you leave me so you do me wrong.

Romeo. Tut, I have left myself, I am not here,
This is not Romeo, he's some other where.

Benvolio. Tell me in sadness, who is that you love?   *200*

Romeo. What! shall I groan and tell thee?

Benvolio. Groan? why no, but sadly tell me who.

Romeo. Bid a sick man in sadness make his will—
Ah, word ill urg'd to one that is so ill.
In sadness, cousin, I do love a woman.   *205*

Benvolio. I aim'd so near when I suppos'd you lov'd.

Romeo. A right good markman! and she's fair I love.

Benvolio. A right fair mark, fair coz, is soonest hit.

Romeo. Well, in that hit you miss. She'll not be hit
With Cupid's arrow. She hath Dian's wit,   *210*
And in strong proof of chastity well arm'd
From Love's weak childish bow she lives uncharm'd.
She will not stay the siege of loving terms,
Nor bid th' encounter of assailing eyes,
Nor ope her lap to saint-seducing gold.   *215*
O she is rich in beauty, only poor
That when she dies, with beauty dies her store.

Benvolio. Then she hath sworn that she will still live chaste?

Romeo. She hath, and in that sparing makes huge waste,
For Beauty, starv'd with her severity,   *220*

Cuts beauty off from all posterity.
She is too fair, too wise, wisely too fair,
To merit bliss by making me despair.
She hath forsworn to love, and in that vow
Do I live dead that live to tell it now.   *225*

Benvolio. Be rul'd by me, forget to think of her.

Romeo. O teach me how I should forget to think.

Benvolio. By giving liberty unto thine eyes,
Examine other beauties.

Romeo.   'Tis the way   *230*
To call hers, exquisite, in question more.
These happy masks that kiss fair ladies' brows,
Being black, puts us in mind they hide the fair.
He that is strucken blind cannot forget
The precious treasure of his eyesight lost.   *235*
Show me a mistress that is passing fair—
What doth her beauty serve but as a note
Where I may read who pass'd that passing fair?
Farewell, thou canst not teach me to forget.

Benvolio. I'll pay that doctrine or else die in debt.   *240*

                                                    Exeunt.

❧ Scene Second ❧

Enter Capulet, County Paris and the Clown.

Capulet. But Montague is bound as well as I
In penalty alike, and 'tis not hard, I think,
For men so old as we to keep the peace.

Paris. Of honorable reck'ning are you both,
And pity 'tis you liv'd at odds so long.   *5*
But now, my lord, what say you to my suit?

Capulet. But saying o'er what I have said before—
My child is yet a stranger in the world,
She hath not seen the change of fourteen years.
Let two more summers wither in their pride   *10*
Ere we may think her ripe to be a bride.

Paris. Younger than she are happy mothers made.

Capulet. And too soon marr'd are those so early made.
Earth hath swallow'd all my hopes but she—
She's the hopeful lady of my earth.   *15*
But woo her, gentle Paris, get her heart,
My will to her consent is but a part.
And she agreed, within her scope of choice
Lies my consent and fair according voice.
This night I hold an old accustom'd feast,   *20*
Whereto I have invited many a guest
Such as I love, and you among the store
One more, most welcome, makes my number more.
At my poor house look to behold this night
Earth-treading stars that make dark heaven light.   *25*
Such comfort as do lusty young men feel
When well-apparel'd April on the heel

168 proof: *experience* **169 view:** *sight* **muffled:** *blindfolded* **still:** *always* **170 his will:** *to make us fall in love* **174–179 brawling love ... sleep;** *cf. n.* **177 seeming:** *Q1; Q2 seeing* **179 Still-waking:** *ever-wakeful* **182 coz:** *cousin* **187 propagate:** *multiply* **191 Being purg'd:** *when the smoke has cleared away* **196 Soft:** *wait a moment* **197 And if:** *if* **198 left:** *Q2 lost; cf. n.* **200 sadness:** *seriousness (Romeo quibbles on 'sorrow')* **that:** *she whom* **202 sadly:** *seriously* **203 Bid a ... make:** *Q1; Q2 A ... makes* **204 ill urg'd:** *inopportunely mentioned* **209 in ... you miss:** *right in general but not in this case* **210 Dian's wit:** *The goddess Diana's wisdom to remain a virgin* **211 proof:** *armor* **212 From:** *by* **213 stay:** *endure* **216–217 rich ... store;** *cf. n.* **220 starv'd with:** *killed by*

223 merit ... despair: *i.e. earn salvation through chastity* **224 forsworn:** *sworn not* **231 call ... in question:** *contemplate* **236 passing:** *surpassingly* **237, 238 note ... fair:** *reminder of a fairer mistress* **240 pay ... debt:** *give that instruction despite the cost* **SD County:** *count* **Clown:** *countryman, peasant (Capulet's servant)* **1 bound:** *bonded (to keep the peace)* **4 reck'ning:** *reputation* **9 fourteen years:** *see I.3.11; cf. n.* **13 marr'd ... made;** *cf. n.* **14 Earth ... she:** *i.e. my other children are buried* **15 earth:** *body (since she will perpetuate his line)* **19 according:** *consenting* **20 feast:** *the rhyme indicates the common Elizabethan pronunciation 'fest'* **22 store:** *gathering* **26 lusty:** *vigorous*

Of limping Winter treads, e'en such delight
Among fresh fennel buds shall you this night
Inherit at my house—hear all, all see,   30
And like her most whose merit most shall be;
Which, on more view of many, mine (being one)
May stand in number though in reck'ning none.
Come, go with me. Go sirrah, trudge about
Through fair Verona. Find those persons out   35
Whose names are written there, and to them say
My house and welcome on their pleasure stay.

          Exeunt [Capulet and Paris].

 Servant. Find them out whose names are written?
Here it is written that the shoemaker should meddle with   40
his yard and the tailor with his last, the fisher with his pencil
and the painter with his nets. But I am sent to find those
persons whose names are here writ, and can never find what
names the writing person hath here writ. I must to the
learned. In good time!   45

        Enter Benvolio and Romeo.

 Benvolio. Tut man, one fire burns out another's burning,
One pain is lessen'd by another's anguish;
Turn giddy and be holp by backward turning,
One desp'rate grief cures with another's languish.
Take thou some new infection to thy eye   50
And the rank poison of the old will die.
 Romeo. Your plantain leaf is excellent for that.
 Benvolio. For what, I pray thee?
 Romeo.   For your broken shin.
 Benvolio. Why Romeo, art thou mad?   55
 Romeo. Not mad, but bound more than a madman is,
Shut up in prison, kept without my food,
Whipp'd and tormented, and—Godden, good fellow.
 Servant. Godgigoden. I pray sir, can you read?
 Romeo. Ay, mine own fortune in my misery.   60
 Servant. Perhaps you have learn'd it without book.
But I pray, can you read anything you see?
 Romeo. Ay, if I know the letters and the language.
 Servant. Ye say honestly, rest you merry!
 Romeo. Stay fellow, I can read.   65

        He reads the letter.

Signior Martino and his wife and daughters,
County Anselm and his beauteous sisters,
The lady widow of Vitruvio,
Signior Placentio and his lovely nieces,
Mercutio and his brother Valentine,   70
Mine uncle Capulet, his wife and daughters,
My fair niece Rosaline and Livia,
Signior Valentio and his cousin Tybalt,
Lucio and the lively Helena.

A fair assembly, whither should they come?   75
 Servant. Up—
 Romeo. Whither? to supper?
 Servant. To our house.
 Romeo. Whose house?
 Servant. My master's.   80
 Romeo. Indeed I should have ask'd thee that before.
 Servant. Now I'll tell you without asking. My master is the
great rich Capulet, and if you be not of the house of Mon-
tagues, I pray come and crush a cup of wine. Rest you merry!

               [Exit.]

 Benvolio. At this same ancient feast of Capulet's   85
Sups the fair Rosaline, whom thou so loves,
With all th' admired beauties of Verona.
Go thither and with unattainted eye
Compare her face with some that I shall show,
And I will make thee think thy swan a crow.   90
 Romeo. When the devout religion of mine eye
Maintains such falsehood, then turn tears to fires,
And these who, often drown'd, could never die,
Transparent heretics, be burnt for liars.
One fairer than my love? th' all-seeing Sun   95
Ne'er saw her match since first the world begun.
 Benvolio. Tut, you saw her fair none else being by,
Herself pois'd with herself in either eye.
But in that crystal scales let there be weigh'd
Your lady's love against some other maid   100
That I will show you shining at this feast,
And she shall scant show well that now seems best.
 Romeo. I'll go along, no such sight to be shown,
But to rejoice in splendor of mine own.   *[Exeunt.]*

      ❧ SCENE THIRD ❧

    Enter Capulet's Wife and Nurse.

 Wife. Nurse, where's my daughter? call her forth to me.
 Nurse. Now by my maidenhead at twelve year old, I bade
her come. What! lamb, what! ladybird. God forbid, where's
this girl? What! Juliet.

        Enter Juliet.

 Juliet. How now, who calls?   5
 Nurse. Your mother.
 Juliet. Madam, I am here, what is your will?
 Wife. This is the matter. Nurse, give leave awhile, we must
talk in secret. Nurse, come back again, I have remember'd me,
thou's hear our counsel. Thou knowest my daughter's of a   10
pretty age?
 Nurse. Faith, I can tell her age unto an hour.
 Wife. She's not fourteen.
 Nurse. I'll lay fourteen of my teeth (and yet to my teen
be it spoken, I have but four) she's not fourteen. How long   15
is it now to Lammas-tide?

28 e'en: Q2 *euen* (silently emended throughout) 29 fennel: *a bridal flower* (supposedly
an aphrodisiac) 30 Inherit: *possess* 32 Which: *with whom* (referring to 'her') on:
Q2 *one* mine: *my daughter* 33 none: *quibble on 'One is no number'* (proverbial; compare
Sonnet 136) 34 sirrah: *term of address to an inferior* (the servant) 40–42 shoemaker
. . . nets; *cf. n.* 40 meddle: *busy himself* 41 yard: *measuring rod* pencil: *brush* 45
In good time: *in the nick of time* 48 holp: *helped* 49 languish: *suffering* 52
plantain leaf: *medication; cf. n.* 54 broken: *with the skin broken* 56–58 bound . . .
tormented; *cf. n.* 58 Godden: *good e'en* (good evening, used after noon) 59 Godgigoden: *God give ye good e'en* 61 without book: *by heart* 64 rest you merry: *God keep
you merry* SD letter: *document* 66–74 Signior Martino . . . Helena: *prose in Q1-
2* 68 Vitruvio: *Q1-2 Vtruuio* 72 and: *Q1; Q2 omits; cf. n.*

77 to supper; *cf. n.* 81 thee: *Q1; Q2 you; see I.2.72; cf. n.* 84 crush *finish off, drink
down; cf. n.* 85 ancient: *i.e. 'old accustom'd'* (I.2.20) 88 unattainted: *uninfected, unprejudiced* 91-4 devout religion . . . heretics; *cf. n.* 93 these: *i.e. my eyes* 94 Transparent:
bright (quibble on 'easily detected') 98 pois'd: *weighted* 100 lady's love: *i.e. lady-
love* 102 scant: *scarcely* 2–4 Now . . . Juliet; *cf. n.* 3 ladybird: *sweetheart* (literally, a small beetle) SD Juliet; *cf. n.* 8 matter: *business* give leave: *leave us* 10 thou's:
thou shalt counsel: *secret consultation* 11 a pretty age; *cf. n.* 12 an: *so Q2; Q1 a* 14
lay: *wager* teen: *sorrow* 16 Lammas-tide: *Lammas-time* (August 1); *cf. n.*

Wife. A fortnight and odd days.

Nurse. Even or odd, of all days in the year, come Lammas
Eve at night shall she be fourteen. Susan and she (God rest all
Christian souls) were of an age. Well, Susan is with God, she
was too good for me. But as I said, on Lammas Eve at night
shall she be fourteen, that shall she, marry, I remember it well.
'Tis since the earthquake now eleven years, and she was wean'd
(I never shall forget it) of all the days of the year upon that
day, for I had then laid wormwood to my dug, sitting in the
sun under the dove-house wall. My lord and you were then at
Mantua—nay, I do bear a brain. But as I said, when it did
taste the wormwood on the nipple of my dug and felt it bitter
(pretty fool! to see it tetchy and fall out with the dug), 'Shake!'
quoth the dovehouse; 'twas no need, I trow, to bid me trudge.
And since that time it is eleven years, for then she could stand
high-lone. Nay, by th' rood, she could have run and waddled
all about, for even the day before she broke her brow, and
then my husband (God be with his soul, 'a was a merry man)
took up the child. 'Yea,' quoth he, 'dost thou fall upon thy *35*
face? Thou wilt fall backward when thou hast more wit, wilt
thou not, Jule?' And by my holidam, the pretty wretch left crying and said 'Ay.' To see now how a jest shall come about! I
warrant and I should lie a thousand years I never should forget
it. 'Wilt thou not, Jule?' quoth he, and pretty fool, it stinted
and said 'Ay.'

Wife. Enough of this, I pray thee hold thy peace.

Nurse. Yes madam. Yet I cannot choose but laugh—to think
it should leave crying and say 'Ay.' And yet I warrant it had
upon it brow a bump as big as a young cock'rel's stone (a *45*
perilous knock) and it cried bitterly. 'Yea,' quoth my husband,
'fall'st upon thy face? Thou wilt fall backward when thou comest
to age, wilt thou not, Jule?' It stinted and said 'Ay.'

Juliet. And stint thou too, I pray thee, Nurse, say I.

Nurse. Peace, I have done. God mark thee to his *50*
grace, thou was the prettiest babe that e'er I nurs'd. And I
might live to see thee married once, I have my wish.

Wife. Marry, that 'marry' is the very theme
I came to talk of. Tell me, daughter Juliet,
How stands your dispositions to be marry'd? *55*

Juliet. It is an honor that I dream not of.

Nurse. An honor! were not I thine only nurse I would say
thou hadst suck'd wisdom from thy teat.

Wife. Well, think of marriage now. Younger than you
Here in Verona, ladies of esteem, *60*
Are made already mothers. By my count,
I was your mother much upon these years
That you are now a maid. Thus then in brief,
The valiant Paris seeks you for his love.

Nurse. A man, young lady, lady, such a man as all *65*
the world. Why, he's a man of wax.

Wife. Verona's summer hath not such a flower.

Nurse. Nay he's a flower, in faith a very flower.

Wife. What say you, can you love the gentleman?

This night you shall behold him at our feast, *70*
Read o'er the volume of young Paris' face
And find delight writ there with Beauty's pen,
Examine every married lineament
And see how one another lends content,
And what obscur'd in this fair volume lies *75*
Find written in the margent of his eyes.
This precious book of love, this unbound lover,
To beautify him only lacks a cover.
The fish lives in the sea, and 'tis much pride
For fair-without the fair-within to hide. *80*
That book in many's eyes doth share the glory
That in gold clasps locks in the golden story.
So shall you share all that he doth possess,
By having him making yourself no less.

 Nurse. No less! nay, bigger! women grow by men. *85*

 Wife. Speak briefly, can you like of Paris' love?

 Juliet. I'll look to like, if looking liking move,
But no more deep will I endart mine eye
Then your consent gives strength to make it fly.

Enter Servingman.

 Servingman. Madam, the guests are come, supper serv'd *90*
up, you call'd, my young lady ask'd for, the Nurse curs'd in
the pantry, and everything in extremity. I must hence to wait,
I beseech you follow straight.   *[Exit.]*

 Wife. We follow thee. Juliet, the County stays.

 Nurse. Go girl, seek happy nights to happy days. *Exeunt.*

❧ SCENE FOURTH ❧

*Enter Romeo, Mercutio, Benvolio, with five or six other Maskers,
Torchbearers.*

 Romeo. What! shall this speech be spoke for our excuse,
Or shall we on without apology?

 Benvolio. The date is out of such prolixity.
We'll have no Cupid hoodwink'd with a scarf,
Bearing a Tartar's painted bow of lath, *5*
Scaring the ladies like a crowkeeper,
⟨Nor no without-book prologue, faintly spoke
After the prompter, for our entrance⟩.
But let them measure us by what they will,
We'll measure them a measure and be gone. *10*

 Romeo. Give me a torch! I am not for this ambling.
Being but heavy, I will bear the light.

 Mercutio. Nay gentle Romeo, we must have you dance.

 Romeo. Not I, believe me. You have dancing shoes
With nimble soles, I have a soul of lead *15*

23 **since . . . eleven years;** *cf. n.* 27 **bear a brain:** *keep my memory* 29 **tetchy:**
fretful **fall out:** *quarrel* **the dug:** *so Q2; Q1 Dugge* 'Shake!'; *cf. n.* 30 **I trow:**
I assure you 32 **high-lone:** *quite alone* **rood:** *cross* 33 **broke:** *broke the skin
of* 34 **'a:** *he* 36 **wit:** *sense* 37 **by my holidam:** *a mild oath; cf. n.*
38 **come about:** *come true* 40 **stinted:** *stopped* 45 **it brow:** *its brow* **stone:** *testicle*
50 **mark:** *elect* 52 **once:** *some day* 55 **How . . . to be:** *how are you disposed toward
being* 56, 57 **honor:** *Q1; Q2 houre* 58 **thy:** *i.e. the Nurse's* 62–63 **I was
your mother . . . maid;** *cf. n.* 66 **of wax:** *perfectly beautiful* (like a wax
figure)

70 **This night . . . feast;** *cf. n.* 73 **married:** *harmonious* 74 **content:** *a pleasing impression* 76 **margent:** *margin* (where explanatory notes were written) 77 **unbound:** *without binding* (quibble on 'unattached') 78 **cover:** *binding* (quibble on 'wife') 79 **lives
in the sea:** *i.e. is not yet hooked* 82 **clasps:** *fastenings on the binding* (quibble on 'embraces') 86 **like of:** *be pleased with* 87 **look:** *be prepared* 89 **it:** *Q1; Q2
omits* 90 **the guests are come;** *cf. n.* 92 **in extremity:** *at the breaking point* 93
straight: *immediately* 94 **stays:** *waits* **SD Mercutio;** *cf. n.* **Torchbearers;** *cf. n.*
1 **this speech;** *cf. n.* 4 **hoodwink'd:** *blindfolded* 5 **Tartar's painted bow;** *cf. n.* **of
lath:** *i.e. imitation* 6 **crowkeeper:** *boy archer employed as scarecrow* 7, 8 ⟨Nor . . .
entrance⟩; *cf. n.* 7 **without-book:** *memorized* **prologue:** *see The Prologue; cf. n.* 8
After: *with assistance from* **entrance:** *here trisyllabic* 9 **measure us:** *find out about
us* 10 **measure them a measure:** *dance with them a stately dance* 11 **ambling:** *dancing*
(compared to a horse's gait) 12–21 **heavy . . . bound;** *cf. n.*

So stakes me to the ground I cannot move.
   Mercutio. You are a lover, borrow Cupid's wings
And soar with them above a common bound.
   Romeo. I am too sore enpierced with his shaft
To soar with his light feathers, and so bound   20
I cannot bound a pitch above dull woe.
Under love's heavy burthen do I sink.
   Mercutio. And to sink in it should you burthen love—
Too great oppression for a tender thing.
   Romeo. Is love a tender thing? it is too rough,   25
Too rude, too boist'rous, and it pricks like thorn.
   Mercutio. If love be rough with you, be rough with love:
Prick love for pricking and you beat love down.
Give me a case to put my visage in.
A visor for a visor! what care I   30
What curious eye doth cote deformities?
Here are the beetle brows shall blush for me.
   Benvolio. Come, knock and enter, and no sooner in
But every man betake him to his legs.
   Romeo. A torch for me! let wantons light of heart   35
Tickle the senseless rushes with their heels,
For I am proverb'd with a grandsire phrase—
I'll be a candle-holder and look on.
The game was ne'er so fair, and I am dun.
   Mercutio. Tut, dun 's the mouse, the constable's own word. 40
If thou are Dun we 'll draw thee from the mire
Of (save your reverence) love, wherein thou stick'st
Up to the ears. Come, we burn daylight, ho!
   Romeo. Nay that 's not so.
   Mercutio.   I mean, sir, in delay   45
We waste our lights in vain. Lights, lights by day!
Take our good meaning, for our judgment sits
Five times in that ere once in our five wits.
   Romeo. And we mean well in going to this mask,
But 'tis no wit to go.   50
   Mercutio.   Why? may one ask.
   Romeo. I dreamt a dream tonight.
   Mercutio.   And so did I.
   Romeo. Well, what was yours?
   Mercutio.   That dreamers often lie.   55
   Romeo. In bed asleep while they do dream things true.
   Mercutio. O, then I see Queen Mab hath been with you.
She is the fairies' midwife, and she comes
In shape no bigger than an agate stone
On the forefinger of an alderman,   60
Drawn with a team of little *atomi*
Over men's noses as they lie asleep;
Her wagon spokes made of long spinners' legs,
The cover of the wings of grasshoppers,
Her traces of the smallest spider web,   65

Her collars of the moonshine's wat'ry beans,
Her whip of cricket's bone, the lash of philome,
Her wagoner a small grey-coated gnat
Not half so big as a round little worm
Prick'd from the lazy finger of a maid;   70
Her chariot is an empty hazel nut,
Made by the joiner squirrel or old grub,
Time out a mind the fairies' coachmakers.
And in this state she gallops night by night
Through lovers' brains and then they dream of love,   75
On courtiers' knees that dream on cursies straight,
O'er lawyers' fingers who straight dream on fees,
O'er ladies' lips who straight on kisses dream,
Which oft the angry Mab with blisters plagues
Because their breaths with sweetmeats tainted are.   80
Sometime she gallops o'er a courtier's nose
And then dreams he of smelling out a suit,
And sometime comes she with a tithe-pig's tail
Tickling a parson's nose as 'a lies asleep—
Then he dreams of another benefice.   85
Sometimes she driveth o'er a soldier's neck
And then dreams he of cutting foreign throats,
Of breaches, ambuscadoes, Spanish blades,
Of healths five fadom deep; and then anon
Drums in his ear, at which he starts and wakes,   90
And being thus frighted swears a prayer or two
And sleeps again. This is that very Mab
That plats the manes of horses in the night
And bakes the elflocks in foul sluttish hairs
Which once entangled much misfortune bodes.   95
This is the hag, when maids lie on their backs,
That presses them and learns them first to bear,
Making them women of good carriage.
This is she—
   Romeo.   Peace, peace, Mercutio, peace!   100
Thou talk'st of nothing.
   Mercutio.   True, I talk of dreams.
Which are the children of an idle brain,
Begot of nothing but vain phantasy,
Which is as thin of substance as the air   105
And more inconstant than the wind, who woos
E'en now the frozen bosom of the North,
And being anger'd puffs away from thence,
Turning his face to the dew-dropping South.
   Benvolio. This wind you talk of blows us from ourselves.   110
Supper is done, and we shall come too late.
   Romeo. I fear too early, for my mind misgives
Some consequence yet hanging in the stars
Shall bitterly begin his fearful date
With this night's revels, and expire the term   115
Of a despised life clos'd in my breast
By some vile forfeit of untimely death.

21 pitch: *height reached by a falcon before swooping on its prey*   **29 case:** *mask*   **30 A . . . visor:** *a mask for a masklike face*   **31 cote:** *quote, observe*   **32 shall:** *that shall*   **35 wantons:** *triflers*   **36 rushes:** *the usual floor-covering before carpets*   **37 proverb'd . . . phrase:** *supplied with an old man's proverb; cf. n.*   **38 candle-holder:** *onlooker*   **39 game:** *quarry* (quibble on 'gambling')   **dun:** *Q2 dum; Q1 done; dark, ugly* (pun on 'done,' finished); *cf. n.*   **40 dun 's the mouse:** *keep quiet, lie low* (proverbial)   **constable's own word:** *i.e. when lying in wait for an arrest*   **41 Dun:** *proverbial name for a horse; cf. n.*   **42 Of:** *Q1; Q2 Or*   **save your reverence:** *begging your pardon*   **43 burn daylight:** *waste time*   **44 Nay:** *Romeo quibbles on 'waste torchlight by day'*   **not so:** *since it is now after dark*   **47 good:** *correct*   **47, 48 judgment . . . wits;** *cf. n.*   **48 five wits:** *Q2 fine wits*   **49 mask:** *masking party*   **50 no wit:** *unwise*   **52 tonight:** *last night*   **57 Queen Mab,** *midwife; cf. n.*   **58–95 She is . . . bodes:** *prose in Q2; verse in Q1*   **59 agate stone;** *cf. n.*   **61 atomi:** *Q1; Q2 ottamie; atoms, tiny creatures; cf. n.*   **63 spinners:** *spiders*

66 wat'ry: *since the moon was thought to cause dew*   **67 philome:** *film, gossamer*   **69 worm:** *idleness was suppose to breed maggots in the fingers*   **70 maid:** *Q1; Q2 man; cf. n.*   **72 joiner:** *cabinetmaker*   **73 a:** *of*   **74 state:** *pomp*   **76 cursies:** *curtsies*   **80 sweetmeats:** *kissing-comfits* (for perfuming the breath)   **82 suit;** *cf. n.*   **83 tithe-pig:** *every tenth pig born* (due the parson as church tax)   **84 'a:** *he*   **88 ambuscadoes:** *ambushes*   **89 fadom:** *fathoms* (old plural)   **anon:** *presently*   **94 elflocks:** *cakes of tangled hair* (supposedly the work of elves)   **95 entangled:** *Q2 untangled*   **96 hag:** *incubus*   **97 bear:** *bear children* (quibble on 'support a man')   **98 carriage:** *here pronounced 'carri-age'; cf. n.*   **103 idle:** *empty*   **104 phantasy:** *imagination*   **109 face:** *Q1; Q2 side*   **110 ourselves:** *i.e. our present intentions*   **113 consequence:** *future event*   **114 his:** *its*   **date** *period, duration*   **115–117 expire . . . death;** *cf. n.*

But He that hath the stirrage of my course
Direct my sail. On, lusty gentlemen.
    Benvolio. Strike drum.   *120*

They march about the stage, and Servingmen come forth with
napkins.

    1. Servingman. Where's Potpan that he helps not to take
away? He shift a trencher! he scrape a trencher!
    2. Servingman. When good manners shall lie in one or two
men's hands, and they unwash'd too, 'tis a foul thing.
    1. Servingman. Away with the join-stools, remove the   *125*
court-cubbert, look to the plate. Good thou, save me a piece
of marchpane, and as thou loves me let the porter let in
Susan Grindstone and Nell. Anthony and Potpan!
    3. Servingman. Ay boy, ready.
    1. Servingman. You are look'd for and call'd for, ask'd   *130*
for and sought for in the great chamber.
    4. Servingman. We cannot be here and there too. Cheerly,
boys, be brisk awhile and the longer liver take all.
                                        Exeunt [Servingmen].

Enter ⟨old Capulet with⟩ all the Guests and Gentlewomen to the
Maskers.

    Capulet. Welcome gentlemen, ladies that have their toes
Unplagu'd with corns will walk a bout with you.   *135*
Ah my mistresses, which of you all
Will now deny to dance? She that makes dainty,
She I'll swear hath corns. Am I come near ye now?
Welcome gentlemen, I have seen the day
That I have worn a visor and could tell   *140*
A whispering tale in a fair lady's ear
Such as would please. 'Tis gone, 'tis gone, 'tis gone.
You are welcome, gentlemen. Come musicians, play.
                            Music plays and they dance.
A hall, a hall! give room! And foot it, girls.
More light! you knaves, and turn the tables up,   *145*
And quench the fire, the room is grown too hot.
Ah sirrah, this unlook'd-for sport comes well.
Nay sit, nay sit, good cousin Capulet,
For you and I are past our dancing days.
How long is 't now since last yourself and I   *150*
Were in a mask?
    2. Capulet.   Berlady, thirty years.
    Capulet. What! man, 'tis not so much, 'tis not so much,
'Tis since the nuptial of Lucentio
(Come Pentecost as quickly as it will)   *155*
Some five and twenty years, and then we mask'd.
    2. Capulet. 'Tis more, 'tis more, his son is elder, sir,
His son is thirty.
    Capulet.   Will you tell me that?

His son was but a ward two years ago.   *160*
    Romeo. What lady 's that which doth enrich the hand
Of yonder knight?
    Servant. I know not, sir.
    Romeo. O she doth teach the torches to burn bright.
It seems she hangs upon the cheek of night   *165*
As a rich jewel in an Ethiop's ear—
Beauty too rich for use, for earth too dear.
So shows a snowy dove trooping with crows
As yonder lady o'er her fellows shows.
The measure done, I'll watch her place of stand,   *170*
And touching hers make blessed my rude hand.
Did my heart love till now? forswear it, Sight!
For I ne'er saw true beauty till his night.
    Tybalt. This by his voice should be a Montague.
Fetch me my rapier, boy. What! dares the slave   *175*
Come hither cover'd with an antic face
To fleer and scorn at our solemnity?
Now by the stock and honor of my kin,
To strike him dead I hold it not a sin.
    Capulet. Why, how now! kinsman, wherefore storm you so? *180*
    Tybalt. Uncle, this is a Montague, our foe,
A villain that is hither come in spite
To scorn at our solemnity this night.
    Capulet. Young Romeo is it?
    Tybalt.   'Tis he, that villain Romeo.   *185*
    Capulet. Content thee, gentle coz, let him alone.
'A bears him like a portly gentleman,
And, to say truth, Verona brags of him
To be a virtuous and well-govern'd youth.
I would not for the wealth of all this town   *190*
Here in my house do him disparagement.
Therefore be patient, take no note of him.
It is my will, the which if thou respect,
Show a fair presence and put off these frowns,
An ill-beseeming semblance for a feast.   *195*
    Tybalt. It fits when such a villain is a guest,
I'll not endure him.
    Capulet.   He shall be endur'd.
What! goodman boy, I say he shall. Go to!
Am I the master here or you? Go to!   *200*
You 'll not endure him! God shall mend my soul,
You 'll make a mutiny among my guests!
You will set cock-a-hoop! You 'll be the man!
    Tybalt. Why Uncle, 'tis a shame.
    Capulet.   Go to, go to!   *205*
You are a saucy boy. *[Aside.]* Is 't so indeed?
This trick may chance to scathe you. I know what,
You must contrary me! Marry, 'tis time—
Well said, my hearts. You are a princox, go!
Be quiet or— More light, more light! For shame!   *210*
I'll make you quiet— What! cheerly, my hearts.
    Tybalt. Patience perforce with willful choler meeting

118 stirrage: *steerage*   **119 sail:** *Q1; Q2* sute,   **SD They march … napkins:** *for staging see notes*   **121–133 Where's Potpan … take all;** *cf. n.*   **122 trencher:** *wooden platter*   **125 join:** *fabricated by a joiner*   **126 court-cubbert:** *court-cupboard, sideboard* **plate** *tableware*   **127 marchpane:** *marzipan (an almond candy)*   **131 great chamber:** *hall used for social occasions*   **133 the longer … all:** *i.e. lets be cheerfully resigned (proverbial)*   **SD Enter … to the Maskers;** *cf. n.*   **135 walk a bout:** *tread a measure* **a bout:** *Q2* about   **137 makes dainty:** *affects fastidiousness*   **138 Am I … Now?:** *Have I hit the truth?*   **144 A hall:** *clear the floor*   **145 knaves:** *fellows* **tables:** *hinged leaves on trestles*   **147 sirrah:** *here used familiarly*   **148 cousin:** *used of any but nearest relatives* **cousin Capulet:** *probably Capulet's uncle (see I.2.71)*   **151 Were in:** *i.e. wore*   **152 Berlady:** *By our Lady (the Virgin Mary)*   **154 nuptial:** *wedding*   **155 Pentecost:** *Whitsunday (seventh Sunday after Easter)*

160 ward: *minor in charge of a guardian*   **169 shows:** *appears*   **175 slave:** *base fellow*   **176 antic face:** *grotesque mask*   **177 fleer:** *sneer* **solemnity:** *festivity*   **186 Content thee:** *calm thyself*   **187 portly:** *of good deportment, well mannered*   **191 disparagement:** *indignity*   **192 patient:** *calm, forbearing*   **194 presence:** *demeanor*   **199 goodman boy:** *a contemptuous phrase; cf. n.* **Go to:** *get out*   **201 mend:** *amend, purge, save*   **202 mutiny:** *disturbance*   **203 set cock-a-hoop:** *be utterly reckless; cf. n.*   **SD Aside;** *cf. n.*   **207 trick:** *i.e. of brawling* **scathe:** *harm*   **208 contrary:** *stressed — ́ —*   **209 princox:** *coxcomb, conceited youth*   **212 Patience perforce:** *enforced self-control (proverbial)*

Makes my flesh tremble in their diff'rent greeting.
I will withdraw, but this intrusion shall,
Now seeming sweet, convert to bitt'rest gall.   *Exit.*   215
     Romeo. If I profane with my unworthiest hand
This holy shrine, the gentle sin is this,
My lips, two blushing pilgrims, ready stand
To smooth that rough touch with a tender kiss.
     Juliet. Good pilgrim, you do wrong your hand too much,   220
Which mannerly devotion shows in this,
For saints have hands that pilgrims hands do touch,
And palm to palm is holy palmers' kiss.
     Romeo. Have not saints lips and holy palmers too?
     Juliet. Ay pilgrim, lips that they must use in prayer.   225
     Romeo. O then dear saint, let lips do what hands do—
They pray, grant thou, lest faith turn to despair.
     Juliet. Saints do not move, though grant for prayers' sake.
     Romeo. Then move not while my prayer's effect I take.
Thus from my lips, by thine, my sin is purg'd.   230
     Juliet. Then have my lips the sin that they have took.
     Romeo. Sin from my lips? O trespass sweetly urg'd!
Give me my sin again.
     Juliet.   You kiss by th' book.
     Nurse. Madam, your mother craves a word with you.   235
     Romeo. What is her mother?
     Nurse.   Marry bachelor,
Her mother is the lady of the house,
And a good lady, and a wise and virtuous.
I nurs'd her daughter that you talk'd withal.   240
I tell you, he that can lay hold of her
Shall have the chinks.
     Romeo.   Is she a Capulet?
O dear account! my life is my foe's debt.
     Benvolio. Away, be gone, the sport is at the best.   245
     Romeo. Ay, so I fear, the more is my unrest.
     Capulet. Nay gentlemen, prepare not to be gone,
We have a trifling foolish banquet towards.
                              (They whisper in his ear.)
Is it e'en so? why then I thank you all.
I thank you, honest gentlemen. Good night.   250
More torches here! Come on then, let's to bed.
Ah, sirrah, by my fay, it waxes late,
I'll to my rest.

     ⟨*Exeunt [Capulet and most of the others.]*⟩

     Juliet. Come hither, Nurse. What is yond gentleman?
     Nurse. The son and heir of old Tiberio.   255
     Juliet. What 's he that now is going out of door?
     Nurse. Marry, that I think be young Petruchio.
     Juliet. What 's he that follows here that would not dance?
     Nurse. I know not.
     Juliet. Go ask his name. If he be married   260
My grave is like to be my wedding bed.

     Nurse. His name is Romeo, and a Montague,
The only son of your great enemy.
     Juliet. My only love sprung from my only hate!
Too early seen unknown, and known too late!   265
Prodigious birth of love it is to me
That I must love a loathed enemy.
     Nurse. What 's this? what's this?
     Juliet.   A rhyme I learn'd e'en now
Of one I danc'd withal.   270
                    One calls within, 'Juliet!'
     Nurse.   Anon, anon!
Come, let's away, the strangers all are gone.   *Exeunt.*

          [Enter Chorus.]

     CHORUS. *Now old Desire doth in his deathbed lie,*
And young Affection gapes to be his heir.
That fair for which Love groan'd for and would die,   275
With tender Juliet match'd, is now not fair.
Now Romeo is belov'd and loves again,
Alike bewitched by the charm of looks;
But to his foe suppos'd he must complain,
And she steal love's sweet bait from fearful hooks.   280
Being held a foe, he may not have access
To breathe such vows as lovers use to swear;
And she, as much in love, her means much less
To meet her new beloved anywhere.
But passion lends them pow'r, time means, to meet,   285
Temp'ring extremities with extreme sweet.   *[Exit.]*

ACT SECOND ❧ SCENE FIRST

     Enter Romeo alone.

     Romeo. Can I go forward when my heart is here?
Turn back, dull earth, and find thy center out.   *[Retires.]*

     Enter Benvolio with Mercutio.

     Benvolio. Romeo, my cousin Romeo! Romeo!
     Mercutio. He 's wise and on my life hath stol'n him home
to bed.   5
     Benvolio. He ran this way and leapt this orchard wall.
Call, good Mercutio.
     Mercutio.   Nay I 'll conjure too.
Romeo! humors! madman! passion! lover!
Appear thou in the likeness of a sigh.   10
Speak but one rhyme and I am satisfy'd,
Cry but 'Ay me!' pronounce but 'love' and 'dove,'
Speak to my goship Venus one fair word,
One nickname for her purblind son and heir,
Young Abram Cupid, he that shot so true   15

213 **diff'rent:** *hostile*   **greeting:** *encounter*   216–229 **If I profane . . . I take:** *the lovers' first dialogue forms a sonnet*   217 **shrine:** *i.e. Juliet's hand*   217–219 **the gentle sin . . . kiss** *cf. n.*   218–224 **pilgrims . . . palmers** *cf. n.*   218 **ready:** *Q1; Q2 did readie; for text see V.3.102; cf. n.*   221 **mannerly:** *well mannered, polite*   222 **saints:** *images of saints*   228 **move . . . sake:** *initiate action, though they do answer prayers*   229 **effect:** *fulfillment*   230 **Thus . . . purg'd;** *cf. n.*   232 **urg'd:** *mentioned*   234 **by th' book:** *authoritatively*   236 **What:** *who*   240 **withal:** *with*   242 **the chinks:** *plenty of coin*   244 **dear:** *grievous* (quibble on 'costly')   **is my foe's debt:** *is owed to my foe* (i.e. is in Juliet's power)   248 **foolish:** *humble*   **banquet:** *refreshments, supper*   **towards:** *in preparation*   250 **honest:** *honorable*   252 **fay:** *faith*   257 **be:** *may be* (subjunctive)   **Petruchio;** *cf. n.*

264 **sprung:** *descended*   266 **Prodigious:** *monstrous, ill-omened*   271 **Anon:** *right away*   273–286 **Now old Desire . . . sweet;** *cf. n.*   273 **old Desire:** *i.e. for Rosaline*   274 **gapes:** *is eager*   275 **Love:** *i.e. the lover*   278 **Alike:** *i.e. both he and she*   286 **extremities:** *hardships*   **extreme:** *stressed ́ —*   1 **forward:** *i.e. away from Juliet*   2 **earth . . . center:** *body . . . heart; cf. n.*   **SD Retires:** *i.e. hides behind a pillar or stage property*   4 **He's;** *cf. n.*   8 **conjure:** *call up a spirit by incantation*   9 **Romeo . . . lover;** *cf. n.*   **humors:** *moods, whims*   10 **in . . . sigh:** *in form of mist*   12 **pronounce:** *Q1; Q2 prouaunt*   **dove:** *Q1; Q1 day*   13 **goship:** *gossip, friend, confidant*   14 **purblind:** *totally blind*   **heir:** *Q1; Q2 her*   15 **Abram:** *beggarly, hypocritical* (like an Abraham Man); *cf. n.*

When King Cophetua lov'd the beggar maid.
He heareth not, he stirreth not, he moveth not:
The ape is dead and I must conjure him.
I conjure thee by Rosaline's bright eyes,
By her high forehead and her scarlet lip,   20
By her fine foot, straight leg and quiv'ring thigh,
And the demesnes that there adjacent lie,
That in thy likeness thou appear to us.
    Benvolio. And if he hear thee thou wilt anger him.
    Mercutio. This cannot anger him. 'Twould anger him   25
To raise a spirit in his mistress' circle
Of some strange nature, letting it there stand
Till she had laid it and conjur'd it down—
That were some spite. My invocation
Is fair and honest, in his mistress' name   30
I conjure only but to raise up him.
    Benvolio. Come, he hath hid himself among these trees
To be consorted with the hum'rous night.
Blind is his love and best befits the dark.
    Mercutio. If love be blind love cannot hit the mark.   35
Now will he sit under a medlar tree
And wish his mistress were that kind of fruit
As maids call medlars when they laugh alone.
O Romeo, that she were— O that she were
An open-arse or thou a pop'rin pear.   40
Romeo, good night. I 'll to my truckle-bed,
This field-bed is too cold for me to sleep.
Come, shall we go?
    Benvolio.   Go then, for 'tis in vain
To seek him here that means not to be found.   45
                    Exeunt [Benvolio and Mercutio].
    Romeo. He jests at scars that never felt a wound.
But soft, what light through yonder window breaks?
It is the East and Juliet is the sun.
Arise fair Sun and kill the envious Moon,
Who is already sick and pale with grief   50
That thou her maid art far more fair than she.
Be not her maid, since she is envious,
Her vestal liv'ry is but sick and green,
And none but fools do wear it, cast it off.

                    [Enter Juliet at the window.]

It is my lady! O it is my love!   55
O that she knew she were!
She speaks yet she says nothing, what of that?
Her eye discourses, I will answer it.
I am too bold, 'tis not to me she speaks.
Two of the fairest stars in all the heaven,   60
Having some business, do entreat her eyes
To twinkle in their spheres till they return.
What if her eyes were there, they in her head?
The brightness of her cheek would shame those stars

As daylight doth a lamp; her eye in heaven   65
Would through the airy region stream so bright
That birds would sing and think it were not night.
See how she leans her cheek upon her hand!
O that I were a glove upon that hand
That I might touch that cheek.   70
    Juliet.   Ay me!
    Romeo.   She speaks.
O speak again, bright angel, for thou art
As glorious to this night, being o'er my head,
As is a winged messenger of Heaven   75
Unto the white-upturned wond'ring eyes
Of mortals that fall back to gaze on him
When he bestrides the lazy puffing clouds
And sails upon the bosom of the air.
    Juliet. O Romeo, Romeo, wherefore art thou Romeo?   80
Deny thy father and refuse thy name;
Or if thou wilt not, be but sworn my love
And I'll no longer be a Capulet.
    Romeo. Shall I hear more or shall I speak at this?
    Juliet. 'Tis but thy name that is my enemy,   85
Thou art thyself, though not a Montague.
What's Montague? it is nor hand nor foot
Nor arm nor face, O be some other name
Belonging to a man.
What 's in a name? that which we call a rose   90
By any other word would smell as sweet.
So Romeo would, were he not Romeo call'd,
Retain that dear perfection which he owes
Without that title. Romeo, doff thy name,
And for thy name, which is no part of thee,   95
Take all myself.
    Romeo.   I take thee at thy word.
Call me but Love and I 'll be new baptiz'd,
Henceforth I never will be Romeo.
    Juliet. What man art thou that thus bescreen'd in night   100
So stumblest on my counsel?
    Romeo.   By a name
I know not how to tell thee who I am.
My name, dear saint, is hateful to myself
Because it is an enemy to thee.   105
Had I it written, I would tear the word.
    Juliet. My ears have yet not drunk a hundred words
Of thy tongue's utt'ring, yet I know the sound.
Art thou not Romeo, and a Montague?
    Romeo. Neither, fair maid, if either thee dislike.   110
    Juliet. How cam'st thou hither, tell me, and wherefore?
The orchard walls are high and hard to climb,
And the place death, considering who thou art,
If any of my kinsmen find thee here.
    Romeo. With Love's light wings did I o'erperch these walls.
For stony limits cannot hold Love out,
And what Love can do, that dares Love attempt.
Therefore thy kinsmen are no stop to me.
    Juliet. If they do see thee they will murther thee.
    Romeo. Alack, there lies more peril in thine eye   120
Than twenty of their swords, look thou but sweet

16 **King Cophetua:** *a ballad character; cf. n.* 18 **dead:** *playing dead (like a performing ape)* **conjure him:** *i.e. to raise his ghost* 26 **circle:** *magic ring (quibble on 'pudendum')* 27 **strange:** *belonging to another person* 28 **conjur'd:** *stressed* — ́ 29 **spite:** *injury* **invocation:** *here five syllables; see I.4.98; cf. n.* 33 **consorted:** *associated* **hum'rous:** *moist (quibble on 'moody')* 36 **medlar:** *a fruit resembling a small brown apple (symbol of pudendum)* 40 **open-arse:** *Q2 open; Q1 open Et cætera; medlar; cf. n.* **pop'rin pear;** *cf. n.* 41 **truckle-bed:** *a low bed trundled by day under a standing bed* 42 **field-bed:** *bed on the bare ground* 46 **Romeo:** *for staging see notes* 47 **soft:** *hush* 49 **Moon:** *Diana (goddess of chastity)* 53 **vestal:** *virgin* **green:** *pale, sickly (as from green-sickness; compare III.5.156)* **SD Enter ... window;** *cf. n.* **window;** *cf. n.* 60 **stars:** *planets* 61 **do:** *Q1; Q2 to* 62 **spheres:** *orbits; cf. n.*

66 **stream:** *shine* 78 **puffing:** *up-swelling, inflating; cf. n.* 80 **wherefore:** *why* 86 **though not:** *even if thou wert not* 87–89 **What's Montague ... a man;** *cf. n.* 93 **owes:** *owns* 101 **counsel:** *secret thought* 106 **written:** *in writing* 110 **dislike:** *displease* 115 **o'erperch:** *fly over* 118 **stop:** *obstacle*

And I am proof against their enmity.
    Juliet. I would not for the world they saw thee here.
    Romeo. I have night's cloak to hide me from their eyes,
And but thou love me, let them find me here.   125
My life were better ended by their hate
Than death prorogued, wanting of they love.
    Juliet. By whose direction found'st thou out this place?
    Romeo. By Love, that first did prompt me to inquire.
He lent me counsel, and I lent him eyes.   130
I am no pilot, yet wert thou as far
As that vast shore wash'd with the farthest sea,
I should adventure for such marchandise.
    Juliet. Thou know'st the mask of night is on my face,
Else would a maiden blush bepaint my cheek   135
For that which thou hast heard me speak tonight.
Fain would I dwell on form—fain, fain deny
What I have spoke. But farewell compliment.
Dost thou love me? I know thou wilt say 'Ay,'
And I will take thy word. Yet if thou swear'st   140
Thou mayst prove false—at lovers' perjuries
They say Jove laughs. O gentle Romeo,
If thou dost love pronounce it faithfully—
Or if thou think'st I am too quickly won,
I 'll frown and be perverse and say thee nay,   145
So thou wilt woo; but else, not for the world.
In truth, fair Montague, I am too fond,
And therefore thou mayst think my havior light,
But trust me, gentleman, I'll prove more true
Than those that have more cunning to be strange.   150
I should have been more strange, I must confess,
But that thou overheard'st, ere I was ware,
My true-love passion. Therefore pardon me,
And not impute this yielding to light love,
Which the dark night hath so discovered.   155
    Romeo. Lady, by yonder blessed moon I vow,
That tips with silver all these fruit-tree tops—
    Juliet. O swear not by the moon, th' inconstant moon.
That monthly changes in her circl'd orb,
Lest that thy love prove likewise variable.   160
    Romeo. What shall I swear by?
    Juliet.   Do not swear at all,
Or if thou wilt, swear by thy gracious self,
Which is the god of my idolatry,
And I'll believe thee.   165
    Romeo.   If my heart's dear love—
    Juliet. Well, do not swear. Although I joy in thee
I have no joy of this contract tonight.
It is too rash, too unadvis'd, too sudden,
Too like the lightning, which doth cease to be   170
Ere one can say 'It lightens.' Sweet, good night.
This bud of love by Summer's rip'ning breath
May prove a beauteous flow'r when next we meet.
Good night, good night! As sweet repose and rest
Come to they heart as that within my breast.   175
    Romeo. O wilt thou leave me so unsatisfy'd?

Juliet. What satisfaction canst thou have tonight?
Romeo. Th' exchange of thy love's faithful vow for mine.
Juliet. I gave thee mine before thou didst request it,
And yet I would it were to give again.   180
    Romeo. Wouldst thou withdraw it? for what purpose, love?
    Juliet. But to be frank and give it thee again.
And yet I wish but for the thing I have,
My bounty is as boundless as the sea,
My love as deep—the more I give to thee   185
The more I have, for both are infinite.
I hear some noise within. Dear love, adieu—

                                  [*Nurse calls within.*]

Anon, good Nurse! Sweet Montague, be true.
Stay but a little, I will come again.   [*Exit.*]
    Romeo. O blessed blessed night! I am afear'd,   190
Being in night, all this is but a dream
Too flatt'ring sweet to be substantial.

                            [*Enter Juliet again.*]

Juliet. Three words, dear Romeo, and good night indeed.
If that thy bent of love be hon'rable,
Thy purpose marriage, send me word tomorrow   195
By one that I 'll procure to come to thee
Where and what time thou wilt perform the rite,
And all my fortunes at thy foot I 'll lay
And follow thee my lord throughout the world.
    Nurse. [*Within.*] Madam!   200
    Juliet. I come, anon. But if thou mean'st not well,
I do beseech thee—
    Nurse. [*Within.*] Madam!
    Juliet.   By and by I come.
—To cease thy strife and leave me to my grief.   205
Tomorrow will I send.
    Romeo. So thrive my soul.
    Juliet.   A thousand times good night.

                                                        [*Exit.*]

    Romeo. A thousand times the worse to want thy light!
Love goes toward love as schoolboys from their books,   210
But love from love toward school with heavy looks.

                            Enter Juliet again.

Juliet. Hist Romeo, hist! O for a falkner's voice
To lure this tassel-gentle back again.
Bondage is hoarse and may not speak aloud,
Else would I tear the cave where Echo lies   215
And make her airy tongue more hoarse than mine
With repetition of my Romeo.
    Romeo. It is my soul that calls upon my name.
How silver-sweet sound lovers' tongues by night,
Like softest music to attending ears.   220
    Juliet. Romeo—
    Romeo.   My dear?
    Juliet.   What a clock tomorrow
Shall I sent to thee?
    Romeo.   By the hour of nine.   225

---

122 **proof:** *armored*   125 **but:** *unless*   127 **prorogued:** *postponed*   133 **adventure:** *take the risk* (of searching)   137 **Fain:** *gladly*   138 **compliment** *convention*   146 **So:** *provided that*   147 **fond:** *foolishly affectionate*   148 **havior:** *Q1; Q2* behauior   **light:** *immodest*   150 **more cunning:** *Q1; Q2* coying   **strange:** *distant, reserved*   155 **Which:** *relates to 'yielding'*   **discovered:** *revealed*   159 **circl'd:** *Q2* circle; *Q1* circled   **circl'd orb:** *the sphere of the moon* (see II.1.62; *cf. n.*)   168 **contract:** *exchange of vows* (stressed — ´);   *cf. n.*   169 **unadvis'd:** *unconsidered*

182 **frank:** *free-handed, generous*   **SD within:** *off stage*   192 **substantial:** *real; here pronounced 'substanti-al'; see I.4.98; cf. n.*   194 **thy bent of love:** *the object of thy love*   196 **procure:** *arrange*   200, 203 **Nurse:** *Q2 omits*   **By and by:** *immediately*   205 **strife:** *striving* (to woo)   207 **So thrive my soul:** *as I hope to be saved*   212 **falkner:** *falconer*   213 **tassel-gentle:** *tercel-gentle (male peregrine falcon)*   214 **Bondage is hoarse:** *i.e. being under my parents' control I must whisper*   216 **mine:** *Q2 omits*   220 **attending:** *listening*   222 **dear:** *Q2* Neece; *cf. n.*

Juliet. I will not fail, 'tis twenty year till then.
I have forgot why I did call thee back.
    Romeo. Let me stand here till thou remember it.
    Juliet. I shall forget, to have thee still stand there,
Rememb'ring how I love thy company.   *230*
    Romeo. And I 'll still stay, to have thee still forget,
Forgetting any other home but this.
    Juliet. 'Tis almost morning. I would have thee gone,
And yet no farther than a wanton's bird
That lets it hop a little from his hand,   *235*
Like a poor pris'ner in his twisted gyves,
And with a silken threed plucks 't back again,
So loving-jealous of his liberty.
    Romeo. I would I were thy bird.
    Juliet.   Sweet, so would I,   *240*
Yet I should kill thee with much cherishing.
Good night, good night!
    Romeo.   Parting is such sweet sorrow
That I shall say good night till it be morrow.
    Juliet. Sleep dwell upon thine eyes, peace in thy breast— *245*
Would I were sleep and peace, so sweet to rest!   *[Exit.]*
    Romeo. The grey-ey'd Morn smiles on the frowning Night,
Check'ring the eastern clouds with streaks of light,
And fleckled Darkness like a drunkard reels
From forth Day's path and Titan's burning wheels.   *250*
Hence will I to my ghostly Friar's close cell,
His help to crave and my dear hap to tell.   *Exit.*

❧ Scene Second ❧

Enter Friar alone with a basket.

    Friar. Now ere the sun advance his burning eye
The day to cheer and night's dank dew to dry,
I must upfill this osier cage of ours
With baleful weeds and precious-juiced flowers.
The Earth that 's Nature's mother is her tomb,   *5*
What is her burying grave, that is her womb,
And from her womb children of divers kind
We sucking on her natural bosom find,
Many for many virtues excellent,
None but for some and yet all different.   *10*
O mickle is the powerful grace that lies
In plants, herbs, stones and their true qualities,
For nought so vile that on the earth doth live
But to the earth some special good doth give,
Nor ought so good but, strain'd from that fair use,   *15*
Revolts from true birth, stumbling on abuse.
Virtue itself turns vice being misapplied,
And vice sometime by action dignified.

Enter Romeo.

Within the infant rind of this weak flower

Poison hath residence and med'cine power,   *20*
For this, being smelt, with that part cheers each part,
Being tasted, stays all senses with the heart.
Two such opposed kings encamp them still
In man as well as herbs, Grace and rude Will,
And where the worser is predominant   *25*
Full soon the canker Death eats up that plant.
    Romeo. Good morrow, Father.
    Friar.   *Benedicite!*
What early tongue so sweet saluteth me?
Young son, it argues a distemper'd head   *30*
So soon to bid good morrow to thy bed.
Care keeps his watch in every old man's eye,
And where Care lodges Sleep will never lie.
But where unbruised Youth with unstuff'd brain
Doth couch his limbs, there golden Sleep doth reign.   *35*
Therefore thy earliness doth me assure
Thou art uprous'd with some distemp'rature.
Or if not so (then here I hit it right)
Our Romeo hath not been in bed tonight.
    Romeo. That last is true, the sweeter rest was mine.   *40*
    Friar. God pardon sin! wast thou with Rosaline?
    Romeo. With Rosaline, my ghostly Father? No.
I have forgot that name and that name's woe.
    Friar. That 's my good son. But where hast thou been then?
    Romeo. I 'll tell thee ere thou ask it me again.   *45*
I have been feasting with mine enemy,
Where on a sudden one hath wounded me
That 's by me wounded. Both our remedies
Within thy help and holy physic lies.
I bear no hatred, blessed man, for lo   *50*
My intercession likewise steads my foe.
    Friar. Be plain, good son, and homely in thy drift,
Riddling confession finds but riddling shrift.
    Romeo. Then plainly know my heart's dear love is set
On the fair daughter of rich Capulet;   *55*
As mine on hers, so hers is set on mine;
And all combin'd, save what thou must combine
By holy marriage. When and where and how
We met, we woo'd and made exchange of vow
I 'll tell thee as we pass. But this I pray,   *60*
That thou consent to marry us today.
    Friar. Holy Saint Francis! what a change is here!
Is Rosaline, that thou didst love so dear,
So soon forsaken? Young men's love then lies
Not truly in their hearts but in their eyes.   *65*
Jesu Maria! what a deal of brine
hath wash'd thy sallow cheeks for Rosaline,
How much salt water thrown away in waste
To season love, that of it doth not taste.
The sun not yet thy sighs from heaven clears,   *70*
Thy old groans yet ring in mine ancient ears.
Lo! here upon they cheek the stain doth sit
Of an old tear that is not wash'd off yet.

234 wanton: *capricious child*   **237 silken threed:** *silken thread; cf. n.*   **243 Romeo:** *Q2 omits*   **242–246 Good night ... rest;** *cf. n.*   **247 Romeo:** *in Q2 before l.246*   **247–250 The grey-ey'd Morn ... wheels;** *cf. n.*   **248 Check'ring:** *Q1; Q2 Checking; cf. n; variegating*   **249 fleckled:** *dappled*   **250 Titan:** *i.e. the sun, offspring of the Titan Hyperion* **wheels:** *i.e. of the sun's chariot (compare III.2.1-4)*   **251 Hence:** *from here* **ghostly:** *spiritual, holy* **close:** *narrow*   **252 dear hap:** *good fortune*   **1 advance:** *raise*   **3 osier cage:** *willow basket*   **11 mickle:** *great* **grace:** *divine power*   **15 strain'd:** *constrained, perverted* **SD Enter Romeo;** *cf. n.*

21 that part: *its odor* **cheers:** *revives* **each part:** *of the body*   **22 stays:** *suspends*   **24 Grace:** *virtue* **Will:** *desire, lust*   **26 canker:** *cankerworm*   **28 Benedicite:** *God bless you (the final e rhymes with me)*   **30, 37 distemper'd, distemp'rature;** *cf. n.*   **34 unstuff'd:** *empty (of care)*   **42 ghostly:** *spiritual*   **49 physic:** *healing power (through the sacrament of marriage)*   **51 intercession:** *petition* **steads:** *benefits*   **52 homely:** *simple* **drift:** *narrative*   **53 shrift:** *absolution*   **57 combin'd:** *united*   **69 season:** *preserve as by salting (quibble on 'flavor')*   **71 ring:** *Q2 ringing*   **73 yet:** *the rhyme indicates the common Elizabethan pronunciation 'yit'*

If e'er thou wast thyself and these woes thine,
Thou and these woes were all for Rosaline.   *75*
And art thou chang'd? Pronounce this sentence then:
Women may fall when there 's no strength in men.
   Romeo. Thou chid'st me oft for loving Rosaline—
   Friar. For doting, not for loving, pupil mine.
   Romeo. And bad'st me bury love—   *80*
   Friar.   Not in a grave,
To lay one in another out to have.
   Romeo. I pray thee chide me not. Her I love now
Doth grace for grace and love for love allow.
The other did not so.   *85*
   Friar.   O she knew well
Thy love did read by rote that could not spell.
But come, young waverer, come go with me,
In one respect I 'll thy assistant be,
For this alliance may so happy prove   *90*
To turn your households' rancor to pure love.
   Romeo. O let us hence! I stand on sudden haste.
   Friar. Wisely and slow, they stumble that run fast.   *Exeunt.*

❧ SCENE THIRD ❧

Enter Benvolio and Mercutio.

   Mercutio. Where the devil should this Romeo be?
came he not home tonight?
   Benvolio. Not to his father's, I spoke with his man.
   Mercutio. Why that same pale hard-hearted wench, that
Rosaline, torments him so that he will sure run mad.   *5*
   Benvolio. Tybalt, the kinsman to old capulet, hath sent a
letter to his father's house.
   Mercutio. A challenge, on my life.
   Benvolio. Romeo will answer it.
   Mercutio. Any man that can write may answer a letter.   *10*
   Benvolio. Nay, he will answer the letter's master how he
dares, being dared.
   Mercutio. Alas poor Romeo, he is already dead—stabb'd
with a white wench's black eye, run though the ear with a
love song, the very pin of his heart cleft with the blind   *15*
bow-boy's butt-shaft. And is he a man to encounter Tybalt?
   Benvolio. Why what is Tybalt?
   Mercutio. More than Prince of Cats. O he 's the courageous
Captain of Compliments. He fights as you sing prick-song—
keeps time, distance and proportion. He rests his minim   *20*
rests—one, two and the third in your bosom. The very butcher
of a silk button, a duelist, a duelist! a gentleman of the very
first house, of the first and second cause. Ah the immortal
passado! The *punto reverso!* the *hai!*
   Benvolio. The what?   *25*
   Mercutio. The pox of such antic, lisping, affecting fantasticoes. These new tuners of accent! 'By Jesu, a very good blade!

a very tall man! a very good whore!' Why, is not this a lamentable thing, grandsire, that we should be thus afflicted with
these strange flies, these fashion-mongers, these pardon-me's,   *30*
who stand so much on the new form that they cannot sit at
ease on the old bench? O their bones, their bones!

Enter Romeo.

   Benvolio. Here comes Romeo, here comes Romeo.
   Mercutio. Without his roe, like a dried herring. O flesh,
flesh, how art thou fishified! Now is he for the numbers that   *35*
Petrarch flowed in. Laura to his lady was a kitchen wench
(marry, she had a better love to berhyme her!), Dido a dowdy,
Cleopatra a gypsy, Helen and Hero hildings and harlots,
Thisbe a grey eye or so but not to the purpose. Signior
Romeo, *bon jour.* There 's a French salutation to your   *40*
French slop. You gave us the counterfeit fairly last night.
   Romeo. Good morrow to you both. What counterfeit did
I give you?
   Mercutio. The slip, sir, the slip, can you not conceive?
   Romeo. Pardon, good Mercutio, my business was great,   *45*
and in such a case as mine a man may strain courtesy.
   Mercutio. That 's as much as to say, such a case as yours
constrains a man to bow in the hams.
   Romeo. Meaning, to cursy?
   Mercutio. Thou hast most kindly hit it.   *50*
   Romeo. A most courteous exposition.
   Mercutio. Nay I am the very pink of courtesy.
   Romeo. Pink for flower?
   Mercutio. Right.
   Romeo. Why then is my pump well flower'd.   *55*
   Mercutio. Sure wit! Follow me this jest now till thou hast
worn out thy pump, that when the single sole of it is worn
the jest may remain after the wearing solely singular.
   Romeo. O single-sol'd jest, solely singular for the singleness!
   Mercutio. Come between us, good Benvolio, my wits faint.   *60*
   Romeo. Swits and spurs! swits and spurs! or I'll cry a match.
   Mercutio. Nay, if our wits run the wild goose chase, I am
done. For thou hast more of the wild goose in one of thy wits
than (I am sure) I have in my whole five. Was I with you
there for the goose?   *65*
   Romeo. Thou wast never with me for anything when thou
wast not there for the goose.
   Mercutio. I will bite thee by the ear for that jest.
   Romeo. Nay good goose, bite not.
   Mercutio. Thy wit is a very bitter sweeting, it is a most   *70*
sharp sauce.
   Romeo. And is it not, then, well serv'd in to a sweet goose?
   Mercutio. O here 's a wit of cheveril, that stretches from an
inch narrow to an ell broad.

---

76 sentence: *proverb*   **83 Her:** *she whom*   **84 grace:** *favor*   **87 read:** *recite*   **89 In one respect:** *for one reason*   **92 stand on:** *insist upon*   **1 should:** *might*   **2 tonight:** *last night*   **4, 5 Why . . . run mad;** *cf. n.*   **9 answer:** *accept*   **12 dared:** *challenged*   **15 pin:** *peg holding the mark in the target's center*   **16 bow-boy:** *Cupid* **butt-shaft:** *unbarbed arrow for practice at the butts*   **18 Prince of Cats;** *cf. n.*   **19 Compliments** *polite formalities* **as you sing prick-song:** *i.e. precisely (as from written music)*   **20 distance:** *interval* **proportion:** *rhythm* **minim:** *rests short pauses (a minim being the shortest note)*   **21, 22 butcher . . . button;** *cf. n.*   **23 house:** *school of fencing* **first and second cause;** *cf. n.*   **24 passado . . . hai:** *fencing terms; cf. n.*   **26 antic:** *absurd*   **26, 27 fantasticoes:** *Q1; Q2 phantacies* **accent:** *language*

28 tall: *brave*   **29 grandsire:** *old man (who would disapprove of affectation)*   **30 flies:** *parasites* **pardon:** *Q1; Q2 pardons*   **31 form:** *fashion (quibble on 'bench')*   **32 bones;** *cf. n.*   **34 roe:** *spawn (quibble on 'sperm')* **like a dried herring:** *i.e. good-for-nothing*   **36 Laura:** *Petrarch's beloved, to whom he addressed his sonnets*   **37 dowdy:** *slut*   **38 gypsy:** *Egyptian (thus of dark complexion)* **hildings:** *good-for-nothings, baggages*   **41 slop:** *baggy breeches*   **44 slip:** *slang for counterfeit coin* **conceive:** *understand*   **46 case:** *quibble on 'pudendum'*   **49 cursy:** *curtsy*   **50 kindly:** *naturally, aptly*   **55 flower'd:** *pinked, perforated (pun on 'floored')*   **58 solely singular:** *all alone*   **59 single-sol'd:** *thin, contemptible (quibble on 'souled')* **solely singular:** *only unique* **singleness:** *feebleness*   **60 faint:** *Q2 faints; Q1 faile*   **61 Swits:** *switch* **Swits and spurs:** *i.e. urge your horse faster* **cry a match:** *claim to have won the contest*   **62 wild goose chase;** *cf. n.*   **64 with you:** *even with you*   **67 goose:** *quibble on 'prostitute'*   **68 bite . . . ear:** *as a sign of affection*   **70 sweeting:** *sweet-flavored apple*   **72 well serv'd in:** *sour sauce with sweet meat being proverbial*   **73 cheveril:** *an elastic leather made from kidskin*   **74 ell:** *45 inches*

Romeo. I stretch it out for that word 'broad,' which added   *75*
to the goose proves thee far and wide a broad goose.

Mercutio. Why, is not this better now than groaning for
love? Now art thou sociable, now art thou Romeo, now art
thou what thou art by Art as well as by Nature, for this
driveling love is like a great natural that runs lolling   *80*
up and down to hide his bauble in a hole.

Benvolio. Stop there, stop there!

Mercutio. Thou desirest me to stop in my tale against the
hair.

Benvolio. Thou wouldst else have made thy tale large.   *85*

Mercutio. O thou art deceived! I would have made it short,
for I was come to the whole depth of my tale and meant
indeed to occupy the argument no longer.

> *Enter Nurse and her Man.*

Romeo. Here 's goodly gear—a sail, a sail!

Mercutio. Two, two—a shirt and a smock.   *90*

Nurse. Peter!

Peter. Anon.

Nurse. My fan, Peter.

Mercutio. Good Peter, to hide her face, for her fan 's the
fairer face.   *95*

Nurse. God ye good morrow, gentlemen.

Mercutio. God ye good den, fair gentlewoman.

Nurse. Is it good den?

Mercutio. 'Tis no less, I tell ye, for the bawdy hand of
the dial is now upon the prick of noon.   *100*

Nurse. Out upon you! what a man are you?

Romeo. One, gentlewoman, that God hath made, himself
to mar.

Nurse. By my troth, it is well said, 'For himself to mar,'
quoth 'a? Gentlemen, can any of you tell me where I may   *105*
find the young Romeo?

Romeo. I can tell you, but young Romeo will be older when
you have found him than he was when you sought him. I am
the youngest of that name, for fault of a worse.

Nurse. You say well.   *110*

Mercutio. Yea, is the worst well? Very well took, i' faith,
wisely, wisely.

Nurse. If you be he, sir, I desire some confidence
with you.

Benvolio. She will endite him to some supper!   *115*

Mercutio. A bawd, a bawd, a bawd! So ho!

Romeo. What hast thou found?

Mercutio. No hare, sir, unless a hare, sir, in a lenten pie,
that is something stale and hoar ere it be spent.

> *⟨He walks by them and sings.⟩*

An old hare hoar, and an old hare hoar, is very   *120*
　good meat in Lent,
But a hare that is hoar is too much for a score
　when it hoars ere it be spent.

Romeo, will you come to your father's? We 'll to dinner
thither.   *125*

Romeo. I will follow you.

Mercutio. Farewell, ancient lady. Farewell, lady. 'Lady,
lady—'   *Exeunt ⟨Benvolio [and] Mercutio⟩.*

Nurse. I pray you, sir, what saucy merchant was this that
was so full of his ropery?   *130*

Romeo. A gentleman, Nurse, that loves to hear himself talk,
and will speak more in a minute than he will stand to in a
month.

Nurse. And 'a speak anything against me, I 'll take him down,
and 'a were lustier than her is, and twenty such Jacks.   *135*
And if I cannot I 'll find those that shall. Scurvy knave! I am
none of his flirt-jills, I am none of his skains-mates.

> *⟨She turns to Peter her Man.⟩*

And thou must stand by too, and suffer every knave to use me
at his pleasure!   *140*

Peter. I saw no man use you at his pleasure. If I had, my
weapon should quickly have been out. I warrant you, I dare
draw as soon as another man—if I see occasion in a good
quarrel and the law on my side.

Nurse. Now afore God, I am so vex'd that every part about   *145*
me quivers. Scurvy knave! Pray you sir, a word. And as I told
you, my young lady bid me inquire you out. What she bid me
say, I will keep to myself—but first let me tell ye, if ye should
lead her in a fool's paradise (as they say) it were a very gross kind
of behavior (as they say), for the gentlewoman is young, and
therefore if you should deal double with her, truly it were an ill
thing to be offer'd to any gentlewoman and very weak dealing.

Romeo. Nurse, commend me to thy lady and mistress.
I protest unto thee—

Nurse. Good heart! and i' faith, I will tell her as much.   *155*
Lord, Lord, she will be a joyful woman.

Romeo. What wilt thou tell her, Nurse? Thou dost not
mark me.

Nurse. I will tell her, sir, that you do protest, which as
I take it is a gentleman-like offer.   *160*

Romeo. Bid her devise some means to come to shrift
this afternoon,
And there she shall at Friar Lawrence' cell
Be shriv'd and marry'd. Here is for thy pains.

Nurse. No truly, sir, not a penny.   *165*

Romeo. Go to! I say you shall.

Nurse. This afternoon, sir? Well, she shall be there.

Romeo. And stay good Nurse, behind the abbey wall
Within this hour my man shall be with thee
And bring thee cords made like a tackled stair,   *170*
Which to the high topgallant of my joy
Must be my convoy in the secret night.
Farewell, be trusty and I'll quit thy pains.

---

75 **broad:** *obvious*   79 **Art:** *acquired polish*   **Nature:** *inborn ability*   80 **natural:**
born fool, idiot   81 **bauble:** *a court fool's baton or scepter* (quibble on 'phallus')   83
tale: *pun on 'tail'*   83, 84 **against the hair:** *against the grain* (quibble on 'pubic
hair')   85 **large:** *indecent*   87 **whole:** *pun on 'hole'*   88 **occupy:** *quibble on 'copulate'; cf. n.*   **SD Enter … Man;** *cf. n.*   89 **goodly gear:** *i.e. matter for jest* (the
Nurse)   90 **shirt:** *i.e. a man*   **smock:** *chemise* (i.e. a woman)   91 **Peter:** *the Nurse's
servant*   93 **fan;** *cf. n.*   97 **God ye good den:** *God give ye good e'en*   100 **prick:**
point (quibble on 'phallus')   101 **Out upon you:** *an expression of indignation*   102
made: *created* (quibble on 'caused'; play on 'make' and 'mar'; see I.2.13; cf. n.)   104
By my troth: *upon my word*   109 **fault:** *default, lack*   113 **confidence:** *malapropism
for 'conference'*   115 **endite:** *intentional malapropism for 'invite'*   116 **bawd:** *go-between*   **So ho:** *the hunter's cry on rousing a hare*   118 **lenten:** *i.e. without meat*   119
stale: *quibble on 'prostitute'*   **hoar:** *mouldy* (pun on 'whore')   **spent:** *consumed*

127, 128 **'Lady, lady':** *from the ballad of 'Chaste Susanna'; cf. n.*   129 **merchant:** *chap, fellow*   130 **ropery:** *rascally talk* (worthy of the hangman's rope)   132 **stand to:** *live up
to*   135 **Jacks:** *knaves*   137 **flirt-jills:** *flirty wenches*   **skains-mates:** *'knives'-mates, cut-
throats*   151 **double:** *deceitfully*   152 **weak:** *contemptible*   153 **commend me:** *convey my
respects*   154 **protest:** *declare*   157 **mark:** *heed*   161, 162 **Bid … afternoon;**
cf. n.   164 **shriv'd:** *absolved*   170 **tackled stair:** *rope ladder*   171 **topgallant:** *the upper-
most of three sections of a mast*   172 **convey:** *conveyance*   173 **quit:** *requite*

Farewell, commend me to thy mistress.

    Nurse. Now God in Heaven bless thee! Hark you, sir.

    Romeo. What say'st thou, my dear Nurse?   *175*

    Nurse. Is your man secret? did you ne'er hear say,

'Two may keep counsel, putting one away'?

    Romeo. I warrant thee, my man 's as true as steel.

    Nurse. Well sir, my mistress is the sweetest lady. Lord, Lord!
when 'twas a little prating thing—O, there is a nobleman   *180*
in town, one Paris, that would fain lay knife aboard, but she,
good soul, had as lieve see a toad, a very toad, as see him. I
anger her sometimes and tell her that Paris is the properer
man, but I 'll warrant you, when I say so she looks as pale
as any clout in the versal world. Doth not rosemary and   *185*
Romeo begin both with a letter?

    Romeo. Ay Nurse, what of that? Both with an *R*.

    Nurse. Ah, mocker, that's the dog-name. *R* is for the—
No, I know it begins with some other letter—and she hath
the prettiest sententious of it, of you and rosemary, that   *190*
it would do you good to hear it.

    Romeo. Commend me to thy lady.   ⟨*Exit.*⟩

    Nurse. Ay, a thousand times. Peter!

    Peter. Anon.

    Nurse. Before and apace.   *Exeunt.*

❧ SCENE FOURTH ❧

Enter Juliet.

Juliet. The clock struck nine when I did send the Nurse.
In half an hour she promis'd to return.
Perchance she cannot meet him—that 's not so.
O she is lame! Love's heralds should be thoughts,
Which ten items faster glides than the sun's beams   *5*
Driving back shadows over low'ring hills.
Therefore do nimble-pinion'd doves draw Love,
And therefore hath the wind-swift Cupid wings.
Now is the sun upon the highmost hill
Of this day's journey, and from nine till twelve   *10*
Is three long hours, yet she is not come.
Had she affections and warm youthful blood
She 'ld be as swift in motion as a ball:
My words would bandy her to my sweet love,
And his to me—but old folks, many feign as they were dead: *15*
Unwieldy, slow, heavy and pale as lead.

Enter Nurse [and Peter].

O God, she comes! O honey Nurse, what news?
Hast thou met with him? Send thy man away.

    Nurse. Peter, stay at the gate.   *[Exit Peter.]*

    Juliet. Now good sweet Nurse—O Lord, why look'st *20*
thou sad?
Though news be sad, yet tell them merrily;
If good, thou sham'st the music of sweet news
By playing it to me with so sour a face.

    Nurse. I am aweary, give me leave awhile.   *25*
Fie, how my bones ache! what a jaunce have I!

    Juliet. I would thou hadst my bones and I thy news.
Nay come, I pray thee, speak! Good, good Nurse, speak!

    Nurse. Jesu, what haste! can you not stay awhile?
Do you not see that I am out of breath?   *30*

    Juliet. How art thou out of breath when thou hast breath
To say to me that thou art out of breath?
Th' excuse that thou dost make in this delay
Is longer than the tale thou dost excuse.
Is thy news good or bad? Answer to that.   *35*
Say either, and I 'll stay the circumstance.
Let me be satisfy'd, is 't good or bad?

    Nurse. Well, you have made a simple choice, you know not
how to choose a man. Romeo? No, not he. Though his face
be better than any man's, yet his leg excels all men's—and *40*
for a hand and a foot and a body, though they be not to be
talk'd on, yet they are past compare. He is not the flower of
courtesy, but I 'll warrant him as gentle as a lamb. Go thy
ways, wench, serve God. What! have you din'd at home?

    Juliet. No, no. But all this did I know before.   *45*
What says he of our marriage, what of that?

    Nurse. Lord, how my head aches! what a head have I!
It beats as it would fall in twenty pieces.
My back a t'other side—ah, my back, my back!
Beshrew your heart for sending me about   *50*
To catch my death with jauncing up and down.

    Juliet. I' faith, I 'm sorry that thou art not well.
Sweet, sweet, sweet Nurse, tell me, what says my love?

    Nurse. Your love says like an honest gentleman,
And a courteous, and a kind, and a handsome,   *55*
And I warrant a virtuous—Where is your mother?

    Juliet. Where is my mother? why, she is within.
Where should she be? How oddly thou repliest:
'Your love says like an honest gentleman,
"Where is your mother?" '   *60*

    Nurse.   O God's Lady dear!
Are you so hot? Marry come up, I trow.
Is this the poultice for my aching bones?
Henceforward do your messages yourself.

    Juliet. Here 's such a coil! Come, what says Romeo?   *65*

    Nurse. Have you got leave to go to shrift today?

    Juliet. I have.

    Nurse. Then hie you hence to Friar Lawrence' cell,
There stays a husband to make you a wife.
Now comes the wanton blood up in your cheeks,   *70*
They 'll be in scarlet straight at any news.
Hie you to church. I must another way,
To fetch a ladder by the which your love
Must climb a bird's nest soon when it is dark.
I am the drudge and toil in your delight,   *75*
But you shall bear the burthen soon at night.
Go, I'll to dinner. Hie you to the cell.

    Juliet. Hie to high fortune! Honest Nurse, farewell.   *Exeunt.*

---

173 mistress: *here trisyllabic*   **176 secret:** *trustworthy*   **178 I:** *Q2 omits*   **181 fain:** *gladly* **lay knife aboard:** *i.e. as in boarding a vessel*   **182 lieve:** *lief, gladly*   **183 properer:** *handsomer*   **185 clout:** *piece of cloth* **versal** *universal* **rosemary:** *see IV.4.114; cf. n.*   **186 a letter:** *the same letter*   **188 dog-name:** *because the R sound suggest a dog's growling*   **190 sententious:** *malapropism for 'sentences' (sayings)*   **195 apace:** *quickly*   **7 nimble-pinion'd:** *swift-winged* **Love:** *Venus*   **12 affections:** *natural emotions*   **14 bandy:** *bat, toss*   **15 And his ... dead:** *this line is apparently a fourteener; see II.3.161, 162; cf. n.*

25 leave: *permission (to rest)*   **26 jaunce:** *jaunt; cf. n.*   **36 circumstance:** *details*   **38 simple:** *foolish*   **49 a:** *on*   **50 Beshrew:** *confound*   **54 honest:** *honorable*   **61 God's Lady dear:** *the Virgin Mary*   **62 Marry come up:** *an expression of angry impatience*   **65 coil:** *fuss*   **68 hie:** *hasten*   **70 wanton:** *uncontrolled*   **71 straight:** *immediately*   **74 soon:** *at once*   **76 soon at night:** *this very night*

❧ SCENE FIFTH ❧

Enter Friar and Romeo.

Friar. So smile the Heav'ns upon this holy act
That after-hours with sorrow chide us not!

Romeo. Amen, amen. But come what sorrow can,
It cannot countervail th' exchange of joy
That one short minute gives me in her sight.   5
Do thou but close our hands with holy words,
Then love-devouring Death do what he dare—
It is enough I may but call her mine.

Friar. These violent delights have violent ends,
And in their triumph die like fire and powder,   10
Which as they kiss consume. The sweetest honey
Is loathsome in his own deliciousness
And in the taste confounds the appetite.
Therefore love moderately, long love doth so,
Too swift arrives as tardy as too slow.   15

Enter Juliet ⟨somewhat fast and embraceth Romeo⟩.

Here comes the lady. O, so light a foot
Will ne'er wear out the everlasting flint.
A lover may bestride the gossamers
That idles in the wanton summer air,
And yet not fall, so light is Vanity.   20

Juliet. Good even to my ghostly confessor.

Friar. Romeo shall thank thee, daughter, for us both.

Juliet. As much to him, else is his thanks too much.

Romeo. Ah Juliet, if the measure of thy joy?
Be heap'd like mine, and that thy skill be more   25
To blazon it, then sweeten with thy breath
This neighbor air and let rich music's tongue
Unfold th' imagin'd happiness that both
Receive in either by this dear encounter.

Juliet. Conceit, more rich in matter than in words,   30
Brags of his substance, not of ornament.
They are but beggars that can count their worth,
But my true love is grown to such excess
I cannot sum up sum of half my wealth.

Friar. Come, come with me, and we will make short work,
For by your leaves you shall not stay alone
Till Holy Church incorporate two in one.   ⟨*Exeunt.*⟩

ACT THIRD ❧ SCENE FIRST

Enter Mercutio, Benvolio and Men.

Benvolio. I pray thee good Mercutio, let 's retire. The day is
hot, the Capels are abroad, and if we meet we shall not scape
a brawl, for now these hot days in the mad blood stirring.

Mercutio. Thou art like one of these fellows that, when he
enters the confines of a tavern, claps me his sword upon the   5
table and says, 'God send me no need of thee'—and by the
operation of the second cup draws him on the drawer, when
indeed there is no need.

Benvolio. Am I like such a fellow?

Mercutio. Come, come, thou art as hot a Jack in thy   10
mood as any in Italy, and as soon moved to be moody and
as soon moody to be moved.

Benvolio. And what to?

Mercutio. Nay, and there were two such we should have none
shortly, for one would kill the other. Thou?—why thou   15
wilt quarrel with a man that hath a hair more or a hair less in
his beard than thou hast. Thou wilt quarrel with a man for
cracking nuts, having no other reason but because thou hast
hazel eyes. What eye but such an eye would spy out such a
quarrel? Thy head is as full of quarrels as an egg is full of   20
meat, and yet thy head hath been beaten as addle as an egg
for quarreling. Thou hast quarrel'd with a man for coughing in
the street, because he hath waken'd thy dog that hath lain
asleep in the sun. Didst thou not fall out with a tailor for wearing his new doublet before Easter? with another for tying   25
his new shoes with old riband? And yet thou wilt tutor me
from quarreling!

Benvolio. And I were so apt to quarrel as thou art, any man
should buy the fee-simple of my life for an hour and a quarter.

Mercutio. The fee-simple? O simple!   30

Enter Tybalt, Petruchio and others.

Benvolio. By my head, here comes the Capulets.

Mercutio. By my heel, I care not.

Tybalt. Follow me close, for I will speak to them.
Gentlemen, good den, a word with one of you.

Mercutio. And but one word with one of us? Couple it   35
with something. Make it a word and a blow.

Tybalt. You shall find me apt enough to that, sir, and you
will give me occasion.

Mercutio. Could you not take some occasion without giving?

Tybalt. Mercutio, thou consort'st with Romeo.   40

Mercutio. Consort? What! dost thou make us minstrels? And
thou make minstrels of us, look to hear nothing but discords.
Here 's my fiddlestick, here 's that shall make you dance.
Zounds, consort!

Benvolio. We talk here in the public haunt of men.   45
Either withdraw unto some private place
Or reason coldly of your grievances
Or else depart. Here all eyes gaze on us.

Mercutio. Men's eyes were made to look, and let them gaze.
I will not budge for no man's pleasure, I.   50

Enter Romeo.

Tybalt. Well, peace be with you, sir, here comes my man.

Mercutio. But I 'll be hang'd sir, if he wear your livery.
Marry, go before to field, he 'll be your follower,
Your worship in that sense may call him 'man.'

3 what: *whatever* **4 countervail:** *counterbalance* **13 confounds:** *destroys* **18 gossamers:** *spiders' threads floating on the wind* **19 wanton:** *sportive* **20 Vanity:** *earthly joy* **21 confessor:** *stressed ´ — —* **23 As much:** *the same (i.e. 'Good even')* **24 measure:** *measuring pot or basket* **25 that:** *if* **26 blazon:** *describe (as a coat of arms in heraldic terms)* **27 music's:** Q2 *musicke* **30 Conceit:** *understanding* **34 sum up sum:** *add up the total* **37 Holy Church:** *see II.1.168; cf. n.* **SD Men:** *servants* **1, 2 I pray . . . abroad:** *for text see II.3.4-6; cf. n.* **2 Capels:** *stressed ´ — (see V.1.18)* **are:** Q1; Q2 *omits* **5 me:** *ethical dative* **6, 7 by . . . cup:** *when he feels the effect of his second drink*

7 draws him: *draws his sword* **drawer:** *tapster, waiter* **10 Jack:** *fellow* **11 mood:** *temper* **moved . . . moody:** *inclined to be angry* **12 moody . . . moved:** *angry at being provoked* **14 and:** *if* **18 reason:** *pun on 'raisin'* **21 addle:** *muddled, confused (quibble on 'rotten')* **25 doublet:** *jacket* **26 riband:** *ribbon* **29 fee-simple:** *possession in perpetuity of land or real property* **for . . . quarter:** *i.e. for very little* **SD Petruchio:** *one of Capulet's guests (see I.4.257)* **32 heel:** *pun on 'heal' (health, salvation)* **40 consort'st:** *dost associate (Mercutio quibbles on 'play music together')* **41 Consort:** *company of musicians* **43 fiddlestick:** *i.e. his sword* **44 Zounds:** *by God's (i.e. Christ's) wounds* **47 coldly:** *coolly, dispassionately* **52 livery:** *Mercutio quibbles on man in the sense of 'servant'* **53 field:** *i.e. for dueling* **follower:** *quibble on 'servant'*

Tybalt. Romeo, the love I bear thee can afford   55
No better term than this, thou art a villain.
   Romeo. Tybalt, the reason that I have to love thee
Doth much excuse the appertaining rage
To such a greeting. Villain am I none,
Therefore farewell, I see thou know'st me not.   60
   Tybalt. Boy, this shall not excuse the injuries
That thou hast done me, therefore turn and draw.
   Romeo. I do protest I never injur'd thee,
But love thee better than thou canst devise
Till thou shalt know the reason of my love.   65
And so, good Capulet (which name I tender
As dearly as mine own) be satisfy'd.
   Mercutio. O calm, dishon'rable, vile submission!
Alla stoccatho carries it away!
Tybalt, you ratcatcher, will you walk?   70
   Tybalt. What wouldst thou have with me?
   Mercutio. Good King of Cats, nothing but one of your nine
lives, that I mean to make bold withal and (as you shall use
me hereafter) dry-beat the rest of the eight. Will you pluck
your sword out of his pilcher by the ears? Make haste, lest   75
mine be about your ears ere it be out.
   Tybalt. I am for you.
   Romeo. Gentle Mercutio, put thy rapier up.
   Mercutio. Come sir, your *passado!*   [*They fight.*]
   Romeo. Draw, Benvolio, beat down their weapons.   80
Gentlemen, for shame forbear this outrage.
Tybalt, Mercutio! the Prince expressly hath
Forbid this bandying in Verona streets.
Hold, Tybalt! Good Mercutio!
   ⟨*Tybalt under Romeo's arm thrusts Mercutio in, and flies.*⟩   85
   Mercutio. I am hurt.
A plague a both houses, I am sped.
Is he gone and hath nothing?
   Benvolio. What! art thou hurt?
   Mercutio. Ay, ay, a scratch, a scratch, marry, 'tis enough.   90
Where is my page? Go villain, fetch a surgeon.   [*Exit Page.*]
   Romeo. Courage man, the hurt cannot be much.
   Mercutio. No, 'tis not so deep as a well nor so wide as a
church door, but 'tis enough, 'twill serve—ask for me tomor-
row and you shall find me a grave man. I am peppered,   95
I warrant, for this world. A plague a both your houses!
Zounds! A dog, a rat, a mouse, a cat, to scratch a man to
death! A braggart, a rogue, a villain that fights by the book of
arithmetic! Why the devil came you between us? I was hurt
under your arm.   100
   Romeo. I thought all for the best.
   Mercutio. Help me into some house, Benvolio,
Or I shall faint. A plague a both your houses.
They have made worms' meat of me.
I have it, and soundly too. Your houses!   105
                    Exeunt [*Mercutio and Benvolio*].
   Romeo. This gentleman, the Prince's near ally,

My very friend, hath got this mortal hurt
In my behalf, my reputation stain'd
With Tybalt's slander—Tybalt, that an hour
Hath been my cousin. O sweet Juliet,   110
Thy beauty hath made me effeminate,
And in my temper soften'd valor's steel.

                    Enter Benvolio.

   Benvolio. O Romeo, Romeo, brave Mercutio's dead.
That gallant spirit hath aspir'd the clouds,
Which too untimely here did scorn the earth.   115
   Romeo. This day's black fate on moe days doth depend,
This but begins the woe others must end.

                    ⟨*Enter Tybalt.*⟩

   Benvolio. Here comes the furious Tybalt back again.
   Romeo. He gay in triumph, and Mercutio slain!
Away to Heav'n, respective lenity,   120
And fire-ey'd Fury be my conduct now!
Now Tybalt, take the 'villain' back again
That late thou gav'st me, for Mercutio's soul
Is but a little way above our heads,
Staying for thine to keep him company.   125
Either thou or I or both must go with him.
   Tybalt. Thou wretched boy that didst consort him here
Shalt with him hence.
   Romeo.   This shall determine that.
                    They fight. Tybalt falls.

   Benvolio. Romeo, away, be gone!   130
The Citizens are up and Tybalt slain.
Stand not amaz'd, the Prince will doom thee death
If thou art taken. Hence, be gone, away!
   Romeo. O I am Fortune's fool!
   Benvolio.   Why dost thou stay?   135
                    Exit Romeo.

                    Enter Citizens.

   Citizens. Which way ran he that kill'd Mercutio?
Tybalt, that murtherer, which way ran he?
   Benvolio. There lies that Tybalt.
   Citizen.   Up sir, go with me.
I charge thee in the Prince's name obey.   140

                    Enter Prince, old Montague, Capulet, their Wives and all.

   Prince. Where are the vile beginners of this fray?
   Benvolio. O noble Prince, I can discover all
Th' unlucky manage of this fatal brawl.
There lies the man, slain by young Romeo,
That slew thy kinsman, brave Mercutio.   145
   Capulet's Wife. Tybalt, my cousin! O my brother's child!
O Prince! O husband! O the blood is spill'd
Of my dear kinsman! Prince, as thou art true,
For blood of ours shed blood of Montague.

---

56 villain: *base person*   **58 appertaining . . . To:** *appropriate . . . to*   **rage:** *i.e. my lack of rage*   **61 Boy:** *see I.4.199; cf. n.*   **64 devise:** *imagine*   **66 tender:** *cherish*   **69 Alla stoccatho:** *Q2* Alla stucatho; *cf. n.*   **carries it away:** *winds the day*   **70, 72 ratcatcher, King of Cats:** *see II.3.21; cf. n.*   **74 dry-beat:** *thrash (without drawing blood)*   **75 pilcher:** *scabbard (metaphor from 'pilch,' a leather garment)*   **ears:** *i.e. hilt*   **79 passado:** *see II.3.24; cf. n.*   **83 bandying:** *exchanging blows, brawling*   SD ⟨**Tybalt . . . flies**⟩: *Q2* Away Tybalt   **thrusts . . . in:** *stabs*   **87 sped:** *dispatched*   **95 peppered:** *i.e. finished*   **98, 99 book of arithmetic:** *rules of fencing theory*   **106 ally:** *kinsman*

107 very: *true*   **112 temper:** *state of mind (quibble on 'temper' of steel)*   **soften'd:** *rather than hardened (in the tempering process)*   **113 brave:** *noble, excellent*   **114 aspir'd:** *mounted to*   **116 moe:** *more (in number)*   **depend:** *impend, hang over*   **119 He gay:** *Q2* He gan; *Q1* A liue; *cf. n.*   **120 respective:** *considerate (of Tybalt's blood-tie with Juliet)*   **121 ey'd:** *Q1; Q2* end   **conduct:** *conductor, guide*   **129 This:** *i.e. his sword*   **131 up:** *up in arms*   **132 amaz'd:** *confounded*   **doom:** *condemn to*   **134 fool:** *dupe, plaything*   **136 Citizens:** *Q2* Citti; *cf. n.*   **139 Citizen:** *Q2* Citi   SD **all:** *including the Prince's Train*   **142 discover:** *uncover, reveal*   **143 manage:** *conduct, proceeding*   **147 O husband:** *Q2* O Cozen, husband

O cousin, cousin!   150
    Prince. Benvolio, who began this bloody fray?
    Benvolio. Tybalt here slain, whom Romeo's hand did slay.
Romeo that spoke him fair bid him bethink
How nice the quarrel was and urg'd withal
Your high displeasure. All this uttered   155
With gentle breath, calm look, knees humbly bow'd,
Could not take truce with the unruly spleen
Of Tybalt, deaf to peace, but that he tilts
With piercing steel at bold Mercutio's breast,
Who all as hot turns deadly point to point   160
And with a martial scorn with one hand beats
Cold death aside and with the other sends
It back to Tybalt, whose dexterity
Retorts it. Romeo he cries aloud,
'Hold, friends! Friends, part!' and swifter than his tongue   165
His agile arm beats down their fatal points
And 'twixt them rushes; underneath whose arm
An envious thrust from Tybalt hit the life
Of stout Mercutio; and then Tybalt fled,
But by and by comes back to Romeo,   170
Who had but newly entertain'd revenge,
And to 't they go like lightning; for ere I
Could draw to part them was stout Tybalt slain,
And as he fell did Romeo turn and fly.
This is the truth or let Benvolio die.   175
    Capulet's Wife. He is a kinsman to the Montague,
Affection makes him false, he speaks not true.
Some twenty of them fought in this black strife,
And all those twenty could but kill one life.
I beg for justice, which thou, Prince, must give—   180
Romeo slew Tybalt, Romeo must not live.
    Prince. Romeo slew him, he slew Mercutio.
Who now the price of his dear blood doth owe?
    Montague. Not Romeo, Prince, he was Mercutio's friend.
His fault concludes but what the law should end—   185
The life of Tybalt.
    Prince.   And for that offence
Immediately we do exile him hence.
I have an int'rest in your hate's proceeding,
My blood for your rude brawls doth lie a-bleeding.   190
But I 'll amerce you with so strong a fine
That you shall all repent the loss of mine.
I will be deaf to pleading and excuses,
Nor tears nor prayers shall purchase out abuses.
Therefore use none. Let Romeo hence in haste,   195
Else when he 's found that hour is his last.
Bear hence this body and attend our will.
Mercy but murders, pardoning those that kill.   *Exeunt.*

❧ Scene Second ❧

Enter Juliet alone.

    Juliet. Gallop apace, you fiery-footed steeds,
Towards Phoebus' lodging. Such a wagoner
As Phaeton would whip you to the West
And bring in cloudy Night immediately.
Spread thy close curtain, love-performing Night,   5
That runaway's eyes may wink and Romeo
Leap to these arms untalk'd of and unseen.
Lovers can see to do their am'rous rites
By their own beauties, or if Love be blind
It best agrees with night. Come, civil Night,   10
Thou sober-suited matron all in black,
And learn me how to lose a winning match
Play'd for a pair of stainless maidenhoods.
Hood my unmann'd blood bating in my cheeks
With thy black mantle till strange love grow bold,   15
Think true love acted simple modesty.
Come Night, come Romeo, come thou day in night,
For thou wilt lie upon the wings of Night
Whiter than new snow upon a raven's back.
Come gentle Night, come loving black-brow'd Night,   20
Give me my Romeo. And when I shall die
Take him and cut him out in little stars,
And he will make the face of heav'n so fine
That all the world will be in love with Night
And pay no worship to the garish Sun.   25
O I have bought the mansion of a love
But not possess'd it, and though I am sold
Not yet enjoy'd. So tedious is this day
As is the night before some festival
To an impatient child that hath new robes   30
And may not wear them. O here comes my Nurse—

Enter Nurse with cords.

And she brings news, and every tongue that speaks
But Romeo's name speaks heav'nly eloquence.
Now Nurse, what news? What hast thou there,
The cords that Romeo bid thee fetch?   35
    Nurse.   Ay, ay, the cords.
    Juliet. Ay me, what news? why dost thou wring thy hands?
    Nurse. Ah weraday, he 's dead, he 's dead, he 's dead!
We are undone, lady, we are undone.
Alack the day! he 's gone, he 's kill'd, he 's dead.   40
    Juliet. Can Heaven be so envious?
    Nurse.   Romeo can,
Though Heav'n cannot. O Romeo, Romeo!
Who ever would have thought it? Romeo!
    Juliet. What divel art thou that dost torment me thus?   45
This torture should be roar'd in dismal Hell.
Hath Romeo slain himself? Say thou but 'Ay.'
And that bare vowel 'I' shall poison more
Than the death-darting eye of cockatrice.

153 fair: *civilly* **bethink:** *consider* **154 nice:** *trivial* **withal:** *at the same time* **157 take truce with:** *come to terms with* **spleen:** *quarrelsomeness* **158 tilts:** *thrusts* **161, 162 one hand ... the other;** *cf. n.* **164 Retorts:** *throws back* **Romeo he:** *duplicated subject* **166 agile:** *Q1; Q2 aged* **169 stout:** *brave* **170 by and by:** *immediately* **171 entertain'd:** *considered* **183 Who ... owe:** *i.e. who now must pay for Tybalt's death* **184 Montague:** *Q2 Capu.; cf. n.* **188 exile:** *here and elsewhere accented 'exile'* **189 hate's:** *Q1; Q2 hearts* **190 My blood:** *since Mercutio was the Prince's kinsman* **191 amerce:** *punish by fine* **192 mine:** *i.e. my blood* **193 I:** *Q1; Q2 It* **194 purchase out:** *buy pardon for* **198 Mercy ... kill;** *cf. n.*

1–31 Gallop apace ... wear them: *cf. n.* **1 steeds:** *the horses of the sun god Phoebus Apollo* **3 Phaeton:** *son of Phoebus* **6 runaway:** *i.e. the sun; cf. n.* **wink:** *shut (i.e. cause darkness).* **9 By:** *Q2 And by; for text see V.3.103; cf. n.* **Love:** *Cupid* **10 civil:** *sober, decorous* **14 Hood:** *cover, blindfold (term from falconry)* **unmann'd:** *untrained (of a falcon; quibble on 'without a man')* **bating:** *fluttering the wins* **17 Night:** *pun on 'knight'* **25 garish:** *glaring* **SD Enter Nurse with cords;** *cf. n.* **cords:** *a rope ladder* **38 weraday:** *weladay, alas* **41 envious:** *malicious* **48 bare vowel 'I':** *the Elizabethan spelling of 'ay'* **49, 50 eye, I:** *puns on 'ay'* **49 cockatrice:** *basilisk; cf. n.*

I am not I if there be such an 'Ay,'   *50*
Or those eyes shut that makes thee answer 'Ay.'
If he be slain say 'Ay' or if not 'No,'
Brief sounds determine my weal or woe.

    Nurse. I saw the wound, I saw it with mine eyes
(God save the mark!) here on his manly breast.   *55*
A piteous corse, a bloody piteous corse,
Pale, pale as ashes, all bedaub'd in blood,
All in gore blood, I sounded at the sight.

    Juliet. O break, my heart! poor bankrout, break at once!
To prison, eyes, ne'er look on liberty.   *60*
Vile earth to earth resign, end motion here,
And thou and Romeo press one heavy bier.

    Nurse. O Tybalt, Tybalt, the best friend I had!
O courteous Tybalt, honest gentleman,
That ever I should live to see thee dead!   *65*

    Juliet. What storm is this that blows so contrary?
Is Romeo slaughter'd and is Tybalt dead?
My dearest cousin and my dearer lord?
Then dreadful trumpet sound the general doom,
For who is living if those two are gone?   *70*

    Nurse. Tybalt is gone and Romeo banished.
Romeo that kill'd him, he is banished.

    Juliet. O God! did Romeo's hand shed Tybalt's blood?

    Nurse. It did, it did! alas the day, it did!

    Juliet. O serpent heart, hid with a flow'ring face!   *75*
Did ever dragon keep so fair a cave?
Beautiful tyrant, fiend angelical!
Dove-feather'd raven, wolvish-rav'ning lamb!
Despised substance of divinest show!
Just opposite to what thou justly seem'st,   *80*
A damned saint, an honorable villain!
O Nature, what hadst thou to do in Hell
When thou didst bow'r the spirit of a fiend
In mortal Paradise of such sweet flesh?
Was ever book containing such vile matter   *85*
So fairly bound? O that deceit should dwell
In such a gorgeous palace!

    Nurse. There 's no trust, no faith, no honesty in men,
All perjur'd, all forsworn, all dissemblers.
Ah, where 's my man? Give me some *aqua vitae*,   *90*
These griefs, these woes, these sorrows make me old.
Shame come to Romeo.

    Juliet.   Blister'd be thy tongue
For such a wish! He was not born to shame,
Upon his brow Shame is asham'd to sit,   *95*
For 'tis a throne where Honor may be crown'd
Sole monarch of the universal earth.
O what a beast was I to chide at him!

    Nurse. Will you speak well of him that kill'd your cousin?

    Juliet. Shall I speak ill of him that is my husband?   *100*
Ah poor my lord, what tongue shall smooth thy name
When I thy three-hours wife have mangled it?

But wherefore villain, didst thou kill my cousin?
That villain-cousin would have kill'd my husband.
Back, foolish tears, back to your native spring,   *105*
Your tributary drops belong to Woe,
Which you mistaking offer up to Joy.
My husband lives that Tybalt would have slain,
And Tybalt 's dead that would have slain my husband.
All this is comfort, wherefore weep I then?   *110*
Some word there was, worser than Tybalt's death,
That murder'd me. I would forget it fain,
But O it presses to my memory
Like damned guilty deeds to sinners' minds:
'Tybalt is dead and Romeo banished.'   *115*
That 'banished,' that one word 'banished,'
Hath slain ten thousand Tybalts. Tybalt's death
Was woe enough if it had ended there,
Or if sour Woe delights in fellowship
And needly will be rank'd with other Griefs,   *120*
Why follow'd not (when she said 'Tybalt 's dead')
'Thy father' or 'Thy mother,' nay, or both,
Which modern lamentation might have mov'd?
But with a rear-ward following Tybalt's death,
'Romeo is banished'—to speak that word   *125*
Is father, mother, Tybalt, Romeo, Juliet,
All slain, all dead. 'Romeo is banished!'
There is no end, no limit, measure, bound,
In that word's death, no words can that woe sound.
Where is my father and my mother, Nurse?   *130*

    Nurse. Weeping and wailing over Tybalt's corse.
Will you go to them? I will bring you thither.

    Juliet. Wash they his wounds with tears? Mine shall be
spent,
When theirs are dry, for Romeo's banishment.   *135*
Take up those cords. Poor ropes, you are beguil'd
(Both you and I) for Romeo is exil'd.
He made you for a highway to my bed,
But I a maid die maiden-widowed.
Come cords, come Nurse. I 'll to my wedding bed,   *140*
And Death, not Romeo, take my maidenhead!

    Nurse. Hie to your chamber, I 'll find Romeo
To comfort you, I wot well where he is.
Hark ye, your Romeo will be here at night.
I 'll to him, he is hid at Lawrence' cell.   *145*

    Juliet. O find him! Give this ring to my true knight
And bid him come to take his last farewell.   *Exeunt.*

❧ SCENE THIRD ❧

Enter Friar.

    Friar. Romeo, come forth! come forth, thou fearful man.
Affliction is enamor'd of thy parts
And thou art wedded to Calamity.

⟨*Enter Romeo.*⟩

    Romeo. Father, what news? what is the Prince's doom?

---

51 those: *Romeo's* **shut:** *Q2* shot   **53 determine:** *decide*   **55 God save the mark:** *God forbid*   **56 corse:** *corpse*   **58 gore:** *a clot of*   **sounded:** *swounded, swooned*   **59 bankrout:** *bankrupt*   **break:** *quibble on 'declare insolvent'*   **61 Vile earth** *wretched body*   **resign:** *yield thyself up to*   **69 general doom:** *Day of Judgment*   **75–81 O serpent heart . . . villain:** *see I.1.174-179; cf. n.*   **76 keep:** *guard*   **cave:** *i.e. containing treasure*   **77 tyrant:** *desperado, villain*   **78 Dove-feather'd:** *Q2* Rauenous doue-feathered; *for text see V.3.103; cf. n.*   **79 substance:** *reality*   **show:** *appearance*   **80 justly:** *truly*   **81 damned:** *Q2* dimme   **83 bow'r:** *lodge*   **89 forsworn, all:** *Q2* forsworn, all naught, all; *cf. n.*   **90 aqua vitae:** *spirits*   **101 smooth:** *speak well of* (antithetic to *mangled*)

120 needly: *of necessity*   **123 modern:** *ordinary*   **124 rear-ward:** *rear guard*   **129 sound:** *utter, express* (quibble on 'fathom')   **134 spent:** *shed*   **143 wot:** *know*   **SD Enter Friar:** *So Q1; Q2* Enter Frier and Romeo; *cf. n.*   **2 parts:** *qualities, endowments*   **4 doom:** *judgment*

What Sorrow craves acquaintance at my hand   5
That I yet know not?
 Friar.   Too familiar
Is my dear son with such sour company.
I bring thee tidings of the Prince's doom.
 Romeo. What less than doomsday is the Prince's doom?   10
 Friar. A gentler judgement vanish'd from his lips,
Not body's death but body's banishment.
 Romeo. Ha! banishment! Be merciful, say 'death,'
For exile hath more terror in his look
Much more, than death. Do not say 'banishment.'   15
  Friar. Here from Verona art thou banished.
Be patient, for the world is broad and wide.
 Romeo. There is no world without Verona walls,
But Purgatory, torture, Hell itself.
Hence banished is banish'd from the world,   20
And world's exile is death. Then 'banished'
Is death misterm'd. Calling death 'banished'
Thou cut'st my head off with a golden ax
And smil'st upon the stroke that murders me.
 Friar. O deadly sin! O rude unthankfulness!   25
Thy fault our law calls death, but the kind Prince,
Taking thy part, hath rush'd aside the law
And turn'd that black word 'death' to 'banishment.'
This is dear mercy and thou see'st it not.
 Romeo. 'Tis torture and not mercy. Heav'n is here   30
Where Juliet lives, and every cat and dog
And little mouse, every unworthy thing,
Live here in Heaven and may look on her,
But Romeo may not. More validity,
More honorable state, more courtship lives   35
In carrion flies than Romeo—they may seize
On the white wonder of dear Juliet's hand
And steal immortal blessing from her lips,
Who e'en in pure and vestal modesty
Still blush, as thinking their own kisses sin,   40
But Romeo may not, he is banished.
Flies may do this but I from this must fly,
They are free men but I am banished.
And say'st thou yet that exile is not death?
Hadst thou no poison mix'd, no sharp-ground knife,   45
No sudden mean of death, though ne'er so mean,
But 'banished' to kill me? 'Banished!'
O Friar, the damned use that word in Hell,
Howling attends it. How hast thou the heart,
Being a divine, a ghostly confessor,   50
A sin-absolver and my friend profess'd,
To mangle me with that word 'banished'?
 Friar. Thou fond mad man, hear me a little speak.
 Romeo. O thou wilt speak again of banishment.
 Friar. I 'll give thee armor to keep off that word,   55
Adversity's sweet milk, Philosophy,
To comfort thee though thou art banished.
 Romeo. Yet 'banished'? Hang up philosophy!
Unless philosophy can make a Juliet,

Displant a town, reverse a prince's doom,   60
It helps not, it prevails not. Talk no more.
 Friar. O then I see that mad men have no ears.
 Romeo. How should they, when that wise men have no eyes?
 Friar. Let me dispute with thee of thy estate.
 Romeo. Thou canst not speak of that thou dost not feel.   65
Wert thou as young as I, Juliet thy love,
An hour but marry'd, Tybalt murdered,
Doting like me and like me banished,
Then mightst thou speak—then mightst thou tear thy hair.
And fall upon the ground as I do now,   70
Taking the measure of an unmade grave.

      ⟨*Nurse knocks [within.]*⟩
 Friar. Arise, one knocks! good Romeo, hide thyself.
 Romeo. Not I, unless the breath of heartsick groans
Mistlike infold me from the search of eyes.

      ⟨*She knocks again.*⟩
 Friar. Hark! how they knock. Who 's there? Romeo, arise,   75
Thou wilt be taken. Stay a while! Stand up. *Loud knock.*
Run to my study— By and by! God's will,
What simpleness is this? I come, I come!   *Knock.*
Who knocks so hard? whence come you? what 's your will?

       Enter Nurse.

 Nurse. Let me come in and you shall know my errand.   80
I come from Lady Juliet.
 Friar.   Welcome then.
 Nurse. O holy Friar, O tell me, holy Friar,
Where is my lady's lord, where 's Romeo?
 Friar. There on the ground, with his own tears made drunk.
 Nurse. O he is even in my mistress' case,
Just in her case! O woeful sympathy,
Piteous predicament—e'en so lies she
Blubb'ring and weeping, weeping and blubb'ring.
Stand up, stand up! stand and you be a man,   90
For Juliet's sake, for her sake, rise and stand.
Why should you fall into so deep an O?   ⟨*He rises.*⟩
 Romeo. Nurse—
 Nurse.   Ah sir! ah sir! death 's the end of all.
 Romeo. Spak'st thou of Juliet? how is it with her?   95
Doth not she think me an old murtherer
Now I have stain'd the childhood of our joy
With blood remov'd but little from her own?
Where is she? and how doth she? and what says
My conceal'd lady to our cancel'd love?   100
 Nurse. O she says nothing, sir, but weeps and weeps,
And now falls on her bed and then starts up,
And Tybalt calls and then on Romeo cries
And then down falls again.
 Romeo.   As if that name   105
Shot from the deadly level of a gun
Did murther her, as that name's cursed hand
Murder'd her kinsman. O tell me, Friar, tell me,
In what vile part of this anatomy

---

7 **familiar:** *here pronounced 'famili-ar'; see I.4.98; cf. n.* **11 vanish'd:** *was breathed, issued* **18 without:** *outside* **21 world's:** *from this world* **27 rush'd:** *thrust* **29 dear:** *rare, unusual* **34 validity:** *value* **35 courtship:** *courtliness (quibble on 'wooing')* **41–44 But Romeo ... death:** *for text see II.1.247-250; cf. n.* **46 mean:** *means* **so mean:** *so base* **50 confessor:** *stressed ´ – —* **53 Thou:** *Q1; Q1 Then* **fond:** *foolish* **58 Yet:** *still*

60 Displant: *uproot* **61 prevails:** *avails* **64 dispute:** *discuss* **estate:** *situation* **65 that:** *that which* **SD** ⟨*Nurse knocks*⟩ *Q2* Enter Nurse, and knocke **SD** (*She knocks again*) *Q2* They knock **SD Loud knock:** *Q2* Slud knock **77 By and by:** *immediately* **78 simpleness:** *folly* **86 case:** *quibble on 'pudendum'* **87 woeful sympathy:** *agreement in woe* **89 Blubb'ring:** *weeping hard* **90 and:** *if* **92 O:** *moan, lament (quibble on 'pudendum'; compare II.1.24)* **96 old:** *experienced, hardened* **100 conceal'd:** *secret (since the marriage is not known; stressed ´ – — to jingle with cancel'd)* **106 level:** *line of aim* **109 anatomy:** *body*

Doth my name lodge? tell me, that I may sack   *110*
The hateful mansion.

⟨*He offers to stab himself, and Nurse snatches the dagger away.*⟩

Friar.   Hold thy desp'rate hand!
Art thou a man? thy form cries out thou art—
Thy tears are wom'nish, thy wild acts denote
Th' unreasonable fury of a beast.   *115*
Unseemly woman in a seeming man,
And ill-beseeming beast in seeming both,
Thou hast amaz'd me. By my holy order,
I thought thy disposition better temper'd.
Hast thou slain Tybalt? wilt thou slay thyself?   *120*
And slay thy lady that in thy life lives
By doing damned hate upon thyself?
Why rail'st thou on thy birth, the Heav'n and earth?
Since birth and Heav'n and earth all three do meet
In thee at once, which thou at once wouldst lose.   *125*
Fie, fie! thou sham'st thy shape, thy love, thy wit,
Which like a usurer abound'st in all
And usest none in that true use indeed
Which should bedeck thy shape, thy love, thy wit.
Thy noble shape is but a form of wax   *130*
Digressing from the valor of a man;
Thy dear love sworn, but hollow perjury,
Killing that love which thou has vow'd to cherish;
Thy wit (that ornament to shape and love,
Misshapen in the conduct of them both)   *135*
Like powder in a skill-less soldier's flask
Is set afire by thine own ignorance,
And thou dismember'd with thine own defence.
What! rouse thee, man, thy Juliet is alive,
For whose dear sake thou wast but lately dead—   *140*
There art thou happy. Tybalt would kill thee,
But thou slew'st Tybalt—there art thou happy.
The law that threaten'd death becomes thy friend
And turns it to exile—there art thou happy.
A pack of blessings light upon thy back,   *145*
Happiness courts thee in her best array,
But like a misbehav'd and sullen wench
Thou pouts upon thy fortune and they love.
Take heed, take heed, for such die mis'rable.
Go get thee to thy love as was decree'd,   *150*
Ascend her chamber, hence and comfort her.
But look thou stay not till the watch be set,
For then thou canst not pass to Mantua,
Where thou shalt live till we can find a time
To blaze your marriage, reconcile your friends,   *155*
Beg pardon of the Prince and call thee back
With twenty hundred thousand times more joy
Than thou went'st forth in lamentation.
Go before, Nurse, commend me to thy lady,
And bid her hasten all the house to bed,   *160*
Which heavy sorrow makes them apt unto.
Romeo is coming.

Nurse. O Lord, I could have stay'd here all the night
To hear good counsel, O what learning is!
My lord, I 'll tell my lady you will come.   *165*
Romeo. Do so, and bid my sweet prepare to chide.
         ⟨*Nurse offers to go in and turns again.*⟩
Nurse. Here sir, a ring she bid me give you, sir.
Hie you, make haste, for it grows very late.
Romeo. How well my comfort is reviv'd by this!
Friar. Go hence, good night.   ⟨*Exit Nurse.*⟩   *170*
         And here stands all your state:
Either be gone before the watch be set
Or by the break of day disguis'd from hence.
Sojourn in Mantua. I'll find out your man,
And he shall signify from time to time   *175*
Every good hap to you that chances here.
Give me thy hand, 'tis late. Farewell, good night.
Romeo. But that a joy past joy calls out on me,
It were a grief so brief to part with thee.
Farewell.   *Exeunt.*

❧ SCENE FOURTH ❧

Enter old Capulet, his Wife and Paris.

Capulet. Things have fall'n out, sir, so unluckily
That we have had no time to move our daughter.
Look you, she lov'd her kinsman Tybalt dearly,
And so did I. Well, we were born to die.
'Tis very late, she 'll not come down tonight.   *5*
I promise you, but for your company
I would have been abed an hour ago.
Paris. These times of woe afford no times to woo.
Madam, good night, commend me to your daughter.
Wife. I will, and know her mind early tomorrow.   *10*
Tonight she 's mew'd up to her heaviness.
⟨*Paris offers to go in, and Capulet calls him again.*⟩
Capulet. Sir Paris, I will make a desp'rate tender
Of my child's love. I think she will be rul'd
In all respects by me; nay more, I doubt it not.
Wife, go you to her ere you go to bed,   *15*
Acquaint her here of my son Paris' love
And bid her (mark you me?) on Wednesday next—
But soft, what day is this?
Paris.   Monday, my lord.
Capulet. Monday. Ha, ha! Well, Wednesday is too soon.   *20*
A Thursday let it be—a Thursday, tell her,
She shall be marry'd to this noble earl.
Will you be ready? do you like this haste?
We 'll keep no great ado—a friend or two—
For hark you, Tybalt being slain so late,   *25*
I may be thought we held him carelessly,
Being our kinsman, if we revel much.
Therefore we 'll have some half a dozen friends
And there an end. But what say you to Thursday?
Paris. My lord, I would that Thursday were tomorrow.   *30*
Capulet. Well, get you gone, a Thursday be it then.

SD **Nurse:** *in the modern theater usually the Friar*   119 **temper'd:** *mixed, balanced*   121 **lives:** *Q1; Q2* lies   122 **damned:** *since suicide is an unforgivable sin*   126 **wit:** *judgment, reason*   127 **Which:** *who*   128 **usest:** *quibble on 'lend at interest'*   131 **Digressing:** *deviating*   141 **There:** *in that respect*   148 **pouts upon:** *Q2* puts up; *Q1* frownst upon   150 **decree'd:** *arranged*   152 **watch:** *guard set: posted (at the city gates)*   155 **blaze:** *proclaim*   **friends:** *relatives, families*   161 **apt:** *inclined*

SD **again:** *back*   171 **here . . . state:** *here is the situation*   172, 173 **Either be gone . . . hence;** *cf. n.*   178 **But that:** *were it not that*   179 **were:** *would be*   **brief:** *hastily*   2 **move:** *urge, persuade*   6 **promise:** *assure*   11 **mew'd up to:** *shut up with (a 'mew' being a falcon's cage)*   **heaviness:** *sorrow*   SD **again:** *back*   12 **desp'rate tender:** *reckless offer; cf. n.*   16 **son:** *intended son-in-law*   21 **A:** *on*   22 **earl:** *nobleman, count*

Go you to Juliet ere you go to bed,
Prepare her, Wife, against this wedding day.
Farewell, my lord. Light to my chamber, ho!
Afore me, it is so very late   35
That we may call it early by and by.
Good night.   *Exeunt.*

❧ SCENE FIFTH ❧

Enter Romeo and Juliet ⟨at the window⟩.

Juliet. Wilt thou be gone? it is not yet near day,
It was the nightingale and not the lark
That pierc'd the fearful hollow of thine ear,
Nightly she sings on yond pomegranate tree.
Believe me, love, it was the nightingale.   5
   Romeo. It was the lark, the herald of the morn,
No nightingale. Look love, what envious streaks
Do lace the sev'ring clouds in yonder East—
Night's candles are burnt out and jocund Day
Stands tiptoe on the misty mountain tops.   10
I must be gone and live or stay and die.
   Juliet. Yond light is not daylight, I know it, I.
It is some meteor that the sun exhal'd
To be to thee this night a torchbearer
And light thee on thy way to Mantua.   15
Therefore stay yet, thou need'st not to be gone.
   Romeo. Let me be tane, let me be put to death,
I am content, so thou wilt have it so.
I'll say yon grey is not the Morning's eye—
'Tis but the pale reflex of Cynthia's brow;   20
Nor that is not the lark whose notes do beat
The vaulty heav'n so high above our heads.
I have more care to stay than will to go.
Come death, and welcome! Juliet wills it so.
How is 't, my soul? let 's talk, it is not day.   25
   Juliet. It is, it is! hie hence, be gone away.
It is the lark that sings so out of tune,
Straining harsh discords and unpleasing sharps.
Some say the lark makes sweet division,
This doth not so for she divideth us.   30
Some say the lark and loathed toad chang'd eyes,
O now I would they had chang'd voices too,
Since arm from arm that voice doth us affray,
Hunting thee hence with hunt's-up to the day.
O now be gone, more light and light it grows.   35
   Romeo. More light and light—more dark and dark our woes.

Enter Nurse ⟨hastily⟩.

Nurse. Madam!
Juliet. Nurse?
Nurse. Your lady mother's coming to your chamber.

The day is broke, be wary, look about.   [*Exit.*]   40
   Juliet. Then window, let day in and let life out.
   Romeo. Farewell, farewell! one kiss, and I'll descend.
                                          ⟨*He goeth down.*⟩
Juliet. Art thou gone so, love? Lord, my husband, friend,
I must hear from thee every day i' th' hour,
For in a minute there are many days—   45
O by this count I shall be much in years
Ere I again behold my Romeo.
   Romeo. Farewell.
I will omit no opportunity
That may convey my greetings, love, to thee.   50
   Juliet. O think'st thou we shall ever meet again?
   Romeo. Ay, doubt it not, and all these woes shall serve
For sweet discourses in our times to come.
   Juliet. O God! I have an ill-divining soul,
Methinks I see thee, now thou art so low,   55
As one dead in the bottom of a tomb.
Either my eyesight fails or thou look'st pale.
   Romeo. And trust me, love, in my eye so do you—
Dry Sorrow drinks our blood. Adieu, adieu!   *Exit.*
   Juliet. O Fortune, Fortune! all men call thee fickle.   60
If thou art fickle, what dost thou with him
That is renowm'd for faith? Be fickle, Fortune,
For then I hope thou wilt not keep him long
But send him back—

Enter Capulet's Wife.

Wife.   Ho daughter! are you up?   65
   Juliet. Who is 't that calls? it is my lady mother,
Is she not down so late or up so early?
What unaccustom'd cause procures her hither?
                           ⟨*She goeth down from the window.*⟩
   Wife. Why how now, Juliet?
Juliet.   Madam I am not well.   70
   Wife. Evermore weeping for your cousin's death?
What! wilt thou wash him from his grave with tears?
And if thou couldst, thou couldst not make him live,
Therefore have done. Some grief shows much of love,
But much of grief shows still some want of wit.   75
   Juliet. Yet let me weep for such a feeling loss.
   Wife. So shall you feel the loss, but not the friend
Which you weep for.
Juliet.   Feeling so the loss,
I cannot choose but ever weep the friend.   80
   Wife. Well girl, thou weep'st not so much for his death
As that the villain lives which slaughter'd him.
   Juliet. What villain, madam?
Wife.   That same villain Romeo.
   Juliet. [*Aside.*] 'Villain' and he be many miles asunder. 85
God pardon him, I do with all my heart,
And yet no man like he doth grieve my heart.
   Wife. That is because the traitor murd'rer lives.
   Juliet. Ay madam, from the reach of these my hands,
Would none but I might venge my cousin's death!   90

---

33 **against:** *in readiness for* 35 **Afore me:** *on my word* (a mild oath) SD **(at the window):** Q2 *aloft* 1-36 **Wilt thou be gone . . . dark:** *our woes; cf. n.* 3 **fearful:** *apprehensive* 7 **envious:** *malicious* 8 **lace:** *streak* 13 **meteor:** *supposedly the ignition of vapors exhaled from the earth* **exhal'd:** Q2 *exhale;* Q1 *exhales; drew up; cf. n.* 17 **tane:** *taken* 18 **so:** *if* 20 **reflex:** *reflected light* **Cynthia:** *the moon* 23 **care:** *concern, desire* 28 **sharps:** *shrill high notes* 29 **division:** *modulation, melody* 31 **Some say . . . eyes;** *cf. n.* **chang'd:** Q2 *change; exchanged* 33 **arm from arm:** *from one another's arms* **affray:** *startle* 34 **hunt's-up:** *morning song* (to waken hunters or a new-married wife) SD **Nurse:** *so Q1;* Q2 *Madame and Nurse; cf. n.* 37-40 **Madam . . . look about:** *for staging see; cf. n.*

41 **life:** *i.e. Romeo* 43 **my:** Q1; Q2 *ay* **friend:** *lover* 46 **count:** *method of reckoning time* 52 **Ay:** Q2 *I* (usually here interpreted as the pronoun) 54 **ill-divining:** *prophesying mischance* 59 **Dry . . . blood:** *since grief was thought to exhaust the blood* 62 **renowm'd;** *cf. n.* 67 **down:** *lying down, abed* 68 **procures:** *brings* SD **(She . . . window):** *for staging see; cf. n.* 76 **feeling:** *heartfelt* 78 **Which:** *whom* 86 **him:** Q2 *omits* 87 **like:** *so much as*

Wife. We will have vengeance for it, fear thou not.
Then weep no more, I'll send to one in Mantua,
Where that same banish'd runagate doth live.
Shall give him such an unaccustom'd dram
That he shall soon keep Tybalt company,   *95*
And then I hope thou wilt be satisfy'd.
   Juliet. Indeed I never shall be satisfy'd
With Romeo till I behold him—dead—
Is my poor heart so for a kinsman vex'd.
Madam, if you could find out but a man   *100*
To bear a poison, I would temper it
That Romeo should upon receipt thereof
Soon sleep in quiet. O how my heart abhors
To hear him nam'd and cannot come to him
To wreak the love I bore my cousin   *105*
Upon his body that hath slaughter'd him.
   Wife. Find thou the means and I'll find such a man.
But now I'll tell thee joyful tidings, girl.
   Juliet. And joy comes well in such a needy time.
What are they, I beseech your ladyship?   *110*
   Wife. Well, well, thou hast a careful father, child,
One who to put thee from thy heaviness
Hath sorted out a sudden day of joy
That thou expects not nor I look'd not for.
   Juliet. Madam, in happy time, what day is that?   *115*
   Wife. Marry, my child, early next Thursday morn
The gallant, young and noble gentleman,
The County Paris, at Saint Peter's Church
Shall happily make thee there a joyful bride.
   Juliet. Now by Saint Peter's Church and Peter too,   *120*
He shall not make me there a joyful bride.
I wonder at this haste, that I must wed
Ere he that should be husband comes to woo.
I pray you tell my lord and father, madam,
I will not marry yet, and when I do, I swear   *125*
It shall be Romeo, whom you know I hate,
Rather than Paris. These are news indeed!
   Wife. Here comes your father, tell him so yourself,
And see how he will take it at your hands.

          Enter Capulet and Nurse.

   Capulet. When the sun sets the earth doth drizzle dew,   *130*
But for the sunset of my brother's son
It rains downright.
How now, a conduit, girl? what! still in tears?
Evermore showering? In one little body
Thou counterfeits a bark, a sea, a wind: *135*
For still thy eyes, which I may call the sea,
Do ebb and flow with tears; the bark thy body is,
Sailing in this salt flood; the winds, thy sighs,
Who, raging with thy tears and they with them.
Without a sudden calm will overset   *140*
Thy tempest-tossed body. How now, Wife,
Have you deliver'd to her our decree?
   Wife. Ay sir, but she will none, she gives you thanks,

I would the fool were marry'd to her grave.
   Capulet. Soft! take me with you, take me with you, Wife.
How! will she none? doth she not give us thanks?
Is she not proud? doth she not count her blest,
Unworthy as she is, that we have wrought
So worthy a gentleman to be her bride?
   Juliet. Not proud you have, but thankful that you have.   *150*
Proud can I never be of what I hate,
But thankful e'en for hate that is meant love.
   Capulet. How, how, how, how, chopt-logic? What is this?
'Proud' and 'I thank you' and 'I thank you not'
And yet 'not proud'? Mistress minion you,   *155*
Thank me no thankings nor proud me no prouds,
But fettle your fine joints 'gainst Thursday next
To go with Paris to Saint Peter's Church,
Or I will drag thee on a hurdle thither.
Out! you green-sickness carrion, out! you baggage,   *160*
You tallow-face!
   Wife.   Fie, fie—what! are you mad?
   Juliet. Good father, I beseech you on my knees,
        ⟨*She kneels down.*⟩
Hear me with patience but to speak a word.
   Capulet. Hang thee! young baggage, disobedient wretch!   *165*
I tell thee what, get thee to church a Thursday
Or never after look me in the face.
Speak not, reply not, do not answer me!
My fingers itch. Wife, we scarce thought us blest
That God had lent us but this only child,   *170*
But now I see this one is one too much
And that we have a curse in having her.
Out on her, hilding!
   Nurse.   God in Heaven bless her!
You are to blame, my lord, to rate her so.   *175*
   Capulet. And why, my Lady Wisdom? Hold your tongue,
Good Prudence; smatter with your gossips, go!
   Nurse. I speak no treason.
   Capulet.   O—Godigoden!
   Nurse. May not one speak?   *180*
   Capulet.   Peace! you mumbling fool.
Utter your gravity o'er a goship's bowl,
For here we need it not.
   Wife.   You are too hot.
   Capulet. God's bread! it makes me mad.   *185*
Day, night—work, play—
Alone, in company—still my care hath been
To have her match'd; and having now provided
A gentleman of noble parentage,
Or fair demesnes, youthful and nobly limb'd,   *190*
Stuff'd, as they say, with honorable parts,
Proportion'd as one's thought would wish a man—
And then to have a wretched puling fool,

---

93 **runagate:** *renegade, fugitive*   94 **Shall:** *who shall*   98 **dead:** *to be construed with both him and heart*   101 **temper:** *mix (quibble on 'mitigate')*   102 **That:** *so that*   105 **wreak:** *avenge (quibble on 'express')*   110 **I:** *Q2 omits*   111 **careful:** *provident*   113 **sorted out:** *arranged for*   114 **nor I look'd not for:** *intensifying double negative*   115 **in happy time:** *bow opportune*   131 **brother:** *brother-in-law*   133 **conduit:** *fountain (sometimes made in the shape of a human figure)*   139 **Who:** *which*   143 **will none:** *will have none of it*

145 **take me with you:** *let me understand you*   148 **wrought:** *arranged for*   149 **bride:** *bridegroom*   153 **chopt-logic:** *sophistical argument*   155 **minion:** *hussy*   157 **fettle:** *make ready* **'gainst:** *in preparation for*   159 **hurdle:** *a sledge for dragging traitors to execution*   160 **green-sickness:** *anemia affecting adolescent girls* **carrion:** *lump of flesh*   161 **tallow:** *i.e. yellowish-white*   173 **hilding:** *baggage*   175 **rate:** *berate; see III.4.12; cf. n.*   177 **smatter:** *prate*   179, 180 **Capulet, Nurse;** *cf. n.*   179 **Godigoden:** *God give ye good e'en*   182 **goship:** *gossip (originally a godparent or sponsor at a baptism)* **bowl:** *christening cup*   185 **God's bread:** *the Host (the consecrated bread of the Eucharist)* **Day, night—work, play;** *cf. n.*   190 **demesnes:** *domains, landed property* **limb'd:** *Q2 liand; Q1 trainde; cf. n.*   191 **parts:** *qualities*   193 **puling:** *whimpering*

A whining mammet, in her fortune's tender
To answer 'I'll not wed, I cannot love,   *195*
I am too young, I pray you pardon me!'
But and you will not wed I'll pardon you—
Graze where you will, you shall not house with me.
Look to 't, think on 't, I do not use to jest.
Thursday is near, lay hand on heart, advise.   *200*
And you be mine, I'll give you to my friend,
And you be not, hang, beg, starve, die in the streets,
For by my soul I'll ne'er acknowledge thee
Nor what is mine shall never do thee good.
Trust to 't, bethink you, I'll not be forsworn.   *Exit.*
   Juliet. Is there no Pity sitting in the clouds
That sees into the bottom of my grief?
O sweet my mother, cast me not away,
Delay this marriage for a month, a week,
Or if you do not, make the bridal bed   *210*
In that dim monument where Tybalt lies.
   Wife. Talk not to me, for I'll not speak a word,
Do as thou wilt, for I have done with thee.   *Exit.*
   Juliet. O God! O Nurse, how shall this be prevented?
My husband is on earth, my faith in Heaven.   *215*
How shall that faith return again to earth
Unless that husband send it me from Heaven
By leaving earth? Comfort me, counsel me!
Alack, alack, that Heav'n should practice stratagems
Upon so soft a subject as myself!   *220*
What say'st thou? hast thou not a word of joy?
Some comfort, Nurse.
   Nurse.   Faith, here it is:
Romeo is banish'd, and all the world to nothing
That he dares ne'er come back to challenge you,   *225*
Or if he do it needs must be by stealth.
Then since the case so stands as now it doth,
I think it best you marry'd with the County.
O he 's a lovely gentleman!
Romeo 's a dishclout to him. An eagle, madam,   *230*
Hath not so green, so quick, so fair an eye
As Paris hath. Beshrew my very heart,
I think you 're happy in this second match,
For it excels your first, or if 't did not
Your first is dead—or 'twere as good he were,   *235*
As living here and you no use of him.
   Juliet. Speak'st thou from thy heart?
   Nurse. And from my soul too, else beshrew them both.
   Juliet. Amen.
   Nurse. What?   *240*
   Juliet. Well, thou hast comforted me marvelous much.
Go in and tell my lady I am gone,
Having displeas'd my father, to Lawrence' cell
To make confession and to be absolv'd.
   Nurse. Marry I will, and this is wisely done.   *[Exit.]*
               ⟨*Juliet looks after Nurse.*⟩
   Juliet. Ancient damnation! O most wicked fiend!

Is it more sin to wish me thus forsworn,
Or to dispraise my lord with that same tongue
Which she hath prais'd him with above compare
So many thousand times? Go counselor,   *250*
Thou and my bosom henceforth shall be twain.
I'll to the Friar to know his remedy,
If all else fail, myself have power to die.   *Exit.*

ACT FOURTH ❧ SCENE FIRST

Enter Friar and County Paris.

   Friar. On Thursday, sir? the time is very short.
   Paris. My father Capulet will have it so,
And I am nothing slow to slack his haste.
   Friar. You say you do not know the lady's mind?
Uneven is the course, I like it not.   *5*
   Paris. Immoderately she weeps for Tybalt's death,
And therefore have I little talk'd of love,
For Venus smiles not in a house of tears.
Now sir, her father counts it dangerous
That she do give her sorrow so much sway,   *10*
And in his wisdom hastes our marriage
To stop the inundation of her tears,
Which, too much minded by herself alone,
May be put from her by society.
Now do you know the reason of this haste.   *15*
   Friar. [*Aside.*] I would I knew not why it should be
slow'd!
Look sir, here comes the lady toward my cell.

Enter Juliet.

   Paris. Happily met, my lady and my wife.
   Juliet. That may be, sir, when I may be a wife.   *20*
   Paris. That 'may be' must be, love, on Thursday next.
   Juliet. What must be shall be.
   Friar.   That's a certain text.
   Paris. Come you to make confession to this Father?
   Juliet. To answer that, I should confess to you.   *25*
   Paris. Do not deny to him that you love me.
   Juliet. I will confess to you that I love him.
   Paris. So will ye, I am sure, that you love me.
   Juliet. If I do so, it will be of more price
Being spoke behind your back than to your face.   *30*
   Paris. Poor soul, thy face is much abus'd with tears.
   Juliet. The tears have got small victory by that,
For it was bad enough before their spite.
   Paris. Thou wrong'st it more than tears with that report.
   Juliet. That is no slander, sir, which is a truth,   *35*
And what I spake, I spake it to my face.
   Paris. Thy face is mine, and thou hast slander'd it.
   Juliet. It may be so, for it is not mine own.
Are you at leisure, holy Father, now,
Or shall I come to you at evening mass?   *40*
   Friar. My leisure serves me, pensive daughter, now.

---

194 **mammet:** *doll, puppet* (from 'Mahomet,' thought of as an idol) **in her fortune's tender:** *on the offer of good fortune*   196 **pardon you:** *quibble on 'give leave to depart'*   199 **do not use:** *am not accustomed*   200 **advise:** *be advised, consider*   205 **be forsworn:** *break my oath*   211 **monument:** *burial vault*   215 **faith:** *marriage vow*   219 **stratagems:** *dreadful deeds*   224 **all the world to nothing:** *i.e. the odds are very great*   225 **challenge:** *claim*   230 **dishclout:** *dishcloth* **to:** *in comparison to*   231 **green:** *a color much admired in eyes* **quick:** *lively*   232 **Beshrew:** *curse*   236 **here:** *i.e. in this world* **SD (Juliet):** *Q1 She*   246 **Ancient damnation:** *damned old woman*

247 **forsworn:** *i.e. by breaking the marriage vow*   2 **father:** *intended father-in-law*   3 **nothing slow:** *extremely reluctant* (intensifying double negative)   5 **Uneven:** *irregular*   7 **talk'd:** *Q2 talke*   29 **price:** *value*   31 **abus'd:** *disfigured*   33 **spite:** *injury*   36 **to my face:** *frankly* (quibble on 'about my face')   40 **evening mass:** *cf. n.*   41 **pensive:** *sorrowful*

My lord, we must entreat the time alone.

Paris. God shield I should disturb devotion.
Juliet, on Thursday early will I rouse ye.   45
Till then, adieu, and keep this holy kiss.   *Exit.*

Juliet. O shut the door! and when thou hast done so,
Come weep with me—past hope, past cure, past help.

Friar. O Juliet, I already know thy grief,
It strains me past the compass of my wits.   50
I hear thou must, and nothing may prorogue it,
On Thursday next be marry'd to this County.

Juliet. Tell me not, Friar, that thou hear'st of this,
Unless thou tell me how I may prevent it.
If in thy wisdom thou canst give no help,   55
Do thou but call my resolution wise
And with this knife I'll help it presently.
God join'd my heart and Romeo's, thou our hands,
And ere this hand by thee to Romeo's seal'd
Shall be the label to another deed,   60
Or my true heart with treacherous revolt
Turn to another, this shall slay them both.
Therefore out of thy long-experienc'd time
Give me some present counsel, or behold
'Twixt my extremes and me this bloody knife   65
Shall play the umpeer, arbitrating that
Which the commission of thy years and art
Could to no issue of true honor bring.
Be not so long to speak, I long to die
If what thou speak'st speak not of remedy.   70

Friar. Hold daughter, I do spy a kind of hope
Which craves as desperate an execution
As that is desp'rate which we would prevent.
If rather than to marry County Paris
Thou hast the strength of will to slay thyself,   75
Then is it likely thou wilt undertake
A thing like death to chide away this shame,
That cop'st with Death himself to scape from it,
And if thou dar'st I'll give thee remedy.

Juliet. O bid me leap, rather than marry Paris,   80
From off the battlements of any tower
Or walk in thievish ways, or bid me lurk
Where serpents are; chain me with roaring bears,
Or hide me nightly in a charnel house,
O'ercover'd quite with dead men's rattling bones,   85
With reeky shanks and yellow chapless skulls;
Or bid me go into a new-made grave
And hide me with a dead man in his shroud—
Things that to hear them told have made me tremble—
And I will do it without fear or doubt   90
To live an unstain'd wife to my sweet love.

Friar. Hold, then. Go home, be merry, give consent
To marry Paris. Wednesday is tomorrow.
Tomorrow night look that thou lie alone,
Let not the Nurse lie with thee in thy chamber.   95
Take thou this vial, being then in bed,
And this distilling liquor drink thou off,

When presently through all thy veins shall run
A cold and drowsy humor—for no pulse
Shall keep his native progress, but surcease;   100
No warmth, no breath shall testify thou livest;
The roses in thy lips and cheeks shall fade
To wanny ashes, thy eyes' windows fall
Like Death when he shuts up the day of life.
Each part, depriv'd of supple government,   105
Shall stiff and stark and cold appear like death,
And in this borrow'd likeness of shrunk death
Thou shalt continue two and forty hours
And then awake as from a pleasant sleep.
Now when the bridegroom in the morning comes   110
To rouse thee from thy bed, there art thou dead.
Then as the manner of our country is.
In thy best robes uncover'd on the bier
Thou shall be borne to that same ancient vault
Where all the kindred of the Capulets lie.   115
In the meantime, against thou shalt awake,
Shall Romeo by my letters know our drift,
And hither shall he come; and he and I
Will watch thy waking, and that very night
Shall Romeo bear thee hence to Mantua.   120
And this shall free thee from this present shame
If no inconstant toy nor wom'nish fear
Abate thy valor in the acting it.

Juliet. Give me, give me! O tell not me of fear!

Friar. Hold, get you gone. Be strong and prosperous   125
In this resolve. I'll send a friar with speed
To Mantua with my letters to thy lord.

Juliet. Love give me strength! and strength shall help
afford.
Farewell, dear Father.   *Exeunt.*

❧ SCENE SECOND ❧

Enter Capulet, his Wife, Nurse and Servingmen, two or three.

Capulet. So many guests invite as here are writ.
                                                [Exit a Servingman.]
Sirrah, go hire me twenty cunning cooks.

Servingman. You shall have none ill, sir, for I'll try if they
can lick their fingers.

Capulet. How canst thou try them so?   5

Servingman. Marry sir, 'tis an ill cook that cannot lick his
own fingers; therefore he that cannot lick his fingers goes not
with me.

Capulet. Go, be gone.   ⟨*Exit Servingman.*⟩
We shall be much unfurnish'd for this time.   10
What, is my daughter gone to Friar Lawrence?

Nurse. Ay forsooth.

Capulet. Well, he may chance to do some good on her,
A peevish self-will'd harlotry it is.

Enter Juliet.

42 entreat: *ask to have*   **43 shield:** *prevent, forbid*   **47 cure:** *Q1; Q2 care*   **50 prorogue:** *postpone*   **59 label:** *i.e. a wax seal; cf. n.*   **deed:** *quibble on 'act'*   **63 present:** *immediate*   **65 umpeer:** *umpire; cf. n.*   **66 commission:** *authority*   **74 slay:** *Q1; Q2 stay*   **76 chide:** *drive*   **77 cop'st:** *wouldst negotiate*   **81 thievish:** *full of thieves*   **83 charnel house:** *bone vault; cf. n.*   **85 reeky:** *rankly moist*   **chapless:** *Q1; Q2 chapels; jawless*   **87 shroud:** *Q2 omits*   **90 unstain'd:** *stressed ̲ ̲ ̲*   **96 distilling:** *distilled*

98 drowsy: *sleep inducing*   **humor:** *fluid*   **99 native progress:** *natural motion*   **surcease: shall cease**   **100 breath:** *Q2 breast*   **102 wanny:** *Q2 many; cf. n.*   **104 supple government:** *the faculty of supple movement*   **107 two and forty hours:** *cf. n.*   **112 uncover'd:** *with face uncovered*   **113, 114 Thou shall ... lie:** *for text see II.1.247-250; cf. n.*   **116 letters:** *letter*   **drift:** *plot*   **121 toy:** *crotchet (i.e. unreasoning aversion)*   **SD Servingmen:** *see I.4.1 SD; cf. n.*   **2 cunning:** *skillful*   **10 unfurnish'd:** *unprovisioned*   **14 peevish:** *silly*   **harlotry:** *wench*   **it:** *she (used affectionately)*

Nurse. See where she comes from shrift with merry look.   *15*
Capulet. How now my headstrong, where have you been
gadding?
   Juliet. Where I have learnt me to repent the sin
Of disobedient opposition
To you and your behests, and am enjoin'd   *20*
By holy Lawrence to fall prostrate here   〈*She kneels down.*〉
To beg your pardon. Pardon, I beseech you,
Henceforward I am ever rul'd by you.
   Capulet. Send for the County, go, tell him of this.
I'll have this knot knit up tomorrow morning.   *25*
   Juliet. I met the youthful lord at Lawrence' cell
And gave him what becomed love I might,
Not stepping o'er the bounds of modesty.
   Capulet. Why, I am glad on 't, this is well. Stand up.
This is as 't should be. Let me see the County.   *30*
Ay marry, go, I say, and fetch him hither.
Now afore God, this reverend holy Friar,
All our whole city is much bound to him.
   Juliet. Nurse, will you go with me into my closet
To help me sort such needful ornaments   *35*
As you think fit to furnish me tomorrow?
   Wife. No, not till Thursday, there is time enough.
   Capulet. Go Nurse, go with her, we'll to church tomorrow.
                Exeunt 〈*Nurse and Juliet*〉
   Wife. We shall be short in our provision,   *40*
'Tis now near night.
   Capulet.   Tush, I will stir about,
And all things shall be well, I warrant thee, Wife.
Go thou to Juliet, help to deck up her.
I'll not to bed tonight, let me alone,   *45*
I'll play the huswife for this once. What ho!
They are all forth. Well, I will walk myself
To County Paris, to prepare up him
Against tomorrow. My heart is wondrous light
Since this same wayward girl is so reclaim'd.   *Exeunt.*

❧ Scene Third ❧

Enter Juliet and Nurse.

Juliet. Ay those attires are best. But gentle Nurse,
I pray thee leave me to myself tonight,
For I have need of many orisons
To move the Heav'ns to smile upon my state,
Which well thou know'st is cross and full of sin.   *5*

Enter Capulet's Wife.

Wife. What, are you busy, ho? need you my help?
Juliet. No madam, we have cull'd such necessaries
As are behoofeful for our state tomorrow.
So please you, let me now be left alone,
And let the Nurse this night sit up with you,   *10*
For I am sure you have your hands full all
In this so sudden business.
   Wife.   Good night,

Get thee to bed and rest, for thou hast need.
                Exeunt [Wife and Nurse].
   Juliet. Farewell! God knows when we shall meet again.   *15*
I have a faint cold fear thrills through my veins
That almost freezes up the heat of life.
I'll call them back again to comfort me.
Nurse!—What should she do here?
My dismal scene I needs must act alone.   *20*
Come, vial.
What if this mixture do not work at all?
Shall I be marry'd then tomorrow morning?
No, no! this shall forbid it, lie thou there.
What if it be a poison which the Friar   *25*
Subtly hath minister'd to have me dead,
Lest in this marriage he should be dishonor'd
Because he marry'd me before to Romeo?
I fear it is, and yet methinks it should not,
For he hath still been tried a holy man.   *30*
How if, when I am laid into the tomb,
I wake before the time that Romeo
Come to redeem me? There 's a fearful point!
Shall I not then be stiffled in the vault,
To whose foul mouth no healthsome air breathes in,   *35*
And there die strangled ere my Romeo comes?
Or if I live, is it not very like
The horrible conceit of death and night
Together with the terror of the place—
As in a vault, an ancient receptacle,   *40*
Where for this many hundred years the bones
Of all my bury'd ancestors are pack'd,
Where bloody Tybalt yet but green in earth
Lies fest'ring in his shroud, where as they say
At some hours in the night spirits resort—   *45*
Alack, alack, is it not like that I
So early waking—what with loathsome smells
And shrieks like mandrakes torn out of the earth,
That living mortals hearing them run mad—
O if I wake, shall I not be distraught,   *50*
Environed with all these hideous fears,
And madly play with my forefathers' joints
And pluck the mangled Tybalt from his shroud
And in this rage with some great kinsman's bone
As with a club dash out my desp'rate brains?   *55*
O look! methinks I see my cousin's ghost
Seeking out Romeo that did spit his body
Upon a rapier's point. Stay Tybalt, stay!
Romeo, Romeo, Romeo! Here's drink—I drink to thee.
        〈*She falls upon her bed within the curtains.*〉

❧ Scene Fourth ❧

Enter Capulet's Wife and Nurse 〈*with herbs*〉.

Wife. Hold, take these keys and fetch more spices, Nurse.
Nurse. They call for dates and quinces in the pastry.

---

25 knot: *bond of wedlock* **27 becomed:** *befitting* **33 bound:** *indebted* **34 closet:**
private room **35 sort:** *select* **SD Exeunt (Nurse and Juliet):** *for staging see; cf. n.* **44**
up: *completely* **46 huswife:** *housewife, hussy (pronounced 'huzzif')* **3 orisons:** *pray-*
ers **4 state:** *condition* **5 cross:** *contrary* **8 behooveful:** *useful* **state:** *ceremony,*
pomp

16 faint: *causing faintness* **20 dismal:** *unlucky* **24 this, thou:** *i.e. her dagger* **26**
minister'd: *provided* **30 still:** *always* **tried:** *proved* **34 stiffled:** *stifled* (pronounced
with a short *i*) **38 conceit:** *idea* **40 As:** *namely* **receptacle:** *stressed* ‒́ ‒ ‒́ ‒ **41**
this: *these* (old plural) **43 green:** *freshly, recently* **48 mandrakes:** *cf. n.* **50 distraught:**
distracted, driven mad **54 rage:** *madness* **SD curtains:** *i.e. of the rear stage* **2**
pastry: *pastry room, pantry*

Enter old Capulet.

Capulet. Come, stir, stir, stir! the second cock hath crow'd,
The curfew bell hath run, 'tis three a clock.
Look to the bak'd meats, good Angelica,   5
Spare not for cost.
    Nurse.   Go you cot-quean, go,
Get you to bed. Faith, you'll be sick tomorrow
For this night's watching.
    Capulet. No, not a whit. What! I have watch'd ere now   10
All night for lesser cause, and ne'er been sick.
    Wife. Ay, you have been a mouse-hunt in your time,
But I will watch you from such watching now.
                    Exeunt Wife and Nurse.
    Capulet. A jealous hood, a jealous hood!

Enter three or four ⟨Servingmen⟩ with spits and logs and baskets.

Now fellow, what is there?   15
    1. Servingman. Things for the cook, sir, but I know not
what.
    Capulet. Make haste, make haste.   [*Exit 1. Servingman.*]
                    Sirrah, fetch drier logs.
Call Peter, he will show thee where they are.   20
    2. Servingman. I have a head, sir, that will find out logs
And never trouble Peter for the matter.   ⟨*Exit.*⟩
    Capulet. Mass! and well said, a merry whoreson, ha!
Thou shalt be loggerhead. Good faith, 'tis day,   *Play music.*
The County will be here with music straight,   25
For so he said he would. I her him near.
Nurse! Wife! What ho! What! Nurse, I say.

Enter Nurse.

Go waken Juliet, go and trim her up,
I'll go and chat with Paris. Hie, make haste,
Make haste, the bridegroom he is come already.   30
Make haste, I say.   [*Exit.*]
    Nurse. Mistress! what! mistress. Juliet! Fast, I warrant her,
she.
Why! lamb, why! lady. Fie, you slugabed.
Why! love. I say! madam. Sweetheart! Why! bride.   35
What, not a word? You take your pennyworths now.
Sleep for a week, for the next night I warrant
The County Paris hath set up his rest
That you shall rest but little. God forgive me!
Marry and amen! How sound is she asleep.   40
I needs must wake her. Madam, madam, madam!
Ay, let the County take you in your bed,
He'll fright you up, i' faith. Will it not be?
What! dressed and in your clothes and down again?
I must needs wake you. lady! lady! lady!   45
Alas, alas! Help, help! my lady 's dead.
O weraday that ever I was born!
Some *aqua vitae*, ho! My lord, my lady!

⟨*Enter Capulet's Wife.*⟩

Wife. What noise is here?
Nurse.   O lamentable day!   50
Wife. What is the matter?
Nurse.   Look, look! O heavy day!
Wife. O me, O me! my child, my only life!
Revive, look up, or I will die with thee.
Help, help! Call help!   55

Enter Capulet.

Capulet. For shame, bring Juliet forth, her lord is come.
Nurse. She's dead, deceas'd, she's dead, alack the day!
Wife. Alack the day! she's dead, she's dead, she's dead!
Capulet. Ha! let me see her. Out alas! she's cold.
Her blood is settled and her joints are stiff,   60
Life and these lips have long been separated.
Death lies on her like an untimely frost
Upon the sweetest flow'r of all the field.
    Nurse. O lamentable day!
    Wife.   O woeful time!   65
    Capulet. Death, that hath tane her hence to make me wail,
Ties up my tongue and will not let me speak.

Enter Friar and the County.

Friar. Come, is the bride ready to go to church?
Capulet. Ready to go but never to return.
O son, the night before thy wedding day   70
Hath Death lain with thy wife. There she lies,
Flow'r as she was, deflowered by him.
Death is my son-in-law, Death is my heir:
My daughter he hath wedded. I will die
And leave him all: life, living—all is Death's.   75
    Paris. Have I thought long to see this morning's face,
And doth it give me such a sight as this?
    ⟨*All at once cry out and wring their hands.*⟩
    Wife. Accurs'd, unhappy, wretched, hateful day!
Most miserable hour that e'er Time saw
In lasting labor of his pilgrimage!   80
But one—poor one, one poor and loving child—
But one thing to rejoice and solace in,
And cruel Death hath catch'd it from my sight!
    Nurse. O woe! O woeful, woeful, woeful day!
Most lamentable day, most woeful day   85
That ever ever I did yet behold.
O day, O day, O day! O hateful day!
Never was seen so black a day as this.
O woeful day! O woeful day!
    Paris. Beguil'd, divorced, wronged, spited, slain!   90
Most detestable Death, by thee beguil'd,
By cruel cruel thee quite overthrown!
O love! O life! not life, but love in death!
    Capulet. Despis'd, distressed, hated, martyr'd, kill'd!
Uncomfortable Time, why cam'st thou now   95
To murther, murther our solemnity?
O child, O child! my soul and not my child!
Dead art thou. Alack! my child is dead,
And with my child my joys are buried.
    Friar. Peace, ho! for shame! confusion's cure lives not   100
In these confusions. Heaven and yourself

5 **bak'd meats:** *meat pies* **Angelica:** *the Nurse* 7 **cot-quean:** *man meddling with woman's work* (literally 'cottage-wife') 9 **watching:** *staying awake* 12 **mouse-hunt:** *woman-chaser* 13 **watch:** *prevent* 14 **hood:** *hud, ninny; cf. n.* **SD (Servingmen)** Q1 *Servingman; see I.4.1 SD; cf. n.* 20 **Peter;** *cf. n.* 23 **Mass:** *by the mass* **whoreson:** *rascal.* 24 **loggerhead:** *blockhead* **faith** Q2 *father* 32 **Nurse:** *for staging see; cf. n.* **Fast:** *fast asleep* 36 **pennyworths:** *i.e. of sleep* (pronounced 'penn'orths') 38 **set up his rest:** *firmly resolved; cf. n.* 47 **weraday:** *weladay, alas*

60 **settled:** *congealed* 75 **living:** *property* 76 **thought long:** *expected, hoped* **long:** Q2 *loue* 83 **catch'd:** *snatched* 91 **detestable:** *stressed* – ́ – – ́ 95 **Uncomfortable:** *discomforting* 100 **confusion:** *disaster* **cure:** Q2 *care*

Had part in this fair maid; now Heav'n hath all,
And all the better is it for the maid.
Your part in her you could not keep from death,
But Heav'n keeps his part in eternal life.   *105*
The most you sought was her promotion,
For 'twas your Heaven she should be advanc'd.
And weep ye now, seeing she is advanc'd
Above the clouds as high as Heav'n itself?
O in this love you love your child so ill   *110*
That you run mad, seeing that she is well.
She's not well marry'd that lives marry'd long,
But she's best marry'd that dies marry'd young.
Dry up your tears and stick your rosemary
On this fair corse, and as the custom is,   *115*
And in her best array, bear her to church;
For though fond Nature bids us all lament,
Yet Nature's tears are Reason's merriment.

   Capulet. All things that we ordained festival
Turn from their office to black funeral—   *120*
Our instruments to melancholy bells,
Our wedding cheer to a sad burial feast,
Our solemn hymns to sullen dirges change,
Our bridal flow'rs serve for a bury'd corse,
And all things change them to the contrary.   *125*

   Friar. Sir go you in, and madam go with him,
And go, Sir Paris. Everyone prepare
To follow this fair corse unto her grave.
The Heav'ns do low'r upon you for some ill,
Move them no more by crossing their high will.   *130*

          ⟨*They all but the Nurse go forth, casting*
          rosemary on her and shutting the curtains.

        Enter Musicians.⟩

   1. Musician. Faith, we may put up our pipes and be gone.
   Nurse. Honest good fellows, ah put up, put up!
For well you know this is a pitiful case.
   1. Musician. Ay, by my troth, the case may be amended.

                                  Exit Nurse.

        Enter Peter.

   Peter. Musicians, O Musicians—'Heart's Ease,'   *135*
'Heart's Ease.' O and you will have me live, play 'Heart's
Ease.'
   1. Musician. Why 'Heart's Ease'?
   Peter. O Musicians, because my heart itself plays 'My Heart
is Full'—O play me some merry dump to comfort me.   *140*
   Musicians. Not a dump, we, 'tis no time to play now.
   Peter. You will not then?
   1. Musician. No.
   Peter. I will then give it you soundly.
   1. Musician. What will you give us?   *145*
   Peter. No money, on my faith, but the gleek. I will give
you the 'Minstrel.'

   1. Musician. Then will I give you the 'Serving Creature.'
   Peter. Then will I lay the serving-creature's dagger on
your pate. I will carry no crotchets. I'll *re* you, I'll *fa* you,   *150*
do you note me?
   1. Musician. And you *re* us and *fa* us you note us.
   2. Musician. Pray you put up your dagger and put out your
wit. Then have at you with my wit.
   Peter. I will dry-beat you with an iron wit and put up   *155*
my iron dagger. Answer me like men:

    When griping griefs the heart doth wound,
    (And doleful dumps the mind oppress,)
    Then music with her silver sound—

Why 'silver sound'? Why 'music with her silver sound'?   *160*
What say you, Simon Catling?
   1. Musician. Marry, sir, because silver hath a sweet sound.
   Peter. Prates. What say you, Hugh Rebeck?
   2. Musician. I say 'silver sound' because musicians sound
for silver.   *165*
   Peter. Prates too. What say you, James Sound-post?
   3. Musician. Faith, I know not what to say.
   Peter. O I cry you mercy, you are the singer. I will 'say'
for you. It is 'music with her silver sound' because musicians
have no gold for sounding.   *170*

   —*Then music with her silver sound*
   With speedy help doth lend redress.

                                  Exit.

   1. Musician. What a pestilent knave is the same!
   2. Musician. Hang him, Jack. Come, we'll in here, tarry for
the mourners, and stay dinner.   *Exeunt.*

ACT FIFTH ❧ SCENE FIRST

       Enter Romeo.

   Romeo. If I may trust the flatt'ring truth of sleep
My dreams presage some joyful news at hand.
My bosom's lord sits lightly in his throne,
And all this day an unaccustom'd spirit
Lifts me above the ground with cheerful thoughts.   *5*
I dreamt my lady came and found me dead
(Strange dream that gives a dead man leave to think!)
And breath'd such life with kisses in my lips
That I reviv'd and was an emperor.
Ah me! how sweet is love itself possess'd   *10*
When but love's shadows are so rich in joy.

     Enter Romeo's Man ⟨*Balthasar, booted*⟩.

News from Verona! How now, Balthasar?
Dost thou not bring me letters from the Friar?
How doth my lady? Is my father well?
How fares my Juliet? That I ask again,   *15*

107 advance'd: *i.e. in rank by marriage* **108 advanc'd:** *raised* **111 well:** *i.e. in Heaven* **114 rosemary;** *cf. n.* **117 fond:** *Q2 some* **Nature:** *natural feeling* **120 office:** *function* **122 cheer:** *food* **SD (They all … Musicians):** *Q2 Exeunt manet cf. n.* **131 put up our pipes:** *put away our instruments (proverbial for 'cease')* **133 case:** *event* **134 case:** *quibble on 'instrument case'* **amended:** *bettered* **SD Nurse:** *Q2 omnes* **SD Peter:** *Q2 Will Kemp cf. n.* **135 'Heart's Ease':** *a popular tune called for in the old play Misogonus* **139–140 'My Heart is Full';** *cf. n.* **dump:** *mournful tune* **144 give it you:** *let you have it* **soundly:** *forcefully (quibble on 'with sounds')* **146 gleek:** *jeer* **146, 147 give you:** *call you (as in a formal insult; compare II.3.29; cf. n.)*

150 carry: *endure* **crotchets:** *whims (quibble on 'quarter notes')* **re … fa you;** *cf. n.* **151 note:** *pay attention to* **152 note us:** *set us to music* **153 put out:** *display* **157–159 When … sound;** *cf. n.* **158 dumps:** *sorrows* **161 Catling:** *lute string of catgut* **163 Prates:** *the subject 'he' is understood* **Rebeck:** *three-stringed fiddle* **166 Sound-post:** *peg supporting the body of a stringed instrument* **168 cry you mercy:** *beg your pardon* **170 sounding:** *playing* **175 stay:** *wait for* **1 flatt'ring:** *illusive* **3 bosom's lord:** *i.e. heart* **11 shadows:** *images* **SD booted:** *i.e. for riding* **15 fares my Juliet:** *Q1; Q2 doth my Lady Juliet; cf. n.*

For nothing can be ill if she be well.
  Balthasar. Then she is well and nothing can be ill.
Her body sleeps in Capels' monument,
And her immortal part with angels lives.
I saw her laid low in her kindred's vault   20
And presently took post to tell it you.
O pardon me for bringing these ill news,
Since you did leave it for my office, sir.
  Romeo. Is it in so? Then I defy you, stars!
Thou know'st my lodging. Get me ink and paper   25
And hire post horses. I will hence tonight.
  Balthasar. I do beseech you, sir, have patience,
Your looks are pale and wild and do import
Some misadventure.
  Romeo.   Tush, thou art deceiv'd.   30
Leave me and do the thing I bid thee do.
Hast thou no letters to me from the Friar?
  Balthasar. No my good lord.
  Romeo.   No matter, get thee gone
And hire those horses. I'll be with thee straight.   35
                            Exit ⟨Balthasar⟩.

Well Juliet, I will lie with thee tonight.
Let's see for means. O mischief, thou art swift
To enter in the thoughts of desp'rate men.
I do remember an apothecary,
And hereabouts 'a dwells (which late I noted)   40
In tatter'd weeds with overwhelming brows,
Culling of simples. Meager were his looks,
Sharp misery had worn him to the bones.
And in his needy shop a tortoise hung,
An alligator stuff'd and other skins   45
Of ill-shap'd fishes; and about his shelves
A beggarly account of empty boxes,
Green earthen pots, bladders and musty seeds,
Remnants of packthread and old cakes of roses
Were thinly scatter'd to make up a show.   50
Noting this penury, to myself I said,
'And if a man did need a poison now
Whose sale is present death in Mantua,
Here lives a caitiff wretch would sell it him.'
O this same thought did but forerun my need,   55
And this same needy man must sell it me.
As I remember, this should be the house,
Being holy day, the beggar's shop is shut.
What ho! apothecary!

           ⟨*Enter apothecary.*⟩

  Apothecary.   Who calls so loud?   60
  Romeo. Come hither man, I see that thou art poor.
Hold, there is forty ducats. Let me have
A dram of poison, such soon-speeding gear
As will disperse itself through all the veins
That the life-weary taker may fall dead,   65
And that the trunk may be discharg'd of breath
As violently as hasty powder fired
Doth hurry from the fatal cannon's womb.

  Apothecary. Such mortal drugs I have, but Mantua's law
Is death to any he that utters them.   70
  Romeo. Art thou so bare and full of wretchedness,
And fear'st to die? Famine is in thy cheeks,
Need and oppression starveth in thy eyes,
Contempt and begg'ry hangs upon thy back.
The world is not thy friend not the world's law,   75
The world affords no law to make thee rich—
Then be not poor, but break it and take this.
  Apothecary. My poverty but not my will consents.
  Romeo. I pay thy poverty and not thy will.
  Apothecary. Put this in any liquid thing you will   80
And drink it off, and if you had the strength
Of twenty men it would dispatch you straight.
  Romeo. There is thy gold—worse poison to men's souls,
Doing more murther in this loathsome world
Than these poor compounds that thou mayst not sell.   85
I sell thee poison, thou hast sold me none.
Farewell, buy food and get thyself in flesh.
Come cordial, and not poison, go with me
To Juliet's grave, for there must I use thee.   *Exeunt.*

❧ Scene Second ❧

Enter Friar John.

  John. Holy Franciscan Friar! brother, ho!

Enter Lawrence.

  Lawrence. This same should be the voice of Friar John.
Welcome from Mantua, what says Romeo?
Or if his mind be writ give me his letter.
  John. Going to find a barefoot brother out,   5
One of our order to associate me,
Here in this city visiting the sick,
And finding him, the searchers of the town,
Suspecting that we both were in a house
Where the infectious pestilence did reign,   10
Seal'd up the doors and would not let us forth,
So that my speed to Mantua there was stay'd.
  Lawrence. Who bare my letter then to Romeo?
  John. I could not sent it (here it is again)
Nor get a messenger to bring it thee,   15
So fearful were they of infection.
  Lawrence. Unhappy fortune! By my brotherhood,
The letter was not nice but full of charge,
Of dear import, and the neglecting it
May do much danger. Friar John, go hence,   20
Get me an iron crow and bring it straight
Unto my cell.
  John. Brother, I'll go and bring it thee.   *Exit.*
  Lawrence. Now must I to the monument alone,
Within this three hours will fair Juliet wake.   25
She will beshrew me much that Romeo
Hath had no notice of these accidents—
But I will write again to Mantua

---

18 monument: *burial vault*   **21 took post:** *traveled by post horse*   **24 in:** *e'en cf. n.* **defy:** *Q1; Q2 denie*   **27 patience:** *here pronounced 'pati-ence'; see I.4.98; cf. n.*   **41 weeds:** *clothes* **overwhelming:** *beetling*   **42 simples:** *medicinal herbs.*   **47 account:** *reckoning, number*   **49 cakes of roses:** *caked rose petals (for use as perfume)*   **54 caitiff:** *miserable*   **62 ducats:** *gold coins*   **63 gear:** *stuff*   **66 trunk:** *body*

70 utters: *gives out*   **73 starveth in:** *look out hungrily from*   **79 pay:** *Q1; Q2 pray*   **88 cordial:** *restorative*   **SD Enter Friar John:** *so Q1; Q2 Enter Frier John to Frier Lawrence; cf. n.*   **6 associate:** *accompany; cf. n.*   **8 searchers:** *health officers*   **11 Seal'd up the doors:** *cf. n.*   **12 stay'd:** *stopped*   **18 nice:** *trivial* **charge:** *weight, importance*   **21 crow:** *crowbar*   **26 beshrew:** *censure*

And keep her at my cell till Romeo come.
Poor living corse, clos'd in a dead man's tomb.   *Exit.*

❧ SCENE THIRD ❧

Enter Paris and his Page ⟨with flowers and sweet water⟩.

Paris. Give me thy torch, boy, hence and stand aloof.
Yet put it out, for I would not be seen.
Under yond yew trees lay thee all along,
Holding thy ear close to the hollow ground,
So shall no foot upon the churchyard tread   5
(Being loose, unfirm with digging up of graves)
But thou shalt hear it. Whistle then to me
As signal that thou hear'st something approach.
Give me those flowers, do as I bid thee, go.
    Page. I am almost afraid to stand alone   10
Here in the churchyard, yet I will adventure.   *[Retires.]*
                    ⟨*Paris strews the tomb with flowers.*⟩
Paris. Sweet flow'r, with flow'rs thy bridal bed I strew.
O woe, thy canopy is dust and stones
Which with sweet water nightly I will dew,
Or wanting that, with tears distill'd by moans.   15
The obsequies that I for thee will keep
Nightly shall be to strew thy grave and weep.   *Whistle Page.*
The boy gives warning something doth approach.
What cursed foot wanders this way tonight
To cross my obsequies and true love's rite?   20
What! with a torch? Muffle me, night, awhile.   *[Retires.]*

*Enter Romeo and Balthasar ⟨with a torch, a mattock and a crow
of iron⟩.*

Romeo. Give me that mattock and the wrenching iron.
Hold, take this letter, early in the morning
See thou deliver it to my lord and father.   25
Give me the light. Upon thy life I charge thee,
Whate'er thou hear'st or see'st, stand all aloof
And do not interrupt me in my course.
Why I descend into this bed of Death
Is partly to behold my lady's face,   30
But chiefly to take thence from her dead finger
A precious ring—a ring that I must use
In dear employment. Therefore hence, be gone.
But if thou jealous dost return to pry
In what I farther shall intend to do,   35
By Heaven I will tear thee joint by joint
And strew this hungry churchyard with thy limbs.
The time and my intents are savage-wild,
More fierce and more inexorable far.
Than empty tigers or the roaring sea.   40
    Balthasar. I will be gone sir, and not trouble ye.
    Romeo. So shalt thou show me friendship. Take thou that,
Live and be prosperous. And farewell, good fellow.
    Balthasar. For all this same I'll hid me hereabout,
His looks I fear and his intents I doubt.   *[Retires.]*   45

Romeo. Thou detestable maw, thou womb of death,
Gorg'd with the dearest morsel of the earth,
Thus I enforce thy rotten jaws to open,
And in despite I'll cram thee with more food.
                    ⟨*Romeo opens the tomb.*⟩
Paris. This is that banish'd haughty Montague   50
That murder'd my love's cousin (with which grief
It is supposed the fair creature died)
And here is come to do some villainous shame
To the dead bodies. I will apprehend him.
Stop thy unhallow'd toil, vile Montague!   55
Can vengeance be pursu'd further than death?
Condemned villain, I do apprehend thee.
Obey and go with me, for thou must die.
    Romeo. I must indeed and therefore came I hither.
Good gentle youth, tempt not a desp'rate man,   60
Fly hence and leave me. Think upon these gone,
Let them affright thee. I beseech thee, youth,
Put not another sin upon my head
By urging me to fury. O be gone!
By Heav'n, I love thee better than myself,   65
For I come hither arm'd against myself.
Stay not, be gone! live, and hereafter say
A mad man's mercy bid thee run away.
    Paris. I do defy thy conjuration
And apprehend thee for a felon here.   70
    Romeo. Wilt thou provoke me? then have at thee, boy!
                    ⟨*They fight.*⟩
    Page. O Lord, they fight! I will go call the watch.   *[Exit.]*
    Paris. O I am slain! I thou be merciful
Open the tomb, lay me with Juliet.
    Romeo. In faith, I will. Let me peruse this face.   75
Mercutio's kinsman, noble County Paris!
What said my man when my betossed soul
Did not attend him as we rode? I think
He told me Paris should have marry'd Juliet.
Said he not so? or did I dream it so?   80
Or am I mad, hearing him talk of Juliet,
To think it was so? O give me thy hand,
One writ with me in sour Misfortune's book.
I'll bury thee in a triumphant grave.
A grave? O no, a lanthorn, slaughter'd youth,   85
For here lies Juliet, and her beauty makes
This vault a feasting presence full of light.
Death, lie thou there, by a dead man interr'd.
How oft when men are at the point of death
Have they been merry—which their keepers call   90
A lightning before death. O how may I
Call this a lightning? O my love, my wife!
Death that hath suck'd the honey of thy breath
Hath had no power yet upon thy beauty.
Thou art not conquer'd—Beauty's ensign yet   95
Is crimson in thy lips and in thy cheeks,
And Death's pale flag is not advanced there.

---

3 **yew:** *Q1; Q2* young **yew trees:** *symbolic of mourning* **all along:** *at full length* 11
adventure: *take the risk* 13 **canopy:** *covering* 14 **sweet:** *perfumed* 20 **cross:**
thwart 21 **Muffle:** *hide* **SD Balthasar:** *Q1; Q2* Peter; *cf. n.* 33 **dear:** *im-*
portant 34 **jealous:** *suspicious* 45 **doubt:** *suspect*

46 **detestable:** *stressed* ´– – – ´– – **maw:** *stomach* **womb:** *belly* 49 **despite:** *defi-*
ance **SD tomb:** *represented by the rear stage* 69 **conjuration:** *Q2* commiration; *Q1*
coniurations; *entreaty* 72 **Page:** *Q2 omits; Q1* Boy 84 **triumphant:** *magnifi-*
cent 85 **lanthorn:** *lantern (windowed dome)* 87 **feasting:** *festive* **presence:** *presence*
chamber 88 **Death:** *i.e. Paris' body* 90 **keepers:** *nurses* 92 **lightning:** *lightening of*
spirits (quibble on 'shedding of light')

Tybalt, ly'st thou there in thy bloody sheet?
O what more favor can I do to thee
Than with that hand that cut thy youth in twain   100
To sunder his that was thine enemy?
Forgive me, cousin. Ah dear Juliet,
Why art thou yet so fair? shall I believe
That unsubstantial Death is amorous
And that the lean abhorred monster keeps   105
Thee here in dark to be his paramour?
For fear of that I still will stay with thee
And never from this pallet of dim Night
Depart again, here, here will I remain
With worms that are thy chambermaids, O here   110
Will I set up my everlasting rest
And shake the yoke of inauspicious stars
From this world-weary'd flesh. Eyes look your last,
Arms take your last embrace, and lips (O you
The doors of breath) seal with a righteous kiss   115
A dateless bargain to engrossing Death!
Come bitter conduct, come unsav'ry guide,
Thou desp'rate pilot, now at once run on
The dashing rocks thy seasick weary bark.
Here's to my love! O true apothecary,   120
Thy drugs are quick. Thus with a kiss I die. ⟨*Falls.*⟩

Enter Friar with lanthorn, crow and spade.

Friar. Saint Francis be my speed! how oft tonight
Have my old feet stumbled at graves. Who 's there?
Balthasar. Here's one, a friend, and one that knows you
well.   125
Friar. Bliss be upon you. Tell me, good my friend,
What torch is yond that vainly lends his light
To grubs and eyeless skulls? as I discern,
It burneth in the Capels' monument.
Balthasar. It doth so, holy sir, and there 's my master.   130
One that you love.
Friar.   Who is it?
Balthasar.   Romeo.
Friar. How long hath he been there?
Balthasar.   Full half an hour.   135
Friar. Go with me to the vault.
Balthasar.   I dare not, sir,
My master knows not but I am gone hence,
And fearfully did menace me with death
If I did stay to look on his intents.   140
Friar. Stay then, I'll go alone. Fear comes upon me,
O much I fear some ill unthrifty thing.
Balthasar. As I did sleep under this yew tree here
I dreamt my master and another fought
And that my master slew him.   [*Exit*].   145
Friar.   Romeo!
⟨*Friar stoops and looks on the blood and weapons.*⟩
Alack alack, what blood is this which stains
The stony entrance of this sepulcher?
What mean these masterless and gory swords   150
To lie discolor'd by this place of peace?

Romeo, O pale! Who else? what! Paris too?
And steep'd in blood? Ah what an unkind hour
Is guilty of this lamentable chance.
The lady stirs.   ⟨*Juliet rises.*⟩   155
Juliet. O comfortable Friar, where is my lord?
I do remember well where I should be
And there I am, where is my Romeo?
Friar. I hear some noise, lady, come from that nest
Of death, contagion and unnatural sleep.   160
A greater power than we can contradict
Hath thwarted our intents, come, come away.
Thy husband in thy bosom there lies dead,
And Paris too. Come, I'll dispose of thee
Among a sisterhood of holy nuns.   165
Stay not to question, for the watch is coming.
Come go, good Juliet, I dare no longer stay.   *Exit.*
Juliet. Go get thee hence, for I will not away.
What 's here? a cup clos'd in my true love's hand!
Poison I see hath been his timeless end.   170
O churl, drunk all and left no friendly drop
To help me after? I will kiss thy lips,
Haply some poison yet doth hang on them
To make me die with a restorative.
Thy lips are warm.   175

Enter Page and Watch.

Chief Watchman. Lead boy, which way?
Juliet. Yea noise? then I 'll be brief. O happy dagger.
This is thy sheath—there rust and let me die.
                    ⟨*She stabs herself and falls.*⟩
Page. This is the place, there where the torch doth burn.
Chief Watchman. The ground is bloody, search about   180
the churchyard.
Go, some of you, whoe'er you find attach.
                    [*Exeunt some of the Watch.*]
Pitiful sight! here lies the County slain,
And Juliet bleeding, warm and newly dead,
Who here hath lain this two days buried.   185
Go tell the Prince, run to the Capulets,
Raise up the Montagues, some others search.
                    [*Exeunt others of the Watch.*]
We see the ground whereon these woes do lie,
But the true ground of all these piteous woes
We cannot without circumstance descry.   190

Enter Romeo's Man [and a Watchman].

2. Watchman. Here's Romeo's man, we found him in the
churchyard.
Chief Watchman. Hold him in safety till the Prince come
hither.

Enter Friar and another Watchman.

3. Watchman. Here is a friar that trembles, sighs and weeps,
We took this mattock and this spade from him
As he was coming from this churchyard's side.
Chief Watchman. A great suspicion, stay the friar too.

---

103 **shall I believe:** *Q2 I will beleeue, Shall I beleeue; cf. n.*   108 **pallet;** *cf. n.*   109–121
Depart again . . . I die: *for text see II.1.247-250; cf. n.*   111 **rest:** *repose* (for quibble see
IV.4.34; cf.n)   116 **dateless:** *endless* **engrossing:** *buying up in gross, monopolizing*   117
conduct: *guide*   122 **speed:** *aid, protector*   123 **stumbled:** *an ill omen*   127 **vainly:**
uselessly   142 **unthrifty:** *unlucky*   143 **yew:** *Q2 yong*

153 **unkind:** *unnatural, degenerate* (stressed ⌣ —)   156 **comfortable:** *comforting*   170
timeless: *untimely*   171 **churl:** *miser*   179 **Page:** *Q2 Watch boy*   182 **attach:** *arrest*   185 **this:** *these*   188 **woes:** *i.e. piteous bodies* **ground:** *basis, cause*   190 **circumstance:** *details*   198 **stay:** *detain*

Enter the Prince ⟨with [Citizens and] others⟩.

Prince. What misadventure is so early up
That calls our person from our morning rest?   200

Enter Capels.

Capulet. What should it be that is so shriek'd abroad?
Wife. The people in the street cry 'Romeo,'
Some 'Juliet' and some 'Paris,' and all run
With open outcry toward our monument.
Prince. What fear is this which startles in our ears?   205
Chief Watchman. Sovereign, here lies the County Paris slain,
And Romeo dead, and Juliet, dead before,
Warm and new kill'd.
Prince. Search, seek, and know how this foul murder comes.
Chief Watchman. Here is a friar and slaughter'd Romeo's   210
man.
With instruments upon them fit to open
These dead men's tombs.
Capulet. O Heav'ns! O Wife, look how our daughter bleeds!
This dagger hath mistane, for lo his house   215
Is empty on the back of Montague,
And it mis-sheathed in my daughter's bosom.
Wife. O me! this sight of death is as a bell
That warns my old age to a sepulcher.

Enter Montague.

Prince. Come Montague, for thou art early up   220
To see thy son and heir now early down.
Montague. Alas my liege, my wife is dead tonight,
Grief of my son's exile hath stopp'd her breath.
What futher woe conspires against mine age?
Prince. Look and thou shalt see.   225
Montague. O thou untaught! what manners is in this,
To press before thy father to a grave?
Prince. Seal up the mouth of outrage for a while
Till we can clear these ambiguities
And know their spring, their head, their true descent,   230
And then will I be gen'ral of your woes
And lead you e'en to death. Meantime forbear,
And let mischance be slave to patience.
Bring forth the parties of suspicion.
Friar. I am, the greatest, able to do least,   235
Yet most suspected, as the time and place
Doth make against me, of this direful murther;
And here I stand both to impeach and purge
Myself condemned and myself excus'd.
Prince. Then say at once what thou dost know in this.   240
Friar. I will be brief, for my short date of breath
Is not so long as is a tedious tale.
Romeo there dead was husband to that Juliet,
And she there dead, that Romeo's faithful wife,
I marry'd them; and their stol'n marriage day   245
Was Tybalt's doomsday, whose untimely death
Banish'd the new-made bridegroom from this city,
For whom and not for Tybalt Juliet pin'd.

You to remove that siege of grief from her
Betroth'd and would have marry'd her perforce   250
To County Paris. Then comes she to me
And with wild looks bid me devise some mean
To rid her from this second marriage,
Or in my cell there would she kill herself.
Then gave I her, so tutor'd by my art,   255
A sleeping potion which so took effect
As I intended, for it wrought on her
The form of death. Meantime I writ to Romeo
That he should hither come as this dire night
To help to take her from her borrow'd grave,   260
Being the time the potion's force should cease.
But he which bore my letter, Friar John,
Was stay'd by accident and yesternight
Return'd my letter back. Then all alone
At the prefixed hour of her waking   265
Came I to take her from her kindred's vault,
Meaning to keep her closely at my cell
Till I conveniently could send to Romeo.
But when I came some minute ere the time
Of her awak'ning, here untimely lay   270
The noble Paris and true Romeo dead.
She wakes, and I entreated her come forth
And bear this work of Heav'n with patience,
But then a noise did scare me from the tomb
And she too desp'rate would not go with me,   275
But as it seems did violence on herself.
All this I know, and to the marriage
Her nurse is privy; and if aught in this
Miscarry'd by my fault, let my old life
Be sacrific'd some hour before his time   280
Unto the rigor of severest law.
Prince. We still have known thee for a holy man.
Where 's Romeo's man? what can he say to this?
Balthasar. I brought my master news of Juliet's death,
And then in post he came from Mantua   285
To this same place, to this same monument.
This letter he early bid me give his father
And threaten'd me with death, going in the vault,
If I departed not and left him there.
Prince. Give me the letter, I will look on it.   290
Where is the County's page that rais'd the watch?
Sirrah, what made your master in this place?
Page. He came with flow'rs to strew his lady's grave
And bid me stand aloof, and so I did.
Anon comes one with light to ope the tomb,   295
And by and by my master drew on him,
And then I ran away to call the watch.
Prince. This letter doth make good the Friar's words—
Their course of love, the tidings of her death;
And here he writes that he did buy a poison   300
Of a poor pothecary, and therewithal
Came to this vault to die and lie with Juliet.
Where be these enemies? Capulet! Montague!
See what a scourge is laid upon your hate
That Heav'n finds means to kill your joys with love.   305
And I for winking at your discords too

SD Citizens; *cf. n.*   SD Enter Capels; *cf. n.*   201 shriek'd: *Q2* shrike   202 The people:
Q2 O the people; *for text see V.3.103; cf. n.*   205 our: *Q2* your; *i.e. the Prince's* (royal
plural)   210 slaughter'd: *Q2* Slaughter   215 mistane: *mistaken, gone astray*   219 warns:
summons   228 Seal up: *for staging see; cf. n.* mouth of outrage: *immoderate clamor-
ing*   234 of: *under*   236 as: *considering how*   237 make against: *implicate*   238
purge: *exonerate*   241 date of breath: *time of life*   244 that: *Q1; Q2* thats

259 as this: *this*   267 closely: *secretly*   278 privy: *secretly accessory*   285 in post:
posthaste   292 made: *was doing*   301 therewithal: *therewith, along with that*   306,
307 And I for winking ... punish'd: *see I.1.92, 93; cf. n.*

Have lost a brace of kinsmen. All are punish'd.
    Capulet. O brother Montague, give me thy hand.
This is my daughter's jointure, for no more
Can I demand.   *310*
    Montague.   But I can give thee more,
For I will ray her statue in pure gold
That whiles Verona by that name is known
There shall no figure at such rate be set
As that of true and faithful Juliet.   *315*
    Capulet. As rich shall Romeo's by his lady's lie,
Poor sacrifices of our enmity.

    Prince. A glooming peace this morning with it brings,
The Sun for sorrow will not show his head.
Go hence to have more talk of these sad things: *320*
Some shall be pardon'd and some punished.
For never was a story of more woe
Than this of Juliet and her Romeo.   *[Exeunt.]*

❧ FINIS ❧

---

307 a brace of kinsmen: *i.e. Mercutio and Paris*   **309 jointure:** *marriage settlement;*
cf. n.   **312 ray:** *array, bedeck* (i.e. gild); *cf. n.*   **314 rate:** *value*

NOTES

The Prologue. Here and in several other plays Shakespeare employs the classical device of commenting on his theme through a Prologue spoken by an actor called the Chorus. He satirizes the convention at I.4.7–8.

12. *two hours.* It was possible to perform an Elizabethan play in approximately such a short space of time chiefly because of the absence, in an Elizabethan public playhouse, of pauses for dropping a curtain or shifting scenery. Shakespeare mentions the same length of time in the Prologue to *Henry VIII,* where the Chorus advises certain members of the audience that they 'may see away their shilling Richly in two short hours.' (Shakespeare quotations are from G. L. Kittredge's edition of 1936.)

I.i. In Elizabethan editions of *Romeo and Juliet* there are no act and scene divisions, which originate with Shakespeare's 18th-century editors. The present edition retains the traditional divisions, except at three points where the action is continuous. See notes at II.1.46, and IV.4.32.

I.i.1–11. *coals . . . move.* Sampson's and Gregory's quibbles and puns on *coals, colliers, choler, draw* ('draw swords,' 'pull,' and 'extract'), *collar* ('harness' and 'hangman's noose'), and *moved* ('angered,' 'impelled,' and 'removed') represent a kind of wit popular in the 1590s. Compare I.4.12-21.

I.i.16. *take the wall.* Since there were no sidewalks and Renaissance street were usually narrow and littered with filth, in passing someone it was courteous to 'give the wall' to him but insulting to 'take the wall' of him, thus causing him to step into the gutter in the middle of the street.

I.i.39. *bite my thumb.* A defiantly insulting gesture made by snicking the thumbnail from under the upper teeth.

I.i. SD. *Benvolio . . .* This name, meaning literally in Italian 'I wish well,' is one of Shakespeare's additions to his source material.

I.i.56–76. *Yes, better, sir . . . seek a foe.* The action of these lines, omitted from Q1, is represented in that edition by the following stage direction: 'They draw. To them enters Tybalt. They fight. To them the Prince, old Montague and his Wife, old Capulet and his Wife, and other Citizens, and part them.'

I.i.69. *Citizens.* Editors usually include an Officer with the Citizens entering after l. 68, on the evidence of Q2's speech heading *Offi.* However, this would appear to be the Q2 compositor's misreading of *Citti.,* the parts of ll. 69, 70 being 'confused cries' to be assigned to various supernumeraries in the crowd of Citizens. Compare the Q2 speech heading *Citti.* at III.1.136.

I.i.71. *long sword.* Capulet calls for the old fashioned medieval weapon rather than the newfangled rapier introduced from the continent to England in Elizabethan times. See II.3.24 Cf. n.

I.i.SD. *Enter old Montague . . . Wife.* Editors usually follow Q2 in locating this direction after l. 81, but the dialogue indicates that Montague is already on stage by l. 80.

I.i.92, 93. *If ever you disturb . . . the peace.* According to Renaissance political theory, the Prince's clemency at this point is an error of civil policy, as he himself later recognizes. (Compare III.1.198 cf. n. and V.3.306-307.) Machiavelli, for example, in discussing the problem of restoring unity to a divided city, lists three courses of action open to the civil governor: 'the one is to put the leaders [of the opposing factions] to death . . . or to banish them from the city, or to reconcile them to each other under a pledge not to offend again. Of these three ways, the last is the worst, being the least certain and effective; for it is impossible that, after dissensions that have caused so much bloodshed and other outrages, a forced peace should be enduring. The parties meeting each other daily face to face will with difficulty abstain from mutual insults, and in their daily intercourse fresh causes for quarrel will constantly occur.' (*Discourses on the First Ten Books of Titus Livius, 3,* 27, in *The Prince and the Discourses,* Modern Library ed., New York, 1940, p. 490.)

I.i.127–138. *Many a morning . . . remove.* Montague's description of his son's romantic melancholy parodies the posturing required of the courtly lover. Compare Rosalind's description of 'a man in love' (*As You Like it,* III.2.367–379) and Ophelia's account of Hamlet's 'madness,' which Polonius pronounces to be 'the very ecstasy of love' (*Hamlet,* II.1.86–111).

I.i.145. *so secret and so close.* Like a true courtly lover, Romeo cherishes the precept laid down by Andreas Capellanus in *The Art of Courtly Love* (c. 1184), 'Qui non celat, amare non potest' (He who does not conceal his love cannot love). See E. C. Pettet, *Shakespeare and the Romance Tradition,* London, 1949, p. 114.

I.i.174–179. *brawling love . . . sleep.* The oxymorons and balanced antitheses of these lines are characteristic of Elizabethan sonnets written in the tradition of Petrarchan love poetry. Juliet employs similar conceits at III.2.75-81.

I.i.198. *left.* Editors usually follow Q2 in here reading *lost,* but in his edition of 1875 P. A. Daniel emends the Q2 reading to *left,* citing two other instances in Shakespeare of a compositor's confusing *left* and *lost* through the similarity in Elizabethan script of *e* to *o* and of *f* to long *s.* The emendation to *left* reveals Romeo's play on Benvolio's *leave* in l. 197, and emphasizes the neo-Platonic idea that Romeo's soul has left his body.

I.i.216–217. *rich . . . store.* That is, rich as she is in beauty, she is poor in that (being chaste) she will leave no children after death to inherit and perpetuate her wealth of beauty. Compare Sonnets 1-14.

I.ii.13. *marr'd . . . made.* Capulet uses the common Elizabethan antithesis of 'make' and 'mar' (compare II.3.102), and through a pun on 'married' plays on the proverbial expression, 'Soon married, soon marred.' Compare Parolles: 'A young man married is a man that's marr'd' (*All's Well That Ends Well,* II.3.298).

I.ii.40–42. *shoemaker . . . nets.* The Servant's confusion in the matter of tools and his bawdy quibble on *meddle* are the stock in trade of Elizabethan clowns.

I.ii.52. *plaintain leaf.* This was popularly believed to cure poisonous infections but was also applied to cuts and bruises. Romeo implies that Benvolio's proposed cure of love by counterinfection will be no more efficacious than a barked shin, since the same medication cures both ailments.

I.ii.56–58. *bound . . . tormented.* Romeo describes the customary Elizabethan treatment of lunatics. Compare Malvolio's treatment in *Twelfth Night* (III.4 and IV.2).

I.ii.72. *and.* Since the Q2 text from about I.2.55 to I.3.32 was printed from an uncorrected exemplar of Q1, Q2's omission of *and* at I.2.72 and the Q2 reading *you* at l. 81 would appear to be the compositor's errors of transmission. Accordingly, at I.2.72 and 81 the present editor prints the Q1 variants *and* and *thee,* the only substantive readings. Two other Q2 variants within this passage (*an* at I.3.12—Q1 *a*—and *the* at l. 29—omitted from Q1) are accepted as necessary corrections of the substantive Q1 text. See G. I. Duthie, 'The Text of Shakespeare's *Romeo and Juliet,' Studies in Bibliography, 4* (1952), pp. 22-3.

I.ii.77. *to supper.* Editors usually shift this phrase to the Servant's speech immediately following. However, the present editor follows Edward Dowden, who retains the Q2 arrangement in his edition of 1900, interpreting Romeo's 'Whither? to supper?' as an interruption of the Servant's 'Up—to our house.' Since Q1 is the only substantive source of this section of the text, the passage may well be corrupt beyond editorial redemption.

I.i.84. *crush.* The expression 'to crush' a cup of wine or a pot of ale was proverbial. Compare Shallow: 'By the mass, you'll crack a quart together' (2 *Henry IV,* V.3.57).

I.i.91–4. *devout religion . . . heretics.* Conceits based on the idea of love as religion are typical of Petrarchan love poetry. Romeo uses the same convention when he first meets Juliet (see I.4.218–224 cf. n.).

I.iii.2–4. *Now . . . Juliet.* Since the 18th century, editors have generally printed this and the Nurse's other speeches in I.3 as verse. However, both aesthetic considerations and bibliographical evidence suggest that their prose arrangement in Q2 and Q1 is more probably correct than incorrect. See Richard Hosley, 'The Corrupting Influence of the Bad Quarto on the Received Text of *Romeo and Juliet,' Shakespeare Quarterly, 4* (1953), 24-5. This article will be hereafter referred to as 'The Received Text.'

I.iii.SD. *Juliet.* Since Juliet was born on Lammas Eve or July 31 (see l. 20), her name is appropriate to her birth month.

I.iii.11. *a pretty age.* To Elizabethans a girl's fourteenth birthday made her ripe for marriage. See T. W. Baldwin, *Shakespeare's Five-Act Structure,* The University of Illinois Press, 1947, pp. 773–5.

I.iii.16. *Lammas-tide.* The *Lammas* (literally 'loaf-mass') was an old English harvest festival at which loaves of bread made from the new wheat were consecrated.

I.iii.23. *since . . . eleven years.* If this is a topical allusion to the earthquake felt in London on April 6, 1580, it may date *Romeo and Juliet* as early as 1591.

I.iii.29. *'Shake!'.* The action of the dovehouse at the moment of the earthquake, as though spoken by the personified dovehouse.

I.iii.37. *by my holidam.* This expression was originally an oath by a sacred relic, *holidam* being a form of *halidom,* 'sanctity, holy relic.' The form *holidam* was often misunderstood as 'Holy Dame,' the Virgin Mary.

I.iii.62, 63. *I was your mother . . . maid.* Since the sight of her daughter's bleeding body will be as a bell that warns her old age to a sepulcher (V.3.218, 219), this remark by Capulet's Wife that she is around twenty-eight years old is evidently a falsehood.

I.iii.70. *This night . . . feast.* Editors usually stop this line with a period, but

in Q2 it is lightly connected by a comma with the following six lines, the verbs of which are apparently futures prophesying how Juliet will fall in love rather than imperatives commanding her to fall in love.

I.iii.90. *the guests are come.* On the domestic arrangements of the Capulet household see Tucker Brooke, 'Shakespeare Remembers his Youth in Stratford,' in *Essays on Shakespeare and Other Elizabethans*, Yale University Press, 1948, pp. 32–4.

I.iv.SD. *Mercutio.* This name (from Brooke's *Romeus and Juliet*) suggests the mercurial qualities of Shakespeare's character, although it is etymologically unrelated to the Italian Mercurio. The original form in da Porto and Bandello is Marcuccio, and affectionate diminutive having approximately the value of 'cunning little Marco.'

I.iv.SD. *Torchbearers.* In the Elizabethan production from which the text of Q1 derives, these supernumeraries were apparently cut to a single Page. Similarly, the 'two or three' Servingmen of IV.2.SD and the 'three of four' of IV.4.14 SD are in each case cut to a single Servingman in Q1.

I.iv.1. *this speech.* It was the Elizabethan custom for a costumed messenger to deliver a speech introducing Maskers and apologizing for their joining a festivity without invitation. The Maskers have been discussing such a speech, which Benvolio rejects as prolix and out of date.

I.iv.5. *Tartar's painted bow.* This is the Roman or Cupid's bow, shaped like the line of the upper lip, as distinguished from the English bow, shaped like the segment of a circle.

I.iv.7, 8. ⟨*Nor . . . entrance*⟩. These two lines from Q1 are incorporated in the text of the present edition on the assumption that they stood in Shakespeare's foul papers but were overlooked by the Q2 compositor. Another theory is that Shakespeare added them to the promptbook version (represented by Q1) of his original text (represented by Q2). See H. R. Hoppe's edition of 1947, p. vi. The references to prologue and prompter harmonize with Shakespeare's habit of alluding to practices of the stage, and the trisyllabic *entrance* accords with similar pronunciations of *mistress* at II.3.173 and III.5.155.

I.iv.12–21. *heavy . . . bound.* Like the word-play of Sampson and Gregory (see notes on I.1.1.–11), Romeo's and Mercutio's puns and quibbles on *heavy* ('melancholy' and 'ponderous'), *light* (opposed to 'dark' and 'heavy'), *sole* and *soul*, *soar* and *sore*, and *bound*. ('tied,' 'limit'; and 'leap') were considered witty in the 1590s. They are followed by bawdy quibbles on *burthen*, *thing*, *prick*, and *case* (ll. 23–9). There is a good deal more of the same in II.3.

I.iv.37. *proverb'd . . . phrase.* Romeo is thinking of some such proverb as 'A good candle-holder proves a good gamester,' since by looking on and not gambling he can lose nothing.

I.iv.39. *dun.* Editors usually emend Q2's *dum* to Q1's *done,* but since the variant spelling *dun* for 'done' does not appear in Q2, *dum* would appear to be the compositor's error for *dun,* 'dark.' Romeo, of course, is playing on *fair* and punning on 'done.'

I.iv.41. *Dun.* This was a quasi-proper name for any horse, whether or not actually a dun. The phrase 'Dun's in the mire,' meaning 'Things are at a standstill,' was the name of an indoor winter game in which a heavy log representing a horse stuck in the mud was hauled out by the players.

I.iv.47, 48. *judgment . . . wits.* Judgment was one of the five inner or spiritual senses, as distinguished from the five outer or physical senses (here 'our five wits'). Mercutio means that the single mental faculty of judgment (which in quibbling about daylight Romeo neglects to use) can apprehend his intended meaning five times as well as can all five of the physical senses.

I.iv.57. *Queen Mab, midwife.* The name *Mab* (which Ben Jonson uses for the Fairy Queen in his *Althorp Entertainment*) is probably a variant of Maeve, the heroic queen of Celtic legend. Mercutio calls her *midwife* (here pronounced 'middif') because she is that fairy who assists at the birth of men's dreams, 'the children of an idle brain, Begot of nothing but vain phantasy' (ll.103, 104).

I.iv.59. *agate stone.* That is, the tiny figure often carved in the agate set in a seal ring. Compare Falstaff on the diminutive size of his Page: 'I was never manned with an agate till now' (2 *Henry IV*, I.2.14).

I.iv.61. *atomi.* Editors usually follow the Q3 editor in emending Q2's *ottamie* to *atomies*, but Hoppe restores Q1's *atomi*, plural of Latin *atomus*, atom. (In Shakespeare's time the Latin plural *atomi* developed into the English singular *atomy*, atom, mote.) Q2's *ottamie* is evidently the compositor's misreading of *attomie* in Shakespeare's foul papers. Moreover, the variant forms in the two editions prove that the Q2 reading was not contaminated by Q1.

I.iv.70. *maid.* This Q1 reading would appear to be supported by Q2's *man*. Since the Q2 compositor occasionally misread *ie* as *n* and final *d* as *e*, *man* is apparently his misreading of *maid*. (Compare the compositor's misreading of *gaie* as *gan* at III.1.119, and of *exhald* as *exhale* at III.5.13) It is possible, however, that *man* is a misreading of *maie*, 'may, maiden,' corrupted in Q1 to *maid*. For the latter suggestion the present editor is indebted to Mr. H. R. Hoppe.

I.iv.82. *suit.* That is, a petition to the monarch which will enable the courtier

to extort a fee from the petitioner in return for interceding, or pretending to intercede, in his behalf.

I.iv.98. *carriage.* In Shakespeare's time pronunciation of the suffixes *-iage*, *-ion*, *-ial*, *-iar*, and *-ience* could be monosyllabic or disyllabic, depending on the metrical context. Disyllabic pronunciations of these suffixes (especially *-ion*) occur throughout *Romeo and Juliet*, but only one example of each is glossed. *carri-age* (I.4.98), *invocati-on* (II.1.29), *substanti-al* (II.1.192), *famili-ar* (III.3.7), and *pati-ence* (V.1.27). See Helge Kökeritz, *Shakespeare's Pronunciation*, Yale University Press, 1953, pp. 256, 293–4.

I.iv.115, 117. *expire . . . death.* Romeo compares the length of his life to the term of a bond or mortgage for which his life itself is security. If the *consequence* of which he has a premonition brings the bond's term to a close, in default of payment he will have to forfeit his life.

I.iv.SD. *They march . . . napkins.* The traditional scene division at this point accords with the modern custom of a curtain drop but obscures the continuity of action and fluidity of scene in an Elizabethan public playhouse, where the marching of the Maskers symbolizes a change of scene from the street outside Capulet's house to a hall within it. The Maskers retire to the back or sides of the forestage during the Servingmen's short scene (I.4.121–133), stepping forward at l. 133 when the dance party enters 'to' them.

I.iv.121–133. *Where's Potpan . . . take all.* Editors usually assign these six speeches to three Servingmen, but there are actually four, in Q2 unconventionally numbered *Ser.*, *1.*, *2.*, and *3.*, rather than *1. Ser.*, *2.*, *3.*, and *4.* The present editor follows the numbering in Dowden's edition.

I.iv.SD. *Enter . . . to the Maskers.* Since Capulet's feast is not a masquerade, masks are worn only by Romeo and his friends, the uninvited guests. See I.4.1. cf. n. and I.4.218–224 cf. n.

I.iv.199. *goodman boy.* This is a double insult, since *goodman* was the title of a farmer or other person beneath the rank of gentleman but above that of laborer, and *boy* was used contemptuously of a green youngster, or one treated as such.

I.iv.203. *set cock-a-hoop.* This means literally, set the *cock* (spigot) on the *hoop* (of the barrel), thus letting the liquor flow freely. The same image for disorder appears at I.1.100 in the expression 'set abroach.'

I.iv.SD. *Aside.* Capulet successively interrupts his quarrel with Tybalt in order to reply to a guest (l. 206), to compliment other guests (l. 209), to order his servants (l. 210), and to encourage the dancing (l. 211).

I.iv.217–219. *the gentle sin . . . kiss.* In atonement for the *rough* sin of profaning Juliet's hand by touching it with his own, Romeo proposes the *gentle sin* of kissing her hand.

I.iv.218–224. *pilgrims . . . palmers.* Although in da Porto's novella Romeo attends a Capelletti masquerade costumed as a nymph, in Shakespeare's play Capulet's feast is not a masquerade and Romeo is not costumed, as a pilgrim or otherwise. Shakespeare's conceit of Romeo as a pilgrim visiting the shrine of his love is suggested by the name Romeo itself, for in Italian it means literally 'Romer' or 'Rome-bound pilgrim.' In the Middle Ages the word was originally used in Palestine and elsewhere to designate pilgrims from Italy, but it ultimately grew to refer to a pilgrim's destination rather than his place of origin. In the *Vita Nuova* Dante distinguishes among the 'three separate denominations proper unto those who undertake journeys to the glory of God. They are called *Palmers* who go beyond the seas eastward [to Jerusalem], whence often they bring palm-branches. And *Pilgrims* [in addition to the general sense of "religious travelers"] . . . are they who journey unto the holy House of Gallicia; seeing that no other apostle was buried so far from his birth-place as was the blessed Saint James [Santiago de Compostela]. And there is a third sort who are called *Romers* [*romei*, plural *of romeo*]; in that they go . . . unto Rome.' (*La Vita Nuova*, XL, tr. D. G. Rossetti.)

I.iv.230. *Thus . . . purg'd.* It was not unusual for partners in an Elizabethan dance to kiss. Compare Ariel's song: 'Come unto these yellow sands, And then take hands. Curtsied when you have and kiss'd, The wild waves whist, Foot it featly here and there . . .' (*The Tempest*, I.2.442–446).

I.iv.257. *Petruchio.* Here and in *The Taming of the Shrew* Shakespeare spells the name Petruccio with a *ch* in order to retain the soft Italian *c* in English. However, since the *i* in Petruccio is not vocalic, this English phonetic spelling results in the traditional mispronunciation 'Petruchi-o.'

I.iv.273–286. *Now old Desire . . . sweet.* According to Senecan tradition, this 'chorus' should precede rather than follow the act division. See Baldwin, *Shakespeare's Five-Act Structure*, p. 744.

II.i.2. *earth . . . center.* As everything on earth tends toward its center, so Romeo's body gravitates toward his heart, which has remained with Juliet.

II.i.4. *He's.* Here and at III.1.112, III.1.196, and III.5.39, the present editor prints the contracted form of Q2's *is*; and elsewhere the contracted forms of *am* (II.4.53), *are* (III.5.222), *would* (II.4.13), and *it* (II.1.222 and III.5.223).

II.i.9. *Romeo . . . lover.* Since it was believed that a spirit could not speak

until properly addressed, Mercutio in his parody of invocation follows the custom of reciting various names in the hope that the right one will cause the spirit to appear and speak. Hamlet does the same in addressing his father's ghost (*Hamlet*, I.4.47, 48).

II.i.15. *Abram.* An *Abram* or Abraham Man was 'one of a class of pretended lunatics who wandered over England seeking alms, after the dissolution of the religious houses' (OED); and thus the term became slang for a cheat or hypocrite. Since Cupid's blindness is misleading (considering his accuracy as an archer) and since he caused King Cophetua to fall in love with a beggar maid, Mercutio describes the god of love by reference to the typical Elizabethan hypocritical beggar. Editors have also explained *Abraham* (the reading of both Q2 and Q1) as alluding to the Old Testament Patriarch (*Abraham* in Hebrew meaning 'Father of Multitudes'), as a variant of *auburn* (i.e. 'auburn-haired'; see *Coriolanus*, II.3.17), and as an error for *Adam,* in allusion to the proverbial archer Adam Bell (see *Much Ado About Nothing*, I.1.216–218). For the editorial principle involved in the retention of this Q2 reading, see 'The Received Text,' pp.18–19.

II.i.16. *King Cophetua.* This hero of a popular Elizabethan ballad fell in love with and married a wandering beggar girl named Penelophon—or Zenelophon, as the name appears in *Love's Labour's Lost* (IV.1.69). On Cophetua's first sight of Penelophon, Cupid, 'The blinded boy, that shoots so trim, From heaven down did hie; He drew a dart and shot at him, In place where he did lie.' (Thomas Percy, *Reliques of Ancient English Poetry*, ed. 1839, vol. 1, bk. II, no. 6)

II.i.40. *open-arse.* Q1's *Et cætera* (euphemistic for 'pudendum') is the traditional reading here, but in adopting it editors usually suppress Q2's *or* and fail to recognize that if l. 40 is to scan properly the word omitted after Q2's *open* must be a monosyllable. Thus the metrical as well as the semantic context requires the reading *open-arse,* an old name for the medlar tree or 'that kind of fruit As maids call medlars when they laugh alone' (ll. 37, 38). Chaucer's Reeve uses it in referring to the fact that the medlar is not worth eating until overripe and slightly decayed: 'This white top writeth myne olde yeris; Myn herte is also mowled [mouldy] as myne heris, But if [unless] I fare as dooth an *open-ers.*' ('The Reeve's Prologue,' in *The Poetical Works of Chaucer*, ed. F. N. Robinson, Boston, 1933, p. 66.) For the editorial principle involved in this emendation, see 'The Received Text,' pp. 20–1.

II.i.38. *pop'rin pear.* The *poppering pear* was so called after its place of origin, the town of Poperinghe in Flanders. Mercutio here couples it with *open-arse* to indicate two different varieties of the same essential kind, Romeo and Rosaline. There may also be quibble on 'phallus'; see Kökeritz, *Shakespeare's Pronunciation*, pp.136–8.

II.i.46. *Romeo.* Here the traditional scene division again obscures the Elizabethan fluidity of scene and continuity of action, emphasized by the rhyme of *wound* with *found.* Romeo, who is usually visible to the audience during Mercutio's raillery (ll. 9–41), now comes forward from his hiding place, and the scene of the forestage changes from a street outside the wall to the orchard within it.

II.i.SD. *Enter . . . window.* Editors usually follow Capell (1768) in locating this entrance (omitted from Q2 and Q1) after II.1.46. However, since the light at the window is the twilight glow of dawn (the East) and since Juliet herself is the sun, its imminent rising designates in metaphor her anticipated appearance at the window. Only after Romeo has invoked the sun to rise (l. 49) and to cast off Diana's livery (l. 54) does the 'sun' actually 'rise': Juliet enters at the window, causing Romeo's triple exclamation of delight at first catching sight of his beloved (ll. 55, 56). Thus Romeo's 'invocation' is Shakespeare's preparation for an effective entrance by Juliet, an ironic echo of Mercutio's parody of invocation in the immediately preceding lines, and a transitional device functioning as a buffer between Mercutio's ribaldry in the first part of II.1 and Juliet's 'true-love passion' (l. 146) in the latter part of that scene. See Richard Hosley, 'Juliet's Entrance,' *The Times Literary Supplement*, May 22, 1953, p. 333.

II.i.SD. *window.* Although in a proscenium-arch theater Juliet usually here enters on a 'balcony,' in an Elizabethan public playhouse she enters on the upper stage, representing her window. Compare the Q1 and Q2 directions at III.5.1. For structural details of the upper stage, rear stage, and forestage in various Elizabethan public theaters, see C. Walter Hodges, *The Globe Restored*, London, 1953.

II.i.62. *spheres.* In medieval and Renaissance astronomy the erratic motions of the planets (and of the moon) were explained according to the Ptolemaic system, in which each planet is carried about the earth by a hollow crystalline sphere concentric with the earth. The general notion persisted a century or more after publication of the Copernican hypothesis (1543).

II.i.78. *puffing.* Editors usually emend Q2's *puffing* to Q1's *pacing*, but the Q2 reading apparently alludes to the personification of winds in old maps as cloud-shaped heads puffing air from distended cheeks. It is possible, however, that *puffing* is the Q2 compositor's misreading of *passing,* Hoppe's emendation. For discussion of the three readings see Duthie, 'The Text of Shakespeare's *Romeo and Juliet*,' pp. 24–6, and Hosley, 'The Received Text,' p. 19 and n. 23.

II.i.87–89. *What's Montague . . . a man.* Editors usually correct these lines by conflating them with the variant Q1 text, but since it is not entirely clear that Q2 is corrupt, the present editor follows Hoppe in reprinting the text as it stands in Q2.

II.i.168. *contract.* Juliet uses this legal term because according to Elizabethan law the lovers have entered into a formal betrothal contract. Such a betrothal was often legally binding as a marriage, although it did not morally license consummation of the marriage until a member of the clergy had performed the nuptial ceremony (compare II.5.36–7). See David P. Harding, 'Elizabethan Betrothals and *Measure for Measure*,' *The Journal of English and Germanic Philology*, *49* (1950), 149–50.

II.i.222. *dear.* Hoppe here restores Q2's *Neece.* However, except for the OED's one doubtful example from around 1470, there is no record of the word 'niece' used as a form of address to an unrelated woman; and the independent emendations of both the F2 editor (to *sweete*) and the Q4 editor (to *Deere*) show that the Q2 reading was considered corrupt in the early 17th century. Since *c* was a common compositor's error for *r*, it seems likely that the Q2 compositor misread *deere* as *Neece.* For Q2's *My Neece* Q1 has *Madame.*

II.i.237. *silken threed.* The Q2 spelling *threed* indicates a common Elizabethan pronunciation of 'thread.' This pronunciation in turn suggests that *threed* is stressed, that *plucks it* is monosyllabic, and that Q1's monosyllabic variant *silke* (the traditional reading) is an error for *silken.*

II.i.242–246. *Good night . . . rest.* Editors here follow the Q4 editor and Pope (1723) in printing the Q1 assignment of ll. 242, 243 to Juliet and of ll. 245, 246 to Romeo. However, in view of the Q1 reporter's recurrent errors of speech assignment (see H. R. Hoppe, *The Bad Quarto of Romeo and Juliet*, Cornell University Press, 1948, pp. 125–6), the present editor reprints the text as it stands in Q2, with the addition from Q3 of Romeo's omitted speech heading to the second half of l. 242 and the shift of his heading at l. 246 to l. 247. For a detailed account of the Q1 and Q2 errors here involved, see 'The Received Text,' pp. 26–8; Clifford Leech, 'Notes on . . . the Received Text of *Romeo and Juliet*,' *Shakespeare Quarterly*, *5* (1954), 94–5; and Richard Hosley, The "Good Night, Good Night" Sequence in *Romeo and Juliet*,' *ibid.*, pp. 96–98.

II.i.247–250. *The grey-ey'd Morn . . . wheels.* These four lines constitute Shakespeare's revision of an original version, which he failed to delete from his manuscript and which was therefore set up by the Q2 compositor as a duplication of the revision (see Text and Date). Since 1723 editors have followed Pope and the Q4 editor in deleting the original version from Romeo's speech in II.1 and in assigning the revised version to the Friar at the beginning of II.2. However, since the original version stands in Romeo's speech two lines before the end of II.1, the passage would appear to belong to him; and the present editor follows the F2 editor and Rowe (1709) in assigning it to Romeo. The image of the 'grey-ey'd Morn' is echoed by Romeo at III.5.19 ('I'll say yon grey is not the Morning's eye'); and the imagery of the passage is generally akin both to that used by Romeo at II.1.48, 49 and III.5.7–10 and by other characters apropos of Romeo at I.1.112, 113, I.1.130–132, and III.2.1–25; whereas the Friar never elsewhere alludes to classical mythology or personifies Day or Night or their aspects in the Homeric manner. The Q1 assignment of the passage to the Friar is apparently the reporter's memorial error. For detailed discussion of this 'revisional duplication' and of others at III.3.41–44, IV.1.113, 114, and V.3.109–121. Duplications of a single word or phrase are listed in the note to V.3.103.

II.i.248. *Check'ring.* This Q1 reading suggests that Q2's *Checking* in the revised Q2 version of the grey-ey'd Morn' passage is a misprint for *Checkring,* the reading of the original Q2 version.

II.ii.SD. *Enter Romeo.* Editors occasionally follow Pope in locating this entrance after l. 26, but the location of the entrance in Q2 is a calculated irony: Romeo, who is to be the victim of *Poison*, enters just before the word is mentioned (l. 20) and overhears the Friar's homily on *Grace* and *rude Will.*

II.ii.30, 37. *distemper'd, distemp'rature.* Both words suggest the idea of mental disturbance as a result of the four bodily humors being disproportionately mixed or tempered.

II.iii.4, 5. *Why . . . run mad.* Editors usually follow Q2 in arranging this prose passage and that at III.1.1–2 as verse, but in each use Q2 appears to have been contaminated by the erroneous arrangement in Q1. See 'The Received Text,' pp.23–4.

II.iii.18. *Prince of Cats.* Tybalt or Tibert (Tebaldo in da Porto and Bandello) is the name of the cat in the medieval French cycle of animal satires concerning Reynard the Fox. In III.1 Mercutio repeats his joke by calling Tybalt 'ratcatcher' (l. 70) and 'King of Cats' (l. 72).

II.iii.21, 22. *butcher . . . button.* Tybalt is such an accurate fencer that he can pink any button he chooses on his opponent's jacket.

II.iii.23. *first and second cause.* These were, according to the code of the

duello, two of the various grounds for a gentleman's recognizing an affront to his honor and therefore challenging the offender to a duel. (Compare Mercutio's use of the phrase in the Q1 version of his death-speech, p. 160.) See Touchstone's satire on such quarreling in *As You Like It* (V.4.48–98), and compare Armado's complaints against Cupid: 'The first and second cause will not serve my turn; the passado he respects not, the duello he regards not. His disgrace is to be called boy, but his glory is to subdue men' (*Loves Labour's Lost*, I.2.157–160). Compare also Peter's quarreling with the Musicians (IV.5.144–156).

II.iii.24. *passado . . . hai.* The *passado* (Italian *passata*, 'pass,' 'thrust') is a lunging thrust involving the passing of one foot before the other while delivering the attack. The *punto reverso* (Italian *punta reversa*, 'point reversed') is a back-handed thrust delivered from the left side of the attacker's body. The word *hai* (Italian, 'thou hast [it]') means a home thrust or death blow. See Horace S. Craig, 'Dueling Scenes and Terms in Shakespeare's Plays,' *University of California Publications in English*, 9 (1940), 1–28. Craig also discusses the medieval long sword, and distinguishes between the rapier-and-dagger swordplay of the young gallants and the sword-and-buckler swashbuckling of the servants.

II.iii.32. *bones.* Mercutio derides the fashion-mongers because the old seats are too hard for their bones, which are presumably afflicted with syphilis—'The Neapolitan bone-ache . . . the curse dependent on those that war for a placket' (*Troilus and Cressida*, II.3.15–17). There may also be a pun on French 'bons,' since the *pardon-me's* affectedly interlard their speech with foreign expressions.

II.iii.62. *wild goose chase.* This is a horse race in which the rider who can seize the lead must be followed cross-country wherever he goes.

II.iii.88. *occupy.* This word's sense of 'copulate' is alluded to by Doll Tearsheet: 'God's light! these villains will make the word [captain] as odious as the word "occupy," which was an excellent good word before it was ill sorted' (*2 Henry IV*, II.4.122–125).

II.iii.SD. *Enter . . . Man.* Editors usually follow Q2 in locating this direction after 'Here's goodly gear' (l. 89), but the Q2 location would appear to be due to the compositor's having reproduced the erroneous location in Q1. The present editor follows the location in F1. See 'The Received Text,' pp. 21–2.

II.iii.93. *fan.* It was the extreme of fashion for a lady to use a fan so large that a servant was required to carry it.

II.iii.127, 128. *'Lady, lady'.* Mercutio quotes from the refrain of a popular ballad on Susanna and the Elders: 'A woman fair and virtuous: Lady, lady, Why should we not of her learn thus To live godly?' Compare Sir Toby Belch: 'Tilly-vally, lady! "There dwelt a man in Babylon, lady, lady!"' (*Twelfth Night*, II.3.70, 71).

II.iii.161, 162. *Bid . . . afternoon.* Editors usually print 'Bid her devise' as a separate dimeter line, but the line as it stands in Q2 appears to be a fourteener. There is another fourteener at II.4.15.

II.iv.26. *jaunce.* This may be the Q2 compositor's misreading of 'jaunte' or a colloquial development form the plural form 'jaunts.'

III.i.69. *Alla stoccatho.* Editors usually emend Q2's *Alla stucatho* to *Alla stoccata*, an Italian fencing term meaning 'at the thrust,' the *stoccata* (from 'stocco,' *rapier*) being a thrust delivered with the fingernails up. However, since *stoccado* was a common Elizabethan variant of *stoccata*, Q1's *Allastockado* preserves essentially the correct reading, for Q2's *stucatho* (or *stocatho*, misread by the compositor) would appear to reproduce Shakespeare's phonetic spelling of *stoccado*, the *th* being an attempt to render the Spanish fricative *d*, as in *renegatho* (*Twelfth Night*, III.2.61). Compare Shallow's *stoccadoes* in *The Merry Wives of Windsor* (II.1.193). Mercutio uses the expression figuratively for Tybalt's blustering.

III.i.119. *He gay.* Editors usually emend Q2's *He gan* to Q1's 'A liue' (i.e. alive), but the present editor follows Hoppe in interpreting *gan* as the Q2 compositor's misreading of *gaie*, a variant spelling of *gay*. Compare the compositor's error two lines later of *end* for *eied* (III.1.121).

III.i.136. *Citizens.* Editors usually interpret Q2's *Citti*, as designating a single Citizen (as at l. 139), but ll. 136, 137 would appear to be spoken by two different Citizens. Compare I.1.69 cf. n.

III.i.161, 162. *one hand . . . the other.* The swordplay here described is of the sword-and-dagger variety, in which the left hand, holding a dagger or wearing a mailed gauntlet, parries the attack and the right hand thrusts with the rapier. See note on II.3.27.

III.i.184. *Montague.* This traditional emendation of the Q2 speech heading *Capulet* was first made by the Q4 editor. Hoppe restores the Q2 reading, but the passage in question (ll. 184-186) seems dramatically more appropriate to Montague and its assignment to him has the theatrical advantage of giving one of Romeo's parents something to say in a scene where they would otherwise remain mute.

III.i.198. *Mercy . . . kill.* The unwiseness of a clement civil policy is discussed by Machiavelli, who writes that a prince 'must not mind incurring the charge of cruelty for the purpose of keeping his subjects united and faithful; for, with a very few examples, he will be more merciful than those who, from excess of

tenderness, allow disorders to arise, from whence spring bloodshed and rapine; for these as a rule injure the whole community, while the executions carried out by the prince injure only individuals.' (*The Prince*, ch. 17, Modern Library ed., p. 60.) Compare notes on I.1.92, 93.

III.ii.1–31. *Gallop apace . . . wear them.* This passage is occasionally called Juliet's serenade or evening song.

III.ii.3. *Phaeton.* The son of Phoebus Apollo, Phaeton was permitted by his father to drive the chariot of the sun. However, he was unable to control the horses, which ran away with him, drawing the sun so close to the earth as to dry up large areas which are now the great deserts. To prevent the universe from being destroyed, Jupiter was forced to kill Phaeton with a thunderbolt. See Ovid, *Metamorphoses*, II.1–328 (Loeb ed.)

III.ii.6. *runaway.* The meaning is not clear. If *runaway* alludes to the Phaeton myth, it probably designates the sun, which Juliet wishes would move faster (as when it ran away with Phaeton) so as to bring in night earlier than usual. This interpretation is supported by Lorenzo's use of the word: 'But come at once; For the close night doth play the *runaway*, And we are stay'd for at Bassanio's feast' (*The Merchant of Venice*, II.6.48–50).

III.ii.SD. *Enter Nurse with cords.* In place of this direction Q1 has 'Enter Nurse wringing her hands, with the ladder of cords in her lap.' Presumably in the production on which the Q1 text is based the Nurse was here 'discovered' seated in the rear stage. In Q1 Juliet's serenade is cut to four lines, and the Q2 phrase 'O here comes my Nurse' is omitted.

III.ii.49. *cockatrice.* The cockatrice or basilisk was a fabulous serpent whose glance was supposed to be fatal. Compare Sir Toby Belch: 'This will so fright them both [Cesario and Sir Andrew Aguecheek] that they will kill one another by the look, like *cockatrices*' (*Twelfth Night*, III.4.178, 179).

III.ii.89. *forsworn all.* Editors usually correct Q2's long and awkward line 'All perjur'd, all forsworn, all naught, all dissemblers' by rearranging the lineation of ll. 88, 89. However, the present editor retains the Q2 lineation and omits the phrase 'all naught' as a first thought which Shakespeare had neglected to delete from his foul papers. See V.3.103 cf. n.

III.iii.SD. *Enter Friar.* Q1's separate entrances for the Friar and Romeo accord with the Q2 text and apparently reflect the bookkeeper's correction (in the promptbook) of the original direction in Shakespeare's foul papers, 'Enter Friar and Romeo.' In an Elizabethan public theater the Friar and Romeo enter 'at several doors' on the forestage, representing the Friar's cell. Compare note on V.2.SD.

III.iii.172, 171. *Either be gone . . . hence.* That is, be gone from hence, disguised, either before the watch be set or (at the latest) by the break of day.

III.iv.12. *desp'rate tender.* Capulet's negotiation for a marriage de convenance without his daughter's consent reflects the strict parental authority exercised by Elizabethans in arranging marriages for their children. (See Charles T. Prouty, *The Sources of Much Ado About Nothing*, Yale University Press, 1950, pp. 44–5). Such authority helps to explain Capulet's anger in III.5, where Juliet, who of course cannot marry Paris because she is already married to Romeo, seems to Capulet to be rejecting a 'good' match out of sheer wilfulness. On the concern of fathers for their daughters' marriages, compare Leonato in *Much Ado About Nothing*, Polonius in *Hamlet*, Brabantio in *Othello*, and Prospero in *The Tempest*.

III.v.1–36. *Wilt thou be gone . . . dark our woes.* These lines compose an aubade or dawn song, a traditional verse form of the troubadours celebrating the hour of parting between two lovers at dawn. As here, the aubade is often a duet in which the lovers debate whether dawn is actually at hand. As an example of Shakespeare's functional use of a conventional verse form, Romeo and Juliet's aubade may be compared with their sonnet at I.4.216–229.

III.v.13. *exhal'd.* Editors usually emend Q2's *exhale* to Q1's *exhales*, but the Q2 reading would appear to be the compositor's error for *exhald*. For a list of the Q2 compositor's recurrent misreadings of final *d* as *e*, see 'The Received Text,' p. 20, n. 27.

III.v.31. *Some say . . . eyes.* Because the beautiful-voiced lark has ugly eyes, whereas the croaking toad has beautiful ones.

III.v.SD. *Nurse.* The Q2 direction 'Enter Madam and Nurse' probably stood in Shakespeare's foul papers as a marginal direction, 'Enter Nurse. Madam'—that is, Enter the Nurse, calling 'Madam'; and accordingly the direction was amplified to 'Enter Madam and Nurse' and duplicated in the text as '*Nur.* Madam.' See Sir Walter Greg, *The Editorial Problem in Shakespeare*, Oxford, 1942, p. 61, n. 2.

III.v.37–40. *Madam . . . look about.* In a proscenium-arch theater the Nurse usually delivers the warning from offstage. But in the Elizabethan production represented by Q1, it was apparently shifted to l. 59 in order to 'cover' Juliet's descent from the upper stage. In such a method of staging the Nurse enters on the forestage. See III.5.SD cf. n.

III.v.62. *renowm'd.* This Q2 spelling indicates an Elizabethan pronunciation emphasizing the etymology of 'renown,' from Old French *renomer.*

III.v.SD. ⟨*She goeth down from the window*⟩. This Q1 stage direction indicates that in an Elizabethan public playhouse Juliet here descends from the upper to the lower stage by means of the tiring-house stairs, and thus that the balance of III.5 is played on the lower rather than the upper level. The text in Q2 and the present edition reproduces the original version of Shakespeare's foul papers. After the Wife's entrance and speech at l. 64, Juliet expresses her surprise in soliloquy (ll. 65–7), exits from the upper stage after l. 67, descends to the lower level, and re-enters 'to' the Wife on the rear stage or the forestage; at which point the scene of the lower stage (having changed on the Wife's entrance from orchard to house) changes from a location outside Juliet's bedroom to one inside it. However, Shakespeare's original version is unstageworthy in that it involves a pause in the action of eight or ten seconds during Juliet's descent. The text in Q1, on the other hand, in part reflects the promptbook version of the staging. In that edition the Nurse's warning is shifted from its Q2 position at III.5.37–40 to l. 59, and Juliet's soliloquies at ll. 60–4 and 65–7 are eliminated. Thus Juliet begins her descent simultaneously with Romeo's exit at l. 59, the descent being 'covered' by the dialogue and stage business of the Nurse's and the Wife's calling Juliet and knocking at her door. At l. 67 Juliet re-enters to the Wife and Nurse on the rear stage or the forestage, where the action proceeds. (If she enters on the rear stage, the players must subsequently 'flow out' to the forestage in order to play the 'upbraiding' scene with Capulet.) In Otway's restoration version entitled *The History and Fall of Caius Marius*, this staging problem was solved by representing a garden scene (see Hazelton Spencer, *Shakespeare Improved*, Harvard University Press, 1927, p. 295); and in the 18th century Romeo and Juliet were 'brought in *tête à tête* [*sic*] on the platform of the stage' (from a contemporary account cited by A. C. Sprague, *Shakespeare and the Actors*, Harvard University Press, 1944, p. 308). In a modern proscenium-arch theater, the problem posed by this transition of scene is usually solved by representing the interior rather than the exterior of Juliet's bedroom, which the Wife enters by a door at l. 67 after Romeo has left by the window at l. 42. In this method of staging, the Q2 text requires no alteration. For a more detailed account, see Richard Hosley, 'The Use of the Upper Stage in *Romeo and Juliet*,' *Shakespeare Quarterly*, 5 (1954).

III.v.179, 180. *Capulet, Nurse.* The present editor here follows the traditional assignment of speeches, based on the corrections of the Q4 editor and Capell (1768). In Q2 Capulet's 'O—Godigoden!' (l. 179) and the Nurse's 'May not one speak?' (l. 180) are printed on separate lines without speech headings, and the reading *Father* stands as part of the 'text proper' immediately before 'O—Godigoden!' That *Father* is an error for the speech heading *Fa.* (used regularly for Capulet from l. 161 to his exit) is corroborated by the Q1 assignment of 'O—Godigoden!' to Capulet, it being clear from variations in text and spelling that Q2 was not here contaminated by Q1. If the Nurse's heading was missing from Shakespeare's foul papers, the Q2 compositor may have misinterpreted Capulet's heading as text in order to set right the sequence of speech headings.

III.v.185. *Day, night—work, play.* For this reading Q2 has 'Day, night, hour, tide, time, work, play.' Some editors reprint the Q2 text verbatim and others conflate it with the variant text of Q1, but Hoppe's deletion of 'hour, tide, time' provides a good reading with a minimum of alteration and accords with the metrical pattern. Since Shakespeare's foul papers had probably been messily rewritten at this point, the text may well be corrupt beyond editorial redemption.

III.v.190. *lim'd.* Editors usually emend Q2's *laind* to Q1's *trainde*, but the Q2 reading would appear to be the compositor's misreading of *limd*. Compare the Q2 spelling *lims* for 'limbs' at II.2.35 and V.3.37. For some of the Q2 compositor's recurrent misreadings of words with minim letters, see 'The Received Text,' p. 20, n. 28.

IV.i.40. *evening mass.* During the Middle Ages the mass was occasionally performed in the afternoon or evening, and the custom, although prohibited in the 16th century, lingered on in some localities long after the Renaissance.

IV.i.59. *label.* This was a strip of ribbon or parchment attached to the bottom of a deed or other legal document. There was a separate label for each party to the agreement, who impressed his seal in a ball of soft wax enclosing the lower end of the label.

IV.i.65. *umpeer.* This Q2 spelling indicates an Elizabethan pronunciation emphasizing the etymology of 'umpire,' from Middle English *noumpere* and Old French *nompere* (modern *non-pair*, 'peerless, nonpareil'). (The *n* of *noumpere* was transferred to the indefinite article by the same process of 'separation' whereby *a naddre* became *an addre*, 'an adder.')

IV.i.83. *charnel house.* This was a vault or shed attached to the church in which were deposited the bones tossed up in the common practice of digging new graves on the site of old. Compare *Hamlet*, V.1.

IV.i.102. *wanny.* Editors usually emend Q2's *many* to F2's *mealy* or Q4's

paly, but the present editor follows Hoppe in interpreting *many* as the Q2 compositor's misreading of *wany*. an Elizabethan spelling variant of *wanny*.

IV.i.107. *two and forty hours.* Shakespeare may have derived this figure for the duration of Juliet's sleep from Painter's novella, where it is described as 'forty hours at the least.' However, forty-two hours cannot be interpreted literally, being too long a period to allow Juliet to awaken early Thursday morning and too short for Friday. The most satisfactory time scheme of the play dates the beginning of the action Sunday morning. Capulet's feast is held Sunday night (I.4), and Romeo and Juliet part at dawn on Monday (II.1). During Monday the lovers are married (II.5) and Mercutio and Tybalt are killed (III.1). The lovers spend Monday night together, and on Tuesday at dawn Romeo departs for Mantua (III.5). During Tuesday Juliet obtains the potion from the Friar (IV.1) and Capulet enthusiastically advances the marriage from Thursday to Wednesday (IV.2). Tuesday night (a day ahead of the Friar's plan) Juliet drinks the potion (IV.3) and Wednesday morning is discovered apparently dead (IV.4). Late Wednesday afternoon Balthasar notifies Romeo of Juliet's death (V.1), and Romeo returns to Verona that same evening, arriving at the tomb after midnight Wednesday (V.3). Thus the action ends early Thursday morning, Juliet apparently having slept somewhat over twenty-four hours.

IV.ii.SD. *Exeunt* ⟨*Nurse and Juliet*⟩. Act IV illustrates the possibilities in an Elizabethan public playhouse of rapidly alternating the action between forestage and rear stage. At IV.2.38 Juliet and the Nurse exit from the forestage, to be discovered a moment later on the rear stage at the beginning of IV.3. During the potion scene (IV.3) Juliet comes out on the forestage to talk with the Wife and to deliver the potion speech, but at the end of the scene she retires to the rear stage and 'falls upon her bed within the curtains,' which are then closed so that the scene of domestic preparation may be played on the forestage (IV.4.1–31). At IV.4.32 the Nurse opens the curtains of the rear stage, where Juliet is discovered apparently dead (see IV.4.32 cf. n.). The lamentation scene (IV.4.32–175) is then played on the forestage. For an argument that the potion scene and the lamentation scene cannot be played upon the upper stage, see 'The Use of the Upper Stage in *Romeo and Juliet*.'

IV.iii.48. *mandrakes.* The *mandrake* or *mandragora* is a plant with opiate properties (see *Othello*, III.3.373), the root of which is often forked so as to resemble the legs of a human being. It had fabulous virtues in magic and medicine, and when pulled from the earth was supposed to shriek and cause hearers to go mad or die. For this reason dogs were supposedly harnessed to draw it from the ground.

IV.iv.14. *hood.* This would appear to be a variant spelling of 'hud' (cover, shell, husk), used metaphorically in the sense of 'an empty person.' Compare the Q2 spelling *hudwincki* for 'hoodwink'd' at I.4.4. Some editors, interpreting *hood* as the suffix indicating generality as in 'womanhood,' hyphenate *jealous hood* and gloss it as 'jealousy,' the abstract for the concrete.

IV.iv.20. *Peter.* In Q1 this name appears as *Will*, presumably because Will Kemp had played the part of Peter (see note on IV.4.134). The present editor is indebted to Mr. Cyrus Hoy for calling his attention to this variant.

IV.iv.32. *Nurse.* At this point the traditional scene division again obscures the continuity of action and fluidity of scene in an Elizabethan public theater, and has induced editors to direct the Nurse offstage at IV.4.31, only to re-enter immediately at l. 32. The Nurse, however, remains on the forestage and after Capulet's exit at l. 31 opens the curtains of the rear stage, where Juliet is discovered lying on her bed; and thus the scene of the forestage changes from a location outside Juliet's bedroom to one (in conjunction with the rear stage) inside it. For a more detailed account, see 'The Use of the Upper Stage in *Romeo and Juliet*.'

IV.iv.38. *set up his rest.* This expression, from the card game of primero, means literally 'staked his reserve.' There is probably also a pun on 'wrest,' wresting instrument, tuning key. See Kökeritz, *Shakespeare's Pronunciation*, p. 140.

IV.iv.114. *rosemary.* Being an evergreen, rosemary symbolizes remembrance and was accordingly used at both weddings and funerals. See Philip Williams, 'The Rosemary Theme in *Romeo and Juliet*,' *Modern Language Notes*, 68 (1953), 400–3. Compare II.3.185 and IV.4.SD.

IV.iv.SD. *They all ... Musicians.* Editors usually follow the Q4 editor in directing the Musicians to enter with Paris and the Friar at IV.4.67. However, the Q1 directions at l. 130 support the evidence of Q2, where *Exeunt* is apparently designed for Capulet, the Wife, Paris, and the Friar, but the singular *manet* for the Nurse, indicating that she is the only actor to remain on stage at IV.4.130 and thus that the Musicians do not enter until this point. See Richard Hosley, 'A Stage Direction in *Romeo and Juliet*,' *The Times Literary Supplement*, June 13, 1952, p. 391.

IV.iv.SD. *Peter.* The reading of Q2 indicates that the role of Peter was probably played by Will Kemp, the famous comic actor of Shakespeare's company. The name 'Will' is also used for Peter in Q1 (see note on IV.4.17). From speech

headings in *Much Ado About Nothing* it appears that Kemp also played the part of Dogberry.

IV.iv.139, 140. *'My Heart is Full'.* Editors usually follow the Q4 editor in emending this Q2 reading to 'My heart is full of woe,' which has been identified as a line from the anonymous song 'A Pleasant New Ballad of Two Lovers.' This emendation may be correct, but it has the appearance of a sophistication by the Q4 editor. The present editor reprints the substance of the Q2 text and punctuation, interpreting 'My heart is Full' as the name of the tune (real or imaginary) which Peter's 'heart itself' is playing. This is, to 'comfort' him, Peter wishes the Musicians to play 'Heart's Ease,' a 'merry dump' which will counteract his heart's sorrowful tune. Peter's use of the term 'dump' is of course a malapropism.

IV.iv.150. *re . . . fa . . . you.* With *re* Peter quibbles on 'ray' (beray, befoul and with *fa* on 'fay' (cleanse, polish). In this context 'ray' and 'fay' probably also mean 'to beat.' See Kökeritz, *Shakespeare's Pronunciation,* pp. 105–6.

IV.iv.157-159. *When . . . sound.* These lines are from 'In Commendation of Music,' a song by Richard Edwards printed in a popular Elizabethan miscellany, *The Paradise of Dainty Devices* (1576).

V.i.15. *fares my Juliet.* The Q2 reading 'How doth my Lady Juliet' would appear to involve the compositor's duplication of part of the immediately preceding line, 'How doth my Lady'; and if so, Q1, in here reading 'How fares my Juliet,' probably preserves the text of Shakespeare's foul papers. See Sir Walter Greg, *Principles of Emendation in Shakespeare,* British Academy Shakespeare Lecture, London, 1928, p. 52, n. 28.

V.i.24. *in.* This Q2 spelling indicates an unstressed Elizabethan pronunciation of 'e'en.'

V.ii.SD. *Enter Friar John.* This Q1 direction and the Q2 dialogue of ll. 1–3 suggest that Q2's 'Enter Lawrence' after l. 1 is the book-keeper's correction in Shakespeare's foul papers of the original direction before l. 1, 'Enter Friar John to Friar Lawrence.' The book-keeper, however, apparently did not delete the last three words of the original direction. In an Elizabethan public playhouse John and Lawrence enter 'severally' on the forestage, representing the Friar's cell. Compare with note on III.3.1 SD.

V.ii.6. *associate.* It was generally required that a friar should not travel unless accompanied by a fellow-member of his order.

V.ii.11. *Seal'd up the doors.* This was a frequent occurrence during the London plagues of Shakespeare's time.

V.iii.SD. *Balthasar.* The erroneous Q2 designation of Romeo's servant as Peter may be due to the servant's being so named in *Romeus and Juliet* (ultimately after the Italian Pietro, Juliet's servant in da Porto but Romeo's in Bandello), or to Will Kemp's doubling in the parts of Balthasar and the Nurse's servant Peter, whose character is Shakespeare's invention. See note on IV.4.129 SD.

V.iii.103. *shall I believe.* The Q2 phrase 'I will believe' is omitted from the present edition as a first thought which had not been deleted from Shakespeare's foul papers and which was therefore printed in Q2 immediately before its revision, 'Shall I believe.' Other short undeleted first thoughts omitted from the present edition are *Cozen* (III.1.147), *And* (III.2.9), *Rauenous* (III.2.78), *all naught* (III.2.89), and *O* (V.3.202). See 'The Received Text,' p. 28 and n. 43.

V.iii.108. *pallet.* Editors usually follow the Q3 editor in emending Q2's *pallat* to *pallace.* However, the Q2 reading is a common Elizabethan spelling variant of *pallet,* an image which supports the theme that Juliet's wedding bed is indeed her grave. Compare 1.4.261, III.5.144, IV.4.71 and V.3.28.

V.iii.SD. *Citizens.* This addition to Q2's direction 'Enter Prince' is suggested both by Q1's 'with others' and by the Wife's reference in Q2 to people running toward the monument (ll. 201–203) Moreover, the appearance of the Citizens at this point has a symbolic value which rounds out the theme of civil disorder. Here and at III.1.144 the Prince is presumably attended by the Train mentioned at I.1.SD.

V.iii.SD. *Enter Capels.* In Q2 this stage direction is duplicated after l. 201 as 'Enter Capulet and his Wife.' The first direction is presumably the book-keeper's correction of the second, Shakespeare's erroneously located original direction.

V.iii.228. *Seal up.* G. B. Harrison suggests that at this point the curtains of the rear stage are closed to conceal the three bodies (*Shakespeare: Major Plays and the Sonnets,* New York, 1948). In the modern theater such concealment is unnecessary, since at this point the play is usually cut to its closing speeches, around V.3.303.

V.iii.309. *jointure.* This is the marriage portion or dowry settled on a bride by the bridegroom's family against the event of her husband's prior decease.

V.iii.312. *ray.* Editors usually emend Q2's *raie* to *raise,* the reading of Brooke's *Romeus and Juliet,* which in turn would seem to be supported by Q1's *erect.* However, since Romeo's statue is to 'lie' by the side of Juliet's (l. 316), it is clear that in Shakespeare's play the proposed 'statues' are high relief figures on sarcophagi.

The Tragedy of Julius Caesar

Edited by
LAWRENCE MASON

Dramatis Personae

JULIUS CAESAR
OCTAVIUS CAESAR ⎫
MARCUS ANTONIUS ⎬ *Triumvirs after the*
M. AEMILIUS LEPIDUS ⎭ *Death of Julius Caesar*
CICERO ⎫
PUBLIUS ⎬ *Senators*
POPILUS LENA ⎭
MARCUS BRUTUS ⎫
CAIUS CASSIUS
CASCA
TREBONIUS ⎬ *Conspirators against*
LIGARIUS   *Julius Caesar*
DECIUS BRUTUS
METELLUS CIMBER
CINNA ⎭
FLAVIUS AND MARULLUS, *Tribunes*
ARTEMIDORUS, *a Sophist of Cnidos*
A SOOTHSAYER
CINNA, *a Poet*
ANOTHER POET

LUCILIUS ⎫
TITINIUS
MESSALA ⎬ *Friends to Brutus and Cassius*
YOUNG CATO
VOLUMNIUS ⎭
VARRO ⎫
CLITUS
CLAUDIUS
STRATO ⎬ *Servants to Brutus*
LUCIUS
DARDANIUS ⎭
PINDARUS, *Servant to Cassius*

CALPURNIA, *Wife to Caesar*
PORTIA, *Wife to Brutus*

COMMONERS, OR PLEBEIANS, OF ROME; SENATORS,
    GUARDS, ATTENDANTS, ETC.

SCENE—*Act I-IV, Scene i, at Rome; Act IV, Scenes ii
    and iii, near Sardis, in Asia Minor; Act V, the plains
    near Philippi, in Macedonia.*

The Tragedy of Julius Cæsar

INTRODUCTION

SOURCES OF THE PLAY

There were, of course, earlier plays in Elizabethan England on the subject of Cæsar's career (Henslowe's Diary attests their popularity in the 1590s) and they may well have influenced Shakespeare's work. For a careful study of these possibilities, see H. M. Ayres' 'Shakespeare's *Julius Cæsar* in the Light of Some Other Versions' (Pub. Mod. Lang. Assoc. of America, 1910). Dr. A. Boecker also has put forward an elaborate effort to establish Shakespeare's indebtedness to Orlando Pescetti's 'Il Cesare,' a tragedy running to nearly four thousand lines of verse and published in Verona in 1594, 2d ed. 1604 ('A Probable Italian Source of Shakespeare's *Julius Cæsar*,' N. Y. Univ. Dissertation, 1913). But after all due allowances have been made for this sort of influence, and for the less important possibility of indebtedness to classic authors such as Appian, it still remains true that the great source of the play is 'The Lives of the Noble Grecians and Romanes, Compared together by that grave learned Philosopher and Historiographer, Plutarke of Chæronea: Translated out of Greeke into French by Iames Amyot . . . and out of French into Englishe, by *Thomas North*. Imprinted at London . . . 1579,' 2d ed. 1595, 3d ed. 1603. To this famous and splendid monument of Elizabethan prose Shakespeare owes the whole action or plot of the play, the separate incidents, many personal details of characterization, some few errors in fact, and occasional verbal suggestions: but his supreme skill in selecting, rejecting, combining, and arranging historical material has rarely been shown to better advantage than in his handling of the three 'Lives' on which he drew,—those, namely, of Cæsar, Brutus, and Antony; while his power of poetic and dramatic transformation will appear upon comparing Act III, Scene i with the following typical passage from North:

'For these things, they may seem to come by chance: but the place where the murther was prepared, and where the Senate were assembled, and where also there stood up an image of *Pompey* dedicated by him selfe amongest other ornaments which he gave unto the Theater: all these were manifest proofes, that it was the ordinaunce of some god that made this treason to be executed, specially in that very place. It is also reported that Cassius (though otherwise hee did favour the doctrine of *Epicurus*) beholding the image of *Pompey*, before they entred into the action of their traiterous enterprise; hee did softly call upon it to aide him. But the instant danger of the present time, taking away his former reason, did sodainly put him into a furious passion, and made him like a man halfe besides him selfe. Now *Antonius*, that was a faithfull friend to *Cæsar*, and a valiant man besides of his handes, him *Decius Brutus Albinus* entertained out of the Senate house, having begunne a long tale of set purpose. So *Cæsar* comming into the house, all the Senate stood up on their feete to doe him honor. The part of Brutus company and confederates stoode round about Cæsars chayre, and part of them

also came towardes him, as though they made sute with *Metellus Cimber*, to call home his brother againe from banishment: and thus prosecuting still their sute, they followed *Cæsar*, till hee was set in his chaire. Who, denying their petitions, and being offended with them one after an other, because the more they were denied the more they pressed upon him, and were the earnester with him: *Metellus* at length, taking his gowne with both his hands, pulled it over his necke, which was the signe given the confederats to set upon him. Then *Casca*, behinde him, strake him in the necke with his sword, howbeit the wound was not great nor mortall, because it seemed the feare of such a devilish attempt did amaze him and take his strength from him, that he killed him not at the first blow. But *Cæsar* turning straight unto him, caught hold of his sword, and held it hard: & they both cried out, *Cæsar* in Latin: O vile traitor Casca, what doest thou? And Casca in Greeke to his brother, brother, helpe mee. At the beginning of this stur, they that were present, not knowing of the conspiracy, were so amazed with the horrible sight they saw: they had no power to flie, neither to helpe him, not so much, as once to make an outcry. They on the other side that had conspired his death compassed him in on everie side with their swords drawen in their hands, that *Cæsar* turned him no where but hee was stricken at by some, and still had naked swords in his face, and was hacked and mangled among them, as a wilde beast taken of hunters. For it was agreede among them, that every man should give him a wound, because all their parts should be in this murther: and then *Brutus* gave him one. . . . Men report also, that *Cæsar* did still defende him selfe against the rest, running every way with his body: but when he saw *Brutus* with his sword drawen in his hand, then he pulled his gowne over his head, and made no more resistaunce, and was driven either casually, or purposedly, by the counsell of the conspirators, against the base whereupon Pompeys image stoode, which ran all of a goare bloud till he was slain. Thus it seemed that the image tooke just revenge of Pompeys enemy, being throwen downe on the ground at his feete, and yeelding up his ghost there, for the number of wounds he had upon him. For it is reported, that he had three and twenty wounds upon his body: and divers of the conspirators did hurt themselves, striking one body with so many blowes. When *Cæsar* was slaine, the Senate (though *Brutus* stood in the middest amongst them, as though he would have saied somewhat touching this fact) presently ran out of the house, and flying, filled all the city with marvellous feare and tumult.' (From 'The Life of Julius Cæsar,' North's 2d ed., 1595, as quoted by Furness, pp. 300, 301.)

THE HISTORY OF THE PLAY

The earliest extant version of Shakespeare's *Julius Cæsar* is that found in the famous First Folio collected edition of his plays, published in 1623, which therefore necessarily forms the basis of all modern texts; for the only known Quarto editions belong to the late Restoration period and so, unfortunately, have little critical value for the solution of the problems presented by the original text. It seems fairly certain now that *Julius Cæsar* was written and first produced in 1599, for on the twenty-first of September in that year a German traveller witnessed a performance of what was presumably Shakespeare's play at the Globe Theatre (cf. 'Londoner Theater und Schauspiele im Jahre 1599,' G. Binz, *Anglia*, xxii, 456, 1899). The next performance that we can date seems to have taken place at court early in 1613, the next at St. James', January 31, 1636-7, and the next at the Cockpit, November 13, 1638; but that the popularity of the play was far greater than these meagre records suggest is attested by various kinds of evidence, from Henslowe's effort to capitalize its success by producing a rival Cæsar play, in 1602, to Digges' striking tribute prefixed to the First Folio.[1]

After the Restoration, *Julius Cæsar* is one of the three Shakespearean dramas listed by Downes ('Roscius Anglicanus,' 1708) among the 'Principal Old Stock Plays' given by Killigrew's company in the 1660s. Charles Hart (d. 1683), grandson of Shakespeare's sister Joan, was the great Brutus of this period, and was succeeded by the famous Thomas Betterton (1635?-1710); it is Betterton's cast that is given in the six Quarto editions published between 1684 and 1691, evidently printed as playgoers' guides (cf. 'Quarto Editions of *Julius Cæsar*,' by Miss H. C. Bartlett, *The Library*, 1913).

It is worthy of note that *Julius Cæsar* is one of the few Shakespearean plays that escaped mutilation at the hands of so-called adapters or revisers, during the seventeenth and eighteenth centuries, for the abortive efforts in 1719 and 1722 had no success or significance (cf. F. W. Kilbourne's 'Alterations and Adaptations of Shakespeare,' Boston, 1906). A plausible sketch by Miss C.

Porter ('How Shakespeare Set and Struck the Scene for *Julius Cæsar* in 1599,' *Mod. Lang. Notes,* 1916) gives a pleasant glimpse into Elizabethan stage procedure, and William Winter's 'Shakespeare on the Stage' (Second Series, 1915) supplies many illuminating hints about the stage 'business' in succeeding and modern productions; while Brander Matthews ('Shaksperian Stage Traditions' in 'Shaksperian Studies,' Columbia Univ. Press, 1916) gives a spirited picture of the Meiningen company's remarkable presentation of the Forum scene and Antony's oration.

In the early eighteenth century Robert Wilks (1665?-1732), the friend of Farquhar, was a brilliant Antony, while Barton Booth (1681-1733) and James Quin (1693-1766) excelled as Brutus. Garrick never acted in *Julius Cæsar*, but his rival, Spranger Barry (1719-1777), was a most moving Antony. The famous Peg Woffington (1714?-1760) appeared as Portia in several performances about 1750, but because the part is such a minor one it has not been taken by many great actresses since then. Coming down to the nineteenth century, we find all the greatest actors appearing in the play. The Kembles and Young, Macready and Davenport, Wallack, Charles Kean, J. B. Booth, Samuel Phelps, and Beerbohm Tree have all presented one or more of the four leading rôles. The first American performance was given at Charleston, S. C., April 20, 1774. Edwin Forrest and John Edward McCullough are also associated with the play, as are Tyrone Power, William Faversham, and Robert Bruce Mantell in our own time; but the crowning achievement in America's production of *Julius Cæsar* will always be the magnificent double triumph of Edwin Booth and Lawrence Barrett, in the '60s, '70s, and '80s, with honorable mention, perhaps, of Richard Mansfield's sombre portrayal of Brutus' tragic loneliness, beginning October 14, 1902. It is not easy nowadays to realize the power and effectiveness attributed by tradition to these great players of the past, but fortunately it is still possible to gain some impression of Edwin Booth's thrilling personal magnetism and manifest genius from the inspired portrait by John S. Sargent in the Players' Club, New York City.

---

1 'The Shakespeare Allusion-Book' lists ten (should be eleven? Digges, p. 318, is not indexed) references to *Julius Cæsar* down to 1649, and twenty-five more between 1650 and 1700.

ACT FIRST   SCENE FIRST

[Rome. A Street]
Enter Flavius, Marullus, and certain Commoners over the Stage.

Flav. Hence! home, you idle creatures, get you home:
Is this a holiday? What! know you not,
Being mechanical, you ought not walk
Upon a labouring day without the sign
Of your profession? Speak, what trade art thou?   *5*
    Car. Why, sir, a carpenter.
    Mar. Where is thy leather apron, and thy rule?
What dost thou with thy best apparel on?
You, sir, what trade are you?
    Cob. Truly, sir, in respect of a fine workman,   *10*
I am but, as you would say, a cobbler.
    Mar. But what trade art thou? Answer me directly.
    Cob. A trade, sir, that, I hope, I may use with a safe
conscience; which is, indeed, sir, a mender of bad soles.
    Mar. What trade, thou knave? thou naughty knave,   *15*
what trade?
    Cob. Nay, I beseech you, sir, be not out with me:
yet, if you be out, sir, I can mend you.
    Mar. What mean'st thou by that? Mend me, thou
saucy fellow?   *20*
    Cob. Why, sir, cobble you.
    Flav. Thou art a cobbler, art thou?
    Cob. Truly, sir, all that I live by is with the awl: I meddle
with no tradesman's matters, nor women's matters, but with
awl. I am, indeed, sir, a surgeon to old shoes; when they   *25*
are in great danger, I recover them. As proper men as ever
trod upon neat's leather have gone upon my handiwork.
    Flav. But wherefore art not in thy shop to-day?
Why dost thou lead these men about the streets?
    Cob. Truly, sir, to wear out their shoes, to get myself   *30*
into more work. But, indeed, sir, we make holiday to see
Cæsar and to rejoice in his triumph.
    Mar. Wherefore rejoice? What conquest brings he home?
What tributaries follow him to Rome
To grace in captive bonds his chariot wheels?   *35*
You blocks, you stones, you worse than senseless things!
O you hard hearts, you cruel men of Rome,
Knew you not Pompey? Many a time and oft
Have you climb'd up to walls and battlements,
To towers and windows, yea, to chimney-tops,   *40*
Your infants in your arms, and there have sat
The livelong day, with patient expectation,
To see great Pompey pass the streets of Rome:
And when you saw his chariot but appear,
Have you not made a universal shout,   *45*
That Tiber trembled underneath her banks,
To hear the replication of your sounds.
Made in her concave shores?
And do you now put on your best attire?
And do you now cull out a holiday?   *50*
And do you now strew flowers in his way,

That comes in triumph over Pompey's blood?
Be gone!
Run to your houses, fall upon your knees,
Pray to the gods to intermit the plague   *55*
That needs must light on this ingratitude.
    Flav. Go, go, good countrymen, and for this fault
Assemble all the poor men of your sort;
Draw them to Tiber banks, and weep your tears
Into the channel, till the lowest stream   *60*
Do kiss the most exalted shores of all.

             Exeunt all the Commoners.
See whether their basest metal be not mov'd;
They vanish tongue-tied in their guiltiness.
Go you down that way towards the Capitol;
This way will I. Disrobe the images   *65*
If you do find them deck'd with ceremonies.
    Mar. May we do so?
You know it is the feast of Lupercal.
    Flav. It is no matter; let no images
Be hung with Cæsar's trophies. I'll about   *70*
And drive away the vulgar from the streets:
So do you too where you perceive them thick.
These growing feathers pluck'd from Cæsar's wing
Will make him fly an ordinary pitch,
Who else would soar above the view of men   *75*
And keep us all in servile fearfulness.   *Exeunt.*

SCENE SECOND

[A Public Place]
Enter [in solemn procession, with music] Cæsar, Antony for the
course, Calpurnia, Portia, Decius, Cicero, Brutus, Cassius, Casca,
[a great crowd following, among them] a Soothsayer: after them
Marullus and Flavius.

    Cæs. Calpurnia!
    Casca.   Peace, ho! Cæsar speaks.   *[Music ceases.]*
    Cæs.   Calpurnia!
    Cal. Here, my lord.
    Cæs. Stand you directly in Antonius' way   *5*
When he doth run his course. Antonius!
    Ant. Cæsar, my lord.
    Cæs. Forget not, in your speed, Antonius,
To touch Calpurnia; for our elders say,
The barren, touched in this holy chase,   *10*
Shake off their sterile curse.
    Ant.   I shall remember:
When Cæsar says 'Do this,' it is perform'd.
    Cæs. Set on; and leave no ceremony out.   *[Music.]*
    Sooth. Cæsar!   *15*
    Cæs. Ha! Who calls?
    Casca. Bid every noise be still: peace yet again!
             [Music ceases.]
    Cæs. Who is it in the press that calls on me?
I hear a tongue, shriller than all the music,
Cry 'Cæsar.' Speak; Cæsar is turn'd to hear.   *20*

SCENE ONE S. d. Marullus; *cf. n.*   **3 mechanical:** *of the laboring class*   **walk:** *go about the streets*   **4, 5 sign . . . profession:** *artisan's garb and implements*   **10 in respect of:** *in comparison with*   **11 cobbler:** *bungler*   **12 directly:** *plainly, without evasion*   **15 naughty:** *wicked, worthless*   **17 out:** *out of temper*   **18 be out:** *have hole in shoe*   **23 with awl;** *cf. n.*   **26 proper:** *goodly, worthy*   **27 neat's leather:** *cowhide*   **32 triumph;** *cf. n.*   **45 her;** *cf. n.*   **46 replication:** *echo*   **50 cull out:** *choose this as*

52 Pompey's blood; *cf. n. on line 32*   **66 ceremonies:** *ceremonial trappings*   **68 Lupercal;** *cf. n.*   **74 pitch:** *height, as of a hawk's flight*   **8 in . . . speed:** *as you run*   **11 sterile curse:** *affliction of barrenness*   **14 Set on:** *proceed, advance*

Sooth. Beware the ides of March.

Cæs.   What man is that?

Bru. A soothsayer bids you beware the ides of March.

Cæs. Set him before me; let me see his face.

Cas. Fellow, come from the throng; look upon Cæsar.   25

Cæs. What sayst thou to me now? Speak once again.

Sooth. Beware the ides of March.

Cæs. He is a dreamer; let us leave him: pass.

               Sennet. Exeunt all but Brutus and Cassius.

Cas. Will you go see the order of the course?

Bru. Not I.   30

Cas. I pray you, do.

Bru. I am not gamesome: I do lack some part
Of that quick spirit that is in Antony.
Let me not hinder, Cassius, your desires;
I'll leave you.   35

Cas. Brutus, I do observe you now of late:
I have not from your eyes that gentleness
And show of love as I was wont to have:
You bear too stubborn and too strange a hand
Over your friend that loves you.   40

Bru.   Cassius,
Be not deceiv'd: if I have veil'd my look,
I turn the trouble of my countenance
Merely upon myself. Vexed I am
Of late with passions of some difference,   45
Conceptions only proper to myself,
Which give some soil perhaps to my behaviours;
But let not therefore my good friends be griev'd,—
Among which number, Cassius, be you one,—
Nor construe any further my neglect,   50
Than that poor Brutus, with himself at war,
Forgets the shows of love to other men.

Cas. Then, Brutus, I have much mistook your passion;
By means whereof this breast of mine hath buried
Thoughts of great value, worthy cogitations.   55
Tell me, good Brutus, can you see your face?

Bru. No, Cassius; for the eye sees not itself,
But by reflection, by some other things.

Cas. 'Tis just:
And it is very much lamented, Brutus,   60
That you have no such mirrors as will turn
Your hidden worthiness into your eye,
That you might see your shadow. I have heard
Where many of the best respect in Rome,—
Except immortal Cæsar,—speaking of Brutus,   65
And groaning underneath this age's yoke,
Have wish'd that noble Brutus had his eyes.

Bru. Into what dangers would you lead me, Cassius,
That you would have me seek into myself
For that which is not in me?   70

Cas. Therefore, good Brutus, be prepar'd to hear;
And, since you know you cannot see yourself
So well as by reflection, I, your glass,

Will modestly discover to yourself
That of yourself which you yet know not of.   75
And be not jealous on me, gentle Brutus:
Were I a common laugher, or did use
To stale with ordinary oaths my love
To every new protester; if you know
That I do fawn on men and hug them hard,   80
And after scandal them; or if you know
That I profess myself in banqueting
To all the rout, then hold me dangerous.

                        Flourish, and shout.

Bru. What means this shouting? I do fear the people
Choose Cæsar for their king.   85

Cas.   Ay, do you fear it?
Then must I think you would not have it so.

Bru. I would not, Cassius; yet I love him well.
But wherefore do you hold me here so long?
What is it that you would impart to me?   90
If it be aught toward the general good,
Set honour in one eye and death i' the other,
And I will look on both indifferently;
For let the gods so speed me as I love
The name of honour more than I fear death.   95

Cas. I know that virtue to be in you, Brutus,
As well as I do know your outward favour.
Well, honour is the subject of my story.
I cannot tell what you and other men
Think of this life; but, for my single self,   100
I had as lief not be as live to be
In awe of such a thing as I myself.
I was born free as Cæsar; so were you:
We both have fed as well, and we can both
Endure the winter's cold as well as he: 105
For once, upon a raw and gusty day,
The troubled Tiber chafing with her shores,
Cæsar said to me, 'Dar'st thou, Cassius, now
Leap in with me into this angry flood,
And swim to yonder point?' Upon the word,   110
Accoutred as I was, I plunged in
And bade him follow; so, indeed he did.
The torrent roar'd, and we did buffet it
With lusty sinews, throwing it aside
And stemming it with hearts of controversy;   115
But ere we could arrive the point propos'd,
Cæsar cried, 'Help me, Cassius, or I sink!'
I, as Æneas, our great ancestor,
Did from the flames of Troy upon his shoulder
The old Anchises bear, so from the waves of Tiber 120
Did I the tired Cæsar. And this man
Is now become a god, and Cassius is
A wretched creature and must bend his body
If Cæsar carelessly but nod on him.
He had a fever when he was in Spain,   125
And when the fit was on him, I did mark
How he did shake; 'tis true, this god did shake;
His coward lips did from their colour fly,

---

21 ides of March: *March fifteenth*   **S. d. Sennet:** *trumpet signal for procession to move*   **29 order of the course:** *progress of the running*   **32 gamesome:** *fond of sport*   **33 quick:** *lively*   **36 do observe:** *have had occasion to notice*   **37 that:** *the same*   **39, 40 handle your friend too stiffly and distantly*   **42 Be not deceiv'd:** *do not misjudge me*   **44 Merely:** *altogether*   **45 of . . . difference:** *conflicting*   **46 proper:** *belonging, relating*   **47 soil:** *blemish*   **50 construe:** *read meaning into*   **54 By . . . whereof:** *because of which mistake*   **59 just:** *true, right*   **64 respect:** *standing*   **67 had . . . eyes:** *had his eyes about him*

76 jealous on: *suspicious of*   **78 stale:** *make cheap*   **ordinary:** *customary*   **79 protester:** *loud-mouthed pretender*   **81 scandal:** *defame*   **82 profess myself:** *make protestations*   **S. d. Flourish:** *trumpet call*   **93 indifferently:** *impartially*   **94 speed:** *favor, prosper*   **97 favour:** *appearance*   **107 with:** *against*   **111 Accoutred:** *clad*   **115 hearts of controversy:** *contesting courage*   **128 his lips forsook their normal redness as cowardly soldiers forsake their flag*

And that same eye whose bend doth awe the world
Did lose his lustre; I did hear him groan;   *130*
Ay, and that tongue of his that bade the Romans
Mark him and write his speeches in their books,
Alas! it cried, 'Give me some drink, Titinius',
As a sick girl. Ye gods, it doth amaze me,
A man of such a feeble temper should   *135*
So get the start of the majestic world,
And bear the palm alone.   *Shout. Flourish.*
    Bru.   Another general shout!
I do believe that these applauses are
For some new honours that are heap'd on Cæsar.   *140*
    Cas. Why, man, he doth bestride the narrow world
Like a Colossus; and we petty men
Walk under his huge legs, and peep about
To find ourselves dishonourable graves.
Men at some time are masters of their fates: *145*
The fault, dear Brutus, is not in our stars,
But in ourselves, that we are underlings.
Brutus and Cæsar: what should be in that 'Cæsar'?
Why should that name be sounded more than yours?
Write them together, yours is as fair a name;   *150*
Sound them, it doth become the mouth as well;
Weigh them, it is as heavy; conjure with 'em,
'Brutus' will start a spirit as soon as 'Cæsar'.
Now, in the names of all the gods at once,
Upon what meat doth this our Cæsar feed,   *155*
That he is grown so great? Age, thou art sham'd!
Rome, thou hast lost the breed of noble bloods!
When went there by an age, since the great flood,
But it was fam'd with more than with one man?
When could they say, till now, that talk'd of Rome,   *160*
That her wide walks encompass'd but one man?
Now is it Rome indeed and room enough,
When there is in it but one only man.
O, you and I have heard our fathers say,
There was a Brutus once that would have brook'd   *165*
Th' eternal devil to keep his state in Rome
As easily as a king.
    Bru. That you do love me, I am nothing jealous;
What you would work me to, I have some aim:
How I have thought of this and of these times,   *170*
I shall recount hereafter; for this present,
I would not, so with love I might entreat you,
Be any further mov'd. What you have said
I will consider; what you have to say
I will with patience hear, and find a time   *175*
Both meet to hear and answer such high things.
Till then, my noble friend, chew upon this:
Brutus had rather be a villager
Than to repute himself a son of Rome
Under these hard conditions as this time   *180*
Is like to lay upon us.
    Cas.   I am glad

That my weak words have struck but thus much show
Of fire from Brutus.
    Bru. The games are done and Cæsar is returning.   *185*
    Cas. As they pass by, pluck Casca by the sleeve,
And he will, after his sour fashion, tell you
What hath proceeded worthy note to-day.

          Enter Cæsar and his Train.

    Bru. I will do so. But, look you, Cassius,
The angry spot doth glow on Cæsar's brow,   *190*
And all the rest look like a chidden train:
Calpurnia's cheek is pale, and Cicero
Looks with such ferret and such fiery eyes
As we have seen him in the Capitol,
Being cross'd in conference by some senators.   *195*
    Cas. Casca will tell us what the matter is.
    Cæs. Antonius!
    Ant. Cæsar.
    Cæs. Let me have men about me that are fat;
Sleek-headed men and such as sleep o' nights.   *200*
Yond Cassius has a lean and hungry look;
He thinks too much: such men are dangerous.
    Ant. Fear him not, Cæsar, he's not dangerous;
He is a noble Roman, and well given.
    Cæs. Would he were fatter! but I fear him not: *205*
Yet if my name were liable to fear,
I do not know the man I should avoid
So soon as that spare Cassius. He reads much;
He is a great observer, and he looks
Quite through the deeds of men; he loves no plays,   *210*
As thou dost, Antony; he hears no music;
Seldom he smiles, and smiles in such a sort
As if he mock'd himself, and scorn'd his spirit
That could be mov'd to smile at anything.
Such men as he be never at heart's ease   *215*
Whiles they behold a greater than themselves,
And therefore are they very dangerous.
I rather tell thee what is to be fear'd
Than what I fear, for always I am Cæsar.
Come on my right hand, for this ear is deaf,   *220*
And tell me truly what thou think'st of him.
          Sennet. Exeunt Cæsar and his Train [except Casca].
    Casca. You pull'd me by the cloak; would you speak
with me?
    Bru. Ay, Casca; tell us what hath chanc'd to-day,
That Cæsar looks so sad.   *225*
    Casca. Why, you were with him, were you not?
    Bru. I should not then ask Casca what had chanc'd.
    Casca. Why, there was a crown offered him; and, being
offered him, he put it by with the back of his hand, thus;
and then the people fell a-shouting.   *230*
    Bru. What was the second noise for?
    Casca.   Why, for that too.
    Cas. They shouted thrice: what was the last cry for?
    Casca. Why, for that too.
    Bru. Was the crown offered him thrice?   *235*
    Casca. Ay, marry, was 't, and he put it by thrice, every

129 bend: *glance*   **130 his:** *its*   **135 temper:** *constitution*   **136 get the start of:** *outstrip*
(in the race of life)   **142 Colossus:** *gigantic statue astride the mouth of the harbor of
Rhodes*   **157 lost . . . bloods:** *lost the art of breeding noble persons*   **158 the great flood:**
Deucalion's, not Noah's   **159 fam'd with:** *famous for*   **161 walks;** *cf. n.*   **162 Rome:**
then often pronounced 'Room'   **165 Brutus:** *Lucius Junius, who expelled the Tarquins, ca.
510 B. C.*   **brook'd:** *tolerated*   **166 state:** *throne, rulership*   **168 nothing:** *not at all*
jealous: *doubtful*   **169 work:** *induce*   **aim:** *inkling*   **172 so:** *if; cf. n.*   **173 mov'd:**
persuaded, urged   **176 meet:** *fit*   **177 chew:** *ponder*   **180 as:** *such as*

193 ferret: *ferret-like, i.e., small and red*   **195 conference:** *debate*   **200 Sleek-headed:**
unruffled by deep plotting   **204 well given:** *well disposed*   **206 my name;** *cf. n.*   **211**
he . . . music; *cf. n.*   **216 Whiles:** *whilst, while*   **225 sad:** *grave, serious*   **236 marry:**
properly an invocation of the Virgin

time gentler than other; and at every putting-by mine
honest neighbours shouted.

Cas. Who offered him the crown?

Casca.   Why, Antony.   240

Bru. Tell us the manner of it, gentle Casca.

Casca. I can as well be hanged as tell the manner of it: it
was mere foolery; I did not mark it. I saw Mark Antony offer
him a crown; yet 'twas not a crown neither, 'twas one of these
coronets; and, as I told you, he put it by once; but, for all *245*
that, to my thinking, he would fain have had it. Then he
offered it to him again; then he put it by again; but, to my
thinking, he was very loath to lay his fingers off it. And then
he offered it the third time; he put it the third time by; and
still as he refused it the rabblement shouted and clapped   *250*
their chopped hands, and threw up their sweaty night-caps, and
uttered such a deal of stinking breath because Cæsar refused
the crown, that it had almost choked Cæsar; for he swounded
and fell down at it: and for mine own part, I durst not laugh,
for fear of opening my lips and receiving the bad air.   *255*

Cas. But soft, I pray you: what! did Cæsar swound?

Casca. He fell down in the market-place, and foamed at
mouth, and was speechless.

Bru. 'Tis very like: he hath the falling-sickness.

Cas. No, Cæsar hath it not; but you, and I,   *260*
And honest Casca, we have the falling-sickness.

Casca. I know not what you mean by that; but I am sure
Cæsar fell down. If the tag-rag people did not clap him and
hiss him, according as he pleased and displeased them, as they
use to do the players in the theatre, I am no true man.   *265*

Bru. What said he, when he came unto himself?

Casca. Marry, before he fell down, when he perceiv'd the
common herd was glad he refused the crown, he plucked me
ope his doublet and offered them his throat to cut. An I had
been a man of any occupation, if I would not have taken him   *270*
at a word, I would I might go to hell among the rogues. And
so he fell. When he came to himself again, he said, if he had
done or said anything amiss, he desired their worships to think
it was his infirmity. Three or four wenches, where I stood,
cried, 'Alas, good soul!' and forgave him with all their hearts: *275*
but there's no heed to be taken of them; if Cæsar had
stabbed their mothers, they would have done no less.

Bru. And after that he came, thus sad, away?

Casca. Ay.

Cas. Did Cicero say anything?   *280*

Casca. Ay, he spoke Greek.

Cas. To what effect?

Casca. Nay, an I tell you that, I'll ne'er look you i' the
face again; but those that understood him smiled at one
another and shook their heads; but, for mine own part,   *285*
it was Greek to me. I could tell you more news too; Marullus
and Flavius, for pulling scarfs off Cæsar's images, are put to
silence. Fare you well. There was more foolery yet, if I could
remember it.

Cas. Will you sup with me to-night, Casca?   *290*

Casca. No, I am promised forth.

Cas. Will you dine with me to-morrow?

Casca. Ay, if I be alive, and your mind hold, and your
dinner worth the eating.

Cas. Good; I will expect you.   *295*

Casca. Do so. Farewell, both.   *Exit.*

Bru. What a blunt fellow is this grown to be!
He was quick mettle when he went to school.

Cas. So is he now in execution
Of any bold or noble enterprise,   *300*
However he puts on this tardy form.
This rudeness is a sauce to his good wit,
Which gives men stomach to digest his words
With better appetite.

Bru. And so it is. For this time I will leave you: *305*
To-morrow, if you please to speak with me,
I will come home to you; or, if you will,
Come home to me, and I will wait for you.

Cas. I will do so: till then, think of the world.

                               Exit Brutus.

Well, Brutus, thou art noble; yet, I see,   *310*
Thy honourable metal may be wrought
From that it is dispos'd: therefore 'tis meet
That noble minds keep ever with their likes;
For who so firm that cannot be seduc'd?
Cæsar doth bear me hard; but he loves Brutus: *315*
If I were Brutus now and he were Cassius,
He should not humour me. I will this night,
In several hands, in at his windows throw,
As if they came from several citizens,
Writings all tending to the great opinion   *320*
That Rome holds of his name; wherein obscurely
Cæsar's ambition shall be glanced at:
And after this let Cæsar seat him sure;
For we will shake him, or worse days endure.   *Exit.*

❧ SCENE THIRD ❧

[A Street]

*Thunder and lightning. Enter [from opposite sides] Casca [with his
sword drawn] and Cicero.*

Cic. Good even, Casca: brought you Cæsar home?
Why are you breathless? and why stare you so?

Casca. Are not you mov'd, when all the sway of earth
Shakes like a thing unfirm? O Cicero!
I have seen tempests, when the scolding winds   *5*
Have riv'd the knotty oaks; and I have seen
The ambitious ocean swell and rage and foam,
To be exalted with the threat'ning clouds:
But never till to-night, never till now,
Did I go through a tempest dropping fire.   *10*
Either there is a civil strife in heaven,
Or else the world, too saucy with the gods,
Incenses them to send destruction.

Cic. Why, saw you anything more wonderful?

Casca. A common slave—you know him well by sight— *15*
Held up his left hand, which did flame and burn

245 **coronets:** *laurel garland of a Lupercal runner*   250 **still:** *always ever*   251 **chopped:**
chopped, callous   253 **swounded:** *fainted*   256 **soft:** *stop, wait*   259 **like:** *likely* **falling-sickness:** *epilepsy*   263 **tag-rag:** *beggarly, common*   265 **true:** *honest*   268 **me:**
expletive 'dative of interest'   269 **ope:** *open* **doublet:** *Elizabethan jacket* **An:** *if*   270
occupation: *artisan's calling*   287, 288 **put to silence:** *dismissed, not killed*   291 **I have**
a previous engagement *(to dine out)*

298 **quick mettle:** *high-spirited*   301 **However:** *notwithstanding that* **tardy form:** *sluggish
manner*   309 **the world:** *public affairs*   312 **that:** *that to which*   315 **bear me hard:**
dislike me   317 **He ... me;** *cf. n.*   318 **several hands:** *different handwritings*   324
or ... endure: *or suffer disastrous consequences of our attempt*   1 **brought:** *escorted*   3
sway: *settled order*   14 **more:** *else (or, extraordinarily)*

Like twenty torches join'd; and yet his hand,
Not sensible of fire, remain'd unscorch'd.
Besides,—I have not since put up my sword,—
Against the Capitol I met a lion,   20
Who glar'd upon me, and went surly by,
Without annoying me; and there were drawn
Upon a heap a hundred ghastly women,
Transformed with their fear, who swore they saw
Men all in fire walk up and down the streets.   25
And yesterday the bird of night did sit,
Even at noon-day, upon the market-place,
Hooting and shrieking. When these prodigies
Do so conjointly meet, let not men say,
'These are their reasons, they are natural';   30
For, I believe, they are portentous things
Unto the climate that they point upon.
    Cic. Indeed, it is a strange-disposed time:
But men may construe things after their fashion,
Clean from the purpose of the things themselves.   35
Comes Cæsar to the Capitol to-morrow?
    Casca. He doth; for he did bid Antonius
Send word to you he would be there to-morrow.
    Cic. Good-night then, Casca: this disturbed sky
Is not to walk in.   40
    Casca.   Farewell, Cicero.   *Exit Cicero.*

Enter Cassius.

    Cas. Who's there?
    Casca.   A Roman.
    Cas.   Casca, by your voice.
    Casca. Your ear is good. Cassius, what night is this!   45
    Cas. A very pleasing night to honest men.
    Casca. Who ever knew the heavens menace so?
    Cas. Those that have known the earth so full of faults.
For my part, I have walk'd about the streets,
Submitting me unto the perilous night,   50
And, thus unbraced, Casca, as you see,
Have bar'd my bosom to the thunder-stone;
And, when the cross blue lightning seem'd to open
The breast of heaven, I did present myself
Even in the aim and very flash of it.   55
    Casca. But wherefore did you so much tempt the heavens?
It is the part of men to fear and tremble
When the most mighty gods by tokens send
Such dreadful heralds to astonish us.
    Cas. You are dull, Casca, and those sparks of life   60
That should be in a Roman you do want,
Or else you use not. You look pale, and gaze,
And put on fear, and cast yourself in wonder,
To see the strange impatience of the heavens;
But if you would consider the true cause   65
Why all these fires, why all these gliding ghosts,
Why birds and beasts, from quality and kind,

Why old men, fools, and children calculate,
Why all these things change from their ordinance,
Their natures, and pre-formed faculties,   70
To monstrous quality,—why, you shall find
That heaven hath infus'd them with these spirits
To make them instruments of fear and warning
Unto some monstrous state.
Now could I, Casca, name to thee a man   75
Most like this dreadful night,
That thunders, lightens, opens graves, and roars
As doth the lion in the Capitol,
A man no mightier than thyself or me
In personal action, yet prodigious grown   80
And fearful as these strange eruptions are.
    Casca. 'Tis Cæsar that you mean; is it not, Cassius?
    Cas. Let it be who it is: for Romans now
Have thews and limbs like to their ancestors;
But, woe the while! our fathers' minds are dead,   85
And we are govern'd with our mothers' spirits;
Our yoke and sufferance show us womanish.
    Casca. Indeed, they say the senators to-morrow
Mean to establish Cæsar as a king;
And he shall wear his crown by sea and land,   90
In every place, save here in Italy.
    Cas. I know where I will wear this dagger then;
Cassius from bondage will deliver Cassius:
Therein, ye gods, you make the weak most strong;
Therein, ye gods, you tyrants do defeat: 95
Nor stony tower, nor walls of beaten brass,
Nor airless dungeon, nor strong links of iron,
Can be retentive to the strength of spirit:
But life, being weary of these worldly bars,
Never lacks power to dismiss itself.   100
If I know this, know all the world besides,
That part of tyranny that I do bear
I can shake off at pleasure.   *Thunder still.*
    Casca.   So can I:
So every bondman is his own hand bears   105
The power to cancel his captivity.
    Cas. And why should Cæsar be a tyrant then?
Poor man! I know he would not be a wolf
But that he sees the Romans are but sheep:
He were no lion, were no! Romans hinds.   110
Those that with haste will make a mighty fire
Begin it with weak straws; what trash is Rome,
What rubbish, and what offal, when it serves
For the base matter to illuminate
So vile a thing as Cæsar! But, O grief,   115
Where hast thou led me? I, perhaps, speak this
Before a willing bondman; then I know
My answer must be made: but I am arm'd,
And dangers are to me indifferent.
    Casca. You speak to Casca, and to such a man   120
That is no fleering tell-tale. Hold, my hand:
Be factious for redress of all these griefs,
And I will set this foot of mine as far

---

18 **sensible of:** *vulnerable by, sensitive to*   22, 23 **drawn … heap:** *crowded together in a* body   26 **bird of night:** *owl*   32 **climate:** *clime, region* **point upon:** *apply to*   33 **strange-disposed:** *of strange character*   34 **after … fashion:** *according to men's own human predilection*   35 **Clean … purpose:** *quite apart from the true meaning*   39 **sky:** *air, state of weather*   45 **what night:** *what a night*   51 **unbraced:** *with doublet open*   52 **thunder-stone:** *supposedly cast from the sky by thunder*   63 **put on:** *exhibit the signs of* **cast … in:** *give way to; cf. n.*   66 **Why:** *i.e., why we have* (or, … *are acting so*)   67 **from … kind:** *far from their proper character and nature*

68 **calculate:** *prophesy; cf. n.*   69 **ordinance:** *ordinary conduct*   74 **monstrous state:** *unnatural state of affairs*   81 **fearful:** *inspiring fear* **eruptions:** *freaks of nature*   85 **woe the while:** *alas for the times*   87 **yoke and sufferance:** *patience under the yoke*   110 **hinds:** *female of red deer; also, servants, rustics*   111–115 *Cf. n.*   118 **My … made:** *I shall have to answer for my words*   121 **That:** *as* **fleering:** *mocking* **Hold, my hand:** *here, take this handclasp as pledge*   122 **factious:** *active* **griefs:** *grievances*

As who goes furthest.
　　Cas. 　　　　　　There's a bargain made. 　　　*125*
Now know you, Casca, I have mov'd already
Some certain of the noblest-minded Romans
To undergo with me an enterprise
Of honourable-dangerous consequence;
And I do know by this they stay for me 　　　*130*
In Pompey's porch: for now, this fearful night,
There is no stir, or walking in the streets;
And the complexion of the element
In favour's like the work we have in hand,
Most bloody, fiery, and most terrible. 　　　*135*
　　Casca. Stand close awhile, for here comes one in haste.
　　Cas. 'Tis Cinna; I do know him by his gait:
He is a friend.

Enter Cinna.

　　　　Cinna, where haste you so?
　　Cin. To find out you. Who's that? Metellus Cimber? 　*140*
　　Cas. No, it is Casca; one incorporate
To our attempts. Am I not stay'd for, Cinna?
　　Cin. I am glad on 't. What a fearful night is this!
There's two or three of us have seen strange sights.
　　Cas. Am I not stay'd for? Tell me. 　　　*145*
　　Cin. 　　　　　　　　Yes, you are.
O Cassius, if you could
But win the noble Brutus to our party—
　　Cas. Be you content. Good Cinna, take this paper,
And look you lay it in the prætor's chair, 　　　*150*
Where Brutus may but find it; and throw this
In at his window; set this up with wax
Upon old Brutus' statue: all this done,
Repair to Pompey's porch, where you shall find us.
Is Decius Brutus and Trebonius there? 　　　*155*
　　Cin. All but Metellus Cimber; and he's gone
To seek you at your house. Well, I will hie,
And so bestow these papers as you bade me.
　　Cas. That done, repair to Pompey's theatre.

　　　　　　　　　　　　　　Exit Cinna.

Come, Casca, you and I will yet ere day 　　　*160*
See Brutus at his house: three parts of him
Is ours already, and the man entire
Upon the next encounter yields him ours.
　　Casca. O, he sits high in all the people's hearts:
And that which would appear offence in us, 　　　*165*
His countenance, like richest alchemy,
Will change to virtue and to worthiness.
　　Cas. Him and his worth and our great need of him
You have right well conceited. Let us go,
For it is after midnight; and ere day 　　　*170*
We will awake him and be sure of him. 　　*Exeunt.*

128 undergo: *undertake* 　**130 by this:** *by this time* 　**131 Pompey's porch;** *cf. n.* 　**133 complexion . . . element:** *visible condition of the sky* 　**136 Stand close:** *avoid notice* 　**141 incorporate:** *joined, affiliated* 　**150 prætor's chair:** *official seat of judge in Roman tribunal* 　**157 hie:** *hasten away* 　**165 countenance:** *patronage, support* 　**alchemy:** *pseudo-science of transmuting metals* 　**169 conceited:** *expressed figuratively*

Act Second ❧ Scene First

Enter Brutus in his Orchard.

　　Bru. What, Lucius! ho!
I cannot, by the progress of the stars,
Give guess how near to day. Lucius, I say!
I would it were my fault to sleep so soundly.
When, Lucius, when? Awake, I say! what, Lucius! 　*5*

Enter Lucius.

　　Luc. Call'd you, my lord?
　　Bru. Get me a taper in my study, Lucius:
When it is lighted, come and call me here.
　　Luc. I will, my lord. 　　　　　*Exit.*
　　Bru. It must be by his death: and, for my part, 　*10*
I know no personal cause to spurn at him,
But for the general. He would be crown'd:
How that might change his nature, there's the question:
It is the bright day that brings forth the adder;
And that craves wary walking. Crown him that, 　*15*
And then, I grant, we put a sting in him
That at his will he may do danger with.
The abuse of greatness is when it disjoins
Remorse from power; and, to speak truth of Cæsar,
I have not known when his affections sway'd 　*20*
More than his reason. But 'tis a common proof,
That lowliness is young ambition's ladder,
Whereto the climber-upward turns his face;
But when he once attains the upmost round,
He then unto the ladder turns his back, 　*25*
Looks in the clouds, scorning the base degrees
By which he did ascend. So Cæsar may:
Then, lest he may, prevent. And, since the quarrel
Will bear no colour for the thing he is,
Fashion it thus; that what he is, augmented, 　*30*
Would run to these and these extremities;
And therefore think him as a serpent's egg
Which hatch'd, would, as his kind, grow mischievous,
And kill him in the shell.

Enter Lucius.

　　Luc. The taper burneth in your closet, sir. 　*35*
Searching the window for a flint, I found
This paper, thus seal'd up; and I am sure
It did not lie there when I went to bed.
　　Bru. Get you to bed again; it is not day.
Is not to-morrow, boy, the ides of March? 　*40*
　　Luc. I know not, sir.
　　Bru. Look in the calendar, and bring me word.
　　Luc. I will, sir.
　　Bru. The exhalations whizzing in the air
Give so much light that I may read by them. 　*45*

　　　　　　Opens the letter, and reads.

'Brutus, thou sleep'st: awake, and see thyself.

Scene First S. d. Orchard: *garden* 　**5 When:** *exclamation of impatience* 　**11 spurn at:** *oppose vindictively* 　**12 general:** *people's sake, public welfare* 　**15 Crown him that;** *cf. n.* 　**19 Remorse:** *mercy, conscience* 　**20 affections:** *passions* 　**21 proof:** *proved experience* 　**26 degrees:** *steps, rungs* 　**28 prevent:** *be beforehand* 　**quarrel:** *attack on him, accusation* 　**29 colour:** *justification* 　**30 Fashion:** *put, formulate* 　**31 these and these:** *such and such* 　**33 as his kind:** *as is the nature of his species* 　**35 closet:** *study* 　**44 exhalations:** *meteors*

Shall Rome, &c. Speak, strike, redress!
Brutus, thou sleep'st: awake!'
Such instigations have been often dropp'd
Where I have took them up.   50
'Shall Rome, &c.' Thus must I piece it out:
Shall Rome stand under one man's awe? What, Rome?
My ancestors did from the streets of Rome
The Tarquin drive, when he was call'd a king.
'Speak, strike, redress!' Am I entreated   55
To speak, and strike? O Rome, I make thee promise:
If the redress will follow, thou receivest
Thy full petition at the hand of Brutus!

Enter Lucius.

Luc. Sir, March is wasted fourteen days.   *Knocking within.*
Bru. 'Tis good. Go to the gate: somebody knocks.   60
                                               [Exit Lucius.]
Since Cassius first did whet me against Cæsar,
I have not slept.
Between the acting of a dreadful thing
And the first motion, all the interim is
Like a phantasma, or a hideous dream: 65
The genius and the mortal instruments
Are then in council; and the state of man,
Like to a little kingdom, suffers then
The nature of an insurrection.

Enter Lucius.

Luc. Sir, 'tis your brother Cassius at the door,   70
Who doth desire to see you.
Bru.   Is he alone?
Luc. No, sir, there are moe with him.
Bru.   Do you know them?
Luc. No, sir; their hats are pluck'd about their ears,   75
And half their faces buried in their cloaks,
That by no means I may discover them.
By any mark of favour.
Bru.   Let 'em enter.   *[Exit Lucius.]*
They are the faction. O conspiracy,   80
Sham'st thou to show thy dangerous brow by night,
When evils are most free? O then by day
Where wilt thou find a cavern dark enough
To mask thy monstrous visage? Seek none, conspiracy;
Hide it in smiles and affability: 85
For if thou path, thy native semblance on,
Not Erebus itself were dim enough
To hide thee from prevention.

Enter the Conspirators, Cassius, Casca, Decius, Cinna, Metellus,
and Trebonius.

Cas. I think we are too bold upon your rest:
Good morrow, Brutus; do we trouble you?   90
Bru. I have been up this hour, awake all night.
Know I these men that come along with you?

Cas. Yes, every man of them; and no man here
But honours you; and every one doth wish
You had but that opinion of yourself   95
Which every noble Roman bears of you.
This is Trebonius.
Bru.   He is welcome hither.
Cas. This, Decius Brutus.
Bru.   He is welcome too.   100
Cas. This, Casca; this, Cinna;
And this, Metellus Cimber.
Bru.   They are all welcome.
What watchful cares do interpose themselves
Betwixt your eyes and night?   105
Cas. Shall I entreat a word?
                              [Brutus and Cassius] whisper.
Dec. Here lies the east: doth not the day break here?
Casca. No.
Cin. O pardon, sir, it doth; and yon grey lines
That fret the clouds are messengers of day.   110
Casca. You shall confess that you are both deceiv'd.
Here, as I point my sword, the sun arises;
Which is a great way growing on the south,
Weighing the youthful season of the year.
Some two months hence up higher toward the north   115
He first presents his fire; and the high east
Stands, as the Capitol, directly here.
Bru. Give me your hands all over, one by one.
Cas. And let us swear our resolution.
Bru. No, not an oath: if not the face of men,   120
The sufferance of our souls, the time's abuse,—
If these be motives weak, break off betimes,
And every man hence to his idle bed;
So let high-sighted tyranny range on,
Till each man drop by lottery. But if these,   125
As I am sure they do, bear fire enough
To kindle cowards and to steel with valour
The melting spirits of women, then, countrymen,
What need we any spur but our own cause
To prick us to redress? what other bond   130
Than secret Romans, that have spoke the word
And will not palter? and what other oath
Than honesty to honesty engag'd,
That this shall be, or we will fall for it?
Swear priests and cowards and men cautelous,   135
Old feeble carrions and such suffering souls
That welcome wrongs: unto bad causes swear
Such creatures as men doubt; but do not stain
The even virtue of our enterprise,
Nor th' insuppressive mettle of our spirits,   140
To think that or our cause or our performance
Did need an oath; when every drop of blood
That every Roman bears, and nobly bears,
Is guilty of a several bastardy,

58 **Thy full petition:** *full measure of what thou askest*   59 **fourteen;** *cf. n.*   61, 62
Cf. n.   64 **motion:** *instigation, inception*   65 **phantasma:** *vision, phantasmagoria*   66
genius: *the guardian spirit, within man* **mortal instruments:** *human faculties*   70
brother: *he had married Brutus' sister, Junia*   73 **moe:** *more, others*   79 **mark of favour:**
trait of countenance   80 **faction:** *band of conspirators*   86 **path:** *walk, proceed* **native:**
natural **on:** *being on*   87 **Erebus:** *gloomy region leading to Hades (the name signifies*
'darkness')   88 **prevention:** *being forestalled*   89 **bold:** *i.e., in intruding*

93 **and no:** *and there is no*   110 **fret:** *chequer*   112 **as:** *where*   113 **growing on:**
tending toward   114 **Weighing:** *on account of*   118 **all over:** *successively*   120 **face of**
men: *mute appeal in the people's looks*   121 **sufferance:** *suffering, distress* **the ... abuse:**
abuses of the time   122 **betimes:** *before it's too late*   124 **high-sighted:** *haughty*   125
lottery: *arbitrary decree*   129 **What:** *why*   131 **Than secret:** *than that of resolute*   132
palter: *play fast and loose*   135 **cautelous:** *crafty, deceitful*   136 **carrions:** *wretches no*
better than soulless carcasses **suffering:** *long-suffering*   139 **even:** *just*   140 **insup-**
pressive: *irrepressible*   141 **or ... or:** *either ... or*   144 *Is individually condemned as*
illegitimate

If he do break the smallest particle   145
Of any promise that hath pass'd from him.
    Cas. But what of Cicero? Shall we sound him?
I think he will stand very strong with us.
    Casca. Let us not leave him out.
    Cin.   No, by no means.   150
    Met. O let us have him; for his silver hairs
Will purchase us a good opinion
And buy men's voices to commend our deeds:
It shall be said his judgment rul'd our hands;
Our youths and wildness shall no whit appear,   155
But all be buried in his gravity.
    Bru. O name him not: let us not break with him;
For he will never follow anything
That other men begin.
    Cas.   Then leave him out.   160
    Casca. Indeed he is not fit.
    Dec. Shall no man else be touch'd but only Cæsar?
    Cas. Decius, well urg'd. I think it is not meet,
Mark Antony, so well belov'd of Cæsar,
Should outlive Cæsar: we shall find of him   165
A shrewd contriver; and you know, his means,
If he improve them, may well stretch so far
As to annoy us all; which to prevent,
Let Antony and Cæsar fall together.
    Bru. Our course will seem too bloody, Caius Cassius,   170
To cut the head off and then hack the limbs,
Like wrath in death and envy afterwards;
For Antony is but a limb of Cæsar.
Let us be sacrificers, but not butchers, Caius.
We all stand up against the spirit of Cæsar;   175
And in the spirit of men there is no blood:
O then that we could come by Cæsar's spirit,
And not dismember Cæsar! But, alas,
Cæsar must bleed for it. And, gentle friends,
Let's kill him boldly, but not wrathfully;   180
Let's carve him as a dish fit for the gods,
Not hew him as a carcass fit for hounds:
And let our hearts, as subtle masters do,
Stir up their servants to an act of rage,
And after seem to chide 'em. This shall make   185
Our purpose necessary and not envious;
Which so appearing to the common eyes,
We shall be call'd purgers, not murderers.
And, for Mark Antony, think not of him;
For he can do no more than Cæsar's arm   190
When Cæsar's head is off.
    Cas.   Yet I fear him;
For in the ingrafted love he bears to Cæsar—
    Bru. Alas, good Cassius, do not think of him.
If he love Cæsar, all that he can do   195
Is to himself: take thought, and die for Cæsar.
And that were much he should, for he is given
To sports, to wildness, and much company.
    Treb. There is no fear in him; let him not die:
For he will live, and laugh at this hereafter.   *Clock strikes.*   200
    Bru. Peace! count the clock.

    Cas.   The clock hath stricken three.
    Treb. 'Tis time to part.
    Cas.   But it is doubtful yet
Whether Cæsar will come forth to-day or no;   205
For he is superstitious grown of late,
Quite from the main opinion he held once
Of fantasy, of dreams, and ceremonies.
It may be, these apparent prodigies,
The unaccustom'd terror of this night,   210
And the persuasion of his augurers,
May hold him from the Capitol to-day.
    Dec. Never fear that: if he be so resolv'd,
I can o'ersway him; for he loves to hear
That unicorns may be betray'd with trees,   215
And bears with glasses, elephants with holes,
Lions with toils, and men with flatterers;
But when I tell him he hates flatterers,
He says he does, being then most flattered.
Let me work;   220
For I can give his humour the true bent,
And I will bring him to the Capitol.
    Cas. Nay, we will all of us be there to fetch him.
    Bru. By the eighth hour: is that the uttermost.
    Cin. Be that the uttermost, and fail not then.   225
    Met. Caius Ligarius doth bear Cæsar hard,
Who rated him for speaking well of Pompey:
I wonder none of you have thought of him.
    Bru. Now, good Metellus, go along by him:
He loves me well, and I have given him reasons;   230
Send him but hither, and I'll fashion him.
    Cas. The morning comes upon 's: we'll leave you, Brutus.
And, friends, disperse yourselves; but all remember
What you have said, and show yourselves true Romans.
    Bru. Good gentlemen, look fresh and merrily;   235
Let not our looks put on our purposes,
But bear it as our Roman actors do,
With untir'd spirits and formal constancy:
And so good morrow to you every one.
                         Exeunt. Manet Brutus.

Boy! Lucius! Fast asleep? It is no matter;   240
Enjoy the honey-heavy dew of slumber:
Thou hast no figures nor no fantasies
Which busy care draws in the brains of men;
Therefore thou sleep'st so sound.

               Enter Portia.

    Por.   Brutus, my lord!   245
    Bru. Portia, what mean you? Wherefore rise you now?
It is not for your health thus to commit
Your weak condition to the raw cold morning.
    Por. Nor for yours neither. You've ungently, Brutus,
Stole from my bed; and yesternight at supper   250
You suddenly arose, and walk'd about,
Musing and sighing, with your arms across,
And when I ask'd you what the matter was,

157 **break with:** *broach our plan to*   165 **of:** *in*   166 **shrewd contriver:** *malevolent plotter*   167 **improve:** *make the most of*   168 **annoy:** *seriously injure*   172 **envy:** *vindictiveness*   193 **ingrafted:** *deeply rooted*   196 **Is to:** *concerns, affects, only*   **take thought:** *despond*   197 **that ... should:** *even that would be more than might be expected*   199 **fear:** *cause for fear*

207 **from ... main:** *changed from the general*   209 **apparent:** *manifest*   215 **trees:** *by luring them to drive their horns too firmly into trees*   216 **glasses:** *mirrors, to distract their attention* **holes:** *pitfalls*   217 **toils:** *nets, snares*   221 **humour:** *disposition; cf. n. on line 250*   224 **uttermost:** *latest*   227 **rated:** *berated, reprimanded*   229 **by him:** *by his house*   231 **fashion:** *like modern 'whip into shape'*   238 **formal constancy:** *dignified self-possession*   242 **figures:** *pictures created by imagination*

You star'd upon me with ungentle looks.
I urg'd you further; then you scratch'd your head,   255
And too impatiently stamp'd with your foot;
Yet I insisted, yet you answer'd not,
But with an angry wafture of your hand
Gave sign for me to leave you. So I did,
Fearing to strengthen that impatience   260
Which seem'd too much enkindled, and withal
Hoping it was but an effect of humour,
Which sometime hath his hour with every man.
It will not let you eat, nor talk, nor sleep,
And could it work so much upon your shape   265
As it hath much prevail'd on your condition,
I should not know you, Brutus. Dear my lord,
Make me acquainted with your cause of grief.
  Bru. I am not well in health, and that is all.
  Por. Brutus is wise, and were he not in health,   270
He would embrace the means to come by it.
  Bru. Why, so I do. Good Portia, go to bed.
  Por. Is Brutus sick, and is it physical
To walk unbraced and suck up the humours
Of the dank morning? What! is Brutus sick,   275
And will he steal out of his wholesome bed
To dare the vile contagion of the night,
And tempt the rheumy and unpurged air
To add unto his sickness? No, my Brutus;
You have some sick offence within your mind,   280
Which, by the right and virtue of my place,
I ought to know of; and, upon my knees,
I charm you, by my once-commended beauty,
By all your vows of love, and that great vow
Which did incorporate and make us one,   285
That you unfold to me, your self, your half,
Why you are heavy, and what men to-night
Have had resort to you; for here have been
Some six or seven, who did hide their faces
Even from darkness.   290
  Bru.   Kneel not, gentle Portia.
  Por. I should not need, if you were gentle Brutus.
Within the bond of marriage, tell me, Brutus,
Is it excepted I should know no secrets
That appertain to you? Am I yourself   295
But, as it were, in sort or limitation,
To keep with you at meals, comfort your bed,
And talk to you sometimes? Dwell I but in the suburbs
Of your good pleasure? If it be no more,
Portia is Brutus' harlot, not his wife.   300
  Bru. You are my true and honourable wife,
As dear to me as are the ruddy drops
That visit my sad heart.
  Por. If this were true then should I know this secret.
I grant I am a woman, but, withal,   305
A woman that Lord Brutus took to wife;
I grant I am a woman, but, withal,
A woman well-reputed, Cato's daughter.
Think you I am no stronger than my sex,

Being so father'd and so husbanded?   310
Tell me your counsels, I will not disclose 'em.
I have made a strong proof of my constancy,
Giving myself a voluntary wound,
Here, in the thigh: can I bear that with patience
And not my husband's secrets?   315
  Bru.   O ye gods,
Render me worthy of this noble wife!   *Knock [within]*.
Hark, hark! one knocks. Portia, go in awhile;
And by and by thy bosom shall partake
The secrets of my heart.   320
All my engagements I will construe to thee,
All the charactery of my sad brows.
Leave me with haste.   *Exit Portia.*
             Lucius, who's that knocks?

Enter Lucius and Ligarius.

  Luc. Here is a sick man that would speak with you.   325
  Bru. Caius Ligarius, that Metellus spoke of.
Boy, stand aside. Caius Ligarius! how?
  Lig. Vouchsafe good morrow from a feeble tongue.
  Bru. O what a time have you chose out, brave Caius,
To wear a kerchief! Would you were not sick!   330
  Lig. I am not sick if Brutus have in hand
Any exploit worthy the name of honour.
  Bru. Such an exploit have I in hand, Ligarius,
Had you a healthful ear to hear of it.
  Lig. By all the gods that Romans bow before,   335
I here discard my sickness! Soul of Rome,
Brave son, deriv'd from honourable loins,
Thou, like an exorcist, hast conjur'd up
My mortified spirit. Now bid me run,
And I will strive with things impossible;   340
Yea, get the better of them. What's to do?
  Bru. A piece of work that will make sick men whole.
  Lig. But are not some whole that we must make sick?
  Bru. That must we also. What it is, my Caius,
I shall unfold to thee as we are going   345
To whom it must be done.
  Lig.   Set on your foot,
And with a heart new-fir'd I follow you,
To do I know not what; but it sufficeth
That Brutus leads me on.   *Thunder.*
  Bru.   Follow me then.   *Exeunt.*

❧ Scene Second ❧

[Cæsar's House]
Thunder and lightning. Enter Julius Cæsar in his night-gown.

  Cæs. Nor heaven nor earth have been at peace tonight:
Thrice hath Calpurnia in her sleep cried out,
'Help, ho! They murder Cæsar!' Who's within?

Enter a Servant.

  Serv. My lord!

---

262 **humour**; *cf. n.*   265, 266 (outward) *shape*, (inward) *condition*   273 **physical**: *healthful*   278 **rheumy**: *causing rheumatic diseases* **unpurged**: *unpurified by the sun*   280 **sick offence**: *unhealthy trouble*   283 **charm**: *conjure, entreat*   296 **in . . . limitation**: *only after a fashion or with restrictions*   305 **withal**: *with this saving reservation*   308 **Cato**: *Marcus Porcius Cato, 'of Utica'*

321 **engagements**: *undertakings that I stand committed to* **construe**: *explain*   322 **charactery**: *writing, message*   324 **who's**: *who is it*   328 **Vouchsafe**: *vouchsafe to receive*   330 **kerchief**: *swathing for the head of the sick*   338 **exorcist**: *magician*   339 **mortified**: *deadened*   346 **To whom**: *to him to whom*   SCENE TWO S. d. **night-gown**: *dressing-gown*

Cæs. Go bid the priests do present sacrifice,   5
And bring me their opinions of success.
   Serv. I will, my lord.   *Exit.*

Enter Calpurnia.

   Cal. What mean you, Cæsar? Think you to walk forth?
You shall not stir out of your house to-day.
   Cæs. Cæsar shall forth: the things that threaten'd me   10
Ne'er look'd but on my back; when they shall see
The face of Cæsar, they are vanished.
   Cal. Cæsar, I never stood on ceremonies,
Yet now they fright me. There is one within,
Besides the things that we have heard and seen,   15
Recounts most horrid sights seen by the watch.
A lioness hath whelped in the streets;
And graves have yawn'd and yielded up their dead;
Fierce fiery warriors fought upon the clouds,
In ranks and squadrons and right form of war,   20
Which drizzled blood upon the Capitol;
The noise of battle hurtled in the air,
Horses did neigh, and dying men did groan,
And ghosts did shriek and squeal about the streets.
O Cæsar, these things are beyond all use,   25
And I do fear them.
   Cæs.   What can be avoided
Whose end is purpos'd by the mighty gods?
Yet Cæsar shall go forth; for these predictions
Are to the world in general as to Cæsar.   30
   Cal. When beggars die there are no comets seen;
The heavens themselves blaze forth the death of princes.
   Cæs. Cowards die many times before their deaths;
The valiant never taste of death but once.
Of all the wonders that I yet have heard,   35
It seems to me most strange that men should fear;
Seeing that death, a necessary end,
Will come when it will come.

Enter a Servant.

                               What say the augurers?
   Serv. They would not have you to stir forth to-day.   40
Plucking the entrails of an offering forth,
They could not find a heart within the beast.
   Cæs. The gods do this in shame of cowardice:
Cæsar should be a beast without a heart
If he should stay at home to-day for fear.   45
No, Cæsar shall not; danger knows full well
That Cæsar is more dangerous than he:
We are two lions litter'd in one day,
And I the elder and more terrible:
And Cæsar shall go forth.   50
   Cal.   Alas, my lord,
Your wisdom is consum'd in confidence.
Do not go forth to-day: call it my fear
That keeps you in the house, and not your own.
We'll send Mark Antony to the senate-house,   55
And he shall say you are not well to-day:

Let me, upon my knee, prevail in this.
   Cæs. Mark Antony shall say I am not well;
And, for thy humour, I will stay at home.

Enter Decius.

Here's Decius Brutus, he shall tell them so.   60
   Dec. Cæsar, all hail! Good morrow, worthy Cæsar:
I come to fetch you to the senate-house.
   Cæs. And you are come in very happy time
To bear my greeting to the senators,
And tell them that I will not come to-day: 65
Cannot, is false, and that I dare not, falser;
I will not come to-day: tell them so, Decius.
   Cal. Say he is sick.
   Cæs.   Shall Cæsar send a lie?
Have I in conquest stretch'd mine arm so far   70
To be afeard to tell greybeards the truth?
Decius, go tell them Cæsar will not come.
   Dec. Most mighty Cæsar, let me know some cause,
Lest I be laugh'd at when I tell them so.
   Cæs. The cause is in my will: I will not come;   75
That is enough to satisfy the senate:
But for your private satisfaction,
Because I love you, I will let you know:
Calpurnia here, my wife, stays me at home:
She dreamt to-night she saw my statue,   80
Which, like a fountain with a hundred spouts,
Did run pure blood; and many lusty Romans
Came smiling, and did bathe their hands in it:
And these does she apply for warnings and portents,
And evils imminent; and on her knee   85
Hath begg'd that I will stay at home to-day.
   Dec. This dream is all amiss interpreted;
It was a vision fair and fortunate:
Your statue spouting blood in many pipes,
In which so many smiling Romans bath'd,   90
Signifies that from you great Rome shall suck
Reviving blood, and that great men shall press
For tinctures, stains, relics, and cognizance.
This by Calpurnia's dream is signified.
   Cæs. And this way have you well expounded it.   95
   Dec. I have, when you have heard what I can say;
And know it now: the senate have concluded
To give this day a crown to mighty Cæsar.
If you shall send them word you will not come,
Their minds may change. Besides, it were a mock   100
Apt to be render'd, for some one to say,
'Break up the senate till another time,
When Cæsar's wife shall meet with better dreams.'
If Cæsar hide himself, shall they not whisper,
'Lo, Cæsar is afraid'?   105
Pardon me, Cæsar; for my dear dear love
To your proceeding bids me tell you this,
And reason to my love is liable.
   Cæs. How foolish do your fears seem now, Calpurnia!
I am ashamed I did yield to them.   110
Give me my robe, for I will go.

---

5 present: *immediate*   **6 success:** *the future*   **13 stood on ceremonies:** *laid stress on omens*   **20 right form:** *regular formations*   **22 hurtled:** *emitted sounds of conflict, clashed*   **25 use:** *previous experience*   **28 end:** *accomplishment*   **30 Are to:** *are as applicable to*   **52 confidence:** *over-confidence*

59 humour: *whim, caprice*   **79 stays:** *keeps*   **92 press:** *crowd about*   **93 tinctures:** *healing medicines; cf. n.* **stains:** *assimilable traces* (tinges) *of Cæsar's qualities* **relics:** *i.e., religious benefits* **cognizance:** *heraldic emblems, i.e. social benefits*   **100 mock:** *gibe*   **107 proceeding:** *career*   **108 liable:** *subservient*

Enter Brutus, Ligarius, Metellus, Casca, Trebonius, Cinna,
and Publius.

And look where Publius is come to fetch me.
  Pub. Good morrow, Cæsar.
  Cæs.   Welcome, Publius.   *115*
What, Brutus, are you stirr'd so early too?
Good morrow, Casca. Caius Ligarius,
Cæsar was ne'er so much your enemy
As that same ague which hath made you lean.
What is 't o'clock?   *120*
  Bru.   Cæsar, 'tis strucken eight.
  Cæs. I thank you for your pains and courtesy.

Enter Antony.

See, Antony, that revels long o' nights,
Is notwithstanding up. Good morrow, Antony.
  Ant. So to most noble Cæsar.   *125*
  Cæs.   Bid them prepare within:
I am to blame to be thus waited for.
Now, Cinna; now, Metellus; what, Trebonius,
I have an hour's talk in store for you;
Remember that you call on me to-day: *130*
Be near me, that I may remember you.
  Treb. Cæsar, I will:—*[Aside.]* and so near will I be,
That your best friends shall wish I had been further.
  Cæs. Good friends, go in, and taste some wine with me;
And we, like friends, will straightway go together.   *135*
  Bru. [Aside.] That every 'like' is not 'the same,' O Cæsar,
The heart of Brutus yearns to think upon.   *Exeunt.*

❧ Scene Third ❧

[A Street near the Capitol]
Enter Artemidorus [reading a paper].

  Art. 'Cæsar, beware of Brutus; take heed of Cassius; come
not near Casca; have an eye to Cinna; trust not Trebonius;
mark well Metellus Cimber; Decius Brutus loves thee not; thou
hast wronged Caius Ligarius. There is but one mind in all
these men, and it is bent against Cæsar. If thou beest not   *5*
immortal, look about you: security gives way to conspiracy.
The mighty gods defend thee! Thy lover,

                            Artemidorus.'

Here will I stand till Cæsar pass along,
And as a suitor will I give him this.   *10*
My heart laments that virtue cannot live
Out of the teeth of emulation.
If thou read this, O Cæsar, thou mayest live;
If not, the Fates with traitors do contrive.   *Exit.*

❧ Scene Fourth ❧

[Another part of the same Street, before the house of Brutus]
Enter Portia and Lucius.

  Por. I prithee, boy, run to the senate-house;
Stay not to answer me, but get thee gone.
Why dost thou stay?
  Luc.   To know my errand, madam.
  Por. I would have had thee there, and here again,   *5*
Ere I can tell thee what thou shouldst do there.
O constancy, be strong upon my side;
Set a huge mountain 'tween my heart and tongue;
I have a man's mind, but a woman's might.
How hard it is for women to keep counsel!   *10*
Art thou here yet?
  Luc.   Madam, what shall I do?
Run to the Capitol, and nothing else?
And so return to you, and nothing else?
  Por. Yes, bring me word, boy, if thy lord look well,   *15*
For he went sickly forth; and take good note
What Cæsar doth, what suitors press to him.
Hark, boy! what noise is that?
  Luc. I hear none, madam.
  Por.   Prithee, listen well: *20*
I heard a bustling rumour, like a fray,
And the wind brings it from the Capitol.
  Luc. Sooth, madam, I hear nothing.

Enter the Soothsayer.

  Por. Come hither, fellow: which way hast thou been?
  Sooth. At mine own house, good lady.   *25*
  Por. What is 't o'clock?
  Sooth.   About the ninth hour, lady.
  Por. Is Cæsar yet gone to the Capitol?
  Sooth. Madam, not yet: I go to take my stand,
To see him pass on to the Capitol.   *30*
  Por. Thou hast some suit to Cæsar, hast thou not?
  Sooth. That I have, lady: if it will please Cæsar
To be so good to Cæsar as to hear me,
I shall beseech him to befriend himself.
  Por. Why, know'st thou any harm's intended towards him?   *35*
  Sooth. None that I know will be, much that I fear may
chance.
Good morrow to you. Here the street is narrow:
The throng that follows Cæsar at the heels,
Of senators, of prætors, common suitors,   *40*
Will crowd a feeble man almost to death:
I'll get me to a place more void, and there
Speak to great Cæsar as he comes along.   *Exit.*
  Por. I must go in. Ay me! how weak a thing
The heart of woman is. O Brutus,   *45*
The heavens speed thee in thine enterprise!
Sure, the boy heard me.—Brutus hath a suit
That Cæsar will not grant.—O, I grow faint.—
Run, Lucius, and commend me to my lord;
Say I am merry: come to me again,   *50*
And bring me word what he doth say to thee.   *Exeunt.*

---

136 *Cf. n.*   **137 yearns:** *grieves*   **6 security gives way:** *unguardedness yields opportu-*
nity   **7 lover:** *friend*   **12 Out . . . teeth:** *free from the bite*   **emulation:** *grudging jealousy*

23 Sooth: *in truth*   **42 void:** *open*

ACT THIRD ❧ SCENE FIRST

[Before the Capitol]

Flourish. Enter Cæsar, Brutus, Cassius, Casca, Decius, Metellus,
Trebonius, Cinna, Antony, Lepidus, Artemidorus, [Popilius,]
Publius, the Soothsayer [and Others].

Cæs. [*To the Soothsayer.*] The ides of March are come.

Sooth. Ay, Cæsar; but not gone.

Art. Hail, Cæsar! Read this schedule.

Dec. Trebonius doth desire you to o'er-read,
At your best leisure, this his humble suit.   5

Art. O Cæsar, read mine first; for mine's a suit
That touches Cæsar nearer. Read it, great Cæsar.

Cæs. What touches us ourself shall be last serv'd.

Art. Delay not, Cæsar; read it instantly.

Cæs. What, is the fellow mad?   10

Pub.   Sirrah, give place.

Cæs. What, urge you your petitions in the street?
Come to the Capitol.

     [Cæsar goes up to the Senate-House, the rest following.]

Pop. I wish your enterprise to-day may thrive.

Cas. What enterprise, Popilius?   15

Pop.   Fare you well.

     [Advances to Cæsar.]

Bru. What said Popilius Lena?

Cas. He wish'd to-day our enterprise might thrive.
I fear our purpose is discovered.

Bru. Look, how he makes to Cæsar: mark him.   20

Cas. Casca, be sudden, for we fear prevention.
Brutus, what shall be done? If this be known,
Cassius or Cæsar never shall turn back,
For I will slay myself.

Bru.   Cassius, be constant: 25
Popilius Lena speaks not of our purposes;
For, look, he smiles, and Cæsar doth not change.

Cas. Trebonius knows his time; for, look you, Brutus,
He draws Mark Antony out of the way.

     [Exeunt Antony and Trebonius.]

Dec. Where is Metellus Cimber? Let him go,   30
And presently prefer his suit to Cæsar.

Bru. He is address'd; press near and second him.

Cin. Casca, you are the first that rears your hand.

Cæs. Are we all ready? What is now amiss,
That Cæsar and his senate must redress?   35

Met. Most high, most mighty, and most puissant Cæsar,
Metellus Cimber throws before thy seat
A humble heart,—   *[Kneeling.]*

Cæs.   I must prevent thee, Cimber.
These couchings and these lowly courtesies,   40
Might fire the blood of ordinary men,
And turn pre-ordinance and first decree
Into the law of children. Be not fond,
To think that Cæsar bears such rebel blood
That will be thaw'd from the true quality   45
With that which melteth fools; I mean sweet words,

Low-crooked curtsies, and base spaniel fawning.
Thy brother by decree is banished:
If thou dost bend and pray and fawn for him,
I spurn thee like a cur out of my way.   50
Know, Cæsar doth not wrong, nor without cause
Will he be satisfied.

Met. Is there no voice more worthy than my own,
To sound more sweetly in great Cæsar's ear
For the repealing of my banish'd brother?   55

Bru. I kiss thy hand, but not in flattery, Cæsar;
Desiring thee, that Publius Cimber may
Have an immediate freedom of repeal.

Cæs. What, Brutus!

Cas.   Pardon, Cæsar; Cæsar, pardon: 60
As low as to thy foot doth Cassius fall,
To beg enfranchisement for Publius Cimber.

Cæs. I could be well mov'd if I were as you;
If I could pray to move, prayers would move me:
But I am constant as the northern star,   65
Of whose true-fix'd and resting quality
There is no fellow in the firmament.
The skies are painted with unnumber'd sparks,
They are all fire and every one doth shine,
But there's but one in all doth hold his place: 70
So, in the world; 'tis furnish'd well with men,
And men are flesh and blood, and apprehensive;
Yet in the number I do know but one
That unassailable holds on his rank,
Unshak'd of motion: and that I am he   75
Let me a little show it, even in this,
That I was constant Cimber should be banish'd,
And constant do remain to keep him so.

Cin. O Cæsar,—

Cæs.   Hence! Wilt thou lift up Olympus?   80

Dec. Great Cæsar,—

Cæs.   Doth not Brutus bootless kneel?

Casca. Speak, hands, for me!   *They stab Cæsar.*

Cæs. Et tu, Brute? Then fall, Cæsar!   *Dies.*

Cin. Liberty! Freedom! Tyranny is dead!   85
Run hence, proclaim, cry it about the streets.

Cas. Some to the common pulpits, and cry out,
'Liberty, freedom, and enfranchisement!'

Bru. People and senators, be not affrighted;
Fly not; stand still; ambition's debt is paid.   90

     [Exeunt all but the Conspirators and Publius.]

Casca. Go to the pulpit, Brutus.

Dec.   And Cassius too.

Bru. Where's Publius?

Cin. Here, quite confounded with this mutiny.

Met. Stand fast together, lest some friend of Cæsar's   95
Should chance—

Bru. Talk not of standing. Publius, good cheer;
There is no harm intended to your person,
Nor to no Roman else; so tell them, Publius.

Cas. And leave us, Publius; lest that the people,   100
Rushing on us, should do your age some mischief.

SCENE FIRST S. d. *Before . . . Capitol; cf. n.*   **3 schedule:** *written scroll*   **8 serv'd:** *attended to*   **25 constant:** *unmoved*   **31 prefer:** *present, offer*   **32 address'd:** *ready*   **40 couchings:** *prostrations* **courtesies:** *bowings*   **42 pre-ordinance:** *what is already ordained*   **43 law of children:** *arbitrary uncertainty* **fond:** *foolish*   **44 rebel:** *ungovernable*   **46 With:** *by*

47 Low-crooked: *low-bending* **curtsies:** *same as 'courtesies,' line 40* **spaniel:** *servile, obsequious*   **51, 52** *Cf. n.*   **55 repealing:** *free, unconditional recall*   **58 freedom of repeal:** *free, unconditional recall*   **64** *Cf. n.*   **66 resting:** *stationary*   **68 painted:** *decorated*   **72 apprehensive:** *intelligent*   **74 holds on:** *maintains* **rank:** *position*   **82 bootless:** *unavailingly*   **87 common pulpits:** *public rostra*   **97 good cheer:** *be of good cheer, undismayed*

Bru. Do so; and let no man abide this deed
But we the doers.   [*Exit Publius.*]

Enter Trebonius.

Cas. Where is Antony?
Tre.   Fled to his house amaz'd.   *105*
Men, wives, and children stare, cry out, and run,
As it were doomsday.
Bru.   Fates, we will know your pleasures.
That we shall die, we know; 'tis but the time
And drawing days out, that men stand upon.   *110*
Casca. Why, he that cuts off twenty years of life
Cuts off so many years of fearing death.
Bru. Grant that, and then is death a benefit:
So are we Cæsar's friends, that have abridg'd
His time of fearing death. Stoop, Romans, stoop,   *115*
And let us bathe our hands in Cæsar's blood
Up to the elbows, and besmear our swords:
Then walk we forth, even to the market-place;
And waving our red weapons o'er our heads,
Let's all cry, 'Peace, freedom, and liberty!'   *120*
Cas. Stoop, then, and wash. How many ages hence
Shall this our lofty scene be acted over,
In states unborn and accents yet unknown!
Bru. How many times shall Cæsar bleed in sport,
That now on Pompey's basis lies along,   *125*
No worthier than the dust!
Cas.   So oft as that shall be,
So often shall the knot of us be call'd
The men that gave their country liberty.
Dec. What, shall we forth?   *130*
Cas.   Ay, every man away:
Brutus shall lead; and we will grace his heels
With the most boldest and best hearts of Rome.

Enter a Servant.

Bru. Soft, who comes here? A friend of Antony's.
Serv. Thus, Brutus, did my master bid me kneel;   *135*
Thus did Mark Antony bid me fall down;
And, being prostrate, thus he bade me say:
Brutus is noble, wise, valiant, and honest;
Cæsar was mighty, bold, royal, and loving:
Say I love Brutus, and I honour him;   *140*
Say I fear'd Cæsar, honour'd him, and lov'd him.
If Brutus will vouchsafe that Antony
May safely come to him, and be resolv'd
How Cæsar hath deserv'd to lie in death,
Mark Antony shall not love Cæsar dead   *145*
So well as Brutus living; but will follow
The fortunes and affairs of noble Brutus
Thorough the hazards of this untrod state
With all true faith. So says my master Antony.
Bru. Thy master is a wise and valiant Roman;   *150*
I never thought him worse.
Tell him, so please him come unto this place,
He shall be satisfied; and, by my honour,
Depart untouch'd.

Serv.   I'll fetch him presently.   *Exit Servant.*
Bru. I know that we shall have him well to friend.
Cas. I wish we may: but yet have I a mind
That fears him much; and my misgiving still
Falls shrewdly to the purpose.

Enter Antony.

Bru. But here comes Antony. Welcome, Mark Antony.   *160*
Ant. O mighty Cæsar! dost thou lie so low?
Are all thy conquests, glories, triumphs, spoils,
Shrunk to this little measure? Fare thee well.
I know not, gentlemen, what you intend,
Who else must be let blood, who else is rank: *165*
If I myself, there is no hour so fit
As Cæsar's death's hour, nor no instrument
Of half that worth as those your swords, made rich
With the most noble blood of all this world.
I do beseech ye, if ye bear me hard,   *170*
Now, whilst your purpled hands do reek and smoke,
Fulfil your pleasure. Live a thousand years,
I shall not find myself so apt to die:
No place will please me so, no mean of death,
As here by Cæsar, and by you cut off,   *175*
The choice and master spirits of this age.
Bru. O Antony! beg not your death of us.
Though now we must appear bloody and cruel,
As, by our hands and this our present act,
You see we do, yet see you but our hands   *180*
And this the bleeding business they have done:
Our hearts you see not; they are pitiful;
And pity to the general wrong of Rome—
As fire drives out fire, so pity pity—
Hath done this deed on Cæsar. For your part,   *185*
To you our swords have leaden points, Mark Antony:
Our arms in strength of malice, and our hearts
Of brothers' temper, do receive you in
With all kind love, good thoughts, and reverence.
Cas. Your voice shall be as strong as any man's   *190*
In the disposing of new dignities.
Bru. Only be patient till we have appeas'd
The multitude, beside themselves with fear,
And then we will deliver you the cause
Why I, that did love Cæsar when I struck him,   *195*
Have thus proceeded.
Ant.   I doubt not of your wisdom.
Let each man render me his bloody hand:
First, Marcus Brutus, will I shake with you;
Next, Caius Cassius, do I take your hand;   *200*
Now, Decius Brutus, yours; now yours, Metellus;
Yours, Cinna; and, my valiant Casca, yours;
Though last, not least in love, yours, good Trebonius.
Gentlemen all,—alas! what shall I say?
My credit now stands on such slippery ground,   *205*
That one of two bad ways you must conceit me,
Either a coward or a flatterer.
That I did love thee, Cæsar, O 'tis true:

103 abide: *pay the penalty for*   **106 wives:** *women*   **110 drawing . . . out:** *prolonging their life*   **stand upon:** *lay stress on, worry about*   **125 Pompey's basis:** *pedestal of Pompey's statue*   **along:** *outstretched*   **128 knot:** *group*   **143 resolv'd:** *convinced, satisfied*   **148 Thorough:** *throughout*   **untrod:** *novel, precarious*   **152 so please him:** *if he is willing to*

156 well to friend: *as a good friend*   **158, 159 still . . . purpose:** *always proves only too well grounded*   **165 let blood:** *bled, for medical purposes*   **rank:** *diseased from surfeiting*   **172 Live:** *if I live*   **173 apt:** *ready, fit*   **174 mean:** *means*   **175 by Cæsar:** *beside Cæsar*   **187 malice:** *power (but not wish) to harm; cf. n.*   **191 disposing . . . dignities:** *distributing . . . offices*

If then thy spirit look upon us now,
Shall it not grieve thee dearer than thy death,   210
To see thy Antony making his peace,
Shaking the bloody fingers of thy foes,
Most noble, in the presence of thy corse?
Had I as many eyes as thou hast wounds,
Weeping as fast as they stream forth thy blood,   215
It would become me better than to close
In terms of friendship with thine enemies.
Pardon me, Julius. Here wast thou bay'd, brave hart;
Here didst thou fall; and here thy hunters stand,
Sign'd in thy spoil, and crimson'd in thy lethe.   220
O world, thou wast the forest to this hart,
And this, indeed, O world, the heart of thee.
How like a deer, stricken by many princes,
Dost thou here lie!
    Cas. Mark Antony,—   225
    Ant.   Pardon me, Caius Cassius:
The enemies of Cæsar shall say this;
Then, in a friend, it is cold modesty.
    Cas. I blame you not for praising Cæsar so;
But what compact mean you to have with us?   230
Will you be prick'd in number of our friends,
Or shall we on, and not depend on you?
    Ant. Therefore I took your hands, but was indeed
Sway'd from the point by looking down on Cæsar.
Friends am I with you all, and love you all,   235
Upon this hope, that you shall give me reasons
Why and wherein Cæsar was dangerous.
    Bru. Or else were this a savage spectacle.
Our reasons are so full of good regard
That were you, Antony, the son of Cæsar,   240
You should be satisfied.
    Ant.   That's all I seek:
And am moreover suitor that I may
Produce his body to the market-place,
And in the pulpit, as becomes a friend,   245
Speak in the order of his funeral.
    Bru. You shall, Mark Antony.
    Cas.   Brutus, a word with you.
[Aside to Brutus.] You know not what you do; do not consent
That Antony speak in his funeral: 250
Know you how much the people may be mov'd
By that which he will utter?
    Bru.   By your pardon;
I will myself into the pulpit first,
And show the reason of our Cæsar's death: 255
What Antony shall speak, I will protest
He speaks by leave and by permission,
And that we are contented Cæsar shall
Have all true rites and lawful ceremonies.
It shall advantage more than do us wrong.   260
    Cas. I know not what may fall; I like it not.
    Bru. Mark Antony, here, take you Cæsar's body.
You shall not in your funeral speech blame us,
But speak all good you can devise of Cæsar,

And say you do 't by our permission;   265
Else shall you not have any hand at all
About his funeral; and you shall speak
In the same pulpit whereto I am going,
After my speech is ended.
    Ant.   Be it is;   270
I do desire no more.
    Bru. Prepare the body then, and follow us.
                    Exeunt all but Antony.
    Ant. O pardon me, thou bleeding piece of earth,
That I am meek and gentle with these butchers;
Thou art the ruins of the noblest man   275
That ever lived in the tide of times.
Woe to the hand that shed this costly blood!
Over thy wounds now do I prophesy,—
Which like dumb mouths do ope their ruby lips,
To beg the voice and utterance of my tongue,—   280
A curse shall light upon the limbs of men;
Domestic fury and fierce civil strife
Shall cumber all the parts of Italy:
Blood and destruction shall be so in use,
And dreadful objects so familiar,   285
That mothers shall but smile when they behold
Their infants quarter'd with the hands of war,—
All pity chok'd with custom of fell deeds;
And Cæsar's spirit, ranging for revenge,
With Ate by his side come hot from hell,   290
Shall in these confines with a monarch's voice
Cry 'Havoc! and let slip the dogs of war;
That this foul deed shall smell above the earth
With carrion men, groaning for burial.

        Enter Octavius' Servant.

You serve Octavius Cæsar, do you not?   295
    Serv. I do, Mark Antony.
    Ant. Cæsar did write for him to come to Rome.
    Serv. He did receive his letters, and is coming;
And bid me say to you by word of mouth—   *[Seeing the body.]*
O Cæsar!—   300
    Ant. Thy heart is big, get thee apart and weep.
Passion, I see, is catching; for mine eyes,
Seeing those beads of sorrow stand in thine,
Began to water. Is thy master coming?
    Serv. He lies to-night within seven leagues of Rome.   305
    Ant. Post back with speed, and tell him what hath chanc'd:
Here is a mourning Rome, a dangerous Rome,
No Rome of safety for Octavius yet;
Hie hence and tell him so. Yet, stay awhile;
Thou shalt not back till I have borne this corpse   310
Into the market-place; there shall I try,
In my oration, how the people take
The cruel issue of these bloody men;
According to the which thou shalt discourse
To young Octavius of the state of things.   315
Lend me your hand.   *Exeunt [with Cæsar's body].*

---

213 corse: *corpse*   **216 close:** *unite*   **218 bay'd:** *brought to bay* **hart:** *stag* (on obvious play on words)   **220 Sign'd ... spoil:** *bearing the bloody mark of thy slaughter* **lethe:** *death (?)* **222 this:** *all that he has just been saying* **228 modesty:** *moderation* **231 prick'd in number:** *marked in the list* **239 good regard:** *what deserves approbation* **244 Produce:** *carry forth* **246 order:** *course* **253 By ... pardon:** *pardon me a moment, and I'll explain* **256 protest:** *announce*

276 tide of times: *ebb and flow of human existence* **287 quarter'd:** *hewn into pieces* **288 custom ... deeds:** *the mere frequency of cruel actions* **290 Ate:** *goddess of discord* **291 confines:** *regions* **292 Havoc:** *the signal for killing without sparing* **let slip:** *unleash* **dogs of war:** *cf. n.* **293 That:** *so that* **294 With rotting corpses, too numerous for the burial that they grievously demand* **302 Passion:** *emotion* **313 issue:** *deed* **314 the which:** *the way in which people act*

❧ Scene Second ❧

[The Forum]

Enter Brutus and [presently] goes into the Pulpit, and Cassius, with
the Plebeians.

Plebeians. We will be satisfied: let us be satisfied.

Bru. Then follow me, and give me audience friends.
Cassius, go you into the other street,
And part the numbers.
Those that will hear me speak, let 'em stay here;   5
Those that will follow Cassius, go with him;
And public reasons shall be rendered
Of Cæsar's death.

First Ple.   I will hear Brutus speak.

Sec. Ple. I will hear Cassius, and compare their reasons,   10
When severally we hear them rendered.

          [Exit Cassius, with some of the Plebeians.]

Third Ple. The noble Brutus is ascended: silence!

Bru. Be patient till the last.

Romans, countrymen, and lovers, hear me for my cause, and
be silent, that you may hear: believe me for mine honour,   15
and have respect to mine honour, that you may believe: censure
me in your wisdom, and awake your senses, that you may the
better judge. If there be any in this assembly, any dear friend
of Cæsar's, to him I say, that Brutus' love to Cæsar was no
less than his. If then that friend demand why Brutus rose   20
against Cæsar, this is my answer: Not that I loved Cæsar less,
but that I loved Rome more. Had you rather Cæsar were living, and die all slaves, than that Cæsar were dead, to live all
free men? As Cæsar loved me, I weep for him; as he was fortunate, I rejoice at it; as he was valiant, I honour him; but, as he   25
was ambitious, I slew him. There is tears, for his love; joy, for
his fortune; honour, for his valour; and death, for his ambition. Who is here so base that would be a bondman? If any,
speak; for him have I offended. Who is here so rude that
would not be a Roman? If any, speak; for him have I of-   30
fended. Who is here so vile that will not love his country? If
any, speak; for him have I offended. I pause for a reply.

All. None, Brutus, none.

Bru. Then none have I offended. I have done no more
to Cæsar, than you shall do to Brutus. The question of his   35
death is enrolled in the Capitol; his glory not extenuated,
wherein he was worthy, nor his offences enforced, for which
he suffered death.

Enter Mark Antony, with Cæsar's body.

Here comes his body, mourned by Mark Antony: who, though
he had no hand in his death, shall receive the benefit of his   40
dying, a place in the commonwealth; as which of you shall
not? With this I depart: that, as I slew my best lover for the
good of Rome, I have the same dagger for myself, when it
shall please my country to need my death.

All. Live, Brutus! live! live!   45

First Ple. Bring him with triumph home unto his house.

Sec. Ple. Give him a statue with his ancestors.

Third Ple. Let him be Cæsar.

Fourth Ple.   Cæsar's better parts
Shall be crown'd in Brutus.   50

First Ple. We'll bring him to his house with shouts and
clamours.

Bru. My countrymen,—

Sec. Ple.   Peace! silence! Brutus speaks.

First Ple. Peace, ho!   55

Bru. Good countrymen, let me depart alone,
And, for my sake, stay here with Antony.
Do grace to Cæsar's corpse, and grace his speech
Tending to Cæsar's glories, which Mark Antony,
By our permission, is allow'd to make.   60
I do entreat you, not a man depart,
Save I alone, till Antony have spoke.   *Exit.*

First Ple. Stay, ho! and let us hear Mark Antony.

Third Ple. Let him go up into the public chair;
We'll hear him. Noble Antony, go up.   65

Ant. For Brutus' sake, I am beholding to you.   *[Goes up.]*

Fourth Ple. What does he say of Brutus?

Third Ple.   He says, for Brutus' sake,
He finds himself beholding to us all.

Fourth Ple. 'Twere best he speak no harm of Brutus here.   70

First Ple. This Cæsar was a tyrant.

Third Ple.   Nay, that's certain:
We are bless'd that Rome is rid of him.

Sec. Ple. Peace! let us hear what Antony can say.

Ant. You gentle Romans,—   75

All.   Peace, ho! let us hear him.

Ant. Friends, Romans, countrymen, lend me your ears;
I come to bury Cæsar, not to praise him.
The evil that men do lives after them,
The good is oft interred with their bones;   80
So let it be with Cæsar. The noble Brutus
Hath told you Cæsar was ambitious;
If it were so, it was a grievous fault,
And grievously hath Cæsar answer'd it.
Here, under leave of Brutus and the rest,—   85
For Brutus is an honourable man;
So are they all, all honourable men,—
Come I to speak in Cæsar's funeral.
He was my friend, faithful and just to me:
But Brutus says he was ambitious;   90
And Brutus is an honourable man.
He hath brought many captives home to Rome,
Whose ransoms did the general coffers fill:
Did this in Cæsar seem ambitious?
When that the poor have cried, Cæsar hath wept;   95
Ambition should be made of sterner stuff:
Yet Brutus says he was ambitious;
And Brutus is an honourable man.
You all did see that on the Lupercal
I thrice presented him a kingly crown,   100
Which he did thrice refuse: was this ambition?
Yet Brutus says he was ambitious;
And, sure, he is an honourable man.
I speak not to disprove what Brutus spoke,
But here I am to speak what I do know.   105
You all did love him once, not without cause:
What cause withholds you then to mourn for him?
O judgment, thou art fled to brutish beasts,
And men have lost their reason. Bear with me;

---

4 *And divide the throng*   **13** *Give me a patient hearing, till I finish*   **29 rude:** *uncivi-*
lized   **35 question of:** *official inquest into*   **enrolled:** *recorded*   **36 extenuated:** *belit-*
tled   **37 enforced:** *unduly stressed, strained*

69 beholding: *indebted*   **84 answer'd:** *atoned for*   **93 general coffers:** *public trea-*
sury   **99 on the Lupercal:** *on the day of the Lupercalia*

My heart is in the coffin there with Cæsar,   *110*
And I must pause till it come back to me.
    First Ple. Methinks there is much reason in his sayings.
    Sec. Ple. If thou consider rightly of the matter,
Cæsar has had great wrong.
    Third Ple.   Has he, masters?   *115*
I fear there will a worse come in his place.
    Fourth Ple. Mark'd ye his words? He would not take the
crown;
Therefore 'tis certain he was not ambitious.
    First Ple. If it be found so, some will dear abide it.   *120*
    Sec. Ple. Poor soul, his eyes are red as fire with weeping.
    Third Ple. There's not a nobler man in Rome than Antony.
    Fourth Ple. Now mark him; he begins again to speak.
    Ant. But yesterday the word of Cæsar might
Have stood against the world; now lies he there,   *125*
And none so poor to do him reverence.
O masters, if I were dispos'd to stir
Your hearts and minds to mutiny and rage,
I should do Brutus wrong, and Cassius wrong,
Who, you all know, are honourable men.   *130*
I will not do them wrong; I rather choose
To wrong the dead, to wrong myself, and you,
Than I will wrong such honourable men.
But here's a parchment with the seal of Cæsar;
I found it in his closet; 'tis his will.   *135*
Let but the commons hear this testament—
Which, pardon me, I do not mean to read—
And they would go and kiss dead Cæsar's wounds,
And dip their napkins in his sacred blood,
Yea, beg a hair of him for memory,   *140*
And, dying, mention it within their wills,
Bequeathing it as a rich legacy
Unto their issue.
    Fourth Ple. We'll hear the will: read it, Mark Antony.
    All. The will, the will! we will hear Cæsar's will!   *145*
    Ant. Have patience, gentle friends; I must not read it:
It is not meet you know how Cæsar lov'd you.
You are not wood, you are not stones, but men:
And, being men, hearing the will of Cæsar,
It will inflame you, it will make you mad.   *150*
'Tis good you know not that you are his heirs;
For if you should, O what would come of it?
    Fourth Ple. Read the will! we'll hear it, Antony;
You shall read us the will, Cæsar's will.
    Ant. Will you be patient? Will you stay awhile?   *155*
I have o'ershot myself to tell you of it.
I fear I wrong the honourable men
Whose daggers have stabb'd Cæsar; I do fear it.
    Fourth Ple. They were traitors: honourable men!
    All. The will! the testament!   *160*
    Sec. Ple. They were villains, murderers. The will! read the
will.
    Ant. You will compel me then to read the will?
Then make a ring about the corpse of Cæsar,
And let me show you him that made the will.   *165*
Shall I descend? And will you give me leave?
    All. Come down.

    Sec. Ple. Descend.
    Third Ple. You shall have leave.
    Fourth Ple. A ring; stand round.   *170*
    First Ple. Stand from the hearse; stand from the body.
                                     [Antony comes down.]
    Sec. Ple. Room for Antony, most noble Antony.
    Ant. Nay, press not so upon me; stand far off.
    All. Stand back! room! bear back!
    Ant. If you have tears, prepare to shed them now.   *175*
You all do know this mantle: I remember
The first time ever Cæsar put it on;
'Twas on a summer's evening, in his tent,
That day he overcame the Nervii.
Look, in this place ran Cassius' dagger through: *180*
See what a rent the envious Casca made:
Through this the well-beloved Brutus stabb'd;
And, as he pluck'd his cursed steel away,
Mark how the blood of Cæsar follow'd it,
As rushing out of doors, to be resolv'd   *185*
If Brutus so unkindly knock'd or no;
For Brutus, as you know, was Cæsar's angel:
Judge, O you gods, how dearly Cæsar lov'd him.
This was the most unkindest cut of all;
For when the noble Cæsar saw him stab,   *190*
Ingratitude, more strong than traitors' arms,
Quite vanquish'd him: then burst his mighty heart;
And, in his mantle muffling up his face,
Even at the base of Pompey's statue,
Which all the while ran blood, great Cæsar fell.   *195*
O, what a fall was there, my countrymen!
Then I, and you, and all of us fell down,
Whilst bloody treason flourish'd over us.
O now you weep, and I perceive you feel
The dint of pity; these are gracious drops.   *200*
Kind souls, what, weep you when you but behold
Our Cæsar's vesture wounded? Look you here,
Here is himself, marr'd, as you see, with traitors.
    First Ple. O piteous spectacle!
    Sec. Ple. O noble Cæsar!   *205*
    Third Ple. O woeful day!
    Fourth Ple. O traitors! villains!
    First Ple. O most bloody sight!
    Sec. Ple. We will be revenged.
    [All.] Revenge!—About!—Seek!—Burn!   *210*
Fire!—Kill!—Slay! Let not a traitor live!
    Ant. Stay, countrymen,—
    First Ple. Peace there! Hear the noble Antony.
    Sec. Ple. We'll hear him, we'll follow him, we'll die with
him!   *215*
    Ant. Good friends, sweet friends, let me not stir you up
To such a sudden flood of mutiny.
They that have done this deed are honourable:
What private griefs they have, alas, I know not,
That made them do it; they are wise and honourable,   *220*
And will, no doubt, with reasons answer you.
I come not, friends, to steal away your hearts:
I am no orator, as Brutus is;
But, as you know me all, a plain blunt man,
That love my friend; and that they know full well   *225*

124, 125 word … world: *his bare assertion would have carried his point against the world*   **126** *And there are none so humble as to show him any respect*   **136 commons:** *common people*   **139 napkins:** *handkerchiefs*

179 That day: *on the day on which; cf. n.*   **187 angel:** *dear as his guardian spirit*   **200 dint:** *impression*

That gave me public leave to speak of him.
For I have neither wit, nor words, nor worth,
Action, nor utterance, nor the power of speech,
To stir men's blood: I only speak right on;
I tell you that which you yourselves do know,   *230*
Show you sweet Cæsar's wounds, poor poor dumb mouths,
And bid them speak for me: but were I Brutus,
And Brutus Antony, there were an Antony
Would ruffle up your spirits, and put a tongue
In every wound of Cæsar, that should move   *235*
The stones of Rome to rise and mutiny.
 All. We'll mutiny.
 First Ple. We'll burn the house of Brutus.
 Third Ple. Away, then! Come, seek the conspirators.
 Ant. Yet hear me, countrymen; yet hear me speak.   *240*
 All. Peace, ho!—Hear Antony, most noble Antony!
 Ant. Why, friends, you go to do you know not what.
Wherein hath Cæsar thus deserv'd your loves?
Alas, you know not: I must tell you then.
You have forgot the will I told you of.   *245*
 All. Most true. The will! Let's stay and hear the will.
 Ant. Here is the will, and under Cæsar's seal.
To every Roman citizen he gives,
To every several man, seventy-five drachmas.
 Sec. Ple. Most noble Cæsar! We'll revenge his death.   *250*
 Third Ple. O royal Cæsar!
 Ant. Hear me with patience.
 All. Peace, ho!
 Ant. Moreover, he hath left you all his walks,
His private arbours, and new-planted orchards,   *255*
On this side Tiber; he hath left them you,
And to your heirs for ever; common pleasures,
To walk abroad and recreate yourselves.
Here was a Cæsar! When comes such another?
 First Ple. Never, never! Come, away, away!   *260*
We'll burn his body in the holy place,
And with the brands fire the traitors' houses.
Take up the body.
 Sec. Ple. Go fetch fire.
 Third Ple. Pluck down benches.   *265*
 Fourth Ple. Pluck down forms, windows, anything.
      Exeunt Plebeians [with the body].
 Ant. Now let it work: mischief, thou art afoot;
Take thou what course thou wilt!

    Enter Servant.

       How now, fellow!
 Serv. Sir, Octavius is already come to Rome.   *270*
 Ant. Where is he?
 Serv. He and Lepidus are at Cæsar's house.
 Ant. And thither will I straight to visit him.
He comes upon a wish. Fortune is merry,
And in this mood will give us anything.   *275*
 Serv. I heard him say Brutus and Cassius
Are rid like madmen through the gates of Rome.
 Ant. Belike they had some notice of the people,
How I had mov'd them. Bring me to Octavius.   *Exeunt.*

---

228 **Action, nor utterance:** *orator's powers of gesticulation and elocution* 229 **right on:**
with simple straightforwardness 234 **ruffle:** *stir* 249 **drachmas:** *Greek coins:*
cf. n. 256 **this;** *cf. n.* 257 **pleasures:** *pleasure-grounds* (in which) 266 **forms:** *long*
seats 274 **upon a wish:** *as if at my wish*

     ❧ Scene Third ❧
      [A Street]
 Enter Cinna, the Poet, and after him the Plebeians.

 Cin. I dreamt to-night that I did feast with Cæsar,
And things unluckily charge my fantasy:
I have no will to wander forth of doors,
Yet something leads me forth.
 First Ple. What is your name?   *5*
 Sec. Ple. Whither are you going?
 Third Ple. Where do you dwell?
 Fourth Ple. Are you a married man, or a bachelor?
 Sec. Ple. Answer every man directly.
 First Ple. Ay, and briefly.   *10*
 Fourth Ple. Ay, and wisely.
 Third Ple. Ay, and truly, you were best.
 Cin. What is my name? Whither am I going? Where do I
dwell? Am I a married man, or a bachelor? Then, to answer
every man directly and briefly, wisely and truly: wisely I say, *15*
I am a bachelor.
 Sec. Ple. That's as much as to say, they are fools that marry;
you'll bear me a bang for that, I fear. Proceed; directly.
 Cin. Directly, I am going to Cæsar's funeral.
 First Ple. As a friend or an enemy?   *20*
 Cin. As a friend.
 Sec. Ple. That matter is answered directly.
 Fourth Ple. For your dwelling, briefly?
 Cin. Briefly, I dwell by the Capitol.
 Third Ple. Your name, sir, truly?   *25*
 Cin. Truly, my name is Cinna.
 Sec. Ple. Tear him to pieces; he's a conspirator!
 Cin. I am Cinna the poet, I am Cinna the poet!
 Fourth Ple. Tear him for his bad verses, tear him for his
bad verses!   *30*
 Cin. I am not Cinna the conspirator!
 Sec. Ple. It is no matter, his name's Cinna; pluck but his
name out of his heart, and turn him going.
 Third Ple. Tear him, tear him! Come, brands, ho! Fire-
brands! To Brutus', to Cassius'; burn all. Some to Decius' *35*
house, and some to Casca's; some to Ligarius'. Away! Go!
      Exeunt all the Plebeians.

Act Fourth ❧ Scene First

   [A Room in Antony's House]
 Antony, Octavius, and Lepidus [seated at a table].

 Ant. These many then shall die; their names are prick'd.
 Oct. Your brother too must die; consent you, Lepidus?
 Lep. I do consent.
 Oct.   Prick him down, Antony.
 Lep. Upon condition Publius shall not live,   *5*
Who is your sister's son, Mark Antony.
 Ant. He shall not live; look, with a spot I damn him.
But, Lepidus, go you to Cæsar's house;
Fetch the will hither, and we shall determine

---

2 **unluckily ... fantasy:** *weigh upon my fancy ominously* 12 **you were best:** *it would be*
best for you 18 **bear me a bang:** *get a blow from me* 23 **For:** *now for* 7 **with ...**
him: *by a mark 'pricked' opposite his name, I condemn him*

How to cut off some charge in legacies.　　　　　*10*

Lep. What, shall I find you here?

Oct. Or here or at the Capitol.　　　　　*Exit Lepidus.*

Ant. This is a slight unmeritable man,

Meet to be sent on errands: is it fit,

The three-fold world divided, he should stand　　　　　*15*

One of the three to share it?

Oct.　　　　　So you thought him;

And took his voice who should be prick'd to die,

In our black sentence and proscription.

Ant. Octavius, I have seen more days than you:　　　　　*20*

And though we lay these honours on this man,

To ease ourselves of divers slanderous loads,

He shall but bear them as the ass bears gold,

To groan and sweat under the business,

Either led or driven, as we point the way;　　　　　*25*

And having brought our treasure where we will,

Then take we down his load, and turn him off,

Like to the empty ass, to shake his ears,

And graze in commons.

Oct.　　　　　You may do your will;　　　　　*30*

But he's a tried and valiant soldier.

Ant. So is my horse, Octavius; and for that

I do appoint him store of provender.

It is a creature that I teach to fight,

To wind, to stop, to run directly on,　　　　　*35*

His corporal motion govern'd by my spirit.

And, in some taste, is Lepidus but so;

He must be taught, and train'd, and bid go forth;

A barren-spirited fellow; one that feeds

On objects, arts and imitations　　　　　*40*

Which, out of use and stal'd by other men,

Begin his fashion: do not talk of him

But as a property. And now, Octavius,

Listen great things: Brutus and Cassius

Are levying powers; we must straight make head;　　　　　*45*

Therefore let our alliance be combin'd,

Our best friends made, and our best means stretch'd out;

And let us presently go sit in council,

How covert matters may be best disclos'd,

And open perils surest answered.　　　　　*50*

Oct. Let us do so: for we are at the stake,

And bay'd about with many enemies;

And some that smile have in their hearts, I fear,

Millions of mischiefs.　　　　　*Exeunt.*

❧ SCENE SECOND ❧

[Camp near Sardis. Before Brutus' Tent]
Drum. Enter Brutus, Lucilius, [Lucius,] and the Army. Titinius and Pindarus meet them.

Bru. Stand, ho!

Lucil. Give the word, ho! and stand!

Bru. What now, Lucilius! is Cassius near?

Lucil. He is at hand; and Pindarus is come

To do you salutation from his master.　　　　　*5*

Bru. He greets me well. Your master, Pindarus,

In his own change, or by ill officers,

Hath given me some worthy cause to wish

Things done, undone; but, if he be at hand,

I shall be satisfied.　　　　　*10*

Pin.　　　　　I do not doubt

But that my noble master will appear

Such as he is, full of regard and honour.

Bru. He is not doubted. A word, Lucilius;

How he receiv'd you, let me be resolv'd.　　　　　*15*

Lucil. With courtesy and with respect enough;

But not with such familiar instances,

Nor with such free and friendly conference,

As he hath us'd of old.

Bru.　　　　　Thou hast describ'd　　　　　*20*

A hot friend cooling. Ever note, Lucilius,

When love begins to sicken and decay,

It useth an enforced ceremony.

There are no tricks in plain and simple faith;

But hollow men, like horses hot at hand,　　　　　*25*

Make gallant show and promise of their mettle;

But when they should endure the bloody spur,

They fall their crests, and, like deceitful jades,

Sink in the trial. Comes his army on?

Lucil. They mean this night in Sardis to be quarter'd;　　　　　*30*

The greater part, the horse in general,

Are come with Cassius.

Bru.　　　　　Hark! he is arriv'd.

Low march within.

March gently on to meet him.

Enter Cassius and his Powers.

Cas. Stand, ho!　　　　　*35*

Bru. Stand, ho! Speak the word along.

[First Officer.] Stand!

[Sec. Officer.] Stand!

[Third Officer.] Stand!

Cas. Most noble brother, you have done me wrong.　　　　　*40*

Bru. Judge me, you gods! Wrong I mine enemies?

And, if not so, how should I wrong a brother?

Cas. Brutus, this sober form of yours hides wrongs;

And when you do them—

Bru.　　　　　Cassius, be content;　　　　　*45*

Speak your griefs softly: I do know you well.

Before the eyes of both our armies here,

---

10 **cut . . . charge:** *reduce some expenditures* (by killing the legatees)　　13 **unmeritable:** *without merit*　　15 **The . . . divided:** *if the world is to be divided into three parts*　　19 *In the black sentence of our proscription*　　28 **empty:** *unladen, worthless*　　29 **commons:** *public pasture*　　33 **appoint:** *assign*　　35 **wind:** *turn*　　37 **taste:** *measure, degree*　　39 **barren-spirited:** *lacking initiative*　　40 **objects:** *objects of interest, in general; cf. n.*　　**arts:** *works of art; cf. n.*　　**imitations:** *conventional forms, empty counterfeits*　　41 **stal'd:** *outworn, made stale*　　42 **Begin his fashion:** *rare to him the height of fashion*　　43 **property:** *instrument, tool*　　44 **Listen:** *hear*　　45 **powers:** *armed forces*　　**make head:** *raise an army*　　46 **combin'd:** *confirmed*　　47 **made:** *made sure*　　**stretch'd out:** *strained to the utmost*　　49 **covert:** *hidden*　　**disclos'd:** *discovered*　　50 **answered:** *faced, met*　　51, 52 *Cf. n.*

1 **Stand:** *halt*　　2 **Give the word:** *pass along the command*　　7 *Owing to a change in himself, or through misconduct of subordinates*　　13 **full . . . honour:** *worthy of honorable regard*　　17 **familiar instances:** *marks of familiarity*　　25 **hollow:** *insincere*　　**hot at hand:** *fiery at the start, only*　　28 **fall:** *let fall, lower*　　**jades:** *worthless nags*　　29 **Sink . . . trial:** *fail in the pinch*　　31 **the horse in general:** *all the cavalry*　　34 **gently:** *slowly*　　43 **sober form:** *calm behavior*　　46 **softly:** *gently*

Which should perceive nothing but love from us,
Let us not wrangle: bid them move away;
Then in my tent, Cassius, enlarge your griefs,   50
And I will give you audience.
   Cas.   Pindarus,
Bid our commanders lead their charges off
A little from this ground.
   Bru. Lucilius, do you the like; and let no man   55
Come to our tent till we have done our conference.
Let Lucius and Titinius guard our door.   *Exeunt.*

❦ SCENE THIRD ❦

[Within the Tent of Brutus]
[Enter] Brutus and Cassius.

   Cas. That you have wrong'd me doth appear in this:
You have condemn'd and noted Lucius Pella
For taking bribes here of the Sardians;
Wherein my letters, praying on his side,
Because I knew the man, were slighted off.   5
   Bru. You wrong'd yourself to write in such a case.
   Cas. In such a time as this it is not meet
That every nice offence should bear his comment.
   Bru. Let me tell you, Cassius, you yourself
Are much condemn'd to have an itching palm;   10
To sell and mart your offices for gold
To underservers.
   Cas.   I an itching palm!
You know that you are Brutus that speaks this,
Or, by the gods, this speech were else your last.   15
   Bru. The name of Cassius honours this corruption,
And chastisement doth therefore hide his head.
   Cas. Chastisement!
   Bru. Remember March, the ides of March remember:
Did not great Julius bleed for justice' sake?   20
What villain touch'd his body, that did stab,
And not for justice? What! shall one of us,
That struck the foremost man of all this world
But for supporting robbers, shall we now
Contaminate our fingers with base bribes,   25
And sell the mighty space of our large honours
For so much trash as may be grasped thus?
I had rather be a dog, and bay the moon,
Than such a Roman.
   Cas.   Brutus, bay not me;   30
I'll not endure it: you forget yourself,
To hedge me in. I am a soldier, I,
Older in practice, abler than yourself
To make conditions.
   Bru.   Go to; you are not, Cassius.   35
   Cas. I am.
   Bru. I say you are not.

   Cas. Urge me no more, I shall forget myself;
Have mind upon your health; tempt me no further.
   Bru. Away, slight man!   40
   Cas. Is 't possible?
   Bru.   Hear me, for I will speak.
Must I give way and room to your rash choler?
Shall I be frighted when a madman stares?
   Cas. O ye gods, ye gods! Must I endure all this?   45
   Bru. All this! ay, more: fret till your proud heart break;
Go show your slaves how choleric you are,
And make your bondmen tremble. Must I budge?
Must I observe you? Must I stand and crouch
Under your testy humour? By the gods,   50
You shall digest the venom of your spleen,
Though it do split you; for, from this day forth,
I'll use you for my mirth, yea, for my laughter,
When you are waspish.
   Cas.   Is it come to this?   55
   Bru. You say you are a better soldier:
Let it appear so; make your vaunting true,
And it shall please me well. For mine own part,
I shall be glad to learn of noble men.
   Cas. You wrong me every way; you wrong me, Brutus;   60
I said an elder soldier, not a better:
Did I say, 'better'?
   Bru.   If you did, I care not.
   Cas. When Cæsar liv'd, he durst not thus have mov'd me.
   Bru. Peace, peace! you durst not so have tempted him.   65
   Cas. I durst not?
   Bru. No.
   Cas. What, durst not tempt him?
   Bru.   For your life you durst not.
   Cas. Do not presume too much upon my love;   70
I may do that I shall be sorry for.
   Bru. You have done that you should be sorry for.
There is no terror, Cassius, in your threats;
For I am arm'd so strong in honesty
That they pass by me as the idle wind,   75
Which I respect not. I did send to you
For certain sums of gold, which you denied me;
For I can raise no money by vile means:
By heaven, I had rather coin my heart,
And drop my blood for drachmas, than to wring   80
From the hard hands of peasants their vile trash
By any indirection. I did send
To you for gold to pay my legions,
Which you denied me: was that done like Cassius?
Should I have answer'd Caius Cassius so?   85
When Marcus Brutus grows so covetous,
To lock such rascal counters from his friends,
Be ready, gods, with all your thunderbolts;
Dash him to pieces!
   Cas.   I denied you not.   90
   Bru. You did.
   Cas.   I did not: he was but a fool
That brought my answer back. Brutus hath riv'd my heart.
A friend should bear his friend's infirmities,
But Brutus makes mine greater than they are.   95

---

50 **enlarge:** *set forth fully*   Scene Three S. d.; *cf. n.*   2 **noted:** *stigmatized*   4
praying . . . side: *interceding for him*   5 **slighted off:** *tossed slightingly aside*   8 **nice:**
trivial   **bear . . . comment:** *be censured*   10 **condemn'd to have:** *blamed for having*   11
mart: *market*   16 **honours . . . corruption:** *sanctions this corrupt practice*   21, 22 **What
. . . justice:** *cf. n.*   24 **robbers:** *his dishonest favorites*   26, 27 *Cf. n.*   28 **bay:** *bark
at*   30 *Cf. n.*   33 **practice:** *experience*   34 **make conditions:** *determine the proper
treatment of subordinates* (referring to lines 1–5)   35 **Go to:** *Nonsense!*

39 **Have . . . health:** *have regard for your safety*   48 **budge:** *flinch*   49 **observe:** *pay
humble reverence to*   76 **respect:** *heed*   82 **indirection:** *dishonesty, crooked dealing*   87
rascal counters: *worthless pelf*   93 **riv'd:** *cleft*

Bru. I do not, till you practise them on me.

Cas. You love me not.

Bru.   I do not like your faults.

Cas. A friendly eye could never see such faults.

Bru. A flatterer's would not, though they do appear   *100*
As huge as high Olympus.

Cas. Come, Antony, and young Octavius, come,
Revenge yourselves alone on Cassius,
For Cassius is aweary of the world;
Hated by one he loves; brav'd by his brother;   *105*
Check'd like a bondman; all his faults observ'd,
Set in a note-book, learn'd, and conn'd by rote,
To cast into my teeth. O, I could weep
My spirit from mine eyes. There is my dagger,
And here my naked breast; within, a heart   *110*
Dearer than Pluto's mine, richer than gold:
If that thou be'st a Roman, take it forth;
I, that denied thee gold, will give my heart:
Strike, as thou didst at Cæsar; for, I know,
When thou didst hate him worst, thou lov'dst him better   *115*
Than ever thou lov'dst Cassius.

Bru.   Sheathe your dagger:
Be angry when you will, it shall have scope;
Do what you will, dishonour shall be humour.
O Cassius, you are yoked with a lamb   *120*
That carries anger as the flint bears fire,
Who, much enforced, shows a hasty spark,
And straight is cold again.

Cas.   Hath Cassius liv'd
To be but mirth and laughter to his Brutus,   *125*
When grief and blood ill-temper'd vexeth him?

Bru. When I spoke that I was ill-temper'd too.

Cas. Do you confess so much? Give me your hand.

Bru. And my heart too.

Cas.   O Brutus!   *130*

Bru.   What's the matter?

Cas. Have not you love enough to bear with me,
When that rash humour which my mother gave me
Makes me forgetful?

Bru.   Yes, Cassius; and from henceforth   *135*
When you are over-earnest with your Brutus,
He'll think your mother chides, and leave you so.

Poet. [Within.] Let me go in to see the generals;
There is some grudge between 'em, 'tis not meet
They be alone.   *140*

Lucil. [Within.] You shall not come to them.

Poet. [Within.] Nothing but death shall stay me.

Enter a Poet [followed by Lucilius, Titinius, and Lucius].

Cas. How now! What's the matter?

Poet. For shame, you generals! What do you mean?
Love, and be friends, as two such men should be;   *145*
For I have seen more years, I'm sure, than ye.

Cas. Ha, ha! how vilely doth this cynic rime!

Bru. Get you hence, sirrah; saucy fellow, hence!

Cas. Bear with him, Brutus; 'tis his fashion.

Bru. I'll know his humour, when he knows his time: *150*
What should the wars do with these jigging fools?
Companion, hence!

Cas.   Away, away: be gone!   *Exit Poet.*

Bru. Lucilius and Titinius, bid the commanders
Prepare to lodge their companies to-night.   *155*

Cas. And come yourselves, and bring Messala with you,
Immediately to us.   *[Exeunt Lucilius and Titinius.]*

Bru.   Lucius, a bowl of wine!   *[Exit Lucius.]*

Cas. I did not think you could have been so angry.

Bru. O Cassius, I am sick of many griefs.   *160*

Cas. Of your philosophy you make no use,
If you give place to accidental evils.

Bru. No man bears sorrow better: Portia is dead.

Cas. Ha? Portia?

Bru. She is dead.   *165*

Cas. How 'scap'd I killing when I cross'd you so?
O insupportable and touching loss!
Upon what sickness?

Bru.   Impatient of my absence,
And grief that young Octavius with Mark Antony   *170*
Have made themselves so strong;—for with her death
That tidings came:—with this she fell distract,
And, her attendants absent, swallow'd fire.

Cas. And died so?

Bru.   Even so.   *175*

Cas.   O ye immortal gods!

Enter Boy [Lucius], with wine and tapers.

Bru. Speak no more of her. Give me a bowl of wine.
In this I bury all unkindness, Cassius.   *Drinks.*

Cas. My heart is thirsty for that noble pledge.
Fill, Lucius, till the wine o'erswell the cup;   *180*
I cannot drink too much of Brutus' love.   *[Drinks.]*

Bru. Come in, Titinius.   *[Exit Lucius.]*

Enter Titinius and Messala.

Welcome, good Messala.
Now sit we close about this taper here,
And call in question our necessities.   *185*

Cas. Portia, art thou gone?

Bru.   No more, I pray you.
Messala, I have here received letters,
That young Octavius and Mark Antony
Come down upon us with a mighty power,   *190*
Bending their expedition towards Philippi.

Mes. Myself have letters of the self-same tenour.

Bru. With what addition?

Mes. That by proscription and bills of out-lawry,
Octavius, Antony, and Lepidus,   *195*
Have put to death an hundred senators.

Bru. Therein our letters do not well agree;
Mine speak of seventy senators that died
By their proscriptions, Cicero being one.

Cas. Cicero one?   *200*

Mes.   Cicero is dead,

---

105 brav'd: *blusteringly taunted*   **106 Check'd:** *scolded*   **107 learn'd ... rote:** *studied, and learned by heart*   **111 Dearer:** *worth more*   **Pluto's;** *cf. n.*   **118 it ... scope:** *your anger shall not be opposed*   **119 dishonour ... humour:** *your dishonorable deeds shall be ignored as caprices*   **120-123** *Cf. n.*   **126 blood ill-temper'd:** *disordered condition*   **147 cynic:** *so called because Diogenes affected rudeness*

150 I'll listen to his folly when he learns the proper time for it   **151 jigging:** *doggerel rhyming*   **152 Companion:** *base fellow*   **155 lodge ... to-night:** *encamp for the night*   **162 give ... accidental:** *admit the power of casual*   **168 upon:** *of*   **169 Impatient of:** *unable to endure*   **170 grief;** *cf. n.*   **172 fell distract:** *became distracted*   **185 call in question:** *bring up for discussion*   **191 Bending ... expedition:** *directing their march*

And by that order of proscription.
Had you your letters from your wife, my lord?
  Bru. No, Messala.
  Mes. Nor nothing in your letters writ of her?   205
  Bru. Nothing, Messala.
  Mes.   That, methinks, is strange.
  Bru. Why ask you? Hear you aught of her in yours?
  Mes. No, my lord.
  Bru. Now, as you are a Roman, tell me true.   210
  Mes. Then like a Roman bear the truth I tell:
For certain she is dead, and by strange manner.
  Bru. Why, farewell, Portia. We must die, Messala:
With meditating that she must die once,
I have the patience to endure it now.   215
  Mes. Even so great men great losses should endure.
  Cas. I have as much of this in art as you,
But yet my nature could not bear it so.
  Bru. Well, to our work alive. What do you think
Of marching to Philippi presently?   220
  Cas. I do not think it good.
  Bru.   Your reason?
  Cas.   This is it:
'Tis better that the enemy seek us:
So shall he waste his means, weary his soldiers,   225
Doing himself offence; whilst we, lying still,
Are full of rest, defence, and nimbleness.
  Bru. Good reasons must, of force, give place to better.
The people 'twixt Philippi and this ground
Do stand but in a forc'd affection;   230
For they have grudg'd us contribution:
The enemy, marching along by them,
By them shall make a fuller number up,
Come on refresh'd, new-added, and encourag'd;
From which advantage shall we cut him off,   235
If at Philippi we do face him there,
These people at our back.
  Cas.   Hear me, good brother.
  Bru. Under your pardon. You must note beside,
That we have tried the utmost of our friends,   240
Our legions are brim-full, our cause is ripe:
The enemy increaseth every day;
We, at the height, are ready to decline.
There is a tide in the affairs of men,
Which, taken at the flood, leads on to fortune;   245
Omitted, all the voyage of their life
Is bound in shallows and in miseries.
On such a full sea are we now afloat;
And we must take the current when it serves,
Or lose our ventures.   250
  Cas.   Then, with your will, go on;
We'll along ourselves, and meet them at Philippi.
  Bru. The deep of night is crept upon our talk,
And nature must obey necessity,
Which we will niggard with a little rest.   255
There is no more to say?
  Cas.   No more. Good-night:

Early to-morrow will we rise, and hence.
  Bru. Lucius!

                Enter Lucius.

        My gown.   *[Exit Lucius.]*   260
            Farewell, good Messala:
Good-night, Titinius. Noble, noble Cassius,
Good-night, and good repose.
  Cas.   O my dear brother!
This was an ill beginning of the night: 265
Never come such division 'tween our souls!
Let it not, Brutus.
  Bru.   Everything is well.
  Cas. Good-night, my lord.
  Bru.   Good-night, good brother.   270
  Tit.   }
  Mes. } Good-night, Lord Brutus.
  Bru.   Farewell, every one.
              Exeunt [all but Brutus].

        Enter Lucius, with the gown.

Give me the gown. Where is thy instrument?
  Luc. Here in the tent.   275
  Bru.   What, thou speak'st drowsily?
Poor knave, I blame thee not; thou art o'er-watch'd.
Call Claudius and some other of my men;
I'll have them sleep on cushions in my tent.
  Luc. Varro! and Claudius!   280

        Enter Varro and Claudius.

  Var. Calls my lord?
  Bru. I pray you, sirs, lie in my tent and sleep:
It may be I shall raise you by and by
On business to my brother Cassius.
  Var. So please you, we will stand and watch your pleasure.   285
  Bru. I will not have it so; lie down, good sirs;
It may be I shall otherwise bethink me.
           [Varro and Claudius lie down.]
Look, Lucius, here's the book I sought for so;
I put it in the pocket of my gown.
  Luc. I was sure your lordship did not give it me.   290
  Bru. Bear with me, good boy, I am much forgetful
Canst thou hold up thy heavy eyes awhile,
And touch thy instrument a strain or two?
  Luc. Ay, my lord, an 't please you.
  Bru.   It does, my boy: 295
I trouble thee too much, but thou art willing.
  Luc. It is my duty, sir.
  Bru. I should not urge thy duty past thy might;
I know young bloods look for a time of rest.
  Luc. I have slept, my lord, already.   300
  Bru. It was well done, and thou shalt sleep again;
I will not hold thee long: if I do live,
I will be good to thee.   *Music, and a Song.*
This is a sleepy tune: O murderous slumber,
Lay'st thou thy leaden mace upon my boy,   305
That plays thee music? Gentle knave, good-night;

---

206 **Nothing, Messala;** *cf. n.*   214 **once:** *some day*   217 **art:** *theory*   219 **alive:** *which concerns the living*   228 **force:** *necessity*   230 *Are friendly to us only under compulsion*   234 **new-added:** *newly augmented*   240 *That we have drawn on our friends to the utmost*   246 **Omitted:** *if it is neglected*   247 **bound in:** *confined to*   250 **ventures:** *investments*   251 **with your will:** *according to your preference*   255 *So to nature's need we will dole out a little rest*

277 **knave:** *boy* **o'er-watch'd:** *worn out by lack of sleep*   283 **raise:** *rouse*   285 **watch:** *wakefully await*   291 **much:** *very*   293 *Play a tune or two on thy lute*   304 **murderous:** *because rendering apparently lifeless*   305 **leaden:** *dull and heavy* **mace:** *bailiff's staff for arresting people*

I will not do thee so much wrong to wake thee.
If thou dost nod, thou break'st thy instrument;
I'll take it from thee; and, good boy, good-night.
Let me see, let me see; is not the leaf turn'd down   *310*
Where I left reading? Here it is, I think.

       Enter the Ghost of Cæsar.

How ill this taper burns. Ha! Who comes here?
I think it is the weakness of mine eyes
That shapes this monstrous apparition.
It comes upon me. Art thou anything?   *315*
Art thou some god, some angel, or some devil,
That mak'st my blood cold and my hair to stare?
Speak to me what thou art.
     Ghost. Thy evil spirit, Brutus.
     Bru.   Why com'st thou?   *320*
     Ghost. To tell thee thou shalt see me at Philippi.
     Bru. Well; then I shall see thee again?
     Ghost.   Ay, at Philippi.
     Bru. Why, I will see thee at Philippi then.   *[Exit Ghost.]*
Now I have taken heart, thou vanishest: *325*
Ill spirit, I would hold more talk with thee.
Boy, Lucius! Varro! Claudius! Sirs, awake!
Claudius!
     Luc. The strings, my lord, are false.
     Bru. He thinks he still is at his instrument.   *330*
Lucius, awake!
     Luc. My lord!
     Bru. Didst thou dream, Lucius, that thou so criedst out?
     Luc. My lord, I do not know that I did cry.
     Bru. Yes, that thou didst. Didst thou see anything?   *335*
     Luc. Nothing, my lord.
     Bru. Sleep again, Lucius. Sirrah, Claudius! Fellow thou,
awake!
     Var. My lord!
     Clau. My lord!   *340*
     Bru. Why did you so cry out, sirs, in your sleep?
     Both. Did we, my lord?
     Bru.   Ay: saw you anything?
     Var. No, my lord, I saw nothing.
     Clau.   Nor I, my lord.   *345*
     Bru. Go, and commend me to my brother Cassius:
Bid him set on his powers betimes before,
And we will follow.
     Both. It shall be done, my lord.   *Exeunt.*

ACT FIFTH ❧ SCENE FIRST

[The Plains of Philippi]
Enter Octavius, Antony, and their Army.

     Oct. Now, Antony, our hopes are answered:
You said the enemy would not come down,
But keep the hills and upper regions;
It proves not so; their battles are at hand;
They mean to warn us at Philippi here,   *5*

Answering before we do demand of them.
     Ant. Tut, I am in their bosoms, and I know
Wherefore they do it: they could be content
To visit other places; and come down
With fearful bravery, thinking by this face   *10*
To fasten in our thoughts that they have courage;
But 'tis not so.

       Enter a Messenger.

     Mess.   Prepare you, generals:
The enemy comes on in gallant show;
Their bloody sign of battle is hung out,   *15*
And something to be done immediately.
     Ant. Octavius, lead your battle softly on,
Upon the left hand of the even field.
     Oct. Upon the right hand I; keep thou the left.
     Ant. Why do you cross me in this exigent?   *20*
     Oct. I do not cross you; but I will do so.   *March.*

       Drum. Enter Brutus, Cassius, and their Army.

     Bru. They stand, and would have parley.
     Cas. Stand fast, Titinius: we must out and talk.
     Oct. Mark Antony, shall we give sign of battle?
     Ant. No, Cæsar, we will answer on their charge.   *25*
Make forth; the generals would have some words.
     Oct. *[To his troops.]* Stir not until the signal.
     Bru. Words before blows: is it so, countrymen?
     Oct. Not that we love words better, as you do.
     Bru. Good words are better than bad strokes, Octavius.   *30*
     Ant. In your bad strokes, Brutus, you give good words:
Witness the hole you made in Cæsar's heart,
Crying, 'Long live! Hail, Cæsar!'
     Cas.   Antony,
The posture of your blows are yet unknown;   *35*
But for your words, they rob the Hybla bees,
And leave them honeyless.
     Ant.   Not stingless too!
     Bru. O yes, and soundless too;
For you have stol'n their buzzing, Antony,   *40*
And very wisely threat before you sting.
     Ant. Villains! you did not so when your vile daggers
Hack'd one another in the sides of Cæsar:
You show'd your teeth like apes, and fawn'd like hounds,
And bow'd like bondmen, kissing Cæsar's feet;   *45*
Whilst damned Casca, like a cur, behind
Struck Cæsar on the neck. O you flatterers!
     Cas. Flatterers! Now, Brutus, thank yourself:
This tongue had not offended so to-day,
If Cassius might have rul'd.   *50*
     Oct. Come, come, the cause: if arguing make us sweat,
The proof of it will turn to redder drops.
Look:
I draw a sword against conspirators;
When think you that the sword goes up again?   *55*

---

312 **How … burns:** *accepted sign of an apparition's presence*   *315* **upon:** *towards*   *317*
stare: *stand on end*   *1* **answered:** *fulfilled*   *4* **battles:** *battalions*   *5* **warn:** *summon,*
challenge

7 **bosoms:** *secrets*   *10* **fearful bravery:** *cowardly bravado*   **face:** *pretense*   *15* **bloody …**
battle: *signal for immediate combat*   *18* **even:** *equally divided*   *20* **exigent:** *emer-*
gency   *21* **but … so:** *but I shall do as I said*   *22* **parley:** *conference*   *25* **answer …**
charge: *fight when they attack*   *26* **Make forth:** *step forward*   *31* **In … strokes:** *while*
delivering foul blows   *35* **posture:** *nature (?)*   **are:** *a plural by attraction*   *36* **Hybla:**
town in Sicily, famous for its honey   *44* **show'd … apes:** *simulated smiles of affection, like*
favorite pets   *47* **flatterers:** *treacherous hypocrites*   *51* **the cause:** *let's get down to business*

Never, till Cæsar's three-and-thirty wounds
Be well aveng'd; or till another Cæsar
Have added slaughter to the sword of traitors.
   Bru. Cæsar, thou canst not die by traitors' hands,
Unless thou bring'st them with thee.   *60*
   Oct.   So I hope;
I was not born to die on Brutus' sword.
   Bru. O, if thou wert the noblest of thy strain,
Young man, thou couldst not die more honourable.
   Cas. A peevish schoolboy, worthless of such honour,   *65*
Join'd with a masquer and a reveller.
   Ant. Old Cassius still!
   Oct.   Come, Antony; away!
Defiance, traitors, hurl we in your teeth.
If you dare fight to-day, come to the field;   *70*
If not, when you have stomachs.
                   Exeunt Octavius, Antony, and Army.
   Cas. Why now, blow wind, swell billow, and swim bark!
The storm is up, and all is on the hazard.
   Bru. Ho, Lucilius: hark, a word with you.
   Lucil. [*Standing forth.*]   My lord?   *75*
                [Brutus and Lucilius talk apart.]
   Cas. Messala.
   Mes. [*Standing forth.*] What says my general?
   Cas.   Messala,
This is my birth-day; as this very day
Was Cassius born. Give me thy hand, Messala: *80*
Be thou my witness that against my will,
As Pompey was, am I compell'd to set
Upon one battle all our liberties.
You know that I held Epicurus strong,
And his opinion; now I change my mind,   *85*
And partly credit things that do presage.
Coming from Sardis, on our former ensign
Two mighty eagles fell, and there they perch'd,
Gorging and feeding from our soldiers' hands;
Who to Philippi here consorted us: *90*
This morning are they fled away and gone,
And in their stead do ravens, crows, and kites
Fly o'er our heads, and downward look on us,
As we were sickly prey: their shadows seem
A canopy most fatal, under which   *95*
Our army lies, ready to give up the ghost.
   Mes. Believe not so.
   Cas.   I but believe it partly,
For I am fresh of spirit and resolv'd
To meet all perils very constantly.   *100*
   Bru. Even so, Lucilius.
   Cas.   Now, most noble Brutus,
The gods to-day stand friendly, that we may,
Lovers in peace, lead on our days to age!
But since the affairs of men rest still incertain,   *105*
Let's reason with the worst that may befall.
If we do lose this battle, then is this
The very last time we shall speak together:

What are you, then, determined to do?
   Bru. Even by the rule of that philosophy   *110*
By which I did blame Cato for the death
Which he did give himself—(I know not how,
But I do find it cowardly and vile,
For fear of what might fall, so to prevent
The time of life)—arming myself with patience,   *115*
To stay the providence of some high powers
That govern us below.
   Cas.   Then, if we lose this battle,
You are contented to be led in triumph
Thorough the streets of Rome?   *120*
   Bru. No, Cassius, no: think not, thou noble Roman,
That ever Brutus will go bound to Rome;
He bears too great a mind: but this same day
Must end that work the ides of March begun;
And whether we shall meet again I know not.   *125*
Therefore our everlasting farewell take:
For ever, and for ever, farewell, Cassius.
If we do meet again, why, we shall smile;
If not, why then this parting was well made.
   Cas. For ever, and for ever, farewell, Brutus.   *130*
If we do meet again, we'll smile indeed;
If not, 'tis true this parting was well made.
   Bru. Why, then, lead on. O, that a man might know
The end of this day's business, ere it come!
But it sufficeth that the day will end,   *135*
And then the end is known. Come, ho! away!   *Exeunt.*

❧ SCENE SECOND ❧

[The Same. The Field of Battle]
Alarum. Enter Brutus and Messala.

   Bru. Ride, ride, Messala, ride, and give these bills
Unto the legions on the other side.   *Loud alarum.*
Let them set on at once, for I perceive
But cold demeanour in Octavius' wing,
And sudden push gives them the overthrow.   *5*
Ride, ride, Messala: let them all come down.   *Exeunt.*

❧ SCENE THIRD ❧

[Another part of the Field]
Alarums. Enter Cassius and Titinius.

   Cas. O look, Titinius, look, the villains fly!
Myself have to mine own turn'd enemy:
This ensign here of mine was turning back;
I slew the coward, and did take it from him.
   Tit. O Cassius! Brutus gave the word too early;   *5*
Who, having some advantage on Octavius,
Took it too eagerly: his soldiers fell to spoil,
Whilst we by Antony are all enclos'd.

Enter Pindarus.

   Pin. Fly further off, my lord, fly further off;

---

56 **three-and-thirty;** *cf. n.*   63 **strain:** *race*   65 **peevish:** *silly*   **such honour:** *i.e., that of dying on Brutus' sword*   67 **Old ... still:** *you are still the same old Cassius*   71 **stomachs:** *courage*   79 **as:** *a colloquial expletive*   82 **As Pompey:** *at the battle of Pharsalia, 48 B. C.*   84 **held ... strong:** *believed Epicurus right in disregarding omens*   87 **former ensign:** *banner at the front of our column*   90 **consorted:** *accompanied*   94 **As:** *as if*   **sickly prey:** *so sick as soon to be their prey*   95 **fatal:** *fateful, doom-foreboding*   103 **The gods:** *may the gods*   106 **reason with:** *consider*

111 **Cato:** *of Utica; committed suicide, 46 B. C.*   116 **stay:** *await, submit to*   121-125 *Cf. n.*   1 **bills:** *written orders*   2 **side:** *wing, commanded by Cassius*   4 **cold demeanour:** *faint-heartedness*   2 **mine own:** *my own troops*   4 **coward:** *i.e., the standard-bearer*

Mark Antony is in your tents, my lord: *10*
Fly, therefore, noble Cassius, fly far off.
   Cas. This hill is far enough. Look, look, Titinius;
Are those my tents where I perceive the fire?
   Tit. They are, my lord.
   Cas.   Titinius, if thou lovest me,   *15*
Mount thou my horse, and hide thy spurs in him,
Till he have brought thee up to yonder troops
And here again; that I may rest assur'd
Whether yond troops are friend or enemy.
   Tit. I will be here again, even with a thought.   *Exit.*   *20*
   Cas. Go, Pindarus, get higher on that hill;
My sight was ever thick; regard Titinius,
And tell me what thou not'st about the field.

                      [Pindarus ascends the hill.]

This day I breathed first; time is come round,
And where I did begin, there shall I end;   *25*
My life is run his compass. Sirrah, what news?
   Pin. [Above.] O my lord!
   Cas. What news?
   Pin. [Above.] Titinius is enclosed round about
With horsemen, that make to him on the spur;   *30*
Yet he spurs on. Now they are almost on him:
Now, Titinius! Now some light; O, he lights too:
He's ta'en.   *Shout.*
           And hark, they shout for joy.
   Cas. Come down; behold no more.   *35*
O, coward that I am, to live so long,
To see my best friend ta'en before my face!

          Enter Pindarus [below].

Come hither, sirrah:
In Parthia did I take thee prisoner;
And then I swore thee, saving of thy life,   *40*
That whatsoever I did bid thee do,
Thou shouldst attempt it. Come now, keep thine oath;
Now be a freeman; and with this good sword,
That ran through Cæsar's bowels, search this bosom.
Stand not to answer; here, take thou the hilts;   *45*
And, when my face is cover'd, as 'tis now,
Guide thou the sword.—Cæsar, thou art reveng'd,
Even with the sword that kill'd thee.   *[Dies.]*
   Pin. So, I am free; yet would not so have been,
Durst I have done my will. O Cassius,   *50*
Far from this country Pindarus shall run,
Where never Roman shall take note of him.   *Exit.*

          Enter Titinius and Messala.

   Mes. It is but change, Titinius; for Octavius
Is overthrown by noble Brutus' power,
As Cassius' legions are by Antony.   *55*
   Tit. These tidings will well comfort Cassius.
   Mes. Where did you leave him?
   Tit.   All disconsolate.
With Pindarus his bondman, on this hill.
   Mes. Is not that he that lies upon the ground?   *60*

   Tit. He lies not like the living. O my heart!
   Mes. Is not that he?
   Tit.   No, this was he, Messala.
But Cassius is no more. O setting sun,
As in thy red rays thou dost sink to night,   *65*
So in his red blood Cassius' day is set.
The sun of Rome is set. Our day is gone;
Clouds, dews, and dangers come; our deeds are done.
Mistrust of my success hath done this deed.
   Mes. Mistrust of good success hath done this deed.   *70*
O hateful error, melancholy's child,
Why dost thou show to the apt thoughts of men
The things that are not? O error, soon conceiv'd,
Thou never com'st unto a happy birth,
But kill'st the mother that engender'd thee.   *75*
   Tit. What, Pindarus! Where art thou, Pindarus?
   Mes. Seek him, Titinius, whilst I go to meet
The noble Brutus, thrusting this report
Into his ears; I may say, thrusting it:
For piercing steel and darts envenomed   *80*
Shall be as welcome to the ears of Brutus
As tidings of this sight.
   Tit.   Hie you, Messala,
And I will seek for Pindarus the while.   *[Exit Messala.]*
Why didst thou send me forth, brave Cassius?   *85*
Did I not meet thy friends, and did not they
Put on my brows this wreath of victory,
And bid me give it thee? Didst thou not hear their shouts?
Alas, thou hast misconstru'd everything.
But, hold thee, take this garland on thy brow;   *90*
Thy Brutus bid me give it thee, and I
Will do his bidding. Brutus, come apace,
And see how I regarded Caius Cassius.
By your leave, gods: this is a Roman's part:
Come, Cassius' sword, and find Titinius' heart.   *Dies.*   *95*

Alarum. Enter Brutus, Messala, Young Cato, Strato, Volumnius,
                    and Lucilius.

   Bru. Where, where, Messala, doth his body lie?
   Mes. Lo, yonder: and Titinius mourning it.
   Bru. Titinius' face is upward.
   Cato.   He is slain.
   Bru. O Julius Cæsar, thou art mighty yet!   *100*
Thy spirit walks abroad, and turns our swords
In our own proper entrails.   *Low alarums.*
   Cato.   Brave Titinius!
Look whether he have not crown'd dead Cassius!
   Bru. Are yet two Romans living such as these?   *105*
The last of all the Romans, fare thee well!
It is impossible that ever Rome
Should breed thy fellow. Friends, I owe more tears
To this dead man than you shall see me pay.—
I shall find time, Cassius, I shall find time.—   *110*
Come therefore, and to Thasos send his body:
His funerals shall not be in our camp,
Lest it discomfort us. Lucilius, come;

---

20 even with: *quick as*   **22 thick:** *dull, imperfect*   **26 is . . . compass:** *has completed its cycle*   **32 lights:** *alight, dismount*   **39 Parthia:** *in Crassus' disastrous campaign, in 53 B. C.*   **40 swore thee:** *made thee swear*   **saving of:** *in return for my sparing*   **43 freeman:** *Cassius' death will free him from slavery*   **44 search:** *probe*   **52 take note of:** *see*   **53 change:** *exchange*

68 our . . . done: *all is over*   **70 Mistrust . . . success:** *misgivings about the outcome of my errand*   **71 melancholy's child:** *result of despondency*   **72 apt:** *impressionable*   **90 hold thee:** *wait a moment*   **92 apace:** *quickly*   **94 By . . . gods:** *a proud apology for taking his fate into his own hands*   **102 proper:** *individual*   **108 fellow:** *equal*   **111 Thasos:** *isle near Thrace*   **113 discomfort:** *dishearten*

And come, young Cato;—let us to the field.
Labeo and Flavius, set our battles on: *115*
'Tis three o'clock; and, Romans, yet ere night
We shall try fortune in a second fight.   *Exeunt.*

❧ SCENE FOURTH ❧

[Another part of the Field]
Alarum. Enter Brutus, Messala, Cato, Lucilius, and Flavius.

Bru. Yet, countrymen, O yet hold up your heads!
  Cato. What bastard doth not? Who will go with me?
I will proclaim my name about the field:
I am the son of Marcus Cato, ho!
A foe to tyrants, and my country's friend;   *5*
I am the son of Marcus Cato, ho!
  [Bru.] And I am Brutus, Marcus Brutus, I;
Brutus, my country's friend; know me for Brutus!
           [Exit Brutus, fighting. Cato is slain.]
  Lucil. O young and noble Cato, art thou down?
Why, now thou diest as bravely as Titinius,   *10*
And may'st be honour'd being Cato's son.
  First Sold. Yield, or thou diest.
  Lucil.   Only I yield to die:
There is so much, that thou wilt kill me straight:
Kill Brutus, and be honour'd in his death.   *15*
  First Sold. We must not. A noble prisoner!
  Sec. Sold. Room, ho! Tell Antony, Brutus is ta'en.
  First Sold. I'll tell the news: here comes the general.

Enter Antony.

Brutus is ta'en, Brutus is ta'en, my lord.
  Ant. Where is he?   *20*
  Lucil. Safe, Antony; Brutus is safe enough:
I dare assure thee that no enemy
Shall ever take alive the noble Brutus:
The gods defend him from so great a shame!
When you do find him, or alive or dead,   *25*
He will be found like Brutus, like himself.
  Ant. This is not Brutus, friend; but, I assure you,
A prize no less in worth. Keep this man safe,
Give him all kindness: I had rather have
Such men my friends than enemies. Go on,   *30*
And see whether Brutus be alive or dead;
And bring us word, unto Octavius' tent,
How everything is chanc'd.   *Exeunt.*

❧ SCENE FIFTH ❧

[Another part of the Field]
Enter Brutus, Dardanius, Clitus, Strato, and Volumnius.

Bru. Come, poor remains of friends, rest on this rock.
  Cli. Statilius show'd the torch-light; but, my lord,
He came not back: he is or ta'en or slain.
  Bru. Sit thee down, Clitus: slaying is the word;
It is a deed in fashion. Hark thee, Clitus.   *[Whispers.]*   *5*
  Cli. What, I, my lord? No, not for all the world.
  Bru. Peace, then: no words.
  Cli.   I'll rather kill myself.
  Bru. Hark thee, Dardanius.   *[Whispers.]*
  Dar.   Shall I do such a deed?   *10*
  Cli. O, Dardanius!
  Dar. O, Clitus!
  Cli. What ill request did Brutus make to thee?
  Dar. To kill him, Clitus. Look, he meditates.
  Cli. Now is that noble vessel full of grief,   *15*
That it runs over even at his eyes.
  Bru. Come hither, good Volumnius: list a word.
  Vol. What says my lord?
  Bru.   Why this, Volumnius:
The ghost of Cæsar hath appear'd to me   *20*
Two several times by night; at Sardis once,
And this last night here in Philippi fields.
I know my hour is come.
  Vol.   Not, so, my lord.
  Bru. Nay, I am sure it is, Volumnius.   *25*
Thou seest the world, Volumnius, how it goes;
Our enemies have beat us to the pit: *Low alarums.*
It is more worthy to leap in ourselves,
Than tarry till they push us. Good Volumnius,
Thou know'st that we two went to school together: *30*
Even for that our love of old, I prithee,
Hold thou my sword-hilts whilst I run on it.
  Vol. That's not an office for a friend, my lord.
            Alarum still.
  Cli. Fly, fly, my lord: there is no tarrying here!
  Bru. Farewell to you; and you; and you, Volumnius.   *35*
Strato, thou hast been all this while asleep;
Farewell to thee too, Strato. Countrymen,
My heart doth joy that yet, in all my life,
I found no man but he was true to me.
I shall have glory by this losing day   *40*
More than Octavius and Mark Antony
By this vile conquest shall attain unto.
So fare you well at once; for Brutus' tongue
Hath almost ended his life's history;
Night hangs upon mine eyes; my bones would rest,   *45*
That have but labour'd to attain this hour.
         Alarum. Cry within, 'Fly, fly, fly!'
  Cli. Fly, my lord, fly!
  Bru.   Hence: I will follow.
       [Exeunt Clitus, Dardanius, and Volumnius.]
I prithee, Strato, stay thou by thy lord:
Thou art a fellow of a good respect;   *50*

116, 117 **three o'clock ... second fight;** *cf. n.*   **2 What ... not:** *Who is so base-born as not to do so?*   **7 [Bru.];** *cf. n.*   **13 Only ... die:** *I yield only in order that I may die*   **14, 15** *Cf. n.*

1 poor remains of: *few surviving*   **2, 3** *Cf. n.*   **15 noble vessel;** *cf. n. Tim. 2.21*   **27 pit:** *brink of destruction*   **43 at once:** *once for all; or, all of you*   **43, 44 Brutus' ... history:** *Brutus' life will end with this very speech, almost*   **46** *Cf. Psalm 90.10*

Thy life hath had some smatch of honour in it:
Hold then my sword, and turn away thy face,
While I do run upon it. Wilt thou, Strato?
    Stra. Give me your hand first: fare you well, my lord.
    Bru. Farewell, good Strato.—Cæsar, now be still;   55
I kill'd not thee with half so good a will.   *Dies.*

Alarum. Retreat. Enter Antony, Octavius, Messala, Lucilius, and
the Army.

    Oct. What man is that?
    Mes. My master's man. Strato, where is thy master?
    Stra. Free from the bondage you are in, Messala;
The conquerors can but make a fire of him;   60
For Brutus only overcame himself,
And no man else hath honour by his death.
    Lucil. So Brutus should be found. I thank thee, Brutus,
That thou hast prov'd Lucilius' saying true.
    Oct. All that serv'd Brutus, I will entertain them.   65
Fellow, wilt thou bestow thy time with me?
    Stra. Ay, if Messala will prefer me to you.
    Oct. Do so, good Messala.
    Mes. How died my master, Strato?

    Stra. I held the sword, and he did run on it.   70
    Mes. Octavius, then take him to follow thee
That did the latest service to my master.
    Ant. This was the noblest Roman of them all;
All the conspirators save only he
Did that they did in envy of great Cæsar;   75
He only, in a general honest thought
And common good to all, made one of them.
His life was gentle, and the elements
So mix'd in him that Nature might stand up
And say to all world, 'This was a man!'   80
    Oct. According to his virtue let us use him,
With all respect and rites of burial.
Within my tent his bones to-night shall lie,
Most like a soldier, order'd honourably.
So, call the field to rest; and let's away   85
To part the glories of this happy day.   *Exeunt omnes.*

✣ FINIS ✣

76, 77 *Cf. n.*   **78 gentle:** *that of a true gentleman* **elements:** *as microcosm, man was believed to be composed of earth, air, fire, and water, mingled in due proportions*   **81 use:** *treat*   **84 Most like:** *as best befits* **order'd:** *arrayed*   **85 field:** *troops in the field*   **86 part:** *share*

51 smatch: *smack, flavor*   **61 only:** *alone*   **65 entertain:** *employ*   **66 bestow ... with:** *devote thy time to*   **67 prefer:** *recommend, transfer*

NOTES

I.i.S.d. *Marullus.* The Folios spell this name incorrectly, 'Murellus.' The emendation, based on Plutarch and other conclusive ancient authorities, is Theobald's. On similar grounds, certain other orthographical vagaries have been corrected in most of the modern editions: e.g., the Folios print 'Calphurnia,' 'Antonio,' 'Claudio,' 'Varrus,' etc. On the other hand, 'Decius Brutus' for 'Decimus' is a genuine confusion of identity which Shakespeare took over from North's Plutarch (see Sources of the Play).

I.i.23. *with awl.* The original Folio pointing and spelling of the text will serve to suggest a further pun not obvious in the modern texts: 'I meddle with no Tradesmans matters, nor womens matters; but withal I am indeed Sir, a Surgeon to old shoes.'

I.i.32. *triumph.* This triumph celebrated Cæsar's defeat of the sons of Pompey at the battle of Munda, in Spain, March 17, B. C. 45, and was the first such recognition of a Roman's victory over any but a foreign foe.—Shakespeare throughout has compressed the historical duration of the play's action considerably, in the interests of dramatic effectiveness: so here he has this triumph coincide with the festival of the Lupercalia, February 15, B. C. 44; in Act III he places the murder, the funeral orations, and the arrival of Octavius all on the same day, whereas in reality some two months elapsed between the earliest and the latest of these events; and in Act V he combines in a single action the two battles of Philippi, which really were separated by a thee-week interval. See further, for the use of 'Double Time' in this play, the note on II.i.61, 62.

I.i.45. *her.* 'Father Tiber' would seem to demand a masculine pronoun, and Rowe accordingly, followed by several other editors, changed 'her' to 'his' in this line and line 48; but Elizabethan usage was less strict than classical, and Shakespeare's laxity was not a special peculiarity of his own.

I.i.68. *Lupercal.* Ancient Roman festival of purification and expiation, celebrated February 15, and believed to give new life and fruitfulness to fields, flocks, and human beings. After due sacrifices had been offered, the chosen young men, called 'Luperci,' ran around the Palatine hill and struck with their thongs of goatskin those who stood in their way, thus warding off barrenness. These thongs were called 'februa,' from 'februare, to purify'; the day, 'dies februatus'; and the whole month, 'februarius.'

I.ii.161. *walks.* The famous and spacious paved Roman Ways, such as the 'Via Appia,' 'Via Sacra,' 'Via Flaminia,' etc., are here put for the city itself, by synecdoche. Or, another sound explanation is based on III.ii.254; 'walks' thus would signify the parks and promenades forming the outlying suburbs of the city. Rowe's emendation, 'walls,' though widely accepted, is unnecessary and prosaic.

I.ii.172. The punctuation in this line is that of Pope's second edition, and has been generally adopted; but the Folio gives a perfectly plausible reading without emendation: 'I would not so (with love I might entreat you) Be any further moved.'

I.ii.206. *my name.* A Latin idiom, meaning 'I myself, Cæsar.' For parallels from Virgil, Milton, and the Bible, cf. R. C. Browne's note on *Paradise Lost*, II, 964, in the Clarendon Press edition of *English Poems by John Milton*, 1906.

I.ii.211. *he hears no music.* Cf. *Merchant of Venice*, V.I.91-93.

I.ii.317. *He should not humour me.* 'He,' as is shown by the 'he' in the preceding line and the 'his' in the following, refers to Brutus, not to Cæsar. Cassius then says: 'If I had Brutus' standing with Cæsar and Brutus only mine, Brutus should not (as easily as I mean to beguile him into doing so) talk me into forgoing the advantages afforded by Cæsar's favor.'

I.iii.63. *cast yourself in wonder.* 'Plunge head-long into, abjectly abandon yourself to, unreasoning wonder.' Cf. 'cast down,' and the etymology of 'abject.' There is no need for emendation, though 'case' has been widely accepted.

I.iii.68. *Why old men, fools, and children calculate.* This line has occasioned much discussion. Many editors emend it thus: 'Why old men fool, and children calculate,' i.e., 'Why the wise are foolish and the foolish wise.' But against this emendation may be urged the facts that 'old men' are not always 'wise,' in Shakespeare or elsewhere, and that the unaltered text affords an acceptable meaning: 'Why dotards, idiots, and infants so far depart from their ordinary characteristics as to utter the profound truths of divination.'

I.iii.111, 115. 'The idea seems to be that, as men start a huge fire with worthless straws or shavings, so Cæsar is using the degenerate Romans of the time, to set the whole world ablaze with his own glory.' (Hudson.)

I.iii.131. *Pompey's porch.* A magnificent colonnade or portico surrounding an open area which contained avenues of sycamore trees, fountains, and statues; it was attached to Pompey's theatre (line 159), in the Campus Martius, the first stone theatre to be erected in Rome.

II.i.15. *Crown him that.* 'Once make him *that*—i.e., once let him become the full-grown adder—by crowning him, and then I realize that we shall be rendering

actual a peril (sting) which now is only potential and latent.' Emendations seem unnecessary, though many have been proposed and few editors retain the Folio and Quarto punctuation given in the present text.

II.i.59. *fourteen.* This is Theobald's generally accepted emendation of the Folio and Quarto reading, 'fifteen.' To Brutus (line 40) it is still the night of the fourteenth. If 'fifteen' days were indeed 'wasted,' i.e., gone, then the ides too would be gone,—which is just what the Soothsayer points out that they are *not* (III.i.2).

II.i.61, 62. Literally interpreted, this statement is incredible, if we stop to reflect that a month has passed since I. ii; Brutus then can mean merely 'I have not slept well.' But as a rule we do *not* stop to reflect thus mathematically, and so we have the impression that 'Cassius first did whet' Brutus 'against Cæsar' only a night or two before and that Brutus' sleeplessness has not been superhumanly protracted; for seemingly 'Brought you Cæsar home?' (I.iii.1) means home from the Lupercal (I.ii), and Casca himself in I. iii is returning from his dinner engagement on the night of the Lupercal (I.ii.291), so that I. iii apparently follows I. ii without any interval; while II. i apparently follows I. iii with almost equal immediacy, for in their last conversation (on stage: I.ii.305-309) Brutus and Cassius arranged to meet again at Brutus' home 'to-morrow,' and hence (II.i.70 ff.) we have their first meeting (on stage) since that time. This device, whereby Shakespeare secures an *impression* of rapid, uninterruptedly continuous action while unobtrusively supplying to *reflection* all needed data for the determination of the actual historical intervals involved, is known as the phenomenon of 'Double Time,' and is well shown further in Acts IV and V of this play. The Short or Dramatic Time-scheme maintains the tension of the passion, while the Long or Historic Time-scheme satisfies the requirements of the analytical reason; but, needless to say, this curious phenomenon is noticeable only in the study, never in the theatre. (Cf. 'Shakespeare's Legerdemain with Time in *Julius Cæsar*,' *Poet Lore*, XI, 1899.)

II.i.262. *humour.* There were supposed to be four fundamental 'humours' or fluids (from the Latin humor,' liquid) in the human body, viz., blood, phlegm, yellow bile, and black bile; and an over-proportion of one of these elements in the system made the disposition predominantly sanguine, phlegmatic, choleric, or melancholy, respectively. So, to the mediæval and renaissance mind, 'humour' might mean literally 'moisture,' as in line 278; or it might account for mental or physical disorder, as in the present line; or it might refer to the more trivial temperamental eccentricity resulting from the fundamental derangement, as in II. ii. 59.

II.ii.93. *For tinctures, stains, relics, and cognizance.* The generally accepted interpretation explains these terms in the very spirit of Calpurnia's dream, i.e., as the appropriate concomitants of martyrdom; but surely nothing could be further from Cæsar's desire or Decius' intention. Consequently, the gloss attempts to give meanings more in keeping with the manifest purpose of Decius as shown in the rest of his speech, and with the obvious requirements of the situation: i.e., Cæsar's blood is to provide metaphorical living blessings, rather than literal physical souvenirs of death.

II.ii.136. *That every 'like' is not 'the same.'* The heart of Brutus grieves to realize that specious resemblance is not genuine identity; that appearances (of friendship, as in the amicable ceremony of taking wine together) are deceptive; that the conspirators, who seem 'like friends' (line 135), are so far from being truly Cæsar's friends that they are on the very point of putting him to death.

III.i.S.d. *Before the Capitol.* In the original texts there is no stage direction in this scene before 'They stab Cæsar,' at line 83, other than the opening direction: 'Flourish. Enter Cæsar, Brutus,' and the rest. Yet lines 11, 12 show that the action takes place outdoors; while lines 35, 90, 125, 130, etc., as well as the familiar tradition and all pictorial representations, show that the murder takes place indoors. Of course, there was no difficulty here on the Elizabethan stage: the action of the first 12 lines would take place on the fore-stage, and then Cæsar would withdraw and seat himself on the dais or inner stage at the rear, with the Senators grouped about him and the approaching conspirators between him and the audience. Except for the standardization of the text established by the almost unbroken succession of editors who have left this dilemma unamended, there would seem to be no reason why the procedure followed in the precisely similar dilemma in IV.ii and iii should not be adopted here: there the action outside Brutus' tent is assigned to a brief Scene Two, while the action inside the tent is very properly assigned to a long separate scene, Scene Three. It must be remembered that *all* the Scene-divisions in this play have had to be determined by modern editors, there being nothing but Act-divisions in the Folios after the initial 'Scæna Prima.'

Capitol. Shakespeare placed the killing of Cæsar in the Capitol on account of the established popular and literary tradition to that effect; cf., e.g., Chaucer, *The Monkes Tale*, 713-718, and *Hamlet*, III. ii. 100-103. In reality Cæsar was assassinated in the Curia Pompeiana, a great hall adjoining the portico of Pompey's theatre (cf. note on I.III.126). This Curia was used for meetings of the Senate and was destroyed in the grief and rage over Cæsar's death, but the colossal statue of Pompey which it had contained (cf. line 125) was saved.

III.i.47, 48. *Know, Cæsar doth not wrong.* Ben Jonson quoted in his *Discoveries*, first printed in 1641, an alternative version of this line: 'Cæsar did never wrong but with just cause.' Jonson ridiculed this sentence as an 'Irish bull'—unjustly: for 'wrong' means not only 'error, mistake,' but also 'harm, injury' (as in line 260 in this very scene). Some few editors have incorporated Jonson's version of this line in the text, following it up with 'Nor without cause will he be satisfied,' on the hypothesis that Jonson was quoting either an early Quarto version which has since disappeared, or at least the acting version current in Shakespeare's lifetime which was unwarrantably changed by the editors of the First Folio.

III.i.59. *If I could pray to move, prayers would move me.* 'If I were as weak as you are, and in the position of looking up to someone more powerful than myself and entreating him to change his mind, why then I should perhaps be weak enough likewise to change my own mind on account of mere empty entreaties; but happily I am as far above one alternative as the other, for,' etc.

III.i.174. This line has given the commentators much trouble, and many emendations have been proposed for the puzzling phrase 'in strength of malice'—such as 'exempt from malice,' 'in strength of amity,' etc. If the Folio reading is to be preserved unchanged, the word 'malice' must clearly be emptied of all its usual meaning, for Brutus could never have applied such a term to any action by the conspirators after his overwhelming repudiation of 'envy' and similar emotions in II. i. 170-191; and the word 'malice,' free from its usual sinister implications, apparently does occur elsewhere in Shakespeare (e.g., *Macbeth*, III.ii.16, 28, and perhaps *John*, II.i.259), and is recognized by the Oxford Dictionary, in the sense of 'power, capacity.' But even so, that interpretation gives a very inferior meaning to the phrase now under discussion, little better than tautology and not very appropriate to the spirit of the context. The present editor therefore ventures to suggest as an emendation here 'instranged' (of the use of which *N. E. D.* gives an example dated 1586), a variant of 'enstranged' (*N. E. D.*: Caxton, 1483), meaning 'estranged, far removed, deprived,' etc. This rare word, 'instranged,' unfamiliar to the compositor's eye or ear, would be very naturally sophisticated into 'in strength,' while it supplies exactly the sense needed in the passage; viz., 'Our arms free from malice, and our hearts of brothers' temper, do receive you in,' etc.

III.i.273. *dogs of war.* Most editors explain the 'dogs' literally and specifically as 'fire, sword, and famine,' on the strength of *Henry V*, I. Prologue 8. But why should not the phrase be merely a general poetic metaphor—on the analogy of 'dove of peace'—designed to suggest all the nameless horrors that result when the destructive energies of ruthless warfare are unpent?

III.ii.178. *That day he overcame the Nervii.* It was in the summer of 57 B.C. that this most warlike of Belgic tribes was defeated, in the battle of the Sambre. The Nervii made a successful surprise attack, and only Cæsar's personal bravery saved the day. Cf. *De Bello Gallico*, II.15-28. This victory is prominently featured in North's Plutarch (see Sources of the Play), and was celebrated at Rome with unprecedented thanksgivings and rejoicings.

III.ii.247. *drachmas.* These were Greek silver coins, of a value impossible to compute accurately in terms of modern currency. In purchasing power the bequest would perhaps be equivalent to-day to something over $100 per citizen.

III.ii.254. *On this side Tiber.* The gardens lay across the Tiber from the Forum in which Antony was speaking, but 'on this side' from the French and English standpoint of Amyot and North—whom Shakespeare too literally follows.

IV.i. 37. *one that feeds On objects, arts, and imitations Which, out of use and stal'd by other men, Begin his fashion.* The Folio text here is at least as satisfactory as any emendation, if the punctuation makes it evident that the disputed 'objects, arts, and imitations' are immediately defined by the restrictive relative clause that follows. Despite his unbridled passions, Antony is eminently a practical politician—as witness the form of Cassius' bribe offered to him after Brutus' futile expression of idealism (III.i.192, 193); and witness also his masterly manipulation of the conspirators and the mob, in III. i and III. ii. He scorns Lepidus then for so lacking personality, initiative, shrewdness, and judgment that he takes even the superficial embellishments of life at second hand, unable to distinguish between the true values and the sham. (Staunton's emendation would substitute 'abjects,' meaning 'discarded scraps,' and 'orts,' meaning 'leavings.')

IV.i.48, 49. *we are at the stake, And bay'd about with many enemies.* This refers to the very popular but very brutal Elizabethan amusement of bear-baiting, wherein the bear was chained to a stake in the center of the 'bear-garden' or arena (the best-known one was situated close by the Globe Theatre) and attacked by a number of dogs.

IV.iii.S.d. For the 'Enter' of modern editions the Folios and Quartos have 'Manet' or 'Manent.' I.e., as explained in the note on III. i.S.d., no new scene was necessary here on the Elizabethan stage: the armies marched off and Brutus and Cassius simply 'remained' in conference, but the locality none the less was supposed to shift to the inside of Brutus' tent.

IV.iii.20, 21. *What villain touch'd his body, that did stab, And not for justice?* 'What one of the conspirators was such a villain that he stabbed Cæsar from any other motive than for justice's sake?' Brutus means, of course, to imply that there was none such then, and they must be doubly careful to avoid giving ground for any such imputation now.

IV.iii.25, 26. The infinite spiritual extent of true honor is contrasted with the petty material extent of a handful of money.

IV.iii.28. *Brutus, bay not me.* 'Bay' (Theobald's widely accepted emendation of the Folio reading 'bait') is a savage and threatening quibble on Cassius' part: 'Don't bark at me, Brutus, and don't bring me to bay either (cf. note on IV.i.51, 52), hedging me in with snarling accusations and goading me on with taunts, or I'll turn on you and then it will be the worse for you.' 'Bait' can be given almost the same interpretation, with reference to bear-baiting, but misses the neat repartee in the repeated 'bay.'

IV.iii.101. *Pluto's.* As god of the infernal regions, Pluto might well be supposed to command great wealth. As Milton says, 'Let none admire That riches grow in Hell; that soil may best Deserve the precious bane.' Many editors, however, prefer to follow Pope in reading 'Plutus',' the god of riches. Confusion between the two occurred in classical times as well as in Elizabethan.

IV.iii.109-112. This badly mixed metaphor can be straightened out if we punctuate 'lamb,—' and interpret 'That' as 'With one that, with a man who,' thus: 'O Cassius, you are associated with a mere lamb,—with a man whose anger is as negative and latent as the fire in a flint, which needs a hard blow before showing any flame at all and even then yields only a momentary spark.'

IV.iii.152. *grief.* The grammatical construction breaks down here (though the sense is clear enough), unless we (1) construe 'grief' with 'impatient of' in the preceding line, thus: 'Unable to endure my absence and her own sorrow over Antony's success'; or (2) read 'grieved' for 'grief,' thus: 'Impatient and grieved, in this situation she fell distract,' etc.

IV.iii.183. *Nothing, Messala.* Various more or less plausible attempts have been made to defend Brutus from this most unpleasant appearance of deceiving Messala in order to win applause for his fortitude under affliction, but the best way out of the difficulty lies in accepting the suggestion of J. Resch that two alternative versions of Brutus' stoical conduct have been accidentally taken over into the Folio text from the MS. or prompt-book copy.

V.i. 53. *three-and-thirty.* According to North's Plutarch the number of Cæsar's wounds was three-and-twenty, and several editors have followed Theobald in making the somewhat meticulous correction.

V.i.111-115. In these lines Brutus has been charged by many critics with flatly contradicting his declaration against suicide in lines 111, 112; but the inconsistency disappears if the significance of lines 122, 123 be grasped (by a proper interpretation of 'Must') as merely restating the stoical fatalism of lines 116, 117, for Brutus really says simply this: 'No, Cassius, you are an Epicurean and do not understand, and I cannot take the time now to explain things to you. No, I bear too great a mind ever to go bound to Rome: *but (my mere human mind does not have to settle this point, for) this same day Must (i.e., will certainly) end that work the ides of March begun.*' I.e., 'I do not have to alter my resolution against suicide for Fate will decide, and to-day either we shall kill Cæsar's usurping successors as we killed Cæsar himself, or we shall ourselves die fighting and thus even the score, pay the reckoning, for Cæsar's death.' This, as Hunter points out, is Brutus' expression of mere speculative theory; if, like Hamlet, he does not live up to his professed principles and abstract resolution when the actual test comes, that is but part of his tragic failure.

V. iii.109,110. The 'second fight' really took place twenty days later. Cf. note on I.i.32.

V.iv.7. No speaker's name precedes this speech in the Folios, and it is accordingly assigned to Brutus on the strength of modern editorial authority only. Some editors, however, would assign it to Lucilius, in order to prepare the audience for his assumption of the rôle of Brutus in lines 7, 8 below.

V.iv.13,14. Many editors supply a stage direction *[Offering money]* to explain 'There is so much'; but surely there would be little sense in offering to give part, where all would naturally fall to his slayer. So Lucilius presumably meant simply this: 'I yield only to ensure dying at once: and there is so much reason for my death and so much advantage in it for you that you will doubtless kill me immediately; for you have only to kill me, i.e., Brutus, in order to win great honor and rewards.'

V.v.2, 3.   This passage is somewhat obscure without its original context in North's Plutarch: 'Brutus thought that there was no great number of men slain in battle: and to know the truth of it, there was one called Statilius, that promised to go through his enemies, for otherwise it was impossible to go see their camp: and from thence, if all were well, that he would lift up a torch-light in the air, and then return again with speed to him.'—*Life of Brutus.*

V.v.71, 72.   'He consented to join them only on impersonal principles of honor and in the hope of promoting the welfare of all.'

THE TEXT OF THE PRESENT EDITION

The text of the present volume is, by permission of the Oxford University Press, that of the Oxford Shakespeare, edited by the late W. J. Craig, except for the following deviations:

1. The stage directions of the Folio have been restored as far as possible, with necessary modern additions in square brackets.

2. The punctuation, especially in the use of exclamation points, has been modernized, and the spelling of Calpurnia brought into conformity with current usage.

3. The only significant verbal departures—usually in the direction of a return to the Folio—are listed below, the readings adopted in the present text being placed before the colon while Craig's readings follow it; and Folio authority is given wherever involved:

I.i.	62	whether: whe'r (F where)
	ii.161	walks F: walls
	iii.111	these F: those
II.i.	73	moe F: more
	287	you are F: are you
	296	or F: of
	ii. 80	statue F: statua
III.i.	34	*Cæs.* F: *Casca*
	220	lethe (F1 Lethee F4 Lethe): leth
	223	stricken F2, 3, 4: strucken (F1 stroken)
ii.S.d.et pas.		*Plebeians* F: *Citizens*
	194	statue F: statua
IV.i.	40	objects, arts F: abject orts
	iii.14	speaks (speakes F): speak
	111	Pluto's F: Plutus'
V.iii.	65	to night F: to-night
	104	whether: whe'r (F where)
	111	Thasos: Thassos (F Tharsus)
	iv.19	Brutus is ta'en, Brutus is ta'en, my Lord F: Brutus is ta'en, my lord
	31	whether: whe'r (F where)

The Tragedy of Hamlet

PRINCE OF DENMARK

Edited by TUCKER BROOKE

and

JACK RANDALL CRAWFORD

Dramatis Personae

CLAUDIUS, *the new King of Denmark*

HAMLET, *Son to the late, and Nephew to
the present King*

FORTINBRAS, *Prince of Norway*

POLONIUS, *a Lord and High Official
(probably Lord Chamberlain)*

LAERTES, *his Son*

HORATIO, *the Friend of Hamlet*

VOLTIMAND
CORNELIUS
ROSENCRANTZ } *Courtiers*
GUILDENSTERN
OSRIC

MARCELLUS, *a Danish Officer*

FRANCISCO } *Soldiers on sentry duty*
BERNARDO

REYNALDO, *Servant to Polonius*

A NORWEGIAN CAPTAIN

PLAYERS ON TOUR

TWO CLOWNS, GRAVEDIGGERS

ENGLISH AMBASSADORS, A PRIEST,
a GENTLEMAN, SOLDIERS, SAILOR,
MESSENGER, AND VARIOUS ATTENDANTS

GERTRUDE, *Queen of Denmark
and Mother of Hamlet*

OPHELIA, *Daughter of Polonius*

GHOST *of Hamlet's father*

SCENE—*The royal castle of Elsinore (Helsingør),
Denmark, and its environs.*

The Tragedy of Hamlet

INTRODUCTION

SOURCES OF THE PLAY

There are two early references to the name 'Hamlet,' or 'Amleth,' one (spelled in Irish fashion 'Amhlaide') in *The Annals of Ireland by the Four Masters*,[1] under the year 917, and the other (spelled 'Amlothi') in Snorri's *Prose Edda*, about three centuries later.[2] The outline of the story of Hamlet, as we are familiar with it, is first found in the *Historia Danica* of Saxo Grammaticus, a Danish chronicler who lived at the end of the twelfth century.[3]

Saxo's version contains the following elements in common with Shakespeare's: the murder of Hamlet's father by the latter's ambitious brother; the mother's incestuous marriage with the murderer; the son's feigned madness, or "folly," for the purpose of carrying out his revenge; a foreshadowing of the character of Ophelia by the girl thrown in Hamlet's way that the true state of his mind may be discovered; a foreshadowing of the character of Polonius; the scene between mother and son,[4] the voyage to England with two companions, during which Hamlet alters the letter, and the companions are put to death in his stead; Hamlet's return to kill his uncle, a deed which he accomplishes. The ending differs.

François de Belleforest published about 1570 a free translation of Saxo's Hamlet story in French prose in the fifth book of his *Histoires Tragiques*. Although many editions of this appeared in France before 1600, there is no evidence of an English version before the publication by Thomas Pavier of the *Hystorie of Hamblet* in 1608. This English translation differs in a few particulars from Belleforest, and these differences seem to be due to the influence of Shakespeare's play. Thus, in Belleforest the counsellor who acts the spy during Amleth's (Hamlet's) interview with his mother, conceals himself under a bed-quilt, upon which Amleth leaps when entering the room and so discovers the eavesdropper. In the *Hystorie,* the counsellor hides behind the arras, as in the play. Again, Hamblet, at the moment of this discovery, calls out "A rat! A rat!," of which there is no trace in Belleforest.

There is another, and more direct, source for Shakespeare's play, *viz.,* an earlier play by another author on the same subject. The evidence for the existence of such a work is as follows: In 1589 was published Greene's *Menaphon* with a prefatory epistle by Thomas Nashe "to the Gentlemen Students of both Vniuersities." In this epistle, Nashe briefly reviews contemporary literature and refers to "whole Hamlets, I should say Handfuls, of tragical speeches," linking this remark with a reference to Seneca.

The next reference to an early play of Hamlet is from the *Diary* of Philip Henslowe,[5] the theatrical manager, for the year 1594.

"Ye 9 of June 1594. R[eceive]d. at hamlet, viijs". At this time the Lord Chamberlain's and the Lord Admiral's men were playing for Henslowe at the theatre at Newington Butts. The former company was the one to which Shakespeare belonged.

Lodge's *Wit's Misery, and the World's Madness,* published in 1596, contains this passage: The devil, Hate-Virtue, is 'a foul lubber, . . . and looks pale as the visard of the ghost, which cried so miserably at the *Theator,* like an oyster-wife, *Hamlet reuenge.'*

The cumulative evidence is conclusive for the existence of a play on the subject of Hamlet at an earlier date than any at which Shakespeare can have been concerned with it. The general consensus of opinion is that this earlier play was by Thomas Kyd, the author of the *Spanish Tragedie.* Nashe's preface to Greene's *Menaphon,* already alluded to, contains a punning reference to "the Kid in Aesop." Kyd's known plays show marked Senecan influence.[6] The probability that Kyd was the author of the earlier *Hamlet* is further substantiated by resemblances between the *Spanish Tragedie* and Shakespeare's *Hamlet.* In both the motive is revenge; the ghost of the victim relates his story; the hero feigns madness; in each play there is a faithful friend named Horatio; each contains a play within a play; the innocent and guilty alike are involved in the catastrophes.

Although no actual trace of this earlier play has been found, most scholars believe that a German manuscript, dated October 27, 1710, and published in 1781, preserves some material from the original version. This manuscript is possibly a modernized copy of an older one which was first translated when a troupe of English actors visited Germany at the end of the sixteenth century.[7] The German play is entitled, *Der Bestrafte Brudermord oder: Prinz Hamlet aus Dänemark. (Fratricide Punished, or Prince Hamlet of Denmark.)* It opens with an allegorical prologue which shows unmistakable Senecan influence. Likewise Polonius is here called Corambus, which corresponds with his name 'Corambis' in the First Quarto. For the most part, this German play is exceedingly crude and coarse, although the outline of the plot action follows Shakespeare's closely. It is, however, devoid of literary merit.

To sum up: the story of Hamlet was taken by Belieforest from Saxo's chronicle. Shakespeare received it either from Belleforest, direct, or from an earlier unknown publication of the translation of Belleforest of which the *Hystorie of Hamblet* is a later version, or (as is most likely) he founded his play on an earlier tragedy which was probably by Thomas Kyd. The traces of Senecan influence in Shakespeare's Hamlet are due either to this earlier play or to the general and common influence of Seneca upon Elizabethan tragic playwrights.

---

1 Cf. the Introduction to Gollancz's *Hamlet in Iceland,* p. li.

2 For an attempt to reconstruct the primitive plot see the last chapter in *The Literary History of Hamlet. I, The Early Tradition,* by Kemp Malone (1923).

3 For most of the materials here referred to see Sir Israel Gollancz, *The Sources of Hamlet,* 1926.

4 Cf. *Hamlet,* III. iv.

5 The entry differs from those Henslowe made when the play mentioned was a new one.

6 He was also the translator of a Seneca-like tragedy entitled *Cornelia,* by the French tragic writer Garnier.

7 The earliest reference known to a performance of *Hamlet* by English actors in Germany is in the year 1626.

History of the Play

The stage history of *Hamlet* is practically that of the English-speaking stage itself. Almost all the great actors of England and America, from Shakespeare's day to this, have appeared as the Prince. In addition, for the past one hundred years, it has been frequently played in the principal European countries. It is safe to say that no other play of Shakespeare's has been more often performed.

Richard Burbage, the leading actor of Shakespeare's company, was undoubtedly the first Hamlet. From the meagre accounts of his style of acting which have survived, we may infer that, like subsequent great interpreters of the part, he was distinguished for the ease and naturalness of his art. The famous lines at the opening of III.ii., 'Speak the speech, I pray you, as I pronounced it to you, trippingly on the tongue,' *etc.* may indeed be a defense of Burbage's style against the more flamboyant method of his great rival, Edward Alleyn.[8] Burbage died three years after Shakespeare and left the rôle of Hamlet for Joseph Taylor, who performed it with applause at the Globe and Blackfriars playhouses until the closing of the theatres in 1642.

After the Restoration, Thomas Betterton achieved great fame in this rôle. He was instructed in his interpretation by Sir William Davenant, who had seen the Blackfriars' company act the play. Betterton for the first time introduced scenery into *Hamlet,* and, if we are to trust the Quarto of 1676, established many of the traditions subsequently followed in acting versions.

David Garrick was the leading interpreter of Hamlet during the middle portion of the eighteenth century. He first appeared in the part on November 16, 1734, and continued to play it many times until he left the stage in 1776. Garrick introduced alterations of his own into the text, one of which was the omission of the churchyard scene (V.i.), but he was not followed by others in this.[9] The latter years of the eighteenth century saw what many to this day consider must have been the greatest Hamlet of them all, John Philip Kemble, with his sister, Mrs. Siddons, as Ophelia. Kemble restored the text as written by Shakespeare and abolished the Garrick innovations.

The nineteenth century witnessed, in England and America, a number of excellent Hamlets, of whom the best remembered are Edmund Kean, Macready, Samuel Phelps, Fletcher, Edwin Booth, Sir Henry Irving, Wilson Barrett, Sir Herbert Tree, Martin Harvey, Sir Johnston Forbes-Robertson, and E. H. Sothern. Later interpretations by John Barrymore, John Gielgud, and Maurice Evans have made theatrical history. The supposed innovation of 'Hamlet in modern dress' in the late 1920's aroused much controversy till it was recalled that the play was so acted in Shakespeare's time, and even in Garrick's.[10] Ten years later the admirable full-length *Hamlet* of Margaret Webster and Maurice Evans freshened appreciation and vindicated the staying powers both of the play and the audiences.

Many of the most artistic and remarkable of the modern productions of *Hamlet* have been produced in Russia, where it has had a special vogue, beginning with the novel and historic presentation designed by Gordon Craig for the Art Theatre in Moscow. Nor is there any indication that the popularity of this play upon the stage has dimmed. It still remains the test of the summit of achievement for the art of a tragic actor.

---

8 Because of the different stage conditions and different conception of oratory, all Elizabethan acting would have seemed formalized to us rather than naturalistic. See Alfred Harbage, 'Elizabethan Acting,' PMLA, Sept., 1939.

9 See G. W. Stone, 'Garrick's Long Lost Alteration of *Hamlet,*' PMLA, Sept., 1934.
10 See Max Huhner, 'Hamlet in Modern Dress,' *Poet Lore,* 1926.

ACT FIRST ❦ SCENE FIRST

[Elsinore. Platform of the Castle]
Enter Bernardo and Francisco, two Sentinels.

Ber. Who's there?
Fran. Nay, answer me; stand, and unfold yourself.
Ber. Long live the king!
Fran. Bernardo?
Ber. He.   5
Fran. You come most carefully upon your hour.
Ber. 'Tis now struck twelve; get thee to bed, Francisco.
Fran. For this relief much thanks; 'tis bitter cold,
And I am sick at heart.
Ber. Have you had quiet guard?   10
Fran.   Not a mouse stirring.
Ber. Well, good night.
If you do meet Horatio and Marcellus,
The rivals of my watch, bid them make haste.

Enter Horatio and Marcellus.

Fran. I think I hear them. Stand, ho! Who is there?   15
Hor. Friends to this ground.
Mar.   And liegemen to the Dane.
Fran. Give you good night.
Mar.   O, farewell, honest soldier.
Who hath reliev'd you?   20
Fran.   Bernardo hath my place.
Give you good night   *Exit Francisco.*
Mar.   Holla! Bernardo!
Ber.   Say,—
What, is Horatio there?
Hor.   A piece of him.   25
Ber. Welcome, Horatio; welcome, good Marcellus.
Mar. What, has this thing appear'd again to-night?
Ber. I have seen nothing.
Mar. Horatio says 'tis but our fantasy,   30
And will not let belief take hold of him
Touching this dreaded sight twice seen of us.
Therefore I have entreated him along
With us to watch the minutes of this night,
That if again this apparition come,   35
He may approve our eyes and speak to it.
Hor. Tush, tush! 'twill not appear.
Ber.   Sit down awhile,
And let us once again assail your ears,
That are so fortified against our story,
What we have two nights seen.   40
Hor.   Well, sit we down,
And let us hear Bernardo speak of this.
Ber. Last night of all,
When yond same star that's westward from the pole   45
Had made his course t' illume that part of heaven
Where now it burns, Marcellus and myself,
The bell then beating one,—

Enter Ghost.

Mar. Peace! break thee off; look, where it comes again!
Ber. In the same figure, like the king that's dead.   50
Mar. Thou art a scholar; speak to it, Horatio.
Ber. Looks 'a not like the king? mark it, Horatio.
Hor. Most like: it harrows me with fear and wonder.
Ber. It would be spoke to.
Mar.   Question it, Horatio.   55
Hor. What art thou that usurp'st this time of night,
Together with that fair and warlike form
In which the majesty of buried Denmark
Did sometimes march? by heaven I charge thee, speak!
Mar. It is offended.   60
Ber.   See! it stalks away.
Hor. Stay! speak, speak! I charge thee, speak!   *Exit Ghost.*
Mar. 'Tis gone, and will not answer.
Ber. How now, Horatio! you tremble and look pale.
Is not this something more than fantasy?   65
What think you on 't?
Hor. Before my God, I might not this believe
Without the sensible and true avouch
Of mine own eyes.
Mar.   Is it not like the king?   70
Hor. As thou art to thyself:
Such was the very armor he had on
When he the ambitious Norway combated;
So frown'd he once, when, in an angry parle,
He smote the sleaded pole-axe on the ice.   75
'Tis strange.
Mar. Thus twice before, and jump at this dead hour,
With martial stalk hath he gone by our watch.
Hor. In what particular thought to work I know not;
But in the gross and scope of my opinion,   80
This bodes some strange eruption to our state.
Mar. Good now, sit down, and tell me, he that knows,
Why this same strict and most observant watch
So nightly toils the subject of the land;
And why such daily cast of brazen cannon,   85
And foreign mart for implements of war;
Why such impress of shipwrights, whose sore task
Does not divide the Sunday from the week;
What might be toward, that this sweaty haste
Doth make the night joint-laborer with the day: 90
Who is 't that can inform me?
Hor.   That can I;
At least, the whisper goes so. Our last king,
Whose image even but now appear'd to us,
Was, as you know, by Fortinbras of Norway,   95
Thereto prick'd on by a most emulate pride,
Dar'd to the combat; in which our valiant Hamlet
(For so this side of our known world esteem'd him,)
Did slay this Fortinbras; who by a seal'd compact,
Well ratified by law and heraldry,   100
Did forfeit with his life all those his lands

S.d. Platform: *level space on castle ramparts*   **3 Long ... king!;** *cf. n.*   **14 rivals:** *partners*   **16 Friends ... Dane;** *cf. n.*   **18 Give you:** *God give you*   **26 piece;** *cf. n.*   **30 fantasy:** *imagination*   **36 approve:** *confirm*   **39 assail your ears;** *i.e., try to tell you*   **46 his;** *cf. n.*

51 scholar; *cf. n.*   **52 'a:** *dialect form of 'he'* (sometimes 'it')   **mark:** *observe closely*   **54 It ... to;** *cf. n.*   **59 sometimes:** *formerly*   **68 sensible:** *involving the use of one of the senses*   **avouch:** *assurance*   **74 parle:** *verbal encounter*   **75 sleaded:** *weighted* (as a sledge-hammer)   **pole-axe:** *battle-ax;* cf. n.   **77 jump:** *just*   **79 thought:** *train of thinking*   **80 gross and scope:** *general drift*   **82 Good now;** *cf. n.*   **84 toils:** *causes to toil*   **subject:** *people, subjects*   **85 cast:** *founding*   **86 mart:** *traffic*   **87 impress:** *enforced service*   **89 toward:** *in preparation*   **96 prick'd on:** *incited*   **emulate:** *ambitious*   **98 this side ... world;** *i.e., all Europe*   **100 law and heraldry;** *cf. n.*

Which he stood seiz'd of, to the conqueror;
Against the which a moiety competent
Was gaged by our king, which had return'd
To the inheritance of Fortinbras,   105
Had he been vanquisher; as, by the same cov'nant,
And carriage of the article design'd,
His fell to Hamlet. Now, sir, young Fortinbras,
Of unimproved mettle hot and full,
Hath in the skirts of Norway here and there   110
Shark'd up a list of lawless resolutes,
For food and diet, to some enterprise
That hath a stomach in 't; which is no other,
As it doth well appear unto our state,
But to recover of us by strong hand   115
And terms compulsatory, those foresaid lands
So by his father lost. And this, I take it,
Is the main motive of our preparations,
The source of this our watch and the chief head
Of this post-haste and romage in the land.   120
      «*Ber.* I think it be no other but e'en so;
Well may it sort that this portentous figure
Comes armed through our watch, so like the king
That was and is the question of these wars.
      Hor. A mote it is to trouble the mind's eye.   125
In the most high and palmy state of Rome,
A little ere the mightiest Julius fell,
The graves stood tenantless and the sheeted dead
Did squeak and gibber in the Roman streets.
[Astounding portents fill'd the element,]   130
As stars with trains of fire and dews of blood,
Disasters in the sun; and the moist star
Upon whose influence Neptune's empire stands
Was sick almost to doomsday with eclipse;
And even the like precurse of fear'd events,   135
As harbingers preceding still the fates
And prologue to the omen coming on,
Have heaven and earth together demonstrated
Unto our climatures and countrymen.»

Enter Ghost again.

But, soft, behold! lo, where it comes again!   140
I'll cross it, though it blast me. Stay, illusion!
If thou hast any sound, or use of voice,
Speak to me!   *It spreads his arms.*
If there be any good thing to be done,
That may to thee do ease and grace to me,   145
Speak to me!
If thou art privy to thy country's fate,
Which happily foreknowing may avoid,
O speak!
Or if thou hast uphoarded in thy life   150

Extorted treasure in the womb of earth,
For which, they say, you spirits oft walk in death,
                                                              The cock crows.
Speak of it: stay, and speak! Stop it, Marcellus.
      Mar. Shall I strike at it with my partisan?
      Hor. Do, if it will not stand.   155
      Ber.   'Tis here!
      Hor.   'Tis here!
                                                              Exit Ghost.
      Mar. 'Tis gone!
We do it wrong, being so majestical,
To offer it the show of violence;   160
For it is, as the air, invulnerable,
And our vain blows malicious mockery.
      Ber. It was about to speak when the cock crew.
      Hor. And then it started like a guilty thing
Upon a fearful summons. I have heard,   165
The cock, that is the trumpet to the morn,
Doth with his lofty and shrill-sounding throat
Awake the god of day; and at his warning,
Whether in sea or fire, in earth or air,
Th' extravagant and erring spirit hies   170
To his confine; and of the truth herein
This present object made probation.
      Mar. It faded on the crowing of the cock.
Some say that ever 'gainst that season comes
Wherein our Saviour's birth is celebrated,   175
This bird of dawning singeth all night long
And then, they say, no spirit dare stir abroad;
The nights are wholesome; then no planets strike,
No fairy takes, nor witch hath power to charm,
So hallow'd and so gracious is that time.   180
      Hor. So have I heard and do in part believe it.
But, look, the morn in russet mantle clad,
Walks o'er the dew of yon high eastward hill.
Break we our watch up; and by my advice
Let us impart what we have seen to-night   185
Unto young Hamlet, for, upon my life,
This spirit, dumb to us, will speak to him.
Do you consent we shall acquaint him with it,
As needful in our loves, fitting our duty?
      Mar. Let's do 't, I pray; and I this morning know   190
Where we shall find him most conveniently.   *Exeunt.*

❧ Scene Second ❧

[The King's Council Chamber]
Flourish. Enter Claudius King of Denmark, Gertrude the Queen
[members of the] Council as Polonius and his son Laertes,
[Voltimand and Cornelius,] Hamlet, cum aliis.

      King. Though yet of Hamlet our dear brother's death
The memory be green, and that it us befitted
To bear our hearts in grief and our whole kingdom
To be contracted in one brow of woe,

---

102 **seiz'd of:** *possessed of; cf. n.*   103 **moiety competent:** *equal amount*   104 **gaged:** *staked*   106 **cov'nant;** *cf. n.*   107 **carriage:** *import*   **design'd:** *drawn up*   109 **unimproved mettle:** *untested courage*   **hot and full:** *exceedingly ardent*   110 **skirts:** *outskirts*   111 **Shark'd up:** *picked up at haphazard*   **list;** *cf.n.*   **resolutes:** *desperadoes*   113 **stomach;** *cf. n.*   116 **compulsatory:** *involving compulsion*   119 **head:** *origin*   120 **romage:** *commotion, bustle*   121–139 *Not in Folio*   122 **sort:** *fit*   125 **mote:** *minute particle of dust*   126 **palmy state:** *flourishing sovereignty*   130 **Astounding ... element;** *cf. n.*   131 **As:** *such as*   132 **Disasters:** *unfavorable omens*   **moist star: moon**   134 **sick ... doomsday;** *cf. n.*   135 **precurse:** *heralding*   **fear'd;** *cf. n.*   136 **still:** *constantly*   137 **prologue:** *introduction*   **omen:** *catastrophe*   139 **climatures;** *cf. n.*   141 **cross:** *meet, face*   **S.d. his:** *its (the ghost's)*   145 **[do] grace:** *do honor to*   148 **happily:** *haply*   150 **uphoarded;** *cf. n.*

154 **partisan;** *cf. n.*   166 **cock;** *cf. n.*   170 **extravagant:** *vagrant*   **erring:** *wandering*   **hies:** *hastens*   171 **confine:** *place of confinement*   172 **probation:** *proof*   173–180 *Cf. n.*   175 **'gainst that:** *by the time that*   179 **planets strike:** *cf. n.*   180 **takes:** *bewitches*   180 **gracious:** *instinct with goodness*   182 **russet:** *gray or reddish-brown (betokening dull weather)*   **I.ii.S.d. Flourish:** *a trumpet call*   **cum aliis;** *cf. n.*   4 **one brow of woe:** *unanimity of sorrow*

Yet so far hath discretion fought with nature   5
That we with wisest sorrow think on him,
Together with remembrance of ourselves.
Therefore our sometime sister, now our queen,
Th' imperial jointress of this warlike state,
Have we, as 'twere with a defeated joy,   10
With an auspicious and a dropping eye,
With mirth in funeral and with dirge in marriage,
In equal scale weighing delight and dole,
Taken to wife. Nor have we herein barr'd
Your better wisdoms, which have freely gone   15
With this affair along. For all, our thanks.
Now follows that you know young Fortinbras,
Holding a weak supposal of our worth,
Or thinking by our late dear brother's death
Our state to be disjoint and out of frame,   20
Colleagued with this dream of his advantage,
He hath not fail'd to pester us with message,
Importing the surrender of those lands
Lost by his father with all bands of law
To our most valiant brother. So much for him.   25
Now for ourself and for this time of meeting.
Thus much the business is: we have here writ
To Norway, uncle of young Fortinbras,
Who, impotent and bed-rid, scarcely hears
Of this his nephew's purpose, to suppress   30
His further gait herein in that the levies,
The lists and full proportions are all made
Out of his subject; and we here dispatch
You, good Cornelius, and you, Voltimand,
For bearers of this greeting to old Norway,   35
Giving to you no further personal power
To business with the king more than the scope
Of these delated articles allow.
Farewell and let your haste commend your duty.

    Cor. }
    Vol. } In that and all things will we show our duty.   40

    King. We doubt is nothing: heartily farewell.

                    Exeunt Voltimand and Cornelius.
And now, Laertes, what's the news with you?
You told us of some suit; what is't, Laertes?   45
You cannot speak of reason to the Dane,
And lose your voice. What wouldst thou beg, Laertes,
That shall not be my offer, not thy asking?
The head is not more native to the heart,
The hand more instrumental to the mouth,   50
Than is the throne of Denmark to thy father.
What wouldst thou have, Laertes?

    Laer.   Dread my lord,
Your leave and favor to return to France;
From whence though willingly I came to Denmark,   55
To show my duty in your coronation,

Yet now, I must confess, that duty done,
My thoughts and wishes bend again toward France
And bow them to your gracious leave and pardon.
    King. Have you your father's leave? What says Polonius?   60
    Pol. He hath, my lord, «wrung from me my slow leave
By laborsome petition, and at last
Upon his will I seal'd my hard consent.»
I do beseech you, give him leave to go.
    King. Take thy fair hour, Laertes; time be thine,   65
And thy best graces spend it at thy will.
But now, my cousin Hamlet, and my son,—
    Ham. [*Aside.*] A little more than kin, and less than kind.
    King. How is it that the clouds still hang on you?
    Ham. Not so, my lord; I am too much i' th' sun.   70
    Queen. Good Hamlet, cast thy nighted color off,
And let thine eye look like a friend on Denmark.
Do not for ever with thy vailed lids
Seek for thy noble father in the dust.
Thou know'st 'tis common; all that lives must die,   75
Passing through nature to eternity.
    Ham. Ay, madam, it is common.
    Queen.   If it be,
Why seems it so particular with thee?
    Ham. Seems, madam! Nay, it is; I know not 'seems.'   80
'Tis not alone my inky cloak, good mother,
Nor customary suits of solemn black,
Nor windy suspiration of forc'd breath,
No, nor the fruitful river in the eye,
Nor the dejected havior of the visage,   85
Together with all forms, moods, shapes of grief
That can denote me truly. These indeed seem,
For they are actions that a man might play:
But I have that within which passes show;
These but the trappings and the suits of woe.   90
    King. 'Tis sweet and commendable in your nature, Hamlet,
To give these mourning duties to your father.
But, you must know, your father lost a father;
That father lost, lost his, and the survivor bound
In filial obligation for some term   95
To do obsequious sorrow; but to perséver
In obstinate condolement is a course
Of impious stubbornness; 'tis unmanly grief.
It shows a will most incorrect to heaven,
A heart unfortified, a mind impatient,   100
An understanding simple and unschool'd:
For what we know must be and is as common
As any the most vulgar thing to sense,
Why should we in our peevish opposition
Take it to heart? Fie! 'tis a fault to heaven,   105
A fault against the dead, a fault to nature,
To reason most absurd, whose common theme
Is death of fathers, and who still hath cried,
From the first corse till he that died to-day,
'This must be so.' We pray you, throw to earth   110

9 **jointress:** *joint possessor*   10 **defeated:** *dispirited*   11 **an auspicious:** *one happy* **a dropping:** *one tearful*   13 **dole:** *grief*   17 **Now . . . know:** *I must next inform you*   18 **weak supposal:** *low opinion*   20 **disjoint:** *at loose ends* **frame:** *order*   21 **Colleagued . . . advantage:** *conspired with himself to profit by this imaginary opportunity*   23 **Importing:** *bearing as its purport*   24 **bands:** *assurances*   31 **gait:** *proceeding* **in that:** *because*   32 **proportions:** *supplies, forces*   33 **his subject:** *liegemen of Norway*   38 **delated:** *expressly stated*   47 **lose your voice:** *speak to no purpose*   49 **native:** *closely and congenitally connected*   50 **instrumental:** *serviceable*   53 **Dread my lord:** *my revered lord*   54 **leave and favor:** *kind permission*

59 **leave and pardon:** *indulgence* [to depart]   61–63 **wrung, etc.;** *not in Folio*   63 **hard:** *given with difficulty*   66 **graces:** *virtues*   67 **cousin:** *nephew*   68 **kin . . . kind;** *cf. n.*   70 **i' th' sun;** *cf. n.*   73 **vailed:** *down-cast*   75 **common:** *the common lot*   79 **particular:** *personal*   83 **windy suspiration:** *tempestuous sighing* **forc'd:** *against one's will*   84 **fruitful:** *copious*   85 **havior:** *behavior*   87 **denote:** *portray*   94 **bound:** *was bound*   96 **obsequious:** *dutiful*   97 **condolement:** *sorrowing*   99 **incorrect to:** *unchastened toward*   103 **vulgar . . . sense:** *common experience*   109 **corse:** *corpse*   110 **throw to earth:** *drop* (like a burden on one's back)

This unprevailing woe, and think of us
As of a father; for let the world take note,
You are the most immediate to our throne,
And with no less nobility of love
Than that which dearest father bears his son   115
Do I impórtune you. For your intent
In going back to school in Wittenberg,
It is most retrograde to our desire;
And we beseech you, bend you to remain
Here in the cheer and comfort of our eye,   120
Our chiefest courtier, cousin, and our son.
    Queen. Let not thy mother lose her prayers, Hamlet.
I pray thee, stay with us; go not to Wittenberg.
    Ham. I shall in all my best obey you, madam.
    King. Why, 'tis a loving and a fair reply!   125
Be as ourself in Denmark.—Madam, come.
This gentle and unforc'd accord of Hamlet
Sits smiling to my heart; in grace whereof,
No jocund health that Denmark drinks to-day,
But the great cannon to the clouds shall tell,   130
And the king's rouse the heavens shall bruit again,
Re-speaking earthy thunder. Come away.
                        Flourish. Exeunt all but Hamlet.
    Ham. O that this too too solid flesh would melt,
Thaw and resolve itself into a dew!
Or that the Everlasting had not fix'd   135
His canon 'gainst self-slaughter! O God! God!
How weary, stale, flat, and unprofitable
Seem to me all the uses of this world.
Fie on 't! ah, fie! 'tis an unweeded garden,
That grows to seed; things rank and gross in nature   140
Possess it merely. That it should come to this!
But two months dead! nay, not so much, not two.
So excellent a king, that was to this
Hyperion to a satyr; so loving to my mother
That he might not beteem the winds of heaven   145
Visit her face too roughly. Heaven and earth!
Must I remember? why, she would hang on him,
As if increase of appetite had grown
By what it fed on; and yet, within a month,—
Let me not think on 't! Frailty, thy name is woman.   150
A little month; or ere those shoes were old
With which she follow'd my poor father's body,
Like Niobe, all tears; why she,—
O God! a beast, that wants discourse of reason,
Would have mourn'd longer,—married with my uncle,   155
My father's brother, but no more like my father
Than I to Hercules. Within a month,
Ere yet the salt of most unrighteous tears
Had left the flushing in her galled eyes,
She married. O most wicked speed, to post   160
With such dexterity to incestuous sheets.
It is not, nor it cannot come to, good.—
But break, my heart, for I must hold my tongue.

                    Enter Horatio, Marcellus and Bernardo.

    Hor. Hail to your lordship!
    Ham.   I am glad to see you well.   165
Horatio! or I do forget myself.
    Hor. The same, my lord, and your poor servant ever.
    Ham. Sir, my good friend; I'll change that name with you.
And what make you from Wittenberg, Horatio?
Marcellus?   170
    Mar. My good lord,—
    Ham. I am very glad to see you. [To Bernardo.] Good even,
sir.
But what, in faith, make you from Wittenberg?
    Hor. A truant disposition, good my lord.   175
    Ham. I would not hear your enemy say so,
Nor shall you do my ear that violence,
To make it truster of your own report
Against yourself; I know you are no truant.
But what is your affair in Elsinore?   180
We'll teach you to drink deep ere you depart.
    Hor. My lord, I came to see your father's funeral.
    Ham. I prithee, do not mock me, fellow-student.
I think it was to see my mother's wedding.
    Hor. Indeed, my lord, it follow'd hard upon.   185
    Ham. Thrift, thrift, Horatio! the funeral bak'd meats
Did coldly furnish forth the marriage tables.
Would I had met my dearest foe in heaven
Or ever I had seen that day, Horatio!
My father, methinks I see my father.   190
    Hor. Where, my lord?
    Ham.   In my mind's eye, Horatio.
    Hor. I saw him once; 'a was a goodly king.
    Ham. 'A was a man! take him for all in all,
I shall not look upon his like again.   195
    Hor. My lord, I think I saw him yesternight.
    Ham. Saw? Who?
    Hor. My lord, the king your father.
    Ham.   The king, my father?
    Hor. Season your admiration for a while   200
With an attent ear, till I may deliver,
Upon the witness of these gentlemen,
This marvel to you.
    Ham.   For God's love, let me hear.
    Hor. Two nights together had these gentlemen,   205
Marcellus and Bernardo, on their watch,
In the dead waste and middle of the night,
Been thus encounter'd: a figure like your father,
Armed at point exactly, cap-a-pe,
Appears before them, and with solemn march   210
Goes slow and stately by them. Thrice he walk'd
By their oppress'd and fear-surprised eyes,
Within his truncheon's length; whilst they, distill'd
Almost to jelly with the act of fear,
Stand dumb and speak not to him. This to me   215
In dreadful secrecy impart they did,
And I with them the third night kept the watch;

111 unprevailing: *unavailing*   113 most immediate: *next in succession*   116 importune: *entreat; cf. n.*   117 Wittenberg; *cf. n.*   118 retrograde: *contrary*   119 bend: *incline*   131 rouse: *revelry, 'carousing'* bruit: *echo*   134 resolve: *dissolve*   136 cannon: *divine law*   138 uses: *usages*   141 merely: *entirely*   144 Hyperion; *cf. n.*   145 beteem: *allow*   153 Niobe; *cf. n.*   154 discourse of reason: *reasoning power*   159 left the flushing: *ceased to produce redness* galled: *sore with weeping*   160 post: *hasten*   161 dexterity: *facility*

166 forget myself; *cf. n.*   168 change that name: *share the name of friend*   175 disposition: *temperament*   181 to drink deep; *cf. n.*   186 bak'd meats: *meat pies; cf. n.*   187 coldly: *when cold*   188 dearest: *direst*   189 Or: *before*   200 Season: *temper, qualify* admiration: *wonder*   201 attent: *attentive*   207 waste; *cf. n.*   209 at point: *in full readiness* cap-a-pe: *from head to foot*   213 truncheon: *officer's' staff* distill'd: *melted*   214 act: *operation*

Where, as they had deliver'd, both in time,
Form of the thing, each word made true and good,
The apparition comes. I knew your father;   220
These hands are not more like.

Ham.   But where was this?

Mar. My lord, upon the platform where we watch.

Ham. Did you not speak to it?

Hor.   My lord, I did;   225
But answer made it none; yet once methought
It lifted up it head and did address
Itself to motion, like as it would speak;
But even then the morning cock crew loud,
And at the sound it shrunk in haste away   230
And vanish'd from our sight.

Ham.   'Tis very strange.

Hor. As I do live, my honor'd lord, 'tis true;
And we did think it writ down in our duty
To let you know of it.   235

Ham. Indeed, indeed, sirs, but this troubles me.
Hold you the watch to-night?

All.   We do, my lord.

Ham. Arm'd, say you?

All.   Arm'd, my lord.   240

Ham.   From top to toe?

All. My lord, from head to foot.

Ham. Then saw you not his face.

Hor. O yes, my lord; he wore his beaver up.

Ham. What! look'd he frowningly?   245

Hor. A countenance more in sorrow than in anger.

Ham. Pale or red?

Hor. Nay, very pale.

Ham.   And fix'd his eyes upon you?

Hor. Most constantly.   250

Ham.   I would I had been there.

Hor. It would have much amaz'd you.

Ham.   Very like.
Stay'd it long?

Hor.   While one with moderate haste   255
Might tell a hundredth.

Both.   Longer, longer.

Hor. Not when I saw 't.

Ham.   His beard was grizzled, no?

Hor. It was, as I have seen it in his life,   260
A sable silver'd.

Ham.   I will watch to-night;
Perchance 'twill walk again.

Hor.   I warr'nt it will.

Ham. If it assume my noble father's person,   265
I'll speak to it, though hell itself should gape
And bid me hold my peace. I pray you all,
If you have hitherto conceal'd this sight,
Let it be tenable in your silence still;
And whatsomever else shall hap to-night,   270
Give it an understanding, but no tongue.
I will requite your loves. So, fare you well.
Upon the platform, 'twixt eleven and twelve,
I'll visit you.

All.   Our duty to your honor.   275

227 it: *its; cf. n.*   **244 beaver:** *face-guard of a helmet*   **256 tell:** *count* **hundredth:** *hundred (a Norse form)*   **259 grizzled:** *grey*   **261 sable:** *heraldic term for black*   **269 Let . . . tenable:** *see that you keep it*   **270 whatsomever:** *whatever*

Ham. Your loves, as mine to you. Farewell.

                    Exeunt [all but Hamlet].

My father's spirit in arms! all is not well;
I doubt some foul play. Would the night were come!
Till then sit still, my soul: foul deeds will rise,
Though all the earth o'erwhelm them, to men's eyes.   *Exit.*

❧ SCENE THIRD ❧

[Polonius' Apartment in the Castle]
Enter Laertes and Ophelia, his sister.

Laer. My necessaries are embark'd; farewell:
And, sister, as the winds give benefit
And convoy is assistant, do not sleep,
But let me hear from you.

Oph.   Do you doubt that?   5

Laer. For Hamlet, and the trifling of his favor,
Hold it a fashion and a toy in blood,
A violet in the youth of primy nature,
Forward, not permanent, sweet, not lasting,
The perfume and suppliance of a minute;   10
No more.

Oph.   No more but so?

Laer.   Think it no more:
For nature crescent does not grow alone
In thews and bulk, but as this temple waxes,   15
The inward service of the mind and soul
Grows wide withal. Perhaps he loves you now,
And now no soil nor cautel doth besmirch
The virtue of his will; but you must fear.
His greatness weigh'd, his will is not his own,   20
⟨For he himself is subject to his birth⟩.
He may not, as unvalu'd persons do,
Carve for himself, for on his choice depends
The safety and health of this whole state;
And therefore must his choice be circumscrib'd   25
Unto the voice and yielding of that body
Whereof he is the head. Then if he says he loves you,
It fits your wisdom so far to believe it
As he in his particular act and place
May give his saying deed; which is no further   30
Than the main voice of Denmark goes withal.
Then weigh what loss your honor may sustain,
If with too credent ear you list his songs,
Or lose your heart, or your chaste treasure open
To his unmaster'd importunity.   35
Fear it, Ophelia, fear it, my dear sister;
And keep you in the rear of your affection,
Out of the shot and danger of desire.
The chariest maid is prodigal enough
If she unmask her beauty to the moon;   40
Virtue itself 'scapes not calumnious strokes;

2 give benefit: *are favorable*   **3 convoy:** *means of conveyance*   **7 fashion:** *mere form* **toy in blood:** *passing amorous fancy*   **8 violet;** *cf. n.* **primy:** *spring-like*   **9 Forward:** *precocious*   **10 suppliance:** *diversion*   **14 crescent:** *growing*   **15 thews:** *bodily strength* **temple:** *body*   **17 withal:** *also*   **18 soil:** *blemish* **cautel:** *trickery*   **19 virtue of his will:** *his virtuous intentions*   **21 not in Quarto**   **22 unvalu'd:** *untitled*   **26 voice and yielding:** *approval and compliance*   **29 place:** *position as a prince; cf. n.* **30 deed:** *effect*   **33 credent:** *trustful* **list:** *listen to*   **35 unmaster'd:** *unrestrained*   **39 chariest:** *most scrupulous*

The canker galls the infants of the spring
Too oft before their buttons be disclos'd,
And in the morn and liquid dew of youth
Contagious blastments are most imminent.   45
Be wary then; best safety lies in fear:
Youth to itself rebels, though none else near.

    Oph. I shall the effect of this good lesson keep,
As watchman to my heart. But, good my brother,
Do not, as some ungracious pastors do,   50
Show me the steep and thorny way to heaven,
Whiles, like a puff'd and reckless libertine,
Himself the primrose path of dalliance treads,
And recks not his own rede.

    Laer.   O fear me not.   55

Enter Polonius.

I stay too long, but here my father comes.
A double blessing is a double grace;
Occasion smiles upon a second leave.

    Pol. Yet here, Laertes? aboard, aboard, for shame!
The wind sits in the shoulder of your sail,   60
And you are stay'd for. There, my blessing with thee!
And these few precepts in thy memory
Look thou chará cter. Give thy thoughts no tongue,
Nor any unproportion'd thought his act.
Be thou familiar, but by no means vulgar;   65
Those friends thou hast, and their adoption tried,
Grapple them unto thy soul with hoops of steel;
But do not dull thy palm with entertainment
Of each new-hatch'd, unfledg'd comráde. Beware
Of entrance to a quarrel, but, being in,   70
Bear 't that th' opposed may beware of thee.
Give every man thy ear, but few thy voice;
Take each man's censure, but reserve thy judgment.
Costly thy habit as thy purse can buy,
But not express'd in fancy; rich, not gaudy;   75
For the apparel oft proclaims the man,
And they in France of the best rank and station
Are of a most select and generous clef in that.
Neither a borrower, nor a lender be;
For loan oft loses both itself and friend,   80
And borrowing dulleth edge of husbandry.
This above all: to thine own self be true,
And it must follow, as the night the day,
Thou canst not then be false to any man.
Farewell; my blessing season this in thee!   85

    Laer. Most humbly do I take my leave, my lord.

    Pol. The time invites you; go, your servants tend.

    Laer. Farewell, Ophelia; and remember well
What I have said to you.

    Oph.   'Tis in my memory lock'd,   90
And you yourself shall keep the key of it.

    Laer. Farewell.   *Exit Laertes.*

    Pol. What is 't, Ophelia, he hath said to you?

    Oph. So please you, something touching the Lord Hamlet.

    Pol. Marry, well bethought: 95
'Tis told me, he hath very oft of late
Given private time to you; and you yourself
Have of your audience been most free and bounteous.
If it be so,—as so 'tis put on me,
And that in way of caution,—I must tell you,   100
You do not understand yourself so clearly
As it behoves my daughter and your honor.
What is between you? give me up the truth.

    Oph. He hath, my lord, of late made many tenders
Of his affection to me.   105

    Pol. Affection! pooh! you speak like a green girl,
Unsifted in such perilous circumstance.
Do you believe his tenders, as you call them?

    Oph. I do not know, my lord, what I should think.

    Pol. Marry, I'll teach you: think yourself a baby,   110
That you have ta'en these tenders for true pay,
Which are not sterling. Tender yourself more dearly;
Or (not to crack the wind of the poor phrase,
Running it thus) you'll tender me a fool.

    Oph. My lord, he hath impórtun'd me with love   115
In honorable fashion.

    Pol. Ay, fashion you may call it. Go to, go to.

    Oph. And hath given countenance to his speech, my lord,
With almost all the holy vows of heaven.

    Pol. Ay, springes to catch woodcocks. I do know,   120
When the blood burns, how prodigal the soul
Lends the tongue vows: these blazes, daughter,
Giving more light than heat, extinct in both,
Even in their promise, as it is a-making,
You must not take for fire. From this time   125
Be somewhat scanter of your maiden presence;
Set your entreatments at a higher rate
Than a command to parley. For Lord Hamlet,
Believe so much in him: that he is young,
And with a larger tether may he walk   130
Than may be given you. In few, Ophelia,
Do not believe his vows, for they are brokers,
Not of that dye which their investments show,
But mere implorators of unholy suits,
Breathing like sanctified and pious bawds,   135
The better to beguile. This is for all:
I would not, in plain terms, from this time forth,
Have you so slander any moment leisure,
As to give words or talk with the Lord Hamlet.
Look to 't, I charge you; come your ways.   140

    Oph. I shall obey, my lord.   *Exeunt.*

---

42 canker: *caterpillar* **galls:** *injures* **infants:** *young plants*   **43 buttons:** *buds* **disclos'd:** *opened*   **44 liquid dew:** *while the dew is still fresh*   **45 blastments:** *blights*   **50 ungracious:** *graceless*   **52 puff'd:** *bloated from excess*   **53 primrose path:** *path of pleasure*   **54 recks:** *heeds* **rede:** *counsel* **fear me not:** *don't worry about me*   **57 double;** *cf. n.*   **58 Occasion:** *opportunity* **smiles upon:** *favors me with*   **60 wind ... of;** *cf. n.*   **62 precepts;** *cf. n.*   **63 character:** *inscribe*   **64 unproportion'd:** *inordinate*   **65 familiar:** *friendly*   **68 dull thy palm:** *make yourself less sensitive to true friendship*   **69 unfledg'd:** *immature*   **73 censure:** *opinion*   **75 express'd in fancy:** *singular in design*   **78 generous:** *aristocratic* **clef:** *musical key, tone; cf. n.*   **81 husbandry:** *thrift*   **85 season this:** *make my admonition palatable*   **86 tend:** *are in waiting*

97 private time: *time in private visits*   **99 put on:** *impressed on*   **104 tenders:** *offers; cf. n.*   **106 green:** *inexperienced*   **107 Unsifted:** *untried* **circumstance:** *state of affairs*   **112 sterling:** *legal currency*   **114 Running;** *cf. n.*   **120 springes:** *snares* **woodcocks;** *cf. n.*   **127 entreatments:** *interviews*   **131 In few:** *briefly*   **132 brokers:** *go-betweens, procurers*   **133 investments:** *vestments, clothes*   **134 implorators:** *solicitors*   **135 bawds;** *cf. n.*   **138 slander:** *bring reproach upon*

❧ SCENE FOURTH ❧

[The Platform of the Castle]
Enter Hamlet, Horatio, and Marcellus.

Ham. The air bites shrewdly; it is very cold.
Hor. It is a nipping and an eager air.
Ham. What hour now?
Hor.   I think it lacks of twelve.
Mar. No, it is struck.   5
Hor. Indeed? I heard it not: it then draws near the season
Wherein the spirit held his wont to walk.

A flourish of trumpets, and two pieces [of ordnance] go off.

What does this mean, my lord?
Ham. The king doth wake to-night and takes his rouse,
Keeps wassail, and the swaggering up-spring reels;   10
And, as he drains his draughts of Rhenish down,
The kettle-drum and trumpet thus bray out
The triumph of his pledge.
Hor.   Is it a custom?
Ham. Ay, marry, is 't: 15
But to my mind, though I am native here
And to the manner born, it is a custom
More honor'd in the breach than the observance.
«This heavy-headed revel east and west
Makes us traduc'd and tax'd of other nations;   20
They clepe us drunkards, and with swinish phrase
Soil our addition; and indeed it takes
From our achievements, though perform'd at height,
The pith and marrow of our attribute.
So, oft it chances in particular men,   25
That for some vicious mole of nature in them,
As, in their birth, (wherein they are not guilty,
Since nature cannot choose his origin),
By the o'ergrowth of some complexion,
Oft breaking down the pales and forts of reason,   30
Or by some habit that too much o'er-leavens
The form of plausive manners; that these men,
Carrying, I say, the stamp of one defect,
Being nature's livery, or fortune's star,—
His virtues else, be they as pure as grace,   35
As infinite as man may undergo,
Shall in the general censure take corruption
From that particular fault. The dram of eale
Doth all the noble substance oft adulter
To his own scandal.»   40

Enter Ghost.

Hor.   Look, my lord, it comes!
Ham. Angels and ministers of grace defend us!
Be thou a spirit of health or goblin damn'd,
Bring with thee airs from heaven or blasts from hell,

Be thy intents wicked or charitable,   45
Thou com'st in such a questionable shape
That I will speak to thee. I'll call thee Hamlet,
King, father, royal Dane! O answer me:
Let me not burst in ignorance, but tell
Why thy canóniz'd bones, hearsed in death,   50
Have burst their cerements; why the sepulchre,
Wherein we saw thee quietly inurn'd,
Hath op'd his ponderous and marble jaws,
To cast thee up again? What may this mean,
That thou, dead corse, again in cómplete steel   55
Revisits thus the glimpses of the moon,
Making night hideous; and we fools of nature
So horridly to-shake our disposition
With thoughts beyond the reaches of our souls?
Say, why is this? wherefore? what should we do?   60

Ghost beckons Hamlet.

Hor. It beckons you to go away with it,
As if it some impartment did desire
To you alone.
Mar.   Look, with what courteous action
It waves you to a more removed ground: 65
But do not go with it.
Hor.   No, by no means.
Ham. It will not speak. Then, I will follow it.
Hor. Do not, my lord.
Ham.   Why, what should be the fear?   70
I do not set my life at a pin's fee;
And for my soul, what can it do to that,
Being a thing immortal as itself?
It waves me forth again; I'll follow it.
Hor. What if it tempt you toward the flood, my lord,   75
Or to the dreadful summit of the cliff
That beetles o'er his base into the sea,
And there assume some other horrible form,
Which might deprive your sovereignty of reason
And draw you into madness? think of it;   80
«The very place puts toys of desperation,
Without more motive, into every brain
That looks so many fadoms to the sea
And hears it roar beneath.»
Ham. It waves me still. Go on! I'll follow thee.   85
Mar. You shall not go, my lord.
Ham.   Hold off your hands!
Hor. Be rul'd; you shall not go.
Ham.   My fate cries out,
And makes each petty arture in this body   90
As hardy as the Némean lion's nerve.
Still am I call'd. Unhand me, gentlemen!
By heaven, I'll make a ghost of him that lets me.
I say, away!—Go on! I'll follow thee.

Exeunt Ghost and Hamlet.

Hor. He waxes desperate with imagination.   95

---

2 **eager**: *sharp*   9 **wake**: *hold a revel by night*   10 **Keeps wassail**: *holds a drinking-bout*   **up-spring**: *wild dance of German origin*   11 **Rhenish**: *Rhine wine*   13 **pledge**: *toast*   19-40 *Not in Folio*   20 **traduc'd and tax'd**: *defamed and censured*   21 **clepe**: *call*   **swinish phrase**: *name of 'pigs'*   22 **Soil our addition**: *blemish our good name*   23 **at height**: *to the maximum*   24 **attribute**: *reputation*   26 **mole**: *blemish*   29 **complexion**: *natural tendency, 'humor'*   30 **pales**: *defensive enclosures*   31 **o'er-leavens**: *makes too light*   32 **plausive**: *pleasing*   34 **nature's livery**: *a natural attribute*   **fortune's star**: *the position in which one is placed by fortune*   35 **His**; *cf. n.*   36 **undergo**: *bear the weight of*   38 **dram**: *minute quantity*   **eale**: *e'il, evil*   39 **oft adulter**; *cf. n.*   40 **scandal**: *shame*   42 **ministers of grace**: *messengers of God*   43 **spirit of health**: *good spirit*   **goblin**: *evil spirit*

46 **questionable**: *inviting question*   50 **canoniz'd**: *buried according to the Church's rule*   **hearsed**: *coffined*   51 **cerements**: *waxen grave-clothes*   52 **inurn'd**: *interred; cf. n.*   56 **glimpses of the moon**: *the earth by night*   57 **fools of nature**: *stupid in nature's presence*   58 **to-shake our disposition**: *shatter our composure*   59 **reaches**: *capacities*   62 **impartment**: *communication*   71 **at . . . fee**: *at even a trifling value*   75 **flood**: *sea*   77 **beetles**: *overhangs threateningly*   79 **deprive . . . reason**: *dethrone reason from its sovereignty*   81-84 **The . . . beneath**; *not in Folio*   81 **toys of desperation**: *whims involving thoughts of self-destruction*   83 **fadoms**: *fathoms*   90 **arture**: *artery*   91 **Nemean lion's**; *cf. n.*   **nerve**: *sinew, tendon*   93 **lets**: *hinders*

Mar. Let's follow; 'tis not fit thus to obey him.
Hor. Have after. To what issue will this come?
Mar. Something is rotten in the state of Denmark.
Hor. Heaven will direct it.
Mar.   Nay, let's follow him.   *Exeunt.*

❧ Scene Fifth ❧

[*A more remote Part of the Platform*]
Enter Ghost and Hamlet.

Ham. Whither wilt thou lead me? speak; I'll go no further.
Ghost. Mark me.
Ham.   I will.
Ghost.   My hour is almost come,
When I to sulphurous and tormenting flames   *5*
Must render up myself.
Ham.   Alas, poor ghost.
Ghost. Pity me not, but lend thy serious hearing
To what I shall unfold.
Ham.   Speak; I am bound to hear.   *10*
Ghost. So art thou to revenge, when thou shalt hear.
Ham. What?
Ghost. I am thy father's spirit,
Doom'd for a certain term to walk the night,
And for the day confin'd to fast in fires,   *15*
Till the foul crimes done in my days of nature
Are burnt and purg'd away. But that I am forbid
To tell the secrets of my prison-house,
I could a tale unfold whose lightest word
Would harrow up thy soul, freeze thy young blood,   *20*
Make thy two eyes, like stars, start from their spheres,
Thy knotted and combined locks to part,
And each particular hair to stand an end,
Like quills upon the fretful porpentine.
But this eternal blazon must not be   *25*
To ears of flesh and blood. List, list, oh list!
If thou didst ever thy dear father love—
Ham. O God!
Ghost. Revenge his foul and most unnatural murther.
Ham. Murther!   *30*
Ghost. Murther most foul, as in the best it is;
But this most foul, strange, and unnatural.
Ham. Haste me to know 't, that I, with wings as swift
As meditation or the thoughts of love,
May sweep to my revenge.   *35*
Ghost.   I find thee apt;
And duller shouldst thou be than the fat weed
That roots itself in ease on Lethe wharf,
Wouldst thou not stir in this. Now, Hamlet, hear:
'Tis given out that, sleeping in my orchard,   *40*
A serpent stung me. So the whole ear of Denmark
Is by a forged process of my death
Rankly abus'd; but know, thou noble youth,
The serpent that did sting thy father's life
Now wears his crown.   *45*

Ham.   O my prophetic soul!
My uncle?
Ghost. Ay, that incestuous, that adulterate beast,
With witchcraft of his wit, with traitorous gifts,—
O wicked wit and gifts, that have the power   *50*
So to seduce!—won to his shameful lust
The will of my most seeming-virtuous queen.
O Hamlet, what a falling-off was there!
From me, whose love was of that dignity
That it went hand in hand even with the vow   *55*
I made to her in marriage; and to decline
Upon a wretch whose natural gifts were poor
To those of mine!
But virtue, as it never will be mov'd,
Though lewdness court it in a shape of heaven,   *60*
So lust, though to a radiant angel link'd,
Will sate itself in a celestial bed,
And prey on garbage.
But, soft! methinks I scent the morning air;
Brief let me be. Sleeping within my orchard,   *65*
My custom always of the afternoon,
Upon my secure hour thy uncle stole,
With juice of cursed hebona in a vial,
And in the porches of my ears did pour
The leperous distilment; whose effect   *70*
Holds such an enmity with blood of man
That swift as quicksilver it courses through
The natural gates and alleys of the body,
And with a sudden vigor it doth posset
And curd, like eager droppings into milk,   *75*
The thin and wholesome blood. So did it mine;
And a most instant tetter bark'd about,
Most lazar-like, with vile and loathsome crust,
All my smooth body.
Thus was I, sleeping, by a brother's hand,   *80*
Of life, of crown, of queen, at once dispatch'd;
Cut off even in the blossoms of my sin,
Unhousel'd, disappointed, unanel'd,
No reckoning made, but sent to my account
With all my imperfections on my head.   *85*
[*Ham.*] O horrible! O horrible! most horrible!
[*Ghost.*] If thou hast nature in thee, bear it not;
Let not the royal bed of Denmark be
A couch for luxury and damned incest.
But, howsomever thou pursu'st this act,   *90*
Taint not thy mind, nor let thy soul contrive
Against thy mother aught. Leave her to heaven,
And to those thorns that in her bosom lodge,
To prick and sting her. Fare thee well at once!
The glow-worm shows the matin to be near,   *95*
And 'gins to pale his uneffectual fire;
Adieu, adieu, adieu! Remember me.   *Exit.*
     Ham. O all you host of heaven! O earth! What else?
And shall I couple hell? O fie! Hold, hold, my heart!

---

97 issue: *outcome*   **21 spheres:** *orbits*   **22 knotted:** *neatly arranged* **combined:** *smoothly combed*   **23 an:** *on*   **24 porpentine:** *porcupine*   **25 eternal blazon:** *revelation of eternity; cf. n.*   **29 unnatural:** *i.e., for one brother to kill another*   **36 apt:** *ready to learn*   **37 fat weed:** *cf. n.*   **38 Lethe:** *cf. n.* **wharf:** *bank*   **40 orchard:** *garden*   **42 process:** *narrative*   **43 abus'd:** *deceived*

48 adulterate: *adulterous*   **68 hebona:** *yew, notorious for its poisonous properties, but henbane and ebony are also involved*   **70 leperous:** *causing leprosy*   **73 gates and alleys:** *streets and lanes; cf. n.*   **74 posset:** *curdle*   **75 eager:** *sour*   **77 instant:** *instantaneous* **tetter:** *skin eruption* **bark'd about:** *covered (as with bark)*   **78 lazar-like:** *leprous-like*   **81 dispatch'd:** *bereft*   **83 Unhousel'd:** *without having received the Holy Communion* **disappointed:** *unprepared* **unanel'd:** *without having received extreme unction*   **84 reckoning:** *confession and absolution*   **86 O horrible:** *cf. n.*   **89 luxury:** *lasciviousness*   **95 matin:** *morning*   **96 uneffectual:** *heatless*

And you, my sinews, grow not instant old,   *100*
But bear me stiffly up. Remember thee?
Ay, thou poor ghost, while memory holds a seat
In this distracted globe. Remember thee?
Yea, from the table of my memory
I'll wipe away all trivial fond records,   *105*
All saws of books, all forms, all pressures past,
That youth and observation copied there;
And thy commandment all alone shall live
Within the book and volume of my brain,
Unmix'd with baser matter: yes, by heaven!   *110*
O most pernicious woman!
O villain, villain, smiling, damned villain!
My tables! Meet it is I set it down,
That one may smile, and smile, and be a villain;
At least I'm sure it may be so in Denmark.   *[Writing.]* *115*
So, uncle, there you are. Now to my word.
It is, 'Adieu, adieu! remember me.'
I have sworn 't.
    Hor. and Mar. within. My lord! my lord!

        Enter Horatio and Marcellus.

    Mar.   Lord Hamlet!   *120*
    Hor. Heaven secure him!
    Ham.   So be it!
    Hor. Illo, ho, ho, my lord!
    Ham. Hillo, ho, ho, boy! come, bird, come.
    Mar. How is 't, my noble lord?   *125*
    Hor.   What news, my lord?
    Ham. O wonderful!
    Hor.   Good my lord, tell it.
    Ham. No; you will reveal it.
    Hor. Not I, my lord, by heaven!   *130*
    Mar.   Nor I, my lord.
    Ham. How say you, then? would heart of man once think it?
But you'll be secret?
    Both.   Ay, by heaven, my lord.
    Ham. There's ne'er a villain dwelling in all Denmark, *135*
But he's an arrant knave.
    Hor. There needs no ghost, my lord, come from the grave,
To tell us this.
    Ham.   Why, right; you are in the right;
And so, without more circumstance at all,   *140*
I hold it fit that we shake hands and part;
You, as your business and desire shall point you,—
For every man hath business and desire,
Such as it is,—and, for my own poor part,
I will go pray.   *145*
    Hor. These are but wild and whirling words, my lord.
    Ham. I am sorry they offend you, heartily;
Yes, faith, heartily.
    Hor.   There's no offence, my lord.
    Ham. Yes, by Saint Patrick, but there is, Horatio, *150*
And much offence, too. Touching this vision here,
It is an honest ghost, that let me tell you.
For your desire to know what is between us,

O'ermaster 't as you may. And now, good friends,
As you are friends, scholars, and soldiers,   *155*
Give me one poor request.
    Hor. What is 't, my lord? we will.
    Ham. Never make known what you have seen tonight.
    Both. My lord, we will not.
    Ham.   Nay, but swear 't.   *160*
    Hor.   In faith,
My lord, not I.
    Mar.   Nor I, my lord, in faith.
    Ham. Upon my sword.
    Mar.   We have sworn, my lord, already. *165*
    Ham. Indeed, upon my sword, indeed.
    Ghost. Swear.   *Ghost cries under the stage.*
    Ham. Ha, ha, boy! sayst thou so? art thou there, true-penny?
Come on,—you hear this fellow in the cellarage,—
Consent to swear.   *170*
    Hor.   Propose the oath, my lord.
    Ham. Never to speak of this that you have seen.
Swear by my sword.
    Ghost. Swear.
    Ham. Hic et ubique? then we'll shift our ground.   *175*
Come hither, gentlemen, and lay your hands
Again upon my sword. Swear by my sword
Never to speak of this that you have heard.
    Ghost. Swear by his sword.
    Ham. Well said, old mole! canst work i' th' earth so fast? *180*
A worthy pioner! once more remove, good friends.
    Hor. O day and night, but this is wondrous strange!
    Ham. And therefore as a stranger give it welcome.
There are more things in heaven and earth, Horatio,
Than are dreamt of in your philosophy.   *185*
But come;
Here, as before, never, so help you mercy,
How strange or odd soe'er I bear myself,—
As I perchance hereafter shall think meet
To put an antic disposition on,—   *190*
That you, at such times seeing me, never shall,
With arms encumber'd thus, or this head-shake,
Or by pronouncing of some doubtful phrase,
As, 'Well, well, we know,' or, 'We could, an if we would;'
Or, 'If we list to speak,' or, 'There be, an if they might;' *195*
Or such ambiguous giving out, to note
That you know aught of me. This do swear,
So grace and mercy at your most need help you.
    Ghost. Swear.   *[They swear.]*
    Ham. Rest, rest, perturbed spirit! So, gentlemen,   *200*
With all my love I do commend me to you:
And what so poor a man as Hamlet is
May do t' express his love and friending to you,
God willing, shall not lack. Let us go in together;
And still your fingers on your lips, I pray.   *205*
The time is out of joint. O cursed spite,
That ever I was born to set it right!
Nay, come, let's go together.   *Exeunt.*

---

103 distracted globe: *confused head* **104 table:** *writing-tablet* **105 fond:** *foolish* **106 saws:** *maxims* **pressures:** *impressions—as of a seal* **116 word:** *watch-word* **123 Illo, ho, ho:** *falconer's hunting call* **124 come, bird, come:** *call which falconers use to their hawk in the air* **136 arrant:** *thoroughgoing* **140 circumstance:** *formality* **146 whirling:** *eddying, incoherent* **150 Saint Patrick:** *cf. n.* **152 honest ghost:** *cf. n.*

154 O'ermaster 't: *conquer it* **168 true-penny:** *honest fellow* **173 sword;** *cf. n.* **175 Hic et ubique:** *here and everywhere* **181 pioner:** *digger, miner* **185 your;** *cf. n.* **189 meet:** *proper* **190 antic:** *fantastic* **192 encumber'd:** *folded; cf. n.* **193 doubtful:** *ambiguous* **194 an if:** *an intensive form of if* **196 to note:** *to give a sign* **206 spite:** *vexatious circumstance*

ACT SECOND ❧ SCENE FIRST

Polonius' Apartment in the Castle
Enter old Polonius with his man [Reynaldo].

Pol. Give him this money and these notes, Reynaldo.
Rey. I will, my lord.
Pol. You shall do marvel's wisely, good Reynaldo,
Before you visit him, to make inquire
Of his behavior.   *5*
Rey.   My lord, I did intend it.
Pol. Marry, well said, very well said. Look you, sir,
Inquire me first what Danskers are in Paris;
And how, and who, what means, and where they keep,
What company, at what expense; and finding   *10*
By this encompassment and drift of question
That they do know my son, come you more nearer
Than your particular demands will touch it.
Take you, as 'twere, some distant knowledge of him;
As thus, 'I know his father, and his friends,   *15*
And in part him.' Do you mark this, Reynaldo?
Rey. Ay, very well, my lord.
Pol. 'And in part him; but,' you may say, 'not well:
But if 't be he I mean, he's very wild,
Addicted so and so'; and there put on him   *20*
What forgeries you please: marry, none so rank
As may dishonor him; take heed of that;
But, sir, such wanton, wild, and usual slips
As are companions noted and most known
To youth and liberty.   *25*
Rey.   As gaming, my lord?
Pol. Ay, or drinking, fencing, swearing,
Quarrelling, drabbing,—you may go so far.
Rey. My lord, that would dishonor him.
Pol. Faith, no, as you may season it in the charge.   *30*
You must not put another scandal on him,
That he is open to incontinency.
That's not my meaning; but breathe his faults so quaintly
That they may seem the taints of liberty,
The flash and outbreak of a fiery mind,   *35*
A savageness in unreclaimed blood,
Of general assault.
Rey.   But, my good lord,—
Pol. Wherefore should you do this?
Rey.   Ay, my lord,   *40*
I would know that.
Pol.   Marry, sir, here's my drift;
And I believe it is a fetch of warrant.
You laying these slight sullies on my son,
As 'twere a thing a little soil'd i' th' working,   *45*
Mark you,
Your party in converse, him you would sound,
Having ever seen in the prenominate crimes

The youth you breathe of guilty, be assur'd,
He closes with you in this consequence: *50*
'Good sir,' or so, or 'friend,' or 'gentleman,'
According to the phrase or the addition
Of man and country—
Rey.   Very good, my lord.
Pol. And then, sir, does 'a this,—'a does,—what was   *55*
I about to say? By the mass I was about to say something.
Where did I leave?
Rey. At 'closes in the consequence,'
At 'friend or so,' and 'gentleman.'
Pol. At 'closes in the consequence'? Ay, marry;   *60*
He closes thus: 'I know the gentleman;
I saw him yesterday, or th' other day,
Or then, or then, with such or such; and, as you say,
There was 'a gaming, there o'ertook in 's rouse,
There falling out at tennis'; or perchance,   *65*
'I saw him enter such a house of sale,'
Videlicet, a brothel, or so forth.
See you now;
Your bait of falsehood takes this carp of truth;
And thus do we of wisdom and of reach,   *70*
With windlasses and with assays of bias,
By indirections find directions out.
So by my former lecture and advice
Shall you my son. You have me, have you not?
Rey. My lord, I have.   *75*
Pol.   God be wi' ye; fare ye well.
Rey. Good my lord!
Pol. Observe his inclination in yourself.
Rey. I shall, my lord.
Pol. And let him ply his music.   *80*
Rey.   Well, my lord.
Pol. Farewell!   *Exit Reynaldo.*

Enter Ophelia.

                      How now, Ophelia! what's the matter?
Oph. O my lord, my lord! I have been so affrighted.
Pol. With what, i' th' name of God?   *85*
Oph. My lord, as I was sewing in my closet,
Lord Hamlet, with his doublet all unbrac'd,
No hat upon his head; his stockings foul'd,
Ungarter'd, and down-gyved to his ankle;—
Pale as his shirt, his knees knocking each other,   *90*
And with a look so piteous in purport
As if he had been loosed out of hell
To speak of horrors, he comes before me.
Pol. Mad for thy love?
Oph.   My lord, I do not know;   *95*
But truly I do fear it.
Pol.   What said he?
Oph. He took me by the wrist and held me hard;
Then goes he to the length of all his arm,
And, with his other hand thus o'er his brow,   *100*
He falls to such perusal of my face

1 notes: *instructions*   **3 marvel's:** *marvelously*   **4 inquire:** *investigation*   **8 Danskers:**
Danes   **9 keep:** *live*   **11 encompassment:** *'talking round' a subject*   **question:** *conversa-*
tion   **13 particular demands:** *concrete questions*   **14 Take:** *assume*   **20 put on:** *im-*
pute to   **21 forgeries:** *invented tales* **rank:** *excessive*   **23 wanton:** *unrestrained*   **28**
drabbing: *wenching*   **30 season:** *flavor* **charge:** *accusation*   **32 incontinency:** *habitual*
loose behavior   **33 breathe . . . quaintly:** *hint . . . cleverly*   **34 taints of liberty:** *blemishes*
due to high spirits   **36 savageness:** *wildness* **unreclaimed:** *untamed*   **37 Of general**
assault: *to which all are liable*   **43 fetch of warrant:** *justifiable trick*   **44 sullies:** *blem-*
ishes   **45** *Cf. n.*   **48 prenominate:** *aforesaid*

50 closes . . . consequence: *confides in you as follows*   **57 leave:** *leave off*   **64 o'ertook**
in 's rouse: *unable to hold his liquor*   **67 Videlicet:** *namely*   **70 reach:** *resourceful-*
ness   **71 windlasses:** *roundabout ways* **assays of bias:** *indirect approaches*   **72 indirec-**
tions: *devious courses* **directions:** *the straight facts*   **73 lecture:** *instruction*   **78 in**
yourself: *for yourself*   **80 ply:** *keep up*   **86 closet:** *sitting room*   **87 doublet:** *close-*
fitting coat **unbrac'd:** *unfastened*   **89 down-gyved:** *hanging down like gyves or fet-*
ters   **101 perusal:** *scrutiny*

As 'a would draw it. Long stay'd he so.
At last, a little shaking of mine arm,
And thrice his head thus waving up and down,
He rais'd a sigh so piteous and profound   *105*
As it did seem to shatter all his bulk
And end his being. That done, he lets me go,
And with his head over his shoulder turn'd,
He seem'd to find his way without his eyes,
For out o' doors he went without their help,   *110*
And to the last bended their light on me.
    Pol. Come, go with me. I will go seek the king.
This is the very ecstasy of love,
Whose violent property fordoes itself
And leads the will to desperate undertakings   *115*
As oft as any passion under heaven
That does afflict our natures. I am sorry.
What! have you given him any hard words of late?
    Oph. No, my good lord; but, as you did command,
I did repel his letters and denied   *120*
His acccss to me.
    Pol.   That hath made him mad.
I am sorry that with better heed and judgment
I had not coted him. I fear'd he did but trifle,
And meant to wrack thee, but beshrew my jealousy!   *125*
By heaven, it is as proper to our age
To cast beyond ourselves in our opinions
As it is common for the younger sort
To lack discretion. Come, go we to the king.
This must be known, which, being kept close, might move   *130*
More grief to hide than hate to utter love.
Come.   *Exeunt.*

❧ Scene Second ❧

[The Lobby in the Castle]
Flourish. Enter King and Queen, Rosencrantz and Guildenstern,
cum aliis.

    King. Welcome, dear Rosencrantz and Guildenstern.
Moreover that we much did long to see you,
The need we have to use you did provoke
Our hasty sending. Something have you heard
Of Hamlet's transformation. So I call it,   *5*
Sith nor th' exterior nor the inward man
Resembles that it was. What it should be,
More than his father's death, that thus hath put him
So much from th' understanding of himself,
I cannot dream of. I entreat you both,   *10*
That being of so young days brought up with him,
And since so neighbor'd to his youth and havior,
That you vouchsafe your rest here in our court
Some little time; so by your companies
To draw him on to pleasures and to gather,   *15*
So much as from occasion you may glean,
«Whether aught to us unknown afflicts him thus,»

That, open'd, lies within our remedy.
    Queen. Good gentlemen, he hath much talk'd of you;
And sure I am two men there are not living   *20*
To whom he more adheres. If it will please you
To show us so much gentry and good will
As to expend your time with us awhile,
For the supply and profit of our hope,
Your visitation shall receive such thanks   *25*
As fits a king's remembrance.
    Ros.   Both your majesties
Might, by the sovereign power you have of us,
Put your dread pleasures more into command
Than to entreaty.   *30*
    Guil.   But we both obey,
And here give up ourselves in the full bent,
To lay our service freely at your feet
To be commanded.
    King. Thanks, Rosencrantz and gentle Guildenstern.   *35*
    Queen. Thanks, Guildenstern and gentle Rosencrantz;
And I beseech you instantly to visit
My too much changed son. Go, some of you,
And bring these gentlemen where Hamlet is.
    Guil. Heavens make our presence and our practices   *40*
Pleasant and helpful to him!
    Queen.   Ay, amen!

Exeunt Rosencrantz and Guildenstern [attended].
Enter Polonius.

    Pol. Th' ambassadors from Norway, my good lord,
Are joyfully return'd.
    King. Thou still hast been the father of good news.   *45*
    Pol. Have I, my lord? Assure you, my good liege,
I hold my duty as I hold my soul,
Both to my God and to my gracious king;
And I do think—or else this brain of mine
Hunts not the trail of policy so sure   *50*
As it hath us'd to do—that I have found
The very cause of Hamlet's lunacy.
    King. O speak of that! that do I long to hear.
    Pol. Give first admittance to th' ambassadors;
My news shall be the fruit to that great feast.   *55*
    King. Thyself do grace to them, and bring them in.
                                      [Exit Polonius.]
He tells me, my dear Gertrude, he hath found
The head and source of all your son's distemper.
    Queen. I doubt it is no other but the main:
His father's death and our o'erhasty marriage.   *60*
    King. Well, we shall sift him.

Enter Polonius, Voltimand, and Cornelius.

                                Welcome, my good friends!
Say, Voltimand, what from our brother Norway?
    Volt. Most fair return of greetings and desires.
Upon our first, he sent out to suppress   *65*
His nephew's levies, which to him appear'd
To be a preparation 'gainst the Polack;

---

106 bulk: *frame*   **113 ecstasy:** *madness*   **114 property:** *nature* **fordoes:** *destroys*   **124 coted:** *observed* (obsolete form of 'quote')   **125 wrack:** *ruin* **beshrew:** *curse* **jealousy:** *suspicion, mistrust*   **126 our age:** *us old folk*   **127 cast ... ourselves:** *be over subtle*   **131 More ... love;** *cf. n.*   **11 of so young days:** *from such early youth; cf. n.*   **12 neighbor'd ... havior:** *near in age and occupation*   **13 vouchsafe your rest:** *please to reside*   **17 not in Folio***

18 open'd: *revealed*   **22 gentry:** *courtesy*   **24 supply and profit:** *aid and successful outcome*   **26 as ... remembrance:** *as is suitable to a king's gratitude*   **32 in the full bent:** *to the utmost degree* (an archery term)   **47, 48** *Cf. n.*   **50 policy:** *conduct of public affairs*   **55 fruit:** *dessert*   **59 main:** *chief point*   **64 desires:** *good wishes*   **65 Upon our first;** *cf. n.*

But, better look'd into, he truly found
It was against your highness: whereat griev'd
That so his sickness, age, and impotence   70
Was falsely borne in hand, sends out arrests
On Fortinbras; which he in brief obeys,
Receives rebuke from Norway, and, in fine,
Makes vow before his uncle never more
To give th' assay of arms against your majesty.   75
Whereon old Norway, overcome with joy,
Gives him three thousand crowns in annual fee,
And his commission to employ those soldiers,
So levied as before, against the Polack;
With an entreaty, herein further shown,   *[Giving a paper.]*
That it might please you to give quiet pass
Through your dominions for this enterprise,
On such regards of safety and allowance
As therein are set down.
    King.   It likes us well;   85
And at our more consider'd time we'll read,
Answer, and think upon this business.
Meantime we thank you for your well-took labor.
Go to your rest; at night we'll feast together.
Most welcome home.   *Exeunt Ambassadors.*   90
    Pol.   This business is well ended.
My liege, and madam, to expostulate
What majesty should be, what duty is,
Why day is day, night night, and time is time,
Were nothing but to waste night, day, and time.   95
Therefore, since brevity is the soul of wit,
And tediousness the limbs and outward flourishes,
I will be brief. Your noble son is mad.
Mad call I it; for to define true madness,
What is 't but to be nothing else but mad?   100
But let that go.
    Queen.   More matter, with less art.
    Pol. Madam, I swear I use no art at all.
That he is mad, 'tis true; 'tis true 'tis pity;
And pity 'tis 'tis true: a foolish figure,   105
But farewell it, for I will use no art.
Mad let us grant him, then; and now remains
That we find out the cause of this effect,
Or rather say, the cause of this defect,
For this effect defective comes by cause.   110
Thus it remains, and the remainder thus.
Perpend.
I have a daughter (have while she is mine)
Who, in her duty and obedience, mark,
Hath given me this. Now, gather and surmise.   115
                        [Reads] The Letter.

*To the celestial, and my soul's idol, the most beautified
Ophelia.—*

That's an ill phrase, a vile phrase; 'beautified' is a vile phrase;
but you shall hear. Thus:

    In her excellent white bosom, these, &c.—   120

    Queen. Came this from Hamlet to her?
    Pol. Good madam, stay awhile; I will be faithful.

    Doubt thou the stars are fire;
      Doubt that the sun doth move;
    Doubt truth to be a liar;   125
      But never doubt I love.
      *O dear Ophelia! I am ill at these numbers: I have not art
to reckon my groans; but that I love thee best, O most best,
believe it. Adieu.*
      Thine evermore, most dear lady, whilst this machine is to   130
him,

                              Hamlet.

This in obedience hath my daughter shown me,
And more above,—hath his solicitings,
As they fell out by time, by means, and place,   135
All given to mine ear.
    King.   But how hath she
Receiv'd his love?
    Pol.   What do you think of me?
    King. As of a man faithful and honorable.   140
    Pol. I would fain prove so. But what might you think,
When I had seen this hot love on the wing,—
As I perceiv'd it, (I must tell you that)
Before my daughter told me,—what might you,
Or my dear majesty, your queen here, think,   145
If I had play'd the desk or table-book,
Or given my heart a winking, mute and dumb,
Or look'd upon this love with idle sight?
What might you think? No, I went round to work,
And my young mistress thus I did bespeak: 150
'Lord Hamlet is a prince, out of thy star;
This must not be:' and then I prescripts gave her,
That she should lock herself from his resort,
Admit no messengers, receive no tokens.
Which done, she took the fruits of my advice;   155
And he, repelled,—a short tale to make,—
Fell into a sadness, then into a fast,
Thence to a watch, thence into a weakness,
Thence to a lightness, and by this declension
Into the madness wherein now he raves,   160
And all we mourn for.
    King.   Do you think 'tis this?
    Queen. It may be, very like.
    Pol. Hath there been such a time,—I'd fain know that,—
That I have positively said, ' 'Tis so,'   165
When it prov'd otherwise?
    King.   Not that I know.
    Pol. Take this from this, if this be otherwise.
                [Pointing to his head and shoulder.]
If circumstances lead me, I will find
Where truth is hid, though it were hid indeed   170
Within the center.
    King.   How may we try it further?

---

71 borne in hand: *deluded*   **73 in fine:** *in conclusion*   **75 assay:** *trial*   **77**
Cf. n.   **78 his commission;** *cf. n.*   **83 regards . . . allowance;** *cf. n.*   **85 likes:**
pleases   **86 consider'd:** *fit for considering*   **92 expostulate:** *set forth one's views*   **96**
wit: *judgment, understanding*   **97 flourishes:** *embellishments*   **105 figure:** *figure of rheto-*
ric   **112 Perpend:** *consider*   **116 beautified:** *beautiful,* or, *accomplished*   **120 these;**
cf. n.

127 ill at: *unskilled at making* **numbers:** *verses*   **128 reckon:** *number metrically,*
scan   **130 machine:** *bodily frame*   **134 more above:** *more too*   **135 fell out:** *occur*
red **means:** *opportunities of access*   **147 winking:** *a short nap, i.e., allowed my heart to*
connive   **149 round:** *straightforwardly*   **150 bespeak:** *address*   **151 out of thy star:**
above the position allotted thee by fortune   **152 prescripts:** *positive orders*   **158 watch:**
state of sleeplessness   **159 lightness:** *lightheadedness* **declension:** *downward course*   **171**
center: *middle point of the earth*

Pol. You know sometimes he walks four hours together
Here in the lobby.

Queen.   So he does indeed.   *175*

Pol. At such a time I'll loose my daughter to him.
Be you and I behind an arras then.
Mark the encounter; if he love her not,
And be not from his reason fallen thereon,
Let me be no assistant for a state,   *180*
But keep a farm and carters.

King.   We will try it.

Enter Hamlet reading on a book.

Queen. But look, where sadly the poor wretch comes
reading.

Pol. Away! I do beseech you, both away.   *185*
I'll board him presently. O, give me leave.

Exeunt King and Queen.

How does my good Lord Hamlet?

Ham. Well, God-a-mercy.

Pol. Do you know me, my lord?

Ham. Excellent well. You are a fishmonger.   *190*

Pol. Not I, my lord.

Ham. Then I would you were so honest a man.

Pol. Honest, my lord?

Ham. Ay, sir; to be honest, as this world goes, is to be
one man picked out of ten thousand.   *195*

Pol. That's very true, my lord.

Ham. For if the sun breed maggots in a dead dog, being
a god kissing carrion,—Have you a daughter?

Pol. I have, my lord.

Ham. Let her not walk i' the sun. Conception is a blessing,
but as your daughter may conceive, friend, look to 't.

Pol. [*Aside.*] How say you by that? Still harping on my
daughter. Yet he knew me not at first; 'a said I was a fishmonger. 'A is far gone; and truly in my youth I suffered much
extremity for love, very near this. I'll speak to him again.   *205*
What do you read, my lord?

Ham. Words, words, words.

Pol. What is the matter, my lord?

Ham. Between who?

Pol. I mean the matter that you read, my lord.   *210*

Ham. Slanders, sir: for the satirical rogue says here that old
men have grey beards, that their faces are wrinkled, their eyes
purging thick amber and plum-tree gum, and that they have a
plentiful lack of wit, together with most weak hams. All which,
sir, though I most powerfully and potently believe, yet I hold
it not honesty to have it thus set down; for yourself, sir, shall
grow old as I am, if, like a crab, you could go backward.

Pol. [*Aside.*] Though this be madness, yet there is method
in 't. Will you walk out of the air, my lord?

Ham. Into my grave?   *220*

Pol. Indeed, that 's out of the air. [*Aside.*] How pregnant
sometimes his replies are! a happiness that often madness hits
on, which reason and sanity could not so prosperously be delivered of. I will leave him and suddenly contrive the means of
meeting between him and my daughter. My honorable   *225*
lord, I will most humbly take my leave of you.

Ham. You cannot take from me anything that I will more
willingly part withal,—except my life, except my life, except
my life.

Pol. Fare you well, my lord.   [*Going.*]   *230*

Ham. These tedious old fools!

Enter Guildenstern and Rosencrantz.

Pol. You go to seek the Lord Hamlet? There he is.

Ros. [*To Polonius.*] God save you, sir!   [*Exit Polonius.*]

Guil. My honored lord!

Ros. My most dear lord!   *235*

Ham. My excellent good friends! How dost thou,
Guildenstern? Ah, Rosencrantz! Good lads, how do you both?

Ros. As the indifferent children of the earth.

Guild. Happy in that we are not over happy; on
Fortune's cap we are not the very button.   *240*

Ham. Nor the soles of her shoe?

Ros. Neither, my lord.

Ham. Then you live about her waist, or in the middle of
her favors?

Guil. Faith, her privates we.   *245*

Ham. In the secret parts of Fortune? O, most true; she
is a strumpet. What news?

Ros. None, my lord, but that the world's grown honest.

Ham. Then is doomsday near; but your news is not true.
⟨Let me question more in particular. What have you, my   *250*
good friends, deserved at the hands of Fortune, that she
sends you to prison hither?

Guil. Prison, my lord!

Ham. Denmark's a prison.

Ros. Then is the world one.   *255*

Ham. A goodly one; in which there are many confines,
wards, and dungeons, Denmark being one o' the worst.

Ros. We think not so, my lord.

Ham. Why, then, 'tis none to you; for there is nothing
either good or bad but thinking makes it so. To me it   *260*
is a prison.

Ros. Why, then your ambition makes it one; 'tis too
narrow for your mind.

Ham. O God, I could be bounded in a nutshell, and
count myself a king of infinite space, were it not that I   *265*
have bad dreams.

Guil. Which dreams, indeed, are ambition, for the very
substance of the ambitious is merely the shadow of a dream.

Ham. A dream itself is but a shadow.

Ros. Truly, and I hold ambition of so airy and light a   *270*
quality that it is but a shadow's shadow.

Ham. Then are our beggars bodies, and our monarchs and
outstretched heroes the beggars' shadows. Shall we to the
court? for, by my fay, I cannot reason.

Both. We'll wait upon you.   *275*

Ham. No such matter. I will not sort you with the rest of
my servants, for, to speak to you like an honest man, I am
most dreadfully attended.⟩ But, in the beaten way of friendship, what make you at Elsinore?

Ros. To visit you, my lord; no other occasion.   *280*

---

177 arras: *hanging tapestry*   **186 board:** *accost* **presently:** *immediately*   **190 fish-**
monger; *cf. n.*   **198 god kissing;** *cf. n.*   **208 matter:** *substance*   **209 Between who?;**
cf. n.   **213 purging:** *discharging* **amber . . . gum;** *cf. n.*   **216 honesty:** *de-*
cency   **221–222 pregnant:** *full of meaning* **happiness:** *appropriateness*   **223 prosper-**
ously: *successfully*

228 withal: *with*   **238 indifferent:** *ordinary, average*   **239, 240 on . . . button;**
cf. n.   **247 strumpet;** *cf. n.*   **250–278 Let me . . . attended;** *not in Quarto*   **271**
quality: *nature*   **272 beggars bodies;** *cf. n.*   **273 outstretched:** *strutting*   **274 fay:**
faith **reason:** *argue*   **275 wait upon:** *attend*   **276 sort:** *class*   **278 beaten:** *well-*
worn, reliable

Ham. Beggar that I am, I am even poor in thanks, but I thank you: and sure, dear friends, my thanks are too dear a halfpenny. Were you not sent for? Is it your own inclining? Is it a free visitation? Come, come, deal justly with me: come, come; nay, speak.   *285*

Guil. What should we say, my lord?

Ham. Why anything, but to the purpose. You were sent for; and there is a kind of confession in your looks which your modesties have not craft enough to color. I know the good king and queen have sent for you.   *290*

Ros. To what end, my lord?

Ham. That you must teach me. But let me conjure you, by the rights of our fellowship, by the consonancy of our youth, by the obligation of our ever-preserved love, and by what more dear a better proposer could charge you withal, be even   *295* and direct with me, whether you were sent for or no.

Ros. [*Aside to Guildenstern.*] What say you?

Ham. Nay, then, I have an eye of you. If you love me, hold not off.

Guil. My lord, we were sent for.   *300*

Ham. I will tell you why; so shall my anticipation prevent your discovery, and your secrecy to the king and queen moult no feather. I have of late,—but wherefore I know not,—lost all my mirth, forgone all custom of exercises; and indeed it goes so heavily with my disposition that this goodly frame, the   *305* earth, seems to me a sterile promontory; this most excellent canopy, the air, look you, this brave o'erhanging firmament, this majestical roof fretted with golden fire, why, it appeareth nothing to me but a foul and pestilent congregation of vapors. What a piece of work is a man! How noble in reason! how   *310* infinite in faculties! in form and moving how express and admirable! in action how like an angel! in apprehension how like a god! the beauty of the world, the paragon of animals. And yet to me what is this quintessense of dust? Man delights not me; no, nor woman neither, though by your smiling you seem   *315* to say so.

Ros. My lord, there was no such stuff in my thoughts.

Ham. Why did ye laugh, then, when I said 'man delights not me'?

Ros. To think, my lord, if you delight not in man, what lenten entertainment the players shall receive from you. We coted them on the way; and hither are they coming, to offer you service.

Ham. He that plays the king shall be welcome, his majesty shall have tribute of me; the adventurous knight shall use his foil and target; the lover shall not sigh gratis; the humorous   *325* man shall end his part in peace; ⟨the clown shall make those laugh whose lungs are tickle o' the sere;⟩ and the lady shall say her mind freely, or the blank verse shall halt for 't. What players are they?

Ros. Even those you were wont to take delight in, the   *330* tragedians of the city.

Ham. How chances it they travel? Their residence, both in reputation and profit, was better both ways.

Ros. I think their inhibition comes by the means of the late innovation.   *335*

Ham. Do they hold the same estimation they did when I was in the city? Are they so followed?

Ros. No, indeed are they not.

⟨*Ham.* How comes it? Do they grow rusty?

Ros. Nay, their endeavor keeps in the wonted pace: but   *340* there is, sir, an aery of children, little eyases, that cry out on the top of question, and are most tyrannically clapped for 't. These are now the fashion, and so berattle the common stages (so they call them) that many wearing rapiers are afraid of goose-quills, and dare scarce come thither.   *345*

Ham. What, are they children? who maintains 'em? how are they escoted? Will they pursue the quality no longer than they can sing? Will they not say afterwards, if they should grow themselves to common players (as it is most like, if their means are no better) their writers do them wrong to make   *350* them exclaim against their own succession?

Ros. Faith, there has been much to-do on both sides, and the nation holds it no sin to tarre them to controversy. There was for a while no money bid for argument, unless the poet and the player went to cuffs in the question.   *355*

Ham. Is 't possible?

Guil. O, there has been much throwing about of brains.

Ham. Do the boys carry it away?

Ros. Ay, that they do, my lord—Hercules and his load too.⟩

Ham. It is not very strange; for my uncle is king of   *360* Denmark, and those that would make mouths at him while my father lived give twenty, forty, fifty, a hundred ducats apiece for his picture in little. 'Sblood, there is something in this more than natural, if philosophy could find it out.   *A flourish.*

Guil. There are the players.   *365*

Ham. Gentlemen, you are welcome to Elsinore. Your hands! come then; th' appurtenance of welcome is fashion and ceremony. Let me comply with you in this garb, lest my extent to the players (which, I tell you, must show fairly outwards) should more appear like entertainment than yours. You are   *370* welcome; but my uncle-father and aunt-mother are deceived.

Guil. In what, my dear lord?

Ham. I am but mad north-north-west. When the wind is southerly, I know a hawk from a handsaw.

Enter Polonius.

Pol. Well be with you, gentlemen!   *375*

Ham. Hark you, Guildenstern, and you too! at each ear a hearer. That great baby you see there is not yet out of his swaddling-clouts.

Ros. Happily he is the second time come to them, for they say an old man is twice a child.   *380*

Ham. I will prophesy he comes to tell me of the players;

282, 283 too dear a halfpenny; *cf. n.*   **284 free:** *voluntary*   **289 color:** *disguise*   **292 conjure:** *adjure*   **293 consonancy:** *harmony*   **295 better proposer:** *more skillful exhorter* **even:** *straightforward*   **298 have an eye of you:** *have an eye upon you*   **301 prevent:** *precede*   **302 discovery:** *disclosure*   **307 brave:** *splendid*   **308 fretted:** *adorned*   **311 faculties:** *powers* **express:** *well-modelled*   **312 apprehension:** *understanding*   **314 quintessence;** *cf. n.*   **317 stuff:** *matter*   **320 lenten:** *meagre*   **321 coted:** *passed*   **325 foil and target:** *sword and shield*   **325–326 humorous man:** *actor of whimsical characters;* *cf. n.*   **326–327 the clown . . . sere;** *not in Quarto*   **327 tickle o' the sere:** *yield easily to any impulse;* *cf. n.*   **328 halt:** *limp*   **332 residence:** *remaining at headquarters*

334 inhibition: *hindrance*   **335 innovation;** *cf. n.*   **336 estimation:** *reputation*   **337 the city;** *cf. n.*   **339–359 How comes it . . . his load too;** *not in Quarto*   **341 aery:** *nest;* *cf. n.*   **eyases:** *young hawks* **cry . . . question:** *deal pungently with the latest gossip*   **342 tyrannically:** *outrageously*   **343 berattle:** *decry* **common stages;** *cf. n.*   **344 many wearing rapiers:** *many men of quality*   **344–345 afraid of goose-quills:** *afraid of being satirized;* *cf. n.*   **346 escoted:** *maintained* **quality:** *profession*   **349 common players:** *professional players*   **351 succession:** *future, inheritance*   **353 tarre:** *incite*   **354 argument:** *subject-matter, plot*   **355 cuffs:** *blows*   **358 carry it away:** *carry the day*   **359 Hercules and his load;** *cf. n.*   **361 mouths:** *grimaces*   **363 in little:** *in a miniature* **'Sblood:** *God's blood*   **367 appurtenance:** *proper accompaniment*   **368 comply:** *observe the formalities of courtesy* **garb:** *manner* **extent:** *showing of kindness*   **370 entertainment:** *hospitality*   **374 handsaw;** *cf. n.*   **378 swaddling-clouts:** *bandages in which newborn children were wrapped*

mark it.—You say right, sir; o' Monday morning. 'Twas then indeed.

Pol. My lord, I have news to tell you.

Ham. My lord, I have news to tell you. When Roscius   *385*
was an actor in Rome,—

Pol. The actors are come hither, my lord.

Ham. Buzz, buzz!

Pol. Upon my honor,—

Ham. Then came each actor on his ass,—   *390*

Pol. The best actors in the world, either for tragedy,
comedy, history, pastoral, pastoral-comical, historical-pastoral,
⟨tragical-historical, tragical-comical-historical-pastoral,⟩ scene individable,
or poem unlimited: Seneca cannot be too heavy, nor
Plautus too light. For the law of writ and the liberty,   *395*
these are the only men.

Ham. O Jephthah, judge of Israel, what a treasure hadst
thou!

Pol. What a treasure had he, my lord?

Ham. Why,   *400*

One fair daughter and no more,
The which he loved passing well.

Pol. [*Aside.*] Still on my daughter.

Ham. Am I not i' the right, old Jephthah?

Pol. If you call me Jephthah, my lord, I have a daughter   *405*
that I love passing well.

Ham. Nay, that follows not.

Pol. What follows, then, my lord?

Ham. Why,

As by lot, God wot.   *410*

And then, you know,

It came to pass, as most like it was.—

The first row of the pious chanson will show you more, for
look where my abridgment comes.

                  Enter four or five Players.

You are welcome, masters; welcome, all. I am glad to see thee   *415*
well. Welcome, good friends. O, my old friend? Why thy face
is valanced since I saw thee last: com'st thou to beard me in
Denmark? What, my young lady and mistress! By 'r lady, your
ladyship is nearer to heaven than when I saw you last by the
altitude of a chopine. Pray God, your voice, like a piece   *420*
of uncurrent gold, be not cracked within the ring. Masters,
you are all welcome. We'll e'en to 't like French falconers, fly
at anything we see: we'll have a speech straight. Come, give
us a taste of your quality; come, a passionate speech.

Player. What speech, my good lord?   *425*

Ham. I heard thee speak me a speech once, but it was never
acted; or, if it was, not above once; for the play, I remember,
pleased not the million; 'twas caviary to the general: but it was
(as I received it, and others, whose judgments in such matters

cried in the top of mine) an excellent play, well digested in the
scenes, set down with as much modesty as cunning. I remember
one said there were no sallets in the lines to make the matter
savory, nor no matter in the phrase that might indict the
author of affection; but called it an honest method, «as wholesome
as sweet, and by very much more handsome than   *435*
fine.» One speech in 't I chiefly loved; 'twas Æneas' tale to
Dido; and thereabout of it especially, where he speaks of
Priam's slaughter. If it live in your memory, begin at this line:
let me see, let me see:—

The rugged Pyrrhus, like th' Hyrcanian beast,—   *440*

'Tis not so. It begins with Pyrrhus:—

The rugged Pyrrhus, he, whose sable arms,
Black as his purpose, did the night resemble
When he lay couched in the ominous horse,
Hath now this dread and black complexion smear'd   *445*
With heraldry more dismal. Head to foot
Now is he total gules, horridly trick'd
With blood of fathers, mothers, daughters, sons,
Bak'd and impasted with the parching streets,
That lend a tyrannous and a damned light   *450*
To their lords' murther. Roasted in wrath and fire,
And thus o'er-sized with coagulate gore,
With eyes like carbuncles, the hellish Pyrrhus
Old grandsire Priam seeks.

«So proceed you.»   *455*

Pol. 'Fore God, my lord, well spoken! with good accent
and good discretion.

   Player.   *Anon, he finds him*
Striking too short at Greeks; his antique sword,
Rebellious to his arm, lies where it falls,   *460*
Repugnant to command. Unequal match'd,
Pyrrhus at Priam drives, in rage strikes wide;
But with the whiff and wind of his fell sword
Th' unnerved father falls. ⟨*Then senseless Ilium,*⟩
Seeming to feel this blow, with flaming top   *465*
Stoops to his base, and with a hideous crash
Takes prisoner Pyrrhus' ear: for lo, his sword,
Which was declining on the milky head
Of reverend Priam, seem'd i' th' air to stick.
So as a painted tyrant Pyrrhus stood,   *470*
And like a neutral to his will and matter,
Did nothing.
But as we often see against some storm
A silence in the heavens, the rack stand still,
The bold winds speechless and the orb below   *475*
As hush as death, anon the dreadful thunder
Doth rend the region; so, after Pyrrhus' pause,
A roused vengeance set him new a-work;

---

385 Roscius; *cf. n.*   **388 Buzz, buzz:** *an exclamation of contempt*   **393 scene individable;**
cf. n.   **394–395 poem unlimited;** *cf. n.*   **394 Seneca;** *cf. n.*   **395 Plautus;** *cf. n.*   **law**
of writ and the liberty; *cf. n.*   **397 Jephthah:** *hero of an old ballad quoted below*   **412**
'as most like it was': *as was most probable*   **413 row:** *stanza, or column of print* **chanson:**
song **414 abridgment:** *something to cut short my talk*   **417 valanced:** *'curtained,' with*
a beard **420 chopine:** *a Venetian raised shoe worn by women*   **421 uncurrent:** *not*
passable as lawful coinage **cracked . . . ring;** *cf. n.* **423 straight:** *immediately* **428**
caviary . . . general; *cf. n.*

430 cried in the top of: *spoke with a louder voice of authority than* **digested:** *ar-*
ranged   **431 modesty:** *moderation* **cunning:** *skill in technique*   **432, 433 sallets . . .**
savory; *cf. n.*   **433 indict:** *convict* **affection:** *affectation*   **434–435 as wholesome . . .**
fine; *not in Folio* **435 handsome;** *cf. n.* **fine:** *elaborately fashioned*   **436 Æneas' tale**
to Dido; *cf. n.*   **440 Hyrcanian;** *cf. n.*   **444 ominous horse;** *cf. n.*   **447 total**
gules: *red all over* **trick'd:** *spotted*   **449 impasted:** *made into a crust*   **452 o'er-sized:**
covered with something like size, a kind of glue   **453 carbuncles:** *glittering red stones, ru-*
bies   **461 Repugnant to:** *resisting*   **463 fell:** *cruel*   **464 senseless:** *incapable of feel-*
ing   **470 painted tyrant:** *picture of an oppressor* **a neutral:** *one indifferent* **matter:**
task   **473 against:** *just before*   **474 rack:** *mass of cloud*   **476 anon:** *presently*   **477**
region: *the air*

And never did the Cyclops' hammers fall
On Mars's armor, forg'd for proof eterne,   480
With less remorse than Pyrrhus' bleeding sword
Now falls on Priam.
Out, out, thou strumpet Fortune! All you gods,
In general synod take away her power,
Break all the spokes and fellies from her wheel,   485
And bowl the round nave down the hill of heaven
As low as to the fiends!

Pol. This is too long.
Ham. It shall to the barber's, with your beard. Prithee, say
on: he's for a jig or a tale of bawdry, or he sleeps. Say on;   490
come to Hecuba.

Player. *But who, O who, had seen the mobled queen—*

Ham. 'The mobled queen'?
Pol. That's good; ('mobled queen' is good.)

Player. *Run barefoot up and down, threat'ning the flames*
With bisson rheum,—a clout upon that head
Where late the diadem stood, and for a robe,
About her lank and all o'er-teemed loins,
A blanket, in the alarm of fear caught up,—
Who this had seen, with tongue in venom steep'd,   500
'Gainst Fortune's state would treason have pronounc'd.
But if the gods themselves did see her then,
When she saw Pyrrhus make malicious sport
In mincing with his sword her husband's limbs,
The instant burst of clamor that she made   505
(Unless things mortal move them not at all)
Would have made milch the burning eyes of heaven
And passion in the gods.

Pol. Look! wh'er he has not turned his color and has tears
in 's eyes. Prithee, no more.   510
Ham. 'Tis well. I'll have thee speak out the rest of this
soon. Good my lord, will you see the players well bestowed?
Do you hear, let them be well used, for they are the abstract
and brief chronicles of the time. After your death you were better have a bad epitaph than their ill report while you live.   515
Pol. My lord, I will use them according to their desert.
Ham. God's bodkin, man, much better! Use every man after
his desert, and who shall 'scape whipping? Use them after your
own honor and dignity: the less they deserve, the more merit
is in your bounty. Take them in.   520
Pol. Come, sirs.
Ham. Follow him, friends: we'll hear a play tomorrow. *Exit*
Polonius [with all the Players but the First.] Dost thou hear me,
old friend; can you play the Murther of Gonzago?
Player. Ay, my lord.   525
Ham. We'll ha 't to-morrow night. You could, for a need,
study a speech of some dozen or sixteen lines, which I would
set down and insert in 't, could you not?
Player. Ay, my lord.

Ham. Very well. Follow that lord, and look you mock   530
him not. *[Exit Player. To Rosencrantz and Guildenstern.]* My good
friends, I'll leave you till night. You are welcome to Elsinore.
Ros. Good my lord!
Ham. Ay, so! Goodbye to you!
     Exeunt [Ros. and Guil.]. Manet Hamlet.
        Now I am alone.   535
O what a rogue and peasant slave am I!
Is it not monstrous that this player here,
But in a fiction, in a dream of passion,
Could force his soul so to his own conceit
That from her working all the visage wann'd,   540
Tears in his eyes, distraction in 's aspect,
A broken voice, and his whole function suiting
With forms to his conceit? and all for nothing!
For Hecuba?
What's Hecuba to him or he to Hecuba,   545
That he should weep for her? What would he do
Had he the motive and the cue for passion
That I have? He would drown the stage with tears,
And cleave the general ear with horrid speech,
Make mad the guilty and appal the free,   550
Confound the ignorant, and amaze indeed
The very faculties of eyes and ears.
Yet I,
A dull and muddy-mettled rascal, peak,
Like John-a-dreams, unpregnant of my cause,   555
And can say nothing; no not for a king,
Upon whose property and most dear life
A damn'd defeat was made. Am I a coward?
Who calls me villain? breaks my pate across?
Plucks off my beard and blows it in my face?   560
Tweaks me by the nose? gives me the lie i' th' throat,
As deep as to the lungs? Who does me this, ha?
'Swounds, I should take it, for it cannot be
But I am pigeon-liver'd, and lack gall
To make oppression bitter, or ere this   565
I should ha' fatted all the region kites
With this slave's offal. Bloody, bawdy villain!
Remorseless, treacherous, lecherous, kindless villain!
⟨O! vengeance!⟩
Why, what an ass am I! This is most brave   570
That I, the son of a dear murthered,
Prompted to my revenge by heaven and hell,
Must like a whore unpack my heart with words,
And fall a-cursing like a very drab,
A scullion! Fie upon it, foh!   575
About, my brains!—Hum,—. I have heard,
That guilty creatures sitting at a play
Have by the very cunning of the scene
Been struck so to the soul that presently
They have proclaim'd their malefactions;   580
For murther, though it have no tongue, will speak

479 Cyclops': *Vulcan's workmen's*   **480 proof eterne:** *eternal impenetrability*   **484 synod:** *assembly*   **485 fellies:** *the pieces of wood of which the circumference is made*   **486 nave:** *hub*   **490 jig:** *lively dance, often accompanied by coarse comic verses or dialogue*   **492 mobled:** *muffled*   **496 bisson rheum:** *blinding tears* **clout:** *piece of cloth*   **498 o'er-teemed:** *exhausted by excessive child-bearing*   **507 milch:** *milky, moist*   **509 turned . . . color:** *grown pale*   **512 bestowed:** *lodged*   **513 abstract:** *summary*   **517 God's bodkin,** *cf. n.*   **524 Gonzago,** *cf. n.*   **526, 527 for a need:** *in case of necessity*   **some dozen or sixteen lines;** *cf. n.*

S.d. Manet: *remains on the stage*   **537 peasant:** *base*   **539 conceit:** *imagination*   **540 wann'd:** *grew pale*   **542 function:** *action of the body* **suiting:** *fitting*   **543 forms:** *bodily expression*   **547 cue;** *cf. n.*   **549 horrid:** *horrible*   **550 free:** *free from offence, guiltless*   **554 muddy-mettled:** *dull-spirited* **peak:** *mope about*   **555 John-a-dreams:** *dreamy fellow; cf. n.* **unpregnant of:** *not quickened by*   **557 property;** *cf. n.*   **558 defeat:** *destruction*   **563 'Swounds:** *God's wounds*   **564 But:** *but that* **pigeon-liver'd:** *meek; cf. n.*   **565 make oppression bitter:** *make me feel the bitterness of oppression*   **566 region kites:** *vultures of the air*   **568 kindless:** *unnatural*   **571 murthered;** *cf. n.*   **575 scullion:** *the lowest household servant*   **576 About, my brains:** *let me think less wildly*

With most miraculous organ. I'll have these players
Play something like the murther of my father
Before mine uncle. I'll observe his looks,
I'll tent him to the quick. If 'a do blench,   *585*
I know my course. The spirit that I have seen
May be a de'il, and the de'il hath power
T' assume a pleasing shape;—yea, and perhaps
Out of my weakness and my melancholy
(As he is very potent with such spirits)   *590*
Abuses me to damn me. I'll have grounds
More relative than this. The play's the thing
Wherein I'll catch the conscience of the king.   *Exit.*

ACT THIRD ❧ SCENE FIRST

A Room in the Castle
Enter King, Queen, Polonius, Ophelia, Rosencrantz, Guildenstern,
and Lords.

King. And can you by no drift of conference
Get from him why he puts on this confusion,
Grating so harshly all his days of quiet
With turbulent and dangerous lunacy?
    Ros. He does confess he feels himself distracted,   *5*
But from what cause 'a will by no means speak.
    Guil. Nor do we find him forward to be sounded,
But with a crafty madness keeps aloof,
When we would bring him on to some confession
Of his true state.   *10*
    Queen.   Did he receive you well?
    Ros. Most like a gentleman.
    Guil. But with much forcing of his disposition.
    Ros. Niggard of question, but of our demands
Most free in his reply.   *15*
    Queen.   Did you assay him
To any pastime?
    Ros. Madam, it so fell out that certain players
We o'er-raught on the way; of these we told him,
And there did seem in him a kind of joy   *20*
To hear of it. They are about the court,
And, as I think, they have already order
This night to play before him.
    Pol.   'Tis most true;
And he beseech'd me to entreat your majesties   *25*
To hear and see the matter.
    King. With all my heart; and it doth much content me
To hear him so inclin'd.
Good gentlemen, give him a further edge,
And drive his purpose into these delights.   *30*
    Ros. We shall, my lord.
                         Exeunt Ros. and Guil.
    King.   Sweet Gertrude, leave us too;
For we have closely sent for Hamlet hither,
That he, as 'twere by accident, may here
Affront Ophelia.   *35*

Her father and myself (lawful espials)
Will so bestow ourselves that, seeing unseen,
We may of their encounter frankly judge,
And gather by him, as he is behav'd,
If 't be th' affliction of his love or no   *40*
That thus he suffers for.
    Queen.   I shall obey you.
And for your part, Ophelia, I do wish
That your good beauties be the happy cause
Of Hamlet's wildness; so shall I hope your virtues   *45*
Will bring him to his wonted way again,
To both your honors.
    Oph.   Madam, I wish it may.
                             [Exit Queen.]
    Pol. Ophelia, walk you here. Gracious, so please you,
We will bestow ourselves. *[To Ophelia.]* Read on this book,   *50*
That show of such an exercise may color
Your loneliness. We are oft to blame in this;
'Tis too much prov'd that with devotion's visage
And pious action we do sugar o'er
The devil himself.   *55*
    King. *[Aside.]*   O 'tis too true!
How smart a lash that speech doth give my conscience!
The harlot's cheek, beautied with plastering art,
Is not more ugly to the thing that helps it
Than is my deed to my most painted word.   *60*
O heavy burthen!
    Pol. I hear him coming; let's withdraw, my lord.
                    Exeunt [King and Polonius].

Enter Hamlet.

    Ham. To be, or not to be, that is the question.
Whether 'tis nobler in the mind to suffer
The slings and arrows of outrageous fortune,   *65*
Or to take arms against a sea of troubles
And by opposing end them. To die: to sleep.
No more; and by a sleep to say we end
The heart-ache and the thousand natural shocks
That flesh is heir to: 'tis a consummation   *70*
Devoutly to be wish'd. To die: to sleep.
To sleep? perchance to dream. Ay, there's the rub;
For in that sleep of death what dreams may come,
When we have shuffled off this mortal coil,
Must give us pause. There's the respect   *75*
That makes calamity of so long life;
For who would bear the whips and scorns of time,
Th' oppressor's wrong, the proud man's contumely,
The pangs of dispriz'd love, the law's delay,
The insolence of office, and the spurns   *80*
That patient merit of th' unworthy takes,
When he himself might his quietus make
With a bare bodkin? Who would fardels bear,
To grunt and sweat under a weary life,
But that the dread of something after death,   *85*

---

585 tent: *probe* **blench:** *start aside* **587 de'il:** *devil* **592 relative:** *relevant, to the purpose* **1 drift of conference:** *turn of the conversation* **2 confusion:** *distraction* **3 Grating:** *harassing* **7 forward:** *ready, disposed* **13 forcing of his disposition:** *constraint* **14 Niggard of question:** *sparing of conversation; cf. n.* **16 assay:** *tempt* **19 o'er-raught:** *overtook* **29 edge:** *incitement* **32 closely:** *privately* **35 Affront:** *meet*

36 espials: *spies* **38 frankly:** *freely* **45 wildness:** *madness* **49 Gracious . . . you:** *if it please your Grace* **51 exercise:** *religious devotion* **53 too much prov'd:** *found by too frequent experience* **59 to:** *in comparison with* **the thing:** *the beautifying cosmetic* **63 Cf. n.** **66 take . . . troubles;** *cf. n.* **72 rub:** *obstacle* **74 shuffled off:** *sloughed off* **mortal coil:** *turmoil of mortal life* **75 give us pause:** *cause us to hesitate* **respect:** *consideration* **76 Cf. n.** **77 For who would bear, etc.;** *cf. n.* **79 dispriz'd:** *held in contempt* **80 office:** *people holding official position* **spurns:** *insults* **82 quietus:** *release from life* **83 bare bodkin;** *cf. n.* **fardels:** *burdens*

The undiscover'd country from whose bourn
No traveller returns, puzzles the will,
And makes us rather bear those ills we have
Than fly to others that we know not of?
Thus conscience does make cowards of us all,   *90*
And thus the native hue of resolution
Is sicklied o'er with the pale cast of thought,
And enterprises of great pitch and moment
With this regard their currents turn awry,
And lose the name of action.—Soft you now!   *95*
The fair Ophelia! Nymph, in thy orisons
Be all my sins remember'd.

Oph.   Good my lord,
How does your honor for this many a day?

  Ham. I humbly thank you; well, well, well.   *100*

  Oph. My lord, I have remembrances of yours,
That I have longed long to re-deliver;
I pray you now, receive them.

    Ham.   No, not I.
I never gave you aught.   *105*

  Oph. My honor'd lord, you know right well you did;
And, with them, words of so sweet breath compos'd
As made the things more rich. Their perfume lost,
Take these again, for to the noble mind
Rich gifts wax poor when givers prove unkind.   *110*
There, my lord.

  Ham. Ha, ha! are you honest?

  Oph. My lord!

  Ham. Are you fair?

  Oph. What means your lordship?   *115*

  Ham. That if you be honest and fair, your honesty should
admit no discourse to your beauty.

  Oph. Could beauty, my lord, have better commerce than
with honesty?

  Ham. Ay, truly; for the power of beauty will sooner trans-   *120*
form honesty from what it is to a bawd than the force of honesty can translate beauty into his likeness. This was sometime a
paradox, but now the time gives it proof. I did love you once.

  Oph. Indeed, my lord, you made me believe so.

  Ham. You should not have believed me, for virtue cannot so   *125*
inoculate our old stock but we shall relish of it. I loved you not.

  Oph. I was the more deceived.

  Ham. Get thee to a nunnery. Why wouldst thou be a
breeder of sinners? I am myself indifferent honest, but yet I
could accuse me of such things that it were better my mother   *130*
had not borne me. I am very proud, revengeful, ambitious,
with more offences at my beck than I have thoughts to put
them in, imagination to give them shape, or time to act them
in. What should such fellows as I do crawling between earth
and heaven? We are arrant knaves all; believe none of us.   *135*
Go thy ways to a nunnery.—Where's your father?

  Oph. At home, my lord.

  Ham. Let the doors be shut upon him, that he may play
the fool nowhere but in 's own house. Farewell.

  Oph. O help him, you sweet heavens!   *140*

  Ham. If thou dost marry, I'll give thee this plague for thy
dowry: be thou as chaste as nice, as pure as snow, thou shalt
not escape calumny. Get thee to a nunnery. Go; farewell. Or if
thou wilt needs marry, marry a fool; for wise men know well
enough what monsters you make of them. To a nunnery,   *145*
go, and quickly too. Farewell.

  Oph. O heavenly powers, restore him!

  Ham. I have heard of your paintings too, well enough. God
hath given you one face, and you make yourselves another.
You jig, you amble, and you lisp. You nickname God's   *150*
creatures, and make your wantonness your ignorance. Go to,
I'll no more on 't; it hath made me mad. I say, we will have
no mo marriage. Those that are married already, all but one,
shall live; the rest shall keep as they are. To a nunnery, go.

                      Exit Hamlet.

  Oph. O what a noble mind is here o'erthrown!   *155*
The courtier's, soldier's, scholar's, eye, tongue, sword;
Th' expectancy and rose of the fair state,
The glass of fashion and the mould of form,
Th' observ'd of all observers, quite, quite down!
And I, of ladies most deject and wretched,   *160*
That suck'd the honey of his music vows,
Now see that noble and most sovereign reason,
Like sweet bells jangled, out of tune and harsh;
That unmatch'd form and feature of blown youth
Blasted with ecstasy. O woe is me,   *165*
T' have seen what I have seen, see what I see!

          Enter King and Polonius.

  King. Love! his affections do not that way tend;
Nor what he spake, though it lack'd form a little,
Was not like madness. There's something in his soul
O'er which his melancholy sits on brood,   *170*
And I do doubt, the hatch and the disclose
Will be some danger; which for to prevent,
I have in quick determination
Thus set it down: he shall with speed to England
For the demand of our neglected tribute.   *175*
Haply the seas and countries different
With variable objects shall expel
This something-settled matter in his heart,
Whereon his brain's still-beating puts him thus
From fashion of himself. What think you on 't?   *180*

  Pol. It shall do well: but yet do I believe
The origin and commencement of his grief
Sprung from neglected love. How now, Ophelia!
You need not tell us what Lord Hamlet said;
We heard it all. My lord, do as you please;   *185*
But if you hold it fit, after the play
Let his queen mother all alone entreat him
To show his grief. Let her be round with him,
And I'll be plac'd (so please you) in the ear
Of all their conference. If she find him not,   *190*

---

86 bourn: *boundary*   **87 No traveller returns;** *cf. n.* **puzzles:** *frustrates*   **90 conscience:** *the ability to think*   **91 native hue:** *healthy complexion*   **92 cast:** *tinge*   **93
pitch and moment:** *elevation and importance*   **94 regard:** *consideration* **currents:**
courses   **96 orisons:** *prayers*   **99 for this many a day:** *all this long time*   **112 honest:**
sincere   **116 honest:** *here in special sense of 'chaste'*   **118 commerce:** *intercourse*   **123
paradox:** *absurdity* **time:** *present age*   **126 inoculate:** *engraft; cf. n.* **relish:** *taste*   **128
nunnery;** *cf. n.*   **129 indifferent:** *tolerably*   **132 beck:** *command*   **136 Where's your
father;** *cf. n.*

148 your paintings: *i.e., that women paint their faces*   **150 nickname:** *travesty; cf. n.* **make
your wantonness your ignorance:** *affect ignorance as a mask for wantonness*   **152 on 't:**
of it   **153 mo:** *more*   **157 expectancy and rose:** *hope and pride*   **158 glass:** *mirror* **mould:** *model*   **162 sovereign:** *supreme*   **164 feature:** *proportion of the whole body*
('stature' in Q 2) **blown:** *full-blown*   **165 Blasted:** *withered*   **171 disclose:** *opening of
the shell, coming to life*   **177 variable objects:** *variety of interests*   **178 something-settled:**
somewhat settled   **179 still-beating:** *constant hammering*   **180 fashion of himself:** *his
ordinary manner*   **190 find:** *see through, interpret*

To England send him, or confine him where
Your wisdom best shall think.
 King.   It shall be so.
Madness in great ones must not unwatch'd go.   *Exeunt.*

  ❧ Scene Second ☙

A Hall in the Castle
Enter Hamlet and three of the Players.

 Ham. Speak the speech, I pray you, as I pronounced it to
you, trippingly on the tongue; but if you mouth it, as many of
our players do, I had as lief the town-crier spoke my lines.
Nor do not saw the air too much with your hand, thus; but
use all gently, for in the very torrent, tempest, and (as I may 5
say) whirlwind of your passion, you must acquire and beget a
temperance that may give it smoothness. O it offends me to
the soul to hear a robustious periwig-pated fellow tear a passion to tatters, to very rags, to split the ears of the groundlings,
who for the most part are capable of nothing but inex- 10
plicable dumb-shows and noise. I would have such a fellow
whipped for o'er-doing Termagant. It out-herods Herod: pray
you, avoid it.
 Player. I warrant your honor.
 Ham. Be not too tame neither, but let your own discretion
be your tutor. Suit the action to the word, the word to the
action, with this special observance, that you o'erstep not the
modesty of nature; for anything so overdone is from the purpose of playing, whose end, both at the first and now, was and
is to hold, as 'twere, the mirror up to nature, to show virtue 20
her own feature, scorn her own image, and the very age and
body of the time his form and pressure. Now this overdone, or
come tardy off, though it makes the unskilful laugh, cannot
but make the judicious grieve, the censure of the which one
must in your allowance o'erweigh a whole theater of others. 25
O there be players that I have seen play and heard others
praise, and that highly (not to speak it profanely) that, neither
having the accent of Christians nor the gait of Christian,
pagan, nor man, have so strutted and bellowed that I have
thought some of nature's journeymen had made men and 30
not made them well, they imitated humanity so abominably.
 Player. I hope we have reformed that indifferently with us,
sir.
 Ham. O reform it altogether. And let those that play your
clowns speak no more than is set down for them; for there 35
be of them that will themselves laugh, to set on some quantity
of barren spectators to laugh too, though in the mean time
some necessary question of the play be then to be considered.
That's villainous, and shows a most pitiful ambition in the
fool that uses it. Go, make you ready. 40
              Exeunt Players.

Enter Polonius, Guildenstern, and Rosencrantz.

How now, my lord? will the king hear this piece of work?
 Pol. And the queen too, and that presently.
 Ham. Bid the players make haste.   *Exit Polonius.*
Will you two help to hasten them?
 Ros. Ay, my lord.   45
             Exeunt they two.

 Ham. What, ho! Horatio!

    Enter Horatio.

 Hor. Here, sweet lord, at your service.
 Ham. Horatio, thou art e'en as just a man
As e'er my conversation cop'd withal.
 Hor. O, my dear lord,—   50
 Ham.   Nay, do not think I flatter;
For what advancement may I hope from thee,
That no revénue hast but thy good spirits
To feed and clothe thee? Why should the poor be flatter'd?
No, let the candied tongue lick ábsurd pomp, 55
And crook the pregnant hinges of the knee
Where thrift may follow fawning. Dost thou hear?
Since my dear soul was mistress of her choice
And could of men distinguish, her election
Hath seal'd thee for herself; for thou hast been 60
As one, in suffering all, that suffers nothing,
A man that fortune's buffets and rewards
Hast ta'en with equal thanks; and bless'd are those
Whose blood and judgment are so well co-mingled
That they are not a pipe for fortune's finger 65
To sound what stop she please. Give me that man
That is not passion's slave, and I will wear him
In my heart's core, ay, in my heart of heart,
As I do thee. Something too much of this.
There is a play to-night before the king. 70
One scene of it comes near the circumstance
Which I have told thee of my father's death.
I prithee, when thou seest that act afoot,
Even with the very comment of thy soul
Observe my uncle. If his occulted guilt 75
Do not itself unkennel in one speech,
It is a damned ghost that we have seen,
And my imaginations are as foul
As Vulcan's stithy. Give him heedful note,
For I mine eyes will rivet to his face, 80
And after we will both our judgments join
In censure of his seeming.
 Hor.   Well, my lord,
If 'a steal aught the whilst this play is playing,
And 'scape detecting, I will pay the theft. 85
 Ham. They are coming to the play. I must be idle.
Get you a place.
Enter King, Queen, Polonius, Ophelia, Rosencrantz, Guildenstern,
and other Lords attendant, with his Guard carrying torches.
   Danish March. Sound a Flourish. 90

---

2 trippingly: *rapidly, but with neat articulation* **mouth:** *speak loudly with false emphasis*
and indistinctness **6 acquire and beget:** *achieve yourself and inspire in your hearers* 7
temperance: *moderation* **8 robustious:** *boisterous* **periwig-pated:** *wearing a wig* 9
groundlings; *cf. n.* **10 capable of:** *able to enjoy* 10, 11 **inexplicable dumb-shows;**
cf. n. **12 Termagant;** *cf. n.* **out-herods Herod;** *cf. n.* **18 from:** *alien to* 21, 22
very age . . . pressure: *even the contemporary and actual quality of the present time* 22
pressure: *impressed character, stamp* **23 come tardy off:** *inadequately done* 24 **the**
which one: *one of whom* **25 allowance:** *estimation* **30 journeymen:** *laborers not yet*
masters of their trade **35, 36 there be of them:** *there are some; cf. n.* **37 barren:** *barren*
of wit

48 just: *fair-minded, righteous* **49 cop'd withal:** *came in contact with* **55 candied:**
flattering **lick:** *pay court to* (like a dog) **absurd:** *silly* **56 pregnant hinges:** *easily bent*
joints **57 thrift:** *profit* **59 election:** *choice* **60 seal'd:** *registered unchangeably* 64
blood: *passions* **co-mingled;** *cf. n.* **66 stop:** *a hole in wind instruments for controlling*
the sound; cf. n. **74 very comment:** *most intense observation* **75 occulted:** *hidden*
76 itself unkennel: *come to light* (like a fox driven from its hole) **in one speech;**
cf. n. **79 Vulcan;** *cf. n.* **stithy:** *blacksmith's shop, forge* **82 censure:** *careful criticism*
seeming: *appearance* **86 be idle:** *act mad; cf. n.*

King. How fares our cousin Hamlet?

Ham. Excellent, i' faith; of the chameleon's dish.
I eat the air, promise-crammed. You cannot feed capons so.

King. I have nothing with this answer, Hamlet.
These words are not mine.   *95*

Ham. No, nor mine now. *[To Polonius.]* My lord, you
played once i' th' university, you say?

Pol. That did I, my lord, and was accounted a good actor.

Ham. What did you enact?

Pol. I did enact Julius Cæsar. I was killed i' the Capitol. *100*
Brutus killed me.

Ham. It was a brute part of him to kill so capital a calf
there. Be the players ready?

Ros. Ay, my lord; they stay upon your patience.

Queen. Come hither, my dear Hamlet, sit by me.   *105*

Ham. No, good mother, here's metal more attractive.

Pol. *[To the King.]* O ho! do you mark that?

Ham. Lady, shall I lie in your lap?

Oph. No, my lord.

⟨*Ham.* I mean, my head upon your lap?   *110*

Oph. Ay, my lord.⟩

Ham. Do you think I meant country matters?

Oph. I think nothing, my lord.

Ham. That's a fair thought to lie between maids' legs.

Oph. What is, my lord?   *115*

Ham. Nothing.

Oph. You are merry, my lord.

Ham. Who, I?

Oph. Ay, my lord.

Ham. O God, your only jig-maker. What should a man *120*
do but be merry? for look you how cheerfully my mother
looks, and my father died within's two hours.

Oph. Nay, 'tis twice two months, my lord.

Ham. So long? Nay, then, let the de'il wear black, for I'll
have a suit of sables. O heavens! die two months ago, and *125*
not forgotten yet? Then there's hope a great man's memory
may outlive his life half a year; but, by 'r lady, 'a must build
churches then, or else shall 'a suffer not thinking on with the
hobby-horse, whose epitaph is, 'For, O! for, O! the hobby-
horse is forgot.'   *130*

Hautboys play. The dumb-show enters.

*Enter a King and a Queen very lovingly, the Queen embracing
   him. She kneels and makes show of protestation unto him.
   He takes her up and declines his head upon her neck; lays
   him down upon a bank of flowers. She, seeing him asleep,
   leaves him. Anon comes in a fellow, takes off his crown,
   kisses it, and pours poison in the King's ears, and exit. The
   Queen returns, finds the King dead, and makes passionate ac
   tion. The Poisoner, with some two or three Mutes, comes in
   again, seeming to lament with her. The dead body is carried
   away. The Poisoner wooes the Queen with gifts; she seems
   loath and unwilling awhile, but in the end accepts his love.*
                                          Exeunt.

Oph. What means this, my lord?

Ham. Marry, this is miching Malicho; it means mischief.

Oph. Belike this show imports the argument of the play. *145*

Enter Prologue.

Ham. We shall know by this fellow. The players cannot
keep counsel; they'll tell all.

Oph. Will 'a tell us what this show meant?

Ham. Ay, or any show that you will show him. Be not you *150*
ashamed to show, he'll not shame to tell you what it means.

Oph. You are naught, you are naught. I'll mark the play.

Pro. For us and for our tragedy,
    Here stooping to your clemency,
    We beg your hearing patiently.   *155*

Ham. Is this a prologue, or the posy of a ring?

Oph. 'Tis brief, my lord.

Ham. As woman's love.

Enter [Player] King and Queen.

[P.] King. *Full thirty times hath Phœbus' cart gone
round*   *160*
*Neptune's salt wash and Tellus' orbed ground,
And thirty dozen moons with borrow'd sheen
About the world have times twelve thirties been,
Since love our hearts and Hymen did our hands
Unite commutual in most sacred bands.*   *165*

   [P.] Queen. *So many journeys may the sun and moon
Make us again count o'er ere love be done!
But, woe is me! you are so sick of late,
So far from cheer and from your former state,
That I distrust you. Yet though I distrust,*   *170*
*Discomfort you, my lord, it nothing must;
«For women fear too much, even as they love,»
And women's fear and love hold quantity,
In neither aught, or in extremity.
Now what my love is, proof hath made you know;*   *175*
*And as my love is siz'd, my fear is so.
«Where love is great, the littlest doubts are fear;
Where little fears grow great, great love grows there.»*

   [P.] King. *Faith, I must leave thee, love, ad shortly too.
My operant powers their functions leave to do,*   *180*
*And thou shalt live in this fair world behind,
Honor'd, belov'd; and haply one as kind
For husband shalt thou—*

   [P.] Queen.   *O confound the rest!
Such love must needs be treason in my breast.*   *185*
*In second husband let me be accurst;
None wed the second but who kill'd the first.*

Ham. [Aside.] That's wormwood, wormwood.

   [P.] Queen. *The instances that second marriage move
Are base respects of thrift, but none of love;*   *190*
A second time I kill my husband dead,

---

92 chameleon's dish; *cf. n.*   **94 have nothing with:** *can make nothing of*   **100 Julius Cæsar;** *cf. n.* **Capitol;** *cf. n.*   **102 brute part:** *stupid act*   **104 stay upon:** *wait for* **patience:** *leisure*   **110, 111** *not in Quarto*   **112 country matters:** *uncouth conduct; cf.*   **120 your only jig-maker:** *I am the best jig-maker there is; cf. n. on II. ii. 502.*   **122 within's:** *within this*   **123 twice two months;** *cf. n.*   **125 suit of sables:** *suit of rich fur; cf. n.*   **128 suffer not thinking on:** *be forgotten*   **129 hobby-horse:** *one of the participants in the morris dance; cf. n.* **S. d. Hautboys:** *wooden double-reed instruments of high pitch* **S. d. Mutes:** *actors without speaking parts* (but here all are mutes)

144 miching Malicho: *skulking mischief; cf. n.*   **145 imports the argument:** *amounts to a synopsis*   **147 counsel:** *secret*   **151 naught:** *wanton*   **154 stooping:** *bowing*   **156 posy:** *motto*   **159 cart:** *chariot*   **161 wash:** *sea* **Tellus';** *cf. n.*   **162 borrow'd sheen:** *reflected light*   **165 commutual:** *an intensive form of 'mutual'*   **170 I distrust you:** *I have misgivings on your account*   **172, 177–178** *not in Folio*   **173 quantity:** *proportion*   **174 In ... extremity:** *nothing of either, or else an excess*   **180 operant:** *vital*   **189 instances:** *motives, inducements* **move:** *suggest*

When second husband kisses me in bed.
   [P.] King. *I do believe you think what now you speak,*
But what we do determine oft we break.
Purpose is but the slave to memory,   195
Of violent birth, but poor validity;
Which now, like fruit unripe, sticks on the tree,
But fall unshaken when they mellow be.
Most necessary 'tis that we forget
To pay ourselves what to ourselves is debt;   200
What to ourselves in passion we propose,
The passion ending, doth the purpose lose.
The violence of either grief or joy
Their own enactures with themselves destroy;
Where joy most revels grief doth most lament,   205
Grief joys, joy grieves, on slender accident.
This world is not for aye, nor 'tis not strange
That even our loves should with our fortunes change,
For 'tis a question left us yet to prove
Whether love lead fortune or else fortune love.   210
The great man down, you mark his favorite flies;
The poor advanc'd makes friends of enemies.
And hitherto doth love on fortune tend,
For who not needs shall never lack a friend;
And who in want a hollow friend doth try   215
Directly seasons him his enemy.
But, orderly to end where I begun,
Our wills and fates do so contrary run
That our devices still are overthrown,
Our thoughts are ours, their ends none of our own.   220
So think thou wilt no second husband wed,
But die thy thoughts when thy first lord is dead.
   [P.] Queen. *Nor earth to me give food, nor heaven*
      light!
Sport and repose lock from me day and night!   225
«To desperation turn my trust and hope!
An anchor's cheer in prison be my scope!»
Each opposite that blanks the face of joy
Meet what I would have well, and it destroy!
Both here and hence pursue me lasting strife,   230
If, once a widow, every I be wife!

Ham. If she should break it now!

   [P.] King. *'Tis deeply sworn. Sweet, leave me here awhile;*
My spirits grow dull, and fain I would beguile
The tedious day with sleep.   *Sleeps.*   235
   [P.] Queen   *Sleep rock thy brain;*
And never come mischance between us twain!   *Exit.*

Ham. Madam, how like you this play?
Queen. The lady doth protest too much, methinks.
Ham. O, but she'll keep her word.   240
King. Have you heard the argument? Is there no offence in 't?
Ham. No, no, they do but jest,—poison in jest. No offence i' th' world.
King. What do you call the play?
Ham. The Mouse-trap. Marry, how? Tropically. This play is the image of a murther done in Vienna. Gonzago is the duke's

name; his wife, Baptista. You shall see anon. 'Tis a knavish piece of work: but what of that? Your majesty and we that have free souls, it touches us not. Let the galled jade wince, our withers are unwrung.   250

       Enter [Player as] Lucianus.

This is one Lucianus, nephew to the king.
   Oph. You are as good as a chorus, my lord.
   Ham. I could interpret between you and your love, if I could see the puppets dallying.
   Oph. You are keen, my lord, you are keen.   255
   Ham. It would cost you a groaning to take off mine edge.
   Oph. Still better, and worse.
   Ham. So you must take your husbands. Begin, murtherer; leave thy damnable faces, and begin. Come; the croaking raven doth bellow for revenge.   260

   Luc. *Thoughts black, hands apt, drugs fit, and time agreeing;*
Confederate season, else no creature seeing.
Thou mixture rank, of midnight weeds collected,
With Hecate's ban thrice blasted, thrice infected,   265
Thy natural magic and fire property,
On wholesome life usurps immediately.
       Pours the poison in his ears.

   Ham. 'A poisons him i' the garden for his estate. His name's Gonzago. The story is extant, and written in very choice Italian. You shall see anon how the murtherer gets the 270 love of Gonzago's wife.
   Oph. The king rises.
   ⟨Ham. What, frighted with false fire?⟩
   Queen. How fares my lord?
   Pol. Give o'er the play.   275
   King. Give me some light! Away!
   Pol. Lights, lights, lights!
       Exeunt all but Hamlet and Horatio.

Ham. *Why, let the stricken deer go weep,*
   The hart ungalled play,
For some must watch while some must sleep: 280
   Thus runs the world away.

Would not this, sir, and a forest of feathers (if the rest of my fortunes turn Turk with me) with two Provincial roses on my razed shoes, get me a fellowship in a cry of players?
   Hor. Half a share.   285
   Ham. A whole one, I.

For thou dost know, O Damon dear,
   This realm dismantled was
Of Jove himself; and now reigns here
   A very, very—pajock.   290

   Hor. You might have rimed.

---

249 galled jade: *horse sore from chafing* **withers:** *shoulders*   **250 unwrung:** *not galled*   **252 chorus:** *in Elizabethan drama one who speaks a prologue summarizing the action*   **253 interpret;** *cf. n.*   **258 So . . . husbands;** *cf. n.*   **259 the croaking . . . revenge;** *cf. n.*   **263 Confederate season:** *time conspiring to assist*   **265 Hecate;** *cf. n.*   **273 not in Quarto**   **275 Give o'er:** *stop*   **278 deer go weep;** *cf. n.*   **282 forest of feathers:** *an allusion to the plumes worn by actors*   **283 turn Turk:** *play the renegade*   **Provincial roses:** *rosettes imitating the damask rose; cf. n.*   **284 razed:** *slashed, i.e., with cuts or openings*   **fellowship:** *partnership*   **cry:** *company; cf. n.*   **285 share:** *i.e., in the profits of the company; cf. n.*   **287 Damon;** *cf. n.*   **290 pajock:** *scarecrow; cf. n.*

196 validity: *strength*   **204 enactures:** *fulfilments*   **215 hollow:** *insincere*   **220 ends:** *results*   **223 Nor . . . nor:** *neither . . . nor*   **225 Sport:** *pleasure; cf. n.*   **226, 227 not in Folio**   **227 anchor's:** *anchorite's*   **228 opposite:** *contrary thing*   **blanks:** *blanches, makes pale*   **245 Tropically:** *figuratively; cf. n.*   **246 image:** *representation*   **246, 247 duke's name;** *cf. n.*

Ham. O good Horatio, I'll take the ghost's word for a thousand pound. Didst perceive?

Hor. Very well, my lord.

Ham. Upon the talk of the poisoning?   295

Hor. I did very well note him.

Ham. Ah, ha! Come, some music! come, the recorders!

For if the king like not the comedy,
Why then, belike he likes it not, perdy.

Come, some music!   300

Enter Rosencrantz and Guildenstern.

Guil. Good my lord, vouchsafe me a word with you.

Ham. Sir, a whole history.

Guil. The king, sir,—

Ham. Ay, sir, what of him?

Guil. Is in his retirement marvellous distempered.   305

Ham. With drink, sir?

Guil. No, my lord, with choler.

Ham. Your wisdom should show itself more richer to signify this to the doctor; for, for me to put him to his purgation would perhaps plunge him into more choler.   310

Guil. Good my lord, put your discourse into some frame, and start not so wildly from my affair.

Ham. I am tame, sir; pronounce.

Guil. The queen, your mother, in most great affliction of spirit, hath sent me to you.   315

Ham. You are welcome.

Guil. Nay, good my lord, this courtesy is not of the right breed. If it shall please you to make me a wholesome answer, I will do your mother's commandment; if not, your pardon and my return shall be the end of my business.   320

Ham. Sir, I cannot.

Ros. What, my lord?

Ham. Make you a wholesome answer. My wit's diseased; but, sir, such answer as I can make, you shall command; or, rather, as you say, my mother. Therefore no more, but to   325 the matter. My mother, you say,—

Ros. Then, thus she says: your behavior hath struck her into amazement and admiration.

Ham. O wonderful son, that can so 'stonish a mother! But is there no sequel at the heels of this mother's admiration?   330 Impart.

Ros. She desires to speak with you in her closet ere you go to bed.

Ham. We shall obey, were she ten times our mother. Have you any further trade with us?   335

Ros. My lord, you once did love me.

Ham. And do still, by these pickers and stealers.

Ros. Good my lord, what is your cause of distemper? You do surely bar the door upon your own liberty, if you deny your griefs to your friend.   340

Ham. Sir, I lack advancement.

Ros. How can that be when you have the voice of the king himself for your succession in Denmark?

Enter the Players, with recorders.

Ham. Ay, sir, but 'While the grass grows,'—the proverb is something musty.—O, the recorders! Let me see one. To   345 withdraw with you,—Why do you go about to recover the wind of me, as if you would drive me into a toil?

Guil. O! my lord, if my duty be too bold, my love is too unmannerly.

Ham. I do not well understand that. Will you play upon   350 this pipe?

Guil. My lord, I cannot.

Ham. I pray you.

Guil. Believe me, I cannot.

Ham. I do beseech you.   355

Guil. I know no touch of it, my lord.

Ham. It is as easy as lying. Govern these ventages with your fingers and thumb, give it breath with your mouth, and it will discourse most eloquent music. Look you, these are the stops.

Guil. But these cannot I command to any utterance of   360 harmony. I have not the skill.

Ham. Why, look you now, how unworthy a thing you make of me. You would play upon me; you would seem to know my stops; you would pluck out the heart of my mystery; you would sound me from my lowest note to the top of   365 my compass. And there is much music, excellent voice, in this little organ, yet cannot you make it speak. 'Sblood, do you think I am easier to be played on than a pipe? Call me what instrument you will, though you can fret me, yet you cannot play upon me.   370

Enter Polonius.

God bless you, sir!

Pol. My lord, the queen would speak with you, and presently.

Ham. Do you see yonder cloud that's almost in shape of a camel?   375

Pol. By the mass, and 'tis like a camel, indeed.

Ham. Methinks it is like a weasel.

Pol. It is backed like a weasel.

Ham. Or like a whale?

Pol. Very like a whale.   380

Ham. Then I will come to my mother by and by. *[Aside.]* They fool me to the top of my bent. *[Aloud.]* I will come by and by.

Pol. I will say so.   *Exit.*

Ham. By and by is easily said. Leave me, friends.   385

[Exeunt all but Hamlet.]

'Tis now the very witching time of night,
When churchyards yawn and hell itself breathes out
Contagion to this world. Now could I drink hot blood,
And do such bitter business as the day   390
Would quake to look on. Soft! now to my mother!
O heart, lose not thy nature; let not ever
The soul of Nero enter this firm bosom.
Let me be cruel, not unnatural;
I will speak daggers to her, but use none.   395
My tongue and soul in this be hypocrites:

---

297 recorders: *wind instruments of the flute type*   **299 perdy:** *a corruption of par dieu*   **305 distempered:** *disordered; cf. n.*   **307 choler:** *anger; cf. n.*   **309 purgation:** *purging; cf. n.*   **311 frame:** *sensible form*   **313 pronounce:** *speak*   **317 of the right breed:** *pure-bred, genuine; cf. n.*   **318 wholesome:** *sincere*   **337 pickers and stealers:** *hands; cf. n.*   **339 liberty:** *freedom of action*   **342 voice:** *vote*

344 'While ... grows'; *cf. n.*   **346 withdraw with:** *speak privately with*   **recover the wind of:** *get advantage of; cf. n.*   **347 toil:** *snare*   **356 know no touch:** *have no skill at all; cf. n.*   **357 ventages:** *holes, stops*   **366 compass:** *range of voice*   **369 fret;** *cf. n.*   **381 by and by:** *at once*   **382 top ... bent:** *limit of my endurance; cf. n.*   **386 witching:** *when spells are cast*   **393 Nero;** *cf. n.*

How in my words somever she be shent,
To give them seals never, my soul, consent!   *Exit.*

❧ Scene Third ❧

[A Room in the Castle]
Enter King, Rosencrantz, and Guildenstern.

King. I like him not, nor stands it safe with us
To let his madness range. Therefore prepare you.
I your commission will forthwith dispatch,
And he to England shall along with you.
The terms of our estate may not endure   5
Hazard so near us as doth hourly grow
Out of his braves.
Guil.   We will ourselves provide.
Most holy and religious fear it is
To keep those many many bodies safe   10
That live and feed upon your majesty.
Ros. The single and peculiar life is bound
With all the strength and armor of the mind
To keep itself from noyance; but much more
That spirit upon whose weal depends and rests   15
The lives of many. The cesse of majesty
Dies not alone, but like a gulf doth draw
What's near it with it. It is a massy wheel,
Fix'd on the summit of the highest mount,
To whose huge spokes ten thousand lesser things   20
Are mortis'd and adjoin'd; which, when it falls,
Each small annexment, petty consequence,
Attends the boisterous ruin. Never alone
Did the king sigh, but with a general groan.
King. Arm you, I pray you, to this speedy voyage;   25
For we will fetters put about this fear,
Which now goes too free-footed.
Ros.   We will haste us.   *Exeunt Gent[lemen].*

Enter Polonius.

Pol. My lord, he's going to his mother's closet.
Behind the arras I'll convey myself   30
To hear the process. I'll warr'nt she'll tax him home;
And, as you said, and wisely was it said,
'Tis meet that some more audience than a mother,
Since nature makes them partial, should o'erhear
The speech, of vantage. Fare you well, my liege.   35
I'll call upon you ere you go to bed
And tell you what I know.
King.   Thanks, dear my lord.

Exit [Polonius].

O my offence is rank, it smells to heaven!
It hath the primal eldest curse upon 't;   40
A brother's murther. Pray can I not.
Though inclination be as sharp as will,

My stronger guilt defeats my strong intent,
And, like a man to double business bound,
I stand in pause where I shall first begin,   45
And both neglect. What if this cursed hand
Were thicker than itself with brother's blood,
Is there not rain enough in the sweet heavens
To wash it white as snow? Whereto serves mercy
But to confront the visage of offence?   50
And what's in prayer but this twofold force,
To be forestalled, ere we come to fall,
Or pardon'd, being down? Then I'll look up;
My fault is past. But, O, what form of prayer
Can serve my turn? 'Forgive me my foul murther?'   55
That cannot be, since I am still possess'd
Of those effects for which I did the murther,
My crown, mine own ambition, and my queen.
May one be pardon'd and retain th' offence?
In the corrupted currents of this world   60
Offence's gilded hand may shove by justice,
And oft 'tis seen the wicked prize itself
Buys out the law; but 'tis not so above.
There is no shuffling, there the action lies
In his true nature, and we ourselves compell'd   65
Even to the teeth and forehead of our faults
To give in evidence. What then? what rests?
Try what repentance can. What can it not?
Yet what can it, when one cannot repent?
O wretched state! O bosom black as death!   70
O limed soul, that struggling to be free
Art more engag'd! Help, angels! make assay!
Bow, stubborn knees; and heart with strings of steel
Be soft as sinews of the new-born babe.
All may be well.   *He kneels.*   75

Enter Hamlet.

Ham. Now might I do it pat, now 'a is praying!
And now I'll do 't. And so 'a goes to heaven;
And so am I reveng'd? That would be scann'd.
A villain kills my father, and for that,
I, his sole son, do this same villain send   80
To heaven.
Why, this is hire and salary, not revenge
'A took my father grossly, full of bread,
With all his crimes broad blown, as flush as May;
And how his audit stands who knows save heaven?   85
But in our circumstance and course of thought
'Tis heavy with him. And am I then reveng'd,
To take him in the purging of his soul,
When he is fit and season'd for his passage?
No.   90
Up, sword, and know thou a more horrid hent;
When he is drunk asleep, or in his rage,

---

397 How . . . somever; *cf.* I. v. 90 **shent:** *rebuked* **398 give them seals:** *confirm them by making words into deeds* **1 like him not:** *distrust him* **2 range:** *rove, roam* **3 forthwith dispatch:** *prepare at once* **5 terms:** *condition* **7 braves:** *defiances; cf. n.* **9 fear:** *caution* **12 single and peculiar:** *individual and private* **14 noyance:** *harm* **15 weal:** *welfare* **16 cesse:** *decease* **17 gulf:** *whirlpool* **18 it is a massy wheel,** *etc.; cf. n.* **22 annexment:** *appendage* **23 Attends:** *accompanies* **25 Arm:** *prepare* **31 process:** *interview* **tax . . . home:** *censure effectually* **32 as you said;** *cf. n.* **35 of vantage:** *in addition* **40 primal:** *primeval; cf. n.*

47 thicker than itself: *made more than double its normal thickness* **50 confront:** *oppose directly* **52 forestalled:** *prevented in anticipation* **57 effects:** *i.e., things acquired by an action* **58 ambition:** *i.e., the realization of ambition (so also offence in 59)* **61 gilded hand:** *hand using bribes of gold* **62 wicked prize:** *reward of wickedness* **63 Buys out:** *corrupts* **64 shuffling:** *trickery* **lies:** *used in its legal sense; cf. n.* **66 teeth and forehead:** *very face* **67 rests:** *remains* **71 limed:** *caught with bird-lime* **72 engag'd:** *entangled* **76 pat:** *to a nicety; cf. n.* **78 would:** *requires to* **scann'd:** *examined, considered* **82 hire and salary:** *i.e., a reward; cf. n.* **83 full of bread:** *without opportunity to fast* **84 broad blown:** *in full bloom* **flush:** *lusty* **85 audit:** *account* **86 in . . . thought:** *according to our vague ideas* **89 passage:** *i.e., to the other world* **91 know . . . hent:** *let me grasp you at a more horrid moment*

Or in th' incestuous pleasure of his bed,
At game a-swearing, or about some act
That has no relish of salvation in 't.   95
Then trip him, that his heels may kick at heaven,
And that his soul may be as damn'd and black
As hell, whereto it goes. My mother stays.—
This physic but prolongs thy sickly days.   *Exit.*

    King [rising]. My words fly up, my thoughts remain below.
Words without thoughts never to heaven go.   *Exit.*

❧ SCENE FOURTH ❧

[The Queen's Closet]
Enter Queen and Polonius.

    Pol. 'A will come straight. Look you lay home to him.
Tell him his pranks have been too broad to bear with,
And that your Grace hath screen'd and stood between
Much heat and him. I'll silence me e'en here.
Pray you, be round with him.   5
    Ham. (within.) Mother, mother, mother!
    Queen.   I'll warrant you;
Fear me not. Withdraw, I hear him coming.
        [Polonius hides behind the arras.]

Enter Hamlet

    Ham. Now, mother, what's the matter?
    Queen. Hamlet, thou hast thy father much offended.   10
    Ham. Mother, you have my father much offended.
    Queen. Come, come, you answer with an idle tongue.
    Ham. Go, go, you question with a wicked tongue.
    Queen. Why, how now, Hamlet!
    Ham.   What's the matter now? 15
    Queen. Have you forgot me?
    Ham.   No, by the rood, not so.
You are the queen, your husband's brother's wife;
And,—would it were not so!—you are my mother.
    Queen. Nay then, I'll set those to you that can speak.   20
    Ham. Come, come, and sit you down; you shall not budge.
You go not till I set you up a glass
Where you may see the inmost part of you.
    Queen. What wilt thou do? thou wilt not murther me?
Help, help, ho!   25
    Pol. What, ho! help! help! help!
    Ham. How now! a rat? Dead, for a ducat, dead!
        Kills Polonius [through the arras].
    Pol. O, I am slain!
    Queen.   O me, what hast thou done?
    Ham. Nay, I know not. Is it the king?   30
    Queen. O, what a rash and bloody deed is this!
    Ham. A bloody deed! almost as bad, good mother,
As kill a king, and marry with his brother.
    Queen. As kill a king?
    Ham.   Ay, lady, 'twas my word.   35
        [Lifts up the arras and discovers Polonius.]
Thou wretched, rash, intruding fool, farewell!
I took thee for thy better. Take thy fortune;

---

95 relish: *flavor*   **99** physic: *medicine, i.e., the postponement*   **1** lay home: *talk plainly*   **2** broad: *free, unrestrained*   **4** heat: *anger*   silence me: *withdraw into silence*   **17** rood: *cross*   **27** for: *i.e., I wager*

Thou find'st to be too busy is some danger.
[To the Queen.] Leave wringing of your hands. Peace! sit
you down,   40
And let me wring your heart; for so I shall
If it be made of penetrable stuff,
If damned custom have not braz'd it so
That it be proof and bulwark against sense.
    Queen. What have I done that thou dar'st wag thy tongue   45
In noise so rude against me?
    Ham.   Such an act
That blurs the grace and blush of modesty,
Calls virtue hypocrite, takes off the rose
From the fair forehead of an innocent love   50
And sets a blister there, makes marriage vows
As false as dicers' oaths. O, such a deed
As from the body of contraction plucks
The very soul, and sweet religion makes
A rhapsody of words! Heaven's face does glow,   55
Yea, this solidity and compound mass,
With tristful visage as against the doom,
Is thought-sick at the act.
    Queen.   Ay me! what act,
That roars so loud and thunders in the index?   60
    Ham. Look here, upon this picture, and on this,
The counterfeit presentment of two brothers.
See what a grace was seated on this brow:
Hyperion's curls, the front of Jove himself,
An eye like Mars, to threaten and command,   65
A station like the herald Mercury
New-lighted on a heaven-kissing hill,
A combination and a form indeed,
Where every god did seem to set his seal,
To give the world assurance of a man.   70
This was your husband. Look you, now, what follows.
Here is your husband, like a mildew'd ear
Blasting his wholesome brother. Have you eyes?
Could you on this fair mountain leave to feed,
And batten on this moor? Ha! have you eyes?   75
You cannot call it love, for at your age
The heyday in the blood is tame, it's humble,
And waits upon the judgment; and what judgment
Would step from this to this? «Sense sure you have,
Else could you not have motion; but sure that sense   80
Is apoplex'd, for madness would not err,
Nor sense to ecstasy was ne'er so thrall'd
But it reserv'd some quantity of choice
To serve in such a difference.» What devil was 't
That thus hath cozen'd you at hoodman-blind?   85
«Eyes without feeling, feeling without sight,
Ears without hands or eyes, smelling sans all,
Or but a sickly part of one true sense
Could not so mope.»
O shame! where is thy blush? Rebellious hell,   90

---

43 braz'd it: *made it brazen*   **44** proof and bulwark: *an impenetrable defence*   sense: *feeling*   **53** contraction: *marriage contract*   **55** rhapsody: *meaningless string*   glow: *blush*   **56** this solidity and compound mass: *the solid and composite earth*   **57** tristful: *sad*   doom: *doomsday*   **60** index: *table of contents, prelude*   **62** counterfeit presentment: *portrayed likeness*   **64** front: *forehead*   **66** station: *poise*   **72** ear: *ear of wheat*   **75** batten: *grow fat*   moor: *a barren upland*   **77** heyday: *youthful high spirits*   **79** Sense: *control of the physical senses*   **79–84** Sense . . . difference: *not in Folio*   **81** apoplex'd: *atrophied*   **82** thrall'd: *enslaved*   **83** quantity of choice: *power to choose*   **85** cozen'd: *cheated*   hoodman-blind: *blind man's buff*   **86–89** *not in Folio*   **87** sans: *without*   **89** mope: *act aimlessly*

If thou canst mutine in a matron's bones,
To flaming youth let virtue be as wax
And melt in her own fire: proclaim no shame
When the compulsive ardor gives the charge,
Since frost itself as actively doth burn,   *95*
And reason panders will.
    Queen.   O Hamlet, speak no more!
Thou turn'st mine eyes into my very soul;
And there I see such black and grained spots
As will not leave their tinct.   *100*
    Ham.   Nay, but to live
In the rank sweat of an enseamed bed,
Stew'd in corruption, honeying and making love
Over the nasty sty,
    Queen.   O speak to me no more!   *105*
These words like daggers enter in my ears.
No more, sweet Hamlet!
    Ham.   A murtherer and a villain;
A slave that is not twentieth part the tithe
Of your precedent lord; a vice of kings;   *110*
A cutpurse of the empire and the rule,
That from a shelf the precious diadem stole,
And put it in his pocket!
    Queen.   No more!

                Enter Ghost.

    Ham. A king of shreds and patches,—   *115*
Save me, and hover o'er me with your wings,
You heavenly guards! What would your gracious figure?
    Queen. Alas! he's mad!
    Ham. Do you not come your tardy son to chide,
That, laps'd in time and passion, lets go by   *120*
Th' important acting of your dread command?
O, say.
    Ghost.   Do not forget. This visitation
Is but to whet thy almost blunted purpose.
But, look, amazement on thy mother sits.   *125*
O, step between her and her fighting soul.
Conceit in weakest bodies strongest works.
Speak to her, Hamlet.
    Ham.   How is it with you, lady?
    Queen. Alas, how is 't with you,   *130*
That you do bend your eye on vacancy
And with th' incorporal air do hold discourse?
Forth at your eyes your spirits wildly peep;
And, as the sleeping soldiers in th' alarm,
Your bedded hair, like life in excrements,   *135*
Start up and stand an end. O gentle son,
Upon the heat and flame of thy distemper
Sprinkle cool patience. Whereon do you look?
    Ham. On him, on him! Look you, how pale he glares!
His form and cause conjoin'd, preaching to stones,   *140*
Would make them capable.—Do not look upon me;

Lest with this piteous action you convert
My stern effects. Then what I have to do
Will want true color,—tears perchance for blood.
    Queen. To whom do you speak this?   *145*
    Ham.   Do you see nothing there?
    Queen. Nothing at all; yet all that is I see.
    Ham. Nor did you nothing hear?
    Queen.   No, nothing but ourselves.
    Ham. Why, look you there! look, how it steals away!   *150*
My father, in his habit as he liv'd!
Look, where he goes, even now, out at the portal.   *Exit Ghost.*
    Queen. This is the very coinage of your brain:
This bodiless creation ecstasy
Is very cunning in.   *155*
    Ham.   ⟨Ecstasy!⟩
My pulse, as yours, doth temperately keep time,
And makes as healthful music. It is not madness
That I have utter'd. Bring me to the test,
And I the matter will re-word, which madness   *160*
Would gambol from. Mother, for love of grace,
Lay not that flattering unction to your soul,
That not your trespass but my madness speaks.
It will but skin and film the ulcerous place,
Whiles rank corruption, mining all within,   *165*
Infects unseen. Confess yourself to heaven;
Repent what's past; avoid what is to come;
And do not spread the compost on the weeds
To make them ranker. Forgive me this my virtue,
For in the fatness of these pursy times   *170*
Virtue itself of vice must pardon beg,
Yea, curb and woo for leave to do him good.
    Queen. O Hamlet, thou hast cleft my heart in twain.
    Ham. O throw away the worser part of it,
And live the purer with the other half.   *175*
Good night; but go not to my uncle's bed;
Assume a virtue, if you have it not.
«That monster, custom, who all sense doth eat
Of habits evil, is angel yet in this,
That to the use of actions fair and good   *180*
He likewise gives a frock or livery
That aptly is put on.» Refrain to-night,
And that shall lend a kind of easiness
To the next abstinence: «the next more easy;
For use almost can change the stamp of nature,   *185*
And either [tame] the devil or throw him out
With wondrous potency.» Once more, good night,
And when you are desirous to be bless'd,
I'll blessing beg of you. For this same lord,
I do repent; but heaven hath pleas'd it so,   *190*
To punish me with this, and this with me,
That I must be their scourge and minister.
I will bestow him, and will answer well
The death I gave him. So, again, good night.
I must be cruel only to be kind: *195*

91 mutine: *rise in mutiny*   **94 charge:** *command*   **96 panders:** *ministers to the gratifications of*   **99 grained:** *ingrained*   **100 leave their tinct:** *lose their color*   **102 enseamed:** *greasy*   **103 honeying:** *talking sweetly*   **109 tithe:** *tenth part* (i.e., not one two-hundredth)   **110 precedent:** *former* **vice:** *buffoon; cf. n.*   **111 cutpurse:** *pickpocket*   **115 shreds and patches;** *cf. n.*   **120 laps'd in time and passion:** *frittering away time and energy*   **121 important:** *urgent*   **127 Conceit:** *imagination*   **132 incorporal:** *incorporeal*   **135 bedded:** *smooth, flatly brushed* **hair:** *hairs* **life in excrements:** *dead tissue come alive*   **136 an end:** *on end*   **140 conjoin'd:** *united*   **141 capable:** *capable of feeling*

142 convert: *translate*   **143 My stern effects:** *the sternness of my deeds*   **144 want true color:** *not be what it should*   **151 habit . . . liv'd:** *familiar costume*   **154 Ecstasy;** *not in Quarto*   **160 re-word:** *repeat word for word*   **161 gambol from:** *skip away from* **grace:** *God*   **162 unction:** *salve*   **165 mining:** *undermining*   **170 fatness:** *grossness* **pursy:** *corpulent*   **172 curb and woo:** *bow and beg* **him;** *i.e., vice*   **178–182 That . . . put on;** *not in Folio*   **179 evil:** *'deuill' in Quarto*   **180 use:** *habitual practice*   **184–187 the next . . . potency;** *not in Folio*   **186 tame;** *cf. n.*   **188 be bless'd:** *become blessed*   **193 answer:** *account for*

Thus bad begins and worse remains behind.
«One word more, good lady.»

    Queen.   What shall I do?

    Ham. Not this, by no means, that I bid you do:

Let the bloat king tempt you again to bed,   200
Pinch wanton on your cheek, call you his mouse;
And let him, for a pair of reechy kisses,
Or paddling in your neck with his damn'd fingers,
Make you to ravel all this matter out,
That I essentially am not in madness,   205
But mad in craft. 'Twere good you let him know;
For who that's but a queen, fair, sober, wise,
Would from a paddock, from a bat, a gib,
Such dear concernings hide? who would do so?
No, in despite of sense and secrecy,   210
Unpeg the basket on the house's top,
Let the birds fly, and, like the famous ape,
To try conclusions in the basket creep,
And break your own neck down.

    Queen. Be thou assur'd, if words be made of breath,   215
And breath of life, I have no life to breathe
What thou hast said to me.

    Ham. I must to England; you know that?

    Queen.   Alack!

I had forgot. 'Tis so concluded on.   220

    Ham. «There's letters seal'd, and my two school-fellows,
Whom I will trust as I will adders fang'd,
They bear the mandate; they must sweep my way
And marshal me to knavery. Let it work,
For 'tis the sport to have the enginer   225
Hoist with his own petar; and 't shall go hard
But I will delve one yard below their mines,
And blow them at the moon. O 'tis most sweet,
When in one line two crafts directly meet!»
This man shall set me packing.   230
I'll lug the guts into the neighbor room.—
Mother, good night indeed.—This counsellor
Is now most still, most secret, and most grave,
Who was in life a foolish prating knave.
Come, sir, to draw toward an end with you.   235
Good night, mother.   *Exit Hamlet tugging in Polonius.*

❦ Scene Fifth ❦

[A Room in the Castle]
Enter King and Queen, with Rosencrantz and Guildenstern.

    King. There's matter in these sighs, these profound heaves,
You must translate. 'Tis fit we understand them.
Where is your son?

    Queen. «Bestow this place on us a little while.»

        [Exeunt Rosencrantz and Guildenstern.]

Ah, mine own lord, what have I seen to-night!   *5*

    King. What, Gertrude? How does Hamlet?

    Queen. Mad as the sea and wind, when both contend
Which is the mightier. In his lawless fit,
Behind the arras hearing something stir,
Whips out his rapier cries, 'A rat! a rat!'   *10*
And in this brainish apprehension kills
The unseen good old man.

    King.   O heavy deed!

It had been so with us had we been there.
His liberty is full of threats to all;   *15*
To you yourself, to us, to every one.
Alas, how shall this bloody deed be answer'd?
It will be laid to us, whose providence
Should have kept short, restrain'd, and out of haunt,
This mad young man. But so much was our love,   *20*
We would not understand what was most fit,
But like the owner of a foul disease,
To keep it from divulging, let it feed
Even on the pith of life. Where is he gone?

    Queen. To draw apart the body he hath kill'd,   *25*
O'er whom his very madness, like some ore
Among a mineral of metals base,
Shows itself pure. 'A weeps for what is done.

    King. O Gertrude, come away!
The sun no sooner shall the mountains touch   *30*
But we will ship him hence; and this vile deed
We must with all our majesty and skill
Both countenance and excuse. Ho, Guildenstern!

    Enter Rosencrantz and Guildenstern.

Friends both, go join you with some further aid.
Hamlet in madness hath Polonius slain,   *35*
And from his mother's closet hath he dragg'd him.
Go seek him out; speak fair, and bring the body
Into the chapel. I pray you haste in this.

        Exeunt Gentlemen.

Come, Gertrude, we'll call up our wisest friends;
And let them know both what we mean to do   *40*
And what's untimely done. [So, haply, slander,]
«Whose whisper o'er the world's diameter,
As level as the cannon to his blank
Transports his poison'd shot, may miss our name,
And hit the woundless air.» O, come away!   *45*
My soul is full of discord and dismay.   *Exeunt.*

❦ Scene Sixth ❦

[Another Room in the Castle]
Enter Hamlet.

    Ham. Safely stowed.

    Gentlemen within. Hamlet! Lord Hamlet!

---

197 One ... lady; *not in Folio*   **200 bloat:** *bloated*   **201 wanton:** *wantonly*   **202 reechy:** *greasy*   **203 paddling:** *playing fondly*   **205 essentially:** *in my essential nature*   **208 paddock:** *toad*   **gib:** *tom-cat*   **209 dear concernings:** *affairs dearly concerning one*   **212 the famous ape;** *cf. n.*   **213 conclusions:** *experiments*   **214 down:** *in the fall*   **221–229** *not in Folio*   **223 mandate:** *command*   **sweep my way:** *clear my path*   **224 marshal:** *conduct*   **225 enginer:** *maker of military engines, sapper*   **226 Hoist:** *blown up*   **petar:** *small bomb*   **226–227 't shall ... will:** *it shall not be for lack of trying if I do not*   **230 set me packing;** *cf. n.*   **III.v.s.d.** *From this point to the end of Act Fourth, the act and scene divisions differ from those traditionally employed; cf. note to IV.i.s.d. The traditional numbering is indicated within square brackets in the running heads.*   **1 heaves:** *prolonged sighs*

4 *Not in Folio; cf. n.*   **7 Mad as the sea and wind;** *cf. n.*   **11 brainish apprehension:** *insane illusion*   **13 heavy:** *grievous*   **18 providence:** *foresight*   **19 short:** *tethered*   **out of haunt:** *out of company*   **23 divulging:** *becoming known*   **27 mineral:** *mine*   **37 fair:** *courteously*   **41 So, haply, slander;** *cf. n.*   **42–45 Whose ... air;** *not in Folio*   **42 diameter:** *extent from side to side*   **43 level:** *straight*   **blank:** *white spot in the centre of a target*

Ham. What noise? who calls on Hamlet?
O, here they come.

Enter Rosencrantz and Guildenstern.

Ros. What have you done, my lord, with the dead body?   *5*
Ham. Compounded it with dust, whereto 'tis kin.
Ros. Tell us where 'tis, that we may take it thence
And bear it to the chapel.
Ham. Do not believe it.
Ros. Believe what?   *10*
Ham. That I can keep your counsel and not mine own.
Besides, to be demanded of a sponge, what replication should
be made by the son of a king?
Ros. Take you me for a sponge, my lord?
Ham. Ay, sir, that soaks up the king's countenance, his   *15*
rewards, his authorities. But such officers do the king best
service in the end. He keeps them, like an ape an apple, in
the corner of his jaw; first mouthed, to be last swallowed.
When he needs what you have gleaned, it is but squeezing you,
and, sponge, you shall be dry again.   *20*
Ros. I understand you not, my lord.
Ham. I am glad of it. A knavish speech sleeps in a foolish
ear.
Ros. My lord, you must tell us where the body is, and
go with us to the king.   *25*
Ham. The body is with the king, but the king is not
with the body. The king is a thing—
Guil. A thing, my lord!
Ham. Of nothing. Bring me to him. ⟨Hide fox, and all
after.⟩   *Exeunt.*   *30*

❧ Scene Seventh ❧

[Another Room in the Castle]
Enter King and two or three.

King. I have sent to seek him and to find the body.
How dangerous is it that this man goes loose!
Yet must not we put the strong law on him:
He's lov'd of the distracted multitude,
Who like not in their judgment but their eyes;   *5*
And where 'tis so, th' offender's scourge is weigh'd,
But never the offence. To bear all smooth and even,
This sudden sending him away must seem
Deliberate pause. Diseases desperate grown
By desperate appliance are reliev'd   *10*
Or not at all.

Enter Rosencrantz.

       How now! what hath befall'n?
Ros. Where the dead body is bestow'd, my lord,
We cannot get from him.
King.   But where is he?   *15*
Ros. Without, my lord, guarded, to know your pleasure.
King. Bring him before us.
Ros. Ho, Guildenstern! bring in my lord.

Enter Hamlet and Guildenstern.

King. Now, Hamlet, where's Polonius?
Ham. At supper.   *20*
King. At supper! Where?
Ham. Not where he eats, but where 'a is eaten. A certain
convocation of politic worms are e'en at him. Your worm is
your only emperor for diet: we fat all creatures else to fat us,
and we fat ourselves for maggots. Your fat king and your lean   *25*
beggar is but variable service,—two dishes, but to one table.
That's the end.
«*King.* Alas, alas!
Ham. A man may fish with the worm that hath eat of a
king, and eat of the fish that hath fed of that worm.»   *30*
King. What dost thou mean by this?
Ham. Nothing, but to show you how a king may go a
progress through the guts of a beggar.
King. Where is Polonius?
Ham. In heaven. Send thither to see. If your messenger   *35*
find him not there, seek him i' th' other place yourself. But,
indeed, if you find him not within this month, you shall
nose him as you go up the stairs into the lobby.
King. [To some Attendants.] Go seek him there.
Ham. 'A will stay till you come.   *40*
                     [Exeunt Attendants.]
King. Hamlet, this deed, for thine especial safety,—
Which we do tender, as we dearly grieve
For that which thou hast done,—must send thee hence
⟨With fiery quickness.⟩ Therefore prepare thyself.
The bark is ready and the wind at help,   *45*
Th' associates tend, and everything is bent
For England.
Ham.   For England?
King.   Ay, Hamlet.
Ham.   Good.   *50*
King. So is it, if thou knew'st our purposes.
Ham. I see a cherub that sees them. But, come; for
England! Farewell, dear mother.
King. Thy loving father, Hamlet.
Ham. My mother. Father and mother is man and wife,   *55*
man and wife is one flesh, and so, my mother. Come, for
England!   *Exit.*
King. Follow him at foot; tempt him with speed aboard.
Delay it not, I'll have him hence to-night.
Away! for everything is seal'd and done   *60*
That else leans on th' affair. Pray you, make haste.
           [Exeunt Rosencrantz and Guildenstern.]
And, England, if my love thou hold'st at aught,—
As my great power thereof may give thee sense,
Since yet thy cicatrice looks raw and red
After the Danish sword, and thy free awe   *65*
Pays homage to us,—thou mayst not coldly set
Our sovereign process, which imports at full,
By letters cóngruing to that effect,
The present death of Hamlet. Do it, England;
For like the hectic in my blood he rages,   *70*

---

12 to be demanded of: *on being questioned by* **replication:** *reply*   **15 countenance:**
favor   **16 authorities:** *offices of authority*   **17 like an ape an apple;** *cf. n.*   **26 The**
. . . body; *cf. n.*   **29, 30 Hide fox, and all after:** *signal cry in a children's game; cf. n.*   **6**
scourge: *punishment*   **7 bear:** *execute*   **smooth and even:** *pleasantly and equably*   **9**
Deliberate pause: *judicially considered*   **10 appliance:** *remedy*

23 convocation: *assembly; cf. n.* **politic:** *crafty*   **26 variable service:** *variety of*
courses   **28–30** *not in Folio*   **33 progress:** *state journey*   **44 With fiery quickness;**
not in Quarto   **46 bent:** *prepared*   **58 at foot:** *close behind*   **61 leans on:** *depends*
upon   **63 thereof may give thee sense:** *may make you think of it*   **64 cicatrice:**
scar   **65 free awe:** *awe still felt but no longer enforced by arms*   **66 set:** *esteem*   **67**
process: *formal command*   **68 congruing:** *agreeing*   **70 hectic:** *wasting fever*

And thou must cure me. Till I know 'tis done,
Howe'er my haps, my joys were ne'er begun.   *Exit.*

❧ SCENE EIGHTH ❧

[Open Country near the Castle]
Enter Fortinbras with his army over the stage.

For. Go, captain, from me greet the Danish king.
Tell him that by his licence Fortinbras
Craves the conveyance of a promis'd march
Over his kingdom. You know the rendezvous.
If that his majesty would aught with us,   *5*
We shall express our duty in his eye,
And let him know so.
     Cap.   I will do 't, my lord.
     For. Go softly on.   *Exit [with army, leaving Captain].*

«Enter Hamlet, Rosencrantz, &c.

Ham. Good sir, whose powers are these?   *10*
Cap. They are of Norway, sir.
Ham. How purpos'd, sir, I pray you?
Cap. Against some part of Poland.
Ham. Who commands them, sir?
Cap. The nephew to old Norway, Fortinbras.   *15*
Ham. Goes it against the main of Poland, sir,
Or for some frontier?
Cap. Truly to speak, and with no addition,
We go to gain a little patch of ground
That hath in it no profit but the name.   *20*
To pay five ducats, five, I would not farm it;
Nor will it yield to Norway or the Pole
A ranker rate, should it be sold in fee.
     Ham. Why, then the Polack never will defend it.
     Cap. Yes, it is already garrison'd.   *25*
     Ham. Two thousand souls and twenty thousand ducats
Will not debate the question of this straw.
This is th' imposthume of much wealth and peace,
That inward breaks, and shows no cause without
Why the man dies. I humbly thank you, sir.   *30*
     Cap. God be wi' you, sir.   *[Exit.]*
     Ros.   Will 't please you go, my lord?
     Ham. I'll be with you straight. Go a little before.
     [Exeunt all except Hamlet.]
How all occasions do inform against me   *35*
And spur my dull revenge! What is a man,
If his chief good and market of his time
Be but to sleep and feed? A beast, no more.
Sure he that made us with such large discourse,
Looking before and after, gave us not   *40*
That capability and godlike reason
To fust in us unus'd. Now, whether it be
Bestial oblivion, or some craven scruple
Of thinking too precisely on th' event

(A thought, which, quarter'd, hath but one part wisdom,   *45*
And ever three parts coward) I do not know
Why yet I live to say 'This thing's to do,'
Sith I have cause and will and strength and means
To do 't. Examples gross as earth exhort me:
Witness this army of such mass and charge,   *50*
Led by a delicate and tender prince,
Whose spirit with divine ambition puff'd
Makes mouths at the invisible event,
Exposing what is mortal and unsure
To all that fortune, death and danger dare,   *55*
Even for an egg-shell. Rightly to be great
Is not to stir without great argument,
But greatly to find quarrel in a straw
When honor's at the stake. How stand I then,
That have a father kill'd, a mother stain'd,   *60*
Excitements of my reason and my blood,
And let all sleep, while, to my shame, I see
The imminent death of twenty thousand men,
That for a fantasy and trick of fame
Go to their graves like beds, fight for a plot   *65*
Whereon the numbers cannot try the cause,
Which is not tomb enough and continent
To hide the slain? O, from this time forth,
My thoughts be bloody, or be nothing worth!   *Exit»*

ACT FOURTH ❧ SCENE FIRST

[A Room in the Castle]
Enter Queen, Horatio, and a Gentleman.

Queen. I will not speak with her.
Gent. She is importunate, indeed distract:
Her mood will needs be pitied.
     Queen.   What would she have?
     Gent. She speaks much of her father; says she hears   *5*
There's tricks i' th' world; and hems, and beats her heart;
Spurns enviously at straws, speaks things in doubt
That carry but half sense. Her speech is nothing,
Yet the unshaped use of it doth move
The hearers to collection. They aim at it,   *10*
And botch the words up fit to their own thoughts;
Which, as her winks and nods and gestures yield them,
Indeed would make one think there might be thought,
Though nothing sure, yet much unhappily.
     Hor. 'Twere good she were spoken with, for she may strew
Dangerous conjectures in ill-breeding minds.
     Queen. Let her come in.   *[Exit Gentleman.]*
To my sick soul, as sin's true nature is,
Each toy seems prologue to some great amiss.
So full of artless jealousy is guilt,   *20*
It spills itself in fearing to be split.

Enter Ophelia distracted.

72 haps: *fortunes*   **3 the conveyance of:** *escort during the course of*   **6 in his eye:** *in his presence*   **9 softly:** *slowly*   **9–69** *not in Folio*   **10 powers:** *troops*   **16 main:** *chief part*   **18 no addition:** *without adding fine words*   **23 ranker:** *richer*   **sold in fee:** *sold absolutely*   **27 debate:** *bring to a settlement*   **straw:** *trifling matter*   **28 imposthume:** *abscess*   **37 market of:** *way to dispose of*   **39 large discourse:** *latitude of comprehension*   **42 fust:** *become mouldy*   **43 Bestial oblivion:** *animal-like forgetfulness*   **44 event:** *outcome*

47 to do; *i.e., still undone*   **49 gross:** *weighty*   **50 charge:** *expense*   **57 argument:** *cause*   **61 Excitements:** *incentives*   **64 trick:** *trifle*   **67 continent:** *(a sufficient) receptacle*   **Scene First, S. d.;** *cf. n.*   **2 importunate:** *persistent*   **6 tricks:** *deceptions*   **7 Spurns:** *kicks* **enviously:** *spitefully* **in doubt:** *ambiguous*   **9 unshaped:** *artless*   **10 collection:** *inference* **aim:** *guess*   **12 Which:** *the words* **yield them:** *interpret her words*   **14 nothing:** *not at all* **much:** *very*   **16 ill-breeding:** *plotting ill*   **19 great amiss:** *calamity*   **20 artless jealousy:** *foolish anxiety*   **21 spills:** *ruins* **S. d.** *Cf. n.*

Oph. Where is the beauteous majesty of Denmark?
Queen. How now, Ophelia!   *She sings.*

Oph.   *How should I your true love know*
           From another one?   25
      By his cockle hat and staff,
           And his sandal shoon.

Queen. Alas! sweet lady, what imports this song?
Oph. Say you? nay, pray you, mark.   *Song.*

      He is dead and gone, lady,   30
           He is dead and gone;
      At his head a grass-green turf;
           At his heels a stone.

O, ho!
Queen. Nay, but Ophelia,—   35
Oph. Pray you, mark.

      White his shroud as the mountain snow,—

                        Enter King.

      Queen. Alas! look here, my lord.

Oph.   *Larded all with sweet flowers;*   *Song.*
      Which bewept to the ground did—not—go   40
           With true-love showers.

King. How do you, pretty lady?
Oph. Well, God 'ild you! They say the owl was a baker's
daughter. Lord! we know what we are, but know not what we
may be. God be at your table!   45
King. Conceit upon her father.
Oph. Pray, let's have no words of this; but when they ask
you what it means, say you this:

      To-morrow is Saint Valentine's day,
           All in the morning betime,   50
      And I a maid at your window,
           To be your Valentine.
      Then up he rose, and donn'd his clo'es,
           And dupp'd the chamber door;
      Let in the maid, that out a maid   55
           Never departed more.

King. Pretty Ophelia!
Oph. Indeed, la, without an oath, I'll make an end on 't:

      By Gis and by Saint Charity,
           Alack, and fie for shame!   60
      Young men will do 't, if they come to 't;
           By Cock they are to blame.
      Quoth she, before you tumbled me,
           You promis'd me to wed.

He answers: 65

      So would I ha' done, by yonder sun,
           An thou hadst not come to my bed.

King. How long hath she been thus?
Oph. I hope all will be well. We must be patient; but I
cannot choose but weep to think they would lay him i' th'   70

cold ground. My brother shall know of it: and so I thank you
for your good counsel. Come, my coach! Good night, ladies;
good night, sweet ladies; good night, good night.   *Exit.*
      King. Follow her close. Give her good watch, I pray you.

                                            [Exit Horatio.]
O, this is the poison of deep grief; it springs   75
All from her father's death. O Gertrude, Gertrude!
When sorrows come, they come not single spies,
But in battalions. First, her father slain;
Next, your son gone, and he most violent author
Of his own just remove; the people muddied,   80
Thick and unwholesome in their thoughts and whispers
For good Polonius' death,—and we have done but greenly,
In hugger-mugger to inter him; poor Ophelia
Divided from herself and her fair judgment,
Without the which we are pictures, or mere beasts.   85
Last, and as much containing as all these,
Her brother is in secret come from France,
Feeds on his wonder, keeps himself in clouds,
And wants not buzzers to infect his ear
With pestilent speeches of his father's death;   90
Wherein necessity, of matter beggar'd,
Will nothing stick our person to arraign
In ear and ear. O my dear Gertrude, this,
Like to a murdering-piece, in many places
Gives me superfluous death.   *A noise within.*   95
      ⟨*Queen.*   Alack! what noise is this?⟩
      King. «Attend!»

                  Enter a Messenger.

Where are my Switzers? Let them guard the door.
What is the matter?
      Mess.   Save yourself, my lord!   100
The ocean, overpeering of his list,
Eats not the flats with more impetuous haste
Than young Laertes, in a riotous head,
O'erbears your officers. The rabble call him lord,
And as the world were now but to begin,   105
Antiquity forgot, custom not known,
The ratifiers and props of every word,
They cry, 'Choose we! Laertes shall be king!'
Caps, hands, and tongues applaud it to the clouds,
'Laertes shall be king, Laertes king!'   110
                                        A noise within.
      Queen. How cheerfully on the false trail they cry!
O, this is counter, you false Danish dogs!
      King. The doors are broke.

                  Enter Laertes with others.

Laer. Where is this king? Sirs, stand you all without.
All. No, let's come in.   115
Laer.   I pray you, give me leave.
All. We will! we will!
Laer.   I thank you: keep the door. *[Mob retires.]*
O thou vile king!

---

26 **cockle hat:** *pilgrim's hat; cf. n.*   27 **shoon:** *shoes*   39 **Larded:** *garnished*   40
did—not—go; *cf. n.*   43 **God 'ild:** *God reward* **owl was a baker's daughter;** *cf. n.*
54 **dupp'd:** *opened*   59 **by Gis:** *by Jesus*   62 **Cock:** *perversion of 'God' in oaths*

80 **remove:** *removal* **muddied:** *stirred up*   82 **greenly:** *foolishly*   83 **In hugger-**
mugger: *secretly*   88 **wonder:** *doubt* **in clouds:** *in gloom, or, invisible*   89 **buzzers:**
tale-bearers   91 **Wherein:** *i.e., in which pestilent speeches* **necessity:** *poverty (of argu-*
ment)   92 **nothing stick:** *not at all hesitate*   93 **In ear and ear:** *in many ears*   94
murdering-piece: *small 'anti-personnel' cannon*   98 **Switzers:** *Swiss guards; cf. n.*   101
overpeering: *rising above* **list:** *boundary*   103 **head:** *hostile advance*   112 **counter:** *fol-*
lowing the trail in a direction opposite to that which the game has taken

Give me my father.   *120*

   Queen.   Calmly, good Laertes.

   Laer. That drop of blood that's calm proclaims me bastard,
Cries cuckold to my father, brands the harlot
Even here, between the chaste unsmirched brows
Of my true mother.   *125*

   King.   What is the cause, Laertes,
That thy rebellion looks so giantlike?
Let him go, Gertrude; do not fear our person.
There's such divinity doth hedge a king
That treason can but peep to what it would,   *130*
Acts little of his will. Tell me, Laertes,
Why thou art thus incens'd. Let him go, Gertrude.
Speak, man.

   Laer. Where is my father?

   King.   Dead.   *135*

   Queen.   But not by him.

   King. Let him demand his fill.

   Laer. How came he dead? I'll not be juggled with.
To hell, allegiance! vows, to the blackest devil!
Conscience and grace, to the profoundest pit!   *140*
I dare damnation. To this point I stand,
That both the worlds I give to negligence.
Let come what comes! only I'll be reveng'd
Most throughly for my father.

   King.   Who shall stay you?   *145*

   Laer. My will, not all the world:
And for my means, I'll husband them so well,
They shall go far with little.

   King.   Good Laertes,
If you desire to know the certainty   *150*
Of your dear father, is 't writ in your revenge,
That, swoopstake, you will draw both friend and foe,
Winner and loser?

   Laer. None but his enemies.

   King.   Will you know them then?   *155*

   Laer. To his good friends thus wide I'll ope my arms;
And like the kind life-rendering pelican,
Repast them with my blood.

   King.   Why, now you speak
Like a good child and a true gentleman.   *160*
That I am guiltless of your father's death,
And am most sensibly in grief for it,
It shall as level to your judgment peer
As day does to your eye.

   A noise within. [Voices.] Let her come in.   *165*

   Laer. How now! what noise is that?

                Enter Ophelia.

O heat, dry up my brains! tears seven times salt,
Burn out the sense and virtue of mine eye!
By heaven, thy madness shall be paid with weight,
Till our scale turn the beam. O rose of May!   *170*
Dear maid, kind sister, sweet Ophelia!
O heavens! is 't possible a young maid's wits

Should be as mortal as an old man's life?
⟨Nature is fine in love, and where 'tis fine
It sends some precious instance of itself   *175*
After the thing it loves.⟩

   Oph. They bore him barefac'd on the bier;
       Hey non nonny, nonny, hey nonny;
       And in his grave rain'd many a tear—

Fare you well, my dove!   *180*

   Laer. Hadst thou thy wits, and didst persuade revenge,
It could not move thus.

   Oph. You must sing, a-down a-down,
       And you call him a-down-a.

O how the wheel becomes it! It is the false steward that   *185*
stole his master's daughter.

   Laer. This nothing's more than matter.

   Oph. There's rosemary, that's for remembrance; pray you,
love, remember: and there is pansies, that's for thoughts.

   Laer. A document in madness, thoughts and   *190*
remembrance fitted.

   Oph. There's fennel for you, and columbines; there's rue for
you, and here's some for me; we may call it herb of grace o'
Sundays. O, you must wear your rue with a difference. There's
a daisy; I would give you some violets, but they withered   *195*
all when my father died. They say he made a good end.

         For bonny sweet Robin is all my joy.

   Laer. Thought and affliction, passion, hell itself,
She turns to favor and to prettiness.

   Oph.   *And will 'a not come again?*   *Song.*
       And will 'a not come again?
         No, no, he is dead;
         Go to thy deathbed,
       He never will come again.
       His beard was as white as snow   *205*
       All flaxen was his poll,
         He is gone, he is gone,
         And we castaway moan:
       God ha' mercy on his soul!

And of all Christian souls, I pray God. God be wi' you!   *210*
                     Exit Ophelia

   Laer. Do you see this, O God?

   King. Laertes, I must cómmune with your grief,
Or you deny me right. Go but apart,
Make choice of whom your wisest friends you will,   *215*
And they shall hear and judge 'twixt you and me.
If by direct or by collateral hand
They find us touch'd, we will our kingdom give,
Our crown, our life, and all that we call ours
To you in satisfaction; but if not,   *220*
Be you content to lend your patience to us,

---

123 **cuckold:** *husband with an unfaithful wife*   130 **peep:** *look from tiptoe* (as over a hedge)   140 **grace:** *God's grace*   142 **both the worlds:** *this world and the next*   146 **My will:** *as regards my will*   150 **certainty:** *the real truth*   152 **swoopstake:** *indiscriminately; cf. n.*   157 **life-rendering pelican;** *cf. n.*   158 **Repast:** *feed*   162 **sensibly:** *feelingly*   163 **peer:** *show itself*   167 **sense and virtue:** *feeling and power*   169 **paid with weight:** *heavily paid for*   170 **of May:** *early-blooming, delicate*

174–176 *not in Quarto; cf. n.*   178 **Hey non nonny;** *cf. n.*   185 **wheel;** *cf. n.* **false steward;** *cf. n.*   188 **rosemary;** *cf. n.*   189 **pansies;** *cf. n.*   190 **document:** *lesson*   192 **fennel:** *emblem of flattery* **columbines:** *emblems of thanklessness* **rue:** *emblem of repentance; cf. n.*   194 **difference;** *cf. n.* **daisy:** *emblem of dissemblers*   195 **violets:** *emblems of faithfulness*   197 **For ... joy;** *cf. n.*   198 **passion:** *suffering*   199 **favor:** *charm*   206 **poll:** *head* ('pow' in dialect)   208 **castaway:** *bereaved ones*   213 **commune:** *consult*   214 **right:** *equitable treatment*   215 **whom your:** *whichever*   217 **collateral:** *indirect*   218 **touch'd:** *implicated*

And we shall jointly labor with your soul
To give it due content.
   Laer.   Let this be so.
His means of death, his óbscure burial,   225
No trophy, sword, nor hatchment o'er his bones,
No noble rite nor formal ostentation,
Cry,—to be heard as 'twere from heaven to earth,—
That I must call 't in question.
   King.   So you shall;   230
And where th' offence is let the great axe fall.
I pray you go with me.   *Exeunt.*

❧ Scene Second ❧

[Another Room in the Castle]
Enter Horatio with an Attendant.

   Hor. What are they that would speak with me?

   Atten. Seafaring men, sir. They say they have letters for you.
   Hor. Let them come in.   *[Exit Attendant.]*
I do not know from what part of the world
I should be greeted, if not from Lord Hamlet.   5

Enter Sailor.

   Sail. God bless you, sir.
   Hor. Let him bless thee too.
   Sail. 'A shall, sir, an 't please him. There's a letter for you,
sir. It came from th' ambassador that was bound for England,—if your name be Horatio, as I am let to know it is. *10*

   Hor. (reads the letter). *Horatio, when thou shalt have
overlooked this, give these fellows some means to the king: they
have letters for him. Ere we were two days old at sea, a pirate
of very warlike appointment gave us chase. Finding ourselves
too slow of sail, we put on a compelled valor, and in the   15
grapple I boarded them. On the instant they got clear of our
ship, so I alone became their prisoner. They have dealt with me
like thieves of mercy, but they knew what they did; I am to do
a good turn for them. Let the king have the letters I have
sent, and repair thou to me with as much speed as thou   20
wouldst fly death. I have words to speak in thine ear will
make thee dumb; yet are they much too light for the bore of
the matter. These good fellows will bring thee where I am.
Rosencrantz and Guildenstern hold their course for England.
Of them I have much to tell thee. Farewell.*   *25*
                   He that thou knowest thine,
                            Hamlet.

Come, I will give you way for these your letters,
And do 't the speedier that you may direct me
To him from whom you brought them.   *30*
                            Exeunt.

❧ Scene Third ❧

[A Room in the Castle]
Enter King and Laertes.

   King. Now must your conscience my acquittance seal,
And you must put me in your heart for friend,
Sith you have heard, and with a knowing ear,
That he which hath your noble father slain
Pursu'd my life.   5
   Laer.   It well appears; but tell me
Why you proceeded not against these feats,
So crimeful and so capital in nature,
As by your safety, greatness, wisdom, all things,
You mainly were stirr'd up.   10
   King.   O, for two special reasons,
Which may to you perhaps seem much unsinew'd,
But yet to me they 're strong. The queen his mother
Lives almost by his looks, and for myself,—
My virtue or my plague, be it either which,—   15
She's so conjunctive to my life and soul
That, as the star moves not but in his sphere,
I could not but by her. The other motive
Why to a public count I might not go
Is the great love the general gender bear him,   20
Who, dipping all his faults in their affection,
Work like the spring that turneth wood to stone,—
Convert his gyves to graces; so that my arrows,
Too slightly timber'd for so loud a wind,
Would have reverted to my bow again,   25
And not where I had aim'd them.
   Laer. And so have I a noble father lost,
A sister driven into desperate terms,
Whose worth, if praises may go back again,
Stood challenger-on-mount of all the age   30
For her perfections. But my revenge will come.
   King. Break not your sleeps for that. You must not think
That we are made of stuff so flat and dull
That we can let our beard be shook with danger
And think it pastime. You shortly shall hear more.   35
I lov'd your father, and we love ourself,
And that, I hope, will teach you to imagine,—

Enter a Messenger with letters.

⟨How now, what news?
   Mess.   Letters, my lord, from Hamlet.⟩
These to your majesty; this to the queen.   40
   King. From Hamlet? who brought them?
   Mess. Sailors, my lord, they say; I saw them not.
They were given me by Claudio, he receiv'd them
«Of him that brought them.»

---

225 **means:** *manner*   226 **trophy:** *memorial emblem* **hatchment:** *tablet displaying armorial bearings* 227 **ostentation:** *ceremony* 228 **Cry:** *cry out, proclaim* **to be heard:** *so loud as to be heard* 229 **call 't in question:** *demand an explanation* 12 **overlooked:** *perused* 14 **appointment:** *equipment* 20 **repair:** *come* 22 **bore:** *literally, calibre, hence importance* 28 **way:** *passage*

3 **knowing:** *convinced*   5 **Pursu'd:** *sought*   8 **capital:** *punishable by death*   9 **your safety:** *regard for your safety* **greatness:** *position* **wisdom:** *intelligence in general; cf. n.*   10 **mainly:** *strongly* 12 **unsinew'd:** *weak* 15 **be ... which:** *whichever it be* 16 **conjunctive:** *closely united* 18 **could not but by her:** *could not move except beside her, (could not live without her)* 19 **count:** *legal indictment* 20 **general gender:** *common people* 22 **Work;** *cf. n.* **spring;** *cf. n.* 23 **gyves:** *leg-irons, marks of shame* 24 **Too slightly timber'd:** *too light* 25 **reverted:** *returned; cf. n.* 29 **praises ... again;** *cf. n.* 30 **challenger-on-mount:** *mounted challenger, ready in the lists; cf. n.* 38–39 *not in Quarto* 43 **Claudio;** *cf. n.* 44 **Of ... them;** *not in Folio*

King.   Laertes, you shall hear them.—   45
Leave us.   *Exit Messenger.*

     High and mighty, you shall know I am set naked on your
     kingdom. To-morrow shall I beg leave to see your kingly eyes;
     when I shall (first asking your pardon there-unto) recount the
     occasion of my sudden and more strange return.   50

What should this mean? Are all the rest come back?
Or is it some abuse, and no such thing?
    Laer. Know you the hand?
    King.   'Tis Hamlet's character. 'Naked'!
And in a postscript here, he says, 'alone.'   55
Can you advise me?
    Laer. I'm lost in it, my lord. But let him come!
It warms the very sickness in my heart
That I shall live and tell him to his teeth,
'Thus didest thou.'   60
    King.   If it be so, Laertes,—
As how should it be so? how otherwise?—
Will you be rul'd by me?
    Laer.   Ay, my lord;
So you will not o'er-rule me to a peace.   65
    King. To thine own peace. If he be now return'd,
As checking at his voyage, and that he means
No more to undertake it, I will work him
To an exploit now ripe in my device,
Under the which he shall not choose but fall;   70
And for his death no wind of blame shall breathe,
But even his mother shall uncharge the practice
And call it accident.
    «*Laer.*   My lord, I will be rul'd;
The rather, if you could devise it so   75
That I might be the organ.
    King.   It falls right.
You have been talk'd of since your travel much,
And that in Hamlet's hearing, for a quality
Wherein, they say, you shine. Your sum of parts   80
Did not together pluck such envy from him
As did that one, and that, in my regard,
Of the unworthiest siege.
    Laer.   What part is that, my lord?
    King. A very riband in the cap of youth,   85
Yet needful too, for youth no less becomes
The light and careless livery that it wears
Than settled age his sables and his weeds
Importing health and graveness.» Two months since
Here was a gentleman of Normandy.   90
I've seen myself, and serv'd against, the French,
And they can well on horseback; but this gallant
Had witchcraft in 't. He grew unto his seat,
And to such wondrous doing brought his horse,
As had he been incorps'd and demi-natur'd   95
With the brave beast. So far he topp'd my thought,
That I, in forgery of shapes and tricks,
Come short of what he did.

    Laer.   A Norman was 't?
    King. A Norman.   100
    Laer. Upon my life, Lamound.
    King.   The very same.
    Laer. I know him well. He is the brooch indeed
And gem of all the nation.
    King. He made confession of you,   105
And gave you such a masterly report
For art and exercise in your defence,
And for your rapier most especially,
That he cried out, 'twould be a sight indeed
If one could match you. «The scrimers of their nation,   110
He swore, had neither motion, guard, nor eye,
If you oppos'd them.» Sir, this report of his
Did Hamlet so envenom with his envy
That he could nothing do but wish and beg
Your sudden coming o'er, to play with you.   115
Now, out of this,—
    Laer.   What out of this, my lord?
    King. Laertes, was your father dear to you?
Or are you like the painting of a sorrow,
A face without a heart?   120
    Laer.   Why ask you this?
    King. Not that I think you did not love your father,
But that I know love is begun by time,
And that I see, in passages of proof,
Time qualifies the spark and fire of it.   125
«There lives within the very flame of love
A kind of wick or snuff that will abate it,
And nothing is at a like goodness still,
For goodness, growing to a plurisy,
Dies in his own too-much. That we would do,   130
We should do when we would, for this 'would' changes,
And hath abatements and delays as many
As there are tongues, are hands, are accidents;
And then this 'should' is like a spendthrift's sigh,
That hurts by easing. But, to the quick o' th' ulcer:»   135
Hamlet comes back. What would you undertake
To show yourself in deed your father's son
More than in words?
    Laer.   To cut his throat i' th' church.
    King. No place, indeed, should murther sanctuarize;   140
Revenge should have no bounds. But, good Laertes,
Will you do this: keep close within your chamber?
Hamlet return'd shall know you are come home.
We'll put on those shall praise your excellence,
And set a double varnish on the fame   145
The Frenchman gave you,—bring you, in fine, together,
And wager on your heads. He, being remiss,
Most generous, and free from all contriving,
Will not peruse the foils; so that with ease,
Or with a little shuffling, you may choose   150
A sword unbated, and in a pass of practice
Requite him for your father.
    Laer.   I will do 't;

---

47 naked: *without resources*   **52 abuse:** *imposture*   **54 character:** *handwriting*   **67 checking:** *stopping short*   **72 uncharge:** *acquit of guilt*   **practice:** *stratagem*   **74–89 Laer. . . . graveness;** *not in Folio*   **76 organ:** *instrument*   **79 falls:** *happens*   **83 siege:** *rank; cf. n.*   **84 part:** *attribute*   **85 riband:** *ribbon*   **87 livery:** *garb*   **88 weeds:** *garments*   **89 health:** *prosperity*   **92 can well:** *are skilled*   **95 incorps'd and demi-natur'd; cf. n.**   **96 topp'd:** *surpassed*   **97 in . . . tricks: cf. n.**

101 Lamound; *cf. n.*   **105 confession:** *report*   **106 masterly report;** *cf. n.*   **107 art and exercise:** *theory and practice*   **defence:** *science of defence*   **110–112 The scrimers . . . them;** *not in Folio*   **110 scrimers:** *fencers*   **115 play:** *fence; cf. n.*   **124 passages of proof;** *cf. n.*   **126–135** *not in Folio*   **129 plurisy:** *fulness; cf. n.*   **132 abatements:** *diminutions*   **134 spendthrift's sigh;** *cf. n.*   **144 put on:** *instigate*   **those:** *certain persons who*   **147 remiss:** *easy-going*   **149 peruse:** *inspect*   **151 unbated:** *not blunted*   **pass of practice:** *treacherous thrust*

And for that purpose I'll anoint my sword.
I bought an unction of a mountebank   *155*
So mortal that, but dip a knife in it,
Where it draws blood no cataplasm so rare,
Collected from all simples that have virtue
Under the moon, can save the thing from death
That is but scratch'd withal. I'll touch my point   *160*
With this contagion, that if I gall him slightly,
It may be death.
    King.   Let's further think of this,
Weigh what convenience both of time and means
May fit us to our shape. If this should fail,   *165*
And that our drift look through our bad performance,
'Twere better not assay'd. Therefore this project
Should have a back or second, that might hold,
If this should blast in proof. Soft! let me see.
We'll make a solemn wager on your cunnings.   *170*
I ha 't:
When in your motion you are hot and dry,—
As make your bouts more violent to that end,—
And that he calls for drink, I'll have prepar'd him
A chalice for the nonce, whereon but sipping,   *175*
If he by chance escape your venom'd stuck,
Our purpose may hold there. «But stay! what noise?»

          Enter Queen.

⟨How, sweet queen?⟩
    Queen. One woe doth tread upon another's heel,
So fast they follow. Your sister's drown'd, Laertes.   *180*
    Laer. Drown'd! O, where?
    Queen. There is a willow grows aslant a brook,
That shows his hoar leaves in the glassy stream.
There with fantastic garlands did she come
Of crowflowers, nettles, daisies, and long purples,   *185*
That liberal shepherds give a grosser name,
But our cold maids do dead men's fingers call them.
There, on the pendent boughs her coronet weeds
Clambering to hang, an envious sliver broke,
When down her weedy trophies and herself   *190*
Fell in the weeping brook. Her clothes spread wide,
And mermaid-like awhile they bore her up;
Which time she chanted snatches of old tunes,
As one incapable of her own distress,
Or like a creature native and indu'd   *195*
Unto that element; but long it could not be
Till that her garments, heavy with their drink,
Pull'd the poor wretch from her melodious lay
To muddy death.
    Laer.   Alas, then, she is drown'd?   *200*
    Queen. Drown'd, drown'd.
    Laer. Too much of water hast thou, poor Ophelia,
And therefore I forbid my tears; but yet
It is our trick, nature her custom holds,

Let shame say what it will. When these are gone,   *205*
The woman will be out. Adieu, my lord!
I have a speech of fire, that fain would blaze,
But that this folly douts it.   *Exit.*
    King.   Let's follow, Gertrude.
How much I had to do to calm his rage!   *210*
Now fear I this will give it start again.
Therefore let's follow.   *Exeunt.*

ACT FIFTH ❧ SCENE FIRST

[A Churchyard near Elsinore]
Enter two Clowns.

[First] Clo. Is she to be buried in Christian burial when she
wilfully seeks her own salvation?
    Other. I tell thee she is. Therefore make her grave straight.
The crowner hath sat on her and finds it Christian burial.
    Clown. How can that be, unless she drowned herself in   *5*
her own defence?
    Other. Why, 'tis found so.
    Clown. It must be *se offendendo*; it cannot be else. For here
lies the point: if I drown myself wittingly, it argues an act, and
an act hath three branches; it is to act, to do, to perform.   *10*
Argal, she drowned herself wittingly.
    Other. Nay, but hear you, goodman delver,—
    Clown. Give me leave. Here lies the water; good. Here
stands the man; good. If the man go to this water and drown
himself, it is, will he, nill he, he goes; mark you that! But   *15*
if the water come to him and drown him, he drowns not
himself. Argal, he that is not guilty of his own death shortens
not his own life.
    Other. But is this law?
    Clown. Ay, marry, is 't; crowner's quest law.   *20*
    Other. Will you ha' the truth on 't? If this had not been a
gentlewoman, she should have been buried out o' Christian
burial.
    Clown. Why, there thou sayest; and the more pity that great
folk should have countenance in this world to drown or   *25*
hang themselves more than their even Christen. Come, my
spade! There is no ancient gentlemen but gardeners, ditchers,
and grave-makers. They hold up Adam's profession.
    Other. Was he a gentleman?
    Clown. 'A was the first that ever bore arms.   *30*
⟨*Other.* Why, he had none.
    Clown. What! art a heathen? How dost thou understand the
Scripture? The Scripture says, Adam digged; could he dig without arms?⟩ I'll put another question to thee. If thou answerest
me not to the purpose, confess thyself—   *35*
    Other. Go to.
    Clown. What is he that builds stronger than either the
mason, the shipwright, or the carpenter?
    Other. The gallows-maker; for that frame outlives a thou-
sand tenants.   *40*
    Clown. I like thy wit well. In good faith the gallows does

---

154 anoint: *smear*   **155 mountebank;** *cf. n.*   **157 cataplasm:** *poultice*   **158 simples:**
medicinal herbs   **159 moon;** *cf. n.*   **165 our shape:** *part we purpose to act*   **166 drift
. . . performance;** *cf. n.*   **168 a back or second;** *cf. n.*   **169 blast in proof:** *burst when
tested* (as of a cannon)   **170 cunnings:** *skill*   **172 motion:** *bodily exertion*   **175 for
the nonce:** *for the purpose*   **176 stuck:** *thrust*   **177 But . . . noise;** *not in Folio*   **178
Not in Quarto**   **183 hoar:** *greyish-white*   **185 crowflowers:** *buttercups; cf. n.*   **long purples:** *early purple orchids* (orchis mascula)   **186 liberal:** *free-spoken*   **188 coronet:** *garlanded*   **194 incapable:** *having no understanding*   **195 indu'd:** *endowed with qualities
fitting her*   **204 trick:** *hereditary trait*

206 woman; *cf. n.*   **208 douts:** *extinguishes*   **S. d. Clowns;** *cf. n.*   **3 straight:** *at
once*   **4 crowner:** *coroner*   **sat on:** *passed on*   **8 se offendendo;** *cf. n.*   **10 branches:**
divisions   **11 Argal:** *corruption of ergo, therefore*   **12 goodman delver:** *Mr. Sexton*   **20
quest:** *inquest*   **26 even Christen:** *fellow Christian*   **30 bore arms;** *cf. n.*   **30–34 not
in Quarto**   **35 confess thyself;** *cf. n.*   **36 Go to:** *out with it!*

well, but how does it well? It does well to those that do ill.
Now thou dost ill to say the gallows is built stronger than the
church. Argal, the gallows may do well to thee. To 't again;
come!   45

Other. Who builds stronger than a mason, a shipwright,
or a carpenter?

Clown. Ay, tell me that, and unyoke.

Other. Marry, now I can tell.

Clown. To 't.   50

Other. Mass, I cannot tell.

         Enter Hamlet and Horatio afar off.

Clown. Cudgel thy brains no more about it, for your dull
ass will not mend his pace with beating; and when you are
asked this question next, say, 'a grave-maker.' The houses he
makes lasts till doomsday. Go, get thee to Yaughan and   55
fetch me a stoup of liquor.   *[Exit other Clown.]*

         [Clown digs and] sings.

In youth, when I did love, did love,
     Methought it was very sweet.
To contract—oh—the time, for—ah—my behove,
     O methought there—ah—was nothing—ah—meet.   60

Ham. Has this fellow no feeling of his business, that he
sings at grave-making?

Hor. Custom hath made it in him a property of easiness.

Ham. 'Tis e'en so; the hand of little employment hath the
daintier sense.   65

Clown. But age, with his stealing steps,
     Hath claw'd me in his clutch,
     And hath shipp'd me intil the land,
     As if I had never been such.

         [Throws up a skull.]

Ham. That skull had a tongue in it and could sing once.   70
How the knave jowls it to the ground, as if 't were Cain's
jaw-bone, that did the first murther! This might be the pate of
a politician which this ass now o'erreaches, one that would circumvent God, might it not?

Hor. It might, my lord.   75

Ham. Or of a courtier, which could say, 'Good morrow,
sweet lord! How dost thou, good lord?' This might be my
Lord Such-a-one, that praised my Lord Such-a-one's horse
when 'a went to beg it, might it not?

Hor. Ay, my lord.   80

Ham. Why, e'en so, and now my Lady Worm's: chapless,
and knocked about the mazzard with a sexton's spade. Here's
fine revolution, an we had the trick to see 't. Did these bones
cost no more the breeding but to play at loggats with 'em?
Mine ache to think on 't.   85

Clown. A pick-axe and a spade, a spade,   Song.
     For and a shrouding sheet;
     O, a pit of clay for to be made
     For such a guest is meet.

         [Throws up another skull.]

Ham. There's another! Why may not that be the skull of a   90
lawyer? Where be his quiddities now, his quillets, his cases, his
tenures, and his tricks? Why does he suffer this rude knave
now to knock him about the sconce with a dirty shovel,
and will not tell him of his action of battery? Hum! This fellow might be in 's time a great buyer of land, with his   95
statutes, his recognizances, his fines, his double vouchers, his
recoveries. ⟨Is this the fine of his fines, and the recovery of
his recoveries,⟩ to have his fine pate full of fine dirt? Will
his vouchers vouch him no more of his purchases, and
double ones too, than the length and breadth of a pair of   100
indentures? The very conveyances of his lands will scarcely lie
in this box, and must th' inheritor himself have no more, ha?

Hor. Not a jot more, my lord.

Ham. Is not parchment made of sheep skins?

Hor. Ay, my lord, and of calves' skins too.   105

Ham. They are sheep and calves which seek out assurance in
that. I will speak to this fellow. Whose grave 's this, sirrah?

Clown. Mine, sir,

O, a pit of clay for to be made
     For such a guest is meet.   110

Ham. I think it be thine indeed, for thou liest in 't.

Clown. You lie out on 't, sir, and therefore 't is not yours.
For my part, I do not lie in 't, yet it is mine.

Ham. Thou dost lie in 't, to be in 't and say it is thine.
'Tis for the dead, not for the quick. Therefore thou liest.   115

Clown. 'Tis a quick lie, sir. 'Twill away again from me
to you.

Ham. What man dost thou dig it for?

Clown. For no man, sir.

Ham. What woman, then?   120

Clown. For none, neither.

Ham. Who is to be buried in 't?

Clown. One that was a woman, sir; but, rest her soul,
she's dead.

Ham. How absolute the knave is! we must speak by the   125
card, or equivocation will undo us. By the Lord, Horatio,
this three years I have took note of it; the age is grown so
picked that the toe of the peasant comes so near the heel
of the courtier he galls his kibe.—How long hast thou been
grave-maker?   130

Clown. Of all the days i' th' year, I came to 't that day
that our last King Hamlet overcame Fortinbras.

Ham. How long is that since?

Clown. Cannot you tell that? Every fool can tell that. It
was that very day that young Hamlet was born,—he that   135
is mad and sent into England.

Ham. Ay, marry! Why was he sent into England?

Clown. Why, because 'a was mad. 'A shall recover his
wits there; or if 'a do not, 'tis no great matter there.

Ham. Why?   140

Clown. 'Twill not be seen in him there. There the men
are as mad as he.

48 unyoke; *cf. n.*   55 Yaughan; *cf. n.*   56 stoup: *two quart measure*   57 In . . .
love; *cf. n.*   59 contract: *shorten* (with pleasure) behove: *benefit*   60 meet: *good
enough*   63 property of easiness; *cf. n.*   65 sense: *sensibility*   68 intil: *into*   71
jowls: *dashes*   71, 72 Cain's jaw-bone, that: *the jaw-bone of Cain, who; cf. n.*   73
o'erreaches; *cf. n.*   79 went: *went about, attempted; cf. n.*   81 chapless: *lacking the
lower jaw* mazzard: *head*   84 loggats; *cf. n.*

91 quiddities: *subtleties* quillets: *minute distinctions*   92 tenures; *cf. n.*   93 sconce:
head   94 action of battery; *cf. n.*   96 statutes; *cf. n.* recognizances; *cf. n.* fines;
cf. n. vouchers; *cf. n.*   98 recoveries; *cf. n.* fine: *end*   97, 98 Is . . . recoveries; *not
in Quarto*   101 indentures: *mutual agreements; cf. n.*   101 conveyances; *cf. n.*   106
assurance: *security; cf. n.*   125 absolute: *precise*   125, 126 by the card: *with precision;
cf. n.*   127 picked: *fastidious; cf. n.*   129 kibe: *chilblain*

Ham. How came he mad?

Clown. Very strangely, they say.

Ham. How, strangely?   145

Clown. Faith, e'en with losing his wits.

Ham. Upon what ground?

Clown. Why, here in Denmark. I have been sexton here, man and boy, thirty years.

Ham. How long will a man lie i' th' earth ere he rot?   150

Clown. Faith, if 'a be not rotten before 'a die (as we have many pocky corses now-a-days, that will scarce hold the laying in) 'a will last you some eight year or nine year. A tanner will last you nine year.

Ham. Why he more than another?   155

Clown. Why, sir, his hide is so tanned with his trade that 'a will keep out water a great while, and your water is a sore decayer of your whoreson dead body. Here's a skull now hath lien you i' th' earth three-and-twenty years.

Ham. Whose was it?   160

Clown. A whoreson mad fellow's it was. Whose do you think it was?

Ham. Nay, I know not.

Clown. A pestilence on him for a mad rogue! 'a poured a flagon of Rhenish on my head once. This same skull, sir,   165 was Sir Yorick's skull, the king's jester.

Ham. This!

Clown. E'en that.

Ham. ⟨Let me see.⟩ *[Takes the skull.]*—Alas, poor Yorick! I knew him, Horatio; a fellow of infinite jest, of most excellent   170 fancy. He hath bore me on his back a thousand times; and now, how abhorred in my imagination it is! my gorge rises at it. Here hung those lips that I have kissed I know not how oft. Where be your gibes now? your gambols? your songs? your flashes of merriment, that were wont to set the table   175 on a roar? Not one now, to mock, your own grinning; quite chapfallen. Now get you to my lady's chamber, and tell her, let her paint an inch thick, to this favor she must come. Make her laugh at that. Prithee, Horatio, tell me one thing.

Hor. What's that, my lord?   180

Ham. Dost thou think Alexander looked o' this fashion i' th' earth?

Hor. E'en so.

Ham. And smelt so? pah!   *[Puts down the skull.]*

Hor. E'en so, my lord.   185

Ham. To what base uses we may return, Horatio! Why may not imagination trace the noble dust of Alexander till 'a find it stopping a bunghole?

Hor. 'Twere to consider too curiously, to consider so.

Ham. No, faith, not a jot; but to follow him thither with   190 modesty enough, and likelihood to lead it; ⟨as thus:⟩ Alexander died, Alexander was buried, Alexander returneth to dust; the dust is earth. Of earth we make loam, and why of that loam, whereto he was converted, might they not stop a beer-barrel?   195

Imperious Cæsar, dead and turn'd to clay,
Might stop a hole to keep the wind away.
O that that earth, which kept the world in awe,
Should patch a wall t' expel the winter's flaw!

But soft! but soft awhile! Here comes the king.   200

Enter King, Queen, Laertes, [a Priest,] and a Coffin, with Lords attendant.

The queen, the courtiers! Who is this they follow?
And with such maimed rites? This doth betoken
The corse they follow did with desperate hand   205
Fordo it own life. 'Twas of some estate.
Couch we awhile, and mark.   *[Retires with Horatio.]*

Laer. What ceremony else?

Ham.   That is Laertes,
A very noble youth. Mark.   210

Laer. What ceremony else?

Priest. Her obsequies have been as far enlarg'd
As we have warranty. Her death was doubtful,
And but that great command o'ersways the order,
She should in ground unsanctified been lodg'd   215
Till the last trumpet; for charitable prayers,
Shards, flints, and pebbles should be thrown on her.
Yet here she is allow'd her virgin crants,
Her maiden strewments, and the bringing home
Of bell and burial.   220

Laer. Must there no more be done?

Priest.   No more be done.
We should profane the service of the dead
To sing a requiem and such rest to her
As to peace-parted souls.   225

Laer.   Lay her i' th' earth,
And from her fair and unpolluted flesh
May violets spring! I tell thee, churlish priest,
A ministering angel shall my sister be
When thou liest howling.   230

Ham.   What! the fair Ophelia?

Queen. *[Scattering flowers.]* Sweets to the sweet! farewell!
I hop'd thou shouldst have been my Hamlet's wife.
I thought thy bride-bed to have deck'd, sweet maid,
And not have strew'd thy grave.   235

Laer.   O treble woe
Fall ten times treble on that cursed head
Whose wicked deed thy most ingenious sense
Depriv'd thee of. Hold off the earth awhile,
Till I have caught her once more in mine arms.   240
                                                                     Leaps in the grave.
Now pile your dust upon the quick and dead,
Till of this flat a mountain you have made
T' o'er-top old Pelion or the skyish head
Of blue Olympus.   245

Ham. *[Advancing.]* What is he whose grief
Bears such an emphasis? whose phrase of sorrow
Conjures the wandering stars, and makes them stand
Like wonder-wounded hearers? This is I,
Hamlet the Dane.   *Hamlet leaps in after Laertes.*   250

Laer.   The devil take thy soul!
                                                                     [Grapples with him.]

Ham. Thou pray'st not well.

200 awhile; *cf. n.*   **206** Fordo it: *undo its* estate: *rank*   **207** Couch: *remain concealed*   **212** enlarg'd: *extended*   **213** warranty: *warrant* doubtful: *suspicious*   **214** *Cf. n.*   **215** been: *have been; cf. n.*   **217** Shards: *fragments of pottery*   **218** crants: *garland; cf. n.*   **219** strewments: *flowers strewn on a grave*   **225** peace-parted: *piously deceased*   **238** ingenious: *delicately sensitive*   **244** Pelion; *cf. n.*   **248** wandering stars: *planets*   **250** Hamlet the Dane; *cf. n.*

157 sore: *grievous*   **158** whoreson: *plagued*   **159** lien: *lain* three-and-twenty years; *cf. n.*   **166** Sir Yorick's; *cf. n.*   **178** favor: *appearance*   **189** curiously: *minutely*   **191** modesty: *moderation* likelihood: *probability*   **199** flaw: *squall of wind*

I prithee take thy fingers from my throat;
For though I am not splenetive and rash,   255
Yet have I in me something dangerous,
Which let thy wisdom fear. Hold off thy hand!

King. Pluck them asunder.

Queen.   Hamlet! Hamlet!

«*All.* Gentlemen!»   260

Hor.   Good my lord, be quiet.

         [*The Attendants part them, and they come
                         out of the grave.*]

Ham. Why, I will fight with him upon this theme
Until my eyelids will no longer wag.

Queen. O my son, what theme?

Ham. I lov'd Ophelia. Forty thousand brothers   265
Could not with all their quantity of love
Make up my sum. What wilt thou do for her?

King. O, he is mad, Laertes.

Queen. For love of God, forbear him.

Ham. 'Swounds, show me what thou't do.   270
Woo't weep? woo't fight? «woo't fast?» woo't tear thyself?
Woo't drink up eisel? eat a crocodile?
I'll do 't. Dost thou come here to whine?
To outface me with leaping in her grave?
Be buried quick with her, and so will I.   275
And if thou prate of mountains, let them throw
Millions of acres on us, till our ground,
Singeing his pate against the burning zone,
Make Ossa like a wart! Nay, an thou'lt mouth,
I'll rant as well as thou.   280

Queen.   This is mere madness,
And thus a while the fit will work on him.
Anon, as patient as the female dove,
When that her golden couplets are disclos'd,
His silence will sit drooping.   285

Ham.   Hear you, sir.
What is the reason that you use me thus?
I lov'd you ever,—but it is no matter.
Let Hercules himself do what he may,
The cat will mew and dog will have his day.   *Exit.*   290

King. I pray thee, good Horatio, wait upon him.

                     [*Exit Horatio.*]

[*To Laertes.*] Strengthen your patience in our last night's
speech.
We'll put the matter to the present push.—
Good Gertrude, set some watch over your son.   295
This grave shall have a living monument.
An hour of quiet shortly shall we see;
Till then, in patience our proceeding be.   *Exeunt.*

❧ SCENE SECOND ❧

[*The Hall in the Castle*]
Enter Hamlet and Horatio.

Ham. So much for this, sir; now shall you see the other.
You do remember all the circumstance?

Hor. Remember it, my lord!

Ham. Sir, in my heart there was a kind of fighting
That would not let me sleep. Methought I lay   5
Worse than the mutines in the bilboes. Rashly,—
And prais'd be rashness for it (let us know,
Our indiscretion sometimes serves us well
When our deep plots do pall; and that should learn us
There's a divinity that shapes our ends,   10
Rough-hew them how we will)—

Hor.   That is most certain.

Ham. Up from my cabin,
My sea-gown scarf'd about me, in the dark
Grop'd I to find out them, had my desire,   15
Finger'd their packet, and in fine withdrew
To mine own room again; making so bold
(My fears forgetting manners) to unseal
Their grand commission, where I found, Horatio,
(Ah, royal knavery!) an exact command,—   20
Larded with many several sorts of reasons
Importing Denmark's health and England's too,
With, ho! such bugs and goblins in my life,—
That, on the supervise, no leisure bated,
No, not to stay the grinding of the axe,   25
My head should be struck off.

Hor.   Is 't possible?

Ham. Here's the commission: read it at more leisure.
But wilt thou hear now how I did proceed?

Hor. I beseech you.   30

Ham. Being thus be-netted round with villainies,
Ere I could make a prologue to my brains
They had begun the play. I sat me down,
Devis'd a new commission, wrote it fair.—
I once did hold it, as our statists do,   35
A baseness to write fair and labor'd much
How to forget that learning, but, sir, now
It did me yeoman's service. Wilt thou know
Th' effect of what I wrote?

Hor.   Ay, good my lord.   40

Ham. An earnest conjuration from the king,
As England was his faithful tributary,
As love between them like the palm might flourish,
As peace should still her wheaten garland wear
And stand a comma 'tween their amities,   45
And many such-like 'As'es of great charge,
That, on the view and knowing of these contents,
Without debatement further, more or less,
He should those bearers put to sudden death,
Not shriving-time allow'd.   50

Hor.   How was this seal'd?

Ham. Why, even in that was heaven ordinant.
I had my father's signet in my purse,
Which was the model of that Danish seal.—
Folded the writ up in the form of th' other,   55
Subscrib'd it, gave 't th' impression, plac'd it safely,

---

255 **splenetive:** *quick-tempered*   269 **forbear him:** *leave him alone*   271 **Woo't:** *wilt thou*   272 **eisel:** *vinegar* (associated with gall)   278 **burning zone:** *'coelum igneum,' heavenly region of fire*   284 **golden couplets;** *cf. n.*   292 **in:** *in the thought of*   294 **present push:** *immediate trial*   296 **living:** *lasting*

6 **mutines:** *mutineers*   **bilboes:** *shackles*   9 **pall:** *fail*   14 **sea-gown;** *cf. n.*   16 **Finger'd:** *pilfered*   23 **bugs . . . life;** *cf. n.*   24 **supervise:** *perusal*   **bated:** *deducted*   31 **be-netted:** *ensnared*   32, 33 **prologue . . . play;** *cf. n.*   35 **statists:** *statesmen*   38 **yeoman's service:** *good and faithful service*   44 **wheaten garland:** *emblem of peace*   45 **comma:** *bond of connection; cf. n.*   46 **'As'es;** *cf. n.*   50 **shriving-time:** *time for absolution*   52 **ordinant:** *controlling*   54 **model:** *exact likeness*   56 **Subscrib'd:** *signed*   **impression:** *i.e., of the seal*

The changeling never known. Now, the next day
Was our sea-fight, and what to this was sequent
Thou know'st already.

    Hor. So Guildenstern and Rosencrantz go to 't.   60

    Ham. ⟨Why, man, they did make love to this employment;⟩
They are not near my conscience. Their defeat
Does by their own insinuation grow.
'Tis dangerous when the baser nature comes
Between the pass and fell-incensed points   65
Of mighty opposites.

    Hor.   Why, what a king is this!

    Ham. Does it not, think thee, stand me now upon?
He that hath kill'd my king and whor'd my mother,
Popp'd in between th' election and my hopes,   70
Thrown out his angle for my proper life,
And with such cozenage—is 't not perfect conscience
⟨To quit him with this arm? and is 't not to be damn'd
To let this canker of our nature come
In further evil?   75

    Hor. It must be shortly known to him from England
What is the issue of the business there.

    Ham. It will be short. The interim is mine,
And a man's life's no more than to say 'One.'
But I am very sorry, good Horatio,   80
That to Laertes I forgot myself,
For by the image of my cause I see
The portraiture of his. I'll court his favors:
But sure the bravery of his grief did put me
Into a towering passion.   85

    Hor.   Peace! who comes here?⟩

Enter young Osric.

    Osr. Your lordship is right welcome back to Denmark.

    Ham. I humbly thank you, sir. *[Aside to Horatio.]*
Dost know this water-fly?

    Hor. [Aside to Hamlet.] No, my good lord.   90

    Ham. [Aside to Horatio.] Thy state is the more gracious, for
'tis a vice to know him. He hath much land, and fertile. Let a
beast be lord of beasts, and his crib shall stand at the king's
mess. 'Tis a chough, but, as I say, spacious in the possession
of dirt.   95

    Osr. Sweet lord, if your lordship were at leisure, I should
impart a thing to you from his majesty.

    Ham. I will receive it, sir, with all diligence of spirit. Put
your bonnet to his right use; 'tis for the head.

    Osr. I thank your lordship. It is very hot.   100

    Ham. No, believe me, 'tis very cold; the wind is northerly.

    Osr. It is indifferent cold, my lord, indeed.

    Ham. But yet methinks it is very sultry and hot for my
complexion.

    Osr. Exceedingly, my lord. It is very sultry, as 'twere,   105
—I cannot tell how. But, my lord, his majesty bade me signify
to you that 'a has laid a great wager on your head. Sir, this
is the matter,—

    Ham. I beseech you, remember—

[Hamlet moves him to put on his hat.]

    Osr. Nay, good my lord, for my ease, in good faith. «Sir,   110
here is newly come to court Laertes,— believe me, an absolute
gentleman, full of most excellent differences, of very soft society and great showing. Indeed, to speak feelingly of him, he is
the card or calendar of gentry, for you shall find in him
the continent of what part a gentleman would see.   115

    Ham. Sir, his definement suffers no perdition in you;
though, I know, to divide him inventorially would dozy th'
arithmetic of memory, and yet but yaw neither, in respect of
his quick sail. But, in the verity of extolment, I take him
to be a soul of great article, and his infusion of such dearth   120
and rareness as, to make true diction of him, his semblable
is his mirror, and who else would trace him his umbrage,
nothing more.

    Osr. Your lordship speaks most infallibly of him.

    Ham. The concernancy, sir? why do we wrap the   125
gentleman in our more rawer breath?

    Osr. Sir?

    Hor. Is 't not possible to understand in another tongue?
You will to 't, sir, really.

    Ham. What imports the nomination of this gentleman?   130

    Osr. Of Laertes?

    Hor. His purse is empty already. All 's golden words are
spent.

    Ham. Of him, sir.

    Osr. I know you are not ignorant—   135

    Ham. I would you did, sir; yet in faith, if you did, it
would not much approve me. Well, sir.»

    Osr. You are not ignorant of what excellence Laertes is—

    «*Ham.* I dare not confess that, lest I should compare with
him in excellence; but to know a man well were to know   140
himself.

    Osr. I mean, sir,» for his weapon; «but in the imputation
laid on him by them, in his meed he's unfellowed.»

    Ham. What's his weapon?

    Osr. Rapier and dagger.   145

    Ham. That's two of his weapons, but,—well.

    Osr. The king, sir, hath wagered with him six Barbary
horses, against the which he has impawned, as I take it, six
French rapiers and poniards, with their assigns; as girdle,
hanger, and so. Three of the carriages, in faith, are very   150
dear to fancy, very responsive to the hilts, most delicate
carriages and of very liberal conceit.

    Ham. What call you the carriages?

    «*Hor.* I knew you must be edified by the margent, ere
you had done.»   155

    Osr. The carriages, sir, are the hangers.

    Ham. The phrase would be more germane to the matter, if
we could carry a cannon by our sides. I would it might be
hangers till then. But, on; six Barbary horses against six French
swords, their assigns, and three liberal-conceited carriages;   160

---

110 **my ease;** *cf. n.*   110–137 *not in Folio*   111 **absolute:** *perfect*   112 **differences:**
distinguishing features **soft:** *gentle*   114 **card:** *map*   116 **definement:** *description* **per-**
dition: *loss*   117 **divide inventorially:** *catalogue* **dozy:** *make giddy*   118 **yaw:** *stagger;*
cf. n. **neither:** *too*   120 **great article:** *large scope* **infusion:** *character imparted by na-*
ture   121 **semblable:** *like*   122 **trace:** *follow* **umbrage:** *shadow*   125 **concernancy:**
relevance   126 **more rawer:** *too unskilled*   128 **another tongue;** *cf. n.*   129 **You will**
to 't: *You will acquire the art*   130 **nomination:** *naming*   137 **approve me:** *commend*
me   139–143 *not in Folio*   139 **compare with:** *vie with*   142 **imputation:** *reputa-*
tion   143 **meed:** *merit, worth* **unfellowed:** *without an equal*   148 **impawned:**
staked   149 **assigns:** *appurtenances*   150 **hanger:** *strap from which a sword is suspended* **car-**
riages: *hangers*   151 **dear to fancy:** *unusual in design* **delicate:** *finely wrought*   152 **liberal**
conceit: *tasteful design*   154, 155 *not in Folio*   154 **margent;** *cf. n.*

---

57 **changeling:** *substitute*   61, 73–86 *not in Quarto*   63 **insinuation:** *intrusion*   65
fell-incensed: *cruelly angered; cf. n.*   66 **opposites:** *opponents*   68 **stand ... upon:**
vitally concern   70 **election;** *cf. n.*   71 **angle:** *fishing-hook* **proper:** *own*   72 **cozen-**
age: *cheating*   84 **bravery:** *ostentatious display*   89 **water-fly;** *cf. n.*   94 **mess;**
cf. n. **chough:** *small chattering bird*   109 **remember;** *cf. n.*

that's the French bet against the Danish. Why is this all impawned, as you call it?

Osr. The king, sir, hath laid that in a dozen passes between yourself and him, he shall not exceed you three hits. He hath laid on twelve for nine, and it would come to immediate   *165* trial, if your lordship would vouchsafe the answer.

Ham. How if I answer no?

Osr. I mean, my lord, the opposition of your person in trial.

Ham. Sir, I will walk here in the hall. If it please his majesty, it is the breathing time of day with me. Let the foils   *170* be brought, the gentleman willing, and the king hold his purpose, I will win for him an I can; if not, I will gain nothing but my shame and the odd hits.

Osr. Shall I deliver you so?

Ham. To this effect, sir, after what flourish your nature will.

Osr. I commend my duty to your lordship.

Ham. Yours, yours. *[Exit Osric.]* He does well to commend it himself; there are no tongues else for 's turn.

Hor. This lapwing runs away with the shell on his head.

Ham. 'A did comply, sir, with his dug before 'a sucked   *180* it. Thus has he—and many more of the same bevy, that I know the drossy age dotes on—only got the tune of the time and outward habit of encounter, a kind of yesty collection which carries them through and through the most fond and winnowed opinions; and do but blow them to their trial, the   *185* bubbles are out.

«*Enter a Lord.*

Lord. My lord, his majesty commended him to you by young Osric, who brings back to him that you attend him in the hall. He sends to know if your pleasure hold to play with Laertes, or that you will take longer time.   *190*

Ham. I am constant to my purposes; they follow the king's pleasure. If his fitness speaks, mine is ready, now or whensoever, provided I be so able as now.

Lord. The king and queen and all are coming down.

Ham. In happy time.   *195*

Lord. The queen desires you to use some gentle entertainment to Laertes before you fall to play.

Ham. She well instructs me.   *[Exit Lord.]*»

Hor. You will lose this wager, my lord.

Ham. I do not think so. Since he went into France, I   *200* have been in continual practice. I shall win at the odds, but thou wouldst not think how ill all 's here about my heart. But it is no matter.

Hor. Nay, good my lord,—

Ham. It is but foolery, but it is such a kind of gaingiving   *205* as would perhaps trouble a woman.

Hor. If your mind dislike anything, obey it. I will forestall their repair hither and say you are not fit.

Ham. Not a whit, we defy augury; there is special providence in the fall of a sparrow. If it be now, 'tis not to come;   *210* if it be not to come, it will be now; if it be not now, yet it will come: the readiness is all. Since no man has aught of what he leaves, what is 't to leave betimes? «*Let be.*»

Enter King, Queen, Laertes and Lords, with other Attendants with foils and gauntlets. A table and flagons of wine on it.

King. Come, Hamlet, come, and take this hand from me.
    [The King puts the hand of Laertes into that of Hamlet.]
Ham. Give me your pardon, sir. I've done you wrong;   *215*
But pardon 't, as you are a gentleman.
This presence knows, and you must needs have heard,
How I am punish'd with a sore distraction.
What I have done,
That might your nature, honor, and exception   *220*
Roughly awake, I here proclaim was madness.
Was 't Hamlet wrong'd Laertes? Never Hamlet.
If Hamlet from himself be ta'en away,
And when he's not himself does wrong Laertes,
Then Hamlet does it not; Hamlet denies it.   *225*
Who does it then? His madness. If 't be so,
Hamlet is of the faction that is wrong'd;
His madness is poor Hamlet's enemy.
⟨Sir, in this audience,⟩
Let my disclaiming from a purpos'd evil   *230*
Free me so far in your most generous thoughts,
That I have shot my arrow o'er the house,
And hurt my brother.
Laer.   I am satisfied in nature,
Whose motive in this case should stir me most   *235*
To my revenge; but in my terms of honor
I stand aloof, and will no reconcilement
Till by some elder masters of known honor
I have a voice and precedent of peace,
To keep my name ungor'd. But till that time,   *240*
I do receive your offer'd love like love,
And will not wrong it.
Ham.   I embrace it freely,
And will this brothers' wager frankly play.
Give us the foils. ⟨Come on.⟩   *245*
Laer.   Come, one for me.
Ham. I'll be your foil, Laertes. In mine ignorance
Your skill shall, like a star i' th' darkest night,
Stick fiery off indeed.
Laer.   You mock me, sir.   *250*
Ham. No, by this hand.
King. Give them the foils, young Osric. Cousin Hamlet,
You know the wager?
Ham.   Very well, my lord;
Your Grace has laid the odds o' th' weaker side.   *255*
King. I do not fear it. I have seen you both;
But since he is better'd, we have therefore odds.
Laer. This is too heavy; let me see another.
Ham. This likes me well. These foils have all a length?
Osr. Ay, my good lord.   *Prepare to play.*   *260*
King. Set me the stoups of wine upon that table.
If Hamlet give the first or second hit,
Or quit in answer of the third exchange,
Let all the battlements their ordnance fire.
The king shall drink to Hamlet's better breath;   *265*
And in the cup an union shall he throw,

165 twelve for nine; *cf. n.*.   170 breathing time: *exercise period*   179 lapwing: *plover, a vivacious little bird* with . . . head: *almost before he is hatched*   180 comply: *use fine language*   182 drossy: *frivolous* tune: *mood*   183 outward . . . encounter: *superficial mannerisms* yesty: *frothy*   185 fond and winnowed; *cf. n.*   S.d. *not in Folio*   195 In happy time: *at an appropriate time*   205 gaingiving: *foreboding*

217 presence: *royal assembly*   220 exception: *disapproval*   224 *Not in Quarto*   234 satisfied in nature; *cf. n.*   239 voice: *opinion*   240 ungor'd: *uninjured*   247 foil; *cf. n.*   249 Stick . . . off: *stand out in relief*   263 quit; *cf. n.*   266 union: *pearl*

Richer than that which four successive kings
In Denmark's crown have worn. Give me the cups;
And let the kettle to the trumpet speak,
The trumpet to the cannoneer without,   *270*
The cannons to the heavens, the heaven to earth:
'Now the king drinks to Hamlet!'   *Trumpets*
               Come, begin!   *the while.*
And you, the judges, bear a wary eye.
    Ham. Come on, sir.   *275*
    Laer.   Come, my lord.   *They play.*
    Ham.   One.
    Laer.   No.
    Ham.   Judgment.
    Osr. A hit, a very palpable hit.   *280*
            «Drum, trumpets and shot.
            Flourish. A piece goes off.»
    Laer.   Well; again.
    King. Stay; give me drink. Hamlet, this pearl is thine.
Here's to thy health. Give him the cup.
        ⟨*Trumpets sound; and shot goes off.*⟩
    Ham. I'll play this bout first; set it by awhile.
Come.—*[They play.]* Another hit! What say you?   *285*
    Laer. ⟨A touch, a touch,⟩ I do confess 't.
    King. Our son shall win.
    Queen.   He's fat and scant of breath.
Here, Hamlet, take my napkin, rub thy brows.
The queen carouses to thy fortune, Hamlet.   *290*
            [Takes Hamlet's cup.]
    Ham. Good madam!
    King.   Gertrude, do not drink!
    Queen. I will, my lord; I pray you, pardon me.
    King. [Aside.] It is the poison'd cup! it is too late.
    Ham. I dare not drink yet, madam. By and by.   *295*
    Queen. Come, let me wipe thy face.
    Laer. My lord, I'll hit him now.
    King.   I do not think 't.
    Laer. [Aside.] And yet it is almost against my conscience.
    Ham. Come, for the third! Laertes, you but dally;   *300*
I pray you, pass with your best violence.
I am afeard you make a wanton of me.
    Laer. Say you so? come on.   *Play.*
    Osr. Nothing, neither way.
    Laer. Have at you now.   *In scuffling they change rapiers.*
    King.   Part them! they are incens'd.
    Ham. Nay, come again!   *[The Queen falls.]*
    Osr.   Look to the queen there. Ho!
    Hor. They bleed on both sides. How is it, my lord?
    Osr. How is 't, Laertes?   *310*
    Laer. Why, as a woodcock to mine own springe, Osric.
I am justly kill'd with mine own treachery.
    Ham. How does the queen?
    King.   She sounds to see them bleed.
    Queen. No, no, the drink, the drink! O my dear Hamlet!   *315*
The drink, the drink! I am poison'd.   *[Dies.]*
    Ham. O villainy! Ho! let the door be lock'd.
Treachery! seek it out.   *[Laertes falls.]*
    Laer. It is here, Hamlet. Hamlet, thou art slain;
No medicine in the world can do thee good.   *320*
In thee there is not half an hour's life.

The treacherous instrument is in thy hand,
Unbated and envenom'd. The foul practice
Hath turn'd itself on me. Lo, here I lie,
Never to rise again. Thy mother's poison'd.   *325*
I can no more. The king, the king's to blame.
    Ham. The point envenom'd too?
Then, venom, to thy work!   *Hurts the King.*
    All.   Treason! treason!
    King. O yet defend me, friends; I am but hurt.   *330*
    Ham. Here, thou incestuous, murd'rous, damned Dane,
Drink off this potion! Is thy union here?
Follow my mother.   *King dies.*
    Laer.   He is justly serv'd;
It is a poison temper'd by himself.   *335*
Exchange forgiveness with me, noble Hamlet:
Mine and my father's death come not upon thee,
Nor thine on me!   *Dies.*
    Ham. Heaven make thee free of it! I follow thee.
I am dead, Horatio. Wretched queen, adieu!   *340*
You that look pale and tremble at this chance,
That are but mutes or audience to this act,
Had I but time (as this fell sergeant, death,
Is strict in his arrest) O, I could tell you—
But let it be. Horatio, I am dead;   *345*
Thou liv'st. Report me and my cause aright
To the unsatisfied.
    Hor.   Never believe it!
I am more an antique Roman than a Dane.
Here's yet some liquor left.   *350*
    Ham.   As th' art a man,
Give me the cup! let go! by heaven, I'll have 't!
O good Horatio, what a wounded name
(Things standing thus unknown) shall live behind me.
If thou didst ever hold me in thy heart,   *355*
Absent thee from felicity awhile,
And in this harsh world draw thy breath in pain,
To tell my story.
         A march afar off ⟨*and shout within*⟩
            What warlike noise is this?

         Enter Osric.

    Osr. Young Fortinbras, with conquest come from Poland,
To the ambassadors of England gives
This warlike volley.
    Ham.   O, I die, Horatio;
The potent poison quite o'er-crows my spirit.
I cannot live to hear the news from England,   *365*
But I do prophesy th' election lights
On Fortinbras. He has my dying voice.
So tell him, with th' occurrents, more and less,
Which have solicited—The rest is silence.   *Dies.*
    Hor. Now cracks a noble heart. Good night, sweet prince,   *370*
And flights of angels sing thee to thy rest!
Why does the drum come hither?

Enter Fortinbras, and English Ambassador, with drum, colors, and
             Attendants.

    Fort. Where is this sight?

269 kettle: *kettledrum*   **288 fat:** *out of training*   **289 napkin:** *handkerchief*   **301 pass:**
thrust   **302 wanton:** *pampered child*   **305 S. d.** *Cf. n.*   **314 sounds:** *swoons*

335 temper'd: *compounded*   **343 sergeant:** *sheriff's officer*   **349 Roman;** *cf. n.*   **362
This warlike volley;** *cf. n.*   **364 o'er-crows:** *triumphs over*   **368 occurrents:** *inci-*
dents   **369 solicited:** *moved; cf. n.*   **371 flights:** *troops*

Hor.   What is it you would see?
If aught of woe or wonder, cease your search.   *375*
    Fort. This quarry cries on havoc. O proud death,
What feast is toward in thine eternal cell,
That thou so many princes at a shot
So bloodily hast struck?
    Amb.   The sight is dismal,   *380*
And our affairs from England come too late.
The ears are senseless that should give us hearing,
To tell him his commandment is fulfill'd,
That Rosencrantz and Guildenstern are dead.
Where should we have our thanks?   *385*
    Hor.   Not from his mouth,
Had it th' ability of life to thank you.
He never gave commandment for their death.
But since, so jump upon this bloody question,
You from the Polack wars, and you from England,   *390*
Are here arriv'd, give order that these bodies
High on a stage be placed to the view;
And let me speak to th' yet unknowing world
How these things came about. So shall you hear
Of carnal, bloody, and unnatural acts,   *395*
Of accidental judgments, casual slaughters,
Of deaths put on by cunning and forc'd cause,

And, in this upshot, purposes mistook
Fall'n on th' inventors' heads. All this can I
Truly deliver.   *400*
    Fort.   Let us haste to hear it,
And call the noblest to the audience.
For me, with sorrow I embrace my fortune.
I have some rights of memory in this kingdom,
Which now to claim my vantage doth invite me.   *405*
    Hor. Of that I shall have also cause to speak,
And from his mouth whose voice will draw on more.
But let this same be presently perform'd,
Even while men's minds are wild, lest more mischance
On plots and errors happen.   *410*
    Fort.   Let four captains
Bear Hamlet like a soldier to the stage;
For he was likely, had he been put on,
To have prov'd most royal. And for his passage
The soldiers' music and the rites of war   *415*
Speak loudly for him!
Take up the bodies. Such a sight as this
Becomes the field, but here shows much amiss.
Go bid the soldiers shoot.

                   Exeunt ⟨marching, after the which a peal of
                            ordnance are shot off⟩

❧ FINIS ❧

---

376 quarry: *heap of slain*   **cries on havoc:** *proclaims merciless slaughter; cf. n.*   **392 stage:** *platform*   **396 casual:** *unpremeditated*   **397 forc'd:** *unreal*

404 rights of memory: *ancient claims*   **407 draw on more:** *be seconded by others*   **413 been put on:** *been put to the proof, tried*   **414 royal;** *cf. n.*   **416 Speak;** *cf. n.*

NOTES

At the time of his sudden death in June of 1946, Professor Brooke had completed his work on the text, notes, and glosses for Hamlet, King Lear, Othello *and* I Henry IV. *The editorial tasks which he left unfinished—preparation of some of the final copy for the press, reading of the proofs, compilation of the* Indexes of Words Glossed, *decisions as to certain matters of style and format, and, in the case of* Henry IV, *the rescuing of the text from the prescriptive punctuation of the eighteenth-century editors—have been undertaken by Professor Benjamin Nangle.*

Textual Note. The two authorities for the text of *Hamlet* are the second quarto (separate) edition of the play published in 1604–05 and the version included in the first folio (collected) edition of Shakespeare's dramatic works, published in 1623. The Quarto text, though marred by bad typographical errors, is fundamentally the more reliable, and is usually (but by no means always) to be preferred. In the present book matter which the Folio omits is set within ornamental brackets («). This mainly represents cuts made in the stage version of the play as acted in Shakespeare's time. Matter which the Quarto omits is set within angle brackets (»). This is largely material excised because indiscreet in 1604 or overtopical.

The bad First Quarto of the play, printed in 1603, is untrustworthy, but is occasionally of use in explaining doubtful passages or illustrating early stage practice.

The stage directions here reprinted are those of the Second Quarto, the Folio, and very occasionally of the First Quarto. Necessary amplifications and other essential matter omitted in the original editions are supplied within square brackets([ ]). The early quartos do not divide the play into acts or scenes. Such a division was attempted in the First Folio and was carried out, with some incompleteness and with Latin headings ('Actus Primus. Scaena Prima,' *etc.*) through the first two acts. The act and scene division in the last three acts, and all indications of the place of action, are the work of post-Shakespearean editors, beginning with the Betterton acting text of 1676.

In Shakespeare's usage it was optional to give full syllabic value to the ending *-ed* of past verbal forms or (as is usually done now) to contract this ending with the preceding syllable. In the present text final *-ed* must always be pronounced as a separate syllable in order to preserve the original rhythm of the verse. Where rhythm requires the contracted form, the spelling *-'d* is used.

Shakespeare accented a number of words on syllables which now do not bear the accent, and sometimes his practice in this matter was inconsistent. Where an unusual accentuation is required, it is indicated by an acute mark over the stressed vowel, as in *canóniz'd.*

Obsolete words and words used in now unusual senses are explained in footnotes the first time they appear in the text. Repetitions are not noted and when they occur should be checked by the Index of Words Glossed at the end of the volume.

The critical and general notes in the present section are announced by the symbol, *cf. n.* ('confer notam'), at the bottom of the page of text to which each has reference. Names in parentheses at the end of notes indicate the authority for the information. No effort has been made to give precise credit either for information that has become common property or for that which, so far as known, is new in the present edition.

The Actors' Names. The first list of *dramatis personae* is found in the edition of 1676, which indicates the roles assumed by the actors of Thomas Betterton's company during Restoration performances of the play.

I.i.s.d. *Enter Bernardo and Francisco.* That is, they meet as the scene opens. The early editions regularly spell 'Barnardo,' which represents the Elizabethan pronunciation of the name.

I.i.3. *Long . . . king!* The pass-word or reply to the sentry's challenge.

I.i.16, 17. *Friends . . . Dane.* When challenged by Francisco (who is now off duty) Horatio and Marcellus reply 'Friends' and 'Countrymen,' and are not asked for the pass-word. Like *Denmark* in line 58 below and *Dane* in line 46 of the next scene, *Dane* here means the king of Denmark.

I.i.26. *piece.* A humorous expression equivalent to 'something like him.'

I.i.46. *his.* Regularly used for 'its.' The latter form had not yet come into common use.

I.i.51. *scholar.* Scholars (and particularly scholars of Dr. Faustus' university, Wittenberg) had special competence to deal with spirits.

I.i.54. *It . . . to.* It was believed that a ghost could not speak until spoken to.

I.i.75. *sleaded pole-axe.* The first two Quartos agree in spelling 'sleaded pollax'; the Folio has 'sledded Pollax.' There seems to be no allusion to the Poles or

'Polacks' mentioned later in the play, though the Folio compositor may have thought so.

I.i.82. *Good now.* Interjectional expression denoting entreaty.

I.i.100. *law and heraldry.* The forms of both the common law and the law of arms having been duly observed. Nobles who signed binding agreements were wont to attach heraldic seals.

I.i.101, 102. *lands . . . seiz'd of.* What Fortinbras staked was not his kingdom, but his personal landed possessions.

I.i.106. *cov'nant.* The Folio reading. Q2 has 'comart,' probably a misreading of Shakespeare's handwriting.

I.i.111. *list.* Literally, a special catalogue of the soldiers of a force; here used in the sense of an indiscriminately chosen crowd.

I.i.113. *hath a stomach.* I.e., gives an opportunity for courage. With a quibble on the literal meaning.

I.i.131. The Quarto compositor (our only authority here) seems to have inadvertently skipped a line, perhaps because it began in the same way as 132. The line here conjecturally substituted is based upon the passage Shakespeare was remembering, where Plutarch writes (in North's translation) 'concerning the fires in the element [*i.e.,* sky] and spirits running up and down in the night' before Cæsar's death.

I.i.134. *sick . . . doomsday.* Perhaps a reference to the Biblical account in Matthew 24. 29: 'Immediately after the tribulation of those days shall the sun be darkened, and the moon shall not give her light.'

I.i.135. *fear'd.* The Quarto has 'feare.' Final 'e' and 'd' were often indistinguishable in Elizabethan handwriting.

I.i.139. *climatures.* A rare derivative from 'climate,' here meaning about as much as 'latitudes.' The passage is an echo of *Julius Cæsar*, I.iii.31, 32, where Casca says of the omens:

'For I believe they are portentous things
Unto the climate that they point upon.'

I.i.150. *uphoarded.* If while alive a person had hidden gold and placed it under a charm, it was necessary, for his soul's quiet, to release it from the spell. (Illustrated by Steevens from Dekker's *Knight's Conjuring,* 1607.)

I.i.154. *partisan.* A long-handled spear with a blade having one or more lateral cutting projections.

I.i.167. *cock.* It was a tradition that at cockcrow spirits returned to their confines.

I.i.174–181. This beautiful passage of (apparently unrecorded) folklore, preserved in the bad first Quarto as well as in the two good texts, is quite irrelevant to the business of the scene. It is clearly not Christmas at Elsinore and the spirits do stir abroad. Perhaps Shakespeare wrote it in anticipation of a Christmas court performance of the play, at which it would have been both appropriate and reassuring to the audience.

I.i.179. *planets strike.* The malignant aspects of planets, according to the pseudo-science of astrology, were supposed to be able to injure incautious travellers by night.

I.ii.s.d. *cum aliis.* With such other characters as the theatre manager may think proper (an author's note). The same vague phrase occurs in II.ii.s.d. This stage direction, following that in Q2, seems to define the scene as a meeting of the new king and queen with an administrative board similar to the Elizabethan Privy Council (Dover Wilson). The business transacted is suitable to such a meeting.

I.ii.68. *kin . . . kind.* I.e., more than his actual kinship and less than a natural relation. 'Kind' is here used equivocally for 'natural' and also for 'affectionate.' A proverbial expression occurring elsewhere in Elizabethan literature.

I.ii.70. *i' th' sun.* Probably Hamlet means he is too much in the unwelcome sunshine of the King's favor. The reply is purposely enigmatical. There is a quibble on 'sun' and 'son.'

I.ii.116. *importune.* The early editions agree in reading *impart toward(s)*; but to impart toward a person with nobility of love has never been intelligible English and the passage has never been adequately explained. The emendation suggested is, graphically, not unlikely. Shakespeare seems to have been prone to improperly doubled consonants. In the *Sonnets* (set up from his autograph probably) one finds such spellings as 'crittick,' 'pittifull,' 'widdowed,' 'boddies,' 'immitated,' *etc.* If he wrote 'importtune' here, it could have been very easily read as 'impart tow'd.' For the phrase 'importune with love' compare the next scene, line 110.

I.ii.117. *Wittenberg.* A famous German university, founded in 1502.

I.ii.144. *Hyperion.* The Titanic sun god, but here used for Apollo.

I.ii.153. *Niobe.* A daughter of Tantalus, who boasted that she had more sons and daughters than Leto. Consequently Apollo and Artemis slew her children with arrows, and she herself was turned by Zeus into a stone upon Mount Sipylus in Lydia, where she shed tears all the summer long.

I.ii.166. *forget myself. I.e.,* or I have lost the knowledge even of myself.

I.ii.181. *to drink deep.* The Second Quarto reading, 'for to drink,' may well be what Shakespeare wrote.

I.ii.186. *bak'd meats.* It was an old custom to have a feast as part of the funeral ceremonies.

I.ii.207. *waste.* It here means emptiness, the time when no living thing was seen.

I.ii.227. *it head.* The neuter possessive, *it,* is not infrequent in Shakespeare, doubtless to avoid the ambiguity of *his.* See note on I.i.46.

I.iii.8. *violet.* Early violets were proverbial examples of transitory things.

I.iii.29. *place.* Instead of *particular act and place* the Folio reads 'peculiar Sect and force.'

I.iii.57. *double blessing. I.e.,* because Laertes had already taken leave of his father and received his blessing.

I.iii.60. *wind . . . in the shoulder of.* Wind blowing from a stern quarter, hence 'behind,' 'favorable.'

I.iii.62. *precepts.* Many parallels for several of these precepts have been discovered. The most striking are Lord Burghley's instructions to his son, Robert Cecil (printed in J. Strype, *Annals of the Reformation, etc.,* 1824, IV, pp. 475–479).

I.iii.78. *clef.* That is, the best bred Frenchmen are noted for striking the perfect tone in dress. Shakespeare uses the word twice elsewhere, spelling it 'cliff.' The early texts virtually agree in misprinting the line: 'Are (Q2 Or) of a most select and generous (Q1 generall) chiefe (F cheff) in that.' It has long been regarded as a puzzle.

I.iii.104. *tenders.* Polonius, in l. 111, uses 'tenders' in the sense of promises to pay, which, as he says, are not legal currency. In line 112 the word means 'value' and in line 114 *tender me* may mean 'present me with' or 'exhibit yourself as'; but by that time Polonius has lost control of the word.

I.iii.114. *Running.* The figure is that of making a horse broken-winded by over-riding. The word is the happy guess of nineteenth-century editors, Dyce and Collier. The Quarto reads 'Wrong' and the Folio 'Roaming.' (In Elizabethan handwriting 'w' may look very much like 'ru.')

I.iii.120. *woodcocks.* The woodcock was supposed to be a witless bird easily snared.

I.iii.135. *bawds.* One of the famous emendations of Lewis Theobald (1688–1744); 'bonds' in the original texts.

I.iv.35. *His.* So the text reads and it requires no change. Hamlet's attention turns from the group (*these men,* l. 32) to the typical individual.

I.iv.39. *oft adulter.* Another well known *crux.* The Second Quarto (again the only authority) reads *of a doubt* and has been variously emended. The reading here accepted is that of S. A. Tannenbaum (*Shaksperian Scraps,* 1933, p. 115). 'Adulter' for adulterate is a well established form, though not known to be used by Shakespeare elsewhere. If his manuscript abbreviated the last syllable in the common way (*oft adoult'*), the Quarto misprint is very easily explained.

I.iv.52. *inurn'd.* Put in an urn such as the Romans used for the ashes of their dead. There is a sharp inconsistency between this image and the previous one of bones bursting their cerements, but Shakespeare has the same confusion in *Henry V,* I.ii.232, 233 f.:

> lay these bones in an unworthy urn,
> Tombless, with no remembrance over them.

(Both the Quartos read 'interr'd.')

I.iv.91. *Nemean lion's.* One of the powerful monsters slain by Hercules.

I.v.25. *blazon.* Literally, to portray armorial bearings in their proper colors.

I.v.37. *the fat weed . . . Lethe wharf.* No particular weed, but an image of the absolute in vegetable nonchalance and inactivity. The Quarto reading, *rootes,* in line 38 is better than the Folio *rots.*

I.v.38. *Lethe.* A river (sometimes called a lake) of the Greek underworld, whose waters gave forgetfulness of the past to those who drank of them.

I.v.73. *gates and alleys.* Shakespeare here implies as much as was then known touching the circulation of the blood (Hudson).

I.v.86. *O horrible, etc.* The early texts print this line as part of the Ghost's speech, but the tradition of the stage is probably correct in assigning it to Hamlet. It was so spoken by, among others, Garrick, Kemble, and Irving. Betterton probably omitted it, for it is marked for omission in the Quarto of 1676.

I.v.150. *Saint Patrick.* He was the keeper of purgatory; the patron saint of all blunders and confusion (Moberly); he banished serpents from Ireland, hence he was the proper saint to take cognizance of the report that a serpent stung

Hamlet's father (Dowden). If Hamlet's oath requires any explanation, the first surmise appears the more probable.

I.v.152. *honest ghost. I.e.,* an actual ghost, and not the devil or an evil spirit in disguise. Note Hamlet's doubt upon this point later.

I.v.173. *sword.* It was customary to swear upon the sword, because the hilt made the form of the cross. Such an oath was binding both in military honor and in religion.

I.v.185. *your.* Does not mean Horatio's philosophy, but refers to philosophy in general. The Folio reads 'our.'

I.v.192. *With arms encumber'd thus, or this head-shake.* Mimicry goes with this, as Hamlet first folds his arms smugly and then nods his head.

II.i.45. *As 'twere a thing a little soil'd i' th' working.* As if Laertes were a gay new garment slightly smudged by the tailor's hands.

II.i.131. *More grief to hide than hate to utter love.* Polonius' syntax is more than usually overstrained as he attempts the oracular riming couplet. His meaning is: This love of Hamlet's must be made known, because if we kept it secret, more trouble might arise from its concealment than can displeasure from its revealing.

II.ii.11. *being of so young days brought up with him.* Rosencrantz and Guildenstern are noblemen who had been selected (as Kittredge remarks) to be Hamlet's schoolmates and playfellows when they were all children. Nothing indicates that they have been at the university. They appear to have been summoned to court from their country estates, quite in Queen Elizabeth's manner, and they arrive in some apprehension.

II.ii.47. *I hold my duty as I hold my soul, etc.* I think my duty, to both God and King, as important as my soul.

II.ii.65. *Upon our first.* Perhaps on hearing the first of the 'delated articles' mentioned in I.ii.38.

II.ii.77. *Gives him three thousand crowns in annual fee.* This line as here printed from the Folio has a Shakespearean rhythm that is destroyed in the Quarto version, 'Gives him threescore thousand crowns,' *etc.* Probably the Quarto printer felt, as modern editors have, that 3,000 crowns was not enough to wage a war; but an annual pension of that amount was a handsome encouragement (about equal to the thousand pounds Queen Elizabeth allowed her impoverished premier earl, the Earl of Oxford), and there is no reason to suppose that Norway means to subsidize the expedition. In any case, 60,000 crowns *in annual fee* (yearly income) would be fantastic.

II.ii.78. *his commission to employ those soldiers.* Something like the 'letters of marque' which make the difference between a privateer and a pirate.

II.ii.83. *regards . . . allowance. I.e.,* terms securing the safety of the country and regulating the passage of troops through it (Clarendon).

II.ii.120. *these, &.* That is, 'Deliver these lines.' The passage imitates the superscription of an Elizabethan letter.

II.ii.190. *fishmonger.* The word is probably used here in some cant coarse sense.

II.ii.198. *god kissing.* Bishop Warburton (1698–1779) suggested this emendation for 'good kissing' in the early editions. The sun's rays were supposed to engender maggots in dead flesh. Compare the reference to 'Titan' the sun god in *I Henry IV,* II.iv.108ff.

II.ii.209. *Between who?* Hamlet deliberately misunderstands 'matter' to mean a cause of dispute.

II.ii.213. *amber . . . gum.* In reference to the exudings from the weak eyes of old men.

II.ii.239, 240. *on . . . button.* That is, we have not reached the summit of good fortune.

II.ii.247. *strumpet.* Because of Fortune's fickleness.

II.ii.272. *beggars bodies. I.e.,* if ambition is but a shadow, then monarchs and heroes, who have attained ambition, are in possession only of a shadow; whereas beggars, who have not attained ambition, at least possess something material—*i.e.,* their bodies. But every beggar may long for ambition—a shadow—and hence the monarchs and heroes who are in possession of their ambitions, are but the beggars' shadows—*i.e.,* have this shadow for which the beggar longs in vain.

II.ii.282, 283. *too dear a halfpenny.* A little too dear. Even my poor thanks are worth more than the visitation for which I am thanking you, for that is not a genuine kindness.

II.ii.314. *quintessence.* A term in alchemy. The fifth essence of ancient and mediæval philosophy, supposed to be the substance of which the heavenly bodies were composed, and to be actually latent in all things: hence, pure essence or extract, essential part of a thing (O. E. D.)

II.ii.325, 326. *humorous man.* It would appear that there is particular reference here to the audience's interruption of Macilente's part in Jonson's *Every Man out of his Humour* when Shakespeare's company first produced that play in

1599. The following passage on the clown, like Hamlet's rebuke in III.ii.34ff., is doubtless pointed at Will Kempe, the popular comic actor and dancer, who left the company in displeasure shortly before Shakespeare's *Hamlet* was produced.

II.ii.327. *tickle o' the sere.* Literally, the 'sere' is the catch of a gunlock that holds the hammer. Hence a trigger that goes off at a light touch. The Folio spells: 'tickled a' th' sere'.

II.ii.335. *the late innovation.* The new popularity of the companies of child-actors, the Children of the Queen's Chapel and Children of Paul's, both of which re-opened their theatres about 1600.

II.ii.337. *the city.* London is meant. What follows is highly topical and refers to conditions during the 'War of the Theatres' of 1600 and 1601.

II.ii.341. *aery of children.* The Children of the Queen's Chapel are particularly meant.

II.ii.343. *common stages.* The public theatres, such as the Globe, which were less aristocratic than the private houses occupied by the children.

II.ii.344, 345. *afraid of goose-quills.* The goose-quills are the pens of satirical dramatists, especially Ben Jonson. His *Poetaster*, acted by the Chapel Children in 1601, is full of ridicule of the adult players, with whom he had temporarily quarrelled.

III.ii.359. *Hercules and his load.* The reference may be to the sign of the Globe Theatre which represented Hercules carrying the globe. The sign itself was an allusion to the story of Hercules relieving Atlas.

II.ii.374. *I know a hawk from a handsaw.* I know one thing from another. An old proverb. (A 'handsaw' is a hernshaw or heron.)

II.ii.385. *Roscius.* A famous Roman actor of Cicero's time, whose intellectual capacities lifted him above the stigma usually attached to his profession.

II.ii.393, 394. *scene individable.* A play which follows the classical rules relating to the three unities of time, place, and action.

II.ii.394. *poem unlimited.* A play which disregarded the unities. *Seneca.* A Roman writer of rhetorical tragedies (died 65 A.D.) whose plays were during the Renaissance considered models of classic technique. *Plautus.* A Roman comic dramatist of the third century B.C. who ranked with Terence as the model for comedy. Imitated by Shakespeare in *The Comedy of Errors.*

II.ii.395. *law of writ and the liberty.* Polonius may be only repeating the distinction between 'scene individable' and 'poem unlimited' above. It is possible that *law of writ* refers to rehearsed performances following the written text, and *liberty* to plays in which the dialogue was extemporized by the actors, as in the Italian *commedia dell' arte.*

II.ii.421. *Cracked . . . ring.* Having the circle broken that surrounds the sovereign's head on a coin. Here used quibblingly for a voice that has changed and hence is 'cracked' in its 'ring' or purity of tone. It is, of course, a boy actor of women's parts that Hamlet is addressing.

II.ii.428. *Caviary . . . general.* I.e., a delicacy (caviar) for which the general public had no relish.

II.ii.432, 433. *no sallets . . . savory.* No ribaldry to spice the lines.

II.ii.435. *handsome.* I.e., its beauty was not that of elaborate diction or polish, but that of structure and proportion.

II.ii.436. *Æneas' tale to Dido.* The passage inserted here should be compared with Marlowe's *Dido, Queen of Carthage* (1594), II.i.213 ff. It is a matter of critical dispute whether Shakespeare intended this passage as burlesque or whether he selected deliberately the earlier turgid romantic style to contrast with his more realistic dramatic method in this scene. The Marlowe play had been acted by the 'little eyases' (Children of the Chapel) and was probably still in their repertoire in 1601.

II.ii.440. *Hyrcanian beast.* The tiger. So described by Virgil. CF. *Æneid*, IV. 367.

II.ii.444. *ominous horse.* The wooden horse in which the Greeks lay hidden until the Trojans dragged it within the walls.

II.ii.517. *God's bodkin.* A corruption of an oath 'by God's body.'

II.ii.524. *the Murther of Gonzago.* No such play is recorded, but S. A. Tannenbaum has dealt with two historical murders in the Gonzaga family (*Shakspere Assoc. Bull.*, xvi, 1941, 169–74).

II.ii.527. *some dozen or sixteen lines.* A colloquial way of indicating an uncertain small number, as we say 'ten or twelve' (Hamlet has not yet written the speech). So Baxter says: 'When he had been a preacher about twelve or sixteen years.'

II.ii.548. *cue.* A technical stage term for the last words of an actor's line to which another actor replied.

II.ii.556. *John-a-dreams.* Armin's *Nest of Ninnies* (1608) contains the following definition: 'His name is John, indeed, says the cynic; but neither John-a-nods, nor John-a-dreams, yet either as you take it, for he is simply simple without tricks.'

II.ii.558. *property.* His crown, his wife, everything, in short, which he might be said to be possessed of, except his life (Furness).

II.ii.565. *pigeon-liver'd.* It was believed that pigeons were gentle because they had no gall.

II.ii.572. *murthered.* Pronounce in three syllables. Only the bad First Quarto has 'father', which is not needed.

III.i.14. *Niggard of question, etc.* This report differs wholly from the facts. Rosencrantz and Guildenstern are not malign, but they have to save their faces.

III.i.63. *To be, or not to be.* To live or die. This is the lowest point that Hamlet's melancholy reaches. In the suspense with which he awaits the outcome of his test, he loses the glad assurance with which he closed Act II (the day before), and allows himself to wonder how any sensitive person can consent to endure the humiliations of life. He argues, however, in general terms, not in terms of his own situation.

III.i.66. *take . . . troubles.* Many commentators have felt that this line contains a badly mixed metaphor and consequently have suggested various unnecessary emendations. The phrase 'sea of troubles,' in the sense of a 'mass of troubles,' however, occurs elsewhere in Elizabethan literature. Cf. Greene's *Mamillia*, ed. Grosart, vol. II., p. 18; "hauing himself escaped the sea of trouble and care," and Dekker's *The Wonder of a Kingdome*, ed. 1873. vol. IV., p. 230:

> *I never heard mongst all your Romane spirits,*
> *That any held so bravely up his head,*
> *In such a sea of troubles (that come rouling*
> *One on anothers necke) as Lotti doth.*

III.i.76. *makes calamity of so long life.* Makes affliction (*i.e.*, the afflicted person) live so long.

III.i.77. *For who would bear, etc.* The miseries specified are more those of man in general than of the Prince of Denmark. (In line 79 the Quarto reads *despiz'd*.)

III.i.83. *a bare bodkin.* This may mean 'a mere pin' or 'an unsheathed dagger.' The former is more forceful.

III.i.87. *No traveller returns.* The ghost is ignored. In this soliloquy Hamlet's mind is curiously stripped of the religious ideas and implications which usually mark it.

III.i.125, 126. *virtue cannot so inoculate our old stock.* A figure from the grafting of apples, with a hint at Eve's apple and original sin. Acquired virtue may be grafted on the old sinful tree ('stock'), but the fruit will still taste of man's fall.

III.i.128. *Get thee to a nunnery.* For which Ophelia's devotional apparatus and attitude qualify her. The sense of futility expressed in the preceding soliloquy here turns to misanthropy.

III.i.136. *Where's your father?* Hamlet here sees Polonius, and in line 153 ('all but one') he sees the king. There is no reason to believe that he is aware of their presence earlier.

III.i.150. *nickname.* I.e., by painting your face and by your fashionable affectations you turn human beings (God's creatures) into figures that bear the same resemblance to reality that a nickname does to a Christian name. Or possibly this is an allusion to the Elizabethan court fashion of giving animal names to the various courtiers.

III.ii.9. *groundlings.* The inferior portion of the audience who paid a penny for standing room in the yard or pit. *Hamlet* was written for a courtly, not a popular, audience, and perhaps in deliberate effort to establish the prestige which the 'little eyases' were endangering.

III.ii.10, 11. *inexplicable dumb-shows.* Pantomimes illustrating the subsequent action of the play, such as began each act of *Gorboduc* and other early tragedies.

III.ii.12. *Termagant.* A noisy character representing a supposed god of the Saracens in some of the mystery plays.

III.ii.12. *out-herods Herod.* I.e., outdoes even the extravagant acting of Herod, the most violent and declamatory figure in the mystery plays. Cf. the stage direction in the Coventry play of the *Magi and Herod*, 'Here Herod rages in the pageant, and in the street also.'

III.ii.35, 36. *there be of them, etc.* Examples of gags and stage business introduced by clowns are found in a contemporary anonymous play, *The Pilgrimage to Parnassus*, Act V, ll. 680 ff.: 'if thou canst but draw thy mouth awry, lay thy leg over thy staff, saw a piece of cheese asunder with thy dagger, lap up drink on the earth, I warrant thee they'll laugh mightily.'

III.ii.64. *co-mingled.* The Folio reading. Q2 has *comedled* (commeddled), which would mean the same thing.

III.ii.65. *a pipe for fortune's finger, etc.* This image of the 'recorder' is elaborately developed later in the scene, ll. 344 ff.

III.ii.76. *in one speech.* While one speech of the play is being spoken. Claudius is not expected to make a speech (cf. lines 79–86 below), but to betray his guilt by the look on his face.

III.ii.79. *Vulcan.* He was the armorer of the gods.

III.ii.86. *be idle.* In Hall's Chronicle, the phrase 'idle and weak in his wit' occurs (*O.E.D.*).

III.ii.92. *chameleon's dish.* It was believed that chameleons fed on air. (Hamlet takes the King's question in the sense, 'How are you being fed?')

III.ii.100. *Julius Cæsar.* The universities gave many representations within their walls of plays in Latin and occasionally English. A Latin play on Cæsar's death by Richard Edes was acted at Christ Church, Oxford, in 1582. See also the title-page of the 1603 Quarto of Hamlet.

III.ii.102. *Capitol.* The murder of Cæsar actually took place in the Theatre of Pompey, which stood in the Campus Martius. Shakespeare transfers the scene to the Capitol both in *Julius Cæsar* and in *Antony and Cleopatra.*

III.ii.112. *country.* For the hidden pun see Farmer & Henley, *Slang and its Analogues,* ii. p. 230.

III.ii.123. *twice two months.* This implies that about two months have passed since the opening of the play (cf. I.ii.142). Most of this time elapsed in the interval between Act I and Act II.

III.ii.124, 125. *I'll have a suit of sables.* Hamlet's persiflage is ambiguous. Sable fur was brown and connoted not mourning but wealth and elegance, but 'sable' as an adjective in heraldry meant black. The sense of the double talk is perhaps (1) Let the devil now wear my black mourning, for I'll be dressed like a normal prince; (2) Let the devil wear black, for I shall be dressed just like him.

III.ii.129. *hobby-horse.* In the morris dance, a figure of a horse made of light material and fastened around the waist of a performer, who went through various antics. The quotation here may be from a ballad perhaps satirizing Puritan opposition to May-games.

III.ii.144. *miching Malicho.* The Quarto has *munching Mallico.* The second word is usually taken to be Spanish 'malbecho,' which does mean 'mischief' or 'misdeed.' Eric Partridge ('Some Romany Words,' London *Times Literary Supplement,* Dec. 26, 1936) argues for a Gypsy origin.

III.ii.161. *Tellus'.* The goddess of the earth, who received and nourished the sown seed. *Orbed ground* is the round earth.

III.ii.225. *Sport and repose.* Here the objects of the verb.

III.ii.245. *Tropically.* By means of a trope or figure of speech; but the bad First Quarto prints 'Trapically,' which (with reference to the Mousetrap) is what Hamlet secretly means.

III.ii.246, 247. *duke's name.* In the First Quarto the leading characters are called Duke and Duchess. In the Second Quarto and the Folio, except for this line, they are always King and Queen.

III.ii.253. *interpret.* At puppet shows or 'motions' the dialogue was spoken by a person concealed behind the stage. This was called 'interpreting.' The classic example is the 'motion' of Hero and Leander presented by Lanthorn Leatherhead in Jonson's *Bartholomew Fair* (1614), V.iv.

III.ii.258. *So you must take your husbands.* That is, 'for better, for worse.' The good texts here have 'mistake' for *must take,* found only in the bad First Quarto.

III.ii.259, 260. *the croaking . . . revenge.* Parody of a non-Shakespearean play of 1594, *The True Tragedy of Richard the Third* (Malone *Society* reprint, ll. 1892f.)

The screeking raven sits croking for revenge,
Whole herds of beasts come bellowing for revenge.

III.ii.265. *Hecate.* Diana, in her aspect as infernal goddess, was regarded as the queen of witches. Pronounce 'Hecat's'.

III.ii.278. *deer go weep.* It was a popular belief that the deer, when badly wounded, retires from the herd and goes apart to weep and die. See *As You Like It,* II.i.34–41.

III.ii.283. *Provincial roses.* So called from Provins, a town forty miles from Paris.

III.ii.284. *cry.* Literally, a pack of hounds—here, troop or company.

III.ii.285. *share.* Theatrical companies were organized on a profit-sharing basis. The controlling members were called 'sharers' and the original 'shares' could be subdivided.

III.ii.287. *Damon.* An allusion to the classical story of the friendship of Damon and Pythias (or Phintias), dramatized by Richard Edwards in a play printed in 1571.

III.ii.290. *pajock.* 'A king of shreds and patches,' as Hamlet calls him a little later (iv.115). The word has nothing to do with peacock, but is the same that Spenser uses, in the form 'patchock' or 'patchcock' to describe the degenerate English in Ireland. The realm, Hamlet says, has been 'dismantled' of his father (as if gorgeous raiment had been removed), and now they have in his place a ragamuffin. (The *O.E.D.* has conjecturally explained this, but editors have ignored the explanation.)

III.ii.305. *distempered.* This word was used both of mental and of bodily disorder. Hamlet pretends to understand it in the latter sense.

III.ii.307. *choler.* The other meaning of 'choler' is bilious disorder, and so again Hamlet pretends to misunderstand it.

III.ii.309. *purgation.* Another word of double meaning: (1) clearing from the accusation or suspicion of guilt; (2) purging in the medical sense.

III.ii.317, 318. *this courtesy is not of the right breed.* Guildenstern does not think Hamlet to be mad and he knows that he is being laughed at. Here, with real dignity, he withdraws from the conversation and leaves Rosencrantz to take it up.

III.ii.337. *pickers and stealers.* An allusion to the phrase in the Catechism, 'To keep my hands from picking and stealing.'

III.ii.344. *'While . . . grows.'* A proverb of frequent occurrence. Cf. Heywood's *Proverbs* "while the grass groweth the horse sterveth," and Whetstone's *Promos and Cassandra* (1578), "Whylst grass doth growe, oft sterves the seely steede."

III.ii.346. *recover the wind of.* A hunting term, meaning to frighten the game by approaching in the direction of the wind.

III.ii.356. *I know no touch of it.* Guildenstern is emphatic. Wind instruments were not in favor with fine gentlemen. They distorted the mouth.

III.ii.369. *fret.* Frets are stops of instruments of the lute or guitar kind. Hamlet also uses it quibblingly to mean 'annoy.'

III.ii.382. *the top of my bent.* An expression derived from archery; the bow has its 'bent' when it is drawn as far as it can be. Compare II.ii.32.

III.ii.393. *Nero.* He murdered his mother, Agrippina.

III.iii.7. *braves.* The Quarto reading is 'browes,' for which the Folio substitutes (apparently in desperation) 'Lunacies.' The word here accepted is an ancient anonymous conjecture, independently revived in *Yale Review* (March, 1935, p. 620) and in the Parrott-Craig ed. (1938).

III.iii.18. *It is a massy wheel, etc.* This passage is an interesting development of the earlier image of Fortune's wheel (II.ii.485–487).

III.iii.32. *as you said.* Polonius knows that the proposal came from himself. Compare III.i.186–190.

III.iii.40. *primal.* The curse of Cain. Cf. Genesis 4. 11: 'And now art thou cursed from the earth, which hath opened her mouth to receive thy brother's blood from thy hand.'

III.iii.64. *lies.* Is sustainable as an action at law.

III.iii.76. *pat.* This famous word is not in the Quarto text, which has 'but' instead.

III.iii.82. *hire and salary.* The Folio reading. Q2 has 'base and silly.'

III.iv.110. *vice.* The Vice was a stock character in the Moralities and Interludes. Although personifying the weaker side of human nature, he was represented as a buffoon and supplied much of the comic element in these plays.

III.iv.115. *A king of shreds and patches.* A mock king dressed in oddments of costume, such as one might see in a peasant folk-play. This line points the contrast with the ghost, who here enters in peaceful dress—'in his nightgown,' or robe of velvet and fur, according to Q1.

III.iv.186. *tame.* A word has dropped out of the Quarto text.

III.iv.212. *The famous ape.* The moral of this unidentified parable is that the Queen will destroy herself, if she allows Hamlet's secrets (the birds) to get abroad or attempts to introduce herself into his business.

III.iv.230. *packing.* A pun: (1) preparing for my journey; (2) plotting, using my wits (Dover Wilson).

III.v.4. The Folio text indicates that the King enters alone to the Queen after Hamlet has dragged out Polonius' body (without any change of scene).

III.v.7. *Mad as the sea and wind, etc.* The queen's report attempts to free Hamlet of responsibility for Polonius' death. She does not really think him mad, but avoids doing what Hamlet has instructed her not to do. See III.iv.199–207.

III.v.41. *So, haply, slander.* Added by Theobald and Capell.

III.vi.17. *like an ape an apple.* A composite reading suggested by Farmer. The Second Quarto has 'like an apple,' the Folio 'like an Ape,' the bad First Quarto 'as an Ape doth nuttes.'

III.vi.26. *The . . . body.* A passage about which there have been many conjectures. If Hamlet is not designedly talking mere nonsense, a possible interpretation is: "The King is still alive (*i.e.,* with *his* body), but he is not with the dead body (*i.e.,* of Polonius)."

III.vi.29, 30. *a thing . . . of nothing.* Quoting the Prayer Book version of Psalm 144. 4, 'Man is like a thing of nought.'

III.vi.30. *Hide fox, and all after.* Added in the Folio, probably to motivate Hamlet's sudden rush from the stage. Compare that of King Lear, *Lear,* IV.vi.198, 199.

III.vii.23. *convocation.* Perhaps an allusion to the famous Diet or convocation of the dignitaries of the German Empire held at Worms in 1521. It was before this Diet that Martin Luther was summoned to appear.

IV.i.s.d. Here the Folio omits the Gentleman, no doubt, as Collier suggested, to avoid the employment of another actor. A time interval of about a month

occurs at this point, and this is the logical place to begin Act IV. Most editors continue the eighteenth century act division, which begins Act IV with III.v, because it has become conventional. (This was apparently Betterton's division, being indicated in the text of 1676.)

IV.i.S.d. The direction in the First Quarto of 1603 is, 'Enter Ofelia playing on a lute, and her haire downe, singing.' This is the basis for the traditional stage-business.

IV.i.26. *cockle hat.* The cockle hat, staff, and sandals were the guise of a pilgrim and often the disguise of a lover. Cf. Romeo's costume at the ball in *Romeo and Juliet.* The hat was so called from the custom of putting cockle-shells upon pilgrims' hats. The shell was used to denote that the pilgrim had been to the shrine of St. James of Compostella in Spain.

IV.i.40. *did—not—go.* The word *not* breaks the rhythm of the song and is perhaps Ophelia's comment on the lack of ceremonious burial for Polonius.

IV.i.43, 44. *owl ... daughter.* There is an old mediæval legend that a baker's daughter was turned into an owl for refusing bread to our Lord (Douce).

IV.i.98. *Switzers.* The Pope and the kings of France employed Swiss mercenaries as guards. The term 'Switzer' gradually became almost synonymous with 'guard.'

IV.i.152. *swoopstake.* A gambling term used when the winner clears the board of all the stakes.

IV.i.157. *life-rendering pelican.* It was a common belief that the pelican fed its young with its own blood. It was thus an emblem of family devotion.

IV.i.174–176. *Nature is fine in love, etc.* When we love, nature refines or subtilizes us so that some precious part of ourselves goes like an 'instance' (memento or farewell gift) after what we love. Thus Ophelia's wits have followed Polonius in death.

IV.i.178. *Hey non nonny.* Such meaningless refrains are common in old songs. Cf. 183, 'a-down.'

IV.i.185. *wheel.* Although this word is usually rendered 'burden,' 'refrain,' it is possible that Ophelia is referring to singing at the spinning wheel.

IV.i.185. *false steward.* This ballad or story is unknown.

IV.i.188. *rosemary.* Flower symbolism was an elaborate system in mediæval and Elizabethan England. Cf. *The Handfull of Pleasant Delights* (1584):

> *Rosemarie* is for remembrance,
> betweene vs daie and night:
> Wishing that I might alwaies haue
> you present in my sight.

Rosemary was often strewn on biers. Cf. *Winter's Tale,* IV.iv.74.

IV.i.189. *pansies.* French, *pensées;* a country emblem of love and courtship.

IV.i.193. *herb of grace.* Simply another popular name for rue. Cf. *Richard II,* III.iv.109, 110:

> *I'll set a bank of rue, sour herb of grace;*
> *Rue, even for ruth, here shortly shall be seen.*

IV.i.194. *difference.* An heraldic bearing, distinguishing the arms of one branch of the same family from another. Ophelia implies that for the Queen rue signifies the remembrance of things to be repented, for herself regret.

IV.i.197. *For ... joy.* The music for this song is contained in Anthony Holborne's *Citharn Schoole* (1597) and other collections. The words have not been found.

IV.iii.9. *As by your safety, greatness, wisdom, all things.* The Quarto adds *els* (else) at the end of the line, a weak superfluity probably due to scribe or compositor. The Folio keeps *else,* but omits *greatness* to make the line scan.

IV.iii.22. *Work.* The Second Quarto reading, certainly correct. The Folio has 'Would,' probably the printer's accidental anticipation of that word in line 25. Shakespeare would not willingly, and no editor should, put 'Would ... wood' in the same line.

IV.iii.22. *spring.* There are several springs in England whose water is so heavily charged with lime that they will petrify with a deposit of lime any object placed in them. There is one at King's Newnham in Warwickshire and another at Knaresborough in Yorkshire.

IV.iii.25. *reverted.* I.e., the 'loud wind' of popular affection for Hamlet would have caused Claudius' shafts to recoil upon himself.

IV.iii.29. *praises ... again.* I.e., if praises may return to what is now no more, *viz.,* Ophelia's former charms.

IV.iii.30. *challenger-on-mount.* I.e., her worth challenged all the age to deny her perfection.

IV.iii.43. *Claudio.* A character who does not appear in the play. Cf. IV.ii.29.

IV.iii.83. *siege.* Literally 'seat,' thence 'rank,' because people sat at table in order of precedence.

IV.iii.95. *incorps'd and demi-natur'd.* I.e., like a Centaur, half horse, half man. Literally, of one body with and half partaking of the nature of his horse.

IV.iii.97. *in ... tricks.* I.e., I cannot describe so many proofs of dexterity as he performed.

IV.iii.101. *Lamound.* So the Folio calls him; the Quarto 'Lamord.'

IV.iii.106. *masterly report.* A report describing Laertes as a master of fence.

IV.iii.115. *to play with you.* That he might fence with you. Not understanding, the Folio adopts the easier reading, 'to play with him.'

IV.iii.124. *passages of proof.* Instances from practical experience of the world.

IV.iii.129. *plurisy.* Often used where today one would say 'plethora' (because of a false association with Latin *plus*).

IV.iii.134. *spendthrift's sigh.* A satisfactory paraphrase has not been suggested. The general meaning is probably that the recognition of a 'should' when it is too late is like a wasteful or supererogatory sigh of the spendthrift who recalls his lost opportunities. The sighs are also spendthrifts on the old notion that each one drained blood from the heart (cf. *M.N.D.,* III.ii.98).

IV.iii.155. *mountebank.* These men were quack-doctors who journeyed from town to town selling miraculous remedies and forbidden poisons. The classical account of their procedure is given in Ben Jonson's play, *Volpone,* Act II. sc. ii.

IV.iii.159. *moon.* It was believed that to gather herbs by moonlight added to their medicinal value. It is possible, however, that here the meaning is simple 'on earth.'

IV.iii.166. *that our drift look through our bad performance.* If our design should become visible by the bad execution of the plot. The image is apparently of the moon looking through thin clouds.

IV.iii.168. *a back or second.* Support or auxiliary. The king and Laertes are bungling plotters, unused and by temperament unsuited to the niceties of crime.

IV.iii.185. *crowflowers.* It is probable that Shakespeare is still carrying on his flower symbolism in the garlands worn by Ophelia. Thus the crowflower was also called 'the fair maid of France'; long purples were said to represent the cold hand of death; nettles meant 'stung to the quick'; and the daisy sometimes imported 'pure virginity' or 'spring of life' (Parkinson).

IV.iii.206. *woman.* I.e., when these tears are shed the woman in me, what I have inherited from my mother, will have come out.

V.i.S.d. *Clowns.* The term applies both to peasants and to actors of low comedy rôles. It seems likely that this scene was inspired by a local incident which occurred when Shakespeare was in his sixteenth year. Katharine Hamlet (*sic*), spinster, was drowned in the River Avon, Dec. 17, 1579, and the coroner's jury sat on her for eight weeks, at last finding it Christian burial. (See E. I. Fripp, *Shakespeare Studies,* 1930, pp. 128–136; and for text of the inquest *Minutes & Accounts of the Corporation of Stratford-upon-Avon,* 1926, vol. iii. p. 50.)

V.i.8. *se offendendo.* The clown's mistake for *se defendendo,* which would itself be a mistake, since this was the verdict in the case of justifiable homicide, not, of course, suicide.

V.i.29. *bore arms.* A quibble on bearing a coat of arms and the literal meaning.

V.i.35. *confess thyself.* Half of an old proverb. The rest was 'and be hanged.' Or possibly 'confess thyself a fool.'

V.i.48. *unyoke.* Literally, 'you may then free your cattle from the yoke'; hence, 'call it a day's work.'

V.i.55. *Yaughan.* Phonetic Danish for 'John' (Johan). The name is in the Folio text, but not in the Quarto, which reads simply, 'Go, get thee *in', etc.* It may be a local joke, added by the actors. Jonson's *Alchemist,* acted by Shakespeare's company at the Blackfriars theatre in 1610, refers to 'an ale-house darker than deaf John's' as if the latter were well and unfavorably known. If Yaughan and deaf John kept the same establishment, this reference cannot be earlier than 1609, when Shakespeare's company began using the Blackfriars.

V.i.57. *In ... love.* This song, by Lord Vaux, is found in Tottel's *Miscellany* (1557) under the title *The aged louer renounceth loue,* although the Clown sings a confused and blundering version of it.

V.i.63. *property of easiness.* I.e., custom has made it natural to him to take his task easily.

V.i.71, 72. Legend asserted that Cain slew Abel with the jaw-bone of an ass.

V.i.73. *o'erreaches.* A quibble on two meanings: (1) 'paws over,' (2) 'outwits.' This is the Quarto reading; the Folio has 'o'er-offices.'

V.i.79. *went to beg it.* This is the reading of the Second Quarto, justified by *O.E.D. (Go* 34,b). The Folio changes 'went' to 'meant,' which looks like a printer's emendation.

V.i.84. *loggats.* A game in which thick sticks are thrown to lie as near as possible to a stake fixed in the ground or to a block of wood on a floor.

V.i.92. *tenures.* The act, right, or manner of holding, as real estate, property of a superior; manner in, or period for, which anything is had and enjoyed. As the present passage shows, Shakespeare's knowledge of legal terminology was

broad, but it was not extraordinary for his time or minutely professional. (See P. S. Clarkson and C. T. Warren, *The Law of Property in Shakespeare and the Elizabethan Drama*, 1942.)

V.i.94. *action of battery.* Right to sue for an unlawful attack by beating and wounding.

V.i.96. *statutes.* Particular modes of recognizance or acknowledgment for securing debts, which thereby became a charge upon the party's land (Ritson).

V.i.96. *recognizances.* Bonds or obligations of record testifying the recognizor to owe to the recognizee a certain sum of money.

V.i.96. *vouchers.* Persons who are called upon to warrant a tenant's title.

V.i.97. *fines, recoveries.* Processes by which entailed estates were commonly transferred from one party to another.

V.i.100. *the length . . . indentures.* That is, a couple of his legal papers will cover all the ground he has left; *i.e.,* his grave.

V.i.101. *conveyances.* Documents by which transference of property is effected.

V.i.106. *assurance.* Also used with quibble on its legal meaning 'evidence of the conveyance or settlement of property.'

V.i.125, 126. *by the card.* The card on which the thirty-two points of the mariner's compass are marked.

V.i.126, 127. *this three years . . . the age is grown so picked.* There is a temptation to associate this with the era of social sophistication which became strikingly articulate in Jonson's *Every Man in his Humor* (1598). Compare the talk of contemporary drama in II.ii.339 ff.

V.i.159. *three-and-twenty years.* We have here further testimony in support of the Clown's earlier statement (lines 134, 135, 149, 150 f.) that Hamlet was about thirty years old. This is evidently purposed and is not contradicted by anything else in the play. Shakespeare may, however, have begun with the idea of a younger prince and have been brought to emphasize his maturity at the end, both by the way the character developed and by the consideration that Richard Burbage (born about 1567) was outgrowing youthful parts.

V.i.166. *Sir Yorick's.* The text follows the Quarto. Yorick was not a knight, but, from the Clown at least, may well rate the honorific awarded to country parsons and bachelors of arts. The name might be meant for George (Georg) as pronounced in Danish. Relations between London and Denmark were close in Queen Elizabeth's reign, and grew closer when James I, with his Danish queen, came to the throne in 1603.

V.i.200. *but soft awhile!* This, the reading of the Second Quarto, is probably what Shakespeare first wrote. The Folio version, 'but soft, aside,' works the necessary business of stepping aside into the line, but that action is covered by line 228.

V.i.214. *And but that great command o'ersways the order.* Except that sovereign power (the king's command) prevails over the rules of the religious order to which the priest belongs. (He corroborates the suspicion of the Clowns in lines 24–30.) Here as elsewhere in the play, the tone is Catholic. In Q2 the priest's two speeches are assigned to '*Doct.,*' whatever that may mean.

V.i.215. *should . . . been lodg'd.* This old-fashioned construction, perfectly normal in earlier English, was modernized in the Folio 'should . . . have lodg'd.'

V.i.218. *crants.* German *Kranz* (singular, not plural). Garlands appear to have been borne before the bodies of unmarried women to the grave, and were hung up in church.

V.i.244. *Pelion.* Pelion, Olympus, and Ossa (l. 279) are three mountains in the north of Thessaly. The Titans, warring with the gods, are said to have attempted to pile Ossa on Pelion in an effort to scale Olympus.

V.i.250. *Hamlet the Dane.* Thus naming himself, he asserts his royal rank and further infuriates Laertes. The stage direction accompanying this line is found only in the bad First Quarto.

V.i.284. *golden couplets.* The dove lays but two eggs and the young, when first disclosed, are covered with a yellow down. Cf. III.i.168 f.

V.ii.14. *sea-gown.* 'A coarse, high-collared and short-sleeved gown, reaching down to the mid leg, and used most by seamen and sailors' (Onions).

V.ii.23. *bugs . . . life. I.e.,* with such enumeration of bugbears and imaginary terrors if Hamlet were allowed to live.

V.ii.32, 33. *prologue . . . play. I.e.,* before I had formed any real plan, my brains had begun their work.

V.ii.45. *comma.* A symbol of relation between two parts of the same whole.

V.ii.46. *'As'es.* A quibble on 'as,' the conditional particle, and 'ass,' the beast of burden.

V.ii.65. *pass and fell-incensed points.* Hendiadys: the angrily thrusting sword points.

V.ii.70. *election.* The Danish throne was elective.

V.ii.89. *water-fly.* Used for a vain or idly busy person, but probably also with reference to the gaudy attire of the foolish courtier.

V.ii.94. *mess.* 'One of the groups of persons, normally four, into which the company at a banquet was divided' (Onions).

V.ii.109. *remember.* The phrase 'remember thy courtesy' (*i.e.,* remember that you are bareheaded) was a conventional one for 'be covered.' Cf. *Love's Labour's Lost,* V.i.82.

V.ii.110. *my ease.* This again was the conventional apologetic reply for declining the invitation of 'remember thy courtesy.'

V.ii.118. *yaw.* Nautical figure: to make way sideward, as from bad steering.

V.ii.127. *another tongue.* Any tongue but his own.

V.ii.154. *edified by the margent.* Equivalent to looking up a word in the glossary. It was customary to print explanatory matter in the margins of Elizabethan books.

V.ii.165. *twelve for nine.* The exact details of this wager are a matter of doubt.

V.ii.185. *fond and winnowed.* So the Folio, meaning perhaps 'foolish and trite (well sifted).' The Quarto reads *prophane and trennowed,* the latter word being an easy misreading of 'winnowed.' This portion of the play was largely unintelligible to the printers of both the early texts.

V.ii.234. *satisfied in nature.* Though his natural anger as a son is satisfied with Hamlet's explanation, yet his artificial honor as a courtier requires that the matter shall be adjudicated.

V.ii.247. *foil.* That which sets something off to advantage, with a quibble on the meaning 'fencing foil.'

V.ii.263. *quit. I.e.,* requite Laertes' winning of the first two bouts be gaining the third.

V.ii.306.S.d. The usual method of representing upon the stage this exchange of rapiers is as follows: With a quick thrust Hamlet disarms Laertes. As the foil drops, Hamlet places his foot upon it, and, with a bow, offers Laertes his own in exchange. Courtesy compels Laertes to accept this, after which Hamlet stoops, picks up Laertes' foil from the ground, and resumes the bout. For a technical discussion see James L. Jackson, 'The Exchange of Weapons in *Hamlet*' (*Mod. Lang. Notes,* Jan., 1942).

V.ii.350. *Roman.* It was a Roman custom to follow masters in death. See *Julius Caesar,* V. iii; *A. & C.,* IV. xii.

V.ii.362. *This warlike volley.* This suggests that the 'shout' mentioned in the Folio s.d. at line 352 should be 'shot.'

V.ii.369. *solicited.* The sentence is left unfinished.

V.ii.376. *cries on havoc.* Originally, to give an army the order 'havoc!' as the signal for pillaging.

V.ii.414. *royal.* The word is very strongly stressed, almost drawn out to three syllables. The Folio weakens by changing it to 'royally.'

V.ii.416. *Speak.* A command: let music, *etc.,* speak.

The Tragedy of Othello

THE MOOR OF VENICE

Edited by TUCKER BROOKE
and
LAWRENCE MASON

Dramatis Personae

OTHELLO, *the Moor*

BRABANTIO, *Father to Desdemona*

CASSIO, *an honorable Lieutenant*

IAGO, *a Villain ['ancient' or standard-bearer,
    and third in command to Othello]*

RODERIGO, *a gulled Gentleman*

DUKE OF VENICE

SENATORS

MONTANO, *Governor of Cyprus*

GENTLEMEN OF CYPRUS

LODOVICO } *two noble Venetians [Kinsman and*
GRATIANO } *Brother, respectively, to Brabantio]*

SAILORS

CLOWN, *[in Othello's retinue]*

DESDEMONA, *Wife to Othello
    [and Daughter to Brabantio]*

EMILIA, *Wife to Iago*

BIANCA, *a Courtesan*

MESSENGERS, HERALD OFFICERS, MUSICIANS,
    AND ATTENDANTS

SCENE—*Act I, at Venice; Acts II-V,
    at a sea-port (Famagosta) in Cyprus.*

The Tragedy of Othello

INTRODUCTION

SOURCES OF THE PLAY

Furness cites two actual historical personages who have been named as possible models for Shakespeare's Othello. (1) Christopher Moro, a heroic Venetian general, returned to Venice in 1508 from the lord-lieutenancy of Cyprus, after the failure of 'an hypothetical' or threatened Turkish attack on the island, in mourning for his recently deceased wife. (2) San Pietro di Bastelica, an Italian adventurer of great distinction in the service of France, in 1563 returned abruptly from a mission to Constantinople (to beg assistance for the Corsicans from the Turks) because of artfully circulated reports of his innocent wife's infidelity; thereupon, after a scene of mingled tenderness and ferocity on his part and gentle submission on hers, he asked pardon upon his knees for the deed he was about to commit and then deliberately strangled her with her handkerchief. The stories of both these personages may well have been retailed in England within Shakespeare's hearing and so may have influenced him; but the chief accepted source for the play remains a prose tale by Cinthio.

Giovanbattista Giraldi, called Cinthio, was a sixteenth-century novelist, poet, dramatist, and university professor of Ferrara who compiled, and published at Monteregale, Sicily, in 1565, an edifying 'philosophical' work wherein ten moral virtues or their opposites are illustrated by ten appropriate tales apiece,—thence entitled *Hecatommithi (The Hundred Fables).* The seventh novel of the third decade is the source of *Othello;* but Shakespeare, unless we credit him with a knowledge of Italian or French (a French translation appeared in 1583) or Spanish (a Spanish translation appeared in 1590), seemingly gained his acquaintance with the *Hecatommithi* at second hand, for no English translation of the work in the sixteenth or seventeenth centuries is known to us.

Cinthio gives a name to none of his prototypes of Shakespeare's characters except the heroine, who is called 'Disdemona.' Othello is simply 'the Moor,' Iago 'the Ensign,' Cassio 'the Captain of the troop' or 'the Captain,' Emilia 'the Ensign's wife,' and Bianca 'a courtesan,' while Brabantio, Lodovico, Gratiano, Montano, Roderigo, the Duke, and the Clown do not appear, and on the other hand 'the Captain of the troop' is provided with an unnamed wife. Cinthio's narrative may be summarized thus, for the sake of the instructive lesson it affords in Shakespeare's method of plot-construction:—

Despite parental opposition, Disdemona loved and married a valiant Moor who had rendered distinguished military service to the Venetian state, and the two lived happily together in Venice for some time, till the Senate appointed the Moor to the command of the troops being sent out as a new garrison for Cyprus. Rather than be separated from her husband, Disdemona insisted upon sharing the perils of the voyage. They accordingly set sail and in due time 'with a perfectly tranquil sea arrived safely at Cyprus.'[1] Now a wicked Ensign among the soldiery, of whose

wife Disdemona became very fond, fell passionately in love with the Moor's wife and 'bent all his thoughts to achieve his conquest; . . . but she, whose every wish was centred in the Moor, had no thought for this Ensign more than for any other man.' The Ensign, ascribing his failure to a certain Captain of a troop to whom Disdemona had always shown great kindness, because of the Moor's affection for him, determined to revenge himself by bringing about the death of the Captain and destroying the Moor's love for the lady. 'Not long afterwards it happened that the Captain, having drawn his sword upon a soldier of the guard, and struck him,' was punished by being deprived of his rank; Disdemona's impulsive intercession thereupon, out of mere friendliness and concern lest her husband should 'lose so dear a friend,' gave the wicked Ensign a hint upon which he promptly acted by dexterously insinuating to the Moor, 'after feigning at first great reluctance to say aught that might displease,' that the lady sought the Captain's restoration to favor for her own sake, 'and all the more since she has taken an aversion to your blackness.' The enraged husband's demand for positive proof was temporarily satisfied by lies and promises, and afterwards 'the villain resolved on a new deed of guilt.

'Disdemona often used to go to visit the Ensign's wife, and remained with her a good part of the day. Now the Ensign observed that she carried about with her a handkerchief, which he knew the Moor had given her, finely embroidered in the Moorish fashion. Then he conceived the plan of taking this kerchief from her secretly, and thus laying the snare for her final ruin. The Ensign had a little daughter, a child three years of age, who was much loved by Disdemona, and one day, when the unhappy lady had gone to pay a visit at the house of this vile man, he took the little child up in his arms and carried her to Disdemona, who took her and pressed her to her bosom; whilst at the same instant this traitor, who had extreme dexterity of hand, drew the kerchief from her sash so cunningly that she did not notice him.'

After this 'it seemed as if fate conspired with the Ensign to work the death of the unhappy Disdemona.' The handkerchief was dropped in the Captain's apartment and found by him; the Moor was made to witness a conversation in which the Ensign's pantomime seemed to indicate that the Captain was confessing everything; Disdemona naturally failed to produce the handkerchief when it was called for; and the Moor, wholly convinced now, 'fell to meditating how he should put his wife to death, and likewise the Captain, so that their death should not be laid to his charge.' 'The Ensign's wife, who knew the whole truth, but dared not, from fear of her husband, disclose a single circumstance,' tried to warn Disdemona indirectly, but the Ensign pointed out to the Moor the Captain's wife 'standing at a window, where she could be seen by all the passers-by in the street,' with the handkerchief in her possession, and the doom of the two innocent victims was sealed. 'After much entreating and being richly paid,' the Ensign

---

1 The quotations are taken from Taylor's translation, 1855, as reprinted by Furness.

finally overcame his fears and one dark night assaulted the Captain, who was 'on his way to visit a courtesan,' and with one blow cut off his right leg at the thigh; only the wounded man's vigorous sword-play and the speedy response to his cries for assistance saved his life.

Then the Ensign and the Moor 'consulted of one means and another—poison and daggers—to kill poor Disdemona, but could resolve on nothing. At length the Ensign said, "A plan comes to my mind, which will give you satisfaction and raise cause for no suspicion. It is this: the house in which you live is very old, and the ceiling of your chamber has many cracks; I propose we take a stocking filled with sand, and beat Disdemona with it till she dies; thus will her body bear no signs of violence. When she is dead we can pull down a portion of the ceiling, and thus make it seem as if a rafter falling on her head had killed the lady. Suspicion cannot rest on you, since all men will impute her death to accident." This cruel counsel pleased the Moor, and he only waited for a fitting time to execute the plot. One night, when he and Disdemona had retired to bed, the Ensign, whom the Moor had concealed in a closet which opened into the chamber, raised a noise in the closet, according to a concerted plan; whereat the Moor said to his wife, "Did you not hear that noise?"

' "Indeed I heard it," she replied.

' "Rise," said the Moor, "and see what 'tis."

'The unhappy Disdemona rose from bed, and the instant she approached the closet, out rushed the Ensign, and being strong and of stout nerve, he beat her cruelly with the bag of sand across her back; upon which Disdemona fell to the ground, scarce able to draw her breath; but with the little voice she had left, she called upon the Moor for aid. But the Moor, leaping from bed, exclaimed, "Thou wickedest of women, thus has thy falseness found its just reward." . . . The wretched lady, hearing these words, and feeling that she was near her end (for the Ensign had given her another blow), appealed to the justice of Heaven, since justice here had failed her, in proof of her fidelity and truth; and as she was thus calling Heaven to witness, the wicked Ensign inflicted a third blow, under which she sank lifeless on the floor. Then the Ensign and the Moor, laying Disdemona on the bed and wounding her head, pulled down part of the ceiling of the chamber as they had arranged; whereupon the Moor began to call aloud for help, exclaiming that the house was falling. Hearing this uproar, the neighbors all came running up, and there found Disdemona lying dead beneath a rafter,—a sight which, from the good life of that poor lady, did fill all hearts with sorrow.'

The two murderers escaped detection for the time being, but remorse finally caused the Moor so to hate his accomplice that, kept from slaying him by fear of consequences, he deprived him of his rank and dismissed him. In revenge the Ensign told the Captain, now going about on a wooden leg, that it was the Moor who had cut off his leg and killed Disdemona. They both repeated these charges before the Senate; and the Moor was thereupon brought pinioned to Venice, tortured, imprisoned, and 'condemned to perpetual banishment, in which he was eventually slain by the kinsfolk of Disdemona, as he merited. The Ensign returned to his own country, and following up his wonted villainy,' lodged a false accusation against a companion, for which he was tortured so violently to make him prove his charges that 'his body rup-

tured' and 'he died a miserable death. Thus did Heaven revenge the innocence of Disdemona.'

THE HISTORY OF THE PLAY

On the strength of Malone's assertion, backed by a now generally credited reference in the Revels Books,[2] the composition of *Othello* is assigned to the year 1604; but no printed version is known to have appeared for eighteen years after that time, until the First Quarto was published by Thomas Walkley, in 1622, having been licensed 6 October 1621. This is the latest in date of all Shakespearean quarto first editions of single plays before the appearance of the famous collected edition of the plays by Heminge and Condell, known as the First Folio, in 1623; and indeed Walkley's advance knowledge of the forthcoming folio publication probably accounts for this quarto issue as an attempt to make something out of his single holding while there was yet time.

Richard Burbage, the leading tragedian of Shakespeare's company, won great fame in the rôle of Othello, as attested by tributes in verse upon his death in 1619. The title-page of the First Quarto assures us that the play had 'beene diuerse times acted at the Globe, and at the Black Friers, by his Maiesties Seruants,' but the *Shakspere Allusion Book* records only two performances between 1604 and 1622: one attended by the German Ambassador at the Globe, 30 April 1610, and the other before Prince Charles (later Charles I), his sister the Princess Elizabeth, and her fiancé the Elector Palatine, presumably at Whitehall, in 1612 or 1613. Three other performances can be definitely dated before the closing of the theatres, in 1642; viz., 22 November 1629; 6 May 1635, 'att the bla: ffryers'; and 8 December 1636, before the King and Queen at Hampton Court; but other references show that the play's popularity was far greater than these meager surviving accounts would indicate. There was a notable production at Oxford in September 1610, when *Othello* was given along with Jonson's then new comedy, *The Alchemist,* to the scandalous delight of the students. In the *Allusion Book's* 'List of Shakspere's Works, arranged according to the number of allusions to each' during the period from 1591 to 1700, *Hamlet* leads with 95 references, and *Othello* stands fifth with 56.[3]

The modern era on the English stage begins with the reopening of the theatres at the Restoration, when actresses and painted scenery were first introduced as regular features of public performances. Here *Othello* figures conspicuously, for on the eighth of December 1660, at the Red Bull, the first woman to appear on the public stage in England played the part of Desdemona. The experiment was undertaken with some misgivings, as Jordan's defensive prologue shows:

> *In this reforming age*
> *We have intents to civilize the Stage.*
> *Our 'women' are defective, and so siz'd*
> *You'd think they were some of the Guard disguiz'd;*
> *For (to speak truth) men act, that are between*

---

2 The entry, recording the performance of the play at court, reads: 'By the King's Majesty's Players. Hallowmas Day, being the first of November [1604], a play in the banqueting house at Whitehall called *The Moor of Venice.*'

3 G. E. Bentley, *Shakespeare and Jonson: their Reputations in the Seventeenth Century Compared,* p. 109, places *Othello* second only to *The Tempest* among Shakespeare's works in seventeenth-century reputation.

Forty and fifty, Wenches of fifteen;
With bone so large, and nerve so incomplyant,
When you call Desdemona, enter Giant.

As might be expected, Pepys has some interesting remarks on Restoration performances of *Othello*: '1660, October 11.—To the Cockpitt to see 'The Moore of Venice,'' which was well done. Burt acted the Moore; by the same token, a very pretty lady that sat by me, called out, to see Desdemona smothered.' '1669, February 6.—To the King's playhouse, and there in an upper box . . . did see 'The Moor of Venice': but ill acted in most parts; Mohun, which did a little surprise me, not acting Iago's part by much so well as Clun used to do: nor another, Hart's[4] which was Cassio's; nor indeed, Burt doing the Moor's so well as I once thought he did.' These actors belonged to Sir William Davenant's[5] Drury Lane company; in one cast in 1663, with the above named, Cartwright, a great Falstaff, played Brabantio and Mrs. Hughes Desdemona.

Othello remained a particular favorite throughout the Restoration and Queen Anne periods, largely owing to the genius of the great Thomas Betterton (1635?-1710). Steele's tribute in the *Tatler* to Betterton's 'wonderful agony' in the last three acts, is familiar, and Colley Cibber's summary often quoted: 'Betterton was an actor as Shakespeare was an author, both without competitors, formed for the mutual assistance and illustration of each other's genius' (Genest I, 492). Genest's record shows that *Othello* was produced practically every season during the period covered, 1660-1830, and, what is more significant still, produced in its original form, when almost every other Shakespearean or Elizabethan play was presented only in some mutilated 'adaptation' or 'revision.'

Betterton's mantle descended upon Barton Booth (1681-1/33), whose Othello was considered by Colley Cibber his best rôle. Like Betterton, he probably played the part in the court-dress of the period. His successor, Quin, who dominated the stage till Garrick's triumphal entry in 1741, appeared in an English military uniform, a large powdered wig, and white gloves; when the latter were removed, the sudden disclosure of his blackened hands made emphatic Othello's alien race. David Garrick (1717-1779) made one of his few failures when he attempted the rôle of Othello, in spite of his great success as Hamlet, Macbeth, and Lear, and wisely avoided the part. Barry's splendid impersonation of the Moor, and Macklin's and Henderson's of Iago, save the credit of the performances of this period. Even Kemble failed to costume Othello properly, while his wonderful sister, Mrs. Siddons, was a far better Lady Macbeth than Desdemona. Edmund Kean won from all critics the most complete and superlative

approval ever accorded any interpreter of Othello's part. The descriptions of his performance make one wonder at the change that has come over actors (or audiences?) in our own time. As is well known, Kean fell stricken upon the shoulder of his son Charles (playing Iago) during what was to have been his farewell appearance at Covent Garden, 25 March 1833, and died a few weeks later. He was the first to present Othello as a light brown or bronzed Moor instead of as a jet-black negro; and he was also a very fine Iago. Junius Brutus Booth played Iago to Kean's Othello in a notable competitive performance at Drury Lane, 20 February 1817, and later, chiefly in America, created an interesting if not wholly convincing interpretation of the Moor as a case of Oriental racial characteristics slowly overcoming an artificial Christian civilization. William C. Macready (1793-1873), who was the first to costume Othello with complete correctness, was really greater as Iago. Sir Henry Irving's first appearance as Othello, 14 February 1876, at the London 'Lyceum,' was too untrammeled by tradition to be appreciated; but on 2 May 1881, he began a brilliantly successful engagement at the 'Lyceum' with Edwin Booth, the two actors alternating the rôles of Othello and Iago at successive performances, to the Desdemona of Ellen Terry, the Cassio of William Terriss, and the Roderigo of Arthur Wing Pinero. Booth's Othello far surpassed Irving's, but the two were perhaps evenly matched as Iago. The famous Italian actor, Tommaso Salvini, was also thrilling audiences in Europe and America in the '70s and '80s by the almost animal passionateness of his interpretation of Othello's jealousy. Sir Johnston Forbes-Robertson essayed Othello in 1898, and again, with Gertrude Elliott as Desdemona, in May 1913; but his Othello was inferior to his Hamlet. Sir Herbert Beerbohm Tree produced *Othello* in London, in April 1912, with his usual scenic elaboration, Laurence Irving playing the part of Iago and Phyllis Neilson-Terry that of Desdemona.

America may claim at least two very great performers of the two rôles (for most great Othellos have also been great Iagos), in Edwin Forrest (1806-1872) and Edwin Booth (1833-1893), while John Edward McCullough (1837-1885) was also successful. Richard Mansfield steadily declined to attempt the part, on the ground that he could add nothing to Salvini's performance. E. H. Sothern appeared early in his career as Roderigo in one of McCullough's last performances, and William Faversham gave a deserving but unsuccessful performance in 1913. One of the other impressive productions was that of the New York Theatre Guild (1943), directed by Margaret Webster, with Paul Robeson as Othello and Jose Ferrer as Iago.

---

4 Shakespeare's grandnephew.
5 Shakespeare's godson (?).

ACT FIRST ❧ SCENE FIRST

[Venice. A Street]
Enter Roderigo and Iago.

Rod. Tush! Never tell me! I take it much unkindly
That thou, Iago, who hast had my purse
As if the strings were thine, shouldst know of this.
 Iago. 'Sblood, but you will not hear me!
If ever I did dream of such a matter,   5
Abhor me.
 Rod. Thou told'st me thou didst hold him in thy hate.
 Iago. Despise me if I do not. Three great ones of the city,
In personal suit to make me his lieutenant,
Off-capp'd to him; and, by the faith of man   10
(I know my price), I am worth no worse a place.
But he, as loving his own pride and purposes,
Evades them with a bombast circumstance
Horribly stuff'd with epithets of war;
«And, in conclusion,»   15
Nonsuits my mediators; for, 'Certes,' says he,
'I have already chose my officer.'
And what was he?
Forsooth, a great arithmetician,
One Michael Cassio, a Florentine   20
(A fellow almost damn'd in a fair wife),
That never set a squadron in the field,
Nor the division of a battle knows
More than a spinster,—unless the bookish theoric,
Wherein the toged consuls can propose   25
As masterly as he. Mere prattle, without practice,
Is all his soldiership; but he, sir, had the election,
And I (of whom his eyes had seen the proof
At Rhodes, at Cyprus, and on other grounds
Christian and heathen) must be-lee'd and calm'd   30
By Debitor-and-Creditor. This counter-caster,
He, in good time, must his lieutenant be,
And I—God bless the mark!—his Moorship's ancient.
 Rod. By heaven, I rather would have been his hangman.
 Iago. Why, there's no remedy. 'Tis the curse of service.   35
Preferment goes by letter and affection,
And not by old gradation, where each second
Stood heir to the first. Now, sir, be judge yourself,
Whether I in any just term am affin'd
To love the Moor.   40
 Rod.   I would not follow him then.
 Iago. O sir, content you.
I follow him to serve my turn upon him;
We cannot be all masters, nor all masters
Cannot be truly follow'd. You shall mark   45
Many a duteous and knee-crooking knave,
That (doting on his own obsequious bondage)

Wears out his time much like his master's ass,
For nought but provender, and when he's old,—cashier'd!
Whip me such honest knaves. Others there are   50
Who, trimm'd in forms and visages of duty,
Keep yet their hearts attending on themselves,
And throwing but shows of service on their lords,
Do well thrive by 'em, and when they have lin'd their coats
Do themselves homage. Those fellows have some soul,   55
And such a one do I profess myself. For, sir,
It is as sure as you are Roderigo,
Were I the Moor, I would not be Iago.
In following him, I follow but myself;
Heaven is my judge, not I for love and duty,   60
But seeming so for my peculiar end,
For when my outward action does demónstrate
The native act and figure of my heart
In complement extern, 'tis not long after
But I will wear my heart upon my sleeve   65
For daws to peck at. I am not what I am.
 Rod. What a full fortune does the thick-lips owe,
If he can carry't thus!
 Iago.   Call up her father.
Rouse him, make after him, poison his delight,   70
Proclaim him in the street, incense her kinsmen,
And though he in a fertile climate dwell,
Plague him with flies; though that his joy be joy,
Yet throw such chances of vexation on't
As it may lose some color.   75
 Rod. Here is her father's house. I'll call aloud.
 Iago. Do; with like timorous accent and dire yell
As when (by night and negligence) the fire
Is spied in populous cities.
 Rod. What, ho, Brabantio! Signior Brabantio, ho!   80
 Iago. Awake! what, ho, Brabantio! thieves! thieves! thieves!
Look to your house, your daughter, and your bags!
Thieves! thieves!

Brabantio at a window, above.

 Bra. What is the reason of this terrible summons?
What is the matter there?   85
 Rod. Signior, is all your family within?
 Iago. Are your doors lock'd?
 Bra.   Why, wherefore ask you this?
 Iago. 'Zounds, sir, you're robb'd!—For shame, put on your
gown!—   90
Your heart is burst, you have lost half your soul.
Even now, now, very now, an old black ram
Is tupping your white ewe. Arise, arise!
Awake the snorting citizens with the bell,
Or else the devil will make a grandsire of you.   95
Arise, I say.
 Bra.   What! have you lost your wits?
 Rod. Most reverend signior, do you know my voice?
 Bra. Not I. What are you?

4 'Sblood; *cf. n.*   **5 matter:** *i.e., the marriage of Othello and Desdemona*   **8 Three great ones;** *cf. n.*   **10 Off-capp'd:** *doffed their caps*   **11 price:** *value*   **13 bombast circumstance:** *inflated circumlocution; cf. n.*   **15 Not in Folio; see 'Textual Note'**   **16 Nonsuits:** *rebuffs*   **Certes:** *positively*   **20 Florentine;** *cf. n.*   **21 Cf. n.**   **23 division ... battle:** *disposition of a battle-line*   **24 unless:** *except, unless you count*   **bookish theoric:** *book-taught theory*   **25 toged consuls:** *councillors in their togas or robes of peace*   **propose:** *converse, discourse*   **27 election:** *appointment*   **30 be-lee'd and calm'd;** *cf. n.*   **31 Cf. n.**   **32 in good time:** *(phrase of contempt), forsooth*   **33 God ... mark;** *cf. n.*   **ancient:** *ensign; cf. n.*   **36 letter:** *commendatory letter, influence*   **affection:** *favoritism*   **37 old gradation:** *the old order of seniority*   **39 in any ... affin'd;** *cf. n.*   **43 to serve ... him:** *to use him for my own advantage*

50 Whip me, etc.: *i.e., I think they should be whipped*   **51 visages:** *outward semblances*   **54 lin'd their coats:** *filled their pockets*   **60 not I:** *i.e., I do not do it*   **61 seeming so:** *seeming loving and dutiful*   **peculiar:** *private*   **63 native act:** *innate operation*   **figure:** *configuration*   **64 complement extern:** *outward counterpart*   **'tis ... But:** *'twill not be long before*   **67 owe:** *possess*   **68 carry't:** *get away with it*   **70 Rouse him;** *cf. n.*   **74 chances of vexation:** *vexatious accidents*   **75 As:** *that*   **78 by night and negligence:** *amid nocturnal repose*   **89, 90 For shame ... gown;** *cf. n.*   **94 snorting:** *snoring*

Rod. My name is Roderigo.   *100*
  Bra.   The worser welcome!
I have charg'd thee not to haunt about my doors.
In honest plainness thou hast heard me say
My daughter is not for thee; and now, in madness,
Being full of supper and distempering draughts,   *105*
Upon malicious bravery dost thou come
To start my quiet.
  Rod. Sir, sir, sir!
  Bra.   But thou must needs be sure,
My spirit and my place have in them power   *110*
To make this bitter to thee.
  Rod.   Patience, good sir.
  Bra. What tell'st thou me of robbing? This is Venice.
My house is not a grange.
  Rod.   Most grave Brabantio,   *115*
In simple and pure soul I come to you.
  Iago. 'Zounds, sir, you are one of those that will not serve
God if the devil bid you. Because we come to do you service
and you think we are ruffians, you'll have your daughter cov-
ered with a Barbary horse; you'll have your nephews   *120*
neigh to you; you'll have coursers for cousins and gennets
for germans.
  Bra. What profane wretch art thou?
  Iago. I am one, sir, that come to tell you, your daughter
and the Moor are now making the beast with two backs.   *125*
  Bra. Thou art a villain.
  Iago.   You are—a senator.
  Bra. This thou shalt answer. I know thee, Roderigo.
  Rod. Sir, I will answer anything. But, I beseech you,
⟨If't be your pleasure and most wise consent   *130*
(As partly, I find, it is) that your fair daughter,
At this odd-even and dull watch o' th' night,
Transported with no worse nor better guard
But with a knave of common hire, a góndolier,
To the gross clasps of a lascivious Moor—   *135*
If this be known to you, and your allowance,
We then have done you bold and saucy wrongs.
But if you know not this, my manners tell me
We have your wrong rebuke. Do not believe
That, from the sense of all civility,   *140*
I thus would play and trifle with your reverence.
Your daughter (if you have not given her leave,
I say again) hath made a gross revolt,
Tying her duty, beauty, wit and fortunes
In an extravagant and wheeling stranger   *145*
Of here and everywhere. Straight satisfy yourself.⟩
If she be in her chamber or your house,
Let loose on me the justice of the state
For thus deluding you.
  Bra.   Strike on the tinder, ho!   *150*
Give me a taper! call up all my people!
This accident is not unlike my dream.
Belief of it oppresses me already.
Light, I say! light!   *Exit.*
  Iago.   Farewell, for I must leave you.   *155*

It seems not meet nor wholesome to my place
To be produc'd (as, if I stay, I shall)
Against the Moor; for I do know the state
(However this may gall him with some check)
Cannot with safety cast him; for he's embark'd   *160*
With such loud reason to the Cyprus wars,
Which even now stand in act, that, for their souls,
Another of his fathom they have not
To lead their business. In which regard,
Though I do hate him as I do hell's pains,   *165*
Yet for necessity of present life,
I must show out a flag and sign of love,
Which is indeed but sign. That you shall surely find him,
Lead to the Sagittary the raised search,
And there will I be with him. So, farewell.   *Exit.*   *170*

*Enter [below] Brabantio in his night gown, and Servants with
torches.*

  Bra. It is too true an evil. Gone she is,
And what's to come of my despised time
Is nought but bitterness. Now, Roderigo,
Where didst thou see her? O unhappy girl!
With the Moor, sayst thou? Who would be a father!   *175*
How didst thou know 'twas she? O, she deceives me
Past thought. What said she to you? Get mo tapers!
Raise all my kindred! Are they married, think you?
  Rod. Truly, I think they are.
  Bra. O heaven! How got she out? O treason of the   *180*
blood!
Fathers, from hence trust not your daughters' minds
By what you see them act. Is there not charms
By which the property of youth and maidhood
May be abus'd? Have you not read, Roderigo,   *185*
Of some such thing?
  Rod.   Yes, sir, I have indeed.
  Bra. Call up my brother. O, would you had had her!
Some one way, some another! Do you know
Where we may apprehend her and the Moor?   *190*
  Rod. I think I can discover him, if you please
To get good guard and go along with me.
  Bra. Pray, lead me on. At every house I'll call;
I may command at most. Get weapons, ho!
And raise some special officers of night.   *195*
On, good Roderigo. I'll deserve your pains.   *Exeunt.*

✄ Scene Second ✄

[Another Street. Before the Sagittary]
Enter Othello, Iago, and Attendants with torches.

  Iago. Though in the trade of war I have slain men,
Yet do I hold it very stuff o' th' conscience
To do no contriv'd murder. I lack iniquity
Sometimes to do me service. Nine or ten times

---

106 **bravery:** *bravado*   107 **start:** *disturb*   114 **grange:** *lonely farmhouse*   120 **nephews:** *grandchildren*   121 **coursers:** *swift and spirited horses* **gennets:** *small Spanish horses*   122 **germans:** *near relatives*   124, 125 *Cf. n.*   127 **a senator;** *cf. n.*   130–146 *Not in Quarto; see 'Textual Note'*   132 *Cf.n.*   136 **your allowance:** *what you approve of*   140 **from ... all:** *deprived of all regard for*   145 **extravagant and wheeling:** *vagabond and itinerant; cf. n.*

157 **produc'd:** *brought forward as witness*   159 **check:** *rebuke*   160 **cast:** *dismiss embark'd:** *engaged, committed*   161 **loud reason:** *pressing necessity* **Cyprus wars;** *cf. n.*   162 **stand in act:** *are actually under way*   163 **fathom:** *capacity*   169 **Sagittary:** *an inn; cf. n.* **S.d. night gown:** *dressing robe*   172 **what's ... time:** *the remainder of my wretched life*   174 **unhappy;** *cf. n.*   177 **mo:** *more*   184 **property:** *nature*   188 **brother:** *i.e., Gratiano*   195 **officers of night:** *night watchmen*   2 **stuff:** *substance, essence*   3 **contriv'd:** *premeditated*

I had thought t' have yerk'd him here under the ribs.   5
    Oth. 'Tis better as it is.
    Iago.   Nay, but he prated,
And spoke such scurvy and provoking terms
Against your Honor
That with the little godliness I have   10
I did full hard forbear him. But, I pray, sir,
Are you fast married? Be assur'd of this,
That the magnifico is much belov'd,
And hath in his effect a voice potential
As double as the duke's. He will divorce you,   15
Or put upon you what restraint and grievance
The law, with all his might to enforce it on,
Will give him cable.
    Oth.   Let him do his spite.
My services which I have done the Signory   20
Shall out-tongue his complaints. 'Tis yet to know
(Which when I know that boasting is an honor
I shall promulgate), I fetch my life and being
From men of royal siege, and my demerits
May speak unbonneted to as proud a fortune   25
As this that I have reach'd. For know, Iago,
But that I love the gentle Desdemona,
I would not my unhoused free condition
Put into circumscription and confine
For the sea's worth. But, look! what lights come yond?   30
    Iago. Those are the raised father and his friends.
You were best go in.
    Oth.   Not I. I must be found.
My parts, my title, and my perfect soul
Shall manifest me rightly. Is it they?   35
    Iago. By Janus, I think no.

       Enter Cassio with lights, Officers and torches.

    Oth. The servants of the duke, and my lieutenant.
The goodness of the night upon you, friends!
What is the news?
    Cas.   The duke does greet you, general,   40
And he requires your haste-post-haste appearance,
Even on the instant.
    Oth.   What's the matter, think you?
    Cas. Something from Cyprus, as I may divine.
It is a business of some heat. The galleys   45
Have sent a dozen sequent messengers
This very night at one another's heels,
And many of the consuls, rais'd and met,
Are at the duke's already. You have been hotly call'd for;
When being not at your lodging to be found,   50
The Senate sent above three several quests
To search you out.
    Oth.   'Tis well I'm found by you.
I will but spend a word here in the house,
And go with you.   *[Enters the Sagittary.]*   55
    Cas.   Ancient, what makes he here?

    Iago. Faith, he to-night hath boarded a land carrack.
If it prove lawful prize, he's made for ever.
    Cas. I do not understand.
    Iago.   He's married.   60
    Cas.   To who?
    Iago. Marry, to—

            [Re-enter Othello.]

        Come, captain, will you go?
    Oth.   Have with you.
    Cas. Here comes another troop to seek for you.   65
    Iago. It is Brabantio. General, be advis'd;
He comes to bad intent.

   Enter Brabantio, Roderigo, and others, with lights and weapons.

    Oth.   Holla! stand there!
    Rod. Signior, it is the Moor.
    Bra.   Down with him! Thief!   70
              [They draw on both sides.]
    Iago. You, Roderigo! Come, sir, I am for you.
    Oth. Keep up your bright swords, for the dew will rust 'em.
Good signior, you shall more command with years
Than with your weapons.
    Bra. O thou foul thief! Where hast thou stow'd my   75
daughter?
Damn'd as thou art, thou hast enchanted her;
For I'll refer me to all things of sense,
⟨If she in chains of magic were not bound,⟩
Whether a maid so tender, fair, and happy,   80
So opposite to marriage that she shunn'd
The wealthy curled darlings of our nation,
Would ever have (t'incur a general mock)
Run from her guardage to the sooty bosom
Of such a thing as thou—to fear, not to delight.   85
⟨Judge me the world, if 'tis not gross in sense
That thou hast practis'd on her with foul charms,
Abus'd her delicate youth with drugs or minerals
That weaken motion. I'll have't disputed on.
'Tis probable, and palpable to thinking.   90
I therefore apprehend and do attach thee⟩
For an abuser of the world, a practiser
Of arts inhibited and out of warrant.
Lay hold upon him. If he do resist,
Subdue him at his peril.   95
    Oth.   Hold your hands,
Both you of my inclining and the rest.
Were it my cue to fight, I should have known it
Without a prompter. Wh'er will you that I go
To answer this your charge?   100
    Bra.   To prison, till fit time
Of law and course of direct session
Call thee to answer.
    Oth.   What if I do obey?
How may the duke be therewith satisfied,   105
Whose messengers are here about my side

---

5 yerk'd: *struck* (with dagger) **him;** *cf. n.*   **13 magnifico:** *title of Venetian nobles* **14, 15** *Cf. n.*   **18 give ... cable:** *permit* **19 his spite:** *whatever spite urges* **20 Signory:** *governing body of Venice* **21 'Tis yet to know:** *i.e., the world doesn't yet know* **24 siege:** *rank* **demerits:** *deserts* **25** *Cf. n.* **28 unhoused;** *cf. n.* **29 confine:** *confinement* **34 parts:** *abilities* **perfect:** *blameless* **36 Janus:** *two-faced Roman god of beginnings* **S.d.;** *cf. n.*   **45 heat:** *urgency* **46 sequent:** *successive* **48 consuls:** *senators*

57 carrack: *large merchant vessel* **58 lawful prize;** *cf. n.* **59–61** *Cf. n.* **62 Marry;** *cf. n.* **72 Keep up:** *keep sheathed* **78 of sense:** *capable of judgment* **84 guardage:** *guardian's shelter* **86 Judge ... world:** *let the world judge* **gross in sense:** *manifest to the reason* **89 motion:** *inward impulse* (cf. I.iii.355) **have't disputed on:** *refer it to specialists* **93 out of warrant:** *unwarranted* **99 Wh'er:** *whither* **102 course ... session:** *due order of special procedure*

Upon some present business of the state
To bring me to him?

   Off.   'Tis true, most worthy signior.
The duke's in council, and your noble self,   *110*
I am sure, is sent for.

   Bra.   How? The duke in council!
In this time of the night! Bring him away.
Mine's not an idle cause. The duke himself,
Or any of my brothers of the state,   *115*
Cannot but feel this wrong as 'twere their own;
For if such actions may have passage free,
Bondslaves and pagans shall our statesmen be.   *Exeunt.*

❧ SCENE THIRD ❧

[The Doge's Palace]

Enter Duke and Senators, set at a table with lights and Attendants.

   Duke. There is no composition in these news
That gives them credit.

   1. Sen.   Indeed, they are disproportion'd.
My letters say a hundred and seven galleys.

   Duke. And mine, a hundred forty.   *5*

   2. Sen.   And mine, two hundred.
But though they jump not on a just account
(As in these cases, where the aim reports,
'Tis oft with difference), yet do they all confirm
A Turkish fleet, and bearing up to Cyprus.   *10*

   Duke. Nay, it is possible enough to judgment.
I do not so secure me in the error,
But the main article I do approve
In fearful sense.

   Sailor within. What, ho! what, ho! what, ho!   *15*

   Off. A messenger from the galleys.

Enter Sailor.

   Duke.   Now! The business?

   Sail. The Turkish preparation makes for Rhodes.
So was I bid report here to the state
⟨By Signior Angelo⟩.   *20*

   Duke. How say you by this change?

   1.Sen.   This cannot be,
By no assay of reason. 'Tis a pageant
To keep us in false gaze. When we consider
Th'importancy of Cyprus to the Turk,   *25*
And let ourselves again but understand
That as it more concerns the Turk than Rhodes,
So may he with more facile question bear it,
⟨For that it stands not in such warlike brace,
But altogether lacks th'abilities   *30*
That Rhodes is dress'd in—if we make thought of this,
We must not think the Turk is so unskilful
To leave that latest which concerns him first,
Neglecting an attempt of ease and gain
To wake and wage a danger profitless.⟩   *35*

   Duke. Nay, in all confidence, he's not for Rhodes.

   Off. Here is more news.

Enter a Messenger.

   Mess. The Ottomites, reverend and gracious,
Steering with due course toward the isle of Rhodes,
Have there injointed them with an after fleet⟨.   *40*

   1. Sen. Ay, so I thought. How many, as you guess?

   Mess.⟩Of thirty sail; and now they do re-stem
Their backward course, bearing with frank appearance
Their purposes toward Cyprus. Signior Montano,
Your trusty and most valiant servitor,   *45*
With his free duty recommends you thus,
And prays you to believe him.

   Duke. 'Tis certain then, for Cyprus.
Marcus Luccicos is not here in town?

   1. Sen. He's now in Florence.   *50*

   Duke. Write from us: wish him post-post-haste dispatch.

   1. Sen. Here comes Brabantio and the valiant Moor.

Enter Brabantio, Othello, Cassio, Iago, Roderigo, and Officers.

   Duke. Valiant Othello, we must straight employ you
Against the general enemy Ottoman.
[To Brabantio.]. I did not see you. Welcome, gentle signior;   *55*
We lack'd your counsel and your help to-night.

   Bra. So did I yours. Good your Grace, pardon me.
Neither my place nor aught I heard of business
Hath rais'd me from my bed, nor doth the general care
Take hold on me, for my particular grief   *60*
Is of so floodgate and o'erbearing nature
That it engluts and swallows other sorrows
And it is still itself.

   Duke.   Why, what's the matter?

   Bra. My daughter! O my daughter!   *65*

   All.   Dead?

   Bra.   Ay, to me.
She is abus'd, stol'n from me, and corrupted
By spells and medicines bought of mountebanks;
For nature so preposterously to err   *70*
⟨Being not deficient, blind, or lame of sense,⟩
Sans witchcraft could not.

   Duke. Whoe'er he be that in this foul proceeding
Hath thus beguil'd your daughter of herself
And you of her, the bloody book of law   *75*
You shall yourself read in the bitter letter
After your own sense; yea, though our proper son
Stood in your action.

   Bra.   Humbly I thank your Grace.
Here is the man, this Moor; whom now, it seems,   *80*
Your special mandate for the state affairs
Hath hither brought.

   All.   We are very sorry for't.

   Duke [to Othello]. What, in your own part, can you
say to this?   *85*

   Bra. Nothing but 'This is so.'

   Oth. Most potent, grave, and reverend signiors,
My very noble and approv'd good masters:
That I have ta'en away this old man's daughter,
It is most true; true, I have married her.   *90*

117, 118 *Cf. n.*   **Scene Third S.d. Enter . . . Attendants;** *cf. n.*   **1 composition:** *consistency*   **7 jump:** *agree*   **just:** *exact*   **8 aim:** *conjecture*   **11 to judgment:** *when judicially considered*   **12–15** *Cf. n.*   **23 assay of reason:** *reasonable test* **pageant:** *feigned show*   **24 in false gaze:** *looking in the wrong direction*   **28 with . . . it:** *carry it with less effort*   **29 brace:** *readiness*   **35 wake and wage:** *start and carry through*

40 after: *reserve*   **46 recommends:** *informs*   **51** *Cf. n.*   **61 floodgate:** *torrential*   **69 mountebanks:** *itinerant vendors of nostrums; cf. n.*   **72 Sans:** *without* **could not:** *would be impossible*   **75–77** *Cf. n.*   **77 proper:** *own*   **78 Stood . . . action:** *were involved by your charge*   **84 part:** *behalf*   **87 ff.** *Cf. n.*   **88 approv'd:** *esteemed*

The very head and front of my offending
Hath this extent, no more. Rude am I in my speech,
And little bless'd with the soft phrase of peace,
For since these arms of mine had seven years' pith
Till now some nine moons wasted, they have us'd *95*
Their dearest action in the tented field;
And little of this great world can I speak
More than pertains to feats of broil and battle,
And therefore little shall I grace my cause
In speaking for myself. Yet, by your gracious patience *100*
I will a round unvarnish'd tale deliver
Of my whole course of love: what drugs, what charms,
What conjuration, and what mighty magic,
(For such proceedings am I charg'd withal)
I won his daughter. *105*
 Bra.   A maiden never bold;
Of spirit so still and quiet, that her motion
Blush'd at herself! And she, in spite of nature,
Of years, of country, credit, everything,
To fall in love with what she fear'd to look on! *110*
It is a judgment maim'd and most imperfect
That will confess perfection so could err
Against all rules of nature, and must be driven
To find out practices of cunning hell,
Why this should be. I therefore vouch again *115*
That with some mixtures powerful o'er the blood,
Or with some dram conjur'd to this effect,
He wrought upon her.
 Duke.   To vouch this is no proof,
Without more certain and more overt test *120*
Than these thin habits and poor likelihoods
Of modern seeming do prefer against him.
 1. Sen. But, Othello, speak.
Did you by indirect and forced courses
Subdue and poison this young maid's affections? *125*
Or came it by request and such fair question
As soul to soul affordeth?
 Oth.   I do beseech you,
Send for the lady to the Sagittary,
And let her speak of me before her father. *130*
If you do find me foul in her report,
⟨The trust, the office I do hold of you,⟩
Not only take away, but let your sentence
Even fall upon my life.
 Duke.   Fetch Desdemona hither. *135*
         Exit two or three.
 Oth. Ancient, conduct them. You best know the place.
         [Exit Iago.]
And till she come, as truly as to heaven
⟨I do confess the vices of my blood,⟩
So justly to your grave ears I'll present
How I did thrive in this fair lady's love, *140*
And she in mine.
 Duke. Say it, Othello.
 Oth. Her father lov'd me; oft invited me,
Still question'd me the story of my life

From year to year, the battles, sieges, fortunes *145*
That I have pass'd.
I ran it through, even from my boyish days
To th' very moment that he bade me tell it.
Wherein I spake of most disastrous chances,
Of moving accidents by flood and field, *150*
Of hair-breadth 'scapes i' th' imminent deadly breach,
Of being taken by the insolent foe
And sold to slavery, of my redemption thence
And portance in my traveller's history.
Wherein of antres vast and deserts idle, *155*
Rough quarries, rocks and hills whose heads touch heaven,
It was my hint to speak (such was the process),
And of the Cannibals that each other eat,
The Anthropophagi, and men whose heads
Do grow beneath their shoulders. This to hear *160*
Would Desdemona seriously incline;
But still the house-affairs would draw her thence,
Which ever as she could with haste dispatch
She'd come again, and with a greedy ear
Devour up my discourse. Which I observing, *165*
Took once a pliant hour and found good means
To draw from her a prayer of earnest heart
That I would all my pilgrimage dilate,
Whereof by parcels she had something heard,
But not intentively. I did consent; *170*
And often did beguile her of her tears,
When I did speak of some distressful stroke
That my youth suffer'd. My story being done,
She gave me for my pains a world of sighs.
She swore, i' faith, 'twas strange, 'twas passing strange; *175*
'Twas pitiful, 'twas wondrous pitiful.
She wish'd she had not heard it, yet she wish'd
That heaven had made her such a man. She thank'd me,
And bade me, if I had a friend that lov'd her,
I should but teach him how to tell my story, *180*
And that would woo her. Upon this heat I spake.
She lov'd me for the dangers I had pass'd,
And I lov'd her that she did pity them.
This only is the witchcraft I have us'd.
Here comes the lady; let her witness it. *185*

    Enter Desdemona, Iago, and the rest.

 Duke. I think this tale would win my daughter too.
Good Brabantio,
Take up this mangled matter at the best.
Men do their broken weapons rather use
Than their bare hands. *190*
 Bra.   I pray you, hear her speak.
If she confess that she was half the wooer,
Destruction on my head, if my bad blame
Light on the man! Come hither, gentle mistress.
Do you perceive in all this noble company *195*
Where most you owe obedience?
 Des.   My noble father,
I do perceive here a divided duty.

---

91 head and front: *i.e., the most glaring part* **95 wasted:** *past, ago* **102–105 what . . .
won:** *with what drugs, etc., I won* **104 withal:** *with* **107 motion;** *cf. n.* **115 vouch:**
assert **121 thin habits:** *insubstantial appearances* **122 modern:** *mere, trivial* **124
forced:** *violent* **126 question:** *conversation* **143 invited me:** *entertained me as
guest* **144 Still:** *constantly*

154 portance: *behavior; cf. n.* **155 antres:** *caves* **157 hint:** *cue* **process:** *narrative* **159 Anthropophagi, etc.;** *cf. n.* **166 pliant:** *suitable* **168 dilate:** *relate in
full* **169 by parcels:** *piecemeal* **170 intentively:** *with undistracted attention* **181
Upon this heat:** *while the iron was hot; cf. n.* **188 at the best:** *as best you may*

To you I am bound for life and education.
My life and education both do learn me   *200*
How to respect you: you are the lord of duty,
I am hitherto your daughter. But here's my husband;
And so much duty as my mother show'd
To you, preferring you before her father,
So much I challenge that I may profess   *205*
Due to the Moor my lord.
    Bra.   God be with you! I have done.
Please it your Grace, on to the state affairs.
I had rather to adopt a child than get it.
Come hither, Moor: *210*
I here do give thee that with all my heart
⟨Which, but thou hast already, with all my heart⟩
I would keep from thee. For your sake, jewel,
I am glad at soul I have no other child,
For thy escape would teach me tyranny,   *215*
To hang clogs on 'em. I have done, my lord.
    Duke. Let me speak like yourself and lay a sentence,
Which, as a grise or step, may help these lovers
«Into your favor.»
When remedies are past, the griefs are ended   *220*
By seeing the worst, which late on hopes depended.
To mourn a mischief that is past and gone
Is the next way to draw more mischief on.
What cannot be preserv'd when Fortune takes,
Patience her injury a mockery makes.   *225*
The robb'd that smiles steals something from the thief;
He robs himself that spends a bootless grief.
    Bra. So let the Turk of Cyprus us beguile,
We lose it not so long as we can smile.
He bears the sentence well that nothing bears   *230*
But the free comfort which from thence he hears;
But he bears both the sentence and the sorrow
That, to pay grief, must of poor patience borrow.
These sentences, to sugar, or to gall,
Being strong on both sides, are equivocal: *235*
But words are words; I never yet did hear
That the bruis'd heart was pierced through the ear.
Beseech you, now to the affairs of state.
    Duke. The Turk with a most mighty preparation makes for
Cyprus. Othello, the fortitude of the place is best known   *240*
to you; and though we have there a substitute of most allowed
sufficiency, yet opinion, a sovereign mistress of effects,
throws a more safer voice on you. You must therefore be
content to slubber the gloss of your new fortunes with this
more stubborn and boisterous expedition.   *245*
    Oth. The tyrant custom, most grave senators,
Hath made the flinty and steel couch of war
My thrice-driven bed of down. I do agnize
A natural and prompt alacrity
I find in hardness, and do undertake   *250*
These present wars against the Ottomites.
Most humbly therefore bending to your state,

I crave fit disposition for my wife,
Due reference of place and exhibition,
With such accommodation and besort   *255*
As levels with her breeding.
    Duke.   If you please,
Be't at her father's.
    Bra.   I'll not have it so.
    Oth. Nor I.   *260*
    Des.   Nor I. I would not there reside,
To put my father in impatient thoughts
By being in his eye. Most gracious duke,
To my unfolding lend your prosperous ear,
And let me find a charter in your voice   *265*
T'assist my simpleness.
    Duke.   What would you? Speak.
    Des. That I did love the Moor to live with him,
My downright violence and storm of fortunes
May trumpet to the world. My heart's subdu'd   *270*
Even to the very quality of my lord.
I saw Othello's visage in his mind,
And to his honors and his valiant parts
Did I my soul and fortunes consecrate.
So that, dear lords, if I be left behind,   *275*
A moth of peace, and he go to the war,
The rites for which I love him are bereft me,
And I a heavy interim shall support
By his dear absence. Let me go with him.
    Oth. Your voices, lords! Beseech you, let her will   *280*
Have a free way. I therefore beg it not
To please the palate of my appetite,
Nor to comply with heat the young affects
In my distinct and proper satisfaction,
But to be free and bounteous to her mind;   *285*
And heaven defend your good souls that you think
I will your serious and great business scant
For she is with me. No, when light-wing'd toys
Of feather'd Cupid seel with wanton dulnes
My speculative and offic'd instruments,   *290*
That my disports corrupt and taint my business,
Let housewives make a skillet of my helm,
And all indign and base adversities
Make head against my estimation!
    Duke. Be it as you shall privately determine,   *295*
Either for her stay or going. Th' affair cries haste,
And speed must answer. You must hence to-night.
    «*Des.* To-night, my lord?
    Duke.   This night.»
    Oth.   With all my heart.   *300*
    Duke. At ten i' the morning here we'll meet again.
Othello, leave some officer behind,
And he shall our commission bring to you;
With such things else of quality or respect
As doth concern you.   *305*

---

200 learn: *teach*   **209 get:** *beget*   **215 escape:** *escapade*   **218 grise:** *nair*   **220–237** *Cf. n.*   **220 griefs:** *distresses of mind, anxieties*   **221 which:** (refers to 'griefs')   **223 next:** *nearest* **more mischief:** *cf. n.*   **224, 225** *Cf. n.*   **227 bootless:** *unavailing*   **228 let:** *i.e., suppose*   **230 sentence:** *adage* (with pun on 'court sentence')   **234, 235 to sugar . . . sides:** *cf. n.*   **237 pierced:** *probed, touched*   **238** *Cf. n.*   **242 opinion . . . effects:** *reputation, a great producer of results*   **245 slubber:** *sully*   **248 driven:** *sifted* **agnize:** *acknowledge*   **249 alacrity:** *congeniality, hearty sympathy*   **250 hardness:** *austerity*

254 reference: *assignment* **exhibition:** *allowance*   **255 besort:** *suitable retinue*   **264 unfolding:** *explanation* **prosperous:** *favoring*   **265 charter:** *official sanction*   **269 storm:** *forcible seizure*   **271 quality:** *profession*   **276 moth,** *etc.; cf. n.*   **280 voices:** *favorable votes*   **283 heat . . . affects:** *lust which the young incline to*   **284 distinct and proper:** *separate and personal; cf. n.*   **286 defend:** *forbid*   **288 For:** *because* **toys:** *trifles*   **289 seel;** *cf. n.*   **290 speculative . . . instruments:** *eyes which should see and perform duties; cf. n.*   **292 skillet:** *kettle* **helm:** *helmet*   **293 indign:** *unworthy*   **294 Make head:** *take arms* **estimation:** *fame*   **301 ten;** *cf. n.*   **304 quality or respect:** *general importance or detail* (almost 'genus' and 'species')

Oth.   Please your Grace, my ancient.
A man he is of honesty and trust.
To his conveyance I assign my wife,
With what else needful your good Grace shall think
To be sent after me.   *310*
     Duke.   Let it be so.
Good night to every one. *[To Brabantio.]* And, noble
signior,
If virtue no delighted beauty lack,
Your son-in-law is far more fair than black.   *315*
     1. Sen. Adieu, brave Moor! use Desdemona well.
     Bra. Look to her, Moor, if thou hast eyes to see:
She has deceiv'd her father, and may thee.
     Oth. My life upon her faith!
                    Exeunt [Duke, Senators, Officers, &c.].
                          Honest Iago,   *320*
My Desdemona must I leave to thee:
I prithee, let thy wife attend on her;
And bring her after in the best advantage.—
Come, Desdemona; I have but an hour
Of love, of worldly matters and direction   *325*
To spend with thee. We must obey the time.
                    Ex. Moor and Desdemona.
     Rod. Iago!
     Iago. What sayst thou, noble heart?
     Rod. What will I do, think'st thou?
     Iago. Why, go to bed, and sleep.   *330*
     Rod. I will incontinently drown myself.
     Iago. Well, if thou dost, I shall never love thee after it.
Why, thou silly gentleman?
     Rod. It is silliness to live when to live is a torment; and
then have we a prescription to die when death is our   *335*
physician.
     Iago. ⟨O, villainous!⟩ I ha' looked upon the world for four
times seven years, and since I could distinguish between a
benefit and an injury, I never found a man that knew how to
love himself. Ere I would say I would drown myself for   *340*
the love of a guinea-hen, I would change my humanity
with a baboon.
     Rod. What should I do? I confess it is my shame to be so
fond, but it is not in my virtue to amend it.
     Iago. Virtue! a fig! 'Tis in ourselves that we are thus or   *345*
thus. Our bodies are gardens, to the which our wills are gardeners; so that if we will plant nettles or sow lettuce, set hyssop
and weed up thyme, supply it with one gender of herbs or distract it with many, either to have it sterile with idleness or
manured with industry, why, the power and corrigible   *350*
authority of this lies in our wills. If the balance of our lives
had not one scale of reason to poise another of sensuality, the
blood and baseness of our natures would conduct us to most
preposterous conclusions. But we have reason to cool our raging motions, our carnal stings, our unbitted lusts, whereof   *355*
I take this that you call love to be a sect or scion.
     Rod. It cannot be.
     Iago. It is merely a lust of the blood and a permission of
the will. Come, be a man. Drown thyself? Drown cats and

blind puppies. I profess me thy friend, and I confess me   *360*
knit to thy deserving with cables of perdúrable toughness. I
could never better stead thee than now. Put money in thy
purse. Follow these wars; defeat thy favor with an usurped
beard. I say, put money in thy purse. It cannot be that Desdemona should long continue her love unto the Moor,—put   *365*
money in thy purse,—nor he his to her. It was a violent commencement, and thou shalt see an answerable sequestration.
Put but money in thy purse. These Moors are changeable in
their wills. Fill thy purse with money. The food that to him
now is as luscious as locusts, shall be to him shortly as   *370*
acerb as the coloquintida. ⟨She must change for youth.⟩ When
she is sated with his body, she will find the error of her
choice. «She must have change, she must.» Therefore put
money in thy purse. If thou wilt needs damn thyself, do it a
more delicate way than drowning. Make all the money   *375*
thou canst. If sanctimony and a frail vow betwixt an erring barbarian and a supersubtle Venetian be not too hard for my wits
and all the tribe of hell, thou shalt enjoy her: therefore make
money. A pox o' drowning! 'tis clean out of the way. Seek
thou rather to be hanged in compassing thy joy than to be   *380*
drowned and go without her.
     Rod. Wilt thou be fast to my hopes ⟨if I depend on the
issue⟩?
     Iago. Thou art sure of me. Go, make money. I have told
thee often, and I tell thee again and again, I hate the Moor.   *385*
My cause is hearted: thine hath no less reason. Let us be conjunctive in our revenge against him. If thou canst cuckold him, thou
dost thyself a pleasure, me a sport. There are many events in the
womb of time which will be delivered. Traverse! go! provide thy
money! We will have more of this to-morrow. Adieu.   *390*
     Rod. Where shall we meet i' th' morning?
     Iago. At my lodging.
     Rod. I'll be with thee betimes.
     Iago. Go to; farewell. Do you hear, Roderigo?
     «*Rod.* What say you?   *395*
     Iago. No more of drowning, do you hear?
     Rod. I am chang'd.» ⟨I'll sell all my land.⟩
     Iago. «Go to; farewell. Put money enough in your purse.»
                    Exit Roderigo.
Thus do I ever make my fool my purse;
For I mine own gain'd knowledge should profane,   *400*
If I would time expend with such a snipe
But for my sport and profit. I hate the Moor,
And it is thought abroad that 'twixt my sheets
He's done my office. I know not if't be true,
But I, for mere suspicion in that kind,   *405*
Will do as if for surety. He holds me well.
The better shall my purpose work on him.
Cassio's a proper man. Let me see now.—
To get his place, and to plume up my will
In double knavery: how? how? Let's see.—   *410*
After some time t'abuse Othello's ear
That he is too familiar with his wife.

---

314 **delighted:** *delighting*   317, 318 *Cf. n.*   331 **incontinently:** *immediately*   341
change: *exchange*   348 **gender:** *kind*   350 **manured:** *cultivated* **corrigible authority:** *correcting control*   351 **balance:** *weighing instrument*   352 **poise:** *offset, counterbalance*   355 **motions:** *impulses* **unbitted:** *unbridled*   356 **sect:** *variety* **scion:** *off-
shoot*

361 **perdúrable:** *most durable*   362 **stead:** *aid*   363 **defeat thy favor:** *disguise thy
face* **usurped:** *false*   367 **answerable sequestration:** *similarly hasty parting*   370 **locusts:** *cassia fistula, a sweet fruit*   371 **acerb:** *bitter* **coloquintida:** *an intensely bitter drug*
(imported from Cyprus)   376 **erring:** *roving; cf. n. on I.i.145*   386 **hearted:** *deep-seated
in the heart* **conjunctive:** *united*   387 **cuckold him:** *seduce his wife*   389 **Traverse:**
march   394 **Go to:** *come, come!*   403–406 **it is . . . surety:** *cf. n.*   405 **in that kind:**
of that sort   408 **proper:** *fine, good-looking*   410 **double knavery:** *cf. n.*
411 **abuse:** *deceive*

He has a person and a smooth dispose
To be suspected, fram'd to make women false;
The Moor a free and open nature too,   *415*
That thinks men honest that but seem to be so,
And will as tenderly be led by th' nose
As asses are.
I have't! it is engender'd! Hell and night
Must bring this monstrous birth to the world's light.   *420*

                         Exit.

ACT SECOND ❧ SCENE FIRST

[Famagosta, capital of Cyprus. An open place near the quay]
Enter Montano, Governor of Cyprus, with two other Gentlemen.

    Mon. What from the cape can you discern at sea?
    1. Gent. Nothing at all. It is a high-wrought flood;
I cannot 'twixt the haven and the main
Descry a sail.
    Mon. Methinks the wind does speak aloud at land;   *5*
A fuller blast ne'er shook our battlements.
If it hath ruffian'd so upon the sea,
What ribs of oak, when mountains melt on them,
Can hold the mortise? What shall we hear of this?
    2. Gent. A segregation of the Turkish fleet;   *10*
For do but stand upon the foaming shore,
The chidden billow seems to pelt the clouds;
The wind-shak'd surge, with high and monstrous mane,
Seems to cast water on the burning bear
And quench the guards of th' ever-fixed pole.   *15*
I never did like molestation view
On the enchafed flood.
    Mon.   If that the Turkish fleet
Be not enshelter'd and embay'd, they are drown'd.
It is impossible they bear it out.   *20*

               Enter a third Gentleman.

    3. Gent. News, lads! our wars are done.
The desperate tempest hath so bang'd the Turks
That their designment halts. A noble ship of Venice
Hath seen a grievous wrack and sufferance
On most part of their fleet.   *25*
    Mon. How! is this true?
    3. Gent.   The ship is here put in,
La Veronesa. Michael Cassio,
Lieutenant to the warlike Moor Othello,
Is come on shore; the Moor himself at sea,   *30*
And is in full commission here for Cyprus.
    Mon. I am glad on't; 'tis a worthy governor.
    3. Gent. But this same Cassio, though he speak of comfort
Touching the Turkish loss, yet he looks sadly
And prays the Moor be safe, for they were parted   *35*
With foul and violent tempest.
    Mon.   Pray heaven he be;
For I have serv'd him, and the man commands

Like a full soldier. Let's to the seaside, ho!
As well to see the vessel that's come in   *40*
As to throw out our eyes for brave Othello,
⟨Even till we make the main and th' aerial blue
An indistinct regard.⟩
    3. Gent.   Come, let's do so;
For every minute is expectancy   *45*
Of more arrivance.

                 Enter Cassio.

    Cas. Thanks to the valiant of this warlike isle,
That so approve the Moor! And let the heavens
Give him defence against the elements,
For I have lost him on a dangerous sea.   *50*
    Mon. Is he well shipp'd?
    Cas. His bark is stoutly timber'd, and his pilot
Of very expert and approv'd allowance.
Therefore my hopes, not surfeited to death,
Stand in bold cure.   *55*
    Messenger within. A sail!—a sail!—a sail!

               Enter a Messenger.

    Cas. What noise?
    Mess. The town is empty. On the brow o' th' sea
Stand ranks of people, and they cry, 'A sail!'
    Cas. My hopes do shape him for the governor.   *60*

                        A shot.

    2. Gent. They do discharge the shot of courtesy.
Our friends, at least.
    Cas.   I pray you, sir, go forth,
And give us truth who 'tis that is arriv'd.
    2. Gent. I shall.   *Exit.*   *65*
    Mon. But, good lieutenant, is your general wiv'd?
    Cas. Most fortunately. He hath achiev'd a maid
That paragons description and wild fame;
One that excels the quirks of blazoning pens,
And in th' essential vesture of creation   *70*
Does tire the ingen-giver.

               Enter 2. Gentleman.

             Now, who has put in?
    2. Gent. 'Tis one Iago, ancient to the general.
    Cas. He's had most favorable and happy speed.
Tempests themselves, high seas, and howling winds,   *75*
The gutter'd rocks, and congregated sands,
Traitors ensteep'd to clog the guiltless keel,
As having sense of beauty, do omit
Their mortal natures, letting go safely by
The divine Desdemona.   *80*
    Mon.   What is she?
    Cas. She that I spoke of, our great captain's captain,
Left in the conduct of the bold Iago,
Whose footing here anticipates our thoughts
A sennight's speed. Great Jove, Othello guard,   *85*
And swell his sail with thine own powerful breath,

---

413 dispose: *manner*   **Scene First S.d.;** *cf. n.*   **3 main:** *open ocean; cf. n.*   **9 hold the mortise:** *remain unshattered*   **10 segregation:** *dispersal*   **15 guards:** *two stars in Ursa Minor* **pole:** *pole-star*   **16 molestation:** *disturbance*   **20 bear it out:** *ride it out*   **23 designment:** *enterprise*   **24 sufferance:** *disaster*   **28 La Veronesa:** *'The Lady of Verona'* (the ship's name); *cf. n.*

39 full: *thorough*   **42, 43** *till the sea and sky become indistinguishable*   **46 more arrivance:** *further arrivals*   **53** *Of very allowed and approved expertness*   **54–56** *Cf. n.*   **56 Messenger;** *cf. n.*   **68 paragons:** *surpasses*   **69 quirks:** *subtleties* **blazoning:** *extolling*   **70** *in the beauties of soul with which nature has clothed her*   **71 ingen-giver;** *cf. n.*   **76 gutter'd:** *jagged*   **77 ensteep'd:** *submerged*   **79 mortal:** *deadly*   **83 conduct:** *escort*   **85 sennight's:** *week's*

That he may bless this bay with his tall ship,
Make love's quick pants in Desdemona's arms,
Give renew'd fire to our extinced spirits,
«And bring all Cyprus comfort»!   90

Enter Desdemona, Iago, Emilia, and Roderigo [with Attendants].

        O! behold,
The riches of the ship is come ashore.
Ye men of Cyprus, let her have your knees.
Hail to thee, lady! and the grace of heaven,
Before, behind thee, and on every hand,   95
Enwheel thee round!
    Des.   I thank you, valiant Cassio.
What tidings can you tell me of my lord?
    Cas. He is not yet arriv'd; nor know I aught
But that he's well, and will be shortly here.   100
    Des. O, but I fear! How lost you company?
                    [Cry] within. 'A sail!—a sail!"
    Cas. The great contention of the sea and skies
Parted our fellowship. But hark! a sail.   *[Guns heard.]*
    2. Gent. They give their greeting to the citadel: 105
This likewise is a friend.
    Cas.   «So speaks this voice.» ⟨See for the news!⟩
                          [Exit 2. Gentleman.]
Good ancient, you are welcome. *[Kisses Emilia.]* Welcome,
mistress.
Let it not gall your patience, good Iago,   110
That I extend my manners. 'Tis my breeding
That gives me this bold show of courtesy.
    Iago. Sir, would she give you so much of her lips
As of her tongue she oft bestows on me,
You'd have enough.   115
    Des.   Alas, she has no speech.
    Iago. In faith, too much.
I find it still when I have list to sleep.
Marry, before your ladyship, I grant,
She puts her tongue a little in her heart,   120
And chides with thinking.
    Emil. You have little cause to say so.
    Iago. Come on, come on! You are pictures out o' doors,
Bells in your parlors, wild cats in your kitchens
Saints in your injuries, devils being offended,   125
Players in your housewifery, and housewives in your beds.
    Des. O fie upon thee, slanderer!
    Iago. Nay, it is true, or else I am a Turk.
You rise to play and go to bed to work.
    Emil. You shall not write my praise.   130
    Iago.   No, let me not.
    Des. What wouldst thou write of me, if thou shouldst praise
me?
    Iago. O gentle lady, do not put me to't,
For I am nothing if not critical.   135
    Des. Come on; assay. There's one gone to the harbor?
    Iago. Ay, madam.
    Des. I am not merry, but I do beguile
The thing I am be seeming otherwise.
Come, how wouldst thou praise me?   140

    Iago. I am about it, but indeed my invention comes from
my pate as birdlime does from frieze. It plucks out brains and
all. But my muse labors, and thus she is deliver'd.

    If she be fair and wise.—Fairness and wit:
    The one's for use, the other useth it.   145

    Des. Well prais'd! How if she be black and witty?
    Iago.

    If she be black, and thereto have a wit,
    She'll find a white that shall her blackness fit.

    Des. Worse and worse.   150
    Emil. How if fair and foolish?
    Iago.

    She never yet was foolish that was fair,
    For even her folly help'd her to an heir.

    Des. These are old fond paradoxes to make fools laugh   155
i' th' alehouse. What miserable praise hast thou for her that's
foul and foolish?
    Iago.

    There's none so foul and foolish thereunto
    But does foul pranks which fair and wise ones do.   160

    Des. O heavy ignorance that praises the worst best! But
what praise couldst thou bestow on a deserving woman indeed?
one that, in the authority of her merits, did justly put on
the vouch of very malice itself?
    Iago.   165

    She that was ever fair and never proud,
    Had tongue at will and yet was never loud;
    Never lack'd gold and yet went never gay,
    Fled from her wish and yet said 'Now I may';
    She that being anger'd, her revenge being nigh,   170
    Bade her wrong stay and her displeasure fly;
    She that in wisdom never was so frail
    To change the cod's head for the salmon's tail;
    She that could think and ne'er disclose her mind,
    ⟨*See suitors following and not look behind:*⟩   175
    She was a wight, if ever such wights were,—

    Des. To do what?
    Iago.

    To suckle fools and chronicle small beer.

    Des. O most lame and impotent conclusion! Do not   180
learn of him, Emilia, though he be thy husband. How say you,
Cassio? Is he not a most profane and liberal counsellor?
    Cas. He speaks home, madam. You may relish him more
in the soldier than in the scholar.
    Iago [aside]. He takes her by the palm. Ay, well said,   185
whisper! With as little a web as this will I ensnare as great a
fly as Cassio. Ay, smile upon her, do! I will gyve thee in thine
own courtship. *[Cassio speaks to Desdemona in dumbshow.]* You
say true, 'tis so, indeed. If such tricks as these strip you out

---

93 **knees:** *obeisance* 96 **Enwheel:** *encircle* 107 **So . . . news;** *cf. n.* 111 **extend:**
elaborate 118 **list:** *inclination* 123 **pictures:** *i.e., paint your faces* 124 **Bells:** *jan-
glers* 125 **Saints . . . injuries:** *adopt a saintly air when saying spiteful things* 126 **housewifery, housewives;** *cf. n.* 136 **assay:** *essay, attempt* 139 **The . . . am:** *my real feeling*

141 **invention:** *imagination* 142 **frieze:** *rough woolen cloth* 146 **black:** *brunette* 149 **white:** *quibble on 'wight' (cf. line 176)* 154 **folly:** *lewdness* 155 **fond:**
foolish 157 **foul:** *ugly* 163 **put on:** *clothe herself in* 164 **vouch:** *favorable testimony* 167 **Had tongue at will:** *was good at talking* 173 *As to mistake show for substance
(?); cf. n.* 179 **chronicle, etc.:** *keep petty household accounts* 182 **liberal:** *licentious* 183 **home:** *to the point* 184 **in the:** *in the character of* 185 **said:** *done* 187,
188 **I . . . courtship;** *cf. n.* 187 **gyve:** *fetter* 188 **courtship:** *courtliness*

of your lieutenantry, it had been better you had not kissed   *190*
your three fingers so oft, which now again you are most apt to
play the sir in. Very good! well kissed! an excellent courtesy!
'tis so, indeed. Yet again your fingers to your lips? would they
were clyster-pipes for your sake!   *Trumpets within.*
The Moor! I know his trumpet.   *195*

    Cas. 'Tis truly so.
    Des. Let's meet him and receive him.
    Cas. Lo, where he comes!

           Enter Othello and Attendants.

    Oth. O my fair warrior!
    Des.   My dear Othello!   *200*
    Oth. It gives me wonder great as my content
To see you here before me. O my soul's joy,
If after every tempest come such calms,
May the winds blow till they have waken'd death!
And let the laboring bark climb hills of seas   *205*
Olympus-high, and duck again as low
As hell's from heaven! If it were now to die,
'Twere now to be most happy, for I fear
My soul hath her content so absolute
That not another comfort like to this   *210*
Succeeds in unknown fate.
    Des.   The heavens forbid
But that our loves and comforts should increase
Even as our days do grow.
    Oth.   Amen to that, sweet powers!   *215*
I cannot speak enough of this content.
It stops me here. It is too much of joy;
And this, and this, the greatest discords be   *They kiss.*
That e'er our hearts shall make!
    Iago [aside]. O! you are well tun'd now,   *220*
But I'll set down the pegs that make this music,
As honest as I am.
    Oth.   Come, let us to the castle.—
News, friends! Our wars are done. The Turks are drown'd.
How does my old acquaintance of his isle?—   *225*
Honey, you shall be well desir'd in Cyprus;
I have found great love amongst them. O my sweet,
I prattle out of fashion, and I dote
In mine own comforts. I prithee, good Iago,
Go to the bay and disembark my coffers.   *230*
Bring thou the master to the citadel;
He is a good one, and his worthiness
Does challenge much respect. Come, Desdemona!
Once more, well met at Cyprus!

     Ex. Othello and Desdemona [with all except Iago and Roderigo].

    Iago [to Rod.]. Do thou meet me presently at the harbor.   *235*
Come hither. If thou be'st valiant (as they say base men being
in love have then a nobility in their natures more than
is native to them), list me. The lieutenant to-night watches on
the court of guard. First, I must tell thee this: Desdemona is
directly in love with him.   *240*
    Rod. With him? Why, 'tis not possible.

    Iago. Lay thy finger thus, and let they soul be
instructed. Mark me with what violence she first loved the
Moor but for bragging and telling her fantastical lies. And will
she love him still for prating? Let not thy discreet heart   *245*
think it. Her eye must be fed; and what delight shall she have
to look on the devil? When the blood is made dull with the
act of sport, there should be, again to inflame it, and to give
satiety a fresh appetite, loveliness in favor, sympathy in years,
manners, and beauties; all which the Moor is defective in.   *250*
Now, for want of these required conveniences, her delicate tenderness will find itself abused, begin to heave the gorge, disrel-
ish and abhor the Moor. Very nature will instruct her in it,
and compel her to some second choice. Now, sir, this granted
(as it is a most pregnant and unforced position), who   *255*
stands so eminently in the degree of this fortune as Cassio
does? A knave very voluble, no farder conscionable than in
putting on the mere form of civil and humane seeming for
the better compassing of his salt and hidden affections?
⟨Why, none; why, none.⟩ A subtle, slippery knave, a   *260*
finder-out of occasions, that has an eye can stamp and counterfeit advantages, though true advantage never present itself.
⟨A devilish knave!⟩ Besides, the knave is handsome, young,
and hath all those requisites in him that folly and green
minds look after. A pestilent complete knave! and the   *265*
woman has found him already.
    Rod. I cannot believe that in her. She's full of most bless'd
condition.
    Iago. Bless'd fig's end! The wine she drinks is made of
grapes. If she had been bless'd, she would never have loved the
Moor. ⟨Bless'd pudding!⟩ Didst thou not see her paddle
with the palm of his hand? ⟨Didst not mark that?⟩
    Rod. Yes, ⟨that I did;⟩ but that was but courtesy.
    Iago. Lechery, by this hand! an index and obscure prologue
to the history of lust and foul thoughts. They met so near   *275*
with their lips that their breaths embraced together. ⟨Villainous
thoughts, Roderigo!⟩ When these mutualities so marshal the
way, hard at hand comes the ⟨master and⟩ main exercise,
the incorporate conclusion. ⟨Pish!⟩ But, sir, be you ruled by
me: I have brought you from Venice. Watch you to-night. For
your command, I'll lay't upon you. Cassio knows you not. I'll
not be far from you. Do you find some occasion to anger Cassio, either by speaking too loud, or tainting his discipline, or
from what other cause you please which the time shall more
favorably minister.   *285*
    Rod. Well.
    Iago. Sir, he is rash and very sudden in choler, and haply
«with his truncheon» may strike at you. Provoke him that
he may, for even out of that will I cause these of Cyprus to
mutiny, whose qualification shall come into no true taste again
but by the displanting of Cassio. So shall you have a shorter
journey to your desires by the means I shall then have to
prefer them, and the impediment most profitably removed
without the which there were no expectation of our prosperity.
    Rod. I will do this, if you can bring it to any opportunity.   *295*

---

242 thus: *on the lips* (i.e., be silent)   **252 heave the gorge:** *be nauseated*   **255 pregnant:**
obvious   **257 voluble:** *fickle* **farder:** *further* **conscionable:** *conscientious*   **259
salt:** *lewd*   **260 A subtle, slippery knave;** *cf. n.*   **266 found him:** *recognized his qualities*   **268 condition:** *quality*   **277 mutualities:** *intimacies* **marshal:** *lead*   **279 incorporate:** *carnal*   **281 command:** *authorization*   **283 tainting:** *disparaging*   **285
minister:** *provide*   **287 in choler:** *when enraged*   **290 qualification:** *pacifica-
tion*   **290 true taste:** *satisfactory state; cf. n.*   **293 prefer:** *promote*   **295 if you can;**
cf. n.

---

191 apt: *ready*   **192 sir:** *gallant*   **194 clyster-pipes:** *tubes for injections*   **199 warrior:**
(because he finds her among the soldiers)   **209 content:** *blissful happiness*   **217 here:**
in his heart   **221 set ... pegs:** *untune the strings by loosening; cf. n.*   **226 well desir'd:**
much sought after   **231 master:** *ship's captain*   **238 list:** *hear*   **239 court:** *post*

Iago. I warrant thee. Meet me by and by at the citadel. I must fetch his necessaries ashore. Farewell.

Rod. Adieu.   *Exit.*

Iago. That Cassio loves her, I do well believe't;
That she loves him, 'tis apt, and of great credit.   *300*
The Moor (howbeit that I endure him not)
Is of a constant, noble, loving, nature;
And I dare think he'll prove to Desdemona
A most dear husband. Now, I do love her too,—
Not out of absolute lust (though peradventure   *305*
I stand accountant for as great a sin),
But partly led to diet my revenge,
For that I do suspect the lusty Moor
Hath leap'd into my seat; the thought whereof
Doth like a poisonous mineral gnaw my inwards,   *310*
And nothing can nor shall content my soul
Till I am even'd with him, wife for wife,—
Or failing so, yet that I put the Moor
At least into a jealousy so strong
That judgment cannot cure. Which thing to do,   *315*
If this poor trash of Venice, whom I thrash
For his quick hunting, stand the putting-on,
I'll have our Michael Cassio on the hip,
Abuse him to the Moor in the rank garb
(For I fear Cassio with my night-cap too),   *320*
Make the Moor thank me, love me, and reward me
For making him egregiously an ass
And practising upon his peace and quiet
Even to madness. 'Tis here, but yet confus'd:
Knavery's plain face is never seen till us'd.   *Exit.*

❧ SCENE SECOND ❧

[A Street]
Enter Othello's Herald, with a proclamation.

Her. It is Othello's pleasure, our noble and valiant general, that, upon certain tidings now arrived, importing the mere perdition of the Turkish fleet, every man put himself into triumph; some to dance, some to make bonfires, each man to what sport and revels his addiction leads him; for, besides *5* these beneficial news, it is the celebration of his nuptial. So much was his pleasure should be proclaimed. All offices are open, and there is full liberty ⟨of feasting⟩ from this present hour of five till the bell have tolled eleven. Heaven bless the isle of Cyprus and our noble general Othello!   *Exit.* *10*

❧ SCENE THIRD ❧

The 'Court of Guard' or Guard-post]
Enter Othello, Desdemona, Cassio, and Attendants.

Oth. Good Michael, look you to the guard to-night.
Let's teach ourselves that honorable stop,

Not to outsport discretion.

Cas. Iago hath direction what to do;
But, notwithstanding, with my personal eye   *5*
Will I look to't.

Oth.   Iago is most honest.
Michael, good night. To-morrow with your earliest
Let me have speech with you.
[To Desdemona.].   Come, my dear love. *10*
The purchase made, the fruits are to ensue;
The profit's yet to come 'twixt me and you.
Good night.   *Ex. Othello and Desdemona [and Attendants].*

Enter Iago.

Cas. Welcome, Iago; we must to the watch.

Iago. Not this hour, lieutenant; 'tis not yet ten o'clock. *15*
Our general cast us thus early for the love of his Desdemona,
—who let us not therefore blame. He hath not yet made wanton the night with her, and she is sport for Jove.

Cas. She's a most exquisite lady.

Iago. And, I'll warrant her, full of game.   *20*

Cas. Indeed, she is a most fresh and delicate creature.

Iago. What an eye she has! Methinks it sounds a parley of provocation.

Cas. An inviting eye, and yet methinks right modest.

Iago. And when she speaks, is it not an alarum to love? *25*

Cas. She is indeed perfection.

Iago. Well, happiness to their sheets! Come, lieutenant, I have a stoup of wine, and here without are a brace of Cyprus gallants that would fain have a measure to the health of black Othello.   *30*

Cas. Not to-night, good Iago. I have very poor and unhappy brains for drinking. I could well wish courtesy would invent some other custom of entertainment.

Iago. O they are our friends. But one cup. I'll drink for you.   *35*

Cas. I have drunk but one cup to-night, and that was craftily qualified too, and, behold, what innovation it makes here. I am unfortunate in the infirmity, and dare not task my weakness with any more.

Iago. What, man! 'tis a night of revels. The gallants *40*
desire it.

Cas. Where are they?

Iago. Here at the door. I pray you, call them in.

Cas. I'll do't; but it dislikes me.   *Exit*

Iago. If I can fasten but one cup upon him,   *45*
With that which he hath drunk to-night already,
He'll be as full of quarrel and offence
As my young mistress' dog. Now, my sick fool Roderigo,
Whom love hath turn'd almost the wrong side out,
To Desdemona hath to-night carous'd   *50*
Potations pottle-deep; and he's to watch.
Three lads of Cyprus, noble swelling spirits,
That hold their honors in a wary distance,
The very elements of this warlike isle,
Have I to-night fluster'd with flowing cups,   *55*
And they watch too. Now, 'mongst this flock of drunkards,

---

300 apt … credit: *natural and very credible*   **306 accountant:** *accountable*   **307 diet:** *feed*   **310 mineral:** *drug*   **316, 317 whom … hunting:** *cf. n.*   **317 putting-on:** *urging; cf. n.*   **319 rank garb:** *grossest fashion*   **323 practising upon:** *using wiles against*   **324 to madness:** *to the point of driving him mad*   **2, 3 mere perdition:** *complete destruction*   **3, 4 put … triumph:** *give himself up to celebrating the occasion*   **5 addiction:** *inclination; cf. n.*   **7 offices:** *storerooms, kitchens*   **9 tolled;** *cf. n.*   **SCENE THIRD;** *cf. n.*   **2 stop:** *caution (musical figure)*

17 who: *whom (Othello)*   **22 parley:** *trumpet-call*   **25 alarum:** *summons*   **27 Well, etc.;** *cf. n.*   **28 stoup:** *large measure (often two quarts)*   **37 qualified:** *diluted*   **innovation:** *disturbance*   **37 here:** *in my head*   **44 dislikes me:** *is distasteful to me*   **51 pottle-deep:** *to the bottom of the tankard*   **53 Cf. n.**   **54 elements:** *typical representatives*

Am I to put our Cassio in some action
That may offend the isle. But here they come.
If consequence do but approve my dream,
My boat sails freely, both with wind and stream.   60

*Enter Cassio, Montano, and Gentlemen [Boys following with
wine].*

    Cas. 'Fore God, they have given me a rouse already.
    Mon. Good faith, a little one. Not past a pint, as I am a
soldier.
    Iago. Some wine, ho!
[Sings]

    And let me the canikin clink, clink;   65
    And let me the canikin clink.
      A soldier's a man;
      O man's life's but a span;
    Why then let a soldier drink.

Some wine, boys!   70
    Cas. 'Fore God, an excellent song.
    Iago. I learned it in England, where indeed they are most
potent in potting. Your Dane, your German, and your swag-
bellied Hollander,—drink, ho!—are nothing to your English.
    Cas. Is your Englishman so exquisite in his drinking?   75
    Iago. Why, he drinks you with facility your Dane dead
drunk. He sweats not to overthrow your Almain. He gives
your Hollander a vomit ere the next pottle can be filled.
    Cas. To the health of our general!
    Mon. I am for it, lieutenant; and I'll do you justice.   80
    Iago. O sweet England!
[Sings]

    King Stephen was and—a worthy peer,
      His breeches cost him but a crown.
    He held them sixpence all too dear,
      With that he call'd the tailor lown.   85
    He was a wight of high renown,
      And thou art but of low degree.
    'Tis pride that pulls the country down,
      Then take thine owd cloak about thee.

Some wine, ho!   90
    Cas. 'Fore God, this is a more exquisite song than the
other.
    Iago. Will you hear't again?
    Cas. No; for I hold him to be unworthy of his place that
does those things. Well, God's above all; and there be souls   95
must be saved, and there be souls must not be saved.
    Iago. It's true, good lieutenant.
    Cas. For mine own part,—no offence to the general, nor
any man of quality,—I hope to be saved.
    Iago. And so do I too, lieutenant.   100
    Cas. Ay; but, by your leave, not before me. The lieutenant
is to be saved before the ancient. Let's have no more of
this; let's to our affairs. God forgive us our sins! Gentlemen,
let's look to our business. Do not think, gentlemen, I am
drunk. This is my ancient; this is my right hand, and   105

this is my left hand. I am not drunk now. I can stand well
enough, and I speak well enough.
    Gent. Excellent well.
    Cas. Why, very well, then. You must not think then that I
am drunk.   *Exit.*   110
    Mon. To the platform, masters. Come, let's set the watch.
    Iago. You see this fellow that is gone before.
He is a soldier fit to stand by Cæsar
And give direction; and do but see his vice.
'Tis to his virtue a just equinox,   115
The one as long as th' other. 'Tis pity of him.
I fear the trust Othello puts him in,
On some odd time of his infirmity,
Will shake this island.
    Mon.   But is he often thus?   120
    Iago. 'Tis evermore the prologue to his sleep:
He'll watch the horologe a double set,
If drink rock not his cradle.
    Mon.   It were well
The general were put in mind of it.   125
Perhaps he sees it not, or his good nature
Prizes the virtue that appears in Cassio,
And looks not on his evils. Is not this true?

Enter Roderigo.

    Iago [aside to him]. How now, Roderigo?
I pray you, after the lieutenant. Go!   *Exit Roderigo.*   130
    Mon. And 'tis great pity that the noble Moor
Should hazard such a place as his own second
With one of an ingraft infirmity.
It were an honest action to say
So to the Moor.   135
    Iago.   Not I, for this fair island:
I do love Cassio well, and would do much
                    [Cry] 'Help! Help!' *within.*
To cure him of this evil. But hark! what noise?

Enter Cassio, driving in Roderigo.

    Cas. Zounds! You rogue, you rascal!
    Mon. What's the matter, lieutenant?   140
    Cas. A knave teach me my duty! I'll beat the knave
into a twiggen bottle.
    Rod. Beat me?
    Cas. Dost thou prate, rogue?   *[Striking Roderigo.]*
    Mon. [Staying him.] Nay, good lieutenant. I pray you,   145
sir, hold your hand.
    Cas. Let me go, sir, or I'll knock you o'er the mazzard.
    Mon. Come, come; you're drunk.
    Cas. Drunk!   *They fight.*
    Iago [aside to Roderigo]. Away, I say! Go out, and cry a   150
mutiny.   *Exit Roderigo.*
Nay, good lieutenant! God's will, gentlemen!
Help, ho! Lieutenant! Sir Montano! sir!
Help, masters! Here's a goodly watch indeed!
                        A bell rung.
Who's that that rings the bell? *Diablo,* ho!   155
The town will rise. God's will! lieutenant, hold!
You will be sham'd for ever.

59 *Cf. n.*   **61 rouse:** *bumper*   **65 canikin:** *little can or mug (an affectionate diminutive);
cf. n.*   **73 potent in potting:** *mighty in drinking*   **73, 74 swag-bellied:** *fat-
paunched*   **77 Almain:** *German*   **80 do you justice:** *keep pace with you in drinking*   **85 lown:** *loon, lout*   **89 owd:** *old*

111 platform: *rampart*   **115 just equinox:** *exact equivalent (virtue and vice are equal in
him)*   **122** *Cf. n.*   **133 ingraft:** *firmly rooted*   **142 twiggen bottle;** *cf. n.*   **147
mazzard:** *head*   **155 Diablo;** *cf. n.*

Enter Othello and Gentlemen with weapons.

Oth.   What is the matter here?

Mon. Zounds! I bleed still. I am hurt to the death.

Oth. Hold, for your lives!   160

Iago. Hold, hold lieutenant! Sir Montano! gentlemen!

Have you forgot all sense of place and duty?

Hold! the general speaks to you; hold for shame!

Oth. Why, how now, ho! from whence arises this?

Are we turn'd Turks, and to ourselves do that   165

Which heaven has forbid the Ottomites?

For Christian shame put by this barbarous brawl.

He that stirs next to carve for his own rage

Holds his soul light; he dies upon his motion.

Silence that dreadful bell! it frights the isle   170

From her propriety. What's the matter, masters?

Honest Iago, that looks dead with grieving,

Speak, who began this? On thy love, I charge thee.

Iago. I do not know. Friends all but now, even now,

In quarter and in terms like bride and groom   175

Devesting them for bed; and then, but now

(As if some planet had unwitted men)

Swords out, and tilting one at other's breast,

In opposition bloody. I cannot speak

Any beginning to this peevish odds,   180

And would in action glorious I had lost

These legs that brought me to a part of it!

Oth. How came it, Michael, you were thus forgot?

Cas. I pray you, pardon me; I cannot speak.

Oth. Worthy Montano, you were wont be civil.   185

The gravity and stillness of your youth

The world hath noted, and your name is great

In mouths of wisest censure. What's the matter,

That you unlace your reputation thus

And spend your rich opinion for the name   190

Of a night-brawler? give me answer to't.

Mon. Worthy Othello, I am hurt to danger.

Your officer, Iago, can inform you

(While I spare speech, which something now offends me)

Of all that I do know; nor know I aught   195

By me that's said or done amiss this night,

Unless self-charity be sometime a vice,

And to defend ourselves it be a sin

When violence assails us.

Oth.   Now, by heaven,   200

My blood begins my safer guides to rule,

And passion, having my best judgment collied,

Assays to lead the way. Zounds! If I stir,

Or do but lift this arm, the best of you

Shall sink in my rebuke. Give me to know   205

How this foul rout began, who set it on;

And he that is approv'd in this offence,

Though he had twinn'd with me—both at a birth—

Shall lose me. What! in a town of war,

Yet wild, the people's hearts brimful of fear,   210

To manage private and domestic quarrels

In night, and on the court and guard of safety!

'Tis monstrous. Iago, who began't?

Mon. If partially affin'd, or leagu'd in office,

Thou dost deliver more or less than truth,   215

Thou art no soldier.

Iago.   Touch me not so near.

I had rather have this tongue cut from my mouth

Than it should do offence to Michael Cassio;

Yet I persuade myself, to speak the truth   220

Shall nothing wrong him. Thus it is, general.

Montano and myself being in speech,

There comes a fellow crying out for help,

And Cassio following him with determin'd sword

To execute upon him. Sir, this gentleman   225

Steps in to Cassio, and entreats his pause.

Myself the crying fellow did pursue,

Lest by his clamor (as it so fell out)

The town might fall in fright. He, swift of foot,

Outran my purpose, and I return'd the rather   230

For that I heard the clink and fall of swords,

And Cassio high in oath, which till to-night

I ne'er might say before. When I came back

(For this was brief), I found them close together,

At blow and thrust, even as again they were   235

When you yourself did part them.

More of this matter can I not report,

But men are men; the best sometimes forget.

Though Cassio did some little wrong to him,

As men in rage strike those that wish them best,   240

Yet surely Cassio, I believe, receiv'd

From him that fled some strange indignity,

Which patience could not pass.

Oth.   I know, Iago,

Thy honesty and love doth mince this matter,   245

Making it light to Cassio. Cassio, I love thee;

But never more be officer of mine—

Enter Desdemona, with others.

Look, if my gentle love be not rais'd up!—

[*To Cassio.*] I'll make thee an example.

Des.   What's the matter?   250

Oth. All's well now, sweeting. Come away to bed.—

Sir, for your hurts, myself will be your surgeon.

Lead him off.   [*Montano is led off.*]

Iago, look with care about the town,

And silence those whom this vile brawl distracted.   255

Come, Desdemona; 'tis the soldiers' life,

To have their balmy slumbers wak'd with strife.

Ex. Moor, Desdemona, and Attendants.

Iago. What! are you hurt, lieutenant?

Cas. Ay, past all surgery.

Iago. Marry, God forbid!   260

Cas. Reputation, reputation, ⟨reputation! O!⟩ I have lost my reputation. I have lost the immortal part «sir,» of myself, and what remains is bestial. My reputation, ⟨Iago, my reputation!⟩

Iago. As I am an honest man, I thought you had received some bodily wound. There is more sense in that than   265 in reputation. Reputation is an idle and most false imposition, oft got without merit, and lost without deserving. You have

---

162 *Cf. n.*   **166** *Cf. n.*   **168 carve for:** *satisfy*   **171 From her propriety:** *out of her very being*   **175 In ... terms:** *on a footing*   **180 odds:** *quarrel*   **188 censure:** *judgment*   **189 unlace:** *undo*   **190 opinion:** *good name*   **194 something:** *somewhat* **offends:** *harms*   **202 collied:** *blackened (as with coal)*   **206 rout:** *riot*   **207 approv'd:** *convicted*   **211 manage:** *set on foot*   **212 on ... safety:** *cf. n.*

214 partially affin'd: *bound by partiality*   **230 rather:** *sooner*   **239 him:** *i.e., Montano*   **266 imposition:** *adjunct*

lost no reputation at all, unless you repute yourself such
a loser. What, man! there are ways to recover the general
again. You are but now cast in his mood (a punishment   *270*
more in policy than in malice), even so as one would beat his
offenceless dog to affright an imperious lion. Sue to him again,
and he is yours.

Cas. I will rather sue to be despised than to deceive so
good a commander with so slight, so drunken, and so   *275*
indiscreet an officer. ⟨Drunk! and speak parrot! and squabble,
swagger, swear, and discourse fustian with one's own shadow!⟩
O thou invisible spirit of wine! if thou hast no name to be
known by, let us call thee devil!

Iago. What was he that you followed with your sword?   *280*
What had he done to you?

Cas. I know not.

Iago. Is't possible?

Cas. I remember a mass of things, but nothing distinctly;
a quarrel, but nothing wherefore. O God! that men should   *285*
put an enemy in their mouths to steal away their brains; that
we should, with joy, revel, pleasure, and applause, transform
ourselves into beasts.

Iago. Why, but you are now well enough. How came
you thus recovered?   *290*

Cas. It hath pleased the devil drunkenness to give place to
the devil wrath. One unperfectness shows me another, to make
me frankly despise myself.

Iago. Come, you are too severe a moraler. As the time,
the place, and the condition of this country stands, I could   *295*
heartily wish this had not so befallen, but since it is as it is,
mend it for your own good.

Cas. I will ask him for my place again. He shall tell me I
am a drunkard. Had I as many mouths as Hydra, such an
answer would stop them all. To be now a sensible man, by   *300*
and by a fool, and presently a beast! ⟨O strange!⟩ Every
inordinate cup is unblessed and the ingredience is a devil.

Iago. Come, come; good wine is a good familiar creature
if it be well used. Exclaim no more against it. And, good
lieutenant, I think you think I love you.   *305*

Cas. I have well approved it, sir. I drunk!

Iago. You or any man living may be drunk at some time.
I'll tell you what you shall do. Our general's wife is now the
general. I may say so in this respect, for that he has devoted
and given up himself to the contemplation, mark, and   *310*
denotement of her parts and graces. Confess yourself freely to
her; importune her help to put you in your place again She is
of so free, so kind, so apt, so blessed a disposition, that she
holds it a vice in her goodness not to do more than she is
requested. This broken joint between you and her husband   *315*
entreat her to splinter; and my fortunes against any lay worth
naming, this crack of your love shall grow stronger than it was
before.

Cas. You advise me well.

Iago. I protest, in the sincerity of love and honest kind-   *320*
ness.

Cas. I think it freely; and betimes in the morning will I
beseech the virtuous Desdemona to undertake for me. I am
desperate of my fortunes if they check me here.

Iago. You are in the right. Good night, lieutenant; I   *325*
must to the watch.

Cas. Good night, honest Iago!   *Exit Cassio.*

Iago. And what's he, then, that says I play the villain,
When this advice is free I give and honest,
Probal to thinking and indeed the course   *330*
To win the Moor again? For 'tis most easy
Th' inclining Desdemona to subdue
In any honest suit; she's fram'd as fruitful
As the free elements. And then for her
To win the Moor,—were't to renounce his baptism,   *335*
All seals and symbols of redeemed sin,
His soul is so enfetter'd to her love,
That she may make, unmake, do what she list,
Even as her appetite shall play the god
With his weak function. How am I, then a villain   *340*
To counsel Cassio to this parallel course
Directly to his good? Divinity of hell!
When devils will their blackest sins put on,
They do suggest at first with heavenly shows,
As I do now; for while this honest fool   *345*
Plies Desdemona to repair his fortunes,
And she for him pleads strongly to the Moor,
I'll pour this pestilence into his ear
That she repeals him for her body's lust;
And, by how much she strives to do him good,   *350*
She shall undo her credit with the Moor.
So will I turn her virtue into pitch,
And out of her own goodness make the net
That shall enmesh them all.

Enter Roderigo.

     How now, Roderigo?   *355*

Rod. I do follow here in the chase, not like a hound
that hunts, but one that fills up the cry. My money is almost
spent; I have been to-night exceedingly well cudgelled; and I
think the issue will be, I shall have so much experience
for my pains; and so, with no money at all and a little   *360*
more wit, return again to Venice.

Iago. How poor are they that have not patience!
What wound did ever heal but by degrees?
Thou know'st we work by wit and not by witchcraft,
And wit depends on dilatory time.   *365*
Does't not go well? Cassio has beaten thee,
And thou by that small hurt hast cashiered Cassio.
Though other things grow fair against the sun,
Yet fruits that blossom first will first be ripe.
Content thyself awhile. By the mass, 'tis morning;   *370*
Pleasure and action make the hours seem short.
Retire thee; go where thou art billeted.
Away, I say; thou shalt know more hereafter.
Nay, get thee gone.   *Exit Roderigo.*
     Two things are to be done: *375*
My wife must move for Cassio to her mistress—
I'll set her on—;
Myself awhile to draw the Moor apart,
And bring him jump when he may Cassio find

---

270 mood: *temporary feeling*   **276 speak parrot:** *use words irrationally*   **277 discourse fustian:** *talk nonsense*   **294 moraler:** *moralizer*   **299 Hydra;** *cf. n.*   **303 familiar:** *domestic*   **310, 311 denotement:** *observation*   **316 splinter:** *bind with splints* **lay:** *wager*

330 Probal: *probable*   **333 fruitful:** *bountiful*   **340 function:** *charcater*   **341 parallel:** *straight; cf. n.*   **343 put on:** *instigate*   **344 suggest:** *tempt*   **349 repeals:** *recalls to favor*   **357 cry:** *pack of hounds (i.e., I merely go through the motions)*   **379 jump:** *precisely*

Soliciting his wife. Ay, that's the way.   *380*
Dull not device by coldness and delay.   *Exit.*

ACT THIRD ❧ SCENE FIRST

[Before the Citadel]
Enter Cassio with Musicians.

Cas. Masters, play here, I will content your pains.
Something that's brief, and bid 'Good morrow, general.'
                              They play, and enter the Clown.
  Clo. Why, masters, ha' your instruments been at
Naples, that they speak i' th' nose thus?
  Mus. How, sir? how?   *5*
  Clo. Are these, I pray, called wind-instruments?
  Mus. Ay, marry, are they, sir.
  Clo. O! thereby hangs a tail.
  Mus. Whereby hangs a tale, sir?
  Clo. Marry, sir, by many a wind-instrument that I know. *10*
But, masters, here's money for you; and the general so likes
your music that he desires you, of all loves, to make no more
noise with it.
  Mus. Well, sir, we will not.
  Clo. If you have any music that may not be heard, to't *15*
again; but (as they say) to hear music the general does not
greatly care.
  Mus. We ha' none such, sir.
  Clo. Then put up your pipes in your bag, for I'll away.
Go; vanish into air; away!   *Exeunt Musicians. 20*
  Cas. Dost thou hear, my honest friend?
  Clo. No, I hear not your honest friend; I hear you.
  Cas. Prithee, keep up thy quillets. There's a poor piece of
gold for thee. If the gentlewoman that attends the
general's wife be stirring, tell her there's one Cassio entreats *25*
her a little favor of speech. Wilt thou do this?
  Clo. She is stirring, sir. If she will stir hither, I shall seem to
notify unto her.
Cas. «Do, good my friend.   *Exit Clown.*

Enter Iago.

               In happy time, Iago.   *30*
  Iago. You ha' not been a-bed, then?
  Cas. Why, no. The day had broke
Before we parted. I ha' made bold, Iago,
To send in to your wife. My suit to her
Is that she will to virtuous Desdemona   *35*
Procure me some accéss.
  Iago.   I'll send her to you presently;
And I'll devise a mean to draw the Moor
Out of the way, that your converse and business
May be more free.   *40*
  Cas. I humbly thank you for't.   *Exit Iago.*
                   I never knew
A Florentine more kind and honest.
            Enter Emilia.
  Emil. Good morrow, good lieutenant. I am sorry

For your displeasure; but all will soon be well.   *45*
The general and his wife are talking of it,
And she speaks for you stoutly. The Moor replies
That he you hurt is of great fame in Cyprus
And great affinity, and that in wholesome wisdom
He might not but refuse you; but he protests he loves you, *50*
And needs no other suitor but his likings
«To take the saf'st occasion by the front»
To bring you in again.
  Cas.   Yet, I beseech you,
If you think fit, or that it may be done,   *55*
Give me advantage of some brief discourse
With Desdemona alone.
  Emil.   Pray you, come in.
I will bestow you where you shall have time
To speak your bosom freely.   *60*
  ⟨*Cas.*   I am much bound to you.⟩
                          Exeunt.

❧ SCENE SECOND ❧

[A Room in the Citadel]
Enter Othello, Iago, and other Gentlemen.

  Oth. These letters give, Iago, to the pilot,
And by him do my duties to the state.
That done, I will be walking on the works;
Repair there to me.
  Iago.   Well, my good lord, I'll do't.   *5*
  Oth. This fortification, gentlemen, shall we see't?
  Gent. We wait upon your lordship.   *Exeunt.*

❧ SCENE THIRD ❧

[The garden of the Citadel]
Enter Desdemona, Cassio, and Emilia.

  Des. Be thou assur'd, good Cassio, I will do
All my abilities in thy behalf.
  Emil. Good madam, do. I know it grieves my husband,
As if the case were his.
  Des. O that's an honest fellow! Do not doubt, Cassio, *5*
But I will have my lord and you again
As friendly as you were.
  Cas.   Bounteous madam,
Whatever shall become of Michael Cassio,
He's never anything but your true servant.   *10*
  Des. O, sir, I thank you. You do love my lord.
You have known him long; and be you well assur'd
He shall in strangeness stand no farther off
Than in a politic distance.
  Cas.   Ay, but, lady,   *15*
That policy may either last so long,
Or feed upon such nice and waterish diet,
Or breed itself so out of circumstances,
That, I being absent and my place supplied,
My general will forget my love and service.   *20*

S.d. **Clown**; *cf. n.*   **3, 4** *Cf. n.*   **12 of all loves:** *for goodness' sake*   **23 qillets:**
quibbles   **25 stirring:** *up and dressed* (in the morning)   **30 In happy time:** *well
met*   **37 presently:** *immediately*   **43 Florentine;** *cf. n.*

45 displeasure: *misfortune*   **49 affinity:** *family connection*   **52** *Cf. n.*   **60 bosom:**
private thoughts and feelings   **2 state;** *cf. n.*   **13 strangeness:** *estrangement*   **16–18** *Cf. n.*
17 nice: *finical*   **waterish:** *watered, thin*

Des. Do not doubt that. Before Emilia here
I give thee warrant of thy place. Assure thee,
If I do vow a friendship, I'll perform it
To the last article. My lord shall never rest;
I'll watch him tame, and talk him out of patience;   *25*
His bed shall seem a school, his board a shrift;
I'll intermingle everything he does
With Cassio's suit. Therefore be merry, Cassio;
For thy solicitor shall rather die
Than give thy cause away.   *30*

      Enter Othello and Iago [at a distance].

Emil. Madam, here comes my lord.
Cas. Madam, I'll take my leave.
Des. Why, stay, and hear me speak.
Cas. Madam, not now. I am very ill at ease,
Unfit for mine own purposes.   *35*
      Des. Well, do your discretion.   *Exit Cassio.*
Iago. Ha! I like not that.
Oth.   What dost thou say?
Iago. Nothing, my lord; or if—I know not what.
Oth. Was not that Cassio parted from my wife?   *40*
Iago. Cassio, my lord? No, sure, I cannot think it,
That he would steal away so guilty-like,
Seeing you coming.
      Oth.   I do believe 'twas he.
Des. How now, my lord!   *45*
I have been talking with a suitor here,
A man that languishes in your displeasure.
      Oth. Who is't you mean?
      Des. Why, your lieutenant, Cassio. Good my lord,
If I have any grace or power to move you,   *50*
His present reconciliation take;
For if he be not one that truly loves you,
That errs in ignorance and not in cunning,
I have no judgment in an honest face.
I prithee call him back.   *55*
      Oth.   Went he hence now?
      Des. Yes, faith; so humbled,
That he has left part of his griefs with me.
I suffer with him. Good love, call him back.
      Oth. Not now, sweet Desdemon. Some other time.   *60*
Des. But shall't be shortly?
      Oth.   The sooner, sweet, for you.
Des. Shall't be to-night at supper?
      Oth.   No, not to-night.
Des. To-morrow dinner then?   *65*
      Oth.   I shall not dine at home.
I meet the captains at the citadel.
      Des. Why then, to-morrow night, or Tuesday morn;
On Tuesday noon, or night; on Wednesday morn.
I prithee name the time, but let it not   *70*
Exceed three days. I' faith, he's penitent;
And yet his trespass, in our common reason
(Save that they say, the wars must make examples
Out of their best), is not almost a fault
T' incur a private check. When shall he come?   *75*
Tell me, Othello. I wonder in my soul,

What you could ask me that I should deny,
Or stand so mammering on. What? Michael Cassio,
That came a-wooing with you, and so many a time,
When I have spoke of you dispraisingly,   *80*
Hath ta'en your part; to have so much to do
To bring him in! By'r Lady, I could do much—
      Oth. Prithee, no more! Let him come when he will.
I will deny thee nothing.
      Des.   Why, this is not a boon.   *85*
'Tis as I should entreat you wear your gloves,
Or feed on nourishing dishes, or keep you warm,
Or sue to you to do a peculiar profit
To your own person. Nay, when I have a suit
Wherein I mean to touch your love indeed,   *90*
It shall be full of poise and difficúlty,
And fearful to be granted.
      Oth.   I will deny thee nothing.
Whereon, I do beseech thee, grant me this,
To leave me but a little to myself.   *95*
      Des. Shall I deny you? No. Farewell, my lord.
      Oth. Farewell, my Desdemona. I'll come to thee straight.
      Des. Emilia, come. Be it as your fancies teach you.
Whate'er you be, I am obedient.
      Exeunt Desdemona and Emilia. *100*
      Oth. Excellent wretch! Perdition catch my soul
But I do love thee! and when I love thee not,
Chaos is come again.
      Iago. My noble lord,—
      Oth.   What does thou say, Iago?   *105*
      Iago. Did Michael Cassio, when you woo'd my lady,
Know of your love?
      Oth. He did, from first to last. Why dost thou ask?
      Iago. But for a satisfaction of my thought.
No further harm.   *110*
      Oth.   Why of thy thought, Iago?
      Iago. I did not think he had been acquainted with her.
      Oth. O yes; and went between us very oft.
      Iago. Indeed?
      Oth. Indeed? ay, indeed. Discern'st thou aught in that?   *115*
Is he not honest?
      Iago.   Honest, my lord?
      Oth.   Honest? ay, honest.
      Iago. My lord, for aught I know.
      Oth. What dost thou think?   *120*
      Iago.   Think, my lord?
      Oth.   Think, my lord?
By heaven, he echoes me,
As if there were some monster in his thought
Too hideous to be shown.—Thou didst mean something.   *125*
I heard thee say but now, thou lik'st not that,
When Cassio left my wife. What didst not like?
And when I told thee he was of my counsel
In my whole course of wooing, thou criedst, 'Indeed?'
And didst contract and purse thy brow together,   *130*
As if thou then hadst shut up in thy brain
Some horrible conceit. If thou dost love me,
Show me thy thought.
      Iago. My lord, you know I love you.

---

21 doubt: *fear*   **25 watch him tame;** *cf. n.*   **26 shrift:** *confessional*   **36 do your discretion:** *do what seems to you discreet*   **68 to-morrow ... morn;** *cf. n.*   **74 not almost:** *almost not, scarcely*

78 mammering: *hesitating*   **82 in:** *into favor*   **91 poise:** *weight*   **101 wretch:** *expression of utmost fondness*   **103** *Cf. n.*   **106** *Cf. n.*   **128 of my counsel:** *in my confidence*   **132 conceit:** *idea*

Oth.   I think thou dost;   *135*
And, for I know thou'rt full of love and honesty,
And weigh'st thy words before thou give 'em breath,
Therefore these stops of thine fright me the more;
For such things in a false disloyal knave
Are tricks of custom, but in a man that's just   *140*
They are close delations, working from the heart
That passion cannot rule.
     Iago.   For Michael Cassio,
I dare be sworn I think that he is honest.
     Oth. I think so too.   *145*
     Iago.   Men should be what they seem;
Or those that be not, would they might seem none!
     Oth. Certain, men should be what they seem.
     Iago. Why then, I think Cassio's an honest man.
     Oth. Nay, yet there's more in this.   *150*
I pray thee, speak to me as to thy thinkings,
As thou dost ruminate, and give thy worst of thoughts
The worst of words.
     Iago.   Good my lord, pardon me;
Though I am bound to every act of duty,   *155*
I am not bound to that all slaves are free to.
Utter my thoughts? Why, say they are vile and false;
As where's that palace whereinto foul things
Sometimes intrude not? who has a breast so pure
But some uncleanly apprehensions   *160*
Keep leets and law-days, and in session sit
With meditations lawful?
     Oth. Thou dost conspire against thy friend, Iago,
If thou but think'st him wrong'd, and mak'st his ear
A stranger to thy thoughts.   *165*
     Iago.   I do beseech you,
Though I perchance am vicious in my guess
(As, I confess, it is my nature's plague
To spy into abuses, and oft my jealousy
Shapes faults that are not)—I entreat you then,   *170*
From one that so imperfectly conjects,
You'd take no notice, nor build yourself a trouble
Out of my scattering and unsure observance.
It were not for your quiet nor your good,
Nor for my manhood, honesty, or wisdom,   *175*
To let you know my thoughts.
     Oth.   «Zounds!» ⟨What dost thou mean?⟩
     Iago. Good name in man, and woman, dear my lord,
Is the immediate jewel of our souls.
Who steals my purse steals trash. 'Tis something, nothing;   *180*
'Twas mine, 'tis his, and has been slave to thousands;
But he that filches from me my good name
Robs me of that which not enriches him,
And makes me poor indeed.
     Oth. By heaven, I'll know thy thought.   *185*
     Iago. You cannot, if my heart were in your hand;
Nor shall not, whilst 'tis in my custody.
     Oth. Ha!
     Iago.   O beware, my lord, of jealousy!
It is the green-ey'd monster which doth mock   *190*

The meat it feeds on. That cuckold lives in bliss
Who, certain of his fate, loves not his wronger;
But, O, what damned minutes tell she o'er
Who dotes, yet doubts; suspects, yet strongly loves!
     Oth. O misery!   *195*
     Iago. Poor and content is rich, and rich enough,
But riches fineless is as poor as winter
To him that ever fears he shall be poor.
Good God, the souls of all my tribe defend
From jealousy.   *200*
     Oth.   Why, why is this?
Think'st thou I'd make a life of jealousy,
To follow still the changes of the moon
With fresh suspicions? No; to be once in doubt
Is once to be resolv'd. Exchange me for a goat   *205*
When I shall turn the business of my soul
To such exsufflicate and blown surmises,
Matching thy inference. 'Tis not to make me jealous
To say my wife is fair, feeds well, loves company,
Is free of speech, sings, plays, and dances well.   *210*
Where virtue is, these are more virtuous.
Nor from mine own weak merits will I draw
The smallest fear or doubt of her revolt;
For she had eyes and chose me. No, Iago.
I'll see before I doubt; when I doubt, prove;   *215*
And, on the proof, there is no more but this:
Away at once with love or jealousy!
     Iago. I am glad of this; for now I shall have reason
To show the love and duty that I bear you
With franker spirit. Therefore (as I am bound)   *220*
Receive it from me—I speak not yet of proof.
Look to your wife. Observe her well with Cassio.
Wear your eye thus, not jealous nor secure.
I would not have your free and noble nature
Out of self-bounty be abus'd. Look to't!   *225*
I know our country disposition well;
In Venice they do let God see the pranks
They dare not show their husbands. Their best conscience
Is not to leave undone, but keep unknown.
     Oth. Dost thou say so?   *230*
     Iago. She did deceive her father, marrying you:
And when she seem'd to shake and fear your looks,
She lov'd them most.
     Oth.   And so she did.
     Iago.   Why, go to, then.   *235*
She that so young could give out such a seeming,
To seel her father's eyes up close as oak,—
He thought 'twas witchcraft—but I am much to blame.
I humbly do beseech you of your pardon
For too much loving you.   *240*
     Oth.   I am bound to thee for ever.
     Iago. I see, this hath a little dash'd your spirits.
     Oth. Not a jot, not a jot.
     Iago.   I' faith, I fear it has.
I hope you will consider what is spoke   *245*
Comes from my love. But I do see you're mov'd.
I am to pray you not to strain my speech
To grosser issues nor to large reach

138 stops: *pauses, reticences*   **140 tricks of custom:** *habitual tricks*   **141 close delations:** *covert, involuntary accusations*   **147 seem none;** *cf. n.*   **160 But:** *but therein*   **161 leets:** *synonymous with 'law-days'* (**keep leet:** *hold court*)   **167 Though:** *supposing, granting that*   **vicious:** *wrong*   **171 conjects:** *imagines; cf. n.*   **173 scattering:** *random*   **179 our souls;** *cf. n.*   **190, 191 mock . . . feeds on:** *tantalizes its victim*

195 O misery; *cf. n.*   **197 fineless:** *endless*   **205 resolv'd:** *freed from uncertainty*   **207 exsufflicate:** *puffed up, empty; cf. n.*   **220 as I am bound:** *this being my duty*   **225 self-bounty:** *inherent generosity*   **226 country:** *native*

Than to suspicion.

    Oth. I will not.   250

    Iago.   Should you do so, my lord,

My speech should fall into such vile success

As my thoughts aim not at. Cassio's my trusty friend—

My lord, I see you're mov'd.

    Oth.   No, not much mov'd.   255

I do not think but Desdemona's honest.

    Iago. Long live she so! and long live you to think so!

    Oth. And, yet, how nature erring from itself,—

    Iago. Ay, there's the point: as (to be bold with you)

Not to affect many proposed matches   260

Of her own clime, complexion, and degree,

Whereto, we see, in all things nature tends—

Foh! one may smell, in such a will, most rank,

Foul disproportion, thoughts unnatural.

But pardon me; I do not in position   265

Distinctly speak of her, though I may fear

Her will, recoiling to her better judgment,

May fall to match you with her country forms

And happily repent.

    Oth.   Farewell, farewell.   270

If more thou dost perceive, let me know more.

Set on thy wife to observe. Leave me, Iago.

    Iago. My lord, I take my leave.   *[Going.]*

    Oth. Why did I marry? This honest creature, doubtless,

Sees and knows more, much more, than he unfolds.   275

    Iago [returning]. My lord, I would I might entreat your honor

To scan this thing no further; leave it to time.

Though it be fit that Cassio have his place

(For sure he fills it up with great ability),   280

Yet if you please to hold him off awhile,

You shall by that perceive him and his means.

Note if your lady strain his entertainment

With any strong or vehement importunity;

Much will be seen in that. In the mean time,   285

Let me be thought too busy in my fears,

As worthy cause I have to fear I am,

And hold her free, I do beseech your honor.

    Oth. Fear not my government.

    Iago. I once more take my leave.   *Exit.* 290

    Oth. This fellow's of exceeding honesty,

And knows all qualities, with a learned spirit

Of human dealing. If I do prove her haggard,

Though that her jesses were my dear heartstrings,

I'd whistle her off and let her down the wind,   295

To prey at fortune. Haply, for I am black,

And have not those soft parts of conversation

That chamberers have, or for I am declin'd

Into the vale of years (yet that's not much)—

She's gone, I am abus'd, and my relief   300

Must be to loathe her. O curse of marriage!

That we can call these delicate creatures ours,

And not their appetites. I had rather be a toad,

And live upon the vapor of a dungeon,

Than keep a corner in the thing I love   305

For others' uses. Yet, 'tis the plague of great ones;

Prerogativ'd are they less than the base.

'Tis destiny unshunnable, like death:

Even then this forked plague is fated to us

When we do quicken.   310

                          Look, where she comes!

If she be false, O then heaven mocks itself.

I'll not believe't.

Enter Desdemona and Emilia.

    Des.   How now, my dear Othello?

Your dinner and the generous islanders   315

By you invited do attend your presence.

    Oth. I am to blame.

    Des.   Why is your speech so faint?

Are you not well?

    Oth. I have a pain upon my forehead here.   320

    Des. Faith, that's with watching; 'twill away again.

Let me but bind your head; within this hour

It will be well.

    Oth.   Your napkin is too little.

    [He puts the handkerchief from him, and it drops.]

Let it alone. Come, I'll go in with you.   325

    Des. I am very sorry that you arc not well.

                         Exeunt Othello and Desdemona.

    Emil. I am glad I have found this napkin.

This was her first remembrance from the Moor.

My wayward husband hath a hundred times   330

Woo'd me to steal it, but she so loves the token

(For he conjur'd her she should ever keep it)

That she reserves it evermore about her

To kiss and talk to. I'll have the work ta'en out

And give't Iago.   335

What he will do with it heaven knows, not I.

I nothing know, but for his fantasy—

Enter Iago.

    Iago. How now! what do you here alone?

    Emil. Do not you chide. I have a thing for you.

    Iago. A thing for me? It is a common thing—   340

    Emil. Ha?

    Iago. To have a foolish wife.

    Emil. O, is that all? What will you give me now

For that same handkerchief?

    Iago.   What handkerchief?   345

    Emil. What handkerchief?

Why, that the Moor first gave to Desdemona;

That which so often you did bid me steal.

    Iago. Hast stol'n it from her?

    Emil. No, faith. She let it drop by negligence,   350

And, to th' advantage, I, being here, took't up.

Look, here it is.

    Iago.   A good wench! give it me.

    Emil. What will you do with't, that you have been so earnest   355

---

252 success: *consequences*   **256 honest:** *virtuous*   **265 position:** *formal logical thesis*   **267 recoiling:** *adjusting itself*   **268 fall:** *chance*   **country forms:** *the types she has been accustomed to*   **269 happily:** *perhaps*   **282 means:** *the methods he uses*   **283 strain his entertainment:** *urge his reinstatement*   **288 free:** *guiltless*   **289 government:** *self control*   **292 qualities:** *kinds of people*   **292, 293 learned . . . dealing:** *mind expert in human intercourse*   **293–296** *Cf. n.*   **297 soft . . . conversation:** *effeminate talents in social intercourse*   **298 chamberers:** *wanton courtiers*

307 Prerogativ'd: *privileged, protected*   **309 forked plague:** *cuckold's horns*   **310 When . . . quicken:** *in prenatal life*   **315 generous:** *noble, of gentle birth*   **321 watching:** *lack of sleep*   **322 your head;** *cf. n.*   **324 napkin:** *handkerchief*   **330 a hundred times;** *cf. n.*   **334 work ta'en out:** *embroidery copied*   **344 handkerchief;** *cf. n.*

To have me filch it?

Iago.   Why, what's that to you? *[Snatches it.]*

  Emil. If it be not for some purpose of import,
Give me't again. Poor lady, she'll run mad
When she shall lack it.   360

  Iago. Be not acknown on't. I have use for it.
Go, leave me.   *Exit Emilia.*
I will in Cassio's lodging lose this napkin,
And let him find it. Trifles light as air
Are to the jealous confirmations strong   365
As proofs of holy writ; this may do something.
⟨The Moor already changes with my poison.⟩
Dangerous conceits are in their natures poisons,
Which at the first are scarce found to distaste,
But, with a little act upon the blood,   370
Burn like the mines of sulphur. I did say so.
Look, where he comes!

Enter Othello.

          Not poppy, nor mandragora,
Nor all the drowsy syrups of the world,
Shall ever medicine thee to that sweet sleep   375
Which thou ow'dst yesterday.

  Oth.   Ha! ha! false to me?

  Iago. Why, how now, general? No more of that.

  Oth. Avaunt! be gone! Thou hast set me on the rack.
I swear 'tis better to be much abus'd   380
Than but to know't a little.

  Iago.   How now, my lord?

  Oth. What sense had I of her stol'n hours of lust?
I saw't not, thought it not, it harm'd not me.
I slept the next night well, was free and merry;   385
I found not Cassio's kisses on her lips.
He that is robb'd, not wanting what is stol'n,
Let him not know't and he's not robb'd at all.

  Iago. I am sorry to hear this.

  Oth. I had been happy if the general camp,   390
Pioners and all, had tasted her sweet body,
So I had nothing known. O, now for ever
Farewell the tranquil mind! farewell content!
Farewell the plumed troops and the big wars
That make ambition virtue! O, farewell!   395
Farewell the neighing steed, and the shrill trump,
The spirit-stirring drum, th' ear-piercing fife,
The royal banner, and all quality,
Pride, pomp, and circumstance of glorious war!
And, O ye mortal engines, whose wide throats   400
Th' immortal Jove's great clamor counterfeit,
Farewell! Othello's occupation's gone!

  Iago. Is't possible, my lord?

  Oth. Villain, be sure thou prove my love a whore,
Be sure of it! Give me the ocular proof;   405
Or by the worth of man's eternal soul,
Thou hadst been better have been born a dog
Than answer my wak'd wrath.

  Iago.   Is't come to this?

  Oth. Make me to see't; or, at the least, so prove it   410

That the probation bear no hinge nor loop
To hang a doubt on, or woe upon thy life!

  Iago. My noble lord,—

  Oth. If thou dost slander her and torture me,
Never pray more. Abandon all remorse;   415
On horror's head horrors accumulate;
Do deeds to make heaven weep, all earth amaz'd;
For nothing canst thou to damnation add
Greater than that.

  Iago.   O grace! O heaven defend me!   420
Are you a man? Have you a soul or sense?
God be wi' you! Take mine office. O wretched fool!
That liv'st to make thine honesty a vice.
O monstrous world! Take note, take note, O world,
To be direct and honest is not safe.   425
I thank you for this profit, and from hence
I'll love no friend, sith love breeds such offence.

  Oth. Nay, stay. Thou shouldst be honest.

  Iago. I should be wise, for honesty's a fool,
And loses that it works for.   430

  ⟨*Oth.*   By the world,
I think my wife be honest and think she is not;
I think that thou art just and think thou art not.
I'll have some proof. Her name, that was as fresh
As Dian's visage, is now begrim'd and black   435
As mine own face. If there be cords or knives,
Poison or fire or suffocating streams,
I'll not endure it. Would I were satisfied!

  Iago.⟩ I see, sir, you are eaten up with passion.
I do repent me that I put it to you.   440
You would be satisfied?

  Oth.   Would? Nay, I will!

  Iago. And may; but how? How satisfied, my lord?
Would you, the supervisor, grossly gape on,
Behold her topp'd?   445

  Oth.   Death and damnation! O!

  Iago. It were a tedious difficulty, I think,
To bring them to that prospect. Damn them, then,
If ever mortal eyes do see them bolster
More than their own. What then? how then?   450
What shall I say? Where's satisfaction?
It is impossible you should see this,
Were they as prime as goats, as hot as monkeys,
As salt as wolves in pride, and fools as gross
As ignorance made drunk. But yet, I say,   455
If imputation, and strong circumstances,
Which lead directly to the door of truth,
Will give you satisfaction, you may have't.

  Oth. Give me a living reason she's disloyal.

  Iago. I do not like the office;   460
But sith I am enter'd in this cause so far
(Prick'd to't by foolish honesty and love),
I will go on. I lay with Cassio lately;
And, being troubled with a raging tooth,
I could not sleep.   465
There are a kind of men so loose of soul

361 Be . . . on't: *admit no knowledge of it*   **370 with . . . act:** *after brief operation*   **371
I did say so:** *just as I was saying!*   **373 mandragora:** *mandrake, a narcotic*   **387 wanting:**
missing   **391 Pioners:** *miners, military menials*   **399 circumstance:** *ceremony*   **400
engines:** *cannon*   **wide;** *cf. n.*   **401 great clamor:** *thunder*

411 probation: *proof*   **hinge nor loop:** *pivot nor strap*   **415 remorse:** *compunction*   **416
accumulate:** *pile up*   **426 profit:** *profitable lesson*   **427 sith:** *since*   **434 Her;** *cf. n.*
440 put: *confided*   **449 bolster:** *bed (together)*   **453 prime:** *ardent*   **454 in pride:**
in heat   **456 imputation . . . circumstances:** *opinion based on strong circumstantial evidence*   **459 living:** *real, not sham*

That in their sleeps will mutter their affairs.
One of this kind is Cassio.
In sleep I heard him say, 'Sweet Desdemona,
Let us be wary, let us hide our loves!'   470
And then, sir, would he gripe and wring my hand,
Cry out 'Sweet creature!' and then kiss me hard,
As if he pluck'd up kisses by the roots
That grew upon my lips; then laid his leg
Over my thigh, and sigh'd, and kiss'd; and then   475
Cried, 'Cursed fate, that gave thee to the Moor!'
   Oth. O monstrous! monstrous!
   Iago.   Nay, this was but his dream.
   Oth. But this denoted a foregone conclusion.
   Oth. 'Tis a shrewd doubt, though it be but a dream;   480
And this may help to thicken other proofs
That do demonstrate thinly.
   Oth.   I'll tear her all to pieces!
   Iago. Nay, but be wise. Yet we see nothing done;
She may be honest yet. Tell me but this: 485
Have you not sometimes seen a handkerchief
Spotted with strawberries in your wife's hand?
   Oth. I gave her such a one. 'Twas my first gift.
   Iago. I know not that; but such a handkerchief
(I am sure it was your wife's) did I to-day   490
See Cassio wipe his beard with.
   Oth.   If 't be that,—
   Iago. If it be that, or any that was hers,
It speaks against her with the other proofs.
   Oth. O that the slave had forty thousand lives!   495
One is too poor, too weak, for my revenge.
Now do I see 'tis true. Look here, Iago;
All my fond love thus do I blow to heaven.

                             [Hisses contemptuously.]
'Tis gone.
Arise, black vengeance, from thy hollow cell!   500
Yield up, O love, thy crown and hearted throne
To tyrannous hate. Swell, bosom, with thy fraught,
For 'tis of aspics' tongues!
   Iago.   Pray, be content.
   Oth. O blood! Iago, blood!   505
   Iago. Patience, I say. Your mind, perhaps, may change.
   Oth. Never ⟨Iago. Like to the Pontic sea,
Whose icy current and compulsive course
Ne'er feels retiring ebb, but keeps due on
To the Propontic and the Hellespont,   510
Even so my bloody thoughts, with violent pace,
Shall ne'er look back, ne'er ebb to humble love,
Till that a capable and wide revenge
Swallow them up.   *He kneels.*
             Now, by yond marble heaven,⟩   515
In the due reverence of a sacred vow
I here engage my words.
   Iago.   Do not rise yet.   *Kneels.*
Witness, you ever-burning lights above!
You elements that clip us round about!   520
Witness that here Iago doth give up

The execution of his wit, hands, heart,
To wrong'd Othello's service! Let him command,
And to obey shall be in me remorse,
What bloody work soever.   *[They rise.]* 525
   Oth.   I greet thy love,
Not with vain thanks, but with acceptance bounteous,
And will upon the instant put thee to't.
Within these three days let me hear thee say
That Cassio's not alive.   530
   Iago. My friend is dead; 'tis done as you request.
But let her live.
   Oth.   Damn her, lewd minx! O, damn her!
Come, go with me apart. I will withdraw
To furnish me with some swift means of death   535
For the fair devil. Now art thou my lieutenant.
   Iago. I am your own for ever.   *Exeunt.*

❧ Scene Fourth ❧

[Before the Citadel]
Enter Desdemona, Emilia, and the Clown.

   Des. Do you know, sirrah, where Lieutenant Cassio lies?
   Clo. I dare not say he lies anywhere.
   Des. Why, man?
   Clo. He is a soldier, and for one to say a soldier lies is
stabbing.   5
   Des. Go to! Where lodges he?
   ⟨*Clo.* To tell you where he lodges is to tell you where I lie.
   Des. Can anything be made of this?⟩
   Clo. I know not where he lodges, and for me to devise a
lodging, and say he lies here or he lies there, were to lie in   10
mine own throat.
   Des. Can you inquire him out, and be edified by report?
   Clo. I will catechize the world for him; that is, make
questions, and by them answer.
   Des. Seek him. Bid him come hither; tell him I have   15
moved my lord in his behalf, and hope all will be well.
   Clo. To do this is within the compass of man's wit, and
therefore I will attempt the doing it.   *Exit Clown.*
   Des. Where should I lose that handkerchief, Emilia?
   Emil. I know not, madam.   20
   Des. Believe me, I had rather have lost my purse
Full of cruzadoes; and but my noble Moor
Is true of mind, and made of no such baseness
As jealous creatures are, it were enough
To put him to ill thinking.   25
   Emil.   Is he not jealous?
   Des. Who, he? I think the sun where he was born
Drew all such humors from him.
   Emil.   Look where he comes!
   Des. I will not leave him now till Cassio   30
Be call'd to him.

              Enter Othello.

         How is't with you, my lord?
   Oth. Well, my good lady. *[Aside.]* O hardness to
dissemble!—

---

479 **foregone conclusion:** *a previous experience*   480 **shrewd doubt:** *ground for dire suspicion; cf. n.*   481 **thicken:** *give substance to*   487 **Spotted:** *embroidered*   493 **any that;** *cf. n.*   495 **the slave:** *Cassio*   500 **hollow cell:** *underground prison*   502 **fraught:** *freight, burden*   503 **aspics:** *asps', venomous snakes'* **content:** *quiet*   507-515 *Cf. n.*   513 **capable:** *comprehensive*   515 **marble:** *inflexible*   520 **clip:** *enclose*

522 **execution:** *exercise*   524 **remorse:** *conscience*   528 **to't:** *to the test*   12 **be edified by report:** *make intelligent use of what you hear*   22 **cruzadoes:** *Portuguese gold coins*

How do you, Desdemona?   *35*
   Des.   Well, my good lord.
   Oth. Give me your hand. This hand is moist, my lady.
   Des. It yet has felt no age nor known no sorrow.
   Oth. This argues fruitfulness and liberal heart:
Hot, hot, and moist. This hand of yours requires   *40*
A séquester from liberty, fasting and prayer,
Much castigation, exercise devout;
For here's a young and sweating devil here
That commonly rebels. 'Tis a good hand,
A frank one.   *45*
   Des.   You may, indeed, say so,
For 'twas that hand that gave away my heart.
   Oth. A liberal hand! The hearts of old gave hands,
But our new heraldry is hands not hearts.
   Des. I cannot speak of this. Come now, your promise.   *50*
   Oth. What promise, chuck?
   Des. I have sent to bid Cassio come speak with you.
   Oth. I have a salt and sorry rheum offends me.
Lend me thy handkerchief.
   Des.   Here, my lord.   *55*
   Oth. That which I gave you.
   Des.   I have it not about me.
   Oth. Not?
   Des.   No, 'faith, my lord.
   Oth.   That is a fault.   *60*
That handkerchief
Did an Egyptian to my mother give.
She was a charmer and could almost read
The thoughts of people. She told her, while she kept it,
'Twould make her amiable and subdue my father   *65*
Entirely to her love, but if she lost it
Or made a gift of it, my father's eye
Should hold her loathly, and his spirits should hunt
After new fancies. She dying gave it me;
And bid me, when my fate would have me wive,   *70*
To give it her. I did so,—and take heed on't;
Make it a darling like your precious eye.
To lose or give't away were such perdition
As nothing else could match.
   Des.   Is't possible?   *75*
   Oth. 'Tis true. There's magic in the web of it.
A sibyl, that had number'd in the world
The sun to course two hundred compasses,
In her prophetic fury sew'd the work.
The worms were hallow'd that did breed the silk,   *80*
And it was dy'd in mummy which the skilful
Conserv'd of maidens' hearts.
   Des.   I' faith? is't true?
   Oth. Most veritable; therefore look to't well.
   Des. Then would to God that I had never seen it!   *85*
   Oth. Ha? wherefore?
   Des. Why do you speak so startingly and rash?
   Oth. Is't lost? is't gone? Speak! Is't out o' the way?
   Des. Heaven bless us!
   Oth.   Say you?   *90*

   Des. It is not lost: but what an if it were?
   Oth. How!
   Des. I say, it is not lost.
   Oth.   Fetch't, let me see't.
   Des. Why, so I can, sir, but I will not now.   *95*
This is a trick to put me from my suit.
Pray you, let Cassio be receiv'd again.
   Oth. Fetch me that handkerchief. My mind misgives.
   Des. Come, come;
You'll never meet a more sufficient man.   *100*
   «*Oth.* The handkercher!
   Des.   I pray, talk me of Cassio.»
   Oth. The handkerchief!
   Des.   A man that all his time
Hath founded his good fortunes on your love,   *105*
Shar'd dangers with you,—
   Oth. The handkerchief!
   Des.   I' faith, you are to blame.
   Oth. Zounds!   *Exit Othello.*
   Emil. Is not this man jealous?   *110*
   Des. I ne'er saw this before.
Sure, there's some wonder in this handkerchief.
I am most unhappy in the loss of it.
   Emil. 'Tis not a year or two shows us a man.
They are all but stomachs, and we all but food.   *115*
They eat us hungerly, and when they are full
They belch us. Look you! Cassio and my husband.

          Enter Iago and Cassio.

   Iago. There is no other way; 'tis she must do't.
And, lo, the happiness! Go and impórtune her.
   Des. How now, good Cassio? what's the news with you?   *120*
   Cas. Madam, my former suit. I do beseech you
That by your virtuous means I may again
Exist, and be a member of his love
Whom I with all the office of my heart
Entirely honor. I would not be delay'd.   *125*
If my offence be of such mortal kind
That nor my service past, nor present sorrows,
Nor purpos'd merit in futurity,
Can ransom me into his love again,
But to know so must be my benefit.   *130*
So shall I clothe me in a forc'd content,
And shut myself up in some other course
To fortune's alms.
   Des.   Alas, thrice-gentle Cassio,
My advocation is not now in tune.   *135*
My lord is not my lord; nor should I know him,
Were he in favor as in humor alter'd.
So help me every spirit sanctified,
As I have spoken for you all my best
And stood within the blank of his displeasure   *140*
For my free speech. You must awhile be patient.
What I can do I will, and more I will
Than for myself I dare. Let that suffice you.
   Iago. Is my lord angry?
   Emil.   He went hence but now,   *145*

41 séquester: *separation*   **48, 49** *Cf. n.*   **51 chuck:** *chick* (term of endearment)   **53 sorry rheum:** *distressing discharge* (of eye or nose); *cf. n.*   **63 charmer:** *witch*   **77 sibyl:** *inspired prophetess*   **78 course . . . compasses:** *make . . . revolutions*   **81 mummy:** *drug made from embalmed bodies*   **84 Most veritable;** *cf. n.*   **87 startingly and rash:** *impetuously and fast*

113 *Cf. n.*   **115 but . . . but:** *merely . . . merely*   **119 the happiness:** *what luck!*   **124 office:** *duty*   **127 nor . . . nor:** *neither . . . nor*   **130 But:** *merely*   **132 shut . . . in:** *confine myself to*   **133 To . . . alms:** *in pursuit of fortune's favor*   **137 humor:** *disposition*   **140 blank:** *range* (literally, target)

And certainly in strange unquietness.
   Iago. Can he be angry? I have seen the cannon,
When it hath blown his ranks into the air,
And, like the devil, from his very arm
Puff'd his own brother,—and can he be angry?   *150*
Something of moment then. I will go meet him;
There's matter in't indeed, if he be angry.
   Des. I prithee, do so.   *Exit [Iago.]*
                       Something, sure, of state,
Either from Venice, or some unhatch'd practice   *155*
Made démonstrable here in Cyprus to him,
Hath puddled his clear spirit; and in such cases
Men's natures wrangle with inferior things,
Though great ones are their object. 'Tis even so;
For let our finger ache, and it endues   *160*
Our other healthful members ev'n to that sense
Of pain. Nay, we must think men are not gods,
Nor of them look for such observancy
As fits the bridal. Beshrew me much, Emilia,
I was (unhandsome warrior as I am)   *165*
Arraigning his unkindness with my soul;
But now I find I had suborn'd the witness,
And he's indicted falsely.
   Emil. Pray heaven it be state-matters, as you think,
And no conception, nor no jealous toy   *170*
Concerning you.
   Des. Alas the day! I never gave him cause.
   Emil. But jealous souls will not be answer'd so.
They are not ever jealous for the cause,
But jealous for they are jealous. 'Tis a monster   *175*
Begot upon itself, born on itself.
   Des. Heaven keep that monster from Othello's mind!
   Emil. Lady, amen.
   Des. I will go seek him. Cassio, walk hereabout.
If I do find him fit, I'll move your suit   *180*
And seek to effect it to my uttermost.
   Cas. I humbly thank your ladyship.
              Exeunt Desdemona and Emilia.

            Enter Bianca.

   Bian. 'Save you, friend Cassio!
   Cas.   What make you from home?
How is it with you, my most fair Bianca?   *185*
I' faith, sweet love, I was coming to your house.
   Bian. And I was going to your lodging, Cassio.
What! keep a week away? seven days and nights?
Eight score eight hours? and lovers' absent hours,
More tedious than the dial eight score times?   *190*
O weary reckoning!
   Cas.   Pardon me, Bianca,
I have this while with leaden thoughts been press'd,
But I shall, in a more continuate time,
Strike off this score of absence. Sweet Bianca,   *195*
        [giving her Desdemona's handkerchief]
Take me this work out.

   Bian.   O Cassio! whence came this?
This is some token from a newer friend;
To the felt absence now I feel a cause;
Is't come to this? ⟨Well, well.⟩   *200*
   Cas.   Go to, woman!
Throw your vile guesses in the devil's teeth,
From whence you have them. You are jealous now
That this is from some mistress, some remembrance.
No, by my faith, Bianca.   *205*
   Bian.   Why, whose is it?
   Cas. I know not, sweet. I found it in my chamber.
I like the work well. Ere it be demanded
(As like enough it will), I'd have it copied.
Take it and do't; and leave me for this time.   *210*
   Bian. Leave you? wherefore?
   Cas. I do attend here on the general,
And think it no addition nor my wish
To have him see me woman'd.
   ⟨*Bian.*   Why, I pray you?   *215*
   Cas. Not that I love you not.⟩
   Bian.   But that you do not love me.
I pray you, bring me on the way a little
And say if I shall see you soon at night.
   Cas. 'Tis but a little way that I can bring you,   *220*
For I attend here; but I'll see you soon.
   Bian. 'Tis very good. I must be circumstanc'd.   *Exeunt.*

ACT FOURTH ❧ SCENE FIRST

[Before the Citadel]
Enter Othello and Iago.

   Iago. Will you think so?
   Oth.   Think so, Iago!
   Iago.   What!
To kiss in private?
   Oth.   An unauthoriz'd kiss.   *5*
   Iago. Or to be naked with her friend abed
An hour or more, not meaning any harm?
   Oth. Naked abed, Iago, and not mean harm?
It is hypocrisy against the devil.
They that mean virtuously, and yet do so,   *10*
The devil their virtue tempts, and they tempt heaven.
   Iago. So they do nothing, 'tis a venial slip.
But if I give my wife a handkerchief,—
   Oth. What then?
   Iago. Why, then, 'tis hers, my lord; and, being hers,   *15*
She may, I think, bestow't on any man.
   Oth. She is protectress of her honor too.
May she give that?
   Iago. Her honor is an essence that's not seen.
They have it very oft that have it not;   *20*
But for the handkerchief,—
   Oth. By heaven, I would most gladly have forgot it.
Thou said'st (O it comes o'er my memory
As doth the raven o'er the infected house,

---

155 unhatch'd practice: *undeveloped plot*   **157 puddled:** *muddied, disturbed*   **160 endues:** *brings*   **163 observancy:** *tender devotion*   **164 Beshrew:** *a mild imprecation*   **165 unhandsome ... am:** *i.e., failing in this test to be a 'fair warrior' (cf. II.i.194)*   **170 conception:** *fancy*   **toy:** *whim*   **183 'Save:** *God save, preserve in health*   **188 keep a week away:** *cf. n.*   **189 Eight score eight:** *168 (seven times twenty-four)*   **194 continuate:** *uninterrupted*

213 no ... wish: *neither advantageous nor desirable*   **214 woman'd:** *accompanied by a woman*   **222 be circumstanc'd:** *yield to circumstances*   **9 hypocrisy against:** *an attempt to cheat*   **20 Cf. n.**   **22 Cf. n.**

Boding to all) he had my handkerchief.   25
  Iago. Ay, what of that?
  Oth.   That's not so good now.
  Iago.   What
If I had said I had seen him do you wrong?
Or heard him say (as knaves be such abroad,   30
Who having, by their own importunate suit
Or voluntary dotage of some mistress,
Convinced or supplied them, cannot choose
But they must blab)—
  Oth.   Hath he said anything?   35
  Iago. He hath, my lord; but be you well assur'd,
No more than he'll unswear.
  Oth.   What hath he said?
  Iago. Faith, that he did—I know not what he did.
  Oth. What? what?   40
  Iago. Lie—
  Oth.   With her?
  Iago.   With her, on her—what you will.
  Oth. Lie with her! lie on her! We say, lie on her, when
they belie her. Lie with her? Zounds, that's fulsome!   45
Handkerchief!—confessions!—handkerchief! ⟨To confess, and be
hanged for his labor. First, to be hanged, and then to confess:
I tremble at it. Nature would not invest herself in such
shadowing passion without some instruction. It is not words that
shake me thus. Pish! Noses, ears, and lips. Is't possible?—   50
Confess!—Handkerchief!—O devil!⟩   *Falls in a trance.*
  Iago. Work on,
My medicine, work! Thus credulous fools are caught;
And many worthy and chaste dames even thus,
All guiltless, meet reproach. What, ho! my lord!   55
My lord, I say! Othello!

        Enter Cassio.

          How now, Cassio!
  Cas. What's the matter?
  Iago. My lord is fallen into an epilepsy.
This is his second fit; he had one yesterday.   60
  Cas. Rub him about the temples.
  Iago.   «No, forbear.»
The lethargy must have his quiet course.
If not he foams at mouth, and by and by
Breaks out to savage madness. Look! he stirs.   65
Do you withdraw yourself a little while,
He will recover straight. When he is gone,
I would on great occasion speak with you.   *[Exit Cassio.]*
How is it, general? Have you not hurt your head?
  Oth. Dost thou mock me?   70
  Iago.   I mock you! no, by heaven.
Would you would bear your fortunes like a man!
  Oth. A horned man's a monster and a beast.
  Iago. There's many a beast then, in a populous city,
And many a civil monster.   75
  Oth. Did he confess?
  Iago.   Good sir, be a man.
Think every bearded fellow that's but yok'd
May draw with you. There's millions now alive

That nightly lie in those unproper beds   80
Which they dare swear peculiar. Your case is better.
O, 'tis the spite of hell, the fiend's arch-mock,
To lip a wanton in a sécure couch,
And to suppose her chaste. No, let me know;
And knowing what I am, I know what she shall be.   85
  Oth. O, thou art wise, 'tis certain.
  Iago.   Stand you awhile apart;
Confine yourself but in a patient list.
Whilst you were here o'erwhelmed with your grief
(A passion most unsuiting such a man),   90
Cassio came hither. I shifted him away,
And laid good 'scuse upon your ecstasy;
Bade him anon return and here speak with me,
The which he promis'd. Do but encave yourself,
And mark the fleers, the gibes, and notable scorns   95
That dwell in every region of his face;
For I will make him tell the tale anew,
Where, how, how oft, how long ago, and when
He has, and is again to cope your wife.
I say, but mark his gesture. Marry, patience;   100
Or I shall say you're all in all in spleen,
And nothing of a man.
  Oth.   Dost thou hear, Iago?
I will be found most cunning in my patience,
But—dost thou hear?—most bloody.   105
  Iago.   That's not amiss;
But yet keep time in all. Will you withdraw?

                [Othello goes apart.]

Now will I question Cassio of Bianca,
A housewife that by selling her desires
Buys herself bread and clothes. It is a creature   110
That dotes on Cassio (as 'tis the strumpet's plague
To beguile many and be beguil'd by one).
He, when he hears of her, cannot refrain
From the excess of laughter. Here he comes.

        Enter Cassio.

As he shall smile, Othello shall go mad;   115
And his unbookish jealousy must cónstrue
Poor Cassio's smiles, gestures, and light behavior
Quite in the wrong. *[Aloud.]* How do you now,
lieutenant?
  Cas. The worser that you give me the addition   120
Whose want even kills me.
  Iago. Ply Desdemona well, and you are sure on't.
[Speaking lower.] Now, if this suit lay in Bianca's power, How
quickly should you speed!
  Cas.   Alas! poor caitiff!   125
  Oth. Look how he laughs already!
  Iago. I never knew a woman love man so.
  Cas. Alas! poor rogue! I think, i' faith, she loves me.
  Oth. Now he denies it faintly, and laughs it out.
  Iago. Do you hear, Cassio?   130
  Oth.   Now he impórtunes him
To tell it o'er. Go to! well said, well said.

---

33 Convinced: *overcome* (those who needed importuning) **supplied:** *satisfied* (those who doted voluntarily) **43–51** *Cf. n.* **63 his:** *its* **73 horned man:** *a deceived husband* **75 civil:** *civilian* **78 yok'd:** *yoked in matrimony* **79 draw:** *draw the same cart, endure the same ignominy*

80 unproper: *not their own* **81 peculiar:** *their own* **83 lip:** *kiss* **sécure:** *carefree* **85 what she shall be:** *i.e., what I am to call her* **88 patient list:** *the bounds of patience* **92 ecstasy:** *fit* **94 encave:** *conceal* **99 cope:** *encounter* **101, 102 all ... man;** *cf. n.* **107 keep time:** *proceed fittingly* **116 unbookish:** *unskilled* **120 addition:** *title* **124 speed:** *prosper* **125 caitiff:** *wretch* (used pityingly) **126** *Cf. n.*

Iago. She gives it out that you shall marry her.
Do you intend it?

Cas. Ha, ha, ha!   *135*

Oth. Do you triumph, Roman? do you triumph?

Cas. I marry her! ⟨what? a customer?⟩ I prithee, bear some charity to my wit; do not think it so unwholesome. Ha, ha, ha!

Oth. So, so, so, so. Laugh that wins!   *140*

Iago. Faith, the cry goes you shall marry her.

Cas. Prithee, say true.

Iago. I am a very villain else.

Oth. Have you scored me? Well!

Cas. This is the monkey's own giving out. She is per-   *145*
suaded I will marry her, out of her own love and flattery, not out of my promise.

Oth. Iago beckons me. Now he begins the story.

Cas. She was here even now; she haunts me in every place. I was t'other day talking on the sea bank with certain   *150*
Venetians, and thither comes the bauble, and falls me thus about my neck—

Oth. Crying, 'O dear Cassio!' as it were. His gesture imports it.

Cas. So hangs and lolls and weeps upon me; so hales   *155*
and pulls me. Ha, ha, ha!

Oth. Now he tells how she plucked him to my chamber. O, I see that nose of yours, but not that dog I shall throw it to.

Cas. Well, I must leave her company.

Iago. Before me! look where she comes!   *160*

Cas. 'Tis such another fitchew! marry, a perfumed one!

Enter Bianca.

What do you mean by this haunting of me?

Bian. Let the devil and his dam haunt you! What did you mean by that same handkerchief you gave me even now? I was a fine fool to take it. I must take out the work? A likely   *165*
piece of work, that you should find it in your chamber and not know who left it there! This is some minx's token, and I must take out the work! There, give it your hobby-horse, wheresoever you had it. I'll take out no work on't.

Cas. How now, my sweet Bianca? how now? how now?   *170*

Oth. By heaven, that should be my handkerchief!

Bian. An you'll come to supper to-night, you may. An you will not, come when you are next prepared for.   *Exit.*

Iago. After her! after her!

Cas. Faith, I must. She'll rail i' the street else.   *175*

Iago. Will you sup there?

Cas. Faith, I intend so.

Iago. Well, I may chance to see you, for I would very fain speak with you.

Cas. Prithee, come; will you?   *180*

Iago. Go to! Say no more.   *Exit Cassio.*

Oth. [*advancing*]. How shall I murder him, Iago?

Iago. Did you perceive how he laughed at his vice?

Oth. O Iago!

Iago. And did you see the handkerchief?   *185*

Oth. Was that mine?

⟨*Iago.* Yours, by this hand. And to see how he prizes the foolish woman your wife! She gave it him, and he hath given it his whore.⟩

Oth. I would have him nine years a-killing. A fine   *190*
woman! a fair woman! a sweet woman!

Iago. Nay, you must forget that.

Oth. Ay, let her rot and perish, and be damned to-night, for she shall not live. No, my heart is turned to stone. I strike it, and it hurts my hand. O, the world has not a sweeter   *195*
creature. She might lie by an emperor's side and command him tasks.

Iago. Nay, that's not your way.

Oth. Hang her! I do but say what she is. So delicate with her needle! An admirable musician! O, she will sing the   *200*
savageness out of a bear. Of so high and plenteous wit and invention!

Iago. She's the worse for all this.

Oth. O, a thousand, a thousand times. And then, of so gentle a condition!   *205*

Iago. Ay, too gentle.

Oth. Nay, that's certain. But yet the pity of it, Iago!
⟨O, Iago, «the pity» of it, Iago!⟩

Iago. If you be so fond over her iniquity, give her patent to offend; for, if it touches not you, it comes near nobody.   *210*

Oth. I will chop her into messes. Cuckold me—

Iago. O, 'tis foul in her.

Oth. With mine officer!

Iago. That's fouler.

Oth. Get me some poison, Iago, this night. I'll not   *215*
expostulate with her, lest her body and beauty unprovide my mind again. This night, Iago.

Iago. Do it not with poison. Strangle her in her bed, even the bed she hath contaminated.

Oth. Good, good. The justice of it pleases. Very good.   *220*

Iago. And for Cassio, let me be his undertaker.
You shall hear more by midnight.

Oth. Excellent good.   *A trumpet.*
       What trumpet is that same?

Iago. Something from Venice, sure. 'Tis Lodovico,   *225*
Come from the duke; and see, your wife is with him.

Enter Lodovico, Desdemona, and Attendants.

Lod. God save you, worthy general!

Oth.   With all my heart, sir.

Lod. The duke and senators of Venice greet you.
       [*Gives him a letter.*]

Oth. I kiss the instrument of their pleasures.   *230*
       [*Opens the letter and reads.*]

Des. And what's the news, good cousin Lodovico?

Iago. I am very glad to see you, signior.
Welcome to Cyprus.

Lod. I thank you. How does Lieutenant Cassio?

Iago. Lives, sir.   *235*

Des. Cousin, there's fall'n between him and my lord
An unkind breach, but you shall make all well.

Oth. Are you sure of that?

Des. My lord?

Oth. [*reads*]. 'This fail you not to do, as you will'—   *240*

---

136 Roman: *used metaphorically, in association with 'triumph'* **137 customer:** *prostitute* **138 wit:** *intelligence* **unwholesome:** *unsound* **140 Laugh:** *let him laugh* **144 scored:** *notched* **146 flattery:** *self-flattery, delusion* **151 bauble:** *plaything* **161 such another:** *a patronizingly fond intensive, like modern 'such a'* **fitchew:** *amorous creature* (literally, *polecat*) **168 hobby-horse:** *harlot* **172 An:** *if* **173 next:** (implying 'never')

187–189 Cf. n. 198 your way: *the way for you* (to think of her) **208 Cf. n. 209 patent:** *license* **216 unprovide:** *unfit, weaken* **218 Strangle her:** *cf. n.* **221 undertaker:** *caretaker* (i.e., settle him) **240 'This fail you not to do,'** *etc.; cf. n.*

Lod. He did not call. He's busy in the paper.
Is there division 'twixt thy lord and Cassio?
　Des. A most unhappy one. I would do much
T'atone them for the love I bear to Cassio.
　Oth. Fire and brimstone!　　　　　　　　　*245*
　Des.　　　　　　My lord?
　Oth.　　　　　　　　Are you wise?
　Des. What! is he angry?
　Lod.　　　　　May be the letter mov'd him;
For, as I think, they do command him home,　　*250*
Deputing Cassio in his government.
　Des. By my troth, I am glad on't.
　Oth.　　　　　　　　Indeed?
　Des.　　　　　　　　　　My lord?
　Oth. I am glad to see you mad.　　　　　　*255*
　Des.　　　　　　How, sweet Othello?
　Oth. Devil!　　　　　　　*[Strikes her.]*
　Des.　　I have not deserved this.
　Lod. My lord, this would not be believ'd in Venice,
Though I should swear I saw't. 'Tis very much.　*260*
Make her amends, she weeps.
　Oth.　　　　　　O devil, devil!
If that the earth could teem with women's tears,
Each drop she falls would prove a crocodile.
Out of my sight!　　　　　　　　　　　*265*
　Des. *[going].* I will not stay to offend you.
　Lod. Truly, an obedient lady!
I do beseech your lordship, call her back.
　Oth. Mistress!
　Des.　　　My lord?　　　　　　　　*270*
　Oth.　　　　What would you with her, sir?
　Lod. Who, I, my lord?
　Oth. Ay, you did wish that I would make her turn.
Sir, she can turn, and turn, and yet go on,
And turn again. And she can weep, sir, weep;　*275*
And she's obedient, as you say, obedient,
Very obedient.—Proceed you in your tears.—
Concerning this, sir,—O well painted passion!—
I am commanded here—Get you away;
I'll send for you anon.—Sir, I obey the mandate,　*280*
And will return to Venice.—Hence! avaunt!　*[Exit Desdemona.]*
Cassio shall have my place. And, sir, to-night,
I do entreat that we may sup together.
You are welcome, sir, to Cyprus.—Goats and monkeys!　*Exit.*
　Lod. Is this the noble Moor whom our full senate　*285*
Call all-in-all sufficient? Is this the nature
Whom passion could not shake, whose solid virtue
The shot of accident nor dart of chance
Could neither graze nor pierce?
　Iago.　　　　　　He is much chang'd.　*290*
　Lod. Are his wits safe? is he not light of brain?
　Iago. He's that he is. I may not breathe my censure.
What he might be (if what he might he is not)
I would to heaven he were!
　Lod.　　　　　What! strike his wife!　*295*
　Iago. Faith, that was not so well; yet would I knew
That stroke would prove the worst!
　Lod.　　　　　　　　Is it his use?

Or did the letters work upon his blood,
And new-create this fault?　　　　　　*300*
　Iago.　　　　　　Alas, alas!
It is not honesty in me to speak
What I have seen and known. You shall observe him,
And his own courses will denote him so
That I may save my speech. Do but go after　*305*
And mark how he continues.
　Lod. I am sorry that I am deceiv'd in him.　*Exeunt.*

❦ SCENE SECOND ❦

[A Room in the Citadel]
Enter Othello and Emilia.

　Oth. You have seen nothing, then?
　Emil. Nor ever heard, nor ever did suspect.
　Oth. Yes, you have seen Cassio and she together.
　Emil. But then I saw no harm, and then I heard
Each syllable that breath made up between 'em.　*5*
　Oth. What! did they never whisper?
　Emil.　　　　　　Never, my lord.
　Oth. Nor send you out o' the way?
　Emil.　　　　　　Never.
　Oth. To fetch her fan, her gloves, her mask, nor　*10*
nothing?
　Emil. Never, my lord.
　Oth. That's strange.
　Emil. I durst, my lord, to wager she is honest,
Lay down my soul at stake. If you think other,　*15*
Remove your thought. It doth abuse your bosom.
If any wretch have put this in your head,
Let heaven requite it with the serpent's curse!
For if she be not honest, chaste, and true,
There's no man happy; the purest of their wives　*20*
Is foul as slander.
　Oth.　　　　Bid her come hither. Go.　*Exit Emilia.*
She says enough; yet she's a simple bawd
That cannot say as much. This is a subtle whore,
A closet lock and key of villainous secrets;　*25*
And yet she'll kneel and pray. I have seen her do't.

Enter Desdemona and Emilia.

　Des. My lord, what is your will?
　Oth.　　　　　Pray, chuck, come hither.
　Des. What is your pleasure?
　Oth.　　　　　Let me see your eyes;　*30*
Look in my face.
　Des.　　　What horrible fancy's this?
　Oth. *[to Emilia].* Some of your function, mistress.
Leave procreants alone and shut the door;
Cough or cry 'hem' if anybody come.　　　*35*
Your mystery, your mystery. Nay, dispatch.　*Exit Emilia.*
　Des. Upon my knees, what does your speech import?
I understand a fury in your words
«But not the words.»
　Oth. Why, what art thou?　　　　　*40*

244 atone: *reconcile*　**247 Are you wise:** *sardonic; Have you no wisdom?*　**251 govern-**
ment: *office*　**263 teem with:** *be impregnated by*　**264 falls:** *lets fall*　**278 painted**
passion: *simulated emotion*　**298 use:** *custom*

299 blood: *temper*　**14 to wager:** *in pledge that* ('durst' goes with 'Lay down')　**15 other:**
otherwise　**18 serpent's curse:** *cf. Genesis 3.14*　**24 This:** *Emilia*　**25 closet lock and key:**
instrument of concealment　**33 function:** *profession (i.e., of procuress)*　**36 mystery:** *trade*

Des.   Your wife, my lord; your true
And loyal wife.
     Oth.   Come, swear it, damn thyself;
Lest, being like one of heaven, the devils themselves
Should fear to seize thee. Therefore be double damn'd.   45
Swear thou art honest.
     Des.   Heaven doth truly know it.
     Oth. Heaven truly knows that thou art false as hell.
     Des. To whom, my lord? with whom? how am I false?
     Oth. Ah! Desdemon! Away, away, away!   50
     Des. Alas, the heavy day! Why do you weep?
Am I the motive of these tears, my lord?
If haply you my father do suspect
An instrument of this your calling back,
Lay not your blame on me. If you have lost him,   55
Why, I have lost him too.
     Oth.   Had it pleas'd heaven
To try me with afflictions, had they rain'd
All kinds of sores and shames on my bare head,
Steep'd me in poverty to the very lips,   60
Given to captivity me and my utmost hopes,
I should have found in some part of my soul
A drop of patience. But, alas!, to make me
A fixed figure for the time of scorn
To point his slow unmoving fingers at!   65
Yet could I bear that too. Well! very well!
But there, where I have garner'd up my heart,
Where either I must live or bear no life;
The fountain from the which my current runs
Or else dries up: to be discarded thence,   70
Or keep it as a cistern for foul toads
To knot and gender in! Turn thy complexion there,
Patience, thou young and rose-lipp'd cherubin.
I here look grim as hell!
     Des. I hope my noble lord esteems me honest.   75
     Oth. O, ay. As summer flies are in the shambles,
That quicken even with blowing.
O thou black weed, why art so lovely fair?
Thou smell'st so sweet that the sense aches at thee.
Would thou hadst ne'er been born!   80
     Des. Alas, what ignorant sin have I committed?
     Oth. Was this fair paper, this most goodly book,
Made to write 'whore' on? What committed?
⟨Committed! O thou public commoner!
I should make very forges of my cheeks,   85
That would to cinders burn up modesty,
Did I but speak thy deeds. What committed?⟩
Heaven stops the nose at it and the moon winks,
The bawdy wind that kisses all it meets
Is hush'd within the hollow mine of earth,   90
And will not hear't. What committed?
«Impudent strumpet!»
     Des.   By heaven, you do me wrong.
     Oth. Are not you a strumpet?
     Des.   No, as I am a Christian.   95
If to preserve this vessel for my lord

From any other foul unlawful touch
Be not to be a strumpet, I am none.
     Oth. What! not a whore?
     Des.   No, as I shall be sav'd.   100
     Oth. Is't possible?
     Des. O heaven, forgiveness!
     Oth.   I cry you mercy, then.
I took you for that cunning whore of Venice
That married with Othello. You, mistress,   105
That have the office opposite to Saint Peter,
And keep the gate of hell!

Enter Emilia.

           You, you, ay, you!
We have done our course. There's money for your pains.
I pray you, turn the key and keep our counsel.   *Exit.* 110
     Emil. Alas! what does this gentleman conceive?
How do you, madam? how do you, my good lady?
     Des. Faith, half asleep.
     Emil. Good madam, what's the matter with my lord?
     Des. With who?   115
     Emil.   Why, with my lord, madam.
⟨*Des.* Who is thy lord?
     Emil.   He that is yours, sweet lady.
     Des. I have none; do not talk to me, Emilia;
I cannot weep, nor answer have I none,   120
But what should go by water. Prithee, to-night
Lay on my bed our wedding sheets. Remember;
And call thy husband hither.
     Emil.   Here is a change indeed! *Exit.*
     Des. 'Tis meet I should be us'd so, very meet.   125
How have I been behav'd, that he might stick
The small'st opinion on my greatest abuse?

Enter Iago and Emilia.

     Iago. What is your pleasure, madam? How is't with you?
     Des. I cannot tell. Those that do teach young babes
Do it with gentle means and easy tasks.   130
He might have chid me so, for, in good faith,
I am a child to chiding.
     Iago. What is the matter, lady?
     Emil. Alas! Iago, my lord hath so bewhor'd her,
Thrown such despite and heavy terms upon her,   135
As true hearts cannot bear.
     Des. Am I that name, Iago?
     Iago.   What name, fair lady?
     Des. Such as she says my lord did say I was.
     Emil. He call'd her whore. A beggar in his drink   140
Could not have laid such terms upon his callet.
     Iago. Why did he so?
     Des. I do not know. I am sure I am none such.
     Iago. Do not weep, do not weep. Alas the day!
     Emil. Has she forsook so many noble matches,   145
Her father, and her country, and her friends,
To be call'd whore? Would it not make one weep?
     Des. It is my wretched fortune.
     Iago.   Beshrew him for't!

---

52 **motive:** *cause*   58 **they;** *cf. n.*   60 **Steep'd:** *submerged* (cf. 'ensteep'd,' II.i.78)   64, 65 *Cf. n.*   67–70 *Cf. n.*   72 **gender:** *engender, multiply*   **72, 73 Turn ... cherubin;** *cf. n.*   73 **cherubin;** *cf. n.*   74 *Cf. n.*   77 **quicken ... blowing;** *cf. n.*   78, 79 **O thou black weed ... sweet;** *cf. n.*   91, 92 **What ... strumpet;** *cf. n.*

102 **forgiveness:** *grant me power to forgive this!*   103 **cry you mercy:** *ask your pardon* (I *cry to be read:* Cry)   104 **whore of Venice:** *a variety with an international fame*   110 **turn the key:** *open the door*   121 **go by water:** *express itself in tears*   126, 128 **stick ... abuse:** *even slightly regard my worst offence as an offence*   141 **callet:** *basest of low women*

How comes this trick upon him?   *150*
 Des.   Nay, heaven doth know.
 Emil. I will be hang'd if some eternal villain,
Some busy and insinuating rogue,
Some cogging, cozening slave, to get some office
Have not devis'd this slander. I'll be hang'd else.   *155*
 Iago. Fie! there is no such man. It is impossible.
 Des. If any such there be, heaven pardon him!
 Emil. A halter pardon him, and hell gnaw his bones!
Why should he call her whore? who keeps her company?
What place? what time? what form? what likelihood?   *160*
The Moor's abus'd by some outrageous knave,
Some base notorious knave, some scurvy fellow.
O heaven! that such companions thou'dst unfold,
And put in every honest hand a whip
To lash the rascal naked through the world,   *165*
Even from the east to the west!
 Iago.   Speak within doors.
 Emil. O, fie upon him! Some such squire he was
That turn'd your wit the seamy side without,
And made you to suspect me with the Moor.   *170*
 Iago. You are a fool. Go to!
 Des.   O good Iago,
What shall I do to win my lord again?
Good friend, go to him; for, by this light of heaven,
I know not how I lost him. ⟨*Here I kneel.*   *175*
If e'er my will did trespass 'gainst his love,
Either in discourse of thought or actual deed,
Or that mine eyes, mine ears, or any sense
Delighted them in any other form;
Or that I do not yet, and ever did,   *180*
And ever will (though he do shake me off
To beggarly divorcement) love him dearly,
Comfort forswear me! Unkindness may do much;
And his unkindness may defeat my life,
But never taint my love. I cannot say 'whore.'   *185*
It does abhor me now I speak the word;
To do the act that might th' addition earn
Not the world's mass of vanity could make me.⟩
 Iago. I pray you be content. 'Tis but his humor.
The business of the state does him offence   *190*
«And he does chide with you.»
 Des. If 'twere no other,—   *[Trumpets within.]*
 Iago.   'Tis but so, I warr'nt you
Hark how these instruments summon you to supper,
And the great messengers of Venice stay.   *195*
Go in, and weep not. All things shall be well. *Ex. women.*

     Enter Roderigo.

How now, Roderigo?
 Rod. I do not find that thou deal'st justly with me.
 Iago. What in the contrary?
 Rod. Every day thou daffest me with some device, Iago;   *200*
and rather, as it seems to me, thou keepest from me all

conveniency, than suppliest me with the least advantage of hope.
I will indeed no longer endure it, nor am I yet persuaded to
put up in peace what already I have foolishly suffered.
 Iago. Will you hear me, Roderigo?   *205*
 Rod. Faith, I have heard too much, for your words and
performance are no kin together.
 Iago. You charge me most unjustly.
 Rod. ⟨With nought but truth.⟩ I have wasted myself out of
my means. The jewels you have had from me to deliver to   *210*
Desdemona would half have corrupted a votarist. You have told
me she has received them, and returned me expectations and
comforts of sudden respect and acquittance, but I find none.
 Iago. Well, go to! Very well.
 Rod. Very well? go to? I cannot go to, man; nor 'tis not *215*
very well. By this hand, I say 'tis very scurvy, and begin to
find myself fopped in it.
 Iago. Very well.
 Rod. I tell you 'tis not very well. I will make myself known
to Desdemona. If she will return me my jewels, I will give   *220*
over my suit and repent my unlawful solicitation. If not,
assure yourself I will seek satisfaction of you.
 Iago. You have said now?
 Rod. Ay, and said nothing but what I protest intendment of
doing.   *225*
 Iago. Why, now I see there's mettle in thee, and even from
this instant do build on thee a better opinion than ever before.
Give me thy hand, Roderigo. Thou hast taken against me
a most just exception; but yet, I protest, I have dealt most
directly in thy affair.   *230*
 Rod. It hath not appeared.
 Iago. I grant indeed it hath not appeared, and your suspicion is not without wit and judgment. But, Roderigo, if thou
hast that within thee indeed, which I have greater reason to
believe now than ever (I mean purpose, courage, and valor),
this night show it. If thou the next night following enjoyest
not Desdemona, take me from this world with treachery and
devise engines for my life.
 Rod. Well, ⟨what is it?⟩ is it within reason and compass?
 Iago. Sir, there is especial commission come from Venice   *240*
to depute Cassio in Othello's place.
 Rod. Is that true? Why, then Othello and Desdemona return
again to Venice.
 Iago. O, no! he goes into Mauritania, and takes away with
him the fair Desdemona, unless his abode be lingered here   *245*
by some accident; wherein none can be so determinate as the
removing of Cassio.
 Rod. How do you mean, removing of him?
 Iago. Why, by making him uncapable of Othello's place.
Knocking out his brains.   *250*
 Rod. And that you would have me to do!
 Iago. Ay; if you dare do yourself a profit and right. He sups
to-night with a harlotry, and thither will I go to him. He
knows not yet of his honorable fortune. If you will watch
his going thence (which I will fashion to fall out between   *255*
twelve and one), you may take him at your pleasure. I will be
near to second your attempt, and he shall fall between us.

---

150 trick: *vagary* **154 cogging, cozening:** *deceiving, cheating* **156** *Cf. n.* **162 noto-**
rious: *egregious, preëminent* **163 companions:** *base fellows* **unfold:** *expose* **167 within**
doors: *quietly, not from the house-tops* **177 discourse of thought:** *day-dreaming* **178**
that: *if* **183 Comfort . . . me:** *may happiness forsake me* **184 defeat:** *destroy* **186**
It does abhor me: *I feel abhorrence* **188 vanity:** *vain treasure* **191 chide with:** *quarrel*
with, 'take it out on' **195 stay:** *are waiting* **199** *What evidence have you against*
me? **200 daffest me:** *puttest me off*

202 conveniency: *opportunity* **advantage:** *increase, furthering* **204 put up:** *ac-*
cept **205** *Cf. n.* **211 votarist:** *religious devotee, nun* **213 sudden respect:** *immediate*
notice **217 fopped:** *swindled* **223 said:** *finished your speech* **230 directly:** *straightfor-*
wardly **238 engines for:** *plots against* **244 Mauritania:** *supposed land of the Moors;*
cf. n. **245 lingered:** *prolonged* **246 determinate:** *decisive*

Come, stand not amazed at it, but go along with me. I will show you such a necessity in his death that you shall think yourself bound to put it on him. It is now high supper- 260 time, and the night grows to waste. About it.

    Rod. I will hear further reason for this.

    Iago. And you shall be satisfied.   *Exeunt.*

❧ SCENE THIRD ❧

[State Bedroom in the Citadel]
Enter Othello, Lodovico, Desdemona, Emilia, and Attendants.

    Lod. I do beseech you, sir, trouble yourself no further.

    Oth. O pardon me; 'twill do me good to walk.

    Lod. Madam, good night. I humbly thank your ladyship.

    Des. Your honor is most welcome.

    Oth.   Will you walk, sir?—   *5*
O! Desdemona.

    Des. My lord?

    Oth. Get you to bed o' the instant. I will be returned forth-with. Dispatch your attendant there. Look it be done.

    Des. I will, my lord.   *10*

               Exit [Othello, with Lodovico and Attendants].

    Emil. How goes it now? He looks gentler than he did.

    Des. He says he will return incontinent.
He hath commanded me to go to bed,
And bade me to dismiss you.

    Emil.   Dismiss me!   *15*

    Des. It was his bidding. Therefore, good Emilia,
Give me my nightly wearing, and adieu.
We must not now displease him.

    Emil. I would you had never seen him.

    Des. So would not I. My love doth so approve him,   *20*
That even his stubbornness, his checks and frowns,—
Prithee, unpin me,—have grace and favor in them.

    Emil. I have laid those sheets you bade me on the bed.

    Des. All's one. Good faith! how foolish are our minds!
If I do die before thee, prithee, shroud me   *25*
In one of those same sheets.

    Emil.   Come, come, you talk!

    Des. My mother had a maid call'd Barbary:
She was in love, and he she lov'd prov'd mad
And did forsake her. She had a song of 'willow';   *30*
An old thing 'twas, but it express'd her fortune,
And she died singing it. That song to-night
Will not go from my mind. ⟨I have much to do
But to go hang my head all at one side,
And sing it like poor Barbary. Prithee, dispatch.   *35*

    Emil. Shall I go fetch your night-gown?

    Des.   No, unpin me here.
This Lodovico is a proper man.

    Emil. A very handsome man.

    Des. He speaks well.   *40*

    Emil. I know a lady in Venice would have walked barefoot to Palestine for a touch of his nether lip.   *Desdemona sings.*

The poor soul sat sighing by a sycamore tree,—
    Sing all a green willow.
Her hand on her bosom, her head on her knee,—   *45*
    Sing willow, willow, willow.
The fresh streams ran by her, and murmur'd her moans.
    Sing willow, &c.
Her salt tears fell from her, and soften'd the stones.
    Sing willow, &c.   *50*

Lay by these.—

        Willow, willow.

Prithee, hie thee; he'll come anon.

    Sing all a green willow must be my garland.
    Let nobody blame him, his scorn I approve,—   *55*

Nay, that's not next.⟩ Hark! who is it that knocks?

    Emil. It is the wind.

    Des.

    ⟨*I call'd my love false love; but what said he then?*
    Sing willow, &c.   *60*
If I court mo women, you'll couch with mo men.⟩

Now get thee gone. Good night. Mine eyes do itch;
Does that bode weeping?

    Emil.   'Tis neither here nor there.

    ⟨*Des.* I have heard it said so. O these men, these men!   *65*
Dost thou in conscience think (tell me, Emilia)
That there be women do abuse their husbands
In such gross kind?

    Emil.   There be some such, no question.⟩

    Des. Wouldst thou do such a deed for all the world?   *70*

    Emil. Why, would not you?

    Des.   No, by this heavenly light!

    Emil. Nor I neither by this heavenly light. I might do't as well i' th' dark.

    Des. Wouldst thou do such a deed for all the world?   *75*

    Emil. The world is a huge thing. It is a great price for a small vice.

    Des. Good troth, I think thou wouldst not.

    Emil. By my troth, I think I should, and undo't when I had done it. Marry, I would not do such a thing for a joint-   *80*
ring, nor for measures of lawn, nor for gowns, petticoats, nor caps, nor any petty exhibition. But for the whole world? Ud's pity! who would not make her husband a cuckold to make him a monarch? I should venture purgatory for't.

    Des. Beshrew me, if I would do such a wrong   *85*
For the whole world.

    Emil. Why, the wrong is but a wrong i' the world; and having the world for your labor, 'tis a wrong in your own world, and you might quickly make it right.

    Des. I do not think there is any such woman.   *90*

    Emil. Yes, a dozen; and as many to the vantage, as would store the world they played for.
⟨But I do think it is their husbands' faults
If wives do fall. Say that they slack their duties,
And pour our treasures into foreign laps,   *95*
Or else break out in peevish jealousies,
Throwing restraint upon us; or say they strike us,

---

261 **grows to waste:** *is wasting away*   1 *Cf. n.*   2 **pardon me:** *don't mention it*   5
Will you walk: *shall we start?*   9 **Dispatch:** *'dismiss' (Folio)*   12 **incontinent:** *immedi-ately*   24 **All's one:** *no matter*   27 **talk:** *talk idly*   29 **mad:** *inconstant, wild*   31
An old thing 'twas; *cf. n.*   34 **But to:** *not to*

53 **hie thee:** *make haste*   79, 80 **undo't . . . done:** *see lines 86–88*   80, 81 **joint-ring:** *ring made in interlocking halves*   91 **to the vantage:** *to boot, in addition*

Or scant our former having in despite;
Why, we have galls, and though we have some grace,
Yet have we some revenge. Let husbands know   *100*
Their wives have sense like them. They see and smell,
And have their palates both for sweet and sour,
As husbands have. What is it that they do
When they change us for others? Is it sport?
I think it is. And doth affection breed it?   *105*
I think it doth. Is't frailty that thus errs?
It is so too. And have not we affections,
Desires for sport, and frailty as men have?
Then, let them use us well; else let them know,
The ills we do, their ills instruct us so.)   *110*
   Des. Good night, good night! God me such usage send,
Not to pick bad from bad, but by bad mend!   *Exeunt.*

ACT FIFTH ❧ SCENE FIRST

[A Street near Bianca's lodging]
Enter Iago and Roderigo.

   Iago. Here, stand behind this bulk. Straight will he
come.
Wear thy good rapier bare, and put it home.
Quick, quick. Fear nothing; I'll be at thy elbow.
It makes us, or it mars us. Think of that,   *5*
And fix most firm thy resolution.
   Rod. Be near at hand. I may miscarry in't.
   Iago. Here, at thy hand. Be bold, and take thy stand.

                                        [Retires.]

   Rod. I have no great devotion to the deed;
And yet he has given me satisfying reasons.   *10*
'Tis but a man gone. Forth, my sword! he dies.
   Iago. I have rubb'd this young quat almost to the sense,
And he grows angry. Now, whether he kill Cassio,
Or Cassio him, or each do kill the other,
Every way makes my gain. Live Roderigo,   *15*
He calls me to a restitution large
Of gold and jewels that I bobb'd from him,
As gifts to Desdemona.
It must not be. If Cassio do remain,
He has a daily beauty in his life   *20*
That makes me ugly; and, besides, the Moor
May unfold me to him. There stand I in peril.
No, he must die. Be it so! I hear him coming.

Enter Cassio.

   Rod. I know his gait; 'tis he. Villain, thou diest!

                          [Makes a pass at Cassio.]

   Cas. That thrust had been my enemy indeed   *25*
But that my coat is better than thou think'st.
I will make proof of thine.

                          [Draws, and wounds Roderigo.]

   Rod.   O! I am slain!

[Iago from behind wounds Cassio in the leg, and exit.]
   Cas. I am maim'd for ever! Light, ho! murder! murder!

                                        [Falls.]

Enter Othello [at a distance].

   Oth. The voice of Cassio. Iago keeps his word.   *30*
   Rod. O villain that I am!
   Oth.   Hark! 'Tis even so.
   Cas. O, help, ho! light! a surgeon!
   Oth. 'Tis he. O brave Iago, honest and just,
That hast such noble sense of thy friend's wrong!   *35*
Thou teachest me. Minion, your dear lies dead,
And your fate hies apace. Strumpet, I come!
Forth of my heart those charms, thine eyes, are blotted.
Thy bed, lust-stain'd, shall with lust's blood be spotted.

                                        Exit Othello.

Enter Lodovico and Gratiano [at a distance].

   Cas. What ho! no watch? no passage? murder! murder!   *40*
   Gra. 'Tis some mischance. The cry is very direful.
   Cas. O, help!
   Lod. Hark!
   Rod. O wretched villain!
   Lod. Two or three groan. It is a heavy night;   *45*
These may be counterfeits. Let's think't unsafe
To come in to the cry without more help.
   Rod. Nobody come? then shall I bleed to death.
   Lod. Hark!

Enter Iago, with a light.

   Gra. Here's one comes in his shirt, with light and weapons.
   Iago. Who's there? Whose noise is this that cries on murder?
   Lod. We do not know.
   Iago.   Did not you hear a cry?
   Cas. Here, here! For heaven's sake, help me.
   Iago.   What's the matter?   *55*
   Gra. This is Othello's ancient, as I take it.
   Lod. The same indeed. A very valiant fellow.
   Iago. What are you here that cry so grievously?
   Cas. Iago? O, I am spoil'd, undone by villains!
Give me some help.   *60*
   Iago. O my lieutenant! what villains have done this?
   Cas. I think that one of them is hereabout,
And cannot make away.
   Iago.   O treacherous villains!
[To Lodovico and Gratiano.] What are you there? Come   *65*
in, and give some help.
   Rod. O help me here!
   Cas. That's one of them.
   Iago.   O murderous slave! O villain!
                                        [Stabs Roderigo.]

   Rod. O damn'd Iago! O inhuman dog!   *70*
   Iago. Kill men i' the dark! Where be those bloody thieves?
How silent is this town! Ho! murder! murder!
What may you be? are you of good or evil?
   Lod. As you shall prove us, praise us.
   Iago. Signior Lodovico?   *75*
   Lod. He, sir.

---

98 having: *allowance, pin-money* **despite:** *spite* **99 galls:** *spirit to resent injury* **101 sense:** *sensations, feelings* **105 affection:** *inclination* **111 usage:** *code of conduct* **112** *Cf. n.* **1 bulk:** *projecting shelter* **12 quat:** *pimple (cf. modern 'scab')* **sense:** *quick* **15 Live Roderigo:** *if Roderigo live; Cf. n.* **17 bobb'd from him:** *cheated him out of* **20** *Cf. n.* **26 coat:** *i.e., he wore defensive armor under his outer garments*

S.d. Enter Othello; *cf. n.* **36 Minion:** *hussy* **40 passage:** *passers-by* **45 heavy:** *doleful (cf. V.ii.120)* **51 cries on:** *shouts* **65 What:** *who* **74 praise:** *appraise, estimate*

Iago. I cry you mercy. Here's Cassio hurt by villains.

Gra. Cassio?

Iago. How is it, brother?

Cas. My leg is cut in two.   80

Iago.   Marry, heaven forbid!
Light, gentlemen. I'll bind it with my shirt.

Enter Bianca.

Bian. What is the matter, ho? who is't that cried?

Iago. Who is't that cried!

Bian. O my dear Cassio! O my sweet Cassio!   85
Cassio! Cassio!

Iago. O notable strumpet! Cassio, may you suspect
Who they should be that thus have mangled you?

Cas. No.

Gra. I am sorry to find you thus. I have been to seek you.   90

⟨*Iago.* Lend me a garter. So. O for a chair,
To bear him easily hence!⟩

Bian. Alas! he faints! O Cassio, Cassio, Cassio!

Iago. Gentlemen all, I do suspect this trash
To bear a part in this.   95
Patience awhile, good Cassio. ⟨Come, come.⟩
Lend me a light. Know we this face, or no?
Alas! my friend and my dear countryman,
Roderigo? no: yes, sure. O heaven! Roderigo.

Gra. What? of Venice?   100

Iago. Even he, sir. Did you know him?

Gra.   Know him? ay.

Iago. Signior Gratiano? I cry you gentle pardon.
These bloody accidents must excuse my manners,
That so neglected you.   105

Gra.   I am glad to see you.

Iago. How do you, Cassio? O, a chair, a chair!

Gra. Roderigo!   *[A chair brought in.]*

Iago. He. 'Tis he.—O! that's well said; the chair.
Some good man bear him carefully from hence.   110
I'll fetch the general's surgeon. *[To Bianca.]* For you, mistress,
Save you your labor. He that lies slain here, Cassio,
Was my dear friend. What malice was betwixt you?

Cas. None in the world; nor do I know the man.

Iago. *[To Bianca.]* What! look you pale?? O, bear him   115
out o' the air.   *[Casio borne off.]*
Stay you, good gentlemen. Look you pale, mistress?—
Do you perceive the gastness of her eye?—
Nay, if you stare, we shall hear more anon.—
Behold her well; I pray you, look upon her.   120
Do you see, gentlemen? nay, guiltiness
Will speak though tongues were out of use.

Enter Emilia.

Emil. 'Las! what's the matter? what's the matter, husband?

Iago. Cassio has here been set on in the dark
By Roderigo and fellows that are 'scap'd.   125
He's almost slain, and Roderigo dead.

Emil. Alas, good gentlemen! alas, good Cassio!

Iago. This is the fruit of whoring. Pray, Emilia,
Go know of Cassio where he supp'd to-night.—
What! do you shake at that?   130

Bian. He supp'd at my house, but I therefore shake not.

Iago. O, did he so? I charge you, go with me.

Emil. Fie, fie upon thee, strumpet!

Bian. I am no strumpet, but of life as honest
As you that thus abuse me.   135

Emil.   As I! foh! fie upon thee!

Iago. Kind gentlemen, let's go see poor Cassio dress'd.
Come, mistress, you must tell's another tale.
Emilia, run you to the citadel,
And tell my lord and lady what has happ'd.   140
Will you go on afore? *[Aside.]* This is the night
That either makes me or fordoes me quite.

           Exeunt.

❧ Scene Second ❧

[State Bedroom in the Citadel]
Enter Othello with a light, and Desdemona in her bed.

Oth. It is the cause, it is the cause, my soul.
Let me not name it to you, you chaste stars!
It is the cause. Yet I'll not shed her blood,
Nor scar that whiter skin of hers than snow,
And smooth as monumental alablaster.   5
Yet she must die, else she'll betray more men.
Put out the light, and then put out the light.
If I quench thee, thou flaming minister,
I can again thy former light restore,
Should I repent me; but once put out thy light,   10
Thou cunning'st pattern of excelling nature,
I know not where is that Promethean heat
That can thy light relume. When I have pluck'd thy rose,
I cannot give it vital growth again.
It needs must wither. I'll smell it on the tree.   *He kisses her.* 15
O balmy breath, that doth almost persuade
Justice to break her sword! One more, one more.
Be thus when thou art dead, and I will kill thee
And love thee after. Once more, and this the last!
So sweet was ne'er so fatal. I must weep,   20
But they are cruel tears. This sorrow's heavenly,
It strikes where it doth love. She wakes.

Des. Who's there? Othello?

Oth.   Ay, Desdemona.

Des. Will you come to bed, my lord?   25

Oth. Have you pray'd to-night, Desdemona?

Des.   Ay, my lord.

Oth. If you bethink yourself of any crime
Unreconcil'd as yet to heaven and grace,
Solicit for it straight.   30

Des. Alas, my lord, what may you mean by that?

Oth. Well, do it, and be brief. I will walk by.
I would not kill thy unprepared spirit.
No (heaven forfend!), I would not kill thy soul.

Des. Talk you of killing?   35

Oth.   Ay, I do.

Des.   Then heaven

90 I have been to seek you; *cf. n.*   **91 chair:** *a plain chair, probably*   **95** *Cf. n.*   **118**
gastness: *ghastliness*   **129 know:** *learn*

139 *Cf. n.*   **141 Will … afore;** *cf. n.*   **142 fordoes:** *unmakes, destroys*   Scene Sec-
OND S.d. **Enter … bed;** *cf. n.*   **1 It is the cause;** *cf. n.*   **5 alablaster;** *cf. n.*   **12**
Promethean heat: *divine fire; cf. n.*   **13 relume:** *rekindle*   **16 doth;** *cf. n.*   **20 fatal;**
cf. n.   **29 grace:** *God's mercy*   **30 Solicit:** *pray*   **32 by:** *apart*   **34 forfend:** *forbid*

Have mercy on me!
  Oth.   Amen! with all my heart.
  Des. If you say so, I hope you will not kill me.   40
  Oth. Humh!
  Des. And yet I fear you; for you are fatal then
When your eyes roll so. Why I should fear I know not,
Since guiltiness I know not; but yet I feel I fear.
  Oth. Think on thy sins.   45
  Des.   They are loves I bear to you.
  Oth. Ay, and for that thou diest.
  Des. That death's unnatural that kills for loving.
Alas, why gnaw you so your nether lip?
Some bloody passion shakes your very frame.   50
These are porténts, but yet, I hope, I hope,
They do not point on me.
  Oth.   Peace, and be still!
  Des. I will so. What's the matter?
  Oth. That handkerchief which I so lov'd and gave thee   55
Thou gav'st to Cassio.
  Des.   No, by my life and soul!
Send for the man and ask him.
  Oth.   Sweet soul, take heed,
Take heed of perjury. Thou'rt on thy death-bed.   60
  Des. Ay, but not yet to die.
  Oth.   Yes, presently.
Therefore confess thee freely of thy sin;
For to deny each article with oath
Cannot remove nor choke the strong conception   65
That I do groan withal. Thou art to die.
  Des. Then Lord have mercy on me!
  Oth.   I say, amen.
  Des. And have you mercy too! I never did
Offend you in my life; never lov'd Cassio   70
But with such general warranty of heaven
As I might love. I never gave him token.
  Oth. By heaven, I saw my handkerchief in his hand.
O perjur'd woman! thou dost stone my heart,
And mak'st me call what I intend to do   75
A murder, which I thought a sacrifice.
I saw the handkerchief.
  Des.   He found it then.
I never gave it him. Send for him hither;
Let him confess a truth.   80
  Oth.   He has confess'd.
  Des. What, my lord?
  Oth. That he hath—uds death!
  Des.   How? unlawfully?
  Oth. Ay.   85
  Des.   He will not say so.
  Oth.   No; his mouth is stopp'd.
Honest Iago hath ta'en order for't.
  Des. O! my fear interprets. What! is he dead?
  Oth. Had all his hairs been lives, my great revenge   90
Had stomach for them all.
  Des. Alas, he is betray'd and I undone!
  Oth. O strumpet! Weep'st thou for him to my face?
  Des. O, banish me, my lord, but kill me not!
  Oth. Down, strumpet!   95

  Des. Kill me to-morrow; let me live to-night!
  Oth. Nay, an you strive,—
  Des. But half an hour!
  ⟨*Oth.*   Being done, there is no pause.
  Des.⟩ But while I say one prayer!   100
  Oth.   It is too late. *He stifles her.*
  «*Des.* O Lord, Lord, Lord!»
Emilia calls within. My lord, my lord! what, ho! my lord,
my lord!
  Oth. What noise is this? Not dead? not yet quite dead?   105
I that am cruel am yet merciful;
I would not have thee linger in thy pain.
So. so.
  Emil. [*within*]. What, ho! my lord, my lord!
  Oth.   Who's there?   110
  Emil. [*within*]. O! good my lord, I'ld speak a word with
you.
  Oth. Yes; 'tis Emilia.—By and by.—She's dead.
'Tis like she comes to speak of Cassio's death.
The noise was high. Ha! no more moving?   115
Still as the grave. Shall she come in? Were't good?
I think she stirs again: no. What's the best?
If she come in, she'll sure speak to my wife:
My wife! my wife! what wife? I have no wife:
O, insupportable! O heavy hour!   120
Methinks it should be now a huge eclipse
Of sun and moon, and that the affrighted globe
Should yawn at alteration.
  Emil. [*within*].   I do beseech you
That I may speak with you, O good my lord.   125
  Oth. I had forgot thee. O, come in, Emilia!—
Soft, by and by.—Let me the curtains draw.—
Where art thou?   [*Unlocks the door.*]

Enter Emilia.

              What's the matter with thee now?
  Emil. O! my good lord, yonder's foul murders done.   130
  Oth. What! now?
  Emil.   But now, my lord.
  Oth. It is the very error of the moon.
She comes more near the earth than she was wont,
And makes men mad.   135
  Emil. Cassio, my lord, has kill'd a young Venetian
Call'd Roderigo.
  Oth.   Roderigo kill'd!
And Cassio kill'd!
  Emil.   No, Cassio is not kill'd.   140
  Oth. Not Cassio kill'd! then murder's out of tune,
And sweet revenge grows harsh.
  Des. O falsely, falsely murder'd.
  Emil.   O Lord! what cry is that?
  Oth. That? what?   145
  Emil. Out and alas! it is my lady's voice.
Help! help, ho! help! O lady, speak again!
Sweet Desdemona! O sweet mistress, speak!
  Des. A guiltless death I die.
  Emil. O! who has done this deed?   150
  Des. Nobody. I myself. Farewell!

---

65 **conception**; *cf. n.*   71 **general … heaven**: *permission granted by heaven to all*   74 **stone**: *make stony*   83 *Cf. n.*   88 **order**: *measures*   91 **stomach**: *appetite*

99 **Being … pause**: *cf. n.*   115 **The … high**; *cf. n.*   117 **What's the best**: *'what's best to do?'* (Folio)   123 **yawn at alteration**; *cf. n.*   127 **Soft**: *stop, wait*   132 **But**: *just*   133 **error**: *aberration*

Commend me to my kind lord. O farewell!   *She dies.*

Oth. Why, how should she be murder'd?

Emil.   Alas, who knows?

Oth. You heard her say herself it was not I.   *155*

Emil. She said so. I must needs report a truth.

Oth. She's like a liar gone to burning hell.

'Twas I that kill'd her.

Emil.   O the more angel she,

And you the blacker devil.   *160*

Oth. She turn'd to folly, and she was a whore.

Emil. Thou dost belie her, and thou art a devil.

Oth. She was false as water.

Emil.   Thou art rash as fire to say

That she was false. O she was heavenly true.   *165*

Oth. Cassio did top her. Ask thy husband else.

O I were damn'd beneath all depth in hell

But that I did proceed upon just grounds

To this extremity. Thy husband knew it all.

Emil. My husband?   *170*

Oth. Thy husband.

Emil. That she was false to wedlock?

Oth. Ay, with Cassio. Nay, had she been true,

If heaven would make me such another world

Of one entire and perfect chrysolite,   *175*

I'd not have sold her for it.

Emil. My husband?

Oth.   Ay, 'twas he that told me first.

An honest man he is, and hates the slime

That sticks on filthy deeds   *180*

Emil.   My husband?

Oth. What needs this iterance, woman? I say thy husband.

⟨*Emil.* O mistress! villainy hath made mocks with love.

My husband say that she was false?

Oth.   He, woman.   *185*

I say, thy husband; dost understand the word?

My friend, thy husband, honest, honest Iago.⟩

Emil. If he say so, may his pernicious soul

Rot half a grain a day! He lies to the heart.

She was too fond of her most filthy bargain.   *190*

Oth. Ha!

Emil. Do thy worst.

This deed of thine is no more worthy heaven

Than thou wast worthy her.

Oth.   Peace! you were best.   *195*

Emil. Thou hast not half the power to do me harm

As I have to be hurt. O gull! O dolt!

As ignorant as dirt! Thou hast done a deed,—

I care not for thy sword. I'll make thee known,

Though I lost twenty lives. Help! help, ho! help!   *200*

The Moor has kill'd my mistress! Murder! murder!

Enter Montano, Gratiano, Iago, and others.

Mon. What is the matter? How now, general?

Emil. O, are you come, Iago? You have done well,

That men must lay their murders on your neck.

Gra. What is the matter?   *205*

Emil. Disprove this villain if thou be'st a man:

He says thou told'st him that his wife was false.

I know thou didst not. Thou'rt not such a villain.

Speak, for my heart is full.

Iago. I told him what I thought, and told no more   *210*

Than what he found himself was apt and true.

Emil. But did you ever tell him she was false?

Iago. I did.

Emil. You told a lie, an odious damned lie;

Upon my soul, a lie, a wicked lie.   *215*

She false with Cassio! Did you say with Cassio?

Iago. With Cassio, mistress. Go to, charm your tongue.

Emil. I will not charm my tongue; I am bound to speak.

⟨My mistress here lies murder'd in her bed.

All. O heavens forfend!   *220*

Emil. And your reports have set the murder on.

Oth. Nay, stare not, masters. It is true indeed.

Gra. 'Tis a strange truth.

Mon. O monstrous act!

Emil.   Villainy! villainy! villainy!   *225*

I think upon't, I think, I smell't. O villainy!

I thought so then. I'll kill myself for grief.

O villainy, villainy!⟩

Iago. What! are you mad? I charge you, get you home.

Emil. Good gentlemen, let me have leave to speak.   *230*

'Tis proper I obey him, but not now.

Perchance, Iago, I will ne'er go home.

Oth. Oh! Oh! Oh!   *Othello falls on the bed.*

Emil.   Nay, lay thee down and roar,

For thou hast kill'd the sweetest innocent   *235*

That e'er did lift up eye.

Oth.   O! she was foul.

I scarce did know you, uncle. There lies your niece,

Whose breath, indeed, these hands have newly stopp'd.

I know this act shows terrible and grim.   *240*

Gra. Poor Desdemon, I am glad thy father's dead.

Thy match was mortal to him, and pure grief

Shore his old thread a-twain. Did he live now,

This sight would make him do a desperate turn,

Yea, curse his better angel from his side,   *245*

And fall to reprobation.

Oth.   'Tis pitiful; but yet Iago knows

That she with Cassio hath the act of shame

A thousand times committed. Cassio confess'd it;

And she did gratify his amorous works   *250*

With the recognizance and pledge of love

Which I first gave her. I saw it in his hand.

It was a handkerchief, an antique token

My father gave my mother.

Emil. O God! O heavenly God!   *255*

Iago.   Zounds! hold your peace.

Emil. 'Twill out, 'twill out! I hold my peace, sir? No!

No, I will speak as liberal as the north.

Let heaven and men and devils, let them all,

All, all, cry shame against me, yet I'll speak.   *260*

Iago. Be wise, and get you home.

Emil.   I will not.   *[Iago threatens Emilia.]*

Gra.   Fie!

Your sword upon a woman?

---

161 folly: *unchastity*   **174 such another:** *another such* (as large as this one)   **175 chryso-**
lite: *a precious stone, green in color*   **182 iterance:** *repetition*   **183 made mocks with:**
made a dupe of   **197 gull:** *fool*   **205 Gra.** *Cf. n.*

217 charm: *silence, as if by a magic spell*   **227 then;** *cf. n.*   **232** *Cf. n.*   **243 Shore:**
cut   **244 do ... turn:** *commit some desperate deed*   **246 reprobation:** *damna-*
tion   **251 recognizance:** *token*   **254** *Cf. n.*   **258 as ... north:** *as freely and strongly*
as the north wind; cf. n.

Emil. O thou dull Moor! that handkerchief thou speak'st of
I found by fortune and did give my husband,
For often with a solemn earnestness
(More than, indeed, belong'd to such a trifle)
He begg'd of me to steal it.

Iago.   Villainous whore!   *270*

Emil. She give it Cassio? No, alas! I found it,
And I did give't my husband.

Iago.   Filth, thou liest!

Emil. By heaven, I do not. I do not, gentlemen.
O murderous coxcomb! what should such a fool   *275*
Do with so good a wife?

Oth.   Are there no stones in heaven
But what serves for the thunder? Precious villain!

              The Moor runs at Iago. Iago kills his wife.

Gra. The woman falls. Sure, he has kill'd his wife. *Exit Iago.*

Emil. Ay, ay. O lay me by my mistress' side.   *280*

Gra. He's gone, but his wife's kill'd.

Mon. 'Tis a notorious villain. *[To Gratiano.]* Take you this
weapon,
Which I have here recover'd from the Moor.
Come, guard the door without. Let him not pass,   *285*
But kill him rather. I'll after that same villain,
For 'tis a damned slave.   *Ex. Mont. and Gratiano.*

Oth.   I am not valiant neither,
But every puny whipster gets my sword.
But why should honor outlive honesty?   *290*
Let it go all.

Emil.   〈What did thy song bode, lady?
Hark, canst thou hear me? I will play the swan,
And die in music.   *[Sings.]*

     Willow, willow, willow.   *295*

Moor, she was chaste. She lov'd thee, cruel Moor.
So come my soul to bliss as I speak true.
So speaking as I think, I die, I die.   *She dies.*

Oth. I have another weapon in this chamber.
It is a sword of Spain, the ice brook's temper.   *300*
O here it is.—Uncle, I must come forth.

Gra. within. If thou attempt it, it will cost thee dear.
Thou hast no weapon, and perforce must suffer.

Oth. Look in upon me then, and speak to me,
Or, naked as I am, I will assault thee.   *305*

        [Enter Gratiano.]

Gra. What is the matter?

Oth.   Behold! I have a weapon.
A better never did itself sustain
Upon a soldier's thigh. I have seen the day
That with this little arm and this good sword   *310*
I have made my way through more impediments
Than twenty times your stop. But O vain boast!
Who can control his fate? 'Tis not so now.
〈Be not afraid, though you do see me weapon'd.
Here is my journey's end, here is my butt   *315*
And very sea-mark of my utmost sail.

Do you go back dismay'd? 'Tis a lost fear.
Man but a rush against Othello's breast,
And he retires. Where should Othello go?—
Now, how dost thou look now? O ill-starr'd wench!〉   *320*
Pale as thy smock! When we shall meet at compt,
This look of thine will hurl my soul from heaven,
And fiends will snatch at it. Cold, cold, my girl,
Even like thy chastity.
O cursed, cursed slave! Whip me, ye devils,   *325*
From the possession of this heavenly sight!
Blow me about in winds! roast me in sulphur!
Wash me in steep-down gulfs of liquid fire!
O Desdemona! Desdemona! dead!
O! O! O!   *330*

*Enter Lodovico, Montano, Iago [prisoner], and Officers, Cassio in
a chair.*

Lod. Where is this rash and most unfortunate man?

Oth. That's he that was Othello. Here I am.

Lod. Where is that viper? bring the villain forth.

Oth. I looked down towards his feet, but that's a fable.
If that thou be'st a devil, I cannot kill thee.   *[Wounds Iago.]*

Lod. Wring his sword from him.

Iago.   I bleed, sir, but not kill'd.

Oth. I am not sorry neither. I'd have thee live,
For in my sense 'tis happiness to die.

Lod. O thou Othello that wert once so good,   *340*
Fall'n in the practice of a damned slave,
What shall be said to thee?

Oth.   Why, anything:
An honorable murderer, if you will;
For nought did I in hate, but all in honor.   *345*

Lod. This wretch hath part confess'd his villainy.
Did you and he consent in Cassio's death?

Oth. Ay.

Cas. Dear general, I did never give you cause.

Oth. I do believe it, and I ask you pardon.   *350*
Will you, I pray, demand that demi-devil
Why he hath thus ensnar'd my soul and body.

Iago. Demand me nothing. What you know, you know:
From this time forth I never will speak word.

Lod. What! not to pray?   *355*

Gra.   Torments will ope your lips.

Oth. Well, thou dost best.

Lod. Sir, you shall understand what hath befall'n,
Which, as I think, you know not. Here is a letter
Found in the pocket of the slain Roderigo,   *360*
And here another. The one of them imports
The death of Cassio to be undertook
By Roderigo.

Oth. O villain!

Cas.   Most heathenish and most gross!   *365*

Lod. Now here's another discontented paper,
Found in his pocket too; and this, it seems,
Roderigo meant t' have sent this damned villain,
But that, belike, Iago in the nick
Came in and satisfied him.   *370*

---

276 wife; *cf. n.*   **277 stones:** *bolts; cf. n.*   **284 recover'd:** *taken*   **289 whipster:**
(*cf. modern whipper-snapper*) *stripling*   **290 honor:** *mere dignity* **honesty:** *fundamental
righteousness*   **300 ice brook's temper:** *tempered in icy water*   **305 naked:** *unarmed (as
Gratiano supposed)*   **312 stop:** *power of prevention*   **315 butt:** *goal* (*literally, target*)   **316 sea-mark:** *beacon, limit*

317 lost: *wasted, unnecessary*   **318 Man:** *wield* **rush:** *bulrush, reed*   **321 compt:** *reckoning, on the Judgment Day*   **326 possession:** *haunting obsession*   **334** *I look for the devil's
outward sign, a cloven hoof*   **337 I bleed, sir;** *cf. n.*   **341 practice:** *sinister scheme*   **353
Demand me nothing;** *cf. n.*   **369 nick:** *nick of time; cf. n.*

Oth.   O the pernicious caitiff!
How came you, Cassio, by that handkerchief
That was my wife's?
    Cas.   I found it in my chamber;
And he himself confess'd it even now   *375*
That there he dropp'd it for a special purpose
Which wrought to his desire.
    Oth.   O fool! fool! fool!
    Cas. There is besides in Roderigo's letter
How he upbraids Iago that he made him   *380*
Brave me upon the watch, whereon it came
That I was cast: and even but now he spake
(After long seeming dead): Iago hurt him,
Iago set him on.
    Lod. You must forsake this room and go with us.   *385*
Your power and your command is taken off,
And Cassio rules in Cyprus. For this slave,
If there be any cunning cruelty
That can torment him much and hold him long,
It shall be his. You shall close prisoner rest,   *390*
Till that the nature of your fault be known
To the Venetian state. Come, bring him away.
    Oth. Soft you! A word or two ⟨before you go.⟩
I have done the state some service, and they know't;
No more of that. I pray you, in your letters,   *395*
When you shall these unlucky deeds relate,
Speak of them as they are. Nothing extenuate,
Nor set down aught in malice. Then must you speak
Of one that lov'd not wisely but too well;
Of one not easily jealous, but, being wrought,   *400*

Perplex'd in the extreme; of one whose hand
(Like the base Indian) threw a pearl away
Richer than all his tribe; of one whose súbdu'd eyes,
Albeit unused to the melting mood,
Drops tears as fast as the Arabian trees   *405*
Their méd'cinable gum. Set you down this;
And say besides, that in Aleppo once,
Where a malignant and turban'd Turk
Beat a Venetian and traduc'd the state,
I took by the throat the circumcised dog,   *410*
And smote him thus.   *He stabs himself.*
    Lod. O bloody period!
    Gra.   All that's spoke is marr'd.
    Oth. I kiss'd thee ere I kill'd thee. No way but this,
Killing myself to die upon a kiss.   *He dies.*
    Cas. This did I fear, but thought he had no weapon;
For he was great of heart.
    Lod.   *[To Iago.]* O Spartan dog,
More fell than anguish, hunger, or the sea,
Look on the tragic loading of this bed!   *420*
This is thy work. The object poisons sight;
Let it be hid. Gratiano, keep the house,
And seize upon the fortunes of the Moor,
For they succeed to you. To you, lord governor,
Remains the censure of this hellish villain,   *425*
The time, the place, the torture. O, enforce it!
Myself will straight aboard, and to the state
This heavy act with heavy heart relate.   *Exeunt omnes.*

❧ FINIS ❧

---

386 taken off: *revoked*   **397** *Cf. n.*   **400 wrought:** *wrought upon, worked up*

401 Perplex'd: *desperately troubled*   **402 Indian;** *cf. n.*   **406 méd'cinable;** *cf. n.*   **407 Aleppo;** *cf. n.*   **412 period:** *ending, close*   **418 Spartan:** *for fierceness and taciturnity*   **419 fell:** *deadly*   **422 Let it be hid;** *cf. n.*   **423 seize upon:** *take legal possession of*   **424 succeed:** *descend in succession (as nearest relative of Desdemona)*   **426 enforce it:** *make it severe*

NOTES

At the time of his sudden death in June of 1946, Professor Brooke had completed his work on the text, notes, and glosses for Hamlet, King Lear, Othello *and* I Henry IV. *The editorial tasks which he left unfinished—preparation of some of the final copy for the press, reading of the proofs, compilation of the* Indexes of Words Glossed, *decisions as to certain matters of style and format, and, in the case of* I Henry IV, *the rescuing of the text from the prescriptive punctuation of the eighteenth-century editors—have been undertaken by Professor Benjamin Nangle.*

Textual Note. The two authorities for the text of *Othello* are the first separate (quarto) edition, printed in 1622, and the version included in the first collected (folio) edition of Shakespeare's dramatic works, published in 1623. Neither is based directly on the other, though there is some indication that both go back to a common manuscript authority which itself was a derivative from Shakespeare's original. The Quarto text is the shorter by more than 150 lines. These lines (missing in Quarto 1, but nearly all restored in the second Quarto of 1630) are here printed within angle brackets (⟨ ⟩). Some of these (*e.g.*, IV.i.187–189, V.ii.315–321) are clearly accidental omissions; others have the appearance of stage cuts. The much less numerous passages which appear in the first Quarto, but not in the Folio, are here printed within ornamental brackets (« »).

Neither of the 'substantive' texts of *Othello* can be said to be well printed. Each has a rather high proportion of plain typographical error, and there are some passages where a tolerable reading can be secured only by blending what appears to be authentic in either the Quarto or the Folio and ejecting the faults of both. In other places variants are found which are so nearly balanced in merit that it is hard to say which word Shakespeare really wrote. In such conditions it is unlikely that a perfectly scientific and satisfactory edition of *Othello* will ever be produced. However, when the faults of the Quarto are weighed against those of the Folio, it becomes quite certain that the margin of virtue is on the side of the former; and this means, since the early editors had a strong prejudice in favor of the Folio, that a considerable number of readings have had to be eliminated in the present edition which familiarity has endeared, but which reason can no longer justify.

The Quarto marks the act divisions, except Act III. The Folio divides the play correctly into both acts and scenes (with a slight deviation from modern practice at II.iii) and adds 'The Names of the Actors' on the last page. The stage directions are fuller in the Quarto, and these have generally been followed; a very few have been taken from the second Quarto of 1630. Necessary amplifications and other essential matter omitted in the original editions are supplied within square brackets.

In Shakespeare's usage it was optional to give full syllabic value to the ending *-ed* of past verbal forms or (as is generally done now) to contract this ending with the preceding syllable. In the present edition final *-ed* must always be pronounced as a separate syllable in order to preserve the original rhythm of the verse. Where rhythm requires the contracted form, the spelling *'d* is used.

Shakespeare accented a number of words on syllables which do not now bear the accent, and sometimes his practice in this matter was inconsistent. Where an unusual accentuation is required, it is indicated by an acute mark over the stressed vowel, as in *séquester*.

Obsolete words and words employed in now unusual senses are explained in footnotes the first time they occur in the text. Repetitions are not usually noted and when they occur should be sought in the *Index of Words Glossed* at the end of the volume.

The critical and general notes in the present section are announced by the symbol, *cf. n.*, at the bottom of the page of text to which each has relevance. A name at the end of a note (in parentheses) indicates the authority; but no special effort is made to give credit for material which is common property or which is, so far as known, new in the present edition.

I.i.4. *'Sblood.* An oath, contracted from 'God's blood'; as *Zounds,* line 86 below, is a contraction from 'God's wounds,'—the reference in both cases being to Christ (as of one substance with God) on the cross. In 1606 King James I caused an Act to be passed forbidding blasphemy on the stage, and accordingly these oaths are omitted in the Folio edition of the play, while other similar expressions throughout are either omitted or softened; cf. Iago's mild ejaculation in IV.i.160.

I.i.8. *Three great ones.* Three quite mythical characters. Iago was never an open candidate for the office of lieutenant. Neither Othello, Cassio, nor Emilia knows of such a thing, and Iago does not mention it again. He invents this story in order to disarm Roderigo's suspicion that he has been preferring Othello's interests to Roderigo's. (It may be, in spite of line 7, that Iago's vague distaste

for Othello first crystallizes into conscious hate at this moment, when he starts inventing specious reasons for it.)

I.i.13. *bombast circumstance.* Bombast was a cheap kind of cotton stuff used for padding Elizabethan garments; the obvious metaphorical use was very common.

I.i.20. *Florentine.* Iago sneers at Cassio's place of origin because the name connotes what 'Parisian' or 'Bostonian' might.

I.i.21. *A fellow almost damn'd in a fair wife.* Properly punctuated by the Folio as a parenthetical remark. Cassio, says Iago, is a fellow of such effeminate quality that the like could hardly be endured in a fine lady. Here *in* means 'in the person of' and *wife* 'woman' in general. In this description of Cassio Iago is again lying (compare note on II.iii.122) in order to build up Roderigo's belief that Othello has misused him. The obscure feeling called inferiority complex drives him in the same direction. It is evident that Shakespeare had confidence in the ability of the actor of Iago, who thus begins his rôle with two statements that the audience must not be allowed to accept with the full faith Roderigo gives them. (The name of the first impersonator of Iago has not been recorded. In the following generation Joseph Taylor [c. 1586–1653], who also played Hamlet, was famous in the part.)

I.i.30. *belee'd and calm'd.* A nautical metaphor, meaning 'Have the wind (of Othello's favor) taken from my sails: be superseded by this interloper.'

I.i.31. *Debitor-and-Creditor.* A coined name of contempt for Cassio: 'Mr. Bookkeeper.' *counter-caster.* 'One who casts accounts, or reckons by counters'; cf. Iago's earlier term, *arithmetician,* line 19 above. These expressions are all intended to cast contempt on Cassio as a man of books and figures, not of warlike deeds. They are later shown to be contrary to fact, except in that Cassio did apparently possess technical qualifications which Iago lacked.

I.i.33. *God bless the mark!* Originally this was a pious formula to avert the consequences of an evil omen; then, by ironical inversion, it came to be a contemptuous interjection equivalent to 'forsooth' or a mild oath. *ancient.* This spelling represents the way in which the word 'ensign' was pronounced. Cassio and Iago were of higher rank than their titles indicate, for they were staff-officers, the commander-in-chief's immediate aides.

I.i.39. *in any . . . affin'd.* The image is from the old tables or terms of affinity which controlled legal marriage and were posted in churches. Do I stand, asks Iago, in any such close spiritual relationship with the Moor that it it my duty to love him?

I.i.70. *Rouse him.* Like the other pronouns in this line, *him* must refer to Othello, not Brabantio. No actor could read the line adequately otherwise.

I.i.89, 90. *For shame . . . gown!* Iago is simply enjoying this exhibition of the senator in *negligé.*

I.i.124, 125. *your daughter . . . two backs.* Borrowed from Rabelais (Bk. I, ch. 3).

I.i.127. *a senator.* Iago, who belongs to the left politically, and who is exploiting his advantage in being unknown, implies that in answering 'Villain!' with 'Senator!' one is offering a generous *quid pro quo.*

I.i.132. The tedious time about midnight; a 'toss-up,' indeterminate odd or even, as to whether it be the last moments of one day or the first of the next.

I.i.145. *extravagant and wheeling.* There is a reference here to Othello's being a 'soldier of fortune,' not a native of Venice. Venetian law required that the commander-in-chief of Venetian forces should be a politically disqualified alien, so that no political ambition might distract him from the strict performance of his military duties and jeopardize the security of the state.

I.i.161. *Cyprus wars.* The historical date at which the action of the play took place has usually been given as 1570, on the strength of Reed's assertion that in that year 'Mustapha, Selymus' general, attacked Cyprus,' after having effected a junction with another Turkish fleet at Rhodes. But in the play (1) the Turks did not 'attack' Cyprus, and (2) they were reported (I.iii.17–36) as intending to 'attack' Rhodes—which had been in their hands since 1522. The date of the action of the play must therefore be placed between 1471, the year in which the Venetians assumed virtual sovereignty of Cyprus, and 1522, the year in which the Turks became masters of Rhodes. The Turkish expedition described in the play must then have been either too abortive for record in history or entirely fictitious, for none such is known between those dates according to Malone and Reed (Furness, 357); but the 'hypothetical attack' cited in Sources of the Play (1) as 'meditated, according to report' in 1508 (Furness, 374) would satisfy all Shakespeare's requirements.

I.i.169. *the Sagittary.* 'The Sign of the Archer.' Most likely an inn in the neighborhood of the famous Venetian Arsenal.

I.i.174. *unhappy.* Hapless, ill-fated, unfortunate; cf. III.iv.113.

I.ii.5. *him.* Evidently Brabantio, as is made clear in Iago's next speech (line 13 ff.). He has been giving Othello a highly spiced account of Brabantio's comments on the wedding. (Iago never talks of his association with Roderigo.)

I.ii.14, 15. 'And has, in actual effect (though not by law), an influence as weighty as the Duke's own.' Iago was simply 'talking big' in order to alarm Othello by exaggerating Brabantio's importance.

I.ii.25. *speak unbonneted.* Speak on equal terms, without removing the hat as one did in the presence of a superior. 'Uncapped' could be used in the same way. In *Coriolanus*, II.ii.23, *bonneted* has the contrary sense, having hats off in token of humility.

I.ii.28. *unhoused.* Possibly merely 'unmarried'; but probably 'unhampered,' free as the open air; just the opposite of 'cabin'd, cribb'd, confin'd,' *Macbeth* III.iv.27.

I.ii. S.d. *Enter Cassio with lights, Officers and torches.* Perhaps in two groups, each with lights. The emphasis on lighting effects in this scene may indicate that it was meant to be acted indoors at court. A type of drama popular at this period was commonly known as the 'nocturnal' (see W. J. Lawrence, 'Shakespeare from a New Angle,' *Studies*, Dublin, Sept., 1919).

I.ii.58. *lawful prize.* Iago uses metaphors from buccaneering. Desdemona is a *land*-carrack (cf. 'prairie schooner'), and Othello's problem is that of the Elizabethan privateer: Will the prize-court allow him to keep his booty?

I.ii.59–61. *I do not understand.* Contrast III.iii.78 ff., 106 ff. Presumably Cassio, who is punctilious, does not understand himself to be at liberty to avow what he knows.

I.ii.62. *Marry.* The word, originally an oath or ejaculation calling on the Virgin Mary, is here used by Iago to create a pun. For its use as a simple ejaculation, cf. II.iii.261, III.i.10.

I.ii.117, 118. If Othello is allowed to commit such an outrage with impunity, Venice may just as well give up the caste system.

I.iii.S.d. *Enter . . . Attendants.* A typical stage direction. The characters do not literally enter, but are revealed by drawing the curtain of the rear stage.

I.iii.12–15. I do not feel so reassured by the mere discrepancy in detail as not to credit, with dreadful apprehensions, the underlying main point.

I.iii.51. *Write from us, etc.* Command him in our name to use the greatest haste (the Quarto reading).

I.iii.69. *mountebanks.* Brabantio's charge, which he has been gradually elaborating (cf. I.i.183 ff., I.ii.86 ff.), now expresses itself in the language Laertes had used in *Hamlet* IV.iii.155.

I.iii.75–77. *the bloody book of law . . . sense.* Capital punishment shall be imposed according to your own interpretation of the bitter letter of the law.

I.iii.88 ff. For discussion of Shakespeare's use of the oration as a branch of rhetoric see M. B. Kennedy, *The Oration in Shakespeare* (1942).

I.iii.107. *motion.* Desdemona was so still and pure by nature that she couldn't move without blushing.

I.iii.154. *portance . . . history.* These adventures of Othello are closely paralleled by those related in Captain John Smith's *True Travels, Adventures and Observations* (1630). When the play was written Smith had not yet gone to Virginia, but he had suffered all the vicissitudes Othello here mentions.

I.iii.159. *Anthropophagi, etc.* For Shakespeare's information about these creatures see J. Milton French, 'Othello among the Anthropophagi,' *PMLA*, Sept., 1934.

I.iii.181. *Upon this heat.* The Quarto reading. The Folio substitute, 'Upon this hint,' has required so much defence that readers have grown fond of it, but it is probably a scribal or typographical slip occasioned by recollection of line 157, 'It was my hint to speak.' It is unlikely that Shakespeare would employ so banal a phrase twice in twenty-five lines, particularly in a passage of such high finish.

I.iii.220–237. These staccato riming couplets are introduced, as prose is later, for contrast and orchestral effect. After a great movement in blank verse, which is the idiom of youth, romance, and passion, Shakespeare brings in the balanced rime, which is the idiom of age, caution, and experience. The same means are employed in *Romeo and Juliet* as the balcony scene (II.ii) is linked to the scene (II.iii) at Friar Lawrence's cell.

I.iii.223. *more mischief.* Quarto reading. The Folio has 'new mischief.' There are many cases like this in *Othello*, where the merits of the two texts are so closely balanced that an editor must be content to impute to Shakespeare what his own taste selects as slightly the more euphonious or more meaningful.

I.iii.224, 225. Part of the art of the gnomic couplet lay in confusion of the prose order of words. The sense here is: When Fortune takes what cannot be preserved, Patience makes a mockery of Fortune's injury.

I.iii.234, 235. *to sugar . . . sides.* Having converse and opposed powers, capable of either sweetening or embittering.

I.iii.238. In the Folio this line is recast in the form of prose. Shakespeare

may so have written or rewritten it to serve as a transition to the Duke's speech which follows.

I.iii.276. *A moth of peace.* A concentrated metaphor. It suggests the futile fluttering of a moth, its confined sphere indoors, and its triviality; while there is also a kind of pun on Desdemona 'fretting' like a moth in the midst of peace.

I.iii.284. *distinct.* Both the early texts here read 'defunct,' and the obscurity resulting has led to some of the most repellent emendations in the Shakespeare canon. In Elizabethan script 'distinct' and 'defunct' are very similar. Shakespeare is notably fond of the word *distinct* in the present sense of 'separate,' 'individual.' The sense of the passage has been further obscured for modern readers by two Elizabethanisms in the previous line: the omission of the relative after *heat*, and the 'Northern' verbal plural in *affects*, both quite characteristic of Shakespeare.

I.iii.289. *seel.* Folio reading; Quarto 'foyles.' Literally, a hawking term, meaning to sew the lids of a falcon's eyes together in order to restrict the sight while the bird was being trained; thence used metaphorically in a variety of senses, such as to blind, cover, conceal, restrain.

I.iii.290. *speculative and offic'd.* The inferior reading of the Quarto, 'speculative and active,' is interesting. It suggests that someone (probably not Shakespeare) was thinking of the old mediaeval coupling of contemplative and active.

I.iii.301. *ten.* No one is likely ever to know whether Shakespeare set the hour for *ten*, as the Quarto says, or 'nine' as the Folio has it. Perhaps he used a Roman numeral, 'x' or 'ix.'

I.iii.317, 318. It is again optional to prefer the Quarto version:

Look to her, Moor! Have a quick eye to see.
She has deceiv'd her father, may do thee.

I.iii.403–406. *it is . . . surety.* The author's purpose is not to discredit Emilia or Othello, who are clearly innocent, but to show that Iago (unlike Othello) has a morbidly jealous nature and is morbidly seeking to rationalize the obscure hostility he feels.

I.iii.410. *double knavery.* Referring to the two purposes mentioned in the preceding line: to get Cassio's place and *plume up* (pamper) Iago's injured ego. Iago, whose reputation for 'honesty' revolts him as a reflection on his intellect, finds a real solace in picturing himself as a clever knave.

II.i.S.d. The place, not definitely mentioned, is evidently Famagosta, which the Turks captured after a famous siege that lasted from 1569 till 1571. The time is a Saturday afternoon (cf. III.iii.68f.) something over a week (cf. II.i.86) after the close of Act I.

II.i.3. *'twixt the haven and the main.* Between the harbor and the point where the sea fades into the horizon. Folio reading: ' 'twixt the Heauen, and the Maine.'

II.i.28. *La Veronesa.* The early texts have 'A Veronessa' ('A Verennessa'), probably a copyist's or printer's misreading.

II.i.54–56. Therefore, while not foolishly over-confident, I am emboldened to hope for the best. A condensed figure almost incapable of precise literal paraphrase.

II.i.56. *Messenger.* The Folio dispenses with the Messenger, making this speech an off-stage cry and assigning his subsequent speech to one of the gentlemen already on the stage. Throughout this scene, the Quarto and Folio texts are frequently at variance in the stage directions and assignment of speechs to the various characters, reflecting the difficulties of the early producers in coping with the complicated action and crowded stage. The present text generally follows the Quarto, which here, as elsewhere, give more thoughtful attention to these details.

II.i.71. *ingen-giver.* What Shakespeare here wrote has bothered all editors, and evidently bothered the earliest printers. The Folio, attempting to follow copy, produces a nonsense word: 'Do's tyre the Ingeniuer.' The Quarto evades the issue by inventing a flat paraphrase: 'Does beare all excellency.' The suggested emendations of earlier editors have read little sense into the passage. The present reading, assuming that the Folio compositor, faced with utterly illegible copy, dropped a 'g' from the word, renders the sentence plausible. *Ingen* (ingine, engine; Latin *ingenium*) meant native talent, mother wit, the mental and moral qualities which come from nature rather than art, and in Platonic conception belong to the inner rather than the outer beauty. The word in this sense was common in Elizabethan and Jacobean literature, and was even used for the names of characters who, like Ingen in Nathan Field's *Amends for Ladies* (c. 1612), represented

'The fountain of humanity, the prize
Of every virtue, moral and divine:'

In the present passage (as in Field's) the *ingen-giver* is Nature, who by Cassio's image tires herself by the multitude of her benefactions to Desdemona. Lines 70, 72 laud her beauty of soul, as lines 68, 69 do her outward beauty. Cassio was a Florentine, and thereby something of a Platonist.

II.i.107. *So . . . news.* Alternative readings of Quarto and Folio respectively. Each satisfactorily completes the metrical line.

II.i.126. *housewifery, housewives.* Pronounced 'huzzifry,' 'huzzivs.' The modern 'hussy' (merely a phonetic transcription of 'housewife') shows the slur intended.

II.i.169. Probably some cant saying or 'double entendre' gave point to this line in Shakespeare's day.

II.i.187, 188. *I . . . courtship.* The Quarto has 'I will catch you in your own courtesies,' and above (180 f.) '. . . whisper: as little a web as this will ensnare as great a Flee as Cassio.'

II.i.221. *set down the pegs, etc.* Iago develops the musical image suggested by Othello in *discords* (line 213).

II.i.260. *A subtle, slippery knave.* Folio: 'A slipper and subtle knave.' In these prose speeches the two texts exhibit a number of slight variations. The Folio may contain actors' additions. (Note the words in angle brackets.)

II.i.290. *taste.* The first Quarto reading, 'trust,' may be right.

II.i.295. *if you can.* Most editors here read with the Quarto 'if I can'; but the Folio is correct. It is Iago who makes the opportunities.

II.i.316, 317. *whom . . . hunting.* 'Whom I flog to make him hunt faster.' The reference is to beating an ill-trained dog to make him more diligent. Instead of *thrash*, the first Quarto reads 'crush,' the second and the Folio 'trace'; but these yield no tolerable sense, and it seems evident that Roderigo is called 'trash of Venice' only for the sake of a pun.

II.i.317. *stand the putting on.* That is, if Roderigo doesn't break down under the rigor of my discipline. One sense of 'put on' was to lay a hound on the scent (*O.E.D., Put* 46. 1).

II.ii.5. *addiction.* So the second Quarto (1630). This may be Shakespeare's word, but if so was a very early use of it and was not understood by the printer of either the first Quarto (who substitutes 'mind') or the Folio (who spells it 'addition').

II.ii.9. *tolled.* Both Quartos and the Folio read 'told.' See H. Kökeritz, 'Two Sets of Shakespearean Homophones,' *R.E.S.,* Oct., 1943.

II.iii. No new scene was necessary here on the Elizabethan stage, and none is indicated in the Folios or Quartos. Theobald first assigned a new location for the action after the Herald's departure, and Capell first added the caption 'Scene iii.'

II.iii.27. *Well, etc.* Iago gives up the effort to lure Cassio into indiscreet comment on the general's wife.

II.iii.53. *hold their honors in a wary distance.* Are skittish about them; allow none to approach too close.

II.iii.59. *If consequence do but approve my dream.* If the outcome only justifies my hope.

II.iii.65. This song like the next (line 81) need not be credited to Iago's invention. The first was quite possibly an Elizabethan tavern catch, and the second is a mélange of old ballads.

II.iii.122. *He'll watch the horologe a double set.* He'll see the hour-hand of the clock make two complete revolutions; *i.e.,* stay awake for twenty-four hours at a stretch. Iago is expert at adjusting his prevarications to what the traffic will bear. To the civilian Roderigo, in I.i., he can safely picture Cassio as a military nincompoop; to the commander Montano, who doubtless knows Cassio's professional reputation but not his personal habits, he can safely deplore the fact that Cassio is a dipsomaniac, while belauding his military competence.

II.iii.142. *twiggen* (Quarto 'wicker') *bottle.* Either 'slash him till he resembles a Chianti bottle covered with straw net-work' (Booth), or 'beat him till he runs to hide himself in one of the wicker flasks we've just been using' (Hart). Cf. also *Much Ado About Nothing* I.i.216, 217: 'Hang me in a bottle like a cat And shoot at me,' and the note thereon.

II.iii.155. *Diablo.* Oath or exclamation of excitement: 'the Devil!' A typical Jacobean affectation of elegance was this garnishing of the speech with scraps of Spanish.

II.iii.162. *all sense of place and duty.* Since Quarto and Folio agree in the misarrangement, 'all place of sense and duty,' it looks as if both were based on a common source.

II.iii.166. *Which heaven has forbid the Ottomites.* That is, heaven has, through the storm, forbidden the Turks to kill us.

II.iii.212. *on . . . safety.* Guard-post established to secure the general safety. Hendiadys for 'court of guard' (cf. II.i.234).

II.iii.299. *Hydra.* A monster with nine heads. Whenever one was cut off, several new ones replaced it. The destruction of the Lernæan Hydra was the second of the Twelve Labors of Hercules.

II.iii.341 f. *this parallel course Directly to his good.* This course which runs straight in line with his advantage.

III.i. S.d. *Clown.* The Clown here must have been a licensed jester, like Touchstone, in Othello's train: cf. III.iv.1–18. (This stage direction comes from the second Quarto.)

III. i. 3, 4. The Neapolitans spoke Italian with a marked nasal twang.

III.i.43. Iago was a Venetian, Cassio a Florentine. The latter merely means to say, 'I never experienced more honesty and kindness even in one of my own countrymen than in this man' (Malone).

III.i.52. Opportunity, in the fable, had no hair on the back of the head and hence must be grasped by the forelock.

III.ii.2. *state.* The Folio has 'Senate.'

III.iii.16–18. 'He may either of himself think it politic to keep me out of office so long, or he may be satisfied with such slight reasons, or so many accidents may' arise to postpone from time to time his intended re-instatement of me, 'that I may be quite forgotten' (Johnson).

III.iii.25. *watch him tame.* A metaphor drawn from falconry. Hawks were tamed, *i.d.,* their fierce spirit of resistance was broken, by deprivation of sleep.

III.iii.68. *to-morrow . . . morn.* This tell us that the day is Sunday and that the arrival in Cyprus occurred on Saturday. The last four acts of this tragedy cover about thirty-six hours.

III.iii.103. *Chaos is come again.* The most emphatic of assurances. I love you, and will till the world returns to chaos. Thus ends in utter failure the plan Iago outlined in the closing lines of Act II for arousing Othello's jealousy.

III.iii.106. *Did Michael Cassio . . . Know of your love?* Thus Iago starts again, building, as his manner is, on the new fact he has just picked up.

III.iii.147. *seem none.* 'No longer seem, or bear the shape of men' (Johnson).

III.iii.171. *conjects.* A very good word, replaced in the Folio by the commoner 'conceits.' This whole speech is here printed as in the Quarto, which seems to give the earlier version. Note that in lines 104–176 Iago is implying nothing about Desdemona, but is playing on Othello's urgent official need to learn the truth about Cassio's trustworthiness, which had been so strangely impugned by the events of the night before (cf. II. iii.242 ff.).

III.iii.179. *our souls.* The Quarto reading, which seems more authentic than the Folio 'their souls.' In this speech Iago begins slyly to turn his insinuations toward Desdemona, but the speech is merely his ingenious parody of Cassio on reputation (II.iii.262 ff.).

III.iii.195. *O misery!* An objective, not subjective, exclamation. It means 'How intolerable!', and is the comment of a sensitive outsider upon the horrid picture Iago is painting. In line 201 Othello bursts into astonished outcry on perceiving that he is himself being linked with jealousy.

III.iii.207. *exsufflicate.* A coined word, not instanced elsewhere, but a good one. 'Exsufflate' would be normal.

III.iii.293–296. An elaborate metaphor drawn from falconry. A *haggard* was a wild hawk caught when mature and often found to be irreclaimable, unamenable to discipline. A word with such a meaning readily lent itself to use as a term of reproach for a loose woman. *Jesses* were leather leg-straps by which the hawk was fastened to the leash. 'The falconers always let the hawk fly *[whistle her off* = start her] against the wind; if she flies with the wind behind her, she seldom returns. If therefore a hawk was for any reason to be dismissed, she was "let down the wind," and from that time shifted for herself and "preyed at fortune" ' (Johnson).

III.iii.322. *your head.* The Folio substitutes 'it hard,' perhaps because 'yr' (your) in the manuscript was read as 'yt' (it).

III.iii.330. *a hundred times.* One of the numerous hints at the lapse of a considerable amount of time which are dropped in this part of the play to counteract the impression of melodramatic and improbable haste. See note on III.iv.188.

III.iii.344. *handkerchief.* Spelled 'handkercher' always in Quarto, and that was probably Shakespeare's form.

III.iii.400. *wide throats.* Folio: 'rude throats.' In this most famous scene the old prestige of the Folio text sometimes adds the charm of familiarity to the less defensible reading. It is necessary to distinguish between what Shakespeare probably wrote and what Kean and Booth declaimed. *Wide throats* and in the next line *great clamor* (Folio 'dread Clamours') better suit the context and Othello's dignity. The Folio variants suggest that even by 1623 the language of the great speeches had suffered here and there from stagy heightening. (But 'rude' may be an honest misreading of the same manuscript word as *wide*.)

III.iii.434. *Her name.* This reading, *Her,* is based on the second Quarto, correcting 'My' in the Folio. The passage is not in the first Quarto.

III.iii.479. The Folio assigns this line to Othello.

III.iii.493. *any that.* Malone's emendation for 'any, it' in the early texts. In Elizabethan handwriting *yt* was commonly used for both 'that' and 'it.'

III.iii.507–515. Steevens cites Holland's translation of Pliny's *Natural History,* 1601, as the probable source of Shakespeare's assertion about the current of the Pontic or Black Sea (the ancient Pontus Euxinus). The first Quarto omits the passage.

III.iv.48, 49. The commentators have brought to light sufficient early plays on the words 'hearts' and 'hands' (to which might be added Herrick's *Panegerick*

to Sir Lewis Pemberton, lines 37–45) to show that this was a favorite quibble. The meaning is: The joining of hands in marriage formerly meant the giving of hearts also, but nowadays we have a formal outward union of hands without any accompanying inward union of hearts.

III.iv.53. *sorry rheum.* The Quarto has 'sullen rheum,' which may be right.

III.iv.84. *Most veritable.* Said ironically, no doubt. Othello is inventing marvels about the handkerchief to try his wife's conscience. Compare V.ii.253 ff.

III.iv.113. *I am most unhappy in the loss of it.* The admirable Emilia has been unfairly blamed for not confessing the theft of the handkerchief. The next lines explain. Emilia loves and fears and (like everybody else) fundamentally trusts Iago. She has the generous trait of imputing her husband's trying qualities to the general imperfection of men, and has not been depressed to see the great Othello behave in as childish a manner (lines 33–117). She thinks him irritated over the temporary loss of a keepsake, and there is nothing in the situation as she understands it which would oblige her at this point to violate Iago's confidence, disobey his command (III.iii.361), and arouse his anger. Jealousy in her view is a totally irrational passion (lines 173–176) and not worth too much bother.

III.iv.188. *keep a week away.* This passage, Lodovico's arrival with the message from the Senators presupposing their receipt of a report from Othello about the 'Turks' discomfiture (IV.i.230 ff.), Roderigo's 'Every day thou daffest me' (IV.ii.200), and various other points in the play would seem to imply that many days must have elapsed since Othello's arrival in Cyprus; yet an unbroken sequence of time-indications can be cited to show that he landed Saturday afternoon and killed Desdemona Sunday night. In this dilemma (which arises, of course, only in close study of the play, never in witnessing a performance) John Wilson ('Christopher North') in 1850 proposed the theory that Shakespeare consciously or unconsciously employed 'Double Time,' *i.e.*, Dramatic or Short Time and Historic or Long Time: 'Short for maintaining the tension of the passion, Long for a thousand general needs; . . . one for our sympathy with Othello's tempest of heart, one for the verisimilitude of the transaction.' Every playwright does something of the sort, but the method in *Othello* is particularly bold.

IV.i.20. *They have it very oft that have it not.* People often have honor (receive outward respect) who have no honor (possess no inward virtue.)

IV.i.22. *I would most gladly have forgot it.* The purpose of Iago's gross talk now appears. In the brief interval since Othello left the stage (III.iv.109), his normal balance has begun to reassert itself and the slanders have taken on unreality. Iago finds himself in a position of direst peril, and for the moment escapes by so nauseating his victim as to deprive him of the use of his reason.

IV.i.43–51. These are the disjointed ejaculations of an agonized mind on the verge of collapse. There are few phrases in it where the reference is not fairly clear.

IV.i.101, 102. *all . . . man.* Altogether given over to mere passionate impulse, and not a real man.

IV.i.126. This line and all Othello's speeches down to line 181 are supposed to be spoken in his hiding-place, where he is both visible and audible to the audience, but neither visible nor audible to Cassio and Iago.

IV.i.187–189. The omission of this speech in the first Quarto was clearly accidental. That the printer had Iago's speech in his copy is shown by the fact that Othello's preceding speech, which comes at the bottom of a page, is followed by the catchword 'Iag.' Iago's speech is then dropped out, the next page beginning with Othello's subsequent speech. The second Quarto also omits Iago's speech, running Othello's two speeches into one.

IV.i.208. *the pity of it, Iago, etc.* The longer version of this speech in the Folio may be an actor's amplification.

IV.i.218. *Strangle her.* If poison were used, Iago would be an accomplice, and there might be no way to convict Othello of the crime. Moreover, Iago nowhere shows any malice against Desdemona. He may think Othello incapable of strangling her and may mean to give her a chance of life.

IV.i.240. *This fail you not to do, etc.* The regular formula for closing formal orders: 'This fail you not to do, as you will enjoy our favor,' or ' . . . as you will answer to us for any disobedience.'

IV.ii.58. *they.* The Quartos read 'he.' Perhaps Shakespeare wrote 'God' for *heaven* in line 57 and withdrew it as over-bold.

IV.ii.64, 65. This noble image seems to be printed correctly in the first Quarto. The Folio somewhat garbles it:

'The fixed Figure for the time of Scorne,
To point his slow, and mouing finger at,'

and the commentators have garbled it still more. Othello pictures himself as one of the figures on the dial of Scorn's clock, pointed at by Scorn's two hands or 'fingers,'—fingers which move so slowly as not to seem to move at all, and yet move through all eternity.

IV.ii.67–70. Dr. Johnson very strangely objected to this masterly pair of metaphors, the grain-garner and the fountain, elemental food and drink, the two sustaining principles represented by Desdemona, without which Othello cannot live.

IV.ii.72, 73. *Turn . . . cherubin.* Look on that sight and blush! Young and rose-lipped Patience at such a spectacle will become a fire-red cherub.

IV.ii.73. *cherubin.* A plural form used with a singular signification, by a common mistake. That the cherub was traditionally painted with a scarlet countenance is vouched for by Chaucer's phrase, 'a fyr-reed cherubinnes face' (*Prologue*, 624).

IV.ii.74. *I here look grim as hell.* A bleak and tortured line, not to be improved by emendation. Here I stand, says Othello, so unlike the cherubim, so black and desperate.

IV.ii.77. *quicken . . . blowing.* The reference is to the blow-fly, which lays its eggs on meat—*cf.* shambles—and 'again becomes pregnant [quicken] the very instant it has laid a batch of eggs [blowing]' (Deighton).

IV.ii.78, 79. *O thou black weed . . . sweet.* Quarto reading. The Folio, perhaps in an (imperfect) effort to divide the lines evenly, reads:

'O thou weed:
Who art so lovely fair, and smell'st so sweet.'

It remains beautiful, but something precious has been lost.

IV.ii.91, 92. *What . . . strumpet.* These four words, of which the last two are not in the Folio, look like an insertion. If they are omitted, the words before and after form a perfect line.

IV.ii.156. *Fie! there is no such man.* Not a shallow lie, probably, but Iago's confession to himself that mere self-interest would not account for what he is doing.

IV.ii.205. Compare I.i.4. The situation here is very much as at the opening of the play.

IV.ii.244. *Mauritania.* It is on such expressions as this and Iago's 'Barbary' (I.i.111) that those rely who wish to prove that Shakespeare thought of Othello as a bronze-colored Moor, while those who maintain that he conceived of him as a jet-black full-blooded negro cite I.i.67, I.ii.84, III.iii.435, 436, etc. Ignorantly or by intention, Shakespeare has combined distinct ethnic traits to produce the blend of romance and realism that the tragedy called for. (There is no reason to believe that Othello is, as Iago says, returning to Mauritania.)

IV.iii.1. After supper they have been showing Lodovico the living quarters in the Citadel. He is now about to leave.

IV.iii.31. *An old thing 'twas.* As this indicates, the famous 'willow song' which follows was not original with Shakespeare. It was perhaps first written (for a man) by John Heywood, 'the Epigrammatist,' in the reign of Henry VIII. A version exists with Elizabethan music.

IV.iii.112. Not to be corrupted by bad example, but take it as a warning.

V.i.15. *Every way makes my gain.* Wishful thinking. Nothing would now save Iago but for Cassio and Roderigo each neatly to eliminate the other, and nobody ask intelligent questions afterwards.

V.i.20. *a daily beauty in his life.* This shows the collapse of Iago's philosophy. The only daily beauty in Cassio's life is the beauty of loyal devotion to his commander, over which Iago had made so merry in I.i.46 ff.

V.i. S.d. *Enter Othello.* He has seen Lodovico to his lodging and is returning.

V.i.90. *I have been to seek you.* This presumably accounts for Gratiano's absence at the opening of IV.iii.

V.i.95. *To bear a part in this.* So the Quarto. The Folio reads 'To be a party in this injury,' which scans, but is certainly weak.

V.i.139. *Emilia, run you to the citadel.* Iago's purpose here is debatable. Did he wish Emilia to intervene in time to save Desdemona's life? Did he wish her message to shame Othello into a murder he might not otherwise commit?

V.i.141. *Will . . . afore?* Addressed to the 'kind gentlemen' of line 137. The purpose is to leave Iago for a moment alone on the stage. (The Quarto printer did not understand *afore* and substituted 'I pray.')

V.ii.S.d. *Enter . . . bed.* Phrased as in second Quarto (less full in first Quarto and Folio). On the Elizabethan stage Othello would enter and, drawing the curtain before the rear stage, under the balcony, reveal Desdemona in bed asleep.

V.ii.1. *It is the cause.* Probably explained by line 6 below. Desdemona must be destroyed, not from personal vengeance, but because she represents a pernicious principle which, if suffered, will corrupt all mankind.

V.ii.5. *alablaster.* Alabaster, a beautiful white stone used for the finest funeral monuments.

V.ii.12. *Promethean heat.* Prometheus, in classical mythology, stole from heaven the sacred element of fire, originally unobtainable on the earth. Othello

means here that the spark of life, once extinguished, cannot be rekindled without some superhuman agency.

V.ii.16. *doth.* The Folio has 'dost,' less felicitously. Othello is commenting on the breath; he is not addressing or personifying it as the Cavalier poets did.

V.ii.20. *fatal.* Referring to Desdemona's deadliness. Cf. line 6.

V.ii.65. *conception.* The Quarto has 'conceit,' which blurs the terrible figure that Othello uses. His strong purpose is like an unwanted infant ineluctably approaching birth.

V.ii.83. *That he hath—* Othello is unable to go on, but the Folio editor was, replacing the oath *uds death* by 'vs'd thee.'

V.ii.99. *Being . . . pause.* While it is being done, there must be no pause. This is not in the Quarto and would not be missed. Perhaps an editor was working Othello's broken prose into the rhythmical pattern.

V.ii.115. *The noise was high.* Probably referring to the outcry resulting from the attack on Cassio. Othello is accounting to himself for Emilia's disturbing presence outside.

V.ii.123. *yawn at alteration.* Crack open at this monstrous change. Earthquakes were believed to accompany or follow eclipses. These lines, 121–123, recall Othello's earlier saying, III.iii.102, 103.

V.ii.205. *Gra.* The Quarto gives this speech to 'All,' which was probably Shakespeare's careless indication. The Folio editor, not caring for a chorus, decided who was to speak it. He properly left 'All' in line 220.

V.ii.227. *I thought so then.* That is, at IV.ii.152 ff. (but without suspicion then of Iago's guilt).

V.ii.232. *Perchance, Iago, I will ne'er go home.* A line of great poignancy, for Emilia and Iago are fond of each other.

V.ii.254. This statement is inconsistent with III.iv.61, 62, though perhaps reconcilable by casuistry. See note on III.iv.84.

V.ii.258. *No, I will speak as liberal as the north.* So the Folio. The Quarto has 'I'll be in speaking liberal as the air,' which is also good. Shakespearean revision is possible.

V.ii.276. *wife.* The Quarto has 'woman.' *no stones in heaven, etc.* Are there no extra thunderbolts to destroy creatures like Iago?

V.ii.338. *I bleed, sir.* Coldbloodedly ironic. You have drawn blood from me, as you couldn't from a real devil. This accounts for *demi-devil* in line 352.

V.ii.354. *Demand me nothing.* Iago, when caught, has been willing to confess facts (lines 296, 321); but when questioned about motives, he takes refuge in sullen silence, for he has no answer that makes any possible sense to him.

V.ii.370. *nick.* So the first Quarto. The Folio editor found the word inelegant and substituted 'interim,' in which perversion he has been followed by all later editions.

V.ii.398. *Speak of them as they are.* This, the first Quarto reading, is more in character than the Folio's 'Speak of me as I am.'

V.ii.403. *Like the base Indian.* There is no significance in the first Folio spelling, 'Iudean.' Shakespeare is thinking of the savage who throws away a king's ransom because he cannot realize its value. In his mind, probably, were the lines near the beginning of Marlowe's *Jew of Malta:*

> 'Give me the merchants of the Indian mines . . .
> The wealthy Moor that in the eastern rocks
> Without control can pick his riches up,
> And in his house heap pearl like pebble-stones.'

V.ii.407. *med'cinable.* Shakespeare seems to prefer this word, with the accent indicated, to 'medicinal,' which is the Quarto reading.

V.ii.408. *Aleppo.* Aleppo was an important center of English oriental trade. Shakespeare was evidently interested in it; cf. *Macbeth* I.iii.8. A consulate was established there in 1586, 'which became a convenient hospice and sometimes a place of refuge for English travellers.' Shakespeare may have read William Parry's *A New and Large Discourse of the Travels of Sir A. Sherley, etc.,* 1601. Of one of Parry's fellow travellers, George Manwaring, it is recorded that at Aleppo 'a Turk took him by the ear and marched him up and down the street while the bystanders threw stones at him and spat upon him' (S. C. Chew, *The Crescent and the Rose,* pp. 157, 245–246). For more detail see *The Three Brothers, or the Travels and Adventures of Sir Anthony, Sir Robert, & Sir Thomas Sherley,* 1825, p. 35.

V.ii.423. *Let it be hid.* The rear-stage curtain is drawn so that the corpses may rise and walk away. The main stage was not curtained.

The Tragedy of King Lear

Edited by TUCKER BROOKE
and
WILLIAM LYON PHELPS

Dramatis Personae

LEAR, KING OF BRITAIN

KING OF FRANCE

DUKE OF BURGUNDY

DUKE OF ALBANY

DUKE OF CORNWALL

EARL OF KENT

EARL OF GLOUCESTER

EDGAR, *Son to Gloucester*

EDMUND, *Bastard Son to Gloucester*

LEAR'S FOOL

CURAN, *Servant to Gloucester*

OSWALD, *Steward to Goneril*

OLD MAN, *Tenant to Gloucester*

DOCTOR

A CAPTAIN, *in Edmund's service*

A GENTLEMAN, *Attendant on Cordelia*

A HERALD

SERVANTS TO CORNWALL

GONERIL
REGAN } *Daughters to Lear*
CORDELIA

KNIGHTS OF LEAR'S TRAIN, OFFICERS, MESSENGERS, SOLDIERS, AND ATTENDANTS

SCENE—*Prehistoric Britain.*

The Tragedy of King Lear

INTRODUCTION

SOURCES OF THE PLAY

There are two tragic stories in this play: the sorrows of Lear and the subordinate tragedy of Gloucester. The former is one of the oldest and most familiar tales in English literature, given in its general outlines by many of the old chroniclers and romancers.[1] Raphael Holinshed, in his *Chronicles* (Chapters V. and VI. of the *Second Book of the History of England*, 2nd ed., 1587), has nearly all the main facts. He gives the names of the King, the three daughters, and their husbands; the answers of the three, saying how much they loved Lear, with Cordelia's consequent disgrace; the cruelty of the two dukes and duchesses to the King. But in his version, France defeats the two antagonists, restores Lear to the throne, and after his death, Cordelia becomes Queen. There was also an old play, entered in the Stationers' Register, 14 May 1594, *The most famous Chronicle historye of Leire kinge of England and his Three Daughters*. On 8 May 1605, this quite un-Shakespearean and untragical piece was again entered on the Register as *The Tragecall historie of Kinge Leir and his Three Daughters, as it was latelie acted*, and printed in the same year. A number of minor similarities with Shakespeare's tragedy have been pointed out.[2]

The Gloucester story was taken from Sir Philip Sidney's *Arcadia*, 1590. In the second book, chapter 10, there is a narrative called *The pitifull state, and story of the Paphlagonian unkind king, and his kind son, first related by the son, then by the blind father*. This tale gives the essentials of the Gloucester-Edgar-Edmund plot, except as Shakespeare has interwoven them with the history of Lear and his three daughters.

The account of King Lear in Holinshed is brief enough to be quoted here in full, with no changes but in spelling:

'Leir the son of Baldud was admitted ruler over the Britons, in the year of the world 3105, at what time Joas reigned in Judah. This Leir was a prince of right noble demeanor, governing his land and subjects in great wealth. He made the town of Caerlier now called Leicester, which standeth upon the river of Sore. It is written that he had by his wife three daughters without other issue, whose names were Gonorilla, Regan, and Cordeilla, which daughters he greatly loved, but specially Cordeilla the youngest far above the two elder. When this Leir therefore was come to great years, & began to wax unwieldy through age, he thought to understand the affections of his daughters towards him, and prefer her whom he best loved to the succession over the kingdom.

'Whereupon he first asked Gonorilla the eldest, how well she loved him: who calling her gods to record, protested that she

loved him more than her own life, which by right and reason should be most dear unto her. With which answer the father being well pleased, turned to the second, and demanded of her how well she loved him: who answered (confirming her sayings with great oaths) that she loved him more than tongue could express, and far above all other creatures of the world.

'Then called he his youngest daughter Cordeilla before him, and asked of her what account she made of him, unto whom she made this answer as followeth: Knowing the great love and fatherly zeal that you have always borne towards me, (for the which I may not answer you otherwise than I think, and as my conscience leadeth me) I protest unto you, that I have loved you ever, and will continually (while I live) love you as my natural father. And if you would more understand of the love that I bear you, ascertain [assure] your self, that so much as you have, so much you are worth, and so much I love you, and no more. The father being nothing content with this answer, married his two eldest daughters, the one unto Henninus, the duke of Cornwall, and the other unto Maglanus, the duke of Albania, betwixt whom he willed and ordained that his land should be divided after his death, and the one half thereof immediately should be assigned to them in hand: but for the third daughter Cordeilla he reserved nothing.

'Nevertheless it fortuned that one of the princes of Gallia (which now is called France) whose name was Aganippus, hearing of the beauty, womanhood, and good conditions of the said Cordeilla, desired to have her in marriage, and sent over to her father, requiring that he might have her to wife: to whom answer was made, that he might have his daughter, but as for any dower he could have none, for all was promised and assured to her other sisters already. Aganippus notwithstanding this answer of denial to receive any thing by way of dower with Cordeilla, took her to wife, only moved thereto (I say) for respect of her person and amiable virtues. This Aganippus was one of the twelve kings that ruled Gallia in those days, as in the British history it is recorded. But to proceed.

'After that Leir was fallen into age, the two dukes that had married his two eldest daughters, thinking it long yer [ere] the government of the land did come to their hands, arose against him in armor, and reft from him the governance of the land, upon conditions to be continued for term of life: by the which he was put to his portion, that is, to live after a rate assigned to him for the maintenance of his estate, which in process of time was diminished as well by Maglanus as by Henninus. But the greatest grief that Leir took, was to see the unkindness of his daughters, which seemed to think that all was too much which their father had, the same being never so little: in so much, that going from the one to the other, he was brought to that misery, that scarcely they would allow him one servant to wait upon him.

'In the end, such was the unkindness, or (as I may say) the unnaturalness which he found in his two daughters, notwith-

1 See Wilfrid Perrett, *The story of King Lear from Geoffrey of Monmouth to Shakespeare*, 1904. Shakespeare may be presumed to have known, besides Holinshed and the old play mentioned below, the version of John Higgins in *The Mirror for Magistrates* (1574). He appears to have taken the spelling of Cordelia's name and the manner of her death from Spenser's more succinct account (*Faery Queen*, 1509, Bk. ii. canto 10, st. 25–32). For a possible minor source see D. F. Atkinson, 'King Lear—Another Contemporary Account,' *E L H*, 1936, pp. 63–66.

2 W. W. Greg, 'The Date of *King Lear* and Shakespeare's Use of Earlier Versions of the Story,' *The Library*, 1940, pp. 377–400.

standing their fair and pleasant words uttered in time past, that being constrained of necessity, he fled the land, and sailed into Gallia, there to seek some comfort of his youngest daughter Cordeilla whom before time he hated. The lady Cordeilla hearing that he was arrived in poor estate, she first sent to him privily a certain sum of money to apparel himself withal, and to retain a certain number of servants that might attend him in honorable wise, as appertained to the estate which he had borne: and then so accompanied, she appointed him to come to the court, which he did, and was so joyfully, honorably, and lovingly received, both by his son in law Aganippus, and also by his daughter Cordeilla, that his heart was greatly comforted: for he was no less honored, than if he had been king of the whole country himself.

'Now when he had informed his son in law and his daughter in what sort he had been used by his other daughters, Aganippus caused a mighty army to be put in a readiness, and likewise a great navy of ships to be rigged, to pass over into Britain with Leir his father in law, to see him again restored to his kingdom. It was accorded, that Cordeilla should also go with him to take possession of the land, the which he promised to leave unto her, as the rightful inheritor after his decease, notwithstanding any former grant made to her sisters or to their husbands in any manner of wise.

'Hereupon, when this army and navy of ships were ready, Leir and his daughter Cordeilla with her husband took the sea, and arriving in Britain, fought with their enemies, and discomfited them in battle, in the which Maglanus and Henninus were slain: and then was Leir restored to his kingdom, which he ruled after this by the space of two years, and then died, forty years after he first began to reign. His body was buried at Leicester in a vault under the channel of the river of Sore beneath the town.

'Cordeilla the youngest daughter of Leir was admitted Q[ueen] and supreme governess of Britain, in the year of the world 3155, before the building of Rome 54, Uziah then reigning in Judah, and Jeroboam over Israel. This Cordeilla after her father's decease ruled the land of Britain right worthily during the space of five years, in which mean time her husband died, and then about the end of those five years, her two nephews Margan and Cunedag, sons to her aforesaid sisters, disdaining to be under the government of a woman, levied war against her, and destroyed a great part of the land, and finally took her prisoner, and laid her fast in ward, wherewith she took such grief, being a woman of a manly courage, and despairing to recover liberty, there she slew herself, when she had reigned (as before is mentioned) the term of five years.'

In the old play, Cornwall is the husband of Goneril, and appears in a somewhat better light than Regan's consort, the king of Cambria (Wales). But Shakespeare, as is hinted by the very first line of *King Lear*, deliberately made Goneril's husband a great and noble character, one of the finest gentlemen to be found among all his *dramatis personæ*; while Regan's husband has no redeeming features except energy and resolution. The Fool—one of the most remarkable among all Shakespeare's jesters—is

another instance, if any were needed, of the dramatist's original creative power. Our respect for Shakespeare's genius is always heightened when we study his 'originals.' In this case, he took a melodramatic story with a 'happy ending,' and transformed it into a poignant tragedy, not merely of Lear, but of old age.

THE HISTORY OF THE PLAY

The first performance of the play of which we have any record was (on the evidence of the Stationers' Register) in the presence of King James I at Whitehall Palace, 26 December 1606.[3] Lear is mentioned at the time of Burbage's death in 1619 as one of that actor's great parts, but the play, in its genuine form at least, had little popularity in the seventeenth century. Both the Jacobean contemporaneity of its social satire and its archaic, unclassical, and non-Christian setting would have alienated it from Restoration taste, though in 1662 there is an allusion to *King Lear* which seems to indicate that it was well known. In 1681 Nahum Tate made a revision which held the stage for a hundred and forty years, and was used by all the great eighteenth-century players. Edgar and Cordelia are united in marriage, and Kent and Lear live together. Tate's version seems insipid in comparison with Shakespeare's, but it was shaped to fit the fashion of the times, and this was the Lear that Garrick and Kemble played. Tate paid a compliment to Shakespeare in his Prologue:

> *each Rustick knows*
> *'Mongst plenteous Flow'rs a Garland to Compose,*
> *Which strung by his course Hand may fairer Show,*
> *But 'twas a Power Divine first made 'em Grow,*

but his garland contained few of the original flowers, and the Fool was totally omitted.

It was in 1823 that the great actor Edmund Kean, who had often appeared in Tate's version, finally decided to return to the original text, saying to his wife, 'The London audience have no notion of what I can do until they see me over the dead body of Cordelia.' The effect was even greater than he had hoped for. W. C. Macready restored Shakespeare's text more fully, and was notably followed by Samuel Phelps, Henry Irving, and Tommaso Salvini, while the two most admired actresses of the century, Helen Faucit and Ellen Terry, made what they could of Cordelia's brief part. The most notable performance by American actors in the nineteenth century were by Edwin Forrest and Edwin Booth, who successively made an indelible impression on both critics and public. In the twentieth century, the play has been produced frequently in Germany and occasionally in Paris, but notable English performances have been few, while the best-known American production was long that of Robert Mantell, who deserved praise for giving his contemporaries their only opportunity to see the tragedy. Still, there is much truth in what Charles Lamb said over a century ago: 'The Lear of Shakespeare cannot be acted . . . the play is beyond all art.'

---

3 For suggestions concerning the date of composition, which was probably during the preceding year, see notes on I.ii.97,99; III.iv.182; III.vii.81.

ACT FIRST ❧ SCENE FIRST

[King Lear's Palace, Leicester]
Enter Kent, Gloucester, and Edmund.

Kent. I thought the king had more affected the Duke of
Albany than Cornwall.

Glo. It did always seem so to us; but now, in the division
of the kingdom, it appears not which of the dukes he values
most, for equalities are so weighed that curiosity in   5
neither can make choice of either's moiety.

Kent. Is not this your son, my lord?

Glo. His breeding, sir, hath been at my charge. I have so
often blushed to acknowledge him, that now I am brazed to it.

Kent. I cannot conceive you.   10

Glo. Sir, this young fellow's mother could; whereupon she
grew round-wombed and had, indeed, sir, a son for her cradle
ere she had a husband for her bed. Do you smell a fault?

Kent. I cannot wish the fault undone, the issue of it being
so proper.   15

Glo. But I have a son, sir, by order of law, some year elder
than this, who yet is no dearer in my account. Though this
knave came something saucily into the world before he was
sent for, yet was his mother fair. There was good sport at
his making, and the whoreson must be acknowledged.   20
—Do you know this noble gentleman, Edmund?

Edm. No, my lord.

Glo. My Lord of Kent. Remember him hereafter as my
honorable friend.

Edm. My services to your lordship.   25

Kent. I must love you, and sue to know you better.

Edm. Sir, I shall study deserving.

Glo. He hath been out nine years, and away he shall again.
The king is coming.

Sound a sennet. Enter one bearing a coronet; then Lear, then the
Dukes of Albany and Cornwall, next Goneril, Regan, Cordelia
with followers.

Lear. Attend the Lords of France and Burgundy, Gloucester.

Glo. I shall, my liege.

              Exit [with Edmund].

Lear. Meantime we shall express our darker purpose.
Give me the map there. Know we have divided
In three our kingdom; and 'tis our fast intent
To shake all cares and business from our age,   35
Conferring them on younger strengths 〈while we
Unburthen'd crawl toward death. Our son of Cornwall,
And you, our no less loving son of Albany,
We have this hour a constant will to publish
Our daughters' several dowers, that future strife   40
May be prevented now.〉 The «two great» princes, France and
Burgundy,
Great rivals in our youngest daughter's love,

Long in our court have made their amorous sojourn,
And here are to be answer'd. Tell me, my daughters,   45
〈Since now we will divest us both of rule,
Interest of territory, cares of state,〉
Which of you shall we say doth love us most,
That we our largest bounty may extend
Where nature doth with merit challenge. Goneril,   50
Our eldest-born, speak first.

 Gon.   Sir,
I love you more than word can wield the matter;
Dearer than eyesight, space, and liberty;
Beyond what can be valu'd, rich or rare;   55
No less than life with grace, health, beauty, honor;
As much as child e'er lov'd, or father found;
A love that makes breath poor and speech unable;
Beyond all manner of so much I love you.

 Cor. [aside]. What shall Cordelia speak? Love, and be silent.

 Lear. Of all these bounds, even from this line to this,
With shadowy forests and 〈with champains rich'd,
With plenteous rivers and〉 wide-skirted meads,
We make thee lady. To thine and Albany's issues
Be this perpetual. What says our second daughter,   65
Our dearest Regan, wife of Cornwall? «Speak.»

 Reg. I am made of that self metal as my sister,
And prize me at her worth. In my true heart
I find she names my very deed of love.
Only she comes too short, that I profess   70
Myself an enemy to all other joys
Which the most precious square of sense possesses
And find I am alone felicitate
In your dear highness' love.

 Cor. [aside].   Then, poor Cordelia!   75
And yet not so, since I am sure my love's
More richer than my tongue.

 Lear. To thee and thine, hereditary ever,
Remain this ample third of our fair kingdom,
No less in space, validity, and pleasure,   80
Than that conferr'd on Goneril. Now, our joy,
Although our last and least, to whose young love
〈The vines of France and milk of Burgundy
Strive to be interess'd〉 what can you say to draw
A third more opulent than your sisters? 〈Speak.〉   85

 Cor. Nothing, my lord.

 〈*Lear.* Nothing?

 Cor. Nothing.〉

 Lear. Nothing will come of nothing. Speak again.

 Cor. Unhappy that I am, I cannot heave   90
My heart into my mouth. I love your majesty
According to my bond; no more nor less.

 Lear. How, how, Cordelia! Mend your speech a little,
Lest you may mar your fortunes.

 Cor.   Good my lord,   95
You have begot me, bred me, lov'd me. I
Return those duties back as are right fit,
Obey you, love you, and most honor you.
Why have my sisters husbands, if they say

S.d. King Lear's Palace; *cf. n.* **1** affected: *loved* **5, 6** equalities … moiety; *cf. n.*
5 curiosity: *whimsicality* **6** moiety: *Share* **9** brazed: *hardened* **15** proper: *hand-some* **16** some year: *about a year* **18** something: *rather* **18–20** knave, whoreson:
terms of bluff affection **26** sue: *beg* **27** study deserving: *try to be worthy* **28** out:
out of the kingdom **S.d.** sennet: *notes on a trumpet* **33** express: *manifest by external
tokens* our darker purpose: *my purpose which is still somewhat unclarified* **34–51**
Cf. n. **34** fast intent: *fixed purpose* **36–41** while we … now: *not in Quarto.* See
Textual Note **40** several: *respective* **41** prevented: *forestalled* two great: *not in Folio.*
See *Textual Note* France and Burgundy; *cf. n.*

47 Interest: *legal title* **50** Where … challenge; *cf. n.* **54** space: *the external
world* **56** with: *enhanced by* **57** found: *experienced* **58** unable: *impotent* **67**
self: *same* **68** prize … worth: *esteem myself as worthy as she is* **69** *Cf. n.* **70**
Only: *only in this* **72** square; *cf. n.* **73** felicitate: *made happy* **77** More richer;
cf. n. **80** validity: *value* **82** *Cf. n.* **83** milk: *pasture land* **84** interess'd: *given
a share* **92** bond: *obligation of duty*

They love you all? Haply, when I shall wed,   *100*
That lord whose hand must take my plight shall carry
Half my love with him, half my care and duty.
Sure I shall never marry like my sisters
«To love my father all».
    Lear. But goes thy heart with this?   *105*
    Cor.   Ay, my good lord.
    Lear. So young, and so untender?
    Cor. So young, my lord, and true.
    Lear. Let it be so. Thy truth then be thy dower,
For by the sacred radiance of the sun,   *110*
The mysteries of Hecate and the night,
By all the operation of the orbs
From whom we do exist and cease to be,
Here I disclaim all my paternal care,
Propinquity and property of blood,   *115*
And as a stranger to my heart and me
Hold thee from this for ever. The barbarous Scythian,
Or he that makes his generation messes
To gorge his appetite, shall ⟨to my bosom⟩
Be as well neighbor'd, pitied, and reliev'd,   *120*
As thou, my sometime daughter.
    Kent.   Good my liege!—
    Lear. Peace, Kent!
Come not between the dragon and his wrath.
I lov'd her most, and thought to set my rest   *125*
On her kind nursery. Hence, and avoid my sight!
So be my grave my peace, as here I give
Her father's heart from her! Call France. Who stirs?
Call Burgundy.—Cornwall and Albany,
With my two daughters' dowers digest the third.   *130*
Let pride, which she calls plainness, marry her.
I do invest you jointly with my power,
Pre-eminence, and all the large effects
That troop with majesty. Ourself by monthly course,
With reservation of an hundred knights,   *135*
By you to be sustain'd, shall our abode
Make with you by due turn. Only we still retain
The name and all th' additions to a king.
The sway,
Revénue, execution of the rest,   *140*
Beloved sons, be yours: which to confirm,
This coronet part between you.
    Kent.   Royal Lear,
Whom I have ever honor'd as my king,
Lov'd as my father, as my master follow'd,   *145*
As my great patron thought on in my prayers,—
    Lear. The bow is bent and drawn. Make from the shaft.
    Kent. Let it fall rather, though the fork invade
The region of my heart. Be Kent unmannerly
When Lear is mad. What wouldst thou do, old man?   *150*
Think'st thou that duty shall have dread to speak
When power to flattery bows? To plainness honor's bound

When majesty stoops to folly. Reverse thy doom,
And in thy best consideration check
This hideous rashness. Answer my life my judgment: *155*
Thy youngest daughter does not love thee least;
Nor are those empty-hearted whose low sounds
Reverb no hollowness.
    Lear.   Kent, on thy life, no more.
    Kent. My life I never held but as a pawn   *160*
To wage against thine enemies; nor fear to lose it,
Thy safety being the motive.
    Lear.   Out of my sight!
    Kent. See better, Lear, and let me still remain
The true blank of thine eye.   *165*
    Lear. Now, by Apollo,—
    Kent.   Now, by Apollo, king,
Thou swear'st thy gods in vain.
    Lear.   O vassal! miscreant!
                   [Laying his hand on his sword.]
⎰*Alb.* ⎱
⎱*Corn.* ⎰   Dear sir, forbear.⟩   *170*
    Kent. «Do;»
Kill thy physician, and thy fee bestow
Upon the foul disease. Revoke thy doom,
Or whilst I can vent clamor from my throat,   *175*
I'll tell thee thou dost evil.
    Lear.   Hear me, ⟨recreant!⟩
On thine allegiance, hear me!
That thou hast sought to make us break our vow,
Which we durst never yet, and with stain'd pride   *180*
To come betwixt our sentence and our power
(Which nor our nature nor our place can bear):
Our potency made good, take thy reward.
Five days we do allot thee for provision
To shield thee from diseases of the world,   *185*
And on the sixth to turn thy hated back
Upon our kingdom. If on the tenth day following
Thy banish'd trunk be found in our dominions,
The moment is thy death. Away! By Jupiter,
This shall not be revok'd.   *190*
    Kent. Fare thee well, king. Sith thus thou wilt appear,
Freedom lives hence, and banishment is here.
[To Cordelia.] The gods to their dear shelter take thee, maid,
That justly think'st, and hast most rightly said!
[To Regan and Goneril.] And your large speeches may your *195*
deeds approve,
That good effects may spring from words of love.
Thus Kent, O princes, bids you all adieu;
He'll shape his old course in a country new.   *Exit.*

Flourish. Enter Gloucester with France and Burgundy, Attendants.

    Glo. Here's France and Burgundy, my noble lord.   *200*
    Lear. My Lord of Burgundy,
We first address toward you, who with this king

---

100 all: *exclusively*   **101 plight:** *pledge*   **111 Hecate:** *goddess of witchcraft*   **112 operation:** *planetary influence*   **115 property of blood:** *kinship*   **117 this:** *this time*   **118 generation:** *children*   **119 to my bosom:** *in my affections*   **120 neighbor'd:** *held in friendly regard*   **125 set my rest:** *stake my all* (figure from a game)   **126 nursery:** *nursing*   **130 digest:** *assimilate*   **131 plainness:** *frankness* **marry:** *find a husband for*   **133 effects:** *outward marks of royalty*   **134 troop with:** *follow in the train of* **course:** *rotation*   **137 still;** *cf. n.*   **138 additions:** *titles, marks of distinction*   **139 The sway;** *cf. n.*   **142 coronet;** *cf. n.*   **147 Make from:** *get out of the way of*

153 *Cf. n.*   **154 in ... consideration:** *with all the care you can*   **155 Answer my life:** *let my life answer for*   **158 Reverb:** *re-echo; cf. n.*   **161 wage:** *stake*   **164 still:** *always*   **165 blank:** *white spot in center of target*   **166 by Apollo;** *cf. n.*   **169 vassal! miscreant;** *cf. n.*   **179 That;** *cf. n.* **us;** *cf. n.*   **183 Our ... good;** *cf. n.*   **184 Five days;** *cf. n.*   **185 diseases:** *slight vexations, dis-eases; cf. n.*   **188 trunk:** *body*   **190 revok'd;** *cf. n.*   **191 Sith:** *since* **thus:** *i.e., in the character of a despot*   **196 approve:** *make good; cf. n.*   **197 effects:** *(actual) results* **words:** *(mere) words*   **199 shape ... course:** *he his old self*   **S.d. Flourish:** *music of horns*

Hath rivall'd for our daughter. What, in the least,
Will you require in present dower with her,
Or cease your quest of love?   205
  Bur.   Most royal majesty,
I crave no more than hath your highness offer'd,
Nor will you tender less.
  Lear.   Right noble Burgundy,
When she was dear t'us we did hold her so,   210
But now her price is fall'n. Sir, there she stands.
If aught within that little-seeming substance,
Or all of it, with our displeasure piec'd,
And nothing more, may fitly like your Grace,
She's there, and she is yours.   215
  Bur.   I know no answer.
  Lear. Will you, with those infirmities she owes,
Unfriended, new-adopted to our hate,
Dower'd with our curse, and stranger'd with our oath,
Take her or leave her?   220
  Bur.   Pardon me, royal sir;
Election makes not up in such conditions.
  Lear. Then leave her, sir; for, by the power that made me,
I tell you all her wealth.—[*To France.*] For you, great king,
I would not from your love make such a stray   225
To match you where I hate. Therefore, beseech you
T'avert your liking a more worthier way
Than on a wretch whom nature is asham'd
Almost t'acknowledge hers.
  France.   This is most strange!   230
That she, that even but now was your best object,
The argument of your praise, balm of your age,
Most best, most dearest, should in this trice of time
Commit a thing so monstrous to dismantle
So many folds of favor. Sure, her offence   235
Must be of such unnatural degree
That monsters it, or your fore-vouch'd affection
Fall'n into taint;—which to believe of her
Must be a faith that reason without miracle
Could never plant in me.   240
  Cor.   I yet beseech your majesty—
If for I want that glib and oily art
To speak and purpose not (since what I well intend,
I'll do't before I speak)—that you make known
It is no vicious blot, murther, or foulness,   245
No unchaste action or dishonor'd step,
That hath depriv'd me of your grace and favor,
But even for want of that for which I am richer,
A still-soliciting eye, and such a tongue
That I am glad I have not, though not to have it   250
Hath lost me in your liking.
  Lear.   Better thou
Hadst not been born than not t'have pleas'd me better.
  France. Is it but this? a tardiness in nature
Which often leaves the history unspoke   255
That it intends to do? My lord of Burgundy,

What say you to the lady? Love's not love
When it is mingled with regards that stands
Aloof from th'entire point. Will you have her?
She is herself a dowry.   260
  Bur.   Royal King,
Give but that portion which yourself propos'd,
And here I take Cordelia by the hand,
Duchess of Burgundy.
  Lear. Nothing. I have sworn ⟨I am firm⟩.   265
  Bur. [*to Cor.*]. I am sorry, then, you have so lost a father
That you must lose a husband.
  Cor.   Peace be with Burgundy!
Since that respects of fortune are his love,
I shall not be his wife.   270
  France. Fairest Cordelia, that art most rich, being poor;
Most choice, forsaken; and most lov'd, despis'd!
Thee and thy virtues here I seize upon.
Be it lawful, I take up what's cast away.
Gods, gods! 'Tis strange that from their cold'st neglect   275
My love should kindle to inflam'd respect.
Thy dowerless daughter, king, thrown to my chance,
Is queen of us, of ours, and our fair France:
Not all the dukes of waterish Burgundy
Can buy this unpriz'd precious maid of me.   280
Bid them farewell, Cordelia, though unkind.
Thou losest here, a better where to find.
  Lear. Thou hast her, France. Let her be thine, for we
Have no such daughter, nor shall ever see
That face of hers again. Therefore be gone   285
Without our grace, our love, our benison.
Come, noble Burgundy.

     Flourish. Exeunt Lear and Burgundy [Cornwall, Albany,
        Gloucester, and Attendants].

  France. Bid farewell to your sisters.
  Cor. The jewels of our father, with wash'd eyes
Cordelia leaves you. I know you what you are;   290
And like a sister am most loath to call
Your faults as they are nam'd. Use well our father.
To your professed bosoms I commit him;
But yet, alas, stood I within his grace,
I would prefer him to a better place.   295
So farewell to you both.
  Gon. Prescribe not us our duties.
  Reg.   Let your study
Be to content your lord, who hath receiv'd you
At fortune's alms. You have obedience scanted,   300
And well are worth the want that you have wanted.
  Cor. Time shall unfold what plighted cunning hides;
Who covers faults, at last shame them derides.
Well may you prosper!
  France.   Come, my fair Cordelia.   305
                        Ex. France and Cordelia.
  Gon. Sister, it is not little I have to say of what most nearly
appertains to us both. I think our father will hence to-night.

---

203 **in the least:** *at the lowest estimate*   208 **tender:** *offer*   212 *Cf. n.*   213 **piec'd:** *pieced out, amplified*   214 **fitly like:** *properly satisfy*   217 **owes:** *owns*   219 **stranger'd with:** *made a stranger by*   222 **Election, etc.:** *I cannot choose*   225 **stray:** *wandering, truancy*   232 **argument:** *subject*   233 **trice:** *moment*   234 **to dismantle:** *as to strip off*   235 **folds of favor:** *layers of regard; cf. n.*   237 **monsters it:** *makes it abnormal*   238 **Fall'n into taint:** *become blemished* **which;** *cf. n.*   243 **speak and purpose not:** *speak deceitfully* **what . . . intend:** *i.e., when I have a good intention*   245 **murther;** *cf. n.*   249 **still-soliciting:** *perpetually greedy*

257 **to:** *on the subject of*   258 **stands:** (old plural form)   269 **respects:** *considerations*   276 **inflam'd respect:** *warmest deference*   280 **unpriz'd precious:** *precious though unprized*   282 **a better where:** *a better place*   286 **benison:** *blessing*   289 **The jewels;** *cf. n.* **wash'd eyes:** *eyes that see clearly*   291 **like a sister:** *as befits a sister*   292 **as . . . nam'd:** *by their right names*   293 **your professed bosoms:** *the affections you have professed*   295 **prefer:** *commend*   300 **At fortune's alms:** *as a petty gift of chance*   301 **well . . . wanted;** *cf. n.*   302 **plighted:** *folded; cf. n.*

Reg. That's most certain, and with you. Next month with us.

Gon. You see how full of changes his age is. The observa- 310
tion we have made of it hath not been little. He always loved
our sister most; and with what poor judgment he hath now
cast her off appears too grossly.

Reg. 'Tis the infirmity of his age. Yet he hath ever but
slenderly known himself. 315

Gon. The best and soundest of his time hath been but rash.
Then must we look from his age to receive not alone the
imperfections of long-engraffed condition, but therewithal
the unruly waywardness that infirm and choleric years bring
with them. 320

Reg. Such unconstant starts are we like to have from him
as this of Kent's banishment.

Gon. There is further compliment of leavetaking between
France and him; pray you, let us sit together. If our father
carry authority with such disposition as he bears, this last 325
surrender of his will but offend us.

Reg. We shall further think of it.

Gon. We must do something, and i' th' heat.   *Exeunt.*

❧ SCENE SECOND ❧

[Earl of Gloucester's Castle]
Enter Bastard, solus.

Edm. Thou, Nature, art my goddess. To thy law
My services are bound. Wherefore should I
Stand in the plague of custom, and permit
The curiosity of nations to deprive me,
For that I am some twelve or fourteen moonshines 5
Lag of a brother? Why bastard? wherefore base?
When my dimensions are as well compact,
My mind as generous, and my shape as true
As honest madam's issue? Why brand they us
With base? with baseness? bastardy? base, base? 10
Who in the lusty stealth of nature take
More composition and fierce quality
Than doth, within a dull, stale, tired bed,
Go to th'creating a whole tribe of fops,
Got 'tween asleep and wake? Well then, 15
Legitimate Edgar, I must have your land.
Our father's love is to the bastard Edmund
As to th'legitimate. Fine word, 'legitimate'!
Well, my legitimate, if this letter speed
And my invention thrive, Edmund the base 20
Shall taw th'legitimate. I grow, I prosper;
Now, gods, stand up for bastards!

Enter Gloucester.

[Edmund ostentatiously reading a letter.]
Glo. Kent banished thus, and France in choler parted!
And the king gone to-night, prescrib'd his power,
Confin'd to exhibition! All this done 25

Upon the gad! Edmund, how now? What news?

Edm. So please your lordship, none.

Glo. Why so earnestly seek you to put up that letter?

Edm. I know no news, my lord.

Glo. What paper were you reading? 30

Edm. Nothing, my lord.

Glo. No? What needed then that terrible dispatch of it into
your pocket? The quality of nothing hath not such need to hide
itself. Let's see. Come! If it be nothing, I shall not need
spectacles. 35

Edm. I beseech you, sir, pardon me. It is a letter from my
brother that I have not all o'erread, and for so much as I have
perused, I find it not fit for your o'erlooking.

Glo. Give me the letter, sir.

Edm. I shall offend, either to detain or give it. The 40
contents, as in part I understand them, are too blame.

Glo. Let's see! let's see!

Edm. I hope, for my brother's justification, he wrote this
but as an essay or taste of my virtue.

Glo. reads.

This policy and reverence of age makes the world bitter to 45
the best of our times, keeps our fortunes from us till our
oldness cannot relish them. I begin to find an idle and fond
bondage in the oppression of aged tyranny, who sways, not
as it hath power, but as it is suffered. Come to me, that
of this I may speak more. If our father would sleep till I 50
waked him, you should enjoy half his revenue for ever, and
live the beloved of your brother,

                           Edgar.

—Hum! Conspiracy! 'Sleep till I waked him, you should
enjoy half his revenue.'—My son Edgar! Had he a hand 55
to write this? a heart and brain to breed it in? When came
this to you? Who brought it?

Edm. It was not brought me, my lord; there's the cunning
of it. I found it thrown in at the casement of my closet.

Glo. You know the character to be your brother's? 60

Edm. If the matter were good, my lord, I durst swear it
were his; but, in respect of that, I would fain think it were
not.

Glo. It is his.

Edm. It is his hand, my lord; but I hope his heart 65
is not in the contents.

Glo. Has he never before sounded you in this business?

Edm. Never, my lord: but I have heard him oft maintain
it to be fit that, sons at perfect age and fathers declined, the
father should be as ward to the son, and the son manage 70
his revenue.

Glo. O villain, villain! His very opinion in the letter! Abhorred villain! Unnatural, detested, brutish villain! worse than
brutish! Go, sirrah, seek him; I'll apprehend him. Abominable
villain! Where is he? 75

Edm. I do not well know, my lord. If it shall please you to
suspend your indignation against my brother till you can derive
from him better testimony of his intent, you should run a cer-

tain course; where, if you violently proceed against him, mistaking his purpose, it would make a great gap in your own   80
honor, and shake in pieces the heart of his obedience. I dare pawn down my life for him, that he hath writ this to feel my affection to your Honor, and to no other pretence of danger.

Glo. Think you so?

Edm. If your Honor judge it meet, I will place you where   85
you shall hear us confer of this, and by an auricular assurance have your satisfaction; and that without any further delay than this very evening.

Glo. He cannot be such a monster—

«*Edm.* Nor is not, sure.   90

Glo.—to his father, that so tenderly and entirely loves him. Heaven and earth!» Edmund, seek him out; wind me into him, I pray you. Frame the business after your own wisdom. I would unstate myself to be in a due resolution.

Edm. I will seek him, sir, presently, convey the business as   95
I shall find means, and acquaint you withal.

Glo. These late eclipses in the sun and moon portend no good to us. Though the wisdom of nature can reason it thus and thus, yet nature finds itself scourged by the sequent effects. Love cools, friendship falls off, brothers divide. In cities,   100
mutinies; in countries, discord; in palaces, treason; and the bond cracked 'twixt son and father. ⟨This villain of mine comes under the prediction; there's son against father. The king falls from bias of nature; there's father against child. We have seen the best of our time: machinations, hollowness,   105
treachery, and all ruinous disorders, follow us disquietly to our graves.⟩ Find out this villain, Edmund. It shall lose thee nothing. Do it carefully. And the noble and true-hearted Kent banished! his offence, honesty! 'Tis strange!   *Exit.*

Edm. This is the excellent foppery of the world, that,   110
when we are sick in fortune—often the surfeits of our own behavior—we make guilty of our disasters the sun, the moon, and the stars; as if we were villains on necessity, fools by heavenly compulsion, knaves, thieves, and treachers by spherical predominance, drunkards, liars, and adulterers by an enforced obedience of planetary influence, and all that we are evil in by a divine thrusting on: an admirable evasion of whoremaster man, to lay his goatish disposition on the charge of a star! My father compounded with my mother under the dragon's tail, and my nativity was under *ursa major;* so that it follows I   120
am rough and lecherous. «Fut!» I should have been that I am had the maidenliest star in the firmament twinkled on my bastardizing. «Edgar—»

Enter Edgar.

Pat he comes, like the catastrophe of the old comedy.
My cue is villainous melancholy, with a sigh like   125
Tom o' Bedlam.—O, these eclipses do portend these divisions!
⟨*Fa, sol, la, mi.*⟩

Edg. How now, brother Edmund! What serious contemplation are you in?

Edm. I am thinking, brother, of a prediction I read this   130
other day, what should follow these eclipses.

Edg. Do you busy yourself with that?

Edm. I promise you the effects he writes of succeed unhappily; ⟨as of unnaturalness between the child and the parent, death, dearth, dissolutions of ancient amities, divisions in   135
state, menaces and maledictions against king and nobles, needless diffidences, banishment of friends, dissipation of cohorts, nuptial breaches, and I know not what.

Edg. How long have you been a sectary astronomical?

Edm. Come, come!⟩ When saw you my father last?   140

Edg. The night gone by.

Edm. Spake you with him?

Edg. Ay, two hours together.

Edm. Parted you in good terms? Found you no displeasure in him by word nor countenance?   145

Edg. None at all.

Edm. Bethink yourself wherein you may have offended him; and at my entreaty forbear his presence until some little time hath qualified the heat of his displeasure, which at this instant so rageth in him that with the mischief of your person it   150
would scarcely allay.

Edg. Some villain hath done me wrong.

Edm. That's my fear. ⟨I pray you have a continent forbearance till the speed of his rage goes slower, and, as I say, retire with me to my lodging, from whence I will fitly bring you   155
to hear my lord speak. Pray ye, go; there's my key. If you do stir abroad, go armed.

Edg. Armed, brother?

Edm.⟩ Brother, I advise you to the best; «go armed;» I am no honest man if there be any good meaning toward you.   160
I have told you what I have seen and heard, but faintly. Nothing like the image and horror of it. Pray you, away.

Edg. Shall I hear from you anon?

Edm. I do serve you in this business.   *Exit Edgar.*
A credulous father and a brother noble,   165
Whose nature is so far from doing harms
That he suspects none, on whose foolish honesty
My practices ride easy! I see the business.
Let me, if not by birth, have lands by wit.
All with me's meet that I can fashion fit.   *Exit.*

❧ SCENE THIRD ❧

[Duke of Albany's Palace, York(?)]
Enter Goneril, and [Oswald her] Steward.

Gon. Did my father strike my gentleman for chiding of his fool?

Osw. Ay, madam.

Gon. By day and night he wrongs me. Every hour
He flashes into one gross crime or other   5
That sets us all at odds. I'll not endure it.
His knights grow riotous, and himself upbraids us
On every trifle. When he returns from hunting,
I will not speak with him. Say I am sick.

83 **pretence:** *intention*   85, 86 **I will … this;** *cf. n.*   92 **wind me into him;** *cf. n.*   94 **unstate myself:** *give all I am and have*   **due resolution:** *proper certainty*   95 **presently:** *instantly*   **convey:** *manage* (with privacy and discretion)   96 **withal:** *therewith*   97 **These late eclipses;** *cf. n.*   98 **wisdom of nature:** *natural philosophy*   **nature:** *human nature, the world of man*   99 **sequent effects:** *results that follow the eclipses; cf. n.*   104 **falls … nature;** *cf. n.*   110 **excellent foppery:** *exceeding folly*   114 **treachers:** *traitors*   **spherical predominance:** *causative action of the celestial 'spheres'*   117 **thrusting on:** *impulsion*   118 **charge:** *liability*   119 **dragon's tail;** *cf. n.*   120 **ursa major:** *the Great Bear*   127 **Fa, sol, la, mi;** *cf. n.*

137 **diffidences:** *suspicions*   137 **dissipation of cohorts:** *disaffection in the army*   139 **sectary astronomical:** *member of the astronomical sect*   150 **mischief:** *harm*   153 **continent:** *temperate*   162 **image and horror:** *horrible image*   168 **practices:** *treacherous plots*   170 Cf. n.   SCENE THIRD. S.d. *Duke of Albany's Palace; cf. n.*   5 **crime:** *offence*

If you come slack of former services,   *10*
You shall do well. The fault of it I'll answer.

   Osw. He's coming, madam. I hear him.

   Gon. Put on what weary negligence you please,
You and your fellows. I'd have it come to question.
If he distaste it, let him to my sister,   *15*
Whose mind and mine, I know, in that are one,
«Not to be over-rul'd. Idle old man,
That still would manage those authorities
That he hath given away! Now, by my life,
Old fools are babes again, and must be us'd   *20*
With checks as flatteries, when they are seen abus'd.»
Remember what I have said.

   Osw.   Well, madam.

   Gon. And let his knights have colder looks among you.
What grows of it, no matter. Advise your fellows so.   *25*
«I would breed from hence occasions, and I shall,
That I may speak.» I'll write straight to my sister
To hold my very course. Prepare for dinner.   *Exeunt.*

❧ SCENE FOURTH ❧

[The same]
Enter Kent [disguised].

   Kent. If but as well I other accents borrow,
That can my speech defuse, my good intent
May carry through itself to that full issue
For which I raz'd my likeness. Now, banish'd Kent,
If thou canst serve thou dost stand condemn'd,   *5*
So may it come, thy master whom thou lov'st
Shall find thee full of labors.

Horns within. Enter Lear and Attendants.

   Lear. Let me not stay a jot for dinner. Go, get it ready.
[Exit an Attendant.] How now! what are thou?

   Kent. A man, sir.   *10*

   Lear. What dost thou profess? What wouldst thou with us?

   Kent. I do profess to be no less than I seem; to serve him
truly that will put me in trust, to love him that is honest, to
converse with him that is wise and says little, to fear judgment,
to fight when I cannot choose, and to eat no fish.   *15*

   Lear. What art thou?

   Kent. A very honest-hearted fellow, and as poor as the king.

   Lear. If thou be'st as poor for a subject as he's for a king,
thou art poor enough. What wouldst thou?

   Kent. Service.   *20*

   Lear. Whom wouldst thou serve?

   Kent. You.

   Lear. Dost thou know me, fellow?

   Kent. No, sir; but you have that in your countenance
which I would fain call master.   *25*

   Lear. What's that?

   Kent. Authority.

   Lear. What services canst thou do?

   Kent. I can keep honest counsel, ride, run, mar a curious
tale in telling it, and deliver a plain message bluntly. That   *30*
which ordinary men are fit for, I am qualified in, and the
best of me is diligence.

   Lear. How old art thou?

   Kent. Not so young, sir, to love a woman for singing,
nor so old to dote on her for anything. I have years on my   *35*
back forty-eight.

   Lear. Follow me; thou shalt serve me, if I like thee no
worse after dinner. I will not part from thee yet. Dinner, ho!
dinner! Where's my knave, my fool? Go you and call my fool
hither.   *[Exit on Attendant.]*   *40*

Enter Steward [Oswald].

You, you, sirrah, where's my daughter?

   Osw. So please you,—   *Exit.*

   Lear. What says the fellow there? Call the clotpoll back.
[Exit a Knight.] Where's my fool? Ho! I think the world's
asleep. *[Re-enter Knight.]* How now? where's that mongrel?   *45*

   Knight. He says, my lord, your daughter is not well.

   Lear. Why came not the slave back to me when I called
him?

   Knight. Sir, he answered me in the roundest manner, he
would not.   *50*

   Lear. He would not!

   Knight. My lord, I know not what the matter is; but, to my
judgment, your highness is not entertained with that ceremonious affection as you were wont. There's a great abatement of
kindness appears as well in the general dependants as in the   *55*
duke himself also and your daughter.

   Lear. Ha! sayest thou so?

   Knight. I beseech you, pardon me, my lord, if I be
mistaken; for my duty cannot be silent when I think your
highness wronged.   *60*

   Lear. Thou but remember'st me of mine own conception. I
have perceived a most faint neglect of late, which I have rather
blamed as mine own jealous curiosity than as a very pretence
and purpose of unkindness. I will look further into't. But
where's my fool? I have not seen him this two days.   *65*

   Knight. Since my young lady's going into France, sir, the
fool hath much pined away.

   Lear. No more of that. I have noted it well. Go you and
tell my daughter I would speak with her.   *[Exit Knight.]*
Go you, call hither my fool.   *[Exit an Attendant.]*

Enter Steward [Oswald].

O! you sir, you, come you hither, sir. Who am I, sir?

   Osw. My lady's father.

   Lear. 'My lady's father!' my lord's knave! You whoreson dog!
you slave! you cur!

   Osw. I am none of these, my lord; I beseech your pardon.   *75*

   Lear. Do you bandy looks with me, you rascal?

                                     [Striking him.]

   Osw. I'll not be strucken, my lord.

   Kent. Nor tripped neither, you base football player.

                                [Tripping up his heels.]

---

14 question: *discussion*   **17 Idle:** *foolish*   **21 With ... abus'd;** *cf. n.*   **23 Well:** *like
French 'bien'*   **1** *Cf. n.*   **2 defuse:** *disguise, disorder*   **3 carry through:** *accomplish* **issue:** *conclusion*   **4 raz'd:** *erased*   **11 dost ... profess:** *is thy profession*   **15 fish;**
cf. n.   **16** *Cf. n.*

29 curious: *fanciful*   **36 forty-eight;** *cf. n.*   **43 clotpoll:** *blockhead, clodpole*   **55
kindness:** *courtesy*   **61 remember'st ... conception;** *cf. n.*   **62 faint:** *sluggish*   **63
jealous curiosity:** *suspicious punctiliousness*   **very pretence:** *genuine intention*   **76 bandy:**
exchange (an expression from the game of tennis)   **77 strucken:** *(mainly a Northern
form)*   **78 football;** *cf. n.*

Lear. I thank thee, fellow. Thou serv'st me, and I'll love thee.   80

Kent. Come, sir, arise, away! I'll teach you differences! Away, away! If you will measure your lubber's length again, tarry. But away! Go to! have you wisdom! [*Pushes Oswald out.*] So.

Lear. Now, my friendly knave. I thank thee. There's earnest of thy service.   [*Gives him money.*]   85

Enter Fool.

Fool. Let me hire him too. Here's my coxcomb.

Lear. How now, my pretty knave! how dost thou?

Fool. Sirrah, you were best take my coxcomb.

«*Kent.* Why, fool?»

⟨*Lear.* Why, my boy?⟩   90

Fool. Why, for taking one's part that's out of favor. Nay, an thou canst not smile as the wind sits, thou'lt catch cold shortly. There, take my coxcomb. Why, this fellow has banished two on's daughters, and did the third a blessing against his will. If thou follow him, thou must needs wear   95 my coxcomb. How now, nuncle! Would I had two coxcombs and two daughters!

Lear. Why, my boy?

Fool. If I gave them all my living, I'd keep my coxcombs myself. There's mine [*offering the coxcomb to Lear*]; beg   100 another of thy daughters.

Lear. Take heed, sirrah! the whip.

Fool. Truth's a dog must to kennel. He must be whipped out when the Lady-brach may stand by the fire and stink.

Lear. A pestilent gall to me!   105

Fool. Sirrah, I'll teach thee a speech.

Lear. Do.

Fool. Mark it, nuncle:—

Have more than thou showest,
Speak less than thou knowest,   110
Lend less than thou owest,
Ride more than thou goest,
Learn more than thou trowest,
Set less than thou throwest.
Leave thy drink and thy whore,   115
And keep in-a-door,
And thou shalt have more
Than two tens to a score.

Kent. This is nothing, fool.

Fool. Then 'tis like the breath of an unfee'd lawyer. You   120 gave me nothing for 't.—Can you make no use of nothing, nuncle?

Lear. Why, no, boy; nothing can be made out of nothing.

Fool [*to Kent*]. Prithee, tell him, so much the rent of his land comes to. He will not believe a fool.   125

Lear. A bitter fool!

Fool. Dost thou know the difference, my boy, between a bitter fool and a sweet one?

Lear. No, lad. Teach me.

Fool.   130

«*That lord that counsell'd thee*
To give away thy land,
Come place him here by me.
Do thou for him stand.
The sweet and bitter fool   135
Will presently appear;
The one in motley here,
The other found out there.

Lear. Dost thou call me fool, boy?

Fool. All thy other titles thou hast given away. That   140 thou wast born with.

Kent. This is not altogether fool, my lord.

Fool. No, faith! Lords and great men will not let me. If I had a monopoly out, they would have part on't, and ladies too. They will not let me have all the fool to myself; they'll   145 be snatching.» Nuncle, give me an egg, and I'll give thee two crowns.

Lear. What two crowns shall they be?

Fool. Why, after I have cut the egg i' th' middle and eat up the meat, the two crowns of the egg. When thou clovest   150 thy crown i' th' middle and gav'st away both parts, thou bor'st thine ass on thy back o'er the dirt. Thou hadst little wit in thy bald crown when thou gav'st thy golden one away. If I speak like myself in this, let him be whipped that first finds it so.

Fools had ne'er less grace in a year,   155
For wise men are grown foppish,
And know not how their wits to wear,
Their manners are so apish.

Lear. When were you wont to be so full of songs, sirrah?

Fool. I have used it, nuncle, e'er since thou mad'st thy   160 daughters thy mothers; for when thou gav'st them the rod and putt'st down thine own breeches,

Then they for sudden joy did weep,
And I for sorrow sung,
That such a king should play bo-peep,   165
And go the fools among.

Prithee, nuncle, keep a schoolmaster that can teach thy fool to lie. I would fain learn to lie.

Lear. An you lie, sirrah, we'll have you whipped.

Fool. I marvel what kin thou and thy daughters are.   170 They'll have me whipped for speaking true, thou'lt have me whipped for lying; and sometimes I am whipped for holding my peace. I had rather be any kind o' thing than a fool; and yet I would not be thee, nuncle. Thou hast pared thy wit o' both sides, and left nothing i' th' middle. Here comes   175 one o' the parings.

Lear. How now, daughter? what makes that frontlet on? You are too much of late i' th' frown.

Fool. Thou wast a pretty fellow when thou hadst no need to care for her frowning. Now thou art an O without a figure.   180 I am better than thou art now. I am a fool, thou art nothing. [*To Goneril.*] Yes, forsooth, I will hold my tongue. So your face bids me, though you say nothing.

---

81 differences: *quibbling distinctions*   **84 earnest:** *advance wages*   **86 coxcomb:** *fool's cap*   **89, 90** Cf. *n.*   **92 an:** *if*   **94 on's:** *of his*   **96 nuncle:** *mine uncle*   **104 brach:** *hunting-bitch;* cf. *n.*   **105** Cf. *n.*   **109–113 Have ... trowest;** cf. *n.*   **112 goest:** *walkest*   **113 trowest:** *believest*   **114 Set ... trowest:** *stake less than you throw to win*   **116 keep in-a-door:** *stay at home and tend to your business*   **117, 118** Cf. *n.*   **123 nothing ... nothing;** cf. *n. I.i.90*

134 Cf. *n.*   **149 monopoly out;** cf. *n.*   **151 crowns:** *half-shells*   **154 like myself:** *like a fool;* let ... so; cf. *n.*   **155 had ... grace:** *were never less in demand*   **156 foppish:** *fool-like*   **157 wits to wear:** *display their wisdom;* cf. *n.*   **165 play bo-peep;** cf. *n.*   **177 frontlet:** *forehead-band; i.e., frown*   **180 an O without a figure:** *a mere cipher*

Mum, mum;
He that keeps nor crust nor crumb,   *185*
Weary of all, shall want some.

That's a sheeled peascod.   *[Pointing to Lear.]*
  Gon. Not only, sir, this your all-licens'd fool,
But other of your insolent retinue
Do hourly carp and quarrel, breaking forth   *190*
In rank and not-to-be-endured riots.
Sir,
I had thought by making this well known unto you
To have found a safe redress; but now grow fearful,
By what yourself too late have spoke and done,   *195*
That you protect this course, and put it on
By your allowance; which if you should, the fault
Would not 'scape censure, nor the redresses sleep,
Which, in the tender of a wholesome weal,
Might in their working do you that offence,   *200*
Which else were shame, that then necessity
Will call discreet proceeding.
  Fool. For you know, nuncle,

   The hedge-sparrow fed the cuckoo so long,
   That it's had it head bit off by it young.   *205*

So out went the candle, and we were left darkling.
  Lear. Are you our daughter?
  Gon. I would you would make use of your good wisdom
(Whereof I know you are fraught), and put away
These dispositions which of late transport you   *210*
From what you rightly are.
  Fool. May not an ass know when the cart draws the horse?
Whoop, Jug! I love thee.
  Lear. Does any here know me? This is not Lear.
Does Lear walk thus? speak thus? Where are his eyes?   *215*
Either his notion weakens, or his discernings
Are lethargied. Ha! waking? 'tis not so.
Who is it that can tell me who I am?
  Fool. Lear's shadow.
  «*Lear.* I would learn that, for by the marks of sovereignty,   *220*
knowledge and reason, I should be false persuaded I had
daughters.
  Fool. Which they will make an obedient father.»
  Lear. Your name, fair gentlewoman?
  Gon. This admiration, sir, is much o' th' favor   *225*
Of other your new pranks. I do beseech you
To understand my purposes aright,
As you are old and reverend, should be wise.
Here do you keep a hundred knights and squires;
Men so disorder'd, so debosh'd, and bold,   *230*
That this our court, infected with their manners,
Shows like a riotous inn. Epicurism and lust
Makes it more like a tavern or a brothel
Than a grac'd palace. The shame itself doth speak
For instant remedy. Be then desir'd,   *235*
By her that else will take the thing she begs,

A little to disquantity your train,
And the remainders that shall still depend
To be such men as may besort your age,
Which know themselves and you.   *240*
  Lear.   Darkness and devils!
Saddle my horses! call my train together!
Degenerate bastard, I'll not trouble thee.
Yet have I left a daughter.
  Gon. You strike my people, and your disorder'd rabble   *245*
Make servants of their betters.

Enter Albany.

  Lear. Woe, that too late repents!
                  «O, sir, are you come?»
Is it your will? Speak, sir.—Prepare my horses.
Ingratitude, thou marble-hearted fiend,   *250*
More hideous, when thou show'st thee in a child,
Than the sea-monster.
  ⟨*Alb.*   Pray, sir, be patient.⟩
  Lear [To Goneril]. Detested kite! thou liest.
My train are men of choice and rarest parts,   *255*
That all particulars of duty know,
And in the most exact regard support
The worships of their name. O most small fault,
How ugly didst thou in Cordelia show,
Which, like an engine, wrench'd my frame of nature   *260*
From the fix'd place, drew from my heart all love
And added to the gall. O Lear, Lear, Lear!
Beat at this gate that let thy folly in.   *[Striking his head.]*
And thy dear judgment out! Go, go, my people.
  Alb. My lord, I am guiltless, as I am ignorant   *265*
⟨Of what hath mov'd you⟩.
  Lear.   It may be so, my lord.
Hear, Nature, hear! dear goddess, hear!
Suspend thy purpose, if thou didst intend
To make this creature fruitful!   *270*
Into her womb convey sterility,
Dry up in her the organs of increase,
And from her derogate body never spring
A babe to honor her! If she must teem,
Create her child of spleen, that it may live   *275*
And be a thwart, disnatur'd torment to her!
Let it stamp wrinkles in her brow of youth,
With cadent tears fret channels in her cheeks,
Turn all her mother's pains and benefits
To laughter and contempt, that she may feel   *280*
How sharper than a serpent's tooth it is
To have a thankless child! Away, away!   *Exit.*
  Alb. Now, gods that we adore, whereof comes this?
  Gon. Never afflict yourself to know more of it,
But let his disposition have that scope   *285*
As dotage gives it.

Enter Lear.

  Lear. What! fifty of my followers at a clap?

---

186 *Cf. n.*   187 **sheeled peascod:** *empty peapod*   194 **safe redress:** *assured remedy*   196 **protect:** *authorize* **put .. on:** *encourage*   197 **allowance:** *approval*   199 **tender:** *care* **wholesome weal:** *sound public welfare*   205 **it:** *its; cf. n.*   206 **darkling:** *in the dark*   209 **fraught:** *stored*   213 **Whoop . . . thee;** *cf. n.*   216 **notion:** *understanding* **discernings:** *faculties by which he apprehends* (?)   223 **Which they;** *cf. n.*   225 **admiration:** *sign of wonder*   228 **should:** *and therefore should*   230 **disorder'd:** *disorderly* **debosh'd:** *debauched*   232 **Epicurism:** *sensuality*   234 **grac'd:** *gracious*

237 **disquantity:** *reduce*   238 **the remainders:** *those remaining* **depend:** *be in service*   239 **besort:** *befit*   247 **Woe, that:** *woe to him who*   252 **sea-monster;** *cf. n.*   254 **kite:** *buzzard*   258 **worships:** *dignity*   260 **engine:** *lever* **my frame of nature:** *the whole fabric of my natural affection*   273 **derogate:** *degraded*   276 **thwart:** *perverted* **disnatur'd:** *unnatural*   278 **cadent:** *falling*   285, 286 **that scope As;** *cf. n.*   287 *Cf. n.*

Within a fortnight?
  Alb.   What's the matter, sir?
  Lear. I'll tell thee. *[To Goneril.]* Life and death! I am   290
asham'd
That thou hast power to shake my manhood thus,
That these hot tears, which break from me perforce,
Should make thee worth them. Blasts and fogs upon thee!
Th' untented woundings of a father's curse   295
Pierce every sense about thee! Old fond eyes,
Beweep this cause again, I'll pluck ye out,
And cast you, with the waters that you lose,
To temper clay. «Yea, is it come to this?»
⟨Let it be so:⟩ I have another daughter,   300
Who, I am sure, is kind and comfortable.
When she shall hear this of thee, with her nails
She'll flay thy wolvish visage. Thou shalt find
That I'll resume the shape which thou dost think
I have cast off for ever «thou shalt, I warrant thee».   305
                Exit [with Kent and Attendants].
  Gon. Do you mark that?
  Alb. I cannot be so partial, Goneril,
To the great love I bear you,—
  Gon. Pray you, content. What, Oswald, ho!   310
[To the Fool.] You, sir, more knave than fool, after your
master.
  Fool. Nuncle Lear, nuncle Lear! tarry, take thy fool with
thee.

    A fox, when one has caught her,   315
    And such a daughter,
    Should sure to the slaughter,
    If my cap would buy a halter,
    So the fool follows after.   *Exit.*

  ⟨*Gon.* This man hath had good counsel. A hundred knights!   320
'Tis politic and safe to let him keep
At point a hundred knights! Yes, that on every dream,
Each buzz, each fancy, each complaint, dislike,
He may enguard his dotage with their powers,
And hold our lives in mercy. Oswald, I say!   325
  Alb. Well, you may fear too far.
  Gon.   Safer than trust too far.
Let me still take away the harms I fear,
Not fear still to be taken. I know his heart.
What he hath utter'd I have writ my sister.   330
If she sustain him and his hundred knights.
When I have show'd th' unfitness,—⟩

          Enter Steward.

                How now, Oswald?
What! have you writ that letter to my sister?
  Osw. Ay, madam.   335
  Gon. Take you some company, and away to horse.
Inform her full of my particular fear,
And thereto add such reasons of your own
As may compact it more. Get you gone,
And hasten your return. *[Exit Oswald.]* No, no, my lord,   340
This milky gentleness and course of yours

Though I condemn not, yet, under pardon,
You are much more atask'd for want of wisdom
Than prais'd for harmful mildness.
  Alb. How far your eyes may pierce I cannot tell.   345
Striving to better, oft we mar what's well.
  Gon. Nay, then—
  Alb. Well, well; th' event.   *Exeunt.*

❧ SCENE FIFTH ❧

[Near Albany's Palace]
Enter Lear, Kent, and Fool.

  Lear. Go you before to Gloucester with these letters. Acquaint my daughter no further with anything you know than comes from her demand out of the letter. If your diligence be not speedy I shall be there afore you.
  Kent. I will not sleep, my lord, till I have delivered your   5
letter.   *Exit.*
  Fool. If a man's brains were in's heels, were't not in danger
of kibes?
  Lear. Ay, boy.
  Fool. Then, I prithee, be merry. Thy wit shall not go   10
slipshod.
  Lear. Ha, ha, ha!
  Fool. Shalt see thy other daughter will use thee kindly; for
though she's as like this as a crab's like an apple, yet I can
tell what I can tell.   15
  Lear. What canst tell, boy?
  Fool. She will taste as like this as a crab does to a crab.
Thou canst tell why one's nose stands i' th' middle on's face?
  Lear. No.
  Fool. Why, to keep one's eyes of either side's nose, that   20
what a man cannot smell out, he may spy into.
  Lear. I did her wrong,—
  Fool. Canst tell how an oyster makes his shell?
  Lear. No.
  Fool. Nor I neither; but I can tell why a snail has a house.   25
  Lear. Why?
  Fool. Why, to put his head in; not to give it away to his
daughters, and leave his horns without a case.
  Lear. I will forget my nature. So kind a father! Be my
horses ready?   30
  Fool. Thy asses are gone about 'em. The reason why the
seven stars are no mo than seven is a pretty reason.
  Lear. Because they are not eight?
  Fool. Yes, indeed. Thou wouldst make a good fool.
  Lear. To take't again perforce! Monster ingratitude!   35
  Fool. If thou wert my fool, nuncle, I'd have thee beaten
for being old before thy time.
  Lear. How's that?
  Fool. Thou shouldst not have been old till thou hadst
been wise.   40
  Lear. O let me not be mad, not mad, sweet heaven! Keep
me in temper; I would not be mad!

[Enter Gentleman.]

---

295 untented: *unsearchable*   **297 Beweep:** *if you weep for*   **299 temper:** *soften*   **301 comfortable:** *comforting*   **315–319** *Cf. n.*   **322 At point:** *in readiness*   **329 taken:** *i.e., subjected to harm*   **339 compact:** *strengthen*   **341 gentleness and course:** *gentleness of your course* (hendiadys)

343 atask'd: *blamed; cf. n.*   **348 th' event:** *the outcome* (will show)   **1 Gloucester:** *cf. n.*   **8 kibes:** *chilblains*   **11 slipshod:** *in slippers; cf. n.*   **13 kindly:** *pun, with double meaning of 'gently' and 'naturally'*   **14 crab:** *crabapple*   **32 the seven stars:** *the constellation of the Pleiades*   **mo:** *more*   **42 temper:** *mental balance*   **S.d.** *Cf. n.*

How now? Are the horses ready?

    Gent. Ready, my lord.

    Lear. Come, boy.   45

    Fool. She that's a maid now, and laughs at my departure,

Shall not be a maid long, unless things be cut shorter.   *Exeunt.*

ACT SECOND ❧ SCENE FIRST

[Earl of Gloucester's Castle]
Enter Bastard [Edmund] and Curan, meeting.

    Edm. Save thee, Curan.

    Cur. And you, sir. I have been with your father, and given him notice that the Duke of Cornwall and Regan his duchess will be here with him to-night.

    Edm. How comes that?   5

    Cur. Nay, I know not. You have heard of the news abroad? I mean the whispered ones, for they are yet but ear-kissing arguments?

    Edm. Not I. Pray you, what are they?

    Cur. Have you heard of no likely wars toward, 'twixt   *10*
the Dukes of Cornwall and Albany?

    Edm. Not a word.

    Cur. You may do, then, in time. Fare you well, sir.   *Exit.*

    Edm. The duke be here to-night! The better! best!

This weaves itself perforce into my business.   *15*

My father hath set guard to take my brother;

And I have one thing, of a queasy question,

Which I must act. Briefness and fortune, work!

Brother, a word; descend! Brother, I say!

Enter Edgar.

My father watches. O, sir, fly this place!   *20*

Intelligence is given where you are hid.

You have now the good advantage of the night.

Have you not spoken 'gainst the Duke of Cornwall?

He's coming hither, now, i' th' night, i' th' haste,

And Regan with him. Have you nothing said   *25*

Upon his party 'gainst the Duke of Albany?

Advise yourself.

    Edg. I am sure on't, not a word.

    Edm. I hear my father coming. Pardon me;

In cunning I must draw my sword upon you.   *30*

Draw; seem to defend yourself. Now quit you well.—

Yield! Come before my father. Light, ho! here!—

Fly, brother.—Torches! torches!—So, farewell.   *Exit Edgar.*

Some blood drawn on me would beget opinion

Of my more fierce endeavor. *[Wounds his arm.]* I have seen *35*
drunkards

Do more than this is sport. Father! father!

Stop! stop! No help?

Enter Gloucester, and Servants with Torches

    Glo. Now, Edmund, where's the villain?

    Edm. Here stood he in the dark, his sharp sword out,   *40*

Mumbling of wicked charms, conjuring the moon

To stand auspicious mistress.

    Glo.   But where is he?

    Edm. Look, sir, I bleed.

    Glo.   Where is the villain, Edmund?   *45*

    Edm. Fled this way, sir. When by no means he could—

    Glo. Pursue him, ho! Go after!   *[Exeunt some Servants.]*
'By no means' what?

    Edm. Persuade me to the murther of your lordship;

But that I told him the revenging gods   *50*

'Gaint parricides did all their thunders bend,

Spoke with how manifold and strong a bond

The child was bound to th' father. Sir, in fine,

Seeing how loathly opposite I stood

To his unnatural purpose, in fell motion   *55*

With his prepared sword he charges home

My unprovided body, latch'd mine arm;

But when he saw my best alarum'd spirits,

Bold in the quarrel's right, rous'd to th' encounter,

Or whether gasted by the noise I made,   *60*

Full suddenly he fled.

    Glo.   Let him fly far.

Not in this land shall he remain uncaught;

And found—dispatch. The noble duke my master,

My worthy arch and patron, comes to-night.   *65*

By his authority I will proclaim it,

That he which finds him shall deserve our thanks,

Bringing the murderous caitiff to the stake;

He that conceals him, death.

    Edm. When I dissuaded him from his intent,   *70*

And found him pight to do it, with curst speech

I threaten'd to discover him. He replied:

'Thou unpossessing bastard, dost thou think,

If I would stand against thee, would the reposal

Of any trust, virtue, or worth in thee   *75*

Make thy words faith'd? No. What I should deny

(As this I would; ay, though thou didst produce

My very character), I'd turn it all

To thy suggestion, plot, and damned practice;

And thou must make a dullard of the world,   *80*

If they not thought the profits of my death

Were very pregnant and potential spurs

To make thee seek it.'

    Glo.   Strong and fasten'd villain!

Would he deny his letter, ⟨said he⟩? «I never got him.»   *85*

                                Tucket within.

Hark! the duke's trumpets. I know not why he comes.—

All ports I'll bar. The villain shall not 'scape;

The duke must grant me that. Besides, his picture

I will send far and near, that all the kingdom

May have due note of him; and of my land,   *90*

Loyal and natural boy, I'll work the means

To make thee capable.

41, 42 *Cf. n.*   **50 But that;** *cf. n.*   **52 Spoke:** *i.e., and I told him*   **55 fell:** *fierce*   **57 unprovided:** *unguarded* **latch'd:** *caught; cf. n.*   **60 gasted:** *scared*   **64 found—dispatch:** *cf. n.*   **65 arch:** *chief*   **68 caitiff;** *cf. n.*   **71 pight:** *fixed* **curst:** *sharp*   **72 discover:** *expose*   **73 unpossessing:** *incapable of inheriting*   **76 faith'd:** *credited*   **79 suggestion:** *evil prompting* **damned practice:** *damnable trickery*   **82 pregnant:** *inciting*   **84 Strong and fasten'd:** *gross and hardened* **S.d. Tucket:** *trumpet-notes, indicating march-signal*   **87 ports:** *seaports*   **91 natural:** *real, my own*   **92 capable:** *legal heir*

46, 47 *Cf. n.*   **Scene First: S.d.** *Castle; cf. n.*   **1 Save thee:** *God save you* **Curan;** *cf. n.*   **7 ear-kissing arguments:** *subjects to be mentioned only with the lips against the ear*   **10 toward:** *in prospect*   **17 queasy question:** *hazardous trial*   **18 Briefness . . . work;** *cf. n.*   **26 party:** *side*   **27 Advise yourself:** *think carefully*   **31 quit you:** *do your part*

Enter Cornwall, Regan, and Attendants.

Corn. How now, my noble friend! Since I came hither
(Which I can call but now), I have heard strange news.

Reg. If it be true, all vengeance comes too short   95
Which can pursue th' offender. How dost, my lord?

Glo. O, madam, my old heart is crack'd; it's crack'd.

Reg. What! did my father's godson seek your life?
He whom my father nam'd? your Edgar?

Glo. O lady, lady, shame would have it hid.   100

Reg. Was he not companion with the riotous knights that
ended upon my father?

Glo. I know not, madam. 'Tis too bad, too bad.

Edm. Yes, madam, he was of that consort.

Reg. No marvel, then, though he were ill affected.   105
'Tis they have put him on the old man's death,
To have th' expense and waste of his revénues.
I have this present evening from my sister
Been well-inform'd of them, and with such cautions
That if they come to sojourn at my house,   110
I'll not be there.

Corn.   Nor I, assure thee, Regan.
Edmund, I hear that you have shown your father
A child-like office.

Edm.   'Twas my duty, sir.   115

Glo. He did bewray his practice, and receiv'd
This hurt you see, striving to apprehend him.

Corn. Is he pursu'd?

Glo.   Ay, my good lord.

Corn. If he be taken he shall never more   120
Be fear'd of doing harm. Make your own purpose,
How in my strength you please. For you, Edmund,
Whose virtue and obedience doth this instant
So much commend itself, you shall be ours.
Natures of such deep trust we shall much need;   125
You we first seize on.

Edm.   I shall serve you, sir,
Truly, however else.

Glo.   For him I thank your Grace.

Corn. You know not why we came to visit you?   130

Reg. Thus out of season threading dark-ey'd night.
Occasions, noble Gloucester, of some poise,
Wherein we must have use of your advice.
Our father he hath writ, so hath our sister,
Of differences, which I best thought it fit   135
To answer from our home. The several messengers
From hence attend dispatch. Our good old friend,
Lay comforts to your bosom, and bestow
Your needful counsel to our business,
Which craves the instant use.   140

Glo.   I serve you, madam.
Your Graces are right welcome.   *Exeunt, Flourish.*

99 *Cf. n.*   104 consort: *company*   107 expense and waste: *wasteful spending;*
cf. n.   114 child-like: *filial*   116 bewray: *expose*   121 of doing: *lest he do*   Make:
execute   122 How . . . please; *cf. n.*   123 virtue and obedience: *loyal manliness*   125
deep trust: *great fidelity*   132 poise: *weight; cf. n.*   136 from: *away from*   137 From
. . . dispatch; *cf. n.*   140 craves . . . use: *must be dealt with at once*

❧ SCENE SECOND ❧

[Courtyard of Gloucester's Castle]
Enter Kent and Steward [Oswald] severally.

Osw. Good dawning to thee, friend. Art of this house?

Kent. Ay.

Osw. Where may we set our horses?

Kent. I' th' mire.

Osw. Prithee, if thou lov'st me, tell me.   5

Kent. I love thee not.

Osw. Why, then I care not for thee.

Kent. If I had thee in Lipsbury pinfold, I would make thee
care for me.

Osw. Why dost thou use me thus? I know thee not.   10

Kent. Fellow, I know thee.

Osw. What dost thou know me for?

Kent. A knave, a rascal, an eater of broken meats; a base,
proud, shallow, beggarly, three-suited, hundred-pound, filthy,
worsted-stocking knave; a lily-liver'd, action-taking knave; a   15
whoreson, glass-gazing, superserviceable, finical rogue; one-
trunk-inheriting slave; one that wouldst be a bawd, in a way of
good service, and art nothing but the composition of a knave,
beggar, coward, pandar, and the son and heir of a mongrel
bitch: one whom I will beat into clamorous whining if thou   20
deniest the least syllable of thy addition.

Osw. Why, what a monstrous fellow art thou, thus to rail
on one that is neither known of thee nor knows thee!

Kent. What a brazen-faced valet art thou, to deny thou
knowest me! Is it two days since I tripped up thy heels and   25
beat thee before the king? Draw, you rogue; for, though it be
night, yet the moon shines: I'll make a sop o' th' moonshine
of you. *[Drawing his sword.]* «Draw,» you whoreson, cullionly
barber-monger, draw.

Osw. Away! I have nothing to do with thee.   30

Kent. Draw, you rascal! You come with letters against the
king, and take Vanity the puppet's part against the royalty of
her father. Draw, you rogue, or I'll so carbonado your shanks!
Draw, you rascal! come your ways!

Osw. Help, ho! Murther! Help!   35

Kent. Strike, you slave! Stand, rogue, stand! You neat slave,
strike!   *[Beating him.]*

Osw. Help, ho! Murther! murther!

*Enter Edmund with his rapier drawn, Gloucester, the Duke and
Duchess, Servants.*

Edm. How now! What's the matter! ⟨Part!⟩

Kent. With you, goodman boy, if you please! Come, I'll   40
flesh ye! Come on, young master.

Glo. Weapons? arms? What's the matter here?

Corn. Keep peace, upon your lives.
He dies that strikes again. What is the matter?

Reg. The messengers from our sister and the king!   45

Corn. What is your difference? Speak.

Scene Second. S.d. severally: *entering at different doors; cf. n.*   1 Art . . . house: *are you
employed here?*   6 I love thee not: *cf. n.*   8 Lipsbury pinfold; *cf. n.*   13 broken
meats: *scraps*   14 three-suited; *cf. n.*   15 action-taking: *given to lawsuits*   16 glass-
glazing: *fond of the mirror*   superserviceable: *officious*   one-trunk-inheriting: *born to practically nothing*   27 sop o' th' moonshine: *make moonlight shine through you;
cf. n.*   28 cullionly: *knavish*   29 barber-monger: *patron of the barber's shop*   32
Vanity the puppet's: *Vanity, a personified character in the Interludes (Goneril is meant)*   33
carbonado: *slice*   34 your ways: *along (with me)*   36 neat: *over-dressed*   39 Part:
separate yourselves   40 With you; *cf. n.*   goodman: *a plebeian form of address*

Osw. I am scarce in breath, my lord.

Kent. No marvel, you have so bestirred your valor. You cowardly rascal, nature disclaims in thee. A tailor made thee.

Corn. Thou art a strange fellow. A tailor make a man.   *50*

Kent. «Ay» a tailor, sir. A stone-cutter or a painter could not have made him so ill, though they had been but two hours o' th' trade.

Corn. Speak yet, how grew your quarrel?

Osw. This ancient ruffian, sir, whose life I have spar'd   *55*
at suit of his grey beard,—

Kent. Thou worseson zed! thou unnecessary letter! My lord, if you will give me leave, I will tread this unbolted villain into mortar, and daub the wall of a jakes with him. Spare my grey beard, you wagtail!   *60*

Corn. Peace, sirrah!
You beastly knave, know you no reverence?

Kent. Yes, sir; but anger hath a privilege.

Corn. Why art thou angry?

Kent. That such slave as this should wear a sword,   *65*
Who wears no honesty. Such smiling rogues as these,
Like rats, oft bite the holy cords a-twain
Which are too intrinse t'unloose; smooth every passion
That in the natures of their lords rebel,
Bring oil to fire, snow to their colder moods;   *70*
Renege, affirm, and turn their halcyon beaks
With every gale and vary of their masters,
Knowing nought, like dogs, but following.
A plague upon your epileptic visage!
Smoil you my speeches, as I were a fool?   *75*
Goose, if I had you upon Sarum plain,
I'd drive ye crackling home to Camelot.

Corn. What! art thou mad, old fellow?

Glo. How fell you out? say that.

Kent. No cóntraries hold more antipathy   *80*
Than I and such a knave.

Corn. Why dost thou call him knave? What is his fault?

Kent. His countenance likes me not.

Corn. No more, perchance, does mine, nor his, nor hers.

Kent. Sir, 'tis my occupation to be plain.   *85*
I have seen better faces in my time
Than stands on any shoulder that I see
Before me at this instant.

Corn.   This is some fellow,
Who, having been prais'd for bluntness, doth affect   *90*
A saucy roughness, and constrains the garb
Quite from his nature. He cannot flatter, he.
An honest mind and plain, he must speak truth.
An they will take it, so; if not, he's plain.
These kind of knaves I know, which in this plainness   *95*
Harbor more craft and more corrupter ends
Than twenty silly-ducking óbservants,
That stretch their duties nicely.

Kent. Sir, in good faith, in síncere verity,
Under th' allowance of your great aspéct,   *100*
Whose influence, like the wreath of radiant fire

Flickering on Phœbus' front,—

Corn.   What mean'st by this?

Kent. To go out of my dialect, which you discommend so much. I know, sir, I am no flatterer. He that beguiled you   *105*
in a plain accent was a plain knave; which for my part I will not be, though I should win your displeasure to entreat me to 't.

Corn. What was th' offence you gave him?

Osw. I never gave him any.
It pleas'd the king his master very late   *110*
To strike at me upon his misconstruction;
When he, conjunct, and flattering his displeasure,
Tripp'd me behind; being down, insulted, rail'd,
And put upon him such a deal of man,
That worthied him, got praises of the king   *115*
For him attempting who was self-subdu'd;
And, in the fleshment of this dread exploit,
Drew on me here again.

Kent.   None of these rogues and cowards
But Ajax is their fool.   *120*

Corn.   Fetch forth the stocks!
You stubborn ancient knave, you reverent braggart,
We'll teach you.

Kent.   Sir, I am too old to learn.
Call not your stocks for me. I serve the king,   *125*
On whose employment I was sent to you.
You shall do small respects, show too bold malice
Against the grace and person of my master,
Stocking his messenger.

Corn. Fetch forth the stocks! As I have life and honor,   *130*
There shall he sit till noon.

Reg. Till noon! Till night, my lord, and all night too.

Kent. Why, madam, if I were your father's dog,
You should not use me so.

Reg.   Sir, being his knave, I will.   *135*

Corn. This is a fellow of the self-same color
Our sister speaks of. Come, bring away the stocks.

                             Stocks brought out.

Glo. Let me beseech your Grace not to do so.
«His fault is much, and the good king his master   *140*
Will check him for't. Your purpos'd low correction
Is such as vilest and contemned'st wretches
For pilferings and most common trespasses
Are punish'd with.» The king ⟨his master needs⟩ must take it ill,   *145*
That he's so slightly valu'd in his messenger,
Should have him thus restrain'd.

Corn.   I'll answer that.

Reg. My sister may receive it much more worse
To have her gentleman abus'd, assaulted,   *150*
«For following her affairs. Put in his legs.»

                     [Kent is put in the stocks.]
Come, my good lord, away.

                Exit [with all but Gloucester and Kent].

Glo. I am sorry for thee, friend. 'Tis the duke's pleasure,   *155*
Whose disposition, all the world well knows,

---

49 disclaims: *claims no share*   **54 yet:** *however*   **57 zed;** *cf. n.*   **58 unbolted:** *unrefined*   **59 a jakes:** *a privy*   **60 wagtail:** *a nervous and impudent small bird*   **67, 68 holy cords ... to intrinse;** *cf. n.*   **smooth:** *make the way easy for*   **71 Renege:** *deny* **halcyon;** *cf. n.*   **72 gale:** *breeze* **vary:** *vacillation*   **75 Smoil;** *cf. n.*   **76 Sarum:** *Salisbury*   **77 Camelot;** *cf. n.*   **86 better faces;** *cf. n.*   **91 constrains the garb:** *forces the fashion*   **92 from:** *contrary to*   **94 he's plain:** *he forces it on them anyway*   **97 óbservants:** *courtiers*   **98 nicely:** *fastidiously*

102 Flickering on; *cf. n.* **front:** *forehead*   **107 your displeasure;** *cf. n.*   **111 upon his misconstruction:** *having misconstrued my conduct*   **112 conjunct:** *in league*   **113 being down, insulted:** *I being down, he exulted*   **115 worthied:** *covered with dignity*   **117 in ... of:** *to feed the appetite created by*   **120 Ajax;** *cf. n.*   **122 reverent:** *for 'reverend' (old enough to know better)*   **127 small respects:** *little in the way of compliment (ironic)*   **129 Stocking;** *cf. n.*   **141 check:** *reprimand*   **142 vilest and contemned'st;** *cf. n.*   **146, 147** *Cf. n.*

Will not be rubb'd nor stopp'd. I'll entreat for thee.
   Kent. Pray, do not, sir. I have watch'd and travell'd hard.
Some time I shall sleep out, the rest I'll whistle.
A good man's fortune may grow out at heels.   *160*
Give you good morrow!
   Glo. The duke's to blame in this. 'Twill be ill taken.   *Exit.*
   Kent. Good king, that must approve the common saw,
Thou out of heaven's benediction com'st
To the warm sun.   *165*
Approach, thou beacon to this under globe,
That by thy comfortable beams I may
Peruse this letter. Nothing almost sees miracles
But misery. I know 'tis from Cordelia,
Who hath most fortunately been inform'd   *170*
Of my obscured course.
[Reads] . . .

   And shall find time
   From this enormous state, seeking to give
   Losses their remedies.

All weary and o'er-watch'd!   *175*
Take vantage, heavy eyes, not to behold
This shameful lodging.
Fortune, good night. Smile once more; turn thy wheel!

          Sleeps.

❧ SCENE THIRD ❧

Enter Edgar.

   Edg. I heard myself proclaim'd,
And by the happy hollow of a tree
Escap'd the hunt. No port is free; no place,
That guard and most unusual vigilance
Does not attend my taking. Whiles I may 'scape   *5*
I will preserve myself, and am bethought
To take the basest and most poorest shape
That ever penury, in contempt of man,
Brought near to beast. My face I'll grime with filth,
Blanket my loins, elf all my hair in knots,   *10*
And with presented nakedness outface
The winds and persecutions of the sky.
The country gives me proof and precedent
Of Bedlam beggars, who with roaring voices
Strike in their numb'd and mortified bare arms   *15*
Pins, wooden pricks, nails, sprigs of rosemary;
And with this horrible object from low farms,
Poor pelting villages, sheep-cotes, and mills,
Sometime with lunatic bans, sometime with prayers,
Enforce their charity. Poor Turlygod! poor Tom!   *20*
That's something yet. Edgar I nothing am.   *Exit.*

❧ SCENE FOURTH ❧

[Courtyard of Gloucester's Castle]
Enter Lear, Fool, and Gentleman.

   Lear. 'Tis strange that they should so depart from home,
And not send back my messenger.
   Gent.   As I learn'd,
The night before there was no purpose in them
Of this remove.   *5*
   Kent.   Hail to thee, noble master!
   Lear. Ha!
Mak'st thou this shame thy pastime?
   Kent.   ⟨No, my lord.⟩
   Fool. Ha, ha! he wears cruel garters. Horses are tied by   *10*
the head, dogs and bears by th' neck, monkeys by th' loins,
and men by th' legs: when a man's over-lusty at legs, then
he wears wooden nether-stocks.
   Lear. What's he that hath so much thy place mistook
To set thee here?   *15*
   Kent.   It is both he and she,
Your son and daughter.
   Lear. No.
   Kent. Yes.
   Lear. No, I say.   *20*
   Kent. I say, yea.
   «*Lear.* No, no; they would not.
   Kent. Yes, they have.»
   Lear. By Jupiter, I swear, no.
   ⟨*Kent.* By Juno, I swear, ay.   *25*
   Lear.⟩   They durst not do't;
They could not, would not do't. 'Tis worse than murther
To do upon respect such violent outrage.
Resolve me, with all modest haste, which way
Thou mightst deserve, or they impose, this usage,   *30*
Coming from us.
   Kent.   My lord, when at their home
I did commend your highness' letters to them,
Ere I was risen from the place that show'd
My duty kneeling, there came a reeking post,   *35*
Stew'd in his haste, half breathless, panting forth
From Goneril his mistress salutations;
Deliver'd letters, spite of intermission
Which presently they read. On whose contents
They summon'd up their meiny, straight took horse;   *40*
Commanded me to follow and attend
The leisure of their answer, gave me cold looks.
And meeting here the other messenger,
Whose welcome, I perceiv'd, had poison'd mine—
Being the very fellow which of late   *45*
Display'd so saucily against your highness—
Having more man than wit about me, drew.
He rais'd the house with loud and coward cries.
Your son and daughter found this trespass worth
The shame which here it suffers.   *50*
   ⟨*Fool.* Winter's not gone yet, if the wild geese fly that way.

   Fathers that wear rags
     Do make their children blind,

157 rubb'd: *checked*   **158 watch'd:** *lost sleep*   **163 approve:** *illustrate*   **164 heaven's benediction;** *cf. n.*   **168, 169 Nothing . . . misery;** *cf. n.*   **172–174 And . . . remedies;** *cf. n.*   **176 Take vantage:** *use the opportunity* (which sleep offers)   **Scene Third;** *cf. n.*   **10 elf:** *twist*   **14 Bedlam beggars;** *cf. n.*   **17 object:** *spectacle*   **18 pelting:** *contemptible*   **19 bans:** *curses*   **20 Turlygod . . . Tom;** *cf. n.*   **21 Edgar I nothing am:** *as Edgar I am nothing*

10 cruel: *pun on crewel; i.e., worsted*   **13 nether-stocks:** *stockings*   **28 Cf. n.**   **29 Resolve:** *inform*   **31 Coming:** *considering that you came*   **38 spite of intermission:** *making no bones of interrupting me*   **39 On:** *on perceiving*   **40 meiny:** *retinue of attendants*   **43–47 And . . . drew;** *cf. n.*   **53 blind:** *i.e., to filial duty*

But fathers that bear bags
    Shall see their children kind.   55
Fortune, that arrant whore,
Ne'er turns the key to th' poor.

But for all this thou shalt have as many dolors for thy
daughters as thou canst tell in a year.⟩
   Lear. O how this mother swells up toward my heart!   60
Hysterica passio! Down, thou climbing sorrow!
Thy element's below. Where is this daughter?
   Kent. With the earl, sir: here within.
   Lear [to Attendants]. Follow me not. Stay here.   *Exit.*
   Gent. Made you no more offence than what you speak of?   65
   Kent. None.
How chance the king comes with so small a number?
   Fool. An thou hadst been set i' th' stocks for that question,
thou'dst well deserved it.
   Kent. Why, fool?   70
   Fool. We'll set thee to school to an ant, to teach thee there's
no laboring i' th' winter. All that follow their noses are led by
their eyes but blind men; and there's not a nose among twenty
but can smell him that's stinking. Let go thy hold when a
great wheel runs down a hill, lest it break thy neck with fol- 75
lowing; but the great one that goes upward, let him draw
thee after. When a wise man gives thee better counsel,
give me mine again. I would have none but knaves follow it,
since a fool gives it.

That sir which serves and seeks for gain,   80
    And follows but for form,
Will pack when it begins to rain,
    And leave thee in the storm.
But I will tarry, the fool will stay,
    And let the wise man fly: 85
The knave turns fool that runs away;
    The fool no knave, perdy.

   Kent. Where learn'd you this, fool?
   Fool. Not i' th' stocks, fool.

Enter Lear and Gloucester.

   Lear. Deny to speak with me! They are sick! They are   90
weary!
They have travell'd all the night! Mere fetches,
The images of revolt and flying off.
Fetch me a better answer.
   Glo.   My dear lord,   95
You know the fiery quality of the duke;
How unremovable and fix'd he is
In his own course.
   Lear. Vengeance! plague! death! confusion!
What fiery quality? Why, Gloucester, Gloucester!   100
I'd speak with the Duke of Cornwall and his wife.
   ⟨*Glo.* Well, my good lord, I have inform'd them so.
   Lear. Inform'd them! Dost thou understand me, man?⟩
   Glo. Ay, my good lord.
   Lear. The king would speak with Cornwall; the dear father   105
Would with his daughter speak, commands her service.

⟨Are they inform'd of this? My breath and blood!⟩
Fiery duke! Tell the hot duke that Lear—
No, but not yet; may be he is not well.
Infirmity doth still neglect all office   110
Whereto our health is bound. We are not ourselves
When nature, being oppress'd, commands the mind
To suffer with the body. I'll forbear;
And am fall'n out with my more headier will,
To take the indispos'd and sickly fit   115
For the sound man. Death on my state!   *[Looking on Kent.]*
Wherefore
Should he sit here? This act persaudes me
That this remotion of the duke and her
Is practice only. Give me my servant forth.   120
Go tell the duke and's wife I'd speak with them,
Now, presently. Bid them come forth and hear me,
Or at their chamber-door I'll beat the drum
Till it cry sleep to death.
   Glo. I would have all well betwixt you.   *Exit.*   125
   Lear. O, me! my heart, my rising heart! but, down!
   Fool. Cry to it, nuncle, as the cockney did to the eels when
she put 'em i' th' paste alive. She knapped 'em o' th' cox-
combs with stick, and cried, 'Down wantons, down!' 'Twas her
brother that, in pure kindness to his horse, buttered his hay.   130

Enter Cornwall, Regan, Gloucester, Servants.

   Lear. Good morrow to you both.
   Corn.   Hail to your Grace.
                       Kent here set at liberty.
   Reg. I am glad to see your highness.
   Lear. Regan, I think you are. I know what reason   135
I have to think so. If thou shouldst not be glad,
I would divorce me from thy mother's tomb,
Sepúlchuring an adult'ress.-*[To Kent.]* O! are you free?
Some other time for that. Beloved Regan,
Thy sister's naught. O Regan! she hath tied   140
Sharp-tooth'd unkindness, like a vulture, here.
                      [Points to his heart.]
I can scarce speak to thee—thou'lt not believe—
Of how deprav'd a quality—O Regan!
   Reg. I pray you, sir, take patience. I have hope
You less know how to value her desert   145
Than she to scant her duty.
   ⟨*Lear.*   Say, how is that?
   Reg. I cannot think my sister in the least
Would fail her obligation. If, sir, perchance
She have restrain'd the riots of your followers,   150
'Tis on such ground and to such wholesome end
As clears her from all blame.⟩
   Lear. My curses on her!
   Reg.   O, sir, you are old.
Nature in you stands on the very verge   155
Of her confine. You should be rul'd and led
By some discretion that discerns your state
Better than you yourself. Therefore I pray you
That to our sister you do make return.
Say, you have wrong'd her, sir.   160

57 turns the key: *unlocks the door*   **58 dolors:** *pun on dollars*   **59 tell:** *count; also*
'narrate'   **60 mother:** *vertigo*   **60, 61 mother . . . Hysterica passio;** *cf. n.*   **78 none**
but knaves; *cf. n.*   **82 pack:** *hurry off*   **87 perdy:** *by God, pardieu*   **90 Deny:**
refuse   **92 fetches:** *tricks*   **93 flying off:** *desertion*   **106–108** *Cf. n.*

110 office: *duty*   **114 more headier:** *too headstrong*   **119 remotion:** *removal*   **124 cry**
sleep to death: *murder sleep*   **127 cockney:** *city woman*   **128 paste:** *pie-dough*
knapped: *rapped*   **138 Sepúlchring:** *for enclosing*   **140 naught:** *worthless*   **143 qual-**
ity: *manner*   **146 scant;** *cf. n.*   **155, 156 on . . . confine;** *cf. n.*   **156 confine:** *territory*

Lear.   Ask her forgiveness?
Do you but mark how this becomes the house:
'Dear daughter, I confess that I am old.
Age is unnecessary: on my knees I beg
That you'll vouchsafe me raiment, bed, and food.'   *165*
    Reg. Good sir, no more; these are unsightly tricks.
Return you to my sister.
    Lear.   Never, Regan.
She hath abated me of half my train,
Look'd black upon me, struck me with her tongue,   *170*
Most serpent-like, upon the very heart.
All the stor'd vengeances of heaven fall
On her ingrateful top! Strike her young bones,
You taking airs, with lameness!
    Corn.   Fie, sir, fie!   *175*
    Lear. You nimble lightnings, dart your blinding flames
Into her scornful eyes! Infect her beauty,
You fen-suck'd fogs, drawn by the powerful sun,
To fall and blast her pride!
    Reg. O the blest gods! So will you wish on me,   *180*
When the rash mood is on.
    Lear. No, Regan, thou shalt never have my curse.
Thy tender-hefted nature shall not give
Thee o'er to harshness. Her eyes are fierce, but thine
Do comfort and not burn. 'Tis not in thee   *185*
To grudge my pleasures, to cut off my train,
To bandy hasty words, to scant my sizes,
And, in conclusion, to oppose the bolt
Against my coming in. Thou better know'st
The offices of nature, bond of childhood,   *190*
Effects of courtesy, dues of gratitude;
Thy half o' th' kingdom hast thou not forgot,
Wherein I thee endow'd.
    Reg.   Good sir, to th' purpose.
    Lear. Who put my man i' th' stocks?   *195*

                       Tucket within.

    Corn.   What trumpet's that?
    Reg. I know't: my sister's. This approves her letter,
That she would soon be here.

         Enter Steward [Oswald].

             Is your lady come?
    Lear. This is a slave, whose easy-borrow'd pride   *200*
Dwells in the fickle grace of her 'a follows.
Out, varlet, from my sight!
    Corn.   What means your Grace?
    Lear. Who stock'd my servant? Regan, I have good hope
Thou didst not know on 't.   *205*

         Enter Goneril.

             Who comes here? O heavens,
If you do love old men, if your sweet sway
Allow obedience, if you yourselves are old,
Make it your cause. Send down and take my part!
[To Goneril.] Art not asham'd to look upon this beard?   *210*
O Regan, will you take her by the hand?
    Gon. Why not by th' hand, sir? How have I offended?

All's not offence that indiscretion finds
And dotage terms so.
    Lear.   O sides, you are too tough!   *215*
Will you yet hold?—How came my man i' th' stocks?
    Corn. I set him there, sir; but his own disorders
Deserv'd much less advancement.
    Lear.   You? Did you?
    Reg. I pray you, father, being weak, seem so.   *220*
If till the expiration of your month
You will return and sojourn with my sister,
Dismissing half your train, come then to me.
I am now from home, and out of that provision
Which shall be needful for your entertainment.   *225*
    Lear. Return to her? and fifty men dismiss'd!
No, rather I abjure all roofs, and choose
To wage against the enmity o' th' air,
To be a comrade with the wolf and owl:
Necessity's sharp pinch! Return with her?   *230*
Why, the hot-blooded France, that dowerless took
Our youngest born, I could as well be brought
To knee his throne, and, squire-like, pension beg
To keep base life afoot. Return with her?
Persuade me rather to be slave and sumpter   *235*
To this detested groom.
    Gon.   At your choice, sir.
    Lear. I prithee, daughter, do not make me mad.
I will not trouble thee, my child. Farewell.
We'll no more meet, no more see one another;   *240*
But yet thou art my flesh, my blood, my daughter,—
Or rather a disease that's in my flesh,
Which I must needs call mine. Thou art a bile,
A plague-sore, an embossed carbuncle,
In my corrupted blood. But I'll not chide thee.   *245*
Let shame come when it will, I do not call it.
I do not bid the thunder-bearer shoot,
Nor tell tales of thee to high-judging Jove.
Mend when thou canst; be better at thy leisure.
I can be patient; I can stay with Regan,   *250*
I and my hundred knights.
    Reg.   Not altogether so.
I look'd not for you yet, nor am provided
For your fit welcome. Give ear, sir, to my sister;
For those that mingle reason with your passion   *255*
Must be content to think you old, and so—
But she knows what she does.
    Lear.   Is this well spoken?
    Reg. I dare avouch it, sir. What! fifty followers?
Is it not well? What should you need of more?   *260*
Yeah, or so many, sith that both charge and danger
Speak 'gainst so great a number? How, in one house,
Should many people under two commands
Hold amity? 'Tis hard; almost impossible.
    Gon. Why might not you, my lord, receive attendance   *265*
From those that she calls servants, or from mine?
    Reg. Why not, my lord? If then they chanc'd to slack ye,
We could control them. If you will come to me
(For now I spy a danger), I entreat you
To bring but five-and-twenty. To no more   *270*

---

162 the house: *our exalted family*   **169 She . . . train;** *cf. n.*   **abated:** *deprived*   **174 taking:** *possessing, in the sense of malignant*   **172 fall:** *make fall*   **183 tender-hefted:** *sensitive; cf. n.*   **187 sizes:** *allowances*   **201 'a:** *he*   **208 Allow:** *commend (as an example)*

217 disorders: *disorderly acts*   **228 wage:** *wage war*   **235 sumpter:** *packhorse (or its driver)*   **236 groom:** *i.e., Oswald*   **243 bile:** *boil; cf. n.*   **244 embossed:** *swollen*   **255 mingle . . . passion;** *cf. n.*   **260 Is it not well:** *is not that enough?*

Will I give place or notice.

Lear. I gave you all—

Reg.   And in good time you gave it.

Lear. Made you my guardians, my depositaries,

But kept a reservation to be follow'd   275

With such a number. What! must I come to you

With five-and-twenty? Regan, said you so?

    Reg. And speak't again, my lord. No more with me.

    Lear. Those wicked creatures yet do look well-favor'd,

When others are more wicked; not being the worst   280

Stands in some rank of praise. *[To Goneril.]* I'll go with thee.

Thy fifty yet doth double five-and-twenty,

And thou art twice her love.

    Gon.   Hear me, my lord.

What need you five-and-twenty? ten? or five?   285

To follow in a house, where twice so many

Have a command to tend you?

    Reg.   What need one?

    Lear. O reason not the need! Our basest beggars

Are in the poorest thing superfluous.   290

Allow not nature more than nature needs,

Man's life is cheap as beast's. Thou art a lady.

If only to go warm were gorgeous,

Why, nature needs not what thou gorgeous wear'st,

Which scarcely keeps thee warm. But for true need,—   295

You heavens, give me that patience, patience I need!

You see me here, you gods, a poor old man,

As full of grief as age, wretched in both!

If it be you that stirs these daughters' hearts

Against their father, fool me not so much   300

To bear it tamely. Touch me with noble anger,

And let not women's weapons, water-drops,

Stain my man's cheeks! No, you unnatural hags,

I will have such revenges on you both

That all the world shall—I will do such things,—   305

What they are yet I know not,—but they shall be

The terrors of the earth. You think I'll weep?

No, I'll not weep.

I have full cause of weeping, but this heart

                       Storm and Tempest.

Shall break into a hundred thousand flaws   310

Or ere I'll weep. O, fool, I shall go mad.

        Exeunt Lear, Gloucester, Kent, and Fool.

    Corn. Let us withdraw. 'Twill be a storm.

    Reg. This house is little. The old man and his people

Cannot be well bestow'd.

    Gon. 'Tis his own blame; hath put himself from rest,   315

And must needs taste his folly.

    Reg. For his particular, I'll receive him gladly,

But not one follower.

    Gon.   So am I purpos'd.

Where is my Lord of Gloucester?   320

    Corn. Follow'd the old man forth. He is return'd.

                 Enter Gloucester.

    Glo. The king is in high rage.

    ⟨*Corn.*   Whither is he going?

    Glo. He calls to horse; but⟩ will I know not whither.

    Corn. 'Tis best to give him way; he leads himself.   325

    Gon. My lord, entreat him by no means to stay.

    Glo. Alack! the night comes on, and the bleak winds

Do sorely ruffle. For many miles about

There's scarce a bush.

    Reg.   O, sir, to wilful men,   330

The injuries that they themselves procure

Must be their schoolmasters. Shut up your doors.

He is attended with a desperate train,

And what they may incense him to, being apt

To have his ear abus'd, wisdom bids fear.   335

    Corn. Shut up your doors, my lord; 'tis a wild night.

My Regan counsels well. Come out o' th' storm.   *Exeunt.*

ACT THIRD ❧ SCENE FIRST

[The Heath]

Storm still. Enter Kent and a Gentleman at several doors.

    Kent. Who's there, besides foul weather?

    Gent. One minded like the weather, most unquietly.

    Kent. I know you. Where's the king?

    Gent. Contending with the fretful elements;

Bids the wind blow the earth into the sea,   5

Or swell the curled waters 'bove the main,

That things might change or cease. «Tears his white hair,

Which the impetuous blasts, with eyeless rage,

Catch in their fury and make nothing of;

Strives in his little world of man t'out-scorn   10

The to-and-fro-conflicting wind and rain.

This night, wherein the cub-drawn bear would crouch,

The lion and the belly-pinched wolf

Keep their fur dry, unbonneted he runs,

And bids what will take all.»   15

    Kent.   But who is with him?

    Gent. None but the fool, who labors to out-jest

His heart-struck injuries.

    Kent.   Sir, I do know you;

And dare, upon the warrant of my note,   20

Commend a dear thing to you. There is division,

(Although as yet the face of it is cover'd

With mutual cunning) 'twixt Albany and Cornwall,

⟨Who have—as who have not, that their great stars

Thron'd and set high—servants, who seem no less,   25

Which are to France the spies and speculations

Intelligent of our state. What hath been seen,

Either in snuffs and packings of the dukes,

Or the hard rein which both of them have borne

Against the old kind king, or something deeper,   30

Whereof perchance these are but furnishings—⟩

«But, true it is, from France there comes a power

Into this scatter'd kingdom; who already,

Wise in our negligence, have secret feet

---

271 notice: *countenance*   **274 depositaries:** *trustees*   **290 in:** *i.e., in possessing* **super-fluous:** *possessed of more than they need*   **292-295 Thou . . . warm;** *cf. n.*   **300 fool . . . much:** *make me not such a fool*   **310 flaws:** *pieces*   **317 For his particular:** *in regard to himself*   **318-321** *Cf. n.*

327 bleak: *cf. n.*   **328 ruffle:** *bluster*   **334 apt:** *naturally disposed*   **337 storm;** *cf. n.*   **6 main:** *land*   **10 little world of man:** *microcosm; cf. n.*   **12 cub-drawn:** *dry-sucked, ravenous*   **14 unbonneted:** *without a hat*   **20 note:** *observation*   **25 no less:** *no less than true servants*   **26 speculations:** *scouts*   **27 Intelligent:** *giving intelligence*   **28 snuffs:** *resentments* **sackings:** *hidden blots*   **31 furnishings:** *outer coverings; cf. n.*   **33 scatter'd:** *disunited*

In some of our best ports, and are at point   *35*
To show their open banner. Now to you:
If in my credit you dare build so far
To make your speed to Dover, you shall find
Some that will thank you, making just report
Of how unnatural and bemadding sorrow   *40*
The king hath cause to plain.
I am a gentleman of blood and breeding,
And from some knowledge and assurance offer
This office to you.»
    Gent. I will talk further with you.   *45*
    Kent.   No, do not.
For confirmation that I am much more
Than my out-wall, open this purse and take
What it contains. If you shall see Cordelia
(As fear not but you shall), show her this ring,   *50*
And she will tell you who your fellow is
That yet you do not know. Fie on this storm!
I will go seek the king.
    Gent. Give me your hand. Have you no more to say?
    Kent. Few words, but, to effect, more than all yet: *55*
That when we have found the king,—in which your pain
That way, I'll this,—he that first lights on him
Holla the other.   *Exeunt.*

❧ SCENE SECOND ❧

[Another part of the Heath]
Storm still. Enter Lear and Fool.

    Lear. Blow, winds, and crack your cheeks! rage! blow!
You cataracts and hurricanoes, spout
Till you have drench'd the steeples, drown'd the cocks!
You sulphurous and thought-executing fires,
Vaunt-couriers of oak-cleaving thunderbolts,   *5*
Singe my white head! And thou, all-shaking thunder,
Strike flat the thick rotundity o' th' world!
Crack nature's moulds, all germens spill at once
That make ingrateful man!
    Fool. O nuncle, court holy-water in a dry house is better   *10*
than this rain-water out o' door. Good nuncle, in; ask thy
daughters' blessing. Here's a night pities neither wise men
nor fools.
    Lear. Rumble thy bellyful! Spit fire! spout rain!
Nor rain, wind, thunder, fire, are my daughters.   *15*
I tax not you, you elements, with unkindness;
I never gave you kingdom, call'd you children,
You owe me no subscription. Then, let fall
Your horrible pleasure. Here I stand, your slave,
A poor, inform, weak, and despis'd old man.   *20*
But yet I call you servile ministers,
That will with two pernicious daughters join
Your high-engender'd battles 'gainst a head
So old and white as this. O! O! 'tis foul.

    Fool. He that has a house to put's head in has a good   *25*
head-piece.

       The codpiece that will house
         Before the head has any,
       The head and he shall louse;
         So beggars marry many.   *30*
       The man that makes his toe
         What he his heart should make,
       Shall of a corn cry woe,
         And turn his sleep to wake.

For there was never yet fair woman but she made mouths   *35*
in a glass.
    Lear. No, I will be the pattern of all patience.
I will say nothing.

          Enter Kent.

    Kent. Who's there?
    Fool. Marry, here's grace and a codpiece; that's a wise   *40*
man and a fool.
    Kent. Alas, sir, are you here? Things that love night
Love not such nights as these. The wrathful skies
Gallow the very wanderers of the dark,
And make them keep their caves. Since I was man   *45*
Such sheets of fire, such bursts of horrid thunder,
Such groans of roaring wind and rain, I never
Remember to have heard. Man's nature cannot carry
Th' affliction nor the fear.
    Lear.   Let the great gods,   *50*
That keep this dreadful pudder o'er our heads,
Find out their enemies now. Tremble, thou wretch,
That hast within thee undivulged crimes
Unwhipp'd of justice; hide thee, thou bloody hand,
Thou perjur'd, and thou simular of virtue   *55*
That art incestuous. Caitiff, to pieces shake,
That under covert and convenient seeming
Hast practis'd on man's life. Close pent-up guilts,
Rive your concealing continents, and cry
These dreadful summoners grace. I am a man   *60*
More sinn'd against than sinning.
    Kent.   Alack! bare-headed!
Gracious my lord, hard by here is a hovel.
Some friendship will it lend you 'gainst the tempest.
Repose you there while I to this hard house   *65*
(More harder than the stones whereof 'tis rais'd,
Which even but now, demanding after you,
Denied me to come in) return and force
Their scanted courtesy.
    Lear.   My wits begin to turn.   *70*
Come on, my boy. How dost, my boy? Art cold?
I am cold myself. Where is this straw, my fellow?
The art of our necessities is strange,
That can make vile things precious. Come, your hovel.
Poor fool and knave, I have one part in my heart   *75*
That's sorry yet for thee.

---

39 making: *for making*   **41 plain:** *complain*   **43 knowledge and assurance:** *sure knowledge*   **48 my out-wall:** *the servant livery I wear*   **51 fellow:** *companion*   **55 to effect:** *in importance*   **2 hurricanoes:** *water-spouts*   **3 cocks:** *weathercocks on steeples*   **4 thought-executing:** *acting Jove's thought*   **5 Vaunt-couriers:** *advance messengers*   **8 germens:** *seeds*   **10 court holy-water:** *flattery*   **18 subscription:** *allegiance*   **23 high-engender'd battles;** *cf. n.*

27 codpiece: *part of man's dress between the legs*   **30** *Cf. n.*   **31, 32 toe, heart;** *cf. n.*   **40 grace:** *majesty*   **44 Gallow:** *terrify*   **51 pudder:** *'powther' (Q), uproar*   **simular:** *simulator*   **59 Rive:** *split* **continents:** *covers*   **60 grace:** *mercy*   **74 vile;** *cf. n.*

Fool.

He that has and-a little tiny wit,
  With hey, ho, the wind and the rain,
Must make content with his fortunes fit,   80
  Though the rain it raineth every day.

Lear. True, my good boy. Come, bring us to this hovel.
                           Exit [with Kent].

⟨*Fool.* This is a brave night to cool a courtesan.
I'll speak a prophecy ere I go:

When priests are more in ward than matter;   85
When brewers mar their malt with water;
When nobles are their tailors' tutors;
No heretics burn'd but wenches' suitors;
When every case in law is right,
No squire in debt, nor no poor knight;   90
When slanders do not live in tongues;
Nor cutpurses come not to throngs;
When usurers tell their gold i' th' field,
And bawds and whores do churches build:
Then shall the realm of Albion   95
Come to great confusion.
Then comes the time, who lives to see't,
That going shall be us'd with feet.

This prophecy Merlin shall make, for I live before his time.
                                   Exit.⟩

❧ SCENE THIRD ❧

[Gloucester's Castle]
Enter Gloucester and the Bastard, with lights.

Glo. Alack, alack, Edmund! I like not this unnatural dealing.
When I desired their leave that I might pity him, they took
from me the use of mine own house; charged me, on pain of
perpetual displeasure, neither to speak of him, entreat for him,
nor any way sustain him.   5

Edm. Most savage, and unnatural!

Glo. Go to! say you nothing. There is division between the
dukes, and a worse matter than that. I have received a letter
this night. 'Tis dangerous to be spoken; I have locked the
letter in my closet. These injuries the king now bears will   10
be revenged home; there's part of a power already footed. We
must incline to the king. I will look him and privily relieve
him. Go you and maintain talk with the duke, that my charity
be not of him perceived. If he ask for me, I am ill and gone
to bed. If I die for it (as no less is threatened me), the king,   15
my old master, must be relieved. There is strange things
toward, Edmund. Pray you, be careful.   *Exit.*

Edm. This courtesy, forbid thee, shall the duke
Instantly know; and of that letter too.
This seems a fair deserving, and must draw me   20
That which my father loses: no less than all.
The younger rises when the old doth fall.   *Exit.*

❧ SCENE FOURTH ❧

[The Heath. Before a Hovel]
Enter Lear, Kent, and Fool.

Kent. Here is the place, my lord; good my lord, enter.
The tyranny of the open night's too rough
For nature to endure   *Storm still.*
  Lear.   Let me alone.
  Kent. Good my lord, enter here.   5
  Lear.   Wilt break my heart?
  Kent. I'd rather break mine own. Good my lord, enter.
  Lear. Thou think'st 'tis much that this contentious storm
Invades us to the skin. So 'tis to thee;
But where the greater malady is fix'd,   10
The lesser is scarce felt. Thou'dst shun a bear;
But if thy flight lay toward the roaring sea,
Thou'dst meet the bear i' th' mouth. When the mind's free,
The body's delicate. The tempest in my mind
Doth from my senses take all feeling else   15
Save what beats there. Filial ingratitude!
Is it not as this mouth should tear this hand
For lifting food to't? But I will punish home!
No, I will weep no more. ⟨In such a night
To shut me out! Pour on! I will endure.⟩   20
In such a night as this! O Regan, Goneril!
Your old kind father, whose frank heart gave you all,—
O, that way madness lies; let me shun that!
No more of that!
  Kent.   Good my lord, enter here.   25
  Lear. Prithee, go in thyself; seek thine own ease.
This tempest will not give me leave to ponder
On things would hurt me more. But I'll go in.
⟨*[To the Fool.]* In, boy; go first.   *Exit [Fool].*
              You houseless poverty,—   30
  [To Kent.] Nay, get thee in. I'll pray, and then I'll sleep.⟩
Poor naked wretches, wheresoe'er you are,
That bide the pelting of this pitiless storm,
How shall your houseless heads and unfed sides,
Your loop'd and window'd raggedness, defend you   35
From seasons such as these? O! I have ta'en
Too little care of this. Take physic, pomp;
Expose thyself to feel what wretches feel,
That thou mayst shake the superflux to them,
And show the heavens more just.   40
  ⟨*Edg. [within].* Fathom and half, fathom and half!
Poor Tom!⟩
  Fool [within]. Come not in here, nuncle. Here's a spirit.
Help me! help me!
  Kent. Give me thy hand. Who's there?   45
  Fool [within]. A spirit, a spirit! He says his name's poor
Tom.
  Kent. What art thou that dost grumble thee i' th' straw?
Come forth.

Enter Edgar and Fool.

  Edg. Away! the foul fiend follows me! Through the sharp   50
hawthorn blows the cold wind. Hum! Go to thy bed and
warm thee.

78 *Cf. n.*   80-96 *Cf. n.*   87 *Cf. n.*   88 No . . . suitors; *cf. n.*   90 nor no poor knight; *cf. n.*   95, 96 Then . . . feet; *cf. n.*   99 Merlin; *cf. n.*   11 home: *to the hilt*   11 power: *army*   footed: *on foot, landed*   12 look: *look for*

14 delicate: *fastidious*   17 as: *as if*   19-21 *Cf. n.*   21 *Cf. n.*   35 loop'd: *full of holes*   39 shake the superflux: *scatter your superfluities; cf. n.*

Lear. Didst thou give all to thy daughters? And art thou
come to this?

Edg. Who gives anything to poor Tom, whom the foul   55
fiend hath led through fire and ⟨through flame,⟩ through ford
and whirlipool, o'er bog and quagmire? that hath laid knives
under his pillow, and halters in his pew; set ratsbane by his
porridge; made him proud of heart, to ride on a bay trotting-
horse over four-inched bridges, to course his own shadow for a
traitor. Bless thy five wits! Tom's a-cold. ⟨O! do de, do de, do
de.⟩ Bless thee from whirlwinds, starblasting, and taking! Do
poor Tom some charity, whom the foul fiend vexes. There
could I have him now, and there, and there again, and there.

Storm still.

Lear. What! has his daughters brought him to this pass?   65
Couldn'st thou save nothing? Would'st thou give 'em all?

Fool. Nay, he reserved a blanket. Else we had been all
shamed.

Lear. Now all the plagues that in the pendulous air
Hang fated o'er men's faults light on thy daughters!   70

Kent. He hath no daughters, sir.

Lear. Death, traitor! nothing could have súbdu'd nature
To such a lowness, but his unkind daughters.
Is it the fashion that discarded fathers
Should have thus little mercy on their flesh?   75
Judicious punishment! 'twas this flesh begot
Those pelican daughters.

Edg. Pillicock sat on Pillicock-hill:
Halloo, halloo, loo, loo!

Fool. This cold night will turn us all to fools and madmen.   80

Edg. Take heed o' th' foul fiend. Obey thy parents; keep
thy word justly; swear not; commit not with man's sworn
spouse; set not thy sweet heart on proud array. Tom's a-cold.

Lear. What hast thou been?

Edg. A servingman, proud in heart and mind, that curled   85
my hair, wore gloves in my cap, served the lust of my mistress's heart, and did the act of darkness with her; swore as
many oaths as I spake words, and broke them in the sweet
face of heaven; one that slept in the contriving of lust, and
waked to do it. Wine loved I deeply, dice dearly, and in   90
woman outparamoured the Turk: false of heart, light of ear,
bloody of hand; hog in sloth, fox in stealth, wolf in greediness,
dog in madness, lion in prey. Let not the creaking of shoes
nor the rustling of silks betray thy poor heart to woman. Keep
thy foot out of brothels, thy hand out of plackets, thy pen   95
from lenders' books, and defy the foul fiend. Still through
the hawthorn blows the cold wind! Hay no nonny, Dolphin
my boy! my boy, sessa! let him trot by.   *Storm still.*

Lear. Why, thou wert better in thy grave than to answer
with thy uncovered body this extremity of the skies. Is man   100
no more than this? Consider him well. Thou owest the worm
no silk, the beast no hide, the sheep no wool, the cat no
perfume. Ha! here's three on's are sophisticated; thou art the
thing itself. Unaccommodated man is no more but such a
poor, bare, forked animal as thou art. Off, off, you lendings!
Come; unbutton here.   *[Tearing off his clothes.]*

Fool. Prithee, nuncle, be contented. 'Tis a naughty night
to swim in. Now a little fire in a wild field were like an old

lecher's heart; a small spark, all the rest on's body cold. Look!
here comes a walking fire.   *110*

Enter Gloucester with a torch.

Edg. This is the foul fiend Flibbertigibbet. He begins at
curfew, and walks till the first cock. He gives the web and
the pin, squints the eye, an makes the harelip; mildews the
white wheat, and hurts the poor creature of earth.

Swithold footed thrice the old;   *115*
He met the night-mare and her nine-fold;
    Bid her alight,
    And her troth plight,
And aroint thee, witch, aroint thee!

Kent. How fares your Grace?   *120*
Lear. What's he?
Kent. Who's there? What is't you seek?
Glo. What are you there? Your names?
Edg. Poor Tom, that eats the swimming frog, the toad, the
tadpole, the wall-newt, and the water; that in the fury of   *125*
his heart, when the foul fiend rages, eats cow-dung for sallets,
swallows the old rat and the ditch-dog; drinks the green
mantle of the standing pool; who is whipped from tithing to
tithing, and stock-punished, and imprisoned; who hath had
three suits to his back, six shirts to his body,   *130*

Horse to ride, and weapon to wear.
But mice and rats and such small deer
Have been Tom's food for seven long year.

Beware thy follower. Peace, Smulkin! peace, thou fiend.
Glo. What! hath your Grace no better company?   *135*
Edg. The prince of darkness is a gentleman;
Modo he's call'd, and Mahu.
Glo. Our flesh and blood, my lord, is grown so vile,
That it doth hate what gets it.
Edg. Poor Tom's a-cold.   *140*
Glo. Go in with me. My duty cannot suffer
T'obey in all your daughter's hard commands.
Though their injunction be to bar my doors,
And let this tyrannous night take hold upon you,
Yet have I ventur'd to come seek you out   *145*
And bring you where both fire and food is ready.
Lear. First let me talk with this philosopher.
What is the cause of thunder?
Kent.   Good my lord,
Take his offer. Go into the house.   *150*
Lear. I'll talk a word with this most learned Theban.
What is your study?
Edg. How to prevent the fiend, and to kill vermin.
Lear. Let me ask you one word in private.
Kent. Impórtune him once more to go, my lord.   *155*
His wits begin t'unsettle.
Glo.   Canst thou blame him?   *Storm still.*
His daughters seek his death. Ah, that good Kent!
He said it would be thus, poor banish'd man.

---

58 **halters in his pew;** *cf. n.*   60 **course:** *hunt*   62 **taking:** *influence of malignant pow-*
ers   63, 64 **There ... now;** *cf. n.*   69 **pendulous:** *overhanging*   70 **fated:** *by fate's*
will   77 **pelican;** *cf. n.*   78 **Pillicock;** *cf. n.*   97, 98 **Hay ... sessa;** *cf. n.*   102 **cat:**
civet-cat   104 **Unaccommodated:** *unequipped*   108 **wild:** *blustery (cf. II.iv. 336)*

111 **Flibbertigibbet:** *one of Harsnet's devils*   112, 113 **web and the pin:** *eye-disease*   115
Swithold: *St. Withold, St. Vitalis*   **old:** *wold, moor-land*   116 **nine-fold:** *nine follow-*
ers   118 **her troth plight:** *pledge her troth*   119 **aroint:** *get out!*   125 **wall-newt:**
lizard **water:** *water-newt*   126 **sallets:** *salads*   127 **ditch-dog:** *dead dog in a ditch*
128 **standing:** *stagnant* **tithing:** *district*   132 **deer:** *game*   134 **Smulkin;**
cf. n.   142 **in all:** *in every respect*

Thou say'st the king grows mad. I'll tell thee, friend: *160*
I am almost mad myself. I had a son,
Now outlaw'd from my blood—he sought my life
But lately, very late. I lov'd him, friend;
No father his son dearer. True to tell thee,
The grief hath craz'd my wits. What a night's this!   *165*
I do beseech your Grace,—
    Lear.   O, cry you mercy, sir.
Noble philosopher, your company.
    Edg. Tom's a-cold.
    Glo. In, fellow, there, into th' hovel. Keep thee warm.   *170*
    Lear. Come, let's in all.
    Kent.   This way, my lord.
    Lear.   With him!
I will keep still with my philosopher.
    Kent. Good my lord, soothe him. Let him take the fellow.   *175*
    Glo. Take him you on.
    Kent. Sirrah, come on; go along with us.
    Lear. Come, good Athenian.
    Glo.   No words, no words. Hush.
    Edg.   *180*

> *Child Rowland to the dark tower came,*
> *His word was still, Fie, Foh, and fum,*
> *I smell the blood of a British man.*   *Exeunt.*

❧ SCENE FIFTH ❧

[Gloucester's Castle]
Enter Cornwall and Edmund

    Corn. I will have my revenge ere I depart the house.
    Edm. How, my lord, I may be censured, that nature thus
gives way to loyalty, something fears me to think of.
    Corn. I now perceive it was not altogether your brother's
evil disposition made him seek his death; but a provoking   *5*
merit, set a-work by a reprovable badness in himself.
    Edm. How malicious is my fortune that I must repent to
be just! This is the letter he spoke of, which approves him an
intelligent party to the advantages of France. O heavens! that
this treason were not, or not I the detector!   *10*
    Corn. Go with me to the duchess.
    Edm. If the matter of this paper be certain, you have
mighty business in hand.
    Corn. True or false, it hath made thee Earl of Gloucester.
Seek out where thy father is, that he may be ready for our   *15*
apprehension.
    Edm. [*aside*] If I find him comforting the king, it will stuff
his suspicion more fully.—I will persever in my course of loyalty, though the conflict be sore between that and my blood.
    Corn I will lay trust upon thee, and thou shalt find a   *20*
dearer father in my love.   *Exeunt.*

❧ SCENE SIXTH ❧

[A Farmhouse near Gloucester's Castle]
Enter Kent and Gloucester.

    Glo. Here is better than the open air; take it thankfully. I
will piece out the comfort with what addition I can. I will not
be long from you.
    Kent. All the power of his wits have given way to his impa-
tience. The gods reward your kindness!   *Exit [Gloucester].*   *5*

Enter Lear, Edgar, and Fool.

    Edg. Frateretto calls me, and tells me Nero is an angler in
the lake of darkness. Pray, innocent, and beware the foul fiend.
    Fool. Prithee, nuncle, tell me whether a madman be a gentle-
man or a yeoman.
    Lear. A king, a king!   *10*
    ⟨*Fool.* No, he's a yeoman that has a gentleman to his son;
for he's a mad yeoman that sees his son a gentleman before
him.
    Lear.⟩ To have a thousand with red burning spits
Come hizzing in upon 'em,—   *15*
    «*Edg.* The foul fiend bites my back.
    Fool. He's mad that trusts in the tameness of a wolf, a
horse's health, a boy's love, or a whore's oath.
    Lear. It shall be done! I will arraign them straight.
[*To Edgar.*] Come, sit thou here, most learnèd justicer.   *20*
[*To the Fool.*] Thou, sapient sir, sit here. No, you she
foxes!
    Edg. Look, where he stands and glares! Want'st thou eyes?
At trial, madam!

> *Come o'er the broom, Bessy, to me,—*   *25*
> *Fool.*
>   *Her boat hath at leak,*
>   *And she must not speak*
> *Why she dares not come over to thee.*

    Edg. The foul fiend haunts poor Tom in the voice of a   *30*
nightingale. Hoppedance cries in Tom's belly for two white
herring. Croak not, black angel. I have no food for thee.
    Kent. How do you, sir? Stand you not so amaz'd.
Will you lie down and rest upon the cushions?
    Lear. I'll see their trial first. Bring in their evidence.   *35*
[*To Edgar.*] Thou robed man of justice, take thy place;
[*To the Fool.*] And thou, his yoke-fellow of equity,
Bench by his side. [*To Kent.*] You are o' th' commission.
Sit you too.
    Edg. Let us deal justly.   *40*

> *Sleepest or wakest thou, jolly shepherd?*
>   *Thy sheep be in the corn;*
> *And for one blast of thy minikin mouth,*
>   *Thy sheep shall take no harm.*

Purr! the cat is grey.   *45*
    Lear. Arraign her first. 'Tis Goneril, I here take my oath be-
fore this honorable assembly, kicked the poor king her father.
    Fool. Come hither, mistress. Is your name Goneril?
    Lear. She cannot deny it.

161-165 *Cf. n.*   **167 cry you mercy:** *I beg your pardon*   **170-173** *Cf. n.*   **183 British
man:** *cf. n.*   **2 censured:** *judged*   **3 something fears me:** *I somewhat fear*   **5, 6
provoking merit:** *meritorious incitement*   **9 intelligent party:** *conscious accessory*

4 have; *cf. n.*   **4, 5 impatience:** *inability to endure*   **S.d.** *Cf. n.*   **6 Frateretto;**
cf. n.   **7 innocent:** *the Fool*   **15 hizzing:** *whizzing*   **25 broom;** *cf. n.*   **33 amaz'd:**
confused   **38 o' th' commission:** *One of the delegated judges*   **41-44** *Cf. n.*   **43 mini-
kin:** *mignonne, pretty*   **45** *Cf. n.*   **46, 47** *Cf. n.*

Fool. Cry you mercy, I took you for a joint-stool.   50
Lear. And here's another, whose warp'd looks proclaim
What store her heart is made on. Stop her there!
Arms! arms! sword! fire! Corruption in the place!
False justicer, why hast thou let her 'scape?»
    Edg. Bless thy five wits!   55
    Kent. O pity! Sir, where is the patience now
That you so oft have boasted to retain?
    Edg. [aside]. My tears begin to take his part so much,
They'll mar my counterfeiting.
    Lear. The little dogs and all,   60
Trey, Blanch, and Sweet-heart, see, they bark at me.
    Edg. Tom will throw his head at them. Avaunt, you curs!

Be thy mouth or black or white,
Tooth that poisons if it bite;
Mastiff, greyhound, mongrel grim,   65
Hound or spaniel, brach or him,
Or bobtail tike or trundle-tail;
Tom will make them weep and wail:
For, with throwing thus my head,
Dogs leap the hatch, and all are fled.   70

Do de, de, de. Sessa! Come, march to wakes and fairs and
market-towns. Poor Tom, thy horn is dry.
    Lear. Then let them anatomize Regan. See what breeds
about her heart. Is there any cause in nature that makes these
hard hearts? *[To Edgar.]* You, sir, I entertain for one of my   75
hundred; only I do not like the fashion of your garments. You
will say, they are Persian, but let them be changed.
    Kent. Now, good my lord, lie here and rest awhile.
    Lear. Make no noise, make no noise. Draw the curtains: so!
so! We'll go to supper i' th' morning. «So! so! so!»   80
    ⟨*Fool.* And I'll go to bed at noon.⟩

Enter Gloucester.

    Glo. Come hither, friend. Where is the king my master?
    Kent. Here, sir; but trouble him not, his wits are gone.
    Glo. Good friend, I prithee, take him in thy arms.
I have o'erheard a plot of death upon him.   85
There is a litter ready; lay him in't,
And drive toward Dover, friend, where thou shalt meet
Both welcome and protection. Take up thy master:
If thou shouldst dally half an hour, his life,
With thine and all that offer to defend him,   90
Stand in assured loss. Take up, take up;
And follow me, that will to some provision
Give thee quick conduct.
    «*Kent.*   Oppress'd nature sleeps.
This rest might yet have balm'd thy broken sinews,   95
Which, if convenience will not allow,
Stand in hard cure.—*[To the Fool.]* Come, help to bear thy
    master;
Thou must not stay behind.
    Glo.»   Come, come, away.   100
                    Exeunt [all but Edgar].
    «*Edg.* When we our betters see bearing our woes,

We scarcely think our miseries our foes.
Who alone suffers suffers most i' th' mind,
Leaving free things and happy shows behind;   105
But then the mind much sufferance doth o'erskip,
When grief hath mates, and bearing fellowship.
How light and portable my pain seems now,
When that which makes me bend makes the king bow,
He childed as I father'd! Tom, away!   110
Mark the high noises, and thyself bewray
When false opinion, whose wrong thought defiles thee,
In thy just proof repeals and reconciles thee.
What will hap more to-night, safe 'scape the king!
Lurk, lurk!»   *[Exit.]*

❧ Scene Seventh ❧

[Gloucester's Castle]
Enter Cornwall, Regan, Goneril, Bastard [Edmund], and Servants.

    Corn. Post speedily to my lord your husband. Show him
this letter. The army of France is landed. Seek out the traitor
Gloucester.   *[Exeunt some of the Servants.]*
    Reg. Hang him instantly.
    Gon. Pluck out his eyes.   5
    Corn. Leave him to my displeasure. Edmund, keep you our
sister company: the revenges we are bound to take upon your
traitorous father are not fit for your beholding. Advise the
duke, where you are going, to a most festinate preparation.
We are bound to the like. Our posts shall be swift and   10
intelligent betwixt us. Farewell, dear sister; farewell,
my Lord of Gloucester.

Enter Steward [Oswald].

How now? Where's the king?
    Osw. My Lord of GLoucester hath convey'd him hence.
Some five or six and thirty of his knights,   15
Hot questrists after him, met him at gate;
Who, with some other of the lord's dependants,
Are gone with him toward Dover, where they boast
To have well-armed friends.
    Corn.   Get horses for your mistress.   20
    Gon. Farewell, sweet lord, and sister.
    Corn. Edmund, farewell.
              Ex. Goneril, Edmund [and Oswald].
              Go seek the traitor GLoucester,
Pinion him like a thief, bring him before us.   25
                  [Exeunt other Servants.]
Though well we may not pass upon his life.
Without the form of justice, yet our power
Shall do a courtesy to our wrath, which men
May blame but not control.

Enter Gloucester, brought in by two or three.

                Who's there? The traitor?   30
    Reg. Ingrateful fox! 'tis he.
    Corn.   Bind fast his corky arms.
    Glo. What means your Graces? Good my friends, consider

---

50 **joint-stool;** *cf. n.*   63 **or . . . or:** *either . . . or*   66 **brach or him:** *female dog or he-dog; cf. n.*   67 **bobtail tike:** *short-tail cur* **trundle-tail:** *curly-tail*   70 **hatch:** *lower half of the house-door*   71 **wakes:** *church festivals*   75 **entertain:** *employ*   76 **hundred:** *i.e., knights*   77 **Persian;** *cf. n.*   80 *Cf. n.*   81 *Cf. n.*   91 **in assured loss:** *sure to be lost*   93 **conduct:** *guidance*   95 **sinews:** *nerves*   97 **in hard cure:** *hard to cure*

107 **bearing:** *suffering*   108 **portable:** *endurable*   111 **high noises:** *great tumults*   113 **repeals:** *recalls*   114 **What . . . more:** *whatever else*   115 **Lurk, lurk;** *cf. n.*   9 **festinate:** *speedy*   16 **questrists:** *searchers*   33 **corky:** *dry, withered*

You are my guests. Do me no foul play, friends.
   Corn. Bind him, I say   *[Servants bind him.]*   *35*
   Reg.   Hard, hard. O filthy traitor!
   Glo. Unmerciful lady as you are, I'm none.
   Corn. To this chair bind him. Villain, thou shalt find—
                            [Regan plucks his beard.]
   Glo. By the kind gods, 'tis most ignobly done
To pluck me by the beard.   *40*
   Reg. So white, and such a traitor!
   Glo.   Naughty lady,
These hairs which thou dost ravish from my chin
Will quicken and accuse thee. I am your host.
With robbers' hands my hospitable favors   *45*
You should not ruffle thus. What will you do?
   Corn. Come, sir, what letters had you late from France?
   Reg. Be simple-answer'd, for we know the truth.
   Corn. And what confederacy have you with the traitors
Late footed in the kingdom?   *50*
   Reg. To whose hands have you sent the lunatic king?
Speak.
   Glo. I have a letter guessingly set down,
Which came from one that's of a neutral heart,
And not from one oppos'd.   *55*
   Corn.   Cunning.
   Reg.   And false.
   Corn. Where hast thou sent the king?
   Glo.   To Dover.
   Reg. Wherefore to Dover? Wast thou not charg'd at peril— *60*
   Corn. Wherefore to Dover? Let him answer that.
   Glo. I am tied to th' stake, and I must stand the course.
   Reg. Wherefore to Dover?
   Glo. Because I would not see thy cruel nails
Pluck out his poor old eyes, nor thy fierce sister   *65*
In his anointed flesh rash boarish fangs.
The sea, with such a storm as his bow'd head
In hell-black night endur'd, would have buoy'd up,
And quench'd the stelled fires;
Yet, poor old heart, he holp the heavens to rage.   *70*
If wolves had at thy gate howl'd that dern time,
Thou shouldst have said, 'Good porter, turn the key.'
All cruels else subscribe, but I shall see
The winged vengeance overtake such children.
   Corn. See't shalt thou never. Fellows, hold the chair   *75*
Upon those eyes of thine I'll set my foot.
   Glo. He that will think to live till he be old,
Give me some help! O cruel! O you gods!
                     [Gloucester's eye put out.]
   Reg. One side will mock another. Th' other too.
   Corn. If you see vengeance—   *80*
   Servant.   Hold your hand, my lord!
I have serv'd you ever since I was a child,
But better service have I never done you
Than now to bid you hold.
   Reg.   How now, you dog?   *85*
   Serv. If you did wear a beard upon your chin,
I'd shake it on this quarrel. What do you mean—

   Corn. My villain!
   Serv. Nay then, come on, and take the chance of anger.
               Draw and fight. [Cornwall is wounded.]
   Reg. Give me thy sword. A peasant stand up thus!   *90*
           She takes a sword and runs at him behind.
   Serv. O, I am slain! My lord, you have one eye left
To see some mischief on him. O!
   Corn. Lest it see more, prevent it. Out, vile jelly!
Where is thy lustre now?   *95*
   Glo. All dark and comfortless. Where's my son Edmund?
Edmund, enkindle all the sparks of nature
To quit this horrid act.
   Reg.   Out, treacherous villain!
Thou call'st on him that hates thee. It was he   *100*
That made the overture of thy treasons to us,
Who is too good to pity thee.
   Glo. O my follies! Then Edgar was abus'd.
Kind gods, forgive me that, and prosper him!
   Reg. Go thrust him out at gates, and let him smell   *105*
His way to Dover.   *Exit [Attendant] with Gloucester.*
How is't, my lord? How look you?
   Corn. I have receiv'd a hurt. Follow me, lady.
Turn out that eyeless villain. Throw this slave
Upon the dunghill. Regan, I bleed apace: *110*
Untimely comes this hurt. Give me your arm.
               Exeunt [Cornwall and Regan].
   «*2nd Serv.* I'll never care what wickedness I do
If this man come to good.
   3rd Serv.   If she live long,
And, in the end, meet the old course of death,   *115*
Women will all turn monsters.
   2nd Serv. Let's follow the old earl, and get the bedlam
To lead him where he would. His roguish madness
Allows itself to anything.
   3rd. Serv. Go thou. I'll fetch some flax and whites of *120*
eggs
To apply to his bleeding face. Now, heaven help him!   *Exeunt.*»

ACT FOURTH ❧ SCENE FIRST

[The Heath]
Enter Edgar.

   Edg. Yet better thus, and known to be contemn'd,
Than still contemn'd and flatter'd. To be worst,
The lowest and most dejected thing of fortune,
Stands still in esperance, lives not in fear.
The lamentable change is from the best;   *5*
The worst returns to laughter. ⟨Welcome, then,
Thou unsubstantial air that I embrace.
The wretch that thou hast blown unto the worst
Owes nothing to thy blasts.⟩ But who comes here?

Enter Gloucester, led by an old man.

My father, poorly led? World, world, O world!   *10*
But that thy strange mutations make us hate thee,

---

42 Naughty: *wicked*   **44 quicken:** *come to life*   **45 favors:** *features*   **48 simple-answer'd;** *cf. n.*   **53 guessingly:** *expressed in conjectural language*   **62 course:** *an attack in the sport of bear-baiting*   **66 rash:** *push violently, slash; cf. n.*   **67 bow'd;** *cf. n.*   **68 buoy'd:** *surged*   **69 stelled fires:** *fixed stars; cf. n.*   **71 dern:** *dreary*   **73 subscribe:** *sanction; cf. n.*   **81 Hold your hand;** *cf. n.*

98 quit: *requite*   **101 overture:** *exposure*   **115 old:** *familiar, regular*   **117 bedlam:** *bedlam-beggar (Edgar)*   **118 would:** *would be led*   **1 known . . . contemn'd:** *openly despised*   **3 esperance:** *hope*   **6 The . . . laughter;** *cf. n.*   **9 Owes nothing;** *has nothing more to pay*   **10 poorly led;** *cf. n.*   **11, 12 But that . . . age; cf. n.**

Life would not yield to age.

Old Man.   O my good lord!
I have been your tenant, and your father's tenant,
These fourscore years.   *15*

Glo. Away! Get thee away! Good friend, be gone.
Thy comforts can do me no good at all;
Thee they may hurt.

Old Man.   You cannot see your way.

Glo. I have no way, and therefore want no eyes.   *20*
I stumbled when I saw. Full oft 'tis seen,
Our means secure us, and our mere defects
Prove our commodities. O dear son Edgar,
The food of thy abused father's wrath!
Might I but live to see thee in my touch,   *25*
I'd say I had eyes again.

Old Man.   How now! Who's there?

Edg. [aside]. O gods! Who is't can say, 'I am at the worst?'
I am worse than e'er I was.

Old Man.   'Tis poor mad Tom.   *30*

Edg. [aside]. And worse I may be yet. The worst is not.
So long as we can say, 'This is the worst.'

Old Man. Fellow, where goest?

Glo.   Is it a beggar-man?

Old Man. Madman and beggar too.   *35*

Glo. He has some reason, else he could not beg.
I' th' last night's storm I such a fellow saw,
Which made me think a man a worm. My son
Came then into my mind; and yet my mind
Was then scarce friends with him. I have heard more since.   *40*
As flies to wanton boys, are we to th' gods:
They kill us for their sport.

Edg. [aside].   How should this be?
Bad is the trade that must play fool to sorrow,
Angering itself and others.—*[To Gloucester.]* Bless thee, master!

Glo. Is that the naked fellow?

Old Man.   Ay, my lord.

Glo. Then, prithee, get thee gone. If, for my sake,
Thou wilt o'ertake us, hence a mile or twain,
I' th' way toward Dover, do it for ancient love;   *50*
And bring some covering for this naked soul
Which I'll entreat to lead me.

Old Man.   Alack, sir! he is mad.

Glo. 'Tis the times' plague, when madmen lead the blind.
Do as I bid thee, or rather do thy pleasure;   *55*
Above the rest, be gone.

Old Man. I'll bring him the best 'parel that I have,
Come on't what will.   *Exit.*

Glo. Sirrah, naked fellow,—

Edg. Poor Tom's a-cold. *[Aside.]* I cannot daub it further.   *60*

Glo. Come hither, fellow.

Edg. ⟨And yet I must.⟩ Bless thy sweet eyes, they bleed.

Glo. Know'st thou the way to Dover?

Edg. Both stile and gate, horse-way and footpath. Poor
Tom hath been scared out of his good wits. Bless thee, good   *65*
man's son, from the foul fiend! «Five fiends have been in poor
Tom at once: of lust, as Obidicut; Hobbididance, prince of
dumbness; Mahu, of stealing; Modo, of murder; Flibbertigibbet, of mopping and mowing, who since possesses chambermaids and waiting-women. So, bless thee, master!»   *70*

Glo. Here, take this purse, thou whom the heavens' plagues.
Have humbled to all strokes. That I am wretched
Makes thee the happier. Heavens, deal so still!
Let the superfluous and lust-dieted man,   *25*
That slaves your ordinance, that will not see
Because he does not feel, feel your power quickly.
So distribution should undo excess,
And each man have enough. Dost thou know Dover?

Edg. Ay, master.   *30*

Glo. There is a cliff, whose high and bending head
Looks fearfully in the confined deep.
Bring me but to the very brim of it,
And I'll repair the misery thou dost bear
With something rich about me. From that place   *35*
I shall no leading need.

Edg.   Give me thy arm.
Poor Tom shall lead thee.   *Exeunt.*

❧ Scene Second ❧

[Before Albany's Palace]
Enter Goneril and Bastard [Edmund].

Gon. Welcome, my lord! I marvel our mild husband
Not met us on the way.   *Enter Steward [Oswald].*
            Now, where's your master?

Osw. Madam, within; but never man so chang'd.
I told him of the army that was landed;   *5*
He smil'd at it. I told him you were coming;
His answer was, 'The worse!' Of Gloucester's treachery,
And of the loyal service of his son,
When I inform'd him, then he call'd me sot,
And told me I had turn'd the wrong side out.   *10*
What most he should dislike seems pleasant to him;
What like, offensive.

Gon. [To Edmund]. Then shall you go no further.
It is the cowish terror of his spirit
That dares not undertake. He'll not feel wrongs   *15*
Which tie him to an answer. Our wishes on the way
May prove effects. Back, Edmund, to my brother;
Hasten his musters and conduct his powers.
I must change names at home, and give the distaff
Into my husband's hands. This trusty servant   *20*
Shall pass between us. Ere long you are like to hear
(If you dare venture in your own behalf)
A mistress's command. Wear this.   *[Giving a jewel.]*
                    Spare speech;
Decline your head. This kiss, if it durst speak,   *25*
Would stretch thy spirits up into the air.
Conceive, and fare thee well.

Edm. Yours in the ranks of death.

Gon.   My most dear Gloucester!
                        Exit [Edmund].
⟨O the difference of man and man!⟩   *30*
To thee a woman' services are due;

74–78 Cf. n.   74 superfluous and lust-dieted: *over-rich and willful*   75 slaves; *cf. n.*   81 in the confined deep; *cf. n.*   1 Welcome; *cf. n.*   4 never man so chang'd; *cf. n.*   10 turn'd … out: *inverted right and wrong*   14 cowish: *easily cowed*   15 undertake: *assert itself*   16 tie him to: *require*   17 brother: *brother-in-law* (Cornwall)   19 names: *i.e., of husband and wife; cf. n.*   23 mistress's; *cf. n.*   24 Spare speech: *say nothing*   25 Decline: *bend down*   27 Conceive: *interpret my meaning*

22, 23 means … commodities; *cf. n.*   52 Which: *whom* ('who' Q)   60 daub it: *make poor pretence*   69 mopping and mowing: *making grimaces*

My foot usurps my body.

Osw.   Madam, here comes my lord.

                               Exit Steward.

Enter Albany.

Gon. I have been worth the whistling.

Alb.   O, Goneril,   35

You are not worth the dust which the rude wind
Blows in your face. «I fear your disposition.
That nature, which contemns it origin,
Cannot be border'd certain in itself;
She that herself will sliver and disbranch   40
From her material sap, perforce must wither
And come to deadly use.

Gon. No more; the text is foolish.

Alb. Wisdom and goodness to the vile seem vile;
Filths savor but themselves. What have you done?   45
Tigers, not daughters, what have you perform'd?
A father, and a gracious aged man,
Whose reverence even the head-lugg'd bear would lick,
Most barbarous, most degenerate! have you madded.
Could my good brother suffer you to do it?   50
A man, a prince, by him so benefited!
If that the heavens do not their visible spirits
Send quickly down to take these vile offences,
It will come,
Humanity must perforce prey on itself,   55
Like monsters of the deep.»

Gon.   Milk-liver'd man!

That bear'st a cheek for blows, a head for wrongs;
Who hast not in thy brows an eye discerning
Thine honor from thy suffering! «that not know'st   60
Fools do those villains pity who are punish'd
Ere they have done their mischief. Where's thy drum?
France spreads his banners in our noiseless land,
With plumed helm thy state begins to threat,
Whilst thou, a moral fool, sits still, and cries   65
'Alack! why does he so?'»

Alb.   See thyself, devil!

Proper deformity shows not in the fiend
So horrid as in woman.

Gon.   O vain fool!   70

«*Alb.* Thou changed and self-cover'd thing, for shame,
Be-monster not thy feature. Were't my fitness
To let these hands obey my blood,
They are apt enough to dislocate and tear
Thy flesh and bones. Howe'er thou art a fiend,   75
A woman's shape doth shield thee.

Gon. Marry! Your manhood!—Mew!»

Enter a Messenger.

«*Alb.* What news?»

Mess. O my good lord, the Duke of Cornwall's dead;
Slain by his servant, going to put out   80
The other eye of Gloucester.

Alb.   Gloucester's eyes!

Mess. A servant that he bred, thrill'd with remorse,
Oppos'd against the act, bending his sword
To his great master; who, thereat enrag'd,   85
Flew on him, and amongst them fell'd him dead,
But not without that harmful stroke which since
Hath pluck'd him after.

Alb.   This shows you are above,
You justicers, that these are our nether crimes   90
So speedily can venge! But, O poor Gloucester!
Lost he his other eye?

Mess.   Both, both, my lord.

This letter, madam, craves a speedy answer.
'Tis from your sister.   95

Gon. [*aside*].   One way I like this well;
But being widow, and my Gloucester with her,
May all the building in my fancy pluck
Upon my hateful life. Another way
This news is not so tart. [*To Messenger.*] I'll read and answer.   100

                                        Exit.

Alb. Where was his son when they did take his eyes?

Mess. Come with my lady hither.

Alb.   He is not here.

Mess. No, my good lord; I met him back again.

Alb. Knows he the wickedness?   105

Mess. Ay, my good lord. 'Twas he inform'd against him,
And quit the house on purpose that their punishment
Might have the freer course.

Alb.   Gloucester, I live
To thank thee for the love thou show'dst the king   110
And to revenge thine eyes. Come hither, friend.
Tell me what more thou know'st.   *Exeunt.*

❧ Scene Third ❧

[Near Dover]
Enter Kent and a Gentleman.

Kent. Why the King of France is so suddenly gone back
know you no reason?

Gent. Something he left imperfect in the state, which since
his coming forth is thought of; which imports to the kingdom
so much fear and danger that his personal return was most   5
required and necessary.

Kent. Who hath he left behind him general?

Gent. The Marshal of France, Monsieur la Far.

Kent. Did your letters pierce the queen to any demonstration of grief?   10

Gent. Ay, sir; she took them, read them in my presence;
And now and then an ample tear trill'd down
Her delicate cheek. It seem'd she was a queen
Over her passion, who most rebel-like
South to be king o'er her.   15

Kent.   O, then it mov'd her?

Gent. Not to a rage. Patience and sorrow strove

---

32 My ... body; *cf. n.*   **34 worth the whistling;** *cf. n.*   **37 fear:** *fear for*   **38 it:**
it's; cf. n.   **39 border'd certain:** *possessed of fixed limits or standards of conduct*   **40**
sliver and disbranch: *split and seve*   **41 material:** *that of which she is made*   **42 come**
... use: *grow poisonous*   **45** *Cf. n.*   **48 head-lugg'd:** *led about by a muzzle*   **51 A**
man: *i.e., Cornwall* **him:** *i.e., Lear*   **58** *Cf. n.*   **59, 60 discerning ... suffering:**
cf. n.   **61, 62 Fools ... mischief:** *cf. n.*   **63 noiseless:** *peaceful, unready*   **64 state**
... threat; *cf. n.*   **65 moral:** *moralizing*   **68 Proper deformity:** *inherent ugliness*   **70**
vain: *empty*   **71 self-cover'd:** *hypocritical*   **72 Be-monster not thy feature:** *don't let*
your whole appearance become beastly **my fitness:** *what is seemly in me*   **73 blood:** *pas-*
sion   **74 apt:** *ready*   **75 Howe'er:** *notwithstanding that*   **77 Mew:** *cf. n.*

83 remorse: *pity*   **104 back:** *on the way back*   **Scene Third;** *cf. n.*   **11 Ay, sir;**
cf. n.   **14 who:** *which*

Who should express her goodliest. You have seen
Sunshine and rain at once; her smiles and tears
Were like a better way. Those happy smilets   20
That play'd on her ripe lip seem'd not to know
What guests were in her eyes, which parted thence
As pearls from diamonds dropp'd. In brief,
Sorrow would be a rarity most belov'd,
If all could so become it.   25
   Kent.   Made she no verbal question?
   Gent. Faith, once or twice she heav'd the name of 'father'
Pantingly forth, as if it press'd her heart;
Cried, 'Sisters! sisters! Shame of ladies! sisters!
Kent! father! sisters! What, i' th' storm? i' th' night?   30
Let pity not believe 't!' There she shook
The holy water from her heavenly eyes
And clamor-moisten'd hair. Then away she started
To deal with grief alone.
   Kent.   It is the stars,   35
The stars above us, govern our conditions.
Else one self mate and make could no beget
Such different issues. You spoke not with her since?
   Gent. No.
   Kent. Was this before the king return'd?   40
   Gent.   No, since.
   Kent. Well, sir, the poor distressed Lear's i' th' town,
Who sometime, in his better tune, remembers
What we are come about, and by no means
Will yield to see his daughter.   45
   Gent.   Why, good sir?
   Kent. A sovereign shame so elbows him: his own
unkindness,
That stripp'd her from his benediction, turn'd her
To foreign casualties, gave her dear rights   50
To his dog-hearted daughters,—these things sting
His mind so venomously that burning shame
Detains him from Cordelia.
   Gent.   Alack, poor gentleman!
   Kent. Of Albany's and Cornwall's powers you heard not?   55
   Gent. 'Tis so, they are afoot.
   Kent. Well, sir, I'll bring you to our master Lear,
And leave you to attend him. Some dear cause
Will in concealment wrap me up awhile.
When I am known aright, you shall not grieve   60
Lending me this acquaintance. I pray you, go
Along with me.   *Exeunt.*

❧ Scene Fourth ❧

[A Highroad near Dover]
Enter with drum and colors, Cordelia, Gentlemen, Doctor, and
Soldiers.

   Cor. Alack, 'tis he! Why, he as met even now
As mad as the vex'd sea; singing aloud,
Crown'd with rank femiter and furrow weeds,

With hordocks, hemlock, nettles, cuckoo-flowers,
Darnel, and all the idle weeds that grow   5
In our sustaining corn. A century send forth;
Search every acre in the high-grown field,
And bring him to our eye.   *[Exit an Officer.]*
                        What can man's wisdom
In the restoring his bereaved sense?   10
He that helps him take all my outward worth.
   Doct. There is means, madam.
Our foster-nurse of nature is repose,
The which he lacks. That to provoke in him
Are many simples operative, whose power   15
Will close the eye of anguish.
   Cor.   All bless'd secrets,
All you unpublish'd virtues of the earth,
Spring with my tears! be aidant and remediate
In the good man's distress! Seek, seek for him,   20
Lest his ungovern'd rage dissolve the life
That wants the means to lead it.

Enter Messenger.

   Mess.   News, madam.
The British powers are marching hitherward.
   Cor. 'Tis known before. Our preparation stands   25
In expectation of them. O dear father,
It is thy business that I go about!
Therefore great France
My mourning and important tears hath pitied.
No blown ambition doth our arms incite,   30
But love, dear love, and our ag'd father's right,
Soon may I hear and see him!   *Exeunt.*

❧ Scene Fifth ❧

[Regan's Palace, Gloucester]
Enter Regan and Steward [Oswald].

   Reg. But are my brother's powers set forth?
   Osw.   Ay, madam.
   Reg. Himself in person there?
   Osw.   Madam, with much ado.
Your sister is the better soldier.   5
   Reg. Lord Edmund spake not with your lord at home?
   Osw. No, madam.
   Reg. What might import my sister's letter to him?
   Osw. I know not, lady.
   Reg. Faith, he is posted hence on serious matter.   10
It was great ignorance, Gloucester's eyes being out,
To let him live. Where he arrives he moves
All hearts against us. Edmund, I think, is gone,
In pity of his misery, to dispatch
His nighted life; moreover, to descry   15
The strength o' th' enemy.
   Osw. I must needs after him, madam, with my letter.
   Reg. Our troops set forth to-morrow. Stay with us;
The ways are dangerous.

---

20 better way: *like sunshine and rain, but in a nobler way*   **22 which:** *i.e., the 'guests'*
(tears)   **26 verbal question:** *oral conversation*   **31 believe 't;** *cf. n.*   **33 clamor-moist-**
en'd: *wet with lamentation; cf. n.*   **37 mate and make:** *husband and wife*   **43 sometime**
... tune; *cf. n.*   **47 elbows:** *jogs, disquiets*   **50 To foreign casualties:** *to take chances*
among foreigners   **56 so, they:** *true that the*   **3 femiter:** *fumitory, plant with bitter taste*

4 hordocks: *burdocks* (?)   **cuckoo-flowers:** *the ragged robin*   **5 Darnel:** *a coarse*
grass   **idle:** *worthless*   **6 century:** *company of one hundred men*   **15 simples:** *medicinal*
plants   **19 aidant and remediate:** *aiding and remedial*   **29 important:** *importu-*
nate   **Scene Fifth S.d.;** *Cf. n.*   **8 import:** *be the meaning of*

Osw.　　　　　　　I may not, madam.　　　　　20
My lady charg'd my duty in this business.
　　Reg. Why should she write to Edmund? Might not you
Transport her purposes by word? Belike,
Some things—I know not what. I'll love thee much,
Let me unseal the letter.　　　　　　　　　25
　　Osw.　　　　　　Madam, I had rather—
　　Reg. I know your lady does not love her husband.
I am sure of that, and at her late being here
She gave strange eliads and most speaking looks
To noble Edmund. I know you are of her bosom.　　30
　　Osw. I, madam?
　　Reg. I speak in understanding; you are, I know't.
Therefore I do advise you, take this note:
My lord is dead; Edmund and I have talk'd,
And more convenient is he for my hand　　　35
Than for your lady's. You may gather more.
If you do find him, pray you, give him this,
And when your mistress hears thus much from you,
I pray desire her call her wisdom to her.
So, fare you well.　　　　　　　　　40
If you do chance to hear of that blind traitor,
Preferment falls on him that cuts him off.
　　Osw. Would I could meet him, madam! I should show
What party I do follow.
　　Reg.　　　　　Fare thee well.　　　*Exeunt.*　　45

❧ SCENE SIXTH ❧

[The Country near Dover]
Enter Gloucester and Edgar.

　　Glo. When shall I come to th' top of that same hill?
　　Edg. You do climb up it now. Look how we labor.
　　Glo. Methinks the ground is even.
　　Edg.　　　　　　　　Horrible steep.
Hark! do you hear the sea?　　　　　　5
　　Glo.　　　　　No truly.
　　Edg. Why, then your other senses grow imperfect
By your eye's anguish.
　　Glo.　　　　So may it be, indeed.
Methinks thy voice is alter'd, and thou speak'st　　10
In better phrase and matter than thou didst.
　　Edg. Y'are much deceiv'd. In nothing am I chang'd
But in my garments.
　　Glo.　　　　Methinks y'are better spoken.
　　Edg. Come on, sir; here's the place. Stand still.　　15
How fearful
And dizzy 'tis to cast one's eyes so low!
The crows and choughs that wing the midway air
Show scarce so gross as beetles. Half way down
Hangs one that gathers samphire, dreadful trade!　　20
Methinks he seems no bigger than his head.
The fishermen that walk upon the beach.
Appear like mice, and yond tall anchoring bark
Diminish'd to her cock, her cock a buoy

Almost too small for sight. The murmuring surge,　　25
That on th' unnumber'd idle pebble chafes,
Cannot be heard so high. I'll look no more,
Lest my brain turn, and the deficient sight
Topple down headlong.
　　Glo.　　　　Set me where you stand.　　30
　　Edg. Give me your hand. You are now within a foot
Of th' extreme verge. For all beneath the moon
Would I not leap upright.
　　Glo.　　　　Let go my hand.
Here, friend, 's another purse; in it a jewel　　35
Well worth a poor man's taking. Fairies and gods
Prosper it with thee! Go thou further off.
Bid me farewell, and let me hear thee going.
　　Edg. Now fare ye well, good sir.
　　Glo.　　　　With all my heart.　　40
　　Edg. [aside]. Why I do trifle thus with his despair
Is done to cure it.
　　Glo.　　　O you mighty gods!　　*He kneels.*
This world I do renounce, and in your sights
Shake patiently my great affection off.　　45
If I could bear it longer, and not fall
To quarrel with your great opposeless wills,
My snuff and loathed part of nature should
Burn itself out. If Edgar live, O, bless him!
Now, fellow, fare thee well.　　　　　50
　　Edg.　　　　Gone, sir: farewell.

　　　　　　　　He [Gloucester] falls.

[Aside.] And yet I know not how conceit may rob
The treasury of life when life itself
Yields to the theft. Had he been where he thought,
By this had thought been past. Alive or dead?　　55
[To Gloucester.] Ho, you, sir! Friend! Hear you, sir? Speak!—
Thus might he pass indeed; yet he revives.—
What are you, sir?
　　Glo.　　　　Away and let me die.
　　Edg. Hadst thou been aught but gossamer, feathers, air　　60
(So many fathom down precipitating),
Thou'dst shiver'd like an egg; but thou dost breathe,
Hast heavy substance, bleed'st not, speak'st, art sound.
Ten masts at each make not the altitude
Which thou hast perpendicularly fell.　　65
Thy life's a miracle. Speak yet again.
　　Glo. But have I fallen or no?
　　Edg. From the dread summit of this chalky bourn.
Look up a-height! The shrill-gorg'd lark so far
Cannot be seen or heard. Do but look up.　　70
　　Glo. Alack! I have no eyes.
Is wretchedness depriv'd that benefit
To end itself by death? 'Twas yet some comfort,
When misery could beguile the tyrant's rage,
And frustrate his proud will.　　　　75
　　Edg.　　　　Give me your arm.
Up! So. How is't? Feel you your legs? You stand.
　　Glo. Too well, too well.
　　Edg.　　　　This is above all strangeness.
Upon the crown o' th' cliff, what thing was that　　80

---

24 **Some things;** *cf. n.*　26 **I had rather—;** *cf. n.*　29 **eliads:** *aillades, oglings*　30 **of her bosom:** *in her confidence*　33 **take this note:** *speak to her in this key*　39 **desire . . . her:** *i.e., tell her not to be a fool*　12 **deceiv'd:** *mistaken*　18 **choughs:** *bird of the crow family, jackdaw*　20 **samphire:** *samper, used for pickles*　24 **cock:** *cock-boat*

26 **unnumber'd:** *innumerable*　**pebble;** *cf. n.*　28 **deficient sight:** *cf. n.*　41, 42 **Why . . . cure it;** *cf. n.*　47 **opposeless:** *paramount*　48 **snuff;** *cf. n.*　51 **Gone, sir: farewell;** *cf. n.*　52–54 **conceit . . . theft;** *cf. n.*　64 **at each:** *one on another*　68 **summit;** *cf. n.*　**bourn:** *boundary*　69 **shrill-gorg'd:** *high-voiced*

Which parted from you?

Glo.   A poor unfortunate beggar.

Edg. As I stood here below, methought his eyes
Were two full moons; he had a thousand noses,
Horns whelk'd and wav'd like the enridged sea.   85
It was some fiend. Therefore, thou happy father,
Think that the clearest gods, who make them honors
Of men's impossibilities, have preserv'd thee.

Glo. I do remember now. Henceforth I'll bear
Affliction till it do cry out itself   90
'Enough, enough,' and die. That thing you speak of—
I took it for a man—often 'twould say
'The fiend, the fiend.' He led me to that place.

Edg. Bear free and patient thoughts.

Enter Lear, mad.

But who comes here?   95
The safer sense will ne'er accommodate
His master thus.

Lear. No, they cannot touch me for coining. I am the king
himself.

Edg. O thou side-piercing sight!   100

Lear. Nature's above art in that respect. There's your press
money. That fellow handles his bow like a crow-keeper: draw
me a clothier's yard. Look, look! a mouse. Peace, peace! this
piece of toasted cheese will do't. There's my gauntlet; I'll prove
it on a giant. Bring up the brown bills. O! Well flown,   105
bird! I' the clout, i' the clout: hewgh! Give the word.

Edg. Sweet marjoram.

Lear. Pass.

Glo. I know that voice.

Lear. Ha! Goneril, with a white beard! They flatter'd   110
me like a dog, and told me I had white hairs in my beard
ere the black ones were there. To say 'ay' and 'no' to everything
that I said! 'Ay' and 'no' too was no good divinity. When
the rain came to wet me once and the wind to make me chatter, when the thunder would not peace at my bidding, there   115
I found 'em, there I smelt 'em out. Go to! they are not
men o' their words. They told me I was everything. 'Tis a lie:
I am not ague-proof.

Glo. The trick of that voice I do well remember.
Isn't not the king?   120

Lear.   Ay, every inch a king!
When I do stare, see how the subject quakes.
I pardon that man's life. What was thy cause? Adultery? Thou
shalt not die. Die for adultery? No. The wren goes to't, and
the small gilded fly does lecher in my sight. Let copula-   125
tion thrive, for Gloucester's bastard son was kinder to his father than my daughters got 'tween the lawful sheets. To't luxury, pell-mell! for I lack soldiers. Behold yond simpering dame,
whose face between her forks presages snow, that minces virtue,
and does shake the head to hear of pleasure's name: the   130
fitchew nor the soiled horse goes to't with a more riotous appetite. Down from the waist they are centaurs, though women all

above. But to the girdle do the gods inherit, beneath is all the
fiends'. There's hell, there's darkness, there is the sulphurous
pit: burning, scalding, stench, consumption. Fie, fie, fie!   135
pah, pah! Give me an ounce of civet, good apothecary, to
sweeten my imagination. There's money for thee.

Glo. O let me kiss that hand!

Lear. Let me wipe it first. It smells of mortality.

Glo. O ruin'd piece of nature! This great world shall so   140
wear out to naught. Do you know me?

Lear. I remember thine eyes well enough. Dost thou squiny
at me? No, do thy worst, blind Cupid; I'll not love. Read thou
this challenge; mark but the penning of it.

Glo. Were all the letters suns, I could not see.   145

Edg. [aside]. I would not take this from report. It is, and
my heart breaks at it.

Lear. Read.

Glo. What! with the case of eyes?

Lear. O, ho! are you there with me? No eyes in your   150
head, nor no money in your purse? Your eyes are in a heavy
case, your purse in a light. Yet you see how this world goes.

Glo. I see it feelingly.

Lear. What! art mad? A man may see how this world goes
with no eyes. Look with thine ears. See how yond justice   155
rails upon yond simple thief. Hark, in thine ear: change places,
and, handy-dandy, which is the justice, which is the thief?
Thou hast seen a farmer's dog bark at a beggar?

Glo. Ay, sir.

Lear. And the creature run from the cur? There thou   160
mightst behold the great image of authority: a dog's obey'd
in office.
Thou rascal beadle, hold thy bloody hand!
Why dost thou lash that whore? Strip thy own back.
Thou hotly lusts to use her in that kind   165
For which thou whipp'st her. The usurer hangs the cozener.
Through totter'd rags small vices do appear;
Robes and furr'd gowns hide all. ⟨Plate sin with gold,
And the strong lance of justice hurtless breaks;
Arm it in rags, a pigmy's straw does pierce it.   170
None does offend, none, I say none. I'll able 'em.
Take that of me, my friend, who have the power
To seal th' accuser's lips.⟩ Get thee glass eyes;
And, like a scurvy politician, seem
To see the things thou dost not. Now, now, now, now.   175
Pull of my boots; harder, harder. So!

Edg. [aside]. O matter and impertinency mix'd!
Reason in madness!

Lear. If thou wilt weep my fortunes, take my eyes.
I know thee well enough; thy name is Gloucester.   180
Thou must be patient; we came crying hither.
Thou know'st the first time that we smell the air
We waul and cry. I will preach to thee: mark.

Glo. Alack! alack the day!

Lear. When we are born, we cry that we are come   185
To this great stage of fools. This' a good block!
It were a delicate stratagem to shoe
A troop of horse with felt. ⟨I'll put't in proof,⟩

85 whelk'd: *twisted*   86 fiend; *cf. n.*   87 clearest: *most serene*   96 safer: *saner* accommodate: *equip*   101 Nature's above art; *cf. n.*   101, 102 press-money: *money given
to soldiers when pressed into service* crow-keeper; *cf. n.*   103 clothier's yard: *cloth-yard
shaft, used with long bow*   105 brown bills: *halberds, or, men carrying them*   106 clout:
bull's-eye, bit of white cloth used for mark in archery   107 Sweet marjoram: *cf. n.*   111
white hairs: *the marks of wisdom*   113 'Ay' . . . divinity; *cf. n.*   123–137 *Cf. n.*   127
luxury: *lewdness*   129 forks: *legs; cf. n.* minces: *makes an affected show of*   131 fitchew:
polecat soiled: *overfed*   132 centaurs: *cf. n.*

141 Do you; *cf. n.*   142 squiny: *squint*   144 challenge; *cf. n.*   149 case: *sockets*   150 are you . . . me: *so that is it?*   157 handy-dandy; *cf. n.*   162 in office;
cf. n.   163 beadle: *parish police officer*   165 lusts; *cf. n.*   166 usurer: *rapacious or
'grafting' judge* cozener: *petty thief*   167 *Cf. n.*   168 Plate sin; *cf. n.*   171 able:
authorize   172 of me: *on my authority*   177 impertinency: *irrelevant talk*   177, 178
O matter . . . madness; *cf. n.*   186 This': *this is* block: *type of hat; cf. n.*

And when I have stol'n upon these son-in-laws,
Then, kill, kill, kill, kill, kill, kill!   *190*

Enter three Gentlemen.

   Gent. O here he is! lay hand upon him!—Sir,
Your most dear daughter—
   Lear. No rescue? What! a prisoner? I am even
The natural fool of fortune. Use me well;
You shall have ransom. Let me have surgeons;   *195*
I am cut to th' brains.
   Gent.   You shall have anything.
   Lear. No seconds? All myself?
Why this would make ⟨a man,⟩ a man of salt,
To use his eyes for garden water-pots,   *200*
«Ay, and laying autumn's dust.
   Gent.   Good sir,—
   Lear.» I will die bravely like a smug bridegroom.
What! I will be jovial. Come, come! I am a king.
Masters, know you that?   *205*
   Gent. You are a royal one, and we obey you.
   Lear. Then there's life in't. Nay, an you get it, you shall get
it by running. Sa, sa, sa, sa!   *Exit King, running.*
   Gent. A sight most pitiful in the meanest wretch,
Past speaking of in a king! Thou hast one daughter,   *210*
Who redeems nature from the general curse
Which twain have brought her to.
   Edg. Hail, gentle sir!
   Gent.   Sir, speed you. What's your will?
   Edg. Do you hear aught, sir, of a battle toward?   *215*
   Gent. Most sure and vulgar; every one hears that,
Which can distinguish sound.
   Edg.   But, by your favor,
How near's the other army?
   Gent. Near, and on speedy foot. The main descry   *220*
Stands on the hourly thought.
   Edg.   I thank you, sir: that's all.
   Gent. Though that the queen on special cause is here,
Her army is mov'd on.   *Exit.*
   Edg.   I thank you, sir.   *225*
   Glo. You ever-gentle gods, take my breath from me.
Let not my worser spirit tempt me again
To die before you please.
   Edg.   Well pray you, father.
   Glo. Now, good sir, what are you?   *230*
   Edg. A most poor man, made tame to fortune's blows,
Who, by the art of known and feeling sorrows,
Am pregnant to good pity. Give me your hand,
I'll lead you to some biding.
   Glo.   Hearty thanks.   *235*
The bounty and the benison of heaven
To boot, and boot!

Enter Steward [Oswald].

   Osw.   A próclaim'd prize! Most happy!
That eyeless head of thine was first fram'd flesh
To raise my fortunes. Thou old unhappy traitor,   *240*

Briefly thyself remember. The sword is out
That must destroy thee.
   Glo.   Now let thy friendly hand
Put strength enough to't.   *[Edgar interposes.]*
   Osw.   Wherefore, bold peasant,   *245*
Dar'st thou support a publish'd traitor? Hence!
Lest that th' infection of his fortune take
Like hold on thee. Let go his arm.
   Edg. Chill not let go, zir, without vurther 'casion.
   Osw. Let go, slave, or thou diest.   *250*
   Edg. Good gentlemen, go your gait, and let poor volk pass.
And chud ha' bin zwaggered out of my life, 'twould not ha'
bin zo long as 'tis by a vortnight. Nay, come not near th' old
man. Keep out, che vor ye, or ise try whether your costard or
my batoon be the harder. Chill be plain with you.   *255*
   Osw. Out, dunghill!
   Edg. Chill pick your teeth, zir. Come; no matter vor your
foins.   *They fight.*
   Osw. Slave, thou hast slain me. Villain, take my purse.
If ever thou wilt thrive, bury my body;   *260*
And give the letters which thou find'st about me
To Edmund Earl of Gloucester. Seek him out
Upon the British party. O untimely death!
Death!   *He dies.*
   Edg. I know thee well: a serviceable villain,   *265*
As duetous to the vices of thy mistress.
As badness would desire.
   Glo.   What! is he dead?
   Edg. Sit you down, father; rest you.
Let's see his pockets. These letters that he speaks of   *270*
May be my friends. He's dead. I am only sorry
He had no other deaths-man. Let us see.—
Leave, gentle wax! and, manners, blame us not.
To know our enemies' minds, we rip their hearts;
Their papers, is more lawful.   *Reads the letter.*   *275*

    Let our reciprocal vows be remembered. You have many
opportunities to cut him off. If your will want not, time and
place will be fruitfully offered. There is nothing done if he
return the conqueror. Then am I the prisoner, and his bed
my gaol, from the loathed warmth whereof deliver me,   *280*
and supply the place for your labor.
    Your wife (so I would say), your affectionate servant, «*and*
for you her own tormentor,»

                                          Goneril.

O undistinguished space of woman's will!   *285*
A plot upon her virtuous husband's life,
And the exchange my brother! Here, in the sands,
Thee I'll rake up, the post unsanctified
Of murtherous lechers; and in the mature time
With this ungracious paper strike the sight   *290*
Of the death-practis'd duke. For him 'tis well
That of thy death and business I can tell.
   Glo. The king is mad. How stiff is my vile sense,
That I stand up, and have ingenious feeling

190 S.d. Cf. n.   195 ransom; cf. n.   199 man of salt; cf. n.   202 Good sir;
cf. n.   207 life in't: still hope   214 speed you: God prosper you   216 vulgar: common   220 on speedy foot: approaching fast   main descry, etc.; cf. n.   233 pregnant:
ready, receptive   234 biding: abiding place   237 To boot, and boot; cf. n.

241 thyself remember: think of your sins   249 Chill: I will; cf. n.   252 And chud: if
I should   254 che vor ye: I warn you; cf. n.   costard: apple, used jokingly for head   batoon: cudgel; cf. n.   258 foins: thrusts   263 British party; cf. n.   273 Leave: give
leave   277 want not: be not wanting   282, 283 and . . . tormenter;
cf. n.   285 undistinguish'd space: incalculable scope   288 rake up: cover   289 in
. . . time: when the time is ripe   291 death-practis'd: mortally plotted against   293 stiff:
tough.   294 ingenious: conscious

Of my huge sorrows! Better I were distract.   295
So should my thoughts be fenced from my griefs,
And woes by wrong imaginations lose
The knowledge of themselves.   *A drum afar off.*

   Edg.   Give me your hand!
Far off, methinks, I hear the beaten drum.   300
Come, father, I'll bestow you with a friend.

                                                   Exeunt.

❧ SCENE SEVENTH ❧

[A Tent in the French Camp]
Enter Cordelia, Kent, and Doctor [with a Gentleman].

   Cor. O thou good Kent! how shall I live and work
To match thy goodness? My life will be too short,
And every measure fail me.

   Kent. To be acknowledg'd, madam, is o'erpaid.
All my reports go with the modest truth,   5
Nor more nor clipp'd, but so.

   Cor.   Be better suited.
These weeds are memories of those worser hours.
I prithee, put them off.

   Kent.   Pardon me, dear madam.   10
Yet to be known shortens my made intent.
My boon I make it that you know me not
Till time and I think meet.

   Cor. Then be't so, my good lord.—[To the Doctor.]
How does the king?   15

   Doct. Madam, sleeps still.

   Cor.   O you kind gods,
Cure this great breach in his abused nature!
Th' untun'd and jarring senses O wind up
Of this child-changed father!   20

   Doct.   So please your majesty
That we may wake the king? He hath slept long.

   Cor. Be govern'd by your knowledge, and proceed
I' th' sway of your own will. Is he array'd?

   Doct. Ay, madam; in the heaviness of sleep,   25
We put fresh garments on him.

Enter Lear in a chair carried by Servants.

Be by, good madam, when we do awake him;
I doubt not of his temperance.

   «*Cor.*   Very well.

   Doct. Please you, draw near. Louder the music there.»   30

   Cor. O my dear father! Restoration, hang
Thy medicine on my lips, and let this kiss
Repair those violent harms that my two sisters
Have in thy reverence made!

   Kent.   Kind and dear princess!   35

   Cor. Had you not been their father, these white flakes
Had challeng'd pity of them. Was this a face
To be expos'd against the warring winds?
«To stand against the deep dread-bolted thunder
In the most terrible and nimble stroke   40

Of quick cross lightning? to watch—poor pérdu!—
With this thin helm?» Mine enemy's dog,
Though he had bit me, should have stood that night
Against my fire. And wast thou fain, poor father,
To hovel thee with swine and rogues forlorn   45
In short and musty straw? Alack! alack!
'Tis wonder that thy life and wits at once
Had not concluded all. He wakes. Speak to him.

   Doct. Madam, do you; 'tis fittest.

   Cor. How does my royal lord? How fares your   50
majesty?

   Lear. You do me wrong to take me out o' th' grave.
Thou art a soul in bliss; but I am bound
Upon a wheel of fire, that mine own tears
Do scald like molten lead.   55

   Cor.   Sir, do you know me?

   Lear. You are a spirit, I know. Where did you die?

   Cor. Still, still, far wide.

   Doct. He's scarce awake. Let him alone awhile.

   Lear. Where have I been? Where am I? Fair daylight!   60
I am mightily abus'd. I should e'en die with pity
To see another thus. I know not what to say.
I will not swear these are my hands. Let's see.
I feel this pin prick. Would I were assur'd
Of my condition!   65

   Cor.   O look upon me, sir,
And hold your hands in benediction o'er me.
«No, sir,» you must not kneel.

   Lear.   Pray do not mock me.
I am a very foolish fond old man,   70
Fourscore and upward, ⟨not an hour more or less;⟩
And to deal plainly,
I fear I am not in my perfect mind.
Methinks I should know you and know this man;
Yet I am doubtful, for I am mainly ignorant   75
What place this is, and all the skill I have
Remembers not these garments; nor I know not
Where I did lodge last night. Do not laugh at me;
For, as I am a man, I think this lady
To be my child Cordelia.   80

   Cor.   And so I am, ⟨I am.⟩

   Lear. Be your tears wet? Yes, faith. I pray, weep not.
If you have poison for me, I will drink it.
I know you do not love me, for your sisters
Have (as I do remember) done me wrong.   85
You have some cause, they have not.

   Cor.   No cause, no cause.

   Lear. Am I in France?

   Kent.   In your own kingdom, sir.

   Lear. Do not abuse me.   90

   Doct. Be comforted, good madam. The great rage,
You see, is cur'd in him «and yet it is danger
To make him even o'er the time he has lost.»
Desire him to go in; trouble him no more
Till further settling.   95

   Cor. Will't please your highness walk?

   Lear.   You must bear with me.
Pray you now, forget and forgive. I am old and foolish.

---

296 **fenced:** *cf. n.*   **Scene Seventh.** *Cf. n.*   5 **modest:** *measured*   6 **Nor ... clipp'd:** *neither exaggerated nor palliated*   7 **Be better suited:** *dress your self more suitably to your rank*   8 **weeds:** *clothes*   11 **made intent:** *fixed purpose* **Yet ... intent:** *cf. n.*   12 **My boon I make it:** *I ask as a favor*   20 **child-changed:** *cf. n.*   28 **temperance:** *mental balance*   36 **flakes:** *locks of hair*   37, 38 **Was ... winds;** *cf. n.*

41 **pérdu:** *soldier on detached and dangerous sentry duty*   42 **this thin helm:** *only his bare skull*   48 **all:** *entirely*   54 **that:** *so that*   75 **mainly:** *mightily*   92 **cur'd;** *cf. n.*   93 **even o'er:** *smooth out, clear up*

　　　　　　　　　　　Exeunt. Manent Kent and Gent.

«*Gent.* Holds it true, sir, that the Duke of Cornwall was
so slain?　　　　　　　　　　　　　　　　　　　　　　*100*

　Kent. Most certain, sir.

　Gent. Who is conductor of his people?

　Kent. As 'tis said, the bastard son of Gloucester.

　Gent. They say Edgar, his banished son, is with the Earl
of Kent in Germany.　　　　　　　　　　　　　　　　*105*

　Kent. Report is changeable. 'Tis time to look about; the
powers of the kingdom approach apace.

　Gent. The arbitrement is like to be bloody. Fare you well,
sir.　　　　　　　　　　　　　　　　　　　　　　　*[Exit.]*

　Kent. My point and period will be throughly wrought,　*110*
Or well or ill, as this day's battle's fought.　　　　　　*Exit.*

ACT FIFTH ❧ SCENE FIRST

[The British Camp near Dover]
Enter, with drum and colors, Edmund, Regan, Gentlemen, and
Soldiers.

　Edm. Know of the duke if his last purpose hold,
Or whether since he is advis'd by aught
To change the course. He's full of alteration
And self-preproving. Bring his constant pleasure.
　　　　　　　　　　　　　[To one, who goes out.]

　Reg. Our sister's man is certainly miscarried.　　　　*5*

　Edm. 'Tis to be doubted, madam.

　Reg.　　　　　　　　　　　Now, sweet lord,
You know the goodness I intend upon you.
Tell me, but truly, but then speak the truth,
Do you not love my sister?　　　　　　　　　　　　*10*

　Edm.　　　　　　　　In honor'd love.

　Reg. But have you never found my brother's way
To the forefended place?

　«*Edm.*　　　　　　　That thought abuses you.

　Reg. I am doubtful that you have been conjunct　　　*15*
And bosom'd with her, as far as we call hers.»

　Edm. No, by mine honor, madam.

　Reg. I never shall endure her. Dear my lord,
Be not familiar with her.

　Edm.　　　　　　　Fear «me» not.　　　　　　*20*
She and the duke her husband!

　　Enter with drum and colors, Albany, Goneril, Soldiers.

　«*Gon. [aside].* I had rather lose the battle than that sister
Should loosen him and me.»

　Alb. Our very loving sister, well be-met.
Sir, this I heard, the king is come to his daughter,　　*25*
With others whom the rigor of our state
Forc'd to cry out. «Where I could not be honest
I never yet was valiant. For this business,
It touches us, as France invades our land,
Not bolds the king, with others whom, I fear,　　　　*30*
Most just and heavy causes make oppose.

　Edm. Sir, you speak nobly.»

　Reg.　　　　　　　　　Why is this reason'd?

　Gon. Combine together 'gainst the enemy,
For these domestic poor particulars　　　　　　　　*35*
Are not to question here.

　Alb.　　　　　　　　Let's then determine
With th' ancient of war on our proceeding.

　«*Edm.* I shall attend you presently at your tent.»

　Reg. Sister, you'll go with us?　　　　　　　　*40*

　Gon. No.

　Reg. 'Tis most convenient. Pray you, go with us.

　Gon. [aside]. O, ho! I know the riddle. *[Aloud.]* I will go.
　　　　　　　　　　　Exeunt both the Armies.

　　　　　　　　　　Enter Edgar.

　Edg. If e'er your Grace had speech with man so poor,
Hear me one word.　　　　　　　　　　　　　　*45*

　Alb.　　　　　　　I'll overtake you.—Speak.
　　　　　　　　　Exeunt [Edmund, Regan, Congeril].

　Edg. Before you fight the battle, ope this letter.
If you have victory, let the trumpet sound
For him that brought it. Wretched though I seem,
I can produce a champion that will prove　　　　　*50*
What is avouched there. If you miscarry,
Your business of the world hath so an end,
⟨And machination ceases.⟩ Fortune love you!

　Alb. Stay till I have read the letter.

　Edg.　　　　　　　　I was forbid it.　　　*55*
When time shall serve, let but the herald cry,
And I'll appear again.　　　　　　　　　　　　*Exit.*

　Alb. Why, fare thee well. I will o'erlook thy paper.

　　　　　　　　　　Enter Edmund.

　Edm. The enemy's in view; draw up your powers.
Here is the guess of their true strength and forces　　*60*
By diligent discovery; but your haste
Is now urg'd on you.

　Alb.　　　　　　　We will greet the time.
　　　　　　　　　　　　　　　　　　　　Exit.

　Edm. To both these sisters have I sworn my love,
Each jealous of the other as the stung　　　　　　*65*
Are of the adder. Which of them shall I take?
Both? one? or neither? Neither can be enjoy'd
If both remain alive. To take the widow
Exasperates, makes mad, her sister Goneril;
And hardly shall I carry out my side,　　　　　　*70*
Her husband being alive. Now then, we'll use
His countenance for the battle; which being done
Let her who would be rid of him devise
His speedy taking off. As for the mercy
Which he intends to Lear and to Cordelia,　　　　*75*
The battle done, and they within our power,
Shall never see his pardon; for my state
Stands on me to defend, not to debate.　　　　　*Exit.*

⹔ SCENE SECOND ⹔

[A Field between the two Camps]

Alarum. Enter the powers of France over the stage, Cordelia with
her father in her hand, and exeunt. Enter Edgar and Gloucester.

Edg. Here, father, take the shadow of this bush
For your good host; pray that the right may thrive.
If ever I return to you again,
I'll bring you comfort.
   Glo.   Grace go with you, sir!   5
                                         Exit [Edgar].

Alarum and Retreat within. Enter Edgar.

Edg. Away, old man! give me thy hand. Away!
King Lear hath lost, he and his daughter ta'en.
Give me thy hand. Come on.
   Glo. No farther, sir. A man may rot even here.
   Edg. What! in ill thoughts again? Men must endure   10
Their going hence, even as their coming hither.
Ripeness is all. Come on.
   ⟨*Glo.*   And that's true too.⟩   *Exeunt.*

⹔ SCENE THIRD ⹔

[The British Camp, near Dover]

Enter, in conquest, with drum and colors, Edmund; Lear and
Cordelia as prisoners, Soldiers, Captain.

Edm. Some officers take them away! Good guard,
Until their greater pleasures first be known
That are to censure them.
   Cor.   We are not the first
Who, with best meaning, have incurr'd the worst.   5
For thee, oppressed king, I am cast down;
Myself could else out-frown false Fortune's frown.
Shall we not see these daughters and these sisters?
   Lear. No, no ⟨,no, no⟩! Come, let's away to prison.
We two alone will sing like birds i' th' cage.   10
When thou dost ask me blessing, I'll kneel down,
And ask for thee forgiveness. So we'll live,
And pray, and sing, and tell old tales, and laugh
At gilded butterflies, and hear poor rogues
Talk of court news; and we'll talk with them too: 15
Who loses and who wins, who's in, who's out;
And take upon's the mystery of things,
As if we were God's spies; and we'll wear out,
In a wall'd prison, packs and sects of great ones
That ebb and flow by th' moon.   20
   Edm.   Take them away.
   Lear. Upon such sacrifices, my Cordelia,
The gods themselves throw incense. Have I caught thee?
He that parts us shall bring a brand from heaven,
And fire us hence like foxes. Wipe thine eyes.   25
The good years shall devour them, flesh and fell,

Ere they shall make us weep. We'll see 'em starv'd first.
Come.   *Exit [with Cordelia, guarded].*
   Edm. Come hither, captain; hark.
Take thou this note. *[Gives a paper.]* Go follow them to   30
prison.
One step I have advanc'd thee. If thou dost
As this instructs thee, thou dost make thy way
To noble fortunes. Know thou this, that men
Are as the time is; to be tender-minded   35
Does not become a sword. Thy great employment
Will not bear question. Either say thou'lt do't,
Or thrive by other means.
   Capt.   I'll do't, my lord.
   Edm. About it; and write happy when thou'st done.   40
Mark! I say, instantly, and carry it so
As I have set it down.
   «*Capt.* I cannot draw a cart nor eat dried oats.
If it be man's work I'll do't.»   *Exit Captain.*

Flourish. Enter Albany, Goneril, Regan, Soldiers.

   Alb. Sir, you have show'd to-day your valiant strain,   45
And fortune led you well. You have the captives
Who were the opposites of this day's strife.
I do require them of you, so to use them
As we shall find their merits and our safety
May equally determine.   50
   Edm.   Sir, I thought it fit
To send the old and miserable king
To some retention «and appointed guard»,
Whose age has charms in it, whose title more,
To pluck the common bosom on his side,   55
And turn our impress'd lances in our eyes
Which do command them. With him I sent the queen—
My reason all the same; and they are ready
To-morrow, or at further space, t'appear
Where you shall hold your session. «At this time   60
We sweat and bleed, the friend hath lost his friend;
And the best quarrels in the heat are curs'd
By those that feel their sharpness.
The question of Cordelia and her father
Requires a fitter place.»   65
   Alb.   Sir, by your patience,
I hold you but a subject of this war,
Not as a brother.
   Reg.   That's as we list to grace him.
Methinks our pleasure might have been demanded,   70
Ere you had spoke so far. He led our powers,
Bore the commission of my place and person;
The which immediacy may well stand up,
And call itself your brother.
   Gon.   Not so hot!   75
In his own grace he doth exalt himself
More than in your addition.
   Reg.   In my rights,
By me invested, he compeers the best.

Scene Second S.d. *in her hand: his hand clasped in hers; cf. n.*   **1 bush;** *cf. n.*   **12**
Ripeness: *readiness; cf. n.*   **Scene Third. S.d.** *Cf. n.*   **1 Good guard:** *guard them*
well   **2 their greater pleasures;** *cf. n.*   **17, 18** *Cf. n.*   **19 packs and sects;**
cf. n.   **22 sacrifices:** *i.e., of liberty; cf. n.*   **24, 25 He . . . foxes;** *cf. n.*   **26 good**
years; *cf. n.*   **fell:** *skin*

36, 37 Thy . . . question; *cf. n.*   **40 write happy:** *call yourself lucky*   **43** *Cf. n.*   **44**
man's work: *anything a man can do*   **S.d.** *Cf. n.*   **46 led you well:** *was good to you*   **48**
I; *cf. n.*   **53 retention:** *detention*   **55 common bosom:** *affection of the populace*   **56**
impress'd: *enlisted*   **62, 63** *Cf. n.*   **70 demanded:** *inquired*   **73 immediacy:** *position*
as my direct agent   **77 your addition;** *cf. n.*   **79 compeers:** *equals*

Alb. That were the most, if he should husband you.   80
Reg. Jesters do oft prove prophets.
Gon.   Holla, holla!
That eye that told you so look'd but a-squint.
    Reg. Lady, I am not well; else I should answer
From a full-flowing stomach. General,   85
Take thou my soldiers, prisoners, patrimony.
⟨Dispose of them, of me; the whole is thine.⟩
Witness the world, that I create thee here
My lord and master.
    Gon.   Mean you to enjoy him?   90
    Alb. The let-alone lies not in your good will.
    Edm. Nor in thine, lord.
    Alb.   Half-blooded fellow, yes.
    Reg. [to Edmund.]. Let the drum strike, and prove my
title thine.   95
    Alb. Stay yet. Hear reason. Edmund, I arrest thee
On capital treason; and, in thine attaint,
This gilded serpent [pointing to Goneril]. For your claim,
    fair sister,
I bar it in the interest of my wife.   100
'Tis she is sub-contracted to this lord,
And I, her husband, contradict your bans.
If you will marry, make your love to me;
My lady is bespoke.
    ⟨*Gon.*   An interlude!   105
    Alb.⟩ Thou art arm'd, Gloucester. ⟨Let the trumpet sound.⟩
If none appear to prove upon thy person
Thy heinous, manifest, and many treasons,
There is my pledge! [Throws down a glove.] I'll mark it on
thy heart.   110
Ere I taste bread, thou art in nothing less
Than I have here proclaim'd thee.
    Reg.   Sick! O sick!
    Gon. [aside]. If not, I'll ne'er trust medicine.
    Edm. There's my exchange. [Throws down a glove.]   115
What in the world he is
That names me traitor, villain-like he lies.
Call by thy trumpet. He that dares approach,
On him, on you—who not?—I will maintain
My truth and honor firmly.   120
    Alb. A herald, ho!
    «*Edm.*   A herald, ho! a herald!
    Alb.» Trust to thy single virtue; for thy soldiers,
All levied in my name, have in my name
Took their discharge.   125
    Reg.   My sickness grows upon me.
    Alb. She is not well. Convey her to my tent.
                           [Exit Regan, led.]

                 Enter a Herald.

Come hither, herald. Let the trumpet sound,
And read out this.
    «*Capt.* Sound, trumpet!»   *A trumpet sounds.*   130

                 Herald reads.

If any man of quality or degree within the lists of the army

will maintain upon Edmund, supposed Earl of Gloucester, that
he is a manifold traitor, let him appear by the third sound of
the trumpet. He is bold in his defence.

    «*Edm.* Sound!»   *1 Trumpet.*
    Her. Again!   *2 Trumpet.*
    Her. Again!   *3 Trumpet.*
                   Trumpet answers within.

Enter Edgar, armed, at the third sound, a trumpet before him.

    Alb. Ask him his purposes, why he appears
Upon this call o' th' trumpet.
    Her.   What are you?   140
Your name? Your quality? and why you answer
This present summons?
    Edg.   Know, my name is lost,
By treason's tooth bare-gnawn and canker-bit.
Yet am I noble as the adversary   145
I come to cope.
    Alb.   Which is that adversary?
    Edg. What's he that speaks for Edmund earl of
Gloucester?
    Edm. Himself. What sayst thou to him?   150
    Edg.   Draw thy sword,
That, if my speech offend a noble heart,
Thy arm may do thee justice. Here is mine:
Behold, it is the privilege of my tongue,
My oath, and my profession. I protest,   155
Maugre thy strength, youth, place, and eminence,
Despite thy victor sword and fire-new fortune,
Thy valor and thy heart, thou art a traitor,
False to thy gods, thy brother, and thy father,
Conspirant 'gainst this high illustrious prince,   160
And, from th' extremest upward of thy head
To the descent and dust beneath thy feet,
A most toad-spotted traitor. Say thou 'No.'
This sword, this arm, and my best spirits are bent
To prove upon thy heart, whereto I speak,   165
Thou liest.
    Edm.   In wisdom I should ask thy name;
But since thy outside looks so fair and warlike,
And that thy tongue some say of breeding breathes,
⟨What safe and nicely I might well delay⟩   170
By rule of knighthood, I disdain and spurn.
Back do I toss those treasons to thy head,
With the hell-hated lie o'erwhelm thy heart,
Which, for they yet glance by and scarcely bruise,
This sword of mine shall give them instant way,   175
Where they shall rest for ever. Trumpets, speak!
               Alarums. Fights. [Edmund falls.]
    Alb. Save him, save him!
    Gon.   This is mere practice, Gloucester.
By th' law of arms thou wast not bound to answer
An unknown opposite. Thou art not vanquish'd,   180
But cozen'd and beguil'd.
    Alb.   Stop your mouth, dame,

---

80 the most: *the most he could claim; cf. n.*   **85 stomach:** *passion*   **87** *Cf. n.*   **91 let-alone:** *quit-claim; cf. n.*   **94** *Cf. n.*   **97 attaint;** *cf. n.*   **105 An interlude:** *'This is as good as a play'*   **109 mark:** *cf. n.*   **123 single virtue:** *unaided valor*   **131 lists:** *limits, borders*

132 supposed: *putative, soi-distant*   **S.d.** *trumpet: trumpeter*   **144 canker-bit:** *worm-eaten*   **146 cope:** *meet*   **153 mine:** *my sword*   **154 privilege:** *warrant; cf. n.*   **156 Maugre:** *despite*   **162 descent and dust:** *dusty depth (hendiadys)*   **169 say:** *smack, hint*   **170 safe and nicely:** *prudently and fastidiously; cf. n.*   **172, 173 treasons, lie;** *cf. n.*   **182, 183 Stop . . . it;** *cf. n.*

Or with this paper shall I stopple it. ⟨Hold, sir.⟩
Thou worse than any name, read thine own evil.—
No tearing, lady; I perceive you know it.   185
   Gon. Say, if I do. The laws are mine, not thine.
Who can arraign me for't?
   Alb.   Most monstrous!
Know'st thou this paper?
   Gon.   Ask me not what I know.   190
                                          Exit Goneril.
   Alb. Go after her. She's desperate; govern her.
                                  [Exit an Officer.]
   Edm. What you have charg'd me with, that have I done,
And more, much more. The time will bring it out.
'Tis past, and so am I. But what art thou.
That hast this fortune on me? If thou'rt noble,   195
I do forgive thee.
   Edg.   Let's exchange charity.
I am no less in blood than thou art, Edmund;
If more, the more thou'st wrong'd me.
My name is Edgar, and thy father's son.   200
The gods are just, and of our pleasant vices
Make instruments to plague us:
The dark and vicious place where thee he got
Cost him his eyes.
   Edm.   Thou'st spoken right. 'Tis true.   205
The wheel is come full circle; I am here.
   Alb. Methought thy very gait did prophesy
A royal nobleness. I must embrace thee.
Let sorrow split my heart, if ever I
Did hate thee or thy father.   210
   Edg.   Worthy prince, I know't.
   Alb. Where have you hid yourself?
How have you known the miseries of your father?
   Edg. By nursing them, my lord. List a brief tale;
And, when 'tis told, O that my heart would burst!   215
The bloody proclamation to escape
That follow'd me so near—(O our lives' sweetness!
That we the pain of death would hourly die
Rather than die at once!)—taught me to shift
Into a madman's rags, t'assume a semblance   220
That very dogs disdain'd: and in this habit
Met I my father with his bleeding rings,
Their precious stones new lost; became his guide,
Led him, begg'd for him, sav'd him from despair;
Never, (O fault!) reveal'd myself unto him,   225
Until some half hour past, when I was arm'd,
Not sure, though hoping, of this good success.
I ask'd his blessing, and from first to last
Told him my pilgrimage; but his flaw'd heart
(Alack! too weak the conflict to support)   230
'Twixt two extremes of passion, joy and grief,
Burst smilingly.
   Edm.   This speech of yours hath mov'd me,
And shall perchance do good; but speak you on.
You look as you had something more to say.   235
   Alb. If there be more, more woeful, hold it in;
For I am almost ready to dissolve,
Hearing of this.
   «*Edg.*   This would have seem'd a period

To such as love not sorrow; but another   240
To amplify too much, would make much more,
And top extremity. Whilst I was big
In clamor came there in a man,
Who, having seen me in my worst estate,
Shunn'd my abhorr'd society; but then, finding   245
Who 'twas that so endur'd, with his strong arms
He fasten'd on my neck, and bellow'd out
As he'd burst heaven; threw him on my father,
Told the most piteous tale of Lear and him
That ever ear receiv'd; which is recounting   250
His grief grew puissant, and the strings of life
Began to crack. Twice then the trumpets sounded,
And there I left him tranc'd.
   Alb.   But who was this?
   Edg. Kent, sir, the banish'd Kent; who in disguise   255
Follow'd his enemy king, and did him service
Improper for a slave.»

               Enter a Gentleman with a bloody knife.

   Gent. Help, help! O help!
   Edg.   What kind of help?
   ⟨*Alb.*   Speak, man.   260
   Edg.⟩ What means this bloody knife?
   Gent.   'Tis hot, it smokes;
It came even from the heart of—⟨O! she's dead.⟩
   Alb. Who dead? speak, man.
   Gent. Your lady, sir, your lady; and her sister   265
By her is poison'd. She confesses it.
   Edm. I was contracted to them both. All three
Now marry in an instant.
   Edg.   Here comes Kent, sir.

               Enter Kent.

   Alb. Produce the bodies, be they alive or dead.   270
This judgment of the heavens, that makes us tremble,
Touches us not with pity. *[To Kent.]*
                            O! is this he?
The time will not allow the compliment
Which very manners urges.   275
   Kent.   I am come
To bid my king and master aye good-night;
Is he not here?
   Alb.   Great thing of us forgot!
Speak, Edmund, where's the king? and where's Cordelia?   280
          The bodies of Goneril and Regan are brought in.
Seest thou this object, Kent?
   Kent.   Alack! why thus?
   Edm. Yet Edmund was belov'd. The one the other
Poison'd for my sake, and after slew herself.
   Alb. Even so. Cover their faces.   285
   Edm. I pant for life. Some good I mean to do
Despite of mine own nature. Quickly send,
(Be brief in it!) to th' castle, for my writ
Is on the life of Lear and on Cordelia.
Nay, send in time.   290
   Alb.   Run, run! O run!

183 stopple: *close as with a bung or cork*   **190 Ask ... know;** *cf. n.*   **206 I am here;**
cf. n.   **216** *Cf. n.*   **222 rings:** *eye-sockets*   **239 period:** *full stop* (the ultimate)

240–242 but another ... extremity; *cf. n.*   **244, 245 having ... society;** *cf. n.*   **248
threw him;** *cf. n.*   **258–260** *Cf. n.*   **268, 269** *Cf. n.*   **277 aye:** *forever*   **284**
Cf. n.   **288 brief:** *hasty*   **castle:** *Dover Castle*

Edg. To who, my lord? *[To Edmund.]* Who has the
office? Send.
Thy token of reprieve.
    Edm.   Well thought on. Take my sword,   *295*
Give it the captain.
    Alb.   Haste thee, for thy life.
                                  [Exit Edgar.]
    Edm. He hath commission from thy wife and me
To hang Cordelia in the prison, and
To lay the blame upon her own despair,   *300*
That she fordid herself.
    Alb. The gods defend her! Bear him hence awhile.
                          [Edmund is borne off.]

    Enter Lear, with Cordelia in his arms [followed by Edgar,
                  Captain, and others].

    Lear. Howl, howl, howl, howl! O, you are men of stones!
Had I your tongues and eyes, I'd use them so
That heaven's vault should crack. She's gone for ever.   *305*
I know when one is dead, and when one lives.
She's dead as earth. Lend me a looking-glass.
If that her breath will mist or stain the stone,
Why, then she lives.
    Kent.   Is this the promis'd end?   *310*
    Edg. Or image of that horror.
    Alb.   Fall and cease!
    Lear. This feather stirs; she lives! if it be so,
It is a chance which does redeem all sorrows
That ever I have felt.   *315*
    Kent.   O, my good master!
    Lear. Prithee, away.
    Edg.   'Tis noble Kent, your friend.
    Lear. A plague upon you, murderers, traitors all!
I might have sav'd her; now, she's gone for ever!   *320*
Cordelia, Cordelia! stay a little. Ha!
What is't thou sayst? Her voice was ever soft,
Gentle, and low, an excellent thing in woman.
I kill'd the slave that was a-hanging thee.
    Capt. 'Tis true, my lords, he did.   *325*
    Lear.   Did I not, fellow?
I have seen the day, with my good biting falchion
I would have made them skip. I am old now,
And these same crosses spoil me. Who are you?
Mine eyes are not o' th' best. I'll tell you straight.   *330*
    Kent. If fortune brag of two she lov'd and hated,
One of them we behold.
    Lear. ⟨This is a dull sight.⟩ Are you not Kent?
    Kent.   The same,
Your servant Kent. Where is your servant Caius?   *335*
    Lear. He's a good fellow, I can tell you that.
He'll strike, and quickly too. He's dead and rotten.
    Kent. No, my good lord. I am the very man—
    Lear. I'll see that straight.
    Kent. That, from your first of difference and decay,   *340*
Have follow'd your sad steps.

    Lear.   You are welcome hither.
    Kent. Nor no man else. All's cheerless, dark, and deadly.
Your eldest daughters have fordone themselves,
And desperately are dead.   *345*
    Lear.   Ay, so I think.
    Alb. He knows not what he says, and vain is it
That we present us to him.
    Edg.   Very bootless.

             Enter a Messenger.

    Mess. Edmund is dead, my lord.   *350*
    Alb.   That's but a trifle here.
You lords and noble friends, know our intent:
What comfort to this great decay may come
Shall be applied. For us, we will resign,
During the life of this old majesty,   *355*
To him our absolute power.—*[To Edgar and Kent.]*
You, to your rights,
With boot and such addition as your honors
Have more than merited. All friends shall taste
The wages of their virtue, and all foes   *360*
The cup of their deservings. O! see, see!
    Lear. And my poor fool is hang'd! No, no, no life!
Why should a dog, a horse, a rat, have life,
And thou no breath at all? Thou'lt come no more.
Never, never, never, never, never!   *365*
Pray you, undo this button. Thank you, sir.
⟨Do you see this? Look on her! look! her lips!
Look there, look there!⟩ «O, O, O, O.»

                                He dies.
    Edg.   He faints!—My lord, my lord!
    Kent. Break, heart. I prithee, break.   *370*
    Edg.   Look up, my lord.
    Kent. Vex not his ghost. O let him pass! He hates him
That would upon the rack of this tough world
Stretch him out longer.
    Edg.   He is gone, indeed.   *375*
    Kent. The wonder is he hath endur'd so long.
He but usurp'd his life.
    Alb. Bear them from hence. Our present business
Is general woe. *[To Kent and Edgar.]* Friends of my soul,
you twain   *380*
Rule in this realm, and the gor'd state sustain.
    Kent. I have a journey, sir, shortly to go.
My master calls me. I must not say no.
    Edg. The weight of this sad time we must obey;
Speak what we feel, not what we ought to say.   *385*
The oldest hath borne most: we that are young
Shall never see so much, nor live so long.
                  Exeunt, with a dead march.

           ❧ FINIS ❦

---

301 fordid: *slew*   **308 stone:** *mirror*   **310 end:** *Judgment Day*   **311 Or image:** *It is,*
or else the image   **312 Fall and cease;** *cf. n.*   **327, 328 I have . . . skip;** *cf. n.*   **327**
falchion: *broad sword*   **329 these same crosses:** *all these adversities*   **330 tell you**
straight: *recognize you in a moment*   **331, 332** *Cf. n.*   **333 This . . . sight:** *'My eyes are*
certainly bad'   **339 I'll . . . straight:** *you must prove that to me at once*   **340 your first**
. . . decay: *the beginning of your friction and misfortune*

343 Nor . . . else; *cf. n.*   **352 know our intent;** *cf. n.*   **357 You . . . rights;**
cf. n.   **362 fool;** *cf. n.*   **377 usurp'd:** *retained against natural law*   **384 Edg.** *Cf. n.*

NOTES

At the time of his sudden death in June of 1946, Professor Brooke had completed his work on the text, notes, and glosses for Hamlet, King Lear, Othello *and* I Henry IV. *The editorial tasks which he left unfinished—preparation of some of the final copy for the press, reading of the proofs, compilation of the* Indexes of Words Glossed, *decisions as to certain matters of style and format, and, in the case of* I Henry IV, *the rescuing of the text from the prescriptive punctuation of the eighteenth-century editors—have been undertaken by Professor Benjamin Nangle.*

Textual Note. The two authorities for the text of *King Lear* are the version included in the first folio (collected) edition of Shakespeare's dramatic works, published in 1623, and the first quarto (separate) edition, printed in 1608 and advertised on the titlepage for sale 'at the signe of the Pide Bull.' The quarto reprint of this (Q 2), which claims the same date on its titlepage but was produced over ten years later, has only very occasional textual significance. There is no good ground for doubting that Shakespeare wrote every line of *King Lear* to be found in the modern 'conflated' texts, though these contain more than was printed in any single early edition (see note on III.ii.81–97). The first Quarto preserves some three hundred lines which the Folio omitted; these, in the present book, are printed within ornamental brackets (« »). On the other hand, the Quarto omits about a hundred lines found in the Folio, which are here placed within angle brackets (⟨ ⟩). Thus about an eighth of the play is found in one or other of the original texts, but not in both. For the remainder there is no doubt that the Folio is in general the better and safer guide; but in recent years the Quarto has been unduly disparaged.

Very eminent authorities have condemned it as a 'reported' text, made up either from the recollection of actors who had played in *Lear* or from shorthand notes taken during a performance. The same authorities have, on the other hand, given countenance to a theory, proposed by P. A. Daniel in 1885, that the good Folio text was set up from a copy of this same bad Quarto which had been corrected by collation with the theatre manuscript of the play. The two assumptions, which are rather inconsistent with each other, combine to produce the allegation that neither of the two fundamental texts of *King Lear* was printed from a *bona fide* manuscript, and such a conclusion would put the textual integrity of the play as it has come down to us under very grave suspicion. There seems, however, to be no substantial evidence for either of the underlying assumptions.

The Quarto is much too good to be a reported text. Though it abounds in slovenliness of various kinds, it presents a very full and essentially faithful version of the play, such as would be produced by a printer struggling honestly (however ineffectually at times) with a difficult handwriting and yet more difficult style. The two most glaring faults, which have done much to injure its reputation, are its frequent inability to distinguish verse from prose and its scandalously light punctuation. Except at the ends of speeches it uses few stops beyond commas, and runs sentences together in a most abandoned way. Of the lines which are properly blank verse, the Quarto sets up five hundred as plain prose and misdivides a couple of hundred others. (See Edward Hubler, 'The Verse Lining of the First Quarto of *King Lear*', *Parrott Presentation Volume*, 1935, 421–441.)

For these things Shakespeare was largely to blame. His remarkably flexible and sinuous blank verse in *Lear*, his habit of beginning and ending speeches in the middle of lines, and of mingling prose and poetry without warning in the same scene make the division of a passage into its constituent verse units, once the visual distinction has been obscured, a work for none but a trained prosodist. The Folio, though based on a much clearer manuscript, makes many errors of this kind, and the editors of the play have continued through the centuries to make some (see note on IV.vi.123–137). The very badness of the Quarto in these respects is, in the circumstances, rather a testimony of authenticity, for it is not likely that any one but the poet himself would have produced a manuscript as disorderly as the one from which the first Quarto was evidently printed. It must have been a manuscript in which margins and capitalization were so disregarded that verse and prose looked alike, and in which punctuation and legibility were at a minimum. Within two years after the writing of the play no such manuscript is likely to have been in existence except the author's 'foul papers' or personal draft, and it may be surmised that *King Lear* first got into print as a result of the same haul by Thomas Thorpe and his gang which in the next year, 1609, led to the equally unauthorized publication of the *Sonnets* and *Troilus and Cressida*.

The Quarto compositor found his manuscript hard to read and sometimes blundered, or was stopped dead by an illegibility. As is well known, over a hundred of these faults were discovered while the sheets were being printed, and somebody in the printing house corrected or attempted to correct them. (See

W. W. Greg, *The Variants in the First Quarto of 'King Lear,'* 1940.) Often, especially when printing verse as prose and therefore deprived of the check of rhythm, the compositor allowed small words to drop out or get transposed, and sometimes he 'vulgarized,' that is, simplified or paraphrased. These are mainly errors imposed upon him by the difficulty of his 'copy.' But not infrequently he rose above them and came almost as near perfection as the text of *Lear* can come. In Lear's long and passionate speech, 'O reason not the need!' (II.iv.289–309), the Quarto agrees with the Folio altogether in line arrangement and varies in wording in only six cases, one of which is a clear (though slight) Folio error. In Lear's shorter speech, 'Poor naked wretches, wheresoe'er you are' (III.iv.32–40), there is, apart from punctuation and another slight Folio misprint, only one variation, and here it is somewhat doubtful whether the Folio 'pitiless storm' or the Quarto 'pitiless night' is to be preferred. So, in the great speech, 'No, no, no, no! Come, let's away to prison!' (V.iii.9–20), there is no difference of working except that the Quarto omits two of the 'no's' and avoids the Folio's parenthesis-blunder in line 13. The well-rendered speeches are not always Lear's. In the first seventeen lines of Act Fifth, spoken by Edmund and Regan, the Quarto supplies two-and-one-half lines omitted by the Folio, retains a word which the Folio carelessly dropped, and makes two inferior substitutions ('abdication' for 'alteration' and 'I' for 'In'). Otherwise, they are verbally the same.

The passages cited are much above the Quarto's average of correctness, but they are certainly not more untypical than the ones which have been cited to prove its corruptness. It is not likely that Burbage himself could have recited *Lear* from memory with as little error as appears in the better pages of the Quarto text. That such lines could have been so well set down from the recollection of a hireling actor or by any kind of stenography then known exceeds credibility.

If the Quarto is too good to be a reported text, it is too bad to have served as 'copy' for the Folio. Daniel's theory that it was so used does little credit to the good faith of the Folio editors, who on that assumption went out of their way to put one of the 'stolen and surreptitious copies' they were deploring at the base of their purer text. It would be easier to write out clean any average page of *King Lear* than to do the re-lining, re-punctuating, capitalizing, transposing, and substituting of words necessary to make a Quarto page conform to the Folio readings—and the difference to the Folio printer would have been unspeakable. Considering that Heminge and Condell had in their services experts whose business was the making of fair copies, but whose skill in textual collation may well be doubted, it would have been asinine to adopt so cumbrous and dangerous a means of reproducing their theatre manuscript. And why should the editors of the Folio go to the trouble of cutting out the hundreds of undoubtedly Shakespearean lines which only the Quarto prints, while at the same time writing into its pages the lines which it lacks. It would have been a senseless way to proceed, whether considered as a means of giving Shakespeare's works to the word ('cured, and perfect of their limbs,' as they boasted) or as a means of conveniently providing the Folio printer with copy.

It would be a very bigoted editor who would ignore the Quarto text. In the present edition about one hundred and fifty Quarto readings have been accepted as clearly more Shakespearean than their Folio parallels; but, where judgment is difficult between the two texts, the Folio has been preferred, because it is the purer version on the whole and, when it diverges from the original, is more likely to sin in stagy over-heightening than in positive misrepresentation of the poet's meaning. It must be admitted, however, that in some of these cases the preference of the Folio is more the result of prudence and a desire for consistency than of poetic faith. Most of the dubious choices are discussed in the notes.

The Quartos indicate no division of the play into either acts or scenes. The Folio is admirably divided throughout, and is here followed with no change except to translate its Latin 'Actus rimus. Scaena Prima,' *etc.,* to increase the scenes in Act Second from two to four, and regularize the numbering of scenes in Act Fourth. Stage directions are fairly full and accurate in both texts. As usual, those of the Folio show signs of revision by the prompter, and the Quarto wording is here often preferred as more likely to be Shakespeare's. Necessary amplifications and other necessary matter omitted in the original editions are supplied within square brackets ([ ]).

In Shakespeare's usage it was optional to give full syllabic value to the ending *-ed* of past verbal forms or (as is generally done now) to contract this ending with the preceding syllable. In the present edition final *-ed* must always be pronounced as a separate syllable in order to preserve the original rhythm of the verse. Where rhythm requires the contracted form, the spelling *'d* is used.

Shakespeare accented a number of words on syllables which do not now bear the accent, and sometimes his practice in this matter was inconsistent. Where an

unusual accentuation is required, it is indicated by an acute mark over the stressed vowel, as in *revénues*.

Obsolete words and words employed in now unusual senses are explained in footnotes the first time they occur in the text. Repetitions are not usually noted.

The critical and general notes in the following pages are announced by the symbol, *cf. n.*, at the bottom of the page of text to which each has relevance. A name at the end of a note (in parentheses) indicates the authority; but no special effort is made to give credit for material which is common property or which is, so far as known, new in the present edition.

I.i.S.d. *King Lear's Palace.* Shakespeare probably assumed this scene to take place in Leicester, 'Leir-cester,' which, as Holinshed informed him, was built by King Lear and named after him. Leicester is about half way between Liverpool and London in the geographical center of England.

I.i.5, 6 *equalities . . . moiety.* The division is so equal as between these two beneficiaries that neither Albany nor Cornwall could find even frivolous reason for preferring the other's share. We are to understand that Lear's plans for dividing his kingdom into three parts are complete and are known to Kent and Gloucester. Only the formal ratifying ceremony remains. The two noblemen are discussing one of the smaller aspects of the abdication; namely, that in arranging it Lear has not allowed his preference of Albany over Cornwall to appear.

I.i.33–52. This speech is a good text for studying the theory that the Quarto version of the play is a 'reconstruction,' based upon an actor's memory, shorthand notes, or both. The Quarto lacks seven lines that are in the Folio and makes four important verbal substitutions: *'first intent'* (35), *'business of our state'* (36), *'Confirming* them on *younger years'* (37), *'Where merit doth most* challenge *it'* (51). It has three metrically short lines, in addition to the last. Otherwise it is a pretty faithful parallel to the Folio, and as a dramatic unit the shortened speech holds together well.

I.i.42 *France and Burgundy.* Both titles would be anachronisms in the prehistoric period in which *Lear* is set. Shakespeare is probably thinking of the fifteenth-century princes thus entitled whom he had dealt with in *Henry V* and *Henry VI*. See R. A. Law, 'Waterish Burgundy,' *Studies in Philology*, 1936, pp. 222–227.

I.i.51 *Where . . . challenge.* Where natural affection competes with the merit of the recipient as chief motive for my gift.

I.i.70. *she names my very deed of love.* The love she talks about is that which I practise in very deed.

I.i.73. *square.* All the joys that manifest themselves through the various senses are thought of as laid out on an area or 'square' of sensibility as on a map. This seems better than to take *square* as a measuring instrument, a carpenter's square.

I.i.78. *More richer.* The Quarto reading. The phrase occurs also in *Hamlet* III.ii.308. The Folio has 'More ponderous.'

I.i.83. Printed as in the Folio. The Quarto has 'Although the last, not the least in our dear love.'

I.i.138. *still.* The Quarto word. The Folio has 'shall,' possibly copied from 'shall' in the line above.

I.i.140. *The sway.* These words, attached to line 139 in the Folio and prefixed to line 141 in th Quarto, belong metrically to neither.

I.i.143. *coronet.* Perhaps the award intended for Cordelia as best beloved of his children (W. Perrett).

I.i.154. *Reverse thy doom.* Abrogate your decree. The Quarto reading seems clearly better here than the Folio 'Reserve thy state.' The latter could hardly mean anything but 'keep your pomp,' which in lines 138, 139 Lear has done. The Quarto *stoops* is also preferable to the Folio's 'falls' in this line.

I.i.159. *Reverb no hollowness.* There was a proverb, 'Empty vessels have the loudest sounds,' which Kent is applying to the case of Cordleia and her sisters. (The Quarto reading, 'sound reverbs,' may be the better here.)

I.i.167. *by Apollo.* The play is designedly pre-Christian. By Holinshed's chronology Lear lived in the ninth century B.C., before the founding of Rome. He swears by Apollo and Jupiter (190), or their Celtic equivalents, and, as in lines 111–113, by the sun and stars.

I.i.170. *O vassal! miscreant!* Vague terms of opprobrium. The Quarto reading 'Vassal, recreant' might have the preciser meaning, 'perfidious subject.'

I.i.180. *That.* The formal language of judicial sentence: 'for that,' 'forasmuch as.' It depends on *reward* in line 184. The Quarto has 'Since,' which is easier but more colloquial.

I.i.180. *us.* In changing from *me* (line 179) to *us*, Lear marks his assumption of royal dignity and power.

I.i.184. *Our . . . good.* That is, assuming again and asserting the royal power which I have been talking of relinquishing.

I.i.185. *Five days.* So the Folio. The Quarto, which in general gives rather the better version of this speech, has 'four days,' and in line 187 'fift' instead of

sixt. There is a similar inconsistency between 'nine' and 'ten' in *Othello* I.iii.301. The explanation may be that Shakespeare used Roman letters for numerals. In Elizabethan script *v* and *x* often had a preliminary stroke which could cause them to be read *iv, ix.*

I.i.186. *diseases.* The Quarto word. The Folio 'disasters' seems to be a misprint.

I.i.191. *revok'd.* Ironically echoing Kent's word, line 175.

I.i.197. *your large speeches may your deeds approve.* I hope that your deeds will make good your lavish speeches.

I.i.213. *that little-seeming substance.* Her mere physical presence, small as it seems; *i.e.*, Cordelia without dower.

I.i.236. *folds of favor.* Lear's love has been wrapped around Cordelia like a rich oriental garment, fold over fold.

I.i.239. *which.* Of the two alternatives France has just mentioned, he politicly omits to develop the second (namely, that Lear is at fault) and returns to the first, which reflects on Cordelia. (The Quarto gives the better text of this speech.)

I.i.246. *murther.* The early texts agree in putting this word in Cordelia's mouth and there is no reason for questioning it. The atmosphere of the play is primitive. Cordelia may not unnaturally imagine herself suspected of the crime her sisters so easily commit.

I.i.290. *The jewels.* A vocative: O you who are the jewels.

I.i.302. *well . . . wanted.* Well deserve the loss of the inheritance that you have missed.

I.i.303. *plighted.* The image is the same as in line 236 above. The sisters' real purposes are wrapped in fold on fold of cunning. (In the next line *covers* may be read as a plural, like *stands* in line 259.)

I.i.326. *sit.* That is, in order to continue this conversation. There is nothing to be said in favor of the Quarto reading here, 'hit together.'

I.ii.21. *taw.* It can hardly be doubted that this is what Shakespeare wrote. The word *taw*, originally to tan or curry leather, is well illustrated by a line in Jonson's *Bartholomew Fair* (1614) IV.v.78, 'You know where you were taw'd lately, both lash'd and slash'd you were in Bridewell.' The printers, however, could make nothing of it. Instead of *taw th'*, the Folio has 'to'th'' and the Quarto 'tooth'.' The eighteenth-century emendation, 'top the legitimate,' which makes good but not vivid sense, is commonly adopted. One great objection to this has always been that a final 'p' is a very unlikely letter to be overlooked, either in pronunciation or on the written page.

I.ii.24. *prescrib'd.* The folio reading, clearly correct. The quarto has 'subscrib'd.'

I.ii.26. *What news?* In Edmund's letter, of course.

I.ii.41. *too blame.* A common Elizabethan misunderstanding of 'to blame,' *blame* being taken for an adjective (blameworthy).

I.ii.59. *thrown . . . closet.* Shakespeare borrows this device from his play of *Julius Caesar* (II.i.35), where in turn it is borrowed from Plutarch's life of Caesar.

I.ii.78. *should.* More deferential than 'will' or 'shall.'

I.ii.85, 86. *I will . . . this.* Shakespeare makes Edmund repeat the trick Iago had employed in *Othello* IV.i.87ff.

I.ii.92. *wind me into him.* Get into his confidence. The 'ethical dative,' *me*, means 'for my sake.' It was commonly used and often has such light emphasis that it can hardly be paraphrased.

I.ii.97. *These late eclipses.* A topical allusion, connecting the play with the very recent experience of the first spectators. An eclipse of the moon on 27 September 1605 was followed two weeks later (12 October) by an eclipse of the sun.

I.ii.99. *sequent effects.* The next two sentences depict the outburst of suspicion, fear, and brutality that followed the discovery of the Gunpowder Plot, 5 November 1605.

I.ii.104. *falls . . . nature.* Ceases to be governed by the natural instinct (to love one's daughter). A figure from the game of bowls. The 'bias' was the asymmetrical structure of the balls which forced them to roll in a peculiar course.

I.ii.119. *dragon's tail.* Referring to the position of the moon with relation to the long constellation Draco.

I.ii.127. *Fa, sol, la, mi.* This is mere trolling nonsense, based on the notes of the old musical scale.

I.ii.170. *All with me's meet that I can fashion fit.* With me any action is correct which I can make to suit my purpose. In the last six lines Edmund, left alone on the stage, steps out of his character and by a recognized Elizabethan convention speaks objectively and informatively to the audience.

I.iii.S.d. *Duke of Albany's Palace.* Albany was the old name of North Britain, above the Humber River. York, a very ancient city which was the military capital of Roman Britain, would be the natural residence of Goneril and her husband. It is a hundred miles north of Leicester.

I.iii.21. *With . . . abus'd.* The line, found only in the Quarto text, is most

likely incorrect. A sense can be given to it by taking *as* to mean 'as well as' and *abus'd* 'misguided.'

I.iv.1. *If but as well, etc.* That is, if I can disguise my voice as well as I have changed my looks.

I.iv.15. *fish.* Possibly an anachronistic jest meaning 'I am ultra-Protestant,' keyed to the strong anti-Catholic feeling aroused by the Gunpowder Plot.

I.iv.16. *What art thou?* Lear repeats the question Kent has twice humorously evaded (lines 10, 12). Kent evades again.

I.iv.36. *forty-eight.* It has been suggested that Kent's part was specially written to fit John Heminge, one of the 'sharers' in Shakespeare's company and later the senior editor of the Folio. The age of Kent is not suggested by any of the sources and it would fit with Heminge's at the time the play was produced. See T. S. Baldwin, *Organization and Personnel of the Shakespearean Company*, p. 250.

I.iv.61. *remember'st . . . conception.* You remind me of what I have myself thought.

I.iv.78. *football.* Football was a rough game for rough village lads, not regarded as gentleman's sport. It was in special (but not exclusive) vogue in the North (see note on II.ii.75).

I.iv.89, 90. The Quarto is here correct. The Folio accidentally substitutes Lear's speech in line 98.

I.iv.104. *the Lady-brach.* This, one fears, alludes to Goneril. The Quarto has 'Ladie oth'e brach.'

I.iv.105. *A pestilent gall to me.* The Fool's talk rubs me shrewdly where I am sore. Lear, however, whose conscience has begun to hurt him, is not ungrateful for this counter-irritant and encourages it for the distraction it affords.

I.iv.109–113. *Have . . . trowest.* These precepts of wordly wisdom may be paraphrased: Don't display all you have, don't tell all you know, don't lend all you own, don't disregard your own comfort, don't believe all you are told.

I.iv.117, 118. *thou shalt have more Than two tens to a score.* If you do all this, you will have more than maximum felicity.

I.iv.134. *Do thou for him stand.* A masterpiece of indirect arraignment. The king can do no wrong, but the king can stand for the hypothetical lord who counselled the king to the king's own folly.

I.iv.144. *monopoly out.* This alludes to a common commercial abuse in Shakespeare's time. Individuals or companies were granted the exclusive right to trade in various commodities (as wine, sugar, *etc.*), and often thus amassed huge fortunes. The sense of *out* is 'issued in my name.'

I.iv.154. *let . . . so.* Any one who condemns the Fool's reasoning about Lear's distribution of the kingdom must be a knave and deserves whipping.

I.iv.157. *wits to wear.* Behind this nonsense verse, and in other parts of the play, one detects a scornful protest against the new foppery and social extravagance that James I's accession brought in.

I.iv.165. *play bo-peep.* Erratically display and conceal his royal countenance, as a nurse does her face to amuse an infant. This stanza is a parody of a popular pious ballad written by John Careless, one of the martyrs of Queen Mary's time (for text, see H. E. Rollins, *Old English Ballads*, 1920, pp. 47ff.).

I.iv.186. *Weary of all, shall want some.* Tired of possessing everything, shall find himself lacking even the portion that he needs. The story of Lear in a nutshell.

I.iv.205. *it.* An old possessive case, of which Shakespeare seems to have been fond as a relief from the neuter *his,* especially in childish talk.

I.iv.213. *Whoop . . . thee. Jug* was a pet-name for Joan, and the words may be quoted from a current song. They are inspired by Goneril's speech just above, on which the Fool comments: any ass can tell when the cart is drawing the horse; *i.e.,* when the relation of child and father is unnaturally inverted. And then, with sardonic reference to Goneril, he trolls: 'Whoop! how I do love you!'

I.iv.223. *Which they.* The antecedent is not clear. Lear's speech above, badly preserved in the Quarto which alone contains it, was evidently in verse. Only the last line of it now scans.

I.iv.252. *sea-monster.* The dreadful mythological creature who came for

> The virgin tribute paid by howling Troy
> To the sea-monster (Merchant of Venice III.ii.59).

I.iv.285, 286. *that scope As.* Such scope as, whatever scope. The Quarto has the easier 'that scope that.'

I.iv.287. *fifty of my followers at a clap.* The two texts agree in this puzzling line. One might suspect that Lear has discovered, in the brief moment he has been off the stage, that Goneril has somehow liquidated fifty knights, though she has threatened nothing so drastic. However, in the next act (II.iv.223–225) Lear still has his hundred knights, as he has on Goneril's word in line 331 below. It looks as if some change was made in the play at this point. See E. S. Noyes, 'On the Dismissal of Lear's Knights and Goneril's Letter to Regan,' *Philological Quarterly*, 1930, pp. 297–303.

I.iv.315–319. The main virtuosity about this piece of doggerel appears to be that the Fool sings it in rustic dialect, making all the final words rime: ca't her, da'ter, sla'ter, ha'ter, a'ter.

I.iv.343. *atask'd.* For the elaborate bibliographical structure which has been built upon this word, see W. W. Greg, *The Editorial Problem in Shakespeare,* 1942, p. 98. The printer of the Quarto first set up 'alapt,' which can hardly be anything but a misreading of 'ataxt.' The error was discovered while the Quarto was being printed and in certain copies "attaskt" was substituted. The Folio printed 'at task.' 'Tax' and 'task' (the same word originally) were both commonly used in the sense of 'blame.' Shakespeare might have used whichever he liked (and on other occasions employed both with this meaning), but (perhaps only for the sake of rhythm), he preferred to invent a derived form, either 'atax' or 'atask,' which apparently no one else has ever used. The new word seems to have reached the Quarto printer in the form 'ataxt' or the Folio printer in the form 'attaskt' and in each case it made trouble; but it is doubtful whether more can be read into the situation than the presumption that the two texts were set up from different manuscripts.

I.v.1. *Gloucester.* The residence of Regan and Cornwall and capital of the southwestern section of Lear's kingdom. A very ancient city, important in Roman and Anglo-Saxon times, about seventy-five miles southwest of Leicester.

I.v.11. *Thy wit shall not go slipshod.* One of the Fool's poorer and more acid jokes. If men' brains were liable to chilblains like their heels, you would be immune, because you have so little brain. He is desperately attempting to prevent Lear from brooding.

I.v.S.d. The Folio marks the Gentleman's entrance (erroneously) with the rest at the opening of the scene. This is the textual convention known as 'massed entrances.'

I.v.46, 47. *departure . . shorter.* Pronounced in vulgar fashion, 'departer . . . sharter.' This parting obscenity is addressed to the audience after Lear has gone out. (The Fool, it should be remembered, is an adolescent boy.)

II.i.S.d. *Castle.* This is on a treeless and uncultivated heath, a day's ride from the city of Gloucester. Shakespeare was doubtless thinking of one of the British Camps, the remains of which are conspicuous on the crests of hills (*e.g.,* the one near Dorchester on the Thames which he would have passed in going from Stratford to London). Gloucester's castle may appropriately be located in the Vale of the White House or Salisbury Plain or, perhaps more plausibly, in one of the bleaker parts of the Cotswolds, *e.g.,* near Chipping Norton.

II.i.1. *Curan.* A name not found in any of the sources. It is probably suggested by the popular story of Curan and Argentile in William Watson's *Albion's England,* first printed in 1586. Curan seems to be a confidential agent of Gloucester who finds it worth his while to pass on to Edmund the information that he picks up.

II.i.18. *Briefness and fortune, work!* Let me leave it to quick action and luck.

II.i.41, 42. *Mumbling . . . mistress.* A clear effort at pagan atmosphere.

II.i.50. *But that.* That is, he could by no means so persuade me but that (in spite of what he said) I told him.

II.i.57. *latch'd.* Shakespeare is fond of this old word and probably used it here, as the Folio records. The Quarto has 'lancht,' *i.e.,* lanced, a more obvious verb.

II.i.64. *found—dispatch.* When he is found, a quick death to him!

II.i.68. *caitiff.* The Quarto word, more expressive than 'Coward,' which the Folio substitutes.

II.i.99. *He whom my father nam'd.* This tells us by Elizabethan convention that Lear's name was also Edgar; but the reference to 'godson' and the Anglo-Saxon name are both anachronisms.

II.i.107. *expense and waste.* Folio reading. The Quarto text is an interesting illustration of publishers' methods. The printer set up 'these—and wast,' the first part of which (which perhaps should have been printed 'the—se') seems to be an honest confession of failure to make anything of the indecipherable combination 'thexpense.' The Quarto corrector, out of his own head, changed this to 'the wast and spoyle,' which appears in some of the copies.

II.i.122. *How . . . please.* Employing my power as you will.

II.i.132. *poise.* The Folio prints 'prize' and the Quarto printer first set up 'prise,' but this was corrected in certain copies of the Quarto to 'poyse.'

II.i.137. *From . . . dispatch.* Are waiting to be started on their way from here.

II.ii.S.d. Kent and Oswald have both ridden all night. Kent, having arrived a little earlier, is taken by Oswald for a native of the place.

II.ii.6. *I love thee not.* The particular reason for Kent's rage against Oswald appears in scene fourth of this act, lines 32ff.

II.ii.8. *Lipsbury pinfold.* Lipsbury, a place unknown to geographical research, must be a Shakespearean coinage, and can hardly mean anything but 'Lip-Town.' A pinfold is a village pound in which straying beasts are corraled. 'Lipsbury

pinfold,' then, is where one may expect 'lippy' creatures like Oswald, with vagrant tongues and habits, to wind up. Kent says: If I had you in an appropriate place from which you couldn't escape, I would make you care for me. Both the texts print the phrase with perfect correctness, though the printers can hardly have known what it meant.

II.ii.14. *three-suited.* This has been sometimes taken to indicate poverty of wardrobe, but *cf.* III.iv.129, *who hath had three suits to his back,* where Edgar plainly alludes to a former state of affluence. It may refer to a servant's liveries, and thus would be a natural term of contempt applied to Oswald; and Edgar, in the later passage, would refer to the 'enough and to spare' enjoyed by hired servants. At the extortionate price of Elizabethan clothes the possession of three suits was quite beyond the ordinary man. Similarly *hundred-pound* and *worsted-stocking* suggest luxury. Kent is contrasting the pampered lackey's outward exquisiteness with his mental and moral poverty.

II.ii.27. *sop o' th' moonshine.* A sop was bread soaked in wine or other liquid. Kent will make Oswald's body so porous with holes that it will suck up the moonbeams he has just mentioned.

II.ii.40. *With you.* Let me have a word (and a blow) with you. Kent continues to address Oswald, refusing to be diverted by Edmund.

II.ii.57. *zed.* The current name of the letter 'z.' It had an ornate orthographic form, was seldom used (because its work was generally done by 's'), and so is an image of the social parasite.

II.ii.67, 68. *holy cords . . . too intrinse.* The holy cords are the bonds of affection between father and daughters. The idea is repeated in Cleopatra's lines to the asp, *Antony and Cleopatra* V.ii.349, 350:

> With thy sharp teeth this knot intrinsicate
> Of life at once untie.

II.ii.71. *halcyon.* The kingfisher. The popular superstition was that, if a dead kingfisher were hung up, his bill would point toward the quarter from which the wind was blowing.

II.ii.75. *Smoil.* Both the texts read *Smoile* ('smoyle'), a Northern dialect form of 'smile,' meaning presumably 'smile at.' It is used in Tennyson's *Northern Farmer (Old Style),* line 53. It looks as if Oswald was represented on the stage as a somewhat farcical Yorkshireman (*cf.* I.iv.82), and Kent seems to be parodying his accent.

II.ii.77. *Camelot.* Supposed to have been in Somerset (or Cornwall), but the Elizabethans identified it with Winchester and believed that King Arthur's round table was still to be seen there (see the play of *Eastward Hoe.* V.i., composed about a year before *King Lear*). Winchester is about a day's journey by foot from Sarum (Salisbury) Plain. The *goose . . . Camelot* collocation contains an allusion to the unsavory disease known to Shakespeare as 'Winchester goose.' The idea is the same as in lines 9, 10 above.

II.ii.86. *better faces.* Kent's opinion of Cornwall is hinted at in the first lines of the play.

II.ii.102. *Flickering on.* Quarto: 'In flitkering.' Folio: 'On flickering.' 'Flickering' in this sense was perhaps original with Shakespeare; it puzzled the compositors.

II.ii.107. *your displeasure.* 'your Displeasure,' an ironic honorific, modelled on 'your Excellence,' 'your Grace,' etc.

II.ii.120. *Ajax.* According to their own account, Ajax is but a ninny beside them. In *Love's Labor's Lost* V.ii.618, Ajax is runner-up for a place among the Nine Worthies.

II.ii.129. *Stocking.* As a royal messenger, Kent had the immunity of heralds, and the stocks were punishment for low misdemeanors and vulgar malefactors.

II.ii.142. *vilest and contemned'st.* The reading is uncertain. The Quarto, which alone contains the line, originally had 'belest and contaned' which in some copies was changed to 'basest and temnest.' (See Greg, *variants,* p. 54.)

II.ii.146, 147. *That . . . restrain'd.* Here, except that the Folio has 'he' instead of *he's,* the two texts agree in a reading which does not make sense. Perhaps a line dropped out after 146.

II.ii.164. *heaven's benediction.* The proverb, with 'God's blessing' instead of *heaven's benediction,* is, as Kent stays, common; but the instances that have been found do not explain what God's blessing is. Probably, the beneficent rain; and probably the saw was meant to rebuke those who forsake a dull and salutary way of life in search of something more garish. The mention of 'the warm sun' in line 165 motivates Kent's following address to the luminary, which is now about to rise. The whole scene has taken place in the obscure light of dawn.

II.ii.168, 169. *Nothing . . . misery.* This, by admitting, palliates the improbability that Kent should at this time have an unread letter from Cordelia. Shakespeare is fond of the trick. The words mean: The strangest good fortune comes when one is most miserable.

II.ii.172–174. *And . . . remedies.* The last words of Cordelia's letter, offering hope that she may be able to remedy Lear's losses. 'This enormous state' may mean no more than the weighty business of the French crown.

II.iii. In the Folio, Scene Second continues to the end of the act. What modern editors mark as Scene Third has no local designation. It registers the passage of several hours, while Kent sleeps. Edgar simply appears on the front stage, without particular indication of where he is, makes his soliloquy to the audience, and goes out, after which the action of Scene Second resumes in what we call Scene Fourth.

II.iii.14. *Bedlam beggars.* Former inmates of Bedlam (Bethlehem Hospital for the insane) in London, who had been discharged as partially cured, and licensed to solicit charity. This is a contemporary (seventeenth-century) touch.

II.iii.20. *Turlygod . . . Tom.* The Bedlamites solicited their alms under the name of 'Poor Tom' or 'Tom o' Bedlam.' *Turlygod* is spelled in just this way in both the original texts, capitalized and italicized as a proper name. The Quarto, having first printed *'Tuelygod,'* is at pains to correct the 'e' to 'r' on the revised forme. Yet the name has not been found elsewhere. It may be a form of 'twirligig' (whirligig). A word 'grinagod' (also 'grinagog') means one who is always grinning, on the analogy of which 'turligod' would be one always whirling or being whirled about, the sport of chance (*O. E. D.*).

II.iv.28. *To do upon respect such violent outrage.* To outrage decency so violently.

II.iv.43–47. *And . . . drew.* Kent is too angry to be coherent. And I, he means, meeting the other messenger, drew my sword.

II.iv.60, 61. *mother . . . Hysterica passio.* These terms are taken from Harsnet's pamphlet on witchcraft and demoniacal possession, which suggested so much of Edgar's mad talk. See note on III.iv.58. Both the early texts of the play, naturally enough, read 'Historica,' corrected in the fourth Folio of 1685.

II.iv.78. *none but knaves.* The Fool does not accept the opportunist doctrine he has just cynically stated.

II.iv.106–108. Text as in Quarto (corrected forme).

II.iv.146. *scant.* So the Folio. The Quarto has 'slack,' and Shakespeare doubtless wrote one or the other, though strict logic would require a word with the opposite meaning such as 'perform.'

II.iv.155, 156. *on . . . confine.* A very fine figure. Lear's powers (like the owner of an estate) have travelled over all the territory that is theirs and now stand on the extreme edge, viewing that over which they have no control.

II.iv.169. *She . . . train.* See note on I.iv.287 and lines 223–225 below.

II.iv.183. *tender-hefted.* Responsive to the hilt, easily managed. A figure from a knife or other instrument in which the haft or handle easily accommodates itself to the master's use. The term can perhaps be illustrated by Osric's talk about rapiers in *Hamlet* V.ii.147ff.

II.iv.243. *bile.* So spelled in the early editions ('byle,' 'bile') and so commonly pronounced.

II.iv.255. *mingle . . . passion.* Do not receive your wild words at face value, but discount them in the light of reason. The figure, however, is that of mixing a drink.

II.iv.292–295. *Thou . . . warm.* Lear here becomes very modern and proves his point by reference to the costume of a lady of fashion at James I's court. If we assume, he says, that the purpose of gorgeous raiment is to keep the wearer warm, then (1) nature does not need such extravagance of dress, and (2) this dress, cut according to the fashion of the day, hardly keeps the wearer warm anyway.

II.iv.318–321. *So am I . . . return'd.* These speeches are differently assigned in the Quarto, the first to Cornwall and the second to Regan. The Quarto likewise gives Cornwall's speech, line 325, to Regan.

II.iv.327. *bleak.* The Quarto word. Folio, 'high.'

II.iv.337. *storm.* The storm, which plays so large a rôle in Act Third, had no place in the Lear story before Shakespeare. He took it, along with the tale of Gloucester and his sons, from Sidney's *Arcadia* (ed. 1590, Bk.ii, ch. 10). See Sources of the Play.

III.i.10. *little world of man.* Lear, whose rage is in unison with that of the storm, illustrates the metaphysical doctrine that the 'microcosm,' man, lives in a complex harmony with the 'macrocosm' or universe of world of 'things' (see line 7).

III.i.31. *furnishings.* The sentence is incomplete, and, since a Quarto cut here immediately precedes a Folio cut, it is possible that an intermediate line or two may have been omitted by both texts (Greg), but nothing important for the sense seems to have been lost.

III.ii.23. *high-engender'd battles.* Battalions of rain and wind, produced high in the air.

III.ii.30. *So beggars marry many.* So many beggars marry; *i.e.,* before they have a roof over their heads.

III.ii.31, 32. The *toe* stands for Goneril and Regan, the *heart* for Cordelia. He who misplaces his affection upon that which is meanest.

III.ii.74. *vile.* This word is regularly spelled 'vild' or 'vilde' in both the early texts.

III.ii.79. *Must make content with his fortunes fit.* Must fit contentment to his fortunes, be satisfied with what he has.

III.ii.81–97. Comic relief, which at this point is badly needed. It would be unreasonable to suppose that Shakespeare did not write it. It is a parody of the famous prophecy of Merlin, of which one text was printed in Elizabethan texts of Chaucer and in Puttenham's *Art of English Poetry*, 1589, whence Shakespeare may have got it. The first four lines describe conditions current in Shakespeare's England; the next six describe absurdly utopian conditions; and the conclusion (lines 94, 95) is that when these things come together, the realm of Albion will be in great confusion.

III.ii.86. *nobles are their tailors' tutors.* Noblemen spend their time teaching their tailors new fashions.

III.ii.87. *No . . . suitors.* No heretics except lying lovers; no burnings except from venereal disease.

III.ii.89. *nor no poor knight.* And no knight poor.

III.ii.96, 97. *Then . . . feet.* After the imposing build-up, the prophecy ends, as such things often did, in a flat truism: When people walk, they will do it with their feet.

III.ii.98. *Merlin.* A playful anachronism. Merlin was the magician of King Arthur's court. By the chronology Shakespeare followed, the Fool would have lived about 1300 years before his time.

III.iv.19–21. *In such a night . . . In such a night as this!* Consciously antiphonal, it would seem, to the joyous duet of Lorenzo and Jessica: 'in such a night as this . . . in such a night' (*Merchant of Venice* V.i).

III.iv.21. *Your old kind father, whose frank heart gave you all.* Here the Quarto text is better. The Folio, by omitting *you*, gets the conventional count of syllables, but puts the accent on the wrong words. Stress *fath'r*, *frank*, and *gave*.

III.iv.39. *shake the superflux.* The figure is from shaking the branches of an over-laden fruit tree.

III.iv.58. *halters in his pew.* The word *pew* is for the sake of grisly impropriety and to show how ubiquitous the fiend's temptation is. He lays knives under his pillow when he sleeps, puts hangman's nooses in his pew when he prays, sets ratsbane by his porridge when he eats. Lewis Theobald (1688–1744) was the first to show that the allusions to superstitions and fiends in Edgar's simulated ravings were largely taken from Samuel Harsnet's *Declaration of Egregious Popish Impostures*, 1603. Harsnet tells of a man who brought home a new halter and two knives; whereupon the devil 'laid them in the gallery, that some of those that were possessed might either hang themselves with the halter or kill themselves with the blades.' This is doubtless Shakespeare's source, though similar passages are found in Marlowe's *Doctor Faustus* (lines 632ff.) and Spenser's *Faery Queen* (Bk.I, canto ix, st. 22ff.)

III.iv.63, 64. *There . . . now.* He picks at different parts of his body, as if the foul fiend were vexing him in the bites of vermin.

III.iv.77. *pelican.* In the natural history of the time the young pelican is the type of ungrateful progeny, because fostered on its parents' blood.

III.iv.78. *Pillicock.* 'Pelican' suggests to Edgar this vulgar word, which he fancifully distorts into a bird of prey sitting on its hill.

III.iv.97, 98. *Hay . . . sessa.* Essentially as in Quarto. The Folio expands strangely: 'Sayes, suum, mun, nonny, Dolphin my Boy, Boy *Sesey*.' The last word, spelled 'caese' in Quarto, is probably the same exclamation which occurs in III.vi.70, where the Folio spells it 'sese,' and in IV.vi.208.

III.iv.134. *Smulkin.* Smulkin, like Modo and Mahu mentioned below (line 137), was among the devils exorcised in the witch findings discussed in Harsnet's book (see note on line 58 above).

III.iv.161–165. *I had a son, etc.* Edgar, who has been using mad talk as a shield against recognition, becomes almost speechless on hearing this disclosure.

III.iv.170–173. The first line may be from some lost romance; the last two are from the popular ballad of *Jack the Giant-killer*. They are Edgar's mystical way of saying that he sees a dark adventure before him and smells a rat.

III.iv.182. *British man.* 'English man' in the ballad, but there were no Englishmen in Lear's time, and when Shakespeare was writing this play there was a new movement to call all inhabitants of the island 'British' in recognition of the union with Scotland. James I had been proclaimed King of Great Britain, 24 October 1604.

III.vi.4. *have.* The preceding word, *wits*, has caused the verb to take the plural form. Shakespeare was capable of this and both the texts have it so, but it may be a scribal error.

III.vi.S.d. *Enter Lear, etc.* The Quarto has these characters enter with Kent and Gloucester at the opening of the scene, but the Folio arrangement is evidently correct. Edgar has been holding back to avoid recognition by his father. Lear has kept with Edgar, and the Fool with Lear.

III.vi.6. *Frateretto.* Listed by Harsnet with Flibbertigibbet (*cf.* III.iv.111) in

his group of devils. The following allusion to Nero may be a vague recollection of Rabelais (bk. ii.30).

III.vi.25. *broom.* In the old song the word is 'bourn,' brook; but Edgar may be intentionally misquoting, with a hint at witches and broomsticks.

III.vi.40–43. *Sleepest . . . harm.* Based on some version of the nursery rime of 'Little Boy Blue,' as lines 25–28 are based on another popular song. In Edgar's perversion line 43 probably means 'If you give me one kiss.'

III.vi.44. *Purr! the cat is grey.* Hinting that it is an old grey witch who is wheedling the jolly shepherd. Lear seizes the suggestion and identifies her with Goneril.

III.vi.45, 46. *'Tis Goneril . . . father.* So the first Quarto. The second Quarto (perhaps rightly) adds 'she' before *kicked*.

III.vi.49. *joint-stool.* A joint-stool was one made by joiners, as opposed to the usual rough home-made ones. The frequent mention of this article illustrates the scarcity of good furniture in Shakespeare's time. Lear, of course, in his delirium identifies the stool with Goneril.

III.vi.65. *brach or him.* So the early texts. Instead of *him* Sir Thomas Hanmer (1677–1746) conjectured 'lym' in the sense of 'lyme-hound,' bloodhound; but that use is not well supported, and a misreading of manuscript 'l' as 'h' is not likely.

III.vi.76. *Persian.* The customary epithet for gorgeous attire from the days of the Greeks and Romans. At the time *Lear* was written the travels of the Sherley brothers had called attention to the opportunities of trade with Persia.

III.vi.79. *We'll go to supper i' th' morning.* Lear is hungry, but his weariness exceeds his hunger, and by royal decree (*We'll go*) he postpones supper till the morning.

III.vi.80. *And I'll go to bed at noon.* Fool's logic. If supper takes place in the morning, bedtime will come at noon. The words are the last the Fool speaks and they hint a sort of author's apology for closing his career in the middle of the play. if the Fool's part was written for Robert Armin, as many think, there seems less reason for the otherwise plausible theory that the Fool's sudden disappearance and the scantiness of Cordelia's part are both due to the need Shakespeare found to give the two rôles to a single boy actor. On the other hand, if Armin played only the Fool, it seems strange that so conspicuous an actor should have been allowed no appearance in the fourth or fifth act. The likelihood is that Armin, who was not very old, was obliged to undertake the part of Cordelia as well as his normal one, for Goneril and Regan made big demands on the available boys in the company. (It may be too venturous to suggest that these famous words, found only in the Folio, may have been added by Armin himself rather than Shakespeare.)

III.vi.113. *Lurk, lurk!* In the Quarto version (which alone contains this speech) Edgar conceals himself as Cornwall *et al.* enter the stage for Scene Seventh.

III.vii.48. *simple-answer'd.* Straightforward in your reply. The Quarto reads 'Simple answerer.'

III.vii.66. *rash.* Here the Folio, which substitutes 'stick,' seems to be sophisticating. *Rash* was a good old verb, used by Malory of the attack of boars, but was becoming rare in standard English in Shakespeare's time. In printing 'rain' for *rage* in line 70 and 'stern' for *dern* in line 62, the Folio seems again to be preferring the less Shakespearean word.

III.vii.67. *bow'd.* This is a new emendation, but it seems to account for both the Quarto reading 'lou'd' (corrected in some copies to 'lowd') and the Folio 'bare.' A tragi-grotesque quibble with *buoy'd* in the next line is probably intentional.

III.vii.69. *stelled fires.* There is a pun in *stelled*, which suggests both 'stelled,' fixed, and 'stellate,' starry. The shortness of line 69 and the number of hard textual problems both indicate that this speech of Gloucester's puzzled the printers.

III.vii.73. *All cruels else subscribe.* The Folio reading. The Quarto has 'subscrib'd.' The clause is concessive and general: Give sanction and formal allowance, if you like, to all other cruel creatures, yet I shall see, *etc.*

III.vii.81. *Hold your hand, etc.* The intervention of the servant in a vain attempt to prevent his master's crime is not in Sidney's *Arcadia*, upon which this portion of the play is based. It is taken from an actual incident dramatized in the pseudo-Shakespearean play, *A Yorkshire Tragedy*, produced by Shakespeare's company in the late summer or autumn of 1605, and therefore throws light upon the date of composition of *King Lear*. See *Modern Language Notes*, xxvii (1912), p. 62.

IV.i.6. *The . . . laughter.* The familiar image of Fortune's wheel, constantly revolving. Those on its bottom live in the element of tears, those on the top in the element of laughter.

IV.i.10. *poorly led.* So the Folio. Edgar has not yet noticed his father's blind-

ness. The original Quarto reading, 'poorlie, leed,' is probably a misreading of 'poorlie-ledd' and the Quarto corrector's 'parti, eyd' a mere guess.

IV.i.11, 12. *But that . . . age.* Only the strange reversals of worldly fortune make men grow old. The doctrine is similar to that of Matthew Arnold in *The Scholar Gipsy*, stanzas 17–23.

IV.i.22, 23. *Means . . . commodities.* Our resources (or capabilities) make us foolhardy and our bald deficiencies prove to be advantages.

IV.i.74–78. These lines repeat the social philosophy of III.iv.38–40.

IV.i.75. *That slaves your ordinance.* Who tramples underfoot your command (to love one's neighbor as oneself).

IV.i.81. *in the confined deep.* A poetical paraphrase for what the Elizabethans called 'the narrow seas,' the Strait of Dover. (*In* means 'into' or 'down upon.')

IV.ii.1. *Welcome, my lord!* Goneril and Edmund have, of course, made the long journey from Gloucester's castle to York (?) together. As they approach her palace, she bids him welcome there.

IV.ii.4. *never man so chang'd.* One of the most successful minor touches in the play is the development in Albany, who is evidently young and honest, and at the opening stands in confused awe of his majestic wife. Goneril's misjudgment of him is a large factor in her downfall.

IV.ii.19. *names.* The Folio reading. If the Quarto 'arms' is correct, the sense is: I must exchange the distaff for the sword.

IV.ii.23. *mistress's.* There is a quibble on two meanings. Ere long I shall challenge you both as queen and lover. She is doubtless planing to detach Edmund from Cornwall's service to her own.

IV.ii.24. *My . . . body.* To be taken with the preceding line. A woman might justly adore Edmund, but Albany in the rôle of husband is as if the foot presumed to control the whole body. This is the reading of the uncorrected Quarto and is doubtless as Shakespeare wrote it, but it was not understood. The Quarto corrector clarified it vulgarly into 'A fool usurps my bed' and the Folio into 'My fool usurps my body.'

IV.ii.34. *worth the whistling.* Alluding to the proverb, 'It is a poor dog that is not worth the whistling'; that is, there was a time when you thought me worthy of attention.

IV.ii.38. *it.* The purpose of the Quarto corrector in changing *it* to 'ith' is obscure. He can hardly have meant to substitute 'its,' for in 1608 that form was very new and rare. Doubtless he did not understand the passage and took this for another of the *i' th'* abbreviations of 'in the.'

IV.ii.45. *Filths savor but themselves.* To the filthy all things are filthy. Suggested by the Latin proverbs, 'puris omnia pura' and 'pravis omnia prava.'

IV.ii.58. *a head for wrongs.* That is, borne to be made a cuckold.

IV.ii.59, 60. *discerning . . . suffering.* Capable of distinguishing between an advantage and an injury.

IV.ii.61, 62. *Fools . . . mischief.* This is greatly condensed. 'Grant that we are all villains,' Goneril seems to mean; 'yet you are involved with the rest of us, and only fools pity the sort of villain you are, who will allow yourself to be punished for treason before you have done any overt act.'

IV.ii.64. *state . . . threat.* Where, as here, the Folio offers no text for comparison, the true reading of this difficult poetry is often obscure. The Quarto compositor read this as 'thy slayer begins threats,' which in certain copies was altered to 'thy state begins thereat.' The emendation is by Charles Jennens (1700–1773).

IV.ii.77. *Mew!* The 'cat-call' employed by an Elizabethan audience to hiss a bad actor.

IV.iii. This sentimental and undramatic scene is certainly Shakespeare's. Its purpose is to reawaken the audience's sympathy for Cordelia, who has been so long absent from the stage and is now about to appear again. The scene is wholly omitted in the Folio, which, of course, throws out the Folio numbering of the remaining scenes in the act (but see note on Scene Seventh). The Quarto printer made, as usual, several blunders, which previous editors have not been very resourceful in clearing up.

IV.iii.11. *Ay, sir.* Quarto 'I say' (explained by Theobald).

IV.iii.31. *believe't.* Quarto 'be beleeft.' (The repetition of 'be' is probably accidental.)

IV.iii.33. *clamor-moisten'd hair.* Quarto 'clamour moystened her.' In Shakespeare ladies' tresses suffer remarkably when they weep. Compare *King John* III.iv.62ff.:

> Bind up those tresses. O what love I note
> In the fair multitude of those her hairs!
> Where but by chance a silver drop hath fallen,
> Even to that drop ten thousand wiry friends
> Do glue themselves in sociable grief.

IV.iii.43. *sometime . . . tune.* Occasionally, when better in tune, *i.e.*, more rational.

IV.v.S.d. *Regan's Palace.* For the presumable place see note on I.v.1. There

is no reason to suppose that Regan would continue to live in Gloucester's castle (which she complained of as 'little,' II.iv.313). When she speaks of Goneril's 'late being *here*' in line 28, she means 'in this part of the country,' in the South; or else it is a dramatic license which in Shakespeare's theatre would never be detected.

IV.v.24. *Some things.* Perhaps she begins to say that some things are not to be trusted even to Oswald's discretion, but she checks herself.

IV.v.26. *I had rather—.* Without being disrespectful, Oswald makes it clear that he is incorruptible, and Regan drops her plea to see the letter.

IV.vi.26. *pebble.* So in both texts. A collective plural like 'sand.' 'Pebbles' would be cacophonous here.

IV.vi.28. *deficient sight.* A bold use of metonymy. The dizzy man's failing eyesight is put for the man himself.

IV.vi.41, 42. *Why . . . cure it.* The grammar is curiously twisted, but apparently genuine. The two texts agree.

IV.vi.48. *snuff.* The partly consumed wick of a candle, giving smoke rather than light.

IV.vi.51. *Gone, sir: farewell.* The Quarto prints these words following the stage direction (omitted in the Folio) which they here precede. Since they give Gloucester assurance that his instructions have been obeyed, they clearly should be spoken before he leaps.

IV.vi.52–54. *conceit . . . theft.* Mere imagination (conceit) may cause death when there is no will to live.

IV.vi.68. *summit.* A rather rare word in the seventeenth century, often spelled 'sommet' as in French. Shakespeare employs it only here and in two passages of *Hamlet* (I.iv.76, III.iii.19), and the earliest texts generally print it 'Sonnet,' as in the Folio here. The *Lear* Quarto misrepresents it as 'sommons' and the Folio in the earlier *Hamlet* passage as 'Sonnet.'

IV.vi.86. *fiend.* Edgar's purpose is to give Gloucester a sense of the value of his life by persuading him that the evil powers have attempted to destroy him and the good have preserved him.

IV.vi.101. *Nature's above art.* To be taken with Lear's previous speech. A king cannot be arrested for issuing false currency, for the currency is all the king's and bears his image. Therefore nature (royal birth) is better than the counterfeiter's art. Lear then imagines himself in various occupations of his past life: enlisting soldiers, drilling recruits, indulging in the pastime of ratting, challenging an opponent, calling up the reserves in battle, and attending an archery contest. Finally, he sees Edgar and imagines himself a sentinel on duty.

IV.vi.102. *crow-keeper.* Crow-herd, a boy or old man employed to keep crows off planted fields (and equipped with a makeshift bow).

IV.vi.107. *Sweet marjoram.* Described in Nicholas Culpeper's *Complete Herbal* as 'an excellent remedy for the brain' (E. Blunden, *Shakespeare's Significances*, 1929).

IV.vi.113. *'Ay' . . . divinity.* Alluding to St. Paul's words to the Corinthians (2 Cor. I. 18, 19): 'But as God is true, our word toward you was not yea and nay. For the Son of God, Jesus Christ . . . was not yea and nay, but in him was yea.'

IV.vi.123–127. After a line and a half of blank verse matching Gloucester's, Lear reverts to undoubted prose. The Folio made a halfhearted attempt to divide it as poetry and modern editors have gone further, with sad results. It is part of the great irony of the play that this mad barbarian king here interrupts his madness to arraign Jacobean court life.

IV.vi.129. *Whose face between her forks presages snow.* To understand this now it is necessary to read *between her forks* after *snow.*

IV.vi.132. *centaurs.* Hybrids of beast and man. Ben Jonson had the same idea, if not this line, in mind when he called one of the ladies in *The Silent Woman* (1609) Madam Centaur.

IV.vi.141. *Do you.* Quarto reading. Th Folio has 'Do'st thou,' but there seems no reason for Gloucester to speak familiarly to his king at this point.

IV.vi.144. *challenge.* The challenge is addressed to Cupid. Compare the opening of *Much Ado about Nothing* (I.i.32-34), where Beatrice says that Benedick 'challenged Cupid at the flight; and my uncle's fool, reading the challenge, subscribed for Cupid, and challenged him at the bird-bolt.'

IV.vi.157. *handy-dandy.* An expression from a child's game, meaning 'which hand will you have?'—*i.e.*, they both look alike.

IV.vi.162. *in office.* That is, when he has a position of authority. The Quarto has the interesting misprint, 'a dogge, so bade in office,' which is stressed by some critics as evidence that that text depends on hearing rather than the written word. All it means is that the Quarto compositor was here working automatically without his mind on his work and unthinkingly set up the first words suggested by the sounds he was carrying in his head. A subconscious association with 'a dog so bayed' may have put him off the track. The wonder is that the style of *Lear* did not oftener derail him.

IV.vi.165. *lusts.* Second person singular, like *whipp'st* below. Shakespeare was not obliged by current usage to employ the -st form, and did not when it was too cacophonous. (Quarto reading: 'thy bloud hotly lusts.')

IV.vi.167. *Through totter'd rags small vices do appear.* Quarto reading. Here the Folio goes wrong: 'Thorough tatter'd cloathes great Vices do appeare.' But this is cold-blooded perversion by somebody who thought he could improve the text. The meaning is that the smallest vices are seen (and punished) in the poor, but the privileged classes can conceal even the greatest. Shakespeare seems to have preferred the spelling *totter'd* to 'tatter'd,' but both were used.

IV.vi.168. *Plate sin.* Theobald's excellent emendation for the Folio 'Place sinnes.'

IV.vi.177, 178. *O matter . . . madness!* Much the same as Laertes' remark on Ophelia (*Hamlet* IV.i.190): 'A document in madness, thoughts and remembrance fitted.'

IV.vi.185. *block!* One of the remarkable topical anachronisms in the play. Lear (or Gloucester) is wearing one of the flamboyant hats that current fashion prescribed, either the 'copintank' or sugarloaf, or more probably one of the newer type with broad drooping brims. Lear suggests, there would be enough felt in a few of these to shoe a troop of horse, and this sets him off on a mad thought.

IV.vi.S.d. *three Gentlemen.* In the Folio text the frugality of the stage manager has reduced them to one.

Iv.vi.195. *ransom.* He imagines himself on the battlefield and wounded.

Iv.vi.199. *man of salt.* Even a man of salt, whose tears would not be good for the garden.

IV.vi.202. *Good sir.* This speech has had to be supplied from the second Quarto, but it is evident that something has dropped out of the first, which here assigns two consecutive speeches to Lear. In the extant copies of Q 1 no corrections have been noted in sheet I, which contains this part of the play, but, as Q 2 shows no other sign of independent authority, it looks as if it had been printed from a copy of Q 1 which did have this correction (P. A. Daniel).

IV.vi.220. *The main descry, etc.* We expect from hour to hour to get a view of the main body.

IV.vi.237. *To boot, and boot.* A quibble on the two senses of *boot,* one casual, the other spiritual. Gloucester offers Edgar his thanks, wishing him the bounty and benison of heaven *to boot* (in addition) and also, thinking of the deeper meaning, to his soul's *boot.* On em ight paraphrase thus: I give you hearty thanks; I invoke upon you the blessing of heaven also, and the latter (as my thanks are not) is a gift of real profit. The same pun is made, more jocosely, by Autolycus (*Winter's Tale* IV.iv.746f.): 'What an exchange had this been without *boot!* what a *boot* is here with this exchange!

IV.vi.249. *Chill not, etc.* Shakespeare makes Edgar use the Southwestern rustic dialect, which suits him as a Gloucestershire peasant and was familiar to the poet from childhood. It was sometimes called 'Cotswold speech' and became the usual mark of the stage countryman. It is characterized by retention of the old 'ich' for 'I' and the voicing (v, z) of the voiceless spirants, f and s.

IV.vi.254. *che vor ye.* See H. Kökeritz, 'Elizabethan "che vore ye," "I warrant you," ' *Modern Language Notes,* February, 1942. Edgar's dialect may here be slightly wrong.

IV.vi.255. *batoon.* The older English form of French *baton.* The word made trouble. The Quarto printed it 'battero,' reduced in some copies to 'bat.' The folio printed 'Ballow,' a word not otherwise known and probably, like 'battero,' a misreading of 'battoon.' Skeat and Mayhew (*Glossary of Tudor and Stuart Words*) suggest that a 'ballow' might be a quarterstaff made from 'ballow' wood, that is, wood with the bark removed, but this last sense also has very scanty support.

IV.vi.263. *British party.* In the army of the Britons (in opposition to the French). The Folio erroneously prints 'English.'

IV.vi.282, 283. *and . . . tormentor.* One who torments herself with thoughts of you. The Quarto compositor set up what he thought he saw: 'and for you her owne for *Venter.*' The second Quarto and Folio omitted the words entirely (rather than print foolishness, presumably), but they are necessary. Goneril's conclusion is flat without them.

IV.vi.296. *fenced.* Here the Quarto keeps the Shakespearean word, the Folio 'seuer'd' (sever'd) being an easy but trite misreading. If Gloucester were distract, he would have both thoughts and griefs, but they would be fenced or railed off from each other, so that, as he says in the next lines, the griefs (*woes*) would no longer be interpreted by thought and would lose the knowledge of themselves.

IV.vii. As Scene Third of this act is omitted in the Folio, Scenes Fourth, Fifth, and Sixth are naturally there marked 'tertia,' 'quarta,' and 'quinta,' respectively; but the present scene is marked 'septima,' as if there had been no omission. The Folio reduces this scene considerably and combines the Doctor and Gentleman in a single part.

IV.vii.11. *Yet . . . intent.* To be recognized now would limit the scope of my design.

IV.vii.20. *child-changed.* This means both 'changed into a child' and 'changed by the action of his children.'

IV.vii.37, 38. *Was . . . winds?* The Quarto reading. The Folio has 'oppos'd' and 'jarring.' There is a reminiscence, as elsewhere in Shakespeare, of Marlowe's great line. 'Was this the face that launch'd a thousand ships?'

IV.vii.92. *cur'd.* Quarto reading. Folio, 'kill'd.' Here words of opposite sense give the same meaning and there is not a great deal to choose between them.

V.i.16. *as far . . . hers.* To the limit of what she has to give.

V.i.30. *Not bolds, etc.* A confused sentence. Albany apparently means: This business concerns me because France invades Britain, not because France countenances King Lear (in which support of Lear France is joined), with others whom, I fear, righteous and serious causes impel against us. The similarity in meaning as well as form between the two clauses beginning 'with others whom' (lines 26f. and 30f.) is very suspicious.

V.i.35, 36. *For . . . here.* This is not the place to discuss these petty details of domestic friction. (For *particulars* in this sense, *cf.* I.iv.270.) The text is that of the Quarto as emended by Collier and Mitford: *poor* instead of 'dore.' The Folio reads 'For these domestic and particular broils Are not the question here,' which is easy but not very convincing. Shakespeare uses 'broils' to describe tumults of a more violent character than the bickerings Goneril wishes to suggest, and 'particular broils' is a muddy phrase not used elsewhere by Shakespeare. It took quite a number of people to make a broil. If the Folio text were original there would be no accounting for that of the Quarto; but if both rest on a manuscript in which the scribe had carelessly repeated the 'd' of *domestic* in the next word, making 'door' out of *poor,* the compositor or editor of the Folio may have felt justified in rewriting the line according to his own lights.

V.i.43. *riddle.* Since Goneril does not share her knowledge, the riddle remains obscure. This seems to be the meaning. There are two separate British armies which have entered the field successively: a Southern army, commanded by Regan and Edmund, and a Northern army commanded by Albany and Goneril. Regan most surprisingly invites her sister to join Edmund and herself in the Southern camp, and insists that she must come as chaperon (line 42). The 'riddle' Goneril reads is apparently Regan's secret intention to take advantage of her sister's visit to poison her. When we next see them, we find it is Goneril who has poisoned Regan. On the stage the words would be delivered with a sort of wink to the audience, inviting them to watch developments.

V.i.61. *By diligent discovery.* Edmund has been engaged on a reconnaissance. See IV.v.15, 16.

V.ii.S.d. This, except the words, *and exeunt,* is the Quarto stage direction. The Folio version is drier and more technical.

V.ii.1. *bush.* The Folio makes it a 'Tree,' but a bush would be better cover for the old man in a battle.

V.ii.12. *Ripeness is all.* Compare *Hamlet* V.ii.211, 212: '. . . if it be not now, yet it will come: the readiness is all' (Steevens).

V.iii.S.d. The Folio stage direction, probably composed by the stage-manager. Shakespeare may have written the simpler (and insufficient) version of the Quarto: *'Enter Edmund, with Lear and Cordelia prisoners.'*

V.iii.2. *their greater pleasures.* That is, the will of those personages of higher rank (than mine); *i.e.,* Goneril, Regan, and Albany.

V.iii.17, 18. *And take upon's the mystery of things, As if we were God's spies.* Undertake to explain the mysterious ways of providence, as if we were spying on God Himself. This seems to be the only allusion in the play to the Christian God.

V.iii.19. *packs and sects of great ones.* Flocks and flocks of office-holders. The distinguishing thing about all these is that they have no personal existence, but are mere units in a transient crowd. The lowest ones are grouped in packs, like dogs or wolves; the most intelligent in sects, like philosophers.

V.iii.22. *Upon such sacrifices, etc.* A paganized echo of two well-known Scriptural passages: 'The sacrifice of God is a troubled spirit: a broken and contrite heart, O God, shalt thou not despise' (Psalm 51. 17), and 'for with such sacrifices God is well pleased' (Hebrews 13. 16).

V.iii.24, 25. *He . . . foxes.* The last resort for getting foxes from their holes was fire. At Judgment Day the whole world will be subjected to the same treatment. Cordelia and Lear will dwell in their prison secure and united as foxes in their 'earths,' and nothing shall drive them hence but the angel of judgment with his fiery brand.

V.iii.26. *good years.* A vague phrase, perhaps Dutch in origin, suggesting some unnamed malign force. Still current in English dialect as 'The Goodgers.'

V.iii.36, 37. *Thy . . question.* The important service I am offering you cannot be discussed.

V.iii.43. *I cannot draw a cart nor eat dried oats.* I cannot live like a beast of burden: I must better my condition.

V.iii.S.d. As in the Folio, doubtless after the prompter's revision. Shakespeare's more casual way of dealing with such details probably appears in the Quarto version: *'Enter Duke, the two Ladies, and others.'*

V.iii.48. *I.* So the Folio, correctly. The Quarto, doubtless misled by the next line, has 'We.' Albany does not until much later (line 354 below) assume the royal 'We,' as Regan does in line 69. In line 49 *we . . . our* means 'all of us in our council' and 'our general safety.'

V.iii.62, 63. *And the best quarrels in the heat are curs'd By those that feel their sharpness.* Edmund is saying that we are in no mood to judge dispassionately while suffering personal discomfort. He illustrates by a figure from an archery contest, *heat* meaning 'bout' (as in horse-races). A man who has been accidentally struck by one of the *quarrels* (cross-bow arrows) is more likely to curse it than to praise its extraordinary length of flight. Of course there is a quibble on the other sense of 'quarrel.'

V.iii.77. *your addition.* The title you have given him. The Quarto has 'your advancement,' probably a simplification of a rather unusual expression.

V.iii.80. *That were the most, if he should husband you.* The Quarto, followed by most editors, gives this speech to Goneril.

V.iii.87. The line is not in the Quarto, and the Folio reading, 'the walls is thine,' does not make sense. The conjecture, *whole,* is an old one, but anonymous.

V.iii.91. *The let-alone.* Waiver of one's claim, promise to pursue *a laissez-faire* policy; used of land with a clouded title. Goneril, Albany says, has no property in Edmund, no legal position in regard to him.

V.iii.94. The Quarto gives this line to Edmund, changing the words to 'prove my title good.'

V.iii.97. *attaint.* In conjunction with your attainder or accusation of dishonor. The Folio has 'in thy arrest' by influence of the line above.

V.iii.109. *mark.* The Folio reads 'make' and the Quarto 'prove' (probably repeated from line 107). In the Folio word the type is spread so as to suggest that an 'r' may have dropped out in printing.

V.iii.154. *Behold, it is the privilege of my tongue.* So the Quarto. The Folio is confused here, missing both sense and rhythm: 'Behold it is my privilege, The privilege of mine Honours.'

V.iii.170. *What safe and nicely I might well delay.* For the sake of the record. Edmund makes the most of the fact that knights accepted challenges only from opponents of proper rank; but his action, like all his actions, is practical and self-interested. Deprived of military power, arrested as a traitor, and challenged by Albany, he has little to lose in encountering the unknown and a good deal perhaps to gain, since victory in trial by combat cleared the victor of the charges against him.

V.iii.172, 173. *treasons, lie.* Accusations of treason and lying. *Which* in the next line refers to both.

V.iii.182, 183. *Stop . . . stopple it.* Quarto reading. Folio: 'Shut . . . stop it.' It looks as if the Folio editor added the words 'Hold, sir' to complete his metrically deficient line, under the erroneous impression that line 184 is addressed to Edmund.

V.iii.190. *Ask . . . know.* Assigned to Edmund in the Folio.

V.iii.206. *I am here.* At the foot of Fortune's wheel, where his life began.

V.iii.216. *The bloody proclamation to escape.* In order to escape the hue and cry after me as a capital offender. When this sentence resumes after the parenthesis, the construction is altered. Instead of *taught me* in line 219, one would expect something like 'I was obliged.'

V.iii.240–242. *but another . . . extremity.* But if I were to recount another sorrow too fully, it would make much more (sorrow) and exceed the limit of endurance.

V.iii.244, 245. *having . . . society.* When he had seen me as Poor Tom, he had shunned my abhorrent company.

V.iii.248. *threw him.* Threw himself. Theobald's emendation for the Quarto 'threw me.'

V.iii.258–260. *Alb. Speak, man.* The Quarto, omitting this short speech, throws the two questions of Edgar together and gives them as one speech to Albany.

V.iii.268, 269. *Here comes Kent, sir.* The quarto has this and the entrance of Kent follow the words 'Touches us not with pity' (line 272), which would seem to be more effective; but the metrical dove-tailing of speeches indicates that the Folio order was intentional.

V.iii.284. *Poison'd for my sake, and after slew herself.* A fine tumultuous line with a spondaic second foot. Read 'Poison'd for my sáke.'

V.iii.311. *Fall and cease!* Albany invokes the heaven and earth to display the accompaniments of Judgment Day. Fall, heavens! Cease, earth!

V.iii.327, 328. *I have . . . skip.* Reminiscent of *Othello* V.ii.309-312f.:

> *I have seen the day*
> *That with this little arm and this good sword*
> *I have made my way through more impediments*
> *Than twenty times your stop.*

V.iii.331, 332. *If fortune . . . behold.* If the inconstant goddess can boast that she ever consistently loved one man and hated another, then one of those two (the latter) we behold. The meaning is clear if we understand the word 'respectively' before *lov'd.*

V.iii.343. *Nor . . . else.* Kent sees the grisly irony of Lear's words and puns on them: Neither I nor any of the rest of us have well come hither.

V.iii.352. *know our intent.* Albany, as the survivor of those to whom Lear had transferred his absolute power, now assumes the royal prerogative and language in order to return to him what he had resigned.

V.iii.356, 357. *You . . . rights.* That is, I wish you a happy return to the rightful dignities you have been deprived of.

V.iii.362. *my poor fool.* A phrase of tenderness, of course; but more telling if the rôles of Cordelia and the Fool were linked and Lear were felt by the audience to be taking leave of both of them. See note on III.vi.80.

V.iii.384. *Edg.* The Quarto gives this last speech to Albany, who might be expected to close the play, but the Folio is right. It is Edgar's reply to Albany's commission: *Rule in this realm.* Kent replies that he cannot serve because he expects to follow his master in death. Edgar replies that the young must accept the burden of the time and answer its demands by the dictates of their hearts rather than their heads: Speak what we feel, not what we ought (prudentially) to say. He accepts Albany's commission.

The Tragedy of Macbeth

Edited by
EUGENE M. WAITH

Dramatis Personae

DUNCAN, *King of Scotland*

MALCOLM ⎱ *his Sons*
DONALBAIN ⎰

MACBETH ⎱ *Generals of the King's Army*
BANQUO ⎰

MACDUFF
LENNOX
ROSS
MENTETH ⎱ *Noblemen of Scotland*
ANGUS
CATHNESS

FLEANCE, *Son to Banquo*

SIWARD, *Earl of Northumberland,*
General of the English forces

YOUNG SIWARD, *his Son*

SEYTON, *an Officer attending on Macbeth*

BOY, *Son to Macduff*

AN ENGLISH DOCTOR
A SCOTCH DOCTOR
A CAPTAIN
A PORTER
AN OLD MAN
LADY MACBETH
LADY MACDUFF
GENTLEWOMAN ATTENDING ON LADY MACBETH
HECCAT
THREE WITCHES

LORDS, GENTLEMEN, OFFICERS, SOLDIERS,
  MURTHERERS, ATTENDANTS, AND
  MESSENGERS; THE GHOST OF BANQUO,
  AND OTHER APPARITIONS

SCENE—*Scotland; in IV.3, England.*

The Tragedy of Macbeth

INTRODUCTION

TEXT AND DATE

The Tragedie of Macbeth* was first printed in the Folio of 1623, the First Folio. This is the only authoritative text, and is consequently the basis of the present edition. From the early 18th century to the present time many editors, feeling that the Folio text was seriously corrupt, have altered it extensively. The main reasons for this feeling are, first, that the play is abnormally short, suggesting that it was cut; second, that certain passages presenting Heccat (III.5; IV.1.39–43, 136–143), stylistically different from the rest of the play, seem to have been interpolated; and, third, that the lineation of the play is often markedly irregular. Most critics agree that the shortness may be due in part to the special requirements of a court performance, but it cannot be proved that there was a much longer version which was drastically cut, as some have suspected. In fact, it is difficult to imagine what of any importance is missing from the play as it stands. As A. C. Bradley pointed out long ago in his *Shakespearean Tragedy* (London, Macmillan, 1912, pp. 468–9): (1) 'there is no internal evidence of the omission of anything essential to the plot,' (2) Simon Forman, who saw the play in 1611 (see below) mentions nothing we do not find in the Folio; and (3) if extensive cuts were made, their location is extremely puzzling. The question is complicated by the virtual certainty that Shakespeare did not leave the play in its present form. The Heccat passages, referred to above, not only stand out stylistically, but seen to relate *Macbeth* to *The Witch*, a manuscript play by Thomas Middleton, in which Heccat appears, singing two songs indicated in the stage direction of *Macbeth* (III.5.33, IV.1.43). The exact relationship of these plays is uncertain, but it is probable that someone, possibly Middleton himself, added the Heccat passages in the course of revising Shakespeare's play. Although this speculation opens the further possibility that the entire play was substantially altered at the time of this revision, a conservative view limits the changes to the relatively brief interpolations.

It is possible, then, that neither the first nor the second reason for suspecting widespread corruption is valid. Modern editors, such as J. Dover Wilson and Kenneth Muir, argue against the earlier, pessimistic view. The irregular lineation of the Folio, however, presents a difficult problem. If it is not due to the hand of an unskillful reviser, it may be explained as the fantasy of a compositor or as an indication of how the lines should be read. Though I do not brush aside the possibility that the compositor (or a transcriber of the manuscript) rearranged Shakespeare's lines, the alternative explanation seems to me to deserve more consideration than it has been given. For example, Wilson[1] cites the end of II.2 as a place where the compositors 'have obviously been monkeying with the verse-lining . . . in order to fill up their columns.' It may be so, but can we be certain that the Folio printing does not indicate the pauses occasioned by the knocking at the gate and by the anxiety it arouses in Lady Macbeth and

Macbeth? A pause between Macbeth's last two lines seems a necessity, and in each of the other cases where these half-lines appear as separate lines, a marked pause might create an appropriate effect. If the half-lines are combined, as is usually done, the indication of such effects is lost. Here and in a few comparable situations I have retained the separate lines, but have introduced modern echeloning. Another example of a sort of punctuation by line-division is provided by III.2.24, 25, which most editors print as one line. This alteration not only obscures what may again be the indication of a pause, but suggests that *ecstasy* should be crowded into one foot so as to make room in the line for 'Duncan is in his grave.' As they are printed in the Folio, both of these short lines are made up of three feet, and the rhythm and meaning are better served by reading them in that way. Accentuation is adversely affected in another instance, III.1.87, 88, printed by most editors:

> which held you
> So under fortune, which you thought had been
> Our innocent self.

The Folio arrangement, reprinted in this text, suggests the accentuation:

> Which yóu thought hád been oúr innocent sélf.

This reading, with its heavy emphasis on Macbeth's deceptive portrayal of himself, seems to me a good one; it is surely not indicated by the alternative arrangement. One more instance of what may be punctuation by irregular line-division is II.1.9–11. It is natural for Banquo to pause after the word *sleep* before uttering his anguished prayer. Though l. 10 has six feet and l. 11 only four, no rearrangement is entirely satisfactory, and the lines as they stand correspond to a natural musical phrasing.

In the face of such evidence we cannot assume that we shall be getting back to what Shakespeare wrote by rearranging the lines in the closest approximation to iambic pentameter. Since the contrary assumption, that the Folio is always right, is also unwarranted, each irregularity must be considered separately. My aim has been to reproduce the Folio lineation except where I could find no *raison d'être* for an irregularity, or where one could be corrected easily without altering the rhythm or meaning. For example, the Folio prints I.3.142–144 thus:

> This supernaturall solliciting
> Cannot be ill; cannot be good.
> If ill? why hath it giuen me earnest of successe,

This division might be defended as logical, but no damage is done to a good reading of the lines by adding the first foot of l. 144 to the end of l. 143, making them both normal five-foot lines. In some instances, such as III.1.96–102, the familiar modern rearrangement seems a definite improvement over the Folio's senseless irregularity. Here is the passage as the Folio gives it:

---

1. *Macbeth*, Cambridge, Cambridge University Press, 1951, pp. 90–1.

Macb. *I did so:*
And went further, which is now
Our point of second meeting.
Doe you finde your patience so predominant,
In your nature, that you can let this goe?
Are you so Gospell'd, to pray for this good man,
And for his Issue, whose heauie hand
Hath bow'd you to the Graue, and begger'd
Yours for euer?

This erractic lineation in no way clarifies the meaning of the passage, nor does it correspond to any conceivable speech rhythm. In such instances I have reproduced a regularization of the lines.

My conclusion is that the case against the irregular lineation of the Folio is not proven. In a large number of passages, therefore, I have preferred to accept the Folio arrangement as possibly deliberate and meaningful. While there is no guarantee that Shakespeare wrote the lines this way, there is at least a fair chance that they were spoken this way, whereas the regularizations often represent only the prosody of an 18th-century editor. The argument for the procedure I have adopted is strengthened by the fact that comparable irregularities of lineation occur in *Coriolanus* and *Antony and Cleopatra*, which are thought to have been set up from Shakespeare's own manuscripts. I should point out here that because I have not kept the modern regularizations, the line-numbering of this edition often differs slightly from that of the Globe edition, on which many references are based.

There is little obscurity in *Macbeth*. In a very few instances, where it seemed essential for the understanding of a passage, I have accepted emendations, recording the divergence from the Folio at the foot of the page. I have rejected two emendations which have become so familiar that the original forms will shock many readers. *Scorch'd* (III.2.15) is a good word, and has been accepted by several modern editors in preference to Theobald's unnecessary emendation, *scotch'd*. Theobald is also responsible for *weird*, instead of which I have kept *weyard*, the form occuring most often in the Folio. The spelling *weird* never occurs there, and Theobald's diaeresis is an unsatisfactory means of indicating the two syllables clearly required by the meter. Except in such instances as this, where an archaic spelling is a necessary indication of pronunciation, I have used modern American spelling. In punctuating, I have tried to give the modern equivalents of the Elizabethan marks.

The first recorded performance of *Macbeth* is that which the astrologer, Dr. Simon Forman, attended on April 20, 1611. Though his reference to 'women feiries or Nimphes' suggests that he refreshed his memory of the play by reading in Holinshed's *Chronicle*, his account of the performance is extremely interesting as showing what particularly struck one contemporary spectator:

In Mackbeth at the glob[2] 1610[3] the 20 of aprill [Saturday[4]]. ther was to be obserued firste howe Mackbeth and Bancko 2 noble men[5] of Scotland Ridinge thorowe a wod the[r] stode befor them 3 women feiries or Nimphes And Saluted Mackbeth sayinge: 3 tyms vnto him. Haille mackbeth. king of Codor[6] for thou shalt be a kinge but shalt beget No kinges. &c. then said Bancko What all to mackbeth And nothing to

me. Yes said the nimphes Haille to thee Banko thou shalt beget kinges. yet be no kinge And so they departed & cam to the Courte of Scotland to Dunkin king of Scotes and yt was in the dais of Edward the Confessor. And Dunkin bad them both kindly wellcom. And made Mackbeth forth with Prince of Northumberland. and sent him hom to his own castell and appointed mackbeth to prouid for him for he wold Sup with him the next dai at night. & did soe. And mackebeth contrived to kill Dunkin. & thorowe the persuasion of his wife did that night Murder the kinge in his own Castell beinge his guest And ther were many prodigies seen that night & the dai before. And when Mack Beth had murdred the kinge the blod on his handes could not be washed of by Any means. nor from his wiues handes which handled the bluddi daggers in hiding them By which means they became both moch amazed & affronted. the murder being knowen Dunkins 2 sonns fled the on to England the [other to] Walles to saue them selues. they beinge fled they were supposed guilty of the murder of their father which was nothinge so—Then was Mackbeth. Crowned kinge and then be for feare of Banko his old Companion that he should beget kinges but be no kinge him self. he contriued the death to Banko and caused him to be Murdred on the way as he Rode The next night beinge at supper with his noble men whom he had bid to a feaste to the which also Banco should haue com. he began to speake of Noble Banco and to wish that he wer ther. And as he thus did standing vp to drincke a Carouse to him. the ghoste of Banco came and sate down in his cheier behind him. And he turninge About to sit down Again sawe the goste of banco which fronted him so. that he fell in to a great passion of fear & fury. Vtteringe many wordes about his murder by which when they hard that Banco was Murdred they Suspected Mackbet.

Then Mack Dove fled to England to the kinges sonn. And soe they Raised an Army and cam to scotland. and at dun ston Anyse over thrue Mackbet. In the meantyme whille Macdouee was in England Mackbet slewe Mackdoues wife & children. and after in the battelle mackdoue slewe mackbet.

Obserue Also howe Mackbetes quen did Rise in the night in her slepe & walke and talked and confessed all & the docter noted her words.[7]

That the performance seen by Forman was not the first is suggested by what seem to be topical allusions in the play to events of 1606, such as the apparent reference to Garnet in II.3.7. *Macbeth* may have been given at Hampton Court before James I and his royal guest, Christian IV of Denmark, on August 7, 1606; Shakespeare may even have written the play specifically for this occasion.[8] From various bits of evidence it seems most likely that *Macbeth* belongs to the year 1606.

Any editor of Shakespeare is enormously indebted to his predecessors. I wish to acknowledge in particular my debt to Mark Harvey Liddell (New York Doubleday, Page, 1903), George Lyman Kittredge (Boston, Ginn, 1939), J. Dover Wilson (Cambridge, Cambridge University Press, 1947), and Kenneth Muir (London, Methuen, 1951). I am grateful for innumerable suggestions from the general editors of the Yale Shakespeare, Professors Helge Kökeritz and Charles T. Prouty.

---

2. Miswritten 'glod.'
3. A slip for '1611,' as is clear from other entries in the MS.
4. Represented by an astronomical sign for Saturn.
5. Italicized letters indicate expansions of MS contractions.
6. Miswritten 'Codon.'

7. See *Macbeth*, ed. G. L. Kittredge, pp. 240–1; E. K. Chambers, *William Shakespeare*, Oxford, Clarendon Press, 1930, 2, 337–8.
8. Henry N. Paul, *The Royal Play of Macbeth* (New York, Macmillan, 1950, pp. 317–31), adduces persuasive evidence to support this hypothesis.

SOURCES OF THE PLAY

Shakespeare's chief source for *Macbeth* was the second edition (1587) of Raphael Holinshed's *Chronicles of England, Scotland, and Ireland*. The excerpts from 'The Historie of Scotland' printed below illustrate how Shakespeare put together details from various sections of this work. He obviously read in the pages preceding the account of Macbeth about the murder of King Duff by Donwald, and about the sleeplessness of King Kenneth, tormented by guilt after he had murdered his nephew:

But Donwald, not forgetting the reproch which his linage had susteined by the execution of those his kinsmen, whome the king for a spectacle to the people had caused to be hanged, could not but shew manifest tokens of great griefe at home amongst his familie: which his wife perceiuing, ceassed not to trauell with him, till she vnderstood what the cause was of his displeasure. Which at length when she had learned by his owne relation, she as one that bare no lesse malice in hir heart towards the king, for the like cause of hir behalfe, than hir husband did for his friends, counselled him (sith the king oftentimes vsed to lodge in his house without anie gard about him, other than the garrison of the castell, which was wholie at his commandement) to make him awaie, and shewed him the meanes wherby he might soonest accomplish it.

Donwald thus being the more kindled in wrath by the words of his wife, determined to follow hir aduise in the execution of so heinous an act. Whervpon deuising with himselfe for a while, which way hee might best accomplish his cursed intent, at length gat opportunitie, and sped his purpose as followeth. It chanced that the king vpon the daie before he purposed to depart foorth of the castell, was long in his oratorie at his praiers, and there continued till it was late in the night. At the last, comming foorth, he called such afore him as had faithfullie serued him in pursute and apprehension of the rebels, and giuing them heartie thanks, he bestowed sundrie honorable gifts amongst them, of the which number Donwald was one, as he that had beene euer accounted a most faithfull seruant to the king.

At length, hauing talked with them a long time, he got him into his priuie chamber, onelie with two of his chamberlains, who hauing brought him to bed, came foorth againe, and then fell to banketting with Donwald and his wife, who had prepared diuerse delicate dishes, and sundrie sorts of drinks for their reare supper or collation, wherat they sate vp so long, till they had charged their stomachs with such full gorges, that their heads were no sooner got to the pillow, but asleepe they were so fast, that a man might haue remooued the chamber ouer them, sooner than to haue awaked them out of their droonken sleepe.

Then Donwald, though he abhorred the act greatlie in heart, yet through instigation of his wife hee called foure of his seruants vnto him (whome he had made priuie to his wicked intent before, and framed to his purpose with large gifts) and now declaring vnto them, after what sort they should worke the feat, they gladlie obeied his instructions, & speedilie going about the murther, they enter the chamber (in which the king laie) a little before cocks crow, where they secretlie cut his throte as he lay sleeping, without anie buskling at all: and immediatlie by a posterne gate they caried foorth the dead bodie into the fields . . .

Donwald, about the time that the murther was in dooing,

got him amongst them that kept the watch, and so continued in companie with them all the residue of the night. But in the morning when the noise was raised in the kings chamber how the king was slaine, his bodie conueied awaie, and the bed all beraied with bloud; he with the watch ran thither, as though he had knowne nothing of the matter, and breaking into the chamber, and finding cakes of bloud in the bed, and on the floore about the sides of it, he foorthwith slue the chamber-leins, as guiltie of that heinous murther, and then like a mad man running to and fro, he ransacked euerie corner within the castell, as though it had beene to haue seene if he might have found either the bodie, or anie of the murtherers hid in anie priuie place: but at length comming to the posterne gate, and finding it open, he burdened the chamberleins, whome he had slaine, with all the fault, they hauing the keies of the gates committed to their keeping all the night, and therefore it could not be otherwise (said he) but that they were of counsell in the committing of that most detestable murther.

Finallie, such was his ouer earnest diligence in the seuere inquisition and triall of the offendors heerein, that some of the lords began to mislike the matter, and to smell foorth shrewd tokens, that he should not be altogither cleare himselfe. But for so much as they were in that countrie, where he had the whole rule, what by reason of his friends and authoritie togither, they doubted to vtter what they thought, till time and place should better serue therevnto, and heerevpon got them awaie euerie man to his home. For the space of six moneths togither, after this heinous murther thus committed, there appeered no sunne by day, nor moone by night in anie part of the realme, but still was the skie couered with continuall clouds, and sometimes such outragious winds arose, with lightenings and tempests, that the people were in great feare of present destruction. . . .

Monstrous sights also that were seene within the Scotish kingdome that yeere were these: horsses in Louthian, being of singular beautie and swiftnesse, did eate their owne flesh, and would in no wise taste anie other meate. In Angus there was a gentlewoman brought foorth a child without eies, nose, hand, or foot. There was a sparhawke also strangled by an owle. Neither was it anie lesse woonder that the sunne, as before is said, was continuallie couered with clouds for six moneths space. But all men vnderstood that the abhominable murther of king Duffe was the cause heereof . . . (Pp. 150–2).

Thus might he seeme happie to all men, hauing the loue both of his lords and commons: but yet to himselfe he seemed most vnhappie, as he that could not but still liue in continuall feare, least his wicked practise concerning the death of Malcolme Duffe should come to light and knowledge of the world. For so commeth it to passe, that such as are pricked in conscience for anie secret offense committed, haue euer an vnquiet mind. And (as the fame goeth) it chanced that a voice was heard as he was in bed in the night time to take his rest, vttering vnto him these or the like woords in effect: 'Thinke not Kenneth that the wicked slaughter of Malcolme Duffe by thee contriued, is kept secret from the knowledge of the eternall God: thou art he that didst conspire the innocents death, enterprising by traitorous meanes to doo that to thy neighbour, which thou wouldest haue reuenged by cruell punishment in anie of thy subjects, if it had beene offered to thy selfe. It shall therefore come to passe, that both thou thy selfe, and thy

issue, through the iust vengeance of almightie God, shall suffer woorthie punishment, to the infamie of thy house and familie for euermore. For euen at this present are there in hand secret practises to dispatch both thee and thy issue out of the waie, that other maie inioy this kingdome which thou doost indeuour to assure vnto thine issue.'

The king, with this voice being striken into great dread and terror, passed that night without anie sleepe comming in his eies. (P. 158.)

Ten pages later comes the story of Duncan's succession to the throne:

After Malcolme succeeded his nephue Duncane the sonne of his daughter Beatrice: for Malcolme had two daughters, the one which was this Beatrice, being giuen in mariage vnto one Abbanath Crinen, a man of great nobilitie, and thane of the Iles and west parts of Scotland, bare of that mariage the foresaid Duncane; the other called Doada, was maried vnto Sinell the thane of Glammis, by whom she had issue one Makbeth a valiant gentleman, and one that if he had not beene somewhat cruell of nature, might have beene thought most woorthie the gouernement of a realme. On the other part, Duncane was so soft and gentle of nature, that the people wished the inclinations and maners of these two cousins to haue beene so tempered and interchangeablie bestowed betwixt them, that where the one had too much of clemencie, and the other of crueltie, the meane vertue betwixt these two extremities might haue reigned by indifferent partition in them both, so should Duncane haue proued a woorthie king, and Makbeth an excellent capteine.

Holinshed then gives a lengthy account of the rebellion of Makdowald (Shakespeare's 'merciless Macdonwald'), and the wars against Sueno of Norway and Canute of England, in all of which Macbeth and Banquo fought victoriously for Duncan. The three actions are combined in the account given in I.2. Next comes the introduction of Macbeth's ambition for the throne:

After these were the warres that Duncane had with forren enimies, in the seuenth yeere of his reigne. Shortlie after happened a strange and vncouth woonder, which afterward was the cause of much trouble in the realme of Scotland, as ye shall after heare. It fortuned as Makbeth and Banquho iournied towards Fores, where the king then laie, they went sporting by the waie togither without other companie, saue onelie themselues, passing thorough the woods and fields, when suddenlie in the middest of a laund, there met them three women in strange and wild apparell, resembling creatures of elder world, whome when they attentiuelie beheld, woondering much at the sight, the first of them spake and said; 'All haile Makbeth, thane of Glammis' (for he had latelie entered into that dignitie and office by the death of his father Sinell). The second of them said: 'Haile Makbeth thane of Cawder.' But the third said; 'All haile Mackbeth that heereafter shalt be king of Scotland.'

Then Banquho; 'What manner of woman (saith he) are you, that seeme so little fauourable vnto me, whereas to my fellow heere, besides high offices, ye assigne also the kingdome, appointing foorth nothing for me at all?' 'Yes (saith the first of them) we promise greater benefits vnto thee, than vnto him, for he shall reigne in deed, but with an vnluckie end: neither shall he leaue anie issue behind him to succeed in his place,

where contrarilie thou in deed shalt not reigne at all, but of thee those shall be borne which shall gouerne the Scotish kingdome by long order of continuall descent.' Herewith the foresaid women vanished immediatlie out of their sight. This was reputed at the first but some vaine fantasticall illusion by Mackbeth and Banquho, insomuch that Banquho would call Mackbeth in iest, king of Scotland; and Mackbeth againe would call him in sport likewise, the father of manie kings. But afterwards the common opinion was, that these women were either the weird sisters, that is (as ye would say) the goddesses of destinie, or else some nymphs or feiries, indued with knowledge of prophesie by their necromanticall science, bicause euerie thing came to passe as they had spoken. For shortlie after, the thane of Cawder being condemned at Fores of treason against the king committed; his lands, liuings, and offices were giuen of the kings liberalitie to Mackbeth.

The same night after, at supper, Banquho iested with him and said; Now Mackbeth thou hast obteined those things which the two former sisters prophesied, there remaineth onelie for thee to purchase that which the third said should come to passe. Wherevpon Mackbeth reuoluing the thing in his mind, began euen then to deuise how he might atteine to the kingdome: but yet he thought with himselfe that he must tarie a time, which should aduance him thereto (by the diuine prouidence) as it had come to passe in his former preferment. But shortlie after it chanced the king Duncane, hauing two sonnes by his wife which was the daughter of Siward earle of Northumberland, he made the elder of them called Malcolme prince of Cumberland, as it were thereby to appoint him his successor in the kingdome, immediatlie after his decease. Mackbeth sore troubled herewith, for that he saw by this means his hope sore hindered (where, by the old lawes of the realme, the ordinance was, that if he that should succeed were not of able age to take the charge vpon himselfe, he that was next of bloud vnto him should be admitted) he began to take counsell how he might vsurpe the kingdome by force, hauing a iust quarell so to doo (as he tooke the matter) for that Duncane did what in him lay to defraud him of all maner of title and claime, which he might in time to come, pretend vnto the crowne.

The woords of the three weird sisters also (of whom before ye haue heard) greatlie incouraged him hereunto, but speciallie his wife lay sore vpon him to attempt the thing, as she that was verie ambitious, burning in vnquenchable desire to beare the name of a queene. At length therefore, communicating his purposed intent with his trustie friends, amongst whome Banquho was the chiefest, vpon confidence of their promised aid, he slue the king at Enuerns, or (as some say) at Botgosuane, in the sixt years of his reigne. Then hauing a companie about him of such as he had made priuie to his enterprise, he caused himselfe to be proclaimed king, and foorthwith went vnto Scone, where (by common consent) he receiued the inuesture of the kingdome according to the accustomed maner. The bodie of Duncane was first conueied vnto Elgine, & there buried in kinglie wise; but afterwards it was remoued and conueied vnto Colmekill, and there laid in a sepulture amongst his predecessors, in the yeare after the birth of our Sauiour, 1046.

Malcolme Cammore and Donald Bane the sons of king Duncane, for feare of their liues (which they might well know that Mackbeth would seeke to bring to end for his more sure confirmation in the estate) fled into Cumberland, where Malcolme remained, till time that saint Edward the sonne of

Ethelred recouered the dominion of England from the Danish power, the which Edward receiued Malcolme by way of most friendlie enterteinment: but Donald passed ouer into Ireland, where he was tenderlie cherished by the king of that land. Mackbeth, after the departure thus of Duncanes sonnes, vsed great liberalitie towards the nobles of the realme, thereby to win their fauour, and when he saw that no man went about to trouble him, he set his whole intention to mainteine iustice, and to punish all enormities and abuses, which had chanced through the feeble and slouthful administration of Duncane. (Pp. 170–1).

After Holinshed has described some good laws passed by Macbeth at the beginning of his reign, he continues:

These and the like commendable lawes Mackbeth caused to be put as then in vse, gouerning the realme for the space of ten yeares in equall iustice. But this was but a counterfet zeale of equitie shewed by him, partlie against his naturall inclination to purchase thereby the fauour of the people. Shortlie after, he began to shew what he was, in stead of equitie practising crueltie. For the pricke of conscience (as it chanceth euer in tyrants, and such as atteine to anie estate by vnrighteous means) caused him euer to feare, least he should be serued of the same cup, as he had ministred to his predecessor. The woords also of the three weird sisters, would not out of his mind, which as they promised him the kingdome, so likewise did they promise it at the same time vnto the posteritie of Banquho. He willed therefore the same Banquho with his sonne named Fleance, to come to a supper that he had prepared for them, which was in deed, as he had deuised, present death at the hands of certeine murderers, whom he hired to execute that deed, appointing them to meete with the same Banquho and his sonne without the palace, as they returned to their lodgings, and there to slea them, so that he would not haue his house slandered, but that in time to come he might cleare himselfe, if anie thing were laid in his charge vpon anie suspicion that might arise.

It chanced yet by the benefit of the darke night, that though the father were slaine, the sonne yet by the helpe of almightie God reseruing him to better fortune, escaped that danger: and afterwards hauing some inkeling (by the admonition of some friends which he had in the court) how his life was sought no lesse than his fathers, who was slaine not by chancemedlie (as by the handling of the matter Makbeth woould haue had it to appeare) but euen vpon a prepensed deuise: wherevpon to auoid further perill he fled into Wales. (P. 172.)

An account of the Stuart dynasty follows. Shakespeare, at a comparable point in his play, introduces the 'show of eight kings.' Holinshed then describes how Macbeth became suspicious of Macduff:

Neither could he afterwards abide to looke vpon the said Makduffe, either for that he thought his puissance ouer great; either else for that he had learned of certeine wizzards, in whose words he put great confidence (for that the prophesie had happened so right, which the three faries or weird sisters had declared vnto him) how that he ought to take heed of Makduffe, who in time to come should seeke to destroie him.

And suerlie herevpon had he put Makduffe to death, but that a certeine witch, whom hee had in great trust, had told that he should neuer be slaine with man borne of anie woman,

nor vanquished till the wood of Bernane came to the castell of Dunsinane. By this prophesie Makbeth put all feare out of his heart, supposing he might doo what he would, without anie feare to be punished for the same, for by the one prophesie he beleeued it was vnpossible for anie man to vanquish him, and by the other vnpossible to slea him. This vaine hope caused him to doo manie outragious things, to the greeuous oppression of his subiects. At length Makduffe, to auoid peril of life, purposed with himselfe to passe into England, to procure Malcolme Cammore to claime the crowne of Scotland. But this was not so secretlie deuised by Makduffe, but that Makbeth had knowledge giuen him thereof: for kings (as is said) haue sharpe sight like vnto Lynx, and long ears like vnto Midas. For Makbeth had in euerie noble mans house one slie fellow or other in fee with him, to reueale all that was said or doone within the same, by which slight he oppressed the most part of the nobles of his realme.

Immediatlie then, being aduertised whereabout Makduffe went, he came hastily with a great power into Fife, and foorthwith besieged the castell where Makduffe dwelled, trusting to haue found him therein. They that kept the house, without anie resistance opened the gates, and suffered him to enter, mistrusting none euill. But neuertheless Makbeth most cruellie caused the wife and children of Makduffe, with all other whom he found in that castell, to be slaine. Also he confiscated the goods of Makduffe, proclamed him traitor, and confined him out of all the parts of his realme; but Makduffe was alreadie escaped out of danger, and gotten into England vnto Malcolme Cammore, to trie what purchase hee might make by means of his support, to reuenge the slaughter so cruellie executed on his wife, his children, and other friends. At his comming vnto Malcolme, he declared into what great miserie the estate of Scotland was brought, by the detestable crueltie exercised by the tyrant Makbeth, hauing committed manie horrible slaughters and murders, both as well of the nobles as commons, for the which he was hated right mortallie of all his liege people, desiring nothing more than to be deliuered of that intollerable and most heauie yoke of thraldome, which they susteined at such a caitifes hands.

Malcolme hearing Makduffe's woords, which he vttered in verie lamentable sort, for meere compassion and verie ruth that pearsed his sorowfull hart, bewailing the miserable state of his countrie, he fetched a deepe sigh; which Makduffe perceiuing, began to fall most earnestlie in hand with him, to enterprise the deliuering of the Scotish people out of the hands of so cruell and bloudie a tyrant, as Makbeth by too manie plaine experiments did shew himselfe to be: which was an easie matter for him to bring to passe, considering not onelie the good title he had, but also the earnest desire of the people to haue some occasion ministred, whereby they might be reuenged of those notable iniuries, which they dailie susteined by the outragious crueltie of Makbeths misgouernance. Though Malcolme was verie sorowfull for the oppression of his countriemen the Scots, in maner as Makduffe had declared; yet doubting whether he were come as one that ment vnfeinedlie as he spake, or else as sent from Makbeth to betraie him, he thought to haue some further triall, and therevpon dissembling his mind at the first, he answered as followeth.

'I am trulie verie sorie for the miserie chanced to my countrie of Scotland, but though I haue neuer so great affection to relieue the same, yet by reason of certeine incurable vices,

which reigne in me, I am nothing meet thereto. First, such immoderate lust and voluptuous sensualitie (the abhominable founteine of all vices) followeth me, that if I were made king of Scots, I should seeke to defloure your maids and matrones, in such wise that mine intemperancie should be more importable vnto you than the bloudie tyrannie of Makbeth now is.' Heerevnto Makduffe answers: 'This suerlie is a verie euill fault, for manie noble princes and kings haue lost both liues and kingdomes for the same; neuerthelesse there are women enow in Scotland, and therefore follow my counsell. Make thy selfe king, and I shall conueie the matter so wiselie, that thou shalt be so satisfied at thy pleasure in such secret wise, that no man shall be aware thereof.'

Then said Malcolme, 'I am also the most auaritious creature on the earth, so that if I were king, I should seeke so manie waies to get lands and goods, that I would slea the most part of all the nobles of Scotland by surmized accusations, to the end I might inioy their lands, goods, and possessions; and therefore to shew you what mischiefe may insue on you through mine vnsatiable couetousnes, I will rehearse vnto you a fable. There was a fox hauing a sore place on him ouerset with a swarme of flies, that continuallie sucked out hir bloud: and when one that came by and saw this manner, demanded whether she would haue the flies driuen beside hir, she answered no: for if these flies that are alreadie full, and by reason thereof sucke not verie egerlie, should be chased awaie, other that are emptie and fellie an hungred, should light in their places, and sucke out the residue of my bloud farre more to my greeuance than these, which now being satisfied doo not much annoie me. Therefore' saith Malcome, 'suffer me to remaine where I am, least if I atteine to the regiment of your realme, mine vnquenchable auarice may prooue such; that ye would thinke the displeasures which now grieue you, should seeme easie in respect of the vnmeasurable outrage, which might insue through my comming amongst you.'

Makduffee to this made answer, how it was a far woorse fault than the other: 'for auarice is the root of all mischiefe, and for that crime the most part of our kings haue beene slaine and brought to their finall end. Yet notwithstanding follow my counsell, and take vpon thee the crowne. There is gold and riches inough in Scotland to satisfie thy greedie desire.' Then said Malcolme againe, 'I am furthermore inclined to dissimulation, telling of leasings, and all other kinds of deceit, so that I naturallie reioise in nothing so much, as to betraie & deceiue such as put anie trust or confidence in my words. Then sith there is nothing that more becommeth a prince than constancie, veritie, truth, and iustice, with the other laudable fellowship of those faire and noble vertues which are comprehended onelie in soothfastnesse, and that lieng vtterlie ouerthroweth the same; you see how vnable I am to gouerne anie prouince or region: and therefore sith you haue remedies to cloke and hide all the rest of my other vices, I praie you find shift to cloke this vice amongst the residue.'

Then said Makduffe: 'This yet is the woorst of all, and there I leaue thee, and therefore saie; Oh ye vnhappie and miserable Scotishmen, which are thus scourged with so manie and sundrie calamities, ech one aboue other! Ye haue one cursed and wicked tyrant that now reigneth ouer you, without anie right or title, oppressing you with his most bloudie crueltie. This other that hath the right to the crowne, is so replet with the inconstant behauiour and manifest vices of En-

glishmen, that he is nothing woorthie to inioy it: for by his owne confession he is not onelie auaritious, and giuen to vnsatiable lust, but so false a traitor withall, that no trust is to be had vnto anie woord he speaketh. Adieu Scotland, for now I account my selfe a banished man for euer, without comfort or consolation': and with those woords the brackish tears trickled downe his cheekes verie abundantlie.

At the last, when he was readie to depart, Malcolme tooke him by the sleeue, and said: 'Be of good comfort Makduffe, for I haue none of these vices before remembred, but have iested with thee in this manner, onelie to prooue thy mind: for diuerse times heeretofore hath Makbeth sought by this manner of meanes to bring me into his hands, but the more slow I haue shewed my selfe to condescend to thy motion and request, the more diligence shall I vse in accomplishing the same.' Incontinentlie heerevpon they imbraced ech other, and promising to be faithfull the one to the other, they fell in consultation how they might best prouide for all their businesse, to bring the same to good effect. Soone after, Makduffe repairing to the borders of Scotland, addressed his letters with secret dispatch vnto the nobles of the realme, declaring how Malcolme was confederat with him, to come hastilie into Scotland to claime the crowne, and therefore he required them, sith he was right inheritor thereto, to assist him with their powers to recouer the same out of the hands of the wrongfull vsurper.

In the meane time, Malcolme purchased such fauor at king Edwards hands, that old Siward earle of Northumberland was appointed with ten thousand men to go with him into Scotland, to support him in this enterprise, for recouerie of his right. After these newes were spread abroad in Scotland, the nobles drew into two seuerall factions, the one taking part with Makbeth, and the other with Malcolme. Heerevpon insued oftentimes sundrie bickerings, & diuerse light skirmishes: for those that were of Malcolmes side, would not ieopard to ioine with their enimies in a pight field, till his comming out of England to their support. But after that Makbeth perceiued his enimies power to increase, by such aid as came to them foorth of England with his aduersarie Malcolme, he recoiled backe into Fife, there purposing to abide in campe fortified, at the castell of Dunsinane, and to fight with his enimies, if they ment to pursue him; howbeit some of his friends aduised him, that it should be best for him, either to make some agreement with Malcolme, or else to flee with all speed into the Iles, and to take his treasure with him, to the end he might wage sundrie great princes of the realme to take his part, & reteine strangers, in whome he might better trust than in his owne subiects, which stale dailie from him: but he had such confidence in his prophesies, that he beleeued he should neuer be vanquished, till Birnane wood were brought to Dunsinane; nor yet to be slaine with anie man, that should be or was borne of anie woman.

Malcolme following hastilie after Makbeth, came the night before the battell vnto Birnane wood, and when his armie had rested a while there to refresh them, he commanded euerie man to get a bough of some tree or other of that wood in his hand, as big as he might beare, and to march foorth therewith in such wise, that on the next morrow they might come closelie and without sight in this manner within viewe of his enimies. On the morrow when Makbeth beheld them comming in this sort, he first maruelled what the matter ment, but in the end

remembered himselfe that the prophesie which he had heard long before that time, of the comming of Birnane wood to Dunsinane castell, was likelie to be now fulfilled. Neuerthelesse, he brought his men in order of battell, and exhorted them to doo valiantlie, howbeit his enimies had scarselie cast from them their boughs, when Makbeth perceiuing their numbers, betooke him streict to flight, whom Makduffe pursued with great hatred euen till he came vnto Lunfannaine, where Makbeth perceiuing that Makduffe was hard at his backe, leapt beside his horsse, saieng; 'Thou traitor, what meaneth it that thou shouldest thus in vaine follow me that am not appointed to be slaine by anie creature that is borne of a woman, come on therefore, and receiue thy reward which thou hast deserued for thy paines,' and therewithall he lifted vp his swoord thinking to haue slaine him.

But Makduffe quicklie auoiding from his horsse, yer he came at him, answered (with his naked swoord in his hand) saieng: 'It is true Makbeth, and now shall thine insatiable crueltie haue an end, for I am euen he that thy wizzards haue told thee of, who was neuer borne of my mother, but ripped out of her wombe': therewithall he stept vnto him, and slue him in the place. Then cutting his head from his shoulders, he set it vpon a pole, and brought it vnto Malcolme. This was the end of Makbeth, after he had reigned 17 yeeres ouer the Scotishmen. In the beginning of his reigne he accomplished manie woorthie acts, verie profitable to the commonwealth (as ye haue heard), but afterward by illusion of the diuell, he defamed the same with most terrible crueltie. He was slaine in the yeere of the incarnation 1057, and in the 16 yeere of king Edwards reigne ouer the Englishmen. (Pp. 174–6.)

Any reader of these excerpts will observe that Shakespeare departs notably from Holinshed in depicting the characters of Macbeth and Lady Macbeth. Holinshed's description of Donwald and his wife does not account for the departure, and it may be that Shakespeare was influenced by other historians of Scotland. Several scholars, Henry Paul most recently, have suggested that he was familiar with the Latin *Rerum Scoticarum Historia* (1582) by George Buchanan, whose portrayal of Macbeth and Lady Macbeth differs considerably from that of Holinshed. The nature of the difference may be seen from the following brief excerpts in Paul's translation:[1]

For Macbeth had keen intelligence, was absolutely high minded and desirous of great things; had moderation been given to him he would have been worthy of exercise power howsoever great.

• • •

By this dream [in Buchanan the meeting with the witches occurs in a dream] his mind, sick with desire and hope, was so profoundly stirred that he kept turning over with himself all the ways of obtaining the kingdom. [Even before the dream he] cherished in his mind a hidden hope of being king.

• • •

His mind, bold enough of itself, was spurred on by the almost daily taunts of his wife, who shared all of his plans.

• • •

The stings of the king's murder drove his overwrought mind to a precipice, as he turned his rule gained by perfidy into a cruel tyranny.

---

1. See Paul, pp. 213–17; Buchanan, pp. 72–3.

ACT FIRST ❧ SCENE FIRST

Thunder and lightning. Enter three Witches.

1 Witch. When shall we three meet again?
In thunder, lightning, or in rain?
  2 Witch. When the hurlyburly's done,
When the battle's lost and won.
  3 Witch. That will be ere the set of sun.   5
  1 Witch. Where the place?
  2 Witch.   Upon the heath.
  3 Witch. There to meet with Macbeth.
  1 Witch. I come, Graymalkin!
  2 Witch. Paddock calls.   10
  3 Witch. Anon!
  All. Fair is foul, and foul is fair:
Hover through the fog and filthy air.   *Exeunt.*

❧ SCENE SECOND ❧

*Alarum within. Enter King [Duncan], Malcolm, Donalbain,
Lennox, with Attendants, meeting a bleeding Captain.*

Duncan. What bloody man is that? He can report,
As seemeth by his plight, of the revolt
The newest state.
  Malcolm.   This is the sergeant,
Who like a good and hardy soldier fought   5
'Gainst my captivity. Hail, brave friend!
Say to the king the knowledge of the broil
As thou didst leave it.
  Captain.   Doubtful it stood,
As two spent swimmers, that do cling together   10
And choke their art. The merciless Macdonwald—
Worthy to be a rebel, for to that
The multiplying villainies of nature
Do swarm upon him—from the Western Isles
Of kerns and gallowglasses is supplied;   15
And Fortune, on his damned quarrel smiling,
Show'd like a rebel's whore: but all's too weak;
For brave Macbeth—well he deserves that name—
Disdaining Fortune, with his brandish'd steel,
Which smok'd with bloody execution,   20
Like Valor's minion carv'd out his passage
Till he fac'd the slave;
Which nev'r shook hands, nor bade farewell to him,
Till he unseam'd him from the nave to th' chops,
And fix'd his head upon our battlements.   25
  Duncan. O valiant cousin! worthy gentleman!
  Captain. As whence the sun 'gins his reflection
Shipwracking storms and direful thunders break,
So from that spring whence comfort seem'd to come
Discomfort swells. Mark, King of Scotland, mark: 30
No sooner Justice had, with valor arm'd,

Compell'd these skipping kerns to trust their heels,
But the Norweyan lord, surveying vantage,
With furbish'd arms and new supplies of men
Began a fresh assault.   35
  Duncan. Dismay'd not this our captains, Macbeth
and Banquo?
  Captain. Yes, as sparrows eagles,
Or the hare the lion.
If I say sooth, I must report they were   40
As cannons overcharg'd with double cracks,
So they doubly redoubled strokes upon the foe.
Except they meant to bathe in reeking wounds,
Or memorize another Golgotha,
I cannot tell—but I am faint,   45
My gashes cry for help.
  Duncan. So well thy words become thee as thy wounds;
They smack of honor both. Go, get him surgeons.

                              [Exit Captain, attended.]

Enter Ross and Angus.

Who comes here?
  Malcolm.   The worthy Thane of Ross.   50
  Lennox. What a haste looks through his eyes!
So should he look that seems to speak things strange.
  Ross. God save the king!
  Duncan. Whence cam'st thou, worthy thane?
  Ross.   From Fife, great king;   55
Where the Norweyan banners flout the sky
And fan our people cold.
Norway himself, with terrible numbers,
Assisted by that most disloyal traitor,
The Thane of Cawdor, began a dismal conflict,   60
Till that Bellona's bridegroom, lapp'd in proof,
Confronted him with self-comparisons,
Point against point, rebellious arm 'gainst arm,
Curbing his lavish spirit; and to conclude,
The victory fell on us.   65
  Duncan.   Great happiness!
  Ross. That now Sweno, the Norways' king,
Craves composition;
Nor would we deign him burial of his men
Till he disbursed, at Saint Colme's Inch,   70
Ten thousand dollars to our general use.
  Duncan. No more that Thane of Cawdor shall deceive.
Our bosom interest. Go pronounce his present death,
And with his former title greet Macbeth.
  Ross. I'll see it done.   75
  Duncan. What he hath lost noble Macbeth hath won.

                                          Exeunt.

SD Thunder and lightning; *Cf. n.*   **9–13 Graymalkin . . . air;** *Cf. n.*   **11 Anon:** *right away*   **SD Alarum within:** *trumpet call off stage*   **4 sergeant:** *three syllables; Cf. n.*   **12 to that:** *to make him so*   **15 kerns:** *light-armored Irish foot soldiers*   **gallowglasses:** *Irish armor-bearers; F. Gallowgrosses*   **16 quarrel:** *F. Quarry*   **20 execution:** *five syllables*   **21 minion:** (three syllables) *favorite*   **23 Which:** *who; Cf. n.*   **24 he:** *i.e. Macbeth*   **unseam'd:** *ripped*   **nave:** *navel*   **27, 28 As whence . . . thunders break;** *Cf. n.*   **27 reflection:** (four syllables) *shining*   **28 break:** *F omits*

33 surveying vantage: *seeing his chance*   **40 sooth:** *truth*   **41 cracks:** *explosions, i.e. charges*   **43 Except:** *unless*   **reeking:** *steaming*   **44 memorize another Golgotha;** *Cf. n.*   **50 Thane;** *Cf. n.*   **56, 57 flout . . . cold;** *Cf. n.*   **58 Norway:** *the King of Norway*   **60 dismal:** *disastrous*   **61 Bellona:** *goddess of war*   **bridegroom:** *i.e. Macbeth*   **lapp'd in proof:** *clad in tested (proved) armor*   **62 Confronted him with self-comparisons:** *i.e. showed him (Norway) his equal*   **63 rebellious;** *Cf. n.*   **64 lavish:** *insolent*   **67 Norways':** *Norwegians'*   **68 composition:** (five syllables) *a truce*   **70 Saint Colme's Inch:** *the island of Inchcolm in the Firth of Forth*   **71 dollars:** *16th-century German and Spanish currency (thaler)*   **general:** *read 'gen'ral'; Cf. n.*   **72, 73 deceive . . . interest;** *Cf. n.*

❧ Scene Third ❧

Thunder. Enter the three Witches.

1 Witch. Where hast thou been, sister?

2 Witch. Killing swine.

3 Witch. Sister, where thou?

1 Witch. A sailor's wife had chestnuts in her lap,

And munch'd, and munch'd, and munch'd: 'Give me,'   *5*

quoth I:

'Aroint thee, witch!' the rump-fed ronyon cries.

Her husband's to Aleppo gone, master o' th' *Tiger:*

But in a sieve I'll thither sail,

And, like a rat without a tail,   *10*

I'll do, I'll do, and I'll do.

2 Witch. I'll give thee a wind.

1 Witch. Th' art kind.

3 Witch. And I another.

1 Witch. I myself have all the other;   *15*

And the very ports they blow,

All the quarters that they know

I' th' shipman's card.

I'll drain him dry as hay;

Sleep shall neither night nor day   *20*

Hang upon his penthouse lid;

He shall live a man forbid.

Weary sev'nights nine times nine

Shall he dwindle, peak and pine:

Though his bark cannot be lost,   *25*

Yet it shall be tempest-tost.

Look what I have.

2 Witch. Show me, show me.

1 Witch. Here I have a pilot's thumb,

Wrack'd as homeward he did come.   *Drum within.*   *30*

3 Witch. A drum! a drum!

Macbeth doth come.

All. The weyard sisters, hand in hand,

Posters of the sea and land,

Thus do go about, about,   *35*

Thrice to thine, and thrice to mine,

And thrice again, to make up nine.

Peace! the charm's wound up.

Enter Macbeth and Banquo.

Macbeth. So foul and fair a day I have not seen.

Banquo. How far is't call'd to Forres? What are these,   *40*

So wither'd and so wild in their attire,

That look not like th' inhabitants o' th' earth,

And yet are on't? Live you? or are you aught

That man may question? You seem to understand me,

By each at once her choppy finger laying   *45*

Upon her skinny lips. You should be women,

And yet your beards forbid me to interpret

That you are so.

Macbeth.   Speak, if you can: what are you?

1 Witch. All hail, Macbeth! hail to thee, Thane of Glamis!   *50*

2 Witch. All hail, Macbeth! hail to thee, Thane of Cawdor!

3 Witch. All hail, Macbeth, that shall be king hereafter!

Banquo. Good sir, why do you start, and seem to fear

Things that do sound so fair? I' th' name of truth,

Are ye fantastical, or that indeed   *55*

Which outwardly ye show? My noble partner

You greet with present grace and great prediction

Of noble having and of royal hope,

That he seems rapt withal; to me you speak not.

If you can look into the seeds of time,   *60*

And say which grain will grow and which will not,

Speak then to me, who neither beg nor fear

Your favors nor your hate.

1 Witch. Hail!

2 Witch. Hail!   *65*

3 Witch. Hail!

1 Witch. Lesser than Macbeth, and greater.

2 Witch. Not so happy, yet much happier.

3 Witch. Thou shalt get kings, though thou be none.

So, all hail, Macbeth and Banquo!   *70*

1 Witch. Banquo and Macbeth, all hail!

Macbeth. Stay, you imperfect speakers, tell me more.

By Sinel's death I know I am Thane of Glamis;

But how of Cawdor? the Thane of Cawdor lives,

A prosperous gentleman; and to be king   *75*

Stands not within the prospect of belief

No more than to be Cawdor. Say from whence

You owe this strange intelligence, or why

Upon this blasted heath you stop our way

With such prophetic gretting. Speak, I charge you.   *80*

                           Witches vanish.

Banquo. The earth hath bubbles, as the water has,

And these are of them. Whither are they vanish'd?

Macbeth. Into the air, and what seem'd corporal

Melted, as breath into the wind.

Would they had stay'd!   *85*

Banquo. Were such things here as we do speak about?

Or have we eaten on the insane root

That takes the reason prisoner?

Macbeth. Your children shall be kings.

Banquo.   You shall be king.   *90*

Macbeth. And Thane of Cawdor too; went it not so?

Banquo. To th' selfsame tune and words. Who's here?

Enter Ross and Angus.

Ross. The king hath happily receiv'd, Macbeth,

The news of thy success; and when he reads

Thy personal venture in the rebels' fight,   *95*

His wonders and his praises do contend

Which should be thine, or his. Silenc'd with that,

In viewing o'er the rest o' th' selfsame day,

He finds thee in the stout Norweyan ranks,

Nothing afeard of what thyself didst make,   *100*

Strange images of death. As thick as hail

Came post with post, and every one did bear

Thy praises in his kingdom's great defense,

---

7 **Aroint thee:** *begone* **rump-fed:** *fat-rumped* **ronyon:** *term of abuse; literally 'scab'*   **8**
Tiger: *name of a ship*   15 **other:** *i.e. other winds*   16 **ports they blow:** *ports to which*
they blow (?); Cf. n.   18 **card:** *dial of the compass*   21 **penthouse lid:** *eyelid; Cf. n.*   22
forbid: *accursed*   24 **peak:** *waste away*   33 **weyard:** *weird; F. weyward; Cf. n.*   34
Posters: *persons who ride posthaste*   36, 37 **thrice to thine . . . to make up mine;**
Cf. n.   40 **Forres:** *F. Soris*   45 **choppy:** *chapped, cracked*   47 **beards;** *Cf. n.*

55 **fantastical:** *imaginary*   58 **having:** *estate*   59 **rapt withal:** *transported by it*   69
get: *beget*   73 **Sinel:** *Macbeth's father*   83 **corporal:** *corporeal*   87 **insane:** *causing*
insanity as, e.g., hemlock was supposed to do   96, 97 **His wonders . . . Silenc'd with that;**
Cf. n.   101 **images of death:** *i.e. those killed by Macbeth; F. punctuates* death, *as*   101,
102 **hail/Came:** *F. Tale/Can*

And pour'd them down before him.

   Angus.   We are sent   *105*
To give thee from our royal master thanks;
Only to herald thee into his sight,
Not pay thee.

   Ross. And, for an earnest of a greater honor,
He bade me, from him, call thee Thane of Cawdor;   *110*
In which addition, hail, most worthy thane!
For it is thine.

   Banquo.   What, can the devil speak true?

   Macbeth. The Thane of Cawdor lives;
Why do you dress me in borrowed robes?   *115*

   Angus. Who was the thane lives yet;
But under heavy judgment bears that life
Which he deserves to lose.
Whether he was combin'd with those of Norway,
Or did line the rebel with hidden help   *120*
And vantage, or that with both he labor'd
In his country's wrack, I know not;
But treasons capital, confess'd and prov'd,
Have overthrown him.

   Macbeth. [Aside.] Glamis, and Thane of Cawdor: *125*
The greatest is behind.

   [*To Ross and Angus.*] Thanks for your pains.
[*To Banquo.*] Do you not hope your children shall be kings,
When those that gave the Thane of Cawdor to me
Promis'd no less to them?   *130*

   Banquo.   That, trusted home,
Might yet enkindle you unto the crown,
Besides the Thane of Cawdor. But 'tis strange:
And oftentimes, to win us to our harm,
The instruments of darkness tell us truths,   *135*
Win us with honest trifles, to betray's
In deepest consequence.
Cousins, a word, I pray you.

   Macbeth. [Aside.]   Two truths are told,
As happy prologues to the swelling act   *140*
Of the imperial theme.—I thank you, gentleman.—
[*Aside.*] This supernatural soliciting
Cannot be ill, cannot be good; if ill,
Why hath it given me earnest of success,
Commencing in a truth? I am Thane of Cawdor.   *145*
If good, why do I yield to that suggestion
Whose horrid image doth unfix my hair
And make my seated heart knock at my ribs,
Against the use of nature? Present fears
Are less than horrible imaginings: *150*
My thought, whose murther yet is but fantastical,
Shakes so my single state of man
That function is smother'd in surmise,
And nothing is but what is not.

   Banquo. Look how our partner's rapt.   *155*

   Macbeth. [Aside.] If chance will have me king, why,
chance may crown me,

Without my stir.

   Banquo.   New honors come upon him,
Like our strange garments, cleave not to their mold   *160*
But with the aid of use.

   Macbeth. [Aside.]   Come what come may,
Time and the hour runs through the roughest day.

   Banquo. Worthy Macbeth, we stay upon our leisure.

   Macbeth. Give me your favor;   *165*
My dull brain was wrought with things forgotten.
Kind gentlemen, your pains are register'd
Where every day I turn the leaf to read them.
Let us toward the king.
[*To Banquo.*] Think upon what hath chanc'd; and,   *170*
at more time,
The interim having weigh'd it, let us speak
Our free hearts each to other.

   Banquo.   Very gladly.

   Macbeth. Till then, enough. Come, friends.   *Exeunt.*

❧ Scene Fourth ❧

Flourish. Enter King, Lennox, Malcolm, Donalbain, and Attendants.

   Duncan. Is execution done on Cawdor?
Are not those in commission yet return'd?

   Malcolm. My liege, they are not yet come back.
But I have spoke with one that saw him die;
Who did report that very frankly he   *5*
Confess'd his treasons, implor'd your highness' pardon,
And set forth a deep repentance.
Nothing in his life became him
Like the leaving it. He died
As one that had been studied in his death   *10*
To throw away the dearest thing he ow'd
As 'twere a careless trifle.

   Duncan.   There's no art
To find the mind's construction in the face:
He was a gentleman on whom I built   *15*
An absolute trust.

Enter Macbeth, Banquo, Ross, and Angus.

          O worthiest cousin,
The sin of my ingratitude even now
Was heavy on me. Thou art so far before,
That swiftest wing of recompense is slow   *20*
To overtake thee. Would thou hadst less deserv'd,
That the proportion both of thanks and payment
Might have been mine! only I have left to say,
More is thy due than more than all can pay.

   Macbeth. The service and the loyalty I owe,   *25*
In doing it, pays itself.
Your highness' part is to receive our duties;
And our duties are to your throne and state,
Children and servants, which do but what they should,
By doing everything safe toward your love   *30*
And honor.

---

109 earnest: *pledge*   **111 addition:** title   **113 devil:** (one syllable here) *often spelled and pronounced 'divel'*   **120 line:** *reinforce*   **122 wrack:** *ruin*   **131 home:** *to the utmost*   **137 In deepest consequence:** *in matters of gravest importance*   **140 swelling:** *stately; see Henry V, Prologue, 3–4*   **142 soliciting:** *prompting*   **148 seated:** *firmly fixed*   **149 Against . . . nature:** *contrary to natural habit*   **151 murther:** *common Elizabethan variant of 'murder'*   **fantastical:** *imaginary*   **152–155 Shakes . . . rapt;** *Cf. n.*   **152 single state of man;** *Cf. n. single, undivided, unbroken*   **153 function:** *normal activity of mind and body*

160 strange: *unfamiliar, new*   **their mold:** *i.e. the body*   **162, 163 Come . . . day;** *Cf. n.*   **162 runs:** *alternative plural form*   **165 favor:** *pardon*   **166 wrought:** *troubled*   **SD Flourish:** *trumpet fanfare*   **2 Are:** *F. Or*   **in commission:** *charged with the duty*   **10 had been studied:** *had trained himself*   **11 ow'd:** *owned*   **19 before:** *ahead*   **22, 23 That . . . mine;** *Cf. n.*   **23 I have:** *read 'I've'; Cf. n.*   **30 safe toward:** *to guarantee*

Duncan. Welcome hither:
I have begun to plant thee, and will labor
To make thee full of growing. Noble Banquo,
That hast no less deserv'd, nor must be known   35
No less to have done so, let me infold thee
And hold thee to my heart.
     Banquo.   There if I grow,
The harvest is your own.
     Duncan.   My plenteous joys,   40
Wanton is fullness, seek to hide themselves
In drops of sorrow. Sons, kinsmen, thanes,
And you whose places are the nearest, know
We will establish our estate upon
Our eldest, Malcolm, whom we name hereafter   45
The Prince of Cumberland; which honor must
Not unaccompanied invest him only,
But signs of nobleness, like stars, shall shine
On all deservers. From hence to Inverness,
And bind us further to you.   50
     Macbeth. The rest is labor, which is not us'd for you:
I'll be myself the harbinger, and make joyful
The hearing of my wife with your approach;
So, humbly take my leave.
     Duncan.   My worthy Cawdor!   55
     Macbeth. [*Aside.*] The Prince of Cumberland! that is a step
On which I must fall down, or else o'er-leap;
For in my way it lies. Stars, hide your fires;
Let not light see my black and deep desires;
The eye wink at the hand; yet let that be   60
Which the eye fears, when it is done, to see.   *Exit.*
     Duncan. True, worthy Banquo; he is full so valiant,
And in his commendations I am fed:
It is a banquet to me. Let's after him,
Whose care is gone before to bid us welcome: 65
It is a peerless kinsman.   *Flourish. Exeunt.*

❧ SCENE FIFTH ❧

Enter Macbeth's Wife alone, with a letter.

Lady Macbeth. 'They met me in the day of success; and I
have learn'd by the perfect'st report, they have more in them
than mortal knowledge. When I burn'd in desire to question
them further, they made themselves air, into which they vanish'd. Whiles I stood rapt in the wonder of it, came missives   5
from the king, who all-hail'd me, "Thane of Cawdor," by
which title, before, these weyard sisters saluted me, and referred
to me to the coming on of time with "Hail, king that shalt
be!" This have I thought good to deliver thee, my dearest
partner of greatness, that thou mightst not lose the dues of   10
rejoicing by being ignorant of what greatness is promis'd thee.
Lay it to thy heart, and farewell.'
Glamis thou art, and Cawdor, and shalt be
What thou art promis'd. Yet do I fear thy nature;
It is too full o' th' milk of human kindness   15

To catch the nearest way. Thou wouldst be great,
Art not without ambition, but without
The illness should attend it. What thou wouldst highly
That wouldst thou holily; wouldst not play false,
And yet wouldst wrongly win.   20
Thou'dst have, great Glamis, that which cries,
'Thus thou must do,' if thou have it,
And that which rather thou dost fear to do
Than wishest should be undone. Hie thee hither,
That I may pour my spirits in thine ear,   25
And chastise with the valor of my tongue
All that impedes thee from the golden round,
Which Fate and metaphysical aid doth seem
To have thee crown'd withal.

           Enter Messenger.

             What is your tidings?   30
     Messenger. The king comes here tonight.
     Lady Macbeth.   Thou'rt mad to say it.
Is not thy master with him? who, were't so,
Would have inform'd for preparation.
     Messenger. So please you, it is true; our thane is coming;   35
One of my fellows had the speed of him,
Who, almost dead for breath, had scarcely more
Than would make up his message.
     Lady Macbeth.   Give him tending;
He brings great news.   *Exit Messenger.*   40
          The raven himself is hoarse
That croaks the fatal entrance of Duncan
Under my battlements. Come, you spirits
That tend on mortal thoughts, unsex me here,
And fill me from the crown to the toe top-full   45
Of direst cruelty! Make thick my blood,
Stop up th' access and passage to remorse,
That no compunctious visitings of nature
Shake my fell purpose, nor keep peace between
Th' effect and it! Come to my women's breasts,   50
And take my milk for gall, you murth'ring ministers,
Wherever in your sightless substances
You wait on nature's mischief! Come, thick Night,
And pall thee in the dunnest smoke of hell,
That my keen knife see not the wound it makes,   55
Nor Heaven peep through the blanket of the dark,
To cry 'Hold, hold!'

           Enter Macbeth.

      Great Glamis! worthy Cawdor!
Greater than both, by the all-hail hereafter!
Thy letters have transported me beyond   60
This ignorant present, and I feel now
The future in the instant.
     Macbeth.   My dearest love,
Duncan comes here tonight.
     Lady Macbeth.   And when goes hence?   65

---

41 Wanton: *unrestrained*   **44 establish our estate:** *settle the succession*   **46 Prince of Cumberland;** *Cf. n.*   **51 The rest . . . for you;** *Cf. n.*   **rest:** *repose*   **53 your approach:** *i.e. news of your approach*   **5 missives:** *messengers*   **7 weyard:** *F* weyward   **9 deliver:** *report to*   **13 shalt:** *wilt*

16 catch the nearest way: *take the shortest route*   **18 The illness should:** *the wickedness which should*   **19–24 Thou'dst have . . . undone;** *Cf. n.*   **26 chastise:** *stressed* —́ —   **27 round:** *i.e. crown*   **28 metaphysical:** *supernatural*   **34 preparation:** *five syllables*   **36 had the speed of:** *outspeeded*   **41 raven;** *Cf. n.*   **42 entrance:** *perhaps three syllables here*   **44 mortal:** *murderous*   **49, 50 keep . . . it;** *Cf. n.*   **50 it:** *F.* hit   **51 take:** *exchange*   **52 sightless:** *invisible*   **54 pall:** *enshroud*   **dunnest:** *murkiest*   **59 hereafter:** *following, i.e. the third all-hail*

Macbeth. Tomorrow, as he purposes.
  Lady Macbeth.   O, never
Shall sun that morrow see!
Your face, my thane, is as a book where men
May read strange matters. To beguile the time,   *70*
Look like the time; bear welcome in your eye,
Your hand, your tongue: look like th' innocent flower,
But be the serpent under't. He that's coming
Must be provided for; and you shall put
This night's great business into my dispatch;   *75*
Which shall to all our nights and days to come
Give solely sovereign sway and masterdom.
  Macbeth. We will speak further.
  Lady Macbeth.   Only look up clear;
To alter favor ever is to fear.   *80*
Leave all the rest to me.   *Exeunt.*

❧ Scene Sixth ❧

Hoboyes and torches. Enter King, Malcolm, Donalbain, Banquo, Lennox, Macduff, Ross, Angus, and Attendants.

  Duncan. This castle hath a pleasant seat; the air
Nimbly and sweetly recommends itself
Unto our gentle senses.
  Banquo.   This guest of summer,
The temple-haunting martlet, does approve   *5*
By his lov'd mansionry that the heavens' breath
Smells wooingly here; no jutty, frieze,
Buttress, nor coign of vantage, but this bird
Hath made his pendent bed and procreant cradle:
Where they most breed and haunt, I have observ'd   *10*
The air is delicate.

Enter Lady.

  Duncan.   See, see, our honor'd hostess!
The love that follows us sometime is our trouble,
Which still we thank as love. Herein I teach you
How you shall bid God eyld us for your pains,   *15*
And thank us for your trouble.
  Lady Macbeth.   All our service,
In every point twice done, and then done double,
Were poor and single business, to contend
Against those honors deep and broad   *20*
Wherewith your majesty loads our house.
For those of old, and the late dignities
Heap'd up to them, we rest your ermites.
  Duncan. Where's the Thane of Cawdor?
We cours'd him at the heels, and had a purpose   *25*
To be his purveyor; but he rides well,
And his great love, sharp as his spur, hath holp him
To his home before us. Fair and noble hostess,
We are your guest tonight.

70 To beguile: *the time F punctuates* matters, to beguile the time; *Cf. n.*   **75 dispatch:** *management*   **79 clear:** *with unclouded face*   **80 favor:** *facial expression*   **SD Hoboyes:** (phonetic spelling of 'hautboys') *woodwind instruments, related to modern oboe* **torches;** *Cf. n.*   **1 seat:** *situation*   **5 martlet:** *F. Barlet; Cf. n.*   **approve:** *prove*   **6 mansionry:** *home-building*   **7 jutty:** *projection*   **8 coign of vantage:** *advantageous projecting corner*   **9 procreant cradle:** *cradle where he breeds*   **10 most:** *F. must*   **13–16 The love . . . trouble;** *Cf. n.*   **15 eyld:** (probably pronounced 'eeld') *reward*   **19 single:** *trivial*   **23 ermites:** *hermits, i.e. to pray for you*   **25 cours'd:** *rode after*   **26 purveyor:** *stressed ⌣́ — ⌣̀; Cf. n.*   **27 holp:** *helped*

  Lady Macbeth.   Your servants ever   *30*
Have theirs, themselves, and what is theirs, in compt,
To make their audit at your highness' pleasure,
Still to return your own.
  Duncan.   Give me your hand;
Conduct me to mine host: we love him highly,   *35*
And shall continue our graces towards him.
By your leave, hostess.   *Exeunt.*

❧ Scene Seventh ❧

Hoboyes, Torches. Enter a Sewer, and divers Servants with dishes and service over the stage. Then enter Macbeth.

  Macbeth. If it were done, when 'tis done, then 'twere well
It were done quickly. If th' assassination
Could trammel up the consequence, and catch
With his surcease success: that but this blow
Might be the be-all and the end-all—here,   *5*
But here, upon this bank and shoal of time,
We'd jump the life to come. But in these cases
We still have judgment here; that we but teach
Bloody instructions, which being taught, return
To plauge th' inventor. This even-handed justice   *10*
Commends th' ingredients of our poison'd chalice
To our own lips. He's here in double trust:
First, as I am his kinsman and his subject,
Strong both against the deed; then, as his host,
Who should against his murtherer shut the door,   *15*
Not bear the knife myself. Besides, this Duncan
Hath borne his faculties so meek, hath been
So clear in his great office, that his virtues
Will plead like angels, trumpet-tongu'd against
The deep damnation of his taking-off;   *20*
And Pity, like a naked new-born babe,
Striding the blast, or heaven's cherubin, hors'd
Upon the sightless couriers of the air,
Shall blow the horrid deed in every eye,
That tears shall drown the wind. I have no spur   *25*
To prick the sides of my intent, but only
Vaulting ambition, which o'er-leaps itself
And falls on th' other.

Enter Lady.

            How now? What news?
  Lady Macbeth. He has almost supp'd. Why have you   *30*
left the chamber?
  Macbeth. Hath he ask'd for me?
  Lady Macbeth.   Know you not he has?
  Macbeth. We will proceed no further in this business;
He hath honor'd me of late, and I have bought   *35*
Golden opinions from all sorts of people,
Which would be worn now in their newest gloss,
Not cast aside so soon.
  Lady Macbeth.   Was the hope drunk

31 Have . . . in compt: (pronounced 'count') *hold . . . accountable*   **theirs:** *their retainers*   **33 Still:** *always*   **36 our:** *probably disyllabic here*   **SD Sewer:** *chief butler*   **3 trammel up:** *hold, as in a net; hamper*   **4 his surcease;** *Cf. n.*   **5–7 here . . . come;** *Cf. n.*   **6 shoal:** *F. Schoole* (a 17th-century spelling of shoal)   **7 jump:** *risk*   **8 have judgment:** *receive sentence; Cf. n.*   **17 faculties:** *powers*   **18 clear:** *blameless*   **22–3 heaven's . . . air;** *Cf. n.*   **23 sightless:** *invisible*   **27–8 Vaulting ambition . . . on th' other;** *Cf. n.*

Wherein you dress'd yourself? Hath it slept since?   40
And wakes it now to look so green and pale
At what it did so freely? From this time
Such I account thy love. Art thou afeard
To be the same in thine own act and valor
As thou art in desire? Wouldst thou have that   45
Which thou esteem'st the ornament of life,
And live a coward in thine own esteem,
Letting 'I dare not' wait upon 'I would,'
Like the poor cat i' th' adage?
    Macbeth.   Prithee, peace.   50
I dare do all that may become a man;
Who dares do more is none.
    Lady Macbeth.   What beast was't then
That made you break this enterprise to me?
When you durst do it then you were a man;   55
And, to be more than what you were, you would
Be so much more the man. Nor time nor place
Did then adhere, and yet you would make both:
They have made themselves, and that their fitness now
Does unmake you. I have given suck, and know   60
How tender 'tis to love the babe that milks me—
I would, while it was smiling in my face,
Have pluck'd my nipple from his boneless gums,
And dash'd the brains out, had I so sworn
As you have done to this.   65
    Macbeth.   If we should fail?
    Lady Macbeth.   We fail?
But screw your courage to the sticking-place,
And we'll not fail. When Duncan is asleep—
Whereto the rather shall his day's hard journey   70
Soundly invite him—his two chamberlains
Will I with wine and wassail so convince
That memory, the warder of the brain,
Shall be a fume, and the receipt of reason
A limbeck only. When in swinish sleep   75
Their drenched natures lies as in a death,
What cannot you and I perform upon
Th' unguarded Duncan? what not put upon
His spongy officers, who shall bear the guilt
Of our great quell?   80
    Macbeth.   Bring forth men-children only;
For thy undaunted mettle should compose
Nothing but males. Will it not be receiv'd
When we have mark'd with blood those sleepy two
Of his own chamber, and us'd their very daggers,   85
That they have done't?
    Lady Macbeth.   Who dares receive it other,
As we shall make our griefs and clamor roar
Upon his death?
    Macbeth.   I am settled, and bend up   90
Each corporal agent to this terrible feat.
Away, and mock the time with fairest show:
False face must hide what the false heart doth know.   *Exeunt.*

---

49 cat i' th' adage: Cf. n.   **52 do:** F. no; Cf. n.   **54 break:** *broach*   **58 adhere:** *suit*   **59 that their fitness:** *that fitness of time and place*   **60 unmake:** *unnerve*   **68 But:** *only*   **sticking-place:** Cf. n.   **72 convince:** *overpower*   **73–75 memory . . . only:** Cf. n.   **74 receipt:** *receptable*   **75 limbeck:** *alembic, an apparatus formerly used in distilling*   **76 lies:** *lie*   **79 spongy:** *drunken*   **80 quell:** *killing*   **82 mettle:** (same word as 'metal') *substance, spirit*   **83 males:** *pun on 'mails,' the metal rings of which mail armor was composed*   **receiv'd:** *understood*   **87 other:** *otherwise*   **91 corporal agent:** *bodily faculty*   **92 time:** *world;* see I.5.70, 71.

ACT SECOND ❧ SCENE FIRST

Enter Banquo, and Fleance with a torch before him.

Banquo. How goes the night, boy?
Fleance. The moon is down; I have not heard the clock.
Banquo. And she goes down at twelve.
Fleance. I take't, 'tis later, sir.
Banquo.   Hold, take my sword.   5
There's husbandry in heaven;
Their candles are all out. Take thee that too.
A heavy summons lies like lead upon me,
And yet I would not sleep. Merciful powers,
restrain in me the cursed thoughts   10
That nature gives way to in repose.

Enter Macbeth, and a Servant with a torch.

Give me my sword. Who's there?
    Macbeth.   A friend.
    Banquo. What, sir, not yet at rest? The king's a-bed.
He hath been in unusual pleasure,   15
And sent forth great largess to your offices.
This diamond he greets your wife withal,
By the name of most kind hostess, and shut up
In measureless content.
    Macbeth.   Being unprepar'd,   20
Our will became the servant to defect,
Which else should free have wrought.
    Banquo.   All's well.
I dreamt last night of the three weyard sisters:
To you they have show'd some truth.   25
    Macbeth.   I think not of them.
Yet, when we can entreat an hour to serve,
We would spend it in some words upon that business,
If you would grant the time.
    Banquo.   At your kind'st leisure.   30
    Macbeth. If you shall cleave to my consent, when 'tis,
It shall make honor for you.
    Banquo.   So I lose none
In seeking to augment it, but still keep
My bosom franchis'd and allegiance clear,   35
I shall be counsell'd.
    Macbeth.   Good repose the while!
    Banquo. Thanks, sir: the like to you.
                Exit Banquo [with Fleance.]
    Macbeth. Go bid thy mistress, when my drink is ready
She strike upon the bell. Get thee to bed.   40
                  Exit [Servant.]
Is this a dagger which I see before me,
The handle toward my hand? Come, let me clutch thee.
I have thee not, and yet I see thee still.
Art thou not, fatal vision, sensible
To feeling as to sight? or art thou but   45
A dagger of the mind, a false creation,
Proceeding from the heat-oppressed brain?
I see thee yet, in form as palpable
As this which now I draw.

SD torch: *i.e. torchbearer*   **6 husbandry:** *economy*   **7 that:** *i.e. a shield* (?) *or clock*(?)   **8 summons:** *i.e. to sleep*   **16 largess:** *gifts*   **offices:** *servants' quarters*   **18 shut up:** *ended* (his remarks or his day)   **20–22 Being . . . wrought:** Cf. n.   **24 weyard:** F. weyward   **31 cleave . . . 'tis:** *be of my party when the time comes*   **35 franchis'd:** *free of blame*   **44 sensible:** *perceptible*

Thou marshall'st me the way that I was going,   *50*
And such an instrument I was to use.
Mine eyes are made the fools o' th' other senses,
Or else worth all the rest. I see thee still;
And on thy blade and dudgeon gouts of blood,
Which was not so before. There's no such thing: *55*
It is the bloody business which informs
Thus to mine eyes. Now o'er the one half world
Nature seems dead, and wicked dreams abuse
The curtain'd sleep; witchcraft celebrates
Pale Heccat's off'rings; and wither'd Murther,   *60*
Alarum'd by his sentinel, the wolf,
Whose howl's his watch, thus with his stealthy pace,
With Tarquin's ravishing strides, towards his design
Moves like a ghost. Thou sure and firm-set earth,
Hear not my steps, which way they walk, for fear   *65*
Thy very stones prate of my whereabout,
And take the present horror from the time,
Which now suits with it. Whiles I threat he lives:
Words to the heat of deeds too cold breath gives.

             A bell rings.

I go, and it is done; the bell invites me.   *70*
Hear it not, Duncan, for it is a knell
That summons thee to heaven or to hell.

               Exit.

✲ Scene Second ✲

Enter Lady.

Lady Macbeth. That which hath made them drunk hath
made me bold:
What hath quench'd them hath give me fire.
Hark! Peace! It was the owl that shriek'd,
The fatal bellman, which gives the stern'st good night. *5*
He is about it; the doors are open;
And the surfeited grooms do mock their charge
With snores. I have drugg'd their possets,
That death and nature do contend about them,
Whether they live or die.   *10*
 Macbeth. [Within.] Who's there? what, ho!
Lady Macbeth. Alack! I am afraid they have awak'd,
And 'tis not done; th' attempt and not the deed
Confounds us. Hark! I laid their daggers ready;
He could not miss 'em. Had he not resembled   *15*
My father as he slept I had done't.

       Enter Macbeth.

         My husband!
Macbeth. I have done the deed. Didst thou not hear a
noise?
 Lady Macbeth. I heard the owl scream and the crickets *20*
cry.

Did not you speak?
 Macbeth.   When?
 Lady Macbeth.   Now.
 Lady Macbeth.   As I descended? *25*
 Lady Macbeth. Ay.
 Macbeth.   Hark! Who lies i' th' second chamber?
 Lady Macbeth. Donalbain.
 Macbeth. [Looking on his hands.] This is a sorry sight.
 Lady Macbeth. A foolish thought to say a sorry sight. *30*
 Macbeth. There's one did laugh in's sleep,
And one cried 'Murther!' that they did wake each other.
I stood and heard them; but they did say their prayers,
And address'd them again to sleep.
 Lady Macbeth. There are two lodg'd together. *35*
 Macbeth. One cried 'God bless us!' and 'Amen' the other,
As they had seen me with these hangman's hands.
List'ning their fear, I could not say 'Amen,'
When they did say 'God bless us!'
 Lady Macbeth.   Consider it not so deeply. *40*
 Macbeth. But wherefore could not I pronounce 'Amen'?
I had most need of blessing, and 'Amen'
Stuck in my throat.
 Lady Macbeth. These deeds must not be thought
After these ways; so, it will make us mad.   *45*
 Macbeth. Methought I heard a voice cry 'Sleep no more!
Macbeth does murther Sleep,' the innocent Sleep,
Sleep that knits up the ravel'd sleave of care,
The death of each day's life, sore labor's bath,
Balm of hurt minds, great nature's second course, *50*
Chief nourisher in life's feast,—
 Lady Macbeth.   What do you mean?
 Macbeth. Still it cried, 'Sleep no more!' to all the house;
'Glamis hath murther'd sleep, and therefore Cawdor
Shall sleep no more: Macbeth shall sleep no more!' *55*
 Lady Macbeth. Who was it that thus cried? Why worthy
thane,
You do unbend your noble strength to think
So brainsickly of things. Go get some water,
And wash this filthy witness from your hand.   *60*
Why did you bring these daggers from the place?
They must lie there. Go carry them, and smear
The sleepy grooms with blood.
 Macbeth.   I'll go no more.
I am afraid to think what I have done;   *65*
Look on't again I dare not.
 Lady Macbeth.   Infirm of purpose!
Give me the daggers. The sleeping and the dead
Are but as pictures; 'tis the eye of childhood
That fears a painted devil. If he do bleed,   *70*
I'll gild the faces of the grooms withal,
For it must seem their guilt.   *Exit. Knock within.*
 Macbeth.   Whence is that knocking?
How is't with me, when every noise appalls me?
What hands are here? Ha! they pluck out mine eyes. *75*
Will all great Neptune's ocean wash this blood
Clean from my hand? No, this my hand will rather

---

54 **dudgeon:** *handle* **gouts:** *drops* 56 **informs:** *gives information; takes shape* (?) 60
Heccat's off'rings: *offerings to Hecate, the classical goddess of witchcraft* (the phonetic spelling
of F indicates the pronunciation) 61 **Alarum'd:** *aroused* 62 **Whose howl's his watch;**
Cf. n. 63 **Tarquin's;** *Cf. n.* **strides** *F sides* 64 **sure:** *F sowre* 65 **way they:** *F they
may* 67 **present horror:** *i.e. silence* 5 **bellman:** *watchman, town crier; Cf. n.* 8
posset: *a punch made of hot milk curdled with ale or wine* 14 **Confounds:** *ruins* SD
Enter Macbeth; *Cf. n.*

---

37 **As:** *as if* **hangman:** *used loosely for 'executioner'* 48 **knits:** *ties, fastens* **ravel'd:** *frayed,*
disintegrated **sleave:** *slender filament of silk obtained by separating* (sleaving) *thicker*
thread 50 **second course:** *i.e. the main course of an Elizabethan dinner* 58 **unbend:**
relax

The multitudinous seas incarnardine,
Making the green one red.

          Enter Lady.

Lady Macbeth. My hands are of your color, but I shame   80
To wear a heart so white.—   *Knock.*
I hear a knocking at the south entry.
Retire we to our chamber.
A little water clears us of this deed.
How easy is it, then! Your constancy   85
Hath left you unattended.   *Knock.*
              Hark! more knocking.
Get on your night-gown, lest occasion call us,
And show us to be watchers. Be not lost
So poorly in your thoughts.   90
    Macbeth. To know my deed   *Knock.*
                'Twere best not know myself.
Wake Duncan with thy knocking!
                I would thou couldst!
                     Exeunt.

❧ Scene Third ❧

       Enter a Porter. Knocking within.

Porter. Here's a knocking, indeed! If a man were porter of
hell-gate he should have old turning the key. *(Knock.)* Knock,
knock, knock! Who's there, i' th' name of Belzebub? Here's a
farmer that hang'd himself on th' expectation of plenty. Come
in, time-server; have napkins enow about you; here you'll   5
sweat for't. *(Knock.)* Knock, knock! Who's there, in th' other
devil's name? Faith, here's an equivocator, that could swear in
both the scales against either scale; who committed treason
enough for God's sake, yet could not equivocate to heaven. O,
come in, equivocator! *(Knock.)* Knock, knock, knock! Who's   10
there? Faith, here's an English tailor come hither for stealing
out of a French hose. Come in, tailor; here you may roast
your goose. *(Knock.)* Knock, knock! Never at quiet! What
are you? But this place is too cold for hell. I'll devil-porter
it no further. I had thought to have let in some of all pro-   15
fessions, that go the primrose way to th' everlasting bonfire. *(Knock.)*
Anon, anon! I pray you, remember the porter. *[Opens the gate.]*

       Enter Macduff and Lennox.

Macduff. Was it so late, friend, ere you went to bed, that
you do lie so late?
    Porter. Faith, sir, we were carousing till the second cock;   20
and drink, sir, is a great provoker of three things.
    Macduff. What three things does drink especially provoke?
    Porter. Marry, sir, nose-painting, sleep, and urine. Lechery,
sir, it provokes, and unprovokes: it provokes the desire, but it
takes away the performance. Therefore much drink may be   25
said to be an equivocator with Lechery: it makes him, and it
mars him; it sets him on, and it takes him off; it persuades

him, and disheartens him; makes him stand to, and not
stand to; in conclusion, equivocates him in a sleep, and, giving
him the lie, leaves him.   30
    Macduff. I believe drink gave thee the lie last night.
    Porter. That it did, sir, i' the very throat of me; but I
requited him for his lie; and, I think, being too strong to
him, though he took up my legs sometime, yet I made a
shift to cast him.   35

       Enter Macbeth.

    Macduff. Is thy master stirring?
Our knocking has awak'd him; here he comes.
    Lennox. Good morrow, noble sir.
    Macbeth.   Good morrow, both.
    Macduff. Is the king stirring, worthy thane?   40
    Macbeth.   Not yet.
    Macduff. He did command me to call timely on him;
I have almost slipp'd the hour.
    Macbeth.   I'll bring you to him.
      Macduff. I know this is a joyful trouble to you;   45
But yet 'tis one.
    Macbeth. The labor we delight in physics pain.
This is the door.
    Macduff.   I'll make so bold to call,
For 'tis my limited service.   *Exit Macduff.*   50
    Lennox. Goes the king hence today?
    Macbeth.   He does; he did appoint so.
    Lennox. The night has been unruly.
Where we lay, our chimneys were blown down,
And, as they say, lamentings heard i' th' air,   55
Strange screams of death,
And prophesying with accents terrible
Of dire combustion and confus'd events
New hatch'd to th' woeful time.
The obscure bird clamor'd the livelong night.   60
Some say the earth was feverous, and did shake.
    Macbeth. 'Twas a rough night.
    Lennox. My young remembrance cannot parallel
A fellow to it.

       Enter Macduff.

    Macduff.   O horror! horror! horror!   65
Tongue nor heart cannot conceive nor name thee!
    Macbeth.   ⎱
              ⎰ What's the matter?
    Lennox.   ⎰
    Macduff. Confusion now hath made his masterpiece!
Most sacrilegious murther hath broke ope   70
The Lord's anointed temple, and stole thence
The life o' th' building!
    Macbeth.   What is't you say? the life?
    Lennox. Mean you his majesty?
    Macduff. Approach the chamber, and destroy your sight   75
With a new Gorgon. Do not bid me speak.
See, and then speak yourselves.
                Exeunt Macbeth and Lennox.
                Awake! awake!

---

78 incarnardine: *incarnardine, redden*   **85, 86 constancy … unattended:** *firmness has abandoned you*   **88 night-gown:** *dressing gown*   **90 poorly:** *feebly*   **2 should:** *would* **old:** *plenty of* (colloquial)   **3 Belzebub:** *Beelzebub*   **4 farmer;** *Cf. n.*   **4, 5 come in, time-server:** *F. Come in time; Cf. n.*   **5 napkins:** *handkerchiefs* **enow:** *enough*   7 **equivocator;** *Cf. n.*   **11, 12 stealing … hose;** *Cf. n.*   **13 goose:** *smoothing iron; Cf. n.*   **16 anon:** *right away*   **18–21 Was … things:** *F prints as verse*   **20 second cock:** *i.e. about 3 A.M.*

34 took up my legs: *got my feet off the ground* (as in wrestling)   **made a shift:** *contrived*   **35 cast:** *throw; also 'vomit'*   **SD Enter Macbeth;** *Cf. n.*   **43 slipp'd:** *missed*   **47 physics:** *curse*   **50 limited:** *appointed*   **53–61 The night … shake;** *Cf. n.*   **58 combustion:** *tumult, disorder*   **60 obscure bird:** *bird of darkness, the owl*   **64 fellow:** *equal*   **71 Lord's anointed temple:** *anointed body of the king*   **76 Gorgon:** *a monster whose aspect turned the beholder to stone*

Ring the alarum-bell. Murther and treason!
Banquo and Donalbain! Malcolm, awake!   80
Shake off this downy sleep, death's counterfeit,
And look on death itself! up, up, and see
The great doom's image! Malcolm, Banquo,
As from your graves rise up, and walk like sprites,
To countenance this horror! Ring the bell.   85

    Bell rings. Enter Lady.

Lady Macbeth. What's the business,
That such a hideous trumpet calls to parley
The sleepers of the house? speak, speak!
 Macduff.   O gentle lady,
'Tis not for you to hear what I can speak;   90
The repetition in a woman's ear
Would murther as it fell.

    Enter Banquo.

      O Banquo, Banquo,
Our royal master's murther'd!
 Lady Macbeth.   Woe, alas!   95
What, in our house?
 Banquo.   Too cruel anywhere.
 Dear Duff, I prithee contradict thyself,
And say it is not so.

    Enter Macbeth and Lennox.

Macbeth. Had I but died an hour before this chance,   100
I had liv'd a blessed time; for, from this instant
There's nothing serious in mortality;
All is but toys; renown and grace is dead,
The wine of life is drawn, and the mere lees
Is left this vault to brag of.   105

    Enter Malcolm and Donalbain.

 Donalbain. What is amiss?
 Macbeth.   You are, and do not know't:
The spring, the head, the fountain of your blood
Is stopp'd; the very source of it is stopp'd.
 Macduff. Your royal father's murther'd.   110
 Malcolm.   O, by whom?
 Lennox. Those of his chamber, as it seem'd, had done't.
Their hands and faces were all badg'd with blood;
So were their daggers, which unwip'd we found
Upon their pillows. They star'd and were distracted;   115
No man's life was to be trusted with them.
 Macbeth. O, yet I do repent me of my fury,
That I did kill them.
 Macduff.   Wherefore did you so?
 Macbeth. Who can be wise, amaz'd, temp'rate and furious,   120
Loyal and neutral, in a moment? No man.
Th' expedition of my violent love
Outrun the pauser, reason. Here lay Duncan,
His silver skin lac'd with his golden blood;
And his gash'd stabs look'd like a breach in nature   125
For ruin's wasteful entrance; there, the murtherers,
Steep'd in the colors of their trade; their daggers

Unmannerly breech'd with gore. Who could refrain,
That had a heart to love, and in that heart
Courage to make's love known?   130
 Lady Macbeth.   Help me hence, ho!
 Macduff. Look to the lady.
 Malcolm. [*Aside to Donalbain.*] Why do we hold our
tongues.
That most may claim this argument for ours?   135
 Donalbain. [*Aside to Malcolm.*] What should be spoken here,
Where our fate, hid in an auger-hole,
May rush and seize us? Let's away.
Our tears are not yet brew'd.
 Malcolm. [*Aside to Donalbain.*] Nor our strong sorrow   140
Upon the foot of motion.
 Banquo.   Look to the lady.
       [*Lady Macbeth is carried out.*]
And when we have our naked frailties hid,
That suffer in exposure, let us meet,
And question this most bloody piece of work,   145
To know it further. Fears and scruples shake us.
In the great hand of God I stand, and thence
Against the undivulg'd pretence I fight
Of treasonous malice.
 Macduff.   And so do I.   150
 Allduff.   So all.
 Macbeth. Let's briefly put on manly readiness,
And meet i' th' hall together.
 All.   Well contented.
    Exeunt [all but Malcolm and Donalbain.]
 Malcolm. What will you do? Let's not consort with them.   155
To show an unfelt sorrow in an office
Which the false man does easy. I'll to England.
 Donalbain. To Ireland, I; our separated fortune
Shall keep us both safer. Where we are,
There's daggers in men's smiles; the near in blood,   160
The nearer bloody.
 Malcolm.   This murtherous shaft that's shot
Hath not yet lighted, and our safest way
Is to avoid the aim. Therefore, to horse!
And let us not be dainty of leave-taking,   165
But shift away. There's warrant in that theft
Which steals itself when there's no mercy left.   *Exeunt.*

❧ Scene Fourth ❧

Enter Ross with an Old Man.

Old Man. Threescore and ten I can remember well,
Within the volume of which time I have seen
Hours dreadful and things strange, but this sore night
Hath trifled former knowings.
 Ross.   Ha! good father,   5
Thou seest the heavens, as troubled with man's act,
Threatens his bloody stage. By th' clock 'tis day,
And yet dark night strangles the traveling lamp.

---

83 **great doom's image:** *likeness of doomsday* 84 **sprites:** *spirits* 85 **countenance:** *face (?) or accord with (?)* **SD Enter Macbeth and Lennox;** *Cf. n.* 102 **mortality:** *mortal life* 103 **toys:** *trifles* 105 **vault;** *Cf. n.* 113 **badg'd:** *marked with* 122 **expedition:** *speed* 123 **Outrun:** *outran* 124 **lac'd:** *decorated in a lacy pattern* 128 **Unmannerly ... gore;** *Cf. n.* 135 **argument:** *subject* 137, 138 **Where ... seize us;** *Cf. n.* 137 **auger-hole:** *i.e. a small hole* 139–141 **Our tears ... motion;** *Cf. n.* 143 **naked frailties;** *Cf. n.* 148 **pretence:** *design* 152 **briefly:** *quickly* 160 **near:** *nearer* 165 **dainty of:** *particular about* 166 **shift:** *steal* **warrant:** *justification* 4 **trifled:** *made trifles of* 6–24 **Thou ... upon't:** *see II.3.53–61; Cf. n.* 7 **Threatens:** *threaten* **stage;** *Cf. n.* 8 **lamp:** *i.e. the sun*

Is't night's predominance, or the day's shame,
That darkness does the face of the earth entomb,   *10*
When living light should kiss it?
    Old Man.   'Tis unnatural,
Even like the deed that's done. On Tuesday last,
A falcon, tow'ring in her pride of place,
Was by a mousing owl hawk'd at and kill'd.   *15*
    Ross. And Duncan's horses—a thing most strange
and certain—,
Beauteous and swift, the minions of their race,
Turn'd wild in nature, broke their stalls, flung out,
Contending 'gainst obedience, as they would   *20*
Make war with mankind.
    Old Man.   'Tis said they eat each other.
    Ross. They did so, so th' amazement of mine eyes,
That look'd upon't.

Enter Macduff.

                 Here comes the good Macduff.   *25*
How goes the world, sir, now?
    Macduff.   Why see you not?
    Ross. Is't known who did this more than bloody deed?
    Macduff. Those that Macbeth hath slain.
    Ross.   Alas, the day!   *30*
What good could they pretend?
    Macduff.   They were suborn'd.
Malcolm and Donalbain, the king's two sons,
Are stol'n away and fled, which puts upon them
Suspicion of the deed.   *35*
    Ross.   'Gainst nature still!
Triftless ambition, that will ravin up
Thine own life's means! Then 'tis most like
The sovereignty will fall upon Macbeth.
    Macduff. He is already nam'd, and gone to Scone   *40*
To be invested.
    Ross.   Where is Duncan's body?
    Macduff. Carried to Colmekill,
The sacred storehouse of his predecessors
And guardian of their bones.   *45*
    Ross.   Will you to Scone?
    Macduff. No, cousin, I'll to Fife.
    Ross.   Well, I will thither.
    Macduff. Well, may you see things well done there. Adieu!
Lest our old robes sit easier than our new!   *50*
    Ross. Farewell, father.
    Old Man. God's benison go with you, and with those
That would make good of bad, and friends of foes!

Exeunt omnes.

ACT THIRD ❧ SCENE FIRST

Enter Banquo.

Banquo. Thou hast it now: king, Cawdor, Glamis, all,
As the weyard women promis'd; and I fear
Thou play'dst most fouly for't; yet it was said

It should not stand in thy posterity,
But that myself should be the root and father   *5*
Of many kings. If there come truth from them—
As upon thee, Macbeth, their speeches shine—
Why, by the verities on thee made good,
May they not be my oracles as well,
And set me up in hope? But hush, no more.   *10*

Sennet sounded. Enter Macbeth, as king; Lady; Lennox, Ross,
Lords, and Attendants.

    Macbeth. Here's our chief guest.
    Lady Macbeth.   If he had been forgotten.
It had been as a gap in our great feast,
And all-thing unbecoming.
    Macbeth. Tonight we hold a solemn supper, sir,   *15*
And I'll request your presence.
    Banquo.   Let your highness
Command upon me, to the which my duties
Are with a most indissoluble tie
Forever knit.   *20*
    Macbeth. Ride you this afternoon?
    Banquo.   Ay, my good lord.
    Macbeth. We should have else desir'd your good advice—
Which still hath been both grave and prosperous—
In this day's council; but we'll take tomorrow.   *25*
Is't far you ride?
    Banquo. As far, my lord, as will fill up the time
'Twixt this and supper. Go not my horse the better,
I must become a borrower of the night
For a dark hour or twain.   *30*
    Macbeth.   Fail not our feast.
    Banquo. My lord, I will not.
    Macbeth. We hear our bloody cousins are bestow'd
In England and in Ireland, not confessing
Their cruel parricide, filling their hearers   *35*
With strange invention. But of that tomorrow,
When therewithal we shall have cause of state
Craving us jointly. Hie you to horse. Adieu,
Till you return at night. Goes Fleance with you?
    Banquo. Ay, my good lord; our time does call upon's.   *40*
    Macbeth. I wish your horses swift and sure of foot;
And so I do commend you to their backs. Farewell.

Exit Banquo.

Let every man be master of his time
Till seven at night;
To make society the sweeter welcome,   *45*
We will keep ourself till suppertime alone.
While then, God be with you.

Exeunt [all but Macbeth and a Servant.]

                     Sirrah, a word with you.
Attend those men our pleasure?
    Servant.   They are, my lord,   *50*
Without the palace gate.
    Macbeth.   Bring them before us.

Exit Servant.

---

14 tow'ring . . . place; *Cf. n.*   **15 mousing:** *i.e. that normally flies near to the ground*   **18 minions:** *darlings: i.e. best*   **22 eat:** *ate*   **31 pretend:** *intend*   **32 suborn'd:** *induced to commit a crime*   **37 ravin up:** *swallow greedily*   **41 invested:** *robed and crowned*   **43 Colmekill:** *island in the Hebrides now called Iona*   **52 benison:** *blessing*

SD Sennet: *trumpet call*   **14 all-thing:** *wholly*   **15 solemn:** *formal, ceremonious; see III.4.40–42*   **19 indissoluble:** *stressed — ´ — — ˋ —*   **24 still . . . prosperous:** *has always been weighty and profitable*   **28 Go . . . better;** *Cf. n.*   **37 cause of state:** *public business*   **38 Craving us jointly:** *demanding our joint attention*   **45–53 To make . . . safely thus;** *Cf. n.*   **45 sweeter:** *more sweetly*   **47 While then:** *till then*

To be thus is nothing, but to be safely thus.
Our fears in Banquo stick deep,
And in his royalty of nature reigns   55
That which would be fear'd. 'Tis much he dares,
And to that dauntless temper of his mind
He hath a wisdom that doth guide his valor
To act in safety. There is none but he
Whose being I do fear; and under him   60
My genius is rebuk'd, as it is said
Mark Antony's was by Caesar. He chid the sisters
When first they put the name of king upon me,
And bade them speak to him. Then, prophet-like,
They hail'd him father to a line of kings.   65
Upon my head they plac'd a fruitless crown,
And put a barren scepter in my gripe,
Thence to be wrench'd with an unlineal hand,
No son of mine succeeding. If't be so,
For Banquo's issue have I fil'd my mind;   70
For them the gracious Duncan have I murther'd;
Put rancors in the vessel of my peace
Only for them; and mine eternal jewel
Given to the common enemy of man,
To make them kings, the seeds of Banquo kings!   75
Rather than so, come Fate into the list,
And champion me to th' utterance!
                                    Who's there?

                    Enter Servant and two Murtherers.

Now go to the door, and stay there till we call.

                                              Exit Servant.
Was it not yesterday we spoke together?   80
    Murtherers. It was, so please your highness.
    Macbeth.   Well then.
Now have you consider'd of my speeches;
Know that it was he, in the times past,
Which held you so under fortune,   85
Which you thought had been our innocent self.
This I made good to you in our last conference;
Pass'd in probation with you
How you were borne in hand, how cross'd,
The instruments, who wrought with them,   90
And all things else that might to half a soul
And to a notion craz'd say, 'Thus did Banquo.'
    1 Murtherer. You made it known to us.
    Macbeth. I did so; and went further, which is now
Our point of second meeting. Do you find   95
Your patience so predominant in your nature
That you can let this go? Are you so gospel'd
To pray for this good man and for his issue,
Whose heavy hand hath bow'd you to the grave
And beggar'd yours forever?   100
    1 Murderer.   We are men, my liege.
    Macbeth. Ay, in the catalogue ye go for men,
As hounds and greyhounds, mongrels, spaniels, curs,

Shoughs, waterrugs, and demi-wolves, are clipt
All by the name of dogs. The valued file   105
Distinguishes the swift, the slow, the subtle,
The housekeeper, the hunter, every one
According to the gift which bounteous nature
Hath in him clos'd; whereby he does receive
Particular addition, from the bill   110
That writes them all alike; and so of men.
Now, if you have a station in the file,
Not i' th' worst rank of manhood, say't;
And I will put that business in your bosoms,
Whose execution takes your enemy off,   115
Grapples you to the heart and love of us,
Who wear our health but sickly in his life,
Which in his death were perfect.
    2 Murtherer.   I am one, my liege,
Whom the vile blows and buffets of the world   120
Hath so incens'd that I am reckless what
I do to spite the world.
    1 Murtherer.   And I another,
So weary with disasters, tugg'd with Fortune,
That I would set my life on any chance,   125
To mend it or be rid on't.
    Macbeth.   Both of you
Know Banquo was your enemy.
    Murtherers.   True, my lord.
    Macbeth. So is he mine; and in such bloody distance   130
That every minute of his being thrusts
Against my near'st of life; and though I could
With barefac'd power sweep him from my sight
And bid my will avouch it, yet I must not,
For certain friends that are both his and mine,   135
Whose loves I may not drop, but wail his fall
Who I myself struck down. And thence it is
That I to your assistance do make love,
Masking the business from the common eye
For sundry weighty reasons.   140
    2 Murtherer.   We shall my lord,
Perform what you command us.
    1 Murtherer.   Though our lives—
    Macbeth. Your spirits shine through you. Within
this hour at most   145
I will advise you where to plant yourselves,
Acquaint you with the perfect spy o' th' time,
The moment on't, for't must be done tonight,
And something from the palace; always thought
That I require a clearness; and with him,   150
To leave no rubs nor botches in the work,
Fleance his son, that keeps him company,
Whose absence is no less material to me
Than is his father's, must embrace the fate
Of that dark hour. Resolve yourselves apart;   155
I'll come to you anon.

104 Shoughs: *pronounced 'shocks'; shag-haired dogs* **waterrugs:** *shaggy water dogs* **clipt:** *called* **105 valued file:** *list in which value is recorded* **110 addition:** *title* **110, 111 from . . . alike:** *i.e. to distinguish him from the others in the general category of dogs* **118 in:** *during* **121 Hath:** *have* **124 tugg'd with:** *pulled about by* **130 distance:** *enmity* **132 near'st of life:** *most vital parts* **134 avouch:** *justify* **135 For:** *on account of* **136 but wail:** *but I must wail* **146 advise:** *inform* **147 perfect spy:** *exact indication* (literally, 'observation'); *Cf. n.* **148 on't:** *for it* **149 something:** *a little way* **always thought:** *i.e. it must be kept in mind* **150 clearness:** *freedom from suspicion* **151 rubs nor botches:** *roughness nor clumsy patching*

53 but: *unless* **61, 62 My genius . . . Caesar;** *Cf. n.* **61 genius:** *guardian spirit* **rebuk'd** *cowed* **70 fil'd** *defiled* **72 rancors:** *bitter enmities* **vessel of my peace:** *peace is compared to a liquid in a container* **73 jewel:** *i.e. soul* **76 list:** *lists* **77 champion:** *fight* **utterance:** *uttermost* **78 Who's there?:** *a customary phrase to summon the servant* **83 have you:** *you have* **84 Know:** *i.e. now you know* **85 under fortune:** *in distress* **87 made good:** *proved* **88 Pass'd in probation:** *went over the proofs* **89 borne in hand:** *deceived* **92 notion:** *mind* **97 gospel'd:** *so filled with Christian forgiveness*

Murtherers.   We are resolv'd, my lord.
Macbeth. I'll call upon you straight. Abide within.
                                    [*Exeunt Murtherers.*]
It is concluded. Banquo, thy soul's flight,
If it find heaven, must find it out tonight.   [*Exit.*] *160*

❧ SCENE SECOND ❧

Enter Macbeth's Lady and a Servant.

Lady Macbeth. Is Banquo gone from court?
Servant. Ay, madam, but returns again tonight.
Lady Macbeth. Say to the king, I would attend his leisure
For a few words.
Servant.   Madam, I will.   *Exit.* *5*
Lady Macbeth.   Nought's had, all's spent,
Where our desire is got without content.
'Tis safer to be that which we destroy
Than by destruction dwell in doubtful joy.

Enter Macbeth.

How now, my lord? Why do you keep alone,   *10*
Of sorriest fancies your companions making,
Using those thoughts which should indeed have died
With them they think on? Things without all remedy
Should be without regard: what's done is done.
Macbeth. We have scorch'd the snake, not kill'd it: *15*
She'll close and be herself, whilst our poor malice
Remains in danger of her former tooth.
But let the frame of things disjoint, both the worlds suffer,
Ere we will eat our meal in fear, and sleep
In the affliction of these terrible dreams   *20*
That shake us nightly. Better be with the dead,
Whom we, to gain our peace, have sent to peace,
Than on the torture of the mind to lie
In restless ecstasy.
Duncan is in his grave;   *25*
After life's fitful fever he sleeps well.
Treason has done his worst. Nor steel, nor poison,
Malice domestic, foreign levy, nothing
Can touch him further.
Lady Macbeth.   Come on: *30*
Gentle my lord, sleek o'er your rugged looks;
Be bright and jovial among your guests tonight.
Macbeth. So shall I, love, and so, I pray, be you.
Let your remembrance apply to Banquo;
Present him eminence, both with eye and tongue—   *35*
Unsafe the while that we must lave
Our honors in these flattering streams,
And make our faces vizards to our hearts,
Disguising what they are.
Lady Macbeth.   You must leave this.   *40*
Macbeth. O, full of scorpions is my mind, dear wife!
Thou know'st that Banquo and his Fleance lives.
Lady Macbeth. But in them nature's copy's not eterne.
Macbeth. There's comfort yet; they are assailable;

Then be thou jocund. Ere the bat hath flown   *45*
His cloister'd flight, ere to black Heccat's summons
The shard-borne beetle with his drowsy hums
Hath rung night's yawning peal, there shall be done
A deed of dreadful note.
Lady Macbeth.   What's to be done?   *50*
Macbeth. Be innocent of the knowledge, dearest chuck,
Till thou applaud the deed. Come, seeling night,
Scarf up the tender eye of pitiful day,
And with thy bloody and invisible hand
Cancel and tear to pieces that great bond   *55*
Which keeps me pale! Light thickens, and the crow
Makes wing to th' rooky wood.
Good things of day begin to droop and drowse,
Whiles night's black agents to their preys do rouse.
Thou marvell'st at my words; but hold thee still;   *60*
Things bad begun make strong themselves by ill.
So prithee go with me.   *Exeunt.*

❧ SCENE THIRD ❧

Enter three Murtherers.

1 Murtherer. But who did bid thee join with us?
3 Murtherer.   Macbeth.
2 Murtherer. He needs not our mistrust, since he delivers
Our offices and what we have to do
To the direction just.   *5*
1 Murtherer.   Then stand with us.
The west yet glimmers with some streaks of day.
Now spurs the lated traveler apace
To gain the timely inn, and near approaches
The subject of our watch.
3 Murtherer.   Hark! I hear horses.   *10*
Banquo within. Give us a light there, no!
2 Murtherer.   Then 'tis he;
The rest that are within the note of expectation
Already are i' th' court.   *15*
1 Murtherer.   His horses go about.
3 Murtherer. Almost a mile; but he does usually,
So all men do, from hence to th' palace gate
Make it their walk.

Enter Banquo and Fleance with a torch.

2 Murtherer.   A light, a light!   *20*
3 Murtherer.   'Tis he.
1 Murtherer. Stand to't.
Banquo. It will be rain tonight.
1 Murtherer.   Let it come down.
                         [*Strikes out light; stabs Banquo.*]
Banquo. O, treachery! Fly, good Fleance, fly, fly, fly!   *25*
Thou mayst revenge. O slave!   [*Dies. Fleance escapes.*]
3 Murtherer. Who did strike out the light?
1 Murtherer.   Was't not the way?

---

157 Resolve: *yourselves make up your minds*   **15 scorch'd:** *slashed as with a knife;*
Cf. n.   **18 frame of things disjoint:** *structure of the universe fall to pieces*   **both the worlds:** *i.e. celestial and terrestrial*   **24 ecstasy:** *frenzy*   **31 sleek:** *smooth*   **34 remembrance: read 'remembrance'**   **35 Present him eminence:** *do him honor*   **36 Unsafe:** *i.e. though we are unsafe*   **38 vizards:** *masks*   **42 lives:** *live*   [*43 copy:** *pattern; Cf. n.*]

47 shard-borne; *Cf. n.*   **51 chuck:** *familiar term of endearment*   **52 seeling:** *sewing up the eyelids (a term from falconry)*   **55 bond;** *Cf. n.*   **57 rooky:** *filled with rooks*   **3 He needs not our mistrust:** *i.e. we need not distrust him* (the third murderer)   **delivers:** *reports*   **4 offices:** *duties*   **5 To the direction:** *according to the instructions* (of Macbeth)   **14 note of expectation:** *list of expected guests*   **SD Enter Banquo and Fleance:** *See II.3. SD; Cf. n.*

3 Murtherer. There's but one down; the son is fled.
2 Murtherer.   We have lost
Best half of our affair.
1 Murtherer. Well, let's away, and say how much is done.
                                                    Exeunt.

❧ Scene Fourth ❧

*Banquet prepared. Enter Macbeth, Lady, Ross, Lennox, Lords and
Attendants.*

Macbeth. You know your own degrees; sit down.
At first and last, the hearty welcome.
Lords. Thanks to your majesty.
Macbeth. Ourself will mingle with society
And play the humble host.   5
Our hostess keeps her state, but in best time
We will require her welcome.
Lady Macbeth. Pronounce it for me, sir, to all our friends,
For my heart speaks they are welcome.

Enter First Murtherer [to the door].

Macbeth. See, they encounter thee with their hearts' thanks.   10
Both sides are even; here I'll sit i' th' midst.
Be large in mirth; anon, we'll drink a measure
The table round. *[Approaching the door.]* There's blood upon
thy face.
Murtherer. 'Tis Banquo's, then.   15
Macbeth. 'Tis better thee without than he within.
Is he dispatch'd?
Murtherer. My lord, his throat is cut; that I did for him.
Macbeth. Thou art the best o' th' cut-throats;
Yet he's good that did the like for Fleance: 20
If thou didst it, thou art the nonpareil.
Murtherer. Most royal sir—
                              Fleance is 'scap'd.
Macbeth. Then comes my fit again; I had else been perfect;
Whole as the marble, founded as the rock,   25
As broad and general as the casing air.
But now I am cabin'd, cribb'd, confin'd, bound in
To saucy doubts and fears. But Banquo's safe?
Murtherer. Ay, my good lord; safe in a ditch he bides.
With twenty trenched gashes on his head;   30
The least a death to nature.
Macbeth.   Thanks for that.
There the grown serpent lies; the worm that's fled
Hath nature that in time will venom breed,
No teeth for th' present. Get thee gone; tomorrow   35
We'll hear ourselves again.   *Exit Murderer.*
Lady Macbeth.   My royal lord,
You do not give the cheer. The feast is sold
That is not often vouch'd, while 'tis a-making;
'Tis given with welcome. To feed were best at home;   40
From thence, the sauce to meat is ceremony;
Meeting were bare without it.

Enter the Ghost of Banquo, and sits in Macbeth's place.

Macbeth.   Sweet remembrancer!
Now good digestion wait on appetite,
And health on both!   45
Lennox.   May't please your highness sit?
Macbeth. Here had we now our country's honor roof'd,
Were the grac'd person of our Banquo present;
Who may I rather challenge for unkindness
Than pity for mischance!   50
Ross.   His absence, sir,
Lays blame upon his promise. Please't your highness
To grace us with your royal company?
Macbeth. Take table's full.
Lennox.   Here is a place reserv'd, sir.   55
Macbeth.   Where?
Lennox. Here, my good lord. What is't that moves your
highness?
Macbeth. Which of you have done this?
Lords.   What, my good   60
lord?
Macbeth. Thou canst not say I did it; never shake
Thy gory locks at me.
Ross. Gentlemen, rise; his highness is not well.
Lady Macbeth. Sit, worthy friends. My lord is often thus,   65
And hath been from his youth. Pray you, keep seat;
The fit is momentary; upon a thought
He will again be well. If much you note him
You shall offend him and extend his passion;
Feed and regard him not. Are you a man?   70
Macbeth. Ay, and a bold one, that dare look on that
Which might appall the divel.
Lady Macbeth.   O proper stuff!
This is the very painting of your fear;
This is the air-drawn dagger which you said   75
Led you to Duncan. O, these flaws and starts—
Imposters to true fear—would well become
A woman's story at a winter's fire,
Authoriz'd by her grandam. Shame itself!
Why do you make such faces? When all's done   80
You look but on a stool.
Macbeth.   Prithee, see there!
Behold! look! lo! how say you?
Why, what care I? If thou canst nod, speak too.
If charnel houses and our graves must send   85
Those that we bury back, our monuments
Shall be the maws of kites.   *[Exit Ghost.]*
Lady Macbeth.   What! quite unmann'd in folly?
Macbeth. If I stand here, I saw him.
Lady Macbeth.   Fie, for shame!   90
Macbeth. Blood hath been shed ere now, i' th' olden time,
Ere humane statute purg'd the gentle weal;
Ay, and since too, murthers have been perform'd
Too terrible for the ear. The times has been,
That, when the brains were out, the man would die,   95
And there an end. But now they rise again,

1 **degrees:** *ranks*   2 **At first and last:** *once for all*   4–6 **Ourself . . . state;** *Cf. n.*   7
require: *request*   11 **Both sides are even:** *i.e. there are equal numbers on both sides of the
table*   12 **measure:** *large goblet*   13 **Approaching the door;** *Cf. n.*   16 **thee . . .
within:** *outside you than inside him*   21 **nonpareil:** *unequaled one*   26 **broad and general:** *free and unconfined*   **casing:** *surrounding*   30 **trenched:** *cut*   36 **hear ourselves:**
confer   38–40 **The feast . . . welcome;** *Cf. n.*

SD **Enter . . . Banquo;** *Cf. n.*   43 **remembrancer:** *one who reminds another; Cf. n.*   47
had we: *we should have*   **honor roof'd:** *under one roof*   67 **upon a thought:**
in a moment   69 **extend:** *increase*   76 **flaws:** *outbursts*   77 **Imposters:** *false pretend-
ers*   79 **Authoriz'd:** *stressed — ́ —; vouched for*   81 **stool;** *Cf. n.*   85–87 **If charnel
houses . . . kites;** *Cf. n.*   **charnel houses:** *repositories for bones*   92 **humane:** *stressed — ́ —;
both 'human' and 'humane'*   **gentle weal:** *civilized state*   94 **has:** *have*

With twenty mortal murthers on their crowns,
And push us from our stools. This is more strange
Than such a murther is.

   Lady Macbeth.   My worthy lord,   *100*
Your noble friends do lack you.

   Macbeth.   I do forget.
Do not muse at me, my most worthy friends;
I have a strange infirmity, which is nothing
To those that know me. Come, love and health to all;   *105*
Then, I'll sit down. Give me some wine; fill full.

                 Enter Ghost.

I drink to th' general joy o' th' whole table,
And to our dear friend Banquo, whom we miss.
Would he were here! to all, and him, we thirst,
And all to all.   *110*

   Lords.   Our duties, and the pledge.

   Macbeth. Avaunt, and quit my sight! Let the earth
hide thee!
Thy bones are marrowless, thy blood is cold;
Thou hast no speculation in those eyes   *115*
Which thou dost glare with.

   Lady Macbeth.   Think of this, good peers.
But as a thing of custom. 'Tis no other;
Only it spoils the pleasure of the time.

   Macbeth. What man dare, I dare.   *120*
Approach thou like the rugged Russian bear,
The arm'd rhinoceros, or th' Hyrcan tiger;
Take any shape but that, and my firm nerves
Shall never tremble. Or be alive again,
And dare me to the desart with thy sword;   *125*
If trembling I inhabit then, protest me
The baby of a girl. Hence, horrible shadow!
Unreal mock'ry, hence!   *[Exit Ghost.]*
                 Why, so; being gone
I am a man again. Pray you, sit still.   *130*

   Lady Macbeth. You have displac'd the mirth, broke
the good meeting
With most admir'd disorder.

   Macbeth.   Can such things be
And overcome us like a summer's cloud,   *135*
Without our special wonder? You make me strange
Even to the disposition that I owe,
When now I think you can behold such sights,
And keep the natural ruby of your cheeks,
When mine is blanch'd with fear.   *140*

   Ross.   What sights, my lord?

   Lady Macbeth. I pray you, speak not. He grows worse
and worse;
Question enrages him. At once, good night.
Stand not upon the order of your going,   *145*
But go at once.

   Lennox.   Good night; and better health
Attend his majesty!

   Lady Macbeth.   A kind good night to all!

             Exeunt Lords [and Attendants].   *150*

   Macbeth. It will have blood, they say: blood will have blood.
Stones have been known to move and trees to speak;
Augures and understood relations have
By maggot-pies and choughs and rooks brought forth
The secret'st man of blood. What is the night?   *155*

   Lady Macbeth. Almost at odds with morning, which is
which.

   Macbeth. How sayst thou, that Macduff denies his person
At our great bidding?

   Lady Macbeth.   Did you send to him, sir?   *160*

   Macbeth. I hear it by the way; but I will send.
There's not a one of them but in his house
I keep a servant fee'd. I will tomorrow—
And betimes I will—to the weyard sisters.
More shall they speak; for now I am bent to know   *165*
By the worst means the worst. For mine own good
All causes shall give way. I am in blood
Stepp'd in so far that, should I wade no more,
Returning were as tedious as go o'er.
Strange things I have in head that will to hand,   *170*
Which must be acted ere they may be scann'd.

   Lady Macbeth. You lack the season of all natures, sleep.

   Macbeth. Come, we'll to sleep. My strange and self-abuse
Is the initiate fear that wants hard use;
We are yet but young in deed.   *Exeunt.*

❧ SCENE FIFTH ❧

Thunder. Enter the three Witches, meeting Heccat.

   1 Witch. Why, how now, Heccat? You look angerly.

   Heccat. Have I not reason, beldams as you are,
Saucy and overbold? How did you dare
To trade and traffic with Macbeth
In riddles and affairs of death;   *5*
And I, the mistress of your charms,
The close contriver of all harms,
Was never call'd to bear my part,
Or show the glory of our art?
And, which is worse, all you have done   *10*
Hath been but for a wayward son,
Spiteful and wrathful; who, as others do,
Loves for his own ends, not for you.
But make amends now. Get you gone,
And at the pit of Acheron   *15*
Meet me i' th' morning. Thither he
Will come to know his destiny.
Your vessels and your spells provide,
Your charms and every thing beside.
I am for th' air; this night I'll spend   *20*
Unto a dismal and a fatal end.
Great business must be wrought ere noon.
Upon the corner of the moon
There hangs a vap'rous drop profound;

97 murthers: *i.e. wounds*   **103 muse:** *wonder*   **SD Enter Ghost:** *see III.4.SD;* *Cf. n.*   **109 thirst:** *are eager to drink*   **110 all to all:** *all drink to all*   **115 speculation:** *comprehending vision*   **118 of custom:** *usual*   **122 Hyrcan:** *Hyrcanian; Cf. n.*   **123 that:** *i.e. of Banquo* **nerves:** *sinews*   **125 desart:** *desert, i.e. any solitary place*   **126 inhabit:** *live, continue to live* **protest:** *proclaim*   **127 The baby of a girl:** *a baby girl*   **131 displac'd:** *banished*   **132 admir'd:** *wondered at*   **135 overcome:** *pass over*   **136, 137 You … owe;** *Cf. n.*   **140 is:** *are*   **145 Stand … going;** *Cf. n.*

SD Exeunt: *F Exit*   **153 Augures:** *auguries* **understood relations;** *Cf. n.*   **154 maggot-pies:** *magpies* **choughs:** *birds of the crow family*   **156 at odds with:** *disputing with*   **158 How sayst thou:** *what do you say to this*   **161 by the way:** *incidentally*   **171 scann'd:** *considered*   **172 season:** *preservative*   **173 strange and self-abuse:** *strange and self-imposed delusion*   **175 in deed:** *F. indeed*   **SCENE 5;** *Cf. n.*   **2 beldams:** *hags*   **7 close:** *secret*   **15 Acheron:** *a river of Hades*

I'll catch it ere it come to ground;   *25*
And that distill'd by magic sleights
Shall raise such artificial sprites
As by the strength of their illusion
Shall draw him on to his confusion.
He shall spurn fate, scorn death, and bear   *30*
His hopes 'bove wisdom, grace, and fear;
And you all know security
Is mortals' chiefest enemy.

Music and a song. Sing within.
'*Come away, come away,*' *etc.*

Hark! I am call'd; my little spirit, see,
Sits in a foggy cloud, and stays for me.

                        [Exit Heccat.]

  1 Witch. Come, let's make haste; she'll soon be back again.
                            Exeunt.

❧ Scene Sixth ❧

Enter Lennox and another Lord.

  Lennox. My former speeches have but hit your thoughts,
Which can interpret farther. Only I say
Things have been strangely borne. The gracious Duncan
Was pitied of Macbeth. Marry, he was dead!
And the right valiant Banquo walk'd too late;   *5*
Whom you may say—if't please you—Fleance kill'd,
For Fleance fled. Men must not walk too late.
Who cannot want the thought how monstrous
It was for Malcolm and for Donalbain
To kill their gracious father? Damned fact!   *10*
How it did grieve Macbeth! Did he not straight
In pious rage the two delinquents tear,
That were the slaves of drink and thralls of sleep?
Was not that nobly done? Ay, and wisely too;
For 'twould have anger'd any heart alive   *15*
To hear the men deny't. So that I say
He has borne all things well; and I do think
That, had he Duncan's sons under his key—
As, and't please heaven, he shall not—they should find
What 'twere to kill a father; so should Fleance.   *20*
But, peace! for from broad words, and 'cause he fail'd
His presence at the tyrant's feast, I hear
Macduff lives in disgrace. Sir, can you tell
Where he bestows himself?
  Lord.   The son of Duncan,   *25*
From whom this tyrant holds the due of birth,
Lives in the English court, and is receiv'd
Of the most pious Edward with such grace
That the malevolence of fortune nothing
Takes from his high respect. Thither Macduff   *30*
Is gone to pray the holy king, upon his aid
To wake Northumberland and warlike Siward;
That, by the help of these (with Him above

To ratify the work) we may again
Give to our tables meat, sleep to our nights;   *35*
Free from our feasts and banquets bloody knives;
Do faithful homage and receive free honors,
All which we pine for now. And this report
Hath so exasperate the king that he
Prepares for some attempt of war.   *40*
  Lennox.   Sent he to Macduff?
  Lord. He did; and with an absolute 'Sir, not I'
The cloudy messenger turns me his back,
And hums, as who should say, 'You'll rue the time
That clogs me with this answer.'   *45*
  Lennox.   And that well might
Advise him to a caution, t' hold what distance
His wisdom can provide. Some holy angel
Fly to the court of England and unfold
His message ere he come, that a swift blessing   *50*
May soon return to this our suffering country
Under a hand accurs'd!
  Lord.   I'll send my prayers with him!
                            Exeunt.

ACT FOURTH ❧ Scene First

Thunder. Enter the three Witches.

  1 Witch. Thrice the brinded cat hath mew'd.
  2 Witch. Thrice, and once the hedge-pig whin'd.
  3 Witch. Harpier cries; 'tis time, 'tis time.
  1 Witch. Round about the cauldron go;
In the poison'd entrails throw.   *5*
Toad, that under cold stone
Days and nights has thirty-one
Swelt'red venom sleeping got,
Boil thou first i' th' charmed pot.
  All. Double, double, toil and trouble;   *10*
Fire burn, and cauldron bubble.
  2 Witch. Fillet of a fenny snake,
In the cauldron boil and bake;
Eye of newt, and toe of frog,
Wool of bat, and tongue of dog;   *15*
Adder's fork, and blind-worm's sting,
Lizard's leg, and howlet's wing;
For a charm of pow'rful trouble,
Like a hell-broth boil and bubble.
  All. Double, double, toil and trouble;   *20*
Fire burn, and cauldron bubble.
  3 Witch. Scale of dragon, tooth of wolf,
Witches' mummy, maw and gulf
Of the ravin'd salt-sea shark;
Root of hemlock digg'd i' th' dark;   *25*
Liver of blaspheming Jew,
Gall of goat, and slips of yew

27 artificial: *cunning, well-contrived* **sprites:** *spirits*   **29 confusion:** *ruin*   **SD Sing within;** *Cf. n.*   **34 5 Hark . . . for me;** *Cf. n.*   **SCENE 6;** *Cf. n.*   **1 hit:** *coincided with*   **3 borne:** *managed*   **4 of:** *by*   **8 cannot want:** *can avoid*   **monstrous:** *perhaps three syllables here*   **19 and:** *if*   **21 broad:** *frank, outspoken*   **21, 22 fail'd/His presence:** *did not appear*   **25 son:** *F Sonnes*   **28 Edward:** *Edward the Confessor, King of England (1042–66)*   **31 pray . . . upon his aid:** *i.e. ask for his assistance; Cf. n.*

36 Free . . . knives; *Cf. n.*   **37 free:** *not bought by subservience to the tyrant*   **39 exasperate:** *exasperated*   **the:** *F their*   **42 absolute:** *unconditional*   **'Sir, not I':** *Macduff's message*   **43 cloudy:** *frowning*   **45 clogs:** *hampers; Cf. n.*   **1 brinded:** *brindled*   **2 hedge-pig:** *hedgehog; Cf. n.*   **3 Harpier:** *see I.1.8–12; Cf. n.*   **8 Swelt'red:** '*exuded,*' *like sweat*   **12 Fillet:** *slice*   **fenny:** *from the fens*   **16 fork:** *forked tongue*   **blind-worm:** *a small lizard*   **17 howlet:** *owlet*   **23 mummy:** *mummified flesh; Cf. n.*   **maw and gulf:** *stomach; Cf. n.*   **24 ravin'd:** *glutted with prey, or ravenous (?)*

Sliver'd in the moon's eclipse;
Nose of Turk, and Tartar's lips;
Finger of birth-strangled babe   30
Ditch-deliver'd by a drab,
Make the gruel thick and slab.
Add thereto a tiger's chawdron,
For th' ingredients of our cawdron,
  All. Double, double, toil and trouble;   35
Fire burn, and cauldron bubble.
  2 Witch. Cool it with a baboon's blood;
Then the charm is firm and good.

       Enter Heccat and the other three Witches.

  Heccat. O, well done! I commend your pains,
And every one shall share i' th' gains.   40
And now about the cauldron sing,
Like elves and fairies in a ring,
Enchanting all that you put in.

     Music and a song, 'Black Spirits,' etc.
                            [Exit Heccat.]

  2 Witch. By the pricking of my thumbs,
Something wicked this way comes.   45
Open, locks, whoever knocks.

              Enter Macbeth.

  Macbeth. How now, you secret, black, and midnight hags?
What is't you do?
  All.   A deed without a name.
  Macbeth. I conjure you, by that which you profess—   50
Howere you come to know it—answer me.
Though you untie the winds and let them fight
Against the churches; though the yesty waves
Confound and swallow navigation up;
Though bladed corn be lodg'd and trees blown down;   55
Though castles topple on their warders' heads;
Though palaces and pyramids do slope
Their heads to their foundations; though the treasure
Of nature's germens tumble all together,
Even till destruction sicken; answer me   60
To what I ask you.
  1 Witch.   Speak.
  2 Witch.   Demand.
  3 Witch.   We'll answer.
  1 Witch. Say if th' hadst rather hear it from our mouths, 65
Or from our masters?
  Macbeth.   Call 'em; let me see 'em.
  1 Witch. Pour in sow's blood, that hath eaten
Her nine farrow; grease, that's sweaten
From the murderer's gibbet, throw   70
Into the flame.
  All.   Come, high or low;
Thy self and office deftly show.

    Thunder. First Apparition, an Armed Head.

  Macbeth. Tell me, thou unknown power—
  1 Witch.   He knows thy thought: 75
Hear his speech, but say thou nought.
  1 Apparition. Macbeth! Macbeth! Macbeth! beware Macduff;
Beware the Thane of Fife. Dismiss me. Enough.   *He descends.*
  Macbeth. Whate'er thou art, for thy good caution thanks;
Thou hast harp'd my fear aright. But one word more—   80
  1 Witch. He will not be commanded. Here's another,
More potent than the first.

    Thunder. Second Apparition, a Bloody Child.

  2 Apparition. Macbeth! Macbeth! Macbeth!
  Macbeth. Had I three ears, I'd hear thee.
  2 Apparition. Be bloody, bold, and resolute; laugh to scorn. 85
The power of man; for none of woman born
Shall harm Macbeth.   *Descends.*
  Macbeth. Then live, Macduff; what need I fear of thee?
But yet I'll make assurance double sure,
And take a bond of fate. Thou shalt not live;   90
That I may tell pale-hearted fear it lies,
And sleep in spite of thunder.

  Thunder. Third Apparition, a Child Crowned, with a tree in his
                     hand.

                    What is this,
That rises like the issue of a king,
And wears upon his baby brow the round   95
And top of sovereignty?
  All.   Listen, but speak not to't.
  3 Apparition. Be lion-mettled, proud, and take no care
Who chafes, who frets, or where conspirers are.
Macbeth shall never vanquish'd be until   100
Great Birnam wood to high Dunsinane hill
Shall come against him.   *Descend.*
  Macbeth.   That will never be:
Who can impress the forest, bid the tree
Unfix his earth-bound root? Sweet bodements! good!   105
Rebellious head, rise never till the wood
Of Birnam rise, and our high-plac'd Macbeth
Shall live the lease of nature, pay his breath
To time and mortal custom. Yet my heart
Throbs to know one thing: tell me, if your art   110
Can tell so much: shall Banquo's issue ever
Reign in this kingdom?
  All.   Seek to know no more.
  Macbeth. I will be satisfied. Deny me this,
And an eternal curse fall on you! Let me know.   115
Why sinks that cauldron? and what noise is this?
                            Hoboyes.

  1 Witch. Show!
  2 Witch. Show!
  3 Witch. Show!
  All. Show his eyes, and grieve his heart;   120
Come like shadows, so depart.

---

31 Ditch-deliver'd: *born in a ditch* **drab:** *whore* **32 slab:** *thick* **33 chawdron:** *en-trails* **34 cawdron:** *cauldron* **37 baboon's:** *stressed* ‿́ — **SD Enter Heccat ...
Witches;** *Cf.* n. **39–43 O, well done ... you put in;** *Cf.* n. **50 that which you
profess:** *i.e. your magic art* **53 yesty:** *frothy* **55 bladed corn:** *grain not yet in the
ear* **lodg'd:** *beaten flat* **59 germens:** *seeds* (see King Lear, III.2.8) **69 farrow:** *young
pigs* **73 office:** *function* **SD First Apparition;** *Cf.* n.

80 harp'd: *guessed* **SD Second Apparition;** *Cf.* n. **90 bond:** *i.e. further guaranty*
SD Third Apparition; *Cf.* n. **101 Dunsinane:** *stressed* — ‿́ — (here only) **SD
Descend;** *Cf.* n. **104 impress:** *enlist forcibly* **105 bodements:** *prophecies* **106 head:**
F dead; Cf. n. **107 Birnam:** *F Byrnan; Cf.* n. **108 lease of nature:** *normal life-span* **116 sinks that cauldron;** *Cf.* n.

A show of eight Kings and Banquo, [the] last [king] with a glass in his hand.

Macbeth. Thou art too like the spirit of Banquo; down!
Thy crown does sear mine eyeballs. And thy hair,
Thou other gold-bound brow, is like the first.
A third is like the former. Filthy hags!   125
Why do you show me this?—A fourth? Start, eyes!
What, will the line stretch out to th' crack of doom?
Another yet? A seventh? I'll see no more.
And yet the eighth appears, who bears a glass
Which shows me many more; and some I see   130
That twofold balls and treble scepters carry.
Horrible sight! Now, I see, 'tis true,
For the blood-bolter'd Banquo smiles upon me,
And points at them for his.   *[Apparitions vanish.]*
                                     What? is this so?   135
   1 Witch. Ay, sir, all this is so. But why
Stands Macbeth thus amazedly?
Come, sisters, cheer we up his sprites,
And show the best of our delights.
I'll charm the air to give a sound,   140
While you perform your antic round,
That this great king may kindly say,
Our duties did his welcome pay.
                     Music. The Witches dance, and vanish.
   Macbeth. Where are they? Gone? Let this pernicious   145
hour
Stand aye accursed in the calendar!
Come in, without there!

Enter Lennox.

   Lennox.   What's your grace's will?
   Macbeth. Saw you the weyard sisters?   150
   Lennox.   No, my lord.
   Macbeth. Came they not by you?
   Lennox.   No indeed, my lord.
   Macbeth. Infected be the air whereon they ride,
And damn'd all those that trust them! I did hear   155
The galloping of horse. Who was't came by?
   Lennox. 'Tis two or three, my lord, that bring you word
Macduff is fled to England.
   Macbeth.   Fled to England?
   Lennox. Ay, my good lord.   160
   Macbeth. Time, thou anticipat'st my dread exploits;
The flighty purpose never is o'ertook
Unless the deed go with it. From this moment
The very firstlings of my heart shall be
The firstlings of my hand. And even now,   165
To crown my thoughts with acts, be it thought and done:
The castle of Macduff I will surprise,
Seize upon Fife, give to th' edge o' th' sword
His wife, his babes, and all unfortunate souls
That trace him in his line. No boasting like a fool;   170
This deed I'll do before this purpose cool;
But no more sights! Where are these gentlemen?
Come, bring me where they are.   *Exeunt.*

SD A show of eight Kings; *Cf. n.*   **127 crack of doom:** *sound of the trumpet on dooms-*
day   **129 eighth:** *F* eight   glass; *Cf. n.*   **131 twofold ... scepters;** *Cf. n.*   **133 blood-**
bolter'd: *having the hair clotted with blood*   **136–143 Ay, sir, ... his welcome pay;**
Cf. n.   **141 antic:** *fantastic* round: *dance*   **161 exploits:** *stressed* — ́   **162, 163 The**
flighty ... it; *Cf. n.*   **165 firstlings:** *first-born*   **170 trace:** *follow, i.e. are related to*

❧ Scene Second ❧

Enter Macduff's Wife, her Son, and Ross.

   Lady Macduff. What had he done to make him fly the land?
   Ross. You must have patience, madam.
   Lady Macduff.   He had none.
His flight was madness. When our actions do not,
Our fears do make us traitors.   5
   Ross.   You know not
Whether it was his wisdom or his fear.
   Lady Macduff. Wisdom! to leave his wife, to leave his babes,
His mansion, and his titles, in a place
From whence himself does fly? He loves us not;   10
He wants the natural touch. For the poor wren,
The most diminitive of birds, will fight,
Her young ones in her nest, against the owl.
All is the fear and nothing is the love;
As little is the wisdom, where the flight   15
So runs against all reason.
   Ross.   My dearest coz,
I pray you school yourself. But, for your husband,
He is noble, wise, judicious, and best knows
The fits o' th' season. I dare not speak much further;   20
But cruel are the times, when we are traitors
And do not know ourselves, when we hold rumor
From what we fear, yet know not what we fear,
But float upon a wild and violent sea
Each way, and move. I take my leave of you.   25
Shall not be long but I'll be here again.
Things at the worst will cease, or else climb upward
To what they were before. My pretty cousin,
Blessing upon you!
   Lady Macduff. Father'd he is, and yet he's fatherless.   30
   Ross. I am so much a fool, should I stay longer,
It would be my disgrace, and your discomfort:
I take my leave at once.   *Exit Ross.*
   Lady Macduff.   Sirrah, your father's dead;
And what will you do now? How will you live?   35
   Son. As birds do, mother.
   Lady Macduff.   What, with worms and flies?
   Son. With what I get, I mean; and so do they.
   Lady Macduff. Poor bird! thou'dst never fear the net
nor lime,   40
The pit-fall nor the gin.
   Son. Why should I, mother? Poor birds they are not set for.
My father is not dead, for all your saying.
   Lady Macduff. Yes, he is dead. How wilt thou do for a
father?   45
   Son. Nay, how will you do for a husband?
   Lady Macduff. Why, I can buy me twenty at any market.
   Son. Then you'll buy 'em to sell again.
   Lady Macduff. Thou speak'st with all thy wit;
And yet, i' faith, with wit enough for thee.   50
   Son. Was my father a traitor, mother?
   Lady Macduff. Ay, that he was.
   Son. What is a traitor?
   Lady Macduff. Why, one that swears and lies.
   Son. And be all traitors that do so?   55

9 titles: *possessions*   **11 wants:** *lacks*   **12 diminitive:** *diminutive*   **17 coz:** *short for*
'cousin'   **18 school:** *control*   **20 fits:** *disorders*   **34 Sirrah:** *form of address often used by*
parents to children   **40 lime:** *birdlime*   **41 gin:** *snare*   **42 they:** *i.e. traps and snares*

Lady Macduff. Every one that does so is a traitor, and must be hang'd.

Son. And must they all be hang'd that swear and lie?

Lady Macduff. Every one.

Son. Who must hang them?   60

Lady Macduff. Why, the honest men.

Son. Then the liars and swearers are fools, for there are liars and swearers enow to beat the honest men and hang up them.

Lady Macduff. Now God help thee, poor monkey! But how wilt thou do for a father?   65

Son. If he were dead, you'd weep for him. If you would not, it were a good sign that I should quickly have a new father.

Lady Macduff. Poor prattler, how thou talk'st!

Enter a Messenger.

Messenger. Bless you, fair dame! I am not to you known.   70
Though in your state of honor I am perfect.
I doubt some danger does approach you nearly.
If you will take a homely man's advice,
Be not found here; hence, with your little ones.
To fright you thus methinks I am too savage;   75
To do worse to you were fell cruelty,
Which is too nigh your person. Heaven preserve you!
I dare abide no longer.   *Exit Messenger.*

Lady Macduff.   Whither should I fly?
I have done no harm. But I remember now   80
I am in this earthly world, where to do harm
Is often laudable, to do good sometime
Accounted dangerous folly. Why then, alas,
Do I put up that womanly defense,
To say I have done no harm?   85

Enter Murtherers.

    What are these faces?

Murtherer. Where is your husband?

Lady Macduff. I hope in no place so unsanctified
Where such as thou mayst find him.

Murtherer.   He's a traitor.   90

Son. Thou liest, thou shag-hair'd villain.

Murtherer.   What! you egg.
Young fry of treachery!   *[Stabbing him.]*

Son.   He has killed me, mother.
Run away, I pray you!

Exit [Lady Macduff] crying 'Murther.'

❧ Scene Third ❧

Enter Malcolm and Macduff.

Malcolm. Let us seek out some desolate shade, and there
Weep our sad bosoms empty.

Macduff.   Let us rather
Hold fast the mortal sword, and like good men
Bestride our downfall'n birthdom. Each new morn   5
New widows howl, new orphans cry, new sorrows

Strike heaven on the face, that it resounds
As if it felt with Scotland and yell'd out
Like syllable of dolor.

Malcolm.   What I believe I'll wail,   10
What know believe, and what I can redress,
As I shall find the time to friend, I will.
What you have spoke, it may be so perchance.
This tyrant, whose sole name blisters our tongues,
Was once thought honest; you have lov'd him well;   15
He hath not touch'd you yet. I am young; but something
You may discern of him through me, and wisdom
To offer up a weak, poor, innocent lamb
T' appease an angry god.

Macduff. I am not treacherous.   20

Malcolm.   But Macbeth is.
A good and virtuous nature may recoil
In an imperial charge. But I shall crave your pardon
That which you are my thoughts cannot transpose;
Angels are bright still, though the brightest fell.   25
Though all things foul would wear the brows of grace,
Yet grace must still look so.

Macduff.   I have lost my hopes.

Malcolm. Perchance even there where I did find my doubts.
Why in that rawness left you wife and child,   30
Those precious motives, those strong knots of love,
Without leave-taking? I pray you,
Let not my jealousies by your dishonors,
But mine own safeties. You may be rightly just,
Whatever I shall think.   35

Macduff.   Bleed, bleed, poor country!
Great tyranny, lay thou thy basis sure,
For goodness dare not check thee! Wear thou thy wrongs;
The title is affeer'd! Fare thee well, lord,
I would not be the villain that thou think'st   40
For the whole space that's in the tyrant's grasp,
And the rich East to boot.

Malcolm.   Be not offended.
I speak not as in absolute fear of you.
I think our country sinks beneath the yoke;   45
It weeps, it bleeds, and each new day a gash
Is added to her wounds. I think withal,
There would be hands uplifted in my right;
And here from gracious England have I offer
Of goodly thousands. But, for all this,   50
When I shall tread upon the tyrant's head,
Or wear it on my sword, yet my poor country
Shall have more vices than it had before,
More suffer, and more sundry ways than ever,
By him that shall succeed.   55

Macduff.   What should he be?

Malcolm. It is myself I mean; in whom I know
All the particulars of vice so grafted
That, when they shall be open'd, black Macbeth
Will seem as pure as snow, and the poor state   60
esteem him as a lamb, being compar'd

56, 57 Every one … hang'd: *F prints as verse*   **63 enow:** *enough*   **64, 65 Now … father:** *F prints as verse*   **71 in … perfect:** *perfectly acquainted with your honorable station*   **72 doubt:** *fear*   **73 homely:** *humble*   **75 thus methinks:** *F punctuates thus. Me thinkes*   **91 shag-hair'd:** *F shagge-ear'd; Cf. n.*   **4 mortal:** *deadly*   **5 Bestride:** *i.e. in its defense* **birthdom:** *fatherland*

12 to friend: *as a friend; i.e. to be favorable*   **14 sole:** *mere*   **17 discern:** *learn by discernment; Cf. n.*   **22, 23 recoil … charge:** *give way under pressure from a ruler*   **24 transpose:** *alter*   **27 so:** *i.e. like itself*   **30 rawness:** *unprotected condition*   **31 motives:** *persons inspiring love and action*   **33 jealousies:** *suspicions*   **39 affeer'd:** *confirmed; F affear'd*   **49 gracious England:** *i.e. the English king, Edward the Confessor*

With my confineless harms.
 Macduff.   Not in the legions
Of horrid hell can come a divel more damn'd
In evils to top Macbeth.   *65*
 Malcolm.   I grant him bloody,
Luxurious, avaricious, false, deceitful,
Sudden, malicious, smacking of every sin
That has a name. But there's no bottom, none,
In my voluptuousness: your wives, your daughters, *70*
Your matrons, and your maids, could not fill up
The cistern of my lust, and my desire
All continent impediments would o'erbear
That did oppose my will. Better Macbeth
Than such an one to reign.   *75*
 Macduff.   Boundless intemperance
In nature is a tyranny. It hath been
Th' untimely emptying of the happy throne,
And fall of many kings. But fear not yet
To take upon you what is yours; you may *80*
Convey your pleasures in a spacious plenty,
And yet seem cold, the time you may so hoodwink.
We have willing dames enough; there cannot be
That vulture in you, to devour so many
As will to greatness dedicate themselves, *85*
Finding it so inclin'd.
 Malcolm.   With this there grows
In my most ill-compos'd affection such
A stanchless avarice that, were I king,
I should cut off the nobles for their lands, *90*
Desire his jewels and this other's house;
And my more-having would be as a sauce
To make me hunger more, that I should forge
Quarrels unjust against the good and loyal,
Destroying them for wealth.   *95*
 Macduff.   This avarice
Sticks deeper, grows with more pernicious root
Than summer-seeming lust, and it hath been
The sword of our slain kings. Yet do not fear;
Scotland hath foisons to fill up your will *100*
Of your mere own. All these are portable,
With other graces weigh'd.
 Malcolm. But I have none. The king-becoming graces,
As justice, verity, temp'rance, stableness,
Bounty, perseverance, mercy, lowliness, *105*
Devotion, patience, courage, fortitude,
I have no relish of them, but abound
In the division of each several crime,
Acting it many ways. Nay, had I power, I should
Pour the sweet milk of concord into hell, *110*
Uproar the universal peace, confound
All unity on earth.
 Macduff.   O Scotland, Scotland!
 Malcolm. If such a one be fit to govern, speak.
I am as I have spoken.   *115*

 Macduff.   Fit to govern?
No, not to live. O nation miserable!
With an untitled tyrant bloody-scept'red,
When shalt thou see thy wholesome days again,
Since that the truest issue of thy throne *120*
By his own interdiction stands accus'd,
And does blaspheme his breed? Thy royal father
Was a most sainted king; the queen that bore thee,
Oft'ner upon her knees than on her feet,
Died every day she liv'd. Fare thee well! *125*
These evils thou repeat'st upon thyself
Hath banish'd me from Scotland. O my breast,
Thy hope ends here!
 Malcolm.   Macduff, this noble passion,
Child of integrity, hath from my soul *130*
Wip'd the black scruples, reconcil'd my thoughts
To thy good truth and honor. Divelish Macbeth
By many of these trains hath sought to win me
Into his power, and modest wisdom plucks me
From overcredulous haste; but God above *135*
Deal between thee and me! for even now
I put myself to thy direction, and
Unspeak mine own detraction, here abjure
The taints and blames I laid upon myself,
For strangers to my nature. I am yet *140*
Unknown to woman, never was forsworn,
Scarcely have coveted what was mine own,
At no time broke my faith, would not betray
The devil to his fellow, and delight
No less in truth than life. My first false speaking *145*
Was this upon myself. What I am truly
Is thine and my poor country's to command;
Whither indeed, before thy here-approach,
Old Siward, with ten thousand warlike men,
Already at a point, was setting forth. *150*
Now we'll together, and the chance of goodness
Be like our warranted quarrel. Why are you silent?
 Macduff. Such welcome and unwelcome things at once
'Tis hard to reconcile.

Enter a Doctor.

 Malcolm. Well, more anon. Comes the king forth, *155*
I pray you?
 Doctor. Ay, sir; there are a crew of wretched souls
That stay his cure; their malady convinces
The great assay of art. But, at his touch,
Such sanctity hath heaven given his hand, *160*
They presently amend.
 Malcolm.   I thank you, doctor. *Exit [Doctor.]*
 Macduff. What's the disease he means?
 Malcolm.   'Tis call'd the evil.
A most miraculous work in this good king, *165*
Which often, since my here-remain in England,
I have seen him do. How he solicits heaven,
Himself best knows; but strangely-visited people,

---

62 **confineless:** *boundless* 67 **Luxurious:** *lustful* 73 **continent:** *restraining* 81 **Convey:** *arrange secretly* 82 **cold, the time:** *F punctuates* cold. The time. **time:** *see I.5.70; Cf. n.* 88 **affection:** *disposition* 89 **stanchless:** *insatiable* 98 **summer-seeming:** *befitting* (beseeming) *summer, or resembling it* 99 **sword:** *i.e. cause of death* 100 **foisons:** *plentiful supplies* 101 **your mere own:** *what is entirely yours* **portable:** *endurable* 102 **With ... weigh'd:** *i.e. when balanced against other graces* 105 **perseverance:** *read 'persév'rance'* 108 **division:** *variation* 110–112 **Pour ... earth;** *Cf. n.*

121 **interdiction:** *statement of unfitness (legal term)* 125 **Died ... liv'd:** *i.e. was always ready for death; see I Corinthians 15:31* 127 **Hath:** *have* 133 **trains:** *stratagems* 134 **modest:** *marked by moderation* 140 **For:** *as being* 148 **thy:** *F* they 150 **at a point:** *in readiness* 151, 152 **the chance ... quarrel;** *Cf. n.* 158 **stay his cure:** *wait for him to cure them; Cf. n.* 158, 159 **convinces ... art:** *conquers the greatest efforts of medical skill* 161 **presently:** *immediately* 164 **evil:** *see IV.3.157; Cf. n.* 168 **visited:** *afflicted*

All swolne and ulcerous, pitiful to the eye,
The mere despair of surgery, he cures,   *170*
Hanging a golden stamp about their necks,
Put on with holy prayers; and 'tis spoken
To the succeeding royalty he leaves
The healing benediction. With this strange virtue,
He hath a heavenly gift of prophecy,   *175*
And sundry blessings hang about his throne
That speak him full of grace.

Enter Ross.

Macduff.   See who comes here.
Malcolm. My countryman; but yet I know him not.
Macduff. My ever-gentle cousin, welcome hither.   *180*
Malcolm. I know him now. Good God, betimes remove
The means that makes us strangers!
     Ross.   Sir, amen.
Macduff. Stands Scotland where it did?
     Ross.   Alas, poor country.   *185*
Almost afraid to know itself! It cannot
Be call'd our mother, but our grave; where nothing,
But who knows nothing, is once seen to smile;
Where sighs and groans and shrieks that rent the air
Are made, not mark'd; where violent sorrow seems   *190*
A modern ecstasy; the dead man's knell
Is there scarce ask'd for who; and good men's lives
Expire before the flowers in their caps,
Dying or ere they sicken.
     Macduff.   O, relation   *195*
Too nice, and yet too true.
     Malcolm.   What's the newest grief?
Ross. That of an hour's age doth hiss the speaker;
Each minute teems a new one.
     Macduff.   How does my wife?   *200*
Ross. Why, well.
     Macduff.   And all my children?
     Ross.   Well too.
Macduff. The tyrant has not batter'd at their peace?
Ross. No; they were well at peace when I did leave   *205*
'em.
     Macduff. Be not a niggard of your speech: how goes't?
Ross. When I came hither to transport the tidings
Which I have heavily borne, there ran a rumor
Of many worthy fellows that were out;   *210*
Which was to my belief witness'd the rather
For that I saw the tyrant's power afoot,
Now is the time of help; your eye in Scotland
Would create soldiers, make our women fight,
To doff their dire distresses.   *215*
     Malcolm.   Be't their comfort
We are coming thither. Gracious England hath
Lent us good Siward and ten thousand men;
An older and a better soldier none
That Christendom gives out.   *220*
     Ross.   Would I could answer
This comfort with the like! But I have words

That would be howl'd out in the desert air,
Where hearing them should not latch them.
     Macduff.   What concern they?   *225*
The general cause? or is it a fee-grief
Due to some single breast?
     Ross.   No mind that's honest
But in it shares some woe, though the main part
Pertains to you alone.   *230*
     Macduff.   If it be mine,
Keep it not from me; quickly let me have it.
     Ross. Let not your ears despise my tongue forever,
Which shall possess them with the heaviest sound
That ever yet they heard.   *235*
     Macduff.   Humh! I guess at it.
Ross. Your castle is surpris'd; your wife and babes
Savagely slaughter'd. To relate the manner
Were, on the quarry of these murther'd deer,
To add the death of you.   *240*
     Malcolm.   Merciful heaven!
What, man! Ne'er pull your hat upon your brows.
Give sorrow words; the grief that does not speak
Whispers the o'er-fraught heart and bids it break.
     Macduff. My children too?   *245*
Ross. Wife, children, servants, all that could be found.
Macduff. And I must be from thence! My wife kill'd too?
Ross. I have said.
     Malcolm.   Be comforted.
Let's make us med'cines of our great revenge,   *250*
To cure this deadly grief.
     Macduff. He has no children. All my pretty ones?
Did you say all? O hell-kite! All?
What, all my pretty chickens and their dam
At one fell swoop?   *255*
     Malcolm. Dispute it like a man.
     Macduff.   I shall do so;
But I must also feel it as a man.
I cannot but remember such things were,
That were most precious to me. Did heaven look on,   *260*
And would not take their part? Sinful Macduff,
They were all struck for thee! Naught that I am,
Not for their own demerits, but for mine,
Fell slaughter on their souls. Heaven rest them now!
     Malcolm. Be this the whetstone of your sword; let grief   *265*
Convert to anger; blunt not the heart, enrage it.
     Macduff. O, I could play the woman with mine eyes,
And braggart with my tongue. But, gentle heavens,
Cut short all intermission. Front to front
Bring thou this fiend of Scotland and myself;   *270*
Within my sword's length set him; if he scrape,
Heaven forgive him too!
     Malcolm.   This tune goes manly.
Come, go we to the king; our power is ready;
Our lack is nothing but our leave. Macbeth   *275*
Is ripe for shaking, and the powers above
Put on their instruments. Receive what cheer you may;
The night is long that never finds the day.   *Exeunt.*

---

169 swolne: *swollen*   **170 mere:** *utter*   **171 stamp:** *stamped coin*   **180 gentle:** *noble*   **181 betimes:** *speedily*   **191 ecstasy:** *frenzy; Cf. n.*   **194 or ere:** *ere*   **195 relation:** *recital*   **196 nice:** *minutely accurate*   **198 hiss:** *cause to be hissed for giving outdated information*   **199 teems:** *gives birth to*   **210 out:** *i.e. in the field of arms*   **212 power:** *army*   **217 Gracious England:** *see l. 49*   **220 gives out:** *proclaims*

223 would be: *demand to be*   **224 latch:** *catch*   **226 fee-grief:** *private grief*   **234 heaviest:** *most grievous*   **239 quarry:** *game killed in hunting*   **255 swoop:** *i.e. of the hell-kite*   **256 Dispute it:** *contest it (Macbeth's action); i.e. avenge yourself; Cf. n.*   **262 Naught:** *wicked man*   **269 intermission:** *delay*   **273 tune:** *F time*   **274 power:** *army*   **275 Our lack ... leave:** *we need only permission to go*   **277 Put on their instruments:** *arm themselves*

ACT FIFTH ❧ SCENE FIRST

Enter a Doctor of Physic and a Waiting Gentlewoman.

Doctor. I have two nights watch'd with you, but can perceive no truth in your report. When was it she last walk'd?

Gentlewoman. Since his majesty went into the field, I have seen her rise from her bed, throw her nightgown upon her, unlock her closet, take forth paper, fold it, write upon't, 5 read it, afterwards seal it, and again return to bed; yet all this while in a most fast sleep.

Doctor. A great perturbation in nature, to receive at once the benefit of sleep and do the effects of watching! In this slumb'ry agitation, besides her walking and other actual 10 performances, what, at any time, have you heard her say?

Gentlewoman. That, sir, which I will not report after her.

Doctor. You may to me, and 'tis most meet you should.

Gentlewoman. Neither to you nor anyone, having no witness to confirm my speech. 15

Enter Lady, with a taper.

Lo you, here she comes. This is her very guise, and upon my life, fast asleep. Observe her; stand close.

Doctor. How came she by that light?

Gentlewoman. Why, it stood by her. She has light by her continually; 'tis her command. 20

Doctor. You see her eyes are open.

Gentlewoman. Ay, but their sense are shut.

Doctor. What is it she does now? Look how she rubs her hands.

Gentlewoman. It is an accustom'd action with her, to 25 seem thus washing her hands. I have known her continue in this a quarter of an hour.

Lady Macbeth. Yet here's a spot.

Doctor. Hark! she speaks. I will set down what comes from her, to satisfy my remembrance the more strongly. 30

Lady Macbeth. Out, damned spot! out, I say! One; two. Why, then, 'tis time to do't. Hell is murky. Fie, my lord, fie! a soldier, and afeard? What need we fear who knows it, when none can call our power to accompt? Yet who would have thought the old man to have had so much blood in him? 35

Doctor. Do you mark that?

Lady Macbeth. The Thane of Fife had a wife. Where is she now? What, will these hands ne'er be clean? No more o' that, my lord, no more o' that! You mar all with this starting.

Doctor. Go to, go to! You have known what you should 40 not.

Gentlewoman. She has spoke what she should not, I am sure of that. Heaven knows what she has known.

Lady Macbeth. Here's the smell of the blood still. All the perfumes of Arabia will not sweeten this little hand. 45 Oh, oh, oh!

Doctor. What a sigh is there! The heart is sorely charg'd.

Gentlewoman. I would not have such a heart in my bosom for the dignity of the whole body.

Doctor. Well, well, well. 50

Gentlewoman. Pray God it be, sir.

Doctor. This disease is beyond my practice. Yet I have known those which have walk'd in their sleep who have died holily in their beds.

Lady Macbeth. Wash your hands, put on your nightgown, 55 look not so pale. I tell you yet again, Banquo's buried; he cannot come out on's grave.

Doctor. Even so?

Lady Macbeth. To bed, to bed! There's knocking at the gate. Come, come, come, come, give me your hand. What's done 60 cannot be undone. To bed, to bed, to bed!   *Exit Lady.*

Doctor. Will she go now to bed?

Gentlewoman. Directly.

Doctor. Foul whisp'rings are abroad. Unnatural deeds Do breed unnatural troubles. Infected minds 65 To their deaf pillows will discharge their secrets. More needs she the divine than the physician. God, God forgive us all! Look after her; Remove from her the means of all annoyance, And still keep eyes upon her. So, good night. 70 My mind she has mated, and amaz'd my sight. I think, but dare not speak.

Gentlewoman.   Good night, good doctor.

Exeunt.

❧ SCENE SECOND ❧

Drum and colors. Enter Menteth, Cathness, Angus, Lennox, Soldiers.

Menteth. The English power is near, led on by Malcolm, His uncle Siward, and the good Macduff. Revenges burn in them; for their dear causes Would to the bleeding and the grim alarm Excite the mortified man. 5

Angus.   Near Birnam wood Shall we well meet them; that way are they coming.

Cathness. Who knows if Donalbain be with his brother?

Lennox. For certain, sir, he is not. I have a file Of all the gentry: there is Siward's son, 10 And many unrough youths that even now Protest their first of manhood.

Menteth.   What does the tyrant?

Cathness. Great Dunsinane he strongly fortifies. Some say he's mad; others that lesser hate him 15 Do call it valiant fury; but, for certain, He cannot buckle his distemper'd cause Within the belt of rule.

Angus.   Now does he feel His secret murthers sticking on his hands; 20 Now minutely revolts upbraid his faith-breach. Those he commands move only in command, Nothing in love. Now does he feel his title Hang loose about him, like a giant's robe Upon a dwarfish thief. 25

Menteth.   Who then shall blame His pester'd senses to recoil and start, When all that is within him does condemn

3 **into the field:** *i.e. to battle*   4 **nightgown:** *dressing gown*   5 **closet:** *private repository of valuables*   9 **effects of watching:** *actions of a waking condition*   17 **close:** *concealed*   21 **are;** *Cf. n.*   34 **accompt:** *account (and so pronounced)*   40 **Go to, go to:** *come, come* **You:** *i.e. Lady Macbeth*   47 **sorely charg'd:** *heavily burdened*   49 **dignity:** *worth*

56 **on's:** *of his*   68 **annoyance:** *injury (to herself)*   70 **mated:** *bewildered*   1 **power:** *army*   3 **dear:** *heartfelt*   4 **alarm:** *call to battle*   5 **mortified:** *numbed, or even dead*   11 **unrough:** *unbearded*   12 **Protest:** *proclaim*   17 **distemper'd:** *sick, unruly*   21 **minutely:** *(stressed ⏑́ — —) happening every minute*   23 **Nothing:** *not at all*   27 **pester'd:** *troubled*

Itself for being there?

  Cathness.   Well, march we on,   30
To give obedience where 'tis truly ow'd.
Meet we the med'cine of the sickly weal,
And with him pour we in our country's purge
Each drop of us.

  Lennox.   Or so much as it needs   35
To dew the sovereign flower and drown the weeds.
Make we our march towards Birnam.

                       Exeunt marching.

❧ Scene Third ❧

Enter Macbeth, Doctor, and Attendants.

  Macbeth. Bring me no more reports; let them fly all!
Till Birnam wood remove to Dunsinane
I cannot taint with fear. What's the boy Malcolm?
Was he not born of woman? The spirits that know
All mortal consequences have pronounc'd me thus: 5
'Fear not, Macbeth; no man that's born of woman
Shall ere have power upon thee.' Then fly, false thanes,
And mingle with the English epicures!
The mind I sway by and the heart I bear
Shall never sag with doubt nor shake with fear.   10

Enter Servant.

The divel damn thee black, thou cream-fac'd loon!
Where got'st thou that goose look?

  Servant. There is ten thousand—

  Macbeth.   Geese, villain?

  Servant.   Soldiers, sir.   15

  Macbeth. Go prick thy face, and over-red thy fear,
Thou lily-liver'd boy. What soldiers, patch?
Death of thy soul! those linen cheeks of thine
Are counselors to fear. What soldiers, wheyface?

  Servant. The English force, so please you.   20

  Macbeth. Take thy face hence.   *[Exit Servant.]*

                 Seyton!—I am sick at heart
When I behold—Seyton, I say!—This push
Will cheer me ever or disseat me now.
I have liv'd long enough. My way of life   25
Is falne into the sear, the yellow leaf;
And that which should accompany old age,
As honor, love, obedience, troops of friends,
I must not look to have; but, in their steed,
Curses, not loud but deep, mouth-honor, breath,   30
Which the poor heart would fain deny, and dare not.
Seyton!

Enter Seyton.

  Seyton. What's your gracious pleasure?

  Macbeth.   What news more?

  Seyton. All is confirm'd, my lord, which was reported.   35

  Macbeth. I'll fight till from my bones my flesh be hack'd.

Give me my armor.

  Seyton.   'Tis not needed yet.

  Macbeth. I'll put it on.
Send out moe horses, skirr the country round;   40
Hang those that talk of fear. Give me mine armor.
How does your patient, doctor?

  Doctor.   Not so sick, my lord,
As she is troubled with thick-coming fancies
That keep her from her rest.   45

  Macbeth.   Cure her of that!
Canst thou not minister to a mind diseas'd.
Pluck from the memory a rooted sorrow,
Raze out the written troubles of the brain,
And with some sweet oblivious antidote   50
Cleanse the stuff'd bosom of that perilous stuff
Which weighs upon the heart?

  Doctor.   Therein the patient
Must minister to himself.

  Macbeth. Throw physic to the dogs; I'll none of it.   55
Come, put mine armor on. Give me my staff.
Seyton, send out.—Doctor, the thanes fly from me.—
Come, sir, dispatch.—If thou couldst, doctor, cast
The water of my land, find her disease,
And purge it to a sound and pristine health,   60
I would applaud thee to the very echo,
That should applaud again.—Pull't off, I say.—
What rhubarb, cyme, or what purgative drug
Would scour these English hence? Hear'st thou of them?

  Doctor. Ay, my good lord. Your royal preparation   65
Makes us hear something.

  Macbeth.   Bring it after me.
I will not be afraid of death and bane
Till Birnam forest come to Dunsinane.

  Doctor. [Aside.] Were I from Dunsinane away and clear.   70
Profit again should hardly draw me here.   *Exeunt.*

❧ Scene Fourth ❧

Drum and colors. Enter Malcolm, Siward, Macduff, Siward's Son, Menteth, Cathness, Angus, [Lennox, Ross,] and Soldiers marching.

  Malcolm. Cousins, I hope the days are near at hand
That chambers will be safe.

  Menteth.   We doubt it nothing.

  Siward. What wood is this before us?

  Menteth.   The wood of Birnam.   5

  Malcolm. Let every soldier hew him down a bough
And bear't before him: thereby shall we shadow
The numbers of our host, and make discovery
Err in report of us.

  Soldier.   It shall be done.   10

  Siward. We learn no other but the confident tyrant
Keeps still in Dunsinane, and will endure
Our setting down before't.

  Malcolm.   'Tis his main hope;

---

32 med'cine: *physician* **weal:** *state*   **36 dew:** *literally 'water,' figuratively 'make grow'* **sovereign flower:** *Cf. n.*   **3 taint:** *become tainted*   **5 mortal consequences:** *future events in human life*   **9 sway:** *control myself*   **11 cream-fac'd:** *the servant's face is white with fear* **loon:** *rascal, lout*   **16 over-red:** *cover with red*   **17 patch:** *clown, fool*   **23 push:** *crisis, attack*   **24 cheer;** *Cf. n.* **disseat:** *unseat; F. dis-eate*   **26 falne:** *fallen*   **29 steed:** *stead*

40 moe: *more* **skirr:** *scour*   **45 her:** *F omits*   **49 Raze out:** *erase* **written:** *i.e. permanent*   **50 oblivious:** *causing forgetfulness*   **58, 59 cast/The water:** *analyze the urine*   **63 cyme:** *a cathartic; Cf. n.*   **2 chambers will be safe:** *i.e. we can sleep in security*   **7 shadow:** *partially conceal*   **8 discovery:** *reconnaissance*   **13 setting down before:** *laying siege to*

For where there is advantage to be given,   *15*
Both more and less have given him the revolt,
And none serve with him but constrained things
Whose hearts are absent too.
   Macduff.   Let our just censures
Attend the true event, and put we on   *20*
Industrious soldiership.
   Siward.   The time approaches
That will with due decision make us know
What we shall say we have and what we owe.
Thoughts speculative their unsure hopes relate,   *25*
But certain issue strokes must arbitrate,
Towards which advance the war.   *Exeunt marching.*

❧ Scene Fifth ❧

Enter Macbeth, Seyton, and Soldiers, with drums and colors.

Macbeth. Hang out our banners on the outward walls.
The cry is still, 'They come.' Our castle's strength
Will laugh a siege to scorn. Here let them lie
Till famine and the ague eat them up.
Were they not forc'd with those that should be ours,   *5*
We might have met them dareful, beard to beard,
And beat them backward home.
                    A cry within of women.
          What is that noise?
Seyton. It is the cry of women, my good lord.   *[Exit.]*
   Macbeth. I have almost forgot the taste of fears.   *10*
The time has been, my senses would have cool'd
To hear a night-shriek, and my fell of hair
Would at a dismal treatise rouse and stir
As life were in't. I have supp'd full with horrors;
Direness, familiar to my slaughterous thoughts,
Cannot once start me.   *15*

       [Enter Seyton.]

          Wherefore was that cry?
Seyton. The queen, my lord, is dead.
   Macbeth. She should have died hereafter;
There would have been a time for such a word.
Tomorrow, and tomorrow, and tomorrow,   *20*
Creeps in this petty pace from day to day,
To the last syllable of recorded time;
And all our yesterdays have lighted fools
The way to dusty death. Out, out, brief candle!
Life's but a walking shadow, a poor player   *25*
That struts and frets his hour upon the stage,
And then is heard no more. It is a tale
Told by an idiot, full of sound and fury,
Signifying nothing.

       Enter a Messenger.

Thou com'st to use thy tongue; thy story quickly.   *30*

Messenger. Gracious my lord,
I should report that which I say I saw,
But know not how to do't.
   Macbeth.   Well, say, sir.   *35*
   Messenger. As I did stand my watch upon the hill,
I look'd toward Birnam, and anon, methought,
The wood began to move.
   Macbeth.   Liar and slave!
   Messenger. Let me endure your wrath if't be not so: *40*
Within this three mile may you see it coming;
I say, a moving grove.
   Macbeth.   If thou speak'st false,
Upon the next tree shall thou hang alive
Till famine cling thee. If thy speech be sooth,   *45*
I care not if thou dost for me as much.
I pull in resolution and begin.
To doubt th' equivocation of the fiend
That lies like truth. 'Fear not, till Birnam wood
Do come to Dunsinane,' and now a wood   *50*
Comes toward Dunsinane. Arm, arm, and out!
If this which he avouches does appear,
There is nor flying hence, nor tarrying here.
I gin to be aweary of the sun,
And wish th' estate o' th' world were now undone.   *55*
Ring the alarum bell! Blow, wind! come, wrack!
At least we'll die with harness on our back.   *Exeunt.*

❧ Scene Sixth ❧

Drum and colors. Enter Malcolm, Siward, Macduff, and their Army, with boughs.

Malcolm. Now near enough; your leavy screens throw down,
And show like those you are. You, worthy uncle,
Shall with my cousin, your right-noble son,
Lead our first battle. Worthy Macduff and we
Shall take upon's what else remains to do,   *5*
According to our order.
   Siward.   Fare you well.
Do we but find the tyrant's power tonight,
Let us be beaten, if we cannot fight.
   Macduff. Make all our trumpets speak; give them all   *10*
breath.
Those clamorous harbingers of blood and death.
          Exeunt. Alarums continued.

❧ Scene Seventh ❧

Enter Macbeth.

Macbeth. They have tied me to a stake; I cannot fly,
But bearlike I must fight the course. What's he
That was not born of woman? such a one
Am I to fear, or none.

       Enter Young Siward.

Young Siward. What is thy name?   *5*

---

15 **where ... given:** *i.e. where opportunity is offered*   16 **more and less:** *high and low*   19, 20 **Let ... event:** *Let's wait until after the battle to make a true judgment*   19 **censures:** *judgments*   20 **event:** *outcome*   24 **owe:** *own* (in fact, as opposed to what we 'say we have')   25, 26 **Thoughts ... arbitrate;** *Cf. n.*   5 **forc'd:** *reinforced*   12 **fell of hair:** *skin with hair growing on it*   13 **treatise:** *story*   15 **start:** *startle*   18 **should:** *would*   19 **word:** *i.e. the announcement of her death*   25, 26 **Life's ... stage:** *see II.4.7; Cf. n.*

44 **shall:** *shalt*   45 **cling:** *wither*   **sooth:** *truth*   47 **pull in:** *rein in*   **resolution:** *assurance, confidence*   55 **estate o' th' world:** *orderly universe*   56 **wrack:** *ruin*   1 **leavy:** *leafy*   4 **battle:** *part of the army*   2 **bearlike ... course;** *Cf. n.*

Macbeth.   Thou'lt be afraid to hear it.
Young Siward. No; though thou call'st thyself a hotter name
Than any is in hell.
Macbeth.   My name's Macbeth.
Young Siward. The divel himself could not pronounce   *10*
a title
More hateful to mine ear.
Macbeth.   No, nor more fearful.
Young Siward. Thou liest, abhorred tyrant; with my sword
I'll prove the lie thou speak'st.   *15*

            Fight, and Young Siward slain.

Macbeth.   Thou wast born of woman;
But swords I smile at, weapons laugh to scorn,
Brandish'd by man that's of a woman born.   *Exit.*

         Alarums. Enter Macduff.

Macduff. That way the noise is. Tyrant, show thy face!   *20*
If thou be'st slain and with no stroke of mine,
My wife and children's ghosts will haunt me still.
I cannot strike at wretched kerns, whose arms
Are hir'd to bear their staves; either thou, Macbeth,
Or else my sword with an unbatter'd edge   *25*
I sheathe again undeeded. There thou shouldst be.
B this great clatter, one of greatest note
Seems bruited. Let me find him, fortune!
And more I beg not.   *Exit. Alarums.*

         Enter Malcolm and Siward.

Siward. This way, my lord; the castle's gently rend'red;   *30*
The tyrant's people on both sides do fight;
The noble thanes do bravely in the war;
The day almost itself professes yours,
And little is to do.
Malcolm.   We have met with foes   *35*
That strike beside us.
Siward.   Enter, sir, the castle.

              Exeunt. Alarum.

          Enter Macbeth.

Macbeth. Why should I play the Roman fool, and die
On mine own sword? whiles I see lives, the gashes
Do better upon them.   *40*

          Enter Macduff.

Macduff.   Turn, hell-hound, turn!
Macbeth. Of all men else I have avoided thee.
But get thee back, my soul is too much charg'd
With blood of thine already.
Macduff.   I have no words;   *45*
My voice is in my sword, thou bloodier villain
Than terms can give thee out!   *Fight. Alarum.*
Macbeth.   Thou losest labor.
As easy mayst thou the intrenchant air
With thy keen sword impress, as make me bleed.   *50*
Let fall thy blade on vulnerable crests;
I bear a charmed life, which must not yield

To one of woman born.
Macduff.   Despair thy charm;
And let the angel whom thou still hast serv'd   *55*
Tell thee, Macduff was from his mother's womb
Untimely ripp'd.
Macbeth. Accursed be that tongue that tells me so,
For it hath cow'd my better part of man!
And be these juggling fiends no more believ'd,   *60*
That palter with us in a double sense;
That keep the word of promise to our ear,
And break it to our hope. I'll not fight with thee.
Macduff. Then yield thee, coward,
And live to be the show and gaze o' th' time.   *65*
We'll have thee, as our rarer monsters are,
Painted upon a pole, and underwrit,
'Here may you see the tyrant.'
Macbeth.   I will not yield,
To kiss the ground before young Malcolm's feet,   *70*
And to be baited with the rabble's curse.
Though Birnam wood be come to Dunsinane,
And thou oppos'd, being of no woman born,
Yet I will try the last. Before my body
I throw my warlike shield. Lay on, Macduff,   *75*
And damn'd be him that first cries, 'Hold, enough!'

             Exeunt fighting. Alarums.

       Enter fighting, and Macbeth slain.
   Retreat and flourish. Enter, with drum and colors, Malcolm,
        Siward, Ross, Thanes, and Soldiers.

Malcolm. I would the friends we miss were safe arriv'd.
Siward. Some must go off; and yet, by these I see,
So great a day as this is cheaply bought.
Malcolm. Macduff is missing, and your noble son.   *80*
Ross. Your son, my lord, has paid a soldier's debt.
He only liv'd but till he was a man,
The which no sooner had his prowess confirm'd
In the unshrinking station where he fought,
But like a man he died.   *85*
Siward.   Then he is dead?
Ross. Ay, and brought off the field. Your cause of sorrow
Must not be measur'd by his worth, for then
It hath no end.
Siward.   Had he his hurts before?   *90*
Ross. Ay, on the front.
Siward.   Why then, God's soldier be he!
Had I as many sons as I have hairs,
I would not wish them to a fairer death;
And so, his knell is knoll'd.   *95*
Malcolm.   He's worth more sorrow,
And that I'll spend for him.
Siward.   He's worth no more;
They say he parted well, and paid his score,
And so, God be with him! Here comes newer comfort.   *100*

       Enter Macduff, with Macbeth's head.

Macduff. Hail, king! for so thou art. Behold, where stands

SD **Exit;** *Cf. n.*   **23 kerns:** *see I.2.15.*   **24 staves:** *spears*   **28 bruited:** *noised, re-*
ported   **30 rend'red:** *surrendered*   **32 bravely:** *worthily, excellently*   **36 strike beside**
us *deliberately miss us*   SD **Enter Macbeth;** *Cf. n.*   **38 Roman fool:** *i.e. Brutus, An-*
tony, etc.   **39 lives:** *i.e. living enemies*   **49 intrenchant:** *incapable of being cut*

55 still: *always*   **59 better part of man:** *i.e. valor*   **61 palter:** *equivocate*   **67 Painted**
upon a pole: *i.e. with a painted likeness suspended on a pole*   **71 baited:** *i.e. like a bear;*
see V.7.2.; Cf. n.   SD **Retreat:** *trumpet signal to cease pursuit*   **78 go off:** *stage metaphor*
for 'die'   **84 unshrinking station:** *i.e. the station where he did not shrink*   **93 hairs:**
pronounced like 'heirs'   **99 score:** *account*

Th' usurper's cursed head; the time is free.
I see thee compass'd with thy kindgom's pearl,
That speak my salutation in their minds;
Whose voices I desire aloud with mine;   *105*
Hail, King of Scotland!
  All.   Hail, King of Scotland!
            Flourish.

  Malcolm. We shall not spend a large expense of time
Before we reckon with your several loves,
And make us even with you. My thanes and kinsmen,   *110*
Henceforth be earls, the first that ever Scotland
In such an honor nam'd. What's more to do,
Which would be planted newly with the time—
As calling home our exil'd friends abroad

That fled the snares of watchful tyranny,   *115*
Producing forth the cruel ministers
Of this dead butcher and his fiendlike queen,
Who, as 'tis thought, by self and violent hands
Took off her life—this, and what needful else
That calls upon us, by the grace of Grace   *120*
We will perform in measure, time, and place.
So, thanks to all at once and to each one,
Whom we invite to see us crown'd at Scone.
         Flourish. Exeunt omnes.

꘡ FINIS ꘡

---

103 pearl: *i.e. the nobles* **109 several loves:** *devotion of each of you*   **118 self and violent:** *her own violent* **121 in measure:** *in proportion, with proper decorum*

NOTES

I.i.SD. *Thunder and lightning.* The scenes with the witches were probably staged in a spectacular fashion. The witches may have been revealed on the inner stage by drawing back a curtain; each of their appearances is accompanied by stage thunder, which was produced by beating drums or by rolling a heavy ball of iron or stone down an uneven set of steps constructed in the superstructure over the stage. The lightning was made by blowing rosin through a candle flame. A stage mist, made by burning rosin, may have risen through the trap door to make the witches disappear in the 'fog and filthy air' at the end of this scene, as also at I.3.83.

I.i.9–13. *Graymalkin . . . air.* The witches answer the calls of their 'familiars' or attendant spirits, which have assumed the forms of animals. *Graymalkin* is a pet name for a grey cat; *Paddock* means 'toad.' The familiar of the Third Witch, unnamed here, is called *Harpier* in IV.1.3, possibly a corruption of 'harpy.' F ascribes the lines "Paddock calls . . . filthy air" to *All;* the arrangement adopted here is clearly more logical.

I.ii.4. *sergeant.* A title which a commissioned officer might have in the army of Shakespeare's time. Modern editors often unnecessarily change *Captain* to *Sergeant* in the stage directions and speech headings.

I.ii.23. *Which.* Probably refers to Macdonwald, who never took leave of Macbeth until Macbeth killed him. It may refer to Macbeth; it is possible that the omission of some lines has obscured the sense. A touch of grim humor is added by reference to polite forms of leave-taking: 'shook hands,' 'bade farewell.'

I.ii.27, 28. *As whence . . . thunders break.* Storms come out of the east, whence the sun rises.

I.ii.44. *memorize another Golgotha.* Make the field memorable as another 'place of the skull,' the literal meaning of Golgotha, where Christ was crucified.

I.ii.50. *Thane.* A title of nobility in Scotland, corresponding to the English earl.

I.ii.56, 57. *flout . . . cold.* Insult the Scottish sky and chill the people with fear.

I.ii.63. *rebellious.* Sweno, though not a rebel, was assisting rebellion.

I.ii.71. *general.* Here and in many other words such as *prosperous, treasonous, interim,* etc. a lightly accented syllable following a heavily accented syllable may be omitted in pronunciation. Note also that phrases such as 'to the' and 'to his' may be pronounced 'to th'' and 'to's.'

I.ii.72, 73. *deceive . . . interest.* Betray the interests closest to our heart. Here as elsewhere the king uses the royal plural.

I.iii.16. *ports they blow.* The meaning seems to be that she will delay the *Tiger's* arrival in port.

I.iii.21. *penthouse lid.* The eyelid is compared to a penthouse, that is, a lean-to.

I.iii.33. *weyard.* One form of 'weird,' derived from the Old English *wyrd,* 'fate.' F uses the forms *weyard* and *weyward* (possibly by association with 'wayward'), but never 'weird,' which has become familiar because of Theobald's 18th-century emendation. The form *weyard* preserves the original meter. The exact nature of the 'weyard sisters' is left undefined: they are not merely old hags practicing sorcery, nor are they truly fates, as they appear to be in Holinshed's *Chronicle,* one of the chief sources of the play (see Sources of the Play).

I.iii.36. *thrice to thine . . . to make up nine.* The witches probably make obeisances to their familiars.

I.iii.47. *beards.* A beard on a woman was often thought to indicate that she was a witch.

I.iii.96, 97. *His wonders . . . Silenc'd with that.* Since the king is unable to decide whether astonishment or admiration better answers Macbeth's accomplishment, or better expresses his own feeling, he is reduced to silence.

I.iii.152–155. *Shakes . . . rapt.* Here and in a number of other places (notably I.3.152–155, I.4.1–9, I.5.19, 20, I.7.65, 66, II.1.4–11, 13–15, II.2.3–10, 37, 38, II.3.53–61, III.1.47–53, 83–94, III.4.19–23) most modern editors rearrange the lines in order to approximate more closely regular iambic pentameter. See Text and Date.

I.iii.152. *single state of man.* The nature of man is compared to a nation (as in *Julius Caesar,* II.1.65–68), which internal disturbances may reduce to impotence.

I.iii.162, 163. *Come . . . day.* That is, even the roughest day must come to an end. This fatalistic thought is relevant to Macbeth's previous aside.

I.iv.22, 23. *That . . . mine.* That I might have been able to make my thanks and reward proportionate to your desert.

I.iv.23. *I have.* Such contractions as 'I've' were common in Elizabethan speech, but are not always indicated in the spelling. Other examples will be found in I.7.29–65, and elsewhere.

I.iv.46. *Prince of Cumberland.* A Scottish title corresponding to Prince of Wales in England.

I.iv.51. *The rest . . . for you.* Any relaxation of the effort to serve you is in reality a greater effort.

I.v.19–24. *Thou'dst have . . . undone.* That is, Macbeth would have the crown, which demands that he murder in order to have it; and murder is what he rather fears to do than wishes undone.

I.v.41. *raven.* The raven's croaking was traditionally associated with gloom and misfortune.

I.v.49, 50. *keep . . . it.* Peaceably intervene between my purpose and its accomplishment.

I.v.70. *To beguile the time. The time* means here 'the world' or 'the present age'; hence, 'to deceive the world.'

I.vi.SD. *torches.* Torches were often used to indicate that the scene took place at night, though the stage of the Elizabethan public theater, lighted by daylight, was necessarily bright. In this scene Duncan approaches the castle gate in the evening. It is light enough for him to see the building and the birds, but the torches remind us that night, called upon by Lady Macbeth in the preceding scene, is falling.

I.vi.5. *martlet.* In Shakespeare's day *martlet* often meant the house martin, which was supposed to build its nest only in 'fair houses.'

I.vi.13–16. *The love . . . trouble.* Duncan means that just as we gratefully accept the trouble to which our friends put us as a sign of their love, so Lady Macbeth should thank him for the troublesome visit he is paying her.

I.vi.26. *purveyor.* An officer whose duty was to ride ahead and make necessary arrangements.

I.vii.4. *his surcease.* Probably Duncan's death; possibly the arresting of the consequence.

I.vii.5–7. *here . . . come.* That is, we'd enjoy the profits of crime in this present life and take our chances on the next life.

I.vii.8. *have judgment.* That is, we may be punished here by those who follow our example.

I.vii.22–3. *heavens . . . air.* Psalm 18:10 in the Great Bible (1539) reads: 'He rode upon the Cherubins and dyd flye: he came flyenge with the wynges of the wynde.'

I.vii.27–8. *Vaulting ambition . . . on th' other.* Ambition, like an overeager horseman, vaults over the saddle and falls on the other side of the horse. The word 'side,' which would fill out the meter of the line, may have dropped out.

I.vii.49. *cat i' th' adage.* 'The cat would eat fish and would not wet her feet.'

I.vii.52. *do Lady.* Macbeth's reply makes Macbeth's implication clear: to do more than becomes a man is to behave like a beast. The sense of the context thus justifies the emendation.

I.vii.68. *sticking-place.* The metaphor is that of a crossbow, the cord of which must be screwed up to the notch where it sticks.

I.vii.73–75. *memory . . . only.* In Elizabethan physiology memory was thought of as a sort of guard, prepared to warn the brain of attack. It was supposed to be lodged at the base of the skull, reason occupying the upper part. If memory is overcome by fumes of wine rising from the stomach, no warning is given, and the fumes rise to fill the receptacle of reason.

II.i.20–22. *Being . . . wrought.* Our desire to entertain the king was hampered by unpreparedness; otherwise we should have done more.

II.i.62. *Whose howl's his watch.* The wolf's howl tells Murder that it is time to act.

II.i.63. *Tarquin's.* See Shakespeare's *The Rape of Lucrece.*

II.ii.5. *bellman.* A bellman was customarily sent to condemned prisoners the night before their execution.

II.ii.SD. *Enter Macbeth.* F gives Macbeth's entrance before his speech, 'Who's there?' but this is clearly given offstage.

II.iii.4. *farmer.* He had hoarded grain to sell at high prices in a famine; the prospect of a plentiful crop confronted him with ruin.

II.iii.4, 5. *Come in, time-server.* It is logical to expect a phrase here to parallel the later 'come in, equivocator' and 'Come in, tailor.' F's *Come in time* is incomprehensible. J. Dover Wilson, who suggests the emendation adopted here, in his edition of *Macbeth* (Cambridge, Cambridge University Press, 1951, pp. 125–6) says, 'My guess is "come in, time-server," an epithet appropriate to all farmers, who must serve Time in its changes of season and caprices of weather, and to this farmer in its special sense of one who adapts his conduct to the time with an eye to the main chance . . .'

II.iii.7. *equivocator.* Presumably a reference to Henry Garnet, a Jesuit tried and condemned in 1600 for complicity in the Gunpowder Plot. After perjuring himself at the trial, he defended his conduct on the grounds that equivocation was justifiable in certain circumstances.

II.iii.11, 12. *stealing . . . hose.* Trousers (hose) made in the latest French style were so tight-fitting that the tailor got caught in trying to steal cloth as he had done in making the larger ones formerly in fashion. There may be a pun on 'staling' (since *stealing* then had the same pronunciation), 'urinating.'

II.iii.13. *goose.* Possibly continues the *double entendre* on *stealing,* since *goose* also meant a swelling caused by venereal disease.

II.iii.SD. *Enter Macbeth.* The entrance of a character is frequently indicated a few lines before his first speech, to give him time to walk across the large platform stage, and to give characters onstage the chance to see him and comment on his arrival.

II.iii.53–61. *The night . . . shake.* In *Macbeth,* as in many other plays, Shakespeare makes use of the commonly held belief that dire portents and disorders in nature accompany disruptions of the social order, such as the assassination of Duncan.

II.iii.SD. *Enter Macbeth and Lennox.* F indicates an entrance for Ross here, but it is apparent later (II.4.28 ff) that he has not visited Duncan's chamber.

II.iii.105. *vault.* Refers both to a wine cellar and to the earth, with the sky as a roof.

II.iii.128. *Unmannerly . . . gore.* The blood makes *unmannerly* breeches for the daggers, whose proper breeches would be sheathes.

II.iii.137, 138. *Where . . . seize us.* That is, where we may be surprised by fate, hidden in the smallest and least suspected place.

II.iii.139–141. *Our tears . . . motion.* There has not been time yet to weep for our father's death nor to express our sorrow in action.

II.iii.143. *naked frailties.* All except Lennox and Macduff are in dressing gowns.

II.iv.7. *stage.* The frequent comparison of the world to a stage (see V.5.25, 26) had a special appropriateness in the Elizabethan public theater, where the canopy over the stage was called 'the heavens,' while the 'cellarage' beneath it often represented hell.

II.iv.14. *tow'ring . . . place.* Technical terms in falconry: *towering* means circling upward; *place* is the highest point in the falcon's flight.

III.i.28. *Go . . . better.* Unless my horse goes fast enough to make it unnecessary.

III.i.45–53. *To make . . . safely thus.* Neither the lineation nor the punctuation of F makes good sense here. This arrangement of lines was suggested by Kenneth Muir in his edition of *Macbeth* (London, Methuen, 1951).

III.i.61, 62. *My genius . . . Caesar.* See *Antony and Cleopatra,* II.3.20ff.

III.i.147. *perfect spy.* Macbeth apparently intends to send someone with these final pieces of information; it is logical to assume that the Third Murtherer of Scene 3 is that person.

III.ii.15. *scorch'd.* Theobald's 18th-century emendation, *scotch'd,* has become familiar, but is unwarranted; it is merely another spelling of the same word.

III.ii.43. *copy.* May also mean lease, since 'copyhold' was a form of tenure.

III.ii.47. *shard-borne.* It is difficult to tell whether this means 'dung-bred' or 'borne of sealy wings.' The latter seems more probable in this context, which calls attention to the beetle's flight, rather than to its origin.

III.ii.55. *bond.* The prophecy that Banquo's descendants should be kings.

III.iv.4–6. *Ourself . . . state.* Thrones, covered by a canopy, are set up on a dais for the king and queen, probably on the inner stage. On the platform stage is the table for the guests. Macbeth means to sit there with them, while Lady Macbeth will stay on her canopied throne ('keep her state').

III.iv.13. *Approaching the door.* Just as he is about to sit down, Macbeth sees the murderer at the door upstage, some distance from the table, and goes over to confer with him.

III.iv.38–40. *The feast . . . welcome.* That is, a feast where the usual courtesies of the host are omitted seems like a meal sold at an inn.

III.iv.SD. *Enter . . . Banquo.* The ghost may enter at another door than that where Macbeth has been talking, or rise through a trap door beside the table. Macbeth walks back toward the table, but does not at once see the ghost. He first notes that his place is occupied (l. 56), then, recognizing Banquo, supposes that someone has perpetrated a grim practical joke. Simon Forman, who saw *Macbeth* at the Globe in 1611, seems to have been particularly impressed by this scene, which he describes in detail (see Text and Date). His statement that the ghost entered when Macbeth stood up to toast Banquo has puzzled some editors, but the explanation is simple. Forman apparently remembered the second appearance of the ghost (l. 106), when Macbeth has finally gone to his place at the table and proposed a toast. As he turns to sit down (l. 112), he sees the ghost again. Forman's account shows clearly that, although the ghost is invisible to all except Macbeth on the stage, it is intended to be seen by the audience.

III.iv.43. *remembrancer.* The word was used as a title for certain officers of the Exchequer, such as The King's Remembrancer.

III.iv.81. *stool.* The stool was the normal seat for rich and poor in Elizabethan England. Chairs, which were very rare, were reserved for the highest ranking persons present.

III.iv.85–87. *If charnel houses . . . kites.* That is, it may be safer to let kites (birds of prey) eat dead bodies to prevent them from returning to haunt us.

III.iv.122. *Hyrcan.* Hyrcania, south of the Caspian Sea, is often mentioned in classical literature as the habitat of tigers.

III.iv.136, 137. *You . . . owe.* You make me feel unfamiliar with my own disposition.

III.iv.145. *Stand . . . going.* Don't stand on ceremony, the correct order of precedence, etc.

III.iv.153. *understood relations.* Relations as understood by a soothsayer.

III. Scene 5. This scene was probably added by Thomas Middleton or some other contemporary of Shakespeare. The songs indicated in the stage directions here and in IV.1 are found in full in Middleton's *The Witch.* The exact relationship of the two plays has never been determined. See IV. 1.39–43 Cf. n.

III.v.SD. *Sing within.* The second part of this stage direction, *Sing within,* 'Come away, come away,' etc., is printed in F at the end after being interrupted by two spoken lines. Such an arrangement is easy to imagine, since the song, as we have it in *The Witch* (III.3), is in dialogue form, beginning:

> Come away: Come away:
> Heccat: Heccat, Come away } in ye aire.

(See Malone Society Reprint, Oxford, Oxford University Press, 1950, p. 57.) Heccat answers, 'I come, I come,' but she might very well give this answer after ll. 34–5, and then proceed with the rest of the song. Davenant arranged the stage business in this way in his adaptation, which was published in 1674 with the full text of the song.

III.v.34, 35. *Hark . . . for me.* Heccat's words suggest that the attendant spirit appears in a car suspended on ropes and possibly wrapped in some light cloth (the 'foggy cloud'). At the end of the song Heccat gets into the car, and it is drawn up into 'the heavens.'

III. Scene 6. In this scene Lennox and the other Lord describe the results of the action against Macduff planned by Macbeth in III.4. Macduff has already had time to get to England, though the following scene, IV.1, supposedly occurs the day after III.4. There is no logical explanation for this discrepancy.

III.vi.31. *pray . . . upon his aid.* Upon seems to have the force here of 'relying on.' Shakespeare may have had in mind the expression, 'pray in aid,' meaning 'claim assistance' (to which one has some right).

III.vi.36. *Free . . . knives.* That is, free our feasts and banquets from bloody knives.

III.vi.45. *clogs.* The messenger is embarrassed by the answer Macduff makes him return; he is fearful of Macbeth's reaction to it.

IV.i.2. *hedge-pig.* In I.1 the Second Witch's familiar is a toad.

IV.i.23. *mummy.* Embalmed human flesh and powders or liquids made from it, all known as *mummy,* were used in medicine and were also thought to have great magical power.

IV.i.23. *maw and gulf.* Both words mean 'stomach'; *gulf,* by suggesting a yawning chasm, emphasizes the voracious appetite of the shark.

IV.i.SD. *Enter Heccat . . . Witches.* The appearance of Heccat and three more witches was probably a non-Shakespearean addition to the play (see III.5 Cf. n.). No exit is indicated for Heccat, but since she has no lines after l. 43, she probably leaves at this point. The other witches may remain to join in the dance (doubtless another addition) after l. 143.

IV.i.39–43. *O, well done . . . you put in.* These lines, like many in III.5, are iambic tetrameter, whereas the witches elsewhere speak in trochaic tetrameter. This discrepancy is one reason for doubting that they originally belonged in the play. The reference to 'elves and fairies' also strikes a false note.

IV.i.SD. *First Apparition.* Each of the three apparitions rises and then descends through a trap door, probably on the inner stage. The significance of the *Armed Head* is disputable. Some have thought it prefigured the head of Macbeth, cut off by Macduff at the end of the play. It is more likely that it represents Macduff, the adversary of whom Macbeth is here told to beware. As George Lyman Kittredge has pointed out in his edition of *Macbeth* (Boston, Ginn and Co., 1939, p. 189), each of the other apparitions represents a person dangerous to Macbeth; the first apparition should set the pattern. Kittredge also notes that 'the First Apparition should not represent something that comes to pass later than the events foretold by the Second and Third.'

IV.i.SD. *Second Apparition.* Represents Macduff: see V.7.44–5, 56, 57.

IV.i.SD. *Third Apparition.* The child is presumably Malcolm, holding a tree to represent the stratagem by which his army approaches Dunsinane: see V.4.4–9.

IV.i.SD. *Descend.* An imperative verb is often used in Elizabethan stage directions.

IV.i.106. *head.* Macbeth presumably refers again to Macduff, whose 'armed head' is the one potential threat to his security. F's *Rebellious dead* has been interpreted by some as evidence that Macbeth is thinking of Banquo, whom he mentions at l. 111; but *Rebellious dead* would seem to be plural, and, in any case, Banquo cannot well be called 'rebellious.' It is more likely that *head* was mistakenly printed as *dead*.

IV.i.107. *Birnam.* The modern form of this name, suggested by F *Byrnam* at its first mention (l. 101), has been kept throughout, though F spells it more often with a final *n* (as here) or *ne*. Deviations from F's spelling of the name are not elsewhere noted.

IV.i.116. *sinks that cauldron.* The cauldron is lowered by a machine through one of the trap doors.

IV.i.SD. *A show of eight Kings.* The stage direction as printed in F, *A shew of eight Kings, and Banquo last, with a glasse in his hand,* contradicts l. 129, where it is clear that the last king carries the glass. Various reconstructions of the stage business have been made, with corresponding emendations of the text. The emendation adopted here suits the following hypotheses: It seems likely that the kings enter at one side of the stage and move across to the other in a dignified and spectacular procession. They probably remain in sight until l. 134, where Banquo 'points at them,' after which they may *vanish* with him in a stage mist, as the witches do. Since they are all Banquo's descendants, he may precede them onto the stage, standing aside where Macbeth can note their resemblance to him (l. 122).

However this *show* was staged, it is certain that it had a special topical importance as a compliment to King James, before whom the play was probably first given (see Henry N. Paul, *The Royal Play of Macbeth,* New York, Macmillan, 1950, pp. 162–82, 317–31). The Stuarts claimed their descent from Banquo, and James was the ninth Stuart sovereign. His mother, Mary, Queen of Scots, whom Queen Elizabeth forced to abdicate, was the eighth. Faced with the delicate problem of presenting this controversial member of the family, Shakespeare may, as Paul suggests (p. 179) have created a deliberate ambiguity about the eighth 'king,' who may have appeared on the stage heavily shrouded and carrying the glass before his face. In this way various members of the audience would be free to assume that the mysterious figure represented the ill-fated Mary (the eighth 'king' in the generic sense of the word) or her fortunate son (the eighth male sovereign), who could not, however, be plainly depicted without *lèse majesté.* Shakespeare may have seen the drawing of the Stuart genealogical tree published during Mary's lifetime in John Leslie's *De Origine, Moribus, et Rebus Gestis Scotorum* (Rome, 1578), showing the series of 'eight kings' descended from Banquo. On this tree, Mary is the eighth.

IV.i.129. *glass.* Presumably a magic glass in which the future can be seen.

IV.i.131. *twofold . . . scepters.* The ball is part of the royal regalia; *twofold* probably refers to England and Scotland, united under James; the *treble scepters* probably indicate that James is king of England, Scotland, and Ireland.

IV.i.136–143. *Ay, sir . . . his welcome pay.* The meter and the spirit of these lines again seem out of keeping. They were probably added with the Heccat material.

IV.i.162, 163. *The flighty . . . it.* Unless intentions are translated into deeds, they remain forever out of reach.

IV.ii.91. *shag-hair'd.* Refers to the long, unkempt hair of the Elizabethan ruffian.

IV.iii.17. *discern.* Macduff may learn something about Macbeth through Malcolm's plight, and he may even learn the *wisdom* of betraying Malcolm to Macbeth. The unexpected suggestion of the latter part of the sentence makes it at first obscure. Most editors change *discern* to *deserve,* but by this emendation the second half of the sentence is cast adrift: Macduff doesn't *deserve* wisdom.

IV.iii.109–111. *Pour . . . earth. Concord, peace,* and *unity* have not only their general significance here but also a special topical reference, since these were the avowed goals of James I's foreign and domestic policy.

IV.iii.150, 151. *the chance . . . quarrel.* That is, may the chance of good fortune equal the justness of our cause.

IV.iii.157. *stay his cure.* Edward the Confessor was thought to be able to heal 'the king's evil' (scrofula) by his touch. The passage is presumably an indirect compliment to James I, who claimed the same healing power.

IV.iii.190. *ecstasy.* Probably alludes to the sham fits of people pretending to be 'possessed.' Several such cases were known in Shakespeare's day.

IV.iii.255. *dispute it.* Sometimes interpreted as 'contend with your sorrow,' but notice that Malcolm has just urged Macduff to express his sorrow (l. 242).

V.i.21. *are.* The plural, though not strictly grammatical, is probably due to the thought of the two eyes, both unseeing.

V.ii.36. *sovereign flower.* Suggests both 'flower of true sovereignty' (as opposed to usurping weeds) and 'healing, restorative flower' (as opposed to noxious weeds).

V.iii.24. *cheer.* In Shakespeare's day, as still in many dialects, 'chair' had the same pronunciation. There is therefore a pun on 'chair' which relates *cheer* to *disseat.*

V.iii.63. *cyme.* Probably refers to the 'cymes' or tops of the colewort, often taken as a cathartic. May be a misprint for 'cinne,' another spelling of 'senna,' also a cathartic.

V.iv.25, 26. *Thoughts . . . arbitrate.* That is, optimistic speculation is mere wishful thinking; battle will decide the issues.

V.vii.2. *bearlike . . . course.* The comparison is to the popular Elizabethan sport of bear-baiting, in which a bear, tied to a post, was attacked by dogs. A *course* was one round or bout.

V.vii.SD. *Exit.* Here, or possibly after l. 29, the body of Young Siward must be removed, for at l. 86 we learn that he has been 'brought off the field.' Whether or not the body is still onstage when Macduff enters, it is clear that he does not see it, nor does the elder Siward when he enters (l. 30). The entire scene is an excellent example of the fluidity of Elizabethan staging. Different localities are suggested in rapid succession by the use of different parts of the stage. Macduff apparently enters at some distance from the place where Macbeth has killed Young Siward; when Malcolm and the elder Siward enter, they probably head for the inner stage, which may represent the gates of the castle; when Macbeth re-enters, the action is presumably away from the inner stage again, suggesting another part of the field of battle; the entrance of l. 77 may be in the inner stage to indicate that it is inside the castle. Because of the size and the facilities of the stage this panoramic action can be continuous and the pace rapid.

V.vii.SD. *Enter Macbeth.* Many editors begin a new scene here, and some begin another new scene after line 76. The explanation in the preceding note should make it clear why such scene division was unnecessary in writing for the Elizabethan stage.

The Tragedy of Antony and Cleopatra

Edited by
PETER G. PHIALAS

Dramatis Personae

MARK ANTONY ⎫
OCTAVIUS CAESAR ⎬ *Triumvirs*
M. AEMILIUS LEPIDUS ⎭

DOMITIUS ENOBARBUS ⎫
VENTIDIUS │
EROS │
SCARUS ⎬ *Friends to Antony*
DERCETAS │
DEMETRIUS │
PHILO ⎭

MAECENAS ⎫
AGRIPPA │
DOLABELLA │
PROCULEIUS ⎬ *Friends to Caesar*
THIDIAS │
GALLUS ⎭

MENAS ⎫
MENECRATES ⎬ *Friends to Pompey*
VARRIUS ⎭

TAURUS, *Lieutenant General to Caesar*
CANIDIUS, *Lieutenant General to Antony*
ROMAN OFFICER UNDER VENTIDIUS
A SCHOOLMASTER

ALEXAS ⎫
MARDIAN │
SELEUCUS ⎬ *Attendants on Cleopatra*
DIOMEDES ⎭

A SOOTHSAYER
A CLOWN

CLEOPATRA, *Queen of Egypt*
OCTAVIA, *Sister to Caesar, and Wife to Antony*
CHARMIAN ⎫
IRAS ⎬ *Attendants on Cleopatra*

OFFICERS, SOLDIERS, MESSENGERS, ATTENDANTS

The Tragedy of Antony and Cleopatra

INTRODUCTION

1. THE DATE

The earliest record of *Antony and Cleopatra* appears in the Stationers' Register, where under date of May 20, 1608, Edward Blount, the publisher, entered his copy of the play. On the basis of indirect evidence, however, it appears that the play had been completed a year or two earlier. For instance, it probably served as the model for the revision which Samuel Daniel made in his play *Cleopatra* before republishing it in 1607. In this revised edition of his play Daniel replaced much of the relation of events by dialogue, gave greater parts to Iras and Charmian, and introduced Diomedes and Dercetas, the latter in the scene in which he brings Antony's sword to Caesar. Daniel had published *Cleopatra* in 1594, 1599, 1601, and 1602, but only in the edition of 1607 did he make the alterations which brought a portion of his play nearer Shakespeare's tragedy. There is good reason to believe, then, that *Antony and Cleopatra* was the impetus and model for Daniel's revisions, and that therefore it must have been completed in or before 1607 (see note on IV.11.SD).

Echoes of *Antony and Cleopatra* can be heard also in Barnabe Barnes' *The Devil's Charter,* first acted on February 2, 1607, and printed in October of the same year. In a brief passage of the play reference is made to 'Aspiks,' 'Cleopatra's birds,' 'Egyptian slime,' 'Nylus,' 'Ptolemies wife'; and there is the stage direction, 'He putteth to either of their brests an Aspike.' Such echoes may not constitute proof but they support the view that *Antony and Cleopatra* had appeared in 1607 if not earlier. How much earlier the play had been written can be fixed by the dates of two plays, from one of which Shakespeare seems to have borrowed Antony's image of the dragonish cloud (IV.10.3–9). The two plays are George Chapman's *Monsieur D'Olive* (1606) and his *Bussy D'Ambois* (1607). In the latter play appears the passage:

> *and like empty clouds,*
> *In which our faulty apprehensions forge*
> *The forms of dragons, lions, elephants,*
> *When they hold no proportion.*[1]

Perhaps more appropriate as Shakespeare's source is a passage in the earlier play where, as in Antony's image, the central thought is the decline of great men's fortunes:

> *Our great men*
> *Like to a mass of clouds that now seem like*
> *An elephant, and straightways like an ox,*
> *And then a mouse. . . .*[2]

Since the dates of the two plays are 1606 and 1607, we may fix 1606 as the earliest date for *Antony and Cleopatra*. And there is

1 *The Plays of George Chapman*, ed. T. M. Parrott (London, George Routledge & Sons, 1910), III.1.23-6.
2 *Ibid.,* II.2.91-4.

support for such conclusion from internal evidence. On the basis of metrical tests *Antony and Cleopatra* follows *Macbeth,* whose date is 1606. The date of the play, then, is 1606 or 1607.

2. THE TEXT

Though Edward Blount entered his copy in the Stationers' Register in 1608, the play does not appear to have been printed until much later, and the earliest text we possess is that of the First Folio (1623). The probability is strong that this text was set up from a fair copy of Shakespeare's manuscript before its excessive length had been trimmed for stage performance. In support of this theory may be cited the peculiarly Shakespearean misspellings, misprints, and colloquial abbreviations in the text which are duplicated in good quartos or even in Folio texts believed to be based on Shakespeare's manuscripts (New Cambridge Shakespeare, ed. J. D. Wilson, pp. 124–30). Furthermore the stage directions are so precise and demanding, even fussy, and at the same time impracticable, that they appear to be the work of the author rather than those of a promptbook used in an actual performance.

The view that the text was not based on that of a promptbook is supported by the presence of textual irregularities which the prompter might be thought to have eliminated. For instance he would have assigned the speeches at IV.5.1,4,9 to *Soldier,* not to *Eros,* and he would not have retained Dolabella as the speaker at V.1.34,38, since he is not on the stage at the time. It is also likely that he would have eliminated the duplication of the speech prefix *Eno.* at II.7.147,152, and of *Proc.* at V.2.37,40. These are errors due to forgetfulness on the part of Shakespeare or his scribe, and though they appear insignificant, the prompter could not have allowed them to stand since they would have obscured the meaning of the passages involved.

The text contains other irregularities, most of which may be laid to the compositor. In I.2.58–64 he took six lines from Charmian's speech and set them up as a separate speech and prefixed it *Alexas.* The name *Alexas* occurs in Charmian's speech, but the compositor mistook it for a speech prefix, printed it as such, and transferred to it that portion of Charmian's speech which followed it. On the other hand the speech prefix at IV.4.9,10 shows the compositor making the reverse error. Here he mistook the speech prefix *Anthony* for part of Cleopatra's speech and printed:

> Cleo. *Nay, Ile helpe too, Ant'ony,*
> *What's this for? Ah let be, let be, thou art*
> *The Armourer of my heart: False, false this, this,*
> *Sooth-law Ile helpe: Thus it must bee.*

Anthony was the prefix for the speech 'Ah . . . this, this,' which Shakespeare probably wrote in the margin of his manuscript. The compositor literally inserted it between two of Cleopatra's speeches; and having eliminated one speech prefix, he was forced to cancel a second to avoid duplication. Consequently, he struck off the prefix *Cleo.* from the line 'Sooth-law . . . bee,' and added the line to the rest, making one speech out of three.

One last error in speech prefixes may claim comment. In II.1, where Menas and Menecrates appear together, the Folio prefixes *Mene.* all speeches not spoken by Pompey or Varrius, the other two characters in the scene. This, however, renders Menas mute, although two of Pompey's speeches (ll. 38–45, 51–61) are addressed to him and he is three times called by name in them. Far from being mute, then, Menas may claim those speeches prefixed *Mene.* which Pompey seems to be answering, that is, ll. 20, 22, 38–45. The speeches have been reassigned by editors in a variety of ways, the least satisfactory being that in the New Cambridge Shakespeare, where Professor Dover Wilson, following Johnson's hint, assigned all speeches prefixed *Mene.* to Menas. Professor Wilson believes that *Mene.* stands for Menas since the latter is once called Menes in the Folio (II.7.17SD). But even if his name were Menes, the argument would not be conclusive since *Mene.* could stand for either name. Nor is it likely that Shakespeare would have prefixed Menas' (or Menes') speeches *Mene.* in a scene shared with Menecrates. Even in ll.6 and 7, where Menecrates does not appear, Menas' speeches are prefixed *Men.*

It may be argued that the compositor failed to distinguish between *Mene.* and *Men.* in Shakespeare's manuscript, and having set up *Mene.* for the first two speeches, he proceeded to do the same for the rest. That the speeches belong to two different, if not opposite, personalities is suggested by their content and tone. In the first two Menecrates calmly and philosophically recommends prudence and patience to the overconfident Pompey, whereas in the remaining speeches the pragmatic Menas thrusts before his master urgent facts of military and political nature. Menas is the pirate who in a later scene offers to slit the triumvirs' throats so that his master might rule the world alone. To such a character one is scarcely tempted to attribute the lines:

> we, ignorant of ourselves
> Beg often our own harms, which the wise powers
> Deny us for our good; so find we profit
> By losing of our prayers.

The text of the present edition is based on the First Folio, to which it adheres in all important matters. Of minor changes, the most important deal with punctuation and spelling, both of which have been modernized. In the matter of proper names a distinction has been made between spelling and form: the latter is retained throughout, whereas the spelling has been slightly changed in a few cases. Among proper names whose form is preserved is *Mesena* (II.2.192), which editors unnecessarily change to *Misenum*, although it is clear that Shakespeare is following North's spelling of *Misena*. Also restored is the Shakespearean *Thidias* (III.10) which in many editions is metamorphosed into *Thyreus* (Plutarch, *Thyrsus*). Shakespeare is not as careless in his spelling of proper names as we are occasionally asked to believe. In our play he reproduces so accurately such difficult names as Hipparchus, Proculeius, Seleucus, Ventidius (Ventigius), and Menecrates (also Menacrates) that when his

spelling differs from North's we may reasonably conclude that the compositor is responsible for most, if not all, such variations. For instance there is no reason why Shakespeare should have written *Orades* instead of *Orodes*, *Medena* instead of *Modena*; the only plausible explanation for such spelling is that the compositor misread Shakespeare's manuscript. Consequently I have emended the Folio spelling of such names, as for instance *Tourus* to *Taurus*, *Brandusium* to *Brundusium*, *Orades* to *Orodes*, *Medena* to *Modena*, *Licoania* to *Lycaonia*, *Action* (*Actiom*) to *Actium*, *Cidrus* (*Sidnis*) to *Cydnus*. I have also changed *Anthony* to *Antony*, since the latter represents more clearly the pronunciation and is in fact the spelling given in *Julius Caesar*.

Another matter in which the present text adheres to the Folio is lineation. Much has been said in defense of regularizing what appears to be mislineation in the text of Shakespearean plays. In such defense the arguments are based on the unwarranted assumption that in all verse passages, even in the late plays, Shakespeare wrote nothing but precise iambic pentameter. That this is not so the text of *Antony and Cleopatra* makes very clear. In a play whose pervasive quality is spaciousness and freedom we are not surprised to find what may be called irregular lines; for it is clear that here, as elsewhere, the dramatist was concerned far more with rhythm and pause than with metrical consistency. Yet editors have rearranged his lines even when the change involved was a minute one. For instance, in the opening scene of the play the Folio prints ll. 58–60 in the following manner:

> No messenger but thine, and all alone tonight
> We'll wander through the streets, and note
> The qualities of people.

It is true that l. 58 stretches beyond the regular five feet. But it is no great matter; and certainly if we read *messenger* as dissyllabic the line may pass for a respectable pentameter. Some editors, however, print the lines to read as follows:

> No messenger but thine, and all alone
> Tonight we'll wander through the streets, and note
> The qualities of people.

Since both lines (58, 59) can be read as pentameters (we may read *We'll* 'We will') the change is unnecessary; but it is also unfortunate, and indeed unacceptable, since by placing *tonight* at the beginning of l. 59 editors give it the primary emphasis and furthermore make it modify *we'll wander* exclusively, whereas in fact it modifies *all alone* as well and rhythmically belongs with it. Finally, what reason can the compositor have had for making such a small change in Shakespeare's manuscript? If the Folio reading is what Shakespeare wrote, it should remain inviolate.

A similar instance is I.3.122–124, which the Folio prints as follows:

> Be strew'd before your feet:
>   Ant. Let vs go.
> Come: Our separation so abides and flies

Finding l. 123 excessively long, Pope and subsequent editors regularized it by adding its first foot to the end of l. 122. Again, it is difficult to discover for what reason the compositor would have made such a small change, assuming that Shakespeare wrote *Come* at the end of l. 122. If, as we learn elsewhere, the compositor was troubled by long pentameters, some of them too long for his column, why should he have lengthened l. 123 by adding

a word taken from a half-line? On the contrary, he often divides a long pentameter into half-lines, as for instance I.3.42, which the Folio prints as two lines:

> *But bid farewell, and goe:*
> *When you sued staying,*

This is the compositor's most frequent departure from Shakespeare's lineation, and in the present text such half-lines are re-united into a single pentameter.

Not all short lines, however, can be so explained and regularized. To be sure, it is generally safe to combine into a single pentameter two consecutive half-lines. But what of single short lines? Take for instance two such lines separated by a regular pentameter, as in II.2.18–21:

> Ant. *If we compose well heere, to Parthia:*
> *Harke* Ventidius.
>   Caesar. *I do not know Mecenas, aske* Agrippa.
>   Lep. *Noble Friends:*

Since the passage apparently violates 18th-century prosody, editors have regularized it into the following:

>   Ant. *If we compose well here, to Parthia:*
> *Hark Ventidius.*
>   *Caesar.*   *I do not know,*
> *Maecenas; ask Agrippa.*
>   *Lep.*   *Noble friends,*

The change is, of course, unnecessary and indeed unfortunate, for the Folio reading is unquestionably superior, and for the following reasons. First, 'Hark, Ventidius' is a short line not a half-line; that is, it is not the first half of a pentameter. It is independent of the following speech, and in fact its brevity is intended to suggest an awkward pause between the two speeches, perhaps even the distance separating Caesar and Antony on the stage. Second, the regularization breaks up l. 20, which is a precise iambic pentameter: it interrupts the flow of its musical phrasing, by separating *Maecenas* from the preceding clause, with which it surely belongs. And finally the regularization disregards the long pause very clearly marked by the colon at the end of the short line 'Noble friends,' a pause which indicates Lepidus' apprehension and hesitation. The phrase commands a pause, it would seem, for its import must go home to both Antony and Caesar. The two words are not, I believe, a portion of the preceding pentameter but a line in themselves.

Another irregularity in the Folio text is the presence of prose passages which, we are convinced, Shakespeare wrote as verse. Why the compositor made the change is not always clear, but in most cases he did so to conserve space. Now and then he refuses to set up half lines but instead runs them together with a portion of the following pentameter. But in doing so he loses control of the verse lines and is therefore forced to print the remainder of the speech as prose. An instance of such practice is the following passage (I.5.69–76):

> Alex. *I Madam, twenty seuerall Messengers.*
> *Why do you send so thicke?*
>   Cleo. *Who's borne that day when I forget to send to An-*
> thonie, *shall dye a Begger. Inke and paper* Charmian. *Wel-*
> come my good Alexas. *Did I* Charmian, *euer loue Caesar so?*
>   Char. *Oh that braue Caesar!*

In fairness to the compositor it must be said that he may have been confused by revisions in the margin of Shakespeare's manuscript. Whatever the cause of the Folio lineation, I believe that we may profitably rearrange the lines on the assumption that Cleopatra's speech was written in verse. Such an assumption is strongly supported not only by the context but also by Charmian's half-line which is of sufficient length to complete the terminal half-line of Cleopatra's speech. A similar instance is II.1.1–8, a portion of which the Folio prints as prose:

> Pom. *If the great Gods be iust, they shall assist*
> *The deeds of iustest men.*
>   Mene. *Know worthy* Pompey, *that what they do delay,*
> *they do not deny.*
>   Pom. *Whiles we are sutors to their Throne, decayes the*
> *thing we sue for.*
>   Mene. *We ignorant of our selues,*
> *Begge often our owne harmes, which the wise Powres*

Here we may assume that the lines printed as prose were written in verse by Shakespeare, and for the following reasons. The ellipsis in the second speech and the inversion in the third are strong evidence against prose; and the initial half-line 'We ignorant of our selues' presupposes a terminal half-line in the preceding speech, since no other reason can be cited for its length. Going back over the passage we may assume that 'Know worthy *Pompey*' is a half-line completing the terminal half-line of the preceding speech. But the compositor again refuses to give it a whole line in his column and instead adds to it a portion of the following pentameter. Unfortunately in doing so he is forced to print the remainder of the speech in prose; and having disturbed the verse lines of one speech, he proceeds to do the same in the following speech as well. Then he comes upon a familiar landmark, the initial half-line of Menecrates' speech in l. 7, which he prints correctly as well as the remainder of the passage.

It is clear, then, that convincing reasons may be adduced for preserving the Folio lineation of most apparently mislineated passages and in effect for seeing that it is superior to any other; and also for regularizing the lineation of a few speeches where we may be certain the compositor departed from Shakespeare's manuscript. We may not, in other words, follow a blanket policy but must treat each passage separately.

Finally it will be seen that the present edition dispenses with the traditional act and scene divisions which in other editions mark the action of the play. Aside from being absent in the Folio text and therefore without authority, such formal divisions are scarcely admissible in a play where fluidity of scene and smoothness of action are of first importance. However, in order to facilitate reference to lines in this and other editions and to critical works, I have noted the act and scene divisions at the top of each page. Since I have combined the battle scenes in Acts III and IV and since in general I have retained the Folio lineation, my line numbering is slightly different from that of other editions.

In preparing the present edition I have received aid from other editors of *Antony and Cleopatra*, particularly from J. D. Wilson, M. R. Ridley, G. L. Kittredge (Boston, Ginn and Co., 1941), and H. H. Furness (Philadelphia, J. B. Lippincott Co., 1907). To all I wish to acknowledge my debt. And I am especially grateful to the general editors of the Yale Shakespeare, Professors Charles T. Prouty and Helge Kökeritz, for their help and kindness to me.

SOURCES OF THE PLAY

The source of *Antony and Cleopatra* is Plutarch's *Lives of the Noble Grecians and Romans Compared Together,* first printed in 1579. Although North did not go to the Greek original but instead turned into English Jacques Amyot's French translation, his version of the *Lives* shows a startling fidelity to the original. And it appears that this fidelity may have been due in part to the instantaneous attraction North must have felt for Plutarch, whom he reverently calls 'Philosopher and Historiographer.' The attraction, with its attendant fidelity, was repeated a few years later when Shakespeare laid his hand on North's translation. As an additional source a small claim has been advanced for Samuel Daniel's play *Cleopatra* (1595), and it is possible that Shakespeare borrowed a few details from it. But from Plutarch he took all the incidents which make up the drama of Antony's decline and death, and he took also the main characters and much of the language, this last coming to him in the gorgeous prose of North's Elizabethan translation.

In reorganizing the events into a tragedy Shakespeare made no use of those incidents which dealt with the rise in Antony's fortunes, although he often makes reference to them in order to establish the hero's nobility and achievements. He selected, abridged, and rearranged only those episodes which in some way affected or reflected Antony's relationship with Cleopatra, for, unlike Plutarch, he was composing a tragedy in which two lovers played equal parts. It follows, then, that Shakespeare established his own balance in the roles of these two and consequently redistributed the concentration of interest.

Plutarch's main characters served Shakespeare as prototypes which he elaborated by means of emphasis and detail, but the elaboration did not always involve profound change. For instance, in depicting Antony Shakespeare did not find it necessary to alter the lines of the character he had found in North. Plutarch, no less than Shakespeare, was primarily concerned with the enigma of character, in the case of Antony with the juxtaposition in him of strength and weakness in their highest degree. To Plutarch it seemed that Antony illustrated a saying by Plato that 'from great minds, both great vertues and great vices do procede'; and he presented him, as Shakespeare did in the play, in what might be called a tragic equilibrium, a balance between his virtues and the ignoble deeds by which he destroyed himself. But there is this difference between the two characterizations: whereas Plutarch's Antony in the end bows before the moral principles he has violated, Shakespeare's reaffirms his adherence to the values he has espoused, the values by which he has lived, loved, and apparently lost.

In the characterization of Cleopatra Shakespeare departed significantly from Plutarch, who saw her only as another agent in Antony's tragedy. In Plutarch she is not a tragic character: the tragedy is Antony's and his alone. Shakespeare, on the other hand, elevates her to that position, and in Act V presents her in the process of apprehending the tragic experience. But the tragic dignity with which she is invested does not change her. On the contrary, the supreme fascination of the closing moments derives from the juxtaposition in her of the alluring temptress and the tragic heroine. Their tragic vision, then, changes neither Antony nor Cleopatra, and in this particular fact lies Shakespeare's most significant departure from Plutarch. Whereas the philosophic historiographer presents the world of Egypt in opposition to the world of Rome and in the death of Antony and Cleopatra emphasizes the operation of the moral laws they have violated, the dramatist merely juxtaposes the two worlds, and against the death of his hero and heroine he places the triumph of their devotion to the principles by which they have lived.

The most striking correspondence between the play and its source is in language. North's prose, not far removed from poetry, came conveniently to Shakespeare's hand, and he was content on occasion to lift whole passages of it and transfer them to his play. For instance, Enobarbus' description of Cleopatra's first visit to Antony seems little more than a transcription in blank verse of North's lines:

Therefore when she was sent vnto by diuers letters, both from Antonius him selfe, and also from his frendes, she made so light of it, and mocked Antonius so much, that she disdained to set forward otherwise, but to take her barge in the riuer of Cydnus, the poope whereof was of gold, the sailes of purple, and the owers of siluer, which kept stroke in rowing after the sounde of the musicke of flutes, howboyes, citherns, violls, and such other instruments as they played vpon in the barge. And now for the person of her selfe: she was layed vnder a pauillion of cloth of gold of tissue, apparelled and attired like the goddesse Venus, commonly drawen in picture: and hard by her, on either hand of her, pretie faire boyes apparelled as painters doe set forth god Cupide, with litle fannes in their hands, with the which they fanned wind vpon her. Her Ladies and gentlewomen also, the fairest of them were apparelled like the nymphes Nereides (which are the mermaides of the waters) and like the Graces, some stearing the helme, others tending the tackle and ropes of the barge, out of the which there came a wonderfull passing sweete sauor of perfumes, that perfumed the wharfes side, pestered with innumerable multitudes of people. Some of them followed the barge all alongest the riuers side: others also ranne out of the citie to see her comming in. So that in thend, there ranne such multitudes of people one after an other to see her, that Antonius was left post alone in the market place, in his Imperiall seate to geue audience: and there went a rumor in the peoples mouthes, that the goddesse Venus was come to play with the god Bacchus, for the generall good of all Asia. (Pp. 981–2).

A comparison of the passage with II.2.224–253 of the play will show how much and how minutely Shakespeare borrowed from this description. But it will show also that Shakespeare's additions, though few, make a great deal of difference. In describing Cleopatra's barge Shakespeare makes the winds *lovesick* with the perfumed sails, and the water *amorous* of the oars' strokes. Another fanciful touch by which Shakespeare vivifies the scene occurs in the description of the deserted Antony. Plutarch says that so many people had gone out to see Cleopatra 'that Antonius was left post alone in the market place to geue audience.' This in Shakespeare becomes:

        and Antony,
Enthron'd i' th' market-place, did sit alone,
Whistling to th' air.

Other instances of verbal correspondence may be cited, among them the Soothsayer's colloquy with Antony (II.3.12–36), Antony's dying speech (IV.11.61–69), and the Seleucus episode (V.2.168–206). Such borrowing from his prose may be a compliment to North, but it is not, of course, a defect in the play. The passages borrowed were elevated to blank verse, and they were so vitally and smoothly fitted to their contexts that they give the reader no reason to question their origin.

Enter Demetrius and Philo.

Philo. Nay, but this dotage of our general's
O'erflows the measure: those his goodly eyes,
That o'er the files and musters of the war
Have glow'd like plated Mars, now bend, now turn
The office and devotion of their view   5
Upon a tawny front. His captain's heart,
Which in the scuffles of great fights hath burst
The buckles on his breast, reneges all temper,
And is become the bellows and the fan
To cool a gypsy's lust.   10

*Flourish. Enter Antony, Cleopatra, her Ladies, the train, with
Eunuchs fanning her.*

                      Look! where they come:
Take but good note, and you shall see in him
The triple pillar of the world transform'd
Into a strumpet's fool. Behold and see.

Cleopatra. If it be love indeed, tell me how much.   15

Antony. There's beggary in the love that can be reckon'd.

Cleopatra. I'll set a bourn how far to be belov'd.

Antony. Then must thou needs find out new heaven, new
earth.

Enter a Messenger.

Messenger. News, my good lord, from Rome.

Antony.   Grates me, the sum.

Cleopatra. Nay, hear them, Antony.
Fulvia, perchance, is angry: or, who knows
If the scarce-bearded Caesar have not sent
His powerful mandate to you, 'Do this, or this;   25
Take in that kingdom, and enfranchise that.
Perform't, or else we damn thee.'

Antony.   How, my love?

Cleopatra. Perchance? nay, and most like:
You must not stay here longer, your dismission   30
Is come from Caesar; therefore hear it, Antony.
Where's Fulvia's process? Caesar's I would say? both?
Call in the messengers. As I am Egypt's queen,
Thou blushest, Antony, and that blood of thine
Is Caesar's homager: else so thy cheek pays shame   35
What shrill-tongu'd Fulvia scolds. The messengers!

Antony. Let Rome in Tiber melt, and the wide arch
Of the rang'd empire fall! Here is my space.
Kingdoms are clay: our dungy earth alike
Feeds beast as man; the nobleness of life   40
Is to do thus: when such a mutual pair
And such a twain can do't, in which I bind,
On pain of punishment, the world to weet
We stand up peerless.

Cleopatra.   Excellent falsehood!   45
Why did he marry Fulvia and not love her?
I'll seem the fool I am not. Antony will be himself.

Antony. But stirr'd by Cleopatra.
Now, for the love of Love and her soft hours,
Let's not confound the time with conference harsh;   50
There's not a minute of our lives should stretch
Without some pleasure now. What sport tonight?

Cleopatra. Hear the ambassadors.

Antony.   Fie, wrangling queen!
Whom everything becomes, to chide, to laugh,   55
To weep: whose every passion fully strives
To make itself (in thee) fair and admir'd.
No messenger but thine, and all alone tonight
We'll wander through the streets, and note
The qualities of people. Come, my queen.   60
Last night you did desire it. Speak not to us.

                              Exeunt with the train.

Demetrius. Is Caesar with Antonius priz'd so slight?

Philo. Sir, sometimes when he is not Antony
He comes too short of that great property
Which still should go with Antony.   65

Demetrius.   I am full sorry
That he approves the common liar, who
Thus speaks of him at Rome; but I will hope
Of better deeds tomorrow. Rest you happy!   *Exeunt.*

*Enter Enobarbus, a Soothsayer, Charmian, Iras, Mardian the
eunuch, and Alexas.*

Charmian. Lord Alexas, sweet Alexas, most anything Alexas,
almost most absolute Alexas, where's the soothsayer that you
prais'd so to th' queen? O, that I knew this husband, which,
you say, must change his horns with garlands.

Alexas. Soothsayer!   5

Soothsayer. Your will?

Charmian. Is this the man? Is't you, sir, that know things?

Soothsayer. In nature's infinite book of secrecy a little I
can read.

Alexas. Show him your hand.   10

Enobarbus. Bring in the banket quickly: wine enough
Cleopatra's health to drink.

Charmian. Good sir, give me good fortune.

Soothsayer. I make not, but foresee.

Charmian. Pray then, foresee me one.   15

Soothsayer. You shall be yet far fairer than you are.

Charmian. He means in flesh.

Iras. No, you shall paint when you are old.

Charmian. Wrinkles forbid!

Alexas. Vex not his prescience, be attentive.   20

Charmian. Hush!

Soothsayer. You shall be more beloving than belov'd.

Charmian. I had rather heat my liver with drinking.

Alexas. Nay, hear him.

Charmian. Good now, some excellent fortune: let me be   25
married to three kings in a forenoon, and widow them all: let
me have a child at fifty, to whom Herod of Jewry may do

---

4 **plate:** *clothed in armor*   5 **office:** *service*   6 **tawny front:** *dark face*   8 **reneges:** *renounces*   **temper:** *self-restraint*   10 **gypsy's;** *Cf. n.*   13 **triple pillar;** *Cf. n.*   14 **fool:** *dupe*   16 **beggary;** *Cf. n.*   17 **bourn:** *boundary*   21 **Grates:** *irritates*   **the sum: be brief*   23 **Fulvia:** *Antony's wife*   24 **scarce-bearded;** *Cf. n.*   26 **Take in:** *conquer*   **enfranchise:** *set free*   29 **most like:** *without doubt*   30 **dismission:** *dismissal*   32 **process:** *summons*   34 **homager:** *vassal*   38 **rang'd:** *'well-ordered'; or possibly, 'far-flung'*   41 **mutual:** *with equal love for each other*   43 **to weet:** *to know, to acknowledge*   47 **I'll seem . . . not:** *I'll pretend I am foolish enough to believe you (which I am not really)*

50 **confound:** *waste*   51 **stretch:** *pass, be protracted*   56 **whose:** *F who (F refers throughout to the First Folio of 1623)*   **passion:** *emotion*   58–60 **all alone . . . people;** *Cf. n.*   60 **qualities:** *characteristics*   64 **property:** *distinctive quality*   67 **approves:** *proves true*   69 **Rest you happy:** *May God keep you happy*   SD **Enter Enobarbus:** *begins I.2; Cf. n.*   2 **absolute:** *perfect*   4 **change . . . garlands;** *Cf. n.*   11 **banket:** *banquet, dessert*   23 **heat . . . drinking;** *Cf. n.*   27 **Herod of Jewry;** *Cf. n.*

homage. Find me to marry me with Octavius Caesar, and
companion me with my mistress.

Soothsayer. You shall outlive the lady whom you serve.   *30*

Charmian. O excellent! I love long life better than figs.

Soothsayer. You have seen and prov'd a fairer former fortune
Than that which is to approach.

Charmian. Then belike my children shall have no names.
Prithee, how many boys and wenches must I have?   *35*

Soothsayer. If every of your wishes had a womb,
And fertile every wish, a million.

Charmian. Out, fool! I forgive thee for a witch.

Alexas. You think none but your sheets are privy to your
wishes.   *40*

Charmian. Nay, come, tell Iras hers.

Alexas. We'll know all our fortunes.

Enobarbus. Mine, and most of our fortunes, tonight, shall
be—drunk to bed.

Iras. There's a palm presages chastity, if nothing else.   *45*

Charmian. E'en as the o'erflowing Nilus presageth famine.

Iras. Go, you wild bedfellow, you cannot soothsay.

Charmian. Nay, if an oily palm be not a fruitful prognostication, I cannot scratch mine ear. Prithee, tell her but a worky-
day fortune.   *50*

Soothsayer. Your fortunes are alike.

Iras. But how, but how? give me particulars.

Soothsayer. I have said.

Iras. Am I not an inch of fortune better than she?

Charmian. Well, if you were but an inch of fortune   *55*
better than I, where would you choose it?

Iras. Not in my husband's nose.

Charmian. Our worser thoughts Heavens mend! Alexas,
come, his fortune, his fortune. O, let him marry a woman
that cannot go, sweet Isis, I beseech thee, and let her die   *60*
too, and give him a worse, and let worse follow worse, till
the worst of all follow him laughing to his grave, fifty-fold a
cuckold. Good Isis, hear me this prayer, though thou deny
me a matter of more weight: good Isis, I beseech thee.

Iras. Amen, dear goddess, hear that prayer of the people.   *65*
For, as it is a heart-breaking to see a handsome man loose-wiv'd,
so it is a deadly sorrow to behold a foul knave uncuckolded.
Therefore, dear Isis, keep decorum, and fortune him accordingly.

Charmian. Amen.

Alexas. Lo, now, if it lay in their hands to make me a   *70*
cuckold, they would make themselves whores, but they'ld do't.

Enter Cleopatra.

Enobarbus. Hush! here comes Antony.

Charmian.   Not he, the queen.

Cleopatra. Saw you my lord?

Enobarbus.   No, lady.   *75*

Cleopatra.   Was he not here?

Charmian. No, madam.

Cleopatra. He was dispos'd to mirth, but on the sudden
A Roman thought hath struck him. Enobarbus!

Enobarbus. Madam?   *80*

Cleopatra. Seek him, and bring him hither. Where's Alexas?

Alexas. Here, at your service. My lord approaches.

Enter Antony, with a Messenger [and Attendants].

Cleopatra. We will not look upon him. Go with us.
                *Exeunt [Cleopatra, Enobarbus, Alexas, Iras,
                    Charmian, Soothsayer, and Attendants].*

Messenger. Fulvia thy wife first came into the field.

Antony. Against my brother Lucius?   *85*

Messenger. Ay:
But soon that war had end, and the time's state
Made friends of them, jointing their force 'gainst Caesar,
Whose better issue in the war from Italy
Upon the first encounter drave them.   *90*

Antony.   Well, what worst?

Messenger. The nature of bad news infects the teller.

Antony. When it concerns the fool, or coward. On.
Things that are past are done with me. 'Tis thus:
Who tells me true, though in his tale lie death,   *95*
I hear him as he flatter'd.

Messenger.   Labienus—
This is stiff news—hath with his Parthian force
Extended Asia: from Euphrates his conquering
Banner shook from Syria to Lydia   *100*
And to Ionia, whilst—

Antony.   Antony, thou wouldst say.

Messenger. O, my lord.

Antony.   Speak to me home.
Mince not the general tongue, name   *105*
Cleopatra as she is call'd in Rome:
Rail thou in Fulvia's phrase, and taunt my faults
With such full license as both truth and malice
Have power to utter. O, then we bring forth weeds
When our quick minds lie still, and our ills told us   *110*
Is as our earing. Fare thee well awhile.

Messenger. At your noble pleasure.   *Exit Messenger.*

Antony. From Sicyon, ho, the news! Speak there!

1. Attendant. The man from Sicyon, is there such an one?

2. Attendant. He stays upon your will.   *115*

Antony.   Let him appear.
These strong Egyptian fetters I must break,
Or lose myself in dotage.

Enter another Messenger, with a letter.

                What are you?

2. Messenger. Fulvia thy wife is dead.   *120*

Antony.   Where died she?

2. Messenger. In Sicyon:
Her length of sickness, with what else more serious
Importeth thee to know, this bears.   *[Gives a letter.]*

Antony. Forbear me.   *[Exit 2. Messenger.]*   *125*
There's a great spirit gone! Thus did I desire it:

28, 29 companion me: *i.e. as the wife of a triumvir*   31 I ... figs; *Cf. n.*   32 prov'd: *experienced*   34 shall have no names: *will be bastards*   35 wenches: *girls*   37 fertile: *F foretell*   38 for: *because you are*   39 privy to: *secretly aware of*   45 presages chastity: *because it is dry and cool*   48 oily palm: *believed to indicate wantonness*   48, 49 fruitful prognostication: *sign of fertility*   49, 50 worky-day: *ordinary*   59–64 come ... thee: *F assigns passage to Alexas; cf. n.*   60 cannot go: *cannot walk (cannot be pregnant?)*   64 Isis; *Cf. n.*   66 loose-wiv'd: *married to a wanton*   74 Saw: *F saue*   79 A Roman thought: *thought inspired by Roman virtue*

87 time's state: *situation at that moment*   88 jointing: *uniting (cf. Cymbeline, V.4.145, jointed)*   89 issue: *success*   96 as: *as if*   97 Labienus; *Cf. n.*   99–103 Extended ... lord; *Cf. n.*   99 Extended: *taken possession of*   100 Lydia; *Cf. n.*   104 home: *plainly*   105 Mince: *extenuate* general tongue: *common report*   110 minds: *F windes*   110, 111 our ills ... earing; *Cf. n.*   111 earing: *ploughing* SD Exit Messenger: *F reads 'Enter another Messenger' after this direction*   113 ho: *F how*   114 1. Attendant: *F 1. Mess.*   115 2. Attendant: *F 2. Mess.* stays upon your will: *awaits your command*   118 lose myself: *become lost*   120 2. Messenger: *F 3. Mess.*   124 Importeth: *concerns*   125 Forbear me: *leave me*

What our contempts doth often hurl from us
We wish it ours again. The present pleasure,
By revolution low'ring, does become
The opposite of itself: she's good, being gone;　　　　130
The hand could pluck her back that shov'd her on.
I must from this enchanting queen break off:
Ten thousand harms, more than the ills I know,
My idleness doth hatch.

Enter Enobarbus.

　　　　　　　　　How now, Enobarbus!　　　　135
Enobarbus. What's your pleasure, sir?
Antony. I must with haste from hence.
Enobarbus. Why, then, we kill all our women. We see how
mortal an unkindness is to them; if they suffer our departure
death's the word.　　　　140
Antony. I must be gone.
Enobarbus. Under a compelling occasion let women die. It
were pity to cast them away for nothing, though between them
and a great cause they should be esteemed nothing. Cleopatra,
catching but the least noise of this, dies instantly: I have　　　　145
seen her die twenty times upon far poorer moment. I do
think there is mettle in death which commits some loving
act upon her, she hath such a celerity in dying.
Antony. She is cunning past man's thought.
Enobarbus. Alack, sir, no; her passions are made of　　　　150
nothing but the finest part of pure love. We cannot call her
winds and waters sighs and tears: they are greater storms and
tempests than almanacs can report. This cannot be cunning
in her; if it be, she makes a shower of rain as well as Jove.
Antony. Would I had never seen her!　　　　155
Enobarbus. O, sir, you had then left unseen a wonderful
piece of work which not to have been blessed withal would
have discredited your travel.
Antony. Fulvia is dead.
Enobarbus. Sir?　　　　160
Antony. Fulvia is dead.
Enobarbus. Fulvia!
Antony. Dead.
Enobarbus. Why, sir, give the gods a thankful sacrifice: when
it pleaseth their deities to take the wife of a man from him, it
shows to man the tailors of the earth: comforting therein, that
when old robes are worn out there are members to make new.
If there were no more women but Fulvia, then had you indeed
a cut, and the case to be lamented. This grief is crown'd with
consolation; your old smock brings forth a new petticoat, and
indeed the tears live in an onion that should water this sorrow.
Antony. The business she hath broached in the state
Cannot endure my absence.
Enobarbus. And the business you have broach'd here
cannot be without you, especially that of Cleopatra's,　　　　175
which wholly depends on your abode.
Antony. No more light answers. Let our officers
Have notice what we purpose. I shall break
The cause of our expedience to the queen,
And get her leave to part. For not alone　　　　180

The death of Fulvia, with more urgent touches,
Do strongly speak to us, but the letters too
Of many our contriving friends in Rome
Petition us at home. Sextus Pompeius
Hath given the dare to Caesar, and commands　　　　185
The empire of the sea. Our slippery people,
Whose love is never link'd to the deserver
Till his deserts are past, begin to throw
Pompey the Great and all his dignities
Upon his son, who, high in name and power,　　　　190
Higher than both in blood and life, stands up
For the main soldier; whose quality going on,
The sides o' th' world may danger. Much is breeding,
Which, like the courser's hair, hath yet but life,
And not a serpent's poison. Say our pleasure,　　　　195
To such whose place is under us, requires
Our quick remove from hence.
Enobarbus.　　I shall do't.　　　　　　*[Exeunt.]*

Enter Cleopatra, Charmian, Alexas, and Iras.

Cleopatra. Where is he?
Charmian.　　　　I did not see him since.
Cleopatra. See where he is, who's with him, what he does:
I did not send you. If you find him sad,
Say I am dancing; if in mirth, report　　　　5
That I am sudden sick. Quick, and return.　　*[Exit Alexas.]*
Charmian. Madam, methinks, if you did love him dearly,
You do not hold the method to enforce
The like from him.
Cleopatra.　　What should I do, I do not?　　　　10
Charmian. In each thing give him way, cross him in
nothing.
Cleopatra. Thou teachest like a fool: the way to lose him.
Charmian. Tempt him not so too far. I wish, forbear.
In time we hate that which we often fear.　　　　15

Enter Antony.

But here comes Antony.
Cleopatra.　　　　I am sick and sullen.
Antony. I am sorry to give breathing to my purpose.
Cleopatra. Help me away, dear Charmian, I shall fall.
It cannot be thus long, the sides of nature　　　　20
Will not sustain it.
Antony.　　　Now, my dearest queen—
Cleopatra. Pray you, stand farther from me.
Antony.　　　　　　What's the matter?
Cleopatra. I know by that same eye there's some good news.
What says the married woman? You may go.
Would she had never given you leave to come!
Let her not say 'tis I that keep you here,
I have no power upon you: hers you are.
Antony. The gods best know—　　　　30
Cleopatra.　　　　O, never was there queen
So mightily betray'd: yet at the first
I saw the treasons planted.

129 By . . . low'ring: *Cf. n.*　**134 idleness:** *trifling, dotage*　**142 a compelling occasion:**
F a compelling an occasion　**145 noise:** *rumor*　**146 poorer moment:** *less cause*　**147
mettle:** *vigor*　**154 Jove:** *Jupiter Pluvius, the rain god of the Romans*　**166 tailors of the
earth:** *the gods*　**169 cut:** *blow*　**172 broached:** *set in motion*　**176 abode:**
stay　**178 break:** *tell*　**179 expedience:** *haste, sudden departure*　**180 part:** *depart*

181 touches: *concerns*　**183 contriving:** *scheming*　**184 Sextus Pompeius;** *Cf. n.*　**185
Hath:** *F Haue*　**188–190 throw . . . Upon:** *transfer*　**191, 192 stands up For:** *aspires
to be*　**192 main:** *foremost*　**quality:** *condition, character*　**193 sides:** *frame*　**danger:**
endanger　**194 courser's hair;** *Cf. n.*　**196 place:** *F places*　**SD Enter Cleopatra:**
begins I.3　**3 who's:** *F whose*　**4 I did not send you:** *let him not know I sent you*　**sad:**
serious　**10 I do not:** *that I am not doing*　**14 Tempt:** *test, try*　**I wish, forbear:** *I wish
you would forbear*　**18 breathing:** *utterance*　**20 sides of nature:** *human frame*　**26
married woman:** *Fulvia*　**woman? You may go:** *F woman you may go?*

Antony.　　　　　　Cleopatra—
Cleopatra. Why should I think you can be mine and true, *35*
(Though you in swearing shake the throned gods)
Who have been false to Fulvia? Riotous madness,
To be entangled with those mouth-made vows,
Which break themselves in swearing.
　　Antony.　　　　　　Most sweet queen— *40*
Cleopatra. Nay, pray you, seek no color for your going,
But bid farewell, and go: when you su'd staying
Then was the time for words: no going then,
Eternity was in our lips and eyes,
Bliss in our brows' bent: none our parts so poor *45*
But was a race of heaven. They are so still,
Or thou, the greatest soldier of the world,
Art turn'd the greatest liar.
　　Antony.　　　　　　How now, lady?
　　Cleopatra. I would I had thy inches; thou shouldst know *50*
There were a heart in Egypt.
　　Antony.　　　　　　Hear me, queen:
The strong necessity of time commands
Our services awhile, but my full heart
Remains in use with you. Our Italy *55*
Shines o'er with civil swords; Sextus Pompeius
Makes his approaches to the port of Rome;
Equality of two domestic powers
Breed scrupulous faction: the hated, grown to strength,
Are newly grown to love: the condemn'd Pompey, *60*
Rich in his father's honor, creeps apace
Into the hearts of such as have not thriv'd
Upon the present state, whose numbers threaten;
And quietness, grown sick of rest, would purge
By any desperate change. My more particular, *65*
And that which most with you should safe my going,
Is Fulvia's death.
　　Cleopatra. Though age from folly could not give me
freedom,
It does from childishness. Can Fulvia die? *70*
　　Antony. She's dead, my queen.
Look here, and at thy sovereign leisure read
The garboils she awak'd: at the last, best,
See when and where she died.
　　Cleopatra.　　　　　　O most false love! *75*
Where be the sacred vials thou shouldst fill
With sorrowful water? Now I see, I see,
In Fulvia's death, how mine receiv'd shall be.
　　Antony. Quarrel no more, but be prepar'd to know
The purposes I bear: which are or cease *80*
As you shall give th' advice. By the fire
That quickens Nilus' slime, I go from hence
Thy soldier, servant, making peace or war
As thou affects.
　　Cleopatra.　　　　Cut my lace, Charmian, come, *85*
But let it be, I am quickly ill, and well—
So Antony loves.

Antony.　　　　　　My precious queen, forbear,
And give true evidence to his love which stands
An honorable trial. *90*
　　Cleopatra.　　　　So Fulvia told me.
I prithee, turn aside and weep for her,
Then bid adieu to me, and say the tears
Belong to Egypt. Good now, play one scene
Of excellent dissembling, and let it look *95*
Like perfect honor.
　　Antony.　　　　You'll heat my blood; no more.
　　Cleopatra. You can do better yet: but this is meetly.
　　Antony. Now, by my sword—
　　Cleopatra.　　　　And target. Still he mends. *100*
But this is not the best. Look, prithee, Charmian
How this Herculean Roman does become
The carriage of his chafe.
　　Antony.　　　　I'll leave you, lady.
　　Cleopatra. Courteous lord, one word: *105*
Sir, you and I must part, but that's not it:
Sir, you and I have lov'd, but there's not it:
That you know well: something it is I would—
O, my oblivion is a very Antony,
And I am all forgotten. *110*
　　Antony.　　　　But that your royalty
Holds idleness your subject, I should take you
For idleness itself.
　　Cleopatra.　　　'Tis sweating labor
To bear such idleness so near the heart *115*
As Cleopatra this. But, sir, forgive me,
Since my becomings kill me when they do not
Eye well to you. Your honor calls you hence;
Therefore be deaf to my unpitied folly,
And all the gods go with you. Upon your sword *120*
Sit laurel victory, and smooth success
Be strew'd before your feet!
　　Antony.　　　　　Let us go.
Come. Our separation so abides and flies,
That thou residing here, goes yet with me *125*
And I hence fleeting here remain with thee.
Away!　　　　　　　　　　　　　　*Exeunt.*

Enter Octavius [Caesar], reading a letter, Lepidus, and their train.

　　Caesar. You may see, Lepidus, and henceforth know,
It is not Caesar's natural vice to hate
Our great competitor. From Alexandria
This is the news: he fishes, drinks, and wastes
The lamps of night in revel: is not more manlike *5*
Than Cleopatra, nor the queen of Ptolemy
More womanly than he. Hardly gave audience
Or vouchsaf'd to think he had partners. You
Shall find there a man who is th' abstract of all faults,
That all men follow. *10*
　　Lepidus.　　　　I must not think
There are evils enow to darken all his goodness:

41 color: *pretext*　42 su'd staying: *begged to stay*　45 brows' bent: *arch of the eye-brows*　none our parts: *none of our parts*　46 race of heaven: *of heavenly flavor*　51 heart in Egypt: *heart* (courage) *in Cleopatra*　55 in use with you: *yours to keep and enjoy*　56 civil swords: *swords drawn in civil war*　59 scrupulous faction: *quarrel over small differences*　60 condemn'd: *stressed* ´ —　63 state: *government*　64, 65 grown . . . change; *Cf. n.*　65 particular: *personal concern*　66 safe: *make safe*　73 garboils: *brawls*　at the last, best: *the last and best news*　76 sacred vials; *Cf. n.*　80 are: *exist*　81, 82 By the fire . . . slime; *Cf. n.*　85 lace: *lace of her bodice*　87 So: *provided*

89 his love which: *the love of one who*　91 told me: *taught me*　98 meetly: *fairly good*　99 by my sword: *F by sword.*　100 target: *shield*　102, 103 How . . . chafe; *Cf. n.*　109, 110 O . . . forgotten; *Cf. n.*　111 But that: *if it were not that*　112 idleness: *frivolousness*　117 becomings: *graces*　118 Eye well: *appear well*　SD Enter Octavius: *begins I.4*　3 Our: *F One*　competitor: *associate*　6 queen of Ptolemy; *Cf. n.*　7, 12 More . . . goodness; *Cf. n.*　8 vouchsaf'd: *F vouchsafe*　9 abstract: *epitome; F abstracts*　12 enow: *enough*

His faults in him seem as the spots of heaven,
More fiery by night's blackness; hereditary
Rather than purchas'd: what he cannot change   *15*
Than what he chooses.

    Caesar. You are too indulgent. Let's grant it is not
Amiss to tumble on the bed of Ptolemy,
To give a kingdom for a mirth, to sit
And keep the turn of tippling with a slave,   *20*
To reel the streets at noon, and stand the buffet
With knaves that smells of sweat. Say this becomes him
(As his composure must be rare indeed
Whom these things cannot blemish)—yet must Antony
No way excuse his foils, when we do bear   *25*
So great weight in his lightness. If he fill'd
His vacancy with his voluptuousness,
Full surfeits and the dryness of his bones
Call on him for't. But to confound such time
That drums him from his sport, and speaks as loud   *30*
As his own state and ours, 'tis to be chid
As we rate boys who, being mature in knowledge,
Pawn their experience to their present pleasure,
And so rebel to judgment.

       Enter a Messenger.

    Lepidus.   Here's more news.   *35*
    Messenger. Thy biddings have been done, and every hour,
Most noble Caesar, shalt thou have report
How 'tis abroad. Pompey is strong at sea,
And it appears he is belov'd of those
That only have fear'd Caesar: to the ports   *40*
The discontents repair, and men's reports
Give him much wrong'd.
    Caesar.   I should have known no less.
It hath bin taught us from the primal state
That he which is was wish'd until he were;   *45*
And the ebb'd man, ne're lov'd till ne're worth love,
Comes dear'd by being lack'd. This common body,
Like to a vagabond flag upon the stream,
Goes to and back, lacking the varying tide,
To rot itself with motion.   *50*
    Messenger.   Caesar, I bring thee word,
Menecrates and Menas, famous pirates,
Makes the sea serve them, which they ear and wound
With keels of every kind. Many hot inroads
They make in Italy; the borders maritime   *55*
Lack blood to think on't, and flush youth revolt;
No vessel can peep forth, but 'tis as soon
Taken as seen: for Pompey's name strikes more
Than could his war resisted.
    Caesar.   Antony,   *60*

Leave thy lascivious wassails. When thou once
Was beaten from Modena, where thou slew'st
Hirsius and Pansa, consuls, at thy heel
Did famine follow, whom thou fought'st against,
(Though daintily brought up) with patience more   *65*
Than savages could suffer. Thou didst drink
The stale of horses and the gilded puddle
Which beasts would cough at: thy palate then did deign
The roughest berry on the rudest hedge;
Yea, like the stag, when snow the pasture sheets,   *70*
The barks of trees thou brows'd. On the Alps
It is reported thou didst eat strange flesh,
Which some did die to look on. And all this—
(It wounds thine honor that I speak it now)—
Was borne so like a soldier that thy cheek   *75*
So much as lank'd not.
    Lepidus.   'Tis pity of him.
    Caesar. Let his shames quickly
Drive him to Rome. 'Tis time we twain
Did show ourselves i' th' field, and to that end   *80*
Assemble we immediate council. Pompey
Thrives in our idleness.
    Lepidus.   Tomorrow, Caesar,
I shall be furnish'd to inform you rightly
Both what by sea and land I can be able   *85*
To front this present time.
    Caesar.   Till which encounter,
It is my business too. Farewell.
    Lepidus. Farewell, my lord. What you shall know meantime
Of stirs abroad, I shall beseech you, sir,   *90*
To let me be partaker.
    Caesar.   Doubt not, sir;
I knew it for my bond.   *Exeunt.*

      Enter Cleopatra, Charmian, Iras, and Mardian

    Cleopatra. Charmian!
    Charmian. Madam?
    Cleopatra. Ha, ha! Give me to drink mandragora.
    Charmian. Why, madam?
    Cleopatra. That I might sleep out this great gap of time   *5*
My Antony is away.
    Charmian.   You think of him too much.
    Cleopatra. O! 'tis treason.
    Charmian.   Madam, I trust, no so.
    Cleopatra. Thou, eunuch Mardian.
    Mardian.   What's your highness' pleasure?   *10*
    Cleopatra. Not now to hear thee sing. I take no pleasure
In aught an eunuch has. 'Tis well for thee,
That, being unseminar'd, thy freer thoughts
May not fly forth of Egypt. Has thou affections?   *15*
    Mardian. Yes, gracious madam.
    Cleopatra. Indeed?
    Mardian. Not in deed, madam, for I can do nothing
But what indeed is honest to be done:
Yet have I fierce affections, and think   *20*
What Venus did with Mars.

15 purchas'd: *acquired*   **19 mirth:** *entertainment*   **20 keep the turn of:** *take turns*   **21, 22 stand . . . knaves:** *condescend to exchange blows with the riffraff*   **22 smells:** *old plural form in* s *is common in Shakespeare; see l. 53 below*   **23 composure:** *disposition*   **25 foils:** *disgraces; cf. n.*   **25, 26 when . . . lightness:** *when his levity affects us so seriously*   **27 vacancy:** *leisure*   **29 Call on:** *call to account*   **confound:** *put to ill use*   **30 drums:** *calls as drum calls to battle*   **30, 31 speaks . . . ours:** *speaks of weighty matters of triumvirate*   **32 rate:** *scold.* **mature in knowledge:** *old enough to know*   **33 Pawn . . . pleasure:** *gratify their desires against their judgment*   **41 discontents:** *discontented*   **42 Give him:** *represent him as*   **44 bin:** *been.* **primal:** *primeval*   **46 ebb'd:** *declined in fortune.* **ne're:** *ne'er*   **47 Comes dear'd:** *F Comes fear'd*   **48 vagabond:** *shifty* **flag:** *iris*   **49 lacking:** *lackeying, following like a lackey*   **53 ear:** *plough*   **56 Lack blood:** *turn pale* **flush:** *vigorous*   **58, 59 strikes . . . resisted;** *Cf. n.*

61 wassails: *revels*   **61–76 When . . . lank'd not;** *Cf. n.*   **67 stale:** *urine* **gilded:** *of a golden color*   **71 brows'd:** *browsed'st*   **76 lank'd not:** *did not grow thin*   **79 we:** *F me*   **85 can be able:** *can muster*   **86 front:** *face*   **93 bond:** *duty, obligation*   **SD Enter Cleopatra:** *begins I.5*   **3 mandragora:** *mandrake, a narcotic*   **14 unseminar'd:** *unsexed*   **15 affections:** *passions*

Cleopatra.   O Charmian,
Where think'st thou he is now? Stands he, or sits he?
Or does he walk? or is he on his horse?
O happy horse, to bear the weight of Antony!   25
Do bravely, horse, for wot'st thou whom thou mov'st?
The demi-Atlas of this earth, the arm
And burgonet of men. He's speaking now,
Or murmuring "Where's my serpent of old Nile?"
(For so he calls me). Now I feed myself   30
With most delicious poison. Think on me,
That am with Phoebus' amorous pinches black,
And wrinkled deep in time? Broad-fronted Caesar,
When thou wast here above the ground, I was
A morsel for a monarch, and great Pompey   35
Would stand and make his eyes grow in my brow;
There would he anchor his aspect and die
With looking on his life.

      Enter Alexas from Antony.

   Alexas.   Sovereign of Egypt, hail!
   Cleopatra. How much unlike art thou Mark Antony!   40
Yet, coming from him, that great med'cine hath
With his tinct gilded thee.
How goes it with my brave Mark Antony?
   Alexas. Last thing he did, dear queen,
He kiss'd—the last of many doubled kisses—   45
This orient pearl. His speech sticks in my heart.
   Cleopatra. Mine ear must pluck it thence.
   Alexas.   'Good friend,' quoth he,
'Say, the firm Roman to great Egypt sends
This treasure of an oyster; at whose foot,   50
To mend the petty present, I will piece
Her opulent throne with kingdoms. All the East,
(Say thou) shall call her mistress.' So he nodded,
And soberly did mount an arm-gaunt steed,
Who neigh'd so high that what I would have spoke   55
Was beastly dumb'd by him.
   Cleopatra.   What was he, sad or merry?
   Alexas. Like to the time o' th' year between the extremes
Of hot and cold, he was nor sad nor merry.
   Cleopatra. O well-divided disposition! Note him,   60
Note him, good Charmian, 'tis the man; but note him.
He was not sad, for he would shine on those
That make their looks by his. He was not merry,
Which seem'd to tell them his remembrance lay
In Egypt with his joy; but between both.   65
O heavenly mingle! Be'st thou sad or merry,
The violence of either thee becomes,
So does it no man else. Met'st thou my posts?
   Alexas. Ay, madam, twenty several messengers.
Why do you send so thick?   70
   Cleopatra.   Who's born that day
When I forget to send to Antony,
Shall die a beggar. Ink and paper, Charmian.
Welcome, my good Alexas. Did I, Charmian,
Ever love Caesar so?   75

   Charmian.   O, that brave Caesar.
   Cleopatra. Be chok'd with such another emphasis!
Say, the brave Antony.
   Charmian.   The valiant Caesar!
   Cleopatra. By Isis, I will give thee bloody teeth,   80
If thou with Caesar paragon again
My man of men.
   Charmian.   By your most gracious pardon,
I sing but after you.
   Cleopatra.   My salad days,   85
When I was green in judgment, cold in blood,
To say as I said then. But come, away,
Get me ink and paper.
He shall have every day a several greeting,
Or I'll unpeople Egypt.   *Exeunt.*

      Enter Pompey, Menecrates, and Menas, in warlike manner.

   Pompey. If the great gods be just, they shall assist
The deeds of justest men.
   Menecrates.   Know, worthy Pompey,
That what they do delay, they not deny.
   Pompey. Whiles we are suitors to their throne, decays   5
The thing we sue for.
   Menecrates.   We, ignorant of ourselves,
Beg often our own harms, which the wise powers
Deny us for our good: so find we profit
By losing of our prayers.   10
   Pompey.   I shall do well:
The people love me, and the sea is mine;
My powers are crescent, and my auguring hope
Says it will come to th' full. Mark Antony
In Egypt sits at dinner, and will make   15
No wars without doors. Caesar gets money where
He loses hearts: Lepidus flatters both,
Of both is flatter'd: but he neither loves,
Nor either cares for him.
   Menas. Caesar and Lepidus are in the field.   20
A mighty strength they carry.
   Pompey. Where have you this? 'Tis false.
   Menas.   From Silvius, sir.
   Pompey. He dreams: I know they are in Rome together,
Looking for Antony. But all the charms of love,   25
Salt Cleopatra, soften thy wan'd lip!
Let witchcraft join with beauty, lust with both!
Tie up the libertine in a field of feasts,
Keep his brain fuming; Epicurean cooks
Sharpen with cloyless sauce his appetite,   30
That sleep and feeding may prorogue his honor
Even till a Lethe'd dullness—

      Enter Varrius.

       How now, Varrius!
   Varrius. This is most certain that I shall deliver:
Mark Antony is every hour in Rome   35
Expected. Since he went from Egypt 'tis
A space for farther travel.

26 wot'st: *knowest*   **27 demi-Atlas;** *Cf. n.*   **28 burgonet:** *helmet*   **33 Broad-fronted:** *with broad forehead*   **35 great Pompey;** *Cf. n.*   **37 aspect:** *look (stressed — ́—)*   **SD Antony:** *F Caesar*   **41 that great med'cine;** *Cf. n.*   **42 tinct:** *tincture, color*   **43 brave:** *splendid*   **49 firm:** *constant*   **51 mend:** *improve* **piece:** *piece out*   **54 arm-gaunt:** *worn thin with hard campaign service*   **56 dumb'd:** *silenced; F dumbe*   **60 disposition:** *mood*   **61 the man:** *the very man*   **68 posts:** *messengers*   **70 thick:** *in quick succession*

81 paragon: *compare*   **85 salad days:** *inexperienced youth*   **SD Enter Pompey:** *begins II.1.3-6*   **Know ... for;** *Cf. n.*   **3 worthy:** *noble*   **8 powers:** *forces*   **13 crescent:** *growing* **auguring:** *prophesying*   **20, 23, 46 Menas:** *F Mene; see Introduction, 2*   **26 Salt:** *lustful* **wan'd:** *faded*   **30 cloyless:** *which will not satiate*   **31, 32 prorogue ... dullness:** *suspend completely his sense of honor*   **32 Lethe'd;** *Cf. n.*   **34 that:** *what* **deliver:** *report*   **36, 37 'tis ... travel:** *there has been time for a longer journey*

Pompey.   I could have given less matter
A better ear. Menas, I did not think
This amorous surfeiter would have donn'd his helm   40
For such a petty war: his soldiership
Is twice the other twain. But let us rear
The higher our opinion, that our stirring
Can from the lap of Egypt's widow pluck
The ne're lust-wearied Antony.   45
    Menas.   I cannot hope
Caesar and Antony shall well greet together;
His wife that's dead did trespasses to Caesar,
His brother warr'd upon him, although I think
Not mov'd by Antony.   50
    Pompey.   I know not, Menas,
How lesser enmities may give way to greater.
Were't not that we stand up against them all,
'Twere pregnant they should square between themselves,
For they have entertained cause enough   55
To draw their swords: but how the fear of us
May ciment their divisions and bind up
The petty difference, we yet not know.
Be't as our gods will have't! It only stands
Our lives upon, to use our strongest hands.   60
Come, Menas.   *Exeunt.*

          Enter Enobarbus and Lepidus.

Lepidus. Good Enobarbus, 'tis a worthy deed,
And shall become you well, to entreat your captain
To soft and gentle speech.
    Enobarbus.   I shall entreat him
To answer like himself: if Caesar move him,   5
Let Antony look over Caesar's head,
And speak as loud as Mars. By Jupiter,
Were I the wearer of Antonio's beard,
I would not shave't today.
    Lepidus. 'Tis not a time for private stomaching.   10
    Enobarbus. Every time serves for the matter that is then
born in't.
    Lepidus. But small to greater matters must give way.
    Enobarbus. Not if the small come first.
    Lepidus. Your speech is passion: but pray you stir   15
No embers up. Here comes the noble Antony.

        Enter Antony and Ventidius.

Enobarbus. And yonder, Caesar.

    Enter Caesar, Maecenas, and Agrippa.

Antony. If we compose well here, to Parthia:
Hark, Ventidius.
    Caesar. I do not know, Maecenas; ask Agrippa.   20
    Lepidus. Noble friends:
That which combin'd us was most great, and let not
A leaner action rend us. What's amiss,
May it be gently heard. When we debate

Our trivial difference loud, we do commit   25
Murther in healing wounds. Then, noble partners,
The rather for I earnestly beseech,
Touch you the sourest points with sweetest terms,
Nor curstness grow to th' matter.
    Antony.   'Tis spoken well.   30
Were we before our armies, and to fight,
I should do thus.   *Flourish.*
    Caesar. Welcome to Rome.
    Antony.   Thank you.
    Caesar.   Sit.   35
    Antony.   Sit, sir.
    Caesar.   Nay, then.
    Antony. I learn, you take things ill which are not so:
Or being, concern you not.
    Caesar.   I must be laugh'd at   40
If, or for nothing or a little, I
Should say myself offended, and with you
Chiefly i' th' world; more laugh'd at that I should
Once name you derogately, when to sound your name
It not concern'd me.   45
    Antony. My being in Egypt, Caesar, what was't to you?
    Caesar. No more than my residing here at Rome
Might be to you in Egypt: yet, if you there
Did practice on my state, your being in Egypt
Might be my question.   50
    Antony.   How intend you, practic'd?
    Caesar. You may be pleas'd to catch at mine intent
By what did here befall me. Your wife and brother
Made wars upon me, and their contestation
Was theme for you, you were the word of war.   55
    Antony. You do mistake your business; my brother
never
Did urge me in his act: I did inquire it,
And have my learning from some true reports
That drew their swords with you. Did he not rather   60
Discredit my authority with yours,
And make the wars alike against my stomach,
Having alike your cause? Of this my letters
Before did satisfy you. If you'll patch a quarrel,
As matter whole you have to make it with,   65
It must not be with this.
    Caesar.   You praise yourself
By laying defects of judgment to me, but
You patch'd up your excuses.
    Antony.   Not so, not so;   70
I know you could not lack, I am certain on't,
Very necessity of this thought, that I,
Your partner in the cause 'gainst which he fought,
Could not with graceful eyes attend those wars
Which fronted mine own peace. As for my wife,   75
I would you had her spirit in such another:
The third o' th' world is yours, which with a snaffle
You may pace easy, but not such a wife.

42, 43 rear ... opinion: *prize ourselves more highly*   44 Egypt's widow: *Cleopatra, young King Ptolemy's widow*   46 hope: *suppose*   47 greet together: *commune amicably*   49 His brother: *Lucius Antonius; cf. n.* warr'd: *F wan'd*   54 pregnant: *very proba-ble* square: *quarrel*   57 ciment: *cement (stressed ⏑ —)*   59, 60 It only ... upon: *Cf. n.* SD Enter Enobarbus: *begins II.2*   2 to entreat: *read 't'entreat'*   5 like himself: *as befits his character*   9 would not shave't: *would dare him (Caesar) to pluck it; cf. n.*   10 stomaching: *resentment*   18 compose: *come to an agreement*   19 Hark: *F Hearke; cf. n.*

29 curstness: *ill humor* grow to: *to be added to*   41 or ... or: *either ... or*   44 derogately: *disparagingly* sound: *mention*   49 practice on: *plot against*   50 question: *concern*   51 intend: *mean*   55 Was theme for you: *was undertaken in your behalf and interest* word: *watchword*   58 urge me: *use my name*   59 reports: *reporters*   62 stomach: *desire*   63 Having ... cause: *since I had the same cause as you (to be displeased with him)*   64 patch: *make out of, i.e. start a quarrel*   65 you have to: *Cf. n.*   74 graceful ... attend: *regard favorably*   75 fronted: *opposed*   77 snaffle: *bridle bit*   78 pace easy: *control easily*

Enobarbus. Would we had all such wives, that the men
might go to wars with the women! 80

Antony. So much uncurbable, her garboils, Caesar,
Made out of her impatience—which not wanted
Shrodenesse of policy too—I grieving grant
Did you too much disquiet; for that you must
But say I could not help it. 85

Caesar. I wrote to you:
When rioting in Alexandria you
Did pocket up my letters, and with taunts
Did gibe my missive out of audience.

Antony. Sir, 90
He fell upon me, ere admitted, then:
Three kings I had newly feasted, and did want
Of what I was i' th' morning; but next day
I told him of myself, which was as much
As to have ask'd him pardon. Let this fellow 95
Be nothing of our strife: if we contend,
Out of our question wipe him.

Caesar. You have broken
The article of your oath, which you shall never
Have tongue to charge me with. 100

Lepidus. Soft, Caesar.

Antony. No, Lepidus, let him speak.
The honor is sacred which he talks on now,
Supposing that I lack'd it. But on, Caesar,
The article of my oath— 105

Caesar. To lend me arms and aid when I requir'd them
The which you both denied.

Antony. Neglected, rather:
And then when poison'd hours had bound me up
From mine own knowledge. As nearly as I may, 110
I'll play the penitent to you. But mine honesty
Shall not make poor my greatness, nor my power
Work without it. Truth is that Fulvia,
To have me out of Egypt, made wars here;
For which myself, the ignorant motive, do 115
So far ask pardon as befits mine honor
To stoop in such a case.

Lepidus. 'Tis noble spoken.

Maecenas. If it might please you, to enforce no further
The griefs between ye: to forget them quite 120
Were to remember that the present need
Speaks to atone you.

Lepidus. Worthily spoken, Maecenas.

Enobarbus. Or, if you borrow one another's love for
the instant, you may, when you hear no more words of 125
Pompey, return it again: you shall have time to wrangle in
when you have nothing else to do.

Antony. Thou art a soldier only; speak no more.

Enobarbus. That truth should be silent I had almost forgot.

Antony. You wrong this presence; therefore speak no more.

Enobarbus. Go to, then; your considerate stone.

Caesar. I do not much dislike the matter, but

The manner of his speech: for't cannot be
We shall remain in friendship, our conditions
So diff'ring in their acts. Yet, if I knew 135
What hoop should hold us staunch, from edge to edge
O' th' world I would pursue it.

Agrippa. Give me leave, Caesar.

Caesar. Speak, Agrippa.

Agrippa. Thou hast a sister by the mother's side, 140
Admir'd Octavia; great Mark Antony
Is now a widower.

Caesar. Say not so, Agrippa:
If Cleopatra heard you, your reproof
Were well deserv'd of rashness. 145

Antony. I am not married, Caesar: let me hear
Agrippa further speak.

Agrippa. To hold you in perpetual amity,
To make you brothers, and to knit your hearts
With an unslipping knot, take Antony 150
Octavia to his wife: whose beauty claims
No worse a husband than the best of men: whose
Virtue and whose general graces speak
That which none else can utter. By this marriage,
All little jealousies which now seem great, 155
And all great fears, which now import their dangers,
Would then be nothing. Truths would be tales,
Where now half tales be truths: her love to both
Would each to other and all loves to both
Draw after her. Pardon what I have spoke, 160
For 'tis a studied, not a present thought,
By duty ruminated.

Antony. Will Caesar speak?

Caesar. Not till he hears how Antony is touch'd
With what is spoke already. 165

Antony. What power is in Agrippa,
If I would say, 'Agrippa, be it so,'
To make this good?

Caesar. The power of Caesar,
And his power unto Octavia. 170

Antony. May I never
To this good purpose that so fairly shows
Dream of impediment! Let me have thy hand;
Further this act of grace, and from this hour
The heart of brothers govern in our loves 175
And sway our great designs.

Caesar. There's my hand.
A sister I bequeath you, whom no brother
Did ever love so dearly. Let her live
To join our kingdoms and our hearts, and never 180
Fly off our loves again.

Lepidus. Happily, amen.

Antony. I did not think to draw my sword 'gainst Pompey,
For he hath laid strange courtesies and great
Of late upon me. I must thank him only, 185
Lest my remembrance suffer ill report;
At heel of that, defy him.

Lepidus. Time calls upon's.

81 garboils: *disturbances* 83 Shrodenesse: *shrewdness* 89 missive: *messenger* 92 I
had: *read 'I'd'* 92, 93 did want . . . morning: *lacked mastery of myself which I had possessed
in the morning* 94 told him of myself: *explained my condition to him* 96 nothing
of: *irrelevant to* 97 question: *debate* 103, 104 The honor . . . it; *Cf. n.* 110 From
mine own knowledge: *(kept me) from khowing what I was doing* 111–113 But . . . without
it; *Cf. n.* 113, 114 Fulvia . . . here; *Cf. n.* 120 griefs: *grievances* 122 atone: *reconcile.* 123 Worthily: *nobly* 130 presence: *august company* 131 Go to, then: *very well*
considerate stone: *I will think but remain dumb as a stone*

134 conditions: *dispositions* 140 by the mother's side; *Cf. n.* 143 not so: *F not,
say* 144 reproof: *F proofe* 145 deserv'd of rashness: *deserved because of your rashness
(in speaking as you do)* 155 jealousies: *suspicions* 156 import: *carry with them*
157, 158 Truths . . . truths; *Cf. n.* 161 present: *sudden* 172 so fairly shows: *looks so
promising* 184 strange: *rare* 186 remembrance: *memory of favors shown*

Of us must Pompey presently be sought,
Or else he seeks out us.   *190*
    Antony.   Where lies he?
    Caesar. About the Mount Mesena.
    Antony. What is his strength by land?
    Caesar. Great and increasing:
But by sea he is an absolute master.   *195*
    Antony. So is the fame.
Would we had spoke together! Haste we for it:
Yet, ere we put ourselves in arms, dispatch we
The business we have talk'd of.
    Caesar.   With most gladness;   *200*
And do invite you to my sister's view,
Whither straight I'll lead you.
    Antony. Let us, Lepidus, not lack your company.
    Lepidus. Noble Antony, not sickness should detain me.
                 Flourish. Exit omnes. Mane[n]t
                 Enobarbus, Agrippa, Maecenas.
    Maecenas. Welcome from Egypt, sir.   *205*
    Enobarbus. Half the heart of Caesar, worthy Maecenas. My
honourable friend, Agrippa.
    Agrippa. Good Enobarbus.
    Maecenas. We have cause to be glad that matters are so well
digested. You stayed well by't in Egypt.   *210*
    Enobarbus. Ay, sir, we did sleep day out of countenance,
and made the night light with drinking.
    Maecenas. Eight wild boars roasted whole at a breakfast: and
but twelve persons there. Is this true?
    Enobarbus. This was but as a fly by an eagle: we had   *215*
much more monstrous matter of feast, which worthily
deserved noting.
    Maecenas. She's a most triumphant lady, if report be square
to her.
    Enobarbus. When she first met Mark Antony, she purs'd *220*
up his heart, upon the river of Cydnus.
    Agrippa. There she appear'd indeed, or my reporter devis'd
well for her.
    Enobarbus. I will tell you.
The barge she sat in, like a burnish'd throne   *225*
Burnt on the water: the poop was beaten gold,
Purple the sails, and so perfumed that
The winds were lovesick with them; the oars were silver,
Which to the tune of flutes kept stroke, and made
The water which they beat to follow faster,   *230*
As amorous of their strokes. For her own person,
It beggar'd all description; she did lie
In her pavilion, cloth of gold of tissue,
Orepicturing that Venus where we see
The fancy outwork nature. On each side her   *235*
Stood pretty dimpled boys, like smiling Cupids,
With divers-color'd fans whose wind did seem
To glow the delicate cheeks which they did cool,
And what they undid did.
    Agrippa.   O, rare for Antony!   *240*
    Enobarbus. Her gentlewomen, like the Nereides,
So many mermaids tended her i' th' eyes,
And made their bends adornings. At the helm
A seeming mermaid steers: the silken tackle
Swell with the touches of those flower-soft hands   *245*
That yarely frame the office. From the barge
A strange invisible perfume hits the sense
Of the adjacent wharfs. The city cast
Her people out upon her: and Antony,
Enthron'd i' th' market place, did sit alone,   *250*
Whistling to th' air; which, but for vacancy,
Had gone to gaze on Cleopatra too
And made a gap in nature.
    Agrippa.   Rare Egyptian!
    Enobarbus. Upon her landing, Antony sent to her,   *255*
Invited her to supper: she replied,
It should be better he became her guest,
Which she entreated. Our courteous Antony,
Whom ne're the word of 'No' woman hard speak,
Being barber'd ten times o're, goes to the feast,   *260*
And for his ordinary pays his heart
For what his eyes eat only.
    Agrippa.   Royal wench!
She made great Caesar lay his sword to bed;
He plough'd her, and she cropp'd.   *265*
    Enobarbus.   I saw her once
Hop forty paces through the public street;
And having lost her breath, she spoke, and panted
That she did make defect perfection,
And, breathless, power breathe forth.   *270*
    Maecenas. Now Antony must leave her utterly.
    Enobarbus. Never; he will not:
Age cannot wither her, nor custom stale
Her infinite variety: other women cloy
The appetites they feed, but she makes hungry   *275*
Where most she satisfies. For vildest things
Become themselves in her, that the holy priests
Bless her when she is riggish.
    Maecenas. If beauty, wisdom, modesty, can settle
The heart of Antony, Octavia is   *280*
A blessed lottery to him.
    Agrippa.   Let us go.
Good Enobarbus, make yourself my guest
Whilst you abide here.
    Enobarbus.   Humbly, sir, I thank you.   *Exeunt.*

       Enter Antony, Caesar, Octavia between them.

    Antony. The world and my great office will sometimes
Divide me from your bosom.
    Octavia.   All which time
Before the gods my knee shall bow my prayers
To them for you.   *5*
    Antony.   Good night, sir. My Octavia
Read not my blemishes in the world's report:

---

189 **Of:** *by* **presently:** *immediately*   192 **Mesena:** *Misenum, a harbor in southern Italy*   196 **fame:** *rumor*   200 **most:** *greatest*   201 **do:** *I do*   206 **Half . . . Caesar;** *Cf. n.*   210 **disgested:** *digested* **stayed well by't:** *kept it up*   213 **Eight wild boars;** *Cf. n.*   215 **by:** *in comparison with*   218 **triumphant:** *magnificent* **square:** *just, fair*   220 **purs'd up:** *pocketed*   221 **Cydnus:** *F Sidnis; V.2.272, Cidrus*   222 **devis'd:** *invented*   224–235 **I will . . . nature;** *Cf. n.*   231 **For:** *as for*   233 **cloth of gold of tissue:** *rich cloth interwoven with thread of gold*   234 **Orepicturing:** *surpassing the picture of*   235 **outwork:** *excel*   238 **glow:** *make hot; F gloue*   239 **what they undid did;** *Cf. n.*

242 **tended . . . eyes:** *waited upon her every wish*   243 **made . . . adornings;** *Cf. n.*   246 **yarely:** *nimbly.* **frame:** *perform*   259 **hard:** *heard*   261 **ordinary:** *dinner.*   262 **eat:** *ate*   269 **That:** *so that* **defect perfection:** *she made her defective (because panting) speech perfection*   270 **breathe:** *did breathe*   273 **stale:** *make stale*   274 **infinite variety;** *Cf. n.*   276 **vildest:** *vilest*   278 **riggish:** *wanton*   281 **lottery:** *prize*   SD **Enter Antony:** *begins II.3*

I have not kept my square, but that to come
Shall all be done by th' rule. Good night, dear lady.
  Octavia. Good night, sir.   *10*
  Caesar. Good night.   *Exit [with Octavia].*

    Enter Soothsayer.

  Antony. Now, sirrah; you do wish yourself in Egypt?
  Soothsayer. Would I had never come from thence, nor you
thither!
  Antony. If you can, your reason?   *15*
  Soothsayer. I see it in my motion, have it not in my tongue,
But yet hie you to Egypt again.
  Antony. Say to me, whose fortunes shall rise higher,
Caesar's or mine?
  Soothsayer. Caesar's.   *20*
Therefore, O Antony, stay not by his side.
Thy demon, that thy spirit which keeps thee, is
Noble, courageous, high, unmatchable,
Where Caesar's is not. But near him thy angel
Becomes a fear, as being o'repower'd; therefore   *25*
Make space enough between you.
  Antony.   Speak this no more.
  Soothsayer. To none but thee: no more but when to thee.
If thou dost play with him at any game
Thou art sure to lose; and of that natural luck   *30*
He beats thee 'gainst the odds. Thy luster thickens
When he shines by: I say again, thy spirit
Is all afraid to govern thee near him,
But he away, 'tis noble.
  Antony.   Get thee gone: *35*
Say to Ventidius I would speak with him. *Exit [Soothsayer].*
He shall to Parthia. Be it art or hap,
He hath spoken true. The very dice obey him,
And in our sports my better cunning faints
Under his chance; if we draw lots he speeds,   *40*
His cocks do win the battle still of mine
When it is all to nought: and his quails ever
Beat mine, inhoop'd, at odds. I will to Egypt:
And though I make this marriage for my peace,
I' th' east my pleasure lies. O, come Ventidius,   *45*

    Enter Ventidius.

You must to Parthia; your commission's ready:
Follow me, and receive't.   *Exeunt.*

   Enter Lepidus, Maecenas, and Agrippa.

  Lepidus. Trouble yourselves no further: pray you hasten
Your generals after.
  Agrippa.   Sir, Mark Antony
Will e'ne but kiss Octavia, and we'll follow.
  Lepidus. Till I shall see you in your soldier's dress, *5*
Which will become you both, farewell.
  Maecenas.   We shall,
As I conceive the journey, be at Mount
Before you, Lepidus.

  Lepidus.   Your way is shorter; *10*
My purposes do draw me much about:
You'll win two days upon me.
  Both. Sir, good success!
  Lepidus. Farewell.   *Exeunt.*

  Enter Cleopatra, Charmian, Iras, and Alexas.

  Cleopatra. Give me some music: music, moody food
Of us that trade in love.
  Attendant.   The music, ho!

    Enter Mardian the eunuch.

  Cleopatra. Let it alone, let's to billiards: come, Charmian.
  Charmian. My arm is sore; best play with Mardian. *5*
  Cleopatra. As well a woman with an eunuch play'd
As with a woman. Come, you'll play with me, sir?
  Mardian. As well as I can, madam.
  Cleopatra. And when good will is show'd, though't come
too short   *10*
The actor may plead pardon. I'll none now.
Give me mine angle; we'll to th' river: there,
My music playing far off, I will betray
Tawny-finn'd fishes; my bended hook shall pierce
Their slimy jaws; and as I draw them up   *15*
I'll think them every one an Antony,
And say, 'Ah, ha! y'are caught.'
  Charmian.   'Twas merry when
You wager'd on your angling; when your diver
Did hang a salt-fish on his hook, which he   *20*
With fervency drew up.
  Cleopatra.   That time! O times!
I laugh'd him out of patience: and that night
I laugh'd him into patience, and next morn,
Ere the ninth hour, I drunk him to his bed;   *25*
Then put my tires and mantles on him, whilst
I wore his sword Philippan.

    Enter a Messenger.

     O, from Italy!
Ram thou thy fruitful tidings in mine ears,
That long time have bin barren.   *30*
  Messenger.   Madam, madam—
  Cleopatra. Antonio's dead:
If thou say so villain, thou kill'st thy mistress:
But well and free, if thou so yield him,
There is gold and here   *35*
My bluest veins to kiss, a hand that kings
Have lipp'd and trembl'd kissing.
  Messenger. First, madam, he is well.
  Cleopatra. Why, there's more gold.
But sirrah mark, we use   *40*
To say the dead are well: bring it to that,
The gold I give thee will I melt and pour
Down thy ill-uttering throat.
  Messenger. Good madam, hear me.

---

8 square: *bounds of prudence* **12 sirrah:** *familiar form of 'sir,' used sometimes contemptuously,*
sometimes affectionately **16 I see . . . tongue;** *Cf. n.* **22–25 Thy demon . . . o'repow-**
er'd; *Cf. n.* **29–34 If . . . 'tis noble;** *Cf. n.* **31 thickens:** *grows dim* **32 by:** *near*
by **34 away:** *F alway* **SD Ventidius:** *F Ventigius; III.1, Ventidius* **37 art:** *mag-*
ic **hap:** *chance* **39 better cunning:** *superior skill* **40 speeds:** *is successful* **41 His**
cocks; *Cf. n.* **42 When . . . nought;** *Cf. n.* **43 inhoop'd:** *confined in hoops* **SD**
Enter Lepidus: *begins II.4* **8 at Mount:** *at the Mount (i.e. Misenum)*

11 much about: *in a roundabout way* **SD Enter Cleopatra:** *begins II.5* **1 moody:**
melancholy **13 betray:** *snare* **14 Tawny-finn'd:** *F Tawny fine* **17–21 'Twas . . .**
drew up; *Cf. n.* **26 tires:** *head-dresses* **27 Philippan;** *Cf. n.* **32–35 Antonio's . . .**
here; *Cf. n.* **34 yield:** *report* **38 well:** *in heaven* **41 bring it to that:** *say that that*
is your meaning

Cleopatra.   Well, to go, I will;   45
But there's no goodness in thy face; if Antony
Be free and healthful, so tart a favor
To trumpet such good tidings! if not well,
Thou shouldst come like a Fury crown'd with snakes
Not like a formal man.   50
    Messenger.   Will't please you hear me?
    Cleopatra. I have a mind to strike thee ere thou speak'st:
Yet, if thou say Antony lives, 'tis well,
Or friends with Caesar, or not captive to him,
I'll set thee in a shower of gold, and hail   55
Rich pearls upon thee.
    Messenger.   Madam, he's well.
    Cleopatra.   Well said.
    Messenger. And friends with Caesar.
    Cleopatra.   Th'art an honest man.   60
    Messenger. Caesar and he are greater friends than ever.
    Cleopatra. Make thee a fortune from me.
    Messenger.   But yet, madam—
    Cleopatra. I do not like 'but yet,' it does allay
The good precedence; fie upon 'but yet!'   65
'But yet' is as a gaoler to bring forth
Some monstrous malefactor. Prithee, friend,
Pour out the pack of matter to mine ear,
The good and bad together: he's friends with Caesar,
In state of health, thou say'st, and thou say'st, free.   70
    Messenger. Free, madam! no; I made no such report:
He's bound unto Octavia.
    Cleopatra.   For what good turn?
    Messenger. For the best turn i' th' bed.
    Cleopatra.   I am pale, Charmian.
    Messenger. Madam, he's married to Octavia.
    Cleopatra. The most infectious pestilence upon thee!
                            Strikes him down.
    Messenger. Good madam, patience.
    Cleopatra.   What say you?
                              Strikes him.
Hence, horrible villain, or I'll spurn thine eyes   80
Like balls before me; I'll unhair thy head:
                    She hales him up and down.
Thou shalt be whipp'd with wire, and stew'd in brine,
Smarting in ling'ring pickle.
    Messenger.   Gracious madam,
I that do bring the news made not the match.   85
    Cleopatra. Say 'tis not so, a province I will give thee,
And make thy fortunes proud: the blow thou hadst
Shall make thy peace for moving me to rage,
And I will boot thee with what gift beside
Thy modesty can beg.   90
    Messenger.   He's married, madam.
    Cleopatra. Rogue, thou hast liv'd too long.
                              Draw a knife.
    Messenger.   Nay, then I'll run.
What mean you, madam? I have made no fault.   *Exit.*
    Charmian. Good madam, keep yourself within yourself;   95
The man is innocent.
    Cleopatra. Some innocents 'scape not the thunderbolt.

Melt Egypt into Nile! and kindly creatures
Turn all to serpents! Call the slave again:
Though I am mad, I will not bite him. Call!   100
    Charmian. He is afeard to come.
    Cleopatra.   I will not hurt him.
                            [Exit Charmian.]
These hands do lack nobility, that they strike
A meaner than myself; since I myself
Have given myself the cause. Come hither, sir.   105

          Enter [Charmian and] the Messenger again.

Though it be honest, it is never good
To bring bad news: give to a gracious message
An host of tongues, but let ill tidings tell
Themselves when they be felt.
    Messenger.   I have done my duty.   110
    Cleopatra. Is he married?
I cannot hate thee worser than I do
If thou again say 'Yes.'
    Messenger.   He's married, madam.
    Cleopatra. The gods confound thee! dost thou hold   115
there still?
    Messenger. Should I lie, madam?
    Cleopatra.   O, I would thou didst,
So half my Egypt were submerg'd and made
A cesterne for scal'd snakes. Go, get thee hence;   120
Hadst thou Narcissus in thy face, to me
Thou wouldst appear most ugly. He is married?
    Messenger. I crave your highness' pardon.
    Cleopatra.   He is married?
    Messenger. Take no offense that I would not offend you;   125
To punish me for what you make me do
Seems much unequal; he's married to Octavia.
    Cleopatra. O, that his fault should make a knave of thee,
That art not what th'art sure of. Get thee hence;
The marchandise which thou has brought from Rome   130
Are all too dear for me.
Lie they upon thy hand, and be undone by 'em!
                          [Exit Messenger.]
    Charmian. Good your highness, patience.
    Cleopatra. In praising Antony I have disprais'd Caesar.
    Charmian. Many times, madam.   135
    Cleopatra. I am paid for't now. Lead me from hence.
I faint. O Iras! Charmian! 'Tis no matter.
Go to the fellow, good Alexas; bid him
Report the feature of Octavia: her years,
Her inclination, let him not leave out   140
The color of her hair. Bring me word quickly.   *[Exit Alexas.]*
Let him forever go—let him not—Charmian!
Though he be painted one way like a Gorgon,
The other way's a Mars. *[To Mardian.]* Bid you Alexas
Bring me word how tall she is. Pity me, Charmian,   145
But do not speak to me. Lead me to my chamber.   *Exeunt.*

---

98 kindly: *benign*   **107 gracious:** *pleasing*   **115 confound:** *destroy*   **119 So:** *even though*   **120 cesterne:** *cistern*   **121 Narcissus;** *Cf. n.*   **125 Take ... you;** *Cf. n.*   **127 much unequal:** *very unjust*   **129 That ... sure of;** *Cf. n.*   **132 Lie ... hand:** *may they remain unsold (your merchandise)*   **undone:** *ruined*   **140 inclination:** *disposition*   **142 him:** *i.e. Antony*   **144 way's:** *way as*

---

47 so tart a favor: *so sour a countenance*   **50 formal:** *normally shaped*   **60 honest: worthy*   **65 precedence:** *earlier report*   **66 gaoler:** *jailer*   **80 spurn:** *kick.*   SD **hales: drags**   **89 boot thee:** *make amends to thee*   **what:** *whatever*   **90 modesty:** *moderation*

Flourish. Enter Pompey at one door, with drum and trumpet: at another Caesar, Lepidus, Antony, Enobarbus, Maecenas, Agrippa, Menas, with Soldiers marching.

Pompey. Your hostages I have, so have you mine;
And we shall talk before we fight.

 Caesar.   Most meet
That first we come to words, and therefore have we
Our written purposes before us sent;   *5*
Which if thou hast consider'd, let us know
If 'twill tie up thy discontented sword,
And carry back to Sicily much tall youth
That else must perish here.

 Pompey.   To you all three, *10*
The senators alone of this great world,
Chief factors for the gods, I do not know
Wherefore my father should revengers want,
Having a son and friends, since Julius Caesar,
Who at Philippi the good Brutus ghosted,   *15*
There saw you laboring for him. What was't
That mov'd pale Cassius to conspire? And what
Made the all-honor'd, honest Roman, Brutus,
With the arm'd rest, courtiers of beauteous freedom,
To drench the capitol, but that they would   *20*
Have one man but a man? And that is it
Hath made me rig my navy, at whose burthen
The anger'd ocean foams, with which I meant
To scourge th' ingratitude that despiteful Rome
Cast on my noble father.   *25*

 Caesar.   Take your time.

 Antony. Thou canst not fear us, Pompey, with thy sails;
We'll speak with thee at sea. At land, thou know'st
How much we do o'recount thee.

 Pompey.   At land, indeed, *30*
Thou dost o'recount me of my father's house:
But since the cuckoo builds not for himself,
Remain in't as thou mayst.

 Lepidus.   Be pleas'd to tell us—
For this is from the present—how you take   *35*
The offers we have sent you.

 Caesar.   There's the point.

 Antony. Which do not be entreated to,
But weigh what it is worth embrac'd.

 Caesar. And what may follow to try a larger fortune. *40*

 Pompey. You have made me offer
Of Sicily, Sardinia; and I must
Rid all the sea of pirates; then, to send
Measures of wheat to Rome; this 'greed upon,
To part with unhack'd edges, and bear back   *45*
Our targes undinted.

 Omnes.   That's our offer.

 Pompey.   Know, then,
I came before you here a man prepar'd
To take this offer; but Mark Antony   *50*
Put me to some impatience. Though I lose

The praise of it by telling, you must know,
When Caesar and your brother were at blows,
Your mother came to Sicily and did find
Her welcome friendly.   *55*

 Antony.   I have heard it, Pompey,
And am well studied for a liberal thanks
Which I do owe you.

 Pompey.   Let me have your hand:
I did not think, sir, to have met you here.   *60*

 Antony. The beds i' th' east are soft; and thanks to you,
That call'd me timelier than my purpose hither,
For I have gain'd by't.

 Caesar.   Since I saw you last,
There's a change upon you.   *65*

 Pompey. Well, I know not
What counts harsh Fortune casts upon my face,
But in my bosom shall she never come
To make my heart her vassal.

 Lepidus.   Well met here. *70*

 Pompey. I hope so, Lepidus. Thus we are agreed:
I crave our composition may be written
And seal'd between us.

 Caesar.   That's the next to do.

 Pompey. We'll feast each other ere we part, and let's *75*
Draw lots who shall begin.

 Antony.   That will I, Pompey.

 Pompey. No, Antony, take the lot:
But, first or last, your fine Egyptian cookery
Shall have the fame. I have heard that Julius Caesar *80*
Grew fat with feasting there.

 Antony.   You have heard much.

 Pompey. I have fair meanings, sir.

 Antony.   And fair words to them.

 Pompey. Then, so much have I heard;   *85*
And I have heard Apollodorus carried—

 Enobarbus. No more of that: he did so.

 Pompey.   What, I pray you?

 Enobarbus. A certain queen to Caesar in a mattress.

 Pompey. I know thee now; how far'st thou, soldier? *90*

 Enobarbus.   Well;
And well am like to do, for I perceive
Four feasts are toward.

 Pompey.   Let me shake thy hand;
I never hated thee: I have seen thee fight,   *95*
When I have envied thy behavior.

 Enobarbus. Sir, I never lov'd you much, but I ha'
prais'd ye
When you have well deserv'd ten times as much
As I have said you did.   *100*

 Pompey.   Enjoy thy plainness,
It nothing ill becomes thee.
Aboard my galley I invite you all:
Will you lead, lords?

 All.   Show's the way, sir.   *105*

 Pompey.   Come.

   Exeunt. Mane[n]t Enobarbus and Menas.

SD Enter Pompey: *begins II.6* **3 meet:** *proper* **9 tall:** *sturdy, courageous* **12 factors:** *agents* **15 ghosted:** *appeared as a ghost to* **18 Made the all-honor'd:** *F Made all-honor'd* **21 is:** *F his* **27 fear** *frighten* **28 speak:** *meet in conflict* **31 o'recount;** *Cf. n.* **30–33 At land . . . mayst;** *Cf. n.* **32 cuckoo:** *the cuckoo never builds a nest but lays its eggs in the nests of other birds* **33 mayst:** *canst* **35 from the present:** *irrelevant to the present purpose* **39 embrac'd:** *if accepted* **40 to . . . fortune;** *Cf. n.* **45 To part . . . edges:** *to depart without battle* **46 targes:** *shields* **47 Omnes:** *i.e. Caesar, Antony, Lepidus*

54, 55 Your . . . friendly; *Cf. n.* **57 am well . . . thanks:** *I am ready to thank you very much* **62 timelier:** *earlier* **67 counts;** *Cf. n.* **72 composition:** *agreement* **80 Shall . . . fame:** *shall have the opportunity to show that it deserves its reputation; shall win the prize* **87 more of that:** *F more that* **93 toward:** *in prospect* **102 nothing:** *not at all* **105 All:** *i.e. the triumvirs*

Menas. Thy father, Pompey, would ne're have made this treaty. You and I have known, sir.

Enobarbus. At sea, I think.

Menas. We have, sir.   *110*

Enobarbus. You have done well by water.

Menas. And you by land.

Enobarbus. I will praise any man that will praise me; though it cannot be denied what I have done by land.

Menas. Nor what I have done by water.   *115*

Enobarbus. Yes, something you can deny for your own safety; you have been a great thief by sea.

Menas. And you by land.

Enobarbus. There I deny my land service. But give me your hand, Menas; if our eyes had authority, here they   *120* might take two thieves kissing.

Menas. All men's faces are true, whatsomere their hands are.

Enobarbus. But there is never a fair woman has a true face.

Menas. No slander; they steal hearts.

Enobarbus. We came hither to fight with you.   *125*

Menas. For my part, I am sorry it is turn'd to a drinking. Pompey doth this day laugh away his fortune.

Enobarbus. If he do, sure he cannot weep't back again.

Menas. Y' have said, sir. We looked not for Mark Antony here: pray you, is he married to Cleopatra?   *130*

Enobarbus. Caesar's sister is call'd Octavia.

Menas. True, sir; she was the wife of Caius Marcellus.

Enobarbus. But she is now the wife of Marcus Antonius.

Menas. Pray ye, sir?

Enobarbus. 'Tis true.   *135*

Menas. Then is Caesar and he for ever knit together.

Enobarbus. If I were bound to divine of this unity, I would not prophesy so.

Menas. I think the policy of that purpose made more in the marriage than the love of the parties.   *140*

Enobarbus. I think so too. But you shall find the band that seems to tie their friendship together will be the very strangler of their amity: Octavia is of a holy, cold, and still conversation.

Menas. Who would not have his wife so?

Enobarbus. Not he that himself is not so: which is Mark   *145* Antony. He will to his Egyptian dish again: then shall the sighs of Octavia blow the fire up in Caesar, and, as I said before, that which is the strength of their amity shall prove the immediate author of their variance. Antony will use his affection where it is. He married but his occasion here.   *150*

Menas. And thus it may be. Come, sir, will you aboard? I have a health for you.

Enobarbus. I shall take it, sir: we have us'd our throats in Egypt.

Menas. Come, let's away.   *Exeunt.*

Music plays. Enter two or three Servants, with a banket.

1. [Servant.] Here they'll be, man. Some o' their plants are ill-rooted already; the least wind i' th' world will blow them down.

2. [Servant.] Lepidus is high-color'd.

1. [Servant.] They have made him drink alms-drink.

2. [Servant.] As they pinch one another by the   *5* disposition, he cries out, 'No more'; reconciles them to his entreaty, and himself to th' drink.

1. [Servant.] But it raises the greater war between him and his discretion.

2. [Servant.] Why, this it is to have a name in great   *10* men's fellowship. I had as live have a reed that will do me no service as a partisan I could not heave.

1. [Servant.] To be call'd into a huge sphere and not to be seen to move in't are the holes where eyes should be, which pitifully disaster the cheeks.   *15*

A sennet sounded. Enter Caesar, Antony, Pompey, Lepidus, Agrippa, Maecenas, Enobarbus, Menas, with other Captains.

Antony. Thus do they, sir: they take the flow o' th' Nile
By certain scales i' th' pyramid; they know
By th' height, the lowness, or the mean, if dearth
Or foison follow. The higher Nilus swells
The more it promises: as it ebbs, the seedsman   *20*
Upon the slime and ooze scatters his grain,
And shortly comes to harvest.

Lepidus. Y' have strange serpents there?

Antony. Ay, Lepidus.

Lepidus. Your serpent of Egypt is bred now of your   *25*
mud by the operation of your sun: so is your crocodile.

Antony. They are so.

Pompey. Sit—and some wine! A health to Lepidus!

Lepidus. I am not so well as I should be, but I'll ne're out.

Enobarbus. Not till you have slept; I fear me you'll be   *30*
in till then.

Lepidus. Nay, certainly, I have heard the Ptolemies' pyramises
are very goodly things; without contradiction I have heard that.

Menas. Pompey, a word.

Pompey.   Say in mine ear, what is't?   *35*

Menas. Forsake thy seat, I do beseech thee, captain,

          Whispers in's ear.

And hear me speak a word.

Pompey.   Forbear me till anon.
This wine for Lepidus!

Lepidus. What manner o' thing is your crocodile?   *40*

Antony. It is shap'd, sir, like itself, and it is as broad as it
hath breadth; it is just so high as it is, and moves with it own
organs. It lives by that which nourisheth it, and the elements
once out of it, it transmigrates.

Lepidus. What color is it of?   *45*

Antony. Of it own color too.

Lepidus. 'Tis a strange serpent.

Antony. 'Tis so, and the tears of it are wet.

Caesar. Will this description satisfy him?

Antony. With the health that Pompey gives him, else he   *50*
is a very epicure.   *[Menas whispers again.]*

Pompey. Go hang, sir, hang! Tell me of that? away!
Do as I bid you. Where's this cup I call'd for?

---

108 **known:** *met*   120 **authority:** *i.e. to arrest criminals*   121 **take:** *arrest*   **two thieves kissing:** *our hands clasping (with perhaps a glance at ll. 116, 117)*   122 **true:** *honest.*   **whatsomere:** *whatsome'er*   129 **Y' have said:** *you are perfectly right*   134 **Pray ye, sir?:** *phrase expressing surprise and incredulity*   137 **unity:** *compact*   139 **made more in:** *had more to do with*   143 **conversation:** *demeanor, disposition*   149, 150 **will use . . . is:** *will keep loving where he now loves, i.e. in Egypt*   150 **occasion:** *convenience*   SD **Music plays:** *begins II.7.*   1 **o' their:** *F o' th' their*   1 **plants:** *pun on two meanings: 'young trees,' and 'soles of the feet'*

4 **alms-drink:** *toast drunk for one too infirm to answer a pledge*   5 **As . . . disposition:** *whenever they start a quarrel*   11 **live:** *lief*   12 **partisan:** *spear, pike*   13–15 **To be call'd . . . cheeks;** *Cf. n.*   15 **disaster:** *ruin*   SD **sennet:** *set of notes on trumpet announcing the approach or entrance of an important person*   **Menas:** *F Menes*   17 **scales:** *graduations*   18 **dearth:** *scarcity*   19 **foison:** *abundance*   29 **I'll ne're out:** *I'll never give up*   32 **pyramises;** *Cf. n.*   33 **goodly:** *handsome*   SD **Whisper . . . ear:** *F prints SD after anon, l. 38*   42 **it own:** *its own*   43 **elements:** *principle of life*   44 **transmigrates:** *dies (with facetious allusion to doctrine of transmigration of souls)*

Menas. If for the sake of merit thou wilt hear me,
Rise from thy stool.   55
   Pompey.   I think th' art mad. The matter?
   Menas. I have ever held my cap off to thy fortunes.
   Pompey. Thou hast serv'd me with much faith. What's else
to say?
Be jolly, lords.   60
   Antony.   These quicksands, Lepidus,
Keep off them, for you sink.
   Menas. Wilt thou be lord of all the world?
   Pompey.   What sayst thou?
   Menas. Wilt thou be lord of the whole world? That's twice.
   Pompey. How should that be?
   Menas.   But entertain it,
And though thou think me poor, I am the man
Will give thee all the world.
   Pompey.   Hast thou drunk well?   70
   Menas. No, Pompey, I have kept me from the cup.
Thou art, if thou dar'st be, the earthly Jove:
Whatere the ocean pales or sky inclips
Is thine, if thou wilt ha't.
   Pompey.   Show me which way.   75
   Menas. These three world-sharers, these competitors,
Are in thy vessel. Let me cut the cable,
And when we are put off fall to their throats:
All there is thine.
   Pompey.   Ah, this thou shouldst have done,   80
And not have spoke on't. In me 'tis villainy;
In thee't had bin good service. Thou must know
'Tis not my profit that does lead mine honor;
Mine honor it. Repent that ere thy tongue
Hath so betray'd thine act. Being done unknown,   85
I should have found it afterwards well done,
But must condemn it now. Desist, and drink.
   Menas. [Aside.] For this,
I'll never follow thy pall'd fortunes more.
Who seeks and will not take when once 'tis offer'd   90
Shall never find it more.
   Pompey.   This health to Lepidus!
   Antony. Bear him ashore. I'll pledge it for him, Pompey.
   Enobarbus. Here's to thee, Menas!
   Menas.   Enobarbus, welcome!   95
   Pompey. Fill till the cup be hid.
   Enobarbus. There's a strong fellow, Menas.
   Menas. Why?
   Enobarbus. A' bears the third part of the world, man;
see'st not?   100
   Menas. The third part then is drunk; would it were all,
That it might go on wheels!
   Enobarbus. Drink thou; increase the reels.
   Menas. Come.
   Pompey. This is not yet an Alexandrian feast.   105
   Antony. It ripens towards it. Strike the vessels, ho!
Here's to Caesar!
   Caesar.   I could well forbear't.
It's monstrous labor, when I wash my brain

And it grows fouler.   110
   Antony.   Be a child o' th' time.
   Caesar. Possess it, I'll make answer:
But I had rather fast from all four days
Than drink so much in one.
   Enobarbus. Ha! my brave emperor;   115
Shall we dance now the Egyptian Bacchanals,
And celebrate our drink?
   Pompey.   Let's ha't, good soldier.
   Antony. Come, let's all take hands,
Till that the conquering wine hath steep'd our sense   120
In soft and delicate Lethe.
   Enobarbus.   All take hands.
Make battery to our ears with the loud music;
The while I'll place you; then the boy shall sing.
The holding every man shall bear as loud   125
As his strong sides can volley.
             Music plays. Enobarbus places them hand in hand.

    The Song
   Come, thou monarch of the vine,
   Plumpy Bacchus, with pink eyne!
   In thy fats our cares be drown'd,   130
   With thy grapes our hairs be crown'd.
     Cup us, till the world go round,
     Cup us, till the world go round!

   Caesar. What would you more? Pompey, good night.
Good brother,   135
Let me request you off: our graver business
Frowns at this levity. Gentle lords, let's part;
You see we have burnt our cheeks; strong Enobarb
Is weaker than the wine, and mine own tongue
Splits what it speaks; the wild disguise hath almost   140
Antick'd us all. What needs more words? Good night.
Good Antony, your hand.
   Pompey. I'll try you on the shore.
   Antony.   And shall, sir. Give's your hand.
   Pompey. O, Antony, you have my father's house,   145
But, what, we are friends! Come down into the boat.
   Enobarbus. Take heed you fall not. Menas, I'll not on shore.
           [Exeunt Pompey, Caesar, Antony, and Attendants.]
   Menas. No, to my cabin.
These drums! these trumpets, flutes! what!
Let Neptune hear we bid a loud farewell   150
To these great fellows. Sound and be hang'd! Sound out!
              Sound a flourish with drums.
   Enobarbus. Hoo! says a. There's my cap.
   Menas. Hoa! noble captain! Come.   *Exeunt.*

Enter Ventidius, as it were in triumph, the dead body of Pacorus
borne before him.

   Ventidius. Now, darting Parthia, art thou struck; and now
Pleas'd fortune does of Marcus Crassus' death

112 Possess it: *drink it off*   **I'll . . . answer:** *I'll drink to your pledge*   **115 brave:** *magnifi-*
cent   **121 Lethe:** *forgetfulness*   **123 Make battery:** *to assault*   **125 The holding:** *the*
burden or refrain of the song   **bear:** *keep going (the refrain);* F *beate*   **129 pink:** *small, half-*
closed **eyne:** *eyes*   **130 fats:** *vats*   **136 request you off:** *beg you to come away*   **138**
we have: *read 'we've'*   **140 Splits:** F *Spleet's*   **speaks:** *the* F *speakest:* **141 Antick'd**
us: *turned us into grotesque buffoons*   **143 I'll try . . . shore;** *Cf. n.*   **144 Give's:** F
giues   **145 father's:** F *Father*   **147 Take heed . . . out;** *Cf. n.*   **150 hear we:** F *heere*
a we **a loud:** F *aloud*   **SD Enter Ventidius:** *begins III.1.*   **1 darting Parthia;**
Cf. n. **struck:** *defeated;* F *stroke*

57 I have . . . fortunes: *I have ever been your faithful follower*   **67 But entertain it:** *only*
accept it (the idea)   **70 Hast . . . well?:** *Are you drunk?*   **73 pales:** *encloses* **inclips:**
embraces   **76 competitors:** *partners*   **89 pall'd:** *weakened*   **99 A':** *he*   **101 then**
is: F *then he is*   **101, 102 would . . . wheels;** *Cf. n.*   **103 reels:** *revels; cf. n.*   **106**
Strike the vessels: *broach the wine casks*   **109 monstrous:** *abnormal*

Make me revenger. Bear the king's son's body
Before our army. Thy Pacorus, Orodes,
Pays this for Marcus Crassus.   5
   Roman.   Noble Ventidius,
Whilst yet with Parthian blood thy sword is warm,
The fugitive Parthians follow. Spur through Media,
Mesopotamia, and the shelters whither
The routed fly: so thy grand captain Antony   10
Shall set thee on triumphant chariots and
Put garlands on thy head.
   Ventidius.   O Silius, Silius,
I have done enough. A lower place, note well,
May make too great an act. For learn this, Silius,   15
Better to leave undone than by our deed
Acquire too high a fame when him we serve's away.
Caesar and Antony have ever won
More in their officer than person. Sossius,
One of my place in Syria, his lieutenant,   20
For quick accumulation of renown,
Which he achiev'd by th' minute, lost his favor.
Who does i' th' wars more than his captain can
Becomes his captain's captain: and ambition,
The soldier's virtue, rather makes choice of loss   25
Than gain which darkens him.
I could do more to do Antonius good,
But 'twould offend him; and in his offense
Should my performance perish.
   Roman.   Thou hast, Ventidius, that   30
Without the which a soldier and his sword
Grants scarce distinction. Thou wilt write to Antony?
   Ventidius. I'll humbly signify what in his name
That magical word of war, we have effected;
How, with his banners and his well-paid ranks,   35
The ne're-yet-beaten horse of Parthia
We have jaded out o' th' field.
   Roman.   Where is he now?
   Ventidius. He purposeth to Athens, whither, with what haste
The weight we must convey with's will permit   40
We shall appear before him. On, there; pass along.
                                     Exeunt.

   Enter Agrippa at one door, Enobarbus at another.

   Agrippa. What! are the brothers parted?
   Enobarbus. They have dispatch'd with Pompey; he is gone;
The other three are sealing. Octavia weeps
To part from Rome; Caesar is sad, and Lepidus,
Since Pompey's feast, as Menas says, is troubl'd   5
With the green-sickness.
   Agrippa.   'Tis a noble Lepidus.
   Enobarbus. A very fine one. O, how he loves Caesar!
   Agrippa. Nay, but how dearly he adores Mark Antony!
   Enobarbus. Caesar? Why, he's the Jupiter of men.   10
   Agrippa. What's Antony? The god of Jupiter.
   Enobarbus. Spake you of Caesar? How! the non-pareil!
   Agrippa. O, Antony! O thou Arabian bird!

   Enobarbus. Would you praise Caesar, say, 'Caesar': go no
further.   15
   Agrippa. Indeed, he plied them both with excellent praises.
   Enobarbus. But he loves Caesar best; yet he loves Antony.
Hoo! hearts, tongues, figures, scribes, bards, poets, cannot
Think, speak, cast, write, sing, number—hoo!—
His love to Antony. But as for Caesar,   20
Kneel down, kneel down, and wonder.
   Agrippa.   Both he loves.
   Enobarbus. They are his shards, and he their beetle.
                           [Trumpets within.]
This is to horse. Adieu, noble Agrippa.
   Agrippa. Good fortune, worthy soldier, and farewell.   25

   Enter Caesar, Antony, Lepidus, and Octavia.

   Antony. No further, sir.
   Caesar. You take from me a great part of myself;
Use me well in't. Sister, prove such a wife
As my thoughts make thee, and as my farthest band
Shall pass on thy approof. Most noble Antony,   30
Let not the piece of virtue, which is set
Betwixt us as the cyment of our love
To keep it builded, be the ram to batter
The fortress of it: for better might we
Have lov'd without this mean, if on both parts   35
This be not cherish'd.
   Antony.   Make me not offended
In your distrust.
   Caesar.   I have said.
   Antony.   You shall not find,   40
Though you be therein curious, the least cause
For what you seem to fear. So, the gods keep you,
And make the hearts of Romans serve your ends!
We will here part.
   Caesar. Farewell, my dearest sister, fare thee well: 45
The elements be kind to thee, and make
Thy spirits all of comfort! fare thee well.
   Octavia. My noble brother!
   Antony. The April's in her eyes; it is love's spring,
And these the showers to bring it on. Be cheerful.   50
   Octavia. Sir, look well to my husband's house; and—
   Caesar.   What, Octavia?
   Octavia. I'll tell you in your ear.
   Antony. Her tongue will not obey her heart, nor can
Her heart obey her tongue; the swan's-down feather   55
That stands upon the swell at full of tide
And neither way inclines.
   Enobarbus. *[Aside.]* Will Caesar weep?
   Agrippa.   He has a cloud in's face.
   Enobarbus. He were the worse for that were he a horse;   60
So is he, being a man.
   Agrippa.   Why, Enobarbus,
When Antony found Julius Caesar dead,
He cried almost to roaring; and he wept
When at Philippi he found Brutus slain.   65
   Enobarbus. That year, indeed, he was troubl'd with a
rheum;

4, 5 **Thy Pacorus ... Crassus;** *Cf. n.*   4 **Orodes:** *F Orades*   5 **this:** *i.e. death*   6
Roman; *Cf. n.*   14 **A lower place:** *a subordinate*   17 **serve's:** *F serues*   22 **by th'
minute:** *incessantly*   26 **darkens:** *obscures (his superior)*   28 **his offense:** *my offending
him*   30–32 **Thou hast ... distinction;** *Cf. n.*   37 **jaded:** *wearied*   **SD Enter
Agrippa** *begins III.2*   1 **parted:** *departed*   2 **dispatch'd:** *completed their business*   3
sealing: *signing and sealing agreements*   6 **green-sickness;** *Cf. n.*   7 **'Tis;** *Cf. n.*   11
Agrippa: *F Ant.*   13 **Arabian bird;** *Cf. n.*

18 **figures:** *F figure*   19 **cast:** *calculate*   23 **shards:** *'wing cases,' here 'wings'*   29, 30
as my ... approof; *Cf. n.*   30 **pass:** *pledge*   32 **cyment:** *cement (stressed ´— —)*   41
curious: *minutely inquiring*   46 **elements;** *Cf. n.*   55–57 **the swan's-down ... inclines;**
Cf. n   56 **at full:** *F at the full*   59, 60 **He has ... horse;** *Cf. n.*   67 **rheum:** *cold*

What willingly he did confound he wail'd,
Believe't, till I wept too.

   Caesar.   No, sweet Octavia,   70
You shall hear from me still; the time shall not
Out-go my thinking on you.

   Antony.   Come, sir, come;
I'll wrestle with you in my strength of love:
Look, here I have you; thus I let you go,   75
And give you to the gods.

   Caesar.   Adieu; be happy!

   Lepidus. Let all the number of the stars give light
To thy fair way!

   Caesar.   Farewell, farewell! *Kisses Octavia.*   80

   Antony.   Farewell!

                   Trumpets sound. Exeunt.

        Enter Cleopatra, Charmian, Iras, and Alexas.

   Cleopatra. Where is the fellow?

   Alexas.   Half afeard to come.

   Cleopatra. Go to, go to. Come hither, sir.

        Enter the Messenger as before.

   Alexas.   Good majesty,
Herod of Jewry dare not look upon you   5
But when you are well pleas'd.

   Cleopatra.   That Herod's head
I'll have; but how, when Antony is gone
Through whom I might command it? Come thou near.

   Messenger. Most gracious majesty!   10

   Cleopatra.   Didst thou behold Octavia?

   Messenger. Ay, dread queen.

   Cleopatra.   Where?

   Messenger.   Madam, in Rome;
I look'd her in the face, and saw her led   15
Between her brother and Mark Antony.

   Cleopatra. Is she as tall as me?

   Messenger.   She is not, madam.

   Cleopatra. Didst hear her speak? is she shrill-tongu'd or low?

   Messenger. Madam, I heard her speak; she is low-voic'd.   20

   Cleopatra. That's not so good. He cannot like her long.

   Charmian. Like her! O Isis! 'tis impossible.

   Cleopatra. I think so, Charmian: dull of tongue, and
dwarfish!
What majesty is in her gait? Remember,   25
If ere thou look'st on majesty.

   Messenger.   She creeps;
Her motion and her station are as one;
She shows a body rather than a life,
A statue than a breather.   30

   Cleopatra.   Is this certain?

   Messenger. Or I have no observance.

   Charmian.   Three in Egypt
Cannot make better note.

   Cleopatra.   He's very knowing,   35
I do perceive't. There's nothing in her yet.
The fellow has good judgment.

   Charmian.   Excellent.

   Cleopatra. Guess at her years, I prithee.

   Messenger. Madam, she was a widow.   40

   Cleopatra. Widow! Charmian, hark.

   Messenger. And I do think she's thirty.

   Cleopatra. Bear'st thou her face in mind? is't long or round?

   Messenger. Round even to faultiness.

   Cleopatra. For the most part, too, they are foolish that are   45
so.
Her hair, what color?

   Messenger. Brown, madam: and her forehead
As low as she would wish it.

   Cleopatra.   There's gold for thee: 50
Thou must not take my former sharpness ill.
I will employ thee back again; I find thee
Most fit for business. Go, make thee ready;
Our letters are prepar'd.   *[Exit Messenger.]*

   Charmian.   A proper man.   55

   Cleopatra. Indeed, he is so: I repent me much
That so I harried him. Why, methinks, by him
This creature's no such thing.

   Charmian.   Nothing, madam.

   Cleopatra. The man hath seen some majesty, and should   60
know.

   Charmian. Hath he seen majesty? Isis else defend,
And serving you so long!

   Cleopatra. I have one thing more to ask him yet, good
Charmian: 65
But 'tis no matter; thou shalt bring him to me
Where I will write. All may be well enough.

   Charmian. I warrant you, madam.   *Exeunt.*

        Enter Antony and Octavia.

   Antony. Nay, nay, Octavia, not only that,
That were excusable, that and thousands more
Of semblable import, but he hath wag'd
New wars 'gainst Pompey; made his will, and read it
To public ear,   5
Spoke scantly of me; when perforce he could not
But pay me terms of honor, cold and sickly
He vented them; most narrow measure lent me;
When the best hint was given him, he not took't,
Or did it from his teeth.   10

   Octavia.   O my good lord,
Believe not all, or if you must believe,
Stomach not all. A more unhappy lady,
If this division chance, ne're stood between,
Praying for both parts: 15
The good gods will mock me presently,
When I shall pray 'O, bless my lord and husband';
Undo that prayer, by crying out as loud,
'O, bless my brother!' Husband win, win brother,
Prays and destroys the prayer; no midway   20
'Twixt these extremes at all.

   Antony.   Gentle Octavia,
Let your best love draw to that point which seeks
Best to preserve it. If I lose mine honor

68 confound: *destroy*   **69 wept:** *F Weepe*   **71 still:** *continually*   **SD Enter Cleopatra:** *begins III.3*   **5 Herod:** *fierce tyrant of miracle plays*   **7, 8 That . . . have;** *Cf. n.*   **26 look'st:** *look'dst; cf. n.*   **28 station:** *manner of standing*   **29 shows:** *appears to be*

43 long or round; *Cf. n.*   **48 Brown;** *Cf. n.*   **49 As low . . . it;** *Cf. n.*   **55 proper:** *handsome*   **57 harried:** *maltreated*   **by him:** *according to his report*   **SD Enter Antony:** *begins III.4*   **3 semblable:** *similar*   **4 made . . . read it;** *Cf. n.*   **8 vented:** *uttered*   **narrow measure lent me:** *gave me little credit*   **9 took't:** *F look't*   **10 from his teeth:** *grudgingly*   **16 presently:** *instantly*

I lose myself: better I were not yours   25
Than yours so branchless. But, as you requested,
Yourself shall go between's; the mean time, lady,
I'll raise the preparation of a war
Shall stain your brother; make your soonest haste,
So your desires are yours.   30
   Octavia.   Thanks to my lord.
The Jove of power make me, most weak, most weak,
Your reconciler! Wars 'twixt you twain would be
As if the world shall cleave, and that slain men
Should soader up the rift.   35
   Antony. When it appears to you where this begins,
Turn your displeasure that way; for our faults
Can never be so equal that your love
Can equally move with them. Provide your going;
Choose your own company, and command what cost   40
Your heart has mind to.   *Exeunt.*

     Enter Enobarbus and Eros.

   Enobarbus. How now, friend Eros!
   Eros. There's strange news come, sir.
   Enobarbus. What, man?
   Eros. Caesar and Lepidus have made wars upon Pompey.
   Enobarbus. This is old: what is the success?   5
   Eros. Caesar, having made use of him in the wars 'gainst
Pompey, presently denied him rivality, would not let him par-
take in the glory of the action, and not resting here, accuses
him of letters he had formerly wrote to Pompey; upon his own
appeal seizes him: so the poor third is up, till death enlarge his
confine.
   Enobarbus. Then, world, thou hast a pair of chaps, no more;
And throw between them all the food thou hast,
They'll grind the one the other. Where's Antony?
   Eros. He's walking in the garden—thus, and spurns   15
The rush that lies before him; cries, 'Fool, Lepidus!'
And threats the throat of that his officer
That murdred Pompey.
   Enobarbus.   Our great navy's rigg'd.
   Eros. For Italy and Caesar. More, Domitius;   20
My lord desires you presently: my news
I might have told hereafter.
   Enobarbus.   'Twill be naught;
But let it be. Bring me to Antony.
   Eros. Come, sir.   *Exeunt.*

    Enter Agrippa, Maecenas, and Caesar.

   Caesar. Contemning Rome, he has done all this and more
In Alexandria; here's the manner of't:
I' th' market place, on a tribunal silver'd,
Cleopatra and himself in chairs of gold
Were publicly enthron'd: at the feet sat   5
Caesarion, whom they call my father's son,
And all the unlawful issue that their lust
Since then hath made between them. Unto her

He gave the stablishment of Egypt; made her
Of Lower Syria, Cyprus, Lydia, absolute queen.   10
   Maecenas. This in the public eye?
   Caesar. I' th' common show place, where they exercise.
His sons he there proclaim'd the kings of kings;
Great Media, Parthia, and Armenia
He gave to Alexander; to Ptolemy he assign'd   15
Syria, Cilicia, and Phoenicia. She
In th' habiliments of the goddess Isis
That day appear'd, and oft before gave audience,
As 'tis reported, so.
   Maecenas. Let Rome be thus inform'd.   20
   Agrippa. Who, queasy with his insolence already,
Will their good thoughts call from him.
   Caesar.   The people knows it,
And have now receiv'd his accusations.
   Agrippa. Who does he accuse?   25
   Caesar. Caesar, and that, having in Sicily
Sextus Pompeius spoil'd, we had not rated him
His part o' th' isle; then does he say, he lent me
Some shipping unrestor'd; lastly, he frets
That Lepidus of the triumvirate should be depos'd;   30
And, being, that we detain all his revenue.
   Agrippa. Sir, this should be answer'd.
   Caesar. 'Tis done already, and the messenger gone.
I have told him Lepidus was grown too cruel;
That he his high authority abus'd,   35
And did deserve his change: for what I have conquer'd,
I grant him part: but then, in his Armenia,
And other of his conquer'd kingdoms, I
Demand the like.
   Maecenas.   He'll never yield to that.   40
   Caesar. Nor must not then be yielded to in this.

    Enter Octavia, with her train.

   Octavia. Hail, Caesar, and my lord; hail, most dear Caesar!
   Caesar. That ever I should call thee castaway!
   Octavia. You have not call'd me so, nor have you cause.
   Caesar. Why have you stol'n upon us thus? You come not
Like Caesar's sister; the wife of Antony
Should have an army for an usher, and
The neighs of horse to tell of her approach
Long ere she did appear; the trees by th' way
Should have borne men, and expectation fainted,   50
Longing for what it had not; nay, the dust
Should have ascended to the roof of heaven,
Rais'd by your populous troops. But you are come
A market-maid to Rome, and have prevented
The ostentation of our love, which, left unshown,   55
Is often left unlov'd: we should have met you
By sea and land, supplying every stage
With an augmented greeting.
   Octavia.   Good my lord,
To come thus was I not constrain'd, but did it   60
On my free will. My lord, Mark Antony,
Hearing that you prepar'd for war, acquainted

26 branchless: *mutilated*   **29 Shall stain:** *that will stain*   **34 that:** *repeats as if*   **35 soader:** *solder*   **41 has:** *F he's*   **SD Enter Enobarbus:** *begins III.5*   **5 success:** *outcome*   **8 presently:** *immediately.* **rivality:** *partnership*   **9, 10 upon his own appeal:** *on his own (Caesar's) accusation*   **10 is up:** *imprisoned*   **11 enlarge his confine:** *set him free*   **12 Then, world, thou hast:** *F Then would thou hadst* **chaps:** *jaws*   **14 the one the other:** *F the other*   **17 that his officer:** *that officer of his; cf. n.*   **19 navy's:** *F Nauies* **SD Enter Agrippa:** *begins III.6*   **1 contemning:** *scorning* **he has:** *read 'he's'*   **3 tribunal:** *raised platform*   **6 my father's son;** *Cf. n.*

9 stablishment: *government, rule*   **10 Lydia;** *Cf. n.*   **12-19 I' th' common . . . so;** *Cf. n.*   **13 he there:** *F hither* **the kings:** *F the King*   **17 Isis:** *See I.2.60 cf. n. above*   **21 queasy:** *nauseated*   **27 spoil'd:** *despoiled of his territories* **rated him:** *assigned to him*   **30 triumvirate:** *F Triumpherate*   **31 revenue:** *stressed* — – —   **36 I have:** *read 'I've'*   **48 horse:** *horses*   **55-56 The ostentation . . . unlov'd;** *Cf. n.*

My grieved ear withal: whereon, I begg'd
His pardon for return.
    Caesar.   Which soon he granted,   *65*
Being an abstract 'tween his lust and him.
    Octavia. Do not say so, my lord.
    Caesar.   I have eyes upon him,
And his affairs come to me on the wind.
Where is he now?   *70*
    Octavia.   My lord, in Athens.
    Caesar. No, my most wronged sister; Cleopatra
Hath nodded him to her. He hath given his empire
Up to a whore, who now are levying
The kings o' th' earth for war. He hath assembl'd   *75*
Bocchus the King of Libya, Archelaus
Of Cappadocia, Philadelphos, King
Of Paphlagonia, the Thracian king, Adallas,
King Manchus of Arabia, King of Pont,
Herod of Jewry, Mithridates, King   *80*
Of Comageat, Polemon and Amintas,
The Kings of Mede and Lycaonia;
With a more larger list of scepters.
    Octavia. Ay me, most wretched,
That have my heart parted betwixt two friends   *85*
That do afflict each other!
    Caesar.   Welcome hither:
Your letters did withhold our breaking forth,
Ti!l we perceiv'd both how you were wrong led
And we in negligent danger. Cheer your heart;   *90*
Be you not troubl'd with the time, which drives
O're your content these strong necessities,
But let determin'd things to destiny
Hold unbewail'd their way. Welcome to Rome,
Nothing more dear to me. You are abus'd   *95*
Beyond the mark of thought, and the high gods,
To do you justice, makes his ministers
Of us and those that love you. Best of comfort,
And ever welcome to us.
    Agrippa.   Welcome, lady.   *100*
    Maecenas. Welcome, dear madam.
Each heart in Rome does love and pity you;
Only th' adulterous Antony, most large
In his abominations, turns you off,
And gives his potent regiment to a trull,   *105*
That noises it against us.
    Octavia.   Is it so, sir?
    Caesar. Most certain. Sister, welcome; pray you,
Be ever know to patience. My dear'st sister!   *Exeunt.*

Enter Cleopatra and Enobarbus.

    Cleopatra. I will be even with thee, doubt it not.
    Enobarbus. But why, why, why?
    Cleopatra. Thou hast forspoke my being in these wars,

And sayst it is not fit.
    Enboarbus.   Well, is it, is it?   *5*
    Cleopatra. Is't not denounc'd against us? Why should not we
Be there in person?
    Enobarbus. [Aside.]   Well, I could reply:
If we should serve with horse and mares together,
The horse were merely lost; the mares would bear   *10*
A soldier and his horse.
    Cleopatra.   What is't you say?
    Enobarbus. Your presence needs must puzzle Antony;
Take from his heart, take from his brain, from's time,
What should not then be spar'd. He is already   *15*
Traduc'd for levity, and 'tis said in Rome
That Photinus an eunuch and your maids
Manage this war.
    Cleopatra.   Sink Rome, and their tongues rot
That speak against us! A charge we bear i' th' war,   *20*
And as the president of my kingdom will
Appear there for a man. Speak not against it;
I will not stay behind.

Enter Antony and Canidius.

    Enobarbus.   Nay, I have done.
Here comes the emperor.   *25*
    Antony.   Is it not strange, Canidius,
That from Tarentum and Brundusium
He could so quickly cut the Ionian sea,
And take in Toryne? You have heard on't, sweet?
    Cleopatra. Celerity is never more admir'd   *30*
Than by the negligent.
    Antony.   A good rebuke,
Which might have well becom'd the best of men
To taunt at slackness. Canidius, we
Will fight with him by sea.   *35*
    Cleopatra.   By sea! What else?
    Canidius. Why will my lord do so?
    Antony.   For that he dares us to't.
    Enobarbus. So hath my lord dar'd him to single fight.
    Canidius. Ay, and to wage this battle at Pharsalia,   *40*
Where Caesar fought with Pompey. But these offers,
Which serve not for his vantage, he shakes off;
And so should you.
    Enobarbus.   Your ships are not well mann'd;
Your mariners are muleters, reapers, people   *45*
Ingross'd by swift impress; in Caesar's fleet
Are those that often have 'gainst Pompey fought:
Their ships are yare, yours, heavy: no disgrace
Shall fall you for refusing him at sea,
Being prepar'd for land.   *50*
    Antony.   By sea, by sea.
    Enobarbus. Most worthy sir, you therein throw away
The absolute soldiership you have by land,
Distract your army, which doth most consist
Of war-mark'd footmen, leave unexecuted   *55*
Your own renowned knowledge, quite forgo

63 withal: *with it*   **64 pardon:** *permission*   **66 Being an abstract … him;** *Cf. n.*
73 He hath given: *read 'He'th giv'n'*   **74 who:** *i.e. Antony and Cleopatra*   **76 Libya:**
North Africa exclusive of Egypt   **77 Cappadocia:** *Roman province in East Asia Minor*   **78**
Paphlagonia: *Roman province in North Asia Minor* **Adallas:** *F Adullas*   **79 Manchus:** *F*
Mauchus **Pont:** *Pontus*   **81 Comageat:** *Comagene*   **82 Mede:** *Media*
Lycaonia: *Roman province in South Asia minor; F Licoania*   **86 do:** *F does* **afflict:** *clash*
with   **89 wrong led;** *Cf. n.*   **90 negligent danger:** *danger which we neglected*   **96**
mark: *range (metaphor from archery)*   **97 makes his;** *Cf. n.*   **103 large:** *unrestrained*   **105 potent regiment:** *powerful rule* **trull:** *harlot*   **106 noises it:** *is clamorous*   **109 Be … patience:** *remain calm at all times*   **SD Enter Cleopatra:** *begins*
III.7   **3 forspoke:** *spoken against*

5 it is: *F it it*   **6 Is't not denounc'd:** *F If not, denounc'd; cf. n.* **denounc'd:** *proclaimed,
declared*   **10 merely:** *utterly*   **13 puzzle:** *paralyze*   **16–18 'tis said … war;**
Cf. n.   **20 charge:** *responsibility*   **27 Tarentum:** *Taranto* **Brundusium:** *Brin-
disi*   **29 take in:** *capture* **Toryne:** *F Troine; l. 68, Toryne* **on't:** *of it*   **38 For that:**
because   **45 muleters:** *mule-drivers; F Militers*   **46 Ingross'd:** *gathered* **impress:** *con-
scription*   **48 yare:** *light, easy to handle*   **49 fall:** *befall*   **53 absolute soldiership:**
perfect generalship   **54 Distract:** *divide*

The way which promises assurance, and
Give up yourself merely to chance and hazard
From firm security.
   Antony.   I'll fight at sea.   *60*
   Cleopatra. I have sixty sails, Caesar none better.
   Antony. Our overplus of shipping will we burn;
And with the rest full-mann'd, from th' head of Actium
Beat th' approaching Caesar. But if we fail,
We then can do't at land.   *65*

           Enter a Messenger.

           Thy business?
   Messenger. The news is true, my lord, he is descried;
Caesar has taken Toryne.
   Antony. Can he be there in person? 'tis impossible;
Strange that his power should be. Canidius,   *70*
Our nineteen legions thou shalt hold by land,
And our twelve thousand horse. We'll to our ship:
Away, my Thetis!

           Enter a Soldier.

        How now, worthy soldier?
   Soldier. O noble emperor, do not fight by sea;   *75*
Trust not to rotten planks: do you misdoubt
This sword and these my wounds? Let th' Egyptians
And the Phoenicians go a-ducking; we
Have us'd to conquer standing on the earth
And fighting foot to foot.   *80*
   Antony.   Well, well: away!
      Ex[eunt] Antony, Cleopatra, and Enobarbus.
   Soldier. By Hercules, I think I am i' th' right.
   Canidius. Soldier, thou art: but his whole action grows
Not in the power on't: so our leader's led,
And we are women's men.   *85*
   Soldier.   You keep by land
The legions and the horse whole, do you not?
   Canidius. Marcus Octavius, Marcus Justeius,
Publicola, and Caelius are for sea;
But we keep whole by land. This speed of Caesar's   *90*
Carries beyond belief.
   Soldier.   While he was yet in Rome
His power went out in such distractions
As beguil'd all spies.
   Canidius.   Who's his lieutenant, hear you?   *95*
   Soldier. They say, one Taurus.
   Canidius.   Well I know the man.

           Enter a Messenger.

   Messenger. The emperor calls Canidius.
   Canidius. With news the time's with labor,
And throws forth each minute some.   *Exeunt.*

     Enter Caesar [and Taurus] with his army, marching.

   Caesar. Taurus!
   Taurus. My lord?
   Caesar. Strike not by land,
Keep whole, provoke not battle
Till we have done at sea. Do not exceed   *5*
The prescript of this scroll: our fortune lies
Upon this jump.   *[Exeunt.]*

       Enter Antony and Enobarbus.

   Antony. Set we our squadrons on yond side o' th' hill,
In eye of Caesar's battle; from which place
We may the number of the ships behold   *10*
And so proceed accordingly.   *[Exeunt.]*

*Canidius marcheth with his land army one way over the stage,
and Taurus, the lieutenant of Caesar, the other way. After their
going in is heard the noise of a sea fight.*

      Alarum. Enter Enobarbus.

   Enobarbus. Naught, naught, all naught! I can behold no
longer.
Th' Antoniad, the Egyptian admiral,
With all their sixty, fly and turn the rudder: *15*
To see't mine eyes are blasted.

        Enter Scarus.

   Scarus. Gods and goddesses, all the whole synod of them!
   Enobarbus. What's thy passion?
   Scarus. The greater cantle of the world is lost
With very ignorance; we have kiss'd away   *20*
Kingdoms and provinces.
   Enobarbus.   How appears the fight?
   Scarus. On our side like the token'd pestilence,
Where death is sure. Yon ribald-rid nag of Egypt
(Whom leprosy o'ertake), i' th' midst o' th' fight,   *25*
When vantage like a pair of twins appear'd,
Both as the same, or rather ours the elder,
The breese upon her, like a cow in June,
Hoists sails and flies.
   Enobarbus.   That I beheld: *30*
Mine eyes did sicken at the sight, and could not
Endure a further view.
   Scarus.   She once being loof'd,
The noble ruin of her magic, Antony,
Claps on his sea-wing, and (like a doting mallard) *35*
Leaving the fight in heighth, flies after her:
I never saw an action of such shame;
Experience, manhood, honor, ne're before
Did violate so itself.
   Enobarbus.   Alack, alack!   *40*

        Enter Canidius.

   Canidius. Our fortune on the sea is out of breath,
And sinks most lamentably. Had our general

---

63 **head:** *headland* **Actium:** *on the coast of Epirus*   67 **descried:** *seen*   70 **power:** *forces*   73 **Thetis:** *sea goddess*   75–80 **O noble emperor ... foot;** *Cf. n.*   77 **th' Egyptians:** *read 'the Egyptians'*   83, 84 **his whole action ... on't;** *Cf. n.*   84 **leader's led:** *F Leaders leade*   85 **men:** *servants*   88 **Canidius:** *F Ven.*   91 **Carries:** *makes headway*   93 **distractions:** *detachments*   96 **Taurus:** *F Towrus*   99 **time's:** *F times*   100 **throws forth;** *Cf. n.*

SD **Enter Caesar:** *begins III.8*   5 **exceed:** *depart from*   6 **prescript:** *orders*   7 **jump:** *hazard*   9 **battle:** *troops in battle array*   10 **may:** *can*   12 **Naught:** *ruined, lost*   14 **admiral:** *flagship*   18 **passion:** *cause of your troubled mind*   19 **cantle:** *portion*   20 **With:** *by, through* **very:** *absolute* **we have:** *read 'we've'*   23 **like the token'd pestilence;** *Cf. n.*   24 **ribald-rid:** *licentious; F ribaudred*   28 **breese:** *gadfly*   33 **being loof'd;** *Cf. n.*   35 **mallard:** *drake, eager to follow his mate*

Been what he knew himself, it had gone well:
O, he has given example for our flight
Most grossly by his own.   45
   Enobarbus. Ay, are your thereabouts? Why, then, good
night, indeed.
   Canidius. Toward Peloponnesus are they fled.
   Scarus. 'Tis easy to't.
And there I will attend what further comes.   50
   Canidius.   To Caesar will I render
My legions and my horse; six kings already
Show me the way of yielding.
   Enobarbus.   I'll yet follow
The wounded chance of Antony, though my reason   55
Sits in the wind against me.   *[Exeunt.]*

       Enter Antony with Attendants.

   Antony. Hark! the land bids me tread no more upon't;
It is asham'd to bear me. Friends, come hither:
I am so lated in the world that I
Have lost my way for ever. I have a ship
Laden with gold, take that, divide it: fly,   5
And make your peace with Caesar.
   Omnes.   Fly? not we.
   Antony. I have fled myself, and have instructed cowards
To run and show their shoulders. Friends, be gone;
I have myself resolv'd upon a course   10
Which has no need of you. Be gone.
My treasure's in the harbor. Take it. O,
I follow'd that I blush to look upon:
My very hairs do mutiny, for the white
Reprove the brown for rashness, and they them   15
For fear and doting. Friends, be gone; you shall
Have letters from me to some friends that will
Sweep your way for you. Pray you, look not sad,
Nor make replies of loathness; take the hint
Which my despair proclaims; let that be left   20
Which leaves itself; to the seaside straightway;
I will possess you of that ship and treasure.
Leave me, I pray, a little: pray you now,
Nay, do so; for, indeed, I have lost command,
Therefore I pray you. I'll see you by and by. *Sits down.*   25

   Enter Cleopatra, led by Charmian, [Iras,] and Eros.

   Eros. Nay, gentle madam, to him, comfort him.
   Iras. Do, most dear queen.
   Charmian. Do! Why, what else?
   Cleopatra. Let me sit down. O Juno!
   Antony. No, no, no, no, no.   30
   Eros. See you here, sir?
   Antony. O fie, fie, fie!
   Charmian. Madam!
   Iras. Madam, O good empress!
   Eros. Sir, sir!   35
   Antony. Yes, my lord, yes. He at Philippi kept
His sword e'ne like a dancer, while I struck

The lean and wrinkled Cassius; and 'twas I
That the mad Brutus ended: he alone
Dealt on lieutenantry, and no practice had   40
In the brave squares of war: yet now—No matter.
   Cleopatra. Ah, stand by.
   Eros. The queen, my lord, the queen.
   Iras. Go to him, madam, speak to him;
He's unqualited with very shame.   45
   Cleopatra. Well then, sustain me: O!
   Eros. Most noble sir, arise, the queen approaches:
Her head's declin'd, and death will seize her, but
Your comfort makes the rescue.
   Antony. I have offended reputation,   50
A most unnoble swerving.
   Eros.   Sir, the queen.
   Antony. O, whither hast thou led me, Egypt? See,
How I convey my shame out of thine eyes
By looking back what I have left behind   55
Stroy'd in dishonor.
   Cleopatra.   O my lord, my lord.
Forgive my fearful sails: I little thought
You would have follow'd.
   Antony.   Egypt, thou knew'st too well 60
My heart was to thy rudder tied by th' strings,
And thou shouldst tow me after. O're my spirit
The full supremacy thou knew'st, and that
Thy beck might from the bidding of the gods
Command me.   65
   Cleopatra. O, my pardon!
   Antony.   Now I must
To the young man send humble treaties, dodge
And palter in the shifts of lowness, who
With half the bulk o' th' world play'd as I pleas'd,   70
Making and marring fortunes. You did know
How much you were my conqueror, and that
My sword, made weak by my affection, would
Obey it on all cause.
   Cleopatra.   Pardon, pardon!   75
   Antony. Fall not a tear, I say; one of them rates
All that is won and lost. Give me a kiss;
Even this repays me.
We sent our schoolmaster; is a come back?
Love, I am full of lead. Some wine   80
Within there, and our viands! Fortune knows
We scorn her most when most she offers blows.   *Exeunt.*

   Enter Caesar, Agrippa, Dolabella, [Thidias,] with others.

   Caesar. Let him appear that's come from Antony.
Know you him?
   Dolabella. Caesar, 'tis his schoolmaster:
An argument that he is pluck'd, when hither
He sends so poor a pinion of his wing   5
Which had superfluous kings for messengers
Not many moons gone by.

       Enter Ambassador from Antony.

---

43 Been ... himself: *been true to himself as shown in the past*   **44 he has:** F 'his ha's'
cf. n.   **49 to't:** F *toot*   **51 render:** *surrender*   **55 chance:** *fortunes*   **SD Enter
Antony:** *begins III.9*   **3 lated:** *belated*   **7 Omnes:** *i.e. attendants*   **9 show their
shoulders:** *show their backs*   **13 that:** *what*   **18 Sweep your way:** *make easy your reconcilement to Caesar*   **19 hint:** *occasion*   **20 that:** F *them*   **24, 25 I have lost ... you;**
Cf. n.   **37 His sword ... dancer;** *Cf. n.*   **struck:** F *strooke*

38 lean ... Cassius; *Cf. n.*   **40 Dealt on lieutenantry:** *fought by proxy*   **41 squares:**
squadrons   **45 unqualited:** *unmanned*   **48 seize:** F *cease*   **but:** *unless*   **53–55 How
... dishonor;** *Cf. n.*   **62 tow:** F *stowe*   **69 palter:** *shuffle, play tricks*   **the shifts of
lowness:** *tricks of a man humbled by fortune*   **76 Fall:** *let fall*   **rates:** *is worth*   **79
schoolmaster;** *Cf. n.*   **a:** *he*   **SD Enter Caesar:** *begins III.10.*   **Thidias;** *Cf. n.*   **4
argument:** *proof*   **SD Enter Ambassador;** *Cf. n.*

Caesar.   Approach and speak.
Ambassador. Such as I am, I come from Antony:
I was of late as petty to his ends   *10*
As is the morn dew on the myrtle leaf
To his grand sea.
    Caesar.   Be't so. Declare thine office.
    Ambassador. Lord of his fortunes he salutes thee, and
Requires to live in Egypt; which not granted,   *15*
He lessens his requests, and to thee sues
To let him breathe between the heavens and earth,
A private man in Athens: this for him.
Next, Cleopatra does confess thy greatness,
Submits her to thy might, and of thee craves   *20*
The circle of the Ptolemies for her heirs,
Now hazarded to thy grace.
    Caesar.   For Antony,
I have no ears to his request. The queen
Of audience nor desire shall fail, so she   *25*
From Egypt drive her all-disgraced friend,
Or take his life there: this if she perform,
She shall not sue unheard. So to them both.
    Ambassador. Fortune pursue thee!
    Caesar.   Bring him through the bands.   *30*
                        [Exit Ambassador.]
[To Thidias.] To try thy eloquence, now 'tis time; dispatch.
From Antony win Cleopatra; promise,
And in our name, what she requires; add more,
From thine invention, offers. Women are not
In their best fortunes strong, but want will perjure   *35*
The ne're-touch'd vestal. Try thy cunning, Thidias;
Make thine own edict for thy pains, which we
Will answer as a law.
    Thidias.   Caesar, I go.
    Caesar. Observe how Antony becomes his flaw,   *40*
And what thou think'st his very action speaks
In every power that moves.
    Thidias.   Caesar, I shall.   *Exeunt.*

       Enter Cleopatra, Enobarbus, Charmian, and Iras.

Cleopatra. What shall we do, Enobarbus?
Enobarbus.   Think, and die.
Cleopatra. Is Antony or we in fault for this?
Enobarbus. Antony only, that would make his will
Lord of his reason. What though you fled   *5*
From that great face of war, whose several ranges
Frighted each other? Why should he follow?
The itch of his affection should not then
Have nick'd his captainship, at such a point,
When half to half the world oppos'd, he being   *10*
The mered question. 'Twas a shame no less
Than was his loss, to course your flying flags,
And leave his navy gazing.
    Cleopatra.   Prithee, peace.

       Enter the Ambassador, with Antony.

Antony. Is that his answer?   *15*

Ambassador. Ay, my lord.
    Antony. The queen shall then have courtesy,
So she will yield us up.
    Ambassador.   He says so.
    Antony. Let her know't.   *20*
To the boy Caesar send this grizzled head,
And he will fill thy wishes to the brim
With principalities.
    Cleopatra.   That head, my lord?
    Antony. To him again. Tell him he wears the rose   *25*
Of youth upon him, from which the world should note
Something particular: his coin, ships, legions,
May be a coward's, whose ministers would prevail
Under the service of a child as soon
As i' th' command of Caesar. I dare him therefore   *30*
To lay his gay caparisons apart,
And answer me declin'd, sword against sword,
Ourselves alone. I'll write it: follow me.
               [Exeunt Antony and Ambassador.]
    Enobarbus. Yes, like enough, high-battl'd Caesar will
Unstate his happiness, and be stag'd to th' show   *35*
Against a sworder! I see men's judgments are
A parcel of their fortunes, and things outward
Do draw the inward quality after them
To suffer all alike. That he should dream,
Knowing all measures, the full Caesar will   *40*
Answer his emptiness! Caesar, thou hast subdu'd
His judgment too.

       Enter a Servant.

Servant.   A messenger from Caesar.
    Cleopatra. What! no more ceremony? See! my women
Against the blown rose may they stop their nose   *45*
That kneel'd unto the buds. Admit him, sir.   *[Exit Servant.]*
    Enobarbus. Mine honesty and I begin to square.
The loyalty well held to fools does make
Our faith mere folly: yet he that can endure
To follow with allegiance a fall'n lord,   *50*
Does conquer him that did his master conquer,
And earns a place i' th' story.

       Enter Thidias.

Cleopatra.   Caesar's will?
Thidias. Hear it apart.
    Cleopatra.   None but friends: say boldly.   *55*
    Thidias. So, haply, are they friends to Antony.
    Enobarbus. He needs as many, sir, as Caesar has,
Or needs not us. If Caesar please, our master
Will leap to be his friend: for us, you know
Whose he is we are, and that is Caesar's.   *60*
    Thidias.   So.
Thus then, thou most renown'd, Caesar entreats
Not to consider in what case thou stand'st
Further than he is Caesar.
    Cleopatra.   Go on: right royal.   *65*

10–12 as petty ... sea; *Cf. n.*   **21 circle:** *crown*   **22 Now ... grace:** *now lost unless you show favor or mercy*   **25 so:** *provided*   **26 friend:** *lover*   **30 bands:** *troops*   **40 becomes his flaw:** *behaves in his disgrace*   **41, 42 what thou ... moves;** *Cf. n.*   **SD Enter Cleopatra:** *begins III.11*   **4 will:** *desire*   **6 ranges:** *lines of battle*   **8 affection:** *passion*   **9 nick'd:** *made a fool of; cf. n.*   **11 mered question:** *definite cause*   **12 course:** *chase*   **SD Enter the Ambassador:** *see III.9.79; cf. n.*

27 Something particular: *some personal exploit*   **28 ministers:** *agents*   **31 caparisons:** *equipment*   **32 declin'd:** *in my fallen fortunes*   **34 high-battl'd:** *possessed of a victorious army*   **35 Unstate:** *strip of state and importance*   **be stag'd to th' show:** *be shown on the stage in public view*   **36 sworder:** *gladiator*   **37 parcel:** *part*   **39 To suffer all alike:** *so that all deteriorate at the same rate*   **40 all measures:** *both good and bad fortune*   **SD Thidias:** *see III.10.1; cf. n.*   **56 haply:** *very likely*   **59 for:** *as for*   **62 Caesar:** *F caesars*

Thidias. He knows that you embrace not Antony
As you did love, but as you fear'd him.
    Cleopatra.   O!
    Thidias. The scars upon your honor therefore he
Does pity, as constrained blemishes,   70
Not as deserv'd.
    Cleopatra.   He is a god, and knows
What is most right. Mine honor was not yielded,
But conquer'd merely.
    Enobarbus.   To be sure of that,   75
I will ask Antony. Sir, sir, thou art so leaky,
That we must leave thee to thy sinking, for
Thy dearest quit thee.   *Exit Enobarbus.*
    Thidias.   Shall I say to Caesar
What you require of him? for he partly begs   80
To be desir'd to give. It much would please him
That of his fortunes you should make a staff
To lean upon. But it would warm his spirits
To hear from me you had left Antony,
And put yourself under his shroud,   85
The universal landlord.
    Cleopatra.   What's your name?
    Thidias. My name is Thidias.
    Cleopatra.   Most kind messenger,
Say to great Caesar this: in deputation   90
I kiss his conqu'ring hand; tell him I am prompt
To lay my crown at's feet, and there to kneel.
Tell him from his all-obeying breath I hear
The doom of Egypt.
    Thidias.   'Tis your noblest course.   95
Wisdom and fortune combating together,
If that the former dare but what it can,
No chance may shake it. Give me grace to lay
My duty on your hand.
    Cleopatra.   Your Caesar's father oft,   100
When he hath mus'd of taking kingdoms in,
Bestow'd his lips on that unworthy place,
As it rain'd kisses.

       Enter Antony and Enobarbus.

    Antony.   Favors? By Jove that thunders!
What are thou, fellow?   105
    Thidias.   One that but performs
The bidding of the fullest man and worthiest
To have command obey'd.
    Enobarbus.   You will be whipp'd.
    Antony. Approach there! Ah, you kite! Now, gods   110
and divels!
Authority melts from me. Of late, when I cried 'Ho!'
Like boys unto a muss, kings would start forth,
And cry, 'Your will?' Have you no ears? I am
Antony yet. Take hence this Jack and whip him.   115

       Enter a Servant.

    Enobarbus. 'Tis better playing with a lion's whelp
Than with an old one dying.
    Antony.   Moon and stars!
Whip him. Were't twenty of the greatest tributaries

That do acknowledge Caesar, should I find them   120
So saucy with the hand of—she here, what's her name,
Since she was Cleopatra? Whip him, fellows,
Till, like a boy, you see him cringe his face
And whine aloud for mercy. Take him hence.
    Thidias. Mark Antony—   125
    Antony.   Tug him away: being whipp'd,
Bring him again. This Jack of Caesar's shall
Bear us an arrant to him.

       Exeunt [Attendants] with Thidias.

You were half blasted ere I knew you: ha?
Have I my pillow left unpress'd in Rome,   130
Forborne the getting of a lawful race,
And by a gem of women, to be abus'd
By one that looks on feeders?
    Cleopatra.   Good my lord—
    Antony. You have been a boggler ever: 135
But when we in our viciousness grow hard—
O misery on't!—the wise gods seel our eyes,
In our own filth drop our clear judgments, make us
Adore our errors, laugh at's while we strut
To our confusion.   140
    Cleopatra.   O! is't come to this?
    Antony. I found you as a morsel, cold upon
Dead Caesar's trencher; nay, you were a fragment
Of Cneius Pompey's; besides what hotter hours,
Unregist'red in vulgar fame, you have   145
Luxuriously pick'd out; for I am sure
Though you can guess what temperance should be,
You know not what it is.
    Cleopatra.   Wherefore is this?
    Antony. To let a fellow that will take rewards   150
And say 'God quit you!' be familiar with
My playfellow, your hand, this kingly seal
And plighter of high hearts. O, that I were
Upon the hill of Basan to outroar
The horned herd! for I have savage cause,   155
And to proclaim it civilly were like
A halter'd neck which does the hangman thank
For being yare about him.

       Enter a Servant with Thidias.

                Is he whipp'd?
    Servant. Soundly, my lord.   160
    Antony.   Cried he? and begg'd a pardon?
    Servant. He did ask favor.
    Antony. If that thy father live, let him repent
Thou wast not made his daughter; and be thou sorry
To follow Caesar in his triumph, since   165
Thou hast bin whipp'd for following him: henceforth,
The white hand of a lady fever thee,
Shake thou to look on't. Get thee back to Caesar,
Tell him thy entertainment: look thou say
He makes me angry with him. For he seems   170
Proud and disdainful, harping on what I am,

80 require: *request*   **85 shroud:** *protection*   **93 from his:** *read 'from's'* **all-obeying:** *which all obey*   **101 taking ... in:** *conquering*   **103 As:** *as if*   **111 divels:** *devils*   **112 me. Of late, when:** *F me of late. When*   **113 muss:** *scramble*   **115 Jack:** *impudent fellow*

123 cringe: *distort*   **127 This:** *F The*   **128 arrant:** *errand*   **131 getting:** *begetting*   **132 abus'd:** *tricked*   **133 feeders:** *servants*   **135 boggler:** *fickle creature*   **137 seel:** *sew up; cf. n.*   **139 at's:** *at us*   **140 confusion:** *destruction*   **143 trencher:** *wooden platter*   **145 vulgar fame:** *common report*   **146 Luxuriously:** *lasciviously*   **151 quit:** *requite*   **153 plighter:** *pledger*   **153–155 O, that ... herd;** *Cf. n.*   **155 savage cause:** *cause enough to go mad*   **158 yare:** *quick*   **161 a:** *he*   **167 fever thee:** *may it (the lady's white hand) throw you into a fever*   **169 thy entertainment:** *your reception (here)*

Not what he knew I was. He makes me angry,
And at this time most easy 'tis to do't,
When my good stars, that were my former guides,
Have empty left their orbs and shot their fires   *175*
Into th' abysm of hell. If he mislike
My speech and what is done, tell him he has
Hipparchus, my enfranched bondman, whom
He may at pleasure whip, or hang, or torture,
As he shall like, to quit me. Urge it thou: *180*
Hence with thy stripes, be gone!   *Exit Thidias.*
     Cleopatra.   Have you done yet?
     Antony. Alack! our terrene moon is now eclips'd,
And it portends alone the fall of Antony.
     Cleopatra. I must stay his time.   *185*
     Antony. To flatter Caesar, would you mingle eyes
With one that ties his points?
     Cleopatra.   Not know me yet?
     Antony. Cold-hearted toward me?
     Cleopatra.   Ah! dear, if I be so,   *190*
From my cold heart let heaven engender hail,
And poison it in the source, and the first stone
Drop in my neck: as it determines, so
Dissolve my life. The next Caesarion smite
Till by degrees the memory of my womb,   *195*
Together with my brave Egyptians all,
By the discandying of this pelleted storm,
Lie graveless, till the flies and gnats of Nile
Have buried them for prey!
     Antony.   I am satisfied.   *200*
Caesar sets down in Alexandria, where
I will oppose his fate. Our force by land
Hath nobly held; our sever'd navy too
Have knit again, and fleet, threat'ning most sealike.
Where hast thou been, my heart? Dost thou hear, lady?   *205*
If from the field I shall return once more
To kiss these lips, I will appear in blood;
I and my sword will earn our chronicle:
There's hope in't yet.
     Cleopatra.   That's my brave lord!   *210*
     Antony. I will be treble-sinew'd, hearted, breath'd,
And fight maliciously: for when mine hours
Were nice and lucky, men did ransom lives
Of me for jests; but now I'll set my teeth,
And send to darkness all that stop me. Come,   *215*
Let's have one other gaudy night: call to me
All my sad captains; fill our bowls once more:
Let's mock the midnight bell.
     Cleopatra.   It is my birth-day:
I had thought t' have held it poor. But, since my lord   *220*
Is Antony again, I will be Cleopatra.
     Antony. We will yet do well.
     Cleopatra. Call all his noble captains to my lord.
     Antony. Do so, we'll speak to them; and tonight I'll force
The wine peep through their scars. Come on, my queen;   *225*
There's sap in't yet. The next time I do fight

I'll make death love me, for I will contend
Even with his pestilent scythe.   *Exeunt [all but Enobarbus].*
     Enobarbus. Now he'll outstare the lightning. To be furious
Is to be frighted out of fear, and in that mood   *230*
The dove will peck the estridge; and I see still,
A diminution in our captain's brain
Restores his heart. When valor preys on reason
It eats the sword it fights with. I will seek
Some way to leave him.   *Exit.*

     Enter Caesar, Agrippa, and Maecenas, with his army,
          Caesar reading a letter.

     Caesar. He calls me boy, and chides as he had power
To beat me out of Egypt. My messenger
He hath whipp'd with rods, dares me to personal combat,
Caesar to Antony. Let the old ruffian know
I have many other ways to die; meantime   *5*
Laugh at his challenge.
     Maecenas.   Caesar must think
When one so great begins to rage, he's hunted
Even to falling. Give him no breath, but now
Make boot of his distraction: never anger   *10*
Made good guard for itself.
     Caesar.   Let our best heads know
That tomorrow the last of many battles
We mean to fight. Within our files there are,
Of those that serv'd Mark Antony but late,   *15*
Enough to fetch him in. See it done,
And feast the army; we have store to do't,
And they have earn'd the waste. Poor Antony!   *Exeunt.*

     Enter Antony, Cleopatra, Enobarbus, Charmian, Iras,
          Alexas, with others.

     Antony. He will not fight with me, Domitius?
     Enobarbus.   No.
     Antony. Why should he not?
     Enobarbus. He thinks, being twenty times of better fortune,
He is twenty men to one.   *5*
     Antony.   Tomorrow, soldier,
By sea and land I'll fight: or I will live,
Or bathe my dying honor in the blood
Shall make it live again. Woo't thou fight well?
     Enobarbus. I'll strike, and cry 'Take all.'   *10*
     Antony.   Well said; come on
Call forth my household servants; let's tonight
Be bounteous at our meal.

     Enter three or four Servitors.

          Give my thy hand,
Thou hast bin rightly honest, so hast thou,   *15*
Thou, and thou, and thou: you have serv'd me well,
And kings have been your fellows.
     Cleopatra.   What means this?
     Enobarbus. 'Tis one of those odd tricks which sorrow shoots
Out of the mind.   *20*
     Antony.   And thou art honest too.

175 orbs: *spheres; cf. n.*   **178 Hipparchus;** *Cf. n.*   **enfranched:** *freed*   **180 quit:** *pay back*   **Urge:** *mention*   **183 our terrene ... eclips'd;** *Cf. n.*   **187 one ... points:** *his valet*   **193 determines:** *melts*   **196 brave:** *noble*   **198 discandying:** *dissolving; F discandering*   **201 sets:** *sits*   **204 fleet:** *are afloat*   **207 in blood:** *both 'covered with blood' and 'in full vigor' (said of a stag)*   **208 earn our chronicle:** *earn a place in history*   **212 maliciously:** *fiercely*   **213 nice:** *in a light mood (wanton?)*   **216 gaudy:** *festive, with joyous revel*   **226 There's ... yet:** *there is life in it still*

228 Even: *read 'e'en'*   **231 estridge;** *Cf. n*   **233 preys on:** *F prays in*   **SD Enter Caesar:** *begins IV.1*   **10 Make boot:** *take advantage*   **16 fetch him in:** *capture him (surround him)*   **SD Enter Antony:** *begins IV.2*   **7 or:** *either*   **9 Woo't:** *wilt*   **10 'Take all';** *Cf. n.*

I wish I could be made so many men,
And all of you clapp'd up together in
An Antony, that I might do you service
So good as you have done.   25
    Omnes.   The gods forbid!
    Antony. Well, my good fellows, wait on me tonight:
Scant not my cups, and make as much of me
As when mine empire was your fellow too,
And suffer'd my command.   30
    Cleopatra.   What does he mean?
    Enobarbus. To make his followers weep.
    Antony.   Tend me tonight;
May be it is the period of your duty:
Haply, you shall not see me more, or if,   35
A mangled shadow. Perchance tomorrow
You'll serve another master. I look on you
As one that takes his leave. Mine honest friends,
I turn you not away, but like a master
Married to your good service, stay till death: 40
Tend me tonight two hours, I ask no more,
And the gods yield you for't!
    Enobarbus.   What mean you, sir,
To give them this discomfort? Look, they weep,
And I, an ass, am onion-ey'd; for shame,   45
Transform us not to women.
    Antony.   Ho, ho, ho!
Now, the witch take me, if I meant it thus!
Grace grow where those drops fall! My hearty friends,
You take me in too dolorous a sense,   50
For I spake to you for your comfort, did desire you
To burn this night with torches. Know, my hearts,
I hope well of tomorrow, and will lead you
Where rather I'll expect victorious life
Than death and honor. Let's to supper, come,   55
And drown consideration.   *Exeunt.*

    Enter a company of Soldiers.

    1. Soldier. Brother, good night: tomorrow is the day.
    2. Soldier. It will determine one way: fare you well.
Heard you of nothing strange about the streets?
    1. Soldier. Nothing. What news?
    2. Soldier. Belike 'tis but a rumor. Good night to you.   5
    1. Soldier. Well, sir, good night.

    They meet other Soldiers.

    2. Soldier. Soldiers, have careful watch.
    3. Soldier. And you. Good night, good night.
       They place themselves in every corner of the stage.
    4. Soldier. Here we: and if tomorrow
Our navy thrive, I have an absolute hope   10
Our landmen will stand up.
    3. Soldier.   'Tis a brave army,
And full of purpose.
       Music of the hautboys is under the stage.
    4. Soldier.   Peace! what noise?

    1. Soldier.   List, list!   15
    2. Soldier. Hark!
    1. Soldier.   Music i' th' air.
    3. Soldier.   Under the earth.
    4. Soldier. It signs well, does it not?
    3. Soldier.   No.   20
    1. Soldier.   Peace, I say!
What should this mean?
    2. Soldier. 'Tis the god Hercules, whom Antony lov'd,
Now leaves him.
    1. Soldier.   Walk; let's see if other watchmen   25
Do hear what we do.
    2. Soldier.   How now, masters!   *[They] speak together.*
    Omnes. How now? How now? Do you hear this?
    1. Soldier. Ay; is't not strange?
    3. Soldier. Do you hear, masters? do you hear?   30
    1. Soldier. Follow the noise so far as we have quarter.
Let's see how it will give off.
    Omnes. Content. 'Tis strange.   *Exeunt.*

    Enter Antony and Cleopatra, with others.

    Antony. Eros! mine armor, Eros!
    Cleopatra.   Sleep a little.
    Antony. No, my chuck. Eros, come; mine armor, Eros.

    Enter Eros [with armor].

Come, good fellow, put thine iron on:
If fortune be not ours today, it is   5
Because we brave her. Come.
    Cleopatra.   Nay, I'll help too.
What's this for?
    Antony.   Ah, let be, let be; thou art
The armorer of my heart: false, false; this, this.   10
    Cleopatra. Sooth—la, I'll help: thus it must be.
    Antony. Well, well, we shall thrive now.
Seest thou, my good fellow? Go, put on thy defenses.
    Eros. Briefly, sir.
    Cleopatra.   Is not this buckled well?   15
    Antony.   Rarely, rarely:
He that unbuckles this, till we do please
To daff't for our repose, shall hear a storm.
Thou fumblest, Eros, and my queen's a squire
More tight at this than thou: dispatch. O love,   20
That thou couldst see my wars today, and knew'st
The royal occupation, thou shouldst see
A workman in't.

    Enter an armed Soldier.

       Good morrow to thee; welcome;
Thou look'st like him that knows a warlike charge: 25
To business that we love we rise betime,
And go to't with delight.
    Soldier. A thousand, sir, early though't be, have on their
Riveted trim, and at the port expect you.
       Shout. Trumpets flourish.

---

26 **Omnes:** *i.e. servants*   30 **suffer'd:** *submitted to*   33 **Tend:** *wait on*   34 **period:** *end*   35 **Haply:** *very likely*   42 **yield:** *repay, reward*   49 **Grace:** *virtue*   51 **comfort:** *encouragement*   **SD Enter a company:** *begins IV.3*   1–33 **Brother . . . 'Tis strange;** *Cf. n.*   5 **Belike:** *very likely*   8, 12 **3. Soldier:** *F 1*   9, 14 **4. Soldier:** *F 2; l. 19, 4*   12 **brave:** *splendid*

19 **It signs well:** *it is a good omen*   23 **'Tis . . . Hercules;** *Cf. n.*   27 **masters:** *gentlemen*   31 **so far . . . quarter:** *to the limits of our post*   32 **give off:** *end*   **SD Enter Antony:** *begins IV.4*   3 **chuck:** *chick*   7 **Nay . . . must be;** *Cf. n.*   10 **false:** *wrong*   11 **Sooth:** *in truth*   17 **daff't:** *doff it, put it off; F daft*   20 **tight:** *able*   23 **workman:** *expert craftsman*   25 **charge:** *duty*   26 **betime:** *early*   29 **Riveted trim:** *armor*   **port:** *gate*

Enter Captains and Soldiers.

Captain. The morn is fair. Good morrow, general.   30
All. Good morrow, general.
Antony.   'Tis well blown, lads.
This morning, like the spirit of a youth
That means to be of note, begins betimes.
So, so; come, give me that: this way; well said.   35
Fare thee well, dame; whate're becomes of me
This is a soldier's kiss: *[Kisses her.]* rebukable
And worthy shameful check it were, to stand
On more mechanic compliment. I'll leave thee
Now like a man of steel. You that will fight,   40
Follow me close; I'll bring you to't. Adieu.
        Exeunt [all but Cleopatra and Charmian].
Charmian. Please you, retire to your chamber.
Cleopatra.   Lead me.
He goes forth gallantly. That he and Caesar might   45
Determine this great war in single fight!
Then, Antony—but now—Well, on.   *Exeunt.*

Trumpets sound. Enter Antony and Eros [a Soldier meeting them].

Soldier. The gods make this a happy day to Antony!
Antony. Would thou and those thy scars had once prevail'd
To make me fight at land!
Soldier.   Hadst thou done so,
The kings that have revolted and the soldier   5
That has this morning left thee would have still
Follow'd thy heels.
Antony.   Who's gone this morning?
Soldier.   Who?
One ever near thee: call for Enobarbus,   10
He shall not hear thee, or from Caesar's camp
Say, 'I am none of thine.'
Antony. What sayst thou?
Soldier.   Sir, he is with Caesar.
Eros. Sir, his chests and treasure he has not with him.   15
Antony. Is he gone?
Soldier. Most certain.
Antony. Go, Eros, send his treasure after; do it;
Detain no jot, I charge thee: write to him—
I will subscribe—gentle adieus and greetings;   20
Say that I wish he never find more cause
To change a master. O, my fortunes have
Corrupted honest men! Dispatch. Enobarbus!
                            [Exeunt.]

Flourish. Enter Agrippa, Caesar, with Enobarbus and Dolabella.

Caesar. Go forth, Agrippa, and begin the fight:
Our will is Antony be took alive;   25
Make it so known.
Agrippa.   Caesar, I shall.   *[Exit.]*
Caesar. The time of universal peace is near:
Prove this a prosp'rous day, the three-nook'd world
Shall bear the olive freely.   30

Enter a Messenger.

Messenger. Antony is come into the field.
Caesar. Go charge Agrippa
Plant those that have revolted in the vant,
That Antony may seem to spend his fury
Upon himself.   *Exeunt [Caesar and his train].*   35
Enobarbus. Alexas did revolt, and went to Jewry on
Affairs of Antony; there did dissuade
Great Herod to incline himself to Caesar,
And leave his master Antony: for this pains
Caesar hath hang'd him. Canidius and the rest   40
That fell away have entertainment, but
No honorable trust. I have done ill,
Of which I do accuse myself so sorely
That I will joy no more.

Enter a Soldier of Caesar's

Soldier. Enobarbus, Antony   45
Hath after thee sent all thy treasure, with
His bounty overplus. The messenger
Came on my guard, and at my tent is now
Unloading of his mules.
Enobarbus.   I give it you.   50
Soldier. Mock not, Enobarbus,
I tell you true: best you saf'd the bringer
Out of the host. I must attend mind office,
Or would have done't myself. Your emperor
Continues still a Jove.   *Exit.*   55
Enobarbus. I am alone the villain of the earth,
And feel I am so most. O Antony,
Thou mine of bounty, how wouldst thou have paid
My better service, when my turpitude
Thou dost so crown with gold! This blows my heart: 60
If swift thought break it not, a swifter mean
Shall outstrike thought; but thought will do't, I feel.
I fight against thee! No: I will go seek
Some ditch, wherein to die; the foul'st best fits
My latter part of life.   *Exit.*   65

Alarum. Drums and trumpets. Enter Agrippa.

Agrippa. Retire, we have engag'd ourselves too far.
Caesar himself has work, and our oppression
Exceeds what we expected.   *Exit.*

Alarums. Enter Antony, and Scarus wounded.

Scarus. O my brave emperor, this is fought indeed!
Had we done so at first, we had droven them home   70
With clouts about their heads.
Antony.   Thou bleed'st apace.
Scarus. I had a wound here that was like a *T,*
But now 'tis made an *H.*   *[Retreat sounded a]far off.*
Antony.   They do retire.   75
Scarus. We'll beat 'em into bench holes. I have yet
Room for six scotches more.

Enter Eros.

30 Captain: F *Alexas*   **32 'Tis well blown:** *the day begins (blossoms) well*   **35 well said:** *well done;* F *well-sed*   **38 check:** *reproof*   **39 mechanic compliment:** *vulgar, common leave-taking*   **SD Trumpets sound:** *begins IV.5*   **1, 4, 9 Soldier;** *Cf. n.*   **SD [Exeunt]:** F *Exit*   **SD Flourish;** *Cf. n.*   **29 three-nook'd:** *three-cornered (Europe, Asia, Africa)*

33 vant: *vaunt, van*   **36–40 Alexas … him;** *Cf. n.*   **37 dissuade:** *persuade away from*   **41 have entertainment:** *are employed (in Caesar's army)*   **48 on my guard:** *while I was on guard*   **52 saf'd:** *conducted safely*   **53 office:** *duty*   **60 blows:** *causes it to swell (with pain)*   **62 outstrike:** *strike sooner* **thought:** *sorrow, grief* **SD Alarum;** *Cf. n.*   **66 engag'd … far:** *involved ourselves too deeply in enemy's forces*   **67 our oppression:** *pressure on us*   **70 we had:** *read 'we'd'*   **73, 74 a T … an H;** *Cf. n.*   **74 Retreat sounded:** F *Far off after heads, l. 70*   **76 bench holes:** *privy holes*   **77 scotches:** *slashes*

Eros. They are beaten, sir, and our advantage serves
For a fair victory.
Scarus.   Let us score their backs,   *80*
And snatch 'em up as we take hares behind:
'Tis sport to maul a runner.
Antony.   I will reward thee
Once for thy sprightly comfort and tenfold
For thy good valor. Come thee on.   *85*
Scarus.   I'll halt after.

                               Exeunt.

Alarum. Enter Antony again in a march; Scarus, with others.

Antony. We have beat him to his camp: run one before
And let the queen know of our gests. Tomorrow,
Before the sun shall see's, we'll spill the blood
That has today escap'd. I thank you all,
For doughty-handed are you, and have fought   *5*
Not as you serv'd the cause, but as't had been
Each man's like mine; you have shown all Hectors.
Enter the city, clip your wives, your friends,
Tell them your feats, whilst they with joyful tears
Wash the congealment from your wounds, and kiss   *10*
The honor'd gashes whole.

Enter Cleopatra

                    [To Scarus.] Give me thy hand
To this great fairy I'll commend thy acts,
Make her thanks bless thee. O thou day o' th' world!
Chain mine arm'd neck; leap thou, attire and all,   *15*
Through proof of harness to my heart, and there
Ride on the pants triumphing.
Cleopatra.   Lord of lords!
O infinite virtue! com'st thou smiling from
The world's great snare uncaught?   *20*
Antony.   My nightingale,
We have beat them to their beds. What, girl! though gray
Do something mingle with our younger brown, yet ha' we
A brain that nourishes our nerves, and can
Get goal for goal of youth. Behold this man;   *25*
Commend unto his lips thy favoring hand:
Kiss it, my warrior: he hath fought today
As if a god, in hate of mankind, had
Destroy'd in such a shape.
Cleopatra.   I'll give thee, friend,   *30*
An armor all of gold; it was a king's.
Antony. He has deserv'd it, were it carbuncl'd
Like holy Phoebus' car. Give me thy hand:
Through Alexandria make a jolly march;
Bear our hack'd targets like the men that owe them.   *35*
Had our great palace the capacity
To camp this host, we all would sup together
And drink carouses to the next day's fate,
Which promises royal peril. Trumpeters,
With brazen din blast you the city's ear,   *40*
Make mingle with our rattling tabourines,

That heaven and earth may strike their sounds together,
Applauding our approach.   *Exeunt.*

Enter a Sentry and his company; Enobarbus follows.

Sentry. If we be not reliev'd within this hour,
We must return to th' court of guard: the night
Is shiny, and they say we shall embattle
By th' second hour i' th' morn.
   1. Watch. This last day was a shrewd one to's.   *5*
   Enobarbus. O, bear me witness, night—
   2. Watch. What man is this?
   1. Watch.   Stand close and list him.
   Enobarbus. Be witness to me, O thou blessed moon,
When men revolted shall upon record   *10*
Bear hateful memory: poor Enobarbus did
Before thy face repent!
   Sentry.   Enobarbus!
   2. Watch. Peace: hark further.
   Enobarbus. O sovereign mistress of true melancholy,   *15*
The poisonous damp of night disponge upon me,
That life, a very rebel to my will,
May hang no longer on me. Throw my heart
Against the flint and hardness of my fault,
Which, being dried with grief, will break to powder,   *20*
And finish all foul thoughts. O Antony!
Nobler than my revolt is infamous
Forgive me in thine own particular,
But let the world rank me in register
A master leaver and a fugitive.   *25*
O Antony! O Antony!   *[Dies.]*
   1. Watch.   Let's speak to him.
   Sentry. Let's hear him, for the things he speaks
May concern Caesar.
   2. Watch.   Let's do so. But he sleeps.   *30*
   Sentry. Swoonds rather, for so bad a prayer as his
Was never yet for sleep.
   1. Watch.   Go we to him.
   2. Watch. Awake, sir, awake, speak to us.
   1. Watch.   Hear you, sir?   *35*
   Sentry. The hand of death hath raught him.
                         Drums afar off.
Hark! the drums demurely wake the sleepers.
Let us bear him to the court of guard: he is of note.
Our hour is fully out.
   2. Watch. Come on, then; he may recover yet.   *40*
                                 Exeunt.

Enter Antony and Scarus, with their army.

Antony. Their preparation is today by sea;
We please them not by land.
Scarus.   For both, my lord.
Antony. I would they'd fight i' th' fire or i' th' air;
We'ld fight there too. But this it is; our foot   *5*
Upon the hills adjoining to the city

---

86 halt: *limp*   **SD Alarum:** *begins IV.6 cf. n.*   **2 gests:** *exploits; F guests*   **7 shown:** *shown yourselves*   **8 clip:** *embrace*   **13 fairy:** *enchantress*   **14 O thou . . . world:** *thou light-giver to the world (likening Cleopatra to the sun).*   **16 proof of harness:** *armor of proof*   **17 triumphing:** *stressed —́*   **19 virtue:** *valor*   **21 My:** *F Mine*   **22 We have:** *read 'we've'*   **24 nerves:** *sinews*   **25 Get goal . . . youth:** *win as many points from youth as they from us*   **26 Commend:** *commit* **favoring:** *F savoring*   **33 Phoebus' car:** *chariot of the sun*   **35 targets:** *shields* **owe:** *own*

SD Enter a Sentry: *begins IV.7; cf. n.*   **2 court of guard:** *guardroom*   **3 embattle:** *draw up in battle array*   **5 shrewd:** *wicked*   **8 close:** *in concealment*   **10 record:** *stressed —́*   **16 disponge:** *squeeze out*   **20 dried with grief;** *cf. n.*   **23 in . . . particular:** *yourself*   **24 in register:** *in its record of human conduct*   **25 master leaver:** *runaway servant*   **31 Swoonds:** *swoons*   **36 raught:** *reached, seized*   **37 demurely:** *with subdued sound*   **SD Enter Antony:** *begins IV.8; cf. n.*

Shall stay with us. Order for sea is given,
They have put forth the haven,
Where their appointment we may best discover
And look on their endeavor.   *Exeunt.*   *10*

                Enter Caesar and his army.

  Caesar. But being charg'd, we will be still by land.
Which, as I take't, we shall; for his best force
Is forth to man his galleys. To the vales,
And hold our best advantage!   *Exeunt.*

                Enter Antony and Scarus.

  Antony. Yet they are not join'd.   *15*
Where yond pine does stand, I shall discover all.
I'll bring thee word straight how 'tis like to go.   *Exit.*
  Scarus. Swallows have built
In Cleopatra's sails their nests. The augurers
Say they know not, they cannot tell, look grimly,   *20*
And dare not speak their knowledge. Antony
Is valiant and dejected, and by starts
His fretted fortunes give him hope and fear
Of what he has and has not.

            Alarum afar off, as at a sea fight.

                Enter Antony.

  Antony.   All is lost!   *25*
This foul Egyptian hath betrayed me:
My fleet hath yielded to the foe, and yonder
They cast their caps up and carouse together
Like friends long lost. Triple-turn'd whore! 'tis thou
Hast sold me to this novice, and my heart   *30*
Makes only wars on thee. Bid them all fly:
For when I am reveng'd upon my charm,
I have done all. Bid them all fly, be gone.   *[Exit Scarus.]*
O sun! thy uprise shall I see no more;
Fortune and Antony part here, even here   *35*
Do we shake hands. All come to this? The hearts
That spaniel'd me at heels, to whom I gave
Their wishes, do discandy, melt their sweets
On blossoming Caesar; and this pine is bark'd,
That overtopp'd them all. Betray'd I am.   *40*
O this false soul of Egypt! this grave charm,
Whose eye beck'd forth my wars, and call'd them home,
Whose bosom was my crownet, my chief end,
Like a right gypsy hath at fast and loose
Beguil'd me to the very heart of loss.   *45*
What, Eros! Eros!

                Enter Cleopatra.

                Ah, thou spell! Avaunt!
  Cleopatra. Why is my lord enrag'd against his love?
  Antony. Vanish, or I shall give thee thy deserving,
And blemish Caesar's triumph. Let him take thee,   *50*

And hoist thee up to the shouting plebians;
Follow his chariot, like the greatest spot
Of all thy sex. Most monsterlike, be shown
For poor'st diminitives, for dolts, and let
Patient Octavia plough thy visage up   *55*
With her prepared nails.   *Exit Cleopatra.*
                        'Tis well th' art gone,
If it be well to live; but better 'twere
Thou fell'st into my fury, for one death
Might have prevented many. Eros, ho!   *60*
The shirt of Nessus is upon me; teach me,
Alcides, thou mine ancestor, thy rage.
Let me lodge Lichas on the horns o' th' moon,
And with those hands that grasp'd the heaviest club
Subdue my worthiest self. The witch shall die.   *65*
To the young Roman boy she hath sold me, and I fall
Under this plot; she dies for't. Eros, ho!   *Exit.*

          Enter Cleopatra, Charmian, Iras, [and] Mardian.

  Cleopatra. Help me, my women! O, he's more mad
Than Telamon for his shield; the boar of Thessaly
Was never so emboss'd.
  Charmian. To th' monument! There lock yourself,
And send him word you are dead.   *5*
The soul and body rive not more in parting
Than greatness going off.
  Cleopatra.   To th' monument!
Mardian, go tell him I have slain myself;
Say that the last I spoke was 'Antony,'   *10*
And word it, prithee, piteously. Hence, Mardian,
And bring me how he takes my death. To th' monument!
                                Exeunt.

                Enter Antony and Eros.

  Antony. Eros, thou yet behold'st me?
  Eros.   Ay, noble lord.
  Antony. Sometime we see a cloud that's dragonish,
A vapor sometime like a bear or lion,
A tower'd citadel, a pendant rock,   *5*
A forked mountain, or blue promontory
With trees upon't, that nod unto the world
And mock our eyes with air: thou hast seen these signs;
They are black vesper's pageants.
  Eros.   Ay, my lord.   *10*
  Antony. That which is now a horse, even with a thought
The rack dislimns, and makes it indistinct,
As water is in water.
  Eros.   It does, my lord.
  Antony. My good knave, Eros, now thy captain is   *15*
Even such a body: here I am Antony,
Yet cannot hold this visible shape, my knave.
I made these wars for Egypt, and the queen—
Whose heart I thought I had, for she had mine,
Which whilst it was mine had annex'd unto't   *20*

9 **appointment:** *nature and deployment of their ships*   **SD Enter Caesar;** *Cf. n.*   11
still: *quiet*   12 **shall:** *i.e. remain quiet*   **SD Enter Antony;** *Cf. n.*   15 **join'd:** *joined
in battle*   18–21 **Swallows … knowledge;** *Cf. n.*   19 **augurers:** *F Auguries*   23
fretted: *checkered, varied*   **SD Alarum … fight:** *F prints at end of l. 14*   29 **Triple-
turn'd:** *Julius Caesar's, Cneius Pompey's, and Antony's mistress*   32 **charm:** *enchantress*   37
spaniel'd: *F panelled*   38 **discandy:** *dissolve*   41 **grave charm:** *evil-working enchantress*   42 **beck'd:** *beckoned*   43 **my crownet, my chief end;** *Cf. n.*   44 **right:**
true   45 **loss:** *ruin*   47 **Avaunt!:** *be gone!*

54 **diminitives:** *diminutives; undersized, weak creatures*   **dolts:** *fools; Cf. n.*   61 **shirt of
Nessus;** *Cf. n.*   62 **Alcides:** *Hercules*   65 **worthiest:** *noblest*   66 **she hath:** *read
'she'th'*   **SD Enter Cleopatra:** *begins IV.9*   1 **he's:** *read 'he is.'*   2 **Telamon;**
Cf. n. **boar of Thessaly;** *Cf. n.*   3 **emboss'd:** *enraged, foaming at the mouth*   4 **To
th' monument;** *Cf. n.*   6 **rive:** *rend*   **SD Enter Antony:** *begins IV.10*   9 **black …
pageants;** *Cf. n.*   11 **even:** *read 'e'en.'*   12 **rack:** *drifting cloud* **dislimns:** *unpaints,
paints out*   15 **knave:** *fellow*   18 **Egypt:** *the Queen of Egypt*

A million moe, now lost—she, Eros, has
Pack'd cards with Caesar, and false-play'd my glory
Unto an enemy's triumph.
Nay, weep not, gentle Eros; there is left us
Ourselves to end ourselves.   25

Enter Mardian.

O, thy vilde lady; she has robb'd me of my sword.
    Mardian. No, Antony,
My mistress lov'd thee, and her fortunes mingl'd
With thine entirely.
    Antony. Hence, saucy eunuch, peace. She hath betray'd me
And shall die the death.
    Mardian. Death of one person can be paid but once,
And that she has discharg'd. What thou wouldst do
Is done unto thy hand: the last she spake
Was 'Antony! most noble Antony!'   35
Then in the midst a tearing groan did break
The name of Antony; it was divided
Between her heart and lips: she rend'red life,
Thy name so buried in her.
    Antony.   Dead, then?   40
    Mardian.   Dead.
    Antony. Unarm, Eros, the long day's task is done,
And we must sleep. *[To Mardian.]* That thou depart'st hence
safe,
Does pay thy labor richly; go.   *Exit Mardian.*   45
                    Off, pluck off:
The sevenfold shield of Ajax cannot keep
The battery from my heart. O, cleave, my sides!
Heart, once be stronger than thy continent,
Crack thy frail case! Apace, Eros, apace.   50
No more a soldier: bruised pieces, go;
You have bin nobly borne. From me awhile.

                                             Exit Eros.

I will o'retake thee, Cleopatra, and
Weep for my pardon. So it must be, for now
All length is torture: since the torch is out,   55
Lie down and stray no farther. Now all labor
Mars what it does; yea, very force entangles
Itself with strength: seal then, and all is done.
Eros!—I come, my queen. Eros! Stay for me.
Where souls do couch on flowers, we'll hand in hand,   60
And with our sprightly port make the ghosts gaze:
Dido and her Aeneas shall want troops,
And all the haunt be ours. Come, Eros! Eros!

Enter Eros.

    Eros. What would my lord?
    Antony.   Since Cleopatra died,   65
I have liv'd in such dishonor that the gods
Detest my baseness. I, that with my sword
Quarter'd the world, and o're green Neptune's back
With ships made cities, condemn myself to lack
The courage of a woman, less noble mind   70
Than she which by her death our Caesar tells

'I am conqueror of myself.' Thou art sworn, Eros,
That when the exigent should come—which now
Is come indeed—when I should see behind me
Th' inevitable prosecution of disgrace and horror,   75
That on my command thou then wouldst kill me.
Do't, the time is come. Thou strik'st not me,
'Tis Caesar thou defeat'st. Put color in thy cheek.
    Eros. The gods withhold me!
Shall I do that which all the Parthian darts,   80
Though enemy, lost aim and could not?
    Antony.   Eros,
Wouldst thou be window'd in great Rome and see
Thy master thus with pleach'd arms, bending down
His corrigible neck, his face subdu'd   85
To penetrative shame, whilst the wheel'd seat
Of fortunate Caesar, drawn before him, branded
His baseness that ensu'd?
    Eros.   I would not see't.
    Antony. Come, then; for with a wound I must be cur'd.   90
Draw that thy honest sword, which thou hast worn
Most useful for thy country.
    Eros.   O, sir! pardon me.
    Antony. When I did make thee free, swor'st thou not then
To do this when I bade thee? Do't at once,   95
Or thy precedent services are all
But accidents unpurpos'd. Draw and come.
    Eros. Turn from me then that noble countenance
Wherein the worship of the whole world lies.
    Antony. Lo thee!   100
    Eros. My sword is drawn.
    Antony.   Then let it do at once
The thing why thou hast drawn it.
    Eros.   My dear master,
My captain, and my emperor, let me say,   105
Before I strike this bloody stroke, farewell.
    Antony. 'Tis said, man, and farewell.
    Eros. Farewell, great chief. Shall I strike now?
    Antony. Now, Eros.
    Eros. Why there then.   110
Thus do I escape the sorrow of Antony's death.

                                             Kills himself.

    Antony. Thrice-nobler than myself!
Thou teachest me, O valiant Eros, what
I should, and thou couldst not. My queen and Eros
Have by their brave instruction got upon me   115
A nobleness in record; but I will be
A bridegroom in my death, and run into't
As to a lover's bed. Come, then; and, Eros,
Thy master dies thy scholar: to do thus

                                             [Falls on his sword.]

I learn'd of thee. How! not dead? not dead?   120
The guard, ho! O, dispatch me!

Enter [Dercetas and] guard.

    1. Guard. What's the noise?

---

21 **moe:** *more*   22, 23 **Pack'd . . . triumph;** *Cf. n.*   26 **vilde:** *vile* **sword:** *soldierly strength and courage*   38 **rend'red:** *gave up*   49 **thy continent:** *thy case, that which holds thee in*   55 **length:** *prolongation of life*   58 **seal:** *put the seal of death upon*   61 **port:** *bearing*   62 **want troops:** *lack admirers among the departed souls*   64 **all . . . ours:** *we shall be the center of attraction there*   69 **to lack:** *in that I lack*

73 **exigent:** *emergency*   75 **inevitable prosecution:** *unavoidable pursuit*   78 **defeat'st:** *frustratest*   84 **pleach'd:** *folded*   85 **corrigible:** *submissive*   86 **penetrative:** *penetrating*   88 **His baseness that ensu'd:** *the baseness of one who (as captive) followed (the chariot)*   91 **honest:** *honorable*   96 **precedent:** *former*   **SD Kills himself:** *F prints SD after Eros, l. 109*   115, 116 **Have . . . record:** *have won from me a noble position in history*   121 **ho!:** *F how?* **SD Enter [Dercetas and];** *Cf. n.*

Antony.   I have done my work ill, friends.
O, make an end of what I have begun.
  2. Guard. The star is fall'n.   *125*
  1. Guard.   And time is at his period.
  All. Alas, and woe!
  Antony.   Let him that loves me strike me dead.
  1. Guard. Not I.
  2. Guard. Nor I.   *130*
  3. Guard. Nor any one.   *Exeunt [Guards].*
  Dercetas. Thy death and fortunes bid thy followers fly.
This sword but shown to Caesar, with this tidings,
Shall enter me with him.

Enter Diomedes.

  Diomedes. Where's Antony?   *135*
  Dercetas.   There, Diomed, there.
  Diomedes. Lives he? Wilt thou not answer, man?
                     [Exit Dercetas.]
  Antony. Art thou there, Diomed? Draw thy sword, and give
me
Sufficing strokes for death.   *140*
  Diomedes.   Most absolute lord,
My mistress Cleopatra sent me to thee.
  Antony. When did she send thee?
  Diomedes.   Now, my lord.
  Antony.   Where is she?
  Diomedes. Lock'd in her monument. She had a prophesying
fear
Of what hath come to pass: for when she saw—
Which never shall be found—you did suspect
She had dispos'd with Caesar, and that your rage   *150*
Would not be purg'd, she sent you word she was dead;
But fearing since how it might work hath sent
Me to proclaim the truth, and I am come,
I dread, too late.
  Antony. Too late, good Diomed. Call my guard, I prithee.
  Diomedes. What, ho! the emperor's guard!
The guard, what ho! Come, your lord calls!

Enter four or five of the guard of Antony.

  Antony. Bear me, good friends, where Cleopatra bides;
'Tis the last service that I shall command you.
  1. Guard. Woe, woe are we, sir, you may not live to wear
All your true followers out.
  All.   Most heavy day!
  Antony. Nay, good my fellows, do not please sharp fate
To grace it with your sorrows. Bid that welcome
Which comes to punish us, and we punish it   *165*
Seeming to bear it lightly. Take me up;
I have led you oft; carry me now, good friends,
And have my thanks for all.   *Exeunt, bearing Antony.*

Enter Cleopatra and her maids aloft, with Charmian and Iras.

  Cleopatra. O Charmian, I will never go from hence.
  Charmian. Be comforted, dear madam.
  Cleopatra.   No, I will not.
All strange and terrible events are welcome,
But comforts we despise; our size of sorrow,   *5*

Proportion'd to our cause, must be as great
As that which makes it.

Enter [below] Diomedes.

     How now? is he dead?
  Diomedes. His death's upon him, but not dead.
Look out o' th' other side your monument;   *10*
His guard have brought him thither.

Enter [below] Antony [borne by] the guard.

  Cleopatra.   O sun!
Burn the great sphere thou mov'st in; darkling stand
The varying shore o' th' world. O Antony,
Antony, Antony! Help, Charmian, help, Iras, help;   *15*
Help, friends below, let's draw him hither.
  Antony.   Peace!
Not Caesar's valor hath o'rethrown Antony,
But Antony's hath triumph'd on itself.
  Cleopatra. So it should be,   *20*
That none but Antony should conquer Antony,
But woe 'tis so.
  Antony. I am dying, Egypt, dying; only
I here importune death awhile, until
Of many thousand kisses the poor last   *25*
I lay upon thy lips.
  Cleopatra.   I dare not, dear,
Dear my lord, pardon: I dare not,
Lest I be taken: not th' imperious show
Of the full-fortun'd Caesar ever shall   *30*
Be brooch'd with me, if knife, drugs, serpents have
Edge, sting, or operation. I am safe:
Your wife Octavia, with her modest eyes
And still conclusion, shall acquire no honor
Demuring upon me. But come, come, Antony—   *35*
Help me, my women—we must draw thee up.
Assist, good friends.
  Antony.   O, quick, or I am gone.
  Cleopatra. Here's sport indeed! How heavy weighs my lord!
Our strength is all gone into heaviness;   *40*
That makes the weight. Had I great Juno's power,
The strong-wing'd Mercury should fetch thee up
And set thee by Jove's side. Yet come a little,
Wishers were ever fools. O, come, come, come.
           They heave Antony aloft to Cleopatra.
And welcome, welcome! Die when thou hast liv'd,   *45*
Quicken with kissing: had my lips that power,
Thus would I wear them out.
  All.   A heavy sight!
  Antony. I am dying, Egypt, dying.
Give me some wine, and let me speak a little.   *50*
  Cleopatra. No, let me speak, and let me rail so high
That the false huswife Fortune break her wheel,
Provok'd by my offense.
  Antony.   One word, sweet queen.
Of Caesar seek your honor with your safety. O!   *55*
  Cleopatra. They do not go together.

---

126 period: *end*   **134 Shall . . . him:** *will successfully recommend me to him*   **149 found:** *found true*   **150 dispos'd:** *come to terms*   **151 purg'd:** *cleared away, pacified*   **164 To grace it:** *by honoring it*   **SD Exeunt:** *F Exit*   **SD Enter Cleopatra:** *begins IV.11*

13 sphere: *see III.11.175; cf. n.*   **darkling:** *in darkness*   **14 varying:** *ever changing*   **29 imperious show:** *imperial triumph*   **31 brooch'd:** *adorned*   **34 still conclusion:** *calm inference*   **40 heaviness:** *play on double meaning: 'weight' and 'sorrow'*   **SD They heave . . . Cleopatra;** *Cf. n.*   **45 when;** *Cf. n.*   **46 Quicken:** *revive*   **52 huswife:** *hussy, strumpet*   **53 Provok'd:** *incited*

Antony.   Gentle, hear me:
None about Caesar trust, but Proculeius.
    Cleopatra. My resolution and my hands I'll trust,
None about Caesar.   60
    Antony. The miserable change now at my end
Lament nor sorrow at; but please your thoughts
In feeding them with those my former fortunes
Wherein I liv'd, the greatest prince o' th' world,
The noblest: and do now not basely die,   65
Not cowardly put off my helmet to
My countryman. A Roman by a Roman
Valiantly vanquish'd. Now my spirit is going,
I can no more.
    Cleopatra.   Noblest of men, woo't die?   70
Hast thou no care of me? shall I abide
In this dull world, which in thy absence is
No better than a sty? O, see, my women,   *[Antony dies.]*
   The crown o' th' earth doth melt. My lord!
O, wither'd is the garland of the war,   75
The soldier's pole is fall'n: young boys and girls
Are level now with men: the odds is gone,
And there is nothing left remarkable
Beneath the visiting moon.   *[Swoons.]*
    Charmian.   O, quietness, lady!   80
    Iras. She is dead too, our sovereign.
    Charmian.   Lady!
    Iras.   Madam!
    Charmian. O madam, madam, madam!
    Iras. Royal Egypt! Empress!   85
    Charmian. Peace, peace, Iras!
    Cleopatra. No more, but in a woman, and commanded
By such poor passion as the maid that milks
And does the meanest chares. It were for me
To throw my scepter at the injurious gods,   90
To tell them that this world did equal theirs
Till they had stol'n our jewel. All's but naught;
Patience is sottish, and impatience does
Become a dog that's mad: then is it sin
To rush into the secret house of death   95
Ere death dare come to us? How do you, women?
What, what, good cheer? Why, how now, Charmian?
My noble girls! Ah, women, women! look,
Our lamp is spent, it's out. Good sirs, take heart:
We'll bury him, and then, what's brave, what's noble,   100
Let's do't after the high Roman fashion,
And make death proud to take us. Come, away.
This case of that huge spirit now is cold.
Ah, women, women! Come; we have no friend
But resolution, and the briefest end.   105
                Exeunt, bearing off Antony's body.

Enter Caesar, Agrippa, Dolabella, Maecenas, [Gallus, Proculeius,]
            with his Council of War.

    Caesar. Go to him, Dolabella, bid him yield;
Being so frustrate, tell him

He mocks the pauses that he makes.
    Dolabella. Caesar, I shall.   *[Exit.]*

     Enter Dercetas, with the sword of Antony.

    Caesar. Wherefore is that? And what art thou that dar'st   5
Appear thus to us?
    Dercetas.   I am call'd Dercetas,
Mark Antony I serv'd, who best was worthy
Best to be serv'd: whilst he stood up and spoke
He was my master, and I wore my life   10
To spend upon his haters. If thou please
To take me to thee, as I was to him
I'll be to Caesar; if thou pleasest not,
I yield thee up my life.
    Caesar.   What is't thou sayst?   15
    Dercetas. I say, O Caesar, Antony is dead.
    Caesar. The breaking of so great a thing should make
A greater crack. The round world
Should have shook lions into civil streets,
And citizens to their dens. The death of Antony   20
Is not a single doom; in the name lay
A moity of the world.
    Dercetas.   He is dead, Caesar;
Not by a public minister of justice,
Nor by a hired knife; but that self hand   25
Which writ his honor in the acts it did,
Hath, with the courage which the heart did lend it,
Splitted the heart. This is his sword;
I robb'd his wound of it; behold it stain'd
With his most noble blood.   30
    Caesar.   Look you sad, friends?
The gods rebuke me, but it is tidings
To wash the eyes of kings.
    Agrippa.   And strange it is,
That nature must compel us to lament   35
Our most persisted deeds.
    Maecenas. His taints and honors wag'd equal with him.
    Agrippa. A rarer spirit never
Did steer humanity: but you, gods, will give us
Some faults to make us men. Caesar is touch'd.   40
    Maecenas. When such a spacious mirror's set before him,
He needs must see himself.
    Caesar.   O Antony!
I have follow'd thee to this; but we do launch
Diseases in our bodies. I must perforce   45
Have shown to thee such a declining day,
Or look on thine: we could not stall together
In the whole world. But yet let me lament
With tears as sovereign as the blood of hearts
That thou, my brother, my competitor   50
In top of all design, my mate in empire,
Friend and companion in the front of war,
The arm of mine own body and the heart
Where mine his thoughts did kindle, that our stars,
Unreconciliable, should divide our equalness to this.   55
Hear me, good friends—

        Enter an Egyptian.

61–68 The miserable … vanquish'd; *Cf. n.*   **70 woo't:** *wilt thou*   **76 pole:** *garlanded Maypole, central point of sports; cf. n.*   **77 odds:** *difference*   **78 remarkable:** *noteworthy, distinguished*   **87 in:** *even; Cf. n.*   **89 chares:** *chores*   **93 sottish:** *foolish*   **99 lamp:** *source of our light*   **sirs:** *addressed to the women*   **100 brave:** *fine*   **101 do't:** *read 'do it'*   **SD Enter Caesar:** *begins V.1; instead of Maecenas F prints Menas*   **2 frustrate:** *baffled*

3 He mocks … makes: *he makes his own delay ridiculous*   **19 civil streets:** *streets of cities*   **22 moity:** *moiety, half*   **25 self:** *selfsame*   **34, 38 Agrippa;** *Cf. n.*   **36 persisted:** *persistently pursued*   **37 wag'd equal:** *were evenly matched*   **44 launch:** *lance*   **47 stall:** *dwell*   **50 competitor:** *partner*   **51 top of all design:** *loftiest enterprise*

But I will tell you at some meeter season:
The business of this man looks out of him;
We'll hear him what he says. Whence are you?
    Egyptian. A poor Egyptian yet. The queen my mistress,   *60*
Confin'd in all she has, her monument,
Of thy intents desires instruction,
That she preparedly may frame herself
To th' way she's forc'd to.
    Caesar.   Bid her have good heart;   *65*
She soon shall know of us, by some of ours,
How honorable and how kindly we
Determine for her; for Caesar cannot live
To be ungentle.
    Egyptian.   So the gods preserve thee!   *Exit.*   *70*
    Caesar. Come hither, Proculeius. Go and say
We purpose her no shame: give her what comforts
The quality of her passion shall require,
Lest in her greatness by some mortal stroke
She do defeat us. For her life in Rome   *75*
Would be eternal in our triumph. Go,
And with your speediest bring us what she says,
And how you find of her.
    Proculeius.   Caesar, I shall.   *Exit Proculeius.*
    Caesar. Gallus, go you along.   *[Exit Gallus.]*   *80*
                Where's Dolabella,
To second Proculeius?
    All.   Dolabella!
    Caesar. Let him alone, for I remember now
How he's employ'd: he shall in time be ready.   *85*
Go with me to my tent, where you shall see
How hardly I was drawn into this war,
How calm and gentle I proceeded still
In all my writings. Go with me, and see
What I can show in this.   *Exeunt.*

    Enter Cleopatra, Charmian, Iras, and Mardian.

    Cleopatra. My desolation does begin to make
A better life. 'Tis paltry to be Caesar:
Not being Fortune, he's but Fortune's knave,
A minister of her will: and it is great
To do that thing that ends all other deeds,   *5*
Which shackles accidents, and bolts up change,
Which sleeps, and never palates more the dung,
The beggar's nurse and Caesar's.

    Enter Proculeius.

    Proculeius. Caesar sends greeting to the Queen of Egypt
And bids thee study on what fair demands   *10*
Thou mean'st to have him grant thee.
    Cleopatra.   What's thy name?
    Proculeius. My name is Proculeius.
    Cleopatra.   Antony
Did tell me of you, bade me trust you, but   *15*
I do not greatly care to be deceiv'd,
That have no use for trusting. If your master
Would have a queen his beggar, you must tell him

That majesty, to keep decorum, must
No less beg than a kingdom: if he please   *20*
To give me conquer'd Egypt for my son,
He gives me so much of mine own as I
Will kneel to him with thanks.
    Proculeius.   Be of good cheer;
Y'are fall'n into a princely hand, fear nothing.   *25*
Make your full reference freely to my lord,
Who is so full of grace that it flows over
On all that need. Let me report to him
Your sweet dependency, and you shall find
A conqueror that will pray in aid for kindness   *30*
Where he for grace is kneel'd to.
    Cleopatra.   Pray you, tell him
I am his fortune's vassal, and I send him
The greatness he has got. I hourly learn
A doctrine of obedience, and would gladly   *35*
Look him i' th' face.
    Proculeius.   This I'll report, dear lady.
Have comfort, for I know your plight is pitied
Of him that caus'd it.

    [Roman soldiers enter behind Cleopatra.]

You see how easily he may be surpris'd.   *40*
Guard her till Caesar come.
    Iras. Royal queen!
    Charmian. O Cleopatra! thou art taken, queen.
    Cleopatra. Quick, quick, good hands.   *[Draws a dagger.]*
    Proculeius.   Hold, worthy lady,   *45*
hold!

    [Seizes and disarms her.]

Do not yourself such wrong, who are in this
Reliev'd, but not betray'd.
    Cleopatra. What of death, too, that rids our dogs of
languish?   *50*
    Proculeius. Cleopatra, do not abuse my master's bounty by
Th' undoing of yourself: let the world see
His nobleness well acted, which your death
Will never let come forth.
    Cleopatra.   Where art thou, death?   *55*
Come hither, come! come, come, and take a queen
Worth many babes and beggars!
    Proculeius.   O, temperance, lady.
    Cleopatra. Sir, I will eat no meat, I'll not drink, sir;
If idle talk will once be necessary,   *60*
I'll not sleep neither. This mortal house I'll ruin,
Do Caesar what he can. Know, sir, that I
Will not wait pinion'd at your master's court,
Nor once be chastis'd with the sober eye
Of dull Octavia. Shall they hoist me up   *65*
And show me to the shouting varletry
Of censuring Rome? Rather a ditch in Egypt
Be gentle grave unto me! rather on Nilus' mud
Lay me stark nak'd, and let the water flies
Blow me into abhorring! rather make   *70*

57 meeter: *more fitting*   **58 looks out of him:** *shows itself in his eyes*   **63 frame:** *adapt*   **68 live:** *F leaue*   **73 passion:** *passionate grief*   **76 eternal:** *eternally recorded (in history)*   **83 All:** *i.e. Agrippa and Maecenas*   **87 hardly:** *unwillingly*   **89 writings:** *dispatches (to Antony); cf. n.*   **SD Enter Cleopatra:** *begins V.2*   **4 minister:** *agent*   *6* **bolts up:** *fetters*   **7 never ... dung:** *no longer tastes the fruits of this vile earth*

26 Make your ... freely: *Cf. n.*   **reference:** *appeal*   **29 dependency:** *submission*   *30* **will pray ... kindness;** *Cf. n.*   **SD Roman ... Cleopatra;** *Cf. n.*   **40, 41 You see ... come;** *Cf. n.*   **45 worthy:** *noble*   **50 languish:** *sufferings*   **52 undoing:** *destruction*   **58 temperance:** *moderation*   **63 pinion'd:** *with wings clipped*   **64 chastis'd:** *stressed ́ —*   **66 varletry:** *rabble; F Varlotarie*

My country's high pyramides my gibbet,
And hang me up in chains!
    Proculeius.   You do extend
These thoughts of horror further than you shall
Find cause in Caesar.   *75*

                    Enter Dolabella.

    Dolabella.   Proculeius,
What thou hast done thy master Caesar knows,
And he hath sent for thee; as for the queen,
I'll take her to my guard.
    Proculeius.   So, Dolabella,   *80*
It shall content me best: be gentle to her.
[To Cleopatra.] To Caesar I will speak what you shall please,
If you'll employ me to him.
    Cleopatra.   Say, I would die.   *Exit Proculeius.*
    Dolabella. Most noble empress, you have heard of me? *85*
    Cleopatra. I cannot tell.
    Dolabella.   Assuredly you know me.
    Cleopatra. No matter, sir, what I have heard or known.
You laugh when boys or women tell their dreams;
Is't not your trick?   *90*
    Dolabella.   I understand not, madam.
    Cleopatra. I dreamt there was an Emperor Antony:
O, such another sleep, that I might see
But such another man.
    Dolabella.   If it might please ye—   *95*
    Cleopatra. His face was as the heavens, and therein stuck
A sun and moon, which kept their course and lighted
The little O, th' earth.
    Dolabella.   Most sovereign creature—
    Cleopatra. His legs bestrid the ocean; his rear'd arm *100*
Crested the world: his voice was propertied
As all the tuned spheres, and that to friends;
But when he meant to quail and shake the orb,
He was as rattling thunder. For his bounty,
There was no winter in't; an autumn it was   *105*
That grew the more by reaping: his delights
Were dolphinlike, they show'd his back above
The element they liv'd in: in his livery
Walk'd crowns and crownets; realms and islands were
As plates dropp'd from his pocket.   *110*
    Dolabella.   Cleopatra—
    Cleopatra. Think you there was or might be such a man
As this I dreamt of?
    Dolabella.   Gentle madam, no.
    Cleopatra. You lie, up to the hearing of the gods.   *115*
But if there be or ever were one such,
It's past the size of dreaming: nature wants stuff
To vie strange forms with fancy, yet to imagine
An Antony were nature's piece 'gainst fancy,
Condemning shadows quite.   *120*
    Dolabella.   Hear me, good madam.
Your loss is as yourself, great; and you bear it
As answering to the weight: would I might never
O'retake pursu'd success, but I do feel,

By the rebound of yours, a grief that smites   *125*
My very heart at root.
    Cleopatra.   I thank you, sir.
Know you what Caesar means to do with me?
    Dolabella. I am loath to tell you what I would you knew.
    Cleopatra. Nay, pray you, sir—   *130*
    Dolabella.   Though he be honorable—
    Cleopatra. He'll lead me then in triumph?
    Dolabella. Madam, he will; I know't.

    Flourish. Enter Proculeius, Caesar, Gallus, Maecenas,
            and others of his train.

    All. Make way there! Caesar!
    Caesar. Which is the Queen of Egypt?   *135*
    Dolabella. It is the emperor, madam.   *Cleopatra kneels.*
    Caesar. Arise, you shall not kneel.
I pray you, rise, rise, Egypt.
    Cleopatra. Sir, the gods will have it thus,
My master and my lord I must obey.   *140*
    Caesar. Take to you no hard thoughts;
The record of what injuries you did us,
Though written in our flesh, we shall remember
As things but done by chance.
    Cleopatra.   Sole sir o' th' world, *145*
I cannot project mine own cause so well
To make it clear, but do confess I have
Been laden with like frailties which before
Have often sham'd our sex.
    Caesar.   Cleopatra, know,   *150*
We will extenuate rather than enforce:
If you apply yourself to our intents,
Which towards you are most gentle, you shall find
A benefit in this change; but if you seek
To lay on me a cruelty, by taking   *155*
Antony's course, you shall bereave yourself
Of my good purposes, and put your children
To that destruction which I'll guard them from,
If thereon you rely. I'll take my leave.
    Cleopatra. And may through all the world: 'tis yours, *160*
and we,
Your scutcheons and your signs of conquest, shall
Hang in what place you please. Here, my good lord.
    Caesar. You shall advise me in all for Cleopatra.
    Cleopatra. [Giving a scroll.] This is the brief of money, *165*
plate, and jewels.
I am possess'd of: 'tis exactly valued,
Not petty things admitted. Where's Seleucus?
    Seleucus. Here, Madam.
    Cleopatra. This is my treasurer; let him speak, my lord, *170*
Upon his peril, that I have reserv'd
To myself nothing. Speak the truth, Seleucus.
    Seleucus. Madam, I had rather seel my lips
Than to my peril speak that which is not.
    Cleopatra. What have I kept back?   *175*
    Seleucus. Enough to purchase what you have made known.
    Caesar. Nay, blush not, Cleopatra; I approve
Your wisdom in the deed.
    Cleopatra.   See, Caesar! O, behold

---

98 O, th' earth: *F o' th' earth*   **101 Crested:** *surmounted* **was propertied:** *as harmonious* **103 quail:** *terrify* **orb:** *earth* **105 an autumn:** *F an Anthony it was: read* '*twas*' **106–108 his delights ... liv'd in;** *Cf. n.*   **109 crownets:** *coronets* **110 plates:** *silver coins* **116 or ever:** *F nor euer* **118 To vie ... fancy:** *to compete with imagination in the creation of wonderful forms* **118–120 yet ... quite;** *Cf. n.*

146 project: *set forth; stressed — —*   **151 enforce:** *stress (them)* **156 bereave:** *deprive* **162 scutcheons:** *armorial bearings, signs of victory* **165 brief:** *list* **173 seel:** *sew up; see III.11.137; cf. n.*

How pomp is follow'd; mine will now be yours,   *180*
And, should we shift estates, yours would be mine.
The ingratitude of this Seleucus does
Even make me wild. O slave, of no more trust
Than love that's hir'd. What! goest thou back? thou shalt
Go back, I warrant thee; but I'll catch thine eyes   *185*
Though they had wings: slave, soulless villain, dog!
O rarely base!
     Caesar.   Good queen, let us entreat you.
     Cleopatra. O Caesar! what a wounding shame is this,
That thou, vouchsafing here to visit me,   *190*
Doing the honor of thy lordliness
To one so meek, that mine own servant should
Parcel the sum of my disgraces by
Addition of his envy. Say, good Caesar,
That I some lady trifles have reserv'd,   *195*
Immoment toys, things of such dignity
As we greet modern friends withal; and say,
Some nobler token I have kept apart
For Livia and Octavia, to induce
Their mediation; must I be unfolded   *200*
With one that I have bred? The gods! it smites me
Beneath the fall I have. *[To Seleucus.]* Prithee, go hence,
Or I shall show the cinders of my spirits
Through th' ashes of my chance. Wert thou a man,
Thou wouldst have mercy on me.   *205*
     Caesar.   Forbear, Seleucus.
     Cleopatra. Be it known that we, the greatest, are
misthought
For things that others do; and, when we fall,
We answer others' merits in our name,   *210*
Are therefore to be pitied.
     Caesar.   Cleopatra,
Not what you have reserv'd, nor what acknowledg'd,
Put we i' th' roll of conquest: still be 't yours,
Bestow it at your pleasure, and believe   *215*
Caesar's no merchant to make prize with you
Of things that merchants sold. Therefore be cheer'd,
Make not your thoughts your prisons: no, dear queen,
For we intend so to dispose you as
Yourself shall give us counsel. Feed, and sleep: *220*
Our care and pity is so much upon you
That we remain your friend; and so, adieu.
     Cleopatra. My master, and my lord!
     Caesar.   Not so. Adieu.
          Flourish. Exeunt Caesar and his train.
     Cleopatra. He words me, girls, he words me,   *225*
That I should not be noble to myself;
But, hark thee, Charmian.   *[Whispers.]*
     Iras. Finish, good lady, the bright day is done,
And we are for the dark.
     Cleopatra.   Hie thee again: *230*
I have spoke already, and it is provided;
Go, put it to the haste.
     Charmian.   Madam, I will.

180 How ... follow'd: *how unfaithful are the servants of the great*   181 shift estates: *exchange places*   183 Even: *read 'e'en'*   193 Parcel the sum: *add to the sum total*   195 lady: *feminine*   196 Immoment: *valueless* dignity: *value*   197 modern: *ordinary*   199 Livia: *Octavius Caesar's wife*   200 unfolded: *betrayed*   201 With: *by*   204 chance: *fortune*   208 misthought: *misjudged*   210 merits in our name: *faults committed in our name*   215 Bestow: *make use of*   216 make prize: *bargain*   225 words me: *tries to delude me with words*

          Enter Dolabella.

     Dolabella. Where is the queen?
     Charmian.   Behold, sir.   *[Exit.]*   *235*
     Cleopatra.   Dolabella!
     Dolabella. Madam, as thereto sworn by your command,
Which my love makes religion to obey,
I tell you this: Caesar through Syria
Intends his journey; and within three days   *240*
You with your children will he send before.
Make your best use of this. I have perform'd
Your pleasure and my promise.
     Cleopatra. Dolabella, I shall remain your debtor.
     Dolabella. I your servant.   *245*
Adieu, good queen; I must attend on Caesar.
     Cleopatra. Farewell, and thanks.   *Exit [Dolabella].*
                    Now, Iras, what think'st thou?
Thou, an Egyptian puppet, shall be shown
In Rome, as well as I; mechanic slaves   *250*
With greasy aprons, rules, and hammers shall
Uplift us to the view; in their thick breaths,
Rank of gross diet, shall we be enclouded
And forc'd to drink their vapor.
     Iras.   The gods forbid!   *255*
     Cleopatra. Nay, 'tis most certain, Iras. Saucy lictors
Will catch at us, like strumpets, and scald rimers
Ballad us out o' tune: the quick comedians
Extemporally will stage us and present
Our Alexandrian revels. Antony   *260*
Shall be brought drunken forth, and I shall see
Some squeaking Cleopatra boy my greatness
I' th' posture of a whore.
     Iras.   O, the good gods!
     Cleopatra. Nay, that's certain.   *265*
     Iras. I'll never see 't! for I am sure my nails
Are stronger than mine eyes.
     Cleopatra. Why, that's the way to fool their preparation,
And to conquer their most absurd intents.

          Enter Charmian.

Now, Charmian.   *270*
Show me, my women, like a queen: go fetch
My best attires. I am again for Cydnus
To meet Mark Antony. Sirrah Iras, go.
Now, noble Charmian, we'll dispatch indeed,
And when thou hast done this chare I'll give thee leave   *275*
To play till doomsday. Bring our crown and all.
          [Exit Iras.] A noise within.
Wherefore's this noise?

          Enter a Guardsman.

     Guardsman.   Here is a rural fellow
That will not be denied your highness' presence:
He brings you figs.   *280*
     Cleopatra. Let him come in.   *Exit Guardsman.*
                    What poor an instrument
May do a noble deed! he brings me liberty.
My resolution's plac'd, and I have nothing

250 mechanic: *engaged in manual labor*   257 scald: *scurvy*   258 Ballad: *F Ballads* quick: *quick-witted*   262 Some ... greatness; *Cf. n.*   263 posture: *behavior*   266 my: *F mine*   275 thou hast: *read 'thou'st'* chare: *chore*   284 plac'd: *fixed*

Of woman in me; now from head to foot 285
I am marble-constant: now the fleeting moon
No planet is of mine.

Enter Guardsman and Clown [bringing in a basket].

Guardsman. This is the man.
Cleopatra. Avoid, and leave him. *Exit Guardsman.*
Hast thou the pretty worm of Nilus there, 290
That kills and pains not?
Clown. Truly, I have him: but I would not be the party
that should desire you to touch him, for his biting is immortal; those that do die of it do seldom or never recover.
Cleopatra. Remember'st thou any that have died on't? 295
Clown. Very many, men and women too. I heard of one of
them no longer than yesterday—a very honest woman, but
something given to lie, as a woman should not do but in the
way of honesty—how she died of the biting of it, what pain
she felt. Truly, she makes a very good report o' th' worm; 300
but he that will believe all that they say shall never be saved
by half that they do: but this is most falliable, the worm's an
odd worm.
Cleopatra. Get thee hence; farewell.
Clown. I wish you all joy of the worm. 305
[*Sets down the basket.*]
Cleopatra. Farewell.
Clown. You must think this, look you, that the worm will
do his kind.
Cleopatra. Ay, ay; farewell.
Clown. Look you, the worm is not to be trusted but in 310
the keeping of wise people: for indeed there is no goodness in
the worm.
Cleopatra. Take thou no care, it shall be heeded.
Clown. Very good: give it nothing, I pray you, for it is not
worth the feeding. 315
Cleopatra. Will it eat me?
Clown. You must not think I am so simple but I know the
devil himself will not eat a woman: I know that a woman is a
dish for the gods, if the devil dress her not. But, truly, these
same whoreson devils do the gods great harm in their 320
women, for in every ten that they make, the devils mar five.
Cleopatra. Well, get thee gone, farewell.
Clown. Yes, forsooth: I wish you joy o' th' worm.
Exit.

[*Enter Iras, with a robe, crown, etc.*]

Cleopatra. Give me my robe, put on my crown; I have
Immortal longings in me. Now no more 325
The juice of Egypt's grape shall moist this lip.
Yare, yare, good Iras; quick. Methinks I hear
Antony call: I see him rouse himself
To praise my noble act. I hear him mock
The luck of Caesar, which the gods give men 330
To excuse their after wrath. Husband, I come:
Now to that name my courage prove my title!
I am fire and air; my other elements
I give to baser life. So, have you done?
Come then, and take the last warmth of my lips. 335

Farewell, kind Charmian; Iras, long farewell.
[Kisses them. Iras falls and dies.]
Have I the aspic in my lips? Dost fall?
If thou and nature can so gently part,
The stroke of death is as a lover's pinch,
Which hurts, and is desir'd. Dost thou lie still? 340
If thus thou vanishest, thou tell'st the world
It is not worth leave-taking.
Charmian. Dissolve, thick cloud and rain, that I may say
The gods themselves do weep.
Cleopatra. This proves me base: 345
If she first meet the curled Antony,
He'll make demand of her, and spend that kiss
Which is my heaven to have. Come, thou mortal wretch,
With thy sharp teeth this knot intrinsicate
Of life at once untie: poor venomous fool, 350
Be angry, and dispatch. O, couldst thou speak,
That I might hear thee call great Caesar ass
Unpolicied.
Charmian. O eastern star!
Cleopatra. Peace, peace! 355
Dost thou not see my baby at my breast,
That sucks the nurse asleep?
Charmian. O, break! O, break!
Cleopatra. As sweet as balm, as soft as air, as gentle—
O Antony!—Nay, I will take thee too. 360
[Applying another asp to her arm.]
What should I stay— *Dies.*
Charmian. In this vile world? So, fare thee well.
Now boast thee, death, in thy possession lies
A lass unparalell'd. Downy windows, close,
And golden Phoebus never be beheld 365
Of eyes again so royal! Your crown's awry;
I'll mend it, and then play—

Enter the Guard, rushing in.

1. Guard. Where is the queen?
Charmian. Speak softly, wake her not.
1. Guard. Caesar hath sent— 370
Charmian. Too slow a messenger.
[Applies an asp.]
O, come apace, dispatch; I partly feel thee.
1. Guard. Approach, ho! All's not well: Caesar's beguil'd.
2. Guard. There's Dolabella sent from Caesar; call him.
1. Guard. What work is here! Charmian, is this well done?
Charmian. It is well done, and fitting for a princess
Descended of so many royal kings.
Ah, soldier. *Charmian dies.*

Enter Dolabella.

Dolabella. How goes it here?
2. Guard. All dead. 380
Dolabella. Caesar, thy thoughts
Touch their effects in this: thyself art coming
To see perform'd the dreaded act which thou
So sought'st to hinder.

Enter Caesar and all his train marching.

SD Clown: *rustic* **289 Avoid:** *withdraw* **290 worm:** *serpent* **293, 294 immortal:**
blunder for 'mortal' **297 honest:** *respectable* **302 falliable:** *he means 'infallible'* **313**
heeded: *guarded* **327 Yare:** *quick* **330, 331 The luck ... wrath;** *Cf. n.* **333, 334**
my other ... life; *Cf. n.* **334 baser life:** *human, mortal life*

337 aspic: *asp* **348 mortal:** *deadly* **349 intrinsicate:** *intricate* **353 Unpolicied:**
unskilled **362 vile:** *F wilde* **366 awry:** *F away* **SD rushing in:** *F rustling in, and*
Dolabella **382 Touch their effects:** *find fulfillment*

All.   A way there!—a way for Caesar!   *385*
Dolabella. O, sir, you are too sure an augurer:
That you did fear is done.
    Caesar.   Bravest at the last,
She level'd at our purposes, and being royal
Took her own way. The manner of their deaths?   *390*
I do not see them bleed.
    Dolabella.   Who was last with them?
    1. Guard. A simple countryman that brought her figs:
This was his basket.
    Caesar.   Poison'd then.   *395*
    1. Guard.   O Caesar!
This Charmian liv'd but now; she stood, and spake:
I found her trimming up the diadem
On her dead mistress; tremblingly she stood,
And on the sudden dropp'd.   *400*
    Caesar.   O noble weakness!
If they had swallow'd poison 'twould appear
By external swelling: but she looks like sleep,
As she would catch another Antony
In her strong toil of grace.   *405*
    Dolabella.   Here, on her breast,
There is a vent of blood, and something blown;

The like is on her arm.
    1. Guard. This is an aspic's trail,
And these fig leaves have slime upon them, such   *410*
As th' aspic leaves upon the caves of Nile.
    Caesar. Most probable
That so she died: for her physician tells me
She hath pursu'd conclusions infinite
Of easy ways to die. Take up her bed,   *415*
And bear her women from the monument.
She shall be buried by her Antony.
No grave upon the earth shall clip in it
A pair so famous. High events as these
Strike those that make them; and their story is   *420*
No less in pity than his glory which
Brought them to be lamented. Our army shall,
In solemn show, attend this funeral,
And then to Rome. Come, Dolabella, see
High order in this great solemnity.   *Exeunt omnes.*

❧ FINIS ❧

---

387 That: *what*   **389 level'd:** *aimed, guessed*   **398 trimming up:** *straightening*   405
toil: *net, snare* **grace:** *beauty*   **407 vent:** *discharge* **blown:** *swollen*

413–415 for her physician ... die; *Cf. n.*   **414 conclusions:** *experiments*   **418 clip:** *embrace*

NOTES

I.i.10. *gypsy's.* The word carries a double meaning here: Cleopatra is called an Egyptian (gypsies were believed to have come from Egypt) and also a hussy.

I.i.13. *triple pillar.* One of the triumvirs, on whom, as on pillars, the world rested.

I.i.16. *beggary.* Like other polysyllabic words (e.g. *infinite*, I.2.8; *amorous*, II.2.231; etc.), it syncopates the medial unstressed syllable when scansion so requires; such words should therefore be read 'begg'ry,' 'inf'nite,' etc. See Helge Kökeritz, *Shakespeare's Pronunciation* (New Haven, Yale University Press, 1953), pp. 25 ff., 283 ff.

I.i.24. *scarce-bearded.* Octavius was then twenty-three. Cf. 'the young man' (III.9.68), 'the boy Cæsar' (III.11.21).

I.i.58. *all alone . . . people.* 'And sometime also, when he would goe vp and downe the citie disguised like a slaue in the night, & would peere into poore mens windowes & their shops, and scold and brawle with them within the house: Cleopatra would be also in a chamber maides array, & amble vp and downe the streets with him, so that oftentimes Antonius bare away both mockes & blowes.' North's *Plutarch* (1579), p. 983.

I.ii.SD. *Enter Enobarbus.* The Folio entry includes Lamprius, Rannius, and Lucillius, all mute characters appearing nowhere else in the play. Lamprius was probably suggested to Shakespeare by Lampryas, Plutarch's grandfather, who related to him the anecdote of Antony's feasts. North, p. 982.

I.ii.4. *change . . . garlands.* 'Take horns (symbol of wife's unfaithfulness) in exchange for garlands (those of marriage).' Many editors read *charge*, 'to load,' in which case the meaning might be: 'to load his horns with garlands, to wear garlands on his horns.'

I.ii.23. *heat . . . drinking.* The liver being the seat of the passion of love, Charmian prefers to heat her liver with wine rather than with unrequited love.

I.ii.27. *Herod of Jewry.* Herod of Judea, who was represented as a fierce and blustering tyrant in the old miracle plays. Charmian prays for a son who would command such a tyrant's homage.

I.ii.31. *I . . . figs.* A difficult line. It may be a proverbial expression, with *figs* carrying one of several meanings, for which see the Arden Shakespeare, ed. M. R. Ridley (London, Methuen and Co., 1954), p. 12. Or it may be a phallic allusion, as J. D. Wilson suggests in the Cambridge Shakespeare (Cambridge, Cambridge University Press, 1950), p. 146.

I.ii.59–64. *come . . . thee.* The compositor mistook *Alexas* for a speech prefix. See Introduction, 2.

I.ii.60. *Isis.* Originally the Egyptian goddess of earth and fertility.

I.ii.97. *Labienus.* Quintus Labienus, having joined Brutus and Cassius in 44 B.C., was by them dispatched to seek aid from Orodes, King of Parthia. At this point he is commanding the Parthian army jointly with Orodes' son Pacorus.

I.ii.99–103. *Extended . . . lord.* Thus in F. Editors normalize passage into strict pentameter, so that the three lines end with *Euphrates, Syria,* and *lord.*

I.ii.100. *Lydia.* Ancient country in western part of Asia Minor.

I.ii.110, 111. *Our ills . . . earing.* 'Having our faults told us is as salutary to us as ploughing is to weed-grown fields.' For a highly suggestive analysis of the passage see Norman H. Pearson's essay '*Antony and Cleopatra*' in *Shakespeare: Of an Age and for All Time*, The Yale Shakespeare Festival Lectures, ed. Charles T. Prouty, (Hamden, Conn., The Shoe String Press, 1954), pp. 138 ff.

I.ii.129. *By . . . low'ring.* Carried to a progressively lower place in our estimation by the turn of the wheel of circumstance. Cf. *King Lear*, V.3.206.

I.ii.184. *Sextus Pompeius.* Younger son of Pompey the Great. He was proscribed by the triumvirs, but taking advantage of the quarrels between Octavius and Antony he was able to seize Sicily and command the sea.

I.ii.194. *courser's hair.* Horse hairs laid in stagnant water were believed to come to life in the shape of worms or small serpents.

I.iii.64, 65. *grown . . . change.* Ill through inactivity (peace), it would restore itself to health through blood-letting (war). 'Purge' often carries the meaning of letting blood, as in *2 Henry IV*, IV.1.68.

I.iii.76. *sacred vials.* Bottles of tears allegedly placed in the urn of loved ones. Cf. *The Two Noble Kinsmen*, I.5.5.

I.iii.81, 82. *By the fire . . . slime.* 'By the sun, which wakes to life Nile's mud' (causing spontaneous generation). Cf. II.7.25, 26.

I.iii.102, 103. *How . . . chafe.* How becomingly this descendant of Hercules conducts himself in his rage; how he acts the part of another Hercules Furens.

I.iii.109, 110. *O . . . forgotten.* My forgetfulness is like Antony, who is the epitome of utter forgetfulness, and I have forgotten all even as I am by all forgotten.

I.iv.6. *queen of Ptolemy.* Cleopatra, according to Egyptian custom, had married her brother Ptolemy, whom she is said to have poisoned.

I.iv.7–12. *More . . . goodness.* Thus in F. Editors rearrange passage into regular pentameter, making the lines end with *Or, there, faults,* and *are.*

I.iv.24. *foils.* Some editors print *soils*, an unnecessary emendation since 'soils' or 'disgraces' is precisely the meaning of *foils* in the context. Cf. F. H. Stratman, *Middle English Dictionary*; *The Tempest*, III.1.55.

I.iv.58, 59. *strikes . . . resisted.* Is more powerful than his actual warfare if it were opposed.

I.iv.61–76. *When . . . lank's not.* 'And therefore it was a wonderfull example to the souldiers, to see Antonius that was brought vp in all finenes and superfluitie, so easily to drinke puddle water, and eate wild frutes and rootes: and moreouer it is reported, that euen as they passed the Alpes, they did eate the barcks of trees, and such beasts, as neuer man tasted of their flesh before.' North, pp. 977, 978.

I.v.27. *demi-Atlas.* Antony and Caesar each carry half the globe on their shoulders; Lepidus does not count.

I.v.35. *great Pompey.* Not Pompey the Great but his son Cneius Pompey.

I.v.41. *that great med'cine.* The elixir which conferred immortality and changed base metals into gold: here meaning Antony.

II.i.3–6. *Know . . . for.* F prints passage as prose. See Introduction, 2.

II.i.32. *Lethe'd.* Oblivious; as if, like the dead crossing into Hades, he had drunk Lethe's water, which caused complete and utter forgetfulness.

II.i.49. *His brother.* 'Nowe Antonius delighting in these fond and childish pastimes, verie ill newes were brought him from two places. The first from Rome, that his brother Lucius, and Fuluia his wife, fell out first betwene them selues, and afterwards fell to open warre with Caesar . . .' North, p. 983.

II.i.59, 60. *It only . . . upon.* Only it is a matter of life and death for us.

II.ii.9. *would not shave't.* Plucking a man's beard was an invitation to quarrel. Cf. *Hamlet*, II.2.600; *King Lear*, III.7.86, 87.

II.ii.19. *Hark.* The F spelling *Hearke* may stand for *Hark* or *Harkee*, i.e. 'Hark ye.'

II.ii.65. *you have to.* Rowe and subsequent editors emend 'you have not to,' arguing that Antony would not admit that Caesar had a more serious grievance to 'patch a quarrel' with. The insertion of *not* may obviate Antony's alleged admission, but it does not clarify the meaning of ll. 64–66. The F lines mean: 'If you insist on starting (patching) a quarrel, you cannot do so with this particular complaint inasmuch as you have more serious complaints (matter whole) to do it with.'

II.ii.103, 104. *The honor . . . it.* The keeping of an oath is a sacred point of honor, which I am now accused of violating.

II.ii.111–113. *But . . . without it.* As my power shall not cause me to overlook my duty, neither shall my honesty (which dictates apology) sacrifice my dignity.

II.ii.113, 114. *Fulvia . . . here.* 'By them he was informed, that his wife Fuluia was the only cause of this warre: who being of a peeuish, crooked, and troublesome nature, had purposely raised this vprore in Italie, in hope thereby to withdraw him from Cleopatra.' North, pp. 983–984.

II.ii.140. *by the mother's side.* Octavia was in fact the daughter of both Caesar's parents, though Plutarch calls her his sister 'not by one mother, for she came of Ancharia, & Caesar him self afterwards of Accia.' North, p. 984.

II.ii.157, 158. *Truths . . . truths.* True reports of trouble would be dismissed as mere gossip, whereas now every rumor is accepted as the truth.

II.ii.206. *Half . . . Caesar.* Maecenas and Agrippa were equally loved by Octavius.

II.ii.213. *Eight wild boars.* Lampryas, Plutarch's grandfather, had heard from one Philotas, a physician, an eye-witness account of the 'wonderfull sumptuous charge and preparation of one only supper. When he was in the kitchen, and saw a world of diuersities of meates, and amongst others, eight wilde boares rosted whole: he began to wonder at it, and sayd, sure you haue a great number of ghests to supper. The cooke fell a laughing, and answered him, no (quoth he) not many ghestes, nor aboue twelue in all.' North, p. 982.

II.ii.224–253. *I will . . . nature.* A phonetic transcription of this famous description as it was spoken in Shakespeare's day is given in Kökeritz, *Shakespeare's Pronunciation*, p. 368.

II.ii.239. *what they undid did.* They cooled the cheeks even as they made them glow with apparent warmth.

II.ii.243. *made . . . adornings.* 'Their beautiful forms bending gracefully

toward her seemed like adornments to her person.' Some editors read *adorings* and interpret: 'They did her observance in the posture of adoration as if she had been Venus.'

II.ii.274. *infinite variety.* The phrase occurs in Florio's Montaigne, in a passage contrasting the weaknesses of present 'indiscreet writers' with the excellence of Plutarch. *The Essays of Montaigne* (New York, The Modern Library, 1933), p. 108.

II.iii.16. *I see . . . tongue.* I have intuitive knowledge of it but cannot express it.

II.iii.22–25. *Thy demon . . . o'repower'd.* 'With Antonius there was a soothsayer or astronomer of Aegypt . . . [who] told Antonius plainly, that his fortune (which of it selfe was excellent good, and very great) was altogether bleamished, and obscured by Caesars fortune: and therefore he counselled him vtterly to leaue his company, and to get him as farre from him as he could. For thy Demon said he, (that is to say, the good angell and spirit that kepeth thee) is affraied of his: and being coragious & high when he is alone, becometh fearefull and timerous when he commeth neere vnto the other.' North, p. 985.

II.iii.29–34. *If . . . 'tis noble.* 'But in all other maner of sportes and exercises, wherein they passed the time away the one with the other: Antonius was euer inferior vnto Caesar, and alway lost, which grieued him much.' North, p. 985.

II.iii.41. *His cocks.* 'Oftentimes when they were disposed to see cockefight, or quailes that were taught to fight one with an other: Caesars cockes or quailes did euer ouercome.' North, p. 985.

II.iii.42. *When . . . nought.* When the odds are everything to nothing in my favor.

II.v.18–21. *'Twas . . . drew up.* 'Antonius then threw in his line and Cleopatra straight commaunded one of her men to diue vnder water before Antonius men, and to put some old salte fish vpon his baite, like vnto those that are brought out of the contrie of Pont.' North, p. 983.

II.v.27. *Philippan.* The sword with which Antony had triumphed over Brutus and Cassius at Philippi in 42 B.C.

II.v.32–35. *Antonio's . . . here.* Thus in F. Some editors rearrange lines into regular pentameters, the three resulting lines ending with *villain, free, here.*

II.v.121. *Narcissus.* A beautiful youth in mythology who fell in love with his own face when he saw its reflection in the water.

II.v.125. *Take . . . you.* Do not be angry with me because I do not wish to offend you.

II.v.129. *That . . . sure of.* Who are not what you are certain Antony is, a deceiver and a knave.

II.vi.29. *o'recount.* Antony means 'outnumber,' whereas in the following line Pompey means 'cheat.'

II.vi.30–33. *At land . . . mayst.* 'Afterwards when Pompeys house was put to open sale, Antonius bought it: but when they asked him money for it, he made it very straung, and was offended with them, and writeth him selfe that he would not goe with Caesar into the warres of Africk, bicause he was not well recompenced for the seruice he had done him before.' North, p. 975.

II.vi.40. *to . . . fortune.* If you risk war in an attempt to gain more than we offer you.

II.vi.54, 55. *Your . . . friendly.* 'Furthermore, Sextus Pompeius had delt verie frendly with Antonius, for he had curteously receiued his mother, when she fled out of Italie with Fuluia.' North, p. 984.

II.vi.67. *counts.* Marks or lines, like those on tally sticks, by which Fortune has recorded her dealings with him.

II.vii.13–15. *To be call'd . . . cheeks.* Being in a position of pre-eminence but unable to dominate or exert influence is like having holes in the place of eyes, which would give a hideous appearance to the cheeks.

II.vii.32. *pyramises.* Lepidus' own unsteady plural. Although *pyramis* (Greek form) and even *pyrame* (taking *pyramis* or *pyrames* as a plural) were common, the plural was *pyramides*, the form Cleopatra uses below, V.2.71.

II.vii.101, 102. *would . . . wheels.* I wish the whole world were drunk so that it might run on wheels, that is, smoothly.

II.vii.103. *reels.* A contraction of *revels* not, as some editors believe, 'the world's reeling.' Cf. *Hamlet*, I.4.10, where *reels* is again a noun, that is, a contraction of *revels* not a verb. For further comment see Kökeritz, *Shakespeare's Pronunciation*, p. 189.

II.vii.143. *I'll try . . . shore.* I'll continue the drinking match with you on the shore.

II.vii.147–151. *Take heed . . . out.* F prints these lines as a single speech by Enobarbus.

III.i.1. *darting Parthia.* The Parthian cavalry was noted for its arrows, and one of its favorite maneuvers was to send a shower of them as it retreated.

III.i.4–5. *Thy Pacorus . . . Crassus.* 'In the mean time, Ventidius once againe ouercame Pacorus, (Orodes sonne King of Parthia) in a battell fought in the contrie of Cyrrestica, he being come againe with a great armie to inuade Syria: at which battell was slaine a great number of the Parthians, & among them Pacorus, the kings owne sonne slaine. This noble exployt as famous as euer any was, was a full reuenge to the Romanes, of the shame and losse they had receiued before by the death of Marcus Crassus.' North, p. 985.

III.i.6. *Roman.* Some editors give this and subsequent speeches the speech heading *Silius,* who is addressed by name in l. 13.

III.i.30–32. *Thou hast . . . distinction.* You possess discretion, without which a man's generalship confers no great distinction on him.

III.ii.6. *green-sickness.* Bilious hue peculiar to lovesick maidens. Lepidus is ironically reported as lovesick for Caesar and Antony.

III.ii.7. *'Tis 'It'* is here used contemptuously to refer to Lepidus.

III.ii.13. *Arabian bird.* The unique phoenix, believed by the ancients to fly from Arabia to the temple of Helios in Egypt once every five hundred years in order to bury there its father's body.

III.ii.29, 30. *as my . . . approof.* Such as I would pledge my utmost you will prove.

III.ii.46. *elements.* Perhaps more than merely a wish for favorable weather. Caesar wishes that the four *elements* believed to constitute the whole world may be propitious to her.

III.ii.55–57. *the swan's-down . . . inclines.* Octavia's emotions, that is, her love of Antony and her devotion to Octavius, are as delicately balanced as a swan's-down feather on the water at the height of the flood and just before the ebb begins.

III.ii.59, 60. *He has . . . horse.* A horse with a dark face; one with no white on it. M. R. Ridley (Arden Shakespeare) quotes *The Two Noble Kinsmen*, V.4.63, to show that the absence of a white mark indicated ill temper.

III.iii.7, 8. *That . . . have.* '. . . also he tooke from other kings their lawfull realmes: (as from Antigonus King of the Iewes, whom he openly beheaded, where neuer King before had suffred like death).' North, p. 986. Another reference may be to the beheading of Cicero by Antony's men. Antony placed Cicero's head over the pulpit for orations, which was 'a fearfull and horrible sight vnto the Romanes, who thought they saw not Ciceroes face, but an image of Antonius life and disposicion.' North, p. 937.

III.iii.26. *look'st.* For such F forms as *look'st* (look'dst) see Kökeritz, *Shakespeare's Pronunciation*, p. 303.

III.iii.43. *long or round.* A long face denoted prudence and wariness; a round one foolishness, indiscretion, instability.

III.iii.48. *Brown.* Brown was not associated with beauty. 'Why, i' faith, methinks she's too low for a high praise, too brown for a fair praise and too little for a great praise.' *Much Ado about Nothing*, I.1.144–146.

III.iii.49. *As low . . . it.* A high forehead was a mark of beauty. Mercutio speaks of Rosaline's 'high forehead and her scarlet lip.' *Romeo and Juliet*, II.1.20.

III.iv.4. *made . . . read it.* Antony is suggesting that Octavius made promises as Julius Caesar had done in his own will. Here Shakespeare departs from Plutarch, who records that Octavius, taking possession of Antony's will, read and attacked it in public. Cf. North, p. 997.

III.v.17. *that his officer.* Titius, Antony's lieutenant, who is reported to have slain Pompey.

III.vi.6. *my father's son.* Caesarion, son of Julius Caesar and Cleopatra. Octavius was adopted as a son by Julius Caesar in his will.

III.vi.10. *Lydia.* So in North. Plutarch gives *Libya*, whose King Bocchus appears in l. 76 below.

III.vi.12–19. *I' th' common . . . so.* 'For he assembled all the people in the show place, where younge men doe exercise them selues, and there vpon a high tribunall siluered, he set two chayres of gold, the one for him selfe, and the other for Cleopatra, and lower chaires for his children: then he openly published before the assembly, that first of all he did establish Cleopatra Queene of Aegypt, of Cyprvs, of Lydia, and of the lower Syria, and at that time also, Caesarion king of the same Realmes.... Now for Cleopatra, she did not onely weare at that time (but at all other times els when she came abroad) the apparell of the goddesse Isis, and so gaue audience vnto all her subiects, as a new Isis.' North, p. 996.

III.vi.55, 56. *The ostentation . . . unlov'd.* The display of our (Caesar's) love, which (love), if not exhibited, is often thought to be unfelt.

III.vi.66. *Being an abstract . . . him.* Variously interpreted. Perhaps the most satisfactory explanation is: 'Your return being a short-cut (abstract) between him and his lust, that is the easiest way to satisfy his desires.' Some editors read *obstruct* (as substantive) and taking it to refer to Octavia interpret: 'You being an obstruction to the satisfaction of his lust.'

III.vi.89. *wrong led.* Some editors emend F reading to *wrong'd* on the doubtful theory that the compositor misread Shakespeare's 'wronged,' inserted a space and added an *l.* But Shakespeare very probably would have written 'wrongd,' which makes the compositor's misreading difficult if not impossible.

III.vi.97. *makes his.* Some editors read *make them* or *make their.* But *makes* (plural) is probably what Shakespeare wrote, and its singular form may be responsible for *his.*

III.vii.6. *Is't not denounc'd.* Some editors retain F reading and are thereby forced to give obscure sense.

III.vii.16–18. *'tis said . . . war.* 'And Caesar sayde furthermore, that Antonius was not Maister of him selfe, but that Cleopatra had brought him beside him selfe, by her charmes and amorous poysons: and that they that should make warre with them, should be Mardian the Euenuke, Photinus, and Iras, a Woman of Cleopatraes bedchamber, that friseled her heare, and dressed her head, and Charmion, the which were those that ruled all the affaires of Antonius Empire.' North, p. 998.

III.vii.75–80. *O noble emperor . . . foot.* 'Now, as he was setting his men in order of battel, there was a Captaine, & a valliant man, that had serued Antonius in many battels & conflicts, & had all his body hacked & cut: who as Antonius passed by him, cryed vnto him, & sayd: O, noble Emperor, how commeth it to passe that you trust to these vile brittle shippes? what, doe you mistrust these woundes of myne, and this sword? let the Aegyptians & Phaenicians fight by sea, and set vs on the maine land, where we vse to conquer, or to be slayne on our feete.' North, p. 1000.

III.vii.83, 84. *his whole action . . . on't.* His plan of action does not make use of his military power with greatest advantage.

III.vii.100. *throws forth.* Most editors read *throes forth* (an extremely rare verb) and interpret 'gives painful birth to,' with a reference to *The Tempest,* II.1. 248, 249, where the Folio reads *throwes* for *throes:*

> *The setting of thine eye and cheek proclaim*
> *A matter from thee, and a birth indeed*
> *Which throes thee much to yield.*

But here the word means '*causes* thee pain, the pain of a difficult birth,' a sense inadmissible in the context of our passage.

III.viii.23. *like the token'd pestilence.* Like the plague when its (usually red) spots have appeared on a patient's skin.

III.viii.33. *being loof'd.* 'Having brought her boat's head toward the wind so that she could sail away'; the word is now spelled 'luff.'

III.viii.44. *he has.* The F reading *his ha's* is retained by some editors. For support of F reading see J. C. Maxwell, 'Shakespeare's Manuscript of Antony and Cleopatra,' *Notes and Queries,* 196, 337.

III.ix.24, 25. *I have lost . . . you.* Since I have lost the power and authority to order you, I entreat you (to leave me).

III.ix.37. *His sword . . . dancer.* Since dancers in Shakespeare's day wore a light sword or rapier as ornaments, Antony means that Caesar wore *his* sword for ornament only.

III.ix.38. *lean . . . Cassius.* Cf. 'Yond Cassius has a lean and hungry look.' *Julius Caesar,* I.2.201.

III.ix.54–56. *How . . . dishonor.* How I try to remove my shame from your eyes by turning from them and looking at my past which now lies in ruins.

III.ix.79. *schoolmaster.* Euphronius, the tutor of Antony's children by Cleopatra.

III.x.SD. *Thidias.* So in Folio. Many editors print North's *Thyreus* (Plutarch has *Thyrsus*) throughout the scene.

III.x.SD. *Enter Ambassador.* Many editors print 'Enter Euphronius, Ambassador from Antony' and prefix his speeches accordingly.

III.x.10–12. *as petty . . . sea.* 'As petty (of as little importance) to his plans and purposes as is the morning dewdrop to those of the ocean.' Some editors read 'its grand sea,' while others take *his* to mean 'its' and interpret: 'to its (the drewdrop's) grand sea, from which it is exhaled.' Another interpretation is: 'to his (Antony's) full tide of prosperity.'

III.x.41, 42. *what thou . . . moves.* What you think is the meaning and purpose of his every act. What we may forecast concerning his state of mind by observing his present behavior.

III.xi.9. *nick'd.* Cut short, like a fool's hair, thereby placing a mark of folly upon it. Cf. 'His man with scissors nicks him like a fool,' *Comedy of Errors,* V.1.178. 'To nick' means also 'to get the better of,' 'to cheat,' a *nick* being 'a winning throw in the game of hazard.' Cf. Arden Shakespeare, p. 139.

III.xi.137. *seel.* A term taken from falconry and meaning to sew up a hawk's eyes by way of preparing it for the use of the hood.

III.xi.153–155. *O, that . . . herd.* Cf. Psalm 12:12, 13. Antony calls himself a horned cuckold surrounded by Cleopatra's lovers.

III.xi.175. *orbs.* The nine concentric spheres in which the seven planets, the fixed stars, and the *primum mobile* moved about the earth in the Ptolemaic system. Cf. Cleopatra's line, IV.11.12, 13: 'O sun! Burn the great sphere thou mov'st in.'

III.xi.178. *Hipparchus.* Not a loyal follower. 'This Theophilus was the father of Hipparchus, who was had in great estimation about Antonius. He was the first of all his infranchised bondmen that reuolted from him, and yelded vnto Caesar, and afterwardes went and dwelt at Corinthe.'' North, p. 1002.

III.xi.183. *Our terrene . . . eclips'd.* 'Our earthly goddess of the moon, that is, Cleopatra, has changed, darkened, portending evil.' In her final moments Cleopatra takes leave of her planet, the moon, V.2.286, 287. Mr. Leslie Hotson interprets 'terrene moon' as the Mediterranean fleet of Antony and Cleopatra which has just been defeated by Caesar's smaller but battle-tested navy. See his *Shakespeare's Sonnets Dated* (London, 1949), pp. 7, 8.

III.xi.231. *estridge.* A goshawk, not ostrich. A dove pecking an ostrich is an incongruous image, whereas a dove pecking a goshawk or falcon is more appropriate, and in fact the expression appears in Shakespeare, *3 Henry VI,* I.4.40, 41:

> *So cowards fight when they can fly no further;*
> *So doves do peck the falcon's piercing talons.*

IV.ii.10. *'Take all.'* Deliberately ambiguous: 'fight desperately' and 'surrender.'

IV.iii.1–33. *Brother . . . 'Tis strange.* 'Furthermore, the selfe same night within a little of midnight, when all the citie was quiet, full of feare, and sorrowe, thinking what would be the issue and ende of this warre: it is said that sodainly they heard a maruelous sweete harmonie of sundrie sortes of instrumentes of musicke, with the crie of a multitude of people, as they had bene dauncing, and had song as they vse in Bacchus feastes, with mouinges and turninges after the maner of Satyres: & it seemed that this daunce went through the city vnto the gate that opened to the enemies, & that all the troupe that made this noise they heard, went out of the city at that gate. Now, such as in reason sought the depth of the interpretation of this wonder, thought that it was the god vnto whom Antonius bare singular deuotion to counterfeate and resemble him, that did forsake them.' North, pp. 1005, 1006.

IV.iii.23. *'Tis . . . Hercules.* Although in Plutarch the god here forsaking Antony is Bacchus, Shakespeare substituted Hercules, the more appropriately to forecst Antony's defeat on the morrow. Cf. I.3.102, and North, p. 971: "Now it had bene a speeche of old time, that the familie of the Antonii were discended from one Anton, the sonne of Hercules, whereof the familie tooke name."

IV.iv.7–11. *Nay . . . must be.* The Folio prints the whole as a single speech by Cleopatra. See Introduction, 2.

IV.v.1, 4, 9. *Soldier.* The Folio prefixes these speeches *Eros,* but Shakespeare intended the speaker to be the soldier, who also has the speeches at ll. 14, 17. That these are all his speeches is made clear by III.7.75 ff.

IV.v.SD. *Flourish.* Some editors begin Scene 6 here, interrupting the continuity of action in the field.

IV.v.36–40. *Alexas . . . him.* 'For Alexas Laodician, who was brought into Antonius house and fauor by meanes of Timagenes, and afterwards was in greater credit with him, then any other Grecian: (for that he had alway bene one of Cleopatraes ministers to win Antonius, and to ouerthrow all his good determinations to vse his wife Octauia well) him Antonius had sent vnto Herodes King of Iurie, hoping still to keepe him his frend, that he should not reuolt from him. But he remained there, and betrayed Antonius. For where he should haue kept Herodes from reuolting from him, he perswaded him to turne to Caesar: & trusting King Herodes, he presumed to come in Caesars presence. Howbeit Herodes did him no pleasure: for he was presently taken prisoner, and sent in chaines to his owne contrie, & there by Caesars commaundement put to death.' North, p. 1004.

IV.v.SD. *Alarum.* With this stage direction some editors begin Scene 7.

IV.v.73, 74. *a T . . . and H.* Pun on 'ache,' pronounced 'aitch' in Shakespeare's time when a noun.

IV.vi.SD. *Alarum.* With this stage direction some editors begin Scene 8.

IV.vii.SD. *Enter a Sentry.* With this stage direction some editors begin Scene 9.

IV.vii.20. *dried with grief.* It was believed that with each sigh the heart lost a drop of blood. Cf. *Hamlet,* IV.3.134, 135: 'And then this "should" is like a spendthrift sigh That hurts by easing.'

IV.viii.SD. *Enter Antony.* With this stage direction some editors begin Scene 10.

IV.viii.SD. *Enter Caesar.* With this stage direction some editors begin Scene 11.

IV.viii.SD. *Enter Antony.* With this stage direction some editors begin Scene 12.

IV.viii. 18–21. *Swallows . . . knowledge.* 'The admirall galley of Cleopatra, was called Antoniade, in the which there chaunced a maruelous ill signe. Swallowes had bred vnder the poope of her shippe, & there came others after them that draue away the first, & plucked downe their neasts.' Shakespeare simplified the augury, perhaps influenced by North's marginal note: 'An ill signe, foreshewed by swallowed breding in Cleopatraes shippe.' North, p. 999.

IV.viii. 43. *my crownet, my chief end.* 'My coronet, the chief reward of all my efforts.' 'Crown' was used in the sense of fulfillment, the last, final achievement.

IV.viii.54. *dolts.* Some editors read *doits*, in which case they doubtfully interpret *diminitives* as 'small coins.' *Doit* was a copper coin of small value, originally of Dutch origin. See Sir William A. Craigie, *A Dictionary of the Older Scottish Tongue* (London, 1937), 2, 182. Shakespeare uses the word in *The Tempest*, II.2.31, 32: 'When they will not give a doit to relieve a lame beggar.'

IV.viii.61. *shirt of Nessus.* A poisoned shirt innocently brought to Hercules by his servant Lichas, which caused him such pain that he threw Lichas to the sky (whence he fell into the sea) and had himself burnt on a pyre on Mount Oeta. Before sending the shirt to her husband, Deianira dipped it in the blood of the Centaur Nessus, recently slain by Hercules, believing the dying Centaur's assurance that she would thereby preserve her husband's love.

IV.ix.2. *Telamon.* Ajax, son of Telamon, went mad when Achilles' shield was denied him and given instead to Ulysses.

IV.ix.2. *boar of Thessaly.* The ferocious boar sent by Artemis to ravage Caledon and slain by Meleager.

IV.ix.4. *To th' monument.* 'Furthermore, Cleopatra had long before made many sumptuous tombes and monumentes, as well as for excellencie of workemanshippe, as for height and greatness of building, ioyning hard to the temple of Isis. Thither she caused to be brought all the treasure & pretious things she had of the auncient kings her predecessors: as gold, siluer, emerods, pearles, ebbanie, iuorie, and sinnamon, and besides all that, a maruelous number of torches, faggots, and flaxe.' North, p. 1005.

IV.x.9. *black . . . pageants.* Shows that precede or announce the coming of night. Extremely elaborate and costly, pageants honored important events or persons, the best known being the annual pageant honoring the inauguration of the Lord Mayor of London.

IV.x.21–22. *Packed . . . triumph.* 'Stacked the cards against me and in Caesar's favor, and played falsely causing my enemy to win (*triumph*) and me to lose the glory I had staked.' *Triumph*, early form of 'trump,' enriches the metaphor by suggesting that Cleopatra betrayed Antony by playing the wrong card (*false-play'd*) to Caesar's trump.

IV.x.SD. *Enter [Dercetas and].* Dercetas probably enters with the guard. The Folio prefixes speech ll. 132–134 *Dercetus*, that at l. 136 *Decre.*, and prints *Decretas* at V.1.SD, and *Dec.* at V.1.7.

IV.xi.SD. *They heave . . . Cleopatra.* The physical problems involved in raising the dying Antony to the upper stage representing Cleopatra's monument may be in fact solved by a description of the same action in Samuel Daniel's 1607 version of *Cleopatra*. Miss Joan Rees offers the attractive theory that Daniel's description is a reminiscence of an actual production of *Antony and Cleopatra*. For Daniel's passage and further comments see Joan Rees, 'An Elizabethan Eyewitness of Antony and Cleopatra,' *Shakespeare Survey, 6* (1953), 91–93. Cf. also Roy Walker, 'Antony and Cleopatra,' (London) *Times Literary Supplement*, May 29, 1953, p. 349.

IV.xi.45. *when.* So in F. Pope and later editors print *where*. The sense of the F reading is: 'Die after you have lived once more,' an interpretation supported by 'quicken with kissing.'

IV.xi.61–68. *The miserable . . . vanquish'd.* 'When he had dronke, he earnestly prayed her, and perswaded her, that she would seeke to saue her life, if she could possible, without reproache and dishonor: and that chiefly she should trust Proculeius aboue any man else about Caesar. And as for him selfe, that she should not lament nor sorrowe for the miserable chaunge of his fortune at the end of his dayes: but rather that she would thinke him the more fortunate, for the former triumphes & honors he had receiued, considering that while he liued he was the noblest and greatest Prince of the world, & that now he was ouercome, not cowardly, but valiantly, a Romane by an other Romane.' North, pp. 1006, 1007.

IV.xi.76. *pole.* Another interpretation, given by Schmidt and some editors, is 'lodestar,' a sense made acceptable by IV.10.125, above.

IV.xi.87. *in.* Contracted, weakly stressed form of *even*, which appears also as *e'ne*, *e'ene*, or *ev'n*. See Kökeritz, *Shakespeare's Pronunciation*, pp. 203, 204.

V.i.34, 38. *Agrippa.* The Folio assigns these two speeches to Dolabella, who in fact is not on the stage, having left it at l. 4. Theobald and subsequent editors assign them to Agrippa.

V.i.89. *writings.* 'Then he called for all his frendes, and shewed them the letters Antonius had written to him, and his aunsweres also sent him againe, during their quarrell and strife: & how fiercely and prowdly the other answered him, to all iust and reasonable matters he wrote vnto him.' North, p. 1007.

V.ii.26. *Make your . . . freely.* Entrust yourself and your fortunes wholly and without fear.

V.ii.30. *will pray . . . kindness.* Will ask for help in looking for opportunities to do kind acts.

V.ii.SD. *Roman . . . Cleopatra.* This incident, as well as the entire scene, takes place inside the monument, and it is now generally agreed that it was acted on the main stage. See The Arden Shakespeare, pp. 251–257; C. W. Hodges, *The Globe Restored* (London, Ernest Benn, 1953), pp. 59, 60.

V.ii.40, 41. *You see . . . come.* Although the Folio heads these lines *Pro.*, some editors have assigned them to Gallus, who presumably leads the soldiers who surprise Cleopatra. Such a drastic emendation was called for by the necessity to eliminate the duplication of the speech heading *Pro.*, and the choice of Gallus was dictated by the fact that in the preceding scene Caesar sends him to the monument shortly after Proculeius. The editors have been influenced also by North's account of the incident, although there Proculeius is the one who surprises Cleopatra while Gallus holds her in conversation. It is possible that Gallus does lead the soldiers who surprise Cleopatra, although there is no evidence in the Folio for his presence on the scene until the stage direction following line 133. But if he does appear on the stage he must remain mute, and the lines in question must be spoken by Proculeius, for the duplication of the speech heading was caused not by careless speech distribution but by the omission of at least a speech. And for such an assumption we have good evidence. The duplication occurs at the precise point in the text where a crucial stage direction should be forthcoming, and it is reasonable to assume that such a stage direction appeared in the poet's manuscript. For in the matter of stage directions, both as to frequency and detail, our play is almost unique. And the absence of a stage direction here suggests strongly that something else in the manuscript may have been omitted as well at this point, perhaps a speech or two. Mr. Ridley's view (Arden ed., p. 254) that Proculeius is unaware of Caesar's little plot against Cleopatra and that therefore the lines are spoken by Gallus, who is privy to it, must be rejected. Proculeius could not mistake Caesar's lines addressed to him before he leaves for Cleopatra's monument (V.1.72–76):

> give her what comforts
> The quality of her passion shall require,
> Lest in her greatness by some mortal stroke
> She do defeat us. For her life in Rome
> Would be eternal in our triumph.

On the other hand, sending Gallus seems like an afterthought, and Caesar gives him no instructions whatever.

V.ii.106–108. *his delights . . . liv'd in.* He kept himself above (superior to) the pleasures in which he lived just as the dolphin keeps its back above the water.

V.ii.118–120. *yet . . . quite.* Yet to imagine an actual Antony, to accept him as a product of Nature, would be to place Nature above fancy since he would excel (and put to shame) even fancy's most outlandish creations.

V.ii.262. *Some . . . greatness.* 'Some boy actor with squeaking voice will burlesque my greatness.' Until the second half of the 17th century female parts were acted by boys on the English stage.

V.ii.330–331. *The luck . . . wrath.* Caesar's good fortune, the sort of excessively good luck which the envious gods use as an excuse (since good fortune may lead to pride) for striking a man (with such luck) down.

V.ii.333, 334. *my other . . . life.* Since of the four elements (earth, fire, air, water) thought to constitute the human body only air and fire were associated with immortality, Cleopatra bequeaths the other two to mortal, that is human, life.

V.ii.413–415. *for her physician . . . die.* 'So when she had dayly made diuers and sundrie proofes, she found none of all them she had proued so fit, as the biting of an Aspicke, the which only causeth a heauines of the head, without swounding or complaining, and bringeth a great desire also to sleepe, with a little swet in the face, and so by litle and litle taketh away the sences and vitall powers, no liuing creature perceiuing that the pacientes feele any paine.' North, p. 1004.

The Tragedy of Coriolanus

Edited by
TUCKER BROOKE

Dramatis Personae

CAIUS MARTIUS, *later named Coriolanus*

COMINIUS ⎱
TITUS LARTIUS ⎰ *Roman Generals*

MENENIUS AGRIPPA, *Friend to Coriolanus*

SICINIUS VELUTUS ⎱
JUNIUS BRUTUS ⎰ *Tribunes of the People*

YOUNG MARTIUS, *Son to Coriolanus*

A ROMAN HERALD

TULLUS AUFIDIUS, *General of the Volscians*

LIEUTENANT TO AUFIDIUS

CONSPIRATORS WITH AUFIDIUS

A ROMAN, *named Nicanor*

A VOLSCIAN, *named Adrian*

A CITIZEN OF ANTIUM

TWO VOLSCIAN GUARDS

VOLUMNIA, *Mother to Coriolanus*

VIRGILIA, *Wife to Coriolanus*

VALERIA, *A noble Lady of Rome*

GENTLEWOMAN, *Attendant of Virgilia*

ROMAN AND VOLSCIAN SENATORS, PATRICIANS, AEDILES, LICTORS, SOLDIERS, CITIZENS, MESSENGERS, SERVANTS TO AUFIDIUS, AND OTHER ATTENDANTS

SCENE—*Rome and the Volscian country to the south, with the towns of Corioli and Antium.*

The Tragedy of Coriolanus

INTRODUCTION

The chief and almost sole source of *Coriolanus,* as of Shakespeare's other Roman plays, is North's translation of Plutarch's *Lives,* which was first printed in 1579 and reached its third edition in 1603. About 550 lines of North's prose are woven into the text of *Coriolanus,* and the verbal adherence of the poet to the translator is even closer than it is in the earlier Plutarchan plays of *Julius Cæsar* and *Antony and Cleopatra.* The two principal characters, Coriolanus and Volumnia, owe most to Plutarch, though Shakespeare has given to each of them distinguishing traits hardly implied by his original. Virgilia, Menenius, and the Tribunes, on the other hand, are developed out of very slight suggestions. North only once mentions Virgilia's name and affords us no clue to her character. He says nothing of Menenius' friendship for Coriolanus, and names him only in the following account of his famous fable:

When the Plebeians were threatening to withdraw from Rome, North says: 'The Senate, being afeared of their departure, did send unto them certain of the pleasantest old men and the most acceptable to the people among them. Of those Menenius Agrippa was he who was sent for chief man of the message from the Senate. He, after many good persuasions and gentle requests made to the people on the behalf of the Senate, knit up his oration in the end with a notable tale, in this manner. That on a time all the members of man's body did rebel against the belly, complaining of it, that it only remained in the midst of the body, without doing anything, neither did bear any labour to the maintenance of the rest: whereas all other parts and members did labour painfully, and were very careful to satisfy the appetites and desires of the body. And so the belly, all this notwithstanding, laughed at their folly, and said: "It is true, I first receive all meats that nourish man's body: but afterwards I send it again to the nourishment of other parts of the same." "Even so" (quoth he) "O you, my masters, and citizens of Rome: the reason is a like between the Senate and you. For matters being well digested, and their counsels thoroughly examined, touching the benefit of the commonwealth, the Senators are cause of the common commodity that cometh unto every one of you." These persuasions pacified the people.'

The most famous declamatory passages in *Coriolanus* are precisely those in which Shakespeare has most closely reproduced the prose of North. They are Coriolanus' indictment of the mob (III.i.83-172), his speech to Aufidius in the latter's house at Antium (IV.v.66-103), and Volumnia's successful appeal for Rome (V.iii.97ff.). These are the emotional crises of the play. They are singular examples of the tact with which at this period of his career Shakespeare could transfer a fine and living picture from narrative to drama and from prose to poetry with the maximum of fidelity and an irreducible minimum of remoulding. North thus reports the speeches of Coriolanus and Aufidius:

"Tullus rose presently from the board, and, coming towards him, asked him what he was, and wherefore he came. Then Martius unmuffled himself, and after he had paused a while, making no answer, he said unto him. "If thou knowest me not yet, Tullus, and, seeing me, dost not perhaps believe me to be the man I am in deed, I must of necessity bewray my self to be that I am. I am Caius Martius, who hath done to thy self particularly, and to all the Volsces generally, great hurt and mischief, which I cannot deny for my surname of Coriolanus that I bear. For I never had other benefit nor recompense of all the true and painful service I have done, and the extreme dangers I have been in, but this only surname: a good memory and witness of the malice and displeasure thou shouldst bear me. Indeed the name only remaineth with me: for the rest envy and cruelty of the people of Rome have taken from me, by the sufferance of the dastardly nobility and magistrats, who have forsaken me, and let me be banished by the people. This extremity hath now driven me to come as a poor suitor to take thy chimney hearth, not of any hope I have to save my life thereby. For if I had feared death, I would not have come hither to have put my life in hazard: but pricked forward with spite and desire I have to be revenged of them that thus have banished me, whom now I begin to be avenged on, putting my person between my enemies. Wherefore, if thou hast any heart to be wreaked of the injuries thy enemies have done thee, speed thee now, and let my misery serve thy turn, and so use it, as my service may be a benefit to the Volsces: promising thee, that I will fight with better good-will for all you, than ever I did when I was against you, knowing that they fight more valiantly, who know the force of their enemy, than such as have never proved it. And if it be so that thou dare not, and that thou art weary to prove fortune any more: than am I also weary to live any longer. And it were no wisdom in thee to save the life of him, who hath been heretofore thy mortal enemy, and whose service now can nothing help nor pleasure thee." Tullus, hearing what he said, was a marvellous glad man, and, taking him by the hand, he said unto him: "Stand up, O Martius, and be of good cheer, for in proffering thyself unto us thou dost us great honour: and by this means thou mayest hope also of greater things at all the Volsces' hands." So he feasted him for that time, and entertained him in the honourablest manner he could, talking with him in no other matters at that present: but within few days after, they fell to consultation together in what sort 'they should begin their wars.'

Comparison of this passage with its Shakespearean counterpart (IV.v.48-173) shows that while the speech of Coriolanus is virtually all Plutarch, the speeches of Aufidius are almost wholly original with Shakespeare. They offer an instructive contrast in style and an admirable illustration of the manner in which Shakespeare could make dramatic adaptation go hand in hand with dramatic originality.

In the handling of incident Shakespeare treats Plutarch with the same appreciative discrimination as in the writing of dialogue. Seven scenes of the play are independent of North, and Plutarchan incidents are not infrequently altered to the advantage of

dramatic economy, as when Shakespeare makes Coriolanus' year-long squabbles with the Plebeians all focus upon the election to the Consulship. But when the Plutarchan story is good drama as it stands, the poet hardly tampers with it at all.

For the fable of Menenius, as told in the play (I.i.77-147) it has been pointed out that Shakespeare appears to have made use of a version more detailed than that which Plutarch gives. This is found in William Camden's *Remaines of a Greater Worke, Concerning Britain,* published in 1605. It will be seen on comparison with North's narrative, quoted on page 158, that the following account, as given by Camden, has a number of verbal similarities with Shakespeare's lines which are absent from North and can hardly have been accidental:—'All the members of the body conspired against the stomacke, as against the swallowing gulfe of all their labors; for whereas the eies beheld the eares heard, the handes labored, the feete traveled, the tongue spake, and all partes performed their functions, onely the stomacke lay ydle and consumed all. Hereuppon they ioyntly agreed al to forbeare their labors, and to pine away their lasie and publike enemy. One day passed over, the second followed very tedious, but the third day was so grievous to them all, that they called a common Counsel; The eyes waxed dimme, the feete could not support the body, the armes waxed lasie, the tongue faltered, and could not lay open the matter; Therefore they all with one accord desired the advise of the Heart. There Reason layd open before them, that hee against whome they had proclaimed warres, was the cause of all this their misery: For he as their common steward, when his allowances were withdrawne, of necessitie withdrew theirs fro them, as not receiving that he might allow. Therefore it were a farre better course to supply him, than that the limbs should faint with hunger. So by the perswasion of Reason, the stomacke was served, the limbes comforted, and peace re-established. Even so it fareth with the bodies of Common-weales. . . .'

THE HISTORY OF THE PLAY

Coriolanus is the latest in date of Shakespeare's tragedies. The evidence of style and several unusually persuasive internal allusions[1] point to its composition in 1608 or 1609, immediately after *Antony and Cleopatra.* Of the stage history of the play before the Restoration we have no knowledge whatever.[2] Indeed the earliest positive allusion to it is found in the licensing notice of previously uncopyrighted Shakespearean plays, entered on the book of the Stationers' Company by the publishers of the Shakespeare Folio, November 8, 1623. Here *Coriolanus* is named first among the eight tragedies 'not formerly entred to other men.' In the Folio of 1623, and the three following Folio editions of Shakespeare, *Coriolanus* is accordingly printed between *Troilus and Cressida* and *Titus Andronicus.* These, with the exception of Tate's alteration, are the only texts of the play published during the seventeenth century.

The manuscript upon which the Folio text of *Coriolanus* was based appears to have been pretty carefully prepared. The play is accurately divided into acts, though not into scenes, and contains rather full and explicit stage directions. The text is certainly faulty

1 See notes on I.i.168; II.ii.106.

2 Jonson's parody of II.ii, 106, however, in *The Silent Woman* is circumstantial evidence that *Coriolanus* was being acted in 1609-1610.

in certain places and the lines are frequently misdivided, but the proportion of error will seem small if one considers the alarming syntactic and metrical peculiarities (those of Shakespeare's last period) with which the printer had to deal. No reason has been found for doubting that the play is wholly Shakespeare's. The text, then, as we have it, would seem to represent a theatre manuscript fully completed by Shakespeare and doubtless occasionally acted by his company, but lacking evidence of the careful revision, abridgment or amplification which popular plays usually received.

Our actual knowledge of the production of *Coriolanus* in any form begins with 1682, when Nahum Tate adapted the tragedy for the Theatre-Royal under the title, *The Ingratitude of a Commonwealth: or, The Fall of Caius Martius Coriolanus.* Tate attempted to inject contemporary interest into the work by giving it an application of the political troubles of the last years of Charles II. 'Upon a close view of this Story,' he says, 'there appear'd in some Passages no small Resemblance with the busie Faction of our own time. And I confess, I chose rather to set the Parallel nearer to Sight than to throw it off at further Distance.'

Through his first four acts Tate follows Shakespeare with reasonable fidelity. The lines are mainly Shakespeare's, though frequently refashioned, and the chief alteration, apart from very drastic cutting, is the quite new presentation of Valeria as 'an affected, talkative, fantastical Lady' after the Restoration mode. The fifth act is almost pure Tate. It develops Aufidius' Lieutenant (*Coriolanus* IV.vii.) as a melodramatic villain and renegade under the name of Nigridius, makes Aufidius an unscrupulous though unsuccessful lover of Virgilia, and closes in a riot of horror. In the final scene at 'Corioles' Menenius, Virgilia, and young Martius are all horribly slain, as well as Nigridius, Aufidius, and Coriolanus, while Volumnia goes furiously mad. It is pleasing to remark that Tate's version does not appear to have been a success.

On November 11, 1719, the Drury Lane Theatre produced an adaptation of *Coriolanus* by John Dennis, which was printed in 1720 with the title, *The Invader of his Country: or, The Fatal Resentment.* This bad play appears to have been acted but three times. Dennis prefaced the printed edition with an indignant letter in which he expostulated against the unfairness with which the management of the theatre had treated him; but the cast, headed by Barton Booth as Coriolanus and Mrs. Porter as Volumnia, was an excellent one, and the failure of the piece to please is well accounted for by the dulness of the adaptation. The play contains extremely few lines recognizable as Shakespeare's, far fewer than Tate's revision, though it shows less than Tate's originality in inventing new plot devices. Dennis opens with the battles at Corioli and closes with a scene in which Coriolanus slays Aufidius and dies in spectacular combat with four Tribunes of the Volsci to an accompaniment of shrieks and lamentations from Volumnia and Virgilia. The most interesting scene is that of the consular election, where adherents of the candidates, Coriolanus and Sempronius, respectively, act out a lively imitation of an English electoral rally.

The theme of the play was next brought upon the English stage by James Thomson, author of the *Seasons,* whose *Coriolanus* was acted at Covent Garden some five months after the poet's death. Thomson's play is independent of Shakespeare's and follows different sources in its treatment of the legend: ignoring Plutarch, Thomson goes to the Roman historians, Livy and Dionysius of Halicarnassus, for his material. Consequently some of the characters appear with different names. Aufidius is called

Attius Tullus, Coriolanus' mother Veturia, and his wife Volumnia. The mere fact that such alterations were possible shows how little the Shakespearean figures were known to the English public of the day.

Thomson's *Coriolanus* was first acted January 13, 1749, and was repeated some ten times by a very notable cast. The famous Quin took the title-rôle and Ryan the hardly less prominent or heroic part of Attius Tullus, while Peg Woffington played Coriolanus' mother and Mrs. Bellamy his wife. Thomson was the first capable English poet to touch the theme of Coriolanus since Shakespeare. His rhetorical tragedy, presenting various types of nobly sensitive souls as the eighteenth century liked to fancy them, seems to us lacking in reality and in dramatic force; but it is a worthy poem of its peculiar kind. It nowhere challenges comparison with Shakespeare, and would hardly come into the history of the latter's play, if the taste of later producers had not brought upon the stage several strange blends of Shakespeare and Thomson.

The earliest of these is ascribed to Thomas Sheridan, manager of the Smock Alley Theatre in Dublin. From thence it was transferred to Covent Garden in London, where it was produced first on December 10, 1754. There was more of Thomson than of Shakespeare in this, and Thomson's names of characters were retained. Coriolanus was played by Sheridan; Attius Tullus, Veturia, and Volumnia by the same distinguished performers who had supported those parts in the 1749 production of Thomson's tragedy. The blend of Shakespeare and Thomson, which had proved decidedly successful in Sheridan's version, became yet more so when John Philip Kemble staged at Drury Lane, February 7, 1789, another adaptation in which the greater part of the material was drawn from Shakespeare. 'In this alteration,' the *European Magazine* said at the time, 'the best parts of Shakespeare and Thomson are retained, and compose a more pleasing drama than that of either author separately.' Kemble's first three acts are wholly from Shakespeare, though much condensed; in acts four and five there is a predominance of Thomson. This piece was many times repeated. Kemble's Coriolanus and the Volumnia

of his sister, Mrs. Siddons, are rated among their greatest parts; and it was in *Coriolanus* that Kemble took his leave of the stage on June 23, 1817.

On June 24, 1820, *Coriolanus,* with Shakespeare's text restored (as was a little falsely asserted), was performed at Drury Lane by Edmund Kean, whose success in this too statuesque rôle did not equal that of Kemble. Rival performances were given at Covent Garden (beginning November 29, 1819) with the title-rôle in the hands of W. C. Macready, who long continued to act the part. John Vandenhoff (from 1823) gave many successful performances of the play throughout England and Scotland, and Samuel Phelps (from 1848) at the Sadler's Wells Theatre in London. Other productions of some note in England have been those of James Anderson (from 1851), Sir Henry Irving (1901), and Sir F. R. Benson. It was the special degree in which this play (particularly with the interpolated borrowings from Thomson) fitted the statuesque acting of Kemble and Mrs. Siddons which gave it its impetus. Its stage value suffered when the Kemble ideal of acting gave place to more romantic and perhaps more subtle conceptions.

Thomson's *Coriolanus* was played at the Southwark Theatre, Philadelphia, on June 8, 1767. The Shakespearean play—that is, presumably, the Kemble version—was first acted in the United States by the Philadelphia Company, June 3, 1796. During the latter half of the nineteenth century the American actors Edwin Booth, John McCullough, and Lawrence Barrett all distinguished themselves as Coriolanus; and the Italian Tommaso Salvini interpreted the part in Boston and other cities during the season of 1885-1886. The American actor who most identified himself with the rôle was, however, Edwin Forrest (1806-1872), whose Coriolanus was perhaps his favorite character and whose statue represents him dressed for that part.

The most notable French production of the play was that of M. Joubé at the Odéon in Paris in 1910. In 1920 the tragedy was acted seven times in Berlin and twice at Lübeck. A total of 103 performances in different German cities has been collected for the period between 1911 and 1920.[3]

---

3 See the list by Dr. E. Mühlbach, Shakespeare-Jahrbuch, 1921, pp. 159-163.

Act First ❧ Scene First

[Rome. A Street]
Enter a Company of mutinous Citizens, with staves, clubs, and other
weapons.

1. Cit. Before we proceed any further, hear me speak.

All. Speak, speak.

1. Cit. You are all resolved rather to die than to famish?

All. Resolved, resolved.

1. Cit. First, you know Caius Martius is chief enemy to   5
the people.

All. We know 't, we know 't.

1. Cit. Let us kill him, and we'll have corn at our own
price. Is 't a verdict?

All. No more talking on 't; let it be done. Away, away!   10

2. Cit. One word, good citizens.

1. Cit. We are accounted poor citizens, the patricians good.
What authority surfeits on would relieve us. If they would
yield us but the superfluity, while it were wholesome, we
might guess they relieved us humanely; but they think we   15
are too dear: the leanness that afflicts us, the object of our
misery, is as an inventory to particularise their abundance;
our sufferance is a gain to them. Let us revenge this with
our pikes, ere we become rakes: for the gods know I speak this
in hunger for bread, not in thirst for revenge.   20

2. Cit. Would you proceed especially against Caius Martius?

All. Against him first: he's a very dog to the commonalty.

2. Cit. Consider you what services he has done for his
country?

1. Cit. Very well; and could be content to give him good   25
report for 't, but that he pays himself with being proud.

2. Cit. Nay, but speak not maliciously.

1. Cit. I say unto you, what he hath done famously, he did
it to that end: though soft-conscienced men can be content to
say it was for his country, he did it to please his mother,   30
and to be partly proud; which he is, even to the altitude
of his virtue.

2. Cit. What he cannot help in his nature, you account a
vice in him. You must in no way say he is covetous.

1. Cit. If I must not, I need not be barren of accusations:
he hath faults, with surplus, to tire in repetition. *Shouts within.*
What shouts are these? The other side o' the city is risen: why
stay we prating here? to the Capitol!

All. Come, come.

1. Cit. Soft! who comes here?   40

Enter Menenius Agrippa.

2. Cit. Worthy Menenius Agrippa; one that hath always
loved the people.

1. Cit. He's one honest enough: would all the rest were so!

Men. What work's, my countrymen, in hand? Where go you.
With bats and clubs? The matter? Speak, I pray you.   45

2. Cit. Our business is not unknown to the senate; they
have had inkling this fortnight what we intend to do, which
now we'll show 'em in deeds. They say poor suitors have
strong breaths: they shall know we have strong arms too.

Men. Why, masters, my good friends, mine honest   50
neighbours,
Will you undo yourselves?

2. Cit. We cannot, sir; we are undone already.

Men. I tell you, friends, most charitable care
Have the patricians of you. For your wants,
Your suffering in this dearth, you may as well   55
Strike at the heaven with your staves as lift them
Against the Roman state, whose course will on
The way it takes, cracking ten thousand curbs
Of more strong link asunder than can ever
Appear in your impediment. For the dearth,   60
The gods, not the patricians, make it, and
Your knees to them, not arms, must help. Alack!
You are transported by calamity
Thither where more attends you; and you slander
The helms o' the state, who care for you like fathers,   65
When you curse them as enemies.

2. Cit. Care for us! True, indeed! They ne'er cared for us
yet: suffer us to famish, and their storehouses crammed with
grain; make edicts for usury, to support usurers; repeal daily
any wholesome act established against the rich, and provide   70
more piercing statutes daily to chain up and restrain the
poor. If the wars eat us not up, they will; and there's all the
love they bear us.

Men. Either you must
Confess yourselves wondrous malicious,   75
Or be accus'd of folly. I shall tell you
A pretty tale: it may be you have heard it;
But, since it serves my purpose, I will venture
To scale 't a little more.

2. Cit. Well, I'll hear it, sir; yet you must not think to fob
off your disgrace with a tale; but, an 't please you, deliver.

Men. There was a time when all the body's members
Rebell'd against the belly; thus accus'd it:
That only like a gulf it did remain
I' the midst o' the body, idle and unactive,   85
Still cupboarding the viand, never bearing
Like labour with the rest, where th' other instruments
Did see and hear, devise, instruct, walk, feel,
And, mutually participate, did minister
Unto the appetite and affection common   90
Of the whole body. The belly answer'd,—

2. Cit. Well, sir, what answer made the belly?

Men. Sir, I shall tell you.—With a kind of smile,
Which ne'er came from the lungs, but even thus—
For, look you, I may make the belly smile   95
As well as speak—it taintingly replied
To the discontented members, the mutinous parts
That envied his receipt; even so most fitly
As you malign our senators for that
They are not such as you.   100

2. Cit.   Your belly's answer? What!
The kingly crowned head, the vigilant eye,
The counsellor heart, the arm our soldier,
Our steed the leg, the tongue our trumpeter,
With other muniments and petty helps   105

---

15 guess: *think*   **16 are too dear:** *cost too much*   **object:** *spectacle*   **17 particularise:**
itemize   **18 sufferance:** *suffering*   **27 2. Cit.;** *cf. n.*   **31 to be partly:** *in part in order*
to be   **36 to . . . repetition:** *which it would weary one to list over*   **45 bats:** *heavy sticks*

58 curbs: *restraining chains*   **64 more:** *more calamity*   **65 helms:** *pilots*   **79 scale 't;**
cf. n.   **81 disgrace:** *unfavored treatment*   **84 gulf:** *devouring whirlpool*   **89 partici-**
pate: *cooperating*   **94 Which . . . lungs;** *cf. n.*   **96 taintingly:** *effectively; cf. n.*   **98**
his receipt: *what he received*   **103 counsellor heart;** *cf. n.*   **105 muniments:** *furnishings*

In this our fabric, if that they—
    Men. What then?—
'Fore me, this fellow speaks! what then? what then?
    2. Cit. Should by the cormorant belly be restrain'd,   *110*
Who is the sink o' the body,—
    Men. Well, what then?
    2. Cit. The former agents, if they did complain,
What could the belly answer?
    Men. I will tell you;   *115*
If you'll bestow a small, of what you have little,
Patience a while, you'st hear the belly's answer.
    2. Cit. You're long about it.
    Men. Note me this, good friend;
Your most grave belly was deliberate,   *120*
Not rash like his accusers, and thus answer'd:
'True is it, my incorporate friends,' quoth he,
'That I receive the general food at first,
Which you do live upon; and fit is is,
Because I am the store-house and the shop   *125*
Of the whole body: but, if you do remember,
I send it through the rivers of your blood,
Even to the court, the heart, to the seat o' the brain;
And, through the cranks and offices of man,
The strongest nerves and small inferior veins   *130*
From me receive that natural competency
Whereby they live. And though that all at once,
You, my good friends,'—this says the belly, mark me,—
    2. Cit. Ay, sir; well, well.
    Men. 'Though all at once cannot   *135*
See what I do deliver out to each,
Yet I can make my audit up, that all
From me do back receive the flour of all,
And leave me but the bran.' What say you to 't?
    2. Cit. It was an answer: how apply you this?   *140*
    Men. The senators of Rome are this good belly,
And you the mutinous members; for, examine
Their counsels and their cares, digest things rightly
Touching the weal o' the common, you shall find
No public benefit which you receive   *145*
But it proceeds or comes from them to you,
And no way from yourselves. What do you think,
You, the great toe of this assembly?
    2. Cit. I the great toe? Why the great toe?
    Men. For that, being one o' the lowest, basest, poorest,   *150*
Of this most wise rebellion, thou go'st foremost:
Thou rascal, that art worst in blood to run,
Lead'st first to win some vantage.
But make you ready your stiff bats and clubs:
Rome and her rats are at the point of battle;   *155*
The one side must have bale.

    Enter Caius Martius.

    Hail, noble Martius!
    Mar. Thanks.—What's the matter, you dissentious rogues,
That, rubbing the poor itch of your opinion,
Make yourselves scabs?   *160*

    2. Cit. We have ever your good word.
    Mar. He that will give good words to thee will flatter
Beneath abhorring. What would you have, you curs,
That like nor peace nor war? the one affrights you,
The other makes you proud. He that trusts to you,   *165*
Where he should find you lions, finds you hares;
Where foxes, geese: you are no surer, no,
Than is the coal of fire upon the ice,
Or hailstone in the sun. Your virtue is,
To make him worthy whose offence subdues him,   *170*
And curse that justice did it. Who deserves greatness
Deserves your hate; and your affections are
A sick man's appetite, who desires most that
Which would increase his evil. He that depends
Upon your favours swims with fins of lead   *175*
And hews down oaks with rushes. Hang ye! Trust ye?
With every minute you do change a mind,
And call him noble that was now your hate,
Him vile that was your garland. What's the matter,
That in these several places of the city   *180*
You cry against the noble senate, who,
Under the gods, keep you in awe, which else
Would feed on one another? What's their seeking?
    Men. For corn at their own rates; whereof they say
The city is well stor'd.   *185*
    Mar. Hang 'em! They say!
They'll sit by the fire, and presume to know
What's done i' the Capitol; who's like to rise,
Who thrives, and who declines; side factions, and give out
Conjectural marriages; making parties strong,   *190*
And feebling such as stand not in their liking
Below their cobbled shoes. They say there's grain enough!
Would the nobility lay aside their ruth,
And let me use my sword, I'd make a quarry
With thousands of these quarter'd slaves, as high   *195*
As I could pick my lance.
    Men. Nay, these are almost thoroughly persuaded;
For though abundantly they lack discretion,
Yet are they passing cowardly. But, I beseech you,
What says the other troop?   *200*
    Mar. They are dissolv'd: hang 'em!
They said they were an-hungry; sigh'd forth proverbs:
That hunger broke stone walls; that dogs must eat;
That meat was made for mouths; that the gods sent not
Corn for the rich men only. With these shreds   *205*
They vented their complainings; which being answer'd,
And a petition granted them, a strange one,—
To break the heart of generosity,
And make bold power look pale,—they threw their caps
As they would hang them on the horns o' the moon,   *210*
Shouting their emulation.
    Men. What is granted them?
    Mar. Five tribunes to defend their vulgar wisdoms,
Of their own choice: one's Junius Brutus,
Sicinius Velutus, and I know not—'Sdeath!   *215*
The rabble should have first unroof'd the city,

---

109 'Fore me: *by my faith!*   **111 sink:** *cesspool*   **117 you'st:** *you shall*   **119 Note me:** *pray note*   **122 incorporate:** *joined in one body*   **125 shop:** *workshop*   **129 cranks:** *winding passages*   **129 offices:** *kitchen, etc*   **131 competency:** *sufficiency*   **144 weal ... common:** *common weal*   **152 rascal ... blood;** *cf. n.*   **153 Lead'st first:** *art the very leader*   **vantage:** *personal profit*   **156 bale:** *disaster*   **159, 160 rubbing ... scabs;** *cf. n.*

163 Beneath abhorring: *more than can be enough abhorred*   **164 nor ... nor:** *neither ... nor*   **168** *Cf. n.*   **169–171 Your virtue ... did it;** *cf. n.*   **172 affections:** *favorable opinions*   **188 like:** *likely*   **189 side:** *espouse*   **190 parties:** *favored factions*   **191 feebling:** *reducing*   **194 quarry:** *pile of dead*   **196 pick:** *pitch*   **199 passing:** *surpassingly*   **206 vented:** *gave vent to*   **answer'd:** *satisfied*   **208 generosity:** *the gentry*

Ere so prevail'd with me; it will in time
Win upon power, and throw forth greater themes
For insurrection's arguing.
   Men.   This is strange.   220
   Mar. Go; get you home, you fragments!

       Enter a Messenger, hastily.

   Mess. Where's Caius Martius?
   Mar.   Here: what's the matter?
   Mess. The news is, sir, the Volsces are in arms.
   Mar. I am glad on 't; then we shall ha' means to vent   225
Our musty superfluity. See, our best elders.

Enter Sicinius Velutus, Junius Brutus; Cominius, Titus Lartius,
         with other Senators.

   1. Sen. Martius, 'tis true that you have lately told us;
The Volsces are in arms.
   Mar.   They have a leader,
Tullus Aufidius, that will put you to 't.   230
I sin in envying his nobility,
And were I anything but what I am,
I would wish me only he.
   Com.   You have fought together.
   Mar. Were half to half the world by th' ears, and he   235
Upon my party, I'd revolt, to make
Only my wars with him: he is a lion
That I am proud to hunt.
   1. Sen.   Then, worthy Martius,
Attend upon Cominius to these wars.   240
   Com. It is your former promise.
   Mar.   Sir, it is;
And I am constant. Titus Lartius, thou
Shalt see me once more strike at Tullus' face.
What! are thou stiff? stand'st out?   245
   Tit.   No, Caius Martius;
I'll lean upon one crutch and fight with t'other,
Ere stay behind this business.
   Men.   O! true-bred.
   Sen. Your company to the Capitol; where I know   250
Our greatest friends attend us.
   Tit.   *[To Cominius.]* Lead you on:
[To Martius.] Follow Cominius; we must follow you;
Right worthy you priority.
   Com.   Noble Martius!   255
   Sen. [To the Citizens.] Hence! to your homes! be gone.
   Mar.   Nay, let them follow:
The Volsces have much corn; take these rats thither
To gnaw their garners. Worshipful mutiners,
Your valour puts well forth; pray, follow.   260
    Exeunt [Martius, Cominius, Titus, etc.]. Citizens steal away.
          Mane[n]t Sicin. & Brutus.
   Sic. Was ever man so proud as is this Martius?
   Bru. He has no equal.
   Sic. When we were chosen tribunes for the people,—   265
   Bru. Mark'd you his lip and eyes?
   Sic.   Nay, but his taunts.
   Bru. Being mov'd, he will not spare to gird the gods.

   Sic. Bemock the modest moon.
   Bru. The present wars devour him! he is grown   270
Too proud to be so valiant.
   Sic.   Such a nature,
Tickled with good success, disdains the shadow
Which he treads on at noon. But I do wonder
His insolence can brook to be commanded   275
Under Cominius.
   Bru.   Fame, at the which he aims,
In whom already he's well grac'd, cannot
Better be held nor more attain'd than by
A place below the first; for what miscarries   280
Shall be the general's fault, though he perform
To th' utmost of a man; and giddy censure
Will then cry out of Martius 'O! if he
Had borne the business.'
   Sic.   Besides, if things go well,   285
Opinion, that so sticks on Martius, shall
Of his demerits rob Cominius.
   Bru.   Come:
Half all Cominius' honours are to Martius,
Though Martius earn'd them not; and all his faults   290
To Martius shall be honours, though indeed
In aught he merit not.
   Sic.   Let's hence and hear
How the dispatch is made; and in what fashion,
More than his singularity, he goes   295
Upon this present action.
   Bru.   Let's along.   *Exeunt.*

❧ SCENE SECOND ❧

   [Corioli. The Senate-house]
   Enter Tullus Aufidius with Senators of Corioli.

   1. Sen. So your opinion is, Aufidius,
That they of Rome are enter'd in our counsels,
And know how we proceed.
   Auf.   Is it not yours?
What ever have been thought on in this state,   5
That could be brought to bodily act ere Rome
Had circumvention? 'Tis not four days gone
Since I heard thence; these are the words: I think
I have the letter here; yes, here it is.
'They have press'd a power, but it is not known   10
Whether for east, or west: the dearth is great;
The people mutinous, and it is rumour'd,
Cominius, Martius, your old enemy,—
Who is of Rome worse hated than of you,—
And Titus Lartius, a most valiant Roman,   15
These three lead on this preparation
Whither 'tis bent: most likely 'tis for you:
Consider of it.'
   1. Sen.   Our army's in the field:
We never yet made doubt but Rome was ready   20
To answer us.

---

218 **Win upon:** *get ahead of* **power:** *constituted authority*   219 **For ... arguing:** *for insurgents to maintain*   225 **vent:** *dispose of*   234 **half to half:** *one half against the other*   237 **Only ... with him:** *with him alone*   245 **stand'st out:** *do you decline to go?*   260 **puts ... forth:** *shows well* (ironic)   S.d. **Manent:** *remain on the stage*

271 **to be:** *of being*   273, 274 **disdains ... noon;** *cf. n.*   282 **giddy censure:** *fickle opinion*   287 **demerits:** *merits*   295 **singularity:** *peculiar character*   2 **enter'd:** *instructed*   5 **What:** *what designs*   7 **circumvention:** *means to circumvent*   10 **press'd a power:** *levied troops*   16 **preparation:** *expedition*

Auf.   Nor did you think it folly
To keep your great pretences veil'd till when
They needs must show themselves; which in the hatching,
It seem'd, appear'd to Rome. By the discovery   25
We shall be shorten'd in our aim, which was
To take in many towns ere almost Rome
Should know we were afoot.
    2. Sen.   Noble Aufidius,
Take your commission; hie you to your bands;   30
Let us alone to guard Corioli:
If they set down before 's, for the remove
Bring up your army; but I think you'll find
They've not prepar'd for us.
    Auf.   O! doubt not that;   35
I speak from certainties. Nay, more;
Some parcels of their power are forth already,
And only hitherward. I leave your honours.
If we and Caius Martius chance to meet,
'Tis sworn between us we shall ever strike   40
Till one can do no more
    All.   The gods assist you!
    Auf. And keep your honours safe!
    1. Sen.   Farewell.
    2. Sen.   Farewell.   45
    All. Farewell.   *Exeunt omnes.*

❧ SCENE THIRD ❧

[Rome. A Room in Martius's House]
Enter Volumnia and Virgilia, mother and wife to Martius. They
set them down on two low stools and sew.

Vol. I pray you, daughter, sing; or express yourself in a
more comfortable sort. If my son were my husband, I should
freelier rejoice in that absence wherein he won honour than in
the embracements of his bed where he would show most love.
When yet he was but tender-bodied and the only son of   5
my womb, when youth with comeliness plucked all gaze his
way, when for a day of kings' entreaties a mother should not
sell him an hour from her beholding, I, considering how honour would become such a person, that it was no better than
picture-like to hang by the wall, if renown made it not stir,   10
was pleased to let him seek danger where he was like to find
fame. To a cruel war I sent him; from whence he returned, his
brows bound with oak. I tell thee, daughter, I sprang not more
in joy at first hearing he was a man-child than now in first
seeing he had proved himself a man.   15
Vir. But had he died in the business, madam; how then?
Vol. Then his good report should have been my son; I
therein would have found issue. Hear me profess sincerely: had
I a dozen sons, each in my love alike, and none less dear than
thine and my good Martius, I had rather had eleven die   20
nobly for their country than one voluptuously surfeit out of
action.

Enter a Gentlewoman.

Gent. Madam, the Lady Valeria is come to visit you.

Vir. Beseech you, give me leave to retire myself.
Vol. Indeed, you shall not.   25
Methinks I hear hither your husband's drum,
See him pluck Aufidius down by the hair,
As children from a bear the Volsces shunning him:
Methinks I see him stamp thus, and call thus:
'Come on, you cowards! you were got in fear,   30
Though you were born in Rome.' His bloody brow
With his mail'd hand then wiping, forth he goes,
Like to a harvestman that's task'd to mow
Or all or lose his hire.
Vir. His bloody brow! O Jupiter, no blood!   35
Vol. Away, you fool! it more becomes a man
Than gilt his trophy: the breasts of Hecuba,
When she did suckle Hector, look'd not lovelier
Than Hector's forehead when it spit forth blood,
At Grecian sword contemning. Tell Valeria   40
We are fit to bid her welcome.

                                        Exit Gent.

Vir. Heavens bless my lord from fell Aufidius!
Vol. He'll beat Aufidius' head below his knee,
And tread upon his neck.

Enter Valeria with an Usher, and a Gentlewoman.

Val. My ladies both, good day to you.   45
Vol. Sweet madam.
Vir. I am glad to see your ladyship.
Val. How do you both? you are manifest housekeepers.
What are you sewing here? A fine spot, in good faith, How
does your little son?   50
Vir. I thank your ladyship; well, good madam.
Val. He had rather see the swords and hear a drum, than
look upon his schoolmaster.
Val. O' my word, the father's son; I'll swear 'tis a very
pretty boy. O' my troth, I looked upon him o' Wednesday   55
half an hour together: he has such a confirmed countenance. I
saw him run after a gilded butterfly; and when he caught it, he
let it go again; and after it again; and over and over he comes,
and up again; catched it again: or whether his fall enraged
him, or how 'twas, he did so set his teeth and tear it; O! I   60
warrant, how he mammocked it!
Vol. One on 's father's moods.
Val. Indeed, la, 'tis a noble child.
Vir. A crack, madam.
Val. Come, lay aside your stitchery; I must have you   65
play the idle huswife with me this afternoon.
Vir. No, good madam; I will not out of doors.
Val. Not out of doors!
Vol. She shall, she shall.
Vir. Indeed, no, by your patience; I'll not over the   70
threshold till my lord return from the wars.
Vol. Fie! you confine yourself most unreasonably. Come;
you must go visit the good lady that lies in.
Vir. I will wish her speedy strength, and visit her with
my prayers; but I cannot go thither.   75
Vol. Why, I pray you?

---

23 pretences: *designs*   **27 take in:** *capture*   **31 Corioli;** *cf. n.*   **32 remove:** *raising the siege*   **37 parcels:** *portions*   **7 for ... entreaties:** *though kings should entreat for a day*   **9 person:** *beauty of body*   **13 bound with oak;** *cf. n.*   **21, 22 out of action:** *in inactivity*

33 task'd: *assigned the task*   **37 Than ... trophy:** *than gilding becomes his monu-ment*   **40 contemning:** *showing defiance*   **48 housekeepers:** *recluses, stay-at-homes*   **49 spot:** *pattern for embroidery*   **56 confirmed:** *determined*   **57 gilded:** *gold-colored*   **61 mammocked:** *tore in pieces*   **62 on 's:** *of his*   **64 crack:** *lively child*   **66 play ... huswife:** *idle away your time*

Vir. 'Tis not to save labour, nor that I want love.

Val. You would be another Penelope; yet, they say, all the yarn she spun in Ulysses' absence did but fill Ithaca full of moths. Come; I would your cambric were sensible as your   *80* finger, that you might leave pricking it for pity. Come, you shall go with us.

Vir. No, good madam, pardon me; indeed, I will not forth.

Val. In truth, la, go with me; and I'll tell you excellent   *85* news of your husband.

Vir. O, good madam, there can be none yet.

Val. Verily, I do not jest with you; there came news from him last night.

Vir. Indeed, madam?   *90*

Val. In earnest, it's true; I heard a senator speak it. Thus it is: The Volsces have an army forth; against whom Cominius the general is gone, with one part of our Roman power: your lord and Titus Lartius are set down before their city Corioli; they nothing doubt prevailing and to make it brief wars.   *95* This is true, on mine honour; and so, I pray, go with us.

Vir. Give me excuse, good madam; I will obey you in everything hereafter.

Vol. Let her alone, lady: as she is now she will but disease our better mirth.   *100*

Val. In troth, I think she would. Fare you well then. Come, good sweet lady. Prithee, Virgilia, turn thy solemness out o' door, and go along with us.

Vir. No, at a word, madam; indeed I must not. I wish you must mirth.   *105*

Val. Well then, farewell.   *Exeunt Ladies.*

❧ SCENE FOURTH ❧

[Before Corioli]

Enter Martius, Titus Lartius, with Drum and Colours, with Captains and Soldiers, as before the City Corioli: to them a Messenger.

Mar. Yonder comes news: a wager they have met.

Lart. My horse to yours, no.

Mar.   'Tis done.

Lart.   Agreed.

Mar. Say, has our general met the enemy?   *5*

Mess. They lie in view, but have not spoke as yet.

Lart. So the good horse is mine.

Mar.   I'll buy him of you.

Lart. No, I'll nor sell nor give him; lend you him I will For half a hundred years. Summon the town.

Mar. How far off lie these armies?   *10*

Mess.   Within this mile and half.

Mar. Then shall we hear their 'larum, and they ours. Now, Mars, I prithee, make us quick in work, That we with smoking swords may march from hence, To help our fielded friends! Come, blow thy blast.   *15*

They sound a Parley. Enter two Senators with others on the Walls of Corioli.

Tullus Aufidius, is he within your walls?

1. Sen. No, nor a man that fears you less than he: That's lesser than a little.   *Drum afar off.* Hark, our drums   *20* Are bringing forth our youth: we'll break our walls, Rather than they shall pound us up: our gates, Which yet seem shut, we have but pinn'd with rushes; They'll open of themselves. Hark you, far off!   *Alarum far off.* There is Aufidius: list, what work he makes   *25* Amongst your cloven army.

Mar.   O! they are at it!

Lart. Their noise be our instruction. Ladders, ho!

Enter the Army of the Volsces.

Mar. They fear us not, but issue forth their city. Now put your shields before your hearts, and fight   *30* With hearts more proof than shields. Advance, brave Titus: They do disdain us much beyond our thoughts, Which makes me sweat with wrath. Come on, my fellows: He that retires, I'll take him for a Volsce, And he shall feel mine edge.   *35*

Alarum. The Romans are beat back to their trenches. Enter Martius, cursing.

Mar. All the contagion of the south light on you, You shames of Rome! you herd of—Boils and plagues Plaster you o'er, that you may be abhorr'd Further than seen, and one infect another Against the wind a mile! You souls of geese,   *40* That bear the shapes of men, how have you run From slaves that apes would beat? Pluto and hell! All hurt behind; backs red, and faces pale With flight and argu'd fear! Mend and charge home, Or, by the fires of heaven, I'll leave the foe   *45* And make my wars on you; look to 't: come on; If you'll stand fast, we'll beat them to their wives, As they us to our trenches follows.

Another alarum, and Martius follows them to gates, and is shut in.

So, now the gates are ope: now prove good seconds: 'Tis for the followers Fortune widens them,   *50* Not for the fliers: mark me, and do the like.   *Enter the gates.*

1. Sol. Foolhardiness! not I.

2. Sol.   Nor I.   *Alarum continues.*

1. Sol. See, they have shut him in.

All.   To the pot, I warrant him.

Enter Titus Lartius.

Lart. What is become of Martius?

All.   Slain, sir, doubtless.

1. Sol. Following the fliers at the very heels, With them he enters; who, upon the sudden, Clapp'd-to their gates; he is himself alone,   *60* To answer all the city.

Lart.   O noble fellow!

---

77 want: *am lacking in*   **80 sensible:** *sensitive*   **97 Give ... excuse:** *pardon*   99 **disease:** *disturb*   **102, 103 turn ... door:** *banish gravity*   **104 at a word:** *positively*   6 **spoke:** *euphemism for 'fought'*   **15 fielded:** *engaged on the battlefield*

18 less; *cf. n.*   **22 pound ... up:** *impound, confine*   **28 instruction:** *directions for proceeding*   **32 beyond ... thoughts:** *more than we expected*   **36 south:** *south wind* (thought to bring disease)   **40 Against ... mile;** *cf. n.*   **44 Mend:** *reform*   **48 follows;** *cf. n.*   **49 seconds:** *assistants*   **55 pot:** *cooking-pot; i.e. destruction*   **60 himself alone:** *quite alone*   **61 answer:** *withstand*

Who, sensibly, outdares his senseless sword,
And, when it bows, stands up. Thou art left, Martius:
A carbuncle entire, as big as thou art,   65
Were not so rich a jewel. Thou wast a soldier
Even to Cato's wish, not fierce and terrible
Only in strokes; but, with thy grim looks and
The thunder-like percussion of thy sounds,
Thou mad'st thine enemies shake, as if the world   70
Were feverous and did tremble.

Enter Martius, bleeding, assaulted by the Enemy.

1. Sol.   Look, sir!
Lart.   O! 'tis Martius!
Let's fetch him off, or make remain alike.
                    They fight, and all enter the City.

❧ SCENE FIFTH ❧

[Corioli. A Street]
Enter certain Romans, with spoils.

1. Rom. This will I carry to Rome.
2. Rom. And I this.
3. Rom. A murrain on 't! I took this for silver.
                    Exeunt. Alarum continues still afar off.

Enter Martius and Titus, with a Trumpet.

Mar. See Here these movers that do prize their hours
At a crack'd drachme! Cushions, leaden spoons,   5
Irons of a doit, doublets that hangmen would
Bury with those that wore them, these base slaves,
Ere yet the fight be done, pack up. Down with them!
And hark, what noise the general makes! To him!
There is the man of my soul's hate, Aufidius,   10
Piercing our Romans: then, valiant Titus, take
Convenient numbers to make good the city,
Whilst I, with those that have the spirit, will haste
To help Cominius.
Lart.   Worthy sir, thou bleed'st;   15
Thy exercise hath been too violent
For a second course of fight.
Mar.   Sir, praise me not;
My work hath yet not warm'd me: fare you well:
The blood I drop is rather physical   20
Than dangerous to me: to Aufidius thus
I will appear, and fight.
Lart.   Now the fair goddess, Fortune,
Fall deep in love with thee; and her great charms
Misguide thy opposers' swords! Bold gentleman,   25
Prosperity be thy page!
Mar.   Thy friend no less
Than those she places highest! So, farewell.
Lart. Thou worthiest Martius!—   *[Exit Martius.]*
Go, sound thy trumpet in the market-place;   30
Call thither all the officers o' the town,
Where they shall know our mind. Away!   *Exeunt.*

❧ SCENE SIXTH ❧

[Near the Camp of Cominius]
Enter Cominius as it were in retire, with soldiers.

Com. Breathe you, my friends: well fought; we are come off
Like Romans, neither foolish in our stands,
Nor cowardly in retire: believe me, sirs,
We shall be charg'd again. Whiles we have struck,
By interims and conveying gusts we have heard   5
The charges of our friends. The Roman gods,
Lead their successes as we wish our own,
That both our powers, with smiling fronts encountering,
May give you thankful sacrifice.

Enter a Messenger.

                             Thy news?   10
Mess. The citizens of Corioli have issu'd,
And given to Lartius and to Martius battle:
I saw our party to their trenches driven,
And then I came away.
Com.   Though thou speak'st truth,   15
Methinks thou speak'st not well. How long is 't since?
Mess. Above an hour, my lord.
Com. 'Tis not a mile; briefly we heard their drums:
How couldst thou in a mile confound an hour,
And bring thy news so late?   20
Mess.   Spies of the Volsces
Held me in chase, that I was forc'd to wheel
Three or four miles about; else had I, sir,
Half an hour since brought my report.
                    Enter Martius [at a distance].
Com.   Who's yonder,   25
That does appear as he were flay'd? O gods!
He has the stamp of Martius; and I have
Before-time seen him thus.
Mar.   Come I too late?
Com. The shepherd knows not thunder from a tabor,   30
More than I know the sound of Martius' tongue
From every meaner man.
Mar.   Come I too late?
Com. Ay, if you come not in the blood of others,
But mantled in your own.   35
Mar.   O! let me clip ye
In arms as sound as when I woo'd, in heart
As merry as when our nuptial day was done,
And tapers burnt to bedward.
Com.   Flower of warriors.   40
How is 't with Titus Lartius?
Mar. As with a man busied about decrees:
Condemning some to death, and some to exile;
Ransoming him, or pitying, threat'ning th' other;
Holding Corioli in the name of Rome,   45
Even like a fawning greyhound in the leash,
To let him slip at will.
Com.   Where is that slave?
Which told me they had beat you to your trenches?
Where is he? Call him hither.   50

---

63 sensibly: *though sensitive to pain*   64 left: *forsaken*   67 Cato's wish; *cf. n.*   74
make ... alike: *remain to share his fate*   4 movers: *cowards*   5 drachme: *drachma,*
small Greek coin of silver   6 doit: *Dutch copper coin*   6, 7 doublets ... wore them;
cf. n.   20 physical: *beneficial to health*   27 Thy friend: *may prosperity befriend thee*

5 By ... gusts: *from time to time, as winds conveyed the sound.*   6 The Roman gods;
cf. n.   18 briefly: *a short time ago*   19 confound: *use up*   22 that: *so that*   26
as: *as if*   30 tabor: *small drum*   32 From: *from that of*   36 clip: *embrace*   44
pitying: *exempting from ransom*

Mar.   Let him alone;
He did inform the truth; but for our gentlemen,
The common file—a plague! tribunes for them!—
The mouse ne'er shunn'd the cat as they did budge
From rascals worse than they.   55
    Com.   But how prevail'd you?
    Mar. Will the time serve to tell? I do not think.
Where is the enemy? Are you lords o' the field?
If not, why cease you till you are so?
    Com. Martius, we have at disadvantage fought,   60
And did retire to win our purpose.
    Mar. How lies their battle? Know you on which side
They have plac'd their men of trust?
    Com.   As I guess, Martius,
Their bands i' the vaward are the Antiates,   65
Of their best trust; o'er them Aufidius,
Their very heart of hope.
    Mar.   I do beseech you,
By all the battles wherein we have fought,
By the blood we have shed together, by the vows,   70
We have made to endure friends, that you directly
Set me against Aufidius and his Antiates;
And that you not delay the present, but,
Filling the air with swords advanc'd and darts,
We prove this very hour.   75
    Com.   Though I could wish
You were conducted to a gentle bath,
And balms applied to you, yet dare I never
Deny your asking: take your choice of those
That best can aid your action.   80
    Mar.   Those are they
That most are willing. If any such be here—
As it were sin to doubt—that love this painting
Wherein you see me smear'd; if any fear
Lesser his person than an ill report;   85
If any think brave death outweighs bad life,
And that his country's dearer than himself;
Let him, alone, or so many so minded,
Wave thus, to express his disposition,
And follow Martius.   90

They all shout, and wave their swords; take him up in their arms,
                    and cast up their caps.

    [*Soldiers.*] O, me alone! Make you a sword of me!
    [*Mar.*] If these shows be not outward, which of you
But is four Volsces? None of you but is
Able to bear against the great Aufidius
A shield as hard as his. A certain number,   95
Though thanks to all, must I select from all: the rest
Shall bear the business in some other fight,
As cause will be obey'd. Please you to march;
And four shall quickly draw out my command,
Which men are best inclin'd.   100
    Com.   March on, my fellows:
Make good this ostentation, and you shall
Divide in all with us.   *Exeunt.*

❧ SCENE SEVENTH ❧

[The Gates of Corioli]

Titus Lartius, having set a guard upon Corioli, going with drum
and trumpet toward Cominius and Caius Martius, enters with a
Lieutenant, other Soldiers, and a Scout.

    Lart. So; let the ports be guarded: keep your duties,
As I have set them down. If I do send, dispatch
Those centuries to our aid; the rest will serve
For a short holding: if we lost the field,
We cannot keep the town.   5
    Lieu.   Fear not our care, sir.
    Lart. Hence, and shut your gates upon 's.
Our guider, come; to the Roman camp conduct us.   *Exit.*

❧ SCENE EIGHTH ❧

[A Field of Battle between the Roman and the Volscian Camps]
Alarum, as in battle. Enter Martius and Aufidius at several doors.

    Mar. I'll fight with none but thee; for I do hate thee
Worse than a promise-breaker.
    Auf.   We hate alike:
Not Afric owns a serpent I abhor
More than thy fame and envy. Fix thy foot.   5
    Mar. Let the first budger die the other's slave,
And the gods doom him after!
    Auf.   If I fly, Martius,
Halloo me like a hare.
    Mar. Within these three hours, Tullus,   10
Alone I fought in your Corioli walls,
And made what work I pleas'd; 'tis not my blood
Wherein thou seest me mask'd; for thy revenge
Wrench up thy power to the highest.
    Auf.   Wert thou the Hector   15
That was the whip of your bragg'd progeny,
Thou shouldst not 'scape me here.

Here they fight, and certain Volsces come in the aid of Aufidius.
    Martius fights till they be driven in breathless.

Officious, and not valiant, you have sham'd me
In your condemned seconds.   *[Exit.]*

❧ SCENE NINTH ❧   20

[The Roman Camp]

Flourish. Alarum. A retreat is sounded. Enter at one door Cominius,
with the Romans: at another door Martius, with his arm in a scarf.

    Com. If I should tell thee o'er this thy day's work,
Thou 't not believe thy deeds: but I'll report it
Where senators shall mingle tears with smiles,
Where great patricians shall attend and shrug,
I' the end, admire; where ladies shall be frighted,   5
And, gladly quak'd, hear more; where the dull Tribunes,
That, with the fusty plebeians, hate thine honours,
Shall say, against their hearts,

---

54 budge: *shrink*   65 vaward: *vanguard* Antiates: *inhabitants of Antium*   71 endure:
continue   73 delay . . . present: *make present delay*   74 We prove: *that we make trial*
of   85 his person: *personal injury*   91 Cf. *n.*   98 As . . . obey'd: *as occasion re-*
quires   102 ostentation: *show of valor*

1 ports: *gates*   2 centuries: *companies*   (viii) 5 fame and envy: *rivalry in frame*
(?)   16 whip . . . progeny; *cf. n.*   19 condemned seconds: *despised efforts at assist-*
ance   4 attend: *give attention* shrug: *express inability to believe*   6 quak'd: *fearful*

'We thank the gods our Rome hath such a soldier!'
Yet cam'st thou to a morsel of this feast,   *10*
Having fully din'd before.

Enter Titus, with his power, from the pursuit.

Titus Lartius.   O general,
Here is the steed, we the caparison:
Hadst thou beheld—
     Mar.   Pray now, no more: my mother,   *15*
Who has a charter to extol her blood,
When she does praise me grieves me. I have done
As you have done; that's what I can: induc'd
As you have been; that's for my country:
He that has but effected his good will   *20*
Hath overta'en mine act.
     Com.   You shall not be
The grave of your deserving; Rome must know
The value of her own: 'twere a concealment
Worse than a theft, no less than a traducement,   *25*
To hide your doings; and to silence that,
Which, to the spire and top of praises vouch'd,
Would seem but modest. Therefore, I beseech you,—
In sign of what you are, not to reward
What you have done,—before our army hear me.   *30*
     Mar. I have some wounds upon me, and they smart
To hear themselves remember'd.
     Com.   Should they not,
Well might they fester 'gainst ingratitude,
And tent themselves with death. Of all the horses,   *35*
Whereof we have ta'en good, and good store, of all
The treasure, in this field achiev'd and city,
We render you the tenth; to be ta'en forth,
Before the common distribution,
At your only choice.   *40*
     Mar.   I thank you, general;
But cannot make my heart consent to take
A bribe to pay my sword: I do refuse it;
And stand upon my common part with those
That have beheld the doing.   *45*

*A long flourish. They all cry 'Martius! Martius!' cast up their caps
and lances: Cominius and Lartius stand bare.*

     Mar. May these same instruments, which you profane,
Never sound more! When drums and trumpets shall
I' the field prove flatterers, let courts and cities be
Made all of false-fac'd soothing!
When steel grows soft as is the parasite's silk,   *50*
Let him be made an overture for the wars!
No more, I say! For that I have not wash'd
My nose that bled, or foil'd some debile wretch,
Which, without note, here's many else have done,
You shout me forth   *55*
In acclamations hyperbolical;

As if I lov'd my little should be dieted
In praises sauc'd with lies.
     Com.   Too modest are you;
More cruel to your good report than grateful   *60*
To us that give you truly. By your patience,
If 'gainst yourself you be incens'd, we'll put you,
Like one that means his proper harm, in manacles,
Then reason safely with you. Therefore, be it known,
As to us, to all the world, that Caius Martius   *65*
Wears this war's garland; in token of the which,
My noble steed, known to the camp, I give him,
With all his trim belonging; and from this time,
For what he did before Corioli, call him,
With all th' applause and clamour of the host,   *70*
Caius Marius Coriolanus! Bear
The addition nobly ever!

*Flourish. Trumpets sound, and drums.
Omnes. Caius Martius Coriolanus!*

     Cor. I will go wash;
And when my face is fair, you shall perceive
Whether I blush, or no: howbeit, I thank you.   *75*
I mean to stride your steed, and at all times
To undercrest your good addition
To the fairness of my power.
     Com.   So, to our tent;
Where, ere we do repose us, we will write   *80*
To Rome of our success. You, Titus Lartius,
Must to Corioli back: send us to Rome
The best, with whom we may articulate,
For their own good and ours.
     Lart.   I shall, my lord.   *85*
     Cor. The gods begin to mock me. I, that now
Refus'd most princely gifts, am bound to beg
Of my lord general.
     Com.   Take 't; 'tis yours. What is 't?
     Cor. I sometime lay here in Corioli   *90*
At a poor man's house; he us'd me kindly:
He cried to me; I saw him prisoner:
But then Aufidius was within my view,
And wrath o'erwhelm'd my pity: I request you
To give my poor host freedom.   *95*
     Com.   O! well begg'd!
Where he the butcher of my son, he should
Be free as is the wind. Deliver him, Titus.
     Lart. Martius, his name?
     Cor.   By Jupiter! forgot.   *100*
I am weary; yea, my memory is tir'd.
Have we no wine here?
     Com.   Go we to our tent:
The blood upon your visage dries; 'tis time
It should be look'd to: come.   *Exeunt. 105*

---

13 caparison: *the mere accoutrements*   **16 charter:** *privilege* **her blood:** *him whose blood she shares*   **20 effected:** *exhibited in action*   **23 The grave of:** *that which buries or conceals*   **26 silence:** *ignore with silence*   **27 to … vouch'd:** *testified to with utmost praise*   **33 Should they not:** *i.e. hear themselves remembered*   **35 tent:** *cleanse, cure; cf. n.*   **36 good store:** *a goodly number*   **37 in … city:** *acquired both in this battle and in the city*   **45 beheld … doing:** *been present at the fighting*   **49 soothing:** *flattery*   **51 an overture;** *cf. n.*   **53 foil'd:** *have overcome* **debile:** *weak*   **54 note:** *special attention*

57, 58 dieted In: *fed on*   **61 give:** *report*   **63 proper:** *own*   **66 garland:** *i.e., special honor*   **68 his … belonging:** *the trappings that go with him*   **72 addition:** *title of honor*   **74 fair:** *clean*   **77 undercrest:** *maintain as a crest or distinguishing device*   **83 articulate:** *discuss terms*   **90 lay:** *lodged*

❧ SCENE TENTH ❧

[The Camp of the Volsces]
A Flourish. Cornets. Enter Tullus Aufidius, bloody, with two or three Soldiers.

Auf. The town is ta'en!
Sol. 'Twill be deliver'd back on good condition.
Auf. Condition!
I would I were a Roman; for I cannot,
Being a Volsce, be that I am. Condition! 5
What good condition can a treaty find
I' the part that is at mercy? Five times, Martius,
I have fought with thee; so often hast thou beat me,
And wouldst do so, I think, should we encounter
As often as we eat. By th' elements, 10
If e'er again I meet him beard to beard,
He is mine, or I am his: mine emulation
Hath not that honour in 't it had; for where
I thought to crush him in an equal force—
True sword to sword—I'll potch at him some way 15
Or wrath or craft may get him.
Sol. He's the devil.
Auf. Bolder, though not so subtle. My valour's poison'd
With only suffering stain by him; for him
Shall fly out of itself. Nor sleep nor sanctuary, 20
Being naked, sick, nor fane nor Capitol,
The prayers of priests, nor times of sacrifice,
Embarquements all of fury, shall lift up
Their rotten privilege and custom 'gainst
My hate to Martius. Where I find him, were it 25
At home, upon my brother's guard, even there
Against the hospitable canon, would I
Wash my fierce hand in 's heart. Go you to the city;
Learn how 'tis held, and what they are that must
Be hostages for Rome. 30
Sol. Wil not you go?
Auf. I am attended at the cypress grove: I pray you—
'Tis south the city mills—bring me word thither
How the world goes, that to the pace of it
I may spur on my journey. 35
Sol. I shall, sir.

[Exeunt.]

ACT SECOND ❧ SCENE FIRST

[Rome. A Public Place]
Enter Menenius, with the two Tribunes of the people, Sicinius & Brutus.

Men. The augurer tells me we shall have news to-night.
Bru. Good or bad?
Men. Not according to the prayer of the people, for they
love not Martius.
Sic. Nature teaches beasts to know their friends. 5
Men. Pray you, who does the wolf love?
Sic. The lamb.

Men. Ay, to devour him; as the hungry plebeians would the
noble Martius.
Bru. He's a lamb indeed, that baes like a bear. 10
Men. He's a bear indeed, that lives like a lamb. You two are
old men; tell me one thing that I shall ask you.
Both. Well, sir.
Men. In what enormity is Martius poor in, that you two
have not in abundance? 15
Bru. He's poor in no one fault, but stored with all.
Sic. Especially in pride.
Bru. And topping all others in boasting.
Men. This is strange now: do you two know how you are
censured here in the city, I mean of us o' the right-hand file?
Do you?
Both. Why, how are we censured?
Men. Because you talk of pride now,—Will you not be angry?
Both. Well, well, sir; well.
Men. Why, 'tis no great matter; for a very little thief of 25
occasion will rob you of a great deal of patience: give your
dispositions the reins, and be angry at your pleasures; at the
least, if you take it as a pleasure to you in being so. You
blame Martius for being proud?
Bru. We do it not alone, sir. 30
Men. I know you can do very little alone; for your helps are
many, or else your actions would grow wondrous single: your
abilities are too infant-like for doing much alone. You talk of
pride: O that you could turn your eyes towards the napes of
your necks, and make but an interior survey of your good 35
selves! O that you could!
Both. What then, sir?
Men. Why, then you should discover a brace of unmerit-
ing, proud, violent, testy magistrates—alias fools—as any
in Rome. 40
Sic. Menenius, you are known well enough too.
Men. I am known to be a humorous patrician, and one
that loves a cup of hot wine with not a drop of allaying Tiber
in 't; said to be something imperfect in favouring the first complaint; hasty and tinder-like upon too trivial motion; one 45
that converses more with the buttock of the night than with
the forehead of the morning. What I think I utter, and spend
my malice in my breath. Meeting two such wealsmen as you
are,—I cannot call you, Lycurguses,—if the drink you give me
touch my palate adversely, I make a crooked face at it. I 50
cannot say your worships have delivered the matter well when
I find the ass in compound with the major part of your syllables; and though I must be content to bear with those that say
you are reverend grave men, yet they lie deadly that tell you
have good faces. If you see this in the map of my microcosm, 55
follows it that I am known well enough too? What harm can
your bisson conspectuities glean out of this character, if I be
known well enough too?
Bru. Come, sir, come, we know you well enough.
Men. You know neither me, yourselves, nor anything. You 60

---

2 condition: *terms* **5 that:** *what* **7 I':** *from the point of view of* **15 potch:** *poke,*
thrust heedlessly **16 Or wrath:** *in which either wrath* **23 Embarquements:** *embargoes,*
restraints **27 hospitable canon:** *law of hospitality* **32 attended:** *awaited*

14 In . . . poor in: *what fault has Marius in small degree* **18 topping:** *surpassing* **20**
censured: *estimated* **right-hand file:** *conservative, aristocratic party* **25, 26 a very . . .**
occasion: *a very little occasion, acting like a thief* **32 single:** *simple, weak* **34–36 O**
that . . . good selves; *cf. n.* **42 humorous:** *whimsical* **43 allaying Tiber:** *diluting*
water; cf. n. **44 something . . . complaint:** *somewhat hasty in judgment* **45 motion:**
occasion, incitement **45–47 one . . . morning;** *cf. n.* **47, 48 spend . . . breath:** *get rid*
of my ill will by putting it into words **48 wealsmen:** *politicians* **49 Lycurguses:** *great*
lawgivers **50–52 I cannot . . . syllables;** *cf. n.* **55 map . . . microcosm;** *cf. n.* **57**
bisson conspectuities: *blinded sight; cf. n.*

are ambitious for poor knaves' caps and legs: you wear out a good wholesome forenoon in hearing a cause between an orange-wife and a fosset-seller, and then rejourn the controversy of three-pence to a second day of audience. When you are hearing a matter between party and party, if you chance to be   65 pinched with the colic, you make faces like mummers, set up the bloody flag against all patience, and, in roaring for a chamber-pot, dismiss the controversy bleeding, the more entangled by your hearing: all the peace you make in their cause is, calling both the parties knaves. You are a pair of strange ones.   70

Bru. Come, come, you are well understood to be a perfecter giber for the table than a necessary bencher in the Capitol.

Men. Our very priests must become mockers if they shall encounter such ridiculous subjects as you are. When you speak best unto the purpose it is not worth the wagging of your   75 beards; and your beards deserve not so honourable a grave as to stuff a botcher's cushion, or to be entombed in an ass's pack-saddle. Yet you must be saying Martius is proud; who, in a cheap estimation, is worth all your predecessors since Deucalion, though peradventure some of the best of 'em were   80 hereditary hangmen. Good den to your worships: more of your conversation would infect my brain, being the herdsmen of the beastly plebeians: I will be bold to take my leave of you.

                      Brutus and Sicinius [go] aside.

Enter Volumnia, Virgilia, and Valeria.

How now, my as fair as noble ladies,—and the moon, were she earthly, no nobler,—whither do you follow your eyes so   85 fast?

Vol. Honourable Menenius, my boy Martius approaches; for the love of Juno, let's go.

Men. Ha! Martius coming home?

Vol. Ay, worthy Menenius; and with most prosperous   90 approbation.

Men. Take my cap, Jupiter, and I thank thee. Hoo! Martius coming home!

2 Ladies. Nay, 'tis true.

Vol. Look, here's a letter from him: the state hath another, his wife another; and, I think, there's one at home for you.

Men. I will make my very house reel tonight. A letter for me!

Vir. Yes, certain, there's a letter for you; I saw 't.

Men. A letter for me! It gives me an estate of seven   100 years' health; in which time I will make a lip at the physician: the most sovereign prescription in Galen is but empiricutic, and, to this preservative, of no better report than a horse-drench. Is he not wounded? he was wont to come home wounded.

Vir. O! no, no, no.   105

Vol. O! he is wounded, I thank the gods for 't.

Men. So do I too, if it be not too much. Brings a' victory in his pocket? The wounds become him.

Vol. On 's brows, Menenius; he comes the third time home with the oaken garland.   110

Men. Has he disciplined Aufidius soundly?

Vol. Titus Lartius writes they fought together, but Aufidius got off.

Men. And 'twas time for him too, I'll warrant him that: an he had stayed by him I would not have been so fidiused   115 for all the chests in Corioli, and the gold that's in them. Is the senate possessed of this?

Vol. Good ladies, let's go. Yes, yes, yes; the senate has letters from the general, wherein he gives my son the whole name of the war. He hath in this action outdone his former deeds   120 doubly.

Val. In troth there's wondrous things spoke of him.

Men. Wondrous! ay, I warrant you, and not without his true purchasing.

Vir. The gods grant them true!   125

Vol. True! pow, wow.

Men. True! I'll be sworn they are true. Where is he wounded? *[To the Tribunes.]* God save your good worships! Martius is coming home: he has more cause to be proud. *[To Volumnia.]* Where is he wounded?   130

Vol. I' the shoulder, and i' the left arm: there will be large cicatrices to show the people when he shall stand for his place. He received in the repulse of Tarquin seven hurts i' the body.

Men. One i' the neck, and two i' the thigh, there's nine that I know.   135

Vol. He had, before this last expedition, twenty five wounds upon him.

Men. Now, it's twenty-seven: every gash was an enemy's grave.

Hark! The trumpets.   *A shout and flourish.* 140

Vol. These are the ushers of Martius: before him he carries noise, and behind him he leaves tears:
Death, that dark spirit, in 's nervy arm doth lie;
Which, being advanc'd, declines, and then men die.

A Sennet. Trumpets sound. Enter Cominius, the General, and Titus Lartius; between them, Coriolanus, crowned with an oaken garland; with Captains and Soldiers, and a Herald.

Her. Know, Rome, that all alone Martius did fight
Within Corioli gates: where he hath won,
With fame, a name to Caius Martius; these   150
In honour follows Coriolanus.
Welcome to Rome, renowned Coriolanus!   *Sound. Flourish.*

All. Welcome to Rome, renowned Coriolanus!

Cor. No more of this; it does offend my heart:
Pray now, no more.   155

Com.   Look, sir, your mother!

Cor.   O!
You have, I know, petition'd all the gods
For my prosperity.   *Kneels.*

Vol.   Nay, my good soldier, up;   160
My gentle Martius, worthy Caius, and
By deed-achieving honour newly nam'd,—
What is it?—Coriolanus must I call thee?
But O! thy wife!—

Cor.   My gracious silence, hail!   165
Wouldst thou have laugh'd had I come coffin'd home,

---

61 **caps and legs:** *applause and reverence*   62, 63 **orange-wife:** *hawker of oranges* **fosset-seller:** *seller of faucets, taps for barrels* **rejourn:** *postpone*   66 **mummers:** *rustic actors*   66, 67 **set ... flag:** *proclaim violent war*   71, 72 *Cf. n.*   75, 76 **not worth ... beards:** *not worth the effort of opening and closing your mouths*   77 **botcher's:** *patching sailor's*   79 **estimation:** *valuation*   79, 80 **Deucalion:** *The Greek Noah*   81 **Good den:** *good evening*   85 **your eyes:** *the eager looks you cast ahead*   90, 91 **prosperous approbation:** *positive success*   92 **Take ... Jupiter:** *i.e. I throw my cap high in the air*   101 **make a lip at:** *defy*   102 **sovereign:** *efficacious* **empiricutic:** *experimental, quackish* **to:** *in comparison with*   109 **On 's brows:** *i.e. not in his pocket*

115 **fidiused:** *Aufidiused, put in Aufidius' proper place*   117 **possessed:** *informed*   119 **name:** *reputation*   132 **stand ... place:** *seek the consulship*   133 **repulse of Tarquin;** *cf. n.*   134 **nine;** *cf. n.*   143 **nervy:** *muscular*   144 **advanc'd:** *raised* **declines:** *falls*   S.d. **Sennet:** *trumpet signal for a procession to move*   150 **to:** *added to*   165 **My gracious silence;** *cf. n.*

That weep'st to see me triumph? Ah! my dear,
Such eyes the widows in Corioli wear,
And mothers that lack sons.
    Men.   Now, the gods crown thee!   *170*
    Cor. And live you yet? *[To Valeria.]* O my sweet lady,
pardon.
    Vol. I know not where to turn: O! welcome home;
And welcome, general; and y' are welcome all.
    Men. A hundred thousand welcomes: I could weep,   *175*
And I could laugh; I am light, and heavy. Welcome.
A curse begin at very root on 's heart
That is not glad to see thee! You are three
That Rome should dote on; yet, by the faith of men,
We have some old crab-trees here at home that will not   *180*
Be grafted to your relish. Yet, welcome, warriors!
We call a nettle but a nettle, and
The faults of fools but folly.
    Com.   Ever right.
    Cor. Menenius, ever, ever.   *185*
    Her. Give way there, and go on!
    Cor. *[To Volumnia and Virgilia.]* Your hand, and yours:
Ere in our own house I do shade my head,
The good patricians must be visited;
From whom I have receiv'd not only greetings,   *190*
But with them change of honours.
    Vol.   I have liv'd
To see inherited my very wishes,
And the buildings of my fancy: only
There's one thing wanting, which I doubt not but   *195*
Our Rome will cast upon thee.
    Cor.   Know, good mother,
I had rather be their servant in my way
Than sway with them in theirs.
    Com. On, to the Capitol!   *200*
          Flourish, Cornets. Exeunt in state, as before.

    Enter Brutus and Sicinius.

    Bru. All tongues speak of him, and the bleared sights
Are spectacled to see him: your prattling nurse
Into a rapture lets her baby cry
While she chats him; the kitchen malkin pins
Her richest lockram bout her reechy neck,   *205*
Clambering the walls to eye him: stalls, bulks, windows
Are smother'd up, leads fill'd, and ridges hors'd
With variable complexions, all agreeing
In earnestness to see him: seld-shown flamens
Do press among the popular throngs, and puff   *210*
To win a vulgar station; our veil'd dames
Commit the war of white and damask in
Their nicely-gawded cheeks to the wanton spoil
Of Phœbus' burning kisses: such a pother
As if that whatsoever god who leads him   *215*
Were slily crept into his human powers,

And gave him graceful posture.
    Sic.   On the sudden
I warrant him consul.
    Bru.   Then our office may,   *220*
During his power, go sleep.
    Sic. He cannot temperately transport his honours
From where he should begin and end, but will
Lose those he hath won.
    Bru.   In that there's comfort.   *225*
    Sic. Doubt not the commoners, for whom we stand,
But they upon their ancient malice will
Forget with the least cause these new honours,
Which that he'll give them, make I as little question
As he is proud to do 't.   *230*
    Bru.   I heard him swear,
Were he to stand for consul, never would he
Appear i' the market-place, nor on him put
The napless vesture of humility;
Nor, showing, as the manner is, his wounds   *235*
To the people, beg their stinking breaths.
    Sic.   'Tis right.
    Bru. It was his word. O! he would miss it rather
Than carry it but by the suit of the gentry to him
And the desire of the nobles.   *240*
    Sic.   I wish no better
Than have him hold that purpose and to put it
In execution.
    Bru. 'Tis most like he will.
    Sic. It shall be to him then, as our good wills,   *245*
A sure destruction.
    Bru.   So it must fall out
To him or our authorities. For an end,
We must suggest the people in what hatred
He still hath held them; that to 's power he would   *250*
Have made them mules, silenc'd their pleaders, and
Dispropertied their freedoms; holding them,
In human action and capacity,
Of no more soul nor fitness for the world.
Than camels in their war; who have their provand   *255*
Only for bearing burthens, and sore blows
For sinking under them.
    Sic.   This, as you say, suggested
At some time when his soaring insolence
Shall teach the people—which time shall not want,   *260*
If he be put upon 't; and that's as easy
As to set dogs on sheep—will be his fire
To kindle their dry stubble; and their blaze
Shall darken him for ever.

    Enter a Messenger.

    Bru.   What's the matter?   *265*
    Mess. You are sent for to the Capitol. 'Tis thought
That Martius shall be consul.
I have seen the dumb men throng to see him, and
The blind to hear him speak: matrons flung gloves,

173 **I . . . turn;** *cf. n.* **177 begin;** *cf. n.* **180 crab-trees:** *crabapple trees, i.e. the sour tribunes* **181 Be . . . relish:** *be brought to taste like you* **185 Menenius . . . ever:** *still the same Menenius* **191 change:** *a variety* **193 inherited:** *realized, come into my possession* **199 sway with:** *rule* **S.d. Enter, etc.;** *cf. n.* **203 rapture:** *fit* **204 chats:** *gossips about* **malkin:** *wench* **205 lockram:** *linen cloth* **reechy:** *dirty* **206 bulks:** *projecting shelves outside a shop* **207 leads:** *lead-covered roofs* **ridges hors'd:** *roof tops bestridden* **208 variable complexions:** *all types of people* **seld-shown flamens:** *priests who seldom show themselves* **210 popular throngs:** *crowds of rabble* **211 vulgar station:** *place in the mob* **213 nicely-gawded:** *daintily colored* **214 pother:** *hubbub*

222, 223 **He . . . end;** *cf. n.* **227 upon:** *on account of* **234 napless:** *threadbare* 239 **but:** *otherwise than* **245 as . . . wills:** *as we would have it* **248 For an end:** *in short* **249 suggest:** *remind by insinuation* **250 still:** *always* **251 mules:** *beasts of burden* **252 Dispropertied:** *annulled* **255 provand:** *food* **260 teach;** *cf. n.* **261 put upon 't:** *provoked* **262 will . . . fire:** *will be in him like a spark* **264 darken:** *tarnish, remove the gloss from*

Ladies and maids their scarfs and handkerchers　　　270
Upon him as he pass'd; the nobles bended,
As to Jove's statue, and the commons made
A shower and thunder with their caps and shouts:
I never saw the like.
 Bru.   Let's to the Capitol;　　　275
And carry with us ears and eyes for the time,
But hearts for the event.
 Sic.   Have with you.   *Exeunt.*

❧ SCENE SECOND ❧

[The Same. The Capitol]
Enter two Officers to lay cushions, as it were, in the Capitol.

 1. Off. Come, come, they are almost here. How many
stand for consulships?
 2. Off. Three, they say; but 'tis thought of every one
Coriolanus will carry it.
 1. Off. That's a brave fellow; but he's vengeance proud,　　5
and loves not the common people.
 2. Off. Faith, there hath been many great men that have
flattered the people, who ne'er loved them; and there be many
that they have loved, they know not wherefore: so that if they
love they knew not why, they hate upon no better a ground.
Therefore, for Coriolanus neither to care whether they love or
hate him manifests the true knowledge he has in their disposition; and out of his noble carelessness lets them plainly see 't.
 1. Off. If he did not care whether he had their love or no,
he waved indifferently 'twixt doing them neither good nor　　15
harm; but he seeks their hate with greater devotion than they
can render it him; and leaves nothing undone that may fully
discover him their opposite. Now, to seem to affect the malice
and displeasure of the people is as bad as that which he dislikes, to flatter them for their love.　　20
 2. Off. He hath deserved worthily of his country; and his ascent is not by such easy degrees as those who, having been supple and courteous to the people, bonneted, without any further
deed to have them at all into their estimation and report; but
he hath so planted his honours in their eyes, and his actions 25
in their hearts, that for their tongues to be silent, and not confess so much, were a kind of ingrateful injury; to report otherwise were a malice, that, giving itself the lie, would pluck
reproof and rebuke from every ear that heard it.
 1. Off. No more of him; he's a worthy man: make way,　　30
they are coming.

A Sennet. Enter the Patricians, and the Tribunes of the People,
Lictors before them: Coriolanus, Menenius, Cominius the Consul.
Sicinius and Brutus take their places by themselves: Coriolanus
stands.

 Men. Having determin'd of the Volsces, and
To send for Titus Lartius, it remains,
As the main point of this our after-meeting,
To gratify his noble service that　　35
Hath thus stood for his country: therefore, please you,
Most reverend and grave elders, to desire
The present consul, and last general
In our well-found successes, to report
A little of that worthy work perform'd　　40
By Caius Martius Coriolanus, whom
We meet here both to thank and to remember
With honours like himself.
 1. Sen.   Speak, good Cominius:
Leave nothing out for length, and make us think　　45
Rather our state's defective for requital,
Than we to stretch it out. *[To the Tribunes.]* Masters o' the
people,
We do request your kindest ears, and, after,
Your loving motion toward the common body,　　50
To yield what passes here.
 Sic.   We are convented
Upon a pleasing treaty, and have hearts
Inclinable to honour and advance
The theme of our assembly.　　55
 Bru.   Which the rather
We shall be bless'd to do, if he remember
A kinder value of the people than
He hath hereto priz'd them at.
 Men.   That's off, that's off;　　60
I would you rather had been silent. Please you
To hear Cominius speak?
 Bru.   Most willingly;
But yet my caution was more pertinent
Than the rebuke you give it.　　65
 Men.   He loves your people;
But tie him not to be their bedfellow.
Worthy Cominius, speak.

     Coriolanus rises, and offers to go away.
Nay, keep your place.　　70
 Sen. Sit, Coriolanus; never shame to hear
What you have nobly done.
 Cor.   Your honours' pardon:
I had rather have my wounds to heal again
Than hear say how I got them.　　75
 Bru.   Sir, I hope
My words disbench'd you not.
 Cor.   No, sir: yet oft,
When blows have made me stay, I fled from words.
You sooth'd not, therefore hurt not. But your people,　　80
I love them as they weigh—
 Men.   Pray now, sit down.
 Cor. I had rather have one scratch my head i' the sun
When the alarum were struck than idly sit
To hear my nothings monster'd. *Exit Coriolanus.* 85
 Men.   Masters of the people,
Your multiplying spawn how can he flatter,—
That's thousand to one good one,—when you now see

274 **shower**: *i.e. of falling caps*　277 **time**: *the present spectacle*　278 **hearts . . . event**: *i.e. keep our minds intent upon what is to follow*　279 **Have with you**: *let us go*　4 **carry**: *win*　5 **vengeance**: *accursedly*　8 **who**: *i.e. the people*　12 **in**: *concerning*　15 **waved indifferently**: *would waver impartially*　16 **devotion**: *earnestness*　18 **discover**: *manifest* **opposite**: *adversary* **affect**: *aim at, desire*　22 **easy degrees**: *gradual steps*　23 **bonneted**: *with hats off*　28 **giving . . . lie**: *manifesting its own falsehood*　32 **determin'd of**: *reached a decision concerning*

35 **gratify**: *reward*　36 **stood for**: *supported*　39 **well-found**: *auspicious*　43 **like himself**: *worthy of him*　46 **defective**: *insufficient*　47 **Than . . . out**: *than we deficient in seeking to make the largest requital*　50 **motion toward**: *proposal to*　51 **passes**: *is voted* **convented**: *called together*　53 **treaty**: *proposal*　55 **theme**: *subject, i.e. Coriolanus*　57 **bless'd**: *happy*　58 **kinder value**: *more favorable opinion*　60 **off**: *amiss*　77 **disbench'd**: *unseated*　80 **sooth'd**: *flattered*　81 **as they weigh**: *according to their worth*　85 **monster'd**: *grotesquely exaggerated*　88 **That's . . . good one**: *of whom only one in a thousand is good*

He had rather venture all his limbs for honour
Than one on 's ears to hear it? Proceed, Cominius.   90
    Com. I shall lack voice: the deeds of Coriolanus
Should not be utter'd feebly. It is held
That valour is the chiefest virtue, and
Most dignifies the haver: if it be,
The man I speak of cannot in the world   95
Be singly counterpois'd. At sixteen years,
When Tarquin made a head for Rome, he fought
Beyond the mark of others; our then dictator,
Whom with all praise I point at, saw him fight,
When with his Amazonian chin he drove   100
The bristled lips before him. He bestrid
An o'er-press'd Roman, and i' the consul's view
Slew three opposers: Tarquin's self he met,
And struck him on his knee: in that day's feats,
When he might act the woman in the scene,   105
He prov'd best man i' the field, and for his meed
Was brow-bound with the oak. His pupil age
Man-enter'd thus, he waxed like a sea,
And in the brunt of seventeen battles since
He lurch'd all swords of the garland. For this last,   110
Before and in Corioli, let me say,
I cannot speak him home: he stopp'd the fliers,
And by his rare example made the coward
Turn terror into sport: as weeds before
A vessel under sail, so men obey'd,   115
And fell below his stem: his sword, death's stamp,
Where it did mark, it took; from face to foot
He was a thing of blood, whose every motion
Was tim'd with dying cries: alone he enter'd
The mortal gate of the city, which he painted   120
With shunless destiny; aidless came off,
And with a sudden re-enforcement struck
Corioli like a planet. Now all's his:
When by and by the din of war 'gan pierce
His ready sense; then straight his doubled spirit   125
Re-quicken'd what in flesh was fatigate,
And to the battle came he; where he did
Run reeking o'er the lives of men, as if
'Twere a perpetual spoil; and till we call'd
Both field and city ours, he never stood   130
To ease his breast with panting.
    Men.   Worthy man!
    Sen. He cannot but with measure fit the honours
Which we devise him.
    Com.   Our spoils he kick'd at,   135
And look'd upon things precious as they were
The common muck o' the world: he covets less
Than misery itself would give; rewards
His deeds with doing them, and is content
To spend the time to end it.   140
    Men.   He's right noble:
let him be call'd for.

    Sen.   Call Coriolanus.
    Off. He doth appear.

Enter Coriolanus.

    Men. The senate, Coriolanus, are well pleas'd   145
To make thee consul.
    Cor.   I do owe them still
My life and services.
    Men.   It then remains
That you do speak to the people.   150
    Cor.   I do beseech you,
Let me o'erleap that custom, for I cannot
Put on the gown, stand naked, and entreat them,
For my wounds' sake, to give their suffrage: please you,
That I may pass this doing.   155
    Sic.   Sir, the people
Must have their voices; neither will they bate
One jot of ceremony.
    Men.   Put them not to 't:
Pray you, go fit you to the custom, and   160
Take to you, as your predecessors have,
Your honour with your form.
    Cor.   It is a part
That I shall blush in acting, and might well
Be taken from the people.   165
    Bru. [*Aside to Sicinius.*] Mark you that?
    Cor. To brag unto them, thus I did, and thus;
Show them the unaching scars which I should hide,
As if I had receiv'd them for the hire
Of their breath only!   170
    Men.   Do not stand upon 't.
We recommend to you, tribunes of the people,
Our purpose to them; and to our noble consul
Wish we all joy and honour.
    Sen. To Coriolanus come all joy and honour!   175

Flourish Cornets. Then exeunt. Mane[n]t Sicinius and Brutus.

    Bru. You see how he intends to use the people.
    Sic. May they perceive 's intent! He will require them,
As if he did contemn what he requested
Should be in them to give.
    Bru.   Come, we'll inform them   180
Of our proceedings here: on the market-place
I know they do attend us.   [*Exeunt.*]

❧ Scene Third ❧

[The Same. The Forum]
Enter seven or eight Citizens.

    1. Cit. Once, if he do require our voices, we ought not to
deny him.
    2. Cit. We may, sir, if we will.
    3. Cit. We have power in ourselves to do it, but it is a
power that we have no power to do; for if he show us his   5
wounds, and tell us his deeds, we are to put our tongues into

---

94 haver: *possessor*   **96 Be . . . counterpois'd:** *find any single equal*   **97 made . . . for:** *raised an army against*   **98 mark;** *cf. n.*   **100 Amazonian:** *i.e. beardless*   **104 on his knee:** *with such force as to bring him to his knee*   **105 in the scene:** *on the stage*   **108 Man-enter'd:** *entered upon manhood*   **110 lurch'd:** *robbed; cf. n.*   **112 speak him home:** *do him full justice*   **116 fell . . . stem:** *yielded to his course*   **117 took:** *took possession, slew*   **120, 121 painted . . . destiny:** *stained with the blood of those who could not escape their doom*   **124 by and by:** *immediately*   **126 fatigate:** *wearied*   **135 kick'd at:** *scorned*   **136 as:** *as if*   **140 to end it:** *merely to kill time*

155 pass this doing: *omit this action*   **157 voices:** *votes.* **bate:** *abate, waive*   **159 Put . . . to 't:** *do not force the issue*   **160 fit you:** *accommodate yourself*   **162 with your form:** *in the conventional manner*   **170 breath:** *i.e. votes*   **172 recommend:** *entrust*   **173 Our . . . them:** *what we propose to them*   **177 require:** *request*   **178 contemn what:** *scorn that what*   **1 Once:** *once for all*

those wounds and speak for them; so, if he tell us his noble
deeds, we must also tell him our noble acceptance of them.
Ingratitude is monstrous, and for the multitude to be
ingrateful were to make a monster of the multitude; of the   *10*
which we being members, should bring ourselves to be
monstrous members.

    1. Cit. And to make us no better thought of, a little help
will serve; for once we stood up about the corn, he himself
stuck not to call us the many-headed multitude.   *15*

    3. Cit. We have been called so of many; not that our heads
are some brown, some black, some abram, some bald, but that
our wits are so diversely coloured: and truly I think, if all our
wits were to issue out of one skull, they would fly east, west,
north, south; and their consent of one direct way should be   *20*
at once to all the points o' the compass.

    2. Cit. Think you so? Which way do you judge my wit
would fly?

    3. Cit. Nay, your wit will not so soon out as another man's
will; 'tis strongly wedged up in a block-head; but if it were   *25*
at liberty, 'twould, sure, southward.

    2. Cit. Why that way?

    3. Cit. To lose itself in a fog; where being three parts
melted away with rotten dews, the fourth would return for
conscience' sake, to help to get thee a wife.   *30*

    2. Cit. You are never without your tricks: you may, you
may.

    3. Cit. Are you all resolved to give your voices? But that's
no matter, the greater part carries it. I say, if he would incline
to the people, there was never a worthier man.   *35*

    Enter Coriolanus, in a gown of humility, with Menenius.

Here he comes, and in the gown of humility: mark his
behaviour. We are not to stay all together, but to come by
him where he stands, by ones, by twos, and by threes. He's to
make his requests by particulars; wherein every one of us has a
single honour, in giving him our own voices with our own   *40*
tongues: therefore follow me, and I'll direct you how you
shall go by him.

    All. Content, content.   *[Exeunt Citizens.]*

    Men. O, sir, you are not right: have you not known
The worthiest men have done 't?   *45*

    Cor.   What must I say?
'I pray, sir,'—Plague upon 't! I cannot bring
My tongue to such a pace. 'Look, sir, my wounds!
I got them in my country's service, when
Some certain of your brethren roar'd and ran   *50*
From the noise of our own drums.'

    Men.   O me! the gods!
You must not speak of that: you must desire them
To think upon you.

    Cor.   Think upon me! Hang 'em!   *55*
I would they would forget me, like the virtues
Which our divines lose by 'em.

    Men.   You'll mar all:
I'll leave you. Pray you, speak to 'em, I pray you,
In wholesome manner.   *Exit.*   *60*

    Enter two of the Citizens.

    Cor.   Bid them wash their faces,
And keep their teeth clean. So, here comes a brace.
You know the cause, sir, of my standing here?

    1. Cit. We do, sir; tell us what hath brought you to 't.

    Cor. Mine own desert.   *65*

    2. Cit. Your own desert!

    Cor. Ay, not mine own desire.

    1. Cit. How! not your own desire?

    Cor. No, sir, 'twas never my desire yet to trouble the
poor with begging.   *70*

    1. Cit. You must think, if we give you anything, we
hope to gain by you.

    Cor. Well, then, I pray, your price o' the consulship?

    1. Cit. The price is, to ask it kindly.

    Cor. Kindly! sir, I pray, let me ha 't: I have wounds to   *75*
show you, which shall be yours in private. Your good voice,
sir; what say you?

    2. Cit. You shall ha 't, worthy sir.

    Cor. A match, sir. There's in all two worthy voices begged.
I have your alms: adieu.   *80*

    1. Cit. But this is something odd.

    2. Cit. An 'twere to give again,—but 'tis no matter.

    Enter two other Citizens.

    Cor. Pray you now, if it may stand with the tune of your
voices that I may be consul, I have here the customary gown.

    1. Cit. You have deserved nobly of your country, and   *85*
you have not deserved nobly.

    Cor. Your enigma?

    1. Cit. You have been a scourge to her enemies, you have
been a rod to her friends; you have not indeed loved the common people.   *90*

    Cor. You should account me the more virtuous that I have
not been common in my love. I will, sir, flatter my sworn
brother the people, to earn a dearer estimation of them; 'tis a
condition they account gentle: and since the wisdom of their
choice is rather to have my hat than my heart, I will practise   *95*
the insinuating nod, and be off to them most counterfeitly;
that is, sir, I will counterfeit the bewitchment of some popular
man, and give it bountiful to the desirers. Therefore, beseech
you, I may be consul.

    2. Cit. We hope to find you our friend, and therefore   *100*
give you our voices heartily.

    1. Cit. You have received many wounds for your country.

    Cor. I will not seal your knowledge with showing them. I
will make much of your voices, and so trouble you no farther.

    Both. The gods give you joy, sir, heartily!   *[Exeunt.]* *105*

    Cor. Most sweet voices!
Better it is to die, better to starve,
Than crave the hire which first we do deserve.
Why in this wolfish toge should I stand here,
To beg of Hob and Dick, that does appear,   *110*
Their needless vouches? Custom calls me to 't:
What custom wills, in all things should we do 't,
The dust on antique time would lie unswept,

14 once: *once when*   **15 stuck:** *hesitated*   **17 abram:** *auburn*   **20 consent of:**
agreement about   **29 rotten dews:** *infectious vapors*   **31, 32 you may:** *you may have
your joke*   **34 greater part:** *majority*   **39 by particulars:** *individually*   **40 single:**
separate   **57 lose by 'em:** *i.e. vainly seek to propagate in them by preaching*   **60 wholesome:** *sane, reasonable*

S.d. two of the Citizens; *cf. n.*   **73 o':** *for*   **93 of:** *from*   **96 be off:** *bare my
head*   **counterfeitly:** *hypocritically*   **97 bewitchment:** *sorcery*   **97, 98 popular man:**
demagogue   **bountiful:** *bountifully*   **103 seal:** *confirm*   **108 first:** *previously, already*   **109 wolfish toge;** *cf. n.*   **110 Hob . . . appear:** *whatever plebeian appears*   **111
needless vouches:** *unnecessary confirmations*

And mountainous error be too highly heap'd
For truth to o'er-peer. Rather than fool it so,   *115*
Let the high office and the honour go
To one that would do thus. I am half through;
The one part suffer'd, the other will I do.

        Enter three Citizens more.

Here come moe voices.
Your voices: for your voices I have fought;   *120*
Watch'd for your voices; for your voices bear
Of wounds two dozen odd; battles thrice six
I have seen and heard of; for your voices have
Done many things, some less, some more; your voices:
Indeed, I would be consul.   *125*
   1. Cit. He has done nobly, and cannot go without any hon-
est man's voice.
   2. Cit. Therefore let him be consul. The gods give him joy,
and make him good friend to the people!
   All. Amen, amen.   *130*
God save thee, noble consul!   *[Exeunt Citizens.]*
   Cor.   Worthy voices!

     Enter Menenius, with Brutus and Sicinius.

   Men. You have stood your limitation; and the tribunes
Endue you with the people's voice: remains
That, in th' official marks invested, you   *135*
Anon do meet the senate
   Cor.   Is this done?
   Sic. The custom of request you have discharg'd:
The people do admit you, and are summon'd
To meet anon, upon your approbation.   *140*
   Cor. Where? at the senate-house?
   Sic.   There, Coriolanus.
   Cor. May I change these garments?
   Sic. You may, sir.
   Cor. That I'll straight do; and, knowing myself again,   *145*
Repair to the senate-house.
   Men. I'll keep you company. Will you along?
   Bru. We stay here for the people.
   Sir.   Fare you well.
     Exeunt Coriolanus and Menenius.
He has it now; and by his looks, methinks,   *150*
'Tis warm at 's heart.
   Bru.   With a proud heart he wore
His humble weeds. Will you dismiss the people?

      Enter the Plebeians.

   Sic. How now, my masters! have you chose this man?
   1. Cit. He has our voices, sir.   *155*
   Bru. We pray the gods he may deserve your loves.
   2. Cit. Amen, sir. To my poor unworthy notice,
He mock'd us when he begg'd our voices.
   3. Cit.   Certainly,
He flouted us downright.   *160*
   1. Cit. No, 'tis his kind of speech; he did not mock us.
   2. Cit. No one amongst us, save yourself, but says
He us'd us scornfully: he should have show'd us

His marks of merit, wounds receiv'd for 's country.
   Sic. Why, so he did, I am sure.   *165*
   All.   No, no; no man, saw 'em.
   3. Cit. He said he had wounds, which he could show in
private;
And with his hat, thus waving it in scorn,
'I would be consul,' says he: 'aged custom,   *170*
But by your voices, will not so permit me;
Your voices therefore': when we granted that,
Here was, 'I thank you for your voices, thank you,
Your most sweet voices: now you have left your voices,
I have no further with you.' Was not this mockery?   *175*
   Sic. Why either were you ignorant to see 't,
Or, seeing it, of such childish friendliness
To yield your voices?
   Bru.   Could you not have told him.
As you were lesson'd, when he had no power,   *180*
But was a petty servant to the state,
He was your enemy, ever spake against
Your liberties and the charters that you bear
I' the body of the weal; and now, arriving
A place of potency and sway o' the state,   *185*
If he should still malignantly remain
Fast foe to the plebeii, your voices might
Be curses to yourselves? You should have said
That as his worthy deeds did claim no less
Than what he stood for, so his gracious nature   *190*
Would think upon you for your voices and
Translate his malice towards you into love,
Standing your friendly lord.
   Sic.   Thus to have said,
As you were fore-advis'd, had touch'd his spirit   *195*
And tried his inclination; from him pluck'd
Either his gracious promise, which you might,
As cause had call'd you up, have held him to;
Or else it would have gall'd his surly nature,
Which easily endures not article   *200*
Tying him to aught; so, putting him to rage,
You should have ta'en th' advantage of his choler,
And pass'd him unelected.
   Bru.   Did you perceive
He did solicit you in free contempt   *205*
When he did need your loves, and do you think
That his contempt shall not be bruising to you
When he hath power to crush? Why, had your bodies
No heart among you? or had you tongues to cry
Against the rectorship of judgment?   *210*
   Sic.   Have you
Ere now denied the asker? and now again
Of him that did not ask, but mock, bestow
Your su'd-for tongues?
   3. Cit. He's not confirm'd; we may deny him yet.   *215*
   2. Cit. And will deny him:
I'll have five hundred voices of that sound.
   1. Cit. Ay, twice five hundred and their friends to
piece em.
   Bru. Get you hence instantly, and tell those friends,   *220*

---

115 o'er-peer: *peep over the accumulation of tradition* **fool it:** *play the fool* **121 Watch'd:** *done vigil* **133 limitation:** *fixed period of time* **134 remains:** *it remains* **135 marks:** *emblems of authority* **140 upon:** *on the business of* **151 'Tis . . . heart:** *it warms his heart*

176 ignorant to: *so dull as not to* **180 lesson'd:** *instructed* **183 charters:** *privileges* **184 weal:** *commonwealth* **arriving:** *attaining* **198 call'd you up:** *summoned you* **200 article:** *condition* **210 rectorship:** *guiding power* **213 Of:** *upon* **219 piece:** *reinforce*

They have chose a consul that will from them take
Their liberties; make them of no more voice
Than dogs that are as often beat for barking
As therefore kept to do so.

    Sic.　　　　　　　　Let them assemble;　　　　225
And, on a safer judgment, all revoke
Your ignorant election. Enforce his pride,
And his old hate unto you; besides, forget not
With what contempt he wore the humble weed;
How in his suit he scorn'd you; but your loves,　　230
Thinking upon his services, took from you
The apprehension of his present portance,
Which most gibingly, ungravely, he did fashion
After the inveterate hate he bears you.

    Bru.　　　　　　　　Lay　　　235
A fault on us, your tribunes; that we labour'd,—
No impediment between,—but that you must
Cast your election on him.

    Sic.　　　　　　　　Say, you chose him
More after our commandment than as guided　　240
By your own true affections; and that, your minds,
Pre-occupied with what you rather must do
Than what you should, make you against the grain
To voice him consul: lay the fault on us.

    Bru. Ay, spare us not. Say we read lectures to you,　　245
How youngly he began to serve his country,
How long continu'd, and what stock he springs of,
The noble house o' the Martians, from whence came
That Ancus Martius, Numa's daughter's son,
Who, after great Hostilius, here was king;　　250
Of the same house Publius and Quintus were,
That our best water brought by conduits hither;
And Censorinus, that was so surnam'd,—
And nobly nam'd so, twice being censor,—
Was his great ancestor.　　255

    Sic.　　　　　　　　One thus descended,
That hath, beside, well in his person wrought
To be set high in place, we did commend
To your remembrances: but you have found,
Scaling his present bearing with his past,　　260
That he's your fixed enemy, and revoke
Your sudden approbation.

    Bru.　　　　　　　　Say you ne'er had done 't—
Harp on that still—but by our putting on;
And presently, when you have drawn your number,　　265
Repair to the Capitol.

    All.　　　　　　　　We will so; almost all
Repent in their election.　　　　*Exeunt Plebeians.*

    Bru.　　　　　　　　Let them go on;
This mutiny were better put in hazard　　270
Than stay, past doubt, for greater.
If, as his nature is, he fall in rage
With their refusal, both observe and answer
The vantage of his anger.

    Sic.　　　　　　　　To the Capitol, come:　　275

We will be there before the stream o' the people;
And this shall seem, as partly 'tis, their own,
Which we have goaded onward.　　　　*Exeunt.*

ACT THIRD ❧ SCENE FIRST

[Rome. A Street]
Coronets. Enter Coriolanus, Menenius, all the Gentry, Cominius,
Titus Lartius, and other Senators.

    Cor. Tullus Aufidius then had made new head?
    Lart. He had, my lord; and that it was which caus'd
Our swifter composition.

    Cor. So then the Volsces stand but as at first,
Ready, when time shall prompt them, to make road　　5
Upon's again.

    Com.　　　　They are worn, lord consul, so,
That we shall hardly in our ages see
Their banners wave again.

    Cor.　　　　　　　　Saw you Aufidius?　　10
    Lart. On safeguard he came to me; and did curse
Against the Volsces, for they had so vilely
Yielded the town: he is retir'd to Antium.

    Cor. Spoke he of me?
    Lart.　　　　　　He did, my lord.　　15
    Cor.　　　　　　　　How? what?
    Lart. How often he had met you, sword to sword;
That of all things upon the earth he hated
Your person most; that he would pawn his fortunes
To hopeless restitution, so he might　　20
Be call'd your vanquisher.

    Cor.　　　　　　At Antium lives he?
    Lart. At Antium.

    Cor. I wish I had a cause to seek him there,
To oppose his hatred fully. Welcome home.　　25

Enter Sicinius and Brutus.

Behold! these are the tribunes of the people,
The tongues o' the common mouth: I do despise them;
For they do prank them in authority
Against all noble sufferance.

    Sic.　　　　　　　　Pass no further.　　30
    Cor. Ha! what is that?
    Bru. It will be dangerous to go on: no further.
    Cor. What makes this change?
    Men.　　　　　　　　The matter?
    Com. Hath he not pass'd the noble and the common?　　35
    Bru. Cominius, no.
    Cor.　　　　　　Have I had children's voices?
    Senat. Tribunes, give way; he shall to the marketplace.
    Bru. The people are incens'd against him.
    Sic.　　　　　　　　Stop,　　40
Or all will fall in broil.

    Cor.　　　　　　Are these your herd?
Must these have voices, that can yield them now,
And straight disclaim their tongues? What are your offices?

---

226 safer: *more prudent* **227 Enforce:** *lay stress upon* **232 apprehension:** *discernment* **portance:** *behavior* **234 After:** *in accord with* **237 No ... between:** *without admitting any impediment* **253** *Cf. n.* **260 Scaling:** *balancing* **264 putting on:** *urging* **265 drawn ... number:** *collected a sufficient number* **268 Repent in:** *repent of* **270 put in hazard:** *risked* **271 stay ... greater:** *that we should wait for a greater, inevitable hazard* **273, 274 answer ... vantage:** *make use*

1 made new head: *raised a new army* **3 composition:** *coming to terms* **5 road:** *an inroad, raid* **20 To ... restitution:** *beyond hope of redemption* **28 prank them:** *deck themselves*

You being their mouths, why rule you not their teeth?   45
Have you not set them on?
    Men.   Be calm, be calm.
    Cor. It is a purpos'd thing, and grows by plot,
To curb the will of the nobility:
Suffer 't, and live with such as cannot rule   50
Nor ever will be rul'd.
    Bru.   Call 't not a plot:
The people cry you mock'd them, and of late,
When corn was given them gratis, you repin'd;
Scandal'd the suppliants for the people, call'd them   55
Time-pleasers, flatterers, foes to nobleness.
    Cor. Why, this was known before.
    Bru.   Not to them all.
    Cor. Have you inform'd them sithence?
    Bru.   How! I inform   60
them!
    Cor. You are like to do such business.
    Bru.   Not unlike,
Each way, to better yours.
    Cor. Why then should I be consul? By yond clouds,   65
Let me deserve so ill as you, and make me
Your fellow tribune.
    Sic.   You show too much of that
For which the people stir; if you will pass
To where you are bound, you must inquire your way,   70
Which you are out of, with a gentler spirit;
Or never be so noble as a consul,
Nor yoke with him for tribune.
    Men.   Let's be calm.
    Com. The people are abus'd; set on. This palt'ring   75
Becomes not Rome, nor has Coriolanus
Deserv'd this so dishonour'd rub, laid falsely
I' the plain way of his merit.
    Cor.   Tell me of corn!
This was my speech, and I will speak 't again,—   80
    Men. Not now, not now.
    Senat.   Not in this heat, sir, now.
    Cor. Now, as I live, I will. My nobler friends,
I crave their pardons:
For the mutable, rank-scented meiny, let them   85
Regard me as I do not flatter, and
Therein behold themselves: I say again,
In soothing them we nourish 'gainst our senate
The cockle of rebellion, insolence, sedition,
Which we ourselves have plough'd for, sow'd and   90
scatter'd
By mingling them with us, the honour'd number;
Who lack not virtue, no, nor power, but that
Which they have given to beggars.
    Men.   Well, no more.   95
    Senat. No more words, we beseech you.
    Cor.   How! no more!
As for my country I have shed my blood,
Not fearing outward force, so shall my lungs
Coin words till their decay against those measles,   100

Which we disdain should tetter us, yet sought
The very way to catch them.
    Bru.   You speak o' the people,
As if you were a god to punish, not
A man of their infirmity.   105
    Sic.   'Twere well
We let the people know 't.
    Men.   What, what? his choler?
    Cor. Choler!
Were I as patient as the midnight sleep,   110
By Jove, 'twould be my mind!
    Sic.   It is a mind
That shall remain a poison where it is,
Not poison any further.
    Cor.   Shall remain!   115
Hear you this Triton of the minnows? mark you
His absolute 'Shall'?
    Com.   'Twas from the canon.
    Cor.   'Shall!'
O good but most unwise patricians! why,   120
You grave but reckless senators, have you thus
Given Hydra here to choose an officer,
That with his peremptory 'shall,' being but
The horn and noise o' the monster's, wants not spirit
To say he'll turn your current in a ditch,   125
And make your channel his? If he have power,
Then vail your ignorance; if none, awake
Your dangerous lenity. If you are learn'd,
Be not as common fools; if you are not,
Let them have cushions by you. You are plebeians   130
If they be senators; and they are no less,
When, both your voices blended, the great'st taste
Most palates theirs. They choose their magistrate,
And such a one as he, who puts his 'shall,'
His popular 'shall,' against a graver bench   135
Than ever frown'd in Greece. By Jove himself!
It makes the consuls base; and my soul aches
To know, when two authorities are up,
Neither supreme, how soon confusion
May enter 'twixt the gap of both and take   140
The one by th' other.
    Com.   Well, on to the market-place.
    Cor. Whoever gave that counsel, to give forth
The corn o' the store-house gratis, as 'twas us'd
Sometime in Greece,—   145
    Men.   Well, well; no more of that.
    Cor. Though there the people had more absolute power,
I say, they nourish'd disobedience, fed
The ruin of the state.
    Bru.   Why, shall the people give   150
One that speaks thus their voice?
    Cor.   I'll give my reasons,
More worthier than their voices. They know the corn
Was not our recompense, resting well assur'd

---

101 **tetter:** *form an eruption on*   111 **mind:** *resolved opinion*   116 **Triton:** *sea-god*   118
from the canon: *not authorized by law*   122 **Given:** *allowed* **Hydra:** *the many-headed
monster*   124 **horn and noise:** *noisy horn*   127 **vail ... ignorance:** *let your folly submit*   127, 128 **awake ... lenity:** *arouse yourselves from your dangerous mildness*   130
cushions: *i.e. seats in the Senate*   132 **great'st taste:** *predominant taste*   133 **palates:**
smacks of   138 **up:** *established*   140 **gap of both:** *cleavage between the two*   140, 141
take ... other: *use the one to overthrown the other*   154 **our recompense:** *fair payment
from us*

---

48 **purpos'd:** *premeditated*   55 **Scandal'd:** *slandered*   59 **sithence:** *since*   64 **Each
... yours:** *to surpass your doings in every way*   68 **that:** *that defect of character*   73 **yoke:**
join in service   75 **abus'd:** *deceived* **set on:** *incited*   77 **dishonour'd rub:** *shameful
obstruction* **falsely:** *treacherously*   85 **meiny:** *multitude*   86 **Regard ... flatter:** *heed
my unflattering presentation*   89 **cockle:** *noxious weed*   100 **measles:** *disease spots*

They ne'er did service for 't. Being press'd to the war,   *155*
Even when the navel of the state was touch'd,
They would not thread the gates: this kind of service
Did not deserve corn gratis. Being i' the war,
Their mutinies and revolts, wherein they show'd
Most valour, spoke not for them. Th' accusation   *160*
Which they have often made against the senate,
All cause unborn, could never be the motive
Of our so frank donation. Well, what then?
How shall this bosom multiplied digest
The senate's courtesy? Let deeds express   *165*
What's like to be their words: 'We did request it;
We are the greater poll, and in true fear
They gave us our demands.' Thus we debase
The nature of our seats, and make the rabble
Call our cares fears; which will in time break ope   *170*
The locks o' the senate, and bring in the crows
To peck the eagles.
    Men.   Come, enough.
    Bru. Enough, with over-measure,
    Cor.   No, take more: *175*
What may be sworn by, both divine and human,
Seal what I end withal! This double worship,
Where one part does disdain with cause, the other
Insult without all reason; where gentry, title, wisdom,
Cannot conclude, but by the yea and no   *180*
Of general ignorance,—it must omit
Real necessities, and give way the while
To unstable slightness: purpose so barr'd, it follows
Nothing is done to purpose. Therefore, beseech you,—
You that will be less fearful than discreet,   *185*
That love the fundamental part of state
More than you doubt the change on 't, that prefer
A noble life before a long, and wish
To jump a body with a dangerous physic
That's sure of death without it, at once pluck out   *190*
The multitudinous tongue; let them not lick
The sweet which is their poison. Your dishonour
Mangles true judgement, and bereaves the state
Of that integrity which should become 't,
Not having the power to do the good it would,   *195*
For th' ill which doth control 't.
    Bru.   H'as said enough.
    Sic. H'as spoken like a traitor, and shall answer
As traitors do.
    Cor. Thou wretch! despite o'erwhelm thee!   *200*
What should the people do with these bald tribunes?
On whom depending, their obedience fails
To the greater bench. In a rebellion,
When what's not meet, but what must be, was law,
Then were they chosen: in a better hour,   *205*
Let what is meet be said it must be meet,

And throw their power i' the dust.
    Bru. Manifest treason!
    Sic.   This a consul? no.
    Bru. The ædiles, ho!   *210*

        Enter an Ædile.

        Let him be apprehended.
    Sic. Go, call the people; *[Exit Ædile.]* in whose name, myself
Attach thee as a traitorous innovator,
A foe to the public weal: obey, I charge thee,
And follow to thine answer.   *215*
    Cor.   Hence, old goat!
    All. We'll surety him.
    Com.   Ag'd sir, hands off.
    Cor. Hence, rotten thing! or I shall shake thy bones
Out of thy garments.   *220*
    Sic.   Help, ye citizens!

        Enter a rabble of Plebeians with the Ædiles.

    Men. On both sides more respect.
    Sic. Here's he that would take from you all your power.
    Bru. Seize him, ædiles!
    All. Down with him!—down with him!—   *225*
    2. Sen. Weapons!—weapons!—weapons!—

        They all bustle about Coriolanus.

Tribunes!—patricians!—citizens!—What ho!—
Sicinius!—Brutus!—Coriolanus!—Citizens!
    All. Peace!—Peace!—Peace!—Stay!—Hold!—Peace!   *230*
    Men. What is about to be?—I am out of breath;
Confusion's near; I cannot speak. You, tribunes
To the people! Coriolanus, patience!
Speak, good Sicinius.
    Sic.   Hear me, people; peace!   *235*
    All. Let's hear our tribune:—Peace!—   Speak, speak, speak.
    Sic. You are at point to lose your liberties:
Martius would have all from you; Martius,
Whom late you have nam'd for consul.
    Men.   Fie, fie, fie!   *240*
This is the way to kindle, not to quench.
    Sen. To unbuild the city and to lay all flat.
    Sic. What is the city but the people?
    All.   True,
The people are the city.   *245*
    Bru. By the consent of all, we were establish'd
The people's magistrates.
    All.   You so remain.
    Men. And so are like to do.
    Com. That is the way to lay the city flat;   *250*
To bring the roof to the foundation,
And bury all, which yet distinctly ranges,
In heaps and piles of ruin.
    Sic.   This deserves death.
    Bru. Or let us stand to our authority,   *255*
Or let us lose it. We do here pronounce,
Upon the part o' the people, in whose power
We were elected theirs, Martius is worthy
Of present death.
    Sic.   Therefore lay hold of him;   *260*

155 press'd: *enlisted*   **156 navel:** *vital center*   **157 thread:** *pass through*   **162 All ...
unborn:** *causelessly* **motive:** *occasion; cf. n.*   **164 bosom multiplied; cf. n.**   **165, 166
Let ... words:** *let their actions explain what they are likely to say*   **167 poll:** *number*   **174
over-measure:** *excess*   **177 What ... withal:** *may all divine and human sanctities attest
my final assertion*   **180 conclude:** *come to a decision*   **183 unstable slightness:** *petty
whims* **purpose so barr'd;** *where rational action is thus obstructed*   **185 less ... discreet:**
prudent rather than timid   **186, 187 That ... on 't:** *whose devotion to the essentials of good
government exceeds your fear of innovations in politics*   **189 jump:** *put in hazard*   **191
multitudinous tongue:** *i.e. voting power of the rabble*   **196 H'as:** *he has*   **198 answer:**
abide the penalty   **200 despite:** *malice*   **203 greater bench:** *senate*   **204 what's ...
be:** *inevitably necessity, however unfitting*

210 ædiles: *ædiles of the people, assistants to the tribunes*   **213 Attach:** *arrest* **innovator:**
agitator   **217 surety:** *vouch for*   **252 distinctly ranges:** *stretches out intact in separate
buildings*

Bear him to the rock Tarpeian, and from thence
Into destruction cast him.
 Bru.   Ædiles, seize him!
 All Ple. Yield, Martius, yield!
 Men.   Hear me one word;   *265*
Beseech you, tribunes, hear me but a word.
 Æd. Peace, peace!
 Men. Be that you seem, truly your country's friends,
And temperately proceed to what you would
Thus violently redress.   *270*
 Bru.   Sir, those cold ways,
That seem like prudent helps, are very poisonous
Where the disease is violent. Lay hands upon him,
And bear him to the rock. *Coriolanus draws his sword.*
 Cor.   No, I'll die here.   *275*
There's some among you have beheld me fighting:
Come, try upon yourselves what you have seen me.
 Men. Down with that sword! Tribunes, withdraw awhile.
 Bru. Lay hands upon him.
 Men.   Help Martius, help,   *280*
You that be noble; help him, young and old!
 All. Down with him!—down with him!   *Exeunt.*

*In this mutiny the Tribunes, the Ædiles, and the People are beat
in.*

 Men. Go, get you to your house; begone, away!
All will be naught else.   *285*
 2. Sen.   Get you gone.
 Cor.   Stand fast;
We have as many friends as enemies.
 Men. Shall it be put to that?
 Sen.   The gods forbid!   *290*
I prithee, noble friend, home to thy house;
Leave us to cure this cause.
 Men.   For 'tis a sore upon us
You cannot tent yourself: begone, beseech you.
 Com. Come, sir, along with us.   *295*
 Cor. I would they were barbarians,—as they are,
Though in Rome litter'd,—not Romans,—as they are not,
Though calv'd i' the porch o' the Capitol,—
 Men.   Begone;
Put not your worthy rage into your tongue;   *300*
One time will owe another.
 Cor.   On fair ground
I could beat forty of them.
 Men.   I could myself
Take up a brace o' the best of them; yea, the two tribunes. *305*
 Com. But now 'tis odds beyond arithmetic;
And manhood is call'd foolery when it stands
Against a falling fabric. Will you hence,
Before the tag return? whose rage doth rend
Like interrupted waters and o'erbear   *310*
What they are us'd to bear.
 Men.   Pray, you, begone.
I'll try whether my old wit be in request
With those that have but little: this must be patch'd

With cloth of any colour.   *315*
 Com.   Nay, come away.
     Exeunt Coriolanus and Cominius.
 Patri. This man has marr'd his fortune.
 Men. His nature is too noble for the world:
He would not flatter Neptune for his trident,   *320*
Or Jove for 's power to thunder, His heart's his mouth:
What his breast forges, that his tongue must vent;
And, being angry, does forget that ever
He heard the name of death.   *A noise within.*
Here's goodly work!   *325*
 Patri.   I would they were a-bed!
 Men. I would they were in Tiber! What the vengeance!
Could he not speak 'em fair?

   Enter Brutus and Sicinius with the rabble again.

 Sic.   Where is this viper
That would depopulate the city and   *330*
Be every man himself?
 Men.   You worthy tribunes,—
 Sic. He shall be thrown down the Tarpeian rock
With rigorous hands: he hath resisted law,
And therefore law shall scorn him further trial   *335*
Than the severity of the public power.
Which he so sets at nought,
 1. Cit.   He shall well know
The noble tribunes are the people's mouths,
And we their hands.   *340*
 All.   He shall, sure on 't.
 Men.   Sir, sir,—
 Sic. Peace!
 Men. Do not cry havoc, where you should but hunt
With modest warrant.   *345*
 Sic.   Sir, how comes 't that you
Have help to make this rescue?
 Men.   Hear me speak:
As I do know the consul's worthiness,
So can I name his faults.   *350*
 Sic.   Consul! what consul?
 Men. The Consul Coriolanus.
 Bru.   He consul!
 All. No, no, no, no, no.
 Men. If, by the tribunes' leave, and yours, good people, *355*
I may be heard, I would crave a word or two,
The which shall turn you to no further harm
Than so much loss of time.
 Sic.   Speak briefly then;
For we are peremptory to dispatch   *360*
This viperous traitor. To eject him hence
Were but one danger, and to keep him here
Our certain death; therefore it is decreed
He dies to-night.
 Men.   Now the good gods forbid   *365*
That our renowned Rome, whose gratitude
Towards her deserved children is enroll'd
In Jove's own book, like an unnatural dam

---

261 rock Tarpeian; *cf. n.*   **277 seen me:** *seen me do*   **285 naught:** *ruined*   **292 cause:** *disorder, disease*   **297 litter'd:** *whelped, born like beasts*   **301 One . . . another:** *a balance will be struck between this unlucky time and one that will be more favorable*   **306 beyond arithmetic:** *incalculable*   **308 fabric:** *building*   **309 tag:** *rabble*   **310 interrupted:** *obstructed*

314, 315 this . . . colour: *we must use the roughest remedies*   **323 does:** *he does*   **328 speak 'em fair:** *conciliate them*   **336 severity:** *i.e. exposure to severity*   **344 cry havoc:** *give the signal for indiscriminate slaughter*   **345 With . . . warrant:** *as moderation warrants*   **357 turn you to:** *occasion you*   **360 peremptory:** *resolved*   **368 dam:** *mother (of breasts)*

Should now eat up her own!

    Sic. He's a disease that must be cut away.   *370*

    Men. O! he's a limb that has but a disease;
Mortal to cut it off; to cure it easy.
What has he done to Rome that's worthy death?
Killing our enemies, the blood he hath lost,—
Which, I dare vouch, is more than that he hath   *375*
By many an ounce,—he dropp'd it for his country;
And what is left, to lose it by his country,
Were to us all, that do 't and suffer it,
A brand to th' end o' the world.

    Sic.   This is clean kam.   *380*

    Bru. Merely awry: when he did love his country
It honour'd him.

    Men.   The service of the foot,
Being once gangren'd, is not then respected
For what before it was.   *385*

    Bru.   We'll hear no more.
Pursue him to his house, and pluck him thence,
Lest his infection, being of catching nature,
Spread further.

    Men.   One word more, one word.   *390*
This tiger-footed rage, when it shall find
The harm of unscann'd swiftness, will, too late,
Tie leaden pounds to 's heels. Proceed by process;
Lest parties—as he is belov'd—break out,
And sack great Rome with Romans.   *395*

    Bru.   If it were so,—

    Sic. What do ye talk?
Have we not had a taste of his obedience?
Our ædiles smote? ourselves resisted? Come!

    Men. Consider this: he has been bred i' the wars   *400*
Since a' could draw a sword, and is ill school'd
In bolted language; meal and bran together
He throws without distinction. Give me leave,
I'll go to him, and undertake to bring him
Where he shall answer by a lawful form,—   *405*
In peace,—to his utmost peril.

    1. Sen.   Noble tribunes,
It is the humane way: the other course
Will prove too bloody, and the end of it
Unknown to the beginning.   *410*

    Sic.   Noble Meneius,
Be you then as the people's officer.
Masters, lay down your weapons.

    Bru.   Go not home.

    Sic. Meet on the market-place. We'll attend you there: *415*
Where, if you bring not Martius, we'll proceed
In our first way.

    Men. I'll bring him to you.
[*To the Senators.*] Let me desire your company. He must come,
Or what is worst will follow.   *420*

    Sen.   Pray you, let's to him.

                        Exeunt omnes.

❧ SCENE SECOND ❧

[The Same. A Room in Coriolanus's House]
Enter Coriolanus with Nobles.

    Cor. Let them pull all about mine ears; present me
Death on the wheel, or at wild horses' heels;
Or pile ten hills on the Tarpeian rock,
That the precipitation might down stretch
Below the beam of sight; yet will I still   *5*
Be thus to them.

    Noble.   You do the nobler.

    Cor. I muse my mother
Does not approve me further, who was wont
To call them woollen vassals, things created   *10*
To buy and sell with groats, to show bare heads
In congregations, to yawn, be still, and wonder,
When one but of my ordinance stood up
To speak of peace or war.

Enter Volumnia.

                 I talk of you: *15*
Why did you wish me milder? Would you have me
False to my nature? Rather say I play
The man I am.

    Vol.   O! sir, sir, sir,
I would have had you put your power well on   *20*
Before you had worn it out.

    Cor.   Let go.

    Vol. You might have been enough the man you are
With striving less to be so: lesser had been
The thwartings of your dispositions if   *25*
You had not show'd them how you were dispos'd,
Ere they lack'd power to cross you.

    Cor.   Let them hang.

    Vol. Ay, and burn too.

Enter Menenius with the Senators.

    Men. Come, come; you have been too rough, something *30*
too rough;
You must return and mend it.

    Sen.   There's no remedy;
Unless, by not so doing, our good city
Cleave in the midst, and perish.   *35*

    Vol.   Pray be counsell'd.
I have a heart as little apt as yours,
But yet a brain that leads my use of anger
To better vantage.

    Men.   Well said, noble woman!   *40*
Before he should thus stoop to the herd, but that
The violent fit o' the time craves it as physic
For the whole state, I would put mine armour on,
Which I can scarcely bear.

    Cor.   What must I do?   *45*

    Men. Return to the tribunes.

    Cor.   Well, what then? what then?

    Men. Repent what you have spoke.

    Cor. For them! I cannot do it to the gods;

---

372 Mortal: *producing death*   **378 suffer:** *permit*   **379 brand:** *mark of infamy*   **380 clean kam:** *absolutely perverse*   **381 Merely:** *completely*   **383-385 The ... was;** *cf. n.* **392 unscann'd:** *rash, thoughtless*   **393 pounds:** *pound-weights* **process:** *legal method*   **394 parties:** *factions*   **397 talk:** *say*   **402 bolted:** *sifted*

4 precipitation: *steepness*   **5 Below ... sight:** *lower than eyesight can reach*   **8 muse:** *wonder*   **10 woollen vassals:** *coarsely dressed underlings*   **11 groats:** *four-penny coins*   **13 ordinance:** *rank*   **22 Let go:** *No more of that*   **25 thwartings;** *cf. n.* **35 Cleave ... midst:** *break in two*   **37 as little apt:** *as unbending*   **41 but:** *except*

Must I then do 't to them?   *50*
    Vol.   You are too absolute;
Though therein you can never be too noble,
But when extremities speak. I have heard you say,
Honour and policy, like unsever'd friends,
I' the war do grow together: grant that, and tell me,   *55*
In peace what each of them by th' other lose,
That they combine not there.
    Cor.   Tush, tush!
    Men.   A good demand.
    Vol. If it be honour in your wars to seem   *60*
The same you are not,—which, for your best ends,
You adopt your policy,—how is it less or worse,
That it shall hold companionship in peace
With honour, as in war, since that to both
It stands in like request?   *65*
    Cor.   Why force you this?
    Vol. Because that now it lies you on to speak
To the people; not by your own instruction,
Nor by the matter which your heart prompts you,
But with such words that are but rooted in   *70*
Your tongue, though but bastards and syllables
Of no allowance to your bosom's truth.
Now this no more dishonours you at all.
Than to take in a town with gentle words,
Which else would put you to your fortune and   *75*
The hazard of much blood.
I would dissemble with my nature where
My fortunes and my friends at stake requir'd
I should do so in honour: I am in this,
Your wife, your son, these senators, the nobles;   *80*
And you will rather show our general louts
How you can frown than spend a fawn upon 'em,
For the inheritance of their loves and safeguard
Of what that want might ruin.
    Men.   Noble lady!   *85*
Come, go with us; speak fair; you may salve so,
Not what is dangerous present, but the loss
Of what is past.
    Vol.   I prithee now, my son,
Go to them, with this bonnet in thy hand;   *90*
And thus far having stretch'd it,—here be with them,—
Thy knee bussing the stones,—for in such business
Action is eloquence, and the eyes of th' ignorant
More learned than the ears,—waving thy head,
Which often, thus, correcting thy stout heart,   *95*
Now humble as the ripest mulberry
That will not hold the handling: or say to them,
Thou art their soldier, and being bred in broils
Hast not the soft way which, thou dost confess,
Were fit for thee to use as they to claim,   *100*
In asking their good loves; but thou wilt frame

Thyself, forsooth, hereafter theirs, so far
As thou hast power and person.
    Men.   This but done,
Even as she speaks, why, their hearts were yours;   *105*
For they have pardons, being ask'd, as free
As words to little purpose.
    Vol.   Prithee now,
Go, and be rul'd; although I know thou hadst rather
Follow thine enemy in a fiery gulf   *110*
Than flatter him in a bower.

                          Enter Cominius.

                          Here is Cominius.
    Com. I have been i' the market-place; and, sir, 'tis fit
You make strong party, or defend yourself
By calmness or by absence: all's in anger.   *115*
    Men. Only fair speech.
    Com.   I think 'twill serve, if he
Can thereto frame his spirit.
    Vol.   He must, and will.
Prithee now, say you will, and go about it.   *120*
    Cor. Must I go show them my unbarbed sconce?
Must I with my base tongue give to my noble heart
A lie that it must bear? Well, I will do 't:
Yet, where there but this single plot to lose,
This mould of Martius, they to dust should grind it,   *125*
And throw 't against the wind. To the marketplace!
You have put me now to such a part which never
I shall discharge to the life.
    Com.   Come, come, we'll prompt you.
    Vol. I prithee now, sweet son, as thou hast said   *130*
My praises made thee first a soldier, so,
To have my praise for this, perform a part
Thou hast not done before.
    Cor.   Well, I must do 't:
Away, my disposition, and possess me   *135*
Some harlot's spirit! My throat of war be turn'd,
Which quir'd with my drum, into a pipe
Small as an eunuch, or the virgin voice
That babies lulls asleep! The smiles of knaves
Tent in my cheeks, and school-boys' tears take up   *140*
The glasses of my sight! A beggar's tongue
Make motion through my lips, and my arm'd knees,
Who bow'd but in my stirrup, bend like his
That hath receiv'd an alms! I will not do 't,
Lest I surcease to honour mine own truth,   *145*
And by my body's action teach my mind
A most inherent baseness.
    Vol.   At thy choice then:
To beg of thee it is my more dishonour
Than thou of them. Come all to ruin; let   *150*
Thy mother rather feel thy pride than fear
Thy dangerous stoutness, for I mock at death
With as big heart as thou. Do as thou list,
Thy valiantness was mine, thou suck'dst it from me,

51 **absolute:** *positive, peremptory*   53 **but . . . speak:** *except under the command of necessity*   54 **policy:** *craft*   57 **combine:** *join*   62 **adopt:** *adopt as*   65 **stands . . .
request:** *is equally valuable* **force:** *urge*   67 **lies . . . on:** *is incumbent upon you*   68
by . . . instruction: *as your nature teaches you*   70, 71 **are . . . tongue:** *have their roots no
deeper than your tongue; cf. n.*   72 **Of . . . to:** *unapproved by*   74 **take in:** *get possession
of*   75 **put . . . fortune:** *force you to risk the fortune of war*   79 **I am:** *I am at stake*   81
general louts: *the good-for-nothings of the community*   83 **safeguard:** *for the security*   84
that want: *the want of their loves*   87, 88 **Not . . . past;** *cf. n.*   90 **this bonnet:** *that
which Coriolanus wears*   91, 92 **And . . . stones;** *cf. n.*   95 **Which often:** *a conciliatory
gesture which you are to repeat often*   100 **as they:** *as for them*

105 **were:** *would be*   106 **free:** *abundantly*   111 **bower:** *abode of pleasure*   114 **make
. . . party:** *collect many supporters*   121 **unbarbed sconce:** *bared head*   124 **this single
plot:** *my own person*   127 **which:** *as*   128 **discharge . . . life:** *perform naturally*   137
quir'd: *harmonized*   138 **virgin:** *nurse-maid's*   140 **Tent:** *encamp* **take up:** *fill*   141
The . . . sight: *my eyes*   145 **surcease to honour:** *cease to have respect for*   149 **my . . .
dishonour:** *more dishonor for me*   150 **thou:** *for thee to beg*   150–152 **let . . . stoutness:**
let my anxiety concerning thy dangerous obstinacy give place to such pride as thou feelest

But owe thy pride thyself.   *155*
　Cor.　　　　　　　　　Pray, be content:
Mother, I am going to the market-place;
Chide me no more. I'll mountebank their loves,
Cog their hearts from them, and come home belov'd
Of all the trades in Rome. Look, I am going: *160*
Commend me to my wife. I'll return consul,
Or never trust to what my tongue can do
I' the way of flattery further.
　Vol.　　　　　　　　　Do your will.
　　　　　　　　　　　　　　　　　Exit Volumnia.
　Com. Away! the tribunes do attend you: arm yourself *165*
To answer mildly; for they are prepar'd
With accusations, as I hear, more strong
Than are upon you yet.
　Cor. The word is 'mildly.' Pray you, let us go:
Let them accuse me by invention, I   *170*
Will answer in mine honour.
　Men.　　　　　　　Ay, but mildly.
　Cor. Well, mildly be it then. Mildly!   *Exeunt.*

❧ SCENE THIRD ❧

[The Same. The Forum]
Enter Sicinius and Brutus.

　Bru. In this point charge him home, that he affects
Tyrannical power: if he evade us there,
Enforce him with his envy to the people,
And that the spoil got on the Antiates
Was ne'er distributed.—   *5*

Enter an Ædile.

What, will he come?
　Æd.　　　　　He's coming.
　Bru.　　　　　　　How accompanied?
　Æd. With old Menenius, and those senators
That always favour'd him.   *10*
　Sic.　　　　　Have you a catalogue
Of all the voices that we have procur'd,
Set down by the poll?
　Æd.　　　　　I have, 'tis ready.
　Sic. Have you collected them by tribes?   *15*
　Æd.　　　　　　　　　I have.
　Sic. Assemble presently the people hither;
And when they hear me say, 'It shall be so,
I' the right and strength o' the commons,' be it either
For death, for fine, or banishment, then let them, *20*
If I say, fine, cry 'fine,'—if death, cry 'death,'
Insisting on the old prerogative
And power i' the truth o' the cause.
　Æd.　　　　　　　I shall inform them.
　Bru. And when such time they have begun to cry, *25*
Let them not cease, but with a din confus'd
Enforce the present execution
Of what we chance to sentence.
　Æd.　　　　　　　Very well.

　Sic. Make them be strong and ready for this hint, *30*
When we shall hap to give 't them.
　Bru.　　　　　　　Go about it.
　　　　　　　　　　　　　　　　　[Exit Ædile.]
Put him to choler straight. He hath been us'd
Ever to conquer, and to have his worth
Of contradiction: being once chaf'd, he cannot   *35*
Be rein'd again to temperance; then he speaks
What's in his heart; and that is there which looks
With us to break his neck.

Enter Coriolanus, Menenius, and Cominius, with others.

　Sic.　　　　　　Well, here he comes.
　Men. Calmly, I do beseech you.   *40*
　Cor. Ay, as an hostler, that for the poorest piece
Will bear the knave by the volume. The honour'd gods
Keep Rome in safety, and the chairs of justice
Supplied with worthy men! plant love among 's!
Throng our large temples with the shows of peace, *45*
And not our streets with war!
　1. Sen.　　　　　　　Amen, amen.
　Men. A noble wish.

Enter the Ædile with the Plebeians.

　Sic.　Draw near, ye people.
　Æd. List to your tribunes; audience; peace! I say. *50*
　Cor. First, hear me speak.
　Both Tri.　　　　Well, say. Peace, ho!
　Cor. Shall I be charg'd no further than this present?
Must all determine here?
　Sic.　　　　　　I do demand,   *55*
If you submit you to the people's voices,
Allow their officers, and are content
To suffer lawful censure for such faults
As shall be prov'd upon you?
　Cor.　　　　　　　I am content.   *60*
　Men. Lo! citizens, he says he is content:
The warlike service he has done, consider; think
Upon the wounds his body bears, which show
Like graves i' the holy churchyard.
　Cor.　　　　　　Scratches with briers,   *65*
Scars to move laughter only.
　Men.　　　　　　Consider further,
That when he speaks not like a citizen,
You find him like a soldier: do not take
His rougher accents for malicious sounds,   *70*
But, as I say, such as I become a soldier,
Rather than envy you.
　Com.　　　　　Well, well; no more.
　Cor. What is the matter,
That being pass'd for consul with full voice   *75*
I am so dishonour'd that the very hour
You take it off again?
　Sic.　　　　　　Answer to us.
　Cor. Say, then: 'tis true, I ought so.
　Sic. We charge you, that you have contriv'd to take *80*

---

155 **owe:** *own*　158 **mountebank:** *act the quack vendor for*　159 **Cog:** *cheat*　165 **arm yourself:** *prepare*　1 **affects:** *aims at*　3 **Enforce:** *press*　4 **on:** *at the expense of*　13 **by the poll:** *by individual names*　15 **by tribes;** *cf. n.*　27 **present:** *immediate*

34, 35 **have . . . contradiction:** *indulge his love of contradiction in full measure*　37 **looks:** *tends, is calculated*　41 **piece:** *coin*　42 **bear . . . volume:** *submit to be called knave interminably*　53 **this present:** *the present occasion*　54 **determine:** *end*　57 **Allow:** *acknowledge*　70 **accents:** *cf. n.*　72 **envy:** *evidence hostility to*　80 **contriv'd:** *designed*

From Rome all season'd office, and to wind
Yourself into a power tyrannical;
For which you are a traitor to the people.
   Cor. How! Traitor!
   Men.   Nay, temperately; your promise.   *85*
   Cor. The fires i' the lowest hell fold in the people!
Call me their traitor! Thou injurious tribune!
Within thine eyes sat twenty thousand deaths,
In thy hands clutch'd as many millions, in
Thy lying tongue both numbers, I would say   *90*
'Thou liest' unto thee with a voice as free
As I do pray the gods.
   Sic.   Mark you this, people?
   All. To the rock!—to the rock with him!
   Sic.   Peace!   *95*
We need not put new matter to his charge:
What you have seen him do, and heard him speak,
Beating your officers, cursing yourselves,
Opposing laws with strokes, and here defying
Those whose great power must try him; even this,   *100*
So criminal and in such capital kind,
Deserves th' extremest death.
   Bru.   But since he hath
Serv'd well for Rome,—
   Cor.   What do you prate of service?   *105*
   Bru. I talk of that, that know it.
   Cor.   You!
   Men. Is this the promise that you made your mother?
   Com. Know, I pray you,—
   Cor.   I'll know no further: *110*
Let them pronounce the steep Tarpeian death,
Vagabond exile, flaying, pent to linger
But with a grain a day, I would not buy
Their mercy at the price of one fair word,
Nor check my courage for what they can give,   *115*
To have 't with saying 'Good morrow.'
   Sic.   For that he has,—
As much as in him lies,—from time to time
Envied against the people, seeking means
To pluck away their power, as now at last   *120*
Given hostile strokes, and that not in the presence
Of dreaded justice, but on the ministers
That doth distribute it; in the name o' the people,
And in the power of us the tribunes, we,
Even from this instant, banish him our city,   *125*
In peril of precipitation
From off the rock Tarpeian, never more
To enter our Rome gates: i' the people's name,
I say, it shall be so.
   All. It shall be so.—It shall be so.—Let him away.—   *130*
He's banish'd, and it shall be so.
   Com. Hear me, my masters, and my common friends,—
   Sic. He's sentenc'd; no more hearing.
   Com.   Let me speak:
I have been consul, and can show for Rome   *135*
Her enemies' marks upon me. I do love
My country's good with a respect more tender,

More holy, and profound, than mine own life,
My dear wife's estimate, her womb's increase,
And treasure of my loins; then if I would   *140*
Speak that—
   Sic.   We know your drift: speak what?
   Bru. There's no more to be said but he is banish'd,
As enemy to the people and his country.
It shall be so.   *145*
   All.   It shall be so,—it shall be so.
   Cor. You common cry of curs! whose breath I hate
As reek o' the rotten fens, whose loves I prize
As the dead carcasses of unburied men
That do corrupt my air, I banish you;   *150*
And here remain with your uncertainty!
Let every feeble rumour shake your hearts!
Your enemies, with nodding of their plumes,
Fan you into despair! Have the power still
To banish your defenders; till at length   *155*
Your ignorance,—which finds not till it feels,—
Making but reservation of yourselves,—
Still your own foes,—deliver you as most
Abated captives to some nation
That won you without blows! Despising,   *160*
For you, the city, thus I turn my back:
There is a world elsewhere.
               Exeunt Coriolanus, Cominius with others.
               They all shout and throw up their caps.
   Æd. The people's enemy is gone, is gone!
   All. Our enemy is banish'd—he is gone!—Hoo! oo!   *165*
   Sic. Go, see him out at gates, and follow him,
As he hath follow'd you, with all despite;
Give him deserv'd vexation. Let a guard
Attend us through the city.
   All. Come, come,—let's see him out at gates! come!   *170*
The gods preserve our noble tribunes! Come!   *Exeunt.*

ACT FOURTH ❦ Scene First

[Rome. Before a Gate of the City]
Enter Coriolanus, Volumnia, Virgilia, Menenius, Cominius, with
the young Nobility of Rome.

   Cor. Come, leave your tears: a brief farewell: the beast
With many heads butts me away. Nay, mother,
Where is your ancient courage? you were us'd
To say extremity was the trier of spirits;
That common chances common men could bear;   *5*
That when the sea was calm all boats alike
Show'd mastership in floating; fortune's blows,
When most struck home,—being gentle, wounded, craves
A noble cunning: you were us'd to load me
With precepts that would make invincible   *10*
The heart that conn'd them.
   Vir. O heavens! O heavens!
   Cor.   Nay, I prithee, woman,—
   Vol. Now the red pestilence strike all trades in Rome,

---

81 season'd: *time-honored*   **86 fold in:** *encompass*   **87 injurious:** *insulting*   **88 Within:** *although within*   **101 capital kind:** *death-deserving measure*   **112 pent:** *imprisoned*   **linger:** *starve slowly*   **116 To have 't:** *though I could have it*   **119 Envied:** *been malignant*   **121 not:** *not merely*   **123 doth:** *do; cf. n.*

139 estimate: *reputation*   **151 remain:** *do you remain*   **uncertainty:** *inconstancy of mind*   **157 Making . . . of:** *exempting from banishment none but*   **159 Abated:** *crestfallen*   **S.d. with others;** *cf. n.*   **7–9 fortune's . . . cunning:** *cf. n.*   **14 red pestilence:** *plague*

And occupations perish!   *15*

  Cor.   What, what, what!
I shall be lov'd when I am lack'd. Nay, mother,
Resume that spirit, when you were wont to say,
If you had been the wife of Hercules,
Six of his labours you'd have done, and sav'd   *20*
Your husband so much sweat. Cominius,
Droop not; adieu. Farewell, my wife! my mother!
I'll do well yet. Thou old and true Menenius,
Thy tears are salter than a young man's,
And venomous to thine eyes. My sometime general,   *25*
I have seen thee stern, and thou hast oft beheld
Heart-hardening spectacles; tell these sad women
'Tis fond to wail inevitable strokes
As 'tis to laugh at 'em. My mother, you wot well
My hazards still have been your solace; and   *30*
Believe 't not lightly,—though I go alone
Like a lonely dragon, that his fen
Makes fear'd and talk'd of more than seen,—your son
Will or exceed the common or be caught
With cautelous baits and practice.   *35*

  Vol.   My first son,
Whither wilt thou go? Take good Cominius
With thee awhile: determine on some course,
More than a wild exposure to each chance
That starts i' the way before thee.   *40*

  Cor.   O the gods!

  Com. I'll follow thee a month, devise with thee
Where thou shalt rest, that thou mayst hear of us,
And we of thee: so, if the time thrust forth
A cause for thy repeal, we shall not send   *45*
O'er the vast world to seek a single man,
And lose advantage, which doth ever cool
I' the absence of the needer.

  Cor.   Fare ye well:
Thou hast years upon thee; and thou art too full   *50*
Of the wars' surfeits, to go rove with one
That's yet unbruis'd: bring me but out at gate.
Come, my sweet wife, my dearest mother, and
My friends of noble touch, when I am forth,
Bid me farewell, and smile. I pray you, come.   *55*
While I remain above the ground you shall
Hear from me still; and never of me aught
But what is like me formerly.

  Men.   That's worthily
As any ear can hear. Come, let's not weep.   *60*
If I could shake off but one seven years
From these old arms and legs, by the good gods,
I'd with thee every foot.

  Cor.   Give me thy hand:
Come.   *Exeunt.*   *65*

❧ SCENE SECOND ❧

[The Same. A Street near the Gate]
Enter the two Tribunes, Sicinius and Brutus, with the Ædile.

  Sic. Bid them all home; he's gone, and we'll no further.
The nobility are vex'd, whom we see have sided
In his behalf.

  Bru.   Now we have shown our power,
Let us seem humbler after it is done   *5*
Than when it was a-doing.

  Sic.   Bid them home;
Say their great enemy is gone, and they
Stand in their ancient strength.

  Bru.   Dismiss them home.   *10*
                  [Exit Ædile.]
Here comes his mother.

Enter Volumnia, Virgilia, and Menenius.

  Sic.   Let's not meet her.

  Bru.   Why?

  Sic. They say she's mad.

  Bru. They have ta'en note of us: keep on your way.   *15*

  Vol. O! y' are well met. The hoarded plague o' the gods
Requite your love!

  Men.   Peace, peace! be not so loud.

  Vol. If that I could for weeping, you should hear,—
Nay, and you shall hear some. *[To Brutus.]* Will you be gone?

  Vir. [To Sicinius.] You shall stay too. I would I had the power
To say so to my husband.

  Sic.   Are you mankind?

  Vol. Ay, fool; is that a shame? Not but this fool.   *25*
Was not a man my father? Hadst thou foxship
To banish him that strook more blows for Rome
Than thou hast spoken words?

  Sic.   O blessed heavens!

  Vol. More noble blows than ever thou wise words;   *30*
And for Rome's good. I'll tell thee what; yet go:
Nay, but thou shalt stay too: I would my son
Were in Arabia, and thy tribe before him,
His good sword in his hand.

  Sic.   What then?   *35*

  Vir.   What then!
He'd make an end of thy posterity.

  Vol. Bastards and all.
Good man, the wounds that he does bear for Rome!

  Men. Come, come: peace!   *40*

  Sic. I would he had continu'd to his country
As he began, and not unknit himself
The noble knot he made.

  Bru.   I would be had.

  Vol. 'I would he had!' 'Twas you incens'd the rabble: *45*
Cats, that can judge as fitly of his worth.
As I can of those mysteries which heaven
Will not have earth to know.

  Bru.   Pray, let's go.

  Vol. Now, pray, sir, get you gone: *50*

---

15 occupations: *mechanical employments*   **18 Resume:** *recover*   **28 fond:** *as fond, as foolish*   **34 or ... common:** *either do some deed of fame*   **35 With ... practice:** *by the snares and treachery of wily adversaries*   **36 first:** *first and only, eminent*   **39 exposure:** *exposure*   **45 repeal:** *recall*   **47 advantage:** *opportunity to profit by circumstances*   **48 needer:** *him who should utilize the advantage*   **51 wars' surfeits:** *strains from military service*   **54 noble touch:** *proved nobility*   **58 me formerly:** *my former self*   **59 worthily:** *as worthily spoken*

2 have sided: *to have enlisted themselves*   **16 The hoarded ... gods:** *every plague the gods have stored up*   **20 some:** *a part*   **23 say so:** *i.e. command his presence*   **mankind:** *savage, cf. n.*   **26 foxship:** *foxlike cunning*   **27 strook:** *struck*   **31 what:** *something*   **33 Arabia:** *the Arabian desert*   **43 noble knot:** *i.e. bond of faithful service*

You have done a brave deed. Ere you go, hear this:
As far as doth the Capitol exceed
The meanest house in Rome, so far my son,—
This lady's husband here, this, do you see,—
Whom you have banish'd, does exceed you all.   55
    Bru. Well, well, we'll leave you.
    Sic.   Why stay we to be baited
With one that wants her wits?   *Exeunt Tribunes.*
    Vol.   Take my prayers with you.
I would the gods had nothing else to do   60
But to confirm my curses! Could I meet 'em
But once a day, it would unclog my heart
Of what lies heavy to 't.
    Men.   You have told them home,
And, by my troth, you have cause. You'll sup with me? 65
    Vol. Anger's my meat; I sup upon myself,
And so shall starve with feeding. Come, lets go.
Leave this faint puling and lament as I do,
In anger, Juno-like. Come, come, come.
                              Exeunt [Volumnia and Virgilia].
    Men. Fie, fie, fie!   *Exit.* 70

❧ SCENE THIRD ❧

[A Highway between Rome and Antium]
Enter a Roman and a Volsce.

    Rom. I know you well, sir, and you know me: your name I
think is Adrian.
    Vols. It is so, sir: truly, I have forgot you.
    Rom I am a Roman; and my services are, as you are, against
'em: know you me yet?   5
    Vols. Nicanor? No.
    Rom. The same, sir.
    Vols. You had more heard, when I last saw you; but your
favour is well appeared by your tongue. What's the news
in Rome? I have a note from the Volscian state to find   10
you out there: you have well saved me a day's journey.
    Rom. There hath been in Rome strange insurrections: the
people against the senators, patricians, and nobles.
    Vols. Hath been! Is it ended then? Our state thinks not so;
they are in a most warlike preparation, and hope to come   15
upon them in the heat of their division.
    Rom. The main blaze of it is past, but a small thing
would make it flame again. For the nobles receive so to
heart the banishment of that worthy Coriolanus, that they
are in a ripe aptness to take all power from the people   20
and to pluck from them their tribunes for ever. This lies
glowing, I can tell you, and is almost mature for the violent
breaking out.
    Vols. Coriolanus banished!
    Rom. Banished, sir.   25
    Vols. You will be welcome with this intelligence, Nicanor.
    Rom. The day serves well for them now. I have heard it
said, the fittest time to corrupt a man's wife is when she's
fallen out with her husband. Your noble Tullus Aufidius will

appear well in these wars, his great opposer, Coriolanus,   30
being now in no request of his country.
    Vols. He cannot choose. I am most fortunate, thus acciden-
tally to encounter you: you have ended my business, and I will
merrily accompany you home.
    Rom. I shall, between this and supper, tell you most   35
strange things from Rome; all tending to the good of their adversaries. Have you an army ready, say you?
    Vols. A most royal one: the centurions and their charges dis-
tinctly billeted, already in th' entertainment, and to be on foot
at an hour's warning.   40
    Rom. I am joyful to hear of their readiness, and am the
man, I think, that shall set them in present action. So, sir,
heartily will met, and most glad of your company.
    Vols. You take my part from me, sir; I have the most cause
to be glad of yours.   45
    Rom. Well, let us go together.   *Exeunt.*

❧ SCENE FOURTH ❧

[Antium. Before Aufidius' House]
Enter Coriolanus, in mean apparel, disguised and muffled.

    Cor. A goodly city is this Antium. City,
'Tis I that made thy widows: many an heir
Of these fair edifices 'fore my wars
Have I heard groan and drop: then, know me not,
Lest that thy wives with spits and boys with stones   5
In puny battle slay me.

Enter a Citizen.

                          Save you, sir.
    Cit. And you.
    Cor.   Direct me, if it be your will,
Where great Aufidius lies. Is he in Antium?   10
    Cit. He is, and feasts the nobles of the state
At his house this night.
    Cor.   Which is his house, beseech you?
    Cit. This, here before you.
    Cor.   Thank you, sir. Farewell. 15
                                           Exit Citizen.
O world, thy slippery turns! Friends now fast sworn,
Whose double bosoms seems to wear one heart,
Whose hours, whose bed, whose meal, and exercise,
Are still together, who twin, as 'twere, in love
Unseparable, shall within this hour,   20
On a dissension of a doit, break out
To bitterest enmity: so, fellest foes,
Whose passions and whose plots have broke their sleep.
To take the one the other, by some chance,
Some trick not worth an egg, shall grow dear friends   25
And interjoin their issues. So with me:
My birth-place hate I, and my love's upon

58 **With:** *by*   61 **confirm:** *note down for execution*   64 **told . . . home:** *said all there is to say*   68 **faint puling:** *weak whining; cf. n.*   9 **favour:** *face*   **appeared:** *made to appear, manifested*   10 **note:** *instruction*   20 **ripe aptness:** *complete readiness*   22 **glowing:** *i.e. like a spark*   27 **The day:** *the state of affairs*

31 **in no request of:** *unvalued by*   32 **cannot choose:** *cannot fail to appear well*   38, 39 **distinctly billeted:** *carefully enrolled*   **entertainment:** *receipt of pay*   **on foot:** *under arms*   44 **my part:** *the words I should say*   3 **'fore my wars:** *confronting me in battle*   7 **Save:** *God preserve*   10 **lies:** *lodges*   16 **thy . . . turns:** *how inconstant you are*   17 **bosom seems;** *cf. n.*   19 **twin:** *are joined like twins*   21 **dissension . . . doit:** *dispute over the value of half a farthing*   22 **fellest:** *fiercest*   23 **passions:** *violent emotions*   24 **To take . . . other;** *cf. n.*   26 **interjoin their issues:** *intermarry their children (to make the league perpetual).*   27 **hate;** *cf. n.*

This enemy town. I'll enter: if he slay me,
He does fair justice; if he give me way,
I'll do his country service.   *Exit.* 30

❧ Scene Fifth ❧

[The Same. A Hall in Aufidius' House]
Music plays. Enter a Servingman.

1. Serv. Wine, wine, wine! What service is here! I think our
fellows are asleep.   *[Exit.]*

Enter another Servingman.

2. Serv. Where's Cotus? my master calls for him. Cotus! *Exit.*

Enter Coriolanus.

Cor. A goodly house: the feast smells well; but I
Appear not like a guest.   5

Enter the First Servingman.

1. Serv. What would you have, friend? Whence are you?
Here's no place for you: pray, go to the door.   *Exit*
Cor. I have deserv'd no better entertainment,
In being Coriolanus.

Enter Second Servant.

2. Serv. Whence are you, sir? Has the porter his eyes in 10
his head, that he gives entrance to such companions? Pray,
get you out.
Cor. Away!
2. Serv. 'Away!' Get you away.
Cor. Now, th' art troublesome.   15
2. Serv. Are you so brave? I'll have you talked with anon.

Enter Third Servingman. The first meets him.

3. Serv. What fellow's this?
1. Serv. A strange one as ever I looked on: I cannot get
him out o' the house: prithee, call my master to him.
3. Serv. What have you to do here, fellow?   20
Pray you, avoid the house.
Cor. Let me but stand; I will not hurt your hearth.
3. Serv. What are you?
Cor. A gentleman.
3. Serv. A marvellous poor one.   25
Cor. True, so I am.
3. Serv. Pray you, poor gentleman, take up some other
station; here's no place for you; pray you, avoid: come.
Cor. Follow your function; go, and batten on cold bits.
      Pushes him away from him. 30
3. Serv. What, you will not? Prithee, tell my master what a
strange guest he has here.
2. Serv. And I shall.   *Exit Second Servingman.*
3. Serv. Where dwell'st thou?
Cor. Under the canopy.   35
3. Serv. 'Under the canopy!'
Cor. Ay.
3. Serv. Where's that?
Cor. I' the city of kites and crows.

3. Serv. 'I' the city of kites and crows!' What an ass it is! 40
Then thou dwell'st with daws too?
Cor. No; I serve not thy master.
3. Serv. How sir! Do you meddle with my master?
Cor. Ay; 'tis an honester service than to meddle with thy
mistress.   45
Thou prat'st, and prat'st: serve with thy trencher.
Hence.   *Beats him away.*

Enter Aufidius with the [Second] Servingman.

Auf. Where is this fellow?
2. Serv. Here, sir: I'd have beaten him like a dog, but for
disturbing the lords within.   50
Auf. Whence com'st thou? what wouldst thou? Thy name?
Why speak'st not? Speak, man: what's thy name?
Cor. *[Unmuffling.]* If, Tullus,
Not yet thou know'st me, and, seeing me, dost not
Think me for the man I am, necessity   55
Commands me name myself.
Auf.   What is thy name?
Cor. A name unmusical to the Volscians' ears,
And harsh in sound to thine.
Auf.   Say, what's thy name? 60
Thou hast a grim appearance, and thy face
Bears a command in 't; though thy tackle's torn,
Thou show'st a noble vessel. What's thy name?
Cor. Prepare thy brow to frown. Know'st thou me yet?
Auf. I know thee not. Thy name?   65
Cor. My name is Caius Martius, who hath done
To thee particularly, and to all the Volsces,
Great hurt and mischief; thereto witness may
My surname, Coriolanus: the painful service,
The extreme dangers, and the drops of blood   70
Shed for my thankless country are requited
But with that surname; a good memory
And witness of the malice and displeasure
Which thou shouldst bear me: only that name remains;
The cruelty and envy of the people,   75
Permitted by our dastard nobles, who
Have all forsook me, hath devour'd the rest;
And suffer'd me by the voice of slaves to be
Whoop'd out of Rome. Now this extremity
Hath brought me to thy hearth; not out of hope,— 80
Mistake me not,—to save my life; for if
I had fear'd death, of all the men i' the world
I would have 'voided thee; but in mere spite,
To be full quit of those my banishers,
Stand I before thee here. Then if thou hast 85
A heart of wreak in thee, that will revenge
Thine own particular wrongs and stop those maims
Of shame seen through thy country, speed thee straight,
And make my misery serve thy turn: so use it,
That my revengeful services may prove 90
As benefits to thee, for I will fight
Against my canker'd country with the spleen
Of all the under fiends. But if so be

24 **way:** *scope, opportunity*   11 **companions:** *rascals*   21 **avoid:** *get out of*   29 **Follow
. . . function:** *do your proper business* **batten:** *fatten yourself*   36 **canopy:** *sky*

41 **daws:** *jackdaws, fools*   46 **trencher:** *wooden platter*   62 **tackle:** *rigging of ship*   72
memory: *reminder*   79 **Whoop'd:** *hooted*   84 **full quit of:** *fully avenged on*   86
heart of wreak: *vengeful heart*   87, 88 **maims . . . shame:** *disgraceful losses of men or
territory*   92 **canker'd:** *malevolent* **spleen:** *anger*

Thou dar'st not this, and that to prove more fortunes
Th' art tir'd, then, in a word, I also am   95
Longer to live most weary, and present
My throat to thee and to thy ancient malice;
Which not to cut would show thee but a fool,
Since I have ever follow'd thee with hate,
Drawn tuns of blood out of thy country's breast,   100
And cannot live but to thy shame, unless
It be to do thee service.
    Auf.   O Martius, Martius!
Each word thou hast spoke hath weeded from my heart
A root of ancient envy. If Jupiter   105
Should from yond cloud speak divine things,
And say, ' 'Tis true,' I'd not believe them more
Than thee, all noble Martius. Let me twine
Mine arms about that body, where against
My grained ash an hundred times hath broke,   110
And scarr'd the moon with splinters: here I clip
The anvil of my sword, and do contest
As hotly and as nobly with thy love
As ever in ambitious strength I did
Contend against thy valour. Know thou first,   115
I lov'd the maid I married; never man
Sigh'd truer breath; but that I see thee here,
Thou noble thing! more dances my rapt heart
Than when I first my wedded mistress saw
Bestride my threshold. Why, thou Mars! I tell thee,   120
We have a power on foot; and I had purpose.
Once more to hew thy target from thy brawn,
Or lose mine arm for 't. Thou hast beat me out
Twelve several times, and I have nightly since
Dreamt of encounters 'twixt thyself and me;   125
We have been down together in my sleep,
Unbuckling helms, fisting each other's throat,
And wak'd half dead with nothing. Worthy Martius,
Had we no quarrel else to Rome, but that
Thou art thence banish'd, we would muster all   130
From twelve to seventy, and, pouring war
In the bowels of ungrateful Rome,
Like a bold flood o'er-bear. O! come; go in,
And take our friendly senators by the hands,
Who now are here, taking their leaves of me,   135
Who am prepar'd against your territories,
Though not for Rome itself.
    Cor.   You bless me, gods!
    Auf. Therefore, most absolute sir, if thou wilt have
The leading of thine own revenges, take   140
Th' one half of my commission, and set down,
As best thou art experienc'd, since thou know'st
Thy country's strength and weakness, thine own ways;
Whether to knock against the gates of Rome,
Or rudely visit them in parts remote,   145
To fright them, ere destroy. But come in:
Let me commend thee first to those that shall
Say yea to thy desires. A thousand welcomes!

And more a friend than e'er an enemy;
Yet, Martius, that was much. Your hand: most welcome!   *Exeunt.*

        Enter two of the Servingmen.

    1. Serv. Here's a strange alteration!
    2. Serv. By my hand, I had thought to have strucken him
with a cudgel; and yet my mind gave me his clothes made a
false report of him.
    1. Serv. What an arm he has! He turned me about   155
with his finger and his thumb, as one would set up a top.
    2. Serv. Nay, I knew by his face that there was something
in him: he had, sir, a kind of face, methought,—I cannot tell
how to term it.
    1. Serv. He had so; looking as it were,—would I were   160
hanged but I thought there was more in him than I could think.
    2. Serv. So did I, I'll be sworn: he is simply the rarest man
i' the world.
    1. Serv. I think he is; but a greater soldier than he you
wot on.   165
    2. Serv. Who? my master?
    1. Serv. Nay, it's no matter for that.
    2. Serv. Worth six on him.
    1. Serv. Nay, not so neither; but I take him to be the
greater soldier.   170
    2. Serv. Faith, look you, one cannot tell how to say that:
for the defence of a town our general is excellent.
    1. Serv. Ay, and for an assault too.

        Enter the Third Servingman.

    3. Serv. O slaves! I can tell you news; news, you rascals.
    Both. What, what, what? let's partake.   175
    3. Serv. I would not be a Roman, of all nations; I had
as lief be a condemned man.
    Both. Wherefore? wherefore?
    3. Serv. Why, here's he that was wont to thwack our
general, Caius Martius.   180
    1. Serv. Why do you say 'thwack our general?'
    3. Serv. I do not say, 'thwack our general'; but he was
always good enough for him.
    2. Serv. Come, we are fellows and friends: he was ever
too hard for him: I have heard him say so himself.   185
    1. Serv. He was too hard for him,—directly to say the
truth on 't: before Corioli he scotched him and notched
him like a carbonado.
    2. Serv. As he had been cannibally given, he might have
boiled and eaten him too.   190
    1. Serv. But, more of thy news.
    3. Serv. Why, he is so made on here within, as if he were
son and heir to Mars; set at upper end o' the table; no question asked him by any of the senators, but they stand bald before him. Our general himself makes a mistress of him;   195
sanctifies himself with 's hand, and turns up the white o' th'
eye to his discourse. But the bottom of the news is, our general is cut i' the middle, and but one half of what he was yesterday, for the other has half, by the entreaty and grant of the

94 prove ... fortunes: *try your fortune further*   **100 tuns:** *huge barrels*   **105 A root ...
envy:** *one of the old sources of my hate*   **109 where against:** *against which*   **110 grained
ash:** *spear-shaft of tough ash*   **111 clip:** *embrace*   **117 Sigh'd ... breath:** *uttered sincere love
sighs*   **118 dances:** *makes leap*   **rapt:** *enraptured*   **122 brawn:** *brawny arm*   **123 out:**
outright   **128 wak'd:** *I have awaked*   **133 o'er-bear:** *bear all before us; cf. n.*   **139 absolute:** *perfect*   **141 set down:** *determine*

S.d. Enter ... Servingmen; *cf. n.*   **153 gave me:** *misgave me, made me suspect*   **156 set
up:** *start spinning*   **164, 165 he ... on:** *the man you know of, i.e. Audifidius; cf. n.*   **175
let's partake:** *let us share it*   **179 thwack:** *beat*   **186 directly:** *candidly*   **187
scotched:** *slashed*   **notched:** *cut*   **carbonado:** *steak prepared for broiling*   **190 boiled;**
cf. n.   **192 made on:** *made much of, pampered*   **196 sanctifies ... hand:** *fondles his
hand as if it were a saint's relic*   **196, 197 turns ... eye:** *gazes upward in reverence*   **bottom:** *fundamental part*

whole table. He'll go, he says, and sowl the porter of Rome   *200*
gates by the ears: he will mow down all before him, and
leave his passage polled.

  2. Serv. And he's as like to do 't as any man I can imagine.

  3. Serv. Do 't! he will do 't; for—look you, sir—he has as
many friends as enemies; which friends, sir—as it were— *205*
durst not—look you, sir—show themselves—as we term
it—his friends, whilst he's in directitude.

  1. Serv. Directitude! what's that?

  3. Serv. But when they shall see, sir, his crest up again,
and the man in blood, they will out of their burrows, *210*
like conies after rain, and revel all with him.

  1. Serv. But when goes this forward?

  3. Serv. To-morrow; to-day; presently. You shall have the
drum strook up this afternoon; 'tis, as it were, a parcel of their
feast, and to be executed ere they wipe their lips. *215*

  2. Serv. Why, then we shall have a stirring world again.
This peace is nothing but to rust iron, increase tailors, and
breed ballad-makers.

  1. Serv. Let me have war, say I; it exceeds peace as far as
day does night; it's spritely, waking, audible, and full of *220*
vent. Peace is a very apoplexy, lethargy; mulled, deaf, sleepy,
insensible; a getter of more bastard children than war's a
destroyer of men.

  2. Serv. 'Tis so: and as war, in some sort, may be said to
be a ravisher, so it cannot be denied but peace is a great *225*
maker of cuckholds.

  1. Serv. Ay, and it makes men hate one another.

  3. Serv. Reason: because they then less need one another.
The wars for my money. I hope to see Romans as cheap as
Volscians. They are rising, they are rising. *230*

  All. In, in, in, in!   *Exeunt.*

❧ SCENE SIXTH ❧

[Rome. A Public Place]
Enter the two Tribunes, Sicinius and Brutus.

  Sic. We hear not of him, neither need we fear him;
His remedies are tame i' the present peace
And quietness o' the people, which before
Were in wild hurry. Here do we make his friends
Blush that the world goes well, who rather had, *5*
Though they themselves did suffer by 't, behold
Dissentious numbers pestering streets, than see
Our tradesmen singing in their shops and going
About their functions friendly.

Enter Menenius.

  Bru. We stood to 't in good time. Is this Menenius? *10*
  Sic. 'Tis he, 'tis he. O! he is grown most kind
Of late. Hail, sir!
  Men.   Hail to you both!

  Sic. Your Coriolanus is not much miss'd
But with his friends: the commonwealth doth stand, *15*
And so would do, were he more angry at it.

  Men. All's well; and might have both much better, if
He could have temporiz'd.

  Sic.   Where is he, hear you?

  Men. Nay, I hear nothing: his mother and his wife *20*
Hear nothing from him.

Enter three or four Citizens.

  All. The gods preserve you both!

  Sic.   Good den, our neighbours.

  Bru. Good den to you all, good den to you all.

  1. Cit. Ourselves, our wives, and children, on our knees, *25*
Are bound to pray for you both.

  Sic.   Live, and thrive!

  Bru. Farewell, kind neighbours: we wish'd Coriolanus
Had lov'd you as we did.

  All.   Now the gods keep you! *30*

  Both Tri. Farewell, farewell.   *Exeunt Citizens.*

  Sic. This is a happier and more comely time
Than when these fellows ran about the streets
Crying confusion.

  Bru.   Caius Martius was *35*
A worthy officer i' the war; but insolent,
O'ercome with pride, ambitious past all thinking,
Self-loving,—

  Sic.   And affecting one sole throne,
Without assistance. *40*

  Men.   I think not so.

  Sic. We should by this, to all our lamentation,
If he had gone forth consul, found it so.

  Bru. The gods have well prevented it, and Rome
Sits safe and still without him. *45*

Enter on Ædile.

  Æd.   Worthy tribunes,
There is a slave, whom we have put in prison,
Reports, the Volsces with two several powers
Are enter'd in the Roman territories,
And with the deepest malice of the war *50*
Destroy what lies before 'em.

  Men.   'Tis Aufidius,
Who, hearing of our Martius' banishment,
Thrusts forth his horns again into the world;
Which were inshell'd when Martius stood for Rome, *55*
And durst not once peep out.

  Sic. Come, what talk you of Martius?

  Bru. Go see this rumourer whipp'd. It cannot be
The Volsces dare break with us.

  Men.   Cannot be! *60*
We have record that very well it can,
And three examples of the like hath been
Within my age. But reason with the fellow,
Before you punish him, where he heard this,
Lest you shall chance to whip your information, *65*

199, 200 by . . . table: *the whole table uniting both in requesting and granting* **200 sowl:** *drag* **202 leave . . . polled:** *leave headless bodies where he passes* **207 directitude:** *error for 'discreditude,' discredit (?)* **210 in blood:** *in fine fettle* **211 conies:** *rabbits* **213 presently:** *at once* **214 parcel:** *part* **217 nothing:** *good for nothing* **220 audible:** *noisy (?), quick of hearing (?)* **vent:** *opportunity for action* **221 mulled:** *insipid, like warmed and sweetened wine* **222 insensible:** *sluggish, insensitive* **228 Reason:** *that is natural* **230 rising:** *getting up from table* **2 remedies:** *means of reinstatement* **tame:** *languid, ineffectual; cf. n.* **4 hurry:** *turbulence* **7 pestering:** *blocking up* **9 friendly:** *like good friends*

15 But with: *except among* **32 comely:** *gracious* **34 Crying confusion:** *shouting for anarchy* **39 affecting . . . throne:** *aiming at individual sovereignty* **42 by this:** *by this time* **to . . . lamentation:** *to the sorrow of us all* **43 gone forth:** *come out, finally become* **found:** *have found* **54 Thrusts . . . horns;** *cf. n.* **55 inshell'd:** *drawn within the shell* **stood for:** *was champion of* **57 what:** *why*

And beat the messenger who bids beware
Of what is to be dreaded.
    Sic.   Tell not me:
I know this cannot be.
    Bru.   Not possible.   *70*

             Enter a Messenger.

    Mess. The nobles in great earnestness are going
All to the senate-house: some news is coming,
That turns their countenances.
    Sic.   'Tis this slave.—
Go whip him 'fore the people's eyes: his raising;   *75*
Nothing but his report.
    Mess.   Yes, worthy sir,
The slave's report is seconded; and more,
More fearful, is deliver'd
    Sic.   What more fearful?   *80*
    Mess. It is spoke freely out of many mouths—
How probable I do not know—that Martius,
Join'd with Aufidius, leads a power 'gainst Rome,
And vows revenge as spacious as between
The young'st and oldest thing.   *85*
    Sic.   This is most likely!
    Bru. Rais'd only, that the weaker sort may wish
Good Martius home again.
    Sic.   The very trick on 't.
    Men. This is unlikely: *90*
He and Aufidius can no more atone
Than violent'st contrariety.

         Enter [another] Messenger.

    Mess. You are sent for to the senate:
A fearful army, led by Caius Martius,
Associated with Aufidius, rages   *95*
Upon our territories; and have already
O'erborne their way, consum'd with fire, and took
What lay before them.

            Enter Cominius.

    Com. O! you have made good work!
    Men.   What news? what news?
    Com. You have holp to ravish your own daughters, and
To melt the city leads upon your pates,
To see your wives dishonour'd to your noses,—
    Men. What's the news? what's the news?
    Com. Your temples burned in their cement, and   *105*
Your franchises, whereon you stood, confin'd
Into an auger's bore.
    Men.   Pray now, your news?—
You have made fair work, I fear me. Pray, your news?
If Martius should be join'd with Volscians,—   *110*
    Com.   If!
He is their god: he leads them like a thing
Made by some other deity than Nature,
That shapes man better; and they follow him,

Against us brats, with no less confidence   *115*
Than boys pursuing summer butterflies,
Or butchers killing flies.
    Men.   You have made good work,
You, and your apron-men; you that stood so much
Upon the voice of occupation and   *120*
The breath of garlic-eaters!
    Com.   He'll shake
Your Rome about your ears.
    Men.   As Hercules
Did shake down mellow fruit. You have made fair work!   *125*
    Bru. But is this true, sir?
    Com.   Ay; and you'll look pale
Before you find it other. All the regions
Do smilingly revolt; and who resist
Are mock'd for valiant ignorance,   *130*
And perish constant fools. Who is 't can blame him?
Your enemies, and his, find something in him.
    Men. We are all undone unless
The noble man have mercy.
    Com.   Who shall ask it?   *135*
The tribunes cannot do 't for shame; the people
Deserve such pity of him as the wolf
Does of the shepherds: for his best friends, if they
Should say, 'Be good to Rome,' they charg'd him even
As those should do that had deserv'd his hate,   *140*
And therein show'd like enemies.
    Men.   'Tis true:
If he were putting to my house the brand
That should consume it, I have not the face
To say, 'Beseech you, cease.'—You have made fair hands,   *145*
You and your crafts! you have crafted fair!
    Com.   You have brought
A trembling upon Rome, such as was never
So incapable of help.
    Tribunes.   Say not we brought it.   *150*
    Men. How! Was 't we? We lov'd him; but, like beasts
And cowardly nobles, gave way unto your clusters,
Who did hoot him out o' the city.
    Com.   But I fear
They'll roar him in again. Tullus Aufidius,   *155*
The second name of mn, obeys his points
As if he were his officer: desperation
Is all the policy, strength, and defence,
That Rome can make against them.

         Enter a troop of Citizens.

    Men.   Here come the clusters.   *160*
And is Aufidius with him? You are they
That made the air unwholesome, when you cast
Your stinking greasy caps in hooting at
Coriolanus' exile. Now he's coming;
And not a hair upon a soldier's head   *165*
Which will not prove a whip: as many coxcombs
As you threw caps up will he tumble down,

---

72 **coming:** *cf. n.*   84, 85 **And vows ... thing;** *cf. n.*   91 **atone:** *grow reconciled*   97 **O'erborne ... way:** *advanced like a wave*   101 **holp:** *helped*   102 **leads:** *leaden roofs*   103 **to:** *before*   105 **temples ... cement:** *cf. n.*   106 **franchises:** *public rights*   **whereon ... stood:** *which you asserted*   **confin'd ... bore:** *reduced to absolute nullity*

115 **brats:** *mere children*   119 **apron-men:** *artisans, dressed in aprons*   120 **voice of occupation:** *workmen's opinion*   128 **other:** *otherwise*   129 **smilingly:** *gladly*   **who resist:** *those who resist*   139 **charg'd:** *would be urging; cf. n.*   141 **show'd:** *would appear*   145 **made fair hands:** *done fine work*   146 **crafted; cf. n. fair:** *with beautiful results*   152 **clusters:** *crowds*   155 **roar ... again:** *yell with pain as he returns*   156 **second ... men:** *the most famous man except Coriolanus*   **points:** *instructions*   157–159 **desperation ... against them;** *cf. n.*   166 **coxcombs:** *fools' heads*

And pay you for your voices. 'Tis no matter;
If he could burn us all into one coal,
We have deserv'd it.   *170*

   Omnes. Faith, we hear fearful news.

   1. Cit.   For mine own part,
When I said banish him, I said 'twas pity.

   2. Cit. And so did I.

   3. Cit. And so did I; and, to say the truth, so did very   *175*
many of us. That we did we did for the best; and though
we willingly consented to his banishment, yet it was against
our will.

   Com. Y' are goodly things, you voices!

   Men.   You have made   *180*
Good work, you and your cry! Shall 's to the Capitol?

   Com. O! ay; what else?   *Exeunt both.*

   Sic. Go, masters, get you home; be not dismay'd:
These are a side that would be glad to have
This true which they so seem to fear. Go home,   *185*
And show no sign of fear.

   1. Cit. The gods be good to us! Come, masters, let's home.
I ever said we were i' the wrong when we banished him.

   2. Cit. So did we all. But come, let's home. *Exeunt Citizens.*

   Bru. I do not like this news.   *190*

   Sic. Nor I.

   Bru. Let's to the Capitol. Would half my wealth
Would buy this for a lie!

   Sic.   Pray let us go.   *Exeunt Tribunes.*

❧ Scene Seventh ❧

[A Camp at a small distance from Rome]
Enter Aufidius with his Lieutenant.

   Auf. Do they still fly to the Roman?

   Lieu. I do not know what witchcraft's in him, but
Your soldiers use him as the grace 'fore meat,
Their talk at table, and their thanks at end;
And you are darken'd in this action, sir,   *5*
Even by your own.

   Auf.   I cannot help it now,
Unless, by using means, I lame the foot
Of our design. He bears himself more proudlier,
Even to my person, than I thought he would   *10*
When first I did embrace him; yet his nature
In that's no changeling, and I must excuse
What cannot be amended.

   Lieu.   Yet, I wish, sir,—
I mean for your particular,—you had not   *15*
Join'd in commission with him; but either
Had borne the action for yourself, or else
To him had left it solely.

   Auf. I understand thee well; and be thou sure,
When he shall come to his account, he knows not   *20*
What I can urge against him. Although it seems,
And so he thinks, and is no less apparent

To the vulgar eye, that he bears all things fairly,
And shows good husbandry for the Volscian state,
Fights dragon-like, and does achieve as soon   *25*
As draw his sword; yet he hath left undone
That which shall break his neck or hazard mine,
Whene'er we come to our account.

   Lieu. Sir, I beseech you, think you he'll carry Rome?

   Auf. All places yields to him ere he sits down;   *30*
And the nobility of Rome are his:
The senators and patricians love him too:
The tribunes are no soldiers; and their people
Will be as rash in the repeal as hasty
To expel him thence. I think he'll be to Rome   *35*
As is the osprey to the fish, who takes it
By sovereignty of nature. First he was
A noble servant to them, but he could not
Carry his honours even; whether 'twas pride,
Which out of daily fortune ever taints   *40*
The happy man; whether defect of judgment,
To fail in the disposing of those chances
Which he was lord of; or whether nature,
Not to be other than one thing, not moving
From the casque to the cushion, but commanding peace   *45*
Even with the same austerity and garb
As he controll'd the war; but one of these,
As he hath spices of them all, not all,
For I dare so far free him, made him fear'd,
So hated, and so banish'd: but he has a merit   *50*
To choke it in the utterance. So our virtues
Lie in th' interpretation of the time;
And power, unto itself most commendable,
Hath not a tomb so evident as a chair
To extol what it hath done.   *55*
One fire drives out one fire; one nail, one nail;
Rights by rights falter, strengths by strengths do fail.
Come, lets away. When, Caius, Rome is thine,
Thou art poor'st of all; then shortly art thou mine.   *Exeunt.*

Act Fifth ❧ Scene First

[Rome. A Public Place]
Enter Menenius, Cominius, Sicinius, Brutus (the two Tribunes),
with Others.

   Men. No, I'll not go: you hear what he hath said
Which was sometime his general; who lov'd him
In a most dear particular. He call'd me father:
But what o' that? Go, you that banish'd him;
A mile before his tent fall down, and knee   *5*
The way into his mercy. Nay, if he coy'd
To hear Cominius speak, I'll keep at home.

   Com. He would not seem to know me.

---

169 **coal:** *hot ember*   181 **cry:** *pack* (of hounds)   **Shall 's:** *shall we*   184 **a side:** *members of a party* (i.e. patricians)   5 **darken'd:** *dimmed in glory*   **action:** *campaign*   6 **your own;** *your own troops*   7 **using means:** *employing treachery*   12 **no changeling:** *i.e. still what it always was*   15 **particular:** *personal advantage*   16 **commission:** *authority*   17 **borne ... yourself:** *taken the whole command yourself*

23 **bears ... fairly:** *behaves honorably in all respects*   25 **achieve:** *conquer*   26–28 **yet ... account;** *cf. n.*   29 **carry:** *take by force*   30 **sits down:** *besieges*   36, 37 **osprey ... nature;** *cf. n.*   39 **even:** *steadily*   40 **out ... fortune:** *as a result of constant good fortune*   **taints:** *sullies*   42 **disposing:** *exploiting*   44 **Not to be:** *not capable of being*   44, 45 **not moving ... cushion;** *cf. n.*   46 **austerity and garb:** *austere manner*   48 **spices ... not all:** *some flavor of all these faults, but not in full degree*   49 **free:** *acquit*   50 **So:** *and therefore* (i.e. because feared)   50, 51 **but ... utterance;** *cf. n.*   52 **Lie in:** *depend upon*   53–55 *Cf. n.*   57 **Rights ... falter;** *cf. n.*   3 **particular:** *personal relation*   5 **knee:** *crawl on your knees*   6 **coy'd:** *held back, showed reluctance*

Men.   Do you hear?

Com. Yet one time he did call me by my name.   *10*
I urg'd our old acquaintance, and the drops
That we have bled together. Coriolanus
He would not answer to; forbad all names;
He was a kind of nothing, titleless,
Till he had forg'd himself a name o' the fire   *15*
Of burning Rome,

Men.   Why, so: you have made good work!
A pair of tribunes that have rack'd for Rome,
To make coals cheap: a noble memory!

Com. I minded him how royal 'twas to pardon   *20*
When it was less expected: he replied,
It was a bare petition of a state
To one whom they had punish'd.

Men.   Very well.
Could he say less?   *25*

Com. I offer'd to awaken his regard
For 's private friends: his answer to me was,
He could not stay to pick them in a pile
Of noisome musty chaff: he said 'twas folly,
For one poor grain or two, to leave unburnt   *30*
And still to nose th' offence.

Men.   For one poor grain or two!
I am one of those; his mother, wife, his child,
And this brave fellow too, we are the grains:
You are the musty chaff, and you are smelt   *35*
Above the moon. We must be burnt for you.

Sic. Nay, pray, be patient: if you refuse your aid
In this so-never-needed help, yet do not
Upbraid 's with our distress. But, sure, if you
Would be your country's pleader, your good tongue,   *40*
More than the instant army we can make,
Might stop our countryman.

Men.   No; I'll not meddle.

Sic. Pray you, go to him.

Men. What should I do?   *45*

Bru. Only make trial what your love can do
For Rome towards Martius.

Men.   Well; and say that Martius
Return me, as Cominius is return'd,
Unheard; what then?   *50*
But as a discontented friend, grief-shot
With his unkindness? say 't be so?

Sic.   Yet your good will
Must have that thanks from Rome, after the measure
As you intended well.   *55*

Men.   I'll undertake 't:
I think he'll hear me. Yet, to bite his lip,
And hum at good Cominius, much unhearts me.
He was not taken well; he had not din'd:
The veins unfill'd, our blood is cold, and then   *60*
We pout upon the morning, are unapt
To give or to forgive; but when we have stuff'd
These pipes and these conveyances of our blood

With wine and feeding, we have suppler souls
Than in our priestlike fasts: therefore, I'll watch him   *65*
Till he be dieted to my request,
And then I'll set upon him.

Bru. You know the very road into his kindness,
And cannot lose your way.

Men.   Good faith, I'll prove him,   *70*
Speed how it will. I shall ere long have knowledge
Of my success.   *Exit.*

Com.   He'll never hear him.

Sic.   Not?

Com. I tell you he does sit in gold, his eye   *75*
Red as 'twould burn Rome, and his injury
The gaoler to his pity. I kneel'd before him;
'Twas very faintly he said 'Rise'; dismiss'd me
Thus, with his speechless hand: what he would do
He sent in writing after me, what he would not,   *80*
Bound with an oath to yield to his conditions:
So that all hope is vain
Unless his noble mother and his wife,
Who, as I hear, mean to solicit him
For mercy to his country. Therefore let's hence,   *85*
And with our fair entreaties haste them on.   *Exeunt.*

❧ Scene Second ❧

[The Volscian Camp before Rome. The Guards at their stations]
Enter Menenius to the Watch or Guard.

1. Wat. Stay! whence are you?

2 Wat.   Stand! and go back.

Men. You guard like men; 'tis well; but, by your leave,
I am an officer of state, and come
To speak with Coriolanus.   *5*

1. Wat.   From whence?

Men.   From Rome.

1. Wat. You may not pass; you must return: our general
Will no more hear from thence.

2. Wat. You'll see your Rome embrac'd with fire before   *10*
You'll speak with Coriolanus.

Men.   Good my friends,
If you have heard your general talk of Rome,
And of his friends there, it is lots to blanks
My name hath touch'd your ears: it is Menenius.   *15*

1. Wat. Be it so; go back: the virtue of your name
Is not here passable.

Men.   I tell thee, fellow,
Thy general is my lover: I have been
The book of his good acts, whence men have read   *20*
His fame unparallel'd, haply amplified;
For I have ever verified my friends—
Of whom he's chief—with all the size that verity
Would without lapsing suffer: nay, sometimes,
Like to a bowl upon a subtle ground,   *25*
I have tumbled past the throw, and in his praise

---

13 forbad: *prohibited the use of*   **15 o':** *out of*   **18 rack'd:** *strained themselves, worked desperately; cf. n.*   **19 coals:** *cinders, charcoal*   **20 minded:** *reminded*   **22 bare:** *threadbare, poor*   **26 offer'd:** *presumed*   **31 nose:** *smell*   **offence:** *nuisance, offensive matter*   **41 instant:** *capable of being raised at once*   **47 towards:** *in relation to*   **51 grief-shot:** *pierced with grief*   **54, 55 after . . . well:** *proportionate to the goodness of your intention*   **58 unhearts:** *dispirits*   **59 taken well:** *propitiously encountered*

66 dieted to: *fed up auspiciously for*   **71 Speed:** *turn out*   **72 Of . . . success:** *how I shall fare*   **75 in gold:** *on golden throne*   **78 faintly:** *coldly*   **79, 80 what . . . conditions; cf. n.*   **83 Unless:** *unless in the efforts of*   **14 lots of blanks; cf. n.**   **17 passable:** *valid*   **20 book:** *record, that which reports*   **22 verified my friends:** *shown my friends to be my friends; cf. n.*   **23 size:** *exaggeration*   **24 lapsing:** *slipping into falsehood*   **25 subtle:** *temptingly level*   **26 throw:** *distance aimed at*

Have almost stamp'd the leasing. Therefore, fellow,
I must have leave to pass.

   1. Wat. Faith, sir, if you have told as many lies in his
behalf as you have uttered words in your own, you should   *30*
not pass here; no, though it were as virtuous to lie as to
live chastely. Therefore go back.

   Men. Prithee, fellow, remember my name is Menenius,
always factionary on the party of your general.

   2. Wat. Howsoever you have been his liar—as you say   *35*
you have—I am one that, telling true under him, must say
you cannot pass. Therefore go back.

   Men. Has he dined, canst thou tell? for I would not speak
with him till after dinner.

   1. Wat. You are a Roman, are you?   *40*

   Men. I am as thy general is.

   1. Wat. Then you should hate Rome, as he does. Can you,
when you have pushed out your gates the very defender of
them, and, in a violent popular ignorance, given your enemy
your shield, think to front his revenges with the easy groans   *45*
of old women, the virginal palms of your daughters, or with
the palsied intercession of such a decayed dotant as you seem
to be? Can you think to blow out the intended fire your city
is ready to flame in with such weak breath as this? No, you
are deceived; therefore, back to Rome, and prepare for   *50*
your execution: you are condemned, our general has sworn
you out of reprieve and pardon.

   Men. Sirrah, if thy captain knew I were here, he would
use me with estimation.

   1. Wat. Come, my captain knows you not.   *55*

   Men. I mean, thy general.

   1. Wat. My general cares not for you. Back, I say: go, lest
I let forth your half-pint of blood; back, that's the utmost
of your having: back!

   Men. Nay, but, fellow, fellow,—   *60*

                  Enter Coriolanus with Aufidius.

   Cor. What's the matter?

   Men. Now, you companion, I'll say an errand for you: you
shall know how that I am in estimation; you shall perceive that
a Jack guardant cannot office me from my son Coriolanus: guess,
but by my entertainment with him, if thou standest not   *65*
i' the state of hanging, or of some death more long in specta-
torship, and crueller in suffering; behold now presently, and
swound for what's to come upon thee. *[To Coriolanus.]* The
glorious gods sit in hourly synod about thy particular prosperity, and love thee no worse than thy old father Menenius   *70*
does! O my son! my son! thou art preparing fire for us; look
thee, here's water to quench it. I was hardly moved to come to
thee; but being assured none but myself could move thee, I
have been blown out of your gates with sighs; and conjure thee
to pardon Rome, and thy petitionary countrymen. The   *75*
good gods assuage thy wrath, and turn the dregs of it upon this
varlet here; this, who, like a block, hath denied my access to thee.

   Cor. Away!

   Men. How! away!

   Cor. Wife, mother, child, I know not. My affairs   *80*
Are servanted to others: though I owe
My revenge properly, my remission lies
In Volscian breasts. That we have been familiar,
Ingrate forgetfulness shall poison, rather
Than pity note how much. Therefore, begone: *85*
Mine ears against your suits are stronger than
Your gates against my force. Yet, for I lov'd thee,
Take this along; I writ it for thy sake,   *[Gives a paper.]*
And would have sent it. Another word, Menenius,
I will not hear thee speak. This man, Aufidius,   *90*
Was my belov'd in Rome: yet thou behold'st!

   Auf. You keep a constant temper.

             Exeunt [Coriolanus and Aufidius].
             Mane[n]t the Guard and Menenius.

   1. Wat. Now, sir, is your name Menenius?

   2. Wat. 'Tis a spell, you see, of much power.
You know the way home again.   *95*

   1. Wat. Do you hear how we are shent for keeping your
greatness back?

   2. Wat. What cause, do you think, I have to swound?

   Men. I neither care for the world, nor your general: for such
things as you, I can scarce think there's any, y' are so slight.
He that hath a will to die by himself fears it not from another.
Let your general do his worst. For you, be that you are long;
and your misery increase with your age! I say to you, as I was
said to, Away!   *Exit.*

   1. Wat. A noble fellow, I warrant him.   *105*

   2. Wat. The worthy fellow is our general: he's the rock, the
oak, not to be wind-shaken.   *Exit Watch.*

❧ SCENE THIRD ❧

[The Tent of Coriolanus]
Enter Coriolanus and Aufidius.

   Cor. We will before the walls of Rome to-morrow
Set down our host. My partner in this action,
You must report to the Volscian lords, how plainly
I have borne this business.

   Auf.   Only their ends   *5*
You have respected; stopp'd your ears against
The general suit of Rome; never admitted
A private whisper; no, not with such friends
That thought them sure of you.

   Cor.   This last old man,   *10*
Whom with a crack'd heart I have sent to Rome,
Lov'd me above the measure of a father;
Nay, godded me indeed. Their latest refuge
Was to send him; for whose old love I have,
Though I show'd sourly to him, once more offer'd   *15*
The first conditions, which they did refuse,
And cannot now accept, to grace him only
That thought he could do more. A very little

I have yielded to; fresh embassies and suits,
Nor from the state, nor private friends, hereafter   20
Will I lend ear to. Ha! what shout is this?   *Shout within.*
Shall I be tempted to infringe my vow.
In the same time 'tis made? I will not.

Enter Virgilia, Volumnia, Valeria, young Martius,
with Attendants.

My wife comes foremost; then the honour'd mould
Wherein this trunk was fram'd, and in her hand   25
The grandchild to her blood. But out, affection!
All bond and privilege of nature, break!
Let it be virtuous to be obstinate.
What is that curtsy worth? or those doves' eyes,
Which can make gods forsworn? I melt, and am not   30
Of stronger earth than others. My mother bows,
As if Olympus to a molehill should
In supplication nod; and my young boy
Hath an aspect of intercession, which
Great nature cries, 'Deny not.' Let the Volsces   35
Plough Rome, and harrow Italy; I'll never
Be such a gosling to obey instinct, but stand
As if a man were author of himself
And knew no other kin.
   Vir.   My lord and husband!   40
   Cor. These eyes are not the same I wore in Rome.
   Vir. The sorrow that delivers us thus chang'd
Makes you think so.
   Cor.   Like a dull actor now,
I have forgot my part, and I am out,   45
Even to a full disgrace. Best of my flesh,
Forgive my tyranny; but do not say
For that, 'Forgive our Romans.' O! a kiss
Long as my exile, sweet as my revenge!
Now, by the jealous queen of heaven, that kiss   50
I carried from thee, dear, and my true lip
Hath virgin'd it e'er since. You gods! I prate,
And the most noble mother of the world
Leave unsaluted. Sink, my knee, i' the earth;   *Kneels.*
Of thy deep duty more impression show   55
Than that of common sons.
   Vol.   O! stand up bless'd;
Whilst, with no softer cushion than the flint,
I kneel before thee, and unproperly
Show duty, as mistaken all this while   60
Between the child and parent.   *[Kneels.]*
   Cor.   What's this?
Your knees to me! to your corrected son!
Then let the pebbles on the hungry beach
Fillip the stars; then let the mutinous winds   65
Strike the proud cedars 'gainst the fiery sun,
Murd'ring impossibility, to make
What cannot be, slight work.
   Vol.   Thou art my warrior;

I holp to frame thee. Do you know this lady?   70
   Cor. The noble sister of Publicola,
The moon of Rome; chaste as the icicle
That's curdied by the frost from purest snow,
And hangs on Dian's temple: dear Valeria!
   Vol. This is a poor epitome of yours,   75
                     [Pointing to the Child.]
Which by th' interpretation of full time
May show like all yourself.
   Cor.   The god of soldiers,
With the consent of supreme Jove, inform
Thy thoughts with nobleness; that thou mayst prove   80
To shame unvulnerable and stick i' the wars
Like a great sea-mark, standing every flaw,
And saving those that eye thee!
   Vol.   Your knee, sirrah.
   Cor. That's my brave boy!   85
   Vol. Even he, your wife, this lady, and myself
Are suitors to you.
   Cor.   I beseech you, peace:
Or, if you'd ask, remember this before:
The things I have forsworn to grant may never   90
Be held by you denials. Do not bid me
Dismiss my soldiers, or capitulate
Again with Rome's mechanics: tell me not
Wherein I seem unnatural: desire not
To allay my rages and revenges with   95
Your colder reasons.
   Vol.   O! no more, more;
You have said you will not grant us anything;
For we have nothing else to ask but that
Which you deny already: yet we will ask;   100
That, if you fail in our request, the blame
May hang upon your hardness. Therefore, hear us.
   Cor. Aufidius, and you Volsces, mark; for we'll
Hear nought from Rome in private. Your request?
   Vol. Should we be silent and not speak, our raiment   105
And state of bodies would bewray what life
We have led since they exile. Think with thyself
How more unfortunate than all living women
Are we come hither: since that thy sight, which should
Make our eyes flow with joy, hearts dance with comforts,   110
Constrains them weep and shake with fear and sorrow;
Making the mother, wife, and child to see
The son, the husband, and the father tearing
His country's bowels out. And to poor we
Thine enmity's most capital: thou barr'st us   115
Our prayers to the gods, which is a comfort
That all but we enjoy; for how can we,
Alas! how can we for our country pray,
Whereto we are bound, together with thy victory,
Whereto we are bound? Alack! or we must lose   120
The country, our dear nurse, or else thy person,
Our comfort in the country. We must find
An evident calamity, though we had
Our wish, which side should win; for either thou

20 Nor ... friends: *neither from the state nor from private friends*   **24 in ... hand:** *led by the hand*   **37 gosling:** *young goose*   **41 These ... same:** *i.e. I look upon you with different feelings*   **42 thus chang'd:** *in mourning garb; cf. n.*   **45 out:** *at loss for the proper words*   **55 duty:** *dutifulness, respect*   **more ... show;** *cf. n.*   **59 unproperly:** *abnormally*   **60 as mistaken:** *as if the obligation of deference had been misunderstood*   **63 corrected:** *yielding to correction, submissive*   **64 hungry:** *sterile (?), voracious (?)*   **65 Fillip:** *hit against*   **67 Murd'ring:** *annulling*   **68 slight work:** *a trivial task*

73 curdied: *congealed*   **74 dear Valeria;** *cf. n.*   **76 by ... time:** *when full growth has shown what he is*   **79 inform:** *inspire*   **81 stick:** *stand conspicuous*   **82 sea-mark:** *beacon*   **flaw:** *squals of wind*   **83 eye:** *take as guide*   **92 capitulate:** *make terms*   **101 fail in:** *disappoint us in*   **106 state of bodies:** *physical health*   **bewray:** *disclose*   **114 we:** *us*   **115 capital:** *fatal*   **120 or:** *either*   **124 which:** *in determining which.*

Must, as a foreign recreant, be led   125
With manacles through our streets, or else
Triumphantly tread on thy country's ruin,
And bear the palm for having bravely shed
Thy wife and children's blood. For myself, son,
I purpose not to wait on Fortune till   130
These wars determine: if I cannot persuade thee
Rather to show a noble grace to both parts
Than seek the end of one, thou shalt no sooner
March to assault thy country than to tread—
Trust to 't, thou shalt not—on thy mother's womb,   135
That brought thee to this world.
    Vir.   Ay, and mine,
That brought you forth this boy, to keep your name
Living to time.
    Boy.   A' shall not tread on me: 140
I'll run away till I am bigger, but then I'll fight.
    Cor. Not of a woman's tenderness to be,
Requires nor child nor woman's face to see.
I have sat too long.   *[Rising.]*
    Vol.   Nay, go not from us thus.   145
If it were so, that our request did tend
To save the Romans, thereby to destroy
The Volsces whom you serve, you might condemn us,
As poisonous to your honour: no; our suit
Is, that you reconcile them: while the Volsces   150
May say, 'This mercy we have show'd; the Romans,
'This we receiv'd'; and each in either side
Give the all-hail to thee, and cry, 'Be bless'd
For making up this peace!' Thou know'st, great son,
The end of war's uncertain; but this certain,   155
That, if thou conquer Rome, the benefit
Which thou shalt thereby reap is such a name
Whose repetition will be dogg'd with curses;
Whose chronicle thus writ: 'The man was noble,
But with his last attempt he wip'd it out,   160
Destroy'd his country, and his name remains
To th' ensuing age abhorr'd.' Speak to me, son!
Thou hast affected the fine strains of honour,
To imitate the graces of the gods;
To tear with thunder the wide cheeks o' the air,   165
And yet to charge thy sulphur with a bolt
That should but rive an oak. Why dost not speak?
Think'st thou it honourable for a nobleman
Still to remember wrongs? Daughter, speak you:
He cares not for your weeping. Speak thou, boy: 170
Perhaps thy childishness will move him more
Than can our reasons. There is no man in the world
More bound to 's mother; yet here he lets me prate
Like one i' the stocks. Thou hast never in thy life
Show'd thy dear mother any courtesy;   175
When she—poor hen! fond of no second brood—
Has cluck'd thee to the wars, and safely home,
Loaden with honour. Say my request's unjust,
And spurn me back; but if it be not so,

Thou art not honest, and the gods will plague thee,   180
That thou restrain'st from me the duty which
To a mother's part belongs. He turns away:
Down, ladies; let us shame him with our knees.
To his surname Coriolanus longs more pride
Than pity to our prayers. Down: an end;   185
This is the last: so we will home to Rome,
And die among our neighbours. Nay, behold's.
This boy, that cannot tell what he would have,
But kneels and holds up hands for fellowship,
Does reason our petition with more strength   190
Than thou hast to deny 't. Come, let us go:
This fellow had a Volscian to his mother;
His wife is in Corioli, and his child
Like him by chance. Yet give us our dispatch:
I am hush'd until our city be a-fire,   195
And then I'll speak a little.
    Cor.   O, mother, mother!
                    Holds her by the hand silent.
What have you done? Behold! the heavens do ope,
The gods look down, and this unnatural scene
They laugh at. O my mother! mother! O!   200
You have won a happy victory to Rome;
But, for your son, believe it, O believe it,
Most dangerously you have with him prevail'd,
If not most mortal to him. But let it come.
Aufidius, though I cannot make true wars,   205
I'll frame convenient peace. Now, good Aufidius,
Were you in my stead, would you have heard
A mother less, or granted less, Aufidius?
    Auf. I was mov'd withal.
    Cor.   I dare be sworn you were: 210
And, sir, it is no little thing to make
Mine eyes to sweat compassion. But, good sir,
What peace you'll make, advise me: for my part,
I'll not to Rome, I'll back with you: and pray you,
Stand to me in this cause. O mother! wife!   215
    Auf. [Aside.] I am glad thou hast set thy mercy and thy honour
At difference in thee: out of that I'll work
myself a former fortune.
               [The ladies make signs to Coriolanus.]
    Cor.   Ay, by and by;   220
But we will drink together; and you shall bear
A better witness back than words, which we,
On like conditions, would have counterseal'd.
Come, enter with us. Ladies, you deserve
To have a temple built you: all the swords   225
In Italy, and her confederate arms,
Could not have made this peace.   *Exeunt.*

---

125 **foreign recreant:** *one whose treachery has made him a foreigner*   131 **determine:** *end*   133 **end:** *destruction*   142 **Not ... be:** *not to yield to womanly weakness*   153 **all-hail:** *formal acclamation*   160 **attempt:** *undertaking it: his nobility*   163 **fine strains:** *special refinements*   165 **cheeks ... air;** *cf. n.*   166, 167 **And yet ... oak;** *cf. n.*   173 **prate:** *talk without result*   174 **one ... stocks:** *a prisoner who has nothing free but his voice*   175 **courtesy:** *particular favor*

180 **honest:** *honourable*   184 **longs:** *belongs*   189 **for fellowship:** *to keep us company*   190 **Does ... strength:** *has stronger arguments in favor of our petition*   195 **hush'd:** *silent*   204 **most mortal:** *with most mortal results*   206 **convenient:** *a fitting*   209 **withal:** *therewith*   212 **sweat compassion:** *weep with pity*   215 **Stand to:** *support*   219 **a ... fortune:** *a position as great as formerly*   222 **A better witness:** *i.e. a formal document*   223 *If conditions had been reversed, should have been glad to confirm strongly*   226 **her ... arms:** *the weapons of Italy's allies*

❧ SCENE FOURTH ❧

[Rome. A Public Place]
Enter Menenius and Sicinius.

Men. See you yond coign o' the Capitol, yond corner-stone?
Sic. Why, what of that?
Men. If it be possible for you to displace it with your little
finger, there is some hope the ladies of Rome, especially his
mother, may prevail with him. But I say, there is no hope　5
in 't. Our throats are sentenced and stay upon execution.
Sic. Is 't possible that so short a time can alter the condition of a man?
Men. There is differency between a grub and a butterfly; yet
your butterfly was a grub. This Martius is grown from man　10
to dragon: he has wings; he's more than a creeping thing.
Sic. He loved his mother dearly.
Men. So did he me; and he no more remembers his mother
now than an eight-year-old horse. The tartness of his face sours
ripe grapes: when he walks, he moves like an engine, and　15
the ground shrinks before his treading: he is able to pierce a
corslet with his eye; talks like a knell, and his 'hum!' is a battery. he sits in his state, as a thing made for Alexander. What
he bids be done is finished with his bidding. He wants nothing
of a god but eternity and a heaven to throne in.　20
Sic. Yes, mercy, if you report him truly.
Men. I paint him in the character. Mark what mercy his
mother shall bring from him: there is no more mercy in him
than there is milk in a male tiger; that shall our poor city
find: and all this is long of you.　25
Sic. The gods be good unto us!
Men. No, in such a case the gods will not be good unto
us. When we banished him, we respected not them; and, he
returning to break our necks, they respect not us.

Enter a Messenger.

Mess. Sir, if you'd save your life, fly to your house:　30
The plebeians have got your fellow-tribune,
And hale him up and down; all swearing, if
The Roman ladies bring not comfort home,
They'll give him death by inches.

Enter another Messenger.

Sic.　　　　　　　　　　What's the news?　35
Mess. Good news, good news! the ladies have prevail'd,
The Volscians are dislodg'd, and Martius gone.
A merrier day did never yet greet Rome,
No, not th' expulsion of the Tarquins.
Sic.　　　　　　　　　　Friend,　40
Art thou certain this is true? Is 't most certain?
Mess. As certain as I know the sun is fire:
Where have you lurk'd that you make doubt of it?
Ne'er through an arch so hurried the blown tide,
As the recomforted through the gates. Why, hark you!　45
　　　　Trumpets, hautboys, drums beat, all together.
The trumpets, sackbuts, psalteries, and fifes,

Tabors, and cymbals, and the shouting Romans,
Make the sun dance. Hark you!　　　　*A shout within.*
Men.　　　　　　　This is good news:
I will go meet the ladies. This Volumnia　50
Is worth of consuls, senators, patricians,
A city full; of tribunes, such as you,
A sea and land full. You have pray'd well to-day:
This morning for ten thousand of your throats
I'd not have given a doit. Hark, how they joy!　55
　　　　　　Sound still with the shouts.
Sic. First, the gods bless you for your tidings; next,
Accept my thankfulness.
Mess.　　　　　　Sir, we have all
Great cause to give great thanks.
Sic.　　　　　　　They are near the city?　60
Mess. Almost at point to enter.
Sic.　　　　　　　We'll meet them,
And help the joy.　　　　　　　　*Exeunt.*

Enter two Senators, with Ladies, passing over the Stage, with
other Lords.

Sen. Behold our patroness, the life of Rome!
Call all your tribes together, praise the gods,　65
And make triumphant fires; strew flowers before them:
Unshout the noise that banish'd Martius;
Repeal him with the welcome of his mother;
Cry, 'Welcome, ladies, welcome!'
All.　　　　　　　Welcome, ladies,　70
Welcome!　　　　*A flourish with drums and trumpets.*
　　　　　　　　　　　　　　[Exeunt.]

❧ SCENE FIFTH ❧

[Corioli. A Public Place]
Enter Tullus Aufidius, with Attendants

Auf. Go tell the lords o' the city I am here:
Deliver them this paper: having read it,
Bid them repair to the market-place; where I,
Even in theirs and in the commons' ears,
Will vouch the truth of it. Him I accuse　5
The city ports by this hath enter'd, and
Intends to appear before the people, hoping
To purge himself with words: dispatch.

　　　　　　　　　　[Exeunt Attendants.]

Enter three or four Conspirators of Aufidius' faction.

Most welcome!
1. Con. How is it with our general?　10
Auf.　　　　　　　Even so
As with a man by his own alms empoison'd,
And with his charity slain.
2. Con.　　　　　　Most noble sir,
If you do hold the same intent wherein　15
You wish'd us parties, we'll deliver you
Of your great danger.
Auf.　　　　　Sir, I cannot tell:

---

1 **coign:** *keystone*　6 **stay upon:** *await*　9 **differency:** *difference*　15 **engine:** *piece of
artillery*　16 **corslet:** *breastplate*　17 **talks . . . battery;** *cf. n.*　18 **state:** *chair of state*　**as . . . Alexander:** *like a statue of Alexander the Great*　19 **finished . . . bidding:** *as
good as done when he commands it*　20 **throne:** *enthrone himself*　22 **in . . . character:**
as he is　25 **long of:** *on account of*　28 **respected:** *heeded*　34 **by inches:** *by slow
torture*　37 **are dislodg'd:** *have broken camp*　44 **blown:** *swollen; cf. n.*　46 **sackbuts:**
bass wind instrument, trombones　**psalteries:** *stringed instruments, dulcimers*

47 **Make . . . dance;** *cf. n.* S.d. *Cf. n.*　66 **fires:** *bonfires*　67 **Unshout:** *cancel and
retract by your shouts*　**Scene Five Corioli;** *cf. n.*　6 **city ports:** *gates of the city*　8
purge: *clear*　16 **parties:** *to take part*

We must proceed as we do find the people.

3. Con. The people will remain uncertain whilst   20
'Twixt you there's difference; but the fall of either
Makes the survivor heir of all.

Auf.   I know it;
And my pretext to strike at him admits
A good construction. I rais'd him, and I pawn'd   25
Mine honour for his truth: who being so heighten'd,
He water'd his new plants with dews of flattery,
Seducing so my friends; and, to this end,
He bow'd his nature, never known before
But to be rough, unswayable, and free.   30

3. Con. Sir, his stoutness
When he did stand for consul, which he lost
By lack of stooping,—

Auf.   That I would have spoke of:
Being banish'd for 't, he came unto my hearth;   35
Presented to my knife his throat: I took him;
Made him joint-servant with me; give him way
In all his own desires; nay, let him choose
Out of my files, his projects to accomplish,
My best and freshest men; serv'd his designments   40
In mine own person; holp to reap the fame
Which he did end all his; and took some pride
To do myself this wrong: till, at the last,
I seem'd his follower, not partner; and
He wag'd me with his countenance, as if   45
I had been mercenary.

1. Con.   So he did, my lord:
The army marvell'd at it; and, in the last,
When we had carried Rome, and that we look'd
For no less spoil than glory,—   50

Auf.   There was it;
For which my sinews shall be stretch'd upon him.
At a few drops of women's rheum, which are
As cheap as lies, he sold the blood and labour
Of our great action: therefore shall he die,   55
And I'll renew me in his fall. But, hark!

Drums and trumpets sound, with great shouts of the people.

1. Con. Your native town you enter'd like a post,
And had no welcomes home; but he returns,
Splitting the air with noise.

2. Con.   And patient fools,   60
Whose children he hath slain, their base throats tear
With giving him glory.

3. Con.   Therefore, at your vantage,
Ere he express himself, or move the people
With what he would say, let him feel your sword,   65
Which we will second. When he lies along,
After your way his tale pronounc'd shall bury
His reasons with his body.

Auf.   Say no more:

Here come the lords.   70

Enter the Lords of the City.

All Lords. You are most welcome home.

Auf.   I have not deserv'd it.
But, worthy lords, have you with heed perus'd
What I have written to you?

All.   We have.   75

1. Lord.   And grieve to hear 't.
What faults he made before the last, I think,
Might have found easy fines; but there to end
Where he was to begin, and give away
The benefit of our levies, answering us   80
With our own charge, making a treaty where
There was a yielding, this admits no excuse.

Auf. He approaches: you shall hear him.

*Enter Coriolanus, marching with drums and colours; the
Commoners being with him.*

Cor. Hail, lords! I am return'd your soldier;
No more infected with my country's love   85
Than when I parted hence, but still subsisting
Under your great command. You are to know,
That prosperously I have attempted and
With bloody passage led your wars even to
The gates of Rome. Our spoils we have brought home   90
Do more than counterpoise a full third part
The charges of the action. We have made peace
With no less honour to the Antiates
Than shame to the Romans; and we here deliver,
Subscrib'd by the consuls and patricians,   95
Together with the seal o' the senate, what
We have compounded on.

Auf.   Read it not, noble lords;
But tell the traitor, in the highest degree
He hath abus'd your powers.   100

Cor. Traitor! How now?

Auf.   Ay, traitor, Martius.

Cor.   Martius!

Auf. Ay, Martius, Caius Martius. Dost thou think
I'll grace thee with that robbery, thy stol'n name,   105
Coriolanus in Corioli?
You lords and heads o' the state, perfidiously
He has betray'd your business, and given up,
For certain drops of salt, your city Rome,
I say 'your city,' to his wife and mother;   110
Breaking his oath and resolution like
A twist of rotten silk, never admitting
Counsel o' the war, but at his nurse's tears
He whin'd and roar'd away your victory,
That pages blush'd at him, and men of heart   115
Look'd wondering each at others.

Cor.   Hear'st thou, Mars?

Auf. Name not the god, thou boy of tears.

Cor.   Ha!

21 **difference:** *dispute*   24 **pretext:** *design*   25 **good construction:** *justification*   27
By flattery he increased his power in his new environment   30 **free:** *independent*   37 **way:**
freedom of action   39 **files:** *troops*   40, 41 **serv'd . . . person:** *personally assisted him in
his designs*   42 **end:** *garner, store away*   45 **wag'd:** *rewarded*   **countenance:** *patronizing
favor*   48 **in the last:** *finally*   52 **my sinews . . . stretch'd:** *I shall exert all my
force*   53 **rheum:** *tears, liquid secretion*   57 **post:** *messenger*   63 **at . . . vantage:** *as
soon as favorable opportunity arises*   66 **along:** *prostrate*   67 **After . . . pronounc'd:** *your
statement of his case*   68 **His reasons:** *what he might urge in his behalf*

78 **fines:** *penalties*   80 **benefit . . . levies:** *profits of war*   **answering:** *repaying; cf. n.*   81
treaty: *compromise*   82 **yielding:** *complete defeat of the enemy*   85 **infected:** *affected,
contaminated*   88 **prosperously . . . attempted:** *my attempts have prospered*   92 **we
have:** *which we have*   97 **compounded:** *agreed*   112 **twist:** *skein*   112, 113 **never . . .
war:** *permitting no council of war*   115 **That pages:** *so that young boys*   **men of heart:**
valiant men

Auf. No more.   *120*

Cor. Measureless liar, thou hast made my heart
Too great for what contains it. Boy! O slave!
Pardon me, lords, 'tis the first time that ever
I was forc'd to scold. Your judgments, my grave lords,
Must give this cur the lie: and his own notion—   *125*
Who wears my stripes impress'd upon him, that
Must bear my beating to his grave—shall join
To thrust the lie unto him.

1. Lord. Peace, both, and hear me speak.

Cor. Cut me to pieces, Volsces; men and lads,   *130*
Stain all your edges on me. Boy! False hound!
If you have writ your annals true, 'tis there,
That, like an eagle in a dove-cote, I
Flutter'd your Volscians in Corioli:
Alone I did it. Boy!   *135*

Auf.   Why, noble lords,
Will you be put in mind of his blind fortune,
Which was your shame, by this unholy braggart,
'Fore your own eyes and ears?

All Consp.   Let him die for 't.   *140*

All People. Tear him to pieces.—Do it presently.—He killed
my son.—My daughter.—He killed my cousin Marcus.—
He killed my father.

2. Lord. Peace, ho! no outrage: peace!
The man is noble and his fame folds in   *145*
This orb o' the earth. His last offences to us
Shall have judicious hearing. Stand, Aufidius,
And trouble not the peace.

Cor.   O that I had him,
With six Aufidiuses, or more, his tribe,   *150*
To use my lawful sword!

Auf.   Insolent villain!

All. Consp. Kill, kill, kill, kill, kill him!

Draw all the Conspirators, and kill Martius, who falls. Aufidius
stands on him.

Lords.   Hold, hold, hold, hold!

Auf. My noble masters, hear me speak.   *155*

1. Lord.   O Tullus!

2. Lord. Thou hast done a deed whereat valour will weep.

3. Lord. Tread not upon him, masters; all be quiet.
Put up your swords.

Auf. My lords, when you shall know,—as in this rage,   *160*
Provok'd by him, you cannot,—the great danger
Which this man's life did owe you, you'll rejoice
That he is thus cut off. Please it your honours
To call me to your senate, I'll deliver
Myself your loyal servant, or endure   *165*
Your heaviest censure.

1. Lord.   Bear from hence his body;
And mourn you for him! Let him be regarded
As the most noble corse that ever herald
Did follow to his urn.   *170*

2. Lord.   His own impatience
Takes from Aufidius a great part of blame.
Let's make the best of it.

Auf.   My rage is gone,
And I am struck with sorrow. Take him up: *175*
Help, three o' the chiefest soldiers; I'll be one.
Beat thou the drum, that it speak mournfully;
Trail your steel pikes. Though in this city he
Hath widow'd and unchilded many a one,
Which to this hour bewail the injury,   *180*
Yet he shall have a noble memory.

Assist.   *Exeunt, bearing the body of Martius.*
                                   A dead march sounded.

❧ FINIS ❧

---

122 Too ... it: *swollen with indignation till my breast cannot contain it*   **125 notion:**
intelligence   **126 that:** *who*   **134 Flutter'd:** *put to fight*   **147 judicious:** *judicial, le-*
gal   **Stand:** *stay, hold*

162 did owe you: *promised to bring upon you, rendered you liable to*   **164 deliver:** *demon-*
strate   **178 Trail:** *drag on the ground in sign of mourning*   **179 unchilded:** *slain the*
children of

NOTES

I.i.27. *2. Cit.* The Folio gives this line to '*All.*' The later speeches of the Second Citizen, beginning with that at line 46, are transferred by Capell and other editors to the First Citizen on the ground that the Second Citizen has shown himself friendly to Martius. He is, however, a convinced supporter of the people's rights.

I.i.79. *To scale 't a little more.* 'Scale' is probably used in the sense of put it on the scales, weigh its meaning. Compare 'Scaling' in II.iii.257. Theobald has been followed by most editors in emending to 'stale.'

I.i.94. *Which ne'er came from the lungs.* A quiet reflective smile with nothing boisterous about it.

I.i.96. *taintingly.* Modern editors agree in emending to 'tauntingly,' but the belly is not taunting. To taint means to make a successful hit in tilting.

I.i.103. *The counsellor heart.* The heart was supposed to be the seat of reason. Compare line 128.

I.i.152. *Thou rascal, that art worst in blood to run.* You who are in the worst physical condition for running (or other activity). A rascal was a lean, inferior deer, whereas stags were said to be 'in blood' when in good condition. Compare IV.v. 226.

I.i.159, 160. *That, rubbing the poor itch of your opinion, Make yourselves scabs.* There is a pun on 'scabs': (a) scabby sores, (b) good-for-nothing citizens.

I.i.167, 168. *you are no surer, no. Than is the coal of fire upon the ice.* The Thames River was frozen over in the winter of 1608 (a rare phenomenon), and fires were built upon the ice. This figure has therefore been used in dating the play.

I.i.169-171. *Your virtue is, To make him worthy whose offence subdues him, And curse that justice did it.* Your kindness shows itself only in espousing the cause of the punished delinquent and in cursing the justice which made him suffer.

I.i.273, 274. *disdains the shadow Which he treads on at noon.* 'The sun being vertical at noon, a man treads on his own shadow then.' (Arden ed.)

I.ii.31. *Corioli.* The name had been gallicized by Amyot into 'Corioles.' It is retained in this form by North and usually in the Shakespeare Folio. (In the stage direction at the opening of this scene the Folio spells it 'Coriolus.')

I.iii.13. *his brows bound with oak.* Crowned with a wreath of oak leaves. Plutarch (North) records that in an early battle the young Martius saved the life of a Roman soldier. 'Hereupon, after the battle was won, the Dictator did not forget so noble an act, and therefore first of all he crowned Martius with a garland of oaken boughs. For whosoever saveth the life of a Roman, it is a manner among them to honour him with such a garland.'

I.iv.18. *No, nor a man that fears you less than he.* Logical syntax requires 'more' instead of 'less.' Shakespeare frequently makes slips of this sort.

I.iv.40. *Against the wind a mile.* Let the infection be so great as to carry a mile against the wind.

I.iv.48. *As they us to our trenches follows.* As they are now following us to our trenches. Instances of the old northern English plural in –s abound in Shakespeare.

I.iv.66, 67. *Thou wast a soldier Even to Cato's wish.* This passage is a close adaptation of North's words: 'For he was even such another as Cato would have a soldier and a captain to be, not only terrible and fierce to lay about him, but to make the enemy afeared with the sound of his voice and grimness of his countenance.' Shakespeare's transfer of the speech to the mouth of a contemporary of Coriolanus produces a striking anachronism, since Martius lived some three hundred years before Cato the Censor (234-149 B.C.).

I.v.6, 7. *doublets that hangmen would Bury with those that wore them.* An allusion to the Elizabethan custom which made the garments of executed prisoners a perquisite of the hangman. Doublets (jackets) which a hangman would refuse to take would not be worth the plunders' while to steal.

I.vi.6. *The Roman gods.* O you, the gods of Rome! It is not necessary to alter 'The' to 'Ye,' as is commonly done. The reading of the text is an authorized vocative construction in Elizabeth English.

I.vi.91. *[Soldiers.] O, me alone! Make you a sword of me!* The Folio prints the line without indication of speaker, but it is difficult to explain it as part of Martius' speech.

I.viii.15, 16. *Wert thou the Hector That was the whip of your bragg'd progeny.* 'Progeny' means race or stock, and 'whip' the scourge with which punishment is inflicted: 'If you were Hector, the most formidable warrior of your boasted race.' Allusion is made, of course, to the asserted descent of the Romans from the Trojans.

I.ix.35. *tent themselves with death.* Make death the means of cleansing themselves from festering ingratitude.

I.ix.51. *Let him be made an overture for the wars.* Tyrwhitt and most modern editors alter 'an overture' to 'a coverture,' without much assisting the interpretation of the line. The Folio text appears to mean, 'Let an offer of warlike employment be made to him (the parasite).' When soldiers adopt the effeminate ways of courtiers, let us recruit our armies among the latter class.

II.i.34-36. *O that you could turn your eyes towards the napes of your necks, and make but an interior survey of your good selves.* 'The original fable of Æsop, reproduced by Phædrus, IV. 10, was that Jupiter was furnished every man with two wallets, one hanging down on his breast and containing his neighbour's faults, which are always before his eyes, and the other hanging down his back out of sight, and filled with his own faults.' (Arden ed.) A variation of the fable is found in *Troilus and Cressida*, III.iii.151 f., where Ulysses says:

'*Time hath, my lord, a wallet at his back,*
Wherein he puts alms for oblivion.'

II.i.43. *a cup of hot wine with not a drop of allaying Tiber in 't.* This passage apparently suggested Lovelace's famous lines (*To Althæa from Prison*):

'*When flowing cups run swiftly round*
With no allaying Thames.'

II.i.45-47 *one that converts more with the buttock of the night than with the forehead of the morning.* Better acquainted with the last hour of the night than the first hour of the morning.

II.i.50-52. *I cannot say your worships have delivered the matter well when I find the ass in compound with the major part of your syllables.* I cannot compliment you on your statement of the case against Martius when the larger part of what you say cries out 'ass!' against you—cconvicts you of asininity.

II.i.55. *the map of my microcosm.* My face, Menenius' microcosm or little world was himself and his face the map or chart which summarized its characteristics.

II.i.57 *bisson conspectuities.* No other example of 'conspectuities' appears to be known. It is doubtless an intentionally pretentious coinage from Latin *conspectus*, sight. 'The Folio spelling of 'bisson' is 'beesome.'

II.i.71, 72. *come, come, you are well understood to be a perfecter giber for the table than a necessary bencher in the Capitol.* It is well known that you are better fitted to be a jesting table-companion than a serviceable senator.

II.i.133. *the repulse of Tarquin.* Plutarch says (North): 'The first time he went to the wars, being but a stripling, was when Tarquin surnamed the proud (that had been king of Rome, and was driven out for his pride . . .) did come to Rome with all the aid of the Latins, and many other people of Italy . . . who with a great and a mighty army had undertaken to put him into his kingdom again.' The battle referred to, the last of four attempts to restore King Tarquin, occurred in 499 B.C. Shakespeare makes Cominius tell the story of Martius' exploits on this occasion. See II.ii.92 ff.

II.i.134. *there's nine that I know.* Shakespeare often seems resentful of mathematical precision. One would expect a total of ten here. Some commentators improbably suggest that Menenius makes a fresh count to himself, ending with 'One i' the neck,' etc.

II.i.165. *My gracious silence.* Mr. Case (Arden ed.) suggests that Shakespeare may have derived this pretty nickname of Virgilia from North's translation of Plutarch's Life of Numa, where it is stated that the hero 'taught the Romans to reverence one of [the Muses] above all the rest, who was called Tacita, as ye would say *Lady Silence.*'

II.i.173. *I know not where to turn.* I retain, doubtfully, the arrangement of modern editors. The Folio gives lines 171 and 172 to Cominius, not Coriolanus, which would better explain Volumnia's words. if 171 and 172 really belongs to Coriolanus, it is possible that 'I know . . . turn' should also be assigned to him and Volumnia's speech begin 'O! welcome home,' which commences a new line in the Folio.

II.i.177. *A curse begin at very root on 's heart.* May a curse strike home at once to the most vital part! The common emendation, 'begnaw' for 'begin,' is unnecessary.

II.i.S.d. *Enter Brutus and Sicinius.* That is, they now come forward.

II.i.222, 223. *He cannot temperately transport his honours From whence he should begin and end.* He cannot, as a self-restrained man could, derive honor from both the beginning and the completion of his performances. He cannot go an equable pace and conclude with the same honors with which he begins.

II.i.258-260. *This, as you say, suggested At some time when his soaring insolence Shall teach the people.* If we time our incitement to some occasion when his insolence shall confirm it in the people's mind. instead of 'teach' Hanmer suggested 'touch' and Theobald 'reach.' The former is a very plausible correction, but not inevitable.

II.ii.97, 98. *he fought Beyond the mark of others.* In fighting he surpassed all that others could do. Compare note on II.i.133.

II.ii.110. *He lurch'd all swords of the garland.* Evidence for the date of Coriolanus has been found in the fact that Ben Jonson appears to have imitated this passage in the last speech of his *Silent Woman* (1609 or 1610), where Truewit says: 'Well, Dauphine, you have lurch'd your friends of the better half of the garland.'

II.iii.S.d. *Enter two of the Citizens.* The Folio indicates the number as 'three' and assigns the speeches at lines 64, 68, 71, and 81 to '*3. Cit.*'; but Coriolanus alludes to them as 'a brace' (l. 62) and 'two worthy voices' (l. 85).

II.iii.109. *wolfish toge.* Wolf's toga, or garment. Why should I stand here like a wolf in sheep's clothing? The first Folio has 'Wooluish tongue,' and the later Folios 'Woolvish gowne.' One of the best of many emendations is 'woolless toge.'

II.iii.253. *And Censorinus, that was so surnam'd.* This line is omitted by the Folio, evidently by inadvertence, since 254 makes no sense immediately after 252. The present line is Delius' emendation, based upon the words of North in the opening passage of the Life of Coriolanus, which Brutus' speech paraphrases closely. North translates: 'Of the same house were Publius and Quintus, who brought Rome their best water they had by conducts. *Censorinus* also came of that family, *that was so surnamed* because the people had chosen him Censor twice.' It may be that the Folio printer was confused by two consecutive lines beginning with 'And,' and accidentally omitted the first.

III.i.162. *motive.* Johnson's emendation for 'natiue' of the Folio.

III.i.164, 165. *How shall this bosom multiplied digest The senate's courtesy?* This is the Folio reading, which editors have unjustifiably emended. 'This bosom multiplied' means this composite bosom, the bosom of this conglomerate rabble. Compare *King Lear* V.iii.52–55:

'the old and miserable king . . .
Whose age has charms in it, whose title more,
To pluck the common bosom on his side.'

Shakespeare frequently uses 'bosom' for the seat of digestion, or rather the part of the body in which indigestion makes itself felt; thus in *2 Henry IV* I.iii.95-102:

'O thou fond many! . . .
So, so, thou common dog, didst thou disgorge
Thy glutton bosom of the loyal Richard.'

III.i.261. *the rock Tarppeian.* A part of the Capitoline hill, down which condemned criminals were cast to death.

III.i.383-385. *The service of the foot, Being once gangren'd, is not then respected For what before it was.* Menenius is elaborating his statement in lines 371, 372, that the 'disease' in Coriolanus, which causes the plebeians to dislike him, is curable. Brutus, however, interrupts him.

III.ii.25. *The thwartings of.* Theobald's emendation. The Folio reads 'The things of,' which does not make sense. In line 41, below, 'Theobald has again been followed in substituting 'herd' for the 'heart' of the Folio.

III.ii.70, 71. *such words that are but rooted in Your tongue.* The Folio spells 'roated,' which can be interpreted as 'roted,' learned by rote, parrot-like; but one would then expect the following preoposition to be 'on' rather than 'in.'

III.ii.87, 88. *Not what is dangerous present, but the loss Of what is past.* Not only apply a healing salve to the present danger, but also save what you have already lost. 'Salve' in line 86 has a different sense with each of the object clauses.

III.ii.91, 92. *And thus far having stretch'd it,—here be with them.—Thy knee bussing the stones.* Stretching your conciliatory gestures to the point (do this to please their mood) of letting your knee caress the paving stones.

III.iii.15. *Have you collected them by tribes?* This, like the counting of votes 'by the poll' (line 13), was a device to give weight to the plebeian vote. North says: 'And first of all the Tribunes would in any case (whatsoever became of it) that the people would proceed to give their voices by Tribes, and not by hundreds: for by this means the multitude of the poor needy people (and all such rabble as had nothing to lose, and had less regard of honesty before their eyes) came to be of greater force (because their voices were numbered by the poll) than the noble honest citizens, whose persons and purse did dutifully serve the commonwealth in their wars.' The division of Roman citizens into tribes (originally three, finally thirty-five) was democratic, while the division into 193 hundreds (centuriæ) was based upon property qualifications.

III.iii.70. *accents.* Theobald's universally accepted emendation for the Folio's 'Actions.'

III.iii.123. *doth.* An old (southern) plural. The second folio normalized it to 'doc.'

III.iii.S. d. *with others.* The Folio gives this in the remarkably corrupted form, 'with Cumalijs' (i.e. *cum aliis*). The 'others' are the rest of the patricians. The next word, 'They,' refers to the plebeians.

IV.i.7. *fortune's blows, When most struck home,—being gentle, wounded, craves A noble cunning.* 'When Fortune strikes her hardest blows, to be wounded, and yet continue calm, requires a generous policy.' (Johnson.) The construction of the sentence is suddenly changed in the middle (anacoluthon): 'fortune's blows,' originally intended as subject, is left hanging as an 'absolute nominative,' and a new subject, 'being gentle,' is introduced.

IV.ii.24. *mankind.* Sicinius uses the word in the invidious sense in which it was applied to women: virago-like. Volumnia in the next line takes it as meaning 'human' in contrast with the 'foxship' of Sicinius.

IV.ii.68. *Leave this faint puling.* Volumnia addresses Virgilia, who is weeping silently.

IV.iv.17. *Whose double bosoms seems to wear one heart.* The verbal plural in –s (cf. note on I.iv.48), perhaps here used with some idea of the apparent unity of the 'double bosoms.'

IV.iv.24. *To take the one the other.* Construe with 'plots' in line 23: plots by which the one hopes to get the better of the other.

IV.iv.27. *My birth-place hate I.* For 'hate' the Folio misprints 'haue.'

IV.v.133. *o'er-bear.* The Folio has 'o're-beate,' which a few editors defend.

IV.v.S. d. *Enter two of the Servingmen.* That is, the Servingmen, who have been auditors, now advance. Compare II.i.S. d.

IV.v.164. *but a greater soldier than he you wot on.* The Folio reading is 'but a greater soldier than he, you wot one,' i.e., you know one greater soldier (Aufidius) than he. This can be justified, but Dyce's emendation, as given in the text, seems preferable. In any case the servants are speaking cautiously, drawing each other out.

IV.v.190. *boiled.* Culinary editors, led by Pope, alter to 'broiled,' since that is the proper treatment of a 'carbonado' steak.

IV.vi.2. *tame i' the present peace.* Theobald added the preposition. The Folio reads: 'His remedies are tame,. the present peace.'

IV.vi.54. *Thrusts forth his horns again.* The allusion is to the action of a snail. See next line.

IV.vi.72. *some news is coming.* Rowe has been usually followed in altering 'coming' to 'come,' but Shakespeare is fond of the conception of news as gradually unfolded by 'sequent messengers,' whose reports vary and cause uncertainty or suspense. Compare *Othello* I.ii.41 and the opening of the following scene in that play; also *2 Henry IV* I.i.

IV.vi.84, 85. *And vows revenge as spacious as between The young'st and oldest thing.* Vows to include every living thing in his revenge.

IV.vi.105. *Your temples burned in their cement.* Subjected to such conflagration that even the mortar will be consumed. As always in Shakespeare, 'cement' is accented on the first syllable.

IV.vi.139, 140. *they charg'd him even As those should do that had deserv'd his hate.* By asking him to spare Rome his friends would be making common cause with his foes.

IV.vi.146. *you have crafted fair.* A pun on 'crafted' is involved: (a) advanced the crafts' interests, (b) shown your craft.

IV. vi.157, 158. *desperation Is all the policy, strength, and defence, That Rome can make against them.* All that Rome can do against them in the way of either negotiation, offence, or defence is a desperate hope.

IV.vii.26-28. *yet he hath left undone That which shall break his neck or hazard mine, Whene'er we come to our account.* The allusion appears to be to Plutarch's statement that, after Coriolanus had led his army to within forty furlongs of Rome and made great demands on behalf of the Volsci, he omitted to press his advantage and allowed the Romans a respite of thirty days in which to make their answer. 'This,' says North, 'was the first matter wherewith the Volsces (that most envied Martius' glory and authority) did charge Martius with. Among those, Tullus was chief.'

IV.vii.36, 37. *As is the osprey to the fish, who takes it By sovereignty of nature.* The osprey, or fishhawk, was supposed to have a natural power of fascinating fishes. Editors quote several contemporary statements of the belief; e.g., Peele's *Battle of Alcazar* II.iii.:

'I will provide thee with a princely osprey,
That, as she flieth over fish in pools,
The fish shall turn their glittering bellies up.'

IV.vii.44, 45. *not moving From the casque to the cushion.* His nature or disposition not adapting itself to suit the properties of conduct in time of war and time

of peace respectively. The casque is the symbol of the warrior, the cushion of the senator. Compare III.i.130 and stage direction at opening of II.ii.

IV.vii.51, 51. *but he has a merit To choke it in the utterance.* His merit is so great that condemnation of his fault should be silenced ere fully uttered.

IV.vii.53-55. *And power, unto itself most commendable, hath not a tomb so evident as a chair To extol what it hath done.* Power, though (when considered absolutely) most worthily attained, is never so near its grave as when the successful man, seated in the chair of authority, seeks to justify the means by which he has risen.

IV.vii.57. *Rights by rights falter.* One conception of justice hampers another. For 'falter' (Dyce's emendation) the Folio reads 'fouler.' Johnson proposed 'founder.'

V.i.18. *rack'd.* The word is spelled 'wrack'd' in the Folio; and there is probably a play on the sense of 'rack'd' as explained in the footnote and 'wrack'd,' brought all to wrack and ruin.

V.i.79-81. *what he would do He sent in writing after me, what he would not, Bound with an oath to yield to his conditions.* He sent a written statement of what he would and would not do, requiring an oath of unconditional acceptance of these conditions.

V.ii.14. *it is lots to blanks.* It is more likely than not. Lots were the drawings in a lottery, blanks those that carried no prize. The Arden editors have a learned not upon this phrase, the meaning of which is not so simple as it appears.

V.ii.22. *I have ever verified my friends.* The Folio reading, 'verified,' gives a reasonable sense. Many emendations have, however, been proposed and adopted; e.g., magnified, amplified, glorified.

V.ii.82, 83. *my remission lies In Volscian breasts.* In exercising clemency I am no free agent, but must be governed by the feelings of the Volsci.

V.ii.83-85. *That we have been familiar, Ingrate forgetfulness shall poison, rather Than pity note how much.* I shall rather be ungrateful in forgetting our old familiarity than by dwelling upon it allow my pity to be aroused.

V.ii.101. *He that hath a will to die by himself fears it not from another.* One who, like Menenius, would be wiling to slay himself is beyond caring for the death threats of the Watch. Compare line 58, above.

V.iii.42, 43. *The sorrow that delivers us thus chang'd Makes you think so.* Virgilia purposely misconstrues her husband's words. The great alteration, she says, which sorrow has caused in our appearance makes you think you can't believe your eyes.

V.iii.55, 56. *Of thy deep duty more impression show Than that of common sons.* Wishing to emphasize his dutiful respect, Coriolanus bids his knee, not simply touch the ground, but sink into it and leave a deep imprint.

V.iii.74. *dear Valeria.* In Plutarch it is she who suggests to Volumnia and Virgilia the visit to Coriolanus' camp. North speaks of her thus: 'Valeria, Publicola's own sister; the self same Publicola, who did such notable service to the Romans, both in peace and wars, and was dead also certain years before, as we have declared in his life. His sister Valeria was greatly honoured and reverenced among all the romans; and did so modestly and wisely behave herself, that she did not shame nor dishonour the house she came of.'

V.iii.165. *To tear with thunder the wide cheeks o' the air* The allusion is doubtless to the common indication of the winds (north, south, etc.) in old maps as issuing from cherubs' swollen cheeks. In *Richard II*, III.iii.56-58, Shakespeare speaks of

'the elements
Of fire and water, when their thundering shock
At meeting tears the cloudy cheeks of heaven.'

V.iii.166, 167. *And yet to charge the sulphur with a bolt That should but rive an oak.* And yet, with all your terrible show, to commit no inhumanity.

V.iv.17. *talks like a knell, and his 'hum! is a battery.* His conversation bodes death, and his exclamation of impatience is like the sound of cannon.

V.iv.44. *Ne'er through an arch so hurried the blown tide.* The allusion is to the rush of the incoming tide through the old London bridge, which consisted of twenty arches. The same figure is found in *Lucrece*, ll. 1667-1671:

'As through an arch the violent roaring tide
Outruns the eye that doth behold his haste,
Yet in the eddy boundeth in his pride.
Back to the strait that forc'd him on so fast;
In rage sent out, recall'd in rage, being past.'

V.iv.48. *Make the sun dance.* An old popular belief was that the sun danced for joy on Easter morning. It is alluded to by many writers of Shakespeare's time.

V.iv.S.d. Some editors make a new scene of the next six lines.

V.v.S.d. *Corioli.* The text of this scene is inconsistent in locating it, first at Antium, the Volscian capital, and later at Corioli. Professor Gordon's explanation is highly satisfactory: 'Editors are divided whether to place this scene in Antium or Corioli. We should expect it to be Antium. Plutarch makes it Antium. But in line 104 it is explicitly said to be Corioli. On the other hand, ll.57, 84, 91, all point to Antium. We hear in l. 50 that it was Aufidius's native town, which seems to have been Antium (I.vi.72); in l. 84 that Coriolanus has come back to the place he started from, which was Antium; in l. 91 that peace had been made with honour to "the Antiates." The solution seems to me to be this. Shakespeare meant the scene to be Antium, and wrote with Antium in his mind until he came to Aufidius's speech in l. 102. There he was carried away by the magnificent opportunity of placing "Coriolanus in Corioli" (l. 104), and for the rest of the scene thought rather of Corioli than of Antium.'

V.v.80, 81. *answering us With our own charge.* Paying us back only the amount of our expenditure, bringing in no profit. Compare lines 88-89, where Coriolanus estimates that the gains from the expedition amount to one-third more than the costs. The point is that no large indemnity had been secured from the Romans.

THE TEXT OF THE PRESENT EDITION

The text to the present volume is based, by permission of the Oxford University Press, upon that of the Oxford Shakespeare, edited by the late W. J. Craig. Craig's text has been carefully collated with the Shakespeare Folio of 1623, and the following deviations have been introduced:

1. The stage directions of the Folio have been restored. necessary words and directions, omitted by the Folio, are added within square brackets.

2. Punctuation and spelling have been normalized to accord with modern English practice; e.g., anything, everything, warlike, priestlike, hostler, carcasses, scandal'd (instead of any thing, every thing, war-like, priest-like, ostler, carcases, scandall'd). Generally the changes introduced, both in punctuation and in spelling, effect a closer approximation to the Folio form. The form Martius, invariable in the Folio and in North, is restored *passim* in place of Marcius. The Folio abbreviation 'Y' are' is likewise replaced instead of the varying 'you 're,' 'ye 're,' or 'you are' of modern editions.

3. The frequent elisions, characteristic of the Folio text and often necessary for scansion of the lines, have generally been retained; e.g., th' expulsion, th' accusation, is 't, we'll, o' (for *of* or *on*), 's (for *is, his,* or *us*), etc.

4. The following changes of text have been introduced, nearly always in accordance with Folio authority. The readings of the present edition precede the colon, while Craig's readings follow it:

I.i.22   All: First Cit.
   46   2. Cit.: First Cit. (So also in lines 52, 66, 80, 92, 101, 110, 113, 118, 134, 140, 149, 161.)
   96   taintingly: tauntingly
  117   you'st: you'll
  ii.34   prepar'd: prepared
  iii.2   should: would
  iv.48   follows: follow'd
  vi.6   The Roman: Ye Roman
   39   burnt: burn'd
  ix.51   an overture: a coverture

II.i.13   Both: Sic. } Bru.

   37   Both: Bru.
  204   begin; begnaw
  177   virgilia: Valeria
  255   their war: the war
  ii.7   hath: have
  iii.36   the: a(misprint?)
   98   bountiful: bountifully
  104   farther: further
  109   wolfish: woolvish
  110   does: do
  119   moe: more
  156   loves: love
  163   us'd: used
III.i.85   meiny (Meynie F): many
   93   lack: lack'd
  100   their: they
  164   bosom multiplied: bisson multitude

401   a' (a F): he
ii.25   thwartings (things F): thwarting
37   as little: of mettle
137   quir'd: quired
138   an eunuch: a eunuch
iii.86   fold in: fold-in
123   doth: do
IV.i.8   home,—being: home, being
29   'em: them
ii.27   strook: struck (So also in IV.v.231)
iii.9   appeared: approved

iv.17   seems: seem
v.110   an hundred: a hundred
190   boiled: broiled
vi.62   hath: have
72   coming: come
vii.30   yields: yield
V.ii.22   verified: glorified
iii.168   nobleman: noble man
iv.17   'hum!': hum
v.116   others: other

The Life of Timon of Athens

Edited by

STANLEY T. WILLIAMS

Dramatis Personae

TIMON *of Athens*

LUCIUS
LUCULLUS } *flattering Lords*
SEMPRONIUS

VENTIDIUS, *one of Timon's false Friends*

APEMANTUS, *a churlish Philosopher*

ALCIBIADES, *an Athenian Captain*

POET, PAINTER, JEWELLER, MERCHANT
　[AND MERCER]

CERTAIN SENATORS

CERTAIN MASQUERS [*Ladies dressed as Amazons*]

CERTAIN THIEVES

[FLAVIUS, *Steward to Timon*]

FLAMINIUS
[LUCILIUS] } *Servants to Timon*
SERVILIUS

CAPHIS
PHILOTUS
TITUS } *Several Servants to Usurers*
LUCIUS 　[*and to the Lords*]
HORTENSIUS

[PHRYNIA
TIMANDRA } *Mistresses to Alcibiades*]

CUPID

WITH DIVERS OTHER SERVANTS AND ATTENDANTS

[SERVANTS OF VENTIDIUS, AND OF VARRO AND
　ISIDORE (TWO OF TIMON'S CREDITORS)

THREE STRANGERS

AN OLD ATHENIAN

A PAGE

A FOOL]

SCENE—*Athens, and the neighbouring Woods.*

The Life of Timon of Athens

INTRODUCTION

SOURCES OF THE PLAY

The basic legend of Shakespeare's *Timon of Athens* began in antiquity. Early in the fifth century B. C., Timon's picturesque misanthropy was a theme of Greek comic poets. The hero of *The Misanthrope*, by Phrynichus, remarks: 'I live like Timon. I have no wife, no servant, I am irritable and hard to get on with. I never laugh, I never talk, and my opinions are all my own.' From the uncertain realms of casual allusion emerge two later Greek portrayals of the character of Timon: The story of the misanthrope in Plutarch's *Life of Antonius*, and Lucian's comic dialogue, *Timon the Misanthrope*.[1]

How much Plutarch had already yielded Shakespeare we know; here were the geneses of *Julius Cæsar*, *Coriolanus*, and *Antony and Cleopatra*. And if it is believed that *Timon of Athens* was written at about the same time as the last-named tragedy, it is conceivable that the full possibilities of the Timon legend were brought home to Shakespeare in the very act of composing *Antony and Cleopatra*. The dramatist's reliance upon this source is suggested by the following excerpt: 'Antonius, he forsooke the citie and companie of his friends, and built him a house in the sea, & dwelt there, as a man that banished himself from all mens company: saying that he would leade *Timons* life because he had the like wrong offered him, that was before offered vnto *Timon*: and that for the vnthankfulnesse of those he had done good vnto, and whom he tooke to be his friends, he was angrie with all men, and would trust no man. This *Timon* was a citizen of ATHENS, that liued about the war of PELOPONNESUS, as appeareth by *Plato & Aristophanes* comedies: in the which they mocked him, calling him a viper and malicious man vnto mankind, to shun all other mens companies, but the companie of young *Alcibiades*, a bold and insolent youth, whom he would greatly feast and make much of, and kissed him very gladly. *Apemantus* wondering at it, asked him the cause what he meant to make so much of that young man alone, and to hate all others: *Timon* answered him, I do it, said he, because I know that one day he shall do great mischiefe vnto the ATHENIANS.[2] This *Timon* sometimes would haue *Apemantus* in his companie, because he was much like of his nature and conditions, and also followed him in manner of life. On a time when they solemnly celebrated the feasts called Choæ at ATHENS, (to wit, the feasts of the dead where they make sprinklings and sacrifices for the dead) and that they two then feasted together by them selues, *Apemantus* said vnto the other: O here is a trim banquet *Timon*. *Timon* answered again: Yea, said he, so thou wert not here.[3] It is reported of him also, that

this *Timon* on a time (the people being assembled in the market place about dispatch of some affaires) got vp into the pulpit for Orations, where the Oratours commonly vse to speake vnto the people: and silence being made, euery man listening to heare what he would say, because it was a wonder to see him in that place, at length he began to speake in this manner: My Lords of ATHENS, I haue a litle yard at my house where there groweth a figge tree, on the which many citizens have hanged themselues: and because I meane to make some building on the place, I thought good to let you all vnderstand it, that before the figge tree be cut downe, if any of you be desperate, you may there in time go hang your selues.[4] He died in the citie of HALES, and was buried vpon the sea side. Now it chanced so, that the sea getting in, compassed his tombe round about, that no man could come to it: and vpon the same was written this Epitaph:

> Here lies a wretched corse, of wretched soule bereft: Seeke not my name: a plague consume you wicked wretches left.

It is reported that *Timon* himselfe, when he liued, made this Epitaph: for that which is commonly rehearsed, was not his, but made by the Poet Callimachus:

> Here lye I Timon, who aliue all liuing men did hate: Passe by and curse thy fill: but passe, and stay not here thy gate—

It will be observed that the themes of this ancient story have been much expanded and enriched by Shakespeare. The 'vnthankfulnesse of those he had done good vnto,' elaborated, becomes the *motif* for Timon's perversion; and 'young Alcibiades,' with his hatred for Athens, dominates the underplot. Were proof needed, the epitaphs show Shakespeare's dependence upon Plutarch. They are quoted in juxtaposition, but are contradictory. The inclusion of both instead of the selection of one must be due to inadvertence or misunderstanding on the part of the poet. In fact, the more the passage in Plutarch is studied the more certainly does it appear that this or a later work based upon Plutarch, such as Painter's *Palace of Pleasure* (1566),[5] is the dynamic or inspirational source of our play.

Nevertheless, certain incidents can be attributed neither to Plutarch nor Painter. Of basic principles and ideas Plutarch is the source; for other episodes and character portraiture the responsibility is elsewhere. It is probable that one such source was an old Elizabethan comedy of Timon of Athens, acted about 1600. More or less faithful analogues may be found in the old

---

1 Definite references to Timon occur in the comedies of Aristophanes, Plato, and Antiphanes. He is later mentioned by Roman writers, notably Cicero, Seneca, the Elder Pliny, and Strabo. Strabo was the first to allude to Timon's early life of affluence. It is quite certain that the legend had general currency. For full compilations of classical and Elizabethan allusions to the Timon story the reader is referred to Dr. Ernest Hunter Wright's monograph, *The Authorship of Timon of Athens*, Columbia University Press, 1910, and W. H. Clemons; *The Sources of Timon of Athens*, in the Princeton University Bulletin, September, 1904.

2 For Alcibiades' part in *Timon of Athens*, see III. v.; IV. iii; V. iv. Plutarch's *Life of Alcibiades* refers to him as Timon's friend.

3 See *Timon of Athens*, IV. iii. 307 ff.

4 For Shakespeare's use of the incident of the fig-tree, see *Timon of Athens*, V. i. 229-236.

5 The twenty-eighth novel of Painter's *Palace of Pleasure* is of *The strange and beastly nature of Timon of Athens*, based upon Plutarch, and adding only the particular that Timon lived in a desert. We know that the *Palace of Pleasure* furnished the source of *All's Well that Ends Well*, and that it influenced *Romeo and Juliet*. It is, accordingly, unlikely that Shakespeare was unfamiliar with the novel of *Timon of Athens*. The exact porportion of Shakespeare's reference, in writing the tragedy, to Plutarch or Painter is, of course, indeterminable. Perhaps the most reasonable conclusion concerning the matter is that he retained a general recollection of Painter, but that a copy of Plutarch lay before him as he wrote.

play for the following incidents: Timon's betrayal by the parasites; the mock-banquet; Timon's exile; the finding of the gold; and, though less certainly, the episodes of the Old Athenian and Ventidius. Since these incidents occur also in Lucian's *Dialogues*,[6] such evidence proves only that Shakespeare drew either from one or both of these sources. But the mock-banquet and the all-sacrificing steward are to be found in the old play and *not* in Lucian. In the portion of the old play's mock-banquet scene here reprinted (IV. v.), the reader will find much in substance and spirit worthy of comparison with the corresponding scene in Shakespeare's play (III. vi.).

(ACT IV, SCENE V.)

TIMON, LACHES, OBBA, PHILARGURUS, GELASIMUS, PSEUDOCHEUS, DEMEAS, EUTRAPELUS: HERMOGENES, STILPO, SPEUSIPPUS come awhile after.

Tim. *Furnish the table, sette on dainty cheare;*
Timon doth bidde his friends their last farewell.
  Phil. *Thou wisely dost; it is too late to spare*
When all is spent; whom the gods woulde haue
To lieu but poorely, let him bee content.
  Tim. *What man is hee can wayle the losse of wealthe,*
Guarded with such a friendly company?
Ill thriue my gold, it shall not wring one teare
From these mine eies, nor one sigh from my hearte:
My friends sticke close to mee, they will not starte.
  Dem. *Is hee madde? wee. knew him not this morning.*
Hath hee soe soone forgotte an injury?

· · · · · ·

Enter *TIMON*

  Tim. *O happy mee, equall to Joue himselfe!*
I going touche the starres. Breake out, O joy,
And smother not thyselfe within my breast!
Soe many friends, soe many friends I see;
Not one hathe falsifi'de his faith to mee.
What, if I am opprest with pouretie?
And griefe doth vexe mee? fortune left mee poore?
All this is nothing: they releeue my wants;
The one doth promise helpe, another golde,
A thirde a friendly welcome to his house
And entertainement; eache man actes his parte;
All promise counsaile and a faithfull hearte.
  Gelas. *Timon, thou art forgettefull of thy feast.*
  Tim. *Why doe yee not fall to? I am at home:*
Ile standing suppe, or walking, if I please.—
Laches, bring here the artichokes with speede.—
Eutrapelus, Demeas, Hermogenes,

I'le drinke this cuppe, a healthe to all your healths!
  Lach. *Conuerte it into poison, O ye gods!*
Let it bee ratsbane to them!   [Aside.
  Gelas. *What, wilt thou haue the legge or els the winge?*
  Eutr. *Carue yee that capon.*
  Dem. *I will cutte him up,*
And make a beaste of him.
  Phil. *Timon, this healthe to thee.*
  Tim. *Ile pledge you, sir.*
These artichokes doe noe mans pallat please.
  Dem. *I loue them well, by Joue.*
  Tim. *Here, take them, then!*
[Stones painted like to them; and throwes them at them.
Nay, thou shalt haue them, thou and all of yee!
Yee wicked, base, perfidious rascalls,
Thinke yee my hate's soe soone extinguished?
         [TIMON BEATES HERM. aboue all the reste.
  Dem. *O my heade!*
  Herm. *O my cheekes!*
  Phil. *Is this a feaste?*
  Gelas. *Truly, a stony one.*
  Stil. *Stones sublunary haue the same matter with the heauenly.*
  Tim. *If I Joues horridde thunderbolte did holde*
Within my hande, thus, thus would I darte it!
                                    [He hitts HERM.
  Herm. *Woe and alas, my braines are dashed out!*
  Gelas. *Alas, alas, twill neuer bee my happe,*
To trauaile now to the Antipodes!
Ah, that I had my Pegasus but here!
I'de fly away, by Joue.
              [Exeunt (all except TIM. and LACH.)
  Tim. *Yee are a stony generation,*
Or harder, if ought harder may bee founde;
Monsters of Scythia inhospitall,
Nay, very diuells, hatefull to the gods.
  Lach. *Master, they are gone.*
  Tim. *The pox goe with them;*
And whatsoe're the horridde sounding sea
Or earthe produces, whatsoe're accurs'd
Lurks in the house of silent Erebus,
Let it, O, let it all sprawl forth here! here,
Cocytus, flowe, and yee blacke foords of Styx!
Here barke thou, Cerberus! and here, yee troopes
Of cursed Furies, shake your firy brands!
Earth's worse than hell: let hell chaunge place with earth,
And Plutoes regiment bee next the sunne!
  Lach. *Will this thy fury neuer bee appeas'd?*
  Tim. *Neuer, neuer it; it will burne for euer:*
It pleases mee to hate. Goe, Timon, goe,
Banishe thyselfe from mans society;
Farther than hell fly this inhumane city:
If there bee any exile to bee had,
There will I hide my heade.   [Exit.
  Lach. *Ile follow thee through sword, through fire, and deathe;*
If thou goe to the ghosts, Ile bee thy page,
And lacky thee to the pale house of hell:
They misery shall make my faith excell.   [Exit.

---

6 The amount of Shakespeare's obligation to *Timon the Misanthrope* in Lucian's *Dialogues* has been rather widely disputed. When Shakespeare's play was written there existed no English translation of Lucian's *Dialogues*. Unless the tale of Shakespeare's Greek is discredited, he cannot be believed conversant with the original. If he was influenced it must have been through existent French or Italian translations. Shakespeare's tragedy includes no passages traceable to Lucian which cannot as readily be ascribed to the old play or another source of later date than Lucian. Yet the absence of evidence has failed to convince certain critics that Shakespeare was not directly affected by the *Dialogues*. 'The Timon of Shakespeare,' says W. H. Clemons, 'is not the Timon of the academic production; still less is it like the Timon of the popular Elizabethan stories. In the depth and tone of his misanthropy, Lucian's Timon is the true type of Shakespeare's Timon.' (Princeton University Bulletin, September, 1904, 219.) The same writer also calls attention to the likeness in Timon's apostrophes to the gold in Lucian and in Shakespeare (IV. iii. 25 ff.).

Besides similarity of spirit in the two scenes, much has been made of the possible reminiscence of Shakespeare's line: 'One day he gives us diamonds, next day *stones*' (III. vi. 115). Shakespeare's use of the mock-banquet and of the loyal steward, when no such precedent exists in Lucian, argues strongly for his dependence upon the old comedy of *Timon*. Steevens and Malone believed in this indebtedness. Dyce, the editor of the comedy, did not investigate the matter deeply. 'I leave to others,' he says in his introduction, 'a minute discussion of the question, whether or not Shakespeare was indebted to the present piece. I shall merely observe, that I entertain considerable doubts of his having been acquainted with a drama, which was certainly never performed in the metropolis, and which was likely to have been read only by a few of the author's particular friends, to whom manuscripts of it had been presented.' But the inability to state positively that Shakespeare knew the play hardly lessens the significance of the strong parallelism between it and the tragedy. Almost certainly it was a source of *Timon of Athens*.

Besides relying upon these established sources it is conceivable that Shakespeare enjoyed also an acquaintance with certain secondary sources, and it is possible that his interest in the Timon story was increased by its currency in his own time. In Elizabethan literature Timon was regarded as a legitimate and clearly defined type. Robert Greene alludes to him, and Dekker and Nash slur at 'Timonists.' The character crept into Lyly, and Shakespeare himself, in *Love's Labour's Lost* (IV. iii. 170), has an apt reference to the misanthrope: 'And critic Timon laugh at idle toys.' It is possible, though by no means probable, that Shakespeare had read two plays of the Renaissance, Boiardo's *Il Timone* (written about 1494) and Galeotto del Caretto's play of the same name (written about 1497). Both these plays follow Lucian closely, and add little to the Timon story except an underplot. No hint of this underplot is found in the tragedy. As Lucian's version of the tale is reflected in Boiardo and Caretto, so Painter's story has been followed by Sir Richard Barckley in his *Discourse on the Felicitie of Man* (1598). Although Shakespeare may well have been familiar with this book, it is clear that he took nothing from it that he might not have had from Painter's *Palace of Pleasure*.

HISTORY OF THE PLAY

Problematic in sources and authorship, *Timon of Athens* has, in addition, a unique history as a printed and acted play. No quartos exist; the play was first printed in the Folio of 1623 in the section of the Tragedies between *Romeo and Juliet* and *Julius Cæsar*. On November 8, 1623, it was entered by the publishers upon the Stationers' Register as one of the plays 'not formerly entered to other men.'[7] The date of composition of Shakespeare's part can be determined only by internal evidence. Various years have been suggested between 1606 and 1610. The general likeness of the tragedy, in story and tone, to *King Lear* and *Coriolanus* fix it rather definitely in this period; while the theory that the idea of *Timon* occurred to Shakespeare while working on *Antony and Cleopatra* (see Sources of the Play) would place it about 1607-1608, a date upon which there has been some measure of agreement.

The dramatic history of *Timon of Athens* confirms the usual opinion of readers that it is not well suited for representation on the stage. It is, indeed, surprising that dramatic annals record no performance of the play, in its original form, even with only slight alterations, until towards the close of the eighteenth century. During the last quarter of the seventeenth century, however, there began to appear versions and alterations of the tragedy. Some of these included changes designed merely to please the taste of the time; others cut or expanded the original until it was almost unrecognizable; but all retain the central theme of Timon's misanthropy and much, also, of the indelible influence of Shakespeare. These versions, then, together with a few revivals of the play in its original form, constitute the stage-history of *Timon of Athens*.[8]

Probably the first performance of an alteration of *Timon of Athens* occurred in December, 1678, at Dorset Garden, when Thomas Shadwell's version of the play was acted under the title of *Timon of Athens*, or *The Man-Hater*. Thomas Betterton (1635?-1710) played the rôle of Timon. In the Dedication Shadwell says he has made the history of Timon 'into a play.' What changes he thought necessary to accomplish this result may be seen in the following excerpts from Genest: Shadwell 'introduces two ladies,—the one, with whom Timon was on the point of marriage, deserts him in his adversity—the other, whom he had himself deserted, sticks to him to the last—this love business is far from an improvement—Shadwell has likewise spoilt the character of Flavius, and made him desert his master. . . . Considerable additions are made to the part of Apemantus, but on the whole it is altered for the worse—in the 2d act, he is called a snarling stoick. . . .' In the same act Shadwell also 'introduces some proper observations on bad poetry, applicable to his own times.' *The Jew of Venice* (1701) refers to the unpopularity of this production, but Genest declares it to have been the first of many performances of the play: 'It was afterwards revived, and continued on the acting list for many years—Downes indeed says it pleased the Court and City generally.'[9] At least five other productions of Shadwell's version took place between 1678 and 1745. On June 27, 1707, it was acted at the Haymarket Theatre with John Mills (d. 1736) as Timon and John Verbruggen (1688-1707) as Apemantus. Barton Booth (1681-1733) played Alcibiades, while the two female parts, unknown to Shakespeare, of Evandra and Melissa, were taken, respectively, by Mrs. Mary Porter (d. 1765) and Mrs. Bradshaw. Shadwell's version was also known in Ireland, for a record has survived of a performance at the Smock Alley Theater, Dublin, in the year 1715. The next[10] English performance of this version occurred on December 8, 1720, at Drury Lane Theatre, Mills this time acting the part of Apemantus and Booth that of Timon. It was again seen at Covent Garden on May 1, 1733,[11] with James Quin (1693-1766) as

7 No record exists of the acting of *Timon of Athens* before 1623. Nevertheless, the stage directions seem to indicate that the play had been acted. It is possible that the tragedy was presented without success, and was soon withdrawn.

8 The editor has in preparation a monograph supplying further details of the stage-history of the play and also some account of its history in Continental theatres.

9 The success of this version was due partially to the masque added by Henry Purcell.

10 An amateur performance of *Timon of Athens* was given at the Clerkenwell charity school on February 6, 1711. John Honeycott, the master of the school, 'with the children of the school, publicly acted the play called "Timon of Athens," and by tickets signed by himself had invited several people to it.' For this venture Honeycott was rebuked by the Society for Promoting Christian Knowledge, the trustees of the school. (*Notes and Queries* 7th s. iii. See also Secretan's *Life of Robert Nelson*, London, 1860, 130.) Whether this was the original play or Shadwell's version is conjectural.

11 The influence of the play upon the stage at this time is evidenced by the performance on December 5, 1733, of a comedy of three acts, with songs, dealing with the theme of Timon and his false friends, called *Timon in Love, or The Innocent Theft*. This trifle was ascribed to C. J. Kelly.

Apemantus. In connection with the next performance at Drury Lane on March 20, 1740, Genest says that the piece had not been acted in three years, but no record is at hand to prove the inference that the play was acted in 1737. At this revival of 1740 Quin again played Apemantus; Milward was Timon; Henry Woodward (1714-1777) acted the rôle of the Poet; and Mrs. Hannah Pritchard (1711-1768) had the part of Melissa. Shadwell's version was acted again, apparently for the last time, on April 20, 1745, at the Covent Garden Theatre.

A composite version, based upon both Shakespeare and Shadwell, was published in 1768, by James Dance, known to the stage as James Love. This play was acted at about the same time at Richmond in a theatre built by the author and his brother. No record exists, apparently, of a London performance, but *Biographia Dramatica* says that the Richmond production was 'well received.'

An important eighteenth century alteration of *Timon of Athens* was that written by Richard Cumberland, leader of the school of Sentimental Drama. This saccharine version, in which Timon has a daughter Evanthe, beloved by Alcibiades, was acted at Drury Lane on December 4, 1771. Horace Walpole, who saw this production, thought that Cumberland had 'caught the manners and diction of the original so exactly' that it was 'full as bad a play as it was before he corrected it.' Radical changes from Shakespeare occur throughout the play, and the fifth act is almost entirely Cumberland's. In fact, Doran notes that this *Timon* has 'more of Cumberland and less of Shakespeare than the public could welcome.'

Shakespeare and Shadwell formed the basis for still another eighteenth century alteration by Thomas Hull (1728-1808), acted at Covent Garden Theatre on May 13, 1786. Joseph Holman (1764-1817) played Timon and Richard Wroughton (1748-1822) was 'a very good Apemantus.' Hull himself played the part of Flavius, and Mrs. Inchbald (1753-1821) that of Melissa. This production, too, was unsuccessful. It ought, says *The European Magazine* for May, 1786, 'to be consigned to oblivion.' 'The play,' says *Biographia Dramatica*, 'has been coldly received and has not been printed.'

The nineteenth century found less interest in new versions of *Timon of Athens* than in reviving the original play, often with elaborate scenic effects. But the play was always, as a whole, unsuccessful, and it becomes increasingly difficult not to acquiesce heartily in Sheridan's remark that 'it is calculated for the closet only, and cannot produce a great effect in representation.' Similarly Macready writes in his Diary: 'Looked at *Timon of Athens*, but it is (for the stage) only an incident with comments on it. The story is not complete enough—not furnished, I ought to say, with the requisite varieties of passion for a play; it is heavy and monotonous.' The first revival of the play in this century was Edmund Kean's at Drury Lane on October 28, 1816. George Lamb, in his Advertisement to this production, stated: 'The present attempt has been to restore Shakespeare on the stage, with no omissions than such as the refinement of manners rendered necessary.' Kean had the title rôle, and it was certainly due to his genius that the play was acted seven times. B. W. Proctor, in his *Life of Edmund Kean*, praises the effectiveness of the play's latter dialogues when vitalized by Kean's passion, but says that even 'Kean was unable, by dint of his own single strength, to make it popular.' Writing in like vein, the editor of *The New Monthly Magazine* for December, 1816, declares that 'till the conclusion of the third act he [Kean] had very little opportunity of distinguishing himself.' The same magazine also says that 'the

tragedy [is] got up in splendid style; the banquet scene in particular is superb.'

Thirty-five years later, on September 15, 1851, at Sadler's Wells, Samuel Phelps 'produced with great splendor Shakespeare's Timon of Athens, and again made a tremendous effect on playgoers generally in the character of Timon. Old habitués and the critics who remembered Edmund Kean in this character all said Phelps surpassed him.' This production was acted about forty times between its first night and the following Christmas.

On October 11, 1856, Phelps revived the production with new scenery 'not only archæologically correct, but picturesquely beautiful.' Alcibiades' attack upon Athens was 'a masterpiece of effect and contrivance.' This and the earlier rendering of the play concluded 'with a beautiful seaside view, where the tomb of Timon is the conspicuous object, before which the army of the invader is drawn up in reverence.' Frank Marshall, in the *Henry Irving Shakespeare*, says: 'Francis Guest Tomlins, secretary of the original Shakespeare Society, instituted comparisons between the Shakespearean revivals at Sadler's Wells and those by Charles Kean at the Princess's, wholly to the credit of the former. At the head of the Princess's was a showman who as lavishly illustrates Pizarro as Macbeth; at that of Sadler's Wells was an artist who assigned fervour and genius predominance over archæology.' This production of *Timon* pleased Professor Morley, who has recorded his impressions in his *Journal of a London Playgoer*. 'Timon of Athens,' he says, 'is always a poem to the Sadler's Wells audience.' Of Phelps' performance in the rôle of Timon he adds: 'His . . . acting treats the character as an ideal, as the central figure in a mystery. As the liberal Athenian lord, his gestures are large, his movements free—out of himself everything pours, towards himself he will draw nothing.'

When *Timon of Athens* was next acted is uncertain. *The Atheneum* of May 28, 1904, says that Charles Calvert, the actor-manager, staged the tragedy about twenty years after Phelps' production, at Manchester. Professor Ward, however, in his list of Calvert's Shakespearean revivals, begun at the Theatre Royal, Manchester, in 1864, does not include *Timon of Athens*. It is quite possible, then, that the next performance of the play was that at Stratford-on-Avon, in the annual series of Shakespearean plays undertaken by F. R. Benson, beginning Monday, April 18, 1892. *Timon of Athens* was acted three times during the week, once on Friday, and twice on Saturday, the poet's birthday. A three-act version was given. *Timon* was again produced, apparently in similar form, in London, at the Court Theatre, on May 18, 1904, when it enjoyed a run of some ten nights. *The London Times* of May 19 praises the production, but notes that there is 'no "female interest" in the play, and [that] even the ladies Timandra and Phrynia "mistresses to Alcibiades" have been on this occasion virtually reduced to dumb-show.' In conclusion the reviewer adds: 'There is a lovely ballet, and a Cupid who might have strayed out of Offenbach's *Belle Hélène*.' Altogether the *Times* finds this *Timon* 'an olio of attractions.' On the other hand, *The Atheneum* declares that the performance possessed 'little interest beyond that of curiosity.'

Perhaps the earliest performance of *Timon of Athens* in America occurred when an adaptation by N. H. Bannister was acted for the first time at the Franklin Theatre in New York City on April 8, 1839. We are told that Richard Mansfield considered the production of the tragedy, but no proof is available that the play has been recently acted on the American stage except in a series of performances by Mr. Frederick Warde when on tour in 1910.

AUTHORSHIP OF THE PLAY

The exact circumstances of the writing of *Timon of Athens* will probably remain conjectural, but that the play is not wholly Shakespeare's creation is certain. Double authorship is constantly proclaimed by singularities of workmanship and by technical problems involving inconsistencies in character and action. Regular and highly irregular verse, rhymed and unrhymed lines, dignified prose and prose that is absurdly flat follow each other in capricious fashion. Poetry as lofty as that of *King Lear* is linked to doggerel, and scenes unquestionably written by Shakespeare suddenly become inane under the influence of another hand. By means of internal evidence of this character scholars have tried to determine how much of the play was written by Shakespeare and how much by the unknown assistant.

The ascriptions differ in detail, but there is some agreement regarding the portions of the tragedy attributable to Shakespeare. About the first one hundred and seventy-five lines of the play are admittedly his (I. i. 1-203). In the passage between the entrance of Apemantus and that of Alcibiades (I. i. 204-266) only the first ten lines have generally been assigned to Shakespeare.[12] The rest of the scene (267-315) was probably written by Shakespeare, with the exception of about eighteen lines of dialogue between the two lords and Apemantus (286-302).[13] Bad verse and blunders have marked the second scene as non-Shakespearean.[14] The first scene of the second act is Shakespeare's (II. i.). The second scene of this act is, by substantial agreement, conceded to be Shakespeare's as far as the entrance of Apemantus and the Fool (II. ii. 1-57),[15] and there is approximately similar agreement that the episode introduced by this entrance is spurious (58-130).[16] The remainder of the scene, approximately (131-253), is usually attributed to Shakespeare except ten prose lines that intrude upon the verse (203-209).[17] The first three scenes of the third act are probably interpolations (III. i., ii, iii.).[18] The commonplace fourth scene is not genuine (III. iv.),[19] nor is the ill-motivated scene showing Alcibiades before the Senate (III. v.). In the sixth scene (III. vi.) I think we can safely assign only Timon's denunciation (83-115) to Shakespeare, though more considerable portions have sometimes been ascribed to him.[20] 'From the fourth act on,' as Wright says, 'the play may be called Shakespere's.' The first scene of this act is almost certainly his (IV. i.) and about the first thirty lines of the second scene (IV. ii. 1-32) may possibly have been touched by his hand.[21] The important third scene (IV. iii.) has evoked marked differences of opinion. Although it is generally conceded that almost the first three hundred lines are Shakespeare's (IV. iii. 1-316), the exact ending of the interpolated passage that follows (316 ff.) is disputed. Fleay would end it at about line 375, and others have adopted his conclusion; Wright, however, believes that Shakespeare's hand is not again discernible until about line 389. The rest of this episode, as far as the entrance of the Banditti, is conceded to be Shakespeare's (389-424). It has been customary to regard a few lines at the opening and a few lines at the closing of the Banditti episode as spurious, but it is quite possible that the whole passage is genuine (425-485).[22] The rest of the scene is probably interpolated (486-569).[23] The first scene of the fifth act with the possible exception of the introduction (1-52) was written by Shakespeare.[24] The second and fourth scenes are likewise his; only the third scene bears no trace of his workmanship.[25]

Concerning the double authorship of *Timon of Athens* there have arisen three distinct theories:

(1) *Timon of Athens* of the Folio represents Shakespeare's work as interpolated and corrupted by the players. In his lectures of 1815, Coleridge stated his belief that the play was Shakespeare's throughout, and that when first written it was one of the Poet's most complete performances.[26] He explained the unusual versification on the ground that the play had been injured by the actors, and was of the opinion that the editors of 1623 saw only a mutilated copy of the original.[27] This theory would be more tenable if there existed positive proof that the play was frequently acted before 1623. But such proof is not to be had. Opportunity for interpolation by the players was almost certainly limited. This theory has, generally speaking, given way before more vigorous hypotheses.

(2) Shakespeare rewrote or revised an earlier *Timon of Athens*, the work of an inferior dramatist. This theory, having its genesis in a belief of Farmer's that there had been an earlier popular play with Timon as a hero, was first advanced by Knight in 1838: '*Timon* was a play originally produced by an artist very inferior to Shakespeare, [and] probably retained possession of the stage for some time in its first form; . . . It has come down to us not wholly rewritten but so far remodelled that entire scenes of Shakespeare have been substituted for entire scenes of the elder play.'[28] Delius gave this theory its fullest development in 1867.[29]

---

12 Fleay was supported in this belief by Hudson, Rolfe, Gollancz, and White. Wright thinks it likely that Shakespeare was the author of the entire passage.

13 Concerning this passage Fleay argued that the unknown author retained the two lords on the stage to jeer at Apemantus, preparing more naturally for the cynic's entrance in the next scene, when he appears 'dropping after all, discontentedly, like himself.' (I. ii. S. d.) Wright considers the passage Shakespeare's.

14 Among other crudities and errors, Wright mentions the following: Ventidius desires to pay his debt to Timon, thus nullifying the dramatic effect of Timon's later request for Ventidius' aid; and in the last act, senators are announced but do not enter.

15 Fleay, Hudson, Rolfe, Gollancz, White, and Wright agree on this point of division.

16 In this passage occurs a typical problem: The Steward urges the duns to await Timon's answer, and with the words, 'Pray, draw near,' is escorting them off, when Apemantus approaches. Whereupon, one of the duns says, 'Stay, stay!' The Steward leaves, but the duns remain throughout the next episode. Johnson suggests that at this point an entire scene is missing.

17 Wright advances the theory that all of these lines, save one, are Shakespeare's. Gollancz believes lines 57-127 (approximately) to be non-Shakespearean.

18 Wright develops an ingenious theory that the first two of these scenes are Shakespeare's. White holds that Shakespeare wrote some dozen lines in the first scene (III. i. 45-58).

19 Three characters, Titus, Hortensius, and Philotus, appear here for the only time in the play. The introduction of a character called Lucius, apparently not the Lucius of the next act, is also puzzling.

20 Hudson assigns to Shakespeare all lines spoken while Timon is on the stage (24-100).

21 Hudson and Wright include these lines in their ascriptions, but Fleay and Rolfe do not.

22 Hudson maintains that Shakespeare wrote approximately the first four hundred and sixty-four lines of this scene.

23 Wright ascribes to Shakespeare approximately lines 498-529 and 552-565.

24 Wright thinks it possible that Shakespeare wrote these lines, since they constitute the introduction to his own scene.

25 A characteristic problem occurs in this act in connection with the entrance of the Poet and Painter. At IV. iii. 373, Apemantus says: 'Yonder comes a poet and a painter.' Yet these characters do not actually enter until about two hundred lines later at the beginning of the fifth act. Thus the leisurely approach of the Poet and Painter becomes an absurdity. To meet the difficulty Hudson substituted 'parcel of soldiers' for 'poet and painter.' Wright explains the confusion by declaring that Apemantus' words occur in a spurious passage; in this case the premature announcement was made by the interpolator.

26 This was the conviction of many German scholars, among them Schlegel, Gervinus, and Ulrici. Elze, however, believed that parts of the play were due to an old *Timon* (*William Shakespeare*, 1876); Wendlandt thought that *Shakespeare* had left part of the play in rough draft (*Jahrbuch*, 1888); Kullmann suggested that there had been three authors (*Archiv für Litteraturgeschichte*, 1892); and Bulthaupt ascribed only a small part of the play to Shakespeare. 'I conjecture,' says Ulrici, ' . . . that Shakespeare originally made a rapid and hurried sketch of "Timon of Athens," only that this was done with greater hurry and carelessness than usual . . . but subsequently—after the piece had been brought upon the stage—he found himself nevertheless obliged to work out some parts with more care.' (*Shakespeare's Dramatic Art*, Vol. I., p. 523.)

27 A passage in the third act (III. iii. 34-36) may be interpreted as a satire upon the Puritans. Coleridge considered this an actor's interpolation.

28 *Pictorial Edition*, 1838.

29 *Jahrbuch der deutschen Shakespeare Gesellschaft*, 1867, pp. 335 ff.

With slight divergences of opinion Delius' view has been supported by the Cambridge Editors, Staunton, Dyce, Nicholson, Evans, and others. 'The original play,' say the first of these, 'on which Shakespeare worked, must have been written, for the most part, either in prose or in very irregular verse.' Evans' comment may be taken as typical of the theory: 'We assume that during his reading of Plutarch Shakespeare's attention was arrested by the story of Timon; that it struck him that the character of Timon might be made effective for the stage, and not having time or inclination to work up a complete plot into a regular five-act play he availed himself of a "Timon" which was in the hands of the theatre at the time. . . . Accordingly he rewrote about half of it, and hastily revised the rest, leaving this for the most part untouched, but inserting or altering a few lines or phrases here and there. But before he had had time to give the whole a final revision it was called for by the manager, and hurried upon the boards. These assumptions will account both for the general unity of the plan as well as for the signs of incomplete revision observable here and there.[30] In quality of argument, and in the support afforded it by eminent scholars, this theory will probably remain important. It has, however, been overshadowed by the third hypothesis.

(3) Shakespeare wrote the main portions of *Timon of Athens*— which was completed or revised by an inferior dramatist. Verplanck, the American scholar, led the way for this theory in 1847, when he wrote: 'It is like . . . a work left incomplete and finished by another hand, inferior, though not without skill, and working on the conceptions of the greater master.' In the same connection he adds: 'The hypothesis which I should offer . . . is this: Shakespeare adopted the canvas of *Timon's* story as a fit vehicle for poetic satire . . . while, as to the rest, he contented himself with a rapid and careless composition of some scenes and probably on others (such as that of Alcibiades with the Senate) contenting himself with simply sketching out the substance of an intended dialogue to be afterwards elaborated.'[31] In 1869 this conception of the authorship was further discussed by Tschischwitz.[32] The theory culminated in 1874 in the analysis and argument of Fleay who stated strongly his confidence in Shakespeare's priority.[33] He concludes his Essay as follows: 'The *essential* part of this paper is the proof that the Shakespere part of this play was written *before* the other part.' Among the critics who have, in the main, subscribed to this theory are Rolfe, Hudson, Deighton, Gollancz, and Furnivall. Hudson declares that 'whatsoever may be judged of this theory in other respects it seems to make clear work with the question why there should be in this case so great discrepancy of style and execution joined with such general unity of purpose and movement.'[34] Apropos of the second theory, that Shakespeare revised an earlier play, the same critic says: 'Shakespeare's approved severity of taste and strength of judgment at that period of his life, together with his fulness and availability of resource, would hardly have endured to retain certain parts in so crude and feeble a state as we here find them.'[35] This belief in Shake-

speare's priority has grown, and, unless some new subversive evidence appears, can hardly be shaken.[36]

Although the dual authorship of *Timon of Athens* has been long admitted, comparatively little has been done to identify the second author. The inferior parts of the play have been variously ascribed—with meagre evidence, in every case—to Thomas Heywood (d. 1650?), George Wilkins (fl. 1607), John Day (fl.1606), and Cyril Tourneur (1575?-1626). Verplanck surmises that when the play was wanted by Heming and Condell 'some literary artist like Heywood was invited to fill up the accessory and subordinate parts of the play upon the author's own outline, and this was done, or attempted to be done, in the manner of the great original, as far as possible, but with distinction of his varieties of style.[37] Delius believed that both *Pericles* and *Timon* showed the hand of George Wilkins, but his evidence is unconvincing.[38] Wright, in commenting upon this latter theory, declares, with reason, that 'the nearer a reviewer comes to thinking that George Wilkins wrote the regular though wooden verse of the first two acts of *Pericles*, the farther he will be from a belief that the same man wrote the highly irregular verse of the interpolations in *Timon*.'[39]

Fleay does not press his theory strongly, but points out that in ratio of rhyme to blank verse, irregularities of length, and double endings, *Timon of Athens* resembles closely *The Revenger's Tragedy* (1607) by Tourneur. He notes that Tourneur is fond of quoting Latin.

Fleay subjoins passages from *The Revenger's Tragedy* which he finds to be in exactly the strain of the unknown author of *Timon of Athens*,[40] and states positively his belief that 'Cyril Tourneur was the only person connected with the King's Company who could have written the other part of the play.'[41] It should be observed that Fleay's identification of Tourneur as reviser of *Timon* loses force if Tourneur's authorship of *The Revenger's Tragedy* be denied.

---

30 *The Works of William Shakespeare* edited by Henry Irving and Frank A. Marshall, Introduction to *Timon of Athens*.

31 *The Illustrated Shakespeare*, edited by G. C. Verplanck (New York, 1847), Introduction to *Timon of Athens*.

32 *Jahrbuch*, 1869, 160-197.

33 *Transactions of the New Shakspere Society*, 1874.

34 *Shakespeare's Complete Works*, edited by H. N. Hudson, Introduciton to *Timon of Athens*.

35 *Ibid.*

36 E. H. Wright, in *The Authorship of Timon of Athens*, elaborates upon the theory of Shakespeare's priority. Reasoning that nine lines of a ten-line prose passage (II. ii. 198-209) are genuine, Wright is enabled to advance the theory that the germane scenes are also Shakespeare's (III. i., and III. ii.). If these two scenes are spurious, as they have been usually considered, Shakespeare's share of the play has been inadequately motivated. If, on the other hand, these two scenes are from his pen, Shakespeare himself has motivated Timon's misanthropy, and his priority in composition is rendered more likely. (A second apparent gap in the play has been the lack of motivation for the assistance given Timon by Alcibiades. Wright shows how the interpolator tried to close this gap, and suggests how Shakespeare himself may have planned to fill it.) As an additional argument for Shakespeare's priority Wright also notes that every point at which the play follows a source 'falls within a scene that Shakespeare wrote—that every episode or line for which a source is known comes from his pen.' In concluding his argument for Shakespeare's priority Wright says: 'Ten spurious scenes and passages scattered through Shakspere's play and filling one third of it; and Shakspere never using them, never counting on them, never, except to suggest one (III. vi. 51: "Alcibiades is banished.") making a mention of them,—unaware of them. Lift them bodily from the play, and not a word will tell that they were ever in it. The fact is final. Those scenes and passages were no nucleus around which Shakspere built his play. They were extensions to the play he had already built.'

37 *The Illustrated Shakespeare*, edited by G. C. Verplanck, (New York, 1847), Introduction to *Timon of Athens*.

38 *Jahrbuch*, 1867, p. 175.

39 *The Authorship of Timon of Athens*, p. 101.

40 Dodsley's Edition, pp. 322, 384.

41 See *Transactions of the New Shakspere Society*, 1874, pp. 138-139.

ACT FIRST ❧ SCENE FIRST

[Athens. A Hall in Timon's House]
Enter Poet, Painter, Jeweller, Merchant, and Mercer, at several doors.

Poet. Good day, sir.
Pain.   I am glad you're well.
Poet. I have not seen you long: how goes the world?
Pain. It wears, sir, as it grows.
Poet.   Ay, that's well known: 5
But what particular rarity? what strange,
Which manifold record not matches? See,
Magic of bounty! all these spirits thy power
Hath conjur'd to attend. I know the merchant.
Pain. I know them both; th' other's a jeweller.   10
Merch. O, 'tis a worthy lord!
Jew.   Nay, that's most fix'd.
Merch. A most incomparable man, breath'd, as it were,
To an untirable and continuate goodness:
He passes.   15
Jew. I have a jewel here—
Merch. O, pray, let's see't: for the Lord Timon, sir?
Jew. If he will touch the estimate: but, for that—
Poet. 'When we for recompense have prais'd the vile,
It stains the glory in that happy verse   20
Which aptly sings the good.'
Merch. [Looking at the jewel.] 'Tis a good form.
Jew. And rich: here is a water, look ye.
Pain. You are rapt, sir, in some work, some dedication
To the great lord.   25
Poet.   A thing slipp'd idly from me.
Our poesy is as a gum, which oozes
From whence 'tis nourish'd: the fire i' the flint
Shows not till it be struck; our gentle flame
Provokes itself, and, like the current, flies   30
Each bound it chafes. What have you there?
Pain. A picture, sir. When comes your book forth?
Poet. Upon the heels of my presentment, sir.
Let's see your piece.
Pain. 'Tis a good piece.   35
Poet. So 'tis: this comes off well and excellent.
Pain. Indifferent.
Poet.   Admirable: how this grace
Speaks his own standing! what a mental power
This eye shoots forth! how big imagination   40
Moves in this lip! to the dumbness of the gesture
One might interpret.
Pain. It is a pretty mocking of the life.
Here is a touch; is 't good?
Poet.   I'll say of it,   45
It tutors nature: artificial strife
Lives in these touches, livelier than life.

Enter certain Senators [who pass over the stage].

Pain. How this lord is follow'd!
Poet. The senators of Athens: happy man!
Pain. Look, moe!   50
Poet. You see this confluence, this great flood of visitors.
I have, in this rough work, shap'd out a man,
Whom this beneath world doth embrace and hug
With amplest entertainment: my free drift
Halts not particularly, but moves itself   55
In a wide sea of wax: no levell'd malice
Infects one comma in the course I hold;
But flies an eagle flight, bold and forth on,
Leaving no tract behind.
Pain. How shall I understand you?   60
Poet.   I will unbolt to you.
You see how all conditions, how all minds,
As well of glib and slippery creatures as
Of grave and austere quality, tender down
Their services to Lord Timon: his large fortune,   65
Upon his good and gracious nature hanging,
Subdues and properties to his love and tendance
All sorts of hearts; yea, from the glass-fac'd flatterer
To Apemantus, that few things love better
Then to abhor himself: even he drops down   70
The knee before him, and returns in peace
Most rich in Timon's nod.
Pain.   I saw them speak together.
Poet. Sir, I have upon a high and pleasant hill
Feign'd Fortune to be thron'd: the base o' the mount   75
Is rank'd with all deserts, all kind of natures,
That labour on the bosom of this sphere
To propagate their states: amongst them all,
Whose eyes are on this sovereign lady fix'd,
One do I personate of Lord Timon's frame,   80
Whom Fortune with her ivory hand wafts to her;
Whose present grace to present slaves and servants
Translates his rivals.
Pain.   'Tis conceiv'd to scope.
This throne, this Fortune, and this hill, methinks,   85
With one man beckon'd from the rest below,
Bowing his head against the steepy mount
To climb his happiness, would be well express'd
In our condition.
Poet.   Nay, sir, but hear me on.   90
All those which were his fellows but of late,
Some better than his value, on the moment
Follow his strides, his lobbies fill with tendance,
Rain sacrificial whisperings in his ear,
Make sacred even his stirrup, and through him   95
Drink the free air.
Pain.   Ay, marry, what of these?
Poet. When Fortune in her shift and change of mood
Spurns down her late belov'd, all his dependants

SCENE ONE. S. d. and Mercer; *cf. n.*   **2 long:** *for a long time*   **4 grows:** *grows older; cf. n.*   **6, 7 what strange, etc.:** *what unusual event*   **12 fix'd:** *certain*   **13 breath'd:** *inured*   **14 continuate:** *lasting*   **15 passes:** *surpasses*   **18 touch the estimate:** *pay the price of which it is valued*   **19 'When we for recompense,' etc.;** *cf. n.*   **23 water:** *lustre*   **24 rapt:** *transported*   **29–31 our gentle flame . . . chafes;** *cf. n.*   **33 present-ment:** *dedication; cf. n.*   **36 comes off:** *turns out*   **37 Indifferent:** *reasonably well*   **39 standing:** *position (?); cf. n.*   **41 to the dumbness, etc.;** *cf. n.*   **46 artificial strife:** *vying of art with nature*

50 moe: *more*   **52 shap'd out:** *imagine*   **53 beneath world:** *world below*   **54 drift:** *aim*   **55 particularly:** *at any individual person*   **56 wide sea of wax:** *cf. n.* **levell'd:** *designed (?); cf. n.*   **58 forth on:** *forward*   **59 tract:** *tract*   **61 unbolt:** *disclose*   **67 properties:** *appropriates* **tendance:** *service*   **68 glass-facd:** *reflecting, like a mirror, the looks of another*   **76 Is rank'd with all deserts:** *has men of all kinds standing in rows*   **78 states:** *fortunes*   **80 personate:** *represent*   **81 wafts:** *beckons*   **82 present salves:** *im-mediate slaves*   **83 Translates:** *transforms* **to scope:** *to the purpose*   **87 steepy:** *difficult to ascend*   **88, 89 would . . . condition;** *cf. n.*   **94 sacrificial:** *having the character of sacrifice offered to a god*   **97 marry:** *by Mary, an oath*

Which labour'd after him to the mountain's top   *100*
Even on their knees and hands, let him slip down,
Not one accompanying his declining foot.
    Pain. 'Tis common:
A thousand moral paintings I can show,
That shall demonstrate these quick blows of Fortune's   *105*
More pregnantly than words. Yet you do well
To show Lord Timon that mean eyes have seen
The foot above the head.

    Trumpets sound. Enter Lord Timon, addressing himself
    courteously to every suitor. [A Messenger from Ventidius
    talking with him; Lucilius and other servants following.]

    Tim.   Imprison'd is he, say you?
    Mess. Ay, my good lord: five talents is his debt;   *110*
Iis means most short, his creditors most strait:
Your honourable letter he desires
To those have shut him up; which failing,
Periods his comfort.
    Tim.   Noble Ventidius! Well: *115*
I am not of that feather to shake off
My friend when he must need me. I do know him
A gentleman that well deserves a help:
Which he shall have: I'll pay the debt and free him.
    Mess. Your lordship ever binds him.   *120*
    Tim. Commend me to him: I will send his ransom;
And, being enfranchis'd, bid him come to me.
'Tis not enough to help the feeble up,
But to support him after. Fare you well.
    Mess.   All happiness to your honour!   *Exit.* *125*

    Enter an old Athenian.

    Old Ath. Lord Timon, hear me speak.
    Tim.   Freely, good father.
    Old Ath. Thou hast a servant nam'd Lucilius.
    Tim. I have so: what of him?
    Old Ath. Most noble Timon, call the man before thee.   *130*
    Tim. Attends he here, or no? Lucilius!
    Luc. Here, at your lordship's service.
    Old Ath. This fellow here, Lord Timon, this thy creature,
By night frequents my house. I am a man
That from my first have been inclin'd to thrift,   *135*
And my estate deserves an heir more rais'd
Than one which holds a trencher.
    Tim.   Well, what further?
    Old Ath. One only daughter have I, no kin else,
On whom I may confer what I have got: *140*
The maid is fair, o' the youngest for a bride,
And I have bred her at my dearest cost
In qualities of the best. This man of thine
Attempts her love: I prithee, noble lord,
Join with me to forbid him her resort;   *145*
Myself have spoke in vain.
    Tim.   The man is honest.
    Old Ath. Therefore he will be, Timon:
His honesty rewards him in itself;

It must not bear my daughter.   *150*
    Tim.   Does she love him?
    Old Ath. She is young and apt:
Our own precedent passions do instruct us
What levity's in youth.
    Tim. [*To Lucilius.*] Love you the maid?   *155*
    Luc. Ay, my good lord; and she accepts of it.
    Old Ath. If in her marriage my consent be missing,
I call the gods to witness, I will choose
Mine heir from forth the beggars of the world
And dispossess her all.   *160*
    Tim.   How shall she be endow'd,
If she be mated with an equal husband?
    Old Ath. Three talents on the present; in future, all.
    Tim. This gentleman of mine hath serv'd me long:
To build his fortune I will strain a little,   *165*
For 'tis a bond in men. Give him thy daughter:
What you bestow, in him I'll counterpoise,
And make him weigh with her.
    Old Ath.   Most noble lord,
Pawn me to this your honour, she is his.   *170*
    Tim. My hand to thee; mine honour on my promise.
    Luc. Humbly I thank your lordship: never may
That state or fortune fall into my keeping,
Which is not ow'd to you!   *Exit [with old Athenian].*
    Poet. Vouchsafe my labour, and long live your lordship! *175*
    Tim. I thank you; you shall hear from me anon:
Go not away. What have you there, my friend?
    Pain. A piece of painting, which I do beseech
Your lordship to accept.
    Tim.   Painting is welcome.   *180*
The painting is almost the natural man;
For since dishonour traffics with man's nature,
He is but outside: these pencil'd figures are
Even such as they give out. I like your work,
And you shall find I like it: wait attendance   *185*
Till you hear further from me.
    Pain.   The gods preserve ye!
    Tim. Well fare you, gentleman: give me your hand;
We must needs dine together. Sir, your jewel
Hath suffer'd under praise.   *190*
    Jew.   What, my lord! dispraise?
    Tim. A mere satiety of commendations.
If I should pay you for 't as 'tis extoll'd,
It would unclew me quite.
    Jew.   My lord, 'tis rated   *195*
As those which sell would give: but you well know,
Things of like value, differing in the owners,
Are prized by their masters. Believe 't, dear lord,
You mend the jewel by the wearing it.
    Tim. Well mock'd.   *200*

    Enter Apemantus.

    Merch. No, my good lord; he speaks the common tongue,
Which all men speak with him.
    Tim. Look, who comes here: will you be chid?

---

104 moral: *allegorical*   **106 pregnantly:** *clearly*   **107 mean eyes:** *eyes of inferiors*   **110 five talents;** *cf. n.*   **111 strait:** *exacting*   **114 Periods:** *brings to an end*   **136 more rais'd:** *of higher station*   **137 holds a trencher:** *serves at table*   **142 dearest:** *utmost*   **145 her resort:** *visiting her by way of courtship*   **147–150 The man is honest ... daughter;** *cf. n.*

150 bear: *carry as a consequence*   **152 apt:** *pliable*   **153 precedent:** *early*   **160 all:** *altogether*   **166 bond in men:** *obligation of affection among men*   **168 weigh:** *equivalent in wealth*   **170 Pawn:** *if you pledge*   **184 give out:** *profess to be*   **185 wait attendance:** *remain near*   **190, 191 Hath ... dispraise;** *cf. n.*   **194 unclew:** *ruin*   **196 As ... give;** *cf. n.*   **198 by:** *according to*

Jew. We'll bear, with your lordship.

Merch.   He'll spare none.   205

Tim. Good morrow to thee, gentle Apemantus!

Apem. Till I be gentle, stay thou for thy good morrow;
When thou art Timon's dog, and these knaves honest.

Tim. Why dost thou call them knaves? thou know'st
them not.   210

Apem. Are they not Athenians?

Tim. Yes.

Apem. Then I repent not.

Jew. You know me, Apemantus?

Apem. Thou know'st I do; I call'd thee by thy name.   215

Tim. Thou art proud, Apemantus?

Apem. Of nothing so much as that I am not like Timon.

Tim. Whither art going?

Apem. To knock out an honest Athenian's brains.

Tim. That's a deed thou't die for.   220

Apem. Right, if doing nothing be death by the law.

Tim. How likest thou this picture, Apemantus?

Aptem. The best, for the innocence.

Tim. Wrought he not well that painted it?

Apem. He wrought better that made the painter; and   225
yet he's but a filthy piece of work.

Pain. You're a dog.

Apem. Thy mother's of my generation:
what's she, if I be a dog?

Tim. Wilt dine with me, Apemantus?   230

Apem. No; I eat not lords.

Tim. An thou shouldst, thou'dst anger ladies.

Apem. O, they eat lords; so they come by
great bellies.

Tim. That's a lascivious apprehension.   235

Apem. So thou apprehendest it: take it for thy labour.

Tim. How dost thou like this jewel, Apemantus?

Apem. Not so well as plain-dealing, which
will not cost a man a doit.

Tim. What dost thou think 'tis worth?   240

Apem. Not worth my thinking. How now, poet!

Poet. How now, philosopher!

Apem. Thou liest.

Poet. Art not one?

Apem. Yes.   245

Poet. Then I lie not.

Apem. Art not a poet?

Poet. Yes.

Apem. Then thou liest: look in thy last work,
where thou hast feigned him a worthy fellow.   250

Poet. That's not feigned; he is so.

Apem. Yes, he is worthy of thee, and to pay thee for thy
labour: he that loves to be flattered is worthy o' the flatterer.
Heavens, that I were a lord!

Tim. What wouldst do then, Apemantus?   255

Apem. Even as Apemantus does now; hate a lord with
my heart.

Tim. What, thyself?

Apem. Ay.

Tim. Wherefore?   260

Apem. That I had no angry wit to be a lord.

Art not thou a merchant?

Merch. Ay, Apemantus.

Apem. Traffic confound thee, if the gods will not!

Merch. If traffic do it, the gods do it.   265

Apem. Traffic's thy god; and thy god confound thee!

Trumpet sounds. Enter a Messenger.

Tim. What trumpet's that?

Mes. 'Tis Alcibiades, and some twenty horse,
All of companionship.

Tim. Pray, entertain them; give them guide to us.   270
             [Exeunt some Attendants.]

You must needs dine with me: go not you hence
Till I have thank'd you: when dinner's done,
Show me this piece. I am joyful of your sights.

Enter Alcibiades with the rest [of his Company].

Most welcome, sir!   275

Apem.   So, so, there!
Aches contract and starve your supple joints!
That there should be small love 'mongst these sweet knaves,
And all this courtesy! The strain of man's bred out
Into baboon and monkey.   280

Alcib. Sir, you have sav'd my longing, and I feed
Most hungerly on your sight.

Tim.   Right welcome, sir!
Ere we depart, we'll share a bounteous time
In different pleasures. Pray you, let us in.   285
         Exeunt [all except Apemantus].

Enter two Lords.

First Lord. What time o' day is 't, Apemantus?

Apem. Time to be honest.

First Lord. That time serves still.

Apem. The most accursed thou, that still omitt'st it.   290

Sec. Lord. Thou art going to Lord Timon's feast?

Apem. Ay, to see meat fill knaves and wine heat fools.

Sec. Lord. Fare thee well, fare thee well.

Apem. Thou art a fool to bid me farewell twice.

Sec. Lord. Why, Apemantus?   295

Apem. Shouldst have kept one to thyself, for
I mean to give thee none.

First Lord. Hang thyself!

Apem. No, I will do nothing at thy bidding: make thy
requests to thy friend.   300

Sec. Lord. Away, unpeaceable dog, or I'll spurn thee hence!

Apem. I will fly, like a dog, the heels o' the ass.   *[Exit.]*

First Lord. He's opposite to humanity. Come shall we in,
And taste Lord Timon's bounty? he outgoes
The very heart of kindness.   305

Sec. Lord. He pours it out; Plutus, the god of gold,
Is but his steward: no meed, but he repays
Sevenfold above itself; no gift to him,
But breeds the giver a return exceeding
All use of quittance.   310

First Lord.   The noblest mind he carries

269 All of companionship: *all belonging to one party*   **277 Aches;** *cf n.*   **starve:** *paralyze*   **279 strain:** *stock*   **bred out:** *degenerated*   **282 hungerly:** *hungrily*   **284 depart:** *take leave of one another*   **289 serves:** *affords an opportunity*   **301 unpeaceable:** *quarrelsome*   **303 opposite:** *hostile*   **304 outgoes:** *exceeds*   **306 Plutus;** *cf.n.*   **307 meed:** *gift*   **310 use of quittance:** *customary requital*

208 When ... honest; *cf. n.*   **223 innocence:** *stupidity*   **232 An:** *if*   **235 apprehension:** *interpretation*   **238 plain-dealing;** *cf. n.*   **239 doit:** *a former Dutch coin, equivalent to half a farthing, a trifle*   **261 That ... lord;** *cf. n.*

That ever govern'd man.

Sec. Lord. Long may he live in fortunes!
Shall we in?

First Lord. I'll keep you company.   *Exeunt.*

❧ Scene Second ❧

[The Same. A Banqueting-room in Timon's House.]
Hautboys playing loud music. A great banquet served in: and
then, Enter Lord Timon, the States, the Athenian Lords,
Ventidius which Timon redeemed from prison. [Enter Alcibiades.
Flavius and other attending.] Then comes, dropping after
all, Apemantus, discontentedly, like himself.

Ven. Most honour'd Timon,
hath pleas'd the gods to remember my father's age,
And call him to long peace.
He is gone happy, and has left me rich:
Then, as in grateful virtue I am bound   5
To your free heart, I do return those talents,
Doubled with thanks and service, from whose help
I deriv'd liberty.

Tim.   O, by no means,
Honest Ventidius; you mistake my love: 10
I gave it freely ever; and there's none
Can truly say he gives, if he receives:
If our betters play at that game, we must not dare
To imitate them; faults that are rich are fair.

Ven. A noble spirit!   15

[They all stand ceremoniously looking on Timon.]

Tim. Nay, my lords, ceremony was but devis'd at first
To set a gloss on faint deeds, hollow welcomes,
Recanting goodness, sorry ere 'tis shown;
But where there is true friendship, there needs none.
Pray, sit; more welcome are yet to my fortunes   20
Than my fortunes to me.   *[They sit.]*

First Lord. My lord, we always have confess'd it.

Apem. Ho, ho, confess'd it! hang'd it, have you not?

Tim. O, Apemantus, you are welcome.

Apem.   No;   25
You shall not make me welcome:
I come to have thee thrust me out of doors.

Tim. Fie, thou'rt a churl; ye've got a humour there
Does not become a man; 'tis much to blame.
They say, my lords, 'Ira furor brevis est';   30
But yond man is ever angry.
Go, let him have a table by himself;
For he does niether affect company,
Nor is he fit for 't, indeed.

Apem. Let me stay at thine apperil, Timon: 35
I come to observe; I give thee warning on 't.

Tim. I take no heed of thee; thou'rt an
Athenian, therefore, welcome: I myself would
have no power; prithee, let my meat make thee silent.

Apem. I scorn thy meat; 'twould choke me, for I should   40
Ne'er flatter thee. O you gods, what a number

Of men eat Timon, and he sees 'em not!
It grieves me to see so many dip their meat
In one man's blood; and all the madness is,
He cheers them up too.   45
I wonder men dare trust themselves with men:
Methinks they should invite them without knives;
Good for their meat, and safer for their lives.
There's much example for 't; the fellow that
Sits next him now, parts bread with him, and pledges   50
The breath of him in a divided draught.
Is the readiest man to kill him: 't has been prov'd.
If I were a huge man, I should fear to drink at meals,
Lest they should spy my wind-pipe's dangerous notes;
Great men should drink with harness on their throats.   55

Tim. My lord, in heart, and let the health go round.

Sec. Lord. Let it flow this way, my good lord.

Apem. Flow this way! A brave fellow! he keeps his tides well.
Those healths will make thee and thy state look ill, Timon.
Here's that which is too weak to be a sinner,   60
Honest water, which ne'er left man i' the mire:
This and my food are equals; there's no odds:
Feasts are too proud to give thanks to the gods.

Apemantus's Grace

'Immortal gods, I crave no pelf;
I pray for no man but myself: 65
Grant I may never prove so fond,
To trust man on his oath or bond,
Or a harlot for her weeping,
Or a dog that seems a-sleeping,
Or a keeper with my freedom;   70
Or my friends, if I should need 'em.
Amen. So fall to 't:
Rich men sin, and I eat root.'

[Eats and drinks.]

Much good dich they good heart, Apemantus!

Tim. Captain Alcibiades, your heart's in the field now.   75

Alcib. My heart is ever at your service, my lord.

Tim. You had rather be at a breakfast of enemies than a
dinner of friends.

Alcib. So they were bleeding-new, my lord, there's no meat
like 'em: I could wish my best friend at such a feast.   80

Apem. Would all those flatterers were thine enemies, then,
that then thou mightst kill 'em and bid me to 'em!

First Lord. Might we but have that happiness, my lord, that
you would once use our hearts, whereby we might express
some part of our zeals, we should think ourselves for ever   85
perfect.

Tim. O, no doubt, my good friends, but the gods themselves have provided that I shall have much help from you:
how had you been my friends else? why have you that charitable title from thousands, did not you chiefly belong to my   90
heart? I have told more of you to myself than you can with
modesty speak in your own behalf, and thus far I confirm you.
O you gods, think I, what need we have any friends, if we
should ne'er have need of 'em? they were the most needless
creatures living should we ne'er have use for 'em, and   95

Scene Two, S. D. States: *princes* which: *whom* dropping after all: *lingering*   **22, 23**
confess'd ... not; *cf. n.*   **28** humour: *disposition*   **30–45;** *cf. n.*   **30** 'Ira furor
brevis est'; *cf. n.*   **33** affect: *like*   **35** apperil: *risk*   **39** power: *i.e., to make you silent*

47 Methinks ... knives; *cf. n.*   **48** Good: *that would be good*   **54** dangerous notes:
signs of vulnerability   **55** harness: *armor*   **56** in heart: *cheer up*   **67** fond: *foolish*   **74** dich: *do it*   **79** bleeding-new: *freshly killed*   **86** perfect: *satisfied*   **89, 90**
charitable title: *name of endearment*   from: *from among*

would most resemble sweet instruments hung up in cases, that
keep their sounds to themselves. Why, I have often wished myself poorer, that I might come nearer to you. We are born to
do benefits: and what better or properer can we call our own
than the riches of our friends? O, what a precious comfort *100*
'tis, to have so many, like brothers, commanding one another's fortunes! O joy, e'en made away ere 't can be born! Mine eyes cannot
hold out water, methinks: to forget their faults I drink to you.

 Apem. Thou weep'st to make them drink, Timon.

 Sec. Lord. Joy had the like conception in our eyes, *105*
And, at that instant, like a babe, sprung up.

 Apem. Ho, ho! I laugh to think that babe a bastard.

 Third Lord. I promise you, my lord, you mov'd me much.

 Apem Much!   *Sound Tucket.*

 Tim. What means that trump? *110*

Enter Servant.

    How now!

 Serv. Please you, my lord, there are certain ladies most
desirous of admittance.

 Tim. Ladies! What are their wills?

 Serv. There comes with them a forerunner, my lord, *115*
which bears that office, to signify their pleasures.

 Tim. I pray, let them be admitted.

Enter Cupid.

 Cup. Hail to thee, worthy Timon! and to all
That of his bounties taste! The five best senses
Acknowledge thee their patron, and come freely *120*
To gratulate thy plenteous bosom: th' ear,
Taste, touch, and smell, pleas'd from thy table rise;
They only now come but to feast thine eyes.

 Tim. They're welcome all; let 'em have kind admittance:
Music, make their welcome! *[Exit Cupid.]* *125*

 First Lord. You see, my lord, how ample you're beloved.

*[Music.] Enter Cupid with the masque of Ladies [as] Amazons,
 with lutes in their hands, dancing and playing.*

 Apem. Hoy-day, what a sweep of vanity comes this way!
They dance! they are mad women.
Like madness is the glory of this life,
As this pomp shows to a little oil and root. *130*
We make ourselves fools, to disport ourselves,
And spend our flatteries, to drink those men
Upon whose age we void it up again
With poisonous spite and envy.
Who lives, that's not depraved or depraves? *135*
Who dies, that bears not one spurn to their graves
Of their friend's gift?
I should fear those that dance before me now
Would one day stamp upon me: 't has been done;
Men shut their doors against a setting sun. *140*

*The Lords rise from table, with much adoring of Timon; and to
show their loves each singles out an Amazon, and all dance, men
with women, a lofty strain or two to the hautboys, and cease.*

 Tim. You have done our pleasures much grace, fair ladies,
Set a fair fashion on our entertainment,
Which was not half so beautiful and kind;
You have added worth unto 't and lustre,
And entertain'd me with mine own device: *145*
I am to thank you for 't.

 First Lady. My lord, you take us even at the best.

 Apem. Faith, for the worst is filthy, and would not hold
taking, I doubt me.

 Tim. Ladies, there is an idle banquet *150*
Attends you: please you to dispose yourselves.

 All Lad. Most thankfully, my lord.

       Exeunt [Cupid and Ladies].

 Tim. Flavius!

 Flav. My lord?

 Tim.   The little casket bring me hither. *155*

 Flav. Yes, my lord. *[Aside.]* More jewels yet!
There is no crossing him in 's humour;
Else I should tell him—well, i' faith, I should—
When all's spent, he'd be cross'd then, an he could.
'Tis pity bounty had not eyes behind, *160*
That man might ne'er be wretched for his mind. *Exit.*

 First Lord. Where be our men?

 Serv. Here, my lord, in readiness.

 Sec. Lord. Our horses!

Enter Flavius [with the casket].

 Tim. O, my friends! I have one word to say to you; *165*
Look you, my good lord,
I must entreat you, honour me so much
As to advance this jewel; accept it and wear it,
Kind my lord.

 First Lord. I am so far already in your gifts,— *170*

 All. So are we all.

Enter a Servant.

 Serv. My lord, there are certain nobles of the senate
Newly alighted and come to visit you.

 Tim. They are fairly welcome.

 Flav.   I beseech your honour, *175*
Vouchsafe me a word; it does concern you near.

 Tim. Near! why, then, another time I'll hear thee:
I prithee, let's be provided to show them entertainment.

 Flav. [Aside.] I scarce know how.

Enter another Servant.

 Sec. Serv. May it please your honour, Lord Lucius, *180*
Our of his free love, hath presented to you
Four milk-white horses, trapp'd in silver.

 Tim. I shall accept them fairly: let the presents
Be worthily entertain'd.

Enter a third Servant.

    How now! what news? *185*

 Third Serv. Please you, my lord, that honourable gentleman,

101, 102 O joy … born; *cf. n.* 104 Thou weep'st … Timon; *cf. n.* 106 sprung
up: *stirred within us, quickened* S. d. Tucket: *trumpet call* S. d. Enter Cupid; *cf. n.* 121
gratulate: *salute* 126 ample: *fully* S. d. with … Amazons; *cf. n.* 127 Hoy-day:
exclamation of surprise 128 mad women; *cf. n.* 129, 130 Like madness … root;
cf. n. 133 void … up: *vomit* 135 depraved: *vilified* depraves: *vilifies* 136, 137
spurn … gift: *contemptuous blow received from a friend* 140 *Cf. n.*

143 kind: *gracious* 148, 149 hold taking: *endure handling* doubt: *fear* 150 idle:
trifling banquet: *dessert* 151 Attends: *which awaits* 159 *Cf. n.* 160, 161 'Tis pity
… mind; *cf. n.* mind: *magnanimity* 168 advance: *do honor to (by taking it into your
possession)* 174 fairly: *courteously* 176 near: *intimately* 177 *Cf. n.* 184 entertain'd: *accepted*

Lord Lucullus, entreats your company to-morrow to hunt with
him, and has sent your honour two brace of greyhounds.

Tim. I'll hunt with him; and let them be receiv'd,
Not without fair reward.   *190*

Flav.   [Aside.] What will this come to?
He commands us to provide, and give great gifts,
And all out of an empty coffer:
Nor will he know his purse, or yield me this,
To show him what a beggar his heart is,   *195*
Being of no power to make his wishes good.
His promises fly so beyond his state
That what he speaks is all in debt; he owes
For every word: he is so kind that he now
Pays interest for 't; his land's put to their books.   *200*
Well, would I were gently put out of office,
Before I were forc'd out!
Happier he that has no friend to feed
Than such that do e'en enemies exceed.
I bleed inwardly for my lord.   *Exit.*   *205*

Tim.   You do yourselves
Much wrong, you bate too much of your own merits.
Here, my lord, a trifle of our love.

Sec. Lord. With more than common thanks I will receive it.

Third Lord. O, he's the very soul of bounty!   *210*

Tim. And now I remember, my lord, you gave
Good words the other day of a bay courser
I rode on. It is yours, because you lik'd it.

Third Lord. O, I beseech you, pardon me, my lord, in that.

Tim. You may take my word, my lord; I know no man *215*
Can justly praise, but what he does affect:
I weigh my friend's affection with mine own:
I'll tell you true. I'll call to you.

All Lords.   O, none so welcome.

Tim. I take all and your several visitations   *220*
So kind to heart, 'tis not enough to give:
Methinks, I could deal kingdoms to my friends,
And ne'er be weary. Alcibiades,
Thou art a soldier, therefore seldom rich;
It comes in charity to thee: for all thy living   *225*
Is 'mongst the dead, and all the lands thou hast
Lie in a pitch'd field.

Alcib.   Ay, defil'd land, my lord.

First Lord. We are so virtuously bound—

Tim.   And so   *230*
Am I to you.

Sec. Lord. So infinitely endear'd,—

Tim. All to you. Lights, more lights!

First Lord.   The best of happiness,
Honour, and fortunes, keep with you, Lord Timon!   *235*

Tim. Ready for his friends.   *Exeunt Lords.*

Apem.   .   What a coil's here!
Serving of becks and jutting-out of bums!
I doubt whether their legs be worth the sums
That are given for 'em. Friendship's full of dregs: *240*
Methinks, false hearts should never have sound legs.
Thus honest fools lay out their wealth on court'sies.

Tim. Now, Apemantus, if thou wert not sullen,
I would be good to thee.

Apem. No, I'll nothing: for if I should be bribed too,   *245*
there would be none left to rail upon thee; and then thou
wouldst sin the faster. Thou givest so long, Timon, I fear me
thou wilt give away thyself in paper shortly: what needs these
feasts, pomps, and vain-glories?

Tim. Nay, an you begin to rail on society once, I am   *250*
sworn not to give regard to you.
Farewell; and come with better music.   *Exit.*

Apem. So:
Thou wilt not hear me now; thou shalt not then;
I'll lock thy heaven from thee.   *255*
O, that men's ears should be
To counsel deaf, but not to flattery!   *Exit*

ACT SECOND ❧ SCENE SECOND

[Athens. A room in a Senator's House]
Enter a Senator [with papers in his hand].

Sen. And late five thousand: to Varro and to Isidore
He owes nine thousand; besides my former sum,
Which makes it five and twenty. Still in motion
Of raging waste? It cannot hold; it will not.
If I want gold, steal but a beggar's dog   *5*
And give it Timon, why, the dog coins gold:
If I would sell my horse and buy twenty moe
Better than he, why, give my horse to Timon;
Ask nothing, give it him, it foals me, straight,
And able horses. No porter at his gate,   *10*
But rather one that smiles and still invites
All that pass by. It cannot hold; no reason
Can found his state in safety. Caphis, ho!
Caphis, I say!

Enter Caphis.

Caph. Here, sir; what is your pleasure?   *15*

Sen. Get on your cloak, and haste you to Lord Timon;
Importune him for my moneys; be not ceas'd
With slight denial; nor then silenc'd, when—
'Commend me to your master'—and the cap
Plays in the right hand, thus: but tell him,   *20*
My uses cry to me, I must serve my turn
Out of mine own; his days and times are past,
And my reliances on his fracted dates
Have smit my credit: I love and honour him,
But must not break my back to heal his finger: *25*
Immediate are my needs; and my relief
Must not be toss'd and turn'd to me in words,
But find supply immediate. Get you gone:
Put on a most importunate aspect,
A visage of demand; for, I do fear,   *30*
When every feather sticks in his own wing,
Lord Timon will be left a naked gull,
Which flashes now a phoenix. Get you gone.

Caph. I go, sir.

---

194 yield: *grant*   **204 such:** *such friends*   **207 bate:** *deduct*   **218 I'll call to you;**
cf. n.   **220 visitations:** *visits*   **228 defil'd;** *cf. n.*   **229 bound:** *under obliga-*
tion   **237 coil:** *fuss*   **238** *Offering of obeisances and excessive bowing*   **239 legs;** *cf. n.*

248 paper: *bonds*   **252 come . . . music;** *cf. n.*   **255 heaven:** *salvation, good advice*   **1**
late: *lately*   **10 No porter, etc.;** *cf. n.*   **11 still:** *always*   **12 hold:** *continue*   **17 be**
not ceas'd: *do not allow yourself to be silenced*   **21 uses:** *needs*   **23 fracted:** *bro-*
ken   **27 turn'd:** *flung back*   **31 his:** *its (that of the bird to which it belongs); cf. n.*

Sen. 'I go, sir!' Take the bonds along with you,   *35*
And have the dates in compt.
Caph.   I will, sir.
Sen.   Go.   *Exeunt.*

❧ Scene Second ❧

[The Same. A Hall in Timon's House]
Enter Steward [Flavius] with many bills in his hand.

Flav. No care, no stop! so senseless of expense,
That he will neither know how to maintain it,
Nor cease his flow of riot: takes no account
How things go from him; nor resumes no care
Of what is to continue: never mind   *5*
Was to be so unwise, to be so kind.
What shall be done? He will not hear, till feel:
I must be round with him, now he comes from hunting.
Fie, fie, fie, fie!

Enter Caphis, [and the Servants of] Isidore and Varro.

Caph.   Good even, Varro. What,   *10*
You come for money?
Var. Serv.   Is 't not your business too?
Caph. It is: and yours too, Isidore?
Isid. Serv.   It is so.
Caph. Would we were all discharged!   *15*
Var. Serv.   I fear it.
Caph. Here comes the lord!

Enter Timon, and his Train [Alcibiades, Lords, and Others].

Tim. So soon as dinner's done, we'll forth again,
My Alcibiades. With me? what is your will?
Caph. My lord, here is a note of certain dues.   *20*
Tim. Dues! Whence are you?
Caph.   Of Athens here, my lord.
Tim. Go to my steward.
Caph. Please it your lordship, he hath put me off
To the succession of new days this month: *25*
My master is awak'd by great occasion
To call upon his own, and humbly prays you
That with your other noble parts you'll suit
In giving him his right.
Tim.   Mine honest friend,   *30*
I prithee but repair to me next morning.
Caph. Nay, good my lord,—
Tim.   Contain thyself, good friend.
Var. Serv. One Varro's servant, my good lord,—
Isid. Serv.   From Isidore: *35*
He humbly prays your speedy payment.
Caph. If you did know, my lord, my master's wants,—
Var. Serv. 'Twas due on forfeiture, my lord, six weeks
And past.
Isid. Serv. Your steward puts me off, my lord;   *40*
And I am sent expressly to your lordship.
Tim. Give me breath.

I do beseech you, good my lords, keep on;
I'll wait upon you instantly.   *[Exeunt Alcibiades and Lords.]*
    [To Flavius.] Come hither: pray you,   *45*
How goes the world, that I am thus encounter'd
With clamorous demands of date-broke bonds,
And the detention of long-since-due debts,
Against my honour?
Flav.   Please you, gentlemen,   *50*
The time is unagreeable to this business:
Your importunacy cease till after dinner,
That I may make his lordship understand
Wherefore you are not paid.
Tim.   Do so, my friends.   *55*
See them well entertained.   *[Exit.]*
Flav. Pray, draw near.   *Exit.*

Enter Apemantus and Fool.

Caph. Stay, stay, here comes the fool with
Apemantus: let's ha' some sport with 'em.
Var. Serv. Hang him, he'll abuse us.   *60*
Isid. Serv. A plague upon him, dog!
Var. Serv. How dost, fool?
Apem. Dost dialogue with thy shadow?
Var. Serv. I speak not to thee.
Apem. No, 'tis to thyself.   *[To the Fool.]*   *65*
Come away.
Isid. Serv. [To Var. Serv.] There's the fool hangs on your
back already.
Apem. No, thou stand'st single; thou'rt not on him yet.
Caph. Where's the fool now?   *70*
Apem. He last asked the question. Poor rogues, and
usurers' men! bawds between gold and want!
All Serv. What are we, Apemantus?
Apem. Asses.
All Serv. Why?   *75*
Apem. That you ask me what you are, and do not know
yourselves. Speak to 'em, fool.
Food. How do you, gentlemen?
All Serv. Gramercies, good fool: how does your mistress?
Fool. She's e'en setting on water to scald such chickens   *80*
as you are. Would we could see you at Corinth!
Apem. Good! gramercy.

Enter Page.

Fool. Look you, here comes my mistress' page.
Page. [To the Fool.] Why, how now, captain! what do
you in this wise company? How dost thou, Apemantus?   *85*
Apem. Would I had a rod in my mouth, that I might
answer thee profitably.
Page. Prithee, Apemantus, read me the superscription of
these letters: I know not which is which.
Apem. Canst not read?   *90*
Page. No.
Apem. There will little learning die then, that day thou art
hanged. This is to Lord Timon; this is Alcibiades. Go; thou
wast born a bastard, and thou'lt die a bawd.

36 compt: *reckoning, for the calculation of interest due*   **4 resumes:** *takes*   **5, 6 never mind, etc.;** *cf. n.*   **7 hear, till feel:** *listen to warnings till the actual disaster befalls him*   **8 round:** *plain*   **12–14 Varro . . . Isidore;** *cf. n.*   **15 discharged:** *paid*   **18 we'll forth again;** *cf. n.*   **25 To the succession of new days:** *from one day to another*   **26 occasion:** *particular need*   **28 parts:** *endowments*   **suit:** *be consistent*   **31 but:** *only*   **repair:** *return*

47 date-broke: *overdue*   **51 unagreeable:** *unsuitable*   **69 No, thou . . . yet;** *cf. n.*   **71 He:** *he who*   **79 Gramercies:** *God-a-mercy, God reward you*   **81 Corinth:** *(allusively) house of ill fame*   **84 captain:** *a familiar term of address*

Page. Thou wast whelped a dog, and thou shalt famish,   *95*
—a dog's death. Answer not; I am gone.   *Exit.*

    Apem. E'en so thou outrunn'st grace.
Fool, I will go with you to Lord Timon's.

    Fool. Will you leave me there?

    Apem. If Timon stay at home. You three serve three   *100*
usurers?

    All Serv. Ay; would they served us!

    Apem. So would I,—as good a trick as ever hangman
served thief.

    Fool. Are you three usurers' men?   *105*

    All Serv. Ay, fool.

    Fool. I think no usurer but has a fool to his servant: my
mistress is one, and I am her fool. When men come to borrow
of your masters, they approach sadly, and go away merry;
but they enter my mistress' house merrily, and go away   *110*
sadly: the reason of this?

    Var. Serv. I could render one.

    Apem. Do it, then, that we may account thee a whoremaster
and a knave; which notwithstanding, thou shalt be no less
esteemed.   *115*

    Var. Serv. What is a whoremaster, fool?

    Fool. A fool in good clothes, and something like thee. 'Tis a
spirit: sometime 't appears like a lord; sometime like a lawyer;
sometime like a philosopher, with two stones moe than 's
artificial one. He is very often like a knight; and generally,   *120*
in all shapes that man goes up and down in from fourscore
to thirteen, this spirit walks in.

    Var. Serv. Thou art not altogether a fool.

    Fool. Nor thou altogether a wise man: as much foolery
as I have, so much wit thou lack'st.   *125*

    Apem. That answer might have become Apemantus.

    All Serv. Aside, aside; here comes Lord Timon.

         Enter Timon and Steward [Flavius].

    Apem. Come with me, fool, come.

    Fool. I do not always follow lover, elder brother, and
woman; sometime the philosopher.   *130*

         [Exeunt Apemantus and Fool.]

    Flav. Pray you, walk near: I'll speak with you anon.

         Exeunt [Servants].

    Tim. You make me marvel; wherefore, ere this time,
Had you not fully laid my state before me,
That I might so have rated my expense
As I had leave of means?   *135*

    Flav.   You would not hear me,
At many leisures I propos'd.

    Tim.   Go to:
Perchance some single vantages you took,
When my indisposition put you back;   *140*
And that unaptness made your minister,
Thus to excuse yourself.

    Flav.   O my good lord,
At many times I brought in my accounts,
Laid them before you; you would throw them off,   *145*
And say, you found them in mine honesty.
When for some trifling present you have bid me

Return so much, I have shook my head and wept;
Yea, 'gainst the authority of manners, pray'd you
To hold your hand more close: I did endure   *150*
Not seldom, nor no slight checks, when I have
Prompted you in the ebb of your estate
And your great flow of debts. My loved lord,
Though you hear now, too late!—yet now's a time—
The greatest of your having lacks a half   *155*
To pay your present debts.

    Tim.   Let all my land be sold.

    Flav. 'Tis all engag'd, some forfeited and gone,
And what remains will hardly stop the mouth
Of present dues: the future comes apace: *160*
What shall defend the interim? and at length
How goes our reckoning?

    Tim. To Lacedæmon did my land extend.

    Flav. O my good lord, the world is but a word:
Were it all yours to give it in a breath,   *165*
How quickly were it gone!

    Tim.   You tell me true.

    Flav. If you suspect my husbandry or falsehood,
Call me before the exactest auditors,
And set me on the proof. So the gods bless me,   *170*
When all our offices have been oppress'd
With riotous feeders, when our vaults have wept
With drunken spilth of wine, when every room
Hath blaz'd with lights and bray'd with minstrelsy,
I have retir'd me to a wasteful cock,   *175*
And set mine eyes at flow.

    Tim.   Prithee, no more.

    Flav. Heavens, have I said, the bounty of this lord!
How many prodigal bits have slaves and peasants
This night englutted! Who is not Timon's?   *180*
What heart, head, sword, force, means, but is Lord
Timon's?
Great Timon, noble, worthy, royal Timon!
Ah, when the means are gone that buy this praise,
The breath is gone whereof this praise is made: *185*
Feast-won, fast-lost; one cloud of winter showers,
These flies are couch'd.

    Tim.   Come, sermon me no further:
No villainous bounty yet hath pass'd my heart;
Unwisely, not ignobly, have I given.   *190*
Why dost thou weep? Canst thou the conscience lack,
To think I shall lack friends? Secure thy heart;
If I would broach the vessels of my love,
And try the argument of hearts by borrowing,
Men and men's fortunes could I frankly use   *195*
As I can bid thee speak.

    Flav.   Assurance bless your thoughts.

    Tim. And in some sort these wants of mine are crown'd,
That I account them blessings; for by these
Shall I try friends: you shall perceive how you   *200*
Mistake my fortunes; I am wealthy in my friends.
Within there! Flaminius! Servilius!

152 Prompted … in: *reminded … of*   **154 yet now's a time;** *cf. n.*   **155** *The most you have is but half enough*   **168 husbandry:** *management; cf. n.*   **170 set me on:** *put me to* **proof:** *test*   **171 offices:** *parts of house-buildings devoted to purely household matters*   **173 spilth:** *spilling*   **179 bits:** *portions*   **180 englutted:** *swallowed up*   **187 are couch'd:** *go into hiding*   **192 Secure:** *set at ease*   **194 argument:** *summary of subject-matter of a book (figuratively) contents*   **195 frankly:** *freely*   **197 Assurance bless:** *may the actual fact justify*   **198 crown'd:** *glorified*

98 to Lord Timon's; *cf. n.*   **118 sometime:** *at times*   **119 philosopher, etc.;** *cf. n.*   **134 rated:** *alloted*   **135 As … means:** *as my means permitted*   **137 propos'd:** *spoke*   **139 vantages:** *opportunities*   **140 indisposition:** *disinclination*   **141** *And made that disinclination your agent*

Enter three Servants.

Serv. My lord? my lord?

Tim. I will dispatch you severally: you, to Lord Lucius:
to Lord Lucullus you: I hunted with his honour to-day;   205
you, to Sempronius: Commend me to their loves; and, I am
proud, say, that my occasions have found time to use 'em
toward a supply of money: let the request be fifty talents.

Flam. As you have said, my lord.

Flav. [Aside.] Lord Lucius, and Lucullus? hum!   210

Tim. [To another Servant.] Go you, sir, to the senators—
Of whom, even to the state's best health, I have
Deserv'd this hearing—bid 'em send o' the instant
A thousand talents to me.

Flav.   I have been bold,   215
For that I knew it the most general way,
To them to use your signet and your name,
But they do shake their heads, and I am here
No richer in return.

Tim.   Is 't true? can 't be?   220

Flav. They answer, in a joint and corporate voice,
That now they are at fall, want treasure, cannot
Do what they would; are sorry—you are honourable,—
But yet they could have wish'd—they know not—
Something hath been amiss—a noble nature   225
May catch a wrench—would all were well—'tis pity:—
And so, intending other serious matters,
After distasteful looks and these hard fractions,
With certain half-caps and cold-moving nods
They froze me into silence.   230

Tim.   You gods, reward them!
Prithee, man, look cheerly. These old fellows
Have their ingratitude in them hereditary:
Their blood is cak'd, 'tis cold, it seldom flows:
'Tis lack of kindly warmth they are not kind;   235
And nature, as it grows again toward earth,
Is fashion'd for the journey, dull and heavy.
[To a Servant.] Go to Ventidius. [To Flavius.]
Prithee, be not sad;
Thou art true and honest; ingeniously I speak,   240
No blame belongs to thee. [To Servant.] Ventidius lately
Buried his father, by whose death he's stepp'd
Into a great estate: when he was poor,
Imprison'd, and in scarcity of friends,
I clear'd him with five talents: greet from me;   245
Bid him suppose some good necessity
Touches his friend, which craves to be remember'd
With those five talents.   [Exit Servant. To Flavius.]
That had, give 't these fellows
To whom 'tis instant due. Ne'er speak, or think   250
That Timon's fortunes 'mong his friends can sink.

Flav. I would I could not think it: that thought is
bounty's foe;
Being free itself, it thinks all others so.   *Exeunt.*

ACT THIRD ❧ SCENE FIRST

[Athens. A Room in Lucullus's House]
Flaminius waiting to speak with a Lord [Lucullus] from his master,
enters a servant to him.

Serv. I have told my lord of you; he is coming down to
you.

Flam. I thank you, sir.

Enter Lucullus.

Serv. Here's my lord.

Lucul. [Aside.] One of Lord Timon's men? a gift, I   5
warrant. Why, this hits right; I dreamt of a silver basin and
ewer to-night. Flaminius, honest Flaminius; you are very respectively welcome, sir. Fill me some wine.   *[Exit Servant.]*
And how does that honourable, complete, freehearted gentleman of Athens, thy very bountiful good lord and master?   10

Flam. His health is well, sir.

Lucul. I am right glad that his health is well, sir: and what
hast thou there under they cloak, pretty Flaminius?

Falm. Faith, nothing but an empty box, sir; which, in my
lord's behalf, I come to entreat your honour to supply;   15
who, having great and instant occasion to use fifty talents, hath
sent to your lordship to furnish him, nothing doubting your
present assistance therein.

Lucul. La, la, la, la! 'nothing doubting,' says he? Alas, good
lord! a noble gentleman 'tis, if he would not keep so good   20
a house. Many a time and often I ha' dined with him, and
told him on 't; and come again to supper to him, of purpose
to have him spend less; and yet he would embrace no counsel,
take no warning by my coming. Every man has his fault, and
honesty is his: I ha' told him on 't, but I could ne'er get   25
him from 't.

Enter Servant with Wine.

Serv. Please your lordship, here is the wine.

Lucul. Flaminius, I have noted thee always wise.
Here's to thee.

Flam. Your lordship speaks your pleasure.   30

Lucul. I have observed thee always for a towardly, prompt
spirit—give thee thy due—and one that knows what belongs to
reason; and canst use the time well, if the time use thee well:
good parts in thee. [To the Servant.] Get you gone, sirrah.
[Exit Servant.] Draw nearer, honest Flaminius. Thy lord's a   35
bountiful gentleman: but thou art wise; and thou knowest
well enough, although thou comest to me, that this is no time
to lend money, especially upon bare friendship, without security. Here's three solidares for thee: good boy, wink at me, and
say thou saw'st me not. Fare thee well.   40

Flam. Is 't possible the world should so much differ,
And we alive that liv'd? Fly, damned baseness,
To him that worships thee!   [Throwing back the money.]

Lucul. Ha! now I see thou art a fool, and fit
for thy master.   *Exit Lucullus.*   45

Flam. May these add to the number that may scald thee!
Let molten coin be thy damnation,

---

204 **severally:** *separately*   212, 213 **Of whom . . . hearing;** *cf. n.*   **o' the instant:** *immedi-*
ately   221 **corporate:** *belonging to a body of persons*   222 **at fall:** *at a low ebb*   227
intending: *pretending*   228 **fractions:** *fragments*   229 **half-caps:** *half-courteous sa-*
lutes   **cold-moving:** *frigid*   240 **ingeniously:** *ingenuously*   250 **instant:** *immediately*   254 **free:** *liberal*

7 **respectively:** *particularly*   9 **complete:** *accomplished*   25 **honesty:** *generosity*   31
towardly: *docile*   39 **solidares:** *small coins, shillings (?)*   **wink at:** *seem not to see*   42
And we alive that liv'd; *cf. n.*   47 **molten coin;** *cf. n.*

Thou disease of a friend, and not himself!
Has friendship such a faint and milky heart,
It turns in less than two nights? O you gods,   50
I feel my master's passion! This slave, unto his honour,
Has my lord's meat in him:
Why should it thrive and turn to nutriment,
When he is turn'd to poison?
O, may diseases only work upon 't!   55
And, when he's sick to death, let not that part of nature
Which my lord paid for, be of any power
To expel sickness, but prolong his hour!   *Exit.*

❧ SCENE SECOND ❧

[The Same. A Public Place]
Enter Lucius, with three Strangers.

Luc. Who, the Lord Timon? he is my very good friend, and
an honourable gentleman.

First Stran. We know him for no less, though we are but
strangers to him. But I can tell you one thing, my lord, and
which I hear from common rumours: now Lord Timon's   5
happy hours are done and past, and his estate shrinks from
him.

Luc. Fie, no, do not believe it; he cannot want for money.

Sec. Stran. But believe you this, my lord, that, not long ago
one of his men was with the Lord Lucullus to borrow so   10
many talents; nay, urged extremely for't, and showed what
necessity belonged to 't, and yet was denied.

Luc. How!

Sec. Stran. I tell you, denied, my lord.

Luc. What a strange case was that! now, before the gods,   15
I am ashamed on 't. Denied that honourable man! there was
very little honour showed in 't. For my own part, I must
needs confess, I have receivd some small kindnesses from him,
as money, plate, jewels, and such like trifles, nothing comparing to his; yet, had he mistook him and sent to me, I   20
should ne'er have denied his occasion so many talents.

Enter Servilius.

Servil. See, by good hap, yonder's my lord;
I have sweat to see his honour. My honoured lord!

Luc. Servilius! you are kindly met, sir.
Fare thee well: commend me to thy honourable virtuous   25
lord, my very exquisite friend.   *[Going.]*

Servil. May it please your honour, my lord hath sent—

Luc. Ha! what has he sent? I am so much endeared to that
lord; he's ever sending: how shall I thank him, thinkest thou?
And what has he sent now?   30

Servil. He has only sent his present occasion now, my lord;
requesting your lordship to supply his instant use with so
many talents.

Luc. I know his lordship is but merry with me;
He cannot want fifty-five hundred talents.   35

Servil. But in the mean time he wants less, my lord.
If his occasion were not virtuous,
I should not urge it half so faithfully.

Luc. Doth thou speak seriously, Servilius?

Servil. Upon my soul, 'tis true, sir.   40

Luc. What a wicked beast was I to disfurnish myself against
such a good time, when I might ha' shown myself honourable!
how unluckily it happened, that I should purchase the day before for a little part, and undo a great deal of honour! Servilius, now, before the gods, I am not able to do—the more   45
beast, I say:—I was sending to use Lord Timon myself, these
gentlemen can witness; but I would not, for the wealth of Athens, I had done 't now. Commend me bountifully to his good
lordship; and I hope his honour will conceive the fairest of me,
because I have no power to be kind: and tell him this from   50
me, I count it one of my greatest afflictions, say, that I cannot
pleasure such an honourable gentleman. Good Servilius, will
you befriend me so far as to use mine own words to him?

Servil. Yes, sir, I shall.

Luc. I'll look you out a good turn, Servilius.   55
                                          Exit Serviluius.

True, as you said, Timon is shrunk indeed;
And he that's once denied will hardly speed.   *Exit.*

First Stran. Do you observe this, Hostilius?

Sec. Stran.   Ay, too well.

First Stran. Why this is the world's soul; and just of the   60
same piece.
Is every flatterer's spirit. Who can call him
His friend that dips in the same dish? for, in
My knowing, Timon has been this lord's father,
And kept his credit with his purse;   65
Supported his estate; nay, Timon's money
Has paid his men their wages: he ne'er drinks
But Timon's silver treads upon his lip;
And yet—O, see the monstrousness of man
When he looks out in an ungrateful shape!—   70
He does deny him, in respect of his,
What charitable men afford to beggars.

Third Stran. Religion groans at it.

First Stran.   For mine own part,
I never tasted Timon in my life,   75
Nor came any of his bounties over me,
To mark me for his friend; yet, I protest,
For his right noble mind, illustrious virtue,
And honourable carriage,
Had his necessity made use of me,   80
I would have put my wealth into donation,
And the best half should have return'd to him,
So much I love his heart. But, I perceive,
Men must learn now with pity to dispense;
For policy sits above conscience.   *Exeunt.*

---

51 passion: *violent emotion*   **20 mistook:** *misdoubted (?)*   **21 occasion:** *necessity*   **22**
hap: *fortune*   **37 virtuous:** *forcible*

41 disfurnish: *deprive* **against:** *on the eve of*   **43, 44 that I . . . honour:** *cf. n.*   **49**
conceive . . . fairest: *make the most favorable judgment*   **57 speed:** *be successful*   **71 in**
respect of his: *in comparison with his own resources*   **73 Religion:** *proper feeling*   **75**
tasted: *had experience of the qualities of*

❧ Scene Third ❧

[The Same. A Room in Sempronius's House]
Enter a third servant [of Timon's] with Sempronius, another of Timon's friends.

Sem. Must he needs trouble me in 't,—hum! 'bove all
others?
He might have tried Lord Lucius, or Lucullus;
And now Ventidius is wealthy too,
Whom he redeem'd from prison: all these　　　　　5
Owe their estates unto him.
　　Serv.　　　　　My lord,
They have all been touch'd and found base metal, for
They have all denied him.
　　Sem.　　　　　How! have they denied him?　10
Have Ventidius and Lucullus denied him?
And does he send to me? Three? hum!
It shows but little love or judgment in him:
Must I be his last refuge? His friends, like physicians,
Thrice give him over: must I take the cure upon me?　15
He has much disgrac'd me in 't; I'm angry at him,
That might have known my place: I see no sense for't,
But his occasions might have woo'd me first;
For, in my conscience, I was the first man
That e'er received gift from him:　　　　　20
And does he think so backwardly of me now,
That I'll requite it last? No.
So it may prove an argument of laughter
To the rest, and 'mongst lords I be thought a fool.
I'd rather than the worth of thrice the sum,　　　25
He'd sent to me first, but for my mind's sake;
I'd such a courage to do him good. But now return,
And with their faint reply this answer join;
Who bates mine honour shall not know my coin.　*Exit.*
　　Serv. Excellent! Your lordship's a goodly villain. The devil　30
knew not what he did when he made man politic; he crossed
himself by 't: and I cannot think but in the end the villainies
of man will set him clear. How fairly this lord strives to appear
foul! takes virtuous copies to be wicked; like those that under
hot ardent zeal would set whole realms on fire:　　　35
Of such a nature is his politic love.
This was my lord's best hope; now all are fled
Save only the gods. Now his friends are dead,
Doors, that were ne'er acquainted with their wards
Many a bounteous year, must be employ'd　　　40
Now to guard sure their master;
And this is all a liberal course allows;
Who cannot keep his wealth must keep his house.　*Exit.*

❧ Scene Fourth ❧

[The Same. A Hall in Timon's House]
Enter Varro's man [men] meeting others. All Timon's creditors to wait for his coming out. Then enter [servant of] Lucius and Hortensius.

First Var. Serv. Well met; good morrow, Titus and
Hortensius.
　　Tit. The like to you, kind Varro.
　　Hor.　　　　　Lucius!
What, do we meet together?　　　　　5
　　Luc. Serv.　　　　Ay, and I think
One business does command us all; for mine
Is money.
　　Tit. So is theirs and ours.

Enter Philotus.

　　Luc. Serv.　　　　And Sir Philotus too!　　10
　　Phi. Good day at once.
　　Luc. Serv.　　　　Welcome, good brother.
What do you think the hour?
　　Phi.　　　　　Labouring for nine.
　　Luc. Serv. So much?　　　　　15
　　Phi.　　　　Is not my lord seen yet?
　　Luc. Serv.　　　　　　Not yet.
　　Phi. I wonder on 't; he was wont to shine at seven.
　　Luc. Serv. Ay, but the days are waxed shorter with him:
You must consider that a prodigal course　　　20
Is like the sun's; but not, like his, recoverable.
I fear,
'Tis deepest winter in Lord Timon's purse;
This is, one may reach deep enough and yet
Find little.　　　　　25
　　Phi.　　I am of your fear for that.
　　Tit. I'll show you how to observe a strange event.
Your lord sends now for money.
　　Hor.　　　　　Most true, he does.
　　Tit. And he wears jewels now of Timon's gift,　　30
For which I wait for money.
　　Hor. It is against my heart.
　　Luc. Serv.　　　　Mark, how strange it shows,
Timon in this should pay more than he owes:
And e'en as if your lord should wear rich jewels,　　35
And send for money for 'em.
　　Hor. I'm weary of this charge, the gods can witness:
I know my lord hath spent of Timon's wealth,
And now ingratitude makes it worse than stealth.
　　First Var. Serv. Yes, mine's three thousand crowns:　40
what's yours?
　　Luc. Serv. Five thousand mine.
　　First Var. Serv. 'Tis much deep; and it should seem by
the sum,
Your master's confidence was above mine;　　45
Else, surely, his had equall'd.

Enter Flaminius.

　　Tim. One of Lord Timon's men.
　　Luc. Serv. Flaminius! Sir, a word. Pray, is my lord ready
to come forth?

---

8 **touch'd:** *tested as with the touchstone*　15 **Thrice;** *cf. n.*　21 **backwardly:** *perversely*　23 **argument:** *theme*　27 **courage:** *inclination*　28 **faint:** *timid*　30-33 **The devil ... clear;** *cf. n.*　33 **set ... clear:** *place in an innocent light*　34 **copies:** *models*　39 **wards:** *bars*　41 **sure:** *in safety*　43 **keep ... house:** *remain within doors*

11 **at once:** *to all of you together*　21 **Is like the sun's;** *cf. n.*　**recoverable:** *capable of being retraced*　33 **shows:** *appears*　37 **charge:** *commission*

Flam. No, indeed he is not.   50

Tit. We attend his lordship: pray, signify so much.

Flam. I need not tell him that; he knows you are too
diligent.   [*Exit Flaminius.*]

     Enter Steward [Flavius] in a cloak, muffled.

Luc. Serv. Ha! is not that his steward muffled so?   55
He goes away in a cloud: call him, call him.

    Tit. Do you hear, sir?

    Sec. Var. Serv. By your leave, sir.

    Flav. What do ye ask of me, my friend?

    Tit. We wait for certain money here, sir.   60

Flav.   Ay,
If money were as certain as your waiting,
'Twere sure enough
Why then preferr'd you not your sums and bills,
When your false masters eat of my lord's meat?   65
Then they could smile and fawn upon his debts,
And take down the interest into their gluttonous maws.
You do yourselves but wrong to stir me up;
Let me pass quietly:
Believe 't, my lord and I have made an end;   70
I have no more to reckon, he to spend.

    Luc. Serv. Ay, but this answer will not serve.

    Flav. If 'twill not serve, 'tis not so base as you;
For you serve knaves.   [*Exit.*]

    First Var. Serv. How! what does his cashiered worship   75
mutter?

    Sec. Var. Serv. No matter what; he's poor, and that's re-
venge enough. Who can speak broader than he that has no
house to put his head in? such may rail against great building.

     Enter Servilius.

    Tit. O, here's Servilius; now we shall know some answer.   80

    Servil. If I might beseech you, gentlemen, to repair some
other hour, I should derive much from 't; for, take 't of my
soul, my lord leans wondrously to discontent. His comfortable
temper has forsook him; he's much out of health, and keeps
his chamber.   85

    Luc. Serv. Many do keep their chambers are not sick:
And, if it be so far beyond his health,
Methinks he should the sooner pay his debts,
And make a clear way to the gods.

    Servil   Good gods!   90

    Tit. We cannot take this for answer, sir.

    Flam. Within. Servilius, help! my lord! my lord!

     Enter Timon, in a rage [Flaminius following].

    Tim. What! are my doors oppos'd against my passage?
Have I been ever free, and must my house
Be my retentive enemy, my gaol?   95
The place which I have feasted, does it now,
Like all mankind, show me an iron heart?

    Luc. Serv. Put in now, Titus.

    Tit. My lord, here is my bill.

    Luc. Serv. Here's mine.   100

    Hor. And mine, my lord.

    Both Var Serv. And ours, my lord.

    Phi. All our bills.

    Tim. Knock me down with 'em: cleave me to the girdle.

    Luc. Serv. Alas, my lord,—   105

    Tim. Cut my heart in sums.

    Tit. Mine, fifty talents.

    Tim. Tell out my blood.

    Luc. Serv. Five thousand crowns, my lord.

    Tim. Five thousand drops pays that. What yours?—and   110
yours?

    First Var. Serv. My lord,—

    Sec. Var. Serv. My lord,—

    Tim. Tear me, take me; and the gods fall upon you!

                              Exit Timon.

    Hor. Faith, I perceive our masters may throw their caps   115
at their money: these debts may well be called desperate one,
for a madman owes 'em.   *Exeunt.*

     Enter Timon [and Flavius.]

    Tim. They have e'en put my breath from me, the slaves.
Creditors? devils!

    Flav. My dear lord.—   120

    Tim. What if it should be so?

    Flav. My lord,—

    Tim. I'll have it so. My steward!

    Flav. Here, my lord.

    Tim. So fitly? Go, bid all my friends again,   125
Lucius, Lucullus, and Sempronius: all:
I'll once more feast the rascals.

    Flav.   O my lord,
You only speak from your distracted soul;
There is not so much left to furnish out   130
A moderate table.

    Tim.   Be't not in thy care: go.
I charge thee, invite them all: let in the tide
Of knaves once more; my cook and I'll provide.   *Exeunt.*

     ❧ **SCENE FIVE** ❧

    [The Same. The Senate House. The Senate sitting.]
Enter three Senators at one door, Alcibiades meeting them [later],
with attendants.

    First Sen. My lord, you have my voice to it; the fault's
Bloody; 'tis necessary he should die;
Nothing emboldens sin so much as mercy.

    Sec. Sen. Most true; the law shall bruise him.

    Alcib. Honour, health, and compassion to the senate!   5

    First Sen. Now, captain?

    Alcib. I am a humble suitor to your virtues;
For pity is the virtue of the law,
And none but tyrants use it cruelly.
It pleases time and fortune to lie heavy   10
Upon a friend of mine, who in hot blood
Hath stepp'd into the law, which is past depth
To those that without heed do plunge into 't.
He is a man, setting his fate aside,
Of comely virtues: 15
Nor did he soil the fact with cowardice—
An honour in him which buys out his fault—
But, with a noble fury and fair spirit,

---

95 retentive: *confining*   **98 Put in:** *advance a claim*   **104 Knock me down with 'em;** *cf. n.*

115 throw their caps at: *give up for lost*   **S.d.;** *Cf. n.*   **125 fitly:** *at a fitting time*   **126**
Sempronius: *all; cf. n.*   **130 to:** *as to*   **1 voice:** *vote*   **16 fact:** *deed*

Seeing his reputation touch'd to death,
He did oppose his foe: 20
And with such sober and unnoted passion
He did behave his anger, ere 'twas spent,
As if he had but prov'd an argument.
   First Sen. You undergo too strict a paradox.
Striving to make an ugly deed look fair: 25
Your words have took such pains as if they labour'd
To bring manslaughter into form, and set quarrelling
Upon the head of valour; which indeed
Is valour misbegot and came into the world
When sects and factions were newly born.   30
He's truly valiant that can wisely suffer
The worst that man can breathe, and make his wrongs
His outsides, to wear them like his raiment, carelessly,
And ne'er prefer his injuries to his heart,
To bring it into danger.   35
If wrongs be evils and enforce us kill,
What folly 'tis to hazard life for ill!
   Alcib. My lord,—
   First Sen. You cannot make gross sins look clear:
To revenge is no valour, but to bear.   40
   Alcib. My lords, then, under favour, pardon me,
If I speak like a captain.
Why do fond men expose themselves to battle,
And not endure all threats? sleep upon't,
And let the fores quietly cut their throats,   45
Without repugnancy? If there be
Such valour in the bearing, what make we
Abroad? why then, women are more valiant
That stay at home, if bearing carry it;
And the ass more captain then the lion, the fellow   50
Loaden with irons wiser than the judge,
If wisdom be in suffering. O my lords,
As you are great, be pitifully good:
Who cannot condemn rashness in cold blood?
To kill, I grant, is sin's extremest gust;   55
But, in defence, by mercy, 'tis most just.
To be in anger is impiety;
But who is man that is not angry?
Weigh but the crime with this.
   Sec. Sen. You breathe in vain.   60
   Alcib.   In vain! his service done
At Lacedæmon and Byzantium
Were a sufficient briber for his life.
   First Sen. What's that?
   Alcib. I say, my lords, he has done fair service,   65
And slain in fight many of your enemies:
How full of valour did he bear himself
In the last conflict, and made plenteous wounds!
   Sec. Sen. He has made too much plenty with 'em;
He's a sworn rioter; he has a sin that often   70
Drowns him and takes his valour prisoner:
If there were no foes, that were enough
To overcome him: in that beastly fury
He has been known to commit outrages

And cherish factions: 'tis inferr'd to us,   75
His days are foul and his drink dangerous.
   First Sen. He dies.
   Alcib. Hard fate! he might have died in war.
My lords, if not for any parts in him—
Though his right arm might purchase his own time,   80
And be in debt to none—yet, more to move you,
Take my deserts to his and join 'em both:
And, for I know your reverend ages love
Security, I'll pawn my victories, all
My honour to you, upon his good returns.   85
If by this crime he owes the law his life,
Why, let the war receive 't in valiant gore;
For law is strict, and war is nothing more.
   First Sen. We are for law: he dies; urge it no more,
On height of our displeasure: friend or brother,   90
He forfeits his own blood that spills another.
   Alcib. Must it be so? it must not be. My lords,
I do beseech you, know me.
   Sec. Sen. How!
   Alcib. Call me to your remembrances.   95
   Third Sen.   What!
   Alcib. I cannot think but your age has forgot me;
It could not else be I should prove so base
To sue, and be denied such common grace:
My wounds ache at your.   100
   First Sen.   Do you dare our anger?
'Tis in few words, but spacious in effect;
We banish thee for ever.
   Alcib.   Banish me!
Banish your dotage; banish usury,   105
That makes the senate ugly.
   First Sen. If, after two days' shine, Athens contain thee,
Attend our weightier judgment. And, not to swell our spirit,
He shall be executed presently.   *Exeunt [Senators].*
   Alcib. Now the gods keep you old enough,   110
that you may live
Only in bone, that none may look on you!
I'm worse than mad: I have kept back their foes,
While they have told their money and let out
Their coin upon large interest, I myself   115
Rich only in large hurts. All those for this?
Is this the balsam that the usuring senate
Pours into captains' wounds? Banishment!
It comes not ill; I hate not to be banish'd;
It is a cause worthy my spleen and fury,   120
That I may strike at Athens. I'll cheer up
My discontented troops, and lay for hearts.
'Tis honour with most lands to be at odds;
Soldiers should brook as little wrongs as gods.   *Exit*

---

19 touch'd: *wounded*   21 unnoted: *undemonstrative* (?)   22 behave: *control*   24 undergo: *undertake*   34 prefer: *show*   39 clear: *unspotted*   40 *Valor consists not in revenge but in patience*   46 repugnancy: *opposition*   47 make: *do*   49 if bearing carry it; *cf. n.*   50 fellow; *cf. n.*   56 by mercy: *by a merciful condition* (?), *by your leave* (?)   60 breathe in vain: *waste your breath*   63 briber: *advocate*

75 factions: *factious intrigue* inferr'd: *alleged*   83 for: *because*   91 spills: *destroys*   108 Attend: *await* spirit: *anger*   112 Only in bone ... you; *cf. n.*   114 told: *counted*   122 lay for hearts; *cf. n.*

❧ SCENE SIXTH ❧

*[The Same. A Banqueting-room in Timon's House.
Music. Tables set out.] Enter divers Friends at several doors.*

First Lord. The good time of day to you, sir.

Sec. Lord. I also wish it you. I think this honourable lord did but try us this other day.

First Lord. Upon that were my thoughts tiring when we encountered: I hope it is not so low with him as he made   *5* it seem in the trial of his several friends.

Sec. Lord. It should not be, by the persuasion of his new feasting.

First Lord. I should think so: he hath sent me an earnest inviting, which many my near occasions did urge me to   *10* put off; but he hath conjured me beyond them, and I must needs appear.

Sec. Lord. In like manner was I in debt to my importunate business, but he would not hear my excuse. I am sorry, when he sent to borrow of me, that my provision was out.   *15*

First Lord. I am sick of that grief too, as I understand how all things go.

Sec. Lord. Every man here's so. What would he have borrowed of you?

First Lord. A thousand pieces.   *20*

Sec. Lord. A thousand pieces!

First Lord. What of you?

Third Lord. He sent to me, sir,—Here he comes.

Enter Timon and Attendants.

Tim. With all my heart, gentlemen both: and how fare you?

First Lord. Ever at the best, hearing well of your lordship. *25*

Sec. Lord. The swallow follows not summer more willing than we your lordship.

Tim. [Aside.] Nor more willingly leaves winter; such summer-birds are men.—Gentlemen, our dinner will not recompense this long stay: feast your ears with the music awhile, if they *30* will fare so harshly o' the trumpet's sound; we shall to 't presently.

First Lord. I hope it remains not unkindly with your lordship that I returned you an empty messenger.

Tim. O, sir, let it not trouble you.   *35*

Sec. Lord. My noble lord,—

Tim. Ah, my good friend, what cheer?

Sec. Lord. My most honourable lord, I am e'en sick of shame, that, when your lordship this other day sent to me, I was so unfortunate a beggar.   *40*

Tim. Think not on 't, sir.

Sec. Lord. If you had sent but two hours before—

Tim. Let it not cumber your better remembrance.

The banquet brought in.

Come, bring in all together.

Sec. Lord. All covered dishes!   *45*

First Lord. Royal cheer, I warrant you.

Third Lord. Doubt not that, if money and the season can yield it.

First Lord. How do you? What's the news?

Third Lord. Alcibiades is banished: hear you of it?   *50*

First Lord.
Sec. Lord. } Alcibiades banished!

Third Lord. 'Tis so, be sure of it.

First Lord. How? how?

Sec. Lord. I pray you, upon what?   *55*

Tim. My worthy friends, will you draw near?

Third Lord. I'll tell you more anon. Here's a noble feast toward.

Sec. Lord. This is the old man still.

Third Lord. Will 't hold? will 't hold?   *60*

Sec. Lord. It does: but time will—and so—

Third Lord. I do conceive.

Tim. Each man to his stool, with that spur as he would to the lip of his mistress: your diet shall be in all places alike. Make not a city feast of it, to let the meat cool ere we can *65* agree upon the first place: sit, sit. The gods require our thanks.—

You great benefactors sprinkle our society with thankfulness. For your own gifts, make yourselves praised: but reserve still to give, lest your deities be despised. Lend to each man enough, *70* that one need not lend to another, for, were your godheads to borrow of men, men would forsake the gods. Make the meat be beloved more than the man that gives it. Let no assembly of twenty be without a score of villains: if there sit twelve women at the table, let a dozen of them—be as they are. The rest *75* of your fees, O gods,—the senators of Athens, together with the common lag of people,—what is amiss in them, you gods, make suitable for destruction. For these my present friends, as they are to me nothing, so in nothing bless them, and to nothing are they welcome. Uncover, dogs, and lap.   *80*

[The dishes are uncovered and are seen to be full of warm water.]

Some speak. What does his lordship mean?

Some other. I know not.

Tim. May you a better feast never behold,
You knot of mouth-friends! smoke and lukewarm water
Is your perfection. This is Timon's last;   *85*
Who, stuck and spangled with your flatteries,
Washes it off, and sprinkles in your faces

[Throwing the water in their faces.]

Your reeking villainy. Live loath'd, and long,
Most smiling, smooth, detested parasites,
Courteous destroyers, affable wolves, meek bears,   *90*
You fools of fortune, trencher-friends, time's flies,
Cap-and-knee slaves, vapours, and minute-jacks!
Of man and beast the infinite malady
Crust you quite o'er! What, dost thou go?
Soft! take thy physic first—thou too—and thou:—   *95*
Stay, I will lend thee money, borrow none.

[Throws the dishes at them, and drives them out.]

What, all in motion? Henceforth be no feast
Whereat a villain's not a welcome guest.
Burn, house! sink, Athens! henceforth hated be
Of Timon man and all humanity!   *Exit.*   *100*

Enter the Senators, with other Lords.

First Lord. How now, my lords!

---

4 **tiring:** *busily engaged; cf. n.*   10 **many:** *many of*   **near:** *important*   26 **willing:** *willingly*   30, 31 *if they will fare ... sound; cf. n.*   43 **better remembrance:** *remembrance of better things*

58 **toward:** *at hand*   63 **spur:** *incentive, eagerness*   65 **a city feast:** *a formal dinner of municipal functionaries*   76 **fees:** *property (?)*   77 **common lag:** *lowest class*   84 **knot: band   smoke:** *steam*   85 **perfection:** *highest excellence*   91 **time's flies:** *flies of a season; cf. II.ii.187*   92 **minute-jacks;** *cf. n.*   93 **infinite:** *numberless (?)*   95 **Soft! Stay**   100 **Of:** *by*

Sec. Lord. Know you the quality of Lord Timon's fury?

Third Lord. Push! did you see my cap?

Fourth Lord. I have lost my gown.

First Lord. He's but a mad lord, and nought but   *105*
humour sways him. He gave me a jewel th' other day, and
now he has beat it out of my hat. Did you see my jewel?

Third Lord. Did you see my cap?

Sec. Lord. Here 'tis.

Fourth Lord. Here lies my gown.   *110*

First Lord. Let's make no stay.

Sec. Lord. Lord Timon's mad.

Third Lord.   I feel 't upon my bones.

Fourth Lord. One day he gives us diamonds, next day
stones.   *Exeunt the Senators [and others].*

ACT FOURTH *Scene First*

[Without the Walls of Athens.]
Enter Timon.

Tim. Let me look back upon thee. O thou wall,
That girdlest in those wolves, dive in the earth,
And fence not Athens! Matrons, turn incontinent!
Obedience fail in children! Slaves and fools,
Pluck the grave wrinkled senate from the bench,   *5*
And minister in their steads! To general filths
Convert, o' the instant, green virginity!
Do 't in your parents' eyes! Bankrupts, hold fast;
Rather than render back, out with your knives,
And cut your trusters' throats! Bound servants, steal!   *10*
Large-handed robbers your grave masters are,
And pill by law. Maid, to thy master's bed;
Thy mistress is o' the brothel! Son of sixteen,
Pluck the lin'd crutch from thy old limping sire:
With it beat out his brains! Piety and fear,   *15*
Religion to the gods, peace, justice, truth,
Domestic awe, night-rest and neighbourhood,
Instruction, manners, mysteries and trades,
Degrees, observances, customs and laws,
Decline to your confounding contraries,   *20*
And let confusion live! Plagues incident to men,
Your potent and infectious fevers heap
On Athens, ripe for stroke! Thou cold sciatica,
Cripple our senators, that their limbs may halt
As lamely as their manners! Lust and liberty   *25*
Creep in the minds and marrows of our youth,
That 'gainst the stream of virtue they may strive,
And drown themselves in riot! Itches, blains,
Sow all the Athenian bosoms, and their crop
Be general leprosy! Breath infect breath,   *30*
That their society, as their friendship, may
Be merely poison! Nothing I'll bear from thee
But nakedness, thou detestable town!
Take thou that too, with multiplying bans!
Timon will to the woods, where he shall find   *35*

The unkindest beast more kinder than mankind.
The gods confound—hear me, you good gods all!—
The Athenians both within and out that wall!
And grant, as Timon grows, his hate may grow
To the whole race of mankind, high and low!   *40*
                                        Amen. *Exit.*

SCENE SECOND

[Athens. Timon's House]
Enter Steward [Flavius], with two or three servants.

First Serv. Hear you, master steward, where's our master?
Are we undone? cast off? nothing remaining?

Flav. Alack, my fellows, what should I say to you?
Let me be recorded by the righteous gods,
I am as poor as you.   *5*

First Serv.   Such a house broke!
So noble a master fall'n! All gone! and not
One friend to take his fortune by the arm,
And go along with him!

Sec. Serv.   As we do turn our backs   *10*
From our companion thrown into his grave,
So his familiars to his buried fortunes
Slink all away; leave their false vows with him,
Like empty purses pick'd; and his poor self,
A dedicated beggar to the air,   *15*
With his disease of all-shunn'd poverty,
Walks, like contempt, alone. More of our fellows.

Enter other Servants.

Flav. All broken implements of a ruin'd house.

Third Serv. Yet do our hearts wear Timon's livery;
That see I by our faces; we are fellows still,   *20*
Serving alike in sorrow: leak'd in our bark,
And we, poor mates, stand on the dying deck,
Hearing the surges threat: we must all part
Into this sea of air.

Flav.   Good fellows all,   *25*
The latest of my wealth I'll share amongst you.
Wherever we shall meet, for Timon's sake
Let's yet be fellows; let's shake our heads, and say,
As 'twere a knell unto our master's fortunes,
'We have seen better days.' Let each take some.   *30*
Nay, put out all your hands. Not one word more:
Thus part we rich in sorrow, parting poor.
                        [They] embrace and part several ways.
O, the fierce wretchedness that glory brings us.
Who would not wish to be from wealth exempt,
Since riches point to misery and contempt?   *35*
Who would be so mock'd with glory? or to live
But in a dream of friendship?
To have his pomp and all what state compounds
But only painted, like his varnish'd friends?
Poor honest lord, brought low by his own heart,   *40*
Undone by goodness. Strange, unusual blood,
When man's worst sin is he does too much good!

---

103 **Push:** *Pshaw*   106 **humour:** *caprice*   115 **stones;** *cf. n.*   6 **filths:** *strumpets*   7
Convert: *turn*   9 **render back:** *repay*   12 **pill:** *plunder*   14 **lin'd:** *stuffed*   17 **Do-**
mestic awe: *respect for parents* **neighbourhood:** *neighborly feeling*   18 **mysteries:**
crafts   20 **confounding:** *ruinous*   25 **liberty:** *license*   28 **blains:** *sores*   32 **merely:**
entirely   34 **multiplying:** *increasing* **bans:** *curses*

38 **out:** *without*   4 **recorded:** *taken to witness*   12 **familiars . . . fortunes:** *those who
were so intimate with his now buried prosperity*   15 *A beggar devoted by fortune to a homeless
life*   17 **fellows:** *comrades* **S. d. several ways:** *in different directions*   36 **to live:** *desire
to live*   38 **all . . . compounds;** *cf. n.*   41 **blood:** *temper*

Who then dares to be half so kind again?
For bounty, that makes gods, does still mar men.
My dearest lord, blest, to be most accurs'd,   45
Rich only to be wretched, thy great fortunes
Are made thy chief afflictions. Alas, kind lord!
He's flung in rage from this ingrateful seat
Of monstrous friends;
Nor has he with him to supply his life,   50
Or that which can command it.
I'll follow and inquire him out:
I'll ever serve his mind with my best will;
Whilst I have gold I'll be his steward still.   Exit

❧ SCENE THIRD ❧

[Woods and Cave near the Sea-shore]
Enter Timon in the Woods [from the Cave]

Tim. O blessed breeding sun, draw from the earth
Rotten humidity; below thy sister's orb
Infect the air! Twinn'd brothers of one womb,
Whose procreation, residence and birth,
Scarce is dividant, touch them with several fortunes,   5
The greater scorns the lesser: not nature,
To whom all sores lay siege, can bear great fortune
But by contempt of nature.
Raise me this beggar, and deny't that lord,
The senator shall bear contempt hereditary,   10
The beggar native honour.
It is the pasture lards the rother's sides,
The want that makes him lean. Who dares, who dares,
In purity of manhood stand upright,
And say, 'This man's a flatterer'? If one be,   15
So are they all; for every grize of fortune
Is smooth'd by that below: the learned pate
Ducks to the golden fool: all is oblique;
There's nothing level in our cursed natures
But direct villainy. Therefore, be abhorr'd   20
All feasts, societies, and throngs of men!
His semblable, yea, himself, Timon disdains:
Destruction fang mankind! Earth, yield me roots!   *[Digging.]*
Who seeks for better of thee, sauce his palate
With thy most operant poison! What is here?   25
Gold? yellow, glittering, precious gold? No, gods,
I am no idle votarist: roots, you clear heavens!
Thus much of this will make black white, foul fair,
Wrong right, base noble, old young, coward valiant.
Ha, you gods! why this? what this, you gods? Why, this   30
Will lug your priests and servants from your sides,
Pluck stout men's pillows from below their heads:
This yellow slave
Will knit and break religions; bless the accurs'd;
Make the hoar leprosy ador'd; place thieves,   35
And give them title, knee, and approbation,
With senators on the bench: this is it
That makes the wappen'd widow wed again;

She, whom the spital-house and ulcerous sores
Would cast the gorge at, this embalms and spices   40
To the April day again. Come, damned earth,
Thou common whore of mankind, that putt'st odds
Among the rout of nations, I will make thee
Do thy right nature. *March afar off.* Ha! a drum? thou'rt quick,   45
But yet I'll bury thee: thou't go, strong thief,
When gouty keepers of thee cannot stand:
Nay, stay thou out for earnest.   *[Keeping some gold.]*

Enter Alcibiades, with drum and fife, in warlike manner; and
Phrynia and Timandra.

Alcib. What art thou there? speak.
Tim. A beast, as thou art. The canker gnaw thy heart,   50
For showing me again the eyes of man!
Alcib. What is thy name? Is man so hateful to thee,
That art thyself a man?
Tim. I am 'Misanthropos,' and hate mankind.
For thy part, I do wish thou wert a dog,   55
That I might love thee something.
Alcib.   I know thee well,
But in thy fortunes am unlearn'd and strange.
Tim. I know thee too; and more than that I know thee
I not desire to know. Follow thy drum;   60
With man's blood paint the ground, gules, gules:
Religious canons, civil laws are cruel;
Then what should war be? This fell whore of thine
Hath in her more destruction than thy sword
For all her cherubin look.   65
Phry.   Thy lips rot off!
Tim. I will not kiss thee; then the rot returns
To thine own lips again.
Alcib. How came the noble Timon to this change?
Tim. As the moon does, by wanting light to give: 70
But then renew I could not like the moon;
There were no suns to borrow of.
Alcib. Noble Timon, what friendship may I do thee?
Tim. None, but to maintain my opinion.
Alcib. What is it, Timon?   75
Tim. Promise me friendship, but perform none: if thou wilt
not promise, the gods plague thee, for thou art a man: if thou
dost perform, confound thee, for thou art a man!
Alcib. I have heard in some sort of thy miseries.
Tim. Thou saw'st them, when I had prosperity.   80
Alcib. I see them now; then was a blessed time.
Tim. As thine is now, held with a brace of harlots.
Timan. Is this the Athenian minion, whom the world
Voic'd so regardfully?
Tim.   Art thou Timandra?   85
Timan.   Yes.
Tim. Be a whore still; they love thee not that use thee;
Give them diseases, leaving with thee their lust.
Make use of thy salt hours: season the slaves
For tubs and baths; bring down rose-cheeked youth   90

---

49 monstrous: *unnatural*   **50 to supply his life:** *the necessities of life*   **5 dividant:** *divided*   **9 Raise me ... lord;** *cf. n.*   **12 rother's:** *ox's; cf. n.*   **16 grize:** *step*   **17 smooth'd:** *flattered*   **18 oblique:** *indirect*   **22 semblable:** *counterpart*   **23 fang:** *seize*   **25 operant:** *potent*   **27 idle:** *empty* **votarist:** *votary; cf. n.*   **32 Pluck ... heads;** *cf. n.* **stout:** *strong*   **38 wappen'd:** *stale (?)*

39, 40 spital-house ... cast the gorge at: *hospital patients or victims of ulcerous sores would loathe*   **44 Do ... nature;** *cf. n.*   **45 quick:** *living (a pun)*   **48 earnest:** *money paid as an instalment to secure a bargain*   **54 'Misanthropos':** *Hater of Mankind; cf. n.*   **56 something:** *somewhat*   **58 strange:** *unacquainted*   **61 gules:** *the heraldic term for red*   **63 fell:** *deadly*   **79 in some sort:** *in a way*   **83 minion:** *darling*   **84 Voic'd:** *acclaimed* **regardfully:** *respectfully*   **89 salt:** *wanton*

To the tub-fast and the diet.

Timon.   Hang thee, monster!

Alcib. Pardon him, sweet Timandra, for his wits
Are drown'd and lost in his calamities.
I have but little gold of late, brave Timon,   *95*
The want whereof doth daily make revolt
In my penurious band: I have heard and griev'd
How cursed Athens, mindless of thy worth,
Forgetting they great deeds, when neighbour states,
But for thy sword and fortune, trod upon them—   *100*

Tim. I prithee, beat thy drum, and get thee gone.

Alcib. I am thy friend and pity thee, dear Timon.

Tim. How dost thou pity him whom thou dost trouble?
I had rather be alone.

Alcib.   Why, fare thee well: *105*
Here is some gold for thee.

Tim.   Keep it, I cannot eat it.

Alcib. When I have laid proud Athens on a heap—

Tim. Warr'st thou 'gainst Athens?

Alcib. Ay, Timon, and have cause.   *110*

Tim. The gods confound them all in they conquest, and
Thee after, when thou hast conquer'd!

Alcib.   Why me, Timon?

Tim. That by killing of villains thou wast born to conquer
My country.   *115*
Put up thy gold: go on,—here's gold,—go on;
Be as a planetary plague, when Jove
Will o'er some high-vic'd city hang his poison
In the sick air: let not thy sword skip one
Pity not honour'd age for his white beard;   *120*
He is a usurer. Strike me the counterfeit matron;
It is her habit only that is honest,
Herself's a bawd. Let not the virgin's cheek
Make soft thy trenchant sword; for those milkpaps,
That through the window-bars bore at men's eyes,   *125*
Are not within the leaf of pity writ,
But set them down horrible traitors. Spare not the babe,
Whose dimpled smiles from fools exhaust their mercy;
Think it a bastard whom the oracle
Hath doubtfully pronounc'd thy throat shall cut,   *130*
And mince it sans remorse. Swear against objects;
Put armour on thine ears and on thine eyes,
Whose proof nor yells of mothers, maids, nor babes,
Nor sight of priests in holy vestments bleeding,
Shall pierce a jot. There's gold to pay thy soldiers: *135*
Make large confusion; and, thy fury spent,
Confounded by thyself! Speak not, be gone.

Alcib. Hast thou gold yet? I'll take the gold thou giv'st me,
Not all they counsel.

Tim. Dost thou or dost thou not, heaven's curse upon thee!

Phr. ⎱
Timan. ⎰ Give us some gold, good Timon: hast thou more?

Tim. Enough to make a whore forswear her trade,
And to make whores, a bawd. Hold up, you sluts,
Your aprons mountant: you are not oathable;   *145*

Although, I know, you'll swear, terribly swear
Into strong shudders and to heavenly agues
The immortal gods that hear you; spare your oaths,
I'll trust to your conditions: be whores still;
And he whose pious breath seeks to convert you,   *150*
Be strong in whore, allure him, burn him up;
Let your close fire predominate his smoke,
And be no turncoats: yet may your pains, six months,
Be quite contrary: and thatch your poor thin roofs
With burdens of the dead;—some that were hang'd,   *155*
No matter:—wear them, betray with them: whore still;
Paint till a horse may mire upon your face:
A pox of wrinkles!

Phr. ⎱
Timan. ⎰ Well, more gold. What then?   *160*
Believe 't, that we'll do anything for gold.

Tim. Consumptions sow
In hollow bones of man; strike their sharp shins,
And mar men's spurring. Crack the lawyer's voice,
That he may never more false title plead,   *165*
Nor sound his quillets shrilly: hoar the flamen,
That scolds against the quality of flesh
And not believes himself: down with the nose,
Down with it flat; take the bridge quite away
Of him that, his particular to foresee,   *170*
Smells from the general weal: make curl'd-pate ruffians bald;
And let the unscarr'd braggarts of the war
Derive some pain from you: plague all,
That your activity may defeat and quell
The source of all erection. There's more gold: *175*
Do you damn others, and let this damn you,
And ditches grave you all!

Phr. ⎱ More counsel with more money, bounteous
Timan. ⎰ Timon.   *180*

Tim. More whore, more mischief first; I have given you
earnest.

Alcib. Strike up the drum towards Athens! Farewell, Timon:
If I thrive well, I'll visit thee again.

Tim. If I hope well, I'll never see thee more.   *185*

Alcib. I never did thee harm.

Tim. Yes, thou spok'st well of me.

Alcib.   Call'st thou that harm?

Tim. Men daily find it. Get thee away, and take
Thy beagles with thee.   *190*

Alcib.   We but offend him. Strike!

[Drum beats.] Exeunt [Alcibiades, Phrynia, and Timandra].

Tim. That nature, being sick of man's unkindness,
Should yet be hungry! Common mother, thou,   *[Digging.]*
Whose womb unmeasurable, and infinite breast,
Teems, and feeds all; whose self-same mettle,   *195*
Whereof thy proud child, arrogant man, is puff'd,
Engenders the black toad and adder blue,
The gilded newt and eyeless venom'd worm.
With all the abhorred births below crisp heaven
Whereon Hyperion's quickening fire doth shine;   *200*
Yield him, who all thy human sons doth hate,

91 **To the tub-fast and the diet;** *cf. n.*   97 **penurious:** *poverty-stricken*   99 **neighbour:**
neighboring   108 **on:** *in*   117 **planetary plague;** *cf. n.*   121 **counterfeit:** *deceit-*
ful   122 **habit:** *demeanor*   125 **window-bars:** *latticed open-work of the bodice* **bore**
at: *show themselves to*   129 **whom:** *who*   130 **doubtfully:** *ambiguously*   131 **sans:**
without **objects:** *objects of commiseration*   133 **proof:** *impenetrability*   136 **confusion:**
destruction   140 **Dost ... not:** *whether you do or not*   143 **Enough ... bawd;**
cf. n.   145 **mountant:** *rising* **oathable:** *fit to swear a true oath*

149 **conditions:** *characters*   154, 155 **and thatch ... dead;** *cf. n.*   166 **quillets:** *verbal*
niceties **hoar:** *make mouldy* **flamen:** *priest*   170 **particular:** *personal interest*   171
Smells from: *loses the scent of*   177 **grave:** *bury*   185 **hope well:** *attain my hope*   190
beagles: *small variety of hound, used contemptuously of women*   199 **crisp:** *wavy, with*
clouds   200 **Hyperion;** *cf. n.*

From forth thy plenteous bosom, one poor root!
Ensear thy fertile and conceptious womb,
Let it no more bring out ingrateful man!
Go great with tigers, dragons, wolves, and bears;
Teem with new monsters, whom thy upward face   205
Hath to the marbled mansion all above
Never presented!—O, a root! dear thanks!—
Dry up thy marrows, vines, and plough-torn leas;
Whereof ingrateful man, with liquorish draughts
And morsels unctuous, greases his pure mind,   210
That from it all consideration slips!

Enter Apemantus.

More man? Plague, plague!
   Apem. I was directed hither: men report
Thou dost affect my manners, and dost use them.
   Tim. 'Tis then because thou dost not keep a dog,   215
Whom I would imitate: consumption catch thee!
   Apem. This is in thee a nature but infected;
A poor unmanly melancholy sprung
From change of fortune. Why this spade? this place?
This slave-like habit? and these looks of care?   220
Thy flatterers yet wear silk, drink wine, lie soft,
Hug their diseas'd perfumes, and have forgot
That ever Timon was. Shame not these woods
By putting on the cunning of a carper.
Be thou a flatterer now, and seek to thrive   225
By that which has undone thee: hinge thy knee,
And let his very breath whom thou'lt observe
Blow off thy cap; praise his most vicious strain,
And call it excellent. Thou wast told thus;
Thou gav'st thine ears, like tapsters that bade welcome,   230
To knaves and all approachers: 'tis most just
That thou turn rascal; hadst thou wealth again,
Rascals should have 't. Do not assume my likeness.
   Tim. Were I like thee I'd throw away myself.
   Apem. Thou hast cast away thyself, being like thyself,   235
A madman so long, now a fool. What, think'st
That the bleak air, thy boisterous chamberlain,
Will put thy shirt on warm? will these moss'd trees,
That have outliv'd the eagle, page thy heels
And skip when thou point'st out? will the cold brook,   240
Candied with ice, caudle thy morning taste,
To cure the o'er-night's surfeit? Call the creatures
Whose naked natures live in all the spite
Of wreakful heaven, whose bare unhoused trunks
To the conflicting elements expos'd,   245
Answer mere nature; bid them flatter thee;
O, thou shalt find—
   Tim.   A fool of thee. Depart.
   Apem. I love thee better now than e'er I did.
   Tim. I hate thee worse.   250
   Apem.   Why?
   Tim.   Thou flatter'st misery.
   Apem. I flatter not, but say thou art a caitiff.

   Tim. Why dost thou seek me out?
   Apem.   To vex thee.   255
   Tim. Always a villain's office, or a fool's.
Dost please thyself in 't?
   Apem.   Ay.
   Tim.   What! a knave too?
   Apem. If thou didst put this sour-cold habit on   260
To castigate thy pride, 'twere well: but thou
Dost it enforcedly; thou'dst courtier be again,
Wert thou not beggar. Willing misery
Outlives incertain pomp, is crown'd before:
The one is filling still, never complete;   265
The other, at high wish: best state, contentless,
Hath a distracted and most wretched being,
Worse than the worst, content.
Thou shouldst desire to die, being miserable.
   Tim. Not by his breath that is more miserable.   270
Thou art a slave, whom Fortune's tender arm
With favour never clasp'd, but bred a dog.
Hadst thou, like us from our first swath, proceeded
The sweet degrees that this brief world affords
To such as may the passive drudges of it   275
Freely command, thou wouldst have plung'd thyself
In general riot, melted down thy youth
In different beds of lust, and never learn'd
The icy precepts of respect, but follow'd
The sugar'd game before thee. But myself,   280
Who had the world as my confectionary,
The mouths, the tongues, the eyes, and hearts of men
At duty, more than I could frame employment,
That numberless upon me stuck as leaves
Do on the oak, have with one winter's brush   285
Fell from their boughs, and left me open, bare
For every storm that blows: I, to bear this,
That never knew but better, is some burden:
Thy nature did commence in sufferance, time
Hath made thee hard in 't. Why shouldst thou hate men?   290
They never flatter'd thee: what hast thou given?
If thou wilt curse, thy father, that poor rag,
Must be thy subject, who in spite put stuff
To some she beggar and compounded thee
Poor rogue hereditary. Hence, be gone!   295
If thou hadst not been born the worst of men,
Thou hadst been a knave and flatterer.
   Apem.   Art thou proud yet?
   Tim. Ay, that I am not thee.
   Apem.   I, that I was   300
No prodigal.
   Tim.   I, that I am one now:
Were all the wealth I have shut up in thee,
I'd give thee leave to hang it. Get thee gone.
That the whole life of Athens were in this!   305
Thus would I eat it.   *[Eating a root.]*
   Apem.   Here; I will mend thy feast.

               [Offering him a root.]

   Tim. First mend my company; take away thyself.

202 **conceptious:** *fruitful*   206 **marbled:** *shining like marble*   209 **liquorish:** *pleasant*   210 **unctuous:** *oily*   211 **consideraton:** *regard for higher things*   217 **infected:** *affected*   222 **perfumes:** *perfumed mistresses*   224 **cunning:** *profession* **carper:** *censurer*   226 **hinge:** *bend*   227 **observe:** *pay court to*   228 **strain:** *quality*   238 **warm:** *heated moderately*   239 **page:** *follow like a page*   241 **Candied:** *crystallized with frost* **caudle:** *serve as a warm drink*   244 **wreakful:** *revengeful*   246 **Answer mere nature;** *cf. n.*

256–259 **Always ... too;** *cf. n.*   268 *Far worse than the worst condition of life when accompanied by content*   270 **breath:** *voice, advice*   273 **swath:** *swaddling-clothes*   273, 274 **proceeded ... degrees;** *cf. n.*   275 **drudges;** *cf. n.*   281 **confectionary:** *maker of sweet-meats*   283 **frame:** *provide with*   285 **have:** *i.e., and now have* **brush:** *violence*   289 **sufferance:** *suffering*   290 **hard in:** *hardened to*   292 **rag:** *term of contempt, a shabby person*   295 **hereditary:** *by heredity*   305 **That:** *would that*

Apem. So I shall mend mine own, by the lack of thine.

Tim. 'Tis not well mended so, it is but botch'd; 310
If not, I would it were.

Apem. What wouldst thou have to Athens?

Tim. Thee thither in a whirlwind. If thou wilt,
Tell them there I have gold; look, so I have.

Apem. Here is no use for gold. 315

Tim. The best and truest;
For here it sleeps, and does no hired harm.

Apem. Where liest o' nights, Timon?

Tim. Under that 's above me.
Where feed'st thou o' days, Apemantus? 320

Apem. Where my stomach finds meat; or, rather, where
I eat it.

Tim. Would poison were obedient and knew my mind!

Apem. Where wouldst thou send it?

Tim. To sauce thy dishes. 325

Apem. The middle of humanity thou never knewest, but
the extremity of both ends: when thou wast in thy gilt and
thy perfume, they mocked thee for too much curiosity; in
thy rags thou know'st none, but art despised for the contrary.
There's a medlar for thee; eat it. 330

Tim. On what I hate I feed not.

Apem. Dost hate a medlar?

Tim. Ay, though it look like thee.

Apem. An thou hadst hated meddlers sooner, thou shouldst
have loved thyself better now. What man didst thou ever 335
know unthrift that was beloved after his means?

Tim. Who, without those means thou talk'st of, didst
thou ever know beloved?

Apem. Myself.

Tim. I understand thee; thou hadst some means to 340
keep a dog.

Apem. What things in the world canst thou nearest
compare to thy flatterers?

Tim. Women nearest; but men, men are the things
themselves. What wouldst thou do with the world, 345
Apemantus, if it lay in thy power?

Apem. Give it the beasts, to be rid of the men.

Tim. Wouldst thou have thyself fall in the confusion
of men, and remain a beast with the beasts?

Apem. Ay, Timon. 350

Tim. A beastly ambition, which the gods grant thee t' attain
to! If thou wert the lion, the fox would beguile thee: if thou
wert the lamb, the fox would eat thee: if thou wert the fox,
the lion would suspect thee, when peradventure thou wert accused by the ass: if thou wert the ass, thy dulness would 355
torment thee, and still thou livedst but as a breakfast to the
wolf: if thou wert the wolf, thy greediness would afflict thee,
and oft thou shouldst hazard thy life for thy dinner: wert thou
the unicorn, pride and wrath would confound thee, and
make thine own self the conquest of thy fury: wert 360
thou a bear, thou wouldst be killed by the horse: wert
thou a horse, thou wouldst be seized by the leopard: wert thou
a leopard, thou wert german to the lion, and the spots of thy
kindred were jurors on thy life: all thy safety were remotion,

and thy defence absence. What beast couldst thou be, 365
that were not subject to a beast? and what a beast art
thou already, that seest not thy loss in transformation!

Apem. If thou couldst please me with speaking to me, thou
mightst have hit upon it here: the commonwealth of Athens
is become a forest of beasts. 370

Tim. How has the ass broke the wall, that thou art out
of the city?

Apem. Yonder comes a poet and a painter: the plague of
company light upon thee! I will fear to catch it, and give way.
When I know not what else to do, I'll see thee again. 375

Tim. When there is nothing living but thee, thou shalt be
welcome. I had rather be a beggar's dog than Apemantus.

Apem. Thou art the cap of all the fools alive.

Tim. Would thou wert clean enough to spit upon!

Apem. A plague on thee! thou art too bad to curse. 380

Tim. All villains that do stand by thee are pure.

Apem. There is no leprosy but what thou speak'st.

Tim. If I name thee,
I'll beat thee; but I should infect my hands.

Apem. I would my tongue could rot them off! 385

Tim. Away, thou issue of a mangy dog!
Choler does kill me that thou art alive;
I swound to see thee.

Apem. Would thou wouldst burst!

Tim. Away, 390
Thou tedious rogue! I am sorry I shall lose
A stone by thee. *[Throws a stone at him.]*

Apem. Beast!

Tim. Slave!

Apem. Toad! 395

Tim. Rogue, rogue, rogue!
I am sick of this false world, and will love nought
But even the mere necessities upon 't.
Then, Timon, presently prepare thy grave;
Lie where the light foam of the sea may beat 400
Thy grave-stone daily: make thine epitaph,
That death in me at others' lives may laugh.

[Looking on the gold.]

O thou sweet king-killer, and dear divorce
'Twixt natural son and sire! thou bright defiler
Of Hymen's purest bed! thou valiant Mars! 405
Thou ever young, fresh, lov'd, and delicate wooer,
Whose blush doth thaw the consecrated snow
That lies on Dian's lap! thou visible god,
That solder'st close impossibilities,
And mak'st them kiss! that speak'st with every tongue, 410
To every purpose! O thou touch of hearts!
Think thy slave, man, rebels; and by thy virtue
Set them into confounding odds, that beasts
May have the world in empire!

Apem. Would 'twere so! 415
But not till I am dead. I'll say thou'st gold:
Thou wilt be throng'd to shortly.

Tim. Throng'd to!

Apem. Ay.

Tim. Thy back, I prithee. 420

Apem. Live, and love thy misery!

310, 311 'Tis not ... would it were; *cf. n.* 312 What ... Athens; *cf. n.* 328 curiosity: *fastidiousness* 330 medlar; *cf. n.* 336 unthrift: *prodigal* after; *cf. n.* 348 confusion: *ruin* 358, 359 wert thou the unicorn, etc.; *cf. n.* 359 confound: *destroy* 362–364 wert thou ... life; *cf. n.* 363 german: *akin* 364 remotion: *keeping away*

373 Yonder ... painter; *cf. n.* 378 cap: *chief* 388 swound: *swoon* 399 presently: *immediately* 403 dear: *used intensively* 405 Hymen; *cf. n.* 409 close: *closely* (?) 411 touch: *touchstone*

Tim. Long live so, and so die!   *Exit Apemantus.*
              I am quit.
Moe things like men? Eat, Timon, and abhor them.

Enter the Banditti.

First Ban. Where should he have this gold?   425
It is some poor fragment, some slender ort of his remainder;
the mere want of gold, and the falling-from of his friends,
drove him into this melancholy.
     Sec. Ban. It is noised he hath a mass of treasure.
     Third Ban. Let us make the assay upon him: if he care   430
not for 't, he will supply us easily; if he covetously reserve
it, how shall's get it?
     Sec. Ban. True; for he bears it not about him; 'tis hid.
     First Ban. Is not this he?
     All. Where?   435
     Sec. Ban. 'Tis his description.
     Third Ban. He; I know him.
     All. Save thee, Timon.
     Tim. Now, thieves?
     All. Soldiers, not thieves.   440
     Tim. Both too; and women's sons.
     All. We are not thieves, but men that much do want.
     Tim. Your greatest want is, you want much of meat.
Why should you want? Behold, the earth hath roots;
Within this mile break forth a hundred springs;   445
The oaks bear mast, the briers scarlet hips;
The bounteous housewife, nature, on each bush
Lays her full mess before you. Want! why want?
     First Ban. We cannot live on grass, on berries, water,
As beasts and birds and fishes.   450
     Tim. Nor on the beasts themselves, the birds, and fishes;
You must eat men. Yet thanks I must you con
That you are thieves profess'd, that you work not
In holier shapes: for there is boundless theft
In limited professions. Rascal thieves,   455
Here's gold. Go, suck the subtle blood o' the grape,
Till the high fever seethe your blood to froth,
And so 'scape hanging: trust not the physician;
His antidotes are poison, and he slays
Moe than you rob: take wealth and lives together;   460
Do villany, do, since you protest to do 't,
Like workmen. I'll example you with thievery:
The sun's a thief, and with his great attraction
Robs the vast sea: the moon's an arrant thief,
And her pale fire she snatches from the sun: 465
The sea's a thief, whose liquid surge resolves
The moon into salt tears: the earth's a thief,
That feeds and breeds by a composture stol'n
From general excrement: each thing's a thief:
The laws, your curb and whip, in their rough power   470
Have uncheck'd theft. Love not yourselves; away!
Rob one another. There's more gold. Cut throats:
All that you meet are thieves: to Athens go,
Break open shops; nothing can you steal,
But thieves do lose it: steal not less for this   475

I give you; and gold confound you howsoe'er!
Amen.
     Third Ban. Has almost charmed me from my profession by
persuading me to it.
     First Ban. 'Tis in the malice of mankind that he thus   480
advises us; not to have us thrive in our mystery.
     Sec. Ban. I'll believe him as an enemy, and give over my
trade.
     First Ban. Let us first see peace in Athens: there is no time
so miserable but a man may be true.   *Exeunt Thieves.*

Enter the Steward [Flavius] to Timon.

Flav. O you gods!
Is yond despised and ruinous man my lord?
Full of decay and failing? O monument
And wonder of good deeds evilly bestow'd!
What an alteration of honour   490
Has desperate want made!
What viler thing upon the earth than friends
Who can bring noblest minds to basest ends!
How rarely does it meet with this time's guise,
When man was wish'd to love his enemies!   495
Grant I may ever love, and rather woo
Those that would mischief me than those that do!
Has caught me in his eye: I will present
My honest grief unto him, and, as my lord,
Still serve him with my life. My dearest master!   500

[Timon comes forward.]

     Tim. Away! what art thou?
     Flav.   Have you forgot me, sir?
     Tim. Why dost ask that? I have forgot all men;
Then, if thou grant'st thou'rt a man, I have forgot thee.
     Flav. An honest poor servant of yours.   505
     Tim.   Then I know thee not:
I never had an honest man about me, I; all
I kept were knaves, to serve in meat to villains
     Flav. The gods are witness,
Ne'er did poor steward wear a truer grief   510
For his undone lord than mine eyes for you.
     Tim. What, dost thou weep? come nearer; then I love thee,
Because thou art a woman, and disclaim'st
Flinty mankind, whose eyes do never give,
But thorough lust and laughter. Pity's sleeping: 515
Strange times, that weep with laughing, not with weeping!
     Flav. I beg of you to know me, good my lord,
To accept my grief and whilst this poor wealth lasts
To entertain me as your steward still.
     Tim. Had I a steward   520
So true, so just, and now so comfortable?
It almost turns my dangerous nature mild.
Let me behold thy face. Surely this man
Was born of woman.
Forgive my general and exceptless rashness,   525
You perpetual-sober gods! I do proclaim
One honest man—mistake me not—but one;
No more, I pray,—and he's a steward.

423 quit: *rid of you*   426 ort: *fragment*   427 falling-from: *desertion*   430 assay: *trial*   432 shall's: *shall we*   439 Now: *how now*   446 mast: *fruit of the beach, oak, or chestnut* hips: *fruit of the wild rose*   448 mess: *dish (of food)*   452 thanks ... con: *be grateful*   455 limited: *restricted*   461 protest: *vow*   462 example: *furnish with instances*   466, 467 whose liquid ... tears; *cf. n.*   468 composture: *manure*

485 true: *honest*   490 alteration of honour: *change to dishonor*   494 rarely: *finely*   494, 495 How rarely ... enemies; *cf. n.*   496, 497 Grant ... that do; *cf. n.*   514 give: *shed tears*   515 thorough: *through*   519 entertain: *maintain, use*   521 comfortable: *helpful*   525 exceptless: *making no exception*

How fain would I have hated all mankind!   530
And thou redeem'st thyself: but all, save thee,
I fell with curses.
Methinks thou art more honest now than wise;
For, by oppressing and betraying me,
Thou mightst have sooner got another service: 535
For many so arrive at second masters,
Upon their first lord's neck. But tell me true—
For I must ever doubt, though ne'er so sure—
Is not thy kindness subtle, covetous,
If not a usuring kindness and as rich men deal gifts,   540
Excepting in return twenty for one?

Flav. No, my most worthy master; in whose breast
Doubt and suspect, alas, are plac'd too late:
You should have fear'd false times when you did feast:
Suspect still comes when an estate is least.   545
That which I show, heaven knows, is merely love,
Duty and zeal to your unmatched mind,
Care of your food and living; and, believe it,
My most honour'd lord,
For any benefit that points to me,   550
Either in hope, or present, I'd exchange
For this one wish, that you had power and wealth
To requite me by making rich yourself.

Tim. Look thee, 'tis so! Thou singly honest man,
Here, take: the gods out of my misery,   555
Have sent thee treasure. Go, live rich and happy;
But thus condition'd: thou shalt build from men,
Hate all, curse all, show charity to none,
But let the famish'd flesh slide from the bone,
Ere thou relieve the beggar: give to dogs   560
What thou deny'st to men; let prisons swallow 'em,
Debts wither 'em to nothing: be men like blasted woods,
And may diseases lick up their false bloods!
And so, farewell, and thrive.

Flav.   O, let me stay   565
And comfort you, my master.

Tim.   If thou hatest
Curses, stay not: fly, whilst thou'rt blest and free:
Ne'er see thou man, and let me ne'er see thee.   *Exit.*

ACT FIFTH ❦ SCENE FIRST

[The Woods. Before Timon's Cave]
Enter Poet and Painter.

Pain. As I took note of the place, it cannot be far where
he abides.

Poet. What's to be thought of him? Does the rumour hold
for true that he's so full of gold?

Pain. Certain: Alcibiades reports it; Phrynia and Timandra 5
had gold of him: he likewise enriched poor straggling soldiers
with great quantity: 'tis said he gave unto his steward a mighty
sum.

Poet. Then this breaking of his has been but a try for his
friends.   10

Pain. Nothing else: you shall see him a palm in Athens
again, and flourish with the highest. Therefore 'tis not amiss
we tender our loves to him in this supposed distress of his:
it will show honestly in us, and is very likely to load our
purposes with what they travail for, if it be a just and   15
true report that goes of his having.

Poet. What have you now to present unto him?

Pain. Nothing at this time but my visitation: only I
will promise him an excellent piece.

Poet. I must serve him so too, tell him of an intent   20
that's coming towards him.

Pain. Good as the best. Promising is the very air o' the
time: it opens the eyes of expectation: performance is ever the
duller for his act; and, but in the plainer and simpler kind of
people, the deed of saying is quite out of use. To promise 25
is most courtly and fashionable: performance is a kind of
will or testament which argues a great sickness in his judgement that makes it.

Enter Timon from his Cave.

Tim. [Aside.] Excellent workman! Thou canst not paint
a man so bad as is thyself.   30

Poet. I am thinking what I shall say I have provided for
him: it must be a personating of himself; a satire against the
softness of prosperity, with a discovery of the infinite flatteries
that follow youth and opulency.

Tim. [Aside.] Must thou needs stand for a villain in thine 35
own work? Wilt thou whip thine own faults in other men?
Do so, I have gold for thee.

Poet. Nay, let's seek him:
Then do we sin against our own estate,
When we may profit meet, and come too late.   40

Pain. True;
When the day serves, before black-corner'd night,
Find what thou want'st by free and offer'd light.
Come.

Tim. [Aside.] I'll meet you at the turn. What a god's gold, 45
That he is worshipp'd in a baser temple
Than where swine feed!
'Tis thou that rigg'st the bark and plough'st the foam,
Settlest admired reverence in a slave:
To thee be worship! and thy saints for aye   50
Be crown'd with plagues, that thee alone obey!
Fit I meet them.   *[Coming forward.]*

Poet. Hail, worthy Timon!

Pain.   Our late noble master!

Tim. Have I once liv'd to see two honest men?   55

Poet. Sir,
Having often of your open bounty tasted,
Hearing you were retir'd, your friends fall'n off,
Whose thankless natures—O abhorred spirits!
Not all the whips of heaven are large enough—   60
What! to you,
Whose star-like nobleness gave life and influence
To their whole being! I am rapt, and cannot cover
The monstrous bulk of this ingratitude
With any size of words.   65

---

543 **suspect:** *suspicion*   547 **unmatched:** *matchless*   554 **singly:** *uniquely*   557 **thus
condition'd:** *on these conditions*   3, 4 **hold for:** *prove*   11 **try:** *test*

15 **purposes:** *plans*   25 **deed of saying:** *performance of promise*   32 **personating:** *representing*   33 **discovery:** *showing*   42 **black-corner'd;** *cf. n.*   52 **Fit:** *it is fitting
that*   63 **rapt:** *beside myself*

Tim. Let it go naked, men may see 't the better:
You, that are honest, by being what you are,
Make them best seen and known
    Pain.   He and myself
Have travail'd in the great shower of your gifts,   *70*
And sweetly felt it.
    Tim.   Ay, you are honest men.
    Pain. We are hither come to offer you our service.
    Tim. Most honest men! Why, how shall I requite you?
Can you eat roots, and drink cold water? no.   *75*
    Both. What we can do, we'll do, to do you service.
    Tim. Ye're honest men: ye've heard that I have gold;
I am sure you have: speak truth; ye're honest men.
    Pain. So it is said, my noble lord: but therefore
Came not my friend nor I.   *80*
    Tim. Good honest men! Thou draw'st a counterfeit
Best in all Athens: thou'rt indeed the best;
Thou counterfeit'st most lively.
    Pain.   So, so, my lord.
    Tim. E'en so, sir, as I say. And, for thy fiction,   *85*
Why, thy verse swells with stuff so fine and smooth
That thou art even natural in thine art.
But for all this, my honest-natur'd friends,
I must needs say you have a little fault:
Marry, 'tis not monstrous in you; neither wish I   *90*
You take much pains to mend.
    Both.   Beseech your honour
To make it known to us.
    Tim.   You'll take it ill.
    Both. Most thankfully, my lord.   *95*
    Tim.   Will you, indeed?
    Both. Doubt it not, worthy lord.
    Tim. There's never a one of you but trusts a knave
That mightily deceives you.
    Both.   Do we, my lord?   *100*
    Tim. Ay, and you hear him cog, see him dissemble,
Know his gross patchery, love him, feed him,
Keep in your bosom: yet remain assur'd
That he's a made-up villain.
    Pain. I know none such, my lord.   *105*
    Poet.   Nor I.
    Tim. Look you, I love you well; I'll give you gold,
Rid me these villains from your companies:
Hang them or stab them, drown them in a draught,
Confound them by some course, and come to me,   *110*
I'll give you gold enough.
    Both. Name them, my lord, let's know them.
    Tim. You that way, and you this, but two in company:
Each man apart, all single and alone,
Yet an arch-villain keeps him company.   *115*
If, where thou art two villains shall not be,
Come not near him. *[To the Poet.]* If thou would'st not reside
But where one villain is, then him abandon.
Hence, pack! there's gold; you came for gold, ye slaves:
[To Painter.] You have done work for me, there's payment: *120*
hence!
[To Poet.] You are an alchemist, make gold of that:

Out, rascal dogs!
          [Beats them out, and then returns into his cave.]
      Enter Steward [Flavius], and two Senators.

    Flav. It is in vain that you would speak with Timon;
For he is set so only to himself   *125*
That nothing but himself which looks like man,
Is friendly with him.
    First Sen.   Bring us to his cave:
It is our part and promise to the Athenians
To speak with Timon.   *130*
    Sec. Sen.   At all times alike
Men are not still the same: 'twas time and griefs
That fram'd him thus: time, with his fairer hand,
Offering the fortunes of his former days,
The former man may make him. Bring us to him,   *135*
And chance it as it may.
    Flav.   Here is his cave.
Peace and content be here! Lord Timon! Timon!
Look out, and speak to friends. The Athenians,
By two of their most reverend senate, greet thee: *140*
Speak to them, noble Timon.

        Enter Timon out of his Cave.

    Tim. Thou sun, that comfort'st, burn! Speak, and be
hang'd:
For each true word, a blister! and each false
Be as a cauterizing to the root o' the tongue,   *145*
Consuming it with speaking!
    First Sen.   Worthy Timon,—
    Tim. Of none but such as you, and you of Timon.
    Sec. Sen. The senators of Athens greet thee, Timon.
    Tim. I thank them, and would send them back the plague, *150*
Could I but catch it for them.
    First Sen.   O, forget
What we are sorry for ourselves in thee.
The senators will one consent of love
Entreat thee back to Athens; who have thought   *155*
On special dignities, which vacant lie
For thy best use and wearing.
    Sec. Sen.   They confess
Toward thee forgetfulness too general, gross;
Which now the public body, which doth seldom   *160*
Play the recanter, feeling in itself
A lack of Timon's aid, hath sense withal
Of it own fail, restraining aid to Timon;
And send forth us, to make their sorrow'd render,
Together with a recompense more fruitful   *165*
Then their offence can weigh down by the dram;
Ay, even such heaps and sums of love and wealth,
As shall to thee blot out what wrongs were theirs,
And write in thee the figures of their love,
Ever to read them thine.   *170*
    Tim.   You witch me in it,
Surprise me to the very brink of tears:
Lend me a fool's heart and a woman's eyes,
And I'll beweep these comforts, worthy senators.

---

81 counterfeit: *likeness*   **83 lively:** *to the life*   **87 natural:** *pun on 'natural,' a fool*   **101 cog:** *cheat*   **102 patchery:** *roguery*   **104 made-up:** *consummate*   **109 draught:** *cesspool*   **119 pack:** *depart*

125 set . . . to himself: *wrapped up in himself*   **129 part:** *particular business*   **133 fram'd: moulded**   **135 The . . . him:** *may restore him to his former self*   **162 hath . . . withal: has, besides, a realization**   **163 it:** *its*   **fail:** *offence*   **164 sorrow'd render:** *confession of sorrow*   **171 witch:** *bewitch*

First Sen. Therefore so please thee to return with us,   *175*
And of our Athens—thine and ours—to take
The captainship, thou shalt be met with thanks,
Allow'd with absolute power, and thy good name
Live with authority: so soon we shall drive back
Of Alcibiades the approaches wild;   *180*
Who, like a boar too savage, doth root up
His country's peace.
   Sec. Sen.   And shakes his threat'ning sword
Against the walls of Athens.
   First Sen.   Therefore, Timon,—   *185*
   Tim. Well, sir, I will; therefore, I will, sir;
thus:—
If Alcibiades kill my countrymen,
Let Alcibiades know this of Timon,
That Timon cares not. But if he sack fair Athens,   *190*
And take our goodly aged men by the beards,
Giving our holy virgins to the stain
Of contumelious, beastly, mad-brain'd war;
Then let him know, and tell him Timon speaks it,
In pity of our aged and our youth   *195*
I cannot choose but tell him, that I care not,
And let him take 't at worst; for their knives care not
While you have throats to answer: for myself
There's not a whittle in the unruly camp
But I do prize it at my love before   *200*
The reverend'st throat in Athens. So I leave you
To the protection of the prosperous gods,
As thieves to keepers.
   Flav.   Stay not; all's in vain.
   Tim. Why, I was writing of my epitaph;   *205*
It will be seen to-morrow. My long sickness
Of health and living now begins to mend,
And nothing brings me all things. Go, live still;
Be Alcibiades your plague, you his,
And last so long enough!   *210*
   First Sen.   We speak in vain.
   Tim. But yet I love my country, and am not
One that rejoices in the common wrack,
As common bruit doth put it.
   First Sen.   That's well spoke.   *215*
   Tim. Commend me to my loving countrymen,—
   First Sen. These words become your lips as they pass
through them.
   Sec. Sen. And enter in our ears like great triumphers
In their applauding gates.   *220*
   Tim.   Commend me to them;
And tell them, that, to ease them of their griefs,
Their fears of hostile strokes, their aches, losses,
Their pangs of love, with other incident throes
That nature's fragile vessel doth sustain   *225*
In life's uncertain voyage, I will some kindness do them:
I'll teach them to prevent wild Alcibiades' wrath
   Sec. Sen. I like this well; he will return again.
   Tim. I have a tree, which grows here in my close,
That mine own use invites me to cut down,   *230*
And shortly must I fell it: tell my friends,
Tell Athens, in the sequence of degree,

From high to low throughout, that whoso please
To stop affliction, let him take his haste,
Come hither, ere my tree hath felt the axe,   *235*
And hang himself. I pray you, do my greeting.
   Flav. Trouble him no further; thus you still shall find
him.
   Tim. Come not to me again; but say to Athens,
Timon hath made his everlasting mansion   *240*
Upon the beached verge of the salt flood;
Who once a day with his embossed froth
The turbulent surge shall cover: thither come,
And let my grave-stone be your oracle.
Lips, let sour words go by and language end: *245*
What is amiss plague and infection mend!
Graves only be men's works and death their gain!
Sun, hide thy beams! Timon hath done his reign.   *Exit Timon.*
   First Sen. His discontents are unremovably
Coupled to nature.   *250*
   Sec. Sen. Our hope in him is dead: let us return,
And strain what other means is left unto us
In our dear peril.
   First Sen. It requires swift foot.   *Exeunt.*

❧ SCENE SECOND ❧

[Before the Walls of Athens]
Enter two other Senators, with a Messenger.

   First Sen. Thou hast painfully discover'd: are his files
As full as they report?
   Mess.   I have spoke the least:
Besides, his expedition promises
Present approach.   *5*
   Sec. Sen. We stand much hazard, if they bring not Timon.
   Mess. I met a courier, one mine ancient friend,
Whom, though in general part we were oppos'd,
Yet our old love made a particular force,
And made us speak like friends: this man was riding   *10*
From Alcibiades to Timon's cave,
With letters of entreaty, which imported
His fellowship i' the cause against your city,
In part for his sake mov'd.
   First Sen.   Here come our brothers.   *15*

Enter the other Senators [from Timon].

   Third Sen. No talk of Timon, nothing of him expect.
The enemies' drum is heard, and fearful scouring
Doth choke the air with duty. In, and prepare:
Ours is the fall, I fear, our foes the snare.   *Exeunt.*

❧ SCENE THIRD ❧

[The Woods. Timon's Cave, and a rude Tomb seen]
Enter a Soldier in the Woods, seeking Timon.

   Sold. By all description this should be the place.
Who's here? speak, ho! No answer! What is this?

---

178 Allow'd: *sanctioned* **199 whittle:** *small clasp-knive* **202 prosperous:** *propitious* **208 nothing:** *oblivion, death* **213 wrack:** *ruin* **214 bruit:** *rumor* **227 prevent:** *escape* **229 close:** *enclosure* **232 in ... degree:** *one after another according to rank*

234 take ... haste: *make haste* **242 embossed:** *foaming* **252 strain:** *exert to the utmost* **1 painfully discover'd:** *told distressing tidings* **files:** *ranks* **8 in general part:** *in the public cause*

Timon is dead, who hath outstretch'd his span:
Some beast read this; there does not live a man.
Dead, sure; and this his grave. What's on this tomb   5
I cannot read; the character I'll take with wax:
Our captain hath in every figure skill,
An ag'd interpreter, though young in days.
Before proud Athens he's set down by this,
Whose fall the mark of his ambition is.   *Exit.*

⚜ SCENE FOURTH ⚜

[Before the Walls of Athens]

Trumpets sound. Enter Alcibiades with his Powers before Athens.

Alcib. Sound to this coward and lascivious town
Our terrible approach.   *Sounds a parley.*

The Senators appear upon the Walls.

Till now you have gone on and fill'd the time
With all licentious measure, making your wills
The scope of justice; till now myself and such   5
As slept within the shadow of your power
Have wander'd with our travers'd arms, and breath'd
Our sufferance vainly. Now the time is flush,
When crouching marrow, in the bearer strong,
Cries of itself, 'No more:' now breathless wrong   10
Shall sit and pant in your great chairs of ease,
And pursy insolence shall break his wind
With fear and horrid flight.
     First Sen.   Noble and young,
When thy first griefs were but a mere conceit,   15
Ere thou hadst power or we had cause of fear,
We sent to thee, to give thy rages balm,
To wipe out our ingratitude with loves
Above their quantity.
     Sec. Sen.   So did we woo   20
Transformed Timon to our city's love
By humble message and by promis'd means:
We were not all unkind, nor all deserve
The common stroke of war.
     First Sen.   These walls of ours   25
Were not erected by their hands from whom
You have receiv'd your grief: nor are they such
That these great towers, trophies, and schools should fall
For private faults in them.
     Sec. Sen.   Nor are they living   30
Who were the motives that you first went out;
Shame that they wanted cunning in excess
Hath broke their hearts. March, noble lord,
Into our city with thy banners spread:
By decimation, and a tithed death,—   35
If thy revenges hunger for that food
Which nature loathes,—take thou the destin'd tenth,

And by the hazard of the spotted die
Let die the spotted.
     First Sen.   All have not offended;   40
For those that were, it is not square to take,
On those that are, revenges: crimes like lands
Are not inherited. Then, dear countryman,
Bring in thy ranks, but leave without thy rage:
Spare thy Athenian cradle and those kin   45
Which, in the bluster of thy wrath, must fall
With those that have offended: like a shepherd,
Approach the fold and cull th' infected forth,
But kill not all together.
     Sec. Sen.   What thou wilt,   50
Thou rather shalt enforce it with thy smile
Than hew to 't with thy sword.
     First Sen.   Set but thy foot
Against our rampir'd gates, and they shall ope,
So thou wilt send thy gentle heart before,   55
To say thou'lt enter friendly.
     Sec. Sen.   Throw thy glove,
Or any token of thine honour else,
That thou wilt use the wars as thy redress
And not as our confusion, all thy powers   60
Shall make their harbour in our town, till we
Have seal'd thy full desire.
     Alcib.   Then there's my glove;
Descend, and open your uncharged ports:
Those enemies of Timon's and mine own,   65
Whom you yourselves shall set out for reproof,
Fall, and no more: and, to atone your fears
With my more noble meaning, not a man
Shall pass his quarter, or offend the stream
Of regular justice in your city's bounds,   70
But shall be render'd to your public laws
At heaviest answer.
     Both.   'Tis most nobly spoken.
Alcib. Descend, and keep your words.
     [The Senators descend, and open the gates.]

Enter a Messenger.

Mess. My noble general, Timon is dead;
Entomb'd upon the very hem o' the sea;   75
And on his grave-stone this insculpture, which
With wax I brought away, whose soft impression
Interprets for my poor ignorance.

Alcibiades reads the epitaph.

Alcib. 'Here lies a wretched corse, of wretched soul bereft: 80
Seek not my name: a plague consume you wicked caitiffs left!
Here lie I, Timon; who, alive, all living men did hate:
Pass by, and curse thy fill; but pass and stay not here thy gait.'
These well express in thee thy latter spirits:
Though thou abhorr'dst in us our human griefs,   85
Scorn'dst our brain's flow and those our droplets which

---

3 **outstretch'd his span:** *reached the limit of his life*   4 **read;** *cf. n.*   6 **character:** *writing*   7 **travers'd arms:** *folded arms, reversed arms (?)*   8 **flush:** *full*   9 **marrow:** *vigor*   12 **pursy:** *short-winded*   15 **griefs:** *grievances* **conceit:** *fancy*   22 **promis'd means:** *means of promises (?)*   31 **motives:** *agents*   32 **that ... excess:** *at their excessive folly*   35 **tithed:** *involving the slaughter of a tenth*

39 **spotted:** *stained*   41 **square:** *proper*   44 **without:** *outside*   52 **hew to 't:** *cut the way to it*   54 **rampir'd:** *fortified against an attack*   55 **So:** *if only*   62 **seal'd:** *brought to completion*   64 **uncharged:** *unattacked* **ports:** *gates*   67 **atone:** *set at one*   69 **quarter:** *lodging place*   71 **render'd:** *surrendered*   72 **At ... answer:** *to pay the full penalty*   77 **insculpture:** *carved inscription*   80–84 **Here ... gait;** *cf. n.*   80 **corse:** *corpse*   86 **brain's flow:** *tears*

From niggard nature fall, yet rich conceit
Taught thee to make vast Neptune weep for aye
On thy low grave, on faults forgiven. Dead
Is noble Timon, of whose memory   *90*
Hereafter more. Bring me into your city,
And I will use the olive with my sword,

Make war breed peace, make peace stint war, make each
Prescribe to other as each other's leech.
Let our drums strike.   *Exeunt.*

❧ FINIS ❧

---

93 stint: *stop*   **94 leech:** *physician*

NOTES

Dramatis Personæ. In the First Folio the last page of Timon of Athens bears the caption: 'The Actors' Names.' Additions to this list of characters have been placed in brackets. In the Folio Sempronius' name occurs twice. Ventidius is known as Ventigius; Philotus as Philo; and Hortensius as Hortensis.

I.i.S. d. *Enter ... and Mercer.* The stage direction of the Folio has been restored. Many modern editors have changed it to read: *Enter ... Merchant, and others ...* , omitting the 'Mercer.' Whether or not the 'Mercer' speaks during the scene is not made clear by the test of the Folio, since each speech is preceeded by *Mer.*, which may represent, equally well, either 'Merchant' or 'Mercer.'

I.i.4. *It wears, sir, as it grows.* A half-facetious reply to the Poet's greeting: as the world grows older it wears away.

I.i.19. *'When we for recompense,'* etc. A stage direction might be added: 'Reciting to himself,' or 'Reading from his poems.'

I.i.29-31. *our gentle flame ... chafes.* The poet's fancy is self-inspired, and, like a swift stream, it flies away from every boundary which it chafes. 'Bound' refers to the banks of the stream; against these the current 'chafes,' but speeds onward.

I.i.33. *Upon the heels of my presentment, sir.* 'As soon as my book has been presented to Lord Timon.' (Johnson.) In Shakespeare's day, as later, the success of a book often depended upon its patron.

I.i.38, 39. *how this grace Speaks his own standing!* How truly the gracefulness of this figure expresses the dignity of the original!

I.i.41, 42. *to the dumbness of the gesture One might interpret.* To the mute eloquence of this gesture one might easily supply words. This line may allude to the 'interpreter' whose function was to explain the action of the puppet-shows.

I.i.56. *In a wide sea of wax.* The usual explanation that reference is made to use among the ancients of writing-tablets covered with wax, is not wholly satisfactory.

I.i.56-59. *no levell'd malice ... behind.* 'Shakespeare's meaning is, my poem is not a satire written with any particular view, or levelled at any single person; I fly like an eagle into the general expanse of life, and leave not, by any private mischief, the trace of my passage.' (Johnson.) Keightley conjectures that a lacuna exists after 'hold.'

I.i.88, 89. *would ... condition.* 'Would find a striking parallel in our state.' (Schmidt.) Of various interpretations this seems most convincing. However, it is possible that by 'condition' the painter means 'art'; specifically, 'the art of painting.'

I.i.110. *five talents.* About six thousand dollars. A talent was approximately twelve hundred dollars.

I.i.147-150. *The man is honest ... daughter.* 'The meaning of the first line the poet himself expains, or rather unfolds, in the second. "The man is honest!"— True; and for that very cause, and with no additional or extrinsic motive, he will be so. No man can be justly called honest, who is not so for honesty's sake, itself including its reward.' (Coleridge.)

I.i.190, 191. *Hath ... dispraise.* Timon's statement that the jewel has been embarrassingly praised or valued is misunderstood by the jeweller; he interprets 'under praise' as 'dispraise.'

I.i.196. *As ... give.* At a figure which those who sell would be willing to pay.

I.i.208. *When ... honest.* Until you become a dog and these knaves become honest,—remote contingencies!

I.i.238. *plain-dealing.* An allusion to the proverb, 'Plain-dealing is a jewel, but they that use it die beggars.'

I.i.261. *That I had no angry wit to be a lord.* It is possible that the adjective 'angry' is corrupt. As it stands in the text the line seems to express the annoyance of Apemantus at the idea that angry self-derision should not be aroused in him at the fact of his being a lord.

I.i.277. *Aches.* To be scanned as a dissyllable.

I.i.306. *Plutus, the god of gold.* The Greek personification of riches. He was supposed to have been blinded by Zeus so that he might distribute his gifts without choice.

I.ii.22, 23. *confess'd ... not.* In all likelihood an allusion to the proverb of Shakespeare's time: 'Confess and be hanged.'

I.ii.30-45. *They say ... too.* It is difficult to state whether these lines, and others in the play, should be printed as poetry or as prose. Certain modern editors give them as Prose.

I.ii.30. *'Ira furor brevis est.'* Wrath is a brief madness. Horace, *Epistles*, Book I.ii.62.

I.ii.47. *Methinks they should invite them without knives.* The Elizabethan guests were accustomed to bring their knives to feasts. (Ritson.)

I.ii.101, 102. *O joy, ... born.* Timon's tears of joy choke and seem to belie the very happiness that provokes them.

I.ii.104. *Thou weep'st to make them drink, Timon.* The tears you shed so bountifully would be a suitable beverage for the flatterers (rather than the wine they swill). Or, perhaps, the remark is merely a sneer at the incongruity of Timon's weeping while his guests drink.

I.ii.S. d. *Enter Cupid.* I.e., the 'forerunner,' a boy dressed to personate the god of love; as in *As You Like It*, V. iv, one personates Hymen, the god of marriage.

I.ii.S. d. *with the masque of Ladies [as] Amazons.* The masque, a form of histrionic spectacle, was much in vogue during the early seventeenth century. There are masque-like features in *Henry VIII*, *The Winter's Tale*, and *The Tempest*, all written within a few years of *Timon of Athens*. No stage direction occurs at this point in the Folio. Instead, the words clearly required here are by anticipation added to the stage directions after lines 117 and 126. The former reads: 'Sound Tucket. Enter the Maskers of Amazons, with Lutes in their hands, dauncing and playing;' and the latter: 'Enter Cupid with the Maske of Ladies.'

I.ii.128. *they are mad women.* This line may reflect the Puritan spirit of the time. Stubbes' *Anatomie of Abuses* (1583), speaks of 'Dauncers thought to be madmen.' 'There were (saith Ludovicus Vives) from far countries certain men brought into our parts of the world, who, when they saw men daunce, ran away marvellously affraid, crying out and thinking them mad.'

I.ii.129, 130. *Like madness ... root.* 'Just such madness is the glory of this life as the pomp of this feast appears when compared with the philosopher's frugal repast of a little oil and a few roots.' (Clarke.)

I.ii.140. *Men shut their doors against a setting sun.* A proverbial saying, the sense of which is illustrated by a passage in Bacon's essay on Friendship (1625): 'L. Sylla, when he commanded Rome, raised Pompey, after surnamed the Great, to that height, that Pompey vaunted himself for Sylla's over-match. For when he had the consulship for a friend of his against the pursuit of Sylla, and that Sylla did a little resent thereat, and began to speak great, Pompey turned upon him again, and in effect bade him be quiet, for that more men adored the sun rising, than the sun setting.'

I.ii.159. *When all ... could.* There is a quibble on 'cross'd,' and 'crossing' in line 157. 'Cross'd' probably refers to the cross upon many coins of the day. Hence, 'to be crossed' or 'to bear a cross' was a joking expression meaning 'to have ready cash.' Or the quibble may refer to the crossing out of a debt on the creditor's books.

I.ii.160, 161. *'Tis pity ... mind.* In order that bounty might be able to foresee the evils and miseries about to attack it.

I.ii.177. The meaning is illustrated by a parallel passage in *Julius Cæsar*, III.i.6-8:

'O Cæsar, read mine first; for mine's a suit
That touches Cæsar nearer ...
Cæs. What touches us ourself shall be last serv'd.'

I.ii.218. *I'll call to you.* Sandys in the *Shakespeare Society Papers* (vol.iii., p. 23), says that the expression 'I'll call to (i.e., at) your house' is still (1846) employed in the West of England.

I.ii.228. *defil'd.* Used here with a play on 'pitch'd.' Cf. *Henry IV, Part 1*, II.iv.372, 373: 'Pitch ... doth defile.'

I.ii.239. *legs.* Used here with a play upon the two senses of 'limbs' and 'bowings.'

I.ii.252. *come ... music.* 'Come again in a better tone of mind.'

II.i.10. *No porter at his gate.* In Elizabethan days the porter was a stern guardian. Cf. Thomas Dekker's *A Knight's Conjuring*: 'You mistake, if you imagine that Plutoe's *porter* is like one of those big fellows that stand like gyants at lordes gates.'

II.i.31, 32. *When every feather ... gull.* When every creditor has his proper due, Lord Timon will be stripped. 'Gull' is used with a play upon the meanings of 'unfledged bird' and 'dupe.'

II.ii.5, 6. *never ... kind.* Never was mind made to be so unwise, and yet so kind.

II.ii.12-14. *Varro ... Isidore.* The servants are addressed by their masters' names.

II.ii.18. *we'll forth again.* It was an Elizabethan custom to hunt both before and after dinner. While at Kenilworth Castle Queen Elizabeth hunted afternoons.

II.ii.69. *No, thou ... yet.* When Apemantus says 'thou' he speaks to the servant of Varro; 'thou'rt' is addressed to the servant of Isidore.

II.ii.98. *to Lord Timon's.* Almost certainly an error if this scene is laid in Timon's house. Perhaps, however, the action occurs in the street outside.

II.ii.119. *philosopher,* etc. The 'philosopher's stone' or 'great elixir' was, in alchemy, a soluble, solid substance supposed to have the property of transmuting baser metals into silver or gold, and of prolonging life. Cf. *Henry IV, Part 2,* III.ii.289, 290.

II.ii.154. *yet now's a time.* Flavius means that, although too late to save Timon, there is at least an opportunity now to acquaint him with true conditions.

II.ii.168. *If ... falsehood.* Zeugma makes the line awkward. Flavius means: 'If you question my thrift or suspect me of falsehood.'

II.ii.212, 213. *Of whom ... hearing.* 'By whom, by reason of my previous services, I expect my request ('hearing') to be honored, even to the extent of the State's fullest resources.'

III.i.42. *And we alive that liv'd?* In this brief time. 'That we, who only yesterday saw Timon's friends at his feet, should to-day see them spurning him after this man's fashion.'

III.i.47. *Let molten coin be thy damnation.*

'And ladles full of melted gold
Were poured down their throats.'
—Old Ballad, 'The Dead Man's Song.'

Possibly the allusion is to the fate of Marcus Crassus, down whose throat the Parthians poured melted gold.

III.ii.43, 44. *that I ... honour.* Of the many explanations of this passage that of Steevens is the best: 'By purchasing what brought me little honour, I have lost the more honourable opportunity of supplying the wants of my friend.'

III.iii.15. *Thrice.* Johnson's reading. The Folio has 'Thriue,' which some modern editors have adopted. In such a case the allusion would be to the rich and indifferent physician who flourishes at the expense of his patient. Cf. Webster, *Duchess of Malfi,* III.v.7-9

'physicians thus,
With their hands full of money use to give o'er
Their patients.'

III.iii.30-33. *The devil ... clear.* The devil did not appreciate the significance of making man politic. By it he defeated his own purpose, for the villainies of man will, by comparison, make him appear innocent.

III.iv.21. *Is like the sun's.* 'Like him in blaze and splendour' (Johnson.)

III.iv.104. *Knock me down with 'em,* etc. A quibble upon 'bills' in the sense of weapons (i.e., a kind of long-handled axe).

III.iv.S. d. *Enter Timon [and Flavius].* This represents the modern editors' conception of the action. According to the Folio, Flavius does not leave the stage at line 74, and Timon, reentering at the present point, finds him still there.

III.iv.126. *Sempronius: all.* In the First Folio this portion of the line reads: *Sempronius Vllorxa: All.* Of the many conjectures concerning this puzzling corruption the least improbable seems to be that 'Vllorxa' is a printer's error for the name of another character, possibly Ventidius.

III.v.49. *if bearing carry it.* 'If endurance is the greater virtue.'

III.v.50. *fellow.* As in the First Folio. Johnson's plausible reading is 'felon.'

III.v.112. *Only in bone ... you.* 'That you may live to be mere skeletons, and scare men from looking at you.' (Clarke.)

III.v.122. *lay for hearts.* 'Endeavour to win popular affection.' (Clarke.)

III.vi.4. *tiring.* 'A metaphorical application of the language of falconry, in which a hawk was said to tire upon the refuse of her prey, which the falconer threw to her as reward and encouragement.' 'An hawke Tyryth upon rumpes. She fedyth on all manere of flesshe. She gorgith whan she fyllyth her gorge wyth meete.' (The boke of hawkynge, huntyng, and fysshynge by Julianna Berners, ciij.)

III.vi.30, 31. *if they will fare ... sound.* If the anticipated trumpet signal is so harshly delayed. Dinner was announced in great households by the sounding of trumpets. CF. *Othello,* IV.ii.192.

III.vi.92. *minute-jacks.* Contemptible fellows who change their minds every minute. It is possible that the word has reference to the 'Jacks-of-the-Clock,' figures that struck the bells in the old clocks.

III.vi.115. *stones.* There is no evidence in this play that stones were thrown at the guests. In the old play, *Timon,* stones are painted to resemble artichokes and are hurled at the parasites. It is possible that this line is reminiscent of the older play. See Sources of the Play, pp. 1335-1337.

IV.ii.38. *and all what state compounds.* 'All that goes to make up state.'

IV.iii.9. *Raise me ... lord.* 'Give elevation to a beggar, but deny it to a lord.'

IV.iii.12. *rother's.* Singer's emendation for 'Brothers' of the Folio. Holloway's *General Provincial Dictionary* mentions the 'rother market' of Stratford-on-Avon. The sentence, as printed in the Folio runs: 'It is the Pastour Lards, the Brothers sides, The want that makes him leaue.'

IV.iii.27. *idle votarist.* Timon means, presumably: *'My* vows of hate for human wealth are not insincere. The discovery of gold will not send me back to the life I have forsworn.'

IV.iii.32. *Pluck ... heads.* An old custom of drawing away the pillows of dying men to render their deaths easier, and, sometimes, for the inhuman purpose of hastening their departures.

IV.iii.44. *Do thy right nature.* 'Lie in the earth where nature laid thee.' (Johnson.)

IV.iii.54. *'Misanthropos.'* North's Plutarch has this marginal note: 'Antonius followeth the life and example of Timon Misanthropos, the Athenian.'

IV.iii.91. *To the tub-fast and the diet.* An allusion to the sweating cure used by the Elizabethans.

IV.iii.117. *planetary plague.* A reference to a common belief of the time that plagues and pestilences were often due to the malignant influence of the planets. Cf. *King Lear,* I.ii.115, 116: 'By an enforced obedience of planetary influence.' Cf. also *Troilus and Cressida,* I.iii.96-98:

'but when the planets
In evil mixture to disorder wander,
What plagues and what portents! ...'

IV.iii.143. *Enough ... bawd.* 'Enough to make a whore leave whoring, and a bawd leave making whores.' (Johnson.)

IV.iii.154, 155. *and thatch ... dead.* 'Cover your thin heads with false hair taken from dead bodies.' Shakespeare repeatedly attacks the practice of wearing false hair.

IV.iii.200. *Hyperion.* A Titan, the father of Helios, the sun-god. The name is used here, as elsewhere, for the sun itself.

IV.iii.246. *Answer mere nature.* 'Cope with nature in all its stark rigour.' (Deighton.) Cf. *King Lear,* III.iv.99, 100: 'Answer with thy uncovered body this extremity of the skies.'

IV.iii.256-259. *Always ... too.* Timon means that to vex another is the function of a fool or a villain. He has hitherto thought of Apemantus as a fool; Apemantus' 'Ay' leads him to think him also a knave, or villain.

IV.iii.273, 274. *proceeded ... degrees.* Technical terms used at English universities.

IV.iii.275. *drudges.* Mason's reading for 'drugges.' The New English Dictionary, quoting Huloet (1552) says: 'Drudge, or *drugge,* or vile servant in a house, whych doth all the vyle service.'

IV.iii.310, 311. *'Tis not ... would it were.* 'Even then (when mended by lack of *my* company) *your* company, being the company of yourself alone, cannot be said to be *well* mended, but only to be clumsily patched, a mere piece of botchery; if not, I wish you might find it so.'

IV.iii.312. *What ... Athens.* What commission do you wish to give me for Athens?

IV.iii.330. *medlar.* The fruit of the tree Mespilus Germanica, which is like a small brown-skinned apple and is eaten when in a soft, pulpy state. It is used in this passage, as elsewhere in Shakespeare, with a pun upon the word 'meddler.'

IV.iii.336. *after his means.* 'After' may have the significance of 'according to,' or the phrase may mean: 'after his means are gone.'

IV.iii.358, 359. *wert thou the unicorn* , etc. 'It was supposed that unicorns, in their fury, would rush at their enemy blindly, strike their horn against a tree, stick fast, and so be killed.' Cf. *Julius Cæsar,* II.i.215: 'Unicorns may be betray'd with trees.'

IV.iii.362-364. *wert thou ... life.* If you were a leopard, you would be akin to the lion, and your spots would be the cause of your death. The line alludes to the jealousy of the lion, which tolerates no rival.

IV.iii.373. *Yonder comes a poet and a painter.* This mistake is typical of the confused text of the play. The poet and the painter do not enter until the next act. See Authorship of the Play, footnote 15.

IV.iii.405. *Hymen.* The Greek god of marriage and of the marriage song named after him.

IV.iii.466, 467. *whose liquid ... tears.* Alluding to the influence of the moon upon the tides. There existed, too, a popular belief that the moon influenced the weather. In *Hamlet* (I.i.132), the moon is called the 'moist star.'

IV.iii.494, 495. *How rarely ... enemies.* 'How admirably does the injunction to love one's enemies accord with the fashion of the times!' (Rolfe.)

IV.iii.496, 497. *Grant ... that do.* 'Let me rather *woo* or caress those that

would mischief, that *profess to mean me mischief*, than those that *really do me mischief* under false professions of kindness.' (Johnson.) Cf. the Spanish proverb: 'Defend me from my friends, and from my enemies I will defend myself.'

V.i.42. *black-corner'd night*. 'Night shrouding all with the darkness of black corners.'

V.iii.4. *read*. The Folio reading. Warburton suggested 'rear'd,' implying that the rude tomb could not have been erected by man. If 'read' is accepted two interpretations are possible: (1) The line may be part of an inscription on the tomb, or (2) it may be a contemptuous comment from the soldier: 'Let a beast read this; there is no man present who can do so!'

V.iv.80-84. *Here . . . gait*. These lines are a combination of two epitaphs, both appearing in North's Plutarch. Lines 81 and 82 are clearly contradictory. See Sources of the Play, pp. 1335 and 1336.

THE TEXT OF THE PRESENT EDITION

Only the Folio text of *Timon of Athens* has survived. The text of the present volume is, by permission of the Oxford University Press, that of the Oxford Shakespeare, edited by the late W. J. Craig, except for the following deviations:

1. In almost every case the stage directions of the Folio have been restored. A few obvious errors in these have been corrected. Necessary or helpful modern stage directions have been added within square brackets.

2. Craig's punctuation has been normalized, as well as the spelling of a very few words: e.g., villainy (villany), court'sies (curtsies), basin (bason), again (agen).

3. Various changes in wording have been made, usually with the purpose of following more closely the Folio text. In the following list of verbal variations from Craig's text, the new readings precede the colon, while Craig's versions are given after it. When concerned in the change, the Folio authority has been indicated.

[Dramatis Personæ] F (Spelling modernized and modern additions bracketed): Dramatis Personæ (entirely modern).

I.i.50   moe F: more   So also: II.i.7; II.ii.117; IV.iii.400, 439
   186   ye F: you   So also: III.iv.46
   290   most F: more

	302	o' the ass F: of an ass
ii.	34	for 't F: for it
	42	sees 'em not F: sees them not
	102	ere 't F: ere it
	122	Taste, touch, and smell: Taste, touch, smell
	124	They're F: They are
	139	't has F: it has
	158	tell him—well, i' faith, I should—: tell him well, i' faith, I should,
	204	Than such that do F: Than such as do
II.ii.207		'em F: them
	239	ingeniously F: ingenuously
III.i.26		from 't F: from it
ii.	48	done 't F: done it
iii.	24	and 'mongst lords I be thought a fool: and I 'mongst lords be thought a fool. ['I' not in Folio.]
	25	I'd F: I had
	26	He'd: He had
iv.	59	ye F: you
v.	50	fellow F: felon
	113	I'm F: I am
vi.	22	of you F: you (misprint)
IV.ii.36		to live F: so live
	45	blest F: bless'd See also: IV.iii.544
iii.	32	heads F: head
	230	bade F: bid
	351	t' attain F: to attain
	475	not F: no
	498	Has F: He hath
	507	me, I; all: me; ay all
V.i.4		he's F: he is
	15	travail F: travel
	70	travail'd F: travell'd
	117	would'st F: would
	119	you F: ye
	163	it F: its
	168	blot F: block
iii.	4	read F: rear'd
		there F: here

Pericles, Prince of Tyre

Edited by
ALFRED R. BELLINGER

Dramatis Personae

ANTIOCHUS, *King of Antioch*

PERICLES, *Prince of Tyre*

HELICANUS } *two Lords of Tyre*
ESCANES

SIMONIDES, *King of Pentapolis*

CLEON, *Governor of Mitylene*

CERIMON, *a Lord of Ephesus*

THALIARD, *a Lord of Antioch*

PHILEMON, *Servant to Cerimon*

LEONINE, *Servant to Dionyza*

MARSHAL

A PANDAR

BOULT, *his servant*

THE DAUGHTER OF ANTIOCHUS

DIONYZA, *Wife to Cleon*

THAISA, *Daughter to Simonides*

MARINA, *Daughter to Pericles and Thaisa*

LYCHORIDA, *Nurse to Marina*

A BAWD

LORDS, LADIES, KNIGHTS, GENTLEMEN, SAILORS, PIRATES, FISHERMEN, AND MESSENGERS

DIANA

GOWER, *as Chorus*

SCENE—*In various Mediterranean countries.*

Pericles, Prince of Tyre

INTRODUCTION

SOURCES OF THE PLAY

The ultimate source of the story is undoubtedly a pagan Greek romance, probably by a writer of Asia Minor or Egypt, certainly later than the second century B.C., and certainly earlier than the sixth century A.D. It apparently falls somewhere in the first three centuries of the Christian era. The story is laid in the time of Antiochus the Great (second century B.C.), and, though it is full of historical inaccuracies, as will be seen from the notes, it preserves enough reminiscence of the actual conditions to make it almost certain that it came from an age before the break-up of the Roman empire had obliterated all memory of the preceding Greek empire in Asia. The Greek original, of a type familiar from other works, is lost, but it is represented by a great number of Latin manuscripts, bearing the general title *Historia Apollonii regis Tyrii*, which are more or less close translations with a certain amount of later Christian coloring. These vary considerably in content and in age, the earliest being of the ninth century, but the main outline of the story is constant, and is that reproduced in *Pericles, Prince of Tyre*. The original Latin version probably dates from the fifth century A.D. At least two editions were printed before 1500. In the twelfth century, Godfrey of Viterbo used the story in his *Pantheon*, a verse chronicle of events, beginning with Adam. It was partly from this work that Gower borrowed the tale. It was also included, in the thirteenth or fourteenth century, by the anonymous compiler of the *Gesta Romanorum*, which is the basis of Twine's version. From one or other of the Latin manuscripts, from the *Pantheon*, and from the *Gesta Romanorum*, a multitude of variants arose, in a dozen different languages.

John Gower, an English poet, contemporary with Chaucer, wrote, about 1390, the *Confessio Amantis* (first printed, by Caxton, in 1483), a collection of tales illustrating the seven deadly sins. In the Eighth Book, which deals with lechery, occurs the case of Antiochus and his daughter, which serves as an introduction to the whole story of Apollonius. It is written in rhymed tetrameter, like most of the Gower choruses in the play. In lines 271-273 he states his obligation to Godfrey of Viterbo:

'Of a Cronique in daies gon,
The which is cleped [named] Pantheon,
In loves cause I rede thus'—

But he is also influenced by the Latin narrative. There are several instances of his agreement with the *Historia Apollonii regis Tyrii* where he differs from Godfrey, besides certain changes for which he is himself responsible. Gower is one of the immediate sources of the play; the other is 'The Patterne of Painefull Aduentures, Containing the most excellent, pleasant, and variable Historie of the strange accidents that befell vnto Prince Apollonius, the Lady Lucina his wife and Tharsia his daughter. Wherein the vncertaintie of this world, and the fickle state of mans life are liuely described. Gathered into English by Laurence Twine Gentleman.

Imprinted at London by William How. 1576.'[1] This is a translation of the *Gesta Romanorum* version. Twine was an Oxford graduate of some repute as a poet, but, except for the song (cf. n. on V.i.88) and three rhymed riddles in this work, his poetry has disappeared. No copies of the original edition are known to exist, but it was reprinted, once without date, and again in 1607.

As Gower had professed to follow Godfrey, so the play opens with an acknowledgment of Gower as its literary father. This announcement is made through the introduction of the poet himself, talking a villainous counterfeit Middle English, as Chorus. Like Gower, the playwright uses a second source as well, but, in this case, Twine's novel furnished only a few passages. The interview between Cleon and Dionyza, for example (IV.iii., cf. n.), is modelled on the novel, and not on the poem. Here and there incidents and phrases show Twine's influence, but Gower must be acknowledged to be the chief source. When the two differ as to the names of characters, the play (except in the case of Cerimon) prefers the form given by Gower. But there is some originality in the matter of names. Stranguilio, Arthestrathes, and Athenagoras become Cleon, Simonides, and Lysimachus respectively—*metri causa*, one would suppose. Leonine, the keeper of the brothel in Gower (his name doubtless reminiscent of the Latin *leno*) becomes Dionyza's servant, whose earlier name was Theophilus. Boult is invented by the playwright. Gower leaves the hero's wife nameless and calls the daughter Thaise; Thaisa[2] now becomes the mother, while the daughter is named Marina,[3] from her birth at sea. Most important of all, the prince himself, hitherto consistently known as Apollonius, becomes Pericles. It is possible that there may be some recollection of the great Athenian statesman, though there is little enough similarity, but it seems more likely that the name was suggested by Pyrocles, the hero of the romance, *The Countesse of Pembroke's Arcadia written by Philippe Sidnei*, published in 1590. There are other instances of similarity (e.g. I.i.10, 11, cf. n.) which make it probable that Sidney's book was fresh in the playwright's mind.

The consideration of George Wilkins' novel is reserved for Authorship of the Play.

THE HISTORY OF THE PLAY

The literary history of the play begins with the following entry in the Stationers' Registers, in the year 1608:

20 Maij

Entered [to Edward Blount] for his copie under thandes of

---

1 The title is so given by Sidney Lee (Oxford facsimile of *Pericles*, p. 8), apparently on the assumption that it was identical with the later editions except for the imprimatur. The title given in the Stationers' Registers is 'The most excellent variable and pleasant history of the strange adventures of Prince Apollonius, Lucina his wife, and Tharsa his daughter.'

2 In Act III, Scene iv, the Quartos read *Tharsa*; Twine's name for the daughter was Tharsia.

3 But the Quartos of 1609 and 1611 have *MARIANA* on the title-page.

Sir George Buck knight and Master Warden Seton A booke called. *The booke of Pericles prynce of Tyre* vjd.

But Blount did not publish the play, for what reason cannot be determined. It was published in 1609 by Henry Gosson, in two quarto editions. The title-pages of these are identical, but numerous small differences in the text make it clear that one is a reprint of the other. The question of precedence is discussed, by P. Z. Round, in the introductions to the Quarto Facsimiles printed by Pretorius in 1886. He decides, as do the Cambridge editors, in favor of the British Museum copy C. 12h. 5. (distinguished by the first stage direction *Enter Gower*, while the other has *Eneer Gower*) as the First Quarto, and that decision is adopted in the present edition.[4] The Quartos of 1609 were followed by another in 1611, a fourth in 1619, a fifth in 1630, which exhibits two varieties of title-page, and a sixth in 1635. Although excluded from the First Folio, of 1623, and the Second Folio, of 1632, it was included in the second impression of the Third Folio, of 1664, and in the Fourth Folio, of 1685. The first critical edition was that of Nicolas Rowe, in 1709, republished in 1714. Pope rejected the play as spurious, and the next editor of a collective edition to publish it was Malone, in 1780. In 1734, however, two separate 12mo editions appeared, one by R. Walker, the other by J. Tonson. All editors since, escept J. Keightley, in 1864, have printed it. The text of the first Quartos is very corrupt. Not only are misprints common, but occasionally passages of prose are printed in lines like verse, and very often blank verse is run together like prose, or divided without the slightest attention to meter. It seems likely that the source of the text was a shorthand copy, made at a performance. This would explain not only the confusion of prose and verse, but certain verbal errors as well (e.g. *Pompey* for *pompae* II.ii.31). Whatever the source, it is sufficiently apparent that no qualified person reviewed the text before its first printing. Nor did it have the benefit of comparison with a correct copy thereafter, for the subsequent history of the text is a course of careless mistakes, varied with unintelligent corrections, until the last state thereof is worse than the first. Occasionally, but very rarely, a true reading is found in one of the later editions. Rowe began the laudable attempt to make the play intelligible. In this he was followed by Steevens and Malone, who attacked the multitudinous problems with a praise-worthy courage and industry. Very little was overlooked, and every edition since their time has borne the marks of their learned labors. But it was the style of their time for editors to allow themselves licenses in regard to emendation which stricter critical standards would not approve. At times they restore rather what the dramatist ought to have written than what he did write. The state of the text, and the character of the non-Shakespearean parts of the play lend themselves only too readily to emendations of that sort, so that many passages in the Steevens-Malone editions are pretty certainly not what the author wrote, though they are unquestionably much smoother reading. This would do no harm, if it had not proved so much easier to adopt

their results than to form a new text out of the original chaos, that many an unsound conjecture has received the sanction of continued repetition, and become an established part of the play. The result has been assisted by the fact that the critics do not always look for authority before they argue, and more than one ingenious deduction has been made from a conjecture mistaken for a fact. A scholarly, detailed reëxamination of the early copies will untimately yield a better text than is now available.

The first edition presupposes that the play had already been acted. It is generally conceded that it had been acted before the entry in the Stationers' Registers in 1608. Evidence that it was produced as early as 1606 is presented by T. S. Graves (cf. n. on I. iv. 95). The first reference to it was in 1609, in an anonymous rhyme. Several other seventeenth century notices of it strayed into print, but the only two that are worth repeating are the reference of Ben Jonson in 'Come leave the loathed stage' to 'some mouldy tale like Pericles,' and the couplet from Dryden's prologue to Davenant's *Circe*:

> 'Shakespeare's *own Muse her* Pericles *first bore,*
> The Prince of Tyre *was elder than the* Moore.'

Dryden, then, explained the defects of the piece on the ground of Shakespeare's inexperience. In this he was wrong. Jonson merely testifies that the play had more success than it deserved, which would, indeed, be evident enough from the profusion of quarto editions. We hear of its production on May 24, 1619, at the Court, in honor of the French ambassador, and, on June 10, 1631, at the Globe Theatre 'upon the cessation of the plague.' There is no doubt that there were many successful performances of which there is no record. According to Downes,[5] Betterton was 'highly applauded' for his acting in the title rôle, probably in 1659. During the Restoration period, it fell into oblivion, whence it has seldom emerged. In 1738, George Lillo recast the drama, starting with the present Act IV, but making a three-act play of it. The change benefits the play somewhat, in the points of unity and decency, but the new matter is weak. This composite piece, named *Marina*, was presented at the Covent Garden Theatre in 1738. It was acted three times. On October 14, 1854, *Pericles*, with Gower omitted and the brothel scenes expurgated, was produced by Phelps, who took the title rôle. It was received with much enthusiasm, but it is impossible to read the laudatory accounts of Henry Morley and Douglas Jerrold without suspecting that some of their interest was due to the novelty of the production. An account of this performance is given in *The Henry Irving Shakespeare*, Vol. VIII, pp. 264, 265. On October 20, 1882, *Pericles* was presented at Munich, accompanied by music written for the occasion. The genuine parts seem to have been highly successful. It has more recently been included in the repertory of Sir F. R. Benson's company at the Shakespeare Memorial Theatre at Stratford-on-Avon.

AUTHORSHIP OF THE PLAY

During the first century of the play's life, no doubt of its authenticity was expressed except by its exclusion from the First and Second Folios. Rowe included it in his edition of 1709, but

---

4 It should be noted that the facsimile of the First Quarto in the Bodleian Library, published, in 1905, by Sidney Lee, differs from the British Museum copy. The Oxford facsimile has the following divergent readings:

II Gower 24 *And hid in Tent to murdered him* (Q1 *And had intent to murder him;* Q2 *And hid intent to murder him*). (This is noted by the Cambridge editors.)

II.i.110 *pary* (Q1 & 2 *pray*)

II.i.111 *yeat* (Q1 & 2 *yet*)

II.i.136 *di'e* (Q1 *do'e;* Q2 *di'e*)

V.i.34 *sight, hee will* (Q1 *sight see, will;* Q2 *sight, hee will*)

These differences are not important, but the coincidences with the Second Quarto suggest that a full collation of the seven other known copies of the First Quarto would be desirable.

---

5 *Roscius Anglicanus*, p. 18. This was before the formation of Sir William Davenant's company, in which Betterton's great reputation was made.

it was rejected by Pope as spurious, and that view prevailed until Malone, in 1780, in his Supplement to Steevens' Shakespeare of 1778, argued that it was a genuine, though youthful, production of Shakespeare. Steevens at first dissented, but finally, in 1790, adopted the theory of a double authorship. With few exceptions, scholars have now agreed that *Pericles* is only partly the work of Shakespeare, and it is included among his later plays. This leaves three questions for discussion: 1. How much of it is attributable to Shakespeare? 2. Who wrote the rest? 3. Did Shakespeare's contribution precede or follow the work of the other author or authors?

1. The general opinion is that the largely or wholly Shakespearean part begins with Act III, Scene i, that is, that he is the author of the portion dealing with the fortunes of Marina. This is the conclusion to which Tennyson came, anticipating the editors by some years, and his reading of the parts he considered genuine seems to have carried conviction to his hearers. It is also the conclusion of Swinburne, who expresses the utmost enthusiasm for the portion he accepted. But there is still divergence of opinion as to whether Shakespeare had any hand in the first two acts, and whether he wrote all of the last three. Of course, those who hold that his original play on the story of Marina was later completed by another writer—a theory to be discussed presently—must deny him any share in the drama before Marina appears. H. D. Sykes,[6] finding parallels to Wilkins rife in Acts I and II, would therefore insist that Shakespeare had no hand in them, while Frank Harris,[7] in a burst of enthusiasm over the speech beginning

See where she comes apparell'd like the spring

(I.i.12)

concludes that the whole work is Shakespeare's. As a matter of fact, neither of these methods is admissible. If it be once granted, as Sykes maintains, that Shakespeare worked over another writer's play, nothing less than proof that every line of a certain part is the work of the other writer will suffice to prove that Shakespeare has not touched that part at all; while the fact that there are fine passages in the first two acts cannot prove that he wrote the absurdities of Act II, Scene v, for instance, which Steevens condemns so roundly. Coleridge once remarked that Shakespeare's share in the play could be recognized 'even to half a line,' but as he never recorded which half lines he meant, and as subsequent critics show no disposition to agree, it is safest to conclude merely that there are some passages, before the appearance of Marina, which are worthy of the master, but that there are many which are certainly unworthy of him. In the latter half of the play, there are two parts which challenge attention, the Gower choruses and the brothel scenes. It will be observed that the Gower choruses of Acts IV and V, with the exception of that before Act IV, Scene ii, are in pentameter instead of tetrameter, and it has been argued that Shakespeare wrote the five foot lines, but not the four foot: a clear distinction, which though it cannot be considered proved, has enough confirmation from the substance of the choruses to be probable. The brothel scenes are generally held to be by a second or even a third hand. The origin of this theory is a natural desire to believe that Shakespeare did not write scenes so repellent. But extreme measure would be necessary to take all the objectionable scenes out of Shakespeare, and a

candid reading of the ones in this play will show that there is considerable restraint about them, as well as a definite purpose; the illustration of Marina's virtue by the blackness of her surroundings. There are, moreover, definitely Shakespearean touches in such quantity that it is rather the part of prejudice than of scholarship to deny his authorship of them. The only other portion whose authenticity is denied is the vision of Diana (V.i. 270-279). Fleay regarded it as spurious, like the vision in *Cymbeline*, Act V, Scene iv, and recent editors have quoted him with approval. But, whatever may be the reasons for rejecting the passage in *Cymbeline*, it is hard to see why they should be held to apply also to this. The episode cannot be interpolated, for it occurs in the sources and is certainly essential to the plot; and it is so far superior in technique to the average of the non-Shakespearean parts that there seem to be no good grounds for assigning it to the author of them. Even Sykes, an indefatigable searcher for the traces of Wilkins, can find little evidence of him in the rest of Acts III, IV, and V. Our conclusion, then, is that Shakespeare is responsible for occasional passages of the first two acts, and for practically all the rest of the play, excepting the tetrameter Gower choruses.

2. Setting aside, for the moment, the brothel scenes, there are two serious contestants for the authorship of the rest of the play: George Wilkins and Thomas Heywood. Wilkins, of whom practically nothing is known, is certainly the author of a comedy entitled *The Miseries of Enforced Marriage* (1607),[8] besides collaborating with Day and Rowley in *The Travells of Three English Brothers* (1607).[9] The prose works that bear his name are: *The Three Miseries of Barbary; Plague, Famine, Civil War* (1603); *Jests to Make you Merrie; with the conjuring up of Cock Watt the walking Spirit of Newgate*, written in collaboration with Dekker (1607); and, most important for us, *The Painful Adventures of Pericles, Prince of Tyre* (1608). A pamphlet entitled *Two Unnatural Murders* (1605) and the play, *A Yorkshire Tragedy*, published in 1608 with Shakespeare's name attached, have been conjecturally ascribed to him,[10] as also some part in *Law Tricks*,[11] published in 1608 under Day's name, and in *Timon of Athens*[12] (1607-1608?). It will be seen that he was a man of varied, if meagre, talents. There can be no doubt of the close connection between the novel and the play. The title-page of the former announces it to be 'The true History of the Play of *Pericles*,' and the similarities are continual and self-evident. Delius[13] advanced the theory that Wilkins had written the original play, which was revised by Shakespeare, in 1608, whereupon Wilkins produced his novel, which he calls, in the dedication, the 'poore infant of my braine.' It purported to be founded on the play alone, but actually followed also the reprint of Twine's novel in 1607. Delius held that the phrase 'poore infant of my braine' was intended by Wilkins to refer to his origination of the play; he adduced further evidence from a comparison with *The Miseries of Enforced Marriage* and those parts of *Timon* which he took to be Wilkins', finding likenesses, in their common artistic mediocrity, in the mixture of rhyme, blank verse and prose, and in the technique of both prose and verse. Fleay[14] stated rather than proved metrical similarities

6 *Sidelights on Shakespeare*, Stratford-upon-Avon, 1919, pp. 141-203.
7 *The Women of Shakespeare*, London, 1911, pp. 231 ff.

8 Reprinted in Hazlitt's *Dodsley*, Vol. IX.
9 Published with Day's works by G. A. Bullen, 1881.
10 H. D. Sykes, op. cit. pp. 77-98.
11 Robert Boyle, *Transactions of the New Shakespeare Society*, 1882, pp. 323-340.
12 N. Delius, *Jahrbuch der Deutschen Shakespeare-Gesellschaft*, 1867, pp. 335-361. This has little evidence to justify it, and has received no subsequent support.
13 *Jahrbuch*, 1868, pp. 175-204.
14 *Transactions of the New Shakespeare Society*, 1874, pp. 195-241.

looking to the same conclusion, and his result was reinforced, though his method was condemned, by Robert Boyle,[15] who added similarities of language, of substance, and of technique. All this evidence is reviewed, with additions, by H. D. Sykes,[16] who stresses particularly Wilkins' ellipses and his frequent use of verbal antithesis. He has extended the search to the other works of Wilkins, certain and supposed, and has, indeed, collected an imposing number of parallel passages. Moreover, he has made a detailed comparison between the novel and the play, and come to the conclusion that the novel was written before the play, instead of following it. He is obliged, however, by the evidence of the title-page, to assume that Wilkins delayed its publication until after the play, revised by Shakespeare, had been produced. For this he gives no reason. He cites the case of Pericles' harp-playing (cf. II.v.28 and n.), and maintains, besides the greater inherent probability of an Elizabethan play made from a novel than of a novel made from a play, that the passages in common are actually parts of the novel introduced by Wilkins into the play. His arguments are plausible, but not overwhelming. In general it may be said that the case for Wilkins is founded, first on the connection between the novel and the play, and, second, on similarities, largely of language, with Wilkins' other works.

In 1908, D. L. Thomas[17] suggested as the first author of *Pericles* the prolific Thomas Heywood. Thomas attacks the theory of Delius and Boyle, without doing it perfect justice, perhaps, but in a way to show certain weaknesses in it: the fact, for instance, that verbal likenesses are somewhat unsatisfactory unless they accompany likenesses of dramatic technique, and that, to be convincing, the champions of Wilkins ought to show that *Pericles* is verbally more like his works than like those of any other contemporary playwright. Thomas' own argument is largely concerned with dramatic devices, and the larger questions of conception, style and technique. He also cites twenty-three of what he calls 'dictional parallels' between *Pericles* and plays of Heywood, but they are not striking, nor is the number large, considering that two dozen of Heywood's plays are left. The arguments from construction and treatment of incidents are more convincing, but, in the end, they go rather to prove that Heywood could have written *Pericles* than that he did. The question cannot be considered settled until other possibilities have been examined as exhaustively as Wilkins and Heywood, but, at present, the weight of evidence is still in favor of the former.

The brothel scenes are considered as a separate problem by those who regard them as non-Shakespearean. Fleay recognized their superiority to the parts which he assigned to Wilkins, and, to avoid the difficulty, suggested Rowley (with whom Wilkins had collaborated before) as their author. Walker had already suggested Dekker, *faute de mieux*. J. M. Robertson[18] argues for Chapman, as a corollary to his thesis that Chapman wrote similar parts of *Measure for Measure*. But here, the result of the argument is rather possibility than probability. No real similarity with Dekker or Rowley has been brought forward, and the case for Chapman is merely inferred from other conjectural conclusions. Of course, if we admit the scenes to be Shakespeare's, the problem disappears.

3. We have already seen that Sykes believes *Pericles* to be a revision by Shakespeare of another's play. This was the view expressed by Steevens and by Coleridge, who did not name the original author, and it has received the support of many commentators since. A bolder theory, but one with many advocates, is that of Fleay, who believed that Shakespeare originally wrote *The Story of Marina*[19]—that is, the greater part of the last three acts, and then laid it aside, for some reason or other, when it was completed by Wilkins and Rowley. The source of this supposition seems to be a feeling that Shakespeare would have disdained to work over so dull a performance as that of the other author. But for him to have written these acts, whether intending them for the beginning and end, as A. H. Smyth believes,[20] or for the end alone, as they actually became, seems unlikely in the extreme. In either case, it means that Shakespeare deliberately chose a theme which did not readily admit of dramatic unity, and wrote a piece, too short for presentation, with the conclusion complete, and, therefore, as hard as possible for anyone to fill out. To a piece of work so preposterous, in the strict sense of the word, so useless for theatrical purposes, so unsuitable for publication, the history of literature affords, I think, no parallel.[21] Surely the natural explanation is the right one, and we have here, as Coleridge conjectured,[22] an illustration of 'the way in which Shakespeare handled a piece he had to refit for representation.'

---

15 Op. cit.

16 Op. cit. pp. 141-203.

17 *Englische Studien*, 1908, pp. 210-239. The article has received the polite dissent of subsequent scholars.

18 *The Shakespeare Canon*, London, 1923. Part II, pp. 165, 184, 186.

19 The part of the play is printed as a whole by Fleay in the *Transactions of the New Shakespeare Society* for 1874, pp. 211-241. It is preceded (pp. 195-209) by a discussion of his reasons for believeing it to be Shakespeare's original production.

20 *Pericles and Apollonius*, Philadelphia 1898, p. 68.

21 K. Deighton. Introduction to *Pericles*, *The Arden Shakespeare*.

22 H. C. Robinson's Diary, Dec. 28, 1810.

ACT FIRST

Enter Gower.

To sing a song that old was sung,
From ashes ancient Gower is come,
Assuming man's infirmities,
To glad your ear, and please your eyes.
It hath been sung at festivals,   5
On ember-eves, and holy-ales;
And lords and ladies in their lives
Have read it for restoratives:
The purchase is to make men glorious;
Et bonum quo antiquius, eo melius.   10
If you, born in these latter times,
When wit's more ripe, accept my rimes,
And that to hear an old man sing
May to your wishes pleasure bring,
I life would wish, and that I might   15
Waste it for you like taper-light.
This Antioch, then, Antiochus the Great
Built up, this city, for his chiefest seat,
The fairest in all Syria,
I tell you what mine authors say.   20
This king unto him took a fere,
Who died and left a female heir,
So buxom, blithe, and full of face
As heaven had lent her all his grace;
With whom the father liking took,   25
And her to incest did provoke.
Bad child, worse father! to entice his own
To evil should be done by none.
By custom what they did begin
Was with long use account no sin.   30
The beauty of this sinful dame
Made many princes thither frame,
To seek her as a bed-fellow,
In marriage-pleasures play-fellow:
Which to prevent, he made a law,   35
To keep her still, and men in awe,
That whoso ask'd her for his wife,
His riddle told not, lost his life:
So for her many a wight did die,
As yon grim looks do testify.   40
What now ensues, to the judgment of your eye
I give, my cause who best can justify.   *Exit.*

✤ SCENE FIRST ✤

[Antioch. A Room in the Palace]
Enter Antiochus, Prince Pericles, and Followers.

Ant. Young Prince of Tyre, you have at large receiv'd
The danger of the task you undertake.

Per. I have, Antiochus, and, with a soul
Embolden'd with the glory of her praise,
Think death no hazard in this enterprise.   *Music.* 5
Ant. Bring in our daughter, clothed like a bride,
For the embracements even of Jove himself;
At whose conception, till Lucina reign'd,
Nature this dowry gave, to glad her presence,
The senate-house of planets all did sit,   10
To knit in her their best perfections.

Enter Antiochus' Daughter.

Per. See, where she comes apparell'd like the spring,
Graces her subjects, and her thoughts the king
Of every virtue gives renown to men!
Her face the book of praises, where is read   15
Nothing but curious pleasures, as from thence
Sorrow were ever rac'd, and testy wrath
Could never be her mild companion.
You gods, that made me man, and sway in love,
That have inflam'd desire in my breast   20
To taste the fruit of yon celestial tree
Or die in the adventure, be my helps,
As I am son and servant to your will,
To compass such a boundless happiness!
Ant. Prince Pericles,—   25
Per. That would be son to great Antiochus.
Ant. Before thee stands this fair Hesperides,
With golden fruit, but dangerous to be touch'd;
For death-like dragons here affright thee hard:
Her face, like heaven, enticeth thee to view   30
Her countless glory, which desert must gain;
And which, without desert, because thine eye
Presumes to reach, all thy whole heap must die.
Yon sometime famous princes, like thyself,
Drawn by report, adventurous by desire,   35
Tell thee with speechless tongues and semblance pale,
That without covering, save yon field of stars,
Here they stand martyrs, slain in Cupid's wars;
And with dead cheeks advise thee to desist
For going on death's net, whom none resist.   40
Per. Antiochus, I thank thee, who hath taught
My frail mortality to know itself,
And by those fearful objects to prepare
This body, like to them, to what I must;
For death remember'd should be like a mirror,   45
Who tells us life's but breath, to trust it error.
I'll make my will then; and as sick men do,
Who know the world, see heaven, but feeling woe,
Gripe not at earthly joys as erst they did;
So I bequeath a happy peace to you   50
And all good men, as every prince should do;
My riches to the earth from whence they came,
[To the Daughter of Antiochus.]
But my unspotted fire of love to you.
Thus ready for the way of life or death,
I wait the sharpest blow.   55
Ant. Scorning advice, read the conclusion then;
Which read and not expounded, 'tis decreed,

ACT FIRST; *cf. n.* Enter Gower; *cf. n.*   6 ember-eves; *cf. n.* holy-ales: *holidays;*
cf. n.   9 purchase: *gain*   10 Et bonum quo antiquius, eo melius: *and the more ancient
a good thing, the better*   17, 18 Cf. n.   20 Cf. n.   21 fere: *mate* 22, 23 Cf. n.
24 heaven: *i.e. God* 25, 26 Cf. n.   28 should: *which should*   32 frame: *go* 36
still: *always* 38 told not: *not being guessed* 40 Cf. n.   1 Young Prince of Tyre;
cf. n. receiv'd: *learned*

8 Lucina: *the goddess of childbirth*   9 glad her presence: *make her personality glad*   10,
11 Cf. n.   13, 14 Cf. n.   16 curious: *delicate, particular* as: *as though*   17 rac'd:
razed, done away with   27 Hesperides; *cf. n.*   40 For going on: *for fear of going into*

As these before thee, thou thyself shalt bleed.
  Daugh. Of all say'd yet, mayst thou prove prosperous!
Of all say'd yet, I wish thee happiness!   60
  Per. Like a bold champion, I assume the lists,
Nor ask advice of any other thought
But faithfulness and courage.

The Riddle

   'I am no viper, yet I feed   65
On mother's flesh which did me breed;
I sought a husband, in which labour
I found that kindness in a father.
He's father, son, and husband mild,
I mother, wife, and yet his child.   70
How they may be, and yet in two,
As you will live, resolve it you.'

Sharp physic is the last: but, O you powers!
That give heaven countless eyes to view men's acts,
Why cloud they not their sights perpetually,   75
If this be true, which makes me pale to read it?
Fair glass of light, I lov'd you, and could still,
Were not this glorious casket stor'd with ill:
But I must tell you now my thoughts revolt;
For he's no man on whom perfections wait   80
That, knowing sin within, will touch the gate.
You're a fair viol, and your sense the strings,
Who, finger'd to make man his lawful music,
Would draw heaven down and all the gods to hearken;
But being play'd upon before your time,   85
Hell only danceth at so harsh a chime.
Good sooth, I care not for you.
  Ant. Prince Pericles, touch not, upon thy life,
For that's an article within our law,
As dangerous as the rest. Your time's expir'd: 90
Either expound now or receive your sentence.
  Per. Great king,
Few love to hear the sins they love to act;
'Twould braid yourself too near for me to tell it.
Who has a book of all that monarchs do,   95
He's more secure to keep it shut than shown;
For vice repeated is like the wandering wind,
Blows dust in others' eyes, to spread itself;
And yet the end of all is bought thus dear,
The breath is gone, and the sore eyes see clear   100
To stop the air would hurt them. The blind mole casts
Copp'd hills towards heaven, to tell the earth is throng'd
By man's oppression; and the poor worm doth die for 't.
Kings are earth's gods; in vice their law's their will;
And if Jove stray, who dares say Jove doth ill?   105
It is enough you know; and it is fit,
What being more known grows worse, to smother it.
All love the womb that their first being bred,
Then give my tongue like leave to love my head.
  Ant. [Aside.] Heaven, that I had thy head! he has   110
found the meaning;
But I will gloze with him. Young Prince of Tyre,
Though by the tenour of our strict edict,

Your exposition misinterpreting,
We might proceed to cancel off your days;   115
Yet hope, succeeding from so fair a tree
As your fair self, doth tune us otherwise:
Forty days longer we do respite you;
If by which time our secret be undone,
This mercy shows we'll joy in such a son: 120
And until then your entertain shall be
As doth befit our honour and your worth.   *Manet Pericles solus.*
   Per How courtesy would seem to cover sin,
When what is done is like a hypocrite,
The which is good in nothing but in sight!   125
If it be true that I interpret false,
Then were it certain you were not so bad
As with foul incest to abuse your soul;
Where now you're both a father and a son,
By your untimely claspings with your child,—   130
Which pleasure fits a husband, not a father;—
And she an eater of her mother's flesh,
By the defiling of her parent's bed;
And both like serpents are, who though they feed
On sweetest flowers, yet they poison breed.   135
Antioch, farewell! for wisdom sees, those men
Blush not in actions blacker than the night,
Will shun no course to keep them from the light.
One sin, I know, another doth provoke;
Murder's as near to lust as flame to smoke.   140
Poison and treason are the hands of sin,
Ay, and the targets, to put off the shame:
Then, lest my life be cropp'd to keep you clear,
By flight I'll shun the danger which I fear.   *Exit*

Enter Antiochus.

  Ant. He hath found the meaning, for which we mean   145
To take his head.
He must not live to trumpet forth my infamy,
Nor tell the world Antiochus doth sin
In such a loathed manner;
And therefore instantly this prince must die,   150
For by his fall my honour must keep high.
Who attends us there?

Enter Thaliard.

  Thal.   Doth your highness call?
  Ant. Thaliard,
You're of our chamber, and our mind partakes   155
Her private actions to your secrecy;
And for your faithfulness we will advance you.
Thaliard, behold, here's poison, and here's gold;
We hate the Prince of Tyre, and thou must kill him:
It fits thee not to ask the reason why,   160
Because we bid it. Say, is it done?
  Thal. My lord, 'tis done.
  Ant. Enough.

Enter a Messenger.

Let your breath cool yourself telling your haste.

---

59 Of all say'd yet: *more than all who have assayed yet; cf. n.*   **65–70** *Cf. n.*   **82 sense:** *senses*   **94 braid:** *upbraid*   **97–101** *Cf. n.*   **101 would:** *which would*   **102 Copp'd:** *peaked*   **103 poor worm:** *mole*   **104** *Cf. n.*   **110** *Cf. n.*   **112 gloze:** *use fair words*

114–117 *Cf. n.*   **121 entertain:** *entertainment*   **137 Blush:** *who blush*   **142 targets: shields**   **put off:** *turn aside*   **155 partakes:** *imparts*   **164 telling your haste:** *explaining the cause of your haste*

Mess. My lord, Prince Pericles is fled.   *[Exit.]*
Ant.   *[To Thaliard.]* As thou
Wilt live, fly after; and, as an arrow shot
From a well-experienc'd archer hits the mark
His eye doth level at, so thou ne'er return
Unless thou say 'Prince Pericles is dead.'   *170*
    Thal. My lord,
If I can get him within my pistol's length,
I'll make him sure enough: so, farewell to your highness.
    Ant. Thaliard, adieu!   *[Exit Thaliard.]*
                    Till Pericles be dead,
My heart can led no succour to my head.   *Exit.*

❧ SCENE SECOND ❧

[Tyre. A Room in the Palace]

Enter Pericles with his Lords.

Per. Let none disturb us.—*[Aside]* Why should this change
of thoughts,
The sad companion, dull-ey'd melancholy,
Be my so us'd a guest, as not an hour
In the day's glorious walk or peaceful night—   *5*
The tomb where grief should sleep—can breed me quiet?
Here pleasures court mine eyes, and mine eyes shun them,
And danger, which I feared, is at Antioch,
Whose arm seems far too short to hit me here;
Yet neither pleasure's art can joy my spirits,   *10*
Nor yet the other's distance comfort me.
Then it is thus: the passions of the mind,
That have their first conception by mis-dread,
Have after-nourishment and life by care;
And what was first but fear what might be done,   *15*
Grows elder now and cares it be not done.
And so with me: the great Antiochus,—
'Gainst whom I am too little to contend,
Since he's so great can make his will his act,—
Will think me speaking, though I swear to silence;   *20*
Nor boots it me to say I honour him,
If he suspect I may dishonour him;
And what may make him blush in being known,
He'll stop the course by which it might be known.
With hostile forces he'll o'erspread the land,   *25*
And with the ostent of war will look so huge,
Amazement shall drive courage from the state,
Our men be vanquish'd ere they do resist,
And subject punish'd that ne'er thought offence:
Which care of them, not pity of myself,—   *30*
Who am no more but as the tops of trees,
Which fence the roots they grow by and defend them,—
Make both my body pine and soul to languish,
And punish that before, that he would punish.

Enter [Helicanus and] all the Lords to Pericles.

1. Lord. Joy and all comfort in your sacred breast!   *35*
2. Lord. And keep your mind, till you return to us,
Peaceful and comfortable.

172 **length:** *range*   SCENE SECOND S. d. Enter Pericles; *cf. n.*   4 **us'd:** *familiar* as:
that   10 **joy:** *gladden*   16 **cares:** *takes care*   19 **can ... act:** *that he can perform his*
will   21 **boots it me:** *does it avail me*   26 **ostent:** *show*

Hel. Peace, peace! and give experience tongue.
They do abuse the king that flatter him;
For flattery is the bellows blows up sin;   *40*
The thing the which is flatter'd, but a spark,
To which that blast gives heat and stronger glowing;
Whereas reproof, obedient and in order,
Fits kings, as they are men, for they may err:
When Signior Sooth here does proclaim a peace,   *45*
He flatters you, makes war upon your life.
Prince, pardon me, or strike me, if you please;
I cannot be much lower than my knees.   *[Kneeling.]*
    Per. All leave us else; but let your care o'erlook
What shipping and what lading's in our haven,   *50*
And then return to us.   *[Exeunt Lords.]*
                    Helicanus, thou
Hast mov'd us; what seest thou in our looks?
    Hel. An angry brow, dread lord.
    Per. If there be such a dart in prince's frowns,   *55*
How durst thy tongue move anger to our face?
    Hel. How dare the plants look up to heaven, from whence
They have their nourishment?
    Per.   Thou know'st I have power
To take thy life from thee.   *60*
    Hel. I have ground the axe myself;
Do you but strike the blow.
    Per.   Rise, prithee, rise;
Sit down; thou art no flatterer:
I thank thee for it; and heaven forbid   *65*
That kings should let their ears hear their faults hid!
Fit counsellor and servant for a prince,
Who by thy wisdom mak'st a prince thy servant,
What wouldst thou have me do?
    Hel.   To bear with patience   *70*
Such griefs as you yourself do lay upon yourself.
    Per. Thou speak'st like a physician, Helicanus,
That minister'st a potion unto me
That thou wouldst tremble to receive thyself.
Attend me then: I went to Antioch,   *75*
Where as thou know'st, against the face of death
I sought the purchase of a glorious beauty,
From whence an issue I might propagate
Are arms to princes and bring joys to subjects.
Her face was to mine eye beyond all wonder;   *80*
The rest, hark in thine ear, as black as incest;
Which by my knowledge found, the sinful father
Seem'd not to strike, but smooth; but thou know'st this,
'Tis time to fear when tyrants seem to kiss.
Which fear so grew in me I hither fled,   *85*
Under the covering of a careful night,
Who seem'd my good protector; and, being here,
Bethought me what was past, what might succeed.
I knew him tyrannous; and tyrants' fears
Decrease not, but grow faster than the years.   *90*
And should he doubt it, as no doubt he doth,
That I should open to the listening air
How many worthy princes' bloods were shed,
To keep his bed of blackness unlaid ope,
To lop that doubt he'll fill this land with arms,   *95*
And make pretence of wrong that I have done him;

50 **lading:** *cargo*   75 **Attend:** *listen to*   79 **Are arms:** *such as are arms*   83 **smooth:**
flatter   88 **succeed:** *come next*   91 **doubt it:** *suspect*   94 **unlaid ope:** *undiscovered*

When all, for mine, if I may call 't, offence,
Must feel war's blow, who spares not innocence:
Which love to all, of which thyself art one,
Who now reprov'st me for it,— 100
 Hel.   Alas! sir.
 Per. Drew sleep out of mine eyes, blood from my cheeks,
Musings into my mind, with thousand doubts
How I might stop this tempest, ere it came;
And finding little comfort to relieve them, 105
I thought it princely charity to grieve for them.
 Hel. Well, my lord, since you have given me leave to speak,
Freely will I speak. Antiochus you fear,
And justly too, I think, you fear the tyrant,
Who either by public war or private treason 110
Will take away your life.
Therefore, my lord, go travel for a while,
Till that his rage and anger be forgot,
Or till the Destinies do cut his thread of life.
Your rule direct to any; if to me, 115
Day serves not light more faithful than I'll be.
 Per. I do not doubt thy faith;
But should he wrong my liberties in my absence?
 Hel. We'll mingle our bloods together in the earth,
From whence we had our being and our birth. 120
 Per. Tyre, I now look from thee then, and to Tarsus
Intend my travel, where I'll hear from thee,
And by whose letters I'll dispose myself.
The care I had and have of subjects' good
On thee I'll lay, whose wisdom's strength can bear it. 125
I'll take thy word for faith, not ask thine oath;
Who shuns not to break one will sure crack both.
But in our orbs we'll live so round and safe,
That time of both this truth shall ne'er convince,
Thou show'dst a subject's shine, I a true prince. *Exeunt.*

❧ SCENE THIRD ❧

[The Same. An Antechamber in the Palace]
Enter Thaliard solus.

 Thal. So this is Tyre, and this the court. Here must I kill
King Pericles; and if I do not, I am sure to be hanged at
home: 'tis dangerous. Well, I perceive he was a wise fellow,
and had good discretion, that, being bid to ask what he would
of the king, desired he might know none of his secrets: 5
now do I see he had some reason for it; for if a king bid a
man be a villain, he is bound by the indenture of his oath
to be one. Hush! here come the lords of Tyre.

Enter Helicanus, Escanes, with other Lords.

 Hel. You shall not need, my fellow peers of Tyre,
Further to question me of your king's departure: 10
His seal'd commission, left in trust with me,
Doth speak sufficiently he's gone to travel.
 Thal. [Aside.] How! the king gone!
 Hel. If further yet you will be satisfied,
Why, as it were unlicens'd of your loves, 15

He would depart, I'll give some light unto you.
Being at Antioch—
 Thal.   *[Aside.]* What from Antioch?
 Hel. Royal Antiochus—on what cause I know not—
Took some displeasure at him, at least he judg'd so; 20
And doubting lest that he had err'd or sinn'd,
To show his sorrow he'd correct himself;
So puts himself unto the shipman's toil,
With whom each minute threatens life or death.
 Thal. [Aside.] Well, I perceive 25
I shall not be hang'd now, although I would;
But since he's gone, the king it sure must please:
He 'scap'd the land, to perish at the sea.
I'll present myself. *[Aloud.]* Peace to the lords of Tyre.
 Hel. Lord Thaliard from Antiochus is welcome. 30
 Thal. From him I come,
With message unto princely Pericles;
But since my landing I have understood
Your lord hath betook himself to unknown travels,
My message must return from whence it came. 35
 Hel. We have no reason to desire it,
Commended to our master, not to see us:
Yet, ere you shall depart, this we desire,
As friends to Antioch, we may feast in Tyre. *Exeunt.*

❧ SCENE FOURTH ❧

[Tarsus. A Room in the Governor's House]

*Enter Cleon the Governor of Tarsus, with [Dionyza] his wife and
others.*

 Cle. My Dionyza, shall we rest us here,
And by relating tales of others' griefs,
See if 'twill teach us to forget our own?
 Dio. That were to blow at fire in hope to quench it;
For who digs hills because they do aspire 5
Throws down one mountain to cast up a higher.
O my distressed lord! even such our griefs are;
Here they're but felt, and seen with mischief's eyes,
But like to groves, being topp'd, they higher rise.
 Cle. O Dionyza, 10
Who wanteth food, and will not say he wants it,
Or can conceal his hunger till he famish?
Our tongues and sorrows do sound deep
Our woes into the air; our eyes do weep
Till tongues fetch breath that may proclaim them louder; 15
That if heaven slumber while their creatures want,
They may awake their helps to comfort them.
I'll then discourse our woes, felt several years,
And, wanting breath to speak, help me with tears.
 Dio. I'll do my best, sir. 20
 Cle. This Tarsus, o'er which I have the government,
A city on whom plenty held full hand,
For riches strew'd herself even in the streets;
Whose towers bore heads so high they kiss'd the clouds,
And the strangers ne'er beheld but wonder'd at; 25

Whose men and dames so jetted and adorn'd,
Like one another's glass to trim them by:
Their tables were stor'd full to glad the sight,
And not so much to feed on as delight;
All poverty was scorn'd, and pride so great,   30
The name of help grew odious to repeat.
    Dio. O! 'tis too true.
    Cle. But see what heaven can do! By this our change,
These mouths, whom but of late earth, sea, and air
Were all too little to content and please,   35
Although they gave their creatures in abundance,
As houses are defil'd for want of use,
They are now starv'd for want of exercise;
Those palates who, not yet two summers younger,
Must have inventions to delight the taste,   40
Would now be glad of bread, and beg for it;
Those mothers who, to nousle up their babes,
Thought nought too curious, are ready now
To eat those little darlings whom they lov'd.
So sharp are hunger's teeth, that man and wife   45
Draw lots who first shall die to lengthen life.
Here stands a lord, and there a lady weeping;
Here many sink, yet those which see them fall
Have scarce strength left to give them burial.
Is not this true?   50
    Dio. Our cheeks and hollow eyes do witness it.
    Cle. O! let those cities that of plenty's cup
And her prosperities so largely taste,
With their superfluous riots, hear these tears:
The misery of Tarsus may be theirs.   55

Enter a Lord.

    Lord. Where's the lord governor?
    Cle. Here.
Speak out they sorrows which thou bring'st in haste,
For comfort is too far for us to expect.
    Lord. We have descried, upon our neighbouring shore,   60
A portly sail of ships make hitherward.
    Cle. I thought as much.
One sorrow never comes but brings an heir
That may succeed as his inheritor;
And so in ours. Some neighbouring nation,   65
Taking advantage of our misery,
Hath stuff'd these hollow vessels with their power,
To beat us down, the which are down already;
And make a conquest of unhappy me,
Whereas no glory's got to overcome.   70
    Lord. That's the least fear; for by the semblance
Of their white flags display'd, they bring us peace,
And come to us as favourers, not as foes.
    Cle. Thou speak'st like him 's untutor'd to repeat:
'Who makes the fairest show means most deceit.'   75
But bring they what they will and what they can,
What need we fear?
The ground's the lowest and we are half way there.
Go tell their general we attend him here,
To know for what he comes, and whence he comes,   80
And what he craves.

    Lord. I go, my lord.   [*Exit.*]
    Cle. Welcome is peace if he on peace consist;
If wars, we are unable to resist.

Enter Pericles with Attendants.

    Per. Lord governor, for so we hear you are,   85
Let not our ships and number of our men,
Be like a beacon fir'd to amaze your eyes.
We have heard your miseries as far as Tyre,
And seen the desolation of your streets:
Nor come we to add sorrow to your tears,   90
But to relieve them of their heavy load;
And these our ships, you happily may think
Are like the Troyan horse was stuff'd within
With bloody veins, expecting overthrow,
Are stor'd with corn to make your needy bread,   95
And give them life whom hunger starv'd half dead.
    All. The gods of Greece protect you!
And we'll pray for you.
    Per.   Arise, I pray you, rise:
We do not look for reverence, but for love,   100
And harbourage for ourself, our ships, and men.
    Cle. The which when any shall not gratify,
Or pay you with unthankfulness in thought,
Be it our wives, our children, or ourselves,
The curse of heaven and men succeed their evils!   105
Till when—the which, I hope, shall ne'er be seen—
Your Grace is welcome to our town and us.
    Per. Which welcome we'll accept; feast here awhile,
Until our stars that frown lend us a smile.

              Exeunt.

ACT SECOND 🙠

Enter Gower.

Here have you seen a mighty king
His child, iwis, to incest bring;
A better prince and benign lord,
That will prove awful both in deed and word.
Be quiet, then, as men should be,   5
Till he hath pass'd necessity.
I'll show you those in troubles reign,
Losing a mite, a mountain gain.
The good in conversation,
To whom I give my benison,   10
Is still at Tarsus, where each man
Thinks all is writ he speken can;
And, to remember what he does,
Build his statue to make him glorious:
But tidings to the contrary   15
Are brought your eyes; what need speak I?

Dumb Show.

*Enter at one door Pericles talking with Cleon; all the Train with
    them. Enter, at another door, a Gentleman, with a letter to*

---

26 jetted: *walked proudly*   **42 nousle:** *foster, train up*   **61 portly:** *stately*   **70 Where
there is no glory in overcoming**
83 consist: *insist*   **92 happily:** *haply, perhaps*   **93 the Troyan horse;** *cf. n.*   **95** *Cf. n.*
2 iwis: *certainly, indeed*   **9 The good:** *i.e. Pericles*   **conversation:** *behavior*   **10 benison:** *blessing*   **12 writ:** *holy writ, Gospel truth*

Pericles; Pericles shows the letter to Cleon; Pericles gives the
Messenger a reward, and knights him. Exit Pericles
at one door, and Cleon at another.

Good Helicane hath stay'd at home,
Not to eat honey like a drone
From others' labours; for though he strive
To killen bad, keep good alive,   *20*
And to fulfil his prince' desire,
Sends word of all that haps in Tyre:
How Thaliard came full bent with sin
And had intent to murder him;
And that in Tarsus was not best   *25*
Longer for him to make his rest.
He, doing so, put forth to seas,
Where when men been, there's seldom ease;
For now the wind begins to blow;
Thunder above and deeps below   *30*
Make such unquiet, that the ship
Should house him safe is wrack'd and split;
And he, good prince, having all lost,
By waves from coast to coast is tost.
All perishen of man, of pelf,   *35*
Ne aught escapen'd but himself;
Till Fortune, tir'd with doing bad,
Threw him ashore, to give him glad;
And here he comes. What shall be next,
Pardon old Gower, this longs the text.   *[Exit.]*

❧ Scene First ❧

[Pentapolis. An open Place by the Sea-side]

Enter Pericles wet.

Per. Yet cease your ire, you angry stars of heaven!
Wind, rain, and thunder, remember, earthly man
Is but a substance that must yield to you;
And I, as fits my nature, do obey you.
Alas! the sea hath cast me on the rocks,   *5*
Wash'd me from shore to shore, and left my breath
Nothing to think on but ensuing death:
Let it suffice the greatness of your powers
To have bereft a prince of all his fortunes;
And having thrown him from your watery grave,   *10*
Here to have death in peace is all he'll crave.

Enter three Fishermen.

1. Fish. What, ho, Pilch!
2. Fish. Ha! come and bring away the nets.
1. Fish. What, Patch-breech, I say!
3. Fish. What say you, master?   *15*
1. Fish. Look how thou stirrest now! come away, or I'll
fetch thee with a wanion.
3. Fish. Faith, master, I am thinking of the poor men that
were cast away before us even now.
1. Fish. Alas! poor souls; it grieved my heart to hear what *20*

pitiful cries they made to us to help them, when, well-a-day,
we could scarce help ourselves.

3. Fish. Nay, master, said not I as much when I saw the
porpoise how he bounced and tumbled? they say they're half
fish, half flesh; a plague on them! they ne'er come but I look   *25*
to be washed. Master, I marvel how the fishes live in the sea.

1. Fish. Why, as men do a-land; the great ones eat up the
little ones; I can compare our rich misers to nothing so fitly as
to a whale; a' plays and tumbles, driving the poor fry before
him, and at last devours them all at a mouthful. Such whales   *30*
have I heard on o' the land, who never leave gaping till they've
swallowed the whole parish, church, steeple, bells, and all.

Per. [Aside.] A pretty moral.

3. Fish. But master, if I had been the sexton, I would have
been that day in the belfry.   *35*

2. Fish. Why, man?

3. Fish. Because he should have swallowed me too; and
when I had been in his belly, I would have kept such a jangling of the bells, that he should never have left till he cast
bells, steeple, church, and parish, up again. But if the good   *40*
King Simonides were of my mind,—

Per. [Aside.] Simonides!

3. Fish. We would purge the land of these drones, that rob
the bee of her honey.

Per. [Aside.] How from the finny subject of the sea   *45*
These fishers tell the infirmities of men;
And from their watery empire recollect
All that may men approve or men detect!
[Aloud.] Peace be at your labour, honest fishermen.

2. Fish. Honest! good fellow, what's that? if it be a day fits
you, search out of the calendar, and nobody look after it.

Per. Y' may see the sea hath cast me on your coast.

2. Fish. What a drunken knave was the sea, to cast thee in
our way!

Per. A man whom both the waters and the wind,   *55*
In that vast tennis-court, have made the ball
For them to play upon entreats you pity him;
He asks of you, that never us'd to beg.

1. Fish. No, friend, cannot you beg? here's them in our
country of Greece gets more with begging then we can do   *60*
with working.

2. Fish. Canst thou catch any fishes then?

Per. I never practised it.

2. Fish. Nay then thou wilt starve, sure;
for here's nothing to be got now-a-days unless thou canst   *65*
fish for 't.

Per. What I have been I have forgot to know,
But what I am want teaches me to think on;
A man throng'd up with cold; my veins are chill,
And have no more of life than may suffice   *70*
To give my tongue that heat to ask your help;
Which if you shall refuse, when I am dead,
For that I am a man, pray you see me buried.

1. Fish. Die, quoth-a? Now, gods forbid 't! And I have a
gown here; come, put it on; keep thee warm. Now, afore   *75*
me, a handsome fellow! Come, thou shalt go home, and we'll
have flesh for all day, fish for fasting-days, and moreo'er
puddings and flap-jacks; and thou shalt be welcome.

Per. I thank you, sir.

---

23 full bent with sin: *bent upon sin*   **35 All perishen of man:** *all the men perish*   **pelf:**
property   **38 glad:** *gladness*   **40 longs:** *makes too long (?), belongs to (?)*   Scene First
Pentapolis; *cf. n.*   S. d. Enter three Fishermen; *cf. n.*   **12 Pilch;** *cf. n.*   **17 with
a wanion:** *with a vengeance*

48 may men approve: *may put men to the test*   **50-51** *Cf. n.*   **56 tennis-court;** *cf. n.*

2. Fish. Hark you, my friend; you said you could not beg?
Per. I did but crave.   *80*
2. Fish. But crave! Then I'll turn craver too, and so I shall 'scape whipping.
Per. Why, are your beggars whipped, then?
2. Fish. O! not all, my friend, not all; for if all your beggars were whipped, I would wish no better office than   *85*
to be beadle. But, master, I'll go draw up the net.

                              [Exit with Third Fisherman.]
Per. How well this honest mirth becomes their labour!
1. Fish. Hark you, sir; do you know where ye are?
Per. Not well.   *90*
1. Fish. Why, I'll tell you: this is called Pentapolis, and our king the good Simonides.
Per. The good Simonides do you call him?
1. Fish. Ay, sir; and he deserves to be so called for his peaceable reign and good government.   *95*
Per. He is a happy king, since he gains from his subjects the name of good by his government. How far is his court distant from this shore?
1. Fish. Marry, sir, half a day's journey; and I'll tell you, he hath a fair daughter, and to-morrow is her birthday; and   *100*
there are princes and knights come from all parts of the world to joust and tourney for her love.
Per. Were my fortunes equal to my desires, I could wish to make one there.
1. Fish. O! sir, things must be as they may; and what a   *105*
man cannot get, he may lawfully deal for—his wife's soul,—

                    Enter the two Fishermen, drawing up a net.

2. Fish. Help, master, help! here's a fish hangs in the net, like a poor man's right in the law; 'twill hardly come out. Ha! bots on 't, 'tis come at last, and 'tis turned to a rusty armour.
Per. An armour, friends! I pray you, let me see it.   *110*
Thanks, Fortune, yet, that after all my crosses
Thou giv'st me somewhat to repair myself;
And though it was mine own, part of my heritage,
Which my dead father did bequeath to me,
With this strict charge, even as he left his life,   *115*
'Keep it, my Pericles, it hath been a shield
'Twixt me and death';—and pointed to this brace;
'For that it sav'd me, keep it; in like necessity—
The which the gods protect thee from!—it may defend thee.'
It kept where I kept, I so dearly lov'd it;   *120*
Till the rough seas, that spare not any man,
Took it in rage, though, calm'd, have given 't again.
I thank thee for 't; my shipwrack now's no ill,
Since I have here my father gave in his will.
1. Fish. What mean you, sir?   *125*
Per. To beg of you, kind friends, this coat of worth,
For it was sometime target to a king;
I know it by this mark. He lov'd me dearly,
And for his sake I wish the having of it;
And that you'd guide me to your sovereign's court,   *130*
Where with it I may appear a gentleman;

And if that ever my low fortune's better,
I'll pay your bounties; till then rest your debtor.
1. Fish. Why, wilt thou tourney for the lady?
Per. I'll show the virtue I have borne in arms.   *135*
1. Fish. Why, do 'e take it; and the gods give thee good on 't!
2. Fish. Ay, but hark you, my friend; 'twas we that made up this garment through the rough seams of the waters; there are certain condolements, certain vails. I hope, sir, if you   *140*
thrive, you'll remember from whence you had them.
Per. Believe 't, I will.
By your furtherance I am cloth'd in steel;
And spite of all the rupture of the sea,
This jewel holds his building on my arm: *145*
Unto thy value will I mount myself
Upon a courser, whose delightful steps
Shall make the gazer joy to see him tread.
Only, my friend, I yet am unprovided
Of a pair of bases.   *150*
2. Fish. We'll sure provide; thou shalt have my best gown to make thee a pair, and I'll bring thee to the court myself.
Per. Then honour be but a goal to my will!
This day I'll rise, or else add ill to ill.   *[Exeunt.]*

❧ SCENE SECOND ❧

[The Same. A public Way. Platform leading to the Lists. A Pavilion near it, for the reception of the King, Princess, Ladies, Lords, &c.]
Enter Simonides, with attendants, and Thaisa.

King. Are the knights ready to begin the triumph?
1. Lord. They are, my liege;
And stay your coming to present themselves.
King. Return them, we are ready; and our daughter,
In honour of whose birth these triumphs are,   *5*
Sits here, like beauty's child, whom nature gat
For men to see, and seeing wonder at.   *[Exit a Lord.]*
Thai. It pleaseth you, my royal father, to express
My commendations great, whose merit's less.
King. It's fit it should be so; for princes are   *10*
A model, which heaven makes like to itself:
As jewels lose their glory if neglected,
So princes their renowns if not respected.
'Tis now your honour, daughter, to explain
The labour of each knight in his device.   *15*
Thai. Which, to preserve mine honour, I'll perform.

                    The first Knight passes by.

King. Who is the first that doth prefer himself?
Thai. A knight of Sparta, my renowned father;
And the device he bears upon his shield
Is a black Ethiop reaching at the sun;   *20*
The word, *Lux tua vita mihi.*
King. He loves you well that hold his life of you.

---

86 **beadle:** *a parish officer with power over petty offenders*   102 **joust and tourney;** *cf. n.*   105, 106 **what . . . soul;** *cf. n.*   109 **bots:** *a disease of horses;* **bots on 't:** *an oath on the analogy of 'plague on it'*   113 **And though:** *and I thank thee though*   117 **brace;** *cf. n.*   120 **kept:** *lived, stayed*   124 **my father gave:** *what my father gave*   127 **target;** *cf. n.*

133 **pay your bounties:** *repay your generosity*   138, 139 **made up . . . waters:** *brought up through the waves*   140 **condolements:** *satisfactions for loss* **vails:** *gratuities*   144 **In spite of all the sea's destructive power*   145 **holds his building:** *keeps its place*   146 **thy:** *the jewel's*   150 **bases:** *horseman's ornamental skirt*   3 **stay:** *await*   4 **Return them:** *announce to them*   14, 15 *Cf. n.*   15 **labour:** *achievements*   17 **prefer:** *present*   21 **Lux . . . mihi:** *Thy light my life*

The Second Knight.

Who is the second that presents himself?
   Thai. A prince of Macedon, my royal father;
And the device he bears upon his shield   25
Is an arm'd knight that's conquer'd by a lady;
The motto thus, in Spanish, *Piu por dulzura que por fuerza.*

Third Knight.

   King. And what's the third?
   Thai.   The third of Antioch;
And his device, a wreath of chivalry;   30
The word, *Me pompæ provexit apex.*

Fourth Knight.

   King. What is the fourth?
   Thai. A burning torch that's turned upside down;
The word, *Qui me alit me extinguit.*
   King. Which shows that beauty hath his power and will,   35
Which can as well inflame as it can kill.

Fifth Knight.

   Thai. The fifth, an hand environed with clouds,
Holding out gold that's by the touchstone tried;
The motto thus, *Sic spectanda fides.*

Sixth Knight [Pericles].

   King. And what's   40
The sixth and last, the which the knight himself
With such a graceful courtesy deliver'd?
   Thai. He seems to be a stranger; but his present is
A wither'd branch, that's only green at top;
The motto, *In hac spe vivo.*   45
   King. A pretty moral;
From the dejected state wherein he is,
He hopes by you his fortunes yet may flourish.
   1. Lord. He had need mean better than his outward show
Can any way speak in his just commend;   50
For, by his rusty outside he appears
To have practis'd more the whipstock then the lance.
   2. Lord. He well may be a stranger, for he comes
To an honour'd triumph strangely furnished.
   3. Lord. And on set purpose let his armour rust   55
Until this day, to scour it in the dust.
   King. Opinion's but a fool, that makes us scan
The outward habit by the inward man.
But stay, the knights are coming; we'll withdraw
Into the gallery.   60
                           [Exeunt.]

Great shouts, and all cry, 'The mean knight!'

❧ SCENE THIRD ❧

[The Same. A Hall of State. A Banquet prepared]
Enter the King and Knights from tilting [Thaisa, Ladies, Lords, and
Attendants].

   King. Knights,
To say you're welcome were superfluous.
To place upon the volume of your deeds,
As in a title-page, your worth in arms,
Were more than you expect, or more than's fit,   5
Since every worth in show commends itself.
Prepare for mirth, for mirth becomes a feast:
You are princes and my guest.
   Thai. But you, my knight and guest;
To whom this wreath of victory I give,   10
And crown you king of this day's happiness.
   Per. 'Tis more by fortune, lady, than my merit.
   King. Call it by what you will, the day is yours;
And here, I hope, is none that envies it.
In framing an artist art hath thus decreed,   15
To make some good, but others to exceed;
And you're her labour'd scholar. Come, queen o' the feast,—
For, daughter, so you are,—here take your place;
Marshal the rest, as they deserve their grace.
   Knights. We are honour'd much by good Simonides.   20
   King. Your presence glads our days; honour we love,
For who hates honour, hates the gods above.
   Marshal. Sir, yonder is your place.
   Per.   Some other is more fit.
   1. Knight. Contend not, sir; for we are gentlemen   25
That neither in our hearts nor outward eyes
Envy the great nor shall the low despise.
   Per. You are right courteous knights.
   King.   Sit, sir; sit.
   Per. By Jove, I wonder, that is king of thoughts,   30
These cates resist me, she but thought upon.
   Thai. [Aside.] By Juno, that is queen of marriage,
All viands that I eat do seem unsavoury,
Wishing him my meat. *[Aloud.]* Sure, he's a gallant gentleman.
   King. He's but a country gentleman;   35
He has done no more than other knights have done;
He has broken a staff or so; so let it pass.
   Thai. To me he seems like diamond to glass.
   Per. Yon king's to me like to my father's picture,
Which tells me in that glory once he was;   40
Had princes sit, like stars, about his throne,
And he the sun for them to reverence.
None that beheld him, but like lesser lights
Did vail their crowns to his supremacy;
Where now his son's like a glow-worm in the night,   45
The which hath fire in darkness, none in light:
Whereby I see that Time's the king of men;
He's both their parent, and he is their grave,
And gives them what he will, not what they crave.
   King. What, are you merry, knights?   50
   Knights. Who can be other in this royal presence?
   King. Here, with a cup that's stor'd unto the brim,
As you do love, fill to your mistress' lips,
We drink this health to you.

---

27 Piu ... fuerza: *More by sweetness than by force; cf. n.*   **31 Me ... apex:** *The crown of glory has drawn me on*   **34 Qui ... extinguit:** *Who feeds me extinguishes me*   **37 environed with:** *surrounded by*   **38 touchstone;** *cf. n.*   **39 Sic ... fides:** *So should faith be tested*   **45 In ... vivo:** *In this hope I live*   **50 commend:** *commendation*   **54 triumph:** *public festivity*   **55** *He has let his armour rust on purpose*   **58** *Cf. n.* **S.d. mean:** *of undistinguished appearance*

17 And ... scholar; *cf. n.*   **23 Sir ... place;** *cf. n.*   **31** *If I but think of her, these delicacies tempt me not; cf. n.*

Knights.   We thank your Grace.   *55*
King. Yet pause awhile;
Yon knight doth sit too melancholy,
As if the entertainment in our court
Had not a show might countervail his worth.
Note it not you, Thaisa?   *60*
Thai.   What is it
To me, my father?
King.   O, attend, my daughter:
Princes in this should live like gods above,
Who freely give to every one that comes   *65*
To honour them;
And princes not doing so are like to gnats,
Which make a sound, but kill'd are wonder'd at.
Therefore to make his entrance more sweet,
Here say we drink this standing-bowl of wine to him.   *70*
Thai. Alas! my father, it befits not me
Unto a stranger knight to be so bold;
He may my proffer take for an offence,
Since men take women's gifts for impudence.
King. How!   *75*
Do as I bid you, or you'll move me else.
Thai. [*Aside.*] Now, by the gods, he could not please me
better.
King. And further tell him, we desire to know of him,
Of whence he is, his name, and parentage.   *80*
Thai. The king, my father, sir, has drunk to you.
Per. I thank him.
Thai. Wishing it so much blood unto your life.
Per. I thank both him and you, and pledge him freely.
Thai. And further he desires to know of you,   *85*
Of whence you are, your name and parentage.
Per. A gentleman of Tyre, my name, Pericles;
My education been in arts and arms;
Who, looking for adventures in the world,
Was by the rough seas reft of ships and men,   *90*
And after shipwrack, driven upon this shore.
Thai. He thanks your Grace; names himself Pericles,
A gentleman of Tyre,
Who only by misfortune of the seas
Bereft of ships and men, cast on this shore.   *95*
King. Now, by the gods, I pity his misfortune,
And will awake him from his melancholy.
Come, gentlemen, we sit too long on trifles,
And waste the time which looks for other revels.
Even in your armours, as you are address'd,   *100*
Will well become a soldier's dance.
I will not have excuse with saying this,
'Loud music is too harsh for ladies' heads,'
Since they love men in arms as well as beds.   *They dance.*
So this was well ask'd, 'twas so well perform'd.   *105*
Come, sir;
Here's a lady that wants breathing too:
And I have heard, you knights of Tyre
Are excellent in making ladies trip,
And that their measures are as excellent.   *110*

Per. In those that practise them they are, my lord.
King. Oh! that's as much as you would be denied
Of your fair courtesy.   *They dance.*
               Unclasp, unclasp;
Thanks, gentlemen, to all; all have done well,   *115*
[*To Pericles.*] But you the best. Pages and lights, to conduct
These knights unto their several lodgings! Yours, sir,
We have given order be next our own.
Per. I am at your Grace's pleasure.
[*King.*] Princes, it is too late to talk of love,   *120*
And that's the mark I know you level at;
Therefore each one betake him to his rest;
To-morrow all for speeding do their best.   [*Exeunt.*]

❧ SCENE FOURTH ❧

[Tyre. A Room in the Governor's House]
Enter Helicanus and Escanes.

Hel. No, Escanes, know this of me,
Antiochus from incest liv'd not free;
For which, the most high gods not minding longer
To withhold the vengeance that they had in store,
Due to this heinous capital offence,   *5*
Even in the height and pride of all his glory,
When he was seated in a chariot
Of an inestimable value, and his daughter with him,
A fire from heaven came and shrivell'd up
Their bodies, even to loathing; for they so stunk,   *10*
That all those eyes ador'd them ere their fall
Scorn now their hand should give them burial.
Esca. 'Twas very strange.
Hel.   And yet but justice; for though
This king were great, his greatness was no guard   *15*
To bar heaven's shaft, but sin had his reward.
Esca. 'Tis very true.

Enter two or three Lords.

1. Lord. See, not a man in private conference
Or council has respect with him but he.
2. Lord. It shall no longer grieve without reproof.   *20*
3. Lord. And curst be he that will not second it.
1. Lord. Follow me then. Lord Helicane, a word.
Hel. With me? and welcome. Happy day, my lords.
1. Lord. Know that our griefs are risen to the top,
And now at length they overflow their banks.   *25*
Hel. Your griefs! for what? wrong not your prince you love.
1. Lord. Wrong not yourself then, noble Helicane;
But if the prince do live, let us salute him,
Or know what ground's made happy by his breath.
If in the world he live, we'll seek him out;   *30*
If in his grave he rest, we'll find him there;
And be resolv'd he lives to govern us,
Or dead, give's cause to mourn his funeral,
And leave us to our free election.
2. Lord. Whose death's indeed the strongest in our censure:
And knowing this kingdom is without a head,

---

59 countervail: *equal*   **67, 68** *Cf. n.*   **69 entrance:** *joining in our festivity*   **70 standing-bowl:** *bowl with a standard*   **76 move:** *anger*   **87–91** *Cf. n.*   **88 been:** *has been*   **98 on:** *at*   **100 address'd:** *dressed*   **101 Will:** *You will*   **103 Loud music:** *the clash of their armor*   **105 So this was well ask'd:** *I did well to ask this*   **107 breathing:** *exercising*

112, 113 *Cf. n.*   **121 level:** *aim*   **123 To-morrow let all do their best at wooing**   **3 minding:** *being minded*   **9, 10** *Cf. n.*   **11 ador'd:** *which adored*   **26 you:** *whom you*   **32–34** *Cf. n.*   **35 strongest . . . censure:** *most likely in our opinion*

(Like goodly buildings left without a roof
Soon fall to ruin) your noble self,
That best know how to rule and how to reign,
We thus submit unto, our sovereign.   40
    Omnes. Live, noble Helicane!
    Hel. Try honour's cause, forbear your suffrages:
If that you love Prince Pericles, forbear.
Take I your wish, I leap into the seas,
Where's hourly trouble for a minute's ease.   45
A twelvemonth longer let me entreat you
To forbear the absence of your king;
If in which time expir'd he not return,
I shall with aged patience bear your yoke.
But if I cannot win you to this love,   50
Go search like nobles, like noble subjects,
And in your search spend your adventurous worth;
Whom if you find, and win unto return,
You shall like diamonds sit about his crown.
    1. Lord. To wisdom he's a fool that will not yield;   55
And since Lord Helicane enjoineth us,
We with our travels will endeavour.
    Hel. Then you love us, we you, and we'll clasp hands:
When peers thus knit, a kingdom ever stands.   *[Exeunt.]*

❧ SCENE FIFTH ❧

[Pentapolis. A Room in the Palace]
Enter the King reading of a letter at one door; the Knights meet
him.

    1. Knight. Good morrow to the good Simonides.
    King. Knights, from my daughter this I let you know,
That for this twelvemonth she'll not undertake
A married life.
Her reason to herself is only known,   5
Which yet from her by no means can I get.
    1. Knight. May we not get access to her, my lord?
    King. Faith, by no means; she hath so strictly tied
Her to her chamber that 'tis impossible.
One twelve moons more she'll wear Diana's livery;   10
This by the eye of Cynthia hath she vow'd,
And on her virgin honour will not break it.
    3. Knight. Loath to bid farewell, we take our leaves.
                              [Exeunt Knights.]
    King. So,
They are well dispatch'd; now to my daughter's letter.   15
She tells me here, she'll wed the stranger knight,
Or never more to view nor day nor light.
'Tis well, mistress; your choice agrees with mine;
I like that well: nay, how absolute she's in 't,
Not minding whether I dislike or no!   20
Well, I do commend her choice;
And will no longer have it be delay'd.
Soft! here he comes: I must dissemble it.

Enter Pericles.

    Per. All fortune to the good Simonides!

    King. To you as much! Sir, I am beholding to you   25
For your sweet music this last night: I do
Protest my ears were never better fed
With such delightful pleasing harmony
    Per. It is your Grace's pleasure to commend,
Not my desert.   30
    King.   Sir, you are music's master.
    Per. The worst of all her scholars, my good lord.
    King. Let me ask you one thing.
What do you think of my daughter, sir?
    Per. A most virtuous princess.   35
    King. And she is fair too, is she not?
    Per. As a fair day in summer; wondrous fair.
    King. Sir, my daughter thinks very well of you;
Ay, so well that you must be her master,
And she will be your scholar: therefore look to it.   40
    Per. I am unworthy for her schoolmaster.
    King. She thinks not so; peruse this writing else.
    Per. *[Aside.]* What's here?
A letter that she loves the knight from Tyre!
'Tis the king's subtilty to have my life.   45
Oh, seek not to entrap me, gracious lord,
A stranger and distressed gentleman,
That never aim'd so high to love your daughter,
But bent all offices to honour her.
    King. Thou hast bewitch'd my daughter, and thou art   50
A villain.
    Per. By the gods, I have not:
Never did thought of mine levy offence;
Nor never did my actions yet commence
A deed might gain her love or your displeasure.   55
    King. Traitor, thou liest.
    Per.   Traitor!
    King.   Ay, traitor,
    Per. Even in his throat, unless it be the king,
That calls me traitor, I return the lie.   60
    King. *[Aside.]* Now, by the gods, I do applaud his courage.
    Per. My actions are as noble as my thoughts,
That never relish'd of a base descent.
I came unto your court for honour's cause,
And not to be a rebel to her state;   65
And he that otherwise accounts of me,
This sword shall prove he's honour's enemy
    King. No?
Here comes my daughter, she can witness it.

Enter Thaisa.

    Per. Then, as you are as virtuous as fair,   70
Resolve your angry father, if my tongue
Did e'er solicit, or my hand subscribe
To any syllable that made love to you.
    Thai. Why, sir, say if you had,
Who takes offence at that would make me glad?   75
    King. Yea, mistress, are you so peremptory?—
I am glad on 't, with all my heart.   *Aside.*
[Aloud.] I'll tame you; I'll bring you in subjection.
Will you, not having my consent,
Bestow your love and your affections   80

---

37 Like: *as*   **44** Take I: *if I take*   **47** forbear: *bear in patience*   **55** He's a fool *who will not yield to wisdom*   **3, 4** *Cf. n.*   **10, 11** *Cf. n.*

25 beholding: *indebted*   **28** *Cf. n.*   **45** subtilty: *crafty plot*   **49** bent all offices: *directed all his endeavors*   **53** levy: *aim at*   **63** relish'd: *had a taste*   **71** Resolve: *inform*   **76** peremptory: *determined*

Upon a stranger?—who, for aught I know,
May be, nor can I think the contrary,
As great in blood as I myself.—   *Aside.*
[*Aloud.*] Therefore, hear you, mistress; either frame
Your will to mine; and you, sir, hear you,   85
Either be rul'd by me, or I'll make you—
Man and wife:
Nay, come, your hands and lips must seal it too;
And being join'd, I'll thus your hopes destroy;
And for further grief,—God give you joy!   90
What! are you both pleas'd?
    Thai.   Yes, if you love me, sir.
    Per. Even as my life, my blood that fosters it.
    King. What! are you both agreed?
    Ambo. Yes, if 't please your majesty.   95
    King. It pleaseth me so well, that I will see you wed;
And then with what haste you can get you to bed.
                                                 Exeunt.

ACT THIRD ❧

Enter Gower.

Now sleep yslacked hath the rout;
No din but snores the house about,
Made louder by the o'erfed breast
Of this most pompous marriage-feast.
The cat, with eyne of burning coal,   5
Now couches fore the mouse's hole;
And crickets sing at the oven's mouth,
Are the blither for their drouth.
Hymen hath brought the bride to bed,
Where, by the loss of maidenhead,   10
A babe is moulded. Be attent;
And time that is so briefly spent
With your fine fancies quaintly eche;
What's dumb in show I'll plain with speech.

[Dumb Show.]

Enter Pericles and Simonides, at one door with Attendants; a Mes-
senger meets them, kneels, and gives Pericles a letter: Pericles shows
it Simonides; the Lords kneel to Pericles. Then enter Thaisa with
child, with Lychorida a nurse: the King shows her the letter; she
rejoices: she and Pericles take leave of her father, and depart.

By many a dern and painful perch,   15
Of Pericles the careful search
By the four opposing coigns,
Which the world together joins,
Is made with all due diligence
That horse and sail and high expense   20
Can stead the quest. At last from Tyre,—
Fame answering the most strange inquire—
To the court of King Simonides
Are letters brought, the tenour these:
Antiochus and his daughter dead;   25

The men of Tyrus on the head
Of Helicanus would set on
The crown of Tyre, but he will none:
The mutiny he there hastes t' oppress;
Says to 'em, if King Pericles   30
Come not home in twice six moons,
He, obedient to their dooms,
Will take the crown. The sum of this,
Brought hither to Pentapolis,
Yravished the regions round,   35
And every one with claps can sound,
'Our heir-apparent is a king!
Who dream'd, who thought of such a thing?'
Brief, he must hence depart to Tyre:
His queen, with child, makes her desire,—   40
Which who shall cross?—along to go.
Omit we all their dole and woe:
Lychorida, her nurse, she takes,
And so to sea. Their vessel shakes
On Neptune's billow; half the flood   45
Hath their keel cut: but Fortune's mood
Varies again: the grisled north
Disgorges such a tempest forth,
That, as a duck for life that dives,
So up and down the poor ship drives.   50
The lady shrieks, and, well-a-near!
Does fall in travail with her fear;
And what ensues in this fell storm
Shall for itself itself perform.
I nill relate, action may   55
Conveniently the rest convey,
Which might not what by me is told.
In your imagination hold
This stage the ship, upon whose deck
The seas-toss'd Pericles appears to speak.   *[Exit.]*

❧ SCENE FIRST ❧

Enter Pericles, a-shipboard.

    Per. The God of this great vast rebuke these surges,
Which wash both heaven and hell; and thou, that hast
Upon the winds command, bind them in brass,
Having call'd them from the deep. O, still
Thy deafening, dreadful thunders; gently quench   5
Thy nimble, sulphurous flashes. O, how, Lychorida,
How does my queen? Thou storm, venomously
Wilt thou spit all thyself? The seaman's whistle
Is as a whisper in the ears of death,
Unheard. Lychorida! Lucina, O   10
Divinest patroness, and midwife gentle
To those that cry by night, convey thy deity
Aboard our dancing boat; make swift the pangs
Of my queen's travails!

Enter Lychorida [with an Infant].

95 Ambo: *both*   97 *Cf. n.*   1 yslacked hath the rout: *hath quieted the company*   5
eyne: *eyes*   6 fore: *before*   8 *And are the more blithe for their dryness*   13 eche: *eke*
out   15-19 *Cf. n.*   21 stead: *help*   22 *Report answering the most widespread inquiry*
32 dooms: *judgments*   35 Yravished: *delighted*   36 can: *'gan, began to*   45 half . . .
cut: *they have made half the voyage*   51 well-a-near!: *well-a-day!*   53 fell: *fierce*   55
nill: *will not; cf. n.*   55-57 action . . . told; *cf. n.*   SCENE FIRST; *cf. n.*   1 rebuke
these surges; *cf. n.*

                              Now, Lychorida!   15

Lyc. Here is a thing too young for such a place,
Who, if it had conceit, would die, as I
Am like to do: take in your arms this piece
Of your dead queen.

Per.   How, how, Lychorida?   20

Lyc. Patience, good sir; do not assist the storm.
Here's all that is left living of your queen,
A little daughter: for the sake of it,
Be manly, and take comfort.

Per.   O you gods!   25

Why do you make us love your goodly gifts,
And snatch them straight away? We here below
Recall not what we give, and therein may
Vie honour with you.

Lyc.   Patience, good sir,   30

Even for this charge.

Per.   Now, mild may be thy life!

For a more blusterous birth had never babe:
Quiet and gentle thy conditions! for
Thou art the rudeliest welcome to this world   35
That e'er was prince's child. Happy what follows!
Thou hast as chiding a nativity
As fire, air, water, earth, and heaven can make,
To herald thee from the womb; even at the first
Thy loss is more than can thy portage quit,   40
With all thou canst find here. Now, the good gods
Throw their best eyes upon 't!

Enter two Sailors.

1. Sail. What courage, sir? God save you!

Per. Courage enough. I do not fear the flaw;
It hath done to me the worst. Yet for the love   45
Of this poor infant, this fresh new seafarer,
I would it would be quiet.

1. Sail. Slack the bolins there! thou wilt not, wilt thou?
Blow, and split thyself.

2. Sail. But sea-room, and the brine and cloudy billow   50
kiss the moon, I care not.

1. Sail. Sir, your queen must overboard: the sea works high,
the wind is loud, and will not lie till the ship be cleared of the
dead.

Per. That's your superstition.   55

1. Sail. Pardon us, sir; with us at sea it hath been still observed, and we are strong in custom. Therefore briefly yield
her, for she must overboard straight.

Per. As you think meet. Most wretched queen!

Lyc. Here she lies, sir.   60

Per. A terrible child-bed hast thou had, my dear;
No light, no fire: th' unfriendly elements
Forgot thee utterly; nor have I time
To give thee hallow'd to thy grave, but straight
Must cast thee, scarcely coffin'd, in the ooze;   65
Where, for a monument upon thy bones,
And aye-remaining lamps, the belching whale
And humming water must o'erwhelm thy corpse,
Lying with simple shells! O Lychorida!

Bid Nestor bring me spices, ink and paper,   70
My casket and my jewels; and bid Nicander
Bring me the satin coffer: lay the babe
Upon the pillow. Hie thee, whiles I say
A priestly farewell to her: suddenly, woman.

                              [Exit Lychorida.]

2. Sail. Sir, we have a chest beneath the hatches, caulk'd   75
and bitumed ready.

Per. I thank thee. Mariner, say what coast is this?

2. Sail. We are near Tarsus.

Per. Thither, gentle mariner,
Alter thy course for Tyre. When canst thou reach it?   80

2. Sail. By break of day, if the wind cease.

Per. O! make for Tarsus.
There will I visit Cleon, for the babe
Cannot hold out to Tyrus; there I'll leave it
At careful nursing. Go thy ways, good mariner;   85
I'll bring the body presently.   *Exit [followed by Sailors].*

❧ SCENE SECOND ❧

[Ephesus. A Room in Cerimon's House]
Enter Lord Cerimon, with a Servant [and some Persons
who have been shipwrecked].

Cer. Philemon, ho!

Enter Philemon.

Phil. Doth my lord call?

Cer. Get fire and meat for these poor men;
'T has been a turbulent and stormy night.

Ser. I have been in many; but such a night as this   5
Till now I ne'er endur'd.

Cer. Your master will be dead ere you return;
There's nothing can be minister'd to nature
That can recover him. *[To Philemon.]* Give this to
the 'pothecary,   10
And tell me how it works.   *[Exeunt all except Cerimon.]*

Enter two Gentlemen.

1. Gent.   Good morrow.

2. Gent. Good morrow to your lordship.

Cer.   Gentlemen,
Why do you stir so early?   15

1. Gent. Sir,
Our lodgings, standing bleak upon the sea,
Shook as the earth did quake;
The very principals did seem to rend,
And all to topple. Pure surprise and fear   20
Made me to quit the house.

2. Gent. That is the cause we trouble you so early;
'Tis not our husbandry.

Cer.   O, you say well.

1. Gent. But I much marvel that your lordship, having   25
Rich tire about you, should at these early hours
Shake off the golden slumber of repose.
'Tis most strange,

---

17 conceit: *understanding*   **27–29** We . . . you; *cf. n.*   **31** Even . . . charge: *for the sake of the baby*   **40** can . . . quit: *thy safe delivery can atone for*   **44** flaw: *squall*   **48** bolins: *bowlines*   **50** But sea-room and: *only give us sea-room, and though*   **50** cloudy billow: *waves like clouds*   **52** *Cf. n.*

74 suddenly: *swiftly*   **76** bitumed: *pitched*   **80** thy . . . Tyre: *your present course towards Tyre*   **85** At . . . nursing: *to be carefully nursed*   SCENE SECOND Ephesus; *cf. n.*   **19** principals: *frame-work*   **23** husbandry: *thrifty habits*   **26** tire: *bed furnishings*

Nature should be so conversant with pain,
Being thereto not compell'd.   30
   Cer.   I hold it ever,
Virtue and cunning were endowments greater
Than nobleness and riches; careless heirs
May the two latter darken and expend,
But immortality attends the former,   35
Making a man a god. 'Tis known I ever
Have studied physic, through which secret art,
By turning o'er authorities, I have—
Together with my practice—made familiar
To me and to my aid the blest infusions   40
That dwells in vegetives, in metals, stones;
And can speak of the disturbances
That nature works, and of her cures; which doth give me
A more content in course of true delight
Than to be thirsty after tottering honour,   45
Or tie my treasure up in silken bags,
To please the fool and death.
   2. Gent. Your honour has through Ephesus pour'd forth
Your charity, and hundreds call themselves
Your creatures, who by you have been restor'd: 50
And not your knowledge, your personal pain, but even
Your purse, still open, hath built Lord Cerimon
Such strong renown as time shall never decay.

     Enter two or three [Servants] with a chest.

   Serv. So; lift there.
   Cer.   What's that?   55
   Serv.   Sir, even now
Did the sea toss up upon our shore this chest:
'Tis of some wrack.
   Cer.   Set it down; let's look upon 't.
   2. Gent. 'Tis like a coffin, sir.   60
   Cer.   Whate'er it be,
'Tis wondrous heavy. Wrench it open straight;
If the sea's stomach be o'ercharg'd with gold,
'Tis a good constraint of fortune it belches upon us.
   2. Gent. 'Tis so, my lord.   65
   Cer.   How close 'tis caulk'd and bottomed!
Did the sea cast it up?
   Serv. I never saw so huge a billow, sir,
As toss'd it upon shore.
   Cer.   Wrench it open.   70
Soft! it smells most sweetly in my sense.
   2. Gent. A delicate odour.
   Cer. As ever hit my nostril. So, up with it.
O you most potent gods! what's here? a corse!
   2. Gent. Most strange!   75
   Cer. Shrouded in cloth of state; blam'd and entreasur'd
With full bags of spices! A passport too!
Apollo, perfect me in the characters!
   'Here I give to understand,
   If e'er this coffin drives a-land,   80
   I, King Pericles, have lost
This queen worth all our mundane cost.
Who finds her, give her burying;
She was the daughter of a king:

Besides this treasure for a fee,   85
   The gods requite his charity!'
If thou liv'st, Pericles, thou hast a heart
That even cracks for woe! This chanc'd to-night.
   2. Gent. Most likely, sir.
   Cer.   Nay, certainly to-night;   90
For look, how fresh she looks. They were too rough
That threw her in the sea. Make a fire within;
Fetch hither all my boxes in my closet.   *[Exit Second Servant.]*
Death may usurp on nature many hours,
And yet the fire of life kindle again   95
The o'erpress'd spirits. I heard of an Egyptian,
That had nine hours lien dead,
Who was by good appliance recovered.

     Enter one with napkins and fire.

Well said, well said; the fire and cloths.
The rough and woeful music that we have,   100
Cause it to sound, beseech you.
The viol once more;—how thou stirr'st, thou block!
The music there! I pray you, give her air.
Gentlemen,
This queen will live; nature awakes, a warmth   105
Breathes out of her; she hath not been entranc'd
About five hours. See how she 'gins to blow
Into life's flower again.
   1. Gent.   The heavens
Through you increase our wonder and sets up   110
Your fame for ever.
   Cer.   She is alive! behold,
Her eyelids, cases to those heavenly jewels
Which Pericles hath lost,
Begin to part their fringes of bright gold;   115
The diamonds of a most praised water
Doth appear, to make the world twice rich. Live,
And make us weep to hear your fate, fair creature,
Rare as you seem to be!   *She moves.*
   Thai.   O dear Diana!   120
Where am I? Where's my lord? What world is this?
   2. Gent. Is not this strange?
   1. Gent.   Most rare.
   Cer.   Hush, my gentle neighbours!
Lend me your hands; to the next chamber bear her.   125
Get linen; now this matter must be look'd to,
For her relapse is mortal. Come, come;
And Æsculapius guide us!

     They carry her away.   *Exeunt omnes.*

❧ Scene Third ❧

[Tarsus. A Room in Cleon's House]
Enter Pericles, at Tarsus, with Cleon and Dionyza [and Lychorida,
carrying the infant Marina].

   Per. Most honour'd Cleon, I must needs be gone;
My twelve months are expir'd, and Tyrus stands

---

37 **physic:** *the art of healing*   40 **aid:** *assistant; cf. n.*   51 **pain:** *care*   74 **corse:**
corpse   76 **entreasur'd:** *stored up*   78 *Apollo, enable me to read the writing*

88 **to-night:** *last night*   94 **usurp:** *encroach*   96 **o'erpress'd:** *overcome*   97 **lien:**
lain   110 **sets;** *cf. n.*   117 **twice rich;** *cf. n.*   120, 121 *Cf. n.*   127 **is mortal:**
would be fatal   128 **Æsculapius:** *god of healing*

In a litigious peace. You and your lady
Take from my heart all thankfulness; the gods
Make up the rest upon you!   5
    Cer. Your shakes of fortune, though they haunt you mortally,
Yet glance full wanderingly on us.
    Dion.   O your sweet queen!
That the strict fates had pleas'd you had brought her hither, *10*
To have bless'd mine eyes with her!
    Per.   We cannot but obey
The powers above us. Could I rage and roar
As doth the sea she lies in, yet the end
Must be as 'tis. My gentle babe Marina—whom,   *15*
For she was born at sea, I have nam'd so—here
I charge your charity withal, leaving her
The infant of your care, beseeching you
To give her princely training, that she may be
Manner'd as she is born.   20
    Cle.   Fear not, my lord, but think
Your Grace, that fed my country with your corn—
For which the people's prayers still fall upon you—
Must in your child be thought on. If neglection
Should therein make me vile, the common body,   *25*
By you reliev'd, would force me to my duty;
But if to that my nature need a spur,
The gods revenge it upon me and mine,
To the end of generation!
    Per.   I believe you;   30
Your honour and your goodness teach me to 't,
Without your vows. Till she be married, madam,
By bright Diana, whom we honour, all
Unscissor'd shall this hair of mine remain,
Though I show ill in 't. So I take my leave.   *35*
Good madam, make me blessed in your care
In bringing up my child.
    Dion.   I have one myself,
Who shall not be more dear to my respect
Than yours, my lord.   40
    Per.   Madam, my thanks and prayers.
    Cle. We'll bring your Grace e'en to the edge o' the shore;
Then give you up to the mask'd Neptune and
The gentlest winds of heaven.
    Per.   I will embrace   45
Your offer. Come, dearest madam. O! no tears,
Lychorida, no tears:
Look to your little mistress, on whose grace
You may depend hereafter. Come, my lord.   *[Exeunt.]*

❧ SCENE FOURTH ❧

[Ephesus. A Room in Cerimon's House]
Enter Cerimon and Thaisa.

    Cer. Madam, this letter, and some certain jewels,
Lay with you in your coffer; which are
At your command. Know you the character?
    Thai. It is my lord's.

That I was shipp'd at sea, I well remember,   5
Even on my eaning time; but whether there
Deliver'd, by the holy gods,
I cannot rightly say. But since King Pericles,
My wedded lord, I ne'er shall see again,
A vestal livery will I take me to,   *10*
And never more have joy.
    Cer. Madam, if this you purpose as ye speak,
Diana's temple is not distant far,
Where you may abide till your date expire.
Moreover, if you please, a niece of mine   *15*
Shall there attend you.
    Thai. My recompense is thanks, that's all;
Yet my good will is great, though the gift small.
                   Exit [with Cerimon].

ACT FOURTH ❧

Enter Gower.

Imagine Pericles arriv'd at Tyre,
Welcom'd and settled to his own desire.
His woeful queen we leave at Ephesus,
Unto Diana there a votaress.
Now to Marina bend your mind,   5
Whom our fast-growing scene must find
At Tarsus, and by Cleon train'd
In music, letters; who hath gain'd
Of education all the grace,
Which makes her both the heart and place   *10*
Of general wonder. But, alack!
That monster envy, oft the wrack
Of earned praise, Marina's life
Seeks to take off by treason's knife
And in this kind hath our Cleon   *15*
One daughter, and a wench full grown,
Even ripe for marriage-rite; this maid
Hight Philoten, and it is said
For certain in our story, she
Would ever with Marina be: 20
Be 't when she weav'd the sleided silk
With fingers, long, small, white as milk,
Or when she would with sharp needle wound
The cambric, which she made more sound
By hurting it; when to the lute   25
She sung, and made the night-bird mute,
That still records with moan; or when
She would with rich and constant pen
Vail to her mistress Dian; still
This Philoten contends in skill   *30*
With absolute Marina: so
With the dove of Paphos might the crow
Vie feathers white. Marina gets
All priases, which are paid as debts,
And not as given. This so darks   35

---

3 **litigious:** *questionable*   5 **upon:** *to*   6–9 *Cf. n.*   8 **full wanderingly:** *wide of their mark*   24 **neglection:** *neglect*   25 **the common body:** *the citizens*   39 **respect:** *care*   43 **mask'd Neptune:** *the mighty sea appearing calm*

6 **eaning time:** *time of bringing forth*   9 *Cf. n.*   10 **vestal livery;** *cf. n.*   14 **your date expire:** *you die*   10 **heart and place:** *the very center*   18 **Hight:** *named*   21 **sleided:** *raw*   26 **night-bird:** *nightingale*   27 **records:** *sings*   29 **Vail:** *do homage*   31 **absolute:** *perfect*   32 **the dove of Paphos;** *cf. n.*   34, 35 **All . . . given;** *cf. n.*   35 **darks:** *obscures*

In Philoten all graceful marks,
That Cleon's wife, with envy rare,
A present murderer does prepare
For good Marina, that her daughter
Might stand peerless by this slaughter.   40
The sooner her vile thought to stead,
Lychorida, our nurse, is dead:
And cursed Dionyza hath
The pregnant instrument of wrath
Prest for this blow. The unborn event   45
I do commend to your content:
Only I carried winged time
Post on the lame feet of my rime;
Which never could I so convey,
Unless your thoughts went on my way.   50
Dionyza doth appear,
With Leonine, a murtherer.   *Exit.*

❧ Scene First ❧

[Tarsus. An open Place near the Sea-shore]
Enter Dionyza, with Leonine.

Dion. Thy oath remember; thou hast sworn to do 't:
'Tis but a blow, which never shall be known.
Thou canst not do a thing i' the world so soon,
To yield thee so much profit. Let not conscience,
Which is but cold, inflaming love i' thy bosom,   5
Inflame too nicely; nor let pity, which
Even women have cast off, melt thee, but be
A soldier to thy purpose.
   Leon. I'll do 't; but yet she is a goodly creature.
   Dion. The fitter, then, the gods should have her. Here   10
She comes weeping for her only mistress' death.
Thou art resolv'd?
   Leon.   I am resolv'd.

Enter Marina, with a basket of flowers.

Mar. No, I will rob Tellus of her weed,
To strew thy green with flowers; the yellows, blues,   15
The purple violets, and marigolds,
Shall as a carpet hang upon thy grave,
While summer days doth last. Ay me! poor maid,
Born in a tempest, when my mother died,
This world to me is a lasting storm,   20
Whirring me from my friends.
   Dion. How now, Marina! why do you keep alone?
How chance my daughter is not with your? Do not
Consume your blood with sorrowing; you have
A nurse of me. Lord! how your favour's chang'd   25
With this unprofitable woe. Come,
Give me your flowers, ere the sea mar it.
Walk with Leonine; the air is quick there,
And it pierces and sharpens the stomach. Come,
Leonine, take her by the arm, walk with her.   30
   Mar. No, I pray you;

I'll not bereave you of your servant.
   Dion.   Come, come;
I love the king your father, and yourself,
With more than foreign heart. We every day   35
Expect him here; when he shall come and find
Our paragon to all reports thus blasted,
He will repent the breadth of his great voyage;
Blame both my lord and me, that we have taken
No care to your best courses. Go, I pray you;   40
Walk, and be cheerful once again; reserve
That excellent complexion, which did steal
The eyes of young and old. Care not for me;
I can go home alone.
   Mar.   Well, I will go;   45
But yet I have no desire to it.
   Dion. Come, come, I know 'tis good for you.
Walk half an hour, Leonine, at least.
Remember what I have said.
   Leon.   I warrant you, madam.   50
   Dion. I'll leave you, my sweet lady, for a while;
Pray you walk softly, do not heat your blood:
What! I must have care of you.
   Mar.   My thanks, sweet madam.
                                                       [Exit Dionyza.]
Is this wind westerly that blows?   55
   Leon.   South-west.
   Mar. When I was born, the wind was north.
   Leon.   Was 't so?
   Mar. My father, as nurse said, did never fear,
But cried 'Good seamen!' to the sailors, galling   60
His kingly hands haling ropes;
And, clasping to the mast, endur'd a sea
That almost burst the deck.
   Leon. When was this?
   Mar. When I was born: 65
Never were waves nor wind more violent;
And from the ladder-tackle washes off
A canvas-climber. 'Ha!' says one, 'wilt out?'
And with a dropping industry they skip
From stem to stern; the boatswain whistles, and   70
The master calls, and trebles their confusion.
   Leon. Come; say your prayers.
   Mar. What mean you?
   Leon. If you require a little space for prayer,
I grant it. Pray; but be not tedious,   75
For the gods are quick of ear, and I am sworn
To do my work with haste.
   Mar.   Why will you kill me?
   Leon. To satisfy my lady.
   Mar. Why would she have me kill'd?   80
Now, as I can remember, by my troth,
I never did her hurt in all my life.
I never spake bad word, nor did ill turn
To any living creature; believe me, la,
I never kill'd a mouse, nor hurt a fly;   85
I trod upon a worm against my will,
But I wept for it. How have I offended,
Wherein my death might yield her any profit,

36   *All attention to the grace of Philoten*   44 **pregnant:** *ready*   45 **Prest:** *prepared*   47-50 *Cf. n.*   6 **nicely:** *scrupulously*   14 **Tellus:** *Earth*   15 **green:** *grave*   21 **Whirring:** *hurrying*   23 **How chance:** *how comes it*   25 **of:** *in*   **favour:** *face*   27 **it:** *them*   28 **quick:** *invigorating*   29 **stomach:** *spirits*

37 **to all reports:** *equal to all reports*   40 **courses:** *interests*   52 **softly:** *slowly*   61 **haling:** *pulling*   68 **canvas-climber:** *seaman*   69 **dropping:** *dripping wet*

Or my life imply her any danger?

Leon. My commission   90
Is not to reason of the deed, but do 't.

Mar. You will not do 't for all the world, I hope.
You are well favour'd, and your looks foreshow
You have a gentle heart. I saw you lately,
When you caught hurt in parting two that fought;   95
Good sooth, it show'd well in you; do so now;
Your lady seeks my life; come you between,
And save poor me, the weaker.

Leon.   I am sworn,
And will dispatch.   100

Enter Pirates.

1. Pirate. Hold, villain!   *[Leonine runs away.]*
2. Pirate. A prize! a prize!
3. Pirate. Half-part, mates, half-part.
Come, let's have her aboard suddenly.
              Exit [Marina, carried by Pirates].

Enter Leonine.

Leon. These roguing thieves serve the great pirate Valdes; *105*
And they have seiz'd Marina. Let her go;
There's no hope she'll return. I'll swear she's dead,
And thrown into the sea. But I'll see further;
Perhaps they will but please themselves upon her,
Not carry her aboard. If she remain,   *110*
Whom they have ravish'd must by me be slain.   *Exit.*

❧ SCENE SECOND ❧

[Mitylene. A Room in a Brothel]
Enter the three Bawds [i.e. Pandar, Bawd, and Boult].

Pand. Boult.
Boult. Sir?
Pand. Search the market narrowly; Mitylene is full of
gallants; we lost too much money this mart by being too
wenchless.   5
Bawd. We were never so much out of creatures. We have
but poor three, and they can do no more than they can do;
and they with continual action are even as good as rotten.
Pand. Therefore, let's have fresh ones, whate'er we pay for
them. If there be not a conscience to be used in every trade, *10*
we shall never prosper.
Bawd. Thou sayst true; 'tis not the bringing up of poor
bastards, as, I think, I have brought up some eleven—
Boult. Ay, to eleven; and brought them down again. But
shall I search the market?   *15*
Bawd. What else, man? The stuff we have a strong wind
will blow it to pieces, they are so pitifully sodden.
Pand. Thou sayst true; they're too unwholesome, o'
conscience. The poor Transylvanian is dead, that lay with the
little baggage.   *20*
Boult. Ay, she quickly pooped him; she made him roast-
meat for worms. But I'll go search the market.   *Exit.*
Pand. Three or four thousand chequins were as pretty a

proportion to live quietly, and so give over.
Bawd. Why to give over, I pray you? is it a shame to   *25*
get when we are old?
Pand. O! our credit comes not in like the commodity, nor
the commodity wages not with the danger; therefore, if in our
youths we could pick up some pretty estate, 'twere not amiss
to keep our door hatched. Besides, the sore terms we stand   *30*
upon with the gods will be strong with us for giving over.
Bawd. Come, other sorts offend as well as we.
Pand. As well as we! ay, and better too; we offend worse.
Neither is our profession any trade; it's no calling. But here
comes Boult.   *35*

Enter Boult, with the Pirates and Marina.

Boult. Come your ways. My masters, you say she's a virgin?
1. Pirate. O, sir, we doubt it not.
Boult. Master, I have gone through for this piece, you see:
if you like her, so; if not, I have lost my earnest.
Bawd. Boult, has she any qualities?   *40*
Boult. She has a good face, speaks well, and has excellent
good clothes; there's no farther necessity of qualities can
make her be refused.
Bawd. What's her price, Boult?
Boult. I cannot be bated one doit of a thousand pieces.   *45*
Pand. Well, follow me, my masters, you shall have your
money presently. Wife, take her in; instruct her what she has
to do, that she may not be raw in her entertainment.
          [Exeunt Pandar and Pirates.]
Bawd. Boult, take you the marks of her, the colour of her
hair, complexion, height, age, with warrant of her virginity; *50*
and cry, 'He that will give most, shall have her first.' Such a
maidenhead were no cheap thing, if men were as they have
been. Get this done as I command you.
Boult. Performance shall follow.   *Exit.*
Mar. Alack, that Leonine was so slack, so slow!   *55*
He should have struck, not spoke; or that these pirates—
Not enough barbarous—had not o'erboard thrown me
For to seek my mother!
Bawd. Why lament you, pretty one?
Mar. That I am pretty.   *60*
Bawd. Come, the gods have done their part in you.
Mar. I accuse them not.
Bawd. You are lit into my hands, where you are like to live.
Mar. The more my fault
To 'scape his hands where I was like to die.   *65*
Bawd. Ay, and you shall live in pleasure.
Mar. No.
Bawd. Yes, indeed, shall you, and taste gentlemen of all
fashions. You shall fare well; you shall have the difference
of all complexions. What! do you stop your ears?   *70*
Mar. Are you a woman?
Bawd. What would you have me be, an I be not a woman?
Mar. An honest woman, or not a woman.
Bawd. Marry, whip thee, gosling; I think I shall have
something to do with you. Come, you are a young foolish   *75*
sapling, and must be bowed as I would have you.
Mar. The gods defend me!

93 **well favour'd:** *handsome*   103 **Half-part:** *I demand my share*   105 **Valdes;** *cf. n.*
SCENE SECOND Mitylene; *cf. n.*   4 **mart:** *market time*   21 **pooped:** *deceived*   23
chequins: *sequins, gold coins*

24 **give over:** *give up* (the life)   28 **wages not:** *is not equal*   30 **hatched;** *cf. n.*   **S. d.**
Enter Boult, etc.; *cf. n.*   38 **gone through:** *struck a bargain*   39 **earnest:** *advance
payment*   45 **bated one doit:** *reduced a farthing*   48 **raw:** *unskilled* **entertainment:**
occupation

Bawd. If it please the gods to defend you by men, then
men must comfort you, men must feed you, men must stir
you up. Boult's returned.   *80*

[Re-enter Boult.]

Now, sir, hast thou cried her through the market?

Boult. I have cried her almost to the number of her hairs;
I have drawn her picture with my voice.

Bawd. And I prithee, tell me, how dost thou find the inclination of the people, especially of the younger sort?   *85*

Boult. Faith, they listened to me, as they would have heark-
ened to their father's testament. There was a Spaniard's mouth
so watered, that he went to bed to her very description.

Bawd. We shall have him here to-morrow with his best ruff
on.   *90*

Boult. To-night, to-night. But, mistress, do you know the
French knight that cowers i' the hams?

Bawd. Who? Monsieur Veroles?

Boult. Ay, he; he offered to cut a caper at the proclamation;
but he made a groan at it, and swore he would see her to-   *95*
morrow.

Bawd. Well, well; as for him, he brought his disease hither:
here he does but repair it. I know he will come in our
shadow, to scatter his crowns in the sun.

Boult. Well, if we had of every nation a traveller, we should
lodge them with this sign.

Bawd. [*To Marina.*] Pray you, come hither awhile. You have
fortunes coming upon you. Mark me: you must seem to do
that fearfully, which you commit willingly; to despise profit
where you have most gain. To weep that you live as ye do   *105*
makes pity in your lovers; seldom but that pity begets you a
good opinion, and that opinion a mere profit.

Mar. I understand you not.

Boult. O! take her home, mistress, take her home; these
blushes of hers must be quenched with some present practice.

Bawd. Thou sayst true, i' faith, so they must; for your bride
goes to that with shame which is her way to go with warrant.

Boult. Faith, some do, and some do not. But, mistress, if I
have bargained for the joint,—

Bawd. Thou mayst cut a morsel off the spit.   *115*

Boult. I may so?

Bawd. Who should deny it? Come, young one, I like the
manner of your garments well.

Boult. Ay, by my faith, they shall not be changed yet.

Bawd. Boult, spend thou that in the town; report what a   *120*
sojourner we have; you'll lose nothing by custom. When nature
framed this piece, she meant thee a good turn; therefore say
what a paragon she is, and thou has the harvest out of thine
own report.

Boult. I warrant you, mistress, thunder shall not so awake   *125*
the beds of eels as my giving out her beauty stir up the
lewdly-inclined. I'll bring home some to-night.

Bawd. Come your ways; follow me.

Mar. If fires be hot, knives sharp, or waters deep,
Untied I still my virgin knot will keep.   *130*
Diana, aid my purpose!

Bawd. What have we to do with Diana?
Pray you, will you go with us?   *Exeunt.*

101 sign: *inn sign, Marina*   **107 mere:** *sure*   **112 which ... warrant:** *the way which
she is entitled to go*

❧ Scene Third ❧

[Tarsus. A Room in Cleon's House]
Enter Cleon and Dionyza.

Dion. Why, are you foolish? Can it be undone?

Cle. O Dionyza! such a piece of slaughter
The sun and moon ne'er look'd upon.

Dion.   I think
You'll turn a child again.   *5*

Cle. Were I chief lord of all this spacious world,
I'd give it to undo the deed. O lady!
Much less in blood than virtue, yet a princess
To equal any single crown o' the earth
I' the justice of compare. O villain Leonine!   *10*
Whom thou hast poison'd too;
If thou hadst drunk to him 't had been a kindness
Becoming well thy fact; what canst thou say
When noble Pericles shall demand his child?

Dion. That she is dead. Nurses are not the fates,   *15*
To foster it, nor ever to preserve.
She died at night; I'll say so. Who can cross it?
Unless you play the pious innocent,
And for an honest attribute cry out
'She died by foul play.'   *20*

Cle.   O! go to. Well, well,
Of all the faults beneath the heavens, the gods
Do like this worst.

Dion.   Be one of those that think
The pretty wrens of Tarsus will fly hence,   *25*
And open this to Pericles. I do shame
To think of what a noble strain you are,
And of how coward a spirit.

Cle.   To such proceeding
Who ever but his approbation added,   *30*
Though not his prime consent, he did not flow
From honourable sources.

Dion.   Be it so, then;
Yet none does know but you how she came dead,
Nor none can know, Leonine being gone.   *35*
She did distain my child, and stood between
Her and her fortunes; none would look on her,
But cast their gazes on Marina's face,
Whilst ours was blurted at and held a malkin
Not worth the time of day. It pierc'd me thorough;   *40*
And though you call my course unnatural,
You not your child well loving, yet I find
It greets me as an enterprise of kindness
Perform'd to your sole daughter.

Cle.   Heavens forgive it!   *45*

Dion. And as for Pericles,
What should he say? We wept after her hearse,
And even yet we mourn; her monument
Is almost finish'd, and her epitaphs
In glittering golden characters express   *50*
A general praise to her, and care in us

Scene Third; *cf. n.*   **10 I' ... compare:** *by just comparison*   **12 drunk to:** *toasted* (in
poison)   **13 fact:** *misdeed*   **17 cross:** *deny*   **19 attribute:** *reputation*   **26 open:**
reveal   **29–32 To ... sources:** *whoever could approve such a crime, though not party to it,
must be base*   **36 distain:** *put a stain upon*   **39 blurted:** *mocked* **malkin:** *slat-
tern*   **40 the time of day:** *a civil greeting* **thorough:** *through*   **43 greets:** *gratifies*

At whose expense 'tis done.
   Cle.   Thou art like the harpy,
Which, to betray, dost, with thine angel's face,
Seize with thine eagle's talons.   55
   Dion. You are like one that superstitiously
Do swear to the gods that winter kills the flies;
But yet I know you'll do as I advise.   *[Exeunt.]*

❧ SCENE FOURTH ❧

[Before the Monument of Marina at Tarsus]
[Enter Gower.]

   Gower. Thus time we waste, and long leagues make short;
Sail seas in cockles, have, an wish but for 't;
Making—to take your imagination—
From bourn to bourn, region to region.
By you being pardon'd, we commit no crime   5
To use one language in each several clime
Where our scenes seem to live. I do beseech you
To learn of me, who stand i' the gaps to teach you,
The stages of our story. Pericles
Is now again thwarting the wayward seas,   10
Attended on by many a lord and knight,
To see his daughter, all his life's delight.
Old Helicanus goes along. Behind
Is left to govern it, you bear in mind,
Old Escanes, whom Helicanus late   15
Advanc'd in time to great and high estate.
Well-sailing ships and bounteous winds have brought
This king to Tarsus, think his pilot thought,
So with his steerage shall your thoughts grow on,
To fetch his daughter home, who first is gone.   20
Like motes and shadows see them move awhile;
Your ears unto your eyes I'll reconcile.

[Dumb Show.]
Enter Pericles at one door with all his Train; Cleon and Dionyza
at the other. Cleon shows Pericles the tomb; whereat Pericles
makes lamentation, puts on sackcloth, and in a mighty passion
departs. [Exeunt Cleon and Dionyza.]

   Gower. See how belief may suffer by foul show!
This borrow'd passion stands for true old woe;
And Pericles, in sorrow all devour'd,   25
With sighs shot through, and biggest tears o'ershower'd,
Leaves Tarsus and again embarks. He swears
Never to wash his face, nor cut his hairs;
He puts on sackcloth, and to sea. He bears
A tempest, which his mortal vessel tears,   30
And yet he rides it out. Now please you wit
The epitaph is for Marina writ
By wicked Dionyza.

[Reads inscription on Marina's monument.]

The fairest, sweet'st, and best lies here,
Who wither'd in her spring of year: 35
She was of Tyrus the king's daughter,

On whom foul death hath made this slaughter.
Marina was she call'd; and at her birth,
Thetis, being proud, swallow'd some part o' th' earth:
Therefore the earth, fearing to be o'erflow'd,   40
Hath Thetis' birth-child on the heavens bestow'd:
Wherefore she does, and swears she'll never stint,
Make raging battery upon shores of flint.

No visor does become black villainy
So well as soft and tender flattery.   45
Let Pericles believe his daughter's dead,
And bear his courses to be ordered
By Lady Fortune; while our scene must play
His daughter's woe and heavy well-a-day
In her unholy service. Patient then,   50
And think you now are all in Mitylen.   *Exit.*

❧ SCENE FIFTH ❧

[Mitylene. A Street before the Brothel]
Enter two Gentlemen.

   1. Gent. Did you ever hear the like?
   2. Gent. No, nor never shall do in such a place as this, she
being once gone.
   1. Gent. But to have divinity preached there! did you ever
dream of such a thing?   5
   2. Gent. No, no. Come, I am for no more bawdy-houses.
Shall's go hear the vestals sing?
   1. Gent. I'll do anything now that is virtuous; but I am out
of the road of rutting forever.   *Exeunt.*

❧ SCENE SIXTH ❧

[The Same. A Room in the Brothel]
Enter the three Bawds.

   Pand. Well, I had rather than twice the worth of her she
had ne'er come here.
   Bawd. Fie, fie upon her! she is able to freeze the god Priapus, and undo a whole generation; we must either get her ravished, or be rid of her. When she should do for clients her   5
fitment, and do me the kindess of our profession, she has me
her quirks, her reasons, her master-reasons, her prayers, her
knees; that she would make a puritan of the devil if he should
cheapen a kiss of her.
   Boult. Faith, I must ravish her, or she'll disfurnish us   10
of all our cavaliers, and make all our swearers priests.
   Pand. Now, the pox upon her green-sickness for me!
   Bawd. Faith, there's no way to be rid on 't but by the way
to the pox. Here comes the Lord Lysimachus, disguised.
   Boult. We should have both lord and lown if the peevish   15
baggage would but give way to customers.

Enter Lysimachus.

   Lys. How now! How a dozen of virginities?
   Bawd. Now, the gods to-bless your honour!
   Boult. I am glad to see your honour in good health.

---

53 harpy; *cf. n.*   **56, 57** *Cf. n.*   **1 waste:** *do away with*   **2 have, an wish but for
't:** *have what we but wish for*   **4 bourn:** *boundary*   **18 think his pilot thought:** *imagine
your thought is his pilot*   **19 steerage:** *voyage*   **30 tempest:** *storm of mental anguish* **his
. . . vessel:** *the vessel of his life*

39 Thetis: *goddess of the sea*   **42 stint:** *cease*   **3 Priapus:** *the god of fertility and generation*   **6 fitment:** *duty* **has me:** *has, forsooth*   **7 quirks:** *subtle arguments, quibbles*   **9
cheapen:** *bargain for*   **12 green-sickness:** *anæmia*   **15 lown:** *loon, menial*   **18 to-
bless:** *bless entirely*

Lys. You may so; 'tis the better for you that your resorters   20
stand upon sound legs. How now, wholesome iniquity! have
you that a man may deal withal, and defy the surgeon?

Bawd. We have here one, sir, if she would—but there
never came her like in Mitylene.

Lys. If she'd do the deeds of darkness, thou wouldst say.   25

Bawd. Your honour knows what 'tis to say well enough.

Lys. Well; call forth, call forth.

Boult. For flesh and blood, sir, white and red, you shall
see a rose; and she were a rose indeed if she had but—

Lys. What, prithee?   30

Boult. O! sir, I can be modest.

Lys. That dignifies the renown of a bawd no less than it
gives a good report to a number to be chaste.   *[Exit Boult.]*

Bawd. Here comes that which grows to the stalk; never
plucked yet, I can assure you.—   35

[Enter Boult with Marina.]

Is she not a fair creature?

Lys. Faith, she would serve after a long voyage at sea.
Well, there's for you; leave us.

Bawd. I beseech your honour, give me leave; a word, and
I'll have done presently.   40

Lys. I beseech you, do.

Bawd. *[To Marina.]* First, I would have you note, this is
an honourable man.

Mar. I desire to find him so, that I may worthily note him.

Bawd. Next, he's the governor of this country, and a   45
man whom I am bound to.

Mar. If he govern the country, you are bound to him
indeed; but how honourable he is in that I know not.

Bawd. Pray you, without any more virginal fencing, will you
use him kindly? He will line your apron with gold.   50

Mar. What he will do graciously, I will thankfully receive.

Lys. Ha' you done?

Bawd. My lord, she's not paced yet; you must take some
pains to work her to your manage. Come, we will leave his
honour and her together.   55

Lys. Go thy ways. *[Exeunt Bawd and Pandar. Boult retires
to the door.]* Now, pretty one, how long have you been at this
trade?

Mar. What trade, sir?

Lys. Why, I cannot name 't but I shall offend.   60

Mar. I cannot be offended with my trade.
Please you to name it.

Lys. How long have you been of this profession?

Mar. E'er since I can remember.

Lys. Did you go to 't so young? Were you a gamester   65
at five or at seven?

Mar. Earlier too, sir, if now I be one.

Lys. Why, the house you dwell in proclaims you to be a
creature of sale.

Mar. Do you know this house to be a place of such resort,
and will come into 't? I hear say you are of honourable parts,
and are the governor of this place.

Lys. Why, hath your principal made known unto you who
I am?

Mar. Who is my principal?   75

Lys. Why, your herb-woman; she that sets seeds and roots
of shame and iniquity. O! you have heard something of my
power, and so stand aloof for more serious wooing. But I
protest to thee, pretty one, my authority shall not see thee,
or else look friendly upon thee. Come, bring me to some   80
private place; come, come.

Mar. If you were born to honour, show it now;
If put upon you, make the judgment good
That thought you worthy of it.

Lys. How's this? how's this? Some more; be sage.   85

Mar. For me,
That am a maid, though most ungentle fortune
Hath plac'd me in this sty, where, since I came,
Diseases have been sold dearer than physic,
O that the gods   90
Would set me free from this unhallow'd place,
Though they did change me to the meanest bird
That flies i' the purer air!

Lys.   I did not think
Thou couldst have spoke so well; ne'er dream'd thou couldst.
Had I brought hither a corrupted mind,
Thy speech had alter'd it. Hold, here's gold for thee;
Persever in that clear way thou goest,
And the gods strengthen thee!

Mar. The good gods preserve you!   100

Lys. For me, be you thoughten
That I came with no ill intent, for to me
The very doors and windows savour vilely.
Farewell. Thou art a piece of virtue, and
I doubt not but thy training hath been noble.   105
Hold, here's more gold for thee.
A curse upon him, die he like a thief,
That robs thee of thy goodness! If thou dost
Hear from me, it shall be for thy good.

Boult. *[Advancing.]* I beseech your honour, one piece for me.

Lys. Avaunt! thou damned door-keeper. Your house,
But for this virgin that doth prop it, would
Sink and overwhelm you. Away!   *[Exit.]*

Boult. How's this? We must take another course with you.
If your peevish chastity, which is not worth a breakfast in   115
the cheapest country under the cope, shall undo a whole
household, let me be gelded like a spaniel. Come your ways.

Mar. Whither would you have me?

Boult. I must have your maidenhead taken off, or the
common hangman shall execute it. Come your ways. We'll   120
have no more gentlemen driven away. Come your ways, I say.

Enter Bawd.

Bawd. How now! what's the matter?

Boult. Worse and worse, mistress; she has here spoken
holy words to the Lord Lysimachus.

Bawd. O! abominable.   125

Boult. She makes our profession as it were to stink afore
the face of the gods.

Bawd. Marry, hang her up forever!

Boult. The nobleman would have dealt with her like a
nobleman, and she sent him away as cold as a snowball;   130
saying his prayers too.

---

33 **report ... to be chaste:** *reputation of being chaste*   53 **paced:** *trained*   54 **manage:**
control   60 **but ... offend:** *without offense*   71 **parts:** *qualities*

83 **If put upon you:** *if honor was bestowed upon you (and not inherited)*   101 **be you**
thoughten: *think*   104 **piece of virtue:** *virtuous creature*   116 **cope:** *firmament*

Bawd. Boult, take her away; use her at thy pleasure;
crack the glass of her virginity, and make the rest malleable.

    Boult. An if she were a thornier piece of ground than she is,
she shall be ploughed.   *135*

    Mar. Hark, hark, you gods!

    Bawd. She conjures; away with her! Would she had never
come within my doors! Marry, hang you! She's born to undo
us. Will you not got the way of womenkind? Marry, come up,
my dish of chastity with rosemary and bays!   *[Exit.] 140*

    Boult. Come, mistress; come your ways with me.

    Mar. Whither wilt thou have me?

    Boult. To take from you the jewel you hold so dear.

    Mar. Prithee, tell me one thing first.

    Boult. Come now, your one thing.   *145*

    Mar. What canst thou wish thine enemy to be?

    Boult. Why, I could wish him to be my master, or rather,
my mistress.

    Mar. Neither of these are so bad as thou art,
Since they do better thee in their command.   *150*
Thou hold'st a place, for which the pained'st fiend
Of hell would not in reputation change;
Thou art the damned door-keeper to every
Coystril that comes inquiring for his Tib,
To the choleric fisting of every rogue   *155*
Thy ear is liable, thy food is such
As hath been belch'd on by infected lungs.

    Boult. What would you have me do? go to the wars, would
you? where a man may serve seven years for the loss of a leg,
and have not money enough in the end to buy him a   *160*
wooden one?

    Mar. Do anything but this thou doest. Empty
Old receptacles, or common sewers, of filth;
Serve by indenture to the common hangman:
Any of these ways are yet better than this;   *165*
For what thou professest, a baboon, could he speak,
Would own a name too dear. O that the gods
Would safely deliver me from this place!
Here, here's gold for thee.
If that thy master would gain by me,   *170*
Proclaim that I can sing, weave, sew, and dance,
With other virtues, which I'll keep from boast;
And I will undertake all these to teach.
I doubt not but this populous city will
Yield many scholars.   *175*

    Boult. But can you teach all this you speak of?

    Mar. Prove that I cannot, take me home again,
And prostitute me to the basest groom
That doth frequent your house.

    Boult. Well, I will see what I can do for thee; if I can   *180*
place thee, I will.

    Mar. But, amongst honest women.

    Boult. Faith, my acquaintance lies little amongst them. But
since my master and mistress have bought you, there's no
going but by their consent; therefore I will make them   *185*
acquainted with your purpose, and I doubt not but I shall
find them tractable enough. Come; I'll do for thee what
I can; come your ways.   *Exeunt.*

---

133 **malleable:** *able to be moulded*   139 **Marry, come up:** *out upon you!*   140 **with ...
bays:** *with all the trimmings*   150 *Since they benefit thee in their employ*   151 **pained'st:**
most tortured   154 **Coystril:** *knave*   155 **choleric fisting:** *angry buffets*   167 **Would
... dear:** *would think his race too good*

ACT FIFTH ❧

Enter Gower.

Marina thus the brothel 'scapes, and chances
Into an honest house, our story says.
She sings like one immortal, and she dances
As goddess-like to her admired lays;
Deep clerks she dumbs; and with her neeld composes   *5*
Nature's own shape, of bud, bird, branch, or berry,
That even her art sisters the natural roses;
Her inkle, silk, twin with the rubied cherry;
That pupils lacks she none of noble race,
Who pour their bounty on her; and her gain   *10*
She gives the cursed bawd. Here we her place,
And to her father turn our thoughts again,
Where we left him, on the sea. We there him lost,
Whence, driven before the winds, he is arriv'd
Here where his daughter dwells: and on this coast   *15*
Suppose him now at anchor. The city striv'd
God Neptune's annual feast to keep; from whence
Lysimachus our Tyrian ship espies,
His banners sable, trimm'd with rich expense,
And to him in his barge with fervour hies.   *20*
In your supposing once more put your sight
Of heavy Pericles; think this his bark:
Where what is done in action—more, if might—
Shall be discover'd; please you, sit and hark.   *Exit.*

❧ SCENE FIRST ❧

*[On board Pericles' ship, off Mitylene. A pavilion on deck, with a
curtain before it; Pericles within it, reclined on a couch]
Enter Helicanus; to him two Sailors.*

    1. Sail. Where is Lord Helicanus? he can resolve you.
O! here he is.—
Sir, there's a barge put off from Mitylene,
And in it is Lysimachus, the governor,
Who craves to come aboard. What is your will?   *5*

    Hel. That he have his. Call up some gentlemen.

    2. Sail. Ho, gentlemen! my lord calls.

Enter two or three Gentlemen.

    1. Gent. Doth your lordship call?

    Hel. Gentlemen, there is some of worth would come
aboard; I pray, greet him fairly.   *10*

Enter Lysimachus [with Attendants].

    1. Sail. Sir,
This is the man that can, in aught you would,
Resolve you.

    Lys. Hail, reverend sir! The gods preserve you!

    Hel. And you, to outlive the age I am,   *15*
And die as I would do.

---

5 **Deep ... dumbs:** *she silences profound scholars*   **neeld:** *needle*   7 **sisters:** *is near akin to,
very like*   8 **inkle, silk:** *linen or silk thread* (used in embroidery)   9 **That:** *so that*   16 **That:** *so that*   16
striv'd: *outdid itself*   21 **supposing:** *imagination*   22 **heavy:** *sad*   23 **more, if might:**
more would be shown if it were possible   24 **discover'd:** *displayed*   SCENE FIRST:
cf. n.   9 **some of worth:** *some important person*   12 **in aught you would:** *about anything
you want*

Lys.   You wish me well.
Being on shore, honouring of Neptune's triumphs,
Seeing this goodly vessel ride before us,
I made to it to know of whence you are.   *20*
   Hel. First, what is your place?
   Lys. I am the governor of this place you lie before.
   Hel. Sir,
Our vessel is of Tyre, in it the king;
A man who for three months hath not spoken   *25*
To anyone, nor taken sustenance
But to prorogue his grief.
   Lys. Upon what ground is his distemperature?
   Hel. 'Twould be too tedious to repeat;
But the main grief springs from the loss   *30*
Of a beloved daughter and a wife.
   Lys. May we not see him?
   Hel. You may;
But bootless is your sight: he will not speak
To any.   *35*
   Lys. Yet let me obtain my wish.
   Hel. Belhold him. *[Pericles discovered.]* This was a goodly
person,
Till the disaster that, one mortal night,
Drove him to this.   *40*
   Lys. Sir king, all hail! the gods preserve you! Hail, royal sir!
   Hel. It is in vain; he will not speak to you.
   Lord. Sir,
We have a maid in Mitylene, I durst wager,
Would win some words of him.   *45*
   Lys.   'Tis well bethought.
She questionless with her sweet harmony
And other chosen attractions, would allure,
And make a battery through his deafen'd parts
Which now are midway stopp'd: *50*
She is all happy as the fair'st of all,
And with her fellow maids is now upon
The leafy shelter that abuts against
The island's side.   *[Whispers Attendant, who goes out.]*
   Hel. Sure, all's effectless; yet nothing we'll omit,   *55*
That bears recovery's name. But, since your kindess
We have stretch'd thus far, let us beseech you,
That for our gold we may provision have,
Wherein we are not destitute for want,
But weary for the staleness.   *60*
   Lys.   O, sir, a courtesy,
Which if we should deny, the most just God
For every graff would send a caterpillar,
And so inflict our province. Yet once more
Let me entreat to know at large the cause   *65*
Of your king's sorrow.
   Hel.   Sit, sir, I will recount it to you;
But see, I am prevented.

   [Enter Attendant, with Marina, and a young Lady.]

   Lys.   O, here's
The lady that I sent for. Welcome, fair one!   *70*
Is 't not a goodly present?

   Hel.   She's a gallant lady.
   Lys. She's such a one, that were I well assur'd
Came of a gentle kind and noble stock,
I'd wish no better choice, and think me rarely wed.—   *75*
Fair one, all goodness that consists in bounty
Expect even here, where is a kingly patient:
If that thy prosperous and artificial feat
Can draw him but to answer thee in aught,
Thy sacred physic shall receive such pay   *80*
As thy desires can wish.
   Mar.   Sir, I will use
My utmost skill in his recovery,
Provided
That none but I and my companion maid   *85*
Be suffer'd to come near him.
   Lys.   Come, let us leave her;
And the gods make her prosperous!

       The Song.

   Lys. Mark'd he your music?
   Mar.   No, nor look'd on us.   *90*
   Lys. See, she will speak to him.
   Mar. Hail, sir! my lord, lend ear.
   Per. Hum! ha! *[Pushes her away.]*
   Mar. I am a maid,
My lord, that ne'er before invited eyes,   *95*
But have been gaz'd on like a comet; she speaks,
My lord, that, may be, hath endur'd a grief
Might equal yours, if both were justly weigh'd.
Though wayward Fortune did malign my state,
My derivation was from ancestors   *100*
Who stood equivalent with mighty kings;
But time hath rooted out my parentage,
And to the world and awkward casualties
Bound me in servitude.—*[Aside.]* I will desist;
But there is something glows upon my cheek,   *105*
And whispers in mine ear, 'Go not till he speak.'
   Per. My fortunes—parentage—good parentage—
To equal mine!—was it not thus? what say you?
   Mar. I said, my lord, if you did know my parentage,
You would not do me violence.   *110*
   Per. I do think so. Pray you, turn your eyes upon me.
You're like something that—. What country-woman?
Here of these shores?
   Mar.   No, nor of any shores;
Yet I was mortally brought forth, and am   *115*
No other than I appear.
   Per. I am great with woe, and shall deliver weeping.
My dearest wife was like this maid, and such a one
My daughter might have been: my queen's square brows;
Her stature to an inch; as wandlike-straight;   *120*
As silver-voic'd; her eyes as jewel-like,
And cas'd as richly; in pace another Juno;
Who starves the ears she feeds, and makes them hungry,
The more she gives them speech. Where do you live?
   Mar. Where I am but a stranger; from the deck   *125*
You may discern the place.
   Per.   Where were you bred?

---

27 **prorogue**: *prolong*   28 **distemperature**: *disturbance of mind*   34 **bootless . . . sight**: *it will not profit you to see him*   39, 40 *Cf. n.*   47 **questionless**: *undoubtedly*   49, 50 *Cf. n.*   53 **abuts against**: *borders on*   55 **effectless**: *useless*   56 **That . . . name**: *that promises recovery*   63 **graff**: *graft (of trees)*   64 **inflict**: *afflict*   65 **at large**: *fully*

78 **artificial feat**: *feat of art*   **S. d. The Song**; *cf. n.*   101 **equivalent**: *equally powerful*   103 **awkward**: *adverse*

And how achiev'd you these endowments, which
You make more rich to owe?

    Mar. If I should tell my history, it would seem   130
Like lies, disdain'd in the reporting.

    Per. Prithee, speak;
Falseness cannot come from thee, for thou lookest
Modest as justice, and thou seem'st a palace
For the crown'd truth to dwell in. I will believe thee,   135
And make my senses credit thy relation
To points that seem impossible; for thou lookest
Like one I lov'd indeed. What were thy friends?
Didst thou not say when I did push thee back,—
Which was when I perceiv'd thee,—that thou cam'st   140
From good descending?

    Mar.   So indeed I did.

    Per. Report thy parentage. I think thou saidst
Thou hadst been toss'd from wrong to injury,
And that thou thought'st thy griefs might equal mine,   145
If both were open'd.

    Mar.   Some such thing
I said, and said no more but what my thoughts
Did warrant me was likely.

    Per.   Tell thy story;   150
If thine consider'd prove the thousandth part
Of my endurance, thou art a man, and I
Have suffer'd like a girl; yet thou dost look
Like Patience gazing on kings' graves, and smiling
Extremity out of act. What were thy friends?   155
How lost thou them? Thy name, my most kind virgin?
Recount, I do beseech thee. Come, sit by me.

    Mar. My name is Marina.

    Per.   Oh! I am mock'd,
And thou by some incensed god sent hither   160
To make the world to laugh at me.

    Mar.   Patience, good sir,
Or here I'll cease.

    Per.   Nay, I'll be patient.
Thou little know'st how thou dost startle me,   165
To call thyself Marina.

    Mar.   The name
Was given me by one that had some power,
My father, and a king.

    Per.   How! a king's daughter?   170
And call'd Marina?

    Mar.   You said you would believe me;
But, not to be a troubler of your peace,
I will end here.

    Per.   But are you flesh and blood?   175
Have you a working pulse? and are no fairy?
Motion!—Well; speak on. Where were you born?
And wherefore call'd Marina?

    Mar.   Call'd Marina
For I was born at sea.   180

    Per.   At sea! what mother?

    Mar. My mother was the daughter of a king,
Who died the minute I was born,
As my good nurse Lychorida hath oft
Deliver'd weeping.   185

    Per.   O stop there a little.
This is the rarest dream that e'er dull sleep
Did mock sad fools withal. This cannot be
My daughter, buried.—Well; where were you bred?
I'll hear you more, to the bottom of your story,   190
And never interrupt you.

    Mar. You scorn: believe me, 'twere best I did give o'er.

    Per. I will believe you by the syllable
Of what you shall deliver. Yet, give me leave:
How came you in these parts? where were you bred?   195

    Mar. The king my father did in Tarsus leave me,
Till cruel Cleon, with his wicked wife,
Did seek to murther me; and having woo'd
A villain to attempt it, who having drawn to do 't,
A crew of pirates came and rescu'd me;   200
Brought me to Mitylene. But, good sir,
Whither will you have me? Why do you weep? It may be
You think me an imposture; no, good faith;
I am the daughter to King Pericles,
If good King Pericles be.   205

    Per. Ho, Helicanus!

    Hel. Calls my lord?

    Per. Thou art a grave and noble counsellor,
Most wise in general; tell me, if thou canst,
What this maid is, or what is like to be,   210
That thus hath made me weep?

    Hel.   I know not; but
Here's the regent, sir, of Mitylene,
Speaks nobly of her.

    Lys.   She never would tell   215
Her parentage. Being demanded that,
She would sit still and weep.

    Per. O Helicanus! strike me, honour'd sir;
Give me a gash, put me to present pain,
Lest this great sea of joys rushing upon me   220
O'erbear the shores of my mortality,
And drown me with their sweetness. Oh come hither,
Thou that begett'st him that did thee beget;
Thou that wast born at sea, buried at Tarsus,
And found at sea again. O Helicanus!   225
Down on thy knees, thank the holy gods as loud
As thunder threatens us; this is Marina.
What was thy mother's name? tell me but that,
For truth can never be confirm'd enough,
Though doubts did ever sleep.   230

    Mar.   First, sir, I pray,
What is your title?

    Per. I am Pericles of Tyre: but tell me now
My drown'd queen's name, as in the rest you said
Thou hast been godlike perfect: 235
The heir of kingdoms, and another like
To Pericles thy father.

    Mar. Is it no more to be your daughter than
To say my mother's name was Thaisa?
Thaisa was my mother, who did end   240
The minute I began.

    Per. Now, blessing on thee! rise; th' art my child.
Give me fresh garments. Mine own, Helicanus;

129 **to owe:** *by possessing*   136 **relation:** *tale*   137 **To:** *even as far as*   149 **warrant:** *assure*   151, 152 **If … endurance;** *cf. n.*   155 **Extremity out of act:** *so that extreme peril cannot strike*   185 **Deliver'd:** *told*

193 **by the syllable:** *every syllable*   198 **woo'd:** *solicited*   199 **drawn:** *i.e. his sword*   235 **perfect:** *correct*   238 **Is it:** *does it require*   242 **th' art my child;** *cf. n.*

She is not dead at Tarsus, as she should have been,
By savage Cleon; she shall tell thee all;   245
When thou shalt kneel, and justify in knowledge
She is thy very princess. Who is this?
   Hel. Sir, 'tis the governor of Mitylene,
Who, hearing of your melancholy state,
Did come to see you.   250
   Per.   I embrace you.
Give me my robes. I am wild in my beholding.
O heavens! bless my girl. But hark! what music?
Tell Helicanus, my Marina, tell him
O'er, point by point, for yet he seems to dote,   255
How sure you are my daughter. But, what music?
   Hel. My lord, I hear none.
   Per. None!
The music of the spheres! List, my Marina.
   Lys. It is not good to cross him; give him way.   260
   Per. Rarest sounds! Do ye not hear?
   Lys. Music, my lord? I hear.
   Per.   Most heavenly music:
It nips me unto list'ning, and thick slumber
Hangs upon mine eyes; let me rest.   *[Sleeps.]*
   Lys. A pillow for his head!
So, leave him all. Well, my companion friends,
If this but answer to my just belief,
I'll well remember you.

      Diana [appears to Pericles as in a vision].

   Dia. My temple stands in Ephesus; hie thee thither,   270
And do upon mine altar sacrifice.
There, when my maiden priests are met together,
Before the people all,
Reveal how thou at sea didst lose thy wife;
To mourn thy crosses, with thy daughter's, call   275
And give them repetition to the life.
Or perform my bidding, or thou liv'st in woe;
Do it, and happy; by my silver bow!
Awake, and tell thy dream!   *[Disappears.]*
   Per. Celestial Dian, goddess argentine,   280
I will obey thee! Helicanus!
   Hel.   Sir?
   Per. My purpose was for Tarsus, there to strike
The inhospitable Cleon: but I am
For other service first: toward Ephesus   285
Turn our blown sails; eftsoons I'll tell thee why.
[To Lysimachus.] Shall we refresh us, sir, upon your shore,
And give you gold for such provision
As our intents will need?
   Lys. Sir,   290
With all my heart; and when you come ashore,
I have another suit.
   Per.   You shall prevail,
Were it to woo my daughter, for it seems
You have been noble towards her.   295
   Lys.   Sir, lend me your arm.
   Per. Come, my Marina.

                        [Exeunt.]

❧ SCENE SECOND ❧

[Enter Gower.]

   Gower. Now our sands are almost run;
More a little, and then dumb.
This, my last boon, give me,
For such kindness must relieve me,
That you aptly will suppose   5
What pageantry, what feats, what shows,
What minstrelsy, and pretty din,
The regent made in Mitylen
To greet the king. So he thriv'd,
That he is promis'd to be wiv'd   10
To fair Marina; but in no wise
Till he had done his sacrifice,
As Dian bade: whereto being bound,
The interim, pray you, all confound.
In feather'd briefness sails are fill'd,   15
And wishes fall out as they're will'd.
At Ephesus the temple see,
Our king and all his company.
That he can hither come so soon,
Is by your fancy's thankful doom.   *[Exit.]*

❧ SCENE THIRD ❧

*[The Temple of Diana at Ephesus; Thaisa standing near the altar,
as high priestess; a number of Virgins on each side; Cerimon
and other Inhabitants of Ephesus attending]*
*[Enter Pericles, with his Train; Lysimachus, Helicanus, Marina,
and a Lady.]*

   Per. Hail, Dian! to perform thy just command,
I here confess myself the King of Tyre;
Who, frighted from my country, did wed
At Pentapolis the fair Thaisa.
At sea in childbed died she, but brought forth   5
A maid-child call'd Marina; who, O goddess!
Wears yet thy silver livery. She at Tarsus
Was nurs'd with Cleon, whom at fourteen years
He sought to murder; but her better stars
Brought her to Mitylene, 'gainst whose shore   10
Riding, her fortunes brought the maid aboard us,
Where, by her own most clear remembrance, she
Made known herself my daughter.
   Thai.   Voice and favour!
You are, you are—O royal Pericles!—   *[She faints.]* 15
   Per. What means the nun? she dies! help, gentlemen!
   Cer. Noble sir,
If you have told Diana's altar true,
This is your wife.
   Per.   Reverend appearer, no;   20
I threw her overboard with these very arms.
   Cer. Upon this coast, I warrant you.
   Per.   'Tis most certain.
   Cer. Look to the lady. O, she's but overjoy'd.
Early in blustering morn this lady was   25

---

244 **should:** *was reported to*   246 **justify:** *prove*   252 **beholding:** *appearance*   255
dote: *be bewildered*   264 **nips:** *arrests*   267–269 **Well . . . you;** *cf. n.*   S. d. **Diana;**
cf. n.   275 **crosses:** *trials*   276 **to the life:** *exact*   277 **Or:** *either*   280 **argentine:**
silvery   286 **eftsoons:** *soon*   292 **suit:** *petition; cf. n.*

5 **aptly:** *readily*   12 **he:** *Pericles*   14 **confound:** *consider gone*   15 **In feather'd briefness:** *swiftly as wings*   20 **thankful doom:** *decision for which I am thankful*   SCENE
THIRD **The Temple of Diana at Ephesus;** *cf. n.*   11 **Riding:** *modifies 'us'*   15 *Cf. n.*

Thrown upon this shore. I op'd the coffin,
Found there rich jewels; recovered her, and plac'd her
Here in Diana's temple.
    Per.   May we see them?
    Cer. Great sir, they shall be brought you to my house,   *30*
Whither I invite you. Look! Thaisa is
Recovered.
    Thai.   O! let me look!
If he be none of mine, my sanctity
Will to my sense bend no licentious ear,   *35*
But curb it, spite of seeing. O! my lord,
Are you not Pericles? Like him you spake,
Like him you are. Did you not name a tempest,
A birth, and death?
    Per.   The voice of dead Thaisa!   *40*
    Thai. That Thaisa am I, supposed dead
And drown'd.
    Per. Immortal Dian!
    Thai.   Now I know you better.
When we with tears parted Pentapolis,   *45*
The king my father gave you such a ring.   *[Shows a ring.]*
    Per. This, this: no more, you gods! your present kindness
Makes my past miseries sports: you shall do well,
That on the touching of her lips I may
Melt and no more be seen. O! come, be buried   *50*
A second time within these arms.
    Mar.   My heart
Leaps to be gone into my mother's bosom.   *[Kneels to Thaisa.]*
    Per. Look, who kneels here! Flesh of they flesh, Thaisa;
Thy burden at the sea, and call'd Marina,   *55*
For she was yielded there.
    Thai.   Bless'd, and mine own!
    Hel. Hail, madam, and my queen!
    Thai.   I know you not.
    Per. You have heard me say, when I did fly from Tyre,   *60*
I left behind an ancient substitute.
Can you remember what I call'd the man?
I have nam'd him oft.
    Thai.   'Twas Helicanus then.
    Per. Still confirmation!   *65*
Embrace him, dear Thaisa; this is he.
Now do I long to hear how you were found,
How possibly preserv'd, and whom to thank,
Besides the gods, for this great miracle.
    Thai. Lord Cerimon, my lord; this man,   *70*
Through whom the gods have shown their power, that can
From first to last resolve you.
    Per.   Reverend sir,
The gods can have no mortal officer

More like a god than you. Will you deliver   *75*
How this dead queen re-lives?
    Cer.   I will, my lord,
Beseech you first, go with me to my house,
Where shall be shown you all was found with her;
How she came plac'd here in the temple;   *80*
No needful thing omitted.
    Per. Pure Dian! bless thee for thy vision, and
Will offer night-oblations to thee. Thaisa,
This prince, the fair-betrothed of your daughter,
Shall marry her at Pentapolis. And now   *85*
This ornament
Makes me look dismal will I clip to form,
And what this fourteen years no razor touch'd,
To grace thy marriage-day I'll beautify.
    Thai. Lord Cerimon hath letters of good credit, sir,   *90*
My father's dead.
    Per. Heavens make a star of him! Yet there, my queen,
We'll celebrate their nuptials, and ourselves
Will in that kingdom spend our following days;
Our son and daughter shall in Tyrus reign.   *95*
Lord Cerimon, we do our longing stay
To hear the rest untold. Sir, lead 's the way.   *[Exeunt.]*

              Gower.

In Antiochus and his daughter you have heard
Of monstrous lust the due and just reward:
In Pericles, his queen, and daughter, seen—   *100*
Although assail'd with fortune fierce and keen—
Virtue preserv'd from fell destruction's blast,
Led on by heaven, and crown'd with joy at last.
In Helicanus may you well descry
A figure of truth, of faith, of loyalty.   *105*
In reverend Cerimon there well appears
The worth that learned charity aye wears.
For wicked Cleon and his wife, when fame
Had spread their cursed deed, and honour'd name
Of Pericles, to rage the city turn,   *110*
That him and his they in his palace burn:
The gods for murder seemed so content
To punish; although not done, but meant.
So on your patience evermore attending,
New joy wait on you! Here our play has ending.   *[Exit.]*

              ❧ FINIS ❧

---

27 recovered: *revived*   **31 you:** *for you*   **45 parted:** *left*   **49 That:** *if*   **82 bless:** *I bless*   **86** *His hair and beard*   **87 Makes:** *which makes*

NOTES

Dramatis Personæ. No list occurs in any of the Quartos. It appears first after the play in the Third Folio.

Act First. None of the Quartos have any division into acts and scenes. In the Folios the beginning is marked *Actus Primus Scena Prima.* Thereafter the acts, but not the scenes, are indicated. The division into scenes is the work of Malone.

I. Prologue. *Gower.* An English poet, ca. 1330-1408, whose *Confessio Amantis* contained the story of Pericles. See Sources of the Play, p. 1371. Gower appears at the beginning of each act and at the end of the play, as well as before Act IV, Scene iv, and Act V, Scene ii. He speaks the prologue and the epilogue, and, in the character of Chorus, tells such parts of the tale as cannot be presented on the stage. There is another such prologue, epilogue, and chorus in *Henry V*, and in other Elizabethan plays outside of Shakespeare: e.g. Marlowe's *Doctor Faustus.* In Peele's (?) *Locrine* (ca. 1586) Ate introduces each act with dumb show, and supplies the epilogue. In three plays by Heywood, *The Golden Age, The Silver Age,* and *The Brazen Age,* Homer appears as Chorus. The device of a Chorus is apparently one of the features which the Elizabethan drama inherited from the Greek by way of Seneca. But the ancient chorus was present on the stage throughout the play, and its function was to supplement the action by moral observations, or ornament it by purely lyric passages; it was not used, as here, to supply information otherwise inaccessible to the audience.

I. Prologue. 6 *ember-eves.* The eves of ember days: days in each of the four seasons designated for fasting and prayer. The preceding evenings would be devoted to amusement.

holy-ales. The old editions read *Holydayes.* Richard Farmer is responsible for the present conjecture, on the analogy of *church-ales.* The word *holy-ales* is not known to occur elsewhere, but the editors have followed Farmer in a sentimental desire to preserve the semblance of rhyme, which is the one virtue of this prologue.

I. Prologue. 17, 18. *This Antioch, then, Antiochus the Great Built up, this city, for his chiefest seat.* Twine, at the beginning of the *Patterne of Painefull Adventures,* writes, 'The most famous and mightie king Antiochus ... builded the goodly citie of Antiochia in Syria, and called it after his own name, as the chiefest seat of all his dominions.' (Quotations from Twine are according to the text in *Shakespeare's Library,* Part I. Vol. IV, edited by Hazlitt, London, 1875. Quotations from Gower are according to the edition by G. C. Macaulay, Oxford, 1901.) Antioch, on the river Orontes, was actually founded by Seleucus Nicator in 300 B.C., just after the battle of Ipsus, which assured him control of Asia Minor. It was enlarged by Antiochus Soter (280-261 B.C.), from whom it took its name. To Antiochus the Great (223-187 B.C.), here referred to, it owed only some further additions.

I. Prologue. 20. *I tell you what mine authors say.* This citation of authority is in imitatin of Gower, e.g.

> 'the grete Antiochus
> Of whom that Antioche tok
> His ferst name, as seith the bok.'

(*Confessio Amantis,* VIII. 274-276.)

> 'This yonge Prince, as seith the bok.'

(Ibid. 574.)

> 'And telle as the Croniques sein.'

(Ibid. 1546.)

I. Prologue. 22, 23. *Who died and left a female heir, So buxon, blithe, and full of face.* Cf. Milton, *L'Allegro,* 23, 24. 'Filled her with thee, a daughter fair, So buxom, blithe, and debonair.'

I. Prologue. 25, 26. *With whom the father liking took, And her to incest did provoke.* It may be that this slander on the memory of the great Antiochus originated in the fact that in 196-5 B.C. he married his son Antiochus to his daughter Laodice. This marrying of full brothers and sisters was common enough among the Persian kings, but this is the first instance of the practice among the Greek monarchs of Asia Minor, and it may well have created a scandal.

I. Prologue. 40. *As yon grim looks do testify.* In the *Confessio Amantis,* VIII. 363-365, the poet writes that, unless the suitor could guess the riddle,

> 'He scholde in certein lese his hed.
> And thus there weren manye ded,
> Here hevedes stondende [their heads standing] on the gate.'

Evidently Gower here points to the heads of the unlucky suitors, shown on the stage.

I.i.1. *Young Prince of Tyre.* Tyre and Sidon were, from the earliest times, the

chief seaports on the coast of Phœnicia. They were conquered by Alexander the Great, and thereafter were subject to one or other of the Greek dynasties that succeeded him. Tyre passed into the hands of Antiochus the Great for the first time in 221 B.C. For some years it was fought over by him and Ptolemy Philopatris, but, in 199-8 B.C. he got final control of it. It seems to have been governed by a satrap, whose subordinate power may be reflected in the title 'Prince,' which means, here, not the son of a reigning king, but a ruler under the king's authority. It is worth mentioning that in Godfrey of Viterbo's *Pantheon,* the hero is *rex Tyri et Sidonis.*

I.i.10, 11. *The senate-house of planets all did sit, To knit in her their best perfections.* The planets, whose position was supposed to be of prime importance in determining human character and fortune, conspired to make their influence all favorable. Cf. Sidney's *Arcadia,* Book II (concerning the birth of Pyrocles). 'The senate house of the planets was at no time so set, for the decreeing of perfection in a man.'

I.i.13, 14. *Graces her subjects, and her thoughts the king Of every virtue gives renown to men!* Her mind is the sovereign served by the graces and all the virtues that give renown to men.

I.i.27. *Hesperides.* The daughters of Atlas, celebrated in Greek mythology, from whose garden Hercules brought back the golden apples which a dragon had guarded. Here, the name is taken to be that of the garden itself. Because of this line, 'Hesperides' appears in the first list of characters as the name of the princess.

I.i.59. *Of all say'd yet.* This is the Quarto reading. M. Mason conjectures 'In all save that,' meaning that she wishes him well, but does not want him to read the riddle. Mitford conjectures 'Oh false! and yet,' the exclamation addressed to herself because her wishing Pericles well is a betrayal of her father's interest and her own. Steevens, approving Mason's reading, remarks, with point, that one could wish that the only speech the lady makes had been intelligible.

I.i.65-70. *The Riddle.* Gower's version of the riddle is as follows:

> 'With felonie I am upbore,
> I ete and have it noght forbore
> My modres fleissh, whos housebonde
> My fader forto seche I fonde,
> Which is the Sone ek of my wif.'

(*Confessio Amantis,* VIII. 405-9)

The *Historia Apollonii Regis Tyrii* has 'Scelere vehor, maternam carnem vescor, quaero fratrem meum, meae matris filium, uxoris meae virum, nec invenio.' (I am carried away by sin, my mother's flesh I eat, I seek my brother, the son of my mother, the husband of my wife, and find him not.) It must be confessed that the riddle in its present state makes one think very lightly of the ingenuity of the gentlemen whose heads adorned the gate. The belief that young vipers eat their parents goes back to Herodotus III. 190. Cf. Blake, *Tiriel,*

> 'Serpents, not sons, wreathing around the bones of Tiriel!
> Ye worms of death, feasting upon your aged parents' flesh.'

I.i.97-101. *For vice repeated is like the wandering mind, Blows dust in others' eyes, to spread itself; And yet the end of all is bought thus dear, The breath is gone, and the sore eyes see clear To stop the air would hurt them.* As the wind spreads dust abroad, so the reporter of vice shocks the community. Yet when the wind has passed, people know from what quarter to protect themselves against more dust, and, though the informer may perish for it, people once warned of vice may be on their guard against it.

I.i.104. *Kings are earth's gods.* As a matter of fact, Antiochus the Great, like all the house of Seleucus, did receive divine honors from his subjects.

I.i.110. *Heaven, that I had thy head!* No one has yet explained why he did not have his head. If he had made no scruple to execute the previous suitors who had not guessed the riddle, it is astonishing that he hesitated a moment to silence Pericles, whose death was of the utmost importance to him. However, the playwright is not to blame; both Gower and the *Gesta Romanorum* have this cuious delay of the sentence.

I.i.114-117. *Your exposition misinterpreting, We might proceed to cancel off your days; Yet hope, succeeding from so fair a tree As your fair self, doth tune us otherwise.* Since your explanation misinterprets, we might proceed to put you to death, but, judging by your fair appearance, we hope for better things from you, and are inclined to do otherwise.

I.ii. S. d. *Enter Pericles with his Lords.* This is the reading of the Quarto. Either the Lords must be supposed to go out again at the words *Let none disturb us,* or Pericles soliloquizes in their presence. After line 34, the direction *Enter all*

the Lords to Pericles is not easily explained if 'his Lords' are supposed to be already on the stage, yet to have them appear and disappear at his first words would be a dramatic absurdity. It is certainly more convenient to follow the directions of Craig, who makes Pericles enter alone, and speak his first words to *those without.*

I.iii.3. *he was a wise fellow.* This is a reference to Barnabe Riche's *Soldier's Wishe to Britons Welfare, or Captain Skill and Captain Pill,* of 1604: 'I will therefore commende the poet Philipides, who being dimaunded by King Lisimachus, what favour he might doe unto him for that he loved him, made this answere to the King, "that your majestie would never impart unto me any of your secrets." '

I.iii.34. *But since my landing I have understood. Since* is used in a double sense, both temporal and causative. But because after I landed I found out.

I.iv. *Tarsus.* Tarsus in Cilicia lies about ten miles from the sea of Cyprus, and less than a hundred, in a straight line, from Antioch, though perhaps twice that distance by road. It was a part of Antiochus' empire, and would therefore be no safe refuge for an enemy of his. It is not likely that, at this time, it was under a special satrap, such as the governor here depicted, but it was then, as later, 'no mean city.'

I.iv.8, 9. *Here they're but felt, and seen with mischief's eyes, But like to groves, being topped they higher rise.* If the reading is right, it must mean that, at present, the woes of Tarsus are evident only to the sufferers themselves in the light of their own misfortune, but a comparison with other calamities would make them at once better known and harder to bear. For *mischief's* Steevens would read *mistful*; Singer, *mistie*; Walker, *misery's*; Kennear, *weakness*. But *mischief* commonly means 'calamity.' *Topped* means 'trimmed at the top,' which makes the trees grow higher.

I.iv.93. *the Troyan horse.* The huge hollow horse, filled with Greek warriors, which the Trojans unsuspiciously dragged into the town, and which brought about the fall of Troy. The *bloody veins* are, of course, the soldiers inside, intent on shedding blood. The tale of the Trojan horse is given in Gower, *Confessio Amantis,* I. 1060-1189.

I.iv.95. *Are stor'd with corn to make your needy bread.* To make bread for your needy citizens. T. S. Graves, in an article entitled *On the Date and Significance of Pericles,* in *Modern Philology* for January, 1916, points out that a Venetian ambassador in England is said to have gone 'to a play called *Pericles* which cost (him) more than 20 crowns.' Among other circumstances bearing on the date, is the fact that late in the year 1606, and early in 1607, the ambassador was attempting to get grain shipped to Venice, to relieve the famine there. It is Mr. Graves' opinoin that the performance of *Pericles* in question was produced at this time at the expense of the Venetian ambassador, who hoped that the tale of Pericles relieving the distressed citizens would arouse sympathy for his own mission. The arguments of the article are sometimes rather tenuous, but it does furnish an interesting suggestion as to the date of the first performance.

II.i. S. d. *Pentapolis.* Here understood to be one city, but, in fact, the 'Five Cities' of Cyrene, Apollonia, Berenice, Barca and Asinoë, whose territory comprised the northern part of the district known as Cyrenaica, on the north coast of Africa, to the west of Egypt. In the time of Antiochus, it was a possession of Ptolemy, and had no resident monarch.

II.i. S. d. *Enter three Fisherman.* The older versions of the story have one fisherman only. The change acquires an added interest from a comparison with the fishermen who appear at the beginning of the Second Act of the *Rudens* of the Latin dramatist, Plautus. In that case also the scene is on the coast of Cyrenaica, immediately after a great storm in which some of the characters have been shipwrecked. It is another fisherman who draws up out of the sea the wallet containing proof of the heroine's identity, an incident slightly like the netting of the armor in II.i.109. These resemblances may, of course, be accidental, but one is tempted to think that Shakespeare, who was familiar with Plautus (cf. *The Comedy of Errors,* founded on the *Menæchmi,* and *Hamlet* II.ii.394, 395: *Seneca cannot be too heavy, nor Plautus too light*) may have revised this scene, thinking of the similar situation in the *Rudens.* K. Deighton, in the introduction to *Pericles* in the *Arden Shakespeare,* concludes, from considerations of style, that Shakespeare rewrote the scene.

II.i.12. *Pilch.* The name of an outer garment of skin or leather.

II.i.50-51. This passage certainly means nothing as it stands, and requires somewhat violent emendation before it can mean anything. Steevens conjectures the loss of the last line of Pericles' preceding speech, which he restores as follows:

'The day is rough and thwarts your occupations,'

and then reads:

Second Fish. Honest! good fellow, what's that? If it be not a day fits you, scratch it out of the calendar, and nobody will look after it.

This has the merit of sense, if not of probability.

II.i.56. *tennis-court.* The game is, of course, not lawn-tennis, but court-tennis, and Pericles thinks of himself as enclosed on all sides by wind and water. Whatever was the nature of the Greek game of ball, it must be admitted that the phrase is an anachronism in the mouth of a hero of the second century B.C. In Twine's novel, tennis was the game which the king of Pentapolis was playing when Apollonius encountered him. Cf. Sidney's *Arcadia,* Book V, 'In such a shadow . . . mankind lives . . . that . . . they . . . are like tenis bals tossed by the racket of the higher powers.'

II.i.102. *joust and tourney.* The episode is transplanted. The joust is, of course, an anachronism. Both Gower and Twine have the tourneying and dancing in connection with the celebration of Pericles' marriage to Thaisa. Cf. *Confessio Amantis,* VIII. 965. 'Thei jouste first and after daunce.' And *Patterne of Painefull Adventures,* Chap. VII, 'I may not discourse at large of the liberall challenges made and proclaimed at the tilt, barriers, running at the ring, ioco di can, managing fierce horses, running a foote, and daunsing in armour.' It may have been developed, in the play, in deference to the court of James, which affected mediæval chivalry. The discovery of the armor is an innovation of our author.

II.i.105, 106. 'Perhaps the meaning may be this: "What a man cannot accomplish he may lawfully endeavor to obtain"; as, for instance, his wife's affections.' (M. Mason.)

II.i.117. *brace.* Properly armor for the arms. Here apparently extended to mean the whole suit.

II.i.127. *target.* Properly a light shield. Here the whole suit of armor.

II.ii.14, 15. *'Tis now your honour, daughter, to explain The labour of each knight in his device.* In the novel, the shields are presented to the princess by the knights' pages, and she passes them to her father, who explains the mottos to her.

II.ii.27. *Piu,* which is Italian, is an error for the Spanish word *Mas.*

II.ii.38. *touchstone.* A flint-like stone on which gold was rubbed and its purity ascertained by the color of the metal rubbed off.

II.ii.58. There is an obvious inversion here. Either we should punctuate, *The outward habit by, the inward man,* or transpose *outward* and *inward.*

II.iii.17. *And you're her labour'd scholar.* The word *scholar* suggests that the labor was his, yet the preceding lines imply that art makes the artist, so that *labour'd scholar* should mean 'carefully wrought creation.'

II.iii.23. *Sir, yonder is your place.* Cf. Gower, *Confessio Amantis,* VIII. 711-716:

*'At Soupertime natheles
The king amiddes al the pres
Let clepe [called] him up among hem alle,
And bad his Mareschall of halle
To setten him in such degre
That he upon him myhte se.'*

II.iii.31. *These cates resist me, she but thought upon.* Cf. Wilkins' novel: 'Both king and daughter at one instant were so strucke in love with the noblenesse of his woorth that they could not spare so much time to satisfie themselves with the delicacie of their viands for talking of his prayses.'

II.iii.67, 68. *And princes not doing so are like to gnats, Which make a sound, but kill'd are wonder'd at.* When the gnat is killed, one wonders that so small a creature could make so much sound. So it is a matter of wonder that an unworthy prince can make such a stir.

II.iii.87-91. The novel almost exactly reproduces this passage. 'Pericles . . . thus returneth what hee is, that hee was a gentleman of Tyre, his name Pericles, his education beene in Artes and Armes who looking for adventures in the world was by the rough and unconstant Seas most unfortunately bereft both of shippes and men, and after shipwrecke thrown upon that shoare.' This is the first we hear of his looking for adventure; when he left Tyre he was seeking only safety.

II.iii.112, 113. *Oh! that's as much as you would be denied Of your fair courtesy.* That is as much as to say that you desire not to receive the compliment you deserve.

II.iv.9, 10. *A fire from heaven came and shrivell'd up Their bodies.* Neither Antiochus the Great, nor any other Antiochus of whom history speaks, died in such a manner. Antiochus the Great made his son, Seleucus Philopator, joint king, in 188 B.C., and set out on an expedition to the east from which he never returned.

II.iv.32-34. *And be resolv'd he lives to govern us, Or dead, give's cause to mourn his funeral, And leave us to our free election.* This is the reading of the Quarto, and is perfectly intelligible without emendation, though the construction is somewhat loose. It means: And we shall be assured that he lives to govern us, or, if he be dead, do you give us opportunity to mourn his funeral and then allow us to elect his successor.

II.v.3, 4. *for this twelvemonth she'll not undertake A married life.* This little

fiction is described by Clarke as 'quite characteristic of the waggish tendency to stratagem shown by the royal old gentleman.'

II.v.10, 11. *Diana's livery . . . the eye of Cynthia.* Diana is the virgin goddess and also the goddess of the moon, here addressed as Cynthia.

II.v.28. Gower, after his description of the feast of III.iii., has Apollonius exhibit his skill in music (*Confessio Amantis*, VIII. 777-782):

> 'He takth the Harpe and in his wise [skill]
> He tempreth [tuneth] and of such assise
> Singende he harpeth forth withal,
> That as a vois celestial
> Hem thoghte it souneth in here ere,
> As thogh that he an Angel were.'

Variants are given in Wilkins' novel, and in Twine. Some such scene must have been in the playwright's mind, though the play gives no hint of it. Sykes argues from this that the play is founded on the novel (cf. Authorship of the Play, p. 1372), but it is quite as possible that the playwright was following Gower or Twine as that he was following the Wilkins novel. In any case he thought of the incident as part of the plot, and it may have been written into the play and later rejected.

II.v.97. 'I cannot dismiss the foregoing scene, till I have expressed the most supreme contempt of it. Such another gross, nonsensical dialogue would be sought for in vain among the earliest and rudest efforts of the British theatre. It is impossible not to wish that the *Knights* had horsewhipped *Simonides* and that *Pericles* had kicked him off the stage.' (Steevens.)

III. Gower 15-19. *By many a dern and painful perch, Of Pericles the careful search By the four opposing coigns, Which the world together joins, Is made with all due diligence.* The careful search for Pericles is made with all due diligence through the four corners of the world by many a wild and painful journey. A *perch* is literally a measure of land, five yards and a half in length.

III. Gower 55-57. *action may Conveniently the rest convey, Which might not what by me is told.* Action, which could not well convey what I have told, may conveniently convey the rest.

   III.i. The critics are generally agreed that Shakespeare's hand first appears in this scene, and that it is mostly, if not entirely, his. Cf. the storm in *King Lear* III.ii., and at the beginning of *The Tempest*. He may, however, have retouched passages previous to this.

III.i.1. *rebuke these surges.* Cf. Matt. 9. 26, 'Then he arose and rebuked the winds and the sea, and there was a great calm.'

III.i.27-29. *We here below, Recall not what we give, and therein may Vie honour with you.* We mortals do not take back what we give, and, in this respect, may contend for honor with the gods.

III.i.52. *Sir, your queen must overboard.* Many interesting instances of this common superstition have been discovered, the earliest, apparently, being a passage in Plutarch, who describes how Cato's ship was storm-tossed on his return from Thrace because he refused the pleas of his friends to put the ashes of his brother in another vessel.

III.ii. *Ephesus.* A town in Lydia on the east coast of the Mediterranean. The fact that it is some six hundred miles from Tyre, and three hundred to the north, is sufficient evidence of the violence of the storm. It was a part of the empire of Antiochus.

III.ii.40. *my aid.* A reference to the pupil, Machaon, whom Twine makes responsible for Thaisa's recovery.

III.ii.110. *sets.* Shakespeare frequently employs the old northern English plural ending in -s.

III.ii.117. *twice rich.* 'Because it is blessed with the sight not only of the cases with golden fringes, but of the jewels that they contain.' (Sykes.) Cf. *Arcadia*, Book III, 'Her fair lids then hiding her fairer eyes, seemed unto him sweet boxes of mother of pearl, rich in themselves but containing in them far richer jewels.'

III.ii.120, 121. *O dear Diana! Where am I? Where's my lord? What world is this?* The recovery of Thaisa is closely copied from Gower, *Confessio Amantis*, VIII. 1192-1207:

> 'Thei leide hire on a couche softe,
> And with a scheete warmed ofte
> Hire colde brest began to hete,
> Hire herte also to flacke and bete.
> This Maister hath hire every joignt
> With certein oile and balsme enoignt,
> And putte a liquour in hire mouth
> Which is to fewe clerkes couth, [known]
> So that sche coevereth ate laste:
> And ferst hire yhen up sche caste,

> And whan sche more of strengthe cawhte,
> Hire armes bothe forth sche strawhte,
> Hield up hire hond and pitously
> Sche spak and seide, "Ha, wher am I?
> Where is my lord, what world is this?"'

III.iii.6-9. The reading of the First Quarto is: *Your shakes of fortune, though they hant you mortally Yet glance full wonderingly on us.* The Second changes *hant* to *haunt*. This must mean: Your changes of fortune, following you with a fatal persistence, affect us remarkably, also. But this use of *wonderingly* is strange, and it seems better to follow Steevens in reading *wanderingly* in the sense of wandering from the mark. Steevens would also read *shafts* for *shakes*, and *hurt* for *hant*, making a consistent figure.

III.iv.9. We must suppose that the good queen's memory, which had been so shaken that she could not recall the birth of her daughter, had also lost the recollection of her husband's rank and destination. Otherwise, it is hard to see why she did not follow him to Tyre.

III.iv.10. *vestal livery.* Properly the garb of the virgins who served in the temple of Vesta, goddess of the hearth. Here merely the garb of a priestess of the virgin goddess, Diana.

   IV. Gower 32. *the dove of Paphos.* Paphos, a town in Cyprus, was a seat of the worship of Venus, who was said to have risen from the waves there. Doves were sacred to her as the goddess of beauty.

IV. Gower 34, 35. *All praises which are paid as debts And not as given.* All praise her as though they owe the praise, not as though they were bestowing it.

IV. Gower 47-50. *Only I carried winged time Post on the lame feet of my rime Which never could I so convey Unless your thoughts went on my way.* I only conveyed briefly in my verse the idea of the time elapsed, which you would not have understood without my guidance.

IV.i.105. *Valdes.* Malone remarked that the name may probably have been taken from Don Pedro de Valdes, who was an admiral in the Spanish Armada, and, being captured by Drake in 1588, was imprisoned at Dartmouth.

IV.ii. *Mitylene.* The chief town of Lesbos, in the Ægean Sea. It revolted from Antiochus and joined the Romans, who had just begun to concern themselves with Asiatic politics.

IV.ii.30. *hatched.* Closed with a hatch or half door with an open space above, taken as a characteristic of brothels by former editors. But, surely, the context demands a reputable dwelling house.

IV.ii. S. d. *Enter Boult, with the Pirates and Marina.* Seneca Rhetor (*Floruit* 15 A.D.) in one of his illustrative law cases (*Controversiæ* I. 2) gives proof either that this part of the story has an ancient source, or that the situation was not unique, by introducing a virgin, captured by pirates and sold to a procurer.

IV.iii. It is interesting to note the difference between this version and that of Twine in the *Patterne of Painefull Adventures*, Chapter XII. 'But Stranguilio himselfe consented not to this treason, but so soone as hee heard of the foule mischaunce, beeing as it were a mopte [bewildered], and mated with heauinesse and griefe, he clad himselfe in mourning aray, and lamented that wofull case, saying, Alas, in what a mischiefe am I wrapped? what might I doe, or say herein?—Then casting his eies vp towards heauen, O God said hee, thou knowest that I am innocent from the bloud of silly [innocent] Tharsia, which thou hast to require at Dionisiades handes: and therewithall he looked towards his wife, saying: Thou wicked woman, tell me, how hast thou made away prince Apollonius daughter? thou that liuest both to the slaunder of God, and man? Dionisiades answered in manie wordes euermore excusing herselfe, and, moderating the wrath of Stranguilio, shee counterfeited a fained sorrowe by attiring her selfe and her daughter in mourning apparell.' It will be seen that Cleon and Dionyza differ from Stranguilio and Dionysiades in proportion as they resemble Macbeth and Lady Macbeth. There is something of Lady Macbeth in Dionyza in the scene with Leonine, too. We have excellent evidence, then, for concluding that this is a scene which Shakespeare rewrote from a less elaborate and less dramatic original.

IV.iii.53. *harpy.* A mythical, malignant fowl with a human face. Dionyza's face deceives the victims whom she destroys with her talons.

IV.iii.56, 57. *You are like one that superstitiously Do swear to the gods that winter kills the flies.* In fear of the gods you swear that the killing was not of your doing and was beyond your control.

   V.i. In performance of 1854 in which Phelps took the part of Pericles, this recognition scene is the only one which called forth the enthusiasm of John Oxenham, who wrote, in the *Times*, 'This scene was the only opportunity for acting throughout the piece, and Mr. Phelps availed himself of it most felicitously.'

V.i.39, 40. *Till the disaster that, one mortal night, Drove him to this.* Surely, this is meant to refer to the night when his wife died and his daughter was born.

But it was not that night, but the discovery of his daughter's supposed death that 'drove him to this.' The Quartos read *wight* for *night*.

V.i.49, 50. *And make a battery through his deafen'd parts Which now are midway stopp'd.* And force an entrance to his mind through his ears which are now shut.

V.i. S. d. *The Song.* Gower merely records the fact that she sang 'lich an angele,' but Twine gives the following song:

'*Among the harlots foule I walke,*
    yet harlot none am I:
The Rose amongst the Thorns grows,
    and is not hurt thereby.
The thiefe that stole me, sure I thinke,
    is slaine before this time,
A bawd me bought, yet am I not
    defilde by fleshly crime.
Were nothing pleasanter to me,
    than parents mine to know:
I am the issue of a king,
    my bloud from kings doth flow.
I hope that God will mend my state,
    and send a better day.
Leaue off your teares, plucke vp your heart,
    and banish care away.
Shew gladnesse in your countenance,
    cast vp your cheerfull eyes:
That God remaines that once of nought
    created earth and skies.
He will not let in care and thought
    you still to liue, and all for nought.'

It is impossible to tell how much like this was the song in the play, but it is attractive to think of an incidental lyric by Shakespeare, like Ariel's songs in *The Tempest*, on the theme 'The rose amongst the thorns grows and is not hurt thereby.' Druing the song, the others withdraw a little.

V.i.151, 152. *If thine consider'd prove the thousandth part Of my endurance.* If what thou hast endured prove, on consideration, the thousandth part of what I have.

V.i.242. *th' art my child.* The rediscovery of lost children is a very common feature of the romantic dramas of the Greek New Comedy.

V.i.267-269. Malone suggests that these lines should be given to Marina, and that *companion friend* should be read, referring to the *companion maid* of line 85. But it is possible that the whole speech belongs to Helicanus.

V.i.S. d. *Diana.* This appearance of a god in a dream is characteristic, not of ancient drama, but of ancient romance. In Heliodorus, *Æthiopica,* III. ii., Apollo and Diana appear to the hero, Calasiris, in a vision and tell him to return to his own country. In Longus, *Daphnis and Chloe,* IV. 34, Dionysophanes dreams that the Nymphs tell him to exhibit the tokens of Chloe before the people of Mitylene, which leads to the discovery of her identity.

V.i.292. *I have another suit.* As Pericles surmises, he is about to ask for Marina's hand. In Twine's version, as soon as the governor finds that she is of royal parentage, 'using the benefite of the time,' he kneels to Apollonius without more ado, and rises his prospective son-in-law. In Gower, the idea does not seem to have occurred to him until the celebrations attending Apollonius' entry into Mitylene.

V.iii. S. d. *The Temple of Diana at Ephesus.* The first shrine on this location goes back to the eighth centure B.C. and stood until the third century A.D. For its importance, cf. Acts 19. 27. It would make a fine scene for the climax of a pagan romance.

V.iii.15. *You are, you are—O royal Pericles!* Compare the very similar ending of *The Comedy of Errors,* where the Abbess rediscovers the husband from whom she has been parted at sea.

THE TEXT OF THE PRESENT EDITION

The text of the present volume is, by permission of the Oxford University Press, that of the Oxford Shakespeare, edited by the late W. J. Craig, except for the following deviations:

1. The stage directions are those of the First Quarto of 1609, necessary additional words being inserted in square brackets.

2. The punctuation has been altered in many places, and the following changes in spelling have been made: Troyan (Trojan), iwis (I wis), spoken (speken), wanion (wannion), porpoise (porpus), joust (just), curst (crus'd), Oh (O), murtherer (murderer), anything (any thing), forever (for ever), anyone (any one), wandlike-straight (wand-like straight), godlike (god-like), seafarer (sea-farer).

3. The following alterations of the text have been made after collation with the First Quarto, readings of the present edition preceding and those of Craig following the colon. Unless otherwise specified, the readings of this text are those of the First Quarto. F stands for the Third Folio.

I.i.17	rac'd (Q racte): raz'd
I.i.20	have: hath
I.i.38	Here they: They here
I.i.83	man: men
I.i.115	off (F): of
I.ii.106	grieve for them: grieve them
II. Gower 36	escapen'd: escapen
II.i.6	my: me
II.i.73	pray you: pray
II.i.74	forbid 't: forbid
II.i.74	And I: I
II.i.77	all day: holidays
II.i.119	it (Malone): 't
II.i.122	have given: they have given
II.i.124	father gave in his: father's gift in 's
II.i.132	fortune's: fortunes
II.i.139	waters: water
II.i.141	them: it
II.i.142	believe 't: believe it
II.i.144	rupture: rapture
II.i.145	building: biding
II.ii.10	It's: 'Tis
II.ii.34	Qui: Quod
II.ii.37	an: a
II.ii.48	fortunes: fortune
II.iii.12	my: by
II.iii.27	shall: do
II.iii.107	Here's: Here is
II.iii.108	have heard: have often heard
II.iv.14	justice: just
II.iv.26	your: the
II.iv.34	leave: leaves
II.iv.39	know: know'st
II.iv.42	Try: For
II.v.19	nay, how: how
II.v.38	Sir, my daughter: My daughter, sir
II.v.86	I'll: I will
II.v.93	my: or
II.v.97	And then: Then
III. Gower 8	Are: E'er
III. Gower 60	seas-toss'd: sea-tost
III.i.1	The: Then
III.i.28	Vie (Steevens): Use
III.i.50	and: an
III.ii.12	Good morrow: Good morrow, sir
III.ii.41	dwells: dwell
III.ii.53	never: ne'er decay
III.ii.55	What's: What is
III.ii.57	toss up: toss
III.ii.66	bottomed: bitumed
III.ii.70	Wrench: Come, wrench
III.ii.78	in: i'
III.ii.80	drives: drive
III.ii.92	a fire: fire
III.ii.93	my: the
III.ii.96	o'erpress'd: overpress'd
III.ii.98	appliance: appliances
III.ii.110	sets: set
III.ii.117	Doth: Do
III.ii.124	my gentle: gentle
III.iii.6	shakes: shafts, haunt (2d Q): hurt
III.iii.17	leaving: and leave
IV. Gower 23	needle: neeld
IV. Gower 47	carried: carry
IV.i.18	doth: do

IV.i.20   is a: is like a
IV.ii.42 farther: further
IV.ii.94 Ay, he; he: Ay; he
IV.iii.57 Do: Doth
IV.iv.G. 1 long: longest
IV.iv.25 deeds: deed
V.i.9   there is: there's
V.i.10   I pray: I pray ye, him: them
V.i.15   you: you, sir
V.i.49   parts: ports
V.i.64   inflict: afflict
V.i.69   here's: here is
V.i.71   present: presence
V.i.112   You're: You are
V.i.130   If I should: Should I
V.i.133   lookest: look'st
V.i.135   I will believe: I believe

V.i.189   daughter: daughter's
V.i.192   You: You'll, scorn: scorn to
V.i.203   imposture: imposter
V.i.213   Here's: Here is
V.i.236   The: Thou 'rt, like: life
V.i.242   th 'art: thou art
V.i.255   dote: doubt
V.i.263   Music, my lord? I hear: My lord I hear
                                    Music

V.i.277   Or perform: Perform
V.ii.21   overboard: o'erboard
V.ii.24   overjoy'd: o'erjoyed
V.ii.37   spake: speak
V.ii.48   sports: sport
V.ii.82   and: I
V.ii.113 punish: punish them
V.ii.115 has: hath

The Tragedy of Cymbeline

Edited by
SAMUEL B. HEMINGWAY

Dramatis Personae

CYMBELINE, *King of Britain*

CLOTEN, *Son to the Queen by a former Husband*

POSTHUMUS LEONATUS, *a Gentleman, Husband to Imogen*

BELARIUS, *a banished Lord, disguised under the name of Morgan*

GUIDERIUS
ARVIRAGUS
} *Sons to Cymbeline, disguised under the names of Polydore and Cadwal, supposed Sons to Morgan*

PHILARIO, *Friend to Posthumus*
IACHIMO, *Friend to Philario*
} *Italians*

A FRENCH GENTLEMAN, *Friend to Philario*

CAIUS LUCIUS, *General of the Roman Forces*

A ROMAN CAPTAIN

TWO BRITISH CAPTAINS

PISANIO, *Servant to Posthumus*

CORNELIUS, *a Physician*

TWO LORDS OF CYMBELINE'S COURT

TWO GENTLEMEN OF THE SAME

TWO GAOLERS

QUEEN, *Wife to Cymbeline*

IMOGEN, *Daughter to Cymbeline by a former Queen*

HELEN, *a Lady attending on Imogen*

LORDS, LADIES, ROMAN SENATORS, TRIBUNES, a DUTCH GENTLEMAN, a SPANISH GENTLEMAN, a SOOTHSAYER, MUSICIANS, OFFICERS, CAPTAINS, SOLDIERS, MESSENGERS, and other ATTENDANTS

APPARITIONS

SCENE—*Sometimes in Britain, sometimes in Rome.*

The Tragedy of Cymbeline

INTRODUCTION

SOURCES OF THE PLAY

The name Cymbeline, and the political setting of the play, Shakespeare took from Holinshed's *Chronicles of England*. The wager-story, which forms the basis of the Imogen plot, is a familiar one in mediæval literature; Shakespeare seems to have been chiefly indebted for this story to the ninth novel of the second day in Boccaccio's *Decameron*. It is hardly likely that he was familiar with an English version of this story, published possibly in 1603 but probably not before 1620, called *Westward for Smelts*. Other versions of the story which Shakespeare may, or may not, have known in some sixteenth century English form, are the thirteenth century French romances, *King Florus and Fair Jehane*,[1] *Roman de la Violette*, and *Roman del conte de Poitiers*, a fourteenth century French mystery play; as well as scattered German, Scandinavian, and Gaelic versions. An English play printed in 1589, called *The Rare Triumphs of Love and Fortune*, may have suggested some names, characters, and incident for *Cymbeline, The Winter's Tale,* and *The Tempest*. Beaumont and Fletcher's *Philaster* resembles *Cymbeline* in many details; the two plays were written at about the same time, and it is impossible to state definitely which influenced the other. Both plays indicate that a new type of drama was becoming fashionable toward the end of the first decade of the seventeenth century; it is quite conceivable that they were written contemporaneously and in friendly rivalry. The story of Belarius and the kidnapped princes, as well as the final solution of the complicated plot, seems to have been Shakespeare's own invention.[2]

Cimbeline, or Kymbeline, was, according to Holinshed, a descendant of King Lear, and reigned in Britain from 33 B.C. to 2 A.D. He had been educated in Rome and 'knighted' by Cæsar Augustus. His sons were Guiderius and Arviragus. 'Our histories do affirme' that Cymbeline, and his father Tanantius (cf. *Cymbeline* I.i.36) before him, lived at peace with the Romans, 'and continuallie to them paied the tributes which the Britaines had couenanted with Julius Cæsar to paie, yet we find in the Romane writers that after Julius Cæsar's death ... the Britaines refused to paie that tribute: whereat Augustus, being otherwise occupied, was content to winke; howbeit ... at length ... Augustus made prouision to passe with an armie ouer into Britaine, & was come forward vpon his iournie into Gallia Celtica.... But here receiuing aduertisements that the Pannonians ... and the Dalmations ... had rebelled (cf. *Cymbeline* III.i.75–77), he thought it best first to subdue those rebells neere home.' Holinshed is at a loss to know whether to believe 'our histories' or 'the Romane writers,' but he records presently the arrival of an ambassador from Augustus at the court of Cymbeline, who came to bring to the British king the thanks of the emperor 'for that he had kept his allegiance toward the Romane empire.' Later, Guiderius, after his accession, refused to pay a yearly tribute of three thousand crowns. Shakespeare, by attributing this refusal to Cymbeline, hoped to heighten the dramatic and emotional appeal of this singularly mild and uneventful portion of Holinshed's *Chronicle*.

Posthumus's account of the means whereby the British gained the victory (V.iii.5–62) is taken from Holinshed's *Chronicles of Scotland*, which describe the sudden defeat of the Danes by the Scots, in the year 976, through the intervention of a husbandman named Hay, and his two sons.

The plot of Boccaccio's novel may be summarized as follows: Bernabo Lomellino of Genoa, stopping at an inn in Paris, boasts of his wife's virtue and devotion. Ambrogiuolo of Piacenza sneers at woman's virtue, and proves by philosophical argument that all women must be unchaste. Man is not chaste; woman is more frail than man; ergo! Entreaty, flattery, and gifts will win any woman. Bernabo repudiates philosophical argument and reaffirms his faith in his wife, Ginevra. The discussion waxes hot. Bernabo, in his anger, wagers his head against a thousand florins that Ambrogiuolo could not tempt Ginevra to sin. Ambrogiuolo accepts the wager, substituting a sum of money for Bernabo's head, and starts for Genoa. Within three months he must return with indisputable proofs of his triumph over Ginevra's virtue. Just as he is despairing of success he meets a poor woman, to whom Ginevra has been kind, and bribes her to send him into Ginevra's chamber, in her chest, on the pretence that she is about to take a journey and wishes to leave her belongings in Ginevra's care. Night comes; he emerges from the chest, notes the situation of the room, its ornaments and pictures, and approaching the bed he admires the lady's beauty and perceives the mole on her left breast. For further evidence he removes a gown, a ring, and a girdle. Bernabo is not moved by the description of the room, nor by the articles of apparel, but is 'struck to the very heart' when Ambrogiuolo reveals his knowledge of the mole. He sets out for home 'most cruelly incensed against his wife,' and sends ahead a servant with a letter asking Ginevra to meet him on the way. The servant is instructed to murder her when he reaches 'a fit place.' Ginevra persuades the servant to let her escape, disguised as a page, and to carry word to his lord that she is dead. As page to a Catalonian lord she sails for foreign lands, and on her journeys encounters Ambrogiuolo and hears him tell, as a jest, the story of his wager. She arranges to have her husband brought over seas to listen as Ambrogiuolo tells this tale to the Sultan. The truth is then revealed, and after the Sultan has condemn Ambrogiuolo to be smeared with honey and eaten by wasps,[3] they all sit down to a sumptuous banquet. It is only in the early part of the tale, the long-drawn-out angry debate which provides some possible motivation for the story, that Boccaccio's plot surpasses Shakespeare's.

---

1 English translation in *Aucassin and Nicolette and Other Mediæval Romances*, Everyman's Library Edition, E. P. Dutton.

2 For more detailed discussion of these points see Thorndike: *Influence of Beaumont and Fletcher on Shakespeare*, Worcester, Massachusetts, 1901, and Dowden: *Cymbeline*, in *The Arden Shakespeare*, third edition, London, 1918.

3 This episode of the honey and the wasps, not used by Shakespeare in *Cymbeline*, is probably the source of the passage in *The Winter's Tale* (IV. iv. 846 ff.) in which Autolycus threatens the Clown with a similar fate.

HISTORY OF THE PLAY

Cymbeline was first printed in 1623, at the end of the First Folio, among the tragedies, and under the title, *The Tragedie of Cymbeline*. The text was taken from a prompt-book copy, and was divided into acts and scenes; but it was so carelessly printed that it is full of obscure and perplexing readings. In this play Shakespeare seems to have had the assistance of a coadjutor, who was responsible for the Vision of Posthumus in Act V, which is not an integral part of the action, and perhaps for portions of the Belarios plot.

The play was probably first produced in 1610; in style, diction, and versification it resembles the two romantic comedies, *The Winter's Tale* and *The Tempest*, which appeared in 1610 and 1611, respectively. Dr. Simon Forman, astrologer, quack, and theatre-goer, who in his *Book of Plays* kept a record of the plays he attended, gives a synopsis of the plot of '*Cimbalin*' in an undated entry which follows an entry dated May 15, 1611, recording a performance of '*The Winter's Talle* at the glob.' On January 1, 1633/4, '*Cymbeline* was acted at court by the King's players. Well likte by the Kinge.'[4]

Irreverent hands were laid upon *Cymbeline* in 1682 by Tom Durfey, who attempted to fashion it to the taste of his generation under the title, *The Injured Princess or The Fatal Wager*. The names of the characters are changed—Imogen becomes Eugenia, Posthumus is Ursaces, and Iachimo is Shatillion; new characters are introduced, among them Clarina, who is Eugenia's confidante and daughter of Pisanio, and a drunken friend of Cloten's named Iachimo. Pisanio believes in Imogen's guilt; the lascivious Cloten and his ribald friend kidnap Clarina with evil intent; there is little left of Shakespeare's play but the outline of the plot. This perversion of *Cymbeline* held the stage until 1720, when Shakespeare's play was produced at the new Lincoln's Inn Fields Theatre.

But in 1755 another attempt was made, by Charles Marsh, to refashion the 'old and crude' play; and in 1759 still another.

This time the culprit was the Professor of Poetry at Oxford, William Hawkins, M.A., who possessed 'so thorough a veneration for the great Father of the English stage' that he 'retained, in many places, the very language of the original author.' Fortunately 'unprecedented difficulties and discouragements in the theatre' prevented a long run at Covent Garden Theatre. Two years later, in 1761, Garrick made the first of his many appearances as Posthumus in Shakespeare's play. The play ran for sixteen nights, and the *Dramatic Censor* stated that Garrick's astonishing talents were never more happily exerted. In 1767 and 1770 Mrs. Barry played Imogen to Garrick's Posthumus. John Philip Kemble first played Posthumus in 1785; Mrs. Siddons first appeared as Imogen in 1787; and Charles Kemble, who had appeared as Polydore in 1812 played Posthumus in 1825. Macready played Posthumus in 1818. From the time of Garrick on, *Cymbeline* seems to have been a favorite play for one-night, benefit performances. Helen Faucit was one of the great Imogens of the middle of the nineteenth century, and Ellen Terry's 'last great part on the Lyceum stage' was the rôle of Imogen in Henry Irving's gorgeous production in 1896. Irving chose to play the part of Iachimo, and seems to have made an indifferent success in the rôle. Popular enthusiasm was devoted to Miss Terry's Imogen and to the setting by Alma Tadema.

While Garrick and the Kembles were using *Cymbeline* almost yearly in England, the new and struggling theatres in the American colonies and states followed their illustrious example. From 1767 to 1793 eight revivals of *Cymbeline* occurred along our Atlantic seaboard, three in New York, two in Philadelphia, one in Boston, one in Annapolis, and one in Charleston, South Carolina. One hundred years later *Cymbeline* again became popular on the American stage. Mary Shaw Hamblin, who died in 1873, was a famous Imogen in the 1860s. Adelaide Neilson in the 1870s, Modjeska in the 1880s, and Margaret Mather in the 1890s kept the play familiar to American audiences. In 1906 Viola Allen again revived it, and in 1923 Edward H. Sothern and Julia Marlowe added it to their repertoire.[5]

---

4 *Dramatic Records of Sir Henry Herbert, Master of the Revels 1623-1673*, edited by J. Q. Adams, Yale University Press, 1917.

5 For details concerning the various stage adaptations of the play see Fr. Lücke, *Über Bearbeitungen von Shakespeares 'Cymbeline'* (Rostock diss., 1909).

ACT FIRST ❧ SCENE FIRST

[Britain. The Garden of Cymbeline's Palace]
Enter two Gentlemen.

1. Gent. You do not meet a man but frowns: our bloods
No more obey the heavens than our courtiers
Still seem as does the king.
    2. Gent.   But what's the matter?
    1. Gent. His daughter, and the heir of 's kingdom, whom   *5*
He purpos'd to his wife's sole son,—a widow
That late he married,—hath referr'd herself
Unto a poor but worthy gentleman. She's wedded;
Her husband banish'd; she imprison'd: all
Is outward sorrow, though I think the king   *10*
Be touch'd at very heart.
    2. Gent.   None but the king?
    1. Gent. He that hath lost her too; so is the queen,
That most desir'd the match; but not a courtier,
Although they wear their faces to the bent   *15*
Of the king's looks, hath a heart that is not
Glad at the thing they scowl at.
    2. Gent.   And why so?
    1. Gent. He that hath miss'd the princess is a thing
Too bad for bad report; and he that hath her,—   *20*
I mean that married her, alack, good man!
And therefore banish'd—is a creature such
As, to seek through the regions of the earth
For one his like, there would be something failing
In him that should compare. I do not think   *25*
So fair an outward and such stuff within
Endows a man but he.
    2. Gent.   You speak him far.
    1. Gent. I do extend him, sir, within himself,
Crush him together rather than unfold   *30*
His measure duly.
    2. Gent.   What's his name and birth?
    1. Gent. I cannot delve him to the root: his father
Was called Sicilius, who did join his honour
Against the Romans with Cassibelan,   *35*
But had his titles by Tenantius whom
He serv'd with glory and admir'd success,
So gain'd the sur-addition Leonatus;
And had, besides the gentleman in question,
Two other sons, who in the wars o' the time   *40*
Died with their swords in hand; for which their father—
Then old and fond of issue—took such sorrow
That he quit being, and his gentle lady,
Big of this gentleman, our theme, deceas'd
As he was born. The king, he takes the babe   *45*
To his protection; calls him Posthumus Leonatus;
Breeds him and makes him of his bedchamber;
Puts to him all the learnings that his time
Could make him the receiver of; which he took,
As we do air, fast as 'twas minister'd,   *50*
And in 's spring became a harvest; liv'd in court,—

Which rare it is to do,—most prais'd, most lov'd;
A sample to the youngest, to the more mature
A glass that feated them, and to the graver
A child that guided dotards; to his mistress,   *55*
For whom he now is banish'd, her own price
Proclaims how she esteem'd him and his virtue;
By her election may be truly read
What kind of man he is.
    2. Gent.   I honour him,   *60*
Even out of your report. But pray you, tell me,
Is she sole child to the king?
    1. Gent.   His only child.
He had two sons,—if this be worth your hearing,
Mark it,—the eldest of them at three years old,   *65*
I' the swathing clothes the other, from their nursery
Were stol'n; and to this hour no guess in knowledge
Which way they went.
    2. Gent.   How long is this ago?
    1. Gent. Some twenty years.   *70*
    2. Gent. That a king's children should be so convey'd,
So slackly guarded, and the search so slow,
That could not trace them!
    1. Gent.   Howsoe'er 'tis strange,
Or that the negligence may well be laugh'd at,   *75*
Yet is it true, sir.
    2. Gent.   I do well believe you.
    1. Gent. We must forbear. Here comes the gentleman,
The queen, and princess.   *Exeunt.*

Enter the Queen, Posthumus, and Imogen.

    Queen. No, be assur'd you shall not find me, daughter,   *80*
After the slander of most step-mothers,
Evil-ey'd unto you; you're my prisoner, but
Your gaoler shall deliver you the keys
That lock up your restraint. For you, Posthumus,
So soon as I can win the offended king,   *85*
I will be known your advocate; marry, yet
The fire of rage is in him, and 'twere good
You lean'd unto his sentence with what patience
Your wisdom may inform you.
    Post.   Please your highness,   *90*
I will from hence to-day.
    Queen.   You know the peril:
I'll fetch a turn about the garden, pitying
The pangs of barr'd affections, though the king
Hath charg'd you should not speak together.   *Exit.*
    Imo.   O
Dissembling courtesy. How fine this tyrant
Can tickle where she wounds! My dearst husband,
I something fear my father's wrath; but nothing,—
Always reserv'd my holy duty,—what   *100*
His rage can do on me. You must be gone;
And I shall here abide the hourly shot
Of angry eyes, not comforted to live,
But that there is this jewel in the world

1–3 **our bloods … king;** *cf. n.*   3 **Still:** *continually*   6 **purpos'd:** *intended to give in marriage*   7 **referr'd:** *committed*   15 **to the bent:** *according to the inclination*   25 **him … compare:** *him chosen for comparison*   28 **speak him far:** *go far in sounding his praise*   29 **extend him within himself;** *cf. n.*   34 **join his honour:** *honorably join*   35, 36 *Cf. n.*   38 **sur-addition:** *surname*   48 **time:** *years*

54 **feated:** *formed*   56 **her own price:** *what she is willing to pay in suffering*   58 **election:** *choice*   66 **swathing:** *swaddling*   67 **guess in knowledge:** *intelligent guess*   71 **convey'd:** *stolen*   78 **forbear:** *withdraw* **S.d.** *cf. n.*   81 **After the slander:** *in accord with the ill repute*   88 **lean'd:** *should submit*   89 **inform:** *teach*   93 **fetch a turn:** *take a walk*   97 **fine:** *delicately*   99 **something:** *somewhat* **nothing:** *in no way*   100 **Always … duty;** *cf. n.*

That I may see again.   *105*

    Post.   My queen! my mistress!
O lady, weep no more, lest I give cause
To be suspected of more tenderness
Than doth become a man. I will remain
The loyal'st husband that did e'er plight troth.   *110*
My residence in Rome at one Philario's,
Who to my father was a friend, to me
Known but by letter; thither write, my queen,
And with mine eyes I'll drink the words you send,
Though ink be made of gall.   *115*

    Enter Queen.

    Queen.   Be brief, I pray you;
If the king come, I shall incur I know not
How much of his displeasure. *[Aside.]* Yet I'll move him
To walk this way. I never do him wrong
But he does buy my injuries, to be friends   *120*
Pays dear for my offences.   *[Exit.]*

    Post.   Should we be taking leave
As long a term as yet we have to live,
The loathness to depart would grow. Adieu!

    Imo. Nay, stay a little: *125*
Were you but riding forth to air yourself
Such parting were too petty. Look here, love;
This diamond was my mother's; take it, heart;
But keep it till you woo another wife,
When Imogen is dead.   *130*

    Post.   How! how! another?
You gentle gods, give me but this I have,
And cere up my embracements from a next
With bands of death!—Remain, remain thou here
                    [Putting on the ring.]
While sense can keep it on! And, sweetest, fairest,   *135*
As I my poor self did exchange for you,
To your so infinite loss, so in our trifles
I still win of you; for my sake wear this;
It is a manacle of love; I'll place it
Upon this fairest prisoner.   *140*
            [Putting a bracelet on her arm.]

    Imo.   O the gods!
When shall we see again?

    Enter Cymbeline and Lords.

    Post.   Alack! the king!

    Cym. Thou basest thing, avoid! hence, from my sight!
If after this command thou fraught the court   *145*
With thy unworthiness, thou diest. Away!
Thou 'rt poison to my blood.

    Post. [To Imogen]   The gods protect you
And bless the good remainders of the court!
I am gone.   *Exit.*   *150*

    Imo.   There cannot be a pinch in death
More sharp than this is.

    Cym.   O disloyal thing,
That shouldst repair my youth, thou heap'st

A year's age on me.   *155*

    Imo.   I beseech you, sir,
Harm not yourself with your vexation;
I am senseless of your wrath; a touch more rare
Subdues all pangs, all fears.

    Cym.   Past grace? obedience?   *160*

    Imo. Past hope, and in despair; that way, past grace.

    Cym. That mightst have had the sole son of my queen!

    Imo. O bless'd, that I might not! I chose an eagle
And did avoid a puttock.

    Cym. Thou took'st a beggar; wouldst have made my throne
A seat for baseness.

    Imo.   No; I rather added
A lustre to it.

    Cym.   O thou vile one!

    Imo.   Sir,   *170*
It is your fault that I have lov'd Posthumus:
You bred him as my playfellow, and he is
A man worth any woman, overbuys me
Almost the sum he pays.

    Cym.   What! art thou mad?   *175*

    Imo. Almost, sir; heaven restore me! Would I were
A neat-herd's daughter, and my Leonatus
Our neighbour shepherd's son!

    Cym.   Thou foolish thing!

    Enter Queen.

They were again together: you have done   *180*
Not after our command. Away with her,
And pen her up.

    Queen.   Beseech your patience. Peace!
Dear lady daughter, peace! Sweet sovereign,
Leave us to ourselves, and make yourself some comfort   *185*
Out of your best advice.

    Cym.   Nay, let her languish,
A drop of blood a day; and, being aged,
Die of this folly!   *Exit [Cymbeline with Lords].*

    Queen.   Fie! you must give way.   *190*

    Enter Pisanio.

Here is your servant. How now, sir! What news?

    Pis. My lord your son drew on my master.

    Queen.   Ha!
No harm, I trust, is done?

    Pis.   There might have been,   *195*
But that my master rather play'd than fought,
And had no help of anger; they were parted
By gentlemen at hand.

    Queen.   I am very glad on 't.

    Imo. Your son's my father's friend; he takes his part.   *200*
To draw upon an exile! O brave sir!
I would they were in Afric both together,
Myself by with a needle, that I might prick
The goer-back. Why came you from your master?

    Pis. On his command: he would not suffer me   *205*
To bring him to the haven; left these notes
Of what commands I should be subject to,
When 't pleas'd you to employ me.

    Queen.   This hath been

---

108 tenderness: *sensitiveness*   **115** Though ... gall; *cf. n.*   **119–121** I never ... offences; *cf. n.*   **127** term: *period of time*   **124** loathness: *reluctance*   **133, 134** cere up ... death; *cf. n.*   **142** see: *meet*   **144** avoid: *depart*   **145** fraught: *burden (as of a ship)*   **149** remainders: *those who remain*

158 a touch more rare: *a more precious emotion*   **164** puttock: *kite*   **173, 174** overbuys me ... pays; *cf. n.*   **177** neat-herd's: *cowherd's*   **186** advice: *consideration*   **206** bring: *escort*

Your faithful servant; I dare lay mine honour   *210*
He will remain so.
    Pis.   I humbly thank your highness.
    Queen. Pray, walk awhile.
    Imo. [*To Pisanio.*] About some half-hour hence,
I pray you, speak with me. You shall at least   *215*
Go see my lord aboard; for this time leave me.   *Exeunt.*

❧ Scene Second ❧

[The Same]
Enter Cloten and two Lords.

    1. Lord. Sir, I would advise you to shift a shirt; the violence of
action hath made you reek as a sacrifice. Where air comes out, air
comes in; there's none abroad so wholesome as that you vent.
    Clo. If my shirt were bloody, then to shift it.
Have I hurt him?   *5*
    2. Lord. [*Aside.*] No faith; not so much as his patience.
    1. Lord. Hurt him! his body's a passable carcass if he be
not hurt; it is a throughfare for steel if it be not hurt.
    2. Lord. [*Aside.*] His steel was in debt; it went o' the
backside the town.   *10*
    Clo. The villain would not stand me.
    2. Lord. [*Aside.*] No; but he fled forward still, toward your face.
    1. Lord. Stand you! You have land enough of your own;
but he added to your having, gave you some ground.
    2. Lord. [*Aside.*] As many inches as you have oceans. Puppies!
    Clo. I would they had not come between us.
    2. Lord. [*Aside.*] So would I; till you had measured how
long a fool you were upon the ground.
    Clo. And that she should love this fellow and refuse me!
    2. Lord. [*Aside.*] If it be a sin to make a true election,   *20*
she is damned.
    1. Lord. Sir, as I told you always, her beauty and her
brain go not together: she's a good sign, but I have seen small
reflection of her wit.
    2. Lord. [*Aside.*] She shines not upon fools, lest the   *25*
reflection should hurt her.
    Clo. Come, I'll to my chamber. Would there had been
some hurt done!
    2. Lord. [*Aside.*] I wish not so; unless it had been the
fall of an ass, which is no great hurt.   *30*
    Clo. You'll go with us?
    1. Lord. I'll attend your lordship.
    Clo. Nay, come, let's go togeher.
    2. Lord. Well, my lord.   *Exeunt.*

❧ Scene Third ❧

[The same]
Enter Imogen and Pisanio.

    Imo. I would thou grew'st unto the shores of the haven,
And question'dst every sail: if he should write,
And I not have it, 'twere a paper lost,
As offer'd mercy is. What was the last

That he spake to thee?   *5*
    Pis.   It was his queen, his queen!
    Imo. Then wav'd his handkerchief?
    Pis.   And kiss'd it, madam.
    Imo. Senseless linen, happier therein than I!
And that was all?   *10*
    Pis.   No, madam; for so long
As he could make me with this eye or ear
Distinguish him from others, he did keep
The deck, with glove, or hat, or handkerchief,
Still waving, as the fits and stirs of 's mind   *15*
Could best express how slow his soul sail'd on,
How swift his ship.
    Imo.   Thou shouldst have made him
As little as a crow, or less, ere left
To after-eye him.   *20*
    Pis.   Madam, so I did.
    Imo. I would have broke mine eye-strings, crack'd them, but
To look upon him, till the diminution
Of space had pointed him sharp as my needle,
Nay, follow'd him till he had melted from   *25*
The smallness of a gnat to air, and then
Have turn'd mine eye, and wept. But, good Pisanio,
When shall we hear from him?
    Pis.   Be assur'd, madam,
With his next vantage.   *30*
    Imo. I did not take my leave of him, but had
Most pretty things to say; ere I could tell him
How I would think on him at certain hours
Such thoughts and such, or I could make him swear
The shes of Italy should not betray   *35*
Mine interest and his honour, or have charg'd him,
At the sixth hour of morn, at noon, at midnight,
To encounter me with orisons, for then
I am in heaven for him; or ere I could
Give him that parting kiss which I had set   *40*
Betwixt two charming words, comes in my father,
And like the tyrannous breathing of the north
Shakes all our buds from growing.

Enter a Lady.

    Lady.   The queen, madam,
Desires your highness' company.   *45*
    Imo. Those things I bid you do, get them dispatch'd.
I will attend the queen.
    Pis.   Madam, I shall.   *Exeunt.*

❧ Scene Fourth ❧

[Rome. A Room in Philario's House]
Enter Philario, Iachimo, a Frenchman, a Dutchman, and a Spaniard.

    Iach. Believe it, sir, I have seen him in Britain; he was then
of a crescent note, expected to prove so worthy as since he
hath been allowed the name of; but I could then have looked
on him without the help of admiration, though the catalogue

---

213 **walk:** *withdraw*   1 **shift:** *change*   2 **reek:** *steam*   7 **passable:** *affording pas-*
sage   8 **throughfare:** *thoroughfare*   9, 10 *Cf. n.*   11 **stand:** *withstand*   23 **a good**
sign: *fair to look at*   25, 26 *Cf. n.*   4 **As offer'd mercy is;** *cf. n.*

19 **left:** *ceased*   20 **after-eye:** *gaze after*   22 *Cf. n.*   23, 24 **diminution ... space:**
diminution due to space   30 **vantage:** *opportunity*   38 **encounter:** *meet* **orisons:** *pray-*
ers   40–43 *Cf. n.*   41 **charming:** *having in them a charm to preserve him*   2 **crescent**
note: *growing reputation*   4 **admiration:** *wonder*

of his endowments had been tabled by his side and I to   5
peruse him by items.

Phi. You speak of him when he was less furnished than now
he is with that which makes him both without and within.

French. I have seen him in France: we had very many there
could behold the sun with as firm eyes as he.   10

Iach. This matter of marrying his king's daughter,—wherein
he must be weighed rather by her value than his own,—words
him, I doubt not, a great deal from the matter.

French. And then, his banishment.

Iach. Ay, and the approbation of those that weep this   15
lamentable divorce under her colours are wonderfully to
extend him; be it but to fortify her judgment, which else an
easy battery might lay flat, for taking a beggar without less
quality. But how comes it, he is to sojourn with you? How
creeps acquaintance?   20

Phi. His father and I were soldiers together; to whom I
have been often bound for no less than my life. Here comes the
Briton: let him be so entertained amongst you as suits, with
gentlemen of your knowing, to a stranger of his quality.

Enter Posthumus.

I beseech you all, be better known to this gentleman, whom   25
I commend to you, as a noble friend of mine; how worthy
he is I will leave to appear hereafter, rather than story him in
his own hearing.

French. Sir, we have known together in Orleans.

Post. Since when I have been debtor to you for courtesies,   30
which I will be ever to pay and yet pay still.

French. Sir, you o'er-rate my poor kindness. I was glad I did
atone my countryman and you; it had been pity you should
have been put together with so mortal a purpose as then each
bore, upon importance of so slight and trivial a nature.   35

Post. By your pardon, sir, I was then a young traveller;
rather shunned to go even with what I heard than in my every
action to be guided by others' experiences; but, upon my
mended judgment,—if I offend not to say it is mended,—my
quarrel was not altogether slight.   40

French. Faith, yes, to be put to the arbitrement of swords,
and by such two that would by all likelihood have confounded
one the other, or have fallen both.

Iach. Can we, with manners, ask what was the difference?

French. Safely, I think. 'Twas a contention in public, which
may, without contradiction, suffer the report. It was much like
an argument that fell out last night, where each of us fell in
praise of our country mistresses; this gentleman at that time
vouching—and upon warrant of bloody affirmation—his to be
more fair, virtuous, wise, chaste, constant-qualified, and   50
less attemptable, than any the rarest of our ladies in France.

Iach. That lady is not now living, or this gentleman's opinion by this worn out.

Post. She holds her virtue still and I my mind.

Iach. You must not so far prefer her 'fore ours of Italy.   55

Post. Being so far provoked as I was in France, I would
abate her nothing, though I profess myself her adorer, not
her friend.

Iach. As fair and as good—a kind of hand-in-hand
comparison—had been something too fair and too good for   60
any lady in Britain. If she went before others I have seen, as
that diamond of yours outlustres many I have beheld, I
could not but believe she excelled many; but I have not seen
the most precious diamond that is, nor you the lady.

Post. I praised her as I rated her; so do I my stone.   65

Iach. What do you esteem it at?

Post. More than the world enjoys.

Iach. Either your unparagoned mistress is dead, or she's
outprized by a trifle.

Post. You are mistaken; the one may be sold, or given;   70
or if there were wealth enough for the purchase, or merit
for the gift; the other is not a thing for sale, and only the
gift of the gods.

Iach. Which the gods have given you?

Post. Which, by their graces, I will keep.   75

Iach. You may wear her in title yours, but, you know,
strange fowl light upon neighbouring ponds. Your ring may
be stolen, too; so your brace of unprizeable estimations, the
one is but frail and the other casual; a cunning thief, or a that
way accomplished courtier, would hazard the winning both   80
of first and last.

Post. Your Italy contains none so accomplished a courtier
to convince the honour of my mistress, if, in the holding or
loss of that, you term her frail. I do nothing doubt you have
store of thieves; notwithstanding I fear not my ring.   85

Phi. Let us leave here, gentlemen.

Post. Sir, with all my heart. This worthy signior, I thank
him, makes no stranger of me; we are familiar at first.

Iach. With five times so much conversation I should get
ground of your fair mistress, make her go back, even to the   90
yielding, had I admittance and opportunity to friend.

Post. No, no.

Iach. I dare thereupon pawn the moiety of my estate to
your ring, which, in my opinion, o'ervalues it something;
but I make my wager rather against your confidence than her
reputation; and, to bar your offence herein too, I durst attempt
it against any lady in the world.

Post. You are a great deal abused in too bold a persuasion;
and I doubt not you sustain what you're worthy of by your
attempt.   100

Iach. What's that?

Post. A repulse; though your attempt, as you call it,
deserves more,—a punishment too.

Phi. Gentlemen, enough of this; it came in too suddenly; let
it die as it was born, and, I pray you, be better acquainted.   105

Iach. Would I had put my estate and my neighbour's on
the approbation of what I have spoke!

Post. What lady would you choose to assail?

Iach. Yours; whom in constancy you think stands so safe. I
will lay you ten thousand ducats to your ring, that, commend

---

5 tabled: *set down in a list*   **7 furnished:** *equipped*   **8 makes:** *establishes*   **10**
Cf. n.   **12, 13 words him ... matter;** *cf. n.*   **15–17 the approbation ... extend him:**
cf. n.   **18, 19 without less quality:** *with so little rank*   **23 suits:** *accords*   **24 knowing:**
experience   **27 story:** *tell the story of*   **29 known together:** *known each other*   **31 ever**
to pay: *ever under obligation to pay*   **33 atone:** *reconcile*   **35 importance:** *mat-*
ter   **37–38 rather ... experiences;** *cf. n.*   **42 confounded:** *destroyed*   **45, 46 which**
... report; *cf. n.*   **48 country mistresses:** *ladies of our own countries*   **49 upon ...**
affirmation; *cf. n.*   **50 constant-qualified:** *endowed with constancy*   **51 attemptable:**
liable to seduction

57 abate: *depreciate*   **59 hand-in-hand:** *equal*   **65 rated her:** *estimated her value*   **67**
enjoys: *possesses*   **71 or ... or:** *either ... or*   **78 brace:** *pair*   **79 casual:** *subject to*
chance   **83 convince:** *conquer*   **85 fear not:** *fear not for*   **86 leave here:** *stop at this*
point   **88 familiar at first:** *friends from the beginning*   **93 moiety:** *half*   **98 abused:**
deceived   **persuasion:** *belief*   **107 approbation:** *confirmation*

me to the court where your lady is, with no more advantage
than the opportunity of a second conference, and I will bring
from thence that honour of hers which you imagine so
reserved.

 Post. I will wage, against your gold, gold to it: my   *115*
ring I hold dear as my finger: 'tis part of it.

 Iach. You are a friend, and therein the wiser. If you
buy ladies' flesh at a million a dram, you cannot preserve it
from tainting. But I see you have some religion in you, that
you fear.   *120*

 Post. This is but a custom in your tongue; you bear
a graver purpose, I hope.

 Iach. I am the master of your speeches, and would
undergo what's spoken, I swear.

 Post. Will you? I shall but lend my diamond till your *125*
return. Let there be covenants drawn between 's: my
mistress exceeds in goodness the hugeness of your unworthy
thinking; I dare you to this match. Here's my ring.

 Phi. I will have it no lay.

 Iach. By the gods, it is one. If I bring you no sufficient *130*
testimony that I have enjoyed the dearest bodily part of
your mistress, my ten thousand ducats are yours; so is your
diamond too: if I come off, and leave her in such honour as
you have trust in, she your jewel, this your jewel, and my
gold are yours; provided I have your commendation for *135*
my more free entertainment.

 Post. I embrace these conditions; let us have articles betwixt
us. Only, thus far you shall answer: if you make your voyage
upon her and give me directly to understand you have prevail'd, I am no further your enemy; she is not worth our *140*
debate: if she remain unseduced,—you not making it appear
otherwise,— for your ill opinion, and the assault you have
made to her chastity, you shall answer me with your sword.

 Iach. Your hand; a covenant. We will have these things set
down by lawful counsel, and straight away for Britain, lest *145*
the bargain should catch cold and starve. I will fetch my
gold and have our two wagers recorded.

 Post. Agreed.   *[Exeunt Posthumus and Iachimo.]*

 French. Will this hold, think you?

 Phi. Signior Iachimo will not from it. Pray, let us *150*
follow 'em.   *Exeunt.*

❦ Scene Fifth ❦

[Britain. Cymbeline's Palace]
Enter Queen, Ladies, and Cornelius.

 Queen. Whiles yet the dew's on ground, gather those
flowers:
Make haste; who has the note of them?

 1. Lady.   I, madam.

 Queen. Dispatch.   *Exeunt Ladies.* *5*
Now, Master doctor, have you brought those drugs?

 Cor. Pleaseth your highness, ay; here they are, madam:
        [Presenting a small box.]
But I beseech your Grace, without offence,—

My conscience bids me ask,—wherefore you have
Commanded of me these most poisonous compounds, *10*
Which are the movers of a languishing death,
But though slow, deadly?

 Queen.   I wonder, doctor,
Thou ask'st me such a question: have I not been
Thy pupil long? Hast thou not learn'd me how *15*
To make perfumes? distil? preserve? yea, so
That our great king himself doth woo me oft
For my confections? Having thus far proceeded,—
Unless thou think'st me devilish,—is 't not meet
That I did amplify my judgment in *20*
Other conclusions? I will try the forces
Of these thy compounds on such creatures as
We count not worth the hanging,—but none human,—
To try the vigour of them and apply
Allayments to their act, and by them gather *25*
Their several virtues and effects.

 Cor.   Your highness
Shall from this practice but make hard your heart;
Besides, the seeing these effects will be
Both noisome and infectious. *30*

 Queen.   O! content thee.

Enter Pisanio.

[Aside.] Here comes a flattering rascal; upon him
Will I first work: he's for his master,
And enemy to my son. How now, Pisanio!
Doctor, your service for this time is ended; *35*
Take your own way.

 Cor.   *[Aside.]* I do suspect you, madam;
But you shall do no harm.

 Queen.   *[To Pisanio]* Hark thee, a word.

 Cor. [Aside.] I do not like her. She doth think she has *40*
Strange lingering poisons; I do know her spirit,
And will not trust one of her malice with
A drug of such damn'd nature. Those she has
Will stupefy and dull the sense awhile;
Which first, perchance, she'll prove on cats and dogs, *45*
Then afterward up higher; but there is
No danger in what show of death it makes,
More than the locking-up the spirits a time,
To be more fresh, reviving. She is fool'd
With a most false effect; and I the truer, *50*
So to be false with her.

 Queen.   No further service, doctor,
Until I send for thee.

 Cor.   I humbly take my leave. *Exit.*

 Queen. Weeps she still, sayst thou? Dost thou think in time
She will not quench, and let instructions enter
Where folly now possesses? Do thou work:
When thou shalt bring me word she loves my son,
I'll tell thee on the instant thou art then
As great as is thy master; greater, for *60*
His fortunes all lie speechless, and his name
Is at last gasp; return he cannot, nor
Continue where he is; to shift his being
Is to exchange one misery with another,

115 wage: *wager* **117 a friend;** *cf. n.* **121 custom . . . tongue:** *manner of speech* **123 undergo:** *maintain* **129 lay:** *wager* **135–136 provided . . . entertainment;** *cf. n.* **137 articles:** *written agreements* **146 starve:** *die of cold* **3 note of:** *directions concerning*

15 learn'd: *taught* **21 conclusions:** *experiments* **24 vigour:** *power* **31 content thee:** *do not worry* **45 prove:** *test* **47 show:** *appearance* **50 effect:** *outward manifestation* **56 quench:** *cool down* **63 shift . . . being:** *change . . . abode*

And every day that comes comes to decay   65
A day's work in him. What shalt thou expect,
To be depender on a thing that leans,
Who cannot be new built, nor has no friends,
So much as but to prop him?
   [The Queen drops the box; Pisanio takes it up.]
      Thou tak'st up   70
Thou know'st not what; but take it for thy labour:
It is a thing I made, which hath the king
Five times redeem'd from death; I do not know
What is more cordial: nay, I prithee, take it;
It is an earnest of a further good   75
That I mean to thee. Tell thy mistress how
The case stands with her; do 't as from thyself.
Think what a change thou chancest on, but think
Thou hast thy mistress still, to boot, my son,
Who shall take notice of thee. I'll move the king   80
To any shape of thy preferment such
As thou'lt desire; and then myself, I chiefly,
That set thee on to this desert, am bound
To load thy merit richly. Call my women;
Think on my words.   *Exit Pisanio.*
     A sly and constant knave,
Not to be shak'd; the agent for his master,
And the remembrancer of her to hold
The hand-fast to her lord. I have given him that
Which, if he take, shall quite unpeople her   90
Of liegers for her sweet, and which she after,
Except she bend her humour, shall be assur'd
To taste of too.

    Enter Pisanio and Ladies.

   So, so;—well done, well done.
The violets, cowslips, and the primroses   95
Bear to my closet. Fare thee well, Pisanio:
Think on my words.
      Exeunt Queen and Ladies.
 Pis.   And shall do:
But when to my good lord I prove untrue,
I'll choke myself; there's all I'll do for you.   *Exit.*

❧ Scene Sixth ❧

[The Same]
Enter Imogen alone.

 Imo. A father cruel, and a step-dame false;
A foolish suitor to a wedded lady,
That hath her husband banish'd: O! that husband,
My supreme crown of grief! and those repeated
Vexations of it! Had I been thief-stol'n,   5
As my two brothers, happy! but most miserable
Is the desire that's glorious: bless'd be those,
How mean so'er, that have their honest wills,
Which seasons comfort. Who may this be? Fie!

    Enter Pisanio and Iachimo.

 Pis. Madam, a noble gentleman of Rome,   10
Comes from my lord with letters.
 Iach.   Change you, madam?
The worthy Leonatus is in safety,
And greets your highness dearly. *[Presents a letter.]*
 Imo.   Thanks, good sir.   15
You are kindly welcome.
 Iach. [Aside.] All of her that is out of door most rich!
If she be furnish'd with a mind so rare,
She is alone the Arabian bird, and I
Have lost the wager. Boldness be my friend!   20
Arm me, audacity, from head to foot!
Or, like the Parthian, I shall flying fight;
Rather, directly fly.
 Imo. reads: 'He is one of the noblest note, to whose
kindnesses I am most infinitely tied. Reflect upon him
accordingly, as you value your trust. Leonatus.'
So far I read aloud;
But even the very middle of my heart
Is warm'd by the rest, and takes it thankfully.   30
You are as welcome, worthy sir, as I
Have words to bid you; and shall find it so
In all that I can do.
 Iach.   Thanks, fairest lady.
What! are men mad? Hath nature given them eyes   35
To see this vaulted arch, and the rich crop
Of sea and land, which can distinguish 'twixt
The fiery orbs above and the twinn'd stones
Upon the number'd beach? and can we not
Partition make with spectacles so precious   40
'Twixt fair and foul?
 Imo.   What makes your admiration?
 Iach. It cannot be i' the eye, for apes and monkeys
'Twixt two such shes would chatter this way and
Contemn with mows the other; nor i' the judgment,   45
For idiots in this case of favour would
Be wisely definite; nor i' the appetite,—
Sluttery to such neat excellence oppos'd
Should make desire vomit emptiness,
Not so allur'd to feed.   50
 Imo. What is the matter, trow?
 Iach.   The cloyed will,—
That satiate yet unsatisfied desire, that tub
Both fill'd and running,—ravening first the lamb,
Longs after for the garbage.   55
 Imo.   What, dear sir,
Thus raps you? are you well?
 Iach.   Thanks, madam, well.
[To Pisanio.] Beseech you, sir,
Desire my man's abode where I did leave him;   60
He's strange and peevish.
 Pis.   I was going, sir.
To give him welcome.   *Exit.*
 Imo. Continues well my lord? His health, beseech you?

---

65 **decay:** *destroy* 67 *Cf. n.* 74 **cordial:** *reviving* 75 **earnest:** *first payment to bind a bargain* 79 **to boot:** *in addition* 88 **remembrancer:** *reminder* 89 **hand-fast:** *marriage contract* 91 **liegers:** *ambassadors* **sweet:** *lover* 92 **bend her humour:** *change her inclination* 6-9 **most miserable . . . comfort;** *cf. n.*

12 **Change you:** *do you change color?* 17 **out of door:** *outwardly visible* 19 **alone:** *without rival* **Arabian bird:** *phœnix* 22 **Parthian;** *cf. n.* 37-41 **which . . . foul;** *cf. n.* 42 **makes:** *causes* 45 **mows:** *grimaces* 46 **favour:** *beauty* 47 **definite:** *free from hesitation* 48-50 *Cf. n.* 51 **trow:** *I wonder* 54 **ravening:** *ravenously devouring* 55 **after:** *afterwards* 57 **raps:** *transports* 60 **Desire . . . abode:** *ask my man to remain* 61 **strange:** *a stranger*

Iach. Well, madam.   65

Imo. Is he dispos'd to mirth? I hope he is.

Iach. Exceeding pleasant; none a stranger there

So merry and so gamesome: he is called

The Briton reveller.

Imo.   When he was here   70

He did incline to sadness, and oft-times

Not knowing why.

Iach.   I never saw him sad.

There is a Frenchman his companion, one,

An eminent monsieur, that, it seems, much loves   75

A Gallian girl at home; he furnaces

The thick sighs from him, whiles the jolly Briton—

Your lord, I mean—laughs from 's free lungs, cries, 'O!

Can my sides hold, to think that man, who knows

By history, report, or his own proof,   80

What woman is, yea, what she cannot choose

But must be, will his free hours languish for

Assured bondage?'

Imo.   Will my lord say so?

Iach. Ay, madam, with his eyes in flood with laughter: 85

It is a recreation to be by

And hear him mock the Frenchman; but, heavens know,

Some men are much to blame.

Imo.   Not he, I hope.

Iach. Not he; but yet heaven's bounty towards him might   90

Be us'd more thankfully. In himself, 'tis much;

In you,—which I account his beyond all talents,—

Whilst I am bound to wonder, I am bound

To pity too.

Imo.   What do you pity, sir?   95

Iach. Two creatures, heartily.

Imo.   Am I one, sir?

You look on me: what wrack discern you in me

Deserves your pity?

Iach.   Lamentable! What!   100

To hide me from the radiant sun and solace

I' the dungeon by a snuff!

Imo.   I pray you, sir,

Deliver with more openness your answers

To my demands. Why do you pity me?   105

Iach. That others do,

I was about to say, enjoy your—But

It is an office of the gods to venge it,

Not mine to speak on 't.

Imo.   You do seem to know   110

Something of me, or what concerns me; pray you,—

Since doubting things go ill often hurts more

Than to be sure they do; for certainties

Either are past remedies, or, timely knowing,

The remedy then born,—discover to me   115

What both you spur and stop.

Iach.   Had I this cheek

To bathe my lips upon; this hand, whose touch,

Whose every touch, would force the feeler's soul

To the oath of loyalty; this object, which   120

Takes prisoner the wild motion of mine eye,

Firing it only here; should I—damn'd then—

Slaver with lips as common as the stairs

That mount the Capitol; join gripes with hands

Made hard with hourly falsehood,—falsehood, as   125

With labour;—then by-peeping in an eye,

Base and illustrous as the smoky light

That's fed with stinking tallow; it were fit

That all the plagues of hell should at one time

Encounter such revolt.   130

Imo.   My lord, I fear,

Has forgot Britain.

Iach.   And himself. Not I,

Inclin'd to this intelligence, pronounce

The beggary of his change; but 'tis your graces   135

That from my mutest conscience to my tongue

Charms this report out.

Imo.   Let me hear no more.

Iach. O dearest soul! your cause doth strike my heart

With pity, that doth make me sick. A lady   140

So fair,—and fasten'd to an empery

Would make the great'st king double,—to be partner'd

With tom-boys hir'd with that self exhibition

Which your own coffers yield! with diseas'd ventures

That play with all infirmities for gold   145

Which rottenness can lend nature! such boil'd stuff

As well might poison poison! Be reveng'd;

Or she that bore you was no queen, and you

Recoil from your great stock.

Imo.   Reveng'd!   150

How should I be reveng'd? If this be true,—

As I have such a heart, that both mine ears

Must not in haste abuse,—if it be true,

How should I be reveng'd?

Iach.   Should he make me   155

Live like Diana's priest, betwixt cold sheets,

Whiles he is vaulting variable ramps,

In your despite, upon your purse? Revenge it.

I dedicate myself to your sweet pleasure,

More noble than that runagate to your bed,   160

And will continue fast to your affection,

Still close as sure.

Imo.   What ho, Pisanio!

Iach. Let me my service tender on your lips.

Imo. Away! I do condemn mine ears that have   165

So long attended thee. If thou wert honourable,

Thou wouldst have told this tale for virtue, not

For such an end thou seek'st; as base as strange.

Thou wrong'st a gentleman, who is as far

From thy report as thou from honour, and   170

Solicit'st here a lady that disdains

Thee and the devil alike. What ho, Pisanio!

The king my father shall be made acquainted

Of thy assault; if he shall think it fit,

121, 122 **Takes prisoner ... here;** *cf. n.*   121 **motion:** *passion*   126 **by-peeping:** *looking sidelong*   127 **illustrous:** *without lustre*   130 **Encounter such revolt:** *meet such apostasy*   133–137 **Not I ... out;** *cf. n.*   141 **empery:** *empire*   142 **Would ... double:** *which would double the greatest king's domain*   **partner'd:** *associated*   143 **tom-boys:** *wanton women*   **self:** *same*   **exhibition:** *allowance*   144 **ventures:** *chance mistresses*   146 **boil'd stuff:** *women who have been in the sweating tubs for venereal disease*   149 **Recoil:** *fall away*   157 **ramps:** *harlots*   158 **In your despite:** *in scorn of you*   160 **runagate:** *renegade*   162 **Still ... sure:** *always as secretly as faithfully*   166 **attended:** *listened to*

71 **sadness:** *seriousness*   73 **sad:** *serious*   76 **furnaces:** *exhales as from a furnace*   80 **proof:** *experience*   91 **'tis much:** *i.e. heaven's bounty is great*   92 **talents:** *treasures*   98 **wrack:** *ruin*   101 **to hide me:** *to hide oneself*   102 **snuff:** *candle*   112 **doubting:** *suspecting that*   114, 115 **timely knowing ... born;** *cf. n.*   115 **discover:** *reveal*

A saucy stranger in his court to mart   *175*
As in a Romish stew and to expound
His beastly mind to us, he hath a court
He little cares for and a daughter who
He not respects at all. What ho, Pisanio!
    Iach. O happy Leonatus! I may say.   *180*
The credit that thy lady hath of thee
Deserves thy trust, and thy most perfect goodness
Her assur'd credit. Blessed live you long!
A lady to the worthiest sir that ever
Country call'd his; and you his mistress, only   *185*
For the most worthiest fit. Give me your pardon.
I have spoken this, to know if your affiance
Were deeply rooted, and shall make your lord
That which he is, new o'er; and he is one
The truest manner'd; such a holy witch   *190*
That he enchants societies into him;
Half all men's hearts are his.
    Imo.   You make amends.
    Iach. He sits 'mongst men like a descended god:
He hath a kind of honour sets him off,   *195*
More than a mortal seeming. Be not angry,
Most mighty princess, that I have adventur'd
To try your taking of a false report; which hath
Honour'd with confirmation your great judgment
In the election of a sir so rare,   *200*
Which you know cannot err. The love I bear him
Made me to fan you thus; but the gods made you,
Unlike all others, chaffless. Pray, your pardon.
    Imo. All's well, sir. Take my power i' the court for yours.
    Iach. My humble thanks. I had almost forgot   *205*
To entreat your Grace but in a small request,
And yet of moment too, for it concerns
Your lord, myself, and other noble friends,
Are partners in the business.
    Imo.   Pray, what is 't?   *210*
    Iach. Some dozen Romans of us and your lord,
The best feather of our wing, have mingled sums
To buy a present for the emperor;
Which I, the factor for the rest, have done
In France; 'tis plate of rare device, and jewels   *215*
Of rich and exquisite form; their values great;
And I am something curious, being strange,
To have them in safe stowage. May it please you
To take them in protection?
    Imo.   Willingly;   *220*
And pawn mine honour for their safety: since
My lord hath interest in them, I will keep them
In my bedchamber.
    Iach.   They are in a trunk,
Attended by my men; I will make bold   *225*
To send them to you, only for this night;
I must aboard to-morrow.
    Imo.   O! no, no.
    Iach. Yes, I beseech, or I shall short my word
By lengthening my return. From Gallia   *230*
I cross'd the seas on purpose and on promise
To see your Grace.

    Imo.   I thank you for your pains;
But not away to-morrow!
    Iach.   O! I must, madam: *235*
Therefore I shall beseech you, if you please
To greet your lord with writing, do 't to-night:
I have outstood my time, which is material
To the tender of our present.
    Imo.   I will write.   *240*
Send your trunk to me; it shall safe be kept,
And truly yielded you. You're very welcome.   *Exeunt.*

ACT SECOND ❧ SCENE FIRST

[Britain. Cymbeline's Palace]
Enter Cloten and two Lords.

    Clo. Was there ever man had such luck! when I kissed the
jack, upon an up-cast to be hit away! I had a hundred pound
on 't; and then a whoreson jackanapes must take me up for
swearing, as if I borrowed mine oaths of him and might not
spend them at my pleasure.   *5*
    1. Lord. What got he by that? You have broke his pate
with your bowl.
    2. Lord. [Aside.] If his wit had been like him that
broke it, it would have run all out.
    Clo. When a gentleman is disposed to swear, it is not   *10*
for any standers-by to curtail his oaths, ha?
    2. Lord. No, my lord; *[Aside.]* nor crop the ears of them.
    Clo. Whoreson dog! I give him satisfaction! Would he
had been one of my rank!
    2. Lord. [Aside.] To have smelt like a fool.   *15*
    Clo. I am not vexed more at anything in the earth. A
pox on 't! I had rather not be so noble as I am. They dare
not fight with me because of the queen my mother. Every
Jack-slave hath his bellyful of fighting, and I must go up
and down like a cock that nobody can match.   *20*
    2. Lord. [Aside.] You are cock and capon too; and
you crow, cock, with your comb on.
    Clo. Sayest thou?
    2. Lord. It is not fit your lordship should undertake
every companion that you give offence to.   *25*
    Clo. No, I know that; but it is fit I should commit
offence to my inferiors.
    2. Lord. Ay, it is fit for your lordship only.
    Clo. Why, so I say.
    1. Lord. Did you hear of a stranger that's come to   *30*
court to-night?
    Clo. A stranger, and I not know on 't!
    2. Lord. [Aside.] He's a strange fellow himself, and
knows it not.
    1. Lord. There's an Italian come; and 'tis thought,   *35*
one of Leonatus' friends.
    Clo. Leonatus! a banished rascal; and he's another,
whatsoever he be. Who told you of this stranger?
    1. Lord. One of your lordship's pages.

---

175 saucy: *lascivious*   **mart:** *traffic*   **176 stew:** *brothel*   **181 credit . . . of:** *confidence . . .
in*   **187 affiance:** *confidence*   **190 truest manner'd:** *of the soundest morals*   **191 into:**
unto   **209 Are:** *who are*   **214 factor:** *agent*   **217 curious:** *anxious*

238 outstood: *outstayed*   **material:** *important*   **239 tender:** *presentation*   **1, 2 when . . .
away;** *cf. n.*   **3 whoreson jackanapes:** *rascally coxcomb*   **take me up:** *scold me*   **11, 12
curtail, crop;** *cf. n.*   **18, 19 Jack-slave:** *low fellow*   **21, 22 capon . . . comb on;**
cf. n.   **24 undertake:** *give satisfaction to*   **25 companion:** *rascal*

Clo. Is it fit I went to look upon him? Is there no   40
derogation in 't?

1. Lord. You cannot derogate, my lord.

Clo. Not easily, I think.

2. Lord. [*Aside.*] You are a fool, granted; therefore your
issues, being foolish, do not derogate   45

Clo. Come, I'll go see this Italian. What I have lost to-day
at bowls I'll win to-night of him. Come, go.

2. Lord. I'll attend your lordship.

Exit [Cloten].

That such a crafty devil as is his mother
Should yield the world this ass! a woman that   50
Bears all down with her brain, and this her son
Cannot take two from twenty for his heart
And leave eighteen. Alas! poor princess,
Thou divine Imogen, what thou endur'st
Betwixt a father by thy step-dame govern'd,   55
A mother hourly coining plots, a wooer
More hateful than the foul expulsion is
Of thy dear husband, than that horrid act
Of the divorce he'd make. The heavens hold firm
The walls of thy dear honour; keep unshak'd   60
That temple, thy fair mind; that thou mayst stand,
To enjoy thy banish'd lord and this great land!

Exeunt [Lords].

❧ Scene Second ❧

[*A Bedchamber; in one part of it a Trunk*]
Imogen [*reading*] *in her bed; a Lady* [*attending*].

Imo. Who's there? my woman Helen?

Lady.   Please you, madam.

Imo. What hour is it?

Lady.   Almost midnight, madam.

Imo. I have read three hours then; mine eyes are weak;   5
Fold down the leaf where I have left; to bed:
Take not away the taper, leave it burning,
And if thou canst awake by four o' the clock,
I prithee, call me. Sleep has seized me wholly.

[Exit Lady.]

To your protection I commend me, gods!   10
From fairies and the tempters of the night
Guard me, beseech ye!

Sleeps. Iachimo [*comes*] *from the trunk.*

Iach. The crickets sing, and man's o'er-labour'd sense
Repairs itself by rest. Our Tarquin thus
Did softly press the rushes ere he waken'd   15
The chastity he wounded. Cytherea!
How bravely thou becom'st thy bed, fresh lily,
And whiter than the sheets! That I might touch!
But kiss: one kiss! Rubies unparagon'd,
How dearly they do 't! 'Tis her breathing that   20
Perfumes the chamber thus; the flame of the taper
Bows toward her, and would under-peep her lids,

To see the enclosed lights, now canopied
Under these windows, white and azure lac'd
With blue of heaven's own tinct. But my design,   25
To note the chamber: I will write all down:
Such and such pictures; there the window; such
Th' adornment of her bed; the arras, figures,
Why, such and such; and the contents o' the story.
Ah! but some natural notes about her body,   30
Above ten thousand meaner moveables
Would testify, to enrich mine inventory.
O sleep! thou ape of death, lie dull upon her;
And be her sense but as a monument
Thus in a chapel lying. Come off, come off;—   35

[Taking off her bracelet.]

As slippery as the Gordian knot was hard!
'Tis mine; and this will witness outwardly,
As strongly as the conscience does within,
To the madding of her lord. On her left breast
A mole cinque-spotted, like the crimson drops   40
I' the bottom of a cowslip: here's a voucher;
Stronger than ever law could make: this secret
Will force him think I have pick'd the lock and ta'en
The treasure of her honour. No more. To what end?
Why should I write this down, that's riveted,   45
Screw'd to my memory? She hath been reading late
The tale of Tereus; here the leaf's turn'd down
Where Philomel gave up. I have enough:
To the trunk again, and shut the spring of it.
Swift, swift, you dragons of the night, that dawning   50
May bare the raven's eye! I lodge in fear;
Though this a heavenly angel, hell is here.   *Clock strikes.*
One, two three: time, time!

Exit [into trunk].

❧ Scene Third ❧

[*An Ante-chamber adjoining Imogen's Apartments*]
Enter Cloten and Lords.

1. Lord. Your lordship is the most patient man in loss, the
most coldest that ever turned up ace.

Clo. It would make any man cold to lose.

1. Lord. But not every man patient after the noble temper
of your lordship. You are most hot and furious when you win.

Clo. Willing will put any man into courage. If I could get
this foolish Imogen, I should have gold enough. It's almost
morning, is 't not?

1. Lord. Day, my lord.

Clo. I would this music would come. I am advised to give   10
her music o' mornings; they say it will penetrate.

Enter Musicians.

Come on; tune. If you can penetrate her with your fingering,
so; we'll try with tongue too: if none will do, let her remain;
but I'll never give o'er. First, a very excellent good-conceited

---

41 derogation: *disparagement*   **42, 45 derogate:** *do anything derogatory to rank or position,
and (quibblingly) degenerate*   **45 issues:** *acts, offspring*   **52 for his heart:** *to save his
life*   **56 coining:** *fabricating*   **59 he:** *i.e. Cloten*   **6 left:** *stopped*   **14 Our Tarquin:**
cf. n.   **15 press . . . rushes;** *cf. n.*   **16 Cytherea:** *Venus*   **19, 20 But kiss . . . do 't;**
cf. n.

24 windows: *eyelids*   **24, 25 white . . . tinct;** *cf. n.*   **25 tinct:** *color*   **28 arras:** *wall-
tapestry*   **figures:** *carvings*   **29 contents o' the story;** *cf. n.*   **34 sense:** *perception*   **monument:** *effigy*   **36 Gordian knot;** *cf. n.*   **40 cinque-spotted:** *having five spots*   **47
The tale of Tereus;** *cf. n.*   **50, 51 that . . . eye;** *cf. n.*   **52 this;** *i.e. this's*   **53 time;**
cf. n.   **2 turned up ace;** *cf. n.*   **11 penetrate:** *touch the heart*

thing; after, a wonderful sweet air, with admirable rich words to it: and then let her consider.

Song
'Hark! hark! the lark at heven's gate sings,
 And Phœbus 'gins arise,
His steeds to water at those springs   20
 On chalic'd flowers that lies;
And winking Mary-buds begin
 To ope their golden eyes:
With everything that pretty is,
 My lady sweet, arise: 25
  Arise, arise!'

So, get you gone. If this penetrate, I will consider your music the better; if it do not, it is a vice in her ears, which horse-hairs and calves'-guts, nor the voice of unpaved eunuch to boot, can never amend. *[Exeunt Musicians.]* 30

2. Lord. Here comes the king.

Clo. I am glad I was up so late, for that's the reason I was up so early; he cannot choose but take this service I have done fatherly.

Enter Cymbeline and Queen.

Good morrow to your majesty and to my gracious mother. 35

Cym. Attend you here the door of our stern daughter? Will she not forth?

Clo. I have assail'd her with musics, but she vouchsafes no notice.

Cym. The exile of her minion is too new, 40
She hath not yet forgot him; some more time
Must wear the print of his remembrance out,
And then she's yours.

Queen.   You are most bound to the king,
Who lets go by no vantages that may 45
Prefer you to his daughter. Frame yourself
To orderly soliciting, and be friended
With aptness of the season; make denials
Increase your services; so seem as if
You were inspir'd to do those duties which 50
You tender to her; that you in all obey her
Save when command to your dismission tends,
And therein you are senseless.

Clo.   Senseless! not so.

[Enter a Messenger.]

Mess. So like you, sir, ambassadors from Rome; 55
The one is Caius Lucius.

Cym.   A worthy fellow,
Albeit he comes on angry purpose now;
But that's no fault of his: we must receive him
According to the honour of his sender; 60
And towards himself, his goodness forespent on us,
We must extend our notice. Our dear son,
When you have given good morning to your mistress,
Attend the queen and us; we shall have need

To employ you towards this Roman. Come, our queen. 65
    Exeunt [all but Cloten].

Clo. If she be up, I'll speak with her; if not,
Let her lie still, and dream. By your leave, ho! *[Knocks.]*
I know her women are about her. What
If I do line one of their hands? 'Tis gold
Which buys admittance; oft it doth; yea, and makes 70
Diana's rangers false themselves, yield up
Their deer to the stand o' the stealer; and 'tis gold
Which makes the true man kill'd and saves the thief;
Nay, sometime hangs both thief and true man. What
Can it not do and undo? I will make 75
One of her women lawyer to me, for
I yet not understand the case myself.
By your leave.   *Knocks.*

Enter a Lady.

Lady. Who's there, that knocks?

Clo.   A gentleman. 80

Lady.   No more?

Clo. Yes, and a gentlewoman's son.

Lady.   *[Aside.]* That's more
Than some whose tailors are as dear as yours
Can justly boast of. What's your lordship's pleasure? 85

Clo. Your lady's person: is she ready?

Lady.   Ay,
To keep her chamber.

Clo. There's gold for you; sell me your good report.

Lady. How! my good name? or to report of you 90
What I shall think is good?—The princess!

Enter Imogen.

Clo. Good morrow, fairest; sister, your sweet hand.
    [Exit Lady.]

Imo. Good morrow, sir. You lay out too much pains
For purchasing but trouble; the thanks I give
Is telling you that I am poor of thanks 95
And scarce can spare them.

Clo.   Still, I swear I love you.

Imo. If you but said so, 'twere as deep with me:
If you swear still, your recompense is still
That I regard it not.   100

Clo.   This is no answer.

Imo. But that you shall not say I yield being silent
I would not speak. I pray you, spare me: faith,
I shall unfold equal discourtesy
To your best kindness. One of your great knowing 105
Should learn, being taught, forbearance.

Clo. To leave you in your madness, 'twere my sin:
I will not.

Imo. Fools cure not mad folks.

Clo.   Do you call me fool? 110

Imo. As I am mad, I do:
If you'll be patient, I'll no more be mad;
That cures us both. I am much sorry, sir,
You put me to forget a lady's manners,
By being so verbal; and learn now, for all, 115

19 **Phœbus:** *the sun* 21 **chalic'd:** *having cup-like blossoms* 22 **winking:** *with eyes shut* **Mary-buds:** *buds of marigolds* 27 **consider:** *requite* 28, 29 **horse-hairs:** *fiddle-bows* 29 **calves'-guts:** *fiddle-strings* **unpaved:** *unstoned, castrated* 40 **minion:** *favor-ite* 44 **bound:** *under obligation* 46 **Prefer:** *recommend* **Frame:** *prepare* 53 **sense-less:** *incapable of understanding* 55 **So like you:** *if it please you* 61 **his goodness forespent:** *because of his former goodness*

69 **line:** *put money into* 71 **Diana's rangers:** *forest-rangers of Diana, nymphs* **false:** *be-tray* 72 **stand:** *station of huntsman waiting for game* 73 **true:** *honest* 81 **No more?:** *nothing else?* 93 **lay out:** *expend* 98 **'twere as deep:** *it would make as deep an impres-sion* 115 **verbal:** *explicit*

That I, which know my heart, do here pronounce
By the very truth of it, I care not for you;
And am so near the lack of charity,—
To accuse myself,—I hate you; which I had rather
You felt than make 't my boast.   *120*
   Clo.   You sin against
Obedience, which you owe your father. For
The contract you pretend with that base wretch,
One bred of alms and foster'd with cold dishes,
With scraps o' the court, it is no contract, none;   *125*
And though it be allow'd in meaner parties—
Yet who than he more mean?—to knit their souls—
On whom there is no more dependancy
But brats and beggary—in self-figur'd knot;
Yet you are curb'd from that enlargement by   *130*
The consequence o' the crown, and must not foil
The precious note of it with a base slave,
A hilding for a livery, a squire's cloth,
A pantler, not so eminent.
   Imo.   Profane fellow!   *135*
Wert thou the son of Jupiter, and no more
But what thou art besides, thou wert too base
To be his groom; thou wert dignified enough,
Even to the pint of envy, if 'twere made
Comparative for your virtues, to be styl'd   *140*
The under-hangman of his kingdom, and hated
For being preferr'd so well.
   Clo.   The south-fog rot him!
   Imo. He never can meet more mischance than come
To be but nam'd of thee. His meanest garment   *145*
That ever hath but clipp'd his body, is dearer
In my respect than all the hairs above thee,
Were they all made such men. How now, Pisanio!

              Enter Pisanio.

   Clo. 'His garment!' Now, the devil—
   Imo. To Dorothy my woman hie thee presently,—   *150*
   Clo. 'His garment!'
   Imo.   I am sprighted with a fool,
Frighted, and anger'd worse. Go, bid my woman
Search for a jewel that too casually
Hath left mine arm; it was they master's, 'shrew me   *155*
If I would lose it for a revenue
Of any king's in Europe. I do think
I saw 't this morning; confident I am
Last night 'twas on mine arm, I kiss'd it;
I hope it be not gone to tell my lord   *160*
That I kiss aught but he.
   Pis.   'Twill not be lost.
   Imo. I hope so; go, and search.   *[Exit Pisanio.]*
   Clo.   You have abus'd me:
'His meanest garment!'   *165*
   Imo.   Ay, I said so, sir:
If you will make 't an action, call witness to 't.
   Clo. I will inform your father.

   Imo.   Your mother, too:
She's my good lady, and will conceive, I hope,   *170*
But the worst of me. So I leave you, sir,
To the worst of disconent.
   Clo.   I'll be reveng'd.
'His meanest garment!' Well.   *Exit.*

❧ Scene Fourth ❧

[Rome. Philario's House]
Enter Posthumus and Philario.

   Post. Fear it not, sir; I would I were so sure
To win the king as I am bold her honour
Will remain hers.
   Phi.   What means do you make to him?
   Post. Not any, but abide the change of time,   *5*
Quake in the present winter's state and wish
That warmer days would come; in these fear'd hopes,
I barely gratify your love; they failing,
I must die much your debtor.
   Phi. Your very goodness and your company   *10*
O'erpays all I can do. By this, your king
Hath heard of great Augustus; Caius Lucius
Will do 's commission throughly, and I think
He'll grant the tribute, send the arrearages,
Or look upon our Romans, whose remembrance   *15*
Is yet fresh in their grief.
   Post.   I do believe—
Statist though I am none, nor like to be—
That this will prove a war; and you shall hear
The legions now in Gallia sooner landed   *20*
In our not-fearing Britain, than have tidings
Of any penny tribute paid. Our countrymen
Are men more order'd than when Julius Cæsar
Smil'd at their lack of skill, but found their courage
Worthy his frowning at: their discipline,   *25*
Now mingled with their courage, will make known
To their approvers they are people such
That mend upon the world.
   Phi.   See! Iachimo!

             Enter Iachimo.

   Post. The swifest harts have posted you by land,   *30*
And winds of all the corners kiss'd your sails,
To make your vissel nimble.
   Phi.   Welcome, sir.
   Post. I hope the briefness of your answer made
The speediness of your return.   *35*
   Iach.   Your lady
Is one of the fairest that I have look'd upon.
   Post. And therewithal the best; or let her beauty
Look through a casement to allure false hearts
And be false with them.   *40*
   Iach.   Here are letters for you.
   Post. Their tenour good, I trust.

---

128 dependancy: *consequence (of marriage)*   **129** self-figur'd: *formed by themselves*   **130** curb'd: *restrained* enlargement: *liberty*   **131** consequence: *succession* foil: *pollute*   **133** hilding: *rascal* for: *fit only for* squire's cloth: *lackey's dress*   **134** pantler: *pantry servant*   **138** dignified: *given dignity*   **139, 140** made Comparative for: *compared with*   **142** preferr'd: *advanced* south-fog: *cf. n.*   **146** clipp'd: *embraced*   **152** sprighted with: *haunted by*   **167** action: *law-suit*

2 bold: *confident*   **4** means: *intercession*   **5** abide: *await*   **7–9** in these ... debtor; *cf. n.*   **13** throughly: *thoroughly*   **16** grief: *suffering*   **18** Statist: *statesman*   **19** prove: *turn out to be*   **23** order'd: *disciplined*   **26** mingled ... courage: *cf. n.*   **27** approvers: *those who make trial*   **28** mend ... world: *improve with experience*   **30** posted: *conveyed swiftly*   **31** corners: *quarters from which the wind blows*   **34** made: *caused*

Iach.   'Tis very like.
Phi. Was Caius Lucius in the Britain court
When you were there?   45
    Iach.   He was expected then,
But not approach'd.
    Post.   All is well yet.
Sparkles this stone as it was wont? or is 't not
Too dull for your good wearing?   50
    Iach.   If I have lost it,
I should have lost the worth of it in gold.
I'll make a journey twice as far to enjoy
A second night of such sweet shortness which
Was mine in Britain; for the ring is won.   55
    Post. The stone's too hard to come by.
    Iach.   Not a whit,
Your lady being so easy.
    Post.   Make not, sir,
Your loss your sport: I hope you know that we   60
Must not continue friends.
    Iach.   Good sir, we must,
If you keep covenant. Had I not brought
The knowledge of your mistress home, I grant
We were to question further, but I now   65
Profess myself the winner of her honour,
Together with your ring; and not the wronger
Of her or you, having proceeded but
By both your wills.
    Post.   If you can make 't apparent   70
That you have tasted her in bed, my hand
And ring is yours; if not, the foul opinion
You had of her pure honour gains or loses
Your sword or mine or masterless leaves both
To who shall find them.   75
    Iach.   Sir, my circumstances,
Being so near the truth as I will make them,
Must first induce you to believe: whose strength
I will confirm with oath; which, I doubt not,
You'll give me leave to spare, when you shall find   80
You need it not.
    Post.   Proceed.
    Iach.   First, her bedchamber,—
Where I confess I slept not, but profess
Had that was well worth watching,—it was hang'd   85
With tapestry of silk and silver; the story
Proud Cleopatra, when she met her Roman,
And Cydnus swell'd above the banks, or for
The press of boats or pride; a piece of work
So bravely done, so rich, that it did strive   90
In workmanship and value; which I wonder'd
Could be so rarely and exactly wrought,
Since the true life on 't was—
    Post.   This is true;
And this you might have heard of here, by me,   95
Or by some other.
    Iach.   More particulars
Must justify my knowledge.
    Post.   So they must,
Or do your honour injury.   100

Iach.   The chimney
Is south the chamber, and the chimney-piece
Chaste Dian bathing; never saw I figures
So likely to report themselves; the cutter
Was as another nature, dumb; outwent her,   105
Motion and breath left out.
    Post.   This is a thing
Which you might from relation likewise reap,
Being, at it is, much spoke of.
    Iach.   The roof o' the chamber   110
With golden cherubins is fretted; her andirons—
I had forgot them—were two winking Cupids
Of silver, each on one foot standing, nicely
Depending on their brands.
    Post.   This is her honour!   115
Let it be granted you have seen all this,—and praise
Be given to your remembrance,—the description
Of what is in her chamber nothing saves
The wager you have laid.
    Iach.   Then, if you can,   120
Be pale: I beg but leave to air this jewel; see!
                    [*Showing the bracelet.*]
And now 'tis up again; it must be married
To that your diamond; I'll keep them.
    Post.   Jove!
Once more let me behold it. Is it that   125
Which I left with her?
    Iach.   Sir,—I thank her,—that:
She stripp'd it from her arm; I see her yet;
Her pretty action did outsell her gift,
And yet enriched it too. She gave it me, and said   130
She priz'd it once.
    Post.   May be she pluck'd it off
To send it me.
    Iach.   She writes so to you, doth she?
    Post. O! no, no, no, 'tis true. Here, take this too;   135
                    [*Gives the ring.*]
It is a basilisk unto mine eye,
Kills me to look on 't. Let there be no honour
Where there is beauty; truth where semblance; love
Where there's another man; the vows of women
Of no more bondage be to where they are made   140
Than they are to their virtues, which is nothing.
O! above measure false.
    Phi.   Have patience, sir,
And take your ring again; 'tis not yet won:
It may be probable she lost it; or   145
Who knows if one of her women, being corrupted,
Hath stol'n it from her?
    Post.   Very true;
And so I hope he came by 't. Back my ring.
Render to me some corporal sign about her,   150
More evident than this; for this was stolen.
    Iach. By Jupiter, I had it from her arm.
    Post. Hark you, he swears; by Jupiter he swears.
'Tis true; nay, keep the ring; 'tis true: I am sure
She would not lose it; her attendants are   155

---

43 like: *probable*   58 easy: *compliant*   65 question: *debate*   76 my circumstances: *details of my story*   85 watching: *wakefulness*   90 bravely: *excellently*   90, 91 strive ... value; *cf. n.*

104 likely ... themselves; *cf. n.*   104–106 the cutter ... out; *cf. n.*   111 fretted: *embossed*   112 winking: *blind*   114 Depending: *leaning* brands: *torches*   122 up: *put up*   129 outsell: *exceed in value*   136 basilisk: *fabulous serpent, said to kill with its look*   140 bondage: *binding force*   145 probable: *provable*   150 Render: *describe*

All sworn and honourable; they induc'd to steal it!
And by a stranger! No, he hath enjoy'd her;
The cognizance of her incontinency
Is this; she hath bought the name of whore thus dearly.
There, take thy hire; and all the fiends of hell   160
Divide themselves between you!
 Phi.   Sir, be patient:
This is not strong enough to be believ'd
Of one persuaded well of—
 Post.   Never talk on 't;   165
She hath been colted by him.
 Iach.   If you seek
For further satisfying, under her breast,
Worthy the pressing, lies a mole, right proud
Of that most delicate lodging: by my life,   170
I kiss'd it, and it gave me present hunger
To feed again, though full. You do remember
This stain upon her?
 Post.   Ay, and it doth confirm
Another stain, as big as hell can hold,   175
Were there no more but it.
 Iach.   Will you hear more?
 Post. Spare your arithmetic; never count the turns;
Once, and a million!
 Iach.   I'll be sworn,—   180
 Post.   No swearing.
If you will swear you have not done 't, you lie;
And I will kill thee if thou dost deny
Thou 'st made me cuckold.
 Iach.   I'll deny nothing.   185
 Post. O, that I had her here, to tear her limb-meal!
I will go there and do 't, i' the court, before
Her father. I'll do something—   *Exit*
 Phi.   Quite beside
The government of patience! You have won: 190
Let's follow him, and pervert the present wrath
He hath against himself.
 Iach.   With all my heart.   *Exeunt*

❧ SCENE FIFTH ❧

[The Same. Another Room.]
Enter Posthumus.

 Post. Is there no way for men to be, but women
Must be half-workers? We are all bastards;
And that most venerable man which I
Did call my father was I know not where
When I was stamp'd; some coiner with his tools   5
Made me a counterfeit; yet my mother seem'd
The Dian of that time; so doth my wife
The nonpareil of this. O! vengeance, vengeance;
Me of my lawful pleasure she restrain'd
And pray'd me oft forbearance; did it with   10
A pudency so rosy the sweet view on 't
Might well have warm'd old Saturn; that I thought her
As chaste as unsunn'd snow. O! all the devils!

This yellow Iachimo, in an hour,—was 't not?
Or less—at first?—perchance he spoke not, but   15
Like a full-acorn'd boar, a German one,
Cried 'O!' and mounted; found no opposition
But what he look'd for should oppose and she
Should from encounter guard. Could I find out
The woman's part in me! For there's no motion   20
That tends to vice in man but I affirm
It is the woman's part; be it lying, note it,
The woman's; flattering, hers; deceiving, hers;
Lust and rank thoughts, hers, hers; revenges, hers;
Ambitions, covetings, change of prides, disdain,   25
Nice longing, slanders, mutability,
All faults that may be named, nay, that hell knows,
Why, hers, in part, or all; but rather, all;
For even to vice
They are not constant, but are changing still   30
One vice but of a minute old for one
Not half so old as that. I'll write against them,
Detest them, curse them. Yet 'tis greater skill
In a true hate to pray they have their will:
The very devils cannot plague them better.   *Exit.*

ACT THIRD ❧ SCENE FIRST

[Britain. Cymbeline's Palace]
Enter in state, Cymbeline, Queen, Cloten, and Lords, at one door;
and at another, Caius Lucius and Attendants.

 Cym. Now say what would Augustus Cæsar with us?
 Luc. When Julius Cæsar—whose remembrance yet
Lives in men's eyes, and will to ears and tongues
Be theme and hearing ever—was in this Britain,
And conquer'd it, Cassibelan, thine uncle,—   5
Famous in Cæsar's praises, no whit less
Than in his feats deserving it,—for him
And his succession, granted Rome a tribute,
Yearly three thousand pounds, which by thee lately
Is left untender'd.   10
 Queen.   And, to kill the marvel,
Shall be so ever.
 Clo.   There be many Cæsars
Ere such another Julius. Britain is
A world by itself, and we will nothing pay   15
For wearing our own noses.
 Queen.   That opportunity,
Which then they had to take from 's, to resume
We have again. Remember, sir, my liege,
The kings your ancestors, together with   20
The natural bravery of your isle, which stands
As Neptune's park, ribbed and paled in
With oaks unscaleable and roaring waters,
With sands, that will not bear your enemies' boats,
But suck them up to the topmast. A kind of conquest   25
Cæsar made here, but made not here his brag
Of 'came, and saw, and overcame': with shame—
The first that ever touch'd him—he was carried

---

158 cognizance: *visible sign*   **163 strong:** *convincing*   **171 present:** *immediate*   **186 limb-meal:** *limb from limb*   **191 pervert:** *divert*   **8 nonpareil:** *one that has no equal*   **11 pudency:** *modesty*

20 motion: *impulse*   **25 change:** *variety*   **26 Nice:** *lascivious*   **4 hearing:** *tidings*   **21 bravery:** *defiant spirit*   **22 paled:** *fenced*   **23 oaks;** *cf. n.*

From off our coast, twice beaten; and his shipping—
Poor ignorant baubles!—on our terrible seas,　　　　　　30
Like egg-shells mov'd upon their surges, crack'd
As easily 'gainst our rocks: for joy whereof
The fam'd Cassibelan, who was once at point—
O giglot fortune!—to master Cæsar's sword,
Made Lud's town with rejoicing-fires bright,　　　　　35
And Britons strut with courage.

　　　Clo. Come, there's no more tribute to be paid.
Our kingdom is stronger than it was at that time; and, as I
said, there is no moe such Cæsars; other of them may have
crooked noses, but to owe such straight arms, none.　　40

　　　Cym. Son, let your mother end.

　　　Clo. We have yet many among us can gripe as hard as Cassibelan; I do not say I am one, but I have a hand. Why tribute?
why should we pay tribute? If Cæsar can hide the sun from us
with a blanket, or put the moon in his pocket, we will pay　45
him tribute for light; else, sir, no more tribute, pray you now.

　　　Cym. You must know,
Till the injurious Romans did extort
This tribute from us, we were free; Cæsar's ambition—
Which swell'd so much that it did almost stretch　　　50
The sides o' the world—against all colour here
Did put the yoke upon 's; which to shake off
Becomes a warlike people, whom we reckon
Ourselves to be. We do say then to Cæsar,
Our ancestor was tht Mulmutius which　　　　　　55
Ordain'd our laws, whose use the sword of Cæsar
Hath too much mangled; whose repair and franchise
Shall, by the power we hold, be our good deed,
Though Rome be therefore angry. Mulmutius made our laws,
Who was the first of Britain which did put　　　　　60
His brows within a golden crown, and call'd
Himself a king.

　　　Luc.　　　　I am sorry, Cymbeline,
That I am to pronounce Augustus Cæsar—
Cæsar, that hath more kings his servants than　　　65
Thyself domestic officers—thine enemy.
Receive it from me, then: war and confusion
In Cæsar's name pronounce I 'gainst thee: look
For fury not to be resisted. Thus defied,
I thank thee for myself.　　　　　　　　　　70

　　　Cym.　　　　　Thou art welcome, Caius.
Thy Cæsar knighted me; my youth I spent
Much under him; of him I gather'd honour;
Which he to seek of me again, perforce,
Behoves me keep at utterance. I am perfect　　　75
That the Pannonians and Dalmations for
Their liberties are now in arms; a precedent
Which not to read would show the Britons cold:
So Cæsar shall not find them.

　　　Luc.　　　　　　Let proof speak.　　　80

　　　Clo. His majesty bids you welcome. Make pastime with us
a day or two, or longer; if you seek us afterwards in other
terms, you shall find us in our salt-water girdle; if you beat us
out of it, it is yours; if you fall in the adventure, our crows
shall fare the better of you; and there's an end.　　　85

　　　Luc. So, sir.

　　　Cym. I know your master's pleasure and he mine:
All the remain is 'Welcome!'　　　　　　　*Exeunt*

❧ SCENE SECOND ❧

[The Same]
Enter Pisanio, reading of a letter.

　　　Pis. How! of adultery! Wherefore write you not
What monster's her accuser? Leonatus!
O master! what a strange infection
Is fall'n into thy ear! What false Italian—
As poisonous-tongued as handed—hath prevail'd　　5
On thy too ready hearing? Disloyal! No:
She's punish'd for her truth, and undergoes,
More goddess-like than wife-life, such assaults
As would take in some virtue. O my master!
Thy mind to her is now as low as were　　　　10
Thy fortunes. How! that I should murder her?
Upon the love and truth and vows which I
Have made to thy command? I, her? her blood?
If it be so to do good service, never
Let me be counted serviceable. How look I,　　　15
That I should seem to lack humanity
So much as this fact comes to? *[Reads.]* 'Do 't: the letter
That I have sent her by her own command
Shall give thee opportunity':—O damn'd paper!
Black as the ink that's on thee. Senseless bauble,　　20
Art thou a feodary for this act, and look'st
So virgin-like without? Lo! here she comes.
I am ignorant in what I am commanded.

Enter Imogen

　　　Imo. How now, Pisanio!

　　　Pis. Madam, here is a letter from my lord.　　　25

　　　Imo. Who? thy lord? that is my lord, Leonatus.
O! learn'd indeed were that astronomer
That knew the stars as I his characters;
He'd lay the future open. You good gods,
Let what is here contain'd relish of love,　　　　30
Of my lord's health, of his content, yet not
That we two are asunder; let that grieve him,—
Some griefs are med'cinable; that is one of them,
For it doth physic love,—of his content,
All but in that! Good wax, they leave. Bless'd be　　35
You bees that make these locks of counsel! Lovers
And men in dangerous bonds pray not alike;
Though forfeiters you cast in prison, yet
You clasp young Cupid's tables. Good news, gods!
[Reads.] 'Justice, and your father's wrath, should he take me　40
in his dominion, could not be so cruel to me, as you, O the
dearest of creatures, would even renew me with your eyes.
Take notice that I am in Cambria, at Milford-Haven; what
your own love will out of this advise you, follow. So, he

---

30 baubles: *toys*　**33 at point:** *about*　**34 giglot:** *harlot*　**35 Lud's town:** *London*　**39 moe:** *more*　**40 owe:** *own*　**48 injurious:** *insolent*　**51 against all colour:**
with no pretence of right　**56 whose use:** *the operation of which*　**57 franchise:** *free
exercise*　**74 he to seek:** *his seeking*　**75 keep at utterance:** *vindicate*　**perfect:** *well-
assured*　**80 proof speak:** *trial show*

88 remain: *rest*　**9 take in:** *subdue*　**10 to:** *in comparison with*　**17 fact:** *crime*　**21
feodary:** *accomplice*　**23 I am ignorant:** *i.e. I shall appear to be ignorant*　**27 astronomer:** *astrologer*　**28 characters:** *handwriting*　**30 relish:** *have a taste*　**34 For . . .
love;** *cf. n.*　**36, 37 Lovers . . . alike;** *cf. n.*　**39 Cupid's tables:** *love-letters*　**41, 42
as you . . . eyes;** *cf. n.*

wishes you all happiness, that remains loyal to his vow, and   45
your, increasing in love,

                        LEONATUS POSTHUMUS.'

O! for a horse with wings! Hearest thou, Pisanio?
He is at Milford-Haven; read, and tell me
How far 'tis thither. If one of mean affairs   50
May plod it in a week, why may not I
Glide thither in a day? Then, true Pisanio,—
Who long'st, like me, to see thy lord; who long'st,—
O! let me 'bate,—but not like me; yet long'st,
But in a fainter kind:—O! not like me,   55
For mine's beyond beyond; say, and speak thick,—
Love's counsellor should fill the bores of hearing,
To the smothering of the sense,—how far it is
To this same blessed Milford; and, by the way,
Tell me how Wales was made so happy as   60
T' inherit such a haven; but, first of all,
How we may steal from hence, and, for the gap
That we shall make in time, from our hence-going
And our return, to excuse; but first, how get hence.
Why should excuse be born or ere begot?   65
We'll talk of that hereafter. Prithee, speak,
How many score of miles may we well ride
'Twixt hour and hour?
    Pis.   One score 'twixt sun and sun,
Madam, 's enough for you, and too much too.   70
    Imo. Why, one that rode to 's execution, man,
Could never go so slow: I have heard of riding wagers,
Where horses have been nimbler than the sands
The run i' the clock's behalf. But this is foolery;
Go bid my woman feigns a sickness; say   75
She'll home to her father; and provide me presently
A riding-suit, no costlier than would fit
A franklin's housewife.
    Pis.   Madam, you're best consider.
    Imo. I see before me, man; nor here, nor here,   80
Nor what ensues, but have a fog in them,
That I cannot look through. Away, I prithee;
Do as I bid thee. There's no more to say;
Accessible is none but Milford way.   *Exeunt.*

❦ SCENE THIRD ❦

[Wales. A mountainous Country with a Cave]
Enter [from the Cave] Belarius, Guiderius, and Arviragus.

    Bel. A goodly day not to keep house, with such
Whose roof's as low as ours! Stoop, boys; this gate
Instructs you how to adore the heavens, and bows you
To a morning's holy office; the gates of monarchs
Are arch'd so high that giants may jet through   5
And keep their impious turbans on, without
Good morrow to the sun. Hail, thou fair heaven!
We house i' the rock, yet use thee not so hardly
As prouder livers do.
    Gui.   Hail, heaven!   10

    Arv.   Hail, heaven!
    Bel. Now for our mountain sport. Up to yond hill;
Your legs are young; I'll tread these flats. Consider,
When you above perceive me like a crow,
That it is place which lessens and sets off;   15
And you may then revolve what tales I have told you
Of courts, of princes, of the tricks in war;
This service is not service, so being done;
But being so, allow'd: to apprehend thus
Draws us a profit from all things we see,   20
And often, to our comfort, shall we find
The sharded beetle in a safer hold
Than is the full-wing'd eagle. O! this life
Is nobler than attending for a check,
Richer than doing nothing for a bribe,   25
Prouder than rusting in unpaid-for silk;
Such gain the cap of him that makes 'em fine,
Yet keeps his book uncross'd; no life to ours.
    Gui. Out of your proof you speak; we, poor unfledg'd,
Have never wing'd from view o' the nest, nor know not   30
What air's from home. Haply this life is best,
If quiet life be best; sweeter to you
That have a sharper known, well corresponding
With your stiff age; but unto us it is
A cell of ignorance, travelling a-bed,   35
A prison for a debtor that not dares
To stride a limit.
    Arv.   What should we speak of
When we are old as you? when we shall hear
The rain and wind beat dark December, how   40
In this our pinching cave shall we discourse
The freezing hours away? We have seen nothing;
We are beastly, subtle as the fox for prey,
Like warlike as the wolf for what we eat;
Our valour is to chase what flies; our cage   45
We make a choir, as doth the prison'd bird,
And sing our bondage freely.
    Bel.   How you speak!
Did you but know the city's usuries
And felt them knowingly; the art o' the court,   50
As hard to leave as keep, whose top to climb
Is certain falling, or so slippery that
The fear's as bad as falling; the toil of the war,
A pain that only seems to seek out danger
I' the name of fame and honour; which dies i' the search,   55
And hath as oft a slanderous epitaph
As record of fair act; nay, many times,
Doth ill deserve by doing well; what's worse,
Must curtsy at the censure: O boys! this story
The world may read in me; my body's mark'd   60
With Roman swords, and my report was once
First with the best of note; Cymbeline lov'd me,
And when a soldier was the theme, my name
Was not far off; then was I as a tree
Whose boughs did bend with fruit, but, in one night,   65
A storm or robbery, call it what you will,

---

50 of mean affairs: *an ordinary business*   **54 'bate:** *abate, qualify*   **56 thick:** *fast*   **61 inherit:** *possess*   **65** *Cf. n.*   **73, 74 sands … behalf;** *cf. n.*   **78 franklin's:** *freehold-er's*   **79 you're best:** *it were best for you*   **80-82 I see … through;** *cf. n.*   **1 keep house:** *stay in the house*   **5 jet:** *strut*

18, 19 This service … allow'd; *cf. n.*   **19 apprehend:** *understand*   **22 sharded:** *with imperfect wings*   **hold:** *place*   **24 attending:** *doing service*   **check:** *rebuke*   **27, 28** *Cf. n.*   **31 Haply:** *perhaps*   **37 stride a limit:** *pass a bound*   **41 pinching:** *cold*   **43 beastly:** *like mere beasts*   **44 Like:** *as*   **55 which … search;** *cf. n.*   **61 report:** *reputation*   **62 with … note:** *among those of highest fame*

Shook down my mellow hangings, nay, my leaves,
And let me bare to weather.
    Gui.   Uncertain favour!
    Bel. My fault being nothing,—as I have told you oft,—   70
But that two villains, whose false oaths prevail'd
Before my perfect honour, swore to Cymbeline
I was confederate with the Romans; so
Follow'd my banishment, and this twenty years
This rock and these demesnes have been my world,   75
Where I have liv'd at honest freedom, paid
More pious debts to heaven than in all
The fore-end of my time. But, up to the mountains!
This is not hunter's language. He that strikes
The venison first shall be the lord o' the feast;   80
To him the other two shall minister;
And we will fear no poison which attends
In place of greater state. I'll meet you in the valleys.
                 Exeunt [Guiderius and Arviragus].
How hard it is to hide the sparks of nature!
These boys know little they are sons to the king;   85
Nor Cymbeline dreams that they are alive.
They think they are mine; and, though train'd up thus meanly
I' the cave wherein they bow, their thoughts do hit
The roofs of palaces, and nature prompts them
In simple and low things to prince it much   90
Beyond the trick of others. This Polydore,
The heir of Cymbeline and Britain, who
The king his father call'd Guiderius,—Jove!
When on my three-foot stool I sit and tell
The warlike feats I have done, his spirits fly out   95
Into my story: say, 'Thus mine enemy fell,
And thus I set my foot on 's neck;' even then
The princely blood flows in his cheek, he sweats,
Strains his young nerves, and puts himself in posture
That acts my words. The younger brother, Cadwal,—   100
Once Arviragus,—in as like a figure,
Strikes life into my speech and shows much more
His own conceiving. Hark! the game is rous'd.
O Cymbeline! heaven and my conscience knows
Thou didst unjustly banish me; whereon,   105
At three and two years old, I stole these babes,
Thinking to bar thee of succession, as
Thou reft'st me of my lands. Euriphile,
Thou wast their nurse; they took thee for their mother,
And every day do honour to her grave: 110
Myself, Belarius, that am Morgan call'd,
They take for nautral father. The game is up.   *Exit.*

❦   SCENE FOURTH   ❦

[Near Milford-Haven]
Enter Pisanio and Imogen.

    Imo. Thou told'st me, when we came from horse, the place
Was near at hand; ne'er long'd my mother so
To see me first, as I have now. Pisanio! man!
Where is Posthumus? What is in thy mind,
That makes thee stare thus? Wherefore breaks that sigh   5

From the inward of thee? One, but painted thus,
Would be interpreted a thing perplex'd
Beyond self-explication; put thyself
Into a havior of less fear, ere wildness
Vanquish my staider senses. What's the matter?   10
Why tender'st thou that paper to me with
A look untender? If 't be summer news,
Smile to 't before; if winterly, thou need'st
But keep that count'nance still. My husband's hand!
That drug-damn'd Italy hath out-craftied him,   15
And he's at some hard point. Speak, man; thy tongue
May take off some extremity, which to read
Would be even mortal to me.
    Pis.   Please you, read;
And you shall find me, wretched man, a thing   20
The most disdain'd of fortune.
    Imo. [Reads.] 'Thy mistress, Pisanio, hath played the strumpet
in my bed; the testimonies whereof lie bleeding in me. I speak
not out of weak surmises, but from proof as strong as my grief
and as certain as I expect my revenge. That part thou, Pisanio,   25
must act for me, if thy faith be not tainted with the breach of
hers. Let thine own hands take away her life; I shall give thee opportunity at Milford-Haven; she hath my letter for the purpose;
where, if thou fear to strike, and to make me certain it is done,
thou art the pandar to her dishonour and equally to me disloyal.'
    Pis. What shall I need to draw my sword? the paper
Hath cut her throat already. No, 'tis slander,
Whose edge is sharper than the sword, whose tongue
Outvenoms all the worms of Nile, whose breath
Rides on the posting winds and doth belie   35
All corners of the world; kings, queens, and states,
Maids, matrons, nay, the secrets of the grave
This viperous slander enters. What cheer, madam?
    Imo. False to his bed! What is it to be false?
To lie in watch there and to think on him?   40
To weep 'twixt clock and clock? if sleep charge nature,
To break it with a fearful dream of him,
And cry myself awake? that's false to 's bed, is it?
    Pis. Alas! good lady.
    Imo. I false! Thy conscience witness! Iachimo,   45
Thou didst accuse him of incontinency;
Thou then look'dst like a villain; now methinks
Thy favour's good enough. Some jay of Italy,
Whose mother was her painting, hath betray'd him:
Poor I am stale, a garment out of fashion,   50
And, for I am richer than to hang by the walls,
I must be ripp'd; to pieces with me! O!
Men's vows are women's traitors! All good seeming,
By thy revolt, O husband! shall be thought
Put on for villainy; not born where 't grows,   55
But worn a bait for ladies.
    Pis.   Good madam, hear me.

---

67 **hangings:** *fruits*   68 **weather:** *storms*   78 **fore-end:** *early part*   101–103 **in as
like . . . conceiving;** *cf. n.*

9 **havior:** *bearing* **wildness:** *madness*   12 **summer:** *i.e. pleasant*   15 **drug-damn'd:** *detestable for its drugs* **out-crafted:** *outwitted by craft*   16 **point:** *predicament*   17 **extremity:** *extreme rigor*   31 **What:** *why*   34 **worms:** *serpents*   35 **posting:**
speeding   38 **What cheer:** *how do you feel?*   40 **in watch:** *awake*   41 **charge:**
seize   48 **favour:** *appearance* **jay:** *showy, light woman*   49 **Whose mother . . . painting;** *cf. n.*   51 **by the walls:** *in clothes presses*   53 **seeming:** *appearance*

Imo. True honest men, being heard like false Æneas,
Were in his time thought false, and Sinon's weeping
Did scandal many a holy tear, took pity   60
From most true wretchedness; so thou, Posthumus,
Wilt lay the leaven on all proper men;
Goodly and gallant shall be false and perjur'd
From thy great fail. Come, fellow, be thou honest;
Do thou thy master's bidding. When thou seest him,   65
A little witness my obedience; look!
I draw the sword myself; take it, and hit
The innocent mansion of my love, my heart.
Fear not, 'tis empty of all things but grief;
Thy master is not there, who was indeed   70
The riches of it: do his bidding; strike.
Thou mayst be valiant in a better cause,
But now thou seem'st a coward.
     Pis.   Hence, vile instrument!
Thou shalt not damn my hand.   75
     Imo.   Why, I must die;
And if I do not by thy hand, thou art
No servant of thy master's. Against self-slaughter
There is a prohibition so divine
That cravens my weak hand. Come, here's my heart   80
(Something's afore 't; soft, soft! we'll no defence)
                                              [*Taking out letters.*]
Obedient as the scabbard. What is here?
The scriptures of the loyal Leonatus
All turn'd to heresy! Away, away!
Corrupters of my faith; you shall no more   85
Be stomachers to my heart. Thus may poor fools
Believe false teachers; though those that are betrayed
Do feel the treason sharply, yet the traitor
Stands in worse case of woe.
And thou, Posthumus, thou that didst set up   90
My disobedience 'gainst the king my father,
And make me put into contempt the suits
Of princely fellows, shalt hereafter find
It is no act of common passage, but
A strain of rareness; and I grieve myself   95
To think, when thou shalt be disedg'd by her
That now thou tir'st on, how thy memory
Will then be pang'd by me. Prithee, dispatch;
The lamb entreats the butcher; where's thy knife?
Thou art too slow to do thy master's bidding,   100
When I desire it too.
     Pis.   O, gracious lady!
Since I receiv'd command to do this business
I have not slept one wink.
     Imo.   Do 't, and to bed then.   105
Pis. I'll wake mine eyeballs first.
     Imo.   Wherefore then
Didst undertake it? Why hast thou abus'd
So many miles with a pretence? this place?
Mine action and thine own? our horses' labour?   110
The time inviting thee? the perturb'd court,
For my being absent?—whereunto I never

Purpose return.—Why hast thou gone so far,
To be unbent when thou hast ta'en thy stand,
The elected deer before thee?   115
     Pis.   But to win time
To lose so bad employment, in the which
I have consider'd of a course. Good lady,
Hear me with patience.
     Imo.   Talk thy tongue weary; speak: 120
I have heard I am a strumpet, and mine ear,
Therein false struck, can take no greater wound,
Nor tent to bottom that. But speak.
     Pis.   Then, madam,
I thought you would not back again.   125
     Imo.   Most like,
Bringing me here to kill me.
     Pis.   Not so, neither;
But if I were as wise as honest, then
My purpose would prove well. It cannot be   130
But that my master is abus'd; some villain,
Some villain, ay, and singular in his art,
Hath done you both this cursed injury.
     Imo. Some Roman courtezan.
     Pis.   No, on my life.   135
I'll give but notice you are dead and send him
Some bloody sign of it; for 'tis commanded
I should do so: you shall be miss'd at court,
And that will well confirm it.
     Imo.   Why, good fellow,   140
What shall I do the while? where bide? how live?
Or in my life what comfort, when I am
Dead to my husband?
     Pis.   If you'll back to the court,—
     Imo. No court, no father; nor no more ado   145
With that harsh, noble, simple nothing!
That Cloten, whose love-suit hath been to me
As fearful as a siege.
     Pis.   If not at court,
Then not in Britain must you bide.   150
     Imo.   Where then?
Hath Britain all the sun that sines? Day, night,
Are they not but in Britain? I' the world's volume
Our Britain seems as of it, but not in 't;
In a great pool a swan's nest: prithee, think   155
There's livers out of Britain.
     Pis.   I am most glad
You think of other place. The ambassador,
Lucius the Roman, comes to Milford-Haven
To-morrow; now, if you could wear a mind   160
Dark as your fortune is, and but disguise
That which, t'appear itself, must not yet be
But by self-danger, you should tread a course
Pretty, and full of view; yea, haply, near
The residence of Posthumus; so nigh at least   165
That though his actions were not visible, yet
Report should render him hourly to your ear
As truly as he moves.

58, 59 Æneas, Sinon; *cf. n.*   **62 proper:** *honest*   **66 witness:** *bear witness to*   **80 That cravens:** *that it makes cowardly*   **82 Obedient:** *receptive to the sword*   **83 scriptures;** *cf. n.*   **86 stomachers;** *cf. n.*   **89 case:** *condition*   **90 set up:** *instigate*   **93 fellows:** *equals*   **94 passage:** *occurrence*   **95 strain of rareness:** *rare impulse*   **96 disedg'd:** *satiated*   **97 tir'st:** *feedest*   **98 pang'd:** *pained*   **dispatch:** *make haste*   **106 wake:** *torture by watching or waking*

114 unbent: *unprepared, bow unbent*   **115 elected:** *chosen*   **123 tent:** *probe*   **132 singular:** *unmatched*   **146** *Cf. n.*   **153, 154 I' the . . . in 't;** *cf. n.*   **156 livers:** *people living*   **160, 161 wear . . . fortune:** *make your mind as impenetrable as your fortune is dark*   **162, 163 That . . . self-danger:** *your identity which cannot yet be revealed without danger to yourself*   **164 Pretty:** *fair*   **view:** *promise*

Imo.   O! for such means:
Though peril to my modesty, not death on 't,   *170*
I would adventure.
    Pis.   Well, then, here's the point:
You must forget to be a woman; change
Command into obedience; fear and niceness—
The handmaids of all women, or more truly   *175*
Woman it pretty self—into a waggish courage;
Ready in gibes, quick-answer'd, saucy, and
As quarrelous as the weasel; nay, you must
Forget that rarest treasure of your cheek,
Exposing it—but, O! the harder heart,   *180*
Alack! no remedy—to the greedy touch
Of common-kissing Titan, and forget
Your laboursome and dainty trims, wherein
You made great Juno angry.
    Imo.   Nay, be brief: *185*
I see into thy end, and am almost
A man already.
    Pis.   First, make yourself but like one.
Forethinking this, I have already fit—
'Tis in my cloak-bag—doublet, hat, hose, all   *190*
That answer to them; would you in their serving,
And with what imitation you can borrow
From youth of such a season, 'fore noble Lucius
Present yourself, desire his service, tell him
Wherein you are happy,—which will make him know,   *195*
If that his head have ear in music,—doubtless
With joy he will embrace you, for he's honourable,
And, doubling that, most holy. Your means abroad,
You have me, rich; and I will never fail
Beginning nor supplyment.   *200*
    Imo.   Thou art all the comfort
The gods will diet me with. Prithee, away;
There's more to be consider'd, but we'll even
All that good time will give us; this attempt
I'm soldier to, and will abide it with   *205*
A prince's courage. Away, I prithee.
    Pis. Well, madam, we must take a short farewell,
Lest, being miss'd, I be suspected of
Your carriage from the court. My noble mistress,
Here is a box, I had it from the queen,   *210*
What's in 't is precious; if you are sick at sea,
Or stomach-qualm'd at land, a dram of this
Will drive away distemper. To some shade,
And fit you to your manhood. May the gods
Direct you to the best!   *215*
    Imo.   Amen. I thank thee.   *Exeunt.*

❧ SCENE FIFTH ❧

[Cymbeline's Palace]
Enter Cymbeline, Queen, Cloten, Lucius, Lords [and Attendants].

    Cym. Thus far; and so farewell.
    Luc.   Thanks, royal sir.
My emperor hath wrote, I must from hence;
And am right sorry that I must report ye
My master's enemy.   *5*
    Cym.   Our subjects, sir,
Will not endure his yoke; and for ourself
To show less sovereignty than they, must needs
Appear unkinglike.
    Luc.   So, sir: I desire of you   *10*
A conduct over land to Milford-Haven.
Madam, all joy befall your Grace, and you.
    Cym. My lords, you are appointed for that office;
The due of honour in no point omit.
So, farewell, noble Lucius.   *15*
    Luc.   Your hand, my lord.
    Clo. Receive it friendly; but from this time forth
I wear it as your enemy.
    Luc.   Sir, the event
Is yet to name the winner. Fare you well.   *20*
    Cym. Leave not the worthy Lucius, good my lords,
Till he have crossed the Severn. Happiness!   *Exit Lucius, &c.*
    Queen. He goes hence frowning; but it honours us
That we have given him cause.
    Clo.   'Tis all the better;   *25*
Your valiant Britons have their wishes in it.
    Cym. Lucius hath wrote already to the emperor
How it goes here. It fits us therefore ripely
Our chariots and horsemen be in readiness;
The powers that he already hath in Gallia   *30*
Will soon be drawn to head, from whence he moves
His war for Britain.
    Queen.   'Tis not sleepy business;
But must be look'd to speedily and strongly.
    Cym. Our expectation that it would be thus   *35*
Hath made us forward. But, my gentle queen,
Where is our daughter? She hath not appear'd
Before the Roman, nor to us hath tender'd
The duty of the day; she looks us like
A thing more made of malice than of duty: *40*
We have noted it. Call her before us, for
We have been too slight in sufferance.   *[Exit an Attendant.]*
    Queen.   Royal sir.
Since the exile of Posthumus, most retir'd
Hath her life been; the cure whereof, my lord,   *45*
'Tis time must do. Beseech your majesty,
Forbear sharp speeches to her; she's a lady
So tender of rebukes that words are strokes,
And strokes death to her.

Enter a Messenger.

    Cym.   Where is she, sir? How   *50*
Can her contempt be answer'd?
    Mes.   Please you, sir,

---

174 Command: *princely manner of authority* **niceness:** *fastidiousness*   **176 it:** *its* **waggish:** *pert*   **180 harder:** *too hard*   **182 common-kissing Titan:** *the sun, who kisses everyone*   **183 laboursome:** *elaborate* **trims:** *apparel*   **189 Forethinking:** *anticipating* **fit:** *prepared*   **191 in their serving:** *with their help*   **195 happy:** *skillful*   **195, 196 which . . . music;** *cf. n.*   **198 doubling:** *in addition to* **Your means abroad:** *as for the expenses of your journey*   **202 diet:** *feed*   **203 even:** *act up to, keep pace with*   **205 soldier to:** *enlisted to* **abide:** *encounter*   **209 carriage:** *abduction*   **213 distemper:** *illness* **To some shade:** *withdraw to some secluded place*

12 your Grace, and you; *cf. n.*   **19 event:** *outcome*   **28 fits:** *behooves* **ripely:** *promptly*   **31 drawn to head:** *gathered into a military force*   **42 slight in sufferance:** *careless in forbearance*

Her chambers are all lock'd, and there's no answer
That will be given to the loudest of noise we make.

    Queen. My lord, when last I went to visit her,   *55*
She pray'd me to excuse her keeping close,
Whereto constrain'd by her infirmity,
She should that duty leave unpaid to you,
Which daily she was bound to proffer; this
She wish'd me to make known, but our great court   *60*
Made me to blame in memory.

    Cym.   Her doors lock'd!
Not seen of late! Grant, heavens, that which I fear
Prove false!   *Exit.*

    Queen.   Son, I say, follow the king.   *65*

    Clo. That man of hers, Pisanio, her old servant,
I have not seen these two days.

    Queen.   Go, look after.   *Exit [Cloten].*
Pisanio, thou that stand'st so for Posthumus!
He hath a drug of mine; I pray his absence   *70*
Proceed by swallowing that, for he believes
It is a thing most precious. But for her,
Where is she gone? Haply, despair hath seiz'd her,
Or, wing'd with fervour of her love, she's flown
To her desir'd Posthumus. Gone she is   *75*
To death or to dishonour, and my end
Can make good use of either; she being down,
I have the placing of the British crown.

Enter Cloten.

How now, my son!

    Clo.   'Tis certain she is fled.   *80*
Go in and cheer the king; he rages, none
Dare come about him.

    Queen. [*Aside.*]   All the better; may
This night forestall him of the coming day!   *Exit Qu[een].*

    Clo. I love and hate her; for she's fair and royal,   *85*
And that she hath all courtly parts more exquisite
Than lady, ladies, woman; from every one
The best she hath, and she, of all compounded,
Outsells them all. I love her therefore; but
Disdaining me and throwing favours on   *90*
The low Posthumus slanders so her judgment
That what's else rare is chok'd, and in that point
I will conclude to hate her, nay, indeed,
To be reveng'd upon her. For, when fools
Shall—   *95*

Enter Pisanio

        Who is here? What! are you packing, sirrah?
Come hither. Ah! you precious pandar. Villain,
Where is thy lady? In a word; or else
Thou art straightway with the fiends.

    Pis.   O! good my lord.   *100*

    Clo. Where is thy lady? or, by Jupiter
I will not ask again. Close villain,
I'll have this secret from thy heart, or rip
Thy heart to find it. Is she with Posthumus?
From whose so many weights of baseness cannot   *105*
A dram of worth be drawn.

    Pis.   Alas! my lord,

How can she be with him? When was she miss'd?
He is in Rome.

    Clo.   Where is she, sir? Come nearer,   *110*
No further halting; satisfy me home
What is become of her?

    Pis. O! my all-worthy lord.

    Clo.   All-worthy villain!
Discover where thy mistress is at once,   *115*
At the next word; no more of 'worthy lord!'
Speak, or thy silence on the instant is
Thy condemnation and thy death.

    Pis.   Then, sir,
This paper is the history of my knowledge   *120*
Touching her flight.   *[Presenting a letter.]*

    Clo.   Let's see 't. I will pursue her
Even to Augustus' throne.

    Pis.   [*Aside.*] Or this, or perish.
She's far enough; and what he learns by this   *125*
May prove his travel, not her danger.

    Clo.   Hum!

    Pis. [*Aside.*] I'll write to my lord she's dead. O Imogen!
Safe mayst thou wander, safe return again!

    Clo. Sirrah, is this letter true?   *130*

    Pis. Sir, as I think.

    Clo. It is Posthumus' hand; I know 't. Sirrah, if thou
wouldst not be a villain, but do me true service, undergo
those employments wherein I should have cause to use thee
with a serious industry, that is, what villainy soe'er I bid thee
do, to perform it directly and truly, I would think thee an
honest man; thou shouldst neither want my means for thy
relief nor my voice for thy preferment.

    Pis. Well, my good lord.

    Clo. Wilt thou serve me? For since patiently and   *140*
constantly thou hast stuck to the bare fortune of that beggar
Posthumus, thou canst not, in the course of gratitude, but
be a diligent follower of mine. Wilt thou serve me?

    Pis. Sir, I will.

    Clo. Give me thy hand; here's my purse. Hast any of   *145*
thy late master's garments in thy possession?

    Pis. I have, my lord, at my lodging the same suit he
wore when he took leave of my lady and mistress.

    Clo. The first service thou dost me, fetch that suit
hither: let it be thy first service; go.   *150*

    Pis. I shall, my lord.   *Exit.*

    Clo. Meet thee at Milford-Haven!—I forgot to ask him
one thing; I'll remember 't anon—even there, thou villain
Posthumus, will I kill thee. I would these garments were come.
She said upon a time,—the bitterness of it I now belch from my
heart,—that she held the very garment of Posthumus in more
respect than my noble and natural person, together with the
adornment of my qualities. With that suit upon my back will I
ravish her: first kill him, and in her eyes; there shall she see my
valour, which will then be a torment to her contempt.   *160*
He on the ground, my speech of insultment ended on his
dead body, and when my lust hath dined,—which, as I say, to
vex her, I will execute in the clothes that she so praised,—to the
court I'll knock her back, foot her home again. She hath despised
me rejoicingly, and I'll be merry in my revenge.   *165*

---

84 forestall him of: *prevent his living to see*   **96 packing:** *departing*   **102 Close:** *secretive*   **111 home:** *thoroughly*   **124 Or ... perish:** *I must give him this or I shall die*   **133 undergo:** *perform*

Enter Pisanio [with the clothes].

Be those the garments?

   Pis. Ay, my noble lord.

   Clo. How long is 't since she went to Milford-Haven?

   Pis. She can scarce be there yet.

   Clo. Bring this apparel to my chamber; that is the second   *170*
thing that I have commanded thee; the third is, that thou
wilt be a voluntary mute to my design. Be but duteous, and
true preferment shall tender itself to thee. My revenge is
now at Milford; would I had wings to follow it. Come, and
be true.   *Exit.*   *175*

   Pis. Thou bidd'st me to my loss; for true to thee
Were to prove false, which I will never be,
To him that is most true. To Milford go,
And find not her whom thou pursu'st. Flow, flow,
You heavenly blessings, on her! This fool's speed   *180*
Be cross'd with slowness; labour be his meed!   *Exit.*

❧ Scene Sixth ❧

[Wales. Before the Cave of Belarius]
Enter Imogen [in boy's clothes].

   Imo. I see a man's life is a tedious one;
I have tir'd myself, and for two nights together
Have made the ground my bed; I should be sick
But that my resolution helps me. Milford,
When from the mountain-top Pisanio show'd thee,   *5*
Thou wast within a ken. O Jove! I think
Foundations fly the wretched; such, I mean,
Where they should be reliev'd. Two beggars told me
I could not miss my way; will poor folks lie,
That have afflictions on them, knowing 'tis   *10*
A punishment or trial? Yes; no wonder,
When rich ones scarce tell true. To lapse in fulness
Is sorer than to lie for need, and falsehood
Is worse in kings than beggars. My dear lord!
Thou are one o' the false ones. Now I think on thee,   *15*
My hunger's gone, but even before I was
At point to sink for food. But what is this?
Here is a path to 't; 'tis some savage hold;
I were best not call, I dare not call, yet famine,
Ere clean it o'erthrow nature, makes it valiant.   *20*
Plenty and peace breeds cowards, hardness ever
Of hardiness is mother. Ho! Who's here?
If anything that's civil, speak; if savage,
Take or lend. Ho! No answer? Then I'll enter.
Best draw my sword; and if mine enemy   *25*
But fear the sword like me, he'll scarcely look on 't.
Such a foe, good heavens!   *Exit [to the cave].*

Enter Belarius, Guiderius, and Arviragus.

   Bel. You, Polydore, have prov'd best woodman, and
Are master of the feast; Cadwal and I
Will play the cook and servant, 'tis our match;   *30*

The sweat of industry would dry and die
But for the end it works to. Come; our stomachs
Will make what's homely savoury; weariness
Can snore upon the flint when resty sloth
Finds the down pillow hard. Now, peace be here,   *35*
Poor house, that keep'st thyself!

   Gui.   I am throughly weary.

   Arv. I am weak with toil, yet strong in appetite.

   Gui. There is cold meat i' the cave; we'll browse on that,
Whilst what we have kill'd be cook'd.   *40*

   Bel. [Looking into the cave.] Stay; come not in;
But that it eats our victuals, I should think
Here were a fairy.

   Gui.   What's the matter, sir?

   Bel. By Jupiter, an angel! or, if not,   *45*
An earthly paragon! Behold divineness
No elder than a boy!

Enter Imogen.

   Imo. Good masters, harm me not:
Before I enter'd here, I call'd; and thought
To have begg'd or bought what I have took. Good troth,   *50*
I have stol'n nought, nor would not, though I had found
Gold strew'd i' the floor. Here's money for my meat;
I would have left it on the board so soon
As I had made my meal, and parted
With prayers for the provider.   *55*

   Gui.   Money, youth?

   Arv. All gold and silver rather turn to dirt!
As 'tis no better reckon'd but of those
Who worship dirty gods.

   Imo.   I see you're angry.   *60*
Know, if you kill me for my fault, I should
Have died had I not made it.

   Bel.   Whither bound?

   Imo. To Milford-Haven.

   Bel. What's your name?   *65*

   Imo. Fidele, sir. I have a kinsman who
Is bound for Italy; he embark'd at Milford:
To whom being going, almost spent with hunger,
I am fall'n in this offence.

   Bel.   Prithee, fair youth,   *70*
Think us no churls, nor measure our good minds
By this rude place we live in. Well encounter'd!
'Tis almost night; you shall have better cheer
Ere you depart, and thanks to stay and eat it.
Boys, bid him welcome.   *75*

   Gui.   Were you a woman, youth,
I should woo hard but be your groom. In honesty
I bid for you, as I do buy.

   Arv.   I'll make 't my comfort
He is a man; I'll love him as my brother;   *80*
And such a welcome as I'd give to him
After long absence, such is yours: most welcome!
Be sprightly, for you fall 'mongst friends.

   Imo.   'Mongst friends,
If brothers. [Aside.] Would it had been so, that they   *85*
Had been my father's sons; then had my prize

---

172 **a voluntary mute to:** *voluntarily silent respecting*   181 **labour be his meed:** *his pains be his reward*   6 **within a ken:** *in sight*   7 **Foundations;** *cf. n.*   12 **lapse:** *fall into sin*   **fulness:** *prosperity*   13 **sorer:** *more grievous*   16 **even:** *just*   20 **clean:** *entirely*   21 **hardness:** *difficulty*   22 **hardiness:** *courage*   23 **civil:** *civilized*   24 **Take or lend;** *cf. n.*   27 **Such a foe;** *cf. n.*   28 **woodman:** *huntsman*   30 **match:** *compact*

34 **snore upon the flint:** *sleep on a bed of stones*   **resty:** *sluggish*   54 **parted:** *departed*   71 **churls:** *boors*   73 **cheer:** *entertainment*   77, 78 **In honesty . . . buy;** *cf. n.*   83 **sprightly:** *cheerful*   86 **prize:** *value, hence importance*

Been less, and so more equal ballasting
To thee, Posthumus.
 Bel.   He wrings at some distress.
 Gui. Would I could free 't!   *90*
 Arv.   Or I, whate'er it be,
What pain it cost, what danger. Gods!
 Bel.   Hark, boys.
             [Whispering.]

 Imo. [Aside.] Great men,
That had a court no bigger than this cave,   *95*
That did attend themselves and had the virtue
Which their own conscience seal'd them,—laying by
That nothing-gift of differing multitudes,—
Could not out-peer these twain. Pardon me, gods!
I'd change my sex to be companion with them,   *100*
Since Leonatus' false.
 Bel.   It shall be so.
Boys, we'll go dress our hunt. Fair youth, come in:
Discourse is heavy, fasting; when we have supp'd,
We'll mannerly demand thee of thy story,   *105*
So far as thou wilt speak it.
 Gui.   Pray, draw near.
 Arv. The night to the owl and morn to the lark less
welcome.
 Imo. Thanks, sir.   *110*
 Arv.   I pray, draw near.   *Exeunt.*

❧ SCENE SEVENTH ❧

[Rome. A Public Place]
Enter two Senators and Tribunes.

 1. Sen. This is the tenour of the emperor's writ:
That since the common men are now in action
'Gainst the Pannonians and Dalmatians,
And that the legions now in Gallia are
Full weak to undertake our wars against   *5*
The fall'n-off Britons, that we do incite
The gentry to this business. He creates
Lucius pro-consul; and to you the tribunes,
For this immediate levy, he commends
His absolute commission. Long live Cæsar!   *10*
 1. Tri. Is Lucius general of the forces?
 2. Sen.   Ay.
 1. Tri. Remaining now in Gallia?
 1. Sen.   With those legions
Which I have spoke of, whereunto your levy   *15*
Must be supplyant, the words of your commission
Will tie you to the numbers and the time
Of their dispatch.
 1. Tri.   We will discharge our duty.   *Exeunt.*

ACT FOURTH ❧ SCENE FIRST

[Wales. The Forest, near the Cave of Belarius]
Enter Cloten.

 Clo. I am near to the place where they should meet, if
Pisanio have mapped it truly. How fit his garments serve me!
Why should his mistress, who was made by him that made the
tailor, not be fit too? the rather,—saving reverence of the
word,—for 'tis said a woman's fitness comes by fits. Therein   *5*
I must play the workman. I dare speak it to myself,—for it is
not vain-glory for a man and his glass to confer in his own
chamber,—I mean, the lines of my body are as well drawn as
his; no less young, more strong, not beneath him in fortunes,
beyond him in the advantage of the time, above him in birth,
alike conversant in general services, and more remarkable in single oppositions, yet this imperceiverant thing loves him in my
despite. What mortality is! Posthumus, thy head, which now is
growing upon thy shoulders, shall within this hour be off, thy
mistress enforced, thy garments cut to pieces before thy face;   *15*
and all this done, spurn her home to her father, who may
happily be a little angry for my so rough usage, but my
mother, having power of his testiness, shall turn all into my
commendations. My horse is tied up safe; out, sword, and to a
sore purpose! Fortune, put them into my hand! This is the   *20*
very description of their meeting place; and the fellow dares
not deceive me.   *Exit.*

❧ SCENE SECOND ❧

[Before the Cave of Belarius]
Enter [from the Cave] Belarius, Guiderius, Arviragus, and Imogen.

 Bel. [To Imogen.] You are not well; remain here in the cave;
We'll come to you after hunting.
 Arv.   *[To Imogen.]* Brother, stay
here;
Are we not brothers?   *5*
 Imo.   So man and man should be,
But clay and clay differs in dignity,
Whose dust is both alike. I am very sick.
 Gui. Go you to hunting; I'll abide with him.
 Imo. So sick I am not, yet I am not well;   *10*
But not so citizen a wanton as
To seem to die ere sick. So please you, leave me;
Stick to your journal course; the breach of custom
Is breach of all. I am ill; but your being by me
Cannot amend me; society is no comfort   *15*
To one not sociable. I am not very sick,
Since I can reason of it; pray you, trust me here,
I'll rob none but myself, and let me die,
Stealing so poorly.
 Gui.   I love thee; I have spoke it;   *20*
How much the quantity, the weight as much,
As I do love my father.
 Bel.   What! how! how!

---

87 **ballasting:** *weight*   89 **wrings:** *writhes*   97, 98 **laying by ... multitudes;**
cf. n.   98 **out-peer:** *surpass*   103 **hunt:** *game*   6 **fall'n-off:** *revolted*   9 **commends:**
delivers   16 **supplyant:** *supplementary*

2 **fit:** *fittingly*   4 **saving reverence:** *begging pardon*   5 **fitness:** *inclination* (used in an
objectionable sense)   10 **time:** *present circumstances*   11 **general services:** *public affairs*   12 **oppositions:** *combats* **imperceiverant:** *undiscerning*   15 **enforced:** *ravished*   16 **spurn:** *kick*   17 **happily:** *perchance*   18 **power of:** *control over*   11
citizen ... wanton: *city-bred spoilt child, "tenderfoot"*   13 **journal:** *daily*   17 **reason:**
talk   21 **How much:** *however much*

Arv. If it be sin to say so, sir, I yoke me
In my good brother's fault: I know not why   25
I love this youth; and I have heard you say,
Love's reason's without reason: the bier at door,
And a demand who is 't shall die, I'd say
'My father, not this youth.'
    Bel.   *[Aside.]* O noble strain!   30
O worthiness of nature! breed of greatness!
Cowards father cowards, and base things sire base:
Nature hath meal and bran, contempt and grace.
I'm not their father; yet who this should be
Doth miracle itself, lov'd before me.   35
'Tis the ninth hour o' the morn.
    Arv.   Brother, farewell.
    Imo. I wish ye sport.
    Arv.   You health. So please you, sir.
    Imo. [Aside.] These are kind creatures. Gods, what lies I   40
have heard!
Our courtiers say all's savage but at court:
Experience, O, thou disprov'st report!
The imperious seas breed monsters, for the dish
Poor tributary rivers as sweet fish.   45
I am sick still, heart-sick. Pisanio,
I'll now taste of thy drug.   *[Swallows some.]*
    Gui.   I could not stir him,
He said he was gentle, but unfortunate;
Dishonestly afflicted, but yet honest.   50
    Arv. Thus did he answer me; yet said hereafter
I might know more.
    Bel.   To the field, to the field!
[To Imogen.] We'll leave you for this time; go in and rest.
    Arv. We'll not be long away.   55
    Bel.   Pray, be not sick,
For you must be our housewife.
    Imo.   Well or ill,
I am bound to you.   *Exit.*
    Bel.   And shalt be ever.   60
This youth, howe'er distress'd, appears he hath had
Good ancestors.
    Arv.   How angel-like he sings!
    Gui. But his neat cookery! he cut our roots
In characters,   65
And sauc'd our broths as Juno had been sick
And he her dieter.
    Arv.   Nobly he yokes
A smiling with a sigh, as if the sigh
Was that it was, for not being such a smile;   70
The smile mocking the sigh, that it would fly
From so divine a temple, to commix
With winds that sailors rail at.
    Gui.   I do note
That grief and patience, rooted in him both,   75
Mingle their spurs together.
    Arv.   Grow, patience!
And let the stinking-elder, grief, untwine
His perishing root with the increasing vine!
    Bel. It is great morning. Come, away!—Who's there?   80

Enter Cloten.

    Clo. I cannot find those runagates; that villain
Hath mock'd me. I am faint.
    Bel.   'Those runagates!'
Means he not us? I partly know him; 'tis
Cloten, the son o' the queen. I fear some ambush.   85
I saw him not these many years, and yet
I know 'tis he. We are held as outlaws: hence!
    Gui. He is but one. You and my brother search
What companies are near; pray you, away;
Let me alone with him.   *[Exeunt Belarius and Arviragus.]*
    Clo.   Soft! What are you
That fly me thus? some villain mountainers?
I have heard of such. What slave art thou?
    Gui.   A thing
More slavish did I ne'er than answering   95
A 'slave' without a knock.
    Clo.   Thou art a robber,
A law-breaker, a villain. Yield thee, thief.
    Gui. To who? to thee? What art thou? Have not I
An arm as big as thine? a heart as big?   100
Thy words, I grant, are bigger, for I wear not
My dagger in my mouth. Say what thou art,
Why I should yield to thee?
    Clo.   Thou villain base,
Know'st me not by my clothes?   105
    Gui.   No, nor thy tailor, rascal,
Who is thy grandfather: he made those clothes,
Which, as it seems, make thee.
    Clo.   Thou precious varlet,
My tailor made them not.   110
    Gui.   Hence then, and thank
The man that gave them thee. Thou art some fool;
I am loath to beat thee.
    Clo.   Thou injurious thief,
Hear but my name, and tremble.   115
    Gui.   What's thy name?
    Clo. Cloten, thou villain.
    Gui. Cloten, thou double villain, be thy name,
I cannot tremble at it; were it Toad, or Adder, Spider,
'Twould move me sooner.   120
    Clo.   To thy further fear,
Nay, to thy mere confusion, thou shalt know
I am son to the queen.
    Gui.   I'm sorry for 't, not seeming
So worthy as thy birth.   125
    Clo.   Art not afeard?
    Gui. Those that I reverence those I fear, the wise;
At fools I laugh, not fear them.
    Clo.   Die the death:
When I have slain thee with my proper hand,   130
I'll follow those that even now fled hence,
And on the gates of Lud's town set your heads:
Yield, rustic mountaineer.   *Fight and exeunt.*

Enter Belarius and Arviragus.

    Bel. No companies abroad?
    Arv. None in the world. You did mistake him, sure.   135

---

30 strain: *lineage*   35 miracle; *cf. n.*   48 stir him: *move him to tell his story*   49
gentle: *of gentle birth*   65 characters: *letters*   76 spurs: *roots*   78 stinking-elder;
cf. n.   79 with ... vine: *i.e. as the vine, patience grows*   80 great morning: *broad day*

96 A 'slave': *i.e. the epithet 'slave'*   105 my clothes; *cf. n.*   109 precious: *arrant*   varlet:
knave   122 mere: *sheer*   130 proper: *own*

Bel. I cannot tell; long is it since I saw him,
But time hath nothing blurr'd those lines of favour
Which then he wore; the snatches in his voice,
And burst of speaking, were as his. I am absolute
'Twas very Cloten.   *140*
 Arv.   In this place we left them:
I wish my brother make good time with him,
You say he is so fell.
 Bel.   Being scarce made up,
I mean, to man, he had not apprehension   *145*
Of roaring terrors; for defect of judgment
Is oft the cause of fear. But see, thy brother.

   Enter Guiderius [with Cloten's head].

 Gui. This Cloten was a fool, an empty purse,
There was no money in 't. Not Hercules
Could have knock'd out his brains, for he had none; *150*
Yet I not doing this, the fool had borne
My head as I do his.
 Bel.   What hast thou done?
 Gui. I am perfect what: cut off one Cloten's head,
Son to the queen after his own report,   *155*
Who call'd me traitor, mountaineer, and swore,
With his own single hand he'd take us in,
Displace our heads where—thank the gods!—they grow,
And set them on Lud's town.
 Bel.   We are all undone. *160*
 Gui. Why, worthy father, what have we to lose,
But that he swore to take, our lives? The law
Protects not us; then why should we be tender
To let an arrogant piece of flesh threat us,
Play judge and executioner all himself,   *165*
For we do fear the law? What company
Discover you abroad?
 Bel.   No single soul
Can we set eye on; but in all safe reason
He must have some attendants. Though his humour *170*
Was nothing but mutation, ay, and that
From one bad thing to worse; not frenzy, not
Absolute madness could so far have rav'd
To bring him here alone. Although, perhaps,
It may be heard at court that such as we   *175*
Cave here, hunt here, are outlaws, and in time
May make some stronger head; the which he hearing,—
As it is like him,—might break out, and swear
He'd fetch us in; yet is 't not probable
To come alone, either he so undertaking,   *180*
Or they so suffering; then, on good ground we fear,
If we do fear this body hath a tail
More perilous than the head.
 Arv.   Let ordinance
Come as the gods foresay it; howsoe'er,   *185*
My brother hath done well.
 Bel.   I had no mind
To hunt this day; the boy Fidele's sickness
Did make my way long forth.
 Gui.   With his own sword, *190*

Which he did wave against my throat, I have ta'en
His head from him; I'll throw 't into the creek
Behind our rock, and let it to the sea,
And tell the fishes he's the queen's son, Cloten:
That's all I reck.   *Exit.* *195*
 Bel.   I fear 'twill be reveng'd.
Would, Polydore, thou hadst not done 't! though valour
Becomes thee well enough.
 Arv.   Would I had done 't,
So the revenge alone pursu'd me! Polydore,   *200*
I love thee brotherly, but envy much
Thou hast robb'd me of this deed; I would revenges,
That possible strength might meet, would seek us through
And put us to our answer.
 Bel.   Well, 'tis done.— *205*
We'll hunt no more to-day, nor seek for danger
Where there's no profit. I prithee, to our rock;
You and Fidele play the cooks; I'll stay
Till hasty Polydore return, and bring him
To dinner presently.   *210*
 Arv.   Poor sick Fidele!
I'll willingly to him; to gain his colour
I'd let a parish of such Clotens blood,
And praise myself for charity.   *Exit.*
 Bel.   O thou goddess! *215*
Thou, divine Nature thou, thyself thou blazon'st
In these two princely boys. They are as gentle
As zephyrs, blowing below the violet,
Not wagging his sweet head; and yet as rough,
Their royal blood enchaf'd, as the rud'st wind, *220*
That by the top doth take the mountain pine,
And make him stoop to the vale. 'Tis wonder
That an invisible instinct should frame them
To royalty unlearn'd, honour untaught,
Civility not seen from other, valour   *225*
That wildly grows in them, but yields a crop
As if it had been sow'd! Yet still it's strange
What Cloten's being here to us portends,
Or what his death will bring us.

   Enter Guiderius.

 Gui.   Where's my brother? *230*
I have sent Cloten's clotpoll down the stream,
In embassy to his mother; his body's hostage
For his return.   *Solemn music.*
 Bel. My ingenious instrument!
Hark! Polydore, it sounds; but what occasion *235*
Hath Cadwal now to give it motion? Hark!
 Gui. Is he at home?
 Bel.   He went hence even now.
 Gui. What does he mean? since death of my dear'st mother
It did not speak before. All solemn things   *240*
Should answer solemn accidents. The matter?
Triumphs for nothing and lamenting toys
Is jollity for apes and grief for boys.
Is Cadwal mad?

Enter Arviragus, with Imogen, [as] dead, bearing her in his arms.

---

138 snatches: *sudden checks* 139 absolute: *certain* 140 very Cloten: *Cloten him-self* 143 fell: *fierce* 144–147 Being scarce ... fear; *cf. n.* 166 For: *because* 169 safe: *sound* 171 nothing but mutation: *for constant change* 179 fetch us in: *capture us* 184 ordinance: *divine decree* 189 way long forth: *walking forth seem long*

195 reck: *care* 202–204 I would ... answer; *cf. n.* 212 gain: *restore* 220 en-chaf'd: *excited* 225 seen from other: *observed in others* 226 wildly: *without cultiva-tion* 231 clotpoll: *thick head* 241 answer: *correspond to* accidents: *occurrences* 242 lamenting toys: *lamentation for trifles* 243 apes: *fools*

Bel.　　　　　Look! here he comes, 　　　　　245
And brings the dire occasion in his arms
Of what we blame him for.
　　Arv.　　　　　　　　The bird is dead
That we have made so much on. I had rather
Have skipp'd from sixteen years of age to sixty, 　　250
To have turn'd my leaping-time into a crutch,
Than have seen this.
　　Gui.　　　　　O, sweetest, fairest lily!
My brother wears thee not the one half so well
As when thou grew'st thyself. 　　　　　255
　　Bel.　　　　　　　O melancholy!
Who ever yet could sound thy bottom? find
The ooze, to show what coast thy sluggish crare
Might easiliest harbour in? Thou blessed thing!
Jove knows what man thou mightst have made; but ay! 　260
Thou diedst, a most rare boy, of melancholy.
How found you him?
　　Arv.　　　　　Stark, as you see:
Thus smiling, as some fly had tickled slumber,
Not as death's dart, being laugh'd at; his right cheek 　265
Reposing on a cushion.
　　Gui.　　　　　Where?
　　Arv.　　　　　　　O' the floor,
His arms thus leagu'd; I thought he slept, and put
My clouted brogues from off my feet, whose rudeness 　270
Answer'd my steps too loud.
　　Gui.　　　　　　Why, he but sleeps:
If he be gone, he'll make his grave a bed;
With female fairies with his tomb be haunted,
And worms will not come to thee. 　　　　275
　　Arv.　　　　　　　　With fairest flowers,
While summer lasts and I live here, Fidele,
I'll sweeten thy sad grave; thou shalt not lack
The flower that's like thy face, pale primrose, nor
The azur'd hare-bell, like thy veins, no, nor 　　280
The leaf of eglantine, whom not to slander.
Out-sweeten'd not thy breath: the ruddock would
With charitable bill,—O bill sore-shaming
Those rich-left heirs, that let their fathers lie
Without a monument,—bring thee all this; 　　285
Yea, and furr'd moss besides, when flowers are none,
To winter-ground thy corse.
　　Gui.　　　　　Prithee, have done,
And do not play in wench-like words with that
Which is so serious. Let us bury him, 　　　290
And not protract with admiration what
Is now due debt. To the grave!
　　Arv.　　　　　Say, where shall's lay him?
　　Gui. By good Euriphile, our mother.
　　Arv.　　　　　　Be 't so: 　　　295
And let us, Polydore, though now our voices
Have got the mannish crack, sing him to the ground,
As once to our mother, use like note and words,
Save that Euriphile must be Fidele.
　　Gui. Cadwal, 　　　　　300
I cannot sing; I'll weep, and word it with thee;

For notes of sorrow out of tune are worse
Than priests and fanes that lie.
　　Arv.　　　　　We'll speak it then.
　　Bel. Great griefs, I see, medicine the less, for Cloten 　305
Is quite forgot. He was a queen's son, boys,
And though he came our enemy, remember
He was paid for that; though mean and mighty, rotting
Together, have one dust, yet reverence—
That angel of the world—doth make distinction 　310
Of place 'tween high and low. Our foe was princely,
And though you took his life, as being our foe,
Yet bury him as a prince.
　　Gui.　　　　　Pray you, fetch him hither.
Thersites' body is as good as Ajax' 　　　315
When neither are alive.
　　Arv.　　　　　If you'll go fetch him,
We'll say our song the whilst. Brother, begin. 　*[Exit Belarius.]*
　　Gui. Nay, Cadwal, we must lay his head to the east;
My father hath a reason for 't. 　　　　320
　　Arv.　　　　　'Tis true.
　　Gui. Come on then, and remove him.
　　Arv.　　　　　　So, begin.
　　Gui. 'Fear no more the heat o' the sun,
　　　　Nor the furious winter's rages; 　　　325
　　　Thou thy wordly task hast done,
　　　　Home art gone, and ta'en thy wages;
　　　Golden lads and girls all must,
　　　As chimney-sweepers, come to dust.
　　Arv. 'Fear no more the frown o' the great, 　　330
　　　　Thou art past the tyrant's stroke:
　　　Care no more to clothe and eat;
　　　　To thee the reed is as the oak:
　　　The sceptre, learning, physic, must
　　　　All follow this, and come to dust. 　　335
　　Gui. 'Fear no more the lightning-flash,
　　Arv. 'Nor the all-dreaded thunder-stone;
　　Gui. 'Fear not slander, censure rash;
　　Arv. 'Thou has finished joy and moan:
　　Both. 'All lovers young, all lovers must 　　340
　　　　Consign to thee, and come to dust.
　　Gui. 'No exorciser harm thee!
　　Arv. 'Nor no withcraft charm thee!
　　Gui. 'Ghost unlaid forbear thee!
　　Arv. 'Nothing ill come near thee! 　　　345
　　Both. 'Quiet consummation have;
　　　　And renowned be thy grave!'

Enter Belarius, with the body of Cloten.

　　Gui. We have done our obsequies. Come, lay him down.
　　Bel. Here's a few flowers, but 'bout midnight, more;
The herbs that have on them cold dew o' the night 　350
Are strewings fitt'st for graves. Upon their faces.
You were as flowers, now wither'd; even so
These herblets shall, which we upon you strew.
Come on, away; apart upon our knees.
The ground that gave them first has them again; 　355
Their pleasures here are past, so is their pain.

Exeunt [Belarius, Guiderius, and Arviragus].

---

251 leaping-time: *youth* 　**258 crare:** *small vessel* 　**260 ay:** *alas* 　**270 clouted brogues:** *heavy shoes studded with hobnails* 　**282 ruddock:** *robin* 　**287 winter-ground:** *cover for the winter* 　**289 wench-like:** *womanish* 　**293 shall's:** *shall we* 　**298 to our mother:** *i.e. as once we sang our mother* 　**like:** *the same*

303 fanes: *temple oracles* 　**305 medicine:** *cure* 　**308 paid:** *punished* 　**315 Thersites' ... Ajax';** *cf. n.* 　**337 thunder-stone:** *thunderbolt* 　**341 Consign:** *subscribe* 　**342 exorciser:** *conjurer* 　**351 Upon ... faces;** *cf. n.*

Imogen awakes.

Imo. Yes, sir, to Milford-Haven; which is the way?
I thank you. By yond bush? Pray, how far thither?
'Ods pittikins! can it be six mile yet?
I have gone all night: Faith, I'll lie down and sleep. 360
[*Seeing the body of Cloten.*] But, soft! no bedfellow!
O gods and goddesses!
These flowers are like the pleasures of the world;
This bloody man, the care on 't. I hope I dream;
For so I thought I was a cave-keeper, 365
And cook to honest creatures; but 'tis not so,
'Twas but a bolt of nothing, shot at nothing,
Which the brain makes of fumes. Our very eyes
Are sometimes like our judgments, blind. Good faith,
I tremble still with fear; but if there be 370
Yet left in heaven as small a drop of pity
As a wren's eye, fear'd gods, a part of it!
The dream's here still; even when I wake, it is
Without me, as within me; not imagin'd, felt.
A headless man! The garments of Posthumus! 375
I know the shap of 's leg, this is his hand,
His foot Mercurial, his Martial thigh,
The brawns of Hercules, but his Jovial face—
Murder in heaven? How! 'Tis gone. Pisanio,
All curses madded Hecuba gave the Greeks, 380
And mine to boot, he darted on thee! Thou,
Conspir'd with that irregulous devil, Cloten,
Hast here cut off my lord. To write and read
Be henceforth treacherous! Damn'd Pisanio
Hath with his forged letters, damn'd Pisanio, 385
From this most bravest vessel of the world
Struck the main-top! O Posthumus! alas!
Where is thy head? where's that? Ay, me! where's that?
Pisanio might have kill'd thee at the heart,
And left this head on. How should this be? Pisanio? 390
'Tis he and Cloten; malice and lucre in them
Have laid this woe here. O! 'tis pregnant, pregnant!
The drug he gave me, which he said was precious
And cordial to me, have I not found it
Murderous to the senses? That confirms it home; 395
This is Pisanio's deed, and Cloten's: O!
Give colour to my pale cheek with thy blood,
That we the horrider may seem to those
Which chance to find us. O! my lord, my lord.

                         [*Falls on the body.*]

Enter Lucius, Captains, [other Officers,] and a Soothsayer.

Cap. To them the legions garrison'd in Gallia, 400
After your will, have cross'd the sea, attending
You here at Milford-Haven with your ships:
They are in readiness.
   Luc.   But what from Rome?
   Cap. The senate hath stirr'd up the confiners 405
And gentlemen of Italy, most willing spirits,
That promise noble service; and they come
Under the conduct of bold Iachimo,
Sienna's brother.
   Luc.   When expect you them? 410

Cap. With the next benefit o' the wind.
   Luc.   This forwardness
Makes our hopes fair. Command our present numbers
Be muster'd; bid the captains look to 't. Now, sir,
What have you dream'd of late of this war's purpose? 415
   Sooth. Last night the very gods show'd me a vision,—
I fast and pray'd for their intelligence,—thus:
I saw Jove's bird, the Roman eagle, wing'd
From the spongy south to this part of the west,
There vanish'd in the sunbeams; which portends 420
Unless my sins abuse my divination,
Success to the Roman host.
   Luc.   Dream often so,
And never false. Soft, ho! what trunk is here
Without his top? The ruin speaks that sometime 425
It was a worthy building. How! a page!
Or dead or sleeping on him? But dead rather,
For nature doth abhor to make his bed
With the defunct, or sleep upon the dead.
Let's see the boy's face. 430
   Cap.   He's alive, my lord.
   Luc. He'll, then, instruct us of this body. Young one,
Inform us of thy fortunes, for it seems
They crave to be demanded. Who is this
Thou mak'st thy bloody pillow? Or who was he 435
That, otherwise than noble nature did,
Hath alter'd that good picture? What's thy interest
In this sad wrack? How came it? Who is it?
Who art thou?
   Imo.   I am nothing; or if not, 440
Nothing to be were better. This was my master,
A very valiant Briton and a good,
That here by mountaineers lies slain. Alas!
There are no more such masters; I may wander
From east to occident, cry out for service, 445
Try many, all good, serve truly, never
Find such another master.
   Luc.   'Lack, good youth!
Thou mov'st no less with thy complaining than
Thy master is bleeding. Say his name, good friend. 450
   Imo. Richard du Champ.—[*Aside.*] If I do lie and do
No harm by it, though the gods hear, I hope
They'll pardon it.—Say you, sir?
   Luc.   Thy name?
   Imo.   Fidele, sir. 455
   Luc. Thou dost approve thyself the very same;
Thy name well fits thy faith, thy faith thy name.
Wilt take thy chance with me? I will not say
Thou shalt be so well master'd, but be sure
No less belov'd. The Roman emperor's letters, 460
Sent by a consul to me, should not sooner
Than thine own worth prefer thee. Go with me.
   Imo. I'll follow, sir. But first, an 't please the gods,
I'll hide my master from the flies, as deep
As these poor pickaxes can dig; and when 465
With wild wood-leaves and weeds I ha' strew'd his grave,
And on it said a century of prayers,
Such as I can, twice o'er, I'll weep and sigh;

359 **'Ods:** *God's* **pittikins:** *diminutive form of pity*   **368 fumes:** *vapors*   377, 378
Cf. *n.*   **380 Hecuba;** *cf. n.*   **382 irregulous:** *lawless*   **392 pregnant:** *obvious*   400
To them: *in addition to them*   **405 confiners:** *inhabitants*

419 **spongy:** *wet*   **421 abuse:** *pervert*   **434 demanded:** *inquired*   **435, 436 otherwise**
... picture; *cf. n.*   **449 complaining:** *mourning*   **456 approve:** *prove*   **463 an 't:**
if it   **465 poor pickaxes:** *i.e. her fingers*   **467 century:** *hundred*

And, leaving so his service, follow you,
So please you entertain me.   470
    Luc.   Ay, good youth,
And rather father thee than master thee.
My friends,
The boy hath taught us manly duties; let us
Find out the prettiest daisied plot we can,   475
And make him with our pikes and partisans
A grave; come, arm him. Boy, he is preferr'd
By thee to us, and he shall be interr'd
As soldiers can. Be cheerful; wipe thine eyes:
Some falls are means the happier to arise.   *Exeunt.*

❧ SCENE THIRD ❧

[Cymbeline's Palace]
Enter Cymbeline, Lords, Pisanio [and Attendants].

    Cym. Again; and bring me word how 'tis with her.
                     [Exit an Attendant.]
A fever with the absence of her son,
A madness, of which her life's in danger. Heavens!
How deeply you at once do touch me. Imogen,   5
The great part of my comfort, gone; my queen
Upon a desperate bed, and in a time
When fearful wars point at me; her son gone,
So needful for this present: it strikes me, past
The hope of comfort. But for thee, fellow,   10
Who needs must know of her departure and
Dost seem so ignorant, we'll enforce it from thee
By a sharp torture.
    Pis.   Sir, my life is yours,
I humbly set it at your will; but, for my mistress,   15
I nothing know where she remains, why gone,
Nor when she purposes return. Beseech your highness,
Hold me your loyal servant.
    1. Lord.   Good my liege,
The day that she was missing he was here;   20
I dare be bound he's true and shall perform
All parts of his subjection loyally. For Cloten,
There wants no diligence in seeking him,
And will, no doubt, be found.
    Cym.   The time is troublesome.   25
[To Pisanio.] We'll slip you for a season; but our jealousy
Does yet depend.
    1. Lord.   So please your majesty,
The Roman legions, all from Gallia drawn,
Are landed on your coast, with a supply   30
Of Roman gentlemen, by the senate sent.
    Cym. Now for the counsel of my son and queen!
I am amaz'd with matter.
    1. Lord.   Good my liege,
Your preparation can affront no less   35
Than what you hear of; come more, for more you're ready:
The want is but to put those powers in motion
That long to move.

    Cym.   I thank you. Let's withdraw;
And meet the time as it seeks us. We fear not   40
What can from Italy annoy us, but
We grieve at chances here. Away!
                     Exeunt [all but Pisanio].
    Pis. I heard no letter from my master since
I wrote him Imogen was slain; 'tis strange;   45
Nor hear I from my mistress, who did promise
To yield me often tidings; neither know I
What is betid to Cloten; but remain
Perplex'd in all: the heavens still must work.
Wherein I am false I am honest; not true to be true: 50
These present wars shall find I love my country,
Even to the note o' the king, or I'll fall in them.
All other doubts, by time let them be clear'd;
Fortune brings in some boats that are not steer'd.   *Exit.*

❧ SCENE FOURTH ❧

[Wales. Before the Cave of Belarius]
Enter Belarius, Guiderius, and Arviragus.

    Gui. The noise is round about us.
    Bel.   Let us from it.
    Arv. What pleasure, sir, find we in life, to lock it
From action and adventure?
    Gui.   Nay, what hope   5
Have we in hiding us? this way, the Romans
Must or for Britons slay us, or receive us
For barbarous and unnatural revolts
During their use, and slay us after.
    Bel.   Sons,   10
We'll higher to the mountains; there secure us.
To the king's party there's no going; newness
Of Cloten's death,—we being not known, not muster'd
Among the bands,—may drive us to a render
Where we have liv'd, and so extort from 's that   15
Which we have done, whose answer would be death
Drawn on with torture.
    Gui.   This is, sir, a doubt
In such a time nothing becoming you,
Nor satisfying us.   20
    Arv.   It is not likely
That when they hear the Roman horses neigh,
Behold their quarter'd fires, have both their eyes
And ears so cloy'd importantly as now,
That they will waste their time upon our note,   25
To know from whence we are.
    Bel.   O! I am known
Of many in the army; many years,
Though Cloten then but young, you see, not wore him
From my remembrance. And, besides, the king   30
Hath not deserv'd my service nor your loves
Who find in my exile the want of breeding,
The certainty of this hard life; aye hopeless
To have the courtesy your cradle promis'd,

---

470 **entertain:** *take into service*   476 **partisans:** *combined spear and battle axe*   477 **arm him:** *carry him (i.e. the body of Cloten) in your arms*   4 **touch:** *wound*   8 **present:** *emergency*   18 **Hold:** *consider*   22 **subjection:** *service as a subject*   23 **wants:** *lacks*   26 **slip you:** *let you go*   **jealousy:** *suspicion*   27 **depend:** *remain in suspense*   33 **amaz'd:** *confused*   **matter:** *affairs of importance*   35 *Cf. n.*

48 **betid:** *befallen*   51 **find:** *reveal*   53 **note:** *notice*   8 **revolts:** *rebels*   9 **During their use:** *while they can use us*   14 **render:** *account*   23 **quarter'd fires:** *camp fires*   24 **cloy'd importantly:** *crammed with matters of importance*   25 **upon our note:** *in noticing us*   33 **aye:** *forever*

But to be still hot summer's tanlings and   *35*
The shrinking slaves of winter.
    Gui.   Than be so
Better to cease to be. Pray, sir, to the army:
I and my brother are not known; yourself,
So out of thought, and thereto so o'ergrown,   *40*
Cannot be question'd.
    Arv.   By this sun that shines,
I'll thither: what thing is it that I never
Did see man die! scarce ever look'd on blood
But that of coward hares, hot goats, and venison!   *45*
Never bestrid a horse, save one that had
A rider like myself, who ne'er wore rowel
Nor iron on his heel! I am asham'd
To look upon the holy sun, to have
The benefit of his bless'd beams, remaining   *50*
So long a poor unknown.
    Gui.   By heavens! I'll go:
If you will bless me, sir, and give me leave,
I'll take the better care, but if you will not,
The hazard therefore due fall on me by   *55*
The hands of Romans.
    Arv.   So say I; amen.
    Bel. No reason I, since of your lives you set
So slight a valuation, should reserve
My crack'd one to more care. Have with you, boys!   *60*
If in your country wars you chance to die,
That is my bed too, lads, and there I'll lie:
Lead, lead.—*[Aside.]* The time seems long; their blood
thinks scorn,
Till it fly out and show them princes born.   *Exeunt.*

ACT FIFTH   SCENE FIRST

[Britain. The Roman Camp]
Enter Posthumus [with a bloody handkerchief].

    Post. Yea, bloody cloth, I'll keep thee, for I wish'd
Thou shouldst be colour'd thus. You married ones,
If each of you should take this course, how many
Must murder wives much better than themselves
For wrying but a little! O Pisanio!   *5*
Every good servant does not all commands;
No bond but to do just ones. Gods! if you
Should have ta'en vengeance on my faults, I never
Had liv'd to put on this; so had you sav'd
The noble Imogen to repent, and struck   *10*
Me, wretch more worth your vengeance. But, alack!
You snatch some hence for little faults; that's love,
To have them fall no more; you some permit
To second ills with ills, each elder worse,
And make them dread it, to the doers' thrift.   *15*
But Imogen is your own; do your best wills,
And make me bless'd to obey. I am brought hither
Among the Italian gentry, and to fight
Against my lady's kingdom; 'tis enough

That, Britain, I have kill'd thy mistress; peace!   *20*
I'll give no wound to thee. Therefore good heavens,
Hear patiently my purpose: I'll disrobe me
Of these Italian weeds, and suit myself
As does a Briton peasant; so I'll fight
Against the part I come with, so I'll die   *25*
For thee, O Imogen! even for whom my life
Is, every breath, a death: and thus, unknown,
Pitied nor hated, to the face of peril
Myself I'll dedicate. Let me make men know
More valour in me than my habits show.   *30*
Gods! put the strength o' the Leonati in me.
To shame the guise o' the world, I will begin
The fashion, less without and more within.   *Exit.*

❧ SCENE SECOND ❧

[Field of Battle between the British and Roman Camps]
Enter Lucius, Iachimo, and the Roman Army at one door and the
Britain army at another; Leonatus Posthumus following like a
poor soldier. They march over and go out. Then enter again
in skirmish, Iachimo and Posthumus; he vanquisheth and
disarmeth Iachimo, and then leaves him.

    Iach. The heaviness and guilt within my bosom
Takes off my manhood: I have belied a lady,
The princess of this country, and the air on 't
Revengingly enfeebles me; or could this carl,
A very drudge of nature's, have subdu'd me   *5*
In my profession? Knighthoods and honours, borne
As I wear mine, are titles but of scorn.
If that thy gentry, Britain, go before
This lout as he exceeds our lords, the odds
Is that we scarce are men and you are gods.   *Exit.*

The battle continues; the Britons fly; Cymbeline is taken. Then
enter, to his rescue, Belarius, Guiderius, and Arviragus.

    Bel. Stand, stand! We have the advantage of the ground.   *10*
The lane is guarded; nothing routs us but
The villainy of our fears.
    Gui. ⎫
    Arv. ⎭   Stand, stand, and fight!

Enter Posthumus, and seconds the Britons. They rescue Cymbeline,
and exeunt. Then enter Lucius, Iachimo, and Imogen.

    Luc. Away, boy, from the troops, and save thyself;   *15*
For friends kill friends, and the disorder's such
As war were hoodwink'd.
    Iach.   'Tis their fresh supplies.
    Luc. It is a day turn'd strangely; or betimes
Let's reinforce, or fly.   *Exeunt.*

---

35 tanlings: *creatures tanned by the sun*   **40 thereto so o'ergrown:** *also so overgrown with hair*   **43 what thing is it:** *what a thing it is*   **54 take ... care:** *have ... protection*   **64 thinks scorn:** *despises everything*   **5 wrying:** *swerving*   **7 No bond:** *there is no obligation*   **9 put on:** *instigate*   **14 elder:** *of later date*   **15** *Cf. n.*

23 weeds: *garments*   **suit:** *dress*   **25 part:** *party*   **30 habits:** *clothes*   **32 guise:** *custom*   **1 heaviness and guilt:** *i.e. the weight of guilt*   **4 carl:** *peasant*   **18 hoodwink'd:** *blindfolded*   **20 betimes:** *quickly*

⚓ SCENE THIRD ⚓

[Another Part of the Field]
Enter Posthumus and a Britain Lord.

Lord. Cam'st thou from where they made the stand?
Post.   I did:
Though you, it seems, come from the fliers.
  Lord.   I did.
   Post. No blame be to you, sir; for all was lost,   5
But that the heavens fought. The king himself
Of his wings destitute, the army broken,
And but the backs of Britons seen, all flying
Through a strait lane; the enemy full-hearted,
Lolling the tongue with slaughtering, having work   10
More plentiful than tools to do 't, struck down
Some mortally, some slightly touch'd, some falling
Merely through fear; that the strait pass was damm'd
With dead men hurt behind, and cowards living
To die with lengthen'd shame.   15
  Lord.   Where was this lane?
   Post. Close by the battle, ditch'd, and wall'd with turf;
Which gave advantage to an ancient soldier,
An honest one, I warrant; who deserv'd
So long a breeding as his white beard came to,   20
In doing this for his country; athwart the lane,
He, with two striplings, lads more like to run
The country base than to commit such slaughter,—
With faces fit for masks, or rather fairer
Than those for preservation cas'd, or shame,   25
Made good the passage; cried to those that fled,
'Our Britain's harts die flying, not our men:
To darkness fleet souls that fly backwards. Stand!
Or we are Romans, and will give you that
Like beasts which you shun beastly, and may save,   30
But to look back in frown: stand, stand!' These three,
Three thousand confident, in act as many,—
For three performers are the file when all
The rest do nothing,—with this word, 'Stand, stand!'
Accommodated by the place, more charming   35
With their own nobleness,—which could have turn'd
A distaff to a lance,—gilded pale looks,
Part shame, part spirit renew'd; that some, turn'd coward
But by example,—O! a sin of war,
Damn'd in the first beginners,—'gan to look   40
The way that they did, and to grin like lions
Upon the pikes o' the hunters. Then began
A stop i' the chaser, a retire, anon
A rout, confusion thick; forthwith they fly
Chickens the way which they stoop'd eagles; slaves,   45
The strides they victors made. And now our cowards—
Like fragments in hard voyages—became
The life o' the need; having found the back door open
Of the unguarded hearts, Heavens! how they wound;
Some slain before; some dying; some their freinds   50
O'er-borne i' the former wave; ten, chas'd by one,
Are now each one the slaughter-man of twenty;

Those that would die or ere resist are grown
The mortal bugs o' the field!
  Lord.   This was strange chance: 55
A narrow lane, an old man, and two boys!
   Post. Nay, do not wonder at it; you are made
Rather to wonder at the things you hear
Than to work any. Will you rime upon 't,
And vent it for a mockery? Here is one: 60
'Two boys, an old man twice a boy, a lane,
Preserv'd the Britons, was the Romans' bane.'
  Lord. Nay, be not angry, sir.
   Post.   'Lack! to what end?
Who dares not stand his foe, I'll be his friend;   65
For if he'll do, as he is made to do,
I know he'll quickly fly my friendship too.
You have put me into rime.
  Lord.   Farewell; you're angry.   *Exit.*
   Post. Still going?—This is a lord! O noble misery!   70
To be i' the field, and ask, 'what news?' of me!
To-day how many would have given their honours
To have sav'd their carcasses! took heel to do 't,
And yet died too! I, in mine own woe charm'd,
Could not find death where I did hear him groan,   75
Nor feel him where he struck: being an ugly monster,
'Tis strange he hides him in fresh cups, soft beds,
Sweet words; or hath more ministers than we
That draw his knives i' the war. Well, I will find him;
For being now a favourer to the Briton,   80
No more a Briton, I have resum'd again
The part I came in; fight I will no more,
But yield me to the veriest hind that shall
Once touch my shoulder. Great the slaughter is
Here made by the Roman; great the answer be   85
Britons must take. For me, my ransom's death;
On either side I come to spend my breath,
Which neither here I'll keep nor bear again,
But end it by some means for Imogen.

Enter two [British] Captains, and Soldiers.

  1. Cap. Great Jupiter be praised! Lucius is taken.   90
'Tis thought the old man and his sons were angels.
  2. Cap. There was a fourth man, in a silly habit,
That gave th' affront with them.
  1. Cap.   So 'tis reported;
But none of 'em can be found. Stand! who is there?   95
   Post. A Roman,
Who had not now been drooping here, if seconds
Had answer'd him.
  2. Cap.   Lay hands on him; a dog!
A leg of Rome shall not return to tell   100
What crows have peck'd them here. He brags his service
As if he were of note: bring him to the king.

*Enter Cymbeline, Belarius, Guiderius, Arviragus, Pisanio, and
Roman Captives. The Captains present Posthumus to Cymbeline, who delivers him over to a Gaoler [then exeunt omnes].*

---

9 **strait:** *narrow*   23 **country base:** *country game of prisoners' base*   24 **fit for:** *i.e.
beautiful enough to be protected by*   25 **shame:** *modesty*   28 **fleet:** *vanish*   28–31
Stand … frown; *cf. n.*   32 **confident:** *in confidence*   33 **file:** *body of troops*   35
more charming: *charming others*   45 **stoop'd:** *plunged*   45, 46 **slaves … made;**
cf. n.   48 **life o' the need:** *what sustained life in time of need*

53 **or ere:** *sooner than*   54 **bugs:** *terrors*   70 **noble misery:** *miserable nobility*   78
more: *other*   80 **now:** *but now*   83 **hind:** *menial*   92 **silly:** *simple*   93 **affront:**
attack   97 **seconds:** *followers*   98 **answer'd:** *supported*

❧ SCENE FOURTH ❧

[Britain. A Prison]
Enter Posthumus and [two] Gaoler[s].

1. Gaol. You shall not now be stol'n, you have locks upon
you;
So graze as you find pasture.
   2. Gaol.   Ay, or a stomach. *[Exeunt Gaolers.]*
   Post. Most welcome, bondage! for thou art a way,   *5*
I think, to liberty. Yet am I better
Than one that's sick o' the gout, since he had rather
Groan so in perpetuity than be cur'd
By the sure physician death, who is the key
To unbar these locks. My conscience, thou art fetter'd   *10*
More than my shanks and wrists: you good gods, give me
The penitent instrument to pick that bolt;
Then, free for ever! Is 't enough I am sorry?
So children temporal fathers do appease;
Gods are more full of mercy. Must I repent?   *15*
I cannot do it better than in gyves,
Desir'd more than constrain'd; to satisfy,
If of my freedom 'tis the main part, take
No stricter render of me than my all.
I know you are more clement than vile men,   *20*
Who of their broken debtors take a third,
A sixth, a tenth, letting them thrive again
On their abatement: that's not my desire;
For Imogen's dear life take mine; and though
'Tis not so dear, yet 'tis a life; you coin'd it;   *25*
'Tween man and man they weigh not every stamp;
Though light, take pieces for the figure's sake:
You rather mine, being yours; and so great powers,
If you will take this audit, take this life,
And cancel these cold bonds. O Imogen!   *30*
I'll speak to thee in silence.   *[Sleeps.]*

*Solemn music. Enter, as in an apparition, Sicilus Leonatus,
father to Posthumus, an old man, attired like a warrior; leading in his hand an ancient matron, his wife, and mother to
Posthumus, with music before them. Then, after other music,
follow the two young Leonati, brothers to Posthumus, with
wounds, as they died in the wars. They circle Posthumus
round, as he lies sleeping.*

Sici.   No more, thou thunder-master, show
      Thy spite on mortal flies:
   With Mars fall out, with Juno chide,
      That thy adulteries   *35*
         Rates and revenges.
   Hath my poor boy done aught but well,
      Whose face I never saw?
   I died whilst in the womb he stay'd
      Attending nature's law: *40*
   Whose father then—as men report,
      Thou orphans' father art—
   Thou shouldst have been, and shielded him
      From this earth-vexing smart.
Moth. Lucina lent not me her aid,   *45*

      But took me in my throes;
   That from me was Posthumus ript,
      Came crying 'mongst his foes,
      A thing of pity!
Sici.   Great nature, like his ancestry,   *50*
      Moulded the stuff so fair,
   That he deserv'd the praise o' the world,
      As great Sicilius' heir.
1. Bro. When once he was mature for man,
      In Britain where was he   *55*
   That could stand up his parallel,
      Or fruitful object be
   In eye of Imogen, that best
      Could deem his dignity?
Moth. With marriage wherefore was he mock'd,   *60*
      To be exil'd, and thrown
   From Leonati seat, and cast
      From her his dearest one,
        Sweet Imogen?
Sici.   Why did you suffer Iachimo,   *65*
      Slight thing of Italy,
   To taint his nobler heart and brain
      With needless jealousy;
   And to become the geck and scorn
      O' the other's villainy?   *70*
2. Bro. For this from stiller seats we came,
      Our parents and us twain,
   That striking in our country's cause
      Fell bravely and were slain;
   Our fealty and Tenantius' right   *75*
      With honour to maintain.
1. Bro. Like hardiment Posthumus hath
      To Cymbeline perform'd:
   Then Jupiter, thou king of gods,
      Why hast thou thus adjourn'd   *80*
   The graces for his merits due,
      Being all to dolours turn'd?
Sici.   Thy crystal window ope; look out;
      No longer exercise
   Upon a valiant race thy harsh   *85*
      And potent injuries.
Moth. Since, Jupiter, our son is good,
      Take off his miseries.
Sici.   Peep through thy marble mansion; help!
      Or we poor ghosts will cry   *90*
   To the shining synod of the rest
      Against thy deity.
Both Bro. Help, Jupiter! or we appeal,
      And from thy justice fly.

*Jupiter descends in thunder and lightining, sitting upon an eagle;
he throws a thunderbolt. The Ghosts fall on their knees.*

Jup. No more, you petty spirits of region low,   *95*
Offend our hearing; hush! How dare you ghosts
Accuse the thunderer, whose bolt, you know,
   Sky-planted, batters all rebelling coasts?
Poor shadows of Elysium, hence; and rest
   Upon your never-withering banks of flowers: *100*

---

1 *Cf. n.*   **4 stomach:** *appetite*   **12 penitent instrument:** *instrument of penance*
13–19 *Cf. n.*   **16 gyves:** *fetters*   **23 abatement:** *diminished capital*   **26 stamp:**
coin   **28 You rather ... yours;** *cf. n.*   **32 thunder-master:** *Jupiter*   **36 Rates:**
chides   **40 Attending:** *awaiting*   **45 Lucina:** *goddess who assists in childbirth*

59 deem: *judge*   **69 geck:** *fool*   **77 hardiment:** *deeds of valor*   **80 adjourn'd:** *delayed*   **82 dolours:** *sorrows*   **91 synod:** *assembly of gods*

Be not with mortal accidents opprest;
  No care of yours it is; you know 'tis ours.
Whom best I love I cross, to make my gift,
  The more delay'd, delighted. Be content;
Your low-laid son our godhead will uplift: *105*
  His comforts thrive, his trials well are spent.
Our Jovial star reign'd at his birth, and in
  Our temple was he married. Rise, and fade!
He shall be lord of Lady Imogen,
  And happier much by his affliction made.   *110*
This tablet lay upon his breast, wherein
  Our pleasure his full fortune doth confine;
and so, away: no further with your din
  Express impatience, lest you stir up mine.
  Mount, eagle, to my palace crystalline.   *Ascends. 115*
    Sici. He came in thunder; his celestial breath
Was sulphurous to smell; the holy eagle
Stoop'd, as to foot us; his ascension is
More sweet than our bless'd fields; his royal bird
Prunes the immortal wing and cloys his beak,   *120*
As when his god is pleas'd.
    All.   Thanks, Jupiter!
    Sici. The marble pavement closes; he is enter'd
His radiant roof. Away! and, to be blest,
Let us with care perform his great behest.   *[The Ghosts] vanish.*
    Post. [*Awakening.*] Sleep, thou hast been a grandsire, and
begot
A father to me; and thou hast created
A mother and two brothers. But—O scorn!—
Gone! they went hence so soon as they were born: *130*
And so I am awake. Poor wretches, that depend
On greatness' favour dream as I have done;
Wake, and find nothing. But, alas! I swerve:
Many dream not to find, neither deserve,
And yet are steep'd in favours; so am I,   *135*
That have this golden chance and know not why.
What fairies haunt this ground? A book? O rare one!
Be not, as is our fangled world, a garment
Nobler than that it covers: let thy effects
So follow, to be most unlike our courtiers,   *140*
As good as promise.   *Reads.*

'Whenas a lion's whelp shall, to himself unknown, without
seeking find, and he embraced by a piece of tender air; and
when from a stately cedar shall be lopped branches, which,
being dead many years, shall after revive, be jointed to the
old stock, and freshly grow, then shall Posthumus end his miseries, Britain be fortunate, and flourish in peace and plenty.'

'Tis still a dream, or else such stuff as madmen
Tongue and brain not; either both or nothing;
Or senseless speaking, or a speaking such   *150*
As sense cannot untie. Be what it is,
The action of my life is like it, which
I'll keep, if but for sympathy.

          Enter Gaoler.

    Gaol. Come, sir, are you ready for death?

    Post. Over-roasted rather; ready long ago.   *155*
    Gaol. Hanging is the word, sir: if you be ready for that,
you are well cooked.
    Post. So, if I prove a good repast to the spectators, the
dish pays the shot.
    Gaol. A heavy reckoning for you, sir; but the comfort is, *160*
you shall be called to no more payments, fear no more tavern-
bills, which are often the sadness of parting, as the procuring
of mirth. You come in faint for want of meat, depart reeling
with too much drink, sorry that you have paid too much; and
sorry that you are paid too much; purse and brain both empty;
the brain the heavier for being too light, the purse too light,
being drawn of heaviness: of this contradiction you shall now
be quit. O! the charity of a penny cord; it sums up thousands
in a trice: you have no true debitor and creditor but it; of
what's past, is, and to come, the discharge. Your neck, sir, *170*
is pen, book and counters; so the acquittance follows.
    Post. I am merrier to die than thou art to live.
    Gaol. Indeed, sir, he that sleeps feels not the toothache; but
a man that were to sleep your sleep, and a hangman to help
him to bed, I think he would change places with his officer;
for look you, sir, you know not which way you shall go.
    Post. Yes, indeed do I, fellow.
    Gaol. Your death has eyes in 's head, then; I have not
seen him so pictur'd: you must either be directed by some
that take upon them to know, or take upon yourself that   *180*
which I am sure you do not know, or jump the after
inquiry on your own peril: and how you shall speed in your
journey's end, I think you'll never return to tell one.
    Post. I tell thee, fellow, there are none want eyes to
direct them the way I am going but such as wink and will *185*
not use them.
    Gaol. What an infinite mock is this, that a man should
have the best use of eyes to see the way of blindness! I am
sure hanging's the way of winking.

          Enter a Messenger.

    Mess. Knock off his manacles; bring your prisoner to the *190*
king.
    Post. Thou bring'st good news; I am called to be made free.
    Gaol. I'll be hang'd, then.
    Post. Thou shalt be then freer than a gaoler; no bolts for
the dead.   *Exeunt [all but Gaoler]. 195*
    Gaol. Unless a man would marry a gallows and beget
young gibbets, I never saw one so prone. Yet, on my
conscience, there are verier knaves desire to live, for all he
be a Roman; and there be some of them too that die
against their wills; so should I, if I were one. I would we were *200*
all of one mind, and one mind good; O! there were
desolation of gaolers an gallowses. I speak against my present
profit, but my wish hath a perferment in 't.   *Exit.*

---

104 delighted: *delightful*   **118 as to foot us:** *as if to seize us in his talons*   **120 Prunes:**
preens **cloys:** *claws*   **123 marble pavement:** *sky*   **133 swerve:** *err*   **137 book:** *writ-*
ing   **138 fangled:** *fond of finery*   **142 Whenas:** *when*   **149 Tongue:** *speak* **brain:**
understand

157 well cooked: *cf. n.*   **159 the dish . . . shot:** *cf. n.*   **178 death:** *i.e. a death's head*
or skull   **180 take upon:** *pretend*   **181 jump:** *risk*   **182 speed:** *fare*   **185 wink:**
shut their eyes   **197 prone:** *eager*   **203 hath a preferment:** *cf. n.*

❧ SCENE FIFTH ❧

[Cymbeline's Tent]
Enter Cymbeline, Belarius, Guiderius, Arviragus, Pisanio, Lords
[Officers, and Attendants].

Cym. Stand by my side, you whom the gods have made
Preservers of my throne. Woe is my heart
That the poor soldier that so richly fought,
Whose rags sham'd gilded arms, whose naked breast
Stepp'd before targes of proof, cannot be found: 5
He shall be happy that can find him, if
Our grace can make him so.
Bel.   I never saw
Such noble fury in so poor a thing;
Such precious deeds in one that promis'd nought   10
But beggary and poor looks—
Cym.   No tidings of him?
Pis. He hath been search'd among the dead and living,
But no trace of him.
Cym.   To my grief, I am   15
The heir of his reward; which I will add
                  [To Belarius, Guiderius, and Arviragus.]
To you, the liver, heart, and brain of Britain,
By whom, I grant, she lives. 'Tis now the time
To ask of whence you are; report it.
Bel.   Sir,   20
In Cambria are we born, and gentlemen:
Further to boast were neither true nor modest,
Unless I add, we are honest.
Cym.   Bow your knees.
Arise, my knights o' the battle: I create you   25
Companions to our person, and will fit you
With dignities becoming your estates.

Enter Cornelius and Ladies.

There's business in these faces. Why so sadly
Greet you our victory? you look like Romans,
And not o' the court of Britain.   30
Cor.   Hail, great king!
To sour your happiness, I must report
The queen is dead.
Cym.   Whom worse than a physician
Would this report become? But I consider,   35
By medicine life may be prolong'd, yet death
Will seize the doctor too. How ended she?
Cor. With horror, madly dying, like her life;
Which, being cruel to the world, concluded
Most cruel to herself. What she confess'd   40
I will report, so please you: these her women
Can trip me if I err, who with wet cheeks
Were present when she finish'd.
Cym.   Prithee, say.
Cor. First, she confess'd she never lov'd you, only   45
Affected greatness got by you, not you;
Married your royalty, was wife to your place;
Abhorr'd your person.
Cym.   She alone knew this;

And, but she spoke it dying, I would not   50
Believe her lips in opening it. Proceed.
Cor. Your daughter, whom she bore in hand to love
With such integrity, she did confess
Was as a scorpion to her sight; whose life,
But that her flight prevented it, she had   55
Ta'en off by poison.
Cym.   O most delicate fiend!
Who is 't can read a woman? Is there more?
Cor. More, sir, and worse. She did confess she had
For you a mortal mineral; which, being took,   60
Should by the minute feed on life, and ling'ring,
By inches waste you; in which time she purpos'd,
By watching, weeping, tendance, kissing, to
O'ercome you with her show; yea, and in time—
When she had fitted you with her craft—to work   65
Her son into the adoption of the crown;
But failing of her end by his strange absence,
Grew shameless-desperate; open'd, in despite
Of heaven and men, her purposes; repented
The evils she hatch'd were not effected: so,   70
Despairing died.
Cym.   Heard you all this, her women?
1. Lady. We did, so please your highness.
Cym.   Mine eyes
Were not in fault, for she was beautiful;   75
Mine ears, that heard her flattery; nor my heart,
That thought her like her seeming: it had been vicious
To have mistrusted her: yet, O my daughter!
That it was folly in me, thou mayst say,
And prove it in thy feeling. Heaven mend all!   80

Enter Lucius, Iachimo, the Soothsayer, and other Roman Prisoners:
Posthumus behind, and Imogen.

Thou com'st not, Caius, now for tribute; that
The Britons have raz'd out, though with the loss
Of many a bold one; whose kinsmen have made suit
That their good souls may be appeas'd with slaughter
Of you their captives, which ourself have granted: 85
So, think of your estate.
Luc. Consider, sir, the chance of war: the day
Was yours by accident; had it gone with us,
We should not, when the blood was cool, have threaten'd
Our prisoners with the sword. But since the gods   90
Will have it thus, that nothing but our lives
May be call'd ransom, let it come; sufficeth,
A Roman with a Roman's heart can suffer;
Augustus lives to think on 't; and so much
For my peculiar care. This one thing only   95
I will entreat; my boy, a Briton born,
Let him be ransom'd; never master had
A page so kind, so duteous, diligent,
So tender over his occasions, true,
So feat, so nurse-like. Let his virtue join   100
With my request, which I'll make bold your highness
Cannot deny; he hath done no Briton harm,

---

5 **targes:** *shields*   13 **search'd:** *sought*   21 **Cambria:** *Wales*   35 **consider:** *remember*
46 **Affected:** *desired*

51 **opening:** *revealing*   52 **bore in hand:** *pretended*   55 **prevented:** *anticipated*   57
delicate: *artful*   60 **mortal mineral:** *deadly poison*   65 **fitted:** *prepared*   77 **vicious:**
wrong   82 **raz'd:** *blotted*   86 **estate:** *situation*   92 **sufficeth:** *it suffices*   95 **peculiar:** *personal*   99 **So tender . . . occasions:** *so considerate in attending to his duties*   100
feat: *dextrous*   **virtue:** *merit*

Though he have serv'd a Roman. Save him, sir,
And spare no blood beside.

    Cym. I have surely seen him;   *105*
His favour is familiar to me. Boy,
Thou hast look'd thyself into my grace,
And art mine own. I know not why nor wherefore
To say, 'live, boy': ne'er thank thy master; live:
And ask of Cymbeline what boon thou wilt,   *110*
Fitting my bounty and thy state, I'll give it;
Yea, though thou do demand a prisoner,
The noblest ta'en.

    Imo.   I humbly thank your highness.

    Luc. I do not bid thee beg my life, good lad;   *115*
And yet I know thou wilt.

    Imo.   No, no: alack!
There's other work in hand. I see a thing
Bitter to me as death; your life, good master,
Must shuffle for itself.   *120*

    Luc.   The boy disdains me,
He leaves me, scorns me; briefly die their joys
That place them on the truth of girls and boys.
Why stands he so perplex'd?

    Cym.   What wouldst thou, boy?   *125*
I love thee more and more; think more and more
What's best to ask. Know'st him thou look'st on? speak;
Wilt have him live? Is he thy kin? thy friend?

    Imo. He is a Roman; no more kin to me
Than I to your highness; who, being born your vassal,   *130*
Am something nearer.

    Cym.   Wherefore ey'st him so?

    Imo. I'll tell you, sir, in private, if you please
To give me hearing.

    Cym.   Ay, with all my heart,   *135*
And lend my best attention. What's thy name?

    Imo. Fidele, sir.

    Cym.   Thou'rt my good youth, my page;
I'll be thy master: walk with me; speak freely.

               [Cymbeline and Imogen converse apart.]

    Bel. Is not this boy reviv'd from death?   *140*

    Arv.   One sand another
Not more resembles;—that sweet rosy lad
Who died, and was Fidele. What think you?

    Gui. The same dead thing alive.

    Bel. Peace, peace! see further; he eyes us not; forbear;   *145*
Creatures may be alike; were 't he, I am sure
He would have spoke to us.

    Gui.   But we saw him dead.

    Bel. Be silent; let's see further.

    Pis.   *[Aside.]* It is my mistress: *150*
Since she is living, let the time run on
To good, or bad.

             [Cymbeline and Imogen come forward.]

    Cym. *[To Imogen.]* Come, stand thou by our side:
Make thy demand aloud.—*[To Iachimo.]* Sir, step you forth;
Give answer to this boy, and do it freely,   *155*
Or, by our greatness and the grace of it,
Which is our honour, bitter torture shall
Winnow the truth from falsehood.—*[To Imogen.]* On, speak
to him.

    Imo. My boon is, that this gentleman may render   *160*
Of whom he had this ring.

    Post.   *[Aside.]* What's that to him?

    Cym. That diamond upon your finger, say
How came it yours?

    Iach. Thou'lt torture me to leave unspoken that   *165*
Which, to be spoke, would torture thee.

    Cym.   How! me?

    Iach. I am glad to be constrain'd to utter that
Which torments me to conceal. By villainy
I got this ring; 'twas Leonatus' jewel,   *170*
Whom thou didst banish, and—which more may grieve thee,
As it doth me—a nobler sir ne'er liv'd
'Twixt sky and ground. Wilt thou hear more, my lord?

    Cym. All that belongs to this.

    Iach.   That paragon, thy daughter,—
For whom my heart drops blood, and my false spirits
Quail to remember,—Give me leave; I faint.

    Cym. My daughter! what of her? Renew thy strength;
I had rather thou shouldst live while nature will
Than die ere I hear more. Strive, man, and speak.   *180*

    Iach. Upon a time,—unhappy was the clock
That struck the hour!—it was in Rome,—accurs'd
The mansion where!—'twas at a feast—O, would
Our viands had been poison'd, or at least
Those which I heav'd to head!—the good Posthumus,—   *185*
What should I say? he was too good to be
Where ill men were; and was the best of all
Amongst the rar'st of good ones;—sitting sadly
Hearing us praise our loves of Italy
For beauty that made barren the swell'd boast   *190*
Of him that best could speak; for feature laming
The shrine of Venus, or straight-pight Minerva,
Postures beyond brief nature; for condition,
A shop of all the qualities that man
Loves woman for; besides that hook of wiving,   *195*
Fairness which strikes the eye.

    Cym.   I stand on fire.
Come to the matter.

    Iach.   All too soon I shall,
Unless thou wouldst grieve quickly. This Posthumus—   *200*
Most like a noble lord in love, and one
That had a royal lover—took his hint;
And, not dispraising whom we prais'd,—therein
He was as calm as virtue,—he began
His mistress' picture; which by his tongue being made,   *205*
And then a mind put in 't, either our brags
Were crack'd of kitchen trulls, or his description
Prov'd us unspeaking sots.

    Cym.   Nay, nay, to the purpose.

    Iach. Your daughter's chastity, there it begins.   *210*
He spake of her as Dian had hot dreams,
And she alone were cold; whereat I, wretch,
Made scruple of his praise, and wager'd with him
Pieces of gold 'gainst this, which then he wore
Upon his honour'd finger, to attain   *215*

---

118 **a thing:** *i.e. the ring on Iachimo's finger*

165 **to leave:** *for leaving*   188 **sadly:** *soberly*   191 **feature:** *proportion of parts* **laming:** *making seem deformed*   192 **shrine:** *statue* **straight-pight:** *erect*   193 **Postures . . . nature;** *cf. n.* **condition:** *character*   194 **shop:** *storehouse*   195 **hook of wiving;** *cf. n.*   207 **crack'd:** *uttered boastfully* **trulls:** *sluts*   208 **unspeaking sots:** *fools incapable of speech*   211 **as:** *as if, in comparison*   213 **Made scruple:** *expressed doubt*

In suit the place of his bed, and win this ring
By hers and mine adultery. He, true knight,
No lesser of her honour confident
Than I did truly find her, stakes this ring;
And would so, had it been a carbuncle   *220*
Of Phœbus' wheel; and might so safely, had it
Been all the worth of 's car. Away to Britain
Post I in this design. Well may you, sir,
Remember me at court, where I was taught
Of your chaste daughter the wide difference   *225*
'Twixt amorous and villainous. Being thus quench'd
Of hope, not longing, mine Italian brain
'Gan in your duller Britain operate
Most vilely; for my vantage, excellent;
And, to be brief, my practice so prevail'd,   *230*
That I return'd with simular proof enough
To make the noble Leonatus mad,
By wounding his belief in her renown
With tokens thus, and thus; averring notes
Of chamber-hanging, pictures, this her bracelet;—   *235*
Oh cunning! how I got it!—nay, some marks
Of secret on her person, that he could not
But think her bond of chastity quite crack'd,
I having ta'en the forfeit. Whereupon,—
Methinks I see him now,—   *240*
    Post. [Coming forward.] Ay, so thou dost,
Italian fiend!—Ay me, most credulous fool,
Egregious murderer, thief, anything
That's due to all the villains past, in being,
To come. O! give me cord, or knife, or poison,   *245*
Some upright justicer. Thou king, send out
For torturers ingenious; it is I
That all the abhorred things o' the earth amend
By being worse than they. I am Posthumus,
That kill'd thy daughter; villain-like, I lie;   *250*
That caus'd a lesser villain than myself,
A sacrilegious thief, to do 't; the temple
Of virtue was she; yea, and she herself.
Spit, and throw stones, cast mire upon me, set
The dogs o' the street to bay me; every villain   *255*
Be call'd Posthumus Leonatus; and
Be villainy less than 'twas! O Imogen!
My queen, my life, my wife! O Imogen,
Imogen, Imogen!
    Imo.   Peace, my lord! hear, hear!   *260*
    Post. Shall's have a play of this? Thou scornful page,
There lie thy part.   *[Striking her: she falls.]*
    Pis.   O, gentlemen, help!
Mine, and your mistress! O! my Lord Posthumus,
You ne'er kill'd Imogen till now. Help, help!   *265*
Mine honour'd lady!
    Cym.   Does the world go round?
    Post. How comes these staggers on me?
    Pis.   Wake, my mistress!
    Cym. If this be so, the gods do mean to strike me   *270*
To death with mortal joy.
    Pis.   How fares my mistress?

    Imo. O! get thee from my sight:
Thou gav'st me poison: dangerous fellow, hence!
Breathe not where princes are.   *275*
    Cym.   The tune of Imogen!
    Pis. Lady,
The gods throw stones of sulphur on me, if
That box I gave you was not thought by me
A precious thing: I had it from the queen.   *280*
    Cym. New matter still?
    Imo.   It poison'd me.
    Cor.   O gods!
I left out one thing which the queen confess'd,
Which must approve thee honest: 'If Pisanio   *285*
Have,' and she, 'given his mistress that confection
Which I gave him for cordial, she is serv'd
As I would serve a rat.'
    Cym.   What's this, Cornelius?
    Cor. The queen, sir, very oft importun'd me   *290*
To temper poisons for her, still pretending
The satisfaction of her knowledge only
In killing creatures vile, as cats and dogs,
Of no esteem; I, dreading that her purpose
Was of more danger, did compound for her   *295*
A certain stuff, which, being ta'en, would cease
The present power of life, but in short time
All offices of nature should again
Do their due functions. Have you ta'en of it?
    Imo. Most like I did, for I was dead.   *300*
    Bel.   My boys,
There was our error.
    Gui.   This is, sure, Fidele.
    Imo. Why did you throw your wedded lady from you?
Think that you are upon a rock; and now   *305*
Throw me again.   *[Embracing him.]*
    Post.   Hang there like fruit, my soul,
Till the tree die!
    Cym.   How now, my flesh, my child!
What, mak'st thou me a dullard in this act?   *310*
Wilt thou not speak to me?
    Imo. [Kneeling.]   Your blessing, sir.
    Bel. [To Guiderius and Arviragus.] Though you did love
this youth, I blame ye not;
You had a motive for 't.   *315*
    Cym.   My tears that fall
Prove holy water on thee! Imogen,
Thy mother's dead.
    Imo.   I am sorry for 't, my lord.
    Cym. O, she was naught; and long of her it was   *320*
That we meet here so strangely; but her son
Is gone, we know not how, nor where.
    Pis.   My lord,
Now fear is from me, I'll speak troth. Lord Cloten,
Upon my lady's missing, came to me   *325*
With his sword drawn, foam'd at the mouth, and swore
If I discover'd not which way she was gone,
It was my instant death. By accident,
I had a feigned letter of my master's
Then in my pocket, which directed him   *330*

216 In suit: *by suing* **221 Of Phœbus' wheel:** *from the wheel of the chariot of the sun* **222 car:** *chariot* **230 practice:** *stratogem* **231 simular:** *specious* **233 renown:** *good name* **234 averring:** *avouching* **248 amend:** *make seem less vile* **253 she herself:** *i.e. virtue hers* **268 staggers:** *dizziness*

276 tune: *voice* **278 stones of sulphur:** *thunderbolts* **291 temper:** *compound* **305 rock:** *precipice* **314 blame ye not:** *i.e. am not surprised* **315 motive:** *reason* **320 naught:** *worthless* **long of:** *because of* **324 troth:** *truth*

To seek her on the mountains near to Milford;
Where, in a frenzy, in my master's garments,
Which he enforc'd from me, away he posts
With unchaste purpose and with oath to violate
My lady's honour; what became of him   *335*
I further know not.
    Gui.   Let me end the story:
I slew him there.
    Cym.   Marry, the gods forfend!
I would not thy good deeds should from my lips   *340*
Pluck a hard sentence: prithee, valiant youth,
Deny 't again.
    Gui.   I have spoke it, and I did it.
    Cym. He was a prince.
    Gui. A most incivil one. The wrongs he did me   *345*
Were nothing princelike; for he did provoke me
With language that would make me spurn the sea
If it could so roar to me. I cut off 's head;
And am right glad he is not standing here
To tell this tale of mine.   *350*
    Cym.   I am sorry for thee:
By thine own tongue thou art condemn'd, and must
Endure our law. Thou'rt dead.
    Imo.   That headless man
I thought had been my lord.   *355*
    Cym.   Bind the offender,
And take him from our presence.
    Bel.   Stay, sir king:
This man is better than the man he slew,
As well descended as thyself; and hath   *360*
More of thee merited than a band of Clotens
Had ever scar for. *[To the Guard.]* Let his arms alone;
They were not born for bondage.
    Cym.   Why, old soldier,
Wilt thou undo the worth thou art unpaid for   *365*
By tasting of our wrath? How of descent
As good as we?
    Arv.   In that he spake too far.
    Cym. And thou shalt die for 't.
    Bel.   We will die all three: *370*
But I will prove that two on 's are as good
As I have given out him. My sons, I must
For mine own part unfold a dangerous speech,
Though, haply, well for you.
    Arv.   Your danger's ours.   *375*
    Guil. And our good his.
    Bel.   Have at it, then, by leave.
Thou hadst, great king, a subject who was call'd Belarius.
    Cym. What of him? he is
A banish'd traitor.   *380*
    Bel.   He it is that hath
Assum'd this age: indeed, a banish'd man;
I know not how a traitor.
    Cym.   Take him hence:
The whole world shall not save him.   *385*
    Bel.   Not too hot:
First pay me for the nursing of thy sons;
And let it be confiscate all so soon
As I have receiv'd it.

    Cym.   Nursing of my sons!   *390*
    Bel. I am too blunt and saucy; here's my knee:
Ere I arise I will prefer my sons;
Then spare not the old father. Mighty sir,
These two young gentlemen, that call me father,
And think they are my sons, are none of mine;   *395*
They are the issue of your loins, my liege,
And blood of your begetting.
    Cym.   How! my issue!
    Bel. So sure as you your father's. I, old Morgan,
Am that Belarius whom you sometime banish'd: *400*
Your pleasure was my mere offence, my punishment
Itself, and all my treason; that I suffer'd
Was all the harm I did. These gentle princes—
For such and so they are—these twenty years
Have I train'd up; those arts they have as I   *405*
Could put into them; my breeding was, sir, as
Your highness knows. Their nurse, Euriphile,
Whom for the theft I wedded, stole these children
Upon my banishment: I mov'd her to 't,
Having receiv'd the punishment before,   *410*
For that which I did then; beaten for loyalty
Excited me to treason. Their dear loss,
The more of you 'twas felt the more it shap'd
Unto my end of stealing them. But, gracious sir,
Here are your sons again; and I must lose   *415*
Two of the sweet'st companions in the world.
The benediction of these covering heavens
Fall on their heads like dew! for they are worthy
To inlay heaven with stars.
    Cym.   Thou weep'st, and speak'st.   *420*
The service that you three have done is more
Unlike than this thou tell'st. I lost my children:
If these be they, I know not how to wish
A pair of worthier sons.
    Bel.   Be pleas'd awhile.   *425*
This gentleman, whom I call Polydore,
Most worthy prince, as yours, is true Guiderius;
This gentleman, my Cadwal, Arviragus,
Your younger princely son; he, sir, was lapp'd
In a most curious mantle, wrought by the hand   *430*
Of his queen mother, which, for more probation,
I can with ease produce.
    Cym.   Guiderius had
Upon his neck a mole, a sanguine star;
It was a mark of wonder.   *435*
    Bel.   This is he,
Who hath upon him still that natural stamp.
It was wise nature's end in the donation,
To be his evidence now.
    Cym.   O! what, am I   *440*
A mother to the birth of three? Ne'er mother
Rejoic'd deliverance more. Blest pray you be,
That, after this strange starting from your orbs,
You may reign in them now. O Imogen!
Thou hast lost by this a kingdom.   *445*
    Imo.   No, my lord;
I have got two worlds by 't. O my gentle brothers!

---

339 forfend: *forbid*   **360-362 hath ... scar for;** *cf. n.*   **382 Assum'd:** *attained*

401 pleasure: *caprice* **mere:** *sole*   **411 beaten:** *i.e. my being beaten*   **412 dear:** *great*   **413, 414 shap'd ... end:** *fitted my purpose*   **421, 422 The service ... tell'st;** *cf. n.*   **429 lapp'd:** *wrapped*   **431 probation:** *proof*   **442 Rejoic'd:** *joyed in*

Have we thus met? O, never say hereafter
But I am truest speaker: you call'd me brother,
When I was but your sister; I you brothers   450
When ye were so indeed.
   Cym.   Did you e'er meet?
   Arv. Ay, my good lord.
   Gui.   And at first meeting lov'd;
Continued so, until we thought he died.   455
   Cor. By the queen's dram she swallow'd.
   Cym.   O rare instinct!
When shall I hear all through? This fierce abridgment
Hath to it circumstantial branches, which
Distinction should be rich in. Where? how liv'd you?   460
And when came you to serve our Roman captive?
How parted with your brothers? how first met them?
Why fled you from the court, and whither? These,
And your three motives to the battle, with
I know not how much more, should be demanded,   465
And all the other by-dependances,
From chance to chance, but nor the time nor place
Will serve our long interrogatories. See,
Posthumus anchors upon Imogen,
And she, like harmless lightning, throws her eye   470
On him, her brothers, me, her master, hitting
Each object with a joy: the counterchange
Is severally in all. Let's quit this ground,
And smoke the temple with our sacrifices.
[To Belarius.] Thou art my brother; so we'll hold thee   475
ever.
   Imo. You are my father too; and did relieve me,
To see this gracious season.
   Cym.   All o'erjoy'd
Saves these in bonds; let them be joyful too,   480
For they shall taste our comfort.
   Imo.   My good master,
I will yet do you service.
   Luc.   Happy be you!
   Cym. The forlorn soldier, that so nobly fought,   485
He would have well becom'd this place and grac'd
The thankings of a king.
   Post.   I am, sir,
The soldier that did company these three
In poor beseeming; 'twas a fitment for   490
The purpose I then follow'd. That I was he,
Speak, Iachimo; I had you down and might
Have made you finish.
   Iach.   *[Kneeling.]* I am down again;
But now my heavy conscience sinks my knee,   495
As then your force did. Take that life, beseech you,
Which I so often owe, but your ring first,
And here the bracelet of the truest princess
That ever swore her faith.
   Post.   Kneel not to me: 500
The power that I have on you is to spare you;
The malice towards you to forgive you. Live,
And deal with others better.
   Cym.   Nobly doom'd:

We'll learn our freeness of a son-in-law;   505
Pardon's the word to all.
   Arv.   You holp us, sir,
As you did mean indeed to be our brother;
Joy'd are we that you are.
   Post. Your servant, princes. Good my lord of Rome,   510
Call forth your soothsayer. As I slept, methought
Great Jupiter, upon his eagle back'd,
Appear'd to me, with other spritely shows
Of mine own kindred: when I wak'd, I found
This label on my bosom; whose containing   515
Is so from sense in hardness that I can
Make no collection of it; let him show
His skill in the construction.
   Luc.   Philarmonus!
   Sooth. Here, my good lord.   520
   Luc.   Read, and declare the meaning.

   Sooth. [Reads.] 'Whenas a lion's whelp shall, to himself
unknown, without seeking find, and be embraced by a
piece of tender air; and when from a stately cedar shall be
lopped branches, which, being dead many years, shall after
revive, be jointed to the old stock, and freshly grow: then
shall Posthumus end his miseries, Britain be fortunate,
and flourish in peace and plenty.'

Thou, Leonatus, art the lion's whelp;
The fit and apt construction of thy name,   530
Being Leo-natus, doth import so much.
[To Cymbeline.] The piece of tender air, thy virtuous
daughter,
Which we call *mollis aer*; and *mollis aer*
We term it *mulier*; which *mulier*, I divine,   535
Is this most constant wife; who, even now,
Answering the letter of the oracle,
Unknown to you, *[To Posthumus.]* unsought, were clipp'd
about
With this most tender air.   540
   Cym.   This hath some seeming.
   Sooth. The lofty cedar, royal Cymbeline,
Personates thee, and thy lopp'd branches point
Thy two sons forth; who, by Belarius stolen,
For many years thought dead, are now reviv'd,   545
To the majestic cedar join'd, whose issue
Promises Britain peace and plenty.
   Cym.   Well;
My peace we will begin. And, Caius Lucius,
Although the victor, we submit to Cæsar,   550
And to the Roman empire; promising
To pay our wonted tribute, from the which
We were dissuaded by our wicked queen;
Whom heavens—in justice both on her and hers—
Have laid most heavy hand.   555
   Sooth. The fingers of the powers above do tune
The harmony of this peace. The vision,
Which I made known to Lucius ere the stroke
Of this yet scarce-cold battle, at this instant
Is full accomplish'd; for the Roman eagle,   560
From south to west on wing soaring aloft,

458 fierce abridgment: *rapid narration*   460 Distinction ... rich in: *cf. n.*   464 your three: *of you three*   466 by-dependances: *side issues*   471 her mater: *i.e. Lucius*   472, 473 the counterchange ... all: *cf. n.*   490 beseeming: *appearance* fitment: *preparation*   493 finish: *die*   504 doom'd: *judged*   505 freeness: *generosity*

513 spritely shows: *ghostly apparitions*   515 containing: *contents*   516 from sense: *incomprehensible*   517 collection: *deduction*   534 mollis aer: *tender air*   538 clipp'd: *clasped*

Lessen'd herself, and in the beams o' the sun
So vanish'd: which foreshow'd our princely eagle,
The imperial Cæsar, should again unite
His favour with the radiant Cymbeline,   *565*
Which shines here in the west.
   Cym.   Laud we the gods;
And let our crooked smokes climb to their nostrils
From our bless'd altars. Publish we this peace
To all our subjects. Set we forward: let   *570*
A Roman and a British ensign wave
Friendly together; so through Lud's town march:

And in the temple of great Jupiter
Our peace we'll ratify; seal it with feasts.
Set on there. Never was a war did cease,   *575*
Ere bloody hands were wash'd, with such a peace.   *Exeunt.*

❧ FINIS ❧

NOTES

I.i.1-3. *our bloods No more obey the heavens than our courtiers Still seem as does the king.* Our dispositions are no more surely governed by the heavens, i.e., the stars, than are the looks of courtiers governed by the expression of the king.

I.i.29. *extend him within himself.* 'My praise however extensive is within his merit.' (Johnson.)

I.i.35, 36. According to Shakespeare, Cassibelan was Cymbeline's uncle, Tenantius Cymbeline's father. Holinshed gives a different genealogy.

I.i.S.d. In the Folio this stage direction is the first in *Scena secunda.* Most modern editors make no change of scene, as there is no change of place or lapse of time.

I.i.100. *Always reserv'd my holy duty.* Never forgetting my sacred filial duty of respect; the modern equivalent would be 'with all due respect to my dear father.'

I.i.115. *Though ink be made of gall.* 'Though the accent falls metrically on *made* I prefer to place it on *be*.' (Furness.)

I.i.119–121. *I never do him wrong But he does buy my injuries, to be friends Pays dear for my offences.* Whenever I do him wrong I make it appear that he has wronged me and force him to buy off my wrath; in order to be friends he is willing to assume the blame and pay dear for my offences.

I.i.133, 134. *cere up my embracements from a next With bands of death.* Folio reads *sear up,* and many former editors have explained the phrase as meaning to dry up, cause to wither etc. Furness points out that the New English Dictionary gives *sear* as a sixteenth and seventeenth century form of *cere* (i.e. to wrap in a shroud of waxed cloth), and feels that the reference to the *bands of death* 'leaves no doubt that the word here alludes to the cerements of death.'

I.i.173, 174. *overbuys me Almost the sum he pays.* 'That is, he gives himself, worth any woman, and gets in return only my almost worthless self.' (Rolfe.)

I.ii.9, 10. 'In order to spare him, Posthumus's steel sneaked roundabout Cloten's body, like a debtor trying to avoid his creditors.' (Delius.) Possibly, however, the reference is to Cloten's sword and his awkwardness in fighting.

I.ii.25, 26. The second lord plays on the word *sign,* interpreting it as constellation, and *reflection* as planetary influence.

I.iii.4. *As offer'd mercy is.* The clause which ends with this phrase is a good example of Shakespeare's elliptical style in *Cymbeline.* Imogen's meaning is obvious, viz. the loss of a letter from Posthumus would be as hard to bear as the loss of a reprieve to a criminal (or possibly as the loss of God's mercy to a sinner).

I.iii.22. *I would have broke mine eye-strings, crack'd them.* The eye-strings, or tendons of the eye, were supposed to crack at the loss of sight.

I.iii.40–43. Utterly worthless are the guesses of editors as to what Imogen's two charming words would have been. As the north wind shakes the buds on the trees and so prevents their growing, so Cymbeline's anger prevents this bud of love from ripening further.

I.iv.10. Dowden quotes *3 Henry VI* II.i.91, 92: 'Nay, if thou be that princely eagle's bird, Show thy descent by gazing 'gainst the sun.'

I.iv.12, 13. *words him . . . a great deal from the matter.* 'Makes the description of him very distant from the truth.' (Johnson.)

I.iv.15–17. *the approbation of those that weep this lamentable divorce under her colours are wonderfully to extend him.* The praise of Posthumus by those friends and followers of Imogen who bewail their separation (those that under her colors weep this lamentable divorce) tends greatly to increase his reputation. The obscurity of this sentence rises from the incorrect position of the phrase 'under her colours,' and from the plural verb 'are' where a singular is required.

I.iv.37–38. *rather shunned to go even with what I heard than in my every action to be guided by others' experience.* Posthumus means apparently that as a young man he preferred to avoid agreeing exactly with all that he heard of being guided in every action by the experience of others.

I.iv.45, 46. *which may, without contradiction, suffer the report.* 'Which may, undoubtedly, he publicly told.' (Johnson.)

I.iv.49. *upon warrant of bloody affirmation.* 'Pledging himself to seal the truth of it with his blood.' (Rolfe.)

I.iv.117. *a friend.* This is the First Folio reading and is intelligible: Iachimo says jocularly 'You are her friend and thus know her too well to risk much on her chastity.' Theobald altered *a friend* to *afraid* and in this reading has been followed by many editors.

I.iv.135–136. *provided I have your commendation for my more free entertainment.* Provided that you will commend me to her generous hospitality.

I.v.67. *To be depender on a thing that leans.* 'To be dependent on one who

is himself dependent on others.' (Furness.) In the light of the two following lines Furness's interpretation seems less satisfactory than Johnson's, 'To be dependent on something that inclines toward its fall.'

I.vi.6-9. *most miserable . . . comfort.* Those who have the most exalted desires are the most miserable of men (because their desires are likely to be unattainable); but happy are they, however humble, who attain their simple desires, for the fact of attainment gives a relish to *(seasons)* comfort.

I.vi.22. *Parthian.* 'The ancient Parthian manner of fighting was to shoot at an adversary while flying or pretending to fly.' (Century Dictionary.)

I.vi.37–41. *which can distinguish . . . foul.* Eyes which can distinguish between one star and another and between two stones of identical appearance as they lie on the beach which is covered by numbers of them. And with such precious spectacles (as our eye) can we not distinguish between fair and foul?

I.vi.48–50. 'Desire when it approached sluttery, and considered it in comparison with such neat excellence, would not only be not so allured to feed, but seized with a fit of loathing would vomit emptiness, would feel the convulsions of disgust, though, being unfed, it had nothing to eject.' (Johnson.)

I.vi.114, 115. *timely knowing, The remedy then born.* 'Upon timely knowledge the remedy is straightway born.' (Dowden.)

I.vi.121, 122. *Takes prisoner . . . here.* 'From her alone does the passion of my eye catch fire.' (Dowden.) Many editors have followed the reading of the later Folios which changed 'Fiering' of the First Folio to 'Fixing.'

I.vi.133–137. *Not I . . . out.* 'It is not I who divulge the utter depths of his change, inclined though I be to impart the news, but 'tis your loveliness that has conjured up this report from the innermost silence of my consciousness.' (Furness.) Probably 'inclined' should rather be taken in the sense of 'because inclined.'

II.i.1, 2. *when I kissed the jack, upon an up-cast to be hit away.* The reference is to the game of bowls. The jack is the small bowl at which the others are aimed. The player 'kisses the jack' when his bowl touches it without moving it. Cloten's bowl was knocked away from this advantageous position by another bowler who rolled straight up.

II.i.11, 12. *curtail, crop.* The verb to curtail is from the obsolete word 'curtal,' meaning a horse with a docked tail; hence the second lord's feeble pun about cropping ears.

II.i.21, 22. *capon . . . comb on.* Both these words refer probably to the fool's cap or coxcomb.

II.ii.14. *Our Tarquin.* 'Our' because Iachimo is an Italian. The story of Tarquin is told by Shakespeare in *The Rape of Lucrece.*

II.ii.15 *press the rushes.* Tread upon the rushes (which, in Shakespeare's own time, were strewn upon the floors).

II.ii.19, 20. Iachimo longs to kiss Imogen's lips, 'rubies unparagon'd,' but obviously is not so foolhardy as to attempt it. The lips themselves do exquisitely, 'dearly,' wht Iachimo longs to do.

II.ii.24, 25. The white and azure refer to the white eyelids with their blue veins. Cf. Keats, *Eve of St. Agnes,* 'And still she slept an azure-lidded sleep.' In both cases 'the blue of heaven' in the eyelids of the sleeper is intended to denote her purity.

II.ii.29. *contents o' the story.* Details of the story pictured on the arras.

II.ii.36. *Gordian knot.* The knot tied by Gordius, king of Phrygia, which was so intricate that no one could untie it. An oracle declared that he who loosed it should be master of Asia. Alexander the Great cut it, and the oracle was fulfilled.

II.ii.47. *The tale of Tereus.* Tereus married Procne. According to some versions of the myth, he tired of her, pretended she was dead, invited her sister Philomela to be his wife, ravished her, and tore out her tongue. Philomela contrived to communicate with Procne. Together they killed Itys, son of Tereus, and served him up in a dish for Tereus to eat. Tereus was changed to a hawk, Procne to a swallow, Philomela to a nightingale.

II.ii.50, 51. *that dawning May bare the raven's eye.* That dawn may open the eye of the raven, a bird that wakes early.

II.ii.53. *time.* Iachimo has heard Imogen ask to be called at four. As the clock strikes he counts 'one, two, three,' and on the fourth stroke shuts the lid of the trunk saying, 'time, time.' (Ingleby.)

II.iii.2. *turned up ace.* The reference is to cutting a pack of cards, upon which occasion only ace is low. Ace and ass were pronounced alike: the first lord is quibbling.

II.iii.142. *south-fog.* 'Southerne winds vnbind humours . . . & they cause heauinesse of wits of feeling: they corrupt and destroye, they heat, and maketh

men fall into sicknesse. And they breed the gout, the falling euill, itch, and the ague.' (*Batman vppon Bartholme*, 1582, lib. xi, chap. 3, quoted by Furness.) Compare *Coriolanus* I.i.36: 'All the contagion of the south light on you!'

II.iv.7–9. *in these fear'd hopes . . . debtor.* If these hopes, which are mixed with fears, are realised, I shall barely have enough to repay your affection; if they are not realised, I shall die much in your debt. Tyrwhitt's emendation, *seared* for *feared*, has been followed by many editors.

II.iv.26. *mingled with their courage.* The First Folio reads 'wing-led with their courages.' Dowden interprets this to mean that wings of their army are led by courageous commanders. All the later Folios correct *wing-led* to read *mingled*, but retain the plural form of courage. The First Folio reading of this passage requires a rather ingenious but far-fetched interpretation.

II.iv.90, 91. *strive In workmanship and value.* In it the workmanship and the intrinsic value strive with each other for preëminence.

II.iv.104. *likely to report themselves.* So lifelike that one might expect them to speak.

II.iv.104–106. *the cutter . . . out.* 'The sculptor was as nature, but as nature dumb; he gave everything that nature gives but breath and motion.' (Johnson.)

III.i.23. 'The sea is made by the figure of speech a park, and the rocks a fence of oaks that pale it in.' (Porter & Clark.)

III.ii.34. *For it doth physic love.* 'Grief in absence keeps love in health and vigour.' (Johnson.)

III.ii.36, 37. *Lovers And men in dangerous bonds pray not alike.* I.e. lovers bless the bees for the wax which seals their letters; prisoners curse the bees for the wax which seals their forfeited bonds.

III.ii.41, 42. *as you . . . eyes.* A carelessly constructed sentence which a multitude of emendations and explanations makes no clearer. Posthumus seems to mean that a loving look from Imogen would renew and revive him, no matter how cruel the law and her father's wrath had been to him. Cf. Romeo: 'Look thou but sweet, And I am proof against their enmity.' (*Romeo and Juliet* II.i.114, 115.)

III.ii.65. *Why should excuse be born or ere begot?* 'Why contrive an excuse before the act is done for which the excuse will be necessary?' (Malone.)

III.ii.73, 74. *sands That run i' the clock's behalf.* 'Sands of the hour-glass that run instead of the clock.' (Collier.)

III.ii.80–82. *I see . . . through.* I see only the course that lies directly before me. Everything else, here, and here, and beyond, is obscure.

III.iii.18, 19. *This service . . . allow'd.* Belarius, in his involved style, is here, I think, expressing sentiments akin to those expressed more clearly in the *Collect for Peace* by the clause 'whose service is perfect freedom.' 'This servile labour of ours is not servile, being done as we do it, but being so done it is approved *(allowed)* or enjoyed by us.'

III.iii.27, 28. Such men receive deference from the tradesmen who made the finery, but their accounts are not cancelled (for all this deference). Theirs is no life compared with ours.

III.iii.55. *which dies i' the search.* Editors disagree about the antecedent of *which*, whether it is *pain*, or *name*, or *fame and honour*. The punctuation of the First Folio would indicate that *fame and honour* were not the antecedents, for there is a comma after *fame*. Whatever the antecedent, the general import of the sentence is clear.

III.iii.101–103. *in as like . . . conceiving.* 'That is, acting my words as graphically as his brother. While Guiderius's gestures reflect the immediate impression of Belarius's tale, Arviragus, a more imaginative hearer, heightens what he hears by his greater energy of conception.' (Herford.) *Figure* is used in the sense of an acted part, as in *Tempest* III.iii.99.

III.iv.49. *Whose mother was her painting.* 'Who was born of her paint-box.' (Hudson.)

III.iv.58, 59. *Æneas, Sinon.* The refernece is to Æneas's desertion of Dido, queen of Carthage; cf. Vergil's *Æneid*, Bk. IV. Sinon, a Greek, with tears and protests deceived the Trojans, and persuaded them to take the wooden horse, filled with Greek soldiers, into the city of Troy.

III.iv.83. *scriptures.* Imogen uses the word literally in reference to the letters of Posthumus, which she implies have been her 'sacred writings'; then she plays on the word, using Holy Scriptures as a synonym of orthodoxy, as opposed to *heresy*, in the next line.

III.iv.86. *stomachers.* Again Imogen plays on words. She removes Posthumus's letters from her bosom, saying that she will no more use them as *stomachers*, as ornamental breast-coverings, worn by women, were called; but she also has in mind the word *stomach* in its significant as *courage*: the letters of Posthumus will never again bring courage to her heart.

III.iv.146. This line lacks one syllable in the Folios. Many editors, following Theobald, correct this defect in metre by adding the word *Cloten* to the end of

the line. Porter and Clark, defending the Folio reading, suggest that the time of the missing word is filled up 'by Imogen's exasperated pause, when she can think of nothing bad enough further, except his name.'

III.iv.153, 154. *I' the world's volume Our Britain seems as of it, but not in 't.* Britain seems like a page torn out of the volume; of it, but not in it.

III.iv.195, 196. *which will make him know, If that his head have ear in music.* Pisanio is, I think, referring to the music of Imogen's voice. Your very telling of your accomplishments will, he says, make him realize one of them if he has a musical ear.

III.v.12. *your Grace, and you.* Perhaps the *you* refers to Cloten, but I think not, for the farewell to Cloten seems to come in line 16, perhaps Lucius means to distinguish between the Queen and the woman, 'all joy to you as Queen and as woman'; or perhaps for *you* we should read *yours.*

III.vi.7. *Foundations.* Used quibbingly for (1) things which are supposedly fixed and permanent, and (2) endowed institutions, such as hospitals. Compare the following clause, 'such, I mean, where they should be relieved.'

III.vi.24. *Take or lend.* Take my life or give me food, or 'Take what I have before (*or* in the sense of *ere*) you give me food.' (Dowden.)

III.vi.27. *Such a foe.* Heavens grant me such a foe!

III.vi.77, 78. *In honesty I bid for you, as I do buy.* Honorably I ask for your favor, as I would honorably pay for it.

III.vi.97, 98. *laying by . . . multitudes.* Dispensing with the worthless tribute of fickle multitudes.

IV.ii.35. *miracle.* The word seems to be used in the sense of *mystery*, and the sentence to mean: The identity of this youth who is loved before me is a mystery.

IV.ii.78. *stinking-elder.* The elder was a tree of ill repute. Judas Iscariot was said to have hanged himself on an elder; black fungus droops from it; and both leaves and blossoms have an unpleasant odor.

IV.ii.105. *my clothes.* Cloten is obviously referring to court apparel in general, not to the clothes of Posthumus which he is wearing.

IV.ii.144–147. *Being scarce . . . fear.* Having scarcely the wits of a man, Cloten was not afraid even of 'roaring terrors' which would terrify an intelligent man, for defect of judgment is often the cause of (not *fear* as Shakespeare carelessly writes but) boldness. The Cambridge editors suggest that a line may have dropped out, and that the original sentence may have had the following purport: 'defect of judgment supplies the place of courage, while true judgment is oft the cause of fear.' Dowden's suggested emendation, *cease* for *cause*, though ingenious, is not convincing. *Cease* has not the true Shakespearean ring in this place.

IV.ii.202–204. *I would . . . answer.* I wish that revenges would seek us out and call us to account, that we might meet them with all possible strength.

IV.ii.315. *Thersites' body is as good as Ajax'.* Thersites, the most deformed in body and mind of all the Greeks at the siege of Troy. Ajax, a Greek warrior, gigantic in body and of great courage. Cf. *Troilus and Cressida.*

IV.ii.351. *Upon . . . faces.* This is apparently a direction from Belarius to scatter the flowers upon the faces of Imogen and Cloten; but Cloten's body is headless. Did Shakespeare forget?

IV.ii.377, 378. His foot as nimble and graceful as that of Mercury, his thigh as mighty as that of Mars, his arms as strong as those of Hercules, his face as majestic as that of Jove. These references to the gods explain the first phrase in the next line, 'Murder in heaven!'

IV.ii.380. *Hecuba.* Wife of Priam, king of Troy. In the player's recitation in *Hamlet* (II.ii.502 ff.), Shakespeare refers to 'the instant burst of clamor that she made' 'when she saw Pyrrhus . . . mincing . . . her husband's limbs.'

IV.ii.435, 436. *otherwise . . . picture.* 'Nature took away the life—who mutilated the body?' (Dowden.)

IV.iii.35. *Your preparation can affront no less.* Your army is prepared to face as many.

V.i.15. *And make them dread it, to the doers' thrift.* None of the many proposed emendations of this line seems necessary. Posthumus means that the sinner who is allowed to 'second ills with ills' begins to dread a future of continuous degeneration, and this fear is 'thrift' or profitable to the 'doer' or sinner.

V.iii.28–31. *Stand . . . frown.* Stand, or we will play the part of the Romans and will give you that beastly death which, like beasts, you are shunning and from which you may save yourselves by looking back defiantly upon the enemy.

V.iii.45, 46. *slaves, The strides they victors made.* This clause is parallel in construction to the preceding one. Those who came as eagles fled as chickens; those who came as victors fled as slaves.

V.iv.1. *You shall not now be stol'n, you have locks upon you.* 'The wit of the Gaoler alludes to the custom of putting a lock on a horse's leg when he is turned out to pasture.' (Johnson.)

V.iv.13–19. Posthumus here soliloquizes on the three steps which man must take to receive pardon and absolution, viz. contrition (ll. 13), penance (ll.

15–17), and satisfaction (ll. 17–19). The meaning of the first four lines is clear. Line 17, *Desir'd more than constrain'd*, refers to the gyves, symbols of his voluntary penance: ll. 17–19 signify that if satisfaction, *to satisfy*, be the main part of salvation, *freedom*, from sin, then the gods may take no less than all which he has and is, if thereby he may be freed.

V.iv.28. *You rather . . . yours.* Men do not weigh every coin they receive, but accept them because of their 'image and superscription'; so, although my life is not so valuable as Imogen's, yet the gods made it in their image and should the more readily, i.e. *rather*, take it in compensation.

V.iv.157. *well cooked.* The reference is to meat which is hung up, either preparatory to cooking or instead of being cooked.

V.iv.159. *the dish . . . shot.* 'The viands (namely, himself) pay the reckoning.' (Furness.)

V.iv.203. *hath a preferment.* Includes a hope for my own advancement.

V.v.193. *Postures beyond brief nature.* Beauties of form that surpass those created by hasty Nature.

V.v.195. *hook of wiving.* Physical beauty, the hook wherewith wives catch husbands.

V.v.360–362. *hath More of thee merited than a band of Clotens Had ever scar for.* Guiderius deserves more from the king than a whole band of men like Cloten for actions for which they hae been scarred in battle.

V.v.421, 422. *The service that you three have done is more Unlike than this thou tell'st.* 'I have the less reason to be incredulous because the actions you have done within my knowledge are more incredible than the story you relate.' (Johnson.)

V.v.460. *Distinction should be rich in.* A clearer statement should bring out fully.

V.v.472, 473. *the counterchange Is severally in all.* 'This is reciprocated by all.' (Rolfe.)

THE TEXT OF THE PRESENT EDITION

The text of the present edition is, by permission of the Oxford University Press, based on that of the Oxford Shakespeare, edited by the late W. J. Craig. Stage directions, when not bracketed, are from the First Folio; bracketed stage directions are modern.

In the following list of variants from the Oxford text, the readings of this edition precede, and Craig's readings follow, the colon. The Folio authority is given wherever involved.

I.i.133	cere: sear Ff
I.i.134	bands: bonds Ff
I.i.154	heap'st Ff: heap'st instead
I.iv.50	constant-qualified: constant, qualified Ff
I.iv.117	a friend Ff: afraid
I.iv.139	understand Ff: understand that
I.v.78	change thou chancest: chance thou changest Ff
I.v.95	primroses: prime-roses Ff
I.vi.24	*Imo. reads* Ff: *Imo.*
I.vi.26	trust Ff: truest
I.vi.143	self exhibition Ff1, 4: self-exhibition Ff2, 3
II.ii.34	sense Ff: senses
II.iii.131	foil Ff: soil
II.iv.7	fear'd Ff: sear'd
II.iv.23	order'd Ff: ordered
II.iv.26	mingled Ff2, 3, 4 (F1 wing-led): winged
II.iv.92	So rarely Ff: rarely
II.v.2	bastards Ff: bastards all
II.v.27	may be named Ff2, 3, 4 (F1 name): man may name
III.i.23	oaks Ff: rocks
III.ii.42	would even Ff: would not even
III.iv.106	mine eyeballs Ff: mine eyeballs blind
III.iv.146	nothing: F1 nothing; F2 nothing? Ff3, 4 nothing Cloten
III.iv.195	will Ff: you'll
III.v.12	your Grace, and you Ff: your Grace. *Qu.* And you!
III.v.54	the loudest of (th' lowd of Ff): the loudest
III.v.115	once, Ff: once
III.vi.82	After long absence Ff: After a long absence
IV.i.17	happily Ff: haply
IV.ii.147	cause of fear Ff: cease of fear
IV.ii.216	thou thyself F1 (thyself Ff2, 3, 4): how thyself
IV.ii.260	but ay: but I Ff
IV.ii.298	to our mother Ff: our mother
V.i.20	mistress; peace Ff: mistress-piece
V.iii.100	leg Ff: lag
V.iv.62	Leonati Ff: Leonati's
V.v.468	interrogatories Ff: inter-gatories

The Winter's Tale

Edited by

FREDERICK E. PIERCE

⚘

Dramatis Personae

LEONTES, *King of Sicilia*

MAMILLIUS, *young Prince of Sicilia*

CAMILLO
ANTIGONUS
CLEOMENES } *Four Lords of Sicilia*
DION

HERMIONE, *Queen to Leontes*

PERDITA, *Daughter to Leontes and Hermione*

PAULINA, *Wife to Antigonus*

EMILIA, *a Lady*

POLIXENES, *King of Bohemia*

FLORIZEL, *Prince of Bohemia*

OLD SHEPHERD, *reputed Father of Perdita*

CLOWN, *his Son*

AUTOLYCUS, *a Rogue*

ARCHIDAMUS, *a Lord of Bohemia*

MOPSA
DORCAS } *Shepherdesses*

OTHER LORDS AND GENTLEMEN AND SERVANTS

SHEPHERDS AND SHEPHERDESSES

A MARINER

A GAOLER

LADIES ATTENDING THE QUEEN

SATYRS FOR A DANCE

TIME, *as Chorus*

SCENE—*Sometimes in Sicilia, sometimes in Bohemia.*

The Winter's Tale

INTRODUCTION

SOURCES OF THE PLAY

The Winter's Tale is an excellent example of a novel turned into a play. That practice was common in Elizabethan times as in recent years; but with this difference, that the drama in Shakespeare's time was usually an improvement on the novel and in our own day is usually a popularized degradation of the original. The novel—or novelette, for it can be read in an hour—from which Shakespeare drew most of the plot of his *Winter's Tale* was *Pandosto: the Triumph of Time* (or *The Historic of Dorastus and Fawnis*), which first appeared in 1588 and was a 'best-seller' for years before Shakespeare dramatized it. At least fourteen editions of it are known to have been issued. Its author was Robert Greene, a brilliant and unfortunate author, who died near the beginning of Shakespeare's career, and died bitterly jealous of that transforming genius which was already giving hints of the masterpieces it could make from other men's crude materials.

In Greene's novel Pandosto, king of Bohemia, with his wife Bellaria entertains as his guest his old friend Egistus, king of Sicilia. Pandosto, like Leontes, becomes jealous, but more slowly and with more reason, for Bellaria, though pure, is imprudent. Franion, his cup-bearer, promises murder and escapes, as does Camillo. Bellaria, like Hermione, is accused, cleared by the oracle, and actually—not apparently—dies on learning the death of her son Garinter. Her little daughter Fawnia is abandoned on the coast of Sicilia, brought up by a shepherd, and loved by Prince Dorastus of that country. Capnio, a faithful old servant of Dorastus, aids the young lovers in their flight, as does Camillo, and brings the shepherd and 'fardel' aboard Dorastus' ship as does Shakespeare's Autolycus. The reception of the lovers at the court of Pandosto and the discovery of Fawnia's identity run closely parallel to the same events in the play, save that Pandosto, before learning Fawnia's parentage, conceives an incestuous love for his own daughter. After Fawnia's marriage Pandosto, grown melancholy with brooding over his sins against those whom he loved best, kills himself.

Shakespeare in recasting Greene's material omitted as too tragic and brutal the incestuous passion and violent death of Pandosto, and threw out as impertinent several paragraphs dealing with the life of the old shepherd. He created the characters of Antigonus, Paulina, and Autolycus, and combined the parts of Franion and Capnio in that of Camillo. He created the statue scene which ends the play, and the scene between Perdita and Polixenes (IV. iv.), for which there were no hints in the prose tale. By interchanging throughout the parts of Bohemia and Sicily he probably meant to veil the extent of his debt to a book that was still popular, although he may have believed that the suddenness of Leontes' jealousy would seem truer to life in a hot-blooded Sicilian than in a native of Central Europe. As is almost inevitable when changing a novel into a play, the action is made more rapid. For example, in the second scene of Act First events which in Greene's novel covered several weeks are made to happen in a single hour. The greatest change, however, and the greatest improvement, is in the conception of character, which throughout is more noble and subtle in Shakespeare than in his forerunner.

The closeness of Shakespeare at times to his original can be shown by comparing Hermione's defence (III.ii.20-119) with the corresponding speech of Bellaria:

'If the deuine powers bee priuy to humane actions (as no doubt they are) I hope my patience shall make fortune blushe, and my vnspotted life shall staine spightfully discredit. For although lying Report hath sought to appeach mine honor, and Suspition hath intended to soyle my credit with infamie: yet where Vertue keepeth the Forte, Report and suspition may assayle, but neuer sack: how I haue led my life before Egistus comming, I appeale Pandosto to the Gods & to thy conscience. What hath passed betwixt him and me, the Gods onely know, and I hope will presently reueale: that I loued Egistus I can not denie: that I honored him I shame not to confesse: to the one I was forced by his vertues, to the other for his dignities. But as touching lasciuious lust, I say Egistus is honest, and hope my selfe to be found without spot: for Franion, I can neither accuse him nor excuse him, for I was not priuie to his departure, and that this is true which I haue heere rehearsed, I referre myselfe to the deuine Oracle.' [ed. Grosart, 4. 260.]

Vague likenesses between *The Winter's Tale* and certain other books have been pointed out; but none are close enough to prove borrowing on Shakespeare's part.

THE HISTORY OF THE PLAY

The Winter's Tale was first 'allowed of,' or officially approved for performance, by Sir George Buck, who assumed office as Master of the Revels in 1610; consequently, although Buck did license plays before taking office, we may reasonably assume that it was not written previous to that year. Yet it was already on the stage by May 15, 1611, for a Dr. Simon Forman saw it acted on that date and has left a written record of the fact with an analysis of the plot. The dance of twelve satyrs in IV. iv. was probably suggested by a similar dance of satyrs in Ben Jonson's *Masque of Oberon*, first acted on the opening day of January, 1611. It seems practically certain, therefore, that the play was finished and first staged in the spring of 1611. It was for several years following a favorite at court, and in 1613 was acted with several other Shakespearean dramas before the Prince Palatine and his bride. No Quarto editions of it exist; apparently it first appeared in print in the Folio of 1623.

After Shakespeare's death the play, despite its beauty, was unpopular and almost unnoticed for over a century, more so than many of the author's other works. Certain fantastic qualities in it—the seacoast of Bohemia, a country which for centuries had no seacoast, and the sixteen-year interval between the third and

fourth acts—jarred on the new age, an age which was more fastidious in such matters than the imaginative Elizabethans had been.

In 1741, however, *The Winter's Tale*—'not acted 100 years,' according to the historian Genest—was revived at Goodman's Fields, and the following year at the more famous theatre of Covent Garden. Soon afterward several adaptations of parts of it were made, the most notable being that of the great actor David Garrick (1717-1779), which was played at Drury Lane theatre in 1756. The play in Garrick's adaptation begins with what was Shakespeare's fourth act. The events of sixteen years earlier are rehearsed for the benefit of the audience in a conversation between Camillo and a gentleman. Then the repentant Leontes comes to Bohemia, takes part with Polixenes and Perdita in the conversation at the shepherd's feast, and assumes the part which Shakespeare gave Camillo of comforting the lovers. Florizel and Perdita do not take ship; and the closing statue scene is in Bohemia. Garrick's version was popular for more than a generation. The prosaic ingenuity with which he dovetailed together parts of Shakespeare's great work is well illustrated in the following passage:

> Perd. *One of these is true,*
> *I think affliction may subdue the cheek,*
> *But not take in the mind.*
>   Leon. *Yea, say you so?*
> *There shall not at your father's house, these sev'n years,*
> *Be born another such.*
>   Flor. *O reverend, Sir!*
> *As you would wish a child of your own youth*

> *To meet his happiness in love, speak for me;*
> *Remember since you ow'd no more to time*
> *Than I do now; and with thought of like affections,*
> *Step forth my advocate.*
>   Leon. *You touch me deep,*
> *Deep, to the quick, sweet prince; alas! alas!*
> *I lost a daughter, that 'twixt heaven and earth*
> *Might thus have stood begetting wonder, as*
> *Yon lovely maiden does—of that no more;—*
> *I'll to the king your father,—this our compact,*
> *Your honour not o'erthrown by your desires,*
> *I am friend to them and you.*

>   *[Exit Leontes and Cleomenes.*

The history of the play during the nineteenth century begins with its revival by John Philip Kemble (1757-1823). In 1802 he presented it with splendid decorations and stage properties, the famous Mrs. Siddons, who was Kemble's sister, taking the part of Hermione. The comedy was revived again in 1856 by Charles Kean (1811-1868) at the Princess's theatre, where Ellen Terry, then a little girl, made her first appearance on the stage as Mamillius. Helen Faucit (1817-1898) about the middle of the century, and Mary Anderson (1859-1940) toward its close, gave brilliant interpretations of the leading female rôles. In 1910 in New York, *The Winter's Tale* was admirably produced under the direction of Mr. Louis Calver, 'with such a stage and accessories as, according to the latest researches, Shakespeare had at his own command.' Another important presentation was the one given by Mr. Granville Barker.

ACT FIRST ❧ SCENE FIRST

[Sicilia. An Antechamber in Leontes' Palace]
Enter Camillo and Archidamus.

Arch. If you shall chance, Camillo, to visit Bohemia, on the like occasion whereon my services are now on foot, you shall see, as I have said, great difference betwixt our Bohemia and your Sicilia.

Cam. I think, this coming summer, the King of Sicilia means to pay Bohemia the visitation which he justly owes him.   *5*

Arc. Wherein our entertainment shall shame us we will be justified in our loves: for, indeed,—

Cam. Beseech you,—

Arch. Verily, I speak it in the freedom of my knowledge: we cannot with such magnificence—in so rare—I know not *10* what to say. We will give you sleepy drinks, that your senses, unintelligent of our insufficience, may, though they cannot praise us, as little accuse us.

Cam. You pay a great deal too dear for what's given freely.

Arch. Believe me, I speak as my understanding instructs *15* me, and as mine honesty puts it to utterance.

Cam. Sicilia cannot show himself over-kind to Bohemia. They were trained together in their childhoods; and there rooted betwixt them then such an affection which cannot choose but branch now. Since their more mature dignities *20* and royal necessities made separation of their society, their encounters, though not personal, have been royally attorneyed with interchange of gifts, letters, loving embassies; that they have seemed to be together, though absent, shook hands, as over a vast, and embraced, as it were, from the ends of *25* opposed winds. The heavens continue their loves!

Arch. I think there is not in the world either malice or matter to alter it. You have an unspeakable comfort of your young Prince Mamillius: it is a gentleman of the greatest promise that ever came into my note.   *30*

Cam. I very well agree with you in the hopes of him. It is a gallant child; one that indeed physics the subject, makes old hearts fresh; they that went on crutches ere he was born desire yet their life to see him a man.

Arch. Would they else be content to die?   *35*

Cam. Yes; if there were no other excuse why they should desire to live.

Arch. If the king had no son, they would desire to live on crutches till he had one.   *Exeunt.*

❧ SCENE SECOND ❧

[A Room of State in the Palace]
Enter Leontes, Hermione, Mamillius, Polixenes, Camillo,
[and Attendants].

Pol. Nine changes of the watery star have been
The shepherd's note since we have left our throne
Without a burden: time as long again
Would be fill'd up, my brother, with our thanks;
And yet we should for perpetuity   *5*
Go hence in debt: and therefore, like a cipher,
Yet standing in rich place, I multiply
With one 'We thank you' many thousands moe
That go before it.

Leon.   Stay your thanks awhile,   *10*
And pay them when you part.

Pol.   Sir, that's to-morrow,
I am question'd by my fears, of what may chance
Or breed upon our absence; that may blow
No sneaping winds at home, to make us say,   *15*
'This is put forth too truly!' Besides, I have stay'd
To tire your royalty.

Leon.   We are tougher, brother,
Than you can put us to 't.

Pol.   No longer stay.   *20*

Leon. One seven-night longer.

Pol.   Very sooth, to-morrow.

Leon. We'll part the time between 's then; and in that
I'll no gainsaying.

Pol.   Press me not, beseech you, so.   *25*
There is no tongue that moves, none, none i' the world,
So soon as yours could win me: so it should now,
Were there necessity in your request, although
'Twere needful I denied it. My affairs
Do even drag me homeward; which to hinder   *30*
Were in your love a whip to me; my stay
To you a charge and trouble: to save both,
Farewell, our brother.

Leon.   Tongue-tied, our queen? speak you.

Her. I had thought, sir, to have held my peace until   *35*
You had drawn oaths from him not to stay. You, sir,
Charge him too coldly: tell him, you are sure
All in Bohemia's well: this satisfaction
The by-gone day proclaim'd: say this to him,
He's beat from his best ward,   *40*

Leon.   Well said, Hermione.

Her. To tell he longs to see his son were strong:
But let him say so then, and let him go;
But let him swear so, and he shall not stay,
We'll thwack him hence with distaffs.   *45*
[To Polixenes.] Yet of your royal presence I'll adventure
The borrow of a week. When at Bohemia
You take my lord, I'll give him my commission
To let him there a month behind the gest
Prefix'd for 's parting: yet, good deed, Leontes,   *50*
I love thee not a jar o' the clock behind
What lady she her lord. You'll stay?

Pol.   No, madam.

Her. Nay, but you will?

Pol.   I may not, verily.   *55*

Her. Verily

---

2 **on foot:** *actively employed*   5 **Bohemia:** *the king of Bohemia*   **visitation:** *visit*   6, 7 **entertainment . . . loves;** *cf. n.*   8 **Beseech:** *I beseech*   9 **freedom:** *privilege*   12 **unintelligent of:** *not perceiving*   17 **Sicilia:** *the king of Sicily*   19 **which:** *as*   20 **branch:** *put forth branches*   21, 22 **encounters:** *meetings*   22 **personal:** *performed in person*   **attorneyed:** *performed by proxy*   23 **that:** *so that*   25 **vast:** *boundless and waste expanse*   25, 26 **from . . . winds;** *cf. n.*   30 **note:** *notice*   32 **physics the subject:** *is medicine to the king's subjects*   1 **watery star:** *moon; cf. n.*   2 **The shepherd's note:** *observed by the shepherd*

6, 7 **like . . . place;** *cf. n.*   8 **moe:** *more*   10 **Stay:** *postpone*   11 **part:** *depart*   14 **that may blow;** *cf. n.*   16 **is put forth:** *has blossomed* (resulted)   19 **put us to 't:** *prove by extreme test*   22 **Very sooth:** *in absolute truth*   23 **between 's:** *between us*   31 **in your love a whip to me:** *an injury to me, though meant in love*   32 **charge:** *expense*   40 **ward:** *fencer's guard*   45 **thwack:** *beat*   46 **adventure:** *venture*   47 **borrow:** *borrowing*   48 **commission:** *permission*   49 **let:** *allow to remain*   **gest:** *date of departure; cf. n.*   50 **good deed:** *indeed*   51 **jar:** *tick*   52 **What lady she:** *any lady whatever*

You put me off with limber vows; but I,
Though you would seek to unsphere the stars with oaths,
Should yet say, 'Sir, no going.' Verily,
You shall not go: a lady's 'verily' 's   60
As potent as a lord's. Will you go yet?
Force me to keep you as a prisoner,
Not like a guest; so you shall pay your fees
When you depart, and save your thanks. How say you?
My prisoner, or my guest? by your dread 'verily,'   65
One of them you shall be.
  Pol.   Your guest, then, madam:
To be your prisoner should import offending;
Which is for me less easy to commit
Than you to punish.   70
  Her.   Not your gaoler then,
But your kind hostess. Come, I'll question you
Of my lord's tricks and yours when you were boys:
You were pretty lordings then.
  Pol.   We were, fair queen,   75
Two lads that thought there was no more behind
But such a day to-morrow as to-day,
And to be boy eternal.
  Her.   Was not my lord
The verier wag o' the two?   80
  Pol. We were as twinn'd lambs that did frisk i' the sun,
And bleat the one at the other: what we chang'd
Was innocence for innocence; we knew not
The doctrine of ill-doing, nor dream'd
That any did. Had we pursu'd that life,   85
And our weak spirits ne'er been higher rear'd
With stronger blood, we should have answer'd heaven
Boldly, 'not guilty;' the imposition clear'd
Hereditary ours.
  Her. By this we gather   90
You have tripp'd since.
  Pol.   ·   O! my most sacred lady,
Temptations have since then been born to 's; for
In those unfledg'd days was my wife, a girl;
Your precious self had then not cross'd the eyes   95
Of my young playfellow.
  Her.   Grace to boot!
Of this make no conclusion, lest you say
Your queen and I are devils; yet, go on:
The offences we have made you do we'll answer;
If you first sinn'd with us, and that with us   100
You did continue fault, and that you slipp'd not
With any but with us.
  Leon.   Is he won yet?
  Her. He'll stay, my lord.   105
  Leon.   At my request he would not.
Hermione, my dearest, thou never spok'st
To better purpose.
  Her.   Never?
  Leon.   Never, but once.   110
  Her. What! have I twice said well? when was 't before?
I prithee tell me; cram 's with praise, and make 's
As fat as tame things: one good deed, dying tongueless,
Slaughters a thousand waiting upon that.

Our priases are our wages: you may ride 's   115
With one soft kiss a thousand furlongs ere
With spur we heat an acre. But to the goal:
My last good deed was to entreat his stay:
What was my first? it has an elder sister,
Or I mistake you: O! would her name were Grace.   120
But once before I spoke to the purpose: when?
Nay, let me have 't; I long.
  Leon.   Why, that was when
Three crabbed months had sour'd themselves to death,
Ere I could make thee open thy white hand   125
And clap thyself my love: then didst thou utter,
'I am yours for ever.'
  Her.   'Tis grace indeed.
Why, lo you now, I have spoke to the purpose twice:
The one for ever earn'd a royal husband,   130
The other for some while a friend.
        [Giving her hand to Polixenes.]
  Leon. [Aside.] Too hot, too hot!
To mingle friendship far is mingling bloods.
I have *tremor cordis* on me: my heart dances;
But not for joy; not joy. This entertainment   135
May a free face put on, derive a liberty
From heartiness, from bounty, fertile bosom,
And well become the agent: 't may, I grant:
But to be paddling palms and pinching fingers,
As now they are, and making practis'd smiles,   140
As in a looking-glass; and then to sigh, as 'twere
The mort o' the deer; O! that is entertainment
My bosom likes not, nor my brows. Mamillius,
Art thou my boy?
  Mam.   Ay, my good lord.   145
  Leon.   I' fecks?
Why, that's my bawcock What! hast smutch'd thy nose?
They say it is a copy out of mine. Come, captain,
We must be neat; not neat, but cleanly, captain:
And yet the steer, the heifer, and the calf,   150
Are all call'd neat. Still virginalling
Upon his palm! How now, you wanton calf!
Art thou my calf?
  Mam.   Yes, if you will my lord.
  Leon. Thou want'st a rough pash and the shoots that I have,
To be full like me: yet they say we are
Almost as like as eggs; women say so,
That will say anything: but were they false
As o'er-dy'd blacks, as wind, as waters, false
As dice are to be wish'd by one that fixes   160
No bourn 'twixt his and mine, yet were it true
To say this boy were like me. Come, sir page,
Look on me with your welkin eye: sweet villain!
Most dear'st! my collop! Can thy dam?—may 't be?—
Affection! thy intention stabs the centre: 165
Thou dost make possible things not so held,

---

57 **limber:** *easily evaded* **58 unsphere, etc;** *cf. n.* **63 pay your fees;** *cf. n.* **82 chang'd:** *exchanged* **88 the imposition, etc.;** *cf. n.* **97 Grace to boot:** *Heavenly Grace help us* **113 tame things:** *well-fed pets* **one good deed, etc;** *cf. n.*

117 heat: *race over* **to the goal:** *to come to the point* **120 would her name were Grace:** *would that that were called a gracious deed!* **126 clap:** *declare by clapping thy hand into mine* **134 tremor cordis:** *trembling of the heart* **136 free:** *innocent* **137 fertile:** *generous* **142 mort o' the deer:** *note on hunter's horn announcing death of the deer* **143 brows;** *cf. n.* **146 I' fecks:** *in faith* **147 bawcock:** *fine lad* **smutch'd:** *soiled* **151 neat:** *cattle* **virginalling:** *playing with fingers; cf. n.* **155 pash:** *head* **shoots:** *horns* **159 o'er-dy'd blacks:** *mourning garments rotten from over-dyeing or worn by hypocritical mourners* **161 bourn:** *boundary* **163 welkin:** *sky-blue* **villain:** *little rogue* **164 my collop:** *a piece of my flesh* **dam:** *mother* **165, 166 Affection … dost;** *cf. n.*

Communicat'st with dreams;—how can this be?—
With what's unreal thou co-active art,
And fellow'st nothing: then, 'tis very credent
Thou mayst co-join with something; and thou dost,   *170*
And that beyond commission, and I find it,
And that to the infection of my brains
And hardening of my brows.

    Pol.   What means Sicilia?
    Her. He something seems unsettled.   *175*
    Pol.   How, my lord!
    Leon. What cheer? how is 't with you, best brother?
    Her.   You look
As if you held a brow of much distraction:
Are you mov'd, my lord?   *180*
    Leon.   No, in good earnest.
How sometimes nature will betray its folly,
Its tenderness, and make itself a pastime
To harder bosoms! Looking on the lines
Of my boy's face, methoughts I did recoil   *185*
Twenty-three years, and saw myself unbreech'd,
In my green velvet coat, my dagger muzzled,
Lest it should bite its master, and so prove,
As ornaments oft do, too dangerous:
How like, methought, I then was to this kernel,   *190*
This squash, this gentleman. Mine honest friend,
Will you take eggs for money?
    Mam.   No, my lord, I'll fight.
    Leon. You will? why, happy man be his dole! My brother,
Are you so fond of your young prince as we   *195*
Do seem to be of ours?
    Pol.   If at home, sir,
He 's all my exercise, my mirth, my matter,
Now my sworn friend and then mine enemy;
My parasite, my soldier, statesman, all: *200*
He makes a July's day short as December,
And with his varying childness cures in me
Thoughts that would thick my blood.
    Leon.   So stands this squire
Offic'd with me. We two will walk, my lord,   *205*
And leave you to your graver steps. Hermione,
How thou lov'st us, show in our brother's welcome:
Let what is dear in Sicily be cheap:
Next to thyself and my young rover, he's
Apparent to my heart.   *210*
    Her.   If you would seek us,
We are yours i' the garden: shall 's attend you there?
    Leon. To your own bents dispose you: you'll be found,
Be you beneath the sky.—*[Aside.]* I am angling now,
Though you perceive me not how I give line.   *215*
Go to, go to!
How she holds up the neb, the bill to him!
And arms her with the boldness of a wife
To her allowing husband!
             [Exeunt Polixenes, Hermione, and Attendants.]
                  Gone already!   *220*
Inch-thick, knee-deep, o'er head and ears a fork'd one!

Go play, boy, play; thy mother plays, and I
Play too, but so disgrac'd a part, whose issue
Will hiss me to my grave: contempt and clamour
Will be my knell. Go play, boy, play. There have been,   *225*
Or I am much deceiv'd, cuckolds ere now;
And many a man there is even at this present,
Now, while I speak this, holds his wife by the arm,
That little thinks she has been sluic'd in 's absence,
And his pond fish'd by his next neighbour, by   *230*
Sir Smile, his neighbour: nay, there's comfort in 't,
Whiles other men have gates, and those gates open'd,
As mine, against their will. Should all despair
That have revolted wives, the tenth of mankind
Would hang themselves. Physic for 't there is none: *235*
It is a bawdy planet, that will strike
Where 'tis predominant; and 'tis powerful, think it,
From east, west, noth, and south: be it concluded,
No barricado for a belly: know 't;
It will let in and out the enemy   *240*
With bag and baggage. Many a thousand on 's
Have the disease, and feel 't not. How now, boy!
    Mam. I am like you, they say.
    Leon.   Why, that 's some comfort.
What! Camillo there!   *245*
    Cam. Ay, my good lord.
    Leon. Go play, Mamillius; thou 'rt an honest man.
                           [Exit Mamillius.]
Camillo, this great sir will yet stay longer.
    Cam. You had much ado to make his anchor hold:
When you cast out, it still came home.   *250*
    Leon.   Didst note it?
    Cam. He would not stay at your petitions; made
His business more material.
    Leon.   Didst perceive it?
[Aside.] They're here with me already, whispering, rounding,   *255*
'Sicilia is a so-forth.' 'Tis far gone,
When I shall gust it last. How came 't, Camillo,
That he did stay?
    Cam.   At the good queen's entreaty.
    Leon. At the queen's, be 't: 'good' should be pertinent;   *260*
But so it is, it is not. Was this taken
By any understaning pate but thine?
For thy conceit is soaking; will draw in
More than the common blocks: not noted, is 't,
But of the finer natures? by some severals   *265*
Of head-piece extraordinary? lower messes
Perchance are to this business purblind? say.
    Cam. Business, my lord! I think most understand
Bohemia stays here longer.
    Leon.   Ha!   *270*
    Cam.   Stays here longer.
    Leon. Ay, but why?
    Cam. To satisfy your highness and the entreaties
Of our most gracious mistress.
    Leon.   Satisfy!   *275*
The entreaties of your mistress! satisfy!

---

170 something: *somewhat*   **191 squash:** *an unripe pea-pod*   **192 take eggs for money:** *allow yourself to be imposed on*   **194 dole:** *lot in life*   **202 childness:** *childish humors* **203 thick my blood:** *thicken my blood, cause melancholy*   **205 Offic'd with:** *in relation to* **210 Apparent:** *heir apparent*   **212 shall 's:** *shall we*   **213 bents:** *inclinations*   **217 neb:** *mouth*   **219 allowing:** *approving*   **221 a fork'd one:** *with forked horns*

223 issue: *outcome*   **236 strike:** *blast*   **237 predominant:** *strongest in influence;* *cf. n.*   **250 came home:** *came back without catching*   **253 material:** *important*   **255 here with me:** *making mocking gestures when mentioning me* **rounding:** *whispering* **257 gust:** *perceive*   **261 taken:** *understood*   **263 conceit:** *intelligence* **soaking:** *capable of absorbing*   **264 blocks:** *heads*   **265 severals:** *individuals*   **266 lower messes:** *men of inferior rank who ate, or messed, at a lower table*

Let that suffice. I have trusted thee, Camillo,
With all the nearest things to my heart, as well
My chamber-councils, wherein, priest-like, thou
Hast cleans'd my bosom: I from thee departed   280
Thy penitent reform'd; but we have been
Deceiv'd in thy integrity, deceiv'd
In that which seems so.

    Cam.   Be it forbid, my lord!

    Leon. To bide upon 't, thou art not honest; or,   285
If thou inclin'st that way, thou art a coward,
Which hoxes honesty behind, restraining
From course requir'd; or else thou must be counted
A servant grafted in my serious trust,
And therein negligent; or else a fool   290
That seest a game play'd home, the rich stake drawn,
And tak'st it all for jest.

    Cam.   My gracious lord,
I may be negligent, foolish, and fearful;
In every one of these no man is free,   295
But that his negligence, his folly, fear,
Among the infinite doings of the world,
Sometime puts forth. In your affairs, my lord,
If ever I were wilful-negligent,
It was my folly; if industriously   300
I play'd the fool, it was my negligence,
Not weighing well the end; if ever fearful
To do a thing, where I the issue doubted,
Whereof the execution did cry out
Against the non-performance, 'twas a fear   305
Which oft infects the wisest: these, my lord,
Are such allow'd infirmities that honesty
Is never free of. But, beseech your Grace,
Be plainer with me; let me know my trespass
By its own visage; if I then deny it,   310
'Tis none of mine.

    Leon.   Ha' not you seen, Camillo,—
But that 's past doubt; you have, or your eye-glass
Is thicker than a cuckold's horn,—or heard,—
For to a vision so apparent, rumour   315
Cannot be mute,—or thought,—for cogitation
Resides not in that man that does not think,—
My wife is slippery! If thou wilt confess,—
Or else be impudently negative,
To have nor eyes, nor ears, nor thought,—then say   320
My wife 's a hobby-horse; deserves a name
As rank as any flax-wench that puts to
Before her troth-plight: say 't and justify 't.

    Cam. I would not be a stander-by, to hear
My sovereign mistress clouded so, without   325
My present vengeance taken: 'shrew my heart,
You never spoke what did become you less
Than this; which to reiterate were sin
As deep as that, though true.

    Leon.   Is whispering nothing?   330
Is leaning cheek to cheek? is meeting noses?

Kissing with inside lip? stopping the career
Of laughter with a sigh?—a note infallible
Of breaking honesty,—horsing foot on foot?
Skulking in corners? wishing clocks more swift?   335
Hours, minutes? noon, midnight? and all eyes
Blind with the pin and web but theirs, theirs only,
That would unseen be wicked? is this nothing?
Why, then the world and all that's in 't is nothing;
The covering sky is nothing; Bohemia nothing;   340
My wife is nothing; nor nothing have these nothings,
If this be nothing.

    Cam.   Good my lord, be cur'd
Of this diseas'd opinion, and betimes;
For 'tis most dangerous.   345

    Leon.   Say it be, 'tis true.

    Cam. No, no, my lord.

    Leon.   It is; you lie, you lie:
I say thou liest, Camillo, and I hate thee;
Pronounce thee a gross lout, a mindless slave,   350
Or else a hovering temporizer, that
Canst with thine eyes at once see good and evil,
Inclining to them both: were my wife's liver
Infected as her life, she would not live
The running of one glass.   355

    Cam.   Who does infect her?

    Leon. Why, he that wears her like her medal, hanging
About his neck, Bohemia: who, if I
Had servants true about me, that bare eyes
To see alike mine honour as their profits,   360
Their own particular thrifts, they would do that
Which should undo more doing: ay, and thou,
His cup-bearer,—whom I from meaner form
Have bench'd and rear'd to worship, who mayst see
Plainly, as heaven sees earth, and earth sees heaven,   365
How I am galled,—mightst bespice a cup,
To give mine enemy a lasting wink;
Which draught to me were cordial.

    Cam.   Sir, my lord,
I could do this, and that with no rash potion,   370
But with a lingering dram that should not work
Maliciously like poison: but I cannot
Believe this crack to be in my dread mistress,
So sovereignly being honourable.
I have lov'd thee,—   375

    Leon.   Make that thy question, and go rot!
Dost think I am so muddy, so unsettled,
To appoint myself in this vexation; sully
The purity and whiteness of my sheets,
Which to preserve is sleep; which being spotted   380
Is goads, thorns, nettles, tails of wasps?
Give scandal to the blood o' the prince my son,
Who I do think is mine, and love as mine,
Without ripe moving to 't? Would I do this?
Could man so blench?   385

    Cam. I must believe you, sir:

---

279 **chamber-councils:** *private affairs*   285 **bide:** *dwell, lay emphasis*   287 **hoxes:** *hamstrings*   289 **grafted in my serious trust:** *whom I have trusted implicityly*   298 **puts forth:** *reveals itself*   304 **execution:** *successful performance later*   313 **eye-glass:** *crystalline lens of the eye*   315 **vision so apparent:** *spectacle so obvious*   318 **slippery:** *inconstant*   318-320 **If . . . thought;** *cf. n.*   321 **hobby-horse:** *immoral woman*   322 **flax-wench:** *female flax-dresser* **puts to:** *sins*   325 **clouded:** *shamefully accused; cf. n.*   326 **present:** *immediate* **'shrew:** *beshrew, curse*

334 **honesty:** *chastity*   337 **pin and web:** *cataracs*   355 **glass:** *hour-glass*   357 **medal,** *cf. n.*   361 **thrifts:** *advantages*   363 **meaner form:** *lower seat*   364 **bench'd:** *given a seat of authority* **worship:** *dignity, honor*   366 **bespice:** *poison*   367 **wink:** *sleep*   370 **rash:** *speedy*   372 **Maliciously:** *violently*   373 **crack:** *flaw*   374 **sovereignly:** *above all others*   376 **question:** *subject for thought*   378 **appoint:** *dress*   384 **ripe moving to 't:** *ample cause for it*   385 **blench:** *start aside from his course*

I do; and will fetch off Bohemia for 't;
Provided that when he 's remov'd, your highness
Will take again your queen as yours at first,
Even for your son's sake; and thereby for sealing   390
The injury of tongues in courts and kingdoms
Known and allied to yours.

    Leon.   Thou dost advise me
Even so as I mine own course have set down:
I'll give no blemish to her honour, none.   395
    Cam. My lord,
Go then; and with a countenance as clear
As friendship wears at feasts, keep with Bohemia,
And with your queen. I am his cupbearer;
If from me he have wholesome beverage,   400
Account me not your servant.
    Leon.   This is all:
Do 't, and thou hast the one half of my heart;
Do 't not, thou split'st thine own.
    Cam.   I'll do 't, my lord.   405
    Leon. I will seem friendly, as thou hast advis'd me.   *Exit.*
    Cam. O miserable lady! But, for me,
What case stand I in? I must be the poisoner
Of good Polixenes; and my ground to do 't
Is the obedience to a master; one   410
Who, in rebellion with himself, will have
All that are his so too. To do this deed
Promotion follows. If I could find example
Of thousands that had struck anointed kings,
And flourish'd after, I'd not do 't; but since   415
Nor brass nor stone nor parchment bears not one,
Let villainy itself forswear 't. I must
Forsake the court: to do 't, or no, is certain
To me a break-neck. Happy star reign now!
Here comes Bohemia.   420

           Enter Polixenes.

    Pol.   This is strange: methinks
My favour here begins to warp. Not speak?—
Good day, Camillo.
    Cam.   Hail, most royal sir!
    Pol. What is the news i' the court?   425
    Cam.   None rare, my lord.
    Pol. The king hath on him such a countenance
As he had lost some province and a region
Lov'd as he loves himself: even now I met him
With customary compliment, when he,   430
Wafting his eyes to the contrary, and falling
A lip of much contempt, speeds from me and
So leaves me to consider what is breeding
That changes thus his manners.
    Cam. I dare not know, my lord.   435
    Pol. How! dare not! do not! Do you know, and dare not
Be intelligent to me? 'Tis thereabouts;
For, to yourself, what you do know, you must,
And cannot say you dare not. Good Camillo
Your chang'd complexions are to me a mirror   440
Which shows me mine chang'd too; for I must be
A party in this alteration, finding

Myself thus alter'd with 't.
    Cam.   There is a sickness
Which puts some of us in distemper; but   445
I cannot name the disease, and it is caught
Of you that yet are well.
    Pol.   How! caught of me?
Make me not sighted like the basilisk:
I have look'd on thousands, who have sped the better   450
By my regard, but kill'd none so. Camillo,—
As you are certainly a gentleman, thereto
Clerk-like experienc'd, which no less adorns
Our gentry than our parents' noble names,
In whose success we are gentle,—I beseech you,   455
If you know aught which does behove my knowledge
Thereof to be inform'd, imprison it not
In ignorant concealment.
    Cam.   I may not answer.
    Pol. A sickness caught of me, and yet I well!   460
I must be answer'd. Dost thou hear, Camillo;
I conjure thee, by all the parts of man
Which honour does acknowledge,—whereof the least
Is not this suit of mine,—that thou declare
What incidency thou dost guess of harm   465
Is creeping toward me; how far off, how near;
Which way to be prevented if to be;
If not, how best to bear it.
    Cam.   Sir, I will tell you;
Since I am charg'd in honour and by him   470
That I think honourable. Therefore mark my counsel,
Which must be even as swiftly follow'd as
I mean to utter it, or both yourself and me
Cry 'lost,' and so good night!
    Pol.   On, good Camillo.   475
    Cam. I am appointed him to murder you.
    Pol. By whom, Camillo?
    Cam.   By the king.
    Pol.   For what?
    Cam. He thinks, nay, with all confidence he swears,   480
As he had seen 't or been an instrument
To vice you to 't, that you have touch'd his queen
Forbiddenly.
    Pol.   O, then my best blood turn
To an infected jelly, and my name   485
Be yok'd with his that did betray the Best!
Turn then my freshest reputation to
A savour, that may strike the dullest nostril
Where I arrive; and my approach be shunn'd,
Nay, hated too, worse than the great'st infection   490
That e'er was heard or read!
    Cam.   Swear his thought over
By each particular star in heaven and
By all their influences, you may as well
Forbid the sea for to obey the moon   495

---

387 fetch off: *make away with*   **390 sealing:** *sealing up, ending*   **391 injury of tongues:** *injury caused by gossip*   **419 break-neck:** *ruinous course*   **431 contrary:** *opposite direction* **falling:** *letting fall*   **437 intelligent:** *communicative* **thereabouts:** *about that*

449 Make me not sighted: *do not represent me as saving eyes*   **basilisk:** *fabulous monster whose glance was fatal*   **450 sped:** *fared*   **451 regard:** *look*   **452 thereto:** *in addition*   **453 Clerk-like:** *like a scholar*   **454 gentry:** *noble birth*   **455 In whose success:** *in succession or descent from whom* **gentle:** *of high rank*   **458 ignorant:** *causing ignorance*   **462 parts:** *traits and qualities*   **465 incidency:** *happening*   **476 him:** *the one*   **482 vice:** *force*   **492 Swear his thought over:** *try to overcome his suspicion by oaths*

As or by oath remove or counsel shake
The fabric of his folly, whose foundation
Is pil'd upon his faith, and will continue
The standing of his body.
    Pol.   How should this grow?   *500*
    Cam. I know not: but I am sure 'tis safer to
Avoid what's grown than question how 'tis born.
If therefore you dare trust my honesty,
That lies enclosed in this trunk, which you
Shall bear along impawn'd, away to-night!   *505*
Your followers I will whisper to the business,
And will by twos and threes at several posterns
Clear them o' the city. For myself, I'll put
My fortunes to your service, which are here
By this discovery lost. Be not uncertain;   *510*
For, by the honour of my parents, I
Have utter'd truth, which, if you seek to prove,
I dare not stand by; nor shall you be safer
Than one condemn'd by the king's own mouth, thereon
His execution sworn.   *515*
    Pol.   I do believe thee:
I saw his heart in 's face. Give me thy hand:
Be pilot to me and thy places shall
Still neighbour mine. My ships are ready and
My people did expect my hence departure   *520*
Two days ago. This jealousy
Is for a precious creature: as she's rare
Must it be great, and, as his person's mighty
Must it be violent, and, as he does conceive
He is dishonour'd by a man which ever   *525*
Profess'd to him, why, his revenges must
In that he made more bitter. Fear o'ershades me:
Good expedition be my friend, and comfort
The gracious queen, part of his theme, but nothing
Of his ill-ta'en suspicion! Come, Camillo;   *530*
I will respect thee as a father if
Thou bear'st my life off hence: let us avoid.
    Cam. It is in mine authority to command
The keys of all the posterns: please your highness
To take the urgent hour. Come, sir, away!   *Exeunt.*

ACT SECOND ❧ SCENE FIRST

[A Room in the Palace]
Enter Hermione, Mamillius, and Ladies.

    Her. Take the boy to you: he so troubles me,
'Tis past enduring.
    First Lady.   Come, my gracious lord,
Shall I be your playfellow?
    Mam.   No, I'll none of you.   *5*
    First Lady. Why, my sweet lord?
    Mam. You'll kiss me hard and speak to me as if
I were a baby still. I love you better.
    Sec. Lady. And why so, my lord?

    Mam.   Not for because   *10*
Your brows are blacker; yet black brows, they say,
Become some women best, so that there be not
Too much hair there, but in a semicircle,
Or a half-moon made with a pen.
    Sec. Lady.   Who taught you this?   *15*
    Mam. I learn'd it out of women's faces. Pray now,
What colour are your eyebrows?
    First Lady.   Blue, my lord.
    Mam. Nay, that's a mock: I have seen a lady's nose
That has been blue, but not her eyebrows.   *20*
    Sec. Lady.   Hark ye;
The queen your mother rounds apace: we shall
Present our services to a fine new prince
One of these days; and then you 'd wanton with us,
If we would have you.   *25*
    First Lady.   She is spread of late
Into a goodly bulk: good time encounter her!
    Her. What wisdom stirs amongst you? Come, sir, now
I am for you again: pray you, sit by us,
And tell 's a tale.   *30*
    Mam.   Merry or sad shall 't be?
    Her. As merry as you will.
    Mam.   A sad tale 's best for winter.
I have one of sprites and goblins.
    Her.   Let's have that, good sir.   *35*
Come on, sit down: come on, and do your best
To fright me with your sprites; you're powerful at it.
    Mam. There was a man,—
    Her.   Nay, come, sit down; then on.
    Mam. Dwelt by a churchyard. I will tell it softly;   *40*
Yond crickets shall not hear it.
    Her. Come on then,
And give 't me in mine ear.

    [Enter Leontes, Antigonus, Lords, and Others,]

    Leon. Was he met there? his train? Camillo with him?
    First Lord. Behind the tuft of pines I met them: never   *45*
Saw I men scour so on their way: I ey'd them
Even to their ships
    Leon.   How blest am I
In my just censure, in my true opinion!
Alack, for lesser knowledge! How accurs'd   *50*
In being so blest! There may be in the cup
A spider steep'd, and one may drink, depart,
And yet partake no venom, for his knowledge
Is not infected; but if one present
The abhorr'd ingredient to his eye, make known   *55*
How he hath drunk, he cracks his gorge, his sides,
With violent hefts. I have drunk, and seen the spider.
Camillo was his help in this, his pandar:
There is a plot against my life, my crown;
All 's true that is mistrusted: that false villain   *60*
Whom I employ'd was pre-employ'd by him:
He has discover'd my design, and I
Remain a pinch'd thing; yea, a very trick
For them to play at will. How came the posterns

496 or . . . or: *either . . . or*   **498 continue:** *last as long as*   **504 trunk:** *body*   **505 impawn'd:** *as a pledge*   **507 posterns:** *small gates in city walls*   **508 Clear them o':** *get them away from*   **510 discovery:** *revelation*   **uncertain:** *undecided*   **518 places:** *official positions*   **526 Profess'd:** *professed friendship*   **528-530** *Cf. n.*   **532 avoid:** *depart*   **Scene One S. d.;** *cf. n.*

12 so that: *provided that*   **24 wanton:** *play*   **29 for you:** *at your service*   **46 scour:** *hasten*   **49 censure:** *judgment*   **50 Alack, for lesser knowledge:** *would I had known less!*   **53 partake no venom;** *cf. n.*   **56 gorge:** *throat*   **57 hefts:** *retchings*   **62 discover'd:** *revealed*   **63 pinch'd:** *ridiculous*   **trick:** *trifle, toy*

So easily open?   65
  First Lord. By his great authority;
Which often hath no less prevail'd than so
On your command.
  Leon.   I know 't too well.
  [To Hermione.] Give me the boy: I am glad you did not   70
nurse him:
Though he does bear some signs of me, yet you
Have too much blood in him.
  Her.   What is this? sport?
  Leon. Bear the boy hence; he shall not come about her;   75
Away with him!—   *[Exit Mamillius, attended.]*
and let her sport herself
With that she's big with; for 'tis Polixenes
Has made thee swell thus.
  Her.   But I'd say he had not,   80
And I'll be sworn you would believe my saying,
Howe'er you lean to the nayward,
  Leon.   You, my lords,
Look on her, mark her well; be but about
To say, 'she is a goodly lady,' and   85
The justice of your hearts will thereto add,
' 'Tis pity she's not honest, honourable:'
Priase her but for this her without-door form,—
Which, on my faith deserves high speech,—and straight
The shrug, the hum or ha, these petty brands   90
That calumny doth use,—O, I am out!—
That mercy does, for calumny will sear
Virtue itself: these shrugs, these hums and ha's,
When you have said 'she 's goodly,' come between,
Ere you can say 'she 's honest.' But be 't known,   95
From him that has most cause to grieve it should be,
She's an adulteress.
  Her.   Should a villain say so,
The most replenish'd villain in the world,
He were as much more villain: you, my lord,   100
Do but mistake.
  Leon.   You have mistook, my lady,
Polixenses for Leontes. O thou thing!
Which I'll not call a creature of thy place,
Lest barbarism, making me the precedent,   105
Should a like language use to all degrees,
And mannerly distinguishment leave out
Betwixt the prince and beggar: I have said
She's an adultress; I have said with whom:
More, she 's a traitor, and Camillo is   110
A federary with her, and one that knows
What she should shame to know herself
But with her most vile principal, that she 's
A bed-swerver, even as bad as those
That vulgars give bold'st titles; ay, and privy   115
To this their late escape.
  Her.   No, by my life,
Privy to none of this. How will this grieve you
When you shall come to clearer knowledge that
You thus have publish'd me! Gentle my lord,   120

You scarce can right me throughly then to say
You did mistake.
  Leon.   No; if I mistake
In those foundations which I build upon,
The centre is not big enough to bear   125
A schoolboy's top. Away with her to prison!
He who shall speak for her is afar off guilty
But that he speaks.
  Her.   There 's some ill planet reigns:
I must be patient till the heavens look   130
With an aspect more favourable. Good my lords,
I am not prone to weeping, as our sex
Commonly are; the want of which vain dew
Perchance shall dry your pities; but I have
That honourable grief lodg'd here which burns   135
Worse than tears drown. Beseech you all, my lords,
With thoughts so qualified as your charities
Shall best instruct you, measure me; and so
The king's will be perform'd!
  Leon.   *[To the Guards.]* Shall I be heard?   140
  Her. Who is 't that goes with me? Beseech your highness,
My women may be with me; for you see
My plight requires it. Do not weep, good fools;
There is no cause: when you shall know your mistress
Has deserv'd prison, then abound in tears   145
As I come out: this action I now go on
Is for my better grace. Adieu, my lord:
I never wish'd to see you sorry; now
I trust I shall. My women, come; you have leave.
  Leon. Go, do our bidding: hence!   150
              [Exeunt Queen guarded, and Ladies.]
  First Lord. Beseech your highness call the queen again.
  Ant. Be certain what you do, sir, lest your justice
Prove violence: in the which three great ones suffer,
Yourself, your queen, your son.
  First Lord.   For her, my lord,   155
I dare my life lay down, and will do 't, sir,
Please you to accept it, that the queen is spotless
I' the eyes of heaven and to you: I mean,
In this which you accuse her.
  Ant.   If it prove   160
She 's otherwise, I'll keep my stables where
I lodge my wife; I'll go in couples with her;
Than when I feel and see her no further trust her;
For every inch of woman in the world,
Ay, every dram of woman's flesh is false,   165
If she be.
  Leon. Hold your peaces!
  First Lord.   Good my lord,—
  Ant. It is for you we speak, not for ourselves.
You are abus'd, and by some putter-on   170
That will be damn'd for 't; would I knew the villain,
I would land-damn him. Be she honour-flaw'd,—
I have three daughters; the eldest is eleven,
The second and the third, nine and some five;
If this prove true, they'll pay for 't: by mine honour,   175

---

82 nayward: *contrary*   **87 honest:** *chaste*   **88 without-door form:** *external appearance*   **91 out:** *wrong, like an actor who has forgotten his part*   **99 replenish'd:** *complete*   **104 place:** *high rank*   **111 federary:** *confederate, accomplice*   **113 principal:** *leader insin*   **114 bed-swerver:** *adultress*   **115 vulgars:** *the vulgar*   **120 publish'd:** *denounced publicly*

121 throughly: *thoroughly*   **125 centre:** *earth*   **127 afar off:** *indirectly*   **131 aspect:** *position and influence of a planet*   **137 qualified:** *moderated*   **138 measure:** *judge*   **143 fools:** *a term of endearment, not contempt*   **146 action:** *legal accusation*   **157 Please you:** *if you please*   **161, 162 I'll ... wife;** *cf. n.*   **170 abus'd:** *deceived* **putter-on:** *instigator, plotter*   **172 land-damn;** *cf. n.*

I'll geld them all; fourteen they shall not see,
To bring false generations: they are co-heirs;
And I had rather glib myself than they
Should not produce fair issue.
    Leon.   Cease! no more.   *180*
You smell this business with a sense as cold
As is a dead man's nose; but I do see 't and feel 't,
As you feel doing thus, and see withal
The instruments that feel.
    Ant.   If it be so,   *185*
We need no grave to bury honesty:
There's not a grain of it the face to sweeten
Of the whole dungy earth.
    Leon.   What! lack I credit?
    First Lord. I had rather you did lack than I, my lord,   *190*
Upon this ground; and more it would content me
To have her honour true than your suspicion,
Be blam'd for 't how you might.
    Leon.   Why, what need we
Commune with you of this, but rather follow   *195*
Our forceful instigation? Our prerogative
Calls not your counsels, but our natural goodness
Imparts this; which if you,—or stupefied
Or seeming so in skill,—cannot or will not
Relish a truth like us, inform yourselves   *200*
We need no more of your advice: the matter,
The loss, the gain, the ordering on 't, is all
Properly ours.
    Ant.   And I wish, my liege,
You had only in your silent judgment tried it,   *205*
Without more overture.
    Leon.   How could that be?
Either thou art most ignorant by age,
Or thou wert born a fool. Camillo's flight,
Added to their familiarity,   *210*
Which was as gross as ever touch'd conjecture,
That lack'd sight only, nought for approbation
But only seeing, all other circumstances
Made up to the deed, doth push on this proceeding:
Yet, for a greater confirmation,—   *215*
For in an act of this importance 'twere
Most piteous to be wild,—I have dispatch'd in post
To sacred Delphos, to Apollo's temple,
Cleomenes and Dion, whom you know
Of stuff'd sufficiency. Now, from the oracle   *220*
They will bring all; whose spiritual counsel had,
Shall stop or spur me. Have I done well?
    First Lord. Well done, my lord.
    Leon. Though I am satisfied and need no more
Than what I know, yet shall the oracle   *225*
Give rest to the minds of others, such as he
Whose ignorant credulity will not
Come up to the truth. So have we thought it good
From our free person she should be confin'd,
Lest that the treachery of the two fled hence   *230*
Be left her to perform. Come, follow us:
We are to speak in public; for this business

Will raise us all.
    Ant. *[Aside.]* To laughter, as I take it,
If the good truth were known.   *Exeunt.*

❧ Scene Second ❧

[At the Gate of a Prison]
Enter Paulina [and Attendants].

    Paul. The keeper of the prison, call to him;
Let him have knowledge who I am.—   *[Exit an Attendant.]*
Good lady,
no court in europe is too good for thee;
What dost thou then in prison?   *5*

    [Enter Attendant with the Gaoler.]

               Now, good sir,
You know me, do you not?
    Gaol.   For a worthy lady
And one whom much I honour.
    Paul.   Pray you then,   *10*
Conduct me to the queen.
    Gaol. I may not, madam: to the contrary
I have express commandment.
    Paul.   Here 's ado,
To lock up honesty and honour from   *15*
The access of gentle visitors! Is 't lawful, pray you,
To see her women? any of them? Emilia?
    Gaol. So please you, madam,
To put apart these your attendants, I
Shall bring Emilia forth.   *20*
    Paul.   I pray now, call her.
Withdraw yourselves.   *[Exeunt Attendants.]*
    Gaol.   And, madam,
I must be present at your conference.
    Paul. Well, be 't so, prithee.   *[Exit Gaoler.]*   *25*
Here's such ado to make no stain a stain
As passes colouring.

    [Enter Gaoler, with Emilia.]

               Dear gentlewoman,
How fares our gracious lady?
    Emil. As well as one so great and so forlorn   *30*
May hold together. On her frights and griefs,—
Which never tender lady hath borne greater,—
She is something before her time deliver'd.
    Paul. A boy?
    Emil.   A daughter; and a goodly babe,   *35*
Lusty and like to live: the queen receives
Much comfort in 't: says, 'My poor prisoner,
I am innocent as you.'
    Paul.   I dare be sworn:
These dangerous unsafe lunes i' the king, beshrew them!   *40*
He must be told on 't, and he shall: the office
Becomes a woman best; I'll take 't upon me.
If I prove honey-mouth'd, let my tongue blister,
And never to my red-look'd anger be
The trumpet any more. Pray you, Emilia,   *45*
Commend my best obedience to the queen:

If she dares trust me with her little babe,
I'll show it to the king and undertake to be
Her advocate to the loud'st. We do not know
How he may soften at the sight of the child: 50
The silence often of pure innocence
Persuades when speaking fails.
    Emil.   Most worthy madam,
Your honour and your goodness is so evident
That your free undertaking cannot miss   55
A thriving issue: there is no lady living
So meet for this great errand. Please your ladyship
To visit the next room, I'll presently
Acquaint the queen of your most noble offer,
Who but to-day hammer'd of this design,   60
But durst not tempt a minister of honour,
Lest she should be denied.
    Paul.   Tell her, Emilia,
I'll use that tongue I have: if wit flow from 't
As boldness from my bosom, let it not be doubted   65
I shall do good.
    Emil.   Now be you blest for it!
I'll to the queen. Please you, come something nearer.
    Gaol. Madam, if 't please the queen to send the babe,
I know not what I shall incur to pass it,   70
Having no warrant.
    Paul.   You need not fear it, sir:
The child was prisoner to the womb, and is
By law and process of great nature thence
Freed and enfranchis'd; not a party to   75
The anger of the king, nor guilty of,
If any be, the trespass of the queen.
    Gaol. I do believe it.
    Paul. Do not you fear: upon mine honour, I
Will stand betwixt you and danger.   *Exeunt.* 80

❧ SCENE THIRD ❧

[A Room in the Palace]
Enter Leontes, Servants, Antigonus, and Lords.

    Leon. Nor night, nor day, no rest; it is but weakness
To bear the matter thus; mere weakness. If
The cause were not in being,—part o' the cause,
She the adultress; for the harlot king
Is quite beyond mine arm, out of the blank   5
And level of my brain, plot-proof; but she
I can hook to me: say, that she were gone,
Given to the fire, a moiety of my rest
Might come to me again. Who 's there?
    First Atten.   *[Advancing.]* My lord?   10
    Leon. How does the boy?
    First Atten. He took good rest to-night;
'Tis hop'd his sickness is discharg'd.
    Leon.   To see his nobleness!
Conceiving the dishonour of his mother,
He straight declin'd, droop'd, took it deeply,   15

Fasten'd and fix'd the shame on 't in himself,
Threw off his spirit, his appetite, his sleep,
And downright languish'd. Leave me solely: go,
See how he fares.   *[Exit Attendant.]*   20
               Fie, fie! no thought of him;
The very thought of my revenges that way
Recoil upon me: in himself too mighty,
And in his parties, his alliance; let him be
Until a time may serve: for present vengeance,   25
Take it on her. Camillo and Polixenes
Laugh at me; make their pastime at my sorrow:
They should not laugh, if I could reach them, nor
Shall she within my power.

         Enter Paulina [with a Child].

    First Lord.   You must not enter.   30
    Paul. Nay, rather, good my lords, be second to me:
Fear you his tyrannous passion more, alas,
Than the queen's life? a gracious innocent soul,
More free than he is jealous.
    Ant.   That 's enough.   35
    Sec. Atten. Madam, he hath not slept to-night; commanded
None should come at him.
    Paul.   Not so hot, good sir;
I come to bring him sleep. 'Tis such as you,
That creep like shadows by him and do sigh   40
At each his needless heavings, such as you
Nourish the cause of his awaking: I
Do come with words as med'cinal as true,
Honest as either, to purge him of that humour
That presses him from sleep.   45
    Leon.   What noise there, ho?
    Paul. No noise, my lord; but needful conference
About some gossips for your highness.
    Leon.   How!
Away with that audacious lady! Antigonus,   50
I charg'd thee that she should not come about me:
I knew she would.
    Ant.   I told her so, my lord,
On your displeasure's peril, and on mine,
She should not visit you.   55
    Leon.   What! canst not rule her?
    Paul. From all dishonesty he can: in this,
Unless he take the course that you have done,
Commit me for committing honour, trust it,
He shall not rule me.   60
    Ant.   La you now! you hear;
When she will take the rein I let her run;
But she'll not stumble.
    Paul.   Good my liege, I come,
And I beseech you, hear me, who professes   65
Myself your loyal servant, your physician,
Your most obedient counsellor, yet that dares
Less appear so in comforting your evils
Than such as most seem yours: I say, I come
From your good queen.   70
    Leon.   Good queen!

55 free: *magnanimous*   **56 thriving issue:** *successful result*   **57 meet:** *well fitted*   **58 presently:** *instantly*   **60 hammer'd of:** *thought over*   **61 minister:** *agent*   **64 wit:** *wisdom*   **5 blank:** *white spot in the middle of target*   **6 level:** *aim*   **8 moiety:** *part, usually half*

16 on: *of*   **19 solely:** *alone*   **31 second:** *lending support*   **41 each:** *each of* **heavings:** *sighings*   **44 humour:** *cf.n.*   **48 gossips:** *godparents for the child*   **59 Commit . . . committing:** *imprison . . . putting in practice*   **68 comforting your evils:** *encouraging your evil acts*

Paul. Good queen, my lord, good queen; I say, good queen;
And would by combat make her good, so were I
A man, the worst about you.
    Leon.   Force her hence.   *75*
    Paul. Let him that makes but trifles of his eyes
First hand me: on mine own accord I'll off;
But first I'll do my errand. The good queen,
For she is good, hath brought you forth a daughter:
Here 'tis; commends it to your blessing.   *80*
                            [Laying down the Child.]
    Leon.   Out!
A mankind witch! Hence with her, out o' door:
A most intelligencing bawd!
    Paul.   Not so;
I am as ignorant in that as you   *85*
In so entitling me, and no less honest
Than you are mad; which is enough, I'll warrant,
As this world goes, to pass for honest.
    Leon.   Traitors!
Will you not push her out? Give her the bastard.   *90*
[To Antigonus.] Thou dotard! thou art woman-tir'd, unroosted
By thy dame Partlet here. Take up the bastard;
Take 't up, I say; give 't to thy crone.
    Paul.   For ever
Unvenerable be thy hands, if thou   *95*
Tak'st up the princess by that forced baseness
Which he has put upon 't!
    Leon.   He dreads his wife.
    Paul. So I would you did; then, 'twere past all doubt,
You'd call your children yours.   *100*
    Leon.   A nest of traitors!
    Ant. I am none, by this good light.
    Paul.   Nor I; nor any
But one that 's here, and that 's himself; for he
The sacred honour of himself, his queen's,   *105*
His hopeful son's, his babe's, betrays to slander,
Whose sting is sharper than the sword's; and will not,—
For, as the case now stands, it is a curse
He cannot be compell'd to 't,—once remove
The root of his opinion, which is rotten   *110*
As ever oak or stone was sound.
    Leon.   A callat
Of boundless tongue, who late hath beat her husband
And now baits me! This brat is none of mine;
It is the issue of Polixenes: *115*
Hence with it; and, together with the dam
Commit them to the fire!
    Paul.   It is yours;
And, might we lay the old proverb to your charge,
'So like you, 'tis the worse.' Behold, my lords,   *120*
Although the print be little, the whole matter
And copy of the father; eye, nose, lip,
The trick of 's frown, his forehead, nay, the valley,
The pretty dimples of his chin and cheek, his smiles,
The very mould and frame of hand, nail, finger: *125*
And thou, good goddess Nature, which hast made it
So like to him that got it, if thou hast

The ordering of the mind too, 'mongst all colours
No yellow in 't; lest she suspect, as he does,
Her children not her husband's.   *130*
    Leon.   A gross hag!
And, lozel, thou art worthy to be hang'd,
That wilt not stay her tongue.
    Ant.   Hang all the husbands
That cannot do that feat, you'll leave yourself   *135*
Hardly one subject.
    Leon.   Once more, take her hence.
    Paul. A most unworthy and unnatural lord
Can do no more.
    Leon.   I'll ha' thee burn'd.   *140*
    Paul.   I care not:
It is a heretic that makes the fire,
Not she which burns in 't. I'll not call you tyrant;
But this most cruel usage of your queen,—
Not able to produce more accusation   *145*
Than your own weak-hing'd fancy,—something savours
Of tyranny, and will ignoble make you,
Yea, scandalous to the world.
    Leon.   On your allegiance,
Out of the chamber with her! Were I a tyrant,   *150*
Where were her life? she durst not call me so
If she did know me one. Away with her!
    Paul. I pray you do not push me; I'll be gone.
Look to your babe, my lord; 'tis yours: Jove send her
A better guiding spirit! What need these hands?   *155*
You, that are thus so tender o'er his follies,
Will never do him good, not one of you.
So, so: farewell; we are gone.   *Exit.*
    Leon. Thou, traitor, hast set on thy wife to this.
My child! away with 't!—even thou, that hast   *160*
A heart so tender o'er it, take it hence
And see it instantly consum'd with fire:
Even thou and none but thou. Take it up straight:
Within this hour bring me word 'tis done,—
And by good testimony,—or I'll seize thy life,   *165*
With what thou else call'st thine. If thou refuse
And wilt encounter with my wrath, say so;
The bastard brains with these my proper hands
Shall I dash out. Go, take it to the fire;
For thou sett'st on thy wife.   *170*
    Ant.   I did not, sir:
These lords, my noble fellows, if they please,
Can clear me in 't.
    First Lord.   We can, my royal liege,
He is not guilty of her coming hither.   *175*
    Leon. You are liars all.
    First Lord. Beseech your highness, give us better credit:
We have always truly serv'd you, and beseech you
So to esteem of us; and on our knees we beg,
As recompense of our dear services   *180*
Past and to come, that you do change this purpose,
Which being so horrible, so bloody, must
Lead on to some foul issue. We all kneel.
    Leon. I am a feather for each wind that blows.
Shall I live on to see this bastard kneel   *185*
And call me father? Better burn it now

---

77 hand: *lay hands on*   **82 mankind:** *mannish*   **83 intelligencing:** *acting as go-between*   **91 woman-tir'd:** *hen-pecked*   **92 dame Partlet:** *lecturing wife; cf. n.*   **96 forced baseness:** *arbitrarily imposed title of bastard*   **112 callat:** *disreputable woman*   **127 got:** *begot*

129 yellow: *the color symbolizing jealousy*   **132 lozel:** *worthless rascal*   **168 proper:** *own*   **172 fellows:** *comrades*   **180 dear:** *loving*

Than curse it then. But, be it; let it live:
It shall not neither.—*[To Antigonus.]* You, sir, come you
hither;
You that have been so tenderly officious   *190*
With Lady Margery, your midwife there,
To save this bastard's life,—for 'tis a bastard.
So sure as this beard 's grey,—what will you adventure
To save this brat's life?
    Ant.   Anything, my lord,   *195*
That my ability may undergo,
And nobleness impose: at least, thus much:
I'll pawn the little blood which I have left,
To save the innocent: anything possible.
    Leon. It shall be possible. Swear by this sword   *200*
Thou wilt perform my bidding.
    Ant.   I will, my lord.
    Leon. Mark and perform it—seest thou!—for the fail
Of any point in 't shall not only be
Death to thyself, but to thy lewd-tongu'd wife,   *205*
Whom for this time we pardon. We enjoin thee,
As thou art liegeman to us, that thou carry
This female bastard hence; and that thou bear it
To some remote and desert place quite out
Of our dominions; and that there thou leave it,   *210*
Without more mercy, to it own protection,
And favour of the climate. As by strange fortune
It came to us, I do in justice charge thee,
On thy soul's peril and thy body's torture,
That thou commend it strangely to some place,   *215*
Where chance may nurse or end it. Take it up.
    Ant. I swear to do this, though a present death
Had been more merciful. Come on, poor babe:
Some powerful spirit instruct the kites and ravens
To be thy nurses! Wolves and bears, they say,   *220*
Casting their savageness aside have done
Like offices of pity. Sir, be prosperous
In more than this deed does require! And blessing
Against this cruelty fight on thy side,
Poor thing, condemn'd to loss!   *Exit [with the Child].*   *225*
    Leon.   No; I'll not rear
Another's issue.

                        Enter a Servant.

    Serv.   Please your highness, posts
From those you sent to the oracle are come
An hour since: Cleomenes and Dion,   *230*
Being well arriv'd from Delphos, are both landed,
Hasting to the court.
    First Lord.   So please you, sir, their speed
Hath been beyond account.
    Leon.   Twenty-three days   *235*
They have been absent: 'tis good speed; foretells
The great Apollo suddenly will have
The truth of this appear. Prepare you, lords;
Summon a session, that we may arraign
Our most disloyal lady; for, as she hath   *240*
Been publicly accus'd, so shall she have
A just and open trial. While she lives

My heart will be a burden to me. Leave me,
And think upon my bidding.   *Exeunt.*

ACT THIRD ❧ SCENE FIRST

[A Town in Sicilia]
Enter Cleomenes and Dion.

    Cleo. The climate's delicate, the air most sweet,
Fertile the isle, the temple much surpassing
The common praise it bears.
    Dion.   I shall report,
For most it caught me, the celestial habits,—   *5*
Methinks I so should term them,—and the reverence
Of the grave wearers. O, the sacrifice!
How ceremonious, solemn, and unearthly
It was i' the offering!
    Cleo.   But of all, the burst   *10*
And the ear-deafening voice o' the oracle,
Kin to Jove's thunder, so surpris'd my sense,
That I was nothing.
    Dion.   If the event o' the journey
Prove as successful to the queen,—O, be 't so!—   *15*
As it hath been to us rare, pleasant, speedy,
The time is worth the use on 't.
    Cleo.   Great Apollo
Turn all to the best! These proclamations,
So forcing faults upon Hermione,   *20*
I little like.
    Dion.   The violent carriage of it
Will clear or end the business: when the oracle,
Thus by Apollo's great divine seal'd up,
Shall the contents discover, something rare   *25*
Even then will rush to knowledge.—
[To an Attendant.] Go:—fresh horses!
And gracious be the issue!   *Exeunt.*

❧ SCENE SECOND ❧

[A Court of Justice]
Enter Leontes, Lords, Officers.

    Leon. This sessions, to our great grief we pronounce,
Even pushes 'gainst our heart: the party tried
The daughter of a king, our wife, and one
Of us too much belov'd. Let us be clear'd
Of being tyrannous, since we so openly   *5*
Proceed in justice, which shall have due course,
Even to the guilt or the purgation.
Produce the prisoner.
    Offi. It is his highness' pleasure that the queen
Appear in person here in court. Silence!   *10*

    [Enter Hermione guarded; Paulina and Ladies attending.]

    Leon. Read the indictment.
    Offi. [Reads.] 'Hermione, queen to the worthy Leontes, King

---

191 Lady Margery: *a contemptuous term*   **193 this:** *Antigonus'*   **203 fail:** *failure*   **211 it:** *its*   **215 commend:** *entrust* **strangely:** *as a stranger*   **223 require:** *deserve*   **225 loss:** *being abandoned*   **234 beyond account:** *unaccountable*   **237 suddenly:** *promptly*

5 habits: *garments*   **14 event:** *outcome*   **22 carriage:** *management*   **28 gracious:** *favorable*   **7 purgation:** *acquittal*

of Sicilia, thou art here accused and arraigned of high treason,
in committing adultery with Polixenes, King of Bohemia, and
conspiring with Camillo to take away the life of our sovereign
lord the king, thy royal husband: the pretence whereof being
by circumstances partly laid open, thou, Hermione, contrary to
the faith and allegiance of a true subject, didst counsel and aid
them, for their better safety, to fly away by night.'

   Her. Since what I am to say must be but that   *20*
Which contradicts my accusation, and
The testimony on my part no other
But what comes from myself, it shall scarce boot me
To say 'Not guilty:' mine integrity
Being counted falsehood, shall, as I express it,   *25*
Be so receiv'd. But thus: if powers divine
Behold our human actions, as they do,
I doubt not then but innocence shall make
False accusation blush, and tyranny
Tremble at patience. You, my lord, best know,—   *30*
Who least will seem to do so,—my past life
Hath been as continent, as chaste, as true,
As I am now unhappy; which is more
Than history can pattern, though devis'd
And play'd to take spectators. For behold me,   *35*
A fellow of the royal bed, which owe
A moiety of the throne, a great king's daughter,
The mother to a hopeful prince, here standing
To prate and talk for life and honour 'fore
Who please to come and hear. For life, I prize it   *40*
As I weigh grief, which I would spare: for honour,
'Tis a derivative from me to mine,
And only that I stand for. I appeal
To your own conscience, sir, before Polixenes
Came to your court, how I was in your grace,   *45*
How merited to be so; since he came,
With what encounter so uncurrent I
Have strain'd, to appear thus: if one jot beyond
The bound of honour, or in act or will
That way inclining, harden'd be the hearts   *50*
Of all that hear me, and my near'st of kin
Cry fie upon my grave!
   Leon.   I ne'er heard yet
That any of these bolder vices wanted
Less impudence to gainsay what they did   *55*
Than to perform it first.
   Her.   That's true enough;
Though 'tis a saying, sir, not due to me.
   Leon. You will not own it.
   Her.   More than mistress of   *60*
Which comes to me in name of fault, I must not
At all acknowledge. For Polixenes,—
With whom I am accus'd,—I do confess
I lov'd him as in honour he requir'd,
With such a kind of love as might become   *65*
A lady like me; with a love even such,
So and no other, as yourself commanded:
Which not to have done I think had been in me

Both disobedience and ingratitude
To you and toward your friend, whose love had spoke,   *70*
Even since it could speak, from an infant, freely
That it was yours. Now, for conspiracy,
I know not how it tastes, though it be dish'd
For me to try how: all I know of it
Is that Camillo was an honest man;   *75*
And why he left your court, the gods themselves,
Wotting no more than I, are ignorant.
   Leon. You knew of his departure, as you know
What you have underta'en to do in 's absence.
   Her. Sir,   *80*
You speak a language that I understand not:
My life stands in the level of your dreams,
Which I'll lay down.
   Leon.   Your actions are my dreams:
You had a bastard by Polixenes,   *85*
And I but dream'd it. As you were past all shame,—
Those of your fact are so,—so past all truth:
Which to deny concerns more than avails; for as
Thy brat hath been cast out, like to itself,
No father owning it,—which is, indeed,   *90*
More criminal in thee than it,—so thou
Shalt feel our justice, in whose easiest passage
Look for no less than death.
   Her.   Sir, spare your threats:
The bug which you would fright me with I seek.   *95*
To me can life be no commodity:
The crown and comfort of my life, your favour,
I do give lost; for I do feel it gone,
But know not how it went. My second joy,
And first-fruits of my body, from his presence   *100*
I am barr'd, like one infectious. My third comfort,
Starr'd most unluckily, is from my breast,
The innocent milk in its most innocent mouth,
Hal'd out to murder: myself on every post
Proclaim'd a strumpet: with immodest hatred   *105*
The child-bed privilege denied, which 'longs
To women of all fashion: lastly, hurried
Here to this place, i' the open air, before
I have got strength of limit. Now, my liege,
Tell me what blessings I have here alive,   *110*
That I should fear to die? Therefore proceed.
But yet hear this; mistake me not; no life,
I prize it not a straw:—but for mine honour,
Which I would free, if I shall be condemn'd
Upon surmises, all proofs sleeping else   *115*
But what your jealousies awake, I tell you
'Tis rigour and not law. Your honours all,
I do refer me to the oracle:
Apollo be my judge!
   First Lord.   This your request   *120*
Is altogether just: therefore, bring forth,
And in Apollo's name, his oracle.   *[Exeunt certain Officers.]*
   Her. The Emperor of Russia was my father:
O! that he were alive, and here beholding

---

16 pretence: *purpose, design*   **23 boot:** *profit*   **34 pattern:** *give examples of*   **35 take:** *bewitch, fascinate*   **36 owe:** *own*   **38 hopeful:** *inspiring hope*   **47 encounter:** *behaviour*   **uncurrent:** *extraordinary*   **48 strain'd:** *transgressed beyond due limits*   **55 gainsay:** *deny*   **60-62 More … acknowledge;** *cf. n.*

77 Wotting: *knowing*   **82** *Cf. n.*   **87 fact:** *deed*   **88 concerns more than avails:** *is more significant than helpful to you*   **92 passage:** *procedure*   **95 bug:** *bugbear*   **96 commodity:** *advantage*   **102 Starr'd most unluckily:** *born under stars of most evil influence*   **105 immodest:** *immoderate*   **107 fashion:** *kinds*   **109 of limit:** *from a limited, or normal, period of recuperation*

His daughter's trial; that he did but see   *125*
The flatness of my misery; yet with eyes
Of pity, not revenge!

      [Enter Officers, with Cleomenes and Dion.]

      Offi. You here shall swear upon this sword of justice,
That you, Cleomenes and Dion, have
Been both at Delphos, and from thence have brought   *130*
This seal'd-up oracle, by the hand deliver'd
Of great Apollo's priest, and that since then
You have not dar'd to break the holy seal,
Nor read the secrets in 't.
      Cleo.
      Dion. } All this we swear.   *135*
      Leon. Break up the seals, and read.
      Offi. [Reads.] 'Hermione is chaste; Polixenes blameless;
Camillo a true subject; Leontes a jealous tyrant; his innocent
babe truly begotten; and the king shall live without an heir *140*
if that which is lost be not found.'
      Lords. Now blessed be the great Apollo!
      Her.   Praised!
      Leon. Hast thou read truth?
      Offi.   Ay, my lord; even so   *145*
As it is here set down.
      Leon. There is no truth at all i' the oracle:
The sessions shall proceed: this is mere falsehood.

      [Enter a Servant.]

      Serv. My lord the king, the king!
      Leon.   What is the business?   *150*
      Ser. O sir! I shall be hated to report it:
The prince your son, with mere conceit and fear
Of the queen's speed, is gone.
      Leon.   How! gone!
      Ser.   Is dead.   *155*
      Leon. Apollo's angry; and the heavens themselves
Do strike at my injustice.   *[Hermione swoons.]*
                How now, there!
      Paul. This news is mortal to the queen:—look down,
And see what death is doing.   *160*
      Leon.   Take her hence:
Her heart is but o'ercharg'd; she will recover:
I have too much believ'd mine own suspicion:
Beseech you, tenderly apply to her
Some remedies for life.—   *165*
      [Exeunt Paulina and Ladies, with Hermione.]
Apollo, pardon
My great profaneness 'gainst thine oracle!
I'll reconcile me to Polixenes,
New woo my queen, recall the good Camillo,
Whom I proclaim a man of truth, of mercy;   *170*
For, being transported by my jealousies
To bloody thoughts and to revenge, I chose
Camillo for the minister to poison
My friend Polixenes: which had been done,
But that the good mind of Camillo tardied   *175*
My swift command; though I with death and with
Reward did threaten and encourage him,

Not doing it, and being done: he, most humane
And fill'd with honour, to my kingly guest
Unclasp'd my practice, quit his fortunes here.   *180*
Which you knew great, and to the certain hazard
Of all incertainties himself commended,
No richer than his honour: how he glisters
Thorough my rust! and how his piety
Does my deeds make the blacker!   *185*

      [Enter Paulina.]

      Paul.   Woe the while!
O, cut my lace, lest my heart, cracking it,
Break too!
      First Lord. What fit is this, good lady?
      Paul. What studied torments, tyrant, hast for me?   *190*
What wheels? racks? fires? What flaying? boiling
In leads, or oils? what old or newer torture
Must I receive, whose every word deserves
To taste of thy most worst? Thy tyranny,
Together working with thy jealousies,   *195*
Fancies too weak for boys, too green and idle
For girls of nine, O! think what they have done,
And then run mad indeed, stark mad; for all
Thy by-gone fooleries were but spices of it.
That thou betray'dst Polixenes, 'twas nothing;   *200*
That did but show thee of a fool, inconstant
And damnable ingrateful; nor was 't much
Thou wouldst have poison'd good Camillo's honour
To have him kill a king; poor trespasses,
More monstrous standing by: whereof I reckon   *205*
The casting forth to crows thy baby daughter
To be or none or little; though a devil
Would have shed water out of fire ere done 't:
Nor is 't directly laid to thee, the death
Of the young prince, whose honourable thoughts,—   *210*
Thoughts high for one so tender,—cleft the heart
That could conceive a gross and foolish sire
Blemish'd his gracious dam: this is not, no,
Laid to thy answer: but the last,—O lords!
When I have said, cry, 'woe!'—the queen, the queen,   *215*
The sweetest, dearest creature's dead, and vengeance for 't
Not dropp'd down yet.
      First Lord.   The higher powers forbid!
      Paul. I say she's dead; I'll swear 't: if word nor oath
Prevail not, go and see: if you can bring   *220*
Tincture or lustre in her lip, her eye,
Heat outwardly, or breath within, I'll serve you
As I would do the gods. But, O thou tyrant!
Do not repent these things, for they are heavier
Than all thy woes can stir: therefore betake thee   *225*
To nothing but despair. A thousand knees
Ten thousand years together, naked, fasting,
Upon a barren mountain, and still winter
In storm perpetual, could not move the gods
To look that way thou wert.   *230*
      Leon.   Go on, go on;
Thou canst not speak too much: I have deserv'd

---

126 flatness: *absoluteness*   **148 mere:** *pure*   **152 conceit:** *imagination*   **153 speed:** *fortune*   **175 tardied:** *delayed*

180 Unclasp'd: *revealed; cf. n.* **practice:** *plotting*   **182 incertainties:** *uncertain events*   **183 glisters:** *glitters*   **184 Thorough:** *through*   **187 lace:** *cord for lacing the bodice*   **194 most worst:** *worst*   **199 spices:** *foretastes*   **201 of:** *as*   **221 Tincture:** *color*   **225 stir:** *i.e., remove from thy guilty record*   **228 still:** *always*

All tongues to talk their bitterest.

First Lord.   Say no more:
Howe'er the business goes, you have made fault   235
I' the boldness of your speech.

Paul.   I am sorry for 't:
All faults I make, when I shall come to know them,
I do repent. Alas! I have show'd too much
The rashness of a woman: he is touch'd   240
To the noble heart. What's gone and what's past help
Should be past grief: do not receive affliction
At my peition; I beseech you, rather
Let me be punish'd, that have minded you
Of what you should forget. Now, good my liege,   245
Sir, royal sir, forgive a foolish woman:
The love I bore your queen,—lo, fool again!—
I'll speak of her no more, nor of your children;
I'll not remember you of my own lord,
Who is lost too: take your patient to you,   250
And I'll say nothing.

Leon.   Thou didst speak but well,
When most the truth, which I receive much better
Than to be pitied of thee. Prithee, bring me
To the dead bodies of my queen and son: 255
One grave shall be for both: upon them shall
The causes of their death appear, unto
Our shame perpetual. Once a day I'll visit
The chapel where they lie, and tears shed there
Shall be my recreation: so long as nature   260
Will bear up with this exercise, so long
I daily vow to use it. Come and lead me
To these sorrows.   *Exeunt.*

❧ SCENE THIRD ❧

[Bohemia. A desert country near the sea]
Enter Antigonus, [with the] Babe; and a Mariner.

Ant. Thou art perfect, then, our ship hath touch'd upon
The deserts of Bohemia?

Mar.   Ay, my lord; and fear
We have landed in ill time: the skies look grimly
And threaten present blusters. In my conscience,   5
The heavens with that we have in hand are angry,
And frown upon 's.

Ant. Their sacred wills be done! Go, get aboard;
Look to thy bark: I'll not be long before
I call upon thee.   10

Mar.   Make your best haste, and go not
Too far i' the land: 'tis like to be loud weather;
Besides, this place is famous for the creatures
Of prey that keep upon 't.

Ant.   Go thou away: 15
I'll follow instantly.

Mar.   I am glad at heart
To be so rid of the business.   *Exit.*

Ant.   Come, poor babe:
I have heard, but not believ'd, the spirits o' the dead   20
May walk again: if such thing be, thy mother

Appear'd to me last night, for ne'er was dream
So like a waking. To me comes a creature,
Sometimes her head on one side, some another;
I never saw a vessel of like sorrow,   25
So fill'd, and so becoming: in pure white robes,
Like very sanctity, she did approach
My cabin where I lay; thrice bow'd before me,
And, gasping to begin some speech, her eyes
Became two spouts: the fury spent, anon   30
Did this break from her: 'Good Antigonus,
Since fate, against thy better disposition,
Hath made thy person for the thrower-out
Of my poor babe, according to thine oath,
Places remote enough are in Bohemia,   35
There weep and leave it crying; and, for the babe
Is counted lost for ever, Perdita,
I prithee, call 't: for this ungentle business,
Put on thee by my lord, thou ne'er shalt see
Thy wife Paulina more': and so, with shrieks,   40
She melted into air. Affrighted much,
I did in time collect myself, and thought
This was so and no slumber. Dreams are toys;
Yet for this once, yea, superstitiously,
I will be squar'd by this. I do believe   45
Hermione hath suffer'd death; and that
Apollo would, this being indeed the issue
Of King Polixenes, it should here be laid,
Either for life or death, upon the earth
Of its right father. Blossom, speed thee well!   50

[Laying down Babe.]

There lie; and there thy character: there these;

[Laying down a bundle.]

Which may, if fortune please, both breed thee, pretty,
And still rest thine. The storm begins: poor wretch!
That for thy mother's fault art thus expos'd
To loss and what may follow. Weep I cannot,   55
But my heart bleeds, and most accurs'd am I
To be by oath enjoin'd to this. Farewell!
The day frowns more and more: thou art like to have
A lullaby too rough. I never saw
The heavens so dim by day. A savage clamour!   60
Well may I get aboard! This is the chase:
I am gone for ever.   *Exit, pursued by a bear.*

[Enter a Shepherd.]

Shep. I would there were no age between ten and three-and-
twenty, or that youth would sleep out the rest; for there is
nothing in the between but getting wenches with child,   65
wronging the ancientry, stealing, fighting. Hark you now!
Would any but these boiled brains of nineteen and two-and-
twenty hunt this weather? They have scared away two of my
best sheep; which I fear the wolf will sooner find than the master: if anywhere I have them, 'tis by the sea-side, browsing   70
of ivy. Good luck, an 't be thy will! what have we here? Mercy
on 's, a barne; a very pretty barne! A boy or a child, I wonder?
A pretty one, a very pretty one; sure some scape: though I am

---

244 minded: *reminded*   **249 remember:** *remind*   **1 perfect:** *certain*   **5 blusters:**
storms   **14 keep:** *live*

36 for: *because*   **43 toys:** *trifles*   **44 superstitiously:** *with religious reverence*   **45
squar'd:** *ruled*   **51 character:** *written means of identification*   **52, 53 Which . . . thine;**
cf. n.   **61 the chase:** *a hunted wild beast*   **63 ten;** *cf. n.*   **66 ancientry:** *old peo-*
ple   **67 boiled brains:** *hot heads*   **72 barne:** *child* **child:** *girl*   **73 scape:**
transgression

not bookish, yet I can read waiting-gentle-woman in the scape.
This has been some stair-work, some trunk-work, some 75
behind-door-work; they were warmer that got this than the
poor thing is here. I'll take it up for pity; yet I'll tarry till my
son come; he hollaed but even now. Whoa, ho, hoa!

Enter Clown.

Clo. Hilloa, loa!

Shep. What! art so near? If thou 'lt see a thing to talk 80
on when thou art dead and rotten, come hither. What ailest
thou, man?

Clo. I have seen two such sights by sea and by land! but I
am not to say it is a sea, for it is now the sky: betwixt the
firmament and it you cannot thrust a bodkin's point. 85

Shep. Why, boy, how is it?

Clo. I would you did but see how it chafes, how it rages,
how it takes up the shore! but that's not to the point. O! the
most pieous cry of the poor souls; sometimes to see 'em, and
not to see 'em; now the ship boring the moon with her 90
mainmast, and anon swallowed with yest and froth, as you'd
thrust a cork into a hogshead. And then for the land-service:
to see how the bear tore out his shoulderbone; how he cried
to me for help and said his name was Antigonus, a nobleman.
But to make an end of the ship: to see how the sea flap- 95
dragoned it: but, first, how the poor souls roared, and the sea
mocked them; and how the poor gentleman roared, and the
bear mocked him, both roaring louder than the sea or weather.

Shep. Name of mercy! when was this, boy?

Clo. Now, now; I have not winked since I saw these 100
sights: the men are not yet cold under water, nor the bear half
dined on the gentleman: he's at it now.

Shep. Would I had been by, to have helped the old man!

Clo. I would you had been by the ship's side, to have
helped her: there your charity would have lacked footing. 105

Shep. Heavy matters! heavy matters! but look thee here, boy.
Now bless thyself: thou mettest with things dying, I with
things new born. Here 's a sight for thee; look thee, bearing-
cloth for a squire's child! Look thee here: take up, take up,
boy; open 't. So, let 's see: it was told me, I should be 110
rich by the fairies: this is some changeling.—Open 't.
What's within, boy?

Clo. You're a made old man: if the sins of your youth are
forgiven you, you're well to live. Gold! all gold!

Shep. This is fairy gold, boy, and 'twill prove so: up 115
with 't, keep it close: home, home, the next way. We are
lucky, boy; and to be so still, requires nothing but secrecy. Let
my sheep go. Come, good boy, the next way home.

Clo. Go you the next way with your findings. I'll go see
if the bear be gone from the gentleman, and how much he 120
hath eaten: they are never curst but when they are hungry.
If there be any of him left, I'll bury it.

Shep. That 's a good deed. If thou mayst discern by that
which is left of him what he is, fetch me to the sight of him.

Clo. Marry, will I; and you shall help to put him i' the 125
ground.

Shep. 'Tis a lucky day, boy, and we'll do good deeds on 't.
     Exeunt.

ACT FOURTH ❦ SCENE FIRST

Enter Time, the Chorus.

Time. I, that please some, try all, both joy and terror
Of good and bad, that make and unfold error,
Now take upon me, in the name of Time,
To use my wings. Impute it not a crime
To me or my swift passage, that I slide 5
O'er sixteen years, and leave the growth untried
Of that wide gap; since it is in my power
To o'erthrow law, and in one self-born hour
To plant and o'erwhelm custom. Let me pass
The same I am, ere ancient'st order was 10
Or what is now receiv'd: I witness to
The times that brought them in; so shall I do
To the freshest things now reigning, and make stale
The glistering of this present, as my tale
Now seems to it. Your patience this allowing, 15
I turn my glass and give my scene such growing
As you had slept between. Leontes leaving,—
The effects of his fond jealousies so grieving,
That he shuts up himself,—imagine me,
Gentle spectators, that I now may be 20
In fair Bohemia; and remember well,
I mention'd a son o' the king's, which Florizel
I now name to you; and with speed so pace
To speak of Perdita, now grown in grace
Equal with wondering: what of her ensues 25
I list not prophesy; but let Time's news
Be known when 'tis brought forth. A shepherd's daughter,
And what to her adheres, which follows after,
Is th' argument of Time. Of this allow,
If ever you have spent time worse ere now: 30
If never, yet that Time himself doth say
He wishes earnestly you never may.

     Exit.

❧ SCENE SECOND ❧

[Bohemia. A Room in the Palace of Polixenes]
Enter Polixenes and Camillo.

Pol. I pray thee, good Camillo, be no more importunate: 'tis
a sickness denying thee anything; a death to grant this.

Cam. It is fifteen years since I saw my country: though I
have for the most part been aired abroad, I desire to lay my
bones there. Besides, the penitent king, my master, hath sent 5
for me; to whose feeling sorrows I might be some allay, or I
o'erween to think so, which is another spur to my departure.

Pol. As thou lovest me, Camillo, wipe not out the rest of
thy services by leaving me now. The need I have of thee thine

S.d. **Clown:** *country bumpkin*   85 **bodkin:** *small pointed instrument*   91 **yest:** *foam*   92 **land-service:** *military, as compared with naval, service; used humorously*   95, 96 **flap-dragoned;** *cf. n.*   108, 109 **bearing-cloth:** *infant's christening robe* **squire's:** *gentleman's*   111 **changeling:** *elfin child left by fairies in place of stolen human one*   114 **well to live:** *well to do*   118 **next:** *nearest*   121 **curst:** *savage*   125 **Marry:** *an exclamation, from the name of the Virgin Mary*

8 **one self-born:** *one and the self-same*   11 **receiv'd:** *accepted*   18 **grieving:** *grieving over*   25 **Equal with wondering:** *as much as in admiration*   26 **list:** *wish to*   28 **adheres:** *is related*   29 **argument:** *subject-matter*   4 **been aired:** *lived*   6 **feeling:** *deeply felt*   7 **o'erween:** *rate myself too highly*

own goodness hath made: better not to have had thee than   *10*
thus to want thee. Thou, having made me businesses which
none without thee can sufficiently manage, must either stay to
execute them thyself or take away with thee the very services
thou hast done; which if I have not enough considered,—as
too much I cannot,—to be more thankful to thee shall be   *15*
my study, and my profit therein, the heaping friendships. Of
that fatal country, Sicilia, prithee speak no more, whose very
naming punishes me with the remembrance of that penitent, as
thou callest him, and reconciled king, my bother; whose loss of
his most precious queen and children are even now to be   *20*
afresh lamented. Say to me, when sawest thou the Prince
Florizel, my son? Kings are no less unhappy, their issue not
being gracious, than they are in losing them when they have
approved their virtues.

Cam. Sir, it is three days since I saw the prince. What   *25*
his happier affairs may be, are to me unknown; but I have
missingly noted he is of late much retired from court, and is
less frequent to his princely exercises than formerly he hath
appeared.

Pol. I have considered so much, Camillo, and with some   *30*
care; so far, that I have eyes under my service which look upon
his removedness; from whom I have this intelligence, that he is
seldom from the house of a most homely shepherd; a man, they
say, that from very nothing, and beyond the imagination of his
neighbours, is grown into an unspeakable estate.   *35*

Cam. I have heard, sir, of such a man, who hath a daughter
of most rare note: the report of her is extended more than can
be thought to begin from such a cottage.

Pol. That's likewise part of my intelligence; but, I fear, the
angle that plucks our son thither. Thou shalt accompany us   *40*
to the place; where we will, not appearing what we are, have
some question with the shepherd; from whose simplicity I
think it not uneasy to get the cause of my son's resort thither.
Prithee, be my present partner in this business, and lay aside
the thoughts of Sicilia.   *45*

Cam. I willingly obey your command.

Pol. My best Camillo!—We must disguise ourselves.   *Exeunt.*

❧ SCENE THIRD ❧

[A Road near the Shepherd's Cottage]
Enter Autolycus, singing.

'When daffodils begin to peer,
   With heigh! the doxy, over the dale,
Why, then comes in the sweet o' the year;
   For the red blood reigns in the winter's pale.

'The white sheet bleaching on the hedge,   *5*
   With heigh! the sweet birds, O, how they sing!
Doth set my pugging tooth on edge;
   For a quart of ale is a dish for a king.
'The lark, that tirra-lirra chants,
   With, heigh! with, heigh! the thrush and the jay,   *10*

Are summer songs for me and my aunts,
   While we lie tumbling in the hay.'

I have served Prince Florizel, and in my time
wore three-pile; but now I am out of service:

'But shall I go mourn for that, my dear?   *15*
   The pale moon shines by night;
And when I wander here and there,
   I then do most go right.

'If tinkers may have leave to live,
   And bear the sow-skin bowget,   *20*
Then my account I well may give,
   And in the stocks avouch it.'

My traffic is sheets; when the kite builds, look to lesser linen.
My father named me Autolycus; who being, as I am, littered
under Mercury, was likewise a snapper-up of unconsidered   *25*
trifles. With die and drab I purchased this caparison, and my
revenue is the silly cheat. Gallows and knock are too powerful
on the highway: beating and hanging are terrors to me: for the
life to come, I sleep out the thought of it. A prize! a prize!

Enter Clown.

Clo. Let me see: Every 'leven wether tods; every tod   *30*
yields pound and odd shilling: fifteen hundred shorn, what
comes the wool to?

Aut. [Aside.] If the springe hold, the cock's mine.

Clo. I cannot do 't without compters, Let me see; what am
I to buy for our sheep-shearing feast? 'Three pound of sugar;   *35*
five pound of currants; rice' what will this sister of mine do
with rice? But my father hath made her mistress of the feast,
and she lays it on. She hath made me four-and-twenty nosegays for the shearers, three-man song-men all, and very good
ones; but they are most of them means and basses: but one   *40*
puritan amongst them, and he sings psalms to hornpipes. I
must have saffron, to colour the warden pies; mace, dates,—
none; that's out of my note:—nutmegs seven; a race or two of
ginger,—but that I may I beg;—four pound of prunes, and as
many of raisins o' the sun.   *45*

Aut. O! that ever I was born!   *[Grovelling on the ground.]*

Clo. I' the name of me!—

Aut. O! help me, help me! pluck but off these rags, and
then death, death!

Clo. Alack, poor soul! thou hast need of more rags to   *50*
lay on thee, rather than have these off.

Aut. O, sir! the loathsomeness of them offends me more
than the stripes I have received, which are mighty ones and
millions.

Clo. Alas, poor man! a million of beating may come to   *55*
a great matter.

Aut. I am robbed, sir, and beaten; my money and apparel
ta'en from me, and these detestable things put upon me.

Clo. What, by a horseman or a footman?

---

16 heaping friendships: *increase of friendly acts*   **23 gracious:** *upright, righteous*   **24 approved:** *tested*   **27 missingly:** *grieving at his absence*   **32 removedness:** *absence* **intelligence:** *news*   **37 note:** *celebrity*   **40 angle:** *fish-hook*   **42 question:** *conversation*   **1 peer:** *show slightly*   **2 doxy:** *beggar's mistress*   **4 winter's pale;** *cf. n.*   **7 pugging:** *thieving*

11 aunts: *mistresses (thieves' slang)*   **14 three-pile:** *most costly kind of velvet*   **20 bowget:** *budget, big wallet*   **23** *Cf. n.*   **24, 25 littered under Mercury;** *cf. n.*   **26** *By means of dice and lewd women I acquired this clothing*   **27 silly cheat:** *petty thieving* **gallows and knock:** *fear of hanging and of the officer's blow*   **30 tods:** *yields a tod, twenty-eight pounds of wool*   **33 springe:** *bird-hunter's noose* **cock:** *woodcock, a slang term for a fool*   **34 compters:** *pieces of metal used in making calculations*   **38 lays it on:** *manages lavishly*   **39 three-man song-men:** *singers of songs in three parts*   **40 means:** *altos*   **41 puritan;** *cf. n.*   **42 saffron:** *orange-red substance used for coloring cookery* **warden:** *made of the warden pear*   **43 note:** *list* **race:** *root*   **45 raisins o' the sun:** *sun-dried grapes*

Aut. A footman, sweet sir, a footman.   60

Clo. Indeed, he should be a footman, by the garments he
hath left with thee: if this be a horseman's coat, it hath seen
very hot service. Lend me thy hand, I'll help thee: come, lend
me thy hand.   *[Helping him up.]*

Aut. O! good sir, tenderly, O!   65

Clo. Alas, poor soul!

Aut. O! good sir; softly, good sir! I fear, sir, my shoulder-
blade is out.

Clo. How now! canst stand?

Aut. Softly, dear sir: *[Picks his pocket.]* good sir, softly.   70
You ha' done me a charitable office.

Clo. Dost lack any money? I have a little money for thee.

Aut. No, good sweet sir: no, I beseech you, sir. I have a
kinsman not past three-quarters of a mile hence, unto whom
I was going: I shall there have money, or anything I want: 75
offer me no money, I pray you! that kills my heart.

Clo. What manner of fellow was he that robbed you?

Aut. A fellow, sir, that I have known to go about with trol-
my-dames: I knew him once a servant of the prince. I cannot
tell, good sir, for which of his virtues it was, but he was   80
certainly whipped out of the court.

Clo. His vices, you would say: there's no virtue whipped out
of the court: they cherish it, to make it stay there, and yet it
will no more but abide.

Aut. Vices, I would say, sir. I know this man well: he   85
hath been since an ape-bearer; then a process-server, a bailiff;
then he compassed a motion of the Prodigal Son, and married
a tinker's wife within a mile where my land and living lies;
and having flown over many knavish professions, he settled
only in rogue: some call him Autolycus.   90

Clo. Out upon him! Prig, for my life, prig: he haunts wakes,
fairs, and bear-baitings.

Aut. Very true, sir; he, sir, he: that's the rogue that put me
into this apparel.

Clo. Not a more cowardly rogue in all Bohemia: if you   95
had but looked big and spit at him, he'd have run.

Aut. I must confess to you, sir, I am no fighter: I am false
of heart that way, and that he knew, I warrant him.

Clo. How do you now?

Aut. Sweet sir, much better than I was: I can stand and   100
walk. I will even take my leave of you, and pace softly towards
my kinsman's.

Clo. Shall I bring thee on the way?

Aut. No, good-faced sir; no, sweet sir.

Clo. Then fare thee well: I must go buy spices for our   105
sheep-shearing.   *Exit.*

Aut. Prosper you, sweet sir! Your purse is not hot enough to
purchase your spice. I'll be with you at your sheep-shearing
too. If I make not this cheat bring out another, and the
shearers prove sheep, let me be unrolled, and my name put   110
in the book of virtue.

   Song. *'Jog on, jog on, the footpath way,*
     And merrily hent the stile-a:
   A merry heart goes all the day,
     Your sad tires in a mile-a.'   *Exit.*   115

❧ SCENE FOURTH ❧

[A Lawn before the Shepherd's Cottage]
Enter Florizel and Perdita.

Flo. These your unusual weeds to each part of you
Do give a life: no shepherdess, but Flora
Peering in April's front. This your sheep-shearing
Is as a meeting of the petty gods,
And you the queen on 't.   5

Per.   Sir, my gracious lord,
To chide at your extremes it not becomes me:
O! pardon, that I name them. Your high self,
The gracious mark o' the land, you have obscur'd
With a swain's wearing, and me, poor lowly maid,   10
Most goddess-like prank'd up. But that our feasts
In every mess have folly, and the feeders
Digest it with a custom, I should blush
To see you so attired,—swoon, I think,
To show myself a glass.   15

Flo.   I bless the time
When my good falcon made her flight across
Thy father's ground.

Per.   Now, Jove afford you cause!
To me the difference forges dread: your greatness   20
Hath not been us'd to fear. Even now I tremble
To think, your father, by some accident,
Should pass this way as you did. O, the Fates!
How would he look, to see his work, so noble,
Vilely bound up? What would he say? Or how   25
Should I, in these my borrow'd flaunts, behold
The sternness of his presence?

Flo.   Apprehend
Nothing but jollity. The gods themselves,
Humbling their deities to love, have taken   30
The shapes of beasts upon them: Jupiter
Became a bull, and bellow'd; the green Neptune
A ram, and bleated; and the fire-rob'd god,
Golden Apollo, a poor humble swain,
As I seem now. Their transformations   35
Were never for a piece of beauty rarer,
Nor in a way so chaste, since my desires
Run not before mine honour, nor my lusts
Burn hotter than my faith.

Per.   O! but, sir,   40
Your resolution cannot hold, when 'tis
Oppos'd, as it must be, by the power of the king.
One of these two must be necessities,
Which then will speak, that you must change this purpose,
Or I my life.   45

Flo.   Thou dearest Perdita,
With these forc'd thoughts, I prithee, darken not
The mirth o' the feast: or I'll be thine, my fair,
Or not my father's; for I cannot be
Mine own, nor anything to any, if   50
I be not thine: to this I am most constant,
Though destiny say no. Be merry, gentle;

78, 79 trol-my-dames: *a game in which balls were 'trolled' through arches set on a board*   **84
no more but abide:** *barely make a brief stay*   **86 ape-bearer:** *showman who carries a
trained monkey*   **87 compassed:** *acquired*   **motion:** *puppet show*   **91 Prig:** *thief*   **110
unrolled:** *stricken from the roll of thieves*   **113 hent:** *get over*

1 weeds: *garments*   **3 Peering:** *appearing*   **front:** *van or beginning*   **7 extremes:** *extra-
vangances of conduct*   **9 mark o' the land:** *landmark or model of the nation*   **10 wearing:**
clothing   **11 prank'd up:** *decked out*   **13 with a custom:** *from force of habit*   **14
swoon;** *cf. n.*   **20 difference:** *difference in rank*   **26 flaunts:** *finery*   **31-34
Cf. n.**   **39 faith:** *fidelity*   **47 forc'd:** *unnatural*

Strangle such thoughts as these with anything
That you behold the while. Your guests are coming:
Lift up your countenance, as it were the day   55
Of celebration of that nuptial which
We two have sworn shall come.
    Per.   O lady Fortune,
Stand you auspicious!
    Flo.   See, your guests approach: 60
Address yourself to entertain them sprightly,
And let's be red with mirth.

*[Enter Shepherd, with Polixenes and Camillo disguised; Clown,
Mopsa, Dorcas, and Others.]*

    Shep. Fie, daughter! when my old wife liv'd, upon
This day she was both pantler, butler, cook;
Both dame and servant; welcom'd all, serv'd all,   65
Would sing her song and dance her turn; now here,
At upper end o' the table, now i' the middle;
On his shoulder, and his; her face o' fire
With labour and the thing she took to quench it,
She would to each one sip. You are retir'd,   70
As if you were a feasted one and not
The hostess of the meeting: pray you, bid
These unknown friends to 's welcome; for it is
A way to make us better friends, more known.
Come, quench your blushes and present yourself   75
That which you are, mistress o' the feast: come on,
And bid us welcome to your sheep-shearing,
As your good flock shall prosper.
    Per. [To Polixenes.]   Sir, welcome:
It is my father's will I should take on me   80
The hostess-ship o' the day. *[To Camillo.]* You're welcome, sir.
Give me those flowers there, Dorcas. Reverend sirs,
For you there's rosemary and rue; these keep
Seeming and savour all the winter long:
Grace and remembrance be to you both,   85
And welcome to our shearing!
    Pol.   Shepherdess,—
A fair one are you,—well you fit our ages
With flowers of winter.
    Per.   Sir, the year growing ancient,   90
Not yet on summer's death, nor on the birth
Of trembling winter, the fairest flowers o' the season
Are our carnations, and streak'd gillyvors,
Which some call nature's bastards: of that kind
Our rustic garden's barren, and I care not   95
To get slips of them.
    Pol.   Wherefore, gentle maiden,
Do you neglect them?
    Per.   For I have heard it said
There is an art which in their piedness shares   100
With great creating nature.
    Pol.   Say there be;
Yet nature is made better by no mean
But nature makes that mean: so, over that art,
Which you say adds to nature, is an art   105

That nature makes. You see, sweet maid, we marry
A gentler scion to the wildest stock,
And make conceive a bark of baser kind
By bud of nobler race: this is an art
Which does mend nature, change it rather, but   110
The art itself is nature.
    Per.   So it is.
    Pol. Then make your garden rich in gillyvors,
And do not call them bastards.
    Per.   I'll not put   115
The dibble in earth to set one slip of them;
No more than, were I painted, I would wish
This youth should say, 'twere well, and only therefore
Desire to breed by me. Here's flowers for you;
Hot lavender, mints, savory, marjoram;   120
The marigold, that goes to bed wi' the sun,
And with him rises weeping: these are flowers
Of middle summer, and I think they are given
To men of middle age. You're very welcome.
    Cam. I should leave grazing, were I of your flock,   125
And only live by gazing.
    Per.   Out, alas!
You'd be so lean, that blasts of January
Would blow you through and through. Now, my fair'st friend,
I would I had some flowers o' the spring that might   130
Become your time of day; and yours, and yours,
That wear upon your virgin branches yet
Your maidenheads growing: O Proserpina!
For the flowers now that frighted thou let'st fall
From Dis's waggon! daffodils,   135
That come before the swallow dares, and take
The winds of March with beauty; violets dim,
But sweeter than the lids of Juno's eyes
Or Cytherea's breath; pale primroses,
That die unmarried, ere they can behold   140
Bright Phœbus in his strength, a malady
Most incident to maids; bold oxlips and
The crown imperial; lilies of all kinds,
The flower-de-luce being one. O! these I lack
To make you garlands of, and my sweet friend,   145
To strew him o'er and o'er!
    Flo.   What! like a corse?
    Per. No, like a bank for love to lie and play on;
Not like a corse; or if,—not to be buried,
But quick and in mine arms. Come, take your flowers: 150
Methinks I play as I have seen them do
In Whitsun pastorals: sure this robe of mine
Does change my disposition.
    Flo.   What you do
Still betters what is done. When you speak, sweet,   155
I'd have you do it ever: when you sing,
I'd have you buy and sell so; so give alms;
Pray so; and, for the ordering your affairs,
To sing them too: when you do dance, I wish you
A wave o' the sea, that you might ever do   160
Nothing but that; move still, still so,
And own no other function: each your doing,

61 Address yourself: *make ready* **sprightly:** *in sprightly manner*   **64 pantler:** *servant
in charge of pantry*   **84 Seeming:** *beauty of shape* **savour:** *fragrance*   **85 Grace and
remembrance;** *cf. n.*   **93 gillyvors:** *gillyflowers, pinks (?)*   **100, 101 There ... nature;**
cf. n.   **103 mean:** *instrument*

116 dibble: *gardener's tool to make holes for planting*   **120** *Cf. n.*   **133 Proserpina;**
cf. n.   **139 Cytherea's:** *Venus's*   **143 crown imperial:** *an imported flower from Asia
Minor, the fritilaria imperialis*   **144 flower-de-luce:** *iris*   **150 quick:** *alive*   **152 Whitsun pastorals;** *cf. n.*   **162 each your doing:** *each act of yours*

So singular in each particular,
Crowns what you are doing in the present deed,
That all your acts are queens.   *165*
    Per.   O Doricles!
Your praises are too large: but that your youth,
And the true blood which fairly peeps through it,
Do plainly give you out an unstain'd shepherd,
With wisdom I might fear, my Doricles,   *170*
You woo'd me the false way.
    Flo.   I think you have
As little skill to fear as I have purpose
To put you to 't. But, come; our dance, I pray.
Your hand, my Perdita: so turtles pair   *175*
That never mean to part.
    Per.   I'll swear for 'em.
    Pol. This is the prettiest low-born lass that ever
Ran on the green-sord: nothing she does or seems
But smacks of something greather than herself;   *180*
Too noble for this place.
    Cam.   He tells her something
That makes her blood look out. Good sooth, she is
The queen of curds and cream.
    Clo.   Come on, strike up.   *185*
    Dor. Mopsa must be your mistress: marry, garlic,
To mend her kissing with.
    Mop.   Now, in good time!
    Clo. Not a word, a word: we stand upon our manners.
Come, strike up.   [*Music.*]   *190*
            Here a dance of Shepherds and Shepherdesses.
    Pol. Pray, good shepherd, what fair swain is this
Which dances with your daughter?
    Shep. They call him Doricles, and boasts himself
To have a worthy feeding; but I have it
Upon his own report and I believe it: *195*
He looks like sooth. He says he loves my daughter:
I think so too; for never gaz'd the moon
Upon the water as he'll stand and read
As 'twere my daughter's eyes; and, to be plain,
I think there is not half a kiss to choose   *200*
Who loves another best.
    Pol.   She dances featly.
    Shep. So she does anything, though I report it
That should be silent. If young Doricles
Do light upon her, she shall bring him that   *205*
Which he not dreams of.

            Enter a Servant.

    Serv. O master! if you did but hear the pedlar at the door,
you would never dance again after a tabor and pipe; no, the
bagpipe could not move you. He sings several tunes faster than
you'll tell money; he utters them as he had eaten ballads   *210*
and all men's ears grew to his tunes.
    Clo. He could never come better: he shall come in: I love a
ballad but even too well, if it be doleful matter merrily set
down, or a very pleasant thing indeed and sung lamentably.
    Serv. He hath songs for man or woman, of all sizes; no   *215*

milliner can so fit his customers with gloves: he has the
prettiest love-songs for maids, so without bawdry, which is
strange; with such delicate burdens of dildos and fadings,
'jump her and thump her'; and where some stretch-mouthed
rascal would, as it were, mean mischief and break a foul gap   *220*
into the matter, he makes the maid to answer, 'Whoop, do me
no harm, good man;' puts him off, slights him with 'Whoop,
do me no harm, good man.'
    Pol. This is a brave fellow.
    Clo. Believe me, thou talkest of an admirable conceited   *225*
fellow. Has he any unbraided wares?
    Serv. He hath ribands of all the colours i' the rainbow;
points more than all the lawyers in Bohemia can learnedly handle, though they come to him by the gross; inkles, caddisses,
cambrics, lawns: why, he sings 'em over, as they were gods   *230*
or goddesses. You would think a smock were a she-angel, he so
chants to the sleeve-hand and the work about the square on 't.
    Clo. Prithee, bring him in, and let him approach singing.
    Per. Forewarn him that he use no scurrilous words in 's
tunes.   [*Exit Servant.*]   *235*
    Clo. You have of these pedlars, that have more in them than
you'd think, sister.
    Per. Ay, good brother, or go about to think.

            Enter Autolycus, singing.

'Lawn as white as driven snow;
Cyprus black as e'er was crow;   *240*
Gloves as sweet as damask roses;
Masks for faces and for noses;
Bugle-bracelet, necklace-amber,
Perfume for a lady's chamber;
Golden quoifs and stomachers,   *245*
For my lads to give their dears;
Pins and poking-sticks of steel;
What maids lack from head to heel:
Come buy of me, come; come buy, come buy;
Buy, lads, or else your lasses cry: *250*
Come buy.'

    Clo. If I were not in love with Mopsa, thou shouldst take
no money of me; but being enthralled as I am, it will also be
the bondage of certain ribands and gloves.
    Mop. I was promised them against the feast; but they   *255*
come not too late now.
    Dor. He hath promised you more than that, or there be
liars.
    Mop. He hath paid you all he promised you: may be he has
paid you more, which will shame you to give him again.   *260*
    Clo. Is there no manners left among maids? will they wear
their plackets where they should bear their faces? Is there not
milking-time, when you are going to bed, or kiln-hole, to whistle off these secrets, but you must be tittle-tattling before all

163 singular: *characteristic of you, unique* **particular:** *detail* **167 large:** *extrava-*
gant **169 give you out:** *declare you* · **173 skill:** *reason* **175 turtles:** *turtle-*
doves **179 sord:** *suard* **183 sooth:** *truth* **194 feeding:** *tract of pasture* **201 an-**
other: *the other* **202 featly:** *nimbly* **208 tabor:** *small drum* **210 tell:** *count* **as:**
as if

218 burdens: *refrains* **218, 219** *Cf. n.* **219 stretch-mouthed:** *foul-mouthed* **224**
brave: *fine* **225 admirable conceited:** *wonderfully witty* **226 unbraided:** *un-*
faded **227 ribands:** *ribbons* **228 points:** *tags with lacings for fastening hose to doublet*
or jacket **229 inkles:** *broad linen tape* **caddisses:** *garters of worsted tape* **230 lawns:**
fine silks **231 smock:** *woman's undergarment* **232 sleeve-hand:** *cuff* **work about the**
square: *embroidery about the bosom* **236 You have of these:** *there are some* **238 go**
about: *make an effort* **240 Cyprus:** *crape* **241 sweet:** *perfumed* **243 Bugle-brace-**
let: *bracelet of tube-shaped glass beads* **245 quoifs:** *women's headdresses* **stomachers:** *orna-*
mental coverings for bosom **247 poking-sticks:** *metal rods to adjust plaits of ruffs* **255**
against: *in time for* **262 plackets:** *openings in petticoats* **263 kiln-hole:** *big fire-place*
where women made malt (?)

our guests? 'Tis well they are whispering: clamour your   *265*
tongues, and not a word more.

Mop. I have done. Come, you promised me a tawdry lace
and a pair of sweet gloves.

Clo. Have I not told thee how I was cozened by the way,
and lost all my money?   *270*

Aut. And indeed, sir, there are cozeners abroad; therefore it
behoves men to be wary.

Clo. Fear not thou, man, thou shalt lose nothing here.

Aut. I hope so, sir; for I have about me many parcels of
charge.   *275*

Clo. What hast here? ballads?

Mop. Pray now, buy some: I love a ballad in print, a-life,
for then we are sure they are true.

Aut. Here's one to a very doleful tune, how a usurer's wife
was brought to bed of twenty money-bags at a burden; and   *280*
how she longed to eat adders' heads and toads carbonadoed.

Mop. Is it true, think you?

Aut. Very true, and but a month old.

Dor. Bless me from marrying a usurer!

Aut. Here's the midwife's name to 't, one Mistress Tale-   *285*
porter, and five or six honest wives' that were present. Why
should I carry lies abroad?

Mop. Pray you now, buy it.

Clo. Come on, lay it by: and let's first see moe ballads; we'll
buy the other things anon.   *290*

Aut. Here's another ballad of a fish that appeared upon the
coast on Wednesday the fourscore of April, forty thousand
fathom above water, and sung this ballad against the hard
hearts of maids: it was thought she was a woman and was
turned into a cold fish for she would not exchange flesh   *295*
with one that loved her. The ballad is very pitiful and as true.

Dor. Is it true too, think you?

Aut. Five justices' hands at it, and witnesses more than my
pack will hold.

Clo. Lay it by too: another.   *300*

Aut. This is a merry ballad, but a very pretty one.

Mop. Let's have some merry ones.

Aut. Why, this is a passing merry one, and goes to the tune
of 'Two maids wooing a man': there's a scarce a maid westward but she sings it: 'tis in request, I can tell you.   *305*

Mop. We can both sing it: if thou 'lt bear a part thou shalt
hear; 'tis in three parts.

Dor. We had the tune on 't a month ago.

Aut. I can bear my part; you must know 'tis my occupation:
have at it with you.   *310*

   Aut. 'Get you hence, for I must go,
Where it fits not you to know.'

Dor. 'Whither?'

Mop. 'O! whither?'

Dor. 'Whither?'   *315*

Mop. 'It becomes thy oath full well,
Thou to me thy secrets tell.'

Dor. 'Me too: let me go thither.'

Mop. 'Or thou go'st to the grange or mill.'

Dor. 'If to either, thou dost ill.'   *320*

Aut. 'Neither.'

Dor. 'What, neither?'

Aut. 'Neither.'

Dor. 'Thou hast sworn my love to be.'

Mop. 'Thou hast sworn it more to me: *325*
Then whither go'st? say whither?'

Clo. We'll have this song out anon by ourselves: my father
and the gentlemen are in sad talk, and we'll not trouble them:
come, bring away thy pack after me. Wenches, I'll buy for you
both. Pedlar, let's have the first choice. Follow me, girls.   *330*

       [Exit with Dorcas and Mopsa.]

Aut. And you shall pay well for 'em.

Song.   *'Will you buy any tape,*
          Or lace for your cape,
     My dainty duck, my dear-a?
          Any silk, any thread,   *335*
          Any toys for your head,
   Of the new'st and fin'st, fin'st wear-a?
          Come to the pedlar;
          Money's a meddler,
   That doth utter all men's ware-a.'   *Exit.*   *340*

[Enter a Servant.]

Serv. Master, there is three carters, three shepherds, three
neat-herds, three swine-herds, that have made themselves all
men of hair; they call themselves Saltiers; and they have a
dance which the wenches say is a gallimaufry of gambols,
because they are not in 't; but they themselves are o' the   *345*
mind,—if it be not too rough for some that know little but
bowling,—it will pelase plentifully.

Shep. Away! we'll none on 't; here has been too much
homely foolery already. I know, sir, we weary you.

Pol. You weary those that refresh us: pray, let's see   *350*
these four threes of herdsmen.

Serv. One three of them, by their own report, sir, hath
danced before the king; and not the worst of the three but
jumps twelve foot and a half by the squier,

Shep. Leave your prating: since these good men are   *355*
pleased, let them come in: but quickly now.

Serv. Why, they stay at door, sir.

Here a dance of twelve Satyrs.

Pol. *[To Shep.]* O father! you'll know more of that hereafter.
[To Camillo.] Is it not too far gone? 'Tis time to part them.
He's simple and tells much. *[To Florizel.]* How now, fair   *360*
shepherd!
Your heart is full of something that does take
Your mind from feasting. Sooth, when I was young,
And handed love as you do, I was wont
To load my she with knacks: I would have ransack'd   *365*
The pedlar's silken treasury and have pour'd it
To her acceptance; you have let him go
And nothing marted with him. If your lass
Interpretation should abuse and call this
Your lack of love or bounty, you were straited   *370*
For a reply, at least if you make a care

265 clamour: *silence*   **267 tawdry lace:** *necklace; cf. n.*   **269 cozened:** *cheated*   **275
charge:** *value*   **277 a-life:** *on my life, dearly*   **281 carbonadoed:** *sliced for broiling*   **290 anon:** *immediately*   **303 passing:** *surpassingly*   **319 grange:** *farmhouse*

328 sad: *serious*   **329 Wenches:** *girls*   **339 meddler:** *a go-between*   **340 utter:** *put in
circulation, market*   **342 neat-herds:** *cowherds*   **343 men of hair:** *men dressed as hairy
satyrs* **Saltiers:** *blunder for satyrs*   **344 gallimaufry:** *hotch-potch*   **354 squier:** *measure*   **364 handed:** *held the hand of*   **365 she:** *lady* **knacks:** *knick-knacks*   **368
marted:** *traded*   **369 Interpretation should abuse:** *should misinterpret*   **370 straited:**
put in straits

Of happy holding her.
   Flo.   Old sir, I know
She prizes not such trifles as these are.
The gifts she looks from me are pack'd and lock'd   375
Up in my heart, which I have given already,
But not deliver'd. O! hear me breathe my life
Before this ancient sir, who, it should seem,
Hath sometime lov'd: I take thy hand; this hand,
As soft as dove's down, and as white as it,   380
Or Ethiopian's tooth, or the fann'd snow
That's bolted by the northern blasts twice o'er.
   Pol. What follows this?
How prettily the young swain seems to wash
The hand was fair before! I have put you out: 385
But to your prostestation: let me hear
What you profess.
   Flo.   Do, and be witness to 't.
   Pol. And this my neighbour too?
   Flo.   And he, and more   390
Than he, and men, the earth, the heavens, and all;
That, were I crown'd the most imperial monarch,
Thereof most worthy, were I the fairest youth
That ever made eye swerve, had force and knowledge
More than was ever man's, I would not prize them   395
Without her love: for her employ them all;
Commend them and condemn them to her service
Or to their own perdition.
   Pol.   Fairly offer'd.
   Cam. This shows a sound affection.   400
   Shep.   But, my daughter,
Say you the like to him?
   Per.   I cannot speak
So well, nothing so well; no, nor mean better:
By the pattern of mine own thoughts I cut out   405
The purity of his.
   Shep.   Take hands; a bargain;
And, friends unknown, you shall bear witness to 't:
I give my daughter to him, and will make
Her portion equal his.   410
   Flo.   O! that must be
I' the virtue of your daughter: one being dead,
I shall have more than you can dream of yet;
Enough then for your wonder. But, come on;
Contract us 'fore these witnesses.   415
   Shep.   Come, your hand;
And, daughter, yours.
   Pol.   Soft, swain, awhile, beseech you.
Have you a father?
   Flo.   I have; but what of him?   420
   Pol. Knows he of this?
   Flo.   He neither does nor shall.
   Pol. Methinks a father
Is, at the nuptial of his son, a guest
That best becomes the table. Pray you, once more,   425
Is not your father grown incapable
Of reasonable affairs? is he not stupid
With age and altering rheums? can he speak? hear?
Know man from man? dispute his own estate?

Lies he not bed-rid? and again does nothing   430
But what he did being childish?
   Flo.   No, good sir:
He has his health and ampler strength indeed
Than most have of his age.
   Pol.   By my white beard,   435
You offer him, if this be so, a wrong
Something unfilial. Reason my son
Should choose himself a wife, but as good reason
The father,—all whose joy is nothing else
But fair posterity,—should hold some counsel   440
In such a business.
   Flo.   I yield all this;
But for some other reasons, my grave sir,
Which 'tis not fit you know, I not acquaint
My father of this business.   445
   Pol.   Let him know 't.
   Flo. He shall not.
   Pol.   Prithee, let him.
   Flo.   No, he must not.
   Shep. Let him, my son: he shall not need to grieve   450
At knowing of thy choice.
   Flo.   Come, come, he must not.
Make our contract.
   Pol. Mark your divorce, young sir,   *[Discovering himself.]*
Whom son I dare not call: thou art too base   455
To be acknowledg'd: thou a sceptre's heir,
That thus affect'st a sheep-hook! Thou old traitor,
I am sorry that by hanging thee I can
But shorten thy life one week. And thou, fresh piece
Of excellent witchcraft, who of force must know   460
The royal fool thou cop'st with,—
   Shep.   O, my heart!
   Pol. I'll have thy beauty scratch'd with briers, and made
More homely than thy state. For thee, fond boy,
If I may ever know thou dost but sigh   465
That thou no more shalt see this knack,—as never
I mean thou shalt,—we'll bar thee from succession;
Not hold thee of our blood, no, not our kin,
Far than Deucalion off: mark thou my words:
Follow us to the court. Thou, churl, for this time,   470
Though full of our displeasure, yet we free thee
From the dead blow of it. And you, enchantment,—
Worthy enough a herdsman; yea, him too,
That makes himself, but for our honour therein,
Unworthy thee,—if ever henceforth thou   475
These rural latches to his entrance open,
Or hoop his body more with thy embraces,
I will devise a death as cruel for thee
As thou art tender to 't.   *Exit.*
   Per.   Even here undone!   480
I was not much afeard; for once or twice
I was about to speak and tell him plainly,
The self-same sun that shines upon his court
Hides not his visage from our cottage, but
Looks on alike. Will 't please you, sir, be gone?   485
I told you what would come of this: beseech you,
Of your own state take care: this dream of mine—

---

375 **looks:** *looks for*   382 **bolted:** *sifted*   398 **perdition:** *destruction*   428 **rheums;** *cf. n.*   429 **dispute:** *discuss* **estate:** *affairs*

437 **Reason:** *it is reasonable*   457 **affect'st:** *aspirest to*   459 **fresh:** *young*   460 **of force:** *of necessity*   461 **cop'st:** *dealest*   464 **state:** *social position* **fond:** *foolish*   469 **Far:** *farther* **Deucalion:** *the Greek Noah*   470 **churl:** *peasant*   472 **dead:** *deadly*

Being now awake, I'll queen it no inch further,
But milk my ewes and weep.
    Cam.   Why, how now, father!   *490*
Speak, ere thou diest.
    Shep. I cannot speak, nor think,
Nor dare to know that which I know. O sir!
You have undone a man of fourscore three,
That thought to fill his grave in quiet, yea,   *495*
To die upon the bed my father died,
To lie close by his honest bones: but now
Some hangman must put on my shroud and lay me
Where no priest shovels in dust. O cursed wretch!
That knew'st this was the prince, and wouldst adventure   *500*
To mingle faith with him. Undone! undone!
If I might die within this hour, I have liv'd
To die when I desire.   *Exit.*
    Flo.   Why look you so upon me?
I am but sorry, not afeard; delay'd,   *505*
But nothing alter'd. What I was, I am:
More straining on for plucking back; not following
My leash unwillingly.
    Cam.   Gracious my lord,
You know your father's temper: at this time   *510*
He will allow no speech, which I do guess
You do not purpose to him; and as hardly
Will he endure your sight as yet, I fear:
Then, till the fury of his highness settle,
Come not before him.   *515*
    Flo.   I not purpose it.
I think, Camillo?
    Cam.   Even he, my lord.
    Per. How often have I told you 'twould be thus!
How often said my dignity would last   *520*
But till 'twere known!
    Flo.   It cannot fail but by
The violation of my faith; and then
Let nature crush the sides o' the earth together
And mar the seeds within! Lift up thy looks: *525*
From my succession wipe me, father; I
Am heir to my affection.
    Cam.   Be advis'd.
    Flo. I am; and by my fancy: if my reason
Will thereto be obedient, I have reason;   *530*
If not, my senses, better pleas'd with madness,
Do bid it welcome.
    Cam.   This is desperate, sir.
    Flo. So call it; but it does fulfil my vow;
I needs must think it honesty. Camillo,   *535*
Not for Bohemia, nor the pomp that may
Be thereat glean'd, for all the sun sees or
The close earth wombs or the profound sea hides
In unknown fathoms, will I break my oath
To this my fair belov'd. Therefore, I pray you,   *540*
As you have ever been my father's honour'd friend,
When he shall miss me,—as, in faith, I mean not
To see him any more,—cast your good counsels
Upon his passion: let myself and fortune
Tug for the time to come. This you may know   *545*

And so deliver, I am put to sea
With her whom here I cannot hold on shore;
And most opportune to our need, I have
A vessel rides fast by, but not prepar'd
For this design. What course I mean to hold   *550*
Shall nothing benefit your knowledge, nor
Concern me the reporting.
    Cam.   O my lord!
I would your spirit were easier for advice,
Or stronger for your need.   *555*
    Flo.   Hark, Perdita.   *[Takes her aside.]*
[To Camillo.] I'll hear you by and by.
    Cam.   He's irremovable,
Resolv'd for flight. Now were I happy if
His going I could frame to serve my turn,   *560*
Save him from danger, do him love and honour,
Purchase the sight again of dear Sicilia
And that unhappy king, my master, whom
I so much thirst to see.
    Flo.   Now, good Camillo,   *565*
I am so fraught with curious business that
I leave out ceremony.
    Cam.   Sir, I think
You have heard of my poor services, i' the love
That I have borne your father?   *570*
    Flo.   Very nobly
Have you deserv'd: it is my father's music
To speak your deeds, not little of his care
To have them recompens'd as thought on.
    Cam.   Well, my lord,   *575*
If you may please to think I love the king
And through him what's nearest to him, which is
Your gracious self, embrace but my direction.
If your more ponderous and settled project
May suffer alteration, on mine honour   *580*
I'll point you where you shall have such receiving
As shall become your highness; where you may
Enjoy your mistress,—from the whom, I see,
There's no disjunction to be made, but by,
As, heavens forfend! your ruin,—marry her;   *585*
And with my best endeavours in your absence
Your discontenting father strive to qualify,
And bring him up to liking.
    Flo.   How, Camillo,
May this, almost a miracle, be done?   *590*
That I may call thee something more than man,
And after that trust to thee.
    Cam.   Have you thought on
A place whereto you'll go?
    Flo.   Not any yet;   *595*
But as the unthought-on accident is guilty
To what we wildly do, so we profess
Ourselves to be the slaves of chance and flies
Of every wind that blows.
    Cam.   Then list to me: *600*
This follows; if you will not change your purpose
But undergo this flight, make for Sicilia,

---

501 mingle faith: *exchange troth-plights*   **507 plucking:** *being pulled*   **527 Am heir to
my affection:** *have an inheritance in my love*   **529 fancy:** *love*   **538 wombs:** *bears within
it*   **545 Tug:** *struggle (as in a tug-of-war)*

551, 552 nor ... reporting: *nor is it my business to tell you*   **557 by and by:** *in just a
minute*   **566 fraught:** *loaded down* **curious:** *causing anxiety*   **585 forfend:** *forbid*   **587 discontenting:** *dissatisfied* **qualify:** *pacify*   **588 bring him up to liking:** *make
him approve your choice*   **596, 597 guilty to:** *to blame for*

And there present yourself and your fair princess,—
For so, I see, she must be,—'fore Leontes;
She shall be habited as it becomes   605
The partner of your bed. Methinks I see
Leontes opening his free arms and weeping
His welcomes forth; asks thee, the son, forgiveness
As 'twere i' the father's person; kisses the hands
Of your fresh princess; o'er and o'er divides him   610
'Twixt his unkindness and his kindness: the one
He chides to hell, and bids the other grow
Faster than thought or time.

Flo.   Worthy Camillo,
What colour for my visitation shall I   615
Hold up before him?

Cam.   Sent by the king your father
To greet him and to give him comforts. Sir,
The manner of your bearing towards him, with
What you as from your father shall deliver,   620
Things known betwixt us three, I'll write you down:
The which shall point you forth at every sitting
What you must say; that he shall not perceive
But that you have your father's bosom there
And speak his very heart.   625

Flo.   I am bound to you.
There is some sap in this.

Cam.   A course more promising
Than a wild dedication of yourselves
To unpath'd waters, undream'd shores, most certain   630
To miseries enough: no hope to help you,
But as you shake off one to take another;
Nothing so certain as your anchors, who
Do their best office, if they can but stay you
Where you'll be loath to be. Besides, you know   635
Prosperity's the very bond of love,
Whose fresh complexion and whose heart together
Affliction alters.

Per.   One of these is true:
I think affliction may subdue the cheek,   640
But not take in the mind.

Cam.   Yea, say you so?
There shall not at your father's house these seven years
Be born another such.

Flo.   My good Camillo,   645
She is as forward of her breeding as
She is i' the rear o' our birth.

Cam.   I cannot say 'tis pity
She lacks instructions, for she seems a mistress
To most that teach.   650

Per.   Your pardon, sir; for this
I'll blush you thanks.

Flo.   My prettiest Perdita!
But O! the thorns we stand upon. Camillo,
Preserver of my father, now of me,   655
The med'cine of our house, how shall we do?
We are not furnish'd like Bohemia's son,
Nor shall appear in Sicilia.

Cam.   My lord,

Fear none of this: I think you know my fortunes   660
Do all lie there: it shall be so my care
To have you royally appointed as if
The scene you play were mine. For instance, sir,
That you may know you shall not want, one word.

[They talk aside.]

Enter Autolycus.

Aut. Ha, ha! what a fool Honesty is! and Trust, his   665
sworn brother, a very simple gentleman! I have sold all my
trumpery: not a counterfeit stone, not a riband, glass, pomander, brooch, table-book, ballad, knife, tape, glove, shoe-tie,
bracelet, horn-ring, to keep my pack from fasting: they throng who
should buy first, as if my trinkets had been hallowed and   670
brought a benediction to the buyer: by which means I saw
whose purse was best in picture; and what I saw, to my good
use I remembered. My clown,—who wants but something to
be a reasonable man,—grew so in love with the wenches' song
that he would not stir his pettitoes till he had both tune and
words; which so drew the rest of the herd to me that all their
other senses stuck in ears: you might have pinched a placket, it
was senseless; 'twas nothing to geld a codpiece of a purse; I
would have filed keys off that hung in chains: no hearing,
no feeling, but my sir's song, and admiring the nothing of it; 680
so that, in this time of lethargy I picked and cut most of
their festival purses; and had not the old man come in with a
whoo-bub against his daughter and the king's son, and scared
my choughs from the chaff, I had not left a purse alive in the
whole army.   685

[Camillo, Florizel, and Perdita come forward.]

Cam. Nay, but my letters, by this means being there
So soon as you arrive, shall clear that doubt.

Flo. And those that you'll procure from King Leontes—
Cam. Shall satisfy your father.

Per.   Happy be you!   690
All that you speak shows fair.

Cam. *[Seeing Autolycus.]* Whom have we here?
We'll make an instrument of this: omit
Nothing may give us aid.

Aut. *[Aside.]* If they have overheard me now, why, hanging.

Cam. How now, good fellow! Why shakest thou so? Fear
not, man; here's no harm intended to thee.

Aut. I am a poor fellow, sir.

Cam. Why, be so still; here's nobody will steal that from
thee; yet, for the outside of thy poverty we must take an   700
exchange; therefore, discase thee instantly,—thou must think,
there's a necessity in 't,—and change garments with this gentleman: though the pennyworth on his side be the worst, yet
hold thee, there's some boot.

Aut. I am a poor fellow, sir.—*[Aside.]* I know ye well   705
enough.

Cam. Nay, prithee, dispatch: the gentleman is half flayed
already.

Aut. Are you in earnest, sir? *[Aside.]* I smell the trick on 't.
Flo. Dispatch, I prithee.   710
Aut. Indeed, I have had earnest; but I cannot with con-
science take it.

610 him: *himself*   615 colour: *pretext*   622 point you forth: *direct you*   sitting: *inter-view*   624 bosom: *inmost secrets*   627 sap: *juice, life*   641 take in: *conquer*   646 forward of her breeding: *superior to her upbringing*   657 furnish'd: *equipped*   658 appear: *appear so*

662 appointed: *fitted out*   667 pomander: *cf. n.*   668 table-book: *notebook*   672 pic-ture: *appearance*   675 pettitoes: *pig's feet*   678 senseless: *insensible*   geld a codpiece: *rob a breeches pocket*   683 whoo-bub: *outcry*   684 choughs: *jackdaws, simpletons*   701 discase: *undress*   703 pennyworth: *bargain*   711 earnest: *part payment in advance*

Cam. Unbuckle, unbuckle.—

        [Florizel and Autolycus exchange garments.]

Fortunate mistress,—let my prophecy

Come home to yc!—you must retire yourself   715

Into some covert: take your sweetheart's hat

And pluck it o'er your brows; muffle your face;

Dismantle you, and, as you can, disliken

The truth of your own seeming; that you may,—

For I do fear eyes over you,—to shipboard   720

Get undescried.

    Per.   I see the play so lies

That I must bear a part.

    Cam.   No remedy.

Have you done there?   725

    Flo.   Should I now meet my father

He would not call me son.

    Cam.   Nay, you shall have no hat.

        [Giving it to Perdita.]

Come, lady, come. Farewell, my friend.

    Aut.   Adieu, sir.   730

    Flo. O Perdita, what have we twain forgot!

Pray you, a word.   *[They converse apart.]*

    Cam. [Aside.] What I do next shall be to tell the king

Of this escape, and whither they are bound;

Wherein my hope is I shall so prevail   735

To force him after: in whose company

I shall review Sicilia, for whose sight

I have a woman's longing.

    Flo.   Fortune speed us!

Thus we set on, Camillo, to the sea-side.   740

    Cam. The swifter speed the better.

      Exit [with Florizel and Perdita].

    Aut. I understand the business; I hear it. To have an open ear, a quick eye, and a nimble hand, is necessary for a cut-purse: a good nose is requisite also, to smell out work for the other senses. I see this is the time that the unjust man doth thrive. What an exchange had this been without boot! what a boot is here with this exchange! Sure, the gods do this year connive at us, and we may do anything extempore. The prince himself is about a piece of iniquity; stealing away from his father with his clog at his heels. If I thought it were a piece 750 of honesty to acquaint the king withal, I would not do 't: I hold it the more knavery to conceal it, and therein am I constant to my profession. Aside, aside: here is more matter for a hot brain. Every lane's end, every shop, church, session, hanging, yields a careful man work.   755

        Enter Clown and Shepherd.

    Clo. See, see, what a man you are now! There is no other way but to tell the king she's a changeling and none of your flesh and blood.

    Shep. Nay, but hear me.

    Clo. Nay, but hear me.   760

    Shep. Go to, then.

    Clo. She being none of your flesh and blood, your flesh and blood has not offended the king; and so your flesh and blood is not to be punished by him. Show those things you found about her; those secret things, all but what she has with 765 her: this being done, let the law go whistle: I warrant you.

    Shep. I will tell the king all, every word, yea, and his son's pranks too; who, I may say, is no honest man neither to his father nor to me, to go about to make me the king's brother-in-law.   770

    Clo. Indeed, brother-in-law was the furthest off you could have been to him, and then your blood had been the dearer by I know not how much an ounce.

    Aut. [Aise.] Very wisely, puppies!

    Shep. Well, let us to the king: there is that in this fardel 775 will make him scratch his beard.

    Aut. [Aside.] I know not what impediment this complaint may be to the flight of my master.

    Clo. Pray heartily he be at palace.

    Aut. [Asie.] Though I am not naturally honest, I am so 780 sometimes by chance: let me pocket up my pedlar's excrement. *[Takes off his false beard.]* How now, rustics! whither are you bound?

    Shep. To the palace, an it like your worship.

    Aut. Your affairs there, what, with whom, the condition 785 of that fardel, the place of your dwelling, your names, your ages, of what having, breeding, and anything that is fitting to be known, discover.

    Clo. We are but plain fellows, sir.

    Aut. A lie; you are rough and hairy. Let me have no 790 lying; it becomes none but tradesmen, and they often give us soldiers the lie; but we pay them for it with stamped coin, not stabbing steel; therefore they do not give us the lie.

    Clo. Your worship had like to have given us one, if you had not taken yourself with the manner.   795

    Shep. Are you a courtier, an 't like you, sir?

    Aut. Whether it like me or no, I am a courtier. Seest thou not the air of the court in these enfoldings? hath not my gait in it the measure of the court? receives not thy nose court-odour from me? reflect I not on thy baseness court-contempt? 800 Think'st thou, for that I insinuate, or toaze from thee thy business, I am therefore no courtier? I am courtier, cap-a-pe, and one that will either push on or pluck back thy business there: whereupon I command thee to open thy affair.

    Shep. My business, sir, is to the king.   805

    Aut. What advocate hast thou to him?

    Shep. I know not, an't like you.

    Clo. Advocate's the court-word for a pheasant: say you have none.

    Shep. None, sir; I have no pheasant, cock nor hen.   810

    Aut. How bless'd are we that are not simple men!

Yet nature might have made me as these are,

Therefore I'll not disdain.

    Clo. This cannot be but a great courtier.

    Shep. His garments are rich, but he wears them not 815 handsomely.

    Clo. He seems to be the more noble in being fantastical: a great man, I'll warrant; I know by the picking on 's teeth.

    Aut. The fardel there? what's i' the fardel?

Wherefore that box?   820

    Shep. Sir, there lies such secrets in this fardel and box which none must know but the king; and which he shall know within this hour if I may come to the speech of him.

---

718 Dismantle: *change your cloak* **disliken:** *disguise* **736 To:** *as to* **737 review:** *see again* **751 withal:** *therewith* **761 Go to:** *go ahead*

775 fardel: *bundle* **781 excrement:** *excrescence, hair* **784 an:** *if* **like:** *please* **787 having:** *wealth* **795 with the manner:** *in the act* **798 enfoldings:** *garments* **799 measure:** *stately tread* **801 insinuate:** *wheedle* **toaze:** *draw out* **802 cap-a-pe:** *from head to foot* **818 picking on 's:** *way he picks his*

Aut. Age, thou hast lost thy labour.

Shep. Why, sir?   *825*

Aut. The king is not at the palace; he is gone aboard a new ship to purge melancholy and air himself: for, if thou be'st capable of things serious, thou must know the king is full of grief.

Shep. So 'tis said, sir, about his son, that should have   *830* married a shepherd's daughter.

Aut. If that shepherd be not now in hand-fast, let him fly: the curses he shall have, the torture he shall feel, will break the back of man, the heart of monster.

Clo. Think you so, sir?   *835*

Aut. Not he alone shall suffer what wit can make heavy and vengeance bitter; but those that are germane to him, though removed fifty times, shall all come under the hangman: which though it be great pity, yet it is necessary. An old sheep-whistling rogue, a ram-tender, to offer to have his daughter   *840* come into grace! Some say he shall be stoned; but that death is too soft for him, say I: draw our throne into a sheep cote! all deaths are too few, the sharpest too easy.

Clo. Has the old man e'er a son, sir, do you hear, an 't like you, sir?   *845*

Aut. He has a son, who shall be flayed alive; then 'nointed over with honey, set on the head of a wasp's nest; then stand till he be three quarters and a dram dead; then recovered again with aqua-vitæ or some other hot infusion; then, raw as he is, and in the hottest day prognostication proclaims, shall he   *850* be set against a brick-wall, the sun looking with a southward eye upon him, where he is to behold him with flies blown to death. But what talk we of these traitorly rascals, whose miseries are to be smiled at, their offences being so capital? Tell me,—for you seem to be honest plain men,—what you   *855* have to the king: being something gently considered, I'll bring you where he is aboard, tender your persons to his presence, whisper him in your behalfs; and if it be in man besides the king to effect your suits, here is a man shall do it.

Clo. He seems to be of great authority: close with him,   *860* give him gold; and though authority be a stubborn bear, yet he is oft led by the nose with gold. Show the inside of your purse to the outside of his hand, and no more ado. Remember, 'stoned,' and 'flayed alive'!

Shep. An 't please you, sir, to undertake the business for   *865* us, here is that gold I have: I'll make it as much more and leave this young man in pawn till I bring it you.

Aut. After I have done what I promised?

Shep. Ay, sir.

Aut. Well, give me the moiety. Are you a party in this   *870* business?

Clo. In some sort, sir: but though my case be a pitiful one, I hope I shall not be flayed out of it.

Aut. O! that's the case of the shepherd's son: hang him, he'll be made an example.   *875*

Clo. Comfort, good comfort! we must to the king and show our strange sights: he must know 'tis none of your daughter nor my sister; we are gone else. Sir, I will give you as much as this old man does when the business is performed; and remain, as he says, your pawn till it be brought you.   *880*

Aut. I will trust you. Walk before toward the sea-side; go on the right hand; I will but look upon the hedge and follow you.

Clo. We are blessed in this man, as I may say, even blessed.

Shep. Let's before as he bids us. He was provided to do us good.   *885*

               [Exeunt Shepherd and Clown.]

Aut. If I had a mind to be honest I see Fortune would not suffer me: she drops booties in my mouth. I am courted now with a double occasion, gold, and a means to do the prince my master good; which who knows how that may turn   *890* back to my advancement? I will bring these two moles, these blind ones, aboard him: if he think it fit to shore them again, and that the complaint they have to the king concerns him nothing, let him call me rogue for being so far officious; for I am proof against that title and what shame else belongs   *895* to 't. To him will I present them: there may be matter in it.

                                Exit.

ACT FIFTH ❧ SCENE FIRST

[Sicilia. A Room in the Palace of Leontes]
Enter Leontes, Cleomenes, Dion, Paulina, Servants.

Cleo. Sir, you have done enough, and have perform'd
A saint-like sorrow: no fault could you make
Which you have not redeem'd; indeed paid down
More penitence than done trespass. At the last,
Do as the heavens have done, forget your evil;   *5*
With them forgive yourself.

Leon.   Whilst I remember
Her and her virtues, I cannot forget
My blemishes in them, and so still think of
The wrong I did myself; which was so much,   *10*
That heirless it hath made my kingdom, and
Destroy'd the sweet'st companion that e'er man
Bred his hopes out of.

Paul.   True, too true, my lord;
If one by one you wedded all the world,   *15*
Or from the all that are took something good,
To make a perfect woman, she you kill'd
Would be unparallel'd.

Leon.   I think so. Kill'd!
She I kill'd! I did so; but thou strik'st me   *20*
Sorely to say I did: it is as bitter
Upon thy tongue as in my thought. Now, good now,
Say so but seldom.

Cleo.   Not at all, good lady:
You might have spoken a thousand things that would   *25*
Have done the time more benefit, and grac'd
Your kindness better.

Paul.   You are one of those
Would have him wed again.

Dion.   If you would not so,   *30*
You pity not the state, nor the remembrance
Of his most sovereign name; consider little
What dangers, by his highness' fail of issue,
May drop upon his kingdom and devour

---

832 hand-fast: *custody*   **837 germane:** *related*   **840 offer:** *presume*   **848 a dram:** *a trifle more*   **849 aqua-vitæ:** *brandy*   **850 prognostication:** *the almanac's forecast of the weather*   **853 what:** *why*   **856 considered:** *given a consideration, bribed*   **857 tender:** *present*   **872 case:** *a pun on the two meanings, situation and skin*

892 aboard him: *aboard his ship*   **shore:** *put on shore*   **22 good now:** *pray you*   **26 done … benefit:** *suited the occasion better*   **33 fail:** *lack*

Incertain lookers-on. What were more holy 35
Than to rejoice the former queen is well?
What holier than for royalty's repair,
For present comfort, and for future good,
To bless the bed of majesty again
With a sweet fellow to 't? 40
    Paul.   There is none worthy,
Respecting her that's gone. Besides, the gods
Will have fulfil'd their secret purposes;
For has not the divine Apollo said,
Is 't not the tenour of his oracle, 45
That King Leontes shall not have an heir
Till his lost child be found? which that it shall,
Is all as monstrous to our human reason
As my Antigonus to break his grave
And come again to me; who, on my life, 50
Did perish with the infant. 'Tis your counsel
My lord should to the heavens be contrary,
Oppose against their wills.—*[To Leontes.]* Care not for issue;
The crown will find an heir: great Alexander
Left his to the worthiest, so his successor 55
Was like to be the best.
    Leon.   Good Paulina,
Who hast the memory of Hermione,
I know, in honour; O! that ever I
Had squar'd me to thy counsel! then, even now, 60
I might have look'd upon my queen's full eyes,
Have taken treasure from her lips,—
    Paul.   And left them
More rich, for what they yielded.
    Leon.   Thou speak'st truth. 65
No more such wives; therefore, no wife: one worse,
And better us'd, would make her sainted spirit
Again possess her corpse and on this stage,—
Where we're offenders now,—appear soul-vex'd,
And begin, 'Why to me?' 70
    Paul.   Had she such power,
She had just cause.
    Leon.   She had; and would incense me
To murder her I married.
    Paul.   I should so: 75
Were I the ghost that walk'd, I'd bid you mark
Her eye, and tell me for what dull part in 't
You chose her; then I'd shriek, that even your ears
Should rift to hear me; and the words that follow'd
Should be 'Remember mine.' 80
    Leon.   Stars, stars!
And all eyes else dead coals. Fear thou no wife;
I'll have no wife, Paulina.
    Paul.   Will you swear
Never to marry but by my free leave? 85
    Leon. Never, Paulina: so be bless'd my spirit!
    Paul. Then, good my lords, bear witness to his oath.
    Cleo. You tempt him over much.
    Paul.   Unless another,
As like Hermione as is her picture, 90
Affront his eye.

    Cleo.   Good madam,—
    Paul.   I have done.
Yet, if my lord will marry,—if you will, sir,
No remedy, but you will,—give me the office 95
To choose you a queen, she shall not be so young
As was your former; but she shall be such
As, walk'd your first queen's ghost, it should take joy
To see her in your arms.
    Leon.   My true Paulina, 100
We shall not marry till thou bidd'st us.
    Paul.   That
Shall be when your first queen 's again in breath;
Never till then.

                    Enter a Servant.

    Ser. One that gives out himself Prince Florizel, 105
Son of Polixenes, with his princess,—she
The fairest I have yet beheld,—desires access
To your high presence.
    Leon.   What with him? he comes not
Like to his father's greatness; his approach, 110
So out of circumstance and sudden, tells us
'Tis not a visitation fram'd, but fore'd
By need and accident. What train?
    Ser.   But few,
And those but mean. 115
    Leon.   His princess, say you, with him?
    Ser. Ay, the most peerless piece of earth, I think,
That e'er the sun shone bright on.
    Paul.   O Hermione!
As every present time doth boast itself 120
Above a better gone, so must thy grave
Give way to what's seen now. Sir, you yourself
Have said and writ so,—but your writing now
Is colder than that theme,—'She had not been,
Nor was not to be equall'd'; thus your verse 125
Flow'd with her beauty once: 'tis shrewdly ebb'd
To say you have seen a better.
    Ser.   Pardon, madam:
The one I have almost forgot—your pardon—
The other, when she has obtain'd your eye, 130
Will have your tongue too. This is a creature,
Would she begin a sect, might quench the zeal
Of all professors else, make proselytes
Of who she but bid follow.
    Paul.   How! not women? 135
    Ser. Women will love her, that she is a woman
More worth than any man; men, that she is
The rarest of all women.
    Leon.   Go, Cleomenes;
Yourself, assisted with your honour'd friends, 140
Bring them to our embracement. Still 'tis strange,
                              Exit [Cleomenes with others].
He thus should steal upon us.
    Paul.   Had our prince—
Jewel of children—seen this hour, he had pair'd
Well with this lord: there was not full a month 145
Between their births.

---

35 **Incertain:** *irresolute* 37 **repair:** *restoration* 42 **Respecting:** *compared with* 60 **squar'd me:** *shaped my conduct* 73 **incense:** *incite* 79 **rift:** *rive, burst* 91 **Affront:** *confront*

S. d. **Servant:** *gentleman-in-waiting* 111 **out of circumstance:** *lacking in ceremony* 112 **fram'd:** *planned in advance* 126 **shrewdly:** *exceedingly* 133 **professors else:** *those who profess other faiths* 140 **with:** *by*

Leon. Prithee, no more: cease! thou know'st
He dies to me again when talk'd of: sure,
When I shall see this gentleman, thy speeches
Will bring me to consider that which may   *150*
Unfurnish me of reason. They are come.

Enter Florizel, Perdita, Cleomenes, and others.

Your mother was most true to wedlock, prince;
For she did print your royal father off,
Conceiving you. Were I but twenty-one,
Your father's image is so hit in you,   *155*
His very air, that I should call you brother,
As I did him; and speak of something wildly
By us perform'd before. Most dearly welcome!
And you, fair princess,—goddess! O, alas!
I lost a couple, that 'twist heaven and earth   *160*
Might thus have stood begetting wonder as
You, gracious couple, do: and then I lost—
All mine own folly—the society,
Amity too, of your brave father, whom,
Though bearing misery, I desire my life   *165*
Once more to look on him.
    Flo.   By his command
Have I here touch'd Sicilia; and from him
Give you all greetings that a king, at friend,
Can send his brother: and, but infirmity,—   *170*
Which waits upon worn times,—hath something seiz'd
His wish'd ability, he had himself
The land and waters 'twixt your throne and his
Measur'd to look upon you, whom he loves—
He bade me say so—more than all the sceptres   *175*
And those that bear them living.
    Leon.   O, my brother!—
Good gentleman,—the wrongs I have done thee stir
Afresh within me, and these thy offices
So rarely kind, are as interpreters   *180*
Of my behind-hand slackness! Welcome hither,
As is the spring to the earth. And hath he too
Expos'd this paragon to the fearful usage—
At least ungentle—of the dreadful Neptune,
To greet a man not worth her pains, much less   *185*
The adventure of her person?
    Flo.   Good my lord,
She came from Libya.
    Leon.   Where the warlike Smalus,
That noble honour'd lord, is fear'd and lov'd?   *190*
    Flo. Most royal sir, from thence; from him, whose daughter
His tears proclaim'd his, parting with her: thence—
A prosperous south-wind friendly—we have cross'd,
To execute the charge my father gave me
For visiting your highness: my best train   *195*
I have from your Sicilian shores dismiss'd;
Who for Bohemia bend, to signify
Not only my success in Libya, sir,
But my arrival and my wife's, in safety
Here where we are.   *200*
    Leon.   The blessed gods
Purge all infection from our air whilst you

Do climate here! You have a holy father,
A graceful gentleman: against whose person,
So sacred as it is, I have done sin: *205*
For which the heavens, taking angry note,
Have left me issueless; and your father's bless'd—
As he from heaven merits it—with you,
Worthy his goodness. What might I have been,
Might I a son and daughter now have look'd on,   *210*
Such goodly things as you!

Enter a Lord.

    Lord.   Most noble sir,
That which I shall report will bear no credit,
Were not the proof so nigh. Please you, great sir,
Bohemia greets you from himself by me;   *215*
Desires you to attach his son, who has—
His dignity and duty both cast off—
Fled from his father, from his hopes, and with
A shepherd's daughter.
    Leon.   Where's Bohemia? speak.   *220*
    Lord. Here in your city; I now came from him:
I speak amazedly, and it becomes
My marvel and my message. To your court
Whiles he was hastening,—in the chase it seems
Of this fair couple,—meets he on the way   *225*
The father of this seeming lady and
Her brother, having both their country quitted
With this young prince.
    Flo.   Camillo has betray'd me;
Whose honour and whose honesty till now   *230*
Endur'd all weathers.
    Lord.   Lay 't so to his charge:
He's with the king your father.
    Leon.   Who? Camillo?
    Lora. Camillo, sir: I spake with him, who now   *235*
Has these poor men in question. Never saw I
Wretches so quake: they kneel, they kiss the earth,
Forswear themselves as often as they speak:
Bohemia stops his ears, and threatens them
With divers deaths in death.   *240*
    Per.   O my poor father!
The heaven sets spies upon us, will not have
Our contract celebrated.
    Leon.   You are married?
    Flo. We are not, sir, nor are we like to be;   *245*
The stars, I see, will kiss the valleys first:
The odds for high and low's alike.
    Leon.   My lord,
Is this the daughter of a king?
    Flo.   She is,   *250*
When once she is my wife.
    Leon. That 'once,' I see, by your good father's speed,
Will come on very slowly. I am sorry,
Most sorry, you have broken from his liking
Where you were tied in duty; and as sorry   *255*
Your choice is not so rich in worth as beauty,
That you might well enjoy her.
    Flo.   Dear, look up:

---

151 Unfurnish: *deprive*   **169** at friend: *on friendly terms*   **170–172** but . . . ability;   **222**
cf. n.   **179** offices: *dutiful acts*   **186** adventure: *risk*   **197** bend: *steer*   amazedly: *in a maze* becomes: *befits*   **223** marvel: *astonishment*   **247** Cf. n.   **256**
worth: *wealth and rank*

Though Fortune, visible an enemy,
Should chase us with my father, power no jot   260
Hath she to change our loves. Beseech you, sir,
Remember since you ow'd no more to time
Than I do now; with thought of such affections,
Step forth mine advocate; at your request
My father will grant precious things as trifles.   265
   Leon. Would he do so, I'd beg your precious mistress,
Which he counts but a trifle.
   Paul.   Sir, my liege,
Your eye hath too much youth in 't: not a month
'Fore your queen died, she was more worth such gazes   270
Than what you look on now.
   Leon.   I thought of her,
Even in these looks I made. *[To Florizel.]* But your petition
Is yet unanswer'd. I will to your father:
Your honour not o'erthrown by your desires,   275
I am friend to them and you; upon which errand
I now go toward him. Therefore follow me,
And mark what way I make: come, good my lord.   *Exeunt.*

❧ SCENE SECOND ❧

[Before the Palace]
Enter Autolycus and a Gentleman.

Aut. Beseech you, sir, were you present at this relation?
   Gent. I was by at the opening of the fardel, heard the old shepherd deliver the manner how he found it: whereupon, after a little amazedness, we were all commanded out of the chamber; only this methought I heard the shepherd say, he found   5
the child.
   Aut. I would most gladly know the issue of it.
   Gent. I make a broken delivery of the business; but the changes I perceived in the king and Camillo were very notes of admiration: they seemed almost, with staring on one   10
another, to tear the cases of their eyes; there was speech in theirdumbness, language in their very gesture; they looked as they had heard of a world ransomed, or one destroyed: a notable passion of wonder appeared in them; but the wisest beholder, that knew no more but seeing, could not say if the   15
importance were joy or sorrow; but in the extremity of the one it must needs be.

Enter another Gentleman.

Here comes a gentleman that haply knows more.
The news, Rogero?
   Sec. Gent. Nothing but bonfires: the oracle is fulfilled;   20
the king's daughter is found: such a deal of wonder is broken out within this hour that ballad-makers cannot be able to express it.

Enter another Gentleman.

Here comes the lady Paulina's steward: he can deliver you more. How goes it now, sir? this news which is called true   25
is so like an old tale, that the verity of it is in strong suspicion: has the king found his heir?

Third Gent. Most true, if ever truth were pregnant by circumstance: that which you hear you'll swear you see, there is such unity in the proofs. The mantle of Queen Hermione,   30
her jewel about the neck of it, the letters of Antigonus found with it, which they know to be his character; the majesty of the creature in resemblance of the mother, the affection of nobleness which nature shows above her breeding, and many other evidences proclaim her with all certainty to be the   35
king's daughter. Did you see the meeting of the two kings?
   Sec. Gent. No.
   Third Gent. Then have you lost a sight, which was to be seen, cannot be spoken of. There might you have beheld one joy crown another, so, and in such manner that, it seemed,   40
sorrow wept to take leave of them, for their joy waded in tears. There was casting up of eyes, holding up of hands, with countenances of such distraction that they were to be known by garment, not by favour. Our king, being ready to leap out of himself for joy of his found daughter, as if that joy were   45
now become a loss, cries, 'O, thy mother, thy mother!' then asks Bohemia forgiveness; then embraces his son-in-law; then again worries he his daughter with clipping her; now he thanks the old shepherd, which stands by like a weather-bitten conduit of many kings' reigns. I never heard of such another   50
encounter, which lames report to follow it and undoes description to do it.
   Sec. Gent. What, pray you, became of Antigonus that carried hence the child?
   Third. Gent. Like an old tale still, which will have matter   55
to rehearse, though credit be asleep and not an ear open. He was torn to pieces with a bear: this avouches the shepherd's son, who has not only his innocence—which seems much —to justify him, but a handkerchief and rings of his that Paulina knows.   60
   First Gent. What became of his bark and his followers?
   Third Gent. Wrecked, the same instant of their master's death, and in the view of the shepherd: so that all the instruments which aided to expose the child were even then lost when it was found. But, O! the noble combat that 'twixt joy   65
and sorrow was fought in Paulina. She had one eye declined for the loss of her husband, another elevated that the oracle was fulfilled: she lifted the princess from the earth, and so locks her in embracing, as if she would pin her to her heart that she might no more be in danger of losing.   70
   First Gent. The dignity of this act was worth the audience of kings and princes, for by such was it acted.
   Third Gent. One of the prettiest touches of all, and that which angled for mine eyes,—caught the water though not the fish,—was when at the relation of the queen's death, with the   75
manner how she came to it,—bravely confessed and lamented by the king,—how attentiveness wounded his daughter: till, from one sign of dolour to another, she did, with an 'alas!' I would fain say, bleed tears, for I am sure my heart wept blood. Who was most marble there changed colour; some swounded,   80
all sorrowed: if all the world could have seen 't, the woe had been universal.
   First Gent. Are they returned to the court?

---

262 **since:** *when*   275 **Your honour not:** *provided your honor be not*   278 **way:** *progress*   9 **notes:** *distinctive marks*   10 **admiration:** *wonder*   11 **cases:** *sockets*   16 **importance:** *import*   **in . . . one:** *one in the highest degree*

28, 29 **pregnant by circumstance:** *made full and convincing by circumstantial detail*   31 **jewel:** *jeweled necklace or similar ornament*   32 **character:** *handwriting*   33 **affection of:** *inclination toward*   44 **favour:** *face*   48 **clipping:** *embracing*   49 **weather-bitten:** *weather-worn; cf. n.*   51 **do:** *describe*   58 **innocence:** *stupidity*   59 **justify:** *confirm*   80 **marble:** *i.e., stony-hearted*   **swounded:** *swooned*

Third Gent. No; the princess hearing of her mother's statue, which is in the keeping of Paulina—a piece many years in 85 doing, and now newly performed by that rare Italian master, Julio Romano; who, had he himself eternity and could put breath into his work, would beguile Nature of her custom, so perfectly he is her ape: he so near to Hermione hath done Hermione that they say one would speak to her and stand 90 in hope of answer: thither with all greediness of affection are they gone, and there they intended to sup.

Sec. Gent. I thought she had some great matter there in hand, for she hath privately, twice or thrice a day, ever since the death of Hermione, visited that removed house. Shall 95 we thither and with our company piece the rejoicing?

First Gent. Who would be thence that has the benefit of access? every wink of an eye some new grace will be born: our absence makes us unthrifty to our knowledge. Let's along.

Exeunt [Gentlemen].

Aut. Now, had I not the dash of my former life in me, 100 would preferment drop on my head. I brought the old man and his son aboard the prince; told him I heard them talk of a fardel and I know not what; but he at that time, overfond of the shepherd's daughter,—so he then took her to be,—who began to be much sea-sick, and himself little better, extremity 105 of weather continuing, this mystery remained undiscovered. But 'tis all one to me; for had I been the finder out of this secret, it would not have relished among my other discredits. Here come those I have done good to against my will, and already appearing in the blossoms of their fortune. 110

Enter Shepherd and Clown.

Shep. Come, boy; I am past moe children, but thy sons and daughters will be all gentlemen born.

Clo. You are well met, sir. You denied to fight with me this other day, because I was no gentleman born: see you these clothes? say you see them not and think me still no gentle- 115 man born: you were best say these robes are not gentleman born. Give me the lie, do, and try whether I am not now a gentleman born.

Aut. I know you are now, sir, a gentleman born.

Clo. Ay, and have been so any time these four hours. 120

Shep. And so have I, boy.

Clo. So you have: but I was a gentleman born before my father; for the king's son took me by the hand and called me brother; and then the two kings called my father brother; and then the prince my brother and the princess my sister 125 called my father father; and so we wept: and there was the first gentleman-like tears that ever we shed.

Shep. We may live, son, to shed many more.

Clo. Ay; or else 'twere hard luck, being in so preposterous estate as we are. 130

Aut. I humbly beseech you, sir, to pardon me all the faults I have committed to your worship, and to give me your good report to the prince my master.

Shep. Prithee, son, do; for we must be gentle, now we are gentlemen. 135

Clo. Thou wilt amend thy life?

Aut. Ay, an it like your good worship.

Clo. Give me thy hand: I will swear to the prince thou art as honest a true fellow as any is in Bohemia.

Shep. You may say it, but not swear it. 140

Clo. Not swear it, now I am a gentleman? Let boors and franklins say it, I'll swear it.

Shep. How if it be false, son?

Clo. If it be ne'er so false, a true gentleman may swear it in the behalf of his friend: and I'll swear to the prince thou art a tall fellow of thy hands and that thou wilt not be drunk; but I know thou art no tall fellow of thy hands and that thou wilt be drunk: but I'll swear it, and I would thou wouldst be a tall fellow of thy hands.

Aut. I will prove so, sir, to my power. 150

Clo. Ay, by any means prove a tall fellow: if I do not wonder how thou darest venture to be drunk not being a tall fellow, trust me not. Hark! the kings and the princes, our kindred, are going to see the queen's picture. Come, follow us: we'll be thy good masters. *Exeunt.*

❧ SCENE THIRD ❧

[A Chapel in Paulina's House]

Enter Leontes, Polixenes, Florizel, Perdita, Camillo, Paulina, Lords, and Attendant.

Leon. O grave and good Paulina, the great comfort
That I have had of thee!

Paul.   What, sovereign sir,
I did not well, I meant well. All my services
You have paid home; but that you have vouch-saf'd, 5
With your crown'd brother and these your contracted
Heirs of your kingdoms, my poor house to visit,
It is a surplus of your grace, which never
My life may last to answer.

Leon.   O Paulina! 10
We honour you with trouble: but we came
To see the statue of our queen: your gallery
Have we pass'd through, not without much content
In many singularities, but we saw not
That which my daughter came to look upon, 15
The statue of her mother.

Paul.   As she liv'd peerless,
So her dead likeness, I do well believe,
Excels whatever yet you look'd upon
Or hand of man hath done; therefore I keep it 20
Lonely, apart. But here it is: prepare
To see the life as lively mock'd as ever
Still sleep mock'd death: behold! and say 'tis well.

[Paulina draws back a curtain, and reveals Hermione as a statue.]

I like your silence: it the more shows off
Your wonder; but yet speak: first you, my liege. 25
Comes it not something near?

Leon.   Her natural posture!
Chide me, dear stone, that I may say, indeed

87 Julio Romano; *cf. n.* eternity: *immortality* 88 custom: *customers, trade* 89 ape: *imitator* 95 removed: *distant* 96 piece: *add to* 98 access: *privilege of admittance* 99 unthrifty to: *careless about the increase of* 108 relished: *tasted well, been pleasing* 113 denied: *refused* 129 preposterous: *blunder for prosperous*

142 franklins: *small landholders* 147 tall: *bold* 154 picture: *painted statue* 155 good masters: *patrons* 11 We honour you with trouble: *our so-called honor but makes you trouble* 13 content: *pleasure* 14 singularities: *curiosities* 22 lively: *to the life*

Thou art Hermione; or rather, thou art she
In thy not chiding, for she was as tender   30
As infancy and grace. But yet, Paulina,
Hermione was not so much wrinkled; nothing
So aged as this seems.

Pol.   O! not by much.

Paul. So much the more our carver's excellence;   35
Which lets go by some sixteen years and makes her
As she liv'd now.

Leon.   As now she might have done,
So much to my good comfort, as it is
Now piercing to my soul. O! thus she stood,   40
Even with such life of majesty,—warm life,
As now it coldly stand,—when first I woo'd her.
I am asham'd: does not the stone rebuke me
For being more stone than it? O, royal piece!
There's magic in thy majesty, which has   45
My evils conjur'd to remembrance, and
From thy admiring daughter took the spirits,
Standing like stone with thee.

Per.   And give me leave,
And do not say 'tis superstition, that   50
I kneel and then implore her blessing. Lady,
Dear queen, that ended when I but began,
Give me that hand of yours to kiss.

Paul.   O, patience!
The statue is but newly fix'd, the colour's   55
Not dry.

Cam. My lord, your sorrow was too sore laid on,
Which sixteen winters cannot blow away,
So many summers dry: scarce any joy
Did ever so long live; no sorrow   60
But kill'd itself much sooner.

Pol.   Dear my brother,
Let him that was the cause of this have power
To take off so much grief from you as he
Will piece up in himself.   65

Paul.   Indeed, my lord,
If I had thought the sight of my poor image
Would thus have wrought you,—for the stone is mine,—
I'd not have show'd it.

Leon.   Do not draw the curtain.   70

Paul. No longer shall you gaze on 't, lest your fancy
May think anon it moves.

Leon.   Let be, let be!
Would I were dead, but that, methinks, already—
What was he that did make it? See, my lord,   75
Would you not deem it breath'd, and that those veins
Did verily bear blood?

Pol.   Masterly done:
The very life seems warm upon her lip.

Leon. The fixture of her eye has motion in 't,   80
As we are mock'd with art.

Paul.   I'll draw the curtain;
My lord's almost so far transported that
He'll think anon it lives.

Leon.   O sweet Paulina!   85
Make me to think so twenty years together:
No settled senses of the world can match

The pleasure of that madness. Let 't alone.

Paul. I am sorry, sir, I have thus far stirr'd you: but
I could afflict you further.   90

Leon.   Do, Paulina;
For this affliction has a taste as sweet
As any cordial comfort. Still, methinks,
There is an air comes from her: what fine chisel
Could ever yet cut breath? Let no man mock me,   95
For I will kiss her.

Paul.   Good my lord, forbear.
The ruddiness upon her lip is wet:
You'll mar it if you kiss it; stain your own
With oily painting. Shall I draw the curtain?   100

Leon. No, not these twenty years.

Per.   So long could I
Stand by, a looker-on.

Paul.   Either forbear,
Quit presently the chapel, or resolve you   105
For more amazement. If you can behold it,
I'll make the statue move indeed, descend,
And take you by the hand; but then you'll think,—
Which I protest against,—I am assisted
By wicked powers   110

Leon.   What you can make her do,
I am content to look on: what to speak,
I am content to hear; for 'tis as easy
To make her speak as move.

Paul.   It is requir'd   115
You do awake your faith. Then, all stand still;
Or those that think it is unlawful business
I am about, let them depart.

Leon.   Proceed:
No foot shall stir.   120

Paul.   Music, awake her: strike! *[Music.]*
'Tis time; descend; be stone no more: approach;
Strike all that look upon with marvel. Come;
I'll fill your grave up: stir; nay, come away;
Bequeath to death your numbness, for from him   125
Dear life redeems you. You perceive she stirs:

                  [Hermione comes down.]

Start not; her actions shall be holy as
You hear my spell is lawful: do not shun her
Until you see her die again, for then
You kill her double. Nay, present your hand: 130
When she was young you woo'd her; now in age
Is she become the suitor!

Leon. *[Embracing her.]* O! she's warm.
If this be magic, let it be an art
Lawful as eating.   135

Pol.   She embraces him.

Cam. She hangs about his neck:
If she pertain to life let her speak too.

Pol. Ay; and make 't manifest where she has liv'd,
Or how stol'n from the dead.   140

Paul.   That she is living,
Were it but told you, should be hooted at
Like an old tale; but it appears she lives,
Though yet she speak not. Mark a little while.
Please you to interpose, fair madam: kneel   145

---

32 nothing: *not nearly*   **44 piece:** *woman*   **65 piece up in himself:** *make up by increas-*
ing his own grief   **68 wrought:** *excited*   **81** *Cf. n.*

93 cordial *restorative*   **105 resolve you:** *prepare yourselves*   **123 upon:** *on*   **130 dou-**
ble: *doubly, twice*

And pray your mother's blessing: Turn, good lady;
Our Perdita is found.

    [Presenting Perdita, who kneels to Hermione.]

  Her.   You gods, look down,
And from your sacred vials pour your graces
Upon my daughter's head! Tell me, mine own,   *150*
Where hast thou been preserv'd? where liv'd? how found
Thy father's court? for thou shalt hear that I,
Knowing by Paulina that the oracle
Gave hope thou wast in being, have preserv'd
Myself to see the issue.   *155*
  Paul.   There's time enough for that;
Lest they desire upon this push to trouble
Your joys with like relation. Go together,
You precious winners all: your exultation
Partake to every one. I, an old turtle,   *160*
Will wing me to some wither'd bough, and there
My mate, that's never to be found again,
Lament till I am lost.
  Leon.   O! peace, Paulina.
Thou shouldst a husband take by my consent,   *165*
As I by thine a wife: this is a match,

And made between 's by vows. Thou hast found mine:
But how, is to be question'd; for I saw her,
As I thought dead, and have in vain said many
A prayer upon her grave. I'll not seek far,—   *170*
For him, I partly know his mind,— to find thee
An honourable husband. Come, Camillo,
And take her by the hand; whose worth and honesty
Is richly noted, and here justified
By us, a pair of kings. Let's from this place.   *175*
What! look upon my brother: both your pardons,
That e'er I put betwen your holy looks
My ill suspicion. This' your son-in-law,
And son unto the king,—whom heavens directing,
Is troth-plight to your daughter. Good Paulina,   *180*
Lead us from hence, where we may leisurely
Each one demand and answer to his part
Perform'd in this wide gap of time since first
We were dissever'd: hastily lead away.   *Exeunt.*

❧ FINIS ❧

---

157 push: *impulse*   **158 relation:** *relating of their adventures*   **160 Partake to:** *share with*   **166 match:** *bargain*

174 richly noted: *thoroughly known* **justified:** *vouched for*   **178 This:** *this is*

NOTES

Dramatis Personæ. This play is one of seven for which, under the caption 'The Names of the Actors,' the First Folio lists the Dramatis Personæ. The words put in brackets are there omitted.

I.i.6, 7 *entertainment . . . loves.* 'Our loving welcome shall atone for our inadequate entertainment.'

I.i.25, 26. *from . . . winds.* 'From the opposite corners of the heavens,' where the winds of the north, east, south, and west were suposed to have the homes.

I.ii.1. *the watery star.* The moon, as cause of the tides, was considered the queen of the waters.

I.ii.6, 7. *like . . . place.* 'As a cipher, though worthless in itself, may, in a significant position change thousands into tens of thousands, so my grateful farewell, though wholly inadequate, increases all previous expressions of gratitude.'

I.ii.14. *that may blow.* This is usually interpreted as a wish. 'May there blow no nipping winds.'

I.ii.49. *gest.* The gests of a royal journey (from the old French *giste*, a bed or lodging) were the houses at which the monarch stopped overnight on his way.

I.ii.58. *unsphere the stars with oaths.* 'Shake the stars from their positions in the heavens by the violence of your oaths.' According to the ancient Ptolemaic theory of astronomy the earth was the center of the universe, and the stars were located in concentric hollow spheres revolving around it.

I.ii.63. *pay your fees.* It was formerly a custom in prisons for a jailer to exact fees from his prisoners.

I.ii.88. *the imposition, etc.* 'Setting aside our hereditary taint of original sin.'

I.ii.113. *one good deed, etc.* 'The failure to praise one good deed prevents the existence of a thousand that would have been inspired by it.'

I.ii.143. *brows.* It was a common saying in Shakespeare's time that an unfaithful wife put horns on her husband's head, or brows. The unsavory joke appears repeatedly.

I.ii.151. *virginalling.* Playing as on the keys of the virginal, an old-time instrument resembling a piano. The word is here, as often, used punningly.

I.ii.165, 166. *Affection . . . dost.* A possible interpretation of this much disputed passage is: 'Love, thy intense passion masters the inmost hearts of women. Thou dost make possible on their part sins not believed to be possible. Thou dost make absent lovers communicate with each other through dreams (how can this be?). Thou dost cause the dreaming woman to make love to the unreal dream-image of her absent paramour, and to embrace nothingness. Then it is very believable that thou mayst bring her to the arms of a lover bodily present; and thou dost.' For another interpretation cf. C. D. Stewart, *Some Textual Difficulties in Shakespeare* (Yale Univeristy Press), pp. 96-109.

I.ii.237. *predominant.* Leontes accepts the theory of astrology that certain stars under the right conditions exercise a powerful influence over human conduct.

I.ii.318-320. *If . . . thought.* 'If thou wilt confess the truth—and to do otherwise thou must be one who impudently denies his possession of eyes or ears or thought—then say that my wife is a loose woman.'

I.ii.325. *clouded.* Shakespeare's language is so figurative that a sharp line cannot always be drawn between metaphors and obsolete meanings. In the present case, which is typical of hundreds, he probably thought of the accusation dimming Hermione's fair reputation as a cloud dims the moon.

I.ii.357. *medal.* Medallions with the portrait of a friend or sweetheart were frequently worn around the neck in Shakespeare's day. Leontes' jealous delirium pictures Hermione with her arms around Polixenes' neck and her living face on his bosom where the medallion with her portrait might hang.

I.ii.528-530. 'May good speed in escaping help me, and bring comfort to the gracious queen, who is part of the subject of his thoughts but in no way the intentional cause of his ill-founded suspicion.' The passage is blind, and may have been garbled in printing.

II.i.S.d. The Folio stage direction reads: 'Enter Hermione, Mamillius, Ladies: Leontes, Antigonus, Lords.' Editors have agreed in placing the entrance of Leontes after line 43. In the Folio text of *The Winter's Tale* stage directions repeatedly mention actors who were probably to be ready when thus mentioned, but who evidently did not appear before the audience until later. In the present edition such stage directions are adapted according to the judgment of later editors.

II.i.53. *partake no venom.* The belief was formerly common that a spider in one's drink made the beverage poisonous if the insect was seen, but not if the insect was unobserved. 'In the cup of my family life,' says Leontes, 'there has been the spider of adultery; but it did not poison my mind with jealous suffering as long as I did not perceive it.'

II.i.161, 162. *I'll . . . wife.* 'I'll consider human beings on a level with horses in morality.'

II.i.172. *land-damn.* Nothing but guesses can be given for the meaning of *land-damn.* It may mean to bury alive under the ground (land), to exile from the land, or it may be equivalent to *landan,* the word for a rural punishment in Gloucestershire for slanderers and adulterers, 'by rustics traversing from house to house along the country side, blowing trumpets and beating drums or pans and kettles.'

II.i.183. While saying this Leontes probably pulls Antigonus' beard or offers him some other minor physical violence.

II.i.211-214. *Which . . . deed.* 'Which was as gross as was ever found by a suspicion (conjecture) that lacked sight [of their crime] only, lacked nought for proof (approbation), except actually seeing them in sin—with all other circumstances pointing (made up) to the deed—all these, etc.'

II.i.218. *Delphos.* The famous oracle of Apollo was at Delphi (or Delphos). Its location was on the mainland, but it is spoken of at the beginning of Act Third as being on an 'isle,' probably because it has been confused with the island of Delos. The play bristles with inaccuracies in history and geography, which the author did not consider out of keeping with its romantic atmosphere, and most of which he merely took over from the novel that served him as his source. In the main the story seems located in the Middle Ages, whereas the oracle belongs to a much earlier pagan period.

II.iii.44. *humour.* It was formerly the general belief that there were four liquids (humours) in the body and that diseases were due to a disproportionate amount of some one of them.

II.iii.92. *dame Partlet.* Dame Pertelote (Partlet) was a curtain-lecturing hen in Chaucer's *Nun's Priest's Tale.*

III.ii.60-62. *More . . . acknowledge.* 'I must not at all acknowledge that I am guilty (mistress) of anything more than [that] which is counted against me as a fault [namely, my innocent hospitality toward Polixenes].'

III.ii.82. 'My life is exposed to the deadly aim (level) of your jealous imaginings.'

III.ii.180. *Unclasp'd.* The meaning 'revealed,' like so many Shakespearean meanings, was probably more metaphorical than literal even in the author's day. In *King Henry IV,* Part I (I.iii.192) Worcester begins his revelation to Hotspur: 'And now I will unclasp a secret book.'

III.iii.52, 53. *Which . . . thine.* 'Which may, if fortune is willing, by their great value inspire people to educate (breed) thee, and still remain thy property.'

III.iii.63. *ten.* Most modern editors put *sixteen* or *nineteen* in the place of *ten,* on the ground that so early an age does not harmonize with all the offences mentioned. But the author was representing an ignorant and excited man who did not choose his words with the calm precision of a Shakespearean commentator.

III.iii.95. *flap-dragoned.* A flap-dragon was a raisin or some other substance floating in a glass of brandy, from which some gallant, wishing to show his dexterity, would snatch it with his mouth. The sea gulped down the ship with the easy dexterity with which a toper would gulp down the flap-dragon.

IV.iii.4. *winter's pale.* 'Pale' with Shakespeare had two frequent and widely different meanings, (1) paleness, and (2) an enclosed space, either one of which here would make sense. Consequently we could interpret the line: 'The red blood of youth and spring reigns in the pale face of winter'; or, 'The red blood reigns in those fields which recently were the enclosed park of winter.'

IV.iii.23. It was a common belief that kites stole small linen articles to use in building their nests. My trade, says Autolycus, is in stealing sheets. Look out for lesser linen when the kites are building, but for sheets when I come by.

IV.iii.24, 25. *littered under Mercury.* Born under the influence of the planet Mercury, he naturally imitated the god Mercury, who was the ancient deity of thieves.

IV.iii.41. *puritan.* The puritans were hostile to the stage and consequently attacked repeatedly by Shakespeare and his fellow dramatists. Their habit of singing psalms was only one of their many traits ridiculed.

IV.iv.14. *swoon.* The original text reads *sworn,* and the emendation *swoon,* though now generally adopted, is not very well in harmony with Perdita's healthful life and courageous character. If Shakespeare wrote *sworn,* Perdita probably meant that Florizel had come with the vowed purpose of showing in his plain clothes the opposite of her rich ones, as printed letters in a looking-glass are shown reading backwards.

IV.iv.31-34. Jupiter became a bull to win the love of Europa; Neptune, a ram when in love with Theophane; and Apollo as a humble shepherd kept the flocks of King Admetus.

IV.iv.85. *Grace and remembrance.* These were symbolized by rue and rosemary respectively. The significance of flowers as emblems of human moods was often mentioned by the Elizabethans, and plays an important part in the mad speeches of Ophelia (*Hamlet,* IV. v.).

IV.iv.100, 101. *There . . . nature.* Their variegated colors are partly the result of the gardener's art in cross-breeding, and not wholly produced by nature.

IV.iv.120. Lavender, savory, and certain varieties of marjoram were flowers recently imported into England from southern Europe. It is probably as natives of a warmer climate that Perdita calls them 'hot' and a few lines later speaks of them as 'flowers of middle summer.'

IV.iv.133. *Proserpina.* While Proserpina was gathering flowers in the meadows of Sicily, Dis, or Pluto, the god of the underworld, rose through the earth in his chariot, seized her, and carried her away to be his queen.

IV.iv.152. *Whitsun pastorals.* A pastoral is a play of country life; and a Whitsun play would be one given at Whitsuntide, the seventh Sunday after Easter, although we have no evidence elsewhere that plays given then were pastorals.

IV.iv.218, 219. Dildos, fadings, 'jump her and thump her' were all catch words from the anything but 'delicate' refrains of certain popular songs and ballads.

IV.iv.267. *tawdry lace.* This necklace or necktie of silk derived its name from Saint Audrey (Ethelreda), who believed a tumor which came in her throat to be a divine judgment on her for her vanity earlier in wearing beautiful necklaces.

IV.iv.428. *altering rheums.* Morbid disarrangement of the four humours (see note on II.iii.44), a condition producing rheumatism, catarrh, and the diseases characteristic of old age.

IV.iv.667. *pomander.* A little ball of perfumes worn in the pocket or about the neck as a preventive against the plague.

V.i.170-172. 'But that the infirmity which comes with age has somewhat stolen from him (seized) the traveling ability which he wishes for.'

V.i.247. Probably, 'the odds are as great against me in my princely rôle of Florizel as they were in my humble rôle of Doricles.'

V.ii.49. Conduits were often in the shape of human figures.

V.ii.87. *Julio Romano.* This Italian painter was born in 1492, the year of America's discovery; and the worship of Apollo's oracle ceased among Mediterranean kings about a thousand years before that. Both Shakespeare and his audience had a sublime indifference to such anachronisms in a well-told story.

V.iii.81. 'Though her eye be fixed, yet it seems to have motion in it.' (Edwards.)

THE TEXT OF THE PRESENT EDITION

The text of the present volume is, by permission of the Oxford University Press, that of the *Oxford Shakespeare,* edited by the late W. J. Craig, except for the following deviations:

1. The stage directions and the list of *dramatis personae* are those of the First Folio, any alterations and additions being enclosed in square brackets. The Folio numbering of scenes in the fourth act has been followed.

2. A few minor changes in punctuation (such as *good now,* for *good now* in V.i.22) and in spelling (such as *primroses* for *prime-roses* in IV.iv.139) have been made.

3. The following alterations, all reversions to the readings of the First Folio, have been made in the text, the reading of the Folio and the present text preceding the colon, and that of Craig following it:

I.ii.84 nor dreamed: no nor dreamed
I.ii.177 *Leon.* What cheer?: *Pol.* What cheer?
I.ii.308 free of. But: free of: but
II.iii.193 this: thy
II.iii.211 it: its
II.iii.223 does: doth
III.ii.191 What flaying? boiling: What flaying? or what boiling
III.ii.263 To: Unto
III.iii.63 ten: sixteen
IV.iv.647 our: her

The Tempest

Edited by
DAVID HORNE

Dramatis Personae

ALONSO, *King of Naples*

SEBASTIAN, *his Brother*

PROSPERO, *the right Duke of Milan*

ANTONIO, *his Brother, the usurping Duke of Milan*

FERDINAND, *son to the King of Naples*

GONZALO, *an honest old Councilor*

ADRIAN }
FRANCISCO } *Lords*

CALIBAN, *a salvage and deformed Slave*

TRINCULO, *a Jester*

STEPHANO, *a drunken Butler*

MASTER OF A SHIP

BOATSWAIN

MARINERS

MIRANDA, *a Daughter to Prospero*

ARIEL, *an airy Spirit*

IRIS
CERES
JUNO } *Spirits*
NYMPHS
REAPERS

SCENE—*A ship at sea and then an uninhabited island.*

The Tempest

INTRODUCTION

TEXT AND DATE

The earliest published text of *The Tempest* is in the First Folio, 1623. It is the first play in that volume and one of the most painstakingly printed: only a handful of indisputable typographical errors can be found, the verse lineation is on the whole well preserved, the stage directions are remarkably full, and the punctuation is admirably consistent.

In spite of the obvious care taken with punctuation by the first editors, it has been felt necessary to assist the modern reader by converting the pointing entirely to present-day usage. For example, colons in the Folio text appear in the present edition as colons, semicolons, exclamation points, dashes, or periods, though usually the colon in the original has the force of the modern exclamation point, which indeed in almost every instance would have been the mark substituted if other considerations had not dictated variety.

Few liberties have been taken with the text. These few have been recorded in the glosses and notes, with the exception of a slight shift in position of a stage direction here and there, as in I.1.33; in the Folio this direction follows line 30. Whenever anything has been added to the text, it has been placed within square brackets.

Throughout the play, though most frequently in Act I, are defective lines (for instance I.2.185, 227, 274, 297, 319; II.1.282, 346; IV.1.13; V.1.70). These lines—short by one, two, or three metrical feet—have sometimes been used as evidence for a theory that Act I as it now stands is a cut version, the cuts having been made at the places where the faulty lines occur. In the absence of bibliographical corroboration, however, there seems no need to believe that the extant version is not as Shakespeare wrote it, particularly since irregular lines can be found in other Shakespearaean plays, and in *The Tempest* the short lines occur at places where a slight pause assists both the sense and the rhythm.

It should also be noted that a few verse lines have been rearranged slightly to make the length of each more regular; see I.2.355-359, 425, 426; II.1.200, 201, 202-207. A few lines here printed as verse are probably prose (for example II.1.205-206); a few other lines set as verse in the Folio now appear as prose (for example II.1.16-17); and Caliban's speech in II.2.170-175 has been set as verse but appears as prose in the Folio.

From the very slight bibliographical evidence available it is not possible to do more than guess at the form of the copy supplied the printer of the Folio. It could well have been a prompt copy that had been carefully edited by one or another member of the acting company. Its division into acts and scenes and the inclusion of a list of actors, as well as the full stage directions and consistent punctuation mentioned above, may indicate merely that the editors wanted the first play in their volume to make a good impression. Almost the only mark of carelessness that one can note, in fact, is the circumstance that some obvious prose lines are set as verse and some verse as prose. Here it is important to observe, however, that for the actor a few lines or even passages of verse set as prose, or vice versa, would surely have made no difference in his reading of those lines, the important thing in delivery being the sense of rhythm of the complete speech and scene. This must have been doubly true on the Shakespearean stage, where, from all we can learn, the actor's delivery was rapid. If anything, such mistakes in lineation argue that the play was set from playhouse prompt copy.

In any event Shakespeare wrote it at least twelve years before it was printed, for the accounts of the Office of Revels contain a note that it was presented on Hallowmas night (November 1), 1611. There is some negative evidence that it was not being played during the summer of 1611, and one of the sources Shakespeare made use of could not have been seen by him before late 1610. Thus the best inference that can be drawn concerning the date of composition is sometime between October 1610 and October 1611. Apart from collaboration in *Henry VIII* and *Two Noble Kinsmen*, it was probably Shakespeare's last effort.

SOURCES OF THE PLAY

The true source of *The Tempest* is Shakespeare's experience in coming to terms with life. The symbols which permeate it lie so deep and so near to the heart of humanity that even if a closely parallel play or narrative were to be unearthed—and this hypothesis is dubious in the extreme—it could only in a very limited sense be called a source. The billowing themes of Shakespeare's tragedies, the nuances of the comedies, the moral philosophy that threads its way through the histories—all are here and thoroughly Shakespearean and so worked into the matrix of the play that one can believe it the full and natural expression of what was most meaningful to Shakespeare in life.

This is not to call *The Tempest* a conscious farewell to a career. It is highly ironical that the one speech in the play that really sounds as though Shakespeare were taking leave of the stage is one of the few which derive from earlier works: Prospero's conjuring of the spirits in V.1.38-62 comes from Ovid's *Metamorphoses* VII.192-219—partly from the original Latin, partly from Arthur Golding's English translation (many editions after 1567). This is typical of the so-called sources of the play—a line here or there, at the most a few brief passages garnered from well-known works.

Two of the most popular works at the time the play was being written—and together with a manuscript letter in circulation among the playwright's friends, perhaps the origin of his initial inspiration—were concerned with a highly romantic and for the religious a nearly miraculous wreck off the Bermudas in July 1609. For several years before, public interest in the new Virginia colony in America had been running high. When a fleet of nine ships under the command of Sir George Somers (or Summers) put to sea on June 2, 1609, considerable fanfare and putting of pen to paper accompanied the great setting forth.

Nothing was heard in England about the results of the voyage (except that one of the ships was supposed lost) until the governor of Virgina, who had sailed with the fleet, returned in 1610. It then became known that off the coast of the 'still-vex'd Bermoothes' (Shakespeare uses the common spelling-equivalent of the Spanish *Bermudez*) the flagship had run into a hurricane and having been forced to enter a sheltered cove was there run aground. No lives had been lost, and the implications of this as they concerned the intrepid colonizers of a savage land were not missed by the morally minded Elizabethans. Among the pamphlets which appeared in 1610 were two containing accounts of the wreck and subsequent survival of the voyagers, both sufficiently close to Shakespeare's play to make it seem almost certain he knew of them: Sylvester Jourdain's *Discovery of the Barmudas* (facsimile by J. Q. Adams, New York, 1940) and the Council of Virginia's *True Declaration of the State of the Colonie in Virginia* (ed. Peter Force as vol. 3 of *Tracts and Other Papers*, Washington, 1844).

Even more than to these 'Bermuda pamphlets' is Shakespeare indebted to a letter written by one William Strachey and brought to England shortly after July 15, 1610. Although this letter was not published (so far as is known) until 1625, when it appeared as 'A True Reportory of the Wracke' in *Purchas His Pilgrimes* (vol. 19 of the Glasgow ed., 1906), Leslie Hotson has demonstrated that it was being circulated among friends of Shakespeare who could very easily have shown it to him. (*I, William Shakespeare*, London, 1937). The whole of the first scene of *The Tempest* seems to derive from Strachey's account, as do I.2.227-238, much of II.1, the appearance of the banquet in III, and a few more scattered passages.

The other works to which Shakespeare might have given acknowledgment may be quickly disposed of. Gonzalo's references in III.3.58-61 to the dewlapped mountaineers and men with heads in their breasts are straight from the most widely read adventure book of the period: the *Travels of Sir John Mandeville*,

III.3. Gonzalo's disquisition on the ideal commonwealth in II.1.154-163 is derived from Montaigne's 'Of Cannibals,' translated by John Florio, 1603. The name *'Setebos'* probably stems from Robert Eden's *History of Travaile*, 1577, in which it is claimed that the Patagonians have a 'great devil' called this. The origin of 'Caliban' cannot be pinned down. It may be simply an anagram of 'can[n]ibal' or it may be related to *cauliban*, a gypsy word for blackness, though Virgil and Pliny both mention savages named 'Chalybeates.' The name 'Prospero' occurs in William Thomas' *The Historie of Italie*, 1549.

All other of the 'sources' which at one time or another have been put forth as the primary source are little more than analogues. Thus certain *scenari* of the Italian commedia dell' arte have points of resemblance with the plot of *The Tempest*; the last word on these may not yet have been said. A play by the German Jakob Ayrer (died 1605) called, in translation, *The Beautiful Sidea*, was formerly hailed by the Germans as the archetype, but anyone who takes the trouble to read it will come to the conclusion that only two salient details lend any point whatever to the supposed connection: (1) a prince is held in thrall by the beautiful Sidea and made to carry logs for her, and (2) his sword is charmed, so that he cannot use it. Although these coincidences are interesting, they do not mean that either play necessarily descends from the other. At the same time the possibility of a lost *tertium quid* cannot be dismissed.

In sum, so far as research can discover, Shakespeare borrowed remarkably little. Research will go on, for it is in the nature of source hunters to believe that by turning pages they will eventually upset all vested notions. Sometimes they are remarkably successful; yet for *The Tempest*, it seems safe to prophesy, the results will hardly be worth the effort. The true sources are the three dozen plays of Shakespeare which preceded it, together with the feelings, deeper than ever plummet sounded, of a man who considered life gravely and wrote it down incomparably.

ACT FIRST ❧ SCENE FIRST

A tempestuous noise of thunder and lightning heard.
Enter a Shipmaster and a Boatswain.

Master. Boatswain!
Boatswain. Here, Master! What cheer?
Master. Good. Speak to th' mariners. Fall to't,
yarely, or we run ourselves aground—bestir, bestir!   *Exit.*

Enter Mariners.

Boatswain. Heigh, my hearts! Cheerly, cheerly, my hearts!   5
Yare, yare! Take in the topsail! Tend to th' Master's whistle!
Blow till thou burst thy wind, if room enough!

Enter Alonso, Sebastian, Antonio, Ferdinand, Gonzalo, and others.

Alonso. Good Boatswain, have care! Where's the Master?
Play the men!
Boatswain. I pray now, keep below.   10
Antonio. Where is the Master, Boson?
Boatswain. Do you not hear him? You mar our labor. Keep
your cabins—you do assist the storm.
Gonzalo. Nay, good, be patient.
Boatswain. When the sea is. Hence! What cares these roar-   15
ers for the name of king? To cabin: silence! trouble us not!
Gonzalo. Good, yet remember whom thou hast aboard.
Boatswain. None that I more love than myself. You are a
councilor. If you can command these elements to silence and
work the peace of the present, we will not hand a rope   20
more; use your authority. If you cannot, give thanks you have
lived so long and make yourself ready in your cabin for the
mischance of the hour, if it so hap. Cheerly, good hearts!
Out of our way, I say.   *Exit.*
Gonzalo. I have great comfort from this fellow: methinks   25
he hath no drowning mark upon him; his complexion is perfect gallows. Stand fast, good fate, to his hanging! Make the
rope of his destiny our cable, for our own doth little advantage.
If he be not born to be hanged, our case is miserable.   *Exeunt.*

Enter Boatswain.

Boatswain. Down with the topmast! yare, lower, lower! Bring
her to try with main-course.   *A cry within.*
A plague upon this howling! They are louder than the weather
or our office.

Enter Sebastian, Antonio, and Gonzalo.

Yet again? What do you here? Shall we give ore and drown?
Have you a mind to sink?   35
Sebastian. A pox o' your throat, you bawling, blasphemous,
incharitable dog!
Boatswain. Work you, then.
Antonio. Hang, cur, hang, you whoreson, insolent noise-
maker; we are less afraid to be drown'd than thou art.   40

Gonzalo. I'll warrant him for drowning, though the ship
were no stronger than a nutshell and as leaky as an unstanched
wench.
Boatswain. Lay her ahold, ahold! Set her two courses off to
sea again; lay her off!   45

Enter Mariners, wet.

Mariners. All lost! To prayers, to prayers, all lost!
[Exeunt Mariners.]
Boatswain. What, must our mouths be cold?
Gonzalo. The king and prince at prayers! Let's assist them,
for our case is as theirs.
Sebastian. I am out of patience.   50
Antonio. We are merely cheated of our lives by drunkards.
This wide-chopp'd rascal, would thou might'st lie drowning the
washing of ten tides.
Gonzalo. He'll be hanged yet, though every drop of water
swear against it and gape at wid'st to glut him.   55
[Exit Boatswain.]
A confused noise within.
[Voices.] 'Mercy on us!' 'We split, we split!' 'Farewell,
my wife and children; farewell, brother!' 'We split! we split!
we split!'
Antonio. Let's all sink with' king.
Sebastian. Let's take leave of him.   60
[Exeunt Sebastian and Antonio.]
Gonzalo. Now would I give a thousand furlongs of sea for
an acre of barren ground; long heath, brown furze, anything.
The wills above be done, but I would fain die a dry death.
Exit.

❧ SCENE SECOND ❧

Enter Prospero and Miranda.

Miranda. If by your art, my dearest father, you have
Put the wild waters in this roar, allay them.
The sky it seems would pour down stinking pitch,
But that the sea, mounting to th' welkin's cheek,
Dashes the fire out. O! I have suffered   5
With those that I saw suffer: a brave vessel—
Who had no doubt some noble creature in her—
Dash'd all to pieces. O the cry did knock
Against my very heart. Poor souls, they perish'd.
Had I bin any god of power, I would   10
Have sunk the sea within the earth, or ere
It should the good ship so have swallow'd, and
The fraughting souls within her.
Prospero.   Be collected:
No more amazement. Tell your piteous heart   15
There's no harm done.
Miranda.   O woe the day!
Prospero.   No harm.
I have done nothing but in care of thee—

ACT I; *Cf. n.*   2 **What cheer:** *what mood are you in* (i.e. optimistic or pessimistic)?   3
Good: *i.e. good cheer; Cf. n.*   4 **yarely:** *quickly*   7 **Blow . . . enough;** *Cf. n.*   9 **Play**
the men: *keep the men moving*   11 **Boson:** *boatswain*   12 **hear him, i.e.:** *hear his whistle;*
see 1. 6 above   14 **good:** *good fellow*   15 **cares;** *Cf. n.* **roarers:** *waves* (to roar was to
bluster and boast as well as to shout)   19 **councilor:** *F* counsellor   23 **Cheerly . . .**
hearts: *spoken to the crew*   25–27 **methinks . . . gallows:** *from an old proverb, 'He that's*
born to be hanged need fear no drowning.'   28 **doth . . . advantage:** *benefits us little*   30
Down . . . topmast; *Cf. n.*   31 **main-course:** *mainsail*

41 **warrant . . . drowning:** *be his guarantee against drowning*   44 **ahold:** *so as to hold the*
wind; Cf. n. **courses:** *sails*   46–50; *Cf. n.*   47 **must . . . cold;** *Cf. n.*   51 **merely:**
utterly, without qualification (cf. *Hamlet,* I.2.141; *As You Like It,* II.7.144)   52 **wide-**
chopp'd: *big-mouthed*   53 **washing . . . tides;** *Cf. n.*   55 **glut:** *gulp*   62 **heath . . .**
furze: *shrubs found growing on wasteland*   4 **welkin's:** *sky's*   5 **fire:** *here disyllabic*   6
brave: *here, as elsewhere in the play, 'admirable.'*   11 **or ere:** *before*   13 **fraughting souls:**
souls who composed her freight   15 **amazement:** *astonished terror* **piteous:** *full of pity*

Of thee my dear one, thee my daughter—who   *20*
Art ignorant of what thou art, nought knowing
Of whence I am, nor that I am more better
Than Prospero, master of a full poor cell,
And thy no greater father.
     Miranda.   More to know   *25*
Did never meddle with my thoughts.
     Prospero.   'Tis time
I should inform thee farther: Lend thy hand
And pluck my magic garment from me. So,
Lie there, my art. Wipe thou thine eyes; have comfort;   *30*
The direful spectacle of the wrack which touch'd
The very virtue of compassion in thee
I have with such provision in mine art
So safely order'd that there is no soil,
No, not so much perdition as an hair,   *35*
Betid to any creature in the vessel
Which thou heard'st cry, which thou saw'st sink. Sit down,
For thou must now know farther.
     Miranda.   You have often
Begun to tell me what I am, but stopp'd   *40*
And left me to a bootless inquisition,
Concluding, 'Stay, not yet.'
     Prospero.   The hour's now come;
The very minute bids thee ope thine ear.
Obey and be attentive. Canst thou remember   *45*
A time before we came unto this cell?
I do not think thou canst, for then thou wast not
Out three years old.
     Miranda.   Certainly, sir, I can.
     Prospero. By what? By any other house, or person?   *50*
Of anything the image tell me, that
Hath kept with thy remembrance.
     Miranda.   'Tis far off,
And rather like a dream than an assurance
That my remembrance warrants. Had I not   *55*
Four or five women once that tended me?
     Prospero. Thou hadst, and more, Miranda; but how is it
That this lives in thy mind? What seest thou else
In the dark backward and abysm of time?
If thou rememb'rest aught ere thou cam'st here,   *60*
How thou cam'st here thou mayst.
     Miranda.   But that I do not.
     Prospero. Twelve year since, Miranda, twelve year since,
Thy father was the Duke of Milan and
A prince of power.   *65*
     Miranda.   Sir, are not you my father?
     Prospero. Thy mother was a piece of virtue and
She said thou wast my daughter—and thy father
Was Duke of Milan—and his only heir
And princess, no worse issued.   *70*
     Miranda.   O the heavens,
What foul play had we that we came from thence?
Or blessed was't we did?
     Prospero.   Both, both, my girl.
By foul play, as thou sayst, were we heav'd thence,   *75*

But blessedly holp hither.
     Miranda.   O my heart bleeds
To think o' th' teen that I have turn'd you to,
Which is from my remembrance; please you, further.
     Prospero. My brother and thy uncle, call'd Antonio—   *80*
I pray thee mark me, that a brother should
Be so perfidious—he whom next thyself
Of all the world I lov'd, and to him put
The manage of my state, as at that time
Through all the signories it was the first,   *85*
And Prospero the prime duke, being so reputed
In dignity, and for the liberal arts
Without a parallel, those being all my study—
The government I cast upon my brother,
And to my state grew stranger, being transported   *90*
And rapt in secret studies; thy false uncle—
Dost thou attend me?
     Miranda.   Sir, most heedfully.
     Prospero. Being once perfected how to grant suits,
How to deny them, who t' advance, and who   *95*
To trash for overtopping, new created
The creatures that were mine, I say, or chang'd 'em,
Or else new form'd 'em, having both the key
Of officer and office, set all hearts i' th' state
To what tune pleas'd his ear, that now he was   *100*
The ivy which had hid my princely trunk,
And suck'd my verdure out on't—thou attend'st not?
     Miranda. O good sir, I do.
     Prospero.   I pray thee, mark me:
I, thus neglecting worldy ends, all dedicated   *105*
To closeness and the bettering of my mind
With that which but by being so retired
Orepriz'd all popular rate, in my false brother
Awak'd an evil nature, and my trust,
Like a good parent, did beget of him   *110*
A falsehood, in its contrary as great
As my trust was, which had indeed no limit,
A confidence sans bound. He, being thus, lorded,
Not only with what my revenue yielded,
But what my power might else exact. Like one   *115*
Who having into truth by telling of it
Made such a sinner of his memory
To credit his own lie, he did believe
He was indeed the duke, out o' th' substitution,
And executing th' outward face of royalty   *120*
With all prerogative—hence, his ambition growing—
Dost thou hear?
     Miranda.   Your tale, sir, would cure deafness.
     Prospero. To have no screen between this part he play'd
And him he play'd it for, he needs will be   *125*
Absolute Milan. Me, poor man, my library
Was dukedom large enough; of temporal royalties
He thinks me now incapable, confederates—
So dry he was for sway—wi' th' King of Naples

22 more better: *Cf. n.*   **23 full:** *very*   **29 magic garment:** *Cf. n.*   **32 virtue:** *essence*   **33 provision:** *foresight*   **34 soil:** *Cf. n.*   **35 perdition:** *destruction*   **hair:** *Cf. n.*   **41 bootless inquisition:** *fruitless inquiry*   **48 Out:** *quite, fully*   **59 backward:** *past*   **63 year . . . year:** *the first year may be dissyllabic*   **64 Milan:** *stressed ´ —*   **67 piece:** *masterpiece*   **70 And princess:** *Cf. n.*

76 holp: *helped*   **78 teen:** *trouble*   **79 from:** *out of*   **85 signories:** *dukedoms*   **86 being:** *probably monosyllabic, as in ll.88, 90.*   **91 secret:** *i.e. magical*   **94 perfected:** *stressed ´ — —*   **96 trash for overtopping:** *Cf. n.*   **98 key:** *play on 'musical key' and 'key for lock'* (cf. present-day 'keys of office')   **100 that:** *so that*   **102 on't:** *of it*   **106 closeness:** *privacy*   **107, 108 With . . . rate:** *Cf. n.*   **113 lorded:** *ruled like a lord, domineered; Cf. n.*   **114 revenue:** *stressed ´ — —*   **115-118 Like . . . lie:** *Cf. n.*   **126 Absolute Milan:** *Duke of Milan*   **Me:** *as for me*   **127 temporal royalties:** *worldly attributes of kingship*   **128 confederates:** *conspires*   **129 dry:** *thirsty*   **sway:** *rule*   **wi' th':** *F with*

To give him annual tribute, do him homage,   *130*
Subject his coronet to his crown and bend
The dukedom, yet unbow'd—alas, poor Milan—
To most ignoble stooping.
    Miranda.   O the heavens!
    Prospero. Mark his condition and th' event, then tell me *135*
If this might be a brother.
    Miranda.   I should sin
To think but nobly of my grandmother.
Good wombs have borne bad sons.
    Prospero.   Now the condition.   *140*
This King of Naples being an enemy
To me inveterate hearkens my brother's suit,
Which was that he in lieu o' th' premises
Of homage and I know not how much tribute
Should presently extirpate me and mine   *145*
Out of the dukedom and confer fair Milan,
With all the honors, on my brother; whereon,
A treacherous army levied, one midnight
Fated to th' purpose did Antonio open
The gates of Milan, and i' th' dead of darkness   *150*
The ministers for th' purpose hurried thence
Me and thy crying self.
    Miranda.   Alack, for pity!
I not rememb'ring how I cried out then
Will cry it ore again—it is a hint   *155*
That wrings mine eyes to't.
    Prospero.   Hear a little further,
And then I'll bring thee to the present business
Which now's upon's, without the which this story
Were most impertinent.   *160*
    Miranda.   Wherefore did they not
That hour destroy us?
    Prospero.   Well demanded, wench.
My tale provokes that question. Dear, they durst not,
So dear the love my people bore me, nor set   *165*
A mark so bloody on the business, but
With colors fairer painted their foul ends.
In few, they hurried us aboard a bark,
Bore us some leagues to sea, where they prepar'd
A rotten carcass of a butt, not rigg'd,   *170*
Nor tackle, sail, nor mast; the very rats
Instinctively have quit it. There they hoist us,
To cry to th' sea that roar'd to us, to sigh
To th' winds whose pity, sighing back again,
Did us but loving wrong.   *175*
    Miranda.   Alack, what trouble
Was I then to you!
    Prospero.   O, a cherubin
Thou wast that did preserve me; thou didst smile,
Infused with a fortitude from heaven,   *180*
When I have deck'd the sea with drops full salt,
Under my burthen groan'd, which rais'd in me
An undergoing stomach, to bear up

Against what should ensue.
    Miranda.   How came we ashore?   *185*
    Prospero. By providence divine.
Some food we had, and some fresh water, that
A noble Neapolitan, Gonzalo,
Out of his charity—who being then appointed
Master of this design—did give us, with   *190*
Rich garments, linens, stuffs, and necessaries
Which since have steaded much; so of his gentleness,
Knowing I lov'd my books, he furnish'd me
From mine own library with volumes that
I prize above my dukedom.   *195*
    Miranda.   Would I might
But ever see that man!
    Prospero. Now I arise:
Sit still and hear the last of our sea-sorrow.
Here in this island we arriv'd, and here   *200*
Have I, thy schoolmaster, made thee more profit
Than other princess can, that have more time
For vainer hours and tutors not so careful.
    Miranda. Heavens thank you for't! And now I pray you,
sir—   *205*
For still 'tis beating in my mind—your reason
For raising this sea storm?
    Prospero.   Know thus far forth:
By accident most strange, bountiful fortune—
Now my dear lady—hath mine enemies   *210*
Brought to this shore; and by my prescience
I find my zenith doth depend upon
A most auspicious star, whose influence
If now I court not but omit, my fortunes
Will ever after droop—here cease more questions.   *215*
Thou art inclin'd to sleep; 'tis a good dullness,
And give it way—I know thou canst not choose.
Come away, servant, come! I am ready now.
Approach, my Ariel. Come!

               Enter Ariel.

    Ariel. All hail, great master, grave sir, hail! I come   *220*
To answer thy best pleasure, be't to fly,
To swim, to dive into the fire, to ride
On the curl'd clouds: to thy strong bidding task
Ariel and all his quality.
    Prospero.   Hast thou, spirit,   *225*
Perform'd to point the tempest that I bade thee?
    Ariel. To every article.
I boarded the king's ship; now on the beak,
Now in the waist, the deck, in every cabin
I flam'd amazement; sometime I'ld divide   *230*
And burn in many places; on the topmast,
The yards and boresprit would I flame distinctly,
Then meet and join. Jove's lightning, the precursors,
O' th' dreadful thunderclaps, more mometary
And sight-outrunning were not; the fire and cracks   *235*

---

135 condition: *the condition of his bargain with Naples* (ll. 141-144)   **138 but:** *otherwise than*   **143 in lieu o':** *in consideration of* **premises:** *conditions*   **145 presently:** *at once* **extirpate:** *stressed* — ´ —   **151 ministers:** *agents*   **155 hint:** *occasion*   **160 impertinent:** *not pertinent, out of place*   **163 demanded:** *asked* **wench:** *young woman*   **168 In few:** *in few words*   **170 carcass of a butt:** *derelict ship* (with butt—'a cask for wine'—cf. present-day derogatory 'tub')   **172 hoist:** *originally the past tense of 'hoise,' to raise with block and tackle*   **175 loving wrong:** *oxymoron*   **183 undergoing stomach:** *enduring courage*

192 steaded much; *cf. the modern 'stood in good stead'*   **198 Now I arise;** *Cf. n.*   **201 made thee more profit:** *made thee profit more, i.e. better educated*   **202 princess;** *Cf. n.*   **210 Now my dear lady:** *refers to fortune*   **212, 213** *Cf. n.*   **216 dullness:** *drowsiness*   **217 give it way:** *do not fight it* **canst not choose;** *Cf.n.*   **218 Come away:** *i.e. from where you are to here*   **223 task:** *put to the test*   **224 all his quality:** *'all others of his profession,' i.e. the other spirits*   **226 to point:** *in every point, exactly*   **230 flam'd amazement:** *caused amazement by my flames*   **232 boresprit:** *bowsprit; the reference is to St. Elmo's fire* **distinctly:** *separately*

Of sulphurous roaring the most mighty Neptune
Seem to besiege, and make his bold waves tremble,
Yea, his dread trident shake.
    Prospero.   My brave spirit!
Who was so firm, so constant, that this coil   240
Would not infect his reason?
    Ariel.   Not a soul
But felt a fever of the mad, and play'd
Some tricks of desperation; all but mariners
Plung'd in the foaming brine and quit the vessel.   245
Then all afire with me the king's son, Ferdinand,
With hair up-staring—then like reeds, not hair—
Was the first man that leapt, cried 'Hell is empty,
And all the divels are here!'
    Prospero.   Why, that's my spirit!   250
But was not this nigh shore?
    Ariel.   Close by, my master.
    Prospero. But are they, Ariel, safe?
    Ariel.   Not a hair perish'd:
On their sustaining garments not a blemish,   255
But fresher than before; and as thou bad'st me,
In troops I have dispers'd them 'bout the isle.
The king's son have I landed by himself,
Whom I left cooling of the air with sighs,
In an odd angle of the isle, and sitting,   260
His arms in this sad knot.
    Prospero.   Of the king's ship,
The mariners, say how thou hast dispos'd,
And all the rest o' th' fleet.
    Ariel.   Safely in harbor   265
Is the king's ship, in the deep nook where once
Thou call'dst me up at midnight to fetch dew
From the still-vex'd Bermoothes; there she's hid,
The mariners all under hatches stow'd,
Who with a charm join'd to their suff'red labor   270
I have left asleep; and for the rest o' th' fleet—
Which I dispers'd—they all have met again
And are upon the Mediterranean flote
Bound sadly home for Naples,
Supposing that they saw the king's ship wrack'd,   275
And his great person perish.
    Prospero.   Ariel, thy charge
Exactly is perform'd; but there's more work.
What is the time o' th' day?
    Ariel.   Past the mid season.   280
    Prospero. At least two glasses. The time 'twixt six and now
Must by us both be spent most preciously.
    Ariel. Is there more toil? Since thou dost give me pains,
Let me remember thee what thou hast promis'd,
Which is not yet perform'd me.   285
    Prospero. How now? moody?
What is't thou canst demand?
    Ariel.   My liberty.
    Prospero. Before the time be out? No more!
    Ariel.   I prithee   290
Remember I have done thee worthy service,

Told thee no lies, made thee no mistakings, serv'd
Without or grudge or grumblings; thou didst promise
To bate me a full year.
    Prospero.   Dost thou forget   295
From what a torment I did free thee?
    Ariel.   No.
    Prospero. Thou dost, and think'st it much to tread the ooze
Of the salt deep,
To run upon the sharp wind of the North,   300
To do me business in the veins o' th' earth
When it is bak'd with frost.
    Ariel.   I do not, sir.
    Prospero. Thou liest, malignant thing! Hast thou forgot
The foul witch Sycorax, who with age and envy   305
Was grown into a hoop? Hast thou forgot her?
    Ariel. No, sir.
    Prospero.   Thou hast. Where was she born?
Speak! Tell me!
    Ariel. Sir, in Argier.   310
    Prospero.   Oh, was she so! I must
Once in a month recount what thou hast bin,
Which thou forget'st. This damn'd witch Sycorax,
For mischiefs manifold and sorceries terrible
To enter human hearing, from Argier   315
Thou know'st was banish'd; for one thing she did
They would not take her life. Is not this true?
    Ariel. Ay, sir.
    Prospero. This blue-ey'd hag was hither brought with child,
And here was left by th' sailor; thou, my slave,   320
As thou report'st thyself, was then her servant,
And for thou wast a spirit too delicate
To act her earthy and abhorr'd commands,
Refusing her grand hests, she did confine thee
By help of her more potent ministers,   325
And in her most unmitigable rage,
Into a cloven pine, within which rift
Imprison'd thou didst painfully remain
A dozen years; within which space she died
And left thee there, where thou didst vent thy groans   330
As fast as mill wheels strike. Then was this island—
Save for the son that she did litter here—
A freckled whelp, hag-born—not honor'd with
A human shape.
    Ariel.   Yes, Caliban her son.   335
    Prospero. Dull thing, I say so: he, that Caliban
Whom now I keep in service. Thou best know'st
What torment I did find thee in; thy groans
Did make wolves howl, and penetrate the breasts
Of ever-angry bears: it was a torment   340
To lay upon the damn'd, which Sycorax
Could not again undo; it was mine art,
When I arriv'd and heard thee, that made gape
The pine and let thee out.
    Ariel. I thank thee, master.   345
    Prospero. If thou more murmur'st, I will rend an oak
And peg thee in his knotty entrails till

---

237 Seem to: *seem'd to* (with -d and t- merged)   **240 coil:** *turmoil*   **243 fever of the mad:** *fit of irrationality*   **247 up-staring:** *standing on end*   **255 sustaining:** *'buoyant,' probably through Ariel's magic*   **268 still-vex'd Bermoothes:** (three syllables) *ever-stormy Bermudas; Cf. n.*   **273 flote:** *wave, billows*   **281 glasses:** *hourglasses*   **283 pains:** *trouble in accomplishing tasks (cf. present-day 'paintstaking')*   **284 remember:** *remind*

292 Told thee . . . made thee: *Cf. n.*   **293 or . . . or:** *either . . . or*   **didst:** *F did*   **294 bate me:** *reduce my service by*   **302 bak'd:** *hardened*   **310 Argier:** *Algiers*   **316 for one thing:** *perhaps 'because of one good thing'*   **319 blue-ey'd:** *Cf. n.*   **322 for:** *because*   **spirit:** *one syllable (probably 'sprite')*   **323 earthy:** *Cf. n.*   **324 hests:** *commands*   **331 mill wheels strike:** *i.e. the water*   **332 she:** *F he*

Thou hast howl'd away twelve winters.
 Ariel.   Pardon, master;
I will be correspondent to command   *350*
And do my spriting, gently.
 Prospero. Do so, and after two days I will discharge thee.
 Ariel. That's my noble master!
What shall I do? Say what! What shall I do?
 Prospero. Go make thyself like a nyumph o' th' sea; be *355*
subject
To no sight but thine and mine, invisible
To every eyeball else. Go take this shape
And hither come in't. Go! Hence with diligence!
           Exit [Ariel].

Awake, dear heart, awake; thou hast slept well; *360*
Awake.
 Miranda.   The strangeness of your story put
Heaviness in me.
 Prospero.   Shake it off! Come on,
We'll visit Caliban, my slave, who never *365*
Yields us kind answer.
 Miranda.   'Tis a villain, sir,
I do not love to look on.
 Prospero.   But as 'tis
We cannot miss him; he does make our fire, *370*
Fetch in our wood, and serves in offices
That profit us. What ho! slave! Caliban!
Thou earth, thou! speak!
Caliban within.   There's wood enough within.
 Prospero. Come forth, I say, there's other business for *375*
thee! Come, thou tortoise! When?

   Enter Ariel like a water nymph.

Fine apparition! My quaint Ariel,
Hark in thine ear.
 Ariel. My lord, it shall be done.   *Exit.*
 Prospero. Thou poisonous slave, got by the divel himself *380*
Upon thy wicked dam, come forth.

    Enter Caliban.

 Caliban. As wicked dew as ere my mother brush'd
With raven's feather from unwholesome fen
Drop on you both! A southwest blow on ye,
And blister you all ore!   *385*
 Prospero. For this be sure tonight thou shalt have cramps,
Side stitches, that shall pen thy breath up; urchins
Shall for that vast of night that they may work
All exercise on thee! Thou shalt be pinch'd
As thick as honeycomb, each pinch more stinging *390*
Than bees that made 'em.
 Caliban.   I must eat my dinner.
This island's mine by Sycorax my mother,
Which thou tak'st from me! When thou camest first
Thou strok'st me, and made much of me; wouldst give me *395*
Water with berries in't, and teach me how
To name the bigger light and how the less,

That burn by day and night; and then I lov'd thee
And show'd thee all the qualities o' th' isle,
The fresh springs, brine pits, barren place and fertile. *400*
Curs'd be I that did so! All the charms
Of Sycorax—toads, beetles, bats—light on you!
For I am all the subjects that you have,
Which first was mine own king, and here you sty me
In this hard rock, whiles you do keep from me *405*
The rest o' th' island.
 Prospero.   Thou most lying slave,
Whom stripes may move, not kindness! I have us'd thee—
Filth as thou art—with human care and lodg'd thee
In mine own cell, till thou didst seek to violate *410*
The honor of my child.
 Caliban. O ho! O ho! would't had been done!
Thou didst prevent me; I had peopl'd else
This isle with Calibans.
 Miranda.   Abhorred slave, *415*
Which any print of goodness wilt not take,
Being capable of all ill: I pitied thee,
Took pains to make thee speak, taught thee each hour
One thing or other; when thou didst not, savage,
Know thine own meaning, but wouldst gabble like *420*
A thing most brutish, I endow'd thy purposes
With words that made them known, but thy vild race—
Though thou didst learn—had that in't which good natures
Could not abide to be with; therefore wast thou
Deservedly confin'd into this rock,   *425*
Who hadst deserv'd more than a prison.
 Caliban. You taught me language and my profit on't
Is, I know how to curse! The red plague rid you
For learning me your language!
 Prospero.   Hag-seed, hence! *430*
Fetch us in fuel, and be quick thou'rt best
To answer other business! Shrug'st thou, malice?
If thou neglect'st or dost unwillingly
What I command, I'll rack thee with old cramps,
Fill all thy bones with aches, make thee roar *435*
That beasts shall tremble at thy din.
 Caliban.   No, 'pray thee!
I must obey; his art is of such power
It would control my dam's god Setebos,
And make a vassal of him.   *440*
 Prospero.   So, slave, hence! *Exit Caliban.*

 Enter Ferdinand; and Ariel, invisible, playing and singing.

     Song
Ariel. *Come unto these yellow sands,*
   and then take hands:
  Curtsied when you have, and kiss'd,
   the wild waves whist,   *445*
  Foot it featly here and there,

---

350 **correspondent:** *submissive* 370 **miss:** *spare* 377 **quaint:** *finely dressed* 380 **got:**
begot 384 **southwest:** *a southwest wind was considered infectious* 387 **urchins:** *goblins
in the shape of hedgehogs (cf. below, II.2.10-12)* 388 **vast:** *immense space* 390 **pinch:**
tormented (perhaps pricked with hedgehog quills) 391 **'em:** *i.e. the (cells of) honey-
comb* 394 **camest:** *F* cam'st 395 **strok'st:** *strok'dst F* stroakst; *Cf. n.* 397 **bigger
. . . less:** *see Gen. 1:16: 'And God made two great lights; the greater light to rule the day, and
the lesser light to rule the night.'*

400 **springs . . . fertile:** *i.e. he showed how to distinguish between useful and useless natural
resources (Arden ed.).* **place;** *Cf. n.* 401 **charms:** *evil spirits charmed by Sycorax* 404
mine: *F* min; *if not a printer's error, the spelling may indicate a pronunciation, with* i *as in
'tin.'* **sty:** *pen me as in a pigsty* 415-426; *Cf. n.* 416 **Which . . . take:** *who will
not take any print (impression).* 422 **vild:** *common spelling (showing pronunciation) of
'vile.'* 423 **good natures:** *those who are naturally good* 428 **red plague:** *bubonic plague
(with red sores)* **rid:** *destroy* 431 **be quick thou'rt best:** *you had better be quick* **thou'rt:**
thou wert 432 **answer:** *attend to* 435 **aches:** *pronounced 'aitches.'* 442-452; *Cf. n.*
445 **whist:** *hushed* 446 **featly:** *gracefully*

        And sweet sprites the burthen bear.

        Burthen, dispersedly.

[Voices.]	'Hark, hark!' 'bowgh wawgh!'	
	'The watch-dogs bark!' 'bowgh wawgh!'	450
Ariel.	Hark, hark! I hear	
	The strain of strutting chanticleer	
	Cry cockadiddle-dow!	

Ferdinand. Where should this music be? i' th' air, or th'
earth?   455
It sounds no more! And sure it waits upon
Some god o' th' island; sitting on a bank,
Weeping again the king my father's wrack,
This music crept by me upon the waters,
Allaying both their fury and my passion   460
With its sweet air; thence I have follow'd it—
Or it hath drawn me rather—but 'tis gone.
No, it begins again.

           Song

  Ariel.   *Full fadom five thy father lies;*
             Of his bones are coral made;   465
             Those are pearls that were his eyes:
             Nothing of him that doth fade,
             But doth suffer a sea change
             Into something rich and strange.
             Sea nymphs hourly ring his knell.   470

           Burthen.

[Voices.]	*Ding dong!*
[Ariel.]	*Hark, now I hear them! Ding-dong, bell.*

Ferdinand. The ditty does remember my drown'd father.
This is no mortal business, nor no sound   475
That the earth owes! I hear it now above me.
  Prospero. The fringed curtains of thine eyes advance,
And say what thou seest yond.
  Miranda.   What is't? a spirit?
Lord, how it looks about! Believe me, sir,   480
It carries a brave form. But 'tis a spirit.
  Prospero. No, wench, it eats and sleeps and hath such senses
As we have, such. This gallant which thou seest
Was in the wrack; and but he's something stain'd
With grief—that's beauty's canker—thou might'st call him 485
A goodly person. He has lost his fellows
And strays about to find 'em.
  Miranda.   I might call him
A thing divine, for nothing natural
I ever saw so noble.   490
  Prospero.   It goes on, I see,
As my soul prompts it! Spirit, fine spirit, I'll free thee
Within two days for this.
  Ferdinand.   Most sure the goddess
On whom these airs attend! Vouchsafe my prayer   495

May know if you remain upon this island,
And that you will some good instruction give
How I may bear me here! My prime request—
Which I do last pronounce—is—O you wonder!—
If you be maid or no?   500
  Miranda.   No wonder, sir,
But certainly a maid.
  Ferdinand.   My language? Heavens!
I am the best of them that speak this speech
Were I but where 'tis spoken.   505
  Prospero.   How? the best?
What wert thou if the King of Naples heard thee?
  Ferdinand. A single thing, as I am now, that wonders
To hear thee speak of Naples! He does hear me,
And that he does, I weep. Myself am Naples,   510
Who with mine eyes—never since at ebb—beheld
The king my father wrack'd.
  Miranda.   Alack, for mercy!
  Ferdinand. Yes, faith, and all his lords, the Duke of Milan
And his brave son being twain.   515
  Prospero. *[Aside.]*   The Duke of Milan
And his more braver daughter could control thee
If now 'twere fit to do't. At the first sight
They have chang'd eyes! Delicate Ariel,
I'll set thee free for this.—A word, good sir;   520
I fear you have done yourself some wrong! A word.
  Miranda. Why speaks my father so ungently? This
Is the third man that ere I saw! The first
That ere I sigh'd for! Pity move my father
To be inclin'd my way.   525
  Ferdinand.   O, if a virgin,
And your affection not gone forth, I'll make you
The Queen of Naples.
  Prospero.   Soft, sir. One word more.
[Aside.] They are both in either's powers! But this swift 530
business
I must uneasy make, lest too light winning
Make the prize light.—One word more! I charge thee
That thou attend me! Thou dost here usurp
The name thou ow'st not and hast put thyself   535
Upon this island as a spy, to win it
From me, the lord on't.
  Ferdinand.   No, as I am a man.
  Miranda. There's nothing ill can dwell in such a temple.
If the ill spirit have so fair a house,   540
Good things will strive to dwell with't.
  Prospero.   Follow me.
Speak not you for him! He's a traitor! Come,
I'll manacle thy neck and feet togeher!
Sea water shalt thou drink; thy food shall be   545
The fresh brook mussels, wither'd roots, and husks
Wherein the acorn cradled. Follow.
  Ferdinand.   No,
I will resist such entertainment till
Mine enemy has more power.   550

---

447 the burthen bear: *F prints 'bear the burthen.'* **SD Burthen, dispersedly:** *refrain, sung from several places on (or just off) the stage. (SD is used throughout to indicate stage direction.)* **458 Weeping again:** *while I was weeping again because of* **460 passion:** *suffering* **464 fadom:** *fathoms* **474 remember:** *recall* **476 owes:** *possesses* **481 brave:** *admirable* **484 and but:** *except that* **something:** *somewhat* **485 that's . . . canker:** *which is the blight that destroys beauty* **486 goodly:** *handsome* **492 Spirit . . . spirit:** *both to be read 'sprite.'*

496 remain: *dwell* **498 bear me:** *conduct myself* **500 maid:** *suggests two pairs of opposites: goddess—mortal, unmarried—married* **508 single:** *solitary, alone, defenseless* **510 that:** *because* **515 his brave son;** *Cf. n.* **517 control thee:** *check your statement, hence refute* **519 chang'd:** *play on 'exchanged' and 'altered'* **521 done . . . wrong:** *euphemism for 'lied'* **532-533 light . . . light:** *play on meanings 'easy' and 'of small account'* **535 ow'st:** *own'st* **549 entertainment:** *treatment*

He draws, and is charmed from moving.

Miranda.   O dear father,
Make not too rash a trial of him, for
He's gentle and not fearful.

Prospero.   What, I say!
My foot my tutor? Put thy sword up, traitor,   555
Who mak'st a show, but dar'st not strike, thy conscience
Is so possess'd with guilt! Come, from thy ward,
For I can here disarm thee with this stick,
And make thy weapon drop.

Miranda.   Beseech you, Father!   560

Prospero. Hence! Hang not on my garments.

Miranda.   Sir,
have pity!
I'll be his surety.

Prospero. Silence! One word more   565
Shall make me chide thee, if not hate thee! What,
An advocate for an imposter? Hush!
Thou think'st there is no more such shapes as he,
Having seen but him and Caliban! Foolish wench,
To th' most of men this is a Caliban,   570
And they to him are angels.

Miranda.   My affections
Are then most humble: I have no ambition
To see a goodlier man.

Prospero.   Come on, obey!   575
Thy nerves are in their infancy again,
And have no vigor in them.

Ferdinand.   So they are.
My spirits, as in a dream, are all bound up:
My father's loss, the weakness which I feel,   580
The wrack of all my friends, nor this man's threats,
To whom I am subdu'd, are but light to me,
Might I but through my prison once a day
Behold this maid! All corners else o' th' earth
Let liberty make use of: space enough   585
Have I in such a prison.

Prospero. [*To Ariel.*] It works! [*To Ferdinand.*]
Come on.
[*To Ariel.*] Thou hast done well, fine Ariel! [*To Ferdinand.*]
Follow me.   590
[*To Ariel.*] Hark what thou else shalt do me.

Miranda.   Be of
comfort.
My father's of a better nature, sir,
Than he appears by speech: this is unwonted   595
Which now came from him.

Prospero.   Thou shalt be as free
As mountain winds; but then exactly do
All points of my command.

Ariel.   To th' syllable.   600

Propero. [*To Ferdinand.*] Come, follow! [*To Miranda.*]
Speak not for him.   *Exeunt.*

ACT SECOND ❧ SCENE FIRST

Enter Alonso, Sebastian, Antonio, Gonzalo, Adrian, Francisco,
and others.

Gonzalo. Beseech you, sir, be merry; you have
cause—
So have we all—of joy, for our escape
Is much beyond our loss; our hint of woe
Is common: every day some sailor's wife,   5
The masters of some merchant, and the merchant
Have just our theme of woe. But for the miracle—
I mean our preservaton—few in millions
Can speak like us! Then wisely, good sir, weigh
Our sorrow with our comfort.   10

Alonso.   Prithee, peace.

Sebastian. He receives comfort like cold porridge.

Antonio. The visitor will not give him ore so.

Sebastian. Look, he's winding up the watch of his wit.
By and by it will strike.   15

Gonzalo. Sir—

Sebastian. One! Tell.

Gonzalo. When every grief is entertain'd that's offer'd, comes
to th' entertainer—

Sebastian. A dollar.   20

Gonzalo. Dolour comes to him indeed. You have spoken
truer than you purpos'd.

Sebastian. You have taken it wiselier than I meant you
should.

Gonzalo. Therefore, my lord—   25

Antonio. Fie, what a spendthrift is he of his tongue.

Alonso. I prithee spare.

Gonzalo. Well, I have done. But yet—

Sebastian. He will be talking.

Antonio. Which, of he or Adrian, for a good wager, first   30
begins to crow?

Sebastian. The old cock.

Antonio. The cock'rel.

Sebastian. Done! The wager?

Antonio. A laughter.   35

Sebastian. A match.

Adrian. Though this island seem to be desert—

Sebastian. Ha ha ha!

Antonio. So! You're paid.

Adrian. Uninhabitable and almost inaccessible—   40

Sebastian. Yet—

Adrian. Yet—

Antonio. He could not miss't.

Adrian. It must needs be of subtle, tender, and delicate
temperance.   45

Antonio. Temperance was a delicate wench.

Sebastian. Ay, and a subtle, as he most learnedly deliver'd.

Adrian. The air breathes upon us here most sweetly.

Sebastian. As if it had lungs, and rotten ones.

---

553 gentle: *a gentleman* **fearful:** *afraid* **555 My . . . tutor;** *Cf. n.* **557 from thy ward:** *lower thy guard* **570, 571 To . . . to:** *compared to* **572 affections:** *feelings* **576 nerves:** *sinews* **579 spirits:** *vital powers*

4 hint: *occasion* **6 some merchant:** *either a vessel or the owner* (or purchaser) *of cargo* **the merchant:** *here, probably, in the latter sense* **12 porridge:** *a stew, often with peas; cf. peace in I. 9 (Arden ed.)* **13 visitor:** *comforter of the sick* (cf. below, ll. 203, 204, and Mat. 25:36) **15 By and by:** *immediately* **17 Tell:** *count* **18;** *Cf. n.* **27 spare me any more talk** **35 A laughter,** *Cf. n.* **38, 39 ;** *Cf. n.* **43 miss't:** *avoid the conventional phraseology* (cf. 1.26 above) **45 temperance:** *temperature, climate* **46 Temperance:** *common Puritan name for a woman* **47 subtle:** *here, 'crafty,' 'sly.'*

Antonio. Or as 'twere perfum'd by a fen.   *50*

Gonzalo. Here is everything advantageous to life.

Antonio. True, save means to live.

Sebastian. Of that there's none, or little.

Gonzalo. How lush and lusty the grass looks! How green!

Antonio. The ground indeed is tawny.   *55*

Sebastian. With an eye of green in't.

Antonio. He misses not much.

Sebastian. No—he doth but mistake the truth totally.

Gonzalo. But the rarity of it is—which is indeed almost beyond credit—   *60*

Sebastian. As many vouch'd rarities are—

Gonzalo. That our garments being—as they were—drench'd in the sea, hold, notwithstanding, their freshness and glosses, being rather new-dy'd than stain'd with salt water.

Antonio. If but one of his pockets could speak, would it *65* not say he lies?

Sebastian. Ay, or very falsely pocket up his report.

Gonzalo. Methinks our garments are now as fresh as when we put them on first in Afric, at the marriage of the king's fair daughter Claribel to the King of Tunis.   *70*

Sebastian. 'Twas a sweet marriage, and we prosper well in our return.

Adrian. Tunis was never grac'd before with such a paragon to their queen.

Gonzalo. Not since widow Dido's time.   *75*

Antonio. Widow! A pox o' that! How came that widow in? Widow Dido!

Sebastian. What if he had said 'widower Aeneas' too? Good lord, how you take it!

Adrian. 'Widow Dido' said you? You make me study of *80* that. She was of Carthage, not of Tunis.

Gonzalo. This Tunis, sir, was Carthage.

Adrian. Carthage?

Gonzalo. I assure you, Carthage.

Antonio. His word is more than the miraculous harp.   *85*

Sebastian. He hath rais'd the wall, and houses too.

Antonio. What impossible matter will he make easy next?

Sebastian. I think he will carry this island home in his pocket and give it his son for an apple.

Antonio. And sowing the kernels of it in the sea, bring *90* forth more islands.

Gonzalo. [*Having pondered.*] Ay.

Antonio. Why, in good time.

Gonzalo. Sir, we were talking that our garments seem now as fresh as when we were at Tunis at the marriage of *95* your daughter, who is now queen.

Antonio. And the rarest that ere came there.

Sebastian. Bate, I beseech you, widow Dido.

Antonio. Oh, widow Dido? Ay, widow Dido!

Gonzalo. Is not, sir, my doublet as fresh as the first day *100* I wore it? I mean, in a sort.

Antonio. That sort was well fish'd for.

Gonzalo. When I wore it at your daughter's marriage—

Alonso. You cram these words into mine ears against

The stomach of my sense. Would I had never   *105*
Married my daughter there, for coming thence
My son is lost and—in my rate—she too,
Who is so far from Italy remov'd
I ne'er again shall see her. O thou mine heir
Of Naples and of Milan, what strange fish   *110*
Hath made his meal on thee?

     Francisco.   Sir, he may live.
I saw him beat the surges under him
And ride upon their backs; he trod the water,
Whose enmity he flung aside, and breasted   *115*
The surge most swolne that met him. His bold head
'Bove the contentious waves he kept, and oared
Himself with his good arms in lusty stroke
To th' shore, that ore his wave-worn basis bowed
As stooping to relieve him. I not doubt   *120*
He came alive to land.

     Alonso. No, no, he's gone.

     Sebastian. Sir, you may thank yourself for this great loss
That would not bless our Europe with your daughter,
But rather loose her to an African,   *125*
Where she at least is banish'd from your eye,
Who hath cause to wet the grief on't.

     Alonso. Prithee peace.

     Sebastian. You were kneel'd to and importun'd otherwise
By all of us, and the fair soul herself   *130*
Weigh'd, between loathness and obedience, at
Which end o' th' beam should bow. We have lost your son,
I fear, for ever: Milan and Naples have
Mo widows in them of this business' making
Than we bring men to comfort them.   *135*
The fault's your own.

     Alonso.   So is the dear'st o' th' loss.

     Gonzalo. My Lord Sebastian,
The truth you speak doth lack some gentleness,
And time to speak it in: you rub the sore   *140*
When you should bring the plaster.

     Sebastian.   Very well.

     Antonio. And most chirurgeonly.

     Gonzalo. It is foul weather in us all, good sir,
When you are cloudy.   *145*

     Sebastian.   *Fowl* weather?

     Antonio.   Very foul.

     Gonzalo. Had I plantation of this isle, my lord—

     Antonio. He'd sow't with nettle seed.

     Sebastian.   Or docks, or mallows.   *150*

     Gonzalo. And were the king on't, what would I do?

     Sebastian. 'Scape being drunk, for want of wine.

     Gonzalo. I' th' commonwealth I would by contraries.
Execute all things; for no kind of traffic
Would I admit; no name of magistrate;   *155*
Letters should not be known; riches, poverty,
And use of service, none; contract, succession,

---

54 lusty: *strong*   **55 tawny:** *brown*   **57 misses not much:** *doesn't misses by much*   **63 glosses;** *Cf. n.*   **74 to:** *for*   **77 Widow Dido;** *Cf. n.*   **85 miraculous harp:** *of Zeus' son, who with his playing raised the walls of Thebes*   **86 houses too:** *i.e. by claiming Carthage still exists as Tunis*   **92 Ay:** *in reaffirmation that Tunis was Carthage* (Kittredge); *F spells it* I   **98 Bate:** *except for*   **101 in a sort:** *after a fashion*   **102 fish'd for;** *Cf. n.*

105 stomach: *inclination* **sense:** *feelings*   **107 rate:** *estimation*   **119 basis:** *trunk*   **120 As:** *as if*   **125 loose:** *mate*   **127 Who ... on't:** *which has reason to shed tears upon the grief revealed in it* **Who hath:** *probably pronounced 'Who'th'*   **131 Weigh'd:** *forced to choose*   **134 Mo:** *more*   **137 dear'st:** *'most dearly loved' and 'of highest worth'* ('what touches one most nearly'—Arden ed.)   **140 time:** *fitting time*   **142 Very well:** *very well spoken* (sarcasm)   **143 chirurgeonly:** *like a surgeon*   **146 Fowl;** *Cf. n. foul i.e. 'a very foul pun'—to be balanced against 'Very well' of l. 143, above*   **148 plantation:** *colonization, purposely misconstrued by Antonio in the next line*   **150 docks, or mallows:** *weeds*   **151 on't:** *of it*   **153-176;** *Cf. n.*   **157 use of service:** *custom of employing servants* **contract:** *stressed* — ́ **succession:** *inheritance*

Bourn, bound of land, tilth, vineyard, none;
No use of metal, corn, or wine, or oil;
No occupation—all men idle, all;   160
And women too, but innocent and pure;
No sovereignty.
   Sebastian. Yet he would be king on't.
   Antonio. The latter end of his commonwealth forgets
the beginning.   165
   Gonzalo. All things in common nature should produce,
Without sweat, or endeavor; treason, felony,
Sword, pike, knife, gun, or need of any engine
Would I not have; but Nature should bring forth
Of it own kind all foison, all abundance,   170
To feed my innocent people.
   Sebastian. No marrying 'mong his subjects?
   Antonio. None, man; all idle: whores and knaves.
   Gonzalo. I would with such perfection govern, sir,
T'excel the Golden Age.   175
   Sebastian.   'Save his Majesty!
   Antonio. Long live Gonzalo!
   Gonzalo.   And—do you mark me, sir?
   Alonso. Prithee no more; thou dost talk nothing to me.
   Gonzalo. I do well believe your Highness, and did it to   180
minister occasion to these gentlemen, who are of such sensible
and nimble lungs that they always use to laugh at nothing.
   Antonio. 'Twas you we laugh'd at.
   Gonzalo. Who in this kind of merry fooling am nothing
to you; so you may continue and laugh at nothing still.   185
   Antonio. What a blow was there given!
   Sebastian. And it had not falne flat-long.
   Gonzalo. You are gentlemen of brave metal; you would
lift the moon out of her sphere, if she would continue in
it five weeks without changing.   190

      Enter Ariel playing solemn music.

   Sebastian. We would so, and then go a-batfowling.
   Antonio. Nay, good my lord, be not angry.
   Gonzalo. No, I warrant you; I will not adventure my discre-
tion so weakly. Will you laugh me asleep? for I am very heavy.
   Antonio. Go sleep, and hear us.   195
      [All sleep but Alonso, Sebastian, and Antonio.]
   Alonso. What, all so soon asleep? I wish mine eyes
Would, with themselves, shut up my thoughts. I find
They are inclin'd to do so.
   Sebastian.   Please you, sir,
Do not omit the heavy offer of it.   200
It seldom visits sorrow, when it doth
It is a comforter.
   Antonio.   We two, my lord,
Will guard your person while you take your rest,
And watch your safety.   205
   Alonso.   Thank you. Wondrous heavy . . .
      [Alonso sleeps. Exit Ariel.]
   Sebastian. What a strange drowsiness possesses them!

   Antonio. It is the quality o' th' climate.
   Sebastian.   Why
Doth it not then our eyelids sink? I find not   210
Myself dispos'd to sleep.
   Antonio.   Nor I: my spirits are nimble.
They fell together all as by consent;
They dropp'd as by a thunderstroke. What might,
Worthy Sebastian? O what might—? No more!   215
And yet, methinks I see it in thy face,
What thou shouldst be; th' occasion speaks thee, and
My strong imagination sees a crown
Dropping upon thy head.
   Sebastian.   What? Art thou waking?   220
   Antonio. Do you not hear me speak?
   Sebastian.   I do, and surely
It is a sleepy language, and thou speak'st
Out of thy sleep! What is it thou didst say?
This is a strange repose, to be asleep   225
With eyes wide open—standing, speaking, moving,
And yet so fast asleep.
   Antonio.   Noble Sebastian,
Thou let'st thy fortune sleep—die rather; wink'st
Whiles thou art waking.   230
   Sebastian.   Thou dost snore distinctly:
There's meaning in thy snores.
   Antonio. I am more serious than my custom—you
Must be so too, if heed me; which to do
Trebles thee ore.   235
   Sebastian.   Well, I am standing water.
   Antonio. I'll teach you how to flow.
   Sebastian.   Do so: to ebb
Hereditary sloth instructs me.
   Antonio.   O,   240
If you but knew how you the purpose cherish
Whiles thus you mock it, how in stripping it
You more invest it! ebbing men indeed—
Most often—do so near the bottom run
By their own fear or sloth.   245
   Sebastian.   Prithee say on;
The setting of thine eye and cheek proclaim
A matter from thee, and a birth, indeed,
Which throes thee much to yield.
   Antonio.   Thus, sir: 250
Although this lord of weak remembrance, this
Who shall be of as little memory
When he is earth'd, hath here almost persuaded—
For he's a spirit of persuasion, only
Professes to persuade—the king his son's alive   255
'Tis as impossible that he's undrown'd
As he that sleeps here swims.
   Sebastian.   I have no hope
That he's undrown'd.
   Antonio. O, out of that 'no hope'   260

---

158 Bourn: *boundary* **tilth:** *tilled land* **168 engine:** *machine used in warfare* **170 it:** *its* **foison:** *plentiful harvest* **175 T'excel:** *as to excel* **176 'Save:** *God save; cf. n.* **179 nothing:** *nonsense* **181 sensible:** *sensitive* **182 nimble:** *active* **183 you:** *i.e. 'noting'* **185 to you:** *compared with you* **187 And:** *if* **falne:** *fallen* **flat-long:** *with the flat of the sword* **188 metal:** *modern 'mettle'* **189 sphere;** *Cf. n.* **189, 190 if . . . changing:** *if it would wait an impossible time* (longer than the lunar month) **191 go a-batfowling:** *Cf. n.* **193, 194 adventure my discretion:** *hazard my reputation* **195 hear us:** *i.e. 'hear us laugh'* **200 omit:** *neglect* **offer:** *invitation* **202–205:** *Cf. n.*

210 sink: *cause to close* **213 consent:** *agreement* **217 speaks thee:** *'proclaims thee king,' or 'speaks to thee'* **229 wink'st:** *i.e. 'art oblivious to thy opportunity'* **231 distinctly:** *explained by the next line* **235 Trebles thee ore:** *triples thy value* **236 standing water:** *unmoving, between ebb and flood* **237 flow:** *rise (like the tide)* **242, 243 stripping . . . invest:** *a clothing metaphor: to invest is to clothe with robes of office* **247 setting:** *rigid expression* **249 throes thee:** *causes thee agony (as of childbirth)* **251 this lord:** *probably Gonzalo, who supported Francisco's account and aroused Antonio's scorn* **253 earth'd:** *buried* **254, 255 For . . . persuade:** *for he's persuasion personified, whose only profession is to persuade* **258 hope;** *Cf. n.*

What great hope have you! No hope that way is
Another way so high a hope that even
Ambition cannot pierce a wink beyond
But doubt discovery there. Will you grant with me
That Ferdinand is drown'd?   265
    Sebastian.   He's gone.
    Antonio.   Then tell me,
Who's the next heir of Naples?
    Sebastian.   Claribel.
    Antonio. She that is Queen of Tunis; she that dwells   270
Ten leagues beyond man's life; she that from Naples
Can have no note, unless the sun were post—
The man i' th' moon's too slow—till new-born chins
Be rough and razorable; she that from whom
We all were sea-swallow'd, though some cast again—   275
And by that destiny—to perform an act
Whereof what's past is prologue, what to come
In yours and my discharge.
    Sebastian.   What stuff is this?
How say you?   280
'Tis true my brother's daughter's Queen of Tunis;
So is she heir of Naples; 'twixt which regions
There is some space.
    Antonio.   A space whose ev'ry cubit
Seems to cry out, 'How shall that Claribel   285
Measure us back to Naples? Keep in Tunis
And let Sebastian wake!' Say this were death
That now hath seiz'd them, why they were no worse
Than now they are; there be that can rule Naples
As well as he that sleeps, lords that can prate   290
As amply and unnecessarily
As this Gonzalo—I myself could make
A chough of as deep chat—O that you bore
The mind that I do! What a sleep were this
For your advancement! Do you understand me?   295
    Sebastian. Methinks I do.
    Antonio.   And how does your content
Tender your own good fortune?
    Sebastian.   I remember
You did supplant your brother Prospero.   300
    Antonio.   True.
And look how well my garments sit upon me,
Much feater than before. My brother's servants
Were then my fellows; now they are my men.
    Sebastian. But for your conscience—   305
    Antonio. Ay, sir, where lies that? If 'twere a kibe
'Twould put me to my slipper; but I feel not
This deity in my bosom; twenty consciences
That stand 'twixt me and Milan, candied be they
And melt, ere they molest! Here lies your brother,   310
No better than the earth he lies upon,
If he were that which now he's like—that's dead—
Whom I with this obedient steel—three inches of it—
Can lay to bed forever; whiles you, doing thus,

To the perpetual wink for aye might put   315
This ancient morsel, this Sir Prudence, who
Should not upbraid our course. For all the rest,
They'll take suggestion as a cat laps milk;
They'll tell the clock to any business that
We say befits the hour.   320
    Sebastian.   Thy case, dear friend,
Shall be my precedent: as thou got'st Milan
I'll come by Naples. Draw thy sword; one stroke
Shall free thee from the tribute which thou payest,
And I the king shall love thee.   325
    Antonio.   Draw together;
And when I rear my hand do you the like,
To fall it on Gonzalo.
    Sebastian.   O, but one word.

    [They converse apart.]

    Enter Ariel with music and song.

    Ariel. My master through his art foresees the danger   330
That you, his friend, are in and sends me forth—
For else his project dies—to keep them living.
        Sings in Gonzalo's ear.

        Song
    While you here do snoring lie,
    Open-ey'd Conspiracy
      His time doth take.   335
    If of life you keep a care,
    Shake off slumber and beware.
      Awake, awake!

    Antonio. Then let us both be sudden.
    Gonzalo. [Awakening.]   Now, good angels,   340
Preserve the king!   *[Shakes Alonso.]*
    Alonso. Why, how now, ho! awake? Why are you drawn?
Wherefore this ghastly looking?
    Gonzalo.   What's the matter?
    Sebastian. Whiles we stood here securing your repose—   345
Even now—we heard a hollow burst of bellowing
Like bulls, or rather lions—did't not wake you?
It struck mine ear most terribly.
    Alonso.   I heard nothing.
    Antonio. O, 'twas a din to fright a monster's ear,   350
To make an earthquake! Sure it was the roar
Of a whole herd of lions.
    Alonso.   Heard you this, Gonzalo?
    Gonzalo. Upon mine honor, sir, I heard a humming—
And that a strange one too—which did awake me.   355
I shak'd you, sir, and cried; as mine eyes open'd
I saw their weapons drawn—there was a noise,
That's verily! 'Tis best we stand upon our guard,
Or that we quit this place. Let's draw our weapons.
    Alonso. Lead off this ground and let's make further search   360
For my poor son.
    Gonzalo.   Heavens keep him from these beasts,
For he is sure i' th' island.
    Alonso.   Lead away.
    Ariel. Prospero, my lord, shall know what I have done.   365
So, king, go safely on to seek thy son.   *Exeunt.*

---

264 But doubt discovery: *without putting out the light of discovery: to 'dout' (do out) was to 'extinguish'* **there a:** *state greater than the kingship of Naples* **272 note:** *information* **post:** *messenger* **275 cast:** *play on the meanings 'disgorged' and 'assigned to parts in a play'; cf. following lines* **278, 279 what ... discharge;** *Cf. n.* **286 Measure:** *journey across* **289 there be that:** *there are those who* **292, 293 I ... chat:** *I could make of myself a jackdaw capable of Gonzalo's prattle* **297 content:** *liking* **298 Tender:** *regard* **303 feater:** *more fitly* **306 kibe:** *chilblain, or sore on heel* **309 candied:** *congealed* **310 molest:** *worry me*

319 tell ... to: *say the time is ripe for* **348 struck:** *F strook*

❧ Scene Second ❧

Enter Caliban with a burthen of wood. A noise of thunder heard.

Caliban. All the infections that the sun sucks up
From bogs, fens, flats on Prosper fall, and make him
By inchmeal a disease! His spirits hear me,
And yet I needs must curse. But they'll nor pinch,
Fright me with urchin-shows, pitch me i' th' mire,   5
Nor lead me like a firebrand in the dark
Out of my way, unless he bid 'em; but
For every trifle are they set upon me,
Sometime like apes that mow and chatter at me
And after bite me, then like hedgehogs which   10
Lie tumbling in my barefoot way and mount
Their pricks at my footfall; sometime am I
All wound with adders, who with cloven tongues
Do hiss me into madness.

                Enter Trinculo.

        Lo, now, lo!   15
Here comes a spirit of his, and to torment me
For bringing wood in slowly! I'll fall flat.
Perchance he will not mind me.

Trinculo. Here's neither bush nor shrub to bear off
any weather at all, and another storm brewing. I hear it   20
sing i' th' wind. Yond same black cloud, yond huge one, looks
like a foul bombard that would shed his liquor. If it should
thunder, as it did before, I know not where to hide my head.
Yond same cloud cannot choose but fall by pailfuls. *[Sees Cali-*
ban.] What have we here, a man? or a fish? dead or alive? A   25
fish. He smells like a fish—a very ancient and fishlike smell—a
kind of, not of the newest, poor-john a strange fish! Were I in
England now—as once I was—and had but this fish painted,
not a holiday fool there but would give a piece of silver; there
would this monster make a man: any strange beast there   30
makes a man! When they will not give a doit to relieve a lame
beggar, they will lay out ten to see a dead Indian. Legg'd like
a man, and his fins like arms! Warm, o' my troth! I do now
let loose my opinion, hold it no longer: this is no fish but an
islander, that hath lately suffered by a thunderbolt.   35
[Thunder.] Alas, the storm is come again! My best way is to
creep under his gaberdine. there is no other shelter hereabout.
Misery acquaints a man with strange bedfellows! I will here
shroud till the dregs of the storm be past. *[Creeps under Caliban's*
garment.]   40

                Enter Stephano singing.

I shall no more to sea, to sea;
Here shall I die ashore.

This is a very scurvy tune to sing at a man's funeral!
Well, here's my comfort.   *Drinks [and then] sings.*

                Song
The master, the swabber, the boatswain, and I,   45

The gunner and his mate
Lov'd Moll, Meg, and Marian, and Margery,
But none of us car'd for Kate.
For she had a tongue with a tang,
Would cry to a sailor, go hang!   50
She lov'd not the savor of tar nor of pitch,
Yet a tailor might scratch her wherere she did itch.
Then to sea, boys, and let her go hang!

This is a scurvy tune, too: but here's my comfort.   *Drinks.*
Caliban. Do not torment me! O!   55
Stephano. What's the matter? Have we divels here? Do you
put tricks upon's with salvages and men of Inde? ha? I have
not 'scap'd drowning to be afeard now of your four legs;
for it hath bin said, 'as proper a man as ever went on four
legs cannot make him give ground,' and it shall be said so   60
again, while Stephano breathes at' nostrils.
Caliban. The spirit torments me! O!
Stephano. This is some monster of the isle with four
legs, who hath got—as I take it—an ague. Where the divel
should he learn our language? I will give him some relief if   65
it be but for that! If I can recover him and keep him tame,
and get to Naples with him, he's a present for any emperor
that ever trod on neat's leather.
Caliban. Do not torment me, prithee! I'll bring my
wood home faster.   70
Stephano. He's in his fit now, and does not talk after the
wisest. He shall taste of my bottle! If he have never drunk
wine afore, it will go near to remove his fit. If I can
recover him and keep him tame, I will not take too much for
him; he shall pay for him that hath him, and that soundly.   75
Caliban. Thou dost me yet but little hurt. Thou wilt anon;
I know it by thy trembling. Now Prosper works upon thee.
Stephano. Come on your ways—open your mouth—here
is that which will give language to you, cat. Open your mouth!
This will shake your shaking, I can tell you, and that soundly.   80
You cannot tell who's your friend. Open your chaps again.
Trinculo. I should know that voice! It should be—but he is
drown'd, and these are divels. O defend me!
Stephano. Four legs and two voices—a most delicate
monster! His forward voice now is to speak well of his friend;
his backward voice is to utter foul speeches and to detract. If
all the wine in my bottle will recover him, I will help his
ague. Come! Amen! I will pour some in thy other mouth.
Trinculo. Stephano!
Stephano. Doth thy other mouth call me? Mercy, mercy!   90
This is a divel and no monster! I will leave him: I have no
long spoon.
Trinculo. Stephano! If thou beest Stephano, touch me
and speak to me, for I am Trinculo—be not afeard—
thy good friend Trinculo.   95
Stephano. If thou beest Trinculo, come forth! I'll pull thee
by the lesser legs. If any be Trinculo's legs, these are they . . .
Thou art very Trinculo indeed! How cam'st thou to be
the siege of this mooncalf? Can he vent Trinculos?
Trinculo. I took him to be kill'd with a thunderstroke. But

---

3 **By inchmeal:** *little by little* (cf. modern 'piecemeal')   6 **firebrand:** *ignis fatuus* (will-o'-
the-wisp)   9 **mow:** *grimace*   19 **bear:** *ward*   22 **bombard:** *leather wine jug*   27
poor-john: *salt hake* (a kind of fish)   28 **painted:** *i.e. on a board to advertise the exhibition*
(cf. *Macbeth* V.7.54-55); Malone cites many references to this practice   31 **makes a man:**
make a man's fortune (with a pun, explained in the following clause)   31 **doit:** *almost
worthless Dutch coin*   32 **dead Indian:** *such as were displayed in England, in the Elizabethan
equivalent of a side show*   37 **gaberdine:** *cloak*   39 **shroud:** *take shelter*   45 **swabber:**
one who kept the ship clean

57 **salvages:** *savages*   66 **recover:** *restore*   68 **neat's leather:** *leather from cattle of the
ox kind*   74, 75 **I . . . him:** *no price will be too high for him*   77 **thy trembling:** *i.e.
Trinculo's*   79 **language . . . cat:** *in reference to an old proverb, 'Liquor will make a cat
speak'*   92 **long spoon:** *in reference to the proverb, 'He that would eat with the devil needs
a long spoon'*   99 **siege:** *excrement*   **mooncalf:** *a mooncalf was a shapeless abortion, thought
to be caused by the action of the moon*

art thou not drown'd, Stephano? I hope now thou art not drown'd! Is the storm over-blown? I hid me under the dead mooncalf's gaberdine, for fear of the storm. And art thou living, Stephano? O Stephano, two Neapolitans 'scap'd?

Stephano. Prithee do not turn me about—my stomach 105 is not constant.

Caliban. These be fine things and if they be not sprites! That's a brave god, and bears celestial liquor. I will kneel to him.

Stephano. How didst thou 'scape? How cam'st thou 110 hither? Swear by this bottle how thou cam'st hither! I escap'd upon a butt of sack which the sailors heaved oreboard, by this bottle! which I made of the bark of a tree with mine own hands since I was cast ashore.

Caliban. I'll swear upon that bottle to be thy true 115 subject, for the liquor is not earthly.

Stephano. Here! Swear then how thou escap'dst.

Trinculo. Swum asore, man, like a duck! I can swim like a duck, I'll be sworn.

Stephano. Here, kiss the book. *[Trinculo drinks.]* 120 Though thou canst swim like a duck, thou art made like a goose.

Trinculo. O Stephano, hast any more of this?

Stephano. The whole butt, man! My cellar is in a rock by th' seaside, where my wine is hid. How now, mooncalf? 125 How does thine ague?

Caliban. Hast thou not dropp'd from heaven?

Stephano. Out o' th' moon, I do assure thee. I was the man i' th' moon, when time was.

Caliban. I have seen thee in her—and I do adore thee! 130 My mistress show'd me thee, and thy dog, and thy bush.

Stephano. Come, swear to that! Kiss the book! I will furnish it anon with new contents! Swear.   *[Caliban drinks.]*

Trinculo. By this good light, this is a very shallow monster! I afeard of him? a very weak monster! The man i' th' moon? 135 A most poor credulous monster! Well drawn, monster, in good sooth.

Caliban. I'll show thee every fertile inch o' th' island—and I will kiss thy foot! I prithee, be my god.

Trinculo. By this light, a most perfidious and drunken 140 monster; when's god's asleep he'll rob his bottle.

Caliban. I'll kiss thy foot. I'll swear myself thy subject.

Stephano. Come on, then—down and swear.

Trinculo. I shall laugh myself to death at this puppy-headed monster! A most scurvy monster! I could find in my 145 heart to beat him—

Stephano. Come, kiss.

Trinculo. But that the poor monster's in drink. An abominable monster!

Caliban. I'll show thee the best springs; I'll pluck thee 150 berries;
I'll fish for thee, and get thee wood enough.
A plague upon the tyrant that I serve!
I'll bear him no more sticks, but follow thee,
Thou wondrous man.   155

Trinculo. A most ridiculous monster, to make a wonder of a poor drunkard.

Caliban. I prithee let me bring thee where crabs grow;
And I with my long nails will dig thee pignuts,
Show thee a jay's nest, and instruct thee how   160
To snare the nimble marmoset; I'll bring thee
To clus'tring filberts, and sometimes I'll get thee
Young scamels from the rock. Wilt thou go with me?

Stephano. I prithee now, lead the way without any more talking. Trinculo, the king and all our company else being 165 drown'd, we will inherit here. Here, bear my bottle! Fellow Trinculo, we'll fill him by and by again.

                              Caliban sings drunkenly.

Caliban. Farewell, master; farewell, farewell!
Trinculo. A howling monster! a drunken monster!

Caliban. [Singing.]   170
No more dams I'll make for fish,
Nor fetch in firing
At requiring,
Nor scrape trenchering, nor wash dish.
'Ban, 'Ban, Ca-Caliban   175
Has a new master—get a new man.

Freedom, high-day! high-day, freedom! freedom, high-day, freedom!
Stephano. O brave monster! lead the way.   *Exeunt.*

ACT THIRD ❧ SCENE FIRST

Enter Ferdinand, bearing a log.

Ferdinand. There be some sports are painful, and their labor
Delight in them sets off; some kinds of baseness
Are nobly undergone, and most poor matters
Point to rich ends. This my mean task
Would be as heavy to me as odious, but   5
The mistress which I serve quickens what's dead
And makes my labors pleasures. O she is
Ten times more gentle than her father's crabbed,
And he's compos'd of harshness. I must remove
Some thousands of these logs and pile them up,   10
Upon a sore injunction. My sweet mistress
Weeps when she sees me work, and says such baseness
Had never like executor. I forget;
But these sweet thoughts do even refresh my labors,
Most busy lest, when I do it.   15

Enter Miranda and Prospero [behind her and unseen].

Miranda.   Alas, now pray you
Work not so hard! I would the lightning had
Burnt up those logs that you are enjoin'd to pile:
Pray set it down and rest you; when this burns
'Twill weep for having wearied you. My father   20
Is hard at study; pray now rest yourself:
He's safe for these three hours.
Ferdinand.   O most dear mistress,
The sun will set before I shall discharge

---

107 and if: *if*   **120 kiss the book:** *joking reference to the custom of kissing the Bible after swearing on it; see l. 115 above.*   **129 when time was:** *once upon a time*   **131 thy dog ... bush:** *in reference to an old tale that the man in the moon was banished there with his dog for gathering brush on Sunday*   **136 drawn:** *drunk*

158 crabs: *crabapples*   **163 scamels:** *probably the bird called the sea mell* (mew).   **167 by and by:** *right away*   **174 trenchering:** *trenchers*   **177 high-day:** *heyday*   **1 be: are** are: *which are*   **painful:** *laborious*   **2 Delight ... off:** *the pleasure they arouse compensates for their labor*   **sets:** F set   **11 Upon ... injunction:** *on pain of severe punishment*   **13 I forget:** *i.e. my task*   **15 lest:** *least*   **Most ... it;** *Cf. n.*   **20 'Twill weep:** *the sap* (or pitch) *will look like tears*

What I must strive to do.   25
  Miranda.   If you'll sit down
I'll bear your logs the while—pray give me that;
I'll carry it to the pile.
  Ferdinand.   No, precious creature,
I had rather crack my sinews, break my back,   30
Then you should such dishonor undergo
While I sit lazy by.
  Miranda.   It would become me
As well as it does you, and I should do it
With much more ease, for my good will is to it   35
And yours it is against.
  Prospero.   Poor worm, thou art infected;
This visitation shows it.
  Miranda. You look wearily.
  Ferdinand. No, noble mistress, 'tis fresh morning with me   40
When you are by at night. I do beseech you,
Chiefly that I might set it in my prayers,
What is your name?
  Miranda.   Miranda. O my father,
I have broke your hest to say so.   45
  Ferdinand.   Admir'd Miranda,
Indeed the top of admiration, worth
What's dearest to the world: full many a lady
I have ey'd with best regard, and many a time
Th' harmony of their tongues hath into bondage   50
Brought my too diligent ear; for several virtues
Have I lik'd several women, never any
With so full soul, but some defect in her
Did quarrel with the noblest grace she ow'd
And put it to the foil. But you, O you,   55
So perfect and so peerless, are created
Of every creature's best.
  Miranda.   I do not know
One of my sex, no woman's face remember
Save from my glass mine own, nor have I seen   60
More that I may call men than you, good friend,
And my dear father: how features are abroad
I am skilless of; but by my modesty—
The jewel in my dower—I would not wish
Any companion in the world but you;   65
Nor can imagination form a shape
Besides yourself to like of. But I prattle
Something too wildly and my father's precepts
I therein do forget.
  Ferdinand.   I am, in my condition,   70
A prince, Miranda—I do think a king—
I would not so—and would no more endure
This wooden slavery than to suffer
The flesh-fly blow my mouth. Hear my soul speak:
The very instant that I saw you did   75
My heart fly to your service, there resides
To make me slave to it and for your sake
Am I this patient log-man.
  Miranda.   Do you love me?
  Ferdinand. O heaven, O earth, bear witness to this sound,   80

And crown what I profess with kind event
If I speak true; if hollowly, invert
What best is boded me to mischief: I,
Beyond all limit of what else i' th' world
Do love, prize, honor you.   85
  Miranda.   I am a fool
To weep at what I am glad of.
  Prospero.   Fair encounter
Of two most rare affections! Heavens rain grace
On that which breeds between 'em.   90
  Ferdinand.   Wherefore weep you?
  Miranda. At mine unworthiness, that dare not offer
What I desire to give and much less take
What I shall die to want. But this is trifling
And all the more it seeks to hide itself   95
The bigger bulk it shows. Hence, bashful cunning,
And prompt me, plain and holy innocence.
I am your wife if you will marry me;
If not I'll die your maid. To be your fellow
You may deny me, but I'll be your servant   100
Whether you will or no.
  Ferdinand.   My mistress, dearest!
And I thus humble ever.
  Miranda.   My husband, then?
  Ferdinand. Ay, with a heart as willing   105
As bondage ere of freedom! Here's my hand.
  Miranda. And mine, with my heart in't; and now farewell
Till half an hour hence.
  Ferdinand.   A thousand thousand!   *Exeunt.*
  Prospero. So glad of this as they I cannot be   110
Who are surpris'd with all, but my rejoicing
At nothing can be more! I'll to my book,
For yet ere supper time must I perform
Much business appertaining.   *Exit.*

❧ Scene Second ❧

Enter Caliban, Stephano, and Trinculo.

  Stephano. Tell not me—when the butt is out we will drink
water, not a drop before; therefore bear up and board 'em.
Servant monster, drink to me.
  Trinculo. Servant monster? The folly of this island!
They say there's but five upon this isle; we are three of them.   5
If th' other two be brain'd like us, the state totters.
  Stephano. Drink, servant monster, when I bid thee.
Thy eyes are almost set in thy head.
  Trinculo. Where should they be set else? He were a brave
monster indeed if they were set in his tail.   10
  Stephano. My man-monster hath drown'd his tongue in sack.
For my part, the sea cannot drown me. I swam ere I could
recover the shore, five and thirty leagues off and on. By this
light thou shalt be my lieutenant, monster, or my standard.

38 visitation: Cf. n.   **45 hest:** command   **46 Admir'd Miranda** *a play on Miranda's name*   **54 ow'd:** owned   **55 put ... foil:** *'challenged it to a fencing match,' with a play on foil in the sense of 'defeat' (OED)*   **56 peerless** F: *peetlesse*   **63 skilless:** ignorant   **70 conditon:** rank   **70-74:** Cf. n.   **74 flesh-fly:** *a fly which lays its eggs in dead flesh* **blow** sully

81 event: outcome   **82 hollowly:** falsely   **82, 83 invert ... mischief:** turn into bad fortune all the good that is to befall me   **84 what:** anything   **99 maid:** play on 'maidservant' and 'unmarried woman'; cf. following line **fellow** mate, equal   **106 bondage ... freedom:** one in bondage ever welcomed freedom   **111 with all:** i.e. all that has happened (or perhaps withal, 'thereby,' is meant)   **2 bear ... 'em:** obvious nautical phraseology   **9 set:** fixed in a stare **were:** would be **brave:** admirable

Trinculo. Your lieutenant, if you list—he's no standard.   *15*

Stephano. We'll not run, Monsieur Monster.

Trinculo. Nor go neither; but you'll lie like dogs, and yet say nothing, neither.

Stephano. Mooncalf, speak once in thy life, if thou beest a good mooncalf.   *20*

Caliban. How does thy honor? Let me lick thy shoe. I'll not serve *him*—he is not valiant.

Trinculo. Thou liest, most ignorant monster! I am in case to justle a constable! Why, thou debosh'd fish, thou, was there ever man a coward that hath drunk so much sack as I   *25* today? Wilt thou tell a monstrous lie, being but half a fish and half a monster?

Caliban. Lo, how he mocks me! Wilt thou let him, my lord?

Trinculo. 'Lord,' quoth he? That a monster should be   *30* such a natural!

Caliban. Lo, lo again! Bite him to death, I prithee!

Stephano. Trinculo, keep a good tongue in your head! If you prove a mutineer—the next tree! The poor monster's my subject and he shall not suffer indignity.   *35*

Caliban. I thank my noble lord. Wilt thou be pleas'd to hearken once again to the suit I made to thee?

Stephano. Marry will I. Kneel and repeat it. I will stand and so shall Trinculo.

Enter Ariel, invisible.

Caliban. As I told thee before, I am subject to a tyrant,   *40* a sorcerer, that by his cunning hath cheated me of the island.

Ariel. Thou liest.

Caliban. [To Trinculo.] Thou liest, thou jesting monkey, thou! I would my valiant master would destroy thee. I do not lie.   *45*

Stephano. Trinculo, if you trouble him any more in's tale, by his hand I will supplant some of your teeth.

Trinculo. Why, I said nothing.

Stephano. Mum, then, and no more! Proceed.

Caliban. I say by sorcery he got this isle   *50*
From me, he got it. If thy greatness will,
Revenge it on him—for I know thou dar'st
But this thing dare not.

Stephano. That's most certain.

Caliban. Thou shalt be lord of it, and I'll serve thee.   *55*

Stephano. How now shall this be compass'd? Canst thou bring me to the party?

Caliban. Yea, yea, my lord, I'll yield him thee asleep
Where thou may'st knock a nail into his head.

Ariel. Thou liest. Thou canst not.   *60*

Caliban. What a pied ninny's this? Thou scurvy patch!
I do beseech thy greatness, give him blows
And take his bottle from him! When that's gone
He shall drink nought but brine, for I'll not show him
Where the quick freshes are.   *65*

Stephano. Trinculo, run into no further danger!
Interrupt the monster one word further and by this hand I'll turn my mercy out o' doors and make a stockfish of thee.

Trinculo. Why what did I? I did nothing! I'll go farther off.

Stephano. Didst thou not say he lied?   *70*

Ariel. Thou liest.

Stephano. Do I so? Take thou that! *[Hits Trinculo.]* As you like this, give me the lie another time.

Trinculo. I did not give the lie! Out o' your wits, and hearing too? A pox o' your bottle. This can sack and drinking   *75* do! A murrain on your monster and the divel take your fingers!

Caliban. Ha ha ha!

Stephano. Now forward with your tale! *[To Trinculo.]* Prithee stand further off.   *80*

Caliban. Beat him enough! After a little time I'll beat him too.

Stephano. Stand farther! *[To Caliban.]* Come, proceed.

Caliban. Why, as I told thee, 'tis a custom with him
I' th' afternoon to sleep; there thou mayst brain him,   *85*
Having first seiz'd his books, or with a log
Batter his skull, or paunch him with a stake,
Or cut his wezand with thy knife. Remember
First to possess his books, for without them
He's but a sot, as I am, nor hath not   *90*
One spirit to command: they all do hate him
As rootedly as I. Burn but his books.
He has brave utensils—for so he calls them—
Which when he has a house he'll deck withal.
And that most deeply to consider is   *95*
The beauty of his daughter: he himself
Calls her a nonpareil. I never saw a woman
But only Sycorax my dam and she;
But she as far surpasseth Sycorax
As great'st does least.   *100*

Stephano.   Is it so brave a lass?

Caliban. Ay, lord, she will become thy bed, I warrant,
And bring thee forth brave brood.

Stephano. Monster, I will kill this man! His daughter and I will be king and queen, save our Graces! and Trinculo and   *105* thyself shall be viceroys! Dost thou like the plot, Trinculo?

Trinculo. Excellent.

Stephano. Give me thy hand; I am sorry I beat thee!
But while thou liv'st keep a good tongue in thy head.

Caliban. Within this half hour will he be asleep.   *110*
Wilt thou destroy him then?

Stephano.   Ay, on my honor.

Ariel. This will I tell my master.

Caliban. Thou mak'st me merry: I am full of pleasure;
Let us be jocund. Will you troll the catch   *115*
You taught me but whilere?

Stephano. At thy request, monster, I will do reason,
any reason. Come on, Trinculo, let us sing.   *Sings.*

*Flout 'em and scout 'em—and scout 'em and flout 'em;
Thought is free.*   *120*

Caliban. That's not the tune.

                Ariel plays the tune on a tabor and pipe.

Stephano. What is this same?

---

15 list: *meaning both 'desire' and 'careen'* **standard:** *meaning both 'ensign' (standard bearer) and 'support' (for Stephano, who, like Caliban, is tipsy)* **16 run:** *double-entendre ('run from an enemy' and 'excrete')* **17 lie:** *double-entendre ('prevaricate' and 'excrete')* **23 case:** *condition* **24 debosh'd** *debauched* **31 natural:** *idiot* **53 thing:** *Trinculo* **61 pied ninny:** *fool in motley* **patch:** *dolt* **65 quick freshes:** *springs* **68 stockfish:** *dried cod which had to be beaten soft before it could be cooked*

76 murrain: *cattle disease* **88 wezand:** *windpipe* **90 sot:** *fool* **93 utensils:** *stressed ⏑ — ⏑* **94 deck withal:** *furnish it with* **95 that:** *that which is* **115 troll the catch:** *sing the song; a catch was 'a round in which one singer catches at the words of another, producing ludicrous effects' (OED)* **116 whilere:** *a while ago* **119 scout:** *F prints cout the first time, scout the second* **SD tabor:** *small drum*

Trinculo. This is the tune of our catch, play'd by the picture
of No-body.

Stephano. If thou beest a man, show thyself in thy   *125*
likeness: if thou beest a divel, take't as thou list.

Trinculo. O forgive me my sins.

Stephano. He that dies pays all debts. I defy thee;
mercy upon on!

Caliban. Art thou afeard?   *130*

Stephano. No, monster, not I.

Caliban. Be not afeard, the isle is full of noises,
Sounds and sweet airs that give delight and hurt not.
Sometimes a thousand twangling instruments
Will hum about mine ears, and sometime voices   *135*
That if I then had wak'd after long sleep
Will make me sleep again; and then in dreaming
The clouds methought would open and show riches
Ready to drop upon me, that when I wak'd
I cried to dream again.   *140*

Stephano. This will prove a brave kingdom to me, where I
shall have my music for nothing.

Caliban. When Prospero is destroy'd.

Stephano. That shall be by and by: I remember the story.

Trinculo. The sound is going away. Let's follow it and   *145*
after do our work.

Stephano. Lead, monster, we'll follow. I would I could see
this taborer; he lays it on.

Trinculo. Wilt come? I'll follow, Stephano.   *Exeunt.*

❧ SCENE THIRD ❧

Enter Alonso, Sebastian, Antonio, Gonzalo, Adrian, Francisco, etc.

Gonzalo. By'r lakin, I can go no further, sir.
My old bones aches; here's a maze trod indeed
Through forthrights and meanders; by your patience,
I needs must rest me.

Alonso.   Old lord, I cannot blame thee   *5*
Who am myself attach'd with weariness
To th' dulling of my spirits; sit down and rest.
Even here I will put off my hope and keep it
No longer for my flatterer: he is drown'd
Whom thus we stray to find and the sea mocks   *10*
Our frustrate search on land. Well, let him go.

Antonio. [To Sebastian.] I am right glad that he's
so out of hope.
Do not for one repulse forgo the purpose
That you resolv'd t' effect.

Sebastian.   The next advantage   *15*
Will we take throughly.

Antonio.   Let it be tonight,
For now they are oppress'd with travel, they
Will not nor cannot use such vigilance   *20*
As when they are fresh.

Sebastian.   I say tonight: no more.

Solemn and strange music, and Prosper on the top, invisible.

Alonso. What harmony is this? My good friends, hark!

Gonzalo. Marvelous sweet music.

*Enter several strange shapes bringing in a basket; and dance about
it with gentle actions of salutations, and inviting the king, etc. to
eat, they depart.*

Alonso. Give us kind keepers, heavens! What were these?   *25*

Sebastian. A living drollery! Now I will believe
That there are unicorns! that in Arabia
There is one tree, the phoenix' throne, one phoenix
At this hour reigning there.

Antonio.   I'll believe both!   *30*
And what does else want credit, come to me
And I'll be sworn 'tis true! Travelers nere did lie,
Though fools at home condemn 'em.

Gonzalo.   If in Naples
I should report this now, would they believe me?   *35*
If I should say I saw such islanders—
For certes these are people of the island—
Who though they are of monstrous shape yet, note,
Their manners are more gentle, kind, than of
Our human generation you shall find   *40*
Many, nay almost any.

Prospero. [Aside.]   Honest lord,
Thou hast said well: for some of you there present
Are worse than divels.

Alonso.   I cannot too much muse   *45*
Such shapes, such gesture, and such sound expressing—
Although they want the use of tongue—a kind
Of excellent dumb discourse.

Prospero. [Aside.]   Praise in departing.

Francisco. They vanish'd strangely.   *50*

Sebastian.   No matter, since
They have left their viands behind, for we have stomachs.
Will't please you taste of what is here?

Alonso.   Not I.

Gonzalo. Faith, sir, you need not fear! When we were   *55*
boys
Who would believe that there were mountaineers
Dewlapp'd like bulls, whose throats had hanging at 'em
Wallets of flesh? or that there were such men
Whose heads stood in their breasts? which now we find   *60*
Each putter out of five for one will bring us
Good warrant of.

Alonso.   I will stand to and feed.
Although my last, no matter, since I feel
The best is past: brother, my lord the duke,   *65*
Stand to and do as we.

*Thunder and lightning. Enter Ariel like a harpy, claps his wings
upon the table, and with a quaint device the banquet vanishes.*

Ariel. You are three men of sin, whom destiny—
That hath to instrument this lower world
And what is in't—the never surfeited sea
Hath caus'd to belch up you, and on this island   *70*

---

123 picture of No-body; *Cf. n.*   **132 noises:** *music*   **1 lakin:** *Ladykin (the Virgin
Mary).*   **2 aches:** *old variant plural from of verb*   **3 forthrights:** *straight paths* **meanders** *windig paths*   **6 attach'd:** *seized*   **7 To th':** *to the point of* **spirits vital
strength**   **11 frustrate:** *vain*   **17 throughly:** *thoroughly* **SD Prosper on the top;**
Cf. n.

25 keepers: *guardian angels*   **26 drollery:** *puppet show*   **28 phoenix;** *Cf. n.*   **36
islanders F:** *islands*   **45 muse:** *marvel at*   **46 gesture:** *bearing*   **49 Praise in departing:** *proverbial: 'Wait until the end of the entertainment before you praise it'*   **61 putter
. . . one;** *Cf. n.* **SD quaint:** *ingenious* **the banquet vanishes** *i.e. under the concealment of
Ariel's wings (cf. Aeneid iii.225-66)*   **68 hath to instrument:** *uses for its own ends*   **69
surfeited;** *Cf. n.*

Where man doth not inhabit, you 'mongst men
Being most unfit to live; I have made you mad,
And even with such-like valor men hang and drown
Their proper selves.

                     [Alonso, etc., draw their swords.]
            You fools! I and my fellows   *75*
Are ministers of fate; the elements
Of whom your swords are temper'd may as well
Wound the loud winds, or with bemock'd-at stabs
Kill the still closing waters as diminish
One dowl that's in my plume! My fellow ministers   *80*
Are like invulnerable—if you could hurt,
Your swords are now too massy for your strengths
And will not be uplifted. But remember—
For that's my business to you—that you three
From Milan did supplant good Prospero,   *85*
Expos'd unto the sea—which hath requit it—
Him and his innocent child; for which foul deed
The powers, delaying—not forgetting—have
Incens'd the seas and shores, yea all the creatures
Against your peace: thee of thy son, Alonso,   *90*
They have bereft and do pronounce by me:
Ling'ring perdition—worse than any death
Can be at once—shall step by step attend
You and your ways, whose wraths to guard you from—
Which here in this most desolate isle else falls   *95*
Upon your heads—is nothing but heart's sorrow
And a clear life ensuing.

He vanishes in thunder; then, to soft music, enter the shapes again
    and dance, with mocks and mows, and carrying out the table.

    Prospero. Bravely the figure of this harpy hast thou
Perform'd, my Ariel; a grace it had, devouring.
Of my instruction hast thou nothing bated   *100*
In what thou hadst to say. So with good life
And observation strange my meaner ministers
Their several kinds have done, my high charms work,
And these, mine enemies, are all knit up
In their distractions; they now are in my power,   *105*
And in these fits I leave them, while I visit
Young Ferdinand—whom they suppose is drown'd—
And his and mine lov'd darling.   *.[Exit.]*
    Gonzalo. I' th' name of something holy, sir, why stand you
In this strange stare?   *110*
    Alonso.   O, it is monstrous! monstrous!
Methought the billows spoke and told me of it;
The winds did sing it to me, and the thunder—
That deep and dreadful organ pipe—pronounc'd
The name of Prosper! It did bass my trespass.   *115*
Therefore my son i' th' ooze is bedded, and
I'll seek him deeper than ere plummet sounded,
And with him there lie mudded.   *Exit.*
    Sebastian.   But one fiend at a time—
I'll fight their legions ore!   *120*
    Antonio.   I'll be thy second.
                Exeunt [Sebastian and Antonio.]

    Gonzalo. All three of them are desperate! Their great
guilt,
Like poison given to work a great time after,
Now 'gins to bite the spirits. I do beseech you,   *125*
That are of suppler joints, follow them swiftly
And hinder them from what this ecstasy
May now provoke them to.
    Adrian.   Follow, I pray you.   *Exeunt omnes.*

ACT FOURTH ❧ SCENE FIRST

Enter Prospero, Ferdinand, and Miranda.

    Prospero. If I have too austerely punish'd you
Your compensation makes amends, for I
Have given you here a third of mine own life,
Or that for which I live, who once again
I tender to thy hand; all thy vexations   *5*
Were but my trials of thy love, and thou
Hast strangely stood the test. Here, afore heaven,
I ratify this my rich gift! O Ferdinand,
Do not smile at me that I boast her off,
For thou shalt find she will outstrip all praise   *10*
And make it halt behind her.
    Ferdinand.   I do believe it
Against an oracle.
    Prospero. Then as my gift and thine own acquisition
Worthily purchas'd, take my daughter; but   *15*
If thou dost break her virgin knot before
All sanctimonious ceremonies may
With full and holy rite be minist'red,
No sweet aspersion shall the heavens let fall
To make this contract grow, but barren hate,   *20*
Sour-ey'd disdain, and discord shall bestrew
The union of your bed with weeds so loathly
That you shall hate it both. Therefore take heed
As Hymen's lamps shall light you.
    Ferdinand.   As I hope   *25*
For quiet days, fair issue, and long life
With such love as 'tis now, the murkiest den,
The most opportune place, the strong'st suggestion
Our worser genius can, shall never melt
Mine honor into lust, to take away   *30*
The edge of that day's celebration
When I shall think or Phoebus' steeds are founder'd,
Or Night kept chain'd below.
    Prospero.   Fairly spoke.
Sit then and talk with her; she is thine own.   *35*
                       [They sit apart.]
What, Ariel! my industrious servant, Ariel!

Enter Ariel.

    Ariel. What would my potent master? Here I am.
    Prospero. Thou and thy meaner fellows your last service

---

74 proper: *own*   **81 dowl:** *feather* **minister:** *agents*   **87 requit it:** *retaliated* (by wrecking Alonso and his party)   **98 clear:** *blameless* **SD mows:** *grimaces* **99 Bravely:** *admirably*   **100 devouring:** *i.e. pretending to eat the food of the banquet*   **101 bated:** *omitted*   **102 with good life:** *like real life*   **116 bass:** *sang the bass harmony of nature's dirge*

125 bite the spirits: *impair the vital powers*   **127 ecstasy:** *madness*   **3 third;** *Cf. n.*   **7 strangely:** *surprisingly well*   **9 boast her off:** *cf. the modern 'show her off'; F of* **11 halt:** *limp*   **14 gift** F: *guest*   **17 sanctimonious:** *holy*   **18 rite** F: *right*   **19 aspersion:** *sprinkling of the dew of blessing*   **28 opportune:** *stressed* — ‿ —   **29 worser genius;** *Cf. n.*   **30 to:** *so as to*   **31 edge:** *keen enjoyment*   **32 Phoebus':** *Apollo, god of the sun* **founder'd:** *gone lame*   **32, 33 or . . . below:** *i.e. eternal day, time standing still*

Did worthily perform, and I must use you
In such another trick. Go bring the rabble—　　　　　　40
Ore whom I give thee power—here to this place.
Incite them to quick motion, for I must
Bestow upon the eyes of this young couple
Some vanity of mine art: it is my promise
And they expect it from me.　　　　　　　　　45
　　Ariel.　　　　　　　　Presently?
　　Prospero. Ay, with a twinck.
　　Ariel. Before you can say 'come' and 'go,'
And breathe twice, and cry 'so, so,'
Each one tripping on his toe　　　　　　　　50
Will be here with mop and mow
Do you love me, master? no?
　　Prospero. Dearly, my delicate Ariel! Do not approach
Till thou dost hear me call.
　　Ariel. Well! I conceive.　　　　　　*Exit.*　55
　　Prospero [Back to Ferdinand.] Look thou be true: do not give
dalliance
Too much the reign; the strongest oaths are straw
To th' fire i' th' blood. Be more abstemious,
Or else good night your vow.　　　　　　　60
　　Ferdinand.　　　　　　I warrant you, sir,
The white cold virgin snow upon my heart
Abates the ardor of my liver.
　　Prospero.　　　　　　Well.
Now come, my Ariel, bring a corollary　　　　65
Rather than want a spirit; appear, and pertly.
No tongue—all eyes—be silent.

　　　　　Soft music. Enter Iris.

　　Iris. Ceres, most bounteous lady, thy rich leas
Of wheat, rye, barley, fetches, oats, and peas;
The turfy mountains where live nibbling sheep,　　70
And flat meads thetch'd with stover, them to keep;
Thy banks with pioned and twilled brims
Which spongy April at thy hest betrims
To make cold nymphs chaste crowns; and thy broom groves
Whose shadow the dismissed bachelor loves,　　75
Being lass-lorn; thy poll-clipp'd vineyard;
And thy sea-marge stirrile, and rocky-hard,
Where thou thyself dost air—the queen o' th' sky,
Whose wat'ry arch and messenger am I,
Bids thee leave these and with her sovereign grace　80
　　　　　　　　　Juno [begins to] descend.
Here on this grass plot in this very place
To come and sport. Her peacocks fly amain.
Approach, rich Ceres, her to entertain.

　　　　　Enter Ceres.

　　Ceres. Hail, many-color'd messenger, that nere
Dost disobey the wife of Jupiter;　　　　　　85

Who with thy saffron wings upon my flowers
Diffusest honey drops, refreshing showers,
And with each end of thy blue bow dost crown
My bosky acres and my unshrubb'd down,
Rich scarf to my proud earth—why hath thy queen　90
Summon'd me hither to this short-grass'd green?
　　Iris. A contact of true love to celebrate
And some donation freely to estate
On the bless'd lovers.
　　Ceres.　　　　　Tell me, heavenly bow,　95
If Venus or her son, as thou dost know,
Do not attend the queen? Since they did plot
The means that dusky Dis my daughter got,
Her and her blind boy's scandal'd company
I have forsworn.　　　　　　　　　　100
　　Iris.　　　　Of her society
Be not afraid; I met her deity
Cutting the clouds towards Paphos, and her son
Dove-drawn with her. Here thought they to have done
Some wanton charm upon this man and maid　　105
Whose vows are that no bedrite shall be paid
Till Hymen's torch be lighted; but in vain:
Mars's hot minion is return'd again;
Her waspish-headed son has broke his arrows,
Swears he will shoot no more but play with sparrows　110
And be a boy right out.
　　Ceres.　　　　　Highest queen of state,
Great Juno comes; I know her by her gait.

　　　　　[Enter Juno.]

　　Juno. How does my bounteous sister? Go with me
To bless this twain, that they may prosperous be　115
And honor'd in their issue.　　　　*They sing.*

　　　　　[Song]
Juno.　　*Honor, riches, marriage, blessing,*
　　　　　Long continuance and increasing,
　　　　　Hourly joys, be still upon you,
　　　　　Juno sings her blessing on you.　　120
Ceres.　*Earth's increase, foison plenty,*
　　　　　Barns and garners never empty,
　　　　　Vines with clust'ring bunches growing,
　　　　　Plants with goodly burthen bowing:
　　　　　Spring come to you at the farthest　　125
　　　　　In the very end of harvest!
　　　　　Scarcity and want shall shun you;
　　　　　Ceres' blessing so is on you.

　　Ferdinand. This is a most majestic vision and
Harmonious charmingly; may I be bold　　130
To think these spirits?
　　Prospero.　　　　Spirits which by mine art
I have from their confines call'd to enact
My present fancies.

40 trick: *ingenious piece of mechanism* (Arden ed.)　**44 vanity:** *illusion*　**46 Presently:**
immediately　**51 mop and mow:** *grimaces*　**55 conceive:** *understand*　**63 liver:** *popu-*
larly supposed to be the origin of the love passions　**65 corollary:** *extra spirit*　**66 pertly:**
promptly　**68 Iris:** *messenger of the gods, uniting gods and man*　**Ceres:** *goddess of agriculture*
and marriage　**69 fetches:** *'vetch,' a leguminous plant*　**71 thetch'd:** *thatched*　**stover**
fodder　**keep:** *provide with fodder*　**72 pioned and twilled;** *Cf. n.*　**73 hest:** *com-*
mand　**74 broom:** *a flowering shrub*　**76 poll-clipp'd F:** *pole-clipt*　**vineyard:** *here tri-*
syllabic　**77 stirrile:** *sterile*　**79 wat'ry arch:** *rainbow*　**messenger:** *Iris was the particular*
messenger of Juno as well as a personification of the rainbow　**80 grace:** *majesty*　**SD Juno**
... descend; *Cf. n.*　**82 amain:** *in full force*

88 bow: *rainbow*　**89 bosky:** *bushy*　**unshrubb'd down:** *rolling, treeless hills*　**93 estate:**
bestow　**98 that:** *by which*　**Dis** *Pluto, who stole Proserpine, Ceres' daughter*　**99 blind**
boy's: *Cupid's*　**scandal'd:** *scandalous*　**103 Paphos:** *one of the seats of worship of*
Venus　**106 bedrite F:** *bed-right*　**108 Mars's hot minion:** *Venus was the mistress of*
Mars; F Marses　**109 waspish-headed:** *spiteful*　**110 sparrows:** *associated with worship*
of Venus　**113 gait:** *royal walk*　**115 prosperous:** *a pun on 'Prospero's' is possible*　**119**
still: *always*　**121** *Ceres speech ascription omitted in F.*　**Earth's:** *here disyllabic (read*
'earthes')　**foison** *abundance of harvest*　**125 Spring ... farthest:** *i.e. eliminating win-*
ter　**130 charmingly:** *magically*

Ferdinand.   Let me live here ever!   *135*
So rare a wond'red father and a wise
Makes this place paradise.

Juno and Ceres whisper, and send Iris on employment.

Prospero.   Sweet now, silence.
Juno and Ceres whisper seriously.
There's something else to do—hush and be mute   *140*
Or else our spell is marr'd.
     Iris. You nymphs, call'd naiads, of the windring brooks,
With your sedg'd crowns and ever-harmless looks,
Leave your crisp channels and on this green land
Answer your summons; Juno does command.   *145*
Come, temperate nymphs, and help to celebrate
A contract of true love: be not too late.

Enter certain nymphs.

You sunburn'd sicklemen of August weary,
Come hither from the furrow and be merry;
Make holiday, your rye-straw hats put on,   *150*
And these fresh nymphs encounter every one
In country footing.

Enter certain reapers, properly habited. They join with the nymphs in a graceful dance, towards the end whereof Prospero starts suddenly and speaks, after which, to a strange hollow and confused noise, they heavily vanish.

Prospero. [*Aside.*] I had forgot that foul conspiracy
Of the beast Caliban and his confederates
Against my life. The minute of their plot   *155*
Is almost come. [*To spirits.*] Well done, avoid! no more.
     Ferdinand. This is strange! Your father's in some passion
That works him strongly.
     Miranda.   Never till this day
Saw I him touch'd with anger so distemper'd.   *160*
     Prospero. You do look, my son, in a mov'd sort,
As if you were dismay'd—be cheerful, sir.
Our revels now are ended: these our actors—
As I foretold you—were all spirits and
Are melted into air, into thin air;   *165*
And like the baseless fabric of this vision
The cloud-capp'd towers, the gorgeous palaces,
The solemn temples, the great globe itself,
Yea, all which it inherit, shall dissolve
And like this insubstantial pageant faded   *170*
Leave not a rack behind: we are such stuff
As dreams are made on, and our little life
Is rounded with a sleep. Sir, I am vex'd;
Bear with my weakness, my old brain is troubled!
Be not disturb'd with my infirmity.   *175*
If you be pleas'd, retire into my cell
And there repose; a turn or two I'll walk
To still my beating mind.

Ferdinand. Miranda. We wish your peace.   *Exeunt.*
     Prospero. Come with a thought! I thank thee, Ariel: *180*
Come!

Enter Ariel.

     Ariel. Thy thoughts I cleave to. What's thy pleasure?
     Prospero.   Spirit,
We must prepare to meet with Caliban.
     Ariel. Ay, my commander. When I presented Ceres   *185*
I thought to have told thee of it, but I fear'd
Lest I might anger thee.
     Prospero. Say again, where didst thou leave these varlets?
     Ariel. I told you, sir, they were red hot with drinking,
So full of valor that they smote the air   *190*
For breathing in their faces, beat the ground
For kissing of their feet, yet always bending
Towards their project. Then I beat my tabor,
At which like unback'd colts they prick'd their ears
Advanc'd their eyelids, lifted up their noses   *195*
As they smelt music; so I charm'd their ears
That calflike they my lowing follow'd, through
Tooth'd briers, sharp furzes, pricking goss, and thorns,
Which ent'red their frail shins. At last I left them
I' th' filthy-mantled pool beyond your cell,   *200*
There dancing up to th' chins, that the foul lake
Orestunk their feet.
     Prospero.   This was well done, my bird.
Thy shape invisible retain thou still.
The trumpery in my house, go bring it hither   *205*
For stale to catch these thieves.
     Ariel.   I go, I go.   *Exit.*
     Prospero. A devil, a born devil, on whose nature
Nurture can never stick, on whom my pains,
Humanely taken, all, all lost, quite lost,   *210*
And, as with age, his body uglier grows,
So his mind cankers. I will plague them all,
Even to roaring!

Enter Ariel, loaden with glistering apparel, etc.

Come, hang them on this line.

Enter Caliban, Stephano, and Trinculo, all wet.

Caliban. Pray you, tread softly, that the blind mole may   *215*
not hear a footfall: we are now near his cell.
     Stephano. Monster, your fairy, which you say is a harmless fairy, has done little better than play'd the Jack with us.
     Trinculo. Monster, I do smell all horse piss, at which my nose is in great indignation.   *220*
     Stephano. So is mine. Do you hear, monster: If I should take a displeasure against you—look you.
     Trinculo. Thou wert but a lost monster.
     Caliban. Good my lord, give me thy favor still.
Be patient, for the prize I'll bring thee to   *225*
Shall hoodwink this mischance. Therefore speak softly;
All's hush'd as midnight yet.

---

136 wond'red: *possessing wonder; cf. 'bearded,' 'blue-eyed,' etc. (Kittredge)* **SD Juno ... employment** *F places this after l. 137* **138 Sweet ... silence:** *to Miranda, who is about to speak* **142 windring:** *perhaps a combination of 'winding' and 'wandering'* **144 crisp:** *rippling land; Cf. n.* **146 temperate:** *chaste* **152 footing:** *dancing* **156 avoid:** *be gone* **160 distemper'd:** *unbalanced, disturbed* **161 sort:** *manner* **169 it inherit:** *possess it* **171 rack:** *moving cloud, with a possible double meaning ('wrack')* **172 on:** *of* **173 rounded with:** *'rounded off by,' or perhaps 'surrounded by.'* **178 beating:** *overwrought*

180 Come ... thought: *be summoned by mental telepathy* **thank thee** *spoken to Ariel before he appears* **185 presented:** *enacted* **186 to have:** *read 't have'* **194 unback'd:** *unbroken* **198 goss:** *gorse* **200 filthy-mantled:** *sufaced with dirty scum* **205 trumpery:** *trash, rubbish* **206 stale:** *decoy* **214 hang ... on:** *F hang on them; in F this speech precedes* **SD line;** *Cf. n.* **218 Jack:** *knave* **226 hoodwink ... mischance:** *'blind you to this misfortune'; the reference is to falconry; F hudwinke*

Trinculo. Ay, but to lose our bottles in the pool!

Stephano. There is not only disgrace and dishonor in that,
monster, but an infinite loss.   230

Trinculo. That's more to me than my wetting! Yet
this is your harmless fairy, monster.

Stephano. I will fetch off my bottle, though I be ore ears for
my labor.

Caliban. Prithee, my king, be quiet. Seest thou here,   235
This is the mouth o' th' cell! no noise and enter.
Do that good mischief which may make this island
Thine own for ever and I thy Caliban
For aye thy foot-licker.

Stephano. Give me thy hand. I do begin to have bloody   240
thoughts.

Trinculo. O King Stephano, O peer! O worthy Stephano!
Look what a wardrobe here is for thee!

Caliban. Let it alone, thou fool, it is but trash.

Trinculo. Oho, monster! We know what belongs to a   245
frippery. O King Stephano!

Stephano. Put off that gown, Trinculo. By this hand,
I'll have that gown!

Trinculo. Thy grace shall have it.

Caliban. The dropsy drown this fool! What do you mean   250
To dote thus on such luggage? Let's alone
And do the murther first: if he awake,
From toe to crown he'll fill our skins with pinches.
Make us strange stuff.

Stephano. Be you quiet, monster! Mistress line, is not   255
this my jerkin? Now is the jerkin under the line! Now, jerkin,
you are like to lose your hair and prove a bald jerkin.

Trinculo. Do, do; we steal by line and level, and't like your
grace.

Stephano. I thank thee for that jest; here's a garment   260
for't: wit shall not go unrewarded while I am king of this country! 'Steal by line and level' is an excellent pass of pate! There's
another garment for't.

Trinculo. Monster, come put some lime upon your fingers,
and away with the rest.   265

Caliban. I will have none on't—we shall lose our time
And all be turn'd to barnacles or to apes
With foreheads villainous low.

Stephano. Monster, lay-to your fingers! Help to bear this
away where my hogshead of wine is, or I'll turn you out   270
of my kingdom! Go to, carry this.

Trinculo. And this.

Stephano. Ay, and this.

*A nosie of hunters heard. Enter divers spirits in shape of dogs and
hounds, hunting them about, Prospero and Ariel setting them on.*

Prospero. Hey, Mountain, hey!

Ariel. Silver! There it goes, Silver!   275

Prospero. Fury, Fury! There, Tyrant, there! Hark, hark!
                    [*Exeunt all but Prospero and Ariel.*]
Go charge my goblins that they grind their joints
With dry convulsions, shorten up their sinews

With aged cramps, and more pinch-spotted make them
Than pard or cat-o'-mountain.   280

Ariel.   Hark, they roar!

Prospero. Let them be hunted soundly! At this hour
Lies at my mercy all mine enemies!
Shortly shall all my labors end, and thou
Shalt have the air at freedom! For a little   285
Follow, and do me service.   *Exeunt.*

ACT FIFTH ❧ SCENE FIRST

Enter Prospero in his magic robes, and Ariel.

Prospero. Now does my project gather to a head;
My charms crack not, my spirtis obey, and Time
Goes upright with his carriage. How's the day?

Ariel. On the sixt hour, at which time, my lord,
You said our work should cease.   5

Prospero.   I did say so
When first I rais'd the tempest. Say, my spirit,
How fares the king and's followers?

Ariel.   Confin'd together
In the same fashion as you gave in charge,   10
Just as you left them; all prisoners, sir,
In the line grove which weather-fends your cell;
They cannot budge till your release. The king,
His brother, and yours, abide all three distracted,
And the remainder mouring over them   15
Brimful of sorrow and dismay, but chiefly
Him that you term'd, sir, the gold old lord, Gonzalo.
His tears runs down his beard like winter's drops
From eaves of reeds. Your charm so strongly works 'em
That if you now beheld them, your affections   20
Would become tender.

Prospero.   Dost thou think so, spirit?

Ariel. Mine would, sir, were I human.

Prospero.   And mine shall.
Hast thou—which art but air—a touch, a feeling   25
Of their afflictions, and shall not myself,
One of their kind, that relish all as sharply,
Passion as they, be kindlier mov'd than thou art?
Though with their high wrongs I am struck to th' quick,
Yet with my nobler reason 'gainst my fury   30
Do I take part: the rarer action is
In virtue than in vengeance; they being penitent,
The sole drift of my purpose doth extend
Not a frown further. Go, release them, Ariel.
My charms I'll break, their senses I'll restore,   35
And they shall be themselves.

Ariel.   I'll fetch them, sir.   *Exit.*

Prospero. Ye elves of hills, brooks, standing lakes, and groves,
And yet that on the sand with printless foot
Do chase the ebbing Neptune and do fly him   40
When he comes back; you demipuppets that

242 O ... peer; *Cf. n.*   246 frippery: *old clothes shop*   251 luggage: *encum-
brance* Let's alone: *let us leave it alone (or perhaps let's is a misprint for 'let't', or alone a
misprint for 'along')*   254 strange stuff: *different cloth* (metaphorically, continuing the
idea of frippery in l. 246)   255-257 Mistress ... bald jerkin; *Cf. n.*   258 we ... level;
Cf. n. and't like: *if it please*   262 pass of pate: *rapier thrust of wit, sally*   264 lime;
Cf. n.   267 barnacles: *probably the barnacle goose, thought to hatch from a sea shell*

280 pard: *leopard* cat-o'-mountain: *catamount, lynx*   3 Goes ... carriage: *walks with
erect carriage, instead of bowing under his burden* How's the day?: *what time is it?*   12
weather-fends: *protects from the weather*   13 your release: *released by you*   19 reeds: *a
thatched roof*   20 affections: *feelings*   25-29 *Cf. n.*   27 all: *fully*   31 rarer:
finer   38-46 Ye elves ... *Prospero draws a circle on the ground as he calls upon the spirits;
see SD below*   41 demipuppets: *half the size of puppets*

By moonshine do the green sour ringlets make,
Whereof the ewe not bites; and you whose pastime
Is to make midnight mushrumps, that rejoice
To hear the solemn curfew, by whose aid,   45
Weak masters though ye be, I have bedimm'd
The noontide sun, call'd forth the mutinous winds,
And 'twixt the green sea and the azur'd vault
Set roaring war; to the dread, rattling thunder
Have I given fire, and rifted Jove's stout oak   50
With his own bolt; the strong-bas'd promontory
Have I made shake and by the spurs puck'd up
The pine and cedar. Graves at my command
Have wak'd their sleepers, op'd and let 'em forth
By my so potent art. But this rough magic   55
I here abjure, and when I have requir'd
Some heavenly music—which even now I do—
To work mine end upon their senses, that
This airy charm is for, I'll break my staff,
Bury it certain fadoms in the earth,   60
And deeper than did ever plummet sound
I'll drown my book.

*Solemn music. Here enters Ariel before, then Alonso, with a
frantic gesture, attended by Gonzalo; Sebastian and Antonio in
like manner attended by Adrian and Francisco. They all enter the
circle which Prospero had made and there stand carm'd; which
Prospero observing, speaks.*

A solemn air and the best comforter
To an unsettled fancy, cure thy brains,
Now useless, boil'd wihin thy skull; there stand,   65
For you are spell-stopp'd.
Holy Gonzalo, honorable man,
Mine eyes, ev'n sociable to the show of thine,
Fall fellowly drops. The charm dissolves apace,
And as the morning steals upon the night,   70
Melting the darkness, so their rising senses
Begin to chase the ignorant fumes that mantle
Their clearer reason. O good Gonzalo,
My true preserver and a loyal sir
To him thou follow'st! I will pay thy graces   75
Home both in word and deed. Most cruelly
Didst thou, Alonso, use me and my daughter.
Thy brother was a furtherer in the act.
Thou art pinch'd for't now, Sebastian. Flesh and blood,
You, brother mine, that entertain'd ambition,   80
Expell'd remorse and nature, who, with Sebastian—
Whose inward pinches, therefore, are most strong—
Would here have kill'd your king: I do forgive thee,
Unnatural though thou art. Their understanding
Begins to swell, and the approaching tide   85
Will shortly fill the reasonable shores
That now lie foul and muddy. Not one of them

That yet looks on me or would know me. Ariel,
Fetch me the hat and rapier in my cell.
I will discase me, and myself present   90
As I was sometime Milan—quickly, spirit!
Thou shalt ere long be free.

Ariel [after fetching the clothes] sings and helps to attire him.

[Song]
*Ariel. Where the bee sucks there suck I;
     In a cowslip's bell I lie;
     There I couch when owls do cry;*   95
     *On the bat's back I do fly
       After summer merrily.
     Merrily, merrily shall I live now
     Under the blossom that hangs on the bough.*

Prospero. Why that's my dainty Ariel! I shall miss thee,   100
But yet thou shalt have freedom—so, so, so.
To the king's ship, invisible as thou art!
There shalt thou find the mariners asleep
Under the hatches. The master and the boatswain
Being awake, enforce them to this place,   105
And presently, I prithee.
Ariel. I drink the air before me and return
Or ere your pulse twice beat.   *Exit.*
Gonzalo. All torment, trouble, wonder, and amazement
Inhabits here! Some heavenly power guide us   110
Out of this fearful country!
Prospero.   Behold, Sir King,
The wronged Duke of Milan, Prospero!
For more assurance that a living prince
Does now speak to thee, I embrace thy body,   115
And to thee and thy company I bid
A hearty welcome.
Alonso.   Where thou beest he or no,
Or some enchanted trifle to abuse me—
As late I have been—I not know. Thy pulse   120
Beats as of flesh and blood, and since I saw thee
Th' affliction of my mind amends, with which
I fear a madness held me! This must crave—
And if this be at all—a most strange story.
Thy dukedom I resign and do entreat   125
Thou pardon me my wrongs. But how should Prospero
Be living and be here?
Prospero.   First, noble friend,
Let me embrace thine age, whose honor cannot
Be measur'd or confin'd.   130
Gonzalo.   Whether this be
Or be not I'll not swear.
Prospero.   You do yet taste
Some subtleties o' th' isle, that will not let you
Believe things certain. Welcome, my friends all,   135
[Aside to Sebastian and Antonio.] But you, my brace
of lords; were I so minded
I here could pluck his Highness' frown upon you
And justify you traitors! At this time

---

42 **green sour ringlets:** *'the underground part* (mycelium) *of a toadstool, which affects the grass roots'* (Arden ed.)   44 **mushrumps:** *mushrooms*   58, 59 **their . . . for:** *the senses of those this airy charm is for*   59 **airy charm:** *play on two meanings of airy ('of the air' and 'of music') and two of charm ('magic' and 'song')*   63 **air:** *melody*   64 **thy:** *Prospero addresses Alonso*   65 **boil'd:** *overwrought;* F boile, *probably a misprint of* e *for* d   68 **sociable:** *sympathetic* **show:** *sight*   69 **Fall:** *let fall, shed*   72 **ignorant fumes:** *fumes that make them ignorant* (oblivious)   75, 76 **pay . . . Home:** *repay your kindness*   77 **Didst:** F Did   80 **entertain'd:** *was host to;* F entertaine   81 **who:** F whom   86 **shores:** *i.e. of reason;* F shore

90 **discase:** *remove my magic robe*   91 **sometime:** *formerly* **Milan:** *Duke of Milan* **After:** *following after*   106 **presently:** *immediately*   108 **Or ere:** *before*   114 **For more assurance:** *to give you more proof.*   118 **Where:** *whether*   119 **enchanted trifle:** *unsubstantial sirit* **abuse:** *deceive*   123 **crave:** *necessitate*   124 **And if:** *if*   129 **age:** *aged body*   134 **subtleties:** *illusions, especially disguised confections*   135 **certain:** *real*   139 **justify:** *prove*

I will tell no tales.   *140*
   Sebastian.   The divel speaks in him!
   Prospero.   No!
For you, most wicked sir, whom to call brother
Would even infect my mouth, I do forgive
Thy rankest fault—all of them—and require   *145*
My dukedom of thee, which perforce I know
Thou must restore.
   Alonso.   If thou beest Prospero
Give us particulars of thy preservation,
How thou hast met us here who three hours since   *150*
Were wrack'd upon this shore, where I have lost—
How sharp the point of this remembrance is—
My dear son Ferdinand.
   Prospero.   I am woe for't, sir.
   Alonso. Irreparable is the loss, and patience   *155*
Says it is past her cure.
   Prospero.   I rather think
You have not sought for help, of whose soft grace
For the like loss I have her sovereign aid,
And rest myself content.   *160*
   Alonso.   You the like loss?
   Prospero. As great to me as late, and supportable
To make the dear loss have I means much weaker
Than you may call to comfort you, for I
Have lost my daughter.   *165*
   Alonso.   A daughter?
O heavens that they were living both in Naples,
The king and queen there; that they were I wish
Myself were mudded in that oozy bed
Where my son lies! When did you lose your daughter?   *170*
   Prospero. In this last tempest. I perceive these lords
At this encounter do so much admire
That they devour their reason and scarce think
Their eyes do offices of truth; their words
Are natural breath; but howsoe'er you have   *175*
Been justled from your senses, know for certain
That I am Prospero and that very duke
Which was thrust forth of Milan, who most strangely
Upon this shore, where you were wrack'd, was landed
To be the lord on't. No more yet of this,   *180*
For 'tis a chronicle of day by day,
Not a relation for a breakfast, nor
Befitting this first meeting. Welcome, sir.
This cell's my court; here have I few attendants,
And subjects none abroad; pray you look in.   *185*
My dukedom since you have given me again
I will requite you with as good a thing,
At least bring forth a wonder to content ye
As much as me my dukedom.

Here Prospero discovers Ferdinand and Miranda playing at chess.

   Miranda. Sweet lord, you play me false.   *190*
   Ferdinand. No, my dearest love,
I would not for the world.
   Mirando. Yes, for a score of kingdoms you should wrangle,

And I would call it fair play.
   Alonso.   If this prove   *195*
A vision of the island, one dear son
Shall I twice lose.
   Sebastian.   A most high miracle.
   Ferdinand. [Seeing Alonso.] Though the seas threaten,
they are merciful.   *200*
I have curs'd them without cause.
   Alonso.   Now all the blessings
Of a glad father compass thee about!
Arise and say how thou cam'st here.
   Miranda.   O wonder!   *205*
How many goodly creatures are there here!
How beauteous mankind is! O brave new world
That has such people in't.
   Prospero.   'Tis new to thee.
   Alonso. What is this maid, with whom thou wast at play?   *210*
Your eld'st acquaintance cannot be three hours!
Is she the goddess that hath sever'd us
And brought us thus together?
   Ferdinand.   Sir, she is mortal,
But by immortal Providence she's mine.   *215*
I chose her when I could not ask my father
For his advice—nor thought I had one. She
Is daughter to this famous Duke of Milan,
Of whom so often I have heard renown
But never saw before, of whom I have   *220*
Receiv'd a second life; and second father
This lady makes him to me.
   Alonso.   I am hers.
But O, how oddly will it sound that I
Must ask my child forgiveness?   *225*
   Prospero.   There sir, stop.
Let us not burthen our remembrance with
A heaviness that's gone.
   Gonzalo.   I have inly wept,
Or should have spoken ere this. Look down, you gods,   *230*
And on this couple drop a blessed crown,
For it is you that have chalk'd forth the way
Which brought us hither.
   Alonso.   I say amen, Gonzalo.
   Gonzalo. Was Milan thrust from Milan, that his issue   *235*
Should become kings of Naples? O rejoice
Beyond a common joy, and set it down
With gold on lasting pillars: in one voyage
Did Claribel her husband find at Tunis,
And Ferdinand her brother found a wife   *240*
Where he himself was lost; Prospero his dukedom
In a poor isle; and all of us ourselves,
When no man was his own.
   Alonso.   Give me your hands.
Let grief and sorrow still embrace his heart   *245*
That doth not wish you joy.
   Gonzalo.   Be it so, amen.

Enter Ariel, with the Master and Boatswain amazedly following.

O look, sir, look, sir, here is more of us!
I prophesied if a gallows were on land

---

150 who: *F* whom   **154 am woe for't:** *grive because of it*   **155 patience:** *fortitude*   **158 grace:** *mercy*   **162 late:** *recent*   **supportable:** *stressed* $\cup\;—\;—\;\cup\;—$ **163 dear:** *great*   **168 that:** *provided that*   **172 admire:** *marvel*   **173 devour their reason:** *their reason is swallowed up by amazement*   **SD Prospero pulls aside the curtain to the inner stage**   **193, 194 Yes … play;** *Cf. n.*

211 eld'st: *longest*   **219 renown:** *excellent report*   **223 am hers:** *accept her as my daughter*   **227 remembrance:** *F* remembrances; *see I.2.202; Cf. n. his own master of himself*   **245 still:** *always*   **SD amazedly:** *as in a maze*

This fellow could not drown! Now, blasphemy, 250
That swear'st grace oreboard, not an oath on shore?
Hast thou no mouth by land? What is the news?
    Boatswain. The best news is that we have safely found
Our king and company: the next, our ship
Which but three glasses since we gave out split 255
Is tight and yare, and bravely rigg'd as when
We first put out to sea.
    Ariel.   Sir, all this service
Have I done since I went.
    Prospero.   My trisksy spirit! 260
    Alonso. These are not natural events, they strengthen
From strange to stranger! Say, how came you hither?
    Boatswain. If I did think, sir, I were well awake,
I'd strive to tell you! We were dead of sleep
And—how we know not—all clapp'd under hatches, 265
Where, but even now, with strange and several noises
Of roaring, shrieking, howling, jingling chains,
And mo diversity of sounds, all horrible,
We wre awak'd—straightway at liberty,
Where we, in all our trim, freshly beheld 270
Our royal, good, and gallant ship, our master
Cap'ring to eye her. On a trice, so please you,
Even in a dream, were we divided from them
And were brought moping hither.
    Ariel.   Was't well done? 275
    Prospero. Bravely, my diligence; thou shalt be free.
    Alonso. This is as strange a maze as ere men trod,
And there is in this business more than nature
Was ever conduct of! Some oracle
Must rectify our knowledge. 280
    Prospero.   Sir, my liege,
Do not infest your mind with beating on
The strangeness of this business; at pick'd leisure,
Which shall be shortly, single I'll resolve you—
Which to you shall seem probable—of every 285
These happen'd accidents; till when be cheerful
And think of each thing well. Come hither, spirit.
Set Caliban and his companions free:
Untie the spell.   *[Exit Ariel.]*
            How fares my gracious sir? 290
There are yet missing of your company
Some few odd lads that you remember not.

*Enter Ariel, driving in Caliban, Stephano, and Trinculo in their
stolne apparel.*

    Stephano. Every man shift for all the rest, and let no man
take care for himself, for all is but fortune—*coragio*, bully-
monster, *coragio!* 295
    Trinculo. If these be true spies which I wear in my head,
here's a goodly sight.
    Caliban. O Setebos, these be brave spirits indeed!
How fine my master is! I am afraid
He will chastise me. 300
    Sebastian.   Ha ha!

What things are these, my Lord Antonio?
Will money buy 'em?
    Antonio.   Very like! One of them
Is a plain fish and no doubt marketable. 305
    Prospero. Mark but the badges of these men, my lords,
Then say if they be true. This misshapen knave
His mother was a witch and one so strong
That could control the moon, make flows and ebbs,
And deal in her command without her pow'r. 310
These three have robb'd me, and this demi-divel,
For he's a bastard one, had plotted with them
To take my life. Two of these fellows you
Must know and own, this thing of darkness I
Acknowledge mine. 315
    Caliban.   I shall be pinch'd to death.
    Alonso. Is not this Stephano, my drunken butler?
    Sebastian. He is drunk now; where had he wine?
    Alonso. And Trinculo is reeling ripe! Where should they
Find this grand liquor that hath gilded 'em? 320
How cam'st thou in this pickle?
    Trinculo. I have bin in such a pickle since I saw you last
that I fear me will never out of my bones; I shall not fear fly-
blowing.
    Sebastian. Why, how now Stephano? 325
    Stephano. O touch me not! I am not Stephano but a cramp.
    Prospero. You'd be king o' the isle, sirrah?
    Stephano. I should have been a sore one then.
    Alonso. This is a strange thing as ere I look'd on.
    Prospero. He is as disproportion'd in his manners 330
As in his shape! Go, sirrah, to my cell;
Take with you your companions—as you look
To have my pardon, trim it handsomely.
    Caliban. Ay, that I will! and I'll be wise hereafter
And seek for grace! What a thrice-double ass 335
Was I to take this drunkard for a god
And worship this dull fool!
    Prospero.   Go to, away!
    Alonso. Hence, and bestow your luggage where you found it.
    Sebastian. Or stole it, rather. 340
           [Exeunt Caliban, Stephano, and Trinculo.]
    Prospero. Sir, I invite your Highness and your train
To my poor cell, where you shall take your rest
For this one night, which, part of it, I'll waste
With such discourse as I not doubt shall make it
Go quick away: the story of my life 345
And the particular accidents gone by
Since I came to this isle; and in the morn
I'll bring you to your ship, and so to Naples,
Where I have hope to see the nuptial
Of these our dear belov'd solemnized, 350
And thence retire me to my Milan, where
Every third thought shall be my grave.

---

255 but three glasses since: *only three hours ago*   **256 yare:** *ready*   **260 tricksy:** *brisk*   *Cf. n.*   **264 of sleep:** *asleep*   **266 several:** *distinct*   **268 mo:** *more*   **270 our trim;** *Cf. n.*   **272 On:** *in*   **274 moping:** *bewildered*   **276 diligence:** *industrious one*   **279 conduct:** *conductor*   **282 infest:** *annoy*   **283 at pick'd leisure:** *at a free moment we will choose*   **284 single:** *privately*   **285 every:** *every one of*   **292 few odd:** *several*   **294 coragio:** *courage*   **bully-monster:** *good fellow of a monster*

306 badges; *Cf. n.*   **307, 308 knave His mother:** *knave's mother*   **309 flows:** *tides*   **310 deal . . . pow'r:** *do all the moon could do without assistance from the moon*   **311 demi-divel:** *half a devil (offspring of a witch and the devil Setebos)*   **319 reeling ripe:** *ripe (ready) for reeling*   **320 gilded:** *common term for 'made drunk'—but in combination with 'grand liquor' probably also a play on the alchemical elixir which was supposed to turn base metals to gold*   **321 pickle:** *drunken state*   **322 pickle:** *brine, in reference to the dousing in the horse pond*   **323 that:** *as*   **323, 324 I . . . fly-blowing:** *i.e. because he was so pickled, flies would not touch him*   **328 sore:** *a pun: 'causing pain' and 'feeling pain'*   **347 accidents:** *incidents*   **350 solemnized:** *stressed — ⌣ — ⌣*

Alonso.   I long
To hear the story of your life, which must
Take the ear strangely.   *355*
     Prospero.   I'll deliver all,
And promise you calm seas, auspicious gales,
And sail so expeditious that shall catch
Your royal fleet far off. My Ariel, chick,
That is thy charge—then to the elements   *360*
Be free, and fare thou well! Please you, draw near.
                             Exeunt omnes.

EPILOGUE

Spoken by Prospero

Now my charms are all o'erthrown,
And what strength I have's mine own,
Which is most faint. Now, 'tis true,
I must be here confin'd by you
Or sent to Naples. Let me not,
Since I have my dukedom got
And pardon'd the deceiver, dwell
In this bare island by your spell,
But release me from my bands
With the help of your good hands!
Gentle breath of yours my sails
Must fill or else my project fails,
Which was to please. Now I want
Spirits to enforce, art to enchant,
And my ending is despair
Unless I be reliev'd by prayer
Which pierces so that it assaults
Mercy itself and frees all faults.
     As you from crimes would pardon'd be,
     Let your indulgence set me free.   *Exit.*

❦ FINIS ❦

356 deliver: *relate*

NOTES

The Actors' Names. Based upon the list of character appended to the Folio text of the play.

councilor. The Folio (cited throughout as F) prints *councellor*; the modern 'councilor,' a member of a council, was earlier spelled 'counselor.'

Act I. F divides this play into acts and scenes throughout.

I.i.3. *Good.* Answering the Boatswain's question, the Master tells him to take heart (be of 'good cheer'). Cf. *cheerly* in l. 5 and 'Cheerly, good hearts' in l. 23. F's punctuation (colons after *Good* and *mariners*) suggests that the meaning is not 'good fellow,' as in l. 17 below, where F has no punctuation after *good*.

I.i.7. *Blow . . . enough.* A bravado taunt to the wind: 'Blow until you burst your belly, so long as we have sea room enough!' Cf. *Pericles*, III.1.49.

I.i.15. *cares.* Variant plural form of verb. Instances of seemingly singular verb and plural subject, as well as many other constructions now considered to be grammatical lapses, are common in Shakespeare and illustrate the fluidity of Elizabethan grammar. That they are not compositor's erros is evidenced by their frequent occurrence in manuscripts.

I.i.30. *Down . . . topmast.* For a discussion of this and other nautical expressions consult the Furness Variorum Edition. Shakespeare uses these terms accurately and precisely.

I.i.44. *ahold.* This may be a variant of a-hull, 'hove-to' (or a printer's error for *a-holl*). See discussion by H. B. Allen, *MLN*, 52 (1937), 96–100, cited in Arden ed. (1954), p. 7.

I.i.45–49. These lines are often arranged by editors as blank verse.

I.i.47. *must . . . cold.* A euphemism for 'must we die?' Some editors insist that here the Boatswain drinks from a bottle, but there is no textual evidence that Antonio's charge in l. 51 is just.

I.i.53. *washing . . . tides.* Pirates were hanged at low-water level in the Thames and left until three tides had washed over their bodies.

I.II.22. *more better.* Double comparative for emphasis, common in Shakespeare and other Elizabethan writers.

I.ii.29. *magic garment.* The cloak which invests Prospero with power over the elements and humans.

I.ii.34. *soil.* F soule, but cf. ll. 34–36 with ll. 254 below, and in II.1.63–106. The alternative is to keep *soule,* follow it with a dash, and assume an anacoluthon.

I.ii.35. *hair.* A possible pun on *hair—heir.* Cf. the talk of Alonso's loss of a daughter and son in II.1.72–110, especially ll. 108–110. Fathers and heirs are much on Prospero's mind; see above, ll. 20–24; below, ll. 66 ff., especially l. 69.

I.ii.70. *And princess.* So F. Most editors emend to 'A princess,' but the F text is syntactically satisfactory.

I.ii.96. *trash for overtopping.* To trash was to check a hound with a long weight. To overtop was to run ahead of the pack.

I.ii.107, 108. *With . . . rate.* I.e. 'with that which, save that it kept me in retirement from the world and my duties, surpassed in value everything the world rates highly.'

I.ii.113. *lorded.* By construing this as an intransitive verb (with OED authority) we may retain the F full stop after *exact* in l. 115. The alternative is to change the preceding or following full stop to a comma and construe *lorded* as a past participle (so OED on this passage): 'he being thus made a lord.'

I.ii.115–118. *Like . . . lie.* I.e. 'like one who, having to make his lie credible by frequently repeating it, has come to believe it himself and so made a sinner of his memory.'

I.ii.198. *Now I arise.* Prospero may have suited the action to the word, though in that case the clause is unnecessary. More probably he refers to the change in his fortune; cf. below, ll. 209, 210, 212.

I.ii.202. *princess.* I.e. 'than any other princess can have made for her.' The word may have been 'princesses' (nouns ending in s were often identical in singular and plural). A third possibility is 'princes.' See Helge Kökeritz, *Shakespeare's Pronunciation* (New Haven, 1953), p. 318.

I.ii.212, 213. A reference to the astrological belief that the position of the stars at the time of an action may determine its outcome.

I.ii.217. *canst not choose.* Having resumed his magic mantle, Prospero has 'charmed' his daughter.

I.ii.268. *still-vex'd Bermoothes.* The only time in the play that the Bermudas are mentioned, in spite of the fact that accounts of a wreck in 1609 off the coast of 'these traditionally stormy isles appear to be among the sources of the play. See Sources of the Play.

I.ii.292. *Told thee . . . made thee.* Inclusion of the second *thee* distorts the rhythm of the line to such an extent that we may safely assume it to be a copyist's

or compositor's error caused by the two preceding phrases 'done thee' and 'Told thee.'

I.ii.319. *blue-ey'd.* Blue veins in the eyelids were thought to be a symptom of pregnancy. Cf. *The Duchess of Malfi*, II.1.67.

I.ii.323. *earthy.* Ariel, a spirit of the air, could not perform deeds partaking wholly of the nature of earth. Each of the four elements—earth, air, fire, and water—was thought to have its own spirits.

I.ii.395. *strok'st.* For the loss of the past tense ending in such consonant clusters see Kökeritz, *Shakespeare's Pronunciation*, p. 303.

I.ii.400. *place.* This may be plural. See note on l. 202 above.

I.ii.415–426. Most editors assign this speech to Prospero, who is a likely candidate, but cf. II.2.131. The kindness and the pity are as characteristic of Miranda as of Prospero.

I.ii.442–453. The song may have been sung to a dance of sea nymphs, hence the reference to sands and waves. The curtsey and kiss were the salutations at the beginning of the dance. F is not clear concerning the lineation of the burden, which has been here slightly altered.

I.ii.515. *his brave son.* This character does not appear in the play. Since F has a comma after *son, his* could refer to the king of Naples were it not for the inescapable fact that Ferdinand could not call himself *brave.*

I.ii.555. *My . . . tutor.* In Shakespeare's day the conception was strong that for a harmonious society everything must find and retain its appointed function. For examples of this homily of the head and foot see Arden ed., p. 40.

II.i.18–20. The obvious pun *dollar—dolour* relies on two meanings of 'entertain': to occupy the attention of, and to provide with food and drink.

II.i.35. *A laughter.* 'The whole number of eggs laid by a fowl before she is ready to sit' (OED), with an obvious quibble on the common meaning of *laughter.*

II.i.38, 39. Editors usually reassign l. 38 to Antonio and l. 39 to Sebastian. The problem may also be resolved by assuming that *you're* is a mistake for *you've,* the loser having to laugh (to cackle like a fowl who has just laid an egg?); or that Sebastian, unable to contain himself, laughed first, and Antonio sarcastically reproved him by pretending he had won.

II.i.63. *glosses.* Probably not a mistake for the singular, as many editors believe, but plural because of the plural *garments*—as one might say, 'Gentlemen, put on your hats,' rather than 'hat.'

II.i.80. *Widow Dido.* Dido is a character in Virgil's *Aeneid.* Gonzalo may have pronounced *Dido* to rhyme with *Widow* and thus aroused Antonio's scorn, increased by Gonzalo's assertion of the continuity of Carthage and the modern Tunis. Tunis is another city, near the site of ancient Carthage.

II.i.102. *fish'd for.* The word *sort* was groped for and well chosen, since (Antonio implies) the doublet is not so fresh as Gonzalo believes; *fish'd* suggests the brine from which Gonzalo has recently pulled himself. A *sort* was a group of things, a gathering, hence possibly a catch of fish.

II.i.146. *Fowl.* Pun on *fowl—foul,* and possibly to be associated with 'fool'; see Kökeritz, *Shakespeare's Pronunciation*, pp. 75, 109, 149. The jest of *fowl—foul* lies in the fact that Gonzalo has been called an 'old cock' (l. 33, above; cf. to l. 35).

II.i.153–176. From Florio's translation of Montaigne, bk. I, ch. 30. See Sources of the Play. Gonzalo is not so serious as the ill-natured Sebastian and Antonio pretend—he is attempting both to divert Alonso from the subject of his grief and to bait Sebastian and Antonio, see ll. 181–183, below.

II.i.176. *'Save.* In 1606 an act was passed prohibiting the jesting use of the name of God on the stage. The omission of 'God' in this line may have been due to this prohibition.

II.i.189. *sphere.* According to the Ptolemaic conception of the universe there were seven planets revolving about the earth, each in its own sphere. The moon's sphere was closest to the earth.

II.i.191. *go a-batfowling.* Hunt birds at night with long clubs (bats). The birds were roused from their sleep in low trees and knocked down as they flew about bewilderedly. Gonzalo is the bird they are knocking down; cf. above, ll. 33, 147, and note to l. 35.

II.i.203–206. The lineation has been slightly altered from F.

II.i.261. *hope.* Sebastian uses the word to mean 'expectation'; Antonio adds the meaning 'desire' (Kittredge).

II.i.277, 278. *what . . . discharge.* What happens in the future will depend on how we discharge our duty to make you king.

III.i.15. *Most . . . it.* Elliptical construction: 'when I am most busy I seem

least busy, because I think these sweet thoughts of Miranda.' It is a summarizing conclusion to the whole speech.

III.i.38. *visitation.* Play on the obvious meaning of the word and its other meaning of bubonic plague, which was thought to be a visitation of the wrath of God on sinful man.

III.i.70–74. The Arden ed. (p. 75) suggests a very satisfying rearrangement of these lines which eliminates the metrical irregularities.

III.ii.123, 124. *picture of No-body.* A printer named John Trundle used a picture of a man without a body as the sign of his shop. In 1606 he sold a play called *No-body and Some-body,* the title page of which bears a picture of this sign (Var. Ed.).

III.iii.SD. *Prosper on the top.* Prospero appears on the upper stage or acting space, looking down upon the action. In F ll. 24, 25 are placed after the SD *Enter . . . depart. Banket* was a common spelling of 'banquet' (a light supper) and indicates the pronunciation.

III.iii.28. *phoenix.* Mythical bird thought to be unique and endowed with the ability to immolate itself and rise from its own ashes.

III.iii.61. *putter . . . one.* In the days when travel to a foreign country was an exceedingly hazardous undertaking, it was the custom of travelers to lay wagers against their safe return, the odds being five to one in favor of the traveler.

III.iii.69. *surfeited.* Should probably be read, *surfeit,* an alternative past participle. Note also other probable contractions in this speech: *being* (monosyllable), *I have* ('I've'), and *even* ('e'en').

IV.i.3. *third.* A good share. Kittredge's conjecture cannot be bettered: Since life consists of past, present, and future, and since Prospero lives for his daughter (l.4), in a sense she is his future, i.e. one-third of his life. In l. 4 *Or* has the effect of 'Or in other words.'

IV.i.29. *worser genius.* It was thought that two spirits, a good and a bad, fought for control of each man.

IV.i.72. *pioned and twilled.* Probably 'trenched' (cf. 'pioner' and 'pioneer,' a digger of trenches) and 'grained' (like twill cloth, e.g.) from the winter weather. A contrast is drawn between the banks of a river in early spring and the same banks covered with April verdure.

IV.i.SD. *Juno . . . descend.* This SD from F is often omitted, on the ground that Juno does not enter until l. 115, but there seems no good reason to doubt the authority of F. From the hints of ll. 41, 84, and 105 it seems likely that a stage machine lowered her sufficiently to provide the spectacle of a flying chariot moving across the stage. She could have been deposited at the proper time to take her entrance cue.

IV.i.144. *land.* This may be 'laund,' a glade, a later form of which is the modern 'lawn.' Cf. *3 Henry VI,* III.1.2.

IV.i.214. *line.* Probably a lime or linden tree (cf. 'line grove' below, V.1.10; and there is good authority elsewhere). The alternative is a clothes line.

IV.i.242. *O . . . peer.* 'In *Oth.,* II.iii.82-89, are two stanzas of a ballad printed in Percy's *Reliques,* entitled "Take thy old cloak about thee"; one of these is as follows: "King Stephen was a worthy peere, His breeches cost him but a crowne,/He held them sixpence all too deere;/Therefore he called the taylor Lowne." Hence Trinculo's remark, "What a wardrobe" ' (Arden ed., p. 107).

IV.i.255–257. *Mistress . . . bald jerkin.* The meaning of this passage is largely dependent on the stage business, which was very likely on the vulgar side. It is necessary to remember that 'under the line,' meaning 'below the equator' (a fitting nautical term in Stephano's mouth) meant also 'under the lime tree' (see note above on l. 217). Although the jerkin could have been a hair or fur jerkin, the point of the jest of ll. 258–260 remains obscure unless we remember that 'loin' and 'line' were homonyms (Kökeritz, *Shakespeare's Pronunciation,* p. 125). The drunken Stephano lifts the jerkin off the line (tree) and passes it between his legs (under the line—loin) with an indecent motion (jerkin'). Losing the hair was one of the supposed effects of syphillis (cf. *Measure for Measure,* I.2.32, 33), hence the *bald* (with double-entendre) jerkin afterward.

IV.i.258. *we . . . level.* Trinculo adds to the puns on *line:* 'by line and level' means by mason's plumb line and level, hency 'by rule,' 'skilfully.' But in view of the preceding business and the proximity of the lime tree, a pun on *steal—stale* is almost inevitable. To stale was to urinate (said of horses, dogs, etc.). The word is ironic in the light of *stale* in l. 209 above.

IV.i.264. *lime.* Still another play on line-linden-lime tree. The reference is to the catching of birds by placing sticky lime on trees.

V.i.25–29. If you, who are composed of nothing but air, have been able to feel some compassion for their troubled state, shall not I, human like themselves and able to experience emotion fully as sharply, be moved more than you to behave as a human and take pity on them?

V.i.193, 194. *Yes . . . play.* I agree that you would not cheat, and even if you disputed over twenty kingdoms (instead of this insignificant game of chess), I would still insist you would not cheat.

V.i.270. *our trim.* An important aspect of the clothes imagery in this play is the fact that no one's clothes sustained as much as a blemish, with the exception of Stephano's and Trinculo's. Here the Boatswain is using a nautical term to express the idea.

V.i.306. *badges.* Either the insignia of Prospero attached to the shoulders of the coats, as was customary on the clothing of retainers, or, figuratively, the stolen coats themselves as badges of their guilt.

Venus and Adonis, Lucrece, and the Minor Poems

The Sonnets

Edited by ALBERT FEUILLERAT
and
EDWARD BLISS REED

Contents

Venus and Adonis, Lucrece, and the Minor Poems

INTRODUCTION

THE SOURCES AND COMPOSITION OF 'VENUS AND ADONIS'

Adonis, the incestuous son of Myrrha by Theias, King of Assyria (or Cinyras), was so beautiful that the goddess of love became enamoured of him. And all the ancient writers who have related the story, from Panyasis and Apollodorus down to Ovid, agree in making the youth respond to Venus's love. So much so that Zeus having decided that during four months Adonis should be left to himself, the eight remaining months being divided between Persephone and Aphrodite, the boy chose to spend with Aphrodite the months at his own disposal. In Shakespeare's poem, on the contrary, Adonis being courted by Venus is indifferent to the love proffered and even manifests unfeigned repugnance.

Critics generally explain this peculiar treatment of the well-known legend by supposing that Shakespeare combined the narrative of the Adonic fable as told in Ovid's *Metamorphoses* (X, 503-759) with another episode borrowed from the same source, viz., the wooing of Hermaphroditus by the nymph Salmacis (*Met.*, IV, 285-588). But the confusion of the two Ovidian stories had certainly been made, in England, before Shakespeare wrote his *Venus and Adonis*. A certain resistance on the part of Adonis is implied in Spenser's description of the arras of Castle Joyous (*Fairy Queen*, III, i, xxxiv-xxxviii); Adonis's bashfulness is taken for granted by Robert Greene in a 'conceited dittie' sung by Infida in *Never too Late* (1590), which tells of Venus's ineffectual courtship of 'sweet Adon' who dares not 'glaunce his eye' on the goddess. The poem ends as follows:

Wilt thou let thy Venus die?
  N'oseres-vous, mon bel amy,
Adon were unkinde say I,
  Je vous en prie, pitie me:

.   .   .   .

To let Venus die for woe,
  N'oseres-vous, mon bel amy,
That doth love sweete Adon so,
  Je vous en prie, pitie me.

And Marlowe, in his *Hero and Leander* (12-14), speaks of Adonis's indifference as if it were a well-known thing:

. . . Venus in her naked glory strove
To please the careless and disdainful eyes
Of proud Adonis, that before her lies.

To these instances might be added Constable's 'Shepherd's Song of Venus and Adonis,' if it were not pretty certain that this piece is an imitation of Shakespeare's poem. There must have existed some common source to these English versions of the legend; but this source I have been unable to discover.

It cannot be doubted, however, that Shakespeare was also acquainted with Ovid's treatment of the theme, for several passages in *Venus and Adonis* echo the Latin text (cf. notes on 615-618, 631, 673-678, 883-884, 1115-1116, 1168, and Dürnhöfer, *Venus and Adonis in Verhältnis zu Ovids Metamorphosen*, pp. 35-38). It is no less certain that Shakespeare used Book VIII (ll. 281-297) of the *Metamorphoses* for the description of the Calydonian boar (cf. note on 619-630). The story of Narcissus and Echo (*Met.*, III) may also have provided a hint for the allusion to Narcissus's infatuation with his own person in lines 161, 162, and for Venus's 'wailing note' in lines 829 and following.

On the other hand, Sir Sidney Lee believes that Shakespeare may have been influenced by some of the Italian writers who treated the same subject early in the sixteenth century, such as Lodovico Dolce (*La Favola d' Adone*, 1545), Metello Giovanni Tarchagnota (*L' Adone*, 1550), Girolamo Parabosco (*La Favola d' Adone*, before 1557). 'There are,' he writes, 'too many details peculiar to Shakespeare's poem and to its Italian predecessors, to preclude the suggestion that Shakespeare was acquainted with the latter and absorbed some of their ornaments and episodes.' But this is, no doubt, crediting Shakespeare with a more intimate knowledge of Italian literature than he probably had. In the same way, Sir Sidney Lee finds that 'in the minute description in Shakespeare's poem of the chase of the hare (673-708), there are curious resemblances to the "Ode de la Chasse" (on a stag hunt) by the French dramatist, Estienne Jodelle, in his (*Œuvres et Mélanges Poétiques* (1974).' I must own that I fail to see where the likeness comes in.

More to the point is the comparison which is sometimes made with Lodge's *Scyllas Metamorphosis*, usually called by its running title, *Glaucus and Scylla*, published in 1589. The subject of Lodge's poem is also borrowed from Ovid and it tells of the unrequited love of a woman wooing a reluctant youth. It contains a passage describing Venus's despair at Adonis's death; the metre is the same as the one adopted by Shakespeare, and there are a few resemblances in thought and imagery (cf. notes on 329-336, 589-590). Lodge's poem may have had some influence upon Shakespeare's choice of his subject.

Marlowe's *Hero and Leander* has also been considered as one of Shakespeare's models, and, indeed, echoes of Marlovian thoughts are distinctly heard in a certain number of passages (cf. notes on 3, 263, 264, 720, 751, 768). But none of the similarities recorded is striking enough to be an indisputable proof of the influence of Marlowe on Shakespeare. *Hero and Leander* was licensed for the press on Sept. 28, 1593—several months after *Venus and Adonis*—and it was not published until 1598. It is not improbable that Shakespeare had read Marlowe's poem in manuscript, but it is impossible to prove that he had.

The metre employed—the six-line stanza rhyming ababcc—is described by Puttenham (*Art of English Poesie*, 1589) as 'most usual,' and it had been in fact adopted by numerous poets, e.g. Gascoigne (*Posies*, 1575), Peele (*Device of the Pageant*, 1585), Nicholas Breton (*The Pilgrimage to Paradise; The Countess of Pembroke's Love*, 1592), Spenser (*Shepherd's Calendar*, 1st Eclogue and part of the 8th Eclogue; *Tears of the Muses; Astrophel*), Lodge (*Scyllas Metamorphosis*). No inference as to the sources can therefore be drawn from Shakespeare's choice of this metre.

Date. In the Dedicatory Letter to Lord Southampton the author speaks of *Venus and Adonis* as 'the first heir of my invention,' and this statement has sometimes been taken as a proof that 'the poem was written or at least designed before Shakespeare undertook any of his dramatic work' (Sidney Lee, *Life*, 142). Some critics have even gone so far as to suppose that the descriptions of the country in *Venus and Adonis* could only have been written while Shakespeare was still in Stratford. But if reminiscences of Shakespeare's rural life are to be found in the poem, echoes of his London life are not absent. The comparison with a dumb play and a chorus (359-360) shows that Shakespeare, as he wrote, was full of his theatrical experience, and lines 507-510 contain an allusion to the plague of 1592-1594. Both the comparison and the allusion are so well embodied in the tale that they render improbable the hypothesis offered by certain scholars that 'the first draught lay in the author's desk through four or five summers, and underwent some retouching before it emerged from the press in its final shape.' It is safe to admit that *Venus and Adonis* was written between August, 1592, when the plague broke out and the theatres were closed, and April 8, 1593, when the poem was entered in the Stationers' Register. Shakespeare, so far, had only been employed in revamping old plays and by the words 'the first heir of my invention' he probably meant that this narrative poem was his first original work as an author.

Venus and Adonis was published in 1593 by R. Field, the printer, himself a Stratford man, with the title-page:

Venus/and Adonis/
Vilia miretur vulgus: mihi flauus Apollo
Pocula Castalia plena ministret aqua.
[Device]
London/Imprinted by Richard Field, and are to be sold at/the signe of the white Greyhound in/Paules Church-yard 1593.

In June, 1594, the book was assigned by Field to Harrison (Arber, ii, 655), and again, in June, 1596, to William Leake (Arber, iii, 65), who held the copyright until the year 1617. At least seven editions were printed in Shakespeare's lifetime, and seven posthumously, viz, 1593, 1594, 1596, 1599 (twice), 1600?, 1602, 1617, 1620, 1627 (Edinburgh), 1680 (twice), 1636, and 1675. For more details, see Sidney Lee's Introduction to the Oxford facsimile.

THE SOURCES AND PUBLICATION OF 'LUCRECE'

The story of Lucrece has been told by numerous writers, the chief versions before Shakespeare's time being those of Dionysius Halicarnassensis (IV, 64, etc.), Diodorus Siculus, Dio Cassius, Ovid (*Fasti*, ii, 721-852), Livy (Bk. I, c. 57-60), Gower (*Confessio Amantis*, Bk. VII), Chaucer (*Legend of Good Women*, 1680-1885), Ser Giovanni Fiorentino (*Il Percorone*, Giorn. xvi, nov. ii), Ban-

dello (*Novelle*, Pt. ii, nov. xxi), Paynter (*Palace of Pleasure*). Several 'ballets' on the subject had also appeared in 1558, 1560, and 1576.

Shakespeare drew from several of these sources. In Ovid he found certain suggestions—the simile of the wolf and the lamb, for instance,—and a few expressions or ideas (cf. notes on 400, 1604, 1732-1733, 1772-1775). But the number of details common to Shakespeare and Livy, and not to be found in Ovid, is much greater, e.g., Tarquin is brought to his bedroom (120-128); Lucrece confesses to her husband that 'a stranger came and lay' on his pillow; Lucrece's friends assure her that though her body is stained her mind is pure (1655-1656 and 1709-1710); Lucrece asks her friends to swear to avenge her (1689, etc.); Lucrece will not let her example serve as an excuse for light women (1714-1715); Brutus asks his 'wondering friends' to swear to help in revenging Lucrece (1843-1848). What pertains to the change of attitude in Brutus is hardly paralleled by what Ovid says of him. The Argument betrays a knowledge of several historical facts not supplied by Ovid. There are also passages where Shakespeare seems to follow Livy more closely than Ovid (cf. notes on 8-9, 437-439, 477-504).

A few details may have been borrowed from Chaucer. The words 'stalk' and 'dishevelled,' applied respectively to Tarquin and Lucrece, are also in *Legend of Good Women* (1780 and 1830). The statement that Brutus carried the dead body to Rome is neither in Livy nor in Ovid. But in Chaucer Lucrece's self-murder takes place at Rome and her body is carried 'on a bere through al the toun' (1865-1866). For other resemblances see notes on 197-210, 596-630, 1261-1267.

Long ago Malone pointed out resemblances between Daniel's *Complaynt of Rosamonde* and *Lucrece*. The list has since been considerably augmented by Ewig (*Shakespeare's Lucrece*). The most striking similarities are recorded in the notes (cf. 26, 117-119, 492, 556, 1261, 1450-1451, 1660 ff.). It seems pretty certain that Shakespeare learned much of Daniel in technique and that he consciously or unconsciously imitated the tone of the *Complaynt*, especially in Lucrece's piteous accents.

Sir Sidney Lee finds that 'Lucrece's apostrophe to Time (939 ff.) suggests indebtedness to two other English poets, Thomas Watson in *Hecatompathia*, 1582 (xlvii and lxxvii), and Giles Fletcher in *Licia*, 1593 (xxviii).' But such apostrophes were commonplace in poetry, their ultimate source being traceable to Ovid's *Tristia* (IV.vi.1-10).

Possibly there is a reminiscence of Virgil in the description of the siege of Troy (cf. note on 1366 ff.).

To sum up: Livy seems to have been the chief source, but Shakespeare used also Ovid and probably Chaucer. For the tone and for a few details he was indebted to contemporary poetry, more particularly to Daniel. But the development of the story is entirely his own.

Metre. There is no reason to suppose that Shakespeare was influenced by any particular poem in the choice of his metre. The seven-line stanza, rhyming ababbcc, or rhyme royal, was perhaps the commonest of all Elizabethan metres. It is thus described by Gascoigne in *Certayne Notes of Instruction*, p. 38 (Arber Reprint): 'Rythme royall is a verse of tenne syllables and seven such verses make a staffe, whereof the first and thirde lines do aunswer (acrosse) in like terminations and rime, the second, fourth, and fifth, do aunswere each other in terminations, and the two last do combine and shut up the sentence: this hath bene called Rithme royall, and surely it is a royall kinde of verse,

serving best for graue discourses.' It was used by Chaucer for several of his tales, for his *Compleint unto Pite* and for his *Troylus and Criseyde* (it is sometimes called Troilus verse on that account), and by Spenser for his *Hymns* and his *Ruins of Time*. For the possibility of Shakespeare having first tried the six-line stanza before fixing his choice upon the rhyme royal, see note on 386-395.

Date. Lucrece was entered in the Stationers' Register on May 9, 1594 (Arber, ii, 648), under the title of *The Ravyshement of Lucrece*, and was printed in the same year with the following title:

LUCRECE
[Device]

London/Printed by Richard Field, for John Harison, and are/to be sold at the signe of the white Greyhound/in Paules Church-yard. 1594.

This is no doubt the 'graver labour' announced in the Epistle Dedicatory of *Venus and Adonis*, and must have been composed between the spring of 1593 and the spring of 1594. Lucrece was not so popular as *Venus and Adonis*, but it 'pleased the wiser sort,' and no less than four other editions were printed in Shakespeare's lifetime (1598, 1600, 1607, 1616). Three other editions appeared in 1624, 1632, and 1655.

'THE PHŒNIX AND THE TURTLE'

In 1601, there appeared a book with the following title:

Loves Martyr/or/Rosalins Complaint./*Allegorically shadowing the truth of Loue*/in the constant Fate of the Phœnix/*and Turtle./*A Poeme interlaced with much varietie and raritie;/*now first translated out of the venerable Italian* Torquato/Caeliano, by Robert Chester./With the true legend of famous King *Arthur*, the last of the nine/Worthies, being the first *Essay* of a new *Brytish* Poet: collected/out of diuerse Authenticall Records./*To these are added some new compositions, of seuerall moderne Writers/whose names are subscribed to their seuerall workes, vpon the/first subject: viz.* the Phœnix *and*/Turtle./*Mar:—Mutare dominum non potest liber notus.*/London/Imprinted for E.B./1601./

The supplementary matter is introduced by a separate title-page:

Hereafter/Follow Diverse/Poeticall Essaies on the former Sub-/iect; viz: the *Turtle* and *Phœnix*./Done by the *best and chiefest of our*/moderne writers, with their names sub-/scribed to their particular workes:/*neuer before extant.*/And (now first) consecrated by them all generally,/*to the loue and merite of the true-noble Knight*/Sir John Salisburie./*Dignum laude virum Musa vetat mori.*/

[Device]

MDCI.

The author, Robert Chester, apparently was a dependent in the household of the knight to whom the book was dedicated. Sir John Salusbury, a Welsh Gentleman of Lleweni, Denbighshire, was born in December, 1566, or January, 1567. He had in his veins a few drops of royal blood, for his mother, Catherine of Berain, was the granddaughter of Sir Roland Velville, illegiti-

mate son of Henry VII. Sir John married (December, 1586) Ursula Stanley, natural daughter of Henry Stanley, fourth Earl of Derby. He was himself a poet, a patron of letters, and a lover of the drama. He was acquainted with Ben Johnson, and probably with Shakespeare, as has been shown by Sir Israel Gollancz in his article 'Contemporary Lines to Heminges and Condell' (*The Times Literary Supplement,* January 26, 1922). In 1595 he came up to London, frequented the Court and was in great favor with Queen Elizabeth, who appointed him one of her Esquires of the Body (March, 1595). In 1601 he was knighted and it was presumably to celebrate this event that Robert Chester issued his *Loves Martyr.*

Chester's work is a hodge-podge of various poems on unconnected subjects—a history of early England, a description of the nine female worthies, a metrical biography of King Arthur, a prayer, love ditties, an account of the plants, trees, fishes, minerals, beasts, reptiles, insects, and birds found in Paphos, a series of 'Cantoes alphabet-wise,' another series of 'Cantoes verbally written' or posies—more or less cleverly introduced into an allegorical poem, turning upon the marriage of Sir John Salusbury (the Turtle) to Ursula Stanley (the Phœnix), and obscurely relating how the two birds having decided to die on a pyre, 'in a manner sacrificingly,' out of their mystical ashes there arose another Phœnix (Salusbury's first child, Jane).[1]

In order to render this homage more valuable, either Robert Chester, or Sir John, or maybe the publisher, asked 'the best and chiefest' among contemporary writers—Shakespeare, John Marston, George Chapman, Ben Jonson, and another person who signed himself 'Ignoto'—to supply a poem on the subject of the Phœnix and Turtle, which poems were collected in the Appendix to *Loves Martyr.*

The contributors did their best to comply with the request and produced a variation on the motive set in *Loves Martyr.* Ignoto insisted upon the denouement which he summed up in the final verse: 'One Phœnix borne, another Phœnix burne.' Marston in his inflated style sang the praises of the 'most exact wondrous creature arising out of the Phœnix and Turtle Doues Ashes.' Chapman chose to marvel at the Turtle's fidelity to his Phœnix, and Ben Jonson celebrated both the constancy of the Turtle and the 'splendor' 'more than mortal' of the Phœnix, who turns out to be a lady full of graces and virtues.

Shakespeare alone of all the contributors does not seem to have clearly understood—and he cannot be blamed—the real meaning of the allegory. He evidently did not discover that the Phœnix and the Turtle were consumed, only in a metaphorical sense, in the flames of their own love, and that they lived again in the person of a beautiful offspring. He made the two birds die 'leaving no posteritie,' and described their obsequies, conducted in the presence of the Eagle, the Swan, and the Crow, as mourners.

This difference in the treatment of the theme is somewhat surprising, and several explanations of it have been offered. Sir Sidney Lee cannot believe that Shakespeare's poem 'was penned for Chester's book. It must have been either devised in an idle hour with merely abstract intention, or it was suggested by the death within the poet's own circle of a pair of devoted lovers.'

---

1 Dr. Grosart, in his edition of Chester's *Loves Martyr,* confidently advanced the idea that the 'allegory shadowed the love of Q. Elizabeth for the earl of Essex.' It is one of the wildest hypotheses of that ingenious critic. Mr. Carleton Brown has discovered a document showing that 'Sir John Salusbury was bitterly opposed to the party of Essex, and therefore was the last person to whom such an allegory as Dr. Grosart constructed would have been dedicated.'

Professor Carleton Brown impressed by 'the frigid and perfunctory tone' of Shakespeare's contribution suggests that the poet's 'relations with Sir John Salusbury were less close than those of Jonson, Marston and Chapman, so that his lines on the Phœnix and Turtle were a matter of courteous compliance rather than a tribute to a personal friend.' Prof. J. Q. Adams supposes that Shakespeare did not trouble 'to read Chester's tedious poem far enough to have unraveled its cryptic meaning,' and he even suspects him of having done his task none too seriously: 'The concluding lines of the Threnos,' adds Prof. Adams, 'may be slyly humorous when the poet calls upon his readers to repair to the urn and

> 'For these dead birds sigh a prayer.'

Shakespeare certainly was a humorist, but what his real intentions were we shall probably never know.[2]

Sources. A. H. R. Fairchild in his interesting study of the *Phœnix and Turtle* has collected numerous traces of the influence of Chaucer and of the symbolism of the Renaissance emblem writers upon both the conception and the style of Shakespeare's poem. 'It has,' writes Mr. Fairchild, 'a twofold source, stanzas i-v especially being suggested by Chaucer's poem, *The Parlement of Foules*, part IV, 323 to the end, the remaining stanzas (vi-xviii) being adapted to these from the emblem literature and conceptions of Shakespeare's period.' Sir Sidney Lee, on the other hand, finds a close affinity with "the imagery of Matthew Roydon's elegy on Sir Philip Sidney, where the turtle-dove and phœnix meet the swan and eagle at the dead hero's funeral and there play rôles somewhat similar to those which Shakespeare assigns the birds in his 'poetical essaie.' " Some of the resemblances with Chaucer's *Parlement of Foules* are striking enough and they are recorded in the notes. But I wonder whether it is necessary to find any particular source at all for Shakespeare's use of the different emblems of the allegory, for they were part of the symbolical language of the time.

Metre. The *Phœnix and Turtle* consists of thirteen quatrains in truncated trochaics rhyming abba. The concluding Threnos consists of five three-line stanzas, in octosyllabic trochaics, each stanza having a single rhyme.

THE PUBLICATION AND AUTHORSHIP OF 'THE PASSIONATE PILGRIM'

In 1599 William Jaggard issued a poetical miscellany under the title of

THE/Passionate/Pilgrime./By W. Shakespeare./
[Device]

At London/Printed for W. Jaggard, and are/to be sold by W. Leake, at the Grey-/hound in Paules Churchyard./1599.

The volume contained twenty lyrical pieces, the last six of which were preceded by a second title-page running thus:

Sonnets/to sundry notes of Musicke./
[Device]

At London/Printed for W. Jaggard, and are/to be sold by W. Leake, at the Grey-/hound in Paules Churchyard/1599.

Out of the twenty poems only five are indisputably by Shakespeare. These are numbers I, II, III, V of *The Passionate Pilgrim* and II of *Sonnets to Sundry Notes*, which are extracted from Shakespeare's Sonnets (Nos. 138 and 144) and from *Love's Labour's Lost* (IV.iii.55-68; IV.ii.104-117; IV.iii.99-118). Four other poems, IV, VI, IX, XI, are on the subject of Venus and Adonis. No XI appeared in 1596 in Bartholomew Griffin's *Fidessa*, and there is no reason to doubt that the sonnet was actually written by the poet to whom it was ascribed. As regards IV, VI, IX, critics are divided. Malone thought that they must be 'essays of the author when he first conceived the notion of writing a poem on the subject of *Venus and Adonis*,' and that 'these little pieces bear the strongest mark of the hand of Shakespeare.' Dowden, likewise, was of opinion that 'nothing in any one of these sonnets forbids the idea of Shakespeare's authorship.' He pointed out that IV and VI recall a passage in *The Taming of the Shrew* (Induction,ii.56-58) and that the words 'brakes' and 'queen of love' appear in IX as well as in *Venus and Adonis*. But as I have shown in note to VI the details of the picture in *The Taming of the Shrew* and in *The Passionate Pilgrim* are different; and the repetition of such ordinary expressions as 'queen of love' and 'brakes' does not prove much. These resemblances might just as well be reminiscences of *Venus and Adonis*, as is suggested by Sir Sidney Lee, who refuses to see there any trace of Shakespeare's workmanship. It should also be noted that IV, VI, and IX are remarkable for their lack of imagery: they scarcely contain any simile and metaphor. The man who wrote them was singularly devoid of imagination, a thing which cannot be said of Shakespeare but which is certainly true of Griffin, as XI and the whole of *Fidessa* demonstrates. It is most probable that the four Venus-Adonis sonnets come from the same hand, that of Bartholomew Griffin.

The other poems in the book—with the exception of VII, X, XIII, XIV, and I, III, IV of *Sonnets to Sundry Notes*, which have nothing Shakespearean about them—have been restored to their owners (cf. notes).

The Passionate Pilgrim met with success. As may be inferred from the title-page of the 1612 edition, a second edition was called for, of which no copy is known to exist. In 1612 Jaggard issued another edition with the following title:

The/Passionate/Pilgrime/or/*Certaine Amorous Sonnets/betweene* Venus *and* Adonis/*newly corrected and aug-/mented/By W. Shake-speare*/The third Edition./Whereunto is newly ad/ded two Love-Epistles, the first/from *Paris* to *Hellen*, and *Hellens* answere backe/againe to *Paris*/Printed for W. Jaggard./1612.

The two additions announced on the title-page were extracted from Heywood's *Troia Britannica*, a collection which Jaggard himself had published in 1609. This piece of unscrupulous effrontery elicited a protest from Heywood which appeared as a postscript to his *Apology for Actors* (1612): "Here likewise I must necessarily insert a manifest injury done to me in that worke by taking the two Epistles of Paris to Helen, and Helen to Paris, and printing them in a lesse volume, under the name of another, which may put the world in an opinion I might steale them from him, and hee to doe himselfe right, hath since published them in his owne name: but as I must acknowledge my lines not worthy his [i.e. Shakespeare's] patronage under whom he [i.e.

Jaggard] hath published them, so the Author [i.e. Shakespeare] I know much offended with M. Jaggard that (altogether unknowne to him) presumed to make so bold with his name." This formal statement proved effective, for Jaggard cancelled the fallacious title-page and issued the remaining copies with a new one from which he omitted Shakespeare's name.

THE AUTHORSHIP OF 'A LOVER'S COMPLAINT'

When Thorpe published Shakespeare's *Sonnets* in 1609 he appended a poem in forty-nine seven-line stanzas, entitled *A Lover's Complaint*, which he gave out as written by William Shakespeare. The metre used is that of *Lucrece*, and it is true that several passages exhibit a felicity of phrase which reminds one of Shakespeare's characteristic sweetness. Yet it is to be doubted whether Thorpe was justified in attributing *A Lover's Complaint* to the author of the *Sonnets*. We know that Elizabethan publishers were not very scrupulous in their ascriptions and the methodical analysis of the poem made by Prof. J. W. Mackail (in *Essays and Studies* by members of the English Association, 1912) seems to prove that Shakespeare could not have written that pathetic but somewhat affected lamentation. The poem contains an unusually high proportion of words not to be found in Shakespeare's authentic work, together with a great number of Latinisms and other syntactical peculiarities. It may be added that the rhythm of many lines is too awkward to have satisfied Shakespeare's subtle ear even in the period of his apprenticeship. For my part, I very strongly question the authenticity of this piece.

Poems

Venus and Adonis

'Vilia miretur vulgus; mihi flavus Apollo
Pocula Castalia plena ministret aqua.'

TO THE RIGHT HONOURABLE HENRY WRIOTHESLEY,
Earl of Southampton, and Baron of Tichfield.

RIGHT HONOURABLE,

   I know not how I shall offend in dedicating my unpolished
lines to your lordship, nor how the world will censure me   5
for choosing so strong a prop to support so weak a burthen:
only, if your honour seem but pleased, I account myself highly
praised, and vow to take advantage of all idle hours, till I have
honoured you with some graver labour. But if the first heir of
my invention prove deformed, I shall be sorry it had   10
so noble a godfather, and never after ear so barren a land, for
fear it yield me still so bad a harvest. I leave it to your honourable survey, and your honour to your heart's content; which I
wish may always answer your own wish and the world's hopeful expectation.   15

Your honour's in all duty,
WILLIAM SHAKESPEARE.

❧

Even as the sun with purple-colour'd face
Had ta'en his last leave of the weeping morn,
Rose-cheek'd Adonis hied him to the chase;
Hunting he lov'd, but love he laugh'd to scorn;
    Sick-thoughted Venus makes amain unto him,   5
    And like a bold-fac'd suitor 'gins to woo him.

'Thrice fairer than myself,' thus she began,
'The field's chief flower, sweet above compare,
Stain to all nymphs, more lovely than a man,
More white and red than doves or roses are;   10
    Nature that made thee, with herself at strife,
    Saith that the world hath ending with thy life.

'Vouchsafe, thou wonder, to alight thy steed,
And rein his proud head to the saddle-bow;
If thou wilt deign this favour, for thy meed   15
A thousand honey secrets shalt thou know:
    Here come and sit, where never serpent hisses;
    And being set, I'll smother thee with kisses:

'And yet not cloy thy lips with loath'd satiety,
But rather famish them amid their plenty,   20
Making them red and pale with fresh variety;
Ten kisses short as one, one long as twenty:

A summer's day will seem an hour but short,
Being wasted in such time-beguiling sport.'

With this she seizeth on his sweating palm,   25
The precedent of pith and livelihood,
And, trembling in her passion, calls it balm,
Earth's sovereign salve to do a goddess good:
    Being so enrag'd, desire doth lend her force
    Courageously to pluck him from his horse.   30

Over one arm the lusty courser's rein,
Under her other was the tender boy,
Who blush'd and pouted in a dull disdain,
With leaden appetite, unapt to toy;
    She red and hot as coals of glowing fire,   35
    He red for shame, but frosty in desire.

The studded bridle on a ragged bough
Nimbly she fastens;—O! how quick is love:—
The steed is stalled up, and even now
To tie the rider she begins to prove: 40
    Backward she push'd him, as she would be thrust,
    And govern'd him in strength, though not in lust.

So soon was she along, as he was down,
Each leaning on their elbows and their hips:
Now doth she stroke his cheek, now doth he frown,   45
And 'gins to chide, but soon she stops his lips;
    And kissing speaks, with lustful language broken,
    'If thou wilt chide, thy lips shall never open.'

He burns with bashful shame; she with her tears
Doth quench the maiden burning of his cheeks;   50
Then with her windy sighs and golden hairs
To fan and blow them dry again she seeks:
    He saith she is immodest, blames her miss;
    What follows more she murthers with a kiss.

Even as an empty eagle, sharp by fast,   55
Tires with her beak on feathers, flesh and bone,
Shaking her wings, devouring all in haste,
Till either gorge be stuff'd or prey be gone;
    Even so she kiss'd his brow, his cheek, his chin,
    And where she ends she doth anew begin.   60

Forc'd to content, but never to obey,
Panting he lies, and breatheth in her face;
She feedeth on the steam, as on a prey,
And calls it heavenly moisture, air of grace;
    Wishing her cheeks were gardens full of flowers,   65
    So they were dew'd with such distilling showers.

Epigraph; *cf. n.*   **Ded.** 1 Wriothesley; *cf. n.*   11 **ear:** *plough*   2 **weeping:** *shedding dew*   3 **Rose-cheek'd;** *cf. n.*   **hied him:** *hastened*   5 **makes amain:** *goes in haste*   9 **Stain;** *cf. n.*   11 **Nature . . . strife;** *cf. n.*   12 **the world . . . life;** *cf. n.*   18 **set:** *seated*

24 **wasted:** *spent*   25 **sweating palm;** *cf. n.*   26 **precedent:** *sign* **livelihood:** *vigor*   37 **ragged:** *rough*   40 **prove:** *attempt*   53 **miss;** *cf. n.*   55 **empty:** *hungry*   56 **Tires;** *cf. n.*   61 **content:** *acquiesce; cf. n.*

Look! how a bird lies tangled in a net,
So fasten'd in her arms Adonis lies;
Pure shame and aw'd resistance made him fret,
Which bred more beauty in his angry eyes: 70
    Rain added to a river that is rank
    Perforce will force it overflow the bank.

Still she entreats, and prettily entreats,
For to a pretty ear she tunes her tale;
Still is he sullen, still he lowers and frets,   75
'Twixt crimson shame and anger ashy-pale;
    Being red, she loves him best; and being white,
    Her best is better'd with a more delight.

Look how he can, she cannot choose but love;
And by her fair immortal hand she swears,   80
From his soft bosom never to remove,
Till he take truce with her contending tears,
    Which long have rain'd, making her cheeks all wet;
    And one sweet kiss shall pay this countless debt.

Upon this promise did he raise his chin   85
Like a dive-dapper peering through a wave,
Who, being look'd on, ducks as quickly in;
So offers he to give what she did crave;
    But when her lips were ready for his pay,
    He winks, and turns his lips another way.   90

Never did passenger in summer's heat
More thirst for drink than she for this good turn.
Her help she sees, but help she cannot get;
She bathes in water, yet her fire must burn:
    'O! pity,' 'gan she cry, 'flint-hearted boy: 95
    'Tis but a kiss I beg; why art thou coy?

'I have been woo'd, as I entreat thee now,
Even by the stern and direful god of war,
Whose sinewy neck in battle ne'er did bow,
Who conquers where he comes in every jar;   100
    Yet hath he been my captive and my slave,
    And begg'd for that which thou unask'd shalt have.

'Over my altars hath he hung his lance,
His batter'd shield, his uncontrolled crest,
And for my sake hath learn'd to sport and dance,   105
To toy, to wanton, dally, smile, and jest;
    Scorning his churlish drum and ensign red,
    Making my arms his field, his tent my bed.

'Thus he that overrul'd I oversway'd,
Leading him prisoner in a red-rose chain: 110
Strong-temper'd steel his stronger strength obey'd
Yet was he servile to my coy disdain.
    O, be not proud, not brag not of thy might,
    For mastering her that foil'd the god of fight!

'Touch but my lips with those fair lips of thine,—   115
Though mine be not so fair, yet are they red,—

The kiss shall be thine own as well as mine:
What seest thou in the ground? hold up thy head:
    Look in mine eyeballs, there thy beauty lies;
    Then why not lips on lips, since eyes in eyes?   120

'Art thou asham'd to kiss? then wink again,
And I will wink; so shall the day seem night;
Love keeps his revels where there are but twain;
Be bold to play, our sport is not in sight:
    These blue-vein'd violets whereon we lean   125
    Never can blab, nor know not what we mean.

'The tender spring upon thy tempting lip
Shows thee unripe, yet mayst thou well be tasted.
Make use of time, let not advantage slip;
Beauty within itself should not be wasted: 130
    Fair flowers that are not gather'd in their prime
    Rot and consume themselves in little time.

'Were I hard-favour'd, foul, or wrinkled-old,
Ill-nurtur'd, crooked, churlish, harsh in voice,
O'erworn, despised, rheumatic, and cold,   135
Thick-sighted, barren, lean, and lacking juice,
    Then mightst thou pause, for then I were not for thee;
    But having no defects, why dost abhor me?

'Thou canst not see one wrinkle in my brow;
Mine eyes are grey and bright, and quick in turning;   140
My beauty as the spring doth yearly grow;
My flesh is soft and plump, my marrow burning;
    My smooth moist hand, were it with thy hand felt,
    Would in thy palm dissolve, or seem to melt.

'Bid me discourse, I will enchant thine ear,   145
Or like a fairy trip upon the green,
Or like a nymph, with long dishevell'd hair,
Dance on the sands, and yet no footing seen:
    Love is a spirit all compact of fire,
    Not gross to sink, but light, and will aspire.   150

'Witness this primrose bank whereon I lie;
These forceless flowers like sturdy trees support me;
Two strengthless doves will draw me through the sky,
From morn till night, even where I list to sport me:
    Is love so light, sweet boy, and may it be   155
    That thou shouldst think it heavy unto thee?

'Is thine own heart to thine own face affected?
Can thy right hand seize love upon thy left?
Then woo thyself, be of thyself rejected,
Steal thine own freedom, and complain on theft.   160
    Narcissus so himself himself forsook,
    And died to kiss his shadow in the brook.

'Torches are made to light, jewels to wear,
Dainties to taste, fresh beauty for the use,
Herbs for their smell, and sappy plants to bear;   165
Things growing to themselves are growth's abuse:

71 **rank;** *cf. n.*　　78 **more:** *greater*　　82 *Cf. n.*　　86 **dive-dapper;** *cf. n.*　　90 **winks:**
shuts his eyes　　91 **passenger:** *traveler*　　100 **jar:** *conflict*　　104 **uncontrolled;**
cf. n.　　114 **foil'd:** *defeated*

129-132 *Cf. n.*　　130 *Cf. n.*　　135 **O'erworn:** *worn out by time*　　136 **Thick-:** *weak-*
148 **footing:** *footprint*　　149 **compact:** *composed*　　150 **aspire:** *ascend*　　157 **affected to:**
in love with　　158 *Cf. n.*　　161 **Narcissus;** *cf. n.*

Seeds spring from seeds, and beauty breedeth beauty;
Thou wast begot; to get it is thy duty.

'Upon the earth's increase why shouldst thou feed,
Unless the earth with thy increase be fed?   *170*
By law of nature thou art bound to breed,
That thine may live when thou thyself art dead;
    And so in spite of death thou dost survive,
    In that thy likeness still is left alive.'

By this the love-sick queen began to sweat,   *175*
For where they lay the shadow had forsook them,
And Titan, tired in the mid-day heat,
With burning eye did hotly overlook them;
    Wishing Adonis had his team to guide,
    So he were like him and by Venus' side.   *180*

And now Adonis with a lazy spright,
And with a heavy, dark, disliking eye,
His louring brows o'erwhelming his fair sight,
Like misty vapours when they blot the sky,
    Souring his cheeks, cries, 'Fie! no more of love: *185*
    The sun doth burn my face; I must remove.'

'Ay me,' quoth Venus, 'young, and so unkind?
What bare excuses mak'st thou to be gone?
I'll sigh celestial breath, whose gentle wind
Shall cool the heat of this descending sun: *190*
    I'll make a shadow for thee of my hairs;
    If they burn too, I'll quench them with my tears.

'The sun that shines from heaven shines but warm,
And lo! I lie between that sun and thee:
The heat I have from thence doth little harm,   *195*
Thine eye darts forth the fire that burneth me;
    And were I not immortal, life were done
    Between this heavenly and earthly sun.

'Art thou obdurate, flinty, hard as steel?
Nay, more than flint, for stone at rain relenteth.   *200*
Art thou a woman's son, and canst not feel
What 'tis to love? how want of love tormenteth?
    O, had thy mother borne so hard a mind,
    She had not brought forth thee, but died unkind.

'What am I that thou shouldst contemn me this?   *205*
Or what great danger dwells upon my suit?
What were thy lips the worse for one poor kiss?
Speak, fair; but speak fair words, or else be mute:
    Give me one kiss, I'll give it thee again,
    And one for interest, if thou wilt have twain.   *210*

'Fie! lifeless picture, cold and senseless stone,
Well-painted idol, image dull and dead,
Statue contenting but the eye alone,
Thing like a man, but of no woman bred:
    Thou art no man, though of a man's complexion,   *215*
    For men will kiss even by their own direction.'

This said, impatience chokes her pleading tongue,
And swelling passion doth provoke a pause;
Red cheeks and fiery eyes blaze forth her wrong;
Being judge in love, she cannot right her cause: *220*
    And now she weeps, and now she fain would speak,
    And now her sobs do her intendments break.

Sometimes she shakes her head, and then his hand;
Now gazeth she on him, now on the ground;
Sometimes her arms infold him like a band: *225*
She would, he will not in her arms be bound;
    And when from thence he struggles to be gone,
    She locks her lily fingers one in one.

'Fondling,' she saith, 'since I have hemm'd thee here
Within the circuit of this ivory pale,   *230*
I'll be a park, and thou shalt be my deer;
Feed where thou wilt, on mountain or in dale:
    Graze on my lips, and if those hills be dry,
    Stray lower, where the pleasant fountains lie.

'Within this limit is relief enough,   *235*
Sweet bottom-grass and high delightful plain,
Round rising hillocks, brakes obscure and rough,
To shelter thee from tempest and from rain:
    Then be my deer, since I am such a park;
    No dog shall rouse thee, though a thousand bark.'   *240*

At this Adonis smiles as in disdain,
That in each cheek appears a pretty dimple:
Love made those hollows, if himself were slain,
He might be buried in a tomb so simple;
    Foreknowing well, if there he came to lie,   *245*
    Why, there Love liv'd and there he could not die.

These lovely caves, these round enchanting pits,
Open'd their mouths to swallow Venus' liking.
Being mad before, how doth she now for wits?
Struck dead at first, what needs a second striking?   *250*
    Poor queen of love, in thine own law forlorn,
    To love a cheek that smiles at thee in scorn!

Now which way shall she turn? what shall she say?
Her words are done, her woes the more increasing;
The time is spent, her object will away,   *255*
And from her twining arms doth urge releasing:
    'Pity,' she cries; 'some favour, some remorse!'
    Away he springs, and hasteth to his horse.

But, lo! from forth a copse that neighbours by,
A breeding jennet, lusty, young, and proud,   *260*
Adonis' trampling courser doth espy,
And forth she rushes, snorts and neighs aloud:
    The strong-neck'd steed, being tied unto a tree,
    Breaketh his rein, and to her straight goes he.

177 Titan: *the sun*   **197, 198** *Cf. n.*   **200 relenteth:** *softens*   **203, 204** *Cf. n.*   **204 unkind:** *unnatural*   **205 this:** *thus*

219 blaze: *publish*   **222 her intendments:** *what she means to say*   **229 Fondling:** *darling*   **231 deer;** *cf. n.*   **235 relief;** *cf. n.*   **236 buttom-grass:** *grass growing in the valleys*   **240 rouse;** *cf. n.*   **247 caves;** *cf. n.*   **257 remorse:** *commiseration*   **259-262** *Cf. n.*   **263, 264** *Cf. n.*

Imperiously he leaps, he neighs, he bounds,   *265*
And now his woven girths he breaks asunder;
The bearing earth with his hard hoof he wounds,
Whose hollow womb resounds like heaven's thunder;
    The iron bit he crushes 'tween his teeth,
    Controlling what he was controlled with.   *270*

His ears up-prick'd; his braided hanging mane
Upon his compass'd crest now stand on end;
His nostrils drink the air, and forth again,
As from a furnace, vapours doth he send:
    His eye, which scornfully glisters like fire,   *275*
    Shows his hot courage and his high desire.

Sometime he trots, as if he told the steps,
With gentle majesty and modest pride;
Anon he rears upright, curvets and leaps,
As who should say, 'Lo! thus my strength is tried;   *280*
    And this I do to captivate the eye
    Of the fair breeder that is standing by.'

What recketh he his rider's angry stir,
His flattering 'Holla,' or his 'Stand, I say'?
What cares he now for curb or pricking spur?   *285*
For rich caparisons or trapping gay?
    He sees his love, and nothing else he sees,
    Nor nothing else with his proud sight agrees.

Look, when a painter would surpass the life,
In limning out a well-proportion'd steed,   *290*
His art with nature's workmanship at strife,
As if the dead the living should exceed;
    So did this horse excel a common one,
    In shape, in courage, colour, pace and bone.

Round-hoof'd, short-jointed, fetlocks shag and long,   *295*
Broad breast, full eye, small head, and nostril wide,
High crest, short ears, straight legs and passing strong,
Thin mane, thick tail, broad buttock, tender hide:
    Look, what a horse should have he did not lack,
    Save a proud rider on so proud a back.   *300*

Sometimes he scuds far off, and there he stares;
Anon he starts at stirring of a feather;
To bid the wind a base he now prepares,
And whe'r he run or fly they know not whether;
    For through his mane and tail the high wind sings,   *305*
    Fanning the hairs, who wave like feather'd wings.

He looks upon his love, and neighs unto her;
She answers him as if she knew his mind;
Being proud, as females are, to see him woo her,
She puts on outward strangeness, seems unkind,   *310*
    Spurns at his love and scorns the heat he feels,
    Beating his kind embracements with her heels.

Then, like a melancholy malcontent,
He vails his tail that, like a falling plume
Cool shadow to his melting buttock lent: *315*
He stamps and bites the poor flies in his fume.
    His love, perceiving how he was enrag'd,
    Grew kinder, and his fury was assuag'd.

His testy master goeth about to take him;
When lo! the unback'd breeder, full of fear,   *320*
Jealous of catching, swiftly doth forsake him,
With her the horse, and left Adonis there.
    As they were mad, unto the wood they hie them,
    Out-stripping crows that strive to over-fly them.

All swoln with chafing, down Adonis sits,   *325*
Banning his boisterous and unruly beast:
And now the happy season once more fits,
That love-sick Love by pleading may be blest;
    For lovers say, the heart hath treble wrong
    When it is barr'd the aidance of the tongue.   *330*

An oven that is stopp'd, or river stay'd,
Burneth more hotly, swelleth with more rage:
So of concealed sorrow may be said;
Free vent of words love's fire doth assuage;
    But when the heart's attorney once is mute,   *335*
    The client breaks, as desperate in his suit.

He sees her coming, and begins to glow,—
Even as a dying coal revives with wind,—
And with his bonnet hides his angry brow;
Looks on the dull earth with disturbed mind,   *340*
    Taking no notice that she is so nigh,
    For all askance he holds her in his eye.

O! what a sight it was, wistly to view
How she came stealing to the wayward boy;
To note the fighting conflict of her hue,   *345*
How white and red each other did destroy:
    But now her cheek was pale, and by and by
    It flash'd forth fire, as lightning from the sky.

Now was she just before him as he sat,
And like a lowly lover down she kneels;   *350*
With one fair hand she heaveth up his hat,
Her other tender hand his fair cheek feels:
    His tenderer cheek receives her soft hand's print,
    As apt as new-fall'n snow takes any dint.

O, what a war of looks was then between them!   *355*
Her eyes petitioners to his eyes suing;
His eyes saw her eyes as they had not seen them;
Her eyes woo'd still, his eyes disdain'd the wooing:
    And all this dumb play had his acts made plain
    With tears, which, chorus-like, her eyes did rain.   *360*

Full gently now she takes him by the hand,
A lily prison'd in a gaol of snow,

272 compass'd: *curved*   279 curvets; *cf. n.*   282 breeder: *female*   283 recketh: *cares for* stir: *agitation*   286 caparisons or trapping; *cf. n.*   289-292 *Cf. n.*   295-298 *Cf. n.*   295 shag: *hairy*   297 passing: *exceedingly*   303 To bid ... base; *cf. n.*   304 whe'r: *whether* whether: *which of the two*   310 strangeness: *coldness*

314 vails: *lowers*   316 fume: *rage*   326 Banning: *cursing*   330 aidance: *help*   329-336 *Cf. n.*   335 heart's attorney; *cf. n.*   342 *Cf. n.*   343 wistly: *attentively*   354 dint: *impression*   359, 360 *Cf. n.*

Or ivory in an alablaster band;
So white a friend engirts so white a foe:
 This beauteous combat, wilful and unwilling,   *365*
 Show'd like two silver doves that sit a-billing.

Once more the engine of her thoughts began:
'O fairest mover on this mortal round,
Would thou wert as I am, and I a man,
My heart all whole as thine, thy heart my wound;   *370*
 For one sweet look thy help I would assure thee,
 Though nothing but my body's bane would cure thee.'

'Give me my hand,' saith he, 'why dost thou feel it?'
'Give me my heart,' saith she, 'and thou shalt have it;
O! give it me, lest thy hard heart do steel it,   *375*
And being steel'd, soft sighs can never grave it:
 Then love's deep groans I never shall regard,
 Because Adonis' heart hath made mine hard.'

'For shame,' he cries, 'let go, and let me go;
My day's delight is past, my horse is gone,   *380*
And 'tis your fault I am bereft him so:
I pray you hence, and leave me here alone:
 For all my mind, my thought, my busy care,
 Is how to get my palfrey from the mare.'

Thus she replies: 'Thy palfrey, as he should,   *385*
Welcomes the warm approach of sweet desire:
Affection is a coal that must be cool'd;
Else, suffer'd, it will set the heart on fire:
 The sea hath bounds, but deep desire hath none;
 Therefore no marvel though thy horse be gone.   *390*

'How like a jade he stood, tied to the tree,
Servilely master'd with a leathern rein!
But when he saw his love, his youth's fair fee,
He held such petty bondage in disdain;
 Throwing the base thong from his bending crest,   *395*
 Enfranchising his mouth, his back, his breast.

'Who sees his true-love in her naked bed,
Teaching the sheets a whiter hue than white,
But, when his glutton eye so full hath fed,
His other agents aim at like delight?   *400*
 Who is so faint, that dare not be so bold
 To touch the fire, the weather being cold?

'Let me excuse thy courser, gentle boy;
And learn of him, I heartily beseech thee,
To take advantage on presented joy;   *405*
Though I were dumb, yet his proceedings teach thee.
 O learn to love; the lesson is but plain,
 And once made perfect, never lost again.'

'I know not love,' quoth he, 'nor will not know it,
Unless it be a boar, and then I chase it;   *410*
'Tis much to borrow, and I will not owe it;

My love to love is love but to disgrace it;
 For I have heard it is a life in death,
 That laughs and weeps, and all but with a breath.

'Who wears a garment shapeless and unfinish'd?   *415*
Who plucks the bud before one leaf put forth?
If springing things be any jot diminish'd,
They wither in their prime, prove nothing worth;
 The colt that's back'd and burthen'd being young
 Loseth his pride and never waxeth strong.   *420*

'You hurt my hand with wringing; let us part,
And leave this idle theme, this bootless chat:
Remove your siege from my unyielding heart;
To love's alarms it will not ope the gate:
 Dismiss your vows, your feigned tears, your flattery;   *425*
 For where a heart is hard, they make no battery.'

'What! canst thou talk?' quoth she, 'hast thou a tongue?
O, would thou hadst not, or I had no hearing!
Thy mermaid's voice hath done me double wrong;
I had my load before, now press'd with bearing: *430*
 Melodious discord, heavenly tune, harsh-sounding,
 Ear's deep-sweet music, and heart's deep-sore wounding.

'Had I no eyes, but ears, my ears would love
That inward beauty and invisible;
Or were I deaf, thy outward parts would move   *435*
Each part in me that were but sensible:
 Though neither eyes nor ears, to hear nor see,
 Yet should I be in love by touching thee.

'Say, that the sense of feeling were bereft me,
And that I could not see, nor hear, nor touch,   *440*
And nothing but the very smell were left me,
Yet would my love to thee be still as much;
 For from the still'tory of thy face excelling
 Comes breath perfum'd that breedeth love by smelling.

'But O! what banquet wert thou to the taste,   *445*
Being nurse and feeder of the other four;
Would they not wish the feast might ever last,
And bid Suspicion double-lock the door,
 Lest Jealousy, that sour unwelcome guest,
 Should, by his stealing in, disturb the feast?'   *450*

Once more the ruby-colour'd portal open'd,
Which to his speech did honey passage yield;
Like a red morn, that ever yet betoken'd
Wrack to the seaman, tempest to the field,
 Sorrow to shepherds, woe unto the birds,   *455*
 Gusts and foul flaws to herdmen and to herds.

This ill presage advisably she marketh:
Even as the wind is hush'd before it raineth,
Or as the wolf doth grin before he barketh,
Or as the berry breaks before it staineth,   *460*

363 alablaster: *alabaster, a stalagmitic white stone* **364 engirts:** *encircles* **367 engine;** *cf. n.* **368 round:** *globe* (the earth) **370** *Cf. n.* **372 bane:** *ruin* **375 steel;** *cf. n.* **376 grave:** *engrave* **388 suffer'd:** *allowed to burn* **396 Enfranchising:** *liberating* **397 naked bed;** *cf. n.*

412 *Cf. n.* **414 all ... breath:** *both in the same breath* **421 wringing:** *squeezing* **424 alarms;** *cf. n.* **430 press'd:** *oppressed, crushed* **433-450** *Cf. n.* **436 sensible:** *capable of sensation* **443 still'tory:** *still (alembic)* **446 four:** *four senses* **449 Jealousy:** *Envy* **456 flaws:** *sudden gusts* **457 advisedly:** *heedfully*

Or like the deadly bullet of a gun,
His meaning struck her ere his words begun.

And at his look she flatly falleth down,
For looks kill love and love by looks reviveth;
A smile recures the wounding of a frown;   *465*
But blessed bankrupt, that by love so thriveth!
     The silly boy, believing she is dead,
     Claps her pale cheek, till clapping makes it red;

And all-amaz'd brake off his late intent,
For sharply he did think to reprehend her,   *470*
Which cunning love did wittily prevent:
Fair fall the wit that can so well defend her!
     For on the grass she lies as she were slain,
     Till his breath breatheth life in her again.

He wrings her nose, he strikes her on the cheeks,   *475*
He bends her fingers, holds her pulses hard,
He chafes her lips; a thousand ways he seeks
To mend the hurt that his unkindness marr'd:
     He kisses her; and she, by her good will,
     Will never rise, so he will kiss her still.   *480*

The night of sorrow now is turn'd to day:
Her two blue windows faintly she up-heaveth,
Like the fair sun, when in his fresh array
He cheers the morn and all the earth relieveth:
     And as the bright sun glorifies the sky,   *485*
     So is her face illumin'd with her eye;

Whose beams upon his hairless face are fix'd,
As if from thence they borrow'd all their shine.
Were never four such lamps together mix'd,
Had not his clouded with his brows' repine;   *490*
     But hers, which through the crystal tears gave light,
     Shone like the moon in water seen by night.

'O! where am I?' quoth she, 'in earth or heaven,
Or in the ocean drench'd, or in the fire?
What hour is this? or morn or weary even?   *495*
Do I delight to die, or life desire?
     But now I liv'd, and life was death's annoy;
     But now I died, and death was lively joy.

'O! thou didst kill me; kill me once again:
Thy eyes' shrewd tutor, that hard heart of thine,   *500*
Hath taught them scornful tricks and such disdain
That they have murder'd this poor heart of mine;
     And these mine eyes, true leaders to their queen,
     But for thy piteous lips no more had seen.

'Long may they kiss each other for this cure!   *505*
O, never let their crimson liveries wear!
And as they last, their verdure still endure,
To drive infection from the dangerous year:
     That the star-gazers, having writ on death,
     May say, the plague is banish'd by thy breath.   *510*

'Pure lips, sweet seals in my soft lips imprinted,
What bargains may I make, still to be sealing?
To sell myself I can be well contented,
So thou wilt buy and pay and use good dealing;
     Which purchase if thou make, for fear of slips   *515*
     Set thy seal-manual on my wax-red lips.

'A thousand kisses buys my heart from me;
And pay them at thy leisure, one by one.
What is ten hundred touches unto thee?
Are they not quickly told and quickly gone?   *520*
     Say, for non-payment that the debt should double,
     Is twenty hundred kisses such a trouble?

'Fair queen,' quoth he, 'if any love you owe me,
Measure my strangeness with my unripe years:
Before I know myself, seek not to know me;   *525*
No fisher but the ungrown fry forbears:
     The mellow plum doth fall, the green sticks fast,
     Or being early pluck'd is sour to taste.

'Look! the world's comforter, with weary gait,
His day's hot task hath ended in the west;   *530*
The owl, night's herald, shrieks, 'tis very late;
The sheep are gone to fold, birds to their nest,
     And coal-black clouds that shadow heaven's light
     Do summon us to part and bid good night.

'Now let me say good night, and so say you;   *535*
If you will say so, you shall have a kiss.'
'Good night,' quoth she; and ere he says adieu,
The honey fee of parting tender'd is:
     Her arms do lend his neck a sweet embrace;
     Incorporate then they seem, face grows to face.   *540*

Till, breathless, his disjoin'd, and backward drew
The heavenly moisture, that sweet coral mouth,
Whose precious taste her thirsty lips well knew,
Whereon they surfeit, yet complain on drouth:
     He with her plenty press'd, she faint with dearth,   *545*
     Their lips together glu'd, fall to the earth.

Now quick desire hath caught the yielding prey,
And glutton-like she feeds, yet never filleth;
Her lips are conquerors, his lips obey,
Paying what ransom the insulter willeth;   *550*
     Whose vulture thought doth pitch the price so high,
     That she will draw his lips' rich treasure dry.

And having felt the sweetness of the spoil,
Which blindfold fury she begins to forage;
Her face doth reek and smoke, her blood doth boil,   *555*
And careless lust stirs up a desperate courage;
     Planting oblivion, beating reason back,
     Forgetting shame's pure blush and honour's wrack.

---

465 **recures:** *cures*   472 *Cf. n.*   478 *Cf. n.*   479 **by her good will:** *of her own ac-cord*   482 **windows;** *cf. n.*   490 **repine:** *discontent*   494 **drench'd:** *immersed*   498 **lively joy:** *life's joy*   506 **liveries;** *cf. n.* **wear:** *wear out*   507-510 *Cf. n.*   507 **verdure:** *freshness*

515 **slips;** *cf. n.*   516 **wax-red;** *cf. n.*   529 **comforter;** *cf. n.*   558 **wrack:** *ruin*

Hot, faint, and weary, with her hard embracing,
Like a wild bird being tam'd with too much handling,   *560*
Or as the fleet-foot roe that's tir'd with chasing,
Or like the froward infant still'd with dandling,
   He now obeys, and now no more resisteth,
   While she takes all she can, not all she listeth.

What wax so frozen but dissolves with tempering,   *565*
And yields at last to every light impression?
Things out of hope are compass'd oft with venturing,
Chiefly in love, whose leave exceeds commission:
   Affection faints not like a pale-fac'd coward,
   But then woos best when most his choice is froward.   *570*

When he did frown, O! had she then gave over,
Such nectar from his lips she had not suck'd.
Foul words and frowns must not repel a lover;
What though the rose have prickles, yet 'tis pluck'd:
   Were beauty under twenty locks kept fast,   *575*
   Yet love breaks through and picks them all at last.

For pity now she can no more detain him;
The poor fool prays her that he may depart:
She is resolv'd no longer to restrain him,
Bids him farewell, and look well to her heart,   *580*
   The which, by Cupid's bow she doth protest,
   He carries thence incaged in his breast.

'Sweet boy,' she says, 'this night I'll waste in sorrow,
For my sick heart commands mine eyes to watch.
Tell me, Love's master, shall we meet to-morrow?   *585*
Say, shall we? shall we? wilt thou make the match?'
   He tells her, no; to-morrow he intends
   To hunt the boar with certain of his friends.

'The boar!' quoth she; whereat a sudden pale,
Like lawn being spread upon the blushing rose,   *590*
Usurps her cheek, she trembles at his tale,
And on his neck her yoking arms she throws;
   She sinketh down, still hanging by his neck,
   He on her belly falls, she on her back.

Now is she in the very lists of love,   *595*
Her champion mounted for the hot encounter:
All is imaginary she doth prove,
He will not manage her, although he mount her;
   That worse than Tantalus' is her annoy,
   To clip Elysium and to lack her joy.   *600*

Even so poor birds, deceiv'd with painted grapes,
Do surfeit by the eye and pine the maw,
Even so she languisheth in her mishaps,
As those poor birds that helpless berries saw.
   The warm effects which she in him finds missing,   *605*
   She seeks to kindle with continual kissing.

But all in vain; good queen, it will not be;
She hath assay'd as much as may be prov'd;
Her pleading hath deserv'd a greater fee;
She's Love, she loves, and yet she is not lov'd.   *610*
   'Fie, fie!' he says, 'you crush me; let me go;
   You have no reason to withhold me so.'

'Thou hadst been gone,' quoth she, 'sweet boy, ere this,
But that thou told'st me thou wouldst hunt the boar.
O, be advis'd! thou know'st not what it is   *615*
With javelin's point a churlish swine to gore.
   Whose tushes never sheath'd he whetteth still,
   Like a mortal butcher, bent to kill.

'On his bow-back he hath a battle set
Of bristly pikes, that ever threat his foes;   *620*
His eyes like glow-worms shine when he doth fret;
His snout digs sepulchres where'er he goes;
   Being mov'd, he strikes whate'er is in his way,
   And whom he strikes his crooked tushes slay.

'His brawny sides, with hairy bristles arm'd,   *625*
Are better proof than thy spear's point can enter;
His short thick neck cannot be easily harm'd;
Being ireful, on the lion he will venture:
   The thorny brambles and embracing bushes,
   As fearful of him part, through whom he rushes.   *630*

'Alas! he naught esteems that face of thine,
To which Love's eyes pay tributary gazes;
Nor thy soft hands, sweet lips, and crystal eyne,
Whose full perfection all the world amazes;
   But having thee at vantage, wondrous dread!   *635*
   Would root these beauties as he roots the mead.

'O, let him keep his loathsome cabin still!
Beauty hath naught to do with such foul fiends:
Come not within his danger by thy will;
They that thrive well take counsel of their friends.   *640*
   When thou didst name the boar, not to dissemble,
   I fear'd thy fortune, and my joints did tremble.

'Didst thou not mark my face? was it not white?
Saw'st thou not signs of fear lurk in mine eye?
Grew I not faint? And fell I not downright?   *645*
Within my bosom, whereon thou dost lie,
   My boding heart pants, beats, and takes no rest,
   But, like an earthquake, shakes thee on my breast.

'For where Love reigns, disturbing Jealousy
Doth call himself Affection's sentinel;   *650*
Gives false alarms, suggesteth mutiny,
And in a peaceful hour doth cry "Kill, kill!"
   Distempering gentle Love in his desire,
   As air and water do abate the fire.

'This sour informer, this bate-breeding spy,   *655*
This canker that eats up Love's tender spring,
This carry-tale, dissentious Jealousy,
That sometime true news, sometime false doth bring,
    Knocks at my heart, and whispers in mine ear
    That if I love thee, I thy death should fear: *660*

'And more than so, presenteth to mine eye
The picture of an angry-chafing boar,
Under whose sharp fangs on his back doth lie
An image like thyself, all stain'd with gore;
    Whose blood upon the fresh flowers being shed   *665*
    Doth make them droop with grief and hang the head.

'What should I do, seeing thee so indeed,
That tremble at the imagination?
The thought of it doth make my faint heart bleed,
And fear doth teach it divination: *670*
    I prophesy thy death, my living sorrow,
    If thou encounter with the boar to-morrow.

'But if thou needs wilt hunt, be rul'd by me;
Uncouple at the timorous flying hare,
Or at the fox which lives by subtilty,   *675*
Or at the roe which no encounter dare:
    Pursue these fearful creatures o'er the downs,
    And on thy well-breath'd horse keep with thy hounds.

'And when thou hast on foot the purblind hare,
Mark the poor wretch, to overshoot his troubles   *680*
How he outruns the winds, and with what care
He cranks and crosses with a thousand doubles:
    The many musits through the which he goes
    Are like a labyrinth to amaze his foes.

'Sometime he runs among a flock of sheep,   *685*
To make the cunning hounds mistake their smell,
And sometime where earth-delving conies keep,
To stop the loud pursuers in their yell,
    And sometime sorteth with a herd of deer;
    Danger deviseth shifts; wit waits on fear: *690*

'For there his smell with others being mingled,
The hot scent-snuffing hounds are driven to doubt,
Ceasing their clamorous cry till they have singled
With much ado the cold fault cleanly out;
    Then do they spend their mouths: Echo replies   *695*
    As if another chase were in the skies.

'By this, poor Wat, far off upon a hill,
Stands on his hinder legs with listening ear,
To hearken if his foes pursue him still:
Anon their loud alarums he doth hear;   *700*
    And now his grief may be compared well
    To one sore sick that hears the passing-bell.

'Then shalt thou see the dew-bedabbled wretch
Turn, and return, indenting with the way;
Each envious briar his weary legs doth scratch,   *705*
Each shadow makes him stop, each murmur stay:
    For misery is trodden on by many,
    And being low never reliev'd by any.

'Lie quietly, and hear a little more;
Nay, do not struggle, for thou shalt not rise: *710*
To make thee hate the hunting of the boar,
Unlike myself thou hear'st me moralize,
    Applying this to that, and so to so;
    For love can comment upon every woe.

'Where did I leave?' 'No matter where,' quoth he;   *715*
'Leave me, and then the story aptly ends:
The night is spent,' 'Why, what of that?' quoth she.
'I am,' quoth he, 'expected of my friends;
    And now 'tis dark, and going I shall fall.'
    'In night,' quoth she, 'desire sees best of all.'   *720*

'But if thou fall, O! then imagine this,
The earth, in love with thee, thy footing trips,
And all is but to rob thee of a kiss.
Rich preys make true men thieves; so do thy lips
    Make modest Dian cloudy and forlorn,   *725*
    Lest she should steal a kiss and die forsworn.

'Now of this dark night I perceive the reason:
Cynthia for shame obscures her silver shine,
Till forging Nature be condemn'd of treason,
For stealing moulds from heaven that were divine;   *730*
    Wherein she fram'd thee in high heaven's despite,
    To shame the sun by day and her by night.

'And therefore hath she brib'd the Destinies,
To cross the curious workmanship of nature,
To mingle beauty with infirmities,   *735*
And pure perfection with impure defeature;
    Making it subject to the tyranny
    Of mad mischances and much misery;

'As burning fevers, agues pale and faint,
Life-poisoning pestilence and frenzies wood,   *740*
The marrow-eating sickness, whose attaint
Disorder breeds by heating of the blood;
    Surfeits, imposthumes, grief, and damn'd despair,
    Swear nature's death for framing thee so fair.

'And not the least of all these maladies   *745*
But in one minute's fight brings beauty under:
Both favour, savour, hue, and qualities,
Whereat the impartial gazer late did wonder,
    Are on the sudden wasted, thaw'd and done,
    As mountain-snow melts with the mid-day sun.   *750*

---

655 bate: *strife*   656 spring: *young shoot*   673-678 *Cf. n.*   673-708 *Cf. n.*   674 Uncouple: *set loose the dogs*   680 overshoot: *pass swiftly over*   682 cranks: *runs in and out* doubles: *sudden turns*   683 musits; *cf. n.*   685-688 *Cf. n.*   693, 694 till . . . out; *cf. n.*   695 spend their mouths; *cf. n.*   696 *Cf. n.*   697-699 *Cf. n.*   701, 702 *Cf. n.*

704 indenting; *cf. n.*   720 *Cf. n.*   724 true: *honest*   725 cloudy; *cf. n.*   726 forsworn; *cf. n.*   730 moulds; *cf. n.*   734 cross: *injure*   736 defeature: *deface-ment*   740 wood: *mad*   741 attaint: *infection*   743 imposthumes: *abscesses*   747 favour: *appearance*

'Therefore, despite of fruitless chastity,
Love-lacking vestals and self-loving nuns,
That on the earth would breed a scarcity
And barren dearth of daughters and of sons,
    Be prodigal: the lamp that burns by night   755
    Dries up his oil to lend the world his light.

'What is thy body but a swallowing grave,
Seeming to bury that posterity
Which by the rights of time thou needs must have,
If thou destroy them not in dark obscurity?   760
    If so, the world will hold thee in disdain,
    Sith in thy pride so fair a hope is slain.

'So in thyself thyself art made away;
A mischief worse than civil home-bred strife,
Or theirs whose desperate hands themselves do slay,   765
Or butcher-sire that reaves his son of life.
    Foul-cankering rust the hidden treasure frets,
    But gold that's put to use more gold begets.

'Nay then,' quoth Adon, 'you will fall again
Into your idle over-handled theme;   770
The kiss I gave you is bestow'd in vain,
And all in vain you strive against the stream;
    For by this black-fac'd night, desire's foul nurse,
    Your treatise makes me like you worse and worse.

'If love have lent you twenty thousand tongues,   775
And every tongue more moving than your own,
Bewitching like the wanton mermaid's songs,
Yet from mine ear the tempting tune is blown;
    For know, my heart stands armed in mine ear,
    And will not let a false sound enter there;   780

'Lest the deceiving harmony should run
Into the quiet closure of my breast;
And then my little heart were quite undone,
In his bedchamber to be barr'd of rest.
    No, lady, no; my heart longs not to groan,   785
    But soundly sleeps, while now it sleeps alone.

'What have you urg'd that I cannot reprove?
The path is smooth that leadeth on to danger;
I hate not love, but your device in love,
That lends embracements unto every stranger.   790
    You do it for increase: O strange excuse!
    When reason is the bawd to lust's abuse.

'Call it not love, for Love to heaven is fled,
Since sweating Lust on earth usurp'd his name;
Under whose simple semblance he hath fed   795
Upon fresh beauty, blotting it with blame;
    Which the hot tyrant stains and soon bereaves,
    As caterpillars do the tender leaves.

'Love comforteth like sunshine after rain,
But Lust's effect is tempest after sun;   800

Love's gentle spring doth always fresh remain,
Lust's winter comes ere summer half be done.
    Love surfeits not, Lust like a glutton dies;
    Love is all truth, Lust full of forged lies.

'More I could tell, but more I dare not say;   805
The text is old, the orator too green.
Therefore, in sadness, now I will away;
My face is full of shame, my heart of teen:
    Mine ears, that to your wanton talk attended,
    Do burn themselves for having so offended.'   810

With this he breaketh from the sweet embrace
Of those fair arms which bound him to her breast,
And homeward through the dark laund runs apace;
Leaves Love upon her back deeply distress'd.
    Look, how a bright star shooteth from the sky,   815
    So glides he in the night from Venus' eye;

Which after him she darts, as one on shore
Gazing upon a late-embarked friend,
Till the wild waves will have him seen no more,
Whose ridges with the meeting clouds contend: 820
    So did the merciless and pitchy night
    Fold in the object that did feed her sight.

Whereat amaz'd, as one that unaware
Hath dropp'd a precious jewel in the flood,
Or stonish'd as night-wanderers often are,   825
Their light blown out in some mistrustful wood;
    Even so confounded in the dark she lay,
    Having lost the fair discovery of her way.

And now she beats her heart, whereat it groans,
That all the neighbour caves, as seeming troubled,   830
Make verbal repetition of her moans;
Passion on passion deeply is redoubled:
    'Ay me!' she cries, and twenty times, 'Woe, woe!'
    And twenty echoes twenty times cry so.

She marking them, begins a wailing note,   835
And sings extemporally a woeful ditty;
How love makes young men thrall and old men dote;
How love is wise in folly, foolish-witty:
    Her heavy anthem still concludes in woe,
    And still the choir of echoes answer so.   840

Her song was tedious, and outwore the night,
For lovers' hours are long, though seeming short:
If pleas'd themselves, others, they think, delight
In such like circumstance, with such like sport:
    Their copious stories, oftentimes begun,   845
    End without audience, and are never done.

For who hath she to spend the night withal,
But idle sounds resembling parasites;
Like shrill-tongu'd tapsters answering every call,
Soothing the humour of fantastic wits?   850

---

751 fruitless; *cf. n.*   **757, 758** *Cf. n.*   **766 reaves:** *bereaves*   **768** *Cf. n.*   **774 treatise:** *discourse*   **782 closure:** *enclosure*   **784 barr'd:** *shut out from, deprived*   **787 reprove:** *disprove*

808 teen: *grief*   **813 laund:** *glade*   **825 stonish'd:** *bewildered*   **826 mistrustful:** *causing mistrust*   **828 discovery;** *cf. n.*   **832 Passion:** *lament*   **837 thrall:** *be slaves*   **844 circumstance:** *circuitous discourse*   **848 parasites;** *cf. n.*

She says, ' 'Tis so': they answer all, ' 'Tis so';
And would say after her, if she said 'No.'

Lo! here the gentle lark, weary of rest,
From his moist cabinet mounts up on high,
And wakes the morning, from whose silver breast   *855*
The sun ariseth in his majesty;
    Who doth the world so gloriously behold,
    That cedar-tops and hills seem burnish'd gold

Venus salutes him with this fair good morrow:
'O thou clear god, and patron of all light,   *860*
From whom each lamp and shining star doth borrow
The beauteous influence that makes him bright,
    There lives a son that suck'd an earthly mother,
    May lend thee light, as thou dost lend to other.'

This said, she hasteth to a myrtle grove,   *865*
Musing the morning is so much o'erworn,
And yet she hears no tidings of her love;
She hearkens for his hounds and for his horn:
    Anon she hears them chant it lustily,
    And all in haste she coasteth to the cry.   *870*

And as she runs, the bushes in the way
Some catch her by the neck, some kiss her face,
Some twine about her thigh to make her stay:
She wildly breaketh from their strict embrace,
    Like a milch doe, whose swelling dugs do ache,   *875*
    Hasting to feed her fawn hid in some brake.

By this she hears the hounds are at a bay;
Whereat she starts, like one that spies an adder
Wreath'd up in fatal folds just in his way,
The fear whereof doth make him shake and shudder;   *880*
    Even so the timorous yelping of the hounds
    Appals her senses, and her spirit confounds.

For now she knows it is no gentle chase,
But the blunt boar, rough bear, or lion proud,
Because the cry remaineth in one place,   *885*
Where fearfully the dogs exclaim aloud:
    Finding their enemy to be so curst,
    They all strain courtesy who shall cope him first.

This dismal cry rings sadly in her ear,
Through which it enters to surprise her heart;   *890*
Who, overcome by doubt and bloodless fear,
With cold-pale weakness numbs each feeling part;
    Like soldiers, when their captain once doth yield,
    They basely fly and dare not stay the field.

Thus stands she in a trembling ecstasy,   *895*
Till, cheering up her senses all dismay'd,
She tells them 'tis a causeless fantasy,
And childish error, that they are afraid;

Bids them leave quaking, bids them fear no more:
And with that word she spied the hunted boar,   *900*

Whose frothy mouth bepainted all with red,
Like milk and blood being mingled both together,
A second fear through all her sinews spread,
Which madly hurries her she knows not wither:
    This way she runs, and now she will no further,   *905*
    But back retires to rate the boar for murther.

A thousand spleens bear her a thousand ways,
She treads the path that she untreads again;
Her more than haste is mated with delays,
Like the proceedings of a drunken brain,   *910*
    Full of respects, yet nought at all respecting,
    In hand with all things, nought at all effecting.

Here kennel'd in a brake she finds a hound,
And asks the weary caitiff for his master,
And there another licking of his wound,   *915*
'Gainst venom'd sores the only sovereign plaster;
    And here she meets another sadly scowling,
    To whom she speaks, and he replies with howling.

When he hath ceas'd his ill-resounding noise,
Another flap-mouth'd mourner, black and grim,   *920*
Against the welkin volleys out his voice;
Another and another answer him,
    Clapping their proud tails to the ground below,
    Shaking their scratch'd ears, bleeding as they go.

Look, how the world's poor people are amaz'd   *925*
At apparitions, signs, and prodigies,
Whereon with fearful eyes they long have gaz'd,
Infusing them with dreadful prophecies;
    So she at these sad sighs draws up her breath,
    And, sighing it again, exclaims on Death.   *930*

'Hard-favour'd tyrant, ugly, meagre, lean,
Hateful divorce of love,'—thus chides she Death,—
'Grim-grinning ghost, earth's worm, what dost thou mean
To stifle beauty and to steal his breath,
    Who when he liv'd, his breath and beauty set   *935*
    Gloss on the rose, smell to the violet?

'If he be dead, O no! it cannot be,
Seeing his beauty, thou shouldst strike at it;
O yes! it may; thou hast no eyes to see,
But hatefully at random dost thou hit.   *940*
    Thy mark is feeble age, but thy false dart
    Mistakes that aim and cleaves an infant's heart.

'Hadst thou but bid beware, then he had spoke,
And, hearing him, thy power had lost his power.
The Destinies will curse thee for this stroke;   *945*
They bid thee crop a weed, thou pluck'st a flower.
    Love's golden arrow at him should have fled,
    And not Death's ebon dart, to strike him dead.

---

854 **cabinet**; *cf. n.*   864 **other**: *others*   866 **Musing**: *wondering*   870 **coasteth**: *approaches*   877 **at a bay**; *cf. n.*   883, 884 *Cf. n.*   887 **curst**: *peevish*   888 **strain courtesy**; *cf. n.* **cope**: *encounter*   889 **cry**; *cf. n.*   891, 892 *Cf. n.*   895 **ecstasy**: *excitement*

907 **spleens**: *whims, sudden motions*   909 **mated**: *baffled*   911 **respects**: *considerations*   912 **In hand with**: *undertaking*   920 **flap-mouth'd**; *cf. n.*   933 **worm**; *cf. n.*   944 **his**: *its*   947 **golden arrow**; *cf. n.*   948 **ebon**: *ebony (i.e. black)*

'Dost thou drink tears, that thou provok'st such weeping?
What may a heavy groan advantage thee?   950
Why hast thou cast into eternal sleeping
Those eyes that taught all other eyes to see?
   Now Nature cares not for thy mortal vigour,
   Since her best work is ruin'd with thy rigour.'

Here overcome, as one full of despair,   955
She vail'd her eyelids, who, like sluices, stopp'd
The crystal tide that from her two cheeks fair
In the sweet channel of her bosom dropp'd;
   But through the flood-gates breaks the silver rain,
   And with this strong course opens them again.   960

Oh, how her eyes and tears did lend and borrow!
Her eye seen in the tears, tears in her eye;
Both crystals, where they view'd each other's sorrow,
Sorrow that friendly sighs sought still to dry;
   But like a stormy day, now wind, now rain,   965
   Sighs dry her cheeks, tears make them wet again.

Variable passions throng her constant woe,
As striving who should best become her grief;
All entertain'd, each passion labours so,
That every present sorrow seemeth chief,   970
   But none is best; then join they all together,
   Like many clouds consulting for foul weather.

By this, far off she hears some huntsman holla;
A nurse's song ne'er pleas'd her babe so well:
The dire imagination she did follow   975
This sound of hope doth labour to expel;
   For now reviving joy bids her rejoice,
   And flatters her it is Adonis' voice.

Whereat her tears began to turn their tide,
Being prison'd in her eye, like pearls in glass;   980
Yet sometimes falls an orient drop beside,
Which her cheek melts, as scorning it should pass,
   To wash the foul face of the sluttish ground,
   Who is but drunken when she seemeth drown'd.

O hard-believing love! How strange it seems   985
Not to believe, and yet too credulous;
Thy weal and woe are both of them extremes;
Despair and hope make thee ridiculous:
   The one doth flatter thee in thoughts unlikely,
   In likely thoughts the other kills thee quickly.   990

Now she unweaves the web that she hath wrought:
Adonis lives, and Death is not to blame;
It was not she that call'd him all to naught,
Now she adds honours to his hateful name;
   She clepes him king of graves, and grave for kings,   995
   Imperious supreme of all mortal things.

'No, no,' quoth she, 'sweet Death, I did but jest;
Yet pardon me, I felt a kind of fear

Whenas I met the boar, that bloody beast,
Which knows no pity, but is still severe;   1000
   Then, gentle shadow,—truth I must confess,—
   I rail'd on thee, fearing my love's decease.

' 'Tis not my fault: the boar provok'd my tongue;
Be wreak'd on him, invisible commander;
'Tis he, foul creature, that hath done thee wrong;   1005
I did but act, he's author of my slander:
   Grief hath two tongues: and never woman yet,
   Could rule them both without ten women's wit.'

Thus hoping that Adonis is alive,
Her rash suspect she doth extenuate;   1010
And that his beauty may the better thrive,
With Death she humbly doth insinuate;
   Tells him of trophies, statues, tombs; and stories
   His victories, his triumphs, and his glories.

'O Jove!' quoth she, 'how much a fool was I,   1015
To be of such a weak and silly mind
To wail his death who lives and must not die
Till mutual overthrow of mortal kind;
   For he being dead, with him is beauty slain,
   And, beauty dead, black chaos comes again.   1020

'Fie, fie, fond love! thou art so full of fear
As one with treasure laden, hemm'd with thieves;
Trifles, unwitnessed with eye or ear,
Thy coward heart with false bethinking grieves.'
   Even at this word she hears a merry horn,   1025
   Whereat she leaps that was but late forlorn.

As falcon to the lure, away she flies;
The grass stoops not, she treads on it so light;
And in her haste unfortunately spies
The foul boar's conquest on her fair delight;   1030
   Which seen, her eyes, as murder'd with the view,
   Like stars asham'd of day, themselves withdrew:

Or, as the snail, whose tender horns being hit,
Shrinks backwards in his shelly cave with pain,
And there, all smother'd up, in shade doth sit,   1035
Long after fearing to creep forth again;
   So, at his bloody view, her eyes are fled
   Into the deep dark cabins of her head:

Where they resign their office and their light
To the disposing of her troubled brain;   1040
Who bids them still consort with ugly night,
And never wound the heart with looks again;
   Who, like a king perplexed in his throne,
   By their suggestion gives a deadly groan,

Whereat each tributary subject quakes;   1045
As when the wind, imprison'd in the ground,
Struggling for passage, earth's foundation shakes,
Which with cold terror doth men's minds confound.

---

956 vail'd: *let fall* **981** orient drop: *pearl* **993** Cf. *n.* **995** clepes: *calls* 996
Imperious supreme: *imperial chief*

1004 wreak'd: *avenged* **1010** suspect: *suspicion* **1012** insinuate: *flatter* **1013** trophies; cf. *n.* **1018** mutual: *general* **1027** lure; cf. *n.* **1028** Cf. *n.* **1041** consort:
associate

This mutiny each part doth so surprise
That from their dark beds once more leap her eyes;   *1050*

And, being open'd, threw unwilling light
Upon the wide wound that the boar had trench'd
In his soft flank; whose wonted lily white
With purple tears, that his wound wept, was drench'd:
    No flower was nigh, no grass, herb, leaf, or weed,   *1055*
    But stole his blood and seem'd with him to bleed.

This solemn sympathy poor Venus noteth,
Over one shoulder doth she hang her head,
Dumbly she passions, franticly she doteth;
She thinks he could not die, he is not dead: *1060*
    Her voice is stopp'd, her joints forget to bow,
    Her eyes are mad that they have wept till now.

Upon his hurt she looks so steadfastly,
That her sight dazzling makes the wound seem three;
And then she reprehends her mangling eye,   *1065*
That makes more gashes where no breach should be:
    His face seems twain, each several limb is doubled;
    For oft the eye mistakes, the brain being troubled.

'My tongue cannot express my grief for one,
And yet,' quoth she, 'behold two Adons dead!   *1070*
My sighs are blown away, my salt tears gone,
Mine eyes are turn'd to fire, my heart to lead:
    Heavy heart's lead, melt at mine eyes' red fire!
    So shall I die by drops of hot desire.

'Alas! poor world, what treasure hast thou lost?   *1075*
What face remains alive that's worth the viewing?
Whose tongue is music now? what canst thou boast
Of things long since, or anything ensuing?
    The flowers are sweet, their colours fresh and trim;
    But true-sweet beauty liv'd and died with him.   *1080*

'Bonnet nor veil henceforth no creature wear!
Nor sun nor wind will ever strive to kiss you:
Having no fair to lose, you need not fear;
The sun doth scorn you, and the wind doth hiss you:
    But when Adonis liv'd, sun and sharp air   *1085*
    Lurk'd like two thieves, to rob him of his fair:

'And therefore would he put his bonnet on,
Under whose brim the gaudy sun would peep;
The wind would blow it off, and, being gone,
Play with his locks: then would Adonis weep;   *1090*
    And straight, in pity of his tender years,
    They both would strive who first should dry his tears.

'To see his face the lion walk'd along
Behind some hedge, because he would not fear him;
To recreate himself when he hath sung,   *1095*
The tiger would be tame and gently hear him;
    If he had spoke, the wolf would leave his prey,
    And never fright the silly lamb that day.

'When he beheld his shadow in the brook,
The fishes spread on it their golden gills;   *1100*
When he was by, the birds such pleasure took,
That some would sing, some other in their bills
    Would bring him mulberries and ripe-red cherries;
    He fed them with his sight, they him with berries.

'But this foul, grim, and urchin-snouted boar,   *1105*
Whose downward eye still looketh for a grave,
Ne'er saw the beauteous livery that he wore;
Witness the entertainment that he gave:
    If he did see his face, why then I know
    He thought to kiss him, and hath kill'd him so.   *1110*

' 'Tis true, 'tis true; thus was Adonis slain:
He ran upon the boar with his sharp spear,
Who did not whet his teeth at him again,
But by a kiss thought to persuade him there;
    And nuzzling in his flank, the loving swine   *1115*
    Sheath'd unaware the tusk in his soft groin.

'Had I been tooth'd like him, I must confess,
With kissing him I should have kill'd him first;
But he is dead, and never did he bless
My mouth with his; the more am I accurst.'   *1120*
    With this she falleth in the place she stood,
    And stains her face with his congealed blood.

She looks upon his lips, and they are pale;
She takes him by the hand, and that is cold;
She whispers in his ears a heavy tale,   *1125*
As if they heard the woeful words she told;
    She lifts the coffer-lids that close his eyes,
    Where, lo! two lamps, burnt out, in darkness lies;

Two glasses where herself herself beheld
A thousand times, and now no more reflect;   *1130*
Their virtue lost, wherein they late excell'd,
And every beauty robb'd of his effect:
    'Wonder of time,' quoth she, 'this is my spite,
    That, thou being dead, the day should yet be light.

'Since thou art dead, lo! here I prophesy,   *1135*
Sorrow on love hereafter shall attend:
It shall be waited on with jealousy,
Find sweet beginning, but unsavoury end;
    Ne'er settled equally, but high or low;
    That all love's pleasure shall not match his woe.   *1140*

'It shall be fickle, false, and full of fraud,
Bud and he blasted in a breathing-while;
The bottom poison, and the top o'erstraw'd
With sweets that shall the truest sight beguile:
    The strongest body shall it make most weak,   *1145*
    Strike the wise dumb and teach the fool to speak.

1052 trench'd: *dug*   **1064** *Cf. n.*   **1078 ensuing:** *future*   **1083 fair:** *beauty*   **1094 fear:** *scare*   **1098 silly:** *harmless*

1105 urchin: *hedgehog*   **1107 beauteous livery:** *outward beauty*   **1110** *Cf. n.*   **1115, 1116** *Cf. n.*   **1125 heavy:** *sad*   **1127 coffer-lids;** *cf. n.*   **1139 settled equally:** *evenly balanced*   **1143 o'erstraw'd:** *overstrewn*

'It shall be sparing and too full of riot,
Teaching decrepit age to tread the measures;
The staring ruffian shall it keep in quiet,
Pluck down the rich, enrich the poor with treasures;   *1150*
   It shall be raging mad, and silly mild,
   Make the young old, the old become a child.

'It shall suspect where is no cause of fear;
It shall not fear where it should most mistrust;
It shall be merciful, and too severe,   *1155*
And most deceiving when it seems most just;
   Perverse it shall be, where it shows most toward,
   Put fear to valour, courage to the coward.

'It shall be cause of war and dire events,
And set dissension 'twixt the son and sire;   *1160*
Subject and servile to all discontents,
As dry cumbustious matter is to fire:
   Sith in his prime Death doth my love destroy,
   They that love best their love shall not enjoy.'

By this, the boy that by her side lay kill'd   *1165*
Was melted like a vapour from her sight,
And in his blood that on the ground lay spill'd,
A purple flower sprung up, chequer'd with white;
   Resembling well his pale cheeks, and the blood
   Which in round drops upon their whiteness stood.   *1170*

She bows her head, the new-sprung flowers to smell,
Comparing it to her Adonis' breath;
And says within her bosom it shall dwell,
Since he himself is reft from her by death:
   She crops the stalk, and in the breach appears   *1175*
   Green dropping sap, which she compares to tears.

'Poor flower,' quoth she, 'this was thy father's guise,
Sweet issue of a more sweet-smelling sire
For every little grief to wet his eyes:
To grow unto himself was his desire,   *1180*
   And so 'tis thine; but know, it is as good
   To wither in my breast as in his blood.

'Here was thy father's bed, here in my breast;
Thou art the next of blood, and 'tis thy right:
Lo! in this hollow cradle take thy rest,   *1185*
My throbbing heart shall rock thee day and night:
   There shall not be one minute in an hour
   Wherein I will not kiss my sweet love's flower.'

Thus weary of the world, away she hies,
And yokes her silver doves; by whose swift aid   *1190*
Their mistress, mounted, through the empty skies
In her light chariot quickly is convey'd;
   Holding their course to Paphos, where their queen
   Means to immure herself and not be seen.

❧ FINIS ❧

THE RAPE OF LUCRECE

TO THE RIGHT HONOURABLE HENRY WRIOTHESLEY
Earl of Southampton and Baron of Tichfield.

The love I dedicate to your lordship is without end; whereof this pamphlet, without beginning, is but a superfluous moiety. The warrant I have of your honourable disposition, not the worth of my untutored lines, makes it assured of acceptance. What I have done is yours; what I have to do is yours;   *5* being part in all I have, devoted yours. Were my worth greater, my duty would show greater; meantime, as it is, it is bound to your lordship, to whom I wish long life, still lengthened with happiness.

       Your lordship's in all duty,   *10*
       WILLIAM SHAKESPEARE

❧

THE ARGUMENT

Lucius Tarquinius (for his excessive pride surnamed Superbus), after he had caused his own father-in-law, Servius Tullius, to be cruelly murdered, and contrary to the Roman laws and customs, not requiring or staying for the people's suffrages, had possessed himself of the kingdom, went, ac-   *5* companied with his sons and other noblemen of Rome, to besiege Ardea. During which siege the principal men of the army meeting one evening at the tent of Sextus Tarquinius, the king's son, in their discourses after supper, every one commended the virtues of his own wife: among whom   *10* Collatinus extolled the incomparable chastity of his wife Lucretia. In that pleasant humour they all posted to Rome; and intending, by their secret and sudden arrival, to make trial of that which every one had before avouched, only Collatinus finds his wife—though it were late in the night—spinning   *15* amongst her maids: the other ladies were all found dancing and revelling, or in several disports. Whereupon the noblemen yielded Collatinus the victory, and his wife the fame. At that time Sextus Tarquinius, being inflamed with Lucrece' beauty, yet smothering his passions for the present, departed with   *20* the rest back to the camp; from whence he shortly after privily withdrew himself, and was, according to his estate, royally entertained and lodged by Lucrece at Collatium. The same night he treacherously stealeth into her chamber, violently ravished her, and early in the morning speedeth away. Lucrece, in   *25* this lamentable plight, hastily dispatcheth messengers, one to Rome for her father, and another to the camp for Collatine. They came, the one accompanied with Junius Brutus, the other with Publius Valerius; and finding Lucrece attired in mourning habit, demanded the cause of her sorrow. She, first   *30* taking an oath of them for her revenge, revealed the actor, and the whole manner of his dealing, and withal suddenly stabbed herself. Which done, with one consent they all vowed to root out the whole hated family of the Tarquins; and, bearing the dead body to Rome, Brutus acquainted the people with the   *35* doer and manner of the vile deed, with a bitter invective

---

1148 measures; *cf. n.*   1157 toward: *yielding*   1162 cumbustious: *combustible*   1168
purple flower; *cf. n.*   1193 Paphos; *cf. n.*

1–7 Cf. n.   1 Lucius Tarquinius; *cf. n.*   7 Ardea; *cf. n.*   11 Collatinus; *cf. n.*   26
messengers; *cf. n.*   28 Junius Brutus; *cf. n.*   29 Publius Valerius; *cf. n.*

against the tyranny of the king; wherewith the people were so
moved, that with one consent and a general acclamation the
Tarquins were all exiled, and the state government changed
from kings to consuls.   40

❧

From the besieged Ardea all in post,
Borne by the trustless wings of false desire,
Lust-breathed Tarquin leaves the Roman host,
And to Collatium bears the lightless fire
Which, in pale embers hid, lurks to aspire,   5
    And girdle with embracing flames the waist
    Of Collatine's fair love, Lucrece the chaste.

Haply that name of chaste unhappily set
This bateless edge on his keen appetite;
When Collatine unwisely did not let   10
To praise the clear unmatched red and white
Which triumph'd in that sky of his delight,
    Where mortal stars, as bright as heaven's beauties,
    With pure aspects did him peculiar duties.

For he the night before, in Tarquin's tent,   15
Unlock'd the treasure of his happy state;
What priceless wealth the heavens had him lent
In the possession of his beauteous mate;
Reck'ning his fortune at such high-proud rate,
    That kings might be espoused to more fame,   20
    But king nor peer to such a peerless dame.

O happiness enjoy'd but of a few!
And, if possess'd, as soon decay'd and done
As is the morning's silver-melting dew
Against the golden splendour of the sun;   25
An expir'd date, cancell'd ere well begun:
    Honour and beauty, in the owner's arms,
    Are weakly fortress'd from a world of harms.

Beauty itself doth of itself persuade
The eyes of men without an orator;   30
What needeth then apology be made
To set forth that which is so singular?
Or why is Collatine the publisher
    Of that rich jewel he should keep unknown
    From thievish ears, because it is his own?   35

Perchance his boast of Lucrece' sov'reignty
Suggested this proud issue of a king;
For by our ears our hearts oft tainted be:
Perchance that envy of so rich a thing,
Braving compare, disdainfully did sting   40
    His high-pitch'd thoughts, that meaner men should vaunt
    That golden hap which their superiors want.

But some untimely thought did instigate
His all-too-timeless speed, if none of those:

His honour, his affairs, his friends, his state,   45
Neglected all, with swift intent he goes
To quench the coal which in his liver glows.
    O rash false heat, wrapp'd in repentant cold!
    Thy hasty spring still blasts, and ne'er grows old.

When at Collatium this false lord arriv'd,   50
Well was he welcom'd by the Roman dame,
Within whose face beauty and virtue striv'd
Which of them both should underprop her fame:
When virtue bragg'd, beauty would blush for shame;
    When beauty boasted blushes, in despite   55
    Virtue would stain that o'er with silver white.

But beauty, in that white intituled,
From Venus' doves doth challenge that fair field;
Then virtue claims from beauty beauty's red,
Which virtue gave the golden age to gild   60
Their silver cheeks, and call'd it then their shield;
    Teaching them thus to use it in the fight,
    When shame assail'd, the red should fence the white.

This heraldry in Lucrece' face was seen,
Argu'd by beauty's red and virtue's white: 65
Of either's colour was the other queen,
Proving from world's minority their right.
Yet their ambition makes them still to fight;
    The sovereignty of either being so great,
    That oft they interchange each other's seat.   70

This silent war of lilies and of roses,
Which Tarquin view'd in her fair face's field,
In their pure ranks his traitor eye encloses;
Where, lest between them both it should be kill'd
The coward captive vanquished doth yield   75
    To those two armies that would let him go,
    Rather than triumph in so false a foe.

Now thinks he that her husband's shallow tongue—
The niggard prodigal that prais'd her so—
In that high task hath done her beauty wrong,   80
Which far exceeds his barren skill to show:
Therefore that praise which Collatine doth owe
    Enchanted Tarquin answers with surmise,
    In silent wonder of still-gazing eyes.

This earthly saint, adored by this devil,   85
Little suspecteth the false worshipper;
For unstain'd thoughts do seldom dream on evil,
Birds never lim'd no secret bushes fear:
So guiltless she securely gives good cheer
    And reverend welcome to her princely guest,   90
    Whose inward ill no outward harm express'd:

For that he colour'd with his high estate,
Hiding base sin in plaits of majesty;
That nothing in him seem'd inordinate,

Save sometime too much wonder of his eye, *95*
Which, having all, all could not satisfy;
 But, poorly rich, so wanteth in his store,
 That, cloy'd with much, he pineth still for more.

But she, that never cop'd with stranger eyes,
Could pick no meaning from their parling looks, *100*
Nor read the subtle-shining secrecies
Writ in the glassy margents of such books:
She touch'd no unknown baits, nor fear'd no hooks;
 Nor could she moralize his wanton sight,
 More than his eyes were open'd to the light. *105*

He stories to her ears her husband's fame,
Won in the fields of fruitful Italy;
And decks with praises Collatine's high name,
Made glorious by his manly chivalry
With bruised arms and wreaths of victory: *110*
 Her joy with heav'd-up hand she doth express,
 And, wordless, so greets heaven for his success.

Far from the purpose of his coming thither,
He makes excuses for his being there:
No cloudy show of stormy blustering weather *115*
Doth yet in this far welkin once appear;
Till sable Night, mother of Dread and Fear,
 Upon the world dim darkness doth display,
 And in her vaulty prison stows the Day.

For then is Tarquin brought unto his bed, *120*
Intending weariness with heavy spright;
For after supper long he questioned
With modest Lucrece, and wore out the night:
Now leaden slumber with life's strength doth fight,
 And every one to rest themselves betake, *125*
 Save thieves, and cares, and troubled minds, that wake.

As one of which doth Tarquin lie revolving
The sundry dangers of his will's obtaining;
Yet ever to obtain his will resolving,
Though weak-built hopes persuade him to abstaining: *130*
Despair to gain doth traffic oft for gaining;
 And when great treasure is the meed propos'd,
 Though death be adjunct, there's no death suppos'd.

Those that much covet are with gain so fond,
That what they have not, that which they possess *135*
They scatter and unloose it from their bond,
And so, by hoping more, they have but less;
Or, gaining more, the profit of excess
 Is but to surfeit, and such griefs sustain,
 That they prove bankrupt in this poor-rich gain, *140*

The aim of all is but to nurse the life
With honour, wealth, and ease, in waning age;
And in this aim there is such thwarting strife,

That one for all, or all for one we gage;
As life for honour in fell battles' rage; *145*
 Honour for wealth; and oft that wealth doth cost
 The death of all, and all together lost.

So that in venturing ill we leave to be
The things we are for that which we expect;
And this ambitious foul infirmity, *150*
In having much, torments us with defect
Of that we have: so then we do neglect
 The thing we have: and, all for want of wit,
 Make something nothing by augmenting it.

Such hazard now must doting Tarquin make, *155*
Pawning his honour to obtain his lust,
And for himself himself he must forsake:
Then where is truth, if there be no self-trust?
When shall he think to find a stranger just,
 When he himself himself confounds, betrays *160*
 To slanderous tongues and wretched hateful days?

Now stole upon the time the dead of night,
When heavy sleep had clos'd up mortal eyes;
No comfortable star did lend his light,
No noise but owls' and wolves' death-boding cries; *165*
Now serves the season that they may surprise
 The silly lambs; pure thoughts are dead and still,
 While lust and murder wake to stain and kill.

And now this lustful lord leap'd from his bed,
Throwing his mantle rudely o'er his arm; *170*
Is madly toss'd between desire and dread;
Th' one sweetly flatters, th' other feareth harm;
But honest fear, bewitch'd with lust's foul charm,
 Doth too too oft betake him to retire,
 Beaten away by brain-sick rude desire. *175*

His falchion on a flint he softly smiteth,
That from the cold stone sparks of fire do fly;
Whereat a waxen torch forthwith he lighteth,
Which must be lode-star to his lustful eye;
And to the flame thus speaks advisedly: *180*
 'As from this cold flint I enforc'd this fire,
 So Lucrece must I force to my desire.'

Here pale with fear he doth premeditate
The dangers of his loathsome enterprise,
And in his inward mind he doth debate *185*
What following sorrow may on this arise:
Then looking scornfully, he doth despise
 His naked armour of still-slaughter'd lust,
 And justly thus controls his thoughts unjust:

'Fair torch, burn out thy light, and lend it not *190*
To darken her whose light excelleth thine;
And die, unhallow'd thoughts, before you blot
With your uncleanness that which is divine;
Offer pure incense to so pure a shrine:

99 cop'd with: *encountered* **100 parling:** *speaking* **102 margents:** *margins* **104 moralize:** *interpret* **104, 105** *Cf. n.* **106-112** *Cf. n.* **111 heav'd-up:** *uplifted* **117-119** *Cf. n.* **117 sable:** *black* **120-123** *Cf. n.* **121 Intending:** *pretending* **122 questioned:** *conversed* **135, 136** *Cf. n.* **138-140** *Cf. n.* **144 gage:** *impawn, hazard*

150-152 *Cf. n.* **160 confounds:** *overthrows* **167 silly:** *harmless* **174 retire:** *retreat* **187, 188** *Cf. n.*

Let fair humanity abhor the deed   *195*
That spots and stains love's modest snow-white weed.

'O shame to knighthood and to shining arms!
O foul dishonour to my household's grave!
O impious act, including all foul harms!
A martial man to be soft fancy's slave!   *200*
True valour still a true respect should have;
    Then my digression is so vile, so base,
    That it will live engraven in my face.

'Yea, though I die, the scandal will survive,
And be an eye-sore in my golden coat;   *205*
Some loathsome dash the herald will contrive,
To cipher me how fondly I did dote;
That my posterity sham'd with the note,
    Shall curse my bones, and hold it for no sin
    To wish that I their father had not been.   *210*

'What win I if I gain the thing I seek?
A dream, a breath, a froth of fleeting joy.
Who buys a minute's mirth to wail a week?
Or sells eternity to get a toy?
For one sweet grape who will the vine destroy?   *215*
    Or what fond beggar, but to touch the crown,
    Would with the sceptre straight be stroken down?

'If Collatinus dream of my intent,
Will he not wake, and in desperate rage
Post hither, this vile purpose to prevent?   *220*
This siege that hath engirt his marriage,
This blur to youth, this sorrow to the sage,
    This dying virtue, this surviving shame,
    Whose crime will bear an ever-during blame?

'O, what excuse can my invention make,   *225*
When thou shalt charge me with so black a deed?
Will not my tongue be mute, my frail joints shake,
Mine eyes forgo their light, my false heart bleed?
The guilt being great, the fear doth still exceed;
    And extreme fear can neither fight nor fly,   *230*
    But coward-like with trembling terror die.

'Had Collatinus kill'd my son or sire,
Or lain in ambush to betray my life,
Or were he not my dear friend, this desire
Might have excuse to work upon his wife,   *235*
As in revenge or quittal of such strife:
    But as he is my kinsman, my dear friend,
    The shame and fault finds no excuse nor end.

'Shameful it is; ay, if the fact be known:
Hateful it is; there is no hate in loving: *240*
I'll beg her love; but she is not her own:
The worst is but denial and reproving:
    My will is strong, past reason's weak removing.

Who fears a sentence, or an old man's saw,
Shall by a painted cloth be kept in awe.'   *245*

Thus, graceless, holds he disputation
'Tween frozen conscience and hot-burning will,
And with good thoughts makes dispensation,
Urging the worser sense for vantage still;
Which in a moment doth confound and kill   *250*
    All pure effects, and doth so far proceed,
    That what is vile shows like a virtuous deed.

Quoth he, 'She took me kindly by the hand,
And gaz'd for tidings in my eager eyes,
Fearing some hard news from the warlike band   *255*
Where her beloved Collatinus lies.
O how her fear did make her colour rise!
    First red as roses that on lawn we lay,
    Then white as lawn, the roses took away.

'And how her hand, in my hand being lock'd,   *260*
Forc'd it to tremble with her loyal fear!
Which struck her sad, and then it faster rock'd,
Until her husband's welfare she did hear;
Whereat she smiled with so sweet a cheer,
    That had Narcissus seen her as she stood,   *265*
    Self-love had never drown'd him in the flood.

'Why hunt I then for colour or excuses?
All orators are dumb when beauty pleadeth;
Poor wretches have remorse in poor abuses;
Love thrives not in the heart that shadows dreadeth: *270*
Affection is my captain, and he leadeth;
    And when his gaudy banner is display'd,
    The coward fights and will not be dismay'd.

'Then, childish fear, avaunt! debating, die!
Respect and reason, wait on wrinkled age!   *275*
My heart shall never countermand mine eye:
Sad pause and deep regard beseem the sage;
My part is youth, and beats these from the stage.
    Desire my pilot is, beauty my prize;
    Then who fears sinking where such treasure lies?'   *280*

As corn o'ergrown by weeds, so heedful fear
Is almost chok'd by unresisted lust.
Away he steals with open listening ear,
Full of foul hope, and full of fond mistrust;
Both which, as servitors to the unjust,   *285*
    So cross him with their opposite persuasion,
    That now he vows a league, and now invasion.

Within his thought her heavenly image sits,
And in the self-same seat sits Collatine:
That eye which looks on her confounds his wits;   *290*
That eye which him beholds, as more divine,
Unto a view so false will not incline;
    But with a pure appeal seeks to the heart,
    Which once corrupted, takes the worser part;

---

196 weed: *dress*   **197-210** *Cf. n.*   **200 fancy's:** *love's*   **202 digression:** *misdeed*   **206, 207** *Cf. n.*   **207 cipher:** *express by a sign*   **217 stroken:** *struck*   **236 quittal:** *requital*

245 painted cloth: *cf. n.*   **248 makes dispensation:** *dispenses*   **249 vantage:** *vantage ground*   **265 Narcissus:** *cf. n.*   **278** *Cf. n.*

And therein heartens up his servile powers,   295
Who, flatter'd by their leader's jocund show,
Stuff up his lust, as minutes fill up hours;
And as their captain, so their pride doth grow,
Paying more slavish tribute than they owe.
    By reprobate desire thus madly led,   300
    The Roman lord marcheth to Lucrece' bed.

The locks between her chamber and his will,
Each one by him enforc'd, retires his ward;
But as they open they all rate his ill,
Which drives the creeping thief to some regard: 305
The threshold grates the door to have him heard;
    Night-wand'ring weasels shriek to see him there;
    They fright him, yet he still pursues his fear.

As each unwilling portal yields him way,
Through little vents and crannies of the place   310
The wind wars with his torch to make him stay,
And blows the smoke of it into his face,
Extinguishing his conduct in this case;
    But his hot heart, which fond desire doth scorch,
    Puffs forth another wind that fires the torch: 315

And being lighted, by the light he spies
Lucretia's glove, wherein her needle sticks:
He takes it from the rushes where it lies,
And griping it, the needle his finger pricks;
As who should say, 'This glove to wanton tricks   320
    Is not inur'd; return again in haste;
    Thou seest our mistress' ornaments are chaste.'

But all these poor forbiddings could not stay him;
He in the worst sense construes their denial:
The door, the wind, the glove, that did delay him,   325
He takes for accidental things of trial;
Or as those bars which stop the hourly dial,
    Who with a ling'ring stay his course doth let,
    Till every minute pays the hour his debt.

'So, so,' quoth he, 'these lets attend the time,   330
Like little frosts that sometime threat the spring,
To add a more rejoicing to the prime,
And give the sneaped birds more cause to sing.
Pain pays the income of each precious thing;
    Huge rocks, high winds, strong pirates, shelves and sands,
    The merchant fears, ere rich at home he lands.'

Now is he come unto the chamber door,
That shuts him from the heaven of his thought,
Which with a yielding latch, and with no more,
Hath barr'd him from the blessed thing he sought.   340
So from himself impiety hath wrought,
    That for his prey to pray he doth begin,
    As if the heavens should countenance his sin.

But in the midst of his unfruitful prayer,
Having solicited the eternal power   345
That his foul thoughts might compass his fair fair,
And they would stand auspicious to the hour,
Even there he starts: quoth he, 'I must deflower;
    The powers to whom I pray abhor this fact,
    How can they then assist me in the act?   350

'Then Love and Fortune be my gods, my guide!
My will is back'd with resolution:
Thoughts are but dreams till their effects be tried;
The blackest sin is clear'd with absolution;
Against love's fire fear's frost hath dissolution.   355
    The eye of heaven is out, and misty night.
    Covers the shame that follows sweet delight.'

This said, his guilty hand pluck'd up the latch,
And with his knee the door he opens wide.
The dove sleeps fast that this night-owl will catch: 360
Thus treason works ere traitors be espied.
Who sees the lurking serpent steps aside;
    But she, sound sleeping, fearing no such thing,
    Lies at the mercy of his mortal sting.

Into the chamber wickedly he stalks,   365
And gazeth on her yet unstained bed.
The curtains being close, about he walks,
Rolling his greedy eyeballs in his head:
By their high treason is his heart misled;
    Which gives the watchword to his hand full soon,   370
    To draw the cloud that hides the silver moon.

Look, as the fair and fiery-pointed sun,
Rushing from forth a cloud, bereaves our sight;
Even so, the curtain drawn, his eyes begun
To wink, being blinded with a greater light: 375
Whether it is that she reflects so bright,
    That dazzleth them, or else some shame supposed,
    But blind they are, and keep themselves enclosed.

O had they in that darksome prison died,
Then had they seen the period of their ill;   380
Then Collatine again, by Lucrece' side,
In his clear bed might have reposed still:
But they must ope, this blessed league to kill,
    And holy-thoughted Lucrece to their sight
    Must sell her joy, her life, her world's delight.   385

Her lily hand her rosy cheek lies under,
Cozening the pillow of a lawful kiss;
Who, therefore angry, seems to part in sunder,
Swelling on either side to want his bliss;
Between whose hills her head entombed is: 390
    Where, like a virtuous monument she lies,
    To be admir'd of lewd unhallow'd eyes.

Without the bed her other fair hand was,
On the green coverlet; whose perfect white
Show'd like an April daisy on the grass,   395

---

303 **retires:** *withdraws*   305 **regard:** *consideration*   313 **conduct:** *guide*   318 **rushes;**
cf. n.   328 **let:** *hinder*   332 **prime:** *spring*   333 **sneaped:** *pinched with frost*   334
income: *arrival*   335 **shelves:** *sandbanks*   341 *Cf. n.*   342 **prey, pray;** *cf. n.*

349 **fact:** *misdeed*   356 **eye of heaven;** *cf. n.*   365 **stalks;** *cf. n.*   380 **period:**
end   386-395 *Cf. n.*   389 **to want:** *as if in anger at being deprived of*

With pearly sweat, resembling dew of night.
Her eyes, like marigolds, had sheath'd their light,
   And canopied in darkness sweetly lay,
   Till they might open to adorn the day.

Her hair, like golden threads, play'd with her breath;   *400*
O modest wantons! wanton modesty!
Showing life's triumph in the map of death,
And death's dim look in life's mortality:
Each in her sleep themselves so beautify,
   As if between them twain there were no strife,   *405*
   But that life liv'd in death, and death in life.

Her breasts, like ivory globes circled with blue,
A pair of maiden worlds unconquered,
Save of their lord no bearing yoke they knew,
And him by oath they truly honoured.   *410*
These worlds in Tarquin new ambition bred;
   Who, like a foul usurper, went about
   From this fair throne to heave the owner out,

What could he see but mightily he noted?
What did he note but strongly he desir'd?   *415*
What he beheld, on that he firmly doted,
And in his will his wilful eye he tir'd.
With more than admiration he admir'd
   Her azure veins, her alablaster skin,
   Her coral lips, her snow-white dimpled chin.   *420*

As the grim lion fawneth o'er his prey,
Sharp hunger by the conquest satisfied,
So o'er this sleeping soul doth Tarquin stay,
His rage of lust by gazing qualified;
Slack'd, not suppress'd; for standing by her side,   *425*
   His eye, which late this mutiny restrains,
   Unto a greater uproar tempts his veins:

And they, like straggling slaves for pillage fighting,
Obdurate vassals fell exploits effecting,
In bloody death and ravishment delighting,   *430*
Nor children's tears nor mother's groans respecting,
Swell in their pride, the onset still expecting:
   Anon his beating heart, alarum striking,
   Gives the hot charge and bids them do their liking.

His drumming heart cheers up his burning eye,   *435*
His eye commends the leading to his hand;
His hand, as proud of such a dignity,
Smoking with pride, march'd on to make his stand
On her bare breast, the heart of all her land;
   Whose ranks of blue veins, as his hand did scale,   *440*
   Left their round turrets destitute and pale.

They, mustering to the quiet cabinet
Where their dear governess and lady lies,
Do tell her she is dreadfully beset,
And fright her with confusion of their cries: *445*

397 marigolds; *cf. n.*   **400** golden threads; *cf. n.*   **402** map: *picture*   **407-409**
Cf. n.   **413** heave: *drive*   **417** tir'd; *cf. n.*   **419** alablaster: *alabaster, white*   **421**
fawneth: *shows delight, as a dog does*   **424** qualified: *abated*   **436 commends:** *en-*
trusts   **437-439** *Cf. n.*   **442** cabinet: *closet*

She, much amaz'd, breaks ope her lock'd-up eyes,
   Who, peeping forth this tumult to behold,
   Are by his flaming torch dimm'd and controll'd.

Imagine her as one in dead of night
From forth dull sleep by dreadful fancy waking,   *450*
That thinks she hath beheld some ghastly sprite,
Whose grim aspect sets every joint a-shaking;
What terror 'tis! but she, in worser taking,
   From sleep disturbed, heedfully doth view
   The sight which makes supposed terror true.   *455*

Wrapp'd and confounded in a thousand fears,
Like to a new-kill'd bird she trembling lies;
She dares not look; yet, winking, there appears
Quick-shifting antics, ugly in her eyes:
Such shadows are the weak brain's forgeries;   *460*
   Who, angry that the eyes fly from their lights,
   In darkness daunts them with more dreadful sights.

His hand, that yet remains upon her breast,
Rude ram to batter such an ivory wall!
May feel her heart,—poor citizen,—distress'd,   *465*
Wounding itself to death, rise up and fall,
Beating her bulk, that his hand shakes withal.
   This moves in him more rage, and lesser pity,
   To make the breach and enter this sweet city.

First, like a trumpet, doth his tongue begin   *470*
To sound a parley to his heartless foe;
Who o'er the white sheet peers her whiter chin,
The reason of this rash alarm to know,
Which he by dumb demeanour seeks to show;
   But she with vehement prayers urgeth still   *475*
   Under what colour he commits this ill.

Thus he replies: 'The colour in thy face,—
That even for anger makes the lily pale,
And the red rose blush at her own disgrace,—
Shall plead for me and tell my loving tale;   *480*
Under that colour am I come to scale
   Thy never-conquer'd fort: the fault is thine,
   For those thine eyes betray thee unto mine.

'Thus I forestall thee, if thou mean to chide:
Thy beauty hath ensnar'd thee to this night,   *485*
Where thou with patience must my will abide,
My will that marks thee for my earth's delight,
Which I to conquer sought with all my might;
   But as reproof and reason beat it dead,
   By thy bright beauty was it newly bred.   *490*

'I see what crosses my attempt will bring;
I know what thorns the growing rose defends;
I think the honey guarded with a sting;
All this, beforehand, counsel comprehends:
But will is deaf and hears no heedful friends;   *495*
   Only he hath an eye to gaze on beauty,
   And dotes on what he looks, 'gainst law or duty.

453 taking: *plight*   **459** antics; *cf. n.*   **467** bulk: *frame*   **471** heartless:
timid   **472** peers: *makes to peep out*   **476, 477, 481** colour; *cf. n.*   **477-504**
Cf. n.   **477-511** *Cf. n.*   **492** *Cf. n.*

'I have debated, even in my soul,
What wrong, what shame, what sorrow I shall breed;
But nothing can affection's course control,   *500*
Or stop the headlong fury of his speed.
I know repentant tears ensue the deed,
   Reproach, disdain, and deadly enmity;
   Yet strive I to embrace mine infamy.'

This said, he shakes aloft his Roman blade,   *505*
Which like a falcon, towering in the skies,
Coucheth the fowl below with his wings' shade,
Whose crooked beak threats if he mount he dies:
So under his insulting falchion lies
   Harmless Lucretia, marking what he tells   *510*
   With trembling fear, as fowl hear falcon's bells.

'Lucrece,' quoth he, 'this night I must enjoy thee:
If thou deny, then force must work my way,
For in thy bed I purpose to destroy thee:
That done, some worthless slave of thine I'll slay,   *515*
To kill thine honour with thy life's decay;
   And in thy dead arms do I mean to place him,
   Swearing I slew him, seeing thee embrace him.

'So thy surviving husband shall remain
The scornful mark of every open eye;   *520*
Thy kinsmen hang their heads at this disdain,
Thy issue blurr'd with nameless bastardy:
And thou, the author of their obloquy,
   Shalt have thy trespass cited up in rimes,
   And sung by children in succeeding times.   *525*

'But if thou yield, I rest thy secret friend:
The fault unknown is as a thought unacted;
A little harm done to a great good end,
For lawful policy remains enacted.
The poisonous simple sometimes is compacted   *530*
   In a pure compound; being so applied,
   His venom in effect is purified.

'Then for thy husband and thy children's sake,
Tender my suit: bequeath not to their lot
The shame that from them no device can take,   *535*
The blemish that will never be forgot;
Worse than a slavish wipe or birth-hour's blot:
   For marks descried in men's nativity
   Are nature's faults, not their own infamy.'

Here with a cockatrice' dead-killing eye   *540*
He rouseth up himself, and makes a pause;
While she, the picture of pure piety,
Like a white hind under the gripe's sharp claws,
Pleads in a wilderness where are no laws,
   To the rough beast that knows no gentle right,   *545*
   Nor aught obeys but his foul appetite.

But when a black-fac'd cloud the world doth threat,
In his dim mist the aspiring mountains hiding,
From earth's dark womb some gentle gust doth get,
Which blows these pitchy vapours from their biding,   *550*
Hindering their present fall by this dividing;
   So his unhallow'd haste her words delays,
   And moody Pluto winks while Orpheus plays.

Yet, foul night-waking cat, he doth but dally,
While in his hold-fast foot the weak mouse panteth: *555*
Her sad behaviour feeds his vulture folly,
A swallowing gulf that even in plenty wanteth:
His ear her prayers admits, but his heart granteth
   No penetrable entrance to her plaining:
   Tears harden lust through marble wear with raining.   *560*

Her pity-pleading eyes are sadly fix'd
In the remorseless wrinkles of his face;
Her modest eloquence with sighs is mix'd,
Which to her oratory adds more grace.
She puts the period often from his place;   *565*
   And midst the sentence so her accent breaks,
   That twice she doth begin ere once she speaks.

She conjures him by high almighty Jove,
By knighthood, gentry, and sweet friendship's oath,
By her untimely tears, her husband's love,   *570*
By holy human law, and common troth,
By heaven and earth, and all the power of both,
   That to his borrow'd bed he make retire,
   And stoop to honour, not to foul desire.

Quoth she, 'Reward not hospitality   *575*
With such black payment as though hast pretended;
Mud not the fountain that gave drink to thee;
Mar not the thing that cannot be amended;
End thy ill aim before thy shoot be ended;
   He is no woodman that doth bend his bow   *580*
   To strike a poor unseasonable doe.

'My husband is thy friend, for his sake spare me;
Thyself art mighty, for thine own sake leave me;
Myself a weakling, do not, then, ensnare me;
Thou look'st not like deceit, do not deceive me.   *585*
My sighs, like whirlwinds, labour hence to heave thee;
   If ever man were mov'd with woman's moans,
   Be moved with my tears, my sighs, my groans.

'All which together, like a troubled ocean,
Beat at thy rocky and wrack-threat'ning heart,   *590*
To soften it with their continual motion;
For stones dissolv'd to water do convert.
O, if no harder than a stone thou art,
   Melt at my tears, and be compassionate!
   Soft pity enters at an iron gate.   *595*

'In Tarquin's likeness I did entertain thee;
Hast thou put on his shape to do him shame?

---

500 **affection:** *passion*   507 **Coucheth:** *causes to crouch*   509 **falchion:** *sword;*
cf. n.   511 **falcon's bells;** *cf. n.*   522 **nameless bastardy;** *cf. n.*   534 **Tender:** *receive*
favorably   537 **Worse … wipe;** *cf. n.*   540 **cockatrice;** *cf. n.*   543 **gripe:** *vulture*

556 **vulture folly;** *cf. n.*   559 **plaining:** *complaint*   565-567 *Cf. n.*   576 **pretended:**
intended   580 **woodman:** *hunter*   586 **heave:** *drive*   592 **convert:** *change*   596-
630 *Cf. n.*

To all the host of heaven I complain me,
Thou wrong'st his honour, wound'st his princely name.
Thou art not what thou seem'st; and if the same,   *600*
    Thou seem'st not what thou art, a god, a king;
    For kings like gods should govern everything.

'How will thy shame be seeded in thine age,
When thus thy vices bud before thy spring!
If in thy hope thou dar'st do such outrage,   *605*
What dar'st thou not when once thou art a king?
O be rememb'red, no outrageous thing
    From vassal actors can be wip'd away;
    Then kings' misdeeds cannot be hid in clay.

'This deed will make thee only lov'd for fear;   *610*
But happy monarchs still are fear'd for love:
With foul offenders thou perforce must bear,
When they in thee the like offences prove:
If but for fear of this, thy will remove;
    For princes are the glass, the school, the book   *615*
    Where subjects' eyes do learn, do read, do look.

'And wilt thou be the school where Lust shall learn?
Must he in three read lectures of such shame?
Wilt thou be glass wherein it shall discern
Authority for sin, warrant for blame,   *620*
To privilege dishonour in thy name?
    Thou back'st reproach against long-living laud,
    And mak'st fair reputation but a bawd.

'Hast thou command? by him that gave it thee,
From a pure heart command thy rebel will: *625*
Draw not thy sword to guard iniquity,
For it was lent thee all that brood to kill.
Thy princely office how canst thou fulfil,
    When, pattern'd by thy fault, foul sin may say,
    He learn'd to sin, and thou didst teach the way?   *630*

'Think but how vile a spectacle it were,
To view thy present trespass in another.
Men's faults do seldom to themselves appear;
Their own transgressions partially they smother:
This guilt would seem death-worthy in thy brother.   *635*
    O how are they wrapp'd in with infamies
    That from their own misdeeds askance their eyes!

'To thee, to thee, my heav'd-up hands appeal,
Not to seducing lust, thy rash relier:
I sue for exil'd majesty's repeal;   *640*
Let him return, and flattering thoughts retire:
His true respect will prison false desire,
    And wipe the dim mist from thy doting eyne,
    That thou shalt see thy state and pity mine.'

'Have done,' quoth he; 'my uncontrolled tide   *645*
Turns not, but swells the higher by this let.

Small lights are soon blown out, huge fires abide,
And with the wind in greater fury fret:
The petty streams that pay a daily debt
    To their salt sovereign, with their fresh falls' haste   *650*
    Add to his flow, but alter not his taste.'

'Thou art,' quoth she, 'a sea, a sovereign king;
And lo! there falls into thy boundless flood
Black lust, dishonour, shame, misgoverning,
Who seek to stain the ocean of thy blood.   *655*
If all these petty ills shall change thy good,
    Thy sea within a puddle's womb is hears'd,
    And not the puddle in thy sea dispers'd.

'So shall these slaves be king, and thou their slave;
Thou nobly base, they basely dignified;   *660*
Thou their fair life, and they thy fouler grave;
Thou loathed in their shame, they in thy pride:
The lesser thing should not the greater hide;
    The cedar stoops not to the base shrub's foot,
    But low shrubs wither at the cedar's root.   *665*

'So let thy thoughts, low vassals to thy state'—
'No more,' quoth he; 'by heaven, I will not hear thee:
Yield to my love; if not, enforced hate,
Instead of love's coy touch, shall rudely tear thee;
That done, despitefully I mean to bear thee   *670*
    Unto the base bed of some rascal groom,
    To be thy partner in this shameful doom.'

This said, he sets his foot upon the light,
For light and lust are deadly enemies:
Shame folded up in blind concealing night,   *675*
When most unseen, then most doth tyrannize.
The wolf hath seiz'd his prey, the poor lamb cries;
    Till with her own white fleece her voice controll'd
    Entombs her outcry in her lips' sweet fold:

For with the nightly linen that she wears   *680*
He pens her piteous clamours in her head,
Cooling his hot face in the chastest tears
That ever modest eyes with sorrow shed.
O that prone lust should stain so pure a bed!
    The spots whereof could weeping purify,   *685*
    Her tears should drop on them perpetually.

But she hath lost a dearer thing than life,
And he hath won what he would lose again;
This forced league doth force a further strife;
This momentary joy breeds months of pain;   *690*
This hot desire converts to cold disdain:
    Pure Chastity is rifled of her store,
    And Lust, the thief, far poorer than before.

Look! as the full-fed hound or gorged hawk,
Unapt for tender smell or speedy flight,   *695*
Make slow pursuit, or altogether balk
The prey wherein by nature they delight;
So surfeit-taking Tarquin fares this night:

---

603 **be seeded:** *grow to maturity*   605 **in thy hope:** *while only an heir*   608 **From vassal actors:** *done by vassals*   629 **pattern'd by thy fault:** *having thy fault as an example*   637 **askance:** *turn aside*   639 **relier:** *ally*   640 **repeal:** *recall from exile*   646 **let:** *obstacle*

677 *Cf. n.*   696 **balk:** *forsake*

His taste delicious, in digestion souring,
Devours his will, that liv'd by foul devouring.   *700*

O deeper sin than bottomless conceit
Can comprehend in still imagination!
Drunken Desire must vomit his receipt,
Ere he can see his own abomination.
While Lust is in his pride, no exclamation   *705*
   Can curb his heat, or rein his rash desire,
   Till like a jade Self-will himself doth tire.

And then with lank and lean discolour'd cheek,
With heavy eye, knit brow, and strengthless pace,
Feeble Desire, all recreant, poor, and meek,   *710*
Like to a bankrupt beggar wails his case:
The flesh being proud, Desire doth fight with Grace,
   For there it revels; and when that decays,
   The guilty rebel for remission prays.

So fares it with this faultful lord of Rome,   *715*
Who this accomplishment so hotly chas'd;
For now against himself he sounds this doom,
That through the length of times he stands disgrac'd;
Besides, his soul's fair temple is defac'd;
   To whose weak ruins muster troops of cares,   *720*
   To ask the spotted princess how she fares.

She says, her subjects with foul insurrection
Have batter'd down her consecrated wall,
And by their mortal fault brought in subjection
Her immortality, and made her thrall   *725*
To living death, and pain perpetual:
   Which in her prescience she controlled still,
   But her foresight could not forestall their will.

Even in this thought through the dark night he stealeth,
A captive victor that hath lost in gain;   *730*
Bearing away the wound that nothing healeth,
The scar that will despite of cure remain;
Leaving his spoil perplex'd in greater pain.
   She bears the load of lust he left behind,
   And he the burthen of a guilty mind.   *735*

He like a thievish dog creeps sadly thence,
She like a wearied lamb lies panting there;
He scowls and hates himself for his offence,
She desperate with her nails her flesh doth tear;
He faintly flies, sweating with guilty fear,   *740*
   She stays, exclaiming on the direful night;
   He runs, and chides his vanish'd, loath'd delight.

He thence departs a heavy convertite,
She there remains a hopeless castaway;
He in his speed looks for the morning light,   *745*
She prays she never may behold the day;
'For day,' quoth she, 'night's scapes doth open lay,

And my true eyes have never practis'd how
To cloak offences with a cunning brow.

'They think not but that every eye can see   *750*
The same disgrace which they themselves behold;
And therefore would they still in darkness be,
To have their unseen sin remain untold;
For they their guilt with weeping will unfold,
   And grave, like water that doth eat in steel,   *755*
   Upon my cheeks what helpless shame I feel.'

Here she exclaims against repose and rest,
And bids her eyes hereafter still be blind.
She wakes her heart by beating on her breast,
And bids it leap from thence where it may find   *760*
Some purer chest to close so pure a mind.
   Frantic with grief thus breathes she forth her spite
   Against the unseen secrecy of night:

'O comfort-killing Night, image of hell!
Dim register and notary of shame!   *765*
Black stage for tragedies and murders fell!
Vast sin-concealing chaos! nurse of blame!
Blind muffled bawd! dark harbour for defame!
   Grim cave of death! whispering conspirator
   With close-tongu'd treason and the ravisher!   *770*

'O hateful, vaporous, and foggy Night!
Since thou art guilty of my cureless crime,
Muster thy mists to meet the eastern light,
Make war against proportion'd course of time;
Or if thou wilt permit the sun to climb   *775*
   His wonted height, yet ere he go to bed,
   Knit poisonous clouds about his golden head.

'With rotten damps ravish the morning air;
Let their exhal'd unwholesome breaths make sick
The life of purity, the supreme fair,   *780*
Ere he arrive his weary noontide prick;
And let thy misty vapours march so thick,
   That in their smoky ranks his smother'd light
   May set at noon and make perpetual night.

'Were Tarquin Night, as he is but Night's child,   *785*
The silver-shining queen he would distain;
Her twinkling handmaids too, by him defil'd,
Through Night's black bosom should not peep again:
So should I have co-partners in my pain;
   And fellowship in woe doth woe assuage,   *790*
   As palmers' chat makes short their pilgrimage.

'Where now I have no one to blush with me,
To cross their arms and hang their heads with mine,
To mask their brows and hide their infamy;
But I alone alone must sit and pine,   *795*
Seasoning the earth with showers of silver brine,

701 conceit: *imagination*   **703 receipt;** *cf. n.*   **710 recreant:** *cowardly*   **714 remission:** *pardon*   **721 princess:** *i.e. Tarquin's soul*   **733 his spoil:** *her whom he has violated*   **741 exclaiming on:** *crying out against*   **743 convertite:** *convert*   **747 scapes:** *wanton acts*

755 grave: *engrave*   **761 close:** *enclose*   **766 Black stage;** *cf. n.*   **768 defame:** *dishonor*   **772 my … crime:** *the inexpiable crime I suffer*   **774 proportion'd:** *regulated*   **778 ravish:** *deflower*   **780 fair:** *beauty*   **781 arrive:** *reach* **prick:** *point, mark*   **786 distain:** *blot*

Mingling my talk with tears, my grief with groans,
Poor wasting monuments of lasting moans.

'O Night! thou furnace of foul-reeking smoke,
Let not the jealous Day behold that face   800
Which underneath thy black all-hiding cloak
Immodestly lies martyr'd with disgrace:
Keep still possession of thy gloomy place,
    That all the faults which in thy reign are made
    May likewise be sepulchred in thy shade.   805

'Make me not object to the tell-tale Day!
The light will show, character'd in my brow,
The story of sweet chastity's decay,
The impious breach of holy wedlock vow:
Yea, the illiterate, that know not how   810
    To cipher what is writ in learned books,
    Will cote my loathsome trespass in my looks.

'The nurse, to still her child, will tell my story,
And fright her crying babe with Tarquin's name;
The orator, to deck his oratory,   815
Will couple my reproach to Tarquin's shame;
Feast-finding minstrels, tuning my defame,
    Will tie the hearers to attend each line,
    How Tarquin wronged me, I Collatine.

'Let my good name, that senseless reputation,   820
For Collatine's dear love be kept unspotted:
If that be made a theme for disputation,
The branches of another root are rotted,
And undeserv'd reproach to him allotted
    That is as clear from this attaint of mine,   825
    As I ere this was pure to Collatine.

'O unseen shame! invisible disgrace!
O unfelt sore! crest-wounding, private scar!
Reproach is stamp'd in Collatinus' face,
And Tarquin's eye may read the mot afar,   830
How he in peace is wounded, not in war.
    Alas! how many bear such shameful blows,
    Which not themselves, but he that gives them knows.

'If, Collatine, thine honour lay in me,
From me by strong assault it is bereft.   835
My honey lost, and I, a drone-like bee,
Have no perfection of my summer left,
But robb'd and ransack'd by injurious theft:
    In thy weak hive a wandering wasp hath crept,
    And suck'd the honey which thy chaste bee kept.   840

'Yet am I guilty of thy honour's wrack;
Yet for thy honour did I entertain him;
Coming from thee, I could not put him back,
For it had been dishonour to disdain him:
Besides, of weariness he did complain him,   845
    And talk'd of virtue: O unlook'd-for evil,
    When virtue is profan'd in such a devil!

'Why should the worm intrude the maiden bud?
Or hateful cuckoos hatch in sparrows' nests?
Or toads infect fair founts with venom mud?   850
Or tyrant folly lurk in gentle breasts?
Or kings be breakers of their own behests?
    But no perfection is so absolute,
    That some impurity doth not pollute.

'The aged man that coffers-up his gold   855
Is plagu'd with cramps and gouts and painful fits;
And scarce hath eyes his treasure to behold,
But like still-pining Tantalus he sits,
And useless barns the harvest of his wits;
    Having no other pleasure of his gain   860
    But torment that it cannot cure his pain.

'So then he hath it when he cannot use it,
And leaves it to be master'd by his young;
Who in their pride do presently abuse it:
Their father was too weak, and they too strong,   865
To hold their cursed-blessed fortune long.
    The sweets we wish for turn to loathed sours
    Even in the moment that we call them ours.

'Unruly blasts wait on the tender spring;
Unwholesome weeds take root with precious flowers;   870
The adder hisses where the sweet birds sing;
What virtue breeds iniquity devours:
We have no good that we can say is ours,
    But ill-annexed Opportunity
    Or kills his life, or else his quality.   875

'O Opportunity! thy guilt is great,
'Tis thou that execut'st the traitor's treason;
Thou sett'st the wolf where he the lamb may get;
Whoever plots the sin, thou point'st the season;
'Tis thou that spurn'st at right, at law, at reason;   880
    And in thy shady cell, where none may spy him,
    Sits Sin to seize the souls that wander by him.

'Thou mark'st the vestal violate her oath;
Thou blow'st the fire when temperance is thaw'd;
Thou smother'st honesty, thou murth'rest troth;   885
Thou foul abettor! thou notorious bawd!
Thou plantest scandal and displacest laud:
    Thou ravisher, thou traitor, thou false thief,
    Thy honey turns to gall, thy joy to grief!

'Thy secret pleasure turns to open shame,   890
Thy private feasting to a public fast,
Thy smoothing titles to a ragged name,
Thy sugar'd tongue to bitter wormwood taste:
Thy violent vanities can never last.
    How comes it, then, vile Opportunity,   895
    Being so bad, such numbers seek for thee?

'When wilt thou be the humble suppliant's friend,
And bring him where his suit may be obtain'd?

---

807 character'd: *inscribed*   811 cipher: *decipher*   812 cote: *note, quote*   825 attaint:
wound to honor   828 crest-wounding; *cf. n.*   830 mot; *cf. n.*

848 intrude: *invade*   850 toads infect; *cf. n.*   858 Tantalus; *cf. n.*   859 barns: *lays
up in a barn*   874 ill-annexed; *cf. n.*   875 Or: *either*   876, etc. *Cf. n.*   879
point'st: *appointest*   892 smoothing: *flattering*

THE RAPE OF LUCRECE

When wilt thou sort an hour great strifes to end?
Or free that soul which wretchedness hath chain'd?   *900*
Give physic to the sick, ease to the pain'd?
    The poor, lame, blind, halt, creep, cry out for thee;
    But they ne'er meet with Opportunity.

'The patient dies while the physician sleeps;
The orphan pines while the oppressor feeds;   *905*
Justice is feasting while the widow weeps;
Advice is sporting while infection breeds:
Thou grant'st no time for charitable deeds:
    Wrath, envy, treason, rape, and murther's rages,
    Thy heinous hours wait on them as their pages.   *910*

'When Truth and Virtue have to do with thee,
A thousand crosses keep them from thy aid:
They buy thy help; but Sin ne'er gives a fee,
He gratis comes; and thou art well appaid
As well to hear as grant what he hath said.   *915*
    My Collatine would else have come to me
    When Tarquin did, but he was stay'd by thee.

'Guilty thou art of murther and of theft,
Guilty of perjury and subornation,
Guilty of treason, forgery, and shift,   *920*
Guilty of incest, that abomination;
An accessary by thine inclination
    To all sins past, and all that are to come,
    From the creation to the general doom.

'Misshapen Time, copesmate of ugly Night,   *925*
Swift subtle post, carrier of grisly care,
Eater of youth, false slave to false delight,
Base watch of woes, sin's pack-horse, virtue's snare;
Thou nursest all, and murthrest all that are;
    O hear me, then, injurious, shifting Time!   *930*
    Be guilty of my death, since of my crime.

'Why hath thy servant, Opportunity,
Betray'd the hours thou gav'st me to repose?
Cancell'd my fortunes, and enchained me
To endless date of never-ending woes?   *935*
Time's office is to fine the hate of foes;
    To eat up errors by opinion bred,
    Not spend the dowry of a lawful bed.

'Time's glory is to calm contending kings,
To unmask falsehood and bring truth to light,   *940*
To stamp the seal of time in aged things,
To wake the morn and sentinel the night,
To wrong the wronger till he render right,
    To ruinate proud buildings with thy hours,
    And smear with dust their glittering golden towers;   *945*

'To fill with worm-holes stately monuments,
To feed oblivion with decay of things,
To blot old books and alter their contents,
To pluck the quills from ancient ravens' wings,

To dry the old oak's sap and cherish springs,   *950*
    To spoil antiquities of hammer'd steel,
    And turn the giddy round of Fortune's wheel;

'To show the beldam daughters of her daughter,
To make the child a man, the man a child,
To slay the tiger that doth live by slaughter,   *955*
To tame the unicorn and lion wild,
To mock the subtle, in themselves beguil'd,
    To cheer the ploughman with increaseful crops,
    And waste huge stones with little water-drops.

'Why work'st thou mischief in thy pilgrimage,   *960*
Unless thou couldst return to make amends?
One poor retiring minute in an age
Would purchase thee a thousand thousand friends,
Lending him wit that to bad debtors lends:
    O, this dread night, wouldst thou one hour come back,   *965*
    I could prevent this storm and shun thy wrack.

'Thou ceaseless lackey to eternity,
With some mischance cross Tarquin in his flight:
Devise extremes beyond extremity,
To make him curse this cursed crimeful night: *970*
Let ghastly shadows his lewd eyes affright,
    And the dire thought of his committed evil
    Shape every bush a hideous shapeless devil.

'Disturb his hours of rest with restless trances,
Afflict him in his bed with bedrid groans;   *975*
Let there bechance him pitiful mischances
To make him moan, but pity not his moans;
Stone him with harden'd hearts, harder than stones;
    And let mild women to him lose their mildness,
    Wilder to him than tigers in their wildness.   *980*

'Let him have time to tear his curled hair,
Let him have time against himself to rave,
Let him have time of Time's help to despair,
Let him have time to live a loathed slave,
Let him have time a beggar's orts to crave,   *985*
    And time to see one that by alms doth live
    Disdain to him disdained scraps to give.

'Let him have time to see his friends his foes,
And merry fools to mock at him resort;
Let him have time to mark how slow time goes   *990*
In time of sorrow, and how swift and short
His time of folly and his time of sport;
    And ever let his unrecalling crime
    Have time to wail the abusing of his time.

'O Time! thou tutor both to good and bad,   *995*
Teach me to curse him that thou taught'st this ill;
At his own shadow let the thief run mad,
Himself himself seek every hour to kill:
Such wretched hands such wretched blood should spill;
    For who so base would such an office have   *1000*
    As slanderous deathsman to so base a slave?

---

899 **sort:** *choose*   905 **pines:** *hungers*   914 **appaid:** *satisfied*   920 **shift:** *stratagem*   925 **copesmate:** *companion*   936 **fine:** *end*   942 **sentinel:** *guard*

950 **cherish;** *cf. n.*   953 **beldam:** *grandmother*   956 **unicorn;** *cf. n.*   962 **retiring:** *returning*   985 **orts:** *refuse*   993 **unrecalling:** *irrevocable*   1001 **slanderous:** *contemptible* **deathsman:** *executioner*

'The baser is he, coming from a king,
To shame his hope with deeds degenerate:
The mightier man, the mightier is the thing
That makes him honour'd, or begets him hate;   *1005*
For greatest scandal waits on greatest state.
    The moon being clouded presently is miss'd,
    But little stars may hide them when they list.

'The crow may bathe his coal-black wings in mire,
And unperceiv'd fly with the filth away;   *1010*
But if the like the snow-white swan desire,
The stain upon his silver down will stay.
Poor grooms are sightless night, kings glorious day.
    Gnats are unnoted wheresoe'er they fly,
    But eagles gaz'd upon with every eye.   *1015*

'Out, idle words! servants to shallow fools,
Unprofitable sounds, weak arbitrators!
Busy yourselves in skill-contending schools;
Debate where leisure serves with dull debaters;
To trembling clients be you mediators: *1020*
    For me, I force not argument a straw,
    Since that my case is past the help of law.

'In vain I rail at Opportunity,
At Time, at Tarquin, and uncheerful Night;
In vain I cavil with my infamy,   *1025*
In vain I spurn at my confirm'd despite;
This helpless smoke of words doth me no right.
    The remedy indeed to do me good,
    Is to let forth my foul defiled blood.

'Poor hand, why quiver'st thou at this decree?   *1030*
Honour thyself to rid me of this shame;
For if I die, my honour lives in thee,
But if I live, thou liv'st in my defame;
Since thou couldst not defend thy loyal dame,
    And wast afeard to scratch her wicked foe,   *1035*
    Kill both thyself and her for yielding so.'

This said, from her be-tumbled couch she starteth,
To find some desperate instrument of death;
But this no slaughter-house no tool imparteth
To make more vent for passage of her breath;   *1040*
Which, thronging through her lips, so vanisheth
    As smoke from Ætna, that in air consumes,
    Or that which from discharged cannon fumes.

'In vain,' quoth she, 'I live, and seek in vain
Some happy mean to end a hapless life: *1045*
I fear'd by Tarquin's falchion to be slain,
Yet for the self-same purpose seek a knife:
But when I fear'd I was a loyal wife:
    So am I now: O no! that cannot be;
    Of that true type hath Tarquin rifled me.   *1050*

'O that is gone for which I sought to live!
And therefore now I need not fear to die.
To clear this spot by death, at least I give

A badge of fame to slander's livery;
A dying life to living infamy.   *1055*
    Poor helpless help, the treasure stol'n away,
    To burn the guiltless casket where it lay?

'Well, well, dear Collatine, thou shalt not know
The stained taste of violated troth;
I will not wrong thy true affection so,   *1060*
To flatter thee with an infringed oath;
This bastard graff shall never come to growth;
    He shall not boast who did thy stock pollute
    That thou art doting father of his fruit.

'Nor shall he smile at thee in secret thought,   *1065*
Nor laugh with his companions at thy state;
But thou shalt know thy interest was not bought
Basely with gold, but stol'n from forth thy gate.
For me, I am the mistress of my fate,
    And with my trespass never will dispense,   *1070*
    Till life to death acquit my forc'd offence.

'I will not poison thee with my attaint,
Nor fold my fault in cleanly-coin'd excuses;
My sable ground of sin I will not paint,
To hide the truth of this false night's abuses;   *1075*
My tongue shall utter all; mine eyes, like sluices,
    As from a mountain-spring that feeds a dale,
    Shall gush pure streams to purge my impure tale.'

By this, lamenting Philomel had ended
The well-tun'd warble of her nightly sorrow,   *1080*
And solemn night with slow sad gait descended
To ugly hell; when, lo! the blushing morrow
Lends light to all fair eyes that light will borrow:
    But cloudy Lucrece shames herself to see,
    And therefore still in night would cloister'd be.   *1085*

Revealing day through every cranny spies,
And seems to point her out where she sits weeping;
To whom she sobbing speaks: 'O eye of eyes!
Why pry'st thou through my window? leave thy peeping;
Mock with thy tickling beams eyes that are sleeping: *1090*
    Brand not my forehead with thy piercing light,
    For day hath naught to do what's done by night.'

Thus cavils she with everything she sees:
True grief is fond and testy as a child,
Who wayward once, his mood with nought agrees: *1095*
Old woes, not infant sorrows, bear them mild;
Continuance tames the one; the other wild,
    Like an unpractis'd swimmer plunging still,
    With too much labour drowns for want of skill.

So she, deep-drenched in a sea of care,   *1100*
Holds disputation with each thing she views,
And to herself all sorrow doth compare;
No object but her passion's strength renews,
And as one shifts, another straight ensues:

Sometime her grief is dumb and hath no words;   *1105*
Sometime 'tis mad and too much talk affords.

The little birds that tune their morning's joy
Make her moans mad with their sweet melody:
For mirth doth search the bottom of annoy;
Sad souls are slain in merry company;   *1110*
Grief best is pleas'd with grief's society:
    True sorrow then is feelingly suffic'd
    When with like semblance it is sympathiz'd.

'Tis double death to drown in ken of shore;
He ten times pines that pines beholding food;   *1115*
To see the salve doth make the wound ache more;
Great grief grieves most at what would do it good;
Deep woes roll forward like a gentle flood,
    Who, being stopp'd, the bounding banks o'erflows;
    Grief dallied with nor law nor limit knows.   *1120*

'You mocking birds,' quoth she, 'your tunes entomb
Within your hollow-swelling feather'd breasts,
And in my hearing be you mute and dumb:
My restless discord loves no stops nor rests;
A woeful hostess brooks not merry guests: *1125*
    Relish your nimble notes to pleasing ears;
    Distress likes dumps when time is kept with tears.

'Come, Philomel, that sing'st of ravishment,
Make thy sad grove in my dishevell'd hair:
As the dank earth weeps at thy languishment,   *1130*
So I at each sad strain will strain a tear,
And with deep groans the diapason bear;
    For burthen-wise I'll hum on Tarquin still,
    While thou on Tereus descant'st better skill.

'And whiles against a thorn thou bear'st thy part   *1135*
To keep thy sharp woes waking, wretched I,
To imitate thee well, against my heart
Will fix a sharp knife to affright mine eye,
Who, if it wink, shall thereon fall and die.
    These means, as frets upon an instrument,   *1140*
    Shall tune our heart-strings to true languishment.

'And for, poor bird, thou sing'st not in the day,
As shaming any eye should thee behold,
Some dark deep desert, seated from the way,
That knows not parching heat nor freezing cold,   *1145*
We will find out; and there we will unfold.
    To creatures stern sad tunes, to change their kinds:
    Since men prove beasts, let beasts bear gentle minds.'

As the poor frightened deer, that stands at gaze,
Wildly determining which way to fly,   *1150*
Or one encompass'd with a winding maze,
That cannot tread the way out readily;
So with herself is she in mutiny,

To live or die which of the twain were better,
    When life is sham'd, and death reproach's debtor.   *1155*

'To kill myself,' quoth she, 'alack! what were it
But with my body my poor soul's pollution?
They that lose half with greater patience bear it
Than they whose whole is swallow'd in confusion.
That mother tries a merciless conclusion,   *1160*
    Who, having two sweet babes, when death takes one,
    Will slay the other and be nurse to none.

'My body or my soul, which was the dearer,
When the one, pure, the other made divine?
Whose love of either to myself was nearer,   *1165*
When both were kept for heaven and Collatine?
Ay me! the bark peel'd from the lofty pine,
    His leaves will wither and his sap decay;
    So must my soul, her bark being peel'd away.

'Her house is sack'd, her quiet interrupted,   *1170*
Her mansion batter'd by the enemy;
Her sacred temple spotted, spoil'd, corrupted,
Grossly engirt with daring infamy:
Then let it not be call'd impiety,
    If in this blemish'd fort I make some hole   *1175*
    Through which I may convey this troubled soul.

'Yet die I will not till my Collatine
Have heard the cause of my untimely death;
That he may vow, in that sad hour of mine,
Revenge on him that made me stop my breath.   *1180*
My stained blood to Tarquin I'll bequeath,
    Which by him tainted, shall for him be spent,
    And as his due writ in my testament.

'Mine honour I'll bequeath unto the knife
That wounds my body so dishonoured.   *1185*
'Tis honour to deprive dishonour'd life;
The one will live, the other being dead:
So of shame's ashes shall my fame be bred;
    For in my death I murther shameful scorn;
    My shame so dead, mine honour is new-born.   *1190*

'Dear lord of that dear jewel I have lost,
What legacy shall I bequeath to thee?
My resolution, love, shall be thy boast,
By whose example thou reveng'd mayst be.
How Tarquin must be us'd, read it in me: *1195*
    Myself, thy friend, will kill myself, thy foe,
    And for my sake serve thou false Tarquin so.

'This brief abridgement of my will I make:
My soul and body to the skies and ground;
My resolution, husband, do thou take;   *1200*
Mine honour be the knife's that makes my wound;
My shame be his that did my fame and confound;
    And all my fame that lives disbursed be
    To those that live, and think no shame of me.

1114 **ken:** *view*   1120 **dallied:** *trifled*   1126 **Relish:** *sing*   1127 **dumps:** *doleful ditties*   1130 **dank:** *damp*   1132 **diapason;** *cf. n.*   1133 **burthen;** *cf. n.*   1134 **Tereus;** *cf. note on 1079* **descant'st;** *cf. n.* **better skill;** *cf. n.*   1139 *Cf. n.*   1140 **frets;** *cf. n.*   1143 **shaming:** *being ashamed*

1155 **death reproach's debtor;** *cf. n.*   1157 *Cf. n.*   1160 **conclusion:** *experiments*   1186 **deprive:** *take away*   1188-1190 *Cf. n.*   1196 **thy foe;** *cf. n.*   1199 *Cf. n.*

'Thou, Collatine, shalt oversee this will;   1205
How was I overseen that thou shalt see it!
My blood shall wash the slander of mine ill;
My life's foul deed, my life's fair end shall free it.
Faint not, faint heart, but stoutly say, "So be it":
    Yield to my hand; my hand shall conquer thee: 1210
    Thou dead, both die, and both shall victors be.'

This plot of death when sadly she had laid,
And wip'd the brinish pearl from her bright eyes,
With untun'd tongue she hoarsely call'd her maid,
Whose swift obedience to her mistress hies;   1215
For fleet-wing'd duty with thought's feathers flies.
    Poor Lucrece' cheeks unto her maid seem so
    As winter meads when sun doth melt their snow.

Her mistress she doth give demure good-morrow,
With soft slow tongue, true mark of modesty,   1220
And sorts a sad look to her lady's sorrow,
For why her face wore sorrow's livery;
But durst not ask of her audaciously
    Why her two suns were cloud-eclipsed so,
    Nor why her fair cheeks over-wash'd with woe.   1225

But as the earth doth weep, the sun being set,
Each flower moisten'd like a melting eye;
Even so the maid with swelling drops gan wet
Her circled eyne, enforc'd by sympathy
Of those fair suns set in her mistress' sky,   1230
    Who in a salt-wav'd ocean quench their light,
    Which makes the maid weep like the dewy night.

A pretty while these pretty creatures stand,
Like ivory conduits coral cisterns filling;
One justly weeps, the other takes in hand   1235
No cause but company of her drops spilling;
Their gentle sex to weep are often willing,
    Grieving themselves to guess at other's smarts,
    And then they drown their eyes or break their hearts:

For men have marble, women waxen minds,   1240
And therefore are they form'd as marble will;
The weak oppress'd, the impression of strange kinds
Is form'd in them by force, by fraud, or skill:
Then call them not the authors of their ill,
    No more than wax shall be accounted evil   1245
    Wherein is stamp'd the semblance of a devil.

Their smoothness, like a goodly champaign plain,
Lays open all the little worms that creep;
In men, as in a rough-grown grove, remain
Cave-keeping evils that obscurely sleep: 1250
Through crystal walls each little mote will peep:
    Though men can cover crimes with bold stern looks,
    Poor women's faces are their own faults' books.

No man inveigh against the wither'd flower,
But chide rough winter that the flower hath kill'd: 1255
Not that devour'd, but that which doth devour,
Is worthy blame. O let it not be hild
Poor women's faults, that they are so fulfill'd
    With men's abuses: those proud lords, to blame,
    Make weak-made women tenants to their shame.   1260

The precedent whereof in Lucrece view,
Assail'd by night with circumstances strong
Of present death, and shame that might ensue
By that her death, to do her husband wrong:
Such danger to resistance did belong,   1265
    That dying fear through all her body spread;
    And who cannot abuse a body dead?

By this, mild patience bid fair Lucrece speak
To the poor counterfeit of her complaining;
'My girl,' quoth she, 'on what occasion break   1270
Those tears from thee, that down thy cheeks are raining?
If thou dost weep for grief of my sustaining,
    Know, gentle wench, it small avails my mood:
    If tears could help, mine own would do me good.

'But tell me, girl, when went'—and there she stay'd   1275
Till after a deep groan—'Tarquin from hence?'—
'Madam, ere I was up,' replied the maid,
'The more to blame my sluggard negligence:
Yet with the fault I thus far can dispense;
    Myself was stirring ere the break of day,   1280
    And, ere I rose, was Tarquin gone away.

'But, lady, if your maid may be so bold,
She would request to know your heaviness.'
'O! peace,' quoth Lucrece; 'if it should be told,
The repetition cannot make it less;   1285
For more it is than I can well express:
    And that deep torture may be call'd a hell,
    When more is felt than one hath power to tell.

'Go, get me hither paper, ink, and pen:
Yet save that labour, for I have them here.   1290
What should I say? One of my husband's men
Bid thou be ready by and by, to bear
A letter to my lord, my love, my dear:
    Bid him with speed prepare to carry it;
    The cause craves haste, and it will soon be writ.' 1295

Her maid is gone, and she prepares to write,
First hovering o'er the paper with her quill:
Conceit and grief an eager combat fight;
What wit sets down is blotted straight with will;
This is too curious-good, this blunt and ill: 1300
    Much like a press of people at a door,
    Throng her inventions, which shall go before.

At last she thus begins: 'Thou worthy lord
Of that unworthy wife that greeteth thee,

1205 oversee; cf. n.   1206 overseen: deceived   1207 slander: disgrace   1219 demure: modest   1220 Cf. n.   1221 sorts: adapts   1222 For why: because   1234 Cf. n.   1235 justly: with just cause   1247 champaign: flat, open

1257 hild: i.e. held   1261 Cf. n.   precedent: proof   1261-1267 Cf. n.   1269 counterfeit: portrait   1272 of my sustaining: which I sustain   1279 dispense: be excused   1298 Conceit: thought   1300 curious-good: well expressed but far-fetched

Health to thy person! next vouchsafe t' afford, 1305
If ever, love, thy Lucrece thou wilt see,
Some present speed to come and visit me.
    So I commend me from our house in grief:
    My woes are tedious, though my words are brief.'

Here folds she up the tenour of her woe, 1310
Her certain sorrow writ uncertainly.
By this short schedule Collatine may know
Her grief, but not her grief's true quality:
She dares not thereof make discovery,
    Lest he should hold it her own gross abuse, 1315
    Ere she with blood had stain'd her stain'd excuse.

Besides, the life and feeling of her passion
She hoards, to spend when he is by to hear her;
When sighs, and groans, and tears may grace the fashion
Of her disgrace, the better so to clear her 1320
From that suspicion which the world might bear her.
    To shun this blot, she would not blot the letter
    With words, till action might become them better.

To see sad sights moves more than hear them told;
For then the eye interprets to the ear 1325
The heavy motion that it doth behold,
When every part a part of woe doth bear:
'Tis but a part of sorrow that we hear;
    Deep sounds make lesser noise than shallow fords,
    And sorrow ebbs, being blown with wind of words. 1330

Her letter now is seal'd, and on it writ
'At Ardea to my lord, with more than haste.'
The post attends, and she delivers it,
Charging the sour-fac'd groom to hie as fast
As lagging fowls before the northern blast. 1335
    Speed more than speed but dull and slow she deems:
    Extremity still urgeth such extremes.

The homely villain curtsies to her low;
And, blushing on her, with a steadfast eye
Receives the scroll without or yea or no, 1340
And forth with bashful innocence doth hie:
But they whose guilt within their bosoms lie
    Imagine every eye beholds their blame;
    For Lucrece thought he blush'd to see her shame:

When, silly groom! God wot, it was defect 1345
Of spirit, life, and bold audacity.
Such harmless creatures have a true respect
To talk in deeds, while other saucily
Promise more speed, but do it leisurely:
    Even so this pattern of the worn-out age 1350
    Pawn'd honest looks, but laid no words to gage.

His kindled duty kindled her mistrust,
That two red fires in both their faces blaz'd;
She thought he blush'd, as knowing Tarquin's lust,
And, blushing with him, wistly on him gaz'd; 1355

Her earnest eye did make him more amaz'd:
    The more she saw the blood his cheeks replenish,
    The more she thought he spied in her some blemish.

But long she thinks till he return again,
And yet the duteous vassal scarce is gone. 1360
The weary time she cannot entertain,
For now 'tis stale to sigh, to weep, and groan:
So woe hath wearied woe, moan tired moan,
    That she her plaints a little while doth stay,
    Pausing for means to mourn some newer way. 1365

At last she calls to mind where hangs a piece
Of skilful painting, made for Priam's Troy;
Before the which is drawn the power of Greece,
For Helen's rape the city to destroy,
Threat'ning cloud-kissing Ilion with annoy; 1370
    Which the conceited painter drew so proud,
    As heaven, it seem'd, to kiss the turrets bow'd.

A thousand lamentable objects there,
In scorn of nature, art gave lifeless life;
Many a dry drop seem'd a weeping tear, 1375
Shed for the slaughter'd husband by the wife:
The red blood reek'd, to show the painter's strife;
    And dying eyes gleam'd forth their ashy lights,
    Like dying coals burnt out in tedious nights.

There might you see the labouring pioner, 1380
Begrim'd with sweat, and smeared all with dust;
And from the towers of Troy there would appear
The very eyes of men through loop-holes thrust,
Gazing upon the Greeks with little lust:
    Such sweet observance in this work was had, 1385
    That one might see those far-off eyes look sad.

In great commanders grace and majesty
You might behold, triumphing in their faces;
In youth quick bearing and dexterity;
And here and there the painter interlaces 1390
Pale cowards, marching on with trembling paces;
    Which heartless peasants did so well resemble,
    That one would swear he saw them quake and tremble.

In Ajax and Ulysses, O, what art
Of physiognomy might one behold! 1395
The face of either cipher'd either's heart;
Their face their manners most expressly told:
In Ajax' eyes blunt rage and rigour roll'd;
    But the mild glance that sly Ulysses lent
    Show'd deep regard and smiling government. 1400

There pleading might you see grave Nestor stand,
As 'twere encouraging the Greeks to fight;
Making such sober action with his hand,
That it beguil'd attention, charm'd the sight.
In speech, it seem'd, his beard, all silver white, 1405

1324 *Cf. n.*   1326 **motion:** *action*   1333 **attends:** *waits*   1338 **homely villain:** *simple bondman*   1342 *Cf. n.*   1345 **silly:** *rustic*   1350 **pattern:** *exemplar*   1355 **wistly:** *intently*

1366 **ff.** *Cf. n.*   1367 **painting;** *cf. n.*   1370 **annoy:** *injury*   1371 **conceited:** *imaginative*   1377 **strife:** *emulation*   1380 **pioner:** *sapper*   1384 **lust:** *pleasure*   1385 **observance:** *observant care*   1396 **cipher'd:** *expressed*   1400 **regard:** *reflection*   **government:** *self-command*   1403 **action:** *gesture*

Wagg'd up and down, and from his lips did fly
Thin winding breath, which purl'd up to the sky.

About him were a press of gaping faces,
Which seem'd to swallow up his sound advice;
All jointly listening, but with several graces,   *1410*
As if some mermaid did their ears entice,
Some high, some low, the painter was so nice;
     The scalps of many, almost hid behind,
     To jump up higher seem'd, to mock the mind.

Here one man's hand lean'd on another's head,   *1415*
His nose being shadow'd by his neighbour's ear;
Here one being throng'd bears back, all boll'n and red;
Another smother'd, seems to pelt and swear;
And in their rage such signs of rage they bear,
     As, but for loss of Nestor's golden words,   *1420*
     It seem'd they would debate with angry swords.

For much imaginary work was there;
Conceit deceitful, so compact, so kind,
That for Achilles' image stood his spear,
Grip'd in an armed hand; himself behind,   *1425*
Was left unseen, save to the eye of mind:
     A hand, a foot, a face, a leg, a head,
     Stood for the whole to be imagined.

And from the walls of strong-besieged Troy,
When their brave hope, bold Hector, march'd to field,   *1430*
Stood many Troyan mothers, sharing joy
To see their youthful sons bright weapons wield;
And to their hope they such odd action yield,
     That through their light joy seemed to appear,—
     Like bright things stain'd—a kind of heavy fear.   *1435*

And, from the strand of Dardan, where they fought,
To Simois' reedy banks the red blood ran,
Whose waves to imitate the battle sought
With swelling ridges; and their ranks began
To break upon the galled shore, and than   *1440*
     Retire again, till meeting greater ranks
     They join and shoot their foam at Simois' banks.

To this well-painted piece is Lucrece come,
To find a face where all distress is stell'd.
Many she sees where cares have carved some,   *1445*
But none where all distress and dolour dwell'd,
Till she despairing Hecuba beheld,
     Staring on Priam's wounds with her old eyes,
     Which bleeding under Pyrrhus' proud foot lies.

In her the painter had anatomiz'd   *1450*
Time's ruin, beauty's wrack, and grim care's reign:
Her cheeks with chaps and wrinkles were disguis'd;
Of what she was no semblance did remain;
Her blue blood chang'd to black in every vein,

Wanting the spring that those shrunk pipes had fed,   *1455*
Show'd life imprison'd in a body dead.

On this sad shadow Lucrece spends her eyes,
And shapes her sorrow to the beldam's woes,
Who nothing wants to answer her but cries,
And bitter words to ban her cruel foes: *1460*
The painter was no god to lend her those;
     And therefore Lucrece swears he did her wrong,
     To give her so much grief and not a tongue.

'Poor instrument,' quoth she, 'without a sound,
I'll tune thy woes with my lamenting tongue,   *1465*
And drop sweet balm in Priam's painted wound,
And rail on Pyrrhus that hath done him wrong,
And with my tears quench Troy that burns so long,
     And with my knife scratch out the angry eyes
     Of all the Greeks that are thine enemies.   *1470*

'Show me the strumpet that began this stir,
That with my nails her beauty I may tear.
Thy heat of lust, fond Paris, did incur
This load of wrath that burning Troy doth bear:
Thy eye kindled the fire that burneth here;   *1475*
     And here in Troy, for trespass of thine eye,
     The sire, the son, the dame, and daughter die.

'Why should the private pleasure of some one
Become the public plague of many moe?
Let sin, alone committed, light alone   *1480*
Upon his head that hath transgressed so;
Let guiltless souls be freed from guilty woe;
     For one's offence why should so many fall,
     To plague a private sin in general?

'Lo! here weeps Hecuba, here Priam dies,   *1485*
Here manly Hector faints, here Troilus swounds,
Here friend by friend in bloody channel lies,
And friend to friend gives unadvised wounds,
And one man's lust these many lives confounds:
     Had doting Priam check'd his son's desire,   *1490*
     Troy had been bright with fame and not with fire.'

Here feelingly she weeps Troy's painted woes;
For sorrow, like a heavy-hanging bell,
Once set on ringing, with his own weight goes;
Then little strength rings out the doleful knell: *1495*
So Lucrece, set a-work, sad tales doth tell
     To pencil'd pensiveness and colour'd sorrow;
     She lends them words, and she their looks doth borrow.

She throws her eyes about the painting round,
And whom she finds forlorn she doth lament: *1500*
At last she sees a wretched image bound,
That piteous looks to Phrygian shepherds lent;
His face, though full of cares, yet show'd content;
     Onward to Troy with the blunt swains he goes,
     So mild, that Patience seem'd to scorn his woes.   *1505*

1407 **purl'd:** *curled*   1414 **mock:** *work illusion in*   1417 **throng'd:** *pressed* **boll'n:** *swollen*   1418 **pelt:** *throw out angry words*   1421 **debate:** *fight*   1423 **compact:** *well composed* **kind:** *natural*   1435 **stain'd:** *tarnished*   1436 **Dardan;** *cf. n.*   1437 **Simois;** *cf. n.*   1440 **galled:** *fretted* **than:** *then*   1444 **stell'd:** *delineated*   1450 **anatomiz'd:** *represented minutely*   1450, 1451 *Cf. n.*

1457 **shadow:** *image*   1479 **moe:** *more*   1486 **swounds:** *swoons*   1488 **unadvised:** *unintentional*   1497 **pencil'd:** *painted*   1501 **wretched image;** *cf. n.*

In him the painter labour'd with his skill
To hide deceit, and give the harmless show
An humble gait, calm looks, eyes wailing still,
A brow unbent that seem'd to welcome woe;
Cheeks neither red nor pale, but mingled so   *1510*
   That blushing red no guilty instance gave,
   Nor ashy pale the fear that false hearts have.

But, like a constant and confirmed devil,
He entertain'd a show so seeming-just,
And therein so ensconc'd his secret evil,   *1515*
That jealousy itself could not mistrust
False-creeping craft and perjury should thrust
   Into so bright a day such black-fac'd storms,
   Or blot with hell-born sin such saint-like forms.

The well-skill'd workman this mild image drew   *1520*
For perjur'd Sinon, whose enchanting story
The credulous old Priam after slew;
Whose words, like wildfire, burnt the shining glory
Of rich-built Ilion, that the skies were sorry,
   And little stars shot from their fixed places,   *1525*
   When their glass fell wherein they view'd their faces.

This picture she advisedly perus'd,
And chid the painter for his wondrous skill,
Saying, some shape in Sinon's was abus'd;
So fair a form lodg'd not a mind so ill: *1530*
And still on him she gaz'd, and gazing still,
   Such signs of truth in his plain face she spied,
   That she concludes the picture was belied.

'It cannot be,' quoth she, 'that so much guile,'—
She would have said,—'can lurk in such a look';   *1535*
But Tarquin's shape came in her mind the while,
And from her tongue 'can lurk' from 'cannot' took:
'It cannot be,' she in that sense forsook,
   And turn'd it thus, 'It cannot be, I find,
   But such a face should bear a wicked mind: *1540*

'For even as subtle Sinon here is painted,
So sober-sad, so weary, and so mild,
As if with grief or travail he had fainted,
To me came Tarquin armed to beguild
With outward honesty, but yet defil'd   *1545*
   With inward vice: as Priam him did cherish,
   So did I Tarquin; so my Troy did perish.

'Look, look, how listening Priam wets his eyes,
To see those borrow'd tears that Sinon sheds!
Priam, why art thou old and yet not wise?   *1550*
For every tear he falls a Troyan bleeds:
His eye drops fire, no water thence proceeds;
   Those round clear pearls of his, that move thy pity,
   Are balls of quenchless fire to burn thy city.

'Such devils steal effects from lightless hell;   *1555*
For Sinon in his fire doth quake with cold,

And in that cold hot-burning fire doth dwell;
These contraries such unity do hold,
Only to flatter fools and make them bold:
   So Priam's trust false Sinon's tears doth flatter,   *1560*
   That he finds means to burn his Troy with water.'

Here, all enrag'd, such passion her assails,
That patience is quite beaten from her breast.
She tears the senseless Sinon with her nails,
Comparing him to that unhappy guest   *1565*
Whose deed hath made herself herself detest:
   At last she smilingly with this gives o'er;
   'Fool, fool!' quoth she, 'his wounds will not be sore.'

Thus ebbs and flows the current of her sorrow,
And time doth weary time with her complaining.   *1570*
She looks for night, and then she longs for morrow,
And both she thinks too long with her remaining:
Short time seems long in sorrow's sharp sustaining:
   Though woe be heavy, yet it seldom sleeps;
   And they that watch see time how slow it creeps.   *1575*

Which all this time hath overslipp'd her thought,
That she with painted images hath spent;
Being from the feeling of her own grief brought
By deep surmise of others' detriment;
Losing her woes in shows of discontent.   *1580*
   It easeth some, though none it ever cur'd,
   To think their dolour others have endur'd.

But now the mindful messenger, come back,
Brings home his lord and other company;
Who finds his Lucrece clad in mourning black;   *1585*
And round about her tear-distained eye
Blue circles stream'd, like rainbows in the sky:
   These water-galls in her dim element
   Foretell new storms to those already spent.

Which when her sad-beholding husband saw,   *1590*
Amazedly in her sad face he stares:
Her eyes, though sod in tears, look'd red and raw,
Her lively colour kill'd with deadly cares.
He hath no power to ask her how she fares:
   Both stood like old acquaintance in a trance,   *1595*
   Met far from home, wondering each other's chance.

At last he takes her by the bloodless hand,
And thus begins: 'What uncouth ill event
Hath thee befall'n, that thou dost trembling stand?
Sweet love, what spite hath thy fair colour spent?   *1600*
Why art thou thus attir'd in discontent?
   Unmask, dear dear, this moody heaviness,
   And tell thy grief, that we may give redress.'

Three times with sighs she gives her sorrow fire,
Ere once she can discharge one word of woe: *1605*
At length address'd to answer his desire,
She modestly prepares to let them know

1514 entertain'd: *kept up* **1516 jealousy:** *suspicion* **1523 wildfire;** *cf. n.* **1525** *Cf. n.* **1526 their glass;** *cf. n.* **1527 advisedly:** *intently* **1544 to beguild;** *cf. n.* **1551 falls:** *sheds*

1585 mourning; *cf. n.* **1588 water-galls;** *cf. n.* **1593 lively:** *living* **1598 uncouth:** *unknown* **1600 spite:** *trouble* **1602 moody:** *gloomy* **1604** *Cf. n.* **1606 address'd:** *ready*

Her honour is ta'en prisoner by the foe;
    While Collatine and his consorted lords
    With sad attention long to hear her words.   *1610*

And now this pale swan in her watery nest
Begins the sad dirge of her certain ending.
'Few words,' quoth she, 'shall fit the trespass best,
Where no excuse can give the fault amending:
In me moe woes than words are now depending;   *1615*
    And my laments would be drawn out too long,
    To tell them all with one poor tired tongue.

'Then be this all the task it hath to say:
Dear husband, in the interest of thy bed
A stranger came, and on that pillow lay   *1620*
Where thou wast wont to rest thy weary head;
And what wrong else may be imagined
    By foul enforcement might be done to me,
    From that, alas! thy Lucrece is not free.

'For in the dreadful dead of dark midnight,   *1625*
With shining falchion in my chamber came
A creeping creature with a flaming light,
And softly cried, "Awake, thou Roman dame,
And entertain my love; else lasting shame
    On thee and thine this night I will inflict,   *1630*
    If thou my love's desire do contradict.

' "For some hard-favour'd groom of thine," quoth he,
"Unless thou yoke thy liking to my will,
I'll murther straight, and then I'll slaughter thee,
And swear I found you where you did fulfil   *1635*
The loathsome act of lust, and so did kill
    The lechers in their deed: this act will be
    My fame, and thy perpetual infamy."

'With this I did begin to start and cry,
And then against my heart he set his sword,   *1640*
Swearing, unless I took all patiently,
I should not live to speak another word;
So should my shame still rest upon record,
    And never be forgot in mighty Rome
    The adulterate death of Lucrece and her groom.   *1645*

'Mine enemy was strong, my poor self weak,
And far the weaker with so strong a fear:
My bloody judge forbade my tongue to speak;
No rightful plea might plead for justice there:
His scarlet lust came evidence to swear   *1650*
    That my poor beauty had purloin'd his eyes;
    And when the judge is robb'd the prisoner dies.

'O, teach me how to make mine own excuse,
Or, at the least, this refuge let me find:
Though my gross blood be stain'd with this abuse,   *1655*
Immaculate and spotless in my mind;
That was not forc'd; that never was inclin'd
    To accessary yieldings, but still pure
    Doth in her poison'd closet yet endure.'

Lo! here the helpless merchant of this loss,   *1660*
With head declin'd, and voice damm'd up with woe,
With sad-set eyes, and wretched arms across,
From lips new-waxen pale begins to blow
The grief away that stops his answer so:
    But, wretched as he is, he strives in vain;   *1665*
    What he breathes out his breath drinks up again.

As through an arch the violent roaring tide
Outruns the eye that doth behold his haste,
Yet in the eddy boundeth in his pride
Back to the strait that forc'd him on so fast;   *1670*
In rage sent out, recall'd in rage, being past:
    Even so his sighs, his sorrows, make a saw,
    To push grief on, and back the same grief draw.

Which speechless woe of his poor she attendeth,
And his untimely frenzy thus awaketh: *1675*
'Dear lord, thy sorrow to my sorrow lendeth
Another power; no flood by raining slaketh.
My woe too sensible thy passion maketh
    More feeling-painful: let it then suffice,
    To drown one woe, one pair of weeping eyes.   *1680*

'And for my sake, when I might charm thee so,
For she that was thy Lucrece, now attend me:
Be suddenly revenged on my foe,
Thine, mine, his own: suppose thou dost defend me
From what is past: the help that thou shalt lend me   *1685*
    Comes all too late, yet let the traitor die;
    For sparing justice feeds iniquity.

'But ere I name him, you, fair lords,' quoth she,—
Speaking to those that came with Collatine,—
'Shall plight your honourable faiths to me,   *1690*
With swift pursuit to venge this wrong of mine;
For 'tis a meritorious fair design
    To chase injustice with revengeful arms:
    Knights, by their oaths, should right poor ladies' harms.

At this request, with noble disposition   *1695*
Each present lord began to promise aid,
As bound in knighthood to her imposition,
Longing to hear the hateful foe bewray'd:
But she, that yet her sad task hath not said,
    The protestation stops. 'O, speak!' quoth she,   *1700*
    'How may this forced stain be wip'd from me?

'What is the quality of mine offence,
Being constrain'd with dreadful circumstance?
May my pure mind with the foul act dispense,
My low-declined honour to advance?   *1705*
May any terms acquit me from this chance?
    The poison'd fountain clears itself again;
    And why not I from this compelled stain?'

With this, they all at once began to stay,
Her body's stain her mind untainted clears;   *1710*
While with a joyless smile she turns away

1615 **depending**: *imminent*   1619 **interest**: *possession*   1620 *Cf. n.*   1645 **adulterate**: *adulterous*   1650 **scarlet**; *cf. n.*   1655, 1656 *Cf. n.*   1660 **ff.** *Cf. n.*

1672, 1673 *Cf. n.*   1689-1691 *Cf. n.*   1697 **imposition**: *command*   1706 **chance**: *mischance*   1709, 1710 *Cf. n.*

The face, that map which deep impression bears
Of hard misfortune, carv'd in it with tears.
  'No, no,' quoth she, 'no dame, hereafter living,
  By my excuse shall claim excuse's giving.'   *1715*

Here with a sigh, as if her heart would break,
She throws forth Tarquin's name. 'He, he,' she says,
But more than 'he' her poor tongue could not speak;
Till after many accents and delays,
Untimely breathings, sick and short assays,   *1720*
  She utters this, 'He, he, fair lords, 'tis he,
  That guides this hand to give this wound to me.'

Even here she sheathed in her harmless breast
A harmful knife, that thence her soul unsheath'd:
That blow did bail it from the deep unrest   *1725*
Of that polluted prison where it breath'd;
Her contrite sighs unto the clouds bequeath'd
  Her winged sprite, and through her wounds doth fly
  Life's lasting date from cancell'd destiny.

Stone-still, astonish'd with this deadly deed,   *1730*
Stood Collatine and all his lordly crew;
Till Lucrece' father, that beholds her bleed,
Himself on her self-slaughter'd body threw;
And from the purple fountain Brutus drew
  The murderous knife, and as it left the place,   *1735*
  Her blood, in poor revenge, held it in chase;

And bubbling from her breast, it doth divide
In two slow rivers, that the crimson blood
Circles her body in on every side,
Who, like a late-sack'd island, vastly stood,   *1740*
Bare and unpeopled in this fearful flood.
  Some of her blood still pure and red remain'd,
  And some look'd black, and that false Tarquin stain'd.

About the mourning and congealed face,
Of that black blood a watery rigol goes,   *1745*
Which seems to weep upon the tainted place:
And ever since, as pitying Lucrece's woes,
Corrupted blood some watery token shows;
  And blood untainted still doth red abide,
  Blushing at that which is so putrefied.   *1750*

'Daughter, dear daughter!' old Lucretius cries,
'That life was mine which thou hast here depriv'd.
If in the child the father's image lies,
Where shall I live now Lucrece is unliv'd?
Thou wast not to this end from me deriv'd.   *1755*
  If children predecease progenitors,
  We are their offspring, and they none of ours.

'Poor broken glass, I often did behold
In thy sweet semblance my old age new born;
But now that fair fresh mirror, dim and old,   *1760*
Shows me a bare-bon'd death by time outworn.
O! from thy cheeks my image thou hast torn,

And shiver'd all the beauty of my glass,
That I no more can see what once I was.

'O Time! cease thou thy course, and last no longer,   *1765*
If they surcease to be that should survive.
Shall rotten death make conquest of the stronger,
And leave the faltering feeble souls alive?
The old bees die, the young possess their hive:
  Then live, sweet Lucrece, live again and see   *1770*
  Thy father die, and not thy father thee!'

By this, starts Collatine as from a dream,
And bids Lucretius give his sorrow place;
And then in key-cold Lucrece' bleeding stream
He falls, and bathes the pale fear in his face,   *1775*
And counterfeits to die with her a space;
  Till manly shame bids him possess his breath
  And live to be revenged on her death.

The deep vexation of his inward soul
Hath serv'd a dumb arrest upon his tongue;   *1780*
Who, mad that sorrow should his use control
Or keep him from heart-easing words so long,
Begins to talk; but through his lips do throng
  Weak words so thick, come in his poor heart's aid,
  That no man could distinguish what he said.   *1785*

Yet sometime 'Tarquin' was pronounced plain,
But through his teeth, as if the name he tore.
This windy tempest, till it blow up rain,
Held back his sorrow's tide to make it more;
At last it rains, and busy winds give o'er: *1790*
  Then son and father weep with equal strife
  Who should weep most, for daughter or for wife.

The one doth call her his, the other his,
Yet neither may possess the claim they lay.
The father says, 'She's mine.' 'O! mine she is,'   *1795*
Replies her husband; 'do not take away
My sorrow's interest; let no mourner say
  He weeps for her, for she was only mine,
  And only must be wail'd by Collatine.'

'O!' quoth Lucretius, 'I did give that life   *1800*
Which she too early and too late hath spill'd.'
'Woe, woe,' quoth Collatine, 'she was my wife,
I ow'd her, and 'tis mine that she hath kill'd.'
'My daughter' and 'my wife' with clamours fill'd
  The dispers'd air, who, holding Lucrece' life,   *1805*
  Answer'd their cries, 'my daughter' and 'my wife.'

Brutus, who pluck'd the knife from Lucrece' side,
Seeing such emulation in their woe,
Began to clothe his wit in state and pride,
Burying in Lucrece' wound his folly's show.   *1810*
He with the Romans was esteemed so
  As silly-jeering idiots are with kings,
  For sportive words and uttering foolish things:

1714, 1715 Cf. n.   1720 Untimely: *irregular*   1732, 1733 Cf. n.   1738 that: *so that*   1740 vastly: *like a waste*   1745 rigol; *cf. n.*   1759 semblance: *likeness*   1761 death: *representation of Death*

1766 surcease: *cease*   1772-1775 Cf. n.   1797 interest; *cf. n.*   1801 late: *recently* spill'd: *destroyed*   1803 ow'd: *owned*   1809, 1810 Cf. n.

But now he throws that shallow habit by,
Wherein deep policy did him disguise;   *1815*
And arm'd his long-hid wits advisedly,
To check the tears in Collatinus' eyes.
'Thou wronged lord of Rome,' quoth he, 'arise:
    Let my unsounded self, suppos'd a fool,
    Now set thy long-experienc'd wit to school.   *1820*

'Why, Collatine, is woe the cure for woe?
Do wounds help wounds, or grief help grievous deeds?
Is it revenge to give thyself a blow
For his foul act by whom they fair wife bleeds?
Such childish humour from weak minds proceeds: *1825*
    Thy wretched wife mistook the matter so,
    To slay herself, that should have slain her foe.

'Courageous Roman, do not steep thy heart
In such relenting dew of lamentations;
But kneel with me and help to bear thy part,   *1830*
To rouse our Roman gods with invocations,
That they will suffer these abominations,
    Since Rome herself in them doth stand disgrac'd,
    By our strong arms from forth her fair streets chas'd.

'Now, by the Capitol that we adore,   *1835*
And by this chaste blood so unjustly stain'd,
By heaven's fair sun that breeds the fat earth's store,
By all our country rights in Rome maintain'd,
And by chaste Lucrece' soul, that late complain'd
    Her wrongs to us, and by this bloody knife,   *1840*
    We will revenge the death of this true wife.'

This said, he struck his hand upon his breast,
And kiss'd the fatal knife to end his vow;
And to his protestation urg'd the rest,
Who, wondering at him, did his words allow: *1845*
Then jointly to the ground their knees they bow;
    And that deep vow, which Brutus made before,
    He doth again repeat, and that they swore.

When they had sworn to this advised doom,
They did conclude to bear dead Lucrece thence;   *1850*
To show her bleeding body thorough Rome,
And so to publish Tarquin's foul offence:
Which being done with speedy diligence,
    The Romans plausibly did give consent
    To Tarquin's everlasting banishment.   *1855*

❧ FINIS ❧

1843-1848 *Cf. n.*   1845 **allow:** *approve*   1850, 1851 *Cf. n.*   1854 **plausibly:** *approvingly*

THE PHŒNIX AND THE TURTLE

Let the bird of loudest lay,
On the sole Arabian tree,
Herald sad and trumpet be,
To whose sound chaste wings obey.

But thou shrieking harbinger,   *5*
Foul precurrer of the fiend,
Augur of the fever's end,
To this troop come thou not near.

From this session interdict
Every fowl of tyrant wing,   *10*
Save the eagle, feather'd king:
Keep the obsequy so strict.

Let the priest in surplice white,
That defunctive music can,
Be the death-divining swan,   *15*
Lest the requiem lack his right.

And thou treble-dated crow,
That thy sable gender mak'st
With the breath thou giv'st and tak'st,
'Mongst our mourners shalt thou go.   *20*

Here the anthem doth commence:
Love and constancy is dead;
Phœnix and the turtle fled
In a mutual flame from hence.

So they lov'd, as love in twain   *25*
Had the essence but in one;
Two distincts, division none:
Number there in love was slain.

Hearts remote, yet not asunder;
Distance, and no space was seen   *30*
'Twixt the turtle and his queen:
But in them it were a wonder.

So between them love did shine,
That the turtle saw his right
Flaming in the phœnix' sight;   *35*
Either was the other's mine.

Property was thus appall'd,
That the self was not the same;
Single nature's double name
Neither two nor one was call'd.   *40*

1 **bird of loudest lay;** *cf. n.*   2 **Arabian tree;** *cf. n.*   3 **trumpet:** *trumpeter*   5 **shrieking harbinger;** *cf. n.*   6 **precurrer:** *forerunner*   9 **interdict:** *forbid*   10 **tyrant wing;** *cf. n.*   14 **defunctive:** *funereal* **can:** *knows*   15 **death-divining;** *cf. n.*   17 **treble-dated;** *cf. n.*   18 **sable:** *black; cf. n.*   25-28 *Cf. n.*   29, 30 *Cf. n.*   32 **But: except** **were:** *would be; cf. n.*   33-36 *Cf. n.*   37-40 *Cf. n.*

Reason, in itself confounded,
Saw division grow together;
To themselves yet either neither,
Simple were so well compounded,

That it cried, 'How true a twain   *45*
Seemeth this concordant one!
Love hath reason, reason none,
If what parts can so remain.'

Whereupon it made this threne
To the phœnix and the dove,   *50*
Co-supremes and stars of love,
As chorus to their tragic scene.

THRENOS

Beauty, truth, and rarity,
Grace in all simplicity,
Here enclos'd in cinders lie.   *55*

Death is now the phœnix' nest;
And the turtle's loyal breast
To eternity doth rest,

Leaving no posterity:
'Twas not their infirmity,   *60*
It was married chastity.

Truth may seem, but cannot be;
Beauty brag, but 'tis not she;
Truth and beauty buried be.

To this urn let those repair   *65*
That are either true or fair;
For these dead birds, sigh a prayer.

THE PASSIONATE PILGRIM

I

When my love swears that she is made of truth,
I do believe her, though I know she lies,
That she might think me some untutor'd youth,
Unskilful in the world's false forgeries.
Thus vainly thinking that she thinks me young,   *5*
Although I know my years be past the best,
I smiling credit her false-speaking tongue,
Outfacing faults in love with love's ill rest.
But wherefore says my love that she is young?
And wherefore say not I that I am old?   *10*
O! love's best habit is a soothing tongue,
And age, in love, loves not to have years told.

Therefore I'll lie with love, and love with me,
Since that our faults in love thus smother'd be.

II

Two loves I have of comfort and despair,
Which like two spirits do suggest me still;
The better angel is a man, right fair,
The worser spirit a woman, colour'd ill.
To win me soon to hell, my female evil   *5*
Tempteth my better angel from my side,
And would corrupt a saint to be a devil,
Wooing his purity with her fair pride:
And whether that my angel be turn'd fiend
Suspect I may, but not directly tell;   *10*
For being both to me, both to each friend,
I guess one angel in another's hell.
    The truth I shall not know, but live in doubt,
    Till my bad angel fire my good one out.

III

Did not the heavenly rhetoric of thine eye,
'Gainst whom the world could not hold argument,
Persuade my heart to this false perjury?
Vows for thee broke deserve not punishment.
A woman I forswore; but I will prove,   *5*
Thou being a goddess, I forswore not thee:
My vow was earthly, thou a heavenly love;
Thy grace being gain'd cures all disgrace in me.
My vow was breath, and breath a vapour is;
Then thou, fair sun, that on this earth dost shine,   *10*
Exhale this vapour vow; in thee it is:
If broken, then it is no fault of mine.
    If by me broke, what fool is not so wise
    To break an oath, to win a paradise?

IV

Sweet Cytherea, sitting by a brook
With young Adonis, lovely, fresh, and green,
Did court the lad with many a lovely look,
Such looks as none could look but beauty's queen.
She told him stories to delight his ear;   *5*
She show'd him favours to allure his eye;
To win his heart, she touch'd him here and there,—
Touches so soft still conquer chastity.
But whether unripe years did want conceit,
Or he refus'd to take her figur'd proffer,   *10*
The tender nibbler would not touch the bait,
But smile and jest at every gentle offer:
    Then fell she on her back, fair queen, and toward:
    He rose and ran away; ah! fool too froward.

V

If love make he forsworn, how shall I swear to love?
O, never faith could hold, if not to beauty vow'd!

---

41 **confounded:** *defeated*   42 *Cf. n.*   43-46 *Cf. n.*   44 **compounded:** *blended*   47, 48 *Cf. n.*   49 **threne:** *dirge*   **Threnos:** *dirge*   53 **rarity:** *uncommon excellence*   I; *Cf. n.*   8 **ill rest:** *poor remnant*

II *Cf. n.*   2 **suggest:** *tempt*   11 *Cf. n.*   III *Cf. n.*   IV *Cf. n.*   9 **conceit:** *understanding*   10 **figur'd:** *made by signs*   V *Cf. n.*

Though to myself forsworn, to thee I'll constant prove;
Those thoughts, to me like oaks, to thee like osiers bow'd.
Study his bias leaves, and makes his book thine eyes,   *5*
Where all those pleasures live that art can comprehend.
If knowledge be the mark, to know thee shall suffice;
Well learned is that tongue that well can thee commend;
All ignorant that soul that sees thee without wonder;
Which is to me some praise, that I thy parts admire: *10*
Thine eye Jove's lightning seems, thy voice his dreadful
    thunder,
Which, not to anger bent, is music and sweet fire.
    Celestial as thou art, O! do not love that wrong,
    To sing heaven's praise with such an earthly tongue.   *15*

VI

Scarce had the sun dried up the dewy morn,
And scarce the herd gone to the hedge for shade,
When Cytherea, all in love forlorn,
A longing tarriance for Adonis made
Under an osier growing by a brook,   *5*
A brook where Adon us'd to cool his spleen:
Hot was the day; she hotter that did look
For his approach, that often there had been.
Anon he comes, and throws his mantle by,
And stood stark naked on the brook's green brim: *10*
The sun look'd on the world with glorious eye,
Yet not so wistly as this queen on him:
    He, spying her, bounc'd in, whereas he stood:
    'O Jove,' quoth she, 'why was not I a flood!'

VII

Fair is my love, but not so fair as fickle;
Mild as a dove, but neither true nor trusty;
Brighter than glass, and yet, as glass is, brittle;
Softer than wax, and yet, as iron, rusty:
    A lily pale, with damask dye to grace her,   *5*
    None fairer, nor none falser to deface her.

Her lips to mine how often hath she join'd,
Between each kiss her oaths of true love swearing!
How many tales to please me hath she coin'd,
Dreading my love, the loss thereof still fearing!   *10*
    Yet in the midst of all her pure protestings,
    Her faith, her oaths, her tears, and all were jestings.

She burn'd with love, as straw with fire flameth;
She burn'd out love, as soon as straw outburneth;
She fram'd the love, and yet she foil'd the framing;   *15*
She bade love last, and yet she fell a-turning.
    Was this a lover, or a lecher whether?
    Bad in the best, though excellent in neither.

VIII

If music and sweet poetry agree,
As they must needs, the sister and the brother,

Then must the love be great 'twixt thee and me,
Because thou lov'st the one, and I the other.
Dowland to thee is dear, whose heavenly touch   *5*
Upon the lute doth ravish human sense;
Spenser to me, whose deep conceit is such
As, passing all conceit, needs no defence.
Thou lov'st to hear the sweet melodious sound
That Phœbus' lute, the queen of music, makes;   *10*
And I in deep delight am chiefly drown'd
Whenas himself to singing he betakes.
    One god is god of both, as poets feign;
    One knight loves both, and both in thee remain.

IX

Fair was the morn when the fair queen of love,
   .   .   .   .
Paler for sorrow than her milk-white dove,
For Adon's sake, a youngster proud and wild;
Her stand she takes upon a steep-up hill: *5*
Anon Adonis comes with horn and hounds;
She, silly queen, with more than love's good will,
Forbade the boy he should not pass those grounds:
'Once,' quoth she, 'did I see a fair sweet youth
Here in these brakes deep-wounded with a boar,   *10*
Deep in the thigh, a spectacle of ruth!
See, in my thigh,' quoth she, 'here was the sore.'
    She showed hers; he saw more wounds than one,
    And blushing fled, and left her all alone.

X

Sweet rose, fair flower, untimely pluck'd, soon vaded,
Pluck'd in the bud, and vaded in the spring!
Bright orient pearl, alack! too timely shaded;
Fair creature, kill'd too soon by death's sharp sting!
    Like a green plum that hangs upon a tree,   *5*
    And falls, through wind, before the fall should be.

I weep for thee, and yet no cause I have;
For why thou left'st me nothing in thy will:
And yet thou left'st me more than I did crave;
For why I craved nothing of thee still: *10*
    O yes, dear friend, I pardon crave of thee,
    Thy discontent thou dist bequeath to me.

XI

Venus, with young Adonis sitting by her
Under a myrtle shade, began to woo him:
She told the youngling how god Mars did try her,
And as he fell to her, so fell she to him.
'Even thus,' quoth she, 'the warlike god embrac'd me,
And then she clipp'd Adonis in her arms;
'Even thus,' quoth she, 'the warlike god unlac'd me,'
As if the boy should use like loving charms.
'Even thus,' quoth she, 'he seized on my lips,'
And with her lips on his did act the seizure;   *10*
And as she fetched breath, away he skips,

---

5 bias: *natural disposition*   **VI** *Cf. n.*   **12 wistly:** *eagerly*   **VII** *Cf. n.*   **5 damask:**
cf. n.   **VIII** *Cf. n.*

3 thee: *cf. n.*   **5 Dowland:** *cf. n.*   **14 One knight:** *cf. n.*   **IX** *Cf. n.*   **X**
Cf. n.   **1 vaded:** *faded*   **XI** *Cf. n.*   **6 clipp'd:** *embraced*   **9-12** *Cf. n.*

And would not take her meaning nor her pleasure.
 Ah! that I had my lady at this bay,
 To kiss and clip me till I run away.

XII

Crabbed age and youth cannot live together:
Youth is full of pleasure, age is full of care;
Youth like summer morn, age like winter weather;
Youth like summer brave, age like winter bare.
Youth is full of sport, age's breath is short;   *5*
 Youth is nimble, age is lame;
Youth is hot and bold, age is weak and cold;
Youth is wild, and age is tame.
Age, I do abhor thee, youth, I do adore thee;
 O, my love, my love is young!   *10*
Age, I do defy thee: O, sweet shepherd, hie thee,
 For methinks thou stay'st too long!

XIII

Beauty is but a vain and doubtful good;
A shining gloss that vadeth suddenly;
A flower that dies when first it 'gins to bud;
A brittle glass that's broken presently:
 A doubtful good, a gloss, a glass, a flower,   *5*
 Lost, vaded, broken, dead within an hour.

And as goods lost are seld or never found,
As vaded gloss no rubbing will refresh,
As flowers dead lie wither'd on the ground,
As broken glass no cement can redress,   *10*
 So beauty blemish'd once 's for ever lost,
 In spite of physic, painting, pain, and cost.

XIV

Good night, good rest. Ah! neither be my share:
She bade good night that kept my rest away;
And daff'd me to a cabin hang'd with care,
To descant on the doubts of my decay.
 'Farewell,' quoth she, 'and come again to-morrow:'   *5*
 Fare well I could not, for I supp'd with sorrow.

Yet at my parting sweetly did she smile,
In scorn or friendship, nill I conster whether:
'T may be, she joy'd to jest at my exile,
'T may be, again to make me wander thither: *10*
 'Wander,' a word for shadows like myself,
 As take the pain, but cannot pluck the pelf.

Lord! how mine eyes throw gazes to the east;
My heart doth charge the watch; the morning rise
Doth cite each moving sense from idle rest.   *15*
Not daring trust the office of mine eyes,

While Philomela sits and sings, I sit and mark,
And wish her lays were tuned like the lark;

For she doth welcome daylight with her ditty,
And drives away dark dismal-dreaming night: *20*
The night so pack'd, I post unto my pretty;
Heart hath his hope, and eyes their wished sight;
 Sorrow chang'd to solace, solace mix'd with sorrow;
 For why, she sigh'd and bade me come to-morrow.

Were I with her, the night would post too soon;   *25*
But now are minutes added to the hours;
To spite me now, each minute seems a moon;
Yet not for me, shine sun to succour flowers!
 Pack night, peep day; good day, of night now borrow:
 Short night, to-night, and length thyself to-morrow.   *30*

SONNETS TO SUNDRY NOTES OF MUSIC

I

It was a lording's daughter, the fairest one of three,
That liked of her master as well as well might be,
Till looking on an Englishman, the fair'st that eye could see,
 Her fancy fell a-turning.

Long was the combat doubtful that love with love did fight,   *5*
To leave the master loveless, or kill the gallant knight:
To put in practice either, alas! it was a spite
 Unto the silly damsel.

But one must be refused; more mickle was the pain
That nothing could be used to turn them both to gain,   *10*
For of the two the trusty knight was wounded with disdain:
 Alas! she could not help it.

Thus art with arms contending was victor of the day,
Which by a gift of learning did bear the maid away;
Then lullaby, the learned man hath got the lady gay;   *15*
 For now my song is ended.

II

On a day, alack the day!
Love, whose month was ever May,
Spied a blossom passing fair,
Playing in the wanton air:
Through the velvet leaves the wind,   *5*
All unseen, 'gan passage find;
That the lover, sick to death,
Wish'd himself the heaven's breath.
'Air,' quoth he, 'thy cheeks may blow;
Air, would I might triumph so!   *10*
But, alas! my hand hath sworn

13 bay: *cf. n.*   **XII** *Cf. n*   **4 brave:** *adorned*   **XIII** *Cf. n.*   **2 vadeth;** *cf. X* 1

7 seld: *seldom*   **XIV** *Cf. n.*   **3 daff'd:** *sent off*   **4 descant:** *comment*   **8 nill:** *will*

not **conster:** *construe*   **whether:** *which of the two*   **14** *Cf. n.*

27 moon: *month*   **30 Short:** *shorten*   **length:** *lengthen*   **I** *Cf. n.*   **1 lording:** *noble-*

man   **2 master:** *teacher*   **II** *Cf. n.*

Ne'er to pluck thee from thy thorn:
Vow, alack! for youth unmeet:
Youth, so apt to pluck a sweet.
Thou for whom Jove would swear   *15*
Juno but an Ethiop were;
And deny himself for Jove,
Turning mortal for thy love.'

III

My flocks feed not,
My ewes breed not,
My rams speed not,
    All is amiss:
Love's denying,   *5*
Faith's defying,
Heart's renying,
    Causer of this.
All my merry jigs are quite forgot,
All my lady's love is lost, God wot: *10*
Where her faith was firmly fix'd in love,
There a nay is plac'd without remove.
One silly cross
Wrought all my loss;
    O frowning Fortune! cursed, fickle dame!   *15*
For now I see
Inconstancy
    More in women than in men remain.
In black mourn I,
All fears scorn I,   *20*
Love hath forlorn me,
    Living in thrall:
Heart is bleeding,
All help needing,
O cruel speeding,   *25*
    Fraughted with gall!
My shepherd's pipe can sound no deal,
My wether's bell rings doleful knell;
My curtal dog, that wont to have play'd,
Plays not at all, but seems afraid;   *30*
My sighs so deep
Procure to weep,
    In howling wise, to see my doleful plight.
How sighs resound
Through heartless ground,   *35*
    Like a thousand vanquish'd men in bloody fight!

Clear well spring not,
Sweet birds sing not,
Green plants bring not
    Forth their dye;   *40*
Herds stand weeping,
Flocks all sleeping,
Nymphs back peeping
    Fearfully:
All our pleasure known to us poor swains,   *45*
All our merry meetings on the plains,
All our evening sport from us is fled,

All our love is lost, for Love is dead.
Farewell, sweet lass,
Thy like ne'er was   *50*
    For a sweet content, the cause of all my moan:
Poor Corydon
Must live alone;
    Other help for him I see that there is none.

IV

Whenas thine eye hath chose the dame,
And stall'd the deer that thou should'st strike,
Let reason rule things worthy blame,
As well as fancy, partial wight:
    Take counsel of some wiser head,   *5*
    Neither too young nor yet unwed.

And when thou com'st thy tale to tell,
Smooth not thy tongue with filed talk,
Lest she some subtle practice smell;
A cripple soon can find a halt;   *10*
    But plainly say thou lov'st her well,
    And set thy person forth to sell.

What though her frowning brows be bent,
Her cloudy looks will clear ere night;
And then too late she will repent   *15*
That thus dissembled her delight;
    And twice desire, ere it be day,
    That which with scorn she put away.

What though she strive to try her strength,
And ban and brawl, and say thee nay,   *20*
Her feeble force will yield at length,
When craft hath taught her thus to say,
    'Had women been so strong as men,
    In faith, you had not had it then.'

And to her will frame all thy ways;   *25*
Spare not to spend, and chiefly there
Where thy desert may merit praise,
By ringing in thy lady's ear:
    The strongest castle, tower, and town,
    The golden bullet beats it down.   *30*

Serve always with assured trust,
And in thy suit be humble true;
Unless thy lady prove unjust,
Seek never thou to choose anew.
    When time shall serve, be thou not slack   *35*
    To proffer, though she put thee back.

The wiles and guiles that women work,
Dissembled with an outward show,
The tricks and toys that in them lurk,
The cock that treads them shall not know.   *40*
    Have you not heard it said full oft,
    A woman's nay doth stand for nought?

III *Cf. n.*   **6 defying:** *rejecting*   **7 renying:** *abjuring*   **26 Fraughted:** *freighted*   **29**
curtal: *having the tail docked*

IV *Cf. n.*   **2 stall'd:** *brought to a standstill*   **8 filed:** *polished*

Think, women love to match with men
And not to live so like a saint:
Here is no heaven; they holy then   45
Begin when age doth them attaint.
　　Were kisses all the joys in bed,
　　One woman would another wed.

But, soft! enough! too much, I fear;
For if my mistress hear my song,
She will not stick to round me on th' ear   50
To teach my tongue to be so long:
　　Yet will she blush, here be it said,
　　To hear her secrets so bewray'd.

V

Live with me, and be my love,
And we will all the pleasures prove
That hills and valleys, dales and fields,
And all the craggy mountains yields.

There will we sit upon the rocks,   5
And see the shepherds feed their flocks,
By shallow rivers, by whose falls
Melodious birds sing madrigals.

There will I make thee a bed of roses,
With a thousand fragrant posies,   10
A cap of flowers, and a kirtle
Embroider'd all with leaves of myrtle.

A belt of straw and ivy buds,
With coral clasps and amber studs;
And if these pleasures may thee move,   15
Then live with me and be my love.

LOVE'S ANSWER

If that the world and love were young,
And truth in every shepherd's tongue,
These pretty pleasures might me move,   20
To live with thee and be thy love.

VI

As it fell upon a day
In the merry month of May,
Sitting in a pleasant shade
Which a grove of myrtles made,
Beasts did leap, and birds did sing,   5
Trees did grow, and plants did spring;
Everything did banish moan,
Save the nightingale alone:
She, poor bird, as all forlorn,
Lean'd her breast up-till a thorn,   10
And there sung the dolefull'st ditty,
That to hear it was great pity:

'Fie, fie, fie!' now would she cry;
'Tereu, Tereu!' by and by;
That to hear her so complain,   15
Scarce I could from tears refrain;
For her griefs, so lively shown,
Made me think upon mine own.
Ah! thought I, thou mourn'st in vain,
None takes pity on thy pain: 20
Senseless trees they cannot hear thee,
Ruthless beasts they will not cheer thee:
King Pandion he is dead,
All thy friends are lapp'd in lead,
All thy fellow birds do sing   25
Careless of thy sorrowing.
Even so, poor bird, like thee,
None alive will pity me.
Whilst as fickle Fortune smil'd,
Thou and I were both beguil'd.   30
　　Every one that flatters thee
Is no friend in misery.
Words are easy, like the wind;
Faithful friends are hard to find:
Every man will be thy friend   35
Whilst thou hast wherewith to spend;
But if store of crowns be scant,
No man will supply thy want.
If that one be prodigal,
Bountiful they will him call,   40
And with such-like flattering,
'Pity but he were a king.'
If he be addict to vice,
Quickly him they will entice;
If to women he be bent,   45
They have him at commandement:
But if Fortune once do frown,
Then farewell his great renown;
They that fawn'd on him before
Use his company no more.   50
He that is thy friend indeed,
He will help thee in thy need:
If thou sorrow, he will weep;
If thou wake, he cannot sleep:
Thus of every grief in heart   55
He with thee does bear a part.
These are certain signs to know
Faithful friend from flattering foe.

A LOVER'S COMPLAINT

From off a hill whose concave womb re-worded
A plaintful story from a sistering vale,
My spirits to attend this double voice accorded,
And down I laid to list the sad-tun'd tale;
Ere long espied a fickle maid full pale,   5

---

51 **round:** *whisper (?)*　　**V** *Cf. n.*　　8 **madrigals:** *ditties*　　**VI** *Cf. n.*　　10 **up-till:** *up against*

23 **Pandion;** *cf. n.*　　24 **lapp'd:** *wrapped*　　43 **addict:** *addicted*　　2 **sistering:** *sisterly, neighboring*　　4 **list:** *listen to*

Tearing of papers, breaking rings a-twain,
Storming her world with sorrow's wind and rain.

Upon her head a platted hive of straw,
Which fortified her visage from the sun,
Whereon the thought might think sometime it saw   *10*
The carcass of a beauty spent and done:
Time had not scythed all that youth begun,
     Nor youth all quit; but, spite of heaven's fell rage,
     Some beauty peep'd through lattice of sear'd age.

Oft did she heave her napkin to her eyne,   *15*
Which on it had conceited characters,
Laund'ring the silken figures in the brine
That season'd woe had pelleted in tears,
And often reading what contents it bears;
     As often shrieking undistinguish'd woe   *20*
     In clamours of all size, both high and low.

Sometimes her levell'd eyes their carriage ride,
As they did battery to the spheres intend;
Sometime diverted, their poor balls are tied
To th' orbed earth; sometimes they do extend   *25*
Their view right on; anon their gazes lend
     To every place at once, and nowhere fix'd,
     The mind and sight distractedly commix'd.

Her hair, nor loose nor tied in formal plat,
Proclaim'd in her a careless hand of pride;   *30*
For some, untuck'd, descended her sheav'd hat,
Hanging her pale and pined cheek beside;
Some in her threaden fillet still did bide,
     And true to bondage would not break from thence,
     Though slackly braided in loose negligence.   *35*

A thousand favours from a maund she drew
Of amber, crystal, and of beaded jet,
Which one by one she in a river threw,
Upon whose weeping margent she was set;
Like usury, applying wet to wet,   *40*
     Or monarch's hands that lets not bounty fall
     Where want cries some, but where excess begs all.

Of folded schedules had she many a one,
Which she perus'd, sigh'd, tore, and gave the flood;
Crack'd many a ring of posied gold and bone,   *45*
Bidding them find their sepulchres in mud;
Found yet moe letters sadly penn'd in blood,
     With sleided silk feat and affectedly
     Enswath'd, and seal'd to curious secrecy.

These often bath'd she in her fluxive eyes,   *50*
And often kiss'd, and often 'gan to tear;
Cried 'O false blood! thou register of lies,
What unapproved witness dost thou bear!
Ink would have seem'd more black and damned here.'

This said, in top of rage the lines she rents,   *55*
Big discontent so breaking their contents.

A reverend man that graz'd his cattle nigh—
Sometime a blusterer, that the ruffle knew
Of court, of city, and had let go by
The swiftest hours, observed as they flew—   *60*
Towards this afflicted fancy fastly drew;
     And, privileg'd by age, desires to know
     In brief the grounds and motives of her woe.

So slides he down upon his grained bat,
And comely-distant sits he by her side;   *65*
When he again desires her, being sat,
Her grievance with his hearing to divide:
If that from him there may be aught applied
     Which may her suffering ecstasy assuage,
     'Tis promis'd in the charity of age.   *70*

'Father,' she says, 'though in me you behold
The injury of many a blasting hour,
Let it not tell your judgment I am old;
Not age, but sorrow, over me hath power:
I might as yet have been a spreading flower,   *75*
     Fresh to myself, if I had self-applied
     Love to myself and to no love beside.

'But woe is me! too early I attended
A youthful suit—it was to gain my grace—
Of one by nature's outwards so commended,   *80*
That maidens' eyes stuck over all his face.
Love lack'd a dwelling, and made him her place;
     And when in his fair parts she did abide,
     She was new lodg'd and newly deified.

'His browny locks did hang in crooked curls,   *85*
And every light occasion of the wind
Upon his lips their silken parcels hurls.
What's sweet to do, to do will aptly find:
Each eye that saw him did enchant the mind,
     For on his visage was in little drawn   *90*
     What largeness thinks in Paradise was sawn.

'Small show of man was yet upon his chin;
His phœnix down began but to appear
Like unshorn velvet on that termless skin
Whose bare out-bragg'd the web it seem'd to wear;   *95*
Yet show'd his visage by that cost more dear,
     And nice affections wavering stood in doubt
     If best were as it was, or best without.

'His qualities were beauteous as his form,
For maiden-tongu'd he was, and thereof free;   *100*
Yet, if men mov'd him, was he such a storm
As oft 'twixt May and April is to see,
When winds breathe sweet, unruly though they be.
     His rudeness so with his authoriz'd youth
     Did livery falseness in a pride of truth.   *105*

---

8 platted … straw: *head covering of plaited straw*   **15 heave:** *raise*   **napkin:** *handkerchief*   **17 Laund'ring:** *washing*   **18 pelleted:** *formed into pellets*   **22, 23** *Cf. n.* **26 lend;** *cf. n.*   **31 sheav'd:** *made of straw*   **36 maund:** *hand-basket*   **45 posied:** *bearing a motto*   **48, 49** *Cf. n.*   **48 sleided:** *sleaved, i.e. separated into filaments*   **feat:** *neatly*   **affectedly:** *with overmuch curiosity*   **50 fluxive:** *flowing*

58 ruffle: *turmoil*   **61 fancy:** *love-sick maid*   **64 grained:** *rough*   **bat:** *staff*   **69 ecstasy:** *transport*   **91 sawn:** *sown*   **94 termless:** *indescribable*   **95 bare:** *nudity*   **105 livery:** *clothe in a livery*

'Well could he ride, and often men would say
"That horse his mettle from his rider takes:
Proud of subjection, noble by the sway,
What rounds, what bounds, what course, what stop he makes!"
And controversy hence a question takes,　　110
　　Whether the horse by him became his deed,
　　Or he his manage by the well-doing steed.

'But quickly on this side the verdict went:
His real habitude gave life and grace
To appertainings and to ornament,　　115
Accomplish'd in himself, not in his case:
All aids, themselves made fairer by their place,
　　Came for additions; yet their purpose'd trim
　　Piec'd not his grace, but were all grac'd by him.

'So on the tip of his subduing tongue　　120
All kind of arguments and question deep,
All replication prompt, and reason strong,
For his advantage still did wake and sleep:
To make the weeper laugh, the laugher weep,
　　He had the dialect and different skill,　　125
　　Catching all passions in his craft of will:

'That he did in the general bosom reign
Of young, of old; and sexes both enchanted,
To dwell with him in thoughts, or to remain
In personal duty, following where he haunted:　　130
Consents bewitch'd, ere he desire, have granted;
　　And dialogu'd for him what he would say,
　　Ask'd their own wills, and made their wills obey.

'Many there were that did his picture get,
To serve their eyes, and in it put their mind;　　135
Like fools that in the imagination set
The goodly objects which abroad they find
Of lands and mansions, theirs in thought assign'd;
　　And labouring in more pleasures to bestow them
　　Than the true gouty landlord which doth owe them.　　140

'So many have, that never touch'd his hand,
Sweetly suppos'd them mistress of his heart.
My woeful self, that did in freedom stand,
And was my own fee-simple, not in part,
What with his art in youth, and youth in art,　　145
　　Threw my affections in his charmed power,
　　Reserv'd the stalk and gave him all my flower.

'Yet did I not, as some my equals did,
Demand of him, nor being desired yielded;
Finding myself in honour so forbid,　　150
With safest distance I mine honour shielded.
Experience for me many bulwarks builded
　　Of proofs new-bleeding, which remain'd the foil
　　Of this false jewel, and his amorous spoil.

'But, ah! who ever shunn'd by precedent　　155
The destin'd ill she must herself assay?
Or forc'd examples, 'gainst her own content,
To put the by-pass'd perils in her way?
Counsel may stop awhile what will not stay;
　　For when we rage, advice is often seen　　160
　　By blunting us to make our wits more keen.

'Nor gives it satisfaction to our blood,
That we must curb it upon others' proof;
To be forbid the sweets that seem so good,
For fear of harms that preach in our behoof.　　165
O appetite! from judgment stand aloof;
　　The one a palate hath that needs will taste,
　　Though Reason weep, and cry "It is thy last."

'For further I could say "This man's untrue,"
And knew the patterns of his foul beguiling;　　170
Heard where his plants in others' orchards grew,
Saw how deceits were gilded in his smiling;
Knew vows were ever brokers of defiling;
　　Thought characters and words merely but art,
　　And bastards of his foul adulterate heart.　　175

'And long upon these terms I held my city,
Till thus he 'gan besiege me: "Gentle maid,
Have of my suffering youth some feeling pity,
And be not of my holy vows afraid:
That's to ye sworn to none was ever said;　　180
　　For feasts of love I have been call'd unto,
　　Till now did ne'er invite, nor ever woo.

' "All my offences that abroad you see
Are errors of the blood, none of the mind;
Love made them not: with acture they may be,　　185
Where neither party is nor true nor kind:
They sought their shame that so their shame did find,
　　And so much less of shame in me remains,
　　By how much of me their reproach contains.

' "Among the many that mine eyes have seen,　　190
Not one whose flame my heart so much was warm'd,
Or my affection put to the smallest teen,
Or any of my leisures ever charm'd:
Harm have I done to them, but ne'er was harm'd;
　　Kept hearts in liveries, but mine own was free,　　195
　　And reign'd, commanding in his monarchy.

' "Look here, what tributes wounded fancies sent me,
Of pallid pearls and rubies red as blood;
Figuring that they their passions likewise lent me
Of grief and blushes, aptly understood,　　200
In bloodless white and the encrimson'd mood;
　　Effects of terror and dear modesty,
　　Encamp'd in hearts, but fighting outwardly.

' "And, lo! behold these talents of their hair,
With twisted metal amorously impleach'd,　　205

---

109 **rounds, bounds, course, stop;** *cf. n.*　　**111, 112** *Cf. n.*　　**114 habitude:** *disposition*　　**115 appertainings:** *belongings*　　**118 additions:** *marks of distinction*　　**127 in the general bosom:** *in all the bosoms*　　**132 dialogu'd:** *expressed*　　**140 owe:** *possess*　　**144 my own fee-simple;** *cf. n.*　　**153 foil;** *cf. n.*

157, 158 *Cf. n.*　　**180 That's:** *that which is*　　**185 acture:** *action*　　**192 teen:** *sorrow*　　**204 talents:** *riches*　　**205 impleach'd:** *intertwined*

I have receive'd from many a several fair,
Their kind acceptance weepingly beseech'd,
With th'annexions of fair gems enrich'd,
    And deep-brain'd sonnets, that did amplify
    Each stone's dear nature, worth, and quality.   210

' "The diamond; why, 'twas beautiful and hard,
Whereto his invis'd properties did tend;
The deep-green emerald, in whose fresh regard
Weak sights their sickly radiance do amend;
The heaven-hu'd sapphire and the opal blend   215
    With objects manifold: each several stone,
    With wit well blazon'd, smil'd or made some moan.

' "Lo! all these trophies of affections hot,
Of pensiv'd and subdu'd desires the tender,
Nature hath charg'd me that I hoard them not,   220
But yield them up where I myself must render,
That is, to you, my origin and ender;
    For these, of force, must your oblations be,
    Since I their altar, you enpatron me.

' "O, then, advance of yours that phraseless hand,   225
Whose white weighs down the airy scale of praise;
Take all these similes to your own command,
Hallow'd with sighs that burning lungs did raise;
What me, your minister, for you obeys,
    Works under you; and to your audit comes   230
    Their distract parcels in combined sums.

' "Lo! this device was sent me from a nun,
Or sister sanctified, of holiest note;
Which late her noble suit in court did shun,
Whose rarest havings made the blossoms dote;   235
For she was sought by spirits of richest coat,
    But kept cold distance, and did thence remove,
    To spend her living in eternal love.

' "But, O my sweet! what labour is 't to leave
The thing we have not, mastering what not strives,   240
Paling the place which did no form receive,
Playing patient sports in unconstrained gyves?
She that her fame so to herself contrives,
    The scars of battle 'scapeth by the flight,
    And makes her absence valiant, not her might.   245

' "O, pardon me, in that my boast is true;
The accident which brought me to her eye
Upon the moment did her force subdue,
And now she would the caged cloister fly;
Religious love put out religion's eye: 250
    Not to be tempted, would she be immur'd,
    And now, to tempt, all liberty procur'd.

' "How mighty then you are! O, hear me tell:
The broken bosoms that to me belong
Have emptied all their fountains in my well,   255

And mine I pour your ocean all among:
I strong o'er them, and you o'er me being strong,
    Must for your victory us all congest,
    As compound love to physic your cold breast.

' "My parts had power to charm a sacred nun,   260
Who, disciplin'd, ay, dieted in grace,
Believ'd her eyes when they t' assail begun,
All vows and consecrations giving place.
O most potential love! vow, bond, nor space,
    In thee hath neither sting, knot, nor confine,   265
    For thou art all, and all things else are thine.

' "When thou impressest, what are precepts worth
Of stale example? When thou wilt inflame,
How coldly those impediments stand forth
Of wealth, of filial fear, law, kindred, fame!   270
Love's arms are peace, 'gainst rule, 'gainst sense, 'gainst shame,
    And sweetens, in the suffering pangs it bears,
    The aloes of all forces, shocks, and fears.

' "Now all these hearts that do on mine depend,
Feeling it break, with bleeding groans they pine;   275
And supplicant their sighs to you extend,
To leave the battery that you make 'gainst mine,
Lending soft audience to my sweet design,
    And credent soul to that strong-bonded oath
    That shall prefer and undertake my troth."   280

'This said, his watery eyes he did dismount,
Whose sights till then were levell'd on my face;
Each cheek a river running from a fount
With brinish current downward flow'd apace.
O how the channel to the stream gave grace,   285
    Who glaz'd with crystal gate the glowing roses
    That flame through water which their hue encloses.

'O father! what a hell of witchcraft lies
In the small orb of one particular tear,
But with the inundation of the eyes   290
What rocky heart to water will not wear?
What breast so cold that is not warmed here?
    O cleft effect! cold modesty, hot wrath,
    Both fire from hence and chill extincture hath.

'For, lo! his passion, but an art of craft,   295
Even there resolv'd my reason into tears;
There my white stole of chastity I daft,
Shook off my sober guards and civil fears;
Appear to him, as he to me appears,
    All melting; though our drops this difference bore, 300
    His poison'd me, and mine did him restore.

'In him a plenitude of subtle matter,
Applied to cautels, all strange forms receives,
Of burning blushes, or of weeping water,
Or swounding paleness; and he takes and leaves,   305
In either's aptness, as it best deceives,

---

210 nature: *properties* 212 invis'd: *invisible* 215 blend: *blended* 217 blazon'd: *explained* 219 tender: *offer* 221 render: *surrender* 224 *Cf. n.* 225 phraseless: *above praise* 229, 230 *Cf. n.* 231 distract: *separated* 234 *Cf. n.* 235 blossoms: *cf. n.* 236 coat: *coat of arms* 241 *Cf. n.* 251, 252 *Cf. n.*

258 congest: *bring together* 273 aloes: *i.e. bitter experiences* 276 supplicant: *entreating* 279 credent: *believing* 280 prefer: *present* 293 cleft effect: *twofold result* 294 extincture: *extinction* 297 daft: *doffed, put off* 303 cautels: *wiles*

To blush at speeches rank, to weep at woes,
Or to turn white and swound at tragic shows:

'That not a heart which in his level came
Could scape the hail of his all-hurting aim,   310
Showing fair nature is both kind and tame;
And, veil'd in them, did win whom he would maim:
Against the thing he sought he would exclaim;
When he most burn'd in heart-wish'd luxury,
He preach'd pure maid, and prais'd cold chastity.   315

'Thus merely with the garment of a Grace
The naked and concealed fiend he cover'd;
That the unexperient gave the tempter place,
Which like a cherubin above them hover'd.

Who, young and simple, would not be so lover'd?   320
Ay me! I fell; and yet do question make
What I should do again for such a sake.

'O that infected moisture of his eye,
O that false fire which in his cheek so glow'd,
O that forc'd thunder from his heart did fly,   325
O that sad breath his spongy lungs bestow'd,
O all that borrow'd motion seeming ow'd,
Would yet again betray the fore-betray'd,
And new pervert a reconciled maid!'

❧ FINIS ❧

---

309 **in his level:** *within his range of fire*   318 **unexperient:** *inexperienced*   327 **seeming ow'd:** *seemingly his own*

NOTES

VENUS AND ADONIS

Epigraph. From Ovid, *Amores*, I. El. xv, 35-36. It is printed on the title page of the original edition. Thus translated by Marlowe: 'Let base conceited wits admire vile things/Fair Phœbus lead me to the Muses' springs.'

Dedicatory Epistle. Henry Wriothesley. Third Earl of Southampton (1573-1624), Shakespeare's patron. He is generally identified with the friend to whom Shakespeare addressed his *Sonnets*.

3. *Rose-cheek'd.* This expression is to be found in Marlowe's *Hero and Leander* (l. 93).

9. *Stain.* In Elizabethan English the word often meant: 'to surpass,' 'to shame.' Cf. *Romeus and Juliet* (Shaks. Soc. 77): 'Whose beauty and whose shape so far the rest did stain.' Here used as a noun: the nymphs looked mean compared to Adonis.

11. *Nature that made thee, with herself at strife.* Nature vied with herself when she created Adonis.

12. *the world hath ending with thy life.* Should Adonis die, Nature would cease to create other beings.

25. *sweating palm.* A moist palm was supposed to be the indication of an amorous disposition (cf., further, l. 143, and *Othello*, III.iv.37-40), whilst a dry hand meant indifference to love.

53. *miss.* I.e. misdeed. A more usual form was 'amiss.' On this line, cf. *Notes and Queries*, 10th Ser., vol. IX (1908), pp. 264, 506.

56. *Tires.* A term of falconry, especially used of hawks tearing their food (from French *tirer*, to pull).

61. *Forc'd to content.* Adonis is obliged to bear contentedly what he cannot avoid.

71. *rank.* Often applied to an overflowing river. Cf. *King John*, V.iv.55.

82. *Till he take truce with her contending tears.* Till he cease to resist the assault of tears.

86. *dive-dapper.* A small water-fowl of the Grebe kind, also called dab-chick or dip-chick.

104. *uncontrolled crest.* The crest was properly the feathers on the top of a helmet, here used for the helmet itself. Shakespeare means that Mars had never bowed his head before a victorious enemy.

129-132. *Make . . . time.* Cf. Ovid, *Ars Am.*, III, 59-80.

130. *Beauty . . . wasted.* Cf. Shakespeare's *Sonnets*, I-VI.

158. *Can thy right hand seize love upon thy left.* A way of saying that Adonis is in love with himself.

161. *Narcissus.* Shakespeare's Adonis has several traits in common with Narcissus.

197,198. *And were . . . sun.* If Venus were not immortal, she would be consumed between the heavenly fire (the sun) and the earthly fire (Adonis).

203, 204. *O, had . . . unkind.* An allusion to Myrrha, Adonis's mother. Cf. Sources and Composition, p. 853.

231. *deer.* A play upon the words 'deer' and 'dear.'

235. *relief.* Not 'food,' as is generally explained, but 'relievo,' said in topography of all prominence above the ground plan. Cf., further, 'bottom-grass,' 'plain,' 'hillocks.' It was a common-place metaphor in Shakespeare's time.

240. *rouse.* I.e. 'drive from cover.' A term used in venery, generally applied to the hart or the deer. But Shakespeare loosely uses it for sundry sorts of animals, and even for the owl (cf. *Twelfth Night*, II.iii.53).

247. *Caves.* I.e. the dimples on Adonis's cheeks.

259-262. Shakespeare may have derived the idea of this passage from Ovid, *Ars Am.*, II, 487-488: 'In furias agitantur equae spatioque remota/Per loca dividuos amne sequuntur equos.'

263, 264. Cf. Marlowe, *Hero and Leander.* 'For as a hot proud horse highly disdains/To have his head controll'd, but breaks the reins,/Spits forth the ringled bit, and with his hoves/Checks the submissive ground.'

279. *Curvets.* A term of the *manege* or science of equitation. A 'curvet' is a movement made by a horse, when he raises his fore legs together, and then, while he is bringing them down, raises his hind legs without touching the ground.

286. *Caparisons or trapping.* Richly embroidered dresses and embellishments used in decorating horses, especially in tourneys and jousts.

289-292. Possibly an allusion to Nicon, 'the famous painter of Greece,' who, according to Topsell (*Fourfooted Beasts*, 222), 'when he had most curiously limbed a horses perfection, and failed in no part of nature or art, but only in placing hairs under his eye, for that only fault he received a disgraceful blame.' (Quoted by Pooler.)

295-298. *Round-hoofed, etc.* Several sources have been proposed for the descrip-

tion of the points of a fine horse: Sylvester's translation of Du Bartas, Blundevill's *Arte of Ryding*, Googe's *Foure Books of Husbandry*, Topsell's *Four-footed Beasts*. Prof. Carleton Brown (*The Library*, 3rd Ser., No. 10, vol. III, 182 ff.) has shown that for such descriptions there was a long literary tradition going back to Roman and Greek times. Cf. Dodge (Neil), *Modern Philology*, IX, 211 ff.; Law (R. A.) *Modern Lang. Notes*, XXVIII, 93.

303. *To bid the wind a base.* He prepares to challenge the wind to strive for superiority in speed. From the game 'base' or 'prisoner's base.' 'To bid base' was a frequent locution. Cf. *Two Gentlemen of Verona*, I.ii.104.

329-336. Cf. Lodge, *Glaucus and Scylla*: 'Themis that knewe that waters long restrained/Breake foorth with greater billowes than the brookes/That swetely float through meades with floures distained,/With cheerefull laies did raise his heavie lookes;/And bad him speake and tell what him agreev'd:/For griefes disclos'd (said she) are soone releev'd.'

335. *Heart's attorney.* I.e. the tongue. In *Richard III* (IV.iv.130) words are compared to 'windy attorneys in their client woes.'

342. *For all askance he holds her in his eye.* He looks at her sideways, watching her movements all the time.

359, 360. These two lines are given as a proof that the poem was written not at Stratford, but when Shakespeare was already familiar with the life of the theatres. A dumb play, or dumb show, was a scene in a tragedy shown pantomimically and representing parts of the story which could not be included, or sometimes giving a summary of the action which was to follow. *Chorus*, a character in the old English drama, who presented or commented upon the tragedy.

367. *Engine of her thoughts.* This description of the tongue occurs also in *Titus Andronicus*, III.i.83: 'that delightful engine of her thoughts.'

370. *My heart . . . wound.* Were my heart as whole as thine and thy heart wounded like mine.

375. *steel.* With probably a pun on 'steel' (harden) and 'steal' (rob).

397. *naked bed.* This expression seems to have been common in the sixteenth century. Its meaning has not been satisfactorily explained. Here the phrase evidently means 'lying naked in bed.'

412. *My love to love is love but to disgrace it.* The only love I bear to love is a strong inclination to disgrace it.

424. *alarms.* Or alarums, signals by which soldiers were warned to take arms.

433-450. *Had I . . . feast.* Wyndham compares this passage with Chapman's *Ovid's Banquet of Sense* (1595).

472. *Fair fall the wit.* May prosperity befall the wit, etc.

478. *To mend the hurt that his unkindness marr'd.* 'A mixture of two phrases, (1) to mend the hurt that his unkindness caused, and (2) to mend what was marred by his unkindness, i.e. to restore her consciousness or colour' (Pooler).

482. *windows.* Shakespeare uses the word both in the sense of 'eye' (*Love's Labour's Lost*, V.ii.880), and of 'eyelid' (*Antony and Cleopatra*, V.ii.364).

506. *liveries.* A livery (Fr. *livrée*) was the distinctive dress worn by the servants and dependants in the household of a nobleman.

507-510. *their verdure, etc.* 'The poet evidently alludes to a practice of his own age, when it was customary, in time of the plague, to strew the rooms of every house with rue and other strong-smelling herbs, to prevent infection' (Malone). There was an outbreak of the plague in August, 1592, and the infection lasted until the spring of 1594. During most of that time the plays were under restraint and the theatres closed. This allusion has been used as a clue to the date of composition of *Venus and Adonis*.

515. *Slips.* It has been supposed that there is a reference to the sense of 'counterfeit money.' It is true that 'slip' sometimes means a 'counterfeit coin,' but the context shows that here 'slip' is taken in its ordinary sense of 'error.' Adonis is making a purchase, and a deed is, therefore, to be drawn; and for fear there should be some omission or error which might be invoked as a cause of non-execution, Adonis will set his seal (i.e. his lips) to the legal instrument (Venus's lips) as a token of performance (cf. line 521).

516. *wax-red.* The seal was impressed on wax affixed to the document.

529. *the world's comforter.* I.e. the sun. Cf., above, l. 484.

565, 566. Cf. Lyly, *Euphues* (Bond's ed., I, 187): 'The tender youth of a childe is like the temperinge of new wax apt to receive any form.'

589, 590. Cf. Lodge, *Glaucus and Scylla.* 'An yvorie shadowed front, . . ./Next which her cheekes appeerd like crimson silk,/Or ruddie rose bespred on whitest milk.'

598. *Manage.* Or *manege*, a term of horsemanship = to train a horse to graceful motions, 'regere et gubernare, propriè est equisonum qui solent equos refractarios, orisque immorigeri, hoc modo domare, fraenoque obsequentes reddere' (Minsheu).

601. *painted grapes.* An allusion to the anecdote reported of Zeuxis by Pliny:

'Zeuxis for proof of his cunning brought upon the scaffold a table, wherein were clusters of grapes so lively painted, that the very birds of the air flew flocking thither for to be pecking at the grapes' (Holland's Pliny, II, 535).

608. *assay'd . . . prov'd.* These words have the same meaning, that of putting a metal to the test. There is besides a play on the word *prove* = 'to test' and 'to feel.'

615-618. *O be advis'd . . . kill.* Cf. Ovid, *Met.,* X, 544-549; 705-707.

619-630. *On his . . . rushes.* Cf. Ovid, *Met.,* VIII, 284-289; 294-295.

626. *Are better proof than thy spear's point can enter.* Are too strong (as an armor tested) for the point of thy spear to enter.

631. Cf. Ovid, *Met.,* X, 547-548.

652. *Kill, kill.* The cry formerly uttered by the English soldiers when they made an onset.

673-678. *But if . . hounds.* Cf. Ovid, *Met.,* X, 537-539.

673-708. See Sources and Composition, p. 853.

683. *Musits,* or musets, are gaps in a hedge through which the hare is accustomed to pass; also the form where the hare hides (cf. French *musse*).

685-688. *Sometime . . . yell.* Cf. Turberville, *Booke of Hunting* (Clarendon Press ed., 165): 'And I have seen hares oftentimes runne into a flocke of sheepe in the field when they are hunted, and would never leave the flocke, until I was forced to couple up my houndes, and fold up the sheepe or sometimes drive them to the cote; and then the hare would forsake them . . . I have seene that would take the grounde like a coney.' (Quoted by Pooler.)

693, 694. *Till they have singled With much ado the cold fault cleanly out.* Till they have with great difficulty distinguished the scent of the animal they hunt from the scent of other animals and thus have corrected the fault they made (a dog is then said to be 'at fault') in losing the scent.

695. *spend their mouths.* A technical term of the chase, 'give tongue.' The same phrase occurs in *Henry V,* II.iv.74, and *Troilus and Cressida,* V.i.88.

696. *As if another chase were in the skies.* Cf. *Titus Andronicus,* II.iii.17-19.

697-699. *By this . . . still.* When the hare 'hath left both hunters and dogs a great way behind her, she getteth to some hill or rising of the earth, there she raiseth herself upon her hinder legs, like a watchman in his tower, observing how far or near the enemy approacheth' (Topsell, *Four-footed Beasts,* 211).

701, 702. *And now . . . passing-bell.* When the hare 'can go no more, needs must her weakness betray her to her foe, and so was her flight and want of rest like a sickness begun before her death, an the Foxes presence like the voyce of a passing-bell' (Topsell, *Four-footed Beasts,* 210).

704. *indenting.* Following a meandering course comparable to the indented line in which the duplicates of a legal document were cut out to make them tally with each other. Topsell has (p. 212): 'The dogs run along with a gallant cry, turning over the doubtful steps; now one way, now another (like the cuts of Indentures, through rough and plain, crooked and straight. . . .'

720. *In night . . . desire sees best of all.* Cf. Marlowe, *Hero and Leander.* 'Dark night is Cupid's day.'

725. *cloudy.* Has here the double meaning of 'covered with clouds' and 'gloomy.'

726. *forsworn.* Since she had vowed to remain chaste.

730. *moulds.* The mould in which Adonis was cast, when he was created.

751. *fruitless chastity.* Cf. Marlowe, *Hero and Leander.* 'A fruitless cold virginity.''

757, 758. *What . . . posterity.* Cf. Sonnet 3, 7–8. Note the strange rime of *posterity* with *obscurity.* It is discussed by Neil Dodge, 'An Obsolete Elizabethan Mode of Rhyming,' *Shakespeare Studies* (University of Wisconsin), 1916.

768. *But gold that's put to use more gold begets.* Cf. Marlowe, *Hero and Leander.* 'Then treasure is abused/When misers keep it: being put to loan/In time it will return us two for one.'

828. *discovery.* Adonis has just been compared (l. 815) to a bright star shooting from the sky; Venus, therefore, remains 'confounded' in the dark, having lost the fair light which might have helped her to find out her way.

848. *parasites.* Those sounds being but echoes to her lamentations seem to flatter her obsequiously.

854. *cabinet.* A diminutive of 'cabin,' a small hut. On this line cf. *Notes and Queries,* 10th Ser., vol. V (January-June, 1906), p. 465; vol. IX (1908), p. 505; vol. X, p. 166.

877. *at a bay.* (French *aux abois*), a term of venery, said of the hounds when they have hunted down their game and bay at it; the expression is also used of the hunted animal when it is obliged to stop and face the hounds.

883, 884. *For now . . . proud.* Cf. Ovid, *Met.,* X, 539-541.

888. *strain courtesy.* The expression means either 'exhibit courtesy reluctantly,' 'fall short of courtesy,' or, on the contrary, 'to be courteous beyond the proper extent.' Here the latter meaning is perferable. Each dog displays an eagerness to let the others go first.

889. *cry.* A term of venery, used of the hounds when they bay. Cf. 'full cry.'

891, 892. *Who, overcome, etc.* 'Her heart overwhelmed with fears withdraws the blood from the limbs, and they in turn refuse their office' (Pooler).

920. *flap-mouth'd.* Having loose, hanging-down lips,—a characteristic point in a swift hound.

933. *worm.* Some commentators give to the word the meaning of 'serpent,' which it sometimes has in Elizabethan English. But is not death naturally associated with the idea of worms?

947. *golden arrow.* Cupid was supposed to have golden arrows to inspire love and leaden ones for disdained lovers.

933. *call'd him all to naught.* Called him a worthless person.

1013. *trophies.* Monuments erected in memory of some victory.

1027. *lure.* A piece of flesh with feathers attached to it, in manner of a bird, used by falconers to recall (or reclaim) a hawk.

1028. *The grass stoops not, she treads on it so light.* Cf. Virgil, *Æneid,* VII, 808-809: 'Illa vel intactae segetis per summa volaret/Gramina nec teneras cursu læsisset aristas.'

1064. *That her sight dazzling makes the wound seem three.* Cf. *3 Henry VI,* II.i.25: 'Dazzle mine eyes, or do I see three suns?'

1110. *He thought . . . him so.* Malone compares this passage with a poem 'De Adoni ab apro interempto,' by Minturno, in which the wound made by the boar is represented as an awkwardly given kiss: 'Ingens me miserum libido capit/Mille suavia dulcia hine capere,/Atque me impulit ingens indomitus.' The idea is from Theocritus.

1115, 1116. *And nuzzling, etc.* Cf. Ovid, *Met.,* X, 715, 716.

1127. *Coffer-lids.* Or lids to coffers, treasure-chests. Possibly cover-lid, or coverlet (French *couvrelit,* the covering of a bed).

1148. *Measures.* A dance, more particularly a stately kind of dance with slow, measured steps. Cf. *Much Ado,* II.i.64, 65, where it is said to be 'mannerly-modest' and 'full of state and ancientry.'

1168. *Purple flower.* According to the legend, Adonis was metamorphosed to an anemone, also called Adonis. Cf. Ovid, *Met.,* X, 731-739.

1193. *Paphos.* A city on the west coast of Cyprus. Venus was said to have landed there when she was born from the sea foam.

LUCRECE

THE ARGUMENT

1-7. It is to be noted that the poem contains nothing corresponding to this part of the argument.

1. *Lucius Tarquinius . . . Superbus.* The last legendary king of Rome (534-510 B.C.). His tyrannical ways and the outrage of his son upon Lucretia caused the people to revolt and led to the expulsion of the Tarquins.

6. *Ardea.* An ancient city of Latium, about twenty-four miles south of Rome, one of the most wealthy in that part of Italy.

11. *Collatinus.* L. Tarquinius, the son of Egerius, resided in the town of Collatia; hence his surname of Collatinus. He was cousin to Tarquinius Superbus, and after the dethronement of the latter he was elected one of the consuls.

26. *dispatcheth messengers, etc.* In the poem, Lucrece sends only one messenger, to her husband.

28. *Junius Brutus.* Lucius Junius, after his father's death, to escape being murdered by Tarquinius Superbus, feigned madness, whence his surname of Brutus.

29. *Publius Valerius.* Surnamed Publicola. He took a prominent part in the dethronement of the Tarquins and was the colleague of Brutus in the consulship.

4. *Collatium.* I.e. Collatia, a city of Latium, about ten miles east of Rome.

8,9. *Haply . . . appetite.* Wyndham compares Ovid, *Fasti,* ii, 765: 'Verba placent, et vox, et quod corrumpere non est:/Quoque minor spes est, hoc magis ille cupit.' But Shakespeare's text is nearer Livy's: 'Cum forma tum spectata castitas incitat.'

14. *aspects.* The position of the stars or planets with respect to one another.

26. *An expir'd date, cancell'd ere well begun.* Cf. Daniel, *Rosamonde* (249): 'Cancelled with Time, will have their date expired.'

47. *liver.* In Shakespeare's days, the liver was supposed to be the seat of love or desire. Cf. *Much Ado,* IV.i.239: 'If ever love had interest in his liver.' Also, *Twelfth Night,* II.iv.105.

49. *spring.* Two meanings are possible: 1, a too early spring is blighted by the cold and cannot grow old; 2, premature shoots (springs) are blighted by the cold and therefore cannot grow. The former is preferable.

52-70. *Within whose face beauty and virtue striv'd, etc.* This passage describes the contention between Beauty and Virtue in terms of heraldry, red being identi-

fied with 'or' or gold and white with silver (more properly 'argent'), two of the metals employed in blazonry. The sense can be paraphrased as follows: At sight of Tarquin, Lucrece changed color several times, her cheeks being by turns red and white (cf. ll. 257-259). When Virtue, whose color is white, appeared to be dominant (bragged), Beauty blushed; but, then, Virtue was jealous and tried to surpass (stain) the 'or' of those blushes with the silver of her paleness. Beauty, who considered she had a right (intituled) to white, then claimed a field silver from Venus's doves. As a retort, Virtue claimed Beauty's red, to which she had also a right, for she had given it to the golden age that men, in that virtuous age, might display it combined with silver on their shield, the shield to be used as a defensive armor when shame assailed.

67. *minority.* Cf. 'golden age' at l. 60. From the days when the world was still young, Beauty and Virtue have thus asserted their rights.

72. *field.* A play on the double meaning of the word: 1, field, heraldic term; 2, field of battle.

82. *owe.* Because he had been a niggard in his praise he had not given the full sum of commendation which he ought to have paid.

88. *lim'd.* Caught by bird-lime. Steevens appositely cites *3 Henry VI*, V.vi.13, 14: 'The bird that hath been limed in a bush/With trembling wings misdoubteth every bush.'

104, 105. *Nor . . . light.* 'Lucrece could see that Tarquin was looking, but not what his looks meant' (Pooler).

106-112. *He stories, etc.* Gower (*Confessio Amantis*) also makes Collatinus the subject of Tarquin's conversation with Lucrece.

117-119. *Till sable . . . Day.* Cf. Daniel, *Rosamonde*: 'Night (mother of sleepe and feare)/Who with her sable mantle friendly covers/The sweet-stolne sport of ioyfull meeting lovers' (439).

120-123. *For . . . questioned.* Cf. Livy: 'Cum post cenam in hospitale cubiculum deductus esset.'

135, 136. *That what, etc.* This passage has been much emended. Quartos 5 to 8 have 'That oft, what'; Staunton conjectured 'For what'; Nicholson, 'That while.' The quarto reading, though not very clear, yields, however, an acceptable sense: Those that covet much are so foolish that they scatter what they have not as well as that which they possess, for in their hope to get more they spend beyond their power.

138-140. *Or, gaining more, etc.* If they succeed in getting more, all their profit is but to have more than is necessary, and to experience the griefs that go with fortune, so that, in the end, in this valueless gain they really are bankrupt.

150-152. *And this . . . we have.* 'Rich men suffering from the disease of ambition are tortured by the thought that they are destitute of what they have, viz. abundance' (Pooler).

187, 188. *Then looking . . lust.* 'He despises his naked or defenceless protection from Lust, now still and slaughtered by Fear' (Wyndham).

197-210. Cf. Chaucer, *Legend of Good Women* (1822-1824): 'Why hastow doon dispite to chevalrye?/Why hastow doon thys lady vylanye?/Allas, of the thys was a vilenous deede!'

206, 207. *Some loathsome . . . dote.* In heraldry there exist special marks of disgrace, called 'abatements,' to denote some 'ungentleman-like, dishonorable, disloyal demeanour, quality or stain in the bearer, whereby the dignity of the Coat-armour' is 'greatly abased' (Guillim, *Display of Heraldry*). They consist of 'diminution and reversing; the first is the blemishing some particular point of the escutcheons by sanguine and tenny [orange], which are stains. Reversing signifies some parts of the charge backward or upside down' (Pinnock's *Catechism of Heraldry*). The figures used for 'abatements of honour' were not of metal, but 'tinged or coloured' either tenny or sanguine.

245. *painted cloth.* Pieces of canvas painted in oil and sued for hangings in Elizabethan houses. They were often painted with Scripture incidents and ornamented with mottoes or moral sentences. (Cf. *1 Henry IV*, IV.ii.22; *Troilus and Cressida*, V.x.46.)

265. *Narcissus.* Cf. note on *Venus and Adonis*, 161.

278. *My part is youth, and beats these from the stage.* probably an allusion to some morality play—such as *Lusty Juventus*—now lost.

318. *rushes.* In old days it was customary to strew the rooms with rushes for carpets.

341. *So from himself impiety hath wrought.* 'His sin has made him so unlike himself' (Pooler).

342. *Prey to pray.* 'A jingle not less disgusting occurs in Ovid's narrative of the same event (*Fasti*, ii, 787) "Hostis, ut hospes, init penetralia Collatina" ' (Steevens).

356. *eye of Heaven.* The sun. Cf. *Richard II*, I.iii.277; III.ii.37.

365. *stalks.* So Chaucer, *Legend of Good Women* (l. 1781): 'And in the night ful thefely gan he stalke.'

386-395. *Her lily hand, etc.* Sir John Suckling has a poem entitled 'A Supple-

ment of an imperfect copy of verses of Mr Wil. Shakespears' (ed. W. C. Hazlitt, I, 27), the first lines of which are, with certain variants, lines 386-395 of Shakespeare's *Lucrece*. The beginning of the poem runs as follows:

> One of her hands, one of her cheeks lay under,
>   Cozening the pillow of a lawful kisse,
> Which therefore swel'd and seem'd to part asunder,
>   As angry to be rob'd of such a blisse:
>   The one lookt pale, and for revenge did long,
>   Whilst t'other blush't, cause it had done the wrong.

2

> Out of the bed the other fair hand was
>   On a green satin quilt, whose perfect white
> Lookt like a Dazie in a field of grasse
>   *And shewed like unmelt snowe unto the sight
>   There lay this pretty perdue, safe to keep
>   The rest o th'body that lay fast asleep.

Thus far Shakespeare.

As we have no reason to suspect Suckling's statement that he had an imperfect copy of Shakespeare's verses, and as several lines differ from the corresponding lines in the authentic version, we may admit that Shakespeare had contemplated writing his *Lucrece* in the six-line stanza of *Venus and Adonis*, but that, for some unknown reason, after having tried a stanza or so, he rejected it and adopted the seven-line stanza. (Cf. B. Nicholson, *Notes and Queries*, 1884, June 7, p. 444.)

397. *marigolds.* The marigold was the emblem of constancy in affection and was said 'to go to bed with the sun' (*Winter's Tale*, IV.iv.121).

400. *golden threads.* Ovid speaks of Lucrece's 'flavi capilli.' Chaucer has 'yellow heer.'

407-409. *Her breasts . . . knew.* Cf. Ovid, *Fasti*, ii, 803-804: "positis urguentur pectora palmis,/Tune primum externa pectora tacta manu.'

417. *tir'd.* Cf. note on *Venus and Adonis*, 56.

437-439. *His hand . . . breast.* Compare Livy's 'sinistra manu mulieris pectore oppresso' with Ovid's 'positis urguentur pectora palmis.'

459. *antics.* Grotesques, or fantastic forms.

476, 477, 481. *colour.* A play on the different meanings of the word: pretext, hue, standard.

477-504. Shakespeare may have found the idea of Tarquin's speech in Livy: 'Tum Tarquinius fateri amorem, orare, miscere precibus minas, versare in omnes partes muliebrem animum.' Ovid has only: 'Instat amans hostis precibus pretioque minisque' (805).

477-511. Cf. Ovid, *Fasti*, ii, 803, and Chaucer, *Legend of Good Women*, ll. 1790 ff.

492. *I know what thorns the growing rose defends.* Cf. Daniel, *Rosamonde*: 'The ungather'd Rose defended with the thornes' (217).

509. *falchion.* A play upon the words falchion and falcon (cf. above, l. 506).

511. *falcon's bells.* Falconers fastened bells, often made of silver, to the legs of their hawks or falcons.

522. *nameless bastardy.* Malone compares *Two Gentlemen of Verona*, III.i.310, 311: 'bastard vertues, that indeed know not their fathers, and therefore have no names.'

537. *Worse than a slavish wipe.* 'More disgraceful than the brand with which slaves were marked' (Malone).

540. *cockatrice.* Or basilisk. 'The cockatrice slayeth also all thing that hath life, with breath and with sight. In his sight no fowl nor bird passeth harmless, and though he be far from the fowl, yet it is burnt and devoured by his mouth' (Bartholomew's *De Propriet. rerum*, translated by Trevisa, Bk. xviii, §8).

556. *vulture folly.* Cf. Daniel, *Rosamonde*: 'vulture ambition' (27).

565-567. *She puts . . . speaks.* Steevens compares *Midsummer Night's Dream*, V.i.100: 'Make periods in the midst of sentences,/Throttle their practised accent in their fears,/And in conclusion dumbly have broke off.'

596-630. Cf. Chaucer, *Legend of Good Women* (1819-1821): 'Tarquinius, thou art a Kynges eyre,/And sholdest, as by lynage and by right,/Doon as a lorde and as a verray knyght.'

677. *The wolf hath seiz'd his prey, the poor lamb cries.* Cf. Ovid, *Fasti*, ii, 800: 'Sed tremit ut quondam stabulis deprensa relictis/Parva, sub infesto cum jacet agna lupo,' and Chaucer, *Legend*, l. 1798: 'Right as a wolf that fynt a lamb alone,/To whom shall she compleyne or make mone?'

703. *receipt.* What he has received, as in *Coriolanus*, I.i.97, 98: 'the mutinous parts/That envied his receipt' (said of the belly).

766. *Black stage.* In the Elizabethan system of staging they often used black

hangings as an appropriate setting for tragedies. Cf. *1 Henry VI*, I.i.1; *Warning for Fair Women*, Ind. 74; *Insatiate Countess* (Marston), IV.v.4.

828. *crest-wounding.* Bringing dishonor to the crest. In heraldry the crest is the ornament of a helmet.

830. *mot.* I.e. motto, a sentence (generally written on a scroll) above or under an escutcheon.

850. *toads infect.* 'A toad is a manner venomous frog, and dwelleth both in water and land . . . his venom is accounted most cold and stonieth' (Bartholomew, *De Propriet. rerum*, Bk. xviii, §17).

858. *Tantalus.* A legendary king of Lydia, who was afflicted in Hades with eternal hunger and thirst.

874. *ill-annexed Opportunity.* I.e. opportunity with its evil adjuncts.

876 ff. *O Opportunity, etc.* All this passage seems to have been strongly influenced by Spenser's *Fairy Queen*. Compare, for instance, the personification of Occasion in Bk. ii, canto iv.

950. *cherish.* Warburton proposed as an emendation 'tarish' (from French *tarir*), dry up. Other commentators give to 'springs' the meaning of 'shoots,' in which case 'cherish' means 'nurture,' 'foster.' But in the whole passage Time is shown as destroying everything.

956. *unicorn.* 'It is a beast of an untameable nature' (Topsell, *Four-footed Beasts*, 557). 'An unicorn is a right cruel beast, and hath that name, for he hath in the middle of the forehead an horn of four foot long' (Bartholomew, *De Propriet. rerum*, Bk. xviii, 90).

1054. *badge.* The badge was a piece of cloth or of silver with the arms of a nobleman worn on the left sleeve by his servants or dependents. For 'livery' cf. note on *Venus and Adonis*, 506.

1074. *sable ground.* The ground, or field, is the surface of a shield on which are represented the ensigns armorial composing a coat of arms. 'Sable' is the heraldic term for black.

1079. *Philomel.* A daughter of King Pandion, who, being dishonored by her brother-in-law, Tereus, was metamorphosed into a nightingale (or swallow).

1086. *Revealing day through every cranny spies.* On this line see *Notes and Queries*, 11th Ser., vol. IV (1911), p. 243.

1094. *True grief is fond and testy as a child.* On this line see W. Cairns, in *Literature* (London), July 29, 1899, vol. V, p. 111.

1132. *diapason.* An air sounding in exact concord, i.e. in octaves.

1133. *burthen.* The burden was a musical figure which consisted in repeating the theme throughout the song, in the bass, and continuing when the singer of the air paused. Then it came to mean simply, as here, the bass or undersong.

1134. *descant'st.* 'To descant: to play or sing an air in harmony with a fixed theme' (N.E.D.).

better skill. I.e. with better skill. So Malone and others. But Wyndham explains more subtly: 'Shakespeare, here, as ever, exhibits a complete grasp of technical terms. He makes Lucrece contrast her sad, monotonous accompaniment of groans—humming on Tarquin still—with the treble descant of the nightingale, complaining in a higher register and with more frequent modulations of the wrong wrought her by Tereus, according to Ovid's tale. The one he compares to a single droning base, chiefly in the diapason or lower octave; the other to the "better skill" or more ingenious artifice of a contrapuntal melody scored above it.'

1139. *Who, if it wink, shall thereon fall and die.* I.e. and my heart, if my eye wink, shall fall on the knife and die.

1140. *frets.* Pieces of wire, or wood, fixed on the finger board of guitars and other similar instruments serving to regulate the fingering.

1155. *death reproach's debtor.* Death alone can discharge the debt to infamy and thus acquit Lucrece.

1157. *But with my body my poor soul's pollution.* It would be only adding the pollution of the soul to the pollution of the body.

1188-1190. *So of . . . new-born.* Like the Phœnix which was supposed to rise again from its own ashes.

1196. *thy foe.* Because she has brought shame upon him.

1199. *My soul and body, etc.* The formula usually used at the beginning of a will.

1205. *oversee.* The overseers of a will were persons appointed to see that the intentions of the deceased were correctly carried out. Note the play upon the word at the following line.

1220. *With soft slow tongue, true mark of modesty.* Cf. *Lear*, V.iii.322, 323, of Cordelia: 'Her voice was ever soft,/Gentle, and low,—an excellent thing in woman.'

1234. *Like ivory conduits coral cisterns filling.* Shakespeare was probably thinking of some fountain. Cf. *As You Like It*, IV.i.133.

1261. *The precedent whereof in Lucrece view.* Cf. Daniel, *Rosamonde*: 'The president whereof presented to my view' (414).

1261-1267. Cf. Chaucer, *Legend of Good Women* (ll. 1814-1818): 'That, what for fere of sklaundre and drede of dethe./She lost att ones bothe wytte and brethe;/And in a swowgh she lay, and woxe so ded,/Men myghten smyten of hir arme or hed,/She feleth nothinge, neither foule ne feyre.'

1324. *To see sad sights moves more than hear them told.* Cf. Horace, *Ars Poet.*, 180-181: 'Segnius irritant animos demissa per aurem/Quam quae sunt oculis subjecta fidelibus.'

1342. *But they, etc.* On this line see *Notes and Queries*, 1874, May 2, p. 343; June 20, p. 484.

1366 ff. *At last, etc.* In Virgil, *Æneid*, I, 454-493, Æneas similarly views scenes from the fall of Troy depicted in a temple of Carthage.

1367. *Painting.* Commentators suppose that Shakespeare had in mind not a picture but a hanging, or painted cloth. Nothing in the text bears out such a supposition.

1436. *Dardan.* An adjective applied to Troy, so called after Dardanus.

1437. *Simois.* A river which flows from Mount Ida, and joins the river Scamander in the plain of Troy.

1450, 1451. *In her . . . reign.* Cf. Daniel, *Rosamonde*: 'Reade in my face the ruines of my youth/The wracke of yeeres upon my aged brow' (253-254).

1501. *wretched image.* I.e. Sinon, a son of Ætinus (or of Sisyphus). He mutilated himself and allowed himself to be taken prisoner by the Trojans, in order to facilitate the introduction of the wooden horse, full of Greeks, into the city of Troy.

1523. *wildfire.* A pyrotechnical composition, burning even under water, and analogous to Greek fire.

1525. *And little stars shot from their fixed places.* Cf. Virgil, *Æneid*, ii, 693-696: 'De caelo lapsa per umbras/Stella facem ducens multa cum luce cucurrit./ Illam, summa super labentem culmina tecti,/Cernimus.' The whole passage is strongly reminiscent of the second book of the Æneid.

1526. *their glass.* I.e. the burnished roof of Priam's palace, which reflected the stars.

1544. *armed to beguild.* So all the quartos, 'beguild' having the meaning of 'to cover as with gold.' Perhaps we should read 'to-beguil'd,' all disguised.

1585. *mourning.* Cf. Ovid, *Fasti*, ii, 817-818: 'Utque vident habitum, quae luctus causa, requirunt/Cui paret exequias.' Also in Chaucer, *Legend*, ll. 1829 ff., and in Bandello (Bk. ii, nov. XXI). This detail is not in Livy.

1588. *water-galls.* A watery appearance in the sky, looked upon as a presage of stormy weather.

1604. *Three times.* Cf. Ovid, *Fasti*, ii, 823: 'Ter conata loqui, ter destitit.'

1620. *A stranger . . . lay.* Cf. Livy: 'Vestigia viri alieni in lecto sunt tuo.'

1650. *Scarlet lust.* Tarquin being the judge is clad in scarlet, hence the epithet is applied to his lust that plays the part of a witness.

1655, 1656. *Though . . . my mind.* Cf. Livy: 'Ceterum corpus est tantum violatum, animus insons.' This is not in Ovid.

1660 ff. Cf. the King's lamentations in Daniel's *Rosamonde* (ll. 792 ff.).

1672, 1673. *Even . . . draw.* 'His sighs make a saw, the tool so called, of his sorrows by pushing grief forwards and drawing it back again; i.e. his sighs gave him only momentary relief, a repetition of ll. 1663-1666, he sighs away his grief and drinks it up again' (Pooler).

1689-1691. *Speaking . . . mine.* Cf. Livy: 'Sed date dextras fidemque, haud impune adultero fore . . . si vos viri estis, . . . dant ordine omnes fidem.' Ovid has only: 'Hoc quoque Tarquinio debebimus' (825).

1709, 1710. *With this . . . clears.* Cf. Livy: 'Consolantur aegram animi . . . mentem peccare, non corpus.' This is not in Ovid.

1714, 1715. *No, no . . . giving.* Cf. Livy, thus translated in Paynter's *Palace of Pleasure*: 'As for my part, though I cleare myself of the offence, my body shall feel the punishment: for no unchast or ill woman shall hereafter impute no dishonest act to Lucrece.' This is not in Ovid.

1732, 1733. Cf. Ovid, *Fasti* (ii, 833-834): 'Ecce super corpus communia damna gementes/Obliti decoris, virque paterque jacent.'

1745. *rigol.* Generally explained 'circle,' a ring, and compared with *2 Henry IV*, IV.v.37, where the crown is called 'this golden rigol.' Malone cites Nashe (*Lenten Stuff*): 'the ringol or ringed circle was compact and chalkt out.' But 'ringol' (German, ringel, ring) is not 'rigol.' I am inclined to believe that we have here a word connected with the French 'rigole,' which means a small channel for water, also a rivulet (cf. Low Latin 'rigora,' 'rigulus' and Italian 'rigolo,' scanalatura).

1772-1775. Cf. note to 1732, 1733.

1797. *sorrow's interest.* Wyndham compares Sonnet XXXI: 'How many a holy and obsequious tear/Hath dear religious love stol'n from mine eye/As interest of the dead.'

1809, 1810. *Began . . . to show.* See note on Argument, 29.

1843-1848. *And kissed . . . swore.* Cf. Livy: 'Cultrum deinde Collatino tradit,

inde Lucretio ac Valerio, stupentibus miraculo rei, unde novum in Bruti pectore ingenium. Ut præceptum erat, jurant.' This is not in Ovid.

1850, 1851. *They did . . . Rome.* This is neither in Ovid nor in Livy. Chaucer (*Legend*, ll. 1861-1866) has: 'Of hir had al the toun of Rome routhe . . ./And openly let cary her, on a bere/Through al the toun.'

THE PHŒNIX AND THE TURTLE

1. *the bird of loudest lay.* It is possible that Shakespeare was thinking of the crane which Chaucer mentions in *Parlement of Foules* (l. 344), 'the crane, the geaunt, with his trompes soune.'

2. *Arabian tree.* The date-palm (Greek φοῖνιξ) which the bird phœnix occupied, hence its name. Cf. *Tempest*, III.iii.29, 30.

5. *shrieking harbinger.* The screech-owl, which foretells evil and death. Cf. Chaucer, *Parlement*, l. 342, 'The oule eeke, that of the dethe the bode bringeth.' Cf. *Midsummer Night's Dream*, II.ii.6-8.

10. *tyrant wing.* I.e. birds of prey. Chaucer, *Parlement*, l. 334, says of the eagle: 'Ther was the tyraunt with his fethers donne.'

15. *death-divining.* It was an ancient belief that the swan sang just before his death. Chaucer, *Parlement*, has: 'The Ialous swan, ayens his deth that singeth.' Cf. *King John*, V.vii.21, 22, and *Othello*, V.ii.292, 293.

17. *treble-dated crow.* The crow, on account of his black color, was a suitable mourner. The crow was believed to live three times three human lives. 'Cornicum ut secla vetusta/Ter tres aetates humanas garrula vincit/Cornix' (Lucretius, V, 1053). The crow was also symbolic of conjugal concord (cf. Alciati, Emblem 38). Hence his presence among the mourners of the faithful pair.

18, 19. *Thy sable gender . . . tak'st.* Probably an allusion to the notion that the raven does not 'conceive by conjunction of male and female, but rather by a kind of billing at the mouth which Pliny (x, 12) mentions as an opinion of the common people' (Swan's *Speculum Mundi*, 1665, p. 397. Quoted by Halliwell.). Two crows were often represented by emblem writers with their bills fast locked one in the other, which probably suggested the idea of conceiving by giving and taking breath.

25-28. *So they loved . . . was slain.* Though the lovers were two, so complete was their union that they looked as if they were one in essence; each was distinct from the other, and yet there was no division between them; in their love the very notion of number was annihilated.

29, 30. *Hearts . . . seen.* This stanza develops the same idea as the preceding one. Though their hearts were remote, because belonging to two different persons, yet they were united; there was a distance between them, since remote, but no space, that is, no division.

32. *But . . . wonder.* 'So extraordinary a phenomenon as "hearts remote" yet "not asunder" would have excited admiration had it been found anywhere else except in these two birds. In them it was not wonderful' (Malone).

33-36. *So . . . mine.* Their love shone so bright that the turtle could see his right, that is, the love due to him, all a-blaze in the ardent eyes of the phœnix: Each was the source of inexhaustible treasure (*mine*) to the other.

37-40. *Property . . . call'd.* Property is a Latinism, 'proprietas,' peculiar or essential quality. Cf. *Richard II*, III.ii.135, 136: 'Sweet love, I see, changing his property/Turns to the sourest and most deadly hate.' 'Property' was appalled to find out that personality had been destroyed, since each lover's identity was merged into the other's, and was no longer itself. There were two names to what was in reality one person; therefore it could neither be said that they were two, since their nature was the same, nor that they were one, for in fact there were two distinct persons.

42. *Saw division grow together.* Reason cannot understand how those which seemed different were now one.

43-46. *To themselves . . . one.* And yet Reason saw that the lovers were different in themselves, for the elements in their several natures were so strongly compounded or blended that Reason could exclaim: 'In this unity, there is a real duality.'

47, 48. *Love . . . remain.* So that Love is right while Reason, which ought to be right, is wrong—since there remains a union where there should be a division.

THE PASSIONATE PILGRIM

I. This is Shakespeare's Sonnet 138, with important variant readings.

II. This is Shakespeare's Sonnet 144, with minor variations.

11. 'Being both friends to me and also to each other.'

III. From *Love's Labour's Lost*, IV.iii.55-68. Lines 2, 9, 10, 11, and 14 contain slight differences from the text of the play.

IV. Author unknown.

V. From *Love's Labour's Lost*, IV.ii.109-117, with certain alterations.

VI. Author unknown. The subject is that of one of the pictures offered to Christopher Sly (*Taming of the Shrew*, I.ii.53-56): 'We will fetch thee straight Adonis painted by the running brook, and Cytherea all in sedges hid.' Sedge is not 'osier' and one might as well see in that difference a proof that the sonnet is not by the same hand as the one that wrote *The Taming of the Shrew.*

VII. Author unknown.

5. *Damask.* A red color resembling that of the damask rose.

VIII. By Richard Barnfield. Appeared in *Poems: in divers Humors* (1598).

3. *Thee.* In Barnfield's *Poems* the sonnet is addressed 'To his friend Master R. L. in praise of music and poetry.' R. L. has been identified as Richard Linche, author of *Diella* (1596).

5. *Dowland.* John Dowland (?1563-?1626), a lute player. He was also a composer and published *Songes or Ayres of Foure Partes with Tableture for the Lute* (1597); *Lacrymae* (1605), etc.

14. *One knight.* Probably Sir George Carey.

IX. Author unknown. The second line of this sonnet appears to have been inadvertently omitted.

X. Author unknown. Unlike IX and XI, this poem is not on the Venus and Adonis theme.

XI. By Bartholomew Griffin. Appeared in *Fidessa more chaste than kind* (1596). In regard to ll. 9-12, which are different in the *Passionate Pilgrim* and in *Fidessa*, Grosart suggested that they were altered so as to be a closer copy of Venus and Adonis. I believe Dowden is right when he says: 'This is a case of hesitation between two treatments of a sonnet-close, the writer being doubtful whether the turn in the thought should take place at the ninth or at the eleventh line.'

9-12. In Griffin's *Fidessa* these four lines are as follows: 'But he a wayward boy refused the offer/And ran away, the beauteous queen neglecting/Showing both folly to abuse her proffer/And all his sex of cowardice detecting.'

13. *At this bay.* For this expression see note on *Venus and Adonis*, 877.

XII. Has been ascribed to Thomas Deloney. It occurs, with four additional stanzas, in his *Garland of Good Will*. Pt. III. The first edition known is dated 1604.

XIII. Author unknown.

XIV. Author unknown.

14. Pooler proposes to read: 'My heart doth charge them watch the morning rise,' which is decidedly an improvement.

SONNETS TO SUNDRY NOTES OF MUSIC

I. Author unknown.

II. From *Love's Labour's Lost*, IV.iii.99-118. The chief alteration is the omission of two lines which are found in the play. This poem was also reprinted in *England's Helicon*, with the title 'The Passionate Shepherds Song.'

III. Author unknown. Previously published in a Collection of Madrigals by Thomas Weelkes (1597). It occurs also in *England's Helicon*, with the title 'The Unknown Shepherd's Complaint.'

IV. Author unknown. Prof. Dowden, in his Introduction to Griggs' facsimile, seems ready to accept Grosart's suggestion that this poem is somehow connected with *Willobie his Avisa*. All that can be said is that the metre is the same in both poems.

V. By Marlowe. It appeared in *England's Helicon* with the signature Chr. Marlowe, and two additional stanzas. In *England's Helicon*, 'Love's Answer,' entitled 'The Nymph's reply to the Shepherd,' has five additional stanzas, and is subscribed 'Ignoto.' It was attributed to Sir Walter Raleigh.

VI. By Richard Barnfield. Cf. *Poems: in divers Humors*, and *England's Helicon*.

23. *Pandion.* A king of Athens and father to Philomela. Cf. note on *Lucrece*, 1079.

A Lover's Complaint

22, 23. *levell'd . . . intend.* Her eyes were aimed at the sky as a gun on its carriage.

26. *Lend.* See *Notes and Queries*, 1884, Feb. 2, Feb. 16, and March 29.

48, 49. *With sleided . . . secrecy.* Letters were often closed with a piece of silk ribbon the ends of which were placed under the wax-seal of the letter the better to ensure secrecy.

109. *Rounds, bounds, course, stop.* Terms of the *manege* meaning respectively: motion in a circle, leap, race, pause.

111, 112. *Whether . . . steed.* It was impossible to say whether the horse owed the gracefulness of its movements to the skill of the rider, or whether the rider appeared so graceful in his training on account of the horse's docility.

144. *Was my own fee-simple.* I had an absolute power over myself.

153. *Foil.* The setting of a jewel; that which makes it conspicuous. It probably refers here to the thin plate of metal which was (and is still) placed under a valueless stone to give it the appearance of a gem.

157, 158. *Or forc'd . . . way.* 'Or insisted on the examples which tell against her own (apparent) happiness in order to hinder herself from pursuing it by realising the past dangers of others' (Wyndham).

224. *Since . . . me.* I am the altar on which I sacrifice to you, and, therefore, you become my patron or goddess.

229, 230. *What . . . you.* Whatever obeys me on your account works under you since I am your minister.

234. *Which . . . shun.* Who lately avoided the courtship of noble suitors.

235. *Blossoms.* According to Malone, 'the flower of the young nobility.'

241. *Paling . . . receive.* 'Making oneself as it were without form or void' (Wyndham). 'Securing within the pale of a cloister that heart which had never received the impression of Love' (Malone).

251, 252. *Not to be tempted . . . procur'd.* She sought the cloister in order not to be tempted, but there she only found the liberty to tempt.

The Text of the Present Edition

The text of the present volume is based, by permission of the Oxford University Press, upon that of the Oxford Shakespeare, edited by W. J. Craig, except for the following changes:

1. Punctuation and spelling have been normalized to accord with modern English practice, e.g. forgo (forego), warlike (war-like).

2. Characteristic old forms (e.g., murther, Troyan) and euphonic abbreviations (e.g. th'annexions) are retained.

3. The following alterations in Craig's text have been made, all in conformity with the readings of the First Quartos. The readings of the present edition precede the colon, while Craig's readings follow it.

Venus and Adonis

    188   gone?: gone;
    317   was: is
    484   earth: world
    591   cheek: cheeks
    601   so: as
    896   all: sore
    962   eye: eyes
  1134   thou: you

Lucrece

   135   That: For
   217   stroken: strucken
   319   needle: neeld
   584   look'st: look'dst
   772   cureless: curseless
   812   cote: quote
  1029   foul defiled: foul-defiled
  1145   not: nor
  1338   villain: villein
  1352   her: their
  1544   to beguild: so beguil'd
  1615   woes: woe

Passionate Pilgrim

  XI.14.   run: ran
  XIV.8   scorn or: scorn of   conster: construe

Sonnets to Sundry Notes of Music

  IV. 51   round me on th'ear: ring my ear

Lover's Complaint

   41   lets: let
   47   moe: more
  198   pallid: paled

The Sonnets

INTRODUCTION

The first mention of Shakespeare's sonnets occurs in a little book by Francis Meres entitled *Palladis Tamia, Wit's Treasury*, published in 1598: 'the sweet, witty soul of Ovid lives in mellifluous and honey-tongued Shakespeare, witness his *Venus and Adonis*, his *Lucrece*, his sugared sonnets among his private friends.' 'Among his private friends' means not only that the sonnets were unpublished, but that they were composed for persons with whom he was in intimate relations. The obscurity of many of these poems certainly arises from the fact that they were written for friendly eyes; and accordingly they contain many allusions to persons and events which would be plain enough to Shakespeare's circle, but which would mean little or nothing to outsiders, even in the poet's day.

In *The Passionate Pilgrim*, 1599, were published the first two of Shakespeare's sonnets to appear in print. They were Nos. 138 and 144. Their text differs in several lines from that printed in the first edition of the whole sonnet collection. This first edition, which the present volume follows, was a quarto published by Thomas Thorpe in 1609. It contains a large number of obvious mistakes that ruin the sense; in several cases sonnets that plainly should follow each other are separated; and it is impossible to believe that Shakespeare prepared the text for publication.

This first quarto made no such impression as did Sidney's posthumous sonnet sequence, *Astrophel and Stella*, published in 1591, and it was not until 1640 that a second edition of Shakespeare's sonnets appeared. This was published by John Benson under the title 'Poems written by Wil. Shake-speare, Gent.'; yet it contained, as well, poems by Marlowe, Raleigh, Ben Jonson, Carew, Herrick, Milton, and others. The sonnets were not printed in the order in which they appeared in the quarto of 1609. In many cases they were run together as one continuous poem; and there were added to them, singly or in groups, seventy-four titles, some fairly appropriate, others quite unfitting, and nearly all commonplace. Seven sonnets, including No. 18, 'Shall I compare thee to a summer's day,' and the poem in couplets, No. 126, are omitted from this edition. Plainly it is much inferior to the quarto of 1609. In 1710 both the first and second editions were reprinted. Two editions in a century indicate a lack of interest in the sonnets, especially when their fate is contrasted with the numerous editions and great popularity of many of the plays.

There is further evidence in the manner in which the first editors of Shakespeare neglected these poems. To cite Lee, 'Neither Nicholas Rowe, nor Pope, nor Theobald, nor Hanmer, nor Warburton, nor Capell, nor Dr. Johnson included them in their respective collections of Shakespeare's plays. None of these editors, save Capell, showed any signs of acquaintance with them.' The first critical edition of the sonnets was Malone's, 1780, for which George Steevens supplied some material; and it is indicative of the general attitude towards the sonnets that Steevens himself, in 1793, wrote that 'The strongest act of Parliament that could be framed would fail to compel readers into their service.'

With the rise of the Romantic School, the sonnets found readers, students, and imitators. Wordsworth, Coleridge, and Keats directed attention to them and on the Continent, where also they had suffered neglect, they became a subject of study and criticism. At the present moment, no part of Shakespeare's work arouses more interest or a greater critical discussion, a discussion which unfortunately has arrived at no sure conclusions.

PROBLEMS OF THE SONNETS

The numerous problems presented by this sonnet collection may be grouped under three heads: historical, literary, and autobiographical.

The historical problems are the identification of the men and women of this series, or the events hinted at in such a sonnet as No. 107, Who was W. H.? Is he the same person as the 'beauteous and lovely youth' of the first sonnets? Who was the poet whom Shakespeare considered 'better' and 'worthier' than himself? Who was the dark woman? (Cf. notes, ll. 3, 40, 127.) These questions are perpetually discussed, but never conclusively answered.

The two chief literary problems are: when were these sonnets written and in what order should they be printed? Plainly, from Meres's mention of them in 1598, many of the sonnets were composed long before the appearance of the first quarto in 1609, and just as clearly, many of the sonnets were printed out of their natural order.

In regard to the first question, it has been shown that there are more striking parallels between the sonnets and the earlier plays—*Love's Labour's Lost, Two Gentlemen of Verona, Romeo and Juliet*—than with the later, though the mood of *Troilus and Cressida, Hamlet, Antony and Cleopatra*, is sometimes reflected in this collection. Internal evidence is always dangerous, yet the general impression the sonnets make on the reader by their resemblances to *Venus and Adonis* (1593) and *The Rape of Lucrece* (1594), and by their fluency, their enthusiasm for beauty, their excess of emotion over reflection is that as a whole they are the work of the young Shakespeare. They may be assigned roughly to the years 1593-1598, which would bring them within the period of the greatest vogue of the Elizabethan sonnet. This assumption does not preclude the possibility that some of the sonnets were written much later, even in the reign of James I. Here is one more unsolved problem.

The order of the sonnets is a fascinating study. It has sometimes been assumed that sonnets Nos. 1-125 are all written to or about a lovely youth. It is certain that No. 126, the lyric in couplets, marks a division in the series and that most of the sonnets placed after it concern themselves directly or indirectly with the dark woman; but it does not follow as a corollary that all the sonnets before No. 126 refer to a man. There is no reason

to assume that the original publisher, Thorpe, was close enough to Shakespeare to understand fully the different MSS. out of which he may have combined the whole series. It is easy to see that many of the sonnets are printed in their proper sequence (Nos. 1-17, 40-42 63-65, 78-86, for example), but on the other hand some sonnets are clearly out of their natural order (cf. Nos. 70, 77, 81). It is not at all certain that all of the sonnets before No. 126 must refer to the youth Shakespeare praised, though Thorpe may have thought so or wished the reader to think so. Benson, the publisher of the second edition, would have the reader believe, from the titles affixed to the sonnets in his edition, that nearly all these poems were written to a woman. In five cases when the text of the first edition showed that to be impossible, he altered it, changing 'him' to 'her' and 'friend' or 'boy' to 'love.' (Nos. 101, 104, 108.)

The most disputed problem of all is the autobiographical value of this sequence. Opinions on this matter range from Sir Sidney Lee's conclusion that the sonnets, for all their beauty, are imitative and conventional, to unsubstantiated theories by Frank Harris and Arthur Acheson of the intimate, personal confessions of these poems. Certainly Lee has no difficulty in proving that many of the sonnets are conventional in both theme and treatment. The debates of the eye and heart (Nos. 46, 47) are merely the 'quirks of blazoning pen.' Like the sonnets of Wordsworth and Keats, these poems differ greatly in their content and in their value; and certain quibbling, punning ones, written for the amusement of the moment, seem unworthy of their author. But there are many others which must strike the unprejudiced reader as 'such fair speech as soul to soul affordeth.' Surely in many sonnets we have glimpses of Shakespeare the man. We see a poet who was deeply sensitive to appreciation and friendship, who felt the inferiority of his social position and the discouragements of his art, and who ranged from dejection to exultation, from vulgar ribaldry and cynical indecency to the inspiration of devoted friendship. In part, the inconsistencies in the moods of the sonnets are the inconsistencies of life itself. Shakespeare may not have 'unlocked his heart' in these poems; but surely at times he left the door ajar.

The Sonnet and Elizabethan Sonneteers

It was Petrarch (1304-1374) who made the sonnet the most popular form of the lyric during the fifteenth and sixteenth centuries. Though sonnets had been written before him, notably by Dante, the vogue of Petrarch, overshadowing that of all other lyric poets ancient and modern, was carried far beyond 'this side idolatry.' His themes were love and beauty, a hopeless love thwarted by destiny and death. His followers and imitators were legion. Vagany, in his compendious bibliography of sixteenth-century French and Italian sonneteers, does not include them all, for no man has ever read them all or could survive if he made the attempt.

Before the sonnet reached England, it came to France, where

Ronsard and his contemporaries were deeply influenced by Italian poetry; and in Shakespeare's day it was largely through the French sonneteers that Petrarch affected English writers, though they made direct translations of Italian sonnets as well. The first English sonnets were written by Sir Thomas Wyatt (1503-1542) and Henry Howard, Earl of Surrey (1518-1547), and were first published after their death in *Tottel's Miscellany*, 1557. As might be presumed, both these poets were confirmed admirers of Petrarch, and their sonnets showed it.

The sonnet of Petrarch, commonly called the Italian sonnet, is a poem of fourteen lines divided into two parts of eight and six lines, the octave and the sestet. The octave was written abbaabba, while the sestet could have two or three rhymes, arranged in no fixed order save that the last two lines should not rhyme together. In the octave a thought, an emotion, a picture is completely presented and the verse sentence, so to speak, comes to an end. In the sestet, the explanation, the comment, the summing up of the whole matter is given. Wyatt attempted the Italian form, but found it too difficult to write correctly, and his sonnets end in rhymed couplets. Surrey, more of a stylist, devised a new and simpler form for the sonnet—three quatrains with a concluding couplet, and with no attempt to preserve the division of the octave and sestet. As a simple trial will prove, it is much harder to write a sonnet in the Italian form than to compose three quatrains and a couplet; and as the Elizabethans prized fluency, they preferred Surrey's form. In Shakespeare it reached its greatest beauty so that Surrey's form is now often called the 'Shakespearean' sonnet. It is interesting to notice that at times Shakespeare makes the break in the thought between the eighth and ninth lines that the Italian sonnet writers observed. This will be seen in 'When, in disgrace with fortune and men's eyes,' No. 29, or better still, in several sonnets printed together with the sestet beginning invariably with 'O,' Nos. 21-23, 71, 72, 76.

Apart from Shakespeare, the Elizabethan sonnet sequences most worthy of study are Sidney's *Astrophel and Stella*, 1591, Daniel's *Delia*, 1592, Drayton's *Idea*, 1594, and Spenser's *Amoretti*, 1595. To read them, or even their finest passages, but makes more apparent the supremacy of Shakespeare.

Dedication to the Sonnets

TO · THE · ONLIE · BEGETTER · OF ·
THESE · INSUING · SONNETS ·
MR. W. H. ALL · HAPPINESSE ·
AND · THAT · ETERNITIE ·
PROMISED ·
BY ·
OUR · EVER-LIVING · POET ·
WISHETH ·
THE · WELL-WISHING ·
ADVENTURER · IN ·
SETTING ·
FORTH ·
T. T.

---

1 **Onlie begetter:** *only inspirer* (?); *cf. n.*   3 **Mr. W.H.;** *cf. n.*   10–12 **Adventurer in setting forth:** *publisher*   13 **T.T.;** *cf. n.*

Shakespeare's Sonnets

1

From fairest creatures we desire increase,
That thereby beauty's rose might never die,
But as the riper should by time decease,
His tender heir might bear his memory:
But thou, contracted to thine own bright eyes,   *5*
Feed'st thy light's flame with self-substantial fuel,
Making a famine where abundance lies,
Thyself thy foe, to thy sweet self too cruel.
Thou that art now the world's fresh ornament
And only herald to the gaudy spring,   *10*
Within thine own bud buriest thy content
And, tender churl, mak'st waste in niggarding.
    Pity the world, or else this glutton be,
    To eat the world's due, by the grave and thee.

2

When forty winters shall besiege thy brow,
And dig deep trenches in thy beauty's field,
Thy youth's proud livery, so gaz'd on now,
Will be a tatter'd weed, of small worth held:
Then being ask'd where all thy beauty lies,   *5*
Where all the treasure of thy lusty days,
To say, within thine own deep-sunken eyes,
Were an all-eating shame and thriftless praise.
How much more praise deserv'd thy beauty's use,
If thou couldst answer, 'This fair child of mine   *10*
Shall sum my count, and make my old excuse,'
Proving his beauty by succession thine!
    This were to be new made when thou art old,
    And see thy blood warm when thou feel'st it cold.

3

Look in thy glass, and tell the face thou viewest
Now is the time that face should form another;
Whose fresh repair if now thou not renewest,
Thou dost beguile the world, unbless some mother,
For where is she so fair whose unear'd womb   *5*
Disdains the tillage of thy husbandry?
Or who is he so fond will be the tomb
Of his self-love, to stop posterity?
Thou art thy mother's glass, and she in thee
Calls back the lovely April of her prime;   *10*
So thou through windows of thine age shalt see,
Despite of wrinkles, this thy golden time.
    But if thou live, remember'd not to be,
    Die single, and thine image dies with thee.

4

Unthrifty loveliness, why dost thou spend
Upon thyself thy beauty's legacy?
Nature's bequest gives nothing, but doth lend,
And being frank, she lends to those are free:
Then, beauteous niggard, why dost thou abuse   *5*
The bounteous largess given thee to give?
Profitless usurer, why dost thou use
So great a sum of sums, yet canst not live?
For having traffic with thyself alone,
Thou of thyself thy sweet self dost deceive: *10*
Then how, when Nature calls thee to be gone,
What acceptable audit canst thou leave?
    Thy unus'd beauty must be tomb'd with thee,
    Which used, lives th' executor to be.

5

Those hours, that with gentle work did frame
The lovely gaze where every eye doth dwell,
Will play the tyrants to the very same
And that unfair which fairly doth excel;
For never-resting time leads summer on   *5*
To hideous winter, and confounds him there;
Sap check'd with frost, and lusty leaves quite gone,
Beauty o'ersnow'd and bareness everywhere:
Then, were not summer's distillation left,
A liquid prisoner pent in walls of glass,   *10*
Beauty's effect with beauty were bereft,
Nor it, nor no remembrance what it was:
    But flowers distill'd, though they with winter meet,
    Leese but their show; their substance still lives sweet.

6

Then let not winter's ragged hand deface
In thee thy summer, ere thou be distill'd:
Make sweet some vial; treasure thou some place
With beauty's treasure, ere it be self-kill'd.
That use is not forbidden usury,   *5*
Which happies those that pay the willing loan;
That's for thyself to breed another thee,
Or ten times happier, be it ten for one;
Ten times thyself were happier than thou art,
If ten of thine ten times refigur'd thee;   *10*
Then what could death do, if thou shouldst depart,
Leaving thee living in posterity?
    Be not self-will'd, for thou art much too fair
    To be death's conquest and make worms thine heir.

1. 1-14 *Cf. n.*   5 **contracted:** *betrothed*   6 **Feed'st ... fuel;** *cf. n.*   11 **content:** *desire; cf. n.*   13, 14 **Pity the world ... and thee;** *cf. n.*   3 **livery:** *dress*   4 **weed:** *garment*   11 **old excuse:** *excuse for my old age*   3 **fresh repair:** *healthful state*   5 **unear'd:** *untilled*   7 **fond:** *foolish*   13 **remember'd not to be:** *not caring to be remembered*

4 **frank:** *liberal* **free:** *generous*   2 **gaze:** *object of sight, sight*   4 **unfair:** *deprive of beauty* **fairly:** *in beauty*   6 **confounds:** *destroys*   5. 9, 10 *Cf. n.*   12 **it:** *would it remain*   14 **Leese:** *lose*   1 **ragged:** *rugged*   3 **treasure:** *enrich*   5 **use:** *interest*   6 **happies:** *makes happy*   10 **refigur'd:** *reproduced in appearance*

7

Lo, in the orient when the gracious light
Lifts up his burning head, each under eye
Doth homage to his new-appearing sight,
Serving with looks his sacred majesty;
And having climb'd the steep-up heavenly hill,　　　5
Resembling strong youth in his middle age,
Yet mortal looks adore his beauty still,
Attending on his golden pilgrimage;
But when from highmost pitch, with weary car,
Like feeble age, he reeleth from the day,　　　10
The eyes, 'fore duteous, now converted are
From his low tract, and look another way:
　　　So thou, thyself outgoing in thy noon,
　　　Unlook'd on diest, unless thou get a son.

8

Music to hear, why hear'st thou music sadly?
Sweets with sweets war not, joy delights in joy:
Why lov'st thou that which thou receiv'st not gladly,
Or else receiv'st with pleasure thine annoy?
If the true concord of well-tuned sounds,　　　5
By unions married, do offend thine ear,
They do but sweetly chide thee, who confounds
In singleness the parts that thou shouldst bear.
Mark how one string, sweet husband to another,
Strikes each in each by mutual ordering;　　　10
Resembling sire and child and happy mother,
Who, all in one, one pleasing note do sing:
　　　Whose speechless song, being many, seeming one,
　　　Sings this to thee: 'Thou single wilt prove none.'

9

Is it for fear to wet a widow's eye
That thou consum'st thyself in single life?
Ah! if thou issueless shalt hap to die,
The world will wail thee, like a makeless wife;
The world will be thy widow, and still weep　　　5
That thou no form of thee hast left behind,
When every private widow well may keep
By children's eyes her husband's shape in mind.
Look, what an unthrift in the world doth spend
Shifts but his place, for still the world enjoys it;　　　10
But beauty's waste hath in the world an end,
And kept unus'd, the user so destroys it.
　　　No love toward others in that bosom sits
　　　That on himself such murderous shame commits.

10

For shame deny that thou bear'st love to any,
Who for thyself art so unprovident.
Grant, if thou wilt, thou art belov'd of many,
But that thou none lov'st is most evident;

For thou art so possess'd with murderous hate　　　5
That 'gainst thyself thou stick'st not to conspire,
Seeking that beauteous roof to ruinate
Which to repair should be thy chief desire.
O, change thy thought, that I may change my mind:
Shall hate be fairer lodg'd than gentle love?　　　10
Be, as thy presence is, gracious and kind,
Or to thyself at least kind-hearted prove:
　　　Make thee another self, for love of me,
　　　That beauty still may live in thine or thee.

11

As fast as thou shalt wane, so fast thou grow'st
In one of thine, from that which thou departest;
And that fresh blood which youngly thou bestow'st
Thou mayst call thine when thou from youth convertest.
Herein lies wisdom, beauty and increase;　　　5
Without this, folly, age and cold decay:
If all were minded so, the times should cease
And threescore year would make the world away.
Let those whom Nature hath not made for store,
Harsh, featureless and rude, barrenly perish:　　　10
Look, whom she best endow'd she gave the more;
Which bounteous gift thou shouldst in bounty cherish:
　　　She carv'd thee for her seal, and meant thereby
　　　Thou shouldst print more, nor let that copy die.

12

When I do count the clock that tells the time,
And see the brave day sunk in hideous night;
When I behold the violet past prime,
And sable curls, all silver'd o'er with white;
When lofty trees I see barren of leaves,　　　5
Which erst from heat did canopy the herd,
And summer's green all girded up in sheaves,
Borne on the bier with white and bristly beard,
Then of thy beauty do I question make,
That thou among the wastes of time must go,　　　10
Since sweets and beauties do themselves forsake
And die as fast as they see others grow;
　　　And nothing 'gainst Time's scythe can make defence
　　　Save breed, to brave him when he takes thee hence.

13

O that you were yourself! but, love, you are
No longer yours than you yourself here live:
Against this coming end you should prepare,
And your sweet semblance to some other give:
So should that beauty which you hold in lease　　　5
Find no determination; then you were
Yourself again, after yourself's decease,
When your sweet issue your sweet form should bear.
Who lets so fair a house fall to decay,

---

7. 9-12 *Cf. n.*　**9 highmost pitch:** *highest elevation*　**11 converted:** *turned away*
12 tract: *course*　**13 thyself outgoing ... noon:** *passing beyond your noon of beauty*　**1
Music to hear:** *you whose voice is music*　**10 mutual ordering:** *ordered harmony*
14 'Thou single wilt prove none'; *cf. n.*　**4 makeless:** *mateless*　**5 still:** *continually*　**10 his:** *its*

7 beauteous roof: *your body*　**2 departest:** *takest leave of*　**3 youngly:** *in youth bestow'st:* *layest out, spendest*　**4 convertest:** *changest*　**9 for store:** *for breeding*　**11
Look, ... the more;** *cf. n.*　**2 brave:** *beautiful*　**6 erst:** *formerly*　**9 question make:** *meditate*　**1 yourself;** *cf. n.*　**6 determination:** *end*

Which husbandry in honour might uphold 　　　　　*10*
Against the stormy gusts of winter's day
And barren rage of death's eternal cold?
　　O, none but unthrifts. Dear my love, you know
　　You had a father: let your son say so.

14

Not from the stars do I my judgment pluck;
And yet methinks I have astronomy,
But not to tell of good or evil luck,
Of plagues, of dearths, or seasons' quality;
Nor can I fortune to brief minutes tell, 　　　　　*5*
Pointing to each his thunder, rain, and wind,
Or say with princes of it shall go well,
By oft predict that I in heaven find:
But from thine eyes my knowledge I derive,
And, constant stars, in them I read such art 　　　*10*
As 'Truth and beauty shall together thrive,
If from thyself to store thou wouldst convert;'
　　Or else of thee this I prognosticate:
　　'Thy end is truth's and beauty's doom and date.'

15

When I consider everything that grows
Holds in perfection but a little moment,
That this huge stage presenteth nought but shows
Whereon the stars in secret influence comment;
When I perceive that men as plants increase, 　　　*5*
Cheered and check'd e'en by the self-same sky,
Vaunt in their youthful sap, at height decrease,
And wear their brave state out of memory;
Then the conceit of this inconstant stay
Sets you most rich in youth before my sight, 　　　*10*
Where wasteful Time debateth with Decay,
To change your day of youth to sullied night;
　　And, in all war with Time for love of you,
　　As he takes from you, I engraft you new.

16

But wherefore do not you a mightier way
Make war upon this bloody tyrant, Time?
And fortify yourself in your decay
With means more blessed than my barren rime?
Now stand you on the top of happy hours, 　　　　*5*
And many maiden gardens, yet unset,
With virtuous wish would bear you living flowers
Much liker than your painted counterfeit:
So should the lines of life that life repair,
Which this Time's pencil, or my pupil pen, 　　　　*10*
Neither in inward worth nor outward fair,

Can make you live yourself in eyes of men.
　　To give away yourself, keeps yourself still;
　　And you must live, drawn by your own sweet skill.

17

Who will believe my verse in time to come,
If it were fill'd with your most high deserts?
Though yet, heaven knows, it is but as a tomb
Which hides your life and shows not half your parts.
If I could write the beauty of your eyes 　　　　*5*
And in fresh numbers number all your graces,
The age to come would say, 'This poet lies;
Such heavenly touches ne'er touch'd earthly faces.'
So should my papers, yellow'd with their age,
Be scorn'd, like old men of less truth than tongue, 　*10*
And your true rights be term'd a poet's rage
And stretched metre of an antique song:
　　But were some child of yours alive that time,
　　You should live twice,—in it and in my rime.

18

Shall I compare thee to a summer's day?
Thou art more lovely and more temperate:
Rough winds do shake the darling buds of May,
And summer's lease hath all too short a date:
Sometime too hot the eye of heaven shines, 　　　*5*
And often is his gold complexion dimm'd;
And every fair from fair sometime declines,
By chance, or nature's changing course untrimm'd;
But thy eternal summer shall not fade,
Nor lose possession of that fair thou ow'st, 　　　*10*
Nor shall death brag thou wander'st in his shade,
When in eternal lines to time thou grow'st;
　　So long as man can breathe, or eyes can see,
　　So long lives this, and this gives life to thee.

19

Devouring Time, blunt thou the lion's paws,
And make the earth devour her own sweet brood;
Pluck the keen teeth from the fierce tiger's jaws,
And burn the long-liv'd phœnix in her blood;
Make glad and sorry seasons as thou fleets, 　　　*5*
And do whate'er thou wilt, swift-footed Time,
To the wide world and all her fading sweets;
But I forbid thee one most heinous crime:
O, carve not with thy hours my love's fair brow,
Nor draw no lines there with thine antique pen; 　　*10*
Him in thy course untainted do allow
For beauty's pattern to succeeding men.
　　Yet do thy worst, old Time: despite thy wrong,
　　My love shall in my verse ever live young.

10 husbandry: *thrift*　　**13 unthrifts:** *wastrels*　　**2 have astronomy:** *know astrology*　　**5 tell:** *allot*　　**6 Pointing:** *appointing*　　**8 oft predict:** *frequent predictions*　　**10 art:** *knowledge*　　**12 If from thyself . . . convert;** *cf. n.*　　**14 date:** *end*　　**4 influence;** *cf. n.*　　**6 Cheered and check'd:** *encouraged and repressed*　　**7 Vaunt:** *exult*　　**at height:** *when fully developed*　　**8 And wear . . . memory:** *and outlast the memory of their prime*　　**9 conceit:** *thought*　　**inconstant stay:** *transitory state of being*　　**11 debateth:** *takes counsel with*　　**14 engraft you new:** *renew your beauty* (by my verse)　　**6 unset:** *not planted*　　**8 painted counterfeit:** *portrait*　　**9 lines of life:** *children*　　**10 Which this . . . pupil pen;** *cf. n.*　　**11 fair:** *beauty*

13 To give away yourself: *to beget children*　　**11 rage:** *enthusiasm*　　**12 stretched:** *strained, exaggerated*　　**18. 1-14** *Cf. n.*　　**8 untrimm'd:** *deprived of adornment*　　**10 ow'st:** *ownest*　　**5 fleets:** *hastest*　　**10 antique;** *cf. n.*

20

A woman's face with Nature's own hand painted
Hast thou, the master-mistress of my passion;
A woman's gentle heart, but not acquainted
With shifting change, as is false women's fashion;
An eye more bright than theirs, less false in rolling,   *5*
Gilding the object whereupon it gazeth;
A man in hue all hues in his controlling,
Which steals men's eyes and women's souls amazeth.
And for a woman wert thou first created;
Till Nature, as she wrought thee, fell a-doting,   *10*
And by addition me of thee defeated,
By adding one thing to my purpose nothing.
    But since she prick'd thee out for women's pleasure,
    Mine be thy love, and thy love's use their treasure.

21

So is it not with me as with that Muse
Stirr'd by a painted beauty to his verse,
Who heaven itself for ornament doth use
And every fair with his fair doth rehearse,
Making a couplement of proud compare,   *5*
With sun and moon, with earth and sea's rich gems,
With April's first-born flowers, and all things rare
That heaven's air in this huge rondure hems.
O let me, true in love, but truly write,
And then believe me, my love is as fair   *10*
As any mother's child, though not so bright
As those gold candles fix'd in heaven's air:
    Let them say more that like of hear-say well;
    I will not praise that purpose not to sell.

22

My glass shall not persuade me I am old,
So long as youth and thou are of one date;
But when in thee time's furrows I behold,
Then look I death my days should expiate.
For all that beauty that doth cover thee   *5*
Is but the seemly raiment of my heart,
Which in thy breast doth live, as thine in me:
How can I then be elder than thou art?
O therefore, love, be of thyself so wary
As I, not for myself, but for thee will;   *10*
Bearing thy heart, which I will keep so chary
As tender nurse her babe from faring ill.
    Presume not on thy heart when mine is slain;
    Thou gav'st me thine, not to give back again.

23

As an unperfect actor on the stage,
Who with his fear is put besides his part,
Or some fierce thing replete with too much rage,
Whose strength's abundance weakens his own heart;

So I, for fear of trust, forget to say   *5*
The perfect ceremony of love's rite,
And in mine own love's strength seem to decay,
O'ercharg'd with burden of mine own love's might.
O, let my books be then the eloquence
And dumb presagers of my speaking breast,   *10*
Who plead for love, and look for recompense,
More than that tongue that more hath more express'd.
    O, learn to read what silent love hath writ:
    To hear with eyes belongs to love's fine wit.

24

Mine eye hath play'd the painter and hath stell'd
Thy beauty's form in table of my heart;
My body is the frame wherein 'tis held,
And perspective it is best painter's art.
For through the painter must you see his skill,   *5*
To find where your true image pictur'd lies,
Which in my bosom's shop is hanging still,
That hath his windows glazed with thine eyes.
Now see what good turns eyes for eyes have done:
Mine eyes have drawn thy shape, and thine for me   *10*
Are windows to my breast, where-through the sun
Delights to peep, to gaze therein on thee;
    Yet eyes this cunning want to grace their art,
    They draw but what they see, know not the heart.

25

Let those who are in favour with their stars
Of public honour and proud titles boast,
Whilst I, whom fortune of such triumph bars,
Unlook'd for joy in that I honour most.
Great princes' favourites their fair leaves spread   *5*
But as the marigold at the sun's eye,
And in themselves their pride lies buried,
For at a frown they in their glory die.
The painful warrior famoused for fight,
After a thousand victories once foil'd,   *10*
Is from the book of honour razed quite,
And all the rest forgot for which he toil'd:
    Then happy I, that love and am belov'd,
    Where I may not remove nor be remov'd.

26

Lord of my love, to whom in vassalage
Thy merit hath my duty strongly knit,
To thee I send this written ambassage,
To witness duty, not to show my wit:
Duty so great, which wit so poor as mine   *5*
May make seem bare, in wanting words to show it,
But that I hope some good conceit of thine
In thy soul's thought, all naked, will bestow it;
Till whatsoever star that guides my moving

---

20. 1–14 *Cf. n.*   **7 A man in hue ... controlling:** *cf. n.*   **11 defeated:** *deprived*   **1
Muse:** *poet*   **4 rehearse:** *relate*   **5 Making ... compare:** *joining in proud comparison*   **8 rondure:** *circle*   **4 expiate:** *end*   **13 Presume not on:** *think not to regain*   **2
put besides:** *put out of*

5 fear of trust: *fearing to trust myself (?), lacking all self-confidence (?)*   **10 presagers:**
indicators   **12 that more ... express'd:** *that more eloquently has told of greater devotion*   **1 stell'd:** *placed, engraved (?)*   **2 table:** *surface on which picture is drawn*   **4
perspective:** *cf. n.*   **25. 4 Unlook'd for:** *unexpectedly*   **6 But:** *only*   **7 And in ...
buried:** *their pride soon perishes with them*   **26. 1–14** *Cf. n.*   **3 ambassage:** *message*

Points on me graciously with fair aspect,   10
And puts apparel on my tatter'd loving,
To show me worthy of thy sweet respect:
    Then may I dare to boast how I do love thee;
    Till then, not show my head where thou mayst prove me.

27

Weary with toil, I haste me to my bed,
The dear repose for limbs with travel tir'd;
But then begins a journey in my head
To work my mind, when body's work's expir'd:
For then my thoughts—from far where I abide—   5
Intend a zealous pilgrimage to thee,
And keep my drooping eyelids open wide,
Looking on darkness which the blind do see:
Save that my soul's imaginary sight
Presents thy shadow to my sightless view,   10
Which, like a jewel hung in ghastly night,
Makes black night beauteous and her old face new.
    Lo! thus, by day my limbs, by night my mind,
    For thee, and for myself, no quiet find.

28

How can I then return in happy plight,
That am debarr'd the benefit of rest?
When day's oppression is not eas'd by night,
But day by night, and night by day oppress'd,
And each, though enemies to either's reign,   5
Do in consent shake hands to torture me,
The one by toil, the other to complain
How far I toil, still further off from thee.
I tell the day, to please him, thou art bright
And dost him grace when clouds do blot the heaven: 10
So flatter I the swart-complexion'd night,
When sparkling stars twire not thou gild'st the even.
    But day doth daily draw my sorrows longer,
    And night doth nightly make grief's strength seem stronger.

29

When, in disgrace with fortune and men's eyes,
I all alone beweep my outcast state,
And trouble deaf heaven with my bootless cries,
And look upon myself, and curse my fate,
Wishing me like to one more rich in hope,   5
Featur'd like him, like him with friends possess'd,
Desiring this man's art, and that man's scope,
With what I most enjoy contented least;
Yet in these thoughts myself almost despising,
Haply I think on thee,—and then my state,   10
Like to the lark at break of day arising
From sullen earth, sings hymns at heaven's gate;
    For thy sweet love remember'd such wealth brings
    That then I scorn to change my state with kings.

30

When to the sessions of sweet silent thought
I summon up remembrance of things past,
I sigh the lack of many a thing I sought,
And with old woes new wail my dear times' waste:
Then can I drown an eye, unus'd to flow,   5
For precious friends hid in death's dateless night,
And weep afresh love's long since cancell'd woe,
And moan the expense of many a vanish'd sight:
Then can I grieve at grievances foregone,
And heavily from woe to woe tell o'er   10
The sad account of fore-bemoaned moan,
Which I new pay as if not paid before.
    But if the while I think on thee, dear friend,
    All losses are restor'd and sorrows end.

31

Thy bosom is endeared with all hearts
Which I by lacking have supposed dead;
And there reigns Love, and all Love's loving parts,
And all those friends which I thought buried.
How many a holy and obsequious tear   5
Hath dear religious love stol'n from mine eye,
As interest of the dead, which now appear
But things remov'd that hidden in thee lie!
Thou art the grave where buried love doth live,
Hung with the trophies of my lovers gone,   10
Who all their parts of me to thee did give,
That due of many now is thine alone:
    Their images I lov'd I view in thee,
    And thou—all they—hast all the all of me.

32

If thou survive my well-contented day,
When that churl Death my bones with dust shall cover,
And shalt by fortune once more re-survey
These poor rude lines of thy deceased lover,
Compare them with the bettering of the time,   5
And though they be outstripp'd by every pen,
Reserve them for my love, not for their rime,
Exceeded by the height of happier men.
O, then vouchsafe me but this loving thought:
'Had my friend's Muse grown with this growing age,   10
A dearer birth than this his love had brought,
To march in ranks of better equipage:
    But since he died, and poets better prove,
    Theirs for their style I'll read, his for his love.'

1 **sessions**: *sittings of court*   4 **new wail**: *bewail anew*   6 **dateless**: *endless*   8 **expense**: *loss*   9 **grievances foregone**: *former griefs*   10 **tell**: *count*   1 **endeared**: *made precious*   5 **obsequious**: *dutiful, regardful*   6 **religious**: *devoted*   7 **interest**: *the right, the due*   11 **parts of me**: *claims in me*   12 **That . . . many**: *so that which many once deserved*   13 **Their . . . lov'd**: *the images of those I loved*   1 **my well-contented day**: *the day I shall be well contented with*   5 **bettering . . . time**: *better works of later time*   7 **Reserve**: *retain*   12 **better equipage**: *richer equipment*

33

Full many a glorious morning have I seen
Flatter the mountain-tops with sovereign eye,
Kissing with golden face the meadows green,
Gliding pale streams with heavenly alchemy;
Anon permit the basest clouds to ride   5
With ugly rack on his celestial face,
And from the forlorn world his visage hide,
Stealing unseen to west with this disgrace:
Even so my sun one early morn did shine,
With all-triumphant splendour on my brow;   10
But, out! alack! he was but one hour mine,
The region cloud hath mask'd him from me now.
    Yet him for this my love no whit disdaineth;
    Suns of the world may stain when heaven's sun staineth.

34

Why didst thou promise such a beauteous day,
And make me travel forth without my cloak,
To let base clouds o'ertake me in my way,
Hiding thy bravery in their rotten smoke?
'Tis not enough that through the cloud thou break,   5
To dry the rain on my storm-beaten face,
For no man well of such a salve can speak
That heals the wound and cures not the disgrace:
Nor can thy shame give physic to my grief;
Though thou repent, yet I have still the loss: 10
The offender's sorrow lends but weak relief
To him that bears the strong offence's cross.
    Ah! but those tears are pearl which thy love sheds,
    And they are rich and ransom all ill deeds.

35

No more be griev'd at that which thou hast done:
Roses have thorns, and silver fountains mud;
Clouds and eclipses stain both moon and sun,
And loathsome canker lives in sweetest bud.
All men make faults, and even I in this,   5
Authorising thy trespass with compare,
Myself corrupting, salving thy amiss,
Excusing thy sins more than thy sins are;
For to thy sensual fault I bring in sense,—
Thy adverse party is thy advocate,—   10
And 'gainst myself a lawful plea commence:
Such civil war is in my love and hate,
    That I an accessary needs must be
    To that sweet thief which sourly robs from me.

36

Let me confess that we two must be twain,
Although our undivided loves are one:
So shall those blots that do with me remain,
Without thy help, by me be borne alone.
In our two loves there is but one respect,   5
Though in our lives a separable spite,
Which, though it alter not love's sole effect,
Yet doth it steal sweet hours from love's delight.
I may not evermore acknowledge thee,
Lest my bewailed guilt should do thee shame,   10
Nor thou with public kindness honour me,
Unless thou take that honour from thy name:
    But do not so; I love thee in such sort
    As thou being mine, mine is thy good report.

37

As a decrepit father takes delight
To see his active child do deeds of youth,
So I, made lame by fortune's dearest spite,
Take all my comfort of thy worth and truth;
For whether beauty, birth, or wealth, or wit,   5
Or any of these all, or all, or more,
Entitled in thy parts do crowned sit,
I make my love engrafted to this store:
So then I am not lame, poor, nor despis'd,
Whilst that this shadow doth such substance give   10
That I in thy abundance am suffic'd
And by a part of all thy glory live.
    Look what is best, that best I wish in thee:
    This wish I have; then ten times happy me!

38

How can my Muse want subject to invent,
While thou dost breathe, that pour'st into my verse
Thine own sweet argument, too excellent
For every vulgar paper to rehearse?
O, give thyself the thanks, if aught in me   5
Worthy perusal stand against thy sight;
For who's so dumb that cannot write to thee,
When thou thyself dost give invention light?
Be thou the tenth Muse, ten times more in worth
Than those old nine which rimers invocate;   10
And he that calls on thee, let him bring forth
Eternal numbers to outlive long date.
    If my slight Muse do please these curious days,
    The pain be mine, but thine shall be the praise.

39

O, how thy worth with manners may I sing,
When thou art all the better part of me?
What can mine own praise to mine own self bring?
And what is 't but mine own when I praise thee?
Even for this let us divided live,   5
And our dear love lose name of single one,
That by this separation I may give

---

2 sovereign eye: *eye of a king*   **6 rack:** *clouds in the upper air*   **8 disgrace:** *disfigurement*   **12 region cloud:** *cloud of heaven*   **14 may stain:** *may be obscured* **staineth:** *is obscured*   **4 bravery:** *splendor* **rotten smoke:** *unwholesome mist*   **13, 14 Ah! but those tears . . . ill deeds;** *cf. n.*   **2 fountains:** *springs*   **3 stain:** *dim*   **6 Authorising:** *sanctioning* **with compare:** *by these comparisons*   **7 amiss:** *fault*   **8 Excusing thy sins;** *cf. n.*   **9 sense;** *cf. n.*   **13 accessary:** *accessory, helper*   **14 sourly:** *cruelly*

5 respect: *consideration, regard*   **6 separable:** *dividing, separating*   **13, 14 But do not so . . . good report;** *cf. n.*   **3 dearest spite:** *worst malice*   **37. 5-7** *Cf. n.*   **7 Entitled:** *rightfully*   **8 engrafted:** *added to*   **10 shadow:** *imagination*   **11 suffic'd:** *contented*   **3 argument:** *theme*   **4 rehearse:** *narrate*   **6 against:** *in*   **8 invention:** *creative imagination*   **13 curious:** *fastidious*   **14 pain:** *labour*   **1 with manners:** *becomingly*

That due to thee, which thou deserv'st alone.
O absence! what a torment wouldst thou prove,
Were it not thy sour leisure gave sweet leave   *10*
To entertain the time with thoughts of love,
Which time and thoughts so sweetly doth deceive,
     And that thou teachest how to make one twain,
     By praising him here who doth hence remain.

40

Take all my loves, my love, yea, take them all;
What hast thou then more than thou hadst before?
No love, my love, that thou mayst true love call;
All mine was thine before thou hadst this more.
Then, if for my love thou my love receivest,   *5*
I cannot blame thee for my love thou usest;
But yet be blam'd, if thou thyself deceivest
By wilful taste of what thyself refusest.
I do forgive thy robbery, gentle thief,
Although thou steal thee all my poverty;   *10*
And yet, love knows it is a greater grief
To bear love's wrong than hate's known injury.
     Lascivious grace, in whom all ill well shows,
     Kill me with spites; yet we must not be foes.

41

Those pretty wrongs that liberty commits,
When I am sometimes absent from thy heart,
Thy beauty and thy years full well befits,
For still temptation follows where thou art.
Gentle thou art, and therefore to be won,   *5*
Beauteous thou art, therefore to be assail'd;
And when a woman woos, what woman's son
Will sourly leave her till she have prevail'd?
Ay me! but yet thou mightst my seat forbear,
And chide thy beauty and thy straying youth,   *10*
Who lead thee in their riot even there
Where thou art forc'd to break a twofold truth;—
     Hers, by thy beauty tempting her to thee,
     Thine, by thy beauty being false to me.

42

That thou hast her, it is not all my grief,
And yet it may be said I lov'd her dearly;
That she hath thee, is of my wailing chief,
A loss in love that touches me more nearly.
Loving offenders, thus I will excuse ye: *5*
Thou dost love her, because thou know'st I love her;
And for my sake even so doth she abuse me,
Suffering my friend for my sake to approve her.
If I lose thee, my loss is my love's gain.
And losing her, my friend hath found that loss;   *10*
Both find each other, and I lose both twain,
And both for my sake lay on me this cross:

But here's the joy; my friend and I are one;
Sweet flattery! then she loves but me alone.

43

When most I wink, then do mine eyes best see,
For all the day they view things unrespected;
But when I sleep, in dreams they look on thee,
And darkly bright, are bright in dark directed.
Then thou, whose shadow shadows doth make bright,   *5*
How would thy shadow's form form happy show
To the clear day with thy much clearer light,
When to unseeing eyes thy shade shines so!
How would, I say, mine eyes be blessed made
By looking on thee in the living day,   *10*
When in dead night thy fair imperfect shade
Through heavy sleep on sightless eyes doth stay!
     All days are nights to see till I see thee,
     And nights bright days when dreams do show thee me.

44

If the dull substance of my flesh were thought,
Injurious distance should not stop my way;
For then, despite of space, I would be brought,
From limits far remote, where thou dost stay.
No matter then although my foot did stand   *5*
Upon the furthest earth remov'd from thee;
For nimble thought can jump both sea and land,
As soon as think the place where he would be.
But, ah! thought kills me that I am not thought,
To leap large lengths of miles when thou art gone,   *10*
But that, so much of earth and water wrought,
I must attend time's leisure with my moan;
     Receiving nought by elements so slow
     But heavy tears, badges of either's woe.

45

The other two, slight air and purging fire,
Are both with thee, wherever I abide;
The first my thought, the other my desire,
These present-absent with swift motion slide.
For when these quicker elements are gone   *5*
In tender embassy of love to thee,
My life, being made of four, with two alone
Sinks down to death, oppress'd with melancholy;
Until life's composition be recur'd
By those sweet messengers return'd from thee,   *10*
Who even but now come back again, assur'd
Of thy fair health, recounting it to me:
     This told, I joy; but then no longer glad,
     I send them back again, and straight grow sad.

11 entertain: *pass away*   **13, 14 And that thou teachest ... remain;** *cf. n.*   **40. 1-14** *Cf. n.*   **5 if for:** *if because of (?), if instead of (?)*   **my love receivest:** *receivest the woman I love*   **6 for:** *because*   **8 By wilful taste ... refusest;** *cf. n.*   **14 spites:** *injuries*   **1 liberty:** *license*   **3 chief:** *the main cause*   **7 abuse:** *misuse*   **8 approve:** *like, make trial of (?)*   **11 both twain:** *both the two*

1 wink: *close my eyes*   **2 unrespected:** *unworthy of notice*   **4 darkly:** *in the dark*   **5 whose shadow ... bright:** *whose remembered image makes darkness bright*   **4 where:** *to the place where*   **6 furthest earth remov'd:** *plot of earth most remote*   **9 thought kills me:** *melancholy kills me (?), it kills me to think (?)*   **11 wrought:** *made, created*   **14 badges of either's woe;** *cf. n.*   **9 life's composition:** *union of the four elements*   **recur'd:** *restored*

46

Mine eye and heart are at a mortal war,
How to divide the conquest of thy sight;
Mine eye my heart thy picture's sight would bar,
My heart mine eye the freedom of that right.
My heart doth plead that thou in him dost lie,—   5
A closet never pierc'd with crystal eyes,—
But the defendant doth that plea deny,
And says in him thy fair appearance lies.
To 'cide this title is impanelled
A quest of thoughts, all tenants to the heart;   10
And by their verdict is determined
The clear eye's moiety and the dear heart's part:
     As thus; mine eye's due is thine outward part,
     And my heart's right thine inward love of heart.

47

Betwixt mine eye and heart a league is took,
And each doth good turns now unto the other:
When that mine eye is famish'd for a look,
Or heart in love with sighs himself doth smother,
With my love's picture then my eye doth feast,   5
And to the painted banquet bids my heart;
Another time mine eye is my heart's guest,
And in his thoughts of love doth share a part:
So, either by thy picture or my love,
Thyself away art present still with me;   10
For thou not further than my thoughts canst move,
And I am still with them and they with thee;
     Or, if they sleep, thy picture in my sight
     Awakes my heart to heart's and eye's delight.

48

How careful was I when I took my way,
Each trifle under truest bars to thrust,
That to my use it might unused stay
From hands of falsehood, in sure wards of trust!
But thou, to whom my jewels trifles are,   5
Most worthy comfort, now my greatest grief,
Thou best of dearest and mine only care,
Art left the prey of every vulgar thief.
Thee have I not lock'd up in any chest,
Save where thou art not, though I feel thou art,   10
Within the gentle closure of my breast,
From whence at pleasure thou mayst come and part;
     And even thence thou wilt be stol'n, I fear,
     For truth proves thievish for a prize so dear.

49

Against that time, if ever that time come,
When I shall see thee frown on my defects,
When as thy love hath cast his utmost sum,
Call'd to that audit by advis'd respects;

Against that time when thou shalt strangely pass,   5
And scarcely greet me with that sun, thine eye,
When love, converted from the thing it was,
Shall reasons find of settled gravity;
Against that time do I ensconce me here
Within the knowledge of mine own desert,   10
And this my hand against myself uprear,
To guard the lawful reasons on thy part:
     To leave poor me thou hast the strength of laws,
     Since why to love I can allege no cause.

50

How heavy do I journey on the way,
When what I seek, my weary travel's end,
Doth teach that ease and that repose to say,
'Thus far the miles are measur'd from thy friend!'
The beast that bears me, tired with my woe,   5
Plods dully on, to bear that weight in me,
As if by some instinct the wretch did know
His rider lov'd not speed, being made from thee:
The bloody spur cannot provoke him on
That sometimes anger thrusts into his hide,   10
Which heavily he answers with a groan
More sharp to me than spurring to his side;
     For that same groan doth put this in my mind:
     My grief lies onward, and my joy behind.

51

Thus can my love excuse the slow offence
Of my dull bearer when from thee I speed:
From where thou art why should I haste me thence?
Till I return, of posting is no need.
O, what excuse will my poor beast then find,   5
When swift extremity can seem but slow?
Then should I spur, though mounted on the wind,
In winged speed no motion shall I know:
Then can no horse with my desire keep pace;
Therefore desire, of perfect'st love being made,   10
Shall neigh—no dull flesh—in his fiery race;
But love, for love, thus shall excuse my jade,—
     'Since from thee going he went wilful-slow,
     Towards thee I'll run and give him leave to go.'

52

So am I as the rich, whose blessed key
Can bring him to his sweet up-locked treasure
The which he will not every hour survey,
For blunting the fine point of seldom pleasure.
Therefore are feasts so solemn and so rare,   5
Since, seldom coming, in the long year set,
Like stones of worth they thinly placed are,

---

9 **impanelled:** *enrolled*   10 **quest:** *jury*   12 **moiety:** *share*   4 **himself:** *itself*   4
wards of trust: *place of security*   11 **closure:** *enclosure, confine*   1 **Against:** *in expectation
of*   3 **When as:** *when*   **cast his utmost sum:** *added every item*   4 **advis'd respects:**
careful considerations

5 **strangely:** *like a stranger*   8 **of settled gravity:** *for a grave demeanor*   11 **uprear:** *raise*
(as a witness taking the oath)   8 **being made:** *if directed*   1 **slow offence:** *blameworthy
slowness*   6 **swift extremity:** *extreme speed*   8 **In winged speed . . . know:** *though moving with the speed of wings, I shall not seem to myself to be moving at all*   11 **Shall neigh
. . . fiery race;** *cf. n.*   12 **for love:** *for the sake of his love* (shown by the slow gait)   14
go: *walk*   4 **For:** *for fear of*   **seldom:** *rarely enjoyed*   5 **solemn:** *ceremonious*   7
thinly: *widely separated*

Or captain jewels in the carcanet.
So is the time that keeps you as my chest,
Or as the wardrobe which the robe doth hide,   *10*
To make some special instant special blest
By new unfolding his imprison'd pride.
    Blessed are you, whose worthiness gives scope,
    Being had, to triumph; being lack'd, to hope.

53

What is your substance, whereof are you made,
That millions of strange shadows on you tend?
Since every one hath, every one, one shade,
And you, but one, can every shadow lend.
Describe Adonis, and the counterfeit   *5*
Is poorly imitated after you;
On Helen's cheek all art of beauty set,
And you in Grecian tires are painted new:
Speak of the spring and foison of the year,
The one doth shadow of your beauty show,   *10*
The other as your bounty doth appear;
And you in every blessed shape we know.
    In all external grace you have some part,
    But you like none, none you, for constant heart.

54

O, how much more doth beauty beauteous seem
By that sweet ornament which truth doth give!
The rose looks fair, but fairer we it deem
For that sweet odour which doth in it live.
The canker-blooms have full as deep a dye   *5*
As the perfumed tincture of the roses,
Hang on such thorns, and play as wantonly
When summer's breath their masked buds discloses:
But, for their virtue only is their show,
They live unwoo'd, and unrespected fade;   *10*
Die to themselves. Sweet roses do not so;
Of their sweet deaths are sweetest odours made:
    And so of you, beauteous and lovely youth,
    When that shall vade, my verse distils your truth.

55

Not marble, nor the gilded monuments
Of princes, shall outlive this powerful rime;
But you shall shine more bright in these contents
Than unswept stone, besmear'd with sluttish time
When wasteful war shall statues overturn,   *5*
And broils root out the work of masonry,
Nor Mars his sword nor war's quick fire shall burn
The living record of your memory.
'Gainst death and all-oblivious enmity
Shall you pace forth; your praise shall still find room   *10*

Even in the eyes of all posterity
That wear this world out to the ending doom.
    So, till the judgment that yourself arise,
    You live in this, and dwell in lovers' eyes.

56

Sweet love, renew thy force; be it not said
Thy edge should blunter be than appetite,
Which but to-day by feeding is allay'd,
To-morrow sharpen'd in his former might:
So, love, be thou; although to-day thou fill   *5*
Thy hungry eyes, even till they wink with fulness,
To-morrow see again, and do not kill
The spirit of love with a perpetual dulness.
Let this sad interim like the ocean be
Which parts the shore, where two contracted new   *10*
Come daily to the banks, that, when they see
Return of love, more bless'd may be the view;
    Or call it winter, which, being full of care,
    Makes summer's welcome thrice more wish'd, more rare.

57

Being your slave, what should I do but tend
Upon the hours and times of your desire?
I have no precious time at all to spend,
Nor services to do, till you require.
Nor dare I chide the world-without-end hour   *5*
Whilst I, my sovereign, watch the clock for you,
Nor think the bitterness of absence sour
When you have bid your servant once adieu;
Nor dare I question with my jealous thought
Where you may be, or your affairs suppose,   *10*
But, like a sad slave, stay and think of nought,
Save where you are how happy you make those.
    So true a fool is love that in your will,
    Though you do anything, he thinks no ill.

58

That god forbid that made me first your slave,
I should in thought control your times of pleasure,
Or at your hand the account of hours to crave,
Being your vassal, bound to stay your leisure!
O, let me suffer, being at your beck,   *5*
The imprison'd absence of your liberty;
And patience, tame to sufferance, bide each check,
Without accusing you of injury.
Be where you list, your charter is so strong
That you yourself may privilege your time   *10*
To what you will; to you it doth belong
Yourself to pardon of self-doing crime.
    I am to wait, though waiting so be hell,
    Not blame your pleasure, be it ill or well.

8 captain: *chief* **carcanet:** *necklace*   **9 chest:** *treasure chest*   **12 his . . . pride:** *its gorgeous contents*   **13 scope:** *opportunity*   **3 every one, one shade:** *one shadow apiece*   **5 counterfeit:** *portrait*   **8 tires:** *headdresses*   **9 foison:** *harvest*   **11 bounty:** *generosity*   **14 like none:** *are like none* **none you:** *none are like you*   **5 canker-blooms:** *dogroses, scentless wild roses*   **6 tincture:** *color*   **8 discloses:** *unfolds, opens*   **9 only is their show:** *consists only in their appearance*   **10 unrespected:** *unregarded*   **11 to themselves:** *all alone*   **14 that:** *that beauty, that youth* **vade:** *fade* **distils:** *preserves the essence of*   **7 Nor Mars his:** *neither Mars'*

12 wear this world out: *outlast this world* **ending doom:** *to the judgment day that ends all*   **13 that:** *when*   **10 contracted new:** *but lately betrothed*   **5 world-without-end:** *never ending*   **10 suppose:** *conjecture*   **6 The imprison'd . . . liberty;** *cf. n.*   **7 sufferance:** *suffering* **check:** *rebuke*   **10 privilege:** *authorize*   **12 self-doing:** *done by yourself*

59

If there be nothing new, but that which is
Hath been before, how are our brains beguil'd,
Which, labouring for invention, bear amiss
The second burden of a former child!
O, that record could with a backward look,   *5*
Even of five hundred courses of the sun,
Show me your image in some antique book,
Since mind at first in character was done!
That I might see what the old world could say
To this composed wonder of your frame;   *10*
Whether we are mended, or whe'r better they,
Or whether revolution be the same.
    O, sure I am, the wits of former days
    To subjects worse have given admiring praise.

60

Like as the waves make towards the pebbled shore,
So do our minutes hasten to their end;
Each changing place with that which goes before,
In sequent toil all forwards do contend.
Nativity, once in the main of light,   *5*
Crawls to maturity, wherewith being crown'd,
Crooked eclipses 'gainst his glory fight,
And Time that gave doth now his gift confound.
Time doth transfix the flourish set on youth
And delves the parallels in beauty's brow,   *10*
Feeds on the rarities of nature's truth,
And nothing stands but for his scythe to mow:
    And yet to times in hope my verse shall stand,
    Praising thy worth, despite his cruel hand.

61

Is it thy will thy image should keep open
My heavy eyelids to the weary night?
Dost thou desire my slumbers should be broken,
While shadows, like to thee, do mock my sight?
Is it thy spirit that thou send'st from thee   *5*
So far from home, into my deeds to pry,
To find out shames and idle hours in me,
The scope and tenour of thy jealousy?
O, no! thy love, though much, is not so great:
It is my love that keeps mine eye awake;   *10*
Mine own true love that doth my rest defeat,
To play the watchman ever for thy sake:
    For thee watch I whilst thou dost wake elsewhere,
    From me far off, with others all too near.

62

Sin of self-love possesseth all mine eye
And all my soul and all my every part;

And for this sin there is no remedy,
It is so grounded inward in my heart.
Methinks no face so gracious is as mine,   *5*
No shape so true, no truth of such account;
And for myself mine own worth do define,
As I all other in all worths surmount.
But when my glass shows me myself indeed,
Beated and chopp'd with tann'd antiquity,   *10*
Mine own self-love quite contrary I read;
Self so self-loving were iniquity.
    'Tis thee, myself,—that for myself I praise,
    Painting my age with beauty of thy days.

63

Against my love shall be, as I am now,
With Time's injurious hand crush'd and o'erworn;
When hours have drain'd his blood and fill'd his brow
With lines and wrinkles; when his youthful morn
Hath travell'd on to age's steepy night;   *5*
And all those beauties whereof now he's king
Are vanishing or vanish'd out of sight,
Stealing away the treasure of his spring;
For such a time do I now fortify
Against confounding age's cruel knife,   *10*
That he shall never cut from memory
My sweet love's beauty, though my lover's life:
    His beauty shall in these black lines be seen,
    And they shall live, and he in them still green.

64

When I have seen by Time's fell hand defac'd
The rich-proud cost of outworn buried age;
When sometime lofty towers I see down-raz'd,
And brass eternal slave to mortal rage;
When I have seen the hungry ocean gain   *5*
Advantage on the kingdom of the shore,
And the firm soil win of the watery main,
Increasing store with loss, and loss with store;
When I have seen such interchange of state,
Or state itself confounded to decay;   *10*
Ruin hath taught me thus to ruminate—
That Time will come and take my love away.
    This thought is as a death, which cannot choose
    But weep to have that which it fears to lose.

65

Since brass, nor stone, nor earth, nor boundless sea,
But sad mortality o'ersways their power,
How with this rage shall beauty hold a plea,
Whose action is no stronger than a flower?
O, how shall summer's honey breath hold out   *5*

---

3 labouring for invention: *striving for originality*   **5 record:** *memory*   **8 in character:** *in letters*   **10 composed wonder:** *wonderful composition*   **11 mended:** *advanced beyond our predecessors* **whe'r:** *whether*   **12 whether revolution be the same:** *whether all things come round again*   **4 In sequent toil . . . contend;** *cf. n.*   **5 main:** *flood*   **7 Crooked:** *malignant*   **9 transfix the flourish:** *remove the embellishment*   **10 delves the parallels:** *digs wrinkles*   **13 times in hope:** *future times*   **8 scope and tenour:** *aim and substance*   **11 defeat:** *destroy*

7 do define: *I do define*   **8 As:** *so that* **other:** *others*   **10 Beated and chopp'd:** *battered (?) and chopped; cf. n.* **antiquity:** *old age*   **1 Against:** *when, in anticipation of the time when*   **5 steepy:** *steep, surmounted with difficulty*   **10 confounding:** *destroying*   **12 though:** *though he cuts*   **2 rich-proud . . . age:** *costly and splendid tombs or monuments*   **3 sometime:** *once, formerly*   **4 brass eternal slave:** *eternal brass the slave*   **9 state:** *condition of things*   **10 state itself:** *grandeur*   **13 which:** *this thought which*   **1 Since:** *since there is not*   **4 action:** *vigor*

Against the wrackful siege of battering days,
When rocks impregnable are not so stout,
Nor gates of steel so strong, but Time decays?
O fearful meditation! where, alack,
Shall Time's best jewel from Time's chest lie hid?   10
Or what strong hand can hold his swift foot back?
Or who his spoil of beauty can forbid?
   O, none, unless this miracle have might,
   That in black ink my love may still shine bright.

66

Tir'd with all these, for restful death I cry
As to behold desert a beggar born,
And needy nothing trimm'd in jollity,
And purest faith unhappily forsworn,
And gilded honour shamefully misplac'd,   5
And maiden virtue rudely strumpeted,
And right perfection wrongfully disgrac'd,
And strength by limping sway disabled,
And art made tongue-tied by authority,
And folly—doctor-like—controlling skill,   10
And simple truth miscall'd simplicity,
And captive good attending captain ill:
   Tir'd with all these, from these would I be gone,
   Save that to die, I leave my love alone.

67

Ah! wherefore with infection should he live,
And with his presence grace impiety,
That sin by him advantage should achieve,
And lace itself with his society?
Why should false painting imitate his cheek,   5
And steal dead seeing of his living hue?
Why should poor beauty indirectly seek
Roses of shadow, since his rose is true?
Why should he live, now Nature bankrupt is,
Beggar'd of blood to blush through lively veins?   10
For she hath no exchequer now but his,
And, proud of many, lives upon his gains.
   O, him she stores, to show what wealth she had
   In days long since, before these last so bad.

68

Thus is his cheek the map of days outworn,
When beauty live'd and died as flowers do now,
Before these bastard signs of fair were born,
Or durst inhabit on a living brow;
Before the golden tresses of the dead,   5
The right of sepulchres, were shorn away,
To live a second life on second head;
Ere beauty's dead fleece made another gay:

In him those holy antique hours are seen,
Without all ornament, itself and true,   10
Making no summer of another's green,
Robbing no old to dress his beauty new;
   And him as for a map doth Nature store,
   To show false Art what beauty was of yore.

69

Those parts of thee that the world's eye doth view
Want nothing that the thought of hearts can mend;
All tongues—the voice of souls—give thee that due,
Uttering bare truth, even so as foes commend.
Thy outward thus with outward praise is crown'd;   5
But those same tongues, that give thee so thine own,
In other accents do this praise confound
By seeing farther than the eye hath shown.
They look into the beauty of thy mind,
And that, in guess, they measure by thy deeds;   10
Then,—churls,—their thoughts, although their eyes were kind,
To thy fair flower add the rank smell of weeds:
   But why thy odour matcheth not thy show,
   The soil is this, that thou dost common grow.

70

That thou art blam'd shall not be thy defect,
For slander's mark was ever yet the fair;
The ornament of beauty is suspect,
A crow that flies in heaven's sweetest air.
So thou be good, slander doth but approve   5
Thy worth the greater, being woo'd of time;
For canker vice the sweetest buds doth love,
And thou present'st a pure unstained prime.
Thou hast pass'd by the ambush of young days,
Either not assail'd, or victor being charg'd;   10
Yet this thy praise cannot be so thy praise,
To tie up envy evermore enlarg'd:
   If some suspect of ill mask'd not thy show,
   Then thou alone kingdoms of hearts shouldst owe.

71

No longer mourn for me when I am dead
Than you shall hear the surly sullen bell
Give warning to the world that I am fled
From this vile world, with vilest worms to dwell:
Nay, if you read this line, remember not   5
The hand that writ it; for I love you so,
That I in your sweet thoughts would be forgot,
If thinking on me then should make you woe.
O, if, I say, you look upon this verse,
When I perhaps compounded am with clay,   10
Do not so much as my poor name rehearse,
But let your love even with my life decay;

---

6 **wrackful:** *destructive*   12 **spoil:** *plundering*   3 **needy nothing:** *empty vanity* **trimm'd in jollity:** *decked in finery*   4 **unhappily forsworn:** *unluckily frustrated*   5 **misplac'd:** *bestowed amiss*   8 **disabled:** *rendered helpless*   11 **simplicity:** *folly*   14 **to die:** *by dying*   1 **with infection:** *in this infected world*   4 **lace itself:** *decorate itself*   6 **dead seeing:** *a dead appearance*   7 **indirectly;** *cf. n.*   13 **stores:** *treasures up*   1 **map:** *picture*   3 **bastard signs of fair;** *cf. n.*   6 **The right of sepulchres:** *property belonging to the tomb*

9 **antique hours:** *hours of antiquity*   10 **itself and true:** *natural and sincere*   14 **soil;** *cf. n.* **common:** *too accessible*   70. 1-14 *Cf. n.*   3 **ornament:** *identifying badge* **suspect:** *suspicion, distrust*   5 **approve:** *prove*   6 **woo'd of time:** *wooed by the world*   8 **prime:** *spring, youth*   10 **charg'd:** *attacked*   11 **so thy praise:** *so much thy praise*   12 **To tie up:** *that it will tie up* **enlarg'd:** *at liberty*   13 **mask'd not thy show:** *did not disfigure your beauty*   14 **owe:** *own*   3 **Give warning to the world;** *cf. n.*   7 **would be:** *wish to be*   10 **compounded:** *mixed*   11 **rehearse:** *repeat*

Lest the wise world should look into your moan,
And mock you with me after I am gone.

72

O, lest the world should task you to recite
What merit lived in me, that you should love
After my death,—dear love, forget me quite,
For you in me can nothing worthy prove;
Unless you would devise some virtuous lie,   5
To do more for me than mine own desert,
And hang more praise upon deceased I
Than niggard truth would willingly impart:
O, lest your true love may seem false in this,
That you for love speak well of me untrue,   10
My name be buried where my body is,
And live no more to shame nor me nor you.
    For I am sham'd by that which I bring forth,
    And so should you, to love things nothing worth.

73

That time of year thou mayst in me behold
When yellow leaves, or none, or few, do hang
Upon those boughs which shake against the cold,
Bare ruin'd choirs, where late the sweet birds sang.
In me thou see'st the twilight of such day   5
As after sunset fadeth in the west;
Which by and by black night doth take away,
Death's second self, that seals up all in rest.
In me thou see'st the glowing of such fire,
That on the ashes of his youth doth lie,   10
As the death-bed whereon it must expire,
Consum'd with that which it was nourish'd by.
    This thou perceiv'st, which makes thy love more strong,
    To love that well which thou must leave ere long.

74

But be contented: when that fell arrest
Without all bail shall carry me away,
My life hath in this line some interest,
Which for memorial still with thee shall stay.
When thou reviewest this, thou dost review   5
The very part was consecrate to thee:
The earth can have but earth, which is his due;
My spirit is thine, the better part of me:
So then thou hast but lost the dregs of life,
The prey of worms, my body being dead;   10
The coward conquest of a wretch'd knife,
Too base of thee to be remembered.
    The worth of that is that which it contains,
    And that is this, and this with thee remains.

75

So are you to my thoughts as food to life,
Or as sweet-season'd showers are to the ground;
And for the peace of you I hold such strife
As 'twixt a miser and his wealth is found;
Now proud as an enjoyer, and anon   5
Doubting the filching age will steal his treasure;
Now counting best to be with you alone,
Then better'd that the world may see my pleasure:
Sometime all full with feasting on your sight,
And by and by clean starved for a look;   10
Possessing or pursuing no delight,
Save what is had or must from you be took.
    Thus do I pine and surfeit day by day,
    Or gluttoning on all, or all away.

76

Why is my verse so barren of new pride,
So far from variation or quick change?
Why with the time do I not glance aside
To new-found methods and to compounds strange?
Why write I still all one, ever the same,   5
And keep invention in a noted weed,
That every word doth almost tell my name,
Showing their birth, and where they did proceed?
O, know, sweet love, I always write of you,
And you and love are still my argument;   10
So all my best is dressing old words new,
Spending again what is already spent:
    For as the sun is daily new and old,
    So is my love still telling what is told.

77

Thy glass will show thee how thy beauties wear,
Thy dial how thy precious minutes waste;
The vacant leaves thy mind's imprint will bear,
And of this book this learning mayst thou taste.
The wrinkles which thy glass will truly show   5
Of mouthed graves will give thee memory;
Thou by thy dial's shady stealth mayst know
Time's thievish progress to eternity.
Look! what thy memory cannot contain,
Commit to these waste blanks, and thou shalt find   10
Those children nurs'd, deliver'd from thy brain,
To take a new acquaintance of thy mind.
    These offices, so oft as thou wilt look,
    Shall profit thee and much enrich thy book.

78

So oft have I invok'd thee for my Muse
And found such fair assistance in my verse
As every alien pen hath got my use

---

1 task: *challenge*   **4 prove:** *discover*   **10 untrue:** *untruly*   **11 My name:** *let my name*   **14 should you:** *should you be shamed*   **12 Consum'd with that . . . nourish'd by;** *cf. n.*   **3 interest:** *claim, part*   **4 Which:** *this line which*   **5 reviewest:** *surveyest*   **6 was consecrate:** *that was consecrated*   **12 of thee:** *by thee*   **13 of that:** *of that body*   **is that:** *is that spirit*   **14 that is this:** *that spirit is this poetry*

2 sweet-season'd: *mild*   **3 peace of you:** *peaceful possession of you*   **6 Doubting:** *fearing*   **8 better'd that:** *made happier, more fortunate, because*   **12 had:** *had from you*   **14 Or:** *either*   **or all away:** *or putting all aside, refusing all*   **1 new pride:** *ostentatious novelty*   **6 noted weed:** *well-known dress*   **77. 1-14** *Cf. n.*   **4** *Cf. n.*   **7 shady stealth:** *stealthy shadow*   **10 waste blanks:** *empty pages*   **11, 12** *Cf. n.*   **13 offices;** *cf. n.*   **78. 1-14** *Cf. n.*   **3 As:** *that*   **use:** *habit*

And under thee their poesy disperse.
Thine eyes, that taught the dumb on high to sing   5
And heavy ignorance aloft to fly,
Have added feathers to the learned's wing
And given grace a double majesty.
Yet be most proud of that which I compile,
Whose influence is thine, and born of thee: 10
In others' works thou dost but mend the style,
And arts with thy sweet graces graced be;
    But thou art all my art, and dost advance
    As high as learning my rude ignorance.

79

Whilst I alone did call upon thy aid,
My verse alone had all thy gentle grace;
But now my gracious numbers are decay'd,
And my sick muse doth give another place.
I grant, sweet love, thy lovely argument   5
Deserves the travail of a worthier pen;
Yet what of thee thy poet doth invent
He robs thee of, and pays it thee again.
He lends thee virtue, and he stole that word
From thy behavior; beauty doth he give,   10
And found it in thy cheek; he can afford
No praise to thee but what in thee doth live.
    Then thank him not for that which he doth say,
    Since what he owes thee thou thyself dost pay.

80

O, how I faint when I of you do write,
Knowing a better spirit doth use your name,
And in the praise thereof spends all his might,
To make me tongue-tied, speaking of your fame!
But since your worth,—wide as the ocean is,—   5
The humble as the proudest sail doth bear,
My saucy bark, inferior far to his,
On your broad main doth wilfully appear.
Your shallowest help will hold me up afloat,
Whilst he upon your soundless deep doth ride;   10
Or, being wrack'd, I am a worthless boat,
He of tall building and of goodly pride:
    Then if he thrive and I be cast away,
    The worst was this;—my love was my decay.

81

Or I shall live your epitaph to make,
Or you survive when I in earth am rotten;
From hence your memory death cannot take,
Although in me each part will be forgotten.
Your name from hence immortal life shall have,   5
Though I, once gone, to all the world must die:
The earth can yield me but a common grave,
When you entombed in men's eyes shall lie.
Your monument shall be my gentle verse,
Which eyes not yet created shall o'er-read;   10

And tongues to be your being shall rehearse,
When all the breathers of this world are dead;
    You still shall live,—such virtue hath my pen,—
    Where breath most breathes,—even in the mouths of men.

82

I grant thou wert not married to my Muse,
And therefore mayst without attaint o'erlook
The dedicated words which writers use
Of their fair subject, blessing every book.
Thou art as fair in knowledge as in hue,   5
Finding thy worth a limit past my praise;
And therefore art enforc'd to seek anew
Some fresher stamp of the time-bettering days.
And do so, love; yet when they have devis'd
What strained touches rhetoric can lend,   10
Thou truly fair wert truly sympathiz'd
In true plain words by thy true-telling friend;
    And their gross painting might be better us'd
    Where cheeks need blood; in thee it is abus'd.

83

I never saw that you did painting need,
And therefore to your fair no painting set;
I found, or thought I found, you did exceed
The barren tender of a poet's debt:
And therefore have I slept in your report,   5
That you yourself, being extant, well might show
How far a modern quill doth come too short,
Speaking of worth, what worth in you doth grow.
This silence for my sin you did impute,
Which shall be most my glory, being dumb;   10
For I impair not beauty being mute,
When others would give life, and bring a tomb.
    There lives more life in one of your fair eyes
    Than both your poets can in praise devise.

84

Who is it that says most, which can say more
Than this rich praise,—that you alone are you,
In whose confine immured is the store
Which should example where your equal grew?
Lean penury within that pen doth dwell   5
That to his subject lends not some small glory;
But he that writes of you, if he can tell
That you are you, so dignifies his story.
Let him but copy what in you is writ,
Not making worse what nature made so clear,   10
And such a counterpart shall fame his wit,
Making his style admired everywhere.
    You to your beauteous blessings add a curse,
    Being fond on praise, which makes your praises worse.

---

11 to be: *of future generations*   2 attaint: *disgrace*   6 limit: *mark, goal*   8 time-bettering days: *present greater age*   10 strained: *exaggerated*   11 sympathiz'd: *matched*   4 tender: *offer to pay*   5 in your report: *in describing, praising, you*   7 modern: *ordinary*   14 both your poets; *cf. n.*   3, 4 In whose confine ... equal grew; *cf. n.*   10 clear: *glorious*   11 counterpart: *reproduction* fame: *give fame to*   13 beauteous blessings: *blessings of beauty*   14 Being fond ... praises worse; *cf. n.*

4 under thee: *under thy patronage* disperse: *spread abroad*   9 compile: *compose*   10 influence: *inspiration*   13 advance: *raise*   4 give another place: *yield to another*   5 thy ... argument: *the theme of your beauty*   2 a better spirit; *cf. n.*   8 wilfully: *eagerly*   11 wrack'd: *wrecked*   6 to all the world: *in the world's memory*

85

My tongue-tied Muse in manners holds her still,
Whilst comments of your praise, richly compil'd,
Reserve their character with golden quill,
And precious phrase by all the Muses fil'd.
I think good thoughts, while others write good words,   *5*
And, like unletter'd clerk, still cry 'Amen'
To every hymn that able spirit affords
In polish'd form of well-refined pen.
Hearing you prais'd, I say, ' 'Tis so, 'tis true,'
And to the most of praise add something more;   *10*
But that is in my thought, whose love to you,
Though words come hindmost, holds his rank before.
     Then others for the breath of words respect,
     Me for my dumb thoughts, speaking in effect.

86

Was it the proud full sail of his great verse,
Bound for the prize of all too precious you,
That did my ripe thoughts in my brain inhearse,
Making their tomb the womb wherein they grew?
Was it his spirit, by spirits taught to write   *5*
Above a mortal pitch, that struck me dead?
No, neither he, nor his compeers by night
Giving him aid, my verse astonished.
He, nor that affable familiar ghost
Which nightly gulls him with intelligence,   *10*
As victors of my silence cannot boast;
I was not sick of any fear from thence:
     But when your countenance fill'd up his line,
     Then lack'd I matter; that enfeebled mine.

87

Farewell! thou art too dear for my possessing,
And like enough thou know'st thy estimate:
The charter of thy worth gives thee releasing;
My bonds in thee are all determinate.
For how do I hold thee but by thy granting?   *5*
And for that riches where is my deserving?
The cause of this fair gift in me is wanting,
And so my patent back again is swerving.
Thyself thou gav'st, thy own worth then not knowing,
Or me, to whom thou gav'st it, else mistaking;   *10*
So thy great gift, upon misprision growing,
Comes home again, on better judgment making.
     Thus have I had thee, as a dream doth flatter,
     In sleep a king, but, waking, no such matter.

88

When thou shalt be dispos'd to set me light,
And place my merit in the eye of scorn,
Upon thy side against myself I'll fight,
And prove thee virtuous, though thou art forsworn.
With mine own weakness being best acquainted,   *5*
Upon thy part I can set down a story
Of faults conceal'd, wherein I am attainted;
That thou in losing me shalt win much glory:
And I by this will be a gainer too;
For bending all my loving thoughts on thee,   *10*
The injuries that to myself I do,
Doing thee vantage, double-vantage me.
     Such is my love, to thee I so belong,
     That for thy right myself will bear all wrong.

89

Say that thou didst forsake me for some fault,
And I will comment upon that offence:
Speak of my lameness, and I straight will halt,
Against thy reasons making no defence.
Thou canst not, love, disgrace me half so ill,   *5*
To set a form upon desired change,
As I'll myself disgrace; knowing thy will,
I will acquaintance strangle, and look strange;
Be absent from thy walks; and in my tongue
Thy sweet beloved name no more shall dwell,   *10*
Lest I, too much profane, should do it wrong,
And haply of our old acquaintance tell.
     For thee, against myself I'll vow debate,
     For I must ne'er love him whom thou dost hate.

90

Then hate me when thou wilt; if ever, now;
Now, while the world is bent my deeds to cross,
Join with the spite of fortune, make me bow,
And do not drop in for an after-loss:
Ah! do not, when my heart hath 'scap'd this sorrow,   *5*
Come in the rearward of a conquer'd woe;
Give not a windy night a rainy morrow,
To linger out a purpos'd overthrow.
If thou wilt leave me, do not leave me last,
When other petty griefs have done their spite,   *10*
But in the onset come: so shall I taste
At first the very worst of fortune's might;
     And other strains of woe, which now seem woe,
     Compar'd with loss of thee will not seem so.

91

Some glory in their birth, some in their skill,
Some in their wealth, some in their body's force;
Some in their garments, though new-fangled ill;
Some in their hawks and hounds, some in their horse;

---

1 **in manners:** *modestly*   2 **richly compil'd:** *composed in an elaborate style*   3 **Reserve their character;** *cf. n.*   4 **precious:** *carefully wrought* **fil'd:** *polished*   7 **that able spirit;** *cf. n*   12 **Though words ... before;** *cf. n.* **rank:** *place in line*   13 **respect:** *esteem*   14 **speaking in effect:** *which virtually speak*   3 **inhearse:** *lay as in a coffin*   8 **astonished:** *dismayed*   10 **gulls:** *cheats*   13 **countenance:** *favor*   2 **estimate:** *value*   87. 3 *Cf. n.*   4 **determinate:** *expired*   8 **patent:** *conditional privilege* **swerving:** *turning from me*   11 **upon misprision growing:** *made mistakenly*   1 **set me light:** *estimate me lightly*

6 **Upon thy part:** *in your behalf*   12 **double-vantage:** *doubly reward*   2 **comment:** *discourse*   6 **set a form:** *put a good semblance* **upon desired change:** *on the change you wish in our relations*   8 **acquaintance strangle:** *end our acquaintance* **look strange:** *assume the air of a stranger*   12 **haply:** *perchance*   13 **debate:** *strife*   2 **cross:** *thwart*   4 **drop in:** *come in suddenly*   90. 6 *Cf. n.*   8 **linger out:** *prolong*   11 **onset:** *first attack*   13 **strains:** *emotions*   3 **new-fangled ill:** *fashionably ugly*

And every humour hath his adjunct pleasure,   *5*
Wherein it finds a joy above the rest:
But these particulars are not my measure;
All these I better in one general best.
Thy love is better than high birth to me,
Richer than wealth, prouder than garments' cost,   *10*
Of more delight than hawks or horses be;
And having thee, of all men's pride I boast:
     Wretched in this alone, that thou mayst take
     All this away, and me most wretched make.

92

But do thy worst to steal thyself away,
For term of life thou art assured mine;
And life no longer than thy love will stay,
For it depends upon that love of thine.
Then need I not to fear the worst of wrongs,   *5*
When in the least of them my life hath end.
I see a better state to me belongs
Than that which on thy humour doth depend:
Thou canst not vex me with inconstant mind,
Since that my life on thy revolt doth lie.   *10*
O! what a happy title do I find,
Happy to have thy love, happy to die:
     But what's so blessed-fair that fears no blot?
     Thou mayst be false, and yet I know it not.

93

So shall I live, supposing thou art true,
Like a deceived husband; so love's face
May still seem love to me, though alter'd new,
Thy looks with me, thy heart in other place:
For there can live no hatred in thine eye,   *5*
Therefore in that I cannot know thy change.
In many's looks the false heart's history
Is writ in moods, and frowns, and wrinkles strange,
But heaven in thy creation did decree
That in thy face sweet love should ever dwell;   *10*
Whate'er thy thoughts or thy heart's workings be,
Thy looks should nothing thence but sweetness tell.
     How like Eve's apple doth thy beauty grow,
     If thy sweet virtue answer not thy show!

94

They that have power to hurt and will do none,
That do not do the thing they most do show,
Who, moving others, are themselves as stone,
Unmoved, cold, and to temptation slow;
They rightly do inherit heaven's graces,   *5*
And husband nature's riches from expense;
They are the lords and owners of their faces,
Others but stewards of their excellence.

The summer's flower is to the summer sweet,
Though to itself it only live and die,   *10*
But if that flower with base infection meet,
The basest weed outbraves his dignity:
     For sweetest things turn sourest by their deeds;
     Lilies that fester smell far worse than weeds.

95

How sweet and lovely dost thou make the shame
Which, like a canker in the fragrant rose,
Doth spot the beauty of thy budding name!
O, in what sweets dost thou thy sins enclose!
That tongue that tells the story of thy days,   *5*
Making lascivious comments on thy sport,
Cannot dispraise but in a kind of praise;
Naming thy name blesses an ill report.
O, what a mansion have those vices got
Which for their habitation chose out thee,   *10*
Where beauty's veil doth cover every blot
And all things turn to fair that eyes can see!
     Take heed, dear heart, of this large privilege;
     The hardest knife ill-us'd doth lose his edge.

96

Some say thy fault is youth, some wantonness;
Some say thy grace is youth and gentle sport;
Both grace and faults are lov'd of more and less;
Thou mak'st faults graces that to thee resort.
As on the finger of a throned queen   *5*
The basest jewel will be well esteem'd,
So are those errors that in thee are seen
To truths translated and for true things deem'd.
How many lambs might the stern wolf betray,
If like a lamb he could his looks translate!   *10*
How many gazers mightst thou lead away,
If thou wouldst use the strength of all thy state!
     But do not so; I love thee in such sort,
     As, thou being mine, mine is thy good report.

97

How like a winter hath my absence been
From thee, the pleasure of the fleeting year!
What freezings have I felt, what dark days seen!
What old December's bareness everywhere!
And yet this time remov'd was summer's time,   *5*
The teeming autumn, big with rich increase,
Bearing the wanton burden of the prime,
Like widow'd wombs after their lords' decease:
Yet this abundant issue seem'd to me
But hope of orphans and unfather'd fruit;   *10*
For summer and his pleasures wait on thee,
And, thou away, the very birds are mute:
     Or, if they sing, 'tis with so dull a cheer,
     That leaves look pale, dreading the winter's near.

---

5 humour: *disposition* **adjunct:** *connected*   **7 measure:** *limit* (of joy)   **8 humour:** *mood*   **10 Since that . . . lie:** *since my life would end if you betrayed me*   **94. 1-14** *Cf. n.*   **2 show:** *seem to do*   **6 husband . . . expense:** *do not squander nature's gifts in passion*

94. 9-12 *Cf. n.*   **14** *Cf. n.*   **2 canker:** *cankerworm*   **13 privilege:** *license*   **3 more and less:** *high and low*   **8 translated:** *changed*   **12 state:** *grandeur, beauty* (?)   **96. 13, 14** *Cf. n.*   **5 time remov'd:** *time of absence*   **13 cheer:** *mood*

98

From you have I been absent in the spring,
When proud-pied April, dress'd in all his trim,
Hath put a spirit of youth in everything,
That heavy Saturn laugh'd and leap'd with him.
Yet nor the lays of birds, nor the sweet smell   5
Of different flowers in odour and in hue,
Could make me any summer's story tell,
Or from their proud lap pluck them where they grew:
Nor did I wonder at the lily's white,
Nor praise the deep vermilion in the rose;   10
They were but sweet, but figures of delight,
Drawn after you, you pattern of all those.
     Yet seem'd it winter still, and, you away,
     As with your shadow I with these did play.

99

The forward violet thus did I chide:
Sweet thief, whence didst thou steal thy sweet that smells,
If not from my love's breath? The purple pride
Which on thy soft cheek for complexion dwells
In my love's veins thou hast too grossly dy'd.   5
The lily I condemned for thy hand,
And buds of marjoram had stol'n thy hair;
The roses fearfully on thorns did stand,
One blushing shame, another white despair;
A third, nor red nor white, had stol'n of both,   10
And to his robbery had annex'd thy breath;
But, for his theft, in pride of all his growth
A vengeful canker eat him up to death.
     More flowers I noted, yet I none could see
     But sweet or colour it had stol'n from thee.

100

Where art thou, Muse, that thou forget'st so long
To speak of that which gives thee all thy might?
Spend'st thou thy fury on some worthless song,
Darkening thy power to lend base subjects light?
Return, forgetful Muse, and straight redeem   5
In gentle numbers time so idly spent;
Sing to the ear that doth thy lays esteem
And gives thy pen both skill and argument.
Rise, resty Muse, my love's sweet face survey,
If Time have any wrinkle graven there;   10
If any, be a satire to decay,
And make Time's spoils despised everywhere.
     Give my love fame faster than Time wastes life;
     So thou prevent'st his scythe and crooked knife.

101

O truant Muse, what shall be thy amends
For thy neglect of truth in beauty dy'd?
Both truth and beauty on my love depends;
So dost thou too, and therein dignified.
Make answer, Muse: wilt thou not haply say,   5
'Truth needs no colour, with his colour fix'd;
Beauty no pencil, beauty's truth to lay;
But best is best, if never intermix'd'?
Because he needs no praise, wilt thou be dumb?
Excuse not silence so; for 't lies in thee   10
To make him much outlive a gilded tomb
And to be prais'd of ages yet to be.
     Then do thy office, Muse; I teach thee how
     To make him seem long hence as he shows now.

102

My love is strengthen'd, though more weak in seeming;
I love not less, though less the show appear:
That love is merchandiz'd whose rich esteeming
The owner's tongue doth publish everywhere.
Our love was new, and then but in the spring,   5
When I was wont to greet it with my lays;
As Philomel in summer's front doth sing,
And stops her pipe in growth of riper days:
Not that the summer is less pleasant now
Than when her mournful hymns did hush the night,   10
But that wild music burthens every bough,
And sweets grown common lose their dear delight.
     Therefore, like her, I sometime hold my tongue,
     Because I would not dull you with my song.

103

Alack! what poverty my Muse brings forth,
That having such a scope to show her pride,
The argument, all bare, is of more worth
Than when it hath my added praise beside!
O, blame me not, if I no more can write!   5
Look in your glass, and there appears a face
That over-goes my blunt invention quite,
Dulling my lines and doing me disgrace.
Were it not sinful then, striving to mend,
To mar the subject that before was well?   10
For to no other pass my verses tend
Than of your graces and your gifts to tell;
     And more, much more, than in my verse can sit,
     Your own glass shows you when you look in it.

104

To me, fair friend, you never can be old,
For as you were when first your eye I ey'd,
Such seems your beauty still. Three winters cold
Have from the forests shook three summer's pride,
Three beauteous springs to yellow autumn turn'd   5
In process of the seasons have I seen,
Three April perfumes in three hot Junes burn'd,
Since first I saw you fresh, which yet are green.

---

2 **proud-pied:** *magnificent in many colors* **trim:** *finery*   4 **heavy Saturn:** *Saturn, god of heaviness or melancholy*   7 **summer's story:** *pleasant tale*   9 **wonder at:** *admire*   1 **forward:** *early*   5 **grossly:** *obviously*   6 **for:** *compared with*   7 **buds of marjoram;** *cf. n.*   3 **fury:** *inspiration*   9 **resty:** *indolent*   11 **be . . . decay:** *satirize Time's destruction of beauty*   14 **prevent'st:** *forestall'st*

4 **dignified:** *art dignified*   7 **lay:** *apply, as a color*   8 **if never intermix'd:** *if left to itself*   13 **office:** *work*   1 **seeming:** *appearance*   3 **merchandiz'd:** *cheapened* **esteeming:** *worth*   7 **Philomel:** *the nightingale* **front:** *beginning*   11 **pass:** *end*   13 **sit:** *be contained*   6 **process:** *procession*

Ah! yet doth beauty, like a dial-hand,
Steal from his figure, and no pace perceiv'd: *10*
So your sweet hue, which methinks still doth stand,
Hath motion, and mine eye may be deceiv'd:
    For fear of which, hear this, thou age unbred:
    Ere you were born was beauty's summer dead.

105

Let not my love be call'd idolatry,
Nor my beloved as an idol show,
Since all alike my songs and praises be
To one, of one, still such, and ever so.
Kind is my love to-day, to-morrow kind,   *5*
Still constant in a wondrous excellence;
Therefore my verse, to constancy confin'd,
One thing expressing, leaves out difference.
'Fair, kind, and true,' is all my argument,
'Fair, kind, and true,' varying to other words;   *10*
And in this change is my invention spent,
Three themes in one, which wondrous scope affords.
    'Fair, kind, and true' have often liv'd alone,
    Which three till now never kept seat in one.

106

When in the chronicle of wasted time
I see descriptions of the fairest wights,
And beauty making beautiful old rime,
In praise of ladies dead and lovely knights,
Then, in the blazon of sweet beauty's best,   *5*
Of hand, of foot, of lip, of eye, of brow,
I see their antique pen would have express'd
Even such a beauty as you master now.
So all their praises are but prophecies
Of this our time, all you prefiguring;   *10*
And, for they look'd but with divining eyes,
They had not skill enough your worth to sing:
    For we, which now behold these present days,
    Have eyes to wonder, but lack tongues to praise.

107

Not mine own fears, nor the prophetic soul
Of the wide world dreaming on things to come,
Can yet the lease of my true love control,
Suppos'd as forfeit to a confin'd doom.
The mortal moon hath her eclipse endur'd,   *5*
And the sad augurs mock their own presage;
Incertainties now crown themselves assur'd,
And peace proclaims olives of endless age.
Now with the drops of this most balmy time
My love looks fresh, and Death to me subscribes,   *10*
Since, spite of him, I'll live in this poor rime,
While he insults o'er dull and speechless tribes:

And thou in this shalt find thy monument,
When tyrants' crests and tombs of brass are spent.

108

What's in the brain, that ink may character,
Which hath not figur'd to thee my true spirit?
What's new to speak, what new to register,
That may express my love, or thy dear merit?
Nothing, sweet boy; but yet, like prayers divine,   *5*
I must each day say o'er the very same;
Counting no old thing old, thou mine, I thine,
Even as when first I hallow'd thy fair name.
So that eternal love in love's fresh case
Weighs not the dust and injury of age,   *10*
Nor gives to necessary wrinkles place,
But makes antiquity for aye his page;
    Finding the first conceit of love there bred,
    Where time and outward form would show it dead.

109

O, never say that I was false of heart,
Though absence seem'd my flame to qualify.
As easy might I from myself depart
As from my soul, which in thy breast doth lie:
That is my home of love: if I have rang'd,   *5*
Like him that travels, I return again;
Just to the time, not with the time exchang'd,
So that myself bring water for my stain.
Never believe, though in my nature reign'd
All frailties that besiege all kinds of blood,   *10*
That it could so preposterously be stain'd,
To leave for nothing all thy sum of good;
    For nothing this wide universe I call,
    Save thou, my rose; in it thou art my all.

110

Alas! 'tis true I have gone here and there,
And made myself a motley to the view,
Gor'd mine own thoughts, sold cheap what is most dear,
Made old offences of affections new;
Most true it is that I have look'd on truth   *5*
Askance and strangely; but, by all above,
These blenches gave my heart another youth,
And worse essays prov'd thee my best of love.
Now all is done, have what shall have no end:
Mine appetite I never more will grind   *10*
On newer proof, to try an older friend,
A god in love, to whom I am confin'd.
    Then give me welcome, next my heaven the best,
    Even to thy pure and most most loving breast.

13 in this: *in this verse*   **1 character:** *write*   **3 register:** *record*   **9 in love's fresh case:** *always renewed*   **11 gives . . . place:** *withdraws when wrinkles must come*   **108. 13, 14** *Cf. n.*   **2 qualify:** *moderate*   **5 That:** *thy breast*   **7 Just to the time:** *punctually* **exchang'd:** *changed*   **8 myself bring . . . stain:** *justify my fault (of absence)*   **10 blood:** *temperament*   **11 preposterously:** *unnaturally*   **110. 1, 2** *Cf. n.*   **2 motley:** *jester*   **3 Gor'd:** *wounded*   **4 Made old . . . new:** *offended in forsaking old friends for new*   **7 blenches:** *inconstancies*   **gave . . . youth:** *brought me back to youthful love*   **8 worse essays:** *trials of the worse*   **9 have what . . . end:** *take my unending love*   **10 grind:** *whet*

9 dial-hand: *hand of a watch*   **2 show:** *appear*   **8 difference:** *variety*   **10 varying to other words:** *the thought expressed in other words*   **5 blazon:** *proclaiming*   **8 master:** *possess*   **11 divining:** *prophesying*   **107. 1-4** *Cf. n.*   **5 mortal:** *deadly (?); cf. n.*   **6 presage:** *presentiment*   **10 subscribes:** *submits*

111

O, for my sake do you with Fortune chide,
The guilty goddess of my harmful deeds,
That did not better for my life provide
Than public means which public manners breeds.
Thence comes it that my name receives a brand,   5
And almost thence my nature is subdu'd
To what it works in, like the dyer's hand:
Pity me, then, and wish I were renew'd;
Whilst, like a willing patient, I will drink
Potions of eisel 'gainst my strong infection;   10
No bitterness that I will bitter think,
Nor double penance, to correct correction.
    Pity me, then, dear friend, and I assure ye
    Even that your pity is enough to cure me.

112

Your love and pity doth the impression fill
Which vulgar scandal stamp'd upon my brow;
For what care I who calls me well or ill,
So you o'er-green my bad, my good allow?
You are my all-the-world, and I must strive   5
To know my shames and praises from your tongue;
None else to me, nor I to none alive,
That my steel'd sense or changes right or wrong.
In so profound abysm I throw all care
Of other's voices, that my adder's sense   10
To critic and to flatterer stopped are.
Mark how with my neglect I do dispense:
    You are so strongly in my purpose bred,
    That all the world besides methinks are dead.

113

Since I left you, mine eye is in my mind;
And that which governs me to go about
Doth part his function and is partly blind,
Seems seeing, but effectually is out;
For it no form delivers to the heart   5
Of bird, of flower, or shape, which it doth latch:
Of his quick objects hath the mind no part,
Nor his own vision holds what it doth catch;
For if it see the rud'st or gentlest sight,
The most sweet favour or deformed'st creature,   10
The mountain or the sea, the day or night,
The crow or dove, it shapes them to your feature:
    Incapable of more, replete with you,
    My most true mind thus maketh mine untrue.

114

Or whether doth my mind being crown'd with you,
Drink up the monarch's plague, this flattery?
Or whether shall I say mine eye saith true,
And that your love taught it this alchemy,
To make of monsters and things indigest   5
Such cherubins as your sweet self resemble,
Creating every bad a perfect best,
As fast as objects to his beams assemble?
O, 'tis the first, 'tis flattery in my seeing,
And my great mind most kingly drinks it up: 10
Mine eye well knows what with his gust is 'greeing,
And to his palate doth prepare the cup:
    If it be poison'd, 'tis the lesser sin
    That mine eye loves it and doth first begin.

115

Those lines that I before have writ do lie,
Even those that said I could not love you dearer:
Yet then my judgment knew no reason why
My most full flame should afterwards burn clearer.
But reckoning Time, whose million'd accidents   5
Creep in 'twixt vows, and change decrees of kings,
Tan sacred beauty, blunt the sharp'st intents,
Divert strong minds to the course of altering things;
Alas! why, fearing of Time's tyranny,
Might I not then say, 'Now I love you best,'   10
When I was certain o'er incertainty,
Crowning the present, doubting of the rest?
    Love is a babe; then might I not say so,
    To give full growth to that which still doth grow.

116

Let me not to the marriage of true minds
Admit impediments. Love is not love
Which alters when it alteration finds,
Or bends with the remover to remove:
O, no! it is an ever-fixed mark,   5
That looks on tempests and is never shaken;
It is the star to every wandering bark,
Whose worth's unknown, although his height be taken.
Love's not Time's fool, though rosy lips and cheeks
Within his bending sickle's compass come;   10
Love alters not with his brief hours and weeks,
But bears it out even to the edge of doom.
    If this be error, and upon me prov'd,
    I never writ, nor no man ever lov'd.

117

Accuse me thus: that I have scanted all
Wherein I should your great deserts repay,
Forgot upon your dearest love to call,
Whereto all bonds do tie me day by day;

---

2 guilty goddess . . . deeds: *goddess guilty of . . . deeds*   **5 brand:** *stigma*   **6 subdu'd:** *reduced*   **10 eisel:** *vinegar*   **12 correct correction:** *chastise chastisement, make my correction doubly sure*   **1 impression:** *mark, brand*   **4 o'er-green:** *cover as by a vine or grass* **allow:** *approve*   **112. 7, 8** *Cf. n.*   **10, 11** *Cf. n.*   **12 with . . . dispense:** *I am indifferent to neglect* (by others)   **13 in my purpose bred:** *engrafted in my life*   **14 besides:** *except you*   **3 Doth part his function:** *does but part of its natural work*   **4 effectually:** *practically*   **5 it:** *my eye* **heart:** *mind*   **6 latch:** *catch*   **7 his:** *the eye's*   **8 his own:** *the eye's*   **10 favour:** *countenance*   **113. 14** *Cf. n.*

1 Or whether doth: *is it true that*   **5 indigest:** *formless*   **10 kingly:** *like a king*   **11 what . . . 'greeing:** *what agrees with the mind's taste*   **114. 13, 14** *Cf. n.*   **5 reckoning:** *taking account of*   **12 the rest:** *the future*   **13 so:** *'I love you best'*   **14 To give:** *giving*   **4 remover:** *inconstant* **remove:** *depart*   **8 worth:** *power, influence* **height:** *altitude*   **10 his:** *Time's*   **12 edge of doom:** *judgment day*   **1 scanted:** *grudged*

That I have frequent been with unknown minds,   *5*
And given to time your own dear-purchas'd right;
That I have hoisted sail to all the winds
Which should transport me furthest from your sight.
Book both my wilfulness and errors down,
And on just proof surmise accumulate;   *10*
Bring me within the level of your frown,
But shoot not at me in your waken'd hate;
    Since my appeal says I did strive to prove
    The constancy and virtue of your love.

118

Like as, to make our appetites more keen,
With eager compounds we our palate urge;
As, to prevent our maladies unseen,
We sicken to shun sickness when we purge;
Even so, being full of your ne'er-cloying sweetness,   *5*
To bitter sauces did I frame my feeding;
And, sick of welfare, found a kind of meetness
To be diseas'd, ere that there was true needing.
Thus policy in love, to anticipate
The ills that were not, grew to faults assur'd,   *10*
And brought to medicine a healthful state,
Which, rank of goodness, would by ill be cur'd;
    But thence I learn, and find the lesson true,
    Drugs poison him that so fell sick of you.

119

What potions have I drunk of Siren tears,
Distill'd from limbecks foul as hell within,
Applying fears to hopes, and hopes to fears,
Still losing when I saw myself to win!
What wretched errors hath my heart committed,   *5*
Whilst it hath thought itself so blessed never!
How have mine eyes out of their spheres been fitted,
In the distraction of this madding fever!
O benefit of ill! now I find true
That better is by evil still made better;   *10*
And ruin'd love, when it is built anew,
Grows fairer than at first, more strong, far greater.
    So I return rebuk'd to my content,
    And gain by ill thrice more than I have spent.

120

That you were once unkind befriends me now,
And for that sorrow, which I then did feel,
Needs must I under my transgression bow,
Unless my nerves were brass or hammer'd steel.
For if you were by my unkindness shaken,   *5*
As I by yours, you've pass'd a hell of time;
And I, a tyrant, have no leisure taken
To weigh how once I suffer'd in your crime.

O, that our night of woe might have remember'd
My deepest sense, how hard true sorrow hits,   *10*
And soon to you, as you to me, then tender'd
The humble salve which wounded bosoms fits!
    But that your trespass now becomes a fee;
    Mine ransoms yours, and yours must ransom me.

121

'Tis better to be vile than vile esteem'd,
When not to be receives reproach of being;
And the just pleasure lost, which is so deem'd
Not by our feeling, but by others' seeing:
For why should others' false adulterate eyes   *5*
Give salutation to my sportive blood?
Or on my frailties why are frailer spies,
Which in their wills count bad what I think good?
No, I am that I am, and they that level
At my abuses reckon up their own: *10*
I may be straight though they themselves be bevel;
By their rank thoughts my deeds must not be shown;
    Unless this general evil they maintain,
    All men are bad and in their badness reign.

122

Thy gift, thy tables, are within my brain
Full character'd with lasting memory,
Which shall above that idle rank remain,
Beyond all date, even to eternity:
Or, at the least, so long as brain and heart   *5*
Have faculty by nature to subsist;
Till each to raz'd oblivion yield his part
Of thee, thy record never can be miss'd.
That poor retention could not so much hold,
Nor need I tallies thy dear love to score;   *10*
Therefore to give them from me was I bold,
To trust those tables that receive thee more:
    To keep an adjunct to remember thee
    Were to import forgetfulness in me.

123

No, Time, thou shalt not boast that I do change:
Thy pyramids built up with newer might
To me are nothing novel, nothing strange;
They are but dressings of a former sight.
Our dates are brief, and therefore we admire   *5*
What thou dost foist upon us that is old;
And rather make them born to our desire
Than think that we before have heard them told.
Thy registers and thee I both defy,
Not wondering at the present nor the past,   *10*
For thy records and what we see doth lie,

5 **frequent:** *intimate* **unknown:** *unimportant*   6 **given to time:** *wasted*   10 **on ...
accumulate:** *add suspected to proved offences*   11 **level:** *aim*   1 **Like as:** *just as*   2
eager compounds: *bitter mixtures* **palate urge:** *stimulate the appetite*   7 **welfare:** *good
health*   12 **rank of:** *cloyed with*   2 **limbecks:** *alembics, vessels for distillation*   4 **Still
... win:** *winning new loves but losing the old*   7 **How ... fitted;** *cf. n.*   8 **weigh:**
consider

120. 9, 10 *Cf. n.*   11 **then tender'd:** *then had I tendered*   13 **fee:** *payment, recompense*
121. 3, 4 *Cf. n.*   6 **Give salutation to:** *greet* (as if Shakespere were one of them)   **sportive:**
wanton   8 **in their wills:** *as they please*   11 **bevel:** *oblique*   **122.** 1-14 *Cf. n.*   1
tables: *memorandum book*   3 **idle rank:** *empty row of leaves*   7 **raz'd:** *empty*   9 **poor
retention:** *book that contains little*   10 **tallies ... score;** *cf. n.*   12 **those tables:** *my
memory*   13 **adjunct:** *attendant*   2 **newer:** *more recent*   4 **dressings:** *refashion-
ings*   5 **dates:** *years of life*   **123.** 7, 8 *Cf. n.*   11 **doth lie:** *doth tell us a lie*

Made more or less by thy continual haste.
　This I do vow, and this shall ever be;
　I will be true, despite thy scythe and thee.

124

If my dear love were but the child of state,
It might for Fortune's bastard be unfather'd,
As subject to Time's love or to Time's hate,
Weeds among weeds, or flowers with flowers gather'd.
No, it was builded far from accident;　　　　　　5
It suffers not in smiling pomp, nor falls
Under the blow of thralled discontent,
Whereto the inviting time our fashion calls:
It fears not policy, that heretic,
Which works on leases of short number'd hours,　　10
But all alone stands hugely politic,
That it nor grows with heat, nor drowns with showers.
　To this I witness call the fools of time,
　Which die for goodness, who have liv'd for crime.

125

Were 't aught to me I bore the canopy,
With my extern the outward honouring,
Or laid great bases for eternity,
Which prove more short than waste or ruining?
Have I not seen dwellers on form and favour　　　5
Lose all and more by paying too much rent,
For compound sweet forgoing simple savour,
Pitiful thrivers, in their gazing spent?
No; let me be obsequious in thy heart,
And take thou my oblation, poor but free,　　　10
Which is not mix'd with seconds, knows no art,
But mutual render, only me for thee.
　Hence, thou suborn'd informer! a true soul
　When most impeach'd stands least in thy control.

126

O thou, my lovely boy, who in thy power
Dost hold Time's fickle glass, his sickle hour;
Who hast by waning grown, and therein show'st
Thy lovers withering as thy sweet self grow'st;
If Nature, sovereign mistress over wrack,　　　5
As thou goest onwards, still will pluck thee back,
She keeps thee to this purpose, that her skill
May time disgrace and wretched minutes kill.
Yet fear her, O thou minion of her pleasure!
She may detain, but not still keep, her treasure:　10

Her audit, though delay'd, answer'd must be,
And her quietus is to render thee.

127

In the old age black was not counted fair,
Or if it were, it bore not beauty's name;
But now is black beauty's successive heir,
And beauty slander'd with a bastard's shame:
For since each hand hath put on Nature's power,　　5
Fairing the foul with Art's false borrow'd face,
Sweet beauty hath no name, no holy bower,
But is profan'd, if not lives in disgrace.
Therefore my mistress' brows are raven black,
Her eyes so suited, and they mourners seem　　　10
At such who, not born fair, no beauty lack,
Sland'ring creation with a false esteem:
　Yet so they mourn, becoming of their woe,
　That every tongue says beauty should look so.

128

How oft, when thou, my music, music play'st,
Upon that blessed wood whose motion sounds
With thy sweet fingers, when thou gently sway'st
The wiry concord that mine ear confounds,
Do I envy those jacks that nimble leap　　　　　5
To kiss the tender inward of thy hand,
Whilst my poor lips, which should that harvest reap,
At the wood's boldness by thee blushing stand!
To be so tickl'd, they would change their state
And situation with those dancing chips,　　　　10
O'er whom thy fingers walk with gentle gait,
Making dead wood more bless'd than living lips.
　Since saucy jacks so happy are in this,
　Give them thy fingers, me thy lips to kiss.

129

The expense of spirit in a waste of shame
Is lust in action; and till action, lust
Is perjur'd, murderous, bloody, full of blame,
Savage, extreme, rude, cruel, not to trust;
Enjoy'd no sooner but despised straight;　　　　5
Past reason hunted; and no sooner had,
Past reason hated, as a swallow'd bait,
On purpose laid to make the taker mad:
Mad in pursuit, and in possession so;
Had, having, and in quest to have, extreme;　　　10
A bliss in proof, and prov'd, a very woe;
Before, a joy propos'd; behind, a dream.
　All this the world well knows; yet none knows well
　To shun the heaven that leads men to this hell.

12 Made more or less: *increasing and decreasing, constantly changing*　**1 child of state:** *born of circumstances, accidental*　**2 for:** *because it was*　**4 Weeds ... gather'd;** *cf. n.*　**7 thralled discontent:** *discontent held in subjection*　**8 Whereto:** *to which*　**fashion:** *custom, usage*　**9 policy:** *craft*　**11 hugely politic:** *extremely wise*　**124. 13, 14** *Cf. n.*　**1 Were 't:** *would it be*　**bore the canopy:** *canopy of state; did outward reverence*　**2 With my extern:** *outwardly*　**7 savour:** *perfume*　**8 in their gazing spent:** *wasting themselves in regarding externals*　**10 free:** *whole-hearted*　**11 seconds:** *inferior matter*　**12 render:** *surrender*　**125. 13, 14** *Cf. n.*　**126. 1-12** *Cf. n.*　**2 sickle hour:** *hour when his sickle strikes*　**3 by waning grown:** *with age grown more beautiful*　**5 wrack:** *destruction*　**8 wretched minutes kill:** *kill time's minutes (that bring old age)*　**9 minion:** *darling*

12 quietus: *acquittance of the account*　**127. 1-14** *Cf. n.*　**1 black ... fair;** *cf. n.*　**3 successive:** *legitimate*　**6 Fairing ... face:** *beautifying ugliness by cosmetics*　**10 suited:** *attired*　**11 no beauty lack:** *make themselves beautiful by artifice*　**13 so:** *in such a manner*　**becoming of:** *gracing*　**4 wiry concord:** *harmony of the wires*　**5 jacks;** *cf. n.*　**129. 1-3** *Cf. n.*　**4 extreme:** *violent*　**6 Past:** *beyond all*　**11 in proof:** *when experienced*　**12 propos'd:** *anticipated*

130

My mistress' eyes are nothing like the sun;
Coral is far more red than her lips' red:
If snow be white, why then her breasts are dun;
If hairs be wires, black wires grow on her head.
I have seen roses damask'd, red and white,   5
But no such roses see I in her cheeks;
And in some perfumes is there more delight
Than in the breath that from my mistress reeks.
I love to hear her speak, yet well I know
That music hath a far more pleasing sound: 10
I grant I never saw a goddess go;
My mistress, when she walks, treads on the ground:
    And yet, by heaven, I think my love as rare
    As any she belied with false compare.

131

Thou art as tyrannous, so as thou art,
As those whose beauties proudly make them cruel;
For well thou know'st to my dear doting heart
Thou art the fairest and most precious jewel.
Yet, in good faith, some say that thee behold,   5
Thy face hath not the power to make love groan:
To say they err I dare not be so bold,
Although I swear it to myself alone.
And to be sure that is not false I swear,
A thousand groans, but thinking on thy face,   10
One on another's neck, do witness bear
Thy black is fairest in my judgment's place.
    In nothing art thou black save in thy deeds,
    And thence this slander, as I think, proceeds.

132

Thine eyes I love, and they, as pitying me,
Knowing thy heart torments me with disdain,
Have put on black and loving mourners be,
Looking with pretty ruth upon my pain.
And truly not the morning sun of heaven   5
Better becomes the grey cheeks of the east,
Nor that full star that ushers in the even,
Doth half that glory to the sober west,
As those two mourning eyes become thy face:
O, let it then as well beseem thy heart   10
To mourn for me, since mourning doth thee grace,
And suit thy pity like in every part.
    Then will I swear beauty herself is black,
    And all they foul that thy complexion lack.

133

Beshrew that heart that makes my heart to groan
For that deep wound it gives my friend and me!
Is 't not enough to torture me alone,
But slave to slavery my sweet'st friend must be?

Me from myself thy cruel eye hath taken,   5
And my next self thou harder hast engross'd:
Of him, myself, and thee, I am forsaken;
A torment thrice threefold thus to be cross'd.
Prison my heart in thy steel bosom's ward,
But then my friend's heart let my poor heart bail;   10
Whoe'er keeps me, let my heart be his guard;
Thou canst not then use rigour in my jail:
    And yet thou wilt; for I, being pent in thee,
    Perforce am thine, and all that is in me.

134

So, now I have confess'd that he is thine,
And I myself am mortgag'd to thy will,
Myself I'll forfeit, so that other mine
Thou wilt restore, to be my comfort still:
But thou wilt not, nor he will not be free,   5
For thou art covetous and he is kind;
He learn'd but surety-like to write for me,
Under that bond that him as fast doth bind.
The statute of thy beauty thou wilt take,
Thou usurer, that putt'st forth all to use,   10
And sue a friend came debtor for my sake;
So him I lose through my unkind abuse.
    Him have I lost; thou hast both him and me:
    He pays the whole, and yet am I not free.

135

Whoever hath her wish, thou hast thy *Will*,
And *Will* to boot, and *Will* in over-plus;
More than enough am I that vex thee still,
To thy sweet will making addition thus.
Wilt thou, whose will is large and spacious,   5
Not once vouchsafe to hide my will in thine?
Shall will in others seem right gracious,
And in my will no fair acceptance shine?
The sea, all water, yet receives rain still,
And in abundance addeth to his store;   10
So thou, being rich in *Will*, add to thy *Will*
One will of mine, to make thy large *Will* more.
    Let no unkind 'No' fair beseechers kill;
    Think all but one, and me in that one *Will*.

136

If thy soul check thee that I come so near,
Swear to thy blind soul that I was thy *Will*,
And will, thy soul knows, is admitted there;
Thus far for love my love-suit, sweet, fulfil.
Will will fulfil the treasure of thy love,   5
Ay, fill it full with wills, and my will one.
In things of great receipt with ease we prove
Among a number one is reckon'd none:

5 **damask'd:** *of the shade of a damask rose*   **14 compare:** *comparisons*   **1 so as:** *homely as*   **10 but:** *only on*   **11 One … neck:** *in quick succession*   **4 ruth:** *pity*   **12 suit: attire like:** *alike*   **14 foul:** *ugly*

6 my next self: *my friend* **engross'd:** *gained exclusive possession of*   **10 bail:** *go bail for (?), guard (?)*   **3 other mine:** *other self*   **5 nor he will not be free:** *not does he wish freedom*   **7 He learn'd … me:** *he released me by pledging himself as security*   **9 statute of thy beauty:** *bond giving possession obtained by thy beauty*   **10 to use:** *to interest*   **11 came:** *who became*   **12 my unkind abuse:** *unnatural wrong done to me*   **135. 1-14** *Cf. n.*   **1 check:** *reprove*   **7 receipt:** *capacity*

Then in the number let me pass untold,
Though in thy stores' account I one must be;   *10*
For nothing hold me, so it please thee hold
That nothing me, a something sweet to thee:
    Make but my name thy love, and love that still,
    And then thou lov'st me,—for my name is *Will.*

137

Thou blind fool, Love, what dost thou to mine eyes,
That they behold, and see not what they see?
They know what beauty is, see where it lies,
Yet what the best is take the worst to be.
If eyes, corrupt by over-partial looks,   *5*
Be anchor'd in the bay where all men ride,
Why of eyes' falsehood hast thou forged hooks,
Whereto the judgment of my heart is tied?
Why should my heart think that a several plot
Which my heart knows the wide world's common place?   *10*
Or mine eyes, seeing this, say this is not,
To put fair truth upon so foul a face?
    In things right true my heart and eyes have err'd,
    And to this false plague are they now transferr'd.

138

When my love swears that she is made of truth,
I do believe her, though I know she lies,
That she might think me some untutor'd youth,
Unlearned in the world's false subtleties.
Thus vainly thinking that she thinks me young,   *5*
Although she knows my days are past the best,
Simply I credit her false-speaking tongue:
On both sides thus is simple truth supprest.
But wherefore says she not she is unjust?
And wherefore say not I that I am old?   *10*
O, love's best habit is in seeming trust,
And age in love loves not to have years told:
    Therefore I lie with her, and she with me,
    And in our faults by lies we flatter'd be.

139

O, call not me to justify the wrong
That thy unkindness lays upon my heart;
Wound me not with thine eye, but with thy tongue:
Use power with power, and slay me not by art.
Tell me thou lov'st elsewhere; but in my sight,   *5*
Dear heart, forbear to glance thine eye aside:
What need'st thou wound with cunning, when thy might
Is more than my o'erpress'd defence can bide?
Let me excuse thee: ah! my love well knows
Her pretty looks have been my enemies;   *10*
And therefore from my face she turns my foes,
That they elsewhere might dart their injuries:
    Yet do not so; but since I am near slain,
    Kill me outright with looks, and rid my pain.

140

Be wise as thou art cruel; do not press
My tongue-tied patience with too much disdain;
Lest sorrow lend me words, and words express
The manner of my pity-wanting pain.
If I might teach thee wit, better it were,   *5*
Though not to love, yet, love, to tell me so;
As testy sick men, when their deaths be near,
No news but health from their physicians know;
For, if I should despair, I should grow mad,
And in my madness might speak ill of thee: *10*
Now this ill-wresting world is grown so bad,
Mad slanderers by mad ears believed be.
    That I may not be so, nor thou belied,
    Bear thine eyes straight, though thy proud heart go wide.

141

In faith, I do not love thee with mine eyes,
For they in thee a thousand errors note;
But 'tis my heart that loves what they despise,
Who, in despite of view, is pleas'd to dote.
Nor are mine ears with thy tongue's tune delighted;   *5*
Nor tender feeling to base touches prone.
Nor taste nor smell desire to be invited
To any sensual feast with thee alone:
But my five wits nor my five senses can
Dissuade one foolish heart from serving thee,   *10*
Who leaves unsway'd the likeness of a man,
Thy proud heart's slave and vassal wretch to be:
    Only my plague thus far I count my gain,
    That she that makes me sin awards me pain.

142

Love is my sin, and thy dear virtue hate,
Hate of my sin, grounded on sinful loving:
O, but with mine compare thou thine own state,
And thou shalt find it merits not reproving;
Or, if it do, not from those lips of thine,   *5*
That have profan'd their scarlet ornaments
And seal'd false bonds of love as oft as mine,
Robb'd others' beds' revenues of their rents.
Be it lawful I love thee, as thou lov'st those
Whom thine eyes woo as mine importune thee: *10*
Root pity in thy heart, that when it grows,
Thy pity may deserve to pitied be.
    If thou dost seek to have what thou dost hide,
    By self-example mayst thou be denied!

143

Lo, as a careful housewife runs to catch
One of her feather'd creatures broke away,
Sets down her babe, and makes all quick dispatch
In pursuit of the thing she would have stay;
Whilst her neglected child holds her in chase,   *5*

---

9 untold: *uncounted*   **9 several:** *private*   **138. 1–14** *Cf. n.*   **7 Simply:** *absolutely*   **9**
unjust: *false*   **4 by art:** *by cunning*

4 pity-wanting pain: *unpitied suffering*   **11 ill-wresting:** *maliciously misconstruing*   **9**
five wits; *cf. n.*   **11 unsway'd:** *deprived of self-control (?)*   **14 pain:** *punishment*   **13**
what thou dost hide: *the love you refuse*

Cries to catch her whose busy care is bent
To follow that which flies before her face,
Not prizing her poor infant's discontent:
So runn'st thou after that which flies from thee,
Whilst I thy babe chase thee afar behind;   10
But if thou catch thy hope, turn back to me,
And play the mother's part, kiss me, be kind;
  So will I pray that thou mayst have thy *Will*,
  If thou turn back and my loud crying still.

144

Two loves I have of comfort and despair,
Which like two spirits do suggest me still:
The better angel is a man right fair,
The worser spirit a woman, colour'd ill.
To win me soon to hell, my female evil   5
Tempteth my better angel from my side,
And would corrupt my saint to be a devil,
Wooing his purity with her foul pride.
And whether that my angel be turn'd fiend
Suspect I may, but not directly tell;   10
But being both from me, both to each friend,
I guess one angel in another's hell:
  Yet this shall I ne'er know, but live in doubt,
  Till my bad angel fire my good one out.

145

Those lips that Love's own hand did make,
Breath'd forth the sound that said 'I hate,'
To me that languish'd for her sake:
But when she saw my woeful state,
Straight in her heart did mercy come,   5
Chiding that tongue that ever sweet
Was us'd in giving gentle doom;
And taught it thus anew to greet;
'I hate,' she alter'd with an end,
That follow'd it as gentle day   10
Doth follow night, who like a fiend
From heaven to hell is flown away.
  'I hate' from hate away she threw,
  And sav'd my life, saying—'Not you.'

146

Poor soul, the centre of my sinful earth,
Fool'd by these rebel powers that thee array,
Why dost thou pine within and suffer dearth,
Painting thy outward walls so costly gay?
Why so large cost, having so short a lease,   5
Dost thou upon thy fading mansion spend?
Shall worms, inheritors of this excess,
Eat up thy charge? Is this thy body's end?
Then, soul, live thou upon thy servant's loss,
And let that pine to aggravate thy store;   10
Buy terms divine in selling hours of dross;

Within be fed, without be rich no more:
  So shalt thou feed on Death, that feeds on men,
  And Death once dead, there's no more dying then.

147

My love is as a fever, longing still
For that which longer nurseth the disease;
Feeding on that which doth preserve the ill,
The uncertain sickly appetite to please.
My reason, the physician to my love,   5
Angry that his prescriptions are not kept,
Hath left me, and I desperate now approve
Desire is death, which physic did except.
Past cure I am, now reason is past care,
And frantic-mad with evermore unrest;   10
My thoughts and my discourse as madmen's are,
At random from the truth vainly express'd;
  For I have sworn thee fair, and thought thee bright,
  Who art as black as hell, as dark as night.

148

O me! what eyes hath Love put in my head,
Which have no correspondence with true sight;
Or, if they have, where is my judgment fled,
That censures falsely what they see aright?
If that be fair whereon my false eyes dote,   5
What means the world to say it is not so?
If it be not, then love doth well denote
Love's eye is not so true as all men's: no.
How can it? O, how can Love's eye be true,
That is so vex'd with watching and with tears?   10
No marvel then, though I mistake my view;
The sun itself sees not till heaven clears.
  O cunning Love! with tears thou keep'st me blind,
  Lest eyes well-seeing thy foul faults should find.

149

Canst thou, O cruel! say I love thee not,
When I against myself with thee partake?
Do I not think on thee, when I forgot
Am of myself, all tyrant, for thy sake?
Who hateth thee that I do call my friend?   5
On whom frown'st thou that I do fawn upon?
Nay, if thou lour'st on me, do I not spend
Revenge upon myself with present moan?
What merit do I in myself respect,
That is so proud thy service to despise,   10
When all my best doth worship thy defect,
Commanded by the motion of thine eyes?
  But, love, hate on, for now I know thy mind;
  Those that can see thou lov'st, and I am blind.

---

13 **Will**; *cf. note on Sonnet 135*   **144. 1-14** *Cf. n.*   2 **suggest**: *prompt*   11 **from me**:
away from me **to each**: *to each other*   14 **fire ... out**: *drive out with fire*   **145. 1-14**
Cf. n.   **146. 1, 2** *Cf. n.*   4 **outward walls**: *body*   8 **charge**: *expense*   10 **aggravate**:
increase   11 **terms**: *long periods of time*

6 **kept**: *followed*   7 **approve**: *prove that*   8 **which physic did except**: (Desire) *which
objected to the physic* (of Reason)   4 **censures**: *judges*   10 **watching**: *wakefulness*   2
with thee partake: *take part with thee*   4 **all tyrant**: *you absolute tyrant*   9 **respect**:
prize

150

O, from what power hast thou this powerful might,
With insufficiency my heart to sway?
To make me give the lie to my true sight,
And swear that brightness doth not grace the day?
Whence hast thou this becoming of things ill,   5
That in the very refuse of thy deeds
There is such strength and warrantise of skill,
That, in my mind, thy worst all best exceeds?
Who taught thee how to make me love thee more,
The more I hear and see just cause of hate?   10
O, though I love what others do abhor,
With others thou shouldst not abhor my state:
　　If thy unworthiness rais'd love in me,
　　More worthy I to be belov'd of thee.

151

Love is too young to know what conscience is;
Yet who knows not conscience is born of love?
Then, gentle cheater, urge not my amiss,
Lest guilty of my faults thy sweet self prove:
For, thou betraying me, I do betray   5
My nobler part to my gross body's treason;
My soul doth tell my body that he may
Triumph in love; flesh stays no further reason,
But rising at thy name doth point out thee
As his triumphant prize. Proud of this pride.   10
He is contented thy poor drudge to be,
To stand in thy affairs, fall by thy side.
　　No want of conscience hold it that I call
　　Her 'love' for whose dear love I rise and fall.

152

In loving thee thou know'st I am forsworn,
But thou art twice forsworn, to me love swearing;
In act thy bed-vow broke, and new faith torn,
In vowing new hate after new love bearing.
But why of two oaths' breach do I accuse thee,   5
When I break twenty? I am perjur'd most;
For all my vows are oaths but to misuse thee,
And all my honest faith in thee is lost:
For I have sworn deep oaths of thy deep kindness,

Oaths of thy love, thy truth, thy constancy;   10
And, to enlighten thee, gave eyes to blindness,
Or made them swear against the thing they see;
　　For I have sworn thee fair; more perjur'd I,
　　To swear against the truth so foul a lie!

153

Cupid laid by his brand and fell asleep;
A maid of Dian's this advantage found,
And his love-kindling fire did quickly steep
In a cold valley-fountain of that ground;
Which borrow'd from this holy fire of Love   5
A dateless lively heat, still to endure,
And grew a seething bath, which yet men prove
Against strange maladies a sovereign cure.
But at my mistress' eye Love's brand new-fired,
The boy for trial needs would touch my breast;   10
I, sick withal, the help of bath desired,
And thither hied, a sad distemper'd guest,
　　But found no cure: the bath for my help lies
　　Where Cupid got new fire, my mistress' eyes.

154

The little Love-god lying once asleep
Laid by his side his heart-inflaming brand,
Whilst many nymphs that vow'd chaste life to keep
Came tripping by; but in her maiden hand
The fairest votary took up that fire   5
Which many legions of true hearts had warm'd;
And so the general of hot desire
Was, sleeping, by a virgin hand disarm'd.
This brand she quenched in a cool well by,
Which from Love's fire took heat perpetual,   10
Growing a bath and healthful remedy
For men disease'd; but I, my mistress' thrall,
　　Came there for cure, and this by that I prove,
　　Love's fire heats water, water cools not love.

❧ FINIS ❧

NOTES

DEDICATION

1. *onlie begetter.* Some scholars, notably Lee, argue that 'begetter' here means 'obtainer,' 'procurer'; hence the publisher T. T. is thanking W. H. for finding and delivering to him the MSS. of this sonnet collection. Lee goes further and identifies W. H. as William Hall, a stationer of the period. Mrs. Stopes, practically following Lee's interpretation of 'begetter,' identifies W. H. as William Harvey, the stepfather of the third Earl of Southampton, Shakespeare's friend. The natural rendering of this phrase which recalls the 'only begotten' of the Creed, is 'the one, the only, inspirer.'

3. *W. H.* These initials raise a controversy which many volumes have not yet settled. If we reject Lee's interpretation and believe that a nobleman must be the inspirer of the sonnets praising a youth, the two best candidates are William Herbert, third Earl of Pembroke, and Henry Wriothesley (pronounced 'Rizley'), third Earl of Southampton. Of the two, Southampton seems the better claimant, though Herbert's liaison with Mary Fitton and her subsequent career has led many (especially dramatists) to consider her the heroine of the last group of sonnets. But Herbert came to court as late as 1598 and the sonnets, as a whole, seem to have been written before that year. Southampton is the only patron Shakespeare publicly acknowledged, and the dedication of *Venus and Adonis*, 1593, and *The Rape of Lucrece*, 1594, show that the poet regarded him with gratitude and affection. If, as seems more probable, W. H. was not a great nobleman, other names have been suggested: William Hall, William Harvey (*vide supra*), William Hughes, William Hammond, William Hathaway. It is perfectly evident that Shakespeare must have had many friends whose very names, to say nothing of initials, Time has effaced. All that can be said with certainty of the hero of these sonnets is that he was a youth of better birth and fortune than Shakespeare and that his encouragement and friendship, at a certain period in the poet's career, won Shakespeare's praise and devotion. In his gratitude, Shakespeare, as he said, built in these sonnets an enduring monument; unfortunately for us T. T. wrote its inscription. The best short account of this whole controversy is found in Alden's variorum edition of the sonnets, pp. 464-471, prepared by Frank E. Hill.

13. *T. T.* Thomas Thorpe. Lee describes him as a stationer's assistant, 'holding his own with difficulty for some thirty years in the lowest ranks of the London publishing trade. He merely traded in the "copy" which he procured how he could.' See also R. B. McKerrow, *Dictionary of Printers and Booksellers*, p. 265 f.

SONNETS

1. These first seventeen sonnets are addressed to a beautiful youth whose identity is still a subject of conjecture. They urge him by flattery, expostulation, and argument to marry and perpetuate his beauty in a child.

1. 6. *Feed'st thy light's flame with self-substantial fuel.* Like a candle, you feed your flame by burning your own substance; or, you feed your eyes (light's flame) on the sight of yourself—you see only yourself.

1. 11. *content.* In this line, this word may also mean 'your whole being.'

1. 13, 14. *Pity the world, or else this glutton be, To eat the world's due, by the grave and thee.* This may be paraphrased: Pity the world (by perpetuating your beauty in your children) or glutton-like, you eat your beauty, due the world, by allowing it to perish in the grave and by your failure to beget children.

5. 9, 10. A reference to perfumes extracted from flowers. Compare the close of sonnet 54.

7. 9-12. *But when from highmost pitch, with weary car, Like feeble age, he reeleth from the day, The eyes, 'fore duteous, now converted are From his low tract, and look another way.* Cf. 'All this blanked not Pompey, who told him frankly againe, how men did honour the rising, not the setting of the sunne; meaning thereby, how his owne honor encreased, and Scyllaes diminished.' *Life of Pompey* in *Plutarch's Lives of the Noble Grecians and Romans englished by Sir Thomas North* (1579).

8. 14. *'Thou single wilt prove none.'* 'Perhaps an allusion to the proverbial expression that one is no number.' Dowden. Compare sonnet 136, line 8.

11. 11. *Look, whom she best endow'd she gave the more.* See, to you whom Nature best endowed she gives an added gift.

13. 1. *O that you were yourself.* O that you were yourself forever.

14. 12. *If from thyself to store thou wouldst convert.* If you would turn from living for yourself alone and would beget children.

15. 4. *secret influence.* Astrology taught that there emanated from the stars a power or force (secret influence) which determined the characters and the fortunes of men and states.

16. 10. *Which this Time's pencil, or my pupil pen.* Beeching gives the following paraphrase: 'Neither portraiture ("this Time's pencil," cf. line 8) nor description ("my pupil pen," cf. line 4) can represent you as you are, either in character or beauty.'

18. Sonnets 18-25 form a single series, praising the youth's beauty and declaring the poet's affection for him.

19. 10. *antique pen.* This word, pronounced 'antic,' may mean in this sonnet not merely 'old' (cf. sonnet 106. 7) but also 'a pen that plays pranks, that draws grotesque lines.'

20. This sonnet has hardly the tone in which Shakespeare, the actor, could address a nobleman of high rank.

20. 7. *A man in hue all hues in his controlling.* This line is a source of perpetual debate. The Quarto prints 'all *Hews*,' and some editors have seen here a pun on the name Hughes, even suggesting that this proves 'W. H.' to have been William Hughes. Other editors change the reading 'A man in hue' to 'A native hue' or 'A maiden hue.' Shakespeare has just said that his friend has a woman's gentle heart, an eye that is brighter than a woman's, and in this line, going a step further, he gives to him a man's complexion of such beauty that it overpowers or surpasses the handsome coloring of all others.

24. 4. *perspective.* An optical instrument for viewing objects, a magnifying glass. Notice the pun in the next line, 'through the painter.' Shakespeare is also alluding to the more familiar meaning of perspective. The N. E. D. cites Haydocke, 1598, 'A painter without the perspective was like a doctor without grammar.'

26. By some editors, this sonnet is regarded as an envoi to the preceding twenty-five sonnets. 'This written ambassage' (line 3) may refer to that series; but it may equally well refer to this sonnet only.

34. 13, 14. *Ah! but those tears are pearl which thy love sheds, And they are rich and ransom all ill deeds.* Cf. *Antony and Cleopatra*, III.ix.76-78.

> *Fall not a tear, I say; one of them rates*
> *All that is won and lost. Give me a kiss;*
> *Even this repays me.*

This and the following sonnet may refer to the incident described in sonnets 40-42.

35. 8. *Excusing thy sins more than thy sins are.* Not only the meaning of this line but the correctness of the text itself is a debated question. Q. reads 'their' for 'thy' in both instances; Bullen reads: 'Excusing their sins more than thy sins are.' The present reading is the one most generally adopted. This line and the preceding one may be paraphrased: I am corrupting myself in condoning your fault, for I am so anxious to exculpate you that I offer for you excuses out of all proportion to your sins.

35. 9. *sense.* Not 'reason' but rather 'the senses, the feelings.' The poet's own feelings urge him to excuse the guilt of his friend.

36. 13, 14. *But do not so; I love thee in such sort As thou being mine, mine is thy good report.* But do not dishonor yourself (by showing me kindness in the eyes of the world), for my love has so completely taken possession of you that your good name, your honor, belongs to me. (Note that this same couplet occurs at the close of sonnet 96.)

37. 5-7. Apparently the youth Shakespeare praises is better born, richer, and handsomer than the poet; yet these lines do not prove him to be one of the nobility.

39. 13, 14. *And that thou teachest how to make one twain, By praising him here who doth hence remain.* This may be paraphrased: And because, Absence, you teach me to make of one person two—my friend is away from me and yet I may call him before my memory and seem while praising him to enjoy his presence.

40. There is nothing to prove that the woman of sonnets 40-42 is the 'dark' woman of sonnets 127 ff.

40. 8. *By wilful taste of what thyself refusest.* Dowden paraphrases this: 'By an unlawful union while you refuse loyal wedlock'; Beeching conjectures: 'By taking in wilfulness my mistress whom yet you do not love.'

44. 14. *badges of either's woe.* The poet's heavy tears are the signs of woe of the two elements in his body, earth and water. In the first line of the next sonnet, Shakespeare alludes to the two remaining elements, fire and air. According to the belief of Shakespeare's day, man was composed of these four elements.

51. 11. *Shall neigh—no dull flesh—in his fiery race.* It is possible that the text of this obscure line is corrupt. As it stands, the thought may be expressed as follows: (Desire), no dull, plodding beast, shall neigh like a spirited horse as it rushes on its fiery race to you.

58. 6. *The imprison'd absence of your liberty.* Beeching paraphrases this: 'suffer your absence, which, though it represent liberty to you, means imprisonment to me.'

60. 4. *In sequent toil all forwards do contend.* Toiling and following each other all (the waves) strive onward.

62. 10. This line and the opening lines of the following sonnet give no definite information whatever concerning Shakespeare's age when he wrote these poems. It was a common convention of both English and Continental sonneteers to contrast their wrinkled faces and advanced years with the lovely youth of the person they were praising.

67. 7, 8. *Why should poor beauty indirectly seek Roses of shadow.* In this line 'indirectly' means 'dishonestly.' Shakespeare is inveighing against the fashionable practice of rouging or painting the face. This protest was a common one; it was expressed in many moods, including Hamlet's passionate outburst (*Hamlet* III.i.148ff.).

68. 3. Here the poet attacks the fashionable practice of wearing wigs. According to Stow, the custom of wearing them began in England in 1572.

69. 14. *soil.* The N. E. D. explains the word in this line as 'The solution of the problem.'

70. If this sonnet is addressed to the youth of sonnets 34-35, 40-42, it is plainly out of place, for here the youth's life is pronounced blameless.

71. 2, 3. This alludes to the custom of tolling the church bell when a member of the parish died, one stroke for each year of the deceased.

73. 12. *Consum'd with that which it was nourish'd by.* The wood which fed the fire is now turned to ashes and extinguishes the flame.

77. Apparently this sonnet was either written in a blank book sent to the unknown friend, or else it accompanied such a gift. It is out of place between sonnets 76 and 78 which discuss Shakespeare's own writings.

77. 4. *And of this book this learning mayst thou taste.* Dowden makes the following comment: 'Beauty, Time, and Verse formed the theme of many of Shakespeare's sonnets; now that he will write no more, he commends his friend to his glass, where he may discover the truth about his beauty; to the dial, where he may learn the progress of time; and to this book, which he himself—not Shakespeare—must fill.'

77. 11, 12. *Those children nurs'd, deliver'd from thy brain, To take a new acquaintance of thy mind.* The meaning of these lines may be expressed: Your thoughts, written in the pages ('waste blanks') of this book, will seem new when you reread them, as children, sent out to nurse, are grown and changed when brought back to their parents.

77. 13. *These offices.* The habitual use, in the manner suggested by the poet, of the dial and mirror.

78. This begins a series of nine sonnets in which Shakespeare laments that his friend has turned from Shakespeare's verses to the poetry of a 'better spirit.' Cf. the next note.

80. 2. *Knowing a better spirit doth use your name.* No one has yet established the identity of this 'better spirit' who supplanted Shakespeare in the esteem of his friend and to whom in this sonnet and in the ones immediately following, Shakespeare acknowledges himself far inferior. Attempts have been made to show that the rival poet was Barnes, Chapman, Daniel, Drayton, Jonson, Marston; yet nothing has been proved.

83. 14. *Than both your poets can in praise devise.* That one of these poets must be Shakespeare is quite evident.

84. 3, 4. *In whose confine immured is the store Which should example where your equal grew?* You, in whom is stored up the whole sum of your unexampled beauty.

84. 14. *Being fond on praise, which makes your praises worse.* Being fond of receiving praise which, as it never does you justice, really detracts from you (makes your praises worse).

85. 3. *Reserve their character with golden quill.* This may be paraphrased: (The comments of your praise, l. 2) are written down in a form that will endure (reserve their character), in a beautiful style (with golden quill).

85. 7. *able spirit.* Another reference to the rival poet whose 'hymns' have proved as elusive as his name.

85. 12. *Though words come hindmost, holds his rank before.* This, and the preceding line, may be expressed as follows: Though my words are not equal to your praises sung by another, the loving praise in my mind outranks the tributes of everyone.

87. 3. *The charter of thy worth gives thee releasing.* You do not belong to me because your fine qualities give you the privilege of leaving me.

90. 6. *Come in the rearward of a conquer'd woe.* Attack me after I have defeated one misfortune.

94. It is interesting to compare this sonnet on self-control with Hamlet's famous praise of the man who is not passion's slave (*Hamlet* III.ii.66-89).

94. 9-12. Wyndham paraphrases these lines: 'These self-contained persons may seem to lack generosity; but then, without making voluntary gifts, they give inevitably, even as the summer's flower is sweet to the summer, though it live and die only to itself. Yet let such one beware of corruption.'

94. 14. This line occurs in the anonymous play of *Edward III* (published in 1596), II.i.51. Though the opinion is not unanimous, many Shakespearean scholars believe the sonnet antedates the play, to which Shakespeare has sometimes been thought to have contributed certain scenes.

96. 13, 14. This couplet concludes sonnet 36 where, as many critics observe, it is more in keeping with the general idea of the poem.

99. 7. *buds of marjoram.* The reference may be either to the color of the buds—reddish brown—or to their fragrance.

107. 1-4. The first four lines of this sonnet may be paraphrased: Neither my own fears, nor the divining soul of the world dreaming of the future to which the present shall give way, can overpower the duration of my love, mistakenly supposed to be subject to the fate that limits all things.

107. 5. *mortal moon.* Many scholars find in this sonnet definite allusions to contemporary events. Lee and others believe it celebrates the release of Southampton from prison, 1603. He was set free after the death of Elizabeth, whom contemporary poets celebrated as the moon goddess. ('The mortal moon hath her eclipse endured.') The motto of James I, who released Southampton, was 'Blessed are the peacemakers' (cf. l. 8). To others, the sonnet celebrates the defeat of the Armada, or the reconciliation of Elizabeth with Essex. It is equally possible to read this sonnet as merely one more in the series in which Shakespeare proclaims his devotion to be superior to fate and death.

108. 13, 14. *Finding the first conceit of love there bred, Where time and outward form would show it dead.* Finding the first love still inspired in a face whose appearance of age would make it unlovely to others.

110. 1, 2. These lines refer, probably, though not necessarily, to Shakespeare's career as an actor. They lament, as do the following two sonnets, the associations forced upon him by poverty.

112. 7, 8. *None else to me, nor I to none alive, That my steel'd sense or changes right or wrong.* So far as I am concerned, no one but you (and I live for you alone) can influence my callous feeling to right or wrong.

112. 10, 11. *that my adder's sense To critic and to flatterer stopped are.* This may be a reminiscence of Psalm 58. 4, 5: 'Even like the deaf adder, that stoppeth her ears; Which refuseth to hear the voice of the charmer, charm he never so wisely.'

113. 14. *My most true mind thus maketh mine untrue.* Malone explains this line: 'The sincerity of my affection is the cause of my untruth; i.e., of not seeing objects truly, such as they appear to the rest of mankind.'

114. 13, 14. In line 12, the eye has been compared to the taster for king Mind. If the eye gives him a poisoned cup, it is not such a great sin because the eye drinks the poison first.

119. 7. *How have mine eyes out of their spheres been fitted.* 'How have mine eyes started from their hollows in the fever fits of my disease.' Dowden.

120. 9, 10. *O, that our night of woe might have remember'd My deepest sense, how hard true sorrow hits.* O, that the memory of our night of suffering might have recalled (remember'd) to my inmost soul how hard a blow true sorrow strikes.

121. 3, 4. *And the just pleasure lost, which is so deem'd Not by our feeling, but by others' seeing.* 'And the legitimate pleasure lost, which is deemed vile, not by us who experience it, but by others who look on and condemn.' Dowden. 'And the lawful pleasure lost, which is judged vile from the point of view of others and not from any sense of shame on our part.' Wyndham.

122. In this sonnet Shakespeare explains why he gave away a blank book, a present from his friend. Compare sonnet 77.

122. 10. *Nor need I tallies thy dear love to score.* This line alludes to the old custom of recording by cutting notches (scores) on a stick (tally).

123. 7, 8. *And rather make them born to our desire Than think that we before have heard them told.* 'We regard the wonderful works of to-day as the offspring of our own will, and forget that past ages produced the very same.' Beeching.

124. 4. *Weeds among weeds, or flowers with flowers gather'd.* Time might weed it out with hate or gather it lovingly as a flower.

124. 13, 14. *To this I witness call the fools of time, Which die for goodness, who have liv'd for crime.* Scholars are not agreed as to the meaning of this obscure couplet. 'The fools of time' may be Essex and his followers; the Jesuits, condemned for plotting against the Crown; or any traitors who die piously.

125. 13, 14. *Hence, thou suborn'd informer! a true soul When most impeach'd stands least in thy control.* In this sonnet Shakespeare has asserted that he regards not outward appearance but the heart. Probably there is no personal

reference in 'suborn'd informer'; it means any false idea or detraction of the poet's devotion.

126. The Quarto indicates by brackets that two lines are missing after the final couplet, yet this twelve-line poem, written not in sonnet form but in couplets, is complete as it stands. It serves to mark the conclusion of the sonnets addressed to the friend.

127. The dark woman of the following sonnets is as much a mystery as ever, despite the many pages that editors, critics, and playwrights have devoted to her. Some scholars and dramatists assume her to be a maid of honor of Queen Elizabeth, Mary Fitton, at one time the mistress of William Herbert, Earl of Pembroke. She was evidently attractive, for she was married twice after the Pembroke affair. With the praise of dark beauty in this sonnet compare *Love's Labour's Lost* IV.iii.258-277.

127. 1. *In the old age black was not counted fair.* 'Black' in this sonnet and in the following ones, means 'dark complexioned,' 'brunette'; while 'fair' means both 'light complexioned' and 'beautiful.'

128. 5. *jacks.* 'In the virginal, an upright piece of wood fixed to the key-lever and fitted with a quill which plucked the string as the jack rose when the key was pressed down. Here used as "key." ' Onions.

129. 1-3. *The expense of spirit in a waste of shame Is lust in action; and till action, lust Is perjur'd.* Lust when put into action spends the spirit in a shameful waste; and until it acts, Lust is perjur'd.

135. In this and in the following sonnet, Shakespeare writes a series of puns on the word 'will,' using it as a proper name, as 'wish,' and as 'lust.' Used as a proper name, '*Will* in over-plus; More than enough am I' (ll. 2, 3), refers to Shakespeare; '*Will* to boot,' (l. 2) refers to another man, possibly to the friend of sonnet 133, l. 2.

138. In *The Passionate Pilgrim,* 1599, this sonnet was printed with variations from the present text in eight of its lines. In general, the present version seems the better one and probably represents Shakespeare's revision of the poem published ten years before the collected sonnets appeared.

141. 9. *five wits.* Common sense, imagination, fancy, estimation, memory.

144. This sonnet appeared in *The Passionate Pilgrim,* 1599, with some unimportant changes in text. (Cf. note on sonnet 138.) Drayton's sonnet, 'An evil spirit, your beauty, haunts me still,' published also in 1599, has certain resemblances to this sonnet. That Drayton took a hint from Shakespeare seems more probable than that Shakespeare was indebted to Drayton.

145. This sonnet seems out of place in this series on the 'female evil.' It is written in octosyllabics; and it depicts a woman quite different from that mistress, 'black in deeds,' whose baneful influence upon the poet has been described in the preceding sonnets.

146. 1, 2. *Poor soul, the centre of my sinful earth, Fool'd by these rebel powers that thee array.* In the Quarto, the second line of this couplet is misprinted 'My sinful earth these rebel powers that thee array.' In place of 'My sinful earth,' repeated from the first line, many readings have been proposed, such as: 'Foil'd by'; 'Slave of'; 'Thrall to'; 'Starved by.' The reading of this text is as plausible as any other.

153, 154. These two sonnets are alternative versions of an epigram by Marianus, a Byzantine writer of about the fifth century A.D. There were sixteenth-century translations of this epigram both in Latin and in Italian; in Giles Fletcher's *Licia,* 1593, there is another very free adaptation of it.

THE TEXT OF THE PRESENT EDITION

Although two of the sonnets in this collection, Nos. 138 and 144, were included in *The Passionate Pilgrim,* 1599, the first edition of the sonnets is the quarto which appeared in 1609 and which sold for five pence. This quarto was not sanctioned by Shakespeare; it is full of obvious errors and yet it is the accepted text. By permission, the text of this edition is that of Craig's Oxford Shakespeare, published by the Oxford Press, which follows the first quarto, correcting its mistakes. In a few cases the editor has departed from Craig's text, preferring the reading of the first quarto or some generally accepted emendation. Minor changes of spelling and punctuation are not recorded, but all other variations from Craig's text are given below, where Craig's readings are printed after the colon.

10. 1.	For shame deny	Q: For shame! deny
16. 10.	Which this Time's pencil,:	Which this, Time's pencil,
16. 13.	yourself,	Q: yourself
26. 14.	Till then,	Q: Till then
31. 1.	hearts:	hearts, Q
59. 11.	Whether	Q: Whe'r
66. 14.	Save that to die	Q: Save that, to die
75. 9.	Sometime all	Q: Sometime, all
84. 1.	most,	Q: most?
84. 2.	you,	Q: you?
84. 4.	grew?:	grew.
84. 8.	story.:	story,
85. 3.	Reserve	Q: Deserve
88. 5.	weakness being	Q: weakness, being
110. 9.	have	Q: save
114. 3.	say	Q: say,
141. 6.	feeling	Q: feeling,